GOLDMINE 45 rpm records price guide

8th edition

Dave Thompson

Published by

Krause Publications, a division of F+W Media, Inc.
700 East State Street • Iola, WI 54990-0001
715-445-2214 • 888-457-2873
www.krausebooks.com

To order books or other products call toll-free 1-800-258-0929
or visit us online at www.krausebooks.com

ISBN-13: 9781440248344
ISBN-10: 1440248346

Cover Design by Dean Abatemarco
Designed by Jana Tappa
Edited by Paul Kennedy

Printed in the United States of America

10 9 8 7 6 5 4 3 2 1

Contents

Listings

Acknowledgments

Thanks to everybody who made this edition of the book a reality, most notably the staff of Jupiter Records in Wilmington DE, and Rainbow Records in Newark DE; all at Keystone Record Collectors and the Pennsylvania Music Expo in Lancaster PA; and the host of readers and fellow collectors whose letters and e-mails have kept these listings on their toes.

To Editorial Director Paul Kennedy and Goldmine Editor Pat Prince for setting the wheels in motion, and Database Guru Steve Duberstein for making sure they kept rolling; Amy Thompson, for not complaining when the post-it notes threatened to fill the house; Tamsin Darke and Chris Bentley for their invaluable contributions; and to all the friends and family who lived through the completion of this edition.

Introduction

A Salute to 3 Minutes – or so – of Pure Joy

It's hard to believe, but it's almost 10 years since the last edition of the *Goldmine Price Guide to 45 RPM Records* was published, a decade during which the face of record collecting in America (and elsewhere) has changed almost beyond recognition.

Things were bad in 2009. Twenty years had passed since the music industry of the late 1980s set about abandoning the 45 as the principle means of delivering hit records – replacing it first with cassette singles; then CDs; and, most recently, mp3s. For the first time since the 1940s (when sheet music and 78s still led the charge), young Americans were being introduced to pop music via some of the most soul-less looking media ever deployed to convey, contrarily, what should have been the most exciting sounds around.

Because that's what singles are. Three (or so) minute explosions of joy, fun, electricity and exhilaration; tiny time capsules, any one of which is capable of transporting you back to the moment you first danced, sang, laughed or cried to the music contained within the grooves.

From the moment they were introduced, there was something inherently collectible about 45s – a quality that the format's replacements never managed to accrue. For sure, people do collect cassette and CD singles, but they are in such a minority that even 8-Track fans out-number them. The 45, however, was a massive success from the moment it was introduced, and a lot of people were massively disappointed the moment it was phased out.

People didn't stop collecting

them, however; the problem was, very few new collectors were coming along to join them. And 2009 marked, perhaps, the darkest hour of all.

Record fairs, for so long the lifeblood of the grassroots record collecting hobby, were becoming less regular and less attended all the time, as buyers and sellers alike looked to the Internet to fill the holes in their collection.

Stores were vanishing at record rates – Tower, for so long a colossus in the industry, closed its doors in 2006, smaller "mom-and-pop" style concerns were pulling down the shutters at an epidemic pace.

Even *Goldmine* magazine was affected by the changes, reverting to a monthly schedule after a decade-plus of biweekly issues,

Everywhere you went, the cry went up: Record collecting was dy-

ing. And the 45 was already dead. As recently as 2012, I dropped off a pile of unwanted vinyl at the local branch of a national used books and records chain. The 45s were handed back to me with the words, "we don't take the small ones."

That was then, this is now. Today, the hobby is in the best health it has enjoyed since the early 1980s, and maybe even longer. New vinyl floods the marketplace and even the high street (or, at least, the malls that have replaced it in so many communities) is awash with wax. Classic music reappears on vinyl every week, sometimes (releases from the 90s and beyond) for the first time ever; new releases automatically see daylight on both LP and CD. Even that aforementioned chain store now takes the small ones.

A whole new audience has been wooed, and they in turn have engendered a resurgence in both bricks-and-mortar stores and regular record fairs.

Record Store Day, a barely noticed fledgling when it was first introduced in 2007, is now one of the banner dates on the annual

calendar, so successful in its aims that it now takes place twice a year. And while the majority of the mainstream focus has been targeted toward the revival of the 12-inch LP, its little sibling – the 45 – has risen from the grave as well.

They are not necessarily a force in everyday marketing; new "singles" (if they can even be called that), sadly, are almost exclusively released as downloads today, and the charts, compiled from these sales, respond accordingly.

But the collectors market is awash with new releases, ranging from the flood of colored vinyl, limited editions and reissued rarities that now accompany Record Store Day, to an astoundingly popular series of David Bowie picture disc 45s, each released on the 40th anniversaries of its original 7-inch appearance.

True, the 45 never really died; throughout its years in the mainstream wilderness, the format remained the weapon of choice for any number of independent labels and bands, including such big hitters as Sub Pop, Third Man and the reggae-centric VP, all of whom

built reputations on the quality (and subsequent collectibility) of their releases. But still it has been estimated that no more than 25,000 45s were released in the US throughout the first decade of this century: less than a quarter of the total released during the 1970s.

That statistic is set to double this decade, and it is this persistence that has opened people's eyes to all the 45s that came before them – including people who not only had never previously purchased a 45 before, but who had never even been offered the opportunity.

Again, the major labels began eliminating the format around 1989. Assuming that most fans buy their first records around the age of 9 or 10, that means anybody under the age of 35 very likely missed out on what older music lovers consider one of life's most thrilling rites of passage. They did not need simply to be reintroduced to the format. They needed to discover it.

And they have done so in unprecedented numbers.

This book is dedicated both to them, and to everyone else who kept the faith.

About This Book

It would be impractical, if not impossible, for this volume to list and value every single 45 released in the United States since the format was first introduced, every pop, rock, R&B, folk, jazz, classical, reggae, novelty, comedy, spoken word, easy-listening, children's and oddball release ever to see the light of day.

Likewise, every acetate and promo; likewise every picture sleeve and label variation.

In other words, there *will* be omissions, and a great many of them *are* deliberate.

What this edition strives to do is document every 45 that both precedent and prediction suggest can be considered collectible by the market in general, whether it is one of the hobby's most grandiose one-off rarities, or simply one more entry within a popular artist, or sub-genre's overall catalog.

Within that admittedly grand mission statement, of course, other factors have been taken into consideration.

The listings in this edition end in 1989, the year – as we have already noted – in which it first became apparent that the major labels no longer regarded 45s as a priority. In 1980, around 10,000 45s were released in the US; by mid-decade, that figure had fallen to approximately 6,000; by 1989, it was barely 4,000. The totals continued to dip thereafter, and more and more it was the independent sector that was keeping the numbers as high as they were.

Many of these are themselves highly regarded by collectors, and capable of fetching some remarkable prices. But, just as stamp collecting long ago learned to divide

itself into separate and very well-defined eras, the classics of 1840-1940, and the "modern" age thereafter; and comic collectors have grown even more finicky than that (golden age, silver age, etc), so record collectors, too, are beginning to specialize, drawing a line through their collection at the dawn of the CD era. On the more recent side of that line, singles were increasingly marketed as future collectibles. This volume, on the other hand, focuses on a time when they were produced to be sold, played and enjoyed.

Value, too, comes into play, and, in this edition, we have elected to overlook any record whose valuation in Near Mint condition (see the *Goldmine* Grading Guide later in this section), is below $3 – a bar, of course, that excludes many of the releases that the aforementioned market forces would already have removed from contention.

Also, this catalog DOES NOT LIST Canadian, UK or other foreign releases. Please, before writing to inform us of a glaring omission from our listings, check the small print on the record's actual label or sleeve, particularly the line that gives the country of manufacture.

Neither do we include what an increasing number of correspondents seem to regard as major rarities… indeed, one of the most frequent questions received at *Goldmine* HQ is the one that begins, "I have a copy of such-and-such record, and the labels are on the wrong sides" – that is, the A-side label is on the B-side, and *vice versa*. The question, of course, is "what is it worth?"

It's not an altogether unreasonable query. Errors in coin, stamp and sports cards can often be highly prized, and highly valued, too. Surely it makes sense that what claims to be a copy of Elvis Presley's "In The Ghetto," which instead plays "Any Day Now" (and, when you flip the record over, the opposite) should be similar superscarce?

Well, yes and no. It *is* an error and there probably aren't many of them around. But, and it's a big but, in these cases you simply have… an error. Just one of those niggling flaws that comes from automation, a record slipped into the machine the wrong way up – less an error, then, than a simple foul-up.

Occasionally a collector might want to pick up a mislabeled record for its novelty value. But that, sadly, is all it is – a novelty that is worth no more than a regular pressing, a reminder of a bad split-second at the pressing plant; the vinyl equivalent of buying a pair of pants and discovering they're not the size it says on the label. Keep it as a curio, by all means. But, unless the record itself is a valuable one, never regard it as a family heirloom.

What's New In This Edition?

Fresh emphasis is given to the variety of independent labels that flourished during the late 1970s heyday of punk and New Wave; to the similarly local indies that peopled the rockabilly movement of the late 1950s; and to that vast corpus of soul and R&B obscurities that found new life, and rabid collectibility, across the Atlantic in Britain's Northern Soul movement – a craze that then boomeranged back to these shores, and sent values skyrocketing.

Indeed, it appears symptomatic of many modern collectors that it is genres, as opposed to individual artists, that are currently attracting the most interest.

Of course there is that select handful of performers whose careers will always remain inviolate, with the Beatles certainly leading the way in that respect. Elvis, Phil Spector productions, Pink Floyd, Bruce Springsteen and Bob Dylan follow in their wake, while the deaths, in 2016, of David Bowie and Prince saw those artists, too, ascend to new heights.

But move away from the headline acts, and more collectors than ever seem to be delving into the most obscure corners of the musical movements that may or may not have flourished around the superstars. The glam/glitter rock of the early-mid 1970s, which meant little in the United States at the time, has attracted a wealth of modern-day adherents. Sixties psychedelia, whose fascination constantly ebbs and flows in the marketplace, is currently undergoing some serious flow; and late 1970s punk rock climbs in both value and demand, perhaps as a consequence of the

40th anniversary celebrations that are currently underway.

A number of early 1980s New Wave releases are also becoming increasingly sought after, while the German "Krautrock" movement of the early-mid 1970s, though largely focused on LPs, was also responsible for some now-sought-after 45s.

Country singles from the sixties and seventies, though still widely available for genuinely low prices, are picking up interest, with earlier releases climbing higher still; and finally, we are seeing US collectors at last focus attentions on the small, but delightful, coterie of reggae singles released in this country in the years prior to Bob Marley's breakthrough – names like Prince Buster, Dave & Ansel Collins, Big Youth and Gregory Isaacs. For the first time, this edition has been expanded to include a plethora of ska, rocksteady, reggae and roots 45s, while calypso and mento, too, are at last acknowledged.

All of these movements are reflected within these pages, but so, of course, are those once-hot commodities whose moment has, at least temporarily, passed - eighties heavy metal, for example, and early seventies singer-songwriters.

We may never truly understand exactly what forces lay behind the ups and downs of individual collecting crazes, although even the most rabid opponent of CDs and mp3s should admit that the objects of their scorn have played at least a small part in the return to prominence of the 45, most notably as a consequence of the flood of digital compilations and box sets that have alerted us to old records we might otherwise never have known existed.

Country fans, for example, have been fabulously served by the series of collections released online under the banner of *Armadillo Killer's Odd 45 RPM Country Gems*, an undertaking that has now topped seventy volumes of, indeed, oddities. Lovers of the Texan beat of the late 1950s and early 1960s have been tempted by the 300+ track box set of vintage obscurities released by the German Be! Sharp label; Motown buffs can now purchase the label's entire pre-1972 singles catalog across a series of CD collections; and anybody looking for an instant Northern Soul collection could do a lot worse than pick up the Harmless label's 10CD box set *The Odyssey: A Northern Soul Time Capsule*.

All of which are a joy to own in these most readily available formats. But how many collectors, eyeing their contents (and, in many cases, their cost), set out instead to replicate the discs on original vinyl? Judging from my own conversations and observations in recent years, a lot.

Other collectors, however, create their own wants lists, and build libraries to their own specifications - those who aim to accumulate every individual 45 to make the *Billboard* Top 100, for instance, and don't even baulk at buying two copies of the same release, for those occasions when both sides of a single reached a different place in the chart.

There are those who pursue songs on a single theme (death songs, from "Leader of the Pack" to "Seasons in the Sun," are perennially popular); or that feature a single, unusual instrument. Even more than LPs, singles offer collectors almost unlimited scope to collect

exactly what they need to, and it is our fervent hope that this latest volume of the *Goldmine Price Guide to 45 RPM Records* will tend to all their requirements, both through the material that has carried over from past editions, and all that has been added to this one.

We welcome, too, your comments, additions and, if necessary, corrections. With every new edition of every *Goldmine* price guide, at least one letter will arrive, apprising us of a misprinted catalog number; a misplaced decimal point; even a misspelled name or song title, including some that have passed unnoticed since the very first editions of the book.

Inform us, too, of any omissions that you might spot. Some will, as remarked earlier, be deliberate. But others… who knows? Nobody expects to be informed of an hitherto unknown Elvis Sun single, or a previously undocumented Beatles b-side. But an awful lot of artists have released an awful lot of singles in the years since the 45 format was born, and nobody has listed them all.

One day, we would like to.

How To Use This Book

This book is devoted to two specific types of record: 7-inch singles, or 45s; and 7-inch EPs, or Extended Plays. Of course there are several other formats that can be described as singles, including 10-inch and 12-inch vinyl releases, cassette singles and CD singles. These are beyond the scope of this book.

Listings for 45s and EPs are separate beneath the artist's name. In both cases, they are listed first by record label, and then numerically (not necessarily chronologically) by catalog number.

Several abbreviations are used in the listings:

[DJ]—denotes a promotional release, usually (but not exclusively) intended for radio or press purposes. These records were never intended for public sale.
[M]—a mono recording.
[PS]—Record originally released with picture sleeve.
[S]—a stereo recording.

Both A- and B-sides of each release are noted. Occasionally in the past, this information has been inadvertently flipped. This edition remedies many of these errors; however we welcome additional information. Likewise, we have sought to correct many of the B-sides previously listed as "unknown," but again we welcome corrections.

The year of release and the value in Near Mint condition (see Grading Guide, below) follow. There may then be a further line of text offering additional information on the release.

The Goldmine Grading Guide

Imagine, if you will, stepping back in time to your youth, walking into your local record retailer, and purchasing, on the day of release, the latest single by your favorite artist. Its label will be shiny and unmarked. Its bag will be pristine and uncreased. The vinyl itself will be unplayed and hopefully even untouched. And you're going to do your best to keep it that way.

Of course you'll play it, both sides a few times, and if it comes with a picture sleeve, doubtless you'll turn it over in your hands once or twice. But when you put it on the shelf, or in the box where you keep your records, it still looks as good as new.

In terms of grading your records – assessing their condition, and therefore determining their value according to a generally agreed upon scale – that is Near Mint. A record that has been played, inspected, enjoyed. But which could as easily pass for brand new.

It's an exacting condition, one that allows very little wriggle room. The slightest defect, the merest mark, will send its grade dropping back to Very Good Plus (a full explanation of grading points follows in this introduction), and from there you are on the slippery slope to what remains my own favorite description of a record, by any dealer, anywhere. "It'd be almost perfect if it hadn't been broken in half."

Near Mint is the state in which this volume values its contents.

Lower your sights to any of the grades beneath that, and you might well find bargains galore; but always remember this. A $50 single is only worth that $50 if it lives up to the $50 grade.

Below that, the value dips precipitously, and the piles of old singles, all priced for $1 in your local record store, are probably not worth much more than that. Likewise, the suitcase full of sleeveless oldies that lurks so invitingly in your grandparents' attic. There may well be some finds worth finding therein. There may even be some genuine rarities. But condition is often as important as the music.

Here's how to determine what shape your records are in.

There are eight basic points on the *Goldmine* grading scale—Mint (M), Near Mint (NM), Very Good Plus (VG+), Very Good (VG), Good Plus (G+), Good (G), Fair (F) and Poor (P). Some dealers may insert their own intermediary grades— Near Mint Minus (NM-), for example, or Very Good Double Plus (VG++) but these definitions vary from seller to seller.

Mint (M)

A single grading Mint should be absolutely perfect in every regard. The record has certainly never been played, and might (some collectors say should) never have been removed from its original bag – which itself will also be absolutely pristine. (Unlike LPs and CDs, regu-

lar 7-inch singles were very rarely sold "sealed"; however, 7-inch EPs often were.)

That said, there can be no guarantee against flaws in the actual manufacture of a record, be it an audible pop or a visual smear – either of which could conspire to reduce the grade a little. "Mint," then, is the ultimate caveat emp-tor... Buyer Beware!

Near Mint (NM)

Near Mint is the grade that many dealers prefer to use, suggesting a record that is almost perfect. It is also the highest grade listed in all of the Goldmine price guides, with the understanding that any record that does exceed this standard will be worth significantly more than its stated value.

What can you expect from a Near Mint record? Near-perfection. It may possess the odd minor defect—a tiny (read all-but-invisible) trace of ring wear to the cover, the odd stray fingerprint or, where EPs are concerned, a few silvery lines around the spindle hole in the center of the record.

What there should not be are creases, folds, tears, splits, scratches, scribbles, dings or clicks. If the record was sold with a picture sleeve, it will be present; if it was sold without, it will still be in its original packaging, whether that be a plain sleeve or a company one. In other words, there will be no overt indication whatsoever that

this is anything but a new record that somebody opened before you received it.

Very Good Plus (VG+)

Singles graded as Very Good Plus are generally valued at around 50% of the Near Mint value, the record will clearly have been played and otherwise handled by a previous owner, but it will also have been very well looked after. There may be some visible flaws—scuffs or surface scratches that cannot be felt with a fingertip, but these will not be audible.

A slight warp may be present, but again, it will not affect the music. There will be some wear to the label, and with EPs, more of those silvery lines, but the spindle hole itself will not appear misshapen from repeated plays. The sleeve may show some wear, but nothing that really detracts from its original appearance. Think of it as Near Mint with a few problems.

Very Good (VG)

A single in Very Good condition amplifies the problems found in VG+, and tends to be worth around 25% of the Near Mint value. Expect to hear surface noise in places, particularly during the quieter moments, or during the intro or outro, and scratches elsewhere will be audible. But the record will not skip, and none of these extraneous sounds will overpower the sound of the music itself.

Sure signs of a previous owner will be visible—writing, tape or stickers on either the label or the cover, although not necessarily to the detriment of either—a name written carefully in the top corner of the back cover, for example. (But not an artist's autograph. Personally signed picture sleeves can withstand almost any amount of abuse for as long as the autograph itself remains intact… and genuine. For in these instances, it is oftentimes not the record being sold. It is the signature.)

There will be further wear to the label, and to the picture sleeve, if there is one—the edges will no longer be clean, the seams may show some wear. If there is no picture sleeve, do not expect an original company bag - a generic one, or another label's offering, pulled at random, is more likely. It's still a good looking, nice sounding record, but it once looked and sounded much better.

Very Good Minus (VG-),
Good Plus (G+), Good (G),

Valued at between ten and fifteen percent of the Near Mint value, singles in these grades will continue to amplify the aforementioned problems. Scratches and surface noise will be louder, the grooves will look worn, and there will be some deterioration in the sound. Any picture sleeve will be tatty, with split seams; and any amount of writing might now adorn it.

The record should, however, still be playable; and, if that is all you want it fordo not pass it by. You are unlikely even to recoup the purchase price if and when you come to sell it, but you will still enjoy hearing it.

Poor (P) or Fair (F)

This is the lowest grade. The record will be scratched to pieces, possibly cracked, maybe warped, and will not play through without skipping or sticking.

The tattered, battered sleeve will scarcely hold the record any longer, and might well show signs of some other near-calamity—water damage, for example, or cigarette burns. Nothing about this record recommends itself to a purchaser… unless, of course, you want it. In which case, five percent of its NM value is the maximum you should pay.

Unless, of course, you really want it.

Records Not Included Here

We really have done our best, but the chances are, if you have a large collection, or a particularly specialized one, there will be records that you own which are not featured in this edition.

We will overlook those foreign releases that were discussed earlier this section. To qualify for inclusion in this book, a record must be an official US release. It must have a minimum Near Mint value of $3 and, ultimately, it must adhere to certain (and we will admit it, somewhat random) interpretations of collectibility.

Children's records, for example, are largely omitted – with but a few exceptions, that is a market that has never caught the adult collector's imagination (juvenile collectors, on the other hand, might well disagree), with the result that many record stores will not even accept them for sale, and those that do will have them heaped unwanted for years to come.

Classical 45s, again with a few exceptions, are likewise overlooked - as indeed they were upon release. For reasons that should be apparent to all, classical collectors require full performances of the works they pursue. Three minute extracts rarely interested them back then, and they remain of minimal value today.

Various artist EPs, and budget-priced anonymous cover versions of hit songs also lurk beyond the parameters of this volume. The latter certainly have their fans, but they are few and far between; and besides, even among that number, values tend to be all but negligible.

Other omissions will be noted; many, however, will be documented elsewhere within the Goldmine family of price guides, including specialist guides to country, jazz, promos and doo-wop, and the all-encompassing Standard Catalogue of American Records. However, it is also possible, as stated before, that the record has simply evaded our attentions altogether, so please let us know if you come across such a thing.

Number	Title	Yr	NM

A

A.B. SKHY
MGM

Number	Title	Yr	NM
❑ K14086	Camel Back/Just What I Need	1969	$8
❑ K14086 [PS]	Camel Back/Just What I Need	1969	$15

A-HA
WARNER BROS.

Number	Title	Yr	NM
❑ 7-28500	Cry Wolf/Maybe Maybe	1987	$3
❑ 7-28500 [PS]	Cry Wolf/Maybe Maybe	1987	$3
❑ 7-28684	Hunting High and Low/And You Tell Me (Demo Version)	1986	$4
❑ 7-28684 [PS]	Hunting High and Low/And You Tell Me (Demo Version)	1986	$4
❑ 7-28594	I've Been Losing You/This Alone Is Love	1986	$4
❑ 7-28594 [PS]	I've Been Losing You/This Alone Is Love	1986	$4
❑ 7-27886	Stay on These Roads/You'll End Up Crying	1988	$5
❑ 7-27886 [PS]	Stay on These Roads/You'll End Up Crying	1988	$5
❑ 7-29011	Take On Me/Love Is Reason	1985	$4
❑ 7-29011 [PS]	Take On Me/Love Is Reason	1985	$4
❑ 7-29011 [PS]	Take On Me/Love Is Reason	1985	$20

—*Promo-only comic book gatefold sleeve*

Number	Title	Yr	NM
❑ 7-28305	The Living Daylights/(instrumental)	1987	$5
❑ 7-28305 [PS]	The Living Daylights/(instrumental)	1987	$10

—*Sought-after by European collectors because it has a different picture sleeve than its European counterparts*

Number	Title	Yr	NM
❑ 7-28846	The Sun Always Shines on T.V./Driftwood	1985	$4
❑ 7-28846 [PS]	The Sun Always Shines on T.V./Driftwood	1985	$4

ABACO DREAM
A&M

Number	Title	Yr	NM
❑ 1160	Another Night of Love/Chocolate Pudding	1970	$8
❑ 1081	Life and Death in G and A/Cat Woman	1969	$8

ABBA
ATLANTIC

Number	Title	Yr	NM
❑ 3629	Chiquitita/Lovelight	1979	$4
❑ 3630	Chiquitita (Spanish Version)/I Have a Dream (Spanish Version)	1979	$5
❑ 3372	Dancing Queen/That's Me	1976	$4
❑ 3574	Does Your Mother Know/Kisses of Fire	1979	$4
❑ 3574 [PS]	Does Your Mother Know/Kisses of Fire	1979	$6
❑ 3346	Fernando/Rock Me	1976	$4
❑ 3346	Fernando/Tropical Loveland	1976	$4
❑ 3652	Gimme! Gimme! Gimme! (A Man After Midnight)/The King Has Lost His Crown	1980	$4
❑ PR390 [DJ]	Happy New Year	1980	$15

—*One-sided promo*

Number	Title	Yr	NM
❑ PR380 [DJ]	Happy New Year (mono/stereo)	1980	$15
❑ 3240	Hasta Manana/Ring Ring	1975	$5
❑ 3209	Honey Honey/Dance (While the Music Still Goes On)	1974	$5
❑ 3310	I Do, I Do, I Do, I Do, I Do/Bang-a-Boomerang	1975	$5
❑ 3315	Mamma Mia/Tropical Loveland	1976	$5
❑ 3434	Money, Money, Money/Crazy World	1977	$4
❑ 3826	On and On and On/Lay All Your Love on Me	1981	$4
❑ 89881	One of Us/Should I Laugh or Cry	1983	$3
❑ 89881 [PS]	One of Us/Should I Laugh or Cry	1983	$4
❑ 3265	SOS/Man in the Middle	1975	$5
❑ 3806	Super Trouper/The Piper	1981	$4
❑ 3806 [PS]	Super Trouper/The Piper	1981	$4
❑ 3457	Take a Chance on Me/I'm a Marionette	1978	$4
❑ 3457 [PS]	Take a Chance on Me/I'm a Marionette	1978	$6
❑ 89948	The Day Before You Came/Cassandra	1982	$3
❑ 3776	The Winner Takes It All/Elaine	1980	$4
❑ 3035 [PS]	Waterloo	1974	$20

—*Sleeve is promo only*

Number	Title	Yr	NM
❑ 3035	Waterloo/Watch Out	1974	$5
❑ 3889	When All Is Said and Done/Should I Laugh or Cry	1982	$3
❑ 3889 [PS]	When All Is Said and Done/Should I Laugh or Cry	1982	$3

CBS INTERNATIONAL

Number	Title	Yr	NM
❑ DAS40003 [DJ]	Dame! Dame! Dame!/Gracias Por La Musica	1980	$30

—*The above three are in Spanish, pressed in the U.S. for Hispanic markets; we don't know if stock copies exist*

Number	Title	Yr	NM
❑ DAS40001 [DJ]	Estoy Sonando/Conociendome, Conociendote	1980	$30
❑ DAS40002 [DJ]	Fernando/Al Andar	1980	$30

ABBEY TAVERN SINGERS, THE
HANNA-BARBERA

Number	Title	Yr	NM
❑ 498	Off to Dublin in the Green/The Gallant Forty Twa'	1966	$8

ABBOTT, BILLY, AND THE JEWELS
PARKWAY

Number	Title	Yr	NM
❑ 874	Groovy Baby/Come On Dance with Me	1963	$30
❑ 905	It Isn't Fair/Hey, Good Lookin'	1964	$30

ABBOUD, MONA
PHONOGRAPH

Number	Title	Yr	NM
❑ 100180	The Pretty Little Dolly/I Should've Left The Lites On For Santa	1980	$8

—*Original with green label and red print*

ABDUL, PAULA

Number	Title	Yr	NM
❑ 99282	(It's Just) The Way That You Love Me/(It's Just) The Way That You Love Me (Dub)	1988	$4

—*Originals on black labels*

Number	Title	Yr	NM
❑ 99282	(It's Just) The Way That You Love Me/(It's Just) The Way That You Love Me (Dub)	1988	$3

—*Second pressing on orange labels*

Number	Title	Yr	NM
❑ 99282 [PS]	(It's Just) The Way That You Love Me/(It's Just) The Way That You Love Me (Dub)	1988	$4
❑ 99256	Straight Up/Cold Hearted	1988	$4
❑ 99256	Straight Up/Straight Up (Power Mix)	1988	$3

ABDULLAH
SOUL

Number	Title	Yr	NM
❑ 35051	I Coma Zimba Zio (Here I Stand, The Mighty One)/Why Them, Why Me	1968	$6

ABEL, ALAN
MGM

Number	Title	Yr	NM
❑ 11898	The Story of Santa Claus/Santa and the Doodle-Li-Boop	1954	$30

ABERNATHY, MACK
CMI

Number	Title	Yr	NM
❑ 1988-9	Different Situations/Dos Hermanos Cantina	1988	$6
❑ 1988-8	Slippin' Around/Pocket Rocket Ranger	1988	$6

ABRAHAM AND HIS SONS
REVUE

Number	Title	Yr	NM
❑ 11059	I Can't Do Without You/Your Mother Understood	1970	$60

ABSTRACK REALITY
SPORT

Number	Title	Yr	NM
❑ 104	Love Burns Like a Fire/(Instrumental)	1967	$200

ABSTRACTS, THE
POMPEII

Number	Title	Yr	NM
❑ 66679	Smell the Incense/See the Birdies	1968	$30

AC/DC
ATCO

Number	Title	Yr	NM
❑ 7068	High Voltage/It's a Long Way to the Top	1976	$8
❑ 7086	Problem Child/Let There Be Rock	1977	$8

ATLANTIC

Number	Title	Yr	NM
❑ 3787	Back in Black/What Do You Do for Money Honey	1980	$5
❑ 89532	Danger/Back in Business	1985	$3
❑ 89532 [PS]	Danger/Back in Business	1985	$6
❑ 89722	Flick of the Switch/Badlands	1983	$3
❑ 4029	For Those About to Rock We Salute You/T.N.T.	1982	$4
❑ 4029 [PS]	For Those About to Rock We Salute You/T.N.T.	1982	$8
❑ 89774	Guns for Hire/Landslide	1983	$4
❑ 89136	Heatseeker/Go Zone	1988	$3
❑ 89136 [PS]	Heatseeker/Go Zone	1988	$4
❑ 3617	Highway to Hell/Night Prowler	1979	$6
❑ 3894	Let's Get It Up/Snowballed	1982	$4
❑ 89098	The Way I Wanna Rock 'N' Roll/Kissin' Dynamite	1988	$3
❑ 3644	Touch Too Much/Walk All Over You	1980	$5
❑ 3553	Whole Lotta Rosie/Hell Ain't a Bad Place to Be	1979	$6
❑ 89425	Who Made Who/Guns for Hire (Live)	1986	$3
❑ 89425 [PS]	Who Made Who/Guns for Hire (Live)	1986	$6

ACADEMICS, THE
ANCHO

Number	Title	Yr	NM
❑ 100	At My Front Door/Darla, My Darling	1957	$100
❑ 101	Too Good to Be True/Heavenly Love	1957	$125

—*Reissue of Anchor 101*

ANCHOR

Number	Title	Yr	NM
❑ 101	Too Good to Be True/Heavenly Love	1957	$1000

—*Original edition*

ELMONT

Number	Title	Yr	NM
❑ 1001/2	Drive-In Movie/Something Cool	1958	$70

ACCENTS, THE
BANGAR

Number	Title	Yr	NM
❑ 629	Searchin'/You Don't Love Me	1964	$20
❑ 605	Wherever There's a Will/Howlin' for My Baby	1964	$20

BRUNSWICK

Number	Title	Yr	NM
❑ 55123	I Give My Heart to You/Ching-a-Ling	1959	$20
❑ 55100	Wiggle Waggle/Dreamin' and Schemin'	1958	$20

CHALLENGE

Number	Title	Yr	NM
❑ 59294	Sweet Talk/Tell Me	1965	$15
❑ 59254	Tell Me/Better Watch Out Boy	1964	$20

CHARTER

Number	Title	Yr	NM
❑ 1017	I've Got Better Things to Do/Then He Starts to Cry	1964	$20

—*Featuring Sandi*

COMMERCE

Number	Title	Yr	NM
❑ 5012	Tell Me/Better Watch Out Boy	1964	$30

CORAL

Number	Title	Yr	NM
❑ 62151	Autumn Leaves/Anything You Want Me to Be	1959	$20

C-R-C

Number	Title	Yr	NM
❑ 1017	I've Got Better Things to Do/Then He Starts to Cry	1964	$30

—*Featuring Sandi*

GARRETT

Number	Title	Yr	NM
❑ 4008	Wherever There's a Will/Howlin' for My Baby	1964	$30

JERDEN

Number	Title	Yr	NM
❑ 728	Linda Lou/Stickey	1964	$15

—*Featuring Ron Peterson*

KARATE

Number	Title	Yr	NM
❑ 529	He's the One/On the Run	1966	$20

LIBERTY

Number	Title	Yr	NM
❑ 55813	I Really Love You/What Do You Want to Do (Little Darlin')	1965	$15

MERCURY

Number	Title	Yr	NM
❑ 72154	Enchanted Garden/Tell Me Now	1963	$12

RCA VICTOR

Number	Title	Yr	NM
❑ 74-0127	Love Is a Many-Splendored Thing/Yours Until Tomorrow	1969	$6

VEE JAY

Number	Title	Yr	NM
❑ 484	Our Wonderful Love/A Hundred Walkin' Cats	1963	$8

Number	Title	Yr	NM

ACE
ANCHOR
❏ 21000	How Long/Sniffin' About	1975	$5

ACE IN THE HOLE BAND
❏ 1316	I Don't Want to Talk It Over Anymore/Loneliest Singer in Town	1979	$40
❏ 1309	I Just Can't Go On Dying Like This/Honky Tonk Downstairs	1978	$60
❏ 1313	The Way I Feel About You/ Lonesome Rodeo Cowboy	1978	$50

ACE, JOHNNY
DUKE
❏ 144	Anymore/How Can You Be So Mean	1955	$50
❏ 107	Cross My Heart/Angel	1953	$70
❏ 102	My Song/Follow the Rule	1952	$100
❏ 128	Please Forgive Me/You've Been Gone So Long	1954	$50
❏ 136	Pledging My Love/Anymore	1954	$50
❏ 136	Pledging My Love/No Money	1954	$50
❏ 118	Saving My Love for You/Yes Baby	1953	$50
❏ 148	So Lonely/I'm Crazy	1956	$40
❏ 154	Still Love You So/ Don't You Know	1956	$40
❏ 112	The Clock/Ace's Wild	1953	$70
FLAIR
❏ 1015	Midnight Hours Journey/ Trouble and Me	1953	$200

— *B-side by Earl Forrest*

7-Inch Extended Plays
DUKE
❏ 80 [PS]	Memorial Album	1955	$175
❏ 80	Pledging My Love/Saving My Love for You//Angel/ Please Forgive Me	1955	$175
❏ 81	The Clock/Never Let Me Go// Cross My Heart/My Song	1955	$175
❏ 81 [PS]	Tribute to Johnny Ace	1955	$175

ACE, SONNY
ATLANTIC
❏ 2364	Wooleh Booleh/Chili Peppers	1966	$10

ACE SPECTRUM
ATLANTIC
❏ 3012	Don't Send Nobody Else/Don't Let Me Be Lonely Tonight	1974	$60
❏ 3353	Live and Learn/Just Like in the Movies	1976	$30
❏ 3281	Trust Me/I Just Want to Spend the Night with You	1975	$30
❏ 3296	Without You/Keep Holding On	1975	$50

ACKLIN, BARBARA
BRUNSWICK
❏ 55421	After You/More Ways Than One	1969	$8
❏ 55399	Am I the Same Girl/ Be By My Side	1969	$8
❏ 55319	Fool, Fool, Fool (Look in the Mirror)/Your Sweet Loving	1967	$8
❏ 55486	I Call It Trouble/Love You Are Mine Today	1972	$8
❏ 55447	I Can't Do My Thing/Make the Man Love You	1971	$8
❏ 55440	I Did It/I'm Living with a Memory	1970	$8
❏ 55501	I'm Gonna Bake a Man/I Call It Trouble	1973	$6
❏ 55433	Is It Me/Someone Else's Arms	1970	$8
❏ 55355	I've Got You Baby/ Old Matchmaker	1967	$8
❏ 55465	Lady, Lady, Lady/Stop, Look and Listen	1971	$8
❏ 55379	Love Makes a Woman/ Come and See My Baby	1968	$8
❏ 55412	Seven Days of Night/ Raggedy Ride	1969	$8
CAPITOL
❏ 4061	Give Me Some of Your Sweet Love/Fire Love	1975	$5
❏ 4013	Special Loving/You Gave Him Everything, But I Gave Him Love	1974	$5

ACORNS, THE
UNART
❏ 2006	Angel/I'm Gonna Stick to You	1958	$30
❏ 2015	Please Come Back/ Your Name and Mine	1959	$30

ACUFF, ROY, JR., AND SUE THOMPSON
HICKORY
❏ 1573	Don't Let the Stars Get In Your Eyes/Why You Been Gone	1970	$8
❏ 1558	Talk Back Trembling Lips/ Till I Can't Take It Anymore	1970	$8
❏ 1542	Thoughts/Are You Teasing Me	1969	$10

ACUFF, ROY, JR.
HICKORY
❏ 1476	As Long As I Live/ You, You, You, You	1967	$10
❏ 1349	Baby Just Said Goodbye/ Wabash Cannonball	1965	$12
❏ 1583	Back Down to Atlanta/Outlaw	1970	$8
❏ 1515	Blue Train (Of the Heartbreak Line)/Thru the Windows of Your House	1968	$10
❏ 1398	I Wish It Were Me/Turn That Frown Upside Down	1966	$10
❏ 1551	Looks Like Baby's Gone/ Through the Windows of Your Mind	1969	$10
❏ 1425	Looks Like the Sun Ain't Gonna Shine/Victim of Circumstances	1966	$15

— *As "Roy Junior*

❏ 1505	My World Has Stopped/ Follow Your Drum	1968	$10
❏ 1371	Stand Tall/You Won't Ever See Me Here Again	1966	$10
❏ 1535	The Guy Who Played Bass (So Well in Harlin Mason's Band)/ The Luckiest Guy in the World	1969	$10
❏ 1456	The Lament of the Cherokee Reservation Indian/The Luckiest Guy in the World	1967	$15

HICKORY/MGM
❏ 358	Baby, Maybe, Some Day/ When She's Thirty	1975	$6
❏ 321	California Lady/Take Me Back	1974	$6
❏ 331	Don't Worry 'Bout the Mule/ Precious Memories	1974	$6
❏ 344	Good Morning Country Rain/ Sittin' Around the Campfire	1975	$6
❏ 351	Good Time and T-Bird Wine/Turpentine Blues	1975	$6

ACUFF, ROY
CAPITOL
❏ F3064	Don't Judge Your Neighbors/ Thief Upon the Tree	1955	$30
❏ F2548	Don't Say Goodbye/Sixteen Chickens and a Tambourine	1953	$30
❏ F2901	I'm Planting a Rose/ Streamlined Heartbreaker	1954	$30
❏ F3209	Little Moses/Oh Those Tombs	1955	$30
❏ F2460	Lonesome Joe/Is It Love or Is It Lies?	1953	$30
❏ F2820	Sunshine Special/I Closed My Heart's Door	1954	$30
❏ F2642	Swamp Lily/Sweep Around Your Own Back Door	1953	$30
❏ F3115	That's What Makes the Juke Box Play/Night Spots	1955	$30
❏ F2385	What Will I Do/Tied Down	1953	$30
COLUMBIA
❏ 4-20858	Advice to Joe/When My Money Ran Out	1951	$40
❏ 4-20792	A Plastic Heart/Your Address Unknown	1951	$40
❏ 4-20951	Cheating/Don't Hang Your Dirty Linen on the Line	1952	$30
❏ 4-20828	Doug MacArthur/In the Shadow of the Smokies	1951	$40
❏ 2-357	Lonesome Old River Blues/ It's Just About Time	1949	$50

— *Microgroove 33 1/3 rpm 7-inch single*

❏ 4-20804	Pliney Jane/Baldknob, Arkansas	1951	$40
❏ 4-20912	Ten Little Numbers/My Tears Don't Show	1952	$30
❏ 2-483	The Day They Laid Mary Away/It's All Right Now	1950	$50

— *Microgroove 33 1/3 rpm 7-inch single*

❏ 4-21018	Wonder Is All I Do/She Isn't Guaranteed	1952	$30
DECCA
❏ 9-29748	Crazy Worried Mind/ Along the China Coast	1955	$30
❏ 9-29935	Goodbye Mr. Brown/ Mother Hold Me Tight	1956	$30

— *With Kitty Wells*

❏ 9-30141	I Like Mountain Music/ It's Hard to Love	1956	$30
ELEKTRA
❏ 69937	Fireball Mail/The Stage	1982	$5

— *B-side by Boxcar Willie*

❏ 46515	Freight Train Blues/Don't Worry 'Bout the Walk	1979	$5
❏ 47040	I Can't Help It (If I'm Still in Love with You)/Cold, Cold Heart	1980	$5
❏ 47480	Smokey Mountain Memories/What Have They Done to Them	1982	$5
❏ 45515	That's the Man I'm Looking For/(B-side unknown)	1978	$5
HICKORY
❏ 1636	A Pale Horse and His Ride/ Sing a Country Song	1972	$8
❏ 1097	Come and Knock (On the Door of My Heart)/My Love Came Back to Me	1959	$20
❏ 1519	Don't Be Angry/The Nearest Thing to Heaven Is You	1968	$12
❏ 1113	Don't Know Why/Thanks for Not Telling Me	1960	$15
❏ 1206	Don't Make Me Go to Bed and I'll Be Good/Pins and Needles (In My Heart)	1963	$15
❏ 1271	Do You Wonder Why/Things That Might Have Been	1964	$12
❏ 1191	Fireball Mail/The Great Speckled Bird	1962	$15
❏ 1291	Freight Train Blues/All the World Is Lonely Now	1965	$10
❏ 1394	Golden Treasure/Lost Highway	1966	$10
❏ 1497	I'll Go On Alone/Uncle Pen	1967	$10
❏ 1479	I Love You Because/I'm Movin' On	1967	$10
❏ 1331	I'm Planning a Rose/ Tennessee Central	1965	$10
❏ 1581	Life to Go/Each Season Changes You	1970	$8
❏ 1316	Life to Go/Rising Sun	1965	$12
❏ 1149	Little Mary/Lost John, He's Gone	1961	$15
❏ 1244	Low and Lonely/ Wabash Cannonball	1964	$10
❏ 1134	Mountain Guitar/Till No Longer You Care (For Me)	1960	$15
❏ 1073	Once More/I Don't Care (If You Don't Love Me)	1958	$20
❏ 1365	Pan American/Don't Tell Mama	1966	$10
❏ 1644	Satisfied Mind/Just a Friend	1973	$8
❏ 1160	Six More Days/Willie Boy, The Crippled Boy	1962	$15
❏ 1090	So Many Times/They'll Never Take Her Love from Me	1958	$20
❏ 1627	Somebody Touched Me/Carry Me Back to the Mountains	1972	$8
❏ 1142	Streamlined Cannon Ball/ Time Will Make You Pay	1961	$15
❏ 1223	The Great Titanic/The Birmingham Jail	1963	$15
❏ 1081	The One I Love (Is Gone)/ Searchin' for Happiness	1958	$20
❏ 1178	Wabash Cannonball/Old Age Pension Check	1962	$15
HICKORY/MGM
❏ 348	A Whole Month of Sundays/I Can't Find a Train	1975	$6
❏ 336	Back Down to Atlanta/A Most Reasonable Guy	1974	$6
❏ 314	Back in the Country/Jole Blon	1974	$6
❏ 341	Fireball Mail/Roof Top Lullaby	1975	$6
❏ 319	Old Time Sunshine Song/ This World Can't Stand Long	1974	$6
❏ 355	That's Country/Take Me Home, Country Roads	1975	$6
❏ 362	Walk a Mile in Your Neighbor's Shoes/Waltz in the Wind	1975	$6

AD LIBS, THE
BLUE CAT
❏ 114	Ask Anybody/He Ain't No Angel	1965	$12
❏ 119	On the Corner/Oo-Wee Oh Me Oh My	1965	$10
❏ 102	The Boy from New York City/Kicked Around	1965	$20
CAPITOL
❏ 2944	Love Me/Know All About You	1970	$6
KAREN
❏ 1527	Think of Me/Every Boy and Girl	1966	$30
PHILIPS
❏ 40461	Don't Ever Leave Me/ You're in Love	1967	$8
SHARE
❏ 104	Giving Up/Appreciation	1969	$8
❏ 106	The Boy from New York City/Nothing Worse Than Being Alone	1969	$8

ADAM AND THE ANTS
EPIC
❏ 19-02042	Antmusic/Don't Be Square (Be There)	1981	$5
❏ AE71236 [DJ]	Stand and Deliver/ Beat My Guest	1981	$3
❏ AE71236 [PS]	Stand and Deliver/ Beat My Guest	1981	$3

Number	Title	Yr	NM
ADAM, MIKE AND TIM			
PRESS			
❏ 9728	Little Baby/You're the Reason Why	1964	$12
ADAM'S APPLES			
BRUNSWICK			
❏ 55330	Don't Take It Out on This World/Don't You Want Me Home	1967	$125
ADAMS, ART			
CHERRY			
❏ 1018	Dancing Doll/She Don't Live Here Anymore	1960	$125
ADAMS, BILLY			
APT			
❏ 25072	My Happiness/Big M	1962	$15
CAPITOL			
❏ 4373	Can't Get Enough/The Gods Were Angry With Me	1960	$30
❏ 4308	Count Every Star/Peggy's Party	1959	$30
DECCA			
❏ 30724	Baby I'm Bugged/Short Hair and Turtle Neck Sweater	1958	$40
FERN			
❏ 813	Comic Strip/Call Me	1961	$30
❏ 807	Darling Take My Hand/Tender Years	1961	$30
❏ 808	Tattle Tale/Born to Be a Loser	1961	$30
HOME OF THE BLUES			
❏ 239	Looking for My Baby/Had the Blues	1962	$10
❏ 242	My Happiness/Big M	1962	$30
NAU VOO			
❏ 808	Blue Eyed Ella/Fun House	1959	$80
SUN			
❏ 389	Got My Mojo Workin'/Betty and Dupree	1964	$30
❏ 401	Open the Door, Richard/Rock Me Baby	1966	$30
❏ 391	Trouble in My Mind/Lookin' for Mary Ann	1964	$30
ADAMS, BRYAN			
A&M			
❏ 8651	Christmas Time/Reggae Christmas	1985	$5
—*Red custom label; green vinyl*			
❏ 8651 [PS]	Christmas Time/Reggae Christmas	1985	$6
—*Package" sleeve*			
❏ 8651 [PS]	Christmas Time/Reggae Christmas	1986	$5
—*Sleeve with winter scene*			
❏ 2409	Coming Home/Fits Ya Good	1982	$8
❏ 2553	Cuts Like a Knife/Lonely Nights	1983	$4
❏ 2553 [PS]	Cuts Like a Knife/Lonely Nights	1983	$4
❏ 2249 [DJ]	Give Me Your Love (stereo/mono)	1980	$5
❏ 2249	Give Me Your Love/Wait and See	1980	$10
❏ 2948	Hearts on Fire/The Best Is Yet to Come	1987	$3
❏ 2948 [PS]	Hearts on Fire/The Best Is Yet to Come	1987	$3
❏ 2921 [DJ]	Heat of the Night (4:21) (same on both sides)	1987	$8
—*A 5:07 version appeared on the stock 45s*			
❏ 2921	Heat of the Night/Another Day	1987	$3
❏ 2921 [PS]	Heat of the Night/Another Day	1987	$3
❏ 2729	Heaven/Heaven "Live	1985	$3
❏ 2729 [PS]	Heaven/Heaven "Live	1985	$4
❏ 8653	Heaven/Summer of '69	1985	$3
—*'A&M Memories" reissue*			
❏ 2220 [DJ]	Hidin' from Love (stereo/mono)	1980	$6
❏ 2220	Hidin' from Love/Wait and See	1980	$12
❏ 2791	It's Only Love/The Only One	1985	$3
—*A-side with Tina Turner*			
❏ 2791 [PS]	It's Only Love/The Only One	1985	$3
—*A-side: With Tina Turner*			
❏ 2163	Let Me Take You Dancing/Don't Turn Away	1979	$40
❏ 2163 [DJ]	Let Me Take You Dancing (stereo/mono)	1979	$15

Number	Title	Yr	NM
❏ 2359	Lonely Nights/Don't Look Now	1981	$10
❏ 2359 [DJ]	Lonely Nights (stereo/mono)	1981	$6
❏ 8654	One Night Love Affair/It's Only Love	1985	$3
—*A&M Memories" reissue; B-side with Tina Turner*			
❏ 2770	One Night Love Affair/Lonely Nights	1985	$3
❏ 2770 [PS]	One Night Love Affair/Lonely Nights	1985	$3
❏ 2701	Somebody/Long Gone	1984	$3
❏ 2701 [PS]	Somebody/Long Gone	1984	$4
❏ 8645	Straight from the Heart/Cuts Like a Knife	1985	$3
—*A&M Memories" reissue*			
❏ 2536	Straight from the Heart/One Good Reason	1983	$4
❏ 2536 [PS]	Straight from the Heart/One Good Reason	1983	$4
❏ 2739	Summer of '69/The Best Was Yet to Come	1985	$3
❏ 2739 [PS]	Summer of '69/The Best Was Yet to Come	1985	$3
❏ 2606	The Best Was Yet to Come/I'm Ready	1983	$4
❏ 2574	This Time/Fits Ya Good	1983	$4
❏ 2574 [PS]	This Time/Fits Ya Good	1983	$5
ADAMS, CHARLIE			
COLUMBIA			
❏ 4-21355	Cat'n Around/A Man Was the Cause of It All	1955	$30
❏ 4-21401	Flower of My Heart/Hidin' Out	1955	$30
❏ 4-21300	Gee, But It's Dry in Texas/Waltzing with Sin	1954	$30
❏ 4-21195	Hey Liberace/Will You Love Me When I'm Old	1954	$30
❏ 4-21230	I'll Tickle Your Toeses/You've Wounded the Heart	1954	$30
❏ 4-21443	Pistol Packin' Mama/They Can't Make a Devil Out of My Angel	1955	$30
❏ 4-21524	Sugar Diet/Black Land Blues	1956	$30
DECCA			
❏ 9-46335	If a Beer Bottle Had a Nipple On It/You're Getting Too Old	1951	$30
❏ 9-46391	I Lost an Angel/Without You I'm Lost	1952	$30
❏ 9-46358	I'm Gonna Love You Pretty Baby/I'm Gonna Put My Foot Down	1951	$40
❏ 9-46373	Stop Your Bawlin' Baby/Give Me Back My Kisses	1951	$30
ADAMS, CLIFF			
DOT			
❏ 16385	Funny Kind of Feeling/Keep Off My Mountain	1962	$10
ADAMS, DON			
ATLANTIC			
❏ 4017	Baby Let Your Long Hair Down/Little Girl Blue	1974	$5
❏ 4002	I'll Be Satisfied/All for the Love of a Girl	1973	$5
❏ 4009	I've Already Stayed Too Long/Oh What a Future She Had	1973	$5
❏ 4027	That's Love/I Just Lost My Favorite Girl	1974	$5
JACK O' DIAMONDS			
❏ 1004	Brand New Bed of Roses/Tear Talk	1967	$10
❏ 1015	I Miss You/Just Say You Love Me	1968	$10
❏ 1003	Plant a Little Heartache/Why I Still Love You	1967	$10
❏ 1002	Two of the Usual/Wake Me 100 Years from Now	1967	$10
MUSICOR			
❏ 1136	Big Town Baby/There Are Some Things	1965	$10
❏ 1078	Heartaches Deep in Sorrow/Kill Me with Kindness	1965	$12
❏ 1172	Heartaches Morning, Noon and Night/Painting Pictures	1966	$8
ADAMS, FAYE			
ATLANTIC			
❏ 1007	Sweet Talk/Watch Out, I Told You	1953	$60
HERALD			
❏ 457	Angels Tell Me/Tag Along	1955	$30
❏ 444	Anything for a Friend/Your Love Has My Heart Burning	1955	$30
❏ 489	Anytime, Anyplace, Anywhere/The Hammer Keeps Knockin'	1956	$30
❏ 434	Hurts Me to My Heart/Ain't Gonna Tell	1954	$30
❏ 419	I'll Be True/Happiness to My Soul	1953	$30
❏ 439	I Owe My Heart to You/Love Ain't Nothin' to Play With	1954	$30

Number	Title	Yr	NM
❏ 423	Say a Prayer/Every Day	1954	$30
❏ 512	Shake a Hand/I'll Be True	1958	$30
❏ 416	Shake a Hand/I've Got to Leave You	1953	$40
—*Black vinyl*			
❏ 416	Shake a Hand/I've Got to Leave You	1953	$125
—*Red vinyl*			
❏ 429	Somebody, Somewhere, Someday/Crazy Mixed-Up World	1954	$30
❏ 480	Takin' You Back/Don't Forget to Smile	1956	$30
❏ 470	Teen-Age Heart/Witness to the Crime	1956	$30
IMPERIAL			
❏ 5471	I Have a Twinkle in My Eye/Someone Like You	1957	$30
❏ 5525	When We Kiss/Everything	1958	$30
LIDO			
❏ 606	It Can't Be Wrong/I Waited So Long	1960	$15
❏ 603	That's All Right/It Made Me Cry	1960	$15
SAVOY			
❏ 1606	Cry, You Crazy Heart/Step Up and Rescue Me	1960	$15
WARWICK			
❏ 638	It Can't Be Wrong/It's Nice to Know	1961	$15
❏ 590	Shake a Hand/It Hurts to My Heart	1960	$15
ADAMS, GAYLE			
PRELUDE			
❏ 8046	Baby I Need Your Loving/(B-side unknown)	1982	$70
❏ 8040	Love Fever/(Instrumental)	1981	$4
❏ 8012	Stretch' In Out/Plain Out of Luck	1980	$5
ADAMS, J.T.			
REPUBLIC			
❏ 7020	Christmas Time Is the Best Time/It's Christmas Time	1952	$50
ADAMS, JERRI			
COLUMBIA			
❏ 4-40888	A Little Bit of Kindness/Suddenly (The Meeting)	1957	$15
❏ 4-40279	Alone Together/Two's a Crowd When Only One's in Love	1954	$20
❏ 4-41111	Every Night About This Time/My Heart Tells Me	1958	$15
❏ 4-40415	Guess I Had Too Much to Dream Last Night/Snow Dreams	1955	$20
❏ 4-40615	Happiness Is a Thing Called Joe/Take My Hand, Show Me the Way	1955	$20
❏ 4-40690	If I Forget You/Walk Fast	1956	$20
❏ 4-40992	Looking for Someone to Love/I'm All Right Now	1957	$15
FRATERNITY			
❏ F-874	Ivory Tower/All Around This Heart	1961	$10
7-Inch Extended Plays			
COLUMBIA			
❏ B-9162	(contents unknown)	1956	$15
❏ B-9162 [PS]	It's Cool Inside, Vol. 2	1956	$15
ADAMS, JOHNNY			
ARIOLA AMERICA			
❏ 7701	After All the Good Is Gone/Chasing Rainbows	1978	$5
❏ 7718	Selfish/One Fine Day	1978	$5
ATLANTIC			
❏ 2905	I Wish It Would Rain/You're a Lady	1972	$10
❏ 2834	More Than One Way/You Got Your Kind of Life to Live	1971	$10
❏ 2887	Salt of the Earth/I'll Carry You	1972	$10
GONE			
❏ 5147	Going to the City/I'm Grateful	1964	$60
MODERN			
❏ 1044	One Day/Your Kind of Love	1967	$20
PACEMAKER			
❏ 240	A Place Called Home/Spunky Onions	1965	$30
❏ 255	Let Them Talk/Operator	1965	$30
❏ 249	When I'll Stop Loving You/A Man Will Shed a Few Tears	1965	$30

Number	Title	Yr	NM
PAID			
❏ 117	I'm Afraid to Let You Into My Life/Hell Yes I Cheated	1981	$6
❏ 105	Love Me Now/I Only Want to Be with You	1980	$6
RIC			
❏ 986	A Losing Battle/Who's Gonna Love You	1962	$30
❏ 966	Bells Are Ringing/Teach Me to Forget	1960	$30
❏ 963	Come On/Nowhere to Go	1959	$30
❏ 983	I Solemnly Promise/Life Is Just a Struggle	1961	$30
❏ 961	I Won't Cry/Who Are You	1959	$30
❏ 971	Let the Wind Blow/Someone for Me	1960	$30
❏ 992	Showdown/Tra La La	1962	$30
❏ 980	Wedding Day/O, So Nice	1961	$30
❏ 797	Georgia Mountain Dew/Real Live Livin' Hurtin' Man	1970	$15
❏ 780	I Can't Be All Bad/In a Moment of Weakness	1969	$20
❏ 787	Proud Woman/Real Live Livin' Hurtin' Man	1970	$15

ADAMS, KAY

Number	Title	Yr	NM
CAPITOL			
❏ 3624	Hearts of Stone/I Can, I Can	1973	$8
❏ 3551	Step Aside Girl/Second Hand Sugar Spoon	1973	$8
KING			
❏ 1504	All Around the World/It Just Ain't Love	1955	$30
TOWER			
❏ 235	Anymore/Old Heart Get Ready	1966	$15
❏ 395	Big Mac/Get Out of My Heart	1968	$12
❏ 177	Don't Talk About Trouble to Me/Honky Tonk Heartaches	1965	$20
❏ 470	Good Morning Love/Too Used to Being with You	1969	$10
❏ 360	Husband Stealer/I Let a Stranger (Buy the Wine)	1967	$10
❏ 269	Little Pink Mack/That'll Be the Day	1966	$15
❏ 329	Six Days a-Waiting/Be Nice to Everybody	1967	$12
❏ 445	Someday Maybe You'll Appreciate Me/Gonna Have a Good Time	1968	$12
❏ 305	Trapped/Rocks in My Head	1967	$10
❏ 294	Where Did the Good Times Go/You Taught Me Everything I Know	1966	$10

ADAMS, NANCY

Number	Title	Yr	NM
BUENA VISTA			
❏ 495	Love/Robin Hood	1974	$8
MEGA			
❏ 0076	I'm Leaving You/Pretty Lies	1972	$8
MGM			
❏ 14059	California Dream Boy/One Tiny Taco	1969	$10
RCA VICTOR			
❏ 47-8650	I'm Gonna Build a Fence/Go On!	1965	$15
❏ 47-8410	Lipstick Paint a Smile on Me/I Wanna Hear It from You	1964	$15
❏ 47-8599	Love Is/Little Gold Screw	1965	$15

ADAMS, RICHIE

Number	Title	Yr	NM
BELTONE			
❏ 1011	Two Initials (In a Heart)/What Took You So Long	1961	$20
CONGRESS			
❏ 226	Are You Changing/The King	1964	$20
❏ 248	Every Window in the City/I Ain't Gonna Make It Without You	1965	$20
❏ 217	I Understand/Lookin' for the Blues	1964	$20
❏ 232	Slippin' Away/What Am I	1965	$20
IMPERIAL			
❏ 5856	It's Worth It/Test of Love	1962	$20
❏ 5838	My Prayer of Love/Pakistan	1962	$20
❏ 5806	Something Inside of Me Died/I Got Eyes	1962	$20
MCA			
❏ 41182	The Best of the Rest of Our Lives/Warm	1980	$4
P.I.P.			
❏ 6519	Mamacita/Lisa Lisa	1976	$4
RIBBON			
❏ 6913	Back to School/Don't Go, My Love, Don't Go	1960	$15

Number	Title	Yr	NM
❏ 6910	Lonely One/Tell Me Baby Did You Wait	1960	$15

ADAMS, RUSH

Number	Title	Yr	NM
KING			
❏ 1330	Arizona/Then I'll Be Happy	1954	$30
❏ 1321	Bluebirds Singing in the Rain/Just One Kiss Goodnight	1954	$30
❏ 1270	Counterfeit Heart/Crying for the Carolines	1953	$30
MGM			
❏ K11873	All of You/I Go Out of My Mind	1954	$30
❏ K12051	How Can I Forget/At Last We're Alone	1955	$30
❏ K12145	I Love You to the Point of No Return/Love Plays the Strings of a Banjo	1955	$30
❏ K11834	It Was So Beautiful/Love Can Make an Earthquake	1954	$30
❏ K11953	Only for You/The Rose in Her Hair	1955	$30
❏ K12299	The Best Things in Life Are Free/The Crazy Lips	1956	$20
❏ K12228	The Birds and the Bees/My Buddy's Girls	1956	$20
VIRGO			
❏ 1001	Perfection/Lover (Do You Really, Really Love Me)	1959	$20
ZEPHYR			
❏ 70-014	Dancing in the Streets/Kisses	1957	$30

ADDEO, NICKY

Number	Title	Yr	NM
MELODY			
❏ 1417	Where There Is Love/You Can Depend on Me	1964	$30
REVELATION			
❏ 7-101	Danny Boy/A Lovely Way to Spend An Evening	1964	$500
SAVOY			
❏ 200	Gloria/Bring Back Your Heart	1963	$200
—Black vinyl			
❏ 200	Gloria/Bring Back Your Heart	1963	$400
—Red vinyl			
❏ 200	Gloria/Bring Back Your Heart	1963	$300
—Green vinyl			
SELSOM			
❏ 104	Over the Rainbow/Fool #2	1965	$200

ADDERLEY, CANNONBALL

Number	Title	Yr	NM
BLUE NOTE			
❏ 1737	Autumn Leaves (Part 1)/Autumn Leaves (Part 2)	1959	$12
❏ 1739	One for Daddy-O (Part 1)/One for Daddy-O (Part 2)	1959	$10
❏ 1738	Somethin' Else (Part 1)/Somethin' Else (Part 2)	1959	$12
CAPITOL			
❏ 2698	Country Preacher/Hummin'	1970	$5
❏ 3041	Down in Black Bottom/Get Up Off Your Knees	1971	$5
❏ 5281	Goodbye Charlie/Little Boy with Sad Eyes	1964	$8
❏ 2299	Hamba Nami/Gumba Gumba	1968	$6
❏ 2798	Marabi/Oh Babe	1970	$5
❏ 5374	Matchmaker/Chavaleh	1965	$8
❏ 5648	Money in the Pocket/Hear Me Talking to You	1966	$6
❏ 2064	Oh Babe/Games	1967	$6
❏ 5457	Shake a Lady/Cyclops	1965	$8
❏ 5736	Sticks/Cannon's Theme	1966	$6
❏ 2939	The Price You Got to Pay to Be Free/Run Away Sunshine	1970	$5
❏ 5968	Walk Tall/Do, Do, Do	1967	$6
❏ 5877	Why Am I Treated So Bad/I'm On My Way	1967	$6
FANTASY			
❏ 706	Inside Straight/Saudade	1973	$5
MERCURY			
❏ 71712	Limehouse Blues/Stars Fell on Alabama	1960	$12
RIVERSIDE			
❏ 457	African Waltz/Kelly Blue	1961	$10
❏ 4528	Blue Brass Groove/This Here	1963	$8
❏ 4562	Brother John/Tengo Tango	1964	$8
❏ 4509	Gemini (Part 1)/Gemini (Part 2)	1962	$8
❏ 428	Poor Butterfly (Part 1)/Poor Butterfly (Part 2)	1958	$15
❏ 454	Sack of Woe (Part 1)/Sack of Woe (Part 2)	1960	$10
❏ 465	The Chant (Part 1)/The Chant (Part 2)	1961	$12

Number	Title	Yr	NM
❏ 443	The Word Song/Sassier	1959	$15
❏ 415	Things Are Getting Better (Part 1)/Things Are Getting Better (Part 2)	1958	$15
❏ 432	This Year (Part 1)/This Year (Part 2)	1959	$15

ADDERLEY, TOMMY

Number	Title	Yr	NM
MAR MAR			
❏ 314	Whole Lotta Shakin' Goin' On/I Just Don't Understand	1965	$30

ADDOTTA, KIP

Number	Title	Yr	NM
LAFF			
❏ 024	I Saw Daddy Kissing Santa Claus (same on both sides)	1984	$8

ADDRISI BROTHERS, THE

Number	Title	Yr	NM
BELL			
❏ 45434	Somebody Found Her/Who Do You Think I Am	1974	$4
BRAD			
❏ 03	I'll Be True/Everybody's Happy	1958	$40
BUDDAH			
❏ 579	Does She Do It Like She Dances/Baby, Love Is a Two-Way Street	1977	$4
❏ 566	Slow Dancin' Don't Turn Me On (Short)/Slow Dancin' Don't Turn Me On (Long)	1977	$5
COLUMBIA			
❏ 45705	Lifetime/I Can Count on You	1972	$5
❏ 45610	One Last Time/I Can Feel You	1972	$5
❏ 45521	We've Got to Get It On Again/You Make It All Worthwhile	1972	$5
DEL-FI			
❏ 4116	Cherrystone/Lilies Grow High	1959	$40
❏ 4130	Gonna See My Baby/Ven Ami	1959	$30
❏ 4125	It's Love/Back to the Old Salt Mine	1959	$40
❏ 4120	Saving My Kisses/Un Jarro	1959	$40
ELEKTRA			
❏ 47203	Honey Come Home/Red-Eye Flight	1981	$4
IMPERIAL			
❏ 5715	What a Night for Love/Poor Little Girls	1960	$30
POM POM			
❏ 4160	The Dance Is Over/Socialite	1962	$30
PRIVATE STOCK			
❏ 45,012	Wait for Me/You Made All the Difference	1975	$4
SCOTTI BROTHERS			
❏ 506	As Long As the Music Keeps Playing/(B-side unknown)	1979	$4
❏ 500	Ghost Dancer/Ghost Dancer	1979	$4
❏ 500 [PS]	Ghost Dancer/Ghost Dancer	1979	$6
—Promo-only title sleeve			
VALIANT			
❏ 6058	C'mon Home Baby/Little Miss Sad	1964	$20
❏ 6047	Love Me Baby/The Way You Look at Him	1964	$15
❏ 720	Mr. Love/Side by Side	1965	$15
WARNER BROS.			
❏ 5268	The Dance Is Over (Dance with Me)/Sleeping Beauty	1962	$20
❏ 7249	Time to Love/Good News	1968	$10

ADELPHIS, THE

Number	Title	Yr	NM
RIM			
❏ 2020	Darlin' It's You/Kathleen	1958	$200
—Artist's name listed as "Adelphies			
❏ 2020	Darlin' It's You/Kathleen	1958	$125
—Artist's name spelled correctly as "Adelphis			

ADMIRALS, THE

Number	Title	Yr	NM
KING			
❏ 4782	Close Your Eyes/Give Me Love	1955	$250
❏ 4792	It's a Sad, Sad Feeling/Ow	1955	$60
—With Lucky Millinder			
❏ 4772	Oh Yes/Left with a Broken Heart	1955	$250

Number	Title	Yr	NM

ADMIRATIONS, THE
BRUNSWICK
❑ 55332	Hey Mama/Lonely Street	1967	$30

HULL
| ❑ 1202 | Moonlight/Ain't It Funny | 1965 | $200 |

MERCURY
| ❑ 71521 | The Bells of Roja Rita/ Little Bo Poop | 1959 | $50 |
| ❑ 71883 | To the Aisle/Hey Senorita | 1962 | $200 |

ONE-DERFUL
| ❑ 4851 | Don't Leave Me/All for You | 1967 | $30 |
| ❑ 4849 | Wait Till I Get to Know You/(Instrumental) | 1967 | $30 |

ADORABLES, THE
GOLDEN WORLD
❑ 4	Daddy Please/Deep Freeze	1964	$30
❑ 25	Ooh Boy!/Devil in His Eyes	1965	$100
❑ 10	School's All Over/Be	1964	$30

PEACOCK
| ❑ 1924 | The Drive/Baby, Come and Get It | 1963 | $15 |

ADORNO, PEPI, MAMBO BAND
RAINBOW
| ❑ 267 | Santa Baby Mambo/East of the Sun Mambo | 1954 | $20 |

ADRIAN AND THE SUNSETS
SUNSET
| ❑ 602 | Breakthrough/Cherry Pie | 1963 | $50 |
| ❑ 602 [PS] | Breakthrough/Cherry Pie | 1963 | $120 |

ADVENTURERS, THE (U)
BLUE ROCK
| ❑ 4071 | Something Bad (Is Happening)/ Nobody Can Save Me | 1968 | $8 |

COMPASS
| ❑ 7010 | Easy Baby/(These Days) A Good Girl Is So Hard to Find | 1967 | $8 |

MECCA
| ❑ A-11 | 2 O'Clock Express/Shaggin' | 1960 | $50 |

MIRACLE
| ❑ 1 | 2 O'Clock Express/ October Days | 1960 | $30 |

ADVENTURES, THE
CHRYSALIS
| ❑ 42894 | Send My Love/Lost in Hollywood | 1985 | $4 |

ELEKTRA
❑ 69414	Broken Land/Don't Stand on Me	1988	$3
❑ 69414 [PS]	Broken Land/Don't Stand on Me	1988	$3
❑ 69387	Drowning in the Sea of Love/Stay	1988	$3

AEROSMITH
COLUMBIA
❑ 10516	Back in the Saddle/ Nobody's Fault	1977	$5
❑ 38-08536	Chip Away the Stone/S.O.S.	1989	$4
❑ 10880	Chip Away the Stone (Studio)//S.O.S./Chip Away the Stone (Live)	1979	$6
❑ 10802	Come Together/ Kings and Queens	1978	$5
❑ 10637	Draw the Line/Bright, Light, Fright	1977	$5
❑ 45894	Dream On/Somebody	1973	$6
—Contains a remixed, edited version of A-side			
❑ 10278	Dream On/Somebody	1975	$5
—Contains the full-length version of A-side			
❑ 10727	Get It Up/Milk Cow Blues	1978	$5
❑ 10407	Home Tonight/Pandora's Box	1976	$5
❑ 10359	Last Child/Combination	1976	$5
❑ 46029	Pandora's Box/Same Old Song and Dance	1974	$6
❑ 10105	S.O.S. (Too Bad)/ Lord of the Thighs	1975	$6
❑ 10155	Sweet Emotion/Pandora's Box	1975	$5
❑ 10253	Toys in the Attic/You See Me Crying	1975	$6
❑ 10034	Train Kept a-Rollin'/Spaced	1974	$6
❑ 10206	Walk This Way/ Round and Round	1975	$6
❑ 10449	Walk This Way/Uncle Salty	1976	$5

GEFFEN
❑ 28249	Angel/Girl Keeps Coming Apart	1987	$3
❑ 28249 [PS]	Angel/Girl Keeps Coming Apart	1987	$4
❑ 28240	Dude (Looks Like a Lady)/Simoriah	1987	$3
❑ 28240 [PS]	Dude (Looks Like a Lady)/Simoriah	1987	$5
❑ 22845	Love in an Elevator/Young Lust	1989	$3
❑ 22845 [PS]	Love in an Elevator/Young Lust	1989	$5
❑ 28814	Shela/Gypsy Boots	1986	$4
❑ 28814 [PS]	Shela/Gypsy Boots	1986	$5

AESOP'S FABLES
ATCO
❑ 6508	Girl, I've Got News for You/Yes I'm Back	1967	$8
❑ 6565	Slow and Easy/The Truth	1968	$8
❑ 6523	Take a Step/What's a Man to Do	1967	$8

CADET CONCEPT
❑ 7016	And When It's Over/ What Is Love	1969	$8
❑ 7016	I'm Gonna Make You Love Me/They Go Out and Get It	1968	$8
❑ 7011	Temptation 'Bout to Get Me/What Is Love	1969	$8

AFFECTION COLLECTION, THE
EVOLUTION
| ❑ 1004 | Girl/I'll Be There | 1969 | $15 |
| ❑ 1013 | Watch Her Walk/I Don't Mind | 1969 | $15 |

UNITED ARTISTS
| ❑ 50268 | In Apple Blossom Time/Time Rests Heavy on My Hands | 1968 | $10 |

AFGHAN WHIGS
SUB POP
❑ 32	I Am the Sticks/White Trash Party	1989	$30
❑ 32 [PS]	I Am the Sticks/White Trash Party	1989	$30
—Sub Pop Singles Club, April 1989 (#6)			

AFRICA
ODE
| ❑ ZS7-126 | From Africa with Love/ Savin' All My Love | 1969 | $8 |
| ❑ ZS7-116 | Here I Stand/Widow | 1969 | $8 |

AFRIQUE
MAINSTREAM
| ❑ 5542 | Soul Makossa/Hot Mud | 1973 | $5 |

AGEE, RAY
CELESTE
| ❑ 616 | Merry Christmas My Love/I Want You | 1964 | $10 |
| ❑ 616 | Merry Christmas My Love/ Po-Lee The Polar Bear | 1964 | $10 |

AGGREGATION, THE
LHI
| ❑ 1209 | Sunshine Superman/Maharish | 1968 | $40 |

AHBEZ, EDEN
DEL-FI
| ❑ 4131 | Tobago/The Old Boat | 1959 | $20 |

AIR SUPPLY
ARISTA
❑ 0520	All Out of Love/Old Habits Die Hard	1980	$3
❑ 0692	Even the Nights Are Better/ One Step Closer	1982	$3
❑ 0692 [PS]	Even the Nights Are Better/ One Step Closer	1982	$3
❑ 0564	Every Woman in the World/Chances	1980	$3
❑ 0564	Every Woman in the World/ Having You Near Me	1980	$3
❑ 0564	Every Woman in the World/My Best Friend	1980	$3
❑ 0626	Here I Am (Just When I Thought I Was Over You)/ Don't Turn Me Away	1981	$3
❑ 0626	Here I Am (Just When I Thought I Was Over You)/I've Got Your Love	1981	$3
❑ 9521	Lonely Is the Night/I'd Die for You	1986	$3
❑ 9521 [PS]	Lonely Is the Night/I'd Die for You	1986	$3

❑ 0479	Lost in Love/I Don't Want to Lose You	1980	$3
❑ 9056	Making Love Out of Nothing at All/Late Again	1983	$3
❑ 9056 [PS]	Making Love Out of Nothing at All/Late Again	1983	$3
❑ 0520 [DJ]	Old Habits Die Hard (mono/stereo)	1980	$6
—Interesting promo-only release, as this was not the side that became the hit			
❑ 9542	One More Chance/ Hope Springs Eternal	1986	$3
❑ 9565	Stars in Your Eyes/Put Love in Your Heart	1987	$3
❑ 0655	Sweet Dreams/Don't Turn Me Away	1981	$3
❑ 9667	The Eyes of a Child/Love Is All	1987	$4
❑ 0604	The One That You Love/I Want to Give It All	1981	$3
❑ 0604 [PS]	The One That You Love/I Want to Give It All	1981	$3
❑ 9391	The Power of Love (You Are My Lady)/Sunset	1985	$3
❑ 9391 [PS]	The Power of Love (You Are My Lady)/Sunset	1985	$3
❑ 1004	Two Less Lonely People in the World/What Kind of Girl	1982	$3

AKENS, JEWEL
CAPEHART
| ❑ 5007 | (Dancing) The Mashed Potatoes/ Wee Bit More of Your Lovin' | 1962 | $15 |

COLGEMS
| ❑ 66-1025 | It's a Sin to Tell a Lie/ You Better Move On | 1968 | $8 |
| ❑ 66-1009 | Little Bitty Pretty One/ Born a Loser | 1967 | $12 |

CREST
| ❑ 1098 | (Dancing) The Mashed Potatoes/ Wee Bit More of Your Lovin' | 1962 | $12 |

ERA
❑ 3207	A Slice of the Pie/A Land Where Animals Are People	1969	$8
❑ 3156	A Slice of the Pie/You Better Believe It	1965	$10
❑ 104	Buenos Aires/Mississippi Syrup Sopper	1969	$6
❑ 3142	Georgie Porgie/ Around the Corner	1965	$10
❑ 3164	My First Lonely Night/Mama Take Your Daughter Back	1966	$10
❑ 3141	The Birds and the Bees/Tic Tac Toe	1964	$20

MDM
| ❑ 191 | Christine/Please God | 1988 | $4 |
| —As "Jewel Akens, Mr. Birds and Bees | | | |

AL AND DICK CHILDREN'S CHORUS, THE
CORAL
| ❑ 62157 | We Wish You a Merry Christmas/Santa Cwuz | 1959 | $15 |

ALABAMA
GRT
| ❑ 129 | I Wanna Be with You Tonight/ Lovin' You Is Killin' Me | 1977 | $20 |
| ❑ 129 [PS] | I Wanna Be with You Tonight/ Lovin' You Is Killin' Me | 1977 | $30 |

MDJ
❑ 7906	I Wanna' Come Over/ Get It While It's Hot	1979	$15
—Reissue of Sonny Limbo Int'l. 7906			
❑ 1002 #NAME?	My Home's in Alabama/Some Other Time, Some Other Place	1980	$10
—Jukebox pressing with one B-side			
❑ 1002-R	My Home's in Alabama// Some Other Time, Some Other Place/Why Lady Why	1980	$15
—Regular pressing with two B-sides			

RCA
❑ PB-14165	Can't Keep a Good Man Down/ If It Ain't Dixie (It Won't Do)	1985	$4
❑ PB-13358	Christmas in Dixie/Christmas Is Just a Song for Us This Year	1982	$5
—B-side by Louise Mandrell and R.C. Bannon			
❑ PB-13664	Christmas in Dixie/Never Be One	1983	$4
❑ 5051-7-R	Christmas in Dixie/ Tennessee Christmas	1986	$4
❑ PB-13294	Close Enough to Perfect/Fantasy	1982	$4
❑ PB-13446	Dixieland Delight/A Very Special Love	1983	$4
❑ GB-13786	Dixieland Delight/Lady Down on Love	1984	$3
—Gold Standard Series reissue			

Number	Title	Yr	NM
❏ JK-13446 [DJ]	Dixieland Delight (same on both sides)	1983	$12

—Promo only on blue vinyl

Number	Title	Yr	NM
❏ 5328-7-R	Face to Face/Vacation	1987	$3
❏ 6902-7-R	Fallin' Again/I Saw the Time	1988	$3
❏ 8937-7-R	Fallin' Again/Song of the South	1989	$3

—Gold Standard Series reissue

Number	Title	Yr	NM
❏ GB-13489	Feels So Right/Mountain Music	1983	$3

—Gold Standard Series reissue

Number	Title	Yr	NM
❏ PB-12236	Feels So Right/See the Embers, Feel the Flame	1981	$4
❏ PB-14085	Forty Hour Week (For a Livin')/As Right Now	1985	$4
❏ PB-14085 [PS]	Forty Hour Week (For a Livin')/As Right Now	1985	$5
❏ GB-14350	Forty Hour Week (For a Livin')/Can't Keep a Good Man Down	1986	$3

—Gold Standard Series reissue

Number	Title	Yr	NM
❏ 8948-7-R	High Cotton/"Ole" Baugh Road	1989	$3
❏ 8817-7-R	If I Had You/I Showed Her	1988	$3
❏ PB-13840	If You're Gonna Play in Texas (You Gotta Have a Fiddle in the Band)/I'm Not That Way Anymore	1984	$4
❏ PB-13590	Lady Down on Love/Lovin' Man	1983	$4
❏ PB-12288	Love in the First Degree/Ride the Train	1981	$4
❏ GB-14174	Love in the First Degree/The Closer You Get	1985	$3

—Gold Standard Series reissue

Number	Title	Yr	NM
❏ PB-13019	Mountain Music/Never Be One	1981	$4
❏ PB-13019 [PS]	Mountain Music/Never Be One	1981	$5
❏ PB-12008	My Home's in Alabama/I Wanna Come Over	1980	$4
❏ PB-12008 [PS]	My Home's in Alabama/I Wanna Come Over	1980	$6
❏ PB-12169	Old Flame/I'm Stoned	1981	$4
❏ PB-14281	She and I/The Fans	1986	$4
❏ PB-14281 [PS]	She and I/The Fans	1986	$5
❏ 8744-7-R	Song of the South/(I Wish It Could Always Be) '55	1988	$3
❏ 9083-7-R	Southern Star/Barefootin'	1989	$3
❏ GB-13492	Take Me Down/Close Enough to Perfect	1983	$3

—Gold Standard Series reissue

Number	Title	Yr	NM
❏ PB-13210	Take Me Down/Lovin' You Is Killin' Me	1982	$4
❏ 5222-7-R	Tar Top/If I Could Just See You Now	1987	$3
❏ 5222-7-R [PS]	Tar Top/If I Could Just See You Now	1987	$8

—Promo-only sleeve

Number	Title	Yr	NM
❏ PB-12018	Tennessee River/Can't Forget About You	1980	$4
❏ GB-12369	Tennessee River/Old Flame	1981	$3

—Gold Standard Series reissue

Number	Title	Yr	NM
❏ PB-13524	The Closer You Get/You Turn Me On	1983	$4
❏ GB-14176	(There's a) Fire in the Night/If You're Gonna Play in Texas (You Gotta Have a Fiddle in the Band)	1985	$3

—Gold Standard Series reissue

Number	Title	Yr	NM
❏ PB-13926	(There's A) Fire in the Night/Rock on the Bayou	1984	$4
❏ PB-13992	There's No Way/The Boy	1985	$4
❏ GB-14347	There's No Way/(There's a) Fire in the Night	1986	$3

—Gold Standard Series reissue

Number	Title	Yr	NM
❏ 5003-7-R	Touch Me When We're Dancing/Hanging Up My Travelin' Shoes	1986	$3
❏ PB-13763	When We Make Love/Oklahoma Mountain Dew	1984	$4
❏ GB-12310	Why Baby Why/My Home's in Alabama	1981	$3

—Gold Standard Series reissue

Number	Title	Yr	NM
❏ PB-12091	Why Lady Why/I Wanna Come Over	1980	$4
❏ PB-12091 [PS]	Why Lady Why/I Wanna Come Over	1980	$5

SONNY LIMBO INT'L.

Number	Title	Yr	NM
❏ 7906	I Wanna' Come Over/Get It While It's Hot	1979	$50

SUN

Number	Title	Yr	NM
❏ 1173 [DJ]	I Wanna Be with You Tonight (Standard Version/Edited Version)	1982	$40

—Promo only on yellow vinyl; stock copies were not released

ALABAMA CHRISTIAN MOVEMENT FOR HUMAN RIGHTS CHOIR

TCF

Number	Title	Yr	NM
❏ 2	Do You Hear What I Hear?/The Virgin Mary	1963	$15

ALADDINS, THE

ALADDIN

Number	Title	Yr	NM
❏ 3314	All My Life/So Long, Farewell, Bye Bye	1956	$200
❏ 3358	Help Me/Lord, Show Me	1957	$200
❏ 3298	I Had a Dream Last Night/Get Off My Feet	1955	$200

FRANKIE

Number	Title	Yr	NM
❏ 6	Dot, My Love/My Charlene	1958	$400

WITCH

Number	Title	Yr	NM
❏ 111	Our Love Will Be/Simple Simon	1962	$60
❏ 109	Please Love Me/Munch	1962	$60

ALAIMO, CHUCK

MGM

Number	Title	Yr	NM
❏ 12636	Hop in My Jalop/Rockin' in G	1958	$20
❏ 12449	Leap Frog/That's My Desire	1957	$20
❏ 12508	Local 60-6/How I Love You	1957	$20
❏ 12589	Where's My Baby/Lovers Again	1957	$20

ALAIMO, STEVE

ABC

Number	Title	Yr	NM
❏ 10833	Happy/On the Beach	1966	$15
❏ 10873	Pardon Me (It's My First Day Alone)/Savin' All My Love	1966	$15
❏ 10805	So Much Love/Truer Than True	1966	$15

ABC-PARAMOUNT

Number	Title	Yr	NM
❏ 10712	Blowin' in the Wind/Lady of the House	1965	$15
❏ 10764	Bright Lights Big City/Once a Day	1966	$15
❏ 10680	Cast Your Fate to the Wind/Mais Oui	1965	$15
❏ 10605	Happy/Everybody Knows But Her	1964	$15
❏ 10580	I Don't Know/That's What Love Will Do	1964	$15
❏ 10643	Laughing on the Outside/Tomorrow Is Another Day	1965	$15
❏ 10553	Love Is a Many Splendored Thing/Fade Out	1964	$15
❏ 10540	Love's Gonna Live Here/Let Her Go	1964	$15

ATCO

Number	Title	Yr	NM
❏ 6589	1 x 1 Ain't 2/My Friend	1968	$8
❏ 6797	Can't You See/(On the) Wild Side of Life	1971	$6
❏ 6560	Cuando Yo Vuelvo Ami Tierra/Todavia	1968	$12
❏ 6561	Denver/I Do	1968	$8
❏ 6659	I'm Thankful/Afetr the Smoke Is Gone	1969	$8

—With Betty Wright

Number	Title	Yr	NM
❏ 6732	Melissa/Smilin' in My Sleep	1970	$6
❏ 6710	One Woman/And Then I Tripped Over Your Goodbye	1969	$8
❏ 6620	Thank You for the Sunshine Days/Watching the Trains Go	1968	$8

CHECKER

Number	Title	Yr	NM
❏ 1042	A Lifetime of Loneliness/It's a Long, Long Way to Happiness	1963	$15
❏ 989	All Night Long/I'm Thankful	1961	$15
❏ 981	Big Bad Beulah/I Cried All the Way Home	1961	$15
❏ 1024	Cry Myself to Sleep/One Good Reason	1962	$15
❏ 1047	Don't Let the Sun Catch You Cryin'/I Told You So	1963	$15
❏ 1032	Every Day I Have to Cry/Little Girl	1962	$15
❏ 1006	Mashed Potatoes/Mashed Potatoes (Part 2)	1962	$15
❏ 1054	Michael -- Pt. 1/Michael -- Pt. 2	1963	$15
❏ 1018	My Friend/Going Back to Mary	1962	$15
❏ 998	The Waiting's So Hard/You Got Me Whistling	1961	$15

DADE

Number	Title	Yr	NM
❏ 1800	Home by Eleven/I Wanna Kiss You	1959	$60
❏ 1805	Love Letters/You Can Fall in Love	1959	$60

DICKSON

Number	Title	Yr	NM
❏ 6444/5	Blue Fire/My Heart Never Said Goodbye	1960	$30

ENTRANCE

Number	Title	Yr	NM
❏ 7507	Amerikan Music/Nobody's Fool	1972	$5
❏ 7513	Sand in My Pocket/Gemini	1972	$5
❏ 7503	Thorn in Our Roses/Nobody's Fool	1971	$5
❏ 7501	When My Little Girl Is Smiling/Gemini	1971	$5

IMPERIAL

Number	Title	Yr	NM
❏ 66003	Gotta Lotta Love/Happy Pappy	1963	$15
❏ 5699	My Heart Never Said Goodbye/Blue Fire	1960	$20

MARLIN

Number	Title	Yr	NM
❏ 6064	I Want You to Love Me/Blue Skies	1959	$40
❏ 6067	She's My Baby/Should I Care?	1959	$30
❏ 6103	Spooky/The Redcoats Are Coming	1961	$40

—As "Count Stephen

Number	Title	Yr	NM
❏ 6065	The Weekend's Over/Girls! Girls! Girls!	1959	$30

7-Inch Extended Plays

ABC

Number	Title	Yr	NM
❏ LP-ABCS-531 [PS]	Where the Action Is	1966	$25
❏ LP-ABCS-531	Where the Action Is/Sweet Little Sixteen/500 Miles// Papa's Got a Brand New Bag/ Personality/Blowin' in the Wind	1966	$25

—Jukebox issue; small hole, plays at 33 1/3 rpm

CHECKER

Number	Title	Yr	NM
❏ EP-5135	Don't Cry/I Wake Up Crying//Cry/Don't Let the Sun Catch You Crying	1963	$100
❏ EP-5135 [PS]	(title unknown)	1963	$100

ALAMO, TONY (1)

MGM

Number	Title	Yr	NM
❏ K11353	If I Had Wings/After Your Love	1952	$20
❏ K11380	Merry Christmas Darling/It's Christmas Time	1952	$30
❏ K11415	The Clown/Is It Love You're After	1953	$20

PORT

Number	Title	Yr	NM
❏ 70012	Fabulous/For All We Know	1960	$20

RCA VICTOR

Number	Title	Yr	NM
❏ 47-6288	Girlie, Girlie, Girlie/I Wrote a Song for Your Birthday	1955	$15

ALAMO, TONY (2)

ALAMO

Number	Title	Yr	NM
❏ 334	Something/Dreamer	1986	$4

— With Kim Morris

Number	Title	Yr	NM
❏ 334 [PS]	Something/Dreamer	1986	$4

ALAN, BUDDY, AND DON RICH

CAPITOL

Number	Title	Yr	NM
❏ 2928	Cowboy Convention/We're All Gonna Get Together	1970	$8
❏ 3040	I'm On the Road to Memphis/I'll Be Swingin' You	1971	$8

ALAN, BUDDY

CAPITOL

Number	Title	Yr	NM
❏ 2580	Alabama, Louisiana or Maybe Tennessee/You Can't Make Nothing Out of That But Love	1969	$8
❏ 4075	Another Saturday Night/Nickels, Dimes and Quarters	1975	$6
❏ ST-11019	Best of Buddy Alan	1972	$20
❏ 2715	Big Mama's Medicine Show/When a Man Can't Call His Home a Home	1969	$8
❏ 3944	Call My Number, Call My Name/If I Hurt Her I Know She'll Cry	1974	$6
❏ 4019	Chains/A Whole Lot of Somethin'	1974	$6
❏ 2784	Down in New Orleans/I've Never Had a Dream Come True Before	1970	$8
❏ 3110	Fishin' on the Mississippi/If I Could Love You More	1971	$8
❏ 3346	I'm in Love/The Happiness Song	1972	$8
❏ 3861	I Never Had It So Good/She Always Wears a Yellow Rose	1974	$6
❏ 3146	I Will Drink Your Wine/Doin' the Best I Can	1971	$8
❏ 2653	Lodi/I Wanna Be Wild and Free	1969	$8
❏ 3010	Lookin' Out My Back Door/Corn Liquor	1970	$8
❏ 2852	Santo Domingo/That's Quite a Ride	1970	$8
❏ 4144	Something She's Got/1,000 Miles	1975	$6
❏ 2305	When I Turn Twenty-One/Adios, Farewell, Goodbye, Good Luck, So Long	1968	$8
❏ 2305 [PS]	When I Turn Twenty-One/Adios, Farewell, Goodbye, Good Luck, So Long	1968	$20
❏ 3266	White Line Fever/Another By Your Side	1972	$8

ALAN, LEE
LEE ALAN PRESENTS

Number	Title	Yr	NM
☐ 0(no cat #)	A Trip to Miami	1964	$500

— Interviews with the Beatles; a giveaway with Lee Alan's two-page story of his trip ($200 NM)

ALARM, THE
I.R.S.

Number	Title	Yr	NM
☐ 52828	Absolute Reality/Room at the Top	1986	$3
☐ 52828 [PS]	Absolute Reality/Room at the Top	1986	$4

— Die-cut sleeve with band's name on it

☐ 53259	Presence of Love/My Land, Your Land	1988	$3
☐ 53259 [PS]	Presence of Love/My Land, Your Land	1988	$3
☐ 9924	Sixty-Eight Guns/Pavilion Steps	1984	$4
☐ 9924 [PS]	Sixty-Eight Guns/Pavilion Steps	1984	$4
☐ 73002	Sold Me Down the River	1989	$5
☐ 73002 [PS]	Sold Me Down the River	1989	$5
☐ 52792	Spirit of '76/Reason 36	1986	$3
☐ 52792 [PS]	Spirit of '76/Reason 36	1986	$3
☐ 52736	Strength/Majority	1985	$3
☐ 52736 [PS]	Strength/Majority	1985	$3
☐ 9929	The Deceiver/Second Generation	1984	$4
☐ 9929 [PS]	The Deceiver/Second Generation	1984	$5
☐ 9922	The Stand/Reason 41	1983	$4
☐ 9922 [PS]	The Stand/Reason 41	1983	$10

ALBERT, EDDIE
COLUMBIA

Number	Title	Yr	NM
☐ 4-43850	Don't Think Twice, It's All Right/A Smile Is Just a Frown (Turned Upside Down)	1966	$8
☐ 4-43757	Green Acres/Turn Around	1966	$20
☐ 4-44344	Once Before/Funny Dreams	1967	$8

HICKORY

☐ 1278	Fall Away/Just Waiting	1964	$10
☐ 1326	Men with Broken Hearts/A Man Can Never Go Back Home	1965	$10

KAPP

☐ 108	Come Pretty Little Girl/I'm in Favor of Friendship	1955	$8
☐ 117	Go If You're Going/Just for the Bride and Groom	1955	$15
☐ 134	Little Child/Jenny Kissed Me	1956	$15

— With Sondra Lee

☐ 134 [PS]	Little Child/Jenny Kissed Me	1956	$30
☐ 142	My Amor/You Belong to My Heart	1956	$15

— With Margo

☐ 102	One God/For This I'm Thankful	1954	$15

WONDERLAND

☐ 1776	Our Glorious Commanders/Aura Lee	1975	$8

ALBERT, UREL
CINNAMON

Number	Title	Yr	NM
☐ 786	One Man's Woman at a Time/Just Wait	1974	$10

TOAST

☐ 311	Country and Pop Music/Just Wait	1973	$20

ALBERTI, WILLY

Number	Title	Yr	NM
☐ 45-1888	Marina/Cerasella (Canzone Allegra)	1959	$15

ALBERTS, AL
COLUMBIA

Number	Title	Yr	NM
☐ 42737	Fly Me to the Moon/Before Tomorrow Is Yesterday	1963	$8

CORAL

☐ 62113	By You/High School	1959	$10
☐ 62083	How Soon/Love Is the Tomorrow	1959	$10
☐ 62090	How Soon/Taking a Chance on Love	1959	$10
☐ 62061	My Love/Willingly	1958	$10
☐ 62035	Things I Didn't Say/God's Greatest Gifts	1958	$10

DECCA

☐ 28807	Please Tell Me/Endless	1953	$20

MGM

☐ 12922	Handful of Gold/Blue Bird of Happiness	1960	$12
☐ 12836	Imagination/Handful of Gold	1959	$10

Number	Title	Yr	NM
☐ 12884	South of the Border/No Love But Your Love	1960	$12

PRESIDENT

☐ 715	Blue O'Clock in the Morning/Till Then (I'll Never Again)	1962	$8
☐ 711	Don't Wait for the Hearse/Heaven Needed an Angel	1961	$8
☐ 719	Fly Me to the Moon/Before Tomorrow Is Yesterday	1963	$15
☐ 712	Only on Sunday/Heaven Needed an Angel	1961	$8

SWAN

☐ 4191	Mr. Sandman/Summertime in Venice	1964	$10
☐ 4067	Oh My Papa/Alone	1961	$10

VEE JAY

☐ 568	One Has My Name, The Other Has My Heart/Mala Femina	1963	$20

ALBISTON, TONY
BOGUS

Number	Title	Yr	NM
☐ 1001/2	Mount Shasta/Old Fashioned Couple	1960	$200

ALCATRAZZ
Group featuring YNGWIE J. MALMSTEEM and, later, STEVE VAI, as well as GRAHAM BONNET of Rainbow and MSG fame and members of NEW ENGLAND.
ROCSHIRE

Number	Title	Yr	NM
☐ 95047	Island in the Sun/Hiroshima Mon Amour	1983	$10
☐ 95047 [PS]	Island in the Sun/Hiroshima Mon Amour	1983	$15

ALDA, ALEX
ONE WAY

Number	Title	Yr	NM
☐ 224	The Ballad of Mr. Nixon/Little Pony	1976	$5

TOPIX

☐ 6007 [DJ]	Little Pony (one-sided)	1961	$125

ALDEN AND THE ONE-NIGHTERS
RCA VICTOR

Number	Title	Yr	NM
☐ 47-7490	Love-O-Meter/Theme from Love-O-Meter	1959	$40

ALDRICH, RONNIE
7-Inch Extended Plays
LONDON PHASE 4

Number	Title	Yr	NM
☐ SBG68	Blowin' in the Wind/Do It Again/Time//Mas Que Nada/Theme from "The Fox"/Something Here in My Heart	1968	$10

— Jukebox issue; small hole, plays at 33 1/3 rpm

☐ SBG68 [PS]	This Way "In	1968	$12

ALEXANDER AND THE GREATS
ARVEE

Number	Title	Yr	NM
☐ 5064	Swanee Stomp/Waterlogged	1963	$50

LIMELIGHT

☐ 3040	Do the Mustang/Hot Dang Mustang	1964	$50

ALEXANDER, ARTHUR
BUDDAH

Number	Title	Yr	NM
☐ 492	Every Day I Have to Cry Some/Everybody Needs Somebody to Love	1975	$5
☐ 522	Sharing the Night Together/She'll Throw Stones at You	1976	$5
☐ 602	Sharing the Night Together/She'll Throw Stones at You	1978	$4

DOT

☐ 16387	Anna/I Hang My Head and Cry	1962	$30
☐ 16616	Black Knight/Ole John Amos	1964	$15
☐ 16737	Detroit City/You Don't Care	1965	$15
☐ 16454	I Wonder Where You Are Tonight/Dream Girl	1963	$20
☐ 16509	Pretty Girls Everywhere/Baby Baby	1963	$20
☐ 16554	Where Did Sally Go/Keep Her Guessin'	1963	$20
☐ 16357	Where Have You Been (All My Life)/Soldier of Love	1962	$30

JUDD

☐ 1020	Sally Sue Brown/The Girl That Radiates That Charm	1960	$60

— As "June Alexander

MONUMENT

Number	Title	Yr	NM
☐ 1060	I Need You Baby/Spanish Harlem	1968	$8

MUSIC MILL

☐ 1012	Hound Dog Man's Gone/So Long Baby	1977	$6

SOUND STAGE 7

☐ 2626	Bye Bye Love/Another	1969	$8
☐ 2652	Glory Road/Cry Like a Baby	1970	$8
☐ 2619	Set Me Free/Love's Where Life Begins	1968	$8
☐ 2556	The Other Woman/(Baby) For You	1965	$10
☐ 2572	Turn Around (And Try Me)/Show Me the Road	1966	$10

WARNER BROS.

☐ 7658	Burning Love/It Hurts to Want It So Bad	1972	$6
☐ 7571	I'm Comin' Home/It Hurts to Want It So Bad	1972	$6
☐ 7633	Mr. John/You Got Me Knockin'	1972	$6

ALEXANDER, JOE, AND THE CUBANS
BALLAD

Number	Title	Yr	NM
☐ 1008	Oh Maria/I Hope These Words Will FInd You Well	1954	$1500

ALEXANDER, MAX
CAPROCK

Number	Title	Yr	NM
☐ 116	Little Rome/Rock, Rock, Rock Everybody	1959	$200

ALEXANDER'S TIMELESS BLOOZBAND
KAPP

Number	Title	Yr	NM
☐ 967	Maybe Baby/Power of Your Love	1969	$15

MATAMAT

☐ 101	Love So Strong/Horn Song	1967	$30

UNI

☐ 55044	Love So Strong/Horn Song	1967	$20

ALEXANDRIA, LOREZ
ABC-PARAMOUNT

Number	Title	Yr	NM
☐ 10594	That Far Away Look/Little Boat	1966	$15

ARGO

☐ 5432	Baltimore Oriole/Mother Earth	1963	$20
☐ 5367	I Ain't Got Nothin' But the Blues/Early in the Morning	1960	$20
☐ 5371	I Almost Lost My Mind/Don't Explain	1960	$20

KING

☐ 5206	Love Is Just Around the Corner/Ain't Misbehavin'	1959	$30

PZAZZ

☐ 03	Didn't We/The One You Love Is You	1968	$15
☐ 025	Hey Jude/I Don't Want to Hear It Anymore	1969	$15
☐ 01	I'm Wishin'/Endless	1968	$15
☐ 046	My Way/Hello There Girl	1969	$15
☐ 017	Santa Is Here/Nonchalantly	1968	$15

ALFI AND HARRY
LIBERTY

Number	Title	Yr	NM
☐ 55066	Safari/Cloding Time	1957	$30
☐ 55008	The Trouble with Harry/Little Beauty	1955	$30
☐ 55016	The Word Game Song/Persian on Excursion	1956	$30

ALHONA, RICHIE
FANTASY

Number	Title	Yr	NM
☐ 556	Mama, Mama/The Pagan	1961	$15
☐ 553	One Desire/Young Boy, Young Girl	1961	$40

— Red vinyl

☐ 553	One Desire/Young Boy, Young Girl	1961	$15

— Black vinyl

☐ 553 [PS]	One Desire/Young Boy, Young Girl	1961	$40
☐ 561	The Fool/Teenager Teenager	1962	$15

ALIAS
MERCURY

Number	Title	Yr	NM
☐ 76033	True Love/Danger in the Night	1979	$4

Number	Title	Yr	NM

ALIBI
COMSTOCK
Number	Title	Yr	NM
❑ 1884	Do You Have Any Doubts/ (B-side unknown)	1988	$6
❑ 1833	It Only Hurts When I Cry/ (B-side unknown)	1987	$6

ALICE WONDER LAND
BARDELL
| ❑ 774 | He's Mine (I Love Him, I Love Him, I Love Him)/Cha Linda | 1963 | $30 |

ALIOTTA-HAYNES-JEREMIAH
AMPEX
| ❑ 11012 | Pitter Patter/(B-side unknown) | 1970 | $8 |

— As "Aliotta Haynes

| ❑ 11026 | Tomorrow's Another Day/ One Night Stand | 1971 | $8 |

— As "Aliotta Haynes

SNOW QUEEN
| ❑ 1000 | Lake Shore Drive (L.S.D.)/ Snow Queen | 1973 | $30 |

ALISHA
RCA
❑ 5219-7-R	Into My Secret/Do You Dream About Me	1987	$3
❑ 5219-7-R [PS]	Into My Secret/Do You Dream About Me	1987	$4
❑ 5278-7-R	Into My Secret (Remix)/ (B-side unknown)	1987	$4

VANGUARD
❑ 35244	All Night Passion/Dub All Night	1984	$4
❑ 35262	Baby Talk/One Little Lie	1985	$4
❑ 35263	Stargazing/Boys Will Be Boys	1986	$4
❑ 35254	Too Turned On/ (B-side unknown)	1985	$4

ALIVE AND KICKING
ROULETTE
❑ 7113	Good Ole Lovin' Back Home/Jordan	1971	$5
❑ 7094	London Bridge/You Gave Me Something	1971	$5
❑ 7078	Tighter, Tighter/ Sunday Morning	1970	$5

ALL NIGHT WORKERS, THE
CAMEO
| ❑ 420 | Honey and Wine/God Bless the Child | 1966 | $50 |

MERCURY
| ❑ 72833 | The Collector/Misery | 1968 | $40 |

ROUND SOUND
| ❑ RS-1 | Don't Put All Your Eggs in One Basket/Why Don't You Smile | 1983 | $500 |

— Lou Reed and John Cale co-wrote the B-side of this record

ALL-NITERS, THE
ERIE
| ❑ 02 | Hello (Lonely One)/ Girl Don't Go | 1966 | $30 |
| ❑ 01 | Hey Baby/Talk to Me | 1966 | $30 |

GMA
| ❑ 1 | Summertime Blues/ You Talk Too Much | 1965 | $50 |

ALL POINTS BULLETIN BAND
LCR
| ❑ 10109 | Get Up and Get Down/ (B-side unknown) | 1979 | $10 |
| ❑ 10102 | Sexy Ways-Pretty Legs (Part 1)/Sexy Ways-Pretty Legs (Part 2) | 1975 | $10 |

ALLAN & THE FLAMES
CAMPBELL
| ❑ 225 | Winter Wonderland/ Till The End Of Time | 1960 | $60 |

COLONIAL
| ❑ 7006 | Winter Wonderland/'Till The End of Time | 1960 | $60 |

ALLAN, DAVIE, AND THE ARROWS
CUDE
Number	Title	Yr	NM
❑ 101	War Path/Beyond the Blue	1963	$125

MARC
| ❑ 3223 | War Path/Beyond the Blue | 1963 | $60 |

MGM
❑ 14560	And Evil Did Too/Pleasure Girl	1973	$8
❑ 14650	Apache '73/Run of the Arrow	1973	$8
❑ 14432	Dawn of the 7th Cavalry/ Little Big Horn	1972	$8
❑ 14374	Head Over Heels/Here It Comes	1972	$8
❑ 14299	It's the Little Things You Do/Haven't You Heard	1971	$8

MRC
| ❑ 0901 | Stoked on Surf/Flashback | 1984 | $5 |

PRIVATE STOCK
| ❑ 45,001 | Touch Too Much/We Can Make It Together | 1974 | $6 |

SIDEWALK
| ❑ 1 | Apache '65/Blue Guitar | 1965 | $30 |

TOWER
❑ 116	Apache '65/Blue Guitar	1965	$20
❑ 142	Baby Ruth/I'm Looking Over a Four Leaf Clover	1965	$15
❑ 295	Blue's Theme/Bongo Party	1966	$15

— As "The Arrows featuring Davie Allen

❑ 381	Cycle-Delic/Blue Rides Again	1967	$15
❑ 341	Devil's Angels/Cody's Theme	1967	$15
❑ 133	Moon Dawg '65/ Dance the Freddie	1965	$15
❑ 158	Space Hop/Granny Goose	1965	$15
❑ 267	Wild Angels Theme/UFO	1966	$15
❑ 446	Wild in the Streets/Shape of Things to Come	1968	$15

ALLANSON, SUSIE
20TH CENTURY
| ❑ 2283 | Surrender at Appomattox/ The British Are Coming | 1976 | $6 |

— B-side by Paul Revere and the Raiders

ABC
| ❑ 12219 | Love Is a Satisfied Woman/ Me and Charlie Brown | 1976 | $6 |

ELEKTRA
❑ 46565	I Must Be Crazy/I Can't See Me Without You	1979	$5
❑ 46036	Two Steps Forward and Three Steps Back/I Will Never Leave You	1979	$5
❑ 46503	Without You/Heart to Heart	1979	$5
❑ 46009	Words/We Can Make It Up to Each Other	1979	$5

ENIGMA
| ❑ 75005 | She Don't Love You/ (B-side unknown) | 1987 | $5 |
| ❑ 75001 | Where's the Fire/I Can't Say It on the Radio | 1986 | $5 |

LIBERTY
❑ 1383	Dance the Two Step/You Never Told Me About Goodbye	1980	$4
❑ A-1422	Hearts (Our Hearts)/ Dreamin' Again	1981	$4
❑ 1425	Lay a Little Lovin' on Me/ Love Is Knockin' at My Door	1982	$4
❑ B-1460	Wasn't That Love/Falling in Love for the Last Time	1982	$4

OAK
| ❑ 1001 | Baby, Don't Keep Me Hangin' On/It's Gone | 1977 | $8 |

TNP
❑ 75005	She Don't Love You/ Girls Get Lonely Too	1987	$6
❑ 75005 [PS]	She Don't Love You/ Girls Get Lonely Too	1987	$8
❑ 75001	Where's the Fire/ (B-side unknown)	1986	$6

UNITED ARTISTS
| ❑ 1365 | While I Was Makin' Love to You/Michael | 1980 | $4 |

WARNER BROS.
❑ 8429	Baby, Don't Keep Me Hangin' On/It's Gone	1977	$5
❑ 8473	Baby, Last Night Made My Day/ Will There Really Be a Morning	1977	$5
❑ 8686	Back to the Love/I Want This Feeling to Last	1978	$5
❑ 8534	Maybe Baby/Hide Me in Your Love	1978	$5
❑ 8597	We Belong Together/I Don't Want to Cry Anymore	1978	$5

ALLEN, BARRY
DOT
Number	Title	Yr	NM
❑ 16799	Pretty Paper/Hurry, Santa, Hurry	1965	$30

ALLEN, BILLY
EL DORADO
| ❑ 505 | Butterfly/Oo Wee Baby | 1957 | $30 |

— As "Bill Allen

IMPERIAL
| ❑ 5500 | Please Give Me Something/ Since I Have You | 1958 | $125 |

ALLEN, CLAY
DECCA
| ❑ 9-46360 | A Little Bit of Heaven/If I Live a Thousand Years | 1951 | $30 |
| ❑ 9-46324 | Can't Keep Smiling/Evalina | 1951 | $30 |

TNT
| ❑ 102 | How Many Hearts Have You Broken/Letter's Unclaimed | 1953 | $40 |

ALLEN, DEBORAH
CAPITOL
❑ B-5110	After Tonight/Don't Worry 'Bout Me Baby	1982	$4
❑ B-5186	Don't Stop Lovin' Me/Let's Stop Talkin' About It	1982	$4
❑ 4903	If I Had Known Then/You Never Cross My Mind	1980	$4

RCA
| ❑ JK-13600 [DJ] | Baby I Lied (same on both sides) | 1983 | $12 |

— Promo only on green vinyl

❑ PB-13600	Baby I Lied/Time Is Taking You Away from Me	1983	$4
❑ PB-13600 [PS]	Baby I Lied/Time Is Taking You Away from Me	1983	$5
❑ GB-14356	Baby I Lied/Time Is Taking You Away from Me	1983	$3

— Gold Standard Series" reissue

❑ PB-13921	Heartache and a Half/ It Makes Me Cry	1984	$4
❑ PB-13921 [PS]	Heartache and a Half/ It Makes Me Cry	1984	$5
❑ JK-13921 [DJ]	Heartache and a Half (same on both sides)	1984	$15

— Promo only on red vinyl

❑ PB-13776	I Hurt for You/Cheat the Night	1984	$4
❑ PB-13694	I've Been Wrong Before/ Fool's Paradise	1983	$4
❑ 5136-7-R	Telepathy/You Better Come Back to Me	1987	$4

WARNER BROS.
| ❑ 8271 | Take Me Back/Do You Copy | 1976 | $6 |

ALLEN, JASON
HIT
| ❑ 226 | Everybody Loves a Clown/ You've Got Your Troubles | 1965 | $8 |

— B-side by the Spades

ALLEN, JESSE
BAYOU
| ❑ 011 | Dragnet/Take It Easy | 1953 | $125 |

CORAL
| ❑ 65078 | My Suffering/Let's Party | 1952 | $200 |

IMPERIAL
| ❑ 5256 | Gotta Call That Number/ Gonna Tell My Mama | 1953 | $200 |

— With Audrey Walker

| ❑ 5285 | Sittin' and Wonderin'/I Wonder What's the Matter | 1954 | $250 |
| ❑ 5303 | What a Party/The Things I'm Gonna Do | 1954 | $200 |

ALLEN, JIMMY, AND TOMMY BARTELLA
AL-BRITE
| ❑ 1300 | When Santa Comes Over The Brooklyn Bridge/ What Would You Like To Have For Christmas? | 1959 | $50 |

Number	Title	Yr	NM

ALLEN, LEE
ALADDIN
| ❑ 3334 | Shimmy/Rockin' at Cosmos | 1956 | $30 |

EMBER
❑ 1057	Cat Walk/Creole Alley	1959	$30
❑ 1031	Strollin' with Mr. Lee/ Boppin' at the Hop	1958	$30
❑ 1039	Tic Toc/Chuggin'	1958	$30
❑ 1082	Twistin' with Mr. Lee/ Twist Around the Clock	1962	$20
❑ 1027	Walkin' with Mr. Lee/Promenade	1957	$30

7-Inch Extended Plays
EMBER
| ❑ 103 [PS] | Walkin' with Mr. Lee | 1958 | $250 |
| ❑ 103 | Walkin' with Mr. Lee/ Teen Dream//Promenade/ Big Horn Special | 1958 | $250 |

ALLEN, MILTON
RCA VICTOR
| ❑ 47-7116 | Don't Bug Me Baby/Jamboree | 1957 | $60 |
| ❑ 47-6994 | Love A Love A Lover/Just Look, Don't Touch, She's Mine | 1957 | $40 |

ALLEN, PHYLICIA
CASABLANCA
| ❑ 946 | Colors/Josephine Superstar | 1978 | $8 |

ALLEN, RANCE, GROUP
CAPITOL
❑ 4443	Got to Be Ready/ Reason to Survive	1977	$5
❑ 4512	Peace of Mind/I'm Gonna Make It After All	1977	$5
❑ 4394	Truth Is Marching On/ You're My Everything	1977	$5
❑ 3217	I Belong to You/Wheel of Life	1979	$5
❑ 3226	I'm Coming Back to You/Some People	1980	$5
❑ 3223	Pay Day Is Coming/Where Have All Your Friends Gone	1979	$5
❑ 3221	Smile/Security	1979	$5

TRUTH
| ❑ 3229 | I Give My All to You/What a Day | 1976 | $6 |
| ❑ 3218 | White Christmas/(Instrumental) | 1975 | $8 |

ALLEN, RAY, AND THE UPBEATS
BLAST
| ❑ 204 | Peggy Sue/La Bamba | 1962 | $40 |

SINCLAIR
| ❑ 1004 | Sweet Lorraine/Let Them Talk | 1961 | $60 |

ALLEN, RAY
DCP
| ❑ 1007 | He Don't Love You Anymore/ Please Make Up Your Mind | 1964 | $20 |

MALA
| ❑ 522 | Dondi/That Is My Love | 1966 | $15 |
| ❑ 504 | That Is My Love/Bluebirds Over the Mountain | 1965 | $15 |

ROULETTE
| ❑ 4737 | Hey Ben Go Fly a Kite/Roselina | 1967 | $12 |
| ❑ 4721 | Torna/Al Di La | 1967 | $10 |

ALLEN, REX, AND TEX WILLIAMS
DECCA
| ❑ 9-29254 | This Ole House/ Two Texas Boys | 1954 | $30 |

ALLEN, REX, JR.
IMPERIAL
| ❑ 66288 | Before I Change My Mind (I'm Going Home)/ The World I Live In | 1968 | $15 |

MOON SHINE
❑ 3030	Dream On Texas Ladies/ (B-side unknown)	1984	$5
❑ 3022	Sweet Rosanna/You Sure Could Have Fooled Me	1984	$5
❑ 3017	The Air That I Breathe/ Whiskey Cheer	1983	$5
❑ 3036	When You Held Me in Your Arms/(B-side unknown)	1985	$5

SSS INTERNATIONAL
| ❑ 837 | Country Comfort/The Father Needs a Man | 1971 | $8 |
| ❑ 813 | Wake Up Morning/ You Weren't There | 1970 | $8 |

TNP
| ❑ 75010 | We're Staying Together/ Diamond in the Rough | 1987 | $6 |

WARNER BROS.
❑ GWB 0330	Another Goodbye Song/Goodbye	1976	$4
— Back to Back Hits" reissue; "Burbank" palm trees label			
❑ 8000	Another Goodbye Song/ Yes We Have Love	1974	$6
❑ 49844	Arizona/The One I Sing My Love Songs To	1981	$4
❑ GWB 0368	Can You Hear Those Pioneers/Lonely Street	1979	$4
— Back to Back Hits" reissue			
❑ 8204	Can You Hear Those Pioneers/Streets of Laredo	1976	$5
❑ 29968	Cowboy in a Three Piece Business Suit/Round Up Time	1982	$4
❑ 8418	Don't Say Goodbye/There's No Use Hanging On	1977	$5
❑ 49562	Drink It Down, Lady/ What Was Your Name?	1980	$4
❑ 7788	Goodbye/The Same Old Way	1974	$6
❑ 49020	If I Fell in Love with You/ Pick Up the Pieces	1979	$4
❑ 8354	I'm Getting Good at Missing You (Solitaire)/Don't Say Goodbye	1977	$5
❑ 49128	It's Over/Why Did You Stop Lovin' Me	1980	$4
❑ 8697	It's Time We Talk Things Over/Watch Me Cry	1978	$5
❑ 50035	Last of the Silver Screen Cowboys/Round Up Time	1982	$4
— A-side with Roy Rogers and Rex Allen Sr.			
❑ 50035 [PS]	Last of the Silver Screen Cowboys/Round Up Time	1982	$12
— A-side with Roy Rogers and Rex Allen Sr.			
❑ 8482	Lonely Street/Don't It Make You Want to Go Home	1977	$5
❑ 8095	Lying in My Arms/She Just Said Goodbye	1975	$5
❑ 8786	Me and My Broken Heart/ Lovin' You Is Everything to Me	1979	$5
❑ 8171	Play Me No Sad Songs/ She Just Said Goodbye	1976	$5
❑ 8236	Teardrops in My Heart/ Home Made Love	1976	$5
❑ 7753	The Great Mail Robbery/ Start Again	1973	$6
❑ 8133	Then I'll Be Over You/Paying the Price for Staying Free	1975	$6
❑ 8297	Two Less Lonely People/I Gotta Remember You	1976	$5
❑ 8608	With Love/You Turned It On Again Last Night	1978	$5

ALLEN, REX
BUENA VISTA
❑ F-355	Barefoot Country Boy/ Conversation with a Mule	1960	$20
❑ F-363	Charro Bravo/I Love You So Much It Hurts	1960	$20
❑ F-370	Dodie Ann/Pretty Irish Girl	1960	$20
❑ F-342	I Couldn't Care Less/ Pretty Irish Girl	1959	$20
❑ F-341	Lazy River/Say One for Me	1959	$20
❑ F-351	Staying Young/Forever and Ever	1959	$20
❑ F-358	The Lilacs Grow High/I'm the Man	1960	$20
❑ F-347	The Little Old Church in the Valley/Morgen	1959	$20

DECCA
❑ 732612	Ain't That Beautiful Singing/A Voice	1970	$6
❑ 32072	A Waltz That Never Ends/A Woman (Can Change a Man)	1967	$8
❑ 9-30511	Blue Dream/Blue Light Waltz	1957	$15
❑ 9-29111	Bringing Home the Bacon/I Could Cry My Heart Out	1954	$20
❑ 32401	Bummin' Around/When I Leave This World Behind	1968	$6
❑ 9-28758	Crying in the Chapel/I Thank the Lord	1953	$30
❑ 9-29610	Daddy, You Know What/ The Albino Stallion	1955	$20
❑ 9-30204	Drango/Little White Horse	1957	$15
❑ 9-28998	He Played the Steel Guitar/Somewhere	1954	$30
❑ 9-30833	I Know the Reason Why/ The Mystery of His Way	1959	$15
❑ 9-29168	In the Chapel in the Moonlight/ Chapel of Memories	1954	$20
❑ 32467	It Happens Over and Over Again/Sai Finis	1969	$6
❑ 9-46390	I've Got So Many Million Years (I Can't Count 'Em)/Is He Satisfied	1952	$30
❑ 9-30364	Money, Marbles and Chalk/ Flowers of San Antone	1957	$15
❑ 9-31039	Take Me Lord/Sheltered in the Arms of the Old Rugged Cross	1959	$15
❑ 9-29586	That's What Makes the Juke Box Play/Pedro Gonzales, Tennessee Lopez	1955	$30
❑ 9-29871	The Last Frontier/Sky Boss	1956	$15
❑ 9-29729	The Last Round-Up/I'm a Young Cowboy	1955	$20
❑ 9-27952	The Waltz of the Roses/As Long As the River Flows On	1952	$30
❑ 9-28146	Till the Well Goes Dry/ Rack Up the Balls Boys	1952	$30
❑ 32322	Tiny Bubbles/Jose Villa Lobo Alfredo Thomaso Vincente Lopez	1968	$6
❑ 9-28897	To Be Alone/If God Can Forgive You, So Can I	1953	$30
❑ 9-29397	Tomorrow's Another Day to Cry/ L-O-N-E-S-O-M-E Letter Blues	1955	$20
❑ 9-30066	Trail of the Lonesome Pine/Nothin; to Do	1956	$15
❑ 9-30205	Westward Ho the Wagons/ Wringle Wrangle	1957	$15
❑ 9-28933	Where Did My Snowman Go?/Why Daddy?	1953	$30
❑ 9-88161 [PS]	Where Did My Snowman Go?/Why Daddy?	1953	$40
❑ 9-88161	Where Did My Snowman Go?/Why Daddy?	1953	$20
— Yellow label "Children's Series" release			

MCA
| ❑ 41071 | So Long Duke/At the Rainbow's End | 1979 | $6 |

MERCURY
❑ 57130	Angel to Joe/Cowpoke	1951	$30
❑ 71997	Don't Go Near the Indians/ Touched So Deeply	1962	$12
❑ 62970	I Ain't Gonna Cry No More/I've Drifted	1951	$30
❑ 56190	I'm a Sentimental Fool/ Ten More Miles to Go	1951	$30
❑ 71844	Marines, Let's Go/ Heartaches of a Fool	1961	$10
❑ 56470	Mister and Mississippi/ Lonely Little Robin	1951	$30
❑ 72071	Only the Hangman/ Johnny Travers	1962	$8
❑ 72137	Silver Spoon Lonely Me/To-Ra	1963	$8
❑ 55970	Sparrow in the Tree Top/Always You	1951	$30
❑ 72205	Tear After Tear/I'm Just Killing Time	1964	$8
❑ 72205 [PS]	Tear After Tear/I'm Just Killing Time	1964	$20
❑ 70373	True Blue Lou-Lou-Lou/Save a Little Corner in Your Heart for Me	1954	$30

MUSICOR
| ❑ 1132 | Take It Back and Change It for a Boy/Rodeo Twist | 1965 | $8 |

ALLEN, RICHIE
ERA
| ❑ 3058 | Blue Holiday/Goochie Bamba | 1961 | $30 |

IMPERIAL
❑ 5917	Butterscotch/Sunday Picnic	1963	$20
❑ 5872	Cave Man/Room 304	1962	$30
❑ 5929	Foot Stomp U.S.A./ Skag Along Pete	1963	$30
❑ 5720	Haunted Guitar/In a Persian Market	1961	$30
❑ 5846	Mr. Hobbs (Theme)/ Comin' Back to You	1962	$20
❑ 5701	Sally Ann/Why Did It End	1960	$20
— As "Dickie Allen			
❑ 5683	Stranger from Durango/Redskin	1960	$30
❑ 5941	Surf Beater/The Rising Surf	1963	$20

TOWER
| ❑ 273 | Stranger from Durango/ Nothing Good | 1966 | $15 |

ALLEN, RONNIE
DAPT
| ❑ 205 | Flip You Over/Ronnie's Swanee | 1961 | $50 |

SAN
| ❑ 300 | Gonna Get My Baby/ (B-side unknown) | 1959 | $100 |
| ❑ 209 | High School Love/ (B-side unknown) | 1959 | $100 |

ALLEN, ROSALIE
RCA VICTOR
❑ 47-5308	Bring Your Sweet Self Back to Me/Just Wait Till I Get You Alone	1953	$30
❑ 47-5379	Castaway/My Old Familiar Heartache	1953	$30
❑ 48-0343	Green As Grass/I Wanna Sit	1950	$40
— Original on green vinyl			
❑ 47-4987	I Laughed at Love/I Gotta Have You	1952	$30
❑ 47-4853	It Wasn't God Who Made Honky Tonk Angels/ It'd Surprise You	1952	$30
❑ 48-0403	I've Got the Craziest Feeling/ One and One Is Two	1951	$30
❑ 47-5121	Let Me Share Your Name/ Hard Hearted Woman	1953	$30

Number	Title	Yr	NM
❏ 48-0305	My Dolly Has a Broken Heart/Chocolate Ice Cream Cone	1950	$40

— *Original on green vinyl*

Number	Title	Yr	NM
❏ 47-4425	Shoot Him High Paw/I've Paid	1951	$30
❏ 48-0434	Station L-O-V-E Signing Off/Cranberry Kisses	1951	$30
❏ 47-4683	Tomboy/Hills of Pride	1952	$30

STOP

Number	Title	Yr	NM
❏ 256	Fire on the Mountain/There Goes My World Again	1969	$8

ALLEN, STEVE
BRUNSWICK

Number	Title	Yr	NM
❏ 80230	But Officer/But Baby	1953	$20
❏ 80228	Cinderella/Goldilocks and the Three Bears	1953	$20

CORAL

Number	Title	Yr	NM
❏ 61485	Autumn Leaves/High and Dry	1955	$15
❏ 61565	Don't Be That Way/Sing, Sing, Sing	1956	$15
❏ 61839	Do You Ever Think of Me/I Love You	1957	$12
❏ 61877	Gotta Have Something in the Bank, Frank/The Disc-Jockey's Theme Song	1957	$10
❏ 61376	I'm Glad There Is You/It Can't Be Wrong	1955	$15
❏ 61566	Let's Dance/Goodbye	1956	$15
❏ 61681	Lola's Theme/Conversation	1956	$15
❏ 61909	Pretend You Don't See Him/But I Haven't Got Him	1957	$10
❏ 61707	Star Dust/The Golden Wedding Waltz	1956	$15
❏ 61368	The Ballad of Davy Crockett/Very Square Dance	1955	$15
❏ 61445	The Goo Goo Doll Song/Old Betsy	1955	$15
❏ 61620	Theme from "Picnic"/My Nita, Juanita	1956	$15
❏ 61375	Tonight/Just Stay a Little While	1955	$15
❏ 61573	What Is a Freem?/I Never Harmed an Onion	1956	$15
❏ 61542	What Is a Wife/Memories of You	1956	$15

DOT

Number	Title	Yr	NM
❏ 16457	Gravy Waltz/Preacherman	1963	$8
❏ 15947	Hawaiian Punch/Follow the Leader	1959	$12
❏ 15831	Hula Hoop/Love Theme from "Houseboat"	1958	$10
❏ 16613	I Am the Greatest/Mouth to Mouth Resuscitation	1964	$8
❏ 16408	Mah Mah Limbo/Dream	1962	$8
❏ 15722	Skinny Minnie/Chills	1958	$12
❏ 15891	St. Louis Blues/Ida Sweet as Apple Cider	1959	$10
❏ 16645	Theme from "The Magic Fountain"/Who's Your Sister	1964	$8

DUNHILL

Number	Title	Yr	NM
❏ 4127	Dance Time/Impossible	1968	$6
❏ 4097	Here Comes Sgt. Pepper/Flowers and Love	1967	$20

SIGNATURE

Number	Title	Yr	NM
❏ 12044	Dance Time/Impossible	1960	$12
❏ 12003	Flattery/I Remember It Well	1959	$10

— *With Jayne Meadows*

ALLEN, TONY
ALADDIN

Number	Title	Yr	NM
❏ 3403	Time Won't Wait on You/Holy Smoke, Baby	1957	$30

BETHLEHEM

Number	Title	Yr	NM
❏ 3002	Come-A, Come-A Baby/Just Like Before	1961	$15
❏ 3004	It Hurts Me So/The Trakey-Doo	1962	$15

DIG

Number	Title	Yr	NM
❏ 109	I Found an Angel/I'm Dreaming	1956	$60
❏ 104	It Hurts Me So/Check Yourself	1955	$30

EBB

Number	Title	Yr	NM
❏ 115	Come Back/Why in the World	1957	$30

IMPERIAL

Number	Title	Yr	NM
❏ 5547	Forgive Me/Rockin' Shoes	1958	$20
❏ 5523	Strange Talk/Call My Name	1958	$20

JAMIE

Number	Title	Yr	NM
❏ 1143	Train of Love/God Gave Me You	1959	$20

KENT

Number	Title	Yr	NM
❏ 364	Dreaming/Be My Love, Be My Love	1961	$15

SPECIALTY

Number	Title	Yr	NM
❏ 570	Check Yourself Baby/Especially	1956	$40

ULTRA

Number	Title	Yr	NM
❏ 104	It Hurts Me So/Check Yourself	1955	$40

ALLEN, WARD
D

Number	Title	Yr	NM
❏ 1065	Frisco Waltz/Two Step Polka	1959	$30
❏ 1040	Maple Sugar/Back Up and Push	1959	$30
❏ 1116	Pappy Daily's Breakdown/Bread 'n' Butter	1960	$30

ALLEY CATS, THE
EPIC

Number	Title	Yr	NM
❏ 9778	Lily of the West/I Should Have Stayed at Home Tonight	1965	$15

PHILLES

Number	Title	Yr	NM
❏ 108	Puddin N' Tain (Ask Me Again, I'll Tell You the Same)/Feel So Good	1962	$30

PHILLES/COLLECTABLES

Number	Title	Yr	NM
❏ 3201	Puddin' and Tain/Then He Kissed Me	1985	$6

— *Red vinyl; part of box set "Phil Spector Wall of Sound Series Vol. 2"; B-side by the Crystals*

Number	Title	Yr	NM
❏ 3201	Puddin' and Tain/Then He Kissed Me	1986	$5

— *Black vinyl; B-side by the Crystals*

WHIPPET

Number	Title	Yr	NM
❏ 209	Snap, Crackle and Pop/Last Night	1958	$30
❏ 202	This Thing Called Love/Spang-a-Lang	1957	$30

ALLEY, JIM
AVCO

Number	Title	Yr	NM
❏ 615	Her Memory Is Here Tonight/(B-side unknown)	1975	$8
❏ 606	Her Memory's Gonna Kill Me/If I Didn't Have a Dime	1975	$8

DOT

Number	Title	Yr	NM
❏ 17051	Only Daddy That'll Walk the Line/When You Were Here	1967	$20

ALLIES, THE
REPRISE

Number	Title	Yr	NM
❏ 0674	I Would Love You/The Sound of Children	1968	$30

VALIANT

Number	Title	Yr	NM
❏ 748	I'll Sell My Soul/Burning Glass	1966	$50

ALLISON, FRAN
RCA VICTOR

Number	Title	Yr	NM
❏ 47-3938	The Christmas Tree Angel/Christmas in My Heart	1950	$20

ALLISON, GENE
MONUMENT

Number	Title	Yr	NM
❏ 876	Ev'rybody's Got a Little Problem/Now Hear This	1965	$8

VEE JAY

Number	Title	Yr	NM
❏ 365	Ask/Tell Me Sugar Baby	1960	$20
❏ 317	Everybody But Me/I Believe in Myself	1959	$20
❏ 299	Everything Will Be Alright/I'm a Fool Wanting You	1958	$20
❏ 273	Have Faith/My Heart Remembers	1958	$20
❏ 286	I Don't Know Why/Let's Sit and Talk	1958	$20
❏ 329	I'll Be Waiting for You/Let There Be Women	1959	$20
❏ 305	Tell Me the Truth/Reap What You Sow	1959	$20
❏ 341	Why Do You Treat Me So Cold/Oh Yeah I'm in Love	1960	$20

ALLISON, KEITH
AMY

Number	Title	Yr	NM
❏ 11024	Who Do You Love/Don't Want Nobody But You	1968	$15

COLUMBIA

Number	Title	Yr	NM
❏ 43900	Action/Glitter and Gold	1966	$15
❏ 44853	Birds of a Feather/To Know Her Is to Love Her	1969	$10
❏ 45115	Everybody/Wednesday's Child	1970	$12
❏ 43619	Look at Me/I Ain't Blaming You	1966	$15
❏ 43619 [PS]	Look at Me/I Ain't Blaming You	1966	$30
❏ 44028	Louise/Freeborn Man	1967	$15
❏ 44028 [PS]	Louise/Freeborn Man	1967	$30

WARNER BROS.

Number	Title	Yr	NM
❏ 5681	Sweet Little Rock and Roller/The Girl Can't Help It	1965	$15
❏ 5681 [PS]	Sweet Little Rock and Roller/The Girl Can't Help It	1965	$30

ALLISON, LUTHER
GORDY

Number	Title	Yr	NM
❏ 7137	Part Time Love/Now You Got It	1974	$5
❏ 7128	The Little Red Rooster/Raggedy and Dirty	1973	$5

ALLISONS, THE (1)
COLUMBIA

Number	Title	Yr	NM
❏ 42034	Words/Blue Tears	1961	$10

LONDON

Number	Title	Yr	NM
❏ 1977	Are You Sure/There's One Thing More	1961	$10
❏ 1977 [PS]	Are You Sure/There's One Thing More	1961	$30

SMASH

Number	Title	Yr	NM
❏ 1749	Lessons in Love/Oh My Love	1962	$12

ALLISONS, THE (2)
TIP

Number	Title	Yr	NM
❏ 1011	Surfer Street/Money	1963	$50

ALLMAN AND WOMAN
WARNER BROS.

Number	Title	Yr	NM
❏ 8504	Love Me/Move Me	1977	$5

ALLMAN BROTHERS BAND, THE
Also see ALLMAN AND WOMAN; THE ALLMAN JOYS; DUANE AND GREGG ALLMAN; GREGG ALLMAN; DICKIE BETTS; THE HOUR GLASS.

ARISTA

Number	Title	Yr	NM
❏ 0555	Angeline/So Long	1980	$4
❏ 0584	Mystery Woman/Hell and High Water	1981	$4
❏ 0618	Straight from the Heart/Leavin'	1981	$4
❏ 0618 [PS]	Straight from the Heart/Leavin'	1981	$6
❏ 0643	Two Rights/Never Knew How Much	1981	$4

CAPRICORN

Number	Title	Yr	NM
❏ 0050	Ain't Wastin' Time No More/Blue Sky	1974	$4

— *Back to Back Hits series*

Number	Title	Yr	NM
❏ 0003	Ain't Wastin' Time No More/Melissa	1972	$5
❏ 8003	Black Hearted Woman/Every Hungry Woman	1970	$6
❏ 0326	Can't Take It With You/Sail Away	1979	$4
❏ 0320	Crazy Love/Just Ain't Easy	1979	$4
❏ 0007	Melissa/Blue Sky	1972	$5
❏ 0014	One Way Out/Standback	1972	$5
❏ 8014	Whipping Post/Midnight Rider	1971	$5

7-Inch Extended Plays

ATLANTIC

Number	Title	Yr	NM
❏ SD 7-2-805 [PS]	Beginnings	1973	$20
❏ SD 7-2-805	Black Hearted Woman/Revival (Love Is Everywhere)/Whipping Post/Midnight Rider	1973	$20

— *Jukebox issue; small hole, plays at 33 1/3 rpm*

CAPRICORN

Number	Title	Yr	NM
❏ S CP 0111 [PS]	Brothers and Sisters	1973	$15

— *Part of "Little LP" series (LLP #229)*

Number	Title	Yr	NM
❏ S CP 0111	Come and Go Blues/Wasted Words//Jessica	1973	$15

— *Jukebox issue; small hole, plays at 33 1/3 rpm*

ALLMAN, DUANE AND GREGG
BOLD

Number	Title	Yr	NM
❏ 200	Morning Dew/Morning Dew	1973	$10
❏ 200 [DJ]	Morning Dew/Morning Dew	1973	$30

— *Promo on red vinyl*

ALLMAN, GREGG
ALLMAN BROTHERS BAND and THE ALLMAN JOYS. Also see ALLMAN AND WOMAN.

CAPRICORN

Number	Title	Yr	NM
❏ 0279	Cryin' Shame/One More Try	1977	$4
❏ 0042	Don't Mess Up a Good Thing/Please Call Home	1974	$4

Number	Title	Yr	NM
❏ 0053	Midnight Rider/Don't Mess Up a Good Thing	1975	$4

— *Back to Back Hits series*

Number	Title	Yr	NM
❏ 0035	Midnight Rider/Multi-Colored Lady	1973	$5

EPIC

Number	Title	Yr	NM
❏ 07215	Can't Keep Running/Anything Goes	1987	$3
❏ 07430	Evidence of Love/Anything Goes	1987	$3
❏ 06998	I'm No Angel/Lead Me On	1987	$4
❏ 08041	Slip Away/Every Hungry Woman	1988	$3

7-Inch Extended Plays

CAPRICORN

Number	Title	Yr	NM
❏ S CP 0116 [PS]	Laid Back	1973	$20

— *Part of "Little LP" series (LLP #237)*

ALLMAN JOYS, THE
DIAL

Number	Title	Yr	NM
❏ 4046	Spoonful/You Deserve Each Other	1966	$50

ALLMAN, SHELDON
HIFI

Number	Title	Yr	NM
❏ 593	Walk on the Ground/Radioactive Mama	1960	$15

ORIGINAL SOUND

Number	Title	Yr	NM
❏ 25	Heartbreak Boulevard/Little Black Things	1963	$12

ALLSUP, TOMMY
GRT

Number	Title	Yr	NM
❏ 38	I'll See Him Through/Snowbird	1971	$6

ALMA-KEYS, THE
KISKI

Number	Title	Yr	NM
❏ 2056	Please Come Back to Me/Jumpin' Twist	1962	$300

ALMEIDA, LAURINDO
CAPITOL

Number	Title	Yr	NM
❏ 4863	Lazy River Bossa Nova/Rambing Rose Bossa Nova	1962	$12
❏ 5496	Morituri Theme/Forget Domani	1965	$8

ALMOND, JOHNNY
DERAM

Number	Title	Yr	NM
❏ 85052	Music Machine to R.K./Solar Level	1969	$8

ALMOND, MARC
CAPITOL

Number	Title	Yr	NM
❏ B-44240	Tears Run Rings/Everything I Want Love to Be	1988	$3
❏ B-44240 [PS]	Tears Run Rings/Everything I Want Love to Be	1988	$3

ALMOST BROTHERS, THE
MTM

Number	Title	Yr	NM
❏ B-72062	Birds of a Feather/I Wanna Kiss the Bride	1986	$4
❏ B-72053	Don't Tell Me Love Is Kind/Nighttime Fantasy	1985	$4
❏ B-72079	I Don't Love Her Anymore/Nighttime Fantasy	1986	$4
❏ B-72072	What's Your Name/Adventures in Love	1986	$4

ALPERT, HERB, AND THE TIJUANA BRASS
A&M

Number	Title	Yr	NM
❏ 870	A Banda/Miss Frenchy Brown	1967	$5
❏ 870 [PS]	A Banda/Miss Frenchy Brown	1967	$8
❏ 1962	African Summer/You in Me	1977	$4
❏ 751	All My Loving/El Presidente	1964	$8
❏ 1194	Brasilia/Love Potion #9	1970	$4
❏ 2655	Bullish/Oriental Eyes	1984	$4

— *As "Herb Alpert Tijuana Brass*

Number	Title	Yr	NM
❏ 2655 [PS]	Bullish/Oriental Eyes	1984	$4
❏ 925	Cabaret/Slick	1968	$5
❏ 925 [PS]	Cabaret/Slick	1968	$8
❏ 890	Carmen/A Love So Fine	1967	$5
❏ 890 [PS]	Carmen/A Love So Fine	1967	$8
❏ 850	Casino Royale/Wall Street Rag	1967	$5
❏ 850 [PS]	Casino Royale/Wall Street Rag	1967	$8
❏ 1688	Coney Island/Ratatouille	1975	$4
❏ 1714	El Bimbo/Catfish	1975	$4
❏ 767	El Garbanzo/Mae	1965	$6
❏ 813	Flamingo/So What's New	1966	$6

Number	Title	Yr	NM
❏ 813 [PS]	Flamingo/So What's New	1966	$10
❏ 1526	Fox Hunt/I Can't Go On Living, Baby, Without You	1974	$4
❏ 1420	Last Tango in Paris/Fire and Rain	1973	$4
❏ 823	Mame/Our Day Will Come	1966	$6
❏ 823 [PS]	Mame/Our Day Will Come	1966	$10
❏ 705	Marching Through Madrid/Struttin' with Maria	1963	$8
❏ 1102	Marjorine/Ob-La-Di, Ob-La-Da	1969	$5
❏ 1100	Marjorine/Warm	1969	$5
❏ 711	Mexican Corn/Let It Be Me	1963	$8
❏ 732	Mexican Drummer Man/Great Manolete	1963	$8
❏ 1028	Monday, Monday/Treasure of San Miguel	1969	$5
❏ 1284	Montezuma's Revenge/Darlin'	1971	$4
❏ 1001	My Favorite Things/The Christmas Song	1968	$6
❏ 1001 [PS]	My Favorite Things/The Christmas Song	1968	$10
❏ 1094	Ob-La-Di, Ob-La-Da/Girl Talk	1969	$5
❏ 1852	Promenade/Musique	1976	$4
❏ 1015	She Touched Me/My Favorite Things	1969	$5
❏ 755	South of the Border/Up Cherry Street	1965	$6
❏ 721	Spanish Harlem/A-Mer-I-Ca	1963	$8
❏ 2690	Struttin' on Five/Blow Your Own Horn	1984	$4

— *As "Herb Alpert Tijuana Brass*

Number	Title	Yr	NM
❏ 1261	Summertime/Hurt So Bad	1971	$4
❏ 1261 [PS]	Summertime/Hurt So Bad	1971	$6
❏ 775	Taste of Honey/Third Man Theme	1965	$6
❏ 1237	The Bell That Couldn't Jingle/Las Mananitas	1970	$5
❏ 860	The Happening/Town Without Pity	1967	$5
❏ 860 [PS]	The Happening/Town Without Pity	1967	$8
❏ 703	The Lonely Bull (El Solo Torro)/Acapulco 1922	1962	$10

— *With pale brown label and no horn logo*

Number	Title	Yr	NM
❏ 1159	The Maltese Melody/Country Lake	1969	$5
❏ 742	The Mexican Shuffle/Numero Cinco	1964	$8
❏ 1762	The Whistle Song (Whistlestar)/Carmine	1975	$4
❏ 805	The Work Song/Plucky	1966	$6
❏ 805 [PS]	The Work Song/Plucky	1966	$10
❏ 929	This Guy's in Love with You/A Quiet Tear	1968	$5
❏ 929 [PS]	This Guy's in Love with You/A Quiet Tear	1968	$8
❏ 964	To Wait for Love/Bud	1968	$5
❏ 964 [PS]	To Wait for Love/Bud	1968	$8
❏ 840	Wade in the Water/Mexican Road Race	1967	$5
❏ 840 [PS]	Wade in the Water/Mexican Road Race	1967	$8
❏ 792	What Now My Love/Spanish Flea	1966	$6
❏ 792 [PS]	What Now My Love/Spanish Flea	1966	$10
❏ 760	Whipped Cream/Las Mananitas	1965	$6
❏ 1065	Without Her/Sandbox	1969	$5
❏ 1065 [PS]	Without Her/Sandbox	1969	$6
❏ 1337	Without Her/Zazuiera	1972	$4
❏ 1337 [PS]	Without Her/Zazuiera	1972	$6

7-Inch Extended Plays

Number	Title	Yr	NM
❏ SP412	3rd Man Theme/Cinco De Mayo/Tijuana Taxi//And the Angels Sing/Spanish Flea/A Walk in the Black Forest	1966	$10

— *Jukebox issue; small hole, plays at 33 1/3 rpm*

Number	Title	Yr	NM
❏ SP434	A Banda/"Bud"/Love So Fine//With a Little Help from My Friends/Cowboys and Indians/Carmen	1967	$10

— *Jukebox issue; small hole, plays at 33 1/3 rpm*

Number	Title	Yr	NM
❏ SP446	A Beautiful Friend/Cabaret/Panama//Slick/She Touched Me/The Robin	1968	$10

— *Jukebox issue; small hole, plays at 33 1/3 rpm*

Number	Title	Yr	NM
❏ SP-403	A-Me-Ri-Ca/Surfin' Senorita/Crea Mi Amor//Mexican Corn/Swinger from Seville/Winds of Barcelona	1964	$15

— *Jukebox issue; small hole, plays at 33 1/3 rpm*

Number	Title	Yr	NM
❏ SP424 [PS]	Casino Royale	1966	$12
❏ SP412 [PS]	Going Places	1966	$12
❏ SP424	Gotta Lotta Livin' to Do/Lady Godiva/Bo-Bo//Miss Frenchy Brown/In a Little Spanish Town/Wade in the Water	1966	$10

— *Jukebox issue; small hole, plays at 33 1/3 rpm*

Number	Title	Yr	NM
❏ SP434 [PS]	Herb Alpert's Ninth	1967	$12
❏ SP-403 [PS]	Herb Alpert's Tijuana Brass Volume 2	1964	$15

Number	Title	Yr	NM
❏ SP408	Mexican Shuffle/Up Cherry Street/All My Loving//South of the Border/I've Grown Accustomed to Her Face/Hello, Dolly	1965	$15

— *Stereo jukebox issue; small hole, plays at 33 1/3 rpm*

Number	Title	Yr	NM
❏ SP408 [PS]	South of the Border	1965	$15
❏ SP410	Taste of Honey/Green Peppers/Whipped Cream//Bittersweet Samba/Lollipops and Roses/El Garbanzo	1965	$10

— *Jukebox issue; small hole, plays at 33 1/3 rpm*

Number	Title	Yr	NM
❏ SP446 [PS]	The Beat of the Brass	1968	$12
❏ SP414 [PS]	What Now My Love	1966	$12
❏ SP414	What Now My Love/Freckles/Plucky//Memories of Madrid/So What's New/Brasilia	1966	$10

— *Jukebox issue; small hole, plays at 33 1/3 rpm*

Number	Title	Yr	NM
❏ SP410 [PS]	Whipped Cream and Other Delights	1965	$12

ALPERT, HERB
A&M

Number	Title	Yr	NM
❏ 1446	3 O'Clock Jump/Kalimba	1989	$3
❏ 2757	8" Ball/Lady Love	1985	$3
❏ 2757 [PS]	8" Ball/Lady Love	1985	$4
❏ 2802	African Flame/Lady Love	1985	$3
❏ 2246	Beyond/Keep It Goin'	1980	$4
❏ 2246 [PS]	Beyond/Keep It Goin'	1980	$4
❏ 2929	Diamonds/African Flame	1987	$3
❏ 2929 [PS]	Diamonds/African Flame	1987	$5
❏ 714	Dina/You're Doin' What You Did with Me with Him	1963	$12

— *As "Dore Alpert*

Number	Title	Yr	NM
❏ 2441	Fandango/Coco Loco	1982	$4
❏ 2107	Foreign Natives/Mama Way	1979	$4

— *With Hugh Masekela*

Number	Title	Yr	NM
❏ 2562	Garden Party/Oriental Eyes	1983	$4
❏ 729	I'd Do It All Again/Special Kind of Love	1964	$8

— *As "Dore Alpert*

Number	Title	Yr	NM
❏ 1231	I Need You/The Lady in My Life	1988	$3
❏ 2515	Love Me the Way I Am (Quiereme Tal Como Say)/California Blues	1982	$4
❏ 2356	Magic Man/Fantasy Island	1981	$4
❏ 2356 [PS]	Magic Man/Fantasy Island	1981	$5
❏ 2949	Making Love in the Rain/Rocket to the Moon	1987	$3
❏ 2949 [PS]	Making Love in the Rain/Rocket to the Moon	1987	$3
❏ 2375	Manhattan Melody/You Smile, The Song Begins	1981	$4
❏ 2621	Oriental Eyes/Sundown	1984	$4
❏ 2973	Our Song/African Flame	1987	$3
❏ 2221	Street Life/1980	1980	$4
❏ 2221 [PS]	Street Life/1980	1980	$5
❏ 2573	Sundown/Garden Party	1983	$4
❏ 2632	We Could Be Flying/Come What May	1984	$4

— *With Lani Hall*

ANDEX

Number	Title	Yr	NM
❏ 4036	Summer School/Hully Gully	1959	$10

— *As "Herbie Alpert Sextet*

CARNIVAL

Number	Title	Yr	NM
❏ 701	Tell It to the Birds/Fallout Shelter	1962	$10

— *As "Dore Alpert*

CAROL

Number	Title	Yr	NM
❏ 700	Sweet Georgia Brown/Vipers Blues	1961	

DOT

Number	Title	Yr	NM
❏ 16396	Fallout Shelter/Tell It to the Birds	1962	$10

— *As "Dore Alpert*

RCA VICTOR

Number	Title	Yr	NM
❏ 47-7918	Gotta Get a Girl/Dreamland	1961	$15

— *As "Dore Alpert*

Number	Title	Yr	NM
❏ 47-7988	Little Lost Lover/Won't You Be My Valentine	1962	$15

— *As "Dore Alpert*

ALPERT, HERB/HUGH MASEKELA
HORIZON

Number	Title	Yr	NM
❏ 116	Lobo/African Summer	1978	$4
❏ 115	Skokiaan/African Summer	1978	$4
❏ 115 [PS]	Skokiaan/African Summer	1978	$5

Number	Title	Yr	NM

ALTAIRS, THE
AMY
| ❏ 803 | If You Love Me/Groove Time | 1960 | $30 |

ALTON AND JIMMY
SUN
| ❏ 323 | Have Faith in My Love/No More Crying the Blues | 1959 | $30 |

ALVANS, THE
MAY
| ❏ 102 | Love Is a Game/What Can It Be | 1961 | $200 |

ALVIN AND BILL
FERNWOOD
| ❏ 124 | Typing Jive/How Long | 1960 | $70 |

ALVIN, DAVE
EPIC
| ❏ 34-07394 | Every Night About This Time/Brother on the Line | 1987 | $4 |

ALVIN, JOHNNIE
WARNER BROS.
| ❏ 5024 | Santa Claus Wrecked My 'Lectric Train/Rudolph, the Red-Nosed Reindeer | 1958 | $20 |

AMAZING RHYTHM ACES
ABC
❏ 12142	Amazing Grace (Used to Be Her Favorite Song)/Beautiful Lie	1975	$4
❏ 12369	Ashes of Love/All That I Had Left (With You)	1978	$4
❏ 12359	Burning the Ballroom Down/All That I Had Left (With You)	1978	$4
❏ 12242	Dancin' the Night Away/If I Just Knew What to Say	1976	$4
❏ 12454	Lipstick Traces (On a Cigarette)/Whispering in the Night	1979	$4
❏ 12202	Same Ol' Me/The End Is Not in Sight	1976	$4
❏ 12078	Third Rate Romance/Mystery Train	1975	$5
❏ 12272	Two Can Do It Too/Living in a World Unknown	1977	$4
COLUMBIA
| ❏ 10983 | Love and Happiness/Homestead in My Heart | 1979 | $4 |
WARNER BROS.
| ❏ 49600 | I Musta Died and Gone to Texas/Give Me Flowers While I'm Living | 1980 | $4 |
| ❏ 49543 | Living on Borrowed Time/What Kind of Love Is This | 1980 | $4 |

AMBASSADORS, THE (1)
ARCTIC
❏ 150	Ain't Got the Love of One Girl/Music Makes You Wanna Dance	1969	$10
❏ 156	Can't Take My Eyes Off You/A.W.O.L.	1969	$10
❏ 147	I Really Love You/I Can't Believe You Love Me	1969	$15
❏ 153	Storm Warning/I Dig You Baby	1969	$10
ATLANTIC
❏ 2491	Good Love Gone Bad/Happiness	1968	$10
❏ 2442	(I've Got to Find) Happiness)/I'm So Proud of My Baby	1967	$10
❏ 2547	We Got Love/Never Get Tired of Loving You	1968	$10

AMBASSADORS, THE (2)
DOT
| ❏ 16528 | Surfin' John Brown/Big Breaker | 1963 | $40 |

AMBASSADORS, THE (U)
CUCA
| ❏ 1022 | Christmas Polka/Little Drummer Boy | 1960 | $15 |
SOUND STAGE 7
| ❏ 2588 | If You Don't Know (You Better Ask Somebody)/There's Something on My Baby's Mind | 1967 | $10 |

TIME
| ❏ 1007 | El Grippo/Can't Believe Ya | 1959 | $20 |
TIMELY
| ❏ 1001 | Darling I'm Sorry/Willa-Bea | 1954 | $400 |
UPTOWN
| ❏ 734 | I Need Someone/Bear With Me | 1965 | $30 |

AMBOY DUKES, THE
Also see CACTUS; TED NUGENT.
DISCREET
| ❏ 1199 | Sweet Revenge/Ain't It the Truth | 1974 | $8 |
—As "Ted Nugent and the Amboy Dukes
MAINSTREAM
❏ 676	Baby Please Don't Go/Psalms of Aftermath	1968	$15
❏ 711	Flight of the Byrd/Ivory Castles	1969	$15
❏ 704	For His Namesake/Loaded for Bear	1969	$15
❏ 700	Prodigal Man/Good Natured Emma	1969	$15

AMBROSIA
20TH CENTURY
❏ 2310	Can't Let a Woman/The Brunt	1976	$4
❏ 2207	Holdin' On to Yesterday/Make Us All Aware	1975	$5
❏ 2327	Magical Mystery Tour/Cowboy Star	1977	$5
FULL MOON
| ❏ 49654 | Outside/I Can't Tell You Why | 1981 | $5 |
—B-side by Eagles
SCEPTER
| ❏ 12373 | Shine On/Listen To Her Sing | 1973 | $8 |
WARNER BROS.
❏ 49225	Biggest Part of Me/Livin' on My Own	1980	$4
❏ 49590	Cryin' in the Rain/No Big Deal	1980	$4
❏ 29937	Feelin' Alive Again/For Openers	1982	$4
❏ 29996	How Can You Love Me/Still Not Satisfied	1982	$4
❏ 8640	How Much I Feel/Ready for Amarillo	1978	$5
—With "Burbank..." palm trees label
| ❏ 8640 | How Much I Feel/Ready for Amarillo | 1978 | $4 |
—With white label
| ❏ 8817 | If Heaven Could Find Me/Apothecary | 1979 | $4 |
| ❏ 8699 | Life Beyond L.A./Angola | 1978 | $4 |

AMECHE, JIM
DELTONE
| ❏ 5016 | The First Christmas Tree (Part 1)/The First Christmas Tree (Part 2) | 1964 | $10 |
RIC
| ❏ 137 | The First Christmas Tree (Part 1)/The First Christmas Tree (Part 2) | 1964 | $10 |
| ❏ 137 [PS] | The First Christmas Tree (Part 1)/The First Christmas Tree (Part 2) | 1964 | $15 |

AMEN CORNER
DERAM
| ❏ 85014 | Gin House Blues/I Know | 1967 | $15 |
IMMEDIATE
| ❏ 5013 | If Paradise Is Half As Nice/Hey Hey Girl | 1968 | $10 |

AMERICA
AMERICAN INT'L.
| ❏ 700 | California Dreamin'/See It My Way | 1979 | $5 |
—B-side by FDR
| ❏ 700 [PS] | California Dreamin'/See It My Way | 1979 | $5 |
CAPITOL
❏ 4817	All Around/1960	1980	$4
❏ 4777	All My Life/One Morning	1979	$4
❏ B-5430	(Can't Fall Asleep to a) Lullaby/Fallin' Off the World	1984	$3
❏ B-5275	Cast the Spirit/My Dear	1983	$3

❏ 4950	One in a Million/Hangover	1980	$4
❏ 4752	Only Game in Town/High in the City	1979	$4
❏ B-5398	Special Girl/Unconditional Love	1984	$3
❏ B-5236	The Border/Sometimes Lovers	1983	$3
❏ B-5236 [PS]	The Border/Sometimes Lovers	1983	$3
WARNER BROS.
| ❏ 7555 | A Horse with No Name/Everyone I Meet Is From California | 1972 | $6 |
| ❏ 7650 | A Horse with No Name/I Need You | 1973 | $4 |
—Back to Back Hits" series
❏ 8238	Amber Cascades/Who Loves You	1976	$5
❏ 8118	Daisy Jane/Tomorrow	1975	$5
❏ 7670	Don't Cross the River/To Each His Own	1972	$5
❏ 8397	Don't Cry Baby/Monster	1977	$5
❏ 8373	God of the Sun/Down to the Water	1977	$5
❏ 7580	I Need You/Riverside	1972	$5
❏ 7580 [PS]	I Need You/Riverside	1972	$6
❏ 8048	Lonely People/Mad Dog	1974	$5
❏ 8048 [PS]	Lonely People/Mad Dog	1974	$6
❏ 7725	Muskrat Love/Cornwall Blank	1973	$5
❏ 7694	Only in Your Heart/Moon Song	1973	$5
❏ 8285	She's Beside You/She's a Liar	1976	$5
❏ 7785	She's Gonna Let You Down/Green Monkey	1974	$5
❏ 8086	Sister Golden Hair/Midnight	1975	$5
❏ 7839	Tin Man/In the Country	1974	$5
❏ 8014	Tin Man/In the Country	1974	$4
❏ 8212	Today's the Day/Hideaway (Part 2)	1976	$5
❏ 8157	Woman Tonight/Bell Tree	1975	$5

AMERICAN BEATLES, THE
BYP
| ❏ 1001 | She's Mine/Theme of the American Beetles | 1964 | $30 |
—As "The American Beetles
ROULETTE
| ❏ 4559 | School Days/Hey Hey Girl | 1964 | $20 |
—As "The American Beetles

AMERICAN BLUES, THE
Early incarnation of ZZ TOP.
KARMA
| ❏ 1001 | If I Were a Carpenter/(B-side unknown) | 1967 | $50 |

AMERICAN BREED, THE
ACTA
❏ 827	Anyway You Want Me/Master of My Fate	1968	$8
❏ 811	Bend Me, Shape Me/Mindrocker	1967	$15
❏ 837	Cool It/The Brain	1969	$8
❏ 808	Don't Forget About Me/Short Skirts	1967	$8
❏ 821	Green Light/Don't It Make You Cry	1968	$8
❏ 821 [PS]	Green Light/Don't It Make You Cry	1968	$30
❏ 833	Hunky Funky/Enter Her Majesty	1969	$8
❏ 802	I Don't Think You Know/Give Two Young Lovers a Chance	1967	$8
❏ 830	Private Zoo/Keep the Faith	1968	$8
❏ 804	Step Out of Your Mind/Same Old Thing	1967	$10
❏ 0040	Can't Make It Without You/When I'm With You	1970	$6

AMERICAN COMEDY NETWORK, THE
CRITIQUE
| ❏ 704 | Breaking Up Is Hard on You (a/k/a Don't Take Ma Bell Away from Me)// +3 "Krapco" commercials | 1984 | $5 |

AMERICAN DREAM, THE
AMPEX
| ❏ 11001 | Goodnews/I Ain't Searchin' | 1970 | $10 |
| ❏ 11001 [PS] | Goodnews/I Ain't Searchin' | 1970 | $20 |

AMERICAN EAGLE
DECCA
| ❏ 32833 | Ballad of a Well-Known Gun/On the Rack | 1971 | $12 |
| ❏ 32788 | Family/Gospel | 1971 | $8 |

AMERICAN FOUR, THE
SELMA
| ❏ 2001 | Luci Baines/Soul Food | 1964 | $60 |

AMERICAN SPRING
COLUMBIA

Number	Title	Yr	NM
45834	Fallin' in Love/Shyin' Away	1973	$40
45834 [PS]	Fallin' in Love/Shyin' Away	1973	$70

AMERICA'S CHILDREN
AUDITION

Number	Title	Yr	NM
6106	Swingin' Christmas/The Star	1965	$10

AMES, APRIL
ZEPHYR

Number	Title	Yr	NM
ZR 70-013	Imagination/A Smile Will Go a Long, Long Way	1957	$15

AMES BROTHERS, THE
CORAL

Number	Title	Yr	NM
60804	Absence Makes the Heart Grow Fonder (For Someone Else)/String Along	1952	$15
61005	Always in My Dreams/This Is Fiesta	1953	$15
60967	At the End of a Rainbow/Candy Bar Boogie	1953	$15
60773	Auf Wiedersehn Sweetheart/Break the Bonds That Bind Me	1952	$15
60339	Because/Love's Old Sweet Song	1950	$20
60636	Blind Barnabas/Who Built the Ark	1952	$15
60513	Blue Hawaii/Moon of Manakoora	1951	$20
60212	Blue Prelude/Lorelei	1950	$20
60386	Can Anyone Explain?/Lingering Down the Lane (Ah! La Petit Vin Blanc)	1951	$20
60253	Can Anyone Explain? (No, No, No!)/Sittin' 'N Starin' 'N Rockin'	1950	$20
60399	Clancey Lowered the Boom/More Beer	1951	$20
60633	Deep River/Dry Bones	1952	$15
60870	Do Nothin' Till You Hear from Me/No Moon at All	1952	$15
61127	Don't Believe a Word They Say/Helen Polka	1954	$15
61145	Don't Lie to Me/Don't Believe a Word They Say	1954	$15
60185	Dormi, Dormi/Marianna	1950	$20
60269	Hark! The Herald Angels Sing/It Came Upon a Midnight Clear	1950	$20
60510	Hawaiian War Chant/Sweet Leilani	1951	$20
60885	Home on the Range/Wagon Wheels	1952	$15
60209	Hoop-De-Doo/Stars Are the Windows of Heaven	1950	$20
60617	I Wanna Love You/I'll Still Love You	1952	$15
61060	Lazy River/Stardust	1953	$15
60926	Lonely Wine/Can't I	1953	$15
60387	Lorelei/To Think You've Chosen Me	1951	$20
60352	Loving Is Believing/Music by the Angels (Lyrics by the Lord)	1951	$20
60398	Marianna/(Lift Your Glass) Sing Until the Cows Come Home	1951	$20
60338	Meet Me Tonight in Dreamland/Moonlight Bay	1950	$20
60628	Mother, At Your Feet Is Kneeling/Lovely Lady Dressed in Blue	1952	$15
61723	Mother At Your Feet Is Kneeling/Lovely Lady Dressed in Blue	1956	$15
60846	My Favorite Song/Al-Lee-O! Al-Lee-Ay!	1952	$15
60511	My Little Grass Shack/To You, Sweetheart, Aloha	1951	$20
60404	My Love Serenade/I Love You Much Too Much	1951	$20
60270	Oh, Little Town of Bethlehem/God Rest Ye Merry Gentlemen	1950	$20
60327	Oh Babe/To Think You've Chosen Me	1950	$20
60887	Old Faithful/Tumbling Tumbleweeds	1952	$15
60549	Only, Only You/Everything's Gonna Be Alright	1951	$15
60566	Sentimental Journey/Undecided	1951	$20
60173	Sentimental Me/Blue Prelude	1950	$20
60385	Sentimental Me/Dormi, Dormi	1951	$20
60634	Shadrack/Swing Low, Sweet Chariot	1952	$15
60268	Silent Night/Adeste Fideles	1950	$20
60861	Sing a Song of Santa Claus/Winter's Here Again	1952	$15
60512	Sing Me a Song of the Islands/Song of the Islands	1951	$20
60751	Stardust/Crazy 'Cause I Love You	1952	$15
60388	Stars Are the Window of Heaven/I Don't Mind Being All Alone (When I'm Alone with You)	1951	$20
60888	The Last Round-Up/The Strawberry Roan	1952	$15
60680	The Shiek of Araby/And So I Waited	1952	$15
60333	The Thing/Music by the Angels (Lyrics by the Lord)	1950	$20
60267	The Twelve Days of Christmas/Wassail Song	1950	$20
60300	Thirsty for Your Kisses/I Don't Mind Being All Alone	1950	$20
60363	Three Dollars and Ninety-Eight Cents/More Than I Care to Remember	1951	$20
60337	Till We Meet Again/Tell Me Your Dream	1950	$20
60452	Too Many Women/Sometimes There Must Be Happiness	1951	$20
60489	Wang Wang Blues/Who'll Take My Love	1951	$20
9-60113	White Christmas/Winter Wonderland	1950	$30

— 78 rpm version issued in 1949

EPIC

Number	Title	Yr	NM
9530	Love Me with All Your Heart/Love Is an Ocean of Emotion	1962	$8
9591	Surrender, Surrender/Wrong Man	1963	$8
9630	Washington Square/Knees Up, Mother Brown	1963	$8

MCA

Number	Title	Yr	NM
60005	Sentimental Journey/Undecided	1973	$4

— With Les Brown

RCA VICTOR

Number	Title	Yr	NM
47-6608	49 Shades of Green/Summer Sweetheart	1956	$10
47-7742	A Hayy Pair/Carnival	1960	$8
47-7655	China Doll/Chritsopher Sunday	1959	$10
47-7655 [PS]	China Doll/Chritsopher Sunday	1959	$20
47-7474	Dancin' in the Streets/(Yes I Need) Only Your Love	1959	$12
47-6400	Forever Darling/I'm Gonna Love You	1956	$10
47-6117	Gotta Be This or That/Southern Cross	1955	$10
47-5530	I Can't Believe That You're in Love with Me/Boogie Woogie Maxixe	1953	$15
H7OW-6566/7 [DJ]	I Couldn't Sleep a Wink Last Night/Por Favor	1957	$30

— White label; "Advance Release from New RCA Victor Album Sweet Seventeen

Number	Title	Yr	NM
47-6821	I Only Know One Way to Love You/Did You Ever Get the Roses	1957	$10
47-6720	I Saw Esau/The Game of Love	1956	$10
47-6481	It Only Hurts for a Little While/If You Wanna See Mamie Tonight	1956	$10
47-7365	It's Only a Paper Moon/I Don't Know Why	1958	$10
47-5764	Leave It to Your Heart/Let's Walk and Talk	1954	$12
47-7142	Little Gypsy/In Love	1958	$12
47-5644	Man Is for the Woman Made/The Man with the Banjo	1954	$10
47-7046	Melodie D'Amour/So Little Time	1957	$10
47-6208	My Bonnie Lassie/So Will I	1955	$10
47-5404	My Love, My Life, My Happiness/If You Want My Heart	1953	$15
47-6323	My Love, Your Love/The Next Time It Happens	1955	$10
47-5840	One More Time/Hopelessly	1954	$10
47-7315	Pussy Cat/No One But You	1958	$10
47-7526	Someone Come Home To/Mason-Dixon Line	1959	$12
47-7268	Stay/Little Serenade	1958	$10
47-7801	Suzie Wong/There the Hot Winds Blow	1960	$8
47-6044	Sympathetic Sweet/Sweet Brown-Eyed Baby	1955	$10
47-7604	Take Me Along/What Do I Hear	1959	$10
47-6930	Tammy/Rockin' Shoes	1957	$10
47-5929	There'll Always Be a Christmas/I Got a Cold for Christmas	1954	$10
WY491	There'll Always Be a Christmas/I Got a Cold for Christmas	1954	$10

— From the "Little Nipper" children's series

Number	Title	Yr	NM
WY491 [PS]	There'll Always Be a Christmas/I Got a Cold for Christmas	1954	$15
47-6156	Wrong Again/Merci Beaucoup	1955	$10

7-Inch Extended Plays
CORAL

Number	Title	Yr	NM
EC81060	*Home on the Range/Wagon Wheels/Rye Whiskey/You Are My Sunshine	1955	$25
EC81053	*In the Evening by the Moonlight/Just a Dream of You Dear/Till We Meet Again/You Tell Me Your Dream, I'll Tell You Mine	1954	$25
EC81000	*Star Dust/Lazy River/Wang Wang Blues/The Sheik of Araby	1953	$25
EC81041	*White Christmas/Winter Wonderland/Jolly Old St. Nicholas/Ting-a-Linga-Jingle	1954	$25
EC81043	Absence Makes the Heart Grow Fonder (For Someone Else)/String Along//Auf Wiederseh'n Sweetheart/Thirsty for Your Kisses	1954	$25
EC81041 [PS]	Christmas Greetings from the Ames Brothers	1954	$25
EC81100	Dry Bones/Deep River//Shadrack/Swing Low Sweet Chariot	1956	$25
EC81042 [PS]	Favorite Songs, Vol. 1	1954	$25
EC81043 [PS]	Favorite Songs, Vol. 2	1954	$25
EC81100 [PS]	Favorite Spirituals	1956	$25
EC81060 [PS]	Home on the Range	1955	$25
EC81053 [PS]	In the Evening by the Moonlight	1954	$25
EC81042	My Favorite Song/Blue Prelude//Cruising Down the River/Oh, You Sweet One	1954	$25
EC81000 [PS]	Song Time	1953	$25
EC81054 [PS]	Sweet Leilani	1954	$25
EC81054	To You Sweetheart, Aloha/My Little Grass Shack in Kealakekua, Hawaii//Sweet Leilani/Hawaiian War Chant	1954	$25

RCA VICTOR

Number	Title	Yr	NM
EPA-819	(contents unknown)	1956	$20
EPA-820	(contents unknown)	1956	$20
EPA 3-1541	Deck the Halls/C-H-R-I-S-T-M-A-S/The Night Before Christmas Song/Santa Claus Is Comin' to Town	1957	$20
EPA-4227 [PS]	Destination Moon	1958	$20
ESP-4227 [PS]	Destination Moon	1958	$30
EPA-4227 [M]	Destination Moon/It's Only a Paper Moon//I'm Shooting High/Music from Out of Space	1958	$20
ESP-4227 [S]	Destination Moon/It's Only a Paper Moon//I'm Shooting High/Music from Out of Space	1958	$30
EPA-680	Exactly Like You	1955	$20
EPA-680 [PS]	Exactly Like You/I Only Have Eyes for You//Autumn Leaves/You're Driving Me Crazy	1955	$20
EPA-819 [PS]	Four Brothers, Vol. 1	1956	$20
EPA-820 [PS]	Four Brothers, Vol. 2	1956	$20
SP-45-48 [PS]	French's Mustard Invites You to a Platter Party with the Ames Brothers	1958	$25
547-0329	Gotta Be This or That/Anniversary Song//Love Your Magic Spell Is Everywhere/I Can't Give You Anything But Love	1953	$20

— Part of 2-EP set, EPB-3186

Number	Title	Yr	NM
EPA-4213	I Don't Know Why (I Just Do)/Don't Get Around Much Anymore//For Sentimental Reasons/Oh What It Seemed to Be	1958	$20
EPB3186 [PS]	It Must Be True	1953	$20

— Two-pocket jacket for two-EP set

Number	Title	Yr	NM
EPA-790	It Must Be True/The Alphabet/Ol' Man River//Gotta Be This or That/Anniversary Song/That's the Way Love Goes	1956	$20
EPA-4173 [PS]	Melodie D'Amour	1957	$20
EPA-4173	Melodie d'Amour/Fascination//Sayonara/Around the World	1957	$20
SP-45-48	Moonglow/Rag Mop//Seventeen/Two Sleepy People/When My Sugar Walks Down My Street/I Can't Give You Anything But Love	1958	$25
LPC-112	Moonlight Serenade/And the Angels Sing//Heartaches/It's the Talk of the Town	1961	$25

— Compact 33 Double"; small hole, plays at 33 1/3 rpm

Number	Title	Yr	NM
EPA 2-1541	O Holy Night/What Child Is This//Good King Wenceslas/Go Tell It on the Mountain	1957	$20
EPA-4213 [PS]	Sentimental Mood	1958	$20
EPA 1-1541	Silver Bells/The Christmas Song//Jingle Bells/There'll Always Be a Christmas	1957	$20
EPA-4096 [PS]	Tammy	1957	$20
EPA-4096	Tammy/Not You Not I//That's the Way Love Goes/The Rhythm in My Heart	1957	$20
EPA-790 [PS]	The Ames Brothers	1956	$20
EPA-5020 [PS]	The Ames Brothers (Gold Standard Series)	1958	$20
LPC-112	The Ames Brothers Sing the Best of the Bands	1961	$25
EPA-4320 [PS]	The Best of the Ames Brothers	1958	$20
EPA-571 [PS]	The Man with the Banjo	1955	$20

Number	Title	Yr	NM
❏ EPA-571	The Man with the Banjo/You, You, You//Man, Man Is for the Woman Made/I Can't Believe That You're in Love with Me	1955	$20
❏ EPA 1-1541 [PS]	There'll Always Be a Christmas, Vol. 1	1957	$20
❏ EPA 2-1541 [PS]	There'll Always Be a Christmas, Vol. 2	1957	$20
❏ EPA 3-1541 [PS]	There'll Always Be a Christmas, Vol. 3	1957	$20

AMES, ED

HELLO LYNDON

Number	Title	Yr	NM
❏ RPKM-4426	Hello, Lyndon!/Hello, Lyndon! (Chorus)	1964	$30
❏ RPKM-4426 [PS]	Hello, Lyndon!/Hello, Lyndon! (Chorus)	1964	$60

—Promotional item for Lyndon Johnson's 1964 election campaign

RCA VICTOR

Number	Title	Yr	NM
❏ 74-0156	2001/Son of a Travelin' Man	1969	$6
❏ 74-0678	And I Love You So/The Ship	1972	$4
❏ 47-9517	Apologize/The Wind Will Change Tomorrow	1968	$6
❏ 47-9249	Ballad of the War Wagon/Time, Time	1967	$6
❏ 47-8245	Before I Kiss the World Goodbye/They Were You	1963	$8
❏ 74-0883	Butterflies Are Free/The World Is a Circle	1973	$4
❏ 47-9726	Changing, Changing/Six Words	1969	$6
❏ 47-9864	Chippewa Town/Sing Away the World	1970	$6
❏ 47-8547	Dio Mio/Weaver, Weaver	1965	$8
❏ 74-0726	Distant Drums/Blue Side of Lonesome	1972	$4
❏ 47-8393	Give Me Back My Life/Monica (Love Theme from "The Carpetbaggers")	1964	$8
❏ 47-8871	Gone/There's a Time for Everything	1966	$8
❏ 74-0551	He Gives Us All His Love/Angelica	1971	$5
❏ 74-0329	Honey, What's the Matter/Three Good Reasons	1970	$5
❏ 47-9589	I'll Stay Lonely/All My Love's Laughter	1968	$6
❏ 47-8320	It Only Takes a Moment/The Time Has Come	1964	$8
❏ 47-9319	Let Me So Love/When the Snow Is on the Roses	1967	$6
❏ 74-0800	Lost Horizon/Question Me an Answer	1972	$4
❏ 74-0253	Love of the Common People/Leave Them a Flower	1969	$6
❏ 74-0498	More Than Ever Before/The Day	1971	$5
❏ 47-9002	My Cup Runneth Over/It Seems a Long, Long Time	1966	$8
❏ 47-8231	My Love Is Yours/Somewhere	1963	$8
❏ 47-9178	One Little Girl at a Time/Time, Time	1967	$6
❏ 47-8700	Pretty Is/Melinda	1965	$8
❏ 74-0398	The Answer Is/Sweet, Sweet Reason	1970	$5
❏ SP-45-188 [DJ]	The Ballad Of The Christmas Donkey/Let It Snow! Let It Snow! Let It Snow!	1968	$8
❏ 47-6791	The Bean Song/I'd Give You the World	1957	$15

—As "Eddie Ames"

Number	Title	Yr	NM
❏ 74-0296	Thing Called Love/Today Is the First Day of the Rest of Our Lives	1969	$6
❏ 47-8483	Try to Remember/Love Is Here to Stay	1964	$8
❏ 47-9400	Who Will Answer/My Love Is Gone from Me	1967	$6
❏ 47-9400 [PS]	Who Will Answer/My Love Is Gone from Me	1967	$15

AMES, NANCY

ABC

Number	Title	Yr	NM
❏ 11100	On Green Dolphin Street/Something's Gotten Hold of My Heart	1968	$6

EPIC

Number	Title	Yr	NM
❏ 9885	Dear Hearts and Gentle People/Friends and Lovers Forever	1966	$8
❏ 10003	He Wore the Green Beret/War Is a Card Game	1966	$8
❏ 10056	I Don't Want to Talk About It/Cry Softly	1966	$15
❏ 9874	I've Got a Lot of Love (Left in Me)/Friends and Lovers Forever	1965	$8
❏ 10149	Love's Wine/My Story Book	1967	$8
❏ 9845	Shake a Hand/Funny Thing About It	1965	$8

LIBERTY

Number	Title	Yr	NM
❏ 55598	An Elizabethan Ballad (Part 1)/An Elizabethan Ballad (Part 2)	1963	$10

Number	Title	Yr	NM
❏ 55548	Bonsoir Cher/Cu Cu Rru Cu Cu Paloma	1963	$10
❏ 55762	It Scares Me/Let Tonight Linger On	1965	$10
❏ 55737	Malaguena Salerosa/Cu Cu Ru Cu Cu Paloma	1964	$10

7-Inch Extended Plays

EPIC

Number	Title	Yr	NM
❏ 5-26197 [PS]	As Time Goes By	1967	$12
❏ 5-26197	As Time Goes By/You've Changed/Now Is the Hour//You'll Never Know/How Deep Is the Ocean (How High Is the Sky)/Speak Low	1967	$10

—Jukebox issue; small hole, plays at 33 1/3 rpm

AMES, DE DE

ADVANTAGE

Number	Title	Yr	NM
❏ 185	Break Down the Walls/(B-side unknown)	1987	$6
❏ 175	Dancin' in the Moonlight/(B-side unknown)	1987	$6

—As "Durelle Ames

AMMONS, GENE, AND SONNY STITT

PRESTIGE

Number	Title	Yr	NM
❏ 709	Blues Up and Down/You Can Depend On Me	1951	$30

AMMONS, GENE

ARGO

Number	Title	Yr	NM
❏ 5417	I Can't Stop Loving You/My Babe	1962	$10

DECCA

Number	Title	Yr	NM
❏ 9-28222	Breezy/Somewhere Along the Way	1952	$20
❏ 9-28094	Old Folks/I'll Walk Alone	1952	$20
❏ 227	Anna/Pagan Love Song	1962	$10
❏ 713	Bye Bye/Let It Be	1951	$20
❏ 734	Didn't We/Son of a Preacher Man	1970	$6
❏ 226	I Sold My Heart to the Junkman/Moonglow	1962	$10
❏ 717	I Wanna Be Loved/Gravy	1951	$20
❏ 757	Lady Sings the Blues/Play Me	1973	$6
❏ 214	Twisting the Jug (Part 1)/Twisting the Jug (Part 2)	1962	$15

UNITED

Number	Title	Yr	NM
❏ 175	Big Slam (Part 1)/Big Slam (Part 2)	1955	$20
❏ 164	Stairway to the Stars/Jim Dog	1955	$20
❏ 137	Street of Dreams/The Beat	1954	$20
❏ 185	Traveling Light/Fuzzy	1956	$20

AMON DUUL II

LIBERTY

Number	Title	Yr	NM
❏ 56196	Soda Shop Rock/Archangel's Thunderbird	1970	$6

UNITED ARTISTS

Number	Title	Yr	NM
❏ XW419	Pigman/Mozambique	1974	$5

AMOS 'N' ANDY

COLUMBIA

Number	Title	Yr	NM
❏ 48002	The Lord's Prayer/Little Bitty Baby	1962	$8
❏ 48002 [PS]	The Lord's Prayer/Little Bitty Baby	1962	$10
❏ 42623 [DJ]	The Lord's Prayer/Little Bitty Baby	1962	$8

AMOS, TORI

Also see Y KANT TORI READ.

MEA

Number	Title	Yr	NM
❏ 5290	Baltimore/Walking with You	1980	$800

—As "Ellen Amos

AMY

SCORPION

Number	Title	Yr	NM
❏ 0570	Please Be Gentle/Jump Into My Love	1979	$6

AMY AND THE JARRETTS

HIT

Number	Title	Yr	NM
❏ 151	I Know Johnny Loves Me/Tobacco Road	1964	$10

—B-side by the Roamers

ANACOSTIA

COLUMBIA

Number	Title	Yr	NM
❏ 3-10203	All I Need/One Less Morning	1975	$5
❏ 4-45685	On and Off (Part 1)/(Part 2)	1972	$6
❏ 4-45820	Thick and Thin/I Just Wander	1973	$6

MCA

Number	Title	Yr	NM
❏ 40838	I Can't Stop Loving Her/What Kind of Love	1977	$6

ROULETTE

Number	Title	Yr	NM
❏ 7300	Love Is Never Wrong/(B-side unknown)	1980	$8

TABU

Number	Title	Yr	NM
❏ 5506	Ain't Nothing To It/Anything for You	1978	$5

ANASTASIA

LAURIE

Number	Title	Yr	NM
❏ 3066	Time Bomb/That's My Kind of Love	1960	$30

ANDANTES, THE

DOT

Number	Title	Yr	NM
❏ 16495	My Baby's Gone/No Yo Ru	1963	$30

V.I.P.

Number	Title	Yr	NM
❏ 25006	If You Were Mine/(Like a) Nightmare	1964	$4000

—One of the rarest of all Motown-related 45s. VG 2000; VG+ 3000

ANDERS & PONCIA

KAMA SUTRA

Number	Title	Yr	NM
❏ 240	So It Goes/Virgin of the Night	1967	$15

WARNER BROS.

Number	Title	Yr	NM
❏ 7294	Make a Change (To Something Better)/Lucky	1969	$8
❏ 7271	Take His Love/I'm Beginning to Touch You	1969	$8

ANDERS, BERNIE

KING

Number	Title	Yr	NM
❏ 4833	My Heart Believes/Too Late I Learned	1955	$60

ANDERSEN, ERIC

ARISTA

Number	Title	Yr	NM
❏ 0141	Be True to You/(B-side unknown)	1975	$4
❏ 0121	Ol' 55/Can't Get You Out of My Life	1975	$4

COLUMBIA

Number	Title	Yr	NM
❏ 45730	Blue River/More Often Than Not	1972	$5
❏ 45637	Is It Really Love at All/Pearl's Goodtime Blues	1972	$5

WARNER BROS.

Number	Title	Yr	NM
❏ 7459	Born Again/Rocky Mountain Red	1971	$6
❏ 7408	Lie with Me/Secrets	1970	$6
❏ 7435	Sittin' in the Sunshine/Sunshine & Flowers	1970	$6
❏ 7231	Think About It/So Hard to Fall	1968	$6

ANDERSON, BILL, AND ROY ACUFF

MCA

Number	Title	Yr	NM
❏ 52290	I Wonder If God Likes Country Music/Ride Off Into the Sunset	1983	$4

ANDERSON, BILL, AND JAN HOWARD

DECCA

Number	Title	Yr	NM
❏ 32877	Dis-Satisfied/Knowing You're Mine	1971	$8
❏ 32197	For Loving You/The Untouchables	1967	$8
❏ 32511	If It's All the Same to You/I Thank God for You	1969	$8
❏ 31884	I Know You're Married (But I Love You Still)/Time Out	1966	$10
❏ 32689	Someday We'll Be Together/Who's the Biggest Fool	1970	$8

ANDERSON, BILL, AND MARY LOU TURNER

MCA

Number	Title	Yr	NM
❏ 40852	I'm Way Ahead of You/Just Enough to Make Me Want It All	1978	$4
❏ 40488	Sometimes/Circle in a Triangle	1975	$4
❏ 40533	That's What Made Me Love You/Can We Still Be Friends	1976	$4
❏ 40753	Where Are You Going, Billy Boy/Sad Ole Shade of Gray	1977	$4

ANDERSON, BILL

DECCA

Number	Title	Yr	NM
❑ 31521	8 x 10/One Mile Over – Two Miles Back	1963	$10
❑ 31521 [PS]	8 x 10/One Mile Over – Two Miles Back	1963	$30
❑ 31825	Bright Lights and Country Music/Born	1965	$10
❑ 31743	Certain/You Can Have Her	1965	$10
❑ 9-30993	Dead or Alive/It's Not the End of Everything	1959	$20
❑ 31577	Five Little Fingers/Easy Come -- Easy Go	1964	$10
❑ 31358	Get a Little Dirt on Your Hands/ Down Came the Rain	1962	$15
❑ 32077	Get While the Gettin's Good/ Something to Believe In	1967	$8
❑ 32360	Happy State of Mind/ Time's Been Good to Me	1968	$8
❑ 31999	I Get the Fever/The First Mrs. Jones	1966	$8
❑ 31890	I Love You Drops/Golden Guitar	1966	$10
❑ 31681	In Case You Ever Change Your Mind/Three A.M.	1964	$10
❑ 31404	Mama Sang a Song/ On and On and On	1962	$10
❑ 31630	Me/Cincinnati, Ohio	1964	$10
❑ 32417	Po' Folks' Christmas/ Christmas Time's a-Coming	1968	$8
❑ 32417 [PS]	Po' Folks' Christmas/ Christmas Time's a-Coming	1968	$20
❑ 31262	Po' Folks/Goodbye Cruel World	1961	$15
❑ 31458	Still/You Made It Easy	1963	$10
❑ 32215	Stranger on the Run/Happiness	1967	$8
❑ 9-30773	That's What It's Like to Be Lonesome/Thrill of My Life	1958	$20
❑ 31092	The Tip of My Fingers/ No Man's Land	1960	$15
❑ 31168	Walk Out Backwards/ The Best of Strangers	1960	$15
❑ 32276	Wild Week-End/Fun While It Lasted	1968	$8

MCA

Number	Title	Yr	NM
❑ 40243	Can I Come Home to You/I'm Happily Married	1974	$4
❑ 40404	Country D.J./We Made Love	1975	$4
❑ 40964	Double S/Married Lady	1978	$4
❑ 40304	Every Time I Turn the Radio On/You Are My Story	1974	$4
❑ 40713	Head to Toe/Love Song for Jackie	1977	$4
❑ 51150	Homebody/One Man Band	1981	$4
❑ 40893	I Can't Wait Any Longer/Joanna	1978	$4
❑ 40004	If You Can Live With It (I Can Live Without It)/Let's Fall Apart	1973	$4
❑ 40351	I Still Feel the Same About You/Talk to Me Ohio	1975	$4
❑ 51017	I Want That Feelin' Again/ She Made Me Remember	1980	$4
❑ 40661	Liars One, Believers Zero/ Let Me Whisper Darling One More Time	1976	$4
❑ 41212	Mike Mine Night Time/ Old Me and You	1980	$4
❑ 51052	Mister Peepers/How Married Are You, Mary Ann	1981	$4
❑ 41150	More Than a Bedroom Thing/Love Me and I'll Be Your Best Friend	1979	$4
❑ 40595	Peanuts and Diamonds/ Your Love Blows Me Away	1976	$4
❑ 40794	Still the One/This Ole Suitcase	1977	$4
❑ 40443	Thanks/Why's the Last Time Have to Be the Best	1975	$4
❑ 40070	The Corner of My Life/ Home and Things	1973	$4
❑ 41060	The Dream Never Dies/ One More Sexy Lady	1979	$4
❑ 40992	This Is a Love Song/ Remembering the Good	1979	$4
❑ 51204	Whiskey Made Me Stumble (The Devil Made Me Fall)/ All That Keeps Me Goin'	1981	$4
❑ 40164	World of Make Believe/ Gonna Shine on It Again	1973	$4

SOUTHERN TRACKS

Number	Title	Yr	NM
❑ 1011	Laid Off/Lovin' Tonight	1982	$5
❑ 1067	Sheet Music/Maybe Go Down	1986	$5
❑ 1021	Son of the South/20th Century Fox	1983	$5
❑ 1007	Southern Fried/You Turn the Light On	1982	$5
❑ 1030	Speculation/We May Never Pass This Way Again	1984	$5
❑ 1014	Thank You Darling/ Lovin' Tonight	1983	$5

SWANEE

Number	Title	Yr	NM
❑ 5015	Pity Party/Don't She Look Good	1985	$5
❑ 5018	When You Leave That Way, You Can Never Go Back/Quits	1985	$5
❑ 4013	Wino the Clown/Wild Weekend	1985	$5

TNT

Number	Title	Yr	NM
❑ 9015	City Lights/No Song to Sing	1958	$100
❑ 146	Empty Room/Take Me	1957	$75
❑ 165	Empty Room/Take Me	1958	$70

7-Inch Extended Plays

DECCA

Number	Title	Yr	NM
❑ 7-34330 [PS]	From This Pen	1965	$20
❑ 7-34330	Once a Day/Saginaw, Michigan/City Lights//Po' Folks/ Still/I Don't Love You Anymore	1965	$20

—Jukebox issue; small hole, plays at 33 1/3 rpm

Number	Title	Yr	NM
❑ DL 734534 [PS]	Wild Weekend	1968	$15
❑ DL 734534	Wild Week-End/The Last Thing on My Mind/No One's Gonna Hurt You Anymore// Gentle on My Mind/Sleep/ Won't It Ever Be Morning	1968	$15

—Jukebox issue; small hole, plays at 33 1/3 rpm

ANDERSON, BROTHER JAMES

SUN

Number	Title	Yr	NM
❑ 406	I'm Gonna Move in the Room with the Lord/My Soul Needs Resting	1967	$60

ANDERSON BRUFORD WAKEMAN HOWE

ARISTA

Number	Title	Yr	NM
❑ 9852	Brother of Mine/Vultures	1989	$3

ANDERSON, CAROL

BIG TREE

Number	Title	Yr	NM
❑ 135	Holding On/You Boy	1972	$30

FEE

Number	Title	Yr	NM
❑ 101	Sad Girl/I'll Get Off at the Next Stop	1979	$400

MID-TOWN

Number	Title	Yr	NM
❑ 270	Holding On/It Shouldn't Happen to a Dog	1972	$50
❑ 271	Holding On/You Boy	1972	$40

SOUL "O" SONIC

Number	Title	Yr	NM
❑ 500	Tomorrow Is Not a Promise/ One Man's Woman	1973	$50

ANDERSON, CASEY

AMOS

Number	Title	Yr	NM
❑ 126	I'll Be Your Baby Tonight/ Monsson Season Hungries	1969	$10

ATCO

Number	Title	Yr	NM
❑ 6377	Blues Is a Woman Gone/Say Yes	1965	$20
❑ 6279	Green Rocky Road/This Little Light of Mine	1963	$50
—63			
❑ 6313	More Pretty Girls Than One/ San Francisco Bay Blues	1964	$20

REPRISE

Number	Title	Yr	NM
❑ 0774	God Knows I Love You/ The Things You Do	1967	$10
❑ 0824	Suburbia/Gentle Lovin'	1969	$10

ANDERSON, DEBORAH

COLUMBIA

Number	Title	Yr	NM
❑ 4-45891	Don't Know What's Coming Tomorrow/(B-side unknown)	1973	$6

ANDERSON, ELTON

CAPITOL

Number	Title	Yr	NM
❑ 4830	Shed So Many Tears/ That's How It's Been	1962	$20
❑ 4762	Sick and Tired/Life Problem	1962	$20

LANOR

Number	Title	Yr	NM
❑ 518	Bye Bye Little Angel/ Don't Touch Me Baby	1963	$20
❑ 507	Humpty Dumpty Heart/ Don't Touch Me Baby	1962	$20
❑ 514	I Love You So/(Sorry) I'm Gonna Have to Pass	1963	$20
❑ 509	Sick and Tired/Life Problem	1962	$30
❑ 516	The Crawl (Part 1)/(Part 2)	1963	$20

MERCURY

Number	Title	Yr	NM
❑ 71542	Secret of Love/Cool Down Baby	1959	$30
❑ 71643	Walking Alone/Crying Blues	1960	$30

TREY

Number	Title	Yr	NM
❑ 1011	Secret of Love/Cool Down Baby	1959	$30
❑ 1002	Want a Come Back Home/I Love You	1959	$30

ANDERSON, ERNESTINE

MERCURY

Number	Title	Yr	NM
❑ 71772	A Lover's Question/That's All I Want from You	1961	$8
❑ 71536	Call Me Darling/My Love Will Last	1959	$10
❑ 71960	Hurry Hurry/After the Lights Go Down Low	1962	$8
❑ 71500	I Can Dream, Can't I/I Heard You Cried Last Night	1959	$10
❑ 71423	I Don't See Me in Your Eyes Anymore/Be Mine	1959	$10
❑ 71354	My Man/Wrap Your Troubles in Dreams	1958	$10
❑ 71919	See See Rider/Mound Bayou	1961	$8
❑ 71559	There Are Such Things/ You, You, You	1960	$8

SUE

Number	Title	Yr	NM
❑ 115	I Pity the Fool/You're Not the Guy for Me	1964	$30
❑ 803	The Best Is Yet to Come/ Will I Find My Love Today	1964	$8

ANDERSON, JESSE

CADET

Number	Title	Yr	NM
❑ 5588	Get Loose When You Get Loose/Swing Too High	1968	$10
❑ 5554	True Love Express/ You're Only a Woman	1967	$10

JEWEL

Number	Title	Yr	NM
❑ 835	Help Wanted/Send Me Some Loving	1972	$8

THOMAS

Number	Title	Yr	NM
❑ 805	I Got a Problem/Mighty Mighty	1970	$20
❑ 807	Let Me Back In/ Readings in Astrology	1970	$12

ANDERSON, JOHN

ACE OF HEARTS

Number	Title	Yr	NM
❑ 0500	Swoop Down, Sweet Jesus/ (B-side unknown)	1975	$8

MCA

Number	Title	Yr	NM
❑ 53441	Down in the Orange Grove/The Will of God	1988	$3
❑ 53366	If It Ain't Broke Don't Fix It/ Just to Hold a Little Hand	1988	$3
❑ 53307	It's Hard to Keep This Ship Together/There's Nothing Left for Me to Take for Granted	1988	$3
❑ 53485	Lower on the Hog/The Ballad of Zero and the Tramp	1989	$3
❑ 53226	Somewhere Between Ragged and Right/Just for You	1987	$3
❑ 53155	When Your Yellow Brick Road Turns Blue/Lying in Her Arms	1987	$3
❑ 53155 [DJ]	When Your Yellow Brick Road Turns Blue (same on both sides)	1987	$10

—Promo only on red vinyl

UNIVERSAL

Number	Title	Yr	NM
❑ UVL-66020	Who's Lovin' My Baby/There Was a Time When I Was Alone	1989	$4

WARNER BROS.

Number	Title	Yr	NM
❑ 49582	1959/It Looks Like the Party Is Over	1980	$4
❑ 29497	Black Sheep/Call on Me	1983	$4
❑ 49772	Chicken Truck/I Love You a Thousand Ways	1981	$4
❑ 28502	Countrified/Yellow Creek	1986	$4
❑ 28855	Down in Tennessee/I've Got Me a Woman	1985	$4
❑ 29127	Eye of a Hurricane/ Chicken Truck	1984	$4
❑ 49120	Girl, For You/Your Lying Blue Eyes	1979	$4
❑ 29585	Goin' Down Hill/If a Broken Heart Could Kill	1983	$4
❑ 28639	Honky Tonk Crowd/If I Could Have My Way	1986	$4
❑ 49275	If There Were No Memories/ Shoot Low Sheriff	1980	$4
❑ 49860	I Just Came Home to Count the Memories/Girl, For You	1981	$4
❑ 49699	I'm Just an Old Chunk of Coal (But I'm Gonna Be a Diamond Someday)/Havin' Hard Times	1981	$4
❑ 29002	It's All Over Now/Only Your Love	1985	$4
❑ 8480	I've Got a Feelin' (Somebody Stealin')/It's All the Way Together	1977	$5
❑ 29276	I Wish I Could Write You a Song/The Sun's Gonna Shine (On Our Back Door)	1984	$4
❑ 29385	Let Somebody Else Drive/Mexico	1984	$4
❑ 8863	Low Dog Blues/Girl, for You	1979	$5
❑ 8770	My Pledge of Love/ Why Baby Why	1979	$5
❑ 49191	She Just Started Liking Cheatin' Songs/I Wish I Could Write You a Song	1980	$4
❑ 29207	She Sure Got Away with My Heart/Lonely Is Another State	1984	$4

Number	Title	Yr	NM
❏ 29788	Swingin'/Honky Tonk Saturday Night	1982	$5
❏ 8705	The Girl at the End of the Bar/You're Pleasin' Me	1978	$5
❏ 28916	Tokyo, Oklahoma/Willie's Gone	1985	$4
❏ 28433	What's So Different About You/Life's Little Pleasures	1987	$4
❏ 8585	Whine, Whistle, Whine/If There Were No Memories	1978	$5
❏ 29917	Wild and Blue/Honky Tonk Heart	1982	$4
❏ 50043	Would You Catch a Falling Star/I Danced with San Antonio Rose	1982	$4

ANDERSON, JON
ATLANTIC

Number	Title	Yr	NM
❏ 89997	All in a Matter of Time/Olympia	1982	$4
❏ 3356	Flight of the Moorglade/To the Runner	1976	$5

—Member of Yes

| ❏ 3795 [DJ] | Heart of the Matter (same on both sides) | 1981 | $5 |

—May be promo only

| ❏ 3774 [DJ] | Some Are Born (same on both sides) | 1980 | $5 |

—May be promo only

| ❏ 4054 [DJ] | Surrender (same on both sides) | 1982 | $5 |

—May be promo only

COLUMBIA

| ❏ 38-07766 | Hold On to Love/Sundancing | 1988 | $4 |

ELEKTRA

| ❏ 69580 | Easier Said Than Done/Day of Days | 1985 | $5 |

—Black vinyl

| ❏ 69580 | Easier Said Than Done/Day of Days | 1985 | $12 |

—Green vinyl

ANDERSON, LALE
KING

| ❏ 5478 | (A Ship Will Come) Ein Schiff Wird Kommen/Manchmal Traum Ich Vom Kornfeld | 1961 | $10 |

ANDERSON, LAURIE
ONE TEN

| ❏ (# unknown) | O Superman/Walk the Dog | 1981 | $10 |
| ❏ (# unknown) [PS] | O Superman/Walk the Dog | 1981 | $10 |

WARNER BROS.

| ❏ 28677 | Language Is a Virus/White Lily | 1986 | $4 |
| ❏ 49876 | O Superman/Walk the Dog | 1981 | $5 |

—7-inch 33 1/3 RPM record

| ❏ 49876 [PS] | O Superman/Walk the Dog | 1981 | $5 |

—Includes sleeve and lyric sheet

ANDERSON, LEROY

❏ 9-30403	Bluebells of Scotland/Forgotten Dreams	1957	$10
❏ 9-27875	Blue Tango/Belle of the Ball	1951	$20
❏ 9-29206	Bugler's Holiday/Summer Skies	1954	$15
❏ 9-16021	China Doll/Penny Whistle Song	1953	$20
❏ 9-28776	China Doll/Phantom Regiment	1953	$20
❏ 25581	Clarinet Candy/Lazy Moon	1962	$8
❏ 9-28300	Fiddle-Faddle/A Trumpeter's Holiday	1952	$20
❏ 9-28168	Plink, Plank, Plunk/Serenata	1952	$20
❏ 9-29319	Sandpaper Ballet/Song of the Bells	1954	$15
❏ 9-29050	Serenade/Jazz Pizzicato-Jazz Legato	1954	$15
❏ 9-16000	Sleigh Ride/Promenade	1952	$30
❏ 9-28429	Sleigh Ride/Saraband	1952	$20
❏ 9-28037	The Penny Whistling Song/Horse and Buggy	1952	$20
❏ 9-40201	The Syncopated Clock/The Waltzing Cat	1951	$20
❏ 9-16005	The Syncopated Clock/The Waltzing Cat	1952	$20
❏ 9-28881	The Typewriter/The Girl in Satin	1953	$20

ANDERSON, LES
DECCA

❏ 9-46303	I Was Sorta Wondering/Just Like Two Drops of Water	1951	$30
❏ 9-46352	My Baby Buckaroo/Dimples Dumplins	1951	$30
❏ 9-46370	Tennessee Moon/She's Dynamite in Blue Dungarees	1951	$30
❏ 9-46326	T-T-Tucky Ty/Las Vegas, Nevada	1951	$30

ANDERSON, LIZ, AND LYNN ANDERSON
RCA VICTOR

Number	Title	Yr	NM
❏ 47-9445	Mother, May I/Better Than Life Without You	1968	$8

ANDERSON, LIZ
EPIC

❏ 5-10896	Astrology/Living One Day at a Time	1972	$6
❏ 5-10840	I'll Never Fall in Love Again/You Buy the Wine	1972	$6
❏ 5-10782	It Don't Do No Good to Be a Good Girl/That's What Loving You Has Meant to Me	1971	$6
❏ 5-10952	Time to Love Again/Wearing a Smile	1973	$6

RCA VICTOR

❏ 47-9876	All Day Sucker/Wonder If I'll Feel This Bad Tomorrow	1970	$8
❏ 47-9586	Cry, Cry Again/Me, Me, Me, Me, Me	1968	$8
❏ 74-0166	Excedrin Headache #99/The Rainy Season's Over	1969	$10
❏ 74-0112	Free/Nothing Between Us	1969	$10
❏ 47-8778	Go Now Pay Later/The Bottle Turned into a Blonde	1966	$10
❏ 47-9796	Husband Hunting/All You Add Is Love	1970	$8
❏ 74-0220	If the Creek Don't Rise/Only for Me	1969	$10
❏ 47-9508	Like a Merry-Go-Round/Thanks, But No Thanks	1968	$8
❏ 47-9650	Love Is Ending/Blue Are the Violets	1968	$8
❏ 47-9163	Mama Spank/To the Landlord	1967	$8
❏ 47-8861	So Much for Me, So Much for You/Release Me	1966	$12
❏ 47-9378	Thanks a Lot for Tryin' Anyway/Come Walk in My Shoes	1967	$8
❏ 47-8999	The Wife of the Party/Fairytale	1966	$10
❏ 47-9271	Tiny Tears/Grandma's House	1967	$8
❏ 47-9924	When I'm Not Lookin'/Only for Me	1970	$8

SCORPION

| ❏ 0565 | After You/The World Has Music | 1978 | $5 |

ANDERSON, LYNN, AND JERRY LANE
CHART

| ❏ 1300 | For Better or For Worse/We're Different | 1965 | $10 |

ANDERSON, LYNN
CHART

❏ 1042	Big Girls Don't Cry/I Keep Forgettin'	1968	$8
❏ 1059	Flattery Will Get You Everywhere/A Million Shades of Blue	1968	$8
❏ 5040	He'd Still Love Me/All You Add Is Love	1969	$8
❏ 1430	If I Kiss You (Will You Go Away)/Then Go	1967	$8
❏ 5053	I've Been Everywhere/Penny for Your Thoughts	1970	$8
❏ 1330	My Heart Keeps Walking the Floor/In Person	1966	$10
❏ 5001	Our House Is Not a Home (If It's Never Been Loved in)/Wave Bye-Bye to the Man	1969	$8
❏ 1010	Promises, Promises/It Makes You Happy	1967	$8
❏ 5021	That's a No No/If Silence Is Golden	1969	$8
❏ 1475	Too Much of You/If This Is Love	1967	$10
❏ 1001	Too Much of You/If This Is Love	1967	$8

—Reissue of 1475

| ❏ 5013 | Where's the Playground Bobby/There Oughta Be a Law | 1969 | $8 |

COLUMBIA

❏ 10280	All the King's Horses/If All I Have to Do Is Just Love You	1975	$4
❏ 11374	Blue Baby Blue/The Lonely Hearts Café	1980	$4
❏ 45529	Cry/Simple Words	1972	$4
❏ 45251	Don't Wish Me Merry Christmas/Ding-a-Ling the Christmas Bell	1970	$6
❏ 45251 [PS]	Don't Wish Me Merry Christmas/Ding-a-Ling the Christmas Bell	1970	$8
❏ 45527	Don't Wish Me Merry Christmas/Ding-a-Ling the Christmas Bell	1971	$5
❏ 11296	Even Cowgirls Get the Blues/See Through Me	1980	$4
❏ 45692	Fool Me/What's Made Milwaukee Famous	1972	$4
❏ AE71056 [DJ]	Frosty the Snowman/Don't Wish Me a Merry Christmas	1972	$8

—Christmas Seals record for 1972; promo only

❏ AE71056 [PS]	Frosty the Snowman/Don't Wish Me a Merry Christmas	1972	$15
❏ 10597	He Ain't You/It's Your Love What Keeps Me Going	1977	$4
❏ 10100	He Turns It Into Love Again/Someone to Finish What You Started	1975	$4
❏ 45429	How Can I Unlove You/Don't Say Things You Don't Mean	1971	$4
❏ 11006	I Love How You Love Me/Come As You Are	1979	$4
❏ 10545	I Love What Love Is Doing to Me/Will I Ever Hear Those Church Bells Ring	1977	$4
❏ 10909	Isn't It Always Love/A Child with You Tonight	1979	$4
❏ 10160	I've Never Loved Anyone More/He Worshiped Me	1975	$4
❏ 10809	Last Love of My Life/When You Marry for Money	1978	$4
❏ 45615	Listen to a Country Song/That's What Loving You Has Meant to Me	1972	$4
❏ 10240	Paradise/You've Got It All Together Now	1975	$4
❏ 11104	Sea of Heartbreak/Say You Will	1979	$4
❏ 45918	Sing About Love/Fickle Fortune	1973	$4
❏ 46009	Smile for Me/A Man Like Your Daddy	1974	$4
❏ 45101	Stay There 'Til I Get There/I'd Run a Mile to You	1970	$5
❏ 10401	Sweet Talkin' Man/A Good Old Country Song	1976	$4
❏ 46056	Talkin' to the Wall/I Want to Be a Part of You	1974	$4
❏ 45857	Top of the World/I Wish I Was a Little Girl Again	1973	$4
❏ 10650	We Got Love/Sunshine Man	1977	$4
❏ 10041	What a Man, My Man Is/Everything's Falling in Place	1974	$4
❏ 10467	Wrap Your Love All Around Your Man/I Couldn't Be Lonely (Even If I Wanted To)	1976	$4

MERCURY

❏ 888209-7	Didn't We Shine/We Must Be Doing It Right	1986	$3
❏ 872602-7	How Many Hearts/How Many Hearts (Long Version)	1989	$3
❏ 888597-7	It Goes Without Saying/So Little Love in the World	1987	$3
❏ 872154-7	The Angel Song (Glory to God in the Highest)/When a Child Is Born	1988	$3

—With Butch Baker

| ❏ 872220-7 | What He Does Best/It Goes Without Saying | 1988 | $3 |

PERMIAN

| ❏ 82001 | What I Learned from Loving You/Mr. Sundown | 1983 | $4 |

7-Inch Extended Plays
CHART

| ❏ CH7-1009 [PS] | Best of Lynn Anderson | 1969 | $15 |
| ❏ CH7-1009 | If I Kiss You/Sing Me a Sad Song/No Another Time//Promises Promises/Too Much of You/There Oughta Be a Law | 1969 | $15 |

—Jukebox issue; small hole, plays at 33 1/3 rpm

| ❏ CH7-1028 | The Ways to Love a Man/Wave Bye to the Man/Then Go//Partly Bill/Okie from Muskogee/He Even Woke Me Up | 1970 | $15 |

—Jukebox issue; small hole, plays at 33 1/3 rpm

ANDERSON, MARTY
HIT

| ❏ 216 | One Dyin' and a-Buryin'/I'm Henry VIII, I Am | 1965 | $10 |

—B-side by the Chords (2)

ANDERSON, MICHAEL
A&M

| ❏ 1219 | Sound Alarm/Time to Go Home | 1988 | $4 |

ANDERSON, MILDRED
BLUESVILLE

| ❏ 804 | Person to Person/Connections | 1960 | $20 |

ANDERSON, RANDY
COMSTOCK

| ❏ 1959 | It's Christmas (I Wish You Were Here)/(B-side unknown) | 1988 | $6 |

ANDERSON, SONNY
IMPERIAL

| ❏ 5689 | Our Love Could Never Be/Fool | 1960 | $60 |

Number	Title	Yr	NM

ANDERSON, VICKI
BROWNSTONE

Number	Title	Yr	NM
❑ 4307	Don't Throw Your Love in the Garbage Can/In the Land of Milk and Honey	1972	$6
❑ 4204	I'll Work It Out/In the Land of Milk and Honey	1971	$6
❑ 4202	I'm Too Tough for Mr. Big Stuff/Sound Funky	1971	$6

DELUXE
| ❑ 6201 | Wide Awake in a Dream/Nobody Cares | 1966 | $8 |

KING
| ❑ 6293 | Let It Be Me/Baby, Don't You Know | 1970 | $12 |

—A-side: With James Brown

❑ 6377	Message from the Soul Sisters Part 1/Yesterday	1971	$8
❑ 6109	Tears of Joy/If You Don't Give Me	1967	$8
❑ 6138	That Feelin' Is Real/Baby Don't You Know	1967	$8
❑ 6251	The Answer to Mother Popcorn (I Got a Mother for You)/I'll Work It Out	1969	$8
❑ 6091	Think/Nobody Cares	1967	$8

—A-side: With James Brown

| ❑ 6221 | What the World Needs Now Is Love/I'll Work It Out | 1969 | $8 |
| ❑ 6274 | Wide Awake in a Dream/I Want to Be in the Land of Milk and Honey | 1969 | $8 |

SMASH
| ❑ 1985 | I Love You/Nobody Cares | 1965 | $10 |

TUFF
| ❑ 420 | I Can't Stop Loving You/I Lost a Good Man | 1964 | $10 |

ANDI AND THE BROWN SISTERS
DOOR KNOB

❑ 329	Gently Hold Me/(B-side unknown)	1989	$5
❑ 323	Labor of Love/(B-side unknown)	1989	$5
❑ 331	Lighter Shade of Blue/(B-side unknown)	1989	$5
❑ 337	Shows You What I Know/Lighter Shade of Blue	1989	$5

KILLER
| ❑ 1013 | I'd Do Anything for You, Baby/(B-side unknown) | 1988 | $6 |
| ❑ 115 | This Old Feeling/(B-side unknown) | 1988 | $6 |

ANDREWS, CHRIS
ATCO

| ❑ 6414 | Something On My Mind/To Whom It May Concern | 1966 | $12 |

RCA VICTOR
| ❑ 47-9746 | Pretty Belinda/Maker of Mistakes | 1969 | $8 |

ANDREWS, JULIE
20TH CENTURY FOX

| ❑ 6712 | Star!/Someone to Watch Over Me | 1968 | $6 |
| ❑ 6712 [PS] | Star!/Someone to Watch Over Me | 1968 | $10 |

BUENA VISTA
| ❑ F-434 | Super-cali-fragil-istic-expi-ali-docious/A Spoonful of Sugar | 1965 | $8 |

—A-side with Dick Van Dyke

| ❑ F-434 [PS] | Super-cali-fragil-istic-expi-ali-docious/A Spoonful of Sugar | 1965 | $15 |

LONDON
| ❑ 45-1924 | Lazy Afternoon/Tom Pillibi | 1960 | $12 |

ANDREWS, LEE, AND THE HEARTS
ARGO

| ❑ 1000 | Tear Drops/The Girl Around the Corner | 1957 | $60 |

CASINO
| ❑ 110 | Baby, Come Back/I Wonder | 1958 | $40 |
| ❑ 452 | Try the Impossible/Nobody's Home | 1958 | $600 |

—With playing cards on label

| ❑ 452 | Try the Impossible/Nobody's Home | 1958 | $200 |

—All-black label

CHESS

Number	Title	Yr	NM
❑ 1665	Long Lonely Nights/The Clock	1957	$50

—Sliver-top "chess pieces" label

| ❑ 1665 | Long Lonely Nights/The Clock | 1957 | $20 |

—All-blue label

| ❑ 1675 | Tear Drops/The Girl Around the Corner | 1957 | $30 |

—All-blue label (if a "chess pieces" label exists, we aren't aware of it)

CRIMSON
| ❑ 1015 | I've Had It/Little Bird | 1968 | $8 |
| ❑ 1002 | Oh My Love/Island of Love | 1967 | $8 |

GOTHAM
| ❑ 318 | Bluebird of Happiness/Show Me the Meringue | 1956 | $200 |
| ❑ 320 | Lonely Room/Leona | 1956 | $300 |

GRAND
❑ 157	Long Lonely Nights/The Clock	1962	$15
❑ 156	Teardrops/The Girl Around the Corner	1962	$15
❑ 1001	Cold Gray Dawn/All You Can Do	1968	$8
❑ 1004	Oh My Love/Can't Do Without You	1968	$8

MAIN LINE
| ❑ 102 | Long Lonely Nights/The Clock | 1957 | $400 |

—Green label, no address

| ❑ 102 | Long Lonely Nights/The Clock | 1957 | $200 |

—Black label, Philadelphia address on label

| ❑ 102 | Long Lonely Nights/The Clock | 1962 | $40 |

—Black label, no address

| ❑ 105 | Teardrops/The Girl Around the Corner | 1962 | $15 |

PARKWAY
| ❑ 860 | I'm Sorry, Pillow/Gee, But I'm Lonesome | 1962 | $20 |
| ❑ 866 | Looking Back/Operator | 1963 | $20 |

RAINBOW
| ❑ 252 | Maybe You'll Be There/Baby Come Back | 1954 | $400 |

—Black vinyl

| ❑ 252 | Maybe You'll Be There/Baby Come Back | 1954 | $800 |

—Red vinyl

| ❑ 252 | Maybe You'll Be There/Baby Come Back | 1962 | $10 |

—Reissue with large print

| ❑ 259 | The Bells of St. Mary's/The Fairest | 1954 | $600 |

—Yellow label original

| ❑ 259 | The Bells of St. Mary's/The Fairest | 1962 | $12 |

—Blue label reissue

| ❑ 256 | White Cliffs of Dover/Much Too Much | 1954 | $1500 |

—Yellow label original

| ❑ 256 | White Cliffs of Dover/Much Too Much | 1962 | $10 |

—Blue label reissue

SWAN
| ❑ 4065 | I Miss You So/I've Got to Cry | 1960 | $125 |
| ❑ 4087 | P.S. I Love You/I Cried | 1961 | $200 |

UNITED ARTISTS
❑ 162	Boom/Just Suppose	1959	$30
❑ 151	Maybe You'll Be There/All I Ask Is Love	1958	$30
❑ 123	Try the Impossible/Nobody's Home	1958	$30
❑ 592	Try the Impossible/Nobody's Home	1963	$20
❑ 136	Why Do I/Glad to Be Here	1958	$30

ANDREWS, PATTY
CAPITOL

❑ F3344	Daybreak Blues/I Never Will Marry	1956	$15
❑ F3403	Friendship Ring/Music Drives Me Crazy	1956	$15
❑ F3268	I'll Forgive You/The Rains Came Down	1955	$15
❑ F3228	Suddenly There's a Valley/Booga-Da-Woog	1955	$15
❑ F3495	Too Old to Rock and Roll/Broken	1956	$20

Number	Title	Yr	NM
❑ F3159	Without Love/Where To, My Love?	1955	$15

DECCA
| ❑ 9-27569 | Too Young/Gotta Find Somebody to Love | 1951 | $20 |

ANDREWS, RUBY
ABC

| ❑ 12215 | I Got a Bone to Pick with You/I Don't Know How to Love You | 1976 | $8 |
| ❑ 12286 | I Wanna Be Near You/Cinderfella | 1977 | $8 |

ZODIAC
❑ 1004	Casonova (Your Playing Days Are Over)/I Just Don't Believe It	1967	$10
❑ 1017	Everybody Saw You/Can You Get Away	1970	$15
❑ 1016	Help Yourself (Lover)/All the Way	1969	$15
❑ 1006	Hey Boy Take a Chance on Love/Come to Me	1967	$30
❑ 1022	Hound Dog/Away from the Crowd	1971	$10
❑ 1012	I Let Him Take Me (In His Arms)/I Guess That Don't Make Me a Loser	1968	$15
❑ 1001	Let's Get a Groove Going On (Part 1)/(Part 2)	1967	$125
❑ 1024	My Love Is Coming Down/Good 'n' Plenty	1971	$10
❑ 1010	The Love I Need/Just Loving You	1968	$300
❑ 1023	Whatever It Takes to Please You (Part 1)/(Part 2)	1971	$10

ANDREWS, SHEILA
OVATION

❑ 1128	I Gotta Get Back the Feeling/Diggin' and a Grindin' For His Love	1979	$5
❑ 1146	It Don't Get Better Than This/The Softer You Touch Me The Harder I Fall	1980	$5
❑ 1121	Love Me Like a Woman/It'll Be Love	1979	$5
❑ 1165	Maybe I Should Have Been Listening/(B-side unknown)	1981	$6
❑ 1116	Too Fast for Rapid City/Bigger Fool Than I Am	1978	$5
❑ 1138	What I Had with You/I Gotta Get Back the Feeling	1980	$5

—A-side with Joe Sun

| ❑ 1160 | Where Could You Take Me/Pretty Lies | 1980 | $5 |

ANDREWS SISTERS, THE

Also see PATTY ANDREWS; BING CROSBY.

CAPITOL
❑ F-3583	A Child's Christmas Song/Silver Bells	1956	$20
❑ F-3784	By His Word/I'm Goin' Home	1957	$15
❑ F-3567	Crazy Arms/I Want to Linger	1956	$15
❑ F-3707	Give Me Back My Heart/Stars, Stars	1957	$15
❑ F-4144	I've Got an Invitation to a Dance/My Love Is a Kitten	1959	$10
❑ F-3869	One Mistake/Melancholy Moon	1957	$15
❑ F-3965	Torero/Sunshine	1958	$15

DECCA
❑ 9-27252	A Bushel and a Peck/Guys and Dolls	1950	$20
❑ 9-28342	Adios/Carmen's Boogie	1952	$20
❑ 9-27414	A Penny a Kiss -- A Penny A Hug/Zing Zing, Zoom Zoom	1951	$20
❑ 9-23607	Beat Me Daddy, Eight to the Bar/Scrub Me Mama with a Boogie Beat	1950	$20
❑ 9-23605	Bei Mir Bist Du Schoen/Joseph! Joseph!	1950	$20
❑ 9-27421	Between Two Trees/I Wish I Knew	1951	$20
❑ 9-27878	Blonde Sailor/All the World to Me	1951	$20
❑ 9-27115	Can't We Talk It Over/There Will Never Be Another You	1950	$20
❑ 9-27715	Can We Talk It Over/There Will Never Be Another You	1951	$20
❑ 9-27757	Carioca/Daddy	1951	$20
❑ 9-23722	Christmas Island/Winter Wonderland	1950	$20

—With Guy Lombardo and His Royal Canadians; lines label

| ❑ 9-23722 | Christmas Island/Winter Wonderland | 1955 | $15 |

—With Guy Lombardo and His Royal Canadians; star label

| ❑ 23722 | Christmas Island/Winter Wonderland | 1960 | $10 |

—With Guy Lombardo and His Royal Canadians; color bars label

Number	Title	Yr	NM
❏ 9-28480	Don't Be That Way/ Sing, Sing, Sing	1952	$15
❏ 9-27894	Down in the Valley/ Red River Valley	1951	$20
❏ 9-28116	Dreams Come Tumbling Down/Music Lessons	1952	$20
❏ 9-28482	East of the Sun/In the Mood	1952	$15
❏ 9-28296	Fair Hawaii/Ke Kali Nei Au	1952	$15
❏ 9-28680	Fugue for Tinhorns/ Now That I'm in Love	1953	$20
❏ 9-28297	Good Night, Aloha/Malihini Mele	1952	$15

—Above 4 with Alfred Apaka and His Orchestra

❏ 9-27349	Go West, Young Man/ Along the Navaho Trail	1950	$20
❏ 9-23606	Hold Tight, Hold Tight/ Well Alright	1950	$20
❏ 9-27700	How Many Times/I Used to Love You	1951	$20

— With Tommy Dorsey and His Orchestra

❏ 9-24705	I Can Dream, Can't I?/The Wedding of Lili Marlene	1950	$30

— 78 released in 1949

❏ 9-28276	Idle Chatter/One for the Wonder	1952	$20
❏ 9-27251	I'd Like to Hitch a Ride with Santa Claus/(Sweet Angie) The Christmas Tree Angel	1950	$20
❏ 9-23608	(I'll Be With You) In Apple Blossom Time/Rhumba Boogie	1950	$20

— The above four comprise a box set (9-23) originally issued on 78s

❏ 9-23608	(I'll Be With You) In Apple Blossom Time/Rhumba Boogie	1955	$15

— Black label, star under the first "C" of "Decca

❏ 9-27910	I'm on a Seesaw of Love/ Play Me a Hurtin' Tune	1951	$20

— With Guy Lombardo and His Royal Canadians

❏ 9-27537	I Remember Mama/My Mom	1951	$20
❏ 9-28294	Isle of Golden Dreams/Nalani	1952	$15
❏ 9-27635	It Never Entered My Mind/I'm in Love Again	1951	$20
❏ 9-27007	I Wanna Be Loved/I've Just Got to Get Out of the Habit	1950	$20
❏ 9-28143	Linger Awhile/Wabash Blues	1952	$20

— With Russ Morgan and His Orchestra

❏ 9-27760	Lying in the Way/Love Is Such a Cheat	1951	$20
❏ 9-24748	Merry Christmas Polka/ Christmas Candles	1950	$30

— With Guy Lombardo and His Royal Canadians; from "Album No. A-9-95"; 78 released in 1949

❏ 9-29149	My Love, The Blues and Me/ There's a Rainbow in the Valley	1954	$20
❏ 9-28483	Old Don Juan/The Mambo Man	1952	$15
❏ 9-28481	Piccolo Pete/If I Had a Boy Like You	1952	$15
❏ 9-27310	Sleigh Ride/Telephone Song	1950	$30
❏ 9-27202	The Glory of Love/A Rainy Day Refrain	1950	$20

— With Guy Lombardo and His Royal Canadians

❏ 9-27858	The Three Bells/The Windmill Song	1951	$20
❏ 9-28929	This Little Piggie Went to Market/Love Sends a Little Gift of Roses	1953	$20
❏ 9-27432	Three O'Clock in the Morning/ Lullaby of Broadway	1951	$20
❏ 9-28163	Where Is Your Wandering Mother Tonight/Hang Your Head in Shame	1952	$20

— A-side with Red Foley

❏ 9-28042	Why Worry/That Ever Lovin' Rag	1952	$20
❏ 9-27979	Wondering/Poor Whip-Poor-Will	1952	$20

DOT

❏ 16497	Mr. Bass Man/My Midnight Prison	1963	$8
❏ 16433	Pistol Packin' Mama/Ti-Pi-Tin	1963	$8

KAPP

❏ 309	One, Two, Three, Four/I've Got to Pass Your House	1959	$15

MCA

❏ 60012	Beer Barrel Polka/ Pennsylvania Polka	1973	$4
❏ 60041	Bei Mir Bist Du Schoen/ (I'll Be With You) In Apple Blossom Time	1974	$4
❏ 60040	Boogie Woogie Bugle Boy/ Rum and Coca-Cola	1974	$4
❏ 65020	Christmas Island/ Winter Wonderland	1973	$4

— With Guy Lombardo and His Royal Canadians; black label with rainbow

❏ 65020	Christmas Island/ Winter Wonderland	1980	$3

— With Guy Lombardo and His Royal Canadians; blue label

with rainbow

❏ 60042	Don't Sit Under the Apple Tree/I Can Dream, Can't I?	1974	$4
❏ 65016	Take Me Out to the Ball Game/ In the Good Old Summertime	1973	$4

DOT

❏ DLP807	A Man and a Woman/ Everybody Wants to Be Loved/Theme from "Come September"//Is It Really Over/I Forgot More Than You'll Ever Know/Satin Doll	1967	$10

— Jukebox issue; small hole, plays at 33 1/3 rpm

❏ DLP567 [PS]	Great Country Hits	1963	$15
❏ DLP807 [PS]	Great Performers	1967	$12
❏ DLP567	Tennessee Waltz/Careless Hands/Cold, Cold Heart//I'm Thinking Tonight of My Blue Eyes/Bouquet of Roses/ Your Cheatin' Heart	1963	$15

— Jukebox issue; small hole, plays at 33 1/3 rpm

ANGEL, JOHNNY

EXCELLO

❏ 2077	I Realize/Baby I'm Confessin'	1956	$30

FELSTED

❏ 8633	Lady of Spain/Without Her Heart	1961	$30
❏ 8659	Looking for a Fool/Roller Motion	1962	$30
❏ 8646	Mashed Potatoe Stomp/ One More Tomorrow	1962	$30

GARDENA

❏ 117	All Night Party/Baby, You've Got Soul	1961	$20

IMPERIAL

❏ 5673	Falling Teardrops/Doubt	1960	$50

JAF

❏ 2024	Lonely Nights/Seven Words	1961	$20

LIBERTY

❏ 55895	Summertime Blues/ Biggest Part of Me	1966	$8

POWER

❏ 250	Starlight/The Story of Love	1959	$120

SWAN

❏ 4263	This Is the Night for Love/ You've Been Wrong	1966	$50

VIN

❏ 1004	Teenage Wedding/ Baby, It's Love	1958	$30

ANGEL, JOHNNY (2)

CAPRICE

❏ 2386	The Promise of Love/ Fallin' in Love	1986	$4
❏ 2386 [PS]	The Promise of Love/ Fallin' in Love	1986	$4

ANGEL, JOHNNY T.

BELL

❏ 45472	Tell Laura I Love Her/ The Way I Feel Tonight	1974	$4

YORKSVILLE

❏ 45090	Tell Laura I Love Her/ The Way I Feel Tonight	1974	$6

ANGEL, MARIAN

JUBILEE

❏ 5508	It's Gonna Be Alright/ Tomorrow's Fool	1965	$10

ANGELIC GOSPEL SINGERS, THE

NASHBORO

❏ 946	Glory to the New Born King/ Father, I Stretch My Hands	1968	$8

ANGELLE, LISA

CAPITOL

❏ B-44292	The First Time I Loved Forever//The First Time I Loved Forever/Somewhere I Have Never Travelled	1989	$5
❏ B-44292 [PS]	The First Time I Loved Forever//The First Time I Loved Forever/Somewhere I Have Never Travelled	1989	$5

Number	Title	Yr	NM

EMI AMERICA

❏ B-8294	Bring Back Love/Poor Baby	1985	$6
❏ B-8258	Love, It's the Pits/Biloxi Blue	1985	$6
❏ B-8258 [PS]	Love, It's the Pits/Biloxi Blue	1985	$6

ANGELS, THE (1)

ASCOT

❏ 2139	Irresistible/Cotton Fields	1963	$15

CAPRICE

❏ 121	Cotton Fields/A Moment Ago	1963	$20
❏ 112	Cry Baby Cry/That's All I Ask of You	1962	$30
❏ 116	Everybody Loves a Lover/Blow Joe	1962	$20
❏ 107	'Til/A Moment Ago	1961	$40

—With horizontal "Caprice" logo; B-side listed as "A Moment Ago" but plays as "Cotton Fields

❏ 107	'Til/A Moment Ago	1961	$30

—With semicircular "Caprice" logo

RCA VICTOR

❏ 47-9612 [B]	But for Love/The Boy with the Green Eyes	1968	$10
❏ 47-9246	Go Out and Play/You'll Never Get to Heaven (If You Break My Heart)	1967	$10
❏ 47-9129	I Had a Dream I Lost You/What to Do	1967	$10
❏ 47-9681	Merry Go Round/So Nice (Samba De Verao)	1968	$10
❏ 47-9541	The Medley: Moments to Remember-Theme from A Summer Place-One Summer Night/If I Didn't Love You	1968	$10

SMASH

❏ 1854	I Adore Him/Thank You and Goodnight	1963	$20
❏ 1854 [PS]	I Adore Him/Thank You and Goodnight	1963	$70
❏ 1885	Little Beatle Boy/Java	1964	$30
❏ 1834	My Boyfriend's Back/ (Love Me) Now	1963	$20
❏ 810325-7	My Boyfriend's Back/Thank You and Goodnight	1983	$4

—Reissue in stereo

❏ 1931	World Without Love/The Boy from Crosstown	1964	$20
❏ 1931 [PS]	World Without Love/The Boy from Crosstown	1964	$100
❏ 1870	Wow Wow Wee (He's the Boy for Me)/Snowflakes and Teardrops	1964	$20

ANGELS, THE (2)

GEE

❏ 1024	Glory of Love/It's You I Love Best	1956	$70

GRAND

❏ 121	A Lovely Way to Spend An Evening/You're Still My Baby	1954	$500

—With no address on label

❏ 121	A Lovely Way to Spend An Evening/You're Still My Baby	1954	$60

—With address on label

❏ 115	Wedding Bells/Times Have Changed	1954	$400

—With no address on label

❏ 115	Wedding Bells/Times Have Changed	1954	$60

—With address on label

ANGELS, THE (3)

TAWNY

❏ 101	A Lover's Poem (To Him)/A Lover's Poem (To Her)	1959	$50

ANGIE AND THE CHICKLETTES

APT

❏ 25080	Treat Him Tender Maureen (Now That Ringo Belongs to You)/Tommy	1965	$40

ANGLO-AMERICANS, THE

CHATTAHOOCHIE

❏ 705	The Music Never Stops/ Are You Ready for This?	1966	$40

ANGLOS, THE

ORBIT

❏ 201	Incense/You're Fooling Me	1965	$60

— Steve Winwood is on this record, his first

Number	Title	Yr	NM

SCEPTER

| ❏ 12204 | Since You've Been Gone/A Small Town Boy | 1967 | $30 |

ANGRY SAMOANS
7-Inch Extended Plays
HOMOPHOBIC

| ❏ HOMO-02 | Stupid Jerk/Time to Fuck/The Todd Killings//They Saved Hitler's Cock | 1982 | $10 |

—As "The Queer Pills"

| ❏ HOMO-02 [PS] | Stupid Jerk/Time to Fuck/The Todd Killings//They Saved Hitler's Cock | 1982 | $20 |

—As "The Queer Pills" without "Angry Samoans" rubber-stamped on it

| ❏ HOMO-02 [PS] | Stupid Jerk/Time to Fuck/The Todd Killings//They Saved Hitler's Cock | 1982 | $12 |

—As "The Queer Pills" with "Angry Samoans" rubber-stamp

ANIMALS, THE

Includes "Eric Burdon and the Animals." Also see ERIC BURDON; ERIC BURDON AND WAR; ALAN PRICE.

ABKCO

| ❏ 4037 | Don't Let Me Be Misunderstood/Talkin' About You | 1973 | $4 |
| ❏ 4025 | House of the Rising Sun/Bring It On Home to Me | 1973 | $8 |

—Contains the full-length version of A-side

| ❏ 4038 | I'm Cryin'/Boom Boom | 1973 | $4 |
| ❏ 4026 | We Gotta Get Out of This Place/It's My Life | 1973 | $4 |

I.R.S.

| ❏ 9923 | Love Is For All Time/It's Too Late | 1983 | $5 |

JET

| ❏ XW-1070 | Fire on the Sun/Riverside County | 1977 | $6 |

MGM

❏ 13917	Anything/It's All Meat	1968	$10
❏ 13298	Boom Boom/Blue Feeling	1964	$20
❏ 13298 [PS]	Boom Boom/Blue Feeling	1964	$30
❏ 13339	Bring It On Home to Me/For Miss Caulker	1965	$15
❏ 13339 [PS]	Bring It On Home to Me/For Miss Caulker	1965	$30
❏ CS-11-5	Celebrity Scene: The Animals	1967	$100

—Box set of five singles (13791-13795). Price includes box, all 5 singles, jukebox title strips, bio. Records are sometimes found by themselves, so they are also listed separately.

❏ 13514	Don't Bring Me Down/Cheating	1966	$15
❏ 13791	Don't Bring Me Down/When I Was Young	1967	$15
❏ 13311	Don't Let Me Be Misunderstood/Club A-Go-Go	1964	$20
❏ 13242	Gonna Send You Back to Walker (Gonna Send You Back to Georgia)/Baby, Let Me Take You Home	1964	$20
❏ 13636	Help Me Girl/That Ain't Where It's At	1966	$12
❏ 13274	I'm Crying/Take It Easy Baby	1964	$20
❏ 13274 [PS]	I'm Crying/Take It Easy Baby	1964	$30
❏ 13793	Inside-Looking Out/Help Me Girl	1967	$15
❏ 13468	Inside-Looking Out/You're On My Mind	1966	$15
❏ 13795	It's All Meat/The Other Side of This Life	1967	$15
❏ 13414	It's My Life/I'm Going to Change the World	1965	$15
❏ 13868	Monterey/Ain't That So	1967	$10
❏ 13868 [PS]	Monterey/Ain't That So	1967	$30
❏ 13769	San Franciscan Nights/Good Times	1967	$10
❏ 13769 [PS]	San Franciscan Nights/Good Times	1967	$30
❏ 13794	San Franciscan Nights/Good Times	1967	$15
❏ 13792	See See Rider/Hey Gyp	1967	$15
❏ 13582	See See Rider/She'll Return It	1966	$10

—Starting here, records are by "Eric Burdon and the Animals

| ❏ 13939 | Sky Pilot (Part 1)/Sky Pilot (Part 2) | 1968 | $12 |

—First pressings have black labels

| ❏ 13939 | Sky Pilot (Part 1)/Sky Pilot (Part 2) | 1968 | $8 |

—Second pressings have blue and gold labels

❏ 13264	The House of the Rising Sun/Talkin' About You	1964	$20
❏ 13264 [PS]	The House of the Rising Sun/Talkin' About You	1964	$40
❏ 13382	We Gotta Get Out of This Place/I Can't Believe It	1965	$15

| ❏ 13721 | When I Was Young/A Girl Called Sandoz | 1967 | $10 |

ANIMOTION
CASABLANCA

❏ 884433-7	I Engineer/The Essence	1986	$3
❏ 884433-7 [PS]	I Engineer/The Essence	1986	$3
❏ 884729-7	I Want You/Staring Down the Demons	1986	$3
❏ 884729-7 [PS]	I Want You/Staring Down the Demons	1986	$3
❏ 884916-7	Strange Behavior/One Step Ahead	1986	$4

MERCURY

❏ 880737-7	Let Him Go/Holding You	1985	$3
❏ 880737-7 [PS]	Let Him Go/Holding You	1985	$3
❏ 884659-7	Obsession/Let Him Go	1986	$3

—Reissue

| ❏ 880266-7 | Obsession/Turn Around | 1984 | $3 |
| ❏ 880266-7 [PS] | Obsession/Turn Around | 1984 | $3 |

ANKA, PAUL
ABC-PARAMOUNT

❏ S296-1 [S]	(All of a Sudden) My Heart Sings/(B-side unknown)	1959	$50
❏ 9987 [M]	(All of a Sudden) My Heart Sings/That's Love	1958	$30
❏ S-9987 [S]	(All of a Sudden) My Heart Sings/That's Love	1958	$60
❏ S296-3 [S]	C'est Si Bon/Comme Ci, Comme Ca	1959	$50
❏ 9907	Crazy Love/Let the Bells Keep Ringing	1958	$30
❏ 10220	Dance On Little Girl/I Talk to You	1961	$15
❏ 10220 [PS]	Dance On Little Girl/I Talk to You	1961	$30
❏ 9831	Diana/Don't Gamble with Love	1957	$30
❏ 10132 [M]	Hello Young Lovers/I Love You in the Same Old Way	1960	$20
❏ 10132 [PS]	Hello Young Lovers/I Love You in the Same Old Way	1960	$30
❏ S-10132 [S]	Hello Young Lovers/I Love You in the Same Old Way	1960	$60
❏ 10311	I'd Never Find Another You/Uh Huh	1962	$10
❏ S296-5 [S]	I Love Paris/If You Love Me, Really Love Me	1959	$50

—The above five are jukebox singles excerpting the LP "My Heart Sings

❏ 9855	I Love You, Baby/Tell Me That You Love Me	1957	$40
❏ 10338	I'm Coming Home/Cry	1962	$10
❏ 10011 [M]	I Miss You So/Late Last Night	1959	$20
❏ S-10011 [S]	I Miss You So/Late Last Night	1959	$60
❏ 10011 [PS]	I Miss You So/Late Last Night	1959	$30
❏ 10169	It's Christmas Everywhere/Rudolph, the Red-Nosed Reindeer	1960	$20
❏ 10169 [PS]	It's Christmas Everywhere/Rudolph, the Red-Nosed Reindeer	1960	$30
❏ 10064 [M]	It's Time to Cry/Something Has Changed Me	1959	$20
❏ 10064 [PS]	It's Time to Cry/Something Has Changed Me	1959	$30
❏ S-10064 [S]	It's Time to Cry/Something Has Changed Me	1959	$60
❏ 10022 [M]	Lonely Boy/Your Love	1959	$20
❏ S-10022 [S]	Lonely Boy/Your Love	1959	$60
❏ 10279	Loveland/The Bells at My Wedding	1961	$15
❏ S296-4 [S]	Melodie D'Amour/I Miss You So	1959	$50
❏ 9937	Midnight/Verboten!	1958	$30
❏ 10106 [M]	My Home Town/Something Happened	1960	$20
❏ 10106 [PS]	My Home Town/Something Happened	1960	$30
❏ S-10106 [S]	My Home Town/Something Happened	1960	$60
❏ 10082 [M]	Puppy Love/Adam and Eve	1960	$20
❏ 10082 [PS]	Puppy Love/Adam and Eve	1960	$30
❏ S-10082 [S]	Puppy Love/Adam and Eve	1960	$60
❏ 10040 [M]	Put Your Head on My Shoulder/Don't Ever Leave Me	1959	$20
❏ S-10040 [S]	Put Your Head on My Shoulder/Don't Ever Leave Me	1959	$60
❏ 10040 [PS]	Put Your Head on My Shoulder/Don't Ever Leave Me	1959	$30
❏ 10147 [M]	Summer's Gone/I'd Have to Share	1960	$20
❏ 10147 [PS]	Summer's Gone/I'd Have to Share	1960	$30
❏ S-10147 [S]	Summer's Gone/I'd Have to Share	1960	$60
❏ 10282	The Fools Hall of Fame/Far from the Lights of Town	1961	$15
❏ 10168 [M]	The Story of My Love/Don't Say You're Sorry	1960	$20
❏ 10168 [PS]	The Story of My Love/Don't Say You're Sorry	1960	$30
❏ S-10168 [S]	The Story of My Love/Don't Say You're Sorry	1960	$60
❏ S296-2 [S]	(titles unknown)	1959	$50

| ❏ 10194 | Tonight My Love, Tonight/I'm Just a Fool Anyway | 1961 | $15 |
| ❏ 10194 [PS] | Tonight My Love, Tonight/I'm Just a Fool Anyway | 1961 | $30 |

BUDDAH

❏ 252	Do I Love You/So Long City	1971	$5
❏ 294	Everything's Been Changed/Jubilation	1972	$5
❏ 349	Hey Girl/You and Me Today	1973	$5
❏ 314	Something Good Is Coming/Life Song	1972	$5
❏ 337	While We're Still Young/This Is Your Song	1973	$5

COLUMBIA

| ❏ 04187 | Gimme the Word/No Way Out | 1983 | $3 |

—A-side: With Karla DeVito

❏ 03897	Hold Me 'Til the Mornin' Comes/This Is the First Time	1983	$3
❏ 03897 [PS]	Hold Me 'Til the Mornin' Comes/This Is the First Time	1983	$4
❏ 04407	Second Chance/Walk a Fine Line	1984	$3

FAME

| ❏ XW-345 | Flashback/Let Me Get to Know You | 1973 | $4 |

RCA

❏ PB-11662	As Long As We Keep Believing/Headlines	1979	$4
❏ PB-12225	I've Been Waiting for You All My Life/Think I'm in Love Again	1981	$3
❏ PB-12262	Lady Lay Down/You're Still a Part of Me	1981	$3
❏ PB-11351	Lovely Lady/Brought Up in New York	1978	$4
❏ PB-11351 [PS]	Lovely Lady/Brought Up in New York	1978	$5
❏ PB-11395	This Is Love/I'm By Myself Again	1978	$4
❏ PB-12184	We Love Each Other/Think I'm in Love Again	1981	$3

RCA VICTOR

❏ 47-8030	A Steel Guitar and a Glass of Wine/I Never Knew Your Name	1962	$10
❏ 47-8030 [PS]	A Steel Guitar and a Glass of Wine/I Never Knew Your Name	1962	$30
❏ 47-9228	A Woman Is a Sentimental Thing/That's How Love Goes	1967	$8
❏ 47-9457	Can't Get You Out of My Mind/When We Get There	1968	$8
❏ 47-8441	Cindy Go Home/Ogni Volta	1964	$8
❏ 47-8441 [PS]	Cindy Go Home/Ogni Volta	1964	$20
❏ GB-10180	Diana/Put Your Head on My Shoulders	1975	$4

—Gold Standard Series

❏ 47-8272	Did You Have a Happy Birthday/For No Good Reason at All	1963	$12
❏ 47-8272 [PS]	Did You Have a Happy Birthday/For No Good Reason at All	1963	$30
❏ 47-8097	Eso Beso (That Kiss!)/Give Me Back My Heart	1962	$12
❏ 47-8097 [PS]	Eso Beso (That Kiss!)/Give Me Back My Heart	1962	$30
❏ 47-8662	Every Day a Heart Is Broken/As If There Were No Tomorrow	1965	$8
❏ 47-8662 [PS]	Every Day a Heart Is Broken/As If There Were No Tomorrow	1965	$40
❏ 47-8068	Every Night (Without You)/There You Go	1962	$12
❏ 47-8068 [PS]	Every Night (Without You)/There You Go	1962	$30
❏ VP5-2502 [S]	Falling in Love with You/You're Just in Love	1962	$50

—The above five are 33 1/3 rpm, small hole jukebox singles excerpting the LP "Young, Alive and In Love

❏ 47-8311	From Rocking Horse to Rocking Chair/Cheer Up	1964	$8
❏ 47-8311 [PS]	From Rocking Horse to Rocking Chair/Cheer Up	1964	$20
❏ 47-9648	Goodnight My Love/This Crazy World	1968	$8
❏ 47-9767	Happy/Can't Get You Out of My Mind	1969	$8
❏ 47-8195	Hello Jim/You've Got the Nerve to Call This Love	1963	$12
❏ 47-8195 [PS]	Hello Jim/You've Got the Nerve to Call This Love	1963	$30
❏ 47-8893	I Can't Help Loving You/Can't Get Along Very Well Without Her	1966	$8
❏ VP4-2502 [S]	I Love Life/Aren't You Glad You're You?	1962	$50
❏ 47-8396	In My Imagination/It's Easy to Say	1964	$8
❏ 47-8396 [PS]	In My Imagination/It's Easy to Say	1964	$20
❏ 74-0126	In the Still of the Night/Pickin' Up the Pieces	1969	$8
❏ 47-8839	I Wish/I Went to Your Wedding	1966	$8
❏ 47-8115	Love (Makes the World Go 'Round)/Crying in the Wind	1962	$10
❏ 47-8115 [PS]	Love (Makes the World Go 'Round)/Crying in the Wind	1962	$30

Number	Title	Yr	NM
❏ 47-7977	Love Me Warm and Tender/I'd Like to Know	1962	$10
❏ 47-7977 [PS]	Love Me Warm and Tender/I'd Like to Know	1962	$30
❏ 37-7977	Love Me Warm and Tender/I'd Like to Know	1962	$30

— Compact Single 33" (small hole, plays at LP speed)

Number	Title	Yr	NM
❏ 47-9846	Midnight Mistress/Before It's Too Late-This Land Is Your Land	1970	$8
❏ 47-8349	My Baby's Comin' Home/No, No	1964	$8
❏ 47-8349 [PS]	My Baby's Comin' Home/No, No	1964	$20
❏ 47-9032	Poor Old World/I'd Rather Be a Stranger	1966	$8
❏ GB-10181	Puppy Love/Lonely Boy	1975	$4

— Gold Standard Series

Number	Title	Yr	NM
❏ 74-0164	Sincerely/Next Year	1969	$8
❏ 47-8493	Sylvia/Behind My Smile	1965	$8
❏ 47-8595	The Loneliest Boy in the World/Dream Me Happy	1965	$8
❏ 47-8595 [PS]	The Loneliest Boy in the World/Dream Me Happy	1965	$40
❏ VP3-2502 [S]	This Life of Mine/Life Is Just a Bowl of Cherries	1962	$50
❏ 47-8764	Truly Yours/Oh, Such a Stranger	1965	$8
❏ 47-8237	Wondrous Are the Ways of Love/Hurry Up and Tell Me	1963	$10
❏ 47-8237 [PS]	Wondrous Are the Ways of Love/Hurry Up and Tell Me	1963	$30

RPM

Number	Title	Yr	NM
❏ 472	I Confess/Blau-Wile Deevest Fontaine	1956	$100
❏ 499	I Confess/Blau-Wile Deevest Fontaine	1957	$40

UNITED ARTISTS

Number	Title	Yr	NM
❏ XW-789	Anytime (I'll Be There)/Something About You	1976	$4
❏ XW-896	Happier/Closing Doors	1976	$6

— Canada-only release

Number	Title	Yr	NM
❏ XW-911	Happier/Closing Doors	1976	$4
❏ XW-682	(I Believe) There's Nothing Stronger Than Our Love/Today I Became a Fool	1975	$6

— Canada-only release

Number	Title	Yr	NM
❏ XW-685	(I Believe) There's Nothing Stronger Than Our Love/Today I Became a Fool	1975	$4
❏ XW-615	I Don't Like to Sleep Alone/How Can Anything Be Beautiful After You	1975	$4
❏ XW-615 [PS]	I Don't Like to Sleep Alone/How Can Anything Be Beautiful After You	1975	$4
❏ XW-1158	I Don't Like to Sleep Alone/Times of Your Life	1978	$3

— Reissue

Number	Title	Yr	NM
❏ XW-945	I'll Help You/Never Gonna Fall in Love Like I Fell in Love with You	1977	$4
❏ XW-972	My Best Friend's Wife/Never Gonna Fall in Love Like I Fell in Love with You	1977	$4
❏ XW-569	One Man Woman/One Woman Man/Let Me Get to Know You	1974	$4

— A-side: With Odia Coates

Number	Title	Yr	NM
❏ XW-737	Times of Your Life/Water Runs Deep	1975	$4
❏ XW-737 [PS]	Times of Your Life/Water Runs Deep	1975	$4
❏ XW-1018	Tonight/Everybody Ought to Be in Love	1977	$4

7-Inch Extended Plays

ABC-PARAMOUNT

Number	Title	Yr	NM
❏ A-323	Diana/Puppy Love//Put Your Head on My Shoulder/Lonely Boy	1960	$30
❏ A-240	Down by the Riverside/You Belong to Me//Waiting for You/Walkin' My Baby Back Home	1958	$30
❏ A-323 [PS]	Four Songs from Paul Anka Sings His Big 15	1960	$30
❏ C-296 [PS]	My Heart Sings	1959	$30
❏ A-240 [PS]	Paul Anka, Volume 1	1958	$30
❏ C-296	So It's Goodbye/Les Filles de Paris//Melodie D'Amour/Autumn Leaves	1959	$30

RCA VICTOR

Number	Title	Yr	NM
❏ VLP2575 [PS]	Paul Anka	1962	$20
❏ VLP2575	Teach Me Tonight/Let's Fall in Love/Let's Sit This One Out/I'll See You in My Dreams	1962	$20

— Jukebox issue; small hole, plays at 33 1/3 rpm

JOHNNY NASH

ABC-PARAMOUNT

Number	Title	Yr	NM
❏ 9974	The Teen Commandments/If You Learn to Pray	1958	$30

ANN-MARGRET

ARIOLA

Number	Title	Yr	NM
❏ 7511	Love Rush/For You	1979	$6

AVCO EMBASSY

Number	Title	Yr	NM
❏ 4547	Today/Today	1970	$20

— B-side by Lenny Stack

LHI

Number	Title	Yr	NM
❏ 2	Chico/Sleep in the Grass	1969	$6

— With Lee Hazlewood

Number	Title	Yr	NM
❏ 1	It's a Nice World to Visit/You Turned My Head Around	1969	$6
❏ 5	The Dark End of the Street/Victims of the Night	1969	$6

— With Lee Hazlewood

Number	Title	Yr	NM
❏ 11	Walk Out of My Mind/Hangin' In	1970	$6

— With Lee Hazlewood

MCA

Number	Title	Yr	NM
❏ 41186	Love Rush/For You	1980	$5
❏ 41223	Midnight Message/For You	1980	$5

RCA VICTOR

Number	Title	Yr	NM
❏ 47-8168	Bye Bye Birdie/Take All the Kisses	1963	$10
❏ 47-8168 [PS]	Bye Bye Birdie/Take All the Kisses	1963	$30
❏ VP4-2551 [S]	C'est Si Bon/Please Don't Talk About Me When I'm Gone	1962	$50
❏ 47-8446	He's My Man/Someday Soon	1964	$12
❏ 47-8446 [PS]	He's My Man/Someday Soon	1964	$40
❏ 47-8295	Hey Little Star/Man's Favorite Sport	1963	$12
❏ 47-7857	I Ain't Got Nobody/Lost Love	1961	$15
❏ 37-7857	I Ain't Got Nobody/Lost Love	1961	$30

— Compact Single 33" (small hole, plays at LP speed)

Number	Title	Yr	NM
❏ 47-7894	I Just Don't Understand/I Don't Hurt Anymore	1961	$20
❏ 47-7894 [PS]	I Just Don't Understand/I Don't Hurt Anymore	1961	$30
❏ 37-7894	I Just Don't Understand/I Don't Hurt Anymore	1961	$30

— Compact Single 33" (small hole, plays at LP speed)

Number	Title	Yr	NM
❏ VP5-2551 [S]	Inka Dinka Doo/Begin the Beguine	1962	$50

— The above five are 33 1/3 rpm, small hole jukebox singles excerpting the LP "The Vivacious One"

Number	Title	Yr	NM
❏ 47-7952	It Do Me So Good/Gimme Love	1961	$10
❏ 47-7952 [PS]	It Do Me So Good/Gimme Love	1961	$30
❏ 37-7952	It Do Me So Good/Gimme Love	1961	$30

— Compact Single 33" (small hole, plays at LP speed)

Number	Title	Yr	NM
❏ VP3-2551 [S]	Make Love to Me/Tell Me, Tell Me	1962	$50
❏ 47-8734	Mister Kiss Kiss Bang Bang/What Did I Have That I Don't Have Now	1965	$10
❏ 47-9013	The Swinger/You've Come a Long Way from St. Louis	1966	$10
❏ 47-7986	What Am I Supposed to Do/Let's Stop Kidding Each Other	1962	$10
❏ 47-7986 [PS]	What Am I Supposed to Do/Let's Stop Kidding Each Other	1962	$30

ANNE CHRISTINE

CME

Number	Title	Yr	NM
❏ 4633	Fool, Fool, Fool/Mountain of Lies	1971	$10
❏ 4635	It's Gonna Take a Little Bit Longer/Silver Threads and Golden Needles	1971	$10
❏ 4634	Summer Man/How Important Can It Be	1971	$10

ANNETTE

BUENA VISTA

Number	Title	Yr	NM
❏ 407	Bella Bella Florence/Canzone d'Amoure	1962	$20

— With Marcochi

Number	Title	Yr	NM
❏ 407 [PS]	Bella Bella Florence/Canzone d'Amoure	1962	$200
❏ 436	Bikini Beach Party/The Clyde	1964	$20
❏ 436 [PS]	Bikini Beach Party/The Clyde	1964	$50
❏ 432	Custom City/Rebel Rider	1964	$30
❏ 432 [PS]	Custom City/Rebel Rider	1964	$70
❏ 374	Dream Boy/Please, Please Signore	1961	$20
❏ 374 [PS]	Dream Boy/Please, Please Signore	1961	$40

Number	Title	Yr	NM
❏ 388	Dreamin' About You/Strummin' Song	1961	$20
❏ 388 [PS]	Dreamin' About You/Strummin' Song	1961	$40
❏ 344	Especially for You/My Heart Became of Age	1959	$20
❏ 349	First Name Initial/My Heart Became of Age	1959	$20
❏ 349 [PS]	First Name Initial/My Heart Became of Age	1959	$40
❏ 384	Hawaiian Love Talk/Blue Muu Muu	1961	$20
❏ 384 [PS]	Hawaiian Love Talk/Blue Muu Muu	1961	$60
❏ 405	He's My Ideal/Mr. Piano Man	1962	$20
❏ 405 [PS]	He's My Ideal/Mr. Piano Man	1962	$40
❏ 375	Indian Giver/Mama, Mama Rosa (Where's the Spumoni)	1961	$20
❏ 375 [PS]	Indian Giver/Mama, Mama Rosa (Where's the Spumoni)	1961	$40
❏ 431	Merlin Jones/The Scrambled Egghead	1964	$15

— With Tommy Kirk

Number	Title	Yr	NM
❏ 431 [PS]	Merlin Jones/The Scrambled Egghead	1964	$40
❏ 433	Muscle Beach Party/I Dream About Frankie	1964	$20
❏ 433 [PS]	Muscle Beach Party/I Dream About Frankie	1964	$40
❏ 400	My Little Grass Shack/Hukilau	1962	$20
❏ 354	O Dio Mio/It Took Dreams	1960	$20
❏ 354 [PS]	O Dio Mio/It Took Dreams	1960	$40
❏ 362	Pineapple Princess/Luau Cha Cha Cha	1960	$20
❏ 362 [PS]	Pineapple Princess/Luau Cha Cha Cha	1960	$40
❏ 438	Something Borrowed, Something Blue/How Will I Know My Love	1965	$20
❏ 438 [PS]	Something Borrowed, Something Blue/How Will I Know My Love	1965	$100
❏ 369	Talk to Me Baby/I Love You Baby	1960	$20
❏ 369 [PS]	Talk to Me Baby/I Love You Baby	1960	$40
❏ 414	Teenage Wedding/Walkin' and Talkin'	1962	$30
❏ 414 [PS]	Teenage Wedding/Walkin' and Talkin'	1962	$600
❏ 392	That Crazy Place From Outer Space/Seven Moons (Of Batalayre)	1962	$20

— B-side by Danny Saval and Tom Tryon

Number	Title	Yr	NM
❏ 392 [PS]	That Crazy Place From Outer Space/Seven Moons (Of Batalayre)	1962	$50
❏ 442	The Boy to Love/No One Else Could Be Prouder	1965	$15
❏ 475	The Computer Wore Tennis Shoes/Merlin Jones	1970	$8
❏ 440	The Monkey's Uncle/How Will I Know My Love	1965	$15

— With the Beach Boys backing up

Number	Title	Yr	NM
❏ 440 [PS]	The Monkey's Uncle/How Will I Know My Love	1965	$30
❏ 394	The Truth About Youth/I Can't Do the Sum	1962	$20
❏ 394 [PS]	The Truth About Youth/I Can't Do the Sum	1962	$50
❏ 437	The Wah-Watusi/The Clyde	1964	$15
❏ 359	Train of Love/Tell Me Who's the Girl	1960	$20
❏ 359 [PS]	Train of Love/Tell Me Who's the Girl	1960	$50
❏ 427	Treat Him Nicely/Promise Me Anything	1963	$20
❏ 427 [PS]	Treat Him Nicely/Promise Me Anything	1963	$70
❏ 339	Wild Willie/Lonely Guitar	1959	$20
❏ 339 [PS]	Wild Willie/Lonely Guitar	1959	$40

DISNEYLAND

Number	Title	Yr	NM
❏ 102	How Will I Know My Love/Don't Jump to Conclusions	1958	$40
❏ 102 [PS]	How Will I Know My Love/Don't Jump to Conclusions	1958	$60
❏ 118	Tall Paul/Ma, He's Making Eyes at Me	1959	$30
❏ 114	That Crazy Place in Outer Space/Gold Doubloons and Pieces of Eight	1958	$50

— B-side: "Theme from the Hardy Boys"

EPIC

Number	Title	Yr	NM
❏ 9829	Baby Needs Me Now/Moment of Silence	1965	$30

— With Cecil Null

STARVIEW

Number	Title	Yr	NM
❏ 3001	The Promised Land/In Between and Out of Love	1983	$10
❏ 3001 [PS]	The Promised Land/In Between and Out of Love	1983	$10

TOWER

Number	Title	Yr	NM
❏ 326	What's a Girl to Do/When You Get What You Want	1967	$40

Number	Title	Yr	NM

ANNIE AND THE ORPHANS
CAPITOL

❏ 5144	My Girl's Been Bitten by the Beatle Bug/A Place Called Happiness	1964	$30
❏ 5144 [PS]	My Girl's Been Bitten by the Beatle Bug/A Place Called Happiness	1964	$30

ANQUETTE
LUKE SKYYWALKER

❏ (# unknown)	Ghetto Style/(B-side unknown)	1986	$10

ANT, ADAM
EPIC

❏ ENR-03762	Desparate But Not Serious/(B-side blank)	1983	$8

—One-sided budget release

❏ 34-03688	Desparate But Not Serious/Place in the Country	1983	$4
❏ ENR-03529	Goody Two Shoes/(B-side blank)	1983	$8

—One-sided budget release

❏ 34-03367	Goody Two Shoes/Crackpot History	1982	$4
❏ 15-05538	Goody Two Shoes/Crackpot History	1984	$3

—Golden Oldies" reissue

❏ 34-04461	Puss 'N Boots/Kiss the Drummer	1984	$3
❏ 34-04461 [PS]	Puss 'N Boots/Kiss the Drummer	1984	$4
❏ 34-04337	Strip/Yours, Yours, Yours	1984	$3
❏ 34-04337 [PS]	Strip/Yours, Yours, Yours	1984	$4

ANTELL, PETE
BOUNTY

❏ 103	The Times They Are a-Changin'/Yesterrday and Tomorrow	1965	$20

NEW VOICE

❏ 818	Wanting/Warm Smoke	1967	$10

ANTHONY AND THE SOPHOMORES
ABC

❏ 10844	Heartbreak/I'll Go Through Life Loving You	1966	$30

ABC-PARAMOUNT

❏ 10737	Gee (But I'd Give the World)/It Depends On You	1965	$30
❏ 10770	Get Back to You/Wild for Her	1966	$30

GRAND

❏ 163	Embraceable You/Beautiful Dreamer	1963	$70

JAMIE

❏ 1340	One Summer Night/Work Out	1967	$20
❏ 1330	Serenade (From The Student Prince)/Work Out	1967	$20

JASON SCOTT

❏ 18	Embraceable You/Beautiful Dreamer	1978	$4

MERCURY

❏ 72103	Play Those Oldies Mr. D.J./Clap Your Hands	1963	$70
❏ 72168	Swingin' at the Chariot/Better Late Than Never	1963	$40

ANTHONY, MARK
LA BELLE

❏ 779	Mama's Twistin' with Santa/Music from Studio "D	1962	$15

TABU

❏ ZS4-07959	1919 Main St./Dreams of Love	1988	$3

ANTHONY, MARKUS
R&R

❏ 940	One Night of Love/Call Me	1986	$6
❏ 941	We Gonna Make Love Tonight/(B-side unknown)	1986	$8

ANTHONY, NICK
ABC-PARAMOUNT

❏ 9985	Forbidden Love/My Baby's Gone	1958	$30
❏ 9919	More Than Ever/You're Real Keen, Jelly Bean	1958	$30

Number	Title	Yr	NM

ANTHONY, RAY
CAPITOL

❏ F1196	A Marshmallow World/Where Do I Go from You	1950	$20
❏ F1678	As Time Goes By/At Last	1954	$10

—Reissue

❏ F2104	As Time Goes By/Scatterbrain	1952	$10
❏ F1912	At Last/I'll See You in My Dreams	1952	$12
❏ 4440	Atsa Nice-a/You Know It, You Know It, You Know It	1960	$8
❏ F1280	Autumn Leaves/Mr. Anthony's Boogie	1950	$15
❏ F968	Autumn Nocturne/Tenderly	1950	$15
❏ F2936	A Woman's World/Jambo	1954	$10
❏ F1574	Believing You/One Dance with You	1951	$15
❏ F1352	Be My Love/I Wonder What's Become of Sally	1951	$15
❏ F1956	Bermuda/Broken Hearted	1952	$12
❏ F1857	Brother Fats/I Remember Harlem	1951	$15
❏ F3319	Bullfighter Lament/Rockin' Thru Dixie	1955	$10
❏ F2251	Bunny Hop/Blow, Man, Blow	1952	$15
❏ 4728	Bunny Hop Twist/Tequila with a Twist	1962	$8
❏ F3646	Calypso Dance/Plymouth Rock	1957	$8
❏ F1131	Can Anyone Explain/Shy Coach	1950	$15
❏ 5070	Candy Wrapper/Mr. Novak	1963	$6
❏ F3416	Chubasco (Mexican Storm Song)/Sleepwalker	1956	$8
❏ F859	Count Every Star/Bamboo	1950	$15
❏ F979	Count Every Star/The Darktown Strutters Ball	1950	$15
❏ F2777	Dance My Heart/Somewhere Beyond Tonight	1954	$12
❏ 5714	Danke Schoen/Huapango Mexicana	1966	$6
❏ F1810	Deep Night/With All My Heart and Soul	1951	$15
❏ F1169	Dixie Doodle/All of a Sudden (My Heart Sings)	1950	$15
❏ F2562	Dragnet/Dancing in the Dark	1953	$20
❏ F3261	Flip Flop/Hurricane Anthony	1955	$10
❏ F4227	Fly Now Pay Later/707	1959	$8
❏ F1051	Francie/Mama Told Me to Do the Charleston	1950	$15
❏ 5836	Gallant Men/Around the World	1967	$5
❏ 5654	Goodbye My Love/Merci Cherie	1966	$6
❏ 4513	Gurney Slade Theme/Return to Me	1961	$8
❏ F1190	Harbor Lights/Nevertheless (I'm in Love with You)	1950	$15
❏ 4972	Heartaches/Mexican Market Day	1963	$6
❏ F3029	Heat Wave/Juke Box Special	1955	$12
❏ F1884	Honeydriper/Busman's Holiday	1951	$15
❏ 4834	I Almost Lost My Mind/Trouble in Mind	1962	$8
❏ F3500	I Am in Love/I Love You Samantha	1956	$8
❏ F2293	Idaho/People in Love	1952	$10
❏ F2860	I Don't Hurt Anymore/Cat Dancin'	1954	$10
❏ F1973	I Hear a Rhapsody/For Dancers Only	1952	$10
❏ F1490	I'll Never Know Why/Faithfully Yours	1951	$15
❏ F819	I'll See You in My Dreams/My Baby Is Blue	1950	$15
❏ F1723	I Love the Sunshine in Your Smile/You Blew Out the Flame	1951	$15
❏ F958	In the Mood/Way Down Yonder	1950	$15
❏ 5589	It's Such a Happy Day/Bah-Yoop	1966	$6
❏ 5320	Lady Bird/Tiger Tail	1964	$6
❏ F1073	Lazy Old Tune/Lackawanna Local	1950	$15
❏ F3147	Learning the Blues/Mmmm Marie	1955	$12
❏ 4876	Let Me Entertain You/Wishing Star	1962	$8
❏ 5149	Let's All Do the Swim/Everybody Do the Swim	1964	$6
❏ F3739	Lonely Trumpet/Cello-Phane	1957	$8
❏ F3593	Love is Just Around the Corner/Danciong Lovers	1956	$8
❏ F3335	Madeira/Show Me the Way to Go Home	1955	$10
❏ F2194	Make Believe Dreams/Loaded with Love	1952	$10
❏ F2207	Marilyn/Randles Island	1952	$30
❏ F1739	Mary Rose/Ho Ho	1951	$15
❏ 4603	Moliendo Café/Champs Elysses	1961	$8
❏ F1367	More Than I Care to Remember/Columbia, The Gem of the Ocean	1951	$15
❏ F1502	Mr. Anthony's Blues/Cooks Tour	1951	$15
❏ F1679	Mr. Anthony's Boogie/I Wonder What's Become of Sally	1954	$10

—Reissue

❏ F1835	My Concerto/I'll Remember April	1951	$15
❏ F1249	My Heart Is Out of Town/Harlem Nocturne	1950	$15
❏ F1583	My Truly, Truly Fair/Pretty Eyed Baby	1951	$15
❏ F2678	O Mein Papa (O! My Papa)/Secret Love	1953	$10
❏ F2327	On the Trail/Street Scene	1953	$10
❏ F3176	Pete Kelly's Blues/D.C. 7	1955	$10

Number	Title	Yr	NM

❏ F4041	Peter Gunn/Tango for Two	1958	$10
❏ F2451	Piccadilly Circus/Thunderbird	1953	$10
❏ F923	Sentimental Me/Spaghetti Rag	1950	$15
❏ 5468	Seventh Son/Meeting Over Yonder	1965	$6
❏ F2728	Sign Post/Air Express	1954	$10
❏ F1957	Singin' in the Rain/I Let a Song Go Out of My Heart	1952	$10
❏ F794	Sitting by the Window/Dixie	1949	$20
❏ F1040	Skip to My Lou/Scattered Toys	1950	$15
❏ F2896	Skokiaan/Say Hey	1954	$12
❏ 5418	Skunk in a Trunk/Sabor Ami	1965	$6
❏ 6F-2085	Slaughter on Tenth Avenue (Part I)/Slaughter on Tenth Avenue (Part II)	1952	$12

—Has a maroon rather than purple label

❏ F3096	Sluefoot/Something's Gotta Give	1955	$12
❏ F2637	Sound Off/Another Dawn, Another Day	1953	$12
❏ F1622	Star Dust/Man with a Horn	1951	$15
❏ F1107	Star Dust/Young Man with a Horn	1950	$15
❏ F1654	Tenderly/Autumn Nocturne	1951	$15
❏ F1758	The Fox/Rollin' Home	1951	$15
❏ F1020	The Girl That I Marry/They Say It's Wonderful	1950	$15
❏ F2427	The Hokey Pokey/Bunny Hop	1953	$15
❏ F3676	The Incredible Shrinking Man!/This Could Be the Night	1957	$8
❏ F2002	There Are Such Things/Moonlight Savings Time	1952	$10
❏ F1522	These Things I Offer You (For a Lifetime)/Here's To Your Illusions	1951	$15
❏ F3897	Till There Was You/Big Record	1958	$8
❏ 5026	Toys in the Attic/Oh Steal Away	1963	$6
❏ F2393	True Blue Lou/They Didn't Believe Me	1953	$10
❏ F2058	Trumpet Boogie/You're Driving Me Crazy	1952	$10
❏ F2699	Tuxedo Junction/In the Mood	1954	$10
❏ F4176	Walkin' to Mother's/Bunny Hop	1959	$10
❏ F1664	What Is This Thing Called Love/Harlem Nocturne	1951	$15
❏ F2488	When the Saints Go Marching In/That's My Weakness Now	1953	$10
❏ F933	Where in the World/Candy & Cake	1950	$15
❏ F945	Why/Little Peach from East Orange	1950	$15
❏ 4742	Worried Mind/Al Di La	1962	$8

7-Inch Extended Plays

❏ EAP 1-504	Cooks Tour/Idaho//Jersey Bounce/Thunderbird	1955	$10
❏ SU-2457 [PS]	Dream Dancing Today	1965	$12
❏ SU-2457	Everybody Loves Somebody/A Taste of Honey/Red Roses for a Blue Lady//Are You Lonesome Tonight/You've Lost That Lovin' Feelin'/Dear Heart	1965	$10

—Jukebox issue; small hole, plays at 33 1/3 rpm

❏ SXA-1783 [PS]	I Almost Lost My Mind	1962	$12
❏ SXA-1783	I Almost Lost My Mind/Don't Let the Sun Catch You Cryin'/Midnight Flyer//Prayers/Long Lonely Nights/Trouble in Mind	1962	$10

—Jukebox issue; small hole, plays at 33 1/3 rpm

❏ EAP 1-1181 [PS]	Peter Gunn	1959	$15
❏ EAP 1-1181	Peter Gunn/Fallout//Walkin' to Mothers/Dreamsville	1959	$15

ANTHONY, RAYBURN
AUDIOGRAPH

❏ 459	Dance for a Crystal Ball/(B-side unknown)	1983	$6
❏ 444	Tennessee Whiskey, Texas Women/(B-side unknown)	1983	$6

MERCURY

❏ 55042	I Thought You Were Easy/This One's for You	1978	$4
❏ 55063	It Won't Go Away/Baby Take It from Me	1979	$4
❏ 57024	Married Women/Cheatin' Fire	1980	$4
❏ 55053	Shadows of Love/Fire in the Night	1979	$4
❏ 57006	The Wild Side of Life/I Don't Believe I'll Fall in Love Today	1979	$4

—A-side with Kitty Wells

❏ 57040	What Do You Need with Another Man/Hangin' Out and Holdin' On	1980	$4

MILLION

❏ 19	Memphis Morning/(B-side unknown)	1972	$8

MONUMENT

❏ 1004	I've Worn Out My Welcome Home/Walkin' on My Heart in High Heel Sneakers	1967	$10

Number	Title	Yr	NM
❏ 1023	There'll Be Many Tomorrows (Before I Forget Yesterday)/A Woman Whose Love Is Hard to Keep	1967	$10

POLYDOR

Number	Title	Yr	NM
❏ 14482	Ain't No California/Talk About a Feeling	1978	$5
❏ 14346	Crazy Again/Mother Country Music	1976	$5
❏ 14398	Hold Me/Don't Fall in Love	1977	$5
❏ 14367	If You Don't Like Hank Williams/This Time Marie	1976	$6
❏ 14380	Lonely Eyes/Walkin'	1977	$5
❏ 14457	Maybe I Should've Been Listenin'/This Time Marie	1978	$5
❏ 14423	She Keeps Hangin' On!/Talk About a Feeling	1977	$5

SEVENTY-7

Number	Title	Yr	NM
❏ 905	She Just Laid the Lovin' Right On Me/Walking Tall	1975	$6

SUN

Number	Title	Yr	NM
❏ 333	Alice Blue Gown/St. Louis Blues	1959	$30
❏ 373	Big Dream/How Well I Know	1962	$30
❏ 339	There's No Tomorrow/Who's Gonna Shoe Your Pretty Foot	1960	$30

ANTHONY, TONY
HERALD

Number	Title	Yr	NM
❏ 533	Peek-a-Boo/Lonely One	1959	$40

ANTHONY, VINCE
MIDNIGHT GOLD

Number	Title	Yr	NM
❏ 160	Call Me Friend/Leave Me Tonight	1982	$8
❏ 140	Closing Time/Statue of a Fool	1981	$8

ANTHRAX
MEGAFORCE

Number	Title	Yr	NM
❏ MRS-01	Soldiers of Metal/Howling Furies	1983	$30
❏ MRS-01 [PS]	Soldiers of Metal/Howling Furies	1983	$30

ANTISEEN
7-Inch Extended Plays
AJAX

Number	Title	Yr	NM
❏ 003 [PS]	Blood of Freaks	1988	$13

—*Poster sleeve; 300 made (issued with red vinyl record)*

Number	Title	Yr	NM
❏ 003 [PS]	Blood of Freaks	1988	$8

—*Regular sleeve*

Number	Title	Yr	NM
❏ 003	(contents unknown)	1988	$13

—*Red vinyl; 300 made*

Number	Title	Yr	NM
❏ 003	(contents unknown)	1988	$8

—*Black vinyl*

DEATH TRAIN

Number	Title	Yr	NM
❏ 01	(contents unknown)	1985	$50

—*First pressing, with wrong address crossed out on labels*

Number	Title	Yr	NM
❏ 01	(contents unknown)	1985	$25

—*Second pressing, with corrected address on labels*

Number	Title	Yr	NM
❏ 02	(contents unknown)	1986	$10
❏ 01 [PS]	Drastic	1985	$35

TPOS PRODUCTIONS

Number	Title	Yr	NM
❏ 038	(contents unknown)	1989	$8
❏ 038 [PS]	WXCI Live Radio Broadcast	1989	$8

ANTOINETTE
PARKWAY

Number	Title	Yr	NM
❏ 932	There He Goes/Little Things Mean a Lot	1964	$15

ANTON, SUSAN
COLUMBIA

Number	Title	Yr	NM
❏ 3-10740	Listen to My Smile/My Baby	1978	$6
❏ 3-10740 [PS]	Listen to My Smile/My Baby	1978	$15

ANTONY, MARK
DUKE

Number	Title	Yr	NM
❏ 465	Christmas Together (Part 1)/Christmas Together (Part 2)	1970	$6

AORTA
ATLANTIC

Number	Title	Yr	NM
❏ 2545	Strange/Shape of Things to Come	1968	$30

COLUMBIA

Number	Title	Yr	NM
❏ 44870	Strange/Ode to Missy Mztsfpklk	1969	$10

HAPPY TIGER

Number	Title	Yr	NM
❏ 567	Sandcastles/Willie Jean	1970	$20

APAKA, ALFRED
DECCA

Number	Title	Yr	NM
❏ 31331	Medley: Mele Kalikimaka (Merry Christmas)-Jingle Bells/Silent Night (Polai E)	1961	$15

APHRODITE'S CHILD
PHILIPS

Number	Title	Yr	NM
❏ 40587	End of the World/You Always Stand in My Way	1969	$30
❏ 40536	Other People/Plastics Nevermore	1968	$30

POLYDOR

Number	Title	Yr	NM
❏ 15005	Magic Mirror/I Want to Live	1969	$8

VERTIGO

Number	Title	Yr	NM
❏ 107	Babylon/Break	1973	$20

APOLLO
GORDY

Number	Title	Yr	NM
❏ 7165	Astro Disco (Part 1)/Astro Disco (Part 2)	1979	$4

APOLLO 100
ATCO

Number	Title	Yr	NM
❏ 7001	Dan the Banjo Man/Tidal Wave	1974	$6

MEGA

Number	Title	Yr	NM
❏ 0080	Minuet for a Funky Lady/Telstar	1972	$4
❏ 0069	Symphony #4, 2nd Movement/Reach for the Sky	1972	$4

APPALACHIANS, THE
ABC-PARAMOUNT

Number	Title	Yr	NM
❏ 10464	Big Betty/Hilly-Billy-Ding-Dong-Choo-Choo	1963	$8
❏ 10419	Bony Maronie/It Takes a Man	1963	$10
❏ 10498	Lawdy Miss Clawdy/Over Yonder	1963	$8

APPLE PIE MOTHERHOOD BAND, THE
ATLANTIC

Number	Title	Yr	NM
❏ 2477	Flight Path/Long Live Apple Pie	1968	$8

APPLEJACKS, THE (1)
B.T. PUPPY

Number	Title	Yr	NM
❏ 554	The Son of a Preacher Man/Girl of the Skies	1970	$8

—*As "Dave Appell"*

CAMEO

Number	Title	Yr	NM
❏ 158	Bunny Hop/Night Train Stroll	1959	$20
❏ 170	Circle Dance/Love Scene	1959	$20
❏ 132	Dinner with Drac/No Name Theme	1958	$30
❏ 207	Happy Jose/Noivous	1961	$20

—*As "Dave Appell and His Orchestra"*

Number	Title	Yr	NM
❏ 248	Hippies Waltz/Back in 60 Seconds	1963	$20
❏ 283	Hot Toddy/Dance of the Hours	1963	$20
❏ 110	Love in the Jungle/Chitter Chatter Baby	1957	$30
❏ 149	Mexican Hat Rock/Sophisticated Swing	1958	$30
❏ 149	Mexican Hat Rock/Stop! Red Light	1958	$20
❏ 203	Mexican Hat Twist/Let's Continental	1961	$20
❏ 138	Moonlight Serenade/Walk On	1958	$30
❏ 321	She Loves You/Bongo Beach	1964	$20

—*As "Dave Appell and The Applejacks (Featuring Joe Sher on Drums)*

Number	Title	Yr	NM
❏ 222	Struttin' in the Summertime/Any Time	1962	$20
❏ 184	Theme from The Young Ones/September Song	1960	$20

—*As "Dave Appell and His Orchestra"*

DECCA

Number	Title	Yr	NM
❏ 9-29218	Smarter/My Heart Will Wait for You	1954	$30
❏ 9-29330	Sweet Patootie Pie/Reunion	1954	$30

PRESIDENT

Number	Title	Yr	NM
❏ 1006	Teenage Meeting/Ooh Baby Ooh	1956	$30

TONE-CRAFT

Number	Title	Yr	NM
❏ 200	Ookey-Ook/Honey	1955	$30

—*As "Dave Appell and the Applejacks*

Number	Title	Yr	NM
❏ 202	Where Is My Love/Alrighty	1955	$30

—*As "Dave Appell and the Applejacks*

APPLEJACKS, THE (2)
LONDON

Number	Title	Yr	NM
❏ 9658	Baby Jane/Tell Me When	1964	$15
❏ 9681	Like Dreamers Do/Everybody Fall Down	1964	$20

APPLETREE THEATRE CO.
VERVE FORECAST

Number	Title	Yr	NM
❏ 5071	Hightower Square/Who Do You Think I Am	1967	$15
❏ 5082	Lotus Flower/What a Way to Go	1968	$15

APPRECIATIONS, THE
JUBILEE

Number	Title	Yr	NM
❏ 5525	Afraid of Love/Far from Your Love	1966	$15

SPORT

Number	Title	Yr	NM
❏ 112	It's Better to Cry/Gimme Back My Soul	1967	$200
❏ 108	There's a Place in My Heart/She Never Really Believed Me	1967	$125

APRIL WINE
BIG TREE

Number	Title	Yr	NM
❏ 142	Bad Side of the Moon/Believe in Me	1972	$5
❏ 15006	Come On Along/I'm on Fire for You Baby	1974	$5
❏ 16036	Oowatanite/(B-side unknown)	1975	$5

CAPITOL

Number	Title	Yr	NM
❏ 4802	Before the Dawn/Say Hello	1979	$4
❏ B-5133	Enough Is Enough/Ain't Got Your Love	1982	$4
❏ B-5133 [PS]	Enough Is Enough/Ain't Got Your Love	1982	$5
❏ 4728	Get Ready for Love/Comin' Right Down on Top of Me	1979	$4
❏ B-5153	If You See Kay/Blood Money	1982	$5
❏ 4828	I Like to Rock/Babes in Arms	1980	$4
❏ 4859	Lady's Man/Tonite	1980	$4
❏ A-5001	Sign of the Gypsy Queen/Crash and Burn	1981	$4
❏ A-5001 [PS]	Sign of the Gypsy Queen/Crash and Burn	1981	$5
❏ B-5168	Tell Me Why/Runners in the Night	1982	$4
❏ B-5319	This Could Be the Right One/Really Don't Want Your Love	1984	$3
❏ B-5319 [PS]	This Could Be the Right One/Really Don't Want Your Love	1984	$4

LONDON

Number	Title	Yr	NM
❏ 265	I'm Alive/Rock and Roll Is a Vicious Game	1977	$5
❏ 245	Shot Down/(B-side unknown)	1976	$5

AQUARIAN DREAM
BUDDAH

Number	Title	Yr	NM
❏ 546	Guitar Talk/Look Ahead	1976	$5
❏ 560	Phoenix/Look Ahead	1977	$5
❏ 560 [PS]	Phoenix/Look Ahead	1977	$8

ELEKTRA

Number	Title	Yr	NM
❏ 46523	Are You Ready for Love/Dirty Trick	1979	$4

AQUARIANS
UNI

Number	Title	Yr	NM
❏ 55124	Abela/Jungle Grass	1969	$6

AQUATONES, THE
FARGO

Number	Title	Yr	NM
❏ 1015	Every Time/There's a Long, Long Trail	1960	$30
❏ 1111	My Darling/For You, For You	1960	$30
❏ 1005	My Treasure/My One Desire	1959	$30
❏ 1022	My Treasure/Say You'll Be Mine	1962	$30
❏ 1003	Our First Kiss/The Drive-In	1958	$30
❏ 1002	Say You'll Be Mine/So Fine	1958	$30
❏ 1016	Wanted/Crazy for You	1961	$30

ARATA, TONY
MCA

Number	Title	Yr	NM
❏ 52782	Same Old Story/Rollin'	1986	$4

Number	Title	Yr	NM

NOBLE VISION

| ❏ 106 | Come On Home/Maybe I'm Over You | 1984 | $5 |
| ❏ 108 | Sure Thing/Enjoy the Ride | 1985 | $5 |

ARBORS, THE
CARNEY

| ❏ 1011 | A Symphony for Susan/Love Is the Light | 1966 | $30 |

DATE

❏ 1529	A Symphony for Susan/Love Is the Light	1966	$10
❏ 1546	Dreamer Girl/Just Let It Happen	1967	$12
❏ 1561	Graduation Day/I Win the Whole Wide World	1967	$10
❏ 1645	I Can't Quit Her/Lovin' Tonight (Maybe Tonight)	1969	$10
❏ 1570	Love for All Seasons/With You Girl	1967	$10
❏ 1601	That's the Way It Is/Graduation Day	1968	$12
❏ 1638	The Letter/Most of All	1969	$15
❏ 1651	Touch Me/Motet	1969	$10

MERCURY

| ❏ 72456 | Anybody Here for Love/The Girl with the Heather Green Eyes | 1965 | $15 |

ARCADIA
ATLANTIC

| ❏ 89370 | Say the Word/(Instrumental) | 1986 | $4 |
| ❏ 89370 [PS] | Say the Word/(Instrumental) | 1986 | $4 |

CAPITOL

❏ B-5501	Election Day/She's Moody and Grey; She's Mean and She's Restless	1985	$3
❏ B-5501 [PS]	Election Day/She's Moody and Grey; She's Mean and She's Restless	1985	$3
❏ B-5542	Goodbye Is Forever/Missing	1985	$3
❏ B-5542 [PS]	Goodbye Is Forever/Missing	1985	$4
❏ B-5570	The Flame/Flame Game	1986	$3
❏ B-5570 [PS]	The Flame/Flame Game	1986	$5

ARCHERS, THE
LAURIE

| ❏ 3207 | Hey Rube/Unwind It | 1963 | $20 |

ARCHIBALD
IMPERIAL

❏ 5212	Early Morning Blues/Great Big Eyes	1953	$1500
❏ 5563	Stack-A-Lee/Whispering Hope	1959	$60
❏ 5358	Stack-O-Lee (Part 1)/Stack-O-Lee (Part 2)	1955	$125

ARCHIES, THE
CALENDAR

❏ 63-1006	Bang-Shang-a-Lang/Truck Driver	1968	$8
❏ 63-1006 [PS]	Bang-Shang-a-Lang/Truck Driver	1968	$20
❏ 63-1007	Feelin' So Good (S.K.O.O.B.Y.-D.O.O.)/Love Light	1968	$8
❏ 63-1007 [PS]	Feelin' So Good (S.K.O.O.B.Y.-D.O.O.)/Love Light	1968	$30
❏ 63-1008	Sugar Sugar/Melody Hill	1969	$10

KIRSHNER

❏ 63-5014	A Summer Prayer for Peace/Maybe I'm Wrong	1971	$8
❏ 63-5014 [PS]	A Summer Prayer for Peace/Maybe I'm Wrong	1971	$20
❏ 63-5009	Everything's Alright/Together We Two	1970	$8
❏ 63-5018	Love Is Living in You/Hold On to Lovin'	1972	$8
❏ 63-5021	Strangers in the Morning/Plum Crazy	1972	$8
❏ 63-1009	Sunshine/Over and Over	1970	$8
❏ SP-45-218 [DJ]	Sunshine (same on both sides)	1970	$20

— Promo-only number

| ❏ 63-5011 | Throw a Little Love My Way/This Is Love | 1971 | $8 |
| ❏ 63-5003 | Who's Your Baby/Senorita Rita | 1970 | $8 |

Number	Title	Yr	NM

ARDELLS, THE
EPIC

| ❏ 9621 | Eefananny/Lonely Valley | 1963 | $20 |
| ❏ 9621 [PS] | Eefananny/Lonely Valley | 1963 | $40 |

— Title sleeve with lyrics

MARCO

| ❏ 102 | Every Day of the Week/Roll On | 1961 | $40 |

SELMA

| ❏ 4001 | Seven Lonely Nights/You Can Fall in Love | 1963 | $30 |

ARDEN, TONI
COLUMBIA

| ❏ 4-40019 | All I Desire/Lover's Waltz | 1953 | $20 |

— With the Four Lads

| ❏ 4-39766 | Blow Out the Candle/Where Did the Night Go | 1952 | $20 |
| ❏ 1-760(?) | Can't We Talk It Over/Only a Moment Ago | 1950 | $40 |

— Microgroove 33 1/3 rpm 7-inch single, small hole

| ❏ 4-39208 | Chante Moi/So Deep in Love | 1951 | $20 |
| ❏ 1-937 | Every Moment of My Life/I'm Praying to St. Christopher | 1950 | $40 |

— Microgroove 33 1/3 rpm 7-inch single, small hole

❏ 4-39080	Every Moment of My Life/I'm Praying to St. Christopher	1950	$30
❏ 4-39650	Heart of Stone/There's Always My Heart	1952	$20
❏ 1-377	I Can Dream, Can't I?/A Little Hug, a Little Kiss	1949	$40

— Microgroove 33 1/3 rpm 7-inch single, small hole

❏ 4-40081	I Forgot More Than You'll Ever Know/Any More	1953	$20
❏ 4-40196	In Paris and In Love/Cry, My Heart	1954	$20
❏ 4-39978	It's Only My Heart/F'r Instance	1953	$20
❏ 4-39348	Little Child/Come Back to Sorrento	1951	$20
❏ 1-560(?)	Mother, Mother, Mother/Rain	1950	$40

— Microgroove 33 1/3 rpm 7-inch single, small hole

| ❏ 4-39117 | My Man/Playing Our Song | 1950 | $30 |
| ❏ 1-830(?) | My Tears Won't Dry/And You'll Be Home | 1950 | $40 |

— Microgroove 33 1/3 rpm 7-inch single, small hole

❏ 4-39003	My Tears Won't Dry/And You'll Be Home	1950	$30
❏ 4-39577	Once/Never	1951	$20
❏ 4-39878	Take a Chance/Sweet Forgiveness	1952	$20
❏ 4-40125	Take Me Now/I Wish I Knew	1953	$20
❏ 4-39768	Take My Heart/Tell Your Tale, Nightingale	1952	$20
❏ 4-39525	The Day Isn't Long Enough/I'll Hold You In My Heart	1951	$20
❏ 4-40225	Three Coins in the Fountain/When the Rolling Mountains Meet the Rolling Sea	1954	$20
❏ 4-39271	Too Young/Too Late Now	1951	$20
❏ 1-630(?)	Why/Tonight	1950	$40

— Microgroove 33 1/3 rpm 7-inch single, small hole

❏ 4-39427	Wonder Why/Dark Is the Night	1951	$20
❏ 9-30986	Besame Mucho/Anna	1959	$12
❏ 9-30765	Desire Me/The Window	1958	$12
❏ 31576	In the Summer of His Years/My Heart Is a Chapel	1963	$8
❏ 9-30396	It Takes Only One/Good Morning, Mister Love	1957	$10
❏ 9-30291	Like a Baby/An Empty Heart	1957	$12
❏ 9-30507	Like You/Can You Blame Me	1957	$12
❏ 9-30180	Little by Little/Without Love	1957	$12
❏ 9-30951	Only with You (You Are Me, I Am You)/Your Touch	1959	$10
❏ 9-30628	Padre/All at Once	1958	$15

RCA VICTOR

❏ 47-6346	Are You Satisfied/I Forgot to Remember to Forget	1956	$20
❏ 47-6536	Believe in Love/How Sweet My Love	1956	$15
❏ 47-6142	Beware/I'll Step Aside	1955	$15

AREA CODE (212)
FRIENDS & CO.

| ❏ 131 | Manhattan Shuffle/Daddy | 1979 | $6 |

AREA CODE 615
POLYDOR

| ❏ 14215 | Stone Fox Chase/Sligo | 1973 | $5 |
| ❏ 14012 | Why Ask Why/Ruby | 1969 | $6 |

Number	Title	Yr	NM

ARENA BRASS, THE
7-Inch Extended Plays
EPIC

| ❏ 5-26039 [PS] | The Lonely Bull | 1962 | $12 |
| ❏ 5-26039 | The Lonely Bull/Desafinado/Spanish Harlem//Eso Beso (That Kiss)/Tequila/La Virgen De La Macarena | 1962 | $10 |

— Jukebox issue; small hole, plays at 33 1/3 rpm

ARGENT

Rod Argent's group after THE ZOMBIES broke up.

DATE

| ❏ 1659 | Liar/Schoolgirl | 1970 | $12 |

EPIC

| ❏ 10746 | Celebration/Kingdom | 1971 | $6 |
| ❏ S EPC1243 | Christmas For The Free/God Gave Rock & Roll To You | 1973 | $6 |

— U.K. release

❏ 10972	God Gave Rock and Roll To You/Christmas for the Free	1973	$5
❏ 10852	Hold Your Head Up/Closer to Heaven	1972	$8
❏ 11019	It's Only Money, Part 2/Losing Hold	1973	$5
❏ 11137	Man for All Seasons/Music from the Spheres	1974	$5
❏ 50025	The Coming of Kohoutek/Thunder and Lightning	1974	$5
❏ 10919	Tragedy/He's a Dynamo	1972	$5

ARGO, JUDY
MDJ

❏ 92078	Country Hall of Shame/Night Time Music Man	1979	$6
❏ 51379	He's a Good Man/Why Me	1979	$5
❏ 51379 [PS]	He's a Good Man/Why Me	1979	$8
❏ 4633	Hide Me (In the Shadow of Your Love)/Millionaire Lover	1979	$5

ARGOSY
CONGRESS

| ❏ C-6013 | Mr. Boyd/Imagine | 1969 | $200 |

ARGYLES, THE (2)
BALLY

| ❏ 1030 | Moonbeam/Every Time You Smile | 1957 | $50 |

ARIELS, THE
BRENT

| ❏ 7060 | Feels Like I'm Cryin'/I Love You | 1967 | $70 |

ARISTOCRATS, THE
ARGO

| ❏ 5275 | Maid of the Mist/Vagabonds | 1957 | $30 |

ESSEX

| ❏ 366 | Believe Me/I'm Waiting for Ships | 1954 | $70 |

ARKADE
ABC DUNHILL

❏ 4286	Fool's Way of Lovin'/The Morning of Our Lives	1971	$6
❏ 4247	Sing Out the Love (In My Heart)/Susan	1970	$6
❏ 4268	The Morning of Our Lives/Rhythm of the People	1971	$6
❏ 4268 [PS]	The Morning of Our Lives/Rhythm of the People	1971	$10
❏ 4277	Where You Lead/Sentimental Lisa	1971	$6

ARKANSAS WOODCHOPPER, THE
KAPP

| ❏ 700 | My Daddy Was a Rabbit/Crazy Isaac | 1965 | $20 |

ARLEN, HAROLD, AND "FRIEND

The "Friend" is BARBRA STREISAND.

ARMATRADING, JOAN
A&M

❏ 2868	Angel Man/Rivers on Fire	1986	$4
❏ 2113	Barefoot and Pregnant/Your Letter	1979	$4
❏ 2102	Bottom to the Top/Your Letter	1978	$4
❏ 1898	Down to Zero/Like Fire	1976	$4

Number	Title	Yr	NM
❏ 2538	Drop the Pilot/Business Is Business	1983	$4
❏ 2538 [PS]	Drop the Pilot/Business Is Business	1983	$5
❏ 2622	Frustration/Heaven	1984	$4
❏ 2224	He Wants Up/Show Some Emotion	1980	$4
❏ 2564 [DJ]	(I Love It When You) Call Me Names (same on both sides)	1983	$5

— Stock copies do not exist

❏ 2262	Is It Tomorrow Yet/ Ma-Me-O-Beach	1980	$4
❏ 2400	I Wanna Hold You/Crying	1982	$4
❏ 1235	Living for You/I Really Must Be Going	1988	$4
❏ 1452	Lonely Lady/Together in Words and Music	1973	$4
❏ 1865	Love and Affection/Help Yourself	1976	$5
❏ 2751	Love Grows/Thinking Man	1985	$4
❏ 2240	Me Myself I/Friends	1980	$4
❏ 1994	Show Some Emotion/ No Way Out	1977	$4
❏ 2712	Temptation/Talking to the Wall	1985	$4
❏ 2018	Warm Love/No Way Out	1978	$4
❏ 1914	Water with the Wine/People	1977	$4
❏ 2381	Weakness in Me/Crying	1981	$4

7-Inch Extended Plays

❏ 2391 [DJ]	*Me Myself & I/Tall in the Saddle/Show Some Emotion/ Love and Affection/Rosie/ Back to the Night/People	1980	$5

— White label, small hole, plays at 33 1/3 rpm

❏ 2391 [PS]	Free Joan Armatrading	1980	$5

ARMEN, KAY
DECCA

❏ 9-30932	Anna-Bosha/Only Those in Love	1959	$15
❏ 9-30474	Ha! Ha! Ha! (Chella Lia!)/Till	1957	$20
❏ 9-30318	With This Pen/Don't Be Afraid	1957	$15

MGM

❏ K11967	Bella Notte/La La Lu	1955	$15
❏ K12078	He/Suddenly There's a Valley	1955	$15
❏ K12256	Love Is You/Tenderly He Watches	1956	$15
❏ K12045	The Bible Tells Me So/I Wonder When We'll Ever Know	1955	$15
❏ K11934	Wonder Why/By Candlelight	1955	$15

RCA VICTOR

❏ 47-5160	Smoky Mountain Lullaby/ It's a Sin to Cry Over You	1953	$20

ARMENIAN JAZZ SEXTET
KAPP

❏ 181	Harem Dance/Pretty Girl	1957	$20

ARMS, RUSSELL
EPIC

❏ 5-9083	The "Point of View" Song/The Touch	1954	$15

ERA

❏ 1078	Blue Hawaii/Der Glockenspiel	1958	$15
❏ 3053	Cinco Robles (Five Oaks)/ The World Is Made of Lisa	1961	$10
❏ 1026	Cinco Robles (Five Oaks)/ The World Is Made of Liza	1956	$20
❏ 1059	Hasta La Vista/Walkin' By Your Window	1957	$15
❏ 1018	Is There a Heaven/I Saw a Star	1956	$10
❏ 1048	I Wonder Where's My Darlin'/I'm Tired of Pride	1957	$15
❏ 1033	Share My Love/Evangeline	1957	$15
❏ 1040	The Bridge of San Angelo/ Where Can a Wanderer Go	1957	$15

ARMSTRONG, BILLY, AND THE GENERAL STORE
HILLSIDE

❏ 8107	Christmas Is Bigger in Texas/Tater Pie	1981	$6

ARMSTRONG, BRICE, AND THE AMERICAN GHOULS
DUCHESS

❏ 1020	The Fright Before Christmas/ Happy Ghoul Tide	1962	$30

ARMSTRONG, CHUCK
R&R

❏ 15313	Give Me All Your Sweet Lovin'/She Had the Right	1976	$10

Number	Title	Yr	NM

ARMSTRONG, JIMMY
ENJOY

❏ 1016	Count the Tears/I'm Going to Lock My Heart	1964	$30

SHRINE

❏ 0102	I'm About to Say Goodbye/Mystery	1965	$200

STOP

❏ 105	Close to You/Hanging Out with Early Bird	1965	$200

ARMSTRONG, LOUIS, AND THE MILLS BROTHERS
DECCA

❏ 28984	My Walking Stick/Marie	1953	$20

ARMSTRONG, LOUIS
A&M

❏ 3010	What a Wonderful World/ Game of Love	1988	$4

— B-side by Wayne Fontana and the Mindbenders

❏ 3010 [PS]	What a Wonderful World/ Game of Love	1988	$4

— Good Morning Vietnam" sleeve

ABC

❏ 11126	Hello Brother/The Sunshine of Love	1968	$6
❏ 11075	Hellzapoppin/The Sunshine of Love	1968	$6
❏ 10982	What a Wonderful World/Cabaret	1967	$8

AMSTERDAM

❏ 85019	Everybody's Talkin'/ (B-side unknown)	1970	$5
❏ 85016	Give Peace a Chance/The Creator Has a Master Plan	1970	$8
❏ 85017 [DJ]	Here Is My Heart For Christmas/His Father Wore Long Hair	1970	$12
❏ 85013	We Shall Overcome/ (Instrumental)	1970	$6
❏ 85021	What a Wonderful World/ His Father Wore Long Hair	1971	$5
❏ 173	Bill Bailey/The Creator Has a Master Plan	1971	$6
❏ AFSD5924-1 [S]	Bourbon Street Parade/ Washington and Lee Swing	1960	$10

— Jukebox issue; small hole, plays at 33 1/3 rpm

❏ AFSD5924-2 [S]	(contents unknown)	1960	$10

— Jukebox issue; small hole, plays at 33 1/3 rpm

❏ AFSD5924-3 [S]	(contents unknown)	1960	$10

— Jukebox issue; small hole, plays at 33 1/3 rpm

❏ AFSD5924-4 [S]	Sheik of Araby/Wolverine Blues	1960	$10

— Jukebox issue; small hole, plays at 33 1/3 rpm

❏ AFSD5924-5 [S]	Sweet Georgia Brown/ Limehouse Blues	1960	$10

— Jukebox issue; small hole, plays at 33 1/3 rpm

AVCO EMBASSY

❏ 4562	Miller's Cave/You Can Have Her	1971	$6

BRUNSWICK

❏ 55318	Daydream/Northern Boulevard Blues	1967	$6
❏ 55360	Happy Time/Willkomen	1968	$6
❏ 55395	I Believe/Sunrise, Sunset	1968	$6
❏ 55457	I Believe/You'll Never Walk Alone	1971	$5
❏ 55328	Louie's Dream/Step Down, Brother, Next Case	1967	$6
❏ 55380	Talk to the Animals/I Will Wait for You	1968	$6
❏ 55534	'Twas the Night Before Christmas/(B-side unknown)	1976	$8
❏ 55474	Willkomen/Sunrise, Sunset	1972	$5

BUENA VISTA

❏ F-469	Bibbidi-Bobbidi-Boo/ Zip-a-Dee-Doo-Dah	1968	$20
❏ F-470	Heigh-Ho/When You Wish Upon a Star	1968	$20
❏ F-465	Ten Feet Off the Ground/Bout Time	1968	$20
❏ F-465 [PS]	Ten Feet Off the Ground/Bout Time	1968	$30
❏ F-471	The Ballad of Davy Crocket/ Chim-Chim-Cheree	1968	$30
❏ F-466	The Bare Necessities/Louis	1968	$20
❏ F-489	When You Wish Upon a Star/Zip-a-Dee-Doo-Dah	1972	$10

Number	Title	Yr	NM

COLUMBIA

❏ 40587	A Theme from the Threepenny Opera (Mack the Knife) Back O' Town Blues	1956	$20
❏ 41471	Mack the Knife/The Faithful Hussar	1959	$10
❏ 40711	The Faithful Hussar/ Six Foot Four	1956	$15
❏ 40662	When the Red, Red Robin Comes Bob, Bob, Bobbin' Along/Six Foot Four	1956	$15

DECCA

❏ 28704	April in Portugal/Ramona	1953	$20
❏ 28172	Baby It's Cold Outside/ Stardust (Part 1)	1952	$15
❏ 27190	Baby Won't You Please Come Home/I Surrender Dear (Part 1)	1950	$15
❏ 28169	Back Home Again in Indiana (Part 1)/Way Down Yonder in New Orleans (Part 2)	1952	$15
❏ 28170	Back Home Again in Indiana (Part 2)/Way Down Yonder in New Orleans (Part 1)	1952	$15
❏ 29102	Basin Street Blues (Part 1)/ Basin Street Blues (Part 2)	1954	$20
❏ 27816	Because of You/ Cold, Cold Heart	1951	$20
❏ 28176	Big Daddy Blues/You Can Depend on Me	1952	$15
❏ 30091	Blueberry Hill/That Lucky Old Sun	1956	$15
❏ 28103	Body and Soul (Part 1)/How High the Moon (Part 2)	1952	$15
❏ 28104	Body and Soul (Part 2)/How High the Moon (Part 1)	1952	$15

— Above two with Barney B

❏ 28102	Boff Boff/C Jam Blues	1952	$15
❏ 28524	Chlo-E/Listen to the Mocking Bird	1953	$20
❏ 29710	Christmas Night in Harlem/ Christmas in New Orleans	1955	$20
❏ 27189	Fine and Dandy/I Surrender Dear (Part 2)	1950	$15
❏ 28107	High Society/Baby Won't You Please Come Home	1952	$15
❏ 28173	Honeysuckle Rose/ That's a Plenty	1952	$15
❏ 28099	I Cried for You (Part 1)/ Tea for Two (Part 2)	1952	$15
❏ 28100	I Cried for You (Part 2)/ Tea for Two (Part 1)	1952	$15

— Above two with Velma Middleton

❏ 27481	If You're Just in Love	1951	$20
❏ 30860	I'll String Along with You/ On My Way (Out on My Traveling Shoes)	1959	$10
❏ 30771	I Love Jazz/Mardi Gras March	1958	$10
❏ 9-28076	Indian Love Call/Jeannine	1952	$20

— With Gordon Jenkins and His Orchestra

❏ 27113	La Vie En Rose/C'est Si Bon	1950	$30
❏ 29921	Lazy Bones/Easy Street	1956	$15

— With Gary Crosby

❏ 28097	Lover/Black and Blue	1952	$15
❏ 28098	Mahogany Hall Stomp/ Since I Fell for You	1952	$15
❏ 29280	Muskrat Ramble/Someday You'll Be Sorry	1954	$20
❏ 28174	My Monday Date (Part 1)/ My Monday Date (Part 4)	1952	$15
❏ 28175	My Monday Date (Part 2)/ My Monday Date (Part 3)	1952	$15
❏ 29117	On a Coconut Island/To You Sweetheart Aloha	1954	$20
❏ 28306	Once in a While/Confessin'	1952	$20
❏ 29694	Only You (And You Alone)/ Moments to Remember	1955	$20
❏ 30980	Only You (And You Alone)/ Onkel Satchmo's Lullaby	1960	$10
❏ 28105	On the Sunny Side of the Street (Part 1)/That's My Desire (Part 2)	1952	$15
❏ 28106	On the Sunny Side of the Street (Part 2)/That's My Desire (Part 1)	1952	$15
❏ 27191	Panama (Part 1)/Bugle Call Rag (Part 3)	1950	$15
❏ 27192	Panama (Part 2)/Bugle Call Rag (Part 2)	1950	$15
❏ 29546	Pretty Little Missy/Baby Your Sleep Is Showing	1955	$20
❏ 29421	Sincerely/Pledging My Love	1955	$20
❏ 27254	Sit Down You're Rockin' the Boat/That's What the Man Said	1950	$30
❏ 29256	Skokiaan (Part 1)/ Skokiaan (Part 2)	1954	$20
❏ 28101	Stars Fell on Alabama (Part 1)/ Stars Fell on Alabama (Part 2)	1952	$15
❏ 28108	Steak Face (Part 1)/ Steak Face (Part 2)	1952	$15
❏ 28394	Takes Two to Tango/I Laughed at Love	1952	$20
❏ 27187	That's for Me (Part 1)/ Russian Lullaby (Part 2)	1950	$15
❏ 27188	That's for Me (Part 2)/ Russian Lullaby (Part 1)	1950	$15
❏ 28372	That's My Desire/Baby It's Cold Outside	1952	$20

Number	Title	Yr	NM
❑ 28803	The Dummy Song/ Sittin' in the Sun	1953	$20
❑ 28995	The Gypsy/I Can't Afford to Miss This Dream	1954	$20
❑ 28171	The Hucklebuck/ Stardust (Part 2)	1952	$15
❑ 30309	The Prisoner's Song/ You're a Heavenly Thing	1957	$10
❑ 29153	The Whiffenpoof Song/ Bye and Bye	1954	$20

— With Gordon Jenkins and His Orchestra

❑ 30188	This Younger Generation/ In Pursuit of Happiness	1957	$10
❑ 29352	Trees/Spooks	1954	$20
❑ 27899	When It's Sleepy Time Down South/It's All in the Game	1952	$20

— With Gordon Jenkins and His Orchestra

❑ 27720	(When We Are Dancing) I Get Ideas/A Kiss to Build a Dream On	1951	$20
❑ 28443	White Christmas/ Winter Wonderland	1952	$20

DOT

❑ 15991	Battle Hymn of the Republic/ Lullaby in Ragtime	1959	$12

— With Red Nichols

❑ 15941	The Five Pennies Saints/ Just the Blues	1959	$10

— With Danny Kaye

KAPP

❑ 573	Hello, Dolly!/A Lot of Livin' to Do	1964	$6
❑ 573 [PS]	Hello, Dolly!/A Lot of Livin' to Do	1964	$12
❑ 597	I Still Get Jealous/Someday	1964	$6
❑ 597 [PS]	I Still Get Jealous/Someday	1964	$10
❑ 2145	That's All I Want the World to Remember Me By/Hello, Dolly!	1971	$5

MCA

❑ MSS-35147	What a Wonderful World/ America the Beautiful	1989	$10

— B-side by the San Francisco Boys Chorus

❑ MSS-35147 [PS]	What a Wonderful World/ America the Beautiful	1989	$10

— Special item for the Environmental Defense Fund

❑ 53321	What a Wonderful World/ Dream a Little Dream of Me	1988	$5

— Reissue

MERCURY

❑ 72371	By and By/Faith	1964	$8
❑ 72593	Cheesecake/Bye 'N' Bye	1966	$8
❑ 72495	Circle of Your Arms/ Short But Sweet	1965	$8
❑ 72574	Mame/Tin Roof Blues	1966	$8
❑ 72338	So Long Dearie/ Pretty Little Missy	1964	$8
❑ 72338 [PS]	So Long Dearie/ Pretty Little Missy	1964	$15

MGM

❑ 12809	Someday You'll Be Sorry/ The Beat Generation	1959	$15

RCA VICTOR

❑ 47-4005	Ain't Misbehavin'/ Pennies from Heaven	1950	$20
❑ 47-4006	Saint James Infirmary/ Back o' Town Blues	1950	$20

UNITED ARTISTS

❑ 50617	We Have All the Time in the World/Pretty Little Missy	1969	$6

VERVE

❑ 10154	Top Hat, White Tie and Tails/East of the Sun	1958	$15

7-Inch Extended Plays

ABC

❑ EP-ABCS-650	Cabaret/Dream a Little Dream of Me/The Sunshine of Love// Hello Brother/Fantastic That's You/I Guess I'll Get the Papers and Go Home	1967	$10

— Jukebox issue; small hole, plays at 33 1/3 rpm

❑ EP-ABCS-650 [PS]	What a Wonderful World	1967	$12

COLUMBIA

❑ B-2540	*Mack the Knife/Ain't Misbehavin'/St. Louis Blues	1958	$25
❑ B-2540 [PS]	Louis Armstrong (Hall of Fame Series)	1958	$25

KAPP

❑ KBS969 [PS]	Hello, Dolly!	1964	$12

Number	Title	Yr	NM
❑ KBS969	Hello, Dolly!/Blueberry Hill/Be My Life's Companion/I Still Get Jealous/Hey, Look Me Over/ You Are Woman, I Am Man	1964	$10

— Jukebox issue; small hole, plays at 33 1/3 rpm

ARMSTRONG, VANESSA BELL
JIVE

❑ 1104-7-J	Pressing On/Don't Turn Your Back	1988	$3
❑ 1248-7-J	Something Inside So Strong/Living for You	1989	$3

ARMSTRONG, WAYNE
NSD

❑ 57	Hot Sunday Morning/I Don't Want to Be Alone	1980	$5

ARNAZ, DESI
COLUMBIA

❑ 4-39937	I Love Lucy/There's a Brand New Baby	1953	$50

RCA VICTOR

❑ 47-2866	Babalu/Brazil	1949	$20
❑ 47-2865	Tabu/Cuban Pete	1949	$20
❑ 47-2867	Tico Tico/Peanut Vendor	1949	$20

— The above three comprise a box set

ARNDT, BILL
HIT

❑ 21	Breaking Up Is Hard to Do/Sealed with a Kiss	1962	$8

— B-side by Dick Swift

ARNELL, GINNY
DECCA

❑ 31104	Carnival/We	1960	$20
❑ 31190	Look Who's Talkin'/Tell Me What You Said	1960	$20

MGM

❑ K13362	B-I-L-L Why/A Little Bit of Love Can Hurt	1965	$12
❑ K13177	Dumb Head/How Many Times Can One Heart Break	1963	$15
❑ K13226	He's My Little Devil/I Wish I Knew What Dress to Wear	1964	$15
❑ K13146	I'm Crying Too/Trouble's Back in Town	1963	$15
❑ K13403	I'm Gettin' Mad/I'm So Afraid of Loving You	1965	$10
❑ K13248	Let Me Make You Smile Again/ Yesterday's Memories	1964	$15

WARWICK

❑ 680	Married to You/He Likes Me Better Than Rock and Roll	1962	$30

ARNGRIM, STEFAN
JERDEN

❑ 916	Where Has Christmas Gone?/Cooper's Lagoon	1968	$5

ARNIE'S LOVE
PROFILE

❑ 5066	Date with the Rain/ (Instrumental)	1985	$5

ARNO, AUDREY
DECCA

❑ 31238	La Pachanga/Bei Mir Ist Nix Amore So Im Vorubergehn	1961	$12

ARNOLD, CALVIN
IX CHAINS

❑ 7013	I'm Your Friendly Neighborhood Freak (Part 1)/(Part 2)	1975	$10
❑ 7009	Satisfy My Woman/You'll Do It	1975	$10

SOUND STAGE 7

❑ 45-2506	After the Love Has Gone/ (B-side unknown)	1977	$50

VENTURE

❑ 605	Funky Way/Snatchin' Back	1967	$10
❑ 626	Mama in Law/Miniskirt	1968	$10
❑ 610	Scoobie Doo/Lovely Way to Go	1968	$20

Number	Title	Yr	NM

ARNOLD, EDDY
MGM

❑ 14769	Butterfly/If You Could Only Love Me Now	1974	$4
❑ 14535	If the Whole World Stopped Lovin'/My Son, I Wish You Everything	1973	$4
❑ 14734	I Wish That I Had Loved You Better/Let It Be Love	1974	$4
❑ 14827	Middle of a Memory/I Just Had You on My Mind	1975	$4
❑ 14600	Oh, Oh, I'm Falling in Love Again/Anyway You Want Me	1973	$4
❑ 14672	She's Got Everything I Need/I'm Glad You Happened to Me	1973	$4
❑ 14478	So Many Ways/Once in a While	1972	$5

RCA

❑ PB-13000	All I'm Missing Is You/ Don't It Break Your Heart	1981	$4
❑ PB-12226	Bally-Hoo Days/Two Hearts Beat Better Than One	1981	$4
❑ PB-11257	Country Lovin'/I've So Much to Be Thankful For	1978	$4
❑ PB-13094	Don't Give Up on Me/In Love with Loving You	1982	$4
❑ PB-12136	Don't Look Now (But We Just Fell in Love)/There's Women (Then There's My Woman)	1980	$4
❑ PB-11031	Freedom Ain't the Same as Being Free/Till You Can Make It On Your Own	1977	$4
❑ PB-11668	Goodbye/You're So Good At Lovin' Me	1979	$4
❑ PB-11422	If Everyone Had Someone Like You/You're a Beautiful Place to Be	1978	$4
❑ PB-11752	If I Ever Had to Say Goodbye to You/Love of My Life	1979	$4
❑ PB-11319	I'm the South/You Are My Sunshine	1978	$4
❑ PB-10899	(I Need You) All the Time/I've Never Loved Anyone More	1977	$4
❑ PB-11918	Let's Get It While the Gettin's Good/You Cared Enough (To Give Your Very Best)	1980	$4
❑ PB-10794	Put Me Back Into Your World/Goodnight Irene	1976	$4
❑ PB-12039	That's What I Get for Loving You/Undivided Love	1980	$4
❑ PB-13452	The Blues Don't Care Who's Got 'Em/Wooden Heart	1983	$4
❑ PB-11537	What In Her World Did I Do/Love of My Life	1979	$4
❑ PB-11133	Where Lonely People Go/Penny Arcade	1977	$4

RCA VICTOR

❑ 47-6773	A Dozen Hearts/A Good Lookin' Blonde	1956	$20
❑ 47-4787	A Full Time Job/ Shephard of My Heart	1952	$30
❑ 48-0025	A Heart Full of Love (For a Handful of Kisses)/ Then I Turned and Walked Slowly Away	1949	$60

— Originals on green vinyl

❑ 48-0025	A Heart Full of Love (For a Handful of Kisses)/ Then I Turned and Walked Slowly Away	1949	$30

— Second pressings: Green label, black vinyl

❑ 47-8048	A Little Heartache/ After Loving You	1962	$8
❑ 47-9848	A Man's Kind of Woman/ Living Under Pressure	1970	$5
❑ 47-8207	A Million Years or So/ Just a Ribbon	1963	$8
❑ 48-0002	Anytime/What a Fool I Was	1949	$60

— Originals on green vinyl

❑ 47-9968	A Part of America Died/Call Me	1971	$5
❑ 47-6407	Bayou Baby/Do You Know Where God Lives	1956	$20
❑ 47-7794	Before This Day Ends/ Just Out of Reach	1960	$12
❑ 47-7661	Boot Hill/Johnny Reb, That's Me	1959	$10
❑ 48-0001	Bouquet of Roses/ Texarkana Baby	1949	$60

— Originals on green vinyl

❑ 48-0001	Bouquet of Roses/ Texarkana Baby	1949	$30

— Second pressings: Green label, black vinyl

❑ 48-0001 [PS]	Bouquet of Roses/ Texarkana Baby	1949	$100

— Brown and dark brown title sleeve

❑ 47-4597	Bouquet of Roses/ Texarkana Baby	1952	$30
❑ 48-0175	Bring Roses to Her Now/I Wish I Had a Girl	1950	$60

— Originals on green vinyl

❑ 48-0175	Bring Roses to Her Now/I Wish I Had a Girl	1950	$30

— Second pressings: Green label, black vinyl

Number	Title	Yr	NM
❑ 47-4413	Bundle of Southern Sunshine/Call Her Your Sweetheart	1951	$30
❑ 74-0175	But For Love/My Lady of Love	1969	$5
❑ 47-6601	Casey Jones (The Brave Engineer)/You Were Mine for Awhile	1956	$20
❑ 47-5753	Chapel on the Hill/A Touch of God's Hand	1954	$30
❑ 47-7435	Chip Off the Old Block/I'll Hold You in My Heart (Till I Can Hold You in My Arms)	1959	$10
❑ 47-5905	Christmas Can't Be Far Away/I'm Your Private Santa Claus	1954	$30
❑ 48-0127	C-H-R-I-S-T-M-A-S/Will Santa Come to Shanty Town	1949	$60
— Originals on green vinyl			
❑ 48-0127	C-H-R-I-S-T-M-A-S/Will Santa Come to Shanty Town	1949	$30
— Second pressings: Green label, black vinyl			
❑ PB-10701	Cowboy/Don't Let the Good Times Roll Away	1976	$4
❑ 47-6975	Crazy Dream/Open Your Heart	1957	$15
❑ 48-0342	Cuddle Buggin' Baby/Enclosed, One Broken Heart	1950	$60
— Originals on green vinyl			
❑ 48-0342	Cuddle Buggin' Baby/Enclosed, One Broken Heart	1950	$30
— Second pressings: Green label, black vinyl			
❑ 47-7619	Did It Rain/Sittin' By Sittin' Bull	1959	$12
❑ 47-8102	Does He Mean That Much to You/Tender Touch	1962	$8
❑ 47-8102 [PS]	Does He Mean That Much to You/Tender Touch	1962	$30
❑ 47-4569	Easy on the Eyes/Anything That's Part of You	1952	$30
❑ WP261 [PS]	Eddy Arnold's Favorite Sacred Songs	1950	$30
— Box for records 48-0165, 48-0166 and 48-0167			
❑ 47-5108	Eddy's Song/Condemned Without a Trial	1952	$30
❑ 47-5305	Free Home Demonstration/How's the World Treating You	1953	$30
❑ 47-9889	From Heaven to Heartache/Ten Times Forever More	1970	$5
❑ 47-6905	Gonna Find Me a Bluebird/Little Bit	1957	$15
❑ 47-9368	Here Comes Heaven/Baby That's Loving	1967	$6
❑ 47-9437	Here Comes the Rain, Baby/The World I Used to Know	1968	$6
❑ 48-0167	Hills of Tomorrow/Softly and Tenderly	1950	$60
— Originals on green vinyl			
❑ 48-0167	Hills of Tomorrow/Softly and Tenderly	1950	$30
— Second pressings: Green label, black vinyl			
❑ 48-0030	I'll Hold You in My Heart (Till I Can Hold You in My Arms)/Don't Bother to Cry	1949	$60
— Originals on green vinyl			
❑ 48-0030	I'll Hold You in My Heart (Till I Can Hold You in My Arms)/Don't Bother to Cry	1949	$30
— Second pressings: Green label, black vinyl			
❑ 47-4600	I'll Hold You in My Heart (Till I Can Hold You in My Arms)/Don't Rob Another Man's Castle	1952	$30
❑ 74-0559	I Love You Dear/Long Life, Lots of Happiness	1971	$5
❑ 47-8632	I'm Letting You Go/The Days Gone By	1965	$6
❑ 48-0016	I'm Thinking Tonight of My Blue Eyes/Rockin' Alone	1949	$60
— Originals on green vinyl			
❑ 48-0016	I'm Thinking Tonight of My Blue Eyes/Rockin' Alone	1949	$30
— Second pressings: Green label, black vinyl			
❑ 48-0080	I'm Throwing Rice (At the Girl That I Love)/Show Me the Way Back to Your Heart	1949	$60
— Originals on green vinyl			
❑ 48-0080	I'm Throwing Rice (At the Girl That I Love)/Show Me the Way Back to Your Heart	1949	$30
— Second pressings: Green label, black vinyl			
❑ 47-5525	I Really Don't Want to Know/I'll Never Get Over You	1953	$30
❑ 47-8445	I Thank My Lucky Stars/I Don't Cry No More	1964	$6
❑ 48-0017	It Makes No Difference Now/Molly Darling	1949	$60
— Originals on green vinyl			
❑ 47-4598	It's a Sin/Anytime	1952	$30

Number	Title	Yr	NM
❑ 48-0198	It's a Sin/I Couldn't Believe It Was True	1950	$60
— Originals on green vinyl			
❑ 48-0198	It's a Sin/I Couldn't Believe It Was True	1950	$30
— Second pressings: Green label, black vinyl			
❑ 47-9525	It's Over/No Matter Whose Baby You Are	1968	$6
❑ 47-6001	It Took a Miracle/I Always Have Someone to Turn To	1955	$20
❑ 47-6000	I've Been Thinking/Don't Forget	1955	$20
❑ 48-0476	I Wanna Play House with You/Something Old, Something New	1951	$30
❑ 47-8749	I Want to Go With You/Better Stop Tellin' Lies (About Me)	1965	$8
❑ 47-8749 [PS]	I Want to Go With You/Better Stop Tellin' Lies (About Me)	1965	$20
❑ 48-0300	Little Angel with the Dirty Face/Why Should I Cry?	1950	$60
— Originals on green vinyl			
❑ 48-0300	Little Angel with the Dirty Face/Why Should I Cry?	1950	$30
— Second pressings: Green label, black vinyl			
❑ 47-7040	Little Miss Sunbeam/When He Was Young	1957	$15
❑ 47-7727	Little Sparrow/My Arms Are a House	1960	$10
❑ 47-9080	Lonely Again/Love on My Mind	1967	$6
❑ 74-0641	Lonely People/If It's Alright with You	1972	$5
❑ 74-0747	Lucy/The Last Letter	1972	$5
❑ 47-8679	Make the World Go Away/The Easy Way	1965	$8
❑ 47-8679 [PS]	Make the World Go Away/The Easy Way	1965	$20
❑ 47-5415	Mama, Come Get Your Baby Boy/If I Never Get to Heaven	1953	$30
❑ 48-0425	May the Good Lord Bless and Keep You/I'm Writing a Letter to the Lord	1951	$60
— Originals on green vinyl			
❑ 48-0425	May the Good Lord Bless and Keep You/I'm Writing a Letter to the Lord	1951	$30
— Second pressings: Green label, black vinyl			
❑ 47-9182	Misty Blue/Calling Mary Names	1967	$6
❑ 47-8296	Molly/The Song of the Coo Coo	1963	$8
❑ 47-5192	Moonlight and Roses/Missouri Waltz	1953	$30
❑ 47-6708	Mutual Admiration Society/If'n	1956	$20
— With Jaye P. Morgan			
❑ 47-5020	My Desire/I Want to Thank You Lord	1952	$30
❑ 47-5634	My Everything/Second Fling	1954	$30
❑ 48-0176	My Mother's Sweet Voice/I Wouldn't Trade the Silver	1950	$60
— Originals on green vinyl			
❑ 48-0176	My Mother's Sweet Voice/I Wouldn't Trade the Silver	1950	$30
— Second pressings: Green label, black vinyl			
❑ 47-4954	Older and Bolder/I'd Trade All My Tomorrows (For Just One Yesterday)	1952	$30
❑ 47-6842	One/Do You Love Me	1957	$15
— With Jaye P. Morgan			
❑ 47-7926	One Grain of Sand/The Worst Night of My Life	1961	$10
❑ 48-0083	One Kiss Too Many/The Echo of Your Footsteps	1949	$60
— Originals on green vinyl			
❑ 48-0083	One Kiss Too Many/The Echo of Your Footsteps	1950	$30
— Second pressings: Green label, black vinyl			
❑ 47-7221	Peck a Cheek/Before You Know It	1958	$15
❑ 74-0120	Please Don't Go/Heaven Below	1969	$5
❑ 74-0705	Poison Red Berries/Just Out of Reach	1972	$5
❑ 47-9935	Portrait of My Woman/I Really Don't Want to Know	1970	$5
❑ 74-0282	Since December/Morning of Our Mind	1969	$5
❑ 47-8965	Somebody Like Me/Taking Chances	1966	$6
❑ 47-8965 [PS]	Somebody Like Me/Taking Chances	1966	$15
❑ 47-4273	Somebody's Been Beating My Time/Heart Strings	1951	$30
❑ 47-5197	Someday Somewhere/When I've Done My Best	1953	$30
❑ 47-9801	Soul Deep/(Today) I Started Loving You Again	1969	$6
❑ 47-8363	Sweet Adorable You/Why	1964	$6
❑ 48-0150	Take Me in Your Arms and Hold Me/Mama and Daddy Broke My Heart	1949	$60
— Originals on green vinyl			

Number	Title	Yr	NM
❑ 48-0150	Take Me in Your Arms and Hold Me/Mama and Daddy Broke My Heart	1949	$30
— Second pressings: Green label, black vinyl			
❑ 47-4490	Take My Hand, Precious Lord/Open Thy Merciful Arms	1952	$30
❑ 47-7984	Tears Broke Out on Me/I'll Do As Much for You Someday	1962	$8
❑ 47-7542	Tennessee Stud/What's the Good (Of All This Love)	1959	$10
❑ 47-4245	That Little Boy of Mine/Sinner's Prayer	1951	$30
❑ 47-4599	That's How Much I Love You/A Heart Full of Love	1952	$30
❑ 47-3310	That's How Much I Love You/Chained to a Memory	1949	$30
❑ 48-0174	That Wonderful Mother of Mine/Mother	1950	$60
— Originals on green vinyl			
❑ 48-0174	That Wonderful Mother of Mine/Mother	1950	$30
— Second pressings: Green label, black vinyl			
❑ 47-9027	The Angel and the Stranger/The First Word	1966	$6
❑ 47-6699	The Ballad of Wes Tancred/I Wouldn't Know Where to Begin	1956	$20
❑ 47-6139	The Cattle Call/The Kentuckian Song	1955	$30
❑ 47-7292	The Day You Left Me/Real Love	1958	$15
❑ 47-8818	The Last Word in Lonesome Is Me/Mary Claire Melvina Rebecca Jane	1966	$6
❑ 47-8818 [PS]	The Last Word in Lonesome Is Me/Mary Claire Melvina Rebecca Jane	1966	$15
❑ 48-0165	The Lily of the Valley/Evil, Tempt Me Not	1950	$60
— Originals on green vinyl			
❑ 48-0165	The Lily of the Valley/Evil, Tempt Me Not	1950	$30
— Second pressings: Green label, black vinyl			
❑ 48-0382	The Lovebug Itch/A Prison Without Walls	1950	$60
— Originals on green vinyl			
❑ 48-0382	The Lovebug Itch/A Prison Without Walls	1950	$30
— Second pressings: Green label, black vinyl			
❑ 47-9606	Then You Can Tell Me Goodbye/Apples, Raisins and Roses	1968	$6
❑ 47-5196	The Old Rugged Cross/Have Thine Own Way, Lord	1953	$30
❑ 48-0018	The Prisoner's Song/Seven Years with the Wrong Woman	1949	$60
— Originals on green vinyl			
❑ 48-0018	The Prisoner's Song/Seven Years with the Wrong Woman	1949	$30
— Second pressings: Green label, black vinyl			
❑ 48-0412	There's Been a Change in Me/Tie Me to Your Apron Strings Again	1950	$60
— Originals on green vinyl			
❑ 48-0412	There's Been a Change in Me/Tie Me to Your Apron Strings Again	1950	$30
— Second pressings: Green label, black vinyl			
❑ 48-0042	There's Not a Thing (I Wouldn't Do for You)/Don't Rob Another Man's Castle	1949	$60
— Originals on green vinyl			
❑ 48-0042	There's Not a Thing (I Wouldn't Do for You)/Don't Rob Another Man's Castle	1949	$30
— Second pressings: Green label, black vinyl			
❑ 48-0137	There's No Wings on My Angel/You Know How Talk Gets Around	1949	$60
— Originals on green vinyl			
❑ 48-0137	There's No Wings on My Angel/You Know How Talk Gets Around	1949	$30
— Second pressings: Green label, black vinyl			
❑ 47-8869	The Tip of My Fingers/Long, Long Friendship	1966	$6
❑ 47-8869 [PS]	The Tip of My Fingers/Long, Long Friendship	1966	$15
❑ 47-9667	They Don't Make Love Like They Used To/What a Wonderful World	1968	$6
❑ 47-5805	This Is the Thanks I Get (For Loving You)/Hep Cat Baby	1954	$30
❑ 47-7340	Till You Come Back Again/I'm a Good Boy	1958	$15
❑ WP239 [PS]	To Mother	1950	$30
— Box for records 48-0174, 48-0175 and 48-0176			

Number	Title	Yr	NM
❏ 48-0197	To My Sorrow/Easy Rockin' Chair	1950	$60
— Originals on green vinyl			
❏ 48-0197	To My Sorrow/Easy Rockin' Chair	1950	$30
— Second pressings: Green label, black vinyl			
❏ 47-7143	Too Soon to Know/I Need Somebody	1958	$15
❏ 47-6365	Trouble in Mind/When You Say Goodbye	1955	$20
❏ 47-9265	Turn the World Around/The Long Ride Home	1967	$6
❏ 47-6069	Two Kinds of Love/In Time	1955	$20
❏ 47-7089	Wagon Wheels/You're Made Up for Everything	1957	$15
❏ 47-9993	Welcome to My World/It Ain't No Big Thing	1971	$5
❏ 48-0199	What Is Life Without Love/Be Sure There's No Mistake	1950	$60
— Originals on green vinyl			
❏ 48-0199	What Is Life Without Love/Be Sure There's No Mistake	1950	$30
— Second pressings: Green label, black vinyl			
❏ 47-8516	What's He Doing in My World/Laura Lee	1965	$6
❏ 48-0166	When Jesus Beckons Me Home/Beautiful Isle	1950	$60
— Originals on green vinyl			
❏ 48-0166	When Jesus Beckons Me Home/Beautiful Isle	1950	$30
— Second pressings: Green label, black vinyl			
❏ 47-4243	When My Blue Moon Turns to Gold Again/White Azaleas	1951	$30
❏ 47-4244	When You and I Were Young, Maggie/Roll Along Kentucky Moon	1951	$30
❏ 47-5189	When Your Hair Has Turned to Silver/Angry	1953	$30
❏ 48-0390	White Christmas/Santa Claus Is Comin' to Town	1950	$60
— Originals on green vinyl			
❏ 48-0390	White Christmas/Santa Claus Is Comin' to Town	1950	$30
— Second pressings: Green label, black vinyl			
❏ 47-3311	Will the Circle Be Unbroken/Who, At My Door, Is Standing	1949	$30
❏ 48-0019	Will the Circle Be Unbroken/Who at My Door Is Standing	1949	$60
— Originals on green vinyl			
❏ EPA-5019	Anytime/Just a Little Lovin' (Will Go a Long, Long Way)//The Cattle Call/What Is Life Without Love	1958	$20
❏ EPA-5055 [PS]	Bouquet of Roses	1958	$20
❏ LPC-115	Bouquet of Roses/I'll Hold You In My Heart//Anytime/It's a Sin	1961	$20
— Compact 33 Double" with small hole			
❏ EPA-5055	Bouquet of Roses/I'll Hold You in My Heart (Till I Can Hold You in My Arms)//Texarkana Baby/A Heart Full of Love	1958	$20
❏ 547-0099	Bouquet of Roses/It's a Sin/That's How Much I Love You/Don't Rob Another Man's Castle	1952	$25
— Record 1 of 2-EP set EPB-3027			
❏ VLP2578 [PS]	Cattle Call	1963	$15
❏ EPA473	C-H-R-I-S-T-M-A-S/Will Santy Come to Shanty Town//White Christmas/Santa Claus Is Comin' to Town	1953	$25
❏ VLP2578	Cool Water/Ole Faithful/Sierra Sue//The Wayward Wind/Tumbling Tumbleweeds/Lone Prairie	1963	$15
— Jukebox issue; small hole, plays at 33 1/3 rpm			
❏ EPB3027 [PS]	Country Classics	1952	$25
— Two-pocket jacket for two-EP set (547-0099 and 547-0100)			
❏ 547-0657	Down in the Valley/I Gave My Love a Cherry//The Wayfaring Stranger/Across the Wide Missouri	1955	$25
— Record 2 of 2-EP set EPB-1111			
❏ EPA4109	Each Time You Leave Me/(Gonna Get Myself a) Brand New Sandman//Tennessee Hillbilly Ghost/I'll Be Satisfied	1958	$20
❏ EPA-5019 [PS]	Eddy Arnold (Gold Standard Series)	1958	$20
❏ LPC-115 [PS]	Eddy Arnold Sings Them Again	1961	$20
❏ EPA4109 [PS]	Eddy Arnold Time	1958	$20

Number	Title	Yr	NM
❏ VLP3622	Here Comes My Baby/A Thing Called Sadness/Misty Blue//Don't Touch Me/After the Laughter (Come the Tears)/The Last Word in Lonesome Is Me	1966	$15
❏ 547-0100	I'll Hold You in My Heart (Till I Can Hold You in My Arms)/A Heart Full of Love (For a Handful of Kisses)//Anytime/Texarkana Baby	1952	$25
— Record 2 of 2-EP set EPB-3027			
❏ EPA573 [PS]	I Really Don't Want to Know	1954	$25
❏ EPA573	I Really Don't Want to Know//I'll Never Get Over You//My Everything/Second Fling	1954	$25
❏ VLP3507 [PS]	I Want to Go with You	1966	$15
❏ VLP3507	I Want to Go with You/Somebody Loves You/Don't Forget (I Still Love You)//One Kiss for Old Times' Sake/After Losing You/Pardon Me	1966	$15
— Jukebox issue; small hole, plays at 33 1/3 rpm			
❏ VLP2337 [PS]	Let's Make Memories Tonight	1962	$15
❏ VLP-3753 [PS]	Lonely Again	1967	$15
❏ VLP-3753	Lonely Again/Baby/When Your World Stops//Meet Me at the Altar/Did It Rain/Nobody's Darling But Mine	1967	$15
— Jukebox issue; small hole, plays at 33 1/3 rpm			
❏ VLP3466 [PS]	My World	1965	$15
❏ EPA624	Silver Moon/His Hands//Unchained Melody/Making Believe	1955	$25
❏ VLP3715 [PS]	Somebody Like Me	1966	$15
❏ VLP3715	Somebody Like Me/Lay Some Happiness on Me/There's Always Me//Tip of My Fingers/Love on My Mind/I Love You Drops	1966	$15
— Jukebox EP, small hole, plays at 33 1/3 rpm			
❏ VLP2337	Take Me in Your Arms and Hold Me/I Don't Want to Set the World on Fire/Hey Good Lookin'//Hold Me/Let's Make Memories Tonight/Are You Sincere?	1962	$15
— Jukebox issue; small hole, plays at 33 1/3 rpm			
❏ VLP3622 [PS]	The Last Word in Lonesome	1966	$15
❏ EPA473 [PS]	(title unknown)	1953	$25
❏ 547-0425	Today/Robe of Calvary//I Called on the Master/The Touch of God's Hand	1954	$25
— Record 2 of 2-EP set EPB-3219			
❏ EPA624 [PS]	Top Hits Round-Up	1955	$25
❏ 547-0656	Wanderin'/The Rovin' Gambler/The Lonesome Road//Careless Love/Sometimes I Feel Like a Motherless Child	1955	$25
— Record 1 of 2-EP set EPB-1111			
❏ EPB-1111 [PS]	Wanderin' with Eddy Arnold	1955	$25
— Two-pocket jacket for two-EP set (547-0656 and 547-0657)			
❏ VLP3466	What's He Doin' in My World/I'm Walking Behind You/I'm Letting You Go//As Usual/The Days Gone By/Too Many Rivers	1965	$15
— Jukebox EP, small hole, plays at 33 1/3 rpm			
❏ EPB3219 [PS]	When It's Round-Up Time in Heaven	1954	$25
— Two-pocket jacket for two-EP set (547-0424 and 547-0425)			
❏ 547-0424	When It's Round-Up Time in Heaven/The Chapel on the Hill//'Twas the Dawn of a Beautiful Day/Prayer	1954	$25
— Record 1 of 2-EP set EPB-3219			

ARNOLD, LEE
KIRSHNER

Number	Title	Yr	NM
❏ 4268	A Trucker's Christmas/That Good Old Gospel Music	1976	$5

ARNOLD, P.P.
ATLANTIC

Number	Title	Yr	NM
❏ 2674	Bury Me Down by the River/Give a Hand, Take a Hand	1969	$6

IMMEDIATE

Number	Title	Yr	NM
❏ 5006	If You Think You're Groovy/It Hurts Me Badly	1968	$10
❏ 1901	The First Cut Is the Deepest/Speak to Me	1967	$10

ARNOLD, RICK
LYNN

Number	Title	Yr	NM
❏ 51088	I Must Be Dreaming/(B-side unknown)	1989	$6

ARRIBIANS, THE
J.O.B.

Number	Title	Yr	NM
❏ 1116	To Look at a Star/Working and Gambling	1958	$800

ARROGANTS, THE
LUTE

Number	Title	Yr	NM
❏ 6226	Mirror Mirror/Canadian Sunset	1963	$40

ARS NOVA
ATLANTIC

Number	Title	Yr	NM
❏ 2625	Sunshine and Shadows/Walk on the Sand	1969	$6

ELEKTRA

Number	Title	Yr	NM
❏ 45631	Fields of People/March of the Mad Duke's Circus	1968	$8
❏ 45627	Pavan for My Lady (Fall Winter Summer and Spring)/Zoroaster	1968	$8

ART OF LOVIN'
MAINSTREAM

Number	Title	Yr	NM
❏ 687	Good Times/You've Got the Power	1968	$30

ART OF NOISE
CHINA

Number	Title	Yr	NM
❏ VS4-43134	Dragnet/Acton Art	1987	$4
❏ VS4-43134 [PS]	Dragnet/Acton Art	1987	$5
❏ VS4-43055	Legacy/Opus III	1986	$4
❏ VS4-43055 [PS]	Legacy/Opus III	1986	$4
❏ VS4-42932	Legs/Hoops and Mallets	1985	$4
❏ VS4-42932 [PS]	Legs/Hoops and Mallets	1985	$4
❏ VS4-43002	Paranoimia/Why Me	1986	$4
— A-side with Max Headroom			
❏ VS4-43002 [PS]	Paranoimia/Why Me	1986	$4
❏ VS4-42986	Peter Gunn/Something Always Happens	1986	$4
— A-side featuring Duane Eddy			
❏ VS4-42986 [PS]	Peter Gunn/Something Always Happens	1986	$4

ISLAND

Number	Title	Yr	NM
❏ 99782	Beat Box/Moment in Love	1984	$4
❏ 94999	Close (To the Edit)/Beatbox	1986	$4
— Gold label "Revival of the Fittest" series			
❏ 99754	Close (To the Edit)/Do Donna Do	1984	$4
❏ 99754 [PS]	Close (To the Edit)/Do Donna Do	1984	$5
❏ 99561	Moments in Love/A Time for Fear (Who's Afraid)	1986	$4
— Label credit: Trevor Horn/Paul Morley/Art of Noise			

ARTISTICS, THE
BRUNSWICK

Number	Title	Yr	NM
❏ 55477	Being in Love/It's Those Little Things That Count	1972	$8
❏ 55315	Girl I Need You/Glad I Met You	1967	$8
❏ 55370	Hard to Carry On/Trouble, Heartaches and Pain	1968	$8
❏ 55301	I'm Gonna Miss You/Hope We Have	1966	$8
❏ 55444	(I Want You To) Make My Life Over/Sugar Cane	1971	$8
❏ 55384	Lonely Old World/You Left Me	1968	$8
❏ 55326	Love Song/I'll Always Love You	1967	$8
❏ 55416	Price of Love/Yesterday's Girl	1969	$8
❏ 55493	She's Heaven/Look Out I'm Gonna Get You	1973	$8
❏ 55342	The Chase Is On/One Last Chance	1967	$8
❏ 55404	Walking Tall/What Happened	1969	$8

OKEH

Number	Title	Yr	NM
❏ 7193	Get My Hands on Some Lovin'/I'll Leave It Up to You	1964	$10
❏ 7217	In Another Man's Arms/Patty Cake	1965	$10
❏ 7177	I Need Your Love/What'll I Do	1963	$10
❏ 7243	Loveland/So Much Love in My Heart	1966	$10
❏ 7232	This Heart of Mine/I'll Come Running	1965	$10

Number	Title	Yr	NM
ARTISTS UNITED AGAINST APARTHEID			
MANHATTAN			
❏ B-50026	Let Me See Your I.D. (Street Mix)/(Album Mix)	1986	$5
❏ B-50017	Sun City/Not So Far Away (Dub)	1985	$4
❏ B-50017	Sun City/Not So Far Away (Dub)	1985	$4
ARTS MUSICALE SINGERS			
FOUR JAYS			
❏ 100	I Wonder Where I'll Be Next Christmas/Come Home	1988	$3
❏ 100 [PS]	I Wonder Where I'll Be Next Christmas/Come Home	1988	$3
ARVON, BOBBY			
FIRST ARTISTS			
❏ 41003	From Now On/Drift Away	1978	$5
A'S, THE			
ARISTA			
❏ 0452	After Last Night/Teenage Jerk Off	1979	$4
❏ 0609	A Woman's Got the Power/Heart of America	1981	$4
❏ 0472	Parasite/Words	1979	$4
ASCOTS, THE			
ACE			
❏ 650	I'm Touched/Perfect Love	1962	$30
ARROW			
❏ 736	Easier Said Than Done/Is It Really You	1958	$40
BETHLEHEM			
❏ 3046	Hip Talk/She Did	1962	$20
DUAL-TONE			
❏ 1120	Acapulco Run/The Gladiator	1963	$70
J&S			
❏ 1628/9	What Love Can Do/Everything Will Be Alright	1958	$40
KING			
❏ 5679	I Don't Care One Bit/Tonight	1962	$40
SUPER			
❏ 103	Midnight Hour/Midnight Hour (Part 2)	1966	$30
❏ 102	Monkey See, Monkey Do/You Can't Do That	1966	$30
❏ 104	Put Your Arms Around Me/Sookie Sookie	1966	$30
ASGAERD			
THRESHOLD			
❏ 67010	Friends/Children of a New Born Age	1972	$10
ASHE, CLARENCE			
ABC-PARAMOUNT			
❏ 45-10698	Don't Open the Door on Monday Morning/Close to You	1965	$15
CHESS			
❏ 1896	Trouble I've Had/Dancing in a Dream World	1964	$20
J&S			
❏ 1475/6	Don't Open the Door on Monday Morning/Close to You	1965	$20
❏ 1470/1	Everything Happens to Me/New Broom Sweeps Good	1964	$20
❏ 1469	If I Could Only Lie/Why Have I Had So Much Trouble	1964	$30
❏ 1466	Trouble I've Had/Dancing in a Dream World	1964	$30
ASHES			
VAULT			
❏ 936	Dark on You Now/Roses Gone	1967	$15
❏ 973	Homeward Bound/Sleeping Serenade	1971	$12
❏ 924	Is There Anything I Can Do/Every Little Prayer	1966	$15
ASHFORD AND SIMPSON			
CAPITOL			
❏ B-5468	Babies/Street Corner	1985	$3
❏ B-5468 [PS]	Babies/Street Corner	1985	$3

Number	Title	Yr	NM
❏ B-44404	Cookies and Cake/(B-side unknown)	1989	$4
❏ B-5598	Count Your Blessings/Side Effect	1986	$3
❏ B-5598 [PS]	Count Your Blessings/Side Effect	1986	$3
❏ B-5250	High-Rise/(Instrumental)	1983	$3
❏ B-5250 [PS]	High-Rise/(Instrumental)	1983	$3
❏ B-44326	I'll Be There for You/Way Ahead	1989	$3
❏ B-44326 [PS]	I'll Be There for You/Way Ahead	1989	$3
❏ B-5190	I'll Take the Whole World On/Mighty Mighty Love	1982	$3
❏ B-5310	I'm Not That Tough/Side Effect	1984	$3
❏ B-5310 [PS]	I'm Not That Tough/Side Effect	1984	$3
❏ B-5284	It's Much Deeper/Working Man	1983	$3
❏ B-5284 [PS]	It's Much Deeper/Working Man	1983	$3
❏ B-5146	Love It Away/Street Opera (Part 2)	1982	$3
❏ B-5435	Outta the World/Outta the World (Dub)	1985	$3
❏ B-5435 [PS]	Outta the World/Outta the World (Dub)	1985	$3
❏ B-5397	Solid/Solid (Dub Version)	1984	$3
❏ B-5397 [PS]	Solid/Solid (Dub Version)	1984	$3
❏ B-5109	Street Corner/Make It Work Again	1982	$3
❏ B-5109 [PS]	Street Corner/Make It Work Again	1982	$3
❏ B-5637	What Becomes of Love/It's a Rush	1986	$3
WARNER BROS.			
❏ 8070	Bend Me/Ain't Nothin' But a Name	1975	$4
❏ 8571	By Way of Love's Express/Too Bad	1978	$4
❏ 8514	Don't Cost You Nothing/Let Love Use Me	1978	$4
❏ 8030	Everybody's Got to Give It Up/Over to Where You Are	1974	$4
❏ 8775	Flashback/Ain't It a Shame	1979	$4
❏ 8870	Found a Cure/You Always Could	1979	$4
❏ 49646	Get Out Your Handkerchief/You Never Left Me Alone	1980	$4
❏ 49594	Happy Endings/Make It to the Sky	1980	$4
❏ 7781	Have You Ever Tried It/Time	1974	$4
❏ 7745	(I'd Know You) Anywhere/I'm Determined	1973	$4
❏ 49867	I Need Your Light/It's the Long Run	1981	$4
❏ 8710	Is It Still Good to Ya/As Long As It Holds You	1978	$4
❏ 8179	It'll Come, It'll Come, It'll Come/Caretaker	1976	$4
❏ 8651	It Seems to Hang On/Too Bad	1978	$4
❏ 49805	It Shows in the Eyes/Enough	1981	$4
❏ 49269	Love Don't Make It Right/Finally Got to Me	1980	$4
❏ 49269 [PS]	Love Don't Make It Right/Finally Got to Me	1980	$5
❏ 7811	Main Line/Don't Fight It	1974	$4
❏ 8391	Over and Over/It's You	1977	$4
❏ 8453	Send It/Couldn't Get Enough	1977	$4
❏ 8216	Somebody Told a Lie/It Came to Me	1976	$4
❏ 8337	So So Satisfied/Maybe I Can Find It	1977	$4
❏ 8286	Tried, Tested and Found True/Believe in Me	1976	$4
ASHFORD, NICK			
ABC			
❏ 11260	Let's Go Get Stoned/Dead End Kids	1970	$6
VERVE			
❏ 10599	California Soul/Young Emotions	1968	$8
❏ 10463	I Don't Need No Doctor/Young Emotions	1966	$10
❏ 10493	When I Feel the Need/Young Emotions	1967	$10
ASHLEY, JOHN			
CAPEHART			
❏ 5006	Little Lou/I Need Your Lovin'	1961	$60
DOT			
❏ 15775	Born to Rock/Pickin' on the Wrong Chicken	1958	$60
❏ 15878	My Story/Let the Good Times Roll	1958	$20
SILVER			
❏ 1005	Cry of the Wild Goose/One Love	1960	$30
❏ 1002	I Want to Hear It from You/Seriously in Love	1959	$30
ASHLEY, LEON, AND MARGIE SINGLETON			
❏ 2015	Hangin' On/Four O'Clock	1967	$12
❏ 8000	Love Me or Leave Me (For Love to Find)/Here We Go Again	1969	$10

Number	Title	Yr	NM
MONUMENT			
❏ 990	If Love Has Died/How Can We Divide These Little Hearts	1966	$15
ASHLEY, LEON			
ASHLEY			
❏ 22	Ain't Gonna Worry/Illusions of Life	1969	$10
❏ 2025	Anna, I'm Taking You Home/Curtain of Sadness	1967	$10
❏ 4000	Flower of Love/Prayers Can't Reach Me	1968	$10
❏ 2003	Laura (What's He Got That I Ain't Got)/With the Help of the Wine	1967	$12
❏ 2003	Laura/With the Help of the Wine	1967	$20
— Some early copies have no subtitle on A-side			
❏ 2075	Mental Journey/All I Can Stand	1968	$10
❏ 9000	Walkin' Back to Birmingham/It's All Over But the Crying	1969	$10
❏ 7000	While Your Lover Sleeps/That's Alright	1968	$10
GOLDBAND			
❏ 1104	He'll Never Go/I Was King of the Universe	1960	$30
IMPERIAL			
❏ 5795	It's Alright Baby/Court of Two Sisters	1961	$30
❏ 5759	The Longest Walk/Teenage Angel	1961	$30
ASHLEY, ROBERT			
MERCURY			
❏ 71365	Comic Strip Rock and Roll/The Baby	1957	$60
ASHLEY, TONY			
DECCA			
❏ 32520	I'll Go Crazy/Just a Taste	1969	$70
❏ 32240	I'll Never Be Satisfied/All Along I've Loved You	1967	$30
❏ 32342	We Must Have Love/I Can't Put You Down	1968	$30
ASHTON, GARDNER AND DYKE			
CAPITOL			
❏ 3206	Can You Get It/Oh Lord	1971	$5
❏ 3288	Delirium/Still Got a Long Way to Go	1972	$5
❏ 2981	Hymn to Everyone/Mister Freako	1970	$5
ASHWORTH, ERNEST			
DECCA			
❏ 31292	Be Mine Again/No Room Left for Me	1961	$15
❏ 31085	Each Moment (Spent with You)/Night Time Is Cry Time	1960	$15
❏ 31237	Forever Gone/Life of the Party	1961	$15
HICKORY			
❏ 1609	Another Sleepless Night/Bottle of Blues	1971	$8
❏ 1400	At Ease Heart/The Nearest Thing to Heaven	1966	$12
❏ 1237	A Week in the Country/Heartbreak Avenue	1964	$10
❏ 1304	Because I Cared/Love Has Come My Way	1965	$12
❏ 1647	Dreaming Again/I Wish	1972	$8
❏ 1170	Everybody But Me/(I Just Spent) Another Sleepless Night	1962	$12
❏ 1513	I Feel Better (Than I Meant To)/You Don't Have to Be an Angel Anymore	1968	$10
❏ 1265	I Love to Dance with Annie/My Heart Would Know	1964	$10
❏ 1189	I Take the Chance/King of the Blues	1962	$10
❏ 1358	I Wish/Crazy Me, Foolish You	1966	$10
❏ 1580	Let's Start Talking Before Her Feet Start Walking/My Heart Would Know	1970	$12
❏ 1538	Love, I Finally Found It/King of the Blues	1969	$10
❏ 1466	My Love for You (Is Like a Mountain Range)/You're Tearing My Heart Out	1967	$10
❏ 1281	Pushed in a Corner/Gooder Than Good	1964	$10
❏ 1428	Sad Face/I'm from Missouri	1966	$10
❏ 1599	She's Love/Jesus Is a Soul Man	1971	$8
❏ 1214	Talk Back Trembling Lips/That's How Much I Care	1963	$15
❏ 1484	Tender and True/Back on My Mind Again	1967	$10
❏ 1570	That Look of Good-Bye/A Woman's Touch	1970	$12

Number	Title	Yr	NM
❏ 1325	The D.J. Cried/Scene of Destruction	1965	$12
❏ 1620	Wanted Man/I Love to Dance with Annie	1972	$8
❏ 1528	Where Do You Go (When You Don't Go with Me)/Hocus-Pocus	1969	$10

ASIA

Includes members of KING CRIMSON, EMERSON, LAKE AND PALMER and YES.

GEFFEN

Number	Title	Yr	NM
❏ 29571	Don't Cry/Daylight	1983	$4
❏ 29571 [PS]	Don't Cry/Daylight	1983	$4
❏ 28872	Go/After the War	1985	$3
❏ 28872 [PS]	Go/After the War	1985	$3
❏ 50040	Heat of the Moment/Ride Easy	1982	$4
❏ 50040 [PS]	Heat of the Moment/Ride Easy	1982	$5
❏ 29970	Only Time Will Tell/Time Again	1982	$4
❏ 29970 [PS]	Only Time Will Tell/Time Again	1982	$4
❏ 29871	Sole Survivor/Here Comes the Feeling	1982	$4
❏ 29871 [PS]	Sole Survivor/Here Comes the Feeling	1982	$4
❏ 29475	The Smile Has Left Your Eyes/Lying to Yourself	1983	$4
❏ 29475 [PS]	The Smile Has Left Your Eyes/Lying to Yourself	1983	$4
❏ 28745	Too Late/Wishing	1986	$3

ASLEEP AT THE WHEEL

CAPITOL

Number	Title	Yr	NM
❏ 4187	Bump Bounce Boogie/Fat Boy Rag	1975	$5
❏ 4725	Choo Choo Ch'Boogie/Too Many Bad Habits	1979	$5
❏ 4601	Ghost Dancer/Louisiana	1978	$5
❏ 4357	Miles and Miles of Texas/Blues for Dixie	1976	$5
❏ 4438	Somebody Stole His Body/Let's Face It	1977	$5
❏ 4659	Texas Me & You/One O'Clock Jump	1978	$5
❏ 4115	The Letter That Johnny Walker Read (Part 1)/(Part 2)	1975	$5
❏ 4393	The Trouble with Lovin' Today/Ragtime Annie	1977	$5

EPIC

Number	Title	Yr	NM
❏ 07659	Blowin' Like a Bandit/String of Pars	1987	$3
❏ 07610	Boogie Back to Texas/Tulsa Straight Ahead	1987	$3
❏ 68620	Chattanooga Choo Choo/Sugarfoot Rag	1989	$3
❏ 8-50045	Choo Choo Ch'Boogie/Our Names Aren't Mentioned	1974	$5
❏ 08087	Hot Rod Lincoln/String of Pars	1988	$3
❏ 07125	House of Blue Lights/Big Foot Stomp	1987	$3
❏ 08461	House of Blue Lights/Blowin' Like a Bandit	1988	$3
—Reissue			
❏ 07966	Walk On By/Sugarfoot Rag	1988	$3
❏ 06671	Way Down Texas Way/String of Pars	1987	$3
❏ 06671 [PS]	Way Down Texas Way/String of Pars	1987	$4

MCA

Number	Title	Yr	NM
❏ 51020	Cool as a Breeze/Don't Get Caught Out in the Rain	1980	$4

UNITED ARTISTS

Number	Title	Yr	NM
❏ XW-344	Daddy's Advice/Drivin' Nails in My Coffin	1973	$6
❏ XW-245	Take Me Back to Tulsa/Before You Stop Loving Me	1973	$6

ASPHALT JUNGLE

TEC

Number	Title	Yr	NM
❏ 765	Freakin' Time Pt. 1/Freakin' Time Pt. 2	1980	$4

ASSOCIATION, THE

COLUMBIA

Number	Title	Yr	NM
❏ 45654	Come the Fall/Kicking the Gong Around	1972	$5
❏ 45602	Indian Wells Woman/Darling Be Home Soon	1972	$5

ELEKTRA

Number	Title	Yr	NM
❏ 47094	Dreamer/You Turn the Light On	1980	$4
❏ 47146	Small Town Lovers/Across the Persian Gulf	1981	$4

JUBILEE

Number	Title	Yr	NM
❏ 5505	Babe I'm Gonna Leave You/Baby Can't You Hear Me Call Your Name	1965	$30

RCA VICTOR

Number	Title	Yr	NM
❏ PB-10217	One Sunday Morning/Life Is a Carnival	1975	$4

VALIANT

Number	Title	Yr	NM
❏ 741	Along Comes Mary/Your Own Love	1966	$15
❏ 747	Cherish/Don't Blame It On Me	1966	$15
❏ 755	Pandora's Golden Heebie Jeebies/Standing Still	1966	$10
❏ 755 [PS]	Pandora's Golden Heebie Jeebies/Standing Still	1966	$30
❏ 730	Too Many Mornings/Forty Times	1965	$20

WARNER BROS.

Number	Title	Yr	NM
❏ 7105	Along Comes Mary/Cherish	1968	$8
—"Back to Back Hits" series on "W7" label			
❏ 7429	Along the Way/Traveler's Guide	1970	$6
❏ 7349	Are You Ready?/Dubuque Blues	1969	$8
❏ 7515	Bring Yourself Home/It's Gotta Be Real	1971	$6
❏ 7163	Everything That Touches You/We Love Us	1968	$8
—Orange "WB" label			
❏ 7267	Goodbye Columbus/The Time It Is Today	1969	$8
❏ 7040	Pandora's Golden Heebie Jeebies/Standing Still	1967	$8
❏ 7471	P.F. Sloan/Traveler's Guide	1971	$6
❏ 7229	Six Man Band/Like Always	1968	$8
❏ 7524	That's Racin'/Hate Me Cry (Funny Kind of Song)	1971	$6
❏ 7195	Time for Livin'/Birthday Morning	1968	$8
❏ 7119	Windy/Never My Love	1968	$8
—"Back to Back Hits" series on "W7" label			
❏ 7041	Windy/Sometime	1967	$10

7-Inch Extended Plays

Number	Title	Yr	NM
❏ S1767 [PS]	Greatest Hits	1968	$20
❏ S1767	The Time It Is Today/Everything That Touches You/Along Comes Mary//Enter the Young/No Fair at All/Windy	1968	$20
—Jukebox issue; small hole, plays at 33 1/3 rpm			

ASTAIRE, FRED

DC

Number	Title	Yr	NM
❏ 201 [DJ]	Once A Year Night (same on both sides)	1979	$6

ASTLEY, JON

ATLANTIC

Number	Title	Yr	NM
❏ 88965	Been There, Done That (What's Next Mix)/Welcome to the Circus	1989	$3
❏ 88965 [PS]	Been There, Done That (What's Next Mix)/Welcome to the Circus	1989	$3
❏ 89027	Put This Love to the Test/Been There, Done That	1988	$3
❏ 89027 [PS]	Put This Love to the Test/Been There, Done That	1988	$3

ASTLEY, RICK

RCA

Number	Title	Yr	NM
❏ 9030-1-R	Ain't Too Proud to Beg/I Don't Want to Be Your Lover	1989	$3
❏ 9030-1-R [PS]	Ain't Too Proud to Beg/I Don't Want to Be Your Lover	1989	$3
❏ 8872-1-R	Giving Up on Love/I'll Be Fine	1989	$3
❏ 8872-1-R [PS]	Giving Up on Love/I'll Be Fine	1989	$3
❏ 8663-1-R	It Would Take a Strong Strong Man/You Move Me	1988	$3
❏ 8663-1-R [PS]	It Would Take a Strong Strong Man/You Move Me	1988	$3
❏ 8838-1-R	She Wants to Dance with Me/(Instrumental)	1988	$3
❏ 8838-1-R [PS]	She Wants to Dance with Me/(Instrumental)	1988	$3
❏ 8319-1-R	Together Forever/I'll Never Set You Free	1988	$3
❏ 8319-1-R [PS]	Together Forever/I'll Never Set You Free	1988	$3

ASTORS, THE

STAX

Number	Title	Yr	NM
❏ 170	Candy/I Found Out	1965	$30
❏ 232	Daddy Didn't Tell You/More Power to You	1967	$15
❏ 179	Mystery Woman/In the Twilight Zone	1965	$30
❏ 139	What Can It Be/Just Enough to Hurt Me	1963	$100

ASTRO JETS, THE

IMPERIAL

Number	Title	Yr	NM
❏ 5760	Hide and Seek/Boom-A-Lay	1961	$30

ASTRONAUTS, THE (1)

RCA VICTOR

Number	Title	Yr	NM
❏ 47-8499	Almost Grown/My Sin Is Pride	1965	$30
❏ 47-8194	Baja/Kuk	1963	$30
❏ 47-8298	Competition Coupe/Surf Party	1963	$30
❏ 47-8364	Go Fight for Her/Swim Little Mermaid	1964	$30
❏ 47-8224	Hot Doggin'/Everyone But Me	1963	$30
❏ 47-8224 [PS]	Hot Doggin'/Everyone But Me	1963	$70
❏ 47-9109	I Know You Rider/Better Things	1967	$20
❏ 47-8463	I'm a Fool/Can't You See I Do	1964	$30
❏ 47-8885	In My Car/Main Street	1966	$20
❏ 47-8628	It Doesn't Matter Anymore/The La La La Song	1965	$30
❏ 47-8419	Main Title from Ride the Wild Surf/Around and Around	1964	$30
❏ 47-8545	Tomorrow's Gonna Be Another Day/Razza Matazz	1965	$30

ASTRONAUTS, THE (U)

JAN ELL

Number	Title	Yr	NM
❏ 459	Geneva Twist/Take 17	1962	$40

MERCURY

Number	Title	Yr	NM
❏ 71675	Alabama Jubilee/Gadabout	1960	$15

PALLADIUM

Number	Title	Yr	NM
❏ 610	Come Along Baby/Trying to Get to You	1962	$125

TRIAL

Number	Title	Yr	NM
❏ 3521	Farewell/Chili Charlene	1960	$200

VANRUS

Number	Title	Yr	NM
❏ 1000	Ski Lift/Blues Beat	1962	$40

ASYLUM CHOIR

LEON RUSSELL and Marc Benno.

SHELTER

Number	Title	Yr	NM
❏ 7313	Straight Brother/Tryin' to Stay Alive	1971	$8

SMASH

Number	Title	Yr	NM
❏ 2204	Indian Style/Icicle Star Tree	1969	$8
—As "Asylum Choir"			
❏ 2186	Soul Food/Welcome to Hollywood	1968	$8
—As "Asylum Choir"			

ATCHER, BOB

CAPITOL

Number	Title	Yr	NM
❏ F1258	Blue Christmas/Christmas Island	1950	$30
❏ F1364	Chain Around My Heart/Peek-a-Boo Waltz	1951	$30
❏ F1147	Guilty Conscience/Walk Chicken Walk	1950	$30
❏ F1007	My Pillow Knows/One Kind Word	1950	$30
❏ F975	Smoke Comes Out My Chimney/Ain't You Ashamed	1950	$30

COLUMBIA

Number	Title	Yr	NM
❏ 2-119	Blue Tail Fly/Foggy Foggy Dew	1949	$60
—Microgroove 33 1/3 rpm 7-inch single, small hole			
❏ 4-43524	Buck Private's Lament/Foreclose on a Mortgage	1966	$10
❏ 20620	Bury Me Not on the Lone Prairie/Cowboy's Dream	1949	$10
❏ 4-43365	Flash Flood/Indoor Plumbing	1965	$10
❏ 20618	Home on the Range/Red River Valley	1949	$12
❏ 2-453	I Can't Think of Love Without You/To Make You Mine	1949	$50
—Microgroove 7-inch 33 1/3 rpm single			
❏ 4-43193	I'm Thinking Tonight of My Blue Eyes/Old Fiddler Joe	1964	$10
❏ 20621	I've Got No Use for the Women/Old Chisholm Trail	1949	$10
—The above four probably comprise a 78 rpm album			
❏ 20619	Little Joe the Wrangler/Strawberry Roan	1949	$12
❏ 2-165	Tennessee Border/Don't Rob Another Man's Castle	1949	$60
—Microgroove 33 1/3 rpm 7-inch single			
❏ 2-322	Why Don't You Haul Off and Love Me/The Warm Red Wine	1949	$50
—Microgroove 7-inch 33 1/3 rpm single			
❏ 20611	Why Don't You Haul Off and Love Me/The Warm Red Wine	1949	$15

OKEH

Number	Title	Yr	NM
❏ 6925	The Laughing Record/I'm Thinking Tonight of My Blue Eyes	1952	$40

Number	Title	Yr	NM

ATCHER, RANDY
MGM

Number	Title	Yr	NM
❏ K11954	Flying High/Them Soft Shoulders and Dangerous Curves	1955	$40
❏ K12347	Indian Rock/I'll Be All Smiles Tonight	1956	$40
❏ K12427	I Need You Baby/Give Me Back My Heart	1956	$40

ATKINS
WARNER BROS.

| ❏ 29962 | Easy Street/We Gon' Make You Feel Good | 1982 | $4 |
| ❏ 50037 | Feel It, Don't Fight It/Love Is Growing Stronger | 1982 | $4 |

ATKINS, BIG BEN
GRT

| ❏ 095 | There'll Never Be Another for Me/(B-side unknown) | 1976 | $6 |
| ❏ 161 | We Don't Live Here, We Just Love Here/Baby Blue Eyes | 1978 | $5 |

ATKINS, CHET, AND LES PAUL
RCA

| ❏ PB-11330 | I'm Your Greatest Fan/Hot Toddy | 1978 | $4 |

RCA VICTOR

| ❏ PB-10642 | Moonglow/Avalon | 1976 | $5 |

ATKINS, CHET, AND HANK SNOW
RCA VICTOR

| ❏ 47-5995 | Silver Bell/Old Spinning Wheel | 1954 | $30 |
| ❏ 47-9803 | Wheels/Difficult | 1969 | $8 |

ATKINS, CHET, AND DOC WATSON
RCA

| ❏ PB-12138 | Medley-Tennessee Rag & Beaumont Rag/On My Way to Canaan's Land | 1981 | $4 |

ATKINS, CHET
COLUMBIA

❏ AE71776 [DJ]	East Tennessee Christmas/ Winter Wonderland	1983	$4
❏ 07929	I Still Can't Say Goodbye/ The Mockingbird	1988	$3
❏ 05662	Please Stay Tuned/Some Leather and Lace	1985	$3
❏ CS72712 [DJ]	Sails/My Song	1987	$4
❏ CS72712 [PS]	Sails/My Song	1987	$4
❏ 04859	The Boot and the Stone/Sunrise	1985	$3
❏ 06165	The Official Beach Music/Alicia	1986	$3

RCA

❏ PB-11892	Blind Willie/Dance with Me	1980	$4
❏ PB-12064	I Can Hear Kentucky Calling Me/Strawberry Man	1980	$4
❏ PB-10901	La Chicana/Four in the Morning	1977	$4
— With Danny Davis and Floyd Cramer			
❏ PB-11071	Me and My Guitar/Cascade	1977	$4
❏ PB-12263	Orange Blossom Special/Ready for the Times to Get Better	1981	$4

RCA VICTOR

❏ 47-5565	Barber Shop Rag/ Centipede Boogie	1953	$30
❏ 74-0536	Black Magic Woman/ Wabash Blues	1971	$5
❏ 47-7589	Boo Boo Stick Beat/ Django's Castle	1959	$15
❏ 48-0367	Boogie Man Boogie/Was Bitten By the Same Bug Twice	1950	$60
— Originals on green vinyl			
❏ 48-0367	Boogie Man Boogie/Was Bitten By the Same Bug Twice	1950	$30
— Second pressings: Green label, black vinyl			
❏ 47-6550	Cecilia/The Lady Loves	1956	$20
❏ 48-0142	Centipede Boogie/ Wednesday Night Waltz	1949	$60
— Originals on green vinyl			
❏ 48-0142	Centipede Boogie/ Wednesday Night Waltz	1949	$30
— Second pressings: Green label, black vinyl			
❏ 47-9116	Charlie Brown/What'd I Say	1967	$10
❏ 47-6314	Christmas Carols/Jingle Bells	1955	$20
❏ 47-5300	Country Gentlemen/ The Bells of St. Mary's	1953	$30

Number	Title	Yr	NM
❏ 48-0500	Crazy Rhythm/Hybrid Corn	1951	$30
❏ 48-0089	Dance of the Goldenrod/Telling My Troubles to My Old Guitar	1949	$60
— Originals on green vinyl			
❏ 48-0089	Dance of the Goldenrod/Telling My Troubles to My Old Guitar	1949	$30
— Second pressings: Green label, black vinyl			
❏ 74-0236	Delilah/Ode to Billie Joe	1969	$5
— With Arthur Fiedler and the Boston Pops			
❏ 47-5704	Downhill Drag/Kentucky Derby	1954	$30
❏ 47-8029	Down Home/Melissa	1962	$15
❏ APBO-0146	Fiddlin' Around/Paramaribo	1973	$4
❏ 47-5181	Fig Leaf Rag/High Rockin' Swing	1953	$30
❏ 47-8342	Freight Train/Dobro	1964	$15
❏ PB-10614	Frog Kissin'/Bill Cheatham	1976	$4
❏ 47-8781	From Nashville with Love/Rhythm Guitar	1966	$10
❏ 47-4922	Gallopin' on the Guitar/ (B-side unknown)	1952	$30
❏ 47-5650	Georgia Camp Meeting/ Jealous Hearted Me	1954	$30
— With Minnie Pearl			
❏ 47-4491	Goodbye Blues/Rainbow	1952	$30
❏ 47-8246	Guitar Country/Waitin' for the Evening Train	1963	$15
— With the Anita Kerr Quartet			
❏ 47-5100	Guitar Polka/Dream Train	1952	$30
— With Rosalie Allen			
❏ 48-0062	Guitar Waltz/Barber Shop Rag	1949	$60
— Originals on green vinyl			
❏ 48-0062	Guitar Waltz/Barber Shop Rag	1949	$30
— Second pressings: Green label, black vinyl			
❏ 47-6108	Hey Mr. Guitar/ Unchained Melody	1955	$20
❏ 47-7048	Hidden Charms/ Colonial Ballroom	1957	$20
❏ 47-7796	Hocus Pocus/Theme from The Dark at the End of the Stairs	1960	$15
❏ 47-9578	Huntin' Boots/Blue Angel	1968	$8
❏ 48-0428	Indian Love Call/ Music in My Heart	1951	$60
— Originals on green vinyl			
❏ 48-0428	Indian Love Call/ Music in My Heart	1951	$30
— Second pressings: Green label, black vinyl			
❏ 47-4377	In the Mood/Sweet Bunch of Daisies	1951	$30
❏ 47-9672	Light My Fire/Mrs. Robinson	1968	$8
❏ 47-9824	Love Beads/Passion Flower	1969	$6
❏ 48-0329	Main Street Breakdown/ Under the Hickory Nut Tree	1950	$60
— Originals on green vinyl			
❏ 48-0329	Main Street Breakdown/ Under the Hickory Nut Tree	1950	$30
— Second pressings: Green label, black vinyl			
❏ 47-7891	Man of Mystery/ Windy and Warm	1961	$15
❏ 47-6919	Martinique/Dig These Blues	1957	$20
— With the Rhythm Rockers			
❏ 47-4896	Meet Mr. Callaghan/ Chinatown, My Chinatown	1952	$30
❏ 47-5010	Midnight/Rustic Dance	1952	$30
❏ 47-5956	Mr. Sandman/Set a Spell	1954	$30
❏ 48-0439	My Life with You/A Trinket of Shiny Gold	1951	$30
❏ 47-7684	One Mint Julep/Teensville	1960	$15
❏ 48-0173	One More Chance/ Old Buck Dance	1950	$30
— Originals on green vinyl			
❏ 48-0173	One More Chance/ Old Buck Dance	1950	$30
— Second pressings: Green label, black vinyl			
❏ 47-8927	Prissy/La Fiesta	1966	$10
❏ 47-5813	San Antonio Rose/ Mister Misery	1954	$30
— With Red Kirk			
❏ 47-7747	Slinkey/Rainbow's End	1960	$15
❏ 47-9956	Snowbird/Chaplain in New Shoes	1971	$5
❏ 47-6199	Somebody Stole My Gal/ Shine On Harvest Moon	1955	$20
❏ PB-10448	Sonora/Mostly Mozart	1975	$4
— As "The Atkins String Co.			
❏ 47-4684	Spanish Fandango/ Your Mean Little Heart	1952	$30
❏ 47-9827	Steeplechase Lane/ Love Beads	1970	$5
❏ 47-4931	Tennessee Rag/My Little Girl	1952	$30

Number	Title	Yr	NM
❏ 47-9890	Tennessee Stud/ Cannonball Rag	1970	$5
— With Jerry Reed			
❏ 47-8829	Tennessee Waltz/ Country Gentleman	1966	$10
❏ 48-0402	The Birth of the Blues/Confusin'	1950	$60
— Originals on green vinyl			
❏ 48-0402	The Birth of the Blues/Confusin'	1950	$30
— Second pressings: Green label, black vinyl			
❏ PB-10046	The Entertainer/Dizzy Fingers	1974	$4
❏ 47-9725	Theme from Zorba the Greek/ Those Were the Days	1969	$6
❏ 47-7847	The Slop/Hot Mocking Bird	1961	$15
❏ 47-7847 [PS]	The Slop/Hot Mocking Bird	1961	$30
❏ 47-5484	Three O'Clock in the Morning/City Slicker	1953	$30
❏ 47-6796	Trambone/Blue Echo	1957	$20
❏ 47-8492	Travelin'/Cloudy and Cool	1965	$10
❏ 47-6808	Tricky/Peanut Vendor	1957	$20
— With the Rhythm Rockers			
❏ 47-5638	Wildwood Flower/ Simple Simon	1954	$30

7-Inch Extended Plays

❏ 547-0536	Alabama Jubilee/Have You Ever Been Lonely (Have You Ever Been Blue?)//Caravan/ The Birth of the Blues	1954	$20
— One record of 2-EP set EPB 1090			
❏ EPA-685	Arkansaw Traveler/ Londonderry Air//Ochi Chornya/La Golondrina	1955	$25
❏ EPB1090 [PS]	A Session with Chet Atkins	1954	$25
— Cover for 2-EP set (547-0535, 547-0536)			
❏ 547-0142	Black Mountain Rag/Lover, Come Back to Me//The 3rd Man Theme/Imagination	1952	$25
— One record of 2-EP set EPB 3079			
❏ EPA-686	Blues in the Night/Tenderly// Little Rock Getaway/Tip-Toe Through the Tulips with Me	1955	$25
❏ VLP-2549 [PS]	Caribbean Guitar	1962	$20
❏ EPA-588 [PS]	Chet Atkins and His Guitar	1954	$25
❏ EPA-4194 [PS]	Chet Atkins at Home	1958	$20
❏ EPB3079 [PS]	Chet Atkins' Gallopin' Guitar	1952	$25
— Cover for 2-EP set (547-0141, 547-0142)			
❏ EPA-5052 [PS]	Chet Atkins (Gold Standard Series)	1958	$20
❏ EPA-685 [PS]	Chet Atkins in 3 Dimensions Vol. 1: Folk	1955	$25
❏ EPA-686 [PS]	Chet Atkins in 3 Dimensions Vol. 2: Popular	1955	$25
❏ EPA-687 [PS]	Chet Atkins in 3 Dimensions Vol. 3: Classical	1955	$25
❏ VLP-3531 [PS]	Chet Atkins Picks On the Beatles	1966	$20
❏ LPC-124 [PS]	Chet Atkins Plays Great Movie Themes	1961	$25
❏ EAP 1-1383[PS]	Finger-Style Guitar, Vol. 1	1956	$20
❏ EPA 2-1383[PS]	Finger-Style Guitar, Vol. II	1956	$20
❏ 547-0141	Gallopin' Guitar/Stephen Foster Medley//St. Louis Blues/Hangover Blues	1952	$25
— One record of 2-EP set EPB 3079			
❏ EPA 2-1383	Heartaches/Glow Worm// Malaguena/Waltz in A Flat	1956	$20
❏ EPA-4343 [PS]	Hum and Strum Along with Chet	1959	$20
❏ VLP-3531	I Feel Fine/Can't Buy Me Love/Michelle//A Hard Day's Night/She's a Woman/She Loves You	1966	$20
— Jukebox issue; small hole, plays at 33 1/3 rpm			
❏ EPA-796	Indian Love Call/Memphis Blues//St. Louis Blues/ Black Mountain Rag	1956	$25
❏ EPA-4343	In the Good Old Summertime/ Bill Bailey//Sweet Bunch of Daisies/John Henry	1959	$20
❏ 547-0920	Memphis Blues/12th Street Rag//Gallopin' Guitar/St. Louis Blues	1956	$25
— One record of 2-EP set EPB 1236			
❏ EPA-687	Minuet and Prelude// Intermezzo//Schon Rosmarin/Minute Waltz	1955	$25
❏ 547-0919	Oh By Jingo/Indian Love Call//Alice Blue Gown/ The 3rd Man Theme	1956	$25
— One record of 2-EP set EPB 1236			
❏ EPA-588	Pagan Love Song/ Sunrise Serenade// Beautiful Ohio/Avalon	1954	$25
❏ EPA-594 [PS]	Pickin' the Hits	1955	$25
❏ EPA-4194	Say "Si Si"/Villa// Yankee Doodle Dandy/ You're Just in Love	1958	$20

Number	Title	Yr	NM
❏ 547-0535	South/Indiana//A Gay Ranchero/Frankie and Johnnie	1954	$20

— *One record of 2-EP set EPB 1090*

Number	Title	Yr	NM
❏ EPA-796 [PS]	Stringin' Along with Chet Atkins	1956	$25
❏ EPB1236 [PS]	Stringin' Along with Chet Atkins	1956	$25
❏ EAP 1-1383	Swedish Rhapsody/Liza//Petite Waltz/Unchained Melody	1956	$20
❏ LPC-124	Theme from "The Dark at the Top of the Stairs"/Theme from "Picnic"//Limelight/ Meet Mister Callaghan	1961	$20

— *Compact Double 33"; small hole, plays at 33 1/3 rpm*

Number	Title	Yr	NM
❏ EPA-594	Tweedlee Dee//(The Wallflower) Dance with Me Henry// Cherry Pink and Apple Blossom White/Darling, Je Vous Aime Beaucoup	1955	$25

ATKINSON, SANDY
HIT

Number	Title	Yr	NM
❏ 37	Mama Sang a Song/ Big Girls Don't Cry	1962	$8

— *B-side by the Chellows*

ATLANTA
MCA

Number	Title	Yr	NM
❏ 52671	Can't You Hear the Whistle Blow/Long Ago Shoes	1985	$4
❏ 52552	My Sweet-Eyed Georgia Girl/Dancin' on the Bayou	1985	$4
❏ 52391	Pictures/Long Cool Woman (in a Black Dress)	1984	$4
❏ 52336	Sweet Country Music/ Seven Bridges Road	1984	$4
❏ 52603	Why Not Tonight/ Dancin' on the Bayou	1985	$4
❏ 52452	Wishful Drinkin'/ Blue Side of Grey	1984	$4

MDJ

Number	Title	Yr	NM
❏ 4831	Atlanta Burned Again Last Night/Tumblin' Tumbleweeds	1983	$5
❏ 4832	Dixie Dreaming/Orange Blossom Special-Rocky Top	1983	$5
❏ 4832 [PS]	Dixie Dreaming/Orange Blossom Special-Rocky Top	1983	$12

SOUTHERN TRACKS

Number	Title	Yr	NM
❏ 1087	A Thing Called Love/ (B-side unknown)	1987	$5
❏ 1079	Good Vibrations/We Always Agree on Love	1987	$5
❏ 1097	Look at Us Now!/ (B-side unknown)	1988	$5
❏ 1091	Sad Cliches/We Always Agree on Love	1988	$5
❏ 1074	We Always Agree on Love/ Close Enough for Country	1987	$5

ATLANTA DISCO BAND, THE
ARIOLA AMERICA

Number	Title	Yr	NM
❏ 7611	Bad Luck/Ole Goat	1975	$5
❏ 7615	Do What You Feel/I Am Trying	1976	$5

ATLANTA RHYTHM SECTION
COLUMBIA

Number	Title	Yr	NM
❏ 18-02471	Alien/Southern Exposure	1981	$4

DECCA

Number	Title	Yr	NM
❏ 32928	All in Your Mind/Can't Stand It No More	1972	$8
❏ 33051	Back Up Against the Wall/ It Must Be Done	1973	$8
❏ 32948	Earnestine/Another Man's Woman	1972	$8

MCA

Number	Title	Yr	NM
❏ 40719	All in Your Mind/Earnestine	1977	$5
❏ 40059	Cold Turkey, Tennessee/ Conversation	1973	$6

POLYDOR

Number	Title	Yr	NM
❏ 14262	Angel (What in the World's Come Over Us)/Help Yourself	1975	$4
❏ 2039	Back Up Against the Wall/Large Time	1980	$4
❏ 14289	Bless My Soul/Crazy	1975	$4
❏ 14504	Champagne Jam/ Great Escape	1978	$4
❏ 2079	Conversation/Indigo Passion	1980	$4
❏ 14411	Dog Days/Cuban Crisis	1977	$4
❏ 14568	Do It or Die/My Song	1979	$4
❏ 14248	Doraville/Who Are You Going to Run To	1974	$4
❏ 14339	Free Spirit/Police Police	1976	$4
❏ 14273	Get Your Head Out of Your Heart/Jesus Hearted People	1975	$4
❏ 14459	Imaginary Lover/ Silent Treatment	1978	$4
❏ 14484	I'm Not Gonna Let It Bother Me Tonight/Ballad of Lois Malone	1978	$4

Number	Title	Yr	NM
❏ 2125	Putting My Faith in Love/I Ain't Much	1980	$4
❏ 2142	Silver Eagle/Strictly R & R	1981	$4
❏ 14373	So In to You/Everybody Gotta Go	1977	$4
❏ 14582	Spooky/It's Only Music	1979	$4

— *Unreleased?*

Number	Title	Yr	NM
❏ 2001	Spooky/It's Only Music	1979	$4

ATLANTIC SOUNDS, THE
ATLANTIC

Number	Title	Yr	NM
❏ 2468	Blast Off/Pata Pata	1967	$40
❏ 2492	I Gotta Keep On Gwine/L. David Sloane	1968	$15

ATLANTIC STARR
A&M

Number	Title	Yr	NM
❏ 2392	Circles/Does It Matter	1982	$4
❏ 2392 [PS]	Circles/Does It Matter	1982	$4

— *Not really a picture sleeve, but a blue sleeve with a large hole and the words "Atlantic Starr"*

Number	Title	Yr	NM
❏ 2742	Cool, Calm, Collected/ Island Dream	1985	$3
❏ 2742 [PS]	Cool, Calm, Collected/ Island Dream	1985	$3
❏ 2718	Freak-a-Ristic/Island Dream	1985	$3
❏ 2718 [PS]	Freak-a-Ristic/Island Dream	1985	$4
❏ 2822	If Your Heart Isn't In It/One Love	1986	$3
❏ 2822 [PS]	If Your Heart Isn't In It/One Love	1986	$4
❏ 2849	In the Heat of Passion/ Silver Shadow	1986	$3
❏ 2808	In the Heat of Passion/ Thank You	1986	$3
❏ 2135	(Let's) Rock and Roll/ Gimme Your Lovin'	1979	$4
❏ 2198	Losin' You/Straight to the Point	1979	$4
❏ 2420	Love Me Down/Does It Matter	1982	$4
❏ 2619	More, More, More/ Love Me Down	1984	$4
❏ 2435	Perfect Love/Love Moves	1982	$4
❏ 2435 [PS]	Perfect Love/Love Moves	1982	$4

— *Sleeve similar in format to the "Circles" sleeve*

Number	Title	Yr	NM
❏ 2638	Second to None/I Want Your Love	1984	$4
❏ 2788	Secret Lovers/Thank You	1985	$3
❏ 2340	Send for Me/Does It Matter	1981	$4
❏ 2512	Sexy Dancer/Your Love Finally Ran Out	1982	$4
❏ 2766	Silver Shadow/(Remix)	1985	$3
❏ 2766 [PS]	Silver Shadow/(Remix)	1985	$4
❏ 2065	Stand Up/Don't Abuse My Love	1978	$4
❏ 2364	Think About That/ Does It Matter	1981	$4
❏ 2580	Touch a Four Leaf Clover/Circles	1983	$4
❏ 2580 [PS]	Touch a Four Leaf Clover/Circles	1983	$4
❏ 2312	When Love Calls/Mystery Girl	1981	$4

MANHATTAN

Number	Title	Yr	NM
❏ B-50043	Armed and Dangerous/ (Instrumental)	1986	$3

WARNER BROS.

Number	Title	Yr	NM
❏ 28215	All in the Name of Love/I'm in Love	1987	$3
❏ 28215 [PS]	All in the Name of Love/I'm in Love	1987	$3
❏ 28455	Always//(Instrumental)	1987	$3
❏ 28455 [PS]	Always//(Instrumental)	1987	$3
❏ PRO-S-2663 [DJ]	Always (same on both sides)	1987	$10

— *Heart-shaped red vinyl record in large sleeve; record plays as if it were a 7-inch single*

Number	Title	Yr	NM
❏ 22772	Bring It Back Home Again/I Can't Wait	1989	$3
❏ 27916	Let the Sun In/My Mistake	1988	$3
❏ 27525	My First Love (7" Edit)/My First Love (7" Edit with Dialogue)	1989	$3
❏ 27525 [PS]	My First Love (7" Edit)/My First Love (7" Edit with Dialogue)	1989	$4
❏ 22896	My Sugar/I Can't Wait	1989	$3
❏ 28327	One Lover at a Time/I'm in Love	1987	$3
❏ 28327 [PS]	One Lover at a Time/I'm in Love	1987	$3
❏ 28100	Thankful/Let the Sun In	1988	$3

ATLANTICS, THE
COLUMBIA

Number	Title	Yr	NM
❏ 42877	Greensleeves/Bombera	1963	$30
❏ 43023	War of the World/Bow Man	1964	$30

FARO

Number	Title	Yr	NM
❏ 613	Flame of Love/Tracy	1964	$20

— *B-side by Barry White*

LINDA

Number	Title	Yr	NM
❏ 103	Boo-Hoo-Hoo/Everything Is Gonna Be All Right	1961	$30

RAMPART

Number	Title	Yr	NM
❏ 643	Beaver Shot/Fine, Fine, Fine	1965	$12
❏ 614	Let Me Call You Sweetheart/ Home on the Range	1964	$15
❏ 647	Slopp Dance/Sonny and Cher	1965	$12

ATOMIC ROOSTER
ELEKTRA

Number	Title	Yr	NM
❏ 45745	Devil's Answer/The Rock	1971	$5
❏ 45766	Save Me/Never to Lose	1972	$5
❏ 45800	Stand By Me/Never to Lose	1972	$5
❏ 45727	Tomorrow Night/ Play the Game	1971	$5

ATTITUDE
ATLANTIC

Number	Title	Yr	NM
❏ 89823	Love Me Tonight/ It's Good for Me	1983	$3
❏ 89780	Pump the Nation/ (B-side unknown)	1983	$4
❏ 89879	We Got the Juice/ (Instrumental)	1983	$3

ATTITUDES
DARK HORSE

Number	Title	Yr	NM
❏ 10004	Ain't Love Enough/The Whole World's Crazy	1975	$5
❏ 10004 [PS]	Ain't Love Enough/The Whole World's Crazy	1975	$15
❏ 8452	Good News/In a Stranger's Arms	1977	$4
❏ 10008	Lend a Hand/Honey Don't Leave L.A.	1976	$5
❏ 10011	Sweet Summer Music/ If We Want To	1976	$5
❏ 8404	Sweet Summer Music/ If We Want To	1977	$4

ATTRACTIONS, THE
BELL

Number	Title	Yr	NM
❏ 659	Destination You/Find Me	1967	$30
❏ 690	Why Shouldn't a Man Cry/ Some of Your Time	1967	$30

ATWELL, WINIFRED
COLUMBIA

Number	Title	Yr	NM
❏ 43472	Snow Bells/Flea Circus	1965	$6

ATWOOD THE ELECTRIC ICEMAN
UNI

Number	Title	Yr	NM
❏ 55216	Bossier City/Michoacan	1970	$6

AUDIENCE
ELEKTRA

Number	Title	Yr	NM
❏ 45732	Indian Summer/It Brings a Tear	1971	$5
❏ 45756	I Put a Spell on You/Nancy	1971	$5
❏ 45788	Stand By the Door/ Seven Sore Bruises	1972	$5

AUDREY
PLUS

Number	Title	Yr	NM
❏ 104	Dear Elvis/Dear Elvis (Part 2)	1956	$100

— *Black vinyl; a red vinyl pressing has been reported but is unconfirmed*

AUGER, BRIAN, TRINITY
ATCO

Number	Title	Yr	NM
❏ 6656	A Day in the Life/ Bumpin' On Sunset	1969	$8
❏ 6611	Black Cat/In and Out	1968	$8
❏ 6685	Save the Country/Light My Fire	1969	$8
❏ 6685 [DJ]	Save the Country (long/ short versions)	1969	$15
❏ 6685	Save the Country/The Flesh Failures (Let the Sun Shine In)	1969	$8
❏ 6629	Shadows of You/Road to Cairo	1968	$8

— *With Julie Driscoll*

Number	Title	Yr	NM
❏ 6593 [B]	This Wheel's On Fire/A Kind of Love-In	1968	$20

— *With Julie Driscoll*

RCA VICTOR

Number	Title	Yr	NM
❏ APBO-0085	Happiness Is Just Around the Bend/Inner City Blues	1973	$5
❏ 74-0381	I Wanna Take You Higher/Listen Here	1970	$6
❏ 74-0579	Maria's Wedding/Trouble	1971	$5

— *Group becomes "Oblivion Express*

Number	Title	Yr	NM
❏ 74-0735	Second Wind/Freedom Jazz Dance	1972	$5
❏ APBO-0282	Straight Ahead/ Beginning Again	1974	$5

AUGUST AND DENEEN
ABC

Number	Title	Yr	NM
❏ 11082	We Go Together/Can't Get You Out of My Head	1968	$70

AUGUST, JAN
MERCURY

Number	Title	Yr	NM
❏ 54230	A Day at the Seashore/ Egyptian Ella	1950	$15
❏ 55560	Babalu/Tango of Roses	1950	$15
❏ 707110	Bach Mambo/ Minuet in Mambo	1955	$12
❏ 53950	Besame Mucho/Jan's Jam	1950	$15

—Note: Earlier 5000-series 45s by Jan August, other than those listed, may exist

❏ 53990	Bewitched/Blue Prelude	1950	$15

—With Jerry Murad's Harmonicats

❏ 703570	Circle in the Square/Nobody Wants to Go Home	1954	$10
❏ 54700	Clair de Lune/Scheherazade	1950	$15
❏ 702280	Cow Cow Blues/Martha	1953	$12
❏ 54830	Deep Night/Where Do I Go from Here	1950	$15
❏ 58590	Delicado/Just One of Those Things	1952	$15
❏ 71012-X45	Desert Sunrise/ Nickelodeon Tango	1956	$8
❏ 56540	Dizzy Fingers/Two Lonely Hearts	1951	$15
❏ 70875-X45	Dominique/Lovers and Lollipops	1956	$8
❏ 703200	Esplanada/Silhouettes	1954	$12
❏ 707260	I Never Knew/Skater's Waltz	1955	$10
❏ 51060	Intermezzo/Oye Negra	1950	$20

—78 originally issued in 1948

❏ 30003-X45	Intermezzo/Oye Negra	1957	$8
❏ 54970	Little Gray Home/Down by the Old Mill Stream/Meet Me Tonight in Dreamland	1950	$15
❏ 57810	Ma Belle/Hot Lips	1952	$15
❏ 30000-X45	Malaguena/Miserlou	1957	$8

—Celebrity Series" reissue

❏ 704980	Mambo Is In the Air/ The Love Nest	1954	$10
❏ 59000	Meet Mister Callaghan/ Wish You Were Here	1952	$15

—With Jerry Murad's Harmonicats

❏ 55890	Perfidia/Jan's Cucaracha	1951	$15
❏ 702500	Petite Ballerina/Prince Igor	1953	$10
❏ 57230	San Antonio Rose/ Oriental Blues	1951	$15
❏ 30002-X45	Scheherazade/Clair de Lune	1957	$8

—Celebrity Series" reissue

❏ 700780	Song of Lola/Habanera	1953	$12
❏ 705410	The Crazy Julius (Part 1)/(Part 2)	1955	$12
❏ 54000	The Old Piano Roll Blues/Spain	1950	$15
❏ 71211-X45	The Twilight Theme/ Somehow You Know	1957	$8
❏ 700560	Ti-Pi-Tin/Finesse	1953	$10
❏ 71743	What Is This Thing Called Love/Me and My Shadow	1960	$8
❏ 30001-X45	Where or When/Jalousie	1957	$8

—Celebrity Series" reissue

AULD, GEORGIE
CORAL

Number	Title	Yr	NM
❏ 60558	The Christmas Ball/It Ain't Snowin' Outside	1951	$20

AUSTIN, BILL
HIT

Number	Title	Yr	NM
❏ 06	Dear One/If a Woman Answers	1962	$8
❏ 05	Shout/Dr. Feelgood	1962	$8

—B-side by Jim Porter

❏ 11	Shout! Shout! (Knock Yourself Out)/Hide 'Nor Hair	1962	$8

—B-side by Herbert Hunter

AUSTIN, BOBBY
ATLANTIC

Number	Title	Yr	NM
❏ 2942	Forgotten Footprints/Time for One More Dream	1973	$6

CAPITOL

Number	Title	Yr	NM
❏ 5867	Cupid's Last Arrow/Mary's Merry Go Round	1967	$8

Number	Title	Yr	NM
❏ 2681	For Your Love/(Leaning On) Your Everlasting Love	1969	$8
❏ 2971	Garden of My Mind/When Your Sweet Love Carried On	1970	$8
❏ 2552	Goodbye Again/Play Me a Good Old Country Song	1969	$8
❏ 2152	Is This the Beginning of the End/Sweet Evelina	1968	$8
❏ 4814	I Wouldn't Know Where to Begin/Let It Ring	1962	$10
❏ 2851	Little Boy Don't Live Here Anymore/Scatter Your Seeds to the Wind	1970	$8
❏ 4931	One More Time Around/Heartache, Heartache, Go Away	1963	$10
❏ 4733	Put Me Back Together Again/Look Out Heart	1962	$10
❏ 5923	Some of Us Never Learn/ Feet Keep Walkin'	1967	$8
❏ 2757	The Great Pretender/Tommy Jekyll and Linda Hyde	1970	$8
❏ 2039	This Song Is Just for You/Do-Die	1967	$8

TALLY

Number	Title	Yr	NM
❏ 500	Apartment #9/Going Home to Momma	1966	$20

TRIUNE

Number	Title	Yr	NM
❏ 7208	I'll Run Get You/Carol	1973	$6

AUSTIN, DARLENE
CBT

Number	Title	Yr	NM
❏ 4146	Guilty Eyes/When Do We Stop Starting Over	1986	$6
❏ 4146 [PS]	Guilty Eyes/When Do We Stop Starting Over	1986	$8

MAGI

Number	Title	Yr	NM
❏ 4444	I Had a Heart/ (B-side unknown)	1987	$6

MYRTLE

Number	Title	Yr	NM
❏ 1004	I'm on the Outside Looking In/Heartaches by the Number	1983	$6
❏ 1002	Sunday Go to Cheatin' Clothes/Why Baby Why	1982	$6
❏ 1003	Take Me Tonight/Then You Can Tell Me Goodbye	1982	$6

AUSTIN, DONALD
EASTBOUND

Number	Title	Yr	NM
❏ 603	Crazy Legs/Nan Zee	1973	$8
❏ 608	Sex Plot/Can't Understand the Strain	1973	$8

AUSTIN, GENE
FRATERNITY

Number	Title	Yr	NM
❏ 779	My Blue Heaven/ Lonesome Road	1957	$10

RCA VICTOR

Number	Title	Yr	NM
❏ 47-6969	I Could Write a Book/A Porter's Love Song to a Chambermaid	1957	$10
❏ 47-7117	I'm Not the Braggin' Kind/Wonder	1957	$10
❏ 47-6880	Too Late/That's Love	1957	$15
❏ 47-6880 [PS]	Too Late/That's Love	1957	$30

7-Inch Extended Plays

❏ EPA-4057	(contents unknown)	1957	$15
❏ EPA-4057 [PS]	The Gene Austin Story	1957	$15

AUSTIN, PATTI
ABC

Number	Title	Yr	NM
❏ 11104	Music to My Heart/Love 'Em and Leave 'Em Kind of Love	1968	$20

COLUMBIA

Number	Title	Yr	NM
❏ 45337	Are We Ready for Love/Now That I Know What Loneliness Is	1971	$5
❏ 45906	Being with You/Take a Closer Look	1973	$5
❏ 45410	Black California/All Good Gifts-Day by Day	1971	$5
❏ 45785	Come to Him/Turn On the Music	1973	$5
❏ 45592	Day by Day/Didn't Say a Word	1972	$5
❏ 45499	God Only Knows/Can't Forget the One I Love	1971	$5

CORAL

Number	Title	Yr	NM
❏ 62511	Got to Check You Out/What a Difference a Day Makes	1967	$30
❏ 62455	He's Good Enough for Me/Earl	1965	$30
❏ 62541	I'll Keep Loving You/You're Too Much a Part of Me	1967	$30
❏ 62548	(I've Given) All My Love/ Why Can't We Try It Again	1968	$30

Number	Title	Yr	NM
❏ 62471	I Wanna Be Loved/A Most Unusual Boy	1965	$30
❏ 62500	Leave a Little Love/My Lovelight Ain't Gonna Shine	1966	$30
❏ 62518	Only All the Time/Oh How I Need You Joe	1967	$30
❏ 62478	Someone's Gonna Cry/ You'd Better Know What You're Getting	1966	$125
❏ 62491	Take Your Time/Take Away the Pain Stain	1966	$30

CTI

Number	Title	Yr	NM
❏ 9600	Body Language/ People in Love	1980	$4
❏ 7	In My Life (Part 1)/ In My Life (Part 2)	1973	$5

—With Jerry Butler

❏ 9601	I Want You Tonight/ Love Me Again	1980	$4
❏ 51	Love Me by Name/ You Fooled Me	1978	$4
❏ 33	Say You Love Me/In My Life	1976	$4
❏ 41	We're in Love/Golden Oldies	1977	$4
❏ 59	What's at the End of the Rainbow/In My Life	1978	$4

QWEST

Number	Title	Yr	NM
❏ 29136	All Behind Us Now/Fine Fine Fella (Got to Have You)	1984	$4
❏ 50036	Baby, Come to Me/Solero	1982	$4

—With James Ingram

❏ 49754	Do You Love Me/Solero	1981	$4
❏ 49854	Every Home Should Have One/Solero	1981	$5
❏ 29727	Every Home Should Have One/Solero	1983	$4
❏ 28659	Gettin' Away with Murder/ Anything Can Happen Here	1986	$3
❏ 28935	Honey for the Bees/Hot in the Flames of Love	1985	$3
❏ 29618	How Do You Keep the Music Playing/same (Long Version)	1983	$4

—With James Ingram

❏ 29373	It's Gonna Be Special/Solero	1984	$4
❏ 28573	Only a Breath Away/ Summer Is the Coldest Time of Year	1986	$3
❏ 29234	Shoot the Moon/ Change Your Attitude	1984	$4
❏ 27718	Smoke Gets In Your Eyes/How Long Has This Been Goin' On?	1988	$3
❏ 27718 [PS]	Smoke Gets In Your Eyes/How Long Has This Been Goin' On?	1988	$3
❏ 28788	The Heat of Heat/Hot in the Flames of Love	1986	$3

UNITED ARTISTS

Number	Title	Yr	NM
❏ 50588	I Will Wait for You/Big Mouth	1969	$8
❏ 50520	The Family Tree/ Magical Boy	1969	$8

AUSTIN, SIL
JUBILEE

Number	Title	Yr	NM
❏ 5178	Crossfire (Part 1)/(Part 2)	1955	$20
❏ 5162	Shuffle Board/Sil's Loose	1954	$20
❏ 5153	Stagecoach/Volleyball	1954	$20

MERCURY

Number	Title	Yr	NM
❏ 714080	Applesauce/Vernice Cha Cha	1958	$15
❏ 72238	Back in Your Own Back Yard/Nature Boy	1964	$12
❏ 710270	Birthday Party/ The Last Time	1957	$20
❏ 714420	Danny Boy/Hungry Eye	1959	$15
❏ 711960	Fall Out/Green Blazer	1957	$20
❏ 71977	Golden Twist/Tippin' In	1962	$10
❏ 711150	He's a Real Gone Guy/Dues Day	1957	$20
❏ 713050	Hey Eula/Rainstorm	1958	$15
❏ 71578	One More Time/Satisfied, Satisfied, Satisfied	1960	$10
❏ 71627	Say Lou/Girl with a Foxy Frame	1960	$10
❏ 715430	September Song/ Gone Again	1959	$15
❏ 710770	Seven Days in Barcelona/Pretend	1957	$20
❏ 709630	Slow Walk/Wildwood	1956	$20
❏ 714960	Summertime/Ruby	1959	$15
❏ 71808	The Continental Stroll (Part 1)/(Part 2)	1961	$12
❏ 71693	Why Not/When My Dreamboat Comes Home	1960	$10

SSS INTERNATIONAL

Number	Title	Yr	NM
❏ 747	Honey/Lover's Holiday	1968	$6
❏ 792	Massachusetts/ Tara's Theme	1970	$6

WING

Number	Title	Yr	NM
❏ 900750	Titanic/Sil's Groove	1956	$20

Number	Title	Yr	NM

AUTOGRAPH
RCA

Number	Title	Yr	NM
❏ PB-14231	Blondes in Black Cars/Built for Speed	1985	$4
❏ PB-14055	Send Her to Me/All I'm Gonna Take	1985	$4
❏ 5240-1-R	She Never Looked That Good to Me/Dance All Night	1987	$3
❏ PB-14278	That's the Stuff/Six String Fever	1986	$4
❏ PB-13953	Turn Up the Radio/Thrill of Love	1984	$4
❏ PB-13953 [PS]	Turn Up the Radio/Thrill of Love	1984	$6

AUTOMATIC MAN
ISLAND

Number	Title	Yr	NM
❏ 097	Give It to Me/(B-side unknown)	1978	$5
❏ 063	My Pearl/Newspapers	1977	$5

AUTOSALVAGE
RCA VICTOR

Number	Title	Yr	NM
❏ 47-9506	Parahighway/Rampant Generalities	1968	$15

AUTRY, GENE
COLUMBIA

Number	Title	Yr	NM
❏ 21269	20-20 Vision/You're the Only Good Thing	1954	$20
❏ 20904	Am I a Pastime/I Was Just Walking Out the Door	1952	$20
❏ 21229	Angels in the Sky/A Voice in the Choir	1954	$20
❏ 20814	At Mail Call Today/I'll Be Back	1951	$30

— *Reissue of Columbia 37041 (78)*

Number	Title	Yr	NM
❏ 44632	Back in the Saddle Again/Home on the Range	1968	$8
❏ 4-20084	Back in the Saddle Again/Tumbling Tumbleweeds	1951	$30

— *Reissue of 78 rpm single from 1948, which itself was a reissue*

Number	Title	Yr	NM
❏ 21329	Barney the Bashful Bullfrog/Little Peter Pumpkin Eater	1954	$20
❏ 2-127	Bible on the Table/I Lost My Little Darlin'	1949	$60

— *Microgroove 33 1/3 rpm 7-inch single, small hole*

Number	Title	Yr	NM
❏ 21207	Bimbo/Roly Poly	1954	$20
❏ 1-741(?)	Blue Canadian Rockies/Onteora	1950	$50

— *Microgroove 33 1/3 rpm single*

Number	Title	Yr	NM
❏ 6-741(?)	Blue Canadian Rockies/Onteora	1950	$30
❏ 21252	Closing the Book/My Lazy Day	1954	$20
❏ 39347	Crime Will Never Pay/Gold Can Buy Anything	1951	$20
❏ 20929	Diesel Smoke, Dangerous Curves/Stop Your Gambling	1952	$20
❏ 39808	Don't Believe a Word They Say/God's Little Candles	1952	$20
❏ 40167	Easter Morning/The Horse with the Easter Bonnet	1954	$20
❏ 2-210(?)	Ellie Mae/Sun Flower	1949	$50

— *Microgroove 33 1/3 rpm single*

Number	Title	Yr	NM
❏ 40790	Everyone's a Child at Christmas/You Can See Old Santa Claus	1956	$20
❏ 4-293	Everyone's a Child at Christmas/You Can See Old Santa Claus	1956	$20

— *Yellow label, red print*

Number	Title	Yr	NM
❏ 4-293 [PS]	Everyone's a Child at Christmas/You Can See Old Santa Claus	1956	$30
❏ 39461	Frosty the Snow Man/An Old-Fashioned Tree	1951	$15
❏ 6-742	Frosty the Snow Man/When Santa Claus Gets Your Letter	1950	$30
❏ 1-742	Frosty the Snow Man/When Santa Claus Gets Your Letter	1950	$50

— *Microgroove 33 1/3 rpm single*

Number	Title	Yr	NM
❏ 4-75	Frosty the Snow Man/When Santa Claus Gets Your Letter	1951	$30

— *Yellow label, red print; second number on label is 90072*

Number	Title	Yr	NM
❏ 4-75 [PS]	Frosty the Snow Man/When Santa Claus Gets Your Letter	1951	$30

— *Sleeve was manufactured with a hole in the middle*

Number	Title	Yr	NM
❏ 38907	Frosty The Snowman/When Santa Claus Gets Your Letter	1951	$20

— *Second 45 issue of this song*

Number	Title	Yr	NM
❏ 21527	God's in the Saddle/If Today Were the End of the World	1956	$20
❏ 1-767	Goodnight Irene/Texans Never Cry	1950	$50

— *Microgroove 33 1/3 rpm single*

Number	Title	Yr	NM
❏ 6-767	Goodnight Irene/Texans Never Cry	1950	$30
❏ 40960	Half Your Heart/Darlin' What More Can I Do	1957	$15
❏ 20899	Heartsick Soldier on Heartbreak Ridge/I'm Learning to Live	1952	$20
❏ 4-20377	Here Comes Santa Claus (Down Santa Claus Lane)/An Old-Fashioned Tree	1950	$30

— *Reissue on 45 of a single originally on 78*

Number	Title	Yr	NM
❏ 4-84 [PS]	Here Comes Santa Claus/He's a Chubby Little Fellow	1951	$30

— *Sleeve was manufactured with a hole in the middle*

Number	Title	Yr	NM
❏ 4-84	Here Comes Santa Claus/He's a Chubby Little Fellow	1951	$30

— *Yellow label, red print; second number on label is 90088*

Number	Title	Yr	NM
❏ 20709	I Love You Because/The Last Straw	1950	$30
❏ 21280	I'm a Fool to Care/A Broken Promise Means a Broken Heart	1954	$20
❏ 21358	I'm Innocent/You're an Angel	1955	$20
❏ 21035	I've Lived a Lifetime for You/Story Book of Love	1952	$20
❏ 40135	I Wish My Mom Would Marry Santa Claus/Sleigh Bells	1953	$20
❏ 1-810(?)	Little Johnny Pilgrim/Guffy the Goofy Gobbler	1950	$50

— *Microgroove 33 1/3 rpm single*

Number	Title	Yr	NM
❏ 6-810(?)	Little Johnny Pilgrim/Guffy the Goofy Gobbler	1950	$30
❏ 21144	Love Is So Misleadin'/Don't Send Your Love	1953	$20
❏ 4-150	Merry Texas Christmas, You All!/The Night Before Christmas (In Texas, That Is)	1953	$20

— *Yellow label, red print; second number on label is 90172*

Number	Title	Yr	NM
❏ 4-150 [PS]	Merry Texas Christmas, You All!/The Night Before Christmas (In Texas, That Is)	1953	$30

— *Sleeve was manufactured with a hole in the middle*

Number	Title	Yr	NM
❏ 39371	Mr. and Mississippi/How Long Is Forever	1951	$20
❏ 2-421	Mule Train/A Cowboy's Serenade	1950	$50

— *Microgroove 33 1/3 rpm single*

Number	Title	Yr	NM
❏ 2-258	My Empty Heart/I Wish I Had Stayed Over Yonder	1949	$50

— *Microgroove 33 1/3 rpm single*

Number	Title	Yr	NM
❏ 3-39086	My Heart Cries for You/Teardrops from My Eyes	1950	$40

— *Microgroove 33 1/3 rpm single*

Number	Title	Yr	NM
❏ 4-39086	My Heart Cries for You/Teardrops from My Eyes	1950	$30
❏ 39405	Old Soldiers Never Die/God Bless America	1951	$20
❏ 1-575	Peter Cottontail/Funny Little Bunny	1950	$50

— *Microgroove 33 1/3 rpm single*

Number	Title	Yr	NM
❏ 4-68	Peter Cottontail/Funny Little Bunny	1950	$30

— *Yellow label, red print; second number on label is 90063*

Number	Title	Yr	NM
❏ 4-68 [PS]	Peter Cottontail/Funny Little Bunny	1950	$30

— *Sleeve was manufactured with a hole in the middle*

Number	Title	Yr	NM
❏ 2-484	Poison Ivy/A New Star Is Shining	1950	$50

— *Microgroove 33 1/3 rpm single*

Number	Title	Yr	NM
❏ 39542	Poppy the Puppy/He'll Be Coming Down the Chimney (Like He Always Did Before)	1951	$20
❏ 4-122	Poppy the Puppy/He'll Be Coming Down the Chimney (Like He Always Did Before)	1952	$30

— *Yellow label, red print; second number on label is 90136*

Number	Title	Yr	NM
❏ 4-122 [PS]	Poppy the Puppy/He'll Be Coming Down the Chimney (Like He Always Did Before)	1952	$30

— *Sleeve was manufactured with a hole in the middle*

Number	Title	Yr	NM
❏ 2-336	Santa, Santa, Santa/He's a Chubby Little Fellow	1949	$50

— *Microgroove 33 1/3 rpm single*

Number	Title	Yr	NM
❏ 39464	Santa, Santa, Santa/If It Doesn't Snow on Christmas	1951	$15
❏ 4-176 [PS]	Santa Claus Is Comin' to Town/Up on the Housetop (Ho! Ho! Ho!)	1954	$30
❏ 4-176	Santa Claus Is Comin' to Town/Up on the Housetop (Ho! Ho! Ho!)	1954	$20

— *Yellow label, red print*

Number	Title	Yr	NM
❏ 4-148	Smokey the Bear/Back in the Saddle Again	1953	$20

— *Yellow label, red print; second number on label is 90168*

Number	Title	Yr	NM
❏ 4-148 [PS]	Smokey the Bear/Back in the Saddle Again	1953	$30

— *All sleeves have a hole in the middle*

Number	Title	Yr	NM
❏ 4-103	Sonny the Bunny/Bunny Round-Up	1952	$30

— *Yellow label, red print; second number on label is 90110*

Number	Title	Yr	NM
❏ 39217	Sonny the Bunny/Bunny Roundup Time	1951	$30
❏ 2-550(?)	Take Me Back to My Boots and Saddle/Dust	1950	$50

— *Microgroove 33 1/3 rpm single*

Number	Title	Yr	NM
❏ 20727	That Silver Haired Daddy of Mine/Mississippi Valley Blues	1950	$30

— *Reissue of 78 rpm material*

Number	Title	Yr	NM
❏ 38-06189	The Statue in the Bay/God Bless America	1986	$4
❏ 20775	The Statue in the Bay/The Place Where I Worship	1951	$30
❏ 39543	Thirty-Two Feet -- Eight Little Tails/(Hedrock, Coco and Joe) The Three Little Dwarfs	1951	$20
❏ 4-121	Thirty-Two Feet -- Eight Little Tails/(Hedrock, Coco and Joe) The Three Little Dwarfs	1952	$30

— *Yellow label, red print; second number on label is 90135*

Number	Title	Yr	NM
❏ 4-121 [PS]	Thirty-Two Feet -- Eight Little Tails/(Hedrock, Coco and Joe) The Three Little Dwarfs	1952	$30

— *Sleeve was manufactured with a hole in the middle*

Number	Title	Yr	NM
❏ 21304	When He Grows Tired of You/It Just Don't Seem Like Home	1954	$20
❏ 20865	When It's Springtime in the Rockies/I Don't Want to Set the World on Fire	1951	$30
❏ 39462	When Santa Claus Gets Your Letter/He's a Chubby Little Fellow	1951	$15
❏ 2-350	When the Silver Colorado Turns to Gold/Whirlwinds	1949	$50

— *Microgroove 33 1/3 rpm single*

Number	Title	Yr	NM
❏ J 4-172	Where Did My Snowman Go?/Freddie, the Little Fir Tree	1954	$20
❏ J 4-172 [PS]	Where Did My Snowman Go?/Freddie, the Little Fir Tree	1954	$30
❏ 40092	Where Did My Snowman Go?/Freddie the Little Fir Tree	1953	$20

REPUBLIC

Number	Title	Yr	NM
❏ 001	Back in the Saddle Again/The Last Round-Up	1977	$5
❏ 2002	Santa's Comin' in a Whirlybird/Jingle Bells	1959	$15

AVAK, GEORGE
CINATONE

Number	Title	Yr	NM
❏ 501	Lindy Lou/Long Gone Lonesome Blues	1959	$125

NUGGET

Number	Title	Yr	NM
❏ 1062	How Come He Did It That Way/She's One of a Kind	1971	$10

STARDAY

Number	Title	Yr	NM
❏ 970	Little Pedro/I've Loved You All Over the World	1973	$8

AVALANCHE (1)
ABC

Number	Title	Yr	NM
❏ 12246	Wizard of Love/Sweet Baby Brown Eyes	1977	$5

AVALANCHE (2)
BOBLO

Number	Title	Yr	NM
❏ 527	Feel Like Being Funky?/Hot Ice	1977	$5
❏ 513	Mister Boogie Man/You Know My Love	1976	$5

AVALANCHES, THE
WARNER BROS.

Number	Title	Yr	NM
❏ 5407	Baby, It's Cold Outside/Avalanche	1964	$20

Number	Title	Yr	NM

AVALON, FRANKIE, AND ANNETTE FUNICELLO
PACIFIC STAR

❏ 569	(Together We Can Make a) Merry Christmas/The Night Before Christmas	1981	$5

—*Red vinyl*

❏ 569 [PS]	(Together We Can Make a) Merry Christmas/The Night Before Christmas	1981	$5

AVALON, FRANKIE
AMOS

❏ 127	The Star/Woman Cryin'	1969	$5

BOBCAT

❏ 04103	Such a Miracle/You're the Miracle	1983	$4

CHANCELLOR

❏ 1101	After You've Gone/If You Don't Think I'm Leaving	1962	$10
❏ 1101 [PS]	After You've Gone/If You Don't Think I'm Leaving	1962	$30
❏ 1071	All of Everything/Call Me Anytime	1961	$15
❏ 1071 [PS]	All of Everything/Call Me Anytime	1961	$30
❏ 1115	A Miracle/Don't Let Me Stand in Your Way	1962	$10
❏ 1115 [PS]	A Miracle/Don't Let Me Stand in Your Way	1962	$30
❏ 1065	A Perfect Love/The Puppet Song	1960	$20
❏ 1065 [PS]	A Perfect Love/The Puppet Song	1960	$40
❏ 1139	Beach Party/Don't Stop Now	1963	$20
❏ 1036 [M]	Bobby Sox to Stockings/A Boy Without a Girl	1959	$30

—*Originals have pink labels*

❏ 1036 [M]	Bobby Sox to Stockings/A Boy Without a Girl	1959	$15

—*Reissues have black labels*

❏ 1036 [PS]	Bobby Sox to Stockings/A Boy Without a Girl	1959	$50
❏ S-1036 [S]	Bobby Sox to Stockings/A Boy Without a Girl	1959	$50
❏ 1135	Cleopatra/Heartbeats	1963	$10
❏ 1134	Come Fly with Me/Girl Back Home	1963	$10
❏ 1004	Cupid/Jivin' with the Saints	1957	$30
❏ 1125	Dance the Bossa Nova/Welcome Home	1962	$12
❏ 1125 [PS]	Dance the Bossa Nova/Welcome Home	1962	$30
❏ 1011	Dede Dinah/Ooh La La	1958	$20
❏ 1048	Don't Throw Away All Those Teardrops/Talk, Talk, Talk	1960	$20
❏ 1048 [PS]	Don't Throw Away All Those Teardrops/Talk, Talk, Talk	1960	$40
❏ 1021	Ginger Bread/Blue Betty	1958	$20
❏ 1021 [PS]	Ginger Bread/Blue Betty	1958	$50
❏ 1026	I'll Wait for You/What Little Girl	1958	$20
❏ 1026 [PS]	I'll Wait for You/What Little Girl	1958	$50
❏ 1131	My Ex-Best Friend/First Love Never Dies	1963	$10
❏ 1006	Shy Guy/Teacher's Pet	1957	$30
❏ C-1 [DJ]	Shy Guy/Too Young to Love	1959	$50

—*Promo-only record made for "Acnecare"*

❏ 1095	Sleeping Beauty/The Lonely Bit	1961	$12
❏ 1095 [PS]	Sleeping Beauty/The Lonely Bit	1961	$30
❏ 1056	Togetherness/Don't Let Love Pass You By	1960	$20
❏ 1056 [PS]	Togetherness/Don't Let Love Pass You By	1960	$40
❏ 1087	True, True Love/Married	1961	$10
❏ 1087 [PS]	True, True Love/Married	1961	$30
❏ 1052	Where Are You/Tuxedo Junction	1960	$20
❏ 1052 [PS]	Where Are You/Tuxedo Junction	1960	$40
❏ 1077	Who Else But You/Gotta Get a Girl	1961	$15
❏ 1045 [M]	Why/Swingin' on a Rainbow	1959	$20
❏ 1045 [PS]	Why/Swingin' on a Rainbow	1959	$50

—*Blue background, different picture from Chancellor 1040*

❏ S-1045 [S]	Why/Swingin' on a Rainbow	1959	$50
❏ 1045 [PS]	Why/Swingin' on a Rainbow	1959	$50

—*Red background, same picture as on Chancellor 1040*

❏ 1045 [PS]	Why/Swingin' on a Rainbow	1959	$50

DE-LITE

❏ 907	Beauty School Dropout/Midnight Lady	1978	$4
❏ 907 [PS]	Beauty School Dropout/Midnight Lady	1978	$5
❏ 1584	It's Never Too Late/Where I Leave Off (And You Begin)	1976	$4
❏ 1589	Midnight Lady/Does She Wonder Where I Am	1977	$4
❏ 1591	Splish Splash/When I Said I Love You	1977	$4
❏ 1582	Thank You for That Extra Sunrise/It's His Game	1976	$4

Number	Title	Yr	NM

METROMEDIA

❏ 181	Come On Back to Me Baby/Empty	1970	$5
❏ 192	Heart of Everything/I Want You Near Me	1970	$5

REGALIA

❏ 5508	I'm in the Mood for Love/It's the Same Old Dream	1972	$5

REPRISE

❏ 0697	Dancing on the Stars/But I Do	1968	$8
❏ 0796	Don't You Do It/It's Over	1968	$8
❏ 0826	For Your Love/Why Don't They Understand	1969	$8

UNITED ARTISTS

❏ 728	Again/Don't Make Fun of Me	1964	$10
❏ 800	Moon River/Every Girl Should Get Married	1964	$10
❏ 748	My Love Is Here to Stay/New-Fangled, Jingle-Jangle, Swimming Suit from Paris	1964	$10
❏ 748 [PS]	My Love Is Here to Stay/New-Fangled, Jingle-Jangle, Swimming Suit from Paris	1964	$30
❏ 895	There'll Be Rainbows Again/I'll Take Sweden	1965	$10

X

❏ 06	Trumpet Sorrento/The Rock	1954	$60
❏ 026	Trumpet Tarantella/Dormi, Dormi	1954	$60

7-Inch Extended Plays
CHANCELLOR

❏ B-5000	Shy Guy/The One I Love//Trumpet Instrumental/Undecided	1959	$60
❏ A-5002	Too Young to Love/Into Each Life Some Rain Must Fall//Pretty Eyed Baby/I Can't Begin to Tell You	1959	$60

X

❏ EXA-20	Trumpet Taarantella/Dormi, Dormi (Sleep, My Darling)//Trumpet Sorrento/The Book	1954	$60

AVALONS, THE
ALADDIN

❏ 3336	I Miss You/Love Me	1956	$40

DICE

❏ 90/91	Louella/You Broke Our Hearts	1958	$200

GROOVE

❏ 0141	Chains Around My Heart/Och! She Flew	1956	$200

—*Black vinyl*

❏ 0141	Chains Around My Heart/Och! She Flew	1956	$500

—*Green vinyl*

❏ 0174	It's Funny But It's True/Sugar Sugar	1956	$200

NPC

❏ 302	Begin the Beguine/Malanese	1964	$30

ROULETTE

❏ 4568	Is It the End/Many Things from Your Window	1964	$15

UNART

❏ 2007	Hearts Desire/Ebbtide	1958	$120

AVANT-GARDE, THE
COLUMBIA

❏ 44701	Fly with Me/Revelations Revelations	1968	$8

—*While not issued with a picture sleeve, some stock copies came with a lyric insert. Triple the value if this is included.*

AVANTIS, THE
ASTRA

❏ 1006	Gypsy Surfer/Wax 'Em Down	1963	$50

CHANCELLOR

❏ 1144	Gypsy Surfer/Wax 'Em Down	1963	$30

REGENCY

❏ 108	Do the Surfin' Granny/Surfin' Granny	1964	$50
❏ 110	Phantom Surfer/Lucille	1964	$50

Number	Title	Yr	NM

AVENGERS
CD PRESENTS

❏ 006	Paint It Black/Thin White Line	1983	$6

—*Red vinyl*

❏ 006 [PS]	Paint It Black/Thin White Line	1983	$6

DANGERHOUSE

❏ SFD400	We Are the One//I Believe in Me/Car Crash	1977	$100

—*Black vinyl*

❏ SFD400	We Are the One//I Believe in Me/Car Crash	1977	$70

—*Red vinyl*

❏ SFD400 [PS]	We Are the One//I Believe in Me/Car Crash	1977	$100

—*Crucifix cover (goes with black vinyl record)*

❏ SFD400 [PS]	We Are the One//I Believe in Me/Car Crash	1977	$70

—*Target cover (goes with red vinyl record)*

AVERAGE, JOHNNY, BAND
BEARSVILLE

❏ 49671	Ch Ch Cherie/Gotta Go Home	1981	$5
❏ 49733	Some People/Shake Your Shake	1981	$5

AVERAGE WHITE BAND
ARISTA

❏ 1022	Cupid's in Fashion/(B-side unknown)	1982	$4
❏ 0679	Easier Said Than Done/(B-side unknown)	1982	$4
❏ 0553	For You, For Love/Whatcha 'Gonna Do for Me	1980	$4
❏ 0580	Into the Night/(B-side unknown)	1980	$4
❏ 0515	Let's Go Round Again/Shine	1980	$4

ATLANTIC

❏ 3427	A Star in the Ghetto/What Is Soul?	1977	$4

—*With Ben E. King*

❏ 3500	Big City Lights/She's a Dream	1978	$4
❏ 3388	Cloudy/Love Your Life	1977	$4
❏ 3261	Cut the Cake/Person to Person	1975	$4
❏ 3581	Feel No Fret/Fire Burning	1979	$4
❏ 3444	Fool for You Anyway/The Message	1977	$4

—*With Ben E. King*

❏ 3402	Get It Up/Keepin' It To Myself	1977	$4

—*With Ben E. King*

❏ 3285	If I Ever Lose This Heaven/High Flyin' Woman	1975	$4
❏ 3229	Pick Up the Pieces/Work to Do	1974	$5
❏ 3304	School Boy Crush/Groovin' the Night Away	1975	$4
❏ 3363	Soul Searching/Love of Your Own	1976	$4
❏ 3563	Walk On By/Too Late to Cry	1979	$4
❏ 3614 [DJ]	When Will You Be Mine (same on both sides)	1979	$4

—*May be promo only*

MCA

❏ 40168	This World Has Music/The Jugglers	1973	$5
❏ 40196	Twilight Zone/How Can You Go Home	1974	$5

AVONS, THE (1)
ASTRA

❏ 1023	Baby/Whisper (Softly)	1966	$40

—*Reissue of Hull material*

HULL

❏ 754	A Girl to Call My Own/The Grass Is Greener on the Other Side	1962	$200

—*White label*

❏ 754	A Girl to Call My Own/The Grass Is Greener on the Other Side	1962	$100

—*Brown label*

❏ 722	Baby/Bonnie	1957	$200
❏ 717	Our Love Will Never End/I'm Sending S.O.S.	1956	$200

—*Black label*

❏ 717	Our Love Will Never End/I'm Sending S.O.S.	1956	$60

—*Red label*

❏ 731	What Love Can Do/On the Island	1958	$120

Number	Title	Yr	NM
❏ 728	What Will I Do/Please Come Back to Me	1958	$120
❏ 744	Whisper (Softly)/If I Just (Had My Way)	1961	$125
—White label			
❏ 744	Whisper (Softly)/If I Just (Had My Way)	1961	$125
—Pink label			

AVONS, THE (U)
ABET

Number	Title	Yr	NM
❏ 9419	Talk to Me/Got to Get Used to You	1967	$8

EXCELLO

Number	Title	Yr	NM
❏ 2296	Since I Met You Baby/He's My Hero	1968	$8

GROOVE

Number	Title	Yr	NM
❏ 58-0022	Oh, Gee Baby/Push a Little Harder	1963	$20
❏ 58-0022 [PS]	Oh, Gee Baby/Push a Little Harder	1963	$40
❏ 58-0039	Whatever Happened to Our Love/Tonight Kiss Your Baby Goodbye	1964	$15
❏ 58-0033	Words Written on Water/Rolling Stone	1964	$15

MERCURY

Number	Title	Yr	NM
❏ 71618	We Fell in Love/Pickin' Petals	1960	$20

SOUND STAGE 7

Number	Title	Yr	NM
❏ 2561	Be Good to Your Baby/Just As Long As I Live	1966	$12

AXE
ATCO

Number	Title	Yr	NM
❏ 99850	Heat in the Street/(B-side unknown)	1983	$5
❏ 99823	I Think You'll Remember Tonight/Let the Music Come Back	1983	$4

MCA

Number	Title	Yr	NM
❏ 41073	Hang On/How Come I Love You	1979	$5
❏ 41229	Let Me Know/I Can't Help Myself	1980	$5
❏ 41137	Life's Just an Illusion/How Come I Love You	1979	$5

AXTON, HOYT
20TH FOX

Number	Title	Yr	NM
❏ 6648	Five Dollar Bill/Smoky	1966	$10

A&M

Number	Title	Yr	NM
❏ 1607	Boney Fingers/Life Machine	1974	$5
❏ 1607 [PS]	Boney Fingers/Life Machine	1974	$6
❏ 1541	Boney Fingers/Theme from Buster and Billie	1974	$5
❏ 1864	Evangelina/Jealous Man	1976	$5
❏ 1811	Flash of Fire/Paid in Advance	1976	$4
❏ 1713	In a Young Girl's Mind/Southbound	1975	$5
❏ 1683	Lion in the Winter/No No Song	1975	$5
❏ 1437	Sweet Misery/Less Than the Song	1973	$5
❏ 1497	When the Morning Comes/Billie's Theme	1974	$5

BRIAR

Number	Title	Yr	NM
❏ 100	Georgia Hoss Soldier/Drinking Gourd	1961	$20

CAPITOL

Number	Title	Yr	NM
❏ 3121	Alice in Wonderland/Have a Nice Day	1971	$6
❏ 3167	California Women/Ease Your Pain	1971	$6
❏ 3259	Speed Traps/Hey, Mr. Pilot Man	1972	$6

COLGEMS

Number	Title	Yr	NM
❏ 66-1005	San Fernando/Ten Thousand Sunsets	1967	$10
❏ 66-1005 [PS]	San Fernando/Ten Thousand Sunsets	1967	$30

COLPIX

Number	Title	Yr	NM
❏ 802	Soldier's Last Letter/Speed Trap	1966	$12

ELEKTRA

Number	Title	Yr	NM
❏ 47133	Flo's Yellow Rose/Lion in the Winter	1981	$4

HORIZON

Number	Title	Yr	NM
❏ 351	Greenback Dollar/Crawdad Song	1962	$20
❏ 360	Grizzly Bear/Gypsy Woman	1963	$15
❏ 2	Grizzly Bear/Gypsy Woman	1963	$10
❏ 362	One More Round/Greenback Dollar	1963	$15
❏ 6	The Happy Song/We'll Sing in the Sunshine	1963	$10
❏ 361	This Little Light/Thunder 'N' Lightnin'	1963	$15

JEREMIAH

Number	Title	Yr	NM
❏ 1006	Boozers Are Losers (When the Benders Don't End)/Politicians	1980	$4
❏ 1000	Della and the Dealer/In a Young Girl's Mind	1979	$4
❏ 1005	Evangelina/So Hard to Give It All Up	1980	$4
❏ 1018	If You're a Cowboy/I Collect Hearts	1983	$4
❏ 1016	Pistol Packin' Mama/Fearless the Wonderdog	1982	$4
❏ 1014	She's Too Lazy to Be Crazy/You Do Not Tango	1982	$4
❏ 1011	The Devil/Jealous Man	1981	$4
❏ 1015	There Stands the Glass/James Dean and the Junkman	1982	$4
❏ 1017	Warm Stones and Wild Flowers/Don't Fence Me In	1983	$4
❏ 1008	Where Did the Money Go/Smile As You Go By	1980	$4
❏ 1003	Wild Bull Rider/Torpedo	1979	$4
❏ 1012	Win This One/Ease Your Pain	1981	$4

MCA

Number	Title	Yr	NM
❏ 40731	Little White Moon/Funeral of the King	1977	$5

VEE JAY

Number	Title	Yr	NM
❏ 619	Bring Your Lovin'/Tiger in the Closet	1964	$15
❏ 659	Hush Hush Sweet Charlotte/After You've Gone	1965	$10
❏ 604	L.A. Town/Double Double Dare	1964	$15

AYALA, HANK, AND THE MATADORS
BACK BEAT

Number	Title	Yr	NM
❏ 530	Betty Jo/Handsome	1960	$15
❏ 530 [PS]	Betty Jo/Handsome	1960	$50

AZALEAS, THE
ROMULUS

Number	Title	Yr	NM
❏ 3001	Hands Off/One Drummer Can't Keep Time	1963	$40

AZTEC CAMERA
SIRE

Number	Title	Yr	NM
❏ 29153	All I Need Is Everything/Jump	1984	$4
❏ 29153 [PS]	All I Need Is Everything/Jump	1984	$6
❏ 28155	Deep and Wide and Tall/Bad Education	1987	$3
❏ 28155 [PS]	Deep and Wide and Tall/Bad Education	1987	$4
❏ 29541	Oblivious/Lost Outside the Tunnel	1983	$5
❏ 29269	Oblivious/Queen's Tattoos	1984	$4
❏ 29269 [PS]	Oblivious/Queen's Tattoos	1984	$5
❏ 27819	Somewhere in My Heart/Everybody Is a Number One	1988	$3
❏ 27819 [PS]	Somewhere in My Heart/Everybody Is a Number One	1988	$4

AZTEC TWO-STEP
RCA

Number	Title	Yr	NM
❏ PB-11221	I Wonder If We Tried/Hurting	1978	$5
❏ PB-11313	One Thing I Forgot to Tell You/Hurting	1978	$5
❏ PB-10850	So We Danced/You've Got a Way	1976	$5

RCA VICTOR

Number	Title	Yr	NM
❏ PB-10677	Hey, Little Mama/Step Up to Love	1976	$6
❏ PB-10522	Walking on Air/Humpty Dumpty	1975	$6

AZTECA
COLUMBIA

Number	Title	Yr	NM
❏ 45808	Ain't Got No Special Woman/Can't Take the Funk Out of Me	1973	$6
❏ 45762	Peace Everybody/Mamita Linda	1973	$6

AZTECS, THE
WORLD ARTISTS

Number	Title	Yr	NM
❏ 1029	Da Doo Ron Ron/Hi-Hel Sneakers	1964	$15

AZYMUTH
MILESTONE

Number	Title	Yr	NM
❏ 308	Carnival/Carnival Continued	1979	$5
❏ 309	Dear Limmertz/Papa Song	1980	$5

B

B.B. & Q. BAND, THE
CAPITOL

Number	Title	Yr	NM
❏ 5171	All Night Long/Children of the Night	1982	$4
❏ 5118	Imagination/Hard to Get Around	1982	$4
❏ 4993	On the Beat/Don't Say Goodbye	1981	$4
❏ 5071	Time for Love/Love's What We Should Do	1981	$4

B. BUMBLE AND THE STINGERS
GOLDIES 45

Number	Title	Yr	NM
❏ 2465	Bumble Boogie/School Day Blues	1973	$5

MERCURY

Number	Title	Yr	NM
❏ 72614	Green Hornet Theme/Flight of the Hornet	1966	$10
❏ 72665	Silent Movies/Twelfth Street Rag	1967	$10

RENDEZVOUS

Number	Title	Yr	NM
❏ 186	12th Street Rag/Canadian Sunset	1962	$15
❏ 179	Apple Knocker/The Moon and the Sea	1962	$15
❏ 192	Baby Mash/Night Time Madness	1962	$15
❏ 160	Bee Hive/Caravan	1961	$20
❏ 151	Boogie Woogie/Near You	1961	$20
❏ 140	Bumble Boogie/School Day Blues	1961	$30
❏ 182	Dawn Cracker/Scales	1962	$15
❏ 210	In the Mood/Chicken Chow Mein	1963	$15

B-FATS
ORPHEUS

Number	Title	Yr	NM
❏ B-72664	Music Maestro/Back in the Days	1989	$5

B-52'S, THE
REPRISE

Number	Title	Yr	NM
❏ 22817	Love Shack/Channel Z	1989	$3
❏ 22817 [PS]	Love Shack/Channel Z	1989	$3

WARNER BROS.

Number	Title	Yr	NM
❏ 50064	Deep Sleep/Nip It in the Bud	1982	$4
❏ 49717	Lava/Quiche Lorraine	1981	$12
❏ 29579	Legal Tender/Moon 83	1983	$3
❏ 29971	Mesopotamia/Throw That Beat in the Garbage Can	1982	$3
❏ 49212	Planet Claire/There's a Moon in the Sky (Called the Moon)	1980	$4
❏ 49212 [PS]	Planet Claire/There's a Moon in the Sky (Called the Moon)	1980	$6
❏ 49537	Private Idaho/Party Out of Bounds	1980	$4
❏ 49537 [PS]	Private Idaho/Party Out of Bounds	1980	$6
❏ 29561	Song for a Future Generation/Trism	1983	$3
❏ 29561 [PS]	Song for a Future Generation/Trism	1983	$3
❏ 28561	Summer of Love/Housework	1986	$3
❏ 28561 [PS]	Summer of Love/Housework	1986	$3

B-H-Y
SALSOUL

Number	Title	Yr	NM
❏ 2099	Come As You Are/Opus B-H-Y	1979	$5
❏ 2106	We Funk the Best/I Just Want to Funk (With You)	1979	$5

B.J. AND THE GEMINIS
ATCO

Number	Title	Yr	NM
❏ 6364	Scratch My Back Part 1/Scratch My Back Part 2	1965	$30

B-MOVIE
SIRE

Number	Title	Yr	NM
❏ 28933	Switch On-Switch Off/Just an Echo	1985	$3

B.R.A.T.T.S., THE
TOLLIE

Number	Title	Yr	NM
❏ 9024	Secret Weapon (The British Are Coming)/Jealous Kinda Woman	1964	$30

Number	Title	Yr	NM

B.T. EXPRESS
COAST TO COAST

Number	Title	Yr	NM
❏ ZS5-02630	Let Yourself Go/Cowboy Dancer	1981	$4
❏ ZS4-03246	Star Child (Spirit of the Night)/ This Must Be the Night for Love	1982	$4

COLUMBIA

Number	Title	Yr	NM
❏ 3-10346	Can't Stop Groovin' Now, Wanna Do It Some More/Herbs	1976	$4
❏ 1-11336	Does It Feel Good/ Have Some Fun	1980	$4
❏ 3-10399	Energy to Burn/Make Your Body Move	1976	$4
❏ 3-10582	Funky Music (Don't Laugh at My Funk)/We Got It Together	1977	$4
❏ 1-11249	Give Up the Funk (Let's Dance)/ Better Late Than Never	1980	$4
❏ 1-11200	Heart of Fire/Better Late Than Never	1980	$4
❏ 3-10649	Shout It Out/Ride On B.T.	1977	$4
❏ 11400	Stretch/Just Want to Hold You	1980	$4

ROADSHOW

Number	Title	Yr	NM
❏ 7005	Close to You/(B-side unknown)	1975	$4
❏ 7001	Express/Express (Disco Mix)	1975	$4
❏ 7003	Give It What You Got/ Peace Pipe	1975	$4

SCEPTER

Number	Title	Yr	NM
❏ 12395	Do It ('Til You're Satisfied)/ (Long Version)	1974	$5

BABBITT, BOB
SOUL

Number	Title	Yr	NM
❏ 35101	Gospel Truth/Running Like a Rabbit	1972	$4

BABBITT, HARRY
CORAL

Number	Title	Yr	NM
❏ 60271	Frosty the Snowman/Rudolph the Red-Nosed Reindeer	1950	$20
❏ 60272	Here Comes Santa Claus (Down Santa Claus Lane)/ (All I Want for Christmas Is) My Two Front Teeth	1950	$20
❏ 60555	Thirty-Two Feet -- Eight Little Tails/Hard Rock, Coco and Joe (The Three Little Dwarfs)	1951	$20
❏ 60554	Twas the Night Before Christmas (Part 1)/Twas the Night Before Christmas (Part 2)	1951	$20

BABE RUTH
CAPITOL

Number	Title	Yr	NM
❏ 4219	Say No More/Elusive	1976	$4

HARVEST

Number	Title	Yr	NM
❏ 3553	Wells Fargo/Theme from "For A Few Dollars More	1973	$5

BABES IN TOYLAND
TREEHOUSE

Number	Title	Yr	NM
❏ 017	Dust Cake Boy/Spit to See the Shine	1989	$100

--Green vinyl

Number	Title	Yr	NM
❏ 017	Dust Cake Boy/Spit to See the Shine	1989	$50

--Black vinyl

Number	Title	Yr	NM
❏ 017 [PS]	Dust Cake Boy/Spit to See the Shine	1989	$50

--Same picture sleeve with either color of vinyl

BABIES, THE
ABC DUNHILL

Number	Title	Yr	NM
❏ 4148	I Wanna Testify/Party Time	1968	$15

DUNHILL

Number	Title	Yr	NM
❏ 4101	I'm Not Asking for the World/ Goodbye My Love, Goodbye	1967	$20

BABIT, HI
BI MUSIC

Number	Title	Yr	NM
❏ 132	Dear Mister Santa Claus/ It Makes Me No Never Mind	1973	$5

BABY
CHELSEA

Number	Title	Yr	NM
❏ 3068	Fallen Angel/Baton Rouge	1977	$5
❏ 3057	Where Did All the Money Go/(B-side unknown)	1976	$5

BABY BUGS, THE
VEE JAY

Number	Title	Yr	NM
❏ 594	Bingo/Bingo's Bongo Bingo Party	1964	$30
❏ 594 [PS]	Bingo/Bingo's Bongo Bingo Party	1964	$80

BABY DOLLS, THE
BOOM

Number	Title	Yr	NM
❏ 60002	I Will Do It ('Cause He Wants Me To)/Now That I've Lost You	1966	$10

GAMBLE

Number	Title	Yr	NM
❏ 213	Please Don't Rush Me/ There You Are	1968	$8

HOLLYWOOD

Number	Title	Yr	NM
❏ 1111	Got to Get You Into My Life/Why Can't I Make Him Like You	1960	$50

MASKE

Number	Title	Yr	NM
❏ 103	Go Away Baby/I'm Lonely	1960	$60
❏ 701	Thanks, Mr. DJ/What a Wonderful Love	1961	$120

RCA VICTOR

Number	Title	Yr	NM
❏ 47-7296	Tutti Frutti/Cause I'm in Love	1958	$20

WARNER BROS.

Number	Title	Yr	NM
❏ 5086	Hey Baby/Quiet	1959	$15

BABY EARL AND THE TRINI-DADS
S.P.Q.R.

Number	Title	Yr	NM
❏ 3317	Everybody Do the Ska/Back Slop	1964	$30

BABY FACE LEROY
SAVOY

Number	Title	Yr	NM
❏ 1122	Moonshine Baby/Red Headed Woman	1954	$120
❏ 1501	Moonshine Baby/Red Headed Woman	1956	$100

—Reissue of 1122

BABY GRAND
ARISTA

Number	Title	Yr	NM
❏ 0394 [DJ]	All Night Long (same on both sides)	1979	$5

— May be promo only

Number	Title	Yr	NM
❏ 0293	Bring Me Your Broken Heart/ Lady of My Dreams	1977	$5
❏ 0374	Walk Away Renee/ Much Too Much	1978	$5

BABY HUEY
CURTOM

Number	Title	Yr	NM
❏ 1962	Hard Times/Listen to Me	1971	$12
❏ 1939	Mighty Mighty Children/Mighty Mighty Children (Part 2)	1969	$10

BABY JANE AND THE ROCKABYES
PORT

Number	Title	Yr	NM
❏ 3013	Heartbreak Shop/Dance Till My Feet Get Tired	1964	$40

UNITED ARTISTS

Number	Title	Yr	NM
❏ 593	Get Me to the Church on Time/Hickory Dickory Dock	1963	$20
❏ 560	How Much is That Doggie in the Window/My Boy John	1963	$30
❏ 505	If You Wanna/Oh Johnny	1962	$30

BABY RAY
IMPERIAL

Number	Title	Yr	NM
❏ 66232	Elvira/Just Because	1967	$20
❏ 66216	There's Something On Your Mind/House on Soul Hill	1966	$20

BABYFACE
SOLAR

Number	Title	Yr	NM
❏ B-70022	If We Try/(Instrumental)	1988	$3
❏ B-70009	I Love You Babe/(Instrumental)	1987	$3
❏ ZS4-68966	It's No Crime/(Instrumental)	1989	$3
❏ B-70004	Lovers/Take Your Time	1987	$3
❏ B-70016	Mary Mack/(Instrumental)	1987	$3
❏ ZS4-74003	Tender Lover/(Instrumental)	1989	$3
❏ ZS4-74007	Whip Appeal/(Instrumental)	1989	$3

BABY'S FIRST CHRISTMAS
7-Inch Extended Plays
FISSION

Number	Title	Yr	NM
❏ BFX002	Christmas / Walk With A Winner / Building Up Speed//Purple / Midnight Hour / Frontier	1985	$6
❏ BFX002 [PS]	Christmas / Walk With A Winner / Building Up Speed//Purple / Midnight Hour / Frontier	1985	$6

BABYS, THE
IAlso see JOHN WAITE; BAD ENGLISH.
CHRYSALIS

Number	Title	Yr	NM
❏ 2398	Back on My Feet Again/ Turn Around in Tokyo	1980	$4
❏ 2398 [PS]	Back on My Feet Again/ Turn Around in Tokyo	1980	$6
❏ 2279	Every Time I Think of You/Head First	1978	$5
❏ 2279	Every Time I Think of You/ Please Don't Leave Me Here	1979	$4
❏ 2323	Head First/California	1979	$4
❏ 2132	If You've Got the Time/ Head Above the Waves	1976	$6
❏ 2173	Isn't It Time/Give Me Your Love	1977	$5
❏ 2425	Midnight Rendezvous/ Love Is Just a Mystery	1980	$4
❏ 2495	Postcard/Too Far Gone	1981	$5
❏ 2201	Silver Dreams/And If You Could See Me Cry	1978	$5
❏ 2467	Turn and Walk Away/ Darker Side of Town	1980	$4

BACHARACH, BURT
A&M

Number	Title	Yr	NM
❏ 1222	A House Is Not a Home/ Any Day Now	1970	$5
❏ 845	Alfie/Bond Street	1967	$8
❏ 1241	All Kinds of People/ She's Gone Away	1971	$5
❏ 1241 [PS]	All Kinds of People/ She's Gone Away	1971	$8
❏ 931	Are You There (With Another Girl)/Message to Michael	1968	$6
❏ 1153	Come Touch the Sun/Raindrops Keep Fallin' on My Head	1969	$6
❏ 1064	I'll Never Fall in Love Again/ Pacific Coast Highway	1969	$6
❏ 1921	I Took My Strength from You (I Had None)/Time and Tenderness	1977	$4
❏ 1512	Living Together, Growing Together/Reflections	1974	$4
❏ 1489	Living Together, Growing Together/Something Big	1973	$4
❏ 1290	One Less Bell to Answer/Freefall	1971	$5
❏ 1290 [PS]	One Less Bell to Answer/Freefall	1971	$8
❏ 1004	The Bell That Couldn't Jingle/What the World Needs Now Is Love	1968	$6
❏ 888	The Look of Love/ Reach Out for Me	1967	$8

KAPP

Number	Title	Yr	NM
❏ 657	Don't Go Breaking My Heart/ Trains and Boats and Planes	1965	$8
❏ 685	My Little Red Book/ What's New Pussycat	1965	$8
❏ 532	Saturday Sunshine/And So Goodbye My Love	1963	$8

UNITED ARTISTS

Number	Title	Yr	NM
❏ 50123	The Fox Trot/Ukeatalia	1967	$8

BACHELORS, THE (1)
LONDON

Number	Title	Yr	NM
❏ 20010	Can I Trust You/My Girl	1966	$10
❏ 9793	Chapel in the Moonlight/ The Old Wishing Well	1965	$10
❏ 9793 [PS]	Chapel in the Moonlight/ The Old Wishing Well	1965	$30
❏ 9584	Charmaine/Old Bill	1963	$15
❏ 20071	Diamonds Are Forever/ Where There's a Heartache	1971	$6
❏ 9639	Diane/Happy Land	1964	$15
❏ 9639	Diane/I Believe	1964	$20
❏ 9623	Faraway Places/Is There a Chance	1964	$15
❏ 9672	I Believe/Sweet Lullaby	1964	$15
❏ 9672 [PS]	I Believe/Sweet Lullaby	1964	$30
❏ 9693	I Wouldn't Trade You for the World/Beneath the Willow Tree	1964	$15
❏ 9693 [PS]	I Wouldn't Trade You for the World/Beneath the Willow Tree	1964	$30
❏ 20033	Learn to Live Without You/3 O'Clock Flamingo Street	1967	$8
❏ 20063	Love Is All/The Colours of Love	1970	$6
❏ 9828	Love Me with All of Your Heart/ There's No Room in My Heart	1966	$10
❏ 9762	Marie/You Can Tell	1965	$10
❏ 20027	Marta/Oh How I Miss You	1967	$8
❏ 20051	Punky's Dilemma/ It's a Beautiful Day	1968	$8
❏ 20018	Walk with Faith in Your Heart/ Queen Molly Malone of Ireland	1966	$10
❏ 9632	Whispering/No Light in the Window	1964	$15

Number	Title	Yr	NM

BACHELORS, THE (2)
ALADDIN
❏ 3210	Pretty Baby/Can't Help Loving You	1953	$2500

ROYAL ROOST
❏ 620	I Found Love/You've Lied	1952	$300

BACHELORS, THE (U)
EPIC
❏ 9369	Do the Madison/Bachelor's Club	1960	$15

MGM
❏ 12668	Sometimes/Teenage Memory	1958	$30

NATIONAL
❏ 104	From Your Heart/A Million Teardrops	1957	$30
❏ 115	Today, Tomorrow, Forever/I Want a Girl	1957	$30

POPLAR
❏ 101	After/You Know, I Know (I Love You)	1957	$60

SMASH
❏ 1723	The Day I Met You/Hey Little Girl	1961	$15

BACHMAN-TURNER OVERDRIVE
Also see RANDY BACHMAN; GUESS WHO.

COMPLEAT
❏ 127	For the Weekend/Just Look at Me Now	1984	$4
❏ 137	My Sugaree/(B-side unknown)	1985	$4
❏ 133	My Sugaree/Service with a Smile	1984	$4

MERCURY
❏ 73417	Blue Collar/Hold Back the Water	1973	$5
❏ 73987	Down the Road/A Long Time for a Little While	1978	$4
❏ 73724	Down to the Line/She's a Devil	1975	$4
❏ 73724 [PS]	Down to the Line/She's a Devil	1975	$8
❏ 74062	End of the Line/Jamaica	1979	$4
❏ 73903	Freeways/My Wheels Won't Turn	1977	$4
❏ 73843	Gimme Your Money Please/Four Wheel Drive	1976	$4
❏ 73383	Gimmie Your Money Please/Little Gandy Dancer	1973	$5
❏ 74046	Heaven Tonight/Heartaches	1979	$4
❏ 73683	Hey You!/Flat Broke Love	1975	$4
❏ 73457	Let It Ride/Tramp	1974	$4
❏ 73951	Life Still Goes On (I'm Lonely)/Just for You	1977	$4
❏ 73784	Looking Out for #1/Find Out About Love	1976	$4
❏ 73926	Shotgun Rider/Down, Down	1977	$4
❏ 73766	Take It Like a Man/Woncha Take Me for a While	1976	$4
❏ 73487	Takin' Care of Business/Stonegates	1974	$4

BACHMAN, RANDY
POLYDOR
❏ 14478	Is the Night Too Cold for Dancing/Maybe Again	1978	$6

BACK PORCH MAJORITY, THE
EPIC
❏ 9689	Friends/Hand-Me-Down Things	1964	$10
❏ 9809	Good-Time Joe/Ramblin' Man	1965	$10
❏ 9754	Hey Nelly Nelly/Ol' Dan Tucker	1965	$12
❏ 10036	Honey and Wine/Brother John	1966	$8
❏ 10079	Once Again/Slippery Sal and Dirty Dan, the Oyster Man	1966	$8
❏ 9879	Second Hand Man/That's the Way It's Gonna Be	1965	$10
❏ 9769	Smash Flops/Jack O'Diamonds	1965	$12
❏ 9769 [PS]	Smash Flops/Jack O'Diamonds	1965	$20
❏ 10129	Southtown U.S.A./This Little Light	1967	$8
❏ 9850	The Mighty Mississippi/Song of Hope	1965	$10

BACK STREET CRAWLER
7-Inch Extended Plays
ATCO
❏ PR247 [PS]	Back Street Crawler	1975	$8
❏ PR247 [DJ]	Hoo Doo Woman/All the Girls Are Crazy//Survivor/The Band Plays On	1975	$6
— Small hole, plays at 33 1/3 rpm

BACKROADS
SOUNDWAVES
❏ 4718	He's a Runner/So Close	1983	$5
❏ 4698	So Close/Gonna Stay at Night	1983	$5

BACKTRACK FEATURING JOHN HUNT
GOLDMINE
❏ 11	Mexico/I'm On the Outside	1985	$6

BACKUS, JIM
DICO
❏ 101	I Was a Teenage Reindeer/The Office Party	1959	$30

DORE
❏ 899	Dirty Old Man/Frigid	1974	$5

JUBILEE
❏ 5361	Cave Man/Rock on the Roof	1959	$15
❏ 5351	Cave Man/Why Don't You Go Home for Christmas	1958	$15
❏ 5330	Delicious!/I Need a Vacation	1958	$20
— As "Jim Bakus and Friend"

BACON, GAR
BATON
❏ 248	There's Gonna Be Rockin' Tonight/Y-I-O-U	1957	$70

DALE
❏ 105	Chains of Love/Mary Jane	1957	$30
❏ 108	Dutch Treat/I'll Never Fail You	1958	$40

OKEH
❏ 7115	Marshall, Marshall/Too Young to Love	1959	$30

RKO UNIQUE
❏ 395	Lonesome Wail/You and Your Love	1957	$30

BAD BOY
UNITED ARTISTS
❏ XW1118	I've Had Enough/Disco	1978	$5
❏ XW1063	Shake Me Up/Thinking of You	1977	$5

BAD BOYS, THE
WARNER BROS.
❏ 5605	The Owl and the Pussycat/That's What I'll Do	1965	$15

BAD BRAINS
BAD BRAINS
❏ 01	Pay to Cum/Stay Close to Me	1980	$50
— Black vinyl; colored vinyl versions are not originals

❏ 01 [PS]	Pay to Cum/Stay Close to Me	1980	$50
— With lyric insert; some reissues have a Xerox copy of the original picture sleeve

SST
❏ 065 [PS]	House of Suffering	1986	$20
❏ 065	House of Suffering/(B-side blank)	1986	$10

BAD COMPANY
Also see FREE, PAUL RODGERS; THE FIRM.

ATLANTIC
❏ 88939	Shake It Up/Dangerous Age	1989	$4
❏ 88939 [PS]	Shake It Up/Dangerous Age	1989	$4
❏ 89299	That Girl/If I'm Sleeping	1987	$4
❏ 89355	This Love/Tell It Like It Is	1986	$4
❏ 89355 [PS]	This Love/Tell It Like It Is	1986	$4

SWAN SONG
❏ 70112	Burnin' Sky/Everything I Need	1976	$4
❏ 70015	Can't Get Enough/Little Miss Fortune	1974	$6
❏ 99966	Electricland/Untie the Knot	1982	$5
❏ 99966 [PS]	Electricland/Untie the Knot	1982	$5
❏ 70106	Feel Like Makin' Love/Wild Fire Woman	1975	$6
❏ 71000	Gone, Gone, Gone/Take the Time	1979	$5
❏ 71000 [PS]	Gone, Gone, Gone/Take the Time	1979	$6
❏ 70103	Good Lovin' Gone Bad/Whiskey Bottle	1975	$5
❏ 70109	Honey Child/Fade Away	1976	$4
❏ 70101	Movin' On/Easy on My Soul	1974	$5

BAD ENGLISH
Also see JOHN WAITE; THE BABYS

EPIC
❏ 34-68946	Forget Me Not/Lay Down	1989	$3
❏ 34-73094	Price of Love/The Restless Ones	1989	$4

❏ 34-69082	When I See You Smile/Rockin' Horse	1989	$4

BAD HABITS, THE
PAULA
❏ 370	Bad Wind/Images	1972	$8
❏ 374	Louie, Louie/Touch the Sun	1973	$8
❏ 333	My Baby Specializes/Born on the Bayou	1970	$10
❏ 353	Thank You for the Love/My Days Are Numbered	1971	$10

SCEPTER
❏ 12126	Don't Take My Love Away/Hook Nose and Wooden Legs	1966	$20

BAD MANNERS
PORTRAIT
❏ 37-04602	My Girl Lollipop (My Boy Lollipop)/Falling Out of Love	1984	$5
❏ 37-05725	What the Papers Say/Louie Louie	1985	$5
❏ 37-05725 [PS]	What the Papers Say/Louie Louie	1985	$5

BAD NEWS
EMI
❏ EM36 [PS]	Cashing In on Christmas/Bad News	1987	$6
— Sleeve and record are U.K. imports

❏ EMG36 [PS]	Cashing In on Christmas/Bad News	1987	$10
— Christmas card poster pack sleeve

❏ EM36	Cashing In on Christmas/Bad News	1987	$6

BAD RELIGION
7-Inch Extended Plays
EPITAPH
❏ (# unknown) [PS]	Back to the Known	1985	$30
❏ 1072 [PS]	Bad Religion	1981	$125
❏ 1072	Bad Religion/Politics/Sensory Overload//Slaves/Drastic Actions/World War III	1981	$125
— Red vinyl issues with the title "SUFFER" on the label are bootlegs

BADAROU, WALLY
ISLAND
❏ 99557	Chief Inspector/Spider Woman (Novella Des Nove)	1986	$4
❏ 99530	Spider Woman (Novela Das Nove)/(B-side unknown)	1986	$4

BADD BOYS, THE
EPIC
❏ 10165	Folks in a Hurry/I Told You So	1967	$70

BADFINGER
APPLE
❏ 1864	Apple of My Eye/Blind Owl	1973	$6
❏ P-1864 [DJ]	Apple of My Eye (mono/stereo)	1973	$30
❏ 1844	Baby Blue/Flying	1972	$6
❏ 1844 [PS]	Baby Blue/Flying	1972	$20
❏ 1844 [DJ]	Baby Blue/Flying	1972	$120
— White label

❏ 1815	Come and Get It/Rock of All Ages	1969	$6
❏ 1815	Come and Get It/Rock of All Ages	1969	$8
— With Capitol logo on B-side bottom

❏ 1841	Day After Day/Money	1971	$30
— With star on A-side label

❏ 1841	Day After Day/Money	1971	$6
❏ 1841 [DJ]	Day After Day/Money	1971	$120
— White label

❏ 1803	Maybe Tomorrow/And Her Daddy's a Millionaire	1969	$40
— By "The Iveys"; with star on label

❏ 1803	Maybe Tomorrow/And Her Daddy's a Millionaire	1969	$30
— By "The Iveys"; without star on label

Number	Title	Yr	NM

APPLE/AMERICOM

❏ 1803P/ M-300	Maybe Tomorrow/And Her Daddy's a Millionaire	1969	$600

—By "The Iveys"; four-inch flexidisc sold from vending machines

ELEKTRA

❏ 46022	Lost Inside Your Love/ Come Down Hard	1979	$5
❏ 46025	Love Is Gonna Come At Last/Sail Away	1979	$5

RADIO

❏ 3833	Because I Love You/ Too Hung Up on You	1981	$5
❏ 3793	Hold On/Passin' Time	1981	$5
❏ 3815	I Got You/Rock and Roll Contract	1981	$5

WARNER BROS.

❏ 7801	I Miss You/Shine On	1974	$6

BADLANDS

Also see BLACK SABBATH; OZZY OSBOURNE; KISS.

ATLANTIC

❏ 88888	Dreams in the Dark/Hard Driver	1989	$4

BAEZ, JOAN
A&M

❏ 1703	Blue Sky/Dida	1975	$4
❏ 1884	Caruso/Time Is Passing Us By	1976	$4
❏ 1737	Diamonds and Rust/ Winds of the Old Days	1975	$5
❏ 1516	Forever Young/Guantanamera	1974	$4
❏ 1362	In the Quiet Morning/To Bobby	1972	$4
❏ 1362 [PS]	In the Quiet Morning/To Bobby	1972	$8
❏ 1472	Less Than the Song/Windrose	1973	$4
❏ 1393	Love Song to a Stranger/ Tumbleweed	1972	$4
❏ 1906	O Brother/Still Waters at Night	1977	$4
❏ 1802	Please Come to Boston/ Love Song to a Stranger	1976	$4
❏ 1334	Song of Bangladesh/Prison Trilogy (Billy Rose)	1972	$5
❏ 1334 [PS]	Song of Bangladesh/Prison Trilogy (Billy Rose)	1972	$12
❏ 1454	The Best of Friends/Mary Call	1973	$4

DECCA

❏ 32890	Silent Running/ Rejoice in the Sun	1971	$6

PHILCO-FORD

❏ HP-36	There But For Fortune/ Pack Up Your Sorrows	1969	$30

—4-inch plastic "Hip Pocket Record" with color sleeve

PORTRAIT

❏ 70006	I'm Blowing Away/The Altar Boy and the Sheep	1977	$4
❏ 70032	Light a Light/Michael	1979	$4
❏ 70009	Time Rag/Miracles	1977	$4

RCA VICTOR

❏ 74-0568	The Ballad of Sacco and Vanzetti/Here's to You	1971	$6

VANGUARD

❏ 35012	Banks of the Ohio/Old Blue	1962	$8
❏ 35055	Be Not Too Hard/The North	1967	$8
❏ 35158	Blessed Are/The Brand New Tennessee Waltz	1972	$5
❏ 35114	Carry It On/Rock Salt and Nails	1970	$6
❏ 35098	Four Days Gone/Hickory Wind	1969	$8
❏ 35092	If I Knew/Rock Salt and Nails	1969	$8
❏ 35145	Let It Be/Poor Wayfaring Stranger	1971	$6
❏ 35046	Little Drummer Boy/ Cantique de Noel	1966	$12
❏ 35013	Lonesome Road/Pal of Mine	1962	$8
❏ 35088	Love Is Just a Four-Letter Word/Love Minus Zero-No Limit	1969	$8
❏ SPV-6	Maria Dolores/Plane Wreck at Los Gatos (Deportee)	1971	$4

—Small hole, plays at 33 1/3 rpm

❏ SPV-6 [PS]	Maria Dolores/Plane Wreck at Los Gatos (Deportee)	1971	$4

— The above single and sleeve were a bonus single included with the album "Blessed Are..."; as it is sometimes found apart from the LP, we've made a separate listing, but it was never sold separately at the time

❏ 35026	Medley: With God on Our Side/ Railroad Bill/Rambler Gambler	1964	$8
❏ 35040	Pack Up Your Sorrows/ Swallow Song	1966	$8
❏ 35106	Sweet Sir Galahad/The Ghetto	1970	$6
❏ 35031	There But for Fortune/Daddy You Been On My Mind	1965	$8
❏ 35031 [PS]	There But for Fortune/Daddy You Been On My Mind	1965	$40
❏ 35023	We Shall Overcome/What Have They Done to the Rain	1963	$8

❏ 35018	What Have They Done to the Rain/Danger Waters	1963	$8
❏ 35148	Will the Circle Be Unbroken/ Just a Closer Walk with Thee	1972	$5

BAG, THE
DECCA

❏ 32409	Down and Out/Up in the Mornin'	1968	$8

BAGDADS, THE
DOUBLE SHOT

❏ 133	Bring Back Those Doo-Wopps/Green Power	1968	$20
❏ 128	Let's Talk About the Bad Times/Livin' in Fear	1968	$15
❏ 140	Love Has Two Faces/Jelly	1969	$20

BAGDASARIAN, ROSS
CORAL

❏ 60544	Come On-a My House/Oh Beauty	1951	$40
❏ 60597	The Girl with the Tambourine/ He Says Mu-Humm	1951	$30

LIBERTY

❏ 55462	Armen's Theme/Russian Roulette	1962	$20
❏ 55557	Cecelia/Gotta Get to Your House	1963	$20
❏ 55837	Come On-a My House/ Gotta Get to Your House	1965	$15
❏ 56165	I Treasure Thee/Lie Lie	1969	$15
❏ 55810	La Noche/Naval Maneuver	1965	$15
❏ 55275	Lazy Lovers/One Finger Waltz	1960	$20
❏ 55239	Lotta Bull/(B-side unknown)	1959	$20
❏ 55619	Lucy, Lucy/Scalliwags and Sinners	1963	$20
❏ 55013	The Bold and the Brave/ See a Teardrop Fall	1956	$30
❏ 56004	Walking Birds of Carnaby/Red Wine	1967	$15
❏ 56048	When I Look in Your Eyes/Sands of Time	1968	$15

MERCURY

❏ 70254	Let's Have a Merry, Merry Christmas/Hey Brother, Pour the Wine	1953	$30

BAGELS, THE
WARNER BROS.

❏ 5420	I Wanna Hold Your Hair/ Yeah, Yeah, Yeah, Yeah	1964	$20

BAGGYS, THE
PIPELINE

❏ 501	El Surfer/El Seagull	1963	$50

BAILES, EDDY
CIN KAY

❏ 101	Love Isn't Love (Till You Give It Away)/Houston	1976	$5
❏ 112	Ohio/Honky Tonk Away	1976	$5
❏ 104	Woman, Woman/Down in Texas	1976	$5

BAILEY, DIANE
SWAN

❏ 4079	Golden Idol/Someone Else's Hands	1961	$15
❏ 4086	True Blue Love/ There's a Time	1961	$15

BAILEY, GLEN
YATAHEY

❏ 3024	Designer Jeans/(B-side unknown)	1982	$5
❏ 3024 [PS]	Designer Jeans/(B-side unknown)	1982	$8
❏ 1221	Stompin' on My Heart/ (B-side unknown)	1982	$5

BAILEY, J.R.
CALLA

❏ 158	Love Won't Wear Off/ (Instrumental)	1968	$6

MALA

❏ 12015	Hold Back the Dawn/Too Late	1968	$8

MAM

❏ 3639	Everything I Want I See in You/I Can't See Me Without You	1974	$5
❏ 3635	I'll Always Be Your Lover/ Not Too Long Ago	1974	$5

MIDLAND INT'L

❏ PB-10305	The Entertainer (If They Could Only See Me Now)/You Pass My Love (Like a Moving Train)	1975	$5

RCA

❏ PB-10799	Super Loser/Love Still Remains	1976	$5

SPRING

❏ 3038	I'm Still in Love with You/ (B-side unknown)	1984	$4

TOY

❏ 3805	After Hours/(B-side unknown)	1972	$6
❏ 3801	Love, Love, Love/ (B-side unknown)	1972	$6

UNITED ARTISTS

❏ XW-1215	Alone in the Morning/ Stella by Starlight	1978	$4

BAILEY, JOHNNY
SOUNDWAVES

❏ 4695	What's She Doing to My Mind/This Country Music's Driving Me Crazy	1983	$5

BAILEY, JUDY
COLUMBIA

❏ 11-02045	Slow Country Dancin'/Anything You Can Do (I Can Do Worse)	1981	$4
❏ 18-02505	The Best Bedroom in Town/I'm Guilty of Loving You	1981	$4

WARNER BROS.

❏ 29799	Tender Lovin' Lies/Tryin' Hard Not to Be Easy	1983	$4

WHITE GOLD

❏ 22249	There's a Lot of Good About Goodbye/Comfort	1985	$5

BAILEY, LYNN
E&R

❏ 8101	Too Much, Too Little, Too Late/(B-side unknown)	1981	$6

FRATERNITY

❏ 3376	A Little Light Shines/Love, Peace and Music	1975	$5
❏ 3415	This World/Tupelo Travelin' Show	1977	$5

WARTRACE

❏ 613	Cheater Fever/Small Talk	1980	$6

BAILEY, PEARL
MERCURY

❏ 70926	I Can't Rock and Roll to Save My Soul/The Gypsy Goofed	1956	$20

RCA VICTOR

❏ 74-0510	Close to You/A House Is Not a Home	1971	$5
❏ 74-0435	Mama, a Rainbow/Two by Two	1971	$5

ROULETTE

❏ 4279	Ain't Misbehavin'/Bill Bailey, Won't You Please Come Home	1960	$10
❏ 4016	Bill Bailey, Won't You Please Come Home/C'est Magnifique	1957	$15
❏ 4415	Gee Baby (Ain't I Good to You)/You Gotta Dance	1962	$8
❏ 4167	I Got Rhythm/Summertime	1959	$15
❏ 4781	Look At That Face/Was It a Necessary Evil	1967	$5

BAILEY, PHILIP
COLUMBIA

❏ 38-04679	Easy Lover/Women	1984	$3

—A-side with Phil Collins

❏ 38-04679 [PS]	Easy Lover/Women	1984	$4
❏ 38-06216	Echo My Heart/Special Effect	1986	$3
❏ 38-03968	I Know/The Good Guy's Supposed to Get the Girls	1983	$4
❏ 38-03968 [PS]	I Know/The Good Guy's Supposed to Get the Girls	1983	$5
❏ 38-04607	Photogenic Memory/ Children of the Ghetto	1984	$4
❏ 38-05861	State of the Heart/ Take This With You	1986	$3
❏ 38-05861 [PS]	State of the Heart/ Take This With You	1986	$4
❏ 38-04241	Trapped/Vaya (Go with Love)	1983	$4
❏ 38-04826	Walking on the Chinese Wall/ Children of the Ghetto	1985	$3
❏ 38-04826 [PS]	Walking on the Chinese Wall/ Children of the Ghetto	1985	$4

MYRRH

❏ 9016 [DJ]	Love of God (same on both sides)	1986	$5

MYRRH/A&M

❏ 2725	I Want to Know You/The Wonders of His Love	1985	$4

Number	Title	Yr	NM
❏ 2876	Thank You/All Soldiers	1986	$4

WTG

Number	Title	Yr	NM
❏ 31-08492	Twins (Long)/Twins (Short)	1988	$4

— With Little Richard

BAILEY, RAZZY
ABC

Number	Title	Yr	NM
❏ 10939	Stolen Moments/Re-Enlistment Papers	1967	$15

AQUARIAN

| ❏ 601 | I Hate Hate/Singing Other People's Songs | 1974 | $15 |

— As "Razzy

CAPRICORN

| ❏ 0238 | Grits and Gravy/Peanut Butter | 1975 | $6 |

ERASTUS

| ❏ 528 | Sweet Memories/Love Bump | 1977 | $6 |

MCA

❏ 52628	Fightin' Fire with Fire/To Write a Sad Song	1985	$3
❏ 52547	Modern Day Marriages/New Orleans When It Rains	1985	$3
❏ 52701	Old Blue Yodeler's/Write a Sad Song	1985	$3
❏ 52500	Touchy Situation/Music Takes Me Past the Point	1984	$3

MGM

| ❏ 14728 | I Hate Hate/Singing Other People's Songs | 1974 | $5 |

— As "Razzy

RCA

| ❏ PB-13512 | After the Great Depression/Guess Who's Gonna Be a Dad | 1983 | $4 |
| ❏ JK-13512 [DJ] | After the Great Depression (same on both sides) | 1983 | $10 |

— Promo only on red vinyl

| ❏ PB-11226 | Anywhere There's a Jukebox/Is It Over | 1978 | $4 |
| ❏ JB-13084 | Everytime You Cross My Mind (You Break My Heart) (same on both sides) | 1982 | $15 |

— Promo only on red vinyl

❏ PB-13084	Everytime You Cross My Mind (You Break My Heart)/Tonight She's Gonna Love Me (Like There Was No Tomorrow)	1982	$4
❏ PB-12199	Friends/Anywhere There's a Jukebox	1981	$4
❏ GB-12311	Friends/Lovin' Up a Storm	1981	$3

— Gold Standard Series" reissue

❏ PB-11682	I Ain't Got No Business Doin' Business Today/Conchita	1979	$4
❏ PB-11885	I Can't Get Enough of You/The North Won the War Again Last Night	1979	$4
❏ PB-11536	If Love Had a Face/Natural Love	1979	$4
❏ PB-12120	I Keep Coming Back/True Life Country Music	1980	$4
❏ PB-12120 [PS]	I Keep Coming Back/True Life Country Music	1980	$5
❏ JB-12120 [DJ]	I Keep Coming Back/True Life Country Music	1980	$15

— Promo only on green vinyl

❏ PB-13718	In the Midnight Hour/Mr. Melody Man	1984	$4
❏ PB-13290	Love's Gonna Fall Here Tonight/Singin' Other People's Songs	1982	$4
❏ PB-12062	Lovin' Up a Storm/What's a Little Love Between Friends	1980	$4
❏ PB-12062 [PS]	Lovin' Up a Storm/What's a Little Love Between Friends	1980	$6
❏ JB-12268 [DJ]	Midnight Hauler/Scratch My Back	1981	$15

— Promo only on blue vinyl

| ❏ PB-12268 | Midnight Hauler/Scratch My Back (And Whisper in My Ear) | 1981 | $4 |
| ❏ PB-13359 | Peace on Earth/Let It Snow, Let It Snow, Let It Snow | 1982 | $5 |

— B-side by Charley Pride

| ❏ JK-13359 [DJ] | Peace on Earth (same on both sides) | 1982 | $10 |

— Promo only on green vinyl

| ❏ JK-13383 [DJ] | Poor Boy (same on both sides) | 1982 | $12 |

— Promo only on blue vinyl

| ❏ PB-13383 | Poor Boy/What Time Do You Have to Be Back in Heaven | 1982 | $4 |
| ❏ PB-13007 | She Left Love All Over Me/Blaze of Glory | 1981 | $4 |

Number	Title	Yr	NM
❏ PB-13630	This Is Just the First Day/Night Life	1983	$4
❏ PB-11446	Tonight She's Gonna Love Me (Like There Was No Tomorrow)/Old Love Letters	1978	$4
❏ PB-11954	Too Old to Play Cowboy/9,999,999 Tears	1980	$4
❏ JH-11954 [DJ]	Too Old to Play Cowboy (same on both sides)	1980	$15

— Promo only on green vinyl

| ❏ GB-11990 | What Time Do You Have to Be Back in Heaven/If Love Had a Face | 1980 | $3 |

— Gold Standard Series" reissue

| ❏ PB-11338 | What Time Do You Have to Be Back in Heaven/That's the Way a Cowboy Rocks and Rolls | 1978 | $4 |

SOA

❏ 006	But You Will/(B-side unknown)	1989	$5
❏ 001	If Love Ever Made a Fool/(B-side unknown)	1987	$5
❏ 003	Starting All Over Again/(B-side unknown)	1988	$5

BAILEY, THOMAS
FEDERAL

| ❏ 12559 | Fran/Just Won't Move | 1969 | $15 |
| ❏ 12567 | Wish I Was Back/Percy's Place | 1970 | $125 |

BAINES, VICKI
LOMA

| ❏ 2078 | We Can Find True Love/Sweeter Than Sweet Things | 1967 | $15 |

PARKWAY

| ❏ 966 | Country Girl/Are You Kidding | 1966 | $125 |
| ❏ 957 | Losing You/Got to Run | 1965 | $30 |

BAJA MARIMBA BAND, THE
A&M

❏ 862	Along Comes Mary/Wall Street Rag	1967	$4
❏ 862 [PS]	Along Comes Mary/Wall Street Rag	1967	$5
❏ 1047	Big Red/Ruby '68	1969	$4
❏ 937	Brasilia/Yes Sir, That's My Baby	1968	$4
❏ 1136	Can You Dig It Part 1/Can You Dig It Part 2	1969	$4
❏ 913	Fiddler on the Roof/Sunday Mornin'	1968	$4
❏ 1005	Flyin' High/Les Bicyclettes de Belsize	1968	$4
❏ 892	Foul Play/The Sounds of Silence	1967	$4
❏ 1126	Fresh Air/Wave	1969	$4
❏ 843	Georgy Girl/Cabeza Arriba (Heads Up)	1967	$5
❏ 824	Ghost Riders in the Sky/Sabor A Mi	1966	$5
❏ 1078	I'll Marimba You/I Don't Wanna Walk Without You	1969	$4

— Artist credit: "Julius Wechter & The Baja Marimba Band

| ❏ 975 | Little Prayer/Do You Know the Way to San Jose | 1968 | $4 |

— Artist credit: "Julius Wechter & The Baja Marimba Band

| ❏ 1186 | Picasso Summer/Samba Nuevo | 1970 | $4 |
| ❏ 1281 | Spanish Flea/As Time Goes By | 1971 | $4 |

— Artist credit: "Julius Wechter & The Baja Marimba Band

| ❏ XMAS1 [PS] | The 12 Days Of Christmas/My Favorite Things | 1968 | $20 |

— B-side by We Five

| ❏ XMAS1 [DJ] | The 12 Days Of Christmas/My Favorite Things | 1968 | $15 |

— B-side by We Five

❏ 833	The Cry of the Wild Goose/Spanish Moss	1967	$5
❏ 833 [PS]	The Cry of the Wild Goose/Spanish Moss	1967	$8
❏ 816	The Telephone Song/Portuguese Washerwoman	1966	$5

ALMO

❏ 211	Baja Ska/Samba De Orfeu	1964	$6
❏ 201	Comin' in the Back Door/December's Child	1963	$8
❏ 218	Goin' Out the Side Door/Brasilia	1965	$6
❏ 231	(How Much Is That) Doggie in the Window/Puff (The Magic Dragon)	1966	$6
❏ 203	Moonglow & Theme from Picnic/Acapulco 1922	1964	$6
❏ 206	Pedro's Pouch/Wincle Lamoyan Coan	1964	$6

BELL

| ❏ 45376 | Anytime of the Year/Taco Belle | 1973 | $4 |

Number	Title	Yr	NM
❏ 45339	Theme from "Deep Throat"/Do You Want to Dance	1973	$5

BAKER, MICKEY "GUITAR

Also see MICKEY AND SYLVIA.

ATLANTIC

| ❏ 2042 | Third Man Theme/Baia | 1959 | $15 |

KING

| ❏ 5979 | Do What You Do/Night Blue | 1965 | $12 |
| ❏ 5951 | Side Show/Steam Roller | 1964 | $10 |

MGM

| ❏ 12418 | Spinnin' Rock Boogie/Tricky | 1957 | $30 |

RAINBOW

❏ 299	Bandstand Stomp/Rock with a Sock	1955	$40
❏ 303	Old Devil Moon/Guitarambo	1955	$40
❏ 288	Shake Walkin'/Greasy Spoon	1955	$40

SAVOY

| ❏ 867 | Guitar Mambo/Riverboat | 1952 | $60 |
| ❏ 874 | Love Me Baby/Oh Happy Day | 1953 | $60 |

BAKER, ADAM
AVISTA

❏ 8601	In Love with Her/They Come and They Go	1986	$5
❏ 8704	Standing Invitation/Dixie Nightlife	1987	$5
❏ 8602	Weren't You Listening/Dixie Nightlife	1986	$5

SIGNATURE

| ❏ 22484 | I Can See Him in Her Eyes/(B-side unknown) | 1985 | $6 |

BAKER, ANITA
BEVERLY GLEN

| ❏ 2010 | Angel/Do You Believe Me | 1983 | $5 |
| ❏ 2013 | Feel the Need/Sometimes | 1984 | $5 |

ELEKTRA

❏ 69511	Caught Up in the Rapture/Mystery	1986	$3
❏ 69511 [PS]	Caught Up in the Rapture/Mystery	1986	$4
❏ 69371	Giving You the Best That I Got/Good Enough	1988	$3
❏ 69371 [PS]	Giving You the Best That I Got/Good Enough	1988	$3
❏ 69299	Lead Me Into Love/Good Enough	1989	$3
❏ 69299 [PS]	Lead Me Into Love/Good Enough	1989	$4
❏ 69484	Same Ole Love (365 Days a Year)/(Live Version)	1987	$3
❏ 69484 [PS]	Same Ole Love (365 Days a Year)/(Live Version)	1987	$4
❏ 69557	Sweet Love/Watch Your Step	1986	$3
❏ 69554	Watch Your Step/Mystery	1986	$3

BAKER, B.J.
DECCA

| ❏ 732487 | The Melody Man/Anywhere | 1969 | $8 |

BAKER, BILL
AUDICON

| ❏ 115 | Is It a Dream/I Wanna Know | 1961 | $15 |
| ❏ 118 | To the Aisle/Just to Be Near You | 1961 | $15 |

VIM

| ❏ 515 | Price of Love/Thank Heaven | 1960 | $60 |

BAKER, BOBBY
SWAN

| ❏ 4037 | Baby Blue Eyes/Hush Our Secret | 1959 | $20 |

BAKER, BUTCH
MERCURY

❏ 818379-7	Breakin' In a Broken Heart/Torture	1984	$4
❏ 880020-7	Burn Georgia Burn (There's a Fire in Your Soul)/Bury My Heart (In the Smoky Mountains)	1984	$3
❏ 888543-7	Don't It Make You Wanta Go Home/Your Loving Side	1987	$3
❏ 888926-7	I'll Fall in Love Again/After Losing You	1987	$3
❏ 880653-7	Lady Loves Her Job/Breakin' In a Broken Heart	1985	$3
❏ 874746-7	Our Little Corner/Party People	1989	$3
❏ 870486-7	Party People/After Losing You	1988	$3
❏ 884857-7	That's What Her Memory Is For/After Losing You	1986	$3

Number	Title	Yr	NM
❏ 880836-7	They Ain't Like You Girl/ Lady Loves Her Job	1985	$3
❏ 880256-7	Thinkin' 'Bout Leaving/Bury My Heart (In the Smoky Mountains)	1984	$3
❏ 876226-7	Wonderful Tonight/Party People	1989	$3

BAKER, CARROLL
EXCELSIOR

Number	Title	Yr	NM
❏ 1021	Ain't Nothin' Like a Rainy Night/(B-side unknown)	1981	$6
❏ 1013	Mama What Does Cheatin' Mean/Lover on the Shelf	1981	$6

TEMBO

Number	Title	Yr	NM
❏ 8520	It Always Hurts Like the First Time/(B-side unknown)	1985	$6

BAKER, CHARLES
HIT

Number	Title	Yr	NM
❏ 159	Where You Been/Sha La La	1964	$20

— B-side by the Beasts

BAKER, CHARLIE
LIBERTY

Number	Title	Yr	NM
❏ 55226	Star of Wonder/You Crack Me Up	1959	$30

MUNRAB

Number	Title	Yr	NM
❏ 106	Star of Wonder/You Crack Me Up	1959	$200

BAKER, CHET
7-Inch Extended Plays
PACIFIC JAZZ

Number	Title	Yr	NM
❏ 1222 [B]	Sings	1954	$400

BAKER, DONNIE, AND THE DEMENSIONALS
RAINBOW

Number	Title	Yr	NM
❏ 219	Drinkin' Pop Sodee-Odee (Pop Pop)/Sleepy Time Gal	1953	$70

— Black vinyl

Number	Title	Yr	NM
❏ 219	Drinkin' Pop Sodee-Odee (Pop Pop)/Sleepy Time Gal	1953	$200

— Red vinyl

BAKER, GEORGE, SELECTION
COLOSSUS

Number	Title	Yr	NM
❏ 117	Dear Ann/Fly	1970	$4
❏ 124	I Wanna Love You/Impressions	1970	$4
❏ 112	Little Gren Bag/Pretty Little Dreamer	1970	$5

WARNER BROS.

Number	Title	Yr	NM
❏ 8207	Baby Blue/Morning Sky	1976	$4
❏ 8115	Paloma Blanca/Dreamboat	1975	$4

BAKER, GINGER, 'S AIR FORCE
Also see BLIND FAITH; CREAM.
ATCO

Number	Title	Yr	NM
❏ 6816	Atunde! (We Are Here) Part 1/ Atunde! (We Are Here) Part 2	1971	$5
❏ 6750	Man of Constant Sorrow/Doin' It	1970	$5

BAKER GURVITZ ARMY, THE
ATCO

Number	Title	Yr	NM
❏ 7043	People/(B-side unknown)	1976	$5

JANUS

Number	Title	Yr	NM
❏ 248	4 Phil/Help Me	1975	$5

BAKER, KENNY
DECCA

Number	Title	Yr	NM
❏ 23671	O Little Town Of Bethlehem/It Came Upon A Midnight Clear	1950	$20

ORBIT

Number	Title	Yr	NM
❏ 541	Goodbye Little Star/I'm Gonna Love You	1959	$30

BAKER, LAVERN
ATLANTIC

Number	Title	Yr	NM
❏ 2067	A Help-Each-Other Romance/How Often	1960	$20

— With Ben E. King

Number	Title	Yr	NM
❏ 1057	Bop-Ting-a-Ling/ That's All I Need	1955	$50
❏ 2077	Bumble Bee/My Time Will Come	1960	$20

Number	Title	Yr	NM
❏ 1093	Fee Fee Fi Fo Fum/I'll Do the Same for You	1956	$30
❏ 2267	Fly Me to the Moon/Ain't Gonna Cry No More	1965	$10
❏ 1087	Get Up Get Up (You Sleepyhead)/My Happiness Forever	1956	$30
❏ 1189	Harbor Lights/Whipper Snapper	1958	$30
❏ 2119	Hey, Memphis/Voodoo Voodoo	1961	$20
❏ 1004	How Can You Leave a Man Like This/Soul on Fire	1953	$60
❏ 1150	Humpty Dumpty Heart/ Love Me Right	1957	$30
❏ 1030	I Can't Hold Out Any Longer/I'm Living My Life for You	1954	$50
❏ 1104	I Can't Love You Enough/Still	1956	$30
❏ 2007	I Cried a Tear/Dix-A-Billy	1958	$30
❏ 2109	I Didn't Know I Was Crying/Hurtin' Inside	1961	$20
❏ 2001	It's So Fine/Why Baby Why	1958	$30
❏ 2203	Itty Bitty Girl/Oh, Johnny Oh, Johnny	1963	$15
❏ 2021	I Waited Too Long/ You're Teasing Me	1959	$30
❏ 2137	Must I Cry Again/ No Love So True	1962	$15
❏ 1075	Play It Fair/That Lucky Old Sun	1955	$50
❏ 2099	Saved/Don Juan	1961	$20
❏ 2167	See See Rider/The Story of My Love	1962	$15
❏ 2048	Shake a Hand/Manana	1960	$30
❏ 2033	So High So Low/If You Love Me	1959	$30
❏ 1163	St.Louis Blues/Miracles	1957	$30
❏ 1176	Substitute/Learning to Love	1958	$30
❏ 2041	Tiny Tim/For Love of You	1959	$30
❏ 2186	Trouble in Mind/ Half of Your Love	1963	$15
❏ 1047	Tweedlee Dee/Tomorrow Night	1954	$50
❏ 2059	Wheel of Fortune/ Shadows of Love	1960	$20

BRUNSWICK

Number	Title	Yr	NM
❏ 55297	Batman to the Rescue/ Call Me Darling	1966	$12
❏ 55341	Born to Lose/I Need You So	1967	$8
❏ 55408	I'm the One to Do It/Baby	1969	$6
❏ 55285	Let Me Belong to You/ Pledging My Love	1965	$8
❏ 55291	One Monkey (Don't Stop the Show)/Baby	1966	$8
❏ 55287	Think Twice/Please Don't Hurt Me	1965	$8

— With Jackie Wilson

KING

Number	Title	Yr	NM
❏ 4601	Lost Child/Thunderball Boogie	1953	$60

— B-side by Todd Rhodes

Number	Title	Yr	NM
❏ 4583	Must I Cry Again/Hog Maw and Cabbage Slaw	1952	$60

— B-side by Todd Rhodes

Number	Title	Yr	NM
❏ 4556	Trying/Snuff Dipper	1952	$60

— B-side by Todd Rhodes

7-Inch Extended Plays
ATLANTIC

Number	Title	Yr	NM
❏ 588	*Jim Dandy/Still/Play It Fair/Tra La La (contents unknown)	1957	$100
❏ 566	I Cried a Tear	1956	$125
❏ 617 [PS]	I Cried a Tear	1958	$125
❏ 617	I Cried a Tear/Dix-a-Billy/I Waited Too Long/ You're Teasing Me	1958	$100
❏ 566 [PS]	Tweedle Dee	1956	$125

BAKER, PENNY, AND THE PILLOWS
WITCH

Number	Title	Yr	NM
❏ 123	Bring Back the Beatles/ Gonna Win Him	1964	$30
❏ 123 [PS]	Bring Back the Beatles/ Gonna Win Him	1964	$30

BAKER, RONNIE
LAURIE

Number	Title	Yr	NM
❏ 3164	Land of Love/Time Told Me	1963	$30
❏ 3128	My Story/I Want to Be Loved	1962	$70
❏ 3250	See You in September/ Young at Heart	1964	$30

BAKER, SAM, AND NANCY COHEN
HIT

Number	Title	Yr	NM
❏ 125	Once Upon a Time/No Particular Place to Go	1964	$8

— B-side by Sammie Moore

BAKER, SHARI
HIT

Number	Title	Yr	NM
❏ 175	Don't Forget I Still Love You/ My World's a Blue World	1965	$8

— B-side by Ed Hardin

BAKER SISTERS, THE
MERCURY

Number	Title	Yr	NM
❏ 70980	Little Monster/One By One	1956	$30
❏ 70839	Too Many Teardrops/ Break the String	1956	$30
❏ 71074	Trinidaddy/Careless Love	1957	$30

UNIQUE

Number	Title	Yr	NM
❏ 324	Last Bus Home/If You're Ever Gonna Leave Me	1956	$20

BAKER TWINS, THE
CAMEO

Number	Title	Yr	NM
❏ 324	He's No Good/Words Written on Water	1964	$30

BAKER, WARREN
WARNER BROS.

Number	Title	Yr	NM
❏ 5118	Midnight in Bethlehem/ Little Bitty Baby	1959	$15

BAKER, YVONNE
JAMIE

Number	Title	Yr	NM
❏ 1290	What a Difference Love Makes/ Funny What Time Can Do	1965	$15

BALAAM AND THE ANGEL
VIRGIN

Number	Title	Yr	NM
❏ 99340	I Love the Things You Do to Me/Warm Again	1988	$4

BALANCE
PORTRAIT

Number	Title	Yr	NM
❏ 24-02826	American Dream/I'm Through Loving You	1982	$4
❏ 24-02177	Breaking Away/It's So Strange	1981	$4
❏ 24-02608	Falling in Love/Fly Through the Night	1981	$4
❏ 24-03083	Slow Motion/Is It Over	1982	$4

BALDRY, LONG JOHN
A&M

Number	Title	Yr	NM
❏ 1041	It's Too Late Now/Long and Lonely Nights	1969	$8
❏ 974	When the Sun Comes Shining Through/Wise to the Ways of the World	1968	$8

ASCOT

Number	Title	Yr	NM
❏ 2229	Bring My Baby Back to Me/Cuckoo	1967	$10
❏ 2236	Only a Fool Breaks His Own Heart/Let Him Go	1967	$10

EMI AMERICA

Number	Title	Yr	NM
❏ 8024	A Thrill Is a Thrill/Find You	1979	$4

UNITED ARTISTS

Number	Title	Yr	NM
❏ 50141	Bring My Baby Back to Me/Cuckoo	1967	$10

WARNER BROS.

Number	Title	Yr	NM
❏ 7506	Don't Try to Lay No Boogie-Woogie on the King of Rock N Roll/Mr. Rubin	1971	$6
❏ 7516	Don't Try to Lay No Boogie-Woogie on the King of Rock N Roll/same (Part 2)	1971	$6
❏ 7098	Hey Lord You Made the Night Too Long/Let the Heartaches Begin	1967	$8
❏ 7184	Hold Back the Daybreak/ Since I Lost You Baby	1968	$6
❏ 7597	Iko Iko/You Can't Judge a Book by Its Cover	1972	$6
❏ 7617	Mother Ain't Dead/You Can't Judge a Book by Its Cover	1972	$6

BALIN, MARTY
CHALLENGE

Number	Title	Yr	NM
❏ 9156	I Specialize in Love/ You're Alive with Love	1962	$60

EMI AMERICA

Number	Title	Yr	NM
❏ 8093	Atlanta Lady (Something About Your Love)/Lydia	1981	$4
❏ 8160	Do It for Love/Heart of Stone	1983	$4
❏ 8160 [PS]	Do It for Love/Heart of Stone	1983	$5
❏ 8084	Hearts/Freeway	1981	$4
❏ 8084 [PS]	Hearts/Freeway	1981	$5
❏ 8153	What Love Is/Will You Forever	1983	$4
❏ 8153 [PS]	What Love Is/Will You Forever	1983	$5

Number	Title	Yr	NM

BALL, KENNY
BELL
| ❏ 45412 | Make Love to Me/ Smile, Smile, Smile | 1973 | $5 |

DECCA
| ❏ 32083 | Greenback Theme/Red Square | 1967 | $8 |

GUYDEN
| ❏ 2054 | Samantha/I Still Love You All | 1961 | $20 |

JERDEN
| ❏ 776 | 900 Miles/(I Wonder) What Becomes of Life | 1965 | $30 |

KAPP
❏ 531	55 Days at Peking/Rondo	1963	$10
❏ 581	From Russia with Love/ Acapulco 1922	1964	$10
❏ 554	Heartaches/High Hopes	1963	$12
❏ 451	March of the Siamese Children/Villa	1962	$10
❏ 442	Midnight in Moscow/ American Patrol	1962	$15
❏ KJB-11	Midnight in Moscow/The Green Leaves of Summer	1964	$6
❏ KJB-11 [PS]	Midnight in Moscow/The Green Leaves of Summer	1964	$10
❏ 483	So Do I/All Through the Night	1962	$12
❏ 509	Sukiyaki/Hazelmere	1963	$10
❏ 509	Sukiyaki/Nuages	1963	$10
❏ 460	The Green Leaves of Summer/I Shall Not Be Moved	1962	$10
❏ 494	The Payoff/Coronet Chop Suey	1962	$10

BALL, MARCIA
CAPITOL
| ❏ 4591 | Good Times, Good Music, Good Friends/Train to Dixie | 1978 | $5 |
| ❏ 4633 | I'm a Fool to Care/50 Words or Less | 1978 | $5 |

BALLACK, ROBERT JOHN
ROULETTE
| ❏ 7133 | Ain't No Use/Givin' Up Givin' You Up | 1972 | $5 |
| ❏ 7122 | Sweet Sounds of Music/I'm Comin' to Get You | 1972 | $5 |

BALLADEERS, THE
DEL-FI
❏ 4127	Durant Jail/Turtle Dove	1959	$30
❏ 4138	Hurtin'/Roll Call Company "J	1960	$30
❏ 4123	Morning Star/Tom Gets the Last Laugh	1959	$30

ERA
| ❏ 3069 | A Long Way from Home/ Wedding John Doe | 1962 | $20 |

BALLADS, THE
VEE JAY
| ❏ 714 | I Can't See Your Love (Vocal)/(Instrumental) | 1966 | $30 |

VENTURE
| ❏ 615 | God Bless Our Love/My Baby Knows How to Love Her Man | 1968 | $30 |

— Original pressings call the group "The Ballards

❏ 615	God Bless Our Love/My Baby Knows How to Love Her Man	1968	$20
❏ 630	Goodnight My Love/ Hey Diddle Diddle	1969	$20
❏ 625	I Love You Yeah/You're the One	1968	$20
❏ 637	The Gift of Love/I Wish I Knew	1969	$20

BALLARD, FLORENCE
ABC
❏ 11074	Goin' Out of My Head/It Doesn't Matter How I Say It	1968	$40
❏ 11144	Love Ain't Love/Forever Faithful	1968	$40
❏ 11144 [PS]	Love Ain't Love/Forever Faithful	1968	$100

BALLARD, HANK, AND THE MIDNIGHTERS
CHESS
| ❏ 2111 | Love, Why Is It Taking You So Long/I'm a Junkie for My Baby's Love | 1971 | $6 |

KING
❏ 5713	All the Things in Life That Please You/The Rising Tide	1963	$20
❏ 6228	Are You Lonely for Me Baby/ With Our Sweet Lovin' Self	1969	$10
❏ 5550	Big Red Sunset/Can't You See -- I Need a Friend	1961	$20

❏ 5703	Bring Me Your Love/ She's the One	1962	$20
❏ 6244	Butter Your Popcorn/ Funky Soul Train	1969	$20
❏ 5821	Buttin' In/I'm Leavin'	1963	$20
❏ 5729	Christmas Time for Everyone But Me/Santa Claus Is Coming	1963	$20
❏ 6246	Come On with It/Blackenized	1969	$20
❏ 5245	Cute Little Ways/A House with No Windows	1959	$30
❏ 5931	Daddy Rolling Stone/ What's Your Name	1964	$20
❏ 5860	Don't Fall in Love with Me/I'm So Mad with You	1964	$20
❏ 5835	Don't Let Temptation Turn You Around/Have Mercy, Have a Little Pity	1964	$20
❏ 5593	Do You Know How to Twist/Broadway	1962	$20
❏ 5578	Do You Remember/I'm Gonna Miss You	1961	$20
❏ 5677	Dream World/When I Need You	1962	$20
❏ 5341	Finger Poppin' Time/I Love You, I Love You So-o-o	1960	$30
❏ 6131	Funky's Soul Train/Which Way Should I Turn	1967	$15
❏ 5635	Good Twistin' Tonight/I'm Young	1962	$20
❏ 6092	Here Comes the Hurt/ Dance Till It Hurt Cha	1967	$15
❏ 5746	How Could You Leave Your Man Alone/Walkin' and Talkin'	1963	$20
❏ 6196	How You Gonna Get Respect (When You Haven't Cut Your Process Yet)/ Teardrops on Your Letter	1968	$10

— As "Hank Ballard Along With The Dapps

❏ 5275	I Could Love You/Never Knew	1959	$30
❏ 5884	I Don't Know How to Do But One Thing/These Two Young Girls	1964	$20
❏ 6177	I'm Back to Stay/ Come On Wit' It	1968	$15
❏ 6001	I'm Just a Fool and Everybody Knows/Do It Zulu Style	1965	$15
❏ 6031	I'm Ready/Togetherness	1966	$15
❏ 5601	It's Twistin' Time/ Autumn Breeze	1962	$20
❏ 5655	I Want to Thank You/ Excuse Me	1962	$20
❏ 6055	I Was Born to Move/ He Came Alone	1966	$15
❏ 5954	Let's Get the Show on the Road/A Winner Never Quits	1964	$20
❏ 5400	Let's Go, Let's Go, Let's Go/If You'd Forgive Me	1960	$30
❏ 5459	Let's Go Again (Where We Went Last Night)/ Deep Blue Sea	1961	$30
❏ 5289	Look at Little Sister/I Said I Wouldn't Beg You	1959	$30
❏ 5963	One Monkey Don't Stop No Show/What Can I Tell You	1964	$20
❏ 5996	Poppin' the Whip/You, Just You	1965	$15
❏ 5693	Shaky Mae/I Love and Care for You	1962	$20
❏ 6018	Sloop and Slide/My Sun Is Going Down	1966	$15
❏ 5901	Stay Away from My Baby/ She's Got a Whole Lot of Soul	1964	$20
❏ 5215 [M]	Sugaree/Rain Down Tears	1959	$30
❏ S-5215 [S]	Sugaree/Rain Down Tears	1959	$60
❏ 5171	Teardrops on Your Letter/The Twist	1959	$40
❏ 5513	The Big Frog/Doin' Everything	1961	$20

— B-side by Henry Moore

❏ 5312	The Coffee Grind/Waiting	1960	$30
❏ 5491	The Continental Walk/ What Is This I See	1961	$30
❏ 5491 [PS]	The Continental Walk/ What Is This I See	1961	$100
❏ 5974	The Handwriting on the Wall/I Done It	1964	$20
❏ 5430	The Hoochi Coochi Coo/I'm Thinking of You	1960	$30
❏ 5719	The House on the Hill/ That Low-Down Move	1963	$20
❏ 5510	The Switch-A-Roo/The Float	1961	$20
❏ 5798	Those Lonely, Lonely Feelings/It's Love, Baby	1963	$20
❏ 6332	Work With Me Annie/ Sexy Ways	1970	$10

PEOPLE
| ❏ 604 | Teardrops on Your Letter/ Annie Had a Baby | 1972 | $5 |
| ❏ 606 | With Your Sweet Lovin' Self/ Finger Poppin' Time | 1972 | $5 |

POLYDOR
| ❏ 14128 | Finger Poppin' Time/ From the Love Side | 1972 | $5 |

SILVER FOX
| ❏ 23 | Sunday Morning Coming Down/Love Made a Fool of Me | 1970 | $6 |

STANG
❏ 5058	Hey There Sexy Lady/ (Instrumental)	1975	$5
❏ 5061	Let's Go Skinny Dipping/ Love On Love	1975	$5
❏ 5053	Let's Go Streaking/Let's Go Streaking (Part 2)	1974	$5

7-Inch Extended Plays
KING
❏ 436	(contents unknown)	1959	$120
❏ 435 [PS]	Singin' and Swingin', Vol. 1	1959	$120
❏ 436 [PS]	Singin' and Swingin', Vol. 2	1959	$120
❏ 435	Teardrops on Your Letter/ The Twist/Cute Little Ways/ House with No Windows	1959	$120

BALLARD, KENNY
KAPP
| ❏ 602 | Mr. Magic/Oh How I Cried | 1964 | $30 |

BALLARD, LARRY
CAPITOL
❏ 4247	Booze the Blues Away/I'm Gone	1976	$5
❏ 4352	Honky Tonk Heaven/ Someone That I Can Forget	1976	$5
❏ 4391	Mother Texas/One More Hurtin' Song	1977	$5
❏ 4309	Send Her On Home to Me/The Silver Eagle	1976	$5

BALLARD, RUSS
Member of ARGENT.
EMI AMERICA
❏ 8275	The Fire Still Burns/Hold On	1985	$3
❏ 8275 [PS]	The Fire Still Burns/Hold On	1985	$3
❏ 8217	Two Silhouettes/ Playing with Fire	1984	$4

EPIC
❏ 51002	Breakdown/Rock and Roll Lover	1981	$4
❏ 50883	On the Rebound/Riding with the Angels	1980	$4
❏ 50542	Treat Her Right/What Does It Take	1978	$4
❏ 50211	Winning/Here I Am	1976	$4

BALLEW, MICHAEL
LIBERTY
| ❏ 1447 | Pretending Fool/Ain't No Future in Loving You | 1982 | $4 |

BALLIN' JACK
COLUMBIA
❏ 45464	Ballin' the Jack/Hold On	1971	$5
❏ 45698	Playin' the Game/I'm the One You Need	1972	$4
❏ 45312	Super Highway/Only a Tear	1971	$5

MERCURY
| ❏ 73429 | Sunday Morning/This Song | 1973 | $5 |
| ❏ 73401 | Thunder/Try to Relax | 1973 | $5 |

BALLOON FARM, THE
LAURIE
| ❏ 3445 | Hurry Up Sundown/ Farmer Brown | 1968 | $10 |

BALTIMORA
MANHATTAN
❏ B-50029	Living in the Background/ Chinese Restaurant	1986	$3
❏ B-50018	Tarzan Boy/Tarzan Boy (Dub)	1985	$3
❏ B-50018 [PS]	Tarzan Boy/Tarzan Boy (Dub)	1985	$10

BALTIMORE AND OHIO MARCHING BAND, THE
JUBILEE
❏ 5592	Lapland/Condition Red	1967	$6
❏ 5672	Little Arrows/(B-side unknown)	1969	$5
❏ 5644	Sgt. Crunch/Typsy Gypsy	1968	$5
❏ 5614	The B&O Marching Band Song/The Wanderer	1968	$5

BALTINEERS, THE
TEENAGE
| ❏ 1000 | Moments Like This/New Love | 1956 | $300 |
| ❏ 1002 | Tears in My Eyes/Joe's Calypso | 1956 | $300 |

BAMA
FREE FLIGHT
| ❏ PB-11629 | Touch Me When We're Dancing/Turning the Tables | 1979 | $5 |

Number	Title	Yr	NM

BAMA BAND
COMPLEAT

Number	Title	Yr	NM
❏ 152	I've Changed My Mind/Stone Cold Country	1986	$4
❏ 150	Shop Shop/Too Voodoo	1985	$5
❏ 163	Suddenly Single/Save the Dress	1987	$4
❏ 144	What Used to Be Crazy/White Cadillac	1985	$4
❏ 144 [PS]	What Used to Be Crazy/White Cadillac	1985	$5

MERCURY

Number	Title	Yr	NM
❏ 872048-7	I Got a Rocket in My Pocket/Ellen B.	1988	$3
❏ 870603-7	Southern Accent/It's Gotta Be Love	1988	$3
❏ 872650-7	When We Get Back to the Farm/(B-side unknown)	1989	$4

OASIS

Number	Title	Yr	NM
❏ 1	Dallas/A Cowboy's Welcome Home	1982	$6
❏ 2	Tijuana Sunrise/It Sure Feels Like Love Tonight	1983	$6

SOUNDWAVES

Number	Title	Yr	NM
❏ 4707	Tijuana Sunrise/It Sure Feels Like Love Tonight	1983	$5

BAMBAATAA, AFRIKA, AND THE SOUL SONIC FORCE
TOMMY BOY

Number	Title	Yr	NM
❏ 831	Looking for the Perfect Beat/(Instrumental)	1982	$6
❏ 823	Planet Rock/(Instrumental)	1982	$15

— *Original has orange labels*

Number	Title	Yr	NM
❏ 823	Planet Rock/(Instrumental)	1982	$6

— *Second edition has light blue labels*

BAN-LONS, THE
FIDELITY

Number	Title	Yr	NM
❏ 4051	Highest Mountain/Hey Baby	1959	$200
❏ 4056	I Like It/Hey Good Lookin'	1959	$200

BANANA AND THE BUNCH
WARNER BROS.

Number	Title	Yr	NM
❏ 7626	Back in the U.S.A./My True Life Blues	1972	$5
❏ 7621	My True Life Blues/Vanderbilt's Lament	1972	$5

BANANA BOYS
UNI

Number	Title	Yr	NM
❏ 55194	Come Into My Life/What Will Your Mama Say	1970	$10

BANANA SPLITS, THE
DECCA

Number	Title	Yr	NM
❏ 32536	Pretty Painted Carousel/Long Live Love	1969	$15
❏ 32536 [PS]	Pretty Painted Carousel/Long Live Love	1969	$30
❏ 32429	The Tra-La-La Song (One Banana, Two Banana)/Toy Piano Melody	1968	$15
❏ 32429 [PS]	The Tra-La-La Song (One Banana, Two Banana)/Toy Piano Melody	1968	$30
❏ 32391	We're the Banana Splits/Wait Til Tomorrow	1968	$15

7-Inch Extended Plays
KELLOGG'S/HANNA-BARBERA

Number	Title	Yr	NM
❏ 34579	Doin' the Banana Split/I Enjoy Being a Boy (In Love with You)//The Beautiful Calliopa/Let Me Remember You Smiling	1969	$25
❏ 34578	The Tra La La Song/That's the Pretty Part of You//It's a Good Day for a Parade/The Very First Kid on My Block	1969	$25

BANANARAMA
LONDON

Number	Title	Yr	NM
❏ 886119-7	A Trick of the Night/Cut Above the Rest	1986	$3
❏ 886119-7 [PS]	A Trick of the Night/Cut Above the Rest	1986	$3
❏ PRO468-7 [DJ]	A Trick of the Night (same on both sides)	1986	$6
❏ 810127-1	Cruel Summer/Cruel Dub	1984	$4
❏ 886492-7	Help/Lananeeneenoonoo	1989	$4
❏ 886492-7 [PS]	Help/Lananeeneenoonoo	1989	$4
❏ LD201	He Was Really Sayin' Something/Give Us Back Our Cheap Fares	1982	$5

Number	Title	Yr	NM
❏ 886212-7	I Can't Help It/Mr. Sleaze	1987	$3
❏ 886212-7 [PS]	I Can't Help It/Mr. Sleaze	1987	$3
❏ 886165-7	I Heard a Rumour/Clean Cut Boy	1987	$3
❏ 886165-7 [PS]	I Heard a Rumour/Clean Cut Boy	1987	$3
❏ 886342-7	Love, Truth and Honesty/Strike It Rich	1988	$3
❏ 886342-7 [PS]	Love, Truth and Honesty/Strike It Rich	1988	$3
❏ 886255-7	Love in the First Degree/Ecstasy	1988	$3
❏ 886255-7 [PS]	Love in the First Degree/Ecstasy	1988	$3
❏ 886080-7	More Than Physical/Scarlett	1986	$3
❏ 886080-7 [PS]	More Than Physical/Scarlett	1986	$3
❏ 810112-7	Shy Boy (Don't It Make You Feel Good)/Give Us Back Our Cheap Fares	1983	$4
❏ 810112-7 [PS]	Shy Boy (Don't It Make You Feel Good)/Give Us Back Our Cheap Fares	1983	$4
❏ 882019-7	The Wild Life/The State I'm In	1984	$3
❏ 882019-7 [PS]	The Wild Life/The State I'm In	1984	$3

BANBARRA
UNITED ARTISTS

Number	Title	Yr	NM
❏ XW-734	Shack Up Part 1/Shack Up Part 2	1975	$4

BANCHEE
ATLANTIC

Number	Title	Yr	NM
❏ 2708	I Just Don't Know/Train of Life	1970	$10

POLYDOR

Number	Title	Yr	NM
❏ 14104	Searcher's Life//3/4 Song	1971	$10

BAND AID
COLUMBIA

Number	Title	Yr	NM
❏ 38-04749	Do They Know It's Christmas?/Feed the World	1984	$5
❏ 38-04749 [PS]	Do They Know It's Christmas?/Feed the World	1984	$5

BAND AID II
POLYDOR

Number	Title	Yr	NM
❏ FEED2	Do They Know It's Christmas?/(Instrumental)	1989	$5

— *New version of Band Aid single, unreleased in U.S. for legal reasons*

Number	Title	Yr	NM
❏ FEED2 [PS]	Do They Know It's Christmas?/(Instrumental)	1989	$5

BAND OF ANGELS
MUMS

Number	Title	Yr	NM
❏ ZS86035	He's Not There/So Hard Living Without You	1975	$6

RCA VICTOR

Number	Title	Yr	NM
❏ PB-10452	Will You Still Love Me Tomorrow/Every Minute	1975	$6

BAND OF GOLD
RCA

Number	Title	Yr	NM
❏ PB-14019	In Love Again (Medley)/(Vocal Theme)	1985	$4
❏ PB-13933	Love Songs Are Back Again (Edited)/(Instrumental)	1984	$4

— *This is the actual song without the interwoven medley*

Number	Title	Yr	NM
❏ PB-13866	Medley: Love Songs Are Back Again (Edited)/Medley: Love Songs Are Back Again	1984	$4
❏ PB-14129	Medley: This Is Our Time/Never Let You Go	1985	$4

BAND, THE
Also see ROBBIE ROBERTSON; LEVON HELM; RICK DANKO.
CAPITOL

Number	Title	Yr	NM
❏ 3758	Ain't Got No Home/Get Up Jake	1973	$5
❏ 3433	Don't Do It/Rag Mama Rag	1972	$5
❏ 4361	Georgia on My Mind/The Night They Drove Old Dixie Down	1976	$4
❏ 3500	Hang Up My Rock & Roll Shoes/Caledonia Mission	1972	$5
❏ 3199	Life Is a Carnival/The Moon Struck One	1971	$6
❏ 4230	Ophelia/Hobo Jungle	1976	$4
❏ 2269	The Weight/I Shall Be Released	1968	$8

— *First pressing credits "Jaime Robbie Robertson, Rick Danko, Richard Manuel, Garth Hudson, Levon Helm*

Number	Title	Yr	NM
❏ 3828	Third Man Theme/W.S. Walcott Medicine Show	1974	$5

Number	Title	Yr	NM
❏ 2870	Time to Kill/The Shape I'm In	1970	$6
❏ 4316	Twilight/Acadian Driftwood	1976	$4

WARNER BROS.

Number	Title	Yr	NM
❏ 8592	Out of the Blue/The Well	1978	$4

BAND WITHOUT A NAME, THE
SIDEWALK

Number	Title	Yr	NM
❏ 913	Theme from "Thunder Alley"/Time After Time	1967	$30

TOWER

Number	Title	Yr	NM
❏ 246	Turn On Your Love Light/Perfect Girl	1966	$20
❏ 246 [PS]	Turn On Your Love Light/Perfect Girl	1966	$40

BANDANA
WARNER BROS.

Number	Title	Yr	NM
❏ 29226	All I Wanna Do (Is Make Love to You)/Outside Lookin' In	1984	$4
❏ 29315	Better Our Hearts Should Bend (Than Break)/Ocean of Love	1984	$4
❏ 50045	Cheatin' State of Mind/They Call It Love	1982	$4
❏ 49872	Guilty Eyes/Whatta I Gotta Do	1981	$4
❏ 29831	I Can't Get Over You (Gettin' Over Me)/Come to Me	1982	$4
❏ 29029	It's Just Another Heartache/Heat of the Night	1985	$4
❏ 28939	Lovin' Up a Storm/Good Groove	1985	$4
❏ 29524	Outside Lookin' In/Ocean of Love	1983	$4
❏ 28721	Touch Me/Heat of the Night	1986	$4

BANDIT
ARIOLA AMERICA

Number	Title	Yr	NM
❏ 7731	One Way Love/I'm a Rocker	1979	$5

BANDIT BAND, THE
MCA

Number	Title	Yr	NM
❏ 41294	Deliverance of the Wildwood Flower/Ride Concrete Cowboy Ride	1980	$5

— *B-side by Roy Rogers and the Sons of the Pioneers*

PEGASUS

Number	Title	Yr	NM
❏ 108	Do You Wanna Fall in Love/(B-side unknown)	1987	$6

BANDS OF GOLD
SMASH

Number	Title	Yr	NM
❏ 2058	It's Over/You Won't Change Me	1966	$30

BANDWAGON, THE
BELL

Number	Title	Yr	NM
❏ 953	(Blame It) On the Pony Express/Never Let Her Go	1971	$6
❏ 902	Sweet Inspiration/Pride Comes Before Fall	1970	$6

EPIC

Number	Title	Yr	NM
❏ 10255	Baby Make Your Own Sweet Music/On the Day We Fell in Love	1967	$8
❏ 10352	Breakin' Down the Walls of Heartache/Dancin' Master	1968	$8
❏ 10442	Don't Let It In/When Love Has Gone Away	1969	$8
❏ 10412	I Ain't Lying/You	1968	$8

— *Artist credit: "Johnny Johnson and the Bandwagon*

BANDY, CHARLIE
RCI

Number	Title	Yr	NM
❏ 2379	I Better Go Home (While I Still Got a Home)/(B-side unknown)	1984	$6
❏ 2391	Love You Right Out of My Mind/(B-side unknown)	1984	$6
❏ 2386	Tenamock Georgia/All I See Is You	1984	$6

SOUNDWAVES

Number	Title	Yr	NM
❏ 4611	It Was Love What It Was/Somewhere in Kentucky	1981	$5
❏ 4629	Pyramid of Cans/Till You Can Make It on Your Own	1981	$5
❏ 4596	Talk Back Trembling Lips/From Cotton to Satin	1981	$5
❏ 4674	To Make a Short Story Long/Divorce Looks Good on You	1982	$5

BANDY, MOE, AND JOE STAMPLEY
COLUMBIA

Number	Title	Yr	NM
❏ 38-04756	Daddy's Honky Tonk/Wild and Crazy Guys	1985	$4

Number	Title	Yr	NM
❏ 60508	Hey Joe (Hey Moe)/Two Beers Away	1981	$4
❏ 11147	Holding the Bag/When It Comes to Cowgirls	1979	$5

—As "Moe and Joe"

Number	Title	Yr	NM
❏ 18-02198	Honky Tonk Queen/Partners in Rhyme	1981	$4
❏ 38-04843	Still on a Roll/He's Back in Texas	1985	$4
❏ 11244	Tell Ole I Ain't Here, He Better Get On Home/Only the Names Have Been Changed	1980	$4
❏ 38-04601	The Boy's Night Out/Alive and Well	1984	$4
❏ 38-04601 [PS]	The Boy's Night Out/Alive and Well	1984	$5
❏ 38-04477	Where's the Dress/Wildlife Sanctuary	1984	$4

BANDY, MOE
COLUMBIA

Number	Title	Yr	NM
❏ 38-05438	Barroom Roses/That's All She Needed to Hear	1985	$4
❏ 10974	Barstool Mountain/To Cheat or Not to Cheat	1979	$5
❏ 38-05689	Can't Leave That Woman Alone/Where Do You Take a Broken Heart	1985	$4
❏ 10558	Cowboys Ain't Supposed to Cry/Till I Stop Needing You	1977	$5
❏ 11395	Following the Feeling/Mexico Winter	1980	$4

—A-side with Judy Bailey

Number	Title	Yr	NM
❏ 10265	Hank Williams, You Wrote My Life/I'm the Honky-Tonk on Losers Avenue	1975	$5
❏ 10361	Here I Am Drunk Again/What Happened to Our Love	1978	$5
❏ 11090	I Cheated Me Right Out of You/Honky Tonk Merry-Go-Round	1979	$5
❏ 10487	I'm Sorry for You, My Friend/A Four Letter Fool	1977	$5
❏ 38-03625	I Still Love You in the Same Ol' Way/Drivin' Me Back to You	1983	$4
❏ 10889	It's a Cheating Situation/Try My Love On for Size	1979	$5
❏ 38-04353	It Took a Lot of Drinkin' (To Get That Woman Over Me)/In Mexico	1984	$4
❏ 38-03970	Let's Get Over Them Together/In Love	1983	$4

—A-side with Becky Hobbs

Number	Title	Yr	NM
❏ 11-02039	My Woman Loves the Devil Out of Me/Today I Almost Stopped Loving You	1981	$4
❏ 11184	One of a Kind/The Bitter with the Sweet	1980	$4
❏ 38-03309	Only If There Is Another You/Your Memory Is Showing All Over Me	1982	$4
❏ 10619	She Just Loved the Cheatin' Out of Me/Up to Now I've Wanted Everything But You	1977	$5
❏ 18-02966	She's Not Really Cheatin' (She's Just Gettin' Even)/The All American Dream	1982	$4
❏ 10428	She Took More Than Her Share/Then You Can Let Me Go (Out of Your Mind)	1976	$5
❏ 10671	Soft Lights and Hard Country Music/There's Nobody Home on the Range Anymore	1978	$5
❏ 18-02735	Someday Soon/She's Playing Hard to Forget	1982	$4
❏ 10735	That's What Makes the Juke Box Play/Are We Making Love or Just Making Friends	1978	$5
❏ 10313	The Biggest Airport in the World/I Think I've Got a Love On for You	1976	$5
❏ 11255	The Champ/She Took Out the Outlaw in Me	1980	$4
❏ 10820	Two Lonely People/I Never Miss a Day (Missing You)	1978	$5
❏ 38-04466	Woman Your Love/Texas Saturday Night	1984	$4

CURB

Number	Title	Yr	NM
❏ 10504	Americana/What Goes Around	1988	$3
❏ 10510	Ashes in the Wind/Hittin' Close to Home	1988	$3
❏ 10537	Brotherly Love/Charlie	1989	$3
❏ 10513	I Just Can't Say No to You/Nobody Gets Off in This Town	1988	$3
❏ 10524	Many Mansions/Yuppie Love	1989	$3
❏ B-76750	Pardon Me (Haven't We Loved Somewhere Before)/The Rarest Flowers	1989	$4

—A-side with Becky Hobbs

Number	Title	Yr	NM
❏ 10555	This Night Won't Last Forever/Ain't Nothin' Gonna Slow This Train Down	1989	$3

FOOTPRINT

Number	Title	Yr	NM
❏ 1006	I Just Started Hatin' Cheatin' Songs Today/How Far Do You Think We Would Go	1974	$10

GRC

Number	Title	Yr	NM
❏ 2070	Bandy the Rodeo Clown/I'm Looking for a New Way to Love You	1975	$6
❏ 2055	Don't Anyone Make Love at Home Anymore/Somebody That Good	1975	$6
❏ 2024	Honky Tonk Amnesia/Cowboys and Playboys	1974	$6
❏ 2006	I Just Started Hatin' Cheatin' Songs Today/How Far Do You Think We Would Go	1974	$6
❏ 2036	It Was Always So Easy (To Find an Unhappy Woman)/I Wouldn't Cheat on Her If She Was Mine	1974	$6

MCA

Number	Title	Yr	NM
❏ 52950	One Man Band/Ridin' Her Memory Down	1986	$3
❏ 53033	Till I'm Too Old to Die Young/You Can't Straddle the Fence	1987	$3

SATIN

Number	Title	Yr	NM
❏ SA-009	Hey, There My Friend/You're Part of Me	1966	$30

—As "Moe Bandy & The Mavericks"

Number	Title	Yr	NM
❏ SA-003	Lonely Girl/Too Many Times Before	1965	$40

—As "The Mavericks"/"Vocal: Moe Bandy"

SHANNON

Number	Title	Yr	NM
❏ 804	Hanging On to One/Rain Making Baby of Mine	1972	$8
❏ 806	Somebody Nobody Knows/Sweet Memory	1972	$8

BANG
CAPITOL

Number	Title	Yr	NM
❏ 3816	Feels Nice/Slow Down	1974	$4
❏ 3622	Must Be Love/Love Sonnet	1973	$4

BANG TANGO
MCA

Number	Title	Yr	NM
❏ 53753	Breaking Up a Heart of Stone/Don't Stop Now	1989	$4

BANGLES
COLUMBIA

Number	Title	Yr	NM
❏ 38-68744	Be with You/Let It Go	1989	$3
❏ 38-68533	Eternal Flame/What I Meant to Say	1989	$3
❏ 38-04634	Going Down to Liverpool/Dover Beach	1984	$5
❏ 38-04770	Hero Takes a Fall (Remix)/Tell Me	1985	$12
❏ 38-04770 [PS]	Hero Takes a Fall (Remix)/Tell Me	1985	$12
❏ 38-04479	Hero Takes a Fall/Where Were You When I Needed You	1984	$5
❏ 38-05886	If She Knew What She Wants/Not Like You	1986	$3
❏ 38-05886 [PS]	If She Knew What She Wants/Not Like You	1986	$3
❏ 38-08090	In Your Room/Bell Jar	1988	$3
❏ 38-08090 [PS]	In Your Room/Bell Jar	1988	$3
❏ 38-08385	Manic Monday/Hazy Shade of Winter	1988	$3

—Gray label "Golden Oldies" reissue

Number	Title	Yr	NM
❏ 38-05757	Manic Monday/In a Different Light	1986	$3

—A-side written by Prince under pseudonym "Christopher"

Number	Title	Yr	NM
❏ 38-05757 PS]	Manic Monday/In a Different Light	1986	$3
❏ 38-06674	Walking Down Your Street/Let It Go	1987	$3
❏ 38-06674 [PS]	Walking Down Your Street/Let It Go	1987	$3
❏ 38-06257	Walk Like an Egyptian/Angels Don't Fall in Love	1986	$3
❏ 38-08386	Walk Like an Egyptian/Walking Down Your Street	1988	$3

—Gray label "Golden Oldies" reissue

DEF JAM

Number	Title	Yr	NM
❏ 38-07630	Hazy Shade of Winter/She's Lost You	1987	$3

—B-side by Joan Jett and the Blackhearts

Number	Title	Yr	NM
❏ 38-07630 [PS]	Hazy Shade of Winter/She's Lost You	1987	$3

BANGOR FLYING CIRCUS
ABC DUNHILL

Number	Title	Yr	NM
❏ 4220	Come On People/A Change in Our Lives	1969	$6
❏ 4223	Mama Don't You Know/Someday I'll Find	1970	$6

BANGS, THE
DOWNKIDDIE

Number	Title	Yr	NM
❏ 01	Getting Out of Hand/Call On Me	1981	$60

— Yellow label (original)

Number	Title	Yr	NM
❏ 01 [PS]	Getting Out of Hand/Call On Me	1981	$70
❏ 01	Getting Out of Hand/Call On Me	1981	$50

—Blue label

Number	Title	Yr	NM
❏ 01	Getting Out of Hand/Call On Me	1981	$50

— Green label

BANJO BARONS, THE
COLUMBIA

Number	Title	Yr	NM
❏ 42244	I Saw Mommy Kissing Santa Claus/Have Yourself A Merry Little Christmas-Santa Claus Is Comin' To Town	1961	$10

BANKS, PATRYCE "CHOC'LET"
T-ELECTRIC

Number	Title	Yr	NM
❏ 41308	I Waited for Love/Sunshine Love	1980	$5

BANKS AND HAMPTON
WARNER BROS.

Number	Title	Yr	NM
❏ 8344	I'm Gonna Have to Tell Her/We're Moving On	1977	$5
❏ 8199	It's Gotta Be This Way/Wonderful	1976	$5
❏ 8177	Make Due with Whatcha Got/Caught in the Act (Of Gettin' It On)	1976	$5

BANKS, BESSIE
BLUE CAT

Number	Title	Yr	NM
❏ 106	Go Now/It Sounds Like My Baby	1965	$10

SPOKANE

Number	Title	Yr	NM
❏ 4009	Do It Now/(You Should Have Been a) Doctor	1963	$20

TIGER

Number	Title	Yr	NM
❏ 102	Go Now/It Sounds Like My Baby	1964	$30

VERVE

Number	Title	Yr	NM
❏ 10519	I Can't Make It (Without You Baby)/Need You	1967	$20

VOLT

Number	Title	Yr	NM
❏ 4112	Ain't No Easy Way/Try to Leave Me If You Can	1974	$6

WAND

Number	Title	Yr	NM
❏ 163	Do It Now/(You Should Have Been a) Doctor	1964	$15

BANKS, DARRELL
ATCO

Number	Title	Yr	NM
❏ 6484	Angel Baby Don't You Leave Me/Look Into the Eyes of a Fool	1967	$30
❏ 6471	Here Come the Tears/I've Got That Feeling	1967	$30

COTILLION

Number	Title	Yr	NM
❏ 44006	I Wanna Go Home/Love of My Woman	1968	$10

REVILOT

Number	Title	Yr	NM
❏ 201	Open the Door to Your Heart/Our Love Is In the Pocket	1966	$20
❏ 203	Somebody (Somewhere) Needs You/Baby Whatcha Got (For Me)	1966	$20

VOLT

Number	Title	Yr	NM
❏ 4026	Beautiful Feeling/No One Blinder	1969	$12

BANKS, DICK
LIBERTY

Number	Title	Yr	NM
❏ 55145	Dirty Dog/Too Late	1958	$50

BANKS, DOUG
ARGO

Number	Title	Yr	NM
❏ 5483	I Just Keep Dancing/Baby Since You Went Away	1964	$70

GUYDEN

Number	Title	Yr	NM
❏ 2082	Ain't That Just Like a Woman/Never Say Goodbye	1963	$70

Number	Title	Yr	NM
BANKS, EDDIE			
JOSIE			
❏ 804	Sugar Diabetes/ Rock-a-Bye Blues	1956	$50
BANKS, HOMER			
GENIE			
❏ 1000	Hooked by Love/Lady of Stone	1966	$60
MINIT			
❏ 32000	A Lot of Love/Fighting to Win	1966	$30
❏ 32008	Do You Know What/60 Minutes of Your Love	1966	$30
❏ 32020	Hooked by Love/Lady of Stone	1967	$30
BANKS, RON			
CBS ASSOCIATED			
❏ ZS4-04242	Make It Easy on Yourself/ You and Me	1983	$4
❏ ZS4-04142	Truly Bad/(Instrumental)	1983	$4
BANKS, ROSE			
MOTOWN			
❏ 1404	Darling Baby/Right's Alright	1976	$5
❏ 1383	Whole New Thing/What Am I Gonna Do (With My Life)	1976	$5
SOURCE			
❏ 41219	Papa, Daddy Dear/Papa, Daddy Dear (Stone's Fusion)	1980	$4
BANKS, TONY			
ATLANTIC			
❏ 89339	Smilin' Jack Casey/Short Cut to Somewhere	1986	$3
❏ 89820 [DJ]	This Is Love (same on both sides)	1983	$4
— May be promo only			
❏ 88858	Throwback/Thursday the Twelfth	1989	$3
— As "Bankstatement"			
BANNED, THE			
FONTANA			
❏ 1621	Goodbye, Groovy, Goodbye/A Blanket of Sound	1968	$10
❏ 1616	It Couldn't Happen Here/ Annie Went to Ohio	1968	$10
❏ 1616 [PS]	It Couldn't Happen Here/ Annie Went to Ohio	1968	$30
❏ 1604	My Life Is My Own/ Nothing Matters But You	1967	$10
BANNON, R.C.			
CAPITOL			
❏ 3966	Freedom/I Don't Want to Play Games	1974	$6
COLUMBIA			
❏ 11267	If You're Serious About Cheatin'/What's a Nice Girl Like You Doing (Living in a Place Like This)	1980	$4
❏ 10655	It Doesn't Matter Anymore/ All of the Best	1977	$5
❏ 10771	Loveless Hotel/Nightbird	1978	$5
❏ 11210	Lovely Lonely Lady/I've Never Gone to Bed with an Ugly Woman	1980	$4
❏ 10847	Somebody's Gonna Do It Tonight/Got That Lookin' Feelin'	1978	$5
❏ 10570	Southbound/You Make All the Difference in the World	1977	$5
❏ 10714	(The Truth Is) We're Livin' a Lie/Lost at First Sight	1978	$5
❏ 11081	Winners and Losers/Cheatin' on Him, Lovin' on Me	1979	$5
RCA			
❏ PB-13029	Til Something Better Comes Along/You're Bringing Out the Fool in Me	1981	$4
BANTAMS, THE			
DECCA			
❏ 31040	My Swing Is Broke/ Windows of Blue	1959	$20
WARNER BROS.			
❏ 5695	Follow Me/Meet Me Tonight Little Girl	1966	$10
❏ 5868	Good Lovin' Girl/I'm So Lucky	1966	$10

Number	Title	Yr	NM
BAR-KAYS, THE			
MERCURY			
❏ 872954-7	Animal/Time Out	1989	$3
❏ 872954-7 [PS]	Animal/Time Out	1989	$3
❏ 73994	Attitudes/Can't Keep My Hands Off You	1978	$4
❏ 884232-7	Banging the Walls/Gina	1985	$3
❏ 76097	Body Fever/Deliver Us	1981	$4
❏ 76088	Boogie Body Land/Running In and Out of My Life	1980	$4
❏ 888837-7	Certified True/It Be That Way Sometimes	1987	$3
❏ 880045-7	Dirty Dancer/(Instrumental)	1984	$3
❏ 76187	Do It (Let Me See You Shake)/ Feels Like I'm Falling in Love	1982	$4
❏ 870018-7	Don't Hang Up/Contagious	1988	$3
❏ 870018-7 [PS]	Don't Hang Up/Contagious	1988	$3
❏ 818631-7	Freakshow on the Dance Floor/Lovers Should Never Fall in Love	1984	$4
❏ 76143	Freaky Behavior/ Backseat Driver	1982	$4
❏ 76123	Hit and Run/Say It Through Love	1981	$4
❏ 74039	I'll Dance/Angel Eyes	1978	$4
❏ 73971	Let's Have Some Fun/Cozy	1977	$4
❏ 870214-7	Many Mistakes/Contagious	1988	$3
❏ 76015	Move Your Boogie Body/ Love's What It's All About	1979	$4
❏ 880255-7	Sexomatic/Sexomatic (Bonus Beats)	1984	$3
❏ 73833	Shake Your Rump to the Funk/Summer of Our Love	1976	$4
❏ 810435-7	She Talks to Me with Her Body/Anticipation	1983	$4
❏ 74048	Shine/Are You Being Real	1979	$4
❏ 73915	Spellbound/You're So Sexy	1977	$4
❏ 872102-7	Struck by You/Your Place or Mine	1989	$3
❏ 872102-7 [PS]	Struck by You/Your Place or Mine	1989	$3
❏ 76036	Today is the Day/Loving You Is My Occupation	1980	$4
❏ 73888	Too Hot to Stop (Pt. 1)/ Bang Bang (Stick 'Em Up)	1977	$4
STAX			
❏ 3216	Holy Ghost/Monster	1978	$5
VOLT			
❏ 158	A Hard Day's Night/I Want Someone	1968	$6
❏ 4007	Copy Cat/In the Middle	1968	$6
❏ 4081	Dance, Dance, Dance/ Memphis at Sunrise	1972	$5
❏ 4011	Don't Stop Dancing/Don't Stop Dancing (Part 2)	1969	$6
❏ 154	Give Everybody Some/ Don't Do That	1967	$6
❏ 4097	God Is Watching/It Ain't Easy	1973	$5
❏ 4019	Midnight Cowboy/A.J. The Housefly	1969	$6
❏ 4050	Montego Bay/Humpin'	1971	$5
❏ 4033	Song and Dance/I Thank You	1970	$6
❏ 4073	Son of Shaft/Song and Dance	1972	$5
❏ 148	Soul Finger/Knucklehead	1967	$8
BARBARA AND THE BELIEVERS			
CAPITOL			
❏ 5866	When You Wish Upon a Star/ What Can Happen to Me Now	1967	$20
BARBARA AND THE BOYS			
DOT			
❏ 15794	Hooty Sapperticker/Cobra	1958	$20
BARBARA AND THE BROWNS			
STAX			
❏ 150	Big Party/You Belong to Her	1964	$30
❏ 164	I Don't Want Trouble/My Lover	1965	$20
❏ 158	Please Be Honest with Me/In My Heart	1964	$20
BARBARIANS, THE			
JOY			
❏ 290	Hey Little Bird/You've Got to Understand	1964	$60
LAURIE			
❏ 3308	Are You a Boy or Are You a Girl/Take It or Leave It	1965	$30
❏ 3326	Moulty/I'll Keep On Seeing You	1965	$30
❏ 3321	Susie Q/What the New Breed Say	1965	$30
BARBARY, RICHARD			
A&M			
❏ 1019	Call On Me/Like You, Babe	1969	$6

Number	Title	Yr	NM
SPRING			
❏ 701	Get Right/When Johnny Comes Marching Home	1967	$8
BARBEES, THE			
STEPP			
❏ 236	The Wind/Que Pasa	1963	$200
BARBER, CHRIS			
ATLANTIC			
❏ 2016	Hush-a-Bye/You Don't Understand	1959	$15
LAURIE			
❏ 3154	It Looks Like a Big Night Tonight/King Kong	1963	$15
❏ 3022	Petite Fleur/Wild Cat Blues	1958	$20
❏ 3022 [PS]	Petite Fleur/Wild Cat Blues	1958	$30
❏ 3057	Swanee River/ Lonesome	1960	$15
LONDON			
❏ 9571V	The Loneliness of the Long Distance Runner/ Valley of Roses	1963	$15
BARBER, FRANK			
VICTORY			
❏ 1001	Hooked on Big Bands (Glenn Miller Medley)/Hooked on Big Bands (Duke Ellington Medley)	1982	$4
BARBER, GLENN			
CENTURY 21			
❏ 101	Love Songs Just for You/ Go Home Little Girl	1978	$6
❏ 100	What's the Name of That Song?/I Can't Find a Way (To Be Free)	1978	$6
D			
❏ 1017	Hello Sadness/Same Old Fool Tomorrow	1958	$50
❏ 1128	The Window/Another You	1960	$50
GRT			
❏ 071	It Took a Drunk (To Drive God's Message Home)/If I Thought for One Moment	1976	$6
HICKORY			
❏ 1605	Blue Eyes Crying in the Rain/ The World You Live In	1971	$8
❏ 1517	Don't Worry 'Bout the Mule (Just Load the Wagon)/ Reflex Reaction	1968	$8
❏ 1618	Fat Albert/Betty Ann	1971	$8
❏ 1494	Go Home Letter (I Wish That I Were You)/Who Made You That Way	1968	$10
❏ 1533	Gonna Make My Mama Proud of Me/You Can't Get Here from There	1969	$8
❏ 1593	I Committed the Crime/ Six Years and a Day	1971	$8
❏ 1527	I Don't Want No More of the Cheese/Motor Mouth Harry	1969	$8
❏ 1626	I'm the Man on Susie's Mind/ Satan's Painted Woman	1972	$8
❏ 1666	It's a Beautiful Thing/That's How a Coward Tells an Angel	1973	$8
❏ 1568	Poison Red Berries/Abilene	1970	$8
❏ 1557	She Cheats on Me/Who's Taking the Picture	1969	$8
❏ 1576	Where There's Smoke/Al	1970	$8
KIK			
❏ 912	A Woman's Touch/ (B-side unknown)	1981	$6
MMI			
❏ 1029	Everybody Wants to Disco/Most Wanted Man in Tennessee	1979	$6
❏ 1031	Woman's Touch/Most Wanted Man in Tennessee	1979	$6
SIMS			
❏ 148	How Can I Forget You/ Rain Check	1963	$20
STARDAY			
❏ 214	Ain't It Funny/Livin' High and Wide	1955	$60
❏ 699	Dancing Shoes/Knock Knock	1964	$15
❏ 741	Happy Birthday Broken Heart/Let's Take the Fear (Out of Being Close)	1965	$15
❏ 166	Ice Water/Ring Around the Moon	1954	$200
❏ 722	Loneliest Man in Town/ She's Out of Our World	1965	$15
❏ 196	Married Man/Poor Man's Baby	1955	$60
❏ 249	Shadow My Baby/ Feeling No Pain	1956	$300

Number	Title	Yr	NM
676	Stronger Than Dirt/If Anyone Can Show Cause	1964	$15

SUNBIRD

Number	Title	Yr	NM
7551	First Love Feelings/What's the Name of That Song	1980	$5

UNITED ARTISTS

Number	Title	Yr	NM
512	I Can't Stop Part 1/I Can't Stop Part 2	1962	$30
337	Most Beautiful/Night Without End	1961	$30

BARBIERI, GATO
A&M

Number	Title	Yr	NM
1916	Don't Cry Rochelle/Europa (Earth's Cry Heaven's Smile)	1977	$4
1885	Fiesta/Behind the Rain	1976	$5
2141	Firepower/Lions Also Cry	1979	$4
1857	I Want You/(B-side unknown)	1976	$5
2006	Midnight Tango/Nostalgia	1978	$4
2066	Poinciana (Song of the Tree)/Evil Eyes	1978	$4
2189	Secret Fiesta/Sophia	1979	$4

UNITED ARTISTS

Number	Title	Yr	NM
XW-175	Last Tango in Paris/Return Tango	1973	$4

BARBOUR, KEITH
BARNABY

Number	Title	Yr	NM
2036	A Pound of Peaches/Music Sweet Music	1971	$5

EPIC

Number	Title	Yr	NM
10598	Alicia/Sweet Mary Sunday	1970	$6
10575	Bake Me a Woman/If I Could Only Touch You	1970	$6
10486	Echo Park/Here I Am Losing You	1969	$6
10652	In the Quiet of Your Love/My God and I	1970	$6

BARCLAY JAMES HARVEST
HARVEST

Number	Title	Yr	NM
3501	Thank You/Medicine Man	1972	$5

MCA

Number	Title	Yr	NM
40795	Hymn/Our Kid's Kid	1977	$4

POLYDOR

Number	Title	Yr	NM
15104	Crazy City/Child of the Universe	1975	$4
14546	Loving Is Easy (Fantasy)/Turning in Circles	1979	$4

SIRE

Number	Title	Yr	NM
4112	Brother Thrush/Poor Wages	1969	$8
4105	Early Morning/Mr. Sunshine	1969	$8

BARD, ANNETTE
IMPERIAL

Number	Title	Yr	NM
5643	What Difference Does It Make/Alibi	1960	$60

BARDENS, PETE
CAPITOL

Number	Title	Yr	NM
B-44192	Gold/In Dreams	1988	$4
B-44192 [PS]	Gold/In Dreams	1988	$4
B-44080	In Dreams/Many Happy Endings	1987	$4
B-44080 [PS]	In Dreams/Many Happy Endings	1987	$4

BARDEUX
ENIGMA

Number	Title	Yr	NM
B-75047	I Love to Bass/I Love to Bass (Dance Mix)	1989	$4
B-75016	Magic Carpet Ride/When We Kiss	1988	$3
B-75016 [PS]	Magic Carpet Ride/When We Kiss	1988	$5
B-75021	Three Time Lover/Bleeding Heart	1988	$3
B-75018	When We Kiss/Magic Carpet Ride	1988	$3
B-75018 [PS]	When We Kiss/Magic Carpet Ride	1988	$5

BARDS, THE (1)
BURDETTE

Number	Title	Yr	NM
103	I Want You/Freedom Catcher	1971	$8

CAPITOL

Number	Title	Yr	NM
2148	The Owl and the Pussycat/The Light of Love	1968	$10
2148 [PS]	The Owl and the Pussycat/The Light of Love	1968	$30

JERDEN

Number	Title	Yr	NM
907	Good Time Charlie's Got the Blues/Tunesmith	1969	$15

PARROT

Number	Title	Yr	NM
351	Day by Day/Wadda Wadda	1970	$12
337	Good Time Charlie's Got the Blues/Tunesmith	1969	$10
344	Our Love/Jubilation	1970	$10

PICCADILLY

Number	Title	Yr	NM
242	Our Love/Jubilation	1967	$15
224	The Owl and the Pussycat/The Light of Love	1966	$30

BARDS, THE (2)
DAWN

Number	Title	Yr	NM
209	Gravy/Avalon	1954	$250
208	I'm a Wine Drinker/Easy Going Baby	1954	$250

BARE, BOBBY, AND SKEETER DAVIS
RCA VICTOR

Number	Title	Yr	NM
47-8496	A Dear John Letter/Too Used to Being with You	1965	$10

BARE, BOBBY, NORMA JEAN, & LIZ ANDERSON
RCA VICTOR

Number	Title	Yr	NM
47-8963	The Game of Triangles/Bye Bye Bye	1966	$10

BARE, BOBBY
CAPITOL

Number	Title	Yr	NM
F3686	Darling Don't/Life of a Fool	1957	$40
F3557	Down on the Corner of Love/Another Love Has Ended	1956	$40
F3771	The Livin' End/Beggar	1957	$40

COLUMBIA

Number	Title	Yr	NM
04092	Diet Song/Stacy Brown Got Two	1983	$4
02577	Dropping Out of Sight/She Is Gone	1981	$4
11365	Food Blues/Used Cars	1980	$4
10891	Healin'/Love Is a Cold Wind	1979	$4
02895	If You Ain't Got Nothing (You've Got Nothing To Lose)/Golden Memories	1982	$4
03149	(I'm Not) A Candle in the Wind/Cold Day in Hell	1982	$4
03628	It's a Dirty Job/Caught in the Spotlight	1983	$4

— A-side with Lacy J. Dalton

Number	Title	Yr	NM
02038	Learning to Live Again/Appaloosa Rider	1981	$4
03334	Praise the Lord and Send Me the Money/I've Been Rained On Too	1982	$4
10831	Sleep Tight, Good Night Man/Hot Afternoon	1978	$5
02414	Take Me As I Am (Or Let Me Go)/White Freight Liner Blues	1981	$4
11259	Tequila Sheila/Quaaludes Again	1980	$4
10998	Till I Gain Control Again/I'll Feel a Whole Lot Better	1979	$4
10690	Too Many Nights Alone/A Yard Full of Rusty Cars	1978	$5
11408	Willie Jones/If That Ain't Love	1980	$4

EMI AMERICA

Number	Title	Yr	NM
8317	Better Not Look Down/Wait Until Tomorrow	1986	$3
8279	When I Get Home/Party of the First Part	1985	$3

EPIC

Number	Title	Yr	NM
10652	My God and I/In the Quiet of Your Love	1970	$6

— B-side by Keith Barbour

FRATERNITY

Number	Title	Yr	NM
878	Book of Love/Lorena	1961	$30
861	I'm Hanging Up My Rifle/That's Where I Wanna Be	1959	$50
885	Sailor Man/Island of Love	1961	$30
867	Sweet Singing Sam/More Than a Poor Boy Could Give	1960	$40
892	The Day My Rainbow Fell/That Mean Old Clock	1961	$30

MERCURY

Number	Title	Yr	NM
73148	Come Sundown/Woman You Have Been a Friend to Me	1970	$6
73097	How I Got to Memphis/It's Freezing in El Paso	1970	$6
73203	Please Don't Tell Me How the Story Ends/Where Have All the Seasons Gone	1971	$6
73236	Short and Sweet/A Million Miles to the City	1971	$6
73317	Sylvia's Mother/Music City U.S.A.	1972	$6
73279	What Am I Gonna Do/Love Forever	1972	$6

RCA

Number	Title	Yr	NM
PB-10790	Drop Kick Me, Jesus/Baby Wants to Boogie	1976	$6
PB-11673	Hurricane Shirley/Crazy Arms	1979	$5

— B-side by Willie Nelson

Number	Title	Yr	NM
PB-10902	Look Who I'm Cheatin' On Tonight/If You Think I'm Crazy Now (You Should Have Seen Me When I Was a Kid)	1977	$5
PB-10718	Put a Little Lovin' on Me/Those City Lights	1976	$5

RCA VICTOR

Number	Title	Yr	NM
47-8238	500 Miles Away from Home/It All Depends On Linda	1963	$20
PB-10318	Alimony/Daddy's Been Around the House Too Long	1975	$5
47-9568	A Little Bit Later On Down the Line/Don't Do Like I Done, Son (Do What I Say)	1968	$8
PB-10223	Back in Huntsville Again/Warm and Free	1975	$5
47-9098	Charleston Railroad Tavern/Vincennes	1967	$8
47-9191	Come Kiss Me Love/Sandy's Crying Again	1967	$8
PB-10409	Cowboys and Daddys/High Plains Jamboree	1975	$5
APBO-0197	Daddy What If/Restless Wind	1973	$5
GB-10166	Daddy What If/Ride Me Down Easy	1975	$3

— Gold Standard Series issue

Number	Title	Yr	NM
47-8146	Dear Waste Basket/I'd Fight the World	1963	$15
47-8183	Detroit City/Heart of Ice	1963	$20
47-8183 [PS]	Detroit City/Heart of Ice	1963	$30
47-9450	Find Out What's Happening/When Am I Ever Gonna Settle Down	1968	$8
47-8443	Four Strong Winds/Take Me Home	1964	$15
74-0264	God Bless America Again/Baby, What Else Can I Do	1969	$6
47-8358	Have I Stayed Away Too Long/More Than a Poor Boy Can Give	1964	$15
47-8395	He Was a Friend of Mine/When I'm Gone	1964	$15
47-8988	Homesick/Guess I'll Move On Down the Line	1966	$12
47-8083	I Don't Believe I'll Fall in Love Today/To Whom It May Concern	1962	$15
47-8083 [PS]	I Don't Believe I'll Fall in Love Today/To Whom It May Concern	1962	$30
74-0866	I Hate Goodbyes/Fallin' Apart	1973	$6
47-8758	In the Same Old Way/Long Black Veil	1965	$10
47-8571	It's Alright/She Picked a Perfect Day	1965	$10
74-0110	(Margie's At) The Lincoln Park Inn/Rainy Day in Richmond	1969	$6
APBO-0261	Marie Laveau/Mermaid	1974	$5
GB-10496	Marie Laveau/Mermaid	1975	$3

— Gold Standard Series issue

Number	Title	Yr	NM
47-8294	Miller's Cave/Jeannie's Last Kiss	1963	$15
47-8032	Shame on Me/Above and Beyond	1962	$15
AMAO-0119	Shame on Me/Above and Beyond	1973	$5
PB-10096	Singin' in the Kitchen/You Are	1974	$5

— As "Bobby Bare and the Family"

Number	Title	Yr	NM
GB-10495	Singin' in the Kitchen/You Are	1975	$3

— Gold Standard Series issue

Number	Title	Yr	NM
47-8699	Talk Me Some Sense/Delia's Gone	1965	$10
47-9314	The Piney Wood Hills/They Covered Up the Old Swimmin' Hole	1967	$8
47-8851	The Streets of Baltimore/She Took My Sunshine Away	1966	$10
47-9643	The Town That Broke My Heart/My Baby	1968	$8
PB-10556	The Winner/Up Against the Wall Redneck Mother	1976	$5
47-8509	Times Are Gettin' Hard/One Day at a Time	1965	$10
PB-10037	Where'd I Come From/Scarlet Ribbons	1974	$5

— By "Bobby Bare, Jr., and Mommy"

Number	Title	Yr	NM
GB-10497	Where'd I Come From/Scarlet Ribbons	1975	$3

— Gold Standard Series issue

Number	Title	Yr	NM
74-0202	Which One Will It Be/My Frame of Mind	1969	$6

RICE

Number	Title	Yr	NM
5057	Christian Soldier/Dropping Out of Sight	1973	$5

Number	Title	Yr	NM
❑ 5066	I Took a Memory to Lunch/ It's Freezing in St. Paul	1974	$5
❑ 5060	Love Forever/A Million Miles to the City	1973	$5

BARGE, GENE
CHECKER

Number	Title	Yr	NM
❑ 1110	Fine Twine/The "In" Crowd	1965	$10
❑ 839	Way Down Home/Country	1954	$40

LEGRAND

Number	Title	Yr	NM
❑ 1006	Thinking of You/Autumn Leaves	1961	$50

PARAMOUNT

Number	Title	Yr	NM
❑ 0160	Love Theme from "The Godfather"/Gina	1972	$5

BARIN, PETE
SABINA

Number	Title	Yr	NM
❑ 512	Loneliest Guy in the World/ Look Out for Cindy	1962	$40
❑ 504	So Wrong/Broken Heart	1962	$60

BARITONES, THE
DORE

Number	Title	Yr	NM
❑ 501	After School Rock/ Sentimental Baby	1958	$50

BARKER BROTHERS, THE
DECCA

Number	Title	Yr	NM
❑ 9-30811	Lovin' Honey/Sunbeam	1959	$40
❑ 9-30753	Well All Right... Friday Night/ How Can You Tell If It's Love	1958	$40

KENT

Number	Title	Yr	NM
❑ 302	Hey Little Mama/I'm in Love with My Teacher	1958	$125

RCA VICTOR

Number	Title	Yr	NM
❑ 47-8405	Shh, Don't Wake Me Up/I Gotta Know	1964	$30

VALIANT

Number	Title	Yr	NM
❑ 6018	Drifter/Tonight, Baby, Tonight	1962	$15

BARKER, DELBERT
KING

Number	Title	Yr	NM
❑ 5031	Amanda/Broken Heart	1957	$40
❑ 6042	It Can't Last Long/ Color Me Gone	1966	$10
❑ 4951	That's a Sin/No Good, Robin Hood	1956	$40
❑ 5008	Wild Heart/There Must Be a Way	1957	$40

BARKER, FRANCINE
COLUMBIA

Number	Title	Yr	NM
❑ 4-44771	Angels in the Sky/A Love You Can Depend On	1969	$10
❑ 4-44614	Don't You Know Love When You See It/Mr. D.J.	1968	$8
❑ 4-44614 [PS]	Don't You Know Love When You See It/Mr. D.J.	1968	$15
❑ 4-44910	Traces/Angels in the Sky	1969	$15

BARKLEY, BRUCE
COLUMBIA

Number	Title	Yr	NM
❑ 4-21468	Fingertip Rhythm/Lookin' Around	1955	$30
❑ 4-21267	Memphis Blues/Jumpin' Jack	1954	$30
❑ 4-21409	My Blue Heaven/Pretty Baby	1955	$30
❑ 4-21330	Wild Honey/Tantalizin' Rhythm	1954	$30

BARLOW, DEAN, AND THE BACHELORS
EARL

Number	Title	Yr	NM
❑ 102	Baby/(B-side unknown)	1955	$1000
❑ 101	Delores/(B-side unknown)	1955	$1000

BARLOW, JACK
ANTIQUE

Number	Title	Yr	NM
❑ 106	The Man on Page 602/ Vinegar in My Wine	1975	$8

—As "Zoot Fenster"

DIAL

Number	Title	Yr	NM
❑ 4024	Dear Ma/I Love Her Still	1965	$15
❑ 4012	I Love Country Music/ Number One in the Nation	1965	$15

DOT

Number	Title	Yr	NM
❑ 17139	Baby, Ain't That Love/ It Ain't No Big Thing	1968	$8

Number	Title	Yr	NM
❑ 17433	Baby, Don't You Cry None/ You've Still Got a Hold on Me	1972	$8
❑ 17212	Birmingham Blues/Papa Didn't Give Me No Love	1969	$8
❑ 17396	Catch the Wind/Tonight I'm Wantin' You Again	1971	$8
❑ 17343	Child Bride/A Little Friendly Advice	1970	$8
❑ 17366	Dayton, Ohio/Where There Ain't No Fools	1970	$8
❑ 17446	How Much Love Will It Take/That's Enough	1973	$8
❑ 17468	Oh Woman/That's Enough	1973	$8
❑ 17287	Pauline/Singing Country Fool	1969	$8
❑ 17381	Somewhere in Texas/ You Make My World	1971	$8
❑ 17414	They Call the Wind Maria/It's a Long Way Back to Georgia	1972	$8

EPIC

Number	Title	Yr	NM
❑ 10185	El Dorado/Long Green	1967	$15

SOMA

Number	Title	Yr	NM
❑ 1420	After All/49-51	1964	$20
❑ 1175	Step Down/House of Stone	1962	$20

BARLOW, RANDY
CAPITOL

Number	Title	Yr	NM
❑ 3883	Throw Away the Pages/ Hello Pawnshop	1974	$6
❑ 3762	Whiskey River/Nobody Likes to See a Big Man Cry	1973	$6

GAZELLE

Number	Title	Yr	NM
❑ 413	California Lady/We're Crazy	1977	$6
❑ 001	Don't Leave Me Lonely Loving You/For a Few Dollars More	1983	$5
❑ 217	Goodnight My Love/ Don't Worry I'm Okay	1976	$6
❑ 280	Lonely Eyes/One Night Stand	1976	$6
❑ 330	Twenty-Four Hours from Tulsa/The Bottle Took His Wife (And My Wife)	1976	$6
❑ 427	Walk Away with Me/ Johnny Orphan	1977	$6

JAMEX

Number	Title	Yr	NM
❑ 002	Love Was Born/Chester's Eyes	1981	$6

MERCURY

Number	Title	Yr	NM
❑ 72808	Color Blind/St. Clair	1968	$10

PAID

Number	Title	Yr	NM
❑ 116	Dixie Man/Don't Give Up on Me	1980	$5
❑ 133	Love Dies Hard/New York City Cowboys-Deep in the Heart of Texas	1981	$5
❑ 144	Try Me/Why Go Searchin' for Something More	1981	$5
❑ 110	Willow Run/Can't Believe I Fell for That Line	1980	$5

REPUBLIC

Number	Title	Yr	NM
❑ 044	Another Easy Lovin' Night/ Louisiana Delta	1979	$5
❑ 034	Fall in Love with Me Tonight/ One More Time	1978	$5
❑ 049	Lay Back in the Arms of Someone/Musical Hearts	1979	$5
❑ 017	Slow and Easy/Stranger I'm Married	1978	$5
❑ 039	Sweet Melinda/Heaven Here We Come	1979	$5

BARMBY, SHANE
MERCURY

Number	Title	Yr	NM
❑ 874168-7	Let's Talk About Us/ (B-side unknown)	1989	$3

BARNABY BYE
ATLANTIC

Number	Title	Yr	NM
❑ 3266	Can't Live This Way/Happy Was the Day We Met	1975	$5
❑ 2984	I Think I'm Gonna Like It/Dreamer	1973	$5
❑ 3244	Take Me With You/Blonde	1975	$5

BARNES, BENNY
D

Number	Title	Yr	NM
❑ 1052	Gold Records in the Snow/ Happy Little Blue Bird	1959	$70

HALL-WAY

Number	Title	Yr	NM
❑ 1203	A Bar with No Beer/ Headed for Heartbreak	1964	$10
❑ 1207	It's Good to Be Home/ For a Minute There	1965	$10

KAPP

Number	Title	Yr	NM
❑ 859	A Bar with No Beer/ Headed for Heartbreak	1967	$8
❑ 912	Sweet Suzannah/It's My Mind That's Broken	1968	$8

MEGA

Number	Title	Yr	NM
❑ 0071	Woman, Leave My Mind Alone/I'm Just Here to Get My Baby Off My Mind	1972	$5

MERCURY

Number	Title	Yr	NM
❑ 71552	Beggar to a King/The Fastest Gun Alive	1959	$30
❑ 71284	Moon Over My Shoulder/ Lonely Street	1958	$30
❑ 71048	Poor Man's Riches/ Those Who Know	1957	$30
❑ 71057	Poor Old Me/Penalty	1957	$30
❑ 71637	Pretty Little Girl/ Message in the Wind	1960	$30
❑ 71600	That-a Boy Willie/Token of Love	1960	$30
❑ 71896	The World's Worst Loser/I Changed My Mind	1961	$30

MUSICOR

Number	Title	Yr	NM
❑ 1169	Diesel Smoke/That's How I Need You	1966	$8
❑ 1127	Have We Really Tried/ Heartache's Comin'	1965	$8
❑ 1247	I'm Her Lover/Same Old Boat	1967	$8
❑ 1100	Let Me Live As Long As I Can/Tea Leaves Don't Lie	1965	$8
❑ 1277	Let One Call Do It All/ Rosanna Martin	1967	$8
❑ 1194	Stand By Your Window/ You're Not There	1966	$8
❑ 1223	What's the Matter with Me/ Third Time Down	1966	$8

PLAYBOY

Number	Title	Yr	NM
❑ 5808	I've Got Some Gettin' Over You to Do/I'll Drink to That	1977	$8
❑ 6084	Little Brown Paper Bag Blues/(B-side unknown)	1976	$8

RCA VICTOR

Number	Title	Yr	NM
❑ 47-9830	An Old Memory Got in My Eye/You're Everywhere	1970	$6
❑ 74-0271	Pressure Cooker/To the Ones I Love	1969	$6

STARDAY

Number	Title	Yr	NM
❑ 236	Once Again/No Fault of Mine	1956	$40
❑ 262	Poor Man's Riches/ Those Who Know	1956	$40

BARNES, BILLY
UNITED ARTISTS

Number	Title	Yr	NM
❑ 311	C.C. Rider/Here Am I	1961	$30
❑ 218	Home Again/I Wish I Didn't Love You So	1960	$30
❑ 157	I'm Coming to See You/ What Am I Supposed to Do	1959	$30

BARNES, GEORGE
DECCA

Number	Title	Yr	NM
❑ 30398	Tammy/Around the World	1957	$30

MERCURY

Number	Title	Yr	NM
❑ 71968	Transville/Spooky	1962	$40

BARNES, J.J.
BUDDAH

Number	Title	Yr	NM
❑ 120	Evidence/I'll Keep Coming Back	1969	$20

CONTEMPO

Number	Title	Yr	NM
❑ 7003	How Long/The Erroll Flynn	1977	$5

GROOVESVILLE

Number	Title	Yr	NM
❑ 1006	Baby Please Come Back Home/Chains of Love	1967	$20
❑ 1009	Easy Living/(B-side unknown)	1967	$20

INVASION

Number	Title	Yr	NM
❑ 1001	My Baby/(You Still) My Baby	1970	$10

KABLE

Number	Title	Yr	NM
❑ 437	Won't You Let Me Know/My Love Came Tumbling Down	1960	$60

MAGIC TOUCH

Number	Title	Yr	NM
❑ 1000	To An Early Grave/Cloudy Days	1970	$10

MICKAY'S

Number	Title	Yr	NM
❑ 4472	Get a Hold of Yourself/ Lonely No More	1964	$100

REVILOT

Number	Title	Yr	NM
❑ 216	Hold On to It/Now She's Gone	1968	$20
❑ 218	I'll Keep Coming Back/ Sad Day a-Comin'	1968	$20
❑ 222	Our Love Is in the Pocket/ All Your Goodies Are Gone	1968	$100
❑ 225	So-Called Friends/ Now She's Gone	1968	$20

RICH

Number	Title	Yr	NM
❑ 1005	Won't You Let Me Know/My Love Came Tumbling Down	1960	$125
❑ 1737	Won't You Let Me Know/My Love Came Tumbling Down	1962	$30

RIC-TIC

Number	Title	Yr	NM
❑ 115	Day Tripper/Don't Bring Me Bad News	1966	$20
❑ 117	Deeper in Love/Say It	1966	$20
❑ 106	Please Let Me In/I Think I Found a Love	1965	$20

RING

Number	Title	Yr	NM
❑ 101	She Ain't Ready/Poor-Unfortunate Me	1964	$30

VOLT

Number	Title	Yr	NM
❑ 4027	Got to Get Rid of You/Snowflakes	1969	$20

BARNES, JIMMY
GEFFEN

Number	Title	Yr	NM
❑ 28693	I'd Die to Be with You Tonight/Piece of My Heart	1986	$3
❑ 27727	I'm Still on Your Side/Lessons in Love	1988	$3
❑ 27920	Too Much Ain't Enough Love/Do or Die	1988	$3
❑ 27920 [PS]	Too Much Ain't Enough Love/Do or Die	1988	$3
❑ 28749	Working Class Man/Boys Cry Out for War	1986	$3

BARNES, KATHY
MGM

Number	Title	Yr	NM
❑ 14836	Be Honest with Me/Paper Cups	1975	$6
❑ 14797	I'm Available (For You to Hold Me Tight)/Come to Me	1975	$6
❑ 14822	Shhh/I Will	1975	$6

REPUBLIC

Number	Title	Yr	NM
❑ 037	Body Talkin'/(B-side unknown)	1979	$5
❑ 376	Catch the Wind/Starve a Fever	1977	$5
❑ 338	Good 'n' Country/One a Day Heartaches	1976	$5
❑ 021	I'm in Love with Love/Mr. Dream Weaver	1978	$5
❑ 046	Love at First Touch/Looking for Someone to Love	1979	$5
❑ 223	Sleeping with a Memory/Hang My Head	1976	$5
❑ 223 [PS]	Sleeping with a Memory/Hang My Head	1976	$12
❑ 293	Someday Soon/Your Love (Makes Our Love So Easy)	1976	$5
❑ 012	Something's Burning/Take It and Go	1977	$5
❑ 018	That Silver Haired Daddy of Mine/(B-side unknown)	1978	$5
❑ 005	The Sun in Dixie/Can't Make It Without You	1977	$5
❑ 389	Tweedle-O-Twill/There You Go Doin' It Again	1977	$5

BARNES, KATHY AND LARRY
REPUBLIC

Number	Title	Yr	NM
❑ 369	If We Can't Do It Right/(B-side unknown)	1977	$5

BARNES, LARRY
SMASH

Number	Title	Yr	NM
❑ 2004	I Feel Love Comin' On/Rags Is Rags	1965	$15

BARNES, MAX D.
OVATION

Number	Title	Yr	NM
❑ 1149	Cowboys Are Common As Sin/Only for You	1980	$5
❑ 1139	Dear Mr. President/Patricia	1979	$5
❑ 1164	Don't Ever Leave Me Again/Singer of Sad Songs	1981	$5
❑ 1158	Heaven on a Freight Train/Patricia	1980	$5
❑ 1142	Mean Woman Blues/Too Far Gone to Find	1980	$5

POLYDOR

Number	Title	Yr	NM
❑ 14419	Allegheny Lady/All the Way In	1977	$6
❑ 14466	She Loves My Troubles Away/This Workin' Man's Got You	1978	$6

BARNES, SIDNEY
BLUE CAT

Number	Title	Yr	NM
❑ 125	I Hurt on the Other Side/Switchy Walk	1966	$200

CHESS

Number	Title	Yr	NM
❑ 2094	Baloney/Old Times	1970	$12

PARACHUTE

Number	Title	Yr	NM
❑ 521	Hold On I'm Coming/Your Love Is So Good to Me	1978	$4

RED BIRD

Number	Title	Yr	NM
❑ Oct-0054	I Hurt on the Other Side/Switchy Walk	1966	$50

BARNETT, BILLY
TEX

Number	Title	Yr	NM
❑ 105	Tired of Your Honky-Tonk Love/One Day Nearer Home	1957	$250

BARNETT, BOBBY
CIN KAY

Number	Title	Yr	NM
❑ 128	Burn Atlanta Down/Pody and Barbara	1978	$5

COLUMBIA

Number	Title	Yr	NM
❑ 4-44861	Drink Canada Dry/Image on Your Mind	1969	$8
❑ 4-44589	Love Me, Love Me/The End of the Lyin'	1968	$8

K-ARK

Number	Title	Yr	NM
❑ 741	Down, Down Came the World/Too Tough to Die	1967	$12
❑ 839	Home Away from Home/New World Tomorrow	1968	$12
❑ 804	Please Come Home/I Have No Conscience (When Passion Commands)	1968	$10
❑ 915	Stepping Stone/Little Black Cloud	1969	$10
❑ 766	The Losing Kind/A Long Way to Go	1967	$10

RAZORBACK

Number	Title	Yr	NM
❑ 306	This Old Heart/(B-side unknown)	1960	$30

REPRISE

Number	Title	Yr	NM
❑ 20099	Crazy Little Lover/Last of the Angels	1962	$20
❑ 20133	Same Old Love/Temptation's Calling	1962	$20

SIMS

Number	Title	Yr	NM
❑ 231	Cheatin' Kathleen/Best Man	1965	$20
❑ 135	I Fall in Love with Every Pretty Girl I See/She Looks Good to the Crowd	1963	$20
❑ 198	Mismatch/Moaning the Blues	1964	$20
❑ 159	Worst of Luck/Working Man	1963	$20

BARNHILL, JOE
UNIVERSAL

Number	Title	Yr	NM
❑ UVL-66000	Becky Morgan (Cotton Pickin' Time)/For Cryin' Out Loud	1989	$4
❑ UVL-66032	Good As Gone/Becky Morgan (Cotton Pickin' Time)	1989	$3

BARNHILL, LESLEE
REPUBLIC

Number	Title	Yr	NM
❑ 040	Bad Day for a Breakup/I'm Still in Love with You	1979	$5
❑ 022	By Your Side/(B-side unknown)	1978	$5
❑ 014	Let's Call It a Day (And Get On with the Night)/I Love the Way You Do What You Do	1978	$5
❑ 026	Someday I'd Like to Love You When You're Mine/(B-side unknown)	1978	$5

BARNUM, H.B.
CAPITOL

Number	Title	Yr	NM
❑ 2036	Baby, Love Me/The Bad Luck's on Me	1967	$15
❑ 5440	Gimme Some/Don't Forget 127th Street	1965	$15
❑ 5748	Gotta Go/Nobody Wants to Hear Nobody's Trouble	1966	$15
❑ 2317	Happiness/It's Just a Game, Love	1968	$12
❑ 5932	Heartbreaker/Searchin' for My Soul	1967	$30
❑ 5477	I Can't Help It/Dance with Me	1965	$15
❑ 5391	I'm a Man/The Record	1965	$15

ELDO

Number	Title	Yr	NM
❑ 111	Lost Love/Hallelujah	1960	$20

IMPERIAL

Number	Title	Yr	NM
❑ 66011	Backstage/Rented Tuxedo	1964	$15
❑ 5530	Blue Moon/Tia-Juana	1958	$50
❑ 66063	Calypso Blues/Three Room Flat	1964	$15
❑ 66074	Eternal Love/So What	1964	$15
❑ 66046	Skakiaan (Skokiaan)/Ska Drums	1964	$15

RCA VICTOR

Number	Title	Yr	NM
❑ 47-7960	Baby Baby Baby (All the Time)/How Many More Times	1961	$20
❑ 47-8014	Call On Me/Oh My Achin' Back	1962	$20
❑ 47-8112	Lonely Hearts/It Hurts Too Much to Cry	1962	$70

UNITED ARTISTS

Number	Title	Yr	NM
❑ XW338	Theme from "5 on the Back Hand Side"/Keep It Comin'	1973	$5

BARON, ELLIOTT
GOLDEN WORLD

Number	Title	Yr	NM
❑ 11	Man to Man/The Spare Rib	1964	$200

BARONS, THE
BELLAIRE

Number	Title	Yr	NM
❑ 103	The Bandit/Wanderin'	1963	$30

DART

Number	Title	Yr	NM
❑ 126	Lonely Loretta/Lula Mae	1959	$30
❑ 134	Perfect Love/Until the Thirteenth Chime	1960	$30

DECCA

Number	Title	Yr	NM
❑ 29293	Exactly Like You/Forget About Me	1954	$120

DEMON

Number	Title	Yr	NM
❑ 1520	Gravel Gert/The Fight	1959	$20

EPIC

Number	Title	Yr	NM
❑ 9586	Don't Go Away (Pretty Little Girl)/Pledge of a Fool	1963	$40
❑ 10093	Don't Go Away (Pretty Little Girl)/Pledge of a Fool	1966	$20
❑ 9747	Lucky Star/Remember Rita	1964	$200

IMPERIAL

Number	Title	Yr	NM
❑ 5370	Cold Kisses/Searching for You	1955	$120
❑ 5397	Don't Walk Out/Once in a Lifetime	1956	$100
❑ 5343	Eternally Yours/Boom Boom	1955	$120
❑ 5343	Eternally Yours/Boom Boom	1955	$300
—Red vinyl, probably promo only			
❑ 5359	I Know I Was Wrong/My Dream, My Love	1955	$120
❑ 66057	Silence/I Just Go Wild Inside	1964	$20
❑ 5383	So Long My Darling/Crying for You Baby	1956	$120

RCA VICTOR

Number	Title	Yr	NM
❑ 47-9034	Since You're Gone/My Smile Is Bigger (Than Your Smile)	1966	$30

TENDER

Number	Title	Yr	NM
❑ 511	Drawbridge/(B-side unknown)	1958	$20

BAROQUES, THE
CHESS

Number	Title	Yr	NM
❑ 2001	Mary Jane/Iowa, A Girl's Name	1967	$20

BARRABAS
ATCO

Number	Title	Yr	NM
❑ 7059	Desperately/If	1976	$5
❑ 7027	Hi Jack/Susie Wong	1975	$5
❑ 7036	Mellow Blue (Long)/Checkmate	1975	$5

BARRACUDA
RCA VICTOR

Number	Title	Yr	NM
❑ 47-9660	The Dance of St. Francis/Lady Fingers	1968	$30
❑ 47-9660 [PS]	The Dance of St. Francis/Lady Fingers	1968	$50

BARRAN, BOB
SILVER STREAK

Number	Title	Yr	NM
❑ 311	Tom Tom Rock/Mother Goose Hop	1960	$200

BARREL, VIC
ATLANTIC

Number	Title	Yr	NM
❑ 2083	White Christmas/Footing	1960	$15

BARRETT, RICHARD
20TH FOX

Number	Title	Yr	NM
❑ 150	Lovely One/The Snake and the Bookworm	1959	$20

ATLANTIC

Number	Title	Yr	NM
❑ 2142	Some Other Guy/Tricky Dicky	1962	$20
—As "Richie Barrett			

Number	Title	Yr	NM

CRACKERJACK

❏ 4012	Summer's Love/Let Me Down Easy	1963	$20

GONE

❏ 5056	Come Softly to Me/Walking Through Dreamland	1959	$40

—With the Chantels

❏ 5060	Summer's Love/All Is Forgiven	1959	$40

—With the Chantels

METRO

❏ 20006	Lovable/Only One Way	1959	$20

MGM

❏ 12659	Body and Soul/The Party	1958	$40
❏ 12616	Smoke Gets In Your Eyes/Remember Me	1958	$40

SEVILLE

❏ 104	Dream On/I Am Yours	1960	$20

BARRETT, SUSAN

PHILIPS

❏ 40147	Between Two Loves/Chico's Girl	1963	$30
❏ 40247	The Love We Never Knew/No One But You	1964	$30

RCA VICTOR

❏ 47-8888	A Grain of Sand/She Gets Everything She Wants	1966	$30
❏ 47-9384	Sunny/Ev'ry Time We Say Goodbye	1967	$30
❏ 47-9017	Walking Happy/How Can You Hold On to a Dream	1966	$30
❏ 47-9296	What's It Gonna Be/It's No Secret	1967	$60

BARRI, STEVE

RONA

❏ 1003	Down Around the Corner/Please Let It Be You	1961	$50
❏ 1004	I Want Your Love/Story of the Ring	1961	$50
❏ 1005	Two Different Worlds/Don't Run Away from Love	1962	$50

BARRIX, BILLY

CHESS

❏ 1662	Cool Off Baby/Almost	1958	$10000

— This record has been counterfeited; most of these are obvious on sight because neither the typeface nor the blue color matches original Chess 45s of the era, the fake label is glossy and originals aren't, and the publisher information at 3 o'clock is flush left on the originals and centered on the fake. VG 5000; VG+ 7500

BARRON, BLUE

MGM

❏ 10523	Christmas Time/Santa Claus Is Coming To Town	1949	$30
❏ 11375	Santa Claus Lullaby/The Little Match Girl	1952	$30

BARRON KNIGHTS, THE

DECCA

❏ 32160	Lazy Fat People/In the Night	1967	$12

EPIC

❏ 9835	Pop Go the Workers Part 1/Part 2	1965	$15
❏ 50755	The Topical Song/The Big V-asectomy	1979	$5

BARROW, KEITH

COLUMBIA

❏ 3-10846	If It's Love You're Looking For/Joyful Music	1978	$5
❏ 3-10494	Mr. Magic Man/We've Got a Right to Be Wrong	1977	$5
❏ 3-10965	Physical Attraction/Free to Be Me	1979	$5
❏ 3-10394	Precious/(B-side unknown)	1976	$5
❏ 3-10901	Turn Me Up (Part 1)/Turn Me Up (Part 2)	1979	$5

BARRY AND THE HIGHLIGHTS

AIRMASTER

❏ 700	Christmas Bell Rock/Chil-E Baby	1960	$60

BAYE

❏ 511	Christmas Bell Rock/Chil-E Baby	1960	$60

BARRY AND THE TAMERLANES

VALIANT

❏ 6050	A Date with Judy/Pretty Things	1964	$20
❏ 6059	Gee/Don't Cry Cindy	1964	$20
❏ 6034	I Wonder What She's Doing Tonight/Don't Go	1963	$30
❏ 703	I Wonder What She's Doing Tonight/Roberta	1965	$15
❏ 6046	Lucky Guy/I Don't Want to Be Your Clown	1964	$20

BARRY AND THE TOTS

FURY

❏ 1058	Christmas Each Day of the Year/I'm a Happy Little Christmas Tree	1961	$15

BARRY, CLAUDJA

CHRYSALIS

❏ 2313	Boogie Woogie Dancin' Shoes/Love of the Hurtin' Kind	1979	$5

EPIC

❏ 34-06669	Can You Feel My Heartbeat/(Percapella)	1987	$4
❏ 34-06308	Down and Counting/(Dub)	1986	$4
❏ 34-07198	Secret Affair/Dance for Your Life	1987	$4

MIRAGE

❏ 4050	If I Do It to You/Up All Night	1982	$5

SALSOUL

❏ 2046	Dance, Dance, Dance/Why Must a Girl Love Me	1977	$6
❏ 2058	Dancin' Fever/Long Lost Friend	1978	$6
❏ 2023	Sweet Dynamite/Taste of Love	1977	$6
❏ 2065	Take It Easy/Johnny, Johnny, Please Come Home	1978	$6

BARRY, GENE

FELSTED

❏ 8648	Moonlight Gambler/Red Silk Stockings and Green Perfume	1961	$15

BARRY, JAY

ABC-PARAMOUNT

❏ 10154	A Picture of You/Sherry	1960	$20
❏ 10226	Love Bank/Love Spell	1961	$20

BARRY, JEFF

A&M

❏ 1422	Walkin' in the Sun/Whatcha Wanna Do	1973	$5

BELL

❏ 45140	Sweet Saviour/Love Has Never Let Me Down	1971	$6

DECCA

❏ 31089	Lenore/Why Does the Feeling Go Away	1960	$30

RCA VICTOR

❏ 47-7821	All You Need Is a Quarter/Teen Quartet	1960	$30
❏ 47-7477	It's Called Rock & Roll/Hip Couples	1959	$30
❏ 47-7797	The Face from Outer Space/Lovely Lips	1960	$30

RED BIRD

❏ Oct-0026	I'll Still Love You/Our Love Can Still Be Saved	1965	$20

UNITED ARTISTS

❏ 50529	Much Too Young/Where It's At	1969	$8
❏ 440	We Got Love Money Can't Buy/Welcome Home	1962	$20

BARRY, JOE

ABC DOT

❏ 17724	If You Really Want Me To, I'll Go/You're Why I'm So Lonely	1977	$4

JIN

❏ 132	Greatest Moment of My Life/Heartbroken Love	1961	$20
❏ 144	I'm a Fool to Care/I Got a Feeling	1961	$30
❏ 157	Till the End of the World/You Don't Have to Be a Baby to Cry	1962	$20

SMASH

❏ 1702	I'm a Fool to Care/I Got a Feeling	1961	$15
❏ 1745	Little Papoose/Why Did You Say Goodbye	1962	$10
❏ 1710	Teardrops in My Heart/For You Sunshine	1961	$10

BARRY, JOHN

20TH FOX

❏ 472	Theme from "Man in the Middle"/Barney's Blues	1964	$15

CAPITOL

❏ F4212	Snap 'N Whistle/Long Long	1959	$20

COLUMBIA

❏ 43320	A Man Alone/Barbara's Theme	1965	$8
❏ 44891	Midnight Cowboy/Fun City	1969	$6
❏ 45062	On Her Majesty's Secret Service/We Have All the Time in the World	1970	$6
❏ 43544	The Chase/Saturday Night Philosopher	1966	$12
❏ 44721	The Lion in Winter/To Rome	1968	$8
❏ 43801	Theme from Born Free/Goldfinger	1966	$10
❏ 45140	Theme from "The Appointment"/The More Things Change	1970	$6
❏ 43951	Wednesday's Child/Sleep Well, My Darling	1966	$10

DECCA

❏ 31815	A Man Alone (Jazz Version)/A Man Alone (Latin Version)	1965	$10

EPIC

❏ 10865	The Persuaders/The Girl with the Sun in Her Hair	1972	$6

KING

❏ 5495	Black Stockings/Get Lost Jack Frost	1961	$20

MERCURY

❏ 72261	From Russia with Love/007	1964	$15

MGM

❏ 13591	Born Free/Elsa at Play	1966	$8

UNITED ARTISTS

❏ 743	Big Shield/Zulu Stomp	1964	$12
❏ 863	From Russia with Love/James Bond Theme	1965	$10
❏ 791	Goldfinger/Troubadour	1964	$10

WARNER BROS.

❏ 7230	Highway 101/Petula	1968	$6

BARRY, LEN

AMY

❏ 11026	4-5-6 (Now I'm Alone)/Funky Night	1968	$6
❏ 11047	The Child Is Born/Wouldn't It Be Beautiful	1968	$6

CAMEO

❏ 318	Little White House/Hearts Are Trump	1964	$15

DECCA

❏ 31827	1-2-3/Bullseye	1965	$20
❏ 32011	I Struck It Rich/Love Is	1966	$10
❏ 31969	It's That Time of the Year/Happily Ever After	1966	$10
❏ 31889	Like a Baby/Happiness (Is a Girl Like You)	1966	$12
❏ 31788	Lip Sync (To the Tongue Twisters)/At the Hop '65	1965	$12
❏ 31923	Somewhere/It's a Crying Shame	1966	$12
❏ 32054	Would I Love You/You Baby	1966	$10

MERCURY

❏ 72299	Let's Do It Again/Happy Days	1964	$15

PARAMOUNT

❏ 0206	Heaven Plus Earth/I'm Marching to the Music	1973	$5

PARKWAY

❏ 969	Little White House/Hearts Are Trump	1966	$8

RCA VICTOR

❏ 47-9275	All Those Memories/Rainy Side of the Street	1967	$8
❏ 47-9150	Our Song/The Moving Finger Writes	1967	$8
❏ 47-9464	Sweet and Funny/I Like the Way	1968	$8
❏ 47-9348	The ABC's of Love/Come Rain or Shine	1967	$8

SCEPTER

❏ 12284	Bob & Carol & Ted & Alice/In My Present State of Mind	1970	$6

Number	Title	Yr	NM
❏ 12251	Put Out the Fire/Spread It On Like Butter	1969	$8

7-Inch Extended Plays

DECCA

Number	Title	Yr	NM
❏ 7-34346	1-2-3/Would I Love You?/Lip Sync (To the Tongue Twisters)/Bullseye/Treat Her Right/I.O.U.	1965	$25

— Stereo jukebox issue; small hole, plays at 33 1/3 rpm

❏ 7-34346 [PS] 1/2/2003		1965	$25

BARRY, SANDRA
PARKWAY

Number	Title	Yr	NM
❏ 943	We Were Lovers/The End of the Line	1965	$20

BARRY SISTERS, THE
ROULETTE

Number	Title	Yr	NM
❏ 4145	Saturday/Yes, My Darling Daughter	1959	$15

BART, LIONEL
LONDON

Number	Title	Yr	NM
❏ 9505	Give Us A Kiss For Christmas/How Now Brown Cow	1961	$15

BARTEL, LOU
ABC-PARAMOUNT

Number	Title	Yr	NM
❏ 9877	Blue Moon/I'm Gonna Kiss My Baby Goodnight	1957	$30

APOLLO

Number	Title	Yr	NM
❏ 473	I Pray/(Zoom) Give Me Your Tonight	1954	$200

BARTHOLOMEW, DAVE
DECCA

Number	Title	Yr	NM
❏ 48216	Tra La La/Teejim	1951	$120

IMPERIAL

Number	Title	Yr	NM
❏ 5322	Another Mule/I Want to Be with Her	1955	$60
❏ 5835	A Sunday Kind of Love/Honky Tonk Trumpet	1962	$20
❏ 5560	Button Blues/Short Subjects	1959	$30
❏ 5308	Cat Music/Jump Children	1954	$120
❏ 5350	Every Night, Every Day/Four Winds	1955	$60
❏ 5481	Hard Times (The Slop)/Cinderella	1957	$30
❏ 5460	How Could You/Barrel House	1957	$30
❏ 5702	I Cried/Somebody New	1960	$30
❏ 5803	I'm Walkin'/Going to the River	1962	$20
❏ 5408	Lovin' You/Three Time Loser	1956	$40
❏ 5714	People Are Talking/Yeah, Yeah	1961	$30
❏ 5373	Shrimp and Gumbo/An Old Cowhand from a Blues Band	1956	$50
❏ 5273	Texas Hop/When the Saints Go Marchin' In Boogie	1954	$200
❏ 5438	The Monkey/The Shuffling	1957	$30
❏ 5210	Who Drank the Beer While I Was in the Rear/The Rest of My Life	1952	$120

— Dave Bartholomew records on Imperial before 5210 are unconfirmed on 45 rpm.

❏ 5390	Would You/Turn Your Lamp Down Low	1956	$50

KING

Number	Title	Yr	NM
❏ 4585	High Flying Woman/Stormy Weather	1953	$125
❏ 4508	In the Alley/I'll Never Be the Same	1952	$200
❏ 4523	Lawdy, Lawdy, Lawd (Part 1)/Lawdy, Lawdy, Lawd (Part 2)	1952	$200
❏ 4544	My Ding-a-Ling/Bad Habit	1952	$250
❏ 4482	Sweet Home Blues/Twins	1951	$200
❏ 4559	The Golden Rule/Mother Knows Best	1952	$125

BARTLEY, CHRIS
BUDDAH

Number	Title	Yr	NM
❏ 115	I Know We Can Work It Out/(My Baby's) One Wonderful Girl AKA Sugar Baby	1969	$60
❏ 93	I'll Take the Blame/Baby I'm Yours	1969	$30

MUSICOR

Number	Title	Yr	NM
❏ 1437	Tomorrow Keeps Shining on Me/A Man, a Woman	1971	$60

VANDO

Number	Title	Yr	NM
❏ 3000	Baby, It's Wonderful/I'll Be Loving You	1967	$30
❏ 14001	I Found a Goodie/Be Mine Forever	1968	$40

Number	Title	Yr	NM
❏ DV-101	The Sweetest Thing This Side of Heaven/Love Me Baby	1967	$20
❏ 14000	Truer Words Were Never Spoken/This Feeling You Give Me	1968	$40

BARTON, EILEEN
20TH CENTURY FOX

Number	Title	Yr	NM
❏ 417	The Earth Stood Still/Patty Cake, Patty Cake	1963	$8

CORAL

Number	Title	Yr	NM
❏ 9-61227	A Husband/A Wife	1954	$15

— With Johnny Desmond

❏ 9-61247	And Then/I Have to Tell You	1954	$20
❏ 9-61057	Anytime, Anywhere/Toys	1953	$20
❏ 9-61175	Bright Eyed and Bushy Tailed/Twilight Time in Tennessee	1954	$30

— With Jimmy Wakely

❏ 9-60592	Cry/Hold Me Just a Little Longer, Daddy	1951	$30
❏ 9-61530	Cry Me a River/Come Home	1955	$15
❏ 9-61109	Don't Ask Me Why/Way Up There	1953	$20
❏ 9-61459	Here I Am in Love Again/Apollo Umberto Silvano	1955	$15
❏ 9-61413	How Could You Forget Me/He Asked Me	1955	$15
❏ 9-61377	How Ja-Do, How Ja-Do, How Ja-Do (If I Knew You Were Comin' I'd've Baked a Cake)/Fujiyama Mama	1955	$15
❏ 9-61019	I Ain't Gonna Do It/Toys	1953	$20
❏ 9-61657	I'll Be Laughing At My Tears/Spring It Was	1956	$15
❏ 9-61344	I Wish You'd Fall in Love with Me/On a Lonely Walk	1955	$15
❏ 9-60986	Pot Luck/A Pretty Girl Milking Her Cow	1953	$20
❏ 9-60927	Pretend/Too Proud to Cry	1953	$20
❏ 9-61324	Punch/This-a-Way, That-a-Way	1954	$30

— With Jimmy Wakely

❏ 9-61185	Sway/When Mama Calls	1954	$20
❏ 9-61585	Teenage Heart/My Social Hot Dog	1956	$15
❏ 9-61695	Then I'll Be Tired of You/Dumayerry	1956	$15
❏ 9-61337	The Year We Fell in Love/I Don't Want to Mambo Polka	1955	$15

— With Lawrence Welk

❏ 9-60691	To Be Loved by You/Wrong	1952	$30
❏ 9-61609	Too Close for Comfort/The Scene of the Crime	1956	$15
❏ 9-60651	Wishin'/When You're Near Me	1952	$30
❏ 9-61293	Without Love/Happy Birthday, My Darling	1954	$20

EPIC

Number	Title	Yr	NM
❏ 5-9225	Goodnight, My Love/Everybody's Buddy	1957	$10
❏ 5-9252	Hearts Are Funny Things/Watch Out for Your Heart	1957	$12

MERCURY

Number	Title	Yr	NM
❏ 53920	If I Knew You Were Comin' I'd've Baked a Cake/Poco, Loco in the Coco	1950	$50

MGM

Number	Title	Yr	NM
❏ K12758	If I Knew You Were Comin' (I'd've Baked a Cake)/When Love Happens to You	1959	$10

NATIONAL

Number	Title	Yr	NM
❏ 91230	Baby Me/What Will Be, Will Be	1950	$40
❏ 91090	Honey, Honeymoon with Me/Dixieland Fall	1950	$40
❏ 91030	If I Knew You Were Comin' I'd've Baked a Cake/Poco, Loco in the Coco	1950	$60
❏ 91370	I Met Him at One O'Clock/Tell Me	1951	$40
❏ 91120	May I Take Two Giant Steps?/If You Saw What I Saw	1950	$40
❏ 91520	The Syncopated Clock/Lock the Barn Door	1951	$40

UNITED ARTISTS

Number	Title	Yr	NM
❏ 182	That Old Feeling/The Joke (Is Not on Me)	1959	$50
❏ 206	That Old Feeling/The Joke (Is Not on Me)	1960	$40

BARTON, ERNIE
PHILLIPS INTERNATIONAL

Number	Title	Yr	NM
❏ 3541	Open the Door Richard/Shut Your Mouth	1959	$200
❏ 3528	Stairway of Love/Raining the Blues	1958	$30

BARTON, LOU ANN
ELEKTRA

Number	Title	Yr	NM
❏ 47432	Brand New Lover/It Ain't Right	1982	$6

BARTZ, GARY
ARISTA

Number	Title	Yr	NM
❏ 0538	After the Love Has Gone/Keep On Goin' On	1980	$4
❏ 0514	Music/(B-side unknown)	1980	$4

CAPITOL

Number	Title	Yr	NM
❏ 4462	Love Ballad/Macaroni	1977	$5
❏ 4511	Music Is My Sanctuary/Carnaval de l'Esprit	1977	$5
❏ 4600	Shake Your Body (It's the Joint)/Ooh Child	1978	$5

BARY, HENRY
HIT

Number	Title	Yr	NM
❏ 228	One, Two, Three/Get Off of My Cloud	1965	$15

— B-side by the Jalopy Five

BASE, ROB, AND D.J. E-Z ROCK
PROFILE

Number	Title	Yr	NM
❏ 5239	Get On the Dance Floor/Keep It Going Now	1988	$3
❏ 5186	It Takes Two/(Instrumental)	1988	$6
❏ 5275	Turn It Out (Go Base)/Crush	1989	$5

BASH, OTTO
HDS

Number	Title	Yr	NM
❏ 2008	My Babe/Straighten Up and Fly Right	1956	$30

RCA VICTOR

Number	Title	Yr	NM
❏ 47-6426	Later Alligator/Lookout Mountain	1956	$30
❏ 47-6585	The Elvis Blues/Later	1956	$60

BASIA
EPIC

Number	Title	Yr	NM
❏ 34-68608	Promises/From Now On	1989	$3
❏ 34-07730	Time and Tide/Run for Cover	1988	$3

BASIC BLACK AND PEARL
POLYDOR

Number	Title	Yr	NM
❏ 15111	There'll Come a Time, There'll Come a Day/He's a Rebel	1975	$5

BASIE, COUNT, AND SAMMY DAVIS, JR.
VERVE

Number	Title	Yr	NM
❏ 10349	She's a Woman/You're Nobody 'Til Somebody Loves You	1965	$6

BASIE, COUNT, AND JOE WILLIAMS
CLEF

Number	Title	Yr	NM
❏ 89152	Alright, Okay, You Win/When the Sun Goes Down	1955	$20
❏ 89162	April in Paris/Roll 'Em Pete	1956	$20

BASIE, COUNT
BRUNSWICK

Number	Title	Yr	NM
❏ 55344	Bright Lights, Big City/Mercy, Mercy, Mercy	1967	$6
❏ 55352	Green Onions/Hang On Sloopy	1967	$6

CLEF

Number	Title	Yr	NM
❏ 89171	Amazing Love/Magic	1956	$15
❏ 89172	April in Paris/Party Blues	1956	$15
❏ 89112	Basie Goes Wess/Softly, With Feeling	1954	$20
❏ 89169	Big Red/Smack Dab in the Middle	1956	$15
❏ 89070	Blee Blop Blues/Small Hotel	1953	$20
❏ 89120	Cherry Point/Right On	1954	$20
❏ 89101	Count's Organ Blues/Basie Beat	1954	$20
❏ 89149	Every Day/The Comeback	1955	$20
❏ 89147	Ska-Di-De-Dee-Oo/16 Men Swinging	1955	$20
❏ 89137	Stereophonie/I Feel Like a New Man	1955	$20
❏ 89167	Teach Me Tonight/My Baby Upsets Me	1956	$15
❏ 89151	The Comeback (Part 1)/The Comeback (Part 2)	1955	$20
❏ 89086	Tippin' on the QT/Bread	1953	$20
❏ 89131	Two for the Blues/Soft Drink	1955	$20

COLUMBIA

Number	Title	Yr	NM
❏ 6-709	Bluebeard Blues/Golden Bullet	1950	$30
❏ 1-709	Bluebeard Blues/Golden Bullet	1950	$40

— Microgroove 7-inch, 33 1/3 rpm single

| ❏ 6-930(?) | Danny Boy/Neal's Deal | 1950 | $30 |
| ❏ 1-930(?) | Danny Boy/Neal's Deal | 1950 | $40 |

— Microgroove 7-inch, 33 1/3 rpm single

Number	Title	Yr	NM
❏ 39406	Little Pony/Beaver Junction	1951	$30
DOT			
❏ 17201	Hay Burner/That Warm Feeling	1969	$5
MERCURY			
❏ 89028	Goin' to Chicago/Sent for You Yesterday and Here You Come Today	1953	$30
❏ 89033	I Want a Little Girl/Oh, Lady Be Good	1953	$30
❏ 89014	Paradise Squat/Hot Nail Boogie	1953	$30
❏ 89061	Song of the Islands/Royal Garden Blues	1953	$30
RCA VICTOR			
❏ 47-2915	Cheek to Cheek/Bran' New Dolly	1949	$30
❏ 47-2990	Did You See Jackie Robinson Hit That Ball?/Shoutin' Blues	1949	$50
❏ 47-3032	She's a Wine-O/Slider	1949	$30
❏ 47-3107	St. Louis Baby/Normania	1949	$30
REPRISE			
❏ 20170	I Can't Stop Loving You/Nice & Easy	1963	$10
❏ 0240	I Left My Heart in San Francisco/Walk Don't Run	1963	$10
ROULETTE			
❏ 4465	Basie's Jingle Bells/Lullabye of Birdland	1962	$12
❏ 4088	Going to Chicago Blues/Swingin' the Blues	1958	$10
❏ 4226	How Am I to Know/It Had to Be You	1960	$10
❏ 4040	Lil' Darlin'/The Kid from Red Bank	1957	$12
❏ 4109	M Squad Theme/Late Late Show	1958	$10
❏ 4286	Ol' Man River Part 1/Ol' Man River Part 2	1960	$10
❏ 4409	Song of the Islands/Summertime	1962	$12
❏ 4403	The Basie Twist/Trot	1962	$15
UNITED ARTISTS			
❏ 50002	Double-O-Seven/Kingston Calypso	1966	$8
VERVE			
❏ 10318	All of Me/On the Road to Mandalay	1964	$8
❏ 10329	Li'l Ol' Groove Maker/Pleasingly Plump	1964	$8
❏ 10350	My Kind of Town/Watermelon Man	1965	$8
❏ 89177	Only Forever/Move	1957	$15

BASIL, TONI
A&M

Number	Title	Yr	NM
❏ 791	Breakaway/I'm 28	1966	$200
CHRYSALIS			
❏ 2665	Mickey (Spanish)/Thief on the Loose	1982	$5
❏ 2665 [PS]	Mickey (Spanish)/Thief on the Loose	1982	$5
❏ 2638	Mickey/Thief on the Loose	1982	$3
❏ 2638 [PS]	Mickey/Thief on the Loose	1982	$3
❏ VS4-03539	Mickey/Thief on the Loose	1983	$4
— Reissue of 2638, but harder to find			
❏ VS442753	Over My Head/Best Performance	1983	$3
❏ VS442753 [PS]	Over My Head/Best Performance	1983	$3
❏ VS4-03537	Shoppin' from A to Z/Time After Time	1983	$3
❏ VS4-03537 [PS]	Shoppin' from A to Z/Time After Time	1983	$3
❏ VS442711	Street Beat/(B-side unknown)	1983	$3

BASILE, VINNIE
DAVY JONES

Number	Title	Yr	NM
❏ 661	Gypsy Girl/Girl	1968	$30

BASKERVILLE, BOBBY
DOT

Number	Title	Yr	NM
❏ 17066	Gotcha Where I Wantcha/Soul Talk	1968	$10

BASKERVILLE HOUNDS, THE
AVCO EMBASSY

Number	Title	Yr	NM
❏ 4504	Hold Me/Here I Come, Miami	1968	$12
BUDDAH			
❏ 17	Caroline/Last Night on the Back Porch	1967	$10
DOT			
❏ 17037	Baby, Am I Losing/Never on Sunday	1967	$12
❏ 17017	Debbie/Jackie's Theme	1967	$12

Number	Title	Yr	NM
❏ 17004	Space Rock, Part 1/Space Rock, Part 2	1967	$10
TEMA			
❏ 132	All You Had to Do Was Ask/Who Does She Love	1967	$20
❏ 131	Christmas Is Here (But Not For Long)/Make Me Your Man	1966	$20
❏ 131 [PS]	Christmas Is Here (But Not For Long)/Make Me Your Man	1966	$60
❏ 125	Debbie/Jackie's Theme	1966	$20
❏ 135	Hold Me/Here I Come, Miami	1967	$20
❏ 128	Space Rock, Part 1/Space Rock, Part 2	1966	$20

BASS, FONTELLA, AND TINA TURNER
VESUVIUS

Number	Title	Yr	NM
❏ 1002	This Would Make Me Happy/Poor Little Fool	1963	$30

BASS, FONTELLA
BOBBIN

Number	Title	Yr	NM
❏ 140	Honey Bee/Bad Boy	1963	$20
❏ 134	I Don't Hurt Anymore/Brand New Love	1962	$20
CHECKER			
❏ 1097	Don't Mess Up a Good Thing/Baby, What You Want Me to Do	1965	$12
— With Bobby McClure			
❏ 1137	I Surrender/I Can't Rest	1966	$10
❏ 1183	Lucky in Love/Sweet Lovin' Daddy	1967	$10
❏ 1147	Safe and Sound/You'll Never Ever Know	1966	$10
EPIC			
❏ 50341	Soon as I Touched Him/You Can Betcha in Love	1977	$4
PAULA			
❏ 389	Home Wrecker/Now That I've Found a Good Thing	1973	$5
❏ 367	I Need to Be Loved/I Want Everyone to Know	1972	$5
❏ 376	It Sure Is Good/I'm Leaving the Choice to You	1973	$5
❏ 393	Talking About Freedom/It's Hard to Get Back In	1974	$5
❏ 360	Who You Gonna Blame/Hold On This Time	1972	$5

BASS, SAM D.
3J

Number	Title	Yr	NM
❏ 1002	Dumbest Heart in Time/I Just Forgot for Awhile	1980	$6
❏ 1003	How Could I Do This to Me/Get Ready for the Blues	1980	$6
❏ 1005	She Don't Live Here Anymore/On My Mind	1980	$6

BASSEY, SHIRLEY
COLUMBIA

Number	Title	Yr	NM
❏ 40848	Tonight My Heart Is Crying/If I Had a Needle and Thread	1957	$20
EPIC			
❏ 9303	As I Love You/Kiss Me Honey, Honey Kiss Me	1959	$15
MGM			
❏ 12919	'S Wonderful/The Party's Over	1960	$15
UNITED ARTISTS			
❏ 511	Above All Others/As Long As He Needs Me	1962	$10
❏ 50961	And I Love You So/Jezebel	1972	$4
❏ 50229	Big Spender/Dangerous Games	1967	$6
❏ 50770	Breakfast in Bed/Pieces of Dreams	1971	$4
❏ 421	Climb Ev'ry Mountain/Where Are You	1962	$10
❏ X1303	Copacabana/This Is My Life (La Vita)	1979	$4
❏ XW387	Davy/The Trouble with Hello	1974	$4
❏ 50845	Diamonds Are Forever/For the Love of Him	1971	$4
❏ 0146	Diamonds Are Forever/This Is My Love	1973	$4
— Silver Spotlight Series issue			
❏ 50544	Does Anybody Miss Me/We	1969	$5
❏ 50031	Don't Take the Lovers from the World/Take Away	1966	$6
❏ XW854	Everything That Touches You/If I Never Sing Another Song	1976	$4
❏ 50606	Fa Fa Fa (Live for Today)/A Bus That Never Comes	1969	$5
❏ 50833	For All We Know/What's Done Is Done Is Done	1971	$4
❏ 50459	Funny Girl/This Is My Life (La Vita)	1968	$5

Number	Title	Yr	NM
❏ 50071	Give Me Your Love/Who Could Love Me	1966	$6
❏ XW508	Goldfinger/How Can I Tell	1974	$4
❏ 790	Goldfinger/Strange How Love Can Be	1964	$10
❏ 404	I'll Get By/Climb Ev'ry Mountain	1962	$10
❏ 956	It's Yourself/Secrets	1965	$8
❏ 699	I Who Have Nothing/Imagination	1964	$8
❏ 50105	I (Who Have Nothing)/Shirley	1966	$6
❏ 50502	Medley: Goin' Out of My Head-You Go to My Head/I Must Know	1969	$5
❏ X1308	Moonraker-Main Title/Moonraker-End Title	1979	$4
❏ 50682	Sea and Sand/What About Today	1970	$4
❏ XW717	Send In the Clowns/Living	1975	$4
❏ 50698	Something/What Are You Doing the Rest of Your Life	1970	$4
❏ 50129	The Impossible Dream/Do I Look Like a Fool	1967	$6
❏ 50099	The Liquidator/Sunshine	1966	$6
❏ 681	Theme from "The Victors"/How Can You Tell	1964	$8
❏ XW318	This Is My Life/Make the World a Little Younger	1973	$4
❏ XW923	What I Did for Love/Feelings	1976	$4
❏ 503	What Kind of Fool Am I/What Now My Love	1962	$10

BASTARDS, THE
TREEHOUSE

Number	Title	Yr	NM
❏ 014	Frank/Loser	1988	$40
— Burgundy vinyl (200 made)			
❏ 014	Frank/Loser	1988	$10
— Black vinyl (800 made)			
❏ 014 [PS]	Frank/Loser	1988	$10
❏ 011	Who Cares/Shit for Brains	1988	$70
— First 100 on green vinyl (numbered)			
❏ 011	Who Cares/Shit for Brains	1988	$40
— Second 100 on black vinyl (numbered)			
❏ 011 [PS]	Who Cares/Shit for Brains	1988	$50
— Accompanies either of the first two pressings, linoleum block print			
❏ 011	Who Cares/Shit for Brains	1988	$20
— Yellow label, 800 made			
❏ 011 [PS]	Who Cares/Shit for Brains	1988	$20
— Yellow or green sleeve (each the same value)			
❏ 011	Who Cares/Shit for Brains	1988	$10
— White label, 700 made			
❏ 011 [PS]	Who Cares/Shit for Brains	1988	$10
— Mostly pink covers for final 700			

BASTILLES, THE
PHILIPS

Number	Title	Yr	NM
❏ 40453	Tenderly/Vengeance	1967	$30

BATAAN
EPIC

Number	Title	Yr	NM
❏ 50089	The Bottle/When You're Down	1975	$4

BATCHELOR, RUTH
PARKWAY

Number	Title	Yr	NM
❏ 852	Mr. Principal/Lemon Drops Lolly Pops	1962	$20

BATDORF & RODNEY
ARISTA

Number	Title	Yr	NM
❏ 0159	Somewhere in the Night/Ain't It Like Home	1975	$4
ASYLUM			
❏ 11011	All I Need/Between the Ages	1972	$5
❏ 11012	Home Again/Between the Ages	1972	$5
ATLANTIC			
❏ 2863	Can You See Him/Never See His Face Again	1972	$5
❏ 2850	Oh My Surprise/Farm	1972	$5

BATISTE, ROSE
GOLDEN WORLD

Number	Title	Yr	NM
❏ 33	Sweetheart Darling/That's What He Told Me	1966	$40
REVILOT			
❏ 204	I Miss My Baby/Hit and Run	1967	$200
❏ 206	I Still Wait for You/Come Back in a Hurry	1967	$200
RIC-TIC			
❏ 105	Holding Hands/That's What He Told Me	1965	$300

Number	Title	Yr	NM

BATORS, STIV
BOMP!

❏ 124	It's Cold Outside/The Last Year	1979	$10
❏ 124 [PS]	It's Cold Outside/The Last Year	1979	$20

BATS, THE (1)
HBR

❏ 445	Big Bright Eyes/Nothing at All	1965	$12

PARROT

❏ 40013	Listen to My Heart/You Look Good Together	1967	$12

BATS, THE (U)
FLAME

❏ 5155	Batmobile/Batusi	1966	$50

BATTIN, SKIP
AURORA

❏ 159	The Dating Game Theme/Night Time Girl	1966	$20

GROOVE

❏ 58-0055	Searchin'/She Acts Like We Never Have Met	1965	$50
❏ 58-0065	Ten Feet Tall/What's Mine Is Mine	1965	$50

SIGNPOST

❏ 70010 [DJ]	Ballad of Dick Clark (mono/stereo)	1973	$6

— *May be promo only*

BAUGH, PHIL
ERA

❏ 3208	Dizzy/Those Were the Days	1969	$12
❏ 3202	Girl Watcher/Jesse's Theme	1969	$10

LONGHORN

❏ 559	Country Guitar/Chattanooga	1965	$20
❏ 563	One Man Band/Live Wire	1965	$20

BAUM, ALLEN
RED ROBIN

❏ 124	My Kinda Woman/Too Much Competition	1954	$400

BAXTER
PARAMOUNT

❏ 0194	Give It All/197 Three	1973	$8

BAXTER, BAXTER AND BAXTER
AMI

❏ 1315	D.W. Washburn/ (B-side unknown)	1983	$5

SUN

❏ 1167	Lying/Want to Love You More	1981	$4
❏ 1160	Take Me Back to the Country/John	1981	$4

BAXTER, DUKE
MERCURY

❏ 73107	Absolute Zero/Wings of Love	1970	$20

VMC

❏ 750	Don't Hurt Me/(B-side unknown)	1969	$20
❏ 740	Everybody Knows Matilda/I Ain't No Schoo Boy	1969	$8
❏ 749	Superstition Bend/Crosstown Woman She Set Me Free	1969	$10

BAXTER, LES
AMERICAN INT'L.

❏ 145	Dock at Papeete/Bora Bora	1970	$5
❏ 143	Dunwich/Necronomicon	1970	$5

A/S

❏ 4511	La La La/Girl on the Boulevard	1970	$5
❏ 4515	Soolaimon/A Taste of Soul	1970	$5

CAPITOL

❏ F3887	A Farewell to Arms/The Dance from Bonjour Tristesse	1958	$10
❏ F2457	A Little Love/Ruby	1953	$15
❏ 4523	Angelina/Follow Me	1961	$10
❏ F2374	Aprin in Portugal/Suddenly	1953	$15
❏ F2705	Atlantis/The Flirtation Waltz	1954	$15
❏ F2143	Auf Wiedersehn Sweetheart/ Padam Padam	1952	$15
❏ F1493	Because of You/Unless	1951	$20

❏ F1785	Be Mine Tonight/California Moon	1951	$20
❏ F3704	Blue Echo/Designing Woman	1957	$10
❏ F1966	Blue Tango/Please Mr. Sun	1952	$15
❏ 4374	Boomada/Cochi Baba	1960	$10
❏ F3624	Clown on the Eiffel Tower/ Woman's Devotion	1957	$10
❏ F4091	Come Prima/My Heart's in Portugal	1958	$10
❏ F2579	Cornflakes/Elaine	1953	$15
❏ F4032	Dance, Everyone, Dance/A Chance Is All I Ask	1958	$12
❏ F3599	Dream Rhapsody/ Midnight on the Cliffs	1956	$12
❏ F3002	Earth Angel (Will You Be Mine)/Happy Wedding	1954	$15
❏ F2005	Festival/Invitation	1952	$15
❏ F3478	Foreign Interlude/Melodia Loca	1956	$10
❏ F3526	Giant/There's Never Been Anyone Else But You	1956	$10
❏ F2053	Green Grow the Lilacs/A Day Away from You	1952	$15
❏ F1596	How Many Times/Bacoa	1951	$20
❏ F3040	I Ain't Mad at You/Blue Mirage	1955	$15
❏ F2748	If You Were Mine/Douchka	1954	$15
❏ F2479	I Love Paris/Gigi	1953	$15
❏ F2102	I'm Yours/Kiss of Fire	1952	$15
❏ F3841	Invisible Boy/I Never Had a Dream Like This Before	1957	$10
❏ F1839	I Remember You Love/I Only Have One Life to Live	1951	$20
❏ F3768	La Panse/Manhattan	1957	$12
❏ F2106	Lonely Wine/Lost in Meditation	1952	$15
❏ F1731	Longing for You/Sarah Kelly from Plumb Nelly	1951	$20
❏ F4011	Love Song from Houseboat/ Lily of Laguna	1958	$10
❏ F2632	Love Theme from The Robe/Manhattan	1953	$15
❏ F2950	Midnight on the Cliffs/ Dream Rhapsody	1954	$15

— *With Leonard Pennario*

❏ 4489	Pepe/Dolce Par Niente	1960	$10
❏ 4322	Prelude & Ben-Hur Theme/Till Tomorrow	1959	$12
❏ F4249	Sabre Dance/Milord	1959	$10
❏ F2275	Santa Claus' Party/Hang Your Wishes on the Tree	1952	$15
❏ F3798	Search for Paradise/ Ricordate Marcellino	1957	$10
❏ F1887	Somebody's Been Beatin' My Time/I Can't Help It	1951	$20
❏ F1760	Somewhere, Somehow, Someday/Because of You	1951	$15
❏ F1299	Somewhere, Somehow, Someday/Tamberina	1950	$20
❏ F3259	Song of the Bayou/Monika	1955	$15
❏ F3606	Stealin'/I'd Love to Fall Asleep	1956	$10

— *With Line Renaud*

❏ F3404	Tango of the Drums/Sinner Man	1956	$10
❏ F2117	Tears/Please Say You Love Me	1952	$15
❏ F4206	Tell Me, Margarita/ Piccolissima Serenata	1959	$10
❏ F2845	The High and the Mighty/ More Love Than Your Love	1954	$15
❏ F3573	The Left Arm of Buddah/What Happens in Buenos Aires	1956	$10
❏ F3728	The Lonely Whistler/Ruby Lips	1957	$10
❏ F2375	The Lord Is My Shepherd/ My Name Is God	1953	$15
❏ F3336	The Poor People of Paris/ Theme from "Helen of Troy	1956	$20
❏ F3291	The Trouble with Harry/Havana	1955	$15
❏ F2205	Till the End of the World/ The Two-Faced Clock	1952	$15
❏ F3195	Toy Tiger/Shrike	1955	$15
❏ F2568	Tropicana/Julie	1953	$15
❏ F3120	Walke the Town and Tell the People/I'll Never Stop Loving You	1955	$15
❏ F1818	When/If You've Forgotten Me	1951	$20
❏ F2018	Wondering/God's Little Candles	1952	$15

GNP CRESCENDO

❏ 382	And We Were Lovers/ Balan Samba	1967	$8
❏ 425	Flame Tree/Girl from Uganda	1969	$6
❏ 313	Linin' Track/Baion	1964	$8
❏ 399	Live for Life/Free Again	1967	$8

RCA VICTOR

❏ 47-3307	L'Ardente Nuit/Possession	1949	$30

— *RCA sides by "Leslie Baxter and His Orchestra*

❏ 47-3305	Toujours Moi/Fame	1949	$30

REPRISE

❏ 0243	How Shall I Send Thee/Have Yourself a Merry Little Christmas	1963	$30

— *B-side by Frank Sinatra*

❏ 20165	Sail Away Ladies/Due Bonita Bandera	1963	$10
❏ 20159	Theme from "How the West Was Won"/Theme from "Lawrence of Arabia"	1963	$10
❏ 20120	Theme from "The Manchurian Candidate"/ The Manchurian Beat	1962	$10

❏ 20120 [PS]	Theme from "The Manchurian Candidate"/ The Manchurian Beat	1962	$60

7-Inch Extended Plays

CAPITOL

❏ EAP 1-672	*Wake the Town and Tell the People/The Shrike/Toy Tiger/I'll Never Stop Loving You	1955	$15
❏ EAP 1-730 [PS]	The Poor People of Paris	1956	$15
❏ EAP 1-730	The Poor People of Paris/ Theme from "Helen of Troy"// The Trouble with Harry/ If You Can Dream	1956	$15
❏ EAP 1-672 [PS]	Wake the Town and Tell the People	1955	$15

Albums

❏ T288 [M]	Le Sacre Du Sauvage	1954	$40

BAXTER, RONNIE
ATCO

❏ 6093	Drivin' Me Out of My Mind/Afraid of Love	1957	$50

GONE

❏ 5041	Gates of Heaven/ Prisoner of Love	1958	$40
❏ 5050	Is It Because/I Finally Found You	1958	$40
❏ 5058	Is It Because/I Finally Found You	1959	$40
❏ 5084	It's Magic/If You Let Me	1960	$30
❏ 5036	Someone to Love Me/ Gates of Heaven	1958	$40

MARK-X

❏ 8001	It's Magic/If You Let Me	1959	$15

BAY CITY ROLLERS
ARISTA

❏ 0120	Bye Bye Baby/It's for You	1975	$10
❏ 0233	Dedication/Rock N' Roller	1977	$4
❏ 0233 [PS]	Dedication/Rock N' Roller	1977	$5
❏ 0193	Don't Stop the Music (Long)/ Don't Stop the Music (Short)	1976	$6
❏ 0205	I Only Want to Be with You/Write a Letter	1976	$4
❏ 0170	Money Honey/Maryanne	1976	$4
❏ 0170 [PS]	Money Honey/Maryanne	1976	$8
❏ 0149	Saturday Night/Marlina	1975	$4
❏ 0149 [PS]	Saturday Night/Marlina	1975	$6
❏ 0272	The Way I Feel Tonight/ Love Power	1977	$5
❏ 0272	The Way I Feel Tonight/ Sweet Virginia	1977	$5
❏ 0476	Turn On the Radio/Hello and Welcome Home	1979	$4

— *As "The Rollers*

❏ 0363	Where Will I Be Now/If You Were My Woman	1978	$4

BELL

❏ 45618	All of Me Loves All of You/The Bump	1974	$20
❏ 45274	Manana/I Heard You Singing Your Song	1972	$20
❏ 45481	Shang-a-Lang/ (B-side unknown)	1974	$20
❏ 45607	Summerlove Sensation/ (B-side unknown)	1974	$20

BAY RIDGE, THE
ATLANTIC

❏ 2431	Back Track/I Can't Get Her Out of My Mind	1967	$12

BAYOU BOYS, THE
CHECKER

❏ 765	Dinah/Bambalays	1952	$200

BAYSIDERS, THE
EVEREST

❏ 19366	Over the Rainbow/My Bonnie	1960	$20
❏ 19393	The Bells of St. Mary's/ Comin' Thru the Rye	1961	$20
❏ 19386	Trees/Look for the Silver Lining	1960	$20

BE-BOP DELUXE
HARVEST

❏ 4244	Crying to the Sky/ Ships in the Night	1976	$4
❏ 4571	Panic in the World/ Blue As a Jewel	1978	$4
❏ 4151	Sister Seagull/Maid in Heaven	1975	$4

BEACH, BILL

KING

Number	Title	Yr	NM
❏ 4940	Peg Pants/You're Gonna Like My Baby	1956	$200

BEACH BOYS, THE

Also see GLEN CAMPBELL; DAVE AND THE MARKSMEN; BRUCE JOHNSTON; MIKE LOVE; BRIAN WILSON; BRIAN WILSON AND MIKE LOVE; CARL WILSON; DENNIS WILSON.

BROTHER

Number	Title	Yr	NM
❏ 1001	Heroes and Villains/You're Welcome	1967	$15
❏ 1001 [PS]	Heroes and Villains/You're Welcome	1967	$125

—*Not to be confused with Capitol 5826, which is a completely different sleeve*

BROTHER/REPRISE

Number	Title	Yr	NM
❏ 0894	Add Some Music to Your Day/Susie Cincinnati	1970	$8
❏ 1156	California Saga (On My Way to Sunny Californ-I-A)/Funky Pretty	1973	$10
❏ 1321 [DJ]	Child Of Winter (Christmas Song) (mono/stereo)	1974	$30
❏ 1321	Child of Winter (Christmas Song)/Susie Cincinnati	1974	$60
❏ 0998	Cool, Cool Water/Forever	1971	$100
❏ 0104	Darlin'/Wild Honey	1973	$5

—*"Back to Back Hits" series*

❏ 0106	Do It Again/Cottonfields	1973	$5

—*"Back to Back Hits" series*

❏ 1375	Everyone's In Love with You/Susie Cincinnati	1976	$4
❏ 0105	Friends/Be Here in the Morning	1973	$5

—*"Back to Back Hits" series*

❏ 0102	God Only Knows/Caroline, No	1973	$5

—*"Back to Back Hits" series*

❏ 0103	Good Vibrations/Heroes and Villains	1973	$5

—*"Back to Back Hits" series*

❏ 1389	Honkin' Down the Highway/Solar System	1977	$4
❏ 0107	I Can Hear Music/Bluebirds Over the Mountain	1973	$5

—*"Back to Back Hits" series*

❏ 1310	I Can Hear Music/Let the Wind Blow	1974	$10
❏ 0957	It's About Time/Tears in the Morning	1970	$30
❏ 1368	It's O.K./Had to Phone Ya	1976	$4
❏ 1015	Long Promised Road/Deirdre	1971	$30
❏ 1047	Long Promised Road/'Til I Die	1971	$30
❏ 1101	Marcella/Hold On Dear Brother	1972	$40
❏ 1394	Peggy Sue/Hey Little Tomboy	1978	$4
❏ 1138	Sail On Sailor/Only With You	1972	$10
❏ 1325	Sail On Sailor/Only With You	1975	$8
❏ 0929	Slip On Through/This Whole World	1970	$12
❏ 1058	Surf's Up/Don't Go Near the Water	1971	$60
❏ 1336	Wouldn't It Be Nice/Caroline, No	1975	$15
❏ 0101	Wouldn't It Be Nice/Sloop John B	1973	$5

—*"Back to Back Hits" series*

CANDIX

Number	Title	Yr	NM
❏ 301	Surfin'/Luau	1961	$200

—*Label says "Distributed by Era Records Sales, Inc.*

❏ 301	Surfin'/Luau	1961	$300

—*No mention of Era Records on label*

❏ 331	Surfin'/Luau	1962	$200

CAPITOL

Number	Title	Yr	NM
❏ 5561	Barbara Ann/Girl Don't Tell Me	1965	$30
❏ 5561 [PS]	Barbara Ann/Girl Don't Tell Me	1965	$200

—*Glossy finish*

❏ 5561 [PS]	Barbara Ann/Girl Don't Tell Me	1965	$200

—*Non-glossy finish*

❏ 4110	Barbara Ann/Little Honda	1975	$5
❏ 4334	Be True to Your School/Graduation Day	1976	$5
❏ 5069	Be True to Your School/In My Room	1963	$30
❏ 2360	Bluebirds Over the Mountain/Never Learn Not to Love	1968	$15
❏ 2530	Break Away/Celebrate the News	1969	$15
❏ B-5630	California Dreamin'/Lady Liberty	1986	$3
❏ 5464	California Girls/Let Him Run Wild	1965	$30

—*Orange and yellow swirl label*

❏ 5464 [PS]	California Girls/Let Him Run Wild	1965	$50

Number	Title	Yr	NM
❏ 5464	California Girls/Let Him Run Wild	1969	$10

—*Red and orange "target" label*

❏ 5464	California Girls/Let Him Run Wild	1973	$8

—*Orange label with "Capitol" at bottom of label*

❏ 5464	California Girls/Let Him Run Wild	1978	$5

—*Purple label*

❏ 2765	Cottonfields/The Nearest Faraway Place	1970	$30
❏ 5306	Dance, Dance, Dance/The Warmth of the Sun	1964	$30
❏ 5306 [PS]	Dance, Dance, Dance/The Warmth of the Sun	1964	$120
❏ 2068	Darlin'/Here Today	1967	$15
❏ 2068 [PS]	Darlin'/Here Today	1967	$30
❏ 2239	Do It Again/Wake the World	1968	$15
❏ B-44297	Don't Worry Baby/Tequila Dreams	1989	$4

—*A-side: With the Everly Brothers; B-side by Dave Grusin*

❏ B-44297 [PS]	Don't Worry Baby/Tequila Dreams	1989	$12
❏ 5372	Do You Wanna Dance/Please Let Me Wonder	1965	$30
❏ 5372 [PS]	Do You Wanna Dance/Please Let Me Wonder	1965	$50
❏ 2160	Friends/Little Bird	1968	$15
❏ 5118	Fun, Fun, Fun/Why Do Fools Fall in Love	1964	$30

—*A-side songwriter listed as "Brian Wilson*

❏ 5118	Fun, Fun, Fun/Why Do Fools Fall in Love	1964	$30

—*A-side songwriter listed as "Brian Wilson-Mike Love*

❏ 5118 [PS]	Fun, Fun, Fun/Why Do Fools Fall in Love	1964	$50
❏ 5676	Good Vibrations/Let's Go Away for Awhile	1966	$30
❏ 5676 [PS]	Good Vibrations/Let's Go Away for Awhile	1966	$40
❏ 5395	Help Me, Rhonda/Kiss Me, Baby	1965	$30
❏ 5395 [PS]	Help Me, Rhonda/Kiss Me, Baby	1965	$50
❏ 5826 [PS]	Heroes and Villains	1967	$400

—*U.S. picture sleeve for unreleased record. This sleeve, however, was exported and used in other countries.*

❏ 2432	I Can Hear Music/All I Want to Do	1969	$15
❏ 5174	I Get Around/Don't Worry Baby	1964	$30

—*Orange and yellow swirl label*

❏ 5174 [PS]	I Get Around/Don't Worry Baby	1964	$50
❏ 5174	I Get Around/Don't Worry Baby	1969	$15

—*Red and orange "target" label*

❏ 5174	I Get Around/Don't Worry Baby	1972	$8

—*Orange label with "Capitol" at bottom*

❏ 5174	I Get Around/Don't Worry Baby	1978	$5

—*Purple label*

❏ 5174	I Get Around/Don't Worry Baby	1982	$5

—*Black label with colorband*

❏ 4093	Little Honda/Hawaii	1975	$5
❏ 5096	Little Saint Nick/The Lord's Prayer	1963	$40

—*Orange and yellow swirl label*

❏ 5096	Little Saint Nick/The Lord's Prayer	1969	$20

—*Red and orange "target" label*

❏ 5096	Little Saint Nick/The Lord's Prayer	1972	$20

—*Orange label with "Capitol" at bottom of label*

❏ 5096	Little Saint Nick/The Lord's Prayer	1978	$5

—*Purple label*

❏ 5096	Little Saint Nick/The Lord's Prayer	1982	$5

—*Black label with colorband*

❏ PRO2936/7	Salt Lake City/Amusement Parks U.S.A.	1965	$200

—*Courtesy of Downtown Salt Lake City Stores" promotional item*

❏ 5602	Sloop John B/You're So Good to Me	1966	$30

—*Orange and yellow swirl label*

❏ 5602 [PS]	Sloop John B/You're So Good to Me	1966	$40
❏ 5602	Sloop John B/You're So Good to Me	1969	$12

—*Red and orange "target" label*

❏ 5602	Sloop John B/You're So Good to Me	1973	$8

—*Orange label with "Capitol" at bottom of label*

Number	Title	Yr	NM
❏ 5602	Sloop John B/You're So Good to Me	1978	$5

—*Purple label*

❏ 7PRO-79841 [DJ]	Somewhere Near Japan (same on both sides)	1989	$70

—*Vinyl is promo only*

❏ 7PRO-79789 [DJ]	Still Cruisin' (same on both sides)	1989	$70

—*Vinyl is promo only*

❏ 5009	Surfer Girl/Little Deuce Coupe	1963	$30
❏ 4777	Surfin' Safari/409	1962	$30
❏ 4777 [PS]	Surfin' Safari/409	1962	$100
❏ 4932	Surfin' U.S.A./Shut Down	1963	$30

—*Version 1: Brian Wilson listed as composer of "Surfin' U.S.A.*

❏ 4932	Surfin' U.S.A./Shut Down	1963	$30

—*Version 2: Chuck Berry listed as composer of "Surfin' U.S.A.*

❏ 3924	Surfin' U.S.A./The Warmth of the Sun	1974	$5
❏ 4880	Ten Little Indians/County Fair	1962	$40
❏ 4880 [PS]	Ten Little Indians/County Fair	1962	$200
❏ A-5030	The Beach Boys Medley/God Only Knows	1981	$5
❏ 5540	The Little Girl I Once Knew/There's No Other (Like My Baby)	1965	$30
❏ 5540 [PS]	The Little Girl I Once Knew/There's No Other (Like My Baby)	1965	$50
❏ 5312	The Man with All the Toys/Blue Christmas	1964	$40
❏ 5245	When I Grow Up (To Be a Man)/She Knows Me Too Well	1964	$30
❏ 5245 [PS]	When I Grow Up (To Be a Man)/She Knows Me Too Well	1964	$60

—*With green border*

❏ 5245 [PS]	When I Grow Up (To Be a Man)/She Knows Me Too Well	1964	$50

—*With blue border*

❏ 2028	Wild Honey/Wind Chimes	1967	$15
❏ 5706	Wouldn't It Be Nice/God Only Knows	1966	$30

—*Even though it has a higher number, this single was released before "Good Vibrations.*

CAPITOL CUSTOM

Number	Title	Yr	NM
❏ 0(no cat #)	Spirit of America/Boogie Woodie	1963	$200
❏ 0(no cat #) [PS]	Spirit of America/Boogie Woodie	1963	$600

—*Promo for KFWB and opening day of Wallich's Music City South Bay store*

CAPITOL STARLINE

Number	Title	Yr	NM
❏ 6259	Barbara Ann/Little Honda	1978	$4

—*Originals have grayish labels*

❏ 6059	Be True to Your School/In My Room	1965	$20

—*Originals have green swirl labels*

❏ 6289	California Girls/Let Him Run Wild	1981	$3

—*Originals have blue labels*

❏ 6105	Dance, Dance, Dance/The Warmth of the Sun	1967	$15

—*Originals have red and white "target" labels*

❏ 6106	Fun, Fun, Fun/Why Do Fools Fall in Love	1967	$15

—*Originals have red and white "target" labels*

❏ 6132	Good Vibrations/Barbara Ann	1968	$15

—*Originals have red and white "target" labels*

❏ 6081	Help Me, Rhonda/Do You Wanna Dance?	1966	$20

—*Originals have green swirl labels*

❏ 6280	I Get Around/Don't Worry Baby	1981	$3

—*Originals have blue labels*

❏ 6277	Little Saint Nick/The Lord's Prayer	1981	$3

—*Originals have blue labels*

❏ 6295	Sloop John B/You're So Good to Me	1981	$3

—*Originals have blue labels*

❏ 6107	Surfer Girl/Little Deuce Coupe	1967	$15

—*Originals have red and white "target" labels*

❏ 6095	Surfin' Safari/409	1966	$20

—*Originals have green swirl labels*

❏ 6094	Surfin' U.S.A./Shut Down	1966	$20

—*Originals have green swirl labels*

❏ 6060	Ten Little Indians/She Knows Me Too Well	1965	$20

—*Originals have green swirl labels*

Number	Title	Yr	NM

CARIBOU

❏ 02633	Come Go with Me/Don't Go Near the Water	1981	$3
❏ 04913	Getcha Back/Male Ego	1985	$3
❏ 04913 [PS]	Getcha Back/Male Ego	1985	$3
❏ 9032	Goin' On/Endless Harmony	1980	$4
❏ 9029	Good Timin'/Love Surrounds Me	1979	$4
❏ 9026	Here Comes the Night/Baby Blue	1979	$4
❏ 9031	It's a Beautiful Day/Sumahama	1979	$4
❏ 05433	It's Gettin' Late/It's OK	1985	$3
❏ 05433 [PS]	It's Gettin' Late/It's OK	1985	$3
❏ 9030	Lady Lynda/Full Sail	1979	$4
❏ 9033	Livin' with a Heartache/Santa Ana Winds	1980	$4
❏ 9034 [DJ]	School Day (Ring! Ring! Goes the Bell) (same on both sides)	1980	$250
❏ 05624	She Believes in Love Again/It's Just a Matter of Time	1985	$3
❏ 05624 [PS]	She Believes in Love Again/It's Just a Matter of Time	1985	$3

CRITIQUE

❏ 99392	Happy Endings/California Girls	1987	$3

—*A-side with Little Richard*

❏ 99392 [PS]	Happy Endings/California Girls	1987	$5

—*Both the Beach Boy and Little Richard are on the sleeve*

FBI

❏ 7701	East Meets West/Rhapsody	1986	$30

—*With Frankie Valli and the Four Seasons*

ODE

❏ 66016	Wouldn't It Be Nice/The Times They Are a-Changing	1971	$40

—*B-side by Merry Clayton*

X

❏ 301	Surfin'/Luau	1961	$1000

7-Inch Extended Plays

CAPITOL

❏ R-5267 [PS]	4-By the Beach Boys	1964	$70
❏ DU-2545 [PS]	Best of the Beach Boys	1966	$100
❏ SXA-2027 [PS]	Shut Down, Volume 2	1964	$120
❏ SXA-1981 [PS]	Surfer Girl	1963	$175
❏ DU-2545	Surfin' U.S.A./Surfer Girl/Little Deuce Coupe//Fun, Fun, Fun/In My Room/Little Honda	1966	$100

—*Jukebox issue; small hole, plays at 33 1/3 rpm; red and white target "Starline" label*

❏ DU2269 [PS]	The Beach Boys Today!	1965	$100
❏ R-5267	Wendy/Don't Back Down//Little Honda/Hushabye	1964	$75

BEACH BOYS, THE (2)

KAPP

❏ 289	Bathing Beauty/On the Beach at Sunset	1959	$30

BEACH BUMS, THE

ARE YOU KIDDING ME?

❏ 1010	Florida Time/The Ballad of the Yellow Beret	1966	$70

—*B-side credited to "D. Dodger"*

BEACH GIRLS, THE

DYNO VOX

❏ 202	Goin' Places/Skiing in the Snow	1965	$30

VAULT

❏ 905	He's My Surfin' Guy/Bobby's the Boy	1963	$40

BEACH NUTS, THE

BANG

❏ 504	Out in the Sun (Hey-O)/Someday Soon	1965	$60

CORONADO

❏ 131	Surf Ride '65/The Last Ride	1965	$60
❏ 131 [PS]	Surf Ride '65/The Last Ride	1965	$70

BEACHNUTS, THE

BANG

❏ 504	Out in the Sun (Hey-O)/Someday So On	1965	$40

BEACON STREET UNION, THE

Also see EAGLE.

MGM

❏ 13935	Blue Suede Shoes/Four Hundred and Five	1968	$10
❏ 14012	May I Light Your Cigarette/Mayola	1968	$10
❏ 13865	South End Incident/Speed Kills	1967	$12

BEAGLES, THE

ERA

❏ 3132	Let's All Sing Like the Birdies Sing/Deep in the Heart of Texas	1964	$20
❏ 3132 [PS]	Let's All Sing Like the Birdies Sing/Deep in the Heart of Texas	1964	$30

HIT

❏ 113	Can't Buy Me Love/White on White	1964	$15

—*B-side by Fred York*

BEAN, GEORGE

LONDON

❏ 9685	A Sad Story/Er, Um, Er	1964	$10

BEAN, JIM

HUB

❏ 47	Lay, Lady, Lay/(B-side unknown)	1988	$6

BEANS

AVALANCHE

❏ 36011	Bleecker Street Rain/Honky Tonk Refrigerator	1972	$8

BEAR CREEK BAND FEATURING LEONDA

BEAR CREEK

❏ 103	Falling in Love Right & Left/I've Had Enough (Of Romance)	1988	$6

BEARD, DEAN

ATLANTIC

❏ 1137	On My Mind Again/Rakin' and Scrapin'	1957	$50
❏ 1162	Party Party/Stand By Me	1957	$50
❏ 1182	Take Time to Love Me/Hold Me Close	1958	$40

CANDIX

❏ 341	The Day That I Lost You/Villa Acuna	1962	$15

CHALLENGE

❏ 59033	Egad, Charlie Brown/Keeper of the Key	1958	$30
❏ 59048	Holding On to a Memory/Little Lover	1959	$30

EDMORAL

❏ 1011	On My Mind Again/Rakin' and Scrapin'	1956	$200

JOED

❏ 715	Coffee Break/Tropical Nights	1962	$30

SIMS

❏ 299	(Are There) Honkytonks in Heaven/Pocketful of Stardust	1966	$10

WINSTON

❏ 1073	Don't Let the Stars Get In Your Eyes/That's How It Gets Sun Up	1963	$15
❏ 1063	I Don't Know How/The Red Rose	1962	$15
❏ 1075	Smile Pretty for Me Temper/To Me	1963	$15

—*With Bill Graham*

BEARDS, THE

BEARDO

❏ 001/002	Stone Cold Love/Fearless Heart	1988	$6

BEASLEY, JIMMY

MODERN

❏ 996	Don't Feel Sorry for Me/Little Coquette	1956	$30
❏ 991	Ella Jane/No Love for Me	1956	$30
❏ 1023	I Want My Baby/We Three	1957	$30
❏ 1009	My Happiness/Jambalaya	1956	$30
❏ 1018	Thinking of You/You Were Fooling	1956	$30

BEASLEY, WALTER

ELEKTRA

❏ 69522	Back in Love Again/(Instrumental)	1986	$4

MERCURY

❏ 876002-7	Don't Say Goodbye/Tenderness	1989	$3

POLYDOR

❏ 887713-7	Call Me/Nothing But a Thang	1988	$3
❏ 887163-7	I'm So Happy/Jump On It	1987	$3
❏ 887163-7 [PS]	I'm So Happy/Jump On It	1987	$3
❏ 887413-7	On the Edge/Where	1988	$3
❏ 887413-7 [PS]	On the Edge/Where	1988	$3

BEASLEY, WATSON

WARNER BROS.

❏ 49267	Don't Let Your Chance Go Bye/What's On My Mind	1980	$5

BEAST

EVOLUTION

❏ 1028	Communication/Move Mountain	1970	$6

BEASTIE BOYS

Also see COUNTRY MIKE.

CAPITOL

❏ 7PRO-79698	Hey Ladies (same on both sides)	1989	$12

—*Originally issued as a promo only; 44454 came later*

❏ B-44454	Hey Ladies/Shake Your Rump	1989	$5
❏ B-44472	Shadrach/And What You Give Is What You Get	1989	$6

DEF JAM

❏ 38-07020	Brass Monkey/Posse in Effect	1987	$5
❏ 38-05864	Hold It Now, Hit It/Hold It Now, Hit It (Acapulco)	1986	$6
❏ 38-06341	It's the New Style/Paul Revere	1986	$6
❏ 38-06675	She's Crafty/No Sleep Till Brooklyn	1987	$6
❏ 38-06675 [PS]	She's Crafty/No Sleep Till Brooklyn	1987	$10
❏ 38-05683	She's On It/Slow and Low	1985	$5
❏ 38-05683 [PS]	She's On It/Slow and Low	1985	$5
❏ CS72264 [DJ]	Slow and Low (same on both sides)	1986	$15

7-Inch Extended Plays

RAT CAGE

❏ MOTR21	*Beastie Boys/Transit Cop/Jimi/Holy Snappers/Riot Fight/Ode to.../Michelle's Farm/Egg Raid on Mojo	1982	$25
❏ MOTR21 [PS]	Polly Wog Stew	1982	$25

BEASTS, THE

HIT

❏ 159	Sha La La/Where You Been	1964	$20

—*B-side by Charles Baker*

BEAT FARMERS

MCA CURB

❏ 53115	Make It Last/Big Big Man	1987	$4
❏ 53115 [DJ]	Make It Last (same on both sides)	1987	$15

—*Promo only on blue vinyl*

BEAT HAPPENING

K

❏ (# unknown)	Look Around/That Girl	1987	$6
❏ (# unknown) [PS]	Look Around/That Girl	1987	$6

BEAT MERCHANTS, THE

TOWER

❏ 127	So Fine/You Were Made for Me	1965	$20

—*B-side by Freddie and the Dreamers*

BEAT RODEO

COYOTE

❏ 005	What's the Matter/Mimi	1983	$6
❏ 005 [PS]	What's the Matter/Mimi	1983	$6

I.R.S.

❏ 52918	Everything I'm Not/It Could Happen Here	1986	$3
❏ 52918 [PS]	Everything I'm Not/It Could Happen Here	1986	$4

Number	Title	Yr	NM

BEAT, THE
COLUMBIA
❏ 11211	Don't Wait Up for Me/ Working Too Hard	1980	$8
❏ 11161	Let Me Into Your Life/ Walking Out on Love	1979	$8
❏ 02833	Met Her Yesterday/ On the Highway	1982	$8

— As "The Paul Collins Beat

BEATIN' PATH, THE
FONTANA
❏ 1583	The Original Nothing People/I Waited So Long	1967	$30

BEATLE-ETTES, THE
JAMIE
❏ 1270	Dance, Beatle, Dance/We Were Meant to Be Married	1964	$30

JUBILEE
❏ 5472	Only Seventeen/Now We're Together	1964	$30

BEATLES, THE

Also see PETE BEST; GEORGE HARRISON; JOHN LENNON; PAUL McCARTNEY; RINGO STARR.

APPLE
❏ 5222	A Hard Day's Night/I Should Have Known Better	1971	$40

— With star on A-side label

❏ 5222	A Hard Day's Night/I Should Have Known Better	1971	$10

— Without star on A-side label

❏ 5222	A Hard Day's Night/I Should Have Known Better	1975	$20

— With "All Rights Reserved" disclaimer

❏ 5964	All You Need Is Love/ Baby, You're a Rich Man	1971	$40

— With star on A-side label

❏ 5964	All You Need Is Love/ Baby, You're a Rich Man	1971	$10

— Without star on A-side label

❏ 5964	All You Need Is Love/ Baby, You're a Rich Man	1975	$20

— With "All Rights Reserved" disclaimer

❏ 5235	And I Love Her/If I Fell	1971	$40

— With star on A-side label

❏ 5235	And I Love Her/If I Fell	1971	$10

— Without star on A-side label

❏ 5235	And I Love Her/If I Fell	1975	$20

— With "All Rights Reserved" disclaimer

❏ 5150	Can't Buy Me Love/ You Can't Do That	1971	$40

— With star on A-side label

❏ 5150	Can't Buy Me Love/ You Can't Do That	1971	$10

— Without star on A-side label

❏ 5150	Can't Buy Me Love/ You Can't Do That	1975	$20

— With "All Rights Reserved" disclaimer on label

❏ Promo-1970 [DJ]	Dialogue from the Beatles' Motion Picture "Let It Be"	1970	$70
❏ Promo-1970 [DJ]	Dialogue from the Beatles' Motion Picture "Let It Be"	1970	$70
❏ 5371	Eight Days a Week/I Don't Want to Spoil the Party	1971	$40

— With star on A-side label

❏ 5371	Eight Days a Week/I Don't Want to Spoil the Party	1971	$12

— Without star on A-side label

❏ 5371	Eight Days a Week/I Don't Want to Spoil the Party	1975	$20

— With "All Rights Reserved" disclaimer

❏ 2490	Get Back/Don't Let Me Down	1969	$10

— Original: With small Capitol logo on bottom of B-side label

❏ 2490	Get Back/Don't Let Me Down	1969	$10

— With "Mfd. by Apple" on label

❏ 2490	Get Back/Don't Let Me Down	1975	$30

— With "All Rights Reserved" disclaimer

❏ 2056	Hello Goodbye/I Am the Walrus	1971	$40

— With star on A-side label

❏ 2056	Hello Goodbye/I Am the Walrus	1971	$12

— Without star on A-side label

❏ 2056	Hello Goodbye/I Am the Walrus	1975	$30

— With "All Rights Reserved" disclaimer

❏ 5476	Help!/I'm Down	1971	$40

— With star on A-side label

❏ 5476	Help!/I'm Down	1971	$12

— Without star on A-side label

❏ 5476	Help!/I'm Down	1975	$20

— With "All Rights Reserved" disclaimer

❏ 2276	Hey Jude/Revolution	1968	$20

— Original: With small Capitol logo on bottom of B-side label

❏ 2276	Hey Jude/Revolution	1968	$12

— With "Mfd. by Apple" on label

❏ 2276	Hey Jude/Revolution	1975	$30

— With "All Rights Reserved" disclaimer

❏ 5327	I Feel Fine/She's a Woman	1971	$40

— With star on A-side label

❏ 5327	I Feel Fine/She's a Woman	1971	$10

— Without star on A-side label

❏ 5327	I Feel Fine/She's a Woman	1975	$20

— With "All Rights Reserved" disclaimer

❏ 5234	I'll Cry Instead/I'm Happy Just to Dance with You	1971	$40

— With star on A-side label

❏ 5234	I'll Cry Instead/I'm Happy Just to Dance with You	1971	$10

— Without star on A-side label

❏ 5234	I'll Cry Instead/I'm Happy Just to Dance with You	1975	$20

— With "All Rights Reserved" disclaimer

❏ 5112	I Want to Hold Your Hand/I Saw Her Standing There	1971	$40

— With star on label

❏ 5112	I Want to Hold Your Hand/I Saw Her Standing There	1971	$10

— Without star on label

❏ 5112	I Want to Hold Your Hand/I Saw Her Standing There	1975	$30

— With "All Rights Reserved" disclaimer on label

❏ 2138	Lady Madonna/The Inner Light	1971	$40

— With star on A-side label

❏ 2138	Lady Madonna/The Inner Light	1971	$12

— Without star on A-side label

❏ 2138	Lady Madonna/The Inner Light	1975	$30

— With "All Rights Reserved" disclaimer

❏ 2764	Let It Be/You Know My Name (Look Up My Number)	1970	$15

— Original: With small Capitol logo on bottom of B-side label

❏ 2764	Let It Be/You Know My Name (Look Up My Number)	1970	$12

— With "Mfd. by Apple" on label

❏ 2764	Let It Be/You Know My Name (Look Up My Number)	1975	$30

— With "All Rights Reserved" disclaimer

❏ 2764 [PS]	Let It Be/You Know My Name (Look Up My Number)	1970	$125
❏ 5255	Matchbox/Slow Down	1971	$40

— With star on A-side label

❏ 5255	Matchbox/Slow Down	1971	$10

— Without star on A-side label

❏ 5255	Matchbox/Slow Down	1975	$20

— With "All Rights Reserved" disclaimer

❏ 5651	Paperback Writer/Rain	1971	$40

— With star on A-side label

❏ 5651	Paperback Writer/Rain	1971	$10

— Without star on A-side label

❏ 5651	Paperback Writer/Rain	1975	$20

— With "All Rights Reserved" disclaimer

❏ 5810	Penny Lane/Strawberry Fields Forever	1971	$40

— With star on A-side label

❏ 5810	Penny Lane/Strawberry Fields Forever	1971	$10

— Without star on A-side label

❏ 5810	Penny Lane/Strawberry Fields Forever	1975	$20

— With "All Rights Reserved" disclaimer

❏ 2654	Something/Come Together	1969	$125

— Original: With small Capitol logo on bottom of B-side label

❏ 2654	Something/Come Together	1969	$12

— With "Mfd. by Apple" on label

❏ 2654	Something/Come Together	1975	$30

— With "All Rights Reserved" disclaimer

❏ 2531	The Ballad of John and Yoko/Old Brown Shoe	1969	$12

— Original: With small Capitol logo on bottom of B-side label

❏ 2531	The Ballad of John and Yoko/Old Brown Shoe	1969	$12

— With "Mfd. by Apple" on label

❏ 2531 [PS]	The Ballad of John and Yoko/Old Brown Shoe	1969	$125
❏ 2531	The Ballad of John and Yoko/Old Brown Shoe	1975	$30

— With "All Rights Reserved" disclaimer

❏ 2832	The Long and Winding Road/For You Blue	1970	$30

— Original: With small Capitol logo on bottom of B-side label

❏ 2832	The Long and Winding Road/For You Blue	1970	$10

— With "Mfd. by Apple" on label

❏ 2832 [PS]	The Long and Winding Road/For You Blue	1970	$125
❏ 2832	The Long and Winding Road/For You Blue	1975	$30

— With "All Rights Reserved" disclaimer

❏ 5407	Ticket to Ride/Yes It Is	1971	$40

— With star on A-side label

❏ 5407	Ticket to Ride/Yes It Is	1971	$10

— Without star on A-side label

❏ 5407	Ticket to Ride/Yes It Is	1975	$20

— With "All Rights Reserved" disclaimer

❏ 5555	We Can Work It Out/Day Tripper	1971	$40

— With star on A-side label

❏ 5555	We Can Work It Out/Day Tripper	1971	$10

— Without star on A-side label

❏ 5555	We Can Work It Out/Day Tripper	1975	$20

— With "All Rights Reserved" disclaimer

APPLE/AMERICOM
❏ 2490/M-335	Get Back/Don't Let Me Down	1969	$1000

— Four-inch flexi-disc sold in vending machines

❏ 2276/M-221	Hey Jude/Revolution	1969	$300

— Four-inch flexi-disc sold in vending machines; "Hey Jude" is edited to 3:25

❏ 2531/M-382	The Ballad of John and Yoko/Old Brown Shoe	1969	$800

— Four-inch flexi-disc sold in vending machines

ATCO
❏ 6308	Ain't She Sweet/Nobody's Child	1964	$60

— With "Vocal by John Lennon" on left of label

❏ 6308 [PS]	Ain't She Sweet/Nobody's Child	1964	$500

— Sleeves with black and green print are reproductions

❏ 6308	Ain't She Sweet/Nobody's Child	1964	$70

— With "Vocal by John Lennon" under "The Beatles

❏ 6302	Sweet Georgia Brown/Take Out Some Insurance On Me Baby	1964	$200

ATLANTIC
❏ OS-13243	Ain't She Sweet/Sweet Georgia Brown	1983	$10

— Oldies Series

BACKSTAGE
❏ 1155 [DJ]	Crying, Waiting, Hoping/Take Good Care of My Baby	1983	$30
❏ 1155 [DJ]	Crying, Waiting, Hoping/Take Good Care of My Baby	1983	$30
❏ 1112 [DJ]	Like Dreamers Do/ Love of the Loved	1982	$30

— Promotional 45 from "Oui" magazine

Number	Title	Yr	NM
❏ 1112 [DJ]	Like Dreamers Do/ Love of the Loved	1982	$30

—*Promotional 45 from "Oui" magazine*

❏ 1133 [DJ]	Like Dreamers Do/ Three Cool Cats	1983	$30

—*Promotional picture disc*

❏ 1133 [DJ]	Like Dreamers Do/ Three Cool Cats	1983	$30

—*Promotional picture disc*

❏ 1122 [DJ]	Love of the Loved/Memphis	1983	$30

—*Promotional picture disc*

❏ 1122 [DJ]	Love of the Loved/Memphis	1983	$30

—*Promotional picture disc*

BEATLES FAN CLUB

❏ (1967)	Christmastime Is Here Again	1967	$200

—*Postcard*

❏ (1966)	Everywhere It's Christmas	1966	$200

—*Postcard*

❏ (1969) H-2565	Happy Christmas 1969	1969	$50

—*Flexi-disc*

❏ (1969) H-2565 [PS]	Happy Christmas 1969	1969	$70
❏ (1964)	Season's Greetings from the Beatles	1964	$300

—*Tri-fold soundcard*

❏ (1968) H-2041	The Beatles 1968 Christmas Record	1968	$70

—*Flexi-disc*

❏ (1968) H-2041 [PS]	The Beatles 1968 Christmas Record	1968	$75
❏ (1965)	The Beatles Third Christmas Record	1965	$100

—*Flexi-disc*

❏ (1965) [PS]	The Beatles Third Christmas Record	1965	$125

CAPITOL

❏ 5222	A Hard Day's Night/I Should Have Known Better	1964	$40

—*Original: Orange and yellow swirl, without "A Subsidiary Of"... in perimeter label print; first version credited both "Unart" and "Maclen" as publishers*

❏ 5222	A Hard Day's Night/I Should Have Known Better	1964	$40

—*Orange and yellow swirl, without "A Subsidiary Of"... in perimeter label print; second version credited only "Maclen" as publishers*

❏ 5222 [PS]	A Hard Day's Night/I Should Have Known Better	1964	$125
❏ 5222	A Hard Day's Night/I Should Have Known Better	1968	$60

—*Orange and yellow swirl with "A Subsidiary Of"... on perimeter print in white*

❏ 5222	A Hard Day's Night/I Should Have Known Better	1968	$125

—*Orange and yellow swirl with "A Subsidiary Of"... on perimeter print in black*

❏ 5222	A Hard Day's Night/I Should Have Known Better	1969	$75

—*Red and orange "target" label with Capitol dome logo*

❏ 5222	A Hard Day's Night/I Should Have Known Better	1969	$30

—*Red and orange "target" label with Capitol round logo*

❏ 5222	A Hard Day's Night/I Should Have Known Better	1976	$6

—*Orange label with "Capitol" at bottom*

❏ 5222	A Hard Day's Night/I Should Have Known Better	1978	$20

—*Purple label*

❏ 72144	All My Loving/This Boy	1964	$60

—*Orange and yellow swirl; Canadian release that was heavily imported to the U.S.*

❏ 72144	All My Loving/This Boy	1971	$125

—*Canadian number with U.S. labels (red and orange "target" label)*

❏ P5964 [DJ]	All You Need Is Love/ Baby, You're a Rich Man	1967	$250

—*Light green label promo*

Number	Title	Yr	NM
❏ 5964	All You Need Is Love/ Baby, You're a Rich Man	1967	$30

—*Original: Orange and yellow swirl, without "A Subsidiary Of"... in perimeter label print*

❏ P5964 [DJ]	All You Need Is Love/ Baby, You're a Rich Man	1967	$250

—*Light green label promo*

❏ 5964 [PS]	All You Need Is Love/ Baby, You're a Rich Man	1967	$50
❏ 5964	All You Need Is Love/ Baby, You're a Rich Man	1968	$60

—*Orange and yellow swirl label with "A Subsidiary Of" in perimeter print*

❏ 5964	All You Need Is Love/ Baby, You're a Rich Man	1969	$80

—*Red and orange "target" label with Capitol dome logo*

❏ 5964	All You Need Is Love/ Baby, You're a Rich Man	1969	$30

—*Red and orange "target" label with Capitol round logo*

❏ 5964	All You Need Is Love/ Baby, You're a Rich Man	1976	$6

—*Orange label with "Capitol" at bottom*

❏ 5964	All You Need Is Love/ Baby, You're a Rich Man	1978	$20

—*Purple label*

❏ 5235	And I Love Her/If I Fell	1964	$40

—*Original: Orange and yellow swirl, without "A Subsidiary Of"... in perimeter label print; publishers listed as "Unart" and "Maclen*

❏ 5235	And I Love Her/If I Fell	1964	$40

—*Original: Orange and yellow swirl, without "A Subsidiary Of"... in perimeter label print; publishers listed as "Maclen" only*

❏ 5235 [PS]	And I Love Her/If I Fell	1964	$120
❏ 5235	And I Love Her/If I Fell	1968	$60

—*Orange and yellow swirl with "A Subsidiary Of"... on perimeter print in white*

❏ 5235	And I Love Her/If I Fell	1968	$80

—*Orange and yellow swirl with "A Subsidiary Of"... on perimeter print in black*

❏ 5235	And I Love Her/If I Fell	1969	$70

—*Red and orange "target" label with Capitol round logo*

❏ 5235	And I Love Her/If I Fell	1969	$30

—*Red and orange "target" label with Capitol dome logo*

❏ 5235	And I Love Her/If I Fell	1976	$6

—*Orange label with "Capitol" at bottom*

❏ 5235	And I Love Her/If I Fell	1978	$20

—*Purple label*

❏ 5150	Can't Buy Me Love/ You Can't Do That	1964	$40

—*Original: Orange and yellow swirl, without "A Subsidiary Of"... in perimeter label print*

❏ 5150	Can't Buy Me Love/ You Can't Do That	1964	$4000

—*Yellow vinyl (unauthorized); value is conjecture. VG 2000; VG+ 3000*

❏ 5150	Can't Buy Me Love/ You Can't Do That	1964	$2000

—*Yellow and black vinyl (unauthorized); value is conjecture. VG 1000; VG+ 1500*

❏ 5150 [PS]	Can't Buy Me Love/ You Can't Do That	1964	$800

—*One of the rarest Beatles picture sleeves. Numerous counterfeits exist; if in doubt, see an expert.*

❏ 5150	Can't Buy Me Love/ You Can't Do That	1968	$60

—*Orange and yellow swirl label with "A Subsidiary Of" in perimeter print*

❏ 5150	Can't Buy Me Love/ You Can't Do That	1969	$30

—*Red and orange "target" label, dome logo*

❏ 5150	Can't Buy Me Love/ You Can't Do That	1969	$70

—*Red and orange "target" label, round logo*

❏ 5150	Can't Buy Me Love/ You Can't Do That	1976	$6

—*Orange label with "Capitol" at bottom*

❏ 5150	Can't Buy Me Love/ You Can't Do That	1978	$20

—*Purple label*

Number	Title	Yr	NM
❏ 5371	Eight Days a Week/I Don't Want to Spoil the Party	1965	$40

—*Original: Orange and yellow swirl, without "A Subsidiary Of"... in perimeter label print*

❏ 5371 [PS]	Eight Days a Week/I Don't Want to Spoil the Party	1965	$30

—*Die-cut sleeve*

❏ 5371 [PS]	Eight Days a Week/I Don't Want to Spoil the Party	1965	$80

—*Straight-cut sleeve*

❏ 5371	Eight Days a Week/I Don't Want to Spoil the Party	1968	$60

—*Orange and yellow swirl label with "A Subsidiary Of" in perimeter print*

❏ 5371	Eight Days a Week/I Don't Want to Spoil the Party	1969	$70

—*Red and orange "target" label with Capitol dome logo*

❏ 5371	Eight Days a Week/I Don't Want to Spoil the Party	1969	$30

—*Red and orange "target" label with Capitol round logo*

❏ 5371	Eight Days a Week/I Don't Want to Spoil the Party	1976	$6

—*Orange label with "Capitol" at bottom*

❏ 5371	Eight Days a Week/I Don't Want to Spoil the Party	1978	$20

—*Purple label*

❏ 2490	Get Back/Don't Let Me Down	1976	$6

—*Orange label with "Capitol" at bottom*

❏ 2490	Get Back/Don't Let Me Down	1978	$8

—*Purple label; label has reeded edge*

❏ 2490	Get Back/Don't Let Me Down	1983	$6

—*Black label with colorband; "Get Back" replaced by LP version as on Let It Be*

❏ 2490	Get Back/Don't Let Me Down	1988	$5

—*Purple label; label has smooth edge; "Get Back" replaced by LP version as on Let It Be*

❏ P-4506 [DJ]	Girl (mono/stereo)	1977	$200

—*Promo only; all colored vinyl versions are counterfeits*

❏ P-4506 [DJ]	Girl (mono/stereo)	1977	$200

—*Promo only; all colored vinyl versions are counterfeits*

❏ 4506 [PS]	Girl/You're Going to Lose That Girl	1977	$20

—*Sleeve for a single that was never pressed*

❏ 4274	Got to Get You Into My Life/Helter Skelter	1976	$6

—*Original: Orange label with "Capitol" at bottom, George Martin's name not on label*

❏ 4274 [PS]	Got to Get You Into My Life/Helter Skelter	1976	$5
❏ 4274	Got to Get You Into My Life/Helter Skelter	1976	$10

—*Orange label with "Capitol" at bottom, George Martin's name is on label*

❏ 4274	Got to Get You Into My Life/Helter Skelter	1978	$6

—*Purple label; label has reeded edge*

❏ 4274	Got to Get You Into My Life/Helter Skelter	1983	$6

—*Black label with colorband*

❏ 4274	Got to Get You Into My Life/Helter Skelter	1988	$5

—*Purple label; label has smooth edge*

❏ P-4274 [DJ]	Got to Get You Into My Life (mono/stereo)	1976	$50
❏ P-4274 [DJ]	Got to Get You Into My Life (mono/stereo)	1976	$50
❏ P2056 [DJ]	Hello Goodbye/I Am the Walrus	1967	$250

—*Light green label promo*

❏ 2056	Hello Goodbye/I Am the Walrus	1967	$40

—*Original: Orange and yellow swirl, without "A Subsidiary Of"... in perimeter label print; publishing credited to "Maclen" (we're not sure which came first)*

❏ 2056	Hello Goodbye/I Am the Walrus	1967	$40

—*Original: Orange and yellow swirl, without "A Subsidiary Of"... in perimeter label print; publishing credited to "Comet" (we're not sure which came first)*

❏ P2056 [DJ]	Hello Goodbye/I Am the Walrus	1967	$250

—*Light green label promo*

❏ 2056 [PS]	Hello Goodbye/I Am the Walrus	1967	$125

Number	Title	Yr	NM
❑ 2056	Hello Goodbye/I Am the Walrus	1968	$60

—*Orange and yellow swirl label with "A Subsidiary Of" in perimeter print*

❑ 2056	Hello Goodbye/I Am the Walrus	1969	$70

—*Red and orange "target" label with Capitol dome logo*

❑ 2056	Hello Goodbye/I Am the Walrus	1969	$30

—*Red and orange "target" label with Capitol round logo*

❑ 2056	Hello Goodbye/I Am the Walrus	1976	$6

—*Orange label with "Capitol" at bottom*

❑ 2056	Hello Goodbye/I Am the Walrus	1978	$8

—*Purple label; label has reeded edge*

❑ 2056	Hello Goodbye/I Am the Walrus	1983	$6

—*Black label with colorband*

❑ 2056	Hello Goodbye/I Am the Walrus	1988	$5

—*Purple label; label has smooth edge*

❑ 5476	Help!/I'm Down	1965	$40

—*Original: Orange and yellow swirl, without "A Subsidiary Of"... in perimeter label print*

❑ 5476 [PS]	Help!/I'm Down	1965	$80
❑ 5476	Help!/I'm Down	1968	$60

—*Orange and yellow swirl with "A Subsidiary Of"... on perimeter print in white*

❑ 5476	Help!/I'm Down	1968	$125

—*Orange and yellow swirl with "A Subsidiary Of"... on perimeter print in black*

❑ 5476	Help!/I'm Down	1969	$70

—*Red and orange "target" label with Capitol dome logo*

❑ 5476	Help!/I'm Down	1969	$30

—*Red and orange "target" label with Capitol round logo*

❑ 5476	Help!/I'm Down	1976	$6

—*Orange label with "Capitol" at bottom*

❑ 5476	Help!/I'm Down	1978	$20

—*Purple label*

❑ P-4274 [DJ]	Helter Skelter (mono/stereo)	1976	$50
❑ P-4274 [DJ]	Helter Skelter (mono/stereo)	1976	$50
❑ 2276	Hey Jude/Revolution	1976	$6

—*Orange label with "Capitol" at bottom*

❑ 2276	Hey Jude/Revolution	1978	$8

—*Purple label; label has reeded edge*

❑ 2276	Hey Jude/Revolution	1983	$6

—*Black label with colorband*

❑ 2276	Hey Jude/Revolution	1988	$5

—*Purple label; label has smooth edge*

❑ 5327	I Feel Fine/She's a Woman	1964	$40

—*Original: Orange and yellow swirl, without "A Subsidiary Of"... in perimeter label print*

❑ 5327 [PS]	I Feel Fine/She's a Woman	1964	$100
❑ 5327	I Feel Fine/She's a Woman	1968	$60

—*Orange and yellow swirl label with "A Subsidiary Of" in perimeter print*

❑ 5327	I Feel Fine/She's a Woman	1969	$30

—*Red and orange "target" label with Capitol dome logo*

❑ 5327	I Feel Fine/She's a Woman	1969	$70

—*Red and orange "target" label with Capitol round logo*

❑ 5327	I Feel Fine/She's a Woman	1976	$6

—*Orange label with "Capitol" at bottom*

❑ 5327	I Feel Fine/She's a Woman	1978	$20

—*Purple label*

❑ 5234	I'll Cry Instead/I'm Happy Just to Dance with You	1964	$50

—*Original: Orange and yellow swirl, without "A Subsidiary Of"... in perimeter label print*

❑ 5234 [PS]	I'll Cry Instead/I'm Happy Just to Dance with You	1964	$200
❑ 5234	I'll Cry Instead/I'm Happy Just to Dance with You	1968	$70

—*Orange and yellow swirl label with "A Subsidiary Of" in perimeter print*

❑ 5234	I'll Cry Instead/I'm Happy Just to Dance with You	1969	$75

—*Red and orange "target" label with Capitol dome logo*

❑ 5234	I'll Cry Instead/I'm Happy Just to Dance with You	1969	$30

—*Red and orange "target" label with Capitol round logo*

❑ 5234	I'll Cry Instead/I'm Happy Just to Dance with You	1976	$6

—*Orange label with "Capitol" at bottom*

❑ 5234	I'll Cry Instead/I'm Happy Just to Dance with You	1978	$20

—*Purple label*

❑ 5112	I Want to Hold Your Hand/I Saw Her Standing There	1964	$50

—*First pressing credits "Walter Hofer" as B-side publisher*

❑ 5112	I Want to Hold Your Hand/I Saw Her Standing There	1964	$40

—*Second pressing credits "George Pincus and Sons" as B-side publisher*

❑ 5112	I Want to Hold Your Hand/I Saw Her Standing There	1964	$40

—*Third pressings credit "Gil Music" as B-side publisher*

❑ 5112 [PS]	I Want to Hold Your Hand/I Saw Her Standing There	1964	$125

—*Die-cut, crops George Harrison's head in photo*

❑ 5112 [PS]	I Want to Hold Your Hand/I Saw Her Standing There	1964	$125

—*Straight cut, shows all of George Harrison's head*

❑ 5112	I Want to Hold Your Hand/I Saw Her Standing There	1968	$70

—*Orange and yellow swirl label with "A Subsidiary Of" in perimeter print*

❑ 5112	I Want to Hold Your Hand/I Saw Her Standing There	1969	$30

—*Red and orange "target" label, round logo*

❑ 5112	I Want to Hold Your Hand/I Saw Her Standing There	1969	$70

—*Red and orange "target" label, dome logo*

❑ 5112	I Want to Hold Your Hand/I Saw Her Standing There	1976	$10

—*Orange label, "Capitol" logo on bottom*

❑ 5112	I Want to Hold Your Hand/I Saw Her Standing There	1978	$20

—*Purple label*

❑ 5112	I Want to Hold Your Hand/I Saw Her Standing There	1984	$5

—*20th anniversary reissue; black print on perimeter of label (1964 pressings are white)*

❑ 5112 [PS]	I Want to Hold Your Hand/I Saw Her Standing There	1984	$6

—*Same as 1964 sleeve except has "1984" in small print, and Paul McCartney's cigarette is airbrushed out*

❑ 5112 [PS]	I Want to Hold Your Hand/ WMCA Good Guys	1964	$2000

—*Giveaway from New York radio station with photo of WMCA DJs on rear*

❑ P2138 [DJ]	Lady Madonna/The Inner Light	1968	$200

—*Light green label promo*

❑ 2138	Lady Madonna/The Inner Light	1968	$40

—*Original: Orange and yellow swirl, without "A Subsidiary Of"... in perimeter label print*

❑ 2138	Lady Madonna/The Inner Light	1968	$60

—*Orange and yellow swirl label with "A Subsidiary Of" in perimeter print*

❑ P2138 [DJ]	Lady Madonna/The Inner Light	1968	$200

—*Light green label promo*

❑ 2138 [PS]	Lady Madonna/The Inner Light	1968	$125
❑ 2138 [PS]	Lady Madonna/The Inner Light	1968	$30

—*Beatles Fan Club" insert that was issued with above sleeve. Originals are glossy.*

❑ 2138	Lady Madonna/The Inner Light	1969	$70

—*Red and orange "target" label with Capitol dome logo*

❑ 2138	Lady Madonna/The Inner Light	1969	$30

—*Red and orange "target" label with Capitol round logo*

❑ 2138	Lady Madonna/The Inner Light	1976	$6

—*Orange label with "Capitol" at bottom*

❑ 2138	Lady Madonna/The Inner Light	1978	$8

—*Purple label; label has reeded edge*

❑ 2138	Lady Madonna/The Inner Light	1983	$6

—*Black label with colorband*

❑ 2138	Lady Madonna/The Inner Light	1988	$5

—*Purple label; label has smooth edge*

❑ B-5439 [PS]	Leave My Kitten Alone/ Ob-La-Di, Ob-La-Da	1985	$60

—*Sleeve for a record that was never released, not even as a promo*

❑ 2764	Let It Be/You Know My Name (Look Up My Number)	1976	$6

—*Orange label with "Capitol" at bottom*

❑ 2764	Let It Be/You Know My Name (Look Up My Number)	1978	$8

—*Purple label; label has reeded edge*

❑ 2764	Let It Be/You Know My Name (Look Up My Number)	1983	$6

—*Black label with colorband*

❑ 2764	Let It Be/You Know My Name (Look Up My Number)	1988	$5

—*Purple label; label has smooth edge*

❑ B-5189	Love Me Do/P.S. I Love You	1982	$5

—*Original: Orange and yellow swirl label, black print*

❑ B-5189 [PS]	Love Me Do/P.S. I Love You	1982	$5
❑ B-5189	Love Me Do/P.S. I Love You	1983	$6

—*Black label with colorband*

❑ B-5189	Love Me Do/P.S. I Love You	1988	$4

—*Purple label; label has smooth edge*

❑ PB-5189 [DJ]	Love Me Do (same on both sides)	1982	$20
❑ PB-5189 [DJ]	Love Me Do (same on both sides)	1982	$20
❑ 5255	Matchbox/Slow Down	1964	$40

—*Original: Orange and yellow swirl, without "A Subsidiary Of"... in perimeter label print*

❑ 5255 [PS]	Matchbox/Slow Down	1964	$200
❑ 5255	Matchbox/Slow Down	1968	$60

—*Orange and yellow swirl label with "A Subsidiary Of" in perimeter print*

❑ 5255	Matchbox/Slow Down	1969	$70

—*Red and orange "target" label with Capitol dome logo*

❑ 5255	Matchbox/Slow Down	1969	$30

—*Red and orange "target" label with Capitol round logo*

❑ 5255	Matchbox/Slow Down	1976	$6

—*Orange label with "Capitol" at bottom*

❑ 5255	Matchbox/Slow Down	1978	$20

—*Purple label*

❑ 4347	Ob-La-Di, Ob-La-Da/Julia	1976	$8

—*Original: Orange label with "Capitol" at bottom*

❑ 4347 [PS]	Ob-La-Di, Ob-La-Da/Julia	1976	$8

—*Sleeves are individually numbered; very low numbers (under 1000) can fetch premium prices*

❑ 4347	Ob-La-Di, Ob-La-Da/Julia	1978	$8

—*Purple label; label has reeded edge*

❑ 4347	Ob-La-Di, Ob-La-Da/Julia	1983	$6

—*Black label with colorband*

❑ 4347	Ob-La-Di, Ob-La-Da/Julia	1988	$5

—*Purple label; label has smooth edge*

❑ P-4347 [DJ]	Ob-La-Di, Ob-La-Da (mono/stereo)	1976	$50
❑ P-4347 [DJ]	Ob-La-Di, Ob-La-Da (mono/stereo)	1976	$50
❑ 5651	Paperback Writer/Rain	1966	$30

—*Original: Orange and yellow swirl, without "A Subsidiary Of"... in perimeter label print*

❑ 5651 [PS]	Paperback Writer/Rain	1966	$80
❑ 5651	Paperback Writer/Rain	1968	$60

—*Orange and yellow swirl with "A Subsidiary Of"... on perimeter print in white*

❑ 5651	Paperback Writer/Rain	1968	$125

—*Orange and yellow swirl with "A Subsidiary Of"... on perimeter print in black*

❑ 5651	Paperback Writer/Rain	1969	$70

—*Red and orange "target" label with Capitol dome logo*

❑ 5651	Paperback Writer/Rain	1969	$30

—*Red and orange "target" label with Capitol round logo*

❑ 5651	Paperback Writer/Rain	1976	$6

—*Orange label with "Capitol" at bottom*

❑ 5651	Paperback Writer/Rain	1978	$20

—*Purple label*

Number	Title	Yr	NM
❏ P5810 [DJ]	Penny Lane/Strawberry Fields Forever	1967	$300

—Light green promo; most copies have an extra trumpet solo at the end of "Penny Lane

| ❏ P5810 [DJ] | Penny Lane/Strawberry Fields Forever | 1967 | $600 |

—Light green promo; a few copies have no trumpet solo at the end of "Penny Lane

| ❏ 5810 | Penny Lane/Strawberry Fields Forever | 1967 | $30 |

—Original: Orange and yellow swirl, without "A Subsidiary Of"... in perimeter label print; "Penny Lane" time listed as 3:00

| ❏ 5810 | Penny Lane/Strawberry Fields Forever | 1967 | $40 |

—Orange and yellow swirl, without "A Subsidiary Of"... in perimeter label print; "Penny Lane" time listed as 2:57

| ❏ P5810 [DJ] | Penny Lane/Strawberry Fields Forever | 1967 | $300 |

—Light green promo; most copies have an extra trumpet solo at the end of "Penny Lane

| ❏ P5810 [DJ] | Penny Lane/Strawberry Fields Forever | 1967 | $600 |

—Light green promo; a few copies have no trumpet solo at the end of "Penny Lane

| ❏ 5810 [PS] | Penny Lane/Strawberry Fields Forever | 1967 | $125 |
| ❏ 5810 | Penny Lane/Strawberry Fields Forever | 1968 | $60 |

—Orange and yellow swirl label with "A Subsidiary Of" in perimeter print

| ❏ 5810 | Penny Lane/Strawberry Fields Forever | 1969 | $70 |

—Red and orange "target" label with Capitol dome logo

| ❏ 5810 | Penny Lane/Strawberry Fields Forever | 1969 | $30 |

—Red and orange "target" label with Capitol round logo

| ❏ 5810 | Penny Lane/Strawberry Fields Forever | 1976 | $6 |

—Orange label with "Capitol" at bottom

| ❏ 5810 | Penny Lane/Strawberry Fields Forever | 1978 | $20 |

—Purple label

| ❏ 4612 | Sgt. Pepper's Lonely Hearts Club Band-With a Little Help from My Friends/A Day in the Life | 1978 | $8 |

—Original: Purple label; label has reeded edge

| ❏ 4612 [PS] | Sgt. Pepper's Lonely Hearts Club Band-With a Little Help from My Friends/A Day in the Life | 1978 | $30 |
| ❏ 4612 | Sgt. Pepper's Lonely Hearts Club Band-With a Little Help from My Friends/A Day in the Life | 1983 | $6 |

—Black label with colorband

| ❏ 4612 | Sgt. Pepper's Lonely Hearts Club Band-With a Little Help from My Friends/A Day in the Life | 1988 | $5 |

—Purple label; label has smooth edge

❏ P-4612 [DJ]	Sgt. Pepper's Lonely Hearts Club Band-With a Little Help from My Friends (mono/stereo)	1978	$50
❏ P-4612 [DJ]	Sgt. Pepper's Lonely Hearts Club Band-With a Little Help from My Friends (mono/stereo)	1978	$50
❏ 2654	Something/Come Together	1976	$6

—Orange label with "Capitol" at bottom

| ❏ 2654 | Something/Come Together | 1978 | $6 |

—Purple label; label has reeded edge

| ❏ 2654 | Something/Come Together | 1983 | $6 |

—Black label with colorband

| ❏ 2654 | Something/Come Together | 1988 | $5 |

—Purple label; label has smooth edge

| ❏ 2531 | The Ballad of John and Yoko/Old Brown Shoe | 1978 | $6 |

—Purple label; label has reeded edge

| ❏ 2531 | The Ballad of John and Yoko/Old Brown Shoe | 1988 | $6 |

—Purple label; label has smooth edge

❏ PB-5100 [DJ]	The Beatles' Movie Medley/Fab Four on Film	1982	$30
❏ B-5100 [PS]	The Beatles' Movie Medley/Fab Four on Film	1982	$30
❏ PB-5100 [DJ]	The Beatles' Movie Medley/Fab Four on Film	1982	$30

| ❏ B-5100 | The Beatles' Movie Medley/Fab Four on Film | 1982 | $60 |

—Stock copy; not officially released, but some got out by mistake

❏ B-5107	The Beatles' Movie Medley/I'm Happy Just to Dance with You	1982	$5
❏ B-5107 [PS]	The Beatles' Movie Medley/I'm Happy Just to Dance with You	1982	$5
❏ 2832	The Long and Winding Road/For You Blue	1976	$6

—Orange label with "Capitol" at bottom

| ❏ 2832 | The Long and Winding Road/For You Blue | 1978 | $8 |

—Purple label; label has reeded edge

| ❏ 2832 | The Long and Winding Road/For You Blue | 1983 | $6 |

—Black label with colorband

| ❏ 2832 | The Long and Winding Road/For You Blue | 1988 | $5 |

—Purple label; label has smooth edge

| ❏ 5407 | Ticket to Ride/Yes It Is | 1965 | $40 |

—Original: Orange and yellow swirl, without "A Subsidiary Of"... in perimeter label print

| ❏ 5407 [PS] | Ticket to Ride/Yes It Is | 1965 | $125 |
| ❏ 5407 | Ticket to Ride/Yes It Is | 1968 | $60 |

—Orange and yellow swirl with "A Subsidiary Of"... on perimeter print in white

| ❏ 5407 | Ticket to Ride/Yes It Is | 1968 | $125 |

—Orange and yellow swirl with "A Subsidiary Of"... on perimeter print in black

| ❏ 5407 | Ticket to Ride/Yes It Is | 1969 | $70 |

—Red and orange "target" label with Capitol dome logo

| ❏ 5407 | Ticket to Ride/Yes It Is | 1969 | $30 |

—Red and orange "target" label with Capitol round logo

| ❏ 5407 | Ticket to Ride/Yes It Is | 1976 | $6 |

—Orange label with "Capitol" at bottom

| ❏ 5407 | Ticket to Ride/Yes It Is | 1978 | $20 |

—Purple label

❏ P05624 [DJ]	Twist and Shout (same on both sides)	1986	$20
❏ P-B-5624 [DJ]	Twist and Shout (same on both sides)	1986	$20
❏ B-5624	Twist and Shout/There's a Place	1986	$5

—Black label with colorband

| ❏ B-5624 | Twist and Shout/There's a Place | 1988 | $5 |

—Purple label; label has smooth edge

| ❏ 5555 | We Can Work It Out/Day Tripper | 1965 | $40 |

—Original: Orange and yellow swirl, without "A Subsidiary Of"... in perimeter label print

| ❏ 5555 [PS] | We Can Work It Out/Day Tripper | 1965 | $70 |
| ❏ 5555 | We Can Work It Out/Day Tripper | 1968 | $60 |

—Orange and yellow swirl label with "A Subsidiary Of" in perimeter print

| ❏ 5555 | We Can Work It Out/Day Tripper | 1969 | $70 |

—Red and orange "target" label with Capitol dome logo

| ❏ 5555 | We Can Work It Out/Day Tripper | 1969 | $30 |

—Red and orange "target" label with Capitol round logo

| ❏ 5555 | We Can Work It Out/Day Tripper | 1969 | $1500 |

—Red and white "Starline" label (mispress)

| ❏ 5555 | We Can Work It Out/Day Tripper | 1976 | $6 |

—Orange label with "Capitol" at bottom

| ❏ 5555 | We Can Work It Out/Day Tripper | 1978 | $20 |

—Purple label

CAPITOL/EVATONE

| ❏ 420826cs | All My Loving/You've Got to Hide Your Love Away | 1982 | $10 |

—Flexi-disc issued as giveaway by The Musicland Group; "Musicland" version

| ❏ 420826cs | All My Loving/You've Got to Hide Your Love Away | 1982 | $30 |

—Flexi-disc issued as giveaway by The Musicland Group; "Discount" version

| ❏ 420826cs | All My Loving/You've Got to Hide Your Love Away | 1982 | $30 |

—Flexi-disc issued as giveaway by The Musicland Group; "Sam Goody" version

| ❏ 1214825cs | German Medley | 1983 | $70 |

—Flexi-disc given away by House of Guitars in New York

| ❏ 420827cs | Magical Mystery Tour/Here Comes the Sun | 1982 | $10 |

—Flexi-disc issued as giveaway by The Musicland Group; "Musicland" version

| ❏ 420827cs | Magical Mystery Tour/Here Comes the Sun | 1982 | $30 |

—Flexi-disc issued as giveaway by The Musicland Group; "Discount" version

| ❏ 420827cs | Magical Mystery Tour/Here Comes the Sun | 1982 | $30 |

—Flexi-disc issued as giveaway by The Musicland Group; "Sam Goody" version

| ❏ 830771X | Till There Was You/Three Cool Cats | 1983 | $6 |

—Flexi-disc issued as giveaway with a book

CAPITOL STARLINE

| ❏ 6281 | A Hard Day's Night/I Should Have Known Better | 1981 | $8 |

—Originals have blue labels

| ❏ 6300 | All You Need Is Love/Baby You're a Rich Man | 1981 | $8 |

—Originals have blue labels

| ❏ 6283 | And I Love Her/If I Fell | 1981 | $8 |

—Originals have blue labels

| ❏ 6066 | Boys/Kansas City | 1965 | $100 |

—Green swirl label

| ❏ 6066 | Boys/Kansas City | 1971 | $40 |

—Red and orange "target" label

| ❏ 6279 | Can't Buy Me Love/You Can't Do That | 1981 | $8 |

—Originals have blue labels

| ❏ 6064 | Do You Want to Know a Secret/Thank You Girl | 1965 | $120 |

—Green swirl label

| ❏ 6287 | Eight Days a Week/I Don't Want to Spoil the Party | 1981 | $8 |

—Originals have blue labels

| ❏ 6290 | Help!/I'm Down | 1981 | $8 |

—Originals have blue labels

| ❏ 6286 | I Feel Fine/She's a Woman | 1981 | $8 |

—Originals have blue labels

| ❏ 6282 | I'll Cry Instead/I'm Happy Just to Dance with You | 1981 | $8 |

—Originals have blue labels

| ❏ 6278 | I Want to Hold Your Hand/I Saw Her Standing There | 1981 | $30 |

—Originals have blue labels

| ❏ 6062 | Love Me Do/P.S. I Love You | 1965 | $120 |

—Green swirl label

| ❏ 6284 | Matchbox/Slow Down | 1981 | $8 |

—Originals have blue labels

| ❏ 6296 | Paperback Writer/Rain | 1981 | $8 |

—Originals have blue labels

| ❏ 6299 | Penny Lane/Strawberry Fields Forever | 1981 | $8 |

—Originals have blue labels

| ❏ 6063 | Please Please Me/From Me to You | 1965 | $120 |

—Green swirl label

| ❏ 6288 | Ticket to Ride/Yes It Is | 1981 | $8 |

—Originals have blue labels

| ❏ 6061 | Twist and Shout/There's a Place | 1965 | $120 |

—Green swirl label

| ❏ 6293 | We Can Work It Out/Day Tripper | 1981 | $8 |

—Originals have blue labels

COLLECTABLES

❏ 1514	Ask Me Why/Twist and Shout	1982	$3
❏ 1514 [PS]	Ask Me Why/Twist and Shout	1982	$3
❏ 1505	A Taste of Honey/Besame Mucho	1982	$3
❏ 1505 [PS]	A Taste of Honey/Besame Mucho	1982	$3
❏ 1510	Be-Bop-a-Lula/Hallelujah I Love Her So	1982	$3
❏ 1510 [PS]	Be-Bop-a-Lula/Hallelujah I Love Her So	1982	$3
❏ 1520	Cry for a Shadow/Rock and Roll Music	1987	$5

—Despite label credit to The Beatles, B-side is a Peter Best recording

Number	Title	Yr	NM
❏ 1509	Falling in Love Again/Sheila	1982	$3
❏ 1509 [PS]	Falling in Love Again/Sheila	1982	$3
❏ 1502	Hippy Hippy Shake/ Sweet Little Sixteen	1982	$3
❏ 1502 [PS]	Hippy Hippy Shake/ Sweet Little Sixteen	1982	$3
❏ 1519	How'd You Get to Know Her Name/If You Can't Get Her	1987	$10

—*Despite label credit to The Beatles, both are Peter Best recordings*

❏ 1518	I'll Have Everything Too/I'm Checking Out Now Baby	1987	$10

—*Despite label credit to The Beatles, both are Peter Best recordings*

❏ 1516	I'll Try Anyway/I Don't Know Why I Do (I Just Do)	1987	$10

—*Despite label credit to The Beatles, both are Peter Best recordings*

❏ 1501	I'm Gonna Sit Right Down and Cry Over You/Roll Over Beethoven	1982	$3
❏ 1501 [PS]	I'm Gonna Sit Right Down and Cry Over You/Roll Over Beethoven	1982	$3
❏ 1515	I Saw Her Standing There/ Can't Help It "Blue Angel	1982	$3

—*B-side is actually "Reminiscing*

❏ 1515 [PS]	I Saw Her Standing There/ Can't Help It "Blue Angel	1982	$3
❏ 1503	Lend Me Your Comb/ Your Feets Too Big	1982	$3
❏ 1503 [PS]	Lend Me Your Comb/ Your Feets Too Big	1982	$3
❏ 1521	Let's Dance/If You Love Me Baby	1987	$6

—*Despite label credit to The Beatles, A-side is a Tony Sheridan solo recording*

❏ 1513	Long Tall Sally/I Remember You	1982	$3
❏ 1513 [PS]	Long Tall Sally/I Remember You	1982	$3
❏ 1517	She's Not the Only Girl in Town/ More Than I Need Myself	1987	$10

—*Despite label credit to The Beatles, both are Peter Best recordings*

❏ 1512	Talkin' Bout You/Shimmy Shake	1982	$3
❏ 1512 [PS]	Talkin' Bout You/Shimmy Shake	1982	$3
❏ 1506	Till There Was You/Everybody's Trying to Be My Baby	1982	$3
❏ 1506 [PS]	Till There Was You/Everybody's Trying to Be My Baby	1982	$3
❏ 1508	To Know Her Is To Love Her/Little Queenie	1982	$3
❏ 1508 [PS]	To Know Her Is To Love Her/Little Queenie	1982	$3
❏ 1522	What'd I Say/Sweet Georgia Brown	1987	$6

—*Despite label credit to The Beatles, A-side is a Tony Sheridan solo recording*

❏ 1504	Where Have You Been All My Life/Mr. Moonlight	1982	$3
❏ 1504 [PS]	Where Have You Been All My Life/Mr. Moonlight	1982	$3
❏ 1524	Why/I'll Try Anyway	1987	$6

—*Despite label credit to The Beatles, B-side is a Peter Best recording*

DECCA

❏ 31382 [DJ]	My Bonnie/The Saints	1962	$3000

—*By "Tony Sheridan and the Beat Brothers"; ' pink label, star on label under "Decca*

❏ 31382	My Bonnie/The Saints	1962	$15000

—*By "Tony Sheridan and the Beat Brothers"; black label with color bars (all-black label with star under "Decca" should be a counterfeit). VG 7500; VG+ 11,250*

❏ 31382 [DJ]	My Bonnie/The Saints	1962	$3000

—*By "Tony Sheridan and the Beat Brothers"; pink label, star on label under "Decca". VG 1,000; VG+ 2,000*

EVA-TONE

❏ 830771X [DJ]	Til There Was You/Three Cool Cats (both on same side)	1983	$6

—*Red plastic flexidisc; issued as giveaway with a Beatles price guide*

MGM

❏ 13213 [DJ]	My Bonnie (My Bonnie Lies Over the Ocean)/The Saints (When the Saints Go Marching In)	1964	$250

—*The Beatles with Tony Sheridan*

❏ 13213	My Bonnie (My Bonnie Lies Over the Ocean)/The Saints (When the Saints Go Marching In)	1964	$50

—*The Beatles with Tony Sheridan; no reference to LP on label*

❏ 13213	My Bonnie (My Bonnie Lies Over the Ocean)/The Saints (When the Saints Go Marching In)	1964	$60

—*The Beatles with Tony Sheridan; LP number on label*

Number	Title	Yr	NM
❏ 13213 [DJ]	My Bonnie (My Bonnie Lies Over the Ocean)/The Saints (When the saints Go Marching In)	1964	$300

—*The Beatles with Tony Sheridan*

❏ 13213 [PS]	My Bonnie (My Bonnie Lies Over the Ocean)/The Saints (When the saints Go Marching In)	1964	$120

—*The Beatles with Tony Sheridan*

❏ 13227 [DJ]	Why/Cry for a Shadow	1964	$250

—*The Beatles with Tony Sheridan*

❏ 13227	Why/Cry for a Shadow	1964	$200

—*The Beatles with Tony Sheridan*

❏ 13227 [DJ]	Why/Cry for a Shadow	1964	$250

—*The Beatles with Tony Sheridan*

❏ 13227 [PS]	Why/Cry for a Shadow	1964	$400

—*The Beatles with Tony Sheridan*

OLDIES 45

❏ 149	Do You Want to Know a Secret/Thank You Girl	1964	$20
❏ 151	Love Me Do/P.S. I Love You	1964	$20
❏ 150	Please Please Me/ From Me to You	1964	$20
❏ 152	Twist and Shout/There's a Place	1964	$20

SWAN

❏ 4152 [DJ]	I'll Get You (one-sided)	1964	$600
❏ 4152 [DJ]	I'll Get You (one-sided)	1964	$600
❏ 4152 [DJ]	She Loves You/I'll Get You	1963	$500

—*Thick print, no "Don't Drop Out" on label*

❏ 4152 [DJ]	She Loves You/I'll Get You	1963	$450

—*Thin print, "Don't Drop Out" on label*

❏ 4152 [DJ]	She Loves You/I'll Get You	1963	$500

—*Flat white label, no "Don't Drop Out" on label*

❏ 4152	She Loves You/I'll Get You	1963	$600

—*Semi-glossy white label/red print; "Don't Drop Out" not on label*

❏ 4152	She Loves You/I'll Get You	1963	$650

—*Flat white label/red print, "Don't Drop Out" not on label*

❏ 4152	She Loves You/I'll Get You	1963	$650

—*Semi-glossy white label/red print, "Don't Drop Out" on label*

❏ 4152	She Loves You/I'll Get You	1963	$600

—*Semi-glossy white label/blue printing*

❏ 4152 [DJ]	She Loves You/I'll Get You	1963	$500

—*Thick print, no "Don't Drop Out" on label*

❏ 4152 [DJ]	She Loves You/I'll Get You	1963	$450

—*Thin print, "Don't Drop Out" on label*

❏ 4152 [DJ]	She Loves You/I'll Get You	1963	$500

—*Flat white label, no "Don't Drop Out" on label*

❏ 4152	She Loves You/I'll Get You	1964	$50

—*Black label, silver print, "Don't Drop Out" not on label*

❏ 4152	She Loves You/I'll Get You	1964	$40

—*Black label, silver print, "Don't Drop Out" on label*

❏ 4152	She Loves You/I'll Get You	1964	$60

—*Black label, silver print, "Produced by George Martin" on both labels*

❏ 4152	She Loves You/I'll Get You	1964	$60

—*Black label, silver print, "Produced by George Martin" on only one label*

❏ 4152 [PS]	She Loves You/I'll Get You	1964	$120
❏ 4182 [DJ]	Sie Liebt Dich (She Loves You)/I'll Get You	1964	$400

—*White label, "(She Loves You)" under "Sie Liebt Dich*

❏ 4182 [DJ]	Sie Liebt Dich (She Loves You)/I'll Get You	1964	$450

—*White label, "Sie Liebt Dich (She Loves You)" on one line*

❏ 4182	Sie Liebt Dich (She Loves You)/I'll Get You	1964	$200

—*White label, "Sie Liebt Dich (She Loves You)" on one line*

❏ 4182	Sie Liebt Dich (She Loves You)/I'll Get You	1964	$200

—*White label, "(She Loves You)" under "Sie Liebt Dich," narrow print*

❏ 4182	Sie Liebt Dich (She Loves You)/I'll Get You	1964	$200

—*White label, "(She Loves You)" under "Sie Liebt Dich," wide red print*

Number	Title	Yr	NM
❏ 4182	Sie Liebt Dich (She Loves You)/I'll Get You	1964	$175

—*White label, "(She Loves You)" under "Sie Liebt Dich," wide orange print*

❏ 4182 [DJ]	Sie Liebt Dich (She Loves You)/I'll Get You	1964	$400

—*White label, "(She Loves You)" under "Sie Liebt Dich*

❏ 4182 [DJ]	Sie Liebt Dich (She Loves You)/I'll Get You	1964	$450

—*White label, "Sie Liebt Dich (She Loves You)" on one line*

TOLLIE

❏ 9008 [DJ]	Love Me Do/P.S. I Love You	1964	$400
❏ 9008 [DJ]	Love Me Do/P.S. I Love You	1964	$400
❏ 9008	Love Me Do/P.S. I Love You	1964	$60

—*Yellow label, black print (any logo or print variation)*

❏ 9008	Love Me Do/P.S. I Love You	1964	$60

—*Yellow label, blue/green print*

❏ 9008	Love Me Do/P.S. I Love You	1964	$70

—*Black label, silver print*

❏ 9008 [PS]	Love Me Do/P.S. I Love You	1964	$200
❏ 9001	Twist and Shout/There's a Place	1964	$60

—*Yellow label, green print, "tollie" lowercase*

❏ 9001	Twist and Shout/There's a Place	1964	$60

—*Yellow label, black print, "TOLLIE" stands alone*

❏ 9001	Twist and Shout/There's a Place	1964	$60

—*Yellow label, black print, black "tollie" in box*

❏ 9001	Twist and Shout/There's a Place	1964	$70

—*Yellow label, black print, purple "tollie" in box*

❏ 9001	Twist and Shout/There's a Place	1964	$60

—*Yellow label, black print, black "TOLLIE" in thin box*

❏ 9001	Twist and Shout/There's a Place	1964	$80

—*Yellow label, black print, "TOLLIE" in brackets*

❏ 9001	Twist and Shout/There's a Place	1964	$70

—*Yellow label, blue print*

❏ 9001	Twist and Shout/There's a Place	1964	$100

—*Yellow label, purple print*

❏ 9001	Twist and Shout/There's a Place	1964	$100

—*Yellow label, green print, "TOLLIE" uppercase*

❏ 9001	Twist and Shout/There's a Place	1964	$70

—*Black label, silver print*

UNITED ARTISTS

❏ UAEP10029 [DJ]	A Hard Day's Night Open End Interview	1964	$1500
❏ UAEP10029 [DJ]	A Hard Day's Night Open End Interview	1964	$1500
❏ SP-2357 [DJ]	A Hard Day's Night Theatre Lobby Spot	1964	$1500
❏ SP-2357 [DJ]	A Hard Day's Night Theatre Lobby Spot	1964	$1500
❏ ULP-42370	Let It Be Radio Spots	1970	$1200

VEE JAY

❏ Spec. DJ No.8	Ask Me Why/Anna	1964	$10000

—*Though it doesn't fit into any known Vee Jay numbering system (other "Spec. DJ No." records are rumored, but none are confirmed), this is an authentic 1964 promotional release. VG 5000; VG+ 7500*

❏ 587 [DJ]	Do You Want to Know a Secret/Thank You Girl	1964	$600
❏ 587 [DJ]	Do You Want to Know a Secret/Thank You Girl	1964	$600
❏ 587	Do You Want to Know a Secret/Thank You Girl	1964	$60

—*Black rainbow label, oval logo*

❏ 587	Do You Want to Know a Secret/Thank You Girl	1964	$75

—*Plain black label; "Vee Jay" in oval*

❏ 587	Do You Want to Know a Secret/Thank You Girl	1964	$75

—*Plain black label; "VJ" in brackets*

❏ 587	Do You Want to Know a Secret/Thank You Girl	1964	$75

—*Plain black label; "VJ" stands alone*

❏ 587	Do You Want to Know a Secret/Thank You Girl	1964	$60

—*Plain black label; "VEE JAY" stands alone*

❏ 587	Do You Want to Know a Secret/Thank You Girl	1964	$50

—*Plain black label with two horizontal lines; "VJ" in brackets*

Number	Title	Yr	NM
❏ 587	Do You Want to Know a Secret/Thank You Girl	1964	$75

— Yellow label

Number	Title	Yr	NM
❏ 587 [PS]	Do You Want to Know a Secret/Thank You Girl	1964	$120

— Any copy of this claiming to be a "Promotional Copy" is a fake

❏ 587	Do You Want to Know a Secret/Thank You Girl	1964	$50

— Black rainbow label, brackets logo

❏ 522 [DJ]	From Me to You/Thank You Girl	1963	$500
❏ 522	From Me to You/Thank You Girl	1963	$600

— Black rainbow label; "Vee Jay" in oval

❏ 522	From Me to You/Thank You Girl	1963	$900

— Black rainbow label; "VJ" in brackets

❏ 522	From Me to You/Thank You Girl	1963	$800

— Plain black label

❏ 522 [DJ]	From Me to You/Thank You Girl	1963	$500
❏ 498 [DJ]	Please Please Me/Ask Me Why	1963	$1100

— Misspelled "The Beattles

❏ 498	Please Please Me/Ask Me Why	1963	$1600

— Misspelled "The Beattles"; number is "#498

❏ 498	Please Please Me/Ask Me Why	1963	$1500

— Misspelled "The Beattles"; number is "VJ 498

❏ 498	Please Please Me/Ask Me Why	1963	$1600

— Correct spelling; number is "#498

❏ 498	Please Please Me/Ask Me Why	1963	$900

— Correct spelling; number is "VJ 498"; thick print

❏ 498	Please Please Me/Ask Me Why	1963	$2000

— Correct spelling; number is "VJ 498"; brackets label. VG 1000; VG+ 1500

❏ 498 [DJ]	Please Please Me/Ask Me Why	1963	$1100

— Misspelled "The Beattles

❏ 581 [DJ]	Please Please Me/From Me to You	1964	$600

— White label, blue print; "Promotional Copy" on label

❏ 581 [DJ]	Please Please Me/From Me to You	1964	$900

— White label, blue print; no "Promotional Copy" on label

❏ 581 [DJ]	Please Please Me/From Me to You	1964	$600

— White label, blue print; "Promotional Copy" on label

❏ 581 [DJ]	Please Please Me/From Me to You	1964	$900

— White label, blue print; no "Promotional Copy" on label

❏ 581	Please Please Me/From Me to You	1964	$60

— Black rainbow label, oval logo

❏ 581	Please Please Me/From Me to You	1964	$50

— Plain black label with two horizontal lines

❏ 581	Please Please Me/From Me to You	1964	$80

— Plain black label, brackets logo

❏ 581	Please Please Me/From Me to You	1964	$80

— Yellow label

❏ 581	Please Please Me/From Me to You	1964	$160

— White label

❏ 581	Please Please Me/From Me to You	1964	$250

— Purple label

❏ 581 [PS]	Please Please Me/From Me to You	1964	$500
❏ 581	Please Please Me/From Me to You	1964	$70

— Plain black label, "VEE JAY" stands alone

❏ 581	Please Please Me/From Me to You	1964	$75

— Plain black label, "VJ" stands alone

❏ 581	Please Please Me/From Me to You	1964	$70

— Black rainbow label, brackets logo

❏ 581	Please Please Me/From Me to You	1964	$70

— Plain black label, oval logo

❏ 0(no cat #) [PS]	We Wish You a Merry Christmas and a Happy New Year	1964	$100

— Used with any Vee Jay or Tollie Beatles single in 1964-65 holiday season

7-Inch Extended Plays

CAPITOL

❏ R-5365 [PS]	4-By the Beatles	1965	$250
❏ EAP 1-2121 [PS]	Four by the Beatles	1964	$300

Number	Title	Yr	NM
❏ R-5365	Honey Don't/I'm a Loser// Mr. Moonlight/Everybody's Trying to Be My Baby	1965	$100
❏ SXA-2108	I'll Cry Instead/And I Love Her/Slow Down//If I Fell/ Tell Me Why/Matchbox	1964	$400

— 33 1/3 rpm, small hole jukebox edition

❏ SXA-2047	It Won't Be Long/This Boy/All My Loving//Don't Bother Me/All I've Got to Do/I Wanna Be Your Man	1964	$400

— Stereo jukebox edtion; small hole, plays at 33 1/3 rpm

❏ SXA-2047 [PS]	Meet the Beatles	1964	$600

— With all jukebox title strips intact (deduct 33 percent if missing, deduct less if material is there but not intact)

❏ PRO-2548/9 [DJ]	Open End Interview with the Beatles	1964	$800

— 33 1/3 rpm, small hole. Authentic copies have colorband along outside of label.

❏ PRO-2548/9 [PS]	Open End Interview with the Beatles	1964	$1000

— Contains script for interview. Authentic copies are glossy and have a die-cut thumb tab.

❏ SXA-2108 [PS]	Something New	1964	$600

— With all jukebox title strips intact (deduct 33 percent if missing, deduct less if material is there but not intact)

❏ SXA-2080	Thank You Girl/Devil in Her Heart/ Money (That's What I Want)// Long Tall Sally/I Call Your Name/ Please Mister Postman	1964	$400

— 33 1/3 rpm, small hole jukebox edition

❏ SXA-2080 [PS]	The Beatles' Second Album	1964	$600

— With all jukebox title strips intact (deduct 33 percent if missing, deduct less if material is there but not intact)

❏ PRO-2598/9 [DJ]	The Beatles Second Album Open End Interview	1964	$800

— 33 1/3 rpm, small hole; interview plus three songs from the LP

❏ PRO-2598/9 [PS]	The Beatles Second Album Open End Interview	1964	$1000

— Contains script for interview

VEE JAY

❏ 1-903 [DJ]	Misery/Taste of Honey// Ask Me Why/Anna	1964	$400

— White and blue label, all titles the same size

❏ 1-903 [DJ]	Misery/Taste of Honey// Ask Me Why/Anna	1964	$300

— White and blue label, "Ask Me Why" in much larger print

❏ 1-903	Misery/Taste of Honey// Ask Me Why/Anna	1964	$50

— Black rainbow label, oval logo

❏ 1-903 [B]	Misery/Taste of Honey// Ask Me Why/Anna	1964	$150

— Plain black label, oval logo

❏ 1-903 [B]	Misery/Taste of Honey// Ask Me Why/Anna	1964	$150

— Black rainbow label, brackets logo, "Ask Me Why" in much larger print

❏ 1-903 [B]	Misery/Taste of Honey// Ask Me Why/Anna	1964	$100

— Black rainbow label, brackets logo, all titles the same size

❏ 1-903	Misery/Taste of Honey// Ask Me Why/Anna	1964	$250

— Plain black label, brackets logo

❏ 1-903	Misery/Taste of Honey// Ask Me Why/Anna	1964	$175

— Plain black label, "VEE JAY" stands alone

❏ 1-903 [DJ]	Misery/Taste of Honey// Ask Me Why/Anna	1964	$400

— White and blue label, all titles the same size

❏ 1-903 [DJ]	Misery/Taste of Honey// Ask Me Why/Anna	1964	$300

— White and blue label, "Ask Me Why" in much larger print

❏ 1-903 [PS]	Souvenir of Their Visit to America	1964	$75

— Cardboard sleeve

❏ 1-903 [PS]	Souvenir of Their Visit to America	1964	$8000

— Ask Me Why/The Beatles" plugged on promo-only sleeve. VG 4000; VG+ 6000

BEATMASTER
TOMMY BOY

Number	Title	Yr	NM
❏ TB842	Lipservice/(Instrumental)	1984	$5

BEATSTALKERS, THE
PRESS

❏ 5001	Left, Right, Left/Get a Better Hold On	1966	$20

BEATTY, E.C.
COLONIAL

❏ 7003	Ski King/I'm a Lucky Man	1959	$40

BEATTY, SUSI
STARWAY

❏ 1205	Hard Baby to Rock/ Down Home Jubilee	1989	$6
❏ 1206	Heart from a Stone/ Down Home Jubilee	1989	$6

BEAU, BILLY
DOT

❏ 16281	Hey Daddy (I'm Gonna Tell Santa On You)/Santa's Coffee	1961	$50

BEAU BRUMMELS, THE
AUTUMN

❏ 20	Don't Talk to Strangers/ In Good Time	1965	$8
❏ 24	Good Time Music/Sad Little Girl	1965	$8
❏ 8	Laugh, Laugh/Still in Love with You Baby	1965	$20

— White label

❏ 8	Laugh, Laugh/Still in Love with You Baby	1965	$15

— Tan label

RHINO

❏ RNOR4506	Laugh, Laugh/Just a Little	1984	$4
❏ RNOR4506 [PS]	Laugh, Laugh/Just a Little	1984	$4

WARNER BROS.

❏ 7204	Are You Happy/Lift Me	1968	$6
❏ 7260	Cherokee Girl/Deep Water	1969	$6
❏ 7014	Don't Make Promises/ Two Days 'Til Tomorrow	1967	$8
❏ 5848	Fine with Me/Here We Are Again	1966	$8
❏ 7218	I'm a Sleeper/Long Walking Down to Misery	1968	$6
❏ 7079	Magic Hollow/Lower Level	1967	$8
❏ 5813	One Too Many Mornings/ She Reigns	1966	$8

BEAU COUP
AMHERST

❏ 322	Born and Raised on Rock-n-Roll/Jane	1988	$4
❏ 318	Sweet Rachel/Hold on Me	1987	$4

BEAU-K'S, THE
MERCURY

❏ 72157	Packin' Up/Forget Me Not	1963	$10

BEAU-MARKS, THE
MAINSTREAM

❏ 688	Clap Your Hands/Daddy Said	1968	$10

PORT

❏ 70029	Little Miss Twist/ Lovely Little Lady	1962	$20

RUST

❏ 5050	I'll Never Be the Same/ Tender Years	1962	$30
❏ 5035	School Is Out/Classmates	1961	$30

SHAD

❏ 5021	Cause We're in Love/ Billy Went a-Walkin'	1960	$30
❏ 5017	Clap Your Hands/Daddy Said	1960	$30

TIME

❏ 1032	Oh Joan/Rockin' Blues	1961	$40

Number	Title	Yr	NM

BEAUMONT, JIMMY
BANG

❏ 525	I Never Loved Her Anyway/You Got Too Much Going for You	1966	$40
❏ 510	Tell Me/I Feel Like I'm Falling in Love	1965	$30

COLPIX

❏ 607	The End of a Story/ Baion Rhythms	1961	$40

MAY

❏ 112	Ev'rybody's Cryin'/Camera	1961	$30
❏ 136	I'll Always Be in Love with You/Give Her My Best	1963	$30
❏ 115	I Should Have Listened to Mama/Juarez	1962	$30

BEAUREGARDE
INTERNATIONAL ARTISTS

❏ 123	Popcorn Popper/Mama Never Taught Me How to Jelly Roll	1968	$30

BEAVER AND KRAUSE
WARNER BROS.

❏ 7642	Bluebird Canyon Stomp/ Real Slow Drag	1972	$6
❏ 7414	People's Park/Salute to the Vanishing Bald Eagle	1970	$6
❏ 7485	Walkin' By the River/The Saga of the Blue Beaver	1971	$6

BEAVERS, CLYDE
DECCA

❏ 31314	Ain't Gonna Drink No More/I Wanted Heaven	1961	$20
❏ 31173	Here I Am Drunk Again/ My Love Is Real	1960	$20

DOT

❏ 17416	Clyde/Truck Stop Wall	1972	$6
❏ 17438	I Will Love You Until I Die/ Broken Wings Can't Fly	1972	$6
❏ 17382	Last Call for Alcohol/How Can Anything Be So Wrong	1971	$6

HICKORY

❏ 1346	That's You (And What's Left of Me)/Old Tree	1966	$8
❏ 1376	Thirty-Two Years/Train from North to South	1966	$8

TEMPWOOD V

❏ 1039	Still Loving You/Happy Times	1963	$10
❏ 1044	Sukiyaki (I Look Up When I Walk)/Handprints on the Window	1963	$10

BEAVERS, JACKEY
CHECKER

❏ 1119	I Want Somebody/Slingshot	1965	$30

—As "Jackey Beaver

MAINSTREAM

❏ 713	When Something Is Wrong with My Baby/We're Not Too Young to Fall in Love	1969	$70

REVILOT

❏ 208	Love That Never Grows Old/I Need My Baby	1967	$1000

SOUND STAGE 7

❏ 2649	Hey Girl (I Can't Stand to See You Go)/Hold On	1969	$15
❏ ZS71506	Singing a Funky Song (For My Baby)/Hey Girl (I Can't Stand to See You Go)	1972	$10
❏ ZS71502	Someday We'll Be Together/ Lover Come Back	1971	$30

BEAVERS, THE
CAPITOL

❏ F3956	Sack Dress/Rockin' at the Drive-In	1958	$30

BECK, BECKY LEE
CHALLENGE

❏ 59272	I Want a Beatle for Christmas/Puppy Dog	1964	$30

BECK, BOBBY
ABC-PARAMOUNT

❏ 10099	Isle of Capri/Swinging on a Chandelier	1960	$30
❏ 10148	The Door Is Always Open/ You Got All My Love	1960	$30

BECK, BOGERT & APPICE

Also see JEFF BECK; VANILLA FUDGE; CACTUS. (SC1)
Also see JEFF BECK; VANILLA FUDGE; CACTUS.
Also see JEFF BECK; VANILLA FUDGE; CACTUS. (45)

EPIC

❏ 10998	I'm So Proud/Oh to Love You	1973	$8
❏ 11027	Lady/Oh to Love You	1973	$8

BECK FAMILY, THE
LEJOINT

❏ 34003	Can't Shake the Feeling/ Nobody But You	1979	$5
❏ 34005	Falling in Love Again/ (B-side unknown)	1979	$5

BECK, JEFF, AND ROD STEWART
EPIC

❏ 34-05416	People Get Ready/ Back on the Street	1985	$3
❏ 34-05416 [PS]	People Get Ready/ Back on the Street	1985	$3

BECK, JEFF
EPIC

❏ 10157	Beck's Bolero/Hi-Ho Silver Lining	1967	$20
❏ 10390	Blues De Luxe/Ol' Man River	1968	$15
❏ 50276	Come Dancing/Head for Backstage Pass	1976	$4
❏ 50112	Constipated Duck/You Know What I Mean	1975	$6
❏ 10938	Definitely Maybe/ Hi Ho Silver Lining	1973	$12
❏ 34-05595	Gets Us All in the End/ You Know We Know	1985	$4
❏ 10814	Got the Feeling/Situation	1971	$10
❏ 50914	Too Much to Lose/ The FInal Peace	1980	$4

BECKER, GLORIA
REAL

❏ 1304	Sixteen Pounds (Housewife's Lament)/Adios to Mexico City	1956	$30

—A-side is a parody of "Sixteen Tons

BECKHAM, BOB
DECCA

❏ 31337	10,000 Teardrops (And One Broken Heart)/Just Friends	1961	$10
❏ 31432	Building Memories/ Memory Mountain	1962	$8
❏ 31029	Crazy Arms/Beloved	1959	$15
❏ 31029 [PS]	Crazy Arms/Beloved	1959	$30
❏ 31493	Footprints/Midnight	1963	$8
❏ 31239	Forget It/Like a Fool	1961	$10
❏ 31547	Grabbing at Rainbows/ My Heart Would Know	1963	$8
❏ 31607	Helpless/I'll Be Around	1964	$8
❏ 31285	How Soon (Will I Be Seeing You)/I'm Wondering	1961	$10
❏ 31391	I Cry Like a Baby/I'll Take My Chances	1962	$8
❏ 31163	Meet Me Halfway/One More Time	1960	$10
❏ 31089	Only the Broken Hearted/Mais Oui	1960	$10
❏ 30617	Tomorrow/I'm Tired of Everyone But You	1958	$15
❏ 31132	Two Wrongs Don't Make a Right/Nothing Is Forever	1960	$10
❏ 31132 [PS]	Two Wrongs Don't Make a Right/Nothing Is Forever	1960	$30

MONUMENT

❏ 1018	Cherokee Strip/You Really Know How to Hurt a Guy	1967	$6
❏ 1030	Lily White/Look at Them	1967	$6

SMASH

❏ 1990	Slowly Dying/It's My Heart	1965	$8

BECKHAM, CHARLIE
OAK

❏ 1048	Think I'll Go Home/ (B-side unknown)	1988	$6

BECKY AND THE LOLLIPOPS
EPIC

❏ 9736	I Don't Care (What They Say)/My Boyfriend	1964	$15

BEDLAM

Includes RAINBOW and BLACK SABBATH drummer Cozy Powell. (SC1)
Includes RAINBOW and BLACK SABBATH drummer Cozy Powell.
Includes RAINBOW and BLACK SABBATH drummer Cozy Powell. (45)

BEE, CELI
APA

❏ 17011	Blow My Mind/Give It to Me	1979	$6
❏ 17007	Fly Me on the Wings of Love/ You're the Best Thing (That Ever Happened to My Life)	1978	$8
❏ 17012	It's Love/For the Love of My Man	1980	$6
❏ 17008	Love Drops/Can't Let You Go	1979	$6
❏ 17002	One Love/It's Sad	1978	$8
❏ 17001	Superman/Hurt Me, Hurt Me	1977	$8
❏ 17000	Together/Lost in Love	1977	$8

BEE GEES

Also see THE BUNBURYS; BARRY GIBB; MAURICE GIBB; ROBIN GIBB; JIMMY HANNAN.

ATCO

❏ 6909	Alive/Paper Mache, Cabbages and Kings	1972	$5
❏ 6702	Don't Forget to Remember/I Lay Down and Die	1969	$40

—Only issued with this B-side in Canada; not only that, but it's a different mix than the LP version

❏ 6702	Don't Forget to Remember/The Lord	1969	$12
❏ 6847	Don't Wanna Live Inside Myself/Walking Back to Waterloo	1971	$6
❏ 6657	First of May/Lamplight	1969	$8
❏ 6521	Holiday/Every Christian Lion Hearted Man Will Show You	1967	$12
❏ 6824	How Can You Mend a Broken Heart/ Country Woman	1971	$6
❏ 6741	If Only I Had My Mind on Something Else/Sweetheart	1970	$8
❏ 6752	I.O.I.O./Then You Left Me	1970	$8
❏ 6639	I Started a Joke/ Kilburn Towers	1969	$8
❏ 6603	I've Gotta Get a Message to You/Kitty Can	1968	$8
❏ 6795	Lonely Days/Man for All Seasons	1971	$6
❏ 6871	My World/On Time	1972	$5
❏ 6532	(The Lights Went Out in) Massachusetts/Sir Geoffrey Saved the World	1967	$10
❏ 6503	To Love Somebody/ Close Another Door	1967	$10
❏ 6682 [DJ]	Tomorrow Tomorrow (Short Version 3:04)/ (Long Version 4:02)	1969	$15

—On white label with no promo markings

❏ 6682	Tomorrow Tomorrow/ Sun in My Morning	1969	$8
❏ 6548	Words/Sinking Ships	1968	$10

EMMC

❏ 0(no cat #)	A Personal Message from the Bee Gees/The Rescue of Bonnie Prince Wally	1979	$10

—Official Bee Gees Fan Club record; small hole, plays at 33 1/3 rpm

RSO

❏ 867	Boogie Child/Lovers	1976	$4
❏ 501	Charade/Heavy Breathing	1974	$6
❏ 8001	Come On Over/Jive Talkin'	1980	$4

—Reissue series; first time on 45 for A-side

❏ 880	Edge of the Universe/Words	1977	$4
❏ 519	Fanny (Be Tender With My Love)/Country Lanes	1975	$4
❏ 1066	He's a Liar/(Instrumental)	1981	$3
❏ 882	How Deep Is Your Love/Can't Keep a Good Man Down	1977	$4
❏ 1067	Living Eyes/I Still Love You	1981	$3
❏ 8011	Lonely Days/Words	1980	$3

—Reissue series

❏ 859	Love So Right/You Stepped Into My Life	1976	$4
❏ 925	Love You Inside Out/I'm Satisfied	1979	$4
❏ 8019	More Than a Woman/ Night Fever	1980	$4

—Reissue series; first time on 45 for A-side

❏ 408	Mr. Natural/It Doesn't Matter Much to Me	1974	$6
❏ 401	Saw a New Morning/My Life Has Been a Song	1973	$6
❏ RP106 [DJ]	Sgt. Pepper's Lonely Hearts Club Band/With a Little Help from My Friends (stereo/mono)	1978	$20

—As "Lonely Hearts Club Band" (Bee Gees with Peter Frampton and Paul Nicholas); promo only

❏ 907	She's Leaving Home/ Oh! Darling	1978	$4

—B-side by Robin Gibb solo

❏ 815235-7	Someone Belonging to Someone/I Love You Too Much	1983	$3

Number	Title	Yr	NM
❏ 815235-7 [PS]	Someone Belonging to Someone/I Love You Too Much	1983	$6
❏ 8009	Stayin' Alive/How Deep Is Your Love	1980	$3

— Reissue series

❏ 885	Stayin' Alive/If I Can't Have You	1977	$4
❏ 813173-7	The Woman in You/Stayin' Alive	1983	$3
❏ 813173-7 [PS]	The Woman in You/Stayin' Alive	1983	$6
❏ 410	Throw a Penny/I Can't Let Go	1974	$6
❏ 8010	To Love Somebody/How Can You Mend a Broken Heart	1980	$3

— Reissue series

❏ 913	Too Much Heaven/Rest Your Love on Me	1978	$4
❏ 8030	Too Much Heaven/Rest Your Love on Me	1980	$3

— Reissue series

❏ 913A [DJ]	Too Much Heaven (Stereo 3:15)/(Mono 3:15)	1978	$10

— Both sides have edited versions

❏ 8022	Tragedy/Love You Inside Out	1980	$3

— Reissue series

❏ 918 [DJ]	Tragedy (Stereo 4:32)/(Mono 3:42)	1979	$10

— Promo only; both sides are shorter than the 5:01 stock copy

❏ 918	Tragedy/Until	1979	$4
❏ 404	Wouldn't I Be Someone/Elisa	1973	$6

WARNER BROS.

❏ 28139	E.S.P./Overnight	1987	$3
❏ 28139 [PS]	E.S.P./Overnight	1987	$4
❏ 22899	One/Wing and a Prayer	1989	$3
❏ 22899 [PS]	One/Wing and a Prayer	1989	$3

7-Inch Extended Plays

ATCO

❏ SD 37-264	Where Are You/Spicks and Specks/Playdown/Second Hand People/Monday's Rain/Tint of Blue	1968	$30

— Jukebox single; small hole, plays at 33 1/3 rpm

BEE JAY
CLOCK

❏ 1743	I'll Go On/There's No One for Me	1962	$30

BEE, JIMMY
CALLA

❏ 111	Breakin' Up Is Hard to Do/March Funky	1976	$5

BEE, KATHY
LILAC

❏ 1213	Let's Go Party/(B-side unknown)	1988	$6

BEE, MOLLY
CAPITOL

❏ F2494	Doggie on the Highway/I'll Tell My Mommy	1953	$30
❏ F3968	Don't Look Back/Please Don't Talk About Me When I'm Gone	1958	$20
❏ F4064	Five Points of a Star/After You've Gone	1958	$20
❏ F2567	God Bless Us All/This Is My Dog	1953	$30
❏ F2339	Honky Tonk Mountain/Nobody's Lonesome for Me	1953	$30
❏ F2285	I Saw Mommy Kissing Santa Claus/Willy Claus (Little Son of Santa Claus)	1952	$30
❏ F3865	Magic Mirror/I'm Going Steady with a Dream	1957	$20
❏ F2790	Stuffy/In the Pyrenees	1954	$30
❏ F2258	Tennessee Tango/Kids Who Pay	1952	$30
❏ F2396	What'll He Do/Dancing with Someone	1953	$30

CORAL

❏ 9-61357	I Won't Grow Up/False Alarm	1955	$30

DOT

❏ 15517	Since I Met You Baby/I'll Be Waiting for You	1956	$30
❏ 15453	Sweet Shoppe Sweetheart/From the Wrong Side of Town	1956	$30

LIBERTY

❏ 55543	All My Love, All My Life/She's New to You	1963	$15
❏ 55569	I Was Only Kidding/He's My True Love	1963	$15
❏ 55691	Our Secret/He Doesn't Want You	1964	$15
❏ 55631	Some Tears Fall Dry/Johnny Liar	1963	$15

Number	Title	Yr	NM
MGM			
❏ 13694	Almost Persuaded/Heartbreak U.S.A.	1967	$10
❏ 13537	How's the World Treating You/It Keeps Right On a-Hurtin'	1966	$10
❏ 13491	Losing You/Miserable Me	1966	$10
❏ 13864	Sinner's Wine/Fresh Out of Tryin'	1967	$10
❏ 13411	Together Again/I'm Gonna Change Everything	1965	$10

BEEFEATERS, THE
ELEKTRA

❏ 45013 [DJ]	Please Let Me Love You/Don't Be Long	1964	$250
❏ 45013	Please Let Me Love You/Don't Be Long	1964	$500
❏ 45013 [DJ]	Please Let Me Love You/It Won't Be Long	1964	$200

— Group became The Byrds.

BEEHIVES, THE
KING

❏ 5881	I Want to Hold Your Hand/She Loves You	1964	$20

BEERS FAMILY, THE
COLUMBIA

❏ 43916	Three Little Drummers/The Peace Carol	1966	$6

BEES, THE
IMPERIAL

❏ 5320	I Want to Be Loved/Get Away Baby	1954	$300
❏ 5314	Toy Bell/Snatchin' Back	1954	$200

MIRWOOD

❏ 5503	She's An Artist/Leave Me Be	1965	$30

BEETHOVEN SOUL
DOT

❏ 17031	Good Time Gal/The Walls Are High	1967	$8

BEETLES, THE
BLUE CAT

❏ 115	Ain't That Love/Welcome to My Heart	1965	$20

— Also issued as "The Bouquets"

BEGINNING OF THE END, THE
ALSTON

❏ 4604	Come Down Baby - Part 1/Come Down Baby - Part 2	1971	$4
❏ 4607	Doin' the Funky Do/Fishman	1972	$4
❏ 4595	Funky Nassau- Part 1/Funky Nassau - Part 2	1971	$5
❏ 4605	Gee Whiz, It's Christmas/Surrey Ride	1971	$4
❏ 4599	Hey Pretty Girl/Monkey Tamarind	1971	$4

BEL-AIRES, THE (1)
CROWN

❏ 126	Cherry Pie/Tick Tock	1954	$60

FLIP

❏ 303	This Paradise/Let's Party Awhile	1954	$125

— Maroon label

❏ 303	This Paradise/Let's Party Awhile	1954	$125

— Blue label

❏ 304	White Port and Lemon Juice/This Is Goodbye	1955	$125

BEL-AIRES, THE (U)
DECCA

❏ 30631	My Yearbook/Rockin' An' Strollin'	1958	$40

NU SOUND

❏ 1022	Palmeras/Pony Rock	1962	$15

BEL-LARKS, THE
RANSOM

❏ 5001	A Million and One Dreams/(B-side unknown)	1963	$500

Number	Title	Yr	NM
BELAFONTE, HARRY			
CAPITOL			
❏ F1018	A Farewell to Arms/I Still Get a Thrill	1950	$40
❏ F856	Whispering/Sometimes I Feel Like a Motherless Child	1950	$50

COLUMBIA

❏ 18-02396	Forever Young/Something to Hold On To	1981	$4

GEFFEN

❏ 27859	Day-O/Main Titles	1988	$3

— B-side: instrumental from the "Beetlejuice" soundtrack

❏ 27859 [PS]	Day-O/Main Titles	1988	$3

RCA VICTOR

❏ 47-7289	Ain't That Love/The Waiting Game	1958	$8
❏ 47-9406	Annie/I'm Just a Country Boy	1967	$6
❏ 47-4676	A-Roving/Chimney Smoke	1952	$20
❏ 47-6771	Banana Boat (Day-O)/Star-O	1956	$15
❏ 47-6771 [PS]	Banana Boat (Day-O)/Star-O	1956	$30
❏ 47-9542	By the Time I Get to Phoenix/Sleep Late, My Lady Friend	1968	$6
❏ SP-45-181 [DJ]	By the Time I Get to Phoenix/Sleep Late, My Lady Friend	1968	$15

— Promo-only number

❏ 74-0428	Circle 'Round the Sun/Something in the Way She Moves	1971	$5
❏ 47-6788	Come Back Liza/Brown Skin Girl	1956	$10
❏ 47-6790	Danny Boy/Take My Mother Home	1956	$12
❏ 47-6790 [PS]	Danny Boy/Take My Mother Home	1956	$30
❏ 47-7491	Darlin' Cora/Turn Around	1959	$8
❏ 47-7550	Fifteen/'Round the Bay of Mexico	1959	$8
❏ 47-7550 [PS]	Fifteen/'Round the Bay of Mexico	1959	$20
❏ 47-7445	Gotta Travel On/Tarrytown	1959	$8
❏ 47-8513	Hallelujah I Love You So/In the Even' Mama	1965	$6
❏ 47-5617	Hold 'Em Joe/I'm Just a Country Boy	1954	$20
❏ 47-6787	Hosanna/I Adore Her	1956	$10
❏ 47-9075	Hurry Sundown/Mama Look At Bubu	1967	$6
❏ 47-7425	I Heard the Bells on Christmas Day/Mary, Mary	1958	$8
❏ 47-7425 [PS]	I Heard the Bells on Christmas Day/Mary, Mary	1958	$20
❏ 47-6885	Island in the Sun/Cocoanut Woman	1957	$10
❏ 47-8717	Little Bit of Rain/Roll On, Buddy	1965	$6
❏ 74-0145	Lullabye/The Train Song	1969	$5

— With Miriam Makeba

❏ 47-6830	Mama Look a Boo Boo (Shut Your Mouth - Go Away)/Don't Ever Love Me	1957	$15

— Same recording as above, but new A-side title

❏ 47-6830	Mama Look at Bubu/Don't Ever Love Me	1957	$15
❏ 47-6830 [PS]	Mama Look at Bubu/Don't Ever Love Me	1957	$30
❏ 47-6782	Man Piaba/The Fox	1956	$10
❏ 47-6782 [PS]	Man Piaba/The Fox	1956	$30
❏ 47-6783	Man Smart (Woman Smarter)/Chimney Smoke	1956	$10
❏ 47-6783 [PS]	Man Smart (Woman Smarter)/Chimney Smoke	1956	$30
❏ 47-4892	Man Smart (Woman Smarter)/Jerry	1952	$20
❏ 47-7681	March Down to Jordan/Oh Freedom	1960	$8
❏ 47-6735	Mary's Boy Child/Venezuela	1956	$15
❏ 47-6735 [PS]	Mary's Boy Child/Venezuela	1956	$30
❏ 47-5151	Matilda, Matilda/Suzanne	1953	$20
❏ 47-6781	Mo Mary/Lord Randall	1956	$10
❏ APBO-0093	Morningside/So Close	1973	$4
❏ 47-5722	Pretty As A Rainbow/Acorn in the Meadow	1954	$20
❏ 47-5722 [PS]	Pretty As A Rainbow/Acorn in the Meadow	1954	$40
❏ 47-5051	Scarlet Ribbons (For Her Hair)/Shenandoah	1952	$20
❏ 47-5210	Springfield Mountain/Gomen-Nasai	1953	$20
❏ 47-9263	Sunflower/A Strange Song	1967	$6
❏ 47-9263 [PS]	Sunflower/A Strange Song	1967	$10
❏ 47-6458	The Blues Is Man (Part 1)/The Blues Is Man (Part 2)	1956	$15
❏ 47-7176	The Marching Saints/Did You Hear About Jerry?	1958	$8
❏ 47-6249	Troubles/Hello Everybody	1955	$15
❏ 47-6789	Water Boy/Noah	1956	$10
❏ 47-6786	Will His Love Be Like His Rum?/Dolly Dawn	1956	$10
❏ 74-0628	Women/Pastures of Plenty	1971	$5

7-Inch Extended Plays

CAPITOL

Number	Title	Yr	NM
❏ EAP-1-619 [PS]	Close Your Eyes	1955	$20
❏ EAP-1-619	Close Your Eyes/Sometimes I Feel Like a Motherless Child/I Still Get a Thrill/Deep As the River	1955	$20

RCA VICTOR

Number	Title	Yr	NM
❏ EPA 1-1402 [PS]	An Evening with Belafonte, Vol. 1	1956	$15
❏ EPA 2-1402 [PS]	An Evening with Belafonte, Vol. 2	1956	$15
❏ EPA 3-1402 [PS]	An Evening with Belafonte, Vol. 3	1956	$15
❏ EPA4217 [PS]	Ballads by Belafonte	1958	$15
❏ EPA693 [PS]	Belafonte, Act 1	1955	$15
❏ EPA694 [PS]	Belafonte, Act 2	1955	$15
❏ EPA695 [PS]	Belafonte, Act 3	1955	$12
❏ LPC-127 [PS]	Belafonte at Carnegie Hall Highlights	1961	$12
❏ EPA 1-1505 [PS]	Belafonte Sings of the Caribbean, Vol. 1	1957	$12
❏ EPA 2-1505 [PS]	Belafonte Sings of the Caribbean, Vol. 2	1957	$12
❏ EPA768 [PS]	Calypso	1956	$15
❏ EPB1248 [PS]	Calypso	1956	$25

— *Two-pocket jacket for two-EP set*

Number	Title	Yr	NM
❏ SP-45-67	Cocoanut Woman/A Woman Is a Sometime Thing//Turn Around/In the Evenin' Mama	1959	$25
❏ 599-9128	Come Back Liza/Brown Skin Girl//Man Smart (Woman Smarter)/Matilda	1956	$8

— *Side 3 and 18 of 10-EP set SPD-24*

Number	Title	Yr	NM
❏ EPA 3-1402	Come Oh My Love//Eden Was Like This/Shenandoah	1956	$15
❏ EPA 2-1505	(contents unknown)	1957	$10
❏ EPA4217	Cordella Brown/Judy Drownded//Lead Man Holler/Angelique-O	1958	$15
❏ EPA 2-1402	Cu Cu Ru Cu Cu/Paloma//Hava Negela/When the Saints Go Marching In	1956	$15
❏ 547-0899	Day-O/I Do Adore Her//Brown Skin Girl/Dolly Dawn	1956	$10

— *Record 1 of 2-EP set EPB 1248*

Number	Title	Yr	NM
❏ 599-9126	Day-O/I Do Adore Her//Jamaica Farewell/Will His Love Be Like His Rum?	1956	$8

— *Side 1 and 20 of 10-EP set SPD-24*

Number	Title	Yr	NM
❏ LPC-127	Day-o/Jamaica Farewell//Man Smart (Woman Smarter)/Shenandoah	1961	$10

— *Compact 33 Double"; small hole, plays at 33 1/3 rpm*

Number	Title	Yr	NM
❏ EPA768	Day O/Will His Love Be Like His Rum?//Jamaica Farewell/Dolly Dawn	1956	$15
❏ 599-9127	Dolly Dawn/Star O//The Jack-Ass Song/Hosanna	1956	$8

— *Side 2 and 19 of 10-EP set SPD-24*

Number	Title	Yr	NM
❏ EPA 1-1505	Haiti Cherie/Love, Love Alone//Lucy's Door/Scratch, Scratch	1957	$10
❏ EPA412 [PS]	Harry Belafonte Sings "Man Smart" and Other Folk Songs	1952	$15
❏ EPA-4084 [PS]	Island in the Sun	1957	$15
❏ EPA-4084	Island in the Sun/Cocoanut Woman//Lead Man Holler	1957	$15
❏ EPB1022	Mark Twain" and Other Folk Favorites	1954	$25

— *Two-pocket jacket for two-EP set*

Number	Title	Yr	NM
❏ 547-0404	Mark Twain/Man Piaba//Mo Mary/Lord Randall	1954	$10

— *Record 1 of 2-EP set EPB 1022*

Number	Title	Yr	NM
❏ 599-9132	Mark Twain/Tol' My Captain//Man Piaba/The Drummer and the Cook	1956	$8

— *Side 7 and 14 of 10-EP set SPD-24*

Number	Title	Yr	NM
❏ EPA 1-1402	Merci Bon Dieu//The Drummer and the Cook/Danny Boy	1956	$15
❏ VLP2449	Midnight Special//Crawdad Hole//Gotta Travel On/Mule Skinner	1962	$60

— *Jukebox issue; small hole, plays at 33 1/3 rpm; Bob Dylan plays harmonica on the first track*

Number	Title	Yr	NM
❏ 599-9134	Mo Mary/Lord Randall//Delia/Shenandoah	1956	$8

— *Side 9 and 12 of 10-EP set SPD-24*

Number	Title	Yr	NM
❏ EPA412	Shenandoah/Scarlet Ribbons (For Her Hair)//Man Smart (Woman Smarter)/Jerry (This Timber Got to Roll)	1952	$20

— *Black label, outline of dog at right*

Number	Title	Yr	NM
❏ EPA412	Shenandoah/Scarlet Ribbons (For Her Hair)//Man Smart (Woman Smarter)/Jerry (This Timber Got to Roll)	1954	$10

— *Black label, white dog at top*

Number	Title	Yr	NM
❏ EPA694	Sylvie//In That Great Gettin' Up Mornin'/Jump Down, Spin Around	1955	$15

— *With dog on label*

Number	Title	Yr	NM
❏ EPA694	Sylvie//In That Great Gettin' Up Mornin'/Jump Down, Spin Around	1955	$20

— *No dog on label*

Number	Title	Yr	NM
❏ 599-9131	Sylvie//Scarlet Ribbons (For Her Hair)/Unchained Melody	1956	$8

— *Side 6 and 15 of 10-EP set SPD-24*

Number	Title	Yr	NM
❏ EPA693	Take My Mother Home//Unchained Melody/Matilda	1955	$15
❏ SPD-24 [PS]	The Best of Belafonte	1956	$25

— *Box for 10-EP set plus liner-note booklet*

Number	Title	Yr	NM
❏ VLP2449 [PS]	The Midnight Special	1962	$60
❏ 599-9129	Waterboy/Suzanne (Every Night When the Sun Goes Down)//Troubles/In That Great Gettin' Up Mornin'	1956	$8

— *Side 4 and 17 of 10-EP set SPD 24*

BELAIRS, THE
ARVEE

Number	Title	Yr	NM
❏ A-5034	Mr. Moto/Little Brown Jug	1961	$50

BELEW, CARL, AND BETTY JEAN ROBINSON
DECCA

Number	Title	Yr	NM
❏ 32802	All I Need Is You/Funny What a Pair of Fools Will Do	1971	$8
❏ 32871	Hung Up on Lovin' You/Living Under Pressure	1971	$8
❏ 32916	When My Baby Sings His Song/Don't Let That Happen to Us	1972	$8

BELEW, CARL
4 STAR

Number	Title	Yr	NM
❏ 1721	Everytime I'm Kissing You/24 Hour Night	1958	$30
❏ 1715	I Can't Forget/Stop the World	1958	$30

BRUNSWICK

Number	Title	Yr	NM
❏ 9-55071	Everytime I'm Kissing You/Now We're One	1958	$30

DECCA

Number	Title	Yr	NM
❏ 30842	Am I That Easy to Forget/Such Is Life	1959	$15
❏ 31200	Another Lonely Night/I Can't Lose Something (That I Never Had)	1961	$15
❏ 31427	Can't You Hear Me Call Your Name/I Don't Know How I'll Live (And Feel This Way)	1962	$15
❏ 32885	God Is Alive/Buss 22	1971	$8
❏ 31325	I'm So Lonesome/I Have To	1961	$15
❏ 31012	I Wish I'd Never/I Know, But Tell Me Dear It Didn't Happen	1959	$15
❏ 32952	I Won't Care/Happy Harry's Honky Tonk	1972	$8
❏ 32789	Stay Close to Me/I Can Give You What You Want Now	1971	$8
❏ 31273	Stop the World (And Let Me Off)/I Can't Take a Chance	1961	$15
❏ 31140	The End of Time/My Baby's Not Here	1960	$15
❏ 32747	The Fastest Man Alive/Mary	1970	$8
❏ 31086	Too Much to Lose/That's What I Get for Loving You	1960	$15

RCA VICTOR

Number	Title	Yr	NM
❏ 47-8352	Before I Go to Bed/Anna Louise	1964	$12
❏ 47-8744	Boston Jail/I Spent a Week There One Night	1966	$10
❏ 47-8633	Crystal Chandelier/Lonely Hearts Do Foolish Things	1965	$12
❏ 47-9272	Girl Crazy/Turnabout	1967	$10
❏ 47-8058	Hello Out There/Together We Stand	1962	$12
❏ 47-9078	Help Stamp Out Loneliness/I Dream Too Big	1967	$12
❏ 47-9351	Home Away from Home/Too Much to Lose	1967	$12
❏ 47-8406	In the Middle of a Memory/Cheaters Never Prosper	1964	$10
❏ 47-9446	Mary's Little Lamb/Once	1968	$10
❏ 47-8199	My Pride Won't Let Me/I Can't Stand to Look	1963	$10
❏ 47-8010	Odd Man Out/Second Chance	1962	$10
❏ 47-8835	Possum Holler/Pick Up My Marbles and Run Home	1966	$12
❏ 47-8132	Pretty Brown Eyes/The Masquerade Party	1963	$10
❏ 47-8527	She Reads Me Like a Book/Silent Partner	1965	$10
❏ 47-8270	Speak to Me/Big City Girls	1963	$10
❏ 47-8996	Walking Shadow, Talking Memory/I'm Lonesome	1966	$10

7-Inch Extended Plays
4 STAR

Number	Title	Yr	NM
❏ EP-41 [DJ]	Am I That Easy to Forget/Such Is Life/Cry Not for Me/Yes, I Understand	1959	$50

— *B-side by Patsy Cline; sometimes said to be on the "Patsy Cline" label, but it is a 4 Star promo-only item; not issued with cover?*

Number	Title	Yr	NM
❏ EP-43 [DJ]	That's What I Get for Loving You/My Baby's Not Here (In Town Tonight)/How Can I Face Tomorrow/A Church, a Courtroom, Then Goodbye	1959	$50

— *B-side by Patsy Cline; sometimes said to be on the "Patsy Cline" label, but it is a 4 Star promo-only item; not issued with cover?*

BELFAST GYPSIES, THE
LOMA

Number	Title	Yr	NM
❏ 2051	Gloria's Dream/Secret Police	1966	$20
❏ 2060	Portland Town/People, Let's Freak Out	1966	$20

BELL & JAMES
A&M

Number	Title	Yr	NM
❏ 2347	In Spanish Harlem/Lover Call My Name	1981	$5
❏ 2069	Livin' It Up (Friday Night)/Don't Let the Man Get You	1978	$6
❏ 2204	Only Make Believe/Stay	1979	$5
❏ 2185	Shakedown/Nobody Knows It	1979	$5

BELL, ARCHIE, AND THE DRELLS
ATLANTIC

Number	Title	Yr	NM
❏ 2855	Green Power/I Can't Face You Baby	1972	$6
❏ 2793	I Just Want to Fall in Love/Love at First Sight	1971	$6
❏ 2829	Let the World Know/Archie's in Love	1971	$6
❏ 2478	Tighten Up/Dog Eat Dog	1968	$15
❏ 2478	Tighten Up/Tighten Up -- Part 2	1968	$8

BECKET

Number	Title	Yr	NM
❏ 45-4	Any Time Is Right/(B-side unknown)	1981	$4

GLADES

Number	Title	Yr	NM
❏ 1711	Ain't Nothing for a Man in Love/You Never Know What's On a Woman's Mind	1973	$6
❏ 1707	Dancing to Your Music/Count the Ways	1973	$6
❏ 1718	Girls Grow Up Faster Than Boys/Love's Gonna Rain on You	1973	$6

OVIDE

Number	Title	Yr	NM
❏ 228	Tighten Up/Dog Eat Dog	1967	$70

PHILADELPHIA INT'L.

Number	Title	Yr	NM
❏ 3710	Strategy/We Got 'Um Dancin'	1979	$5

PHILADELPHIA INT'L

Number	Title	Yr	NM
❏ 3615	Everybody Have a Good Time/I Bet I Can Do That Dance You're Doin'	1977	$5
❏ 3632	Glad You Could Make It/There's No Other Like You	1977	$5
❏ 3637	I've Been Missing You/It's Hard Not to Love You	1977	$5
❏ 3651	Old People/On the Radio	1978	$5

TSOP

Number	Title	Yr	NM
❏ 4767	I Could Dance All Night/King of the Castle	1975	$5
❏ 4775	Let's Groove (Part 1)/Let's Groove (Part 2)	1976	$5
❏ 4774	The Soul City Walk/King of the Castle	1975	$5

WMOT

Number	Title	Yr	NM
❏ 03057	Touchin' You/(Instrumental)	1982	$5

BELL, CARL, AND THE NORVAIRS
LAURIE

Number	Title	Yr	NM
❏ 3014	Birth of the Beat/Open House in Your Heart	1958	$30

BELL, CHUCK
SUN

Number	Title	Yr	NM
❏ 1161	Crazy Days/I Don't Live There Anymore	1981	$5

Number	Title	Yr	NM

BELL, DELIA
WARNER BROS.

| ❏ 29550 | Coyote Song/Love Pilgrim | 1983 | $4 |
| ❏ 29653 | Flame in My Heart/Good Lord A'Mighty | 1983 | $4 |

BELL, FREDDIE, AND THE BELL BOYS
MERCURY

| ❏ 70919 | Stay Loose, Mother Goose/All Right, OK, You Win | 1956 | $30 |
| ❏ 71075 | Take the First Train Out of Town/Hey There You | 1957 | $30 |

TEEN

| ❏ 101 | Hound Dog/Move Me Baby | 1955 | $60 |
| ❏ 103 | Old Town Hall/5-10-15 Hours | 1955 | $40 |

WING

| ❏ 90066 | Giddy Up a Ding Dong/I Said It and I'm Glad | 1956 | $50 |
| ❏ 90082 | The Hucklebuck/Rompin' and Stompin' | 1956 | $50 |

BELL HOPS, THE
BARB

| ❏ 100 | Angela/Ring Dang Doo Ting-a-Ling | 1958 | $30 |
| ❏ 101/2 | Teenage Years/Carmella | 1958 | $30 |

DECCA

| ❏ 48208 | For the Rest of My Life/It Would Take a Million Years | 1951 | $125 |
| ❏ 48239 | I'm All Yours/Where Is Love | 1951 | $125 |

TIN PAN ALLEY

| ❏ 153 | Please Don't Say No to Me/Merchant Street Blues | 1956 | $200 |

BELL, JAMES
BELL

| ❏ 710 | He Ain't Country/A Friendly Place to Cry | 1968 | $8 |

BELL, JERRY
MCA

| ❏ 51077 | Love Will Make It All Right/Call On Me | 1981 | $4 |

BELL, MADELINE
ASCOT

| ❏ 2180 | Don't Cry My Heart/Daytime | 1965 | $12 |

BRUT

| ❏ 808 | All That Love Went to Waste/A Touch of Class | 1973 | $5 |

MOD

| ❏ 1007 | I'm Gonna Make You Love Me/Picture Me Gone | 1967 | $15 |

PHILIPS

❏ 40539	Finding You, Loving You/Doing Things Together with You	1968	$6
❏ 40517	I'm Gonna Make You Love Me/Picture Me Gone	1968	$8
❏ 40582	Step Inside Love/What I'm Supposed to Do	1969	$6

PYE

| ❏ 71061 | I Always Seem to Wind Up Loving You/Your Smile | 1976 | $4 |

BELL, MAGGIE
ATLANTIC

| ❏ 3018 | After Midnight/Souvenirs | 1974 | $5 |
| ❏ 3040 | Caddo Queen/Oh My My | 1974 | $5 |

SWAN SONG

| ❏ 99907 | Here, There and Everywhere/Put Angels Around You | 1983 | $4 |

—With Bobby Whitlock

| ❏ 99907 [PS] | Here, There and Everywhere/Put Angels Around You | 1983 | $4 |

—With Bobby Whitlock

| ❏ 70105 | Wishing Well/Comin' On Strong | 1975 | $5 |

BELL NOTES, THE
AUTOGRAPH

| ❏ 204 | Little Girl in Blue/Too Young or Too Old | 1960 | $30 |

Number	Title	Yr	NM

CLOCK

| ❏ 71889 | There She Goes/My Pledge to You | 1961 | $30 |

MADISON

| ❏ 136 | Shortnin' Bread/To Each His Own | 1960 | $30 |

TIME

| ❏ 1004 | I've Had It/Be Mine | 1958 | $40 |

—First pressing on blue labels

| ❏ 1004 | I've Had It/Be Mine | 1959 | $30 |

—Later pressings on red labels

❏ 1010	Old Spanish Town/She Went Thataway	1959	$30
❏ 1013	That's Right/Betty Dear	1959	$30
❏ 1017	White Buckskin Sneakers and Checkerboard Socks/No Dice	1959	$30

7-Inch Extended Plays

| ❏ TEP-100 [PS] | I've Had It | 1959 | $125 |
| ❏ TEP-100 | I've Had It/Be Mine//Dream Street/A Sad Guitar | 1959 | $125 |

BELL, RANDY
EPIC

| ❏ 34-04497 | Don't Do Me/Someone's Fantasy | 1984 | $4 |
| ❏ 34-04497 [PS] | Don't Do Me/Someone's Fantasy | 1984 | $4 |

BELL, TOMMY
GOLD SOUND

❏ 8013	Georgiana/Untangle My Mind	1982	$6
❏ 8013 [PS]	Georgiana/Untangle My Mind	1982	$10
❏ 8016	Honky Tonk Crazy/(B-side unknown)	1983	$6

BELL TONES, THE
RAMA

| ❏ 170 | Heart to Heart/The Wedding | 1955 | $200 |

BELL, TRUDY
PHILIPS

| ❏ 40055 | I Remember Jimmy/A Promise and a Kiss Goodnight | 1962 | $15 |
| ❏ 40021 | Willie/This Friend of Mine | 1962 | $15 |

BELL, VINCENT
DECCA

❏ 32659	Airport Love Theme/Marilyn's Theme	1970	$5
❏ 32418	California Summer/A Sinner Kissed An Angel	1968	$6
❏ 32695	Darling Lili/Nikki	1970	$5
❏ 32224	Eleanor/Goin' Out of My Head	1967	$6
❏ 32483	Good Morning Starshine/Because of You	1969	$5
❏ 32530	Les Bicyclettes De Belsize/The Ballad of John and Yoko	1969	$5

VERVE

| ❏ 10308 | Shindig/Whistle Stop | 1963 | $15 |

BELL, VIVIAN
GRT

| ❏ 118 | The Angel in Your Arms/What in the Name of Love | 1977 | $5 |

BELL, WILLIAM
KAT FAMILY

| ❏ 03502 | Bad Time to Break Off/The Truth in Your Eyes | 1983 | $4 |
| ❏ 03995 | Playing Hard to Get/The Truth in Your Eyes | 1983 | $4 |

MERCURY

| ❏ 73922 | Coming Back for More/You I Absolutely Positively Love | 1977 | $4 |
| ❏ 73839 | Tryin' to Love Two/If Sex Was All We Had | 1976 | $5 |

STAX

| ❏ 0106 | All for the Love of a Woman/I'll Be Home | 1971 | $5 |
| ❏ 0067 | All I Have to Do Is Dream/Leave the Girl Alone | 1970 | $5 |

—With Carla Thomas

| ❏ 0198 | All I Need Is Your Love/Gettin' What You Want | 1974 | $5 |
| ❏ 128 | Any Other Way/Please Help Me I'm Falling | 1962 | $30 |

Number	Title	Yr	NM

❏ 0092	A Penny for Your Thoughts/Till My Back Ain't Got No Bone	1971	$5
❏ 248	A Tribute to a King (Otis Redding)/Every Man Oughta Have a Woman	1968	$6
❏ 0054	Born Under a Bad Sign/A Smile Can't Hide a Broken Heart	1969	$5
❏ 174	Crying All By Myself/Don't Stop Now	1965	$15
❏ 146	Don't Make Something Out of Nothing/Who Will It Be Tomorrow	1964	$15
❏ 212	Everybody Loves a Winner/You're Such a Sweet Thing	1967	$8
❏ 237	Everyday Will Be Like a Holiday/Ain't Got No Girl	1967	$8
❏ 0221	Get It While It's Hot/Nobody Walks Away from Love Unhurt	1974	$5
❏ 0044	I Can't Stop/I Need You Woman	1969	$5

—With Carla Thomas

❏ 0015	I Forgot to Be Your Lover/Bring the Curtains Down	1968	$6
❏ 0128	If You Really Love Him/Save Us	1972	$5
❏ 141	I'll Show You!/Monkeying Around	1963	$20
❏ 132	I Told You So/What'Cha Gonna Do	1963	$20
❏ 0017	Left-Over Love/My Baby Specializes	1968	$5

—With Judy Clay

❏ 0157	Livin' on Borrowed Time/The Man in the Street	1973	$5
❏ 0070	Lonely Soldier/Let Me Ride	1970	$5
❏ 0043	Love's Sweet Sensation/Strung Out	1969	$5

—With Mavis Staples

❏ 0038	My Kind of Girl/Happy	1969	$5
❏ 0032	My Whole World Is Falling Down/All God's Children Got Soul	1969	$5
❏ 227	One Plus One/Eloise (Hang On In There)	1967	$8
❏ 0005	Private Number/Love-Eye-Tis	1968	$5

—With Judy Clay

❏ 191	Share What You Got/Marching Off to War	1966	$10
❏ 199	Soldier's Goodbye/Never Like This Before	1966	$12
❏ 138	Somebody Mentioned Your Name/What Can I Do to Forget	1963	$20

WRC

| ❏ 204 | Headline News/Let Him Pay the Band | 1986 | $5 |
| ❏ 202 | I Don't Want to Wake Up (Feelin' Guilty)/Whatever You Want (You Got It) | 1986 | $5 |

—With Janice Bulluck

BELLAMY BROTHERS, THE
ELEKTRA

❏ 47431	For All the Wrong Reasons/This Time	1982	$4
❏ 69999	Get Into Reggae Cowboy/We're Just a Little Ole Country Band	1982	$4
❏ 69850	When I'm Away from You/Long Distance Love Affair	1983	$4

MCA CURB

❏ 53478	Big Love/The Courthouse	1988	$3
❏ 52834	Country Rap/One Too Many Times	1986	$3
❏ 52834 [DJ]	Country Rap (same on both sides)	1986	$15

—Promo only on yellow vinyl

| ❏ 53154 | Crazy from the Heart/White Trash | 1987 | $3 |
| ❏ 52747 [DJ] | Feelin' the Feelin' (same on both sides) | 1985 | $15 |

—Promo only on yellow vinyl

❏ 52747	Feelin' the Feelin'/The Single Man and His Wife	1985	$3
❏ 52380	Forget About We/We're Having Some Fun Now	1984	$3
❏ 53642	Hillbilly Hell/You're My Favorite Star	1989	$3
❏ 53310	I'll Give You All My Love Tonight/Ying Yang	1988	$3
❏ 52518	I Need More of You/Diesel Cafe	1984	$3
❏ 52668	Lie to You for Your Love/Season of the Wind	1985	$3
❏ 52579	Old Hippie/Wheels	1985	$3
❏ 53222	Santa Fe/White Trash	1987	$3
❏ 53719	The Center of My Universe/Hillbilly Hell	1989	$3
❏ 52446	The World's Greatest Lover/Rock-A-Dash	1984	$3
❏ 52917	Too Much Is Not Enough/Restless	1986	$3

—A-side with The Forester Sisters

| ❏ 52917 [DJ] | Too Much Is Not Enough (same on both sides) | 1986 | $15 |

Number	Title	Yr	NM
	—With The Forester Sisters; promo only on red vinyl		

WARNER BROS.

Number	Title	Yr	NM
❏ 8521	Bird Dog/Make Me Over	1978	$4
❏ 8401	Can Somebody Hear Me Now/You Made Me	1977	$4
❏ 49573	Classic Case of the Blues/Lovers Live Longer	1980	$4
❏ 8350	Crossfire/Tiger Lily Lover	1977	$4
❏ 49241	Dancin' Cowboys/Dead Aim	1980	$4
❏ 49639	Do You Love As Good As You Look/Givin' In to Love Again	1980	$4
❏ 8462	Hard Rockin'/Memorabilia	1977	$4
❏ 8220	Hell Cat/I'm the Only Man Left Alive	1976	$4
❏ 8790	If I Said You Have a Beautiful Body Would You Hold It Against Me/Make Me Over	1979	$4
❏ 29645	I Love Her Mind/Lazy Eyes	1983	$4
❏ 49875	It's So Close to Christmas/Let Me Waltz Into Your Heart	1981	$4
❏ 8558	Let's Give Love a Try/Slipping Away	1978	$4
❏ 8169	Let Your Love Flow/Inside My Guitar	1975	$5
❏ 8284	Livin' in the West/Highway 2-18 (Hang On to Your Dreams)	1976	$4
❏ 8692	Lovin' on/My Shy Anne	1978	$4
❏ 29514	Strong Weakness/Doin' It the Hard Way	1983	$4
❏ 49160	Sugar Daddy/I Could Be Makin' Love to You	1980	$4
❏ 49729	They Could Put Me in Jail/Endangered Species	1981	$4
❏ 8627	Tumbleweed and Rosalee/Wild Honey	1978	$4

BELLAMY, DAVID
WARNER BROS.

Number	Title	Yr	NM
❏ 8123	Baby, You're Not a Legend/Nothin' Heavy	1975	$5

BELLAND & SOMERVILLE
BARNABY

Number	Title	Yr	NM
❏ 2009	Sure Seems a Lot Like Sunday/When She's Lovin'	1969	$8

BELLE EPOQUE
BIG TREE

Number	Title	Yr	NM
❏ 16123	Black Is Black/(B-side unknown)	1978	$5
❏ 16109	Miss Broadway/Losing You	1978	$5

SHADY BROOK

Number	Title	Yr	NM
❏ 1040	Miss Broadway/Losing You	1977	$8

BELLE STARS, THE
CAPITOL

Number	Title	Yr	NM
❏ B-44343	Iko Iko/Las Vegas	1989	$4
	—B-side by Hans Zimmer		
❏ 7PRO-79543	Iko Iko (same on both sides)	1989	$6
	—Promo-only number		

WARNER BROS.

Number	Title	Yr	NM
❏ 29672	Sign of the Times/Madness	1983	$4
❏ 29672 [PS]	Sign of the Times/Madness	1983	$6

BELLES, THE
HIT

Number	Title	Yr	NM
❏ 83	Sally Go 'Round the Roses/Be My Baby	1963	$8
	—B-side by the Georgettes		
❏ 101	The Boy Next Door/As Usual	1964	$8
	—B-side by Betty Williams		

BELLS, THE (1)
MGM

Number	Title	Yr	NM
❏ 14533	Child of Mine/He Was Me, He Was You	1973	$4
❏ 14624	Love Once Removed/The Singer	1973	$4

POLYDOR

Number	Title	Yr	NM
❏ 15016	Fly Little White Dove, Fly/Follow the Sun	1970	$4
❏ 15027	I Love You Lady Dawn/Rain	1971	$4
❏ 15039	Lord, Don't You Think It's Time/Easier Said Than Done	1972	$4
❏ 15036	Oh My Love/You You You	1972	$4
❏ 15029	She's a Lady/Sweet Sounds of Music	1971	$4
❏ 15023	Stay Awhile/Sing a Song of Freedom	1971	$5
❏ 15031	To Know You Is To Love You/For Better For Worse	1971	$4

BELLS, THE (2)
RAMA

Number	Title	Yr	NM
❏ 166	What Can I Tell Her Now/Let Me Love You, Love You	1955	$500

BELLTONES, THE
GRAND

Number	Title	Yr	NM
❏ 102	Estelle/Promise Love	1954	$4000
	—VG 2000; VG+ 3000		

BELLUS, TONY
KING

Number	Title	Yr	NM
❏ 5973	Mustang/Goodbye Baby, Goodbye	1964	$15

NRC

Number	Title	Yr	NM
❏ 035	Hey Little Darlin'/Only Your Heart	1959	$30
❏ 045	Hey Little Darlin'/Young Girls	1959	$30
❏ 040	Little Dreams/Young Girls	1959	$30
❏ 051	The End of My Love/The Echo of An Old Song	1960	$30
	—Available on both white and tan labels, no difference in value		
❏ 051 [PS]	The End of My Love/The Echo of An Old Song	1960	$60
❏ 058	The Great Pretender/Give Me a Heart	1960	$30

BELMONTS, THE
DOT

Number	Title	Yr	NM
❏ 17257	Have You Heard-The Worst That Could Happen/Answer Me My Love	1969	$20

LAURIE

Number	Title	Yr	NM
❏ 3631	A Brand New Song/Story Teller	1975	$5
❏ 3080	We Belong Together/Such a Long Way	1961	$40

SABINA

Number	Title	Yr	NM
❏ 509	Ann Marie/Ac-Cent-Tchu-Ate the Positive	1963	$30
❏ 519	C'mon Everybody/Why	1964	$30
❏ 505	Come On Little Angel/How About Me	1962	$30
	—Black label		
❏ 505	Come On Little Angel/How About Me	1962	$30
	—Greenish label		
❏ 507	Diddle-Dee-Dum (What Happens When Your Love Has Gone)/Farewell	1962	$30
❏ 503	Hombre/I Confess	1962	$30
❏ 502	I Need Some One/That American Dance	1961	$30
❏ 513	Let's Call It a Day/Walk On Boy	1963	$30
❏ 517	More Important Things to Do/Walk On Boy	1963	$30
❏ 521	Summertime/Nothing in Return	1964	$30

SABRINA

Number	Title	Yr	NM
❏ 501	Searching for a New Love/Don't Get Around Much Anymore	1961	$30
❏ 500	Tell Me Why/Smoke from Your Cigarette	1961	$30

STRAWBERRY

Number	Title	Yr	NM
❏ 106	Cheek to Cheek/Voyager	1976	$5

SURPRISE

Number	Title	Yr	NM
❏ 1000	Tell Me Why/Smoke from Your Cigarette	1961	$125

UNITED ARTISTS

Number	Title	Yr	NM
❏ 50007	Come with Me/You're Like a Mystery	1966	$30
❏ 966	I Got a Feeling/To Be with You	1965	$30
❏ 904	(Then) I Walked Away/Today My Love Has Gone Away	1965	$30
❏ 809	Wintertime/I Don't Know Why, I Just Do	1965	$30

BELOYD
20TH CENTURY

Number	Title	Yr	NM
❏ 2353	Get Into Your Life/Today All Day	1977	$5

BELUSHI, JOHN
MCA

Number	Title	Yr	NM
❏ 40950	Louie Louie/Money	1978	$5

BELVIN, ANDY
ATCO

Number	Title	Yr	NM
❏ 6289	Travelin' Mood/Flip Flip	1964	$15

CANDIX

Number	Title	Yr	NM
❏ 338	Walking the Blues/Prettiest Girl	1962	$30

VAULT

Number	Title	Yr	NM
❏ 908	Travelin' Mood/Flip Flop	1964	$20

BELVIN, JESSE
ALADDIN

Number	Title	Yr	NM
❏ 3431	Let Me Dream/Sugar Doll	1958	$50

CASH

Number	Title	Yr	NM
❏ 1056	Dry Your Tears/Beware	1957	$125
	—Black and silver label		
❏ 1056	Dry Your Tears/Beware	1957	$30
	—Orange and black label		

CLASS

Number	Title	Yr	NM
❏ 267	I'm Confessin'/Deep in My Heart	1960	$30

HOLLYWOOD

Number	Title	Yr	NM
❏ 1059	Betty My Darling/Dear Heart	1956	$400

IMPACT

Number	Title	Yr	NM
❏ 23	Tonight My Love/Looking for Love	1962	$20

JAMIE

Number	Title	Yr	NM
❏ 1145	Goodnight My Love (Pleasant Dreams)/My Desire	1959	$30

KENT

Number	Title	Yr	NM
❏ 326	Sentimental Reasons/Senorita	1959	$30

KNIGHT

Number	Title	Yr	NM
❏ 2012	Little Darling/Deacon Dan Tucker	1959	$50

MODERN

Number	Title	Yr	NM
❏ 1015	By My Side/Don't Close the Door	1957	$40
❏ 45x1005	Goodnight My Love (Pleasant Dreams)/I Want You With Me Xmas	1956	$60
❏ 45x1005	Goodnight My Love (Pleasant Dreams)/Let Me Love You Tonight	1956	$50
❏ 1013	I Need You So/Senorita	1957	$40
❏ 1027	My Satellite/Just to Say Hello	1957	$40
❏ 1020	Sad and Lonesome/I'm Not Free	1957	$40

MONEY

Number	Title	Yr	NM
❏ 208	I'm Only a Fool/Trouble and Misery	1955	$70

RCA VICTOR

Number	Title	Yr	NM
❏ 47-7387	Funny/Pledging My Love	1958	$30
❏ 47-7596	Give Me Love/I'll Never Be Lonely Again	1959	$30
❏ 47-8040	Guess Who/Funny	1962	$20
❏ 47-7469	Guess Who/My Girl Is Just Enough Woman for Me	1959	$30
❏ 61-7469	Guess Who/My Girl Is Just Enough Woman for Me	1959	$60
	—Living Stereo" (large hole, plays at 45 rpm)		
❏ 47-7543	Here's a Heart/It Could've Been Worse	1959	$30
❏ 47-7675	Something Happens to Me/The Door Is Always Open	1960	$30

RECORDED IN HOLLYWOOD

Number	Title	Yr	NM
❏ 120	Dream Girl/Hang Your Tears Out to Dry	1951	$600
❏ 412	Love Comes Tumbling Down/(B-side unknown)	1953	$400

SPECIALTY

Number	Title	Yr	NM
❏ 435	Confusin' Blues/Baby Don't Go	1952	$100
❏ 550	Gone/One Little Blessing	1955	$60
❏ 559	Where's My Girl/Love, Love of My Life	1955	$60

BEN, LA BRENDA
GORDY

Number	Title	Yr	NM
❏ 7009	Camel Walk/The Chaperone	1962	$60
❏ 7021	I Can't Help It, I Gotta Dance/Just Be Yourself	1963	$60

MOTOWN

Number	Title	Yr	NM
❏ 1033	Camel Walk/Chaperone	1962	$400

BENATAR, PAT
CHRYSALIS

Number	Title	Yr	NM
❏ 43268	All Fired Up/Cool Zero	1988	$3
❏ 43268 [PS]	All Fired Up/Cool Zero	1988	$3
❏ 43301	Don't Walk Away/Lift 'Em On Up	1988	$3
❏ 2529	Fire and Ice/Hard to Believe	1981	$3
❏ 2529 [PS]	Fire and Ice/Hard to Believe	1981	$4

Number	Title	Yr	NM
❑ 2395	Heartbreaker/My Clone Sleeps Alone	1979	$4
❑ 2395 [PS]	Heartbreaker/My Clone Sleeps Alone	1979	$6
❑ 2464	Hit Me with Your Best Shot/Prisoner of Love	1980	$3
❑ 2464 [PS]	Hit Me with Your Best Shot/Prisoner of Love	1980	$4
❑ 2373	If You Think You Know How to Love Me/(B-side unknown)	1979	$8
❑ 42877	Invincible (Theme from Legend of Billie Jean)/(Instrumental)	1985	$4
❑ 42877	Invincible (Theme from The Legend of Billie Jean)/(Instrumental)	1985	$3
— Note slightly altered subtitle			
❑ 42877 [PS]	Invincible (Theme from The Legend of Billie Jean)/(Instrumental)	1985	$4
❑ 42968	Le Bel Age/Walking in the Underground	1986	$3
❑ 43314	Let's Stay Together/Wide Awake in Dreamland	1988	$3
❑ 43314 [PS]	Let's Stay Together/Wide Awake in Dreamland	1988	$3
❑ 03536	Little Too Late/Fight It Out	1983	$3
❑ 03536 [PS]	Little Too Late/Fight It Out	1983	$3
❑ 42688	Looking for a Stranger/I'll Do It	1983	$3
❑ 42688 [PS]	Looking for a Stranger/I'll Do It	1983	$4
❑ 42732	Love Is a Battlefield/Hell Is For Children	1983	$3
❑ 42732 [PS]	Love Is a Battlefield/Hell Is For Children	1983	$3
❑ 42843	Ooh Ooh Song/La Cancion Ooh Ooh	1984	$3
❑ 42843 [PS]	Ooh Ooh Song/La Cancion Ooh Ooh	1984	$4
❑ 2555	Promises in the Dark/Evil Genius	1981	$3
❑ 2555 [PS]	Promises in the Dark/Evil Genius	1981	$4
❑ 42927	Sex as a Weapon/Red Vision	1985	$3
❑ 42927 [PS]	Sex as a Weapon/Red Vision	1985	$4
❑ 2647	Shadows of the Night/The Victim	1982	$3
❑ 2647 [PS]	Shadows of the Night/The Victim	1982	$4
❑ 03541	Shadows of the Night/The Victim	1983	$4
❑ 2487	Treat Me Right/Never Wana Leave You	1981	$3
❑ 2487 [PS]	Treat Me Right/Never Wana Leave You	1981	$4
❑ 42826	We Belong/Suburban King	1984	$3
❑ 42826 [PS]	We Belong/Suburban King	1984	$4
❑ 2419	We Live for Love/So Sincere	1980	$4
❑ 2419 [PS]	We Live for Love/So Sincere	1980	$6

TRACE

Number	Title	Yr	NM
❑ 5293	Day Gig/Last Saturday	1976	$40

BENDER, FREDDIE
PARKWAY

Number	Title	Yr	NM
❑ 876	Miss Daisy De Lite/Let's Twist Again	1963	$20

BENEDICT, ERNIE
RCA VICTOR

Number	Title	Yr	NM
❑ 48-0059	Polka Dots and Polka Dreams/Tzigane Polka	1949	$30
— Original on green vinyl			
❑ 48-0106	When I Comb My Hands (Through the Sands of Texas)/Big and Beautiful	1949	$40
— Original on green vinyl			

BENEKE, TEX/RAY EBERLE/THE MODERNAIRES
COLUMBIA

Number	Title	Yr	NM
❑ JZSP111917/8 [DJ]	And The Bells Rang/Merry Christmas, Baby	1965	$20
— Promo only on green vinyl			

MGM

Number	Title	Yr	NM
❑ 11098	Santa Claus Parade/Root'n Toot'n Santa	1951	$30

BENET, VICKI
DECCA

Number	Title	Yr	NM
❑ 30044	Sam's Song (The Happy Tune)/Tea for Two	1956	$20

LIBERTY

Number	Title	Yr	NM
❑ 55100	After My Laughter Came Tears/Always in My Heart	1957	$20
❑ 55186	Heartstring Melody/Love Me	1959	$15

BENNETT, BOYD
KING

Number	Title	Yr	NM
❑ 5049	Big Boy/Put the Chain on the Door	1957	$30

Number	Title	Yr	NM
❑ 4903	Blue Suede Shoes/Mumbles Blues	1956	$30
❑ 5115	Click Clack/Move	1958	$30
❑ 4853	Desperately/The Most	1955	$30
❑ 1443	Everlovin'/Boogie at Midnight	1955	$40
❑ 5282	High School Hop/Cool Disc Jockey	1959	$30
❑ 4953	Hit That Jive, Jack/Rabbit-Eye Pink and Charcoal Black	1956	$30
❑ 5021	I'm Moving On/Big Jay Shuffle	1957	$30
❑ 4925	Let Me Love You/Groovy Age	1956	$30
❑ 1494	My Boy-Flat Top/Banjo Rock and Roll	1955	$30
❑ 1432	Poison Ivy/You Upset Me Baby	1955	$40
❑ 1201	Precious Little Sweetheart/Wasting My Time	1953	$60
❑ 5097	Sentimental Journey/Boy Meets Girl	1957	$30
❑ 1470	Seventeen/Little Old You-All	1955	$40
— Maroon label			
❑ 1470	Seventeen/Little Old You-All	1955	$40
— Blue label			
❑ 5374	Seventeen/My Boy Flat Top	1960	$30
❑ 5113	Signed, Sealed and Delivered/Her Momma Doesn't Think It's Right	1958	$30
❑ 5738	Teenage Years/Hear Me Talking	1963	$20
❑ 1475	Tennessee Rock and Roll/Oo, Oo, Oo	1955	$30
❑ 1413	Waterloo/I've Had Enough	1954	$40

MERCURY

Number	Title	Yr	NM
❑ 71479	Boogie Bear/A Boy Can Tell	1959	$30
❑ 71813	Coffee Break/The Brain	1961	$30
❑ 71724	Hershey Bar/Big Junior	1960	$30
❑ 71605	It's Wonderful/Amo, Amas, Amat	1960	$30
❑ 71648	Seventeen/Sarasota	1960	$30
❑ 71409	Tight Tights/Tear It Up	1959	$30

7-Inch Extended Plays
KING

Number	Title	Yr	NM
❑ 377 [PS]	Boyd Bennett	1956	$300
❑ 377	(contents unknown)	1956	$250

BENNETT, CLIFF, AND THE REBEL ROUSERS
ABC

Number	Title	Yr	NM
❑ 10842	Got to Get You Into My Life/Baby Each Day	1966	$20

AMY

Number	Title	Yr	NM
❑ 930	If Only You'd Reply/Three Rooms with Running Water	1965	$20

ASCOT

Number	Title	Yr	NM
❑ 2146	Everybody Loves a Lover/My Old Stand By	1964	$20

CAPITOL

Number	Title	Yr	NM
❑ 4621	I'm in Love with You/You've Got What I Like	1961	$60
❑ 5309	One Way Love/I'm in Love with You	1964	$20

BENNETT, JOE, AND THE SPARKLETONES
ABC-PARAMOUNT

Number	Title	Yr	NM
❑ 9837	Black Slacks/Boppin' Rock Boogie	1957	$40
❑ 9885	Cotton Pickin' Rocker/I Dig You Baby	1958	$40
❑ 9959	Do the Stop/Late Again	1958	$40
❑ 9929	Little Turtle/We've Had It	1958	$40
❑ 9867	Penny Loafers and Bobby Socks/Rocket	1957	$40

PARIS

Number	Title	Yr	NM
❑ 530	Bayou Rock/Beautiful One	1959	$40
❑ 537	Boys Do Cry/What the Heck	1959	$30
❑ 546	Softly/What the Heck	1960	$30

BENNETT, LINDA
MERCURY

Number	Title	Yr	NM
❑ 73750	An Old Fashioned Christmas/Daddy Cursed the Day	1975	$5

BENNETT, TONY
BRUT

Number	Title	Yr	NM
❑ 813	All That Love Went to Waste/Some of These Days	1973	$6
❑ 813 [PS]	All That Love Went to Waste/Some of These Days	1973	$6

COLUMBIA

Number	Title	Yr	NM
❑ 43768	A Time for Love/Touch the Earth	1966	$6
❑ 39209	Beautiful Madness/Valentino Tango	1951	$20
❑ 3-39209	Beautiful Madness/Valentino Tango	1951	$30
— Microgroove 7-inch 33 1/3 rpm single			

Number	Title	Yr	NM
❑ 39362	Because of You/I Won't Cry Anymore	1951	$15
❑ 39824	Because of You/I Won't Cry Anymore	1952	$12
❑ 39555	Blue Velvet/Solitaire	1951	$15
❑ 41032	Ca, C'est L'amour/I Never Felt More Like Falling in Love	1957	$10
❑ 42395	Candy Kisses/Have I Told You Lately That I Love You	1962	$8
❑ 40667	Can You Find It in Your Heart/Forget Her	1956	$10
❑ 40272	Cinnamon Sinner/Take Me Back Again	1954	$15
❑ 41520	Climb Ev'ry Mountain/Ask Anyone in Love	1959	$10
❑ 42135	Close Your Eyes/Rules of the Road	1961	$8
❑ 39449	Cold, Cold Heart/While We're Young	1951	$15
❑ 39827	Cold, Cold Heart/While We're Young	1952	$10
❑ 40598	Come Next Spring/Afraid of the Dark	1955	$10
❑ 39910	Congratulations to Someone/Take Me	1953	$15
❑ 31272 [S]	(contents unknown)	1961	$15
❑ 31273 [S]	(contents unknown)	1961	$15
❑ 31274 [S]	(contents unknown)	1961	$15
❑ 31275 [S]	(contents unknown)	1961	$15
❑ 31276 [S]	(contents unknown)	1961	$15
❑ 31563 [S]	(contents unknown)	1962	$15
❑ 31564 [S]	(contents unknown)	1962	$15
❑ 31565 [S]	(contents unknown)	1962	$15
❑ 31566 [S]	(contents unknown)	1962	$15
❑ 31567 [S]	(contents unknown)	1962	$15
— Anyone who can fill in these gaps -- the above 10 all are Columbia "Stereo 7" singles -- please let us know.			
❑ 41157	Crazy Rhythm/The Beat of My Heart	1958	$12
❑ 42886	Don't Wait Too Long/Limehouse Blues	1963	$8
❑ 45157	Everybody's Talkin'/Think How It's Gonna Be	1970	$5
❑ 41237	Firefly/The Night That Heaven Fell	1958	$10
❑ 41237 [PS]	Firefly/The Night That Heaven Fell	1958	$30
❑ 43331	Fly Me to the Moon (In Other Words)/How Insensitive	1965	$6
❑ 44258	For Once in My Life/How Do You Say Auf Wiedersehn	1967	$6
❑ 40726	From the Candy Store on the Corner to the Chapel on the Hill/Happiness Street (Corner Sunshine Square)	1956	$10
❑ 40376	Funny Thing/My Pretty Shoo-Gah	1954	$15
❑ 43715	Georgia Rose/The Very Thought	1966	$6
❑ 39764	Have a Good Time/Please My Love	1952	$15
❑ 39745	Here in My Heart/I'm Lost Again	1952	$15
❑ 40567	How Can I Replace You/Tell Me That You Love Me	1955	$10
❑ 44584	Hushabye Mountain/Hi-Ho	1968	$5
❑ 43220	If I Ruled the World/Take the Moment	1965	$6
❑ 42332	I Left My Heart In San Francisco/Once Upon a Time	1962	$8
❑ 42332 [PS]	I Left My Heart In San Francisco/Once Upon a Time	1962	$20
❑ 45255	I'll Begin Again/I Do Not Know a Day I Did Not Love You	1970	$5
❑ 41595	I'll Bring You a Rainbow/Ask Me (I Know)	1960	$8
❑ 39964	I'm the King of Broken Hearts/No One Will Ever Know	1953	$15
❑ 40965	In the Middle of An Island/I Am	1957	$10
❑ 43073	It's a Sin to Tell a Lie/A Taste of Honey	1964	$8
❑ 41341	It's So Peaceful in the Country/Being True to One Another	1959	$10
❑ 40427	It's Too Soon to Know/Close Your Eyes	1955	$10
❑ 44947	I've Gotta Be Me/A Lonely Place	1969	$5
❑ 42634	I Wanna Be Around/I Will Live My Life for You	1962	$8
❑ 45376	I Want to Be Happy/Tea for Two	1971	$5
❑ 1-670(?)	Let's Make Love/I Can't Give You Anything But Love, Baby	1950	$30
— Microgroove 7-inch 33 1/3 rpm single			
❑ 45073	Little Green Apples/Coco	1970	$5
❑ 41298	Love, Look Away/Blue Moon	1958	$10
❑ 45613	Love/Maybe This Time	1972	$5
❑ 41086	Love Song from Beauty and the Beast/Weary Blues From Waitin'	1957	$10
❑ JZSP112321 [DJ]	Love Theme from "The Sandpiper" (The Shadow of Your Smile) (same on both sides)	1965	$8
— Black vinyl promo			
❑ 45032	MacArthur Park/Before We Say Goodbye	1969	$5
❑ 41860	Marriage-Go-Round/Somebody	1960	$8
❑ 40523	May I Never Love Again/Don't Tell My Why	1955	$10
❑ 45411	More and More/I'm Losing My Mind	1971	$5
❑ AE28 [DJ]	My Favorite Things/I Love the Winter Weather	1970	$8

Number	Title	Yr	NM
❏ AE28 [PS]	My Favorite Things/I Love the Winter Weather	1970	$15

— Theme Song for 1970 Christmas Seals Campaign

Number	Title	Yr	NM
❏ 39187	Once There Lived a Fool/I Can't Give You Anything But Love, Baby	1951	$20
❏ 39826	Once There Lived a Fool/The Valentine Tango	1952	$10
❏ 40907	One for My Baby (And One More for the Road)/No Hard Feelings	1957	$10
❏ 40849	One Kiss Away from Heaven/Sold to the Man with the Broken Heart	1957	$10
❏ 44755	People/They All Laughed	1969	$5
❏ 41691	Put On a Happy Face/Baby, Talk to Me	1960	$8
❏ 39635	Silly Dreamer/Since My Love Has Gone	1952	$15
❏ 40632	Sing You Sinners/Capri in May	1956	$10
❏ 1-800(?)	Sing You Sinners/Kiss You	1950	$30

— Microgroove 7-inch 33 1/3 rpm single

Number	Title	Yr	NM
❏ 6-800(?)	Sing You Sinners/Kiss You	1950	$30
❏ 4-39695	Sleepless/Somewhere Along the Way	1952	$15
❏ 41434	Smile/You Can't Love 'Em All	1959	$12
❏ 40004	Someone Turned the Moon Upside Down/I'll Go	1953	$15
❏ 45109	Something/Eleanor Rigby	1970	$5
❏ 45205	Something/Think How It's Gonna Be	1970	$5
❏ 45523	Somewhere Along the Line/The Summer Knows	1972	$5
❏ 43508	Song from The Oscar/Baby Dream Your Dream	1966	$6
❏ 43508 [PS]	Song from The Oscar/Baby Dream Your Dream	1966	$12
❏ 40121	Stranger in Paradise/Why Does It Have to Be Me	1953	$15
❏ 42219	Tender Is the Night/Comes Once in a Lifetime	1961	$8
❏ 40770	The Autumn Waltz/Just in Time	1956	$12
❏ 41965	The Best Is Yet to Come/Marry Young	1961	$8
❏ 43202	The Best Thing to Be Is a Person/The Brightest Smile in Town	1964	$8
❏ 1-640(?)	The Boulevard of Broken Dreams/I Wanna Be Loved	1950	$30

— Microgroove 7-inch 33 1/3 rpm single

Number	Title	Yr	NM
❏ 39825	The Boulevard of Broken Dreams/I Wanna Be Loved	1952	$12
❏ 41381	The Cool School/You'll Never Get Away from Me	1959	$12
❏ 44443	The Glory of Love/A Fool of Fools	1968	$5
❏ 42779	The Good Life/Spring in Manhattan	1963	$8
❏ 42931	The Little Boy/The Moment of Truth	1963	$8
❏ 40169	There'll Be No Teardrops Tonight/My Heart Won't Say Goodbye	1954	$15
❏ 43431	The Shadow of Your Smile/I'll Only Miss Her When I Think of Her	1965	$6
❏ 42820	This Is All I Ask/True Blue Lou	1963	$8
❏ 41770	Till I Am	1960	$8
❏ 42003	Toot Toot Tootsie (Goodbye)/I'm Coming Virginia	1961	$8
❏ 45573	Twilight World/Easy Come, Easy Go	1972	$5
❏ 45449	Walkabout/How Beautiful Is Night	1971	$5
❏ 43954	What Makes It Happen/Country Girl	1966	$6
❏ 43954 [DJ]	What Makes It Happen/Country Girl	1966	$20

— Orange-vinyl promo issue

Number	Title	Yr	NM
❏ 44855	What the World Needs Now Is Love/Play It Again Sam	1969	$5
❏ 40491	What Will I Tell My Heart/Punch and Judy Love	1955	$10
❏ 42996 [DJ]	When Joanna Loved Me (same on both sides)	1964	$30

— Promo only on red vinyl

Number	Title	Yr	NM
❏ 42996	When Joanna Loved Me/The Kid's a Dreamer	1964	$8
❏ 42996 [PS]	When Joanna Loved Me/The Kid's a Dreamer	1964	$30

— Promo-only title sleeve with red vinyl issue; no number on sleeve

Number	Title	Yr	NM
❏ 45316	(Where Do I Begin) Love Story/I'll Begin Again	1971	$5
❏ 44688	Where Is Love/My Favorite Things	1968	$5
❏ 38-07658	White Christmas/All of My Life	1987	$3
❏ 38-07658 [PS]	White Christmas/All of My Life	1987	$3
❏ 43141	Who Can I Turn To (When Nobody Needs Me)/Waltz for Debby	1964	$8
❏ 44824	Whoever You Are, I Love You/A Place Over the Sun	1969	$5
❏ 38-06138	Why Do People Fall in Love/Moments Like This	1986	$3

MGM

Number	Title	Yr	NM
❏ 14607	My Love/(B-side unknown)	1973	$4

VERVE

Number	Title	Yr	NM
❏ 10690	Living Together, Growing Together/The Good Things in Life	1972	$4
❏ 10702	O Solo Mio/The Good Things in Life	1973	$4
❏ 10714	Tell Her It's Snowing/If I Could Go Back	1973	$4

7-Inch Extended Plays

COLUMBIA

Number	Title	Yr	NM
❏ B-2582	*One for My Baby/I Can't Give You Anything But Love/Solitaire/Once There Lived a Fool	1959	$10
❏ B-9382	*These Foolish Things/I Can't Give You Anything But Love/Boulevard of Broken Dreams/I'll Be Seeing You	1957	$10
❏ ZTEP26851/2	Because of You/In the Middle of an Island/Cold, Cold Heart//From Rags to Riches/Come Next Spring/Can You Find It in Your Heart	1957	$30

— Coca-Cola promotional item

Number	Title	Yr	NM
❏ 7-9173	I Left My Heart in San Francisco/I Wanna Be Around/Quiet Nights of Quiet Stars//The Good Life/A Taste of Honey/The Best Is Yet to Come	1964	$10

— Special Coin Operator Release"; small hole, plays at 33 1/3 rpm

Number	Title	Yr	NM
❏ 7-8800 [PS]	I Wanna Be Around	1964	$12
❏ 7-8800	I Wanna Be Around/The Good Life/Let's Face the Music and Dance//Once Upon a Summertime/Someone to Love/Quiet Night	1964	$10

— Special Coin Operator Release"; small hole, plays at 33 1/3 rpm

Number	Title	Yr	NM
❏ B-9382 [PS]	Tony	1957	$12
❏ ZTEP26851/2 [PS]	Tony Bennett Autographed Edition of Hits	1957	$30

— Coca-Cola promotional item

Number	Title	Yr	NM
❏ B-2582	Tony Bennett (Hall of Fame Series)	1959	$10
❏ 7-9173 [PS]	Tony Bennett's Greatest Hits Volume III	1964	$15
❏ 7-9085 [PS]	Who Can I Turn To	1964	$10
❏ 7-9085	Who Can I Turn To (When Nobody Needs Me)/Wrap Your Troubles in Dreams (And Dream Your Troubles Away)/Autumn Leaves//The Brightest Smile in Town/Listen, Little Girl/The Best Thing to Be Is a Person	1964	$10

— Special Coin Operator Release"; small hole, plays at 33 1/3 rpm

BENNIS, BARBARA
MALA

Number	Title	Yr	NM
❏ 468	Here's My Shoulder/I Wonder What He'll Say	1963	$15

BENNO, MARC
A&M

Number	Title	Yr	NM
❏ 1327	Baby, I Love You/Speak Your Mind	1972	$6
❏ 2184	Chasin' Rainbows/(B-side unknown)	1979	$6
❏ 1387	Southern Woman/Jive Fade Jive	1972	$6

BENNY AND THE BEDBUGS
DCP

Number	Title	Yr	NM
❏ 1008	The Beatle Beat/Roll Over Beethoven	1964	$20
❏ 1008 [PS]	The Beatle Beat/Roll Over Beethoven	1964	$30

BENOIT, DAVID

Number	Title	Yr	NM
❏ 341	Take a Look Inside My Heart/Oslo	1983	$6

BENONI, ARNE
ROUND ROBIN

Number	Title	Yr	NM
❏ 1881	If I Live to Be a Hundred (I'll Die Young)/(B-side unknown)	1989	$6
❏ 1879	Southern Lady/Those Evening Bells	1989	$6
❏ 1879 [PS]	Southern Lady/Those Evening Bells	1989	$8

BENSON, GEORGE, AND EARL KLUGH
WARNER BROS.

Number	Title	Yr	NM
❏ 28244	Dreamin'/Love Theme from "Romeo and Juliet"	1987	$3
❏ 27975	Since You're Gone/Love Theme from "Romeo and Juliet"	1988	$3
❏ 27975 [PS]	Since You're Gone/Love Theme from "Romeo and Juliet"	1988	$4

BENSON, GEORGE
A&M

Number	Title	Yr	NM
❏ 1003	Chattanooga Choo Choo/The Shape of Things to Come	1968	$6
❏ 1057	Don't Let Me Lose This Dream Part 1/Part 2	1969	$6
❏ 8395	Golden Slumbers-You Never Give Me Your Money (Medley)/(B-side unknown)	1971	$6

— May be promo only

Number	Title	Yr	NM
❏ 1128	I Got a Woman Part 1/I Got a Woman Part 2	1969	$6
❏ 1124	My Cherie Amour/Tell It Like It Is	1969	$6

ARISTA

Number	Title	Yr	NM
❏ 0251	The Greatest Love of All/Ali's Theme	1977	$4

— B-side by Michael Masser

Number	Title	Yr	NM
❏ 0251 [PS]	The Greatest Love of All/Ali's Theme	1977	$6

COLUMBIA

Number	Title	Yr	NM
❏ 43684	Summertime/Ain't That Peculiar	1966	$10
❏ 43998	The Man from Toledo/Georgia Stick	1967	$10

CTI

Number	Title	Yr	NM
❏ 47	Hold On, I'm Comin'/Gone	1978	$5
❏ 30	Summertime & 2001 (Part 1)/Summertime & 2001 (Part 2)	1977	$5
❏ 25	Supership/My Latin Brother	1975	$6

GROOVE

Number	Title	Yr	NM
❏ 024	It Should Have Been Me #2/She Makes Me Mad	1954	$50

WARNER BROS.

Number	Title	Yr	NM
❏ 29120	20-20/Shark Bite	1984	$4
❏ 29120 [PS]	20-20/Shark Bite	1984	$4
❏ 8268	Breezin'/Six to Four	1976	$4
❏ 28410	Did You Hear Thunder/Teaser	1987	$3
❏ 8360	Everything Must Change/The Wind and I	1977	$4
❏ 49505	Give Me the Night/Dinorah, Dinorah	1980	$4
❏ 49505 [PS]	Give Me the Night/Dinorah, Dinorah	1980	$5
❏ 8377	Gonna Love You More/Valdez in the Country	1977	$4
❏ 27537	Good Habit/Stephanie	1989	$3
❏ 49051	Hey Girl/Welcome Into My World	1979	$4
❏ 29042	I Just Wanna Hang Around You/Beyond the Sea (La Mer)	1985	$3
❏ 29649	Inside Love (So Personal)/In Search of a Dream	1983	$4
❏ 29649 [PS]	Inside Love (So Personal)/In Search of a Dream	1983	$4
❏ 29442	In Your Eyes/Never Too Far to Fall	1983	$4
❏ 8604	Lady Blue/California P.M.	1978	$4
❏ 8604 [PS]	Lady Blue/California P.M.	1978	$5
❏ 29563	Lady Love Me (One More Time)/Being with You	1983	$4
❏ 27780	Let's Do It Again/Let Go	1988	$3
❏ 27780 [PS]	Let's Do It Again/Let Go	1988	$3
❏ 8759	Love Ballad/You're Never Too Far from Me	1979	$4
❏ 8759 [PS]	Love Ballad/You're Never Too Far from Me	1979	$5
❏ 49570	Love Dance/Love X Love	1980	$4
❏ 49637	Midnight Love Affair/Turn Off the Lamplight	1980	$4
❏ 8542	On Broadway/We As Love	1978	$4
❏ 8542 [PS]	On Broadway/We As Love	1978	$5
❏ 28523	Shiver/Love Is Here Tonight	1986	$3
❏ 8209	This Masquerade/Lady	1976	$5
❏ 49846	Turn Your Love Around/Nature Boy	1981	$4
❏ 49846 [PS]	Turn Your Love Around/Nature Boy	1981	$4
❏ 27658	Twice the Love/(Instrumental)	1989	$3
❏ 27658 [PS]	Twice the Love/(Instrumental)	1989	$3

BENSON, JANE
ATCO

Number	Title	Yr	NM
❏ 6151	Growing Up/Surrendering	1959	$20

BENSON, MATT
STEP ONE

Number	Title	Yr	NM
❏ 406	When Will the Fires End/America	1989	$4

Number	Title	Yr	NM

BENT BOLT AND THE NUTS
MGM

Number	Title	Yr	NM
❏ 13635	Mechanical Man/ Sweet and Sour	1966	$8
❏ 13635 [PS]	Mechanical Man/ Sweet and Sour	1966	$10

BENTLEYS, THE
SMASH

Number	Title	Yr	NM
❏ 1988	Did Anybody Lose a Tear/ Why Didn't I Listen to Mother	1965	$30
❏ 1967	She's My Hot Rod Queen/ Why Does Everybody Want to Hold My Baby	1965	$30

BENTON, BARBI
PLAYBOY

Number	Title	Yr	NM
❏ 6032	Brass Buckles/Put a Little Bit on Me	1975	$5
❏ 6043	Movie Magazine, Stars in Her Eyes/He Looks Just Like His Daddy	1975	$5
❏ 6078	Staying Power/San Diego Serenade	1976	$5
❏ 5802	Take Some and Give Some (And Leave Some Behind)/ Ain't That Just the Way (That Life Goes Down)	1977	$5
❏ 6008	Welcome Stranger/That Country Boy of Mine	1974	$5

BENTON, BROOK, AND DAMITA JO
MERCURY

Number	Title	Yr	NM
❏ 72207	Baby, You've Got It Made/Stop Foolin'	1963	$12

BENTON, BROOK
ALL PLATINUM

Number	Title	Yr	NM
❏ 2364	Can't Take My Eyes Off You/ Weekend with Feathers	1976	$5

BRUT

Number	Title	Yr	NM
❏ 810	Lay Lady Lay/A Touch of Class	1973	$5
❏ 816	South Carolina/ (B-side unknown)	1973	$5

COTILLION

Number	Title	Yr	NM
❏ 44138	A Black Child Can't Smile/ If You Think God Is Dead	1971	$6
❏ 44078	Don't It Make You Want to Go Home/I've Gotta Be Me	1970	$6
❏ 44007	I Just Don't Know What to Do with Myself/Do Your Own Thing	1968	$6
❏ 44152	Movin' Day/Poor Make Believer	1972	$6
❏ 44072	My Way/A Little Bit of Soap	1970	$6
❏ 44130	Please Send Me Someone to Love/She Even Woke Me Up to Say Goodbye	1971	$6
❏ 44031	She Knows What to Do with 'Em/Touch 'Em with Love	1969	$8
❏ 44093	Shoes/Let Me Fix It	1970	$6
❏ 44141	Soul Santa/Let Us All Get Together with the Lord	1971	$8
❏ 44119	Take a Look at Your Hands/ If You Think God Is Dead	1971	$6
❏ 44110	Whoever Finds This, I Love You/Heaven Help Us All	1971	$6

EPIC

Number	Title	Yr	NM
❏ 9177	Love Made Me Your Fool/ Give Me a Sign	1956	$30
❏ 9199	The Wall/All My Love Belongs to You	1957	$30

MERCURY

Number	Title	Yr	NM
❏ 72303	A House Is Not a Home/ Come On Back	1964	$10
❏ 72303 [PS]	A House Is Not a Home/ Come On Back	1964	$30
❏ 72365	Do It Right/Please, Please Make It Easy	1964	$12
❏ 72365 [PS]	Do It Right/Please, Please Make It Easy	1964	$30
❏ 71443	Endlessly/So Close	1959	$20
❏ 872798-7	Endlessly/So Many Ways	1989	$4
❏ 71722	Fools Rush In (Where Angels Fear to Tread)/Someday You'll Want Me to Want You	1960	$15
❏ 71722 [PS]	Fools Rush In (Where Angels Fear to Tread)/Someday You'll Want Me to Want You	1960	$30
❏ 71859	Frankie and Johnny/It's Just a House Without You	1961	$15
❏ 71859 [PS]	Frankie and Johnny/It's Just a House Without You	1961	$30
❏ 72230	Going, Going, Gone/ After Midnight	1963	$10
❏ 72230 [PS]	Going, Going, Gone/ After Midnight	1963	$30
❏ 71962	Hit Record/Thanks to the Fool	1962	$12
❏ 71962 [PS]	Hit Record/Thanks to the Fool	1962	$30

—*Blue background with orange title banner*

Number	Title	Yr	NM
❏ 71962 [PS]	Hit Record/Thanks to the Fool	1962	$40

—*All-orange background with different photo*

Number	Title	Yr	NM
❏ 72055	Hotel Happiness/Still Waters Run Deep	1962	$10
❏ 72055 [PS]	Hotel Happiness/Still Waters Run Deep	1962	$30
❏ 72099	I Got What I Wanted/ Dearer Than Life	1963	$10
❏ 72099 [PS]	I Got What I Wanted/ Dearer Than Life	1963	$30
❏ 71394	It's Just a Matter of Time/Hurtin' Inside	1959	$20
❏ 872796-7	It's Just a Matter of Time/Hurtin' Inside	1989	$4
❏ 72024	Lie to Me/With the Touch of Your Hand	1962	$12
❏ 72024 [PS]	Lie to Me/With the Touch of Your Hand	1962	$30
❏ 72446	Love Me Now/A-Sleepin' at the End of the Bed	1965	$10
❏ 72333	Lumberjack/Don't Do What I Did (Do What I Say)	1964	$10
❏ 72333 [PS]	Lumberjack/Don't Do What I Did (Do What I Say)	1964	$30
❏ 72135	My True Confession/ Tender Years	1963	$10
❏ 72135 [PS]	My True Confession/ Tender Years	1963	$30
❏ 71912	Shadrack/The Lost Penny	1961	$15
❏ 71912 [PS]	Shadrack/The Lost Penny	1961	$30
❏ 71512	So Many Ways/I Want You Forever	1959	$20
❏ 72398	Special Years/Where There's a Will (There's a Way)	1965	$10
❏ 71478	Thank You Pretty Baby/ With All of My Heart	1959	$20
❏ 71820	The Boll Weevil Song/Your Eyes	1961	$15
❏ 71820 [PS]	The Boll Weevil Song/Your Eyes	1961	$30

—*Back of sleeve has six albums pictured*

Number	Title	Yr	NM
❏ 71820 [PS]	The Boll Weevil Song/ Your Eyes	1961	$30

—*Back of sleeve has three albums pictured*

Number	Title	Yr	NM
❏ 71566	The Ties That Bind/ Hither, Thither and Yon	1960	$15
❏ 71566 [PS]	The Ties That Bind/ Hither, Thither and Yon	1960	$30
❏ 71774	Think Twice/For My Baby	1961	$15
❏ 71774 [PS]	Think Twice/For My Baby	1961	$30
❏ 71558	This Time of the Year/ How Many Times	1959	$20
❏ 71730	This Time of the Year/Merry Christmas, Happy New Year	1960	$15
❏ 71554	This Time of the Year/ Nothing in the World	1959	$20
❏ 72266	Too Late to Turn Back Now/ Another Cup of Coffee	1964	$10
❏ 72266 [PS]	Too Late to Turn Back Now/ Another Cup of Coffee	1964	$30
❏ 72177	Two Tickets to Paradise/ Don't Hate Me	1963	$10
❏ 72177 [PS]	Two Tickets to Paradise/ Don't Hate Me	1963	$30
❏ 71925	Walk on the Wild Side/ Somewhere in the Used to Be	1962	$10
❏ 71925 [PS]	Walk on the Wild Side/ Somewhere in the Used to Be	1962	$30

MGM

Number	Title	Yr	NM
❏ 14440	If You've Got the Time/You Take Me Home Honey	1972	$5

OKEH

Number	Title	Yr	NM
❏ 7065	Bring Me Love/Some of My Best Friends	1956	$30

OLDE WORLD

Number	Title	Yr	NM
❏ 1100	Makin' Love Is Good for You/Better Times	1977	$5
❏ 1107	Soft/Glow Love	1978	$5

POLYDOR

Number	Title	Yr	NM
❏ 2015	I Cried for You/ Love Me a Little	1979	$4

RCA VICTOR

Number	Title	Yr	NM
❏ 47-8879	Break Her Heart/In the Evening in the Moonlight	1966	$10
❏ 47-8693	Mother Nature, Father Time/You're Mine	1965	$10
❏ 47-8693 [PS]	Mother Nature, Father Time/You're Mine	1965	$30
❏ 47-7489	Only Your Love/If Only I Had Known	1959	$40
❏ 47-9031	Our First Christmas Together/Silent Night	1966	$15
❏ 47-8995	So True in Life, So True in Love/If You Only Knew	1966	$12
❏ 47-8830	Too Much Good Lovin'/A Sailor Boy's Love Song	1966	$10
❏ 47-9096	Wake Up/All My Love Belongs to You	1967	$8
❏ 47-8944	Where Does a Man Go to Cry/The Roach Song	1966	$10
❏ 47-8768	Where There's Life/ Only a Girl Like You	1965	$10

REPRISE

Number	Title	Yr	NM
❏ 0649	Glory of Love/ Weakness in a Man	1967	$8
❏ 0676	Instead (Of Loving You)/ Lonely Street	1968	$8

STAX

Number	Title	Yr	NM
❏ 0231	Winds of Change/I Keep Thinking to Myself	1974	$5

VIK

Number	Title	Yr	NM
❏ 0311	A Million Miles from Nowhere/Devoted	1957	$30
❏ 0325	Because You Love Me/ Crinoline Skirt	1958	$30
❏ 0336	Crazy in Love with You/I'm Coming Back to You	1958	$30
❏ 0285	I Wanna Do Everything for You/Come On Be Nice	1957	$30

BERGEN, POLLY
COLUMBIA

Number	Title	Yr	NM
❏ 41971	Bye Bye Blackbird/The Happiest Girl in the World	1961	$10
❏ 41675	Do It Yourself/The Party's Over	1960	$12
❏ 41342	He Didn't Call/I Feel Sorry for the Boy	1959	$15
❏ 41617	It Might As Well Be Spring/Four Seasons	1960	$10

RCA VICTOR

Number	Title	Yr	NM
❏ 47-3886	Oh Them Dudes/I Got Tookin'	1950	$20
❏ 47-4022	Out of Sight/Tonda Wanda Hey	1951	$20

BERLIN
COLUMBIA

Number	Title	Yr	NM
❏ 38-05903	Take My Breath Away/ Radar Radio	1986	$3

—*B-side by Georgio Moroder*

Number	Title	Yr	NM
❏ 38-05903 [PS]	Take My Breath Away/ Radar Radio	1986	$3
❏ 38-68719	Take My Breath Away/ Top Gun Anthem	1989	$3

—*Golden Oldies" reissue; B-side by Harold Faltermeyer*

EVATONE

Number	Title	Yr	NM
❏ 13	Masquerade/(B-side blank)	1983	$8

—*Flexi-disc from an issue of Trouser Press*

GEFFEN

Number	Title	Yr	NM
❏ 7-29192	Dancing in Berlin/ Pictures of You	1984	$5
❏ 7-28563	Like Flames/Hideaway	1986	$4
❏ 7-28563 [PS]	Like Flames/Hideaway	1986	$4
❏ 7-29504	Masquerade/Live Sex	1983	$5
❏ 7-29504 [PS]	Masquerade/Live Sex	1983	$5
❏ 7-29747	Sex (I'm a ...)/Tell Me Why	1983	$5
❏ 7-29747 [PS]	Sex (I'm a ...)/Tell Me Why	1983	$8
❏ 7-29638	The Metro/World of Smiles	1983	$5
❏ 7-29638 [PS]	The Metro/World of Smiles	1983	$5

M.A.O.

Number	Title	Yr	NM
❏ F-4	The Metro/Tell Me Why	1981	$30
❏ F-4 [PS]	The Metro/Tell Me Why	1981	$30

ZONE H

Number	Title	Yr	NM
❏ ZOH-001	Matter of Time/Overload	1980	$30
❏ ZOH-001 [PS]	Matter of Time/Overload	1980	$30

ZONE H/I.R.S.

Number	Title	Yr	NM
❏ 9015	Matter of Time/French Reggae	1980	$10

—*Small hole*

Number	Title	Yr	NM
❏ 9015 [PS]	Matter of Time/French Reggae	1980	$10

BERMUDAS, THE
ERA

Number	Title	Yr	NM
❏ 3125	Donnie/Chu Sen Ling	1964	$15

BERNA-DEAN
IMPERIAL

Number	Title	Yr	NM
❏ 5978	Hello/Sleepless Nights	1963	$30
❏ 5840	He's Mine/One Gal in Town, Five Men Hagin' Around	1962	$30
❏ 5792	I Walk in My Sleep/ Little Willie	1961	$30
❏ 5877	Morning, Noon and Night/ The World Keeps Changing	1962	$30
❏ 5950	The President Says Walk/I Wonder	1963	$30

BERNARD, CHRIS
REVUE

Number	Title	Yr	NM
❏ 11053	Good Hearted Woman/Mother	1969	$40

BERNARD, ROD

ARBEE

Number	Title	Yr	NM
❏ 104	Gimme Back My Cadillac/Don't You Think I've Paid Enough	1965	$10
❏ 105	Those Were Our Songs/Just Another Lie	1966	$10

ARGO

Number	Title	Yr	NM
❏ 5327	This Should Go On Forever/Pardon Mr. Gordon	1959	$30

CARL

Number	Title	Yr	NM
❏ 0(# unknown)	Linda Gail/Little Bitta Mama	1957	$30

CRAZY CAJUN

Number	Title	Yr	NM
❏ 9020	Papa Thibodeaux/My Little Jollie Blonde	1978	$5

HALLWAY

Number	Title	Yr	NM
❏ 1917	Diggy Liggy Lo/The Clock	1963	$20
❏ 1915	Forgive/I Want Somebody	1963	$20
❏ 1806	I Had a Girl/Wedding Bells	1963	$20
❏ 1919	Loneliness/Boss Man's Son	1964	$20
❏ 1922	My Own Mother-in-Law/I Might As Well	1964	$20
❏ 1902	Who's Gonna Rock My Baby/Colinda	1962	$20

JIN

Number	Title	Yr	NM
❏ 350	A Winner in Love/I Forgot I Had These Memories of You	1975	$5
❏ 240	Big Mamou/New Orleans Jail	1969	$8
❏ 325	Breaking Up Is Hard to Do/Sometimes I Walk in My Sleep	1975	$5
❏ 232	Congratulations to You Darling/You're the Reason I'm in Love	1968	$8
❏ 307	Don't You Think I've Paid Enough/Somebody Wrote That Song for Me	1974	$5
❏ 376	Go On, Go On/I Never Had the One I Wanted	1976	$5
❏ 373	Mardi Gras in New Orleans/Oh Mother Dear	1976	$5
❏ 338	This Should Go On Forever/I Spent a Week There Last Night	1975	$5
❏ 105	This Should Go On Forever/Pardon, Mr. Gordon	1958	$50
❏ 237	To Have and Hold/Cajun Honey	1968	$8

MERCURY

Number	Title	Yr	NM
❏ 71767	Lonely Hearts Club/Who Knows	1961	$20
❏ 71592	One of These Days/Let's Get Together Tonight	1960	$30
❏ 71507	Shedding Teardrops Over You/One More Chance	1959	$30
❏ 71689	Sttrange Kisses/Just a Memory	1960	$30
❏ 71842	(Tell Me) Sometime/I'm Not Lonely Anymore	1961	$20
❏ 71654	Two Young Fools in Love/Dance Fool Dance	1960	$30

SCEPTER

Number	Title	Yr	NM
❏ 12195	Those Were Our Songs/Recorded in England	1967	$20

TEAR DROP

Number	Title	Yr	NM
❏ 3044	Our Teenage Love/Doing the Oo-Wa-Woo	1966	$10
❏ 3117	This Should Go On Forever/Recorded in England	1969	$8

BERRY, CHUCK

ATCO

Number	Title	Yr	NM
❏ 7203	Oh What a Thrill/California	1979	$4

CHESS

Number	Title	Yr	NM
❏ 1722	Almost Grown/Little Queenie	1959	$40
❏ 1716	Anthony Boy/That's My Desire	1959	$40
❏ 2169	Baby What You Want Me to Do/Shake, Rattle and Roll	1975	$4
❏ 1729	Back in the U.S.A./Memphis Tennessee	1959	$40
❏ 1697	Beautiful Delilah/Vacation Time	1958	$40
❏ 1737	Broken Arrow/Childhood Sweetheart	1959	$50
❏ 1754	Bye Bye Johnny/Worried Life Blues	1960	$30
❏ 1700	Carol/Hey Pedro	1958	$40
❏ 1799	Come On/Go-Go-Go	1961	$30
❏ 1926	Dear Dad/Lonely School Days	1965	$20
❏ 1763	I Got to Find My Baby/Mad Lad	1960	$30
❏ 1853	I'm Talking About You/Diploma for Two	1963	$30
❏ 1779	I'm Talking About You/Little Star	1961	$30
❏ 1943	It Wasn't Me/Welcome Back Pretty Girl	1965	$20
❏ 1943 [PS]	It Wasn't Me/Welcome Back Pretty Girl	1965	$40
❏ 1912	Little Marie/Go Bobby Soxer	1964	$20
❏ 1912 [PS]	Little Marie/Go Bobby Soxer	1964	$50
❏ 1604	Maybellene/Wee Wee Hours	1955	$60
❏ 1866	Memphis/Sweet Little Sixteen	1963	$30
❏ 2131	My Ding-a-Ling/Johnny B. Goode	1972	$6

—All-blue label

Number	Title	Yr	NM
❏ 2131	My Ding-a-Ling/Johnny B. Goode	1972	$4

—Orange and blue label

Number	Title	Yr	NM
❏ 1664	Oh Baby Doll/La Jaunda	1957	$60
❏ 1767	Our Little Rendezvous/Jaguar and Thunderbird	1960	$30
❏ 1916	Promised Land/Things I Used to Do	1964	$20
❏ 1916 [PS]	Promised Land/Things I Used to Do	1964	$60
❏ 1653	School Day (Ring! Ring! Goes the Bell)/Deep Feeling	1957	$60
❏ 1709	Sweet Little Rock and Roll/Joe Joe Gun	1958	$40
❏ 1683	Sweet Little Sixteen/Reelin' and Rockin'	1958	$40
❏ 1610	Thirty Days (To Come Back Home)/Together	1955	$60
❏ 1635	Too Much Monkey Business/Brown Eyed Handsome Man	1956	$60
❏ 1747	Too Pooped to Pop ("Casey")/Let It Rock	1960	$30
❏ 2090	Tulane/Have Mercy Judge	1970	$6
❏ 72680	Back to Memphis/I Do Really Love You	1967	$12
❏ 72643	Club Nitty Gritty/Laugh and Cry	1966	$10
❏ 72748	It Hurts Me Too/Feelin' It	1967	$10
❏ 72963	It's Too Dark in There/Good Looking Woman	1969	$30
❏ 72963 [PS]	It's Too Dark in There/Good Looking Woman	1969	$40
❏ 72840	Louie to Frisco/Ma Dear	1968	$10

PHILCO-FORD

Number	Title	Yr	NM
❏ HP-34	Maybellene/Roll Over Beethoven	1969	$30

—4-inch plastic "Hip Pocket Record" with color sleeve

7-Inch Extended Plays

CHESS

Number	Title	Yr	NM
❏ CH-5118 [PS]	After School Session	1957	$300
❏ EP-5124	Carol/Hey Pedro//Beautiful Delilah/Vacation Time	1958	$125
❏ EP-5124 [PS]	Pickin' Berries	1958	$250
❏ CH-5118	School Day (Ring, Ring Goes the Bell)/Wee Wee Hours// Brown Eyed Handsome Man/ Too Much Monkey Business	1957	$120
❏ EP-5126 [PS]	Sweet Little Rock and Roller	1958	$250
❏ CH-5121 [PS]	Sweet Little Sixteen	1958	$250
❏ CH-5121	Sweet Little Sixteen/Rockin' at the Philharmonic/Reelin' and Rockin'/Guitar Boogie	1958	$125

BERRY, DAVE

LONDON

Number	Title	Yr	NM
❏ 20038	Do I Still Figure in Your Life/Latisha	1968	$8
❏ 9666	Memphis Tennessee/My Baby Left Me	1964	$20
❏ 9698	The Crying Game/Don't Gimme No Lip Child	1964	$20
❏ 9781	This Strange Effect/Now	1965	$20

PARROT

Number	Title	Yr	NM
❏ 40010	Picture Me Gone/Baby's Gone	1967	$10

BERRY, JAN

A&M

Number	Title	Yr	NM
❏ 1957	Little Queenie/That's the Way It Is	1977	$20
❏ 2020	Skateboard Surfin' U.S.A. (Sidewalk Surfin' with Me)/How How I Love You	1978	$20

ODE

Number	Title	Yr	NM
❏ 66034	Don't You Just Know It/Blue Moon Shuffle	1973	$50

—With Brian Wilson on co-lead vocals on A-side

Number	Title	Yr	NM
❏ 66023	Mother Earth/Blue Moon Shuffle	1972	$30
❏ 66120	Sing Sang a Song/Sing Sang a Song (Singalong Version)	1976	$30
❏ 66050	Tinsel Town/Blow Up Music	1974	$30

—As "I Jan I

RIPPLE

Number	Title	Yr	NM
❏ 6101	Tomorrow's Teardrops/My Midsummer Night's Dream	1961	$125

—As "Jan Barry

BERRY, JOHN

DOT

Number	Title	Yr	NM
❏ 16132	Dance with Me Darlin'/Lucy Lou	1960	$15

BERRY, KEN

BARNABY

Number	Title	Yr	NM
❏ 2034	Everyday with You/He'll Have to Go	1971	$8
❏ 2020	Lonely Street/Ain't That a Shame	1970	$8

BERRY KIDS, THE

MGM

Number	Title	Yr	NM
❏ 12379	Go, Go, Go, Right Into Town/Love Me, Love	1956	$100

BERRY, MIKE

CORAL

Number	Title	Yr	NM
❏ 62341	A Tribute to Buddy Holly/Every Little Kiss	1962	$70
❏ 62357	Don't You Think It's Time/Loneliness	1963	$40
❏ 62483	Gonna Fall in Love/It Comes and Goes	1966	$20

EPIC

Number	Title	Yr	NM
❏ 50748	I Am a Rocker/Boogaloo Dues	1979	$4
❏ 50913	Stay Close to Me/One by One	1980	$4

MCA

Number	Title	Yr	NM
❏ 40432	Don't Be Cruel/It's All Over	1975	$5

BERRY, RICHARD

FLAIR

Number	Title	Yr	NM
❏ 1052	Bye Bye/At Last	1954	$70

—With the Dreamers

Number	Title	Yr	NM
❏ 1058	Daddy Daddy/Baby Darling	1954	$70

—With the Dreamers

Number	Title	Yr	NM
❏ 1068	God Gave Me You/Doncha Go	1955	$60
❏ 1016	I'm Still in Love with You/One Little Prayer	1953	$100
❏ 1064	Please Tell Me/Oh Oh Get Out of the Car	1955	$60
❏ 1075	Together/Jelly Roll	1955	$60
❏ 1055	What You Do to Me/The Big Break	1954	$70

FLIP

Number	Title	Yr	NM
❏ 339	Besame Mucho/Do I, Do I	1958	$40
❏ 349	Have Love, Will Travel/No Room	1960	$40
❏ 336	Heaven on Wheels/The Mess Around	1958	$50
❏ 352	I'll Never Ever Love Again/Somewhere There's a Rainbow	1961	$40
❏ 321	Louie, Louie/Rock, Rock, Rock	1957	$50
❏ 321	Louie, Louie/You Are My Sunshine	1957	$70
❏ 327	Sweet Sugar You/Rock, Rock, Rock	1957	$50
❏ 318	Take the Key/No Kissin' and Huggin'	1956	$50

HAPPY TIGER

Number	Title	Yr	NM
❏ 5063	Louie Louie/Rock Rock Rock	1972	$8

K&G

Number	Title	Yr	NM
❏ 9001	I'm Your Fool/In a Really Big Way	1961	$40

RPM

Number	Title	Yr	NM
❏ 465	Angel of My Life/Yama Yama Pretty Mama	1956	$125
❏ 452	Pretty Brown Eyes/I Am Bewildered	1956	$40
❏ 477	Wait for Me/Good Love	1956	$40

SMASH

Number	Title	Yr	NM
❏ 1811	I'm Learning/Empty Chair	1963	$15
❏ 1789	What Good Is a Heart/Everybody's Got a Lover But Me	1963	$15

WARNER BROS.

Number	Title	Yr	NM
❏ 5164	Walk Right In/It's All Right	1960	$60

BERTRAM, BOB

BERTRAM INTERNATIONAL

Number	Title	Yr	NM
❏ 201	A Christmas Aloha for You/I Don't Need a Thing for Christmas	1958	$20

BERU REVUE, BUNNY DRUMS, DA PLIARS, PRETTY POISON, THE HOOTERS & THE VELS

HALF TRACK

Number	Title	Yr	NM
❏ 914	Hang Up Your Stockings/Sleigh Ride	1984	$6

BEST, BILLY, AND THE DITALIANS

MERCURY

Number	Title	Yr	NM
❏ 72923	Baby That Takes the Cake/Time Is Getting Hard Josephine	1969	$8

BEST, PETER (1)

CAMEO

Number	Title	Yr	NM
❏ 391	Boys/Kansas City	1965	$100
❏ 391 [PS]	Boys/Kansas City	1965	$125

Number	Title	Yr	NM
HAPPENING			
❑ 405	If You Can't Get Her/ Don't Play with Me	1964	$180
❑ 1117/8	If You Can't Get Her/The Way I Feel About You	1966	$200
—Label credit: "Best of the Beatles (Peter Best)			
MR. MAESTRO			
❑ 712	Casting My Spell/I'm Blue	1965	$200
—Black vinyl			
❑ 712	Casting My Spell/I'm Blue	1965	$200
—Blue vinyl			
❑ 711	I Can't Do Without You Now/Keys to My Heart	1965	$200
—Label credit: "Best of the Beatles"; black vinyl			
❑ 711	I Can't Do Without You Now/Keys to My Heart	1965	$200
—Label credit: "Best of the Beatles"; blue vinyl			
ORIGINAL BEATLES DRUMMER			
❑ 800	(I'll Try) Anyway/I Wanna Be There	1964	$180
BEST, PETER (2)			
CAPITOL			
❑ 2092	Carousel of Love/Want You	1968	$40
BEST THINGS, THE			
UNITED ARTISTS			
❑ 50027	Chicks Are for Kids/ You May See Me Cry	1966	$10
BETTS, DICKEY			
ARISTA			
❑ 0333	Atlanta's Burning Down/ Mr. Blues Man	1978	$4
❑ 0269	Bougainvilla/Sweet Virginia	1977	$4
CAPRICORN			
❑ 0221	Highway Call/Rain	1975	$5
BEVEL, CHARLES			
A&M			
❑ 1481	Black Santa Claus/Making A Decision (Bring On Sunshine)	1973	$6
❑ 1608	Don't Lie to Me/It Ain't Magic	1974	$5
❑ 1481	Making a Decision/Meet "Mississippi Charles Bevel"	1973	$5
❑ 1501	Sally B. White/Porcupine Meat	1974	$5
BEVERLY			
DERAM			
❑ 7502	Happy New Year/Where The Good Times Are	1966	$12
BEVERLY AND DUANE			
ARIOLA AMERICA			
❑ 7728	Glad I Gotcha Baby/We Got to Stick Together	1978	$5
❑ 7741	Living in a World/Surround Me	1979	$5
❑ 7768	Take a Ride/It's Gonna Be Alright	1979	$5
BEVERLY, FRANKIE, AND THE BUTLERS			
FAIRMOUNT			
❑ 1017	Because of My Heart/I Want to Feel I'm Wanted	1966	$2000
— VG 1000; VG+ 1500			
❑ 1012	She Kissed Me/Don't Cry Little Sad Boy	1966	$200
GAMBLE			
❑ 220	If That's What You Wanted/ Love (Your Pain Goes Deep)	1968	$400
BEVERLY, FRANKIE, 'S RAW SOUL			
GREGAR			
❑ 71-0108	Color Blind/Mother Nature's Been Good to You	1971	$200
❑ 71-0112	People in the Know/ Understanding	1971	$200
❑ 71-0115	Tomorrow May Not Be Your Day/While I'm Alone	1971	$30
BEVERLY SISTERS, THE			
LONDON			
❑ 1731	Blow the Wind Southerly/ Doodle Doo Doo	1957	$15

Number	Title	Yr	NM
❑ 1703	Greensleeves/I'll See You in My Dreams	1956	$15
❑ 1891	Little Donkey/Toy Dream	1960	$15
❑ 1783	Long Black Nylons/ Young Cavalier	1958	$15
❑ 1757	Old Enough to Know/I Remember Mama	1957	$15
❑ 1862	The Little Drummer Boy/ Strawberry Fair	1958	$15
MERCURY			
❑ 71671	Oh Ricky/Only Me	1960	$15
ROULETTE			
❑ 4350	Flight 1203/(B-side unknown)	1961	$15
BI-TONES, THE			
BLUE JAY			
❑ 1000	Oh How I Love You So/Beatnik Girl	1960	$30
BICKEL, BILL, TRIO			
CORAL			
❑ 60307	The Christmas Tree Angel/ Christmas Island	1950	$20
BIDDU ORCHESTRA			
COLOSSUS			
❑ 125	The Sooner I Get to You/ (B-side unknown)	1970	$8
—As "Biddu			
EPIC			
❑ 50387	Funky Tropical/Girl You'll Be a Woman Soon	1977	$4
❑ 50173	I Could Have Danced All Night/Jump for Joy	1975	$4
❑ 50439	Soal Coaxing/Nirvana	1977	$4
❑ 50139	Summer of '42/Northern Dancer	1975	$4
BIG AUDIO DYNAMITE			
Features Mick Jones, formerly of THE CLASH.			
COLUMBIA			
❑ 38-06708	Badrock City/C'mon Every Beatbox	1987	$3
❑ 38-06708 [PS]	Badrock City/C'mon Every Beatbox	1987	$3
—Demonstration -- Not for Sale" on back			
❑ 38-06364	C'Mon Every Beatbox (Edit)/Badrock City	1986	$3
❑ 38-06364 [PS]	C'Mon Every Beatbox (Edit)/Badrock City	1986	$3
❑ 38-06053	E=MC2/A Party	1986	$3
❑ 38-06053 [PS]	E=MC2/A Party	1986	$3
❑ 38-05841 [PS]	Medicine Show	1986	$6
—Demonstration -- Not for Sale" on back			
❑ 38-05841	Medicine Show/This Is Big Audio Dynamite	1986	$3
❑ 38-05841 [PS]	Medicine Show/This Is Big Audio Dynamite	1986	$3
❑ 38-08094	The Other 99/What Happened to Eddie	1988	$3
❑ 38-08094 [PS]	The Other 99/What Happened to Eddie	1988	$3
BIG BEATS, THE			
COLUMBIA			
❑ 41072	Clark's Expedition/Big Boy	1958	$30
BIG BLACK			
HOMESTEAD			
❑ HMS 042	Il Duce/Big Money	1985	$5
❑ HMS 042 [PS]	Il Duce/Big Money	1985	$5
TOUCH & GO			
❑ TG21	Heartbeat/Things to Do/ Today I Can't Believe	1987	$6
❑ TG21 [PS]	Heartbeat/Things to Do/ Today I Can't Believe	1987	$6
❑ TG23	He's a Whore/The Model	1987	$20
❑ TG23 [PS]	He's a Whore/The Model	1987	$20
UNI			
❑ 55099	Come On Down to the Beach/ Love, Sweet Like Sugarcane	1968	$8
❑ 55293	Long Hair/Diggin' What You're Doing	1971	$6
❑ 55337	Mellow/Diggin' What You're Doing	1972	$6
❑ 55051	The Snakecharmer/Come On and Get It Baby	1968	$8

Number	Title	Yr	NM
BIG BLUE WRECKING CREW			
ELEKTRA			
❑ 47253	We Are the Champions/Theme from "New York, New York	1981	$4
❑ 47253 [PS]	We Are the Champions/Theme from "New York, New York	1981	$4
BIG BOPPER			
D			
❑ 1008	Chantilly Lace/The Purple People Eater Meets the Witch Doctor	1958	$250
MERCURY			
❑ 71312	A Teenage Mom/Monkey Song	1958	$70
—As "Jape Richardson			
❑ 71219	Beggar to a King/Crazy Blue	1957	$70
—As "Jape Richardson			
❑ 71375	Big Bopper's Wedding/ Little Red Riding Hood	1958	$20
❑ 71343	Chantilly Lace/The Purple People Eater Meets the Witch Doctor	1958	$30
❑ 71451	It's the Truth, Ruth/That's What I'm Talkin' About	1959	$20
❑ 71482	Pink Petticoats/Time Clock	1959	$20
❑ 71416	Someone's Watching Over You/ Walking Through My Dreams	1959	$20
BIG BOYS			
7-Inch Extended Plays			
BIG BOYS			
❑ BB42480 [PS]	Frat Cars	1980	$60
—Warning: The above has been bootlegged			
❑ BB42480	Frat Cars/Heartbeat// Movies/Mutant Rock	1980	$60
BIG BROTHER			
ALL AMERICAN			
❑ 5718	E.S.P./Brother, Where Are You	1970	$50
BIG BROTHER AND THE HOLDING COMPANY			
Also see JANIS JOPLIN. (45)			
COLUMBIA			
❑ 45502	Black Widow Spider/ Nu Boogaloo Jam	1971	$6
❑ 44626	Piece of My Heart/Turtle Blues	1968	$10
MAINSTREAM			
❑ 657	All Is Loneliness/Blindman	1967	$15
❑ 666	Bye Bye Baby/Intruder	1968	$15
❑ 678	Coo Coo/The Last Time	1968	$15
❑ 662	Down on Me/Call On Me	1967	$15
❑ 675	Women Is Losers/Caterpillar	1968	$100
—This is much rarer than the version with the other flip side			
❑ 675	Women Is Losers/Light Is Faster Than Sound	1968	$15
BIG CHIEF			
BIG CHIEF			
❑ MD777	Brake Torque/Superstupid	1989	$10
—Purple vinyl			
❑ MD777	Brake Torque/Superstupid	1989	$8
—Green vinyl			
❑ MD777 [PS]	Brake Torque/Superstupid	1989	$8
BIG COUNTRY			
MERCURY			
❑ 811450-7	Fields of Fire/Angle Park	1983	$3
❑ 811450-7 [PS]	Fields of Fire/Angle Park	1983	$6
—Fold-out poster sleeve			
❑ 814467-7	In a Big Country/All of Us	1983	$3
❑ 814467-7 [PS]	In a Big Country/All of Us	1983	$6
❑ 884645-7	Look Away/Restless Natives	1986	$3
❑ 884645-7 [PS]	Look Away/Restless Natives	1986	$4
❑ 880412-7	Where the Rose Is Sown/Prairie Rose	1984	$3
❑ 880412-7 [PS]	Where the Rose Is Sown/Prairie Rose	1984	$3
❑ 818834-7	Wonderland/Lost Patrol (Live)	1984	$3
❑ 818834-7 [PS]	Wonderland/Lost Patrol (Live)	1984	$6

Number	Title	Yr	NM

BIG DADDY AND HIS BOYS
KING
❏ 5013	Bacon Fat/Bad Boy	1957	$30

BIG FRANK AND THE ESSENCES
BLUE ROCK
❏ 4012	Secret/I Won't Let Her See Me Cry	1965	$200

PHILIPS
❏ 40283	Secret/I Won't Let Her See Me Cry	1965	$125

BIG GUYS, THE
PALETTE
❏ 5114	Propulsion/(B-side unknown)	1964	$30
❏ 5110	Walkin' the Board/Faith 7	1963	$30

WARNER BROS.
❏ 7047	Hang My Head and Cry/Mr. Cupid (Don't You Call on Me)	1967	$60

BIG MAYBELLE
BRUNSWICK
❏ 55234	Candy/Cry	1962	$15
❏ 55242	Cold, Cold Heart/ Why Was I Born	1963	$15
❏ 55256	Everybody's Got a Home But Me/How Deep Is the Ocean	1963	$15

CHESS
❏ 1967	It's a Man's Man's Man's World/ Big Maybelle Sings the Blues	1966	$10

OKEH
❏ 7053	Ain't No Use/Don't Leave Poor Me	1955	$40
❏ 7069	Gabbin' Blues/New Kind of Mambo	1956	$40
❏ 6931	Gabbin' Blues/Rain Down Rain	1953	$50
❏ 7026	I've Got a Feelin'/ You'll Never Know	1954	$40
❏ 7042	My Big Mistake/I'm Gettin' 'Long Alright	1954	$40
❏ 7009	My Country Man/ Maybelle's Blues	1953	$50
❏ 6998	Send for Me/Jimmy Mule	1953	$50
❏ 7066	Such a Cutie/The Other Night	1956	$40
❏ 6955	Way Back Home/Just Want Your Love	1953	$50
❏ 7060	Whole Lotta Shakin' Goin' On/One Monkey Don't Stop No Show	1955	$40

PARAMOUNT
❏ 0237	Blame It on Your Love/ See See Rider	1973	$6

PORT
❏ 3002	Let Me Go/No Better for You	1965	$15

ROJAC
❏ 112	96 Tears/That's Life	1966	$12
❏ 1969	Don't Pass Me By/ It's Been Raining	1966	$12
❏ 121	Heaven Will Welcome You, Dr. King/Eleanor Rigby	1968	$12
❏ 124	How It Lies/Old Love Never Dies	1968	$8
❏ 115	I Can't Wait Any Longer/Turn the World Around the Other Way	1967	$8
❏ 116	Mama (He Treats Your Daughter Mean)/Keep That Man	1967	$8

SAVOY
❏ 1572	A Good Man Is Hard to Find/Pitiful	1959	$20
❏ 1558	Baby Won't You Please Come Home/Say It Isn't Do	1959	$20
❏ 1536	Blues Early, Early (Part 1)/ Blues Early, Early (Part 2)	1958	$20
❏ 1195	Candy/That's a Pretty Good Love	1956	$30
❏ 1595	I Ain't Got Nobody/ Going Home Baby	1961	$20
❏ 1512	I Don't Want to Cry/All of Me	1957	$20
❏ 1583	I Got It Bad and That Ain't Good/Ramblin' Blues	1960	$20
❏ 1583	I Got It Bad and That Ain't Good/Until the Real Thing Comes Along	1960	$20
❏ 1500	Mean to Me/Tell Me Who	1956	$20
❏ 1527	So Long/Ring Dang Dilly	1957	$20
❏ 1576	Some of These Days/I Understand	1959	$20
❏ 1541	White Christmas/Silent Night	1958	$20

SCEPTER
❏ 1288	I Don't Want to Cry/ Yesterday's Kisses	1965	$15

BIG MOUTH
SPINDIZZY
❏ ZS74004	Where the Master Lives/Too Busy	1972	$6

BIG PIG
A&M
❏ 3014	Breakaway/Hell Bent Heaven	1988	$4
❏ 3014 [PS]	Breakaway/Hell Bent Heaven	1988	$4
❏ 1216	Hungry Town/Charlie	1988	$4
❏ 1216 [PS]	Hungry Town/Charlie	1988	$4

BIG RIC
SCOTTI BROTHERS
❏ ZS4-04239	How Does She Do It/ Weather Girl	1983	$4
❏ ZS4-04084	Take Away/Or What	1983	$4

BIG STAR
ARDENT
❏ 2909	O My Soul/Morphatoo-- I'm in Love with a Girl	1974	$30
❏ 2912	September Gurls/ (B-side unknown)	1974	$30
❏ 2904	Watch the Sunrise/ Don't Lie to Me	1972	$30

—With correct song on B-side. Label has the number "AS-01180" on it.

❏ 2904	Watch the Sunrise/Don't Lie to Me	1972	$60

—B-side plays the song "Thirteen" in error. Label has the number "AS-01127" on it.

❏ 2902	When My Baby's Beside Me/In the Street	1972	$30

BIG THREE, THE
FM
❏ 9001	Come Away/Rider	1963	$20
❏ 3003	The Banjo Song/Winkin' Blinkin' and Nod	1964	$20

—Second issue, distributed by Vee Jay

❏ 9004	The Banjo Song/ Winkin' Blinkin' Nod	1963	$30

—Original issue (possibly promo only), distributed by Roulette

TOLLIE
❏ 9006	The Banjo Song/Winkin' Blinkin' and Nod	1964	$15

—Third issue

BIG TROUBLE
COLUMBIA
❏ 38-07045	All I Need Is You/Semi-Final	1987	$3

—B-side by Georgio Moroder

EPIC
❏ 34-07432	Crazy World/Lipstick	1987	$3
❏ 34-07432 [PS]	Crazy World/Lipstick	1987	$3
❏ 34-07677	When the Love Is Good/Last Kiss	1988	$3
❏ 34-07677 [PS]	When the Love Is Good/Last Kiss	1988	$3

BIG WHEELIE AND THE HUB CAPS
MCA
❏ 40951	Sh-Boom (Life Could Be a Dream)/Touch and Go	1978	$5

SCEPTER
❏ 12375	Elvis Presley Medley/ Chuck Berry Medley	1973	$12
❏ 12392	Leader of the Pack/Redneck Rock and Rollers	1974	$8
❏ 12385	Little Richard Medley/ Over the Mountain	1973	$10

BIKINIS, THE
DOT
❏ 15872	Chop Stick Rock/ A'Right, A'Ready	1958	$50
❏ 15808	Fatima the Dreamer/ Kitchy Koo	1958	$30

ROULETTE
❏ 4073	Bikini/Boogie Rock 'n' Roll	1958	$30

TOP RANK
❏ 2032	Crazy Vibrations/Spunky	1959	$30

BILK, ACKER, AND BENT FABRIC
ATCO
❏ 6378	Alley Cat/Stranger on the Shore	1965	$6

BILK, ACKER
ATCO
❏ 6230	Above the Stars/Soft Sands	1962	$10
❏ 6247	A Taste of Honey/Only You (& You Alone)	1963	$8
❏ 6190	Buona Sera/Corinne, Corinna	1961	$10
❏ 6311	Dream Ska/Ska Face	1964	$8
❏ 6441	La Playa/When You Are There	1966	$6
❏ 6514	Limehouse Blues/Wot Cher (Knocked 'Em In the Old Kent Road)	1967	$6
❏ 6238	Lonely/Lime Light	1962	$10
❏ 6269	Moonlight Tango/Never Love a Stranger	1963	$8
❏ 6217	Stranger on the Shore/ Cieleto Lindo	1962	$15
❏ 6160	Summer Set/Acker's Away	1960	$10
❏ 6323	The Good Life/Theme from Warsaw Concerto	1964	$8
❏ 6282	The Harem/Train Song	1964	$8

PYE
❏ 71078	Aria/The Fool on the Hill	1976	$4

REPRISE
❏ 20090	Dardenella Part 1/ Dardenella Part 2	1962	$20

BILLARD, DOUG, AND THE SOUL PATROL
PARKWAY
❏ 126	Emily/Genuine Jade	1966	$50

BILLION DOLLAR BABIES
Members of ALICE COOPER's band.
POLYDOR
❏ 14406 [DJ]	Too Young (stereo)/ Too Young (mono)	1977	$15
❏ 14406 [DJ]	Too Young (stereo)/ Too Young (mono)	1977	$15

BILLY AND LILLIE
ABC-PARAMOUNT
❏ 10489	Carry Me Across the Threshold/ Why I Love Billy (Lillie)	1963	$40
❏ 10421	Love Me Sincerely/ Whip It To Me Baby	1963	$40

SWAN
❏ 4069	Ain't Comin' Back (To You)/Bananas	1961	$20
❏ 4036	Bells, Bells, Bells/Honeymoonin'	1959	$20
❏ 4051	Free for All/The Ins and Outs of Love	1960	$20
❏ 4005	Happiness/Creepin' Crawlin' Cryin'	1958	$30
❏ 4002	La Dee Dah/The Monster	1957	$40

—SWAN" in all capital letters; B-side by Billy Ford and the Thunderbirds

❏ 4002	La Dee Dah/The Monster	1958	$30

—Only the S in "Swan" is capitalized; B-side by Billy Ford and the Thunderbirds

❏ 4020	Lucky Ladybug/I Promise You	1958	$30
❏ 4042	Terrific Together/Swampy	1959	$20
❏ 4058	That's the Way the Cookie Crumbles (Ah-So)/Over the Mountain, Across the Sea	1960	$20
❏ 4011	The Greasy Spoon/ Hanging On to You	1958	$30
❏ 4030	Tumbled Down/A.H. Thomas the Cat	1959	$20

BILLY AND THE ESSENTIALS
JAMIE
❏ 1239	Over the Weekend/ Maybe You'll Be There	1962	$40
❏ 1229	The Dance Is Over/Steady Girl	1962	$40

LANDA
❏ 691	The Dance Is Over/Steady Girl	1962	$60

MERCURY
❏ 72210	Last Dance/Yes Sir, That's My Baby	1963	$30

SMASH
❏ 2045	Babalu's Wedding Day/ My Way of Saying	1966	$20
❏ 2071	Don't Cry (Sing Along with the Music)/Baby Go Away	1966	$15

SSS INTERNATIONAL
❏ 706	I Wrote a Song/Oh What a Feeling	1967	$15

Number	Title	Yr	NM

BILLY BOY
COOL

❏ 103	I Ain't Got No Money/ Hello Stranger	1953	$1000

—As "Billy Boy Arnold

VEE JAY

❏ 192	Here's My Picture/ You've Got Me Wrong	1956	$50
❏ 171	I Ain't Got You/Don't Stay Out All Night	1956	$100

—Label lists artist as "Billy Boy Arnold

❏ 146	I Wish You Would/I Was Fooled	1955	$100

VIVID

❏ 109	Prisoner's Plea/I Wish You Would	1964	$30

BILLY HILL
REPRISE

❏ 7-22746	I Can't Help Myself (Sugar Pie, Honey Bunch)/Just in Case You Want to Know	1989	$3
❏ 7-22942	Too Much Month at the End of the Money/Rollin' Dice	1989	$3

BILLY JOE AND THE CHECKMATES
DORE

❏ 791	A Man and a Woman/Floatin'	1967	$10
❏ 857	Ambrosia/Newport Beach Concerto	1971	$6
❏ 884	Aphrodisiac (Part 1)/ Aphrodisiac (Part 2)	1973	$5
❏ 728	Bells of Rome/Shadows	1965	$12
❏ 668	Bossville/One More Cup	1963	$15
❏ 652	Chalypso Dancer/My Friend, the Rain	1962	$15
❏ 747	Clair de Looney/Holding Hands	1966	$10
❏ 720	C'mopn Everybody (Part 1)/C'mon Everybody (Part 2)	1964	$15
❏ 892	Flaky (same on both sides)	1974	$5
❏ 697	Forbidden Planet/Slauson, Baby, Slauson	1964	$15
❏ 685	Last Dance/My Friend the Rain	1963	$15
❏ 620	Percolator (Twist)/Round & Round & Round & Round	1961	$20
❏ 680	Shake, Shake, Shake/ Summertime in Venice	1963	$15
❏ 664	Solid Gold Hubcaps/ Laughing Woodpecker	1963	$15
❏ 703	Spotlight Dance/Zip Code	1964	$15
❏ 643	The Chester Drag/Laughing Machine Gunner	1962	$15
❏ 694	The Drifter/Nashville West (One More Time)	1963	$15
❏ 871	Try It, You'll Like It/ Topless Dancer	1972	$5

BILLY SATELLITE
CAPITOL

❏ B-5409	I Wanna Go Back/Rockin' Down the Highway	1984	$4
❏ B-5409 [PS]	I Wanna Go Back/Rockin' Down the Highway	1984	$4
❏ B-5356	Satisfy Me/Turning Point	1984	$4
❏ B-5356 [PS]	Satisfy Me/Turning Point	1984	$4

BILLY THE KID
CYCLONE

❏ 103	What I Feel Is You/Songpainter	1979	$6

KAPP

❏ 261	Apron Strings/I Hardly Know You	1959	$15

BINGHAM, J.B.
UNITED ARTISTS

❏ XW816	All Alone by the Telephone/ Live and You Learn	1976	$20
❏ XW872	She's Gone/Keep On Walking	1976	$20

WARNER BROS.

❏ 7775	Sunshine/Peek-A-Boo	1974	$10

BINKLEY, CAROLYN
COLUMBIA

❏ 43468	I Want a Baby Brother for Christmas/All I Want for Christmas Is My Two Front Teeth	1965	$10
❏ 43468 [PS]	I Want a Baby Brother for Christmas/All I Want for Christmas Is My Two Front Teeth	1965	$20
❏ 4-43918	I Want a Baby Brother for Christmas/Mister Pilot	1966	$10

Number	Title	Yr	NM

BINKLEY, JIMMY
CHANCE

❏ 1134	Hey, Hey Sugar Ray/ Midnite Wail	1953	$200

CHECKER

❏ 835	Messin' Around/You Made a Boo-Boo	1956	$125
❏ 789	Wine, Wine, Wine/ Boogie On the Hour	1954	$200

NOTE

❏ 10002	Why Oh Why/Blue Moon	1957	$300

BIRD WATCHERS, THE
LAURIE

❏ 3399	Turn Around Girl/You Got It	1967	$15

MALA

❏ 527	Girl I've Got News for You/Eddie's Tune	1966	$40
❏ 548	I'm Gonna Do It to You/I Have No Worried Mind	1966	$40
❏ 536	I'm Gonna Love You Anyway/A Little Bit of Lovin'	1966	$40
❏ 555	Mary Mary (It's to You That I Belong)/Cry a Little Bit	1967	$40

BIRDSONG, EDWIN
PHILADELPHIA INT'L

❏ 3670	Phiss-Phizz/Goldmine	1979	$4

POLYDOR

❏ 14095	It Ain't No Fun Being a Welfare Recipient/Uncle Tom Game	1971	$5
❏ 14118	My Father Preaches That God Is the Father of Us All/The Spirit of Do Do	1972	$5
❏ 14058	The Old Messiah/ Use What You Got	1970	$5

—With Doug McClure

❏ 14224	Turn Around Hate (Communicate)/ Down on the Beat	1974	$5

SALSOUL

❏ 7019	Funtaztik/Win Tonight	1982	$4
❏ 7024	She's Wrapped Too Tight (She's a Button Buster)/(Instrumental)	1982	$4

BIRKIN, JANE, AND SERGE GAINSBOURG
FONTANA

❏ 1684	La Decadanse/Les Langues de Chat	1969	$5

BISCAYNES, THE
NORTHRIDGE

❏ 1001	Church Key/Moment of Truth	1963	$70

—B-side by the Surfaris

REPRISE

❏ 20180	Church Key/Moment of Truth	1963	$40

—B-side by the Surfaris

BISHOP, BOB
GOLDISC

❏ 3027	Santa Claus (Don't Pass Me By)/Ann Marie	1961	$30

—As "Bobby Bishop

MALA

❏ 423	Anybody (But You)/ That's Where I Belong	1960	$30

—As "Bobby Bishop

WAYSIDE

❏ 1004	I Hate to Sing and Run/ My Crying Chair	1967	$8

—As "Bobby Bishop

BISHOP, EDDIE
ABC

❏ 10858	Candy Man/What You're Doing to Me	1966	$30

ABC-PARAMOUNT

❏ 10799	What Did He Say?/Call Me	1966	$70

Number	Title	Yr	NM

BISHOP, ELVIN
CAPRICORN

❏ 0243	Calling All Cows/ Juke Joint Jump	1975	$5
❏ 0222	Can't Go Back/Let It Flow	1975	$5
❏ 0252	Fooled Around and Fell in Love/Have a Good Time	1976	$6

—This is actually the second pressing, bit it's harder to find than the first

❏ 0252	Fooled Around and Fell in Love/Slick Titty Boom	1976	$5
❏ 0296	Fooled Around and Fell in Love/Travelin' Shoes	1978	$4
❏ 0313	It's a Feeling/Right Now Is the Hour	1979	$4
❏ 0248	Silent Night (Vocal Version)/(Instrumental)	1975	$8
❏ 0266	Spend Some Time/ Sugar Dumplin	1976	$5
❏ 0256	Struttin' My Stuff/ Grab All the Love	1976	$5
❏ 0237	Sure Feels Good/ Arkansas Line	1975	$5
❏ 0202	Travelin' Shoes/Fishin'	1974	$5

EPIC

❏ 11022	Last Mile/Stealin' Watermelons	1973	$5

FILLMORE

❏ 7003	Don't Fight It, Feel It/ (B-side unknown)	1971	$6
❏ 7004	I Just Got to Go On/ (B-side unknown)	1971	$6
❏ 7002	So Fine/(B-side unknown)	1971	$6

BISHOP, STEPHEN
ABC

❏ 12435	Animal House/Dream Girl	1978	$4
❏ 12435 [PS]	Animal House/Dream Girl	1978	$8
❏ 12406	Everybody Needs Love/ Only the Heart Within You	1978	$4
❏ 12442	Looking for the Right One/I've Never Known a Nite Like This	1979	$4
❏ 12260	On and On/Little Italy	1977	$4
❏ 12232	Save It for a Rainy Day/Careless	1976	$4

MCA

❏ 52814	The Heart Is So Willing/ (instrumental)	1986	$3

WARNER BROS.

❏ 29924	If Love Takes You Away/ Search for Lisa	1982	$4
❏ 29791	It Might Be You (Theme from "Tootsie")/Metamorphosis Blues	1983	$4

—B-side by Dave Grusin

❏ 49595	Send a Little Love My Way/City Girl	1980	$4
❏ 49658	Send a Little Love My Way/City Girl	1981	$4
❏ 29626	Tootsie/Working Girl March	1983	$4

—B-side by Dave Grusin

BISHOP, TERRI
UNITED ARTISTS

❏ XW1194	One More Kiss/My Memories	1978	$6

BIT 'A SWEET
ABC

❏ 11125	The Second Time/2086	1968	$30

MGM

❏ 13695	Out of Sight, Out of Mind/ It Is On, It Is Off	1967	$30

BITE THE WAX GODHEAD
FLYING A

❏ 19763 [PS]	Lookin' For Santa/(I'll Be Glad When) Christmas Is Over	1988	$5

—B-side by the Hungry Dutchmen

❏ 19763	Lookin' For Santa/(I'll Be Glad When) Christmas Is Over	1988	$5

—B-side by the Hungry Dutchmen; red vinyl

BITS AND PIECES
MANGO

❏ 109	Don't Stop the Music/(Remix)	1981	$4

Number	Title	Yr	NM

BITTERSWEET
THREE BEE
| ❏ 0 (no cat #) | Lonely Street/You Can Cry All Night | 1983 | $5 |

BITTERSWEETS, THE
CAMEO
| ❏ 368 | What a Lonely Way to Start the Summertime/Mark My Words | 1965 | $30 |

ORIGINAL SOUND
| ❏ 70 | Another Chance/In the Night | 1967 | $30 |

BIZARROS, THE
CLONE
| ❏ CL-001 | Lady Doubonette/I Bizarro//Without Reason/Nova | 1976 | $40 |

— *Reissue of Gorilla release*

| ❏ CL-001 [PS] | Lady Doubonette/I Bizarro//Without Reason/Nova | 1976 | $60 |

7-Inch Extended Plays
| ❏ CL-003 | Laser Boys/It Hurts, Janey//A New Order | 1978 | $15 |
| ❏ CL-003 [PS] | Laser Boys/It Hurts, Janey//A New Order | 1978 | $20 |

GORILLA
| ❏ NR-7639 | Lady Doubonette/I Bizarro//Without Reason/Nova | 1976 | $15 |

— *Small hole, plays at 33 1/3 rpm*

| ❏ NR-7639 [PS] | Lady Doubonette/I Bizarro//Without Reason/Nova | 1976 | $20 |

BJORN AND BENNY
PLAYBOY
| ❏ 50018 | Another Town, Another Train/I Am Just a Girl | 1973 | $40 |
| ❏ 50014 | Merry-Go-Round/People Need Love | 1972 | $40 |

BLACK, BILL'S COMBO
COLUMBIA
❏ 44867	But It's Alright/Slow Action	1969	$5
❏ 44983	California Dreamin'/Funky Train	1969	$5
❏ 45092	Heaven Knows/One Five One Eight Chelsea	1970	$5

HI
❏ 2291	Almost Persuaded/Back Up and Push	1975	$4
❏ 2027	Blue Tango/Willie	1960	$20
❏ 2027 [PS]	Blue Tango/Willie	1960	$30
❏ 78508	Cashin' In (A Tribute to Luther Perkins)/L.A. Blues	1978	$4
❏ 2085	Come On Home/He'll Have to Go	1964	$10
❏ 2072	Comin' On/Soft Winds	1964	$15
❏ 2168	Creepin' Around/The Son of Hickory Holler's Tramp	1969	$6
❏ 2208	Daylite/Four A.M.	1972	$5
❏ 2064	Do It -- Rat Now/Little Jasper	1963	$15
❏ 2030	Do Lord/When the Roll Is Called Up Yonder	1961	$50

— *Stereo single, small hole, plays at 33 1/3 rpm*

❏ 2026	Don't Be Cruel/Rollin'	1960	$20
❏ 2026 [PS]	Don't Be Cruel/Rollin'	1960	$30
❏ 2031	Down by the Riverside/It Is No Secret (What God Can Do)	1961	$50

— *Stereo single, small hole, plays at 33 1/3 rpm*

❏ 2301	Fire on the Bayou/Memphis Soul	1976	$4
❏ 2028	Hearts of Stone/Royal Blue	1961	$15
❏ 2106	Hey, Good Lookin'/Mountain of Love	1966	$12
❏ 2311	I Can Help/Jump Back Joe	1976	$4
❏ 2079	Little Queenie/Boo Ray	1964	$15
❏ 2069	Monkey-Shine/Love Gone	1963	$15
❏ 2038	Movin'/Honky Train	1961	$15
❏ 2029	Old Time Religion/He's Got the Whole World in His Hands	1961	$50

— *Stereo single, small hole, plays at 33 1/3 rpm*

❏ 2036	Ole Buttermilk Sky/Yogi	1961	$15
❏ 2036 [PS]	Ole Buttermilk Sky/Yogi	1961	$30
❏ 2049	Slippin' and Slidin'/Twist with Me, Baby	1962	$50

— *Stereo single, small hole, plays at 33 1/3 rpm*

❏ 2234	Smokey Bourbon Street/Mighty Fine	1973	$5
❏ 2018	Smokie (Part 2)/Smokie (Part 1)	1959	$30
❏ 2124	Son of Smokie/Peg Leg	1967	$8
❏ 2277	Soul Serenade/Pickin'	1974	$4
❏ 2055	So What/Blues for the Red Boy	1962	$15
❏ 2094	Spootin'/Crazy Feeling	1965	$10
❏ 2077	Tequila/Raunchy	1964	$15

Number	Title	Yr	NM
❏ 2046	The Hucklebuck/Corrina, Corrina	1962	$50

— *Stereo single, small hole, plays at 33 1/3 rpm*

❏ 2283	Truck Stop/Boilin' Cabbage	1975	$4
❏ 2145	Turn On Your Love Life/Ribbon of Darkness	1968	$6
❏ 2042	Twist-Her/My Girl Josephine	1961	$15
❏ 2045	Twist-Her/Night Train	1962	$50

— *Stereo single, small hole, plays at 33 1/3 rpm*

❏ 2052	Twistin' -- White Silver Sands/My Babe	1962	$15
❏ 2052 [PS]	Twistin' -- White Silver Sands/My Babe	1962	$30
❏ 2032	When the Saints Go Marching In/Nobody Knows the Trouble I've Seen	1961	$50

— *Stereo single, small hole, plays at 33 1/3 rpm*

| ❏ 2021 | White Silver Sands/The Wheel | 1960 | $30 |

MEGA
❏ 0070	Harlem Nocturne/Sassy Parts	1972	$5
❏ 0113	Listen to the Music/Memphis Shuffle	1973	$5
❏ 207	Oh Happy Day/Listen to the Music	1974	$4
❏ 0052	Oh Happy Day/Sugar Cured	1971	$5
❏ 0117	Satin Sheets/Memphis Shuffle	1973	$5
❏ 201	Smokie Part 2/Tequila	1973	$5

7-Inch Extended Plays
HI
❏ SBG-48 [PS]	All Timers	1965	$12
❏ SBG-17 [PS]	Bill Black's Greatest Hits	1963	$15
❏ SBG-71	Everyday I Have the Blues/Prowlin'/The Birds and the Bees//Things I Used to Do/Imperial Tempo/Last Train	1968	$10

— *Jukebox issue; small hole, plays at 33 1/3 rpm*

| ❏ SBG-48 | Hey Good Lookin'/Bouquet of Roses/Anytime//I Walk the Line/Half as Much/Love's Gonna Live | 1965 | $10 |

— *Jukebox issue; small hole, plays at 33 1/3 rpm*

❏ HE22002	Honky Tonk/Cherry Pink//Singing the Blues/You Win Again	1961	$50
❏ SBG-41 [PS]	Mr. Beat	1965	$12
❏ SBG-41	Mr. Beat/It's All in the Game/Black Beat/Talk Back Trembling Lips/Spootin'/Oh Lonesome Me	1965	$10

— *Jukebox issue; small hole, plays at 33 1/3 rpm*

| ❏ HSP2 | My Babe/40 Miles of Bad Road/Ain't That Lovin' You Baby//What'd I Say/The Walk/Witchcraft | 1962 | $20 |

— *33 1/3 rpm jukebox single, small hole*

| ❏ SBG-64 | Simon Says/Bright Lights Big City/Red Light//Big Boss Man/Shoo-Be-Doo-Be-Doo-Da-Day/The Horse | 1968 | $10 |

— *Jukebox issue; small hole, plays at 33 1/3 rpm*

❏ HE22002 [PS]	Solid and Raunchy	1961	$50
❏ SBG-71 [PS]	Soulin' the Blues	1968	$12
❏ SBG-57 [PS]	The Beat Goes On	1967	$12
❏ SBG-57	The Beat Goes On/Ode to Billy Joe/Let the Good Times Roll//Funky Broadway/The Letter/A Whiter Shade of Pale	1967	$10

— *Jukebox issue; small hole, plays at 33 1/3 rpm*

❏ HSP2 [PS]	(title unknown)	1962	$20
❏ SBG-64 [PS]	Turn On Your Love Light	1968	$12
❏ SBG-17	White Silver Sands/Josephine/Hearts of Stone//Blue Tango/Ole Buttermilk Sky/Don't Be Cruel	1963	$15

— *Jukebox issue; small hole, plays at 33 1/3 rpm*

LONDON
| ❏ SBG-22 [PS] | Bill Black's Combo Plays Tunes By Chuck Berry | 1964 | $15 |

— *Cover says label is "Hi," but the record is on London*

| ❏ SBG-50 [PS] | Black Lace | 1965 | $12 |

— *Cover says label is "Hi," but the record is on London*

| ❏ SBG-22 | School Days/Roll Over Beethoven/Little Queenie//Thirty Days/Brown Eyed Handsome Man/Memphis, Tennessee | 1964 | $15 |

— *Jukebox issue; small hole, plays at 33 1/3 rpm*

Number	Title	Yr	NM

BLACK BROTHERS, THE
LITTLE DARLIN'
| ❏ 061 | Some of My Best Friends Are Women/Little Girl Blue | 1969 | $12 |

BLACK, CILLA
BELL
| ❏ 726 | Step Inside Love/I Couldn't Take My Eyes Off You | 1968 | $30 |

CAPITOL
❏ 5782	A Fool Am I/For No One	1966	$15
❏ 5674	Alfie/Night Time Is Here	1966	$15
❏ 5763	Don't Answer Me/The Right One Is Left	1966	$15
❏ 5258	It's for You/He Won't Ask Me	1964	$15
❏ 5414	I've Been Wrong Before/My Love Came Home	1965	$15
❏ 5595	Love's Just a Broken Heart/Yesterday	1966	$15
❏ 5595 [PS]	Love's Just a Broken Heart/Yesterday	1966	$40
❏ 5373	One Little Voice/Is It Love	1965	$15

DJM
❏ 70018 [DJ]	Across the Universe (mono/stereo)	1970	$15
❏ 70014	Conversations/London Bridge	1969	$8
❏ 70016	If I Thought You'd Ever Change Your Mind/Conversations	1970	$8
❏ 70015	If I Thought You'd Ever Change Your Mind/It Feels So Good	1970	$8
❏ 70012	Surround Yourself with Sorrow/It'll Never Happen Again	1969	$8
❏ 70007	What the World Needs Now Is Love/Only Forever Will Do	1969	$8
❏ 70011	Without Him/It'll Never Happen Again	1969	$8

EMI
| ❏ 4003 | He Was a Writer/I'll Never Run Out of You | 1974 | $6 |

PRIVATE STOCK
| ❏ 45,077 | Fantasy/It's Now | 1976 | $5 |
| ❏ 45,040 | I'll Take a Tango/To Know Him Is To Love Him | 1975 | $5 |

BLACK, CLINT
RCA
| ❏ 8781-7-R | A Better Man/Winding Down | 1989 | $10 |

— *Mysteriously, this seems to be quite scarce as a stock 45. Promos (with "A Better Man" on both sides) go for less than half this amount.*

| ❏ 9126-7-R | Walkin' Away/Straight from the Factory | 1989 | $3 |

BLACK, CODY
CAPITOL
| ❏ 2807 | Fool in the Wild/I'm Sorry | 1970 | $200 |
| ❏ 2858 | Stop Trying to Do What You See Your Neighbor Do/Ain't No Love Like Your Love | 1970 | $125 |

BLACK FLAG
ALTERNATIVE TENTACLES
| ❏ VIRUS9 | Six Pack/I've Heard It Before/American Waste | 1981 | $12 |
| ❏ VIRUS9 [PS] | Six Pack/I've Heard It Before/American Waste | 1981 | $12 |

— *Manufactured in U.S. for export to the U.K. (standard U.S. issue is on SST)*

POSH BOY
❏ 13	Louie Louie/Damaged 1	1981	$10
❏ 13 [PS]	Louie Louie/Damaged 1	1981	$10
❏ 005	Six Pack/I've Heard It Before/American Waste	1981	$4
❏ 005 [PS]	Six Pack/I've Heard It Before/American Waste	1981	$4
❏ 012	TV Party/I've Got to Run/My Rules	1981	$4

— *Reissue of Unicorn 95006*

| ❏ 012 [PS] | TV Party/I've Got to Run/My Rules | 1981 | $4 |

SST/UNICORN
| ❏ BOGUS 001 | Thirsty and Miserable/Life of Pain (Live) | 1981 | $40 |

— *Promo-only giveaway item for the Liquorice Pizza chain*

| ❏ 95006 | TV Party//I've Got to Run/My Rules | 1981 | $20 |

Number	Title	Yr	NM

BLACK FLAMES, THE
DEF JAM
38-07651	Are You My Woman?/Bring the Noise	1987	$3

—*B-side by Public Enemy*

| 38-07651 [PS] | Are You My Woman?/Bring the Noise | 1987 | $3 |

BLACK HEAT
ATLANTIC
3033	Check It All Out/M & M's	1974	$5
3258	Drive My Car/Questions and Conclusions	1975	$5
2890	Street of Tears/Chip's Funk	1972	$5

BLACK ICE
AMHERST
| 706 | Girl, That's What I Call Love/Making Love in the Rain | 1975 | $6 |

HDM
505	Blind Over You/(B-side unknown)	1978	$8
7701	Push/Fantasize	1977	$8
503	Shake Down Part 1/Shake Down Part 2	1977	$8

MONTAGE
| A-1204 | I Just Wanna Hold You/All About Love | 1981 | $5 |

BLACK IVORY
BUDDAH
489	Feel It/Daily News	1975	$4
506	Love Won't You Stay/Daily News	1975	$4
610	Mainline/(B-side unknown)	1979	$4
443	Will We Ever Come Together/Warm Inside	1975	$4

TODAY
1501	Don't Turn Around/I Keep Asking You Questions	1971	$5
1511	I'll Find A Way (Loneliest Man in Town)/Surrender	1972	$5
1520	Spinning Around/Find the One Who Loves You	1973	$5
1516	Time Is Love/Got to Be There	1972	$5
1524	We Made It/Just Leave Me Some	1973	$5

BLACK, JAY
ATLANTIC
| 3273 | Dolphins/Running Scared | 1975 | $5 |

MIDSONG INT'L
| 72012 | The Part of Me That Needs You Most/You Stole the Music | 1980 | $4 |

MILLENNIUM
| 618 | Love Is In the Air/Please Stay | 1978 | $5 |

PRIVATE STOCK
| 45,058 | Every Time You Walk in the Room/I'd Build a Bridge | 1975 | $5 |

ROULETTE
| 7198 | One Night Affair/Between Two Worlds | 1976 | $6 |

UNITED ARTISTS
| 50116 | What Will My Mary Say/Return to Me | 1967 | $15 |
| 50116 [PS] | What Will My Mary Say/Return to Me | 1967 | $30 |

BLACK, JEANNE
CAPITOL
4566	Commandments of Love/Jimmy Love	1961	$10
4535	Don't Speak to Me/When You're Alone	1961	$12
4654	Heartbreak U.S.A./His Own Little Island	1961	$12
4368	He'll Have to Stay/Under Your Spell Again	1960	$15
4685	Letter to Anya/Guessin' Again	1962	$12
4396	Lisa/Journey of Love	1960	$12
4492	Oh How I Miss You Tonight/Just a Little Bit Lonely	1960	$10
4456	Sleep Walkin'/You'll Find Out	1960	$12

BLACK 'N BLUE
Includes Tommy Thayer, now in KISS.
GEFFEN
| PRO-S-2358 [DJ] | Swing Time/Rockin' on Heaven's Door | 1985 | $6 |
| PRO-S-2358 [PS] | Swing Time/Rockin' on Heaven's Door | 1985 | $8 |

BLACK OAK ARKANSAS
Includes drummer Tommy Aldridge of PAT TRAVERS and WHITESNAKE fame.
ATCO
7019	Back Door Man/Good Stuff	1975	$4
6893	Full Moon Ride/We Help Each Other	1972	$4
7003	Hey Y'all/Sting Me	1974	$4
6925	Hot and Nasty/Hot Rod	1973	$4
6829	Lord Have Mercy on My Soul/Uncle Lijah	1971	$5
6849	Singing the Blues/Hot and Nasty	1971	$5
7015	Taxman/Dixie	1975	$4

MCA
40586	A Fistful of Love/Storm of Passion	1976	$3
40536	Great Balls of Fire/Highway Pirate	1976	$3
40496	Strong Enough to Be Gentle/Ace in the Hole	1975	$4
40621	When the Band Was Singin' "Shakin' All Over"/Bad Boy's Back in School	1976	$3

BLACK, OSCAR
ATLANTIC
| 956 | Love, Love, Love/Troubled Man Blues | 1952 | $200 |

GROOVE
| 0115 | Baby, Please Don't Go/I'll Live My Life Alone | 1955 | $70 |

—*With Sue Allen*

| 0102 | Be My Baby/Ain't Nobody Home But Me | 1955 | $70 |

—*With Sue Allen*

| 012 | I'll Get By/Hold Me Baby | 1954 | $70 |

—*With Sue Allen*

| 0168 | Into Each Heart (Some Tears Must Fall)/If I Cry Tomorrow | 1956 | $60 |

—*With Sue Allen*

| 0130 | Think of Tomorrow/Set a Wedding Day | 1955 | $70 |

—*With Sue Allen and the Four Students*

SAVOY
| 1600 | I Got a Feeling/I'm a Fool to Care | 1961 | $20 |

BLACK PEARL
ATLANTIC
| 2657 | White Devil/Mr. Soul Satisfaction | 1969 | $8 |

BLACK RANDY AND THE METROSQUAD
DANGERHOUSE
| KY724 | I Slept in an Arcade/Give it Up or Turnit a Loose | 1979 | $30 |
| KY724 [PS] | I Slept in an Arcade/Give it Up or Turnit a Loose | 1979 | $40 |

7-Inch Extended Plays
| IDI722 [PS] | Idi Amin | 1978 | $25 |
| IDI722 | Idi Amin Say It Loud (I'm Black and I'm Proud!)/Parts 3 Thru 14/I Wanna Be a Nark | 1978 | $25 |

—*Black vinyl*

| IDI722 | Idi Amin Say It Loud (I'm Black and I'm Proud!)/Parts 3 Thru 14/I Wanna Be a Nark | 1978 | $50 |

—*Green vinyl*

| MO721 [PS] | Trouble at the Cup | 1977 | $35 |
| MO721 | Trouble at the Cup/Loner with a Boner/Sperm Bank Baby | 1977 | $25 |

BLACK SABBATH
Also see OZZY OSBOURNE; DIO; DEEP PURPLE; TRAPEZE.
WARNER BROS.
7530	Iron Man/Electric Funeral	1971	$8
7802	Iron Man/Electric Funeral	1974	$8
49549	Lady Evil/Children of the Sea	1980	$6
7625	Laguna Sunrise/Tomorrow's Dream	1972	$8
7437	Paranoid/Wizard	1970	$10
7764	Sabbath, Bloody Sabbath/Changes	1973	$8
29434	Stonehenge/Trashed	1983	$6

7-Inch Extended Plays
| S2695 | Looking for Today/Sabbath, Bloody Sabbath//Sabbra Cadabra | 1973 | $25 |

—*Jukebox issue; small hole, plays at 33 1/3 rpm*

| S2695 [PS] | Sabbath, Bloody Sabbath | 1973 | $30 |

—*Part of "Little LP" series (#241)*

BLACK SHEEP
With Lou Gramm, pre-FOREIGNER. (45)
CAPITOL
| 4012 | A Little or a Lot/Broken Promises | 1974 | $5 |

CHRYSALIS
| 2038 | Stick Around/Cruisin' | 1974 | $5 |

BLACK, SHELLY
VIGOR
| 1730 | Free and Red Hot (Part 1)/(Part 2) | 1976 | $5 |

BLACK, TERRY, AND LAUREL WARD
KAMA SUTRA
| 540 | Goin' Down/Oh Babe | 1972 | $6 |

BLACK, TERRY
DUNHILL
| 4005 | How Many Guys/Only Sixteen | 1965 | $10 |
| 4046 | Ordinary Girl/Baby's Gone | 1966 | $10 |

TOLLIE
| 9041 | Say It Again/Everyone Can Tell | 1965 | $15 |
| 9041 [PS] | Say It Again/Everyone Can Tell | 1965 | $30 |

BLACK VELVET
EMBER
| 702 | Peace and Love Is the Message/The Clown | 1970 | $10 |

OKEH
| 7330 | Come On Heart/Just Came Back | 1969 | $20 |

BLACK, ZELL
MOTOWN
| 1290 | I Been Had by the Devil/Confession | 1974 | $5 |
| 1281 | I'd Hate Myself in the Morning/Take My Word | 1973 | $5 |

WARNER BROS.
| 8138 | Fly Me Part 1/You Make the Sun Keep Shining | 1975 | $4 |
| 8202 | Fly Me/Ride On Rider | 1976 | $4 |

BLACKBURN, LOU
IMPERIAL
| 5943 | Grand Prix/Jazz-a-Nova | 1963 | $40 |
| 5998 | Two Note Samba/17 Richmond Park | 1963 | $30 |

BLACKBYRDS, THE
FANTASY
914	Dancin' Dancin'/Lonelies for Your Love	1981	$4
729	Do It, Fluid/Summer Love	1974	$5
747	Flyin' High/All I Ask	1975	$4
762	Happy Music/Love So Fine	1976	$4
910	Love Don't Strike Twice/Don't Know What to Say	1981	$4
794	Party Land/In Life	1977	$4
809	Soft and Easy/Something Special	1977	$4
819 [PS]	Supernatural Feeling	1978	$20

—*Promo-only sleeve issued with 2:59 promos of the song*

819	Supernatural Feeling/Looking Ahead	1978	$4
787	Time Is Movin'/Lady	1977	$4
736	Walking in Rhythm/The Baby	1975	$4
904	What We Have Is Right/What's On Your Mind	1980	$4

Number	Title	Yr	NM

BLACKFOOT

Rick Medlocke, both formerly and later of LYNYRD SKYNYRD, was in this group.

ATCO

Number	Title	Yr	NM
❏ 7331	Fly Away/Good Morning	1981	$4
❏ 7313	Gimme, Gimme, Gimme/ In the Night	1980	$4
❏ 7104	Highway Song/Road Fever	1979	$5
❏ 99690	Morning Dew/Livin' in the City	1984	$3
❏ 7338	Searchin'/Payin' For It	1981	$4
❏ 7303 [DJ]	Spendin' Cabbage (stereo/mono)	1980	$6

— May be promo only

❏ 99851	Teenage Idol/Run for Cover	1983	$3
❏ 7207	Train, Train/Baby Blue	1979	$5

ATLANTIC

❏ 89223	Closest Thing to Heaven/ Back on the Streets	1987	$3

— As "Rick Medlocke and Blackfoot"

BLACKFOOT, J.

EDGE

❏ 7006	Bad Weather/Friendship	1987	$4
❏ 7007	Tear Jerker/Taxi	1987	$4

— A-side featuring Ann Hines

SOUND TOWN

❏ 0011	Don't You Feel It Like I Feel It/ You Can't Take It With You	1985	$6
❏ 0015	Hiding Place/Street Girl	1985	$6
❏ 0006	I Stood on the Sidewalk and Cried/One of Those Parties	1984	$6
❏ 0004	Taxi/Where Is Love	1983	$6

BLACKFOOT, J.D.

FANTASY

❏ 741	Twilight/Done on the Ocean	1975	$8

PHILIPS

❏ 40625	Epitaph for a Head/ Who's Nuts, Alfred	1969	$15
❏ 40679	I've Never Seen You/ One Time Woman	1970	$15

BLACKJACK

With Bruce Kulick (later of KISS) and Michael Bolotin (better known as MICHAEL BOLTON). The group on 20th Century is a different band.

20TH CENTURY

❏ 2279	Inland Sea/Joyride	1976	$8

BLACKSMOKE

CHOCOLATE CITY

❏ 006	There It Is/(B-side unknown)	1976	$5

BLACKWELL, DEWAYNE

RANWOOD

❏ 979	I Got Your Number/Lady	1974	$5
❏ 967	Mama Come 'n Get Your Baby Boy/Lady	1974	$5

BLACKWELL, OTIS

ATLANTIC

❏ 1165	Make Ready for Love/ When You're Around	1957	$50
❏ 1178	Turtle Dove/What a Coincidence	1958	$50

CUB

❏ 9107	Sister Twister/Ga Ga	1962	$30

DATE

❏ 1006	Don't Run Away/Handle with Care	1958	$40

GROOVE

❏ 034	Oh, What a Babe/Here I Am	1954	$50

JAY-DEE

❏ 784	Daddy Rolling Stone/ Tears! Tears! Tears!	1953	$60
❏ 798	Go Away Mr. Blues/I'm Comin' Back Baby	1955	$60
❏ 792	I'm Standing at the Doorway/ Nobody Met the Train	1954	$60
❏ 794	My Josephine/Ain't Got No Time	1954	$60
❏ 808	Oh What a Wonderful Time/ Let the Daddy Hold You	1955	$60
❏ 791	On That Power Line/Don't You Know How I Love You	1954	$60

RCA VICTOR

❏ 47-5225	The Fool That I Be/Number 000	1953	$60
❏ 47-5069	Wake You Fool/Please Help Me Find	1952	$60

Number	Title	Yr	NM

BLACKWELLS, THE

GUYDEN

❏ 2020	Oh My Love/Holey Sombrero	1959	$30

HICKORY

❏ 1261	Ballad of a Young Truck Driver/ She Loves the Love I Give Her	1964	$12
❏ 1241	I Won't Be Perfect/ Playin' Heart Strings	1964	$10
❏ 1319	Little Bird/I've Been Waiting	1965	$12

JAMIE

❏ 1150	Always It's You/Honey, Honey	1960	$20
❏ 1150 [PS]	Always It's You/Honey, Honey	1960	$40
❏ 1179	Love or Money/Big Daddy and the Cat	1961	$15
❏ 1146	The Christmas Holiday/ Little Match Girl	1959	$30
❏ 1173	The Christmas Holiday/ Little Match Girl	1960	$20

LIBERTY

❏ 55750	Show Me Around/The Old Coast Road	1964	$10

BLACKWOOD, R.W.

CAPITOL

❏ 4346	Memory Go Round/Freedom Lives in a Country Song	1976	$6
❏ 4302	Sunday Afternoon Boatride in the Park on the Lake/Lookin' at the World Through the Eyes of Love	1976	$6
❏ 4408	We Mighta' Come Over in Different Ships/I Can Feel Love	1977	$6

SCORPION

❏ 0561	Dolly/Counterfeit Cowboy	1978	$6

BLADES, CAROL

GEE

❏ 1029	When Will I Know/What Did I Do Wrong	1957	$200

BLADES OF GRASS, THE

JUBILEE

❏ 5582	Happy/That's What a Boy Likes	1967	$8
❏ 5605	Help/Justah	1967	$8
❏ 5635	I Love You, Alice B. Toklas/ That's What a Boy Likes	1968	$8
❏ 5662	Love Her and Cherish Her/Pageant	1969	$8
❏ 5622	The Way You'll Never Be/ You Turned Off the Sun	1968	$8

BLADES, RUBEN

ELEKTRA

❏ 69731	Buscando America/ (B-side unknown)	1984	$6
❏ 69407	Hopes on Hold/(B-side unknown)	1988	$5
❏ 69584	Move On (Muevete)/Y Seis Del Solo	1985	$5
❏ 69309	'Tas Caliente/Patria	1989	$5

BLAINE, HAL

ABC DUNHILL

❏ 4181	Beverly Drive/Midnight at Fink's	1969	$15

DUNHILL

❏ 4142	Allegro from "Mac Arthur Park"/Drums A-Go-Go	1968	$20
❏ 4049	Bang Bang Rhythm/ Drums A-Go-Go	1966	$20
❏ 4006	La Bamba/Topsy '65	1965	$20
❏ 4091	Love-In (December)/ Wiggy (November)	1967	$20
❏ 4021	Secret Agent Man/ Midnight at Pink's	1966	$20
❏ 4102	The Invaders/Secret Agent Man	1967	$20
❏ 4074	The Swinger/Drums A-Go-Go	1967	$20

MELODY HOUSE

❏ 100	Slow Gate/South of Shreveport	1962	$50

RCA VICTOR

❏ 47-8282	Challenger II/Gear Stripper	1963	$30
❏ 47-8223	Dance with the Surfin' Band/ The Drummer Plays for Me	1963	$30
❏ 47-8147	Hawaii 1963/East Side Story	1963	$30

ROCK-IT

❏ 1000	Alamo Rock/Alamo Rock (Part 2)	1959	$60

BLAIR, KENNY

AWESOME

❏ 119	Lost in Austin/(B-side unknown)	1988	$6
❏ 118	She's Too Good to Be Treated Like This/(B-side unknown)	1988	$6

Number	Title	Yr	NM

BLAIR, TOM

DECCA

❏ 31344	Dolar Bills/Since You Are Gone	1961	$40
❏ 31223	West Coast/With My Hand on My Heart	1961	$40

BLAKE AND HINES

MOTOWN

❏ 1878	Sherry/Movie Queen	1987	$4
❏ 1878 [PS]	Sherry/Movie Queen	1987	$6

BLAKE, COREY

CAPITOL

❏ 4057	How Can I Go On Without You/ Your Love Is Like a Boomerang	1975	$1000

BLAKE, HARRIETTE

LTD

❏ 409	Gee You Are/Unspoken Words	1966	$15
❏ 403	Two of Us/Turn Around Boy	1966	$15

MONUMENT

❏ 1121	I Laughed Till I Cried/ Tell It Like It Is	1968	$8

MUSICOR

❏ 1052	Love Me, Love Me/Wishin'	1965	$15

PARKWAY

❏ 961	Dansero/Why Did Our Love Go Wrong	1965	$20

BLAKE, TOMMY

BUDDY

❏ 107	I'm a Fool/Kool It	1958	$1000

RCA VICTOR

❏ 47-6925	Freedom/Mr. Hoody	1957	$60

SUN

❏ 278	Flatfoot Sam/Lordy Hoody	1957	$125
❏ 300	Sweetie Pie/I Dig You	1958	$300

BLAKELY, WELLINGTON

VEE JAY

❏ 104	Sailor Joe/Gypsy with a Broken Heart	1953	$400

BLANC, MEL

CAPITOL

❏ F1727	10 Little Bottles in the Sink/OKMNX	1951	$40
❏ F2718	I Dess I Dotta Doe/ The Lady Bird Song	1954	$40
❏ F2635	I'm in the Mood for Love/ My Kinda Love	1953	$30
❏ F1853	I Tan't Wait Till Quithmuth/ Christmas Chopsticks	1951	$40
❏ F1360	I Tawt I Taw a Puddy Tat/ Yosemite Sam	1951	$40
❏ F2048	Lord Bless His Soul/Morris	1952	$40
❏ F2764	Money/Polly Pretty Polly	1954	$30
❏ F2470	Somebody Stole My Gal/I Love Me	1953	$30
❏ F1948	That's All Folks!/Wontcha Ever	1952	$40
❏ F3902	The Hat I Got for Christmas Is Too Beeg/Pancho's Christmas	1959	$30
❏ F2261	The Misses Wouldn't Approve/I Tell My Troubles to Joe	1952	$40
❏ F2430	Tia-Juana/Little Red Monkey	1953	$30
❏ F1330	Woody Woodpecker/Trixie and the Piano Pixie	1950	$40

WARNER BROS.

❏ 5156	Blimey/I Can't Fool My Heart	1960	$30
❏ 5129	Tweety's Twistmas Troubles/I Keep Hearing Those Bells	1959	$30

BLANCH, ARTHUR

MC

❏ 5015	The Little Man's Got the Biggest Smile in Town/Another Pretty Country Song	1978	$5

RIDGETOP

❏ 00479	Maybe I'll Cry Over You/ (B-side unknown)	1979	$6

BLANCHARD, JACK, AND MISTY MORGAN

EPIC

❏ 50205	47 Miles (to the Georgia Line)/Motel Time	1976	$4
❏ 50122	Because We Love/It's Me	1975	$4
❏ 50082	Chorus/House	1975	$4

Number	Title	Yr	NM
❏ 11030	Cockroach Stomp/ Carolina Sundown Red	1973	$4
❏ 50023	Down to the End of the Wine/ You Can't Say I Didn't Try	1974	$4
❏ 50181	I'm High on You/Let's Pretend	1975	$4
❏ 11097	Something on Your Mind/Here Today and Gone Tomorrow	1974	$4

MEGA

Number	Title	Yr	NM
❏ 0101	A Handful of Dimes/It Seems Like There Ain't No Going Home	1973	$4
❏ 0082	Miami Sidewalks/Washin' Harry Down the Sink	1972	$4
❏ 0089	Second Tuesday in December/Don't It Make You Want to Go Home	1972	$4
❏ 0114	Shadows of the Leaves/ Sweet Memories	1973	$4
❏ 0046	Somewhere in Virginia in the Rain/If Eggs Had Legs	1971	$4
❏ 0063	The Legendary Chicken Fairy/ The Night We Heard the Voice	1972	$4
❏ 0031	There Must Be More to Life/Fire Hydrant #79	1971	$4

UNITED ARTISTS

Number	Title	Yr	NM
❏ XW1067	Heartaches/You Come So Easy to Me	1977	$4
❏ XW1004	Tennessee Birdwalk/ Living Together	1977	$4

WAYSIDE

Number	Title	Yr	NM
❏ 1024	Bethlehem Steel/No Sign of Love	1969	$6
❏ 00	Big Black Bird (Spirit of Our Love)/ Autumn Song (On a Yellow Day)	1969	$5

—*Reissue of 1028*

Number	Title	Yr	NM
❏ 1028	Big Black Bird (Spirit of Our Love)/ Autumn Song (On a Yellow Day)	1969	$6
❏ 007	Changin' Times/Poor Jody	1969	$5
❏ 013	Humphrey the Camel/A Place in My Mind	1970	$5
❏ 010	Tennessee Bird Walk/ The Clock of St. James	1970	$5

BLANCHARD, JACK
EPIC

Number	Title	Yr	NM
❏ 50245	Hands/Molasses in the Moonlight	1976	$4

BLANCMANGE
ISLAND

Number	Title	Yr	NM
❏ 99887	Blind Vision/Waves	1983	$5
❏ 99929	Living on the Ceiling/Running Thin	1983	$5
❏ 99929 [PS]	Living on the Ceiling/Running Thin	1983	$5

SIRE

Number	Title	Yr	NM
❏ 29202	Don't Tell Me/Get Out of That	1984	$5
❏ 28792	Lose Your Love/John	1986	$4

BLAND, BILLY
OLD TOWN

Number	Title	Yr	NM
❏ 1151	A Little Touch of Your Love/Little Boy Blue	1963	$20
❏ 1114	Busy Little Boy/All I Want to Do Is Cry	1961	$20
❏ 1022	Chicken Hop/Oh You for Me	1956	$30
❏ 1016	Chicken in the Basket/ The Fat Man	1956	$30
❏ 1128	Darling Won't You Think of Me/How Many Hearts	1962	$20
❏ 1143	Doing the Mule/Farmer in the Dell	1963	$20
❏ 1109	Do the Bug with Me/Uncle Bud	1962	$20
❏ 1093	Everything That Shines Ain't Gold/ Keep Talkin' That Sweet Talk	1960	$20
❏ 1098	I Cross My Heart/Steady Kind	1961	$20
❏ 1035	If I Could Be Your Man/I Had a Dream	1957	$30
❏ 1076	Let the Little Girl Dance/ Sweet Thing	1960	$30
❏ 1088	Make Believe Lover/Harmonys	1960	$20
❏ 1124	Mama Stole the Chicken/I Spent My Life Loving You	1962	$20
❏ 1105	My Heart's On Fire/Can't Stop Her from Dancing	1961	$20

ST. LAWRENCE

Number	Title	Yr	NM
❏ 1005	She's Already Married/My Divorce	1965	$15

TIP TOP

Number	Title	Yr	NM
❏ 708	Chicken in the Basket/ Chicken Hop	1958	$30

BLAND, BOBBY, AND B.B. KING
ABC IMPULSE

Number	Title	Yr	NM
❏ 31009	Everyday I Have the Blues/ The Thrill Is Gone	1976	$4
❏ 31006	Let the Good Times Roll/ Strange Things	1976	$4

BLAND, BOBBY
ABC

Number	Title	Yr	NM
❏ 12405	Come Fly with Me/Ain't God Something	1978	$4

Number	Title	Yr	NM
❏ 12189	It Ain't the Real Thing/ Who's Foolin' Who	1976	$4
❏ 12134	I Take It On Home/You've Never Been This Far Before	1975	$4
❏ 12360	Love to See You Smile/I'm Just Your Man	1978	$4
❏ 12330	Sittin' on a Poor Man's Throne/I Intend to Take Your Place	1978	$4
❏ 12280	The Soul of a Man/If I Weren't a Gambler	1977	$4
❏ 12156	Today I Started Loving You Again/Too Far Gone	1976	$4

ABC DUNHILL

Number	Title	Yr	NM
❏ 15003	Ain't No Love in the Heart of the City/Twenty-Four Hour Blues	1974	$5
❏ 4379	Goin' Down Slow/Up and Down World	1974	$5
❏ 15015	I Wouldn't Treat a Dog (The Way You Treated Me)/I Ain't Gonna Be the First to Cry	1974	$5
❏ 4369	This Time I'm Gone for Good/Where Baby Went	1973	$5

DUKE

Number	Title	Yr	NM
❏ 383	Ain't Doing Too Bad (Part 1)/ Ain't Doing Too Bad (Part 2)	1964	$10
❏ 369	Ain't It a Good Thing/ Queen for a Day	1963	$20
❏ 375	Ain't Nothing You Can Do/Honey Child	1964	$20
❏ 338	Ain't That Loving You/ Jelly, Jelly, Jelly	1961	$30
❏ 115	Army Blues/No Blow, No Show	1953	$200
❏ 426	A Touch of the Blues/Shoes	1967	$8
❏ 412	Back in the Same Old Bag Again/I Ain't Myself Anymore	1966	$8
❏ 386	Blind Man/Black Night	1965	$10
❏ 449	Chains of Love/Ask Me 'Bout Nothing (But the Blues)	1969	$8
❏ 327	Cry Cry Cry/I've Been Wrong So Long	1960	$30
❏ 336	Don't Cry No More/How Does a Cheating Woman Feel	1961	$30
❏ 340	Don't Cry No More/Saint James Infirmary	1961	$30
❏ 167	Don't Want No Woman/I Smell Trouble	1957	$40
❏ 472	Do What You Set Out to Do/ Ain't Nothing You Can Do	1972	$8
❏ 432	Driftin' Blues/You Could Read My Mind	1968	$8
❏ 390	Dust Got in Daddy's Eyes/ Ain't No Telling	1965	$12
❏ 170	Farther Up the Road/ Sometime Tomorrow	1957	$40
❏ 402	Good Time Charlie/Good Time Charlie (Part 2)	1966	$8
❏ 447	Gotta Get to Know You/ Baby I'm On My Way	1969	$8
❏ 433	Honey Child/A Piece of Gold	1968	$8
❏ 153	I Can't Put You Down/ You've Got Bad Intentions	1956	$60
❏ 458	If You've Got a Heart/Sad Feeling	1970	$8
❏ 160	I Learned My Lesson/I Don't Believe	1956	$50
❏ 160	I Learned My Lesson/Lead Us On	1956	$50
❏ 314	I'll Take Care of You/That's Why	1959	$30
❏ 466	I'm Sorry/Yum Yum Tree	1971	$8
❏ 477	I'm So Tired/If You Could Read My Mind	1972	$8
❏ 393	I'm Too Far Gone (To Turn Around)/If You Could Read My Mind	1965	$10
❏ 332	I Pity the Fool/Close to You	1961	$30
❏ 310	Is It Real/Someday	1959	$30
❏ 318	Lead Me On/Hold Me Tenderly	1960	$30
❏ 196	Little Boy Blue/Last Night	1958	$30
❏ 460	Lover with a Reputation/ If Love Ruled the World	1970	$8
❏ 105	Lovin' Blues/I.O.U. Blues	1952	$300
❏ 407	Poverty/Building a Fire with Hair	1966	$8
❏ 435	Save Your Love for Me/ Share Your Love with Me	1968	$8
❏ 471	Shape Up or Ship Out/The Love That We Share (Is True)	1971	$8
❏ 377	Share Your Love with Me/ After It's Too Late	1964	$10
❏ 366	Sometimes You Gotta Cry a Little/You're Worth It All	1963	$20
❏ 355	Stormy Monday Blues/ Your Friends	1962	$30
❏ 182	Teach Me/Bobby's Blues	1957	$30
❏ 421	That Did It/Getting Used to the Blues	1967	$8
❏ 480	That's All There Is/I Don't Want Another Mountain to Climb	1973	$8
❏ 360	That's the Way Love Is/Call On Me	1962	$30
❏ 370	The Feeling Is Gone/I Can't Stop Singing	1963	$20
❏ 385	These Hands (Small But Mighty)/Today	1965	$10
❏ 141	Time Out/It's My Life Baby	1955	$70
❏ 344	Turn On Your Love Light/ You're the One (That I Need)	1961	$30
❏ 347	Who Will the Next Fool Be/Blue Moon	1962	$30
❏ 303	Wishing Well/I'm Not Ashamed	1959	$30

KENT

Number	Title	Yr	NM
❏ 378	Love You Baby/Drifting	1962	$10

—*With Ike Turner*

MALACO

Number	Title	Yr	NM
❏ 2133	Angel/I Hear You Thinkin'	1986	$3
❏ 2126	Can We Make Love Tonight/In the Ghetto	1986	$3
❏ 2122	Members Only/I Just Got to Know	1985	$3

MCA

Number	Title	Yr	NM
❏ 52482	Get Real Clean/It's Too Bad	1984	$3
❏ 52136	Here We Go Again/ You're About to Win	1982	$3
❏ 52270	If It Ain't One Thing/Tell Mr. Bland	1983	$3
❏ 52180	Is This the Blues/You're About to Win	1983	$3
❏ 52436	Looking Back/You Got Me Loving You	1984	$3
❏ 41197	Soon as the Weather Breaks/To Be Friends	1980	$4
❏ 41140	Tit for Tat/Come Fly with Me	1979	$4
❏ 51181	What a Difference A Day Makes/ Givin' Up the Streets for Love	1982	$3

WAND

Number	Title	Yr	NM
❏ 1102	Honey, You've Been On My Mind/You've Got Time	1965	$20

BLANE, MARCIE
SEVILLE

Number	Title	Yr	NM
❏ 133	Bobby Did/After the Laughter	1964	$20
❏ 120	Bobby's Girl/Time to Dream	1962	$30

—*Exists with "Seville" logo straight across the top of the label, and with the "Seville" logo curving around the top of the label. No difference in value has yet been noted.*

Number	Title	Yr	NM
❏ 126	Little Miss Fool/Rag Time Sound	1963	$20
❏ 137	The Hurtin' Kind/She'll Break the String	1965	$20
❏ 123	What Does a Girl Do?/ How Can I Tell Him	1963	$20
❏ 130	Why Can't I Get a Guy/Who's Going to Take My Daddy's Place	1963	$20

BLANTON, LOY
SOUNDWAVES

Number	Title	Yr	NM
❏ 4750	California Sleeping/I Wrote the Book	1985	$5
❏ 4744	Christmas at the Jersey Lily Lounge/Ghost Story	1984	$6
❏ 4760	Sailing Home to Me/Run for Your Life Love Affair	1985	$5

BLAST, C.L.
ATLANTIC

Number	Title	Yr	NM
❏ 2596	If I Could See My Baby's Face Again/I'll Take the Case	1969	$30

CLINTONE

Number	Title	Yr	NM
❏ 011	Husband-in-Law/Fools Love	1973	$30
❏ 09	Leftover Love/Fools Love	1973	$30

COTILLION

Number	Title	Yr	NM
❏ 46002	If I Had Loved You More/I've Got to Make It on My Own	1980	$5
❏ 45016	I Wanna Get Down/Let's Do Something Different Tonight	1980	$5

PARK PLACE

Number	Title	Yr	NM
❏ 104	50/50 Love/Boomerang Love	1984	$5

STAX

Number	Title	Yr	NM
❏ 229	Double Up/I'm Glad to Do It	1967	$30

BLASTERS, THE
MCA

Number	Title	Yr	NM
❏ 52378	Blue Shadows/I Can Dream About You	1984	$4

—*B-side by Dan Hartman*

Number	Title	Yr	NM
❏ 52378 [PS]	Blue Shadows/I Can Dream About You	1984	$4

—*Sleeve emphasizes the Dan Hartman hit*

SLASH

Number	Title	Yr	NM
❏ 29678	Barefoot Rock/Bus Station	1983	$3
❏ 29678 [PS]	Barefoot Rock/Bus Station	1983	$3
❏ 29055	Colored Lights/Help You Dream	1985	$4
❏ 29055 [PS]	Colored Lights/Help You Dream	1985	$4
❏ SRS110	I'm Shakin'/No Other Girl	1981	$8
❏ SRS110 [PS]	I'm Shakin'/No Other Girl	1981	$8
❏ 50047	I'm Shakin'/No Other Girl	1982	$3
❏ 50047 [PS]	I'm Shakin'/No Other Girl	1982	$3
❏ 29975	So Long Baby Goodbye/ Border Radio	1982	$3
❏ 29975 [PS]	So Long Baby Goodbye/ Border Radio	1982	$3

Number	Title	Yr	NM

BLAVAT, JERRY
CAMEO
❏ 393	Discophonic Walk/Back to School One More Time	1965	$15

FAVOR
| ❏ 100 | Discophonic Walk/Back to School One More Time | 1965 | $20 |

ROULETTE
| ❏ 7085 | Tasty (To Me)/Oh Be Joyous | 1970 | $8 |

— With the Geatorettes

BLAZE
EPIC
| ❏ 50292 | Silver Heels/Rock 'N' Roll Madness | 1976 | $5 |

BLAZER BOY
IMPERIAL
| ❏ 5199 | Mornin'Train/Joe's Kid Sister | 1952 | $125 |
| ❏ 5244 | Surprise Blues/Waiting for My Baby | 1953 | $125 |

BLEND, THE
MCA
| ❏ 40961 | I'm Gonna Make You Love Me/I Hope You Find Somethin' | 1978 | $5 |
| ❏ 41139 | She Can Take Me/For Crying Out Loud | 1979 | $5 |

BLENDAIRS, THE
TIN PAN ALLEY
| ❏ 252 | My Love Is Just for You/Repetition | 1958 | $200 |

BLENDELLS, THE
RAMPART
| ❏ 641 | La La La La La/Huggies Bunnies | 1964 | $30 |

REPRISE
| ❏ 0340 | Dance with Me/Get Your Baby | 1965 | $30 |
| ❏ 0291 | La La La La La/Huggies Bunnies | 1964 | $30 |

BLENDERS, THE
AFO
| ❏ 305 | Graveyard/It Takes Time | 1962 | $300 |

ALADDIN
| ❏ 3449 | Two Loves/Soda Shop | 1959 | $1500 |

CLASS
| ❏ 236 | My Heart's Desire/Little Rose | 1958 | $50 |

CORTLAND
| ❏ 103 | Everybody's Got a Right/What Have You Got | 1962 | $15 |
| ❏ 102 | Love Is a Treasure/Fisherman | 1962 | $15 |

DECCA
❏ 27587	All I Gotta Do Is Think of You/The Busiest Corner	1951	$300
❏ 48158	Count Every Star/Would I Still Be the One in Your Heart	1950	$300
❏ 48156	Gone/Honeysuckle Rose	1950	$300
❏ 48183	I'm So Crazy For Love/What About Tonight	1950	$300
❏ 48244	My Heart Will Never Forget/You Do the Dreaming	1951	$300
❏ 27403	The Masquerade Is Over/Little Small Town Girl	1951	$400

JAY DEE
| ❏ 780 | Don't Play Around with You/You'll Never Smile Again | 1953 | $200 |

MGM
| ❏ 11488 | I Don't Miss You Anymore/If That's the Way You Want It Baby | 1953 | $400 |
| ❏ 11531 | Please Take Me Back/Isn't It a Shame | 1953 | $400 |

RCA VICTOR
❏ 47-7009	I'm Following You/Since I Kissed My Baby Goodbye	1957	$60
❏ 47-6591	I've Told Every Little Star/Cecilia	1956	$70
❏ 47-6712	Wake Up to Music/New Sensations in Sound	1956	$60

WANGER
| ❏ 189 | Angel/Old MacDonald | 1959 | $30 |

WITCH
❏ 117	Boys Think/Squat and Squirm	1963	$20
❏ 114	Daughter/Everybody's Got a Right	1963	$20
❏ 123	One Time/(B-side unknown)	1964	$20

BLENDTONES, THE
DON-EL
| ❏ 106 | She's Gone/Lights Please | 1961 | $125 |

IMPERIAL
| ❏ 5758 | She's Gone/Lights Please | 1961 | $30 |

SUCCESS
| ❏ 105 | Come On Home/The Slide | 1963 | $50 |
| ❏ 101 | Lovers/Dear Diary | 1963 | $50 |

BLEU LIGHTS, THE
BAYSOUND
| ❏ 67007 | Bony Moronie/Lonely Man's Prayer | 1968 | $40 |
| ❏ 67003 | Forever/They Don't Know My Heart | 1968 | $50 |

BLEVINS, CHUCK
FOXIE
| ❏ 7006 | Sleigh Bell Rock/Singing for You | 1959 | $30 |

BLEYER, ARCHIE
CADENCE
| ❏ 1279 | 'Cause You're My Lover/Nothing to Do | 1955 | $20 |

— By "Archie and Janet Bleyer

❏ 1241	Hernando's Hideaway/S'il Vous Plait	1954	$20
❏ 1338	Hernando's Hideaway/Steam Heat	1957	$15
❏ 1426	Moonlight Serenade/Sunrise Serenade	1962	$10
❏ 1383	Mustafa/Jimmie's Blues	1960	$10
❏ 1313	Strange One/Jocko's Theme	1957	$15

BLIND FAITH
Also see GINGER BAKER'S AIR FORCE; ERIC CLAPTON; STEVE WINWOOD.
POLYDOR
| ❏ 871798-7 | Presence of the Lord/Can't Find My Way Home | 1989 | $4 |

RSO
| ❏ 873 | Presence of the Lord/Can't Find My Way Home | 1977 | $8 |

— First single release from 1969 self-titled album

BLINKY
MOTOWN
| ❏ 1168 | How You Gonna Keep It/This Time Last Summer | 1970 | $125 |
| ❏ 1134 | I Wouldn't Change the Man He Is/I'll Always Love You | 1968 | $8 |

MOWEST
| ❏ 5019 | For Your Precious Love/So Tired | 1972 | $6 |
| ❏ 5033 | T'Ain't Nobody's Bizness If I Do/What More Can I Do | 1973 | $5 |

SOUL
| ❏ 35089 | How You Gonna Keep It/This Time Last Summer | 1971 | $6 |

BLISTERS, THE
LIBERTY
| ❏ 55577 | Shortnin' Bread/Cookie Rockin' in Her Stockings | 1963 | $15 |

TITANIC
| ❏ 5005 | Fifty Mile Hike/Recitation | 1963 | $30 |

BLIXSETH, TIM, AND KATHY WALKER
COMPLEAT
| ❏ 141 | It Can't Be Done/Sometimes I Wish You Didn't Love Me | 1985 | $5 |

BLOCH, RAY
CORAL
❏ 60767	Adeste Fideles/Cantique de Noel	1952	$15
❏ 60768	Here We Come a-Caroling-The First Nowell-God Rest Ye Merry Gentlemen/Joy to the World-Good King Wenceslas-Angels We Haver Heard on High	1952	$15
❏ 60864	Santa Claus Is Comin'/Let It Snow	1952	$15
❏ 60769	Silent Night/Deck the Halls-Away in the Manger-Hark! The Herald Angels Sing	1952	$15
❏ 60863	The Christmas Song/White Christmas	1952	$15

— With Monica Lewis

BLOCH, SONNY
BEE
| ❏ 1000 | Beetle Squash/Leapin' Lizards | 1964 | $15 |

— As "Sonny Bloch's Elephants

NRC
| ❏ 5009 | Buona Natale (Merry Christmas to You)/Little Louie the Elf | 1959 | $20 |
| ❏ 016 | Buona Natale (Merry Christmas to You)/One, Two, Three | 1958 | $20 |

REGAL
| ❏ 7503 | Ask Me No Questions/Hand of Faith | 1958 | $30 |

BLOCK, DOUG
DOOR KNOB
| ❏ 143 | Have Another Drink/It's Only a Matter of Time | 1980 | $6 |

— As "Douglas

REVOLVER
| ❏ 005 | Have Another Drink/It's Only a Matter of Time | 1984 | $6 |

BLODWYN PIG
JETHRO TULL related.
A&M
| ❏ 1158 | Dear Jill/Summer Day | 1969 | $8 |

BLOND
FONTANA
| ❏ 1673 | Deep Inside My Heart/I Will Bring You Flowers in the Morning | 1969 | $15 |
| ❏ 1673 [PS] | Deep Inside My Heart/I Will Bring You Flowers in the Morning | 1969 | $20 |

BLONDIE
CHRYSALIS
❏ 2410	Atomic/Die Young Stay Pretty	1980	$4
❏ 2410 [PS]	Atomic/Die Young Stay Pretty	1980	$5
❏ 42946	Call Me/Atomic	1985	$3

— Silver label reissue

| ❏ 2414 | Call Me/(Instrumental) | 1980 | $3 |
| ❏ 2414 [PS] | Call Me/(Instrumental) | 1980 | $5 |

— Photo of Richard Gere on sleeve.

| ❏ 2414 [PS] | Call Me/(Instrumental) | 1980 | $5 |

— Photo of Deborah Harry on sleeve.

❏ 2220	Denis/I'm On E	1977	$5
❏ 2379	Dreaming/Living in the Real World	1979	$4
❏ 2271	Hanging on the Telephone/Fade Away and Radiate	1978	$5
❏ 2271 [PS]	Hanging on the Telephone/Fade Away and Radiate	1978	$5
❏ CHE-2266	Hanging on the Telephone/Will Anything Happen	1978	$12

— Large hole; "Made in USA" on label, but exported to England

| ❏ 2295 | Heart of Glass/11:59 | 1979 | $4 |

— Standard issue with 3:22 version

| ❏ 2295 [PS] | Heart of Glass/11:59 | 1979 | $4 |
| ❏ 42944 | Heart of Glass/Hanging on the Telephone | 1985 | $3 |

— Silver label reissue; contains a mysterious 4:33 version of "Heart of Glass"

| ❏ CHE-2275 | Heart of Glass/Rifle Range | 1979 | $12 |

— Small hole; "Made in USA" on label, but exported to England; features the original 3:54 LP version complete with "pain in the ass" lyric intact

❏ 2251	I'm Gonna Love You Too/Just Go Away	1978	$5
❏ 2603	Island of Lost Souls/Dragonfly	1982	$3
❏ 2603 [PS]	Island of Lost Souls/Dragonfly	1982	$3
❏ 42945	One Way or Another/Dreaming	1985	$3

— Silver label reissue

| ❏ 2336 | One Way or Another/Just Go Away | 1979 | $4 |
| ❏ CHE-2242 | Picture This/Fade Away and Radiate | 1978 | $10 |

— Small hole; made for export to England; "Picture This" is listed with a time of "2:63"

❏ 2408	The Hardest Part/Sound Asleep	1980	$4
❏ 2408 [PS]	The Hardest Part/Sound Asleep	1980	$5
❏ 2465	The Tide Is High/Suzy and Jeffrey	1980	$3
❏ 2465 [PS]	The Tide Is High/Suzy and Jeffrey	1980	$3

PRIVATE STOCK
| ❏ 45,141 | In the Flesh/Man Overboard | 1977 | $30 |
| ❏ 45,141 [DJ] | In the Flesh (mono/stereo) | 1977 | $10 |

Number	Title	Yr	NM
BLOOD, SWEAT AND TEARS			
ABC			
❏ 12310	Blue Street/Somebody I Trusted	1977	$4
COLUMBIA			
❏ 45008	And When I Die/Sometimes in Winter	1969	$6
❏ 45427	Go Down Gamblin'/Valentine's Day	1971	$5
❏ 45427 [PS]	Go Down Gamblin'/Valentine's Day	1971	$8
❏ 10151	Got to Get You Into My Life/Naked Man	1975	$5
❏ 45204	Hi-De-Ho/The Battle	1970	$5
❏ 44559	I Can't Quit Her/House in the Country	1968	$8
❏ 45477	Lisa, Listen to Me/Cowboys and Indians	1971	$5
❏ 45235	Lucretia Mac Evil/Lucretia's Reprise	1970	$5
❏ 45965	Save Our Ship/Song for John	1973	$5
❏ 45661	So Long Dixie/Alone	1972	$5
❏ 45661 [PS]	So Long Dixie/Alone	1972	$8
❏ 44871	Spinning Wheel/More and More	1969	$6
❏ JBQ501 [Q]	Spinning Wheel/You've Made Me So Very Happy	1973	$25

— Special Coin Operator Release" in quadraphonic; contains the full-length versions of the songs (edited versions are on other 45s)

Number	Title	Yr	NM
❏ 46059	Tell Me That I'm Wrong/Rock Reprise	1974	$5
7-Inch Extended Plays			
❏ 7-30590	*Redemption/Lisa, Listen to Me/A Look to My Heart (duet)/A Look to My Heart (inst.)/For My Lady/Mama Gets High	1971	$10

— Jukebox issue; small hole, plays at 33 1/3 rpm

Number	Title	Yr	NM
❏ 7-30590 [PS]	Blood, Sweat and Tears 4	1971	$15
BLOODROCK			

GRAND FUNK and TERRY KNIGHT related.

Number	Title	Yr	NM
CAPITOL			
❏ 3399	Castle of Thoughts/D.O.A.	1972	$5
❏ 3009	D.O.A./Children's Heritage	1971	$8
❏ 3320	Erosion/Castle of Thoughts	1972	$5
❏ 2736	Fatback/Gotta Find a Way	1970	$6
❏ PRO-6579/81 [DJ]	Help Is On the Way/Bloodrock Interview (By Sol Smaizys/Dennis Gray WXFM-Chicago)	1972	$15
❏ 3451	Help Is On the Way/Thank You Daniel Ellsburg	1972	$5
BLOODSTONE			
EPIC			
❏ 50437	Got to Find Myself Another Baby/Weeping Willow Tree	1977	$4
LONDON			
❏ 1064	Do You Wanna Do a Thing/Save Me	1976	$5
❏ 1038	Girl/Judy, Judy	1972	$5
❏ 1062	Give Me Your Heart/Something's Missing	1975	$5
❏ 1062 [PS]	Give Me Your Heart/Something's Missing	1975	$10
❏ 1059	I Believe You Now/I Need Time	1974	$5
❏ 1061	My Little Lady/Loving You Is Just a Pastime	1975	$5
❏ 1052	Outside Woman/Dumb Dude	1974	$5
❏ 1055	That's Not How It Goes/Everybody Needs Love	1974	$5
❏ 1042	That's the Way We Make Our Music/This Thing Is Heavy	1972	$5
T-NECK			
❏ ZS4-04592	Bloodstone's Party/Feel the Heat	1984	$4
❏ ZS5-03049	Go On and Cry/(Instrumental)	1982	$4
❏ ZS4-04465	Instant Love/It Feels So Good	1984	$4
❏ ZS4-03394	My Love Grows Stronger (Part 1)/(Part 2)	1982	$4
❏ ZS5-02825	We Go a Long Way Back/Nite Time Fun	1982	$4
BLOOM, BOBBY			
EARTH			
❏ E-106	Heidi/Sign of the V	1970	$8
KAMA SUTRA			
❏ 229	Count on Me/Was I Dreamin'	1967	$12
❏ 210	Heart of Town/Make the Radio a Little Louder	1966	$15

— As "Bobby Mann

Number	Title	Yr	NM
❏ 223	Love, Don't Let Me Down/Where Is the Woman	1967	$10

Number	Title	Yr	NM
KAPP			
❏ 710	I Still Remember/Rough and Tough	1965	$15
L&R			
❏ 157	Montego Bay/Try a Little Harder	1970	$6
MAP CITY			
❏ 306	Emergency/Again 'N' Again	1970	$6
MGM			
❏ 14343	I Really Got It Bad for You/Until They Say Mercy	1972	$5
❏ 14212	Make Me Happy/This Thing I've Gotten Into	1970	$5
❏ 14437	Stay on Top/Sha La Boom Boom	1972	$5
❏ 14614	The Island/Oh, I Wish I Knew	1973	$5
❏ 14292	We Need Each Other/You Touch Me	1971	$5
❏ 14246	We're All Goin' Home/Careful Not to Break the Spell	1971	$5
ROULETTE			
❏ 7095	Oh Yesterday/Where Are We Going	1971	$5
WHITE WHALE			
❏ 285	All I Wanna Do Is Dance/Taggin' Along	1968	$8
BLOOMFIELD, MIKE/JOHN PAUL HAMMOND/DR. JOHN			
COLUMBIA			
❏ 45887	I Yi Yi/Pretty Thing	1973	$6
BLOOMFIELD, MIKE/AL KOOPER/STEVE STILLS			
COLUMBIA			
❏ 44657	Season of the Witch/Albert's Shuffle	1968	$6
BLOOMFIELD, MIKE, AND AL KOOPER			
COLUMBIA			
❏ 44678	The Weight/Mama's Temptation	1968	$6
BLOSSOMS, THE			
BELL			
❏ 857	I Ain't Got to Love Nobody Else/Don't Take Your Love	1970	$8
❏ 937	One Step Away/Break Your Promise	1970	$8
CAPITOL			
❏ F4072	Baby Daddy-O/No Other Love	1958	$30
❏ F3878	Little Louie/Have Faith in Me	1958	$30
❏ F3822	Move On/He Promised Me	1957	$40
CHALLENGE			
❏ 9122	Hard to Get/Write Me a Letter	1961	$30
❏ 9109	Son-In-Law/I'll Wait	1961	$30

— B-side by the Coeds

Number	Title	Yr	NM
❏ 9138	The Search Is Over/Big Talking Jim	1962	$30
EEOC			
❏ 8172	Things Are Changing (same on both sides)	1965	$200
❏ 8172 [PS]	Things Are Changing (same on both sides)	1965	$200

— Promotional item for the Equal Employment Opportunity Commission

Number	Title	Yr	NM
EPIC			
❏ 50434	There's No Greater Love (Than Mine for You My Love)/Walking on Air	1977	$5
LION			
❏ 125	Grandma's Hands/Cherish What Is Dear to You	1972	$6
❏ 108	Touchdown/It's All Up to You	1972	$6
MGM			
❏ 13964	Tweedlee Dee/You Got Me Hummin'	1968	$10
ODE			
❏ 106	Cry Like a Baby/Wonderful	1968	$15
❏ 101	Stoney End/Wonderful	1967	$15
❏ 125	Stoney End/Wonderful	1969	$15
OKEH			
❏ 7162	I'm in Love/What Makes Love	1963	$30
REPRISE			
❏ 0639	Deep Into My Heart/Good, Good Lovin'	1967	$20
❏ 0436	Good, Good Lovin'/That's When the Tears Start	1965	$20
❏ 0522	Let Your Love Shine on Me/Deep Into My Heart	1966	$20

Number	Title	Yr	NM
❏ 0475	Lover Boy/My Love, Come Home	1966	$20
BLOW, KURTIS			
MERCURY			
❏ 880170-7	8 Million Stories/A.J. Scratch	1984	$5
❏ 884547-7	A.J. Is Cool/Respect to the King	1986	$5
❏ 884079-7	America/(Dub)	1985	$5
❏ 870328-7	Back by Popular Demand/(Dub)	1988	$5
❏ 880408-7	Basketball/One-Two-Five	1984	$6
❏ DJ562 [DJ]	Christmas Rappin' Part 1/Christmas Rappin' Part 2	1979	$10
❏ 76194	Daydreamin'/Christmas Rappin' Part 1	1982	$5
❏ 76093	Hard Times/Takin' Care of Business	1981	$5
❏ 884269-7	If I Ruled the World/(Dub)	1985	$5
❏ 888004-7	I'm Chillin'/Don't Cha Feel Like Making Love	1986	$5
❏ 76116	It's Gettin' Hot/All I Want in the World	1981	$6
❏ 870992-7	Only the Strong Survive/Still on the Scene	1988	$4
❏ 812687-7	Party Time/(Instrumental)	1983	$5
❏ 76112	Starlife/Way Out West	1981	$6
❏ 810324-7	The Breaks/Christmas Rappin' Part 2	1983	$5
❏ 76075	The Breaks (Part 1)/(Part 2)	1980	$6
❏ 888282-7	The Bronx/Unity Party Jam	1987	$4
❏ 76083	Throughout Your Years (Part 1)/(Part 2)	1980	$6
❏ 76170	Tough (Vocal)/(Instrumental)	1982	$6
POLYDOR			
❏ 881529-1	Basketball/(B-side unknown)	1985	$30
❏ 881529-7	Basketball/(It's) The Game	1985	$6

— B-side by Ralph MacDonald

Number	Title	Yr	NM
BLOW MONKEYS			
RCA			
❏ PB-14325	Digging Your Scene (U.K. Mix)/(U.S. Mix)	1986	$4

— We have no evidence that a U.S. picture sleeve exists

Number	Title	Yr	NM
❏ PB-14325 [PS]	Digging Your Scene (U.K. Mix)/(U.S. Mix)	1986	$30
❏ 5138-7-R	It Doesn't Have to Be This Way/Ask for More	1987	$3
❏ 5138-7-R [PS]	It Doesn't Have to Be This Way/Ask for More	1987	$3
❏ PB-14423	Wicked Ways/Walking the Blue Beat	1986	$3
❏ PB-14423 [PS]	Wicked Ways/Walking the Blue Beat	1986	$5
BLU, NIKKI			
PARKWAY			
❏ 931	(Whoa Whoa) I Love You So/(Instrumental)	1964	$10
BLU, PEGGI			
CAPITOL			
❏ B-44014	All the Way with You/(Remix)	1987	$3

— With Bert Robinson

Number	Title	Yr	NM
❏ B-44014 [PS]	All the Way with You/(Remix)	1987	$3
BLUE			
ROCKET			
❏ 40801	Bring Back the Love/Falling	1977	$6
❏ 40706 [DJ]	Capture Your Heart (mono) (stereo)	1977	$15

— Promo only on blue vinyl

Number	Title	Yr	NM
❏ 40706	Capture Your Heart/The Shepherd	1977	$6
❏ 40762	I'm Alone/Another Night Time Flight	1977	$6
BLUE ANGEL			

Features CYNDI LAUPER.

Number	Title	Yr	NM
POLYDOR			
❏ 2149	I Had a Love/Take a Chance	1980	$10
BLUE BELLES, THE			
ATLANTIC			
❏ 987	The Story of a Fool/Cancel the Call	1953	$200
BLUE, BOBBY			
NITE			
❏ 108	Once Upon a Time/(B-side unknown)	1986	$6
❏ 108 [PS]	Once Upon a Time/(B-side unknown)	1986	$8

Number	Title	Yr	NM

BLUE BOYS, THE
RCA VICTOR

Number	Title	Yr	NM
❏ 47-8687	Evening Bells/Over and Over Again	1965	$15
❏ 47-8609	I Hear Little Rock Calling/I'll Follow Each Rainbow	1965	$15
❏ 47-9418	I'm Not Ready Yet/My Heart's with You	1968	$10
❏ 47-8777	Love Struck Me Down/Pin a Tail on a Donkey and Call Me Jack	1965	$15
❏ 47-9201	My Cup Runneth Over/One for the Lady	1967	$10
❏ 47-8878	Soakin' Up Suds/Nobody Going Nowhere	1966	$12
❏ 47-9039	What Makes That/Gonna Change Everything	1966	$10
❏ 47-9322	Without Love (There Is Nothing)/She's Wild as the Wind	1967	$10

BLUE CHEER
MERCURY

Number	Title	Yr	NM
❏ 872804-7	Summertime Blues/Just a Little Bit	1989	$5

— Reissue

PHILIPS

Number	Title	Yr	NM
❏ 40682	Ain't That the Way/Fool	1970	$8
❏ 40651	All Night Long/Fortunes	1969	$8
❏ 40691	Babji (Twilight Raga)/Fool	1971	$12
❏ 40691	Babji (Twilight Raga)/Pilot	1971	$8
❏ 40561	Feathers from Your Tree/Sun Cycle	1968	$10
❏ 40561 [PS]	Feathers from Your Tree/Sun Cycle	1968	$50
❏ 40664	Hello L.A., Bye-Bye Birmingham/Natural Man	1970	$8
❏ 40516	Summertime Blues/Out of Focus	1968	$15
❏ 40516 [PS]	Summertime Blues/Out of Focus	1968	$30
❏ 40561	Sun Cycle/Albert's Shuffle	1968	$10
❏ 40602	West Coast Child of Sunshine/When It All Gets Old	1969	$8

BLUE DIAMONDS, THE
SAVOY

Number	Title	Yr	NM
❏ 1134	Honey Baby/No Money	1954	$70

BLUE EYED SOUL
CAMEO

Number	Title	Yr	NM
❏ 423	Something New/Tonight I Am King	1966	$30
❏ 401	The Shadow of Your Love/Look Gently at the Rain	1966	$30

BLUE HAZE
A&M

Number	Title	Yr	NM
❏ 1357	Smoke Gets In Your Eyes/Anna Roseanna	1972	$5

BLUE, JAY
IMPERIAL

Number	Title	Yr	NM
❏ 5587	Get Off My Back/The Coolest	1959	$100

BLUE JAYS, THE (1)
MILESTONE

Number	Title	Yr	NM
❏ 2010	Let's Make Love/Rock, Rock, Rock	1962	$30
❏ 2008	Lover's Island/You're Gonna Cry	1961	$50

— Dark blue label

❏ 2008	Lover's Island/You're Gonna Cry	1961	$40

— Green label

❏ 2008	Lover's Island/You're Gonna Cry	1961	$40

— Light blue and white label

❏ 2009	Tears Are Falling/Tree Tall Men	1961	$40

BLUE JAYS, THE (2)
CHECKER

Number	Title	Yr	NM
❏ 782	White Cliffs of Dover/Hey Poppa	1953	$2000

— VG 1000; VG+ 1500

BLUE JAYS, THE (U)
LAURIE

Number	Title	Yr	NM
❏ 3037	Sweet Georgia Brown/J.J.'s Blues	1959	$30

MAP CITY

Number	Title	Yr	NM
❏ 307	Freedom (Where Have You Gone)/(B-side unknown)	1971	$6

PHILIPS

Number	Title	Yr	NM
❏ 40186	Who (Will I Be Today)?/Come On Baby	1964	$20

ROULETTE

Number	Title	Yr	NM
❏ 4169	Practical Joker/Barbara	1959	$30

WARNER BROS.

Number	Title	Yr	NM
❏ 7299	Edgy/I'm Only Dreaming	1969	$6

BLUE MAGIC
ATCO

Number	Title	Yr	NM
❏ 7031	Chasing Rainbows/You Won't Have to Tell Me Goodbye	1975	$5
❏ 7052	Freak-N-Stein/Stop and Get a Hold of Yourself	1976	$5
❏ 7046	Grateful Part 1/Grateful Part 2	1976	$5
❏ 7090	I Waited/Can't Get You Out of My Mind	1978	$4
❏ 6930	Look Me Up/What's Come Over Me	1973	$6
❏ 7014	Love Has Found Its Way to Me/When Ya Coming Home	1975	$6
❏ 6961	Sideshow/Just Don't Want to Be Lonely	1974	$6
❏ 6910	Spell/Guess Who	1972	$6
❏ 6949	Stop to Start/Where Have You Been	1973	$6
❏ 7061	Teach Me (It's Something About Love)/Spark of Love	1976	$5
❏ 7004	Three Ring Circus/Welcome to the Club	1974	$6

CAPITOL

Number	Title	Yr	NM
❏ 4977	Land of Make Believe/Remember November	1981	$6

COLUMBIA

Number	Title	Yr	NM
❏ 38-68900	It's Like Magic/Couldn't Get to Sleep Last Night	1989	$4
❏ 38-69017	Secret Lover/There's a Song in My Head	1989	$4

LIBERTY

Number	Title	Yr	NM
❏ 56146	Can I Say I Love You/One, Two, Three	1969	$10

MIRAGE

Number	Title	Yr	NM
❏ 99914	Magic #/See Through	1983	$8
❏ 99843	See Through/(B-side unknown)	1983	$4
❏ 99869	Since You Been Gone/If You Move You Lose	1983	$4

WMOT

Number	Title	Yr	NM
❏ 4003	Summer Snow/Spark of Love	1976	$5

BLUE MINK
MCA

Number	Title	Yr	NM
❏ 40230	Get Up/Loneliness	1974	$5
❏ 40031	I Can't Find the Answer/By the Devil I Was Tempted	1973	$5

PHILIPS

Number	Title	Yr	NM
❏ 40672	Can You Feel It Baby/(B-side unknown)	1970	$8
❏ 40697	Gasoline Alley Bred/We Have All Been Saved	1971	$8
❏ 40658	Melting Pot/But Not Forever	1969	$8
❏ 40686	Our World/Respects to Mrs. Jones	1970	$8

BLUE NILE, THE
A&M

Number	Title	Yr	NM
❏ 2747	Stay/Saddle the Horses	1985	$4

BLUE NOTES, THE (1)
3 SONS

Number	Title	Yr	NM
❏ 103	WPLJ/While I'm Away	1962	$40

JOSIE

Number	Title	Yr	NM
❏ 800	If You Love Me/There's Something in Your Eyes, Eloise	1956	$200
❏ 814	Letters/With This Pen	1957	$120

— As "Todd Randall and the Blue Notes"

PORT

Number	Title	Yr	NM
❏ 70021	If You Love Me/There's Something in Your Eyes, Eloise	1958	$70

RED TOP

Number	Title	Yr	NM
❏ 135	My Hero/A Good Woman	1963	$40

UNI

Number	Title	Yr	NM
❏ 55132	Got Chills and Cold Thrills/Never Gonna Leave You	1969	$15

Number	Title	Yr	NM
❏ 55201	This Time Will Be Different/Lucky Me	1970	$15

VAL-UE

Number	Title	Yr	NM
❏ 213	My Hero/A Good Woman	1960	$100
❏ 215	Winter Wonderland/O Holy Night	1960	$100

BLUE NOTES, THE (2)
RAMA

Number	Title	Yr	NM
❏ 25	If You'll Be Mine/Too Hot to Handle	1953	$200

BLUE NOTES, THE (U)
20TH CENTURY

Number	Title	Yr	NM
❏ 1213	Blue Star/Pucker Your Lips	1961	$20

DOT

Number	Title	Yr	NM
❏ 15720	Darling of Mine/I Love Her So	1958	$30
❏ 15692	My Steady Girl/Mighty Lou	1958	$30

— B-side by Henry Wilson

TNT

Number	Title	Yr	NM
❏ 150	Darling of Mine/I Love Her So	1958	$40

BLUE ORCHIDS, THE
LONDON

Number	Title	Yr	NM
❏ 9637	Love Hit Me/Don't Make Me Mad	1964	$10
❏ 9669	Oo-Chang-a-Lang/I've Got That Feeling	1964	$10

BLUE OYSTER CULT
COLUMBIA

Number	Title	Yr	NM
❏ 3-10169	Born to Be Wild/(B-side unknown)	1975	$6
❏ 18-02415 [DJ]	Burnin' for You (Long Version) (Short Version)	1981	$5
❏ 18-02415	Burnin' for You/Vengeance (The Pact)	1981	$4
❏ 18-02415 [PS]	Burnin' for You/Vengeance (The Pact)	1981	$8
❏ 4-45598	Cities on Flame with Rock and Roll/Before the Kiss, A Redcap	1972	$10
❏ 38-05845	Dancin' in the Ruins/Shadow Warrior	1986	$3
❏ 3-10046	Dominance and Submission/Career of Evil	1974	$6
❏ 13-03137	(Don't Fear) The Reaper/Burnin' for You	1982	$4

— Reissue

❏ 3-10384	(Don't Fear) The Reaper/Tattoo Vampire	1976	$5
❏ 3-10725	Godzilla (Live Version)/(Studio Version)	1978	$5
❏ AE71156 [DJ]	Godzilla (Live Version)/(Studio Version)	1978	$6
❏ AE71156 [PS]	Godzilla (Live Version)/(Studio Version)	1978	$8
❏ 3-10697	Godzilla/Nosferatu	1978	$5
❏ 3-10659	Goin' Through the Motions/Searchin' for Celine	1977	$5
❏ 4-45879	Hot Rails to Hell/Seven Screaming Diz Busters	1973	$6
❏ 4-45879 [PS]	Hot Rails to Hell/Seven Screaming Diz Busters	1973	$20
❏ 11055	In Thee/Lonely Teardrops	1979	$4
❏ 38-06199	Perfect Water/Spy in the House of Night	1986	$3
❏ 38-04298	Shooting Shark/Dragon Lady	1984	$3
❏ 38-04298 [PS]	Shooting Shark/Dragon Lady	1984	$6
❏ 38-04435	Take Me Away/Let Go	1984	$3
❏ 11-11401	The Marshall Plan/Divine Wind	1980	$4
❏ 3-10560	This Ain't the Summer of Love/Debbie Denise	1977	$5
❏ 3-10841	We Gotta Get Out of This Place/E.T.I. (Extra Terrestrial Intelligence)	1978	$5

BLUE RONDOS, THE
PARKWAY

Number	Title	Yr	NM
❏ 937	Little Baby/Baby I Go for You	1964	$15

BLUE SKY BOYS, THE
RCA VICTOR

Number	Title	Yr	NM
❏ 48-0072	Alabama/You've Branded Your Name on My Heart	1949	$60

— Originals on green vinyl

❏ 48-0370	Drop Your Net/Sunny Side of Life	1950	$50

— Originals on green vinyl

❏ 48-0036	Dust on the Bible/Speak to Me Little Darling	1949	$60

— Originals on green vinyl

Number	Title	Yr	NM
❏ 48-0111	Little Mother of the Hills/Shake Hands with Your Mother	1949	$60
— Originals on green vinyl			
❏ 48-0163	One Cold Winter's Eve/When Heaven Comes Down	1949	$60
— Originals on green vinyl			
STARDAY			
❏ 667	Satisfied Mind/Why Not Confess	1964	$15

BLUE STARS
MERCURY

Number	Title	Yr	NM
❏ 70877X45	Broadway at Basin Street/The Kissing Dance	1956	$10
❏ 70742	Lullaby of Birdland/That's My Girl	1955	$10
❏ 70808	Mambo Italiano/Speak Low	1956	$10

BLUE STEEL
ASYLUM

❏ 47126	Slip Away/Nothing But Time	1981	$6
INFINITY			
❏ 50044	Shark/Baby You Can't Dance	1979	$5

BLUE SWEDE
CAPITOL

❏ 3627	Hooked on a Feeling/Gotta Have Your Love	1973	$8
EMI			
❏ 4065	Dr. Rock and Roll/Gotta Have Your Love	1975	$4
❏ 3627	Hooked on a Feeling/Gotta Have Your Love	1974	$5
❏ 4029	Hush-I'm Alive/Lonely Summer Afternoon	1975	$4
❏ 3893	Silly Milly/Lonely Sunday Afternoon	1974	$4

BLUE THINGS, THE
RCA VICTOR

❏ 47-8860	Doll House/Man on the Street	1966	$30
❏ 47-8692	I Must Be Doing Something Wrong/La Do Da Da	1965	$30
❏ 47-8998	Orange Rooftop of Your Mind/One Hour Cleaners	1966	$30
❏ 47-9203	Twist and Shout/You Can Live in Our Tree	1967	$30
RUFF			
❏ 1000	Mary Lou/Your Turn to Cry	1965	$50
❏ 1002	Pretty Thing/Just Two Days Ago	1965	$50

BLUE TONES, THE
BLUE JAY

❏ 101	I'll Love You Till the End of Time/(Instrumental)	1965	$200
— Reissued on Swan 4200 by "The Royal Teens			

BLUE VELVET BAND, THE
WARNER BROS.

❏ 7320	Hitch-Hiker/Sittin' on Top of the World	1969	$8

BLUE ZOO
RCA

❏ PB-13609	Cry Baby Cry/Off to Market (Dub)	1983	$4

BLUENOTES, THE
BROOKE

❏ 116	Forever on My Mind/I'm Gonna Find Out	1960	$20
❏ 116 [PS]	Forever on My Mind/I'm Gonna Find Out	1960	$40
❏ 111	I Don't Know What It Is/You Can't Get Away from Love	1959	$20
❏ 119	It Had to be You/Summer Love	1960	$20

BLUES BOY WILLIE
ICHIBAN

❏ 166	Let's Go, Let's Go, Let's Go/One More Mile	1989	$4

BLUES BROTHERS
ATLANTIC

❏ 3884	Expressway to Your Heart/Rubber Biscuit	1982	$6

Number	Title	Yr	NM
❏ 3666 [DJ]	Gimme Some Lovin' (same on both sides)	1980	$10
— Promo only on blue vinyl			
❏ 3666	Gimme Some Lovin'/She Caught the Katy	1980	$4
❏ 3666 [PS]	Gimme Some Lovin'/She Caught the Katy	1980	$5
❏ 3802	Going Back to Miami/From the Bottom	1981	$5
❏ 3574	Hey Bartender/(I Got Everything I Need) Almost	1979	$5
❏ 3545	Soul Man/Excusez Moi Mon Cherie	1978	$4
❏ 3545 [PS]	Soul Man/Excusez Moi Mon Cherie	1978	$5
❏ 89492 [DJ]	Soul Man (same on both sides)	1985	$5
— May be promo only			
❏ 3785	Who's Making Love/Perry Mason Theme	1980	$4

BLUES, ELWOOD, REVUE
ATLANTIC

❏ 89062	Land of a Thousand Dances (Part 1)/Land of a Thousand Dances (Part 2)	1988	$5

BLUES IMAGE
ATCO

❏ 6814	Behind Every Man/It's the Truth	1971	$4
❏ 6777	Gas Lamps and Clay/Running the Water	1970	$4
❏ 6718	Lay Your Sweet Love on Me/Outside Was Night	1969	$4

BLUES MAGOOS
ABC

❏ 11283	Gulf Coast Bound/Sea Breeze Express	1970	$8
❏ 11226	Heartbreak Hotel/I Can Feel It (Feelin' Time)	1969	$8
GANIM			
❏ 1000	Who Do You Love/Let Your Love Ride	1968	$50
MERCURY			
❏ 72838	I Can Hear the Grass Grow/Yellow Rose	1968	$10
❏ 72707	I Wanna Be There/Summer Is the Man	1967	$10
❏ 72729	Life Is Just a Cher O'Bowlies/There She Goes	1967	$12
❏ 72692	One by One/Dante's Inferno	1967	$20
❏ 72692 [PS]	One by One/Dante's Inferno	1967	$40
❏ 72660	Pipe Dream/There's a Chance We Can Make It	1967	$20
❏ 72660 [PS]	Pipe Dream/There's a Chance We Can Make It	1967	$40
❏ 72590	Tobacco Road/Sometimes I Think About You	1966	$60
❏ 72622	(We Ain't Got) Nothin' Yet/Gotta Get Away	1966	$30
❏ 872806-7	(We Ain't Got) Nothin' Yet/Pipedream	1989	$3
— Reissue			
VERVE FOLKWAYS			
❏ 5006	People Had No Faces/So I'm Wrong and You Are Right	1966	$30
— As "The Bloos Magoos			
❏ 5006	People Had No Faces/So I'm Wrong and You Are Right	1966	$20
❏ 5044	People Had No Faces/So I'm Wrong and You Are Right	1967	$20

BLUES PROJECT, THE
CAPITOL

❏ 3374	Crazy Girl/Easy Lady	1972	$8
MCA			
❏ 40154	Fly Away/Louisiana Blues	1973	$5
VERVE FOLKWAYS			
❏ 5004	Back Door Man/Violets of Dawn	1966	$20
❏ 5013	Catch the Wind/I Want to Be Your Driver	1966	$20
❏ 5032	I Can't Keep from Crying Sometimes/The Way My Baby Walks	1966	$20
❏ 5019	Where There's Smoke There's Fire/Goin' Down Louisiana	1966	$20
❏ 5019 [PS]	Where There's Smoke There's Fire/Goin' Down Louisiana	1966	$30
VERVE FORECAST			
❏ 5063	Gentle Dreams/Lost in the Shuffle	1967	$15

BLUESTONE
DIMENSION

❏ 1002	Haven't I Loved You Somewhere Before/A Little Thing Like a Golden Ring	1980	$5

BLUNSTONE, COLIN
EPIC

❏ 11004	Andorra/Carolina Goodbye	1973	$5
❏ 10826	Caroline Goodbye/Misty Roses	1972	$5
❏ 10948	I Don't Believe in Miracles/I've Always Had You	1973	$5
❏ 10981	Pay Me Later/I Want Some More	1973	$5
❏ 10868	Say You Don't Mind/Though You Are Far Away	1972	$5
ROCKET			
❏ PB-11356	I'll Never Forget You/You Are the Way for Me	1978	$4
❏ PB-11412	Photograph/Touch and Go	1978	$4

BOARDO, LIZ
MASTER

❏ 03	I Need to Be Loved Again/(B-side unknown)	1987	$5
❏ 02	There's Still Enough of Us/Hangin' On by a Heartache	1987	$5

BOB AND BOBBIE
HIT

❏ 50	Hey Paula/I Saw Linda Yesterday	1963	$8
— B-side by Dave Gibson			

BOB AND EARL
CHENE

❏ 103	The Sissy/(B-side unknown)	1964	$10
CLASS			
❏ 232	Chains of Love/Sweet Pea	1958	$40
❏ 231	Gee Whiz/When She Walks	1958	$40
❏ 213	That's My Desire/You Made a Boo-Boo	1957	$50
❏ 247	That's My Desire/You Made a Boo-Boo	1959	$30
LOMA			
❏ 2004	Everybody Jerk/Just One Look in Your Eyes	1964	$12
MARC			
❏ 104	Harlem Shuffle/I'll Come Running	1963	$30
❏ 105	Puppet on a String/My Woman	1964	$30
MIRWOOD			
❏ 5517	Baby It's Over/Dancin' Everywhere	1966	$8
❏ 5526	I'll Keep Running Back/Baby, Your Time Is My Time	1966	$8
TEMPE			
❏ 102	Don't Ever Leave Me/Oh Baby Doll	1962	$20
UNI			
❏ 55248	Get Ready for the New Day/Honey, Sugar, My Sweet Thing	1970	$6
WHITE WHALE			
❏ 310	Harlem Shuffle/I'll Come Running	1969	$15

BOB AND JERRY
COLUMBIA

❏ 42162	We're the Guys (Who Drove Your Baby Wild)/Dreamy Eyes	1961	$15
MUSICOR			
❏ 1018	Chubby Isn't Chubby Anymore/Nursery Rhym Floks	1962	$15
RENDEZVOUS			
❏ 100	Ghost Satellite/Who's Gonna Cry for Me	1958	$20

BOB AND LUCILLE
DITTO

❏ 126	Eeny-Meeny-Miney-Moe/The Big Kiss	1962	$100
❏ 121	What's the Password/Demon Lover	1962	$80
DOT			
❏ 17327	Dream Baby/Southbound Plane	1969	$8
— As "Bob Regan and Lucille Starr			
KING			
❏ 5631	Eeny-Meeny-Miney-Moe/The Big Kiss	1962	$40

Number	Title	Yr	NM

BOB AND SHERI
SAFARI

❏ 101 [DJ]	The Surfer Moon/Humpty Dumpty	1962	$1000

— *White label*

❏ 101	The Surfer Moon/Humpty Dumpty	1962	$4000

— *Light blue label (other colors and colored vinyl are reproductions or counterfeits). VG 2000; VG+ 3000*

BOB B. SOXX AND THE BLUE JEANS
PHILLES

❏ 110	Why Do Lovers Break Each Other's Heart?/Dr. Kaplan's Office	1963	$30

PHILLES/COLLECTABLES

❏ 3209	Why Do Lovers Break Each Other's Heart/Zip-a-Dee Doo-Dah	1985	$6

— *Gold vinyl*

❏ 3209	Why Do Lovers Break Each Other's Heart/Zip-a-Dee Doo-Dah	1985	$5

— *Black vinyl*

BOBBETTES, THE
ATLANTIC

❏ 2027	Don't Say Goodnight/You Are My Sweetheart	1959	$30
❏ 2069	I Shot Mr. Lee/Untrue Love	1960	$40
❏ 1144	Mr. Lee/Look at the Stars	1957	$30
❏ 1159	Speedy/Come-a Come-a	1957	$30
❏ 1194	The Dream/Um Bow Bow	1958	$30

DIAMOND

❏ 142	Close Your Eyes/Somebody Bad Stole De Wedding Bell	1963	$15
❏ 166	I'm Climbing a Mountain/In Paradise	1964	$15
❏ 189	Love Is Blind/Teddy	1965	$15
❏ 156	My Mamma Said/Sandman	1964	$15

END

❏ 1095	I Don't Like It Like That (Part 1)/I Don't Like It Like That (Part 2)	1961	$30
❏ 1093	Mr. Johnny Q/Teach Me Tonight	1961	$30

GALLANT

❏ 1006	Oh, My Papa/I Cried	1960	$30

GONE

❏ 5112	I Don't Like It Like That (Part 1)/Mr. Johnny Q	1961	$20

JUBILEE

❏ 5427	Over There/Loneliness	1962	$15
❏ 5442	The Broken Heart/Mama, Papa	1962	$15

KING

❏ 5551	Are You Satisfied/Looking for a Lover	1961	$20
❏ 5623	I'm Stepping Out Tonight/My Dearest	1962	$20
❏ 5490	Oh My Papa/Dance With Me Georgie	1961	$20

RCA VICTOR

❏ 47-8983	It's All Over/Happy-Go-Lucky Me	1966	$20
❏ 47-8832	I've Gotta Face the World/Having Fun	1966	$20

TRIPLE-X

❏ 106	Have Mercy Baby/Dance with Me Georgie	1960	$30
❏ 104	I Shot Mr. Lee/Billy	1960	$30

BOBBY AND BUDDY
HIT

❏ 238	Michelle/My Love	1966	$10

— *B-side by Betty York*

❏ 180	Willow Weep for Me/Bless You Little Girl	1965	$8
❏ 246	Woman/Homeward Bound	1966	$8

— *B-side by Sammy and Theodore*

BOBBY AND CONNIE
HIT

❏ 286	Something Stupid/Dedicated to the One I Love	1967	$8

— *B-side by the Chords (2)*

❏ 281	The Beat Goes On/Sock It To Me Baby	1967	$8

— *B-side by the Jalopy Five*

BOBBY AND HIS ORBITS
SEECO

❏ 6005	Felicia/Bandstand Dancing	1959	$100
❏ 6030	Teen Age Love/What Do I Say (When I'm Close to You)	1960	$60

BOBBY AND THE DUKES
PHILIPS

❏ 40293	Ah, Ah, Ah/Come On Along with Me	1965	$30

BOBBY AND THE MIDNITES
ARISTA

❏ 0640	Too Many Lovers/Haze	1981	$5

COLUMBIA

❏ 38-04587	(I Want to Live in) America/City Girls	1984	$5

BOBCAT
ARISTA

❏ 9886	I'm Cool/I'm Serious	1989	$4
❏ 9814	I Need You/Bobcat Has Proven	1989	$4

BOBO, WILLIE
CAPITOL

❏ 4253	Funky Sneakers/Funky Sneakers (Part 2)	1976	$4

COLUMBIA

❏ 10862	Fairytales for Two/Always There	1978	$4

VERVE

❏ 10400	1-2-3 (Uno, Dos, Tres)/Fried Neckbones and Home Fries	1966	$8
❏ 10518	Ain't Too Proud to Beg/Knock on Wood	1967	$6
❏ 10474	Blues in the Closet/Spanish Grease	1967	$8
❏ CS?-5	Celebrity Scene: Willie Bobo	1967	$60

— *Box set of five singles (10472-10476). Price includes box, all 5 singles, jukebox title strips, bio. Records are sometimes found by themselves, so they are also listed separately.*

❏ 10550	Evil Ways/Up, Up and Away	1967	$6
❏ 10476	Fried Neckbones and Home Fries/Feelin' So Good	1967	$8
❏ 10473	Hurt So Bad/Boogaloo in Room 802	1967	$8
❏ 10374	Hurt So Bad/It's Not Unusual	1966	$8
❏ 10593	Move It On Over/Tweedle Dee	1968	$6
❏ 10482	Shing-a-Ling Baby/Juicy	1967	$6
❏ 10475	Sockit To Me/1-2-3 (Uno, Dos, Tres)	1967	$8
❏ 10448	Sockit To Me/Sunshine Superman	1967	$8
❏ 10472	Sunshine Superman/Call Me	1967	$8

BOCKY AND THE VISIONS
PHILIPS

❏ 40242	I'm Pickin' Petals/I'm Not Worth It	1964	$30
❏ 40224	Mojo Hanna/Spirit of '64	1964	$30

BODEANS
SLASH

❏ 28102	Dreams/Ooh	1988	$3
❏ 28102 [PS]	Dreams/Ooh	1988	$3
❏ 28682	Fadeaway/Try and Try	1986	$4
❏ 28179	Only Love/Stella	1987	$3
❏ 28179 [PS]	Only Love/Stella	1987	$3
❏ 28549	She's a Runaway/Still the Night	1986	$4

BOENZEE CRYQUE
CHICORY

❏ 406	Sky Gone Gray/Still in Love with You Baby	1966	$40

UNI

❏ 55012	Sky Gone Gray/Still in Love with You Baby	1967	$30
❏ 55022	Watch the Time/You Won't Believe It's True	1967	$30

BOETCHER, CURT
ELEKTRA

❏ 45834	I Love You More Each Day/Such a Lady	1973	$5

BOFFALONGO
UNITED ARTISTS

❏ 50699	Dancing in the Moonlight/Endless Question	1970	$8

❏ 50656	Please Stay/Mr. Go Away	1970	$8
❏ 50607	Tomorrow Not Today/Mr. Go Away	1969	$8

BOFILL, ANGELA
ARISTA

❏ 0688	Break It to Me Gently/(B-side unknown)	1982	$5

— *May be promo only*

❏ 9270	Can't Slow Down/No Love in Sight	1984	$3
❏ 0662	Holdin' Out for Love/Only Love	1982	$3
❏ 9452	I Don't Wanna Come Down from Love/(B-side unknown)	1985	$4
❏ 9109	I'm On Your Side/Gotta Make It Up to You	1983	$3
❏ 9312	Let Me Be the One/Love Me for Today	1984	$3
❏ 0666	Only Love/Estory Esperando Por El Amor	1982	$6
❏ 0636	Something About You/Time to Say Goodbye	1981	$3
❏ 9156	Special Delivery/Gotta Make It Up to You	1984	$3
❏ 9414	Tell Me Tomorrow/(If You Wanna Love Me) You're On	1985	$3
❏ 1060	Tonight I Give In/Song for a Rainy Day	1983	$6
❏ 9015	Tonight I Give In/Song for a Rainy Day	1983	$3
❏ 1031	Too Tough/Rainbow Inside My Heart	1983	$3
❏ 9339	Who Knows You Better/No Love in Sight	1985	$3

ARISTA/GRP

❏ 2504	Angel of the Night/Rainbow Child	1980	$4
❏ 2500	This Time I'll Be Sweeter/Baby I Need Your Love	1979	$4
❏ 2503	What I Wouldn't Do (For the Love of You)/Rainbow Child	1979	$4

CAPITOL

❏ B-44169	I Just Wanna Stop/Everlasting Love	1988	$3
❏ B-44169 [PS]	I Just Wanna Stop/Everlasting Love	1988	$3
❏ B-44298	Love Is In Your Eyes/I Just Wanna Stop	1989	$3

BOGGS, NOEL
COLUMBIA

❏ 4-21274	How Long/Make Believe Heart	1954	$30
❏ 4-21220	Stealin' Home/Day Sleeper	1954	$30

BOGGUSS, SUZY
CAPITOL

❏ B-44399	Cross My Broken Heart/Hopeless Romantic	1989	$4
❏ B-5669	I Don't Want to Set the World on Fire/Hopeless Romantic	1987	$4
❏ B-44167	I Want to Be a Cowboy's Sweetheart/I Still Love You	1988	$4
❏ B-44045	Love Will Never Slip Away/True North	1987	$4
❏ B-44503	Mr. Santa/I'm at Home on the Range	1989	$5
❏ 7PRO-79788	My Sweet Love Ain't Around (same on both sides)	1989	$6

— *Vinyl is promo only*

❏ B-44270	Somewhere Between/I'm at Home on the Range	1989	$4

BOHANNON
COMPLEAT

❏ 107	Don't Leave Me/Funkville	1983	$4
❏ 103	Make Your Body Move/Come Back My Love	1983	$4
❏ 148	South Africa/South Africa (Special Mix)	1984	$4
❏ 114	Wake Up/Enjoy Your Day	1983	$4

DAKAR

❏ 4551	Bohannon's Beat (Pt. 1)/East Coast Groove	1975	$5
❏ 4554	Dance Your Ass Off/Happy Feeling	1976	$5
❏ 4549	Disco Stomp (Part 1)/Disco Stomp (Part 2)	1975	$5
❏ 4528	Fat Man/Red Bone	1974	$6
❏ 4544	Foot Stompin' Music/Dance with Your Partner	1975	$5
❏ 4560	Gittin' Off/Come Winter	1976	$5
❏ 4534	Happiness/Truck Stop	1976	$6
❏ 4518	Save Their Souls/Stop and Go	1973	$6
❏ 4539	South African Music (Pt. 1)/Have a Good Day	1974	$5
❏ 4521	The Pimpwalk/Happiness	1973	$6

MCA

❏ 53685	House Train/(Instrumental)	1989	$3
❏ 53766	The Gang's All Here/Over the Rainbow	1989	$3

Number	Title	Yr	NM
MERCURY			
❏ 76054	Baby I'm for Real/ Hurry Mr. Sunshine	1980	$4
❏ 73939	Bohannon Disco Symphony/Moving Fast	1977	$4
❏ 74044	Cut Loose/Listen to the Children Play	1979	$4
❏ 76040	Feel Like Dancin'/Funk Walk	1980	$4
❏ 74015	Let's Start the Dance/I Wonder Why	1978	$4
❏ 74035	Me and the Gang/ Summertime Groove	1978	$4
❏ 74085	The Groove Machine/ Love Floats	1979	$4
PHASE II			
❏ 5651	Dance, Dance, Dance All Night/April My Love (Part 1)	1980	$4
❏ 5654	Don't Be Ashame to Call My Name/(B-side unknown)	1981	$4
❏ WS8-02145	Foot Stompin' in the Summertime/(Instrumental)	1981	$4
❏ WS8-02062	Goin' for Another One/ The Happy Dance	1981	$4
❏ ZS5-02897	I've Got the Dance Fever (With Rap Intro)/(Without Intro)	1982	$4
❏ WS9-02573	Let's Start II Dance Again/ Let's Start the Dance	1981	$4
❏ ZS5-02682	Take the Country to New York City (Part 1 and 2)	1982	$4
❏ ZS5-02998	The Party Train (Parts I & II)/Thoughts and Wishes	1982	$4
❏ 5650	Throw Down the Groove (Part I)/Throw Down the Groove (Part II)	1980	$4
BOHEMIAN VENDETTA			
UNITED ARTISTS			
❏ 50174	Talk the Time/Enough	1967	$30
BOILING POINT			
BULLET			
❏ 05	Let's Get Funktafied -- Part I/ Let's Get Funktafied -- Part II	1978	$8
BOLD			
CAMEO			
❏ 430	Gotta Get Some/Robin Hood	1966	$30
DYNOVOICE			
❏ 232	The Train Kept a-Rollin'/Found What I Was Lookin' For	1967	$40
—As "Steve Walker and the Bold"			
BOLGER, RAY			
ARMOUR			
❏ 7799 [PS]	L'il Elfy/Frosty The Snowman	1963	$30
❏ 7799	Li'l Elfy/Frosty The Snowman	1963	$12
BOLIN, TOMMY			
Also see THE JAMES GANG; ZEPHYR; DEEP PURPLE.			
NEMPEROR			
❏ 005	Savannah Woman/ Marching Power	1976	$8
❏ 004	The Grind/Homeward Strut	1976	$8
BOLL WEEVILS, THE			
HIT			
❏ 107	Please Please Me/My Bonnie	1964	$15
BOLT, AL			
CIN KAY			
❏ 103	Family Man/If Today Were a Fish	1976	$5
❏ 102	I'm in Love with My Pet Rock/ Paint Your World Happy	1976	$5
❏ 109	Wait a Minute/Cowboy	1976	$5
BOLTON, MICHAEL			
COLUMBIA			
❏ 38-04823	Everybody's Crazy/She Did the Same Thing	1985	$3
❏ 38-03800	Fools Game/Fighting for My Life	1983	$4
❏ 38-73017	How Am I Supposed to Live Without You/Forever Eyes	1989	$3
❏ 38-04154	I Almost Believed You/ She Did the Same Thing	1983	$4
❏ 38-07680	(Sittin' On) The Dock of the Bay/Call My Name	1988	$3
❏ 38-07680 [PS]	(Sittin' On) The Dock of the Bay/Call My Name	1988	$3
❏ 38-07680 [PS]	(Sittin' On) The Dock of the Bay/Call My Name	1988	$15
—Promo-only sleeve with a message from Mrs. Otis Redding on the back			

Number	Title	Yr	NM
❏ 38-68909	Soul Provider/The Hunger	1989	$3
❏ 38-7322	That's What Love Is All About/Take a Look at My Face	1987	$3
—U.S. editions are missing the usual "0" after the "38			
❏ 38-07794	Wait on Love/I Almost Believed You	1988	$3
❏ 38-07794 [PS]	Wait on Love/I Almost Believed You	1988	$3
❏ 38-07983	Walk Away/The Hunger	1988	$3
BOMBERS			
WEST END			
❏ 1215	(Everybody) Get Dancin'/ Don't Stop the Music	1979	$12
—All-maroon print on silver label; time listed as 3:19; publisher listed as "Highway One Music-BMI"; number in trail-off wax is "WES-1215A-RE			
❏ 1215	(Everybody) Get Dancin'/ Don't Stop the Music	1979	$12
—Mostly black print (except for the West End logo) on silver label; time listed as 3:22; publisher listed as "Mandingo Music-BMI"; "WES-1215-A-70352" in A-side trail-off wax			
❏ 1212	The Mexican/Dance, Dance, Dance	1978	$10
BON-AIRES, THE			
❏ 5077	My Love My Love/Bye Bye	1964	$30
❏ 5097	The Shrine of St. Ceceia/ Jeanie Baby	1965	$30
BON-AIRS, THE			
KING			
❏ 4975	Stop the World/Bermuda	1956	$40
BON BONS, THE			
CORAL			
❏ 62435	Everybody Wants My Boyfriend/Each Time	1964	$60
❏ 62402	What's Wrong with Ringo/ Come On Baby	1964	$70
BON JOVI			
MERCURY			
❏ 870657-7	Bad Medicine/99 in the Shade	1988	$3
❏ 870657-7 [PS]	Bad Medicine/99 in the Shade	1988	$3
❏ 872156-7	Born to Be My Baby/ Love for Sale	1988	$3
❏ 872156-7 [PS]	Born to Be My Baby/ Love for Sale	1988	$3
❏ 872564-7	I'll Be There for You/ Homebound Train	1989	$3
❏ 872564-7 [PS]	I'll Be There for You/ Homebound Train	1989	$3
❏ 880951-7	In and Out of Love/Breakout	1985	$6
❏ 874452-7	Lay Your Hands on Me/ Runaway (Live)	1989	$3
❏ 874452-7 [PS]	Lay Your Hands on Me/ Runaway (Live)	1989	$3
❏ 876070-7	Living in Sin/Love Is War	1989	$3
❏ 876070-7 [PS]	Living in Sin/Love Is War	1989	$3
❏ 888184-7	Livin' on a Prayer/ Wild in the Streets	1986	$3
❏ 888184-7 [PS]	Livin' on a Prayer/ Wild in the Streets	1986	$3
❏ 880736-7	Only Lonely/Always Run to You	1985	$6
❏ 880736-7 [PS]	Only Lonely/Always Run to You	1985	$6
❏ 818958-7	She Don't Know Me/ Burning for Love	1984	$10
❏ 818958-7 [PS]	She Don't Know Me/ Burning for Love	1984	$8
❏ 884299-7	Silent Night/Price of Love	1986	$10
❏ 888467-7	Wanted Dead or Alive/I'd Die for You	1987	$3
❏ 888467-7 [PS]	Wanted Dead or Alive/I'd Die for You	1987	$3
BONADUCE, DANNY			
LION			
❏ 145	Blueberry You/Dreamland	1973	$10
❏ 145 [PS]	Blueberry You/Dreamland	1973	$30
BONAIRS, THE			
DOOTONE			
❏ 325	It's Christmas/I'm Alone Tonight	1953	$200
—B-side by Ernie Tavares Trio			

Number	Title	Yr	NM
BONAPARTE, GONZALES			
MADISON			
❏ 142	Why Is There Christmas/ Christmas Medley	1960	$20
BOND, ANGELO			
ABC			
❏ 12153	He Gained the World (But Lost His Soul)/I Love You for What You Are	1976	$5
❏ 12135	I Love You for What You Are/Eve	1975	$5
BOND, BOBBY			
HICKORY			
❏ 1594	Call of the Blues/Nothing New in Oklahoma	1971	$8
❏ 1566	Houston Blues/Looking for My Tracks	1970	$8
❏ 1630	One More Mile, One More Town/Six White Horses	1972	$8
❏ 1610	Put Me on the Road to the Country/If You're Goin' Girl	1971	$8
MGM			
❏ 13951	Anyway/Mr. and Mrs. Brown	1968	$15
WARNER BROS.			
❏ 7292	If You're Leaving Me/One More Mile, One More Town	1969	$10
BOND, EDDIE			
CORAL			
❏ 62200	Little Black Book/Is My Ring On Your Finger	1960	$20
BOND, GRAHAM			
ASCOT			
❏ 2211	St. James Infirmary/ Wade in the Water	1966	$10
PULSAR			
❏ 2409	Crossroads of Time/Moving Towards the Light	1969	$8
❏ 2405	Love Is the Law/The Naz	1969	$8
❏ 2415	Stiffened Chicken/Water, Water	1969	$8
BOND, JOHNNY, AND LEFTY FRIZZELL			
COLUMBIA			
❏ 40934	Sick, Sober and Sorry/ Lover By Appointment	1957	$20
BOND, JOHNNY, AND RED SOVINE			
STARDAY			
❏ 790	The Gearjammer and the Hobo/Sweet Nellie	1966	$10
BOND, JOHNNY			
20TH FOX			
❏ 156	Gold Rush/The Long Tall Shadow	1959	$15
COLUMBIA			
❏ 21222	10 Little Bottles/They Got Me	1954	$20
❏ 40973	All I Can Do Is Cry/Sale of Broken Hearts	1957	$20
❏ 21082	Anybody's Baby/ Hills of Kentucky	1953	$20
❏ 2-400(?)	A Petal from a Faded Rose/ Put Me to Bed #2	1950	$30
—Microgroove 7-inch, 33 1/3 rpm single			
❏ 21041	Back Street Affair/Our Love Isn't Legal	1952	$20
❏ 20734	Barrel House Bessie/It Ain't Gonna Happen to Me	1950	$30
❏ 21042	Born to Be Bad/#9 Blues	1952	$20
❏ 20876	Broke, Disgusted and Sad/ In Old New Mexico	1952	$20
❏ 21369	Cherokee Waltz/Glad Rags	1955	$20
❏ 2-600(?)	Cherokee Waltz/Mean Mama Boogie	1950	$30
—Microgroove 7-inch, 33 1/3 rpm single			
❏ 2-319	Drowning My Sorrows/Women Make a Fool Out of Me	1950	$30
—Microgroove 7-inch, 33 1/3 rpm single			
❏ 21243	Firewater/Old Man Blues	1954	$20
❏ 40842	Honky Tonk Fever/ Lay It on the Line	1957	$20
❏ 20909	I Found You Out/ Alabama Boogie Boy	1952	$20
❏ 21335	I Lose Again/Everybody Knew the Truth But Me	1954	$20

Number	Title	Yr	NM
❏ 2-210(?)	I'm Biting My Fingernails/I Wish I Had a Nickel	1949	$30

— Microgroove 7-inch, 33 1/3 rpm single

Number	Title	Yr	NM
❏ 20756	I Wanna Do Something For Santa/Jingle Bell Boogie	1950	$30
❏ 21007	I Went to Your Wedding/Our Love Isn't Legal	1952	$20
❏ 21521	Little Rock and Roll/I'll Be Here	1956	$60
❏ 21150	Live and Let Live/I Wonder Where You Are Tonight	1953	$20
❏ 21494	Loaded for Bear/Six of One, Half a Dozen of the Other	1956	$20
❏ 21565	Lonesome Train/Laughing Back the Heartaches	1956	$20
❏ 20948	Louisiana Lucy/The Man Behind the Throttle	1952	$20
❏ 2-532	Love Song in 32 Bars/Tennessee Kentucky & Alabam'	1950	$30

— Microgroove 7-inch, 33 1/3 rpm single

Number	Title	Yr	NM
❏ 21113	Peace Be Still/Ninety & Nine	1953	$20
❏ 40080	Santa Got Stuck in the Chimney/I Said a Prayer for Santa Claus	1953	$20

— With Jimmy Boyd

Number	Title	Yr	NM
❏ 20787	Set 'Em Up Joe/Glad Rags	1951	$30
❏ 20808	Sick, Sober and Sorry/Tennessee Walking Horse	1951	$30
❏ 21424	Somebody's Pushin'/Carolina Waltz	1955	$20
❏ 21294	Stealin'/My Darling Lola Lee	1954	$20
❏ 21186	Sweet Mama Tree Top Tall/Put a Little Sweetness in Your Love	1953	$20
❏ 2-100(?)	Take It or Leave It Baby/Till the End of the World	1949	$30

— Microgroove 7-inch, 33 1/3 rpm single

Number	Title	Yr	NM
❏ 2-100(?)	Tennessee Saturday Night/A Heart Full of Love	1949	$30

— Microgroove 7-inch, 33 1/3 rpm single

Number	Title	Yr	NM
❏ 20844	Ten Trips to the Altar/Keep Your Cotton Pickin' Hands	1951	$30
❏ 21187	Thanks/I Dreamed I Searched Heaven	1953	$20
❏ 41034	That's Just What I'll Do/Broken Doll	1957	$20
❏ 20738	There's a Gold Moon Shining/Cream of Kentucky	1950	$30
❏ 21066	Wildcat Boogie/Let Me Go, Devil	1953	$20
❏ 21160	Wildcat Boogie/Let Me Go, Devil	1953	$20

DITTO

Number	Title	Yr	NM
❏ 120	The Tijuana Jail/Fools Paradise	1959	$15

MGM

Number	Title	Yr	NM
❏ 10751	Heart of Gold/Hey Ho Virginia Reel	1950	$50

REPUBLIC

Number	Title	Yr	NM
❏ 2005	Hot Rod Lincoln/Five Minute Love Affair	1960	$15
❏ 2022	Sadie Was a Lady/Buck Private's Lament	1961	$15
❏ 2010	Side Car Cycle/Like Nothin' Man	1961	$15

SMASH

Number	Title	Yr	NM
❏ 1761	I'll Step Aside/Mister Sun	1962	$10

STARDAY

Number	Title	Yr	NM
❏ 704	10 Little Bottles/Let It Be Me	1964	$8
❏ 826	Bottom of the Bottle/I'm Gonna Raise Cain (While I'm Able)	1968	$8
❏ 847	Down to Your Last Fool/Invitation to the Blues	1968	$8
❏ 758	Fireball/Over the Hill	1966	$8
❏ 665	Have You Seen My Baby/What Have You Done for Me Lately	1964	$8
❏ 776	Hell's Angels/A Way of Life	1966	$8
❏ 916	Here Come the Elephants/Take Me Back to Tulsa	1970	$6
❏ 678	Hot Rod Surfin' Hootlebeatnanny/Don't Mama Count Anymore	1964	$20
❏ 618	How to Succeed with Girls (Without Half-Way Trying)/Don't Mention Her Name	1963	$8
❏ 813	I Ain't Gonna Go/Don't Bite the Hand That's Feeding You	1967	$8
❏ 893	It Only Hurts When I Cry/The Girl Who Carried the Torch for Me	1970	$6
❏ 690	My Wicked, Wicked Ways/Bachelor Bill	1964	$8
❏ 951	Put the Country Back in Country Music/Fly Me, Try Me	1972	$6
❏ 721	Sick, Sober & Sorry/The Man Who Comes Around	1965	$8
❏ 931	The Bottle's Empty/The Late and Great Myself	1971	$6
❏ 731	The Great Figure Eight Race/Sadie Was a Lady	1965	$8
❏ 749	They Got Me/Silent Walls	1966	$8
❏ 649	Three Sheets in the Wind/Let the Tears Begin	1963	$8
❏ 635	True Love (Is Hard to Find)/Cimarron	1963	$8

7-Inch Extended Plays

COLUMBIA

Number	Title	Yr	NM
❏ B-2820	Sick, Sober and Sorry/Love Song in 32 Bars/Ten Little Bottles/Put Me to Bed	1958	$35

REPUBLIC

Number	Title	Yr	NM
❏ 100	(contents unknown)	1960	$25
❏ 100 [PS]	Hot Rod Lincoln	1960	$25

BONDS, GARY U.S.

ATCO

Number	Title	Yr	NM
❏ 6689	The Star/You Need a Personal Manager	1969	$6

BLUFF CITY

Number	Title	Yr	NM
❏ 221	My Love Song/Blue Grass	1974	$5

BOTANIC

Number	Title	Yr	NM
❏ 1002	I'm Glad You're Back/Funky Lies	1968	$8

EMI AMERICA

Number	Title	Yr	NM
❏ 8133	Love's on the Line/Way Back When	1982	$4
❏ 8117	Out of Work/Bring Her Back	1982	$4
❏ 8117 [PS]	Out of Work/Bring Her Back	1982	$5
❏ 8079	This Little Girl/Way Back When	1981	$4
❏ 8079 [PS]	This Little Girl/Way Back When	1981	$5
❏ 8145	Turn the Music Down/Way Back When	1982	$4

LEGRAND

Number	Title	Yr	NM
❏ 1039	Beaches U.S.A./Do the Bumpsie	1965	$12
❏ 1045	Call Me for Christmas/Mixed Up Faculty	1967	$15
❏ 1020	Copy Cat/I'll Change That Too	1962	$20
❏ 1015	Dear Lady/Havin' So Much Fun	1961	$30

— Original title of A-side

Number	Title	Yr	NM
❏ 1015	Dear Lady Twist/Havin' So Much Fun	1962	$20
❏ 1025	Do the Limbo with Me/Where Did That Naughty Little Girl Go	1962	$20
❏ 1041	Due to Circumstances Under My Control/Slow Motion	1966	$12
❏ 1027	I Don't Wanta Wait/What a Dream	1963	$15
❏ 1022	Mixed Up Faculty/I Dig This Station	1962	$20
❏ 1035	Oh Yeah, Oh Yeah/Let Me Go Lover	1965	$10
❏ 1030	Perdido Part 1/Perdido Part 2	1963	$15
❏ 1046	Sarah Jane/What a Crazy World	1967	$10
❏ 1012	School Is In/Trip to the Moon	1961	$20
❏ 1012	School Is In/Trip to the Moon	1971	$8

— Red label reissue

Number	Title	Yr	NM
❏ 1009	School Is Out/One Million Years	1961	$30

— Artist listed as "U.S. Bonds"

Number	Title	Yr	NM
❏ 1009	School Is Out/One Million Years	1961	$20

— Artist listed as "Gary (U.S.) Bonds" as are all later Legrand singles

Number	Title	Yr	NM
❏ 1009 [PS]	School Is Out/One Million Years	1961	$50
❏ 1043	Send Her Back to Me/Workin' for My Baby	1967	$10
❏ 1019	Seven Day Weekend/Gettin' a Groove	1962	$20
❏ 1040	Take Me Back to New Orleans/I'm That Kind of Guy	1966	$10
❏ 1032	The Music Goes Round and Round/Ella Is Yella	1964	$15
❏ 1018	Twist, Twist Senora/Food of Love	1962	$20

MCA

Number	Title	Yr	NM
❏ 52335	One More Time Around the Block, Ophelia/Deadline U.S.A.	1984	$4

— B-side by Shalamar

PHOENIX

Number	Title	Yr	NM
❏ 0071	Standing in the Line of Fire/Wild Nights	1984	$5
❏ 0071 [PS]	Standing in the Line of Fire/Wild Nights	1984	$5

PRODIGAL

Number	Title	Yr	NM
❏ 0612	Grandma's Washboard/Believing You	1975	$5

SUE

Number	Title	Yr	NM
❏ 17	One Broken Heart/Can't Use You in My Business	1970	$6

BONEY M

ATCO

Number	Title	Yr	NM
❏ 7063	Daddy Cool/Lovin' or Leavin'	1976	$5
❏ 7080	Sunny/New York City	1978	$6

ATLANTIC

Number	Title	Yr	NM
❏ 3422	Ma Baker/A Woman Can Change a Man	1977	$5

SIRE

Number	Title	Yr	NM
❏ 1038	Dancing in the Street/Never Change Lovers in the Middle of the Night	1979	$5
❏ 1036	Mary's Boy Child-Oh My Lord/Dancing in the Street	1978	$5
❏ 49144	Mary's Boy Child-Oh My Lord/He Was a Steppenwolf	1979	$6

BONFIRE, MARS

COLUMBIA

Number	Title	Yr	NM
❏ 44772	Faster Than the Speed of Life/She	1969	$10
❏ 44888	In Christina's Arms/Lady Moon Walker	1969	$10

BONNERS, THE

OL

Number	Title	Yr	NM
❏ 110	Ordinary Hero/(B-side unknown)	1988	$6

— As "The Bonner Family

Number	Title	Yr	NM
❏ 126	Way Beyond the Blue/You Haven't Tried Me	1988	$6

BONNEVILLES, THE

More than one group. (45)

BARRY

Number	Title	Yr	NM
❏ 104	Lorraine/Zu Zu	1962	$60

CAPRI

Number	Title	Yr	NM
❏ 102	Give Me Your Love/Until You Say We're Through	1959	$60

MUNICH

Number	Title	Yr	NM
❏ 103	Lorraine/Zu Zu	1960	$300

— Red label

Number	Title	Yr	NM
❏ 103	Lorraine/Zu Zu	1960	$125

— Black label

WHITEHALL

Number	Title	Yr	NM
❏ 30002	I Do/Make Believe Lovin'	1959	$40

BONNEY, GRAHAM

CAPITOL

Number	Title	Yr	NM
❏ 2221	I'll Be Your Baby Tonight/Back from Baltimore	1968	$6
❏ 5624	Super Girl/Hill of Lovin'	1966	$8

MIKE

Number	Title	Yr	NM
❏ 4009	Baby's Gone/Later Tonight	1966	$8

BONNIE AND THE BUTTERFLYS

SMASH

Number	Title	Yr	NM
❏ 1878	I Saw Him Standing There/Dust Storm	1964	$30

BONNIE AND THE LITTLE BOYS BLUE

NIKKI

Number	Title	Yr	NM
❏ 611	Bells/You'd Better Run	1958	$8000

BONNIE AND THE TREASURES

PABLO

Number	Title	Yr	NM
❏ 7014	Davey, I'm So Glad It Rained/The Lonely Surfer	1964	$50

— B-side by the Mid-Americans

PHI-DAN

Number	Title	Yr	NM
❏ 5005	Home of the Brave/Our Song	1965	$50

BONNIE LOU

FRATERNITY

Number	Title	Yr	NM
❏ 812	Friction Heat/I Give My Love to You	1958	$20

KING

Number	Title	Yr	NM
❏ 1506	Barnyard Hop/Miss the Love	1955	$30
❏ 4900	Bo Weevil/Chaperon	1956	$30
❏ 4835	Daddy-O/Dancing in My Socks	1955	$30
❏ 4864	Daddy-O/Miss the Love	1956	$30
❏ 1445	Danger, Heartbreak Ahead/A Rusty Old Halo	1955	$30

Number	Title	Yr	NM
❏ 1476	Drop Me a Line/Old Faithful	1955	$30
❏ 1341	Huckleberry Pie/No One	1954	$30
❏ 5094	I'm Available/Waiting in Vain	1957	$30
❏ 4919	I Turn to You/Lonesome Lover	1956	$30
❏ 5009	I Want You/Easy Love, Easy Kisses	1957	$30
❏ 4895	Little Miss Bobby Sox/Beyond the Shadow of a Doubt	1956	$30
❏ 1272	Papaya Mama/Since You Said Goodbye	1953	$40
❏ 1213	Scrap of Paper/Dancin' with Someone	1953	$40
❏ 1192	Seven Lonely Days/Just Out of Reach	1953	$40
❏ 5865	Seven Lonely Days/Tennessee Wig Walk	1964	$15
❏ 5063	Teeange Wedding/Runnin' Away	1957	$30
❏ 1384	Tell the World/Darlin' Why	1954	$30
❏ 1414	Tennessee Mambo/Train Whistle Blues	1955	$30
❏ 1237	Tennessee Wig Walk/Hand Me Down Heart	1953	$40
❏ 1279	Texas Polka/No Heart at All	1953	$40
❏ 5425	Tweedle Dee/Daddy-O	1960	$20
❏ 1436	Tweedle Dee/Finger of Suspicion	1955	$30
❏ 1373	Two-Step Side Step/Please Don't Laugh When I Cry	1954	$30
❏ 1365	Wait for Me Darling/Blue Tennessee Rain	1954	$30
❏ 1318	Welcome Mat/Don't Stop Kissing Me Goodnight	1954	$30

TODD

Number	Title	Yr	NM
❏ 1073	24 Hours of Loneliness/Be Tender	1962	$15

BONNIE SISTERS, THE
RAINBOW

Number	Title	Yr	NM
❏ 45-344	Confess/Shuga Duga	1956	$40
❏ 45-328	Cry Baby/Broken	1956	$40
❏ 45-328	I Saw Mommy Cha Cha Cha with You Know Who?/Cry Baby	1955	$50
❏ 45-333	Track That Cat/Wandering Heart	1956	$40

BONNIWELL, T.S.
CAPITOL

Number	Title	Yr	NM
❏ 2551	Sleep/Where Am I to Go	1969	$12

BONOFF, KARLA
COLUMBIA

Number	Title	Yr	NM
❏ 1-11206	Baby Don't Go/The Letter	1980	$4
❏ 3-10618	I Can't Hold On/Falling Star	1977	$5
❏ 3-10710	Isn't It Always Love/Rose in the Garden	1978	$5
❏ 18-02805	Personally/Dream	1982	$4
❏ 18-02805 [PS]	Personally/Dream	1982	$5
❏ 18-03172	Please Be the One/Just Walk Away	1982	$4
❏ 38-04472	Somebody's Eyes/Just Walk Away	1984	$4
❏ 38-04472 [PS]	Somebody's Eyes/Just Walk Away	1984	$4
❏ 3-10751	Someone to Lay Down Beside Me/Rose in the Garden	1978	$5
❏ 1-11041	Trouble Again/If He's Even Here	1979	$4
❏ 1-11130	When You Walk in the Room/Never Stop Her Heart	1979	$4

BONZO DOG BAND, THE
IMPERIAL

Number	Title	Yr	NM
❏ 66345	I'm the Urban Spaceman/Canyons of Your Mind	1969	$20
❏ 66373	Mr. Apollo/Ready Made	1969	$20

— As "The Bonzo Dog Doo-Dah Band"

UNITED ARTISTS

Number	Title	Yr	NM
❏ 50809	I'm the Urban Spaceman/Canyons of Your Mind	1971	$10
❏ 50943	Slush/King of Scurf	1972	$20

BONZO GOES TO WASHINGTON
SLEEPING BAG

Number	Title	Yr	NM
❏ SLX13-7 [DJ]	5 Minutes (unknown version) (same on both sides)	1984	$10

— 45 not released commercially

BOOGIE BOYS, THE
CAPITOL

Number	Title	Yr	NM
❏ B-5498	A Fly Girl/(Dub)	1985	$4
❏ B-44146	Body/I'm Comin'	1988	$4
❏ B-5325	Break Dancer/Zodiac	1984	$8
❏ B-5622	Dealin' with Life/(Instrumental)	1986	$4
❏ B-5594	Girl Talk/(Instrumental)	1986	$4
❏ B-5594 [PS]	Girl Talk/(Instrumental)	1986	$4
❏ B-44076	I'm Comin'/(Instrumental)	1987	$4
❏ B-5546	Party Asteroid/Runnin' from Your Love	1986	$4
❏ B-5649	Share My World/Run It	1986	$4
❏ B-5649 [PS]	Share My World/Run It	1986	$4

BOOGIE DOWN PRODUCTIONS
JIVE

Number	Title	Yr	NM
❏ 1098-7-J	My Philosophy/(Instrumental)	1988	$3
❏ 1120-7-J	Stop the Violence/(Instrumental)	1988	$3
❏ 1120-7-J [PS]	Stop the Violence/(Instrumental)	1988	$3

BOOGIE KINGS, THE
MONTEL

Number	Title	Yr	NM
❏ 939	Crying Man/Two Steps from the Blues	1965	$15

PAULA

Number	Title	Yr	NM
❏ 272	Bony Maronie/I've Got Your Number	1967	$10
❏ 260	Tell It Like It Is/Philly Walk	1967	$10

BOOK OF LOVE
SIRE

Number	Title	Yr	NM
❏ 29030	Boy/Book of Love	1985	$4
❏ 28882	I Touch Roses/Lost Souls	1985	$4
❏ 28428	I Touch Roses/Lost Souls	1987	$4
❏ 28428 [PS]	I Touch Roses/Lost Souls	1987	$4
❏ 27667	Lullaby/Oranges and Lemons	1989	$4
❏ 28320	Modigliani/Modigliani (Lost in Your Eyes)	1987	$4
❏ 27858	Pretty Boys and Pretty Girls/Tubular Bells	1988	$4
❏ 27858 [PS]	Pretty Boys and Pretty Girls/Tubular Bells	1988	$4

BOOKENDS, THE
CAPITOL

Number	Title	Yr	NM
❏ 4667	Christmas Kisses/Let Me Walk with You	1961	$20

BOOKER, CHUCKII
ATLANTIC

Number	Title	Yr	NM
❏ DMD1478 [DJ]	That's My Honey (3 versions)	1989	$15
❏ 88841	Touch/(Dub Edit)	1989	$3
❏ 88917	Turned Away/Keep Your Guard Up	1989	$3

BOOKER, JAY
EMI AMERICA

Number	Title	Yr	NM
❏ B-8379	Hot Red Sweater/Mary Mandolin	1987	$3
❏ B-43045	The Mule Won't Move/Brand New Outlaw	1987	$3

BOOKER T. AND PRISCILLA
A&M

Number	Title	Yr	NM
❏ 1487	Crippled Crow/Wild Fox	1973	$5
❏ 1298	The Wedding Song/She	1971	$5

BOOKER T. AND THE MG'S
A&M

Number	Title	Yr	NM
❏ 2394	Don't Stop Your Love/I Came to Love You	1982	$4
❏ 2374	I Want You/You're the Best	1981	$4
❏ 2234	The Best of You/Let's Go Dancin'	1980	$4

— As "Booker T. Jones"

Number	Title	Yr	NM
❏ 2279	Will You Be the One/Cookie	1980	$4

— As "Booker T. Jones"

ASYLUM

Number	Title	Yr	NM
❏ 45424	Grab Bag/Reincarnation	1977	$4
❏ 45392	Sticky Stuff/The Stick	1977	$4

EPIC

Number	Title	Yr	NM
❏ 50031	Evergreen/Song for Casey	1974	$4
❏ 50078	Front Street Rag/Mama Stewart	1975	$4
❏ 50149	Life Is Funny/Tennessee Voodoo	1975	$4

STAX

Number	Title	Yr	NM
❏ 134	Big Train/Burnt Biscuits	1963	$15
❏ 134	Big Train/Home Grown	1963	$15
❏ 196	Booker-Loo/My Sweet Potato	1966	$10
❏ 169	Boot-Leg/Outrage	1965	$10
❏ 0200	Breezy/Neckbone	1974	$5

— As "The MG's"

Number	Title	Yr	NM
❏ 161	Can't Be Still/Terrible Thing	1964	$10
❏ 137	Chinese Checkers/Plum Nellie	1963	$15
❏ 127	Green Onions/Behave Yourself	1962	$30

— Gray label

Number	Title	Yr	NM
❏ 127	Green Onions/Behave Yourself	1962	$20

— Blue label

Number	Title	Yr	NM
❏ 224	Groovin'/Slim Jenkin's Place	1967	$10
❏ 0013	Hang 'Em High/Over Easy	1968	$8
❏ 211	Hip-Hug-Her/Summertime	1967	$12
❏ 0082	Melting Pot/Kinda Easy Like	1970	$6
❏ 142	Mo' Onions/Fannie Mae	1963	$15
❏ 142	Mo' Onions/Tic Tac Toe	1963	$15
❏ 0037	Mrs. Robinson/Soul Clap '69	1969	$8
❏ 236	Silver Bells/Winter Snow	1967	$15
❏ 0049	Slum Baby/Meditation	1969	$8
❏ 0073	Something/Sunday Sermon	1970	$6
❏ 153	Soul Dressing/MG Party	1964	$12
❏ 0001	Soul-Limbo/Heads Or Tails	1968	$8
❏ 0169	Sugarcane/Blackride	1973	$5

— As "The MG's"

Number	Title	Yr	NM
❏ 0028	Time Is Tight/Johnny I Love You	1969	$8

VOLT

Number	Title	Yr	NM
❏ 102	Green Onions/Behave Yourself	1962	$40

BOOM, TAKA
MIRAGE

Number	Title	Yr	NM
❏ 99567	Climate for Love/Love Bank	1986	$3
❏ 99628	Middle of the Night (Edit)/(Album Version)	1985	$3
❏ 99628 [PS]	Middle of the Night (Edit)/(Album Version)	1985	$3
❏ DMD863 [DJ]	Middle of the Night (Long Version) (Long Dub) (Short Version)	1985	$10

PRELUDE

Number	Title	Yr	NM
❏ 8071	To Hell with Him/Love Party	1983	$4

BOOMERANG
RCA VICTOR

Number	Title	Yr	NM
❏ 74-0508	Mockingbird/Montreal Jail	1971	$8

BOOMTOWN RATS, THE
Includes (Sir!) BOB GELDOF

COLUMBIA

Number	Title	Yr	NM
❏ 38-05590	Drag Me Down/Hard Times	1985	$4
❏ 1-11117	I Don't Like Mondays/It's All the Rage	1979	$5
❏ 1-11248	Someone's Looking at You/I Don't Like Mondays (Live)	1980	$5

BOONE, DANIEL
EPIC

Number	Title	Yr	NM
❏ 10787	Daddy Don't You Walk So Fast/Tiger Woman	1971	$5

MERCURY

Number	Title	Yr	NM
❏ 73339	Annabelle/Sleepyhead	1972	$4
❏ 73281	Beautiful Sunday/Truly Julie	1972	$5
❏ 73357	Crying/Sunshine Lover	1973	$4
❏ 73461	Love Spell/Lilly, I Love You	1974	$4
❏ 73428	Skydiver/Do You Thank the Lord	1973	$4

PYE

Number	Title	Yr	NM
❏ 71052	I Think of You/(B-side unknown)	1976	$4

BOONE, DEBBY
WARNER BROS.

Number	Title	Yr	NM
❏ 49176	Are You On the Road to Lovin' Me Again/When It's Just You and Me	1980	$4
❏ 8814	Breakin' In a Brand New Broken Heart/When You're Loved	1979	$4
❏ 8511	California/Hey Everybody	1978	$4
❏ 8511 [PS]	California/Hey Everybody	1978	$4
❏ 49107	Everybody's Somebody's Fool/I'll Never Say Goodbye	1979	$4
❏ 49281	Free to Be Lonely Again/Love Put a Song in My Heart	1980	$4
❏ 8554	God Knows/Baby, I'm Yours	1978	$4
❏ 8554 [PS]	God Knows/Baby, I'm Yours	1978	$4
❏ 8700	In Memory of Your Love/When You're Loved	1978	$4
❏ 49720	It'll Be Him/Too Many Rivers	1981	$4
❏ 8739	My Heart Has a Mind of Its Own/I'd Rather Leave While I'm in Love	1979	$4
❏ 8633	Oh, No, Not My Baby/When You're Loved	1978	$4
❏ 49652	Perfect Fool/Every Day I Have to Cry	1981	$4
❏ 49042	See You in September/Jamie	1979	$4
❏ 49585	Take It Like a Woman/I Wish That I Could Hurt That Way Again	1980	$4

BOONE, PAT

CAPITOL

Number	Title	Yr	NM
❑ 2860	Picking Up Pebbles/ Oh My God	1970	$5
❑ 2763	What Are You Doing the Rest of Your Life/Now I'm Saved	1970	$5

DOT

Number	Title	Yr	NM
❑ 17098	500 Miles/I Had a Dream	1968	$6
❑ 16028	Ain't That a Shame/I'll Be Home	1960	$10
❑ 15377	Ain't That a Shame/ Tennessee Saturday Night	1955	$30
❑ 16474	Always You and Me/ Main Attraction	1963	$10
❑ 16808	A Man Alone/Run to Me, Baby	1966	$8
❑ 16498	Amore Baciami/ Gondoli Gondola	1963	$10
❑ 15660	April Love/When the Swallows Come Back to Capistrano	1957	$20
❑ 16825	As Tears Go By/Judith	1966	$8
❑ 15422	At My Front Door/ No Other Arms	1955	$30
❑ 16707	Baby Elephant Walk/ Say Goodbye	1965	$8
❑ 16658	Beach Girl/Little Honda	1964	$40
❑ 17156	Beyond One Memory/ September Blues	1968	$6
❑ 16006 [M]	Beyond the Sunset/ My Faithful Heart	1959	$20
❑ S-218 [S]	Beyond the Sunset/ My Faithful Heart	1959	$50
❑ 16244	Big Cold Wind/That's My Desire	1961	$15
❑ 16699	Blueberry Hill/Heartaches	1965	$8
❑ 17045	By the Time I Get to Phoenix/Ride Ride Ride	1967	$6
❑ 16190	Cherry Pink and Apple Blossom White/On Both Sides	1961	$15
❑ 16439	Days of Wine and Roses/Meditation	1963	$12
❑ 16152	Dear John/Alabam	1960	$15
❑ 16122	Delia Gone/Candy Street	1960	$15
❑ S-228 [S]	Delia Gone/Candy Street	1960	$50
❑ 15521	Don't Forbid Me/Anastasia	1956	$20
❑ 16034	Don't Forbid Me/April Love	1960	$12
❑ 16871	Five Miles from Home/Don't Put Your Feet in the Lemonade	1966	$8
❑ 15982 [M]	Fools Hall of Fame/The Brightest Wishing Star	1959	$20
❑ 15982 [PS]	Fools Hall of Fame/The Brightest Wishing Star	1959	$40
❑ S-211 [S]	Fools Hall of Fame/The Brightest Wishing Star	1959	$50
❑ 15914 [M]	For a Penny/The Wang Dang Taffy Apple Tango	1959	$20
❑ S-203 [S]	For a Penny/The Wang Dang Taffy Apple Tango	1959	$50
❑ 15490	Friendly Persuasion (Thee I Love)/Chains of Love	1956	$30

—Original on maroon label

Number	Title	Yr	NM
❑ 15490	Friendly Persuasion (Thee I Love)/Chains of Love	1956	$20

—Second pressing on black label

Number	Title	Yr	NM
❑ 15825	Gee, But It's Lonely/ For My Good Fortune	1958	$20
❑ 15435	Gee Whittakers!/Take the Time	1955	$30
❑ 17122	Gonna Find Me a Bluebird/ Deafening Roar of Silence	1968	$6
❑ 16668	Goodbye, Charlie/ Love, Who Needs It	1964	$8
❑ 0(no cat #) [PS]	Great! Great! Great!	1960	$30

—7x7 glossy insert that came with the package containing stereo singles 1520-1524

Number	Title	Yr	NM
❑ 17018	Have You Heard (It's All Over)/Me	1967	$6
❑ 16998	Hurry Sundown/What If They Gave a War and Nobody Came	1967	$6
❑ 16033	I Almost Lost My Mind/ Friendly Persuasion	1960	$10
❑ 15472	I Almost Lost My Mind/I'm in Love with You	1956	$30
❑ 16684	I'd Rather Die Young/I Want It That Way	1964	$8
❑ 15785	If Dreams Came True/That's How Much I Love You	1958	$20
❑ 16576	I Like What You Do/ Never Put It in Writing	1964	$8
❑ 15840	I'll Remember Tonight/ The Mardi Gras March	1958	$20
❑ 15840 [PS]	I'll Remember Tonight/ The Mardi Gras March	1958	$40
❑ 16312	I'll See You in My Dreams/ Pictures in the Fire	1961	$15
❑ 16785	I Love You So Much It Hurts/ Meet Me Tonight in Dreamland	1965	$8
❑ 17027	In the Mirror of Your Mind/ Swanee Is a River	1967	$6
❑ 16416	In the Room/Mexican Joe	1963	$10
❑ 17076	It's a Happening World/Emily	1968	$6
❑ 16836	It Seems Like Yesterday/ Well Remembered, Highly Thought Of Love Affair	1966	$8
❑ 15690	It's Too Soon to Know/A Wonderful Time Up There	1958	$20
❑ 16598	I Understand (Just How You Feel)/Rosemarie	1964	$8
❑ 15457	Long Tall Sally/Just As Long As I'm with You	1956	$30
❑ 16278	Louella (same on both sides)	1961	$30

—Probably a promo only, though it is on the black Dot label with no promo markings

Number	Title	Yr	NM
❑ 16278 [PS]	Louella (same on both sides)	1961	$50

—Title sleeve "Dedicated to Miss Louella Parsons

Number	Title	Yr	NM
❑ 16035	Love Letters in the Sand/A Wonderful Time Up There	1960	$10
❑ 15570	Love Letters in the Sand/Bernardine	1957	$20
❑ 15570 [PS]	Love Letters in the Sand/Bernardine	1957	$40
❑ 16525	Love Me/Mr. Moon	1963	$10
❑ 16498	Main Attraction/Si Si Si	1963	$10
❑ 16738	Mickey Mouse/Time Marches On	1965	$8
❑ 16738	Mickey Mouse/(Welcome) New Lovers	1965	$8
❑ 16209	Moody River/A Thousand Years	1961	$20
❑ 16728	Pearly Shells/Crazy Arms	1965	$8
❑ 16547	Santa's Coming in a Whirleybird/Oh Holy Night	1963	$10
❑ 1521 [S]	Send Me the Pillow You Dream On/Cathy's Clown	1960	$15

—Small hole, plays at 33 1/3 rpm

Number	Title	Yr	NM
❑ 16626	Side by Side/I'll Never Be Free	1964	$8

—By "Pat and Shirley Boone

Number	Title	Yr	NM
❑ 16641	Sincerely/Don't You Just Know It	1964	$8
❑ 16559	Some Enchanted Evening/That's Me	1963	$12
❑ 16368	Speedy Gonzales/The Locket	1962	$15
❑ 1520 [S]	Stagger Lee/El Paso	1960	$15

—Small hole, plays at 33 1/3 rpm

Number	Title	Yr	NM
❑ 15750	Sugar Moon/Cherie, I Love You	1958	$20
❑ 15750 [PS]	Sugar Moon/Cherie, I Love You	1958	$40
❑ 16391	Ten Lonely Guys/Lover's Lane	1962	$10
❑ 16176	The Exodus Song (This Land Is Mine)/There's a Moon Out Tonight	1961	$15
❑ 17056	The Green Kentucky Hills of Home/You Mean All the World to Me	1967	$6
❑ 16494	Tie Me Kangaroo Down Sport/I Feel Like Crying	1963	$10
❑ 16015	To the Center of the Earth Part 1/Part 2	1959	$30
❑ 15443	Tutti Frutti/I'll Be Home	1956	$30
❑ 1522 [S]	Tweedle Dee/The Wayward Wind	1960	$15

—Small hole. plays at 33 1/3 rpm

Number	Title	Yr	NM
❑ 15955 [M]	Twixt Twlve and Twenty/ Rock Boll Weevil	1959	$20
❑ 15955 [PS]	Twixt Twlve and Twenty/ Rock Boll Weevil	1959	$40
❑ S-207 [S]	Twixt Twlve and Twenty/ Rock Boll Weevil	1959	$50
❑ 15338	Two Hearts/Tra La La	1955	$30
❑ 16073	Walking the Floor Over You/Spring Rain	1960	$15
❑ 16073 [PS]	Walking the Floor Over You/Spring Rain	1960	$30
❑ S-221 [S]	Walking the Floor Over You/Spring Rain	1960	$50
❑ 16048	(Welcome) New Lovers/Words	1960	$15
❑ 16048 [PS]	(Welcome) New Lovers/Words	1960	$30
❑ S-220 [S]	(Welcome) New Lovers/Words	1960	$50
❑ 1524 [S]	White Silver Sands/He's Got the Whole World in His Hands	1960	$15

—Small hole, plays at 33 1/3 rpm

Number	Title	Yr	NM
❑ 15545	Why Baby Why/I'm Waiting Just for You	1957	$20
❑ 16933	Wish You Were Here, Buddy/Love for You	1966	$8
❑ 15888 [M]	With the Wind and the Rain in Your Hair/Good Rockin' Tonight	1959	$20
❑ S-200 [S]	With the Wind and the Rain in Your Hair/Good Rockin' Tonight	1959	$50
❑ 16903	Wrath of Grapes/You Don't Need Me Anymore	1966	$8

HITSVILLE

Number	Title	Yr	NM
❑ 6054	Colorado Country Morning/Don't Want to Fall Away from You	1977	$5
❑ 6047	Country Days and Country Nights/Lovelight Comes a-Shining	1976	$5
❑ 6042	Oklahoma Sunshine/ Won't Be Home Tonight	1976	$5
❑ 6037	Texas Woman/It's Gone	1976	$5

LAMB & LION

Number	Title	Yr	NM
❑ 818	It's OK to Be a Kid at Christmas/Don't Let the Season Pass You By	1979	$5

LION

Number	Title	Yr	NM
❑ 126	Empty Chairs/If You're Gonna Make a Fool of Somebody	1972	$5
❑ 119	I Believe in Music/Children Learn What They Live	1972	$5

—With the Boone Family

Number	Title	Yr	NM
❑ 106	Mr. Blue/Song of the Children of Israel (Exodus)	1972	$5

—With the Boone Girls

MC

Number	Title	Yr	NM
❑ 5001	Whatever Happened to the Good Old Honky Tonk/ Ain't Going Down in the Ground Before My Time	1977	$5

MELODYLAND

Number	Title	Yr	NM
❑ 6001	Candy Lips/Young Girl	1974	$5
❑ 6029	Glory Train/U.F.O.	1976	$5
❑ 6018	I'd Do It with You/Yester-Me, Yester-You, Yesterday	1975	$5

—A-side with Shirley Boone

Number	Title	Yr	NM
❑ 6005	Indiana Girl/Young Girl	1975	$5

MGM

Number	Title	Yr	NM
❑ 14242	All for the Love of Sunshine/M.I.A-P.O.W.	1971	$5
❑ 14282	C'mon, Give a Hand/Where There's a Heartache	1971	$5
❑ 14601	Everything Begins and Ends with You/Golden Rocket	1973	$4
❑ 14470	I Saw the Light/Great Speckled Bird	1972	$5
❑ 14521	Tying the Pieces Together/ Hayden Carter	1973	$4
❑ 14521 [PS]	Tying the Pieces Together/ Hayden Carter	1973	$5

REPUBLIC

Number	Title	Yr	NM
❑ 7084	I Need Someone/ Loving You Madly	1954	$30
❑ 7119	My Heart Belongs to You/I Need Someone	1955	$30
❑ 7049	My Heart Belongs to You/ Until You Tell Me So	1953	$30

WARNER BROS.

Number	Title	Yr	NM
❑ 49596	Colorado Country Morning/ Whatever Happened to the Good Old Honky Tonk	1980	$4
❑ 49255	Hostage Prayer/Love's Got a Way of Hanging On	1980	$4
❑ 49097	Midnight/Can You Feel the Love	1979	$4

—By "Pat and Shirley Boone

Number	Title	Yr	NM
❑ 49691	Won't Be Home Tonight/ Throw It Away	1981	$4

7-Inch Extended Plays

DOT

Number	Title	Yr	NM
❑ DEP-1076	*You Can't Be True, Dear/ My Happiness//Now Is the Hour/Side by Side	1959	$20
❑ DEP-1056 [PS]	A Closer Walk with Thee	1957	$25
❑ DEP-1055 [PS]	A Date with Pat Boone	1957	$25
❑ DEP-1062 [PS]	… And a Very Merry Christmas	1957	$35
❑ DEP-1049	At My Front Door/Tennessee Saturday Night//Ain't That a Shame/Two Hearts	1956	$25
❑ DEP-1069	Autumn Leaves/Blueberry Hill// Cold, Cold Heart/St. Louis Blues	1958	$25
❑ DEP-1054	Coax Me A Little/The Mocking Bird In The Willow Tree//Indiana Holiday/Marry Me, Marry Me	1956	$25
❑ DEP-1055	Don't Forbid Me/Why Did I Choose You?//Rock Me Baby/The Fat Man	1957	$25
❑ DEP-1057 [PS]	Four by Pat	1957	$25
❑ DEP-1075	Loyalty/Bourbon Street Blues// Bigger Than Texas/A Fiddle, A Rifle, An Axe and a Bible	1958	$20
❑ DEP-1075 [PS]	Mardi Gras	1958	$20
❑ DEP-1049 [PS]	Pat Boone	1956	$25
❑ DEP-1054 [PS]	Pat Boone Sings Songs from Friendly Persuasion	1956	$25
❑ DEP-1053 [PS]	Pat On Mike	1956	$25
❑ DEP-1076 [PS]	Side by Side	1959	$20

—By "Pat & Shirley Boone

Number	Title	Yr	NM
❑ DEP-1069 [PS]	Star Dust	1958	$25
❑ DEP-1057	Technique/Cathedral in the Pines//Louella/Without My Love	1957	$25
❑ DEP-1053	Treasure of Love/B-I-N-G-O//Hoboken Baby/ Am I Seeing Angels	1956	$25
❑ DEP-1062	White Christmas/Silent Night//Jingle Bells/Santa Claus Is Comin' to Town	1957	$35

BOONES, THE

MOTOWN

Number	Title	Yr	NM
❑ 1389	My Guy/When the Lovelight Starts Shining Through His Eyes	1976	$5
❑ 1314	Please Mr. Postman/Friend	1974	$5

—As "The Pat Boone Family

Number	Title	Yr	NM
❏ 1334	When The Lovelight Starts Shining Through His Eyes/Viva Espana	1975	$5

WARNER BROS.

❏ 8385 [DJ]	Hasta Manana (mono/stereo)	1977	$5
—Stock copy not known to exist			
❏ 8446	He's a Rebel/You Light Up My Life	1977	$6
—B-side by Debby Boone			

BOOT
AGAPE

❏ 9008	Hey Little Girl/Liza Brown	1972	$8

BOOTEE, DUKE
MERCURY

❏ 818809-7	Live Wire (I Want a Girl That Sweats)/Slow Down	1984	$4
❏ 880105-7	Same Day Service/ (B-side unknown)	1984	$4

BOOTH, TONY
CAPITOL

❏ 3356	A Whole Lot of Somethin'/ Nobody's Fool But Yours	1972	$6
❏ 3214	Cinderella/Somebody Called L.A.	1971	$6
❏ 4058	Down at the Corner Bar/ Someone Who Really Does	1975	$5
❏ 4123	Fanny Lee (The Burlesque Queen)/How's Everything	1975	$5
❏ 3795	Happy Hour/Midnight Race	1973	$5
❏ 3853	Lonely Street/It Never Will Be Over for Me	1974	$5
❏ 3441	Lonesome 7-7203/ Congratulations, You're Absolutely Right	1972	$6
❏ 3582	Loving You/What a Liar I Am	1973	$5
❏ 3639	Old Faithful/Don't Let True Love Slip Away	1973	$5
❏ 3723	Secret Love/Someday I'm Gonna Go to Mexico	1973	$5
❏ 3899	There Ain't Enough of Love to Go Around/Someone Who Really Does	1974	$5
❏ 3994	Watch Out for Lucy/ Good As Gone	1974	$5
❏ 3515	When a Man Loves a Woman (The Way That I Love You)/Just a Man	1973	$5
❏ 3943	Workin' at the Car Wash Blues/That Loving Feeling	1974	$5

MGM

❏ 14156	Give Me One Last Kiss and Go/Las Virgenes Road	1970	$8
❏ 14112	Irma Jackson/One Too Many Times	1970	$8

UNITED ARTISTS

❏ XW1028	All Night Long/Fading Tail Lights	1977	$4
❏ XW962	Letting Go/Nothing Seems to Work Anymore	1977	$4
❏ XW906	Somethin' 'Bout You Baby I Like/Lady Alone	1976	$4

BOOTLES, THE
GNP CRESCENDO

❏ 311	I'll Let You Hold My Hand/ Never Till Now	1964	$20

BOOTSY'S RUBBER BAND
WARNER BROS.

❏ 29889	Body Slam!/I'd Rather Be With You	1982	$4
❏ 49013	Bootsy Get Live Part 1/Part 2	1979	$5
❏ 8512	Bootzilla/Vanish in Our Sleep	1978	$6
❏ 8403	Can't Stay Away/ Another Point of View	1977	$6
❏ 49661	F-Encounter/(Instrumental)	1981	$5
—As "Bootsy"			
❏ 8575	Hollywood Squares/ What's a Telephone Bill	1978	$5
❏ 8575 [PS]	Hollywood Squares/ What's a Telephone Bill	1978	$8
❏ 8246	I'd Rather Be with You/ Vanish in Our Sleep	1976	$6
❏ 49708	Is That My Song?/It's a Musical	1981	$5
—As "Bootsy"			
❏ 49599	Mug Push/Scenery	1980	$5
—As "Bootsy"			
❏ 49599 [PS]	Mug Push/Scenery	1980	$6
—As "Bootsy"			
❏ 8291	Psychoticbumpschool/ Vanish in Our Sleep	1976	$6
❏ 8328	The Pinocchio Theory/ Rubber Duckie	1977	$6

Number	Title	Yr	NM

BOOTY PEOPLE
CALLA

❏ 110	Spirit of '76/Anyway I'm Busted	1976	$8

BOP-A-LOOS, THE
MERCURY

❏ 70568	Hearts of Stone/Miracle Mambo	1955	$30
❏ 70569	Sincerely/Cuban Carnival	1955	$30
❏ 70552	Teach Me Tonight/South Parkway Mambo	1955	$30
❏ 70553	Tweedle Dee/Bongo Mambo	1955	$30

BOP-CHORDS, THE
HOLIDAY

❏ 2608	Baby/So Why	1957	$300
—Red label			
❏ 2601	Castle in the Sky/ My Darling to You	1957	$200
—Black label			
❏ 2603	When I Woke Up This Morning/I Really Love You	1957	$200
—Black label			

BOPPERS, THE
FANTASY

❏ 843	There She Goes Again/ Everybody Wants to Be a Star	1977	$8

BORCHERS, BOBBY
ABC

❏ 12075	We've Come As Far As We Can Go Together/Revelation	1975	$6

ABC DOT

❏ 17578	God Bless Robert E. Lee/ The Temptation Is Gone	1975	$6

EPIC

❏ 11093	Alabama Dream Girl/I'll Still Be Loving You This Much	1974	$6
❏ 50687	I Just Wanna Feel the Magic/Old Emotional Me	1979	$4
❏ 50585	Sweet Fantasy/You Are Yesterday	1978	$4
❏ 11073	When Johnny Cash Comes Back to Folsom/I'll Still Be Loving You This Much	1973	$6
❏ 50650	Wishing I Had Listened to Your Song/I've Had a Lovely Time	1979	$4

LONGHORN

❏ 3003	(I Remember When I Thought) Whiskey Was a River/It Was Love What It Was	1987	$5
❏ 3002	It Was Love What It Was/ (B-side unknown)	1987	$5

PLAYBOY

❏ 5803	Cheap Perfume and Candlelight/Hobo's Delight	1977	$5
❏ 5827	I Like Ladies in Long Black Dresses/Shawn	1978	$5
❏ 5823	I Promised Her a Rainbow/ Brass Buckles	1977	$5
❏ 6065	Someone's with Your Wife Tonight, Mister/Hobo's Delight	1976	$5
❏ 6083	They Don't Make 'Em Like That Anymore/I Can't Keep My Hands Off of You	1976	$5
❏ 5816	What a Way to Go/ Lunch-Time Lovers	1977	$5
❏ 6092	Whispers/Just for a Minute	1976	$5

BORDERS, TONY
HALL

❏ 1921	Get Yourself Another Man/Bit by Bit	1964	$40
❏ 1918	Pass the Word/Soft Wind, Soft Voice	1964	$40

HALLWAY

❏ 1817	It'll Be My Song/ Dreamers Prayer	1963	$30

REVUE

❏ 11025	Cheaters Never Win/ Love and a Friend	1968	$30
❏ 11040	I Met Her in Church/ What Kind of Spell	1969	$40
❏ 11054	Polly Wolly/Gentle on My Mind	1970	$30

TCF

❏ 124	Stay By My Side/Love's Been Good to Me	1966	$50

UNI

❏ 55180	Lonely Weekend/ You Better Believe	1969	$20

Number	Title	Yr	NM

BORDERSONG
GREAT NORTHWEST

❏ 704	She's a Good Woman/Morning	1976	$30

BOSSTONES, THE
BOSS

❏ 401	Mope-Itty Mope/ Wings of an Angel	1959	$125
—As "Boss Tones"			
❏ 501	Mope-Itty Mope/ Wings of an Angel	1959	$200
—As "Bosstones"			

V-TONE

❏ 208	Mope-Itty Mope/ Wings of an Angel	1960	$70

BOSTIC, EARL, AND BILL DOGGETT
KING

❏ 4954	Indiana/Bubbins Rock	1956	$20
❏ 4930	Mean to Me/Bo-Do Rock	1956	$20
❏ 5427	Special Delivery Stomp/ Earl's Dog	1960	$10

7-Inch Extended Plays

❏ EP-397	*Bubbins Rock/Indiana/The Bo-Do Rock/Mean to Me	1957	$25
❏ EP-397 [PS]	Bill Doggett -- Earl Bostic	1957	$25

BOSTIC, EARL
KING

❏ 5402	720 in the Books/Just in Time	1960	$15
❏ 5081	A Gay Day/Answer Me	1957	$20
❏ 4454	Always/How Could It Have Been You and I	1951	$40
❏ 5819	Apple Cake/Don't Do It Please	1963	$10
❏ 5699	Autumn Leaves/Anita's Theme	1962	$12
❏ 4723	Blue Skies/Mambolino	1954	$30
❏ 4905	Bugle Call Rag/I'll String Along with You	1956	$20
❏ 4623	Cherokee/The Song Is Ended	1953	$30
❏ 5742	Cherry Pink (And Apple Blossom White)/Your Cheatin' Heart	1963	$10
❏ 4790	Cocktails for Two/When Your Lover Has Gone	1955	$30
❏ 5636	Dark Eyes/People Will Say We're in Love	1962	$12
❏ 4674	Deep Purple/Smoke Rings	1953	$30
❏ 5683	Ducky/Deep in My Heart	1962	$12
❏ 4815	East of the Sun/Dream	1955	$30
❏ 5301	Ebb Tide/Hildegarde	1959	$15
❏ 5711	El Choclo Bossa Nova/ My Reverie	1963	$12
❏ 5317	Elegie/Out of Nowhere	1960	$15
❏ 4765	Embraceable You/Night and Day	1955	$30
❏ 4475	Flamingo/I'm Getting Sentimental Over You	1951	$40
❏ 4829	For All We Know/Beyond the Blue Horizon	1955	$30
❏ 4570	For You/Smoke Gets In Your Eyes	1952	$30
❏ 5944	From Russia with Love/ My Special Dream	1964	$8
❏ 5263	Gondola/Once in a While	1959	$15
❏ 5152	Goodnight Sweetheart/ Indian Boogie Woogie	1958	$20
❏ 4978	Harlem Nocturne/I Hear a Rhapsody	1956	$20
❏ 5961	Hello Dolly/Walk on the Wild Side	1964	$8
❏ 5127	Honeysuckle Rose/Back Beat	1958	$20
❏ 5600	How Deep Is the Ocean/Wrap It	1962	$10
❏ 4491	I Got Loaded/Chains of Love	1951	$50
❏ 4883	I Love You Truly/'Cause You're My Lover	1956	$20
❏ 5209	La Cucaracha Cha Cha/ Dancing in the Dark	1959	$15
❏ 5120	Lester Leaps In/ Pompton Turnpike	1958	$20
❏ 5861	Let's Dance Little Girl/ Summertime	1964	$8
❏ 5309	Let's Move Out/I Burned Your Letter	1960	$15
❏ 4536	Linger Awhile/Velvet Sunset	1952	$30
❏ 5776	Love Letters in the Sand/Tammy	1963	$10
❏ 5345	Make Believe/A Gay Day	1960	$15
❏ 5900	Make Believe/Star Gazer	1964	$8
❏ 4644	Melancholy Serenade/ What, No Pearls?	1953	$30
❏ 4776	Melody of Love/Sweet Lorraine	1955	$30
❏ 4550	Moonglow/Ain't Misbehavin'	1952	$30
❏ 5977	More/Charade	1965	$8
❏ 5661	More Than You Know/ Don't Blame Me	1962	$10
❏ 4699	My Heart at Thy Sweet Voice/Cracked Ice	1954	$30
❏ 5175	My Reverie Cha Cha/Barcarole	1959	$15
❏ 4683	Off Shore/Don't You Do It	1953	$30
❏ 5314	Off Shore/Hello '60	1960	$15
❏ 4845	O Solo Mio/Poeme	1955	$30
❏ 5144	Pinkie/Home Sweet Home Rock	1958	$20
❏ 6254	September Song/ Harlem Nocturne	1969	$5
❏ 5056	She's Funny That Way/Exercise	1957	$20

Number	Title	Yr	NM
4444	Sleep/September Song	1951	$40
4754	Song of the Islands/Liebestraum	1954	$30
5106	Southern Fried/No Name Jive	1958	$20
5839	Telstar Drive/Fast Track	1964	$8
5041	Temptation/September Song	1957	$20
5454	That Old Black Magic/Full Moon and Empty Arms	1961	$12
5955	Theme from The Unforgiven/Dominique	1964	$8
4511	The Moon Is Low/Lover Come Back to Me	1952	$30
5925	The Pink Panther/Lawrence of Arabia	1964	$8
4730	These Foolish Things/Mambostic	1954	$30
4603	The Sheik of Araby/Steamwhistle Jump	1953	$30
5564	The Thrill Is Gone/April in Portugal	1961	$10
5025	Too Fine for Crying/Avalon	1957	$20
5290	Tut-Strut/All the Things You Are	1959	$15
5362	Tuxedo Junction/Polonaise	1960	$15
5136	Twilight Time/Over Waves Rock	1958	$20
5252	White Horse/Dark Eyes	1959	$15
5229	Who Cares/Feeling Cool	1959	$15
5133	Woodchopper's Ball/John's Idea	1958	$20

7-Inch Extended Plays

Number	Title	Yr	NM
EP-415	*720 in the Books/Air Mail Special/Pompton Turnpike/Woodchopper's Ball	1958	$25
EP202	*Always/Linger Awhile/Merry Widow/Earl Blows a Fuse	1953	$30
EP381	*Bugle Call Rag/I'll Sing Along with You/I Love You Truly/'Cause You're My Lover	1956	$25
EP204	*Cherokee/Seven Steps/No Name Blues/Don't You Do It	1953	$30
EP355	*Cherry Bean/Liebestraum/Night and Day/Embraceable You	1955	$25
EP285	*Danube Waves/My Heart at Thy Sweet Voice/Poeme/O Sole Mio	1954	$25
EP203	*Deep Purple/Velvet Sunset/Choppin' It Down/You Go to My Head	1953	$30
EP375	*Dream/Beyond the Blue Horizon/East of the Sun/For All We Know	1956	$25
EP206	*Filibuster/The Sheik of Araby/Smoke Gets in Your Eyes/The Hour of Parting	1953	$30
EP-410	*Jeannine I Dream of Lilac Time/Answer Me/Vienna, My City of Dreams/Make Believe	1958	$25
EP284	*Jungle Drums/The Song Is Ended/Off Shore/Cracked Ice	1954	$25
EP-409	*Just Too Shy/Laura/Josephine/A Gay Day	1958	$25
EP347	*Mambostic/Time on My Hands/Mambolino/Ven-A-Mi	1955	$25
EP363	*Melody of Love/Cocktails for Two/Blue Moon/Remember	1955	$25
EP205	*Moonglow/For You/Blip Boogie/Wrap It Up	1953	$30
EP-416	*Night Train/Stompin' at the Savoy/Honeysuckle Rose/No Name Jive	1958	$25
EP207	*Serenade/Ain't Misbehavin'/Smoke Rings/Steamwhistle Jump	1953	$30
EP-405	*She's Funny That Way/How Deep Is the Ocean/Avalon/September Song	1958	$25
EP201	*Sleep/Earl's Imagination/Lover Come Back to Me/I'm Gettin' Sentimental Over You	1953	$30
EP-406	*Temptation/Sweet Lorraine/Away/Exercise	1958	$25
EP-420 [PS]	Alto Magic in Hi Fi, Vol. 1	1958	$25
EP-421 [PS]	Alto Magic in Hi Fi, Vol. 2	1958	$25
EP-422 [PS]	Alto Magic in Hi Fi, Vol. 3	1958	$25
EP-406 [PS]	Alto-Tude	1958	$25
KEP350	Blue Skies/Ubangi Stomp//Song of the Islands/These Foolish Things	1955	$25
EP381 [PS]	Bostic Blows, Vol. 17	1956	$25
EP-410 [PS]	Bostic Plays	1958	$25
EP-422	C Jam Blues/Wee-Gee Board//The Wrecking Rock/Home Sweet Home Rock	1958	$25
EP-417	(contents unknown)	1958	$25
EP-421	(contents unknown)	1958	$25
EP-419	(contents unknown)	1958	$25
KEP398 [PS]	Earl Bostic, Vol. 18	1957	$25
EP201 [PS]	Earl Bostic and His Alto Sax, Vol. 2	1953	$30
EP202 [PS]	Earl Bostic and His Alto Sax, Vol. 3	1953	$30
EP203 [PS]	Earl Bostic and His Alto Sax, Vol. 4	1953	$30
EP204 [PS]	Earl Bostic and His Alto Sax, Vol. 5	1953	$30
EP205 [PS]	Earl Bostic and His Alto Sax, Vol. 6	1953	$30
EP206 [PS]	Earl Bostic and His Alto Sax, Vol. 7	1953	$30
EP207 [PS]	Earl Bostic and His Alto Sax, Vol. 8	1953	$30
EP245 [PS]	Earl Bostic and His Alto Sax, Vol. 9	1954	$25
EP284 [PS]	Earl Bostic and His Alto Sax, Vol. 10	1954	$25
EP285 [PS]	Earl Bostic and His Alto Sax, Vol. 11	1954	$25
EP347 [PS]	Earl Bostic and His Alto Sax, Vol. 12	1955	$25
EP355 [PS]	Earl Bostic and His Alto Sax, Vol. 14	1955	$25
EP363 [PS]	Earl Bostic and His Alto Sax, Vol. 15	1955	$25
EP-405 [PS]	Earl Bostic Dance Time	1958	$25
EP-409 [PS]	Earl Bostic for Listening and Dancing	1958	$25
EP375 [PS]	Earl Bostic with Strings, Vol. 16	1956	$25
KEP398	Harlem Nocturne/I Hear a Rhapsody//Roses of Picardy/Where or When	1957	$25
EP-414 [PS]	Hits of the Swing Age, Vol. 1	1958	$25
EP-415 [PS]	Hits of the Swing Age, Vol. 2	1958	$25
EP-416 [PS]	Hits of the Swing Age, Vol. 3	1958	$25
EP-445	I Cover the Waterfront//In the Still of the Night/The Thrill Is Gone/The Night Is Young	1959	$20
EP245	Melancholy Serenade/What! No Pearls//The Very Thought of You/Memories	1954	$25
EP-417 [PS]	Showcase of Swinging Dance Hits, Vol. 1	1958	$25
EP-418 [PS]	Showcase of Swinging Dance Hits, Vol. 2	1958	$25
EP-419 [PS]	Showcase of Swinging Dance Hits, Vol. 3	1958	$25
EP-445 [PS]	Sweet Tunes of the Swinging 30s, Volume 1	1959	$20
KEP350 [PS]	The Artistry of Earl Bostic, Vol. 13	1955	$25
EP-420	Twilight Time/Stairway to the Stars//Rockin' with Richard/Be My Love	1958	$25
EP-418	Two O'Clock Jump//Back Beat//John's Idea/Royal Garden Blues	1958	$25

BOSTIC, SAM
ATLANTIC

Number	Title	Yr	NM
89581	Cold Tears/Built for Love	1985	$3
89544	Women Out There Waiting/(B-side unknown)	1985	$3

BOSTICK, CALVIN
CHESS

Number	Title	Yr	NM
1530	Christmas Won't Be Christmas Without You/Four-Eleven Boogie	1952	$200

BOSTON
EPIC

Number	Title	Yr	NM
8-50638	A Man I'll Never Be/Don't Be Afraid	1978	$4
8-50590	Don't Look Back/The Journey	1978	$4
8-50677	Feelin' Satisfied/Used to Bad News	1979	$4
8-50329	Long Time/Let Me Take You Home Tonight	1976	$4
15-02355	More Than a Feeling/Long Time	1981	$3

— Golden Oldies" reissue

Number	Title	Yr	NM
8-50266	More Than a Feeling/Smokin'	1976	$4
15-02365	Peace of Mind/Don't Look Back	1981	$3

— Golden Oldies" reissue

Number	Title	Yr	NM
8-50381	Peace of Mind/Foreplay	1977	$4

MCA

Number	Title	Yr	NM
52756	Amanda/My Destination	1986	$3
52756 [PS]	Amanda/My Destination	1986	$3
53029	Can'tcha Say (You Believe in Me)/Still in Love//Cool the Engines	1987	$3
53029 [PS]	Can'tcha Say (You Believe in Me)/Still in Love//Cool the Engines	1987	$3
53114	Hollyann/To Be a Man	1987	$3
53114 [PS]	Hollyann/To Be a Man	1987	$4
52985	We're Ready/The Launch	1986	$3
52985 [PS]	We're Ready/The Launch	1986	$3

BOSTON CRABS, THE
CAPITOL

Number	Title	Yr	NM
5493	Down in Mexico/Who?	1965	$12

TOWER

Number	Title	Yr	NM
368	Gin House/Leave My Woman Alone	1967	$10

BOSTON POPS ORCHESTRA (FIEDLER)
RCA VICTOR

Number	Title	Yr	NM
49-0515	Sleigh Ride/Serenata	1949	$40

— Originals on red vinyl

Number	Title	Yr	NM
KO7W-1589 [DJ]	White Christmas/(B-side unknown)	1959	$20
WEPR5	Der Rosenkavalier: Waltzes/Faust: Waltzes	1952	$25

— Red vinyl

BOTKIN, PERRY, JR.
A&M

Number	Title	Yr	NM
1990	Bridges/Love Theme from Aspen	1977	$4
1967	Looking for Home/Lovers	1977	$4

DECCA

Number	Title	Yr	NM
30912	The Execution Theme/Waltz of the Hunter	1959	$15

MGM

Number	Title	Yr	NM
14379	Bless the Beasts and Children/Lost	1972	$5
14357	Soley Soley/(B-side unknown)	1972	$5

— As "Perry Botkin, Inc.

VALIANT

Number	Title	Yr	NM
6025	Careless Love/Wabash Cannonball	1962	$10
719	Where Does Love Go (Instrumental)/Where Does Love Go (Vocal)	1965	$8

— B-side by Charles Boyer

BOUCHER, PEGI
HIBACK

Number	Title	Yr	NM
101	The Christmas Clock/Christmas Tree Heaven	1966	$8
101 [PS]	The Christmas Clock/Christmas Tree Heaven	1966	$20

BOUGALIEU
ROULETTE

Number	Title	Yr	NM
4767	Let's Do Wrong/When I Was a Child	1967	$30
4776	Let's Do Wrong/When I Was a Child	1967	$20

BOUQUETS
BLUE CAT

Number	Title	Yr	NM
115	Welcome to My Heart/Ain't That Love	1965	$40

MALA

Number	Title	Yr	NM
472	I Love Him So/No Love at All	1964	$20

BOURGEOIS TAGG
ISLAND

Number	Title	Yr	NM
99372	Cry Like a Baby/15 Minutes in the Sun	1988	$3
99372 [PS]	Cry Like a Baby/15 Minutes in the Sun	1988	$4
99409	I Don't Mind at All/Pencil & Paper	1987	$3
99558	Mutual Surrender (What a Wonderful World)/The Move Up	1986	$3
99521	The Perfect Life/Electric Train	1986	$3
99331	Waiting for the World to Turn/Coma	1988	$3

BOW WOW WOW
RCA

Number	Title	Yr	NM
PB-13291	Baby, Oh No/Cowboy	1982	$5
PB-13291 [PS]	Baby, Oh No/Cowboy	1982	$6
PB-12338	Chihuahua/Golly! Golly! Go Buddy!	1981	$5
PB-12338 [PS]	Chihuahua/Golly! Golly! Go Buddy!	1981	$6
PB-13467	Do You Wanna Hold Me?/What's the Time (Hey Buddy)	1983	$4
PB-13204	I Want Candy/Elimination Dancing	1982	$5
PB-13204 [PS]	I Want Candy/Elimination Dancing	1982	$6
PB-13060	Orang-Outang/Mickey, Put It Down	1982	$5
PB-13060 [PS]	Orang-Outang/Mickey, Put It Down	1982	$6

STUDIO 54

Number	Title	Yr	NM
0 (no cat #) [DJ]	The Mile High Club/C-30. C-60, C-90, Go!	1981	$30

— Promo given out at a show

BOWEN, BILL
METEOR

Number	Title	Yr	NM
5033	Have Myself a Ball/Don't Shoot Me Baby	1956	$2000

BOWEN, JIMMY
CAPEHART

Number	Title	Yr	NM
5005	Teenage Dreamworld/It's Against the Law	1962	$30
5005 [PS]	Teenage Dreamworld/It's Against the Law	1962	$60

Number	Title	Yr	NM
CREST			
❏ 1085	Don't Drop It/Somebody to Love	1961	$30
REPRISE			
❏ 0264	The Biggest Lover in Town/The Big Bus	1964	$12
❏ 0358	The Golden Eagle/Spanish Cricket	1965	$10
❏ 0450	Wonder Mother/Captain Gorgeous	1966	$10
ROULETTE			
❏ 4122	Always Faithful/Wish I Were Tied to You	1958	$30
❏ 4083	By the Light of the Silvery Moon/The Two Step	1958	$30
❏ 4057	Can She Kiss/Keeping You	1958	$30
❏ 4023	Cross Over/It's Shameful	1957	$30
❏ 4017	Ever Since That Night/Don't Tell Me Your Troubles	1957	$30
❏ 4001	I'm Stickin' With You/Ever Lovin' Fingers	1957	$30
— With the Rhythm Orchids			
❏ 4102	My Kind of Woman/Blue Moon	1958	$30
❏ 4224	Oh Yeah! Oh Yeah! Mm Mm/Your Loving Arms	1960	$30
❏ 4010	Warm Up to Me Baby/I Trusted You	1957	$30
TRIPLE D			
❏ 798	I'm Stickin' With You/Party Doll	1956	$1000
— B-side by Buddy Knox			

7-Inch Extended Plays

ROULETTE

Number	Title	Yr	NM
❏ EPR-1-302	I'm Stickin' with You/Warm Up to Me Baby//Raggedy Anne/Ever Since That Night	1957	$250

BOWERS, GEORGE
NTM

Number	Title	Yr	NM
❏ 001	Christopher the Christmas Tree/Lonely Christmas	1971	$8

PARAMOUNT

Number	Title	Yr	NM
❏ 0139	Christopher the Christmas Tree/Lonely Christmas	1971	$6

BOWERS, KENNY
COLUMBIA

Number	Title	Yr	NM
❏ 41049	Weach For The Wafter, Santa/An Ax, An Apple And A Buckskin Jacket	1957	$20

BOWES, MARGIE
DECCA

Number	Title	Yr	NM
❏ 31708	Big City/Watch Me Fall	1964	$8
❏ 31907	Look Who's Lonely/That Completely Destroys My Plans	1966	$8
❏ 31838	Lost/I Can't Love That Way	1965	$8
❏ 32158	Making Believe/A Man Around the House	1967	$8
❏ 31557	Our Things/There's Gotta Be a Way	1963	$8
❏ 32014	Part Time Baby, Full Time Fool/It's Enough to Make a Woman Lose Her Mind	1966	$8
❏ 31644	What In This World (Am I Gonna Do)/Overnight	1964	$8

HICKORY

Number	Title	Yr	NM
❏ 1135	Are You Teasing Me/Judge Not	1960	$20
❏ 1124	Day After Day/Don't Turn On the Lights	1960	$20
❏ 1112	Make a Wish/They Just Don't Know You	1960	$20
❏ 1102	My Love and Little Me/Sweet Night of Love	1959	$20
❏ 1094	Poor Old Heartsick Me/Blue Dream	1959	$20
❏ 1084	Won'cha Come Back to Me/One Broken Heart	1958	$30

MERCURY

Number	Title	Yr	NM
❏ 71897	Always Remember/Lonely Pillow	1961	$10
❏ 71845	Little Miss Belong to No One/Bitter Sweet Kisses	1961	$12
❏ 72090	Think It Over/Within Your Crowd	1963	$10

BOWIE, DAVID, AND MICK JAGGER
EMI AMERICA

Number	Title	Yr	NM
❏ B-8288	Dancing in the Street/(Instrumental)	1985	$3
❏ B-8288 [PS]	Dancing in the Street/(Instrumental)	1985	$3

BOWIE, DAVID
BACKSTREET

Number	Title	Yr	NM
❏ 52024	Cat People (Putting Out Fire)/Paul's Theme (Jogging Chase)	1982	$3
— B-side by Georgio Moroder			
❏ 52024 [PS]	Cat People (Putting Out Fire)/Paul's Theme (Jogging Chase)	1982	$3

DERAM

Number	Title	Yr	NM
❏ 85016	Love You Till Tuesday/Did You Ever Have a Dream	1967	$125

EMI AMERICA

Number	Title	Yr	NM
❏ B-8308	Absolute Beginners/(Dub Mix)	1986	$3
❏ B-8308 [PS]	Absolute Beginners/(Dub Mix)	1986	$4
❏ B-8231	Blue Jean/Dancin' with the Big Boys	1984	$6
— First pressing on blue vinyl			
❏ B-8231	Blue Jean/Dancin' with the Big Boys	1984	$3
— Second pressing on black vinyl			
❏ B-8231 [PS]	Blue Jean/Dancin' with the Big Boys	1984	$3
— Both colors of vinyl have the same picture sleeve			
❏ B-8165	China Girl/Shake It	1983	$3
❏ B-8165 [PS]	China Girl/Shake It	1983	$6
❏ B-8380	Day In Day Out/Julie	1987	$3
❏ B-8380 [PS]	Day In Day Out/Julie	1987	$4
❏ B-8158	Let's Dance/Cat People (Putting Out Fire)	1983	$3
❏ B-8158 [PS]	Let's Dance/Cat People (Putting Out Fire)	1983	$3
❏ BG-8271	Loving the Alien/Don't Look Down	1985	$3
❏ BG-8271 [PS]	Loving the Alien/Don't Look Down	1985	$5
— Gatefold sleeve			
❏ B-8177	Modern Love/Modern Love (Live)	1983	$3
❏ B-8177 [PS]	Modern Love/Modern Love (Live)	1983	$3
❏ B-8251	This Is Not America/(Instrumental)	1984	$3
— With the Pat Metheny Group			
❏ B-8251 [PS]	This Is Not America/(Instrumental)	1984	$3
❏ B-43020	Time Will Crawl/Girls	1987	$3
❏ B-43020 [PS]	Time Will Crawl/Girls	1987	$20
❏ B-8246	Tonight/Tumble and Twirl	1984	$3
❏ B-8246 [PS]	Tonight/Tumble and Twirl	1984	$6
— Fold-out poster sleeve			
❏ B-8190	Without You/Criminal World	1984	$3
❏ B-8190 [PS]	Without You/Criminal World	1984	$3

LONDON

Number	Title	Yr	NM
❏ 20079	The Laughing Gnome/The Gospel According to Tony Day	1973	$60

MERCURY

Number	Title	Yr	NM
❏ 73173 [DJ]	All the Madmen (mono/stereo)	1971	$125
— May be promo only			
❏ 73173 [DJ]	All the Madmen (mono/stereo)	1971	$200
— May be promo only			
❏ 73075	Memory of a Free Festival Part 1/Part 2	1970	$200
❏ 72949	Space Oddity/Wild-Eyed Boy from Freecloud	1969	$60

RCA

Number	Title	Yr	NM
❏ PB-13769	1984/TVC 15	1984	$5
❏ PB-13769 [PS]	1984/TVC 15	1984	$6
❏ PB-12078	Ashes to Ashes/It's No Game	1980	$5
❏ PB-11190	Beauty and the Beast/Sense of Doubt	1978	$8
❏ PB-11017	Be My Wife/The Speed of Life	1977	$8
❏ PB-11585	Boys Keep Swinging/Fantastic Voyage	1979	$6
❏ PB-11661	D.J./Fantastic Voyage	1979	$8
❏ GB-10938	Fame/Golden Years	1977	$3
— Gold Standard Series issue			
❏ JE-12087 [DJ]	Fashion/It's No Game/Teenage Wildlife	1980	$400
❏ JE-12087 [DJ]	Fashion/It's No Game/Teenage Wildlife	1980	$400
❏ PB-12134	Fashion/Scream Like a Baby	1980	$5
❏ PB-11121	Heroes/V-2 Schneider	1977	$8
❏ PB-11724	Look Back in Anger/Repetition	1979	$6
❏ PH-13400	Peace on Earth-Little Drummer Boy/Fantastic Voyage	1982	$5
— A-side with Bing Crosby			
❏ PH-13400 [PS]	Peace on Earth-Little Drummer Boy/Fantastic Voyage	1982	$10
— A-side with Bing Crosby			

Number	Title	Yr	NM
❏ PB-10905	Sound and Vision/A New Career in a New Town	1977	$6
❏ PB-10736	Stay/Word on a Wing	1976	$6
❏ PB-10664	TVC 15/We Are the Dead	1976	$6
❏ PB-13660	White Light-White Heat/Cracked Actor	1983	$5
❏ PB-13660 [PS]	White Light-White Heat/Cracked Actor	1983	$5

RCA VICTOR

Number	Title	Yr	NM
❏ PB-10026	1984/Queen Bitch	1974	$6
❏ 74-0605	Changes/Andy Warhol	1971	$10
— Orange label (original)			
❏ 74-0605	Changes/Andy Warhol	1974	$6
— Tan or gray label			
❏ GB-10468	Changes/Andy Warhol	1975	$4
— Gold Standard Series issue			
❏ APBO-0293	Diamond Dogs/Holy Holy	1974	$12
— Part of U.S. numbering system, but released only outside the U.S.			
❏ JB-10320 [DJ]	Fame (Long Version 4:12)/(Short Version 3:30)	1975	$15
— Promo-only edition; stock copies contain the 3:30 version			
❏ PB-10320	Fame/Right	1975	$6
— Tan label (Indianapolis pressing)			
❏ PB-10320	Fame/Right	1975	$6
— Orange label (West Coast pressing)			
❏ PB-10441	Golden Years/Can You Hear Me	1975	$6
❏ APBO-0028	Let's Spend the Night Together/Lady Grinning Soul	1973	$6
❏ APBO-0160	Sorrow/Amsterdam	1973	$6
❏ 74-0876	Space Oddity/The Man Who Sold the World	1973	$6
❏ 74-0876 [PS]	Space Oddity/The Man Who Sold the World	1973	$30
❏ GB-10470	Space Oddity/The Man Who Sold the World	1975	$4
— Gold Standard Series issue			
❏ 74-0719	Starman/Suffragette City	1972	$6
❏ 74-0719 [PS]	Starman/Suffragette City	1972	$40
❏ APBO-0001	Time/The Prettiest Star	1973	$6
❏ APBO-0001 [PS]	Time/The Prettiest Star	1973	$8000

WARNER BROS.

Number	Title	Yr	NM
❏ 5815	Can't Stop Thinking About Me/And I Say to Myself	1966	$400
— As "David Bowie and the Lower Third"			

7-Inch Extended Plays

RCA VICTOR

Number	Title	Yr	NM
❏ 45-103 [DJ]	David Bowie	1972	$25
❏ 45-103 [PS]	David Bowie	1972	$35
❏ 45-103 [DJ]	Space Oddity/Moonage Daydream//Life on Mars?/It Ain't Easy	1972	$35

BOWLES, RICK
POLYDOR

Number	Title	Yr	NM
❏ 2216	Fool Again/Your Loss	1982	$4
❏ 2209	Too Good to Turn Back Now/Mr. Right	1982	$4

BOWLING, ROGER
MERCURY

Number	Title	Yr	NM
❏ 57049	A Little Bit of Heaven/She Can't Break It to Her Heart	1981	$4
❏ 76135	More Than I Used To/(B-side unknown)	1982	$4

NSD

Number	Title	Yr	NM
❏ 37	Friday Night Fool/There'll Never Be a Love Song	1980	$5
❏ 144	Good Bartender/I've Got to Break the Bottle	1983	$5
❏ 149	Hangout for Your Memory/Then I'll Stop Loving You	1983	$5
❏ 50	I Can't Get Over You/Dig a Little Deeper in the Well	1980	$5
❏ 58	Long Arm of the Law/I Can't Get Over You	1980	$5
❏ 46	The Diplomat/I'm Looking for a Lonely Woman	1980	$5

UNITED ARTISTS

Number	Title	Yr	NM
❏ XW803	I Don't Stand a Chance Anyway/You've Got a Lovin' Comin'	1976	$5
❏ XW715	I Want to See You One More Time/Juke Box Girl	1975	$5

Number	Title	Yr	NM

BOWLING, SHELL
SOUNDWAVES
❏ 4690	Christmas Time Is Coming/ Born on Christmas Day	1982	$5

BOWMAN, CECIL
D
❏ 1085	Curse of Wine/Cotton	1959	$30
❏ 1110	Sweet Cakes and Kisses/ Tea Leaves Don't Lie	1960	$30
❏ 1145	Whispering Lips/Most Beautiful	1960	$30

BOWMAN, DON
MEGA
❏ 0062	Hello D.J. (Part 1)/ Hello D.J. (Part 2)	1972	$6

RCA VICTOR
❏ 47-8384	Chit Atkins, Make Me a Star/I Never Did Finish That Song	1964	$10
❏ 47-8670	Dear Harlan Howard/ Freddy Four Toes	1965	$12
❏ 47-9617	Folsom Prison Blues #2/ House of the Setting Sun	1968	$8
❏ 47-8811	Giddyup Do-nut/Freda on the Freeway	1966	$8
❏ 47-8588	Graduation Day/The Wrong House	1965	$10
❏ 47-8506	I Fell Out of Love with Love/The World's Worst Guitar Picker	1965	$10
❏ 47-9949	I Owe It All to Chet Atkins/Another Puff	1971	$8
❏ 74-0133	Poor Old Ugly Gladys Jones/ The Boll Weevil Air Lives	1969	$8
❏ 47-9576	San Francisco Scene/ Messin' Up My Mind	1968	$8
❏ 47-8990	Surely Not/Dear Sister	1966	$8
❏ 47-8916	The All American Boy/I Get the Feeling We're Through	1966	$8
❏ 47-9290	Tijuana Drum and Bugle Corps/Little Leroy	1967	$8
❏ 47-9783	Top Ten/How Come It Is	1969	$8
❏ 47-9176	What Kind of Fool Am I/ My Voice Is Changing	1967	$8

BOWMAN, JIMMY
SOMA
❏ 1152	Big Red And Cool Yule/ Portrait Of Jenny	1960	$30

BOWSER, DONNIE
BAMBOO
❏ 508	Talk to Me Baby/Tomorrow	1961	$20

DESS
❏ 7004	I Love You Baby/Love So Rare	1957	$50

— As "Little Donnie Bowshier"

ERA
❏ 3029	I Love You Baby/Stone Heart	1960	$20

FRATERNITY
❏ 801	I Love You Baby/Stone Heart	1958	$100

PLAYBACK
❏ 1342	Another One of My Near Mrs./(B-side unknown)	1989	$6

— With Bobby Bare

RIDGEWOOD
❏ 3002	Falling for You/You've Got My Arms to Come Back To	1989	$6

ROBBINS
❏ 1009	I Love You Baby/Stone Heart	1958	$200

SAGE
❏ 274	Got the Best of Me/It's Our Secret	1959	$30
❏ 259	I Love You Baby/Love So Rare	1958	$30

— As "Donnie Bowshier"

❏ 265	I Love You Baby/Stone Heart	1958	$30

BOX TOPS, THE
ARISTA
❏ 9488	Sweet Cream Ladies/ Neon Rainbow	1986	$3

— "Flashback" oldies series

BELL
❏ 865	Come On Honey/You Keep Tightening Up on Me	1970	$8
❏ 923	Let Me Go/Got to Hold on to You	1970	$8

GUSTO
❏ 2112	The Letter/Cry Like a Baby	1981	$4

— Re-recordings

HI
❏ 2242	Hold On Girl/Angel	1973	$6
❏ 2228	It's All Over/Sugar Creek Woman	1972	$6

MALA
❏ 12005	Choo Choo Train/Fields of Clover	1968	$10
❏ 593	Cry Like a Baby/The Door You Closed to Me	1968	$15
❏ 12017	I Met Her in Church/ People Gonna Talk	1968	$10
❏ 12038	I Shall Be Released/I Must Be the Devil	1969	$10
❏ 12040	Soul Deep/The Happy Song	1969	$12
❏ 12035	Sweet Cream Ladies, Forward March/I See Only Sunshine	1968	$10
❏ 565	The Letter/Happy Times	1967	$15
❏ 12042	Turn On a Dream/Together	1969	$10

PHILCO-FORD
❏ HP-27	The Letter/Happy Times	1968	$30

— 4-inch plastic "Hip Pocket Record" with color sleeve

SPHERE SOUND
❏ 77002	Cry Like a Baby/The Door You Closed to Me	1970	$8

— Silver label; reissue

❏ 77001	The Letter/Happy Times	1969	$10

— Blue label; reissue

❏ 77001	The Letter/Happy Times	1970	$8

— Silver label; reissue

STAX
❏ 0199	It's Gonna Be O.K./ Willobee and Dale	1974	$6

BOXCAR WILLIE
❏ 1012	Train Medley/Lonesome Hobo	1980	$8

ELEKTRA
❏ 69937	The Stage/Fireball Mail	1982	$5

— B-side by Roy Acuff

MAIN STREET
❏ 951	Bad News/Lefty Left Us Lonely	1982	$5
❏ 950	Boxcar Blues/Don't Let the Stars Get in Your Eyes	1981	$5
❏ 954	Country Music Nightmare/ Train Medley	1983	$5
❏ 953	Last Train to Heaven/Keep On Rollin' Down the Line	1982	$5
❏ 93021	Luther/Luther (Long Version)	1984	$5
❏ (# unk)	T for Texas/Hobo's Lament	1983	$8

— Gold vinyl

❏ (# unk) [PS]	T for Texas/Hobo's Lament	1983	$10

— Sleeve calls this "Tribute to Jimmie Rodgers"

❏ 93017	The Man I Used to Be/ No More Trains to Ride	1983	$5
❏ 952	We Made Memories/To My Baby I'm a Big Star All the Time	1982	$5

— A-side with Penny DeHaven

❏ 93023	Whine, Whistle, Whine/ Hobo's Lament	1984	$5

ROTO
❏ 7493-1	Boxcar Willie/(B-side unknown)	1976	$40

— As "Marty Martin and the Rangers"; the song from which he took his stage name

BOXER, KARL
DOT
❏ 16853	Hava Nagila/A Piece of the Action	1966	$30

BOY GEORGE
Also see CULTURE CLUB.
VIRGIN
❏ 99272	Don't Take My Mind on a Trip/Girlfriend	1988	$3
❏ 99445	Everything I Own/Use Me	1987	$4
❏ 99445 [PS]	Everything I Own/Use Me	1987	$6
❏ 99390	Live My Life (The Mix)/ (Soul Remix)	1987	$3
❏ 99159	Whisper/Leave in Love	1989	$4

BOY MEETS GIRL
A&M
❏ 2750	Don't Tell Me We Have Nothing/I Wish You Were Here	1985	$4
❏ 2713	Oh Girl/Kissing, Falling, Flying	1985	$3
❏ 2713 [PS]	Oh Girl/Kissing, Falling, Flying	1985	$4
❏ 2741	The Touch/Pieces	1985	$4

RCA
❏ 8807-7-R	Bring Down the Moon/ Restless Dreamer	1989	$3
❏ 8807-7-R [PS]	Bring Down the Moon/ Restless Dreamer	1989	$3
❏ 8691-7-R	Waiting for a Star to Fall/ No Apologies	1988	$3
❏ 8691-7-R [PS]	Waiting for a Star to Fall/ No Apologies	1988	$3

BOYCE, TOMMY, AND BOBBY HART
A&M
❏ 948	Alice Long (You're Still My Favorite Girlfriend)/P.O. Box 9847	1968	$10
❏ 948 [PS]	Alice Long (You're Still My Favorite Girlfriend)/P.O. Box 9847	1968	$30
❏ 919	Goodbye Baby (I Don't Want to See You Cry)/Where Angels Go, Trouble Follows	1968	$10
❏ 919 [PS]	Goodbye Baby (I Don't Want to See You Cry)/Where Angels Go, Trouble Follows	1968	$30
❏ 893	I Wonder What She's Doing Tonight/The Ambushers	1967	$15
❏ 893 [PS]	I Wonder What She's Doing Tonight/The Ambushers	1967	$30
❏ 1031	L.U.V. (Let Us Vote)/I Wanna Be Free	1969	$8
❏ 1031 [PS]	L.U.V. (Let Us Vote)/I Wanna Be Free	1969	$20
❏ 1017	Maybe Somebody Heard/It's All Happening on the Inside	1969	$8
❏ 858	Out and About/My Little Chickadee	1967	$10
❏ 858 [PS]	Out and About/My Little Chickadee	1967	$30
❏ 874	Sometimes She's a Little Girl/Love Every Day	1967	$12
❏ 874 [PS]	Sometimes She's a Little Girl/Love Every Day	1967	$30
❏ 993	We're All Going to the Same Place/6 + 6	1968	$10
❏ 993 [PS]	We're All Going to the Same Place/6 + 6	1968	$10

AQUARIAN
❏ 380	I'll Blow You a Kiss in the Wind/Smilin'	1970	$4
❏ 380 [PS]	I'll Blow You a Kiss in the Wind/Smilin'	1970	$6

BOYCE, TOMMY
A&M
❏ 826	In Case the Wind Should Blow/Simon Smith and the Amazing Dancing Bear	1966	$30
❏ 809	Sunday, The Day Before Monday/The Green Grass (Is Turning Brown)	1966	$20

CAPITOL
❏ 3136	Alice My Sweet/Eve Laurain	1971	$5

CHELSEA
❏ BCBO-0101	Thank God for Rock and Roll/Krush on Kris	1973	$5

— As "Christopher Cloud"

COLPIX
❏ 794	Let's Go Where the Action Is/(Instrumental)	1966	$30

DOT
❏ 16117	The Gypsy Song/ Give Me the Clue	1960	$30

MGM
❏ 13429	Little Suzy Somethin'/ Pee's N' Que's	1965	$20
❏ 13400	Pretty Thing (You Look Out of Sight Tonight)/I Don't Have to Worry 'Bout You	1965	$20

RCA VICTOR
❏ 47-7975	Along Came Linda/ You Look So Lonely	1961	$30
❏ 47-8025	Come Here Joanne/The Way I Used to Do	1962	$30
❏ 47-8208	Don't Be Afraid/A Million Things to Say	1963	$30
❏ 47-8126	Have You Had a Change of Heart/Sweet Little Baby, I Care	1963	$30
❏ 47-8074	I'll Remember Carol/ Too Late for Tears	1962	$30

R-DELL
❏ 111	Betty Jean/I'm Not Sure	1960	$30

WOW
❏ 345	Is It True/Little One	1961	$30

BOYD, BILL, AND HIS COWBOY RAMBLERS
RCA VICTOR
❏ 48-0208	Bandera Waltz/Letters Have No Arms	1950	$50

— Originals on green vinyl

Number	Title	Yr	NM
❏ 48-0067	Blue Danube Waltz/Varsoviana	1949	$50

— Originals on green vinyl

Number	Title	Yr	NM
❏ 48-0335	Come and Get It/Red River Rag	1950	$50

— Originals on green vinyl

Number	Title	Yr	NM
❏ 48-0449	Drifting Texas Sand/Stop Polka	1951	$40
❏ 48-0410	Mean, Mean, Mean/Cuckoo Waltz	1950	$40
❏ 48-0112	Poison Ivy/Pass the Turnip Greens	1949	$50

— Originals on green vinyl

Number	Title	Yr	NM
❏ 48-0172	Texas Blues/Yes You Did	1950	$50

— Originals on green vinyl

Number	Title	Yr	NM
❏ 48-0351	Why Don't You Love Me/Red Lips Kiss My Blues Away	1950	$50

— Originals on green vinyl

Number	Title	Yr	NM
❏ 48-0482	Why Do You Punish Me/Gladiola Waltz	1951	$40

STARDAY

Number	Title	Yr	NM
❏ 289	Big D/Texas Star	1957	$30
❏ 303	Lone Star Rag/Ramblers March	1957	$30

BOYD, EDDIE
ART TONE

Number	Title	Yr	NM
❏ 832	I'm Comin' Home/Operator	1962	$20

BEA & BABY

Number	Title	Yr	NM
❏ 107	Blue Monday Blues/The Blues Is Here to Stay	1959	$20
❏ 108	Come Home/You've Got to Reap What You Sow	1959	$20
❏ 101	I'm Comin' Home/Thank You Baby	1959	$20

CHESS

Number	Title	Yr	NM
❏ 1533	24 Hours/The Tickler	1953	$125

— Black vinyl

Number	Title	Yr	NM
❏ 1533	24 Hours/The Tickler	1953	$400

— Red vinyl

Number	Title	Yr	NM
❏ 1523	Cool Kind Treatment/Rosa Lee Swing	1952	$125
❏ 1621	Don't/Life Gets to Be a Burden	1956	$50
❏ 1576	Driftin'/Rattin' and Runnin' Around	1954	$70
❏ 1573	Hush Baby, Don't You Cry/Came Home This Morning	1954	$70
❏ 1660	I Got a Woman/Hotel Blues	1957	$50
❏ 1674	I Got the Blues/She's the One	1957	$50
❏ 1606	I'm a Prisoner/I've Been Deceived	1955	$60
❏ 1552	That's When I Miss You So/Tortured Soul	1953	$100
❏ 1582	The Story of Bill/Please Help Me	1954	$70
❏ 1541	Third Degree/Back Beat	1953	$200

— Black vinyl

Number	Title	Yr	NM
❏ 1541	Third Degree/Back Beat	1953	$500

— Red vinyl

HERALD

Number	Title	Yr	NM
❏ 406	Lonesome for My Baby/I'm Goin' Downtown	1953	$400

J.O.B.

Number	Title	Yr	NM
❏ 1007	Five Long Years/Blue Coat Man	1952	$200

— Black vinyl

Number	Title	Yr	NM
❏ 1007	Five Long Years/Blue Coat Man	1952	$300

— Red vinyl

Number	Title	Yr	NM
❏ 1114	I Love You/Save Her Doctor	1957	$70
❏ 1009	It's Miserable to Be Alone/I'm Pleading	1953	$300

RCA VICTOR

Number	Title	Yr	NM
❏ 50-0006	What Makes These Things Happen/Chicago Is Just That Way	1950	$120

— Gray label, orange vinyl

BOYD, JIM
RCA VICTOR

Number	Title	Yr	NM
❏ 48-0353	Bear Creek Boogie/The Girl in the Picture	1950	$40

— Originals on green vinyl

Number	Title	Yr	NM
❏ 48-0443	Boogie Bottom Boogie/Dear John	1951	$30
❏ 47-4263	Boogie Woogie Square Dance/Texas Moon Waltz	1951	$30
❏ 48-0047	Dear John/One Heart, One Love	1949	$50

— Originals on green vinyl

Number	Title	Yr	NM
❏ 48-0383	Dixieland Boogie/I Got Along Without You	1950	$40

— Originals on green vinyl

Number	Title	Yr	NM
❏ 48-0093	Dust on My Telephone/Save the Next Waltz for Me	1949	$50

— Originals on green vinyl

Number	Title	Yr	NM
❏ 48-0301	Mule Boogie/We Were Married	1950	$40

— Originals on green vinyl

Number	Title	Yr	NM
❏ 48-0159	Sweetheart of Hawaii/Truck Driver's Boogie	1950	$50

— Originals on green vinyl

Number	Title	Yr	NM
❏ 48-0475	Take Time to Pray/Will You Be Mine	1951	$30
❏ 48-0418	The Big D Boogie/From Here On	1951	$30
❏ 48-0455	Waxahachie Dishwasher Boy/When I'm Beside You	1951	$30
❏ 48-0031	We Were Married/Mule Boogie	1949	$50

— Originals on green vinyl

BOYD, JIMMY
CAPITOL

Number	Title	Yr	NM
❏ 4967	Day Dreamer/I've Got It Made	1963	$12

COLUMBIA

Number	Title	Yr	NM
❏ 41547	Dennis the Menace/Little Josey	1960	$30

— With Rosemary Clooney

Number	Title	Yr	NM
❏ 40756	Don't Forget to Say Your Prayers/Little Dog	1956	$15
❏ 39927	Early Bird/I'll Stay in the House	1953	$20
❏ 39696	God's Little Candles/Owl Lullaby	1952	$20
❏ 40218	I'm So Glad (I'm a Little Boy and You're a Little Girl)/Kitty in the Basket	1954	$20

— With Gayla Peevey

Number	Title	Yr	NM
❏ 40365	I Saw Mommy Do the Mambo (With You Know Who)/Santa Claus Blues	1954	$20
❏ 40070	I Saw Mommy Kissing Santa Claus/Santa Claus Is Coming to Town	1953	$15
❏ 39871	I Saw Mommy Kissing Santa Claus/Thumbelina	1952	$20
❏ 4-152	I Saw Mommy Kissing Santa Claus/Thumbelina	1952	$30

— Yellow-label Children's Series issue; alternate number is 90174

Number	Title	Yr	NM
❏ 4-152 [PS]	I Saw Mommy Kissing Santa Claus/Thumbelina	1952	$30
❏ 40138	I've Got Those "Wake Up Seven-Thirty, Wash Your Ears They're Dirty, Eat Your Eggs and Oatmeal, Rush to School" Blues/Jelly on My Head	1954	$30
❏ 40881	I Wanna Go Steady/Gonna Take My Heart on a Hayride	1957	$15
❏ 40504	I Want a Haircut with a Moon on Top/How Come	1955	$15
❏ 40181	Little Bonny Bunny/Jimmy, Roll Me Gently	1954	$20
❏ 40304	Little Sir Echo/The Little White Duck	1954	$20
❏ 39733	Little Train A-Chuggin'/Needle In, Needle Out	1952	$20
❏ 40253	Ma I Miss Your Apple Pie/Shepherd Boy	1954	$20
❏ 40049	Marco, the Polo Pony/God Bless Us All	1953	$20
❏ 39955	My Bunny and My Sister Sue/Two Easter Sunday Sweethearts	1953	$20
❏ 40007	Playmates/Shoo Fly Pie and Apple Pan Dowdy	1953	$20
❏ 40080	Santa Got Stuck in the Chimney/I Said a Prayer for Santa Claus	1953	$20

— With Johnny Bond

Number	Title	Yr	NM
❏ 4-183 [PS]	Santa Got Stuck in the Chimney/I Said a Prayer for Santa Claus	1953	$30
❏ 4-183	Santa Got Stuck in the Chimney/I Said a Prayer for Santa Claus	1953	$20

— Yellow-label Children's Series issue

Number	Title	Yr	NM
❏ 40072	Silent Night, Holy Night/Frosty the Snowman	1953	$15
❏ 40073	The Little Match Girl/Rudolph, the Red-Nosed Reindeer	1953	$15
❏ 40071	Winter Wonderland/Here Comes Santa Claus	1953	$15

DOT

Number	Title	Yr	NM
❏ 16126	Dusty/Jambalaya	1960	$15

IMPERIAL

Number	Title	Yr	NM
❏ 66166	I Would Never Do That/Lazy Me	1966	$8
❏ 66206	She Chased Me/Will I Cry	1966	$8
❏ 66233	So Young and So Fine/I Would Never Do That	1967	$8

JUBILEE

Number	Title	Yr	NM
❏ 5316	Don't Tempt Me/High School Social	1958	$15

MGM

Number	Title	Yr	NM
❏ 12788	Cream Puff/I Love You So Much	1959	$70

VEE JAY

Number	Title	Yr	NM
❏ 620	All Alone/In Love In Vain	1964	$10
❏ 686	That's What I'll Give to You/My Home Town	1965	$12

BOYD, MIKE
CLARIDGE

Number	Title	Yr	NM
❏ 413	Deep South Carnival Show/Main Street Mission Home	1976	$6
❏ 417	The Leaving Was Easy/Time Wounds All Heels	1976	$6

INERGI

Number	Title	Yr	NM
❏ 305	Love and Hate/Birds and Bees	1978	$6

MBI

Number	Title	Yr	NM
❏ 4815	I'll Always Love You/One Kiss for Old Times' Sake	1977	$6
❏ 4816	Stop and Think It Over/Whiskey	1977	$6
❏ 4817	Whiskey/April's Fool	1977	$6

BOYER, BONNIE
COLUMBIA

Number	Title	Yr	NM
❏ 3-11028	Got to Give In to Love/Never, Never	1979	$4
❏ 1-11112	I Believe in You/Sister Nasty	1979	$4

BOYER TWINS, THE
GUSTO

Number	Title	Yr	NM
❏ 9008	Margaritaville/Oh Ain't It a Beauty	1979	$5

SABRE

Number	Title	Yr	NM
❏ 4516	Three Little Words/(B-side unknown)	1980	$6

BOYFRIENDS, THE
KAPP

Number	Title	Yr	NM
❏ 569	Let's Fall in Love/Oh Lana	1964	$125

BOYLAN, TERENCE
ASYLUM

Number	Title	Yr	NM
❏ 47028	Did She Finally Get to You/Dump It on the River	1980	$5
❏ 45473	Don't Hang Up Those Dancing Shoes/Shame	1978	$5
❏ 45442	Sundown of Fools/Where Are You	1977	$5
❏ 46631	Tell Me/Going Home	1980	$5

BOYS BAND, THE
ELEKTRA

Number	Title	Yr	NM
❏ 47406	Don't Stop Me Baby (I'm on Fire)/We're Lovers	1982	$4
❏ 47406 [PS]	Don't Stop Me Baby (I'm on Fire)/We're Lovers	1982	$5

BOYS CLUB
MCA

Number	Title	Yr	NM
❏ 53649	Danglin' on a String/You're So Right	1989	$3
❏ 53430	I Remember Holding You/It's Alright	1988	$3
❏ 53430 [PS]	I Remember Holding You/It's Alright	1988	$3
❏ 53507	The Loneliest Heart/I Can't Explain It	1989	$3

BOYS DON'T CRY
ATLANTIC

Number	Title	Yr	NM
❏ 89085	We Got the Magic/Love Talk	1987	$3
❏ 89085 [PS]	We Got the Magic/Love Talk	1987	$3
❏ 89196	Who the Am Dam Do You Think You Am/The Cure	1987	$3
❏ 89196 [PS]	Who the Am Dam Do You Think You Am/The Cure	1987	$3

PROFILE

Number	Title	Yr	NM
❏ 5114	Cities on Fire/Lipstick	1986	$4
❏ 5084	I Wanna Be a Cowboy/(Instrumental)	1986	$4

BOYS FROM INDIANA
OLD HERITAGE

Number	Title	Yr	NM
❏ 8812 [PS]	Santa Got Picked Up For A D.U.I./Christmas Time	1988	$5
❏ 8812	Santa Got Picked Up For A D.U.I./Christmas Time	1988	$5

Number	Title	Yr	NM

BOYS NEXT DOOR, THE
ATCO
Number	Title	Yr	NM
❏ 6477	Be Gone Girl/See the Way She's Mine	1967	$15
❏ 6455	Christmas Kiss/The Wildest Christmas	1966	$15
❏ 6443	Mandy/One Face in the Crowd	1966	$15

CAMEO
| ❏ 394 | There Is No Greater Sin/I Could See Me Dancing with You | 1965 | $20 |

SOMA
| ❏ 1439 | Suddenly She Was Gone/Why Be Proud | 1965 | $50 |

BOYS, THE
CAMEO
| ❏ 351 | It Ain't Fair/I Want You | 1965 | $30 |

BOZ
EPIC
| ❏ 10097 | Baby Song/Pinocchio | 1966 | $12 |
| ❏ 10097 [PS] | Baby Song/Pinocchio | 1966 | $20 |

BOZE, CALVIN
ALADDIN
❏ 3079	Beat Street on Saturday Night/Choo Choo Ch'Boogieing My Baby Back Home	1951	$125
❏ 3143	Blue Shuffle/Popside	1952	$70
❏ 3132	Good Time Sue/Keep Your Nose Out of My Business	1952	$70
❏ 3160	Havin' a Time/Shamrock	1953	$60
❏ 3122	Hey, Lawdy Miss Clawdy/My Friend Told Me	1952	$100
❏ 3110	I'm Gonna Steam Off the Stamp/Fish Tail	1952	$100
❏ 3100	I've Got News for You!/I Can't Stop Crying	1951	$100
❏ 3065	Lizzie Lou/Lizzie Lou (Part 2)	1950	$200
❏ 3147	Looped/Blow Man Blow	1952	$70
❏ 3055	Safronia B/Angel City Blues	1950	$200
❏ 3086	Slippin' and Slidin'/Baby, You're Tops with Me	1951	$125
❏ 3072	Stinkin' from Drinkin'/Look Out for Tomorrow Today	1950	$125
❏ 3181	That Other Woman/Shoot De Pistol	1953	$60
❏ 3142	The Blue Tango/The Glory of Love	1952	$70
❏ 3045	Waiting and Drinking/If You Ever Had the Blues	1950	$200

IMPERIAL
| ❏ 5844 | Shamrock/Safronia B | 1962 | $15 |

BRACELETS, THE
CONGRESS
| ❏ 104 | I'll Play Along/Waddle, Waddle | 1962 | $20 |

BRADDOCK, BOBBY
COLUMBIA
| ❏ 4-45265 | Born and Raised in Your Arms/Revelation | 1970 | $8 |

ELEKTRA
❏ 46038	Between the Lines/Happy Hour	1979	$5
❏ 46507	I Did the Right Thing/Moon Fever	1979	$5
❏ 46650	I Love You Whoever You Are/Burnin' Down	1980	$5

MERCURY
❏ 73868	Big Black Telephone/Twiddle	1976	$6
❏ 73816	Gloria the Magnificent/Splidene	1976	$6
❏ 73757	My Better Half/Ruby Is a Groupie	1976	$6

MGM
❏ 14078	Crying at the Mirror/Successful Story	1969	$8
❏ 14042	Every Man's a King/Trash Man	1969	$8
❏ 13737	I Know How to Do It/Get Along	1967	$8
❏ 13843	I'm a Good Girl/Old Faithful	1967	$8
❏ 14017	The Girls in Country Music/Put Me Back Together Again	1968	$8

RCA
| ❏ PB-13529 | Dolly Parton's Hits/It Took a Long Time (To Get Me Over You) | 1983 | $5 |
| ❏ PB-13871 | Willie Where Are You/Avalanche of Romance | 1984 | $4 |

BRADEN, JOHN
A&M
| ❏ 1066 | What a Friend We Have in Jesus/Hand Me Down Man | 1969 | $10 |

BRADFORD, KEITH
MU-SOUND
| ❏ 421 | Lonely People/A Whole Lot of Crying | 1978 | $6 |

SCORPION
| ❏ 0572 | Lonely Coming Down/A Whole Lot of Crying | 1979 | $6 |

BRADING, SUSIE
RIDDLE
| ❏ 1010 | Dream Lover/Standing on the Outside | 1984 | $6 |

BRADLEY, BERRY
HIT
| ❏ 88 | That Sunday, That Summer/Don't Think Twice, It's All Right | 1963 | $8 |

—B-side by Jimmy, Wayne and Betty

BRADLEY, HAROLD
COLUMBIA
❏ 4-42694	Devil Woman/Walk On By	1963	$12
❏ 4-42830	Maria Elena/A La Orilla Del Lago	1963	$10
❏ 4-43043	Sugarfoot Rag/Wildwood Flower	1964	$8

BRADLEY, JAMES
MALACO
| ❏ 1056 | I'm In Too Deep/I Can't Get Enough of Your Love | 1979 | $5 |
| ❏ 2063 | Let's Do It Together/Knowing You're My Everything | 1979 | $5 |

BRADLEY, JAN
CHESS
❏ 1884	Curfew Blues/Pack My Things	1964	$8
❏ 1919	I'm Over You/The Brush-Off	1964	$8
❏ 1845	Mama Didn't Lie/Lovers Like Me	1962	$10
❏ 1897	Please Mr. D.J./Two of a Kind	1964	$8
❏ 1851	These Tears/Baby What Can I Do	1963	$8
❏ 1996	Trust Me/Things a Woman Needs	1967	$6

FORMAL
| ❏ 1048 | Dear Sears and Roebuck/(B-side unknown) | 1963 | $15 |
| ❏ 1044 | Mama Didn't Lie/Lovers Like Me | 1962 | $200 |

HOOTENANNY
| ❏ 1 | Christmas Time (Part 1)/Christmas Time (Part 2) | 1962 | $15 |

BRADLEY, OWEN
CORAL
❏ 9-60908	Baby, I'm Lost Without You/My Heart's Desire	1953	$15
❏ 9-60373	Be My Love/Sentimental Music	1951	$30
❏ 9-60458	Black Maria/Satins and Lace	1951	$20
❏ 9-60378	Blue Danube Waltz/Wine, Women and Song	1951	$20
❏ 9-60434	Blue Eyes Cryin' in the Rain/Strange Little Girl	1951	$30
❏ 9-60294	Boulevard of Broken Dreams/Petite Waltz	1950	$30
❏ 9-60240	Close Your Pretty Eyes/Say When	1950	$30
❏ 9-60839	Come Thou Almighty King/Now the Day Is Over	1952	$20
❏ 9-60275	Deck the Halls/Ring Out the Bells	1950	$30
❏ 9-60604	Fit as a Fiddle/Beautiful Girl	1951	$20
❏ 9-60838	Holy, Holy, Holy/Fight the Good Fight	1952	$20
❏ 9-60734	Horse and Buggy/Phantom Regiment	1952	$15
❏ 9-60360	I Give You My Love/Little Small Town Girl	1951	$30
❏ 9-60293	Is There Somebody Else/I'll Never Be Free	1950	$30
❏ 9-60603	I've Got a Feelin' You're Foolin'/Should I?	1951	$20
❏ 9-60241	I Wanna Be Loved/La Vie En Rose	1950	$30
❏ 9-60892	I Will Still Love You/Beyond the Border	1952	$15
❏ 9-60464	Lazy River/Rose of Rio Grande	1951	$20
❏ 9-60465	Missouri Waltz/Beautiful Ohio	1951	$20
❏ 9-60507	Mister Honky Tonk/Didn't Yer Mother Ever Tell Ya Nothin'	1951	$30
❏ 9-60467	Moonlight on the Colorado/On the Banks of the Wabash	1951	$20
❏ 9-60836	O Come All Ye Faithful/Blest Be the Tie That Binds	1952	$20
❏ 9-60276	O Come All Ye Faithful/The Birthday of the King	1950	$30
❏ 9-60594	Santa Claus Looks Like My Daddy/Uncle Mistletoe	1951	$30
❏ 9-60273	Silent Night/Oh Holy Night	1950	$30
❏ 9-60601	Singin' in the Rain/The Wedding of the Painted Doll	1951	$20
❏ 9-60236	Sit Down and Tell Me Where I Stand with You/Black and White Rag	1950	$30
❏ 9-60466	Swanee River/Down the River of Golden Dreams	1951	$20
❏ 9-60380	Tales from the Vienna Woods/An Artist's Life	1951	$20
❏ 9-60565	Tennessee Blues/Aboard the Sentimental Train	1951	$30
❏ 9-60837	The Church's One Foundation/My Faith Looks Up to Thee	1952	$20
❏ 9-60274	The First Nowell/Joy to the World	1950	$30
❏ 9-60539	The Girls We Never Did Wed/Dreamy Melody	1951	$20
❏ 9-60735	The Penny-Whistle Song/Plink, Plank, Plunk	1952	$15
❏ 9-60314	Wabash Blues/Written Guarantee	1950	$30

DECCA
| ❏ 30450 | Dansero/The Hour of Parting | 1957 | $15 |

— With the Anita Kerr Singers

❏ 28732	Granada/Breeze	1953	$15
❏ 29216	Happy Days and Lonely Nights/Friends and Neighbors	1954	$15
❏ 29233	Melancholy Serenade/I'm Afraid to Say Goodbye	1954	$15
❏ 29816	Moritat/Lights of Vienna	1956	$15
❏ 30564	Sentimental Dream/Big Guitar	1958	$15
❏ 30848	Simple Simon/Little Beaver	1959	$15
❏ 30083	The Italian Theme/Polka Dots and Moonbeams	1956	$15
❏ 30702	Trudie/Warwind	1958	$15
❏ 30363	White Silver Sands/Midnight Blues	1957	$15

BRADSHAW, CAROLYN
ABBOTT
❏ 153	A Man on the Loose/Flavor of the Rio	1954	$30
❏ 141	Marriage of Mexican Joe/Baby, Then You're Catching On	1953	$40
❏ 151	Say No, No, No/It's Still the Same	1954	$30

BRADSHAW, JACK
DECCA
| ❏ 29654 | My Heart, My Heart/Flirting with You | 1955 | $30 |

MAR-VEL
❏ 750	Don't Tease Me/Don't Cause Me to Hate You	1954	$125
❏ 752	It Just Ain't Right/Naughty Girls	1955	$70
❏ 751	Searchin'/My Heart, My Heart	1955	$70

BRADSHAW, TERRY
HEART WARMING
| ❏ 5395 | Getting Free/Less and Less | 1983 | $6 |

MERCURY
❏ 73760	I'm So Lonesome I Could Cry/Making Plans	1976	$5
❏ 73856	Take These Chains from My Heart/Here Comes My Baby Back Again	1976	$5
❏ 73808	The Last Word in Lonesome Is Me/Less and Less	1976	$5

BRADSHAW, TINY
KING
❏ 4376	After You've Gone/Boogie Green	1950	$70
❏ 4747	A Stack of Dollars/Cat Fruit	1954	$50
❏ 4447	Brad's Blues/Two Dry Bones on the Pantry Shelf	1951	$70
❏ 4457	Bradshaw Boogie/Walkin' the Chalk Line	1951	$70
❏ 4417	Breaking Up the House/If You Don't Love Me, Tell Me So	1950	$70
❏ 4397	Butterfly/I'm Going to Have Myself a Ball	1950	$70
❏ 4777	Cat Nap/Stomping Room Only	1955	$50
❏ 4713	Don't Worry 'Bout Me/Overflow	1954	$50
❏ 4357	I Hate You/Well Oh Well	1950	$70
❏ 4467	I'm a High Ballin' Daddy/You Came By	1951	$70
❏ 4757	Light/Choice	1954	$50
❏ 4537	Mailman's Sack/Newspaper Boy Blues	1952	$200
❏ 4787	Phantom Turnpike/Come On	1955	$50
❏ 4687	Powder Puff/Ping Pong	1953	$60
❏ 5114	Short Shorts/Bushes	1958	$30
❏ 4664	South of the Orient/Later	1953	$60
❏ 4727	Spider Web/The Gypsey	1954	$50
❏ 4577	Strange/Soft	1952	$60
❏ 4487	T-99/Long Time Baby	1951	$200
❏ 4621	The Blues Came Pouring In/Heavy Juice	1953	$60
❏ 4497	The Train Kept a-Rollin'/Knockin' Blues	1951	$200

Number	Title	Yr	NM
❑ 4427	Walk That Mess/One, Two, Three, Kick Blues	1951	$70

BRADY BUNCH, THE
PARAMOUNT

Number	Title	Yr	NM
❑ 062	Frosty the Snowman/Silver Bells	1970	$15
❑ 062 [PS]	Frosty the Snowman/Silver Bells	1970	$40
❑ 0229	I'd Love You to Want Me/ Everything I Do	1973	$15

—As "The Brady Bunch Kids

❑ 0167	Time to Change/We'll Always Be Friends	1972	$15
❑ 0141	We Can Make the World a Whole Lot Brighter/ Time to Change	1972	$15

BRADY, JUNE AND GEORGE
ABC-PARAMOUNT

❑ 9893	Sweetheart, Sweetheart/ You're My Love	1958	$30

BRAINBOX
CAPITOL

❑ 2943	Alpha & Omega/Cruel Train	1970	$8

ELEKTRA

❑ 45673	Woman's Gone/Down Man	1969	$8

BRAINS, THE
GREY MATTER

❑ GM1	Money Changes Everything/ Quick with Your Lip	1978	$8
❑ GM1 [PS]	Money Changes Everything/ Quick with Your Lip	1978	$15

—First sleeve: Individual photos on back

❑ GM1 [PS]	Money Changes Everything/ Quick with Your Lip	1978	$8

—Second sleeve: Group photo on back

MERCURY

❑ 76065	Money Changes Everything/ Girl in a Magazine	1980	$4

BRAINSTORM
CALLA

❑ 164	Early in the Morning/Movin'	1970	$30

TABU

❑ ZS85505	Everytime I See You I Go Wild/Loving Just You	1978	$5
❑ ZS85514	Hot for You/Don't Let Me Catch You with Your Groove Down	1979	$5
❑ ZS85503	Loving Just You/The Visitor	1978	$5
❑ QB-10961	Lovin' Is Really My Game (Pt. 1)/(Pt. 2)	1977	$6
❑ QB-10811	Wake Up and Be Somebody/ We Know a Place	1976	$6
❑ ZS85502	We're On Our Way Home (Part 1)/(Part 2)	1978	$5

BRAMLETT, DELANEY
COLUMBIA

❑ 45950	Are You a Beatle or a Rolling Stone/California Rain	1973	$10
❑ 45696	I'm Not Your Lover, I'm Your Lover/Over and Over	1972	$5
❑ 45781	We Can't Be Seen Together/Thank God	1973	$5

CREAM

❑ 8147	What's a Little Love/I Love to Love You	1981	$4

—By "Delaney and Bekka Bramlett

GNP CRESCENDO

❑ 328	Heartbreak Hotel/You Never Looked Sweeter	1964	$20
❑ 339	Liverpool Lou/You Have No Choice	1965	$20
❑ 363	Without Your Love/A Better Man Than Me	1965	$20

INDEPENDENCE

❑ 76	Guess I Must Be Dreaming/Don't Let It	1967	$20

BRANCH, CLIFF
SUTRA

❑ 168	Don't Give Up (On Love)/ (B-side unknown)	1988	$6

BRAND NUBIAN
ELEKTRA

Number	Title	Yr	NM
❑ 69285	Brand Nubian/Feel So Good	1989	$8

BRANDON, BILL

❑ 9001	Stop This Merry-Go-Round/I'm a Believer Now	1972	$30

PRELUDE

❑ 71098	Can't We Just Sit Down (And Talk It Over)/(B-side unknown)	1977	$5
❑ 71105	Special Occasion/ Get It While It's Hot	1978	$5
❑ 71102	We Fell in Love While Dancing/(Long Version)	1978	$5

BRANDON, JOHNNY
LAURIE

❑ 3042	Santa Claus Jr./Theme from Santa Claus Jr.	1959	$15

BRANDON, PATTI
VIK

❑ 0245	Christmas Prayer/Fairyland	1956	$20

BRANDOS, THE
RELATIVITY

❑ 88561-8192-7	In My Dreams/Gettysburg	1987	$5
❑ 88561-8192-7 [PS]	In My Dreams/Gettysburg	1987	$5

BRANDYWINE CHORALE, THE
CORAL

❑ 98126 [PS]	Christmas Is Here Now/ The Old Bell Ringer	1964	$15

— 1964 Christmas Seals promotional record

❑ 98126 [DJ]	Christmas Is Here Now/ The Old Bell Ringer	1964	$10
❑ 62434	Christmas Is Here Now/The Old Bell Ringer (Papa John)	1964	$8

BRANE, SHERRY
E.I.O.

❑ 1129	Falling in Trouble Again/I'm Gonna Make You Love Me	1980	$6

MMI

❑ 1030	Stop! In the Name of Love/ (B-side unknown)	1979	$6

OAK

❑ 1013	It's My Party/(B-side unknown)	1978	$6

TEJAS

❑ 1015	Little Girls Need Daddies/I'm Gonna Make You Love Me	1980	$6

BRANIGAN, LAURA
ATCO

❑ 99280	Come Into My Life/ Believe in Me	1988	$4

— With Joe Esposito

ATLANTIC

❑ 4023	All Night with Me/I Wish We Could Be Alone	1982	$5
❑ 89121	Cry Wolf/Whatever I Do	1988	$3
❑ 3770 [DJ]	Fool's Affair (same on both sides)	1980	$8

— May be promo only

❑ 4048	Gloria/Living a Lie	1982	$4
❑ 89496	Hold Me/Tenderness	1985	$3
❑ 89496 [PS]	Hold Me/Tenderness	1985	$3
❑ 89805	How Am I Supposed to Live Without You/Mama	1983	$3
❑ 89805 [PS]	How Am I Supposed to Live Without You/Mama	1983	$5
❑ 89451	I Found Someone/When	1986	$3
❑ 89451 [PS]	I Found Someone/When	1986	$3
❑ 3807 [DJ]	Looking Out for Number One (same on both sides)	1981	$8

— May be promo only

❑ 89191	Power of Love/Spirit of Love	1987	$3
❑ 89191 [PS]	Power of Love/Spirit of Love	1987	$3
❑ 89676	Self Control/Silent Partners	1984	$3
❑ 89676 [PS]	Self Control/Silent Partners	1984	$3
❑ 89245	Shattered Glass/ Statue in the Rain	1987	$3
❑ 89245 [PS]	Shattered Glass/ Statue in the Rain	1987	$3
❑ 89868	Solitaire/I'm Not the Only One	1983	$3
❑ 89868 [PS]	Solitaire/I'm Not the Only One	1983	$3
❑ 89531	Spanish Eddie/Tenderness	1985	$3
❑ 89531 [PS]	Spanish Eddie/Tenderness	1985	$3

Number	Title	Yr	NM
❑ 3846 [DJ]	Tell Him (same on both sides)	1981	$8

— May be promo only

❑ 89636	The Lucky One/Breaking Out	1984	$3
❑ 89636 [PS]	The Lucky One/Breaking Out	1984	$3
❑ 89608	Ti Amo/Satisfaction	1984	$3
❑ 89608 [PS]	Ti Amo/Satisfaction	1984	$3

BRANNON, KIPPI
MCA

❑ 52202	B.Y.O.B./In My Dreams	1983	$4
❑ 51166	Dreamin'/Slowly	1982	$4
❑ 52096	He Don't Make Me Cry/ Piece of My Heart	1982	$4
❑ 52023	If I Could See You Tonight/I'm So Afraid of Losing You Again	1982	$4

BRANT, BOBBY
EASTWEST

❑ 124	Piano Nellie/I Found a New Love	1959	$125

WHITE ROCK

❑ 1114	Piano Nellie/I Found a New Love	1959	$200

BRASS CONSTRUCTION
CAPITOL

❑ B-5347	Breakdown/We Can Work It Out	1984	$3
❑ B-5500	Give and Take/My Place	1985	$3
❑ B-5425	International/What Is the Law	1984	$3
❑ B-5382	Partyline/We Can Bring It Back	1984	$3
❑ B-5382 [PS]	Partyline/We Can Bring It Back	1984	$3
❑ B-5219	Walkin' the Line/Forever Love	1983	$3
❑ B-5219 [PS]	Walkin' the Line/Forever Love	1983	$3
❑ B-5252	We Can Work It Out/Easy	1983	$3

LIBERTY

❑ B-1473	Attitude/Hotdog	1982	$4
❑ B-1453	Can You See the Light/E.T.C.	1982	$4
❑ 1387	How Do You Do (What You Do to Me)/Don't Try to Change Me	1980	$4

UNITED ARTISTS

❑ XW1204	Celebrate/Top of the World	1978	$5
❑ XW837	Changin'/Love	1976	$5
❑ X1262	Get Up/Perceptions (What's the Right Direction)	1978	$5
❑ XW921	Ha Cha Cha (Funktion)/ Sambo (Conditions)	1976	$5
❑ XW1242	Help Yourself/Pick Yourself Up	1978	$5
❑ XW1120	L-O-V-E-U/Get It Together	1978	$5
❑ XW1160	Movin'/Changin'	1978	$3

— Reissue

❑ XW775	Movin'/Talkin'	1976	$4
❑ X1346	Music Makes You Feel Like Dancing/I Want Some Action	1980	$5
❑ XW957	The Message (Inspiration)/ What's On Your Mind (Expression)	1977	$5
❑ X1371	We Are Brass/I'm Not Gonna Stop	1980	$5

BRASS FEVER
ABC IMPULSE!

❑ 31002	Lady Marmalade/ (B-side unknown)	1975	$5
❑ 31010	Time Is Running Out/ Funky Carnival	1976	$5

BRASS RING, THE
ABC DUNHILL

❑ 4164	For the Love of Ivy/The Theme from The Odd Couple	1968	$6

DUNHILL

❑ 4047	California Dreamin'/ Samba de Orfeu	1966	$6
❑ 4132	Cherry Pink & Apple Blossom White/Adoro (Don't Tempt Me)	1968	$6
❑ 4059	Lapland/Patricia	1966	$6
❑ 4036	Lara's Theme/Secret Love	1966	$6
❑ 4090 [PS]	Love in the Open Air/Wait for Me	1967	$40

— Sleeve says this is "Paul McCartney's first non-Beatles song

❑ 4090	Love in the Open Air/Wait for Me	1967	$30
❑ 4108	Monday, Monday/Flower Ring	1967	$6
❑ 4065	The Dis-Advantages of You/The Dating Game	1967	$6
❑ 4023	The Phoenix Love Theme (Sensa Fine)/Lightning Bug	1966	$6

7-Inch Extended Plays
ABC DUNHILL

❑ LP-DS-50044 [DJ]	Mrs. Robinson/This Guy's in Love with You/For Love of Ivy// Do You Know the Way to San Jose/Love Is Blue/Honey	1969	$15

—Small hole, 33 1/3 rpm jukebox EP

❑ LP-DS-50044 [PS]	Only Love	1969	$15

Number	Title	Yr	NM

BRAVE BELT

Also see RANDY BACHMAN; BACHMAN-TURNER OVERDRIVE.

REPRISE

Number	Title	Yr	NM
❑ 1083	Another Way Out/Dunrobin's Gone	1972	$5
❑ 1039	Holy Train/Crazy Arms-Crazy Eyes	1971	$5

BRAVE NEW WORLD

EPIC

Number	Title	Yr	NM
❑ 10123	It's Tomorrow/Cried	1967	$30

BREAD

ELEKTRA

Number	Title	Yr	NM
❑ 45832	Aubrey/Didn't Even Know Her Name	1973	$4
❑ 45751	Baby I'm-a Want You/Truckin'	1971	$4
❑ 45668	Could I/You Can't Measure the Cost	1969	$6
❑ 45784	Diary/Down on My Knees	1972	$4
❑ 45666	Dismal Day/Anyway You Want Me	1969	$8
❑ 45765	Everything I Own/I Don't Love You	1972	$4
❑ 45389	Hooked on You/Our Lady of Sorrow	1977	$4
❑ 45720	If/Take Comfort	1971	$4
❑ 45720 [PS]	If/Take Comfort	1971	$8
❑ 45701	It Don't Matter to Me/Call on Me	1970	$4
❑ 45701 [PS]	It Don't Matter to Me/Call on Me	1970	$8
❑ 45711	Let Your Love Go/Too Much Love	1971	$4
❑ 45365	Lost Without Your Love/Change of Heart	1976	$4
❑ 45686	Make It With You/Why Do You Keep Me Waiting	1970	$4
— Red, black and white label			
❑ 45686	Make It With You/Why Do You Keep Me Waiting	1970	$4
— Yellow and black label			
❑ 45740	Mother Freedom/Life in Your Love	1971	$4
❑ 45818	Sweet Surrender/Make It By Yourself	1972	$4
❑ 45803	The Guitar Man/Just Like Yesterday	1972	$4

BREAKAWAYS, THE

CAMEO

Number	Title	Yr	NM
❑ 323	That's How It Goes/He Doesn't Love Me	1964	$20

LONDON INT'L.

Number	Title	Yr	NM
❑ 10526	That Boy of Mine/Here She Comes	1963	$15

MELBOURNE

Number	Title	Yr	NM
❑ 1805	Granada/The Flipper	1964	$15

BREAKERS, THE

AMY

Number	Title	Yr	NM
❑ 938	Don't Send Me No Flowers (I Ain't Dead Yet)/Love of My Life	1965	$20

DJB

Number	Title	Yr	NM
❑ 116	Super Jet Rumble/Beach Head	1964	$60
— Revised A-side title			

IMPACT

Number	Title	Yr	NM
❑ 14	Surfin' Tragedy/Surf Bird	1963	$30
— Black vinyl			
❑ 14	Surfin' Tragedy/Surf Bird	1963	$100
— Gold vinyl			

JERDEN

Number	Title	Yr	NM
❑ 789	All My Nights, All My Days/Better for the Both of Us	1966	$30

MARSH

Number	Title	Yr	NM
❑ 206	Balboa Memories/Long Way Home	1963	$60

RIVERTON

Number	Title	Yr	NM
❑ 102	All My Nights, All My Days/Better for the Both of Us	1966	$50

BREAKFAST CLUB

MCA

Number	Title	Yr	NM
❑ 53348	Drive My Car (from "License to Drive")/(Instrumental)	1988	$3
❑ 53273	Expressway to Your Heart/Tongue Tied	1988	$3
❑ 53273 [PS]	Expressway to Your Heart/Tongue Tied	1988	$3

BREAKWATER

ARISTA

Number	Title	Yr	NM
❑ 0542	Say You Love Me Girl/Time	1980	$5
❑ 0518	Splashdown Time/Let Love In	1980	$5
❑ 0404	Work It Out/Feel Your Way	1979	$5

BREATHE

A&M

Number	Title	Yr	NM
❑ 1401	All This I Should Have Known/In All Honesty	1989	$4
❑ 1267	Don't Tell Me Lies/Liberties of Love	1989	$3
❑ 1267 [PS]	Don't Tell Me Lies/Liberties of Love	1989	$3
❑ 2991	Hands to Heaven/Life and Times	1987	$3
❑ 2991 [PS]	Hands to Heaven/Life and Times	1987	$6
❑ 1224	How Can I Fall?/Monday Morning Blues	1988	$3
❑ 1224 [PS]	How Can I Fall?/Monday Morning Blues	1988	$3

BREATHLESS

EMI AMERICA

Number	Title	Yr	NM
❑ 8028	Dead of the Night/Looks Like a Heartache	1980	$5
❑ 8067	Happy Ending/Can You Feel It	1980	$5
❑ 8020	Takin' It Back/Alibis	1979	$5

BRECKER BROTHERS, THE

ARISTA

Number	Title	Yr	NM
❑ 0253	Don't Stop the Music/Finger Lickin' Good	1977	$4
❑ 0365	East River (La-Di-Da)/Funky Sea, Funky Do	1978	$4
❑ 0182	If You Wanna Boogie... Forget It/Slick Stuff	1976	$4
❑ 0122	Sneakin' Up Behind You/Sponge	1975	$4

BREEDLOVE, JIMMY

ATCO

Number	Title	Yr	NM
❑ 6105	I Can Still Hear You Say You Love Me/I Wish I Were Twins	1957	$30
❑ 6094	That's My Baby/Over Somebody Else's Shoulder	1957	$30

EPIC

Number	Title	Yr	NM
❑ 9319	All Is Forgiven/I Say Hello	1959	$30
❑ 9270	Could This Be Love/This Too Shall Pass Away	1958	$30
❑ 9283	Love Is All We Need/Lovable	1958	$30
❑ 9289	Love Is All We Need/Oo-Wee Good Gosh A-Mighty	1958	$30
❑ 9360	To Belong/Waiting for You	1960	$30

OKEH

Number	Title	Yr	NM
❑ 7145	Anytime You Want Me/My Guardian Angel	1962	$15
❑ 7152	Don't Let It Happen/Queen Bee	1962	$15

ROULETTE

Number	Title	Yr	NM
❑ 7010	I Can't Help Lovin' You/I Saw You	1968	$8

7-Inch Extended Plays

RCA CAMDEN

Number	Title	Yr	NM
❑ CEP-447	(contents unknown)	1958	$30

BREEN, BOBBY

CHIC

Number	Title	Yr	NM
❑ 1003	If the Night Could Tell You/Wait	1956	$20
❑ 1013	We Will Make Love/Rainbow	1957	$20

MOTOWN

Number	Title	Yr	NM
❑ 1053	How Can We Tell Him/Better Late Than Never	1964	$30

NRC

Number	Title	Yr	NM
❑ 055	Hawaii Calls/Theme from A Summer Place	1960	$12

BREEZE

ATLANTIC

Number	Title	Yr	NM
❑ 88909	L.A. Posse/Pull a Fast One	1989	$4

BREMERS, BEVERLY

COLUMBIA

Number	Title	Yr	NM
❑ 10451	The Prisoner/Flight 309 to Tennessee	1976	$5
❑ 10180	What I Did for Love/You're Precious to Me	1975	$5

SCEPTER

Number	Title	Yr	NM
❑ 12380	Daddy's Coming Home/A Little Bit of Love	1973	$5
❑ 12315	Don't Say You Don't Remember/Get Smart Girl	1971	$6
❑ 12370	Heaven Help Us/All That's Left Is the Music	1973	$5
❑ 12363	I'll Make You Music/I Made a Man Out of You, Jimmy	1972	$5
❑ 12399	One Day at a Time/Get Up in the Morning	1975	$5
❑ 12391	Sing a Happy Song/Get Smart Girl	1973	$5
❑ 12348	We're Free/Colors of Love	1972	$5
❑ 12348 [PS]	We're Free/Colors of Love	1972	$10
❑ 12332	When Michael Calls/Toy Girl	1971	$5

BRENDA AND HERB (THE EXCITERS)

DRIVE

Number	Title	Yr	NM
❑ 6275	I Who Have Nothing/Sweet Dreamer	1978	$5

H&L

Number	Title	Yr	NM
❑ 4703	I Got a Letter/Satin Doll	1978	$6
❑ 4699	Tonight I'm Gonna Make You a Star/Sweet Dreamer	1978	$6

BRENDA AND THE TABULATIONS

CHOCOLATE CITY

Number	Title	Yr	NM
❑ 004	Home to Myself/Leave Me Alone	1976	$4
❑ 009	(I'm a) Superstar/Take It or Leave It	1977	$4
❑ 012	Let's Go All the Way (Down)/I Keep Coming Back for More	1977	$4

DIONN

Number	Title	Yr	NM
❑ 500	Dry Your Eyes/The Wash	1967	$12
❑ 509	I Can't Get Over You/That's in the Past	1968	$10
❑ 512	That's the Price You Have to Pay/I Wish I Hadn't Done What I Did	1969	$12
❑ 507	To the One I Love/Baby You're So Right	1968	$10
❑ 504	When You're Gone/Hey Boy	1967	$10
❑ 501	Who's Lovin' You/Stay Together Young Lovers	1967	$10

EPIC

Number	Title	Yr	NM
❑ 11059	I'm in Love/Walk On In	1973	$6
❑ 50081	Let Me Be Happy/Little Bit of Love	1975	$4
❑ 10898	Little Bit of Love/Let Me Be Happy	1972	$6
❑ 10954	One Girl Too Late/The Magic of Your Love	1973	$6

PHILCO-FORD

Number	Title	Yr	NM
❑ HP-40	Dry Your Eyes/When You're Gone	1969	$30
— 4-inch plastic "Hip Pocket Record" with color sleeve			

TOP & BOTTOM

Number	Title	Yr	NM
❑ 406	A Child No One Wanted/Scuse Us All	1970	$8
❑ 403	And My Heart Sang (Tra La La)/Lies, Lies, Lies	1970	$8
❑ 408	A Part of You/Where There's a Will	1971	$8
❑ 404	Don't Make Me Over/You've Changed	1970	$8
❑ 401	The Touch of You/Stop Sneaking Around	1969	$8
❑ 411	Why Didn't I Think of That/A Love You Can Depend On	1971	$8

BRENNAN, WALTER

DOT

Number	Title	Yr	NM
❑ 16066	Dutchman's Gold/Back to the Farm	1960	$15
❑ 16066 [PS]	Dutchman's Gold/Back to the Farm	1960	$30
❑ 16136	Space Mice/The Thievin' Stranger	1960	$15
❑ 16136 [PS]	Space Mice/The Thievin' Stranger	1960	$30
❑ 16348	Tribute to a Dog/Life Gets Tee-Jus Don't It	1962	$15

KAPP

Number	Title	Yr	NM
❑ 2126	Grandad/Man Needs to Know	1971	$6

LIBERTY

Number	Title	Yr	NM
❑ 55518	Henry Had A Merry Christmas/White Christmas	1962	$15
❑ 55518 [PS]	Henry Had A Merry Christmas/White Christmas	1962	$30
❑ 55477	Houdini/The Old Kelly Place	1962	$15
❑ 55477 [PS]	Houdini/The Old Kelly Place	1962	$30
❑ 55508	Mama Sang a Song/Who Will Take Gramma	1962	$15
❑ 55436	Old Rivers/The Epic Ride of John B. Glenn	1962	$15

UNITED ARTISTS

Number	Title	Yr	NM
❑ 0055	Old Rivers/Mama Sang a Song	1973	$4
— Silver Spotlight Series issue			

BRENSTON, JACKIE
CHESS

Number	Title	Yr	NM
❏ 1532	Blues Got Me Again/Starvation	1953	$250
❏ 1469	In My Real Gone Rocket/Tuckered Out	1951	$1000
❏ 1496	Leo the Louse/Hi-Ho Baby	1952	$500

FEDERAL

Number	Title	Yr	NM
❏ 12291	Much Later/The Mistreater	1957	$60
❏ 12283	What Can It Be?/Gonna Wait for My Chance	1956	$60

SUE

Number	Title	Yr	NM
❏ 736	Trouble Up the Road/You Ain't the One	1961	$30

BRENT, CAROLYN
CONGRESS

Number	Title	Yr	NM
❏ 213	My Man (Mon Homme)/Rose of Washington Square	1964	$8

BRENT, RONNIE
COLT 45

Number	Title	Yr	NM
❏ 109	Cowboys and Indians/Flow Gently	1959	$30
❏ 101	Crazy Feeling/Shirley Ann	1959	$30

UNITED ARTISTS

Number	Title	Yr	NM
❏ 108	My Sweet Verlene/Love	1958	$50

BRENT, TONY
ROULETTE

Number	Title	Yr	NM
❏ 4113	Girl of My Dreams/Don't Play That Melody	1958	$15

BRENTWOOD
HOT SCHATZ

Number	Title	Yr	NM
❏ 0052	Anything for Your Love/(B-side unknown)	1984	$6
❏ 0051	Love the One You're With/(B-side unknown)	1983	$6

BRESH, THOM, AND LANE BRODY
LIBERTY

Number	Title	Yr	NM
❏ 1487	When It Comes to Love/Somebody Like You	1982	$4

BRESH, TOM
ABC

Number	Title	Yr	NM
❏ 12389	First Encounter of a Close Kind/A Woman Who Will	1978	$4
❏ 12352	Ways of a Woman in Love/Huckleberry Week-End	1978	$4

ABC DOT

Number	Title	Yr	NM
❏ 17738	Smoke, Smoke, Smoke (That Cigarette)/My Lickskillet, Indiana Home	1977	$4
❏ 17720	That Old Cold Shoulder/Start All Over Again	1977	$4

FARR

Number	Title	Yr	NM
❏ 012	Hey Daisy (Where Have All the Good Times Gone)/Where Was I	1976	$6
❏ 004	Home Made Love/California Old Time Song	1976	$6
❏ 009	Sad Country Love Song/While We Make Love Together	1976	$6

KAPP

Number	Title	Yr	NM
❏ 2160	Apple Pie/Where Are You	1972	$8

—B-side by D.B. Cooper

LIBERTY

Number	Title	Yr	NM
❏ B-1502	I'd Love You to Want Me/Somebody Like You	1983	$4
❏ B-1510	Whatever Blows Your Dress Up/Somebody Like You	1983	$4

MGM

Number	Title	Yr	NM
❏ 14824	Soda Pop and Gumball Days/(B-side unknown)	1975	$5

BREWER AND SHIPLEY
A&M

Number	Title	Yr	NM
❏ 996	Dreamin' in the Shade/Tame and Changes	1968	$8
❏ 938	Green Bamboo/Truly Right	1968	$8

—Artist reads "Michael Brewer and Tom Shipley

CAPITOL

Number	Title	Yr	NM
❏ 4105	Brain Damage/Rock and Roll Hostage	1975	$4
❏ 3933	Fair Play/How Are You	1974	$4

KAMA SUTRA

Number	Title	Yr	NM
❏ 567	Black Sky/Fly, Fly Fly	1972	$4
❏ 516	One Toke Over the Line/Oh Mommy	1970	$5
❏ 512	People Love Each Other/Witchi-Tai-To	1970	$4
❏ 539	Shake Off the Demon/Indian Summer	1972	$4
❏ 524	Tarkio Road/Seems Like a Long Time	1971	$4

BREWER, TERESA, AND DON CORNELL
CORAL

Number	Title	Yr	NM
❏ 61027	The Glad Song/What Happened to the Music	1953	$15

BREWER, TERESA
AMSTERDAM

Number	Title	Yr	NM
❏ 85025	A Simple Song/Singing a Doo-Dah Song	1973	$4
❏ 85029	Bo Weevil/Bei Mir Bist Du Schoen (Means That You're Grand)	1974	$4
❏ 85024	Day by Day/Somewhere There's Someone Who Loves You	1972	$4
❏ 85027	Music, Music, Music/School Days	1973	$4
❏ 85028	Music to the Man/Another Useless Day	1973	$4

CORAL

Number	Title	Yr	NM
❏ 61548	A Good Man Is Hard to Find/It's Siesta Time	1956	$10
❏ 62306	Another/I Want You to Worry	1962	$8
❏ 62219	Anymore/That Piano Man	1960	$8
❏ 62219 [PS]	Anymore/That Piano Man	1960	$10
❏ 61636	A Sweet Old Fashioned Girl/Goodbye John	1956	$10
❏ 61590	A Tear Fell/Bo Weevil	1956	$10
❏ 61225	Au Revoir/Danger Signs	1954	$15
❏ 61500	Baby Be My Toy/So Doggone Lonely	1955	$15
❏ 61066	Bell Bottom Blues/Our Heartbreaking Waltz	1953	$15
❏ 60953	Breakin' the Blues/Dancing with Someone	1953	$15
❏ 62126	Bye Bye Baby Goodbye/Chain of Friendship	1959	$10
❏ 62428	Cry Baby/I Hear the Angels Singing	1964	$6
❏ 61805	Empty Arms/The Ricky Tick Song	1957	$12
❏ 60676	Gonna Get Along Without You Now/Roll Them Roly-Poly Eyes	1952	$15
❏ 62236	Have You Ever Been Lonely (Have You Ever Been Blue)/When Do You Love Me	1960	$8
❏ 62084	Heavenly Lover/Fair Weather Sweetheart	1959	$12
❏ 61362	How Important Can It Be?/Pledging My Love	1955	$15
❏ 61776	How Lonely Can One Be/I'm Drowning My Sorrows	1957	$10
❏ 62197	If There Are Stars in My Eyes/How Do You Know It's Love	1960	$8
❏ 62197 [PS]	If There Are Stars in My Eyes/How Do You Know It's Love	1960	$15
❏ 61339	I Gotta Go Get My Baby/What More Is There to Say	1955	$15
❏ 61067	I Guess It Was You All the Time/Baby, Baby, Baby	1953	$15
❏ 60755	I Hear the Bluebells/Kisses on Paper	1952	$15
❏ 61079	I Just Can't Wait Till Christmas/Too Fat for the Chimney	1953	$15
❏ 61700 [PS]	I Love Mickey/Keep Your Cotton Pickin' Hands Off My Baby	1956	$60
❏ 61700	I Love Mickey/Keep Your Cotton Pickin' Hands Off My Baby	1956	$30
❏ 61078	I Saw Mommy Kissing Santa Claus/Ebenezer Scrooge	1953	$15
❏ 61878	It's the Same Old Jazz/Born to Love	1957	$10
❏ 61315	Let Me Go, Lover/The Moon Is On Fire	1954	$15
❏ 61912	Listen My Children/Hush-a-Bye, Wink-a-Bye	1957	$12
❏ 61944	Lost a Little Puppy/Because Him Is a Baby	1958	$10
❏ 61944 [PS]	Lost a Little Puppy/Because Him Is a Baby	1958	$20
❏ 60645	Lovin' Machine/Noodlin' Bay	1952	$15
❏ 61850	Lula Rock-a-Hula/Teardrops in My Heart	1957	$10
❏ 62150	Mexicali Rose/If You Like-A Me	1959	$10
❏ 62265	Milord/I've Got My Fingers Crossed	1961	$8
❏ 61737	Mutual Admiration Society/Crazy with Love	1956	$10
❏ 62167	Peace of Mind/Venetian Sunset	1960	$8
❏ 62167 [PS]	Peace of Mind/Venetian Sunset	1960	$10
❏ 62013	Pickle Up a Doodle/The Rain Falls on Everybody	1958	$10
❏ 61983	Saturday Dance/I Think the World of You	1958	$10
❏ 62278	Sea Shell/Little Miss Belong to No One	1961	$8
❏ 61528	Shoot It Again/You're Telling Our Secrets	1955	$15
❏ 61394	Silver Dollar/I Don't Want to Be Lonely Tonight	1955	$15
❏ 60591	Sing, Sing, Sing/I Don't Care	1952	$15
❏ 61197	Skinnie Minnie (Fish Tart)/I Had Someone Else Before I Had You	1954	$15
❏ 62299	Step Right Up/Pretty Lookin' Boy	1961	$8
❏ 61448	The Banjo's Back in Town/How to Be Very, Very Popular	1955	$15
❏ 62033	The Hula Hoop Song/So Shy	1958	$10
❏ 62057	The One Rose (That's Left in My Heart)/Satellite	1958	$10
❏ 61948	There's Nothing As Lonesome As Saturday Night/Whirlpool	1958	$10
❏ 60873	Till I Waltz Again with You/Hello Bluebird	1952	$15
❏ 61286	Time/My Sweetie Went Away	1954	$15
❏ 69039	Too Fat For The Chimney/I Just Can't Wait Till Christmas	1953	$20

—Maroon label with silver print

Number	Title	Yr	NM
❏ 60994	Too Much Mustard/Into Each Life Some Rain Must Fall	1953	$15
❏ 61366	Tweedlee Dee/Rock Love	1955	$15
❏ 62253	Whippoorwill/Older and Wiser	1961	$8

DOCTOR JAZZ

Number	Title	Yr	NM
❏ WS4-03835	Classic Medley #1/Jimmy Dorsey Medley	1983	$4

LONDON

Number	Title	Yr	NM
❏ 30100	Choo'n Gum/(B-side unknown)	1950	$20
❏ 1085	If You Don't Marry Me/I Wish I Wuz	1951	$20
❏ 1086	Longing for You/Jazz Me Blues	1951	$20
❏ 30023	Music! Music! Music! (Put Another Nickel In)/Copenhagen	1950	$20
❏ 1083	Oceana Roll/Wang Wang Blues	1951	$20

PHILIPS

Number	Title	Yr	NM
❏ 40177	Come On In/Simple Things	1964	$6
❏ 40227	Dang Me (Dern You)/Mama Never Told Me	1964	$6
❏ 40389	Evil on Your Mind/Ain't Had No Lovin'	1966	$6
❏ 40253	Goldfinger/Make Room for One More Fool	1965	$6
❏ 40367	Handle with Care/I Can't Remember Ever Loving You	1966	$6
❏ 40135	He Understands Me/Just Before We Say Goodbye	1963	$8
❏ 40345	Little Bitty Grain of Sand/Little Buddy	1965	$6
❏ 40310	Say Something Sweet to Your Sweetheart/What About Time	1965	$6
❏ 40120	Second Hand Love/Stand-In	1963	$8
❏ 40095	She'll Never Love You/The Thrill Is Gone	1963	$8
❏ 40282	Supercalifragilisticexpialidocious/I've Grown Accustomed to His Face	1965	$6
❏ 40077	The Ballad of Lover's Hill/Not Like a Sister	1962	$8

PROJECT 3

Number	Title	Yr	NM
❏ #100	Come Follow the Band/(B-side unknown)	1982	$4

SIGNATURE

Number	Title	Yr	NM
❏ PB-10100	Am I Asking Too Much of You/Willie Burgundy	1974	$4
❏ PB-10609	Music, Music, Music/Where Did the Good Times Go	1976	$4
❏ WS4-04654	The Pilgrim (Chapter #33)/School Days	1984	$4

SSS INTERNATIONAL

Number	Title	Yr	NM
❏ 735	Step to the Rear/Live a Little	1968	$5
❏ EC81175	(contents unknown)	1959	$15
❏ EC81115 [PS]	Especially for You...	1955	$15
❏ EC81115	How Important Can It Be?/Rock Love//Pledging My Love/Tweedlee Dee	1955	$15
❏ EC81176 [PS]	Teresa Brewer and the Dixieland Band	1959	$15
❏ EC7-81176 [PS]	Teresa Brewer and the Dixieland Band	1959	$25
❏ EC81176 [M]	The Dixieland Band/When the Saints Go Marching In//Bill Bailey, Won't You Please Come Home/Basin Street Blues	1959	$15
❏ EC 7-81176 [S]	The Dixieland Band/When the Saints Go Marching In//Bill Bailey, Won't You Please Come Home/Basin Street Blues	1959	$25
❏ EC81175 [PS]	When Your Lover Has Gone	1959	$15

LONDON

Number	Title	Yr	NM
❏ BEP6041	*The Jazz Me Blues/Longing for You/I Wish I Wuz/If You Don't Marry Me	1952	$25
❏ BEP6039	Music, Music, Music/Copenhagen//Honky Tonkin'/Ol' Man Mose	1952	$25
❏ BEP6039 [PS]	Teresa Brewer	1952	$25
❏ BEP6041 [PS]	Teresa Brewer, Vol. 2	1952	$25

Number	Title	Yr	NM
BRIAN AND BRENDA			
ROCKET			
❏ 40777	Don't Let Love Go/Toronto	1977	$6
❏ 40602	Gonna Do My Best to Love You/(B-side unknown)	1976	$6
❏ 40521	Highly Prized Possession/ You'll Never Rock Alone	1976	$6
❏ 40809	That's All Right Too/ Who Loves You	1977	$6
BRIAN, NEIL			
JAMIE			
❏ 1216	Lucky Coin/A Fool Was I	1962	$30
PARKWAY			
❏ 895	I Made Her Forget/Lilac and Spanish Moss	1964	$30
❏ 886	My Haunted Heart/ Three Rows Over	1963	$30
BRIARWOOD SINGERS, THE			
UNITED ARTISTS			
❏ 686	He Was a Friend of Mine/ Bound for the Freedom Land	1964	$12
❏ 709	Two Brothers/Love Tastes Like Strawberries	1964	$8
BRICK			
BANG			
❏ 735	Ain't Gonna Hurt Nobody/ Honey Chile	1977	$5
❏ 4810	All the Way/Spread Love	1980	$4
❏ 4804	Dancin' Man/We'll Love	1979	$4
❏ 727	Dazz/Southern Sunset	1976	$5
❏ 734	Dusic/Happy	1977	$5
❏ ZS5-03157	Free Dancer/Stick By You	1982	$4
❏ 723	Music Matic/Good High	1976	$5
—*Reissue of Main Street 119*			
❏ ZS5-02246	Sweat (Til You Get Wet)/ Seaside Vibes	1981	$4
❏ 732	That's What It's All About/ Can't Wait (Tick Tock)	1977	$5
❏ ZS5-02599	Wide Open/Seaside Vibes	1981	$4
MAIN STREET			
❏ 119	Music Matic/Good High	1975	$10
BRICKELL, EDIE, & NEW BOHEMIANS			
GEFFEN			
❏ 27580	Circle/Now	1989	$3
❏ 27580 [PS]	Circle/Now	1989	$3
❏ 22937	Love Like We Do/Plain Jane	1989	$3
❏ 22937 [PS]	Love Like We Do/Plain Jane	1989	$3
❏ 27696	What I Am/I Do	1988	$3
❏ 27696 [PS]	What I Am/I Do	1988	$3
BRIDES OF FUNKENSTEIN, THE			
ATLANTIC			
❏ 3556	Amorous/War Ship Touchante	1979	$5
❏ 3498	Disco to Go/When You're Gone	1978	$5
❏ 3658	Mother May I/Didn't Mean to Fall in Love	1980	$8
BRIDGES, ALICIA			
MEGA			
❏ 0104	Golden Boy/Just a Little Lovin'	1973	$8
POLYDOR			
❏ 14539	Body Heat/We Are One	1979	$4
❏ 14483	I Love the Nightlife (Disco 'Round)/Self Applause	1978	$4
❏ 2044	Starchild/Rex the Robot	1979	$5
BRIDGEWATER, DEE DEE			
ATLANTIC			
❏ 3357	Goin' Through the Motions/ Every Man Wants Another Man's Woman	1976	$6
ELEKTRA			
❏ 46031	Bad for Me/Back of Your Mind	1979	$5
❏ 47046	One in a Million (Guy)/Give	1980	$5
BRIEF ENCOUNTER			
CAPITOL			
❏ 4426	In a Very Special Way/ Got a Good Feeling	1977	$10
❏ 4229	What About Love/Get Right Down (And Do It)	1976	$10

Number	Title	Yr	NM
SEVENTY-7			
❏ SE-132	(Don't You See) I'm Crazy About You/We're Gonna Make It	1973	$30
❏ SE123	I'm So Satisfied/Don't Let Them Tell You	1972	$30
BRIGADIERS, THE			
MALA			
❏ 441	The Cry of the Wild Goose/Dixie Brigade	1961	$30
BRIGANDS, THE			
EPIC			
❏ 10011	(Would I Still Be) Her Big Man/I'm a Patient Man	1966	$30
BRIGGS, LILLIAN			
ABC-PARAMOUNT			
❏ 10253	I Want You to Be My Baby/I'm Burning for You	1961	$10
CORAL			
❏ 62193	Be Mine/Not a Soul	1960	$12
❏ 62136	Blues in the Night/Is There a Man in the House	1959	$10
❏ 62156	Hooray for the Rock/ Diddy Boppers	1959	$10
❏ 62223	I Care for You/That's What It's Like to Be Lonesome	1960	$10
EPIC			
❏ 9151	Eddie, My Love/Teens in Jeans from New Orleans	1956	$30
❏ 9141	Follow the Leader/That's the Only Way to Live	1956	$30
❏ 9120	Give Me a Band and My Baby/It Could've Been Me	1955	$40
❏ 9190	I'll Be Gone/Mean Words	1956	$30
❏ 9115	I Want You to Be My Baby/ Don't Stay Away Too Long	1955	$40
❏ 9249	She Sells Sea Shells/I	1957	$20
❏ 9214	Sugar Blues/Boogie Blues	1957	$20
❏ 9166	The Gypsy Goofed/Too Close for Comfort	1956	$30
SUNBEAM			
❏ 104	Come Home/Till We Meet Again	1958	$15
❏ 114	Hey Ba Ba Re Bop/I've Got Your Heart	1958	$15
7-Inch Extended Plays			
EPIC			
❏ B-7163	(contents unknown)	1956	$50
❏ B-7163 [PS]	High Priestess of Rock 'n' Roll	1956	$50
BRIGHT, DICK, YOUTH CHORALE			
AMBITION			
❏ 102	(What's So Funny 'Bout) Peace, Love and Understanding/ Xmas In The Hot Tub	1980	$15
—*B-side by Little Roger and the Goosebumps*			
BRIGHTER SIDE OF DARKNESS			
20TH CENTURY			
❏ 2034	I Owe You Love/Summer Ride	1973	$10
❏ 2002	Love Jones/I'm the Guy	1972	$8
BRIGHTONES, THE			
WARNER BROS.			
❏ 5472	Swim, Swim, Swim/Rumors	1964	$30
BRIKS, THE			
BISMARK			
❏ 1013	Foolish Baby/Can You See Me	1966	$200
DOT			
❏ 16876	Foolish Baby/Can You See Me	1966	$30
BRILEY, JEBRY LEE			
PAID			
❏ 141	Let Your Fingers Do the Walkin'/Riders and Drivers	1982	$6
BRILEY, MARTIN			
MERCURY			
❏ 880245-7	Dangerous Moments/ School for Dogs	1984	$4
❏ 880245-7 [PS]	Dangerous Moments/ School for Dogs	1984	$5
❏ 880680-7	Dirty Windows/It Shouldn't Have to Hurt That Much	1985	$4

Number	Title	Yr	NM
❏ 76137	I Don't Feel Better/Medley	1982	$5
❏ 875137-7	I Don't Feel Better/Medley	1989	$4
❏ 814182-7	One Night with a Stranger/ Say the Word	1983	$4
❏ 76121	Slipping Away/Medley	1981	$5
❏ 812165-7	The Salt in My Tears/Dumb Love	1983	$4
BRIM, JOHN			
CHESS			
❏ 1588	Go Away/That Ain't Right	1955	$200
❏ 1624	I Would Hate to See You Go/You Got Me Where You Want Me	1956	$200
PARROT			
❏ 799	Tough Times/Gary Stomp	1954	$700
—*Black vinyl*			
❏ 799	Tough Times/Gary Stomp	1954	$1200
—*Red vinyl*			
BRIMSTONES, THE			
MGM			
❏ 13653	It's All Over But the Crying/ What Is This Life	1966	$30
WORLD PACIFIC			
❏ 77834	Cold Hearted Woman/I'm in Misery	1966	$40
BRISTOL, JOHNNY			
ATLANTIC			
❏ 3360	Do It to My Mind/Love to Take a Chance to Taste the Wine	1976	$4
❏ 3421	Waiting on Love/ She's So Amazing	1977	$4
❏ 3501	When He Comes (You Will Know)/Strangers in the Dark Corners	1978	$4
❏ 3526	Why Stop Now/When He Comes (You Will Know)	1978	$4
HANDSHAKE			
❏ WS85304	Love No Longer Has a Hold on Me/Until I See You Again	1981	$70
❏ WS85300	My Guy/My Girl//Now	1980	$4
—*A-side with Amii Stewart*			
❏ 02594	Take Me Down/Loving and Free	1981	$4
MGM			
❏ 14715	Hang On In There Baby/ Take Care of You for Me	1974	$5
❏ 14792	Leave My World/All Goodbyes Aren't Good	1975	$5
❏ 14814	Love Takes Tears/ Go On and Dream	1975	$5
POLYDOR			
❏ 813982-7	Hang On In There Baby/ Stand By Me	1983	$3
—*Reissue*			
BRITISH LIONS			
RSO			
❏ 898	Wild in the Streets/Booster	1978	$6
BRITISH WALKERS, THE			
CAMEO			
❏ 466	Shake/That Was Yesterday	1967	$20
CHARGER			
❏ 108	The Girl Can't Help It/ Lonely Lover's Poem	1965	$40
TRY			
❏ 502	Diddley Daddy/I Found You	1964	$40
BRITO, PHIL			
MGM			
❏ 10779	White Christmas/Ave Maria	1950	$20
BRITT, ELTON, AND ROSALIE ALLEN			
RCA VICTOR			
❏ 48-0346	Ashes of Roses/Cotton Candy and a Toy Balloon	1950	$40
—*Originals on green vinyl*			
❏ 47-4752	Fiddlin' Fool/Wallflower Waltz	1952	$30
❏ 48-0405	It Is No Secret (What God Can Do)/A Little Bit Blue	1950	$40
—*Originals on green vinyl*			
❏ 48-0430	Let's Sail Away to Heaven/ You Missed Your Chance	1951	$40

Number	Title	Yr	NM
❏ 48-0396	Mocking Bird Hill/Tomorrow You'll Be Married	1950	$40
— Originals on green vinyl			
❏ 48-0302	Prairie Land Polka/ Acres of Diamonds	1950	$40
— Originals on green vinyl			
❏ 47-5178	Side by Side/Home Came a Sailor	1953	$30
❏ 48-0312	Tell Her You Love Her/ Written Guarantee	1950	$40
— Originals on green vinyl			
❏ 48-0064	Tennessee Yodel Polka/ Swiss Lullaby	1949	$50
— Originals on green vinyl			

BRITT, ELTON

Also see THE BEVERLY HILL BILLIES.

ABC

Number	Title	Yr	NM
❏ 10819	I Still Believe/It Just Happened That Way	1966	$10

ABC-PARAMOUNT

Number	Title	Yr	NM
❏ 10677	Home Sweet Homesick Blues/Now Is the Hour	1965	$15
❏ 10121	Sioux City Sue/Taller Than Trees	1960	$20
❏ 10080	The Convict and the Rose/Lost Highway	1960	$20
❏ 10743	There's a Star Spangled Banner Waving Somewhere/Red Wing	1965	$15

CERTRON

Number	Title	Yr	NM
❏ 10019	Step Into My Soul/ Three Things I'm Not	1970	$10

DECCA

Number	Title	Yr	NM
❏ 31568	Christmas in November/ Jingle Bell Polka	1963	$15

RCA VICTOR

Number	Title	Yr	NM
❏ 48-0164	Blueberry Lane/Wave to Me My Lady	1950	$50
— Originals on green vinyl			
❏ 47-5251	Broken Wings/Cannonball Yodel	1953	$30
❏ 48-0218	Candy Kisses/You'll Be Sorry from Now On	1950	$40
— Originals on green vinyl; reissue of 78			
❏ 48-0143	Chime Bells/Put My Little Shoes Away	1949	$50
— Originals on green vinyl; reissue of 78			
❏ 48-0125	Driftwood on the River/ Tears from the Sky	1949	$50
— Originals on green vinyl			
❏ 47-4532	Five Glasses on a Texas Bar/ The Blacksmith Blues	1952	$30
❏ 47-4630	Fooling Around/I May Hate Myself in the Morning	1952	$30
❏ 47-4786	God's Little Candles/I'm Gonna Walk and Talk with My Lord	1952	$30
❏ 47-5937	Hurts Me to My Heart/ Goodnight Mrs. Jones	1954	$30
❏ 47-6093	I Almost Lost My Mind/ Absent Minded Heart	1955	$30
❏ 48-0378	I'm the One Who Loves You/I'll Find You	1950	$40
— Originals on green vinyl			
❏ 48-0452	It Takes Two of a Kind/ Then I'll Grow Tired of You	1951	$40
❏ 48-0473	Lonely Little Robin/ Lookin' Around	1951	$40
❏ 48-0049	Lorelei/Rainbow in My Heart	1949	$50
— Originals on green vinyl			
❏ 48-0408	Lost and Found Blues/ My Dearest, My Darling	1950	$40
— Originals on green vinyl			
❏ 48-0044	Maybe I'll Cry Over You/ In a Swiss Chalet	1949	$50
— Originals on green vinyl			
❏ 47-5402	Maybe I Was Wrong/I Feel the Blues Comin' On	1953	$30
❏ 47-4988	Merry Texas Christmas, Y'All/ Christmas Will Be Here	1952	$30
❏ 47-6429	One Life, Two Loves/ Lonesome River	1956	$30
❏ 47-5795	One Way Ticket/ Trailing Arbutus	1954	$30
❏ 47-5996	Skater's Yodel/St. Louis Blues Yodel	1955	$30
❏ 47-4472	Summer Kisses/Jackass Blues	1952	$30
❏ 47-5620	Sweet Leilani/If You Should Change Your Mind	1954	$30
❏ 47-5509	That's How the Yodel Was Born/My Heart Was Made for You	1953	$30
❏ 47-6232	The Alpine Milkman/Shame	1955	$30
❏ 47-9658	The Bitter Taste/My California Sunshine Girl	1968	$8

Number	Title	Yr	NM
❏ 47-4531	The Little Boy I Knew/Don't Ever Be Afraid to Go Home	1952	$30
❏ 48-0339	The Stars and Stripes Forever/The Last Straw	1950	$40
— Originals on green vinyl			
❏ 47-5868	To You Sweetheart Aloha/Singing Hills	1954	$30

7-Inch Extended Plays

Number	Title	Yr	NM
❏ EPA-817	Give Me a Pinto Pal/Chime Bells//Cannonball Yodel/ Patent Leather Boots	1956	$20

BROADWAY (1)

HILLTAK

Number	Title	Yr	NM
❏ 7805	This Funk Is Made for Dancing/Love Bandit	1979	$5

BROADWAY SINGERS, THE

HIT

Number	Title	Yr	NM
❏ 214	I'll Never Find Another You/Come Back to Me	1965	$8
— B-side by William Randolph			

BRODY, LANE

EMI AMERICA

Number	Title	Yr	NM
❏ B-8218	Alibis/One Heart Away	1984	$4
❏ B-8283	Baby's Eyes/Anything But My Baby	1985	$4
❏ B-8266	He Burns Me Up/Memory Now	1985	$4
❏ B-8266 [PS]	He Burns Me Up/Memory Now	1985	$5

LIBERTY

Number	Title	Yr	NM
❏ B-1519	Hanging On/If I Were Loving You Now	1984	$4
❏ B-1457	He's Taken/My Side of the Bed	1982	$4
❏ B-1509	It's Another Silent Night/It's a Bad Night for Good Girls	1983	$4
❏ B-1470	More Nights/My Side of the Bed	1982	$4
❏ B-1498	Over You/My Side of the Bed	1983	$4
❏ B-1498 [PS]	Over You/My Side of the Bed	1983	$5

BROGUES, THE

CHALLENGE

Number	Title	Yr	NM
❏ 59311	But Now I'm Fine/Someday	1965	$40
❏ 59316	I Ain't No Miracle Worker/ Don't Shoot Me Down	1965	$40

TWILIGHT

Number	Title	Yr	NM
❏ 408	But Now I'm Fine/Early Bird	1965	$50
❏ 408	But Now I'm Fine/Someday	1965	$50

BROMBERG, DAVID

COLUMBIA

Number	Title	Yr	NM
❏ 45767	Sharon/Hardworkin' John	1973	$8
❏ 45612	The Holdup/Suffer to Sing the Blues	1972	$6

FANTASY

Number	Title	Yr	NM
❏ 812	Battle of Bull Run Medley/I Want to Go Home	1978	$4
❏ 854	Don't Let Your Deal Go Down/My Own House	1979	$4
❏ 785	Such a Night/Bluebirds	1977	$4

BRONSKI BEAT

MCA

Number	Title	Yr	NM
❏ 52831	C'mon! C'mon!/ Something Special	1986	$3
❏ 52831 [PS]	C'mon! C'mon!/ Something Special	1986	$3
❏ 52750	Hit That Perfect Beat/I Gave You Everything	1985	$3
❏ 52750 [PS]	Hit That Perfect Beat/I Gave You Everything	1985	$3
❏ 52494	Smalltown Boy/Memories	1984	$3
❏ 52494 [PS]	Smalltown Boy/Memories	1984	$3
❏ 52565	Why?/Cadillac Car	1985	$3
❏ 52565 [PS]	Why?/Cadillac Car	1985	$3

BRONZETTES, THE

PARKWAY

Number	Title	Yr	NM
❏ 929	Hot Spot/Run, Run, You Little Fool	1964	$15

BROOD, HERMAN

ARIOLA AMERICA

Number	Title	Yr	NM
❏ 805	I Don't Need You/ (B-side unknown)	1980	$5
❏ 7774	Love You Like I Love Myself/Hit	1979	$5
❏ 7754	Saturdaynight/Back (In Y'r Love)	1979	$5

BROOKLYN BRIDGE, THE

BUDDAH

Number	Title	Yr	NM
❏ 193	Day Is Done/Easy Way	1970	$6
❏ 193	Day Is Done/Opposites	1970	$6
❏ 179	Down by the River/Look Again	1970	$6
❏ 162	Free as the Wind/He's Not a Happy Man	1970	$6
❏ 317	I Feel Free (mono/stereo)	1972	$10
— As "The Bridge"; stock copy unknown			
❏ 60	Little Red Boat by the River/From My Window	1968	$6
❏ 293	Man in a Band/Bruno's Place	1972	$8
❏ 230	Wednesday in Your Garden (mono/stereo)	1971	$8
— Stock copy unknown			
❏ 95	Welcome Me Love/ Blessed Is the Rain	1969	$6
❏ 75	Worst That Could Happen/ Your Kite, My Kite	1968	$8

BROOKLYN DREAMS

CASABLANCA

Number	Title	Yr	NM
❏ 994	Hot Lovin' (Summer in the City)/(B-side unknown)	1979	$5
❏ 2313	I Won't Let Go/ Beautiful Dreamer	1981	$5
❏ 2289	Lover in the Night/ Moment in Time	1981	$4
❏ 962	Make It Last/Long Distance	1979	$5
❏ 2272	The Hollywood Knights/ (B-side unknown)	1980	$5

MILLENNIUM

Number	Title	Yr	NM
❏ 610	Music, Harmony and Rhythm/ Old Fashioned Girl	1978	$5
❏ 606	Sad Eyes/Hollywood Circles	1977	$5

BROOKMEYER, BOB, QUINTET

PACIFIC JAZZ

Number	Title	Yr	NM
❏ 642	Santa Claus Blues/ Sweet Like This	1956	$20

BROOKS, ALBERT

ASYLUM

Number	Title	Yr	NM
❏ XMAS1 [DJ]	A Daddy's Christmas (mono/stereo)	1974	$60
❏ XMAS1 [PS]	A Daddy's Christmas (mono/stereo)	1974	$125
❏ XMAS1 [DJ]	A Daddy's Christmas (mono/stereo)	1974	$60

BROOKS, BOBBY

HIT

Number	Title	Yr	NM
❏ 120	A World Without Love/ Chapel of Love	1964	$8
— B-side by the Flower Sisters			
❏ 127	Don't Let the Sun Catch You Crying/I'll Touch a Star	1964	$8
❏ 231	England Swings/A Taste of Honey	1965	$8
— B-side by the Nashville Five			
❏ 199	Hearts Are Funny Things/Goodnight	1965	$8
— B-side by Ed Hardin			
❏ 269	If I Were a Carpenter/ Poor Side of Town	1966	$8
— B-side by Bobby Sims			
❏ 202	I Must Be Seeing Things/Once a Cheater, Always a Cheater	1965	$8
— B-side by Connie Dee			
❏ 143	It Hurts to Be in Love/ Do Wah Diddy Diddy	1964	$20
— B-side by Bobby Cash			
❏ 146	Last Kiss/A Summer Song	1964	$8
❏ 156	Mountain of Love/Be Yourself	1964	$10
— B-side by the Jalopy Five			
❏ 109	See the Funny Little Clown/ My Heart Belongs to Only You	1964	$8
❏ 192	She's Come of Age/ Eight Days a Week	1965	$15
— B-side by the Jalopy Five			
❏ 123	Tell Me Why/Be Anything (But Be Mine)	1964	$8
— B-side by Connie Dee			
❏ 219	What's New Pussycat?/ Down in the Boondocks	1965	$8
— B-side by Ed Hardin			
❏ 176	Wise Like Solomon/ Hold What You've Got	1965	$8
— B-side by Leroy Jones			

Number	Title	Yr	NM

BROOKS BROTHERS BAND, THE
BUCKBOARD

❏ 115	Hurry On Home/ (B-side unknown)	1984	$6

BROOKS BROTHERS, THE
LONDON

❏ 9668	Once in Awhile/Poor Plan	1964	$10

—As "The Brooks

❏ 1987	Warpaint/Sometimes	1961	$20

LONDON INT'L.

❏ 10501	Ain't Gonna Wash for a Week/One Last Kiss	1962	$15
❏ 10515	Too Scared/Tell Tale	1962	$15

BROOKS, CHUCK, AND THE SHARPIES
DUB

❏ 2844	Spinning My Wheels/You Make Me Feel Mean	1958	$300

BROOKS, DONNIE
CHALLENGE

❏ 59331	I Call Your Name/Be Fair	1966	$8
❏ 59344	Pink Carousel/Mission Man	1966	$8

ERA

❏ 3049	All I Can Give/Wishbone	1961	$20
❏ 3194	Blue Soldier/Love Is Funny That Way	1968	$8
❏ 3052	Boomerang/How Long	1961	$20
❏ 3095	Cries My Heart/It's Not That Easy	1962	$20
❏ 3028	Doll House/Round Robin	1960	$20
❏ 3028 [PS]	Doll House/Round Robin	1960	$30
❏ 3063	Goodnight Judy/Your Little Boy's Gone Home	1961	$20
❏ 3004	Lil' Sweetheart/If You're Lookin'	1959	$30
❏ 3042	Memphis/That's Why	1961	$20
❏ 3042 [PS]	Memphis/That's Why	1961	$30
❏ 3018	Mission Bell/Do It for Me	1960	$30
❏ 3071	My Favorite Kind of Face/He Stole Flo	1962	$20
❏ 3077	Oh You Beautiful Doll/ Just a Bystander	1962	$20
❏ 3059	Sweet Lorraine/Up to My Ears in Tears	1961	$20
❏ 3014	The Devil Ain't a Man/ How Long	1960	$30
❏ 3007	White Orchid/Sway and Move with the Beat	1959	$30

HAPPY TIGER

❏ 526	Abracadabra/I Know You as a Woman	1970	$5
❏ 544	Hush/I Know You as a Woman	1970	$5
❏ 579	I'm Gonna Make You Love Me/Pink Carousel	1971	$5
❏ 566	(I Wanna) Have You for Myself/Rub-a-Dub-Dub	1971	$5
❏ 551	My God and I/Pink Carousel	1970	$5

MIDSONG INT'L.

❏ 1007	Big John/Get Fame, Son	1978	$4

OAK

❏ 1019	The Song That I Sing Is For You/Country Dude	1971	$5

REPRISE

❏ 0311	Can't Help Lovin' You/ Pickin' Up the Pieces	1964	$10
❏ 0261	Gone/Girl Machine	1964	$10
❏ 0363	Hey, Little Girl/I Never Get to Love You	1965	$12

YARDBIRD

❏ 8008	Hush/Sunshine, Summertime and Love	1968	$6
❏ 8006	Sunglasses on the Sand/ Sunshine, Summertime and Love	1968	$6
❏ 8010	Tree Trimming Time/ (Instrumental)	1968	$6

BROOKS, DUSTY, AND HIS TONES WITH JUANITA BROWN
SUN

❏ 182	Heaven or Fire/Tears and Wine	1953	$3000

—VG 1500; VG+ 2250

BROOKS, ELKIE
A&M

❏ 1968	Love Potion No. 9/Honey, Can I Put On Your Clothes	1977	$5
❏ 2271	Paint Your Pretty Pictures/ Pull On the Rope	1980	$4

❏ 2068	Since You Went Away/ Too Precious	1978	$4
❏ 1953	Sunshine After the Rain/ You Did Something for Me	1977	$5
❏ 1781	Where Do We Go from Here (Rich Man's Woman)/Roll Me Over	1976	$5

BROOKS, GARTH
CAPITOL

❏ B-44430	If Tomorrow Never Comes/ Nobody Gets Off in This Town	1989	$10
❏ B-44342	Much Too Young (To Feel This Damn Old)/Alabama Clay	1989	$8

BROOKS, JOHN
HIT

❏ 251	Soul and Inspiration/Good Lovin'	1966	$15

—B-side by the Spartas

BROOKS, KAREN, AND JOHNNY CASH
WARNER BROS.

❏ 28979	I Will Dance with You/ Too Bad for Love	1985	$4

BROOKS, KAREN
WARNER BROS.

❏ 29154	A Simple I Love You/Give It Up	1984	$4
❏ 29302	Born to Love You/A Little Common Kindness	1984	$4
❏ 29958	Country Girl/New Way Out	1982	$4
❏ 29789	If That's What You're Thinking/ Every Beat of My Heart	1983	$4
❏ 29225	Tonight I'm Here with Someone Else/Give It Up	1984	$4
❏ 29644	Walk On/Every Beat of My Heart	1983	$4

BROOKS, KIX
AVION

❏ 103	Baby, When Your Heart Breaks Down/(B-side unknown)	1983	$8

CAPITOL

❏ B-44217	I'm On to You/River Don't Roll	1988	$5
❏ B-44275	Sacred Ground/Story of My Life	1988	$5
❏ B-44352	She Does the Walk On By/(B-side unknown)	1989	$6

BROOKS, LILLIAN
KING

❏ 4999	Merry Christmas To Michael/ Twinkle Twinkle Christmas Star	1956	$30

BROOKS, MEL
ASYLUM

❏ 45458	High Anxiety/ Springtime for Hitler	1978	$6

WMOT

❏ WS9- 02909	It's Good to Be the King (Part 1)/(Part 2)	1982	$5

BROOKS, NANCY
ARISTA

❏ 0385	I'm Not Gonna Cry Anymore/ Let's Go Whoop Ti Hoo	1979	$4

BROOKS, RAMONA
MANHATTAN

❏ XW1052	Skinnydippin'/Rhythm Rhapsody	1977	$5

BROOKS, TED
DECCA

❏ 9-46374	The Hot Guitar/Entitled	1951	$40

BROOM, BOBBY
ARISTA

❏ 9259	Beat Freak/Magic Johnson	1984	$4

ARISTA/GRP

❏ 2516	Saturday Night/ Remember When	1981	$5

BROONZY, BIG BILL
CHESS

❏ 1546	Little City Woman/Lonesome	1953	$400

MERCURY

❏ 8271	Hey Hey/Walkin' the Lonesome Road	1952	$40
❏ 8284	Mopper's Blues/I Know She Will	1952	$40
❏ 70039	South Bound Train/Leavin' Day	1953	$30
❏ 71352	Tomorrow/Hey Hey	1958	$30
❏ 8261	Willie Mae Blues/ Hollerin' the Blues	1951	$40

ROTHER BEYOND
CAPITOL

❏ 7PRO-79725	Be My Twin (same on both sides)	1989	$6

—Vinyl is promo only

❏ B-44340	He Ain't No Competition/ Call Me Lonely	1988	$3
❏ B-44340 [PS]	He Ain't No Competition/ Call Me Lonely	1988	$3

BROTHER FOX AND TAR BABY
CAPITOL

❏ 2940	Electric Chair/Steel Dog Man	1970	$12

BROTHER SISTERS, THE
MERCURY

❏ 71195	Alone (Why Must I Be Alone)/ Pass Me the Mustard	1957	$30
❏ 71678	Strawberry Shortcake/Crystal Ball	1960	$30

BROTHER TO BROTHER
SUGAR HILL

❏ 765	Monster Jam (I Want to Funk With You)/(B-side unknown)	1981	$8

TURBO

❏ 048	Chance with You/Joni	1976	$8
❏ 040	Every Nigger Is a Star/ Mother Earth	1974	$8
❏ 039	In the Bottle/The Affair	1974	$8
❏ 049	Leavin' Me/Phattenin'	1976	$8
❏ 045	Let Your Mind Be Free/ (Instrumental)	1976	$8

BROTHERHOOD
MCA

❏ 40916	Change of Pace/Given My Life	1978	$5
❏ 40969	Funk Footin'/Soul Power	1978	$5

BROTHERHOOD OF MAN, THE
BELL

❏ 45456	When Love Catches Up on You/(B-side unknown)	1974	$4

DERAM

❏ 85078	California Sunday Morning/ Do Your Thing	1972	$5
❏ 85056	Love One Another/A Little Bit of Heaven	1970	$6
❏ 85081	Say a Prayer/Follow Me	1972	$5
❏ 85077	Sing in the Sunshine/You and I	1971	$5
❏ 85070	This Boy/You Can Depend on Me	1971	$5
❏ 85065	Where Are You Going To My Love/Living in the Land of Love	1970	$5

PRIVATE STOCK

❏ 45,165	Angelo/All Night	1977	$5
❏ 45,148	Oh Boy (The Mood I'm In)/ (B-side unknown)	1977	$5

PYE

❏ 71066	Save Your Kisses for Me/ Let's Love Together	1976	$5
❏ 71043	Spring of 1912/(B-side unknown)	1976	$6
❏ 71076	Sweet Lady from Georgia/ Sugar Honey Love	1976	$5

BROTHERS AND SISTERS
ODE

❏ 123	Mr. Tambourine Man/The Times They Are a-Changing	1969	$8
❏ 121	The Mighty Quinn/ Chimes of Freedom	1969	$8

BROTHERS BY CHOICE
ALA

❏ 104	Baby You Really Got Me Going/Take a Little More	1979	$5
❏ 110	How Much I Feel/She Puts the Ease Back Into Easy	1980	$5
❏ 108	Oh Darlin'/Why Can't You Make Up Your Mind	1979	$5
❏ 103	She Puts the Ease Back Into Easy/(Instrumental)	1978	$5

BROTHERS CAIN, THE
ACE...

Number	Title	Yr	NM

BROTHERS CAIN, THE — ACTA
- 810 — Better Times/Pupil Alexander — 1967 — $30
- 820 — It Sure Is Groovy/Anyway You Like It — 1968 — $30

MERCURY
- 72437 — In Love with One/Two Wrongs — 1965 — $30

BROTHERS FOUR, THE — COLUMBIA
- 42787 — 55 Days at Peking/All for the Love of a Girl — 1963 — $8
- S731091 [S] — Abilene/Frogg — 1961 — $15
- 44058 — Ain't No More Cane on the Brazos/Shenandoah — 1967 — $6
- 43984 — All I Need Is You/And Then the Sun Came Down — 1967 — $6
- S731092 [S] — Betty and Dupree/Pastures of Plenty — 1961 — $15
- 42256 — Blue Water Line/Summer Days Alone — 1962 — $8
- 42256 [PS] — Blue Water Line/Summer Days Alone — 1962 — $15
- 43825 — Changes/For Emily, Whenever I May Find Her — 1966 — $6
- 41461 — Chicka Mucha Hi Di/Darlin' Won't You Wait — 1959 — $10
- 43317 — Come Kiss Me Love/Lazy Harry's — 1965 — $6
- 42391 — Darlin' Sporty Jenny/Slowly, Slowly — 1962 — $8
- 42507 — Five Weeks in a Balloon/Land of the Midnight Sun — 1962 — $8
- 42507 [PS] — Five Weeks in a Balloon/Land of the Midnight Sun — 1962 — $15
- 42888 — Four Strong Winds/John B. Sails — 1963 — $8
- 41958 — Frogg/Sweet Rosyanne — 1961 — $8
- 41958 [PS] — Frogg/Sweet Rosyanne — 1961 — $15
- 41571 — Greenfields/Angelique-O — 1960 — $8
- 41571 [PS] — Greenfields/Angelique-O — 1960 — $15
- 44278 — Here Today and Gone Tomorrow/No Sad Songs from Me — 1967 — $6
- S731089 [S] — Hey Hey My Honey/Low Bridge — 1961 — $15
- 42927 — Hootenanny Saturday Night/Across the Sea — 1963 — $8
- 43919 — I'll Be Home for Christmas/'Twas the Night Before Christmas — 1966 — $8
- 44578 — I'm Falling Down/Sweet Dreams, Sweet Runaway Child — 1968 — $5
- S731093 [S] — Island Woman/This Land Is Your Land — 1961 — $15

— The above five are "Stereo Seven" 33 1/3 rpm jukebox singles from set "JS 7-25" entitled "Roamin' with the Brothers Four

- 43493 — It Was a Very Good Year/Wild Colonial Boy — 1965 — $6
- 41692 — My Tani/Ellie Lou — 1960 — $8
- 41692 [PS] — My Tani/Ellie Lou — 1960 — $15
- 42142 — My Woman Left Me/Nobody Knows — 1961 — $8
- 43025 — Seven Daffodils/San Francisco Bay Blues — 1964 — $8
- 44832 — Skip a Rope/Strangest Dream — 1969 — $5
- 43211 — Somewhere/Turn Around — 1965 — $6
- 43147 — Take This Hammer/Little Play Soldier — 1964 — $8
- 44175 — The First Time Ever/Walkin' Backwards Down the Road — 1967 — $6
- 41808 — The Green Leaves of Summer/Beautiful Brown Eyes — 1960 — $8
- 41808 [PS] — The Green Leaves of Summer/Beautiful Brown Eyes — 1960 — $15
- S731090 [S] — The Lilies Grow High/Ballad of Sam Hill — 1961 — $15
- 42586 — The Tavern Song/25 Minutes to Go — 1962 — $8
- 42586 [PS] — The Tavern Song/25 Minutes to Go — 1962 — $30
- 42450 — This Train/Summertime — 1962 — $8
- 42450 [PS] — This Train/Summertime — 1962 — $15
- 43404 — Try to Remember/Sakura — 1965 — $6
- 3-42235 — What Child Is This? (Greensleeves)/Christmas Bells — 1961 — $30

— Columbia Single 33" with small hole; orange label

- 4-42235 — What Child Is This? (Greensleeves)/Christmas Bells — 1961 — $10

FANTASY
- 640 — Going Back to Big Sur/Here I Go Again — 1970 — $5

BROTHERS GRIMM, THE — MERCURY
- 72512 — A Man Needs Love/Looky, Looky — 1966 — $10

BROTHERS GUIDING LIGHT FEATURING DAVID — MERCURY
- 73389 — Getting Together/Sweet Stuff — 1973 — $250

BROTHERS JOHNSON, THE — A&M
- 2098 — Ain't We Funkin' Now/Dancin' and Prancin' — 1978 — $4
- 2368 — Dancin' Free/Do It for Love — 1981 — $4
- 1881 — Free and Single/Thunder Thumbs and Lightning Licks — 1976 — $4
- 1851 — Get the Funk Out Ma Face/Tomorrow — 1976 — $4
- 1851 [PS] — Get the Funk Out Ma Face/Tomorrow — 1976 — $6
- 1806 — I'll Be Good to You/The Devil — 1976 — $4
- 1806 [PS] — I'll Be Good to You/The Devil — 1976 — $6
- 2527 — I'm Giving You All My Love/The Real Thing — 1983 — $4
- 2238 — Light Up the Night/Street Wave — 1980 — $4
- 2015 — Love Is/Right On Time — 1978 — $4
- 2689 — Lovers Forever/Hot Mama — 1984 — $4
- 1229 — Party Avenue/Ball of Fire — 1988 — $3
- 2280 — Smilin' On Ya (mono/stereo) — 1980 — $5

— Promo only

- 2216 — Stomp!/Let's Swing — 1980 — $4
- 1949 — Strawberry Letter 23/Dancin' and Prancin' — 1977 — $4
- 1949 [PS] — Strawberry Letter 23/Dancin' and Prancin' — 1977 — $6
- 1949 [DJ] — Strawberry Letter 23 (mono/stereo) — 1977 — $20

— Promo only on red vinyl

- 2254 — Treasure/Celebrations — 1980 — $4
- 2506 — Welcome to the Club/The End of an Era — 1982 — $4

QWEST
- 28877 — Back Against the Wall Part 1/Part 2 — 1985 — $3

BROTHERS, THE — ARGO
- 5318 — Lazy Susan/Deep Sleep — 1958 — $30
- 5329 — Sioux City Sue/Deep Sleep — 1959 — $30

CHECKER
- 995 — My True Love/One Lonely Heart — 1961 — $20

BROWN, CLARENCE "GATEMOUTH" — PEACOCK
- 1662 — Ain't That Dandy/September Song — 1956 — $100
- 1600 — Baby Take It Easy/Just Got Lucky — 1952 — $400
- 1617 — Boogie Uproar/Hurry Back Good News — 1953 — $200
- 1607 — Dirty Work at the Crossroads/You Got Money — 1952 — $250
- 1653 — Gate's Salty Blues/Rock My Blues Away — 1955 — $125
- 1633 — Midnight Hour/For Now So Long — 1954 — $200
- 1637 — Okie Dokie Stomp/Depression Blues — 1954 — $200
- 1619 — Please Tell Me Baby/Gate Walks to Board — 1953 — $200

BROWN, AL — AMY
- 806 — It's True 'Bout Love/Sweet Little Love — 1960 — $30
- 811 — Take Me Back/Mention Me — 1960 — $30
- 804 — The Madison/Mo' Madison — 1960 — $30

BROWN, ALEX — MERCURY
- 880694-7 — (Come On) Shout/Technique — 1985 — $4

ROXBURY
- 2024 — Love Really Hurts Without You/Ride a Wild Horse — 1976 — $5

TANGERINE
- 1001 — I'm in Love/What Would You Do Without Someone to Love — 1971 — $20

BROWN, ARTHUR, THE CRAZY WORLD OF — ATLANTIC
- 2556 — Fire/Rest Cure — 1968 — $10

TRACK
- 2582 — I Put a Spell on You/Nightmare — 1968 — $8

BROWN, BILLY (1) — CHALLENGE
- 59396 — One of the Ten Most Wanted Women/Open Arms — 1969 — $8

COLUMBIA
- 4-41029 — Did We Have a Party/It's Love — 1957 — $50
- 4-20982 — Don't Hold Back/Rich in Love — 1952 — $60
- 4-41297 — Flip Out/Echo Mountain — 1958 — $50
- 4-41100 — Meet Me in the Alley, Sally/I Wanted You — 1958 — $60
- 4-20936 — Tight Wad/I'm Sending Back Everything But Memories — 1952 — $60
- 4-20789 — Trusting Heart/I Hope I Don't Live Long Enough to Lose You — 1951 — $60

DECCA
- 9-29559 — Drunk-Drunk Again/High Heels But No Soul — 1955 — $30

REPUBLIC
- 2012 — Look Out Heart (Here Comes Love)/It Don't Take Long to Learn — 1961 — $20
- 2004 — The Last Letter/Be Honest with Me — 1960 — $20

STARS
- 552 — Did We Have a Party/It's Love — 1957 — $125

BROWN, BILLY (2) — BERNES
- 101 — What It Means to Be an American/Star Spangled Banner — 1979 — $6

BROWN, BUSTER — FIRE
- 1040 — Blues When It Rains/Good News — 1961 — $30
- 1008 — Fannie Mae/Lost in a Dream — 1959 — $30
- 1023 — Is You Is or Is You Ain't My Baby/Don't Dog Your Woman — 1960 — $30
- 1032 — Sincerely/Doctor Brown — 1960 — $30
- 2021 — Sugar Babe/Don't Dog Your Woman — 1962 — $20
- 507 — Sugar Babe/I'm Going -- But I'll Be Back — 1962 — $30
- 1020 — The Madison Shuffle/John Henry — 1960 — $30

RCA VICTOR
- PB-10023 — Eloise/Fallin' Out of Love — 1974 — $5

WHITE WHALE
- 316 — The Proud One/I've Got It Made — 1969 — $10

BROWN, CHARLES — ACE
- 561 — Educated Fool/I Want to Go Back Home — 1959 — $15

— With Amos Milburn

- 599 — Love's Like a River/Boys Will Be Boys — 1960 — $15
- 599 — Love's Like a River/Sing My Blues Tonight — 1960 — $15

ALADDIN
- 3200 — All My Life/Don't Leave Me Poor — 1953 — $70
- 3076 — Black Night/Once There Was a Fool — 1951 — $200

— Charles Brown records on Aladdin prior to 3076 are unconfirmed on 45 rpm

- 3272 — By the Bend of the River/Honey Slipper — 1955 — $40
- 3163 — Evening Shadows/Moonrise — 1953 — $70
- 3220 — Everybody's Got Trouble/I Fool Around with You — 1954 — $50
- 3423 — Hard Times/Ooh, Ooh Sugar — 1958 — $30
- 3116 — Hard Times/Tender Heart — 1952 — $100
- 3290 — Hot Lips and Seven Kisses/Fools' Paradise — 1955 — $40
- 3091 — I'll Always Be in Love with You/The Message — 1951 — $100
- 3235 — Let's Walk/Crying Mercy — 1954 — $50
- 3191 — Lonesome Feeling/I Lost Everything — 1953 — $70
- 3348 — Merry Christmas, Baby/Black Night — 1956 — $30
- 3296 — My Heart Is Mended/Trees, Trees — 1955 — $40
- 3254 — My Silent Love/Foolish — 1954 — $50
- 3366 — Please Believe Me It's a Sin to Tell a Lie — 1957 — $30
- 3316 — Please Don't Drive Me Away/One Minute to One — 1956 — $30
- 3209 — P.S. I Love You/Cryin' and Driftin' Blues — 1953 — $70
- 3138 — See/Without Your Love — 1952 — $100
- 3092 — Seven Long Days/Don't Fool with My Heart — 1951 — $100
- 3342 — Soothe Me/I'll Always Be in Love with You — 1956 — $30
- 3120 — Still Water/My Last Affair — 1952 — $100
- 3176 — Take Me/Rising Sun — 1953 — $70

BLUESWAY
- 61031 — Merry Christmas, Baby/Rainy, Rainy Day — 1969 — $6

CASH
- 1052 — Lost in the Night/I Sold My Heart to the Junkman — 1957 — $40

— B-side by the Basin Street Boys

Number	Title	Yr	NM

EASTWEST

Number	Title	Yr	NM
❏ 106	When Did You Leave Heaven/ We've Got a Lot in Common	1958	$30

GALAXY

Number	Title	Yr	NM
❏ 766	Abraham, Martin, and John/(B-side unknown)	1968	$10
❏ 762	I'm Gonna Push On/ Cry No More	1968	$10

HOLLYWOOD

Number	Title	Yr	NM
❏ 1021	Merry Christmas Baby/ Sleigh Ride	1954	$30

— Charles Brown's first recording of the A-side, released on 78 on Exclusive 254 (1946); B-side by Lloyd Glenn; maroon label

Number	Title	Yr	NM
❏ 1006	Pleading for Your Love/ The Best I Can Do	1954	$50

IMPERIAL

Number	Title	Yr	NM
❏ 5905	Black Night/Drifting Blues	1963	$10
❏ 5830	Fool's Paradise/ Lonesome Feeling	1962	$10
❏ 5961	I'm Savin' My Love for You/ Please Don't Drive Me Away	1963	$10
❏ 5902	Merry Christmas Baby/I Lost Everything	1962	$10

JEWEL

Number	Title	Yr	NM
❏ 814	Christmas in Heaven/ Just a Blessing	1970	$6
❏ 830	I Don't Know/For You	1972	$5
❏ 838	I've Got Your Love/I Just Can't Get Over You	1973	$5
❏ 815	Merry Christmas Baby/Please Come Home for Christmas	1970	$6
❏ 847	Please Come Home for Christmas/Christmas in Heaven	1974	$5

KENT

Number	Title	Yr	NM
❏ 501	Merry Christmas Baby/3 O'Clock Blues	1968	$10

KING

Number	Title	Yr	NM
❏ 5439	Angel Baby/Baby Oh Baby	1961	$15
❏ 5852	Blow Out All the Candles/ Come Home	1964	$10
❏ 5523	Butterfly/This Fool Has Learned	1961	$15
❏ 5946	Christmas Blues/My Most Miserable Christmas	1964	$10
❏ 5947	Christmas Comes (But Once a Year)/Bringin' In a Brand New Year	1964	$10
❏ 5530	Christmas in Heaven/It's Christmas All Year 'Round	1961	$15
❏ 5731	Christmas Questions/ Wrap Yourself in a Christmas Package	1963	$10
❏ 6420	For the Good Times/ Lonesome and Driftin'	1973	$5
❏ 6192	Hang On a Little Longer/ Black Night	1968	$8
❏ 5802	If You Don't Believe I'm Crying/I Wanna Be Close	1963	$10
❏ 5722	I'm Just a Drifter/I Don't Want Your Rambling Letters	1963	$10
❏ 5726	It's Christmas Time/ Christmas Finds Me Lonely	1963	$10
❏ 5464	I Wanna Go Back Home/ My Little Baby	1961	$15

— With Amos Milburn

Number	Title	Yr	NM
❏ 5825	Lucky Dreamer/Too Fine for Crying	1963	$10
❏ 6194	Merry Christmas, Baby/Let's Make Every Day Christmas	1968	$8
❏ 5405	Please Come Home for Christmas/Christmas (Comes But Once a Year)	1960	$15

— B-side by Amos Milburn; original blue label

Number	Title	Yr	NM
❏ 5405	Please Come Home for Christmas/Christmas (Comes But Once a Year)	1970	$6

— B-side by Amos Milburn; black label

Number	Title	Yr	NM
❏ 5570	Without a Friend/If You Play with Cats	1961	$15
❏ 1393	Merry Christmas, Baby/Silent Night	1980	$5

— B-side by Baby Washington

LILLY

Number	Title	Yr	NM
❏ 506	Bon Voyage/Bye and Bye	1962	$10

MAINSTREAM

Number	Title	Yr	NM
❏ 607	Pledging My Love/ Tomorrow Night	1965	$8

NOLA

Number	Title	Yr	NM
❏ 702	Standing on the Outside/I'll Love You (If You Let Me)	1965	$8

SWING TIME

Number	Title	Yr	NM
❏ 259	Be Fair with Me/Sunny Road	1952	$120
❏ 253	I'll Miss You/New Orleans Blues	1952	$120

UNITED ARTISTS

Number	Title	Yr	NM
❏ 0085	Drifting Blues/Black Night	1973	$4

— Silver Spotlight Series issue

Number	Title	Yr	NM
❏ 0086	I Lost Everything/ Lonesome Feeling	1973	$4

— Silver Spotlight Series issue

Number	Title	Yr	NM
❏ XW582	Merry Christmas Baby/ (B-side unknown)	1974	$5

UPSIDE

Number	Title	Yr	NM
❏ PRO 002 [PS]	Santa Claus Boogie	1986	$4
❏ PRO 002	Santa Claus Boogie (one-sided)	1986	$4

— Flexidisc

BROWN, CHARLIE
HIT

Number	Title	Yr	NM
❏ 164	Legend of Daniel Boone/ Ballad of Daniel Boone	1964	$8

— B-side by Ricky Dickens

BROWN, CHUCK AND THE SOUL SEARCHERS
POLYDOR

Number	Title	Yr	NM
❏ 14277	Boogie Up the Nation Pt. 1/Pt. 2	1975	$30

SOURCE

Number	Title	Yr	NM
❏ 40967	Bustin' Loose Part 1/ Bustin' Loose Part 2	1978	$5
❏ 41279	Come On and Boogie Part 1/ Come On and Boogie Part 2	1980	$5
❏ 41013	Game Seven Part 1/ Game Seven Part 2	1979	$5
❏ 41226	Sticks and Stones (But the Funk Will Never Hurt You) Part 1/Part 2	1980	$5

SUSSEX

Number	Title	Yr	NM
❏ 517	Blow Your Whistle/ Funk to the Folks	1974	$30
❏ 627	If It Ain't Funky/Wind Song	1974	$30
❏ 244	It's All in Your Mind/ Soul to the People	1972	$40
❏ 253	Think/1993	1973	$40
❏ 236	We the People/We the People, Pt. 2	1972	$40

BROWN, DANNY JOE
EPIC

Number	Title	Yr	NM
❏ 14-02398	Edge of Sundown/ Run for Your Life	1981	$4

BROWN, DENNIS
A&M

Number	Title	Yr	NM
❏ 2507	Any Day Now/The Handwriting on the Wall	1982	$5
❏ 2313	Foul Play/The World Is Troubled	1981	$5
❏ 2423	Get High on Your Love/ Halfway Up, Halfway Down	1982	$5
❏ 2577	Historical Places/Save a Little Love for Me	1983	$5
❏ 2407	Love Has Found Its Way/ Why Baby Why	1982	$5
❏ 2337	On the Rocks/The World Is Troubled	1981	$5

BROWN, DON
1ST AMERICAN

Number	Title	Yr	NM
❏ 105	Hug on a Thrill/Hold On	1978	$6
❏ 102	Sitting in Limbo/ Romance and Magic	1978	$6

BROWN, FLOYD
ABC DOT

Number	Title	Yr	NM
❏ 17702	Let's Get Acquainted Again/But I Do	1977	$4

BROWN, FRED
HIT

Number	Title	Yr	NM
❏ 60	Can't Get Used to Losing You/Baby Workout	1963	$8

— B-side by Leroy Jones

BROWN, FRED X.
HIT

Number	Title	Yr	NM
❏ 16	The Man Who Shot Liberty Valance/It Keeps Right On a-Hurtin'	1962	$8

BROWN, GENE
DOT

Number	Title	Yr	NM
❏ 15709	Playing with My Heart Again/Big Door	1958	$70

BROWN, GEORGIA
MERCURY

Number	Title	Yr	NM
❏ 884991-7	George Jones on the Jukebox/I Hear You Knocking	1986	$4

— B-side by D.J. Fontana Band

BROWN, JAMES
A&M

Number	Title	Yr	NM
❏ 3022	I Got You (I Feel Good)/ Nowhere to Run	1988	$4

— B-side by Martha and the Vandellas

Number	Title	Yr	NM
❏ 3022 [PS]	I Got You (I Feel Good)/ Nowhere to Run	1988	$4

— Good Morning Vietnam" sleeve

AUGUSTA SOUND

Number	Title	Yr	NM
❏ 94023	Bring It On ... Bring It On/The Night Time Is the Right Time (To Be With the One That You Love)	1983	$4
❏ 94023 [PS]	Bring It On ... Bring It On/The Night Time Is the Right Time (To Be With the One That You Love)	1983	$4

BETHLEHEM

Number	Title	Yr	NM
❏ 3098	A Man Has to Go Back to the Crossroads/The Drunk	1969	$20
❏ 3089	I Loves You Porgy/ Yours and Mine	1969	$20

FEDERAL

Number	Title	Yr	NM
❏ 12311	Baby Cries Over the Ocean/That Dood It	1957	$30
❏ 12316	Begging, Begging/That's When I Lost My Heart	1958	$30
❏ 12316	Begging, Begging/That's When I Lost My Heart	1958	$70
❏ 12361 [M]	Don't Let It Happen to Me/ Good Good Lovin'	1959	$30
❏ S-12361 [S]	Don't Let It Happen to Me/ Good Good Lovin'	1959	$60
❏ 12292	Gonna Try/Can't Be the Same	1957	$30
❏ 12264	I Don't Know/I Feel That Old Feeling Coming On	1956	$30
❏ 12369	I'll Go Crazy/I Know It's True	1960	$30
❏ 12364	It Was You/Got to Cry	1959	$30
❏ 12352 [M]	I've Got to Change/ It Hurts to Tell You	1959	$30
❏ S-12352 [S]	I've Got to Change/ It Hurts to Tell You	1959	$60
❏ 12300	I Walked Alone/You're Mine, You're Mine	1957	$30
❏ 12348	I Want You So Bad/There Must Be a Reason	1959	$30
❏ 12290	I Won't Plead No More/ Chonnie On Chon	1957	$30
❏ 12295	Love or a Game/Messing with the Blues	1957	$30
❏ 12258	Please, Please, Please/ Why Do You Do Me?	1956	$50
❏ 12370	Think/You've Got the Power	1960	$30
❏ 12378	This Old Heart/I Wonder When You're Coming Home	1960	$30
❏ 12337	Try Me/Tell Me What I Did Wrong	1958	$40

KING

Number	Title	Yr	NM
❏ 6280	Ain't It Funky Now (Part 1)/ Ain't It Funky Now (Part 2)	1970	$8
❏ 6025	Ain't That a Groove Part I/ Ain't That a Groove Part II	1966	$15
❏ 6112	America Is My Home -- Part 1/ America Is My Home -- Part 2	1967	$15
❏ 5524	Baby You're Right/I'll Never, Never Let You Go	1961	$20
❏ 6204	Believers Shall Enjoy/Tit for Tat (Ain't No Turning Back)	1968	$12
❏ 5442	Bewildered/If You Want Me	1961	$20
❏ 6071	Bring It Up/Nobody Knows	1967	$15
❏ 6310	Brother Rapp (Part 1) & (Part 2)/Bewildered	1970	$8
❏ 6329	Call Me Super Bad (Part 1 & Part 2)/Call Me Super Bad (Part 3)	1970	$30

— First pressing: Note longer title

Number	Title	Yr	NM
❏ 5698	(Can You) Feel It Part 1/ (Can You) Feel It Part 2	1962	$20
❏ 6110	Cold Sweat -- Part 1/ Cold Sweat -- Part 2	1967	$15
❏ 6033	Come Over Here/Tell Me What You're Gonna Do	1966	$15
❏ 6056	Don't Be a Drop-Out/Tell Me That You Love Me	1966	$15
❏ 5956	Fine Old Foxy Self/Medley	1964	$20
❏ 6290	Funky Drummer (Part 1)/ Funky Drummer (Part 2)	1970	$8
❏ 6122	Get It Together (Part 1)/ Get It Together (Part 2)	1967	$15
❏ 6347	Get Up, Get Into It, Get Involved Pt. 1/Get Up, Get Into It, Get Involved Pt. 2	1971	$8

Number	Title	Yr	NM
❑ 6318	Get Up (I Feel Like Being A) Sex Machine (Part 1)/ Get Up (I Feel Like Being A) Sex Machine (Part 2)	1970	$8
❑ 6213	Give It Up or Turnit A Loose/I'll Lose My Mind	1969	$10
❑ 6198	Goodbye My Love/ Shades of Brown	1968	$10
❑ 5968	Have Mercy Baby/ Just Won't Do Right	1964	$20
❑ 6164	Here I Go/Shhhh	1968	$15
❑ 6339	Hey America/(Instrumental)	1970	$8
❑ 6339 [PS]	Hey America/(Instrumental)	1970	$20
❑ 5876	How Long Darling/Again	1964	$20
❑ 6144	I Can't Stand Myself (When You Touch Me)/There Was a Time	1967	$15
❑ 6363	I Cried/World (Part 2)	1971	$8
❑ 6040	I Don't Care/It Was You	1966	$15
❑ 5466	I Don't Mind/Love Don't Love Nobody	1961	$20
❑ 6224	I Don't Want Nobody to Give Me Nothing (Open Up the Door, I'll Get It Myself) Part 1/Part 2	1969	$10
❑ 6155	I Got the Feelin'/If I Ruled the World	1968	$15
❑ 6015	I Got You (I Feel Good)/I Can't Help It (I Just Do, Do, Do)	1965	$20
❑ 6141	I Guess I'll Have to Cry, Cry, Cry/Just Plain Funk	1967	$15
❑ 6020	I'll Go Crazy/Lost Someone	1966	$15
❑ 6273	I'm Not Demanding (Part 1)/I'm Not Demanding (Part 2)	1969	$10
❑ 6322	I'm Not Demanding (Part 1)/I'm Not Demanding (Part 2)	1970	$8
❑ 6206	In the Middle (Part 2)/Tit for Tat (Ain't No Turning Back)	1969	$10

—A-side: With Marva Whitney

Number	Title	Yr	NM
❑ 5687	It Hurts to Be in Love/You Can Make It If You Try	1962	$20

—With Yvonne Fair

Number	Title	Yr	NM
❑ 6035	It's a Man's Man's Man's World/Is It Yes Or Is It No?	1966	$15
❑ 6292	It's a New Day (Part 1)/ It's a New Day (Part 2)	1970	$8
❑ 6277	It's Christmas Time (Part 1)/ It's Christmas Time (Part 2)	1969	$10
❑ 6037	I've Got Money/Just Won't Do Right	1966	$15
❑ 6255	Let a Man Come In and Do the Popcorn Part One/Sometime	1969	$12
❑ 6293	Let It Be Me/Baby Don't You Know	1970	$8

—A-side: With Vicki Anderson; B-side: Vicki Anderson solo

Number	Title	Yr	NM
❑ 6072	Let's Make Christmas Mean Something This Year (Part 1)/ Let's Make Christmas Mean Something This Year (Part 2)	1967	$15
❑ 6205	Let's Unite the World at Christmas/In the Middle (Part 1)	1968	$12
❑ 6100	Let Yourself Go/Good Rockin' Tonight	1967	$15
❑ 6166	Licking Stick -- Licking Stick (Part 1)/Licking Stick -- Licking Stick (Part 2)	1968	$15
❑ 5710	Like a Baby/Every Beat of My Heart	1963	$20
❑ 6235	Little Groove Maker (Part 1)/Any Day Now	1969	$12
❑ 6235	Little Groove Maker (Part 1)/I'm Shook	1969	$12
❑ 5573	Lost Someone/Cross Firing	1961	$20
❑ 6250	Lowdown Popcorn/ Top of the Stack	1969	$10
❑ 5672	Mashed Potatoes U.S.A./ You Don't Have to Go	1962	$20
❑ 6159	Maybe Good, Maybe Bad (Part 1)/(Part 2)	1968	$20
❑ 6111	Mona Lisa/It Won't Be Me	1967	$70

—Evidently not released or pulled shortly after release

Number	Title	Yr	NM
❑ 6048	Money Won't Change You Part 1/ Money Won't Change You Part 2	1966	$15
❑ 6245	Mother Popcorn (You Got to Have a Mother for Me) Part 1/ Mother Popcorn (You Got to Have a Mother for Me) Part 2	1969	$10
❑ 5842	Oh Baby Don't You Weep (Part 1)/ Oh Baby Don't You Weep (Part 2)	1964	$20
❑ 5842 [PS]	Oh Baby Don't You Weep (Part 1)/ Oh Baby Don't You Weep (Part 2)	1964	$30
❑ 5999	Papa's Got a Brand New Bag Part I/Papa's Got a Brand New Bag Part II	1965	$20
❑ 6275	Part Two (Let a Man Come In and Do the Popcorn)/ Get a Little Hipper	1969	$12
❑ 5853	Please, Please, Please/ In the Wee Wee Hours	1964	$20
❑ 5739	Prisoner of Love/Choo Choo	1963	$20
❑ 6029	Prisoner of Love/I've Got to Change	1966	$15
❑ 6203	Santa Claus Go Straight to the Ghetto/You Know It	1968	$10
❑ 6340	Santa Claus Is Definitely Here to Stay/(Instrumental)	1970	$8
❑ 6340 [PS]	Santa Claus Is Definitely Here to Stay/(Instrumental)	1970	$40
❑ 6187	Say It Loud -- I'm Black and I'm Proud (Part 1)/Say It Loud -- I'm Black and I'm Proud (Part 2)	1968	$10
❑ 6187	Say It Loud -- I'm Black But I'm Proud (Part 1)/Say It Loud -- I'm Black But I'm Proud (Part 2)	1968	$30

—Some copies have the above erroneous title on both sides

Number	Title	Yr	NM
❑ 6216	Shades of Brown (Part 2)/A Talk with the News	1969	$10

—B-side by Steve Soul

Number	Title	Yr	NM
❑ 5657	Shout and Shimmy/ Come Over Here	1962	$20
❑ 5803	Signed, Sealed and Delivered/Waiting in Vain	1963	$20
❑ 5899	So Long/Dancin' Little Thing	1964	$20
❑ 6368	Soul Power Pt. 1/Soul Power Pt 2 & Pt. 3	1971	$8
❑ 6222	Soul Pride (Part 1)/ Soul Pride (Part 2)	1969	$12
❑ 6366	Spinning Wheel (Part 1)/ Spinning Wheel (Part 2)	1971	$8
❑ 5485	Sticky/Suds	1961	$20
❑ 6329	Super Bad (Part 1 & Part 2)/Super Bad (Part 3)	1970	$8
❑ 6065	Sweet Little Baby Boy (Part 1)/ Sweet Little Baby Boy (Part 2)	1966	$15
❑ 6359	Talking Loud and Saying Nothing -- Part 1/Talking Loud and Saying Nothing -- Part 2	1971	$8
❑ 6300	Talkin' Loud and Sayin' Nothing (Part 1)/Talkin' Loud and Sayin' Nothing (Part 2)	1970	$8
❑ 5922	Tell Me What You're Gonna Do/I Don't Care	1964	$20
❑ 5654	Tell Me Why/Say So Long	1962	$20

—With Yvonne Fair

Number	Title	Yr	NM
❑ 5423	The Bells/And I Do Just What I Want	1960	$20
❑ 5829	The Bells/I've Got to Change	1963	$20
❑ 6064	The Christmas Song (Version 1)/ The Christmas Song (Version 2)	1966	$20
❑ 6240	The Popcorn/The Chicken	1969	$10
❑ 5438	The Scratch/Hold It	1961	$20
❑ 5767	These Foolish Things/ Can You Feel It -- Part 1	1963	$20
❑ 6133	The Soul of J.B./Funky Soul #1	1967	$15
❑ 6091	Think/Nobody Cares	1967	$15

—A-side: With Vicki Anderson; B-side: Vicki Anderson solo

Number	Title	Yr	NM
❑ 5952	Think/Try Me	1964	$20
❑ 6044	This Old Heart/How Long Darling	1966	$15
❑ 5995	This Old Heart/It Was You	1965	$15
❑ 5701	Three Hearts in a Tangle/I've Got Money	1962	$20
❑ 6258	World (Part 1)/World (Part 2)	1969	$10

MERCURY

Number	Title	Yr	NM
❑ 885194-7	Get on the Good Foot/Give It Up or Turnit A Loose	1986	$4

—Reissue

Number	Title	Yr	NM
❑ 885190-7	Prisoner of Love/Please, Please, Please	1986	$4

—Reissue

PEOPLE

Number	Title	Yr	NM
❑ 2500	Escape-ism (Part 1)/ Escape-ism (Parts 2 & 3)	1971	$6
❑ 664	Everybody Wanna Be Funky One More Time Pt. 1/ Everybody Wanna Be Funky One More Time Pt. 2	1976	$5
❑ 2501	Hot Pants Pt. 1 (She Got to Use What She Got to Get What She Wants)/Hot Pants Pt. 2	1971	$6

POLYDOR

Number	Title	Yr	NM
❑ 14360	Bodyheat Part 1/Bodyheat Part 2	1976	$5
❑ 14302	Dooley's Junkyard Dogs Part 1/Part 2	1975	$5
❑ 14168	Down and Out in New York City/Mama's Dead	1973	$5
❑ 14465	Eyesight/I Never Never Never Will Forget	1978	$5
❑ 14522	For Goodness Sakes, Look at Those Cakes Part 1/Part 2	1979	$5
❑ 14258	Funky President (People It's Bad)/Coldblooded	1974	$5
❑ 14139	Get On the Good Foot Part 1/ Get On the Good Foot Part 2	1972	$6
❑ 887500-7	(Get Up I Feel Like Being a) Sex Machine/Vincent's Theme	1988	$3

—B-side by Ethan James

Number	Title	Yr	NM
❑ 887500-7 [PS]	(Get Up I Feel Like Being a) Sex Machine/Vincent's Theme	1988	$4

—B-side by Ethan James

Number	Title	Yr	NM
❑ 2129	Get Up Offa That Thing/ It's Too Funky in Here	1980	$5
❑ 14326	Get Up Offa That Thing/ Release the Pressure	1976	$5
❑ 14409	Give Me Some Skin/People Wake Up and Live	1977	$5

—With the J.B.'s

Number	Title	Yr	NM
❑ 2167	Give the Bass Player Some Part 1/Part 2	1981	$5
❑ 14129	Honky Tonk Part 1/ Honky Tonk Part 2	1972	$6

—Artist credit: "James Brown Soul Train

Number	Title	Yr	NM
❑ 14301	Hot (I Need to Be Loved, Loved, Loved, Loved)/ Superbad, Superslick	1975	$5
❑ 14281	Hustle (Dead On It) Part 1/ Hustle (Dead On It) Part 2	1975	$5
❑ 14438	If You Don't Give a Doggone About It/People Who Criticize	1977	$5

—With the New J.B.'s

Number	Title	Yr	NM
❑ 14155	I Got a Bag of My Own/I Know It's True	1972	$40

—Manufactured in U.S. for export

Number	Title	Yr	NM
❑ 14153	I Got a Bag of My Own/ Public Enemy #1	1972	$6
❑ 14162	I Got Ants in My Pants (and I want to dance) Part 1/Part 15 and 16	1973	$5
❑ 871810-7	I Got You (I Feel Good)/Papa's Got a Brand New Bag	1989	$3

—Reissue

Number	Title	Yr	NM
❑ 14304	(I Love You) For Sentimental Reasons/Goodnight My Love	1976	$5
❑ 14100	I'm a Greedy Man Part 1/I'm a Greedy Man Part 2	1971	$6
❑ 14354	I Refuse to Lose/Home Again	1976	$5
❑ 14557	It's Too Funky in Here/ Are We Really Dancing	1979	$5
❑ 2078	Let the Funk Flow/Sometimes That's All There Is	1980	$5
❑ 14460	Love Me Tender/Have a Happy Day	1978	$5

—With the New J.B.'s

Number	Title	Yr	NM
❑ 14088	Make It Funky Part 1/ Make It Funky Part 2	1971	$6
❑ 14098	My Part/Make It Funky, Part 3//Make It Funky, Part 4	1971	$6
❑ 14244	My Thang/Public Enemy No. 1	1974	$5
❑ 871808-7	Out of Sight/Maybe the Last Time	1989	$3

—Reissue

Number	Title	Yr	NM
❑ 14255	Papa Don't Take No Mess Part 1/Part 2	1974	$5
❑ 14161	Santa Claus Goes Straight to the Ghetto/Sweet Little Baby Boy	1972	$6
❑ 14270	Sex Machine Part 1/ Sex Machine Part 2	1975	$5
❑ 14194	Sexy, Sexy, Sexy/ Slaughter Theme	1973	$5
❑ 14540	Someone to Talk To Part 1/ Someone to Talk To Part 2	1979	$5
❑ 2005	Star Generation/Women Are Something Else	1979	$5
❑ 14210	Stoned to the Bone Part 1/ Stoned to the Bone Part 2	1973	$5

—Notice corrected title

Number	Title	Yr	NM
❑ 14210	Stone to the Bone Part 1/ Stone to the Bone Part 2	1973	$10
❑ 14295	Superbad, Superslick Part 1/ Superbad, Superslick Part 2	1975	$5
❑ 14433	Take Me Higher and Groove Me/Summertime	1977	$5

—B-side by Martha and James

Number	Title	Yr	NM
❑ 14109	Talking Loud and Saying Nothing Part 1/Part 2	1972	$6
❑ 14274	Thank You For Letting Me Be Myself And... Part 1/Part 2	1975	$5
❑ 14169	The Boss/Like It Is, Like It Was	1973	$5
❑ 2034	The Original Disco Man/Let the Boogie Do the Rest	1979	$5
❑ 14223	The Payback Part 1/ The Payback Part 2	1974	$5
❑ 14223 [PS]	The Payback Part 1/ The Payback Part 2	1974	$10
❑ 14125	There It Is Part 1/There It Is Part 2	1972	$6
❑ 14487	The Spank/Love Me Tender	1978	$5
❑ 871804-7	Think/Lost Someone	1989	$3

—Reissue

Number	Title	Yr	NM
❑ 14177	Think/Something	1973	$5
❑ 14185	Think/Something	1973	$5
❑ 14157	What My Baby Needs Now Is a Little More Lovin'/This Guy-This Girl's in Love	1972	$6

—With Lyn Collins

Number	Title	Yr	NM
❑ 14193	Woman Part 1/Woman Part 2	1973	$5

SCOTTI BROTHERS

Number	Title	Yr	NM
❑ ZS4-06275	Gravity/Gravity (Dub Mix)	1986	$3
❑ ZS4-06275 [PS]	Gravity/Gravity (Dub Mix)	1986	$3
❑ ZS4-06568	How Do You Stop/House of Rock	1987	$3
❑ ZS4-06568 [PS]	How Do You Stop/House of Rock	1987	$3
❑ ZS4-07783	I'm Real/Tribute	1988	$3
❑ ZS4-07783 [PS]	I'm Real/Tribute	1988	$3
❑ ZS4-68559	It's Your Money $/You and Me	1989	$3
❑ ZS4-07090	Let's Get Personal/ Repeat the Beat	1987	$3
❑ ZS4-05682	Living in America/Farewell	1985	$3

—B-side by Vince Di Cola

Number	Title	Yr	NM
❏ ZS4-05682 [PS]	Living in America/Farewell	1985	$3
❏ ZS4-07975	Static/Godfather Runnin' the Joint	1988	$3
❏ ZS4-08088	Time to Get Busy/Busy J.B.	1988	$3

SMASH

Number	Title	Yr	NM
❏ 1898	Caldonia/Evil	1964	$15
❏ 1898	Caledonia/Evil	1964	$15
❏ 1898 [PS]	Caledonia/Evil	1964	$30
❏ 1975	Devil's Hideaway/Who's Afraid of Virginia Woolf?	1965	$12
❏ 1989	I Got You/Only You	1965	$60
— Withdrawn			
❏ 2064	Let's Go Get Stoned/ Our Day Will Come	1966	$12
❏ 1919	Out of Sight/Maybe the Last Time	1964	$15
❏ 1919 [PS]	Out of Sight/Maybe the Last Time	1964	$50
❏ 1908	The Things That I Used to Do/Out of the Blue	1964	$15
❏ 1908 [PS]	The Things That I Used to Do/Out of the Blue	1964	$50
❏ 2008	Try Me/Papa's Got a Brand New Bag	1965	$10

T.K.

Number	Title	Yr	NM
❏ 1042	Stay with Me/Smokin' and Drinkin'	1981	$4

7-Inch Extended Plays

KING

Number	Title	Yr	NM
❏ EP-430	*Please, Please, Please!/That's When I Lost My Heart/Try Me/ Tell Me What I Did Wrong	1959	$250
❏ 826	(contents unknown)	1963	$100
❏ 826 [PS]	Live at the Apollo	1963	$120
❏ EP-430 [PS]	Please, Please, Please	1959	$400

BROWN, JAMES (2)

MGM

Number	Title	Yr	NM
❏ K11941	Ballad of Davy Crockett/He's a Rocking Horse Cowboy	1955	$20
❏ K12211	Blue Harmonica/ Blessed Art Thou	1956	$15
❏ K12350	Forward Ho/Ghosttown	1956	$15
❏ 11987	The Berry Tree/I Lost When I Found You	1955	$15
❏ 12080	The White Buffalo/It's Lonesome Out Tonight	1955	$15
❏ K12384	Wagon Train/ Goodbye, My Love	1956	$15

BROWN, JERICHO

DEL-FI

Number	Title	Yr	NM
❏ 4103	I Need You/Lonesome Drifter	1958	$30

RKO UNIQUE

Number	Title	Yr	NM
❏ 412	Little Neva/Darling I Love Thee	1957	$40

WARNER BROS.

Number	Title	Yr	NM
❏ 5408	I'll Be Gone/He's Taken My Baby	1964	$10
❏ 5458	I'm Watching You/ Wisdom of a Fool	1964	$10
❏ 5381	Lonely Birthday/Paper Rose and Candy Ring	1963	$10
❏ 5161	Look for a Star/Don't You Know	1960	$15

BROWN, JIM ED, AND HELEN CORNELIUS

RCA

Number	Title	Yr	NM
❏ PB-10967	Born Believer/Here Today and Gone Tomorrow	1977	$5
❏ PB-12220	Don't Bother to Knock/ Dear Memory	1981	$5
❏ PB-11162	Fall Softly Snow/ Natividad (The Nativity)	1977	$6
❏ PB-11672	Fools/I Think About You	1979	$5
❏ PB-10711	I Don't Want to Have to Marry You/Have I Told You Lately That I Love You	1976	$5
❏ GB-11332	I Don't Want to Have to Marry You/Saying Hello, Saying I Love You, Saying Goodbye	1978	$4
— Gold Standard Series" reissue			
❏ PB-11044	If It Ain't Love By Now/ It Takes So Long	1977	$5
❏ PB-11304	If the World Ran Out of Love Tonight/Blue Ridge Mountains Turning Green	1978	$5
❏ PB-11220	I'll Never Be Free/Baby You Know How I Love You	1978	$5
❏ PB-11532	Lying in Love with You/ Let's Take the Long Way Around the World	1979	$5
❏ PB-11927	Morning Comes Too Early/Emotions	1980	$5
❏ PB-10822	Saying Hello, Saying I Love You, Saying Goodbye/ My Heart Cries for You	1976	$5
❏ PB-12037	The Bedroom/Everything Is Changing	1980	$5

BROWN, JIM ED

RCA

Number	Title	Yr	NM
❏ PB-10786	I've Rode with the Best/ Close the Door	1976	$4
❏ PB-10619	Let Me Love You Where It Hurts/I Love You All Over Again	1976	$4
❏ PB-11134	When I Touch Her There/Mexican Joe	1977	$4

RCA Victor

Number	Title	Yr	NM
❏ 74-0785	All I Had to Do/Triangle	1972	$6
❏ 47-9965	Angel's Sunday/Every Mile of the Way	1971	$6
❏ PB-10531	Another Morning/An Old Flame Never Dies	1975	$5
❏ 47-8867	A Taste of Heaven/Paint Me the Color of Your Wall	1966	$8
❏ 47-9858	Baby, I Tried/The Girl Cries at Night	1970	$6
❏ PB-10233	Barroom Pal, Goodtime Gals/ Nearer My Love to You	1975	$5
❏ 47-9329	Bottle, Bottle/It Doesn't Know Any Better	1967	$8
❏ APBO-0059	Broad-Minded Man/Helpin' You Get Over Him	1973	$5
❏ PB-10131	Don Junior/Who's Gonna Love Me	1974	$5
❏ 74-0642	Evening/You Keep Right On Loving Me	1972	$6
❏ PB-10370	Fine Time to Get the Blues/Sweet Song	1975	$5
❏ PB-10047	Get Up I Think I Love You/A Nickel for the Fiddler	1974	$5
❏ 74-0274	Ginger Is Gentle and Waiting for Me/Drink Boys Drink	1969	$6
❏ 74-0712	How I Love Them Old Songs/Close	1972	$6
❏ 47-8566	I Heard from a Memory Last Night/Just to Satisfy You	1965	$6
❏ 47-8644	I'm Just a Country Boy/ To Be or Not to Be	1965	$6
❏ APBO-0267	It's That Time of Night/ If Wishes Were Horses	1974	$5
❏ 47-9810	Lift Ring, Pull Open/ Going Up the Country	1970	$6
❏ 47-9677	Longest Beer of the Night/ What's a Girl Like You	1968	$6
❏ 74-0114	Man and Wife Time/ Healing Hands of Time	1969	$6
❏ 47-9909	Morning/How to Lose a Good Woman	1970	$6
❏ 47-9192	Pop a Top/Too Good to Be True	1967	$8
❏ 74-0509	She's Leavin' (Bonnie, Please Don't Go)/Love Is Worth the Tryin'	1971	$6
❏ APBO-0180	Sometime Sunshine/ Louisiana Woman	1973	$5
❏ 74-0928	Southern Loving/How Long Does It Take a Memory to Drown	1973	$6
❏ 47-9434	The Cajun Stripper/ You'll Never Know	1968	$8
❏ 47-9518	The Enemy/I Just Came from There	1968	$8
❏ 47-8997	The Last Laugh/Party Girl	1966	$8
❏ 74-0190	The Three Bells/ Beyond the Shadow	1969	$6

BROWN, JOCELYN

VINYL DREAMS

Number	Title	Yr	NM
❏ 72	I Wish You Would/(Instrumental)	1984	$5
❏ 71	Somebody Else's Guy/ (Instrumental)	1984	$5

WARNER BROS.

Number	Title	Yr	NM
❏ 28220	Caught in the Act/(Instrumental)	1987	$3
❏ 28698	Ego Maniac/Love's Gonna Get You	1987	$3
❏ 28698 [PS]	Ego Maniac/Love's Gonna Get You	1987	$3
❏ 28889	Love's Gonna Get You/ (Funkhouse Mix)	1985	$3
❏ 28322	Whatever Satisfies You/ Caught in the Act	1987	$3

BROWN, JOE, AND THE BRUVVERS

BELL

Number	Title	Yr	NM
❏ 45364 [DJ]	Hey Mama (mono/stereo)	1973	$6
— May be promo only			

CAMEO

Number	Title	Yr	NM
❏ 241	It Only Took a Minute/All Things Bright and Beautiful	1963	$15

DOT

Number	Title	Yr	NM
❏ 16508	Hava Nagila/That's What Love Will Do	1963	$15

HICKORY

Number	Title	Yr	NM
❏ 1329	Sally Ann/Little Ukulele	1965	$10

JAMIE

Number	Title	Yr	NM
❏ 1298	Lonely Circus/Teardrops in the Rain	1965	$10
❏ 1327	Sea of Heartbreak/ Mrs. O's Theme	1966	$10

KAPP

Number	Title	Yr	NM
❏ 2068	Adieu, Monsieur Le Professeur/ Diamonds of Dew	1969	$6

LONDON INT'L.

Number	Title	Yr	NM
❏ 10517	A Picture of You/A Lay-About's Lament	1962	$20
❏ 10507	What a Crazy World We're Living In/Popcorn	1962	$20

STELLAR

Number	Title	Yr	NM
❏ 1504	Hava Nagila/That's What Love Will Do	1963	$20

VERTIGO

Number	Title	Yr	NM
❏ 201	I Was Lost/Cincinnati Floor	1974	$15
— As "Brown's Home Brew			

WARNER BROS.

Number	Title	Yr	NM
❏ 7055	With a Little Help from My Friends/Won't You Show Me Around	1967	$8

BROWN, JOSIE

RCA VICTOR

Number	Title	Yr	NM
❏ APBO-0209	Both Sides of the Line/Pour a Little Water on the Flowers	1974	$5
❏ PB-10144	He Just Loved You Out of Me/I Can Feel Love	1974	$5
❏ PB-10337	I Break Easy/Lonely Made Me Do It	1975	$5
❏ APBO-0042	Precious Memories Follow Me/After You've Had Me	1973	$5
❏ APBO-0266	Satisfy Me and I'll Satisfy You/Crackerbox Mansion	1974	$5
❏ PB-10002	The Man They Sweep Up Off the Floor/Delta Queen	1974	$5

BROWN, JUDY

SKYLA

Number	Title	Yr	NM
❏ 1122	Dear Santa/Christmas Wedding Day	1961	$15

BROWN, JULIE

SIRE

Number	Title	Yr	NM
❏ 27983	Girl Fight Tonight/Every Boy's Got One	1988	$4
❏ 28251	Trapped in the Body of a White Girl/Will I Make It Through the 80's	1987	$4
❏ 28251 [PS]	Trapped in the Body of a White Girl/Will I Make It Through the 80's	1987	$6

BROWN, LES

CORAL

Number	Title	Yr	NM
❏ 60820	Let It Snow, Let It Snow, Let It Snow/Rain	1952	$20
❏ 62237	Silver Bells/The Stranger	1960	$10

CORAL

Number	Title	Yr	NM
❏ EC85001	*Baby/Speak Low/Rain/Street of Dreams/Brown's Little Jug	1954	$15
❏ EC85001 [PS]	Concert at the Palladium, Vol. 2	1954	$15

BROWN, MARTI

ATLANTIC

Number	Title	Yr	NM
❏ 4003	Let My Love Shine/Love Me Back to Sleep	1973	$5
❏ 4011	The Single Girl and a Married Man/No Rings, No Strings	1973	$5

BROWN, MAX

DOOR KNOB

Number	Title	Yr	NM
❏ 065	Give Me a Chance to Love You/I Could Write a Book	1978	$5
❏ 056	If I May/Hey Cowboy	1978	$5
❏ 077	In My Little Corner of the World/Maybe	1978	$5
❏ 105	Take Good Care of My Love/Call Me Silly	1979	$5
❏ 095	Take Time to Smell the Flowers/Love Away on Me	1979	$5

BROWN, MAXINE (1)

ABC-PARAMOUNT

Number	Title	Yr	NM
❏ 10255	After All We've Been Through Together/My Life	1961	$15
❏ 10315	Forget Him/A Man	1962	$15
❏ 10235	I Don't Need You No More/Think of Me	1961	$15
❏ 10290	I Got a Funny Kind of Feeling/ What I Don't Need	1962	$15
❏ 10343	I Kneel at Your Throne/ If I Knew Then	1962	$15
❏ 10388	Life Goes On Just the Same/If You Have No Real Objections	1962	$15

Number	Title	Yr	NM
❑ 10370	Promise Me Anything/ Am I Falling in Love	1962	$15

AVCO

Number	Title	Yr	NM
❑ 4585	Always and Forever/ Make Love to Me	1971	$5
❑ 4612	Picked Up, Packed and Went Away/(B-side unknown)	1972	$5
❑ 4604	Treat Me Like a Lady/I.O.U.	1972	$5

COMMONWEALTH UNITED

Number	Title	Yr	NM
❑ 3008	I Can't Get Along Without You/Reason to Believe	1970	$6
❑ 3001	We'll Cry Together/ Darling Be Home Soon	1969	$6

EPIC

Number	Title	Yr	NM
❑ 10424	Love in Them There Hills/ From Loving You	1968	$10
❑ 10334	Seems You've Forsaken My Love/Plum Outa Sight	1968	$10

NOMAR

Number	Title	Yr	NM
❑ 103	All in My Mind/Harry, Let's Marry	1960	$20
❑ 106	Funny/Now That You've Gone	1961	$20
❑ 107	Heaven in Your Arms/ Maxine's Place	1961	$20

—B-side by Frankie and the Flips

WAND

Number	Title	Yr	NM
❑ 185	Anything for a Laugh/ One Step at a Time	1965	$8
❑ 135	Ask Me/Yesterday's Kisses	1963	$12
❑ 135 [PS]	Ask Me/Yesterday's Kisses	1963	$60
❑ 142	Coming Back to You/ Since I Found You	1963	$10
❑ 158	I Cry Alone/Put Yourself in My Place	1964	$8
❑ 1145	I Don't Need Anything/ The Secret of Livin'	1967	$8
❑ 1104	If You Gotta Make a Fool of Somebody/You're in Love	1965	$8
❑ 173	It's Gonna Be Alright/You Do Something to Me	1965	$8
❑ 152	Little Girl Lost/You Upset My Soul	1964	$8
❑ 162	Oh No Not My Baby/ You Upset My Soul	1964	$15
❑ 1117	One in a Million/Anything You Do Is Alright	1966	$8
❑ 1179	Soul Serenade/He's the Only Guy I'll Ever Love	1968	$8
❑ 1128	We Can Work It Out/Let Me Give You My Lovin'	1966	$8

BROWN, MAXINE (2)
CHART

Number	Title	Yr	NM
❑ 1061	Sugar Cane Country/ My Biggest Mistake	1968	$8
❑ 1046	Take Time to Know Him/I Want to Thank You	1968	$8

BROWN, MICHAEL
ESTATE

Number	Title	Yr	NM
❑ ZS4-04075	Dancing to Your Music/ (Instrumental)	1983	$4

KAMA SUTRA

Number	Title	Yr	NM
❑ 563 [DJ]	Circles (mono/stereo)	1972	$10
❑ 563	Circles/Premonitions	1972	$125

—May not exist as a stock copy; this is an approximate price range if it does

PORTRAIT

Number	Title	Yr	NM
❑ 12-01047	Love Talk/Love You Back to Me	1981	$5

—With Janice Dempsey

BROWN, NAPPY
ICHIBAN

Number	Title	Yr	NM
❑ 206	Lemon Squeezin' Daddy/ Small Red Apples	1989	$5

SAVOY

Number	Title	Yr	NM
❑ 1562	A Long Time/All Right Now	1959	$30
❑ 1196	Am I/Love Baby	1956	$30
❑ 1588	Apple of My Eye/Baby I Got News for You	1960	$20
❑ 1587	Baby, Cry, Cry, Cry, Baby/ What's Come Over You	1960	$20
❑ 1594	Coal Miner/Honnie-Bonnie	1961	$20
❑ 1616	Didn't You Know/I've Had My Fun	1962	$20
❑ 1598	Don't Be Angry/Any Time Is the Right Time	1961	$20
❑ 1155	Don't Be Angry/It's Really You	1955	$30
❑ 1176	Doodle I Love You/ Sittin' in the Dark	1955	$30
❑ 1582	Down in the Alley/ My Baby Knows	1960	$20
❑ 1579	Give Me Your Love/Too Shy	1959	$30
❑ 1514	Goody Goody Gum Drops/Bye Bye Baby	1957	$30

Number	Title	Yr	NM
❑ 1575	I Cried Like a Baby/So Deep	1959	$30
❑ 1530	If You Need Some Lovin'/I'm in the Mood	1958	$30
❑ 1135	Is It True, Is It True/ Two-Faced Woman	1954	$40
❑ 1551	It Don't Hurt No More/My Baby	1958	$30
❑ 1506	Little by Little/I'm Getting Lonesome	1956	$30
❑ 1621	Lock on the Door/So Glad I Don't Have to Cry No More	1963	$20
❑ 1187	Open Up That Door/ Pleasing You	1956	$30
❑ 1162	Piddly Patter Patter/ There'll Come a Day	1955	$30
❑ 1511	Pretty Girl (Yea Yea Yea)/I'm Gonna Get You	1957	$30
❑ 1547	Skidy Wo/I Cried Like a Baby	1958	$30
❑ 1129	That Man/I Wonder	1954	$40
❑ 1592	The Hole I'm In/ Nobody Can Say	1960	$20
❑ 1569	This Is My Confession/ For Those Who Love	1959	$30

BROWN, ODELL
CADET

Number	Title	Yr	NM
❑ 5570	Mellow Yellow/Quiet Village	1967	$8
❑ 5591	The Look of Love/No More Water in the Well	1968	$8
❑ 5624	The Weight/Think About It	1968	$8

BROWN, PETER
COLUMBIA

Number	Title	Yr	NM
❑ 38-04622	(Love Is Just) The Game/Hot Flash	1984	$4
❑ 38-04381	They Only Come Out at Night/(Instrumental)	1984	$3
❑ 38-04381 [PS]	They Only Come Out at Night/(Instrumental)	1984	$4

DRIVE

Number	Title	Yr	NM
❑ 6286	Can't Be Love-Do It to Me Anyway/West of the North Star	1980	$5
❑ 6278	Crank It Up (Funk Town) Pt. 1/Pt. 2	1979	$5
❑ 6269	Dance with Me/For Your Love	1978	$6
❑ 6258	Do Ya Wanna Get Funky with Me/Burning Love Breakdown	1977	$6
❑ 6274	Fantasy Love Affair/It's True What They Say About Love	1978	$6
❑ 6281	Stargazer/Penguin	1979	$5

RCA

Number	Title	Yr	NM
❑ PB-13413	Baby Gets High/The Love Game	1982	$4

BROWN, RANDY
CHOCOLATE CITY

Number	Title	Yr	NM
❑ 3224	If I Don't Love You/Looking for the Real Thing	1981	$4

PARACHUTE

Number	Title	Yr	NM
❑ 506	I'd Rather Hurt Myself (Than to Hurt You)/I'm Always in the Mood	1978	$5
❑ 526	I Thought of You Today/Use It	1979	$5
❑ 517	I Wanna Make Love to You/ Sweet, Sweet Darling	1978	$5

STAX

Number	Title	Yr	NM
❑ 3227	If I Had It to Do All Over/ Smoking Room	1980	$5

BROWN, RAY, AND THE WHISPERS
GNP CRESCENDO

Number	Title	Yr	NM
❑ 357	Fool, Fool, Fool/Pride	1965	$30

PARKWAY

Number	Title	Yr	NM
❑ 951	20 Miles/Devoted to You	1965	$40

BROWN, ROY
DELUXE

Number	Title	Yr	NM
❑ 3319	Bar Room Blues/ Good Rockin' Man	1951	$200

—Black vinyl

Number	Title	Yr	NM
❑ 3319	Bar Room Blues/ Good Rockin' Man	1951	$400

—Blue vinyl

Number	Title	Yr	NM
❑ 3318	Big Town/Train Time Blues	1951	$200

—Roy Brown singles on DeLuxe before 3318 are unconfirmed on 45 rpm

Number	Title	Yr	NM
❑ 3318	Big Town/Train Time Blues	1951	$400

—Blue vinyl

Number	Title	Yr	NM
❑ 3323	I've Got the Last Laugh Now/Brown Angel	1951	$200

—Black vinyl

Number	Title	Yr	NM
❑ 3323	I've Got the Last Laugh Now/Brown Angel	1951	$400

—Blue vinyl

HOME OF THE BLUES

Number	Title	Yr	NM
❑ 107	Don't Break My Heart/A Man with the Blues	1960	$30
❑ 115	Oh So Wonderful/Sugar Baby	1961	$30
❑ 110	Tired of Being Alone/ Rocking All the Time	1960	$30

IMPERIAL

Number	Title	Yr	NM
❑ 5489	Ain't Gonna Do It/ Sail On Little Girl	1958	$40
❑ 5422	Everybody/Saturday Night	1957	$40
❑ 5510	Hip Shakin' Baby/Be My Love Tonight	1958	$40
❑ 5455	I'm Convicted of Love/I'm Ready to Play	1957	$40
❑ 5439	Let the Four Winds Blow/ Diddy-Y-Diddy-O	1957	$40
❑ 5969	Let the Four Winds Blow/ Diddy-Yi-Diddy-Yo	1963	$30
❑ 5427	Party Doll/I'm Sticking with You	1957	$40
❑ 5469	Tick of the Clock/Slow Down Little Eva	1957	$40

KING

Number	Title	Yr	NM
❑ 5333	Ain't Got No Blues Today/ Adorable One	1960	$30
❑ 4731	Ain't It a Shame/Gal from Kokomo	1954	$70
❑ 4761	Fannie Brown Got Married/ Queen of Diamonds	1955	$60
❑ 4609	Grandpa Stole My Baby/ Money Can't Buy Love	1953	$70
❑ 5218	Hard Luck Blues/Good Looking and Forty	1959	$30
❑ 5207	I Never Had It So Good/ Rinky Dinky Doo	1959	$30
❑ 5178	La-Dee-Dah-Dee/Melinda	1959	$30
❑ 5521	Mighty Mighty Man/ Good Man Blues	1961	$30
❑ 4834	My Little Angel Child/ She's Gone Too Long	1955	$60
❑ 5247	School Bell Rock/Ain't No Rocking No More	1959	$30
❑ 4816	Shake 'Em Up Baby/ Letter to Baby	1955	$60
❑ 4602	Travelin' Man/Hurry, Hurry Baby	1953	$70
❑ 4704	Trouble at Midnight/ Bootlegging Baby	1954	$70
❑ 4743	Worried Life Blues/ Black Diamond	1954	$70

MERCURY

Number	Title	Yr	NM
❑ 73166	It's My Fault Darling/ Love for Sale	1970	$6
❑ 73219	Mail Man Blues/Hunky Funky Woman	1971	$6

BROWN, RUTH
ATLANTIC

Number	Title	Yr	NM
❑ 962	5-10-15 Hours/Be Anything But Be Mine	1952	$60
❑ 2015	5-10-15 Hours/Itty Bitty Girl	1959	$30
❑ 1177	Book of Lies/Just Too Much	1958	$30
❑ 973	Daddy Daddy/Have a Good Time	1952	$60
❑ 2052	Don't Deceive Me/I Burned Your Letter	1960	$30
❑ 1051	Ever Since My Baby's Been Gone/Bye Bye Young Men	1955	$40
❑ 1059	I Can See Everybody's Baby/ As Long As I'm Moving	1955	$40
❑ 2035	I Don't Know/Papa Daddy	1959	$30
❑ 1027	If I Had Any Sense/ Hello Little Boy	1954	$40
❑ 2104	It Tears Me All to Pieces/ Anyone But You	1961	$20
❑ 1102	I Want to Be Loved/ Mom, Oh Mom	1956	$30
❑ 1018	Love Contest/If You Don't Want Me	1954	$40
❑ 1077	Love Has Joined Us Together/I Gotta Have You	1955	$40

—With Clyde McPhatter

Number	Title	Yr	NM
❑ 1125	Lucky Lips/My Heart Is Breaking Over You	1957	$30
❑ 2008	Mama, He Treats Your Daughter Mean/I'll Step Aside	1958	$30
❑ 986	(Mama) He Treats Your Daughter Mean/R.B. Blues	1953	$70
❑ 1036	Oh What a Dream/ Please Don't Freeze	1954	$40
❑ 1082	Old Man River/I Want to Do More	1956	$30
❑ 1023	Sentimental Journey/ It's All in Your Mind	1954	$40
❑ 948	Shine On—Big Bright Moon Shine On/Without My Love	1951	$70

—Ruth Brown records on Atlantic before 948 (except as listed) are unconfirmed on 45 rpm

Number	Title	Yr	NM
❑ 1153	Show Me/I Hope We Meet	1957	$30
❑ 1113	Smooth Operator/I Still Love You	1956	$30
❑ 1044	Somebody Touch Me/ Mambo Baby	1954	$40
❑ 2088	Sure 'Nuff/Here He Comes	1961	$20
❑ 1091	Sweet Baby of Mine/I'm Getting Right	1956	$30

Number	Title	Yr	NM
❏ 2075	Taking Care of Business/Honey Boy	1960	$30
❏ 919	Teardrops from My Eyes/Am I Making the Same Mistake	1950	$400

— This and Atlantic 914 were the label's first two 45s.

Number	Title	Yr	NM
❏ 2064	The Door Is Still Open/What I Wouldn't Give	1960	$30
❏ 1005	The Tears Keep Tumblin' Down/I Would If I Could	1953	$40
❏ 1197	This Little Girl's Gone Rockin'/Why Me	1958	$30
❏ 978	Three Letters/Good for Nothing Joe	1952	$60
❏ 1072	What'd I Say/It's Love Baby (24 Hours of the Day)	1955	$40
❏ 1140	When I Get You Baby/One More Time	1957	$30
❏ 993	Wild Wild Young Men/Mend Your Ways	1953	$50

DECCA

Number	Title	Yr	NM
❏ 31640	Come a Little Closer/I Love Him and I Know It	1964	$10
❏ 31598	What Happened to You/Yes Sir That's My Baby	1964	$10

MAINSTREAM

Number	Title	Yr	NM
❏ 611	On the Good Ship Lollipop/Hurry On Down	1965	$10

PHILIPS

Number	Title	Yr	NM
❏ 40086	He Tells Me with His Eyes/If You Don't Tell Nobody	1963	$15
❏ 40056	Mama (He Treats Your Daughter Mean)/Hold My Hand	1962	$15
❏ 40119	Satisfied/If You Don't Tell Nobody	1963	$15
❏ 40028	Shake a Hand/Say It Again	1962	$15

7-Inch Extended Plays

ATLANTIC

Number	Title	Yr	NM
❏ 585	*Lucky Lips/Mambo Baby/Smooth Operator/Oh What a Dream	1957	$75
❏ 505	Teardrops from My Eyes/5-10-15//Mama He Treats Your Daughter Mean/So Long	1953	$125

BROWN, SAM

A&M

Number	Title	Yr	NM
❏ 1234	Stop/Blue Soldier	1988	$3
❏ 1234 [PS]	Stop/Blue Soldier	1988	$4

BROWN, SHARON

PROFILE

Number	Title	Yr	NM
❏ 5006	I Specialize in Love/(Instrumental)	1982	$5

BROWN, SHEREE

CAPITOL

Number	Title	Yr	NM
❏ B-5079	Get Down, I'm So Bad/I Wanna Be By Your Side	1981	$4
❏ B-5144	Happy Music/Can't Live Without Love	1982	$4
❏ B-5173	Love Only Knows/Tonight	1982	$4

BROWN, SHIRLEY

ABET

Number	Title	Yr	NM
❏ 9444	I Ain't Gonna Tell Nobody/Love Is Built on a Strong Foundation	1974	$15

ARISTA

Number	Title	Yr	NM
❏ 0231	Blessed Is the Woman (With a Man Like Mine)/Lowdown, Dirty, Good Lover	1977	$5
❏ 0334	I Can't Move No Mountains/Honey Babe	1978	$5
❏ 0254	I Need Somebody to Love Me/Givin' Up	1977	$5
❏ 0270	Long on Lovin'/Mighty Good Feeling	1977	$5

MALACO

Number	Title	Yr	NM
❏ 2157	Ain't Nothin' Like the Lovin' We Got/If This Is Goodbye	1989	$5

— With Johnnie Taylor

SOUND TOWN

Number	Title	Yr	NM
❏ 0010	At Christmas Time/(Instrumental)	1984	$5
❏ 0012	Boyfriend/I Don't Play That	1985	$4
❏ 0007	I Don't Play That/Looking for the Real Thing	1984	$4
❏ 0005	Leave the Bridges Standing/Looking for the Real Thing	1984	$4
❏ 0009	This Used to Be Your House/I Don't Play That	1984	$4

STAX

Number	Title	Yr	NM
❏ 3222	After a Night Like This/Crowding In On My Mind	1979	$5
❏ 3224	Dirty Feelin'/Eyes Can't See	1979	$5

TRUTH

Number	Title	Yr	NM
❏ 3223	It Ain't No Fun/I've Got to Go On Without You	1975	$6
❏ 3231	It's Worth a Whisper/Between You and Me	1975	$6
❏ 3206	Woman to Woman/Yes Sir, Brother	1974	$6

BROWN, SKIPPY

CHANCE

Number	Title	Yr	NM
❏ 1129	So Many Days/Tale of Woe	1953	$250

BROWN SUGAR

BULLET

Number	Title	Yr	NM
❏ 711	Loneliness (Will Bring Us Together Again)/Don't Hold Back	1972	$60

CAPITOL

Number	Title	Yr	NM
❏ 4367	Lay Some Lovin' on Me/Don't Tie Me Down	1976	$30
❏ 4198	The Game Is Over (What's the Matter with You)/I'm Going Through Changes Now	1976	$200

CHELSEA

Number	Title	Yr	NM
❏ BCBO- 0239	Dance to the Music/Love Can Bring You Down	1974	$12
❏ BCBO- 0149	Didn't I/Moonlight and Taming You	1973	$12
❏ 78-0125	Loneliness (Will Bring Us Together Again)/Don't Hold Back	1973	$20

DEMAND

Number	Title	Yr	NM
❏ D 45-002	Sweet Symphony/Bye Bye Baby	1978	$15

BROWN, TOMMY

ABC-PARAMOUNT

Number	Title	Yr	NM
❏ 10632	Ain't So/Well, There Goes My Heart	1965	$15

DOT

Number	Title	Yr	NM
❏ 16130	Tra-La-La/Weepin' and Cryin'	1960	$20

GROOVE

Number	Title	Yr	NM
❏ 0132	Don't Leave Me/Won't You Forgive Me	1955	$40
❏ 0143	The Thrill Is Gone/Gambler's Prayer	1956	$40

KING

Number	Title	Yr	NM
❏ 4679	Goodbye, I'm Gone/Since You Left Me Dear	1953	$70
❏ 4658	How Much Do You Think I Can Stand/Fore Day Train	1953	$200

BROWN, WINI

COLUMBIA

Number	Title	Yr	NM
❏ 6-872	A Good Man Is Hard to Find/This Is the Last Time	1950	$40
❏ 1-872	A Good Man Is Hard to Find/This Is the Last Time	1950	$50

—Microgroove 7-inch, 33 1/3 rpm single

JARO

Number	Title	Yr	NM
❏ 77018	Gone Again/Johnny with the Gentle Hand	1960	$30

MERCURY

Number	Title	Yr	NM
❏ 8270	Be Anything -- Be Mine/Heaven Knows Why	1952	$200
❏ 5870	Here in My Heart/Your Happiness Is Mine	1952	$200
❏ 70062	Tear Down the Sky/Can't Stand No More	1953	$125

RCA VICTOR

Number	Title	Yr	NM
❏ 47-6970	Available Lover/It's All in Your Mind	1957	$30

BROWNE, FRIDAY

RCA VICTOR

Number	Title	Yr	NM
❏ 47-9505	Ask Any Woman/Outdoor Seminar	1968	$6

BROWNE, JACKSON

ASYLUM

Number	Title	Yr	NM
❏ 47003	Boulevard/Call It a Loan	1980	$4
❏ 47003 [PS]	Boulevard/Call It a Loan	1980	$5
❏ 11004	Doctor My Eyes/Looking Into You	1972	$5
❏ 69566	For America/Till I Go Down	1986	$3
❏ 69566 [PS]	For America/Till I Go Down	1986	$3
❏ 69764	For a Rocker/Downtown	1984	$3
❏ 69764 [PS]	For a Rocker/Downtown	1984	$3
❏ 45242	Fountains of Sorrow/The Late Show	1975	$4
❏ 45379	Here Come Those Tears Again/Linda Paloma	1976	$4

Number	Title	Yr	NM
❏ 69543	In the Shape of a Heart/Voice of America	1986	$3
❏ 69543 [PS]	In the Shape of a Heart/Voice of America	1986	$6
❏ 69826	Lawyers in Love/Say It Isn't True	1983	$3
❏ 69826 [PS]	Lawyers in Love/Say It Isn't True	1983	$3
❏ 69982	Somebody's Baby/The Crow on the Cradle [w/Graham Nash & David Lindley]	1982	$4
❏ 69982 [PS]	Somebody's Baby/The Crow on the Cradle [w/Graham Nash & David Lindley]	1982	$4
❏ 45485-A/B	Stay/Rosie	1978	$5
❏ 45485-A/B [PS]	Stay/Rosie	1978	$5
❏ 45485-A/C	Stay/The Load-Out	1978	$4
❏ 69791	Tender Is the Night/On the Day	1983	$3
❏ 69791 [PS]	Tender Is the Night/On the Day	1983	$3
❏ 47036	That Girl Could Sing/Of Missing Persons	1980	$4
❏ 45399	The Pretender/Daddy's Tune	1977	$4
❏ 45227	Walking Slow/Before the Deluge	1975	$4

ELEKTRA

Number	Title	Yr	NM
❏ 69284	Anything Can Happen/Lights and Virtues	1989	$5
❏ 69262	Chasing You Into the Light/How Long	1989	$5
❏ 69292	World in Motion/My Personal Revenge	1989	$4

BROWNE, JANN

CURB

Number	Title	Yr	NM
❏ 10568	Tell Me Why/There Ain't No Train	1989	$3

BROWNE, TOM

ARISTA

Number	Title	Yr	NM
❏ 9144	Cruisin'/Mr. Business	1984	$3
❏ 9272	Secret Fantasy/Hit Man	1984	$3

ARISTA/GRP

Number	Title	Yr	NM
❏ 2501	Brother, Brother/Throw Down	1979	$5
❏ 2519	Bye Gones/A Message (Pride and Pity)	1982	$4
❏ 2518	Fungi Mama/Bebopafunkadiscolypso//Come for the Ride	1981	$4
❏ 2506	Funkin' for Jamaica (N.Y.)/Dreams of Lovin' You	1980	$4
❏ 2513	Let's Dance/I Know	1981	$4
❏ 2502	The Closer I Get to You/I Never Was a Cowboy	1979	$5
❏ 2510	Thighs High (Grip Your Hips and Move)/Midnight Interlude	1980	$4

MALACO

Number	Title	Yr	NM
❏ 100	Ain't No Need to Worry/Happy Song	1989	$4

BROWNETTES, THE

KING

Number	Title	Yr	NM
❏ 6153	Baby, Don't You Know/Never Find a Love Like Mine	1968	$30

BROWNMARK

MOTOWN

Number	Title	Yr	NM
❏ 1980	Bang Bang/(instrumental)	1989	$3

BROWNS, THE

FABOR

Number	Title	Yr	NM
❏ 122	Do Memories Haunt You/Jungle Magic	1955	$30
❏ 118	Here Today and Gone Tomorrow/Draggin' Main Street	1955	$30
❏ 112	Why Am I Falling/Itsy Witsy Bitsy Me	1954	$30

RCA VICTOR

Number	Title	Yr	NM
❏ 47-6730	A Man with a Plan/Just a Lot of Sweet Talk	1956	$30

—As "Jim, Maxine and Bonnie Brown

Number	Title	Yr	NM
❏ 47-7427	Beyond the Shadow/This Time I Would Know	1958	$20
❏ 47-9364	Big Daddy/I Will Bring You Water	1967	$8
❏ 47-7820	Blue Christmas/Greenwillow Christmas	1960	$15
❏ 47-7997	Buttons and Bows/Remember Me	1962	$10
❏ 47-8942	Coming Back to You/Gigawachem	1966	$8
❏ 47-7208	Crazy Dreams/Ain't No Way in the World	1958	$20
❏ 47-6629	Do Memories Haunt You/Draggin' Main Street	1956	$30
❏ 47-8423	Everybody's Darlin', Plus Mine/The Outskirts of Town	1964	$8
❏ 47-7969	Foolish Pride/Alpha and Omega	1961	$10
❏ 37-7969	Foolish Pride/Alpha and Omega	1961	$30

—Compact Single 33" (small hole, plays at LP speed)

Number	Title	Yr	NM
47-7866	Ground Hog/Angel's Dolly	1961	$10
37-7866	Ground Hog/Angel's Dolly	1961	$30

— *Compact Single 33" (small hole, plays at LP speed)*

Number	Title	Yr	NM
47-6628	Here Today and Gone Tomorrow/Looking Back to See	1956	$30
47-8838	I'd Just Be Fool Enough/Springtime	1966	$8
47-8495	I Feel Like Crying/No Sad Songs for Me	1965	$8
47-6995	I Heard the Bluebirds Sing/The Last Thing I Want	1957	$20

— *As "Jim, Maxine and Bonnie Brown*

47-9153	I Hear It Now/He Will Set Your Fields on Fire	1967	$8
47-6918	I'm in Heaven/Getting Used to Being Lonely	1957	$20

— *As "Jim, Maxine and Bonnie Brown*

47-6480	I Take the Chance/Goo Goo Da Da	1956	$30

— *As "Jim Edward and Maxine Brown*

47-8066	It's Just a Little Heartache/The Old Master Painter	1962	$10
47-7755	Lonely Little Robin/Margo (The Ninth of May)	1960	$15
61-7755 [S]	Lonely Little Robin/Margo (The Ninth of May)	1960	$30

— *"Living Stereo" (large hole, plays at 45 rpm)*

47-7755 [PS]	Lonely Little Robin/Margo (The Ninth of May)	1960	$30
47-8714	Meadowgreen/One Take Away One	1965	$8
47-6823	Money/It Takes a Long Train with a Red Caboose	1957	$20
47-8242	Oh, No!/Dear Teresa	1963	$10
47-7614	Scarlet Ribbons (For Her Hair)/Blue Bells Ring	1959	$15
61-7614 [S]	Scarlet Ribbons (For Her Hair)/Blue Bells Ring	1959	$30

— *"Living Stereo" (large hole, plays at 45 rpm)*

47-7804	Send Me the Pillow You Dream On/You're So Much a Part of Me	1960	$15
61-7804 [S]	Send Me the Pillow You Dream On/You're So Much a Part of Me	1960	$30

— *"Living Stereo" (large hole, plays at 45 rpm)*

47-7110	The Man in the Moon/True Love Goes Far Beyond	1957	$20
47-8348	Then I'll Stop Loving You/I Know My Place	1964	$8
47-7700	The Old Lamplighter/Teen-Ex	1960	$15
47-7700 [PS]	The Old Lamplighter/Teen-Ex	1960	$30
61-7700 [S]	The Old Lamplighter/Teen-Ex	1960	$30

— *"Living Stereo" (large hole, plays at 45 rpm)*

47-7555	The Three Bells/Heaven Fell Last Night	1959	$15
61-7555 [S]	The Three Bells/Heaven Fell Last Night	1959	$30

— *"Living Stereo" (large hole, plays at 45 rpm)*

47-8198	The Twelfth Rose/Watching My World Fall Apart	1963	$10
47-7780	The Whiffenpoof Song/Brighten the Corner Where You Are	1960	$15
47-7780 [PS]	The Whiffenpoof Song/Brighten the Corner Where You Are	1960	$30
61-7780 [S]	The Whiffenpoof Song/Brighten the Corner Where You Are	1960	$30

— *"Living Stereo" (large hole, plays at 45 rpm)*

47-7917	Whispering Wine/My Baby's Gone	1961	$10
37-7917	Whispering Wine/My Baby's Gone	1961	$30

— *Compact Single 33" (small hole, plays at LP speed)*

47-7311	Would You Care?/The Trot	1958	$20

7-Inch Extended Plays

EPA 1-1438	I Heard the Bluebirds Sing/I'll Hold You in My Heart/The Table Next to Me/My Isle of Golden Dreams	1957	$20
EPA-4352 [PS]	Scarlet Ribbons	1959	$20
EPA-4352	Scarlet Ribbons/I Still Do//Love Me Tender/We Should Be Together	1959	$20
EPA-4347 [PS]	The Browns Sing The 3 Bells	1959	$20
EPA-4364 [PS]	The Old Lamplighter	1960	$20
EPA-4364	The Old Lamplighter/Oh! My Pa-Pa//True Love/The Enchanted Sea	1960	$20
EPA-4347	The Three Bells/Be My Love//The Man in the Moon/This Time I Would Know	1959	$20

BROWNSVILLE STATION

BIG TREE

Number	Title	Yr	NM
16029	I Got It Bad for You/Mama Don't Allow No Parkin'	1974	$4
15005	I'm the Leader of the Gang/Fast Phyllis	1974	$4
15005	I'm the Leader of the Gang/Meet Me on the Fourth Floor	1974	$4
161	Let Your Yeah Be Yeah/Mister Robert	1973	$5
16011	Smokin' in the Boy's Room/Barefootin'	1973	$5

EPIC

50695	Love Stealer/Fever	1979	$4

— *As "Brownsville*

PALLADIUM

H-1075	Be-Bop Confidential/City Life	1970	$30

PRIVATE STOCK

45,149	Lady (Put the Light on Me)/Rockers and Rollers	1977	$6
45,167	The Martian Boogie/Mr. Johnson Sez	1977	$6

WARNER BROS.

7441	Be-Bop Confidential/City Life	1970	$8
7501	That's Fine/Tell Me All About It	1971	$8

BRUBECK, DAVE
ATLANTIC

Number	Title	Yr	NM
3015	Three to Get Ready/Blue Rondo (A La Turk)	1974	$4

COLUMBIA

42675	Bossa Nova U.S.A./Camptown Races	1963	$8
42651	Bossa Nova U.S.A./This Can't Be Love	1962	$10
44834	Broke Blues/Blues Roots	1969	$6
42920	Cable Car/Theme from Elementals	1963	$8
41485	Camptown Races/Shortnin' Bread	1959	$15
31443 [S]	Charles Matthew Hallelujah/Maria	1962	$15
30719 [S]	(contents unknown)	1960	$15
30720 [S]	(contents unknown)	1960	$15
30721 [S]	(contents unknown)	1960	$15
30722 [S]	(contents unknown)	1960	$15
30723 [S]	(contents unknown)	1960	$15
30899 [S]	(contents unknown)	1961	$15
30900 [S]	(contents unknown)	1961	$15
30901 [S]	(contents unknown)	1961	$15
30902 [S]	(contents unknown)	1961	$15
30903 [S]	(contents unknown)	1961	$15
31312 [S]	(contents unknown)	1962	$15
31313 [S]	(contents unknown)	1962	$15
31314 [S]	(contents unknown)	1962	$15
31315 [S]	(contents unknown)	1962	$15
31316 [S]	(contents unknown)	1962	$15

— *Anyone who can fill in these gaps -- the above 15 all are Columbia "Stereo 7" singles -- please let us know.*

42404	Countdown/Eleven Four	1962	$12
42404 [PS]	Countdown/Eleven Four	1962	$20
31446 [S]	Far More Blue/Gone with the Wind	1962	$15
43409	Happy Bandito/Bag O' Heat	1965	$8
40776	Lover/I'm in a Dancin' Mood	1956	$15
43133	Mr. Broadway/Toki's Theme	1964	$8
42068	Paradiddle Joe/Briar Bush	1961	$10
31444 [S]	Someday My Prince Will Come/I'm in a Dancing Mood	1962	$15
42804	Summer Song/Three to Get Ready	1963	$8
41479	Take Five/Blue Rondo A La Turk	1960	$15
31447 [S]	Take the "A" Train/Camptown Races	1962	$15
31445 [S]	Tangerine/The Duke	1962	$15
43663	Three to Get Ready/Done Her Wrong	1966	$8

FANTASY

518	A Foggy Day/Lyons Bust (Theme)	1953	$20
526	Alice in Wonderland/All the Things You Are	1953	$20
514	Always/I Didn't Know What Time It Was	1953	$20
520	At a Perfume Counter/Frenesi	1953	$20

— *The above four records comprised a box set*

513	Avalon/Perfidia	1953	$20
505	Blue Moon/Tea for Two	1952	$20
503	Body & Soul/Let's Fall in Love	1952	$20
504	Indiana/Laura	1952	$20

— *The above four records comprised a box set*

512	Ipca/Let's Fall in Love	1953	$20

— *The above four records comprised a box set*

501	Lullaby in Rhythm/You Stepped Out of a Dream	1952	$20
519	Mam'selle/Me and My Shadow	1953	$20
511	Prelude/Fugue on Bob's Theme	1953	$20

Number	Title	Yr	NM
510	September in the Rain/What Is This Thing Called Love	1953	$20
507	September Song/Sweet Georgia Brown	1952	$20
502	Singing in the Rain/I'll Remember April	1952	$20
517	Somebody Loves Me/Crazy Chris	1953	$20
515	Squeeze Me/How High the Moon	1953	$20
524	Stardust/Lulu's Back in Town	1953	$20
508	'S Wonderful/Spring Is Here	1952	$20

— *The above four records comprised a box set*

558	The Trolley Song/Crazy Chris	1961	$15
509	The Way You Look Tonight/Love Walked In	1953	$20
521	This Can't Be Love/Look for the Silver Lining	1953	$20
516	Too Marvelous for Words/Heart and Soul	1953	$20

— *The above four records comprised a box set*

7-Inch Extended Plays
COLUMBIA

5-2282	*The Duke/Fare Thee Well, Annabelle/Sometimes I'm Happy	1956	$15
5-2067	A Fine Romance/Brother, Can You Spare a Dime	1955	$10

— *Alternate numbers are "B-473-1" and "B-473-4"*

5-1940	Balcony Rock (Beg.)/Le Souk	1955	$10

— *Alternate numbers are "B-435-1" and "B-435-4"*

5-1941	Balcony Rock (Concl.)/Out of Nowhere	1955	$10

— *Alternate numbers are "B-435-2" and "B-435-3"*

B-473 [PS]	Brubeck Time	1955	$12

— *Dual-pocket sleeve for 2067 and 2068*

B-465 [PS]	Dave Brubeck at Storyville: 1954 (Vol. 1)	1955	$12

— *Dual-pocket sleeve for 2016 and 2017*

5-1943	I Want to Be Happy/Don't Worry 'Bout Me	1955	$15

— *Alternate numbers are "B-436-2" and "B-436-3"*

5-2281	Little Girl Blue/Indiana	1956	$15
5-2280	Lover/Love Walked In	1956	$15
5-2016	On the Alamo (Beginning)/Here Lies Love	1955	$10

— *Alternate numbers are "B-465-1" and "B-465-4"*

5-2017	On the Alamo (Conclusion)/Don't Worry 'Bout Me	1955	$10

— *Alternate numbers are "B-465-2" and "B-465-3"*

5-2068	Pennies from Heaven/Why Do I Love You	1955	$10

— *Alternate numbers are "B-473-2" and "B-473-3"*

5-1942	Take the "A" Train/The Song Is You	1955	$10

— *Alternate numbers are "B-436-1" and "B-436-4"*

BRUCE AND TERRY
COLUMBIA

42956	Custom Machine/Makaha at Midnight	1964	$30
43582	Don't Run Away/Girl It's All Right Now	1966	$20
43238	I Love You Model T/Carmen	1965	$30
43055	Summer Means Fun/Yeah!	1964	$30
43479	Thank You Baby/Come Love	1965	$20

BRUCE, ED
EPIC

50645	Angeline/Give My Old Memory a Call	1978	$4
50503	Love Somebody to Death/I Can't Seem to Get the Hang of Telling Her Goodbye	1977	$4
50544	Man Made of Glass/Never Take Candy from a Stranger	1978	$4
50475	Star Studded Nights/Wedding Dress	1977	$4
50613	The Man That Turned My Mama On/Give My Old Memory a Call	1978	$4
50424	When I Die, Just Let Me Go to Texas/I've Not Forgotten Marie	1977	$4

MCA

52295	After All/It Would Take a Fool	1983	$3
41201	Diane/Blue Umbrella	1980	$3
52109	Ever, Never Lovin' You/Theme from "Bret Maverick"	1982	$3
51076	Evil Angel/Easy Temptations	1981	$3
51018	Girls, Women & Ladies/The Last Thing She Said	1980	$3
52251	If It Was Easy/You've Got Her Eyes	1983	$3

Number	Title	Yr	NM
❏ 52036	Love's Found You and Me/I Take the Chance	1982	$3
❏ 52156	My First Taste of Texas/One More Shot of "Old Back Home Again	1983	$3
❏ 52433	Tell 'Em I've Gone Crazy/Birds of Paradise	1984	$3
❏ 41273	The Last Cowboy Song/The Outlaw and the Stranger	1980	$3
❏ 51139	(When You Fall in Love) Everything's a Waltz/Thirty-Nine and Holding	1982	$3

MONUMENT

Number	Title	Yr	NM
❏ 1138	Everybody Wants to Get to Heaven/When a Man Becomes a Man	1969	$6
❏ 1155	Hey Porter/The Love of My Heart	1969	$6
❏ 1118	Song for Jenny/Puzzles	1968	$6

RCA

Number	Title	Yr	NM
❏ 5005-7-R	Fools for Each Other/Memphis Roots	1986	$3

—A-side with Lynn Anderson

Number	Title	Yr	NM
❏ PB-14150	If It Ain't Love/The Migrant	1985	$3
❏ PB-14037	When Givin' Up Was Easy/Texas Girl, I'm Closing In on You	1985	$3

RCA VICTOR

Number	Title	Yr	NM
❏ 47-7842	Flight 303/Spun Gold	1961	$20
❏ 61-7842 [S]	Flight 303/Spun Gold	1961	$40

—Living Stereo" (large hole, plays at 45 rpm)

Number	Title	Yr	NM
❏ 47-9475	I'll Take You Away/Give More Than You Take	1968	$8
❏ 47-9155	Last Train to Clarksville/I'm Getting Better	1967	$8
❏ 47-9553	Painted Girls and Wine/Ninety-Seven More to Go	1968	$8
❏ 47-9394	Shadows of Her Mind/Her Sweet Love and the Baby	1967	$8
❏ 47-9315	The Price I Pay to Stay/If I Could Just Go Home	1967	$8
❏ 47-9044	Walker's Woods/Lonesome Is Me	1966	$8

SUN

Number	Title	Yr	NM
❏ 292	Sweet Woman/Part of My Life	1958	$50

—As "Edwin Bruce

UNITED ARTISTS

Number	Title	Yr	NM
❏ XW204	A House in New Orleans/Good Jelly Jones	1973	$4
❏ XW862	For Love's Own Sake/When Wide Open Spaces and Cowboys Are Gone	1976	$4
❏ XW403	It's Not What She Done/The Devil Ain't a Lonely Woman's Friend	1974	$4
❏ XW732	Mammas Don't Let Your Babies Grow Up to Be Cowboys/It's Not What She's Done (It's What You Didn't Do)	1975	$5
❏ XW811	Sleep All Mornin'/Working Man's Prayer	1976	$4
❏ XW774	The Littlest Cowboy Rides Again/The Feel of Being Gone	1976	$4

WAND

Number	Title	Yr	NM
❏ 156	I'm Gonna Have a Party/Half a Love	1964	$15
❏ 136	It's Coming to Me/The Greatest Man	1963	$15

BRUCE, TOMMY
CAPITOL

Number	Title	Yr	NM
❏ 4403	Ain't Misbehavin'/Got the Water Boilin'	1960	$15
❏ 5354	It's Driving Me Wild/Over Suzanne	1965	$10

BRUCE, VIN
COLUMBIA

Number	Title	Yr	NM
❏ 4-21027	Are You Forgetting/Knocking on the Door	1952	$30
❏ 4-21077	Clair de Lune/Je Laissez Mon Coeur	1953	$30
❏ 4-20923	Danse La Louisianne/Fille	1952	$30
❏ 4-21157	Goodbye to a Sweetheart/I'm Gonna Steal My Baby Back	1953	$30
❏ 4-21271	Here is the Bottle/I Stay	1954	$30
❏ 4-21120	My Mama Said/I'll Stay Single	1953	$30
❏ 4-21189	Oh Ma Belle/La Valse de St. Marie	1953	$30
❏ 4-20973	Sweet Love/I Trusted You	1952	$30
❏ 4-21336	Too Many Girls/Over an Ocean of Golden Dreams	1954	$30

BRUINS, THE
GENERAL AMERICAN

Number	Title	Yr	NM
❏ 721	Go On and Cry/Can't Believe That You've Grown Up	1965	$50

ROULETTE

Number	Title	Yr	NM
❏ 4566	Believe Me/The Slide	1964	$30

BRUNO, BRUCE
ROULETTE

Number	Title	Yr	NM
❏ 4386	Hey Little One/Some Time, Some Place	1961	$30

BRUNSON, TYRONE
BELIEVE IN A DREAM

Number	Title	Yr	NM
❏ ZS4-04330	Fresh/(Club Mix)	1983	$4
❏ ZS4-03937	Hot Line/(Instrumental)	1983	$4
❏ ZS4-03511	Sticky Situation/(Instrumental)	1983	$4

—As "Tyrone 'Tystick' Brunson"

Number	Title	Yr	NM
❏ ZS4-03163	The Smurf/I Need Love	1982	$4

MCA

Number	Title	Yr	NM
❏ 53000	Love Triangle/Freebee	1987	$4
❏ 52892	The Method/(B-side unknown)	1986	$4

BRUSH ARBOR
CAPITOL

Number	Title	Yr	NM
❏ 3672	Alone Again (Naturally)/Washington County	1973	$5
❏ 4118	Billy Ray/Old Fashioned Few	1975	$5
❏ 3538	Brush Arbor Meeting/Bear Creek Dam	1973	$5
❏ 3901	Carpenter of Wood/Daddy Was a Preacher	1974	$5
❏ 3968	Folk, Rock, Pop, Middle of the Road Country Singer/We Need Rain	1974	$5
❏ 3838	On the Road to Julian/Mary's Barn Door	1974	$5
❏ 3468	Proud Mary/Denver Woman	1972	$5
❏ 3733	Trucker and the U.F.O./Song to Mary Anne	1973	$5

MONUMENT

Number	Title	Yr	NM
❏ 45-207	Dreamin'/(B-side unknown)	1977	$5
❏ 8702	Emmylou/One Woman's Man	1976	$5
❏ 45-230	Get Down Country Music/Don't Play That Song Again	1977	$5
❏ 45-247	Learn How to Love Her/Waiting for a Miracle	1978	$5
❏ 45-265	This Magic Moment/All These Feelings	1978	$5

BRUTE FORCE
B.T. PUPPY

Number	Title	Yr	NM
❏ 561	War/Overture to Hello	1970	$8

COLUMBIA

Number	Title	Yr	NM
❏ 44371	Brute's Party/Toys for Tots	1967	$8
❏ 44091	Cudd'ly/In Jim's Garage	1967	$8

WARNER BROS.

Number	Title	Yr	NM
❏ 7224	Adam & Evening/The Purpose of a Circus	1968	$8

BRYAN, DORA
FONTANA

Number	Title	Yr	NM
❏ TF427	All I Want for Christmas Is a Beatle/If I Were a Fairy	1963	$30

—U.K. pressing, one of the first Beatles novelties

BRYAN, WES
CLOCK

Number	Title	Yr	NM
❏ 1013	Honey Baby/So Blue Over You	1959	$30

ROULETTE

Number	Title	Yr	NM
❏ 4289	I Guess I'll Never Know/Melodie D'Amour	1960	$20

UNITED ARTISTS

Number	Title	Yr	NM
❏ 102	Tiny Spacemen/Lonesome Love	1957	$40
❏ 102 [PS]	Tiny Spacemen/Lonesome Love	1957	$70
❏ 122	Wait for Me Baby/Freeze!	1958	$30

BRYANT, ANITA
ANITA BRYANT MINISTRIES

Number	Title	Yr	NM
❏ 1-413	Gospel Medley/Nostalgia Medley	1980	$20

—Small hole, plays at 33 1/3 rpm

Number	Title	Yr	NM
❏ 1-413 [PS]	Gospel Medley/Nostalgia Medley	1980	$20

CARLTON

Number	Title	Yr	NM
❏ ST118-3 [S]	Anyone Would Love You/The Party's Over	1959	$20
❏ 538	A Texan and a Girl from Mexico/He's Not Good Enough for You	1961	$8
❏ 473	Be Good, Be Careful, Be Mine/Dance On	1958	$20
❏ ST118-2 [S]	Hello Young Lovers/Mr. Wonderful	1959	$20
❏ 547	I Can't Do It By Myself/An Angel Cried	1961	$8

Number	Title	Yr	NM
❏ 530	In My Little Corner of the World/Anyone Would Love You	1960	$8
❏ 553	Lonesome for You Mama/A Place Called Happiness	1961	$8
❏ 535	One of the Lucky Ones/Love Look Away	1960	$8
❏ 528	Paper Roses/Mixed Emotions	1960	$8
❏ 523	Promise Me a Rose (A Slight Detail)/Do-Re-Mi	1959	$10
❏ ST118-4 [S]	Promise Me a Rose/Wouldn't It Be Lovely	1959	$20
❏ 518	Six Boys and Seven Girls/The Blessings of Love	1959	$12
❏ ST118-5 [S]	Small World/Love Look Away	1959	$20

—The above five are jukebox singles excerpting the LP "Anita Bryant

Number	Title	Yr	NM
❏ 512	Till There Was You/Little George	1959	$10
❏ 537	Wonderland by Night/Pictures	1960	$8

COLUMBIA

Number	Title	Yr	NM
❏ 43494	Another Year, Another Love, Another Heartache/Everything in the Garden	1965	$6
❏ 42629	A-Sleepin' at the Foot of the Bed/Wishing It Was You	1962	$6
❏ 42803	A Wound Time Can't Erase/Will I Cry in September	1963	$6
❏ 43928	Battle Hymn of the Republic/The Star-Spangled Banner	1966	$6
❏ 44569	Blue Summer/Silver and Blue	1968	$5
❏ 31570 [S]	(contents unknown)	1962	$10
❏ 31571 [S]	(contents unknown)	1962	$10
❏ 31572 [S]	(contents unknown)	1962	$10
❏ 31573 [S]	(contents unknown)	1962	$10
❏ 31574 [S]	(contents unknown)	1962	$10

—Anyone who can fill in these gaps -- the above 5 all are Columbia "Stereo 7" singles -- please let us know.

Number	Title	Yr	NM
❏ 44341	Do You Hear What I Hear/Away in the Manger	1967	$8
❏ 44341 [PS]	Do You Hear What I Hear/Away in the Manger	1967	$12
❏ 42847	Hey Good Lookin'/Bonaparte's Retreat	1963	$6
❏ 42847	Hey Good Lookin'/You're the Only Star (In My Blue Heaven)	1963	$6
❏ 44324	I Don't See Me in Your Eyes Anymore/Happy Time	1967	$5
❏ 43106	Laughing on the Outside/Welcome, Welcome Home	1964	$6
❏ 44654	Let the Heartaches Begin/Sister Sarah	1968	$5
❏ 42515	Moonlight Melody/I'm Not a Child Anymore	1962	$6
❏ 42515 [PS]	Moonlight Melody/I'm Not a Child Anymore	1962	$10
❏ 43436	My Mind's Playing Tricks on Me Again/Just Say Auf Wiedersehn	1965	$6
❏ 42438	One More Time with Billy/Free	1962	$6
❏ 42739	Our Winter Love/Honest John	1963	$6
❏ 44247	Some Sunday in the Middle of the Week/Little Love Words	1967	$5
❏ 44427	Something in Your Smile/Yellow Days	1968	$5
❏ 42257	Step by Step, Little By Little/Cold, Cold Winter	1962	$6
❏ 42257 [PS]	Step by Step, Little By Little/Cold, Cold Winter	1962	$10
❏ 44067	Sticks and Stones/Tomorrow Belongs to Me	1967	$5
❏ 43205	Tell Me/I Don't Understand	1965	$6
❏ 44193	The Man in the Raincoat/Love Is (Everything You Are)	1967	$5
❏ 44193 [PS]	The Man in the Raincoat/Love Is (Everything You Are)	1967	$8
❏ 42148	The Wedding/Seven Kinds of Lonesome	1961	$8
❏ 42148 [PS]	The Wedding/Seven Kinds of Lonesome	1961	$10
❏ 43037	The World of Lonely People/It's Better to Cry Today Than Cry Tomorrow	1964	$6
❏ 44471	Try to Remember/My Cup Runneth Over	1968	$5

DISNEYLAND

Number	Title	Yr	NM
❏ DL-560	The Orange Bird Song/Orange Tree	1971	$8
❏ DL-560 [PS]	The Orange Bird Song/Orange Tree	1971	$20

BRYANT, DON
SOUTHERN TRACKS

Number	Title	Yr	NM
❏ 1048	I Couldn't Wait For Christmas/In Way Over My Heart	1985	$4
❏ 1072	I Couldn't Wait For Christmas/The Only Thing Bad About Christmas	1986	$4

BRYANT, JAY DEE
HERALD

Number	Title	Yr	NM
❏ 570	Come Summer/I Could Have Cried	1962	$40

ISLAND

Number	Title	Yr	NM
❏ 08	I Want to Thank You Baby/Standing Ovation for Love	1975	$40

Number	Title	Yr	NM

BRYANT, JIMMY
CAPITOL
❏ F2057	Bryant's Shuffle/Yodelling Guitar	1952	$30
❏ F2310	Comin' On/Pickin' the Chicken	1952	$30
❏ F2160	Georgia Steel Guitar/ Midnight Ramble	1952	$30
❏ F2762	Hometown Polka/ Jammin' with Jimmy	1954	$30
❏ F1765	Liberty Bell Polka/T-Bone Rag	1951	$30
❏ F2675	Sunset/This Ain't the Blues	1953	$30

IMPERIAL
❏ 66235	Lazy Guitar/Tobacco Road	1967	$12

BRYANT, LEON
DE-LITE
❏ 814	Can I/(B-side unknown)	1981	$5
❏ 832	Finders Keepers/Never	1984	$5
❏ 833	I'm Gonna Put a Spell on You/(B-side unknown)	1984	$5
❏ 811	Mighty Body (Hotsy Totsy)/ Something More	1981	$5

BRYANT, LILLIE
SWAN
❏ 4029	Smokey Grey Eyes/I'll Never Be Free	1959	$15

BRYANT, RAY
ATLANTIC JAZZ
❏ 5102	Let It Be/Shake-A-Lady	1971	$4

CADET
❏ 5639	After Hours/Quizas, Quizas, Quizas	1969	$5
❏ 5580	City Tribal Dance/Little Suzie	1967	$6
❏ 5535	Gotta Travel On/It Was a Very Good Year	1966	$6
❏ 5558	If You Go Away/Slow Freight	1967	$6
❏ 5625	Little Green Apples/ Up Above the Rock	1968	$5
❏ 5615	Mrs. Robinson/Poochie	1968	$5
❏ 5575	Ode to Billie Joe/Ramblin'	1967	$6
❏ 5587	Pata Pata/Doing My Thing	1968	$6
❏ 5598	To Sir with Love/Dinner on the Grounds	1968	$5

COLUMBIA
❏ 42390	After Hours/Tonk	1962	$10
❏ 41761	C Jam Blues (Part 1)/C Jam Blues (Part 2)	1960	$10
❏ 31339 [S]	(contents unknown)	1961	$15
❏ 31340 [S]	(contents unknown)	1961	$15
❏ 31341 [S]	(contents unknown)	1961	$15
❏ 31342 [S]	(contents unknown)	1961	$15
❏ 31343 [S]	(contents unknown)	1961	$15

—Anyone who can fill in these gaps -- the above 5 all are Columbia "Stereo 7" singles -- please let us know.

❏ 41553	Little Suzie (Part 1)/ Little Suzie (Part 2)	1960	$10
❏ 42015	Moonrise/First Lady	1961	$10
❏ 41940	Sack O' Woe/Walk No More	1961	$10
❏ 41628	The Madison Time (Part 1)/ The Madison Time (Part 2)	1960	$10
❏ 41628 [PS]	The Madison Time (Part 1)/ The Madison Time (Part 2)	1960	$20

MCA
❏ 53322	The Madison Time/ Mama Didn't Lie	1988	$3

—B-side by Jan Bradley

❏ 53322 [PS]	The Madison Time/ Mama Didn't Lie	1988	$3

SIGNATURE
❏ 12026	Little Suzie (Part 2)/ Little Suzie (Part 4)	1960	$15

SUE
❏ 801	Glissamba/Joey	1963	$8
❏ 125	Goldfinger/Adalia	1965	$8
❏ 108	Shake a Lady/Blues March	1964	$8

BRYANT, SHARON
WING
❏ 889878-7	Foolish Heart/Saturday Nite	1989	$3
❏ 871722-7	Let Go/Saturday Nite	1989	$3
❏ 871722-7 [PS]	Let Go/Saturday Nite	1989	$3

BRYCE, SHERRY
MCA
❏ 40630	Everything's Coming Up Love/ Let Your Body Speak Your Mind	1976	$5
❏ 40562	Pretty Lies/Honky Tonk Bands	1976	$5

MGM
❏ 14812	Congratulations/ Hang On Feelin'	1975	$6
❏ 14695	Don't Stop Now/Saying What You're Spending It For	1974	$6
❏ 14842	Hang On Feelin'/This Song's for You	1976	$6
❏ 14548	Leaving's Heavy on My Mind/Coffee and Tears	1973	$6
❏ 14793	Love Song/I Love Loving You	1975	$6
❏ 14747	Oh, How Happy/Come On Down to Our House	1974	$6
❏ 14409	One More Time/That's What Loving You Has Done for Me	1972	$6
❏ 14726	Treat Me Like a Lady/ Where Love Has Died	1974	$6

PILOT
❏ 45100	The Lady Ain't for Sale/ Gone, Baby Gone	1977	$5

BRYNDLE
A&M
❏ 1252	Let's Go Home and Start Again/Woke Up This Morning	1971	$12

BRYSON, PEABO, AND REGINA BELLE
ELEKTRA
❏ 69426	Without You/The Higher You Climb	1987	$3

—B-side by Bryson solo

❏ 69426 [PS]	Without You/The Higher You Climb	1987	$3

—B-side by Bryson solo

BRYSON, PEABO, AND ROBERTA FLACK
ATLANTIC
❏ 3803	Love Is a Waiting Game/ More Than Everything	1981	$4

—As "Roberta Flack and Peabo Bryson

❏ 3775	Make the World Stand Still/Only Heaven Can Wait (For Love)	1980	$4

—As "Roberta Flack and Peabo Bryson

CAPITOL
❏ B-5353	I Just Came Here to Dance/ Can We Find Love Again	1984	$3
❏ B-5283	Maybe/Can We Find Love Again	1983	$3
❏ B-5283 [PS]	Maybe/Can We Find Love Again	1983	$3
❏ B-5242	Tonight, I Celebrate My Love/Born to Love	1983	$3
❏ B-5242 [PS]	Tonight, I Celebrate My Love/Born to Love	1983	$5

BRYSON, PEABO
BULLET
❏ 03	I Can Make It Better/Smile	1977	$8

CAPITOL
❏ B-44429	All My Love/Show and Tell	1989	$3
❏ 4694	Crosswinds/Don't Touch Me	1979	$4
❏ 4573	Feel the Fire/A Fool Already Knows	1978	$4
❏ B-5157	Give Me Your Love/You	1982	$4
❏ 4887	I Love the Way You Love/ When Will I Learn	1980	$4
❏ 4656	I'm So Into You/Smile	1978	$4
❏ A-5065	Let the Feeling Flow/ Move Your Body	1981	$4
❏ 7PRO-79852	Lover's Paradise (Edited Version)/(LP Version)	1989	$8

—Vinyl is promo only

❏ 4844	Minute by Minute/Life Is a Child	1980	$4
❏ 4729	She's a Woman/ Spread Your Wings	1979	$4
❏ B-44347	Show and Tell/Meant to Be	1989	$3
❏ B-44347 [PS]	Show and Tell/Meant to Be	1989	$3
❏ B-5098	There's No Guarantee/ Love Is on the Rise	1982	$4
❏ B-5098 [PS]	There's No Guarantee/ Love Is on the Rise	1982	$4
❏ 4989	Turn the Hands of Time/Friction	1981	$4
❏ 4989 [PS]	Turn the Hands of Time/Friction	1981	$5
❏ B-5188	We Don't Have to Talk (About Love)/Turn It On	1982	$4

ELEKTRA
❏ 69492	Catch 22/Only at Night	1987	$3
❏ 69517	Good Combination/Only at Night	1986	$3
❏ 69728	If Ever You're In My Arms Again/ There's No Getting Over You	1984	$3
❏ 69685	Love Always Finds a Way/ (B-side unknown)	1984	$3
❏ 69632	Take No Prisoners (In the Game of Love)/Love Means Forever	1985	$3
❏ 69632 [PS]	Take No Prisoners (In the Game of Love)/Love Means Forever	1985	$3
❏ 69612	There's Nothin' Out There/ She's Over Me	1985	$3

MCA
❏ 52344	D.C. Cab/Knock Me On My Feet	1984	$4

—B-side by Giorgio Moroder

SHOUT
❏ 309	Disco Queen/(Instrumental)	1975	$12

BUBBLE PUPPY, THE
Also see DEMIAN. (SC1)
Also see DEMIAN.
INTERNATIONAL ARTISTS
❏ 133	Beginning/If I Had a Reason	1969	$30
❏ 136	Days of Our Time/Thinkin' About Thinkin'	1969	$30
❏ 128	Hot Smoke and Sasafrass/Lonely	1969	$30
❏ 138	What Do You See/Hurry Sundown	1970	$30
❏ 138 [DJ]	What Do You See/Hurry Sundown	1970	$60

—Green vinyl promo

BUBI AND BOB
SPHINX
❏ 1201	The Mummy/Biscayne Beat	1959	$40

BUCCANEERS, THE
RAINBOW
❏ 211	Dear Ruth/Fine Brown Flame	1953	$800

RAMA
❏ 24	In the Mission of St. Augustine/ You Did Me Wrong	1954	$2000
❏ 21	The Stars Will Remember/ Come Back My Love	1954	$2000

SOUTHERN
❏ 101	Dear Ruth/Fine Brown Flame	1953	$4000

—All copies are on red vinyl. VG 2000; VG+ 3000

BUCCHINO, JOHN
HORN
❏ HR-4	Love Doesn't Always Stick Around/The Big Affair	1980	$5

BUCHANAN AND ANCELL
FLYING SAUCER
❏ 501	The Creature/Meet the Creature	1957	$50

BUCHANAN AND CELLA
ABC-PARAMOUNT
❏ 10033	String Along with Pal-O-Mine/More and More String Along with Pal-O-Mine	1959	$30

BUCHANAN AND GOODMAN
COMIC
❏ 500	Flying Saucer the Third/ The Cha Cha Lesson	1959	$50

LUNIVERSE
❏ 101X	Back to Earth Part 1/ Back to Earth Part 2	1956	$200
❏ 102	Buchanan and Goodman On Trial/Crazy	1956	$50
❏ 105	Flying Saucer The 2nd/ Martian Melody	1957	$50
❏ 107	Santa and the Satellite Part 1/ Santa and the Satellite Part 2	1957	$50
❏ 103	The Banana Boat Story/The Mystery (In Slow Motion)	1957	$50
❏ 108	The Flying Saucer Goes West/Saucer Serenade	1958	$50
❏ 101	The Flying Saucer Part 1/ The Flying Saucer Part 2	1956	$60

—Most labels have the entire word "Luniverse" typeset

❏ 101	The Flying Saucer Part 1/ The Flying Saucer Part 2	1956	$125

—Original labels have a handwritten "L" at the beginning of the printed word "Universe

NOVELTY
❏ 301	Frankenstein of '59/ Frankenstein Returns	1959	$50

BUCHANAN AND GREENFIELD
NOVEL
❏ 711	The Invasion/What a Lovely Party	1964	$40

—Originals have all-red labels

❏ 711	The Invasion/What a Lovely Party	1972	$8

—Red and white label reissue

Number	Title	Yr	NM

BUCHANAN, BILL
GONE
❏ 5032	The Thing/Happy Day	1958	$40

BUCHANAN, ROY
ATLANTIC
❏ 3433	The Circle/(B-side unknown)	1977	$4
❏ 3414	The Circle/Green Onions	1977	$4

POLYDOR
❏ 14174	Filthy Teddy/Thank You Lord	1973	$5
❏ 14149	Haunted House/Cajun	1972	$5
❏ 14178	Sweet Dreams/John's Blues	1973	$5

SWAN
❏ 4088	Mule Train Stomp/Pretty Please	1961	$15

BUCHANAN, WES
COLUMBIA
❏ 4-44760	A Heel That Time Will Wound/Working My Way Through a Heartache	1969	$8
❏ 4-44686	Warm Red Wine/ Letting Me Down	1968	$8

PEP
❏ 114	Give Some Love My Way/Only Fools	1958	$60

BUCK, CHARLIE
TAD
❏ 104	I Wish I Were A Christmas Tree/ We Can't Miss This Christmas	1962	$15

BUCK, GARY
CAPITOL
❏ 2518	Little White Picket Fences/ Love Away My Lovely	1969	$10
❏ 2316	Mister Brown/Winds Don't Blow That Strong	1968	$10
❏ 2804	Wayward Woman of the World/Wildflower	1970	$10

DIMENSION
❏ 1029	Midnight Magic/Kentucky Lady	1982	$5

PETAL
❏ 1310	As Close As We'll Ever Be/ Leave My Baby Alone	1963	$30
❏ 1750	Back Streets of Love/ Night Hawk	1964	$30
❏ 1011	Happy to Be Unhappy/ Saving All My Love for You	1963	$30
❏ 1500	The Wheel Song/ Suite of Sorrow	1964	$30

RCA VICTOR
❏ 74-0479	It Takes Time/I Saw the Light	1971	$8
❏ 74-0826	The Fool/If I'm a Fool for Leaving	1972	$8
❏ PB-10137	What'll I Do/Knowing That She's Leaving	1974	$6

TOWER
❏ 252	Before You Die/Stepping Out of the Picture	1966	$20
❏ 292	Weather Man/Whatever's Right	1966	$20

BUCKACRE
MCA
❏ 40616	Love Never Lasts Forever/ Bound to Be Blue	1976	$4
❏ 40919	Star That Shines/Tear Down the Walls	1978	$4

BUCKAROOS, THE
CAPITOL
❏ 2420	Anywhere U.S.A./ Gathering Dust	1969	$8
❏ 2010	Chicken Pickin'/Apple Jack	1967	$8
❏ 2010 [PS]	Chicken Pickin'/Apple Jack	1967	$20
❏ 2173	I'm Coming Back Home to Stay/I Can't Stop (My Loving You)	1968	$8
❏ 2173 [PS]	I'm Coming Back Home to Stay/I Can't Stop (My Loving You)	1968	$20
❏ 2264	I'm Goin' Back Home Where I Belong/Too Many Chiefs (Not Enough Indians)	1968	$8

BUCKEYES, THE
DELUXE
❏ 6126	Dottie Baby/Begging You Please	1957	$400
❏ 6110	Since I Fell for You/My Only You	1957	$300

BUCKINGHAM, LINDSEY
Also see BUCKINGHAM NICKS; FLEETWOOD MAC. (45)
ASYLUM
❏ 47408	It Was I/Love from Here, Love from There	1982	$4
❏ 47223	Trouble/Mary Lee Jones	1981	$4
❏ 47223 [PS]	Trouble/Mary Lee Jones	1981	$4

ELEKTRA
❏ 69714	Go Insane/Play in the Rain	1984	$3
❏ 69714 [PS]	Go Insane/Play in the Rain	1984	$4
❏ 69675	Slow Dancing/D.W. Suite	1984	$3

WARNER BROS.
❏ 29570	Holiday Road/The Trip (Theme from Vacation)	1983	$4

—B-side by Ralph Burns

BUCKINGHAM NICKS
Also see LINDSEY BUCKINGHAM; FLEETWOOD MAC; STEVIE NICKS.
POLYDOR
❏ 14428	Crying in the Night/Stephanie	1977	$40
❏ 14428 [PS]	Crying in the Night/Stephanie	1977	$70
❏ 14229	Crying in the Night/Without a Leg to Stand On	1974	$60
❏ 14335	Don't Let Me Down Again/Crystal	1976	$40
❏ 14209	Don't Let Me Down Again/ The Races Are Run	1973	$60

BUCKINGHAMS, THE (1)
COLUMBIA
❏ 44533	Back in Love Again/You Misunderstand Me	1968	$8
❏ 44533 [PS]	Back in Love Again/You Misunderstand Me	1968	$15
❏ 44053	Don't You Care/Why Don't You Love Me	1967	$8
❏ 44053 [PS]	Don't You Care/Why Don't You Love Me	1967	$15
❏ 44254	Hey Baby (They're Playing Our Song)/And Our Love	1967	$8
❏ 44254 [PS]	Hey Baby (They're Playing Our Song)/And Our Love	1967	$15
❏ 44923	It's a Beautiful Day/ Difference of Opinion	1969	$8
❏ 45066	It Took Forever/I Got a Feelin'	1970	$8
❏ 44182	Mercy, Mercy, Mercy/ You Are Gone	1967	$8
❏ 44182 [PS]	Mercy, Mercy, Mercy/ You Are Gone	1967	$15
❏ 44378	Susan/Foreign Policy	1967	$8
❏ 44378 [PS]	Susan/Foreign Policy	1967	$15
❏ 44790	This Is How Much I Love You/ Can't You Find the Words	1969	$8
❏ 44790 [PS]	This Is How Much I Love You/ Can't You Find the Words	1969	$15
❏ 44672	Where Did You Come From/ Song of the Breeze	1968	$8
❏ 44672 [PS]	Where Did You Come From/ Song of the Breeze	1968	$15

SPECTRASOUND
❏ 4618	Sweets for My Sweet/ Beginner's Love	1967	$30

U.S.A.
❏ 848	I Call Your Name/Makin' Up and Breakin' Up	1966	$15
❏ 844	I'll Go Crazy/I Don't Wanna Cry	1966	$15
❏ 853	I've Been Wrong/ Love Ain't Enough	1966	$15
❏ 869	Lawdy Miss Clawdy/I Call Your Name	1967	$15
❏ 869	Lawdy Miss Clawdy/Making Up and Breaking Up	1967	$15
❏ 873	Summertime/Don't Want to Cry	1967	$15

BUCKINGHAMS, THE (2)
LAURIE
❏ 3258	Gonna Say Goodbye/ Many Times	1964	$10

SEG-WAY
❏ 1004	Lobo Lobo/Rockin' Piper	1962	$10

BUCKLEY, TIM
DISCREET
❏ 1189	Dolphins/Honey Man	1974	$6
❏ 1311	Wanda Lu/Who Could Deny You	1974	$6

ELEKTRA
❏ 45612	Aren't You the Girl/Strange Street Affair Down Under	1967	$8
❏ 45606	Grief in My Soul/Wings	1966	$8
❏ 45623	Morning Glory/Once I Was	1967	$8
❏ 45618	Once Upon a Time/Lady Give Me Your Heart	1967	$8

WARNER BROS.
❏ 7623	Move with Me/Nighthawkin'	1972	$6

BUCKNER & GARCIA
BGO
❏ 1001	Pac-Man Fever/(Instrumental)	1982	$15

COLUMBIA
❏ 18-02867	Do the Donkey Kong/ (Instrumental)	1982	$4
❏ 18-03167	E.T. (I Love You)/(Instrumental)	1982	$4
❏ 13-03865	Pac-Man Fever/Do the Donkey Kong	1983	$3

—Reissue
❏ 18-02673	Pac-Man Fever/(Instrumental)	1982	$4

HANDSHAKE
❏ 5308	Merry Christmas in the NFL/(Instrumental)	1980	$8

—As "Willis 'The Guard' and Vigorish"

BUCKNER, JOE
VEE JAY
❏ 172	One More Mile/ Straight and Ready	1956	$30

—B-side by Tommy Dean
❏ 141	Why Don't Cha/How Can I Let Her Go	1955	$30

BUCKWHEAT
LONDON
❏ 156	Carmel Mountain Road/ Long Lonely Road	1971	$5
❏ 184	Good Book/Hey Little Girl	1972	$5
❏ 189	I Got to Boogie/I Just Can't Turn My Habit Into Love	1972	$5
❏ 166	Movin' On (Part 1)/ Movin' On (Part 2)	1971	$5
❏ 176	Simple Song of Freedom/I Got to Boogie	1972	$5
❏ 198	Will the Circle Be Unbroken/ Put Out the Light	1973	$5

BUCKWHEAT ZYDECO
ISLAND
❏ 99396	My Li'l Girl (Ma 'Tit Fille)/ On a Night Like This	1987	$4

BUD AND TRAVIS
LIBERTY
❏ 55284	Ballad of the Alamo/The Green Leaves of Summer	1960	$8
❏ 55235	Cloudy Summer Afternoon/E Labas	1959	$10
❏ 55803	Cold Summer/Girl Sittin' Up in a Tree	1965	$6
❏ 55259	Come to the Dance/ Carmen Carmelia	1960	$8
❏ 55713	How Long, How Long Blues/Gimmie Some	1964	$6
❏ 55764	I Talk to the Trees/ Moment in the Sun	1965	$6
❏ 55681	Maria Cristina/Sabras Que Te Quiero	1964	$6
❏ 55221	Poor Boy/Jenny on a Horse	1959	$12
❏ 55612	Tomorrow Is a Long Time/Haiti	1963	$6
❏ 55202	Truly Do/Bonsoir Dame	1959	$10

BUDD, BILLY
20TH CENTURY-FOX
❏ 502	Why Are You Running/ The Girl of the Year	1964	$8

JUBILEE
❏ 5583	Like I Want You Too/ Love Revolution	1967	$8

PAGE ONE
❏ 21025	Alice Long (You're Still My Favorite Girlfriend)/ The Straight Life	1969	$8
❏ 21008	Sweet Lorraine/ Boom Ditty Boom	1968	$8

BUDDIES, THE
COMET
❏ 2143	Hully Gully Baby/ Must Be True Love	1961	$30

DECCA
❏ 30355	A Prom and a Promise/ The Lottery	1957	$20
❏ 29953	Bag of Bones/Every Time the Phone Rings	1956	$20
❏ 31920	Duckman Part 1/ Duckman Part 2	1966	$8
❏ 29840	The Most Happy Fella/Two Skeletons on a Tin Roof	1956	$20

Number	Title	Yr	NM
GLORY			
❏ 230	I Stole Your Heart/I Waited	1955	$200
OKEH			
❏ 7123	Castle of Love/Give Me Your Love	1959	$20
SWAN			
❏ 4073	Spooky Spider/Lebone Delada	1961	$20
❏ 4170	The Beatle/Pulsebeat	1964	$30
TIARA			
❏ 6121	She's a Loser/Heartless	1959	$30

BUDGIE
KAPP

Number	Title	Yr	NM
❏ 2185 [B]	Stranded/Whiskey River	1972	$50
MCA			
❏ 40367 [B]	Honey/I Ain't No Mountain	1975	$50

BUFF, BEVERLY
BETHLEHEM

Number	Title	Yr	NM
❏ 3065	Forgive Me/No Part-Time Love	1963	$20
❏ 3078	From One Set of Arms to Another/Puzzle of Love	1963	$20
❏ 3027	I'll Sign/Used to Be Sweethearts	1962	$20

BUFFALO SPRINGFIELD
ATCO

Number	Title	Yr	NM
❏ 6499	Bluebird/Mr. Soul	1967	$30
❏ 6452	Everybody's Wrong/Burned	1966	$30
❏ 6545	Expecting to Fly/Everydays	1968	$10
❏ 6459	For What It's Worth/Do I Have to Come Right Out and Say It	1967	$20
❏ 6459	For What It's Worth (Stop, Hey, What's That Sound)/Do I Have to Come Right Out and Say It	1967	$15
❏ 6615	Four Days Gone/On the Way Home	1968	$10
❏ 6602	Special Care/Kind Woman	1968	$10

BUFFETT, JIMMY
ABC

Number	Title	Yr	NM
❏ 12143	Big Red/Havana Daydreamin'	1975	$5
❏ 12305	Changes in Latitudes, Changes in Attitudes/Landfall	1977	$4
❏ 12305 [PS]	Changes in Latitudes, Changes in Attitudes/Landfall	1977	$6
❏ 12358	Cheeseburger in Paradise/African Friend	1978	$4
❏ 12113	Door Number Three/Dallas	1975	$5
❏ 11399 [DJ]	He Went to Paris (stereo/mono)	1973	$15

—Number may have been assigned by mistake; double-sided promotional copies are known to exist; regular copies are on ABC Dunhill 4372

Number	Title	Yr	NM
❏ 12391	Livingston Saturday Night/Cowboy in the Jungle	1978	$4
❏ 12428	Manana/The Coast of Marsailles	1978	$4
❏ 12254	Margaritaville/Miss You So Badly	1977	$4
❏ 12200	Something So Feminine About a Mandolin/Woman Goin' Crazy on Caroline Street	1976	$5
❏ 12175	The Captain and the Kid/Cliches	1976	$5
ABC DUNHILL			
❏ 15011	Brand New Country Star/Pencil Thin Moustache	1974	$4
❏ 4385	Come Monday/The Wino and I Know	1974	$5
❏ 15008	Come Monday/The Wino and I Know	1974	$4
❏ 4359	Grapefruit-Juicy Fruit/I Found Me a Home	1973	$4
❏ 4372	He Went to Paris/Peanut Butter Conspiracy	1973	$4
❏ 15029	Presents to Send You/A Pirate Looks at Forty	1975	$4
❏ 4353	The Great Filling Station Hold Up/They Can't Dance Like Carmen No More	1973	$4
❏ 4348	The Great Filling Station Hold Up/Why Don't We Get Drunk	1973	$8
ASYLUM			
❏ 69890	I Don't Know (Spicoli's Theme)/She's My Baby (And She's Out of Control)	1982	$4

—B-side by Palmer & Jost

Number	Title	Yr	NM
BARNABY			
❏ 2023	Captain America/Truckstop Salvation	1970	$10
❏ 2019	He Ain't Free/There Ain't Nothing Soft About Hard Times	1970	$12
❏ 2013	The Christian/Richard Frost	1970	$12
FULL MOON			
❏ 49659	Survive/Send Me Somebody to Love	1981	$4

—B-side by Kathy Walker

Number	Title	Yr	NM
FULL MOON/ASYLUM			
❏ 47073	Hello Texas/Lyin' Eyes [by the Eagles]	1980	$5
MCA			
❏ 41199	Boat Drinks/Survive	1980	$4
❏ 53396	Bring Back the Magic/That's What Living Is to Me	1988	$3
❏ 53396 [PS]	Bring Back the Magic/That's What Living Is to Me	1988	$4
❏ 52333	Brown Eyed Girl/Twelve Volt Man	1984	$4
❏ S45-17084 [DJ]	Christmas In The Caribbean (same on both sides)	1985	$5
❏ 52499	Come to the Moon/Bigger Than the Both of Us	1984	$4
❏ 52932	Creola/You'll Never Work in Dis Bidness Again	1986	$3
❏ 52932 [PS]	Creola/You'll Never Work in Dis Bidness Again	1986	$4
❏ 41109	Fins/Dreamsicle	1979	$4
❏ 52607	Gypies in the Palace/Jolly Mon Sing	1985	$3
❏ 53360	Homemade Music/L'air de la Louisiane	1988	$3
❏ 53360 [PS]	Homemade Music/L'air de la Louisiane	1988	$4
❏ 52050	If I Could Just Get It on Paper/Where's the Party	1982	$4
❏ 52664	If the Phone Doesn't Ring, It's Me/Frank and Lola	1985	$3
❏ 52849	I Love the Now/No Plane on Sunday	1986	$3
❏ 52013	It's Midnight And I'm Not Famous Yet/When Salome Plays the Drum	1982	$4
❏ 51061	It's My Job/Little Miss Magic	1981	$4
❏ 52298	One Particular Harbour/Distantly in Love	1983	$4
❏ 52752	Please Bypass This Heart/Beyond the End	1986	$3
❏ 51105	Stars Fell on Alabama/Growing Older But Not Up	1981	$4
❏ 53675	Take Another Road/Off to See the Lizard	1989	$3
❏ 53035	Take It Back/Floridays	1987	$3
❏ 52438	When the Wild Life Betrays Me/Ragtop Day	1984	$4
❏ 52438 [PS]	When the Wild Life Betrays Me/Ragtop Day	1984	$4
❏ 52550	Who's the Blond Stranger/She's Going Out of My Mind	1985	$3

BUG COLLECTORS, THE
CATCH

Number	Title	Yr	NM
❏ 103	The Beatle Bug/Thief in the Night	1964	$30

BUGALOOS, THE
CAPITOL

Number	Title	Yr	NM
❏ 2946	Senses of Our World/For a Friend	1970	$15

BUGGLES, THE
CARRERE

Number	Title	Yr	NM
❏ ZS5-02759	I Am a Camera/Inner City	1982	$5
ISLAND			
❏ 49209	Clean Clean/Astro Boy (And the Proles on Parade)	1980	$5

BUGGS, THE
SOMA

Number	Title	Yr	NM
❏ 1413	The Buggs vs. The Beatles/She Loves You	1964	$30

BUGS, THE
ASTOR

Number	Title	Yr	NM
❏ 01	Albert Albert/Strangler in the Night	1966	$20
❏ 01 [PS]	Albert Albert/Strangler in the Night	1966	$20
HIT			
❏ 161	Any Way You Want It/Sidewalk Surfin'	1964	$15

—B-side by the Jalopy Five

Number	Title	Yr	NM
❏ 106	She Loves You/Dawn (Go Away)	1964	$15

—B-side by the Chellows

Number	Title	Yr	NM
❏ 111	Twist and Shout/Stay	1964	$15

—B-side by the Chellows

BULLENS, CINDY
CASABLANCA

Number	Title	Yr	NM
❏ 2217	Trust Me/Holding Me Crazy	1979	$4
UNITED ARTISTS			
❏ X1293	Anxious Heart/Time and Changes	1979	$4
❏ XW1248	High School History/Mr. Anonymous	1978	$4
❏ X1261	Survivor/Finally Rockin'	1978	$4

BUNKERS, THE
RCA VICTOR

Number	Title	Yr	NM
❏ 74-0962	They Can't Take That Away from Me/Oh Babe, What Would You Say	1973	$6
❏ 74-0962 [PS]	They Can't Take That Away from Me/Oh Babe, What Would You Say	1973	$10

BUONO, VICTOR
DORE

Number	Title	Yr	NM
❏ 864	Fat Man's Prayer/Bless Me Doctor	1971	$6

BUOYS, THE
POLYDOR

Number	Title	Yr	NM
❏ 14201	Liza's Last Ride/Downtown Singer	1973	$6
SCEPTER			
❏ 12318	Give Up Your Guns/Prince of Thieves	1971	$8
❏ 12331	Tell Me Heaven Is Here/Bloodknot	1971	$8
❏ 12254	These Days/Don't You Know It's Over	1969	$8
❏ 12275	Timothy/It Feels Good	1970	$10
❏ 12275 [PS]	Timothy/It Feels Good	1970	$30

BURDEN, RAY
CULLMAN

Number	Title	Yr	NM
❏ 6407	Christmas Is Here At Last/Santa, Bring Me A Gal	1958	$60

BURDETTE, LEW
DOT

Number	Title	Yr	NM
❏ 15672	Three Strikes and You're Out/Mary Lou	1957	$30

BURDON, ERIC, AND WAR
ABC

Number	Title	Yr	NM
❏ 12244	Magic Mountain/Home Dream	1977	$5
MGM			
❏ 14118	Spill the Wine/Magic Mountain	1970	$6
❏ 14118 [PS]	Spill the Wine/Magic Mountain	1970	$15
❏ 14196	They Can't Take Away Our Music/Home Cookin'	1970	$5

BURDON, ERIC
MGM

Number	Title	Yr	NM
❏ 14296	Headin' for Home/Soledad	1971	$5

—With Jimmy Witherspoon

BURGESS, DAVE
CHALLENGE

Number	Title	Yr	NM
❏ 1001	Don't Cry, For You I Love/Fire in the Eyes	1957	$30

—As "Dave Dupree"

Number	Title	Yr	NM
❏ 59045	Everlovin'/Just for Me	1959	$30
❏ 1002	Flame of Love/Well, It Isn't Fair	1957	$30

—As "Dave Dupree"

Number	Title	Yr	NM
❏ 59037	I Don't Want to Know/Lulu	1959	$30
❏ 1008	I'm Available/Who's Gonna Cry	1957	$30
❏ 59032	Lovey Dovey Baby/I Hang My Head and Cry	1958	$30
❏ 1018	Take This Love/Maybelle	1958	$30

—As "Dave Burgess and the Champs"

Number	Title	Yr	NM
❏ 59101	Without You/Are You Teasing Me	1961	$30
OKEH			
❏ 7002	Don't Put a Dent in My Heart/Judalina	1953	$30
❏ 7044	Gratefully Yours/Too Late for Tears	1954	$30
TAMPA			
❏ 104	Down, Down/Don't Turn Your Back on Love	1955	$30
❏ 105	I Love Paris/Five Foot Two, Eyes of Blue	1955	$30

BURGESS, FRANK
TRUE

Number	Title	Yr	NM
❏ 94	American Man/(B-side unknown)	1988	$6
❏ 96	What It Boils Down To/(B-side unknown)	1989	$6

Number	Title	Yr	NM
BURGESS, SONNY			
PHILLIPS INT'L.			
❏ 3551	Sadie's Back in Town/ Kiss Goodnight	1960	$40
SUN			
❏ 263	Ain't Got a Thing/Restless	1957	$100
❏ 285	My Bucket's Got a Hole in It/Sweet Misery	1958	$60
❏ 304	Thunderbird/Itchy	1958	$40
BURGESS, WILMA			
DECCA			
❏ 31862	Baby/Wait Till the Sun Comes Up	1965	$8
❏ 31941	Don't Touch Me/Turn Around Teardrops	1966	$8
❏ 32811	Everything's Gonna Be Alright/ Until My Dreams Come True	1971	$8
❏ 32105	Fifteen Days/Two Little Rivers of Tears	1967	$8
❏ 32684	Lonely for You/I Don't See Me in Your Eyes Anymore	1970	$8
❏ 32359	Look at the Laughter/ Sweet Promises	1968	$8
❏ 32027	Misty Blue/Ain't Got No Man	1966	$10
❏ 32273	Only a Fool Keeps Hangin' On/Watch the Roses Grow	1968	$8
❏ 32437	Parting (Is Such Sweet Sorrow)/Shine a Little Sun on Me	1969	$8
❏ 32178	Tear Time/(How Can I Write on Paper) What I Feel in My Heart	1967	$8
❏ 32593	The Sun's Gotta Shine/Only Mama That'll Walk the Line	1969	$8
❏ 32522	The Woman in Your Life/ Happiness Is So Hard to Forget	1969	$8
❏ 31826	When You're Not Around/ The Closest Thing to Love	1965	$10
RCA			
❏ PB-11179	Once You Were Mine/I'm Turning You Loose	1977	$5
SHANNON			
❏ 839	A Satisfied Man/ (B-side unknown)	1975	$6
❏ 835	Baby's Not Forgotten/ (B-side unknown)	1975	$6
❏ 810	Feeling the Way a Woman Should/I'll Always Love the Days	1973	$6
❏ 813	I'll Be Your Bridge (Just Lay Me Down)/I'll Always Love the Days	1973	$6
❏ 821	Love Is Here/Sweet Lovin' Baby	1974	$6
UNITED ARTISTS			
❏ 523	Confused/Something Tells Me	1962	$30
BURKE, FIDDLIN' FRENCHIE			
20TH CENTURY			
❏ 2152	Big Mamou/There'll Be Love Tonight in My House	1974	$5
—As "Fiddlin' Frenchie Bourque and the Outlaws			
❏ 2182	Colinda/Pride, You Wouldn't Listen	1975	$5
❏ 2225	The Fiddlin' of Jacques Pierre Bordeaux/Frenchie's Cotton-Eyed Joe	1975	$5
DELTA			
❏ 11332	(Frenchie Burke's) Fire on the Mountain/Let's Go Get Drunk and Be Somebody	1981	$6
BURKE, SOLOMON			
ABC DUNHILL			
❏ 4388	Midnight and You/I Have a Dream	1974	$5
❏ 15009	Midnight and You/I Have a Dream	1974	$4
AMHERST			
❏ 736	Please Don't You Say Goodbye to Me/See That Girl	1978	$4
APOLLO			
❏ 505	A Picture of You/You Can Run But You Can't Hide	1957	$30
❏ 485	Christmas Presents/ When I'm All Alone	1955	$40
❏ 512	For You and Me/Don't You Are My One Love	1957	$30
❏ 491	I'm All Alone/To Thee	1956	$30
❏ 487	I'm in Love/Why Do Me That Way	1956	$30
❏ 511	I Need You Tonight/This Is It	1957	$30
❏ 527	My Heart Is a Chapel/This Is It	1958	$30
❏ 522	They Always Say/Don't Cry	1958	$30
ATLANTIC			
❏ 2314	Baby Come On Home/(No, No, No) Can't Stop Lovin' You Now	1965	$15

Number	Title	Yr	NM
❏ 2196	Can't Nobody Love You/Stupidity	1963	$20
❏ 2131	Cry to Me/I Almost Lost My Mind	1962	$70
❏ 2147	Down in the Valley/I'm Hanging Up My Heart for You	1962	$20
❏ 2241	Everybody Needs Somebody to Love/Looking for My Baby	1964	$20
❏ 2566	Get Out of My Life Woman/What'd I Say	1968	$10
❏ 2226	Goodbye Baby (Baby Goodbye)/Someone to Love Me	1964	$20
❏ 2170	Go On Back to Him/I Said I Was Sorry	1962	$20
❏ 2276	Got to Get You Off My Mind/Peepin'	1965	$20
❏ 2218	He'll Have to Go/Rockin' Soul	1964	$20
❏ 2327	I Feel a Sin Coming On/ Mountain of Pride	1966	$10
❏ 2185	If You Need Me/You Can Make It If You Try	1963	$20
❏ 2157	I Really Don't Want to Know/ Tonight My Heart She Is Crying (Love Is a Bird)	1962	$20
❏ 2459	It's Been a Change/Detroit City	1967	$10
❏ 2507	I Wish I Knew (How It Would Feel to Be Free)/It's Just a Matter of Time Baby	1968	$10
❏ 2308	Only Love (Can Save Me Now)/A Little Girl That Loves Me	1965	$15
❏ 2483	Party People/Need Your Love So Bad	1968	$10
❏ 2369	Presents for Christmas/A Tear Fell	1966	$15
❏ 2527	Save it!/Meet Me in Church	1968	$10
❏ 2299	Someone Is Watching/ Dance, Dance, Dance	1965	$15
❏ 2345	Suddenly/Lawdy Miss Clawdy	1966	$10
❏ 2416	Take Me (Just As I Am)/ Stayed Away Too Long	1967	$10
❏ 2259	The Price/More Rockin' Soul	1964	$20
❏ 2288	Tonight's the Night/ Maggie's Farm	1965	$20
❏ 2359	When She Touches Me/ Woman How Do You Make Me Love You Like I Do	1966	$10
❏ 2180	Words/Home in Your Heart	1963	$20
BELL			
❏ 891	God Knows I Love You/ In the Ghetto	1970	$6
❏ 829	I'm Gonna Stay Right Here/ Generation of Revelations	1969	$8
❏ 783	Proud Mary/What Am I Living For	1969	$8
❏ 806	That Lucky Old Sun/ How Big a Fool	1969	$8
CHESS			
❏ ACH-401	I'll Never Stop Loving You (Never Ever Song)/ The Do Right Song	1976	$6
❏ 2172	Let Me Wrap My Arms Around You/Everlasting Love	1975	$4
INFINITY			
❏ 50046	Sidewalks, Fences and Walls/ Boo-Hoo-Hoo (Cra-Cra-Craya)	1979	$5
MALA			
❏ 420	This Little Ring/I'm Not Afraid	1960	$30
MGM			
❏ 14651	Georgia Up North/Here Comes the Train	1973	$6
❏ 14425	Get Up and Do Something for Yourself/We're Almost Home	1972	$6
❏ 14185	Lookin' Out My Back Door/ All for the Love of Sunshine	1970	$6
❏ 14353	Love's Street and Fool's Road/I Got to Tell It	1972	$6
❏ 14571	Shambala/Love Thy Neighbor	1973	$6
❏ 14221	The Electronic Magnetism (That's Heavy, Baby)/ Bridge of Life	1971	$6
❏ 14402	We're Almost Home/Fight Back	1972	$6
❏ 14402 [PS]	We're Almost Home/Fight Back	1972	$15
PRIDE			
❏ 1022	All I Want for Christmas/I Can't Stop Loving You (Part 1)	1972	$6
❏ 1017	I Can't Stop Loving You (Part 1)/I Can't Stop Loving You (Part 2)	1972	$6
❏ 1028	My Prayer/Ookie Bookie Man	1973	$6
❏ 1038	Sentimental Journey/ Vaya Con Dios	1973	$6
—With Lady Lee			
BURLAND, SASCHA & THE SKIPJACK CHOIR			
COLUMBIA			
❏ 42009	Gorilla Walk/Hole in My Soul	1960	$30
RCA VICTOR			
❏ 47-8277	Have Yourself a Merry Little Christmas/The Chickens Are in the Chimes	1963	$40

Number	Title	Yr	NM
❏ 47-8277 [PS]	Have Yourself a Merry Little Christmas/The Chickens Are in the Chimes	1963	$50
BURNETT, FRANCES			
CORAL			
❏ 62092	Come to Me/So Many Tears	1959	$125
❏ 62164	I Love Him So/Too Proud	1960	$125
❏ 62127	Please Remember Me/ How I Miss You So	1959	$125
❏ 62214	She Was Taking My Baby/Sweetie	1960	$125
DECCA			
❏ 30571	Spin the Wheel/A Promise Made a Fool of Me	1958	$120
BURNETT, T-BONE			
WARNER BROS.			
❏ 29489	Baby Fall Down/Art Movies	1983	$5
❏ 29876	Hold On Tight/Poetry	1982	$6
BURNETTE, BILLY			
A&M			
❏ 1794	Baby/Just Another Love Song	1976	$5
COLUMBIA			
❏ 11380	Don't Say No/Rockin' L.A.	1980	$4
❏ 02527	Let the New Love Begin/I Don't Know Why	1981	$4
❏ 11432	Oh Susan/Sittin' On Ready	1981	$4
❏ 02699	The Bigger the Love/I Don't Know Why	1982	$4
ENTRANCE			
❏ 7515	Broken Hearted/I'm Always Wondering	1972	$5
MCA CURB			
❏ 52626	Ain't It Just Like Love/Guitar Bug	1985	$3
❏ 52749	It's Not Easy/Try Me	1985	$3
❏ 52852	Soldier of Love/Guitar Bug	1986	$3
❏ 52710	Who's Using Your Heart Tonight/It Ain't Over	1985	$3
POLYDOR			
❏ 14549	Believe What You Say/ Mississippi Line	1979	$4
❏ 14530	Dreamin' My Way Back to You/Shoo-Be-Doo	1979	$4
❏ 2024	What's a Little Love Between Friends/Precious Times	1979	$4
WARNER BROS.			
❏ 7327	Frog Prince/One Extreme to the Other	1969	$8
BURNETTE, BILLY JOE			
❏ 1004	Three Flags/(B-side unknown)	1989	$6
GUSTO			
❏ 9009	The Colonel and the King/ Walk Again in the Hills	1978	$15
—May be promo only			
❏ 167	Welcome Home Elvis/Haven't Seen Mama in Years	1977	$8
K-ARK			
❏ 961	Blow Smoke on a Kangaroo/ Have I Told You Lately	1970	$8
❏ 968	Sufferin'/Fickle Hearted Fool	1970	$8
MT. VERNON			
❏ 501	Billy the Kid/I've Got a Heart	1962	$400
❏ 500	Stomp, Shake & Twist/Don't Let Our Love Go Wrong	1962	$800
—As "Billy Barnette			
PARKWAY			
❏ 826	Two Brothers/Marlene	1961	$30
—As "Billy Barnette			
BURNETTE, DORSEY			
ABBOTT			
❏ 190	At a Distance/Jungle Magic	1957	$60
❏ 188	Let's Fall in Love/ The Devil's Queen	1956	$60
CALLIOPE			
❏ 8012	Soon As I Touched Her/ Dear Hearted Children	1977	$6
❏ 8004	Things I Treasure/One Mornin'	1977	$6
CAPITOL			
❏ 3829	Bob, All the Playboys, and Me/The Bootleggers	1974	$5
❏ 3463	Cry Mama/Lonely to Be Alone	1972	$5

Number	Title	Yr	NM
❏ 3887	Daddy Loves You Honey/True Love Means Forgiving	1974	$5
❏ 3678	Darlin' (Don't Come Back)/Sweet Lovin' Woman	1973	$5
❏ 3404	I Just Couldn't Let Her Walk Away/Church Bells	1972	$5
❏ 3529	I Let Another Good One Get Away/Take Your Weapons, Lay 'Em Down	1973	$5
❏ 3307	In the Spring (The Roses Always Turn Red)/The Same Old You, The Same Old He	1972	$5
❏ 3796	It Happens Every Time/Mr. Jukebox, Sing a Lullaby	1973	$5
❏ 3190	Shelby County Penal Farm/Children of the Universe	1971	$5
❏ 3963	What Ladies Can Do (When They Want To)/Tangerine	1974	$5

CEE-JAM

Number	Title	Yr	NM
❏ 16	Bertha Lou/'Til the Law Says Stop	1957	$100

DOT

Number	Title	Yr	NM
❏ 16305	A Country Boy in the Army/A Dying Ember	1961	$20
❏ 16265	The Feminine Touch/Sad Boy	1961	$20

ELEKTRA

Number	Title	Yr	NM
❏ 46586	B.J. Kick-a-Beaux/What Would It Profit Me	1980	$4
❏ 46513	Here I Go Again/What Would It Profit Me	1979	$4

ERA

Number	Title	Yr	NM
❏ 3045	Great Shakin' Fever/That's Me Without You	1961	$20
❏ 3041	Hard Rock Mine/((It's No) Sin	1961	$20
❏ 3019	Hey Little One/Big Rock Candy Mountain	1960	$20
❏ 3025	The Ghost of Billy Malloo/Red Roses	1960	$20
❏ 3012	(There Was a)Tall Oak Tree/Juarez Town	1960	$30

HAPPY TIGER

Number	Title	Yr	NM
❏ 563	One Lump Sum/Call Me Lowdown	1970	$6
❏ 546	To Be a Man/Fly Away and Hurry Home	1970	$6

HICKORY

Number	Title	Yr	NM
❏ 1458	The House That Jack Built/Ain't That Fine	1967	$8

IMPERIAL

Number	Title	Yr	NM
❏ 5756	House with a Tin Roof Top/Circle Rock	1961	$30
❏ 5987	House with a Tin Roof Top/Circle Rock	1963	$20
❏ 5597	Lonely Train/Misery	1959	$30
❏ 5561	Try/You Came as a Miracle	1959	$30
❏ 5668	Way in the Middle of the Night/Your Love	1960	$30

LIBERTY

Number	Title	Yr	NM
❏ 56087	The Greatest Love/Thin Little Simple Little Plain Little Girl	1969	$6

MEL-O-DY

Number	Title	Yr	NM
❏ 113	Little Acorn/Cold As Usual	1964	$20
❏ 118	Long Long Time Ago/Ever Since the World Began	1964	$20

MELODYLAND

Number	Title	Yr	NM
❏ 6031	Ain't No Heartbreak/I Dreamed I Saw	1976	$5
❏ 6019	Lyin' in Her Arms Again/Doggone the Dogs	1975	$5
❏ 6007	Molly (I Ain't Gettin' Any Younger)/She's Feeling Low	1975	$5

MUSIC FACTORY

Number	Title	Yr	NM
❏ 417	I'll Walk Away/Son, You've Got to Make It Alone	1968	$8

REPRISE

Number	Title	Yr	NM
❏ 20093	Castle in the Sky/Boys Keep Hanging Around	1962	$20
❏ 20121	Darling Jane/I'm a Waitin' For Ya Baby	1962	$20
❏ 0246	Four for Texas/Foolish Pride	1963	$20
❏ 0246 [PS]	Four for Texas/Foolish Pride	1963	$50
❏ 20177	Invisible Chains/Pebbles	1963	$20
❏ 20208	One of the Lonely/Where's the Girl	1963	$20

SMASH

Number	Title	Yr	NM
❏ 2039	If You Want to Love Somebody/Teach Me Little Children	1966	$10
❏ 2062	Tall Oak Tree/I Just Can't Be Tamed	1966	$10
❏ 2029	To Remember/In the Morning	1966	$10

BURNETTE, DORSEY AND JOHNNY

CORAL

Number	Title	Yr	NM
❏ 62190	Blues Stay Away from Me/Midnight Train	1960	$200

—As "Johnny and Dorsey Burnette"

IMPERIAL

Number	Title	Yr	NM
❏ 5509	Warm Love/My Honey	1958	$125

—As "Burnette Brothers

REPRISE

Number	Title	Yr	NM
❏ 20153	It Don't Take Much/Hey Sue	1963	$30

BURNETTE, JOHNNY

CAPITOL

Number	Title	Yr	NM
❏ 5023	All Week Long/It Isn't There	1963	$20
❏ 5176	Walkin' Talkin' Doll/Sweet Suzie	1964	$20

CHANCELLOR

Number	Title	Yr	NM
❏ 1116	I Wanna Thank Your Folks/The Giant	1962	$20
❏ 1123	Party Girl/Tag Along	1962	$20

CORAL

Number	Title	Yr	NM
❏ 61869	Drinkin' Wine Spo-Dee-O-Dee/Butterfingers	1957	$300
❏ 61829	Eager Beaver Baby/Touch Me	1957	$300
❏ 61758	Lonesome Train/I Just Found Out	1956	$300
❏ 61675	Midnight Train/Oh Baby Babe	1956	$300
❏ 61651	Tear It Up/You're Undecided	1956	$300
❏ 61719	The Train Kept a-Rollin'/Honey Hush	1956	$250

FREEDOM

Number	Title	Yr	NM
❏ 44011	Gumbo/Me and the Bear	1959	$100
❏ 44001	I'm Restless/Kiss Me	1958	$100
❏ 44017	Sweet Baby Doll/I'll Never Love Again	1959	$100

LIBERTY

Number	Title	Yr	NM
❏ 55318	Big Big World/Ballad of the One Eyed Jacks	1961	$20
❏ 55318 [PS]	Big Big World/Ballad of the One Eyed Jacks	1961	$50
❏ 55416	Clown Shoes/The Way I Am	1962	$20
❏ 55489	Damn the Defiant/Lonesome Waters	1962	$20
❏ 55243	Don't Do It/Patrick Henry	1959	$30
❏ 55258	Dreamin'/Cincinnati Fireball	1960	$30
❏ 55345	Girls/I've Got a Lot of Things to Do	1961	$20
❏ 55379	God, Country and My Baby/Honestly I Do	1961	$20
❏ 55377	Honestly I Do/Fools Like Me	1961	$20
❏ 55298	Little Boy Sad/(I Go) Down to the River	1961	$20
❏ 55298 [PS]	Little Boy Sad/(I Go) Down to the River	1961	$50
❏ 55222	Settin' the Woods on Fire/Kentucky Waltz	1959	$30
❏ 55448	The Fool of the Year/The Poorest Boy in Town	1962	$20

MAGIC LAMP

Number	Title	Yr	NM
❏ 515	Bigger Man/Less Than a Heartache	1964	$60
❏ 515 [PS]	Bigger Man/Less Than a Heartache	1964	$300

SAHARA

Number	Title	Yr	NM
❏ 512	Fountain of Love/What a Summer Day	1964	$20

UNITED ARTISTS

Number	Title	Yr	NM
❏ 0018	Dreamin'/Little Boy Sad	1973	$4

—Silver Spotlight Series issue

7-Inch Extended Plays

LIBERTY

Number	Title	Yr	NM
❏ LSX-1004 [PS]	Dreamin'	1960	$175
❏ LSX-1004	Dreamin'/Love Me//Settin' the Woods on Fire/Please Help Me, I'm Falling	1960	$125
❏ LSX-1011	Little Boy Sad/Don't Do It//You're Sixteen/I Go Down to the River	1961	$125

BURNETTE, ROCKY

EMI AMERICA

Number	Title	Yr	NM
❏ 8050	Baby Tonight/Because of You	1980	$4
❏ 8060	Fallin' in Love (Bein' Friends)/Roll Like a Wheel	1980	$4
❏ 8043	Tired of Toein' the Line/Boogie Down in Mobile, Alabama	1980	$5

THE GOODS

Number	Title	Yr	NM
❏ 93007	Heartstopper/In the Middle of the Night	1982	$5

BURNETTE, SMILEY

ABBOTT

Number	Title	Yr	NM
❏ 154	Chuggin' On Down "66"/Mucho Gusto	1954	$40
❏ 161	That Long White Line/Lazy Locomotive	1954	$40

CAPITOL

Number	Title	Yr	NM
❏ F1746	Can't Go On/I Ain't Done Nothin' to You	1951	$30

Number	Title	Yr	NM
❏ F1165	Catfish/Jackass Mail	1950	$30
❏ F1520	Do the Pines Grow Green in the Valley/I Can't Be Honest	1951	$30
❏ F1347	Hominy Grits/My Lazy Day	1950	$30

STARDAY

Number	Title	Yr	NM
❏ 586	Old Fishin' Pole/It's My Last Day	1962	$20

BURNING SENSATIONS

CAPITOL

Number	Title	Yr	NM
❏ B-5243	Belly of the Whale/Check Your Mail	1983	$5
❏ B-5297	Maria/Not Cloudy at All	1983	$5

BURNS, BRENT

PANTHEON DESERT

Number	Title	Yr	NM
❏ 79	I Hear You Coming Back/Come Away with Me	1978	$8

BURNS, EDDIE

CHECKER

Number	Title	Yr	NM
❏ 790	Biscuit Baking Mama/Superstition	1954	$300

—As "Big Ed and His Combo"

CHESS

Number	Title	Yr	NM
❏ 1672	Treat Me Like I Treat You/Don't Cha Leave Me Baby	1957	$50

DELUXE

Number	Title	Yr	NM
❏ 6024	Hello Miss Jessie Lee/Dealing with the Devil	1953	$200

HARVEY

Number	Title	Yr	NM
❏ 111	Orange Driver/Hard Hearted Woman	1962	$125
❏ 118	Orange Driver/Messin' with My Bread	1962	$40
❏ 115	The Thing to Do/Mean and Evil (Baby)	1962	$40

JVB

Number	Title	Yr	NM
❏ 82	Treat Me Like I Treat You/Don't Cha Leave Me Baby	1957	$125

BURNS, GEORGE

COMPLEAT

Number	Title	Yr	NM
❏ 112	How to Live to Be a Hundred/Katie	1983	$5

MERCURY

Number	Title	Yr	NM
❏ 870286-7	I Wish I Was Eighteen Again/(B-side unknown)	1988	$3

—Reissue

Number	Title	Yr	NM
❏ 57011	I Wish I Was Eighteen Again/One of the Mysteries of Life	1979	$4
❏ 57011 [PS]	I Wish I Was Eighteen Again/One of the Mysteries of Life	1979	$6
❏ 57021	The Arizona Whiz/A Real Good Cigar	1980	$4
❏ 57045	Willie, Won't You Sing a Song with Me/Just Send Me One	1981	$4

BURNS, HUGHIE

C-S-I

Number	Title	Yr	NM
❏ 002	The Family Inn/Tell Me a Good One	1980	$6

BURNS, JACKIE

HONOR BRIGADE

Number	Title	Yr	NM
❏ 5	Something's Missing (It's You)/What's a Daddy	1969	$12
❏ 3	That's What I Get for Being a Woman/I'll Be Your Woman	1969	$12

JMI

Number	Title	Yr	NM
❏ 8	(If Loving You Is Wrong) I Don't Want to Be Right/A World of Lonely Men	1972	$8
❏ 17	One Big Unhappy Family/Gonna Miss Me	1973	$8

BURNS, JETHRO

RCA VICTOR

Number	Title	Yr	NM
❏ 74-0751	Dolly Parton's Sweet on Me/Don't Shoot the Mandolin Player	1972	$8
❏ APBO-0199	Mama Was a Truck Driving Man/Magic Fingers	1973	$8

BURNS, RANDY

MERCURY

Number	Title	Yr	NM
❏ 73198	Living in the Country/17 Years on the River	1971	$6

POLYDOR

Number	Title	Yr	NM
❏ 14143	Hold On/Country Rain	1972	$6

Number	Title	Yr	NM

BURRAGE, HAROLD
ALADDIN

Number	Title	Yr	NM
❏ 3194	Sweet Brown Gal/Way Down Boogie	1953	$70

COBRA

Number	Title	Yr	NM
❏ 5026	Betty Jean/I Cry for You	1958	$60
❏ 5012	Messed Up/I Don't Care Who Knows	1957	$60
❏ 5004	One More Dance/You Eat Too Much	1956	$60
❏ 5018	Satisfied/Stop for the Red Light	1957	$60
❏ 5022	She Knocks Me Out/A Heart	1958	$60

DECCA

Number	Title	Yr	NM
❏ 48175	Hi Ya/I Need You Baby	1950	$125

M-PAC!

Number	Title	Yr	NM
❏ 7211	Baby I'm Alright/Fifty-Fifty	1964	$12
❏ 7225	Got to Find a Way/How You Fix Your Mouth	1965	$15
❏ 7204	Long Ways Together/I'll Take One	1963	$10
❏ 7229	More Power to You/A Long Way Together	1966	$10
❏ 7234	Take Me Now/You Make Me So Happy	1966	$10
❏ 7210	That's a Friend/Everybody's Dancing	1964	$12
❏ 7201	The Master Key/Faith and Understanding	1963	$10

STATES

Number	Title	Yr	NM
❏ 144	Feel So Fine/You're Gonna Cry	1955	$250

— *Red vinyl*

Number	Title	Yr	NM
❏ 144	Feel So Fine/You're Gonna Cry	1955	$120

— *Black vinyl*

VEE JAY

Number	Title	Yr	NM
❏ 318	What You Don't Know/Crying for My Baby	1959	$30

VIVID

Number	Title	Yr	NM
❏ 102	Betty Jean/I Cry for You	1959	$50

BURRELL, KENNY
CADET

Number	Title	Yr	NM
❏ 5597	Blues Fuse/Recapitulation	1968	$6
❏ 5548	Hot Bossa/Mother-in-Law	1966	$6
❏ 5555	The Little Drummer Boy/Silent Night	1966	$8
❏ 281	Freight Trane (Part 1)/Freight Trane (Part 2)	1963	$8

VERVE

Number	Title	Yr	NM
❏ 10618	Burning Spear/The Preacher	1968	$8
❏ 10375	Downstairs/Loie	1966	$8

BURRIS, NEAL
COLUMBIA

Number	Title	Yr	NM
❏ 4-21234	Bonita Chiquita/Put a Little Sweetnin'	1954	$30
❏ 4-21114	Don't Give Me Kisses/You're Stepping Out	1953	$30
❏ 4-21152	For You Alone/What Does It Mean	1953	$30
❏ 4-21026	Honey Baby Blues/Poison Kisses	1952	$30
❏ 4-21081	I Bet My Heart/That's Time for Love	1953	$30
❏ 4-20972	I Broke a Heart/My Heart Needs Yours	1952	$30
❏ 4-21285	Start the Music/Why Life If Life Is Not	1954	$30
❏ 4-20917	There's No Reason/River of Love	1952	$30

KING

Number	Title	Yr	NM
❏ 967	Life's Been So Beautiful/Please Excuse My Manners	1951	$50

BURT, TOM
CAMEO

Number	Title	Yr	NM
❏ 363	OK Girl/All Through the Night	1965	$20

BURTON, JAMES
PHILIPS

Number	Title	Yr	NM
❏ 40137	Swamp Surfer/Everybody Listen to the Dobro	1963	$50

— *As "Jimmy Dobro"*

BURTON, JENNY
ATLANTIC

Number	Title	Yr	NM
❏ 89583	Bad Habits/Let's Get Back to Love	1984	$4
❏ 89526	Dancing for My Love/Nobody Can Tell Me (He Don't Love Me)	1985	$4
❏ 89343	Do You Want It Bad Enuff/Call Me Anytime	1986	$3
❏ 89343 [PS]	Do You Want It Bad Enuff/Call Me Anytime	1986	$3
❏ 89556	Love Runs Deeper Than Pride/Once in a Lifetime	1985	$4
❏ 89660	Strangers in a Strange World/(Instrumental)	1984	$4

— *With Patrick Jude*

Number	Title	Yr	NM
❏ 89660 [PS]	Strangers in a Strange World/(Instrumental)	1984	$4

BURTON, WENDY
COLUMBIA

Number	Title	Yr	NM
❏ 42624	Mommy's Daddy, Daddy's Daddy and Santa Claus/17 Million Bicycles	1962	$10

BUS BOYS
ARISTA

Number	Title	Yr	NM
❏ 0589	Anggie/Did You See Me	1981	$5
❏ 9229	Cleanin' Up the Town/New Shoes	1984	$4
❏ 9229 [PS]	Cleanin' Up the Town/New Shoes	1984	$4
❏ 1007	Last Forever/(B-side unknown)	1982	$5
❏ 9409	The Boys Are Back in Town/Cleanin' Up the Town	1985	$3

— *Flashback" oldies series*

Number	Title	Yr	NM
❏ 1034	The Boys Are Back in Town/I Get Lost	1983	$5

VOSS

Number	Title	Yr	NM
❏ 75730	Hard Work/(Acappella)	1988	$4

BUSH, BILL
RONN

Number	Title	Yr	NM
❏ 17	I'm Waiting/A Velvet Touch	1967	$1500

BUSH, DICK
ERA

Number	Title	Yr	NM
❏ 1067	Hollywood Party/Exactly	1957	$60

BUSH, JOHNNY
DELTA

Number	Title	Yr	NM
❏ 10041	Whiskey River/When My Conscience Hurts the Most	1981	$6

GUSTO

Number	Title	Yr	NM
❏ 9006	She Just Made Me Love You More/Hands Can Say a Lot	1978	$5

MILLION

Number	Title	Yr	NM
❏ 1	I'll Be There/I Can Feel You in His Arms	1972	$8

RCA VICTOR

Number	Title	Yr	NM
❏ APBO- 0041	Green Snakes on the Ceiling/Drinkin' My Baby Right Out of My Mind	1973	$5
❏ 74-0931	Here Comes the World Again/That Rain Makin' Baby of Mine	1973	$5
❏ PB-10070	Home in San Antone/I Can Feel Him Touching You	1974	$5
❏ 74-0867	There Stands the Glass/These Lips Don't Know How to Say Goodbye	1973	$5
❏ APBO- 0240	Toy Telephone/From Tennessee to Texas	1974	$5
❏ APBO- 0306	Wasted Wine/When It's Midnight in Dallas	1974	$5
❏ APBO- 0164	We're Back in Love Again/(Wine Friend of Mine) Stand By Me	1973	$5
❏ 74-0745	Whiskey River/Right Back in Your Arms Again	1972	$5

STARDAY

Number	Title	Yr	NM
❏ 114	My Mind Is a Bridge/Conscience Turn Your Back	1975	$6

STEP ONE

Number	Title	Yr	NM
❏ 369	The Twenty-Fourth Hour/I Can't See Texas from Here	1987	$5

— *With Darrell McCall*

STOP

Number	Title	Yr	NM
❏ 392	City Lights/The Joy of Loving You	1971	$8
❏ 232	Each Time/Tonight We Steal Heaven Again	1968	$8
❏ 396	Mama's Hands/It's All in the Game	1971	$8

Number	Title	Yr	NM
❏ 310	My Cup Runneth Over/Tonight I'm Going Home to an Angel	1969	$8
❏ 380	My Joy/I'm Warm by the Flame	1970	$8
❏ 371	Warmth of the Wine/Daddy Lived in Houston	1970	$8
❏ 160	What a Way to Live/I Can Feel You in His Arms	1968	$8

WARNER BROS.

Number	Title	Yr	NM
❏ 8141	Loud Music and Strong Wine/Sunday Morning	1975	$5

WHISKEY RIVER

Number	Title	Yr	NM
❏ 791	When My Conscience Hurts the Most/Drivin' Nails in My Coffin	1979	$6

BUSH, KATE
EMI

Number	Title	Yr	NM
❏ 5121	December Will Be Magic Again/Warm And Soothing	1980	$12

— *U.K. import*

Number	Title	Yr	NM
❏ 5121 [PS]	December Will Be Magic Again/Warm And Soothing	1980	$20

— *U.K. import*

EMI AMERICA

Number	Title	Yr	NM
❏ B-8386	Cloudbusting/The Man with the Child in His Eyes	1986	$5
❏ B-8386 [PS]	Cloudbusting/The Man with the Child in His Eyes	1986	$8
❏ B-8363	Experiment IV/Wuthering Heights (New Vocal)	1986	$5
❏ B-8363 [PS]	Experiment IV/Wuthering Heights (New Vocal)	1986	$8
❏ B-8302	Hounds of Love/Burning Bridge	1985	$5
❏ B-8302 [PS]	Hounds of Love/Burning Bridge	1985	$8
❏ B-8327	The Big Sky/Not This Time	1986	$5
❏ B-8327 [PS]	The Big Sky/Not This Time	1986	$8
❏ 8006	The Man with the Child in His Eyes/Moving	1978	$6
❏ 8003	Wuthering Heights/Kite	1978	$10
❏ 8003 [PS]	Wuthering Heights/Kite	1978	$20

BUSHKIN, JOE
COLUMBIA

Number	Title	Yr	NM
❏ 39172	Every Day Is Christmas/The Lady Is A Tramp	1951	$20

BUSTERS, THE
ARLEN

Number	Title	Yr	NM
❏ 740	All American Surfer/Pine Tree Hop	1963	$30
❏ 735	Bust Out/Astronaut's	1963	$30
❏ 745	Heartaches/Torrid Zone	1964	$30

UNITED ARTISTS

Number	Title	Yr	NM
❏ 0145	Bust Out/The Green Mosquito	1973	$5

— *Silver Spotlight Series issue; B-side by the Tune Rockers*

BUTANES, THE
ENRICA

Number	Title	Yr	NM
❏ 1007	Don't Forget I Love You/That My Desire	1961	$30

BUTCHER, JON, AXIS
CAPITOL

Number	Title	Yr	NM
❏ B-5549	Between the Lines/(B-side unknown)	1986	$4
❏ B-5693	Goodbye Saving Grace/Partners in Crime	1987	$4
❏ B-5693 [PS]	Goodbye Saving Grace/Partners in Crime	1987	$4
❏ B-44006	Holy War/The Long Way Home	1987	$3
❏ B-44006 [PS]	Holy War/The Long Way Home	1987	$3
❏ B-44334	Send Me Somebody/Division Street	1989	$3
❏ B-44334 [PS]	Send Me Somebody/Division Street	1989	$3
❏ 5534	Sounds of Your Voice/Stop	1985	$4
❏ 5534 [PS]	Sounds of Your Voice/Stop	1985	$4
❏ 7PRO-79642	Waiting for a Miracle (same on both sides)	1989	$8

— *Vinyl is promo only*

Number	Title	Yr	NM
❏ B-44046	Wishes/Prisoners of the Silver Chain	1987	$3
❏ B-44046 [PS]	Wishes/Prisoners of the Silver Chain	1987	$3

POLYDOR

Number	Title	Yr	NM
❏ 821409-7	Don't Say Goodnight/Can't Tell the Dancer from the Dance	1984	$5
❏ 811822-7	It's Only Words/Life Takes a Life	1983	$4

Number	Title	Yr	NM

BUTLER, BOBBY "SOFINE"
IBC

Number	Title	Yr	NM
❏ 0001	Cheaper Crude or No More Food/ Bobby's (Nervous) Breakdown	1979	$6

— White label stock copy

| ❏ 0001 | Cheaper Crude or No More Food/ Bobby's (Nervous) Breakdown | 1979 | $6 |

— Black label

BUTLER, BILLY, AND INFINITY
MEMPHIS

❏ 45-103	I Don't Want to Lose You/Free Yourself	1971	$10

BUTLER, CARL, AND PEARL
CHART

❏ 5191	Heartaches for Lunch/ Fifteen Years Ago	1973	$4
❏ 5160	She Didn't Come Home/ Two of a Kind	1972	$4
❏ 5145	Temptation Keeps Twisting Her Arm/I'm So Close to Loving You	1972	$4

COLUMBIA

❏ 43335	Beers and Tears/Can I Draw the Line	1965	$8
❏ 45228	Bottoms Up/Let the Sun Shine on the People	1970	$5
❏ 43102	Forbidden Street/When the Door Swings Shut	1964	$8
❏ 44252	Guilty of Love/For a Minute	1967	$6
❏ 44447	If You Should Ever Stop Loving Me/If I'd Only Met You First	1968	$6
❏ 43030	I'm Hanging Up the Phone/ Just a Message	1964	$8
❏ 44694	I Never Got Over You/I Started Loving You Again	1968	$6
❏ 43536	Little Mac/Wrong Generation	1966	$8
❏ 43685	Little Pedro/Cell 29	1966	$8
❏ 42778	Loving Arms/Who'll Be Next	1963	$8
❏ 43433	Our Ship of Love/It's Called Cheating	1965	$8
❏ 44587	Punish Me Tomorrow/ Goodbye Tennessee	1968	$6
❏ 43869	Same Old Me Lovin' Same Old You/Dreaming of a Little Cabin	1966	$8
❏ 42892	Too Late to Try Again/ My Tears Don't Show	1963	$8
❏ 44862	We'll Sweep Out the Ashes in the Morning/Your Way of Life	1969	$6
❏ 44043	Wild Goose Chase/Lost	1967	$6

BUTLER, CARL
CAPITOL

❏ F1996	Alone Without You/Vicious Lies	1952	$30
❏ F1813	A String of Empties/You Plus Me	1951	$30
❏ F1891	Blue Million Tears/River of Love	1951	$30
❏ F1335	Heartbreak Express/White Rose	1950	$40
❏ F1701	Linda Lou/No Trespassing	1951	$30
❏ F1541	Our Last Rendezvous/I Live My Life Alone	1951	$30
❏ F2084	Penny for Your Thoughts/ Everything Will Be the Same	1952	$30
❏ F1399	Plastic Man/Country Mile	1951	$30
❏ F1454	Shake, Rattle & Roll/No Guarantee on My Heart	1951	$30
❏ F2158	Stepping on My Heart/I Need You So	1952	$30

COLUMBIA

❏ 4-21353	Angel Band/Hallelujah We Shall Rise	1955	$30
❏ 41263	Baby I'm a-Waitin'/My Cajun Baby	1958	$12
❏ 42593	Don't Let Me Cross Over/ Wonder Drug	1962	$12
❏ 42306	Have You Run Out of Lies/ If I Had Only Met You First	1962	$12
❏ 41997	Honky Tonkitis/You Were the Orchid	1961	$10
❏ 41119	If You've Got the Money (I've Got the Time)/Nothing I'd Rather Do	1958	$10
❏ 41368	I Like to Pretend/Oh, How I Miss You	1959	$10
❏ 41869	I'm a Prisoner of Love/ For the First Time	1960	$10
❏ 4-21455	It's My Sin/Borrowed Love	1955	$30
❏ 41674	The Door/I Know Why I Cry	1960	$10
❏ 4-21407	Wedding Day/If I Could Spend My Heartaches	1955	$30

OKEH

❏ 18012	Crowded Out/My Heart Tells Me	1954	$20
❏ 18018	So Close/It's Wrong to Be Jealous	1954	$20
❏ 18039	That's All Right/I'll Go Steppin' Too	1955	$30

BUTLER, FREDDIE
KAPP

❏ 819	This Thing/There Was a Time	1967	$20

BUTLER, JERRY, AND BRENDA LEE EAGER
MERCURY

❏ 73255	Ain't Understanding Mellow/ Windy City Soul	1971	$6
❏ 73395	Can't Understand It/ How Long Will It Last	1973	$6
❏ 73301	(They Long to Be) Close to You/You Can't Always Tell	1972	$6
❏ 73422	We Were Lovers, We Were Friends/The Love We Had Stays On My Mind	1973	$6

BUTLER, JERRY
ABNER

❏ 1035	A Lonely Soldier/I Found a Love	1960	$40
❏ 1028	Hold Me Darling/Rainbow Valley	1959	$40
❏ 1030	I Was Wrong/Couldn't Go to Sleep	1959	$40
❏ 1024	Lost/One by One	1959	$40

MCA

❏ 52177	Let's Talk It Over/Especially You	1983	$4

— With Stix Hooper; B-side by Stix Hooper solo

MERCURY

❏ 72876	Are You Happy/I Still Love You	1968	$8
❏ 72991	Don't Let Love Hang You Up/ Walking Around in Teardrops	1969	$8
❏ 73015	Got to See If I Can't Get Mommy (To Come Back Home)/I Forgot to Remember	1970	$8
❏ 72850	Hey, Western Union Man/ Just Can't Forget About You	1968	$8
❏ 73210	How Did We Lose It baby/Do You Finally Need a Friend	1971	$6
❏ 73131	How Does It Feel/Special Memory	1970	$8
❏ 73045	I Could Write a Book/ Since I Lost You, Baby	1970	$8
❏ 72648	I Dig You Baby/Some Kinda Magic	1966	$10
❏ 73169	If It's Real What I Feel/Why Are You Leaving Me	1971	$6
❏ 73290	I Only Have Eyes for You/A Prayer	1972	$6
❏ 72764	Lost/You Don't Know What You've Got Until You Lose It	1968	$8
❏ 72592	Love (Oh How Sweet It Is)/Loneliness	1966	$10
❏ 72929	Moody Woman/Go Away -- Find Yourself	1969	$8
❏ 72721	Mr. Dream Merchant/'Cause I Love You So	1967	$10
❏ 73335	One Night Affair/Life's Unfortunate Song	1972	$6
❏ 72898	Only the Strong Survive/Just Because I Really Love You	1969	$8
❏ 872914-7	Only the Strong Survive/Lost	1989	$3

— Reissue

❏ 73443	Power of Love/What Do You Do on a Sunday Afternoon	1973	$6
❏ 73495	Take the Time to Tell Her/High Stepper	1974	$6
❏ 73459	That's How Heartaches Are Made/Too Many Danger Signs	1974	$6
❏ 73241	Walk Easy My Son/Let Me Be	1971	$6
❏ 72960	What's the Use of Breaking Up/Brand New Me	1969	$8
❏ 73101	Where Are You Going/You Can Fly	1970	$8
❏ 72676	Why Do I Lose You/You Walked Into My Life	1967	$10

MISTLETOE

❏ 803	Silent Night/O Holy Night	1974	$5

MOTOWN

❏ 1421	Chalk It Up/I Don't Want Nobody to Know	1977	$5
❏ 1422	It's a Lifetime Thing/Kiss Me Now	1977	$5

— With Thelma Houston

❏ 1414	I Wanna Do It to You/I Don't Wanna Be Reminded	1977	$5
❏ 1403	The Devil in Mrs. Jones/ Don't Wanna Be Reminded	1976	$5
❏ 1403 [PS]	The Devil in Mrs. Jones/ Don't Wanna Be Reminded	1976	$12

PHILADELPHIA INT'L

❏ 3113	Don't Be Ashamed/Best Love I Ever Had	1980	$4
❏ 3673	I'm Glad to Be Back/Nothing Says I Love You Like I Love You	1979	$4
❏ 3656	(I'm Just Thinking About) Cooling Out/Are You Lonely Tonight	1978	$4
❏ 3683	Let's Make Love/Dream World	1979	$4
❏ 3117	Tell Me Girl (Why It Has to End)/ We've Got This Feeling Again	1980	$4

VEE JAY

❏ 707	Believe in Me/Just for You	1965	$15
❏ 375	Find Another Girl/ When Trouble Calls	1961	$20
❏ 715	For Your Precious Love/Give It Up	1966	$15

❏ 396	For Your Precious Love/ Sweet Was the Wine	1961	$20
❏ 588	Giving Up on Love/I've Been Trying	1964	$15
❏ 651	Good Times/I've Grown Accustomed to Her Face	1965	$15
❏ 354	He Will Break Your Heart/ Thanks to You	1960	$30
❏ 696	I Can't Stand to See You Cry/ Nobody Needs Your Love	1965	$15
❏ 390	I See a Fool/I'm a Telling You	1961	$20
❏ 426	Isle of Sirens/Chi Town	1962	$20
❏ 598	I Stand Accused/I Don't Want to Hear Anymore	1964	$15
❏ 598 [PS]	I Stand Accused/I Don't Want to Hear Anymore	1964	$40
❏ 451	Make It Easy on Yourself/ It's Too Late	1962	$20
❏ 405	Moon River/Aware of Love	1961	$20
❏ 711	Moon River/Make It Easy on Yourself	1966	$15
❏ 371	Silent Night/O Holy Night	1960	$30
❏ 526	Strawberries/I Almost Lost My Head	1963	$15
❏ 475	Theme from Taras Bulba (Wishing Star)/You Go Right Through Me	1963	$15
❏ 475 [PS]	Theme from Taras Bulba (Wishing Star)/You Go Right Through Me	1963	$50
❏ 534	Where's the Girl?/How Beautifully You Lie	1963	$15

BUTLER, JIMMY
GEM

❏ 222	Trim Your Tree/Cruelty For Kindness	1954	$60

BUTLER, LARRY
ALLSTAR

❏ 7214	Another Heartache/I Can't Stand It Anymore	1960	$30
❏ 7186	Echoes Fade and Die/ Foolish Affair	1959	$30
❏ 7225	For Goodness Sake/I Walked Away	1961	$30
❏ 7201	I Could Never Be Untrue/I've Got a Right to Cry	1960	$30
❏ 7242	Same Old Way/I'm Crying All the Day	1961	$30
❏ 7193	Stay Out of My Life/ The 13th Notch	1960	$30

DOT

❏ 16767	Ol' Man River/How Do You Say I'm Sorry	1965	$10

IMPERIAL

❏ 66277	Funny Familiar Forgotten Feelings/Break My Mind	1968	$8
❏ 66296	Lady Madonna/Honey	1968	$8
❏ 66239	Lonesome/Sandy	1967	$8

MCA

❏ 51086	Tess (Love Theme)/The Journey	1981	$4

UNITED ARTISTS

❏ XW1017	Another Somebody Done Somebody Wrong Song/High Noon	1977	$5
❏ XW895	Misty Blue/Nashville P.M.	1976	$5
❏ XW809	Theme from "Stay Hungry"/'Til October	1976	$5
❏ XW819	Theme from Stay Hungry/Til October	1976	$5

BUTTERFIELD, PAUL
BEARSVILLE

❏ 49706	Living in Memphis/Footprints on the Windshield (Upside Down)	1981	$4

ELEKTRA

❏ 45609	Come On In/I Got a Mind to Give Up Living	1967	$10
❏ 45016	Got My Mojo Working/ Mellow Down Easy	1964	$10
❏ 45643	In My Own Dream/ (B-side unknown)	1968	$15
❏ 45692	Love March/(B-side unknown)	1970	$15
❏ 45658	Where Did My Baby Go/ In My Own Dream	1969	$10

BUTTERFLYS, THE
RED BIRD

❏ Oct-009	Goodnight Baby/The Swim	1964	$30
❏ Oct-0016	I Wonder/Gee, Baby, Gee	1964	$30

BUTTONS, RED
COLUMBIA

❏ 40384	Bow Wow Wants a Boy for Christmas/Little Johnny Snowball	1954	$20

Number	Title	Yr	NM
BUTTS BAND			
BLUE THUMB			
❏ 263	Get Up, Stand Up/Mike's Blues	1975	$8
❏ 252	I Won't Be Alone Anymore/ Kansas City	1974	$8
❏ 242	Pop a Top/Baja Bus	1973	$8
BUZZCOCKS, THE			
MAGAZINE related. Also see PETE SHELLEY.			
I.R.S.			
❏ 9017	Are Everything/Why, She's a Girl from the Chain Store	1980	$5
❏ 9017 [PS]	Are Everything/Why, She's a Girl from the Chain Store	1980	$5
❏ 9001	Everybody's Happy Nowadays/ Why Can't I Touch It	1979	$6
❏ 9001 [PS]	Everybody's Happy Nowadays/ Why Can't I Touch It	1979	$6
❏ 9010	I Believe/Something's Gone Wrong Again	1980	$5
❏ 9010 [PS]	I Believe/Something's Gone Wrong Again	1980	$5
❏ 9019	Strange Thing/Airwaves Dream	1980	$5
❏ 9019 [PS]	Strange Thing/Airwaves Dream	1980	$5
BYE BYES, THE			
MERCURY			
❏ 71530	Blonde Hair, Blue Eyes, Ruby Red Lips/Do You	1959	$20
BYERS, BRENDA			
MTA			
❏ 171	California in a Dream/ Wear My Shoes	1969	$8
❏ 102	Call Him Back/Voice in the Wind	1966	$10
❏ 116	Don't Remind Me/ Rainbows and Roses	1967	$12
❏ 167	Empty/(B-side unknown)	1969	$8
❏ 108	Follow the Stars/Rush	1966	$10
❏ 177	Homeward Bound/The Other Side of Me	1969	$8
❏ 193	Homeward Bound/The Other Side of Me	1971	$6
❏ 183	I Can't Go On Loving You/Photographs	1970	$8
❏ 189	Little Boys/Oh, It's Gonna Rain	1970	$8
❏ 176	Thank You for Loving Me/Night Life	1969	$8
❏ 160	The Auctioneer/ Rainbows and Roses	1968	$8
❏ 146	The House That Jack Built/ Nobody Knows You When You're Down and Out	1968	$8
BYRAM, JUDY			
REGAL			
❏ 001	One Fire Between Us/ (B-side unknown)	1988	$5
BYRD, BOBBY			
ABC			
❏ 11134	Here Is My Everything/Loving You	1968	$12
— With Vicki Anderson			
BANG			
❏ 562	Whatcha Gonna Do About It/If She's There	1968	$6
BROWNSTONE			
❏ 4203	Hot Pants - I'm Coming, Coming, I'm Coming	1971	$6
❏ 4206	If You Got a Love You Better (Hold On to It)/You Have Got to Change Your Mind	1972	$6
❏ 4209	Sayin' It and Doin' It Are Two Different Things/ Never Get Enough	1972	$6
❏ 4210	Signed, Sealed and Delivered/I Need Help (I Can't Do It Alone)	1973	$6
FEDERAL			
❏ 12486	They Are Sayin'/I Found Out	1963	$20
INTERNATIONAL BROTHERS			
❏ 901	Back from the Dead/ The Way to Get Down	1975	$6
KING			
❏ 6126	Funky Soul #1 (Part 1)/ Funky Soul #1 (Part 2)	1967	$6
❏ 6069	I Found Out/I'll Keep Pressing On	1967	$6
❏ 6378	I Know You Got Soul/It's I Who Love You (It's Not Him Anymore)	1971	$6
❏ 6308	I'm Not to Blame/It's I Who Loves You (It's Not Him Anymore)	1970	$6
❏ 6323	I Need Help (Part 1)/I Need Help (Part 2)	1970	$6
KWANZA/WB			
❏ 7703	On the Move/Try It Again	1973	$6

Number	Title	Yr	NM
SMASH			
❏ 2052	Ain't No Use/Let Me Know	1966	$8
❏ 1928	I'm Lonely/I've Got a Girl	1964	$8
❏ 2018	Lost in the Mood of Changes/ Oh, What a Nite	1966	$8
❏ 1984	Time Will Make a Change/ The Way I Feel	1965	$8
❏ 1903	Write Me a Letter/I Love You So	1964	$8
BYRD, CHARLIE, AND FATHER MALCOLM BOYD			
COLUMBIA			
❏ 43942	It's Christmas Again, Jesus/ It's Morning, Jesus	1966	$8
BYRD, CHARLIE			
COLUMBIA			
❏ 43504	Baby Love/Walk Right In	1966	$8
— With the Lady Byrds			
❏ 44411	Empty Streets/Far Off, Close By	1967	$6
❏ 45099	I'll Never Fall in Love Again/I'll Walk with the Rain	1970	$5
❏ AE12 [DJ]	Let Go (Canto de Ossanha)/ Here's That Rainy Day	1969	$12
❏ 44669	Lullaby from Rosemary's Baby/Happy Together	1969	$6
❏ 43834	The Work Song/Tomorrow Belongs to Me	1966	$8
❏ 44782	Wichita Lineman/I Don't Have to Take It	1969	$6
RIVERSIDE			
❏ 4556	Longing for Bahia/Softly	1963	$10
❏ 4544	Meditation (Meditacao)/ Little Boat (O Barquinho)	1962	$10
❏ 4529	The Duck/One Note Samba	1962	$10
BYRD, CURTIS			
CANDIX			
❏ 340	Pretty Woman/Turn Some More Lights On	1962	$30
BYRD, DONALD			
❏ XW212	Black Byrd/Slop Jar Blues	1973	$5
❏ XW726	Change (Makes You Want to Hustle) Part 1/Part 2	1975	$5
❏ XW510	Cristo Redentor/Black Byrd	1974	$5
❏ XW965	Dancing in the Street/ Onward 'Til Morning	1977	$5
❏ XW965 [PS]	Dancing in the Street/ Onward 'Til Morning	1977	$8
❏ XW783	(Fallin' Like) Dominoes/ Just My Imagination (Runnin' Away with Me)	1976	$5
❏ XW309	Flight Time/Mr. Thomas	1973	$5
❏ XW650	Think Twice/We're Together	1975	$5
❏ XW445	Witch Hunt/Woman of the World	1974	$5
ELEKTRA			
❏ 47419	I Feel Like Lovin' You Today/Butterfly	1982	$4
❏ 47241	I Love Your Love/Falling	1981	$4
❏ 47168	Love Has Come Around/ Love for Sale	1981	$4
❏ 46019	Loving You/Cristo Redentor	1979	$4
❏ 69972	Sexy Dancer/Midnight	1982	$4
❏ 45545	Thank You for Funking Up My Life/Loving You	1978	$4
VERVE			
❏ 10344	Blind Man, Blind Man/You've Been Talkin' 'Bout My Baby	1965	$8
BYRD, GARY			
RCA VICTOR			
❏ APBO-0048	Soul Travelin' Part 1/Part 2	1973	$6
BYRDS, THE			
ASYLUM			
❏ 11019	Cowgirl in the Sand/ Long Live the King	1973	$5
❏ 11016	Full Circle/Long Live the King	1973	$5
COLUMBIA			
❏ 43702	5 D (Fifth Dimension)/ Captain Soul	1966	$15
❏ 43332	All I Really Want to Do/I'll Feel a Whole Lot Better	1965	$20
❏ 43332 [DJ]	All I Really Want to Do (same on both sides)	1965	$125
— Red vinyl promo			
❏ 45514	America's Great National Pastime/Farther Along	1971	$6
❏ 44499	Artificial Energy/You Ain't Going Nowhere	1968	$8
❏ 44990	Ballad of Easy Rider/ Oil in My Lamp	1969	$12
❏ 45259	Chestnut Mare/Just a Season	1970	$6

Number	Title	Yr	NM
❏ 44746	Drug Store Truck Drivin' Man/ Bad Night at the Whiskey	1969	$8
❏ 43578	Eight Miles High/Why	1966	$15
❏ 43578 [PS]	Eight Miles High/Why	1966	$70
❏ 45440	Glory Glory/Citizen Kane	1971	$6
❏ 44362	Goin' Back/Change Is Now	1967	$8
❏ 44157	Have You Seen Her Face/ Don't Make Waves	1967	$12
❏ 44157 [PS]	Have You Seen Her Face/ Don't Make Waves	1967	$50
❏ JZSP116476 [DJ]	He Was a Friend of Mine (same on both sides)	1966	$50
❏ 43332 [DJ]	I'll Feel a Whole Lot Better (same on both sides)	1965	$120
— Red vinyl promo			
❏ 43501	It Won't Be Wrong/Set You Free This Time	1965	$15
❏ 44230	Lady Friend/Old John Robertson	1967	$12
❏ 44868	Lay Lady Lay/Old Blue	1969	$8
❏ 43766	Mr. Spaceman/ What's Happening	1966	$15
❏ 43271 [PS]	Mr. Tambourine Man	1965	$300
— Promo-only sleeve promoting the Byrds' appeance on the TV show Hullabaloo			
❏ 43271	Mr. Tambourine Man/I Knew I'd Want You	1965	$20
❏ 43271 [DJ]	Mr. Tambourine Man (same on both sides)	1965	$200
— Red vinyl promo			
❏ 44054	My Back Pages/ Renaissance Fair	1967	$15
❏ 44643	Pretty Boy Floyd/I Am a Pilgrim	1968	$8
❏ 43987	So You Want to Be a Rock 'N' Roll Star/Everybody's Been Burned	1967	$15
❏ 4-43391 [PS]	The Times They Are a-Changin'/ She Don't Care About Time	1965	$500
— Picture sleeve for unreleased single			
❏ 43424 [DJ]	Turn! Turn! Turn! (To Everything There Is a Season) (same on both sides)	1965	$125
— Red vinyl promo			
❏ 43424	Turn! Turn! Turn! (To Everything There Is a Season)/She Don't Care About Time	1965	$20
❏ 44990	Wasn't Born to Follow/ Ballad of Easy Rider	1969	$8
7-Inch Extended Plays			
❏ ZLP116003/4 [DJ]	A Special Open-End Interview with the Byrds Talking About Their New LP "Fifth Dimension	1966	$120
— Promo-only interview; plays at 33 1/3 rpm			
❏ ZLP116003/4 [PS]	A Special Open-End Interview with the Byrds Talking About Their New LP "Fifth Dimension	1966	$200
COLUMBIA/SCHOLASTIC			
❏ CV10287	Lover of the Bayou/So You Want to Be a Rock and Roll Star// Chimes of Freedom/Goin' Back	1971	$35
❏ CV10287 [PS]	The Byrds	1971	$35
BYRNE, JERRY			
SPECIALTY			
❏ 662	Carry On/Raining	1959	$60
❏ 635	Lights Out/Honey Babe	1958	$60
❏ 651	Why Did You Ever Say Goodbye/You Know I Love You So	1958	$40
BYRNES, EDD			
WARNER BROS.			
❏ 5087	Like I Love You/ Kookie's Mad Pad	1959	$20
— Artist credit: "Edd Byrnes and Friend			
❏ 5087 [PS]	Like I Love You/ Kookie's Mad Pad	1959	$50
— Artist credit: "Edd Byrnes and Friend			
7-Inch Extended Plays			
❏ EA1309	Hot Broad Rock/I Don't Dig You, Kookie/Saturday Night on Sunset Strip/The Kookie Cha-Cha-Cha	1959	$60
BYRON, LORD DOUGLAS			
DOT			
❏ 16685	Surfin' Santa/The Drink That Makes You Shrink	1964	$40
UNION			
❏ 505	Big Bad Ho-Dad/Coffee House	1962	$50
— B-side by the Continentals			

C

C.A. QUINTET, THE
CANDY FLOSS
Number	Title	Yr	NM
❏ 102	Smooth as Silk/Dr. of Philosophy	1968	$100

FALCON
Number	Title	Yr	NM
❏ 71	Blow to My Soul/She's Got to Be True	1967	$125
❏ 70	Mickey's Monkey/I Want You to Love Me Girl	1967	$125

C.A.R.E. SESSION, THE
BUZZARD
Number	Title	Yr	NM
❏ 17021	The Eyes of the Children (same on both sides?)	1985	$6

C.C.S.
BELL
Number	Title	Yr	NM
❏ 45396	The Band Played the Boogie/Hang It On Me	1973	$4

RAK
Number	Title	Yr	NM
❏ ZS74507	Save the World/The Tap Turns On the Water	1972	$5
❏ ZS74502	Walking/Lookin' for Fun	1971	$5
❏ ZS74501	Whole Lotta Love/Boom Boom	1971	$6

C COMPANY FEATURING TERRY NELSON
PLANTATION
Number	Title	Yr	NM
❏ 73	Battle Hymn of Lt. Calley/Routine Patrol	1971	$5

C.K. STRONG
EPIC
Number	Title	Yr	NM
❏ 5-10534	Stormbird/Daddy	1969	$10

C.L. AND THE PICTURES
DUNES
Number	Title	Yr	NM
❏ 2017	Afraid/Mary Go 'Round	1962	$30
❏ 2010	I'm Asking Forgiveness/Let's Take a Ride	1962	$30
❏ 2023	I'm Sorry/That's What's Happening	1963	$30

MONUMENT
Number	Title	Yr	NM
❏ 958	Baby, Not Now/Jigsaw Puzzle	1966	$30
❏ 888	Could This Be Magic/Yolanda	1965	$30
❏ 854	He'll Only Hurt You/Talking About My Baby	1964	$30

C-NOTES, THE
EVERLAST
Number	Title	Yr	NM
❏ 5005	On Your Mark/From Now On	1957	$60

C.O.D.'S, THE
KELLMAC
Number	Title	Yr	NM
❏ 1012	Coming Back Girl/It Must Be Love	1966	$125
❏ 1008	I'm Looking Out for Me/I'll Come Running Back to You	1966	$30
❏ 1003	Michael/Cry No More	1965	$15
❏ 1005	Pretty Baby/I'm a Good Guy	1965	$30

C-QUENTS, THE
CAPETOWN
Number	Title	Yr	NM
❏ 4027	All I Want for Christmas Is You/Merry Christmas, Baby	1962	$300

CABARET VOLTAIRE
ROUGH TRADE
Number	Title	Yr	NM
❏ RT-US-003	Seconds Too Late/Control Addict	1981	$8
❏ RT-US-003 [PS]	Seconds Too Late/Control Addict	1981	$8

CABINEERS, THE
PRESTIGE
Number	Title	Yr	NM
❏ 917	Baby Mine/(B-side unknown)	1953	$400
❏ 904	Each Time/(B-side unknown)	1952	$300

CABOT, SEBASTIAN
MGM
Number	Title	Yr	NM
❏ 13650	It Ain't Me Babe/And Mostly They Sing	1966	$20

CACTUS
With Tim Bogert and Carmen Appice, ex-VANILLA FUDGE.
ATCO
Number	Title	Yr	NM
❏ 6901	Bringing Me Down/Bad Mother Boogie	1972	$6
❏ 6782	Brother Bill/You Can't Judge a Book By Its Cover	1971	$8
❏ 6811	Long Tall Sally/Rock 'n' Roll Christian	1971	$8
❏ 6872	The Booger Man/Cold Bear	1972	$6
❏ 6842	Token Chokin'/Alaska	1971	$8

CADETS, THE
JAN-LAR
Number	Title	Yr	NM
❏ 102	Don't/Car Crash	1960	$70

MODERN
Number	Title	Yr	NM
❏ 969	Annie Met Henry/So Will I	1955	$50
❏ 985	Church Bells May Ring/Heartbreak Hotel	1956	$50
❏ 956	Don't Be Angry/I Cried	1955	$60
❏ 971	Do You Wanna Rock/If It Is Wrong	1956	$125
❏ 1006	Fools Rush In/I'll Be Spinning	1956	$50
❏ 1024	Hands Across the Table/Love Can Do Most Anything	1957	$50

—As "Will Jones and the Cadets
Number	Title	Yr	NM
❏ 1012	Heaven Help Me/Love Bandit	1957	$50
❏ 963	I Cried/Fine Lookin' Baby	1955	$50
❏ 1000	I Got Loaded/Dancin' Dan	1956	$50
❏ 1019	Pretty Evey/Rum, Jamaica Rum	1957	$60

—As "Aaron Collins and the Cadets
Number	Title	Yr	NM
❏ 994	Stranded in the Jungle/I Want You	1956	$50
❏ 1017	Wiggle Waggle Woo/You Belong to Me	1957	$50

SHERWOOD
Number	Title	Yr	NM
❏ 211	One More Chance/I'm Looking for a Job	1960	$60

CADETS, THE (2)
HIT
Number	Title	Yr	NM
❏ 284	Happy Together/There's a Kind of Hush	1967	$8

—B-side by the Chellows

CADILLACS, THE
ARTIC
Number	Title	Yr	NM
❏ 101	Fool/The Right Kind of Lovin'	1964	$125

CAPITOL
Number	Title	Yr	NM
❏ 4825	Groovy, Groovy Love/White Gardenia	1962	$30
❏ 4935	La Bomba/I Saw You	1963	$30

—As "Bobby Ray and the Cadillacs

JOSIE
Number	Title	Yr	NM
❏ 829	Buzz-Buzz-Buzz/Yes, Yes Baby	1957	$50

—As "The Original Cadillacs
Number	Title	Yr	NM
❏ 861	Cool It Fool/Please Mr. Johnson	1959	$40
❏ 857	Copy Cat/Jay Walker	1959	$40
❏ 870	Dumbell/Bad Dan McGoon	1959	$40
❏ 765	Gloria/I Wonder Why	1954	$700

—Original with "joz" logo at top
Number	Title	Yr	NM
❏ 842	Holy Smoke Baby/I Want to Know	1958	$40
❏ 821	Lucy/Hurry Home	1957	$50

—As "The Original Cadillacs
Number	Title	Yr	NM
❏ 820	My Girl Friend/Broken Heart	1957	$60
❏ 846	Peek-a-Book/Oh, Oh Lolita	1958	$40
❏ 836	Speedo Is Back/A' Looka Here	1958	$40
❏ 785	Speedoo/Let Me Explain	1955	$70
❏ 812	Sugar Sugar/About That Girl Named Lou	1957	$50
❏ 773	Sympathy/No Chance	1955	$125
❏ 876	Tell Me Today/It's Love	1960	$40
❏ 883	That's Why/The Boogie Man	1960	$40
❏ 805	The Girl I Love/That's All I Need	1956	$125
❏ 915	Wayward Wanderer/I'll Never Let You Go	1963	$30

—As "The Original Cadillacs
Number	Title	Yr	NM
❏ 778	Widow Lady/Down the Road	1955	$200
❏ 769	Wishing Well/I Want to Know About Love	1954	$500
❏ 798	Woe Is Me/Betty My Love	1956	$60

MERCURY
Number	Title	Yr	NM
❏ 71738	I'm Willing/Thrill Me So	1961	$125

POLYDOR
Number	Title	Yr	NM
❏ 14031	Deep in the Heart of the Ghetto (Part 1)/Deep in the Heart of the Ghetto (Part 2)	1969	$20

—As "The Original Cadillacs

ROULETTE
Number	Title	Yr	NM
❏ 4654	Let's Get Together/She's My Connection	1965	$30

CAFFERTY, JOHN, AND THE BEAVER BROWN BAND
COASTLINE
Number	Title	Yr	NM
❏ 01	Wild Summer Nights/Tender Years	1980	$15
❏ 01 [PS]	Wild Summer Nights/Tender Years	1980	$20

—As "Beaver Brown

NARD'S
Number	Title	Yr	NM
❏ 16880	All Around the World/Welcome Home	1986	$15

—B-side by Mike Cavaliere

SCOTTI BROTHERS
Number	Title	Yr	NM
❏ ZS4-05452	C-I-T-Y/Where the Action Is	1985	$3
❏ ZS4-05452 [PS]	C-I-T-Y/Where the Action Is	1985	$3
❏ ZS4-05774	Heart's on Fire/Small Town Girl	1986	$3

—A-side credited only to "John Cafferty

Number	Title	Yr	NM
❏ ZS4-05774 [PS]	Heart's on Fire/Small Town Girl	1986	$3
❏ ZS4-68957	Heat of the Night/Runnin' Through the Fire	1989	$4
❏ ZS4-04107	On the Dark Side/Wild Summer Nights	1983	$10

—As "Eddie and the Cruisers
Number	Title	Yr	NM
❏ ZS4-04594	On the Dark Side/Wild Summer Nights	1984	$4
❏ ZS4-68999	Pride and Passion/Heat of the Night	1989	$3
❏ ZS4-05668	Small Town Girl/More Than Just One of the Boys	1985	$3
❏ ZS4-05668 [PS]	Small Town Girl/More Than Just One of the Boys	1985	$3
❏ ZS4-07903	Song and Dance/Burn the Roadhouse Down	1988	$3
❏ ZS4-07903 [PS]	Song and Dance/Burn the Roadhouse Down	1988	$3
❏ ZS4-04327	Tender Years/Down on My Knees	1984	$8
❏ ZS4-04682	Tender Years/Down on My Knees	1984	$3
❏ ZS4-04682 [PS]	Tender Years/Down on My Knees	1984	$3
❏ ZS4-04891	Tough All Over/Strangers in Paradise	1985	$3
❏ ZS4-04891 [PS]	Tough All Over/Strangers in Paradise	1985	$3

CAGE, JOHN AND NEUHAUS, MAX
Albums
MASS ART
Number	Title	Yr	NM
❏ M133 [B]	Fontana Mix - Feed	1966	$350

—limited edition of 300, silk screen sleeve by Max Neuhaus

CAGLE, BUDDY
CAPITOL
Number	Title	Yr	NM
❏ 5043	Sing a Sad Song/Love Inside My Door	1963	$15
❏ 5154	The Gold Cup/Afraid to Go	1964	$15

IMPERIAL
Number	Title	Yr	NM
❏ 66218	Apologize/Help's on the Way	1966	$8
❏ 66357	As If I Needed to Be Reminded/Daddy Please	1969	$8
❏ 66187	Be Nice to Everybody/The Wild Side of Life	1966	$8
❏ 66187	Be Nice to Everybody/Too Many Mountains	1966	$8
❏ 66263	Cincinnati Stranger/Waikiki Sand	1967	$8
❏ 66407	Gutar Player (The Ballad of James Burton)/Mud Is to Jump In	1969	$8
❏ 66331	I'll Get Over You/I've Wondered Where She's Been	1968	$8
❏ 66245	Longtime Traveling/Camptown Girl	1967	$8
❏ 66161	Tonight I'm Coming Home/Honky Tonk College	1966	$8

MERCURY
Number	Title	Yr	NM
❏ 72452	Honky Tonkin' Again/We the People (The Great Society)	1965	$10

CAGLE, WADE
SUN
Number	Title	Yr	NM
❏ 360	Groovy Train/Highland Rock	1961	$30

CAIOLA, AL
AVALANCHE
Number	Title	Yr	NM
❏ XW290	And I Love You So/Live and Let Die	1973	$5

RCA VICTOR
Number	Title	Yr	NM
❏ 47-5252	Anna/Cachita	1953	$20
❏ 47-6404	Antilles/Corsage (Her First Corsage)	1955	$20
❏ 47-6101	A Song of India (Mambo)/Rapid Fire (Samba)	1955	$20
❏ 47-5143	Bim Bam Bum/Mambo Jumbo	1953	$20
❏ 47-5400	Cumana/El Cumbanchero	1953	$20
❏ 47-5315	Pianola/The Donkey Serenade	1953	$20
❏ 47-5949	Steel Guitar Rag/Stardust	1954	$20

REGENT
Number	Title	Yr	NM
❏ 7500	Flamenco Love/(B-side unknown)	1956	$20

SUNBEAM
Number	Title	Yr	NM
❏ 121	In the Mood Cha-Cha/Wheel of Fortune	1958	$15

UNITED ARTISTS
Number	Title	Yr	NM
❏ 347	Autumn in Cheyenne/Speak Low	1961	$8
❏ 983	Batman Theme/Karelia	1966	$15
❏ 302	Bonanza/Bounty Hunter	1961	$10
❏ 50237	Bossa Nova Noel/Holiday on Skis	1967	$10

—With Riz Ortolani
Number	Title	Yr	NM
❏ 814	Brash Brannigan/Hunky Funky	1965	$8
❏ 677	Burke's Law Theme/Smoke Signals	1963	$10
❏ 50037	Duel at Diablo/Sugar Me Sweet	1966	$6
❏ 50159	Eight on the Lam!/Sailor from Gibraltar	1967	$6
❏ 438	Experiment in Terror/Sergeants Three March	1962	$10
❏ 882	Forget Domani/Glory Boys	1965	$8
❏ 711	From Russia with Love/Mexican Summer	1964	$10
❏ 855	Gabrielle/Ring of Fire	1965	$8
❏ 545	Guitar Boogie/Kalinka	1963	$8
❏ 586	Gunsmoke/Ciao	1963	$10

Number	Title	Yr	NM
❏ 50252	Here Is Where I Belong/ The Sound of Music	1968	$5
❏ 50070	Hill Country Theme/ Quedate Un Rato Mas	1966	$6
❏ 50519	Infinity Blue/Soul American	1969	$5
❏ 646	La Donna Nel Mondo/Redigo	1963	$8
❏ 577	Mexicali Rose/Mexicali Rose	1963	$8
❏ 747	On the Trail/Wheels West	1964	$8
❏ 50288	Scalphunter's Theme/ Theme for November	1968	$5
❏ 50571	Stiletto/Guitar Woman	1969	$5
❏ 50471	The High Chaparral/Master Jack	1969	$6
❏ 261	The Magnificent Seven/ The Lonely Rebel	1960	$15
❏ 932	Theme from "The Trials of O'Brien"/Walkin' Down the Line	1965	$8
❏ 50214	Tiny Bubbles/Stag or Drag	1967	$6
❏ 787	Tuff Guitar/Hound Dog	1964	$8

CAIROS, THE
SHRINE
| ❏ 111 | Stop Overlooking Me/Don't Fight It | 1966 | $1200 |

CAKE, THE
DECCA
❏ 32235	Fire Fly/Rainbow Wood	1967	$10
❏ 32179	Mockingbird/Baby That's Me	1967	$10
❏ 32347	PT 280/Have You Heard the News 'Bout Miss Molly	1968	$10

CALABRESE, JOANNE, AND DOC GALVEZ
SCEPTER
| ❏ 12238 | God Rest Ye Merry Gentlemen/(Instrumental) | 1968 | $6 |

CALAMITY JANE
COLUMBIA
❏ 18-02715	I've Just Seen a Face/ Midnight Bandit	1982	$4
❏ 38-03229	Love Wheel/Pick Me Up (And Let Me Love Again)	1982	$4
❏ 18-02503	Send Me Somebody to Love/Don't You Leave Love Alone Too Long	1981	$4
❏ 18-02958	Walkin' After Midnight/ Lover to Lover	1982	$4

CALDWELL, BOBBY
Also see CAPTAIN BEYOND.

CLOUDS
❏ 15	Can't Say Goodbye/Down for the Third Time	1979	$5
❏ 21	Coming Down from Love/ Open Your Eyes	1980	$6
❏ 18	My Flame/Come to Me	1979	$6
❏ 11	What You Won't Do for Love/Love Won't Wait	1978	$5

MARLIN
| ❏ 3349 | Alfie/Take Me Back to Then | 1981 | $10 |

MCA
| ❏ 52473 | Don't Quit/Firepower | 1984 | $8 |

PBR
| ❏ 503 | The House Is Rockin'/ When You Awake | 1976 | $30 |

POLYDOR
| ❏ 2212 | All of My Love/Sunny Hills | 1982 | $6 |

CALE, J.J.
LIBERTY
❏ 55931	After Midnight/Slow Motion	1966	$20
❏ 55840	Dick Tracy/It's a Go-Go Place	1965	$20
❏ 55881	Outside Lookin' In/In Our Time	1966	$20

MCA
| ❏ 51095 | Carry On/Deep Dark Dungeon | 1981 | $4 |

MERCURY
| ❏ 76145 | Devil in Disguise/Drifter's Wife | 1982 | $3 |
| ❏ 814497-7 | Losers/Reality | 1983 | $3 |

SHELTER
❏ 7321	After Midnight/Crying Eyes	1972	$6
❏ 40238	Cajun Moon/Starbound	1974	$5
❏ 7314	Crazy Mama/Don't Go to Strangers	1971	$6
❏ 7332	Going Down/Louisiana Women	1973	$6
❏ 62002	Hey Baby/Cocaine	1976	$6
❏ 40366	I Got the Same Old Blues/ Rock and Roll Records	1975	$5
❏ 40290	I'll Be There/Precious Memories	1974	$5
❏ 7326	Lies/Riding Home	1972	$6
❏ 7306	Magnolia/Crazy Mama	1971	$8

CALE, JOHN
Also see THE VELVET UNDERGROUND.

A&M
| ❏ 2329 | Dead or Alive/Honi Soit | 1981 | $10 |

COLUMBIA
| ❏ 4-45266 | Big White Cloud/Gideon's Bible | 1970 | $25 |
| ❏ 4-45154 | Cleo/Fairweather Friend | 1970 | $30 |

REPRISE
| ❏ 1108 | Legs Larry at Television Center/Days of Steam | 1972 | $40 |

CALELLO, CHARLIE
MIDSONG INT'L.
❏ 1014	Sing, Sing, Sing/In the Mood	1979	$5
❏ 72001	Sing, Sing, Sing/In the Mood	1980	$4
—Reissue of 1014			

CALHOUN, LINDA
GRAPE
| ❏ 2004 | I Can Feel Love/Our Tune of Yesterday | 1979 | $8 |

MGM
| ❏ 14810 | Momma, Let Me Find Shelter (In Your Lovin' Arms)/He Kinda Reminds Me of a Song | 1975 | $6 |
| ❏ 14778 | Swinging Songs/(B-side unknown) | 1975 | $6 |

CALICO
UNITED ARTISTS
| ❏ XW806 | Great American Dream/ September Tears | 1976 | $5 |
| ❏ XW907 | Lyin' Again/Summertime Lovin' | 1976 | $5 |

CALIFORNIA
LAURIE
❏ 3651	I'm Just Thinking of You/ Doo-Wop Music	1977	$4
❏ 3612	See You in September/Ivy Ivy	1974	$4
❏ 3639	Song of a Thousand Voices/ Abraham, Martin and John	1976	$4
❏ 3695	Summer Fun Medley/Paris	1981	$4

RCA
| ❏ PB-11769 | Everybody Needs a Little Help/I'm a Poet | 1979 | $12 |

RSO
| ❏ 901 | I Can Hear Music/Love's Supposed to Be That Way | 1978 | $10 |

WARNER BROS.
| ❏ 8253 | Happy in Hollywood/ Music, Music, Music | 1976 | $12 |

CALIFORNIA MUSIC
EQUINOX
| ❏ PB-10120 | Don't Worry Baby/Ten Years' Harmony | 1974 | $20 |
| ❏ PB-10363 | Why Do Fools Fall in Love/ Don't Worry Baby | 1975 | $20 |

CALIFORNIA, RANDY
EPIC
| ❏ 10927 | Walkin' the Dog/Live for the Day | 1972 | $8 |

CALIFORNIANS, THE (2)
FEDERAL
| ❏ 12231 | My Angel/Heavenly Ruby | 1955 | $300 |

CALL, THE
ELEKTRA
❏ 69546	Everywhere I Go/Tore the Old Place Down	1986	$5
❏ 69546 [PS]	Everywhere I Go/Tore the Old Place Down	1986	$5
❏ 69461	I Don't Wanna/Day or Night	1987	$5
❏ 69461 [PS]	I Don't Wanna/Day or Night	1987	$5
❏ 69521	I Still Believe (Great Design)/Even Now	1986	$5

EVA-TONE
| ❏ 16 | The Walls Came Down | 1983 | $8 |
| —Blue flexi-disc contained in Trouser Press | | | |

MCA
| ❏ 53658 | Let the Day Begin/Uncovered | 1989 | $4 |

MERCURY
| ❏ 811487-7 | The Walls Came Down/Upperbirth | 1983 | $5 |
| ❏ 811487-7 [PS] | The Walls Came Down/Upperbirth | 1983 | $6 |

CALLAHAN BROTHERS, THE
COLUMBIA
❏ 4-21001	I Have Shifted Gears/Bluest Blues	1952	$30
❏ 4-20946	I've Had My Share of Sorrow/All Over You	1952	$30
❏ 4-20881	This Crazy, Crazy Feeling/ Blue Letters	1952	$30

CALLENDER, BOBBY
CORAL
| ❏ 62528 | Sweet Song of Life/Vicissitude (Or a Day at Jaffry's) | 1967 | $10 |

ROULETTE
| ❏ 4471 | Little Star/Love and Kisses | 1963 | $20 |

CALLOWAY, LAEL
ABC-PARAMOUNT
| ❏ 9761 | Dear Santa, Have You Had The Measles?/If Santa Was My Daddy | 1956 | $20 |

CALVANES, THE
DECK
| ❏ 579 | Dreamworld/5, 7 or 9 | 1958 | $125 |
| ❏ 580 | My Love Song/Horror Pictures | 1958 | $125 |

DOOTONE
| ❏ 371 | Crazy Over You/Don't Take Your Love from Me | 1956 | $200 |
| ❏ 380 | One More Kiss/Florabelle | 1956 | $200 |

7-Inch Extended Plays
| ❏ 205 | *They Call Me Fool/One More Kiss/Don't Take Your Love from Me/Crazy Over You | 1956 | $400 |

CAMEL
JANUS
| ❏ 262 | Another Night/Lunar Sea | 1976 | $6 |

CAMELOTS, THE
AANKO
| ❏ 1004 | Sunday Kind of Love/ My Imagination | 1963 | $100 |

CAMEO
| ❏ 334 | Don't Leave Me Baby/Love Call | 1964 | $40 |
| —B-side by the Ebonaires | | | |

COMET
| ❏ 930 | Scratch/Charge | 1962 | $20 |

CRIMSON
| ❏ 1001 | Don't Leave Me Baby/The Letter | 1963 | $40 |

EMBER
| ❏ 1108 | Pocahontas/Searching for My Baby | 1964 | $30 |

LAURIE
| ❏ 3239 | Marie/Daddy's Going Away Again | 1964 | $30 |
| —As "The Harps | | | |

LOST-NITE
| ❏ 247 | Don't Leave Me Baby/The Letter | 1963 | $5 |
| —Reissue | | | |

NIX
❏ 101	Lulu/Never Been in Love Before	1961	$30
❏ 541	Dance Girl/That's My Baby	1965	$8
—B-side by the Suns			

TIMES SQUARE
| ❏ 32 | Dance Girl/That's My Baby | 1964 | $12 |
| —B-side by the Suns | | | |

7-Inch Extended Plays
CLIFTON/UGHA
| ❏ EP507/1 | Music to My Ears/Daddy's Going Away//Pocahontas/ Don't Leave Me Baby | 1981 | $5 |
| ❏ EP507/1 [PS] | (title unknown) | 1981 | $5 |

CAMEO
ATLANTA ARTISTS
❏ 884270-7	A Good-Bye/Little Boys-Dangerous Toys	1985	$3
❏ 880744-7	Attack Me With Your Love/ Love You Anyway	1985	$3
❏ 888385-7	Back and Forth/You Can Have the World	1987	$3
❏ 888385-7 [PS]	Back and Forth/You Can Have the World	1987	$3
❏ 888193-7	Candy/She's Strange	1986	$3
❏ 888193-7 [PS]	Candy/She's Strange	1986	$3
❏ 812472-7	Can't Help Falling in Love/For You	1983	$3
❏ 888711-7	Don't Be Lonely/I've Got Your Image	1987	$3
❏ 880169-7	Hangin' Downtown/ Cameo's Dance	1984	$3
❏ 874050-7	Pretty Girls/Pretty Girls (Dub)	1989	$3
❏ 874050-7 [PS]	Pretty Girls/Pretty Girls (Dub)	1989	$3
❏ 888876-7	She's Mine/I've Got Your Image	1987	$3
❏ PRO-272-7 [DJ]	She's Strange (Rap)/(Edit)	1984	$10
❏ 818384-7	She's Strange/Tribute to Bob Marley	1984	$3
❏ 884010-7	Single Life/I've Got Your Image	1985	$3
❏ 872918-7	Single Life/She's Strange	1989	$3
—Reissue			
❏ 872314-7	Skin I'm In/Honey	1988	$3
❏ 872314-7 [PS]	Skin I'm In/Honey	1988	$3
❏ 814077-7	Slow Movin'/For You	1983	$3
❏ 812054-7	Style/Enjoy Your Life	1983	$3
❏ 818870-7	Talkin' Out the Side of Your Neck/Leve-Toi	1984	$3
❏ 884933-7	Word Up/Urban Warrior	1986	$3
❏ 884933-7 [PS]	Word Up/Urban Warrior	1986	$3

Number	Title	Yr	NM
CHOCOLATE CITY			
❏ 3235	Alligator Woman/Soul Away	1982	$4
❏ 3222	Feel Me/Is This the Way	1981	$4
❏ 001	Find My Way/Good Company	1975	$5
❏ 008	Find My Way/Rigor Mortis	1977	$4
❏ 3233	Flirt/Owe It All to You	1982	$4
❏ 3225	Freaky Dancin'/Better Days	1981	$4
❏ 011	Funk Funk/Good Time	1977	$4
❏ 018	Give Love a Chance/Two of Us	1979	$4
❏ 019	I Just Want to Be/The Rock	1979	$4
❏ 3227	I Like It/The Sound Table	1981	$4
❏ 016	Insane/I Want You	1978	$4
❏ 014	It's Over/Inflation	1978	$4
❏ 013	It's Serious/Inflation	1978	$4
❏ 010	Post Mortem/Smile	1977	$4
❏ 3210	Shake Your Pants/I Came for You	1980	$4
❏ 3202	Sparkle/Macho	1979	$4
❏ 3206	We're Goin' Out Tonight/One the One	1980	$4
CAMEOS, THE			
CAMEO			
❏ 123	Merry Christmas/New Year's Eve	1957	$200
DEAN			
❏ 504	Lost Lover/Wait Up	1961	$200
JOHNSON			
❏ 108	Lost Lover/Wait Up	1961	$100
CAMERON, BART			
REVOLVER			
❏ 013	Dark Eyed Lady/(B-side unknown)	1986	$5
❏ 015	Do It for the Love of It/(B-side unknown)	1987	$5
❏ 011	What's Your Name/(B-side unknown)	1986	$5
CAMERON, JIMMY AND VELLA			
REPRISE			
❏ 0483	Lovin' You Is Such a Groove/I Know a Place	1966	$40
UNLIMITED GOLD			
❏ 1422	Mornin' Time/There Is No Other Love	1980	$4
CAMILLE			
EMI			
❏ 5014	White Christmas/Snowbelle	1979	$30
— U.K. import			
CAMP, THE			
SCEPTER			
❏ 12159	Marching/Long Long Trail	1966	$100
CAMPANELLA, DAVID, AND THE DELLCHORDS			
KANE			
❏ 25593	Over the Rainbow/Everything's That Way	1959	$70
CAMPBELL, ARCHIE, AND LITTLE BONNIE			
RCA VICTOR			
❏ 74-0147	Poor Daddy/Old Shep	1969	$8
CAMPBELL, ARCHIE, AND LORENE MANN			
RCA VICTOR			
❏ 47-9691	My Special Prayer/What Am I Living For	1968	$8
❏ 47-9549	Tell It Like It Is/If That's the Only Way	1968	$8
❏ 47-9401	The Dark End of the Street/The Gettin' Place	1967	$8
❏ 47-9615	Warm and Tender Love/Pledging My Love	1968	$8
CAMPBELL, ARCHIE, AND MINNIE PEARL			
RCA VICTOR			
❏ PB-10077	As Soon As I Hang Up the Phone/Nobody's Business	1974	$6
CAMPBELL, ARCHIE			
ELEKTRA			
❏ 45316	Don't Be Born a Man/More or Less	1976	$5
❏ 45452	I Just Found This Hat/The Night Miss Nancy Ann's Hotel for Single Girls Got Burned Down	1977	$5
RCA VICTOR			
❏ 47-8658	Beeping Sleauty/The Drunk	1965	$12
❏ 47-9028	Christmas at the Opry/Christmas Eve in Heaven	1966	$10
❏ APBO-0155	Freedom Ain't the Same As Bein' Free/The House	1973	$6
❏ 47-8866	Golf, Golf, Golf/Mommy's Little Angel	1966	$10
❏ 47-8976	Life Gets Tee-Jus Don't It/The Martins and the Coys	1966	$12
❏ 47-7757	Make Friends/The Twelfth Rose	1960	$15
❏ 47-8422	Most Richly Blessed/Do Lord	1964	$10

Number	Title	Yr	NM
❏ 47-7807	Ol' Man Mose/Don't Jump from the Bridge	1960	$15
❏ 74-0232	Pfft, You Were Gone/Rindercella	1969	$8
❏ 47-9081	The Cockfight/Red Silk	1967	$12
❏ 47-8741	The Men in My Little Girl's Life/Abe Lincoln Comes Home	1965	$10
❏ 47-7660	Trouble in the Amen Corner/Black Is the Color of My True Love's Hair	1960	$15
❏ 47-9257	We Never Get Hungry on Sunday/Roho and the Black Bantam	1967	$10
STARDAY			
❏ 624	A World Full of Women/My Baby's Home	1963	$15
❏ 643	Crying in My Pillow/Don't Let Love Die	1963	$15
❏ 609	Don't You Ever Fret/The Master's Hand	1962	$15
❏ 600	Fools Side of Town/Root Beer	1962	$15
❏ 727	Green Stamps/Three Little Pigs	1965	$10
❏ 557	Sergeant York/Grab a Little Sunshine	1961	$15
❏ 568	Settin' My Tears to Music/Woman's Work Is Never Done	1961	$15
CAMPBELL, CECIL			
MGM			
❏ 12245	Dixieland Rock/Fog Rising on the Mountain	1956	$70
❏ 12118	Steel Guitar Waltz/Comango	1955	$30
RCA VICTOR			
❏ 48-0376	Serenade of the Winds/Proud Papa Polka	1950	$40
— Originals on green vinyl			
❏ 48-0409	Steel Guitar Dig/Spookie Boogie	1951	$40
❏ 48-0499	Steel Guitar Jamboree/You Kept Makin' Eyes at Me	1951	$40
❏ 48-0014	Steel Guitar Ramble/Left All Alone with a Broken Heart	1949	$50
— Originals on green vinyl			
❏ 48-0219	Steel Guitar Ramble/Left All Alone with a Broken Heart	1950	$40
— Reissue of 48-0014; originals on green vinyl			
❏ 48-0340	Steel Guitar Swing/Catawba River	1950	$40
— Originals on green vinyl			
❏ 48-0445	Steel Guitar Wiggle/Coconut Island	1951	$40
❏ 48-0126	Tear Drops/No Where, No Time, No Place	1949	$50
— Originals on green vinyl			
❏ 48-0472	Tennessee Steel Guitar/Paper Roses	1951	$40
❏ 48-0076	Tropical Island/Tar Heel Rag	1949	$50
— Originals on green vinyl			
CAMPBELL, CHOKER			
APT			
❏ 25011	Walk Awhile/Walking on Thin-Soled Shoes	1958	$70
ATLANTIC			
❏ 1038	Have You Seen My Baby/Jackie Mambo	1954	$50
❏ 1014	Last Call for Whiskey/How Could You Do This	1953	$50
FORTUNE			
❏ 808	Frankie and Johnny/Rocking and Jumping	1953	$70
MOTOWN			
❏ 1072	Come See About Me/Pride and Joy	1964	$30
CAMPBELL, EDDIE			
ARTCO			
❏ 45-103	Contagious Love/Why Do You Treat Me Like You Do	1967	$1200
CAMPBELL, EDDIE C.			
ROOSTER BLUES			
❏ 46	Santa's Messin' with the Kid/King of the Jungle	1981	$15
CAMPBELL, GLEN, AND BOBBIE GENTRY			
CAPITOL			
❏ 2745	All I Have to Do Is Dream/Less of Me	1970	$6
❏ 2314	Less of Me/Morning Glory	1968	$6
❏ 2387	Let It Be Me/Little Green Apples	1969	$6
CAMPBELL, GLEN			
ATLANTIC AMERICA			
❏ 99691	A Lady Like You/Tennessee	1984	$3
❏ 99525	Call Home/Sweet 16	1986	$3
❏ 99559	Cowpoke/Rag Doll	1986	$3
❏ 99768	Faithless Love/Scene of the Crime	1984	$3
❏ 99930	I Love How You Love Me/Hang On Baby (Ease My Mind)	1983	$3
❏ 99600	It's Just a Matter of Time/Gene Autry, My Hero	1985	$3
❏ 99600 [PS]	It's Just a Matter of Time/Gene Autry, My Hero	1985	$4

Number	Title	Yr	NM
❏ 99647	(Love Always) Letter to Home/An American Trilogy	1985	$3
❏ 99967	Old Home Town/Heartache #3	1982	$4
❏ 99967 [PS]	Old Home Town/Heartache #3	1982	$4
❏ 99893	On the Wings of My Victory/A Few Good Men	1983	$3
CAPEHART			
❏ 5008	Death Valley/Nothin' Better Than a Pretty Woman	1961	$30
CAPITOL			
❏ 4584	Another Fine Mess/Can You Fool	1978	$4
❏ 5037	As Far As I'm Concerned/Same Old Places	1963	$15
❏ 3926	Bonaparte's Retreat/Too Many Mornings	1974	$5
❏ 3669	Bring Back My Yesterday/Beautiful Love Song	1973	$5
❏ 5773	Burning Bridges/Only the Lonely	1966	$10
❏ 4715	California/Never Tell You No Lies	1979	$4
❏ 5638	Can't You See I'm Tryin'/Satisfied Mind	1966	$10
❏ 4638	Can You Fool/Let's All Sing a Song About It	1978	$4
❏ 2336	Christmas Is for Children/There's No Place Like Home	1968	$8
❏ 4155	Country Boy (You Got Your Feet in L.A.)/Record Collector's Dream	1975	$4
❏ 4990	Divorce Me C.O.D./Dark As a Dungeon	1963	$15
❏ 3062	Dream Baby (How Long Must I Dream)/Here and Now	1971	$6
❏ 2843	Everything a Man Could Ever Need/Norwood (Me and My Guitar)	1970	$6
❏ 2428	Galveston/How Come Every Time I Itch I Wind Up Scratchin' You	1969	$6
❏ 5939	Gentle on My Mind/Just Another Man	1967	$8
— Orange and yellow swirl, without "A Subsidiary Of"... in perimeter label print			
❏ 5939	Gentle on My Mind/Just Another Man	1968	$6
— Orange and yellow swirl label with "A Subsidiary Of" in perimeter print			
❏ 4515	God Must Have Blessed America/Amazing Grace	1977	$4
❏ 5441	Guess I'm Dumb/That's All Right	1965	$120
— A Brian Wilson "Pet Sounds"-like production			
❏ 2076 [PS]	Hey Little One/My Baby's Gone	1968	$15
❏ 4909	Hollywood Smiles/Hooked on Love	1980	$4
❏ 2718	Honey Come Back/Where Do You Go	1970	$6
❏ 4769	Hound Dog Man/Tennessee Home	1979	$4
❏ 3808	Houston (I'm Coming to See You)/Honestly Love	1973	$5
❏ 3509	I Believe in Christmas/New Snow on the Roof	1972	$6
❏ 4959	I Don't Want to Know Your Name/Daisy a Day	1981	$4
❏ 5854	I Gotta Have My Baby Back/Just to Satisfy You	1967	$10
❏ 3548	I Knew Jesus (Before He Was a Star)/On This Road	1973	$5
❏ 4682	I'm Gonna Love You/Love Takes You Higher	1979	$4
❏ 3988	It's a Sin When You Love Somebody/If I Were Loving You	1974	$5
❏ 5360	It's a Woman's World/Tomorrow Never Comes	1965	$15
❏ 2905	It's Only Make Believe/Pave Your Way Into Tomorrow	1970	$6
❏ 3411	I Will Never Pass This Way Again/We All Pull the Load	1972	$6
❏ 5545	Less of Me/Private John Q	1965	$12
❏ 5172	Let Me Tell You About Mary/Through the Eyes of a Child	1964	$15
❏ 4856	Long Black Limousine/Here I Am	1962	$10
❏ 4856 [PS]	Long Black Limousine/Here I Am	1962	$30
❏ 3305	Manhattan, Kansas/Wayfaring Stranger	1972	$6
❏ 4799	My Prayer/Don't Lose Me in the Confusion	1979	$4
❏ 2787	Oh Happy Day/Someone Above	1970	$6
❏ 4925	Oh My Darling/Prima Donna	1963	$15
❏ 3254	Oklahoma Sunday Morning/Everybody's Got to Go There Sometime	1972	$6
❏ 3483	One Last Time/All My Tomorrows	1972	$6
❏ 4288	See You on Sunday/Bloodline	1976	$4
❏ 4865	Somethin' 'Bout You Baby I Like/Late Night Confession	1980	$4
— With Rita Coolidge			
❏ 4376	Southern Nights/William Tell Overture	1976	$4
❏ 5279	Summer, Winter, Spring and Fall/Heartaches Can Be Fun	1964	$15
❏ 5279 [PS]	Summer, Winter, Spring and Fall/Heartaches Can Be Fun	1964	$30
❏ 4445	Sunflower/How High Did We Go	1977	$4
❏ 3123	The Last Time I Saw Her/Bach Talk	1971	$6
❏ 4245	Then You Can Tell Me Goodbye-Don't Pull Your Love/I Miss You Tonight	1976	$4
❏ 4783	Too Late to Worry — Too Blue to Cry/How Do I Tell My Heart Not to Break	1962	$20
❏ 2573	True Grit/Hava Nagila	1969	$6
❏ 2659	Try a Little Kindness/Lonely My Lonely Friend	1969	$6

Number	Title	Yr	NM
❏ 3735	Wherefore and Why/Give Me Back That Old Familiar Feeling	1973	$5
❏ 2494	Where's the Playground Susie/Arkansas	1969	$6
❏ 4986	Why Don't We Just Sleep on It Tonight/It's Your World	1981	$4

— With Tanya Tucker

| ❏ 2302 | Wichita Lineman/Fate of Man | 1968 | $6 |

CAPITOL CREATIVE PRODUCTS

| ❏ 54 | Homeward Bound/(Sittin' On) The Dock of the Bay//Mary in the Morning | 1969 | $8 |

CENECO

| ❏ 1324 | Dreams for Sale/I've Got to Win | 1961 | $30 |
| ❏ 1356 | I Wonder/You, You, You | 1961 | $30 |

COMPLEAT

| ❏ 113 | Letting Go/(Instrumental) | 1983 | $4 |

CREST

| ❏ 1096 | The Miracle of Love/Once More | 1962 | $20 |
| ❏ 1087 | Turn Around, Look at Me/Brenda | 1961 | $30 |

— With last name spelled correctly

| ❏ 1087 | Turn Around, Look at Me/Brenda | 1961 | $40 |

— With last name spelled incorrectly as "Cambpell"

EVEREST

| ❏ 2500 | Delight, Arkansas/Walk Right In | 1969 | $6 |

MCA

| ❏ 41323 | Dream Lover/Bronco | 1980 | $4 |

— A-side with Tanya Tucker

❏ 53426	Heart of the Matter/Light Years	1988	$3
❏ 53218	I Have You/I'm a One Woman Man	1987	$3
❏ 53245	I Remember You/For Sure, For Certain, Forever, For Always	1988	$3
❏ 53493	More Than Enough/Our Movie	1989	$3
❏ 53172	Still Within the Sound of My Voice/In My Life	1987	$3
❏ 53108	The Hand That Rocks the Cradle/Arkansas	1987	$3

— A-side with Steve Wariner

MIRAGE

| ❏ 3845 | I Love My Truck/Melody's Melody | 1981 | $4 |

STARDAY

| ❏ 853 | For the Love of a Woman/Smokey Blue Eyes | 1968 | $8 |

UNIVERSAL

| ❏ UVL-66024 | She's Gone, Gone, Gone/William Tell Overture | 1989 | $4 |

WARNER BROS.

| ❏ 49609 | Any Which Way You Can/Medley from Any Which Way You Can | 1980 | $4 |

— B-side by Texas Opera Company

7-Inch Extended Plays

CAPITOL CREATIVE PRODUCTS

| ❏ SU-752 [PS] | Greatest Hits | 1971 | $12 |

— Part of "Little LP" series (#156)

| ❏ SU-752 | Wichita Lineman/Try a Little Kindness/By the Time I Get to Phoenix//Gentle on My Mind/I Wanna Live/Galveston | 1971 | $10 |

— Stereo jukebox issue; small hole, plays at 33 1/3 rpm

CAMPBELL, JO ANN

ABC-PARAMOUNT

❏ 10335	Amateur Night/I Wish It Would Rain All Summer	1962	$30
❏ 10172	But Maybe This Year/Crazy Daisy	1960	$30
❏ 10224	Eddie My Love/It Wasn't Right	1961	$30
❏ 10300	I Changed My Mind Jack/You Made Me Love You	1962	$30
❏ 10258	Mama Don't Wait/Duane	1961	$30
❏ 10200	Motorcycle Michael/Puka Puka Pants	1961	$30

CAMEO

❏ 223	I'm the Girl from Wolverton Mountain/Sloppy Joe	1962	$30
❏ 237	Let Me Do It My Way/Mr. Fix-It Man	1962	$30
❏ 249	Mother Please/Waitin' for Love	1963	$30

EL DORADO

| ❏ 504 | Forever Young/Come On Baby | 1957 | $50 |
| ❏ 509 | Funny Thing/I Can't Give You Anything But Love | 1957 | $50 |

GONE

❏ 5068	Beach Comber/I Ain't Got No Steady Date	1959	$40
❏ 5049	Happy New Year Baby/Tall Boy	1958	$40
❏ 5037	I Really, Really Love You/I'm Nobody's Baby Now	1958	$40
❏ 5055	Mama/Nervous	1959	$40
❏ 5014	Wait a Minute/I'm in Love with You	1957	$40
❏ 5014	Wait a Minute/I'm in Love with You	1957	$50
❏ 5027	Whassa Matter with You/You-Oo	1958	$40

POINT

| ❏ 4 | I'm Coming Home Late Tonight/Wherever You Go | 1956 | $50 |

CAMPBELL, JOHN

HIT

| ❏ 64 | If You Wanna Be Happy/Ain't That a Shame | 1963 | $8 |

— B-side by the Chellows

CAMPERS, THE

PARKWAY

| ❏ 974 | The Ballad of Batman/The Batmobile | 1966 | $40 |
| ❏ 974 | The Ballad of Batman/The Batmobile | 1966 | $40 |

— Original label credit: "The Camps"

CAMPI, RAY

COLPIX

| ❏ 166 | French Fries/Hear What I Wanna Hear | 1960 | $20 |

D

| ❏ 1047 | The Ballad of Donna and Peggy Sue/A Man I Met (Tribute to The Big Bopper) | 1959 | $50 |

DOMINO

| ❏ 700 | My Screamin' Screamin' Meemie/With You | 1958 | $40 |

DOT

| ❏ 15617 | It Ain't Me/Give That Love to Me | 1957 | $70 |

ROLLIN' ROCK

| ❏ 006 | Eager Boy/Dobroggie | 1978 | $5 |
| ❏ 031 | Merle's Boogie-Woogie-Missouri/Sweet Temptation Guitar Rag | 1980 | $4 |

— With Merle Travis

❏ 019	My Baby Left Me/A Li'l Bit of Heartache	1979	$5
❏ 029	Scrumptious Baby/I Didn't Mean to Be Mean	1980	$4
❏ 014	Sixteen Chicks/Pan American Boogie	1979	$5
❏ 047	Sweet Woman Blues/The Newest Wave	1982	$4
❏ 046	Texas Sands/How Long Can You Feel	1982	$4
❏ 008	Tore Up/If It's All the Same to You	1978	$5
❏ 027	Wrong, Wrong, Wrong/Booze It	1980	$4

TNT

| ❏ 145 | Caterpillar/Play It Cool | 1958 | $300 |

WINSOR

| ❏ 6401 | Billie Jean/Shenandoah | 1964 | $40 |

CANADIAN BEADLES, THE

TIDE

| ❏ 2206 | I'm Coming Home/Love Walk Away | 1964 | $20 |

— As "Vic, Paul and Bruce"

| ❏ 2203 | I Think I'm Gonna Cry/I'll Show You the Way | 1964 | $20 |

CANADIAN SWEETHEARTS, THE

A&M

❏ 798	Adios, Aloha/Too Far Between Kisses	1966	$10
❏ 758	Blowin' in the Wind/We're Gonna Stand on the Mountain	1965	$10
❏ 778	Don't Knock on My Door/Torture Me	1965	$12
❏ 713	Freight Train/Out for Fun	1963	$15
❏ 786	Haunting Me/Soldier Boy	1965	$12
❏ 727	Hootenanny Express/Half-Breed	1964	$15
❏ 768	Lookin' Back to See/The Wayward Wind	1965	$10
❏ 737	Love/Mountain Special	1964	$15

EPIC

| ❏ 5-10377 | Hey Sue/You Were Worth the Wait | 1968 | $8 |
| ❏ 5-10258 | Let's Wait a Little Longer/More Than Money Can Buy | 1968 | $8 |

CANARIES, THE

B.T. PUPPY

| ❏ 557 | I'll Cry Again/Baby Don't Surprise Me | 1970 | $8 |

DIMENSION

| ❏ 1047 | I'm Sorry Baby/Runaround Ronnie | 1965 | $20 |

CANDLELIGHTERS, THE

DELTA

| ❏ 203 | Would You Do the Same for Me/(B-side unknown) | 1958 | $800 |

CANDY AND THE KISSES

CAMEO

| ❏ 355 | Soldier Boy (Of Mine)/Shakin' Time | 1964 | $30 |
| ❏ 336 | The 81/Two Happy People | 1964 | $30 |

DECCA

| ❏ 32415 | Chains of Love/Someone Out There | 1968 | $6 |

SCEPTER

| ❏ 12125 | Sweet and Lovely/Out in the Streets Again | 1965 | $20 |
| ❏ 12136 | Tonight's the Night/The Last Time | 1966 | $15 |

CANDYMEN, THE

ABC

❏ 11077	Candy Man/Crowded Room	1968	$8
❏ 11023	Deep in the Night/Stone Blues Man	1967	$8
❏ 10995	Georgia Pines/Movies in My Mind	1967	$8
❏ 11141	Go and Tell the People/It's Gonna Get Good in a Minute	1968	$8
❏ 11175	I'll Never Forget/Lonely Eyes	1969	$8
❏ 11048	Sentimental Lady/Ways	1968	$8

LIBERTY

| ❏ 56172 | Happy Tonight/Papers | 1970 | $8 |

CANNED HEAT

ALA

| ❏ 1996 | C.C. Shooter/Harley Davidson Blues | 1984 | $5 |

— As "Heat Brothers '84"

ATLANTIC

| ❏ 3010 | One More River to Cross/Highway 401 | 1974 | $4 |
| ❏ 3236 | The Harder They Come/Rock 'N' Roll Show | 1975 | $4 |

LIBERTY

| ❏ 56140 | Change My Ways/Get Off My Back | 1969 | $6 |
| ❏ 56079 | Christmas Blues/The Chipmunk Song | 1968 | $30 |

— B-side with the Chipmunks

❏ 56005	Evil Woman/The World Is a Jug	1967	$8
❏ 56180	Future Blues/Going Up the Country	1970	$6
❏ 56077	Going Up the Country/One Kind Favor	1968	$6
❏ 56077 [PS]	Going Up the Country/One Kind Favor	1968	$20
❏ 56151	Let's Work Together/I'm Her Man	1970	$6
❏ 56217	My Time Ain't Long/Wooly Bully	1970	$6
❏ 56038	On the Road Again/Boogie Music	1968	$6
❏ 56127	Sic 'Em Pigs/Poor Man	1969	$6
❏ 56097	Time Was/Low Down	1969	$6

UNITED ARTISTS

| ❏ 0059 | Going Up the Country/Let's Work Together | 1973 | $4 |

— Silver Spotlight Series" reissue

| ❏ XW243 [DJ] | Harley Davidson Blues (mono/stereo) | 1973 | $6 |

— Stock copy apparently does not exist

| ❏ 50831 | Long Way from L.A./Hill's Stomp | 1971 | $5 |
| ❏ 0058 | On the Road Again/This Was | 1973 | $4 |

— Silver Spotlight Series" reissue

| ❏ 50927 | Sneakin' Around/Cherokee Dance | 1972 | $5 |

CANNIBAL AND THE HEADHUNTERS

AIRES

| ❏ 1001 | Mean So Much/Dance By the Light | 1968 | $20 |

CAPITOL

| ❏ 2393 | Get It On Up (Get Up the Courage)/Mean So Much | 1969 | $20 |

DATE

| ❏ 1516 | La Bamba/Zulu King | 1966 | $20 |
| ❏ 1525 | Land of 1,000 Dances/Love Bird | 1966 | $20 |

RAMPART

❏ 644	Here Comes Love/Nau Ninny Nau	1965	$20
❏ 646	I Need Your Loving/Follow the Music	1965	$20
❏ 642	Land of 1,000 Dances/I'll Show You How to Love Me	1964	$30
❏ 654	Out of Sight/Please Baby Please	1965	$20

CANNIBALS, THE

HIT

| ❏ FREEBEE2 | Christmas Rock 'n' Roll/New Year's Eve Song | 1980 | $10 |

— U.K. import

| ❏ FREEBEE2 [PS] | Christmas Rock 'n' Roll/New Year's Eve Song | 1980 | $10 |

— U.K. import

CANNON, ACE

FERNWOOD

| ❏ 117 | Big Shot/Rest | 1960 | $40 |

— As "Johnny Cannon"

| ❏ 137 | Big Shot/Tie Me to Your Apron Strings Again | 1964 | $30 |
| ❏ 135 | Summertime/Hoe Down Rock | 1963 | $30 |

HI

| ❏ 2148 | Alley Cat/Cannonball | 1968 | $6 |
| ❏ 2166 | Amen/Down By the Riverside | 1969 | $6 |

Number	Title	Yr	NM
❑ 2084	Blue Christmas/Here Comes Santa Claus	1964	$10
❑ 2313	Blue Eyes Crying in the Rain/I'll Fly Away	1976	$4
❑ 2051	Blues (Stay Away from Me)/ Blues in My Heart	1962	$20
❑ 2187	Chicken Fried Soul/Chunck	1971	$5
❑ 2065	Cottonfields/Mildew	1963	$15
❑ 2065 [PS]	Cottonfields/Mildew	1963	$30
❑ 2256	Country Comfort/Closin' Time's a Downer	1973	$4
❑ 78526	Don't It Make My Brown Eyes Blue/Blanket on the Ground	1978	$4
❑ 2199	Easy Loving/Misty Blue	1971	$5
❑ 2081	Empty Arms/Sunday Blues	1964	$12
❑ 2101	Funny (How Time Slips Away)/Saxy Lullaby	1966	$8
❑ 2155	If I Had a Hammer/Soul for Sale	1969	$6
❑ 78516	It Was Almost Like a Song/ (B-side unknown)	1978	$4
❑ 2127	I Walk the Line/Memory	1967	$8
❑ 2261	Last Date/Methilda	1974	$4
❑ 2063	Love Letters/Since I Met You Baby	1963	$15
❑ 2210	Lovesick Blues/Cold, Cold Heart	1972	$5
❑ 2192	Me and Bobby McGee/ Sweet Caroline	1971	$5
❑ 2107	Mocking Bird Rock/Dedicated to the One I Love	1966	$8
❑ 2111	More/Spanish Eyes	1966	$8
❑ 2286	Peace in the Valley/Raunchy	1975	$4
❑ 2089	Sea Cruise/Gold Coins	1965	$8
❑ 2074	Searchin'/Love Letters in the Sand	1964	$10
❑ 2144	Sleep Walk/By the Time I Get to Phoenix	1968	$6
❑ 2070	Swanee River/Moanin' the Blues	1963	$15
❑ 2070 [PS]	Swanee River/Moanin' the Blues	1963	$30
❑ 2078	The Great Pretender/Gone	1964	$10
❑ 2273	There Goes My Everything/ Tennessee Saturday Night	1974	$4
❑ 2231	Tuffer Than Tuff/The Green Door	1973	$4
❑ 2040	Tuff/Sittin' Tight	1961	$20
❑ 2220	Wabash Cannonball/To Get to You	1972	$5
❑ 2299	Walk On By/Malt Liquor	1975	$4
❑ 2136	White Silver Sands/ San Antonio Rose	1967	$8
❑ 2117	Wonderland by Night/ As Time Goes By	1966	$8

LOUIS (LOUISE?)

Number	Title	Yr	NM
❑ 2001	Tuff/Sittin' Tight	1961	$40

SANTO

Number	Title	Yr	NM
❑ 506	Big Shot/Rest	1962	$20
❑ 503	Sugar Blues/38 Special	1962	$20

7-Inch Extended Plays

HI

Number	Title	Yr	NM
❑ SBG36 [PS]	Ace Cannon Live	1965	$15
❑ SBG-60	By the Time I Get to Phoenix/ Green, Green Grass of Home/ Turn On Your Love Light//Sleep Walking/Woman, Woman/Laura (What's He Got That I Ain't Got)	1968	$10

— Jukebox issue; small hole, plays at 33 1/3 rpm

Number	Title	Yr	NM
❑ SBG36	Memphis/Moody River/You Can't Sit Down//Honky Tonk/ Night Wagon/When the Saints Go Marching In	1965	$15

— Jukebox issue; small hole, plays at 33 1/3 rpm

Number	Title	Yr	NM
❑ SBG-60 [PS]	The Incomparable Sax of Ace Cannon	1968	$12

CANNON, FREDDY

AMHERST

Number	Title	Yr	NM
❑ 201	Dance to the Bop/(She's a) Mean Rebel Rouser	1983	$4

CLARIDGE

Number	Title	Yr	NM
❑ 401	Palisades Park/Way Down Yonder in New Orleans	1975	$6
❑ 416	Sugar/Sugar (Part 2)	1976	$6

METROMEDIA

Number	Title	Yr	NM
❑ 262	If You've Got the Time/ Take Me Back	1972	$10

MIASOUND

Number	Title	Yr	NM
❑ 1002	Let's Put the Fun Back in Rock and Roll/Your Mama Ain't Always Right	1981	$5

— With the Belmonts

ROYAL AMERICAN

Number	Title	Yr	NM
❑ 2	Charged-Up, Turned-On Rock-N-Roll Singer/I Ain't Much, But I'm Yours	1970	$10
❑ 288	Strawberry Wine/Blossom Dear	1969	$10

SIRE

Number	Title	Yr	NM
❑ 4103	Beautiful Downtown Burbank/ If You Give Me a Title	1969	$12

SWAN

Number	Title	Yr	NM
❑ 4071	Buzz Buzz A-Diddle It/Opportunity	1961	$20
❑ 4050	Chattanooga Shoe Shine Boy/ Boston "My Home Town	1960	$20
❑ 4050 [PS]	Chattanooga Shoe Shine Boy/ Boston "My Home Town	1960	$40
❑ 4132	Come On and Love Me/ Four Letter Man	1963	$15
❑ 4155	Do What the Hippies Do/ That's the Way Girls Are	1963	$15
❑ 4149	Everybody Monkey/Oh Gloria	1963	$30
❑ 4083	For Me and My Gal/ Blue Plate Special	1961	$20
❑ 4057	Happy Shades of Blue/(Kwa-Na-Va-Ka) Cuernavaca Choo Choo	1960	$20
❑ 4057 [PS]	Happy Shades of Blue/(Kwa-Na-Va-Ka) Cuernavaca Choo Choo	1960	$40
❑ 4061	Humdinger/My Blue Heaven	1960	$20
❑ 4061 [PS]	Humdinger/My Blue Heaven	1960	$40
❑ 4122	If You Were a Rock and Roll Record/The Truth, Ruth	1962	$20
❑ 4066	Muskrat Ramble/ Two Thousand-88	1961	$20
❑ 4066 [PS]	Muskrat Ramble/ Two Thousand-88	1961	$40
❑ 4038	Okefenokee/Kookie Hat	1959	$30
❑ 4106	Palisades Park/June, July and August	1962	$20
❑ 4139	Patty Baby/Betty Jean	1963	$15
❑ 4031	Tallahassee Lassie/You Know	1959	$30
❑ 4096	Teen Queen of the Week/Wild Guy	1962	$20
❑ 4078	Transistor Sister/Walk to the Moon	1961	$20
❑ 4078 [PS]	Transistor Sister/Walk to the Moon	1961	$40
❑ 4043	Way Down Yonder in New Orleans/Fractured	1959	$30
❑ 4043 [PS]	Way Down Yonder in New Orleans/Fractured	1959	$40
❑ 4168	What a Party/Sweet Georgia Brown	1964	$15
❑ 4117	What's Gonna Happen When Summer's Done/Broadway	1962	$20

WARNER BROS.

Number	Title	Yr	NM
❑ 7075	20th Century Fox/ Cincinnati Woman	1967	$30
❑ 5409	Abigail Beecher/All American Girl	1964	$15
❑ 5645	Action/Beachwood City	1965	$20
❑ 5876	A Happy Clown/In My Wildest Dreams	1966	$30
❑ 5666	Let Me Show You Where It's At/The Old Rag Man	1965	$15
❑ 5487	Little Autograph Seeker/Too Much Monkey Business	1964	$15
❑ 5615	Little Miss A-Go-Go/In the Night	1965	$15
❑ 5615 [PS]	Little Miss A-Go-Go/In the Night	1965	$30
❑ 7019	Maverick's Flat/Run to the Poet Man	1967	$30
❑ 5434	OK Wheeler, The Used Car Dealer/Odie Cologne	1964	$15
❑ 5673	She's Something Else/ Little Bitty Corrine	1965	$15
❑ 5448	Summertime U.S.A./Gotta Good Thing Goin'	1964	$15
❑ 5693	The Dedication Song/ Come On, Come On	1966	$15
❑ 5810	The Greatest Show on Earth/Hokie Pokie Girl	1966	$15
❑ 5832	The Laughing Song/Natalie	1966	$15

WE MAKE ROCK & ROLL

Number	Title	Yr	NM
❑ 1604	Sea Cruise/She's a Friday Night Fox	1968	$6

CANNON, JACKIE

CHAN

Number	Title	Yr	NM
❑ 103	Proof of Your Love/Chill Bumps	1961	$50

CHESS

Number	Title	Yr	NM
❑ 1807	Proof of Your Love/Chill Bumps	1961	$20

CANNONS, THE

COMPLEAT

Number	Title	Yr	NM
❑ 105	All Things Made New Again/Watch My Lips	1983	$5
❑ 116	One Step Closer/Strangers Again	1983	$5

MERCURY

Number	Title	Yr	NM
❑ 888869-7	Bet Your Heart (On a Sure Thing)/I'll Save My Love for You	1987	$3
❑ 888048-7	Do You Mind If I Step Into Your Dreams/How Can I Love Now	1986	$3
❑ 888048-7 [PS]	Do You Mind If I Step Into Your Dreams/How Can I Love Now	1986	$4
❑ 888548-7	Love'll Come Looking for You/I'll Save My Love for You	1987	$3

CANO, EDDIE

DUNHILL

Number	Title	Yr	NM
❑ 4075	Amy's Theme/La Bamba	1967	$6
❑ 4072	Monday, Monday/Slip Slip	1967	$6

GNP CRESCENDO

Number	Title	Yr	NM
❑ 172	La Casita/Hava Nagilah	1962	$8
❑ 187	Line for Lyons/Tin Tin Deo	1962	$8

REPRISE

Number	Title	Yr	NM
❑ 20075	A Taste of Honey/Panchita	1962	$8
❑ 20113	Barsonova Brown/Greenfields	1962	$8
❑ 0237	Danke Schoen/Our Day Will Come	1963	$8
❑ 20147	Days of Wine and Roses/ Our Day Will Come	1963	$8
❑ 0382	Tortilla Flats (Part 1)/ Tortilla Flats (Part 2)	1965	$8
❑ 0254	What Now My Love/Theme from Snow Angel	1963	$8

CANTINA BAND, THE

MILLENIUM

Number	Title	Yr	NM
❑ YB-11818	Summer '81 Medley/ Out in California	1981	$8

CANTRELL, LANA

POLYDOR

Number	Title	Yr	NM
❑ 14261	Like a Sunday Morning/ Good Times	1974	$4

RCA VICTOR

Number	Title	Yr	NM
❑ 74-0173	All the Things You Are/If I Say No	1969	$6
❑ 47-8978	Breakfast at Tiffany's/ Since I Fell for You	1966	$6
❑ 47-9089	Confession/Theme from The Sand Pebbles	1967	$6
❑ 74-0268	I Let the Moment Slip By/ Tomorrow Is the First Day of the Rest of My Life	1969	$6
❑ 47-9391	On the Good Ship Lollipop/ When You Wish Upon a Star	1967	$6
❑ 47-9205	Sunshine/How Can I Hurt You	1967	$6
❑ 47-9619	The Good Times We Had/ Catch the Wind	1968	$6
❑ 47-9526	The Music Played/ Just a Little Lovin'	1968	$6

CANYON

16TH AVENUE

Number	Title	Yr	NM
❑ 70433	Hot Nights/Oh, Help Me	1989	$4
❑ 70419	I Guess I Just Missed You/Love Wins	1988	$4
❑ 70415	In the Middle of the Night/Overdue	1988	$4
❑ 70423	Love Is on the Line/Love Wins	1988	$4
❑ 70410	Overdue/In the Middle of the Night	1988	$4

CAP-TANS, THE

ANNA

Number	Title	Yr	NM
❑ 1122	I'm Afraid/Tight Skirts and Crazy Sweaters	1960	$40

CORAL

Number	Title	Yr	NM
❑ 65071	Asking/Who Can I Turn To	1951	$300

DOT

Number	Title	Yr	NM
❑ 15114	I'm So Crazy for Love/ With All My Love	1953	$125

GOTHAM

Number	Title	Yr	NM
❑ 268	I Thought I Could Forget You/ Waiting at the Station	1951	$300
❑ 233	My, My, My, Ain't She Pretty/ Never Be Lonely	1950	$400

CAPALDI, JIM

ATLANTIC

Number	Title	Yr	NM
❑ 89625	I'll Keep Holding On/ Tales of Power	1984	$4
❑ 89799	Living on the Edge/Gifts of Unknown Things	1983	$3
❑ 89849	That's Love/Runaway	1983	$3
❑ 89849 [PS]	That's Love/Runaway	1983	$4
❑ 89783 [DJ]	Tonight You're Mine (same on both sides)	1983	$4

— May be promo only

ISLAND

Number	Title	Yr	NM
❑ 1204	Eve/Going Down Slow All the Way	1972	$6
❑ 055	Goodbye Love/(B-side unknown)	1976	$4
❑ 067	Goodnight and Good Morning/ Short Cut Draw Blood	1976	$4
❑ 003	It's All Right/Whale Meat Again	1974	$5
❑ 025	It's All Up to You/I've Got So Much Lovin'	1975	$5
❑ 045	Love Hurts/Sugar Honey	1976	$4
❑ 1205	Oh How We Danced/ Open Your Heart	1972	$6
❑ 99220	Some Came Running/ Favela Music	1989	$3
❑ 99220 [PS]	Some Came Running/ Favela Music	1989	$3
❑ 99266	Something So Strong/ Child in the Storm	1988	$3
❑ 99266 [PS]	Something So Strong/ Child in the Storm	1988	$3
❑ 1216	Tricky Dicky Rides Again/ Love Is All You Can Try	1973	$5

RSO

Number	Title	Yr	NM
❑ 912	Daughter of the Night/I'm Gonna Do It	1978	$4

CAPEHART, JERRY

CASH

Number	Title	Yr	NM
❑ 1021	Walkin' Stick Boogie/Rollin'	1956	$200

— With Eddie and Hank Cochran

CREST

Number	Title	Yr	NM
❑ 1101	Song of New Orleans/The Young and Blue (Theme)	1962	$60

CAPERS, THE

VEE JAY

Number	Title	Yr	NM
❑ 315	Candy Store Blues/ High School Diploma	1959	$30
❑ 297	Miss You My Dear/ Early One Morning	1958	$30

CAPITAL CITY ROCKETS

Featuring Eric Moore of THE GODZ.

ELEKTRA

Number	Title	Yr	NM
❑ 45855	Breakfast in Bed/Grab Your Honey	1973	$10
❑ 45872	Little Bit O' Fun/Ten Hole Dollars	1973	$12

Number	Title	Yr	NM

CAPITALS, THE
RIDGETOP
Number	Title	Yr	NM
❏ 01080	A Little Ground in Texas/Bridge Over Broadway	1980	$5
❏ 01281	Bridge Over Broadway/Love Him Out of Your Mind	1981	$5
❏ 00779	Me Touchin' You/If I Was Still Sinnin'	1979	$5

CAPITOL SYMPHONY BAND
CAPITOL
| ❏ F984 | Sleigh Ride/Syncopated Clock | 1949 | $20 |

CAPITOLS, THE (1)
KAREN
❏ 1537	Cool Jerk '68/Afro Twist	1968	$10
❏ 1524	Cool Jerk/Hello Stranger	1968	$20
❏ 1536	Cool Pearl/Don't Say Maybe Baby	1967	$12
❏ 1525	I Got to Handle It/Zig Zagging	1966	$10
❏ 1549	I Thought She Loved Me/When You're in Trouble	1969	$10
❏ 1534	Patty Cake/Take a Chance on Me Baby	1967	$10
❏ 1543	Soul Brother, Soul Sister/Ain't That Terrible	1968	$12
❏ 1546	Soul Soul/When You're in Trouble	1969	$12
❏ 1526	We Got a Thing That's In the Groove/Tired Running from You	1966	$10

CAPITOLS, THE (2)
CARLTON
| ❏ 461 | I Let Her Go/I've Got a Girl | 1958 | $600 |

CAPITOLS, THE (U)
GATEWAY
| ❏ 721 | Day By Day/Little Things | 1964 | $300 |
PET
| ❏ 807 | Angel of Love/'Cause I Love You | 1958 | $200 |
TRIUMPH
| ❏ 601 | Three O'Clock Rock/Write Me a Love Letter | 1959 | $40 |

CAPONE, SUSAN
PILGRIM
| ❏ 718 | Click-I-Dee, Click-I-Dee/Maybe Someday | 1956 | $30 |
| ❏ 704 | I'll Be Dancing/Four or Five Hundred Kisses | 1956 | $30 |

CAPRA, RENO
UNITED ARTISTS
| ❏ 50242 | Winter Song/Sancta Maria | 1967 | $8 |

CAPRIS, THE (1)
AMBIENT SOUND
| ❏ ZS5-02697 | There's a Moon Out Again/Morse Code of Love | 1982 | $6 |
LIFETIME
❏ 1001/2	Oh My Darling/Rock Pretty Baby	1961	$125
❏ 101	There's a Moon Out Tonight/Indian Girl	1961	$75
—Pink label original; black vinyl			
❏ 101	There's a Moon Out Tonight/Indian Girl	1961	$200
—Pink label original; red vinyl			
MR. PEEKE
| ❏ 118 | Limbo/From the Vine Came the Grape | 1963 | $30 |
OLD TOWN
❏ 1107	Girl in My Dreams/My Island in the Sun	1961	$40
❏ 1103	Tears in My Eyes/Why Do I Cry	1961	$40
❏ 1094	There's a Moon Out Tonight/Indian Girl	1961	$40
—Light blue label			
❏ 1094	There's a Moon Out Tonight/Indian Girl	1962	$30
—Mostly black label			
❏ 1099	Where I Fell in Love/Some People Think	1961	$40
PLANET
| ❏ 1010 | There's a Moon Out Tonight/Indian Girl | 1958 | $1200 |
SABRE
| ❏ 201/2 | My Promise to You/Bop! Bop! Bop! | 1959 | $200 |
TROMMERS
❏ 101	There's a Moon Out Tonight/Indian Girl	1961	$30
—Red label			
❏ 101	There's a Moon Out Tonight/Indian Girl	1961	$30
—White label (not a promo)			

CAPRIS, THE (2)
| ❏ 1201 | My Weakness/Yes, My Baby, Please! | 1957 | $70 |
GOTHAM
❏ 304	God Only Knows/That's What You're Doing to Me	1954	$600
—Blue label			
❏ 304	God Only Knows/That's What You're Doing to Me	1954	$120
—Red label			
❏ 304	God Only Knows/That's What You're Doing to Me	1956	$100
— Yellow label			
❏ 308	It's a Miracle/Let's Linger Awhile	1956	$120
❏ 306	It Was Moonglow/Too Poor to Love	1955	$200

CAPTAIN AND TENNILLE
A&M
❏ 1912	Can't Stop Dancin'/Mis Canciones (The Good Songs)	1977	$4
❏ 1912 [PS]	Can't Stop Dancin'/Mis Canciones (The Good Songs)	1977	$6
❏ 1970	Circles/1954 Boogie Blues	1977	$4
❏ 1944	Come In from the Rain/We Never Really Said Goodbye	1977	$4
❏ 1944 [PS]	Come In from the Rain/We Never Really Said Goodbye	1977	$6
❏ 1774	Como Yo Quiero Sentorte (The Way I Want to Touch You)/El Rebote de Broddy	1975	$8
❏ 2027	I'm On My Way/We Never Really Said Goodbye	1978	$4
❏ 2027 [PS]	I'm On My Way/We Never Really Said Goodbye	1978	$6
❏ 8600 [PS]	Lonely Night (Angel Face)/Shop Around	1977	$6
❏ 8600	Lonely Night (Angel Face)/Shop Around	1977	$4
—A&M Forget Me Nots" series; green and yellow labels			
❏ 1782	Lonely Night (Angel Face)/Smile for Me One More Time	1976	$4
❏ 1782 [PS]	Lonely Night (Angel Face)/Smile for Me One More Time	1976	$6
❏ 1672	Love Will Keep Us Together/Gentle Stranger	1975	$4
❏ 1672 [PS]	Love Will Keep Us Together/Gentle Stranger	1975	$6
❏ 1870	Muskrat Love/Honey Come Love Me	1976	$4
❏ 1870 [PS]	Muskrat Love/Honey Come Love Me	1976	$6
❏ 1715	Por Amor Vivremos (Love Will Keep Us Together)/Broddy Bounce	1975	$5
❏ 1817	Shop Around/Butterscotch Castle	1976	$4
❏ 1817 [PS]	Shop Around/Butterscotch Castle	1976	$6
❏ 8601	Song of Joy/Wedding Song (There Is Love)	1977	$4
—A&M Forget Me Nots" series; green and yellow labels			
❏ 8601 [PS]	Song of Joy/Wedding Song (There Is Love)	1977	$6
❏ 1725	The Way I Want to Touch You/Broddy Bounce	1975	$4
❏ 1725 [PS]	The Way I Want to Touch You/Broddy Bounce	1975	$6
❏ 1624	The Way I Want to Touch You/Disney Girls	1974	$6
BUTTERSCOTCH CASTLE
| ❏ 01 | The Way I Want to Touch You/Disney Girls | 1974 | $100 |
CASABLANCA
❏ 2247	Amame Una Vez Mas (Do That To Me One More Time)/Deep in the Dark	1980	$8
❏ 2328	Don't Forget Me/Keep Our Love Warm	1981	$4
❏ 2215	Do That To Me One More Time/Deep in the Dark	1979	$4
❏ 2264	Happy Together (A Fantasy)/Baby You Still Got It	1980	$4
❏ 2243	Love on a Shoestring/How Can You Be So Cold	1980	$4
❏ 2320	This Is Not the First Time/Gentle Stranger	1980	$4
JOYCE
| ❏ 101 | The Way I Want to Tocuh You/Disney Girls | 1974 | $50 |

CAPTAIN BEEFHEART
Also see FRANK ZAPPA.
A&M
| ❏ 794 | Diddy Wah Diddy/Who Do You Think You're Fooling | 1966 | $50 |
| ❏ 818 | Moonchild/Here I Am, Here I Always Am | 1966 | $60 |
BUDDAH
| ❏ 108 | Plastic Factory/Where There's Woman | 1969 | $20 |
MERCURY
| ❏ 73494 | I Got Love on My Mind/Upon the My-O-My | 1974 | $15 |

REPRISE
❏ 1068	Click Clack/I'm Gonna Boogalize You Baby	1972	$20
❏ PRO547 [DJ]	Too Much Time/Low Yo Yo Stuff	1973	$30
❏ PRO547 [PS]	Too Much Time/Low Yo Yo Stuff	1973	$50
—Gatefold cardboard sleeve			
❏ 1133	Too Much Time/My Head Is My Only House Unless It Rains	1972	$20
VIRGIN/EPIC
| ❏ 14-03190 | Ice Cream for Crow/Light Reflected Off the Oceans of the Moon | 1982 | $10 |
| ❏ 14-03190 [PS] | Ice Cream for Crow/Light Reflected Off the Oceans of the Moon | 1982 | $20 |

CAPTAIN SKY
AVI
❏ 273	Dr. Rock/Saturday Night Move-Ease	1979	$8
❏ 299	Moon Child/Fearless (In the Pocket)	1979	$8
❏ 225	Wonder Worm/Saturday Night Move-Ease	1978	$8
TEC
| ❏ 768 | Sir Jam a Lot/Elementry School of Funk | 1980 | $6 |

CAPTAIN STUBBY
DECCA
❏ 9-46282	At the Rainbow's End/You Never Say I Love You	1951	$30
❏ 9-46265	Beautiful Morning Glory/Hilegged Hilegged	1950	$40
❏ 9-46315	Bogle to Boogle to Boone/The Hokey Pokey	1951	$30
❏ 9-46371	It's Hard to Be Loved/I Was the Last One to Know	1951	$30
❏ 9-46321	The Gentle Carpenter of Bethlehem/God Put a Rainbow	1951	$30
❏ 9-46384	The Girl in the Gilded Picture Frame/Every Time I Want	1951	$30

CAPTAIN ZAP AND THE MOTORTOWN CUT-UPS
MOTOWN
| ❏ 1151 | The Luney Landing/The Luney Take-Off | 1969 | $30 |

CARA, IRENE
CASABLANCA
| ❏ 811440-7 | Flashdance... What a Feeling/Love Theme from Flashdance | 1983 | $4 |
| —B-side by Helen St. John | | | |
ELEKTRA
| ❏ 69486 | Girlfriends/Dying for Your Love | 1987 | $3 |
GEFFEN
❏ 29328	Breakdance/Cue Me Up	1984	$4
❏ 29396	The Dream (Hold On to Your Dream)/Receiving	1983	$4
❏ 29464	Why Me?/Talk Too Much	1983	$4
❏ 29464 [PS]	Why Me?/Talk Too Much	1983	$4
NETWORK
| ❏ 47950 | Anyone Can See/Why | 1981 | $4 |
| ❏ 48011 | My Baby (He's Something Else)/Slow Down | 1982 | $4 |
RSO
❏ 1034	Fame/Never Alone	1980	$4
❏ 1048	Out Here On My Own (Piano Vocal)/(Orchestral Vocal)	1980	$5
—Tan label			
❏ 1048	Out Here On My Own (Piano Vocal)/(Orchestral Vocal)	1980	$4
—Silver label			

CARAVAN
LONDON
| ❏ 20080 | Headloss/(B-side unknown) | 1973 | $6 |
| ❏ 20065 | Love to Love You/Golf Girl | 1971 | $6 |
VERVE FORECAST
| ❏ 5102 | A Place of My Own/Ride | 1969 | $10 |

CARAVELLES, THE (1)
SMASH
| ❏ 1869 | Have You Ever Been Lonely/Don't Blow Your Cool | 1964 | $15 |
| ❏ 1958 | I Don't Care If the Sun Don't Shine/I Like a Man | 1964 | $15 |

CARAVELLES, THE (U)
JOEY
| ❏ 301 | Falling for You/Shake Baby | 1963 | $200 |
| ❏ 6208 | One Little Kiss/Twistin' Marie | 1962 | $125 |
STARMAKER
| ❏ 1925 | Pink Lips/Angry Angel | 1961 | $30 |

Number	Title	Yr	NM
CARAY, HARRY			
CHURCHILL			
❑ 7714	Take Me Out to the Ball Game/Na Na, Hey Hey (Kiss Him Goodbye)	1978	$10
CARBO, CHIC			
REVUE			
❑ 11019	Touch Me/Biggest Fool in Town	1968	$30
CARBO, CHUCK			
ACE			
❑ 666	Out on a Limb/Getting Out	1962	$15
❑ 631	Tears, Tears and More Tears/I Shouldn't, But I Do	1961	$15
IMPERIAL			
❑ 5423	Honey Bee/That's My Desire	1957	$40
❑ 5479	I Miss You/The Times	1957	$30
❑ 5405	That's the Way to Win My Heart/Goodbye	1956	$30
❑ 5452	The Bells Are Ringing/Poor Boy	1957	$30
INSTANT			
❑ 3240	In the Night/Run. Henry	1962	$15
❑ 3254	Two Tables Away/ What Does It Take	1962	$15
REX			
❑ 1012	Blue Velvet/It's You	1960	$20
❑ 1011	Lucy Brown/A Picture of You	1960	$20
❑ 1003	Promises/Be My Girl	1959	$20
CARDBOARD ZEPPELIN			
LAURIE			
❑ 3433	City Lights/Ten Story Building	1968	$30
CARDINALS, THE (1)			
ATLANTIC			
❑ 1090	Choo Choo/Off Shore	1956	$60
❑ 1067	Come Back My Love/ Two Things I Love	1955	$125
❑ 952	I'll Always Love You/ Pretty Baby Blues	1952	$400
— Cardinals records on Atlantic before 952 are unconfirmed on 45 rpm			
❑ 1079	Lovely Girl/There Goes My Heart to You	1955	$125
❑ 1025	Please Baby/Under a Blanket of Blue	1954	$200
❑ 972	The Bump/She Rocks	1952	$300
❑ 1054	The Door Is Still Open/Misirlou	1955	$100
❑ 1103	The End of the Story/I Won't Make You Cry Anymore	1956	$60
❑ 958	Wheel of Fortune/Kiss Me Baby	1952	$600
CARDINALS, THE (2)			
CHA CHA			
❑ 741	Go Go Baby/Hatchet Face	1966	$30
❑ 740	I Want You/Tomato Juice	1966	$40
❑ 740 [PS]	I Want You/Tomato Juice	1966	$60
❑ 742	Saturday Night/I'm Gonna Tell on You	1966	$30
❑ 748	When You're Away/I'm Gonna Tell on You	1966	$30
CARDINI, GEORGE			
SKYWAY			
❑ 110	Season's Greetings "A Cheerful Hello"/Christmas Kisses	1957	$20
CARDWELL, JACK			
KING			
❑ 1203	Can I/Lonesome Midnight	1953	$30
❑ 1269	Dear Joan/You're Looking for Something	1953	$40
❑ 1339	Diddle Diddle Dumpling/Blue Cave	1954	$30
❑ 1292	I Can't Make Up My Mind/ Walking My Blues Away	1953	$30
❑ 1262	I'm Gonna Write a Song/A Vitamin Called Love	1953	$30
❑ 1241	I'm Not Lazy, I'm Just Tired/ Stop Laughing at Me	1953	$30
❑ 1172	The Death of Hank Williams/Two Arms	1953	$40
❑ 1454	Whadya/Day Done Broke Too Soon	1955	$30
❑ 1357	Whiskey, Women and Loaded Dice/Slap-Ka-Dab	1954	$30
❑ 1381	Will Our Love Fade and Die/ There's a Train Leaving	1954	$30
SANDY			
❑ 1023	All Alone/Blue Lifetime	1959	$20
STARDAY			
❑ 310	Hey, Hey Baby/Once Every Day	1957	$200
CARE PACKAGE			
JUBILEE			
❑ 5599	To Discover/World of Thursday	1967	$10

Number	Title	Yr	NM
CAREFREES, THE			
LONDON INT'L.			
❑ 10615	Paddy Whack/Aren't You Glad You're You	1964	$20
❑ 10614	We Love You Beatles/ Hot Blooded Lover	1964	$30
—Red label			
❑ 10614	We Love You Beatles/ Hot Blooded Lover	1964	$30
—Gold label			
❑ 10614 [PS]	We Love You Beatles/ Hot Blooded Lover	1964	$50
CARETAKERS, THE			
ABC			
❑ 11110	Get Off My Tulips/Bee Side Blues	1968	$15
CARGILL, HENSON			
ARCO			
❑ 6605	Big Town/How Long Is Never	1967	$8
ATLANTIC			
❑ 4016	She Still Comes to Me (To Pour the Wine)/But You Know I Love You	1974	$4
❑ 4007	Some Old California Memory/A Writer of Verses and a Singer of Songs	1973	$4
❑ 4021	Stop and Smell the Roses/ Strawberry Wine	1974	$4
COPPER MOUNTAIN			
❑ 589	Have a Good Day/ (B-side unknown)	1980	$4
❑ 201	Silence on the Line/ Forever in Blue Jeans	1979	$4
ELEKTRA			
❑ 45234	Deep in the Heart of Dixie/ It Hurts the Man	1975	$4
❑ 45273	Something to Hold On To/Now and Then	1975	$4
MEGA			
❑ 0060	I Can't Face the Bed Alone/ Daddy Don't You Walk So Fast	1972	$5
❑ 0074	Oklahoma Hell/She Likes Warm Summer Days	1972	$5
❑ 0030	Pencil Marks on the Wall/ Momma's Waiting	1971	$5
MONUMENT			
❑ 1106	A Candle for Amy/Wild Flower	1968	$6
❑ 1209	Bless 'Em All/How Much Do Mommies Cost?	1970	$6
❑ 1184	Me & Bobby McGee/ What's My Name	1970	$6
❑ 1084	She Thinks I'm On That Train/It Just Don't Take Me Long to Say Goodbye	1968	$6
❑ 1178	Silver Bells/The Little Drummer Boy	1969	$8
❑ 1041	Skip a Rope/Very Well Traveled Man	1967	$6
❑ 1198	The Most Uncomplicated Goodbye I've Ever Heard/ Four Shades of Love	1970	$6
❑ 1158	Then the Baby Came/Hemphill, Kentucky, Consolidated Coal Mine	1969	$6
❑ 1142	This Generation Shall Not Pass/ Little Girls and Little Boys	1969	$6
TOWER			
❑ 400	Picking White Cotton/ Joe, Jesse and I	1968	$8
CARIANS, THE			
INDIGO			
❑ 136	She's Gone/Snooty Friends	1961	$125
MAGENTA			
❑ 04	Only a Dream/Girls	1961	$60
CARLE, BOBBY, AND THE BLENDAIRES			
DECCA			
❑ 30938	I Got It Bad and That Ain't Good/Guaranteed	1959	$40
CARLE, FRANKIE			
❑ LPC-106	(contents unknown)	1961	$10
—Compact 33 Double"; small hole, plays at 33 1/3 rpm			
❑ LPC-106 [PS]	The Golden Touch	1961	$12
CARLILE, TOM			
COLUMBIA			
❑ 4-44372	I Saw the Light/Nightingale	1967	$10
DOOR KNOB			
❑ 180	Back in Debbie's Arms/ Twenty Years Ago	1982	$5
❑ 180 [PS]	Back in Debbie's Arms/ Twenty Years Ago	1982	$8
❑ 167	Catch Me If You Can/ Get It While You Can	1981	$5
❑ 167 [PS]	Catch Me If You Can/ Get It While You Can	1981	$8
❑ 172	Feel/Walk Around the Block, Deanna	1981	$5

Number	Title	Yr	NM
❑ 172 [PS]	Feel/Walk Around the Block, Deanna	1981	$8
❑ 162	Get It While You Can/ M.D. 20/20 High	1981	$5
❑ 157	Gold Cadillac/Lay Down Sally	1981	$5
❑ 187	Green Eyes/No One to Tell My Heartache To	1982	$5
❑ 187 [PS]	Green Eyes/No One to Tell My Heartache To	1982	$8
❑ 176	Hurtin' for Your Love/The Man Who Loved to Drink	1982	$5
❑ 176 [PS]	Hurtin' for Your Love/The Man Who Loved to Drink	1982	$8
❑ 170	Lover (Right Where I Want You)/ Walk Around the Block, Deanna	1981	$5
❑ 170 [PS]	Lover (Right Where I Want You)/ Walk Around the Block, Deanna	1981	$8
CARLIN, GEORGE			
LITTLE DAVID			
❑ 720	Eleven O'Clock News (Part 1)/ Eleven O'Clock News (Part 2)	1971	$6
❑ 736	Head Lines (Part 1)/ Head Lines (Part 2)	1977	$6
RCA VICTOR			
❑ 47-9110	Winderful WINO/Al Sleet, Your Hippy Dippy Weatherman	1967	$10
7-Inch Extended Plays			
ATLANTIC			
❑ EP-PR-409 [DJ]	*Have a Nice Day/Rice Krispies/Second, Third, Fifth, Sixth Announcements/Join the Book Club/Ice Box Man	1981	$10
❑ EP-PR-409 [PS]	A Place for My Stuff	1981	$15
CARLISLE, BELINDA			
I.R.S.			
❑ 52889	I Feel the Magic/From the Heart	1986	$4
❑ 52889 [PS]	I Feel the Magic/From the Heart	1986	$4
❑ 52815	Mad About You/I Never Wanted a Rich Man	1986	$3
❑ 52815 [PS]	Mad About You/I Never Wanted a Rich Man	1986	$3
❑ S45-17262 [PS]	Since You've Gone	1987	$8
❑ S45-17262 [DJ]	Since You've Gone (same on both sides)	1987	$8
MCA			
❑ 53308	Circle in the Sand/We Can Change	1988	$3
❑ 53308 [PS]	Circle in the Sand/We Can Change	1988	$3
❑ 53181	Heaven Is a Place on Earth/ We Can Change	1987	$3
❑ 53181 [PS]	Heaven Is a Place on Earth/ We Can Change	1987	$3
❑ 53377	I Feel Free/Should I Let You In?	1988	$4
❑ 53377 [PS]	I Feel Free/Should I Let You In?	1988	$4
❑ 53242	I Get Weak/Should I Let You In?	1987	$3
❑ 53242 [PS]	I Get Weak/Should I Let You In?	1987	$3
❑ 53706	Leave a Light On/Shades of Michelangelo	1989	$6
—A-side features a guitar solo by George Harrison			
❑ 53783	Summer Rain/Shades of Michelangelo	1989	$3
CARLISLE, BILL			
CHART			
❑ 5117	Can't Get Enough/ (B-side unknown)	1971	$8
❑ 5092	Daddy Won the War on Poverty/Too Many Dollars, Not Enough Sense	1970	$8
❑ 5065	Dirty Old Mine/Big Wheel from Boston	1970	$8
❑ 5044	I'm Movin'/Everything Will Be Alright	1969	$8
COLUMBIA			
❑ 4-41679	Air Brakes/Home Sweet Home	1960	$15
❑ 4-42609	Hand Me Down My Walking Cane/ It Takes All Kinds to Make a World	1962	$12
❑ 4-42049	Too Old to Cut the Mustard/ Have a Drink on Me	1961	$10
❑ 4-42263	Woman Driver/Monkey Business	1962	$10
HICKORY			
❑ 1502	All of This for Sally/ My Name Is Jones	1968	$8
❑ 1254	Big John Henry's Girl/ Shanghai Rooster	1964	$8
❑ 1518	Do You Love Me, Honey/ Don't Hit My Friend	1968	$8
❑ 1418	If It Were You Instead of Me (What Would You Do)/Doctor R.D.	1966	$8
❑ 1383	Take This Country Music and Shove It/No Help Wanted	1966	$8
❑ 1280	The Great Snow Man/Before She Knows I'm Gone	1964	$8
❑ 1483	Th' Wife/Wouldn't Take Your Pistol	1967	$8
❑ 1348	What Kinda Deal Is This/Shot Gun	1965	$8
RCA VICTOR			
❑ 47-7214	Dumb Bunny/Who's-a Gonna Stop Me	1958	$20
❑ 47-7132	The Tiny Space Man/ How Will I Know	1958	$30
VANGUARD			
❑ 35165	I Wanna Be a Country Singer/ That's What I Shoulda Said	1972	$8

Number	Title	Yr	NM

CARLISLE BROTHERS, THE
KING

Number	Title	Yr	NM
❑ 5714	Empty Arms/Rainbow at Midnight	1963	$15

MERCURY

❑ 70951	A Poor Man's Riches/Rainbow at Midnight	1956	$20
❑ 70604	Bargain Day, Half Off/Nine Have Tried	1955	$30
❑ 70484	Busy Body Boogie/The Mainest Thing	1954	$30
❑ 70754	Dangerous Crossing/Run, Boy	1955	$30
❑ 70435	Honey Love/Female Hercules	1954	$30
❑ 70306	I'll Never Love Again/I Need a Little Help	1954	$30
❑ 71035	I'm Rough Stuff/Business Man	1957	$20
❑ 70174	Is Zat You, Myrtle/Something Different	1953	$30
❑ 70544	It's Bedtime Bill/Rusty Old Hale	1955	$30
❑ 6371	I Would If I Could/Patch Up Your Old Love Affair	1952	$40
❑ 70665	Lil' Liza Jane/Teletouch	1955	$30
❑ 6403	Love, Love, Love/Woman Driver	1952	$30
❑ 70712	Middle Age Spread/On My Way to the Show	1955	$30
❑ 70828	Pickin' Peas/Goo-Goo Da Da	1956	$20
❑ 70351	Shake-A-Leg/Let Me Hold Your Little Hand	1954	$30
❑ 70232	Tain't Nice (To Talk Like That)/Unpucker	1953	$30
❑ 6388	Tennessee Memories/True Love	1952	$40
❑ 6348	Too Old to Cut the Mustard/My Happiness Belongs to Someone Else	1951	$40
❑ 71110	Wouldn't You Like To/Ladder of Love	1957	$20

CARLLILE, KATHY
FRONTLINE

| ❑ 705 | Stay Until the Rain Stops/In Front of the Line | 1980 | $6 |
| ❑ 705 [PS] | Stay Until the Rain Stops/In Front of the Line | 1980 | $8 |

CARLO
LAURIE

❑ 3151	Baby Doll/Write Me a Letter	1962	$40
❑ 3175	Five Minutes More/The Story of Love	1963	$40
❑ 3063	Happy Time/Rockin' Rocket	1960	$30
—As "Carlo and Jimmy"			
❑ 3157	Little Orphan Girl/Mairzy Doats	1963	$40

RAFTIS

| ❑ 110 | Claudine/Fever | 1970 | $15 |

CARLOS, WALTER
COLUMBIA

❑ 8-3322 [PS]	A Second Chance for Bach!	1969	$30
—Promo-only sleeve that came with JZSP 139195/6			
❑ 44803	Brandenberg Concerto No. 3 in G Major/Two-Part Invention in F Major	1969	$10
❑ JZSP139195/6 [DJ]	Third Movement, Brandenburg Concerto No. 3 (mono/stereo)	1969	$15
❑ 45033	Third Movement, Brandenburg Concerto No. 4 in D Major/Scarliotta Sonata	1969	$10

CARLSON, PAULETTE
RCA

❑ PB-13745	Can You Fool/I Go to Pieces	1984	$4
❑ JK-13745 [DJ]	Can You Fool (same on both sides)	1984	$10
—Promo only on yellow vinyl			
❑ JK-13599 [DJ]	I'd Say Yes (same on both sides)	1983	$10
—Promo only on yellow vinyl			
❑ PB-13599	I'd Say Yes/Sweeten the Love	1983	$4

CARLTON, CARL
20TH CENTURY

❑ 2601	I Think It's Gonna Be Alright/Let Me Love You Till the Morning Comes	1982	$4
❑ 2513	Let Me Love You Till the Morning Comes/Sexy Lady	1982	$4
❑ 2488	She's a Bad Mama Jama (She's Built, She's Stacked)/This Feeling's Rated X-Tra	1981	$4
❑ 2459	This Feeling's Rated X-Tra/Fighting in the Name of Love	1980	$4

ABC

❑ 12166	Ain't Gonna Tell Nobody (About You)/Live for Today, Not for Tomorrow	1976	$5
❑ 12226	Let's Groove/Live for Today, Not for Tomorrow	1976	$5
❑ 12089	Morning, Noon and Nightime/Our Day Will Come	1975	$5
❑ 12059	Smokin' Room/Signed, Sealed, Delivered, I'm Yours	1974	$5

BACK BEAT

Number	Title	Yr	NM
❑ 598	46 Drums -- 1 Guitar/Why Don't They Leave Us Alone	1968	$6
—As "Little Carl Carlton"			
❑ 588	Competition Ain't Nothin'/Three Way Love	1968	$40
—As "Little Carl Carlton"			
❑ 610	Don't Walk Away/Hold On a Little Longer	1969	$6
❑ 613	Drop By My Place/Two Timer	1970	$6
—As "Little Carl Carlton"			
❑ 630	Everlasting Love/I Wanna Be Your Main Squeeze	1974	$8
❑ 27001	Everlasting Love/I Wanna Be Your Main Squeeze	1974	$5
❑ 617	I Can Feel It/You've Got So Much (To Learn About Love)	1970	$6
❑ 629	It Ain't Been Easy/I Wanna Be Your Main Squeeze	1973	$6
❑ 627	I Won't Let That Chump Break Your Heart/Why Don't They Leave Us Alone	1972	$6
❑ 603	Look at Mary Wonder (How I Got Over)/Bad for Each Other	1969	$6
—As "Little Carl Carlton"			
❑ 619	Sure Miss Loving You/Wild Child	1970	$6
❑ 624	The Generation Gap/Where Have You Been	1972	$6
❑ 621	Wild Child/Look at Mary Wonder (How I Got Over)	1971	$6

CASABLANCA

| ❑ 880949-7 | Private Property/Mama's Boy | 1985 | $3 |
| ❑ 884274-7 | Slipped, Tripped (Fooled Around and Fell in Love)/Hot | 1986 | $3 |

LANDO

| ❑ 8527 | So What/(B-side unknown) | 1965 | $60 |

MERCURY

| ❑ 73969 | Something's Wrong/You, You | 1977 | $4 |

RCA

| ❑ PB-13313 | Baby I Need Your Loving/Everyone Can Be a Star | 1982 | $4 |
| ❑ PB-13406 | Swing That Sexy Thang/Just One Kiss | 1982 | $4 |

CARLTON, LARRY
BLUE THUMB

| ❑ 227 | An American Family/(B-side unknown) | 1973 | $8 |

MCA

❑ S45-17400 [DJ]	Hello Tomorrow (same on both sides)	1987	$6
❑ 53319	Minute by Minute/Hello Tomorrow	1987	$3
❑ 52844	Smiles and Smiles to Go/Carrying You	1986	$3
❑ 52844 [PS]	Smiles and Smiles to Go/Carrying You	1986	$3

UNI

| ❑ 55120 | Moon People/Son of a Preacher Man | 1969 | $8 |
| ❑ 55080 | The Odd Couple/Monday, Monday | 1968 | $10 |

WARNER BROS.

❑ 50019	Sleepwalk/Frenchman's Flat	1982	$4
❑ 29977	Song for Katie/10:00 P.M.	1982	$4
❑ 29590	Tequila/L.A., N.Y.	1983	$4

CARLYLE, RUSS
MERCURY

| ❑ 5760 | Santa Looks Like Daddy/Only You | 1951 | $20 |

CARMACK, HAROLD
DECCA

| ❑ 9-46362 | Down Yonder/Margie | 1951 | $30 |

CARMAN, JENKS (TEX)
CAPITOL

❑ F1822	Another Dream/Hilo March	1951	$30
❑ F2621	Blue Memories/The Caissons Go Rolling Along	1953	$30
❑ F2886	Dixie Cannon Ball/Indian Polka	1954	$30
❑ F2345	Hillbilly Hula/I'm a Poor Lonesome Fellow	1953	$30
❑ F2534	Locust Hill Rag/My Lonely Heart and I	1953	$30
❑ F2067	My Trusting Heart/Don't Feel Sorry for Me	1952	$30
❑ F2752	Samba Stomp/Sweet Luwanna	1954	$30
❑ F1571	Ten Thousand Miles/I Could Love You Baby	1951	$30

DECCA

❑ 9-28771	Hillbilly Hula/New Waikiki Beach	1953	$30
❑ 351	Fire in the Teepee/Learning to Do Without You	1962	$15
❑ 352	Maggie's Twist/I'll Go On Loving You	1962	$15
❑ 272	Wildwood Flower/Honk, Honk, Honk	1960	$15

CARMEL SISTERS, THE
COLPIX

Number	Title	Yr	NM
❑ 767	Go, Go, G.T.O./Sunny Winter	1965	$300
—As "Carol and Cheryl"			

CARMEN, ERIC
Also see CYRUS ERIE; THE QUICK; RASPBERRIES.
ARISTA

❑ 0165	All By Myself/Everything	1975	$4
❑ 0550	All for Love/Tonight You're Mine	1980	$4
❑ 0384	Baby I Need Your Lovin'/Heaven Can Wait	1979	$4
❑ 9736	Boats Against the Current/No Hard Feelings	1988	$3
❑ 0295	Boats Against the Current/Take It or Leave It	1977	$4
❑ 0354	Change of Heart/Hey Deanie	1978	$4
❑ 0435	Haven't We Come a Long Way/End of the World	1979	$4
❑ 0506	It Hurts Too Much/You Need Some Lovin'	1980	$4
❑ 9686	Make Me Lose Control/That's Rock 'N' Roll	1988	$3
❑ 9686 [PS]	Make Me Lose Control/That's Rock 'N' Roll	1988	$3
❑ 0319	Marathon Man/I Think I Found Myself	1978	$4
❑ 0266	She Did It/Someday	1977	$4
❑ 0266 [PS]	She Did It/Someday	1977	$6
❑ 0200	Sunrise/My Girl	1976	$4

GEFFEN

❑ 29032	I'm Through with Love/Maybe My Baby	1985	$3
❑ 29032 [PS]	I'm Through with Love/Maybe My Baby	1985	$3
❑ 29118	I Wanna Hear It from Your Lips/Spotlight	1985	$3
❑ 29118 [PS]	I Wanna Hear It from Your Lips/Spotlight	1985	$3

RCA

| ❑ 5315-7-R | Hungry Eyes/Where Are You Tonight | 1987 | $3 |

CARMICHAEL, BILL
HIT

❑ 45	It's Up to You/Tell Him	1962	$8
—B-side by Peggy Gaines			
❑ 38	Limbo Rock/Don't Hang Up	1962	$8
—B-side by the Dacrons			

CARMICHAEL, SANDY
HIT

| ❑ 35 | Don't Go Near the Indians/Return to Sender | 1962 | $8 |
| —B-side by Ed Hardin | | | |

CARNATIONS, THE
DERBY

| ❑ 789 | Tree in the Meadow/Clown of the Masquerade | 1952 | $400 |

ENRICA

| ❑ 1001 | Gimme, Gimme, Gimme/Love, Open My Heart | 1959 | $30 |

LAURIE

| ❑ 3163 | Punctuation/Funny Time | 1963 | $30 |

LESCAY

| ❑ 3002 | Long Tall Girl/Is There Such a World | 1961 | $125 |

SAVOY

| ❑ 1172 | Angels Sent You to Me/Night Time Is the Right Time | 1955 | $70 |

TERRY-TONE

| ❑ 199 | Barbary Coast/Sleepy Hollow | 1960 | $50 |

UNIVERSITY

| ❑ 606 | Leap Year/A Wing and a Prayer | 1960 | $30 |

CARNE, JUDY
REPRISE

| ❑ 0680 | Sock It To Me/Right, Said Fred | 1968 | $12 |

CARNES, JANIS
RCA

| ❑ PB-12104 | Smoky Places/Midnight Revival | 1980 | $5 |

CARNES, KIM
A&M

❑ 1807 [DJ]	Bad Seed (mono/stereo)	1976	$8
—No stock copies issued			
❑ 1943	Sailin'/He'll Come Home	1977	$5
❑ 1748	Somewhere in the Night/Hang On to Your Airplane (Honeymoon)	1975	$5
❑ 1902	The Last Thing You Ever Wanted to Do/Let Your Love Come Easy	1977	$5

Number	Title	Yr	NM

AMOS

Number	Title	Yr	NM
❏ 167	It's Love That Keeps It All Together/ Long and Lonely Memeories	1971	$8

— *With Dave Ellingson*

❏ 165	I Won't Call You Back/To Love	1971	$8
❏ 166	To Love Somebody/Fell in Love with a Poet	1971	$8

EMI AMERICA

❏ B-8281	Abadabadango/He Makes the Sun Rise (Orpheus)	1985	$3
❏ B-8281 [PS]	Abadabadango/He Makes the Sun Rise (Orpheus)	1985	$3
❏ 8077	Bette Davis Eyes/Miss You Tonight	1981	$4
❏ 8077 [PS]	Bette Davis Eyes/Miss You Tonight	1981	$4
❏ B-8267	Crazy in the Night (Barking at Airplanes)/Oliver (Voice on the Radio)	1985	$3
❏ B-8267 [PS]	Crazy in the Night (Barking at Airplanes)/Oliver (Voice on the Radio)	1985	$3
❏ 8058	Cry Like a Baby/In the Chill of the Night	1980	$4
❏ B-8322	Divided Hearts/You Say You Love Me (But I Know You Don't)	1986	$3
❏ B-8322 [PS]	Divided Hearts/You Say You Love Me (But I Know You Don't)	1986	$3
❏ B-8147	Does It Make You Remember/ Take It on the Chin	1982	$3
❏ B-8147 [PS]	Does It Make You Remember/ Take It on the Chin	1982	$3
❏ A-8087	Draw of the Cards/Break the Rules Tonite (Out of School)	1981	$4
❏ A-8087 [PS]	Draw of the Cards/Break the Rules Tonite (Out of School)	1981	$4
❏ B-8335	I'd Lie to You for Your Love/ Black and White	1986	$4
❏ B-8181	Invisible Hands/I'll Be Here Where the Heart Is	1983	$3
❏ B-8181 [PS]	Invisible Hands/I'll Be Here Where the Heart Is	1983	$3
❏ B-8250	Invitation to Dance/Breakthrough	1984	$3

— *B-side by Haven*

❏ B-8250 [PS]	Invitation to Dance/Breakthrough	1984	$3
❏ B-8202	I Pretend/Hurricane	1984	$3
❏ B-8202 [PS]	I Pretend/Hurricane	1984	$3
❏ 8011	It Hurts So Bad/Lookin' for a Big Night	1979	$5
❏ 8010	Losing Love/Looking for a Big Night	1979	$5
❏ 8069	Mas Amor/Changin'	1980	$8
❏ A-8098	Mistaken Identity/Jamaica Sunday Morning	1981	$4
❏ A-8098 [PS]	Mistaken Identity/Jamaica Sunday Morning	1981	$4
❏ 8045	More Love/Changin'	1980	$4
❏ 8045 [PS]	More Love/Changin'	1980	$6
❏ B-8154	Say You Don't Know Me/ Breakin' Away from Society	1983	$5
❏ 8014	What Am I Gonna Do/ Goodnight Moon	1979	$5

MCA

❏ 53433	Crazy in Love/Blood from the Bandit	1988	$3
❏ 53433 [PS]	Crazy in Love/Blood from the Bandit	1988	$4
❏ S45-17682 [DJ]	Crazy in Love/(New Version)	1988	$5
❏ 53494	Fantastic Fire of Love/ Brass and Batons	1989	$3
❏ 53387	Speed of the Sound of Loneliness/ Blood from the Bandit	1988	$3

CARNES, RICK AND JANIS

ELEKTRA

❏ 69928	Have You Heard/Blue, Only Blue	1982	$4

MCA

❏ 52414	Long Lost Causes/Standing in the Need of Love	1984	$4

WARNER BROS.

❏ 29448	Does He Ever Mention My Name/Silver Eagle	1983	$4
❏ 29656	Poor Girl/Am I Wastin' My Time	1983	$4

CARNEY, ART

COLUMBIA

❏ 40400	'Twas The Night Before Christmas/ Santa And The Doodle-Li-Boop	1954	$30

CARNIVAL

UNITED ARTISTS

❏ 50749	Where There's a Heartache (There Must Be a Heart)/ The Truth About It	1971	$5
❏ 50749 [PS]	Where There's a Heartache (There Must Be a Heart)/ The Truth About It	1971	$15

WORLD PACIFIC

❏ 77932	Laia Ladaia/Calito de Carnival	1969	$6

CARO, NYDIA

ROULETTE

❏ 4588	Ask Me What I Want for Christmas/Hey Johnny What	1964	$15
❏ 4588 [PS]	Ask Me What I Want for Christmas/Hey Johnny What	1964	$30

CAROL AND GERRI

MGM

❏ 13568	How Can I Ever Find the Way/ On You, Heartache Looks Good	1966	$50

CAROL, LINDA AND CATHY

UNITED

❏ 216	Merry Christmas/I Don't Wanna Be Last On Santa's List	1957	$30

CAROLS, THE (1)

LAMP

❏ 2001	My Search Is Over/Keko	1957	$60

CAROLS, THE (2)

SAVOY

❏ 896	Fifty Million Women/I Got a Feelin'	1953	$200

CAROUSEL, THE

ABC

❏ 10953	One Mistake/Only One for Me	1967	$15

TEEN TOWN

❏ 108	I've Been with You/What Will You Do for Me	1969	$20
❏ 116	To Say Goodbye/I Get Along Indefinitely	1969	$20

CAROUSELS, THE

ABC-PARAMOUNT

❏ 10233	Symptoms of Love/ The Hush of Love	1961	$30

AUTUMN

❏ 13	Beneath the Willow/Sail Away	1965	$12

GONE

❏ 5118	If You Want To/Pretty Little Thing	1961	$40

GUYDEN

❏ 2102	I Wanna Fly/Something Else	1964	$15

JAGUAR

❏ 3029	Drive-In Movie/Rendezvous	1959	$70

SPRY

❏ 116	I've Cried Enough/ Did I Cry Enough	1962	$200

CARP

Actor Gary Busey was in this group.

EPIC

❏ 10647	Pine Creek Bridge/Page 258	1970	$8
❏ 10632	Save the Delta Queen/ Mammoth Mountain Blues	1970	$8

CARPENTER, KRIS

DOOR KNOB

❏ 146	My Song Don't Sing the Same/Cheap Wine and Watered Down Whiskey	1981	$5
❏ 203	Oklahoma Heartaches and California Dreams/ You're Leavin' Me	1983	$5
❏ 156	Take Care of Texas/ (B-side unknown)	1981	$5

CARPENTER, MARY CHAPIN

COLUMBIA

❏ 38-07598	A Lot Like Me/Family Hands	1987	$5
❏ 38-07681	Downtown Train/Just Because	1988	$5
❏ 38-68677	How Do/It Don't Bring You	1989	$4

CARPENTERS

A&M

❏ 1940	All You Get from Love Is a Love Song/I Have You	1977	$4
❏ 2405	Beechwood 4-5789/Two Sides	1982	$4
❏ 1978	Calling Occupants of Interplanetary Craft/Can't Smile Without You	1977	$4
❏ 1978 [PS]	Calling Occupants of Interplanetary Craft/Can't Smile Without You	1977	$6
❏ 8629	Calling Occupants of Interplanetary Craft/Don't Cry for Me Argentina	1980	$5
❏ 8629 [PS]	Calling Occupants of Interplanetary Craft/Don't Cry for Me Argentina	1980	$20
❏ 8620	Christmas Song/Merry Christmas Darling	1977	$5

— *Forget Me Nots" green and gold label*

❏ 8620 [PS]	Christmas Song/Merry Christmas Darling	1977	$10
❏ 2700	Do You Hear What I Hear/Little Altar Boy	1984	$12
❏ 1243	For All We Know/Don't Be Afraid	1971	$4
❏ 1243 [PS]	For All We Know/Don't Be Afraid	1971	$6
❏ 1367	Goodbye to Love/Crystal Lullaby	1972	$4
❏ 1367 [PS]	Goodbye to Love/Crystal Lullaby	1972	$6
❏ 1859	Goofus/Boat to Sail	1976	$4
❏ 8667	Honolulu City Lights/I Just Fall in Love Again	1986	$5
❏ 8667 [PS]	Honolulu City Lights/I Just Fall in Love Again	1986	$10
❏ 1322	Hurting Each Other/ Maybe It's You	1972	$4
❏ 1322 [PS]	Hurting Each Other/ Maybe It's You	1972	$6
❏ 2097	I Believe You/B'wana She No Home	1978	$4
❏ 1828	I Need to Be in Love/Sandy	1976	$4
❏ 1351	It's Going to Take Some Time/Flat Baroque	1972	$4
❏ 1351 [PS]	It's Going to Take Some Time/Flat Baroque	1972	$6
❏ 1521	I Won't Last a Day Without You/One Love	1974	$4
❏ 1521 [PS]	I Won't Last a Day Without You/One Love	1974	$6
❏ 2585	Make Believe It's Your First Time/Look to Your Dreams	1983	$4
❏ 2585 [PS]	Make Believe It's Your First Time/Look to Your Dreams	1983	$5
❏ 1236	Merry Christmas Darling/Mr. Guder	1970	$6

— *A-side vocal is different than later releases of this song*

❏ 1236	Merry Christmas Darling/Mr. Guder	1970	$8
❏ 1677	Only Yesterday/Happy	1975	$4
❏ 1677 [PS]	Only Yesterday/Happy	1975	$6
❏ 1646	Please Mister Postman/ This Masquerade	1974	$4
❏ 1646 [PS]	Please Mister Postman/ This Masquerade	1974	$6
❏ 2620	Sailing on the Tide/Your Baby Doesn't Love You Anymore	1984	$4
❏ 1648	Santa Claus Is Coming to Town/ Merry Christmas Darling	1974	$5
❏ 1648 [PS]	Santa Claus Is Coming to Town/ Merry Christmas Darling	1974	$10
❏ 1413	Sing/Druscilla Penny	1973	$4
❏ 1413 [PS]	Sing/Druscilla Penny	1973	$6
❏ 1721	Solitaire/Love Me for What I Am	1975	$4
❏ 1721 [PS]	Solitaire/Love Me for What I Am	1975	$6
❏ 1289	Superstar/Bless the Beasts and Children	1971	$4
❏ 1289 [PS]	Superstar/Bless the Beasts and Children	1971	$6
❏ 2008	Sweet, Sweet Smile/I Have You	1978	$4
❏ 1991	The Christmas Song/ Merry Christmas Darling	1977	$5
❏ 1991 [PS]	The Christmas Song/ Merry Christmas Darling	1977	$8
❏ 1800	There's a Kind of Hush (All Over the World)/(I'm Caught Between) Goodbye and I Love You	1976	$4
❏ 1800 [PS]	There's a Kind of Hush (All Over the World)/(I'm Caught Between) Goodbye and I Love You	1976	$6
❏ 1183	(They Long to Be) Close to You/IKept On Loving You	1970	$5
❏ 2386	Those Good Old Dreams/ When It's Gone	1981	$4
❏ 1142	Ticket to Ride/Your Wonderful Parade	1969	$10
❏ 1468	Top of the World/Heather	1973	$4

— *Originals have brown labels*

❏ 1468	Top of the World/Heather	1973	$3

— *Second pressings have silvery labels*

❏ 1468 [PS]	Top of the World/Heather	1973	$6
❏ 2344	Touch Me When We're Dancing/Because We Are in Love (The Wedding Song)	1981	$4
❏ 2344 [PS]	Touch Me When We're Dancing/Because We Are in Love (The Wedding Song)	1981	$4
❏ 2370	(Want You) Back in My Life Again/Somebody's Been Lyin'	1981	$4
❏ 1217	We've Only Just Begun/ All of My Life	1970	$5
❏ 1217 [PS]	We've Only Just Begun/ All of My Life	1970	$6

MAGIC LAMP

❏ 704	I'll Be Yours/Looking for Love	1967	$2000

— *As "Karen Carpenter", but Richard also was on this record*

7-Inch Extended Plays

A&M

❏ LLP3502	Bacharach-David Hit Medley// Superstar/Let Me Be the One/For All We Know	1971	$20

— *Jukebox issue; small hole, plays at 33 1/3 rpm*

❏ LLP3502 [PS]	Carpenters	1971	$20

— *Part of "Little LP" series (LLP #151)*

❏ LLP4271 [PS]	Close to You	1970	$20

— *Part of "Little LP" series (LLP #125)*

Number	Title	Yr	NM
❑ LLP3519	Fun, Fun, Fun/The End of the World/Da Doo Ron Ron (When He Walked Me Home)/Deadman's Curve// Johnyn Angel/The Night Has a Thousand Eyes/Our Day Will Come/One Fine Day	1973	$25

—Jukebox issue; small hole, plays at 33 1/3 rpm

Number	Title	Yr	NM
❑ LLP4271	Help/Baby It's You/I'll Never Fall in Love Again//Love Is Surrender/Maybe It's You/(They Long to Be) Close to You	1970	$20

—Jukebox issue; small hole, plays at 33 1/3 rpm

Number	Title	Yr	NM
❑ LLP3601 [PS]	The Singles 1969-1973	1973	$25

—Part of "Little LP" series (LLP #238)

Number	Title	Yr	NM
❑ LLP3601	Ticket to Ride/(They Long to Be) Close to You//We've Only Just Begun/Top of the World/ Rainy Days and Mondays	1973	$25

—Jukebox issue; small hole, plays at 33 1/3 rpm

CARPETS, THE

FEDERAL

Number	Title	Yr	NM
❑ 12269	Lonely Me/Chicken Backs	1956	$200
❑ 12257	Why Do I/Let Her Go	1956	$200

CARR, JOE "FINGERS"

Number	Title	Yr	NM
❑ EAP 1-497	(contents unknown)	1954	$10
❑ EAP 1-497 [PS]	Piano Rags	1954	$12

CARR, CATHY

CORAL

Number	Title	Yr	NM
❑ 60907	Heartbroken/Half Pink Boogie	1953	$15
❑ 60988	I Just Can't Get That Melody Out of My Mind/Somebody Told You a Lie	1953	$15
❑ 61092	I'll Cry at Your Wedding/ Cryin' for the Caroline's	1953	$15
❑ 61646	I'll Cry at Your Wedding/ Heartbroken	1956	$10

FRATERNITY

Number	Title	Yr	NM
❑ 793	Doll Baby/Don't Come to My Party	1958	$15
❑ 743	Heart Hideaway/The Boy on Page 35	1956	$20
❑ 782	House of Heartache/ Presents from the Past	1957	$15
❑ 757	It Looks Like Love/Una Momenta	1957	$15
❑ 734	Ivory Tower/Please Please Believe Me	1956	$20
❑ 718	Morning, Noon and Night/ Toward Evening	1955	$30
❑ 750	Oh Baby/Waltzing to the Blues	1956	$20
❑ 765	Wild Honey/Speak for Yourself John	1957	$15

LAURIE

Number	Title	Yr	NM
❑ 3133	Ivory Tower/Should I Believe Him	1962	$10
❑ 3161	I Waded in the Water/ In Place of You	1963	$10
❑ 3206	My Favorite Song/The Ghost of a Broken Heart	1963	$10
❑ 3147	Sailorboy/Next Time a Band Plays a Waltz	1962	$10
❑ 3378	When You Come Home Again/ The Ghost of a Broken Heart	1967	$6

ROULETTE

Number	Title	Yr	NM
❑ 4248	A Little Time/What Do I Do Now	1960	$15
❑ 4125	First Anniversary/With Love	1959	$15
❑ 4383	I Can't Begin to Tell You/ You're Breaking My Heart	1961	$15
❑ 4152 [M]	I'm Gonna Change Him/ The Little Things You Do	1959	$15
❑ SSR-4152 [S]	I'm Gonna Change Him/ The Little Things You Do	1959	$40
❑ 4296	I Want to Be Your Pet/ Golden Locket	1960	$15
❑ 4219	Little Sister/Dark River	1960	$15
❑ 4187	Shy/Personal Secret	1959	$15
❑ 4107	To Know Him Is to Love Him/ Put Away the Invitation	1958	$15

SMASH

Number	Title	Yr	NM
❑ 1726	Footprints in the Snow/ Nein, Nein, Fraulein	1961	$15

CARR, EDDIE LEE

EVERGREEN

Number	Title	Yr	NM
❑ 1092	Big Bad Mama/(B-side unknown)	1989	$5

CARR, JAMES

ATLANTIC

Number	Title	Yr	NM
❑ 2803	Hold On/I'll Put It to You	1971	$15

GOLDWAX

Number	Title	Yr	NM
❑ 332	A Man Needs a Woman/ Stronger Than Love	1968	$20
❑ 343	Everybody Needs Somebody/ Row, Row Your Boat	1969	$20
❑ 338	Freedom Train/That's the Way Love Turned Out for Me	1968	$20
❑ 119	He's Better Than You/Talk Talk	1965	$40
❑ 112	I Can't Make It/Lovers' Competition	1965	$40
❑ 328	I'm a Fool for You/Gonna Send You Back to Georgia	1967	$20
❑ 323	Let It Happen/A Losing Game	1967	$20
❑ 335	Life Turned Her That Way/A Message to Young Lovers	1968	$20
❑ 309	Love Attack/Come Back to Me Baby	1966	$20
❑ 311	Pouring Water on a Drowning Man/Forgetting You	1966	$20
❑ 317	The Dark End of the Street/Lovable Girl	1967	$20
❑ 340	To Love Somebody/ These Ain't Teardrops	1969	$20

CARR, KENNY

KOTTAGE

Number	Title	Yr	NM
❑ 0091	Tell Me/(B-side unknown)	1989	$6
❑ 0090	The Writing on the Wall/ (B-side unknown)	1988	$6

CARR, ROBERTA, AND MARILYN MILLER

EPIC

Number	Title	Yr	NM
❑ 9642	Christmas in the Hills/No Man But a Snowman	1963	$15

CARR, VIKKI

COLUMBIA

Number	Title	Yr	NM
❑ 45208	Ain't No Mountain High Enough/ Call My Heart Your Home	1970	$5
❑ 46033	Borrowed Time/Sleeping Between Two People	1974	$4
❑ 45622	Cabaret/The Big Hurt	1972	$4
❑ 45955	Have You Heard the News/ Leave a Little Room	1973	$5
❑ 10122	Hoy (Today)/El Pajaro Herido	1975	$4
❑ 45454	I Can't Give Back the Love I Feel for You/I've Never Been a Woman Before	1971	$4
❑ 45510	I'd Do It All Again/I'm Gonna Love You	1971	$4
❑ 45296	I'll Be Home/Call My Heart Your Home	1971	$4
❑ AS85 [DJ]	It Came Upon A Midnight Clear/Wind Me Up	1971	$4
❑ AS85 [PS]	It Came Upon A Midnight Clear/Wind Me Up	1971	$8
❑ 45809	Ms. America/We Didn't Know the Time of Day	1973	$4
❑ 10058	One Hell of a Woman/Wind Me Up	1974	$4
❑ 10214	Puttin' Myself in Your Hands (Gettin' Ready to Move)/I Don't Want a Sometimes Man	1975	$4
❑ 45403	Six Weeks Every Summer (Christmas Every Day)/If You Could Read My Mind	1971	$4

LIBERTY

Number	Title	Yr	NM
❑ 56132	Eternity/I Will Wait for Love	1969	$5
❑ 55976	Fly Away/Sunshine	1967	$6
❑ 55736	Forget You/Her Little Heart Went to Loveland	1964	$8
❑ 56062	Happy Together/Dissatisfied Man	1968	$5
❑ 55869	Heartaches/True Love's a Blessing	1966	$6
❑ 55493	He's a Rebel/Be My Love	1962	$30

—Recorded about the same time, and with many of the same musicians, as The Crystals' classic version.

Number	Title	Yr	NM
❑ 55465	I'll Walk the Rest of the Way/Beside a Bridge	1962	$10
❑ 55839	I Only Have Eyes for You/ None But the Lonely Heart	1965	$8
❑ 55917	It Must Be Him/So Nice	1966	$8
❑ 55986	It Must Be Him/That's All	1967	$6
❑ 56185	Make It Rain/Singing My Song	1970	$5
❑ 55897	My Heart Reminds Me (Part 1)/ My Heart Reminds Me (Part 2)	1966	$6
❑ 55620	San Francisco/Irma La Douce	1963	$10
❑ 55620	San Francisco/Look Again	1963	$10
❑ 56026	She'll Be There/Your Heart Is Free Just Like the Wind	1968	$5
❑ 55783	Should I Follow/Don't Talk to Me (Spanish)	1965	$8
❑ 56012	The Lesson/One More Mountain	1968	$5
❑ 56012 [PS]	The Lesson/One More Mountain	1968	$10
❑ 55804	Theme from "Peyton Place"/Unforgettable	1965	$8
❑ 55857	The Silencers/Santiago	1966	$6
❑ 55857 [PS]	The Silencers/Santiago	1966	$10
❑ 56092	With Pen in Hand/Can't Take My Eyes Off You	1969	$5

UNITED ARTISTS

Number	Title	Yr	NM
❑ 0097	It Must Be Him/The Lesson	1973	$4

—Silver Spotlight Series" reissue

Number	Title	Yr	NM
❑ 0098	With Pen in Hand/Eternity	1973	$4

—Silver Spotlight Series" reissue

CARRACK, PAUL

CHRYSALIS

Number	Title	Yr	NM
❑ VS4-43288	Button Off My Shirt/Double It Up	1988	$3
❑ VS4-43164	Don't Shed a Tear/Merilee	1987	$3
❑ VS4-43164 [PS]	Don't Shed a Tear/Merilee	1987	$3
❑ B-23427	I Live by the Groove/Tailfinder	1989	$3
❑ VS4-43204	One Good Reason/All Your Love Is in Vain	1988	$3
❑ VS4-43204 [PS]	One Good Reason/All Your Love Is in Vain	1988	$3
❑ VS4-43252	When You Walk in the Room/ If You See Her Walkin'	1988	$3
❑ VS4-43252 [PS]	When You Walk in the Room/ If You See Her Walkin'	1988	$3

EPIC

Number	Title	Yr	NM
❑ 34-03397	Always Better with You/ Little Unkind	1982	$4
❑ ENR-03266	I Need You/(B-side blank)	1982	$5

—One-sided budget release

Number	Title	Yr	NM
❑ 14-03146	I Need You/Call Me Tonight	1982	$4

CARRASCO, JOE "KING", AND THE CROWNS

GEE BEE

Number	Title	Yr	NM
❑ GB101	Party Weekend/Houston El Mover	1980	$6
❑ GB101 [PS]	Party Weekend/Houston El Mover	1980	$6

LISA

Number	Title	Yr	NM
❑ 1008	Walk It Like You Talk It/ Cucaracha Taco	1984	$8

MCA

Number	Title	Yr	NM
❑ 52081	Don't Let a Woman/ That's the Love	1982	$5
❑ 52039	Wanna Get That Feel (Again)/ Front Me Some Love	1982	$5

CARROLL, ANDREA

BIG TOP

Number	Title	Yr	NM
❑ 3156	It Hurts to Be Sixteen/ Why Am I So Shy	1963	$30
❑ 515	The Doolang/This Time Tomorrow	1964	$50

EPIC

Number	Title	Yr	NM
❑ 9471	Gee Dad/The Charm on My Arm	1961	$30
❑ 9471 [PS]	Gee Dad/The Charm on My Arm	1961	$50
❑ 9438	I've Got a Date with Frankie/ Young and Lonely	1961	$125
❑ 9523	Miss Happiness/Fifteen Shades of Pink	1962	$30
❑ 9450	Please Don't Talk to the Lifeguard/Room of Memories	1961	$30

RCA VICTOR

Number	Title	Yr	NM
❑ 47-8618	Mr. Music Man/Sally Fool	1965	$30

UNITED ARTISTS

Number	Title	Yr	NM
❑ 50039	Hey, Beach Boy/Why Should We Take the Easy Way Out	1966	$40
❑ 982	The World Isn't Big Enough/She Gets Everything She Wants	1966	$30

CARROLL, BERNADETTE

JULIA

Number	Title	Yr	NM
❑ 1106	My Heart Stood Still/ Sweet Sugar Sweet	1962	$20

LAURIE

Number	Title	Yr	NM
❑ 3311	Circus Girl/Don't Hurt Me	1965	$20
❑ 3268	Happy Birthday/ Homecoming Party	1964	$20
❑ 3320	He's Just a Playboy/Try Your Luck	1965	$20
❑ 3238	Party Girl/I Don't Wanna Know	1964	$20
❑ 3278	The Hero/One Little Lie	1964	$20

CARROLL, BOB

OCEAN STATE

Number	Title	Yr	NM
❑ DMS-3	Dreaming Of Christmas/I Want My Santa Claus	1982	$4

—B-side by Lynn Roberts

CARROLL BROTHERS, THE

CAMEO

Number	Title	Yr	NM
❑ 213	Don't Knock the Twist/Bo Diddley	1962	$30
❑ 140	(My Gal Is) Red Hot/ Dearly Beloved	1959	$100
❑ 221	Sweet Georgia Brown/Boot It	1962	$30

FELSTED

Number	Title	Yr	NM
❑ 8550	Movin' Day/I Found You	1959	$30

CARROLL, CORKY

HEAVY

Number	Title	Yr	NM
❑ JT-1001	Skateboard Bill/Pocket Rocket	1977	$12

—Blue vinyl

PACIFIC ARTS

Number	Title	Yr	NM
❑ 103	Tan Punks on Boards/From Pizza Towers to Defeat	1979	$6
❑ 103 [PS]	Tan Punks on Boards/From Pizza Towers to Defeat	1979	$10

CARROLL, DAVID

MERCURY

Number	Title	Yr	NM
❑ 71226X45	A Beautiful Lady in Blue/ The Ski Song	1957	$10
❑ 70642X45	Alabama Jubilee/Baffi	1955	$10
❑ 71000X45	Armen's Theme/Yearning	1956	$10
❑ 71880	Bonita/Mexican Joe	1961	$8
❑ 71459X45	Bouncing Ball/Doodlin' Drummer	1959	$8
❑ 70335X45	Buck Dance/Stomp and Whistle	1954	$15
❑ 71759	By Heck Cha Cha Cha/ Everything's Coming Up Roses	1961	$8

Number	Title	Yr	NM
❑ 71053X45	Cuddle Up a Little Closer/ Li'l Steel Band	1957	$12
❑ 71307X45	Ducky/Do You Ever Think of Me?	1958	$8
❑ 70292X45	Fancy Pants/By Heck	1953	$15
❑ 71152X45	Fascination/Swingin' Sweethearts	1957	$10
❑ 70247X45	Gadabout/Caribbean	1953	$15
❑ 71335X45	Glow-Worm/Let's Dance	1958	$8
❑ 70412X45	Grandpa's Rocker/Mine	1954	$15
❑ 71790	Hand in Hand/Two Way Stretch	1961	$8
❑ 70907X45	Hell's Bells/Cricket	1956	$12
❑ 70444X45	In a Little Spanish Town/ Bumpty-Bump	1954	$15
❑ 71620	In a Little Spanish Town Cha Cha/Third Man Theme	1960	$8
❑ 70717X45	It's Almost Tomorrow/You Are Mine	1955	$10
❑ 71362X45	Live a Little/Have You Ever Been Lonely	1958	$8
❑ 70952X45	Love Theme from "Giant"/ By the Fountains of Rome	1956	$10
❑ 70896X45	Marimba Charleston/Whispering	1956	$10
❑ 70516X45	Melody of Love/La Golondrina	1954	$15
❑ 70521X45	Melody of Love (With Narration)/(Instrumental)	1955	$15
❑ 71703	Midnight Lace/Juke Box Jingle	1960	$8
❑ 70759X45	My Christmas Carol/I'll Be Home for Christmas	1955	$15
❑ 70871X45	Once Upon a Dream/ May in Monaco	1956	$10
❑ 70613X45	The Cuddlin' Song/Scatterbrain	1955	$12
❑ 70658X45	The Girl Upstairs/You're Here My Love	1955	$10
❑ 70822X45	The Little Ballerina/The Beautiful Girls of Vienna	1956	$10
❑ 70860X45	Theme from The Swan/ Miss Powder Puff	1956	$10
❑ 71069X45	The Ship That Never Sailed/I Love You Truly	1957	$10

— With Franklyn MacCormack as narrator

Number	Title	Yr	NM
❑ 70606X45	Till We Meet Again/ The Blue Scarecrow	1955	$10
❑ 70583X45	Two Timin' Gal/Cecelia	1955	$10
❑ 71535X45	Waltzing Matilda/ Sometimes I'm Happy	1959	$8

CARROLL, DELORES, AND THE FOUR TOPS
CHATEAU

Number	Title	Yr	NM
❑ 2002	Everybody Knows/I Just Can't Keep the Tears from Tumblin' Down	1956	$300

CARROLL, IRENE
ARROW

Number	Title	Yr	NM
❑ 712	It's Christmas/The "Let Me" Song	1956	$20

CARROLL, JIM, BAND
ATCO

Number	Title	Yr	NM
❑ 7323	Day and Night/Wicked Gravity	1981	$8
❑ 7314	People Who Died/I Want the Angel	1980	$8

ATLANTIC

Number	Title	Yr	NM
❑ 89687 [DJ]	Sweet Jane (same on both sides)	1984	$6

— Stock copy may not exist

CARROLL, JIM
A&M

Number	Title	Yr	NM
❑ 1329	On and On/I Don't Know	1972	$5
❑ 1360	Save Me/I Got Plenty	1972	$5

CARROLL, JOHNNY
DECCA

Number	Title	Yr	NM
❑ 30013	Hot Rock/Crazy, Crazy	1956	$200
❑ 29941	Wild, Wild Women/ Corrine, Corrina	1956	$200

PHILLIPS INT'L.

Number	Title	Yr	NM
❑ 3520	That's the Way I Love/I'll Wait	1957	$200

SARG

Number	Title	Yr	NM
❑ 144	I'll Think of You/Stars Come Down	1956	$100

WARNER BROS.

Number	Title	Yr	NM
❑ 5042	Bandstand Doll/The Swing	1959	$40
❑ 5080	Lost Without You/Sugar	1959	$40

CARROLL, RONNIE
PHILIPS

Number	Title	Yr	NM
❑ 40110	Say Wonderful Things/ Please Tell Me Your Name	1963	$15
❑ 40388	Tomorrow/Wait for Me	1966	$10

CARROLL, WAYNE
KING

Number	Title	Yr	NM
❑ 5123	Chicken Out/Cindy Lee	1958	$60
❑ 5146	He Cheated/Wall Around Your Heart	1958	$60

CARROW, GEORGE
COLUMBIA

Number	Title	Yr	NM
❑ 4-44161	Angel Baby (Don't You Ever Leave Me)/Bring Back My Heart	1967	$125

— Red label stock copy with correct title

Number	Title	Yr	NM
❑ 4-44161 [DJ]	Angel Baby (You Don't Even Love Me)/Bring Back My Heart	1967	$200

— White label promo with wrong subtitle

Number	Title	Yr	NM
❑ 4-43703	Tiger Prowl/You Are My Sunshine	1966	$20

CARS, THE

Number	Title	Yr	NM
❑ 47080	Don't Tell Me No/ Don't Go to Pieces	1980	$5
❑ 46580	Double Life/Candy-O	1980	$5
❑ 69706	Drive/Stranger Eyes	1984	$3
❑ 47101	Gimme Some Slack/ Don't Go to Pieces	1981	$5
❑ 46014	Good Times Roll/All Mixed Up	1979	$5
❑ 69681	Hello Again/Hello Again (Dub)	1984	$3
❑ 69569	I'm Not the One/Heartbeat City	1986	$3
❑ 46546	It's All I Can Do/Got a Lot on My Head	1979	$4
❑ 46546 [PS]	It's All I Can Do/Got a Lot on My Head	1979	$6
❑ 46063	Let's Go/That's It	1979	$4
❑ 69724	Magic/I Refuse	1984	$3
❑ 45537	My Best Friend's Girl/ Don't Cha Stop	1978	$5
❑ 47250	Shake It Up/Cruiser	1981	$3
❑ 47250 [PS]	Shake It Up/Cruiser	1981	$3
❑ 47433	Since You're Gone/Think It Over	1982	$3
❑ 47433 [PS]	Since You're Gone/Think It Over	1982	$4
❑ 69427	Strap Me In/Door to Door	1988	$3
❑ 69589	Tonight She Comes/ Just What I Needed	1985	$3
❑ 47039	Touch and Go/Down Boys	1980	$4
❑ 69657	Why Can't I Have You/Breakaway	1985	$3

CARSON, JOE
LIBERTY

Number	Title	Yr	NM
❑ 55664	Double Life/Fort Worth Jail	1964	$12
❑ 55614	Helpless/The Last Song (I'm Ever Gonna Sing)	1963	$12
❑ 55578	I Gotta Get Drunk (And I Shore Do Dread It)/Who Will Buy My Memories	1963	$10
❑ 55547	Shoot the Buffalo/Three Little Words Too Late	1963	$10

CARSON, KEN
CAPITOL

Number	Title	Yr	NM
❑ F1260	Gabby the Gobbler/Do You Believe in Santa Claus	1950	$30

— B-side by Santa Claus

CARSON, MARTHA
CAPITOL

Number	Title	Yr	NM
❑ F2477	Ask and You Shall Receive/I Feel It in My Soul	1953	$20
❑ F2145	Beyond the Shadow/I'm Gonna Walk and Talk with the Lord	1952	$20
❑ F2969	Christmas Time Is Here/Peace On Earth (At Christmas Time)	1954	$20
❑ 4437	Everything's All Right/ High on the Hill	1960	$15
❑ F2252	Fear Not/Cryin' Holy Unto the Lord	1952	$20
❑ F2180	He Will Set Your Fields on Fire/ When God Dips His Love	1952	$20
❑ F2825	I Bowed Down/He'll Part the Water	1954	$20
❑ F3045	It's Alright/Counting My Blessings	1955	$20
❑ F2077	I Wanna Rest/Old Blind Barnabas	1952	$20
❑ F2740	Lazarus/Bye & Bye	1954	$20
❑ F1900	Satisfied/Hide Me Rock of Ages	1951	$20
❑ F2634	Singing on the Other Side/I've Got a Better Place to Go	1953	$20
❑ F2342	There's a Higher Power/ Inspiration from Above	1953	$20
❑ F1982	Weighed the Balance/You Sure Do Need Him Now	1952	$20

RCA VICTOR

Number	Title	Yr	NM
❑ 47-6603	All These Things/ Faith Is the Key	1956	$30
❑ 47-6413	David and Goliath/I Want to Rest a Little While	1956	$30
❑ 47-6510	Dixieland Roll/Music Drives Me Crazy	1956	$30
❑ 47-6724	Get That Golden Key/ He Was There	1956	$30
❑ 47-6293	Laugh a Little More/Let the Light Shine on Me	1955	$30
❑ 47-6861	Satisfied/Let the Light Shine on Me	1957	$20

SIMS

Number	Title	Yr	NM
❑ 144	Everybody Needs Somebody/ It Takes a Lot of Lovin'	1963	$12

7-Inch Extended Plays
CAPITOL

Number	Title	Yr	NM
❑ EAP 1-449	*Satisfied/Cryin' Holy Unto the Lord/I Wanna Rest/I'm Gonna Walk and Talk with My Lord	1954	$20
❑ EAP 1-449 [PS]	Gospel Songs	1954	$20

CARSON, MINDY
COLUMBIA

Number	Title	Yr	NM
❑ 4-39889	All the Time and Everywhere/ Barrels 'n Barrels of Roses	1952	$20
❑ 4-39879	('Cause I Love You) That's-a Why/Train of Love	1952	$20

— With Guy Mitchell

Number	Title	Yr	NM
❑ 4-40033	Free Home Demonstration/ Honey-Darlin'	1953	$15
❑ 4-40347	I Didn't Mean to Hear You/ What Am I Gonna Do	1954	$15
❑ 4-40728	I Don't Want to Know/I Took a Stroll in the Park	1956	$10
❑ 4-40057	I Never Let You Cross My Mind/Darlin', Darlin'	1953	$15
❑ 4-41153	I Was Born/Sentimental Touch	1958	$10
❑ 4-40573	Memories Are Made of This/ Cryin' for Your Kisses	1955	$15
❑ 4-40129	Music Box/Crazy, Madly, Wildly in Love	1953	$15
❑ 4-41221	My Foolish Heart/ Knock on Wood	1958	$10
❑ 4-40789	Since I Met You Baby/ Goodnight, My Love	1956	$10
❑ 4-40923	Sugaree/Time and Tears	1957	$10
❑ 4-41021	Sweet Georgia Brown/ Water Wheel	1957	$10
❑ 4-39914	Tell Me You're Mine (Per Un Bacio D'amour)/ The Chop Boy Song	1953	$15
❑ 4-39992	Tell Us Where the Good Times Are/There's Nothing As Sweet As My Baby	1953	$15

— With Guy Mitchell

Number	Title	Yr	NM
❑ 4-40438	The Fish/Bring Me Your Love	1955	$15
❑ 4-40206	This Above All/Speedy Gonzales	1954	$15
❑ 4-39989	Three Red Roses/I Cry Your Name	1953	$15
❑ 4-40857	Time's Runnin' Out on Me/Please Take Back Your Introduction	1957	$10
❑ 4-40537	Wake the Town and Tell the People/Hold Me Tight	1955	$15

JOY

Number	Title	Yr	NM
❑ 242	A Little Love (Will Go a Long, Long Way)/You're the End	1960	$20
❑ 236	Wake the Town and Tell the People/When I Fall in Love	1960	$20

RCA VICTOR

Number	Title	Yr	NM
❑ 47-3725	Be Mine/Little Darlin', Little Angel	1950	$20
❑ 47-4454	Be My Life's Companion/ Tuh Pocket	1952	$20
❑ 47-4039	Button Up Your Overcoat/Together	1951	$20
❑ 47-3204	Candy and Cake/ My Foolish Heart	1950	$20
❑ 47-4316	Christmas Chopsticks/ Doors That Lead to You	1951	$30
❑ 47-4681	Come Out, Come Out, Wherever You Are/Ho Ho	1952	$20
❑ 47-4457	Dance Me Loose/ Allegheny Fiddler	1952	$20
❑ 47-3718	Go to Sleep, Go to Sleep, Go to Sleep/Ask Me No Questions	1950	$20

— With Don Cornell

Number	Title	Yr	NM
❑ 47-4119	Got to Find Somebody to Love/When You and I Were Young Maggie Blues	1951	$20
❑ 47-4259	Hangin' Around with You/ Out in the Cold Again	1951	$20
❑ 47-3944	If I Were a Bell/Just For a While	1950	$20
❑ 47-4088	I'm Late/'Twas Brillig	1951	$40
❑ 47-3801	I Wish, I Wish/I'm Bashful	1950	$20
❑ 47-3017	Lonely Girl/You're Different	1949	$30
❑ 47-4151	Lonely Little Robin/You Only Want Me When You're Lonesome	1951	$20
❑ 47-2950	One More Time/Twelve O'Clock and All Is Well	1949	$30
❑ 47-2980	Song of Surrender/Blame My Absent Minded Heart	1949	$30
❑ 47-3108	Too-Whit! Too-Whoo! (Bring My Loved One to Me)/All the Bees Are Buzzin' Round My Honey	1949	$30
❑ 47-4018	When You Return/Boutenniere	1951	$20

CARSON, WAYNE
DECCA

Number	Title	Yr	NM
❑ 31621	Blue Feeling/It's You, Always It's You	1964	$15
❑ 31531	There's No In Between/ The Traveler	1963	$15

ELEKTRA

Number	Title	Yr	NM
❑ 45358	Barstool Mountain/Keep On	1976	$5
❑ 45407	Bugle Ann/Down to the Riverq	1977	$5
❑ 45348	The Girl That I'm Hung Up On/Keep On	1976	$5

EMH

Number	Title	Yr	NM
❑ 0017	1 Yr 2 Mo 11 Days/The Timing's All Wrong	1983	$5
❑ 0001	Lovin' You Ain't All I Got to Do/Mr. Coachman	1982	$5

MONUMENT

Number	Title	Yr	NM
❑ 8543	All Night Feeling/No Love at All	1972	$6
❑ 8524	Mexican Divorce/Just as Gone	1971	$6
❑ 1152	Soul Deep/Don't Let the Sun Set on You in Tulsa	1969	$8
❑ 8501	Straight/King's Hideaway	1971	$6

Number	Title	Yr	NM

CARTEE, ALAN
GROOVY
❏ 101	Let My Fingers Do the Walking (I'm Your Telephone Man)/ Twenty-Five Women	1977	$8

CARTEE BROTHERS, THE
REPRISE
❏ 0528	Four Quarters on the Football Field/Don't Say Goodbye	1966	$8

CARTER, ANITA
CADENCE
❏ 1333	Blue Doll/Go Away Johnny	1957	$50

CAPITOL
❏ 3194	A Whole Lotta Lovin'/ Loving Him Was Easier	1971	$6
❏ 2994	Tulsa County/Where Is the Start of Lonely	1970	$6

COLUMBIA
❏ 4-21198	Don Juan/There'll Be No Teardrops	1954	$30
❏ 4-21242	Heartless Romance/ Faithless Johnny Lee	1954	$30
❏ 3-10009	Sweet Memories/ Pictures on the Wall	1974	$5

JAMIE
❏ 1154	Mama Don't Cry at My Wedding/Moon Girl	1960	$20
❏ 1167	Tryin' to Forget About You/ That's All I Want from You	1960	$20

MERCURY
❏ 72364	Little Things Mean a Lot/Stop (Being Mean to Your Baby)	1965	$10

RCA VICTOR
❏ 47-6482	A Tear Fell/One Heartache at a Time	1956	$20
❏ 47-6737	Believe It or Not/If I Had a Needle and Thread	1956	$20
❏ 47-6364	False Hearted/I Wear Dark Glasses	1955	$30
❏ 48-0426	Freight Train Blues/ Someone Else, Not Me	1951	$30
❏ 47-6805	He's a Real Gone Guy/Maybe	1957	$20
❏ 47-9156	I Don't Need You Anymore/ You Weren't Ashamed to Kiss Me (Last Night)	1967	$8
❏ 47-6017	I Dreamed of a Hill-Billy Heaven/Making Believe	1955	$30
❏ 48-0461	I'm Cryin'/Right Way, Wrong Way	1951	$30
❏ 47-8923	I'm Gonna Leave You/You Couldn't Get My Love Back	1966	$8
❏ 47-8809	I've Been Loving You Too Long/ Heard the Wind Blow Before	1966	$8
❏ 47-9307	Love Me Now (While I Am Living)/ It's My Life (And I'll Live It)	1967	$8
❏ 47-6228	Mask on Your Heart/ Here We Are Again	1955	$30
❏ 48-0387	Somebody's Cryin'/Johnny's Got a Sweetheart	1950	$50
— Originals on green vinyl			
❏ 47-6129	That's What Makes the Jukebox Play/I'm Sorry If That's the Way You Feel	1955	$30
❏ 47-8674	Twelve O'Clock High/Is It for Me	1965	$10

CARTER, CALVIN
VEE JAY
❏ 439	Mashed Potatoes/Wimoweh	1962	$20
❏ 436	Twisting Bones/Crazy Little Mama Twist	1962	$20
— As "The Cal Carter Singers			

CARTER, CARLENE, AND DAVE EDMUNDS
WARNER BROS.
❏ 49572	Baby Ride Easy/Too Bad About Sandy	1980	$4

CARTER, CARLENE
EPIC
❏ 38-03952	Heart to Heart/One Way Ticket	1983	$4

WARNER BROS.
❏ 49083	Do It in a Heartbeat/ Swap-Meet Rag	1979	$4
❏ 8658	Love Is Gone/Smoke Dreams	1978	$5
❏ 49155	Old Photographs/Two Sides to Every Woman	1980	$4

CARTER, CLARENCE
ABC
❏ 12162	Dear Abby/Love Ain't Here No More	1976	$4
❏ 12094	Everything Comes Up Roses/A Very Special Love Song	1975	$4
❏ 12224	Heart Full of Song/All Messed Up	1976	$4
❏ 12130	I Got Caught/Take It All Off	1975	$4
❏ 12058	Warning/On Your Way Down	1974	$4

ATLANTIC
❏ 2576	Back Door Santa/That Old Time Feeling	1968	$8
❏ 2660	Doin' Our Thing/I Smell a Rat	1969	$6

Number	Title	Yr	NM
❏ 2726	I Can't Leave Your Love Alone/Devil Woman	1970	$6
❏ 2461	I Can't See Myself/ Looking for a Fox	1967	$6
❏ 2875	If You Can't Beat 'Em/ Lonesomest Lonesome	1972	$6
— With Candi Carter			
❏ 2842	I'm the One/Scratch My Back	1971	$6
❏ 2774	It's All in Your Mind/Till I Can't Take It Anymore	1970	$6
❏ 2748	Patches/Say It One More Time	1970	$6
❏ 2508	Slip Away/Funky Fever	1968	$8
❏ 2818	Slipped, Tripped, and Fell in Love/I Hate to Love and Run	1971	$6
❏ 2605	Snatching It Back/Making Love	1969	$6
❏ 2702	Take It Off Him and Put It On Me/A Few Troubles I've Had	1970	$6
❏ 2801	The Court Room/Getting the Bills	1971	$6
❏ 2642	The Feeling Is Right/You Can't Miss What You Can't Measure	1969	$6
❏ 2569	Too Weak to Fight/Let Me Comfort You	1968	$6

FAME
❏ 91006	Back in Your Arms/Holdin' Out	1972	$5
❏ XW330	I'm the Midnight Special/I Got Another Woman	1973	$5
❏ XW415	Love's Trying to Come to You/Heartbreak Woman	1974	$5
❏ XW179	Put On Your Shoes and Walk/I Found Somebody New	1973	$5
❏ XW250	Sixty Minute Man/Mother-in-Law	1973	$5
❏ 1010	Tell Daddy/I Stayed Away Too Long	1966	$15
❏ 1013	Thread the Needle/Don't Make My Baby Cry	1967	$15

ICHIBAN
❏ 116	Doctor C.C./I Stayed Away Too Long	1987	$3
❏ 131	Grandpa Can't Find His Kate/What'd I Say	1988	$3
❏ 106	If You Let Me Take You Home/ So You're Leaving Me	1986	$3
❏ 158	I'm Just Not Good/I'm the Best	1989	$3
❏ 101	Messin' with My Mind/I Was in the Neighborhood	1986	$3
❏ 108	Strokin'/Love Me with Feelin'	1987	$8
❏ 135	Trying to Sleep Tonight/ (B-side unknown)	1988	$3
❏ 164	Why Do I Stay Here and Take This Shit fro You/ It's a Man Down There	1989	$3

RONN
❏ 90	I Couldn't Refuse Your Love/ What Was I Supposed to Do?	1977	$5

VENTURE
❏ 147	Can We Slip Away Again/ If I Were Yours	1981	$4
❏ 145	It's a Monster Thang/ If I Were Yours	1981	$4
❏ 141	Let's Burn/If I Stay	1980	$4

7-Inch Extended Plays
ATLANTIC
❏ EP1021 [DJ]	Bad News/Soul Deep//I Can't Do Without You/I Smell a Rat	1969	$20
— Promo only; white label, large hole			
❏ EP-1020 [DJ]	Look What I Got/I'd Rather Go Blind//Road of Love/Steal Away	1969	$20
— Promo only; white label, large hole			
❏ EP1021 [PS]	Testifyin'	1969	$25
❏ EP-1020 [PS]	The Dynamic Clarence Carter	1969	$25

CARTER FAMILY, THE
❏ 1010	Mrs. Jimmie Rodgers Visits the Carter Family Part 1/Part 2	1956	$50
— With Mrs. Jimmie Rodgers			

COLUMBIA
❏ 4-20986	Amazing Grace/Softly and Tenderly	1952	$30
❏ 4-21316	Are You Afraid to Remember Me/He Went Slippin' Around	1954	$30
❏ 4-45428	A Song to Mama/One More Summer in Virginia	1971	$8
❏ 4-20920	Fair and Tender Ladies/ Foggy Mountain Top	1952	$30
❏ 4-43235	Farewell/You Win Again	1965	$10
❏ 4-44982	If I Live Long Enough/ Break My Mind	1969	$8
❏ 4-20974	I Never Will Marry/The Sun's Gonna Shine in My Back Door	1952	$30
❏ 4-43579	I Walk the Line/For Lovin' Me	1966	$8
❏ 4-21233	Love, Oh Crazy Love/ Time's a Wastin'	1954	$30
❏ 3-10502	My Father's Fiddle/ My Ship Will Sail	1977	$5
❏ 4-44136	Once Around the Briar Patch/Bye Bye	1967	$8
❏ 3-10387	Papa's Sugar/In the Pines (The Longest Train I Ever Saw)	1976	$5

LIBERTY
❏ 55501	Fourteen Carat Nothing/Get Up Early in the Morning	1962	$15

Number	Title	Yr	NM

MERCURY
❏ 870397-7	Dixie Darlin'/Ain't Gonna Work Tomorrow	1988	$4

CARTER, FRED, JR.
MONUMENT
❏ 1022	And You Wonder Why/ It's a Rough Old Road	1967	$8
❏ 1067	Every Stop of the Way/Turn It Around in Your Mind	1968	$8
❏ 993	I Don't Know Why I Keep Loving You/Coffee Cup	1967	$8

CARTER, GAYLORD
SKYWAY
❏ 103	Season's Greetings (A Cheerful Hello)/Season's Greetings (A Cheerful Hello)	1960	$8
— B-side by Pete Pontrelli			

CARTER, HELEN
HICKORY
❏ 1053	Heart Full of Shame/ Sweet Talkin' Man	1956	$30
❏ 1069	I'd Like to Be/He Made You for Me	1957	$30
— With Wiley Barkdull			
❏ 1076	Set the Wedding/What's to Become of Me Now	1958	$30

CARTER, JUNE
COLUMBIA
❏ 4-45338	A Good Man/Straw Upon the Wind	1971	$8
— As "June Carter Cash			
❏ 4-40797	Baby I Tried/I'm All Right Now	1956	$20
❏ 4-43441	Everything Ain't Been Said/A Long Way from the Cotton Fields	1965	$12
❏ 4-43156	Go Away Stranger/I Want You Again	1964	$10
❏ 4-21380	He Don't Love Me Anymore/ Leftover Loving	1955	$30
❏ 4-42864	I Pitched My Tent (On the Old Campground)/Sweet Flowers	1963	$10
❏ 4-21343	Let Me Go Lover/Left Over Mambo	1955	$30
❏ 3-10149	Losin' You/The Shadow of a Lady	1975	$5
— As "June Carter Cash			
❏ 4-21535	Strange Woman/Honey Look What You've Got	1956	$30
❏ 4-43059	Tall Loverman/Without a Love to Call My Own	1964	$10

LIBERTY
❏ 55440	Mama Teach Me/Money	1962	$10
❏ 55504	Overalls and Dungarees/ Waving from the Hill	1962	$10
❏ 55385	The Heel/If I Ever See Him Again	1961	$10

RCA VICTOR
❏ 48-0401	Bashful Rascal/For Crying Out Loud	1950	$40
❏ 48-0146	Crocodile Tears/ Grandma Told Me So	1950	$50
— Originals on green vinyl			
❏ 48-0450	Mommie's Real Pecooliar/A Bucket of Love	1951	$40
❏ 48-0411	The Thing/Winkin' and a Blinkin'	1950	$40

CARTER, LYNDA
EPIC
❏ 8-50624	All Night Long/Put On a Show	1978	$6
❏ 8-50569	Toto (Don't It Feel Like Paradise)/Put On a Show	1978	$6

CARTER, MEL
AMOS
❏ 132	Everything Stops for a Little While/This Is My Life	1970	$6

ARWIN
❏ 123	Sugar/I'm Coming Home	1960	$20

BELL
❏ 775	Another Saturday Night/ Coming From You	1969	$6
❏ 743	Didn't We/I Pretend	1968	$6

CREAM
❏ 8143	Who's Right, Who's Wrong/I Don't Wanna Get Over You	1981	$4

DERBY
❏ 1005	Time of Young Love/ Wonderful Love	1963	$15
❏ 1003	When a Boy Falls in Love/So Wonderful	1963	$15
❏ 1008	Why I Call Her Mine/After the Party, the Meeting Is Sweeter	1964	$15

IMPERIAL
❏ 66138	(All of a Sudden) My Heart Sings/When I Hold the Hand of the One I Love	1965	$8
❏ 66228	As Time Goes By/Look to the Rainbow	1966	$8
❏ 66165	Band of Gold/Detour	1966	$8
❏ 66052	'Deed I Do/What's On Your Mind	1964	$8

Number	Title	Yr	NM
❏ 66101	High Noon/I Just Can't Imagine	1965	$8
❏ 66113	Hold Me, Thrill Me, Kiss Me/Sweet Little Girl	1965	$12
❏ 66078	I'll Never Be Free/The Richest Man Alive	1964	$8
❏ 66148	Love Is All We Need/I Wish I Didn't Love You So	1965	$8
❏ 66208	Take Good Care of Her/Tar and Cement	1966	$8
LIBERTY			
❏ 56000	Be My Love/Look Into My Love	1967	$6
❏ 55970	Edelweiss/For Once in My Life	1968	$6
❏ 56015	Excuse Me/The Other Woman	1968	$6
❏ 55987	Star Dust/Enter Laughing	1967	$6
PRIVATE STOCK			
❏ 45,087	My Coloring Book	1976	$4
❏ 45,057	Put a Little Love Away/Dancing for Dimes	1975	$4
ROMAR			
❏ 716	I Only Have Eyes for You/Treasure of Love	1974	$4
❏ 711	She Is Me/Do Me Wrong, But Do Me	1973	$4
❏ 714	Treasure of Love/Do Me Wrong, But Do Me	1973	$4

CARTER, MOTHER MAYBELLE

Number	Title	Yr	NM
COLUMBIA			
❏ 4-43521	I Told Them What You're Fighting For/San Antonio Rose	1966	$10

CARTER, PAT

Number	Title	Yr	NM
7 ARTS			
❏ 702	What Should I Do/True Love's Untrue	1961	$15
LIBERTY			
❏ 55471	Sweet Young Girl/Lover Doll	1962	$15

CARTER, ROMAN

Number	Title	Yr	NM
JEWEL			
❏ 794	There's Trouble Brewin'/Queen Bee	1968	$6

CARTER SISTERS, THE

Number	Title	Yr	NM
COLUMBIA			
❏ 4-21262	My Destiny/Well I Guess I Told You Off	1954	$30
❏ 4-21138	Wildwood Flower/He's Solid Gone	1953	$30
RCA VICTOR			
❏ 48-0433	Columbus, Ga./I've Got My Share of Trouble	1951	$40
❏ 48-0319	Don't Wait/Down on My Knees	1950	$50
— Originals on green vinyl			
❏ 48-0372	Little Orphan Girl/God Sent My Little Girl	1950	$50
— Originals on green vinyl			
❏ 48-0050	Someone's Last Way/Why Do You Weep Dear Willow	1949	$50
— Originals on green vinyl			
❏ 48-0153	The Day of Wrath/I've Got a Home in Glory	1950	$50
— Originals on green vinyl			
❏ 48-0105	Walk Closer to Me/A Picture, a Ring, and a Curl	1949	$50
— Originals on green vinyl			
❏ 48-0394	Willow Weep for Me/Gotta Find Somebody to Love	1950	$50
— Originals on green vinyl			

CARTER, SONNY

Number	Title	Yr	NM
DOT			
❏ 15921	Crying Over You/My Lonely Life	1959	$40
KING			
❏ 4756	It's Strange but True/I Solemnly Swear	1954	$60
❏ 4739	There Is No Greater Love/Oh Baby	1954	$60

CARTEY, RIC

Number	Title	Yr	NM
ABC-PARAMOUNT			
❏ 10415	Poor Me/Something in My Eye	1963	$15
NRC			
❏ 503	My Heart Belongs to You/Scratching on the Screen	1959	$60
RCA VICTOR			
❏ 47-6828	Heart Throb/I Wancha to Know	1957	$100
❏ 47-6920	Let Me Tell You About Love/Born to Love One Woman	1957	$120
❏ 47-7011	My Babe/Hello Down Easy	1957	$120

CARTON, MARY

Number	Title	Yr	NM
DECCA			
❏ 27348	Christmas in Killarney/Did Santa Claus Come from Ireland	1950	$20

CARTOONE

Number	Title	Yr	NM
ATLANTIC			
❏ 2598	Mr. Poor Man/Knik Knak Man	1969	$8

CARTWRIGHT, LIONEL

Number	Title	Yr	NM
MCA			
❏ 53651	Give Me His Last Chance/Let the Hard Times Roll	1989	$3
❏ 53723	In My Eyes/That's Why They Call It Falling	1989	$3
❏ 53779	I Watched It All (On My Radio)/Hard Act to Follow	1989	$4
❏ 53498	Like Father, Like Son/A Little Lesser Blue	1989	$3

CARVER, JOHNNY

Number	Title	Yr	NM
ABC			
❏ 11425	Country Lullaby/Pass Me By	1974	$5
❏ 12017	Don't Tell (That Sweet Ole Lady of Mine)/'Til We Find It All Again	1974	$5
❏ 12097	Strings/Double Exposure	1975	$5
❏ 11403	Tonight Someone's Falling in Love/Frank and Don, Howard Too, Broadway Joe and You and Me	1973	$5
ABC DOT			
❏ 17640	Afternoon Delight/Double Exposure	1976	$5
❏ 17729	Apartment/Frank and Don, Howard, Too, Broadway Joe and You and Me	1977	$5
❏ 17707	Down at the Pool/Double Exposure	1977	$5
❏ 17685	Living Next Door to Alice/Treat a Lady Like a Tramp	1977	$5
❏ 17661	Love Is Only Love (When Shared by Two)/It Don't Hurt to Be a Dreamer	1976	$5
❏ 17614	Snap, Crackle and Pop/I Can't Go Swimming in Muddy Water	1976	$5
❏ 17576	Start All Over Again/Love Signs	1975	$5
❏ 17675	Sweet City Woman/'Till We Find It All Again	1976	$5
DOT			
❏ 16823	Poverty Stricken Heart/My Future	1966	$20
EPIC			
❏ 5-10760	If You Think That It's All Right/This Town's Not Big Enough	1971	$6
❏ 5-10813	I Start Thinking About You/Preserving Wildlife	1971	$6
❏ 5-10872	I Want You/I'm Talking About You Baby	1972	$6
EQUITY			
❏ 1902	Fingertips/Caribbean Nights	1980	$6
IMPERIAL			
❏ 66213	Fools' Names, Fools' Faces/What If It Happened to You	1966	$15
❏ 66442	Harvey Harrington IV/Sybil's Rights	1970	$8
❏ 66341	Hold Me Tight/My Heart's Been Marching	1968	$8
❏ 66234	I Gotta Go Home/You Are That Something	1967	$15
❏ 66297	I Still Didn't Have the Sense to Go/Feelin' Kinda Sunday in My Thinkin'	1968	$8
❏ 66316	Leaving Again/Does She Still Get Her Way	1968	$8
❏ 66173	One Way or the Other/Think About Her All the Time	1966	$15
❏ 66361	Sweet Wine/With Every Heartbeat	1969	$8
❏ 66389	That's Your Hang Up/Mother-in-Law	1969	$8
❏ 66423	Willie and the Hand Jive/Take Sadie Out to the Country	1969	$8
MCA			
❏ 51072	Tie a Yellow Ribbon Round the Ole Oak Tree/You Really Haven't Changed	1981	$4
MONUMENT			
❏ WS4-03667	Shed a Little Light/Somewhere	1983	$4
TANGLEWOOD			
❏ 1905	S.O.S./Fingertips	1980	$6

CARVETTES, THE

Number	Title	Yr	NM
COPA			
❏ 200-1/2	A Lover's Prayer/Never Gonna Leave Me	1959	$800

CASAMENIT, AL

Number	Title	Yr	NM
COMMAND			
❏ 4107	Sleigh Ride/Jingle Bells	1967	$6
— B-side by Toots Thielmans			

CASANOVA JR.

Number	Title	Yr	NM
PORT			
❏ 70001	Sally Mae/They Call Me Casanova	1958	$600

CASANOVA, TONY

Number	Title	Yr	NM
AMERICAN INT'L.			
❏ 533	Diary of a High School Bride/When I Say Bye Bye	1959	$50
DORE			
❏ 535	Boogie Woogie Feeling/Showdown	1959	$100

CASANOVAS, THE

Number	Title	Yr	NM
APOLLO			
❏ 477	I Don't Want You to Go/Please Be My Love	1955	$200
❏ 523	(I Got a) Good Lookin' Baby/You Are My Queen	1957	$125
❏ 474	It's Been a Long Time/Hush-a-Mecca	1955	$200
❏ 483	My Baby's Love/Sleepy Head Mama	1956	$200
❏ 519	Please Be Mine/For You and You Alone	1957	$125
❏ 471	That's All/Are You for Real	1955	$125

CASAZZA, JIMMY

Number	Title	Yr	NM
ATINA			
❏ 449	Little Drummer Boy/Carol Of The Drums (Disco '77)//All I Want for Christmas Is My Two Front Teeth	1977	$5

CASCADES, THE

Number	Title	Yr	NM
ARWIN			
❏ 132	Cheryl's Going Home/Truly Julie's Blues	1966	$8
❏ 134	Midnight Lace/All's Fair in Love and War	1966	$8
CANBASE			
❏ 714	I Started a Joke/Sweet America	1972	$5
CHARTER			
❏ 1018	She Was Never Mine (To Really Lose)/My Best Girl	1964	$20
❏ 1018	She Was Never Really Mine (To Lose)/My Best Girl	1964	$30
LIBERTY			
❏ 55822	She'll Love Again/I Bet You Won't Stay	1965	$10
LONDON			
❏ 177	Two-Sided Man/The Woman's A Girl	1972	$5
PROBE			
❏ 453	Two-Sided Man/Everyone Is Blossoming	1968	$8
❏ 453 [PS]	Two-Sided Man/Everyone Is Blossoming	1968	$20
RCA VICTOR			
❏ 47-8206	Cinderella/A Little Like Lovin'	1963	$20
❏ 47-8206 [PS]	Cinderella/A Little Like Lovin'	1963	$30
❏ 47-8268	For Your Sweet Love/Jeannie	1963	$15
❏ 47-8402	I Dare You to Cry/Awake	1964	$15
❏ 47-8321	Little Betty Falling Star/Those Were the Good Old Days	1964	$20
SMASH			
❏ 2101	Flying on the Ground/Main Street	1967	$8
❏ 2083	Hey Little Girl of Mine/Blue Hours	1967	$8
UNI			
❏ 55231	April, May, June and July/Big Ugly Sky	1970	$8
❏ 55200	But For Love/Hazel Autumn Cocoa Brown	1970	$8
❏ 55169	Indian River/Big City Country Boy	1969	$8
❏ 55152	Maybe the Rain Will Fall/Naggin' Cries	1969	$8
VALIANT			
❏ 6032	I Wanna Be Your Lover/My First Day Alone	1963	$20
❏ 6028	Shy Girl/The Last Leaf	1963	$20
❏ 6021	There's a Reason/Second Chance	1962	$30

CASEY, AL

Number	Title	Yr	NM
BLUE HORIZON			
❏ 925	Cookin'/Hot Foot	1962	$30
DOT			
❏ 15524	A Fool's Blues/Juice	1956	$40
❏ 15563	Guitar Man/Come What May	1957	$50
HIGHLAND			
❏ 1002	Got the Teenage Blues/(B-side unknown)	1959	$50
LIBERTY			
❏ 55117	Willa Mae/She Gotta Shake	1957	$30
MCI			
❏ 1005	Pink Panther/If I Told You	1965	$20
STACY			
❏ 925	Cookin'/Hot Foot	1962	$20
❏ 971	Cookin'/What Are We Gonna Do in '64	1964	$20
❏ 956	Doin' It/Monte Carlo	1963	$20
❏ 961	Full House/Indian Love Call	1963	$20
❏ 950	Laughin'/Chicken Feathers	1962	$20
❏ 964	Surfin' Blues/Guitars, Guitars, Guitars	1963	$20
❏ 962	Surfin' Hootenanny/Easy Pickin'	1963	$30
— Black vinyl			
❏ 962	Surfin' Hootenanny/Easy Pickin'	1963	$50
— Red vinyl			
UNITED ARTISTS			
❏ 158	The Stinger/Keep Talking	1959	$30

Number	Title	Yr	NM

CASEY, KAREN

WESTERN PRIDE

Number	Title	Yr	NM
❏ 112	Leavin' on Your Mind/Are You Lonesome Tonight?	1980	$6

CASH, ALVIN

CHESS

| ❏ 2098 | Getaway/Saddle Up | 1970 | $8 |

DAKAR

| ❏ 4559 | Doin' the Ali Shuffle/The Feeling | 1976 | $5 |

MAR-V-LUS

❏ 6014	Alvin's Boo-Ga-Loo/Let's Do Some Good Timing	1966	$10
❏ 6009	Boston Monkey/Unwind the Twine	1965	$10
❏ 6019	Different Strokes for Different Folks/The Change	1967	$12
❏ 6015	Doin' the Ali Shuffle/Feel So Good	1967	$12
❏ 6005	The Barracuda/Do It One More Time	1965	$12
❏ 6012	The Philly Freeze/No Deposit No Return	1966	$10
❏ 6002	Twine Time/The Bump	1964	$20

SEVENTY-7

| ❏ 112 | Alvin's Doing His Thing/It's a Party | 1972 | $6 |
| ❏ 118 | Doin' the Creep/Party Time | 1972 | $6 |

SOUND STAGE 7

| ❏ 1509 | Funky Washing Machine/I Don't Want It | 1973 | $6 |

TODDLIN' TOWN

❏ 104	Alvin's Bag/Whip It On Me	1968	$8
❏ 119	Funky '69/Moaning and Groaning	1969	$8
❏ 124	Poppin' Popcorn/(Instrumental)	1969	$8

WESTBOUND

| ❏ 159 | Stone Thing (Part 1)/Stone Thing (Part 2) | 1970 | $8 |

CASH, BOBBY

HIT

| ❏ 143 | Do Wah Diddy Diddy/It Hurts to Be in Love | 1964 | $20 |

—B-side by Bobby Brooks

KING

❏ 5844	Mona Lisa/Teen Love	1964	$40
❏ 5864	Only Make Believe/Run, Fool, Run	1964	$40
❏ 5894	The Answer to My Dreams/I Don't Need Your Love and Kisses	1964	$40

CASH, EDDIE

PEAK

| ❏ 1010 | Come On Home/(B-side unknown) | 1960 | $20 |
| ❏ 1001 | Doing All Right/Land of Promises | 1958 | $120 |

ROULETTE

| ❏ 4380 | Stormy Weather/Lonely Island | 1961 | $15 |

TODD

| ❏ 1057 | Thinkin' Man/Livin' Lovin' Temptation | 1960 | $15 |

CASH, JOE

HIT

| ❏ 17 | A Steel Guitar and a Glass of Wine/Playboy | 1962 | $8 |

—B-side by Peggy Gaines

CASH, JOHNNY, AND JUNE CARTER

COLUMBIA

❏ 45929	Allegheny/We're for Love	1973	$5
❏ 45631	If I Had a Hammer/I Gotta Go	1972	$5
❏ 45064	If I Were a Carpenter/'Cause I Love You	1970	$5
❏ 44158	Long-Legged Guitar Pickin' Man/You'll Be All Right	1967	$6
❏ 10436	Old Time Feeling/Far Side Banks of Jordan	1976	$5
❏ 45890	Praise the Lord and Pass the Soup/The Ballad of Barbara	1973	$5
❏ 45758	The Loving Gift/Help Me Make It Through the Night	1973	$5

CASH, JOHNNY, AND WAYLON JENNINGS

COLUMBIA

❏ 05896	Even Cowgirls Get the Blues/American by Birth	1986	$3
❏ 06287	The Ballad of $40/Field of Diamonds	1986	$3
❏ 10742	There Ain't No Good Chain Gang/I Wish I Was Crazy Again	1978	$5

CASH, JOHNNY

A&M

| ❏ 2291 | The Death of Me/One More Shot | 1980 | $4 |

—With Levon Helm

CACHET

| ❏ 4504 | Wings in the Morning/What on Earth | 1980 | $5 |

| ❏ 4504 [PS] | Wings in the Morning/What on Earth | 1980 | $5 |

COLUMBIA

❏ 44944	A Boy Named Sue/San Quentin	1969	$6
❏ 10623	After the Ball/Calilou	1977	$5
❏ 41251	All Over Again/What Do I Care	1958	$20
❏ 41251 [PS]	All Over Again/What Do I Care	1958	$50
❏ 45740	Any Old Wind That Blows/Kentucky Straight	1972	$5
❏ 45534	A Thing Called Love/Daddy	1972	$5
❏ 45020	Blistered/See Ruby Fall	1969	$6
❏ 43763	Boa Constrictor/Bottom of a Mountain	1966	$6
❏ 42512	Bonanza!/Pick a Bale o' Cotton	1962	$15
❏ 11237	Bull Rider/Lonesome to the Bone	1980	$4
❏ 42665	Busted/Send a Picture of Mother	1963	$10
❏ 42665 [PS]	Busted/Send a Picture of Mother	1963	$30
❏ 45786	Children/Last Summer	1973	$5
❏ 45979	Christmas As I Knew It/That Christmasy Feeling	1973	$5

— With Tommy Cash

| ❏ 11340 | Cold Lonesome Morning/The Cowboy Who Started the Fight | 1980 | $4 |
| ❏ 04860 | Crazy Old Soldier/It Ain't Gonna Worry My Mind | 1985 | $3 |

—A-side: Ray Charles and Johnny Cash; B-side: Ray Charles and Mickey Gilley

| ❏ 44689 | Daddy Sang Bass/He Turned the Water Into Wine | 1968 | $6 |
| ❏ 05594 | Desperados Waiting for a Train/The Twentieth Century Is Almost Over | 1985 | $3 |

—A-side: Willie Nelson/Waylon Jennings/Johnny Cash/Kris Kristofferson; B-side: Nelson, Cash

❏ 41313	Don't Take Your Guns to Town/I Still Miss Someone	1959	$20
❏ 41313 [PS]	Don't Take Your Guns to Town/I Still Miss Someone	1959	$50
❏ 43673	Everybody Loves a Nut/Austin Prison	1966	$6
❏ 03317	Fair Weather Friends/Ain't Gonna Hobo No More	1982	$4
❏ 10048	Father and Daughter, Father and Son/Don't Take Your Love to Town	1974	$5

— With Rosey Nix

❏ 45269	Flesh and Blood/This Side of the Law	1970	$5
❏ 44513	Folsom Prison Blues/The Folk Singer	1968	$6
❏ 44513 [PS]	Folsom Prison Blues/The Folk Singer	1968	$10
❏ 41371	Frankie's Man, Johnny/You, Dreamer, You	1959	$20
❏ 03058	Georgia on a Fast Train/Sing a Song	1982	$4
❏ 10961	(Ghost) Riders in the Sky/I'm Gonna Sit on the Porch and Pick on My Guitar	1979	$5
❏ 10961 [PS]	(Ghost) Riders in the Sky/I'm Gonna Sit on the Porch and Pick on My Guitar	1979	$6
❏ 41920	Girl in Saskatoon/Locomotive Man	1960	$20
❏ 41804	Going to Memphis/Loading Coal	1960	$20
❏ 10817	Gone Girl/I'm Alright Now	1978	$5
❏ 43420	Happy to Be with You/Pickin' Time	1965	$8
❏ 3-38990	Hey Porter/Big River	1964	$40

—Jukebox single, small hole, plays at 33 1/3 rpm; rather than the usual rainbow "target" label of Columbia "Stereo Seven" singles, this one has green labels

| ❏ 08406 | Highwayman/Desperadoes Waiting for a Train | 1988 | $3 |

— Waylon Jennings/Willie Nelson/Johnny Cash/Kris Kristofferson; reissue

| ❏ 04881 | Highwayman/The Human Condition | 1985 | $3 |

—A-side: Willie Nelson/Waylon Jennings/Johnny Cash/Kris Kristofferson; B-side: Nelson, Cash

| ❏ 04881 [PS] | Highwayman/The Human Condition | 1985 | $5 |

—A-side: Willie Nelson/Waylon Jennings/Johnny Cash/Kris Kristofferson; B-side: Nelson, Cash

| ❏ 41427 | I Got Stripes/Five Feet High and Rising | 1959 | $20 |
| ❏ S730427 [S] | I Got Stripes/Five Feet High and Rising | 1959 | $40 |

—Stereo Seven single; small hole, plays at 33 1/3 rpm

❏ 03524	I'll Cross Over Jordan Some Day/We Must Believe in Magic	1983	$4
❏ 11103	I'll Say It's True/Cocaine Blues	1979	$5
❏ 05672	I'm Leaving Now/Easy Street	1985	$3
❏ 04060	I'm Ragged, But I'm Right/Brand New Dance	1983	$4
❏ 31112 [S]	I'm So Lonesome I Could Cry/I Will Miss You When You Go	1961	$40
❏ 42425	In the Jailhouse Now/A Little at a Time	1962	$15
❏ 42425 [PS]	In the Jailhouse Now/A Little at a Time	1962	$30
❏ 4-43145 [DJ]	It Ain't Me, Babe (same on both sides)	1964	$50

—Red vinyl, white label promo

❏ 4-43145	It Ain't Me, Babe/Time and Time Again	1964	$10
❏ 10855	It'll Be Her/It Comes and Goes	1978	$5
❏ 10424	It's All Over/Ridin' on the Cotton Belt	1976	$5

❏ 10888	I Will Rock and Roll with You/A Song for the Life	1979	$5
❏ 10681	I Would Like to See You Again/Lately	1978	$5
❏ 10587	Lady/Hit the Road and Go	1977	$5
❏ S730843 [S]	Loading Coal/Slow Rider	1960	$40
❏ 10177	Look at Them Beans/All Around Cowboy	1975	$5
❏ S730844 [S]	Lumberjack/Dorrance of Ponchartrain	1960	$40
❏ 45339	Man in Black/Little Bit of Yesterday	1971	$5
❏ 43313	Mister Garfield/Streets or Laredo	1965	$8
❏ 02189	Mobile Bay/The Hard Way	1981	$4
❏ 10116	My Old Kentucky Home (Turpentine and Dandelion Wine)/Hard Times Comin'	1975	$5
❏ 31110 [S]	My Shoes Keep Walking Back to You/Time Changes Everything	1961	$40
❏ S730846 [S]	Old Doc Brown/Boss Jack	1960	$40

—The above four are "Stereo Seven" 33 1/3 rpm jukebox singles from set "JS 7-12" and the album "Ride This Train

| ❏ S730847 [S] | One More Ride/Run Softly, Blue River | 1960 | $40 |

—Stereo Seven" 33 1/3 rpm jukebox single from "JS 7-12," but from the album "The Fabulous Johnny Cash

❏ 10321	One Piece at a Time/Go On Blues	1976	$5
❏ 45660	Oney/Country Trash	1972	$5
❏ 43206	Orange Blossom Special/All of God's Children Ain't Free	1965	$8
❏ 45997	Orleans Parish Prison/Jacob Green	1974	$5
❏ 45460	Papa Was a Good Man/I Promise You	1971	$5
❏ 42615	Peace in the Valley/Were You There	1962	$15

— With the Carter Family

| ❏ 45938 | Pick the Wildwood Flower/Diamonds in the Rough | 1973 | $5 |

— With Mother Maybelle and the Carter Family

❏ 31109 [S]	Seasons of My Heart/I Couldn't Keep from Crying	1961	$40
❏ 41618	Seasons of My Heart/Smiling Bill McCall	1960	$20
❏ 41707	Second Honeymoon/Honky Tonk Girl	1960	$20
❏ 45393	Singing in Viet Nam Talking Blues/You've Got a New Light Shining	1971	$5
❏ 10381	Sold Out of Flagpoles/Mountain Lady	1976	$5
❏ 45211	Sonday Morning Coming Down/I'm Gonna Try to Be That Way	1970	$5
❏ 11283	Song of a Patriot/She's a Go-er	1980	$4
❏ 10279	Strawberry Cake/I Got Stripes	1975	$5
❏ 42147	Tennessee Flat Top Box/Tall Men	1961	$15
❏ 42147 [PS]	Tennessee Flat Top Box/Tall Men	1961	$30
❏ 10237	Texas — 1947/I Hardly Ever Sing Beer Drinking Songs	1975	$5
❏ 04428	That's the Truth/Joshua Gone Barbados	1984	$3
❏ 43058	The Ballad of Ira Hayes/Bad News	1964	$12
❏ 60516	The Baron/I Will Dance with You	1981	$4
❏ 42301	The Big Battle/What I've Learned	1962	$15
❏ 42301 [PS]	The Big Battle/What I've Learned	1962	$30
❏ 04513	The Chicken in Black/The Battle of Nashville	1984	$3
❏ 10066	The Lady Came from Baltimore/Lonesome to the Bone	1974	$5
❏ 10483	The Last Gunfighter Ballad/City Jail	1977	$5
❏ 11399	The Last Time/Rockabilly Blues (Texas 1965)	1980	$4
❏ 41481	The Little Drummer Boy/I'll Remember You	1959	$20
❏ 41481 [PS]	The Little Drummer Boy/I'll Remember You	1959	$50
❏ 42880	The Matador/Still in Town	1963	$10
❏ 42880 [PS]	The Matador/Still in Town	1963	$30
❏ 43496	The One on the Right Is On the Left/Cotton Pickin' Hands	1965	$8
❏ 43342	The Sons of Katie Elder/A Certain Kinda Hurtin'	1965	$8
❏ 44288	The Wind Changes/Red Velvet	1967	$6
❏ 04740	They Killed Him/The Three Bells	1985	$3

— With the Carter Family

❏ 31111 [S]	Transfusion Blues/I'd Just Be Fool Enough (To Fall)	1961	$40
❏ 45134	What Is Truth/Sing a Traveling Song	1970	$5
❏ S730845 [S]	When Papa Played the Dobro/Going to Memphis	1960	$40
❏ 11424	Without Love/It Ain't Nothing New Babe	1981	$4

EPIC

| ❏ 50778 | There Ain't No Good Chain Gang/I Wish I Was Crazy Again | 1979 | $5 |

—Johnny Cash/Waylon Jennings

MERCURY

| ❏ 872420-7 | Ballad of a Teenage Queen/Get Rhythm | 1988 | $3 |

— With Roseanne Cash and the Everly Brothers

❏ 870237-7	Cry, Cry, Cry/Get Rhythm	1988	$3
❏ 888838-7	Let Him Roll/My Ship Will Sail	1987	$3
❏ 888719-7	Sixteen Tons/The Ballad of Barbara	1987	$3

Number	Title	Yr	NM
❑ 870688-7	Tennessee Flat Top Box/That Old Wheel	1988	$3

—A-side with Hank Williams, Jr.

Number	Title	Yr	NM
❑ 874562-7	The Last of the Drifters/Water from the Wells of Home	1989	$3

—A-side with Tom T. Hall

Number	Title	Yr	NM
❑ 870010-7	W. Lee O'Daniel (And the Light Crust Dough Boys)/Letters from Homes	1987	$3

SCOTTI BROS.

Number	Title	Yr	NM
❑ 02803	The General Lee/Duelin' Dukes	1982	$4

—Narration on B-side: Sorrell Booke

SMASH

Number	Title	Yr	NM
❑ 884934-7	Sixteen Candles/Rock & Roll (Fais-Do-Do)	1986	$4

—With Jerry Lee Lewis, Roy Orbison and Carl Perkins

Number	Title	Yr	NM
❑ 888142-7	We Remember the King/Class of '55	1987	$4

—With Jerry Lee Lewis, Roy Orbison and Carl Perkins; B-side by Carl Perkins solo

SUN

Number	Title	Yr	NM
❑ 283	Ballad of a Teenage Queen/Big River	1958	$30
❑ 1121	Big River/Come In Stranger	1971	$5
❑ 376	Born to Lose/Blue Train	1962	$30
❑ 7-36/39	Folsom Prison Blues/I Walk the Line	1969	$30

—Premium" on label; possibly a giveaway with specially marked packages of Dr Pepper soda

Number	Title	Yr	NM
❑ 232	Folsom Prison Blues/So Doggone Lonesome	1956	$40
❑ 1103	Get Rhythm/Hey Porter	1969	$6
❑ 331	Goodbye Little Darlin'/You Tell Me	1959	$30
❑ 295	Guess Things Happen That Way/Come In Stranger	1958	$30
❑ 295 [PS]	Guess Things Happen That Way/Come In Stranger	1958	$50
❑ 221	Hey Porter/Cry, Cry, Cry	1955	$50
❑ 279	Home of the Blues/Give My Love to Rose	1957	$40
❑ 309	It's Just About Time/Just Thought You'd Like to Know	1958	$30
❑ 241	I Walk the Line/Get Rhythm	1956	$50
❑ 316	Luther Played the Boogie/Thanks a Lot	1959	$30
❑ 347	Mean Eyed Cat/Port of Lonely Hearts	1960	$30
❑ 355	Oh Lonesome Me/Life Goes On	1961	$30
❑ 334	Straight A's in Love/I Love You Because	1960	$30
❑ 363	Sugartime/My Treasurer	1961	$30
❑ 343	The Story of a Broken Heart/Down the Street to 301	1960	$30
❑ 302	The Ways of a Woman in Love/You're the Nearest Thing to Heaven	1958	$30
❑ 258	Train of Love/There You Go	1956	$40
❑ 392	Wide Open Road/Belshazar	1964	$30

7-Inch Extended Plays

COLUMBIA

Number	Title	Yr	NM
❑ B-13391	*Drink to Me/Five Feet High and Rising/The Man on the Hill/Hank and Joe and Me	1959	$15
❑ B-13392	*Grandfather's Clock/It Could Be You (Instead of Him)/Old Apache Squaw/Don't Step on Mother's Roses	1959	$15
❑ OBS-81221	Don't Take Your Guns to Town/That's Enough//Frankie's Man Johnny/The Troubadour	1959	$50

—Stereo EP with large hole

Number	Title	Yr	NM
❑ 7-9639	Folsom Prison Blues/The Long Black Veil/I Got Stripes//Cocaine Blues/Jackson/Dirty Old Egg-Sucking Dog	1968	$15

—Jukebox issue; small hole, plays at 33 1/3 rpm

Number	Title	Yr	NM
❑ B-12532	Frankie's Man, Johnny/The Troubadour//Don't Take Your Guns to Town/That's Enough	1958	$15
❑ 7-9943 [PS]	Hello, I'm Johnny Cash	1970	$15
❑ B-12841 [PS]	Hymns by Johnny Cash, Vol. I	1959	$15
❑ B-12842 [PS]	Hymns by Johnny Cash, Vol. II	1959	$15
❑ B-12843 [PS]	Hymns by Johnny Cash, Vol. III	1959	$15
❑ B-12843	I Call Him/These Things Shall Pass//He'll Be a Friend/God Will	1959	$15
❑ B-12533	I'd Rather Die Young/One More Ride//Pickin' Time/Shepherd of My Heart	1958	$15
❑ B-12841	It Was Jesus/I Saw a Man//Are All the Children In?/The Old Account	1959	$15
❑ 7-9943	I've Got a Thing About Trains/Wrinkled, Crinkled Wadded Dollar Bill/Southwind//To Beat the Devil/Sing a Traveling Song	1970	$15

—Jukebox issue; small hole, plays at 33 1/3 rpm

Number	Title	Yr	NM
❑ B-14633	I Will Miss You When You Go/I'm So Lonesome I Could Cry//Just One More/Honky Tonk Girl	1960	$15
❑ B-12842	Lead Me Gently Home/Swing Low, Sweet Chariot//Snow in His Hair/Lead Me Father	1959	$15
❑ B-14632	My Shoes Just Keep Walking Back to You/I'd Just Be Fool Enough (To Fall)//Transfusion Blues/Why Do You Punish Me	1960	$15
❑ B-13393	Old Apache Squaw/Don't Step on Mother's Roses//My Grandfather's Clock/It Could Be You	1959	$15
❑ B-14631	Seasons of My Heart/I Feel Better All Over//I Couldn't Keep from Crying/Time Changes Everything	1960	$15
❑ B-13391 [PS]	Songs of Our Soil, Vol. I	1959	$15
❑ B-13392 [PS]	Songs of Our Soil, Vol. II	1959	$15
❑ B-13393 [PS]	Songs of Our Soil, Vol. III	1959	$15
❑ OBS-81221 [PS]	The Fabulous Johnny Cash	1959	$50
❑ B-12531 [PS]	The Fabulous Johnny Cash, Vol. I	1958	$15
❑ B-12532 [PS]	The Fabulous Johnny Cash, Vol. II	1958	$15
❑ B-12533 [PS]	The Fabulous Johnny Cash, Vol. III	1958	$15

SUN

Number	Title	Yr	NM
❑ EPA-112 [PS]	Country Boy	1956	$60
❑ EPA-114 [PS]	His Top Hits	1958	$60
❑ SEP-116 [PS]	Home of the Blues	1959	$60
❑ EPA-111	I Can't Help It/You Win Again//Hey Good Lookin'/I Could Never Be Ashamed	1956	$50
❑ EPA-113 [PS]	I Walk the Line	1958	$60
❑ EPA-113	I Walk the Line/The Wreck of the Old '97//Folsom Prison Blues/Doin' My Time	1958	$35
❑ SEP-117	So Doggone Lonesome/I Was There When It Happened//Cry, Cry, Cry/Remember Me	1958	$35
❑ EPA-114	The Ways of a Woman in Love/Next in Line//Guess Things Happen That Way/Train of Love	1958	$35

CASH, ROSEANNE

COLUMBIA

Number	Title	Yr	NM
❑ 02937	Ain't No Money/The Feelin'	1982	$3
❑ 73054	Black and White/Never Be You	1989	$3
❑ 03868	Blue Moon with Heartache/Ain't No Money	1983	$3

—Golden Oldies" reissue

Number	Title	Yr	NM
❑ 02659	Blue Moon with Heartache/Only Human	1981	$4
❑ 11188	Couldn't Do Nothin' Right/Seeing Is Believing	1980	$4
❑ 05794	Hold On/Never Gonna Hurt	1986	$3
❑ 08399	Hold On/Second to No One	1988	$3

—Reissue

Number	Title	Yr	NM
❑ 08401	I Don't Know Why You Don't Want Me/Never Be You	1988	$3

—Reissue

Number	Title	Yr	NM
❑ 04809	I Don't Know Why You Don't Want Me/What You Gonna Do About It	1985	$3
❑ 04809 [PS]	I Don't Know Why You Don't Want Me/What You Gonna Do About It	1985	$3
❑ 68599	I Don't Want to Spoil the Party/Look What Our Love Is Coming To	1989	$3
❑ 68599 [PS]	I Don't Want to Spoil the Party/Look What Our Love Is Coming To	1989	$3
❑ 07746	If You Change Your Mind/Somewhere Sometime	1988	$3
❑ 03705	It Hasn't Happened Yet/Somewhere in the Stars	1983	$3
❑ 07693	It's Such a Small World/Crazy Baby	1988	$3

—Rodney Crowell and Roseanne Cash; B-side by Crowell

Number	Title	Yr	NM
❑ 03283	I Wonder/Oh Yes I Can	1982	$3
❑ 02463	My Baby Thinks He's a Train/I Can't Resist	1981	$4
❑ 06159	Second to No One/Never Alone	1986	$3
❑ 11426	Seven Year Ache/Blue Moon with Heartache	1981	$4
❑ 03131	Seven Year Ache/My Baby Thinks He's a Train	1982	$3

—Golden Oldies" reissue

Number	Title	Yr	NM
❑ 07624	Tennessee Flat Top Box/Why Don't You Quit Leaving Me Alone	1987	$3
❑ 07200	The Way We Make a Broken Heart/707	1987	$3

CASH, TOMMY

20TH CENTURY

Number	Title	Yr	NM
❑ 2263	Broken Bones/The Ballad of Jack and Lucille	1975	$5

ELEKTRA

Number	Title	Yr	NM
❑ 45258	The Lady Is a Woman/Only a Stone	1975	$5
❑ 45241	The One I Sing My Love Songs To/Goodbye Ringin' in My Ear	1975	$5

EPIC

Number	Title	Yr	NM
❑ 5-10756	I'm Gonna Write a Song/I'm Nowhere Without You	1971	$8
❑ 5-10915	Listen/Fool Maker	1972	$8
❑ 5-10630	One Song Away/The Ramblin' Kind	1970	$8
❑ 5-10540	Six White Horses/I Owe the World to You	1969	$8
❑ 5-10700	So This Is Love/Love Is Gone	1971	$8
❑ 5-10885	That Certain One/A Free Man	1972	$8
❑ 5-10673	The Tears on Lincoln's Face/Only Place for Me	1970	$8

MONUMENT

Number	Title	Yr	NM
❑ 45-286	Don't Give Up on Me/When the Lovin' Starts	1979	$5
❑ 45-274	I'll Be Better Off Alone/Six Feet Tall and Handsome	1979	$5
❑ 45-238	Take My Love to Rita/We Finally Got It Right	1978	$5
❑ 45-222	The Cowboy and the Lady/Lady I Love You	1977	$5
❑ 45-250	The In Crowd/A Lot of Catching Up to Do	1978	$5

MUSICOR

Number	Title	Yr	NM
❑ 1137	Along the Way/Freedom of Livin'	1965	$15
❑ 1109	I Didn't Walk the Line/Where You Came From	1965	$15
❑ 1060	I Guess I'll Love/Why'd She Gone	1965	$15

UNITED ARTISTS

Number	Title	Yr	NM
❑ 50068	All I've Got to Show (For Loving You)/Down, Down, Down	1966	$10
❑ 50246	I'm Not the Boy I Used to Be/Leaving Your World (A Better Place to Live)	1968	$10
❑ 50337	The Sounds of Goodbye/Easy Woman	1968	$10
❑ 50185	Tobacco Road/Wave Goodbye to Me	1967	$10

CASHMAN, PISTILLI AND WEST

ABC

Number	Title	Yr	NM
❑ 11047	But for Love/Song That Never Comes	1968	$8
❑ 11111	My Side of the Sky/You Can Write a Song	1968	$8
❑ 11079	Spring Has a Tear in Her Eye/Little Girl	1968	$8

CAPITOL

Number	Title	Yr	NM
❑ 2863	Midnight Man/Automatic Pilot	1970	$6
❑ 2582	Proud Mary-Dock of the Bay/Sister John	1969	$6
❑ 2747	She Never Looked Better/Goodbye Jo	1970	$6
❑ 2671	Signs/Dolphins	1969	$6
❑ 2462	Some of My Best Friends Are People/Sausalito	1969	$6

CASHMAN, TERRY

BOOM

Number	Title	Yr	NM
❑ 60005	Try Me/Pretty Face	1966	$20

LIFESONG

Number	Title	Yr	NM
❑ 45015	Baby, Baby I Love You/We'll Be Together	1976	$4
❑ 45087	Baseball (America's National Pastime)/Willie, Mickey and "The Duke" (Talkin' Baseball)	1981	$5
❑ 45087 PS]	Baseball (America's National Pastime)/Willie, Mickey and "The Duke" (Talkin' Baseball)	1981	$12
❑ 45117	Cooperstown (The Town Where Baseball Lives)/Baseball Ballet	1983	$5
❑ 45121 [DJ]	Football U.S.A. (same on both sides)	1983	$4

—May be promo only

Number	Title	Yr	NM
❑ 45110	Talkin' Baseball (Atlanta Braves Version)/Baby, Baby I Love You	1982	$4
❑ 45110 [PS]	Talkin' Baseball (Atlanta Braves Version)/Baby, Baby I Love You	1982	$4

—Green "Talkin' Baseball" sleeve with custom sticker

Number	Title	Yr	NM
❑ 45105 [PS]	Talkin' Baseball/Baby, Baby I Love You	1982	$4

—Green "Talkin' Baseball" sleeve with "For Orioles Fans" custom sticker

Number	Title	Yr	NM
❑ 45105	Talkin' Baseball (Baltimore Orioles Version)/Baby, Baby I Love You	1982	$4
❑ 45105 [PS]	Talkin' Baseball (Baltimore Orioles Version)/Baby, Baby I Love You	1982	$5

—Orange sleeve with photo of Cal Ripken Jr.

Number	Title	Yr	NM
❑ 45104CC	Talkin' Baseball (Baseball and the Cubs)/Baby, Baby I Love You	1982	$4
❑ 45106	Talkin' Baseball (Boston Red Sox Version)/Baby, Baby I Love You	1982	$4
❑ 45106 [PS]	Talkin' Baseball (Boston Red Sox Version)/Baby, Baby I Love You	1982	$4

—Green "Talkin' Baseball" sleeve with custom sticker

Number	Title	Yr	NM
❑ 45101	Talkin' Baseball (Cincinnati Reds Version)/Baby, Baby I Love You	1982	$4
❑ 45101 [PS]	Talkin' Baseball (Cincinnati Reds Version)/Baby, Baby I Love You	1982	$4

—Green "Talkin' Baseball" sleeve with custom sticker

Number	Title	Yr	NM
❑ 45099	Talkin' Baseball (Cleveland Indians Version)/Baby, Baby I Love You	1982	$4
❑ 45099 [PS]	Talkin' Baseball (Cleveland Indians Version)/Baby, Baby I Love You	1982	$4

—Green "Talkin' Baseball" sleeve with custom sticker

Number	Title	Yr	NM
❑ 45103	Talkin' Baseball (Detroit Tigers Version)/Baby, Baby I Love You	1982	$4
❑ 45103 [PS]	Talkin' Baseball (Detroit Tigers Version)/Baby, Baby I Love You	1982	$4

—Green "Talkin' Baseball" sleeve with custom sticker

Number	Title	Yr	NM
❑ 45112	Talkin' Baseball (Houston Astros Version)/Baby, Baby I Love You	1982	$4
❑ 45112 [PS]	Talkin' Baseball (Houston Astros Version)/Baby, Baby I Love You	1982	$4
— Green "Talkin' Baseball" sleeve with custom sticker			
❑ 45111	Talkin' Baseball (Kansas City Royals Version)/ Baby, Baby I Love You	1982	$4
❑ 45111 [PS]	Talkin' Baseball (Kansas City Royals Version)/ Baby, Baby I Love You	1982	$4
— Green "Talkin' Baseball" sleeve with custom sticker			
❑ 45098	Talkin' Baseball (Los Angeles Dodgers Version)/ Baby, Baby I Love You	1982	$4
❑ 45098 [PS]	Talkin' Baseball (Los Angeles Dodgers Version)/ Baby, Baby I Love You	1982	$4
— Green "Talkin' Baseball" sleeve with custom sticker			
❑ 45113	Talkin' Baseball (Milwaukee Brewers Version)/Baby, Baby I Love You	1982	$4
❑ 45113 [PS]	Talkin' Baseball (Milwaukee Brewers Version)/Baby, Baby I Love You	1982	$4
— Green "Talkin' Baseball" sleeve with custom sticker			
❑ 45114	Talkin' Baseball (Minnesota Twins Version)/Baby, Baby I Love You	1982	$4
❑ 45114 [PS]	Talkin' Baseball (Minnesota Twins Version)/Baby, Baby I Love You	1982	$4
— Green "Talkin' Baseball" sleeve with custom sticker			
❑ 45115	Talkin' Baseball (Montreal Expos Version)/Baby, Baby I Love You	1982	$4
❑ 45115 [PS]	Talkin' Baseball (Montreal Expos Version)/Baby, Baby I Love You	1982	$4
— Green "Talkin' Baseball" sleeve with custom sticker			
❑ 45108	Talkin' Baseball (New York Mets Version)/Baby, Baby I Love You	1982	$4
❑ 45108 [PS]	Talkin' Baseball (New York Mets Version)/Baby, Baby I Love You	1982	$4
— Green "Talkin' Baseball" sleeve with custom sticker			
❑ 45097	Talkin' Baseball (New York Yankees Version)/ Baby, Baby I Love You	1982	$4
❑ 45097 [PS]	Talkin' Baseball (New York Yankees Version)/ Baby, Baby I Love You	1982	$4
— Green "Talkin' Baseball" sleeve with custom sticker			
❑ 45096	Talkin' Baseball (Philadelphia Phillies Version)/Baby, Baby I Love You	1982	$4
❑ 45096 [PS]	Talkin' Baseball (Philadelphia Phillies Version)/Baby, Baby I Love You	1982	$4
— Green "Talkin' Baseball" sleeve with custom sticker			
❑ 45109	Talkin' Baseball (Pittsburgh Pirates Version)/Baby, Baby I Love You	1982	$4
❑ 45109 [PS]	Talkin' Baseball (Pittsburgh Pirates Version)/Baby, Baby I Love You	1982	$4
— Green "Talkin' Baseball" sleeve with custom sticker			
❑ 45102	Talkin' Baseball (San Francisco Giants Version)/ Baby, Baby I Love You	1982	$4
❑ 45102 [PS]	Talkin' Baseball (San Francisco Giants Version)/ Baby, Baby I Love You	1982	$4
— Green "Talkin' Baseball" sleeve with custom sticker			
❑ 45104CC [PS]	Talkin' Baseball (Special Cubs Version)/Baby, Baby I Love You	1982	$6
— Green "Talkin' Baseball" sleeve with square Chicago Cubs sticker			
❑ 45107	Talkin' Baseball (St. Louis Cardinals Version)/Baby, Baby I Love You	1982	$4
❑ 45107 [PS]	Talkin' Baseball (St. Louis Cardinals Version)/Baby, Baby I Love You	1982	$4
— Green "Talkin' Baseball" sleeve with custom sticker			
❑ 45100	Talkin' Baseball (Texas Rangers Version)/Baby, Baby I Love You	1982	$4
❑ 45100 [PS]	Talkin' Baseball (Texas Rangers Version)/Baby, Baby I Love You	1982	$4
— Green "Talkin' Baseball" sleeve with custom sticker			
❑ 45021	The Dreamer/Football U.S.A.	1977	$4
❑ 45119	The Earl of Baltimore/ Baseball Ballet	1983	$4
❑ 45086	Willie, Mickey and "The Duke" (Talkin' Baseball)/It's So Easy to Sing a Love Song	1980	$5
❑ 45086 [PS]	Willie, Mickey and "The Duke" (Talkin' Baseball)/It's So Easy to Sing a Love Song	1980	$10

METROSTAR

Number	Title	Yr	NM
❑ M-4585-2	There Must Be Something Inside (A Tribute to Pete Rose)/ Baseball's Red Machine (Talkin' Baseball, Cincinnati Reds)	1985	$10

CASHMERES, THE

HEM

Number	Title	Yr	NM
❑ 1000	Show Stopper/Don't Let the Door Hit Your Back	1965	$5000

— VG 2500; VG+ 3750

HERALD

Number	Title	Yr	NM
❑ 474	Little Dream Girl/Do I Upset You	1956	$100

JOSIE

Number	Title	Yr	NM
❑ 894	Life Line/Where Have You Been	1961	$15

LAKE

Number	Title	Yr	NM
❑ 703	Everything's Gonna Be Alright/Four Lonely Nights	1960	$40
❑ 705	Satisfied/Satisfied (Part 2)	1961	$30

LAURIE

Number	Title	Yr	NM
❑ 3078	I Believe in St. Nick/A Very Special Birthday	1960	$50
❑ 3088	I Gotta Go/Singing Waters	1961	$30
❑ 3105	Poppa Said/Bobby Come On Home	1961	$30

MERCURY

Number	Title	Yr	NM
❑ 70617	Don't Let It Happen Again/ Boom Mag-Azeno-Vip Vay	1955	$100
❑ 70501	My Sentimental Heart/ Yes, Yes, Yes	1954	$100
❑ 70679	There's a Rumor/ Second Hand Heart	1955	$100

RELIC

Number	Title	Yr	NM
❑ 1005	Satisfied/Satisfied (Part 2)	1970	$6

CASINOS, THE (1)

FRATERNITY

Number	Title	Yr	NM
❑ 997	Bye Bye Love/Walk Through This World with Me	1967	$10
❑ 1200	Father John/The Old Saloon	1970	$10
❑ 987	Forever and a Night/ How Long Has It Been	1967	$10
❑ 985	It's All Over Now/Tailor Made	1967	$10
❑ 1028	I Wish I Were Anyone But Me/I Just Want to Stay Here	1969	$10
❑ 1250	Loving Her Was Easier/A Restless Wind	1971	$10
❑ 944	She's Out of Sight/The Gallop	1965	$10
❑ 977	Then You Can Tell Me Goodbye/I Still Love You	1967	$15
❑ 1020	These Are the Things We'll Share/Casinos Having Fun	1969	$10
❑ 995	When I Stop Dreaming/ Please Love	1967	$10
❑ 1201	Wisdom of Love/My House	1970	$10

MILLION

Number	Title	Yr	NM
❑ 13	I'm Walking Behind You/ Angels Were All Asleep	1972	$10

— As "Gene Hughes and the Casinos

UNITED ARTISTS

Number	Title	Yr	NM
❑ 50255	Here I Am/Peggy	1968	$12

— As "Gene Hughes and the Casinos

CASINOS, THE (U)

AIRTOWN

Number	Title	Yr	NM
❑ 02	That's the Way/Too Good to Be True	1967	$20

ALTO

Number	Title	Yr	NM
❑ 2002	I Like It Like That/Baby Don't Do It	1961	$40

CASINO

Number	Title	Yr	NM
❑ 111	My Love for You/Why Am I a Fool	1960	$50

CERTRON

Number	Title	Yr	NM
❑ 10015	Coal River/(B-side unknown)	1970	$6

ITZY

Number	Title	Yr	NM
❑ 2	Do You Recall?/The Swim	1964	$60

NAME

Number	Title	Yr	NM
❑ 7739	Do You Recall?/The Swim	1962	$250

OLIMPIC

Number	Title	Yr	NM
❑ 251	Do You Recall?/The Swim	1963	$200

SIMS

Number	Title	Yr	NM
❑ 306	Moon River/Soul Serenade	1966	$15

TERRY

Number	Title	Yr	NM
❑ 115	Gee Whiz/Lovely One	1964	$70
❑ 116	That's the Way/Too Good to Be True	1964	$60

CASLONS, THE

SEECO

Number	Title	Yr	NM
❑ 6078	Anniversary of Love/ (B-side unknown)	1961	$30

CASSADY, LINDA

CIN KAY

Number	Title	Yr	NM
❑ 107	C.B. Widow/Do You Still Want What's Left of Me	1976	$5
❑ 118	Do You Still Want What's Left of Me/(B-side unknown)	1977	$5
❑ 116	I Don't Hurt Anymore/Baby There's Nothing Wrong with Me	1977	$5
❑ 111	If It's Your Song You Sing It/This Isn't Just Another Love Song	1976	$5
❑ 127	Little Teardrops (Are Smarter Than You Think)/(B-side unknown)	1978	$5
❑ 115	Little Things Mean a Lot/ Sounds of Love	1977	$5
❑ 131	Lonely Side of the Bed/ That's the Way It Is	1978	$6
❑ 129	(There's Nothing Like the Love) Between a Woman and a Man/Finer Side of Life	1978	$5

— With Bobby Spears

DOOR KNOB

Number	Title	Yr	NM
❑ 004	C.B. Widow/Do You Still Want What's Left of Me	1975	$8
❑ 158	Tell It to Someone/ (B-side unknown)	1981	$5
❑ 002	Tell It to Someone Who'll Believe It/Jolene	1975	$8

METRO COUNTRY

Number	Title	Yr	NM
❑ 2010	Is Santa Claus a Hippie?/ What Do You Do?	1969	$10

SOUNDWAVES

Number	Title	Yr	NM
❑ 4584	Dusty Raven/Walk a Mile to a Country School	1980	$5
❑ 4602	Hit Man/Don't Stop Before You Get There	1981	$5
❑ 4636	Is That Mountain Worth Climbing/ We Can Touch, But We Don't Feel	1981	$5
❑ 4594	Out You Go/Can You Keep a Secret	1980	$5

CASSIDY, DAVID

BELL

Number	Title	Yr	NM
❑ 45605	Breaking Up Is Hard to Do/ Please Please Me	1974	$8
❑ 45150	Cherish/All I Want to Do Is Touch You	1971	$10
❑ 45150 [PS]	Cherish/All I Want to Do Is Touch You	1971	$12
❑ 45187	Could It Be Forever/Blind Hope	1972	$10
❑ 45187 [PS]	Could It Be Forever/Blind Hope	1972	$12
❑ 45386	Daydream/Can't Go Home Again	1973	$10
❑ 45413	Daydreamer/The Puppy Song	1973	$10
❑ 45220	How Can I Be Sure/Ricky's Tune	1972	$10

MCA

Number	Title	Yr	NM
❑ 41101	Hurt So Bad/Once a Fool	1979	$10
❑ 41101 [PS]	Hurt So Bad/Once a Fool	1979	$15

RCA

Number	Title	Yr	NM
❑ PB-10788	I'll Have to Go Away (Saying Goodbye)/Gettin' It in the Streets	1976	$10
❑ PB-10921	Saying Goodbye Ain't Easy (We'll Have to Go Away)/Rosa's Cantina	1977	$10

RCA VICTOR

Number	Title	Yr	NM
❑ PB-10647	Breakin' Down Again/On Fire	1976	$10
❑ PB-10321	Get It Up for Love/Love In Bloom	1975	$10
❑ PB-10405	This Could Be the Night/Darlin'	1975	$10
❑ PB-10585	Tomorrow/Bedtime	1976	$10

CASSIDY, SHAUN

WARNER BROS.

Number	Title	Yr	NM
❑ 49039	Are You Afraid of Me?/ You're Usin' Me	1979	$4
❑ 8365	Da Doo Ron Ron/Holiday	1977	$4
❑ 8365 [PS]	Da Doo Ron Ron/Holiday	1977	$6
❑ 8533	Do You Believe in Magic/ Teen Dream	1978	$4
❑ 8533 [PS]	Do You Believe in Magic/ Teen Dream	1978	$4
❑ 49154	Heaven in Your Eyes/Star Trek	1980	$4
❑ 8488	Hey Deanie/Strange Sensation	1977	$4
❑ 8488 [PS]	Hey Deanie/Strange Sensation	1977	$4
❑ 8698	Midnight Sun/She's Right	1978	$5
❑ 8698 [PS]	Midnight Sun/She's Right	1978	$5
❑ 8634	Our Night/Right Before Your Eyes	1978	$4
❑ 8634 [PS]	Our Night/Right Before Your Eyes	1978	$4
❑ 49640	So Sad About Us/Cool Fire	1980	$5
— A-side with Todd Rundgren's Utopia			
❑ 8423	That's Rock 'N' Roll/I Wanna Be with You	1977	$4
❑ 8423 [PS]	That's Rock 'N' Roll/I Wanna Be with You	1977	$5

CASSIDY, TED

CAPITOL

Number	Title	Yr	NM
❑ 5503	The Lurch/Wesley	1965	$30
❑ 5503 [PS]	The Lurch/Wesley	1965	$120

CASSINI, DARIO

EPIC

Number	Title	Yr	NM
❑ 9084	Santo Natale/O Holy Night	1954	$20

CASTALEERS, THE

DONNA

Number	Title	Yr	NM
❑ 1349	That's Why I Cry/My Baby's All Right	1961	$30

FELSTED

Number	Title	Yr	NM
❑ 8504	Come Back/Hi-Fi Baby	1958	$60
❑ 8512	Lonely Boy/My Bull Fightin' Baby	1958	$50

PLANET

Number	Title	Yr	NM
❑ 44	That's Why I Cry/My Baby's All Right	1961	$50

Number	Title	Yr	NM

CASTANETS, THE
TCF

Number	Title	Yr	NM
1	I Love Him/Funky Wunky Piano	1963	$10

CASTAWAYS, THE (1)
BEAR

| 2000 | I Feel So Fine/Hit the Road Jack | 1967 | $50 |

FONTANA

| 1626 | Lavender Popcorn/What Kind of Face | 1968 | $20 |
| 1615 | Walking in Different Circles/Just On High | 1968 | $20 |

SOMA

1461	Girl in Love/Should Happen to Me	1966	$15
1442	Goodbye Babe/A Man's Gotta Be a Man	1965	$15
1433	Liar, Liar/Sam	1965	$20
1469	Liar, Liar/Surfin' Bird	1966	$15

—B-side by the Trashmen

TAUNAH

| 7745 | (I) Feel So Fine/Hit the Road Jack | 1967 | $15 |

CASTAWAYS, THE (2)
CAPITOL

| 4340 | The Twitch/Vibrations | 1960 | $15 |

CASTAWAYS, THE (3)
EXCELLO

| 2038 | I Wish/Teasin' | 1954 | $50 |

CASTAWAYS, THE (4)
GNP CRESCENDO

| 310 | Moritat/Pass It Around | 1964 | $10 |
| 302 | Tarzan/Wild Boy | 1963 | $10 |

CASTAWAYS, THE (U)
WITCH

| 124 | Don't You Just Know It/I Go Ape | 1964 | $40 |

CASTELLE, GEORGE
GRAND

| 118 | It's Christmas Time/Over The Rainbow | 1954 | $60 |

CASTELLES, THE
ATCO

| 6069 | Happy and Gay/Hey Baby Baby | 1956 | $125 |

CLASSIC ARTISTS

| 114 | At Christmas Time/One Little Teardrop | 1989 | $4 |

GRAND

| 109 | Baby Can't You See/Over a Cup of Coffee | 1954 | $2000 |

—Blue label original

| 105 | Do You Remember/If You Were the Only Girl | 1954 | $1500 |

—Glossy yellow label original

| 114 | Marcella/I'm a Fool to Care | 1955 | $1200 |

—Cream label original

| 101 | My Girl Awaits Me/Sweetness | 1954 | $2000 |

—Blue label original

| 122 | My Wedding Day/Heavenly Father | 1955 | $7000 |

—Cream label original

| 103 | This Silver Ring/Wonder Why | 1954 | $2000 |

—Glossy yellow label original

CASTELLS, THE
DECCA

| 31967 | Life Goes On/I Thought You'd Like That | 1966 | $20 |

ERA

3098	Clown Prince/Eternal Spring, Eternal Love	1962	$30
3089	Echoes in the Night/The Only One	1962	$30
3102	Little Sad Eyes/Initials	1963	$30
3038	Little Sad Eyes/Romeo	1961	$30
3057	My Miracle/Make Believe Wedding	1961	$30
3083	Oh, What It Seemed to Be/Stand There, Mountain	1962	$30
3048	Sacred/I Get Dreamy	1961	$30
3107	Some Enchanted Evening/What Do Little Girls Dream Of	1963	$30
3073	So This Is Love/On the Street of Tears	1962	$30

LAURIE

| 3444 | I'd Like to Know/Rocky Ridges | 1968 | $10 |

UNITED ARTISTS

| 50324 | Two Lovers/Jerusalem | 1968 | $10 |

WARNER BROS.

| 5445 | Could This Be Magic/Shinny Up Your Own Side | 1964 | $40 |

| 5421 | I Do/Teardrops | 1964 | $100 |

—A-side written and produced by Brian Wilson

| 5486 | Love Finds a Way/Tell Her If I Could | 1964 | $30 |

CASTLE, JOEY
RCA VICTOR

| 47-7283 | That Ain't Nothin' But Right/Come A Little Closer Baby | 1958 | $70 |

CASTLE, TONY
EASTWEST

| 107 | Terry/Young and In Love | 1958 | $40 |

GONE

5099	Salty/Hi Lili, Hi Lo	1961	$30
5099	Salty/Salty, Part 2	1961	$30
5107	Seems Like Old Times/The Loneliest Girl in the World	1961	$30
5105	Sincerely/Tara's Themes	1961	$30

CASTON, BOBBY
ATLAS

| 1103 | Call Me Darling/Why Wasn't I Told | 1958 | $125 |

CASTOR, JIMMY, BUNCH
ATLANTIC

3331	Bom Bom/What's Best	1976	$4
3362	Everything Is Beautiful to Me/The Magic Is in the Music	1976	$4
3045	Everything Man (E-Man)/Heaven Kissed	1974	$5
3369 [DJ]	I Don't Wanna Lose You (mono/stereo)	1976	$5

—May be promo-only

3396	I Love a Mellow Groove/I Don't Want to Lose You	1977	$4
3011	Maggie (Part 1)/Maggie (Part 2)	1974	$5
3451	Magnolia/TR-7	1978	$4
3455	Maximum Stimulation/It Was You	1978	$4
3270	Potential/Daniel	1975	$5
3375	Space Age/Dracula	1976	$4
3316	Supersound/Drifting	1976	$4
3232	The Bertha Butt Boogie (Part 1)/The Bertha Butt Boogie (Part 2)	1975	$5

ATOMIC

| 100 | Somebody Mentioned Your Name/This Girl of Mine | 1957 | $500 |

CAPITOL

2634	Helpless/Make Me	1969	$8
2358	Hey Shorty (Part 1)/Hey Shorty (Part 2)	1968	$8
2487	Psycho Man/The Real McCoy	1969	$8

CATAWBA

| ZS4-05676 | Godzilla/(Instrumental) | 1985 | $4 |

COMPASS

| 7019 | Soul Sister/Rattlesnake | 1968 | $8 |

COTILLION

| 44253 | Don't Do That!/Don't Do That! (Part 2) | 1979 | $4 |
| 45004 | Party People/I Just Wanna Stop | 1979 | $4 |

DECCA

| 31963 | In a Boogaloo Bag (Part 1)/In a Boogaloo Bag (Part 2) | 1966 | $10 |

DREAM

D7-0360	Amazon/She's an Amazon	1984	$5
D7-0359	Don't Cry Out Loud/(Instrumental)	1983	$5
D70361	It Gets to Me/(Instrumental)	1984	$5

DRIVE

| 6271 | Bertha Butt Encounters Vadar/Mystery of Me | 1978 | $4 |

HULL

| 758 | Poor Loser/Oh Suzzana | 1963 | $30 |

LONG DISTANCE

| 701/2 | Stay with Me (Spend the Night)/Can't Help Falling in Love with You | 1980 | $5 |

RCA VICTOR

APBO-0047	How Beautiful You Are/I'm Not a Child Anymore	1973	$5
74-0763	Luther the Anthropod/Party Life	1972	$5
74-0583	My Brightest Day/You Better Be Good	1971	$5
74-0836	Paradise/The First Time Ever I Saw Your Face	1972	$5
48-1024	Say Leroy (The Creature from the Black Lagoon Is Your Father) (Parts 1 & 2)	1972	$5
74-0953	Soul Serenade/Purple Haze-Foxey Lady (Tribute to Jimi Hendrix)	1973	$5
48-1029	Troglodyte (Cave Man)/I Promise to Remember	1972	$6
AMBO-0120	Troglodyte (Cave Man)/Luther the Anthropod	1973	$4

—Gold Standard Series

SALSOUL

| 7058 | E-Man Boogie '83/It's Just Begun | 1983 | $4 |
| 7018 | E-Man Boogie/Any Way, Any Where, Any Time | 1982 | $4 |

SMASH

| 2069 | Hey, Leroy, Your Mama's Calling You/Ham Hocks Espanol | 1966 | $8 |
| 2099 | Leroy Is In the Army/Dry | 1967 | $8 |

WING

| 90078 | I Promise/I Know the Meaning of Love | 1956 | $120 |

CASTROES, THE
GRAND

| 2002 | Dearest Darling/Dance with Me | 1959 | $200 |

CASUAL ASSOCIATION, THE
PARKWAY

| 158 | Georgy Girl/Nickels and Dimes | 1967 | $15 |

CASUALAIRS, THE
CRAIG

| 5001 | Bossa Nova Twist/Cruising | 1962 | $50 |

MONA-LEE

| 136 | At the Dance/Satsfied | 1959 | $50 |

CASUALS, THE (2)
DOT

| 15671 | Hello Love/Till You Come Back to Me | 1957 | $30 |
| 15557 | Somebody Help Me/My Love Song for You | 1957 | $30 |

CASUALS, THE (3)
MAINSTREAM

| 692 | I've Got Something Too/Jesamine (A Butterfly Child) | 1968 | $10 |
| 697 | Touched/Toy | 1968 | $10 |

—As "The British Casuals"

CASUALS, THE (4)
MINARET

| 109 | Money/Big Hammer | 1963 | $20 |

MONUMENT

| 905 | Promise Her Anything (But Give Her Love)/Walk | 1965 | $15 |
| 937 | Walk Away/If You Don't | 1966 | $15 |

SOUND STAGE 7

| 2534 | Mustang 2 + 2/Play Me a Sad Song | 1964 | $20 |

CAT MOTHER AND THE ALL NIGHT NEWS BOYS
POLYDOR

| 14007 | Can You Dance to It/Marie | 1969 | $6 |

—Both of the above were produced by Jimi Hendrix

14002	Good Old Rock 'N Roll/Bad News	1969	$8
14029	Last Go-Round/I Must Be Dreaming	1970	$6
14126	Letter to the President/Ode to Oregon	1972	$6
14138	She Came from a Different World/Three and Me	1972	$6

CATALINAS, THE (1)
Studio band of Los Angeles session pros.

RIC

| 113 | Banzai Wipeout/Beach Walkin' | 1964 | $30 |
| 164 | Boss Barracuda/Surfer Boy | 1965 | $30 |

SIMS

| 134 | Bail Out/Bulletin | 1963 | $20 |

CATALINAS, THE (2)
LITTLE

| 811/2 | Give Me Your Love/Castle of Love | 1957 | $200 |

CATALINAS, THE (U)
20TH FOX

| 299 | Safari/Pretty Little Nashville Girl | 1962 | $40 |
| 286 | Sweetheart/Unchained Melody | 1962 | $40 |

BACK BEAT

| 513 | Speechless/Flying Formation with You | 1958 | $40 |

DEE JAY

| 1010 | Bail Out/Bulletin | 1963 | $50 |

DIAL

| 3008 | Cha Cha Joe/Echo One | 1963 | $15 |

GLORY

| 285 | Marlene/With Your Girl -- Yeah! | 1958 | $30 |

SCEPTER

| 12188 | Tick Tock/You Haven't the Right | 1967 | $20 |

Number	Title	Yr	NM

CATES, GEORGE
CORAL
❏ 9-62011	Acapulco/Caracas	1958	$10
❏ 9-61655	Away All Boats/The Proud and Profane (To Love Ya)	1956	$15
❏ 9-60249	Baseball Polka/On the Beach	1950	$20
❏ 9-60291	Beloved, Be Faithful/Honestly, I Love You	1950	$20
❏ 9-61810	Boy on a Dolphin/Your Kiss	1957	$10
❏ 9-60810	Carmen's Boogie/Babalu	1952	$15
❏ 9-61965	Champagne Time/Madame Zajj	1958	$10
❏ 9-60215	Chug-a-Lug/She's Shimmyin' on the Beach Again	1950	$20
❏ 9-61226	Double-Gated/Athena	1954	$15
❏ 9-60365	Down by the Old Zuyder River/There's More Pretty Girls Than One	1951	$20
❏ 9-61702	Friendly Persuasion/There's Never Been Anyone Else But You	1956	$15
❏ 9-60546	Hi-Diddle-Diddle/Looking for You	1951	$20
❏ 9-61432	If I Had Three Wishes/If We Never Had Said Alone	1955	$15
❏ 9-61774	Last Night/The Poodle Walk	1957	$12
❏ 9-61618	Moonglow and Theme from "Picnic"/Rio Batucada	1956	$15
❏ 9-60326	Silver Bells/Jing-a-Ling, Jing-a-Ling	1950	$20
❏ 9-60302	Sleigh Ride/Tubby the Tuba Song	1950	$20
❏ 9-60627	Snowflakes/River in the Moonlight	1952	$15
❏ 9-60436	The Syncopated Clock/On Top of Old Smokey	1951	$20
❏ 9-60262	Tzena, Tzena, Tzena/They Put the Light Out	1950	$20
❏ 9-61007	When Someone Wonderful Thinks You're Wonderful/Lost	1953	$15
❏ 9-61683	Where There's Life/One Night in Monte Carlo	1956	$15

DOT
❏ 16481	Canadian Sunset/The Flip	1963	$8
❏ 16461	Diamond Head/How the West Was Won	1963	$8
❏ 16581	Ghost Guitar/Peanut Vendor	1964	$8
❏ 16330	In a Little Spanish Town (Twist)/Star Dust	1962	$8
❏ 16376	Third Man Theme/Quiet Village	1962	$8
❏ 16409	Woodchopper's Ball/Poinciana	1962	$8

HAMILTON
❏ 50041	Flowers on the Wall/Cristo Redentor	1966	$8

SIGNATURE
❏ 12005	Give Me All Your Love/So Tired	1959	$10
❏ 12016	My Darling Laura Lee/Waltzing Matilda	1959	$10
❏ 12034	The Dipsy Doodle/Weary Blues	1960	$12

CATES, RONNIE
TERRACE
❏ 7508	For My Very Own/Long Time	1962	$60
❏ 7501	Ol' Man River/Long Time	1961	$60

CATES SISTERS, THE
CAPRICE
❏ 2032	Can't Help It/(B-side unknown)	1977	$5
❏ 2036	I'll Always Love You/Second Chance	1977	$5
❏ 2041	I've Been Loved/Faded Love	1977	$5
❏ 2047	Long Gone Blues/San Antonio Rose	1978	$5
❏ 2051	Lovin' You Off My Mind/Amazing Grace	1978	$5
❏ 2024	Mr. Guitar/Love Is a Beautiful Thing	1976	$5
❏ 2030	Out of My Mind/Run Your Sweet Love By Me	1976	$5
—As "The Cates			
❏ 2038	Throw Out Your Loveline/West Virginia Smile	1977	$5

MCA
❏ 40032	He Fiddled His Way Into My Heart/Crazy Dreams	1973	$8
—As "Marcy and Margie"			

OVATION
❏ 1123	Going Down Slow/Can I See You Tonight	1979	$5
—All on Ovation as "The Cates"			
❏ 1144	Gonna Get Along Without You Now/I've Been Lovin' You Too Long	1980	$5
❏ 1134	Let's Go Through the Motions/Don't Say Love	1979	$5
❏ 1155	Lightnin' Strikin'/Touch and Go	1980	$5
❏ 1126	Make Love to Me/Day After Day	1979	$5
❏ 1126 [PS]	Make Love to Me/Day After Day	1979	$8

CATHEDRAL ORGAN WITH CHIMES
CAPITOL
❏ F95008	Cantique de Noel/It Came Upon a Midnight Clear	1951	$10
—Part of album CDF-9013			
❏ F95007	Silent Night/Adeste Fideles//Joy to the World/Silent Night	1951	$10

Number	Title	Yr	NM

—Part of album CDF-9013
7-Inch Extended Plays
❏ CDF-9013	Christmas Bells	1951	$40
—Includes three records (F95007, F95008, F95009) and box			

CATHY JEAN AND THE ROOMATES
PHILIPS
❏ 40143	Double Trouble/Believe Me	1963	$30
—As "Cathy Jean"			
❏ 40106	My Heart Belongs to Only You/I Only Want You	1963	$30
—As "Cathy Jean"			

VALMOR
❏ 011	I Only Want You/One Love	1961	$30
❏ 09	Make Me Smile Again/Sugar Cake	1961	$30
❏ 07	Please Love Me Forever/Canadian Sunset	1961	$30
—Red label			
❏ 07	Please Love Me Forever/Canadian Sunset	1961	$20
—Black label			
❏ 07 [PS]	Please Love Me Forever/Canadian Sunset	1961	$75
— Sleeve is promo only			
❏ 016	Please Tell Me/Sugar Cake	1962	$30

CAUDELL, LANE
16TH AVENUE
❏ 70411	I Need a Good Woman Bad/Souvenirs	1988	$4
❏ 70403	Souvenirs/The Honeymoon Is Over	1987	$4

CAPITOL
❏ 3526	And Then We Danced/Play On, Play On	1973	$8
❏ 3389	Let Our Love Ride/You, Him and Her	1972	$8

MCA
❏ 40901	Banging on a Star/I Love You Girl	1978	$5
❏ 40996	Love, Hit and Run/Destiny	1979	$5
❏ 40935	Those Eyes/I'm an Empty Man	1978	$5

METROMEDIA
❏ BMBO-0017	Mama, You Know Me Well/Should I Care	1973	$6

PRIVATE STOCK
❏ 45,122	Alabama Boy/(B-side unknown)	1976	$6

CAUTIONS, THE
SHRINE
❏ 104	Watch Your Step/Is It Right	1965	$700

CAVALIERE, FELIX
BEARSVILLE
❏ 0302	Everlasting Love/Future Train	1975	$6
❏ 0300	High Price to Pay/Mountain Men	1974	$5

EPIC
❏ 9-50785	Castles in the Air/Outside Your Window	1979	$4
❏ 9-50880	Good to Have Love Back/Dancin' the Night Away	1980	$4
❏ 9-50829	Only a Lonely Heart Sees/You Turned Me Around	1980	$4

CAVALIERS, THE (1)
RCA VICTOR
❏ 47-9054	Dance Little Girl/Hold On to My Baby	1966	$125
❏ 47-9321	I Really Love You/I've Gotta Find Her	1967	$100

SHRINE
❏ 119	Do What I Need/Tighten Up	1966	$1200

CAVALIERS, THE (U)
APT
❏ 25004	Dance, Dance, Dance/Play By the Rules of Love	1958	$50

CORAL
❏ 62245	Teen Fever/Funky	1961	$15

DECCA
❏ 29556	Somewhere, Sometime, Someday/Honor Bright	1955	$20

GALENA
❏ 1277	Blowin' Smoke/Ten More Miles	1962	$30

MUSIC WORLD
❏ 101	The Magic Age of Sixteen/So Young, So Warm, So Beautiful	1963	$40

NRC
❏ 028	Dreamy Bikini/Charm Bracelet	1959	$20

Number	Title	Yr	NM

CAVALLARO, CARMEN
DECCA
❏ 24141	Silent Night/White Christmas	1950	$15
—78 rpm released in 1947			

CAVE DWELLERS, THE
ABC-PARAMOUNT
❏ 10735	Sinking Feeling/Sling My Rock	1965	$30

CEDAR CREEK
MOON SHINE
❏ 3016	Georgia Mules and Country Boys/(B-side unknown)	1983	$5
❏ 3013	Lonely Heart/(B-side unknown)	1983	$5
❏ 3001	Looks Like a Set-Up to Me/This Old Heart (Is Gonna Rise Again)	1981	$5
❏ 3008	Take a Ride on a Riverboat/(B-side unknown)	1982	$5
❏ 3003	Took It Like a Man, Cried Like a Baby/Dreamin' Thru Another Day	1982	$5

CELEBRATION FEATURING MIKE LOVE
MCA
❏ S45-1986 [DJ]	Almost Summer/Almost Summer (KRTH Version)	1978	$10
—Special promo for Los Angeles radio station			
❏ 40891	Almost Summer/Lookin' Good	1978	$5
❏ 40930	Summer in the City/Island Girl	1978	$4

PACIFIC ARTS
❏ 105	Starbaby/Gettin' Hungry	1979	$10
—As "Celebration			

CELEBRITYS, THE
CAROLINE
❏ 2302	Absent Minded/We Made Romance	1956	$600

CELIBATE RIFLES, THE
BLACK
❏ AFTP001	Merry Xmas Blues/Splatterdance	1986	$30
—B-side by the Saqqara Dogs			

CELLOS, THE
APOLLO
❏ 524	I Beg for Your Love/What's the Matter with You	1958	$70
❏ 516	The Be-Bop Mouse/Girlie That I Love	1957	$60

CELTICS, THE
AL-JACK'S
❏ 0002	Can You Remember/Send Me Someone to Love	1958	$5000
— VG 2500; VG+ 3750			

WAR CONN
❏ 2216	Darline, Darling/Only the Lonely	1962	$400

CENTER, SANDY
RUBY
❏ 260	Come On Baby, It's Christmas/For Me, No Christmas	1957	$20

CENTRAL NERVOUS SYSTEM
LAURIE
❏ 3446	Alice in Wonderland/Something Happened to Me	1968	$10
❏ 3421	It Takes All Kinds/I'm Still Hung Up on You	1968	$10

CENTURIES, THE
CLEOPATRA
❏ 2	The Outer Limits/Polynesian Paradise	1963	$40

CERRITO
SOUNDWAVES
❏ 4826	Bad Moon Rising/Born to Hurt Me	1989	$5
❏ 4818	Daydream/(B-side unknown)	1989	$5
❏ 4814	My Baby Left Me/(B-side unknown)	1989	$5

CERRONE
ATLANTIC
❏ 3625	Call Me Tonight (3:00)/(3:53)	1979	$6
—May only exist as a promo			

COTILLION
❏ 44237	Give Me Love/Look for Love	1978	$6
❏ 44215	Love in C Minor - Pt. 1/Pt. 2	1977	$6
❏ 44230	Supernature/Sweet Drums	1978	$6

Number	Title	Yr	NM
PAVILLION			
❑ ZS5-02962	Back Track (Vocal)/(Instrumental)	1982	$15
❑ 14-03271	Strollin' on Sunday/Anybody Can Do Anything	1982	$20

CETERA, PETER

Number	Title	Yr	NM
FULL MOON			
❑ 49885	Livin' in the Limelight/How Many Times	1981	$5
❑ 50052	On the Line/I Can Feel It	1982	$5
WARNER BROS.			
❑ 7-27712	Best of Times/Only Love Knows Why	1988	$3
❑ 7-27712 [PS]	Best of Times/Only Love Knows Why	1988	$3
❑ 7-28507	Big Mistake/Livin' in the Limelight	1986	$3
❑ 7-28507 [PS]	Big Mistake/Livin' in the Limelight	1986	$3
❑ 7-28662	Glory of Love/On the Line	1986	$3
❑ 7-28662 [PS]	Glory of Love/On the Line	1986	$4

— Peter Cetera's name in pale green letters

Number	Title	Yr	NM
❑ 7-28662 [PS]	Glory of Love/On the Line	1986	$3

— Peter Cetera's name in red letters

Number	Title	Yr	NM
❑ 7-27563	Holding Out/Scheherazade	1989	$3
❑ 7-27563 [PS]	Holding Out/Scheherazade	1989	$3
❑ 7-27824	One Good Woman/One More Story	1988	$3
❑ 7-27824 [PS]	One Good Woman/One More Story	1988	$3
❑ 7-28383	Only Love Knows Why/Evil Eye	1987	$3
❑ 7-28383 [PS]	Only Love Knows Why/Evil Eye	1987	$3

CEYLEIB PEOPLE, THE

Number	Title	Yr	NM
VAULT			
❑ 940	Changes/Ceyladd Seyta	1968	$30

CHACKSFIELD, FRANK

Number	Title	Yr	NM
CORAL			
❑ 9-60966	Little Red Monkey/Roundabouts and Swings	1953	$30
LONDON			
❑ 1368	A Girl Called Linda/Golden Violins	1953	$15
❑ 1797	Arrividerci Roma/Blue Hawaii	1958	$10
❑ 1484	Black Velvet/Misty Valley	1954	$15
❑ 1535	Blue Mirage/Mademoiselle de Paris	1955	$10
❑ 1722	Breath of Spring/Your Love Is My Love	1957	$10
❑ 1964	Conscious/Madeleine	1960	$8
❑ 1772	Costa Brava/Katsumi Love Theme	1958	$12
❑ 1381	Dancing Princess/Golden Tango	1954	$15
❑ 1671	Donkey Cart/Banks of the Seine	1956	$12
❑ 9519	Ebb Tide/Face to Face	1962	$8
❑ 1358	Ebb Tide/Waltzing Bugle Boy	1953	$15
❑ 1439	Fiddler's Boogie/Picnic for Strings	1954	$15
❑ 1530	Glorious/Pavements of Paris	1955	$10
❑ 1636	Lights of Vienna/Cockleshell Heroes	1956	$12
❑ 1841	My Heart's in Portugal/Rodeo	1958	$10
❑ 1901	On the Beach/A Paris Valentine	1959	$10
❑ 9580	Parakeets of Paraguay/Theme from "Lawrence of Arabia"	1963	$8
❑ 1406	Prelude to a Memory/Flirtation Waltz	1954	$15
❑ 1694	Sahara/Fanagalo	1956	$10
❑ 9611	She Loves Me/Will He Like Me	1963	$8
❑ 1487	Smile/Piper in the Heather	1954	$15
❑ 1725	Temptation/Lullaby of the Leaves	1957	$10
❑ 1342	Terry's Theme from "Limelight"/Limelight	1953	$15
❑ 9617	Theme from "A New Kind of Love"/Street of Goodbye	1963	$8
❑ 1990	Theme from "Carnival"/Lullaby in Blue	1961	$8
❑ 9502	Theme from "King of Kings"/Theme from "Francis of Assisi"	1961	$8
❑ 1945	Theme from "The Dark at the Top of the Stairs"/Caroline	1960	$8
❑ 9803	The Phoenix Love Theme/Marriage Lines	1965	$8

CHAD AND JEREMY

Number	Title	Yr	NM
CAPITOL STARLINE			
❑ 6087	A Summer Song/Willow Weep for Me	1966	$8

— Green and white swirl label

Number	Title	Yr	NM
COLUMBIA			
❑ 43277	Before and After/Fare Thee Well	1965	$12
❑ 43277 [PS]	Before and After/Fare Thee Well	1965	$60

— Basically identical to the more common "I Don't Want to Lose You Baby," except that on this sleeve, the blurbs on the front and back begin "Columbia Records Proudly Introduces..."

Number	Title	Yr	NM
❑ 43277 [DJ]	Before and After (same on both sides)	1965	$50

— Promo only on red vinyl

Number	Title	Yr	NM
❑ 43682	Distant Shores/Last Night	1966	$8
❑ 43682 [PS]	Distant Shores/Last Night	1966	$30
❑ 43339	I Don't Wanna Lose You Baby/Pennies	1965	$8
❑ 43339 [PS]	I Don't Wanna Lose You Baby/Pennies	1965	$30

— Basically identical to the "Before and After" sleeve, except that this one has the words "Columbia Records Proudly Presents..." on front and back

Number	Title	Yr	NM
❑ 43414	I Have Dreamed/Should I?	1966	$8
❑ 44379	Painted Dayglow Smile/Editorial	1967	$8
❑ 44660	Paxton Quigley's Had the Course/You Need Feet	1968	$8
❑ 44660 [PS]	Paxton Quigley's Had the Course/You Need Feet	1968	$20

— Promo-only sleeve of a Nazi party rally

Number	Title	Yr	NM
❑ 44525	Sister Marie/Rest in Peace	1968	$8
❑ 43490	Teenage Failure/Early Morning Rain	1965	$8
❑ 43490 [PS]	Teenage Failure/Early Morning Rain	1965	$30
ROCSHIRE			
❑ 95046	Bite the Bullet/How Many Trains	1983	$4
❑ 95050 [DJ]	Bite the Bullet/Interview	1983	$15
❑ 95061	Dreams/Zanzibar Sunset	1983	$4
WORLD ARTISTS			
❑ 1027	A Summer Song/No Tears for Johnny	1964	$10

— As "Chad Stuart and Jeremy Clyde

Number	Title	Yr	NM
❑ 1056	From a Window/My Coloring Book	1965	$10
❑ 1041	If I Loved You/Donna, Donna	1965	$10
❑ 1041 [PS]	If I Loved You/Donna, Donna	1965	$30
❑ 1060	September in the Rain/Only for the Young	1965	$10
❑ 1052	What Do You Want with Me/A Very Good Year	1965	$10

— As "Chad Stuart and Jeremy Clyde

Number	Title	Yr	NM
❑ 1052 [PS]	What Do You Want with Me/A Very Good Year	1965	$60

— As "Chad Stuart and Jeremy Clyde

Number	Title	Yr	NM
❑ 1034	Willow Weep for Me/If She Was Mine	1964	$10
❑ 1034 [PS]	Willow Weep for Me/If She Was Mine	1964	$30

CHAFFIN, ERNIE

Number	Title	Yr	NM
SUN			
❑ 320	Don't Ever Leave Me/Miracle of You	1959	$30
❑ 262	Feelin' Low/Lonesome for My Baby	1957	$40
❑ 275	Laughin' and Jokin'/I'm Lonesome	1957	$40

CHAIN REACTION

Number	Title	Yr	NM
DATE			
❑ 1538	When I Needed You/The Sun	1966	$40

CHAIRMEN OF THE BOARD

Number	Title	Yr	NM
INVICTUS			
❑ 9106	Bittersweet/Elmo James	1972	$5
❑ 9086	Chairman of the Board/When Will She Tell Me She Needs Me	1971	$5
❑ 1268	Everybody Party All Night/Morning Glory	1974	$5
❑ 9122	Everybody's Got a Song to Sing/Working on a Building of Love	1972	$5
❑ 9079	Everything's Tuesday/Patches	1970	$5
❑ 1251	Finder's Keepers/Finder's Keepers (Part 2)	1973	$5
❑ 9074	Give Me Just a Little More Time/Since the Days of Pigtails	1970	$6
❑ 9089	Hanging On (To) A Memory/Tracked and Trapped	1971	$5
❑ 9126	Let Me Down Easy/I Can't Find Myself	1972	$5
❑ 1271	Let's Have Some Fun/Love at First Sight	1974	$5
❑ 1263	Life & Death/Love with Me, Love with Me	1974	$5
❑ 9103	Men Are Getting Scarce/Bravo! Hurray!	1971	$5
❑ 9081 [PS]	Pay to the Piper/Bless You	1970	$10
❑ 9081	Pay to the Piper/Bless You	1970	$5
❑ 1276	The Skin I'm In/Love at First Sight	1975	$5
❑ 9099	Try On My Love for Size/Working on a Building of Love	1971	$5

CHAKIRIS, GEORGE

Number	Title	Yr	NM
CAPITOL			
❑ 5458	Blue Summer/Ship of Fools	1965	$8
❑ 5426	Days of the Waltz/Finding Words for Spring	1965	$8
❑ 5209	Invisible Tears/Not for Me	1964	$8
❑ 4844	Maria/Once Upon a Time	1962	$8
❑ 4892	My Coloring Book/I've Got Your Number	1962	$8

Number	Title	Yr	NM
❑ 5113	My Place/Love Being Here with You	1964	$8
HORIZON			
❑ 356	But Not for Me/Embraceable You	1962	$15
❑ 363	Cool/Embraceable You	1962	$15

CHAKRAS, THE

Number	Title	Yr	NM
REPRISE			
❑ 0859	Agnes Vandalism/City Boy	1969	$20
❑ 0838	Things We Said Today/Just with You	1969	$20

CHALETS, THE

Number	Title	Yr	NM
DART			
❑ 1026	Who's Laughing-Who's Crying/Fat Fat Fat! Mom-Mi-O	1961	$30
LAURIE			
❑ 3348	She's Not the Marrying Type/(Theme from) She's Not the Marrying Type	1966	$15
MUSICNOTE			
❑ 1001	Who's Laughing-Who's Crying/Fat Fat Fat! Mom-Mi-O	1962	$30
TRU-LITE			
❑ 1001	Who's Laughing-Who's Crying/Mom-Mia	1961	$60

CHALLENGERS III, THE

Number	Title	Yr	NM
TRI-PHI			
❑ 1020	Every Day/I Hear an Echo	1963	$60
❑ 1012	Stay/Honey, Honey, Honey	1962	$60

— As "The Challengers III

Number	Title	Yr	NM
❑ 1012	Stay/Honey, Honey, Honey	1962	$40

— As "The Challengers

CHALLENGERS, THE (1)

Number	Title	Yr	NM
GNP CRESCENDO			
❑ 412	Chitty Chitty Bang Bang/Lonely Little Girl	1968	$10
❑ 400	Color Me In/Before You	1968	$10
❑ 380	Milord/What If It Should Rain	1966	$10
❑ 362	The Man from U.N.C.L.E./Summer Nights	1965	$10
❑ 362	The Man from U.N.C.L.E./The Streets of London	1965	$10
❑ 396	The Water Country/Everything to Me	1967	$10
❑ 368	Walk with Me/How Could It	1966	$10
❑ 376	Wipe Out/North Beach	1966	$10
TRIUMPH			
❑ 112	Pipeline/Asphalt Spinner	1966	$40
VAULT			
❑ 900	Bull Dog/Torquay	1963	$30
❑ 918	Channel Nine/Can't Seem to Make You Mine	1965	$30
❑ 904	Foot Tapper/On the Move	1963	$30
❑ 910	Hot Rod Hootenanny/Maybellene	1964	$40
❑ 913	Hot Rod Show/K-39	1964	$40
❑ 902	Moondawg/Tidal Wave	1963	$30

CHALLENGERS, THE (2)

Number	Title	Yr	NM
CHESS			
❑ 1957	Tossin' and Turnin'/Don;t You Know It	1966	$10

CHALLENGERS, THE (3)

Number	Title	Yr	NM
MELATONE			
❑ 1002	I Can Tell/The Mambo Beat	1956	$300

CHALLENGERS, THE (4)

Number	Title	Yr	NM
NIGHT OWL			
❑ 6794	I Wanna Hold You/The Challengers Take a Ride on the Jefferson Airplane	1967	$40

CHALLENGERS, THE (5)

Number	Title	Yr	NM
TRIODEX			
❑ 107	Deadline/Cry of the Wild Goose	1961	$30
❑ 102	Goofus/Lazy Twist	1960	$30

CHALLENGERS, THE (U)

Number	Title	Yr	NM
CUCA			
❑ 1500	Hear My Message/I Wanna Hold You	1968	$8

CHAMBERLAIN, WILT "THE STILT

Number	Title	Yr	NM
END			
❑ 1066	By the River/That's Easy to Say	1960	$30

Number	Title	Yr	NM

CHAMBERLAIN, DAVID
COUNTRY INT'L.
❏ 215	How Do You Like My Memories/(B-side unknown)	1988	$6
❏ 228	I Finally Made It (Where You Told Me to Go)/ Friends in Low Places	1989	$6
❏ 214	I Owe, I Owe (It's Off to Work I Go)/Love Me Tonight (Like There's No Tomorrow)	1988	$6
❏ 217	Too Late for the Show/ (B-side unknown)	1988	$6

CHAMBERLAIN, RICHARD
MCA
❏ 40691	Secret Kingdom/The Slipper and the Rose Waltz	1977	$4

MGM
❏ K13121	All I Have to Do Is Dream/ Hi-Lili, Hi-Lo	1963	$10
❏ K13121 [PS]	All I Have to Do Is Dream/ Hi-Lili, Hi-Lo	1963	$30
❏ K13170	Blue Guitar/They Long to Be Close to You	1963	$10
❏ K13170 [PS]	Blue Guitar/They Long to Be Close to You	1963	$30
❏ K13148	I Will Love You/True Love	1963	$10
❏ K13148 [PS]	I Will Love You/True Love	1963	$30
❏ K13097	Love Me Tender/All I Do Is Dream of You	1962	$10
❏ K13097 [PS]	Love Me Tender/All I Do Is Dream of You	1962	$30
❏ K13205	Stella By Starlight/ Georgia on My Mind	1964	$8
❏ K13205 [PS]	Stella By Starlight/ Georgia on My Mind	1964	$30
❏ K13075	Theme from Dr. Kildare (Three Stars Will Shine Tonight)/A Kiss to Build a Dream On	1962	$10
❏ K13075 [PS]	Theme from Dr. Kildare (Three Stars Will Shine Tonight)/A Kiss to Build a Dream On	1962	$30

CHAMBERS BROTHERS, THE
AVCO
❏ 4638	1-2-3/Looking Back	1974	$4
❏ 4632	Let's Go, Let's Go, Let's Go/ Do You Believe in Magic	1974	$4
❏ 4657	Miss Lady Brown/ Stealin' Watermelons	1975	$4

COLUMBIA
❏ 43957	All Strung Out Over You/ Falling in Love	1967	$6
❏ 44779	Are You Ready/You Got the Power to Turn Me On	1969	$6
❏ 45837	Boogie Children/You Make the Magic	1973	$6
❏ 44986	Have a Little Faith/Baby Takes Care of Business	1969	$5
❏ 45488	Heaven/(By the Hair on) My Chinny Chin Chin	1971	$6
❏ 4-44679	I Can't Turn You Loose/ Do Your Thing	1968	$6
❏ 4-44679 [PS]	I Can't Turn You Loose/ Do Your Thing	1968	$10
❏ 45277	Love, Peace and Happiness/Funky	1970	$5
❏ 45088	Love, Peace and Happiness/ If You Want Me To	1970	$5
❏ 4-45055	Merry Christmas, Happy New Year/Did You Stop to Pray This Morning	1969	$6
❏ 45518	Merry Christmas, Happy New Year/Did You Stop to Pray This Morning	1971	$6
❏ 44080	Please Don't Leave Me/I Can't Stand It	1967	$6
❏ 4-43816	Time Has Come Today (2:37)/Dinah	1966	$15

—A-side is a different recording than the later hit, both vocally and instrumentally

❏ 4-44414	Time Has Come Today (3:05)/People Get Ready	1968	$10

—No reference to the album "The Time Has Come"; despite the listed time, this plays the 4:45 hit version (master number in trail-off ends in "3B"; we're not sure if stock copies list 3:05 and play 3:05, too

❏ 4-44414 [DJ]	Time Has Come Today (3:05) (same on both sides)	1968	$20

—Special Rush Reservice" on label; this plays a 3:05 edit of the long LP version (master numbers in trail-off end in "1B" on one side and "1F" on the other)

❏ 4-44414	Time Has Come Today (4:45)/People Get Ready	1968	$8

--Hit version; label refers to the album "The Time Has Come

❏ 45146	To Love Somebody/Let's Do It	1970	$5
❏ 44890	Wake Up/Everybody Needs Someone	1969	$6
❏ 45394	When the Evening Comes/ New Generation	1971	$5

ROXBURY
❏ 2034	Bring It On Down Front Pretty Mama/Midnight Blue	1976	$5

VAULT
❏ 920	Call Me/Seventeen	1965	$20

❏ 967	House of the Rising Sun/ Blues Get Off My Shoulder	1970	$6
❏ 923	Pretty Girls Everywhere/ Love Me Like the Rain	1966	$15
❏ 945	Shout Part 1/Shout Part 2	1968	$8

CHAMBERS, CARL
PRAIRIE DUST
❏ 8001	Take Me Home with You/ (B-side unknown)	1981	$6

CHAMP, BILLY
ABC-PARAMOUNT
❏ 10518	Believe Me/Hush-A-Bye	1964	$40

CHAMPAGNE BROTHERS, THE
TEARDROP
❏ 3046	Christmas Time Without You/ Snow On The Old Bayou	1964	$15

CHAMPAIGN
COLUMBIA
❏ 11-11433	How 'Bout Us/Spinnin'	1981	$4

CHAMPLAINS, THE
UNITED ARTISTS
❏ 346	Ding Dong/Have You Changed Your Mind	1961	$50

CHAMPLIN, BILL
ELEKTRA
❏ 47456	Sara/One Way Ticket	1982	$4
❏ 47429	Take it Uptown/The Fool Is All	1982	$4
❏ 47240	Tonight Tonight/Without You	1981	$4

FULL MOON/EPIC
❏ 8-50589	What Good Is Love/Yo' Mama	1978	$5

CHAMPS, THE
CHALLENGE
❏ 59086	Alley Cat/Coconut Grove	1960	$30
❏ 59322	Anna/Buckaroo	1965	$20
❏ 9199	Cactus Juice/Roots	1963	$20
❏ 9116	Cantina/Panic Button	1961	$30
❏ 59018	Chariot Rock/Subway	1958	$30
❏ 59007	El Rancho Rock/Midnighter	1958	$30
❏ 9140	Experiment in Terror/ La Cucaracha	1962	$20
❏ 59263	Fraternity Waltz/Kahlua	1964	$20
❏ 59276	French 75/Bright Lights, Big City	1965	$20
❏ 59035	Gone Train/Beatnik	1958	$30
❏ 59103	Hokey Pokey/Jumping Bean	1961	$30
❏ 9162	Limbo Dance/Latin Limbo	1962	$20
❏ 59043	Moonlight Bay/Caramba	1959	$30
❏ 9180	Mr. Cool/3/4 Mash	1963	$20
❏ 59219	San Juan/Jalisco	1963	$20
❏ 59053	Sky High/Double Eagle Rock	1959	$30
❏ 59236	Switzerland/Only the Young	1964	$20
❏ 1016	Tequila/Train to Nowhere	1958	$30
❏ 1016	Tequila/Train to Nowhere	1958	$600

—Blue vinyl (one known to exist)

❏ 9131	Tequila Twist/Limbo Rock	1961	$30
❏ 59097	The Face/Tough Train	1960	$30
❏ 59314	The Man from Durango/ Red Pepper	1965	$20
❏ 9113	The Shoddy Shoddy/Sombrero	1961	$30
❏ 59063	Too Much Tequila/Twenty Thousand Leagues	1960	$30
❏ 59026	Turnpike/Rockin' Mary	1958	$30
❏ 9143	What a Country/I've Just Seen Her	1962	$20

REPUBLIC
❏ 246	Tequila '76 (Long)/ Tequila '76 (Short)	1976	$8
❏ 246 [PS]	Tequila '76 (Long)/ Tequila '76 (Short)	1976	$8

WE'RE BACK
❏ 1	Tequila '77/From Me to You	1977	$8

7-Inch Extended Plays
CHALLENGE
❏ EP-7100 [PS]	Tequila	1958	$175
❏ EP-7100	Tequila/I'll Be There//Train to Nowhere/Lollipop	1958	$175

CHANCE
MERCURY
❏ 884545-7	I Need Some Good News Bad/ She Needs a Man Like Me	1986	$3
❏ 884178-7	She Told Me Yes/Two Hearts Are Better Than One	1986	$3
❏ 880555-7	To Be Lovers/Call It What You Want To (It's Still Love)	1985	$3
❏ 884918-7	What Did You Do with My Heart/ One Too Many Heartaches	1986	$3

CHANCE, JEFF
CURB
❏ 10516	Let It Burn/She Loves Me	1988	$3
❏ 10506	So Far Not So Good/ Hopelessly Falling	1988	$3

CHANCE, NOLAN
CONSTELLATION
❏ 161	Don't Use Me/Just Like the Weather	1965	$120
❏ 144	She's Gone/If He Makes You	1965	$30

CHANCERS, THE
DOT
❏ 15870	Shirley Ann/My One	1958	$40

CHANDELIERS, THE
ANGLE TONE
❏ 521	Blueberry Sweet/ (B-side unknown)	1958	$250

—As "Chandeliers Quintet"

❏ 521	Blueberry Sweet/ (B-side unknown)	1958	$200

—As "Chandeliers"; black vinyl

❏ 521	Blueberry Sweet/ (B-side unknown)	1958	$400

—As "Chandeliers"; colored vinyl

CHANDELLES, THE
DOT
❏ 16553	El Gato/Jetster	1963	$30

CHANDLER, BARBARA
ABC-PARAMOUNT
❏ 10369	Clinging Vine/The Boy You Used to Go With	1962	$30
❏ 10429	Girl Talk/Broken Hearted	1963	$40

CAMEO
❏ 458	I Go/(You Forgot) In the Still of the Night	1967	$10

KAPP
❏ 575	A Lonely New Year/I'm Going Out With The Girls	1964	$15
❏ 555	I Live to Love You/Fool's Errand	1963	$40
❏ 542	It Hurts to Be Sixteen/ Running, Running Johnny	1963	$40

MUSICOR
❏ 1321	How Can I Say No to You/ Pretty Shade of Blue	1968	$10

CHANDLER, BOBBY
OJ
❏ 1000	I'm Serious/If You Love'd Me	1957	$40

CHANDLER, GENE, AND BARBARA ACKLIN
BRUNSWICK
❏ 55387	From the Teacher to the Preacher/Anywhere But Nowhere	1968	$8
❏ 55405	Little Green Apples/ Will I Find You	1969	$8
❏ 55366	Love Won't Start/Show Me the Way to Go	1968	$8

CHANDLER, GENE, AND JERRY BUTLER
MERCURY
❏ 73195	Two and Two (Take This Woman Off the Corner)/ Everybody Is Waiting	1971	$6

CHANDLER, GENE
20TH CENTURY
❏ 2428	Do What Comes So Natural/ That Funky Disco Rhythm	1979	$4
❏ 2411	When You're #1/I'll Remember You	1979	$4

BRUNSWICK
❏ 55413	Eleanor Rigby/ Familiar Footsteps	1969	$8
❏ 55312	Girl Don't Care/My Love	1967	$8
❏ 55394	Teacher, Teacher/ Pit of Loneliness	1968	$8
❏ 55339	There Goes the Lover/ Tell Me What I Can Do	1967	$8
❏ 55383	There Was a Time/Those Were the Good Old Days	1968	$8
❏ 55425	This Bitter Earth/Suicide	1969	$8

CHECKER
❏ 1220	Go Back Home/In My Baby's House	1969	$8
❏ 1155	I Fooled You This Time/ Such a Pretty Thing	1966	$8
❏ 1190	I Won't Need You/No Peace, No Satisfaction	1967	$8
❏ 1165	To Be a Lover/After the Laughter	1967	$8

CHI-SOUND

Number	Title	Yr	NM
❏ 2451	Does She Have a Friend?/Let Me Make Love to You	1980	$4
❏ 2386	Get Down/I'm the Traveling Kind	1978	$4
❏ 1168	Give Me the Cue/Tomorrow We May Not Feel the Same	1978	$4
❏ 1001	I'll Make the Living If You Make the Loving Worthwhile/(B-side unknown)	1982	$5
❏ 2494	I'm Attracted to You/I've Got to Meet You	1981	$4
❏ 2468	Lay Me Gently/You've Been So Good to Me	1980	$4
❏ 2507	Love Is the Answer/Godsend	1981	$4
❏ 2404	Please Sunrise/Greatest Love Ever Known	1979	$4
❏ 2411	When You're #1/I'll Remember You	1979	$5

CONSTELLATION

Number	Title	Yr	NM
❏ 124	A Song Called Soul/You Left Me	1964	$10
❏ 166	Baby That's Love/Bet You Never Thought	1966	$8
❏ 136	Bless Our Love/London Town	1964	$10
❏ 104	From Day to Day/It's No Good for Me	1963	$10
❏ 160	Good Times/No One Can Love You	1965	$8
❏ 164	Here Come the Tears/Soul Hootenanny (Part 2)	1965	$8
❏ 169	I Can Take Care of Myself/If I Can't Save It	1966	$8
❏ 167	(I'm Just a) Fool for You/Buddy Ain't It a Shame	1966	$8
❏ 172	Mr. Big Shot/I Hate to Be the One to Say	1966	$8
❏ 110	Pretty Little Girl/A Little Like Lovin'	1963	$10
❏ 114	Soul Hootenanny (Part 1)/Soul Hootenanny (Part 2)	1964	$12
❏ 112	Think Nothing About It/Wish You Were Here	1964	$10
❏ 141	What Now/If You Can't Be True	1964	$10

CURTOM

Number	Title	Yr	NM
❏ 1986	Baby I Still Love You/I Understand	1973	$5
❏ 1979	Don't Have to Be Lyin' Babe (Part 1)/Don't Have to Be Lyin' Babe (Part 2)	1973	$5
❏ 1992	Without You Here/Just Be There	1973	$5

FASTFIRE

Number	Title	Yr	NM
❏ 7003	Haven't I Heard That Line Before/You'll Never Be Free of Me	1985	$5
❏ 7005	Lucy/Please You Tonight	1986	$5

MERCURY

Number	Title	Yr	NM
❏ 73083	Groovy Situation/Not the Marrying Kind	1970	$6
❏ 73121	Simply Call It Love/Give Me a Chance	1970	$6

Vee Jay

Number	Title	Yr	NM
❏ 536	Baby, That's Love/Man's Temptation	1963	$20
❏ 511	Check Yourself/Forgive Me	1963	$20
❏ 450	Daddy's Home/The Big Lie	1962	$20

—As "The Duke of Earl"

Number	Title	Yr	NM
❏ 416	Duke of Earl/Kissin' in the Kitchen	1961	$30
❏ 416	Duke of Earl/Kissin' in the Kitchen	1962	$30

—Some later pressings as "The Duke of Earl"

Number	Title	Yr	NM
❏ 455	I'll Follow You/You Left Me	1962	$20

—As "The Duke of Earl"

Number	Title	Yr	NM
❏ 461	Tear for Tear/Miracle After Miracle	1962	$20
❏ 440	Walk On with the Duke/London Town	1962	$20

—As "The Duke of Earl"

CHANDLER, JEFF

DECCA

Number	Title	Yr	NM
❏ 9-29345	Always/Everything Happens to Me	1955	$15
❏ 9-29004	I Should Care/More Than Anyone	1954	$20
❏ 9-29175	Lamplight/That's All She's Waiting to Hear	1954	$15
❏ 9-29405	My Prayer/When Spring Comes	1955	$15
❏ 9-29600	Only the Very Young/A Little Love Can Go a Long, Long Way	1955	$15
❏ 9-29532	Shaner Maidel/Foxfire	1955	$15

LIBERTY

Number	Title	Yr	NM
❏ 55092	Half of My Heart/Hold Me	1957	$10

CHANDLER, KENNY

AMY

Number	Title	Yr	NM
❏ 890	I Don't Know Why/Happy to Be Unhappy	1963	$10

CORAL

Number	Title	Yr	NM
❏ 62309	It Might Have Been/Yours and Yours Alone	1962	$10

EPIC

Number	Title	Yr	NM
❏ 9758	Come Softly to Me/S.O.S. (Sweet On Susie)	1965	$8
❏ 10009	I'll Be Coming Back/Sunshine Sweetheart	1966	$8

LAURIE

Number	Title	Yr	NM
❏ 3158	Heart/Wait for Me	1963	$12
❏ 3181	I Tell Myself/I Can't Stand Tears at a Party	1963	$10
❏ 3140	Man on the Run/Leave Me If You Want To	1962	$10

TOWER

Number	Title	Yr	NM
❏ 405	Beyond Love/Charity	1968	$8
❏ 354	Sleep/Nickles and Dimes	1967	$8

UNITED ARTISTS

Number	Title	Yr	NM
❏ 384	Please Mr. Mountain/What Kind of Love Is Yours	1961	$15
❏ 342	The Magic Ring/Drums	1961	$15

CHANDLER, LORRAINE

GIANT

Number	Title	Yr	NM
❏ 703	What Can I Do/Tell Me You're Mine	1966	$70

RCA VICTOR

Number	Title	Yr	NM
❏ 47-9349	I Can't Change/Oh How I Need Your Love	1967	$60
❏ 47-8980	I Can't Hold On/She Don't Want You	1966	$40
❏ 47-8810	What Can I Do/Tell Me You're Mine	1966	$40

CHANEY, HANK

CMI

Number	Title	Yr	NM
❏ 04	Be-Bop-A-Lula "86"/(B-side unknown)	1986	$8

CHANEY, LON

TOWER

Number	Title	Yr	NM
❏ 114	Monster's Holiday/Yuletide Jerk	1964	$30

CHANGIN' TIMES, THE

BELL

Number	Title	Yr	NM
❏ 675	Free Spirit/You Just Seem to Know	1967	$30
❏ 711	Show Me the Way to Go Home/When the Good Sun Shines	1968	$30

PHILIPS

Number	Title	Yr	NM
❏ 40401	Aladdin/All in the Mind of a Young Girl	1966	$20
❏ 40368	Goin' Lovin' with You/I Should Have Brought Her Home	1966	$20
❏ 40341	How Is the Air Up There/Young and Innocent Girl	1965	$30
❏ 40320	Pied Piper/Thank You Babe	1965	$30

CHANGING SCENE, THE

FONTANA

Number	Title	Yr	NM
❏ 1669	Is It Really Worth It/Sing Me Something Pretty	1969	$15

CHANNEL, BRUCE

ELEKTRA

Number	Title	Yr	NM
❏ 46587	One More Last Chance/That's the Truth, Ruth	1980	$4

KING

Number	Title	Yr	NM
❏ 5294	Will I Ever Love Again/Blow Down Baby	1959	$40

LE CAM

Number	Title	Yr	NM
❏ 1117	A Presley Medley/A Man Without a Woman	1977	$5
❏ 122	Going Back to Louisiana/Forget Me Not	1964	$10
❏ 953	Hey! Baby/Dream Girl	1961	$50
❏ 125	My Baby/Blue Monday	1964	$10

MALA

Number	Title	Yr	NM
❏ 12011	California/Water the Family Tree	1968	$10
❏ 579	Mr. Bus Driver/It's Me	1967	$10
❏ 12041	The Web/Mrs. P	1969	$10
❏ 12027	Try Me/Nobody	1968	$10

MEL-O-DY

Number	Title	Yr	NM
❏ 112	That's What's Happenin'/Satisfied Mind	1964	$20

SMASH

Number	Title	Yr	NM
❏ 1769	Come On Baby/Mine Exclusively	1962	$20
❏ 1731	Hey! Baby/Dream Girl	1962	$30
❏ 1792	Oh Baby/Let's Hurt Together	1962	$20
❏ 1780	Stand Tough/Somewhere in This Town	1962	$20
❏ 1780 [PS]	Stand Tough/Somewhere in This Town	1962	$40
❏ 1838	The Dipsy Doodle/Send Her Home	1963	$20
❏ 1838 [PS]	The Dipsy Doodle/Send Her Home	1963	$40

CHANNELS, THE (1)

CHANNEL

Number	Title	Yr	NM
❏ 1006	A Thousand Miles Away/Don't Let the Green Grass Fool You	1974	$10
❏ 1003	Close Your Eyes/Work with Me Annie	1973	$10
❏ 1000	Gloria/You Said You Loved Me	1971	$10

—Black vinyl

Number	Title	Yr	NM
❏ 1000	Gloria/You Said You Loved Me	1971	$30

—Red vinyl

Number	Title	Yr	NM
❏ 1004	Over Again/In My Arms to Stay	1973	$10
❏ 1001	We Belong Together/Hey Girl, I'm in Love with You	1972	$10

FIRE

Number	Title	Yr	NM
❏ 1001	My Heart Is Sad/The Girl Next Door	1959	$60

—As "Earl Lewis and the Channels"

FURY

Number	Title	Yr	NM
❏ 1021	Bye Bye Baby/My Love Will Never Die	1959	$60
❏ 1071	Bye Bye Baby/My Love Will Never Die	1963	$50

GONE

Number	Title	Yr	NM
❏ 5019	Altar of Love/All Alone	1957	$70
❏ 5012	That's My Desire/Stay As You Are	1957	$70

PORT

Number	Title	Yr	NM
❏ 70022	Flames in My Heart/My Lovin' Baby	1961	$30

—Reissue of Whirlin' Disc 109

Number	Title	Yr	NM
❏ 70023	I Really Love You!/What Do You Do	1961	$30

—Reissue of Whirlin' Disc 107

Number	Title	Yr	NM
❏ 70014	The Closer You Are/Now You Know	1960	$30

—Reissue of Whirlin' Disc 100

Number	Title	Yr	NM
❏ 70017	The Gleam in Your Eyes/Stars in the Sky	1960	$30

—Reissue of Whirlin' Disc 102

RARE BIRD

Number	Title	Yr	NM
❏ 5017	She Blew My Mind/Breaking Up Is Hard to Do	1971	$10

WHIRLIN' DISC

Number	Title	Yr	NM
❏ 109	Flames in My Heart/My Lovin' Baby	1957	$200
❏ 107	I Really Love You!/What Do You Do	1957	$200
❏ 100	The Closer You Are/Now You Know	1956	$250

—Block-letter label name; publisher listed as "Bob-Dan Music"

Number	Title	Yr	NM
❏ 100	The Closer You Are/Now You Know	1956	$200

—Block-letter label name; publisher listed as "Spinning Wheel Music"

Number	Title	Yr	NM
❏ 100	The Closer You Are/Now You Know	1956	$125

—Label name is all caps, but not in block letters

Number	Title	Yr	NM
❏ 102	The Gleam in Your Eyes/Stars in the Sky	1956	$200

CHANNELS, THE (2)

ENJOY

Number	Title	Yr	NM
❏ 2001	Sad Song/My Love	1963	$30

GROOVE

Number	Title	Yr	NM
❏ 58-0046	Anything You Do/I've Got My Eyes on You	1964	$30
❏ 58-0061	Old Chinatown/You Can Count on Me	1965	$30

HIT RECORD

Number	Title	Yr	NM
❏ 700	In My Arms to Stay/You Hurt Me	1963	$50

—As "The Channells"

CHANNELS, THE (3)

MERCURY

Number	Title	Yr	NM
❏ 71501	Earthquake/Jungle Lights	1959	$15

CHANSON

ARIOLA AMERICA

Number	Title	Yr	NM
❏ 7717	Don't Hold Back/Did You Ever	1978	$5

Number	Title	Yr	NM

CHANTAYS
DOT
❏ 16492	Monsoon/Scotch Highs	1963	$30
❏ 16440	Pipeline/Move It	1963	$30
❏ 145	Pipeline/Move It	1966	$8

—Reissue; black label

| ❏ 145 | Pipeline/Move It | 1969 | $6 |

—Reissue; orange-red label

DOWNEY
❏ 126	Beyond/I'll Be Back Someday	1964	$30
❏ 108	Monsoon/Scotch Highs	1963	$40
❏ 120	Only If You Care/Love Can Be Cruel	1964	$30
❏ 104	Pipeline/Move It	1963	$70
❏ 116	Space Probe/Continental Missile	1964	$30
❏ 130	Three Coins in the Fountain/Greens	1965	$30

CHANTECLAIRS, THE
DOT
| ❏ 1227 | Baby Please/Someday Love Will Come My Way | 1954 | $80 |
| ❏ 15404 | Believe Me, Beloved/I've Never Been There | 1955 | $70 |

CHANTELS, THE
CARLTON
❏ 555	Look in My Eyes/Glad to Be Back	1961	$30
❏ 564	Still/Well, I Told You	1961	$30
❏ 569	Summertime/Here It Comes Again	1962	$30

END
| ❏ 1103 | Believe Me (My Angel)/I | 1961 | $70 |

—Originally released on Princeton 102 as "The Veneers"

| ❏ 1015 | Every Night/Whoever You Are | 1958 | $40 |

—Gray (white) label

| ❏ 1015 | Every Night/Whoever You Are | 1959 | $30 |

—Multi-color label

| ❏ 1001 | He's Gone/The Plea | 1957 | $100 |

—Black label

| ❏ 1001 | He's Gone/The Plea | 1959 | $30 |

—Multi-color label

❏ 1030	If You Try/Congratulations	1958	$30
❏ 1020	I Love You So/How Could You Call It Off	1958	$50
❏ 1048	I'm Confessin'/Goodbye to Love	1959	$30
❏ 1005	Maybe/Come My Little Baby	1957	$100

—Black label

| ❏ 1005 | Maybe/Come My Little Baby | 1958 | $50 |

—Gray (white) label

| ❏ 1005 | Maybe/Come My Little Baby | 1959 | $30 |

—Multi-color label

❏ 1026	Prayer/Sure of Love	1958	$30
❏ 1105	There's Our Song Again/I'm the Girl	1961	$30
❏ 1069	Whoever You Are/How Could You Call It Off	1960	$30

LUDIX
| ❏ 101 | Eternally/Swamp Water | 1963 | $30 |
| ❏ 106 | That's Why I'm Happy/Some Tears Fall Dry | 1963 | $30 |

RCA VICTOR
| ❏ 74-0347 | I'm Gonna Win Him Back/Love Makes All the Difference in the World | 1970 | $10 |

ROULETTE
| ❏ 7064 | Maybe/He's Gone | 1969 | $10 |

TCF HALL
| ❏ 123 | Take Me As I Am/There's No Forgetting Me | 1965 | $20 |

VERVE
| ❏ 10435 | Indian Giver/It's Just Me | 1966 | $20 |

7-Inch Extended Plays
END
❏ 202 [PS]	C'est Si Bon	1958	$250
❏ 202	(contents unknown)	1958	$125
❏ 201 [PS]	I Love You So	1958	$250
❏ 201	Sure of Love/Prayee/I Love You So/How Could You Call It Off	1958	$175

CHANTERS, THE (1)
COMBO
| ❏ 92 | I Love You/Hot Mamma | 1955 | $400 |
| ❏ 78 | Why/Watts | 1954 | $500 |

DELUXE
❏ 6172	Angel Darling/Five Little Kisses	1958	$60
❏ 6194	My My Darling/At My Door	1961	$50
❏ 6162	My My Darling/I Need Your Tenderness (I Love You Darling)	1958	$60

KEM
| ❏ 2740 | Lonesome Me/Golden Apple | 1955 | $300 |

RPM
| ❏ 415 | Tell Me, Thrill Me/She Wants to Mambo | 1954 | $300 |

CHANTERS, THE (2)
MGM
| ❏ 13750 | Free As A Bird/Bongo, Bongo | 1967 | $6 |

CHANTILLY
F&L
❏ 534	Baby's Walkin'/Have I Got a Heart for You	1984	$5
❏ 520	Better Off Blue/Right Back Loving You Again	1982	$5
❏ 527	Have I Got a Heart for You/Reached	1983	$5
❏ 523	Storm of Love/Whatever Turns You On	1983	$5

JAROCO
| ❏ 51282 | Stumblin' In/Better Off Blue | 1982 | $5 |
| ❏ 31082 | Whatever Turns You On/Storm of Love | 1982 | $5 |

CHANTONES, THE
CAPITOL
| ❏ 4661 | Stormy Weather/Sweet Georgia Brown | 1961 | $30 |

CARLTON
| ❏ 485 | Five Little Numbers/It's Just a Summer Love | 1958 | $40 |

TOP RANK
| ❏ 2066 | Don't Open That Door/Tangerock | 1960 | $30 |

CHANTS, THE (1)
CAMEO
| ❏ 297 | I Could Write a Book/A Thousand Stars | 1964 | $30 |
| ❏ 277 | I Don't Care/Come Go with Me | 1963 | $30 |

INTERPHON
| ❏ 7703 | She's Mine/Then I'll Be Home | 1964 | $20 |

CHANTS, THE (U)
CAPITOL
| ❏ F3949 | Lost and Found/Close Friends | 1958 | $30 |

CHECKER
| ❏ 1209 | Surfside/Chicken 'N' Gravy | 1968 | $8 |

NITE OWL
| ❏ 40 | Heaven and Paradise/When I'm With You | 1960 | $300 |

—Maroon label original

| ❏ 40 | Heaven and Paradise/When I'm With You | 1960 | $50 |

—Black label, black vinyl

VERVE
| ❏ 10244 | Dick Tracy/Choo Choo | 1961 | $30 |

CHAPARRAL BROTHERS, THE
CAPITOL
❏ 2323	Follow Your Dream/The Rain	1968	$8
❏ 2866	Foolin' Around/Life Has Its Little Ups and Downs	1970	$8
❏ 2772	Hello L.A., Bye Bye Birmingham/I Must Have Been Out of My Mind	1970	$8
❏ 2096	He's Looking at You/Leave	1968	$8
❏ 2977	I Believe in You/Let Somebody Love You	1970	$8
❏ 2540	I'm Not Even Missing You/Maybe I Could Find My Way Back Home Again	1969	$8
❏ 2153	Standing in the Rain/Just One More Time	1968	$8

MGM
| ❏ 14501 | Another Piece of the Puzzle/Hell and Half of Georgia | 1973 | $6 |

CHAPARRO, TAMMY
COMPASS
| ❏ 60 | Stay with Me/(B-side unknown) | 1983 | $6 |

CHAPEL, BETTY
MERCURY
| ❏ 5549 | Christmas in Killarney/Rainbow Gal | 1950 | $20 |

CHAPEL, JEAN
CHALLENGE
❏ 59381	Dino's TV Door/If I Never Get You	1967	$8
❏ 59376	Hungry Eyes/Green Paper	1967	$8
❏ 59370	In the Reach of Your Arms/This Waltz Is Mine	1967	$8
❏ 59386	See and Ye Shall Find/I Really Go for You	1968	$8
❏ 59350	Tell It Like It Is/I'm Your Woman	1966	$8

KAPP
| ❏ 2034 | Bluebird Ridge/I Started Loving You Again | 1969 | $6 |
| ❏ 2082 | I'm Your Woman/The Roll Call | 1970 | $6 |

RCA VICTOR
| ❏ 47-6681 | I Won't Be Rockin' Tonight/Welcome to the Club | 1956 | $50 |
| ❏ 47-6892 | Oo-Ba La Baby/I Had a Dream | 1957 | $30 |

SMASH
| ❏ 1829 | Don't Let Go/Your Tender Love | 1963 | $15 |

SUN
| ❏ 244 | I Won't Be Rockin' Tonight/Welcome to the Club | 1956 | $60 |

7-Inch Extended Plays
RCA VICTOR
| ❏ DJ-7 [DJ] | Welcome to the Club/I Won't Be Rockin' Tonight//Love Me Tender/Anyway You Want Me (That's How I Will Be) | 1956 | $250 |

—B-side tracks by Elvis Presley; white label; each side is labeled with the corresponding nuimber for the regular 45 rpm issue

CHAPERONES, THE
JOSIE
| ❏ 880 | Dance with Me/Cruise to the Moon | 1960 | $200 |

—With typographical error listing group as "The Cahperones"

| ❏ 880 | Dance with Me/Cruise to the Moon | 1960 | $30 |

—With correct group name on label

| ❏ 891 | Man from the Moon/Blueberry Sweet | 1961 | $60 |
| ❏ 885 | Shining Star/My Shadow and Me | 1960 | $30 |

CHAPIN, HARRY
BOARDWALK
| ❏ 5700 | Sequel/I Finally Found It Sandy | 1980 | $4 |
| ❏ NB7-11-119 | Story of a Love/Salt and Pepper | 1981 | $4 |

ELEKTRA
❏ 45327	Better Place to Be (Part 1)/Better Place to Be (Part 2)	1976	$4
❏ 45828	Better Place to Be/Winter Song	1973	$4
❏ 45203	Cat's in the Cradle/Vacancy	1974	$4
❏ 45368	Corey's Coming/If My Mary Were Here	1976	$4
❏ 45792	Could You Put Your Light On, Please?/Any Old Kind of Day	1972	$4
❏ 45426	Dance Band on the Titanic/I Wonder What Happened to Him	1977	$4
❏ 45264	Dreams Go By/Sandy	1975	$4
❏ 45524	Flowers Are Red/Jenny	1978	$4
❏ 45236	I Wanna Learn a Love Song/She Sings Songs Without Words	1975	$4
❏ 45497	I Wonder What Would Happen to This World/If You Want to Feel	1978	$4
❏ 45445	My Old Lady/I'll Do It for You, Jane	1977	$4
❏ 45304	Star Tripper/The Rock	1976	$4
❏ 45811	Sunday Morning Sunshine/Burning Herself	1972	$4
❏ 45285	Tangled-Up Puppet/Dirt Get Under the Fingernails	1975	$4
❏ 45770	Taxi/Empty	1972	$5
❏ 45893	What Made America Famous/Old College Avenue	1974	$4
❏ 45874	WOLD/Short Stories	1973	$4

CHAPINS, THE
EPIC
| ❏ 10761 | Workin' On My Life/The Only Thing (You Ever Really Have to Do Is Die) | 1971 | $15 |

ROCK-LAND
| ❏ 664 | Old Time Movies/Not Your Kind | 1966 | $20 |
| ❏ 664 [PS] | Old Time Movies/Not Your Kind | 1966 | $30 |

CHAPMAN, BETH NIELSEN
CAPITOL
| ❏ 4843 | Hazel's Song (Every Time You Leave Me)/If Only I'd Known | 1980 | $6 |

CHAPMAN, CEE CEE
CURB
❏ 10529	Frontier Justice/Love Is a Liar	1989	$3
❏ 10518	Gone But Not Forgotten/Love Is a Liar	1988	$3
❏ 10547	Twist of Fate/Back to Santa Fe	1989	$3

CHAPMAN, GARY
RCA
| ❏ 7601-7-R | Everyday Man/Cecil (Love Goes On) | 1987 | $4 |
| ❏ 5285-7-R | When We're Together/Your Love Stays with Me | 1987 | $4 |

Number	Title	Yr	NM

CHAPMAN, GRADY
IMPERIAL
| ❏ 5611 | Come Away/Let's Talk About Us | 1959 | $15 |
| ❏ 5591 | Garden of Memories/ Tell Me That You Care | 1959 | $15 |

KNIGHT
| ❏ 2003 | Say You Will Be Mine/ Starlight, Starbright | 1958 | $40 |

MERCURY
❏ 71698	Ambush/My Life Would Be Worth Living	1960	$60
❏ 71771	I'll Never Question Your Love/ This, That, 'N the Other	1961	$15
❏ 71632	Sweet Thing/I Know What I Want	1960	$15

MONEY
| ❏ 204 | I Need You So/Don't Blooper | 1955 | $300 |

ZEPHYR
| ❏ 016 | My Love Will Never Change/Smiling | 1957 | $40 |

CHAPMAN, TRACY
ELEKTRA
❏ 7-69356	Baby Can I Hold You/If Not Now	1988	$3
❏ 7-69356 [PS]	Baby Can I Hold You/If Not Now	1988	$4
❏ 7-69273	Crossroads/Born to Fight	1989	$3
❏ 7-69273 [PS]	Crossroads/Born to Fight	1989	$3
❏ 7-69412	Fast Car/For You	1988	$5
❏ 65938	Fast Car/Talkin' 'Bout a Revolution	1989	$3

— *Spun Gold" series*

| ❏ 7-69383 | Talkin' 'Bout a Revolution/ Behind the Wall | 1988 | $3 |
| ❏ 7-69383 [PS] | Talkin' 'Bout a Revolution/ Behind the Wall | 1988 | $4 |

CHARADES, THE
AVA
| ❏ 154 | Please Be My Love Tonight/ (B-side unknown) | 1963 | $40 |

CHARGERS, THE
RCA VICTOR
| ❏ 47-7301 | Old MacDonald/Dandelion | 1958 | $40 |

CHARIOTEERS, THE
COLUMBIA
| ❏ 1-363 | This Side of Heaven/ Hawaiian Sunset | 1949 | $600 |

— *Microgroove 7-inch, 33 1/3 rpm single*

JOSIE
| ❏ 787 | I've Got My Heart on My Sleeve/ Don't Play No Mambo | 1955 | $100 |

MGM
| ❏ 12569 | The Candles/I Didn't Mean to Be Mean to You | 1957 | $100 |

RCA VICTOR
| ❏ 47-6098 | Easy Does It/Tremble, Tremble, Tremble | 1955 | $100 |

CHARIOTS, THE
TIME
| ❏ 1006 | Gloria/A Sunday Morning Love | 1959 | $50 |

CHARISMA
ROULETTE
| ❏ 7096 | Bizwambi/(B-side unknown) | 1971 | $8 |
| ❏ 7075 | What's It Like/(B-side unknown) | 1970 | $8 |

CHARLATANS, THE
KAPP
| ❏ 779 | The Shadow Knows/32-20 | 1967 | $60 |
| ❏ 779 [PS] | The Shadow Knows/32-20 | 1967 | $100 |

PHILIPS
| ❏ 44824 [DJ] | Date: May 19, 1969 | 1969 | $70 |

— *One-sided, promo only*

| ❏ 40610 | High Coin/When I Go Sailin' By | 1969 | $50 |
| ❏ 40610 [PS] | High Coin/When I Go Sailin' By | 1969 | $100 |

— *Sleeve is promo only*

CHARLEE
AMERAMA
| ❏ 5001 | Standing in Your Shoes/ House of the Rising Sun | 1977 | $8 |

CHARLENE
ARIOLA AMERICA
| ❏ 7696 | Are You Free/We Know | 1977 | $5 |

MOTOWN
❏ 1285	All That Love Went to Waste/ Give It One More Try	1973	$8
❏ 1262	Give It One More Try/Relove	1973	$8
❏ 1761	Hit and Run Lover/Last Song	1984	$3
❏ 1492	Hungry/I Won't Remember Ever Loving You	1980	$4
❏ 1611	I've Never Been to Me/ Somewhere in My Life	1982	$3
❏ 1663	I Want to Go Back There Again/Richie's Song	1983	$3
❏ 1734	We're Both in Love with You/I Want the World to Know He's Mine	1984	$3

PRODIGAL
❏ 0633	Freddie/(B-side unknown)	1977	$5
❏ 0633 [PS]	Freddie/(B-side unknown)	1977	$10
❏ 0632	It Ain't Easy Coming Down/ On My Way to You	1977	$5
❏ 0636	I've Never Been to Me/It's Really Nice to Be in Love Again	1977	$30

CHARLES AND CARL
RED ROBIN
| ❏ 137 | Lucky Star/One More Chance | 1955 | $125 |

CHARLES, BOBBY
BEARSVILLE
| ❏ 0010 | Small Town Talk/Save Me Jesus | 1973 | $4 |

CHESS
❏ 1609	Later Alligator/On Bended Knee	1955	$60
❏ 1638	Laura Lee/No Use Knocking	1956	$60
❏ 1670	One Eyed Jack/Yea Yea Baby	1957	$50
❏ 1628	Only Time Will Tell/ Take It Easy. Greasy	1956	$60
❏ 1647	Put Your Arms Around Me/ Why Can't You, Honey	1957	$50
❏ 1617	Why Did You Leave/Don't You Know I Love You	1956	$60

IMPERIAL
❏ 5642	Bye Bye Baby/Those Eyes	1960	$30
❏ 5691	Four Winds/Nothing Sweet As You	1960	$30
❏ 5557	Oh Yeah/Since I Lost You	1958	$30
❏ 5542	Since She's Gone/ At the Jamboree	1958	$30
❏ 5579	The Town Is Talking/ What Can I Do	1959	$30
❏ 5681	What a Party/I Just Want You	1960	$30

JEWEL
❏ 735	Ain't Misbehavin'/ Preacher's Daughter	1964	$10
❏ 728	Everybody's Laughing/ Everybody Knows	1964	$12
❏ 729	Goodnight Irene/I Hope	1964	$10
❏ 740	Oh Lonesome Me/One More Glass of Wine	1964	$10

PAULA
| ❏ 226 | The Walk/Worrying Over You | 1965 | $10 |

CHARLES, DON
WORLD ARTISTS
| ❏ 1031 | She's Mine/Big Talk from a Little Man | 1964 | $10 |

CHARLES, JIMMY
PROMO
❏ 1002	A Million to One/Hop Scotch Hop	1960	$20
❏ 1002	A Million to One/Hop Scotch Polka	1960	$30
❏ 1005	Christmasville U.S.A./A Little White Mouse Called Steve	1960	$20
❏ 1005 [PS]	Christmasville U.S.A./A Little White Mouse Called Steve	1960	$30
❏ 1006	I Wonder How It Feels to Fall in Love/Just Whistle for Me	1961	$20
❏ 1004	Santa Won't Be Blue This Christmas/I Saw Mommy Kissing Santa Claus	1960	$20
❏ 1004 [PS]	Santa Won't Be Blue This Christmas/I Saw Mommy Kissing Santa Claus	1960	$30
❏ 1003	The Age for Love/ Follow the Swallow	1960	$20
❏ 1003 [PS]	The Age for Love/ Follow the Swallow	1960	$30

CHARLES, KIM
MCA
| ❏ 40987 | Want to Thank You/By Any Chance | 1979 | $4 |

CHARLES, LEE
BAMBOO
| ❏ 110 | Girl You Turned Your Back on Me/I Never Want to Lose My Sweet Thing | 1970 | $30 |
| ❏ 111 | Why Do You Have to Go/I Never Want to Lose My Sweet Thing | 1970 | $20 |

BRUNSWICK
| ❏ 55401 | I'll Never Love Again/ Wrong Number | 1969 | $30 |

DAKAR
| ❏ 601 | Then Would You Love Me/ It's All Over Between Us | 1969 | $30 |

HOT WAX
| ❏ 7303 | I Just Want to Be Loved/ Somebody's Gonna Hurt You Like You Hurt Me | 1973 | $8 |

INVICTUS
| ❏ 1260 | Get Your House in Order/ Sittin' on a Time Bomb | 1974 | $8 |

REVUE
| ❏ 11022 | Someone, Somewhere/ Wrong Number | 1968 | $20 |
| ❏ 11007 | Standing on the Outside/ If That Ain't Lovin' You | 1968 | $20 |

CHARLES, RAY, AND BETTY CARTER
ABC-PARAMOUNT
| ❏ 10298 | Baby It's Cold Outside/ We'll Be Together Again | 1962 | $12 |

CHARLES, RAY, AND MILT JACKSON
7-Inch Extended Plays
ATLANTIC
| ❏ 614 | Blue Funk/Cosmic Ray | 1958 | $75 |
| ❏ 614 [PS] | Soul Brothers | 1958 | $75 |

CHARLES, RAY, SINGERS
COMMAND
❏ 4049	Al Di La/Till the End of Time	1964	$6
❏ 4092	Birds of a Feather/Step By Step	1967	$5
❏ 4096	Bless Your Heart/Little By Little and Step By Step	1967	$5
❏ 4082	Blue Roses/My World (Il Mondo)	1966	$5
❏ 4074	Christmas Is a Birthday/A Toy for a Boy	1965	$10
❏ 4090	Don't Cry/There's No Place Like Home	1967	$5
❏ 4070	Hey, Pretty Pussycat/ The Nut Song	1965	$6
❏ 4130	Holly/Summer Warning	1969	$4
❏ 4115	I Can See It Now/Quiz Me	1968	$5
❏ 4085	It's Time to Sing/Promises	1966	$5
❏ 4123	I Wish I Knew How It Would Feel to Be Free/Let Go	1969	$4
❏ 4046	Love Me with All Your Heart/ Sweet Little Mountain Bird	1964	$10

— *The LP title "Something Special for Young Lovers" is in bold, with "The Ray Charles Singers" in tiny print at bottom*

| ❏ 4046 | Love Me with All Your Heart/ Sweet Little Mountain Bird | 1964 | $6 |

— *With the Ray Charles Singers receiving a more "apt" credit*

❏ 4086	Minneapolis/The Bells	1966	$5
❏ 4135	Move Me, O Wondrous Music/I'll Fly Away	1969	$4
❏ 4073	My Love, Forgive Me/My Guitar and My Song	1965	$6
❏ 4057	One More Time/Bluesette	1964	$6
❏ 4079	One of Those Songs/To You	1966	$5
❏ 4105	Take Me Along/Walkin' Lonely	1968	$5
❏ 4103	Then You Can Tell Me Goodbye/Blame It on Me	1968	$5
❏ 4059	This Is My Prayer/A Toy for a Boy	1965	$6

DECCA
| ❏ 30834 | Hip Hop/A Touch of Pink | 1959 | $12 |

MGM
❏ 12507	Around the World/Take a Trip to Memory Lane	1957	$10
❏ 12108	Autumn in New York/ Autumn in Rome	1955	$12
❏ 12068	Autumn Leaves/Early Autumn	1955	$12
❏ 12413	I've Got My Love to Keep Me Warm/When Winter Comes	1957	$10
❏ 12524	Lazy Afternoon/Mountain Greenery	1957	$12
❏ 12606	Let It Snow, Let It Snow, Let It Snow/You're My Girl	1957	$15
❏ 12445	Mam'selle/Madamoiselle de Paris	1957	$10
❏ 12363	Moonlight in Vermont/ Button Up Your Overcoat	1956	$10
❏ 12333	September in the Rain/'Tis Autumn	1956	$10
❏ 12217	Spring Is Here/Spring! Spring! Spring!	1956	$10
❏ 12563	The Things We Did Last Summer/ Shine On Harvest Moon	1957	$10
❏ 12470	When It's Springtime in the Rockies/Lovelier Than Ever	1957	$10

7-Inch Extended Plays
| ❏ X-1503 [PS] | Here's to My Lady, Vol. 1 | 1957 | $12 |
| ❏ X-1503 | Here's to My Lady/You Must Have Been a Beautiful Baby// The Very Thought of You/You're Getting to Be a Habit with Me | 1957 | $10 |

CHARLES, RAY

ABC

Number	Title	Yr	NM
❑ 11291	Don't Change on Me/Sweet Memories	1971	$8
❑ 11090	Eleanor Rigby/Understanding	1968	$8
❑ 11344	Every Saturday Night/Take Me Home, Country Roads	1973	$6
❑ 11308	Feel So Bad/Your Love Is So Doggone Good	1971	$6
❑ 10938	Here We Go Again/Somebody Ought to Write a Book About It	1967	$8
❑ 11337	Hey Mister/There'll Be No Peace Without All Men as One	1972	$6
❑ 11351	I Can Make It Through the Days (But Oh Those Lonely Nights)/Ring of Fire	1973	$6
❑ 10840	I Chose to Sing the Blues/Hopelessly	1966	$8
❑ 11170	If It Wasn't for Bad Luck/When I Stop Dreaming	1969	$8

—With Jimmy Lewis

Number	Title	Yr	NM
❑ 11271	If You Were Mine/Till I Can't Take It Anymore	1970	$8
❑ 11193	I'll Be Your Servant/I Don't Know What Time It Was	1969	$8
❑ 10970	In the Heat of the Night/Somebody's Got to Change	1967	$8
❑ 10901	I Want to Talk About You/Something Inside Me	1967	$8
❑ 11259	Laughin' and Clownin'/That Thing Called Love	1970	$8
❑ 11213	Let Me Love You/I'm Satisfied	1969	$8
❑ 10808	Let's Go Get Stoned/At the Train	1966	$8
❑ 11329	Look What They've Done to My Song, Ma/America the Beautiful	1972	$10
❑ 10865	Please Say You're Fooling/I Don't Need No Doctor	1966	$8
❑ 11251	Someone to Watch Over Me/Claudie Mae	1969	$8
❑ 11133	Sweet Young Thing Like You/Listen, They're Playing Our Song	1968	$8
❑ 11045	That's a Lie/Go On Home	1968	$8
❑ 11045 [PS]	That's a Lie/Go On Home	1968	$20
❑ 11239	We Can Make It/I Can't Stop Loving You Baby	1969	$8
❑ 11317	What Am I Living For/Tired of My Tears	1971	$6

ABC-PARAMOUNT

Number	Title	Yr	NM
❑ 480-4 [S]	A Tear Fell/No One to Cry To	1964	$30
❑ 480-2 [S]	Baby, Don't You Cry/Cry Me a River	1964	$30
❑ 10530	Baby Don't You Cry/My Heart Cries for You	1964	$15
❑ 410-3 [S]	Born to Lose/Just a Little Lovin'	1962	$30
❑ 465-1 [S]	Busted/(B-side unknown)	1963	$30
❑ 10481	Busted/Making Believe	1963	$20
❑ 10739	Crying Time/When My Dreamboat Comes Home	1965	$20
❑ 10615	Cry/Teardrops from My Eyes	1965	$15
❑ 480-1 [S]	Don't Cry Baby/Teardrops from My Eyes	1964	$30
❑ 10405	Don't Set Me Free/The Brightest Smile in Town	1963	$15
❑ 10135	Georgia on My Mind/Carry Me Back to Old Virginny	1960	$20
❑ 410-2 [S]	Half As Much/I Love You So Much It Hurts	1962	$30
❑ 10314	Hide 'Nor Hair/At the Club	1962	$15
❑ 10244	Hit the Road Jack/The Danger Zone	1961	$20
❑ 10330	I Can't Stop Loving You/Born to Lose	1962	$20
❑ 480-3 [S]	I Cried for You/Cry	1964	$30
❑ 10649	I Gotta Woman (Part 1)/I Gotta Woman (Part 2)	1965	$15
❑ 10700	I'm a Fool to Care/Love's Gonna Live Here	1965	$15
❑ 435-4 [S]	Making Believe/Don't Tell Me Your Troubles	1962	$30
❑ 10609	Makin' Whoopee/(Instrumental)	1964	$15
❑ 10557	My Baby Don't Dig Me/Something's Wrong	1964	$15
❑ 10081	My Baby/Who You Gonna Love	1960	$20
❑ 435-5 [S]	Oh, Lonesome Me/Hang Your Head in Shame	1962	$30

—The above five are 33 1/3 rpm, small hole jukebox singles excerpted from the LP "Modern Sounds in Country and Western Music, Volume Two

Number	Title	Yr	NM
❑ 465-3 [S]	Ol' Man River/(B-side unknown)	1963	$30
❑ 465-4 [S]	Ol' Man Time/(B-side unknown)	1963	$30

—The above four are 33 1/3 rpm, 7-inch jukebox singles with small holes, excerpted from the LP "Ingredients in a Recipe for Soul

Number	Title	Yr	NM
❑ 10588	Smack Dab in the Middle/I Wake Up Crying	1964	$15
❑ 435-3 [S]	Someday (You'll Want Me to Want You)/I'll Never Stand in Your Way	1962	$30
❑ 10118	Sticks and Stones/Worried Life Blues	1960	$15
❑ 10435	Take These Chains from My Heart/No Letter Today	1963	$20
❑ 465-2 [S]	That Lucky Old Sun/(B-side unknown)	1963	$30
❑ 10509	That Lucky Old Sun/Ol' Man Time	1963	$15
❑ 10720	The Cincinnati Kid/That's All I Am to You	1965	$15
❑ 10141	Them That Got/I Wonder	1960	$15
❑ 435-1 [S]	(titles unknown)	1962	$30
❑ 435-2 [S]	(titles unknown)	1962	$30
❑ 10785	Together Again/You're Just About to Lose Your Clown	1966	$15
❑ 10663	Without a Song (Part 1)/Without a Song (Part 2)	1965	$15
❑ 410-4 [S]	Worried Mind/It Makes No Difference Now	1962	$30

ATLANTIC

Number	Title	Yr	NM
❑ 2106	Am I Blue/It Should've Been Me	1961	$15
❑ 3473	A Peace That We Never Could Enjoy/Game Number Nine	1978	$5
❑ 1076	Blackjack/Greenbacks	1955	$40
❑ 2174	Carryin' That Load/Feelin' Sad	1963	$10
❑ 3549 [DJ]	Christmas Time (same on both sides)	1978	$6

—May be promo-only

Number	Title	Yr	NM
❑ 2084	Come Rain or Come Shine/Tell Me You'll Wait for Me	1960	$15
❑ 2470	Come Rain or Come Shine/Tell Me You'll Wait for Me	1968	$10
❑ 3762	Compared To What/Now That We've Found Each Other	1980	$5
❑ 1037	Don't You Know/Losing Hand	1954	$40
❑ 5005	Doodlin' (Part 1)/Doodlin' (Part 2)	1960	$20
❑ 1085	Drown in My Own Tears/Mary Ann	1956	$30
❑ 2094	Early in the Morning/A Bit of Soul	1961	$15
❑ 1008	Feelin' Sad/Heartbreaker	1953	$125
❑ 1096	Hallelujah, I Love Her So/What Would I Do Without You	1956	$30
❑ 2055	Heartbreaker/Just for a Thrill	1960	$15
❑ 3443	I Can See Clearly Now/Anonymous Love	1977	$5
❑ 2043	I'm Movin' On/I Believe to My Soul	1959	$15
❑ 1143	It's All Right/Get On the Right Track Baby	1957	$30
❑ 1021	It Should've Been Me/Sinner's Prayer	1954	$60
❑ 1050	I've Got a Woman/Come Back	1954	$60
❑ 1124	I Want to Know/Ain't That Love	1957	$30
❑ 2118	I Wonder Who/Hard Times (No One Knows Better Than I)	1961	$15
❑ 2047	Let the Good Times Roll/Don't Let the Sun Catch You Cryin'	1960	$15
❑ 1108	Lonely Avenue/Leave My Woman Alone	1956	$30
❑ 999	Mess Around/Funny (But I Still Love You)	1953	$200
❑ 1196	My Bonnie/You Be My Baby	1958	$20
❑ 3611	Some Enchanted Evening/20th Century Fox	1979	$5
❑ 1154	Swanee River Rock (Talkin' 'Bout That River)/I Want a Little Girl	1957	$30
❑ 2239	Talkin' 'Bout You/In a Little Spanish Town	1964	$10
❑ 1172	Talkin' 'Bout You/What Kind of a Man Are You	1958	$20
❑ 2022	Tell Me How Do You Feel/That's Enough	1959	$20
❑ 2068	Tell the Truth/Sweet Sixteen Bars	1960	$15
❑ 984	The Sun's Gonna Shine Again/Jumpin' in the Morning	1953	$400
❑ 1063	This Little Girl of Mine/A Fool for You	1955	$40
❑ 2031	What'd I Say (Part I)/What'd I Say (Part II)	1959	$30

BARONET

Number	Title	Yr	NM
❑ 7111	See See Rider/I Used to be So Happy	1960	$15
❑ 7111 [PS]	See See Rider/I Used to be So Happy	1960	$30

COLUMBIA

Number	Title	Yr	NM
❑ 38-04083	Ain't Your Memory Got No Pride at All/I Don't Want No Strangers Sleeping in My Bed	1983	$3
❑ 38-06370	Dixie Moon/A Little Bit of Heaven	1986	$3
❑ 38-04420	Do I Ever Cross Your Mind/They Call It Love	1984	$3
❑ 38-04860	It Ain't Gonna Worry My Mind/Crazy Old Soldier	1985	$3

—A-side with Mickey Gilley; B-side with Johnny Cash

Number	Title	Yr	NM
❑ 38-06172	Pages of My Mind/Slip Away	1986	$3
❑ 38-08393	Seven Spanish Angels/It Ain't Gonna Worry My Mind	1988	$3

—Reissue; A-side with Willie Nelson, B-side with Mickey Gilley

Number	Title	Yr	NM
❑ 38-04715	Seven Spanish Angels/Who Cares	1984	$3

—A-side with Willie Nelson; B-side with Janie Frickie

Number	Title	Yr	NM
❑ 38-03429	String Bean/Born to Love Me	1982	$4
❑ 38-05575	Two Old Cats Like Us/Little Hotel Room	1985	$3

—A-side with Hank Williams, Jr.; B-side with Merle Haggard

Number	Title	Yr	NM
❑ 38-04297	We Didn't See a Thing/I Wish You Were Here Tonight	1983	$3

—A-side with George Jones and Chet Atkins

Number	Title	Yr	NM
❑ 38-04500	Woman (Sensuous Woman)/I Was On Georgia Time	1984	$3

CROSSOVER

Number	Title	Yr	NM
❑ 985	America the Beautiful/Sunshine	1976	$6

—A-side is a different recording than that on the B-side of ABC 11329

Number	Title	Yr	NM
❑ 973	Come Live with Me/Everybody Sing	1973	$5
❑ 981	Living for the City/Then We'll Be Home	1975	$5
❑ 974	Louise/Somebody	1974	$5

IMPULSE!

Number	Title	Yr	NM
❑ 202	I've Got News for You/I'm Gonna Move to the Outskirts of Town	1961	$10
❑ 200	One Mint Julep/Let's Go	1961	$10

RCA

Number	Title	Yr	NM
❑ PB-10800	Oh Lawd, I'm On My Way/Oh Bess, Where's My Bess	1976	$5

ROCKIN'

Number	Title	Yr	NM
❑ 504	Walkin' and Talkin' (To Myself)/I'm Wonderin' and Wonderin'	1952	$300

SITTIN' IN WITH

Number	Title	Yr	NM
❑ 641	Baby Let Me Hear You Call My Name/Guitar Blues	1952	$300

SWING TIME

Number	Title	Yr	NM
❑ 250	Baby, Let Me Hold Your Hand/Lonely Boy	1951	$500

—Ray Charles records on Swing Time before 250 are unconfirmed on 45 rpm

Number	Title	Yr	NM
❑ 300	Baby Let Me Hear You Call My Name/Guitar Blues	1952	$500
❑ 326	The Snow Is Falling/Misery in My Heart	1953	$500

TANGERINE

Number	Title	Yr	NM
❑ 1015	Booty Butt/Sidewinder	1971	$6

TIME

Number	Title	Yr	NM
❑ 1026	I Found My Baby/Guitar Blues	1960	$20
❑ 1054	Why Did You Go/Back Home	1962	$15

WARNER BROS.

Number	Title	Yr	NM
❑ 49608	Beers to You/Cotton-Eyed Clint	1980	$5

—A-side with Clint Eastwood; B-side by Texas Opera Company

7-Inch Extended Plays

ABC

Number	Title	Yr	NM
❑ EP-ABCS625 [PS]	A Portrait of Ray	1968	$30
❑ EP-ABCS625	Eleanor Rigby/Understanding a Sweet Young Thing Like You//The Sun Died/I Won't Leave	1968	$30

—Jukebox issue; small hole, plays at 33 1/3 rpm

ABC-PARAMOUNT

Number	Title	Yr	NM
❑ EP-ABCS520 [PS]	Country and Western Meets Rhythm and Blues	1965	$30
❑ EP-ABCS480-2	Guess I'll Hang My Tears Out to Dry/Teardrops from My Eyes//No One to Cry To/Don't Cry Baby/After My Laughter Came Tears	1964	$30

—Jukebox issue; small hole, plays at 33 1/3 rpm

Number	Title	Yr	NM
❑ EP A-410	I Can't Stop Loving You/Born to Lose//You Don't Know Me/Careless Love	1962	$30
❑ EP-ABCS500	I Gotta Woman Pt. 1/I Gotta Woman Pt. 2/Margie//Baby Don't You Cry/Hide Nor Hair/Hallelujah I Love Her So	1965	$30

—Jukebox issue; small hole, plays at 33 1/3 rpm

Number	Title	Yr	NM
❑ EP A-410 [PS]	Modern Sounds in Country and Western Music	1962	$30
❑ EP-ABCS480-2 [PS]	Sweet and Sour Tears	1964	$30
❑ EP415	Them That Got/Unchain My Heart/Hit the Road Jack//Sticks and Stones/I Wonder/The Danger Zone	1962	$35

—Jukebox issue; small hole, plays at 33 1/3 rpm

Number	Title	Yr	NM
❑ EP-ABCS520	Together Again/I've Got a Tiger by the Tail/Next Door to the Blues//I Don't Care/Blue Moon of Kentucky/Light Out of Darkness	1965	$30

—Jukebox issue; small hole, plays at 33 1/3 rpm

ATLANTIC

Number	Title	Yr	NM
❑ EP607	*A Fool for You/Mary Ann/Blackjack/Lonely Avenue	1958	$125
❑ EP587	*Ain't That Love/Greenbacks/Drown in My Own Tears/Hallelujah I Love Her So	1956	$125
❑ EP619	*Let the Good Times Roll/Come Rain or Come Shine/Don't Let the Sun Catch You Cryin'/Alexander's Ragtime Band	1959	$125
❑ EP597	Doodlin'/Sweet Sixteen Bars	1957	$125
❑ EP619 [PS]	The Genius of Ray Charles	1959	$125
❑ EP597 [PS]	The Great Ray Charles	1957	$125

CHARLES RIVER VALLEY BOYS, THE

ELEKTRA

Number	Title	Yr	NM
❑ 45642	I've Just Seen a Face/Ticket to Ride	1968	$10

Number	Title	Yr	NM
CHARLES, SONNY			
FRATERNITY			
❑ 935	Speechless/These Two Feet	1964	$15
HIGHRISE			
❑ 2006	Always on My Mind/One-Eyed Jacks	1983	$5
❑ 2001	Put It in a Magazine/The Week-End Father Song	1982	$5
RCA VICTOR			
❑ 74-0645	It's Alright in the City/Nicasio	1972	$6
CHARLETTES, THE			
ANGIE			
❑ 1002	The Fight's Not Over/Whatever Happened to Our Love	1963	$30
CHARMAINES, THE			
DOT			
❑ 16351	Where Is the Boy Tonight/On the Wagon	1961	$30
CHARMERS, THE (1)			
ALADDIN			
❑ 3337	All Alone/Johnny My Dear	1956	$70
❑ 3341	He's Gone/Oh! Yes	1956	$70
IMPERIAL			
❑ 5957	All Alone/Johnny My Dear	1963	$15
—Reissue of Aladdin 3337			
CHARMERS, THE (2)			
CENTRAL			
❑ 1002	The Beating of My Heart/Why Does It Have to Be Me	1954	$800
❑ 1006	Tony, My Darling/In the Rain	1954	$1000
LOST-NITE			
❑ 142	The Beating of My Heart/Why Does It Have to Be Me	1954	$8
—Reissue			
TIMELY			
❑ 1009	I Was Wrong/The Mambo	1955	$1000
❑ 1011	The Church on the Hill/Battle Axe	1955	$1000
CHARMERS, THE (U)			
CO-REC			
❑ 101	The Letter/Watch What You Do	1963	$30
JAF			
❑ 2021	Little Fool/Hard to Get	1961	$30
LAURIE			
❑ 3142	My Kind of Love/Johnny	1962	$30
❑ 3173	Shy Guy/I Cried	1963	$30
❑ 3203	Work It Out/Sweet Talk	1963	$30
LOUIS			
❑ 6806	It's a Funny Way We Met/Where's the Boy	1965	$15
PIP			
❑ 8000	Looking for Trouble/After You Walk Me Home	1964	$15
SURE SHOT			
❑ 104	Lessons from the Stars/My Love	1963	$300
CHARMETTES, THE			
HI			
❑ 2003	My Love with All My Heart/Skating in Blue Light	1958	$30
KAPP			
❑ 570	Oozi-Oozi-Ooh/He's a Wise Guy	1964	$30
❑ 547	Please Don't Kiss Me Again/What Is a Tear	1963	$40
MALA			
❑ 491	My Lover Is a Boy Scout/Mailbox	1964	$15
TRI-DISC			
❑ 103	Why Oh Why/On a Night Like Tonight	1962	$30
WORLD ARTISTS			
❑ 1053	Stop the Wedding (Preacher Man)/Sugar Boy	1965	$30
CHARMS, THE			
CHART			
❑ 613	Heart of a Rose/I Offer You	1956	$50
❑ 623	I'll Be True/Boom Diddy Boom Boom	1956	$50
❑ 608	Love's Our Inspiration/Love, Love Stick Stov	1956	$50
DELUXE			
❑ 6034	Bye Bye Baby/Please Believe in Me	1954	$400
❑ 6056	Come to Me Baby/My Baby, Dearest Darling	1954	$200
❑ 6072	Crazy, Crazy Love/Mambo Sh-Mambo	1955	$60

Number	Title	Yr	NM
❑ 6014	Happy Are We/What Do You Know About That	1953	$400
❑ 6062	Hearts of Stone/Who Knows	1954	$60
❑ 6000	Heaven Only Knows/Loving Baby	1953	$500
❑ 6076	Ling, Ting, Tong/Bazoom (I Need Your Lovin')	1955	$60
❑ 6089	One Fine Day/It's You, You, You	1955	$50
❑ 6065	Two Hearts/The First Time We Met	1954	$60
❑ 6082	Whadya Want?/Crazy, Crazy Love	1955	$50
❑ 6087	When We Get Married/Let the Happenings Happen	1955	$50
ROCKIN'			
❑ 516	Heaven Only Knows/Loving Baby	1953	$800
7-Inch Extended Plays			
DELUXE			
❑ EP-357	*Hearts of Stone/Bazoom (I Need Your Lovin')/Ling Ting Tong/Crazy, Crazy Love	1955	$400
❑ EP-357 [PS]	Hits by the Charms	1955	$400
CHARO			
SALSOUL			
❑ 2076	(Mamacita) Donde Esta Santa Claus?/(Instrumental)	1978	$8
CHARTERS, THE			
ALVA			
❑ 1001	I Lost You/My Little Girl	1963	$300
MEL-O-DY			
❑ 104	Trouble Lover/Show Me Some Sign	1962	$2000
MERRY-GO-ROUND			
❑ 103	Lost in a Dream/This Makes Me Mad	1963	$70
TARX			
❑ 1003	My Rose/El Merengue	1962	$125
CHARTS, THE			
EVERLAST			
❑ 5002	Dance Girl/Why Do You Cry	1957	$100
❑ 5001	Deserie/Zoop	1957	$100
❑ 5026	Deserie/Zoop	1963	$30
❑ 5008	I Told You So/All Because of Love	1958	$70
❑ 5010	My Diane/All Because of You	1958	$75
GUYDEN			
❑ 2021	For the Birds/Ooba-Gooba	1959	$30
WAND			
❑ 1112	Deserie/Fell in Love with Your Baby	1966	$30
❑ 1124	Livin' the Night Life/Nobody Made You Love Me	1966	$70
CHASE			
EPIC			
❑ 5-10738	Get It On/River	1971	$5
❑ 5-10775	Handbags and Gladrags/Open Up Wide	1971	$4
❑ 5-10853	I Can Feel It/Cronus (Saturn)	1972	$4
❑ 8-50027	Love Is on the Way/Bochawa	1974	$4
❑ 5-10806	So Many People/Paint It Sad	1971	$4
CHASE, CAROL			
CASABLANCA			
❑ 2321	If You Don't Know Me by Now/Morning Glory	1981	$4
❑ 4502	Sexy Song/Disco Devil	1980	$5
❑ 4501	This Must Be My Ship/It Always Takes a Fool to Fool Around	1979	$5
MCA			
❑ 52296	Love in the Shadows/You're Here to Remember	1983	$4
CHASTAIN, DAWN			
OAK			
❑ 1018	Me Plus You Equals Love/(B-side unknown)	1978	$6
PHONO			
❑ 2646	Boogie Woogie Rock 'n Roll/All I Have to Do Is Dream	1977	$8
PRAIRIE DUST			
❑ 7622	Hey Mister/Ain't No Doubt About It	1978	$6
❑ 7624	How Can You Say You Don't Love Me No More/You and I	1978	$6
SCR			
❑ 164	Love Talks/(B-side unknown)	1979	$5
❑ 178	That's You, That's Me/(B-side unknown)	1979	$5

Number	Title	Yr	NM
CHAVIS BROTHERS, THE			
ASCOT			
❑ 2177	Torture Me/Humpty Dumpty Time	1965	$15
CLOCK			
❑ 1025	I Love You/So Tired	1960	$30
CORAL			
❑ 62270	Old Time Rock and Roll/Baby, Don't Leave Me	1961	$40
—As "The Five Chavis Brothers			
PARKWAY			
❑ 851	Slippin' and Slidin'/Good Old Mountain Dew	1962	$20
CHEAP TRICK			
Also see FUSE.			
COLUMBIA			
❑ 38-06137	Mighty Wings/Dog Fight #3	1986	$3
—B-side by Harold Faltermeyer			
❑ 38-06137 [PS]	Mighty Wings/Dog Fight #3	1986	$3
EPIC			
❑ 9-50743	Ain't That a Shame/Elo Kiddies	1979	$5
❑ 8-50625	California Man/I Want You to Want Me	1978	$10
—B-side was first American issue of version that became a hit on Epic 50680			
❑ 34-04078	Dancing the Night Away/Don't Make Our Love a Crime	1983	$4
❑ 34-04078 [PS]	Dancing the Night Away/Don't Make Our Love a Crime	1983	$5
❑ 34-07965	Don't Be Cruel/I Know What I Want	1988	$3
❑ 34-07965 [PS]	Don't Be Cruel/I Know What I Want	1988	$3
❑ 9-50774	Dream Police/Heaven Tonight	1979	$5
❑ 9-50774 [PS]	Dream Police/Heaven Tonight	1979	$12
❑ AE71206 [DJ]	Everything Works If You Let It (same on both sides)	1980	$5
—Included as an "extra" in the 10-inch version of the EP "Found All the Parts"; sometimes found separately, though it was never sold separately with this number			
❑ 9-50887	Everything Works If You Let It/Way of the World	1980	$5
❑ 34-08097	Ghost Town/Wrong Side of Love	1988	$3
❑ 34-08097 [PS]	Ghost Town/Wrong Side of Love	1988	$3
❑ 34-04216	I Can't Take It/You Talk Too Much	1983	$4
❑ 14-02968	If You Want My Love/Four Letter Word	1982	$5
❑ 15-03845	If You Want My Love/She's Tight	1983	$4
—Reissue			
❑ 34-06540	It's Only Love/Name of the Game	1987	$4
❑ 34-06540 [PS]	It's Only Love/Name of the Game	1987	$5
❑ 8-50680	I Want You to Want Me/Clock Strikes Ten	1979	$4
❑ 8-50680 [PS]	I Want You to Want Me/Clock Strikes Ten	1979	$10
❑ 8-50435	I Want You to Want Me/Oh Boy	1977	$10
❑ 8-50375	Oh, Candy/Daddy Should Have Stayed in High School	1977	$10
❑ 34-03741	Saturday at Midnight/One on One	1983	$4
❑ 34-03233	She's Tight/All I Really Want to Do	1982	$4
❑ 34-03233 [PS]	She's Tight/All I Really Want to Do	1982	$5
❑ 8-50485	Southern Girls/You're All Talk	1977	$10
❑ 19-50942	Stop This Game/Who D'King	1980	$5
❑ 8-50570	Surrender/Auf Wiedersehn	1978	$10
❑ 34-07745	The Flame/Through the Night	1988	$3
—Custom label			
❑ 34-07745 [PS]	The Flame/Through the Night	1988	$3
❑ 19-50970	The World's Greatest Lover/High Priest of Rhythmic Noise	1981	$5
❑ 34-05431	Tonight It's You/Wild, Wild Women	1985	$4
❑ 34-05431 [PS]	Tonight It's You/Wild, Wild Women	1985	$5
—With no B-side listed on back cover			
❑ 34-05431 [PS]	Tonight It's You/Wild, Wild Women	1985	$5
—With B-side listed on back cover			
WARNER BROS.			
❑ 29723	Spring Break/Get Ready	1983	$6

Number	Title	Yr	NM

CHECKER, CHUBBY

20TH CENTURY

Number	Title	Yr	NM
❏ 2075	She's a Bad Woman/ Happiness Is a Girl Like You	1974	$5

ABKCO

❏ 4004	Hey Bobba Needle/Hooka Tooka	1972	$5
❏ 4003	Limbo Rock/Let's Twist Again	1972	$5
❏ 4027	Slow Twistin'/Birdland	1973	$5
❏ 4002	The Huckebuck/Pony Time	1972	$5
❏ 4001	The Twist/Loddy Lo	1972	$5

BUDDAH

❏ 100	Back in the U.S.S.R./Windy Cream	1969	$15

MCA

❏ 52043	Harder Than Diamond/Your Love	1982	$4

PARKWAY

❏ 873	Birdland/Black Cloud	1963	$20
❏ 873 [PS]	Birdland/Black Cloud	1963	$30
❏ 822	Dance the Mess Around/ Good, Good Lovin'	1961	$20
❏ 810	Dancing Dinosaur/Those Private Eyes (Keep Watchin' Me)	1960	$30

— *The existence of both 808 and 810 has been confirmed*

❏ 842	Dancin' Party/Gotta Get Myself Together	1962	$20
❏ 842 [PS]	Dancin' Party/Gotta Get Myself Together	1962	$30
❏ 949	Do the Freddie/(Do the) Discotheque	1965	$30

— *Reissue with new A-side title (number is P-949-C) and probably incorrect B-side title*

❏ 959	Everything's Wrong/ Cu Me La Be-Stay	1965	$60
❏ 907	Hey Bobba Needle/Spread Joy	1964	$20
❏ 907 [PS]	Hey Bobba Needle/Spread Joy	1964	$30
❏ 989	Hey You! Little Boo-Ga-Loo/Pussy Cat	1966	$15
❏ 920	Lazy Elsie Molly/Rosie	1964	$20
❏ 920 [PS]	Lazy Elsie Molly/Rosie	1964	$30
❏ 949	Let's Do the Freddie/ (At the) Discotheque	1965	$15

— *Original A-side title (number is P-949-A) and probably correct B-side title*

❏ 824	Let's Twist Again/Everything's Gonna Be Alright	1961	$20
❏ 824 [PS]	Let's Twist Again/Everything's Gonna Be Alright	1961	$30
❏ 824	Let's Twist Again/Everything's Gonna Be Alright	1961	$200

— *Orange vinyl*

❏ 849	Limbo Rock/Popeye The Hitch-Hiker	1962	$20
❏ 849 [PS]	Limbo Rock/Popeye The Hitch-Hiker	1962	$30
❏ 890	Loddy Lo/Everything's Gonna Be Alright	1963	$20
❏ 890 [PS]	Loddy Lo/Everything's Gonna Be Alright	1963	$28
❏ 890	Loddy Lo/Hooka Tooka	1963	$20
❏ 890 [PS]	Loddy Lo/Hooka Tooka	1963	$30
❏ 04 [DJ]	Love Is Like a Twist/ Peppermint Twist	1962	$50

— *Yellow label, black print, promo only*

❏ 936	Lovely, Lovely (Loverly, Loverly)/ The Weekend's Here	1964	$15
❏ 936 [PS]	Lovely, Lovely (Loverly, Loverly)/ The Weekend's Here	1964	$30
❏ 818	Pony Time/Oh, Susannah	1960	$20
❏ 808	Samson and Delilah/ Whole Lotta Laughin'	1959	$30
❏ 922	She Wants T'Swim/You Better Believe It, Baby	1964	$15
❏ 922 [PS]	She Wants T'Swim/You Better Believe It, Baby	1964	$30
❏ 835	Slow Twistin'/La Paloma Twist	1962	$20

— *Features female vocal by Dee Dee Sharp*

❏ 835 [PS]	Slow Twistin'/La Paloma Twist	1962	$30
❏ 879	Surf Party/Twist It Up	1963	$20
❏ 879 [PS]	Surf Party/Twist It Up	1963	$30
❏ 804	The Class/Schooldays, Oh Schooldays	1959	$40
❏ 830	The Fly/That's the Way It Goes	1961	$20
❏ 830 [PS]	The Fly/That's the Way It Goes	1961	$30
❏ 813	The Huckebuck/Whole Lotta Shakin' Goin' On	1960	$20
❏ 811	The Twist/Toot	1960	$40

— *First pressings have white label with blue print*

❏ 811	The Twist/Toot	1960	$30

— *Second pressings have orange label with black print*

❏ 811 [DJ]	The Twist/Twistin' U.S.A.	1961	$200

— *Promo copy on red vinyl*

❏ 811 [DJ]	The Twist/Twistin' U.S.A.	1961	$200

— *Promo copy on yellow vinyl*

❏ 811	The Twist/Twistin' U.S.A.	1961	$20
❏ 811 [PS]	The Twist/Twistin' U.S.A.	1961	$30
❏ 862	Twenty Miles/Let's Limbo Some More	1963	$20
❏ 862 [PS]	Twenty Miles/Let's Limbo Some More	1963	$30

TIN PAN APPLE

❏ 887571-7 [PS]	The Twist (Yo, Twist!)/(Buffapella)	1988	$3

— *Stupid def vocals" on a Fat Boys record*

Number	Title	Yr	NM
❏ 887571-7 [PS]	The Twist (Yo, Twist!)/(Buffapella)	1988	$3

7-Inch Extended Plays

PARKWAY

❏ 5001 [PS]	Chubby Checker	1961	$75

— *Paper die-cut sleeve*

CHECKERLADS, THE

RCA VICTOR

❏ 47-8986	Shake Yourself Down/ Baby Send for Me	1966	$30

CHECKERS, THE (1)

FEDERAL

❏ 12355	So Fine/Sentimental Heart	1959	$60
❏ 12375	White Cliffs of Dover/ Let Me Come Back	1960	$60

KING

❏ 4558	Flame in My Heart/ Oh, Oh, Oh Baby	1952	$1000
❏ 4626	Ghost of My Baby/I Wanna Know	1953	$800
❏ 5156	Heaven Only Knows/ Nine More Miles	1958	$400
❏ 4710	House with No Windows/ Don't Stop Dan	1954	$500
❏ 4673	I Promise You/You Never Had It So Good	1953	$500
❏ 4751	I Wasn't Thinking, I Was Drinking/Mama's Daughter	1954	$500
❏ 4596	My Prayer Tonight/ Love Wasn't There	1953	$1000
❏ 5592	Over the Rainbow/ Love Wasn't There	1962	$30

— *As "The Original Checkers*

❏ 4719	Over the Rainbow/You've Been Fooling Around	1954	$400
❏ 4764	Trying to Hold My Girl/ Can't Find My Sadie	1955	$500
❏ 4675	White Cliffs of Dover/ Without a Song	1953	$500

CHECKERS, THE (2)

ARVEE

❏ 5035	Skooby Doo (Part 1)/ Skooby Doo (Part 2)	1961	$30
❏ 5037	Swingin' Summer/Skooby Doo	1961	$30

CHECKERS, THE (3)

KING

❏ 5199	Teardrops Are Falling/ Rock-A-Locka	1959	$70

— *Originally released as King 4781 by The Five Wings*

CHECKERS, THE (U)

JERDEN

❏ 710	Black Cat/Soft Blue	1963	$30

SKYLA

❏ 1120	Blue Saturday/Cascade	1961	$30

CHECKMATES LTD., THE

A&M

❏ 1053	Black Pearl/Lazy Susan	1969	$10

— *As "Sonny Charles and the Checkmates Ltd.*

❏ 1040	Love Is All I Have to Give/ Never Should Have Lied	1969	$8
❏ 1130	Proud Mary/Do You Love Your Baby	1969	$8

— *As "Sonny Charles and the Checkmates Ltd.*

❏ 1006	Spanish Harlem/Baby Don't You Get Crazy	1968	$8
❏ 1127	Spanish Harlem/Proud Mary	1969	$8

— *As "Sonny Charles and the Checkmates Ltd.*

CAPITOL

❏ 5603	Do the Walk/Glad for You	1966	$30
❏ 5753	I Can Hear the Rain/Kissin' Her and Cryin' for You	1966	$40
❏ 5814	Please Don't Take My World Away/Mastered the Art of Love	1966	$30
❏ 5922	Walk in the Sunlight/A & I	1967	$30

FANTASY

❏ 823	Greedy for Your Love/ That's How It Feels (When Two People Fall in Love)	1978	$5
❏ 800	Let's Do It/Take All the Time You Need	1977	$5

GREEDY

❏ 111	I'm Laying My Heart on the Line/Make Love to Your Mind	1977	$5

POLYDOR

❏ 14313	All Alone by the Telephone/ Body Language	1976	$5

CHEECH AND CHONG

MCA

❏ 52655	Born in East L.A./I'm a (Modern) Man	1985	$3

Number	Title	Yr	NM
❏ 52655 [PS]	Born in East L.A./I'm a (Modern) Man	1985	$4
❏ 52732	I'm Not Home Right Now/Hot Saki	1985	$3
❏ 52732 [PS]	I'm Not Home Right Now/Hot Saki	1985	$4

ODE

❏ 66038	Basketball Jones/Don't Bug Me	1973	$5
❏ 66038 [PS]	Basketball Jones/Don't Bug Me	1973	$6
❏ 66104	Black Lassie (Featuring Johnny Stash)/Coming Attractions	1974	$4
❏ 66104 [PS]	Black Lassie (Featuring Johnny Stash)/Coming Attractions	1974	$6
❏ 50471	Bloat On (Featuring the Bloaters)/Just Say "Right On	1977	$4
❏ 50471 [PS]	Bloat On (Featuring the Bloaters)/Just Say "Right On	1977	$6
❏ 66102	Earache My Eye (Featuring Alice Bowie)/ Turn That Thing Down	1974	$4
❏ 66102 [PS]	Earache My Eye (Featuring Alice Bowie)/ Turn That Thing Down	1974	$6
❏ 66124	Framed/Pedro's Request	1976	$4
❏ 66115	How I Spent My Summer Vacation, Or A Day at the Beach with Pedro and Man (Part 1/Part 2)	1975	$4
❏ 66021	Santa Claus and His Old Lady/Dave	1971	$8
❏ 66021 [PS]	Santa Claus and His Old Lady/Dave	1971	$15
❏ 50499	Santa Claus and His Old Lady/Rudolph the Red-Nosed Reindeer	1977	$10
❏ 66041	Sister Mary Elephant/ Wink Dinkerson	1974	$5
❏ 66041 [PS]	Sister Mary Elephant/ Wink Dinkerson	1974	$6

CHEERIOS, THE

INFINITY

❏ 011	Ding Dong Honeymoon/ Where Are You Tonight	1961	$400

CHEERS, THE

CAPITOL

❏ F2921	Bazoom (I Need Your Lovin')/Arrividerci	1954	$30
❏ F3219	Black Denim Trousers and Motorcycle Boots/ Some Night in Alaska	1955	$30
❏ F3219	Black Denim Trousers/ Some Night in Alaska	1955	$30

— *Shorter A-side title; we're not sure which came first*

❏ F3075	Can't We Be More Than Friends/Blueberries	1955	$30
❏ F3409	Heaven on Earth/Que Pasa Muchacha	1956	$30
❏ F3146	I Must Be Dreaming/ Fancy Meeting You Here	1955	$30
❏ F2921	I Need Your Lovin' (Bazoom)/Arrividerci	1954	$50
❏ F3353	The Chicken/Don't Do Anything	1956	$30
❏ F3019	Whadaya Want/Bernie's Tune	1955	$30

MERCURY

❏ 71083	Chug Chug Toot Toot/Big Feet	1957	$20
❏ 71100	Two Hearts/You Never Have the Time	1957	$20

— *As "Bert Convy and the Cheers*

NRC

❏ 5003	Hold That Line/Blue Serenade	1958	$20

CHEETAHS, THE

PHILIPS

❏ 40239	Mecca/That Goodnight Kiss	1964	$10

CHELLOWS, THE

HIT

❏ 64	Ain't That a Shame/If You Wanna Be Happy	1963	$8

— *B-side by John Campbell*

❏ 237	Barbara Ann/No Matter What Shape (Your Stomach's In)	1966	$8

— *B-side by the Upsetters*

❏ 37	Big Girls Don't Cry/ Mama Sang a Song	1962	$8

— *B-side by Sandy Atkinson*

❏ 160	Big Man in Town/We Build a 409	1964	$15

— *B-side by the Roamers*

❏ 264	Bus Stop/Cherish	1966	$8
❏ 187	Bye Bye Baby/This Diamond Ring	1965	$8
❏ 220	California Girls/Help!	1965	$15

— *B-side by the Jalopy Five*

❏ 77	Candy Girl/Hello Muddah, Hello Faddah	1963	$8

— *B-side by Dick Martin*

❏ 106	Dawn (Go Away)/She Loves You	1964	$15

— *B-side by the Bugs*

❏ 252	Gloria/Monday, Monday	1966	$15

— *B-side by the Jalopy Five*

❏ 292	Him or Me -- What's It Gonna Be?/Creeque Alley	1967	$8

Number	Title	Yr	NM
—B-side by the Chords (2)			
❏ 308	Holiday/Incense and Peppermints	1967	$8
—B-side by the Chords (2)			
❏ 298	Little Bit o' Soul/I Take It Back	1967	$8
—B-side by Kathy Shannon			
❏ 262	Little Red Riding Hood/Wild Thing	1966	$8
—B-side by the Jalopy Five			
❏ 30	Sherry/Teenage Idol	1962	$8
—As "The Four Chellows"; B-side by Barney Fox			
❏ 295	Somebody to Love/Groovin'	1967	$8
—B-side by the Jalopy Five			
❏ 111	Stay/Twist and Shout	1964	$15
—B-side by the Bugs			
❏ 247	The Cheater/Sure Gonna Miss Her	1966	$8
—B-side by Ed Hardin			
❏ 284	There's a Kind of Hush/Happy Together	1967	$8
—B-side by the Cadets (2)			
❏ 203	The Sun Will Still Shine/Don't Let Me Be Misunderstood	1965	$10
—B-side by the Chords (2)			
❏ 248	Time Won't Let Me/Secret Agent Man	1966	$8
—B-side by Marty Woods			
❏ 51	Walk Like a Man/Send Me Some Lovin'	1963	$8
—B-side by Leroy Jones			
❏ 288	Western Union/Get Me to the World on Time	1967	$8
❏ 241	Working My Way Back to You/These Boots Are Made for Walking	1966	$8
—B-side by Betty Richards			

CHENIER, CLIFTON
BAYOU
Number	Title	Yr	NM
❏ 712	It's Christmas Time/Time Of Crying	1964	$8

CHER
ATCO
Number	Title	Yr	NM
❏ 6704	For What It's Worth/Hangin' On	1969	$6
❏ 6684	I Walk on Gilded Splinters/Chastity's Song	1969	$6
❏ 6868	Lay Baby Lay/(Just Enough to Keep Me) Hangin' On	1972	$5
❏ 6793	Superstar/First Time	1971	$6
CASABLANCA
❏ 2208	Hell on Wheels/Git Down (Guitar Groupie)	1979	$4
❏ 2228	Holdin' Out for Love/Boys and Girls	1979	$4
❏ 965	Take Me Home/My Song (Too Far Gone)	1979	$4
❏ 987	Wasn't It Good/It's Too Late to Love Me Now	1979	$4
COLUMBIA
| ❏ 18-03150 | I Paralyze/Walk With Me | 1982 | $4 |
GEFFEN
❏ 27529	After All (Love Theme from "Chances Are")/Dangerous Times	1989	$3
—A-side with Peter Cetera			
❏ 27529 [PS]	After All (Love Theme from "Chances Are")/Dangerous Times	1989	$5
❏ 22886	If I Could Turn Back Time/Some Guys	1989	$3
❏ 22886 [PS]	If I Could Turn Back Time/Some Guys	1989	$5
❏ 28191	I Found Someone/Dangerous Times	1987	$3
❏ 28191 [PS]	I Found Someone/Dangerous Times	1987	$3
❏ 27742	Main Man/((It's Been Hard Enough) Gettin' Over You	1988	$3
❏ 27742 [PS]	Main Man/((It's Been Hard Enough) Gettin' Over You	1988	$3
❏ 27894	Skin Deep/Perfection	1988	$3
❏ 27894 [PS]	Skin Deep/Perfection	1988	$3
❏ 27986	We All Sleep Alone/Working Girl	1988	$3
❏ 27986 [PS]	We All Sleep Alone/Working Girl	1988	$3
IMPERIAL
❏ 66192	Alfie/She's No Better Than Me	1966	$10
❏ 66114	All I Really Want to Do/I'm Gonna Love You	1965	$15
❏ 66160	Bang Bang (My Baby Shot Me Down)/Needles and Pins	1966	$15
❏ 66160	Bang Bang (My Baby Shot Me Down)/Our Day Will Come	1966	$15
❏ 66217	Behind the Door/Magic in the Air	1966	$12
❏ 66282	Click Song Number One/But I Can't Love You More	1968	$8
❏ 66223	Dream Baby/Mama (When My Dollies Have Babies)	1966	$12
❏ 66081	Dream Baby/Stan Quetzal	1964	$50
—By "Cherilyn			
❏ 66252	Hey Joe/Our Day Will Come	1967	$12
❏ 66307	Take Me for a Little While/A Song Called Children	1968	$8
❏ 66136	Where Do You Go/See See Blues	1965	$15
KAPP
| ❏ 2134 | Classified 1-A/Don't Put It on Me | 1971 | $6 |

Number	Title	Yr	NM
❏ 2184	Don't Hide Your Love/First Time	1972	$4
❏ 2146	Gypsys, Tramps and Thieves/He'll Never Know	1971	$6
—Black label			
❏ 2146	Gypsys, Tramps and Thieves/He'll Never Know	1971	$5
—Multi-color label; white Kapp logo in black box			
❏ 2146	Gypsys, Tramps and Thieves/He'll Never Know	1971	$4
—Multi-color label; black Kapp logo stands alone			
❏ 2171	Living in a House Divided/One Honest Man	1972	$4
❏ 2158	The Way of Love/Don't Put It on Me	1972	$4
MCA
❏ 40039	Am I Blue/How Long Has This Been Going On	1973	$4
❏ 40324	Carousel Man/When You Find Out Where You're Going Let Me Know	1974	$4
❏ 40161	Dark Lady/Two People Clinging to a Thread	1973	$4
❏ 40102	Half-Breed/Melody	1973	$4
❏ 40273	I Saw a Man and He Danced With His Wife/I Hate to Sleep Alone	1974	$4
❏ 40245	Train of Thought/Dixie Girl	1974	$4
UNITED ARTISTS
❏ 0106	All I Really Want to Do/Where Do You Go	1973	$4
—Silver Spotlight Series" reissue			
❏ 0107	Bang Bang (My Baby Shot Me Down)/You Better Sit Down Kids	1973	$4
—Silver Spotlight Series" reissue			
❏ 50974	Old Man River/Our Day Will Come	1972	$4
❏ XW511	Sunny/Alfie	1974	$4
WARNER BROS.
❏ 8263	Borrowed Time/Long Distance Love Affair	1976	$4
❏ 8096	Geronimo's Cadillac/These Days	1975	$4
❏ 8311	Pirate/Send the Man Over	1976	$4
❏ 8366	War Paint and Soft Feathers/Sand the Man Over	1977	$4
WARNER/SPECTOR
❏ 0402	A Love Like Yours/Just Enough to Keep Me Hangin' On	1975	$10
—With Nilsson			
❏ 0400	Baby, I Love You/A Woman's Story	1974	$12

CHEROKEE
ABC
Number	Title	Yr	NM
❏ 11304	Girl, I've Got News for You/All the Way Home	1971	$8

CHEROKEES, THE (1)
CHALLENGE
| ❏ 9135 | Cherokee Stomp/Uprisin' | 1961 | $30 |

CHEROKEES, THE (2)
GRAND
| ❏ 110 | Please Tell Me So/Remember When | 1954 | $1000 |
PEACOCK
| ❏ 1656 | Drip Drip/Is She Real | 1955 | $200 |

CHEROKEES, THE (3)
GUYDEN
| ❏ 2044 | Cherokee/Harlem Nocturne | 1960 | $20 |
| ❏ 2044 [PS] | Cherokee/Harlem Nocturne | 1960 | $40 |

CHEROKEES, THE (4)
MGM
| ❏ 13433 | Dig a Little Deeper/I Will Never Turn My Back on You | 1965 | $30 |
| ❏ 13334 | Seven Daffodils/Wondrous Place | 1964 | $20 |

CHEROKEES, THE (5)
UNITED ARTISTS
| ❏ 367 | My Heavenly Angel/Bed Bug | 1961 | $125 |

CHERRY, DON
COLUMBIA
Number	Title	Yr	NM
❏ 40597	Band of Gold/Rumble Boogie	1955	$20
❏ 40492	Be My Darling Once Again/You Still Mean the Same to Me	1955	$15
❏ 41259	Big Bad Wolf/I Look for a Love	1958	$12
❏ 40705	Ghost Town/I'll Be Around	1956	$10
❏ 40804	Give Me More/The Story of Sherry	1956	$10
❏ 41351	Hasty Heart/The Golden Age	1959	$12
❏ 41014	I Keep Running Away from You/A Ferryboat Named Minerva	1957	$10
❏ 41077	It'll Be Me/Love Me, If You Will	1957	$10
❏ 40885	Mr. Teardrop/April Age	1957	$10
❏ 40421	Tell It To Me Again/Clean Break	1955	$15
❏ 41134	The Glide/Another Time, Another Place	1958	$10
❏ 40828	The Last Dance/Don't You Worry Your Pretty Little Head	1957	$10

Number	Title	Yr	NM
❏ 40958	There's a Place Called Heaven/Fourteen Carat Gold	1957	$10
❏ 40544	What Am I Trying to Forget/Fifty Million Salty Kisses	1955	$15
❏ 40665	Wild Cherry/I'm Still a King to You	1956	$10
DECCA
❏ 28635	All By Myself/If They Should Ask Me	1953	$15
❏ 27717	Belle, Belle, My Liberty Belle/Cara Cara Bella Bella	1951	$15
❏ 27475	Chapel of the Roses/Beautiful Madness	1951	$15
❏ 27535	Don't Cry/Don't Leave Me Now	1951	$15
❏ 27633	Far, Far Away/Star of Hope	1951	$15
—With Eileen Wilson			
❏ 29444	Home Again/Sip of Moonlight	1955	$12
❏ 28477	How Long/Second Star to the Right	1952	$15
❏ 27484	I Apologize/Bring Back the Thrill	1951	$15
❏ 27836	I Can't Help It/Grievin' My Heart Out for You	1951	$15
❏ 28452	I Don't Want to Set the World on Fire/From Your Lips Only	1952	$15
❏ 28768	If You See Sally/I Got to Pass Your House to Get to My House	1953	$15
❏ 27244	I'll Always Love You/Maybe on Sunday	1950	$20
—With Eileen Wilson			
❏ 27944	I'll Sing to You/Your Sentimental Heart	1952	$15
❏ 29005	I'm Through with Love/You Didn't Have to Tell Me	1954	$10
❏ 27245	I Need You So/Can't Seem to Laugh Anymore	1950	$20
❏ 28050	It Doesn't Matter Where I Go/Sentimental Tears	1952	$15
❏ 28368	It's Been So Long, Darling/Silver Dew on the Blue Grass Tonight	1952	$15
❏ 28548	Lover's Quarrel/Changeable	1953	$15
❏ 29142	Lulu's Back in Town/Anyplace, Anytime, Anywhere	1954	$10
❏ 27626	My Life's Desire/I Can See You	1951	$15
❏ 28292	My Name Is Morgan, But It Ain't J.P./Pretty Girl	1952	$15
❏ 27618	Powder Blue/Vanity	1951	$15
❏ 27435	Seven Wonders of the World/When You Return	1951	$15
❏ 27807	The Lamp of Faith/Sin Ain't Nothing	1951	$15
❏ 27755	The Sweetest Waltz/I Will Never Change	1951	$15
❏ 29807	The Thrill Is Gone/Wanted, Someone to Love Me	1956	$10
❏ 28844	Too Long/For Now and Always	1953	$15
❏ 29322	Where Can You Be/I'm Just a Country Boy	1954	$10
❏ 28153	Wonder/My Mother's Pearl	1952	$15
MONUMENT
❏ 1201	Between Winston-Salem and Nashville, Tennessee/Just a Drop of Rain	1970	$6
❏ 45-232	Come Sundown/Love Is Gone for Good	1977	$5
❏ 1147	Days of Sand and Shovels/That Woman's Coming Home	1969	$6
❏ 930	Don't Change/I Love You Drops	1966	$8
❏ 8542	For a Moment You Slipped My Mind/Is It Any Wonder	1972	$5
❏ 8530	Freedom Come, Freedom Go/Have You Ever Been to Georgia	1971	$5
❏ 8603	Going Away Party/The Old Rugged Cross	1974	$5
❏ 1062	Good Morning/Let Me Lead the Way	1968	$6
❏ 971	I Know Love/Married	1966	$8
❏ 1008	I Live to Love You/I Run to the Door	1967	$6
❏ 1156	I'll Catch the Sun/Ain't You Glad You're Living, Joe	1969	$6
❏ 1185	Lilacs in Winter/Look for Me Tomorrow	1970	$6
❏ 880	More I Cannot Do/Sweet Sugar	1965	$8
❏ 45-269	Six Weeks Every Summer, Christmas Every Day/Play Her Back to Yesterday	1978	$5
❏ 1222	Statue of a Fool/Ev'ry Body Else	1970	$6
❏ 1088	Take a Message to Mary/In My Youth	1968	$6
❏ 1027	That Lucky Old Sun/No Hearts and Flowers	1967	$6
❏ 8704	The Good Old Days Are Right Now/Pleasing You (As Long As I Live)	1976	$5
❏ 1045	Theme from "Will Penny" (Lonely Rider)/Here Comes the Rain	1967	$6
❏ 989	There Goes My Everything/I Don't Wanna Go Home	1966	$8
❏ 898	The Story of My Life/Things Called Sadness	1965	$8
❏ 947	Tip of My Fingers/After I'm Number One	1966	$8
❏ 8578	When You Leave Amarillo, Turn Out the Lights/Cajun Fiddler	1973	$5
❏ 1130	Whippoorwill/To Think You've Chosen Me	1969	$6
VERVE
| ❏ 10270 | Then You Can Tell Me Goodbye/When I Found I'd Lost | 1962 | $10 |
WARWICK
| ❏ 597 | Hair of Gold/Somebody Cares for Me | 1960 | $10 |

Number	Title	Yr	NM

CHERRY, NENEH
VIRGIN
❏ 99231	Buffalo Stance/(Electro Ski Mix)	1989	$3
❏ 99231 [PS]	Buffalo Stance/(Electro Ski Mix)	1989	$3
❏ 99154	Manchild/Phoney Ladies	1989	$3
❏ 99154 [PS]	Manchild/Phoney Ladies	1989	$3

CHERRY PEOPLE, THE
ANGEL related.
HERITAGE
❏ 801	And Suddenly/Imagination	1968	$8
❏ 801 [PS]	And Suddenly/Imagination	1968	$20
❏ 810	Feelings/Mr. Hyde	1969	$8
❏ 810 [PS]	Feelings/Mr. Hyde	1969	$20
❏ 807	Gotta Get Back to the Good Life/I'm the One Who Loves You	1968	$8
❏ 807 [PS]	Gotta Get Back to the Good Life/I'm the One Who Loves You	1968	$20
❏ 815	Light of Love/On to Something New	1969	$8

CHERRY SLUSH
U.S.A.
❏ 904	Gotta Take It Easy/Day Don't Come	1968	$30
❏ 895	I Cannot Stop You/Don't Walk Away	1968	$30

CHESNUT, JIM
ABC HICKORY
❏ 54007	California Lady/What Got in the Way	1977	$5
❏ 54038	Get Back to Loving Me/Kinder Than the Last One	1978	$5
❏ 54013	Let Me Love You Now/A Loaf of Bread (A Jug of Wine)	1977	$5
❏ 54003	She's My Woman/Tell Me, Tell Me That You Love Me	1976	$5
❏ 54033	Show Me a Sign/Whiskey Lady	1978	$5
❏ 54021	The Wrong Side of the Rainbow/I'm So Lonely for Your Baby	1977	$5

HICKORY/MGM
❏ 369	Country Love Song/Good Lord, What Happened to the Trains	1976	$6

LIBERTY
❏ 1405	Bedtime Stories/Pick Up the Pieces	1981	$4

MCA
❏ 41106	Let's Take the Time to Fall in Love Again/A Loaf of Bread (A Jug of Wine)	1979	$4

UNITED ARTISTS
❏ 1372	Out Run the Sun/Pick Up the Pieces	1980	$4

CHESNUTT, MARK
AXBAR
❏ 6046	Country Girl/Running Out of Ways to Say I Love You	1986	$20
❏ 6035	Let's Make a Memory One More Time/Welcome Fool	1985	$20
❏ 6061	Since I Drank My Way to Houston/Heartache County	1988	$20

CHESTERFIELDS, THE (1)
A&M
❏ 2041	That Is Rock and Roll/Why Do Fools Fall in Love	1978	$5

CHESTERFIELDS, THE (2)
CHESS
❏ 1559	I'm in Heaven/All Messed Up	1954	$400

CHESTERFIELDS, THE (3)
CUB
❏ 9008	I Got Fired/Meet Me at the Candy Store	1958	$30

CHESTERFIELDS, THE (4)
PHILIPS
❏ 40060	A Dream Is But a Dream/You Walked Away	1962	$200

CHESTNUT, MORRIS
AMY
❏ 981	Too Darned Soulful/You Don't Love Me Anymore	1967	$250

CHESTNUTS, THE
DAVIS
❏ 447	Love Is True/(B-side unknown)	1956	$200

CHEVALIER, DON
TIARA
❏ 1980	Christmas Is For Giving/Christmastime	1980	$4

CHEVALIER, JAY, AND SHELLEY FORD
CREOLE GOLD
❏ 1114	Disco Blues/Super Country USA	1979	$6

CHEVALIER, MAURICE
7-Inch Extended Plays
RCA VICTOR
❏ EPA-5131	Louise/Mimi//Valentine/Walkin' My Baby Back Home	1959	$20

—*Maroon label*

❏ EPA-5131 [PS]	Maurice Chevalier (Gold Standard Series)	1959	$20

—*Maroon label*

CHEVRONS, THE
BRENT
❏ 7015	Little Darlin'/Little Star	1960	$60
❏ 7007	Lullabye/The Day After Forever	1959	$60
❏ 7000	That Comes With Love/Don't Be Heartless	1959	$60

TIME
❏ 1	Come Go with Me/I'm in Love Again	1960	$50

CHI-LITES, THE
BLUE ROCK
❏ 4020	Doing the Snatch/Bassology	1965	$30
❏ 4007	I'm So Jealous/The Mix-Mix Song	1965	$30

BRUNSWICK
❏ 55426	24 Hours of Sadness/You're No Longer Part of My Heart	1970	$8
❏ 55491	A Letter to Myself/Sally	1973	$6
❏ 55483	A Lonely Man/The Man and the Woman (The Boy and the Girl)	1972	$6
❏ 55442	Are You My Woman (Tell Me So)/Troubles A-Comin'	1970	$8
❏ 55522	Don't Burn No Bridges/(Instrumental)	1975	$6

—*With Jackie Wilson*

❏ 55546	First Time/Marriage License	1978	$5
❏ 55450	(For God's Sake) Give More Power to the People/Troubles A-Comin'	1971	$8
❏ 55398	Give It Away/What Do I Wish For	1969	$8
❏ 55462	Have You Seen Her/Yes I'm Ready	1971	$6
❏ 55505	Homely Girl/Never Had It So Good and Felt So Bad	1974	$6
❏ 55502	I Found Someone/Marriage License	1973	$6
❏ 55438	I Like Your Lovin' (Do You Like Mine)/You're No Longer Part of My Heart	1970	$8
❏ 55422	I'm Gonna Make You Love Me/To Change My Love	1969	$8
❏ 55520	It's Time for Love/Here I Am	1975	$6
❏ 55458	I Want to Pay You back (For Loving Me)/Love Uprising	1971	$8
❏ 55414	Let Me Be the Man My Daddy Was/The Twelfth of Never	1969	$8
❏ 55496	My Heart Just Keeps On Breakin'/Just Two Teenage Kids	1973	$6
❏ 55471	Oh Girl/Being in Love	1972	$6
❏ 55500	Stoned Out of My Mind/Someone Else's Arms	1973	$6
❏ 55478	The Coldest Days of My Life (Part 1)/The Coldest Days of My Life (Part 2)	1972	$6
❏ 55525	The Devil Is Doing His Work/I'm Not a Gambler	1976	$6
❏ 55512	There Will Never Be Any Peace (Until God Is Seated at the Conference Table)/Too Good to Be Forgotten	1974	$6
❏ 55515	Toby/That's How Long	1974	$6
❏ 55455	We Are Neighbors/What Do I Wish For	1971	$8
❏ 55489	We Need Order/Living in the Footsteps of Another Man	1972	$6

CHI-SOUND
❏ 2495	All I Wanna Do Is Make Love to You/Round and Round	1981	$4
❏ 2481	Have You Seen Her/Super Mad (About You Baby)	1981	$4
❏ 2472	Heavenly Body/Strung Out	1980	$4
❏ 2600	Hot on a Thing (Called Love)/Whole Lot of Good Lovin'	1982	$4
❏ 2503	Me and You/Tell Me Where It Hurts	1981	$4
❏ 2604	Try My Side (Of Love)/Get Down with Me	1982	$4

DAKAR
❏ 600	Baby It's Time/Price of Love	1968	$15

—*As "Marshall and the Chi-Lites"*

DARAN
❏ 222	I'm So Jealous/The Mix-Mix Song	1964	$125

—*As "The Hi-Lites"*

❏ 011	One by One/You Did That to Me	1964	$125

—*As "The Hi-Lites"*

❏ 0111	Pretty Girl/Love Bandit	1966	$60

—*As "Marshall and the Chi-Lites"*

INPHASION
❏ 7205	Higher/Stay a Little Longer	1979	$5
❏ 7208	The Only One for Me (One in a Million)/You Won't Be Lonely Too Long	1979	$5

LARC
❏ 81023	Bad Motor Scooter/I Just Wanna Hold You	1983	$4
❏ 81015	Bottom's Up/Bottom's Up Groove	1983	$4

MERCURY
❏ 73844	Happy Being Lonely/Love Can Be Dangerous	1976	$5
❏ 73954	If I Had a Girl/I've Got Love on My Mind	1977	$5
❏ 73934	My First Mistake/Stop Still	1977	$5

NUANCE
❏ 752	Hard Act to Follow/(Instrumental)	1985	$4

PRIVATE I
❏ ZS4-04484	Gimme Whatcha Got/Let Today Come Back Tomorrow	1984	$3
❏ ZS4-04365	Stop What You're Doin'/Little Girl	1984	$3

REVUE
❏ 11005	Love Is Gone/Love Me	1967	$15

CHIC
ATLANTIC
❏ 3435	Dance, Dance, Dance (Yowsah, Yowsah, Yowsah)/Sao Paulo	1977	$4
❏ 3469	Everybody Dance/You Can Get By	1978	$4
❏ 89725	Give Me the Lovin'/You Got Some Love for Me	1983	$3
❏ 3584	Good Times/A Warm Summer Night	1979	$4
❏ 3584 [PS]	Good Times/A Warm Summer Night	1979	$5
❏ 89954	Hangin'/Chic (Everybody Say)	1982	$3
❏ 3557	I Want Your Love/(Funny) Bone	1979	$4
❏ 3557 [PS]	I Want Your Love/(Funny) Bone	1979	$5
❏ 3519	Le Freak/Savoir Faire	1978	$4
❏ 3519 [PS]	Le Freak/Savoir Faire	1978	$5
❏ 3638	My Feet Keep Dancing/Will You Cry (When You Hear This Song)	1979	$4
❏ 3620	My Forbidden Lover/What About Me	1979	$4
❏ 3887	Stage Fright/So Fine	1982	$4

ATLANTIC OLDIES SERIES
❏ OS13211	Dance, Dance, Dance (Yowsah, Yowsah, Yowsah)/Everybody Dance	1979	$3

—*Reissue*

❏ OS13216	Good Times/My Forbidden Lover	1980	$3

—*Reissue*

❏ OS13215	Le Freak/I Want Your Love	1980	$3

—*Reissue*

BUDDAH
❏ 583	Dance, Dance, Dance (Yowsah, Yowsah, Yowsah)/Sao Paulo	1977	$30

MIRAGE
❏ 4032	Soup for One/Burn Hard	1982	$4
❏ 4051	Why/Why	1982	$4

—*B-side by Carly Simon*

CHIC-LETS, THE
JOSIE
❏ 919	I Want You to Be My Boyfriend/Don't Goof on Me	1964	$20

CHICAGO
COLUMBIA
❏ 45194	25 or 6 to 4/Where Do We Go from Here	1970	$5
❏ 3-10845	Alive Again/Love Was New	1978	$5
❏ 3-10360	Another Rainy Day in New York City/Hope for Love	1976	$5
❏ 3-10620	Baby, What a Big Surprise/Takin' It On Uptown	1977	$5
❏ 3-10620 [PS]	Baby, What a Big Surprise/Takin' It On Uptown	1977	$20

—*Sleeve appears to be promo only*

❏ 45417	Beginnings/Colour My World	1971	$5
❏ 45417 [PS]	Beginnings/Colour My World	1971	$8
❏ 45011	Beginnings/Poem 58	1969	$6
❏ 10200	Brand New Love Affair/Hideaway	1975	$5
❏ 46062	Call On Me/Prelude to Aire	1974	$5
❏ 45717	Dialogue (Parts 1 and 2)/Now That You've Gone	1972	$5
❏ 45717 [PS]	Dialogue (Parts 1 and 2)/Now That You've Gone	1972	$6
❏ 4-45264 [DJ]	Does Anybody Really Know What Time It Is? (3:17)/(2:53)	1970	$12

—*A-side master number is "JZSP 154094"; B-side master number is "JZSP 154096*

❏ 4-45264	Does Anybody Really Know What Time It Is?/Listen	1970	$5
❏ 4-45264 [PS]	Does Anybody Really Know What Time It Is?/Listen	1970	$12
❏ 45880	Feelin' Stronger Every Day/Jenny	1973	$5
❏ 45331	Free/Free Country	1971	$5
❏ 45331 [PS]	Free/Free Country	1971	$8

Number	Title	Yr	NM
❏ 3-10935	Gone Long Gone/The Greatest Love on Earth	1979	$4
❏ 10092	Harry Truman/Till We Meet Again	1975	$5
❏ 10092 [PS]	Harry Truman/Till We Meet Again	1975	$6
❏ 3-10390	If You Leave Me Now/Together Again	1976	$5
❏ 46020	(I've Been) Searchin' So Long/Byblos	1974	$5
❏ 3-10683	Little One/Till the End of Time	1978	$5
❏ 45370	Lowdown/Loneliness Is Just a Word	1971	$5
❏ 45370 [PS]	Lowdown/Loneliness Is Just a Word	1971	$8
❏ 45127	Make Me Smile/Colour My World	1970	$5
❏ 45127 [PS]	Make Me Smile/Colour My World	1970	$8
❏ 1-11061	Must Have Been Crazy/Closer to You	1979	$4
❏ 10131	Old Days/Hideaway	1975	$5
❏ 45657	Saturday in the Park/Alma Mater	1972	$5
❏ 11-11376	Song for You/The American Dream	1980	$4
❏ 1-11124	Street Player/Window Dreamin'	1979	$4
❏ 3-10737	Take Me Back to Chicago/Policeman	1978	$5
❏ 1-11345	Thunder and Lightning/I'd Rather Be Rich	1980	$4
❏ 10049	Wishing You Were Here/Life Saver	1974	$5

FULL MOON

Number	Title	Yr	NM
❏ 29979	Hard to Say I'm Sorry/Sonny Think Twice	1982	$4
❏ 29911	Love Me Tomorrow/Bad Advice	1982	$4
❏ 29798	What You're Missing/Rescue You	1983	$4

REPRISE

Number	Title	Yr	NM
❏ 27855	I Don't Wanna Live Without Your Love/I Stand Up	1988	$3
❏ 27855 [PS]	I Don't Wanna Live Without Your Love/I Stand Up	1988	$3
❏ 27766	Look Away/Come In from the Night	1988	$3
❏ 27766 [PS]	Look Away/Come In from the Night	1988	$3
❏ 22985	We Can Last Forever/One More Day	1989	$3

WARNER BROS.

Number	Title	Yr	NM
❏ 28628	25 or 6 to 4/One More Day	1986	$3
❏ 28628 [PS]	25 or 6 to 4/One More Day	1986	$3
❏ 29082	Along Comes a Woman/We Can't Stop the Hurtin'	1985	$3
❏ 29214	Hard Habit to Break/Remember the Feeling	1984	$3
❏ 29214 [PS]	Hard Habit to Break/Remember the Feeling	1984	$3
❏ 28424	If She Would Have Been Faithful.../Forever	1987	$3
❏ 28424 [PS]	If She Would Have Been Faithful.../Forever	1987	$3
❏ 29306	Stay the Night/Only You	1984	$3
❏ 29306 [PS]	Stay the Night/Only You	1984	$3
❏ 28512	Will You Still Love Me/25 or 6 to 4	1986	$3

7-Inch Extended Plays

COLUMBIA

Number	Title	Yr	NM
❏ 7-30110	Canon/Once Upon a Time/Mother// Loneliness Is Just a Word/What Else Can I Say/At the Sunrise	1971	$10

—*Jukebox issue; small hole, plays at 33 1/3 rpm*

Number	Title	Yr	NM
❏ 7-KGP24 [PS]	Chicago	1970	$12
❏ 7-30110 [PS]	Chicago III	1971	$12
❏ 7-32400 [PS]	Chicago VI	1973	$12
❏ 7-KGP24	Movin' In/Wake Up Sunshine/To Be Free//West Virginia Fantasies/Colour My World/It Better End Soon, 2nd Movement	1970	$10

—*Jukebox issue; small hole, plays at 33 1/3 rpm*

Number	Title	Yr	NM
❏ 7-32400	What's This World Comin' To/Darlin' Dear//Discovery/In Terms of Two	1973	$10

—*Jukebox issue; small hole, plays at 33 1/3 rpm*

CHICAGO BEARS SHUFFLIN' CREW, THE

RED LABEL

Number	Title	Yr	NM
❏ B-71012	Superbowl Shuffle/(Instrumental)	1985	$5
❏ B-71012 [PS]	Superbowl Shuffle/(Instrumental)	1985	$5

CHICAGO CUBS, THE

CHESS

Number	Title	Yr	NM
❏ 2075	Pennant Fever/Slide	1969	$15
❏ 2075 [PS]	Pennant Fever/Slide	1969	$40

CHICKEN SHACK

Also see CHRISTINE McVIE; features Stan Webb.

BLUE HORIZON

Number	Title	Yr	NM
❏ 302	Maudie/Diary of Your Life	1972	$6
❏ 100	Tears in the Wind/The Things You Put Me Through	1970	$6

DERAM

Number	Title	Yr	NM
❏ 7537	As Time Goes Passing By/(B-side unknown)	1972	$5

EPIC

Number	Title	Yr	NM
❏ 10414	Six Nights in Seven/Worried About My Woman	1968	$12

CHIEFTAINS, THE

ISLAND

Number	Title	Yr	NM
❏ 048	Love Theme from "Barry Lyndon"/Timpan Reel	1976	$6

SHANACHIE

Number	Title	Yr	NM
❏ 702	Cotton Eyed Joe/The Gold Ring	1981	$12

CHIFFONS, THE

BIG DEAL

Number	Title	Yr	NM
❏ 6003	Tonight's the Night/Do You Know	1960	$100

B.T. PUPPY

Number	Title	Yr	NM
❏ 558	Secret Love/Strange, Strange Feeling	1970	$10

BUDDAH

Number	Title	Yr	NM
❏ 171	So Much in Love/Strange, Strange Feeling	1970	$12

LAURIE

Number	Title	Yr	NM
❏ 3195	A Love So Fine/Only My Friend	1963	$15
❏ 3648	Dream, Dream, Dream/Oh My Lover	1976	$12
❏ 3152	He's So Fine/Oh My Lover	1963	$30
❏ 3152	He's So Fine/Oh My Lover	1963	$30

—*Both B-side titles have been confirmed; we're not sure which came first*

Number	Title	Yr	NM
❏ 3377	If I Knew Then/Keep the Boy Happy	1967	$10
❏ 3212	I Have a Boyfriend/I'm Gonna Dry My Eyes	1963	$15
❏ 3497	Love Me Like You're Gonna Lose Me/Three Dips of Ice Cream	1969	$10
❏ 3166	Lucky Me/Why Am I So Shy?	1963	$20
❏ 3364	My Boyfriend's Back/I Got Plenty of Nuttin'	1966	$10
❏ 3630	My Sweet Lord/Main Nerve	1975	$10
❏ 3179	One Fine Day/Why Am I So Shy	1963	$30
❏ 3350	Out of This World/Just a Boy	1966	$10
❏ 3262	Sailor Boy/When Summer's Through	1964	$15
❏ 3357	Stop, Look, Listen/March	1966	$10
❏ 3340	Sweet Talkin' Guy/Did You Ever Go Steady	1966	$20
❏ 3224	Tonight I Met an Angel/Easy to Love	1964	$15
❏ 3318	Tonight I'm Gonna Dream/Heavenly Place	1965	$15
❏ 3275	What Am I Gonna Do with You/Strange, Strange Feeling	1964	$15

REPRISE

Number	Title	Yr	NM
❏ 20103	After Last Night/Doctor of Hearts	1962	$30

RUST

Number	Title	Yr	NM
❏ 5071	Dry Your Eyes/My Block	1963	$30

—*As "The Four Pennies"*

Number	Title	Yr	NM
❏ 5070	When the Boy's Happy (The Girl's Happy Too)/Hockaday, Part 1	1963	$30

—*As "The Four Pennies"*

CHILD, DESMOND, AND ROUGE

CAPITOL

Number	Title	Yr	NM
❏ 4710	Givin' In to My Love/Main Man	1979	$5
❏ 4791	Imitation of Love/Goodbye Baby	1979	$5
❏ 4669	Our Love Is Insane/City in Heat	1979	$8

—*Multicolored swirl vinyl*

Number	Title	Yr	NM
❏ 4669	Our Love Is Insane/City in Heat	1979	$4

—*Black vinyl*

Number	Title	Yr	NM
❏ 4815	Tumble in the Night/Rosa	1980	$5

EPIC

Number	Title	Yr	NM
❏ 34-03278	A Little Romance/Let's Make It Right	1982	$6

CHILDREN, THE

ATCO

Number	Title	Yr	NM
❏ 6633	Maypole/I'll Be Your Sunshine	1968	$30

CINEMA

Number	Title	Yr	NM
❏ 025	Pills/(B-side unknown)	1968	$40

LARAMIE

Number	Title	Yr	NM
❏ 666	Picture Me/(B-side unknown)	1967	$50

MAP CITY

Number	Title	Yr	NM
❏ 304	What If I/Evil Woman	1970	$15

ODE

Number	Title	Yr	NM
❏ 66013	Fire King/Hand of a Lady	1971	$30
❏ 66005	From the Very Start/Such a Fine Night	1970	$30

CHILLIWACK

A&M

Number	Title	Yr	NM
❏ 1395	Ground Hog/Nothin' to Do	1972	$8
❏ 1310	Lonesome Mary/Ridin'	1971	$8

MILLENNIUM

Number	Title	Yr	NM
❏ YB-13115	I Believe/Living in Stereo	1981	$4
❏ YB-11813	My Girl (Gone, Gone, Gone)/Sign Here	1981	$4
❏ YB-13117	Secret Information/Really Don't Mind	1982	$4
❏ YB-13110	Whatcha Gonna Do/Really Don't Mind	1982	$4

MUSHROOM

Number	Title	Yr	NM
❏ 7033	Arms of Mary/I Wanna Be the One	1978	$4
❏ 7028	Baby Blue/Something Better	1977	$4
❏ 7022	California Girl/Reach	1976	$4
❏ 7046	Communication Breakdown/Are You With Me	1980	$4
❏ 7024	Fly By Night/Mary Lou and Me	1977	$4
❏ 7025	Something Better/Rain-O	1977	$4

PARROT

Number	Title	Yr	NM
❏ 357	Everyday/Sundown	1970	$8
❏ 350	I Must Have Been Blind/Chain Train	1970	$8

SIRE

Number	Title	Yr	NM
❏ 718	Come On Over/Time Don't Mean a Thing to You	1975	$5
❏ 716	Crazy Talk/In and Out	1974	$5
❏ 720	If You Want My Love/Train's a-Comin' Back	1975	$5
❏ 723	Last Day in December/Magnolia	1976	$5

CHILTON, ALEX

7-Inch Extended Plays

ORK

Number	Title	Yr	NM
❏ 81978 [B]	The Singer Not the Song	1977	$50

CHIMES, THE (1)

LAURIE

Number	Title	Yr	NM
❏ 3211	Whose Heart Are You Breaking Now/Baby's Coming Home	1963	$20

METRO

Number	Title	Yr	NM
❏ 1	Whose Heart Are You Breaking Now/Baby's Coming Home	1963	$50

TAG

Number	Title	Yr	NM
❏ 445	I'm in the Mood for Love/Only Love	1961	$40
❏ 447	Let's Fall in Love/Dream Girl	1961	$30
❏ 444	Once in Awhile/Oh, How I Love You So	1960	$60

—*B-side is actually by a group called the Bi-Tones, though credited to the Chimes*

Number	Title	Yr	NM
❏ 444	Once in Awhile/Summer Night	1960	$50

—*Maroon label*

Number	Title	Yr	NM
❏ 444	Once in Awhile/Summer Night	1960	$50

—*Light blue label*

Number	Title	Yr	NM
❏ 450	Paradise/My Love	1961	$40

CHIMES, THE (U)

HOUSE OF BEAUTY

Number	Title	Yr	NM
❏ 3	Tears from An Angel's Eyes/(B-side unknown)	1959	$100

LIMELIGHT

Number	Title	Yr	NM
❏ 3000	Cry, Baby, Cry/Angel Child	1963	$30
❏ 3002	Du Wap/Stop, Look and Listen	1963	$30

RESERVE

Number	Title	Yr	NM
❏ 120	When School Starts Again/Nervous Heart	1957	$50

ROYAL ROOST

Number	Title	Yr	NM
❏ 577	Dearest Darling/A Fool Was I	1955	$700

SPECIALTY

Number	Title	Yr	NM
❏ 574	Chop Chop/Pretty Little Girl	1956	$70
❏ 555	Tears on My Pillow/Cindy Lou	1955	$70

CHINA CRISIS

A&M

Number	Title	Yr	NM
❏ 2902	Arizona Sky/Trading in Gold	1987	$4
❏ 2902 [PS]	Arizona Sky/Trading in Gold	1987	$5
❏ 2936	Best Kept Secret/The Instigator	1987	$4

WARNER BROS.

Number	Title	Yr	NM
❏ 28936	Wake Up (King in a Catholic Style)/Blue Sea	1985	$4
❏ 29243	Wishful Thinking/When the Piper Calls	1983	$8
❏ 29304	Working with Fire and Steel/(B-side unknown)	1983	$8

—*May be promo only*

CHINNOCK, BILLY

PARADISE

Number	Title	Yr	NM
❏ 630	The Way She Makes Love/Rock n' Roll Cowboy	1984	$5

Number	Title	Yr	NM

CHIPMUNKS, THE, DAVID SEVILLE AND
DOT
| ❑ 16997 | Apple Picker/Sorry About That, Herb | 1967 | $15 |

LIBERTY
❑ 55734	All My Lovin'/Do You Want to Know a Secret	1964	$20
❑ 55277	Alvin for President/Sack Time	1960	$20
❑ 55277 [PS]	Alvin for President/Sack Time	1960	$50
❑ 55544	Alvin's All Star Chipmunk Band/Old MacDonald Cha Cha Cha	1963	$20
❑ 55544 [PS]	Alvin's All Star Chipmunk Band/Old MacDonald Cha Cha Cha	1963	$50
❑ 55179	Alvin's Harmonica/Mediocre	1959	$30
❑ 55233	Alvin's Orchestra/Copyright 1960	1960	$20
❑ 55233 [PS]	Alvin's Orchestra/Copyright 1960	1960	$50
❑ 55452	America the Beautiful/My Wild Irish Rose	1962	$20
❑ 55246	Coming 'Round the Mountain/Sing a Goofy Song	1960	$20
❑ 55246 [PS]	Coming 'Round the Mountain/Sing a Goofy Song	1960	$50
❑ 55773	Do-Re-Mi/Supercalifragilisticexpialidocious	1965	$15
❑ 55632	Eefin' Alvin/Flip Side	1963	$20
❑ 55832	I'm Henry VIII, I Am/What's New Pussycat	1965	$15
❑ 55424	The Alvin Twist/I Wish I Could Speak French	1962	$20
❑ 55168	The Chipmunk Song/Almost Good	1958	$30

— *Blue-green label*

| ❑ 55168 | The Chipmunk Song/Almost Good | 1958 | $40 |

— *Black label*

| ❑ 55168 | The Chipmunk Song/Almost Good | 1958 | $40 |

— *Dark blue label*

| ❑ 55250 | The Chipmunk Song/Alvin's Harmonica | 1959 | $20 |

— *Blue-green label, no horizontal lines*

| ❑ 55250 [PS] | The Chipmunk Song/Alvin's Harmonica | 1959 | $50 |

— *Sleeve has Chipmunks depicted somewhat like real chipmunks*

| ❑ 55250 | The Chipmunk Song/Alvin's Harmonica | 1961 | $15 |

— *Blue-green label with horizontal lines*

| ❑ 55250 [PS] | The Chipmunk Song/Alvin's Harmonica | 1961 | $40 |

— *Sleeve has Chipmunks depicted as the familiar cartoon characters*

| ❑ 56079 | The Chipmunk Song/Christmas Blues | 1968 | $20 |

— *With Canned Heat*

SUNSET
❑ 61003	Chitty Chitty Bang Bang/Hushabye Mountain	1968	$10
❑ 61003 [PS]	Chitty Chitty Bang Bang/Hushabye Mountain	1968	$20
❑ 61002	Talk to the Animals/My Friend the Doctor	1968	$10
❑ 61002 [PS]	Talk to the Animals/My Friend the Doctor	1968	$20

UNITED ARTISTS
| ❑ 0057 | Alvin's Harmonica/Rudolph, the Red-Nosed Reindeer | 1973 | $8 |

— *Silver Spotlight Series" reissue*

| ❑ 0056 | The Chipmunk Song/Ragtime Cowboy Joe | 1973 | $8 |

— *Silver Spotlight Series" reissue*

| ❑ XW576 | The Chipmunk Song/Rudolph, the Red-Nosed Reindeer | 1974 | $6 |

7-Inch Extended Plays
LIBERTY
❑ LSX-1008	*Alvin's Orchestra/Swanee River/Sing a Goofy Song/Witch Doctor	1960	$35
❑ LSX-1016 [PS]	Christmas with the Chipmunks	1962	$60
❑ LSX-1017 [PS]	Christmas with the Chipmunks, Volume 2	1963	$60
❑ LSX-1007 [PS]	Let's All Sing with the Chipmunks	1960	$60
❑ LSX-1008 [PS]	Sing Again with the Chipmunks	1960	$60
❑ LSX-1007	The Chipmunk Song/Ragtime Cowboy Joe//Alvin's Harmonica/If You Love Me	1960	$35
❑ LSX-1017	Wonderful Day/Christmas Time//Deck The Halls/The Night Before Christmas	1963	$25

CHIPMUNKS, THE
EXCELSIOR
| ❑ SIS1002 | Call Me/Refugee | 1980 | $5 |
| ❑ SIS1002 [PS] | Call Me/Refugee | 1980 | $6 |

RCA
❑ PB-13098	Bette Davis Eyes/Heartbreaker	1982	$4
❑ PB-13098 [PS]	Bette Davis Eyes/Heartbreaker	1982	$4
❑ PB-13374	E.T. and Me/Tomorrow (Theme from "Annie")	1982	$4
❑ PB-13374 [PS]	E.T. and Me/Tomorrow (Theme from "Annie")	1982	$4

Number	Title	Yr	NM
❑ PB-12301	Mamas Don't Let Your Babies Grow Up to Be Chipmunks/Lunchbox	1981	$4

— *With Jerry Reed*

❑ PB-12247	On the Road Again/Coward of the County	1981	$4
❑ PB-12354	The Chipmunk Song/Sleigh Ride	1981	$4
❑ PB-12354 [PS]	The Chipmunk Song/Sleigh Ride	1981	$5

CHIPPS, JIMMY
OVO
| ❑ 1928 | On Santa Claus Island/Christmas Will Be Here | 1964 | $10 |

CHIPS, THE (2)
PHILIPS
| ❑ 40520 | Mixed Up Shook Up Girl/Break It Gently | 1968 | $10 |
| ❑ 40520 [PS] | Mixed Up Shook Up Girl/Break It Gently | 1968 | $50 |

CHIPS, THE (3)
SATELLITE
| ❑ 105 | As You can See/You Make Me Feel So Good | 1961 | $120 |

CHIPS, THE (4)
STRAND
| ❑ 25027 | Darling (I Need Your Love)/You're On My Side | 1961 | $50 |
VENICE
| ❑ 101 | Darling (I Need Your Love)/You're On My Side | 1961 | $120 |

CHIPS, THE (5)
TOLLIE
| ❑ 9042 | Party People/Long Lonely Winter | 1965 | $10 |

CHIPS, THE (U)
EMBER
| ❑ 1077 | What a Lie/Bye, Bye, My Love | 1961 | $30 |

CHOATES, HARRY
D
❑ 1023	Allons A. Lafayette/Draggin' the Fiddle	1958	$30
❑ 1043	Opelousas Waltz/Poor Hobo	1959	$30
❑ 1044	Port Arthur Waltz/Honky Tonk Boogie	1959	$30
❑ 1132	Tondelay/Basil Waltz	1960	$20
STARDAY
❑ 273	Allons a Lafayette/Draggin' the Fiddle	1956	$30
❑ 284	Basile Waltz/Tondellay	1957	$30
❑ 212	Opelousas Waltz/Poor Hobo	1955	$30
❑ 224	Port Arthur Waltz/Honky Tonk Boogie	1956	$30
❑ 187	The Original New Jole Blon (English)/The Original New Jole Blon (French)	1955	$40

CHOCOLATE WATCH BAND, THE
TOWER
| ❑ 373 | Are You Gonna Be There (At the Love-In)/No Way Out | 1967 | $60 |
UPTOWN
| ❑ 740 | Baby Blue/Sweet Young Thing | 1967 | $300 |
| ❑ 749 | Misty Lane/She Weaves a Tender Trap | 1967 | $60 |

CHOIR, THE
CANADIAN AMERICAN
| ❑ 203 | It's Cold Outside/I'm Goin' Home | 1967 | $50 |
INTREPID
| ❑ 75020 | Gonna Have a Good Time Tonight/So Much Love | 1970 | $30 |
ROULETTE
| ❑ 7005 | Changin' My Mind/When You Were With Me | 1968 | $20 |
| ❑ 4738 | It's Cold Outside/I'm Goin' Home | 1967 | $20 |

CHORALS, THE
DECCA
| ❑ 29914 | In My Dreams/Rock and Roll Baby | 1956 | $100 |

CHORDETTES, THE
ATLANTIC
| ❑ 89310 | Lollipop/Never on Sunday | 1986 | $3 |
| ❑ 89310 [PS] | Lollipop/Never on Sunday | 1986 | $3 |
CADENCE
| ❑ 1417 | Adios/White Rose of Athens | 1962 | $10 |
| ❑ 1366 | A Girl's Work Is Never Done/No Wheels | 1959 | $10 |

Number	Title	Yr	NM
❑ 1366 [PS]	A Girl's Work Is Never Done/No Wheels	1959	$30
❑ 1382	All My Sorrows/A Broken Vow	1960	$10
❑ 1291	Born to Be with You/Love Never Changes	1956	$15
❑ 1307	Come Home to My Arms/(Fifi's) Walking the Poodle	1957	$15
❑ 1319	Echo of Love/Like a Baby	1957	$15
❑ 1284	Eddie My Love/Whispering Willie	1956	$15
❑ 1367	Forever/Ho Hum	1959	$10
❑ 1267	Hummingbird/I Told a Lie	1955	$15
❑ 1425	In the Deep Blue Sea/All My Sorrows	1962	$10
❑ 1239	It's You, It's You I Love/True Love Goes On and On	1954	$20
❑ 1299	Lay Down Your Arms/Teen Age Goodnight	1956	$15
❑ 1345	Lollipop/Baby Come-a Back-a	1958	$20
❑ 1259	Lonely Lips/The Dudelsack Song	1955	$15
❑ 1247	Mr. Sandman/I Don't Wanna See You Cryin'	1954	$20
❑ 1341	Photographs/Baby of Mine	1957	$15
❑ 1412	The Exodus Song/Theme from Goodbye Again (Say No More-It's Goodbye)	1961	$10
❑ 1273	The Wedding/I Don't Know, I Don't Care	1955	$15
❑ 1442	True Love Goes On and On/All My Sorrows	1963	$10

COLUMBIA
❑ 39794	A Little Street Where Old Friends Meet//Basin Street Blues + 1	1952	$20
❑ 39793	Carolina Moon//The Anniversary Waltz/Sentimental Journey	1952	$20
❑ 38757	Carry Me Back to Old Virginny/Ballin' the Jack	1950	$20
❑ 39795	Drifting and Dreaming + 1//I'm Drifting Back to Dreamland/Angry	1952	$20
❑ 38759	I'd Love to Live in Loveland (With a Love Like You)/When Day Is Done	1950	$20

— *The above four comprise box set B-201*

❑ 39252	Love Me and the World Is Mine/Lonesome That's All	1951	$20
❑ 39253	Moonlight on the Ganges/Let the Rest of the World Go By	1951	$20
❑ 39796	S'posin'/The Sweetheart of Sigma Chi//Kentucky Babe/In the Sweet Long Ago	1952	$20
❑ 38758	Tell Me Why/Shine On Harvest Moon	1950	$20
❑ 39254	The World Is Waiting for the Sunrise/Love's Old Sweet Song	1951	$20
❑ 38756	When You Were Sweet Sixteen/Moonlight Bay	1950	$20

7-Inch Extended Plays
CADENCE
❑ CEP101	Mr. Sandman/Hummingbird//Born to Be with You/Soft Sands	1956	$20
❑ CEP101 [PS]	The Chordettes	1956	$20
❑ CEP102 [PS]	The Chordettes	1957	$20

CHORDS, THE
ATCO
| ❑ 6213 | Sh-Boom/Little Maiden | 1961 | $20 |

— *As "The Sh-Booms*

ATLANTIC
| ❑ 2074 | Blue Moon/Short Skirts | 1960 | $30 |

— *As "The Sh-Booms*

CASINO
| ❑ 451 | Tears in Your Eyes/Don't Be a Jumpin' Jack | 1958 | $40 |

CAT
| ❑ 112 | A Girl to Love/Hold Me Baby | 1955 | $50 |

— *As "The Chordcats*

| ❑ 117 | Could It Be/Pretty Wild | 1955 | $50 |

— *As "The Sh-Booms*

| ❑ 104 | Sh-Boom/Cross Over the Bridge | 1954 | $120 |
| ❑ 104 | Sh-Boom/Little Maiden | 1954 | $70 |

METRO
| ❑ 20015 | Elephant Walk/Pretty Face | 1959 | $30 |

VIK
| ❑ 0295 | I Don't Want to Set the World on Fire/Lu Lu | 1957 | $40 |

— *As "The Sh-Booms*

CHORDS, THE (2)
HIT
| ❑ 256 | A Groovy Kind of Love/Green Grass | 1966 | $8 |

— *B-side by Ed Hardin*

| ❑ 236 | As Tears Go By/Five O'Clock World | 1966 | $15 |

— *B-side by the McCalls*

| ❑ 342 | Born to Be Wild/Revolution | 1968 | $10 |

— *B-side by the Jalopy Five*

| ❑ 300 | Carrie-Anne/Pleasant Valley Sunday | 1967 | $8 |

— *B-side by the Jalopy Five*

Number	Title	Yr	NM
❏ 292	Creeque Alley/Him or Me -- What's It Gonna Be?	1967	$8

—B-side by the Chellows

❏ 265	Dandy/Sunshine Superman	1966	$8

—B-side by Joe King

❏ 286	Dedicated to the One I Love/Something Stupid	1967	$8

—B-side by Bobby and Connie

❏ 203	Don't Let Me Be Misunderstood/The Sun Will Still Shine	1965	$12

—B-side by the Chellows

❏ 291	Don't You Care/You Got What It Takes	1967	$8
❏ 233	Fever/Make the World Go Away	1965	$8

—B-side by Johnny Singer

❏ 278	Georgy Girl/Nashville Cats	1967	$8

—B-side by the Chellows

❏ 346	Girl Watcher/Those Were the Days	1968	$8

—B-side by Kathy Shannon

❏ 174	Have You Been There/Downtown	1965	$8

—B-side by Betty York

❏ 271	Have You Seen Your Mother, Baby/The Hair on My Chinny Chin Chin	1966	$12

—B-side by the Jalopy Five

❏ 339	Hello, I Love You/Dreams of the Everyday Housewife	1968	$8

—B-side by Bobby Sims

❏ 319	I Can Take or Leave Your Loving/Love Is Blue	1968	$8

—B-side by the New Society Group

❏ 216	I'm Henry VIII, I Am/One Dyin' and a-Buryin'	1965	$10

—B-side by Marty Anderson

❏ 308	Incense and Peppermints/Holiday	1967	$8

—B-side by the Chellows

❏ 326	Lady Madonna/A Beautiful Morning	1968	$8

—B-side by the Classmates

❏ 254	Leaning on the Lamp Post/How Does That Grab You Darlin'	1966	$8

—B-side by Betty Richards

❏ 242	Listen People/Ballad of the Green Berets	1966	$8

—B-side by Herb Eaton

❏ 314	Massachusetts/Pata Pata	1967	$8

—B-side by the Fantastics

❏ 302	Mercy, Mercy, Mercy/Light My Fire	1967	$8

—B-side by the Fantastics

❏ 294	Mirage/Release Me	1967	$8

—B-side by Ed Hardin

❏ 212	Mrs. Brown You've Got a Lovely Daughter/Where Were You	1965	$10
❏ 344	My Special Angel/Over You	1968	$8

—B-side by the Fantastics

❏ 232	Over and Over/We Can Work It Out	1965	$15

—B-side by the Jalopy Five

❏ 282	Pretty Ballerina/Baby I Need Your Lovin'	1967	$8

—B-side by Ed Hardin

❏ 272	Snoopy vs. the Red Baron/That's Life	1966	$8

—B-side by Bobby Sims

❏ 337	Sunshine of Your Love/You Keep Me Hangin' On	1968	$8

—B-side by Leroy Jones

❏ 307	The Letter/Dandelion	1967	$10

—B-side by the Jalopy Five

❏ 263	This Door Swings Both Ways/Mother's Little Helper	1966	$10

—B-side by the Jalopy Five

❏ 335	Turn Around, Look at Me/The Look of Love	1968	$8

—B-side by the Classmates

❏ 163	Two Plus Two/Mr. Lonely	1964	$8

—B-side by Fred York

❏ 303	White Rabbit/Ode to Billie Joe	1967	$8

—B-side by Kathy Shannon

❏ 353	Worst That Could Happen/Son-of-a-Preacher-Man	1969	$8

—B-side by Kathy Shannon

CHOSEN FEW, THE
CANADIAN AMERICAN
❏ 202	Cute Thing/One of Those Songs	1967	$15

CANUSA
❏ 504	Summer's Love/Hey Joe	1967	$20

CO-OP
❏ 511	Summer's Love/(Instrumental)	1967	$15
❏ 510	Why Can't I Love You/La La La La La	1966	$15

DART
❏ 1080	Foolin' Around with Me/We Walk Together	1967	$8

LIBERTY
❏ 55962	Asian Chrome/Earth Above, Sky Below	1967	$12
❏ 55919	Synthetic Man/The Last Man Alive	1966	$10

POWER INTERNATIONAL
❏ 872	Another Goodbye/Forget About the Past	1966	$50

RCA VICTOR
❏ 74-0254	I'll Never Change You/Talk with Me	1969	$8
❏ 74-0217	Maybe the Rain Will Fall/Deeper In	1969	$8

ROULETTE
❏ 7015	Footsee/You Can Never Be Wrong	1968	$8

CHRIS AND LENNY
HAPPY MAN
❏ 821	When Daddy Did the Driving/(B-side unknown)	1989	$6
❏ 821 [PS]	When Daddy Did the Driving/(B-side unknown)	1989	$8

CHRISTIAN, CHRIS, AND BOB BREUNIG
HOME SWEET HOME
❏ 122586	Thinking of You This Christmas/Living The American Dream	1986	$8

—B-side by the Dallas Cowboys '86

CHRISTIAN, CHRIS
HOME SWEET HOME
❏ 001	Christmas All Year 'Round/God Bless the Children	1981	$4

CHRISTIAN, DIANE
BELL
❏ 610	It Happened One Night/Wonderful Guy	1965	$10
❏ 617	Little Boy/Why Don't the Boy Leave Me Alone	1965	$12

SMASH
❏ 1862	Has Anybody Seen My Boyfriend/There's So Much About My Baby	1963	$12

CHRISTIAN, NEIL
RCA VICTOR
❏ 47-8828	That's Nice/She's Got the Action	1966	$8

CHRISTIAN, ROGER
RENDEZVOUS
❏ 195	The Meaning of Merry Christmas/Little Mary Christmas	1962	$30

CHRISTIE
EPIC
❏ 10732	Man of Many Faces/Country Sam	1971	$4
❏ 10695	San Bernadino/Here I Am	1971	$4

CHRISTIE, LOU
ALCAR
❏ 207	Close Your Eyes/Funny Thing	1963	$30

BUDDAH
❏ 149	Are You Getting Any Sunshine/It'll Take Time	1970	$5
❏ 76	Canterbury Road/Saints of Aquarius	1969	$8
❏ 65	Genesis and the Third Verse/Rake Up the Leaves	1968	$8
❏ 116	I'm Gonna Make You Mine/I'm Gonna Get Married	1969	$6
❏ 192	Indian Lady/Glory River	1970	$5
❏ 163	Love Is Over/She Sold Me Magic	1970	$5
❏ 257	Mickey's Monkey/She Sold Me Magic	1971	$30
❏ 312	Shuffle On Down to Pittsburgh/I'm Gonna Get Married	1972	$30
❏ 285	Sing Me, Sing Me/Paper Song	1972	$5
❏ 285 [PS]	Sing Me, Sing Me/Paper Song	1972	$10

—Sleeve appears to be promo only

❏ 231	Waco/Chucky Wagon	1971	$30

—This has been proven to exist

❏ 235	Waco/Lighthouse	1971	$5
❏ 231 [DJ]	Waco (same on both sides)	1971	$6

C&C
❏ 102	The Gypsy Cried/Red Sails in the Sunset	1962	$200

CO & CE
❏ 235	Outside the Gates of Heaven/All That Glitters Isn't Gold	1966	$10

COLPIX
❏ 778	A Teenager in Love/Back Track	1965	$15
❏ 799	Cryin' on My Knees/Big Time	1966	$15
❏ 799 [PS]	Cryin' on My Knees/Big Time	1966	$30
❏ 770	Make Summer Last Forever/Why Did You Do It Baby	1965	$15
❏ 735	Merry-Go-Round/Guitars and Bongos	1964	$15
❏ 753	Pot of Gold/Have I Sinned	1964	$15

COLUMBIA
❏ 44338	Back to the Days of the Romans/Don't Stop Me	1967	$20
❏ 44240	(I Remember) Gina/Escape	1967	$20
❏ 44177	Self Expression/Back to the Days of the Romans	1967	$20
❏ 44062	Shake Hands and Walk Away Cryin'/Escape	1967	$20

EPIC
❏ 8-50244	Summer in Malibu/Ridin' in My Van	1976	$20

LIFESONG
❏ 1775	Theme from "People" (Part 1)/Theme from "People" (Part 2)	1978	$60

—As "Sacco

MGM
❏ 13576	If My Car Could Only Talk/Song of Lita	1966	$10
❏ 13576 [PS]	If My Car Could Only Talk/Song of Lita	1966	$30
❏ 13412	Lightnin' Strikes/Cryin' in the Streets	1965	$20
❏ 13533	Painter/Du Ronda	1966	$10
❏ 13533 [PS]	Painter/Du Ronda	1966	$30
❏ 13623	Since I Don't Have You/Wild Life's in Season	1966	$10

MIDLAND INT'L.
❏ MB-10959	Spanish Wine/Dancing in the Sand	1977	$20

MIDSONG INT'L.
❏ 72013	Don't Knock My Love (Short)/Don't Knock My Love (Long)	1980	$12

—With Pia Zadora

PLATEAU
❏ 4551	Guardian Angels/(B-side unknown)	1981	$50

ROULETTE
❏ 4504	How Many Teardrops/You and I (Have a Right to Cry)	1963	$15
❏ 4554	Maybe You'll Be There/When You Dance	1964	$30
❏ 4527	Shy Boy/It Can Happen	1963	$15
❏ 4545	Stay/There They Go	1964	$20
❏ 4457	The Gypsy Cried/Red Sails in the Sunset	1963	$30

—White label with spokes

❏ 4457	The Gypsy Cried/Red Sails in the Sunset	1963	$20

—Pink label

❏ 4457	The Gypsy Cried/Red Sails in the Sunset	1964	$10

—Orange and yellow label

❏ 4481	Two Faces Have I/All That Glitters Isn't Gold	1963	$20

SLIPPED DISC
❏ 45270	Summer Days/The One and Only Original Sunshine Kid	1976	$20

THREE BROTHERS
❏ 402	Beyond the Blue Horizon/Saddle the Wind	1974	$5
❏ 400	Blue Canadian Rocky Dream/Wilma Lee and Stoney	1973	$8
❏ 405	Hey You Cajun/Sunbeam	1974	$12

CHRISTIE, SUSAN
COLUMBIA
❏ 44327	All I Have to Do Is Dream/Anywhere You Are	1967	$6
❏ 43595	I Love Onions/Take Me As You Find Me	1966	$10
❏ 43595 [PS]	I Love Onions/Take Me As You Find Me	1966	$60
❏ 44117	Tonight You Belong to Me/Toy Balloon	1967	$6

CHRISTMAS ON 45
ROCK MUSIC CO
❏ SANTA1	Christmas On 45/Have Mercy On The Child	1981	$5

—B-side by Holly and the Ivys; U.K. import

❏ SANTA1 [PS]	Christmas On 45/Have Mercy On The Child	1981	$5

—B-side by Holly and the Ivys; U.K. import

CHRISTMAS SPIRIT, THE (1)
DUEL
❏ 503	It's Christmas/A World to Grow Up In	1961	$15

CHRISTMAS SPIRIT, THE (2)
WHITE WHALE
❏ 290	Christmas Is My Time of Year/Will You Still Believe	1968	$100

Number	Title	Yr	NM

CHRISTOPHER (1)

BELL

| ❏ 679 | Hey Girl/Every Boy in the World | 1967 | $20 |

DATE

| ❏ 1664 | Spring/Santa Ana Winds | 1970 | $15 |

CHRISTOPHER, JORDAN

JUBILEE

| ❏ 5440 | Goodbye My Love/Broken Hearted Boy | 1962 | $10 |
| ❏ 5440 [PS] | Goodbye My Love/Broken Hearted Boy | 1962 | $30 |

UNITED ARTISTS

❏ 993	Hello Lover/Taste of Honey	1966	$8
❏ 50049	Put Your Tears Away/World Down on Your Knees	1966	$8
❏ 50131	To Live a Lie/Angelica	1967	$8
❏ 50072	When That I Was (A Little Tiny Boy)/(B-side unknown)	1966	$8

CHRISTOPHER, TONY

HIT

| ❏ 56 | What Will My Mary Say/South Street | 1963 | $8 |

— B-side by the Dacrons

CHRISTY, JUNE

CAPITOL

❏ F2199	Bei Mir Bist Du Schoen/Some Folks Do	1952	$20
❏ F2765	First Thing You Know/Magazines Are Magic	1954	$20
❏ F1647	Get Happy/I'll Remember April	1951	$15

— Reissue

❏ F2432	Great Scot/I Lived When I Met You	1953	$20
❏ F1207	He Can Come Back Any Time He Wants To/A Mile Down the Highway	1950	$30
❏ F3375	I Never Wanna Look Into Those Eyes Again/Look Out Up There	1956	$15
❏ F3471	Intrigue/You Took Advantage of Me	1956	$15
❏ F2384	I've Got a Letter/Let Me Share Your Name	1953	$20
❏ F2163	Live Oak Tree/The Man I Love	1952	$20
❏ F2308	My Heart Belongs to Only You/I Was a Fool	1952	$20
❏ 4864	One Note Samba/Bossa Nova	1963	$8
❏ F3213	Pete Kelly's Blues/Kicks	1955	$15

CHROME, CHEETAH

ORK

| ❏ NYC4 [B] | Still Wanna Die/Take Me Home | 1978 | $20 |

CHUBBY AND THE TURNPIKES

CAPITOL

| ❏ 5840 | I Didn't Try/I Know the Inside Story | 1967 | $40 |

CHUCK-A-LUCKS, THE

BOW

| ❏ 305 | Heaven Knows/Chuck-a-Luck | 1957 | $60 |

JUBILEE

| ❏ 5415 | Tarzan's Date/Unconditional Surrender | 1961 | $30 |

LIN

| ❏ 5014 | The Magic of First Love/Disc Jockey Fever | 1958 | $60 |
| ❏ 5010 | Who Am I?/The Devil's Train | 1958 | $30 |

MEL-O-DY

| ❏ 106 | Sugar Cane Curtain/Dingbat Diller | 1963 | $30 |

WARNER BROS.

| ❏ 5234 | Cotton Pickin' Love/I'm Hospitalized Over You | 1961 | $30 |
| ❏ 5198 | Long John/Pick Up and Deliver | 1961 | $30 |

CHUCK WAGON GANG, THE

COLUMBIA

❏ 4-21021	After Awhile/All God's Children Gonna Rise	1952	$30
❏ 4-21254	Angels Rock Me to Sleep/As the Life of a Flower	1954	$30
❏ 4-21212	A Soul Winner for Jesus/God Put a Rainbow in the Cloud	1954	$30
❏ 4-21097	At the Dawning/When He Calls I'll Fly Away	1953	$30
❏ 4-20998	Blessed Light Shine On/I Know My Saviour Cares	1952	$30
❏ 4-20788	Camping in Canaan's Land/Happy Day	1951	$30
❏ 4-20968	Camping in Canaan's Land/My Home Sweet Home	1952	$30
❏ 2-786	Come Unto Me/I Am Bound to Travel On	1950	$50

— Microgroove 33 1/3 rpm 7-inch single, small hole

| ❏ 4-20969 | Come Unto Me/Shall We Gather at the River | 1952 | $30 |

— The above four comprise a box set

| ❏ 2-293 | Dream Boat/I'll Fly Away | 1949 | $50 |

— Microgroove 33 1/3 rpm 7-inch single, small hole

| ❏ 2-180(?) | Echoes from the Burning Bush/Sinner You'll Miss Heaven | 1949 | $60 |

— Microgroove 33 1/3 rpm 7-inch single, small hole

❏ 4-41324	Endless Joy Is Waiting/My Cathedral of Dreams	1959	$15
❏ 4-41219	Hallelujah, What a Promise/I Want My Light to Shine	1958	$20
❏ 4-21289	Hark the Herald Angels Sing/O Little Town of Bethlehem	1954	$20

— The above four comprise a box set

❏ 4-43234	He Gave Me That Old Time Religion/I'll Never More Stray	1965	$12
❏ 4-20887	Help Me Lord to Stand/Side by Side	1952	$30
❏ 4-20832	He Said If I Be Lifted Up/I'm Telling the World About His Love	1951	$30
❏ 4-40954	He's My Lord and King/Inside the Gate	1957	$20
❏ 4-41135	He Will Answer Prayer/He's a Friend I Can Tell My Troubles To	1958	$20
❏ 4-21133	Hide Me Rock of Ages/There's Glory on the Winning Side	1953	$30
❏ 2-118	If We Never Meet Again/Sunshine Special	1949	$60

— Microgroove 33 1/3 rpm 7-inch single, small hole

❏ 4-41426	I'll Live in Glory/The Lord Is My Shepherd	1959	$15
❏ 4-40834	I'll Walk and Talk with My Lord/When I Looked Up and He Looked Down	1957	$20
❏ 4-21338	I'm a Precious Friend/I Want to Be Ready to Meet Him	1955	$30
❏ 4-21567	I'm Bound for the Kingdom/I'm Gonna Take a Ride	1956	$30
❏ 4-21509	I'm Glory Bound/I've Been with Jesus	1956	$30
❏ 4-21379	In the Garden/In My New Home	1955	$30
❏ 21379	In the Garden/In My New Home	1955	$15
❏ 4-21452	In the Sweet Forever/I've Got Old Time Religion in My Heart	1955	$30
❏ 4-20916	Is Your Name in the Book of Life/I've Changed My Mind	1952	$30
❏ 4-21287	It Came Upon a Midnight Clear/Silent Night	1954	$20
❏ 2-240	Looking for a City/I'll Have a New Life	1949	$60

— Microgroove 33 1/3 rpm 7-inch single, small hole

| ❏ 4-21153 | Love Leads the Way/Home of the Soul | 1953 | $30 |
| ❏ 2-739 | My Home Sweet Home/Springtime in Glory | 1950 | $50 |

— Microgroove 33 1/3 rpm 7-inch single, small hole

| ❏ 2-603 | On and On We Walk Together/No Tears in Heaven | 1950 | $50 |

— Microgroove 33 1/3 rpm 7-inch single, small hole

❏ 4-20967	On and On We Walk Together/Travelling On	1952	$30
❏ 4-43048	Open Up Them Pearly Gates/That We Might Know	1964	$10
❏ 2-443	Perfect Joy/My Soul Shall Live On	1950	$50

— Microgroove 33 1/3 rpm 7-inch single, small hole

| ❏ 2-370 | Shall We Gather at the River/When the Saints Go Marching In | 1950 | $50 |

— Microgroove 33 1/3 rpm 7-inch single, small hole

❏ 4-40912	Sing on the Way/I Know	1957	$20
❏ 4-20768	Somebody Called My Name/Help Me to Be Ready Lord	1950	$30
❏ 2-921	Somebody Called My Name/Help Me to Be Ready Lord	1950	$50

— Microgroove 33 1/3 rpm 7-inch single, small hole

❏ 4-20806	Stormy Waters/Travellin' On	1951	$30
❏ 4-21293	Tattler's Wagon/O Why Not Tonight	1954	$30
❏ 4-21288	The First Noel/It Came Upon A Midnight Clear	1954	$20
❏ 4-21480	There's Gonna Be Shouting and Singing/I'm Gonna See Heaven	1956	$30
❏ 4-41031	There's Gonna Be Singing/I'm Headed for the Promised Land	1957	$20
❏ 4-20964	Way Up in Glory/Walk and Talk with Jesus	1952	$30
❏ 4-21058	We'll Be Happy All the Time/Just a Veil Between	1952	$30
❏ 4-20966	When the Saints Go Marching In/I'm Telling the World About His Love	1952	$30
❏ 4-21542	When the Sun Shines Over Jordan/A Lot of Heaven	1956	$30
❏ 4-21410	Wonderful Saviour/I'll Shout and Shine	1955	$30

CHURCH, EUGENE

CLASS

❏ 254	Miami/I Ain't Goin' for That	1959	$15
❏ 235	Pretty Girls Everywhere/For the Rest of My Life	1958	$30
❏ 266	The Struttin' Kind/That's What's Happenin'	1960	$15

KING

❏ 5610	Light of the Moon/I'm Your Taboo Man	1962	$12
❏ 5545	Mind Your Own Business/You Got the Right Idea	1961	$15
❏ 5715	Sixteen Tons/Time Has Brought About a Change	1963	$12

| ❏ 5589 | That's All I Need/Geneva | 1962 | $12 |

RENDEZVOUS

| ❏ 132 | Good News/Polly | 1960 | $15 |

SPECIALTY

| ❏ 604 | How Long/Open Up Your Heart | 1957 | $30 |

WORLD PACIFIC

| ❏ 77866 | Dollar Bill/U Maka Hanna | 1967 | $20 |

CHURCH STREET FIVE, THE

LEGRAND

| ❏ 1004 | A Nite with Daddy "G" Part 1/Part 2 | 1961 | $30 |

— Purple label original

| ❏ 1004 | A Nite with Daddy "G" Part 1/Part 2 | 1961 | $20 |

— Red, gold and white "shield" label

❏ 1014	Church Street Walk/I'm Gonna Sue	1961	$30
❏ 1021	Daddy G Rides Again/Hey Now	1962	$30
❏ 1010	Fallen Arches/Everybody's Happy	1961	$30
❏ 1026	Moonlight in Vermont/Sing a Song Children	1963	$30

CINDERELLA

MERCURY

❏ 872982-7	Coming Home/Take Me Back	1989	$3
❏ 872982-7 [PS]	Coming Home/Take Me Back	1989	$3
❏ 870644-7	Don't Know What You Got (Till It's Gone)/Fire and Ice	1988	$3
❏ 870644-7 [PS]	Don't Know What You Got (Till It's Gone)/Fire and Ice	1988	$3
❏ 874578-7	Gypsy Road/Jumpin' Jack Flash	1989	$4
❏ 884869-7	Shake Me/Night Songs	1986	$5
❏ 888483-7	Somebody Save Me/Hell on Wheels	1987	$3
❏ 888483-7 [PS]	Somebody Save Me/Hell on Wheels	1987	$3
❏ 872148-7	The Last Mile/Long Cold Winter	1988	$3
❏ 872148-7 [PS]	The Last Mile/Long Cold Winter	1988	$3

CINDERELLAS, THE (1)

COLUMBIA

| ❏ 41540 | The Trouble with Boys/Puppy Dog | 1959 | $20 |

DECCA

| ❏ 30925 | I Was Only 15/You Never Shoulda Gone Away | 1959 | $30 |
| ❏ 30830 | Mr. Dee Jay/Yum Yum Yum | 1959 | $30 |

CINDERELLAS, THE (2)

DIMENSION

| ❏ 1026 | Baby, Baby, I Still Love You/Please Don't Wake Me | 1964 | $50 |

MERCURY

| ❏ 72394 | Fairy Tale/Mr. Happy Love | 1965 | $10 |

CINDERS, THE

ORIGINAL SOUND

| ❏ 43 | I'll Follow You/The Story | 1964 | $10 |

WARNER BROS.

| ❏ 5326 | The Cinnamon Cinder/C'mon Wobble | 1962 | $15 |

CINDY AND LINDY

ABC-PARAMOUNT

| ❏ 9886 | Shakin'/Sittin' It Out | 1958 | $30 |
| ❏ 9847 | The Language of Love/Brigette's Song | 1957 | $30 |

CORAL

❏ 62119	Before and After/Big Bells and Bongo Drummers	1959	$30
❏ 62165	Let's Go Steady/There Are Such Things	1960	$30
❏ 62072	Saturday Night in Tia-Juana/You Can't Mail an Elephant	1959	$30
❏ 62008	The Wonder That Is You/I'll String Along with You	1958	$30

PILGRIM

| ❏ 705 | Hungry Heart/Livin' and Bein' Loved | 1956 | $20 |
| ❏ 702 | Let's Go Steady/The Wedding Is Over | 1956 | $20 |

CINNAMON ANGELS

B.T. PUPPY

| ❏ 559 | Calypso Girl/Let's Be Sweethearts | 1970 | $8 |

CINNAMONS, THE

B.T. PUPPY

| ❏ 503 | I'm Not Gonna Worry/Strange, Strange Feeling | 1964 | $8 |
| ❏ 508 | Mr. Cupid '65/Dance to the Music | 1965 | $8 |

Number	Title	Yr	NM

CIRCUS
METROMEDIA
| ❏ 68-0112 | Feel So Right/Jonah's Fable | 1973 | $5 |
| ❏ 265 | Stop, Wait and Listen/I Need Your Love | 1972 | $6 |

CIRCUS MAXIMUS
Group features JERRY JEFF WALKER
VANGUARD
| ❏ 35063 | Lonely Man/Negative Dreamer Girl | 1968 | $30 |

CISSEL, CHUCK
ARISTA
❏ 0471	Cisselin' Hot/Do You Believe	1979	$8
❏ 0499	Forever/Don't Tell Me You're Sorry	1980	$10
❏ 0650	If I Had the Chance/ (B-side unknown)	1981	$6

—A-side with Marva King

❏ 0525	Lady in My World/Emergency	1980	$20
❏ 0586	Love's Grown Deep/Mimi	1981	$6
❏ 1000	Possessed/(B-side unknown)	1982	$12

CITATIONS, THE
BALLAD
| ❏ 101 | I Will Stand By You/ To Win the Race | 1967 | $125 |
CANADIAN AMERICAN
| ❏ 136 | Mystery of Love/Magic Eyes | 1962 | $40 |

—As "Nicki North and the Citations

DON-EL
| ❏ 113 | It Hurts Me/Kiss in the Night | 1961 | $50 |
EPIC
| ❏ 9603 | Moon Race/Slippin' and Slidin' | 1963 | $30 |
FRATERNITY
| ❏ 910 | The Girl Next Door/Ten Miles from Nowhere | 1963 | $30 |
| ❏ 992 | The Girl Next Door/Ten Miles from Nowhere | 1967 | $15 |
MERCURY
| ❏ 72286 | Chicago/The Stomp | 1964 | $20 |
MGM
| ❏ 13373 | That Girl of Mine/Down Went the Curtain | 1965 | $30 |
PRINCESS
| ❏ 54 | Carmen P./Everybody Philly | 1965 | $40 |
ROULETTE
| ❏ 4623 | Carmen P./Everybody Philly | 1965 | $20 |
SARA
| ❏ 3301 | Moon Race/Slippin' and Slidin' | 1963 | $60 |
SWAN
| ❏ 4062 | Fiddlin' Around/Fire Ritual | 1960 | $50 |
VANGEE
| ❏ 301 | The Girl Next Door/Ten Miles from Nowhere | 1963 | $50 |

CITY BOY
ATLANTIC
| ❏ 3612 | The Day the Earth Caught Fire/Ambition | 1979 | $4 |
MERCURY
❏ 73999	5.7.0.5/Bad for Business	1978	$5
❏ 73999 [PS]	5.7.0.5/Bad for Business	1978	$10
❏ 73858	Hap-Ki-Do Kid/Surgery Hours (Doctor Doctor)	1976	$6
❏ 73835	Haymaking Time/The Greatest Story Ever Told	1976	$6
❏ 73953	I've Been Spun/Goodbye Blue Monday	1977	$6
❏ 74032	What a Night/Goodbye Laurelie	1978	$5

CITY SURFERS, THE
CAPITOL
| ❏ 5002 | Beach Ball/Sun Tan Baby | 1963 | $30 |
| ❏ 5052 | Powder Puff/Fifty Miles to Go | 1963 | $30 |

CITY, THE
CAROLE KING was a member.
ODE
❏ 119	(Hi-De-Ho) That Old Sweet Roll/Why Are You Leaving	1969	$15
❏ 113	Snow Queen/Paradise Alley	1968	$15
❏ 117	That Old Sweet Rule/ Why Are You Leaving	1968	$15

CIX BITS
ENTERPRISE
| ❏ 9087 | Season's Greetings/New Year's Resolution | 1973 | $6 |

Number	Title	Yr	NM

CLAMS, THE
THREE BROTHERS
| ❏ 404 | Close to You/First Time Ever I Saw Your Face | 1974 | $10 |

—LOU CHRISTIE appears on this record

CLANTON, DARRELL
AUDIOGRAPH
| ❏ 479 | I'll Take As Much of You As I Can Get/That's What Cheaters Do | 1984 | $6 |
| ❏ 474 | Lonesome 7-7203/Me-Oh-My | 1983 | $6 |
WARNER BROS.
| ❏ 29185 | I Forgot That I Don't Live Here Anymore/I Told You So | 1984 | $4 |

CLANTON, JIMMY
ACE
❏ 551	A Letter to An Angel/A Part of Me	1958	$30
❏ 585	Another Sleepless Night/I'm Gonna Try	1960	$20
❏ 585 [PS]	Another Sleepless Night/I'm Gonna Try	1960	$40
❏ 8007	Cindy/I Care Enough (To Give the Very Best)	1963	$10
❏ 600	Come Back/Wait	1960	$20
❏ 600 [PS]	Come Back/Wait	1960	$40
❏ 8005	Darkest Street in Town/ Dreams of a Fool	1962	$12
❏ 616	Down the Aisle/No Longer Blue	1961	$20
❏ 616 [PS]	Down the Aisle/No Longer Blue	1961	$40

— With Mary Ann Mobley

❏ 8006	Endless Nights/Another Day, Another Heartache	1963	$12
❏ 8006 [PS]	Endless Nights/Another Day, Another Heartache	1963	$30
❏ 575	Go, Jimmy, Go/I Trusted You	1959	$30

—Normal white label

| ❏ 575 | Go, Jimmy, Go/I Trusted You | 1959 | $30 |

—Purple label

❏ 575 [PS]	Go, Jimmy, Go/I Trusted You	1959	$40
❏ 668	Heart Hotel/Many Dreams	1963	$15
❏ 622	I Just Wanna Make Love/ Don't Look at Me	1961	$20
❏ 622 [PS]	I Just Wanna Make Love/ Don't Look at Me	1961	$40
❏ 537	I Trusted You/That's You Baby	1958	$30
❏ 634	Lucky in Love with You/ Not Like a Brother	1961	$20
❏ 634 [PS]	Lucky in Love with You/ Not Like a Brother	1961	$40
❏ 560	My Love Is Strong/Ship on a Stormy Sea	1959	$20
❏ 567 [M]	My Own True Love/ Little Boy in Love	1959	$20
❏ 567 [S]	My Own True Love/ Little Boy in Love	1959	$40
❏ 567 [PS]	My Own True Love/ Little Boy in Love	1959	$40
❏ 642 [PS]	Teenage Millionaire	1962	$60
❏ 641	Twist On Little Girl/Wayward Love	1962	$20
❏ 641 [PS]	Twist On Little Girl/Wayward Love	1962	$40
❏ 642	Twist On Little Girl/Wayward Love//Green Light/Happy Times	1962	$60
❏ 607	What Am I Gonna Do/If I	1961	$20
❏ 607 [PS]	What Am I Gonna Do/If I	1961	$40
IMPERIAL
| ❏ 66242 | Absence of Lisa/C'mon Jim | 1967 | $8 |
| ❏ 66274 | Calico Junction/I'll Be Loving You | 1968 | $8 |
LAURIE
❏ 3508	Curly/I'll Never Forget Your Love	1969	$12
❏ 3508	Curly/The Girl Who Cried Love (Once Too Often)	1969	$8
❏ 3534	Tell Me/I'll Never Forget Your Love	1969	$8
MALA
| ❏ 516 | Everything I Touch Turns to Tears/That Special Way | 1965 | $12 |
| ❏ 500 | Hurting Each Other/Don't Keep Your Friends Away | 1965 | $10 |
PHILIPS
❏ 40219	Follow the Sun/Lock the Windows	1964	$10
❏ 40208	If I'm a Fool for Loving You/A Million Drums	1964	$10
❏ 40181	I'll Step Aside/I Won't Cry Anymore	1964	$10
SPIRAL
| ❏ 3406 | The Coolest Hot Pants/ (Instrumental) | 1971 | $5 |
STARCREST
| ❏ 78 [DJ] | Old Rock 'N Roller (mono/stereo) | 1978 | $5 |

—May be promo only

| ❏ 078 [DJ] | Old Rock 'N Roller (mono/stereo) | 1978 | $5 |

—May be promo only

STARFIRE
| ❏ 104 | I Wanna Go Home/You Kissed a Fool Goodbye | 1976 | $5 |

Number	Title	Yr	NM

UNITED ARTISTS
| ❏ 0(no cat #) [S] | Teenage Millionaire | 1961 | $40 |

—Cardboard record; B-side promotes the movie of the same name

VIN
| ❏ 1028 | What Am I Living For/ Wedding Blues | 1962 | $10 |

7-Inch Extended Plays
ACE
❏ 101	(contents unknown)	1959	$125
❏ 102	(contents unknown)	1959	$175
❏ 102 [PS]	Thinking of You	1959	$175

CLAPTON, ERIC
Also see BLIND FAITH; CREAM; DEREK AND THE DOMINOS; B.B. KING; THE YARDBIRDS.
ATCO
| ❏ 6784 | After Midnight/Easy Now | 1970 | $6 |
DUCK
❏ 28391	Behind the Sun/Grand Illusion	1987	$3
❏ 29081	Forever Man/Too Bad	1985	$3
❏ 29081 [PS]	Forever Man/Too Bad	1985	$3
❏ 28514	It's in the Way That You Use It/Grand Illusion	1986	$3
❏ 28514 [PS]	It's in the Way That You Use It/Grand Illusion	1986	$3
❏ 29780	I've Got a Rock n' Roll Heart/Man in Love	1983	$4

—Silver label with Duck logo

❏ 29647	Pretty Girl/The Shape You're In	1983	$4
❏ 28986	See What Love Can Do/She's Waiting	1985	$3
❏ 28279	Tearing Us Apart/Hold On	1987	$3

—A-side with Tina Turner

| ❏ 28279 [PS] | Tearing Us Apart/Hold On | 1987 | $3 |
POLYDOR
❏ 887403-7	After Midnight/I Can't Stand It	1988	$3
❏ 887403-7 [PS]	After Midnight/I Can't Stand It	1988	$3
❏ 15056	Bell Bottom Blues/Little Wing	1973	$5

—Reissue of Derek and the Dominos recordings, but under Clapton's name

| ❏ 15049 | Let It Rain/Easy Now | 1972 | $6 |
REPRISE
| ❏ 22732 | Pretending/Before You Accuse Me | 1989 | $3 |
| ❏ 22732 [PS] | Pretending/Before You Accuse Me | 1989 | $3 |
RSO
❏ 1064	Another Ticket/Rita Mae	1981	$4
❏ 1064 [PS]	Another Ticket/Rita Mae	1981	$5
❏ 1051	Blues Power/Early in the Morning	1980	$4
❏ 868	Carnival/Hungry	1976	$4
❏ 861	Hello Old Friend/ All Our Pastimes	1976	$4
❏ 1060	I Can't Stand It/Black Rose	1981	$4
❏ 409	I Shot the Sheriff/ Give Me Strength	1974	$5
❏ 500	I Shot the Sheriff/ Give Me Strength	1974	$4
❏ 886	Lay Down Sally/Next Time You See Her	1978	$4
❏ 910	Promises/Watch Out for Lucy	1978	$4
❏ 509	Swing Low Sweet Chariot/ Pretty Blue Eyes	1975	$4
❏ 928	Tulsa Time/Cocaine	1979	$5

—Studio versions of the two songs

| ❏ 1039 | Tulsa Time/Cocaine | 1980 | $4 |

—Live versions of the two songs

| ❏ 503 | Willie and the Hand Jive/ Main Line Florida | 1975 | $4 |
| ❏ 895 | Wonderful Tonight/ Peaches and Diesel | 1978 | $4 |
WARNER BROS.
| ❏ 29780 | I've Got a Rock n' Roll Heart/Man in Love | 1983 | $5 |

—Original pressing on white WB label

CLAREMONTS, THE
APOLLO
| ❏ 517 | Why Keep Me Dreaming/ Angel of Romance | 1957 | $70 |
| ❏ 751 | Why Keep Me Dreaming/ Angel of Romance | 1963 | $30 |

CLARK, BETTY
MGM
| ❏ 11381 | I Saw Mommy Kissing Santa Claus/You Can Fly | 1952 | $30 |

CLARK, CHRIS

Number	Title	Yr	NM

MOTOWN
❑ 1114	From Head to Toe/The Beginning of the End	1967	$20
❑ 1121	Whisper You Love Me Boy/ The Beginning of the End	1968	$20

V.I.P.
❑ 25031	Do Right, Baby, Do Right/ Don't Be Too Long	1965	$20
❑ 25041	I Love You/I Want to Go Back There Again	1966	$20
❑ 25038	Love's Gone Bad/Put Yourself in My Place	1965	$30

— Same song as above A-side, but with corrected title

❑ 25038	Love's Gone Mad/Put Yourself in My Place	1965	$70

CLARK, CLAUDINE

CHANCELLOR
❑ 1113	Party Lights/Disappointed	1962	$30

— exists on two different labels

❑ 1124	Telephone Game/Walkin' Through a Cemetery	1962	$15
❑ 1130	Walk Me Home/Who Will You Hurt	1963	$15

HERALD
❑ 523	Teenage Blues/Angel of Happiness	1958	$50

JAMIE
❑ 1291	Buttered Popcorn/A Sometimes Thing	1964	$10
❑ 1279	Moon Madness/(The Strength) To Be Strong	1964	$10

CLARK, DAVE, FIVE

CONGRESS
❑ 212	I Knew It All the Time/ That's What I Said	1964	$30
❑ 212 [PS]	I Knew It All the Time/ That's What I Said	1964	$50

EPIC
❑ 10209	A Little Bit Now/You Don't Play Me Around	1967	$20
❑ 10209 [PS]	A Little Bit Now/You Don't Play Me Around	1967	$30
❑ 9739	Any Way You Want It/ Crying Over You	1964	$15
❑ 9882	At the Scene/I Miss You	1966	$15
❑ 9882 [PS]	At the Scene/I Miss You	1966	$30
❑ 9704	Because/Theme Without a Name	1964	$15
❑ 9704 [PS]	Because/Theme Without a Name	1964	$30
❑ 9671	Bits and Pieces/All of the Time	1964	$15
❑ 10547	Bring It On Home to Me/ Darling, I Love You	1969	$20
❑ 10547 [PS]	Bring It On Home to Me/ Darling, I Love You	1969	$30
❑ 9692	Can't You See That She's Mine/No TIme to Lose	1964	$15
❑ 9692 [PS]	Can't You See That She's Mine/No TIme to Lose	1964	$30
❑ 9833	Catch Us If You Can/On the Move	1965	$15
❑ 9833 [PS]	Catch Us If You Can/On the Move	1965	$30
❑ 9763	Come Home/Your Turn to Cry	1965	$15
❑ 9763 [PS]	Come Home/Your Turn to Cry	1965	$30
❑ 9678	Do You Love Me/Chaquita	1964	$15
❑ 10265/60 [DJ]	Everybody Knows/ Best of Both Worlds	1968	$30

— B-side by Lulu; odd promo

❑ 10265	Everybody Knows/Inside and Out	1967	$20
❑ 10265 [PS]	Everybody Knows/Inside and Out	1967	$40
❑ 9722	Everybody Knows (I Still Love You)/Ol' Sol	1964	$15
❑ 9722 [PS]	Everybody Knows (I Still Love You)/Ol' Sol	1964	$30
❑ 9656	Glad All Over/I Know You	1964	$20
❑ 9656 [PS]	Glad All Over/I Know You	1964	$30
❑ 10684	Good Old Rock and Roll (Medley)/One Night	1970	$30
❑ 10684 [PS]	Good Old Rock and Roll (Medley)/One Night	1970	$40
❑ 10635	Here Comes Summer/Five by Five	1970	$20
❑ 10509	If Somebody Loves You/ Best Day's Work	1969	$20
❑ 9811	I Like It Like That/Hurting Inside	1965	$15
❑ 9811 [PS]	I Like It Like That/Hurting Inside	1965	$30
❑ 10114	I've Got to Have a Reason/ Good Time Woman	1966	$15
❑ 10114 [PS]	I've Got to Have a Reason/ Good Time Woman	1966	$30
❑ 9863 [PS]	Over and Over	1965	$400

— Promo-only black and white sleeve

❑ 9863	Over and Over/I'll Be Yours (My Love)	1965	$15
❑ 9863 [PS]	Over and Over/I'll Be Yours (My Love)	1965	$30
❑ 9863 [DJ]	Over and Over (same on both sides)	1965	$50

— Promo only on red vinyl

❑ 9863 [DJ]	Over and Over (same on both sides)	1965	$50

— Promo only on red vinyl

❑ 10476	Paradise (Is Half As Nice)/34-06	1969	$20
❑ 10476 [PS]	Paradise (Is Half As Nice)/34-06	1969	$40
❑ 10325	Please Stay/Forget	1968	$20
❑ 10031	Please Tell Me Why/ Look Before You Leap	1966	$15

Number	Title	Yr	NM
❑ 10031 [PS]	Please Tell Me Why/ Look Before You Leap	1966	$30
❑ 10053	Satisfied with You/ Don't Let Me Down	1966	$15
❑ 10053 [PS]	Satisfied with You/ Don't Let Me Down	1966	$30
❑ 10704	Southern Man/If You Wanna See Me Cry	1971	$50
❑ 10004	Try Too Hard/All Night Long	1966	$15
❑ 10004 [PS]	Try Too Hard/All Night Long	1966	$30
❑ 10768	Won't You Be My Lady/ Into Your Life	1971	$20

EPIC MEMORY LANE
❑ 2234	Any Way You Want It/Can't You See That She's Mine	1972	$4
❑ 2230	Because/Do You Love Me	1972	$4
❑ 2294	Bring It On Home to Me/ If Somebody Loves You	1972	$4
❑ 2316	Come Home/You Got What It Takes	1972	$4
❑ 2225	Glad All Over/Bits and Pieces	1972	$4
❑ 2313	I Like It Like That/Can't You See That She's Mine	1972	$4
❑ 2239	I Like It Like That/Everybody Knows (I Still Love You)	1972	$4
❑ 2248	Over and Over/Catch Us If You Can	1972	$4

JUBILEE
❑ 5476	Chaquita/In Your Heart	1964	$40

RUST
❑ 5078	I Walk the Line/First Love	1964	$50

7-Inch Extended Plays

EPIC
❑ E26221 [PS]	More Greatest Hits	1966	$75
❑ E26185	Over and Over/Can't You See That She's Mine/I Like It Like That//Catch Us If You Can/Because/Glad All Over	1966	$75

— 33 1/3 rpm, small hole, jukebox edition

❑ E26185 [PS]	The Dave Clark Five's Greatest Hits	1966	$75
❑ E26221	Try Too Hard/Please Tell Me Why/ Reelin' and Rockin'//Satisfied with You/At the Scene/All Night Long	1966	$75

— 33 1/3 rpm, small hole, jukebox edition

CLARK, DEE

ABNER
❑ 1037	At My Front Door/Cling-a-Ling	1960	$30
❑ 0(no cat #) [DJ]	Blues Get Off My Shoulder (B-side blank)	1959	$125

— White label; noted as "Special D.J. Release from Latest E.P."

❑ 1029	Hey Little Girl/If It Wasn't for Love	1959	$30
❑ 1029 [PS]	Hey Little Girl/If It Wasn't for Love	1959	$50
❑ 1032	How About That/Blues Get Off My Shoulder	1959	$30

COLUMBIA
❑ 44200	In These Very Tender Moments/Lost Girl	1967	$8

CONSTELLATION
❑ 142	Ain't Gonna Be Your Fool/ In My Apartment	1964	$15
❑ 120	Come Closer/That's My Girl	1964	$200
❑ 108	Crossfire Time/I'm Going Home	1963	$15
❑ 155	I Can't Run Away/She's My Baby	1965	$15
❑ 165	I Don't Need (Nobody Like You)/Hot Potatoe	1966	$15
❑ 113	It's Raining/That's My Girl	1964	$200
❑ 173	Old Fashion Love/I'm Goin' Home	1963	$15
❑ 147	T.C.B./It's Impossible	1965	$15
❑ 132	Warm Summer Breeze/Heartbreak	1964	$15

FALCON
❑ 1002	Gloria/Kangaroo Hop	1957	$40
❑ 1009	Oh Little Girl/Wondering	1958	$50
❑ 1005	Seven Nights/24 Boy Friends	1957	$50

LIBERTY
❑ 56152	24 Hours of Loneliness/Where Did All the Good Times Go	1970	$5

VEE JAY
❑ 443	Dance On Little Girl/Fever	1962	$20
❑ 409	Don't Walk Away from Me/ You're Telling Your Secrets	1961	$20
❑ 394	Gotos Delluvia (Raindrops)/ Livin' with Vivian	1961	$20

— B-side by Al Smith

❑ 532	How Is He Treating You/ The Jones Boy	1963	$20
❑ 487	I'm a Soldier Boy/ Shook Up Over You	1963	$20
❑ 462	I'm Going Back to School/ Nobody But You	1962	$20
❑ 548	Walking My Dog/Nobody But Me	1963	$20

7-Inch Extended Plays

ABNER
❑ 900	(contents unknown)	1959	$120
❑ 900 [PS]	Dee Clark	1959	$120

Number	Title	Yr	NM

CLARK, DOUG, AND THE HOT NUTS

JUBILEE
❑ 5536	Baby Let Me Bang Your Box Part 1/Baby Let Me Bang Your Box Part 2	1966	$30
❑ 5546	Milk the Cow/Go, Doug, Go	1966	$20

CLARK, FRANK

HIT
❑ 69	Those Lazy-Hazy-Crazy Days of Summer/Blue on Blue	1963	$8

— B-side by John Preston

CLARK, GENE

ASYLUM
❑ 45222	Life's Greatest Fool/ From a Silver Petal	1974	$5

COLUMBIA
❑ 43903	Echoes/I Found You	1966	$20
❑ 43903 [PS]	Echoes/I Found You	1966	$300
❑ 44088	Is Yours Mine/So You Say You Lost Your Baby	1967	$20

RSO
❑ 876	Home Run King/Lonely Saturday	1977	$5

CLARK, GUY

RCA
❑ PB-13688	Texas Cookin'/Broken Hearted People	1983	$4
❑ PB-10781	The Last Gunfighter Ballad/Texas Cookin'	1976	$6

RCA VICTOR
❑ PB-10581	Let Him Roll/Rita Ballou	1976	$6
❑ PB-10188	The Ballad of Laverne and Cpt. Flint/Like a Coat from the Cold	1975	$8

WARNER BROS.
❑ 29456	Better Days/Heartbroke	1983	$4
❑ 8714	Fools for Each Other/ Fool on the Roof	1978	$5
❑ 49542	Heartbroke/Who Do You Think You Are	1980	$5
❑ 29595	Homegrown Tomatoes/ Fool in a Mirror	1983	$4
❑ 49853	She's Crazy for Leavin'/ South Coast of Texas	1981	$5
❑ 49740	The Partner Nobody Chose/Heartbroke	1981	$5

CLARK, JAY

CONCORDE
❑ 301	Love Gone Bad/Modern Day Cowboy	1985	$5
❑ 302	Modern Day Cowboy/ Love Gone Bad	1986	$5

CLARK, LUCKY

POLYDOR
❑ 14343	Amy/Lonely Hearts Women	1976	$6
❑ 14393	Everytime Two Fools Collide/ Another Honky Tonk Tonight	1977	$6
❑ 14317	Sing Me a Sad Song/ The Guy with the Girl	1976	$6

CLARK, MICKEY

EVERGREEN
❑ 1051	When I'm Over You (What You Gonna Do)/(B-side unknown)	1987	$5
❑ 1051 [PS]	When I'm Over You (What You Gonna Do)/(B-side unknown)	1987	$8

MONUMENT
❑ WS4-03519	She's Gone to L.A. Again/ The Tequila Express	1983	$5

CLARK, PETULA

ABC DUNHILL
❑ 15019	Loving Arms/I'm the Woman You Need	1974	$5

CORAL
❑ 60971	Song of the Mermaid/Tell Me Truly	1953	$30
❑ 61077	Where Did My Snowman Go/Three Little Kittens	1953	$30

IMPERIAL
❑ 5582	The Little Blue Man/Baby Lover	1959	$30
❑ 5600	Where Do I Go from Here/ Mama's Talkin' Soft	1959	$30

KING
❑ 1371	The Little Shoemaker/Helpless	1954	$30

LAURIE
❑ 3236	Elle Est Finie/J'ai Tout Oublie	1964	$20
❑ 3316	In Love/Darling Cheri	1965	$15
❑ 3259	In Love/The Road	1964	$20
❑ 3156	I Will Follow Him/Darling Cheri	1963	$20

LONDON INT'L.
❑ 10510	I'm Counting on You/ Some Other World	1962	$20
❑ 10504	My Friend the Sea/ With All My Love	1962	$20

Number	Title	Yr	NM
❑ 10516	Tender Love/Whistlin' for the Moon	1962	$20
MGM			
❑ 14708	Come On Home/The Old Fashioned Way	1974	$5
❑ 14577	Gratification/I Can't Remember	1973	$5
❑ 14392	My Guy/Little Bit of Lovin'	1972	$5
❑ 14511	Serenade of Love/I Can't Remember	1973	$5
❑ 14673	Silver Spoon/Fixing to Live	1973	$5
❑ 12049	The Pendulum Song/ Romance in Rome	1955	$30
❑ 14431	Wedding Song (There Is Love)/Song Without End	1972	$5
SCOTTI BROS.			
❑ 02979	Blue Eyes Crying in the Rain/Love Won't Always Pass You By	1982	$4
❑ 03171	Dreamin' with My Eyes Wide Open/Afterglow	1982	$4
WARNER BROS.			
❑ 7244	American Boys/Look to the Sky	1968	$8
❑ 5802	A Sign of the Times/ Time for Love	1966	$10
❑ 7422	Beautiful Sounds/ The Song Is Love	1970	$8
❑ 5882	Color My World/Take Me Home Again	1966	$10
❑ 7216	Don't Give Up/Every Time I See a Rainbow	1968	$8
❑ 7049	Don't Sleep in the Subway/ Here Comes the Morning	1967	$12
❑ 5494	Downtown/You'd Better Love Me	1964	$20
— Originals have red labels with arrows			
❑ 5494	Downtown/You'd Better Love Me	1964	$12
— Later pressings have orange labels			
❑ 7275	Happy Heart/Love Is the Only Thing	1969	$8
❑ 5835	I Couldn't Live Without Your Love/Your Way of Life	1966	$10
❑ 7484	I Don't Know How to Love Him (Superstar)/Maybe	1971	$8
❑ 5612	I Know a Place/Jack and John	1965	$10
❑ 7310	Look at Mine/If Somebody Loves You	1969	$8
❑ 5684	My Love/Where Am I Going	1965	$10
❑ 7073	The Cat in the Window (The Bird in the Sky)/ Fancy Dancin' Man	1967	$12
❑ 7097	The Other Man's Grass Is Always Greener/ At the Crossroads	1967	$10
❑ 7467	The Song of My Life/ Couldn't Sleep	1971	$8
❑ 7002	This Is My Song/High	1967	$10
❑ 5863	Who Am I/Love Is a Long Journey	1966	$10
7-Inch Extended Plays			
❑ S1743	Have Another Dream on Me/ Your Love Is Everywhere/ One in a Million//The Sun Shines Out of Your Shoes/ Days/Why Can't I Cry?	1968	$15
— Jukebox issue; small hole, plays at 33 1/3 rpm			
❑ S1743 [PS]	Petula	1968	$15

CLARK, ROY

Number	Title	Yr	NM
ABC			
❑ 12437	Is It Hot in Here (Or Is It Me)/ Jolly Ho (Happy Hour)	1978	$4
— With Buck Trent			
❑ 12328	Must You Throw Dirt in My Face/Lazy River	1978	$4
❑ 12402	The Happy Days/Shoulder to Shoulder (Arm and Arm)	1978	$4
❑ 12365	Where Have You Been All of My Life/Near You	1978	$4
ABC DOT			
❑ 17530	Dear God/Take Good Care of Her	1974	$4
❑ 17565	Heart to Heart/Someone Cares for You	1975	$4
❑ 17605	If I Had to Do It All Over Again/ It Sure Looks Good on You	1976	$4
❑ 17667	I Have a Dream, I Have a Love/Half a Love	1976	$4
❑ 17626	Think Summer/Whatever Happened to Gauze	1976	$4
❑ 17712	We Can't Build a Fire in the Rain/I'm So Lonesome I Could Cry	1977	$4
CAPITOL			
❑ 5300	Alabama Jubilee/Down Yonder	1964	$10
❑ 5047	Good Time Charlie/ Application for Love	1963	$10
❑ 5664	Hey Sweet Thing/If You Want It, Come and Get It	1966	$12
— With Mary Taylor			
❑ 5233	It's My Way/I'm Forgetting Now	1964	$10
❑ 5565	Malaguena/Overdue Blues	1965	$10
❑ 5512	So Much to Remember/Turn Around and Look Again	1965	$12
❑ 5770	St. Louis Blues/Just a Closer Walk with Thee	1966	$10
❑ 5163	Take Me As I Am/ If You'll Pardon Me	1964	$10

Number	Title	Yr	NM
❑ 4794	Talk About a Party/As Long As I'm Movin'	1962	$15
❑ 4670	Texas Twist/Wildwood Twist	1961	$15
❑ 5445	The Color of Her Love Is Blue/Too Pooped to Pop	1965	$12
❑ 4956	The Tip of My Fingers/ Spooky Movies	1963	$10
❑ 5099	Through the Eyes of a Fool/Sweet Violets	1964	$10
❑ 5350	When the Wind Blows In Chicago/Live Fast, Love Hard, Die Young	1965	$10
CHURCHILL			
❑ 52469	Another Lonely Night With You/(Instrumental)	1984	$4
❑ 94016	Christmas Wouldn't Be Christmas Without You/A Way Without Words	1982	$6
❑ 94016 [PS]	Christmas Wouldn't Be Christmas Without You/A Way Without Words	1982	$6
❑ 94011	Here We Go Again/ Early in the Morning	1982	$5
❑ 94017	I'm a Booger/A Way Without Words	1983	$5
❑ 94002	Paradise Knife and Gun Club/I Don't Care	1982	$5
❑ 94007	Tennessee Saturday Night/ Tumbling Tumbleweeds	1982	$5
❑ 94007 [PS]	Tennessee Saturday Night/ Tumbling Tumbleweeds	1982	$6
❑ 94025	Wildwood Flower/ Southern Nights	1983	$5
DOT			
❑ 17368	A Simple Thing As Love/I'd Fight the World	1971	$5
❑ 17449	Come Live with Me/ Darby's Castle	1973	$5
❑ 17117	Do You Believe This Town/ It Just Happened That Way	1968	$6
❑ 17498	Honeymoon Feelin'/I Really Don't Want to Know	1974	$5
❑ 17413	I'll Take the Time/ Ode to a Critter	1972	$5
❑ 17349	I Never Picked Cotton/ Lonesome Too Long	1970	$5
❑ 17187	Love Is Just a State of Mind/Look to the Sky	1968	$6
❑ 17395	Magnificent Sanctuary Bird/Be Ready	1971	$5
❑ 17299	September Song/ For the Life of Me	1969	$5
❑ 17386	She Cried/Back in the Race	1971	$5
❑ 17480	Somewhere Between Love and Tomorrow/I'll Paint You a Song	1973	$5
❑ 17355	Thank God and Greyhound/Strangers	1970	$5
❑ 17518	The Great Divide/Chomp'n	1974	$5
❑ 17426	The Lawrence Welk--Hee Haw Counter-Revolution Polka/ When the Wind Blows	1972	$5
❑ 17335	Then She's a Lover/Say Amen	1969	$5
❑ 17370	(Where Do I Begin) Love Story/ Theme from "Love Story	1971	$5
HALLMARK			
❑ 0004	But, She Loves Me/ (B-side unknown)	1989	$5
❑ 0001	What a Wonderful World/ (Instrumental)	1989	$5
MCA			
❑ 41122	Caldonia/Four O'Clock in the Morning	1979	$4
❑ 41153	Chain Gang of Love/Why Don't We Go Somewhere and Love	1979	$4
❑ 41288	For Love's Own Sake/They'll Never Take Her Love from Me	1980	$4
❑ 51031	I Ain't Got Nobody/Play Me a Little Traveling Music	1980	$4
❑ 41208	If There Were Only Time for Love/Then I'll Be Over You	1980	$4
❑ 51111	Love Takes Two/ Come Sundown	1981	$4
❑ 51079	She Can't Give It Away/Dig a Little Deeper in the Well	1981	$4
SILVER DOLLAR			
❑ 0001	Tobacco Road/Black Sapphire	1986	$5
❑ 0001 [PS]	Tobacco Road/Black Sapphire	1986	$8
SONGBIRD			
❑ 51167	The Last Word in Jesus Is Us/Shinin' Face	1981	$4
TOWER			
❑ 331	Orange Blossom Special/ The Great Pretender	1967	$8

CLARK, SANFORD

Number	Title	Yr	NM
DOT			
❑ 15516	A Cheat/Usta Be My Baby	1956	$30
❑ 15585	Love Charms/Loo-Be-Doo	1957	$30
❑ 15738	Modern Romance/Travelin' Man	1958	$200
❑ 15534	Oooo Baby/9 Lb. Hammer	1957	$30
❑ 15646	Swanee River Rock/The Man Who Made an Angel Cry	1957	$30
❑ 15481	The Fool/Lonesome for a Letter	1956	$60
— Originals have maroon labels			
❑ 15481	The Fool/Lonesome for a Letter	1956	$30
— Second pressings have black labels			
❑ 15556	The Glory of Love/Darling Dear	1957	$30

Number	Title	Yr	NM
JAMIE			
❑ 1120	Bad Luck/My Jealousy	1959	$30
❑ 1153	Go On Home/Pledging My Love	1960	$30
❑ 1139	I Can't Help It/Son-of-a-Gun	1959	$30
❑ 1107	Sing 'Em Some Blues/ Still as the Night	1958	$30
LHI			
❑ 1213	Love Me Till Then/Farm Labor Camp No. 2	1968	$8
❑ 1203	The Son of Hickory Holler's Tramp/Black Widow Spider	1968	$8
MCI			
❑ 1003	The Fool/Lonesome for a Letter	1956	$200
RAMCO			
❑ 1987	It's Nothing to Me/ Calling All Hearts	1967	$15
❑ 1976	Shades/Once Upon a Time	1966	$15
❑ 1992	The Big Lie/Where's the Floor	1967	$15
❑ 1972	The Fool '66/Step Aside	1966	$20
❑ 1979	They Call Me Country/ Climbin' the Walls	1967	$15
TREY			
❑ 3016	It Hurts Me Too/Guess It's Love	1961	$30
WARNER BROS.			
❑ 5624	Houston/Hard Feelings	1965	$20
❑ 5473	She Taught Me/Just Blessin'	1964	$20

CLARK, STEVE

Number	Title	Yr	NM
MERCURY			
❑ 880234-7	A Place Out in the Country/ We're So Close	1984	$3
❑ 812922-7	It's Not the Fall/Breakin' Up's Supposed to Break Your Heart	1983	$4
❑ 818058-7	That It's All Over Feeling (All Over Again)/Margarita, You're No Lady	1984	$3

CLARKE, ALLAN

Number	Title	Yr	NM
ASYLUM			
❑ 45313	Light a Light/If You Think You Know How to Love Me	1976	$4
ATLANTIC			
❑ 3522	I'm Betting My Life on You/ Who's Goin' Out the Back Door	1978	$4
❑ 3497	I Wasn't Born Yesterday/The Man Who Manufactured Daydreams	1978	$4
❑ 3459	(I Will Be Your) Shadow in the Street/The Passenger	1978	$4
ELEKTRA			
❑ 46617	Slipstream/Imagination's Child	1979	$4
❑ 47019	The Only Ones/Driving the Doomsday Cars	1980	$4
EPIC			
❑ 5-10914	Baby It's Alright with Me/Ruby	1972	$4

CLARKE, STANLEY, AND GEORGE DUKE

Number	Title	Yr	NM
EPIC			
❑ 34-04322	Good Times/Great Danes	1984	$3
❑ 34-04155	Heroes/Atlanta	1983	$3
❑ 14-02397	I Just Want to Love You/ Finding My Way	1981	$3
❑ 19-01052	Sweet Baby/Never Judge a Cover By Its Book	1981	$3
❑ 14-02568	Touch and Go/Wild Dog	1981	$3

CLARKE, STANLEY

Number	Title	Yr	NM
EPIC			
❑ 34-04914	Born in the U.S.A./ Camp Americano	1985	$3
❑ 34-04485	Heaven Sent You/Speedball	1984	$3
❑ 34-06388	I'm Here to Stay/The Boys of Johnson Street	1986	$3
❑ 34-06591	Listen to the Beat of Your Heart/Where Do We Go	1986	$3
— With Angela Bofill			
❑ 14-03038	Straight to the Top/ The Force of Love	1982	$3
❑ 9-50890	We Supply/Underestimation	1980	$3
❑ 34-05584	What If I Should Fall in Love/Stereotypica	1985	$3
NEMPEROR			
❑ 009	Hot Fun/Life Is Just a Game	1976	$4
❑ 001	Lopsy Lu/Vulcan Princess	1974	$4
❑ 002	Silly Putty/Hello Jeff	1975	$4
❑ 7518	Slow Dance/Rock 'n' Roll Jelly	1978	$4
❑ 7523	Together Again (Part 1)/ Together Again (Part 2)	1980	$4
PORTRAIT			
❑ 37-08051	Funny How Time Flies (When You're Having Fun)/If This Bass Could Only Talk	1988	$4

Number	Title	Yr	NM

CLASH, THE
Also see JOE STRUMMER; BIG AUDIO DYNAMITE.

EPIC

Number	Title	Yr	NM
□ AE71178 [DJ]	Gates of the West/Groovy Times	1979	$8

— *Single included with original pressings of the LP "The Clash*

□ AE71178 [DJ]	Gates of the West/Groovy Times	1979	$8

— *Single included with original pressings of the LP "The Clash*

□ 19-51013	Hitsville U.K./Police on My Back	1981	$12
□ 9-50738	I Fought the Law/White Man in Hammersmith Palais	1979	$10
□ ENR-03571	Should I Stay Or Should I Go?/(B-side blank)	1983	$6

— *One-sided budget release*

□ 34-03547	Should I Stay Or Should I Go?/Cool Confusion	1983	$4
□ 34-03547 [PS]	Should I Stay Or Should I Go?/Cool Confusion	1983	$4
□ 14-03034	Should I Stay or Should I Go/First Night Back in London	1982	$8
□ 14-03061	Should I Stay or Should I Go/First Night Back in London	1982	$6
□ 14-03061 [PS]	Should I Stay or Should I Go/First Night Back in London	1982	$6
□ 14-03006	Should I Stay or Should I Go/Inoculated City	1982	$8
□ 19-02055	The Magnificent Seven/The Magnificent Dance	1981	$10
□ 9-50851	Train in Vain (Stand By Me)/London Calling	1980	$5
□ 15-03088	Train in Vain (Stand By Me)/London Calling	1982	$4

— *Reissue; originals have "Memory Lane" flower petals label (gray label $3 NM)*

CLASS-NOTES, THE
HAMILTON

□ 50011	Take It Back/Bessie's House	1959	$70

CLASSIC IV, THE
ALGONQUIN

□ 1650	Limbo Under The Christmas Tree/Early Christmas	1962	$40

TWIST

□ 1001	Island of Paradise/Heavenly Bliss	1962	$125

CLASSIC SULLIVANS, THE
KWANZA

□ 7678	I Don't Want to Lose You/Paint Yourself Into a Corner	1973	$30

CLASSICS IV
ATLANTA RHYTHM SECTION related.

ARLEN

□ 746	Don't Make Me Wait/It's Too Late	1964	$30

CAPITOL

□ 5710	Cry Baby/Pollyanna	1966	$20

— *As "The Classics"*

□ 5816	Little Darlin'/Nothing to Lose	1966	$20

IMPERIAL

□ 66393	Change of Heart/Rainy Day	1969	$6

— *Starting here, "Dennis Yost and the Classics IV*

□ 66378	Everyday With You Girl/Sentimental Lady	1969	$8
□ 66304	Mama's and Papa's/Waves	1968	$8
□ 66424	Midnight/The Comic	1969	$6
□ 66293	Soul Train/Strange Changes	1968	$8
□ 66259	Spooky/Poor People	1967	$8
□ 66328	Stormy/24 Hours of Loneliness	1968	$8
□ 66328	Stormy/Ladies' Man	1968	$30
□ 66439	The Funniest Thing/Nobody Loves You But Me	1970	$6
□ 66352	Traces/Mary, Mary Row Your Boat	1969	$8

LIBERTY

□ 56182	God Knows I Loved Her/We Miss You	1970	$6
□ 56200	Where Did All the Good Times Go/Ain't It the Truth	1970	$6

MGM

□ 14785	My First Day Without You/Lovin' Each Other	1975	$4

MGM SOUTH

□ 7020	I Knew It Would Happen/Love Me or Leave Me Alone	1973	$5
□ 7027	It's Now Winter's Day/Losing My Mind	1974	$5
□ 7016	Save the Sunlight/Make Me Believe It	1973	$5
□ 7002	What Am I Crying For/All in Your Mind	1972	$5

UNITED ARTISTS

□ 50805	Cherry Hill Park/Pick Up the Pieces	1971	$5
□ 50777	Most of All/It's Time for Love	1971	$5
□ 0125	Stormy/Spooky	1973	$4

— *Silver Spotlight Series" reissue*

□ 0126	Traces/Everyday with You Girl	1973	$4

— *Silver Spotlight Series" reissue*

Number	Title	Yr	NM

CLASSICS, THE (1)
DART

□ 1032	Angel Angela/Eenie Minie Mo	1961	$60
□ 1024	Life Is But a Dream, Sweetheart/That's the Way	1961	$200
□ 1015	So in Love/Cinderella	1960	$40

MERCURY

□ 71829	Life Is But a Dream, Sweetheart/That's the Way	1961	$30

MUSICNOTE

□ 118	P.S. I Love You/Wrap Your Troubles in Dreams	1963	$30
□ 1116	Till Then/Eenie Minie Mo	1963	$125

— *Gold vinyl*

□ 1116	Till Then/Eenie Minie Mo	1963	$200

— *Multi-color vinyl*

□ 1116	Till Then/Eenie Minie Mo	1963	$40

— *Black vinyl, blue label*

□ 1116	Till Then/Eenie Minie Mo	1963	$40

— *Black vinyl, yellow label*

MUSICTONE

□ 1114	So in Love/Cinderella	1963	$30
□ 6131	Too Young/Who's Laughing, Who's Crying	1964	$30

PICCOLO

□ 500	I Apologize/Love for Today	1965	$30

STREAM LINE

□ 1028	Life Is But a Dream, Sweetheart/Nuttin' in the Noggin	1961	$30

CLASSICS, THE (2)
STARR

□ 508	Close Your Eyes/Funny Things	1960	$200

— *Reissued on Alcar with Lou Christie's name prominently mentioned*

CLASSICS, THE (3)
JERDEN

□ 742	Till I Met You/It Didn't Take Much	1964	$40

CLASSICS, THE (U)
CLASS

□ 219	If Only the Sky Was a Mirror/Gosh, But This Is Love	1958	$75

CREST

□ 1063	Let Me Dream/You're the Prettiest One	1959	$100

PROMO

□ 1010	Blue Moon/Little Boy Lost	1961	$40

— *As "Herb Lance and the Classics"*

CLASSMATES, THE
HIT

□ 326	A Beautiful Morning/Lady Madonna	1968	$8

— *B-side by the Chords (2)*

□ 338	Classical Gas/People Got to Be Free	1968	$8
□ 345	Suzie-Q/Midnight Confessions	1968	$8

— *B-side by the Jalopy Five*

□ 335	The Look of Love/Turn Around, Look at Me	1968	$8

— *B-side by the Chords (2)*

□ 324	Tighten Up/Cowboys to Girls	1968	$8

— *B-side by the Fantastics*

CLAY, CASSIUS
COLUMBIA

□ 43007	Stand By Me/I Am the Greatest	1964	$30
□ 43007 [PS]	Stand By Me/I Am the Greatest	1964	$60
□ ZSP0 [DJ]	The Prediction/Will the Real Sonny Liston Please Fall Down	1964	$50
□ ZZSP75717/77185 [DJ]	The Prediction/Will the Real Sonny Liston Please Fall Down	1964	$50
□ ZSP75717/77185 [PS]	The Prediction/Will the Real Sonny Liston Please Fall Down	1964	$100

CLAY, CHRIS
VELTONE

□ 111	Santa Under Analysis Part 1/Santa Under Analysis Part 2	1960	$30

CLAY, JENNY
COLUMBIA

□ 4-43217	I Won the Battle (She Won the War)/True Confession	1965	$10
□ 4-43144	White and Red to Blue/Late Hours	1964	$10

Number	Title	Yr	NM

CLAY, JOE
VIK

□ 0211	Duck Tail/Sixteen Chicks	1956	$125
□ 0218	Get On the Right Track/Cracker Jack	1956	$125

CLAY, JUDY
ATLANTIC

□ 2669	Get Together/Sister Pitiful	1969	$6
□ 2697	Greatest Love/Saving All for You	1969	$6

EMBER

□ 1080	More Than You Know/I Thought I'd Gotten Over You	1961	$15
□ 1085	Stormy Weather/Do You Think That's Right	1962	$15

SCEPTER

□ 12157	He's the Kind of Guy/You Busted My Mind	1966	$8
□ 12218	I Want You/He's the Kind of Guy	1968	$8
□ 1281	Lonely People Do Foolish Things/I'm Comin' Home	1964	$8
□ 1273	My Arms Aren't Strong Enough/That's All	1964	$8
□ 12135	The Way You Look Tonight/Haven't You Got What It Takes	1966	$8

STAX

□ 0006	Bed of Roses/Remove the Clouds	1968	$6
□ 0020	It Ain't Long Enough/Give Love to Save Love	1969	$6

CLAY, OTIS
COTILLION

□ 44001	She's About a Mover/You Don't Miss Your Water	1968	$8

ECHO

□ 2002	Check It Out/Messing with My Mind	1975	$10
□ 2003	The Only Way Is Up/Special Kind of Love	1980	$120

GLADES

□ 1736	All I Need Is You/Special Kind of Soul	1976	$10

HI

□ 2206	Home Is Where the Heart Is/Brand New Thing	1972	$6
□ 2239	I Can't Make It Alone/I Didn't Know the Meaning of Pain	1973	$6
□ 2252	If I Could Reach Out/I Die a Little Bit Each Day	1973	$6
□ 2214	Precious Precious/Too Many Hands	1972	$6
□ 2266	Woman Don't Live Here No More/You Can't Escape the Hands of Love	1974	$6

KAYVETTE

□ 5130	All Because of Your Love/Today My World Fell	1977	$5
□ 5133	Let Me In/Sweet Woman's Love	1977	$5

ONE-DERFUL!

□ 4850	A Lasting Love/Got to Find a Way	1967	$8
□ 4852	Don't Pass Me By/That'll Get You What You Want	1968	$8
□ 4846	Flame in Your Heart/It's Easier Said, Than Done	1967	$8
□ 4837	I Paid the Price/Tired of Falling in (And Out of) Love	1966	$10
□ 4841	I Testify/I'm Satisfied	1966	$10
□ 4848	That's How It Is (When You're in Love)/Show Place	1967	$8
□ 4834	Three Is a Crowd/Flame in Your Heart	1965	$10

CLAY, TOM
BIG TOP

□ 3055	The Little Boy/That's All	1960	$30

CHANT

□ 103	Marry Me/(B-side unknown)	1959	$125

MOWEST

□ 5007	Whatever Happened to Love/Baby I Need Your Loving	1971	$4
□ 5002	What the World Needs Now Is Love/Abraham, Martin and John//The Victors	1971	$6

— *Mostly orange label*

□ 5002	What the World Needs Now Is Love/Abraham, Martin and John//The Victors	1971	$5

— *Blue and yellow label*

CLAYTON-THOMAS, DAVID
ATCO

□ 6347	Hey Hey Hey Hey/Walk That Walk	1965	$20

COLUMBIA

□ 45569	Sing a Song/We're All Meat from the Same Bone	1972	$5

DECCA

□ 32556	Say Boss Man/Done Somebody Wrong	1969	$10

EPIC

Number	Title	Yr	NM
❏ 34-03792	I Can't Blame a Broken Heart/ Some Hearts Get All the Breaks	1983	$4

RCA VICTOR

Number	Title	Yr	NM
❏ 74-0966	Hernando's Hideaway/ Harmony Junction	1973	$4
❏ APBO-0296	Take the Money and Run/ Anytime... Babe	1974	$4
❏ APBO-0078	Workin' on the Railroad/ Prof. Longhair	1973	$4

TOWER

Number	Title	Yr	NM
❏ 263	Born with the Blues/Brainwashed	1966	$15
❏ 206	Take Me Back/Out of the Sunshine	1966	$15

CLAYTON, LEE
MCA

Number	Title	Yr	NM
❏ 40151	Bottles of Booze/ Lonesome Whiskey	1973	$6

CLAYTON, MERRY
CAPITOL

Number	Title	Yr	NM
❏ 5164	Beg Me/La La Jace Song	1964	$12
❏ 4984	It's In His Kiss/The Magic of Romance	1963	$10
❏ 5243	This Is My Dream/The Knocks on the Door	1964	$10

MCA

Number	Title	Yr	NM
❏ 41195	Emotion/Let Me Make You Cry a Little Longer	1980	$4

ODE

Number	Title	Yr	NM
❏ 66018	After All This Time/Whatever	1971	$4
❏ 66007	Country Road/Forget It, I Got It	1970	$5
❏ 66003	Gimme Shelter/Good Girls	1970	$5
❏ 66011	Lift Every Voice and Sing/I Ain't Gonna Worry My Life Away	1970	$5
❏ 66030	Oh No, Not My Baby/ Suspicious Minds	1972	$4
❏ 66116	One More Ride/If I Lose	1976	$4
❏ 66024	Southern Man/Oh No, Not My Baby	1972	$4
❏ 66020	Steamroller/After All This Time	1971	$4
❏ 66108	The Acid Queen/ Eyesight to the Blind	1975	$4

—B-side by Richie Havens

| ❏ 66016 | The Times They Are a-Changing/ Wouldn't It Be Nice | 1971 | $40 |

—B-side by the Beach Boys

RCA

Number	Title	Yr	NM
❏ 8917-7-R	Almost Paradise/Hungry Eyes	1989	$3

—B-side with Eric Carmen

CLEAN LIVING
VANGUARD

Number	Title	Yr	NM
❏ 35171	Far North Again/Me and You	1973	$4
❏ 35162	In Heaven There Is No Beer/Backwoods Girl	1972	$5
❏ 35170	Old Time Music/Jenny Regardless	1973	$4

CLEAR LIGHT
ELEKTRA

Number	Title	Yr	NM
❏ 45622	She's Ready to Be Free/ Black Roses	1967	$15
❏ 45626	They Who Have Nothing/ Ballad of Freddie and Larry	1968	$15

CLEE-SHAYS, THE
TRIUMPH

Number	Title	Yr	NM
❏ 65	The Man from U.N.C.L.E./ Dynamite	1966	$30

CLEFS OF LAVENDER HILL, THE
DATE

Number	Title	Yr	NM
❏ 1567	Gimme One Good Reason/ Oh, Say My Love	1967	$30
❏ 1530	One More Time/So I'll Try	1966	$30
❏ 1533	Play with Fire/It Won't Be Long	1966	$30
❏ 1510	Stop! -- Get a Ticket/ First Tell Me Why	1966	$30

THAMES

Number	Title	Yr	NM
❏ 100	Stop! -- Get a Ticket/ First Tell Me Why	1966	$50

CLEFS, THE
CHESS

Number	Title	Yr	NM
❏ 1521	We Three/Ride On	1952	$400

CLEFTONES, THE
GEE

Number	Title	Yr	NM
❏ 1077	Again/Do You	1961	$30
❏ 1016	Can't We Be Sweethearts/ Niki-Hoeky	1956	$50
❏ 1074	Earth Angel/Blues in the Night	1961	$30
❏ 1064	Heart and Soul/How Do You Feel	1961	$30
❏ 1041	Hey Babe/What Did I Do That Was Wrong	1957	$50

Number	Title	Yr	NM
❏ 1080	How Deep Is the Ocean/ Some Kinda Blue	1962	$30
❏ 1067	(I Love You) For Sentimental Reasons/'Deed I Do	1961	$30
❏ 1011	Little Girl of Mine/You're Driving Me Mad	1956	$50
❏ 1048	Lover Boy/Beginners in Love	1958	$40
❏ 1079	Lover Come Back to Me/ There She Goes	1962	$30
❏ 1038	See You Next Year/ Ten Pairs of Shoes	1957	$50
❏ 1025	String Around My Heart/ Happy Memories	1956	$50
❏ 1031	Why You Do Me Like You Do/I Like Your Style of Making Love	1957	$50

OLD TOWN

Number	Title	Yr	NM
❏ 1011	The Masquerade Is Over/ My Dearest Darling	1955	$500

ROULETTE

Number	Title	Yr	NM
❏ 4161	Mish Mash Baby/Cuzin Casanova	1959	$30
❏ 4302	She's Gone/Shadows on the Very Last Row	1960	$30
❏ 4094	Trudy/She's So Fine	1958	$30

WARE

Number	Title	Yr	NM
❏ 6001	She's Forgotten You/ Right from the Git Go	1964	$20

CLEMENT, JACK
ELEKTRA

Number	Title	Yr	NM
❏ 45518	All I Want to Do in Life/It'll Be Her	1978	$4
❏ 45547	Gone Girl/There She Goes	1978	$4
❏ 45474	We Must Believe in Magic/ When I Dream	1978	$4

HALLWAY

Number	Title	Yr	NM
❏ 1796	Time After Time After Time/ My Voice Is Changing	1963	$20

JMI

Number	Title	Yr	NM
❏ 14	She Thinks I Still Care/Never Give a Heartache a Place to Go	1973	$6
❏ 20	Steal Away/(B-side unknown)	1973	$6
❏ 43	The One on the Right Is on the Left/Feet	1974	$6
❏ 10	The One on the Right Is the One on the Left/The Child That's in the Manger	1972	$6

RCA VICTOR

Number	Title	Yr	NM
❏ 47-7602	Whole Lotta Lookin'/Edge of Town	1959	$20

SUN

Number	Title	Yr	NM
❏ 291	Ten Years/Your Lover Boy	1958	$30
❏ 311	The Black Haired Man/Wrong	1958	$30

CLEMENTINO, CLAIRETTE
CAPITOL

Number	Title	Yr	NM
❏ 5081	Adonis/Bless My Soul	1963	$10
❏ 5003	Everywhere/See Me	1963	$10
❏ 5003 [PS]	Everywhere/See Me	1963	$20
❏ 5276	He Don't Want Your Love Anymore/Never Love a Wandering Boy	1964	$12
❏ 5177	Since I Fell in Love with You/ It's Happening to Me	1964	$10

CLEMENTS, BOOTS
WEST

Number	Title	Yr	NM
❏ 705	Back to You/(Instrumental)	1984	$6

—As "George Clements

❏ 711	Back to You/Morning Love	1985	$6
❏ 716	Ghost Riders in the Sky/ Ghost Rider's Symphony	1985	$6
❏ 718	I Can't Find Me/I Keep Thinkin' 'Bout You Everyday	1986	$6
❏ 709	Morning Love/(I Guess I'm) On the Road Again	1984	$6

—As "George Clements

| ❏ 715 | So Long Lady/My World's Just Made for You | 1985 | $6 |
| ❏ 719 | Sukiyaki "My First Lonely Night"/ The Other Side of Love | 1986 | $6 |

CLEMENTS, VASSAR
FLYING FISH

Number	Title	Yr	NM
❏ 4004	There'll Be No Teardrops Tonight/Move	1980	$6

MERCURY

Number	Title	Yr	NM
❏ 73748	Barnyard Boogie/Yakety Bow	1975	$5

SHIKATA

Number	Title	Yr	NM
❏ 10102	I Hear the South/(B-side unknown)	1988	$6

CLEMENTS, ZEKE
MGM

Number	Title	Yr	NM
❏ 11872	Christmas Star/It's Christmas Time	1954	$20

CLEMONS, CLARENCE
COLUMBIA

Number	Title	Yr	NM
❏ 38-04359	A Woman's Got the Power/ Summer on Signal Hill	1984	$5
❏ 38-05795	I Wanna Be Your Hero/ Summer on Signal Hill	1986	$4

CLEVELAND, JAMES (REV.)
SAVOY

Number	Title	Yr	NM
❏ 4322	Abide with Me/My Faith Looks Up to Thee	1969	$10
❏ 4276	Beautiful Garden of Prayer Pt. 1/Pt. 2	1967	$12
❏ 4166	Deep Down in My Heart/ What a Mighty God	1962	$20
❏ 4327	Father I Stretch My Hand to Thee/(B-side unknown)	1970	$10
❏ 4302	Free at Last/Somebody Knows	1969	$10
❏ 4318	God Is Enough/No Cross	1969	$10

— With the Angelic Choir

| ❏ 4285 | God Is Not Dead Pt. 1/Pt. 2 | 1968 | $10 |
| ❏ 4324 | Grace of God/Trouble Don't Last Always | 1969 | $10 |

— With the Angelic Choir

❏ 4141	He's Alright with Me/Just Like He Said He Would	1960	$20
❏ 4211	He's Always Doing Something Good for Me/I've Come a Long Ways	1964	$15
❏ 4321	He's a Miracle Worker (Part 1)/(Part 2)	1969	$12
❏ 4323	How Tedious and Tasteless (Part 1)/(Part 2)	1969	$10

— With the Cleveland Singers

| ❏ 4320 | I Can't Make It Without You/No Night There | 1969 | $10 |

— With Hular Gene Hurley

| ❏ 4316 | I Don't Need Nobody Else/ That's What I Like About Jesus | 1969 | $10 |

— With the Cleveland Singers

| ❏ 4319 | If I Had a Hammer/ Look Up and Live | 1969 | $10 |

— With the Cleveland Singers

❏ 4157	I Need Jesus on My Journey/Love of God	1961	$20
❏ 4256	I Stood on the Banks of Jordan Pt. 1/Pt. 2	1965	$15
❏ 4315	It All Belongs to My Father/ It's In My Heart	1969	$10
❏ 4252	It's Real/Down by the River	1965	$15
❏ 4290	Martin Luther King Memorial Pt. 1/Pt. 2	1968	$20

— With Rev. Lawrence Roberts

❏ 4154	Oh Lord, I'm Satisfied/There's a Brighter Day Somewhere	1961	$20
❏ 4317	Old Ship of Zion/Sweet Hour of Prayer	1969	$10
❏ 4217	Peace Be Still Pt. 1/Pt. 2	1964	$15

— With the Angelic Choir

| ❏ 4372 | Prayer (Part 1)/(Part 2) | 1979 | $12 |
| ❏ 4176 | Sit Down Servant/There Is No Failure in God | 1962 | $15 |

— With the Gospel Chimes

❏ 4192	The Sun Will Shine After Awhile/No Need to Worry	1963	$15
❏ 4230	Two Wings/That Will Be Good Enough for Me	1965	$15
❏ 4269	Without a Song/(B-side unknown)	1966	$10

CLICK, PAUL
BROKUN

Number	Title	Yr	NM
❏ 4709	Smokey, Trucks & C.B. Radio/(B-side unknown)	1976	$6

CLICKETTES, THE
CHECKER

Number	Title	Yr	NM
❏ 1060	I Just Can't Help It/(Instrumental)	1963	$30

DICE

Number	Title	Yr	NM
❏ 100	But Not for Me/I Love You I Swear	1960	$120
❏ 96/97	Lover's Prayer/Grateful	1959	$200

— With distribution by Memo Record Corp.

❏ 96/97	Lover's Prayer/Grateful	1959	$75
❏ 92/93	To Be a Part of You/Because of My Best Friend	1959	$120
❏ 94/95	Warm, Soft and Lovely/ Why Oh Why	1959	$120

GUYDEN

Number	Title	Yr	NM
❏ 2043	Where Is He/The Lone Lover	1960	$40

TUFF

Number	Title	Yr	NM
❏ 373	I Just Can't Help It/(Instrumental)	1964	$30

CLICKS, THE
JOSIE

Number	Title	Yr	NM
❏ 780	Come Back to Me/Peace and Commitment	1955	$300

CLIFF, BENNY
DRIFT

Number	Title	Yr	NM
❏ 1441	Shake Um Um Rock/ The Breaking Point	1959	$3000

—VG 1000; VG+ 2000

Number	Title	Yr	NM
CLIFF, JIMMY			
A&M			
❑ 1167	Come Into My Life/Viet Nam	1970	$8
❑ 1167 [PS]	Come Into My Life/Viet Nam	1970	$15
❑ 1270	Goodbye Yesterday/Let's Seize the Time	1971	$8
❑ 1146	Wonderful World, Beautiful People/Waterfall	1969	$8
❑ 1146 [PS]	Wonderful World, Beautiful People/Waterfall	1969	$15
COLUMBIA			
❑ 38-05716	American Sweet/Reggae Movement	1985	$4
❑ 38-06235	Club Paradise/Third World People	1986	$3
❑ 38-06235 [PS]	Club Paradise/Third World People	1986	$4
❑ 38-05396	Hot Shot/Modern World	1985	$4
❑ 38-07692	Love Me, Love Me/Sunshine in the Music	1988	$4
❑ 38-06135	Seven Day Weekend/Brightest Star	1986	$4
— A-side with Elvis Costello			
❑ 38-03216	Special/Peace Officer	1982	$4
❑ 38-04335	We All Are One/Roots Woman	1984	$4
MANGO			
❑ 7500	The Harder They Come/You Can Get It If You Really Want	1973	$8
MCA			
❑ 51094	Another Summer/It's the Beginning of the End	1981	$5
❑ 51043	I Am the Living/Love Again	1981	$5
❑ 51211	My Philosophy/Shelter of Your Love	1981	$4
REPRISE			
❑ 1177	Black Queen/Born to Win	1973	$6
❑ 1383	The Harder They Come/Viet Nam	1977	$10
VEEP			
❑ 1265	Aim and Ambition/Give and Take	1967	$20
❑ 1276	That's the Way Life Goes/Thank You	1968	$20
CLIFFORD, BUZZ			
CAPITOL			
❑ 5880	Bored to Tears/Swing in My Back Yard	1967	$10
COLUMBIA			
❑ 41876	Baby Sitter Boogie/Driftwood	1960	$30
❑ 41876	Baby Sittin' Boogie/Driftwood	1960	$30
❑ 41876 [PS]	Baby Sittin' Boogie/Driftwood	1960	$60
❑ 41876	Baby Sittin' Boogie/Driftwood	1972	$12
— Gray label			
❑ 41774	Blue Lagoon/Hello, Mr. Moonlight	1960	$30
❑ 41774 [PS]	Blue Lagoon/Mr. Moonlight	1960	$125
— Sleeve calls B-side "Mr. Moonlight"; may be promo only			
❑ 42290	Forever/Magic Circle	1962	$30
❑ 42290 [PS]	Forever/Magic Circle	1962	$60
❑ 42019	I'll Never Forget/The Awakening	1961	$60
❑ 42019 [PS]	I'll Never Forget/The Awakening	1961	$100
❑ 42177	Moving Day/Loneliness	1961	$30
❑ 42177 [PS]	Moving Day/Loneliness	1961	$60
❑ 41979	Three Little Fishes/Just Because	1961	$30
❑ 41979 [PS]	Three Little Fishes/Just Because	1961	$60
DOT			
❑ 17329	(Baby I Could Be) So Good At Loving You/Children Are Crying Aloud	1970	$6
❑ 17344	Procter and Gunther/I Am the River	1971	$6
CLIFFORD, DOUG			
FANTASY			
❑ 686	Latin Music/Take a Train	1972	$5
❑ 686 [PS]	Latin Music/Take a Train	1972	$6
CLIFFORD, MIKE			
AMERICAN INT'L.			
❑ 138	Broken Hearted Man/When Cindy When	1970	$5
❑ 158	Do Your Own Thing/You Better Start Singing Soon	1971	$5
CAMEO			
❑ 381	Before I Loved Her/Shirl Girl	1965	$12
❑ 395	Out in the Country/Courtin'	1966	$10
COLUMBIA			
❑ 41964	Look in Any Window/Uh Huh	1961	$15
❑ 42029	Pretty Little Girl in the Yellow Dress/At Last	1961	$15
❑ 41862	Stranger/Poor Little Girl	1960	$15
❑ 41862 [PS]	Stranger/Poor Little Girl	1960	$40
❑ 42226	When We Marry/Bombay	1961	$15
❑ 42226 [PS]	When We Marry/Bombay	1961	$30
LIBERTY			
❑ 55219	I Don't Know Why/I'm Afraid to Say I Love You	1959	$15
❑ 55207	Should I/Whisper Whisper	1959	$20
— With Patience and Prudence			
SIDEWALK			
❑ 939	Gas Hassle/Mary Jane	1968	$8

Number	Title	Yr	NM
❑ 917	Send Her Flowers/This Time, Time May Be Wrong	1967	$8
UNITED ARTISTS			
❑ 489	Close to Cathy/She's Just Another Girl	1962	$15
❑ 588	Danny's Dream/One Boy Too Late	1963	$12
❑ 794	Don't Make Her Cry/Barbara's Theme	1964	$12
❑ 614	Gee, I Don't Remember/Cotton Dresses	1963	$10
❑ 823	How to Murder Your Wife/Here's To My Lover	1965	$10
❑ 713	It Had Better Be Tonight/All the Colors of the Rainbow	1964	$10
❑ 763	See You in September/One By One, The Roses Died	1964	$10
❑ 557	What to Do with Laurie/That's What They Said	1963	$10
CLIMATES, THE			
HOLIDAY INN			
❑ 2206	Don't Be Cruel/Tell Him Tonite	1967	$15
CLIMAX			
CAROUSEL			
❑ 30050	Hard Rock Group/(B-side unknown)	1971	$5
❑ 30055	Precious and Few/Park Preserve	1971	$5
ROCKY ROAD			
❑ 30064	Caroline This Time/Rainbow Rides Are Free	1972	$4
❑ 30077	It's Gonna Get Better/(B-side unknown)	1974	$4
❑ 30061	Life and Breath/If It Feels Good, Do It	1972	$4
❑ 30055	Precious and Few/Park Preserve	1972	$4
— Reissue of Carousel 30055			
❑ 30074	Walking in the Georgia Rain/(B-side unknown)	1973	$4
CLIMAX BLUES BAND			
SIRE			
❑ 49012	Children of the Nightime/Long Distance Love	1979	$4
❑ 736	Couldn't Get It Right/Sav'ry Gravy	1977	$5
❑ 712	Goin' to New York/I Am Constant	1974	$6
❑ 358	Hey Mama/That's All	1972	$8
❑ 1026	Makin' Love/Gospel Singer	1978	$4
❑ 1031	Mistress Moonshine/Teardrops	1978	$4
❑ 713	Sense of Direction/Losin' the Humbles	1974	$6
❑ 705	Shake Your Love/Mule on the Dole	1973	$8
❑ 49098	Summer Rain/Money in Your Pocket	1979	$4
❑ 747	Together and Free/Berlin Blues	1977	$4
WARNER BROS.			
❑ 50018	Breakdown/Shake It Lucy	1982	$4
❑ 49850	Darlin'/This Time the Singer	1981	$4
❑ 49605	Gotta Have More Love/One for Me and You	1980	$4
❑ 49669	I Love You/Horizontalized	1981	$5
CLIMBERS, THE			
J&S			
❑ 1658	I Love You/Train, Car, Boat or Plane	1957	$800
❑ 1652/3	My Darlin' Dear/Angels in Heaven Know I Love You	1957	$125
CLINE, PATSY			
❑ 1033	Life's Railway to Heaven/If I Could See the World	1978	$5
CORAL			
❑ 61464	A Church, a Courtroom, Then Goodbye/Honky Tonk Merry-Go-Round	1955	$40
❑ 61583	I Love You Honey/Come Right In	1956	$30
❑ 61523	Turn the Cards Slowly/Hidin' Out	1955	$40
❑ 30659	Come On In/Let the Teardrops Fall	1958	$20
❑ 7-34132 [S]	Crazy/Seven Lonely Days	1962	$30
❑ 31317	Crazy/Who Can I Count On	1961	$15
❑ 30794	Dear God/He Will Do for You	1958	$20
❑ 31522	Faded Love/Blue Moon of Kentucky	1963	$10
❑ 7-34130 [S]	Foolin' 'Round/The Wayward Wind	1962	$30
❑ 30929	Got a Lot of Rhythm in My Soul/I'm Blue Again	1959	$30
❑ 31429	Heartaches/Why Can't He Be You	1962	$15
❑ 31671	He Called Me Baby/Bill Bailey Won't You Please Come Home	1964	$12
❑ 30504	I Don't Wanta/Then You'll Know	1957	$20
❑ 31205	I Fall to Pieces/Lovin' in Vain	1961	$15
❑ 25686	I Love You So Much It Hurts/Seven Lonely Days	1966	$15
❑ 31455	Leavin' On Your Mind/Tra Le La Le La Triangle	1963	$12
❑ 31455 [PS]	Leavin' On Your Mind/Tra Le La Le La Triangle	1963	$30
❑ 25699	Lonely Street/You Were Only Fooling (While I Was Falling in Love)	1966	$15
❑ 31616	Love Letters in the Sand/That's How a Heartache Begins	1964	$10

Number	Title	Yr	NM
❑ 31061	Lovesick Blues/How Can I Face Tomorrow	1960	$15
❑ 7-34133	San Antonio Rose/True Love	1962	$30
— The above four are 33 1/3, small hole jukebox singles			
❑ 31354	She's Got You/Strange	1962	$15
❑ 25694	Shoes/Half As Much	1966	$15
❑ 7-34131 [S]	South of the Border (Down Mexico Way)/I Love You So Much It Hurts	1962	$30
❑ 25673	South of the Border/San Antonio Rose	1965	$15
❑ 31406	So Wrong/You're Stronger Than Me	1962	$15
❑ 29963	Stop, Look and Listen/I've Loved and Lost Again	1956	$30
❑ 30542	Stop the World/Walking Dream	1958	$20
❑ 31483	Sweet Dreams (Of You)/Back in Baby's Arms	1963	$10
❑ 25707	That's My Desire/Foolin' 'Round	1967	$15
❑ 31128	There He Goes/Crazy Dream	1960	$15
❑ 30406	Three Cigarettes in an Ashtray/Stranger in My Arms	1957	$20
❑ 30339	Try Again/Today, Tomorrow and Forever	1957	$20
❑ 9-30221	Walkin' After Midnight/A Poor Man's Roses (Or a Rich Man's Gold)	1957	$30
— Black label, star under "Decca			
❑ 9-30221 [PS]	Walkin' After Midnight/A Poor Man's Roses (Or a Rich Man's Gold)	1957	$100
❑ 9-30221	Walkin' After Midnight/A Poor Man's Roses (Or a Rich Man's Gold)	1957	$40
— Black label, lines on either side of "Decca			
❑ 31377	When I Get Thru with You (You'll Love Me Too)/Imagine That	1962	$15
❑ 31377 [PS]	When I Get Thru with You (You'll Love Me Too)/Imagine That	1962	$30
❑ 31552	When You Need a Laugh/I'll Sail My Ship Alone	1963	$10
EVEREST			
❑ 2060	Crazy Dream/There He Goes	1965	$12
❑ 2052	Got a Lot of Rhythm (In My Soul)/Love Me, Love Me, Honey Do	1964	$10
❑ 2031	I Can See an Angel/Just Out of Reach	1963	$15
❑ 20005	I Don't Wanta/I Can't Forget	1962	$20
❑ 2045	In Care of the Blues/If I Could See the World (Through the Eyes of a Child)	1964	$10
❑ 2039	I've Loved and Lost Again/I Love You Honey	1964	$10
❑ 2011	Then You'll Know/Hungry for Love	1963	$15
❑ 2020	Walking After Midnight/That Wonderful Someone	1963	$15
MCA			
❑ 41303	Always/I Sail My Ship Alone	1980	$4
❑ 60063	Crazy/Your Cheatin' Heart	1973	$5
— Reissue; black label with rainbow			
❑ 60063	Crazy/Your Cheatin' Heart	1980	$3
— Reissue; blue label with rainbow			
❑ 60062	I Fall to Pieces/He Called Me Baby	1973	$5
— Reissue; black label with rainbow			
❑ 51038	I Fall to Pieces/True Love	1980	$4
❑ 60102	Pick Me Up on Your Way Down/Crazy Arms	1973	$5
— Reissue; black label with rainbow			
❑ 52052	So Wrong/I Fall to Pieces	1982	$3
— A-side: With Jim Reeves (electronically created duet)			
❑ 52684	Sweet Dreams/Blue Moon of Kentucky	1985	$3
❑ 60061	Walkin' After Midnight/South of the Border (Down Mexico Way)	1973	$5
— Reissue; black label with rainbow			
RCA			
❑ PB-12346	Have You Ever Been Lonely (Have You Ever Been Blue)/Welcome to My World	1981	$3
— With Jim Reeves (electronically created duet)			
STARDAY			
❑ 7030	Walking After Midnight/Lovesick Blues	1965	$10
❑ 8024	Walking After Midnight/Lovesick Blues	1971	$6
7-Inch Extended Plays			
4 STAR			
❑ EP-41 [DJ]	Cry Not for Me/Yes, I Understand//Am I That Easy to Forget/Such Is Life	1959	$50
— B-side by Carl Belew; sometimes said to be on the "Patsy Cline" label, but it is a 4 Star promo-only item; not issued with cover?			
❑ EP-43 [DJ]	How Can I Face Tomorrow/A Church, a Courtroom, Then Goodbye//That's What I Get for Loving You/My Baby's Not Here (In Town Tonight)	1959	$50
— B-side by Carl Belew; sometimes said to be on the "Patsy Cline" label, but it is a 4 Star promo-only item; not issued with cover?			

Number	Title	Yr	NM
CORAL			
❏ EC81159	*Honky Tonk Merry-Go-Round/A Church, a Courtroom, and Then Goodbye/Turn the Cards Slowly/Hidin' Out	1958	$30
❏ EC81159 [PS]	Songs by Patsy Cline	1958	$35
DECCA			
❏ ED2703	*I Fall to Pieces/Lovin' in Vain/Lovesick Blues/There He Goes	1961	$20
❏ ED2757	*Leavin' on Your Mind/Tra Le La Le La Triangle/Half As Much/Lonely Street	1963	$20
❏ ED2719	*She's Got You/Strange/The Wayward Wind/I Love You So Much It Hurts	1962	$20
❏ ED2794	(contents unknown)	1965	$20
❏ ED2802	(contents unknown)	1965	$20
❏ ED2707	Crazy/Foolin' Around/Who Can I Count On/South of the Border	1961	$20
❏ ED2759 [PS]	Dear God	1963	$20
❏ ED2768 [PS]	How Can I Face Tomorrow	1964	$20
❏ ED2768	I'm Blue Again/How Can I Face Tomorrow//I'm Moving Along/Love Love Love Me Honey Do	1964	$20
❏ ED2757 [PS]	Leavin' on Your Mind	1963	$20
❏ ED2802 [PS]	Love Letters in the Sand	1965	$20
❏ ED2542 [PS]	Patsy Cline	1958	$25
❏ ED2703 [PS]	Patsy Cline	1961	$20
❏ ED2707 [PS]	Patsy Cline	1961	$20
❏ ED2729 [PS]	Patsy Cline	1962	$20
❏ ED2794 [PS]	Portrait of Patsy Cline	1965	$20
❏ ED2719 [PS]	She's Got You	1962	$20
❏ ED2770 [PS]	Someday You'll Want Me to Want You	1964	$20
❏ ED2770	Someday You'll Want Me to Want You/Faded Love//When You Need a Laugh/I'll Sail My Ship Alone	1964	$20
❏ ED2729	So Wrong/You're Stronger Than Me//Heartaches/Your Cheatin' Heart	1962	$20
❏ ED2542	That Wonderful Someone/Three Cigarettes (In an Ashtray)//Hungry for Love/Fingerprints	1958	$25

CLINTON, GEORGE

Number	Title	Yr	NM
CAPITOL			
❏ B-5201	Atomic Dog/(Instrumental)	1983	$4
❏ B-5201 [PS]	Atomic Dog/(Instrumental)	1983	$6
❏ B-5504	Bullet Proof/Silly Millimeter	1985	$4
❏ B-5558	Do Fries Go With That Shake!/Pleasure of Exhaustion (Do It Till I Drop)	1986	$4
❏ B-5473	Double Oh-Oh/Bangladesh	1985	$4
❏ B-5473 [PS]	Double Oh-Oh/Bangladesh	1985	$4
❏ B-5222	Get Dressed/Free Alterations	1983	$4
❏ B-5222 [PS]	Get Dressed/Free Alterations	1983	$4
❏ B-5602	Hey Good Lookin' (Remix)/Hey Good Lookin' (Mirror Mix)	1986	$4
❏ B-5332	Last Dance/Get Dressed	1984	$4
❏ B-5332 [PS]	Last Dance/Get Dressed	1984	$4
❏ B-5160	Loopzilla/Pot Sharing Tots	1982	$4
PAISLEY PARK			
❏ 22790	Tweakin'/French Kiss	1989	$4
❏ 27557	Why Should I Dog U Out?/(Instrumental)	1989	$3
❏ 27557 [PS]	Why Should I Dog U Out?/(Instrumental)	1989	$3
❏ PRO-S-3438 [DJ]	Why Should I Dog U Out? (same on both sides?)	1989	$6

CLINTONIAN CUBS, THE

Number	Title	Yr	NM
MY BROTHERS			
❏ 508	She's Just My Size/Confusion	1960	$300

CLIQUE, THE (1)

Number	Title	Yr	NM
CINEMA			
❏ 01	Stay By Me/Splash One	1967	$40
SCEPTER			
❏ 12212	Gotta Get Away/Love Ain't Easy	1967	$30
❏ 12202	Stay By Me/Splash One	1967	$30
WHITE WHALE			
❏ 338	I'm Alive/Sparkle and Shine	1970	$10
❏ 361	Memphis/Southbound Wind	1970	$10
❏ 333	Soul Mate/I'll Hold Out My Hand	1969	$12
❏ 323	Sugar on Sunday/Superman	1969	$20
❏ 312	Superman/Shadow of Your Love	1969	$15

CLIQUE, THE (2)

Number	Title	Yr	NM
ABC-PARAMOUNT			
❏ 10655	She Ain't No Good/Time, Time, Time	1965	$10

CLIQUE, THE (U)

Number	Title	Yr	NM
LAURIE			
❏ 3365	Sun Come Up/Drifter's Melody	1966	$10

CLIQUES, THE

Number	Title	Yr	NM
MODERN			
❏ 987	Girl in My Dreams/I Wanna Know Why	1956	$60
—Blue label			
❏ 987	Girl in My Dreams/I Wanna Know Why	1956	$40
—Black label			
❏ 995	My Desire/I'm in Love with a Gal	1956	$40

CLODFELTER, AMY

Number	Title	Yr	NM
WINSTON			
❏ 1011	Christmas Time/Santa Claus	1957	$20

CLOONEY, ROSEMARY, AND JIMMY BOYD

Number	Title	Yr	NM
COLUMBIA			
❏ 4-39988	Dennis the Menace/Little Josey	1953	$30

CLOONEY, ROSEMARY

Number	Title	Yr	NM
COLUMBIA			
❏ 40625	A Fine Romance/Goodbye	1955	$15
—With Benny Goodman			
❏ 40498	A Touch of the Blues/Love Among the Young	1955	$15
❏ 40159	Bad News/A Dime and a Dollar	1954	$15
—With Guy Mitchell			
❏ 39212	Beautiful Brown Eyes/Shot Gun Boogie	1951	$20
❏ 39631	Be My Life's Companion/Why Don't You	1952	$20
❏ 40031	Blues in the Night/Tenderly	1953	$15
❏ 39813	Blues in the Night/Who Kissed Me Last Night	1952	$20
❏ 39767	Botch-a-Me (Ba-Ba-Baciami Piccina)/On the First Warm Day	1952	$20
❏ 40434	Brahms' Lullaby/Where Will the Dimple Be	1955	$15
❏ 40160	Brave Man/Meet a Happy Guy	1954	$15
—With Guy Mitchell			
❏ 40187	Brave Man/Tomorrow I'll Dream and Remember	1954	$20
❏ 39141	Cherry Pies/Love Means Love	1951	$20
❏ 38988	C-H-R-I-S-T-M-A-S/Bless This House	1950	$30
❏ 40102	C-H-R-I-S-T-M-A-S/Happy Christmas, Little Friend	1953	$20
❏ 40981	Colors/That's How It Is	1957	$15
❏ 50007	Come On-a My House/(B-side unknown)	1954	$10
—Early "Hall of Fame Series" issue			
❏ 39467	Come On-a My House/Rose of the Mountain	1951	$20
❏ 40774	Come Rain or Come Shine/It's a Nuisance Having You Around	1956	$15
❏ 40370	Count Your Blessings Instead of Sheep/White Christmas	1954	$20
❏ 40812	(Don't That Take the) Rag Offen the Bush/Love Is a Feeling	1956	$15
❏ 39980	Dot's Nice -- Donna Fight/It's the Same	1953	$20
—With Marlene Dietrich			
❏ 39591	Find Me/I Only Saw Him Once	1951	$15
❏ 4-21423	Go On By/I Whsiper Your Name	1955	$30
❏ 39710	Half As Much/Poor Whippoorwill	1952	$20
❏ 40808	He'll Be Comin' Down the Chimney/Mommy Can I Keep the Kitten	1956	$15
—With "Her Sister Gail"			
❏ 40723	Hello, Young Lovers/Peachy, Peachy	1956	$15
❏ 40266	Hey There/This Ole House	1954	$20
❏ B-319 [PS]	Hollywood's Best	1952	$15
—Box for records 39852-39855			
❏ 40676	I Could Have Danced All Night/I've Grown Accustomed to Your Face	1956	$15
❏ 39892	If I Had a Penny/You're After My Own Heart	1952	$20
❏ 39535	I'm Waiting Just for You/If Teardrops Were Pennies	1951	$20
❏ 39185	I Still Feel the Same/When Apples Grow on Cherry Trees	1951	$20
❏ 39854	It Might As Well Be Spring/The Continental	1952	$15
—Sides 3 and 6 of B-319			
❏ 40496	It Might As Well Be Spring/When You Wish Upon a Star	1955	$15
❏ 39536	I Wish I Wuz/Mixed Emotions	1951	$20
❏ 40317	(Let's Give) A Christmas Present to Santa Claus/March of the Christmas Toys	1954	$20
—With Jose Ferrer			
❏ 40358	Love, You Didn't Do Right By Me/Gee, I Wish I Was Back in the Army	1954	$15
❏ 39943	Lovely Weather for Ducks/Haven't Got a Worry	1953	$20
❏ 40361	Mambo Italiano/We'll Be Together Again	1954	$20
❏ 40356	Mandy/The Best Things Happen While Dancing	1954	$15
❏ 40835	Mangos/Independent (On My Own)	1957	$15
❏ 40144	Man (Uh-Huh)/Woman (Uh-Huh)	1953	$20
—B-side by Jose Ferrer			
❏ 40616	Memories of You/It's Bad for Me	1955	$15
—With Benny Goodman			
❏ 39333	Mixed Emotions/Kentucky Waltz	1951	$20
❏ 40407	Mr. and Mrs./Marry the Man	1955	$15
—With Jose Ferrer			
❏ 40142	My Baby Rocks Me/When You Love Someone	1953	$20
❏ 39853	On the Atchison, Topeka and the Santa Fe/When You Wish Upon a Star	1952	$15
—Sides 2 and 7 of B-319			
❏ 39855	Over the Rainbow/Sweet Leilani	1952	$15
—Sides 4 and 5 of B-319			
❏ 40579	Pet Me, Poppa/Wake Me	1955	$15
❏ 40534	Sailor Boy Have Talk to Me in English/Go On By	1954	$15
❏ 39158	Sentimental Music/The Face	1951	$20
❏ 40917	Sing Little Birdie Sing/Who Dot Mon, Mon	1957	$15
❏ 40305	Sisters/Love, You Didn't Do Right by Me	1954	$20
—A-side by Betty Clooney			
❏ 40357	Sisters/Snow	1954	$15
—A-side with Betty Clooney			
❏ 40701	Sophisticated Lady/Grievin'	1956	$15
❏ 40024	Stick with Me/Cheegah, Choonem	1953	$20
❏ 39612	Suzy Snowflake/Little Red Riding Hood's Christmas	1951	$20
❏ 4-123 [PS]	Suzy Snowflake/Little Red Riding Hood's Christmas	1951	$30
❏ 4-123	Suzy Snowflake/Little Red Riding Hood's Christmas	1951	$20
—Yellow-label Children's Series record; alternate number is 90137			
❏ 39730	Tenderly/Be Anything (But Be Mine)	1952	$15
—B-side by Champ Butler; part of a various artists 4-record box set			
❏ 39648	Tenderly/Did Anyone Call	1952	$20
❏ 39054	The Place Where I Worship/House of Singing Bamboo	1950	$20
❏ 40161	This Is Greater Than I Thought/Good Intentions	1954	$15
—With Joanne Gilbert			
❏ 41053	Tonight/Love and Affection	1957	$15
❏ 39812	Too Old to Cut the Mustard/Good for Nothing	1952	$20
—A-side with Marlene Dietrich			
❏ 39931	What Would You Do/I Laughed Until I Cried	1953	$20
❏ 40003	When I See You/It Just Happened to Happen to Me	1953	$20
❏ 40355	White Christmas/Count Your Blessings	1954	$15
❏ 4-175 [PS]	Winter Wonderland/Christmas Song	1954	$30
❏ 4-175	Winter Wonderland/Christmas Song	1954	$20
—Yellow-label Children's Series record			
CORAL			
❏ 62137	A Touch of the Blues/I Wish I Were in Love Again	1959	$10
DOT			
❏ 17100	One Less Bell to Answer/Let Me Down Easy	1968	$6
GIBSON MUSICARDS			
❏ 100G 27104 [PS]	Happy Birthday, Dear Mother	1955	$30
—7x7 card that comes with GIB-6... Others are likely to exist, but we haven't documented them yet.			
❏ GIB-6	Happy Birthday, Dear Mother/(B-side blank)	1955	$30
MGM			
❏ 12655	Hey, Madame/You're So Right for Me	1958	$12
—With Jose Ferrer			
❏ 13349	I'm Glad It's You/Love and Learn	1965	$6
❏ 12705	It's a Boy/The Loudenboomer Bird	1958	$10
❏ 12823	I Wonder/For You	1959	$10
❏ 12760	Love Eyes/Flattery	1959	$10
❏ 12654	Morning Music of Montmartre/Give It All You Got	1958	$10
—With Jose Ferrer			
RCA VICTOR			
❏ 47-7806	Danke Schoen/Swing Me	1960	$12
❏ 47-7948	Give Myself a Party/If I Can Stay Away Long Enough	1961	$10
❏ 47-7819	Hey Look Me Over/What Takes My Fancy	1960	$12
❏ 47-7754	Many a Wonderful Moment/Vaya Vaya	1960	$10
❏ 47-7754 [PS]	Many a Wonderful Moment/Vaya Vaya	1960	$20
❏ 47-7887	Theme from Return to Peyton Place/Without Love	1961	$10
❏ 47-7707	Watermelon Heart/Summertime Love	1960	$10
—With Perez Prado			

Number	Title	Yr	NM

REPRISE

Number	Title	Yr	NM
❏ 0327	A Spoonful of Sugar/Stay Awake	1964	$8
❏ 20222	Helo Faithless/A Hundred Years from Today	1963	$8
❏ 20145	I Will Follow Him (Chariot)/The Rose and the Butterfly	1963	$8
❏ 20173	Mixed Emotions/The Prisoner's Song	1963	$8
❏ 20173	The Prisoner's Song/Mixed Emotions	1963	$8

UNITED ARTISTS

❏ 50076	I Need a Broken Heart (Like a Hole in the Head)/'Round and 'Round	1966	$8

7-Inch Extended Plays

COLUMBIA

❏ B-2550	*Be My Life's Companion/Blame It on My Youth/Blues in the Night/Why Fight the Feeling?	1958	$15
❏ B-2524	*Come On-a My House/Mixed Emotions/Mambo Italiano/Tenderly	1957	$15
❏ B-2525	*Hey There/Botch-A-Me/Half as Much/This Ole House	1957	$15
❏ B-10062	(contents unknown)	1957	$15
❏ B-10063	(contents unknown)	1957	$15
❏ B-10061	What Is There to Say?/Don't Ya Go 'Way Mad//How About You/Together	1957	$15
❏ B-1895 [PS]	While We're Young	1954	$15
❏ B-1895	While We're Young/Too Young//Hello, Young Lovers/Young at Heart	1954	$15

CLOVERS, THE

ATLANTIC

❏ 1118	A Lonely Fool/Baby, Baby, Oh My Darling	1956	$40
❏ 1052	Blue Velvet/If You Love Me (Why Don't You Tell Me So)	1955	$70
❏ 1010	Comin' On/The Feeling Is So Good	1953	$200
❏ 1083	Devil or Angel/Hey, Doll Baby	1956	$200

— *Yellow label, no "fan" logo*

❏ 1083	Devil or Angel/Hey, Doll Baby	1956	$50

— *Red label, no "fan" logo*

❏ 1083	Devil or Angel/Hey, Doll Baby	1956	$4000

— *Red label, no "fan" logo; red vinyl; value is conjecture. VG 2000; VG+ 3000*

❏ 934	Don't You Know I Love You/Skylark	1951	$1000
❏ 2129	Drive It Home/The Bootie Green	1961	$30
❏ 944	Fool, Fool, Fool/Needless	1951	$250
❏ 1107	From the Bottom of My Heart/Bring Me Love	1956	$40
❏ 1000	Good Lovin'/Here Goes a Fool	1953	$100
❏ 1129	Here Comes Romance/You Good-Looking Woman	1957	$40
❏ 1046	I Confess/Alrighty, Oh Sweetie	1954	$60
❏ 1139	I-I-I Love You/So Young	1957	$40
❏ 977	I Played the Fool/Hey, Miss Fannie	1952	$250
❏ 1094	Love, Love, Love/Your Tender Lips	1956	$50
❏ 1060	Love Bug/In the Morning Time	1955	$60
❏ 1022	Lovey Dovey/Little Mama	1954	$60
❏ 963	One Mint Julep/Middle of the Night	1952	$125

— *Yellow label, no "fan" logo*

❏ 963	One Mint Julep/Middle of the Night	1961	$30

— *Red label, no "fan" logo*

❏ 1152	There's No Tomorrow/Down in the Alley	1957	$40
❏ 969	Ting-A-Ling/Wonder Where My Baby's Gone	1952	$125
❏ 1175	Wishing for Your Love/All About You	1958	$40

BRUNSWICK

❏ 55249	Love! Love! Love!/The Kickapoo	1963	$15

JOSIE

❏ 992	For Days/Too Long Without Some Loving	1968	$10
❏ 997	Try My Lovin' On You/Sweet Side of a Soulful Woman	1968	$10

POPLAR

❏ 111	The Good Old Summertime/Idaho	1958	$30
❏ 110	The Gossip Wheel/Please Come On to Me	1958	$30

PORT

❏ 3004	Poor Baby/He Sure Could Hypnotize	1965	$12

PORWIN

❏ 1004	It's All in the Game/That's What I Will Be	1963	$20

— *As "Buddy Bailey and the Clovers*

❏ 1001/2	Stop Pretending/One More Time	1963	$20

— *As "Buddy Bailey and the Clovers*

STENTON

❏ 7001	Please Mr. Sun/Gimme, Gimme, Gimme	1961	$100

— *As "Tippie and the Clovermen*

TIGER

❏ 201	Bossa Nova Baby/The Bossa Nova (My Heart Said)	1962	$20

— *As "Tippie and the Clovers*

UNITED ARTISTS

❏ 227	Easy Lovin'/I'm Confessin' That I Love You	1960	$30
❏ 180	Love Potion #9/Stay Awhile	1959	$30
❏ 0133	Love Potion #9/Stay Awhile	1973	$4

— *Silver Spotlight Series" reissue*

❏ 209	One Mint Julep/Lovey	1960	$30
❏ 307	The Honeydripper/Have Gun	1961	$30

WINLEY

❏ 265	I Need You Now/Gotta Quit You	1962	$20
❏ 255	Let Me Hold You/Wrapped Up in a Dream	1961	$20
❏ 265	They're Rockin' Down the Street/Be My Baby	1962	$20

— *As "The Fabulous Clovers*

7-Inch Extended Plays

ATLANTIC

❏ 590	*Love, Love, Love/Devil or Angel/Blue Velvet/From the Bottom of My Heart (contents unknown)	1955	$175
❏ 537		1954	$175
❏ 504	One Mint Julep/Fool, Fool, Fool/Hey, Miss Fannie/I Played the Fool	1953	$250
❏ 590 [PS]	The Clovers	1955	$250
❏ 504 [PS]	The Clovers Sing	1953	$250
❏ 537 [PS]	The Clovers Sing	1954	$250

CLOWER, JERRY

DECCA

❏ 32899	A Bully Has Done Flung a Cravin' On Me/The Chauffeur and the Professor	1971	$6
❏ 32844	Coon Huntin' City/Marcel's Talking Chainsaw/Homecomin' Steaks	1971	$6

MCA

❏ 40423	Bird Huntin' at Uncle Versies/Coon Huntin' Monkey	1975	$6
❏ 40077	I'm That Country//Marcel Says No School Today/Marcel Wins a Bet/Three Footballs and the Game Ain't Fair	1973	$6
❏ 40774	Steel Marbles/Tar Baby-New Gene and the Lion	1977	$5
❏ 41261	The Ike and Mike Contest/Udell and Ole Skeets	1980	$5
❏ 40599	Wanna Buy a Possum/The House I Live In	1976	$5

CLUB NOUVEAU

WARNER BROS.

❏ 7-27774	Envious (Watcha Back Edit)/(B-side unknown)	1988	$4
❏ 7-27852	For the Love of Frances/What's Going 'Round?	1988	$3
❏ 7-27852 [PS]	For the Love of Frances/What's Going 'Round?	1988	$3
❏ 7-27974	Heavy on My Mind/Let Me Go	1987	$4
❏ 7-28101	It's a Cold, Cold World/Listen to the Message	1987	$4
❏ 7-28430	Lean On Me/Pump It Up	1987	$4
❏ 7-28268	Let Me Go/Promises, Promises	1987	$5
❏ 7-28494	Situation #9/Pump It Up	1987	$4
❏ 7-28360	Why You Treat Me So Bad/(Edit Version)	1987	$4

CLUSTERS, THE

END

❏ 1115	Pardon My Heart/Darling Can't You Tell	1962	$50

EPIC

❏ 9330	Forecast of Our Love/Long Legged Maggie	1959	$100

TEE GEE

❏ 102	Pardon My Heart/Darling Can't You Tell	1958	$300

— *No mention of Gone distribution*

❏ 102	Pardon My Heart/Darling Can't You Tell	1958	$300

— *With Gone distribution mentioned; publishing by Emkay Music*

❏ 102	Pardon My Heart/Darling Can't You Tell	1958	$120

— *With Gone distribution mentioned; publishing by Real Gone Music*

COASTERS, THE

AMERICAN INT'L.

❏ 1122	If I Had a Hammer/If I Had a Hammer (Disco Version)	1976	$5

— *As "The World Famous Coasters*

ATCO

❏ 6141	Along Came Jones/That Is Rock and Roll	1959	$30
❏ 6210	Bad Blood/(Ain't That) Just Like Me	1961	$30
❏ 6379	Bell Bottom Slacks and a Chinese Kimono (She's My Little Spodee-O)/Crazy Baby	1965	$30
❏ 6163	Besame Mucho (Part 1)/Besame Mucho (Part 2)	1960	$30
❏ 6132 [M]	Charlie Brown/Three Cool Cats	1959	$30
SD-45-6132 [S]	Charlie Brown/Three Cool Cats	1959	$70

— *Blue label, silver print, "Stereo" under the "O" of "Atco*

❏ 6111	Dance!/Gee, Golly	1958	$50
❏ 6064	Down in Mexico/Turtle Dovin'	1956	$100
❏ 6204	Girls, Girls, Girls (Part 1)/Girls, Girls, Girls (Part 2)	1961	$30
❏ 6341	Hungry/Lady Like	1965	$20
❏ 6098	Idol with the Golden Head/(When She Wants Good Lovin') My Baby Comes to Me	1957	$50
❏ 6192	Little Egypt (Ying-Yang)/Keep On Rolling	1961	$30
❏ 6300	Lovey Dovey/Bad Detective	1964	$20
❏ 6356	Money Honey/Let's Go Get Stoned	1965	$20
❏ 6073	One Kiss Led to Another/Brazil	1956	$70
❏ 6146	Poison Ivy/I'm a Hog for You	1959	$30
❏ 6407	Saturday Night Fish Fry/She's a Yum Yum	1966	$20
❏ 6087	Searchin'/Young Blood	1957	$75

— *Maroon label (first pressing)*

❏ 6087	Searchin'/Young Blood	1957	$30

— *White and yellow label*

❏ 6178	Shoppin' for Clothes/The Snake and the Book Worm	1960	$30
❏ 6287	Speedo's Back in Town/T'Ain't Nothin' to Me	1964	$20
❏ 6104	Sweet Georgia Brown/What Is the Secret of Your Success	1957	$50
❏ 6219	Teach Me How to Shimmy/Ridin' Hood	1962	$30
❏ 6234	The Climb/(Instrumental)	1962	$30
❏ 6251	The P.T.A./Bull Tick Waltz	1962	$30
❏ 6126	The Shadow Knows/Sorry But I'm Gonna Have to Pass	1958	$30
❏ 6186	Thumbin' a Ride/Wait a Minute	1961	$30
❏ 6168	Wake Me, Shake Me/Stewball	1960	$30
❏ 6321	Wild One/I Must Be Dreaming	1964	$20

CHELAN

❏ 2000	Searchin' '75/Young BLood	1975	$5

— *As "The Coasters 2+2*

DATE

❏ 1617	D.W. Washburn/Everybody's Woman	1968	$30
❏ 1607	Everybody's Woman/She Can	1968	$30
❏ 1552	Soul Pad/Down Home Girl	1967	$30

KING

❏ 6389	Cool Jerk/Talkin' 'Bout a Woman	1972	$6
❏ 6385	Love Potion #9/D.W. Washburn	1972	$6
❏ 6404	Soul Pad/D.W. Washburn	1972	$6

SAL WA

❏ 1001	Take It Easy, Greasy/You Move Me	1975	$5

TURNTABLE

❏ 504	Act Right/The World Is Changing	1969	$10

7-Inch Extended Plays

ATCO

❏ 4506	*Charlie Brown/Three Cool Cats/The Shadow Knows/Sorry But I'm Gonna Have to Pass	1959	$175
❏ 4507	Along Came Jones/That Is Rock & Roll//Dance!/Gee, Golly	1959	$175
❏ 4501	Searchin'/Young Blood//(When She Wants Good Lovin') My Baby Comes to Me/Idol with the Golden Head	1958	$175
❏ 4506 [PS]	The Coasters	1959	$175
❏ 4507 [PS]	The Coasters' Top Hits	1959	$175

COBB, JOYCE

TRUTH

❏ 3224	He Just Loved You Out of Me/Lonesome Time in Memphis Town Tonight	1975	$12

COBRAS, THE (1)

ARMADILLO

❏ 79-1	Blow Joe Blow (Crazy 'Bout a Saxophone)/Sugaree	1980	$125

COBRAS, THE (2)

CASINO

Number	Title	Yr	NM
❏ 1309	La La/Goodbye Molly	1963	$100

SWAN

Number	Title	Yr	NM
❏ 4176	La La/Goodbye Molly	1964	$30

COBRAS, THE (3)

MODERN

Number	Title	Yr	NM
❏ 964	Cindy/I Will Return	1955	$200

— *Revised spelling of A-side*

Number	Title	Yr	NM
❏ 964	Sindy/I Will Return	1955	$300

— *Original spelling of A-side*

COBRAS, THE (U)

MONOGRAM

Number	Title	Yr	NM
❏ 519	Thumpin'/Don't Even Know Your Name	1964	$15

STAX

Number	Title	Yr	NM
❏ 148	Shake Up/Restless	1964	$20

COCHRAN BROTHERS

EKKO

Number	Title	Yr	NM
❏ 1005	Guilty Conscience/Your Tomorrow Never Comes	1955	$250
❏ 1003	Mr. Fiddle/Two Blue Singing Stars	1955	$250
❏ 3001	Tired and Sleepy/Fool's Paradise	1956	$300

COCHRAN, CLIFF

ENTERPRISE

Number	Title	Yr	NM
❏ 9109	All the Love You'll Ever Need/I'd Do As Much for You	1974	$6
❏ 9112	She's Only Lonely/Summer Song	1975	$6
❏ 9103	The Way I'm Needing You/Hearts Are Like That, Yes They Are	1974	$6

RCA

Number	Title	Yr	NM
❏ PB-11711	First Thing Each Morning (Last Thing at Night)/100% Chance of Love Tonight	1979	$4
❏ PB-11562	Love Me Like a Stranger/The Rose Is for Today	1979	$4

COCHRAN, EDDIE

CREST

Number	Title	Yr	NM
❏ 1026	Skinny Jim/Half Loved	1956	$300

LIBERTY

Number	Title	Yr	NM
❏ 55166	C'mon Everybody/Don't Ever Let Me Go	1958	$40
❏ 55087	Drive In Show/Am I Blue	1957	$40
❏ 55217	Hallelujah I Love Her So/Little Angel	1959	$40
❏ 55278	Lonely/Sweetie Pie	1960	$30
❏ 55070	Mean When I'm Mad/One Kiss	1957	$40
❏ 55070 [PS]	Mean When I'm Mad/One Kiss	1957	$1500
❏ 55138	Pretty Girl/Theresa	1958	$40
❏ 55056	Sittin' in the Balcony/Dark Lonely Street	1957	$40
❏ 55144	Summertime Blues/Live Again	1958	$40
❏ 55177	Teen Age Heaven/I Remember	1959	$40
❏ 55177	Teenage Heaven/I Remember	1959	$50

— *Note difference in title*

Number	Title	Yr	NM
❏ 55203	The Boll Weevil Song/Somethin' Else	1959	$40
❏ 55242	Three Steps to Heaven/Cut Across Shorty	1960	$50
❏ 55112	Twenty Flight Rock/Cradle Baby	1957	$200
❏ 55389	Weekend/Lonely	1961	$40

UNITED ARTISTS

Number	Title	Yr	NM
❏ 0015	C'mon Everybody/Twenty Flight Rock	1973	$4
❏ 0016	Sittin' in the Balcony/Somethin' Else	1973	$4

— *0014, 0015, 0016 are "Silver Spotlight Series" reissues*

Number	Title	Yr	NM
❏ 0014	Summertime Blues/Cut Across Shorty	1973	$4

7-Inch Extended Plays

LIBERTY

Number	Title	Yr	NM
❏ LEP 2-3061	(contents unknown)	1958	$250
❏ LEP 3-3061	(contents unknown)	1958	$250
❏ LEP 1-3061 [PS]	Singin' to My Baby (Part One)	1958	$250
❏ LEP 3-3061 [PS]	Singin' to My Baby (Part Three)	1958	$250
❏ LEP 2-3061 [PS]	Singin' to My Baby (Part Two)	1958	$250
❏ LEP 1-3061	Sittin' in the Balcony/Proud of You//Stockings and Shoes/Have I Told You Lately That I Love You	1958	$250

COCHRAN, HANK

CAPITOL

Number	Title	Yr	NM
❏ 4635	Ain't Life Hell/I'm Going With You This Time	1978	$5

— *With Willie Nelson*

Number	Title	Yr	NM
❏ 4585	Willie/Uphill All the Way	1978	$4

—*A-side with Merle Haggard*

DOT

Number	Title	Yr	NM
❏ 17361	One Night for Willie/Back to His	1970	$6

ELEKTRA

Number	Title	Yr	NM
❏ 47062	A Little Bitty Tear/He's Got You	1980	$4
❏ 46596	Make the World Go Away/I Don't Do Windows	1980	$4

GAYLORD

Number	Title	Yr	NM
❏ 6431	A Good Country Song/Same Old Hurt	1963	$15

LIBERTY

Number	Title	Yr	NM
❏ 55498	I'd Fight the World/Lucy, Let Your Lovelight Shine	1962	$15
❏ 55520	I Remember/Private John Q	1963	$10
❏ 55402	Lonely Little Mansion/Has Anybody Seen Me Lately	1962	$15
❏ 55461	Sally Was a Good Old Girl/The Picture Behind the Picture	1962	$15
❏ 55644	Tootsie's Orchid Lounge/Go On Home	1963	$10

MONUMENT

Number	Title	Yr	NM
❏ 1033	A Happy Goodbye/Speak Well of Me to the Kids	1967	$6
❏ 994	All of Me Belongs to You/I Just Burned a Dream	1967	$6
❏ 1051	Has Anybody Seen Me Lately/I Woke Up	1968	$6
❏ 1012	It Couldn't Happen to a Nicer Guy/Tootsie's Orchid Lounge	1967	$6

RCA VICTOR

Number	Title	Yr	NM
❏ 47-8694	Hank Today and Him Tomorrow/I'm Alone	1965	$12
❏ 47-8457	I Want to Go with You/Sad Songs and Waltzes	1964	$10
❏ 47-8329	My Baby's His Baby Now/What Kind of Bird Is That	1964	$10
❏ 47-8375	She Always Comes Back to Me/Your Country Boy	1964	$10
❏ 47-8528	Somewhere in My Dreams/Going in Training	1965	$12
❏ 47-8955	That's What I'll Say/I Lie a Lot	1966	$8
❏ 47-8827	The Crying Section/Only You Can Make Me Well	1966	$8
❏ 47-8616	Who's Gonna/Let's Be Different	1965	$10

COCHRAN, JACKIE LEE

ABC-PARAMOUNT

Number	Title	Yr	NM
❏ 9930	Buy a Car/I Want You	1958	$100

JAGUAR

Number	Title	Yr	NM
❏ 3031	Georgia Lee Brown/I Wanna See You	1959	$120

SIMS

Number	Title	Yr	NM
❏ 107	Hip Shakin' Mama/Riverside Jump	1956	$200

SPRY

Number	Title	Yr	NM
❏ 120	Pity Me/Endless Love	1959	$250

VIV

Number	Title	Yr	NM
❏ 988	I Want You/Buy a Car	1958	$200

COCHRAN, WAYNE

BETHLEHEM

Number	Title	Yr	NM
❏ 3097	Hey Jude/Eleanor Rigby	1970	$6

CHESS

Number	Title	Yr	NM
❏ 2029	Get Ready/Hootchie Cootchie Man	1967	$8
❏ 2020	When My Baby Cries/Some-a Your Sweet Lovin'	1967	$8

EPIC

Number	Title	Yr	NM
❏ 10859	Do You Like the Sound of Music/Everybody's Been Cuttin' In on My Groove	1972	$5
❏ 10893	Long, Long Day/Sleepless Nights	1972	$5

KING

Number	Title	Yr	NM
❏ 5874	Cindy Marie/The Coo	1964	$15
❏ 5856	Last Kiss/I Dreamed, I Gambled, I Lost	1964	$15
❏ 6358	Let Me Come with You (Part 1)/Let Me Come with You (Part 2)	1971	$6
❏ 5832	Little Orphan Annie/Monkey, Monkey	1963	$15
❏ 5950	Mr. Lonely/Wrong Number, Wrong Gal	1964	$15

MERCURY

Number	Title	Yr	NM
❏ 72623	Goin' Back to Miami/I'm in Trouble	1966	$10
❏ 72552	Got Down with It/No Rest for the Wicked	1966	$10
❏ 72507	Harlem Shuffle/Somebody Please	1965	$12

SCOTTIE

Number	Title	Yr	NM
❏ 1303	My Little Girl/The Coo	1959	$30

COCK ROBIN

COLUMBIA

Number	Title	Yr	NM
❏ 38-06143	Once We Might Have Known/More Than Willing	1986	$3
❏ 38-07639	The Biggest Fool of All/Blood of a Saint	1987	$3
❏ 38-07639 [PS]	The Biggest Fool of All/Blood of a Saint	1987	$3
❏ 38-05720 [PS]	The Promise You Made	1985	$5

— *Demonstration -- Not for Sale" on back*

Number	Title	Yr	NM
❏ 38-05720	The Promise You Made/Have You Any Sympathy?	1985	$5
❏ 38-05720 [PS]	The Promise You Made/Have You Any Sympathy?	1985	$3
❏ 38-05635 [PS]	Thought You Were On My Side	1985	$5

— *Demonstration -- Not for Sale" on back*

Number	Title	Yr	NM
❏ 38-05635	Thought You Were On My Side/A Little Innocence	1985	$3
❏ 38-05635 [PS]	Thought You Were On My Side/A Little Innocence	1985	$3
❏ 38-04875	When Your Heart Is Weak	1985	$5

— *Demonstration -- Not for Sale" on back*

Number	Title	Yr	NM
❏ 38-04875	When Your Heart Is Weak/Because It Keeps On Working	1985	$3
❏ 38-04875 [PS]	When Your Heart Is Weak/Because It Keeps On Working	1985	$3

COCKBURN, BRUCE

GOLD MOUNTAIN

Number	Title	Yr	NM
❏ 82013	If I Had a Rocket Launcher/Nicaragua	1984	$6
❏ 82009	Lovers in a Dangerous Time/Sahara Gold	1984	$6

MILLENNIUM

Number	Title	Yr	NM
❏ YB-11806	The Coldest Night of the Year/Lord of the Starfields	1981	$6
❏ YB-11798	Tokyo/Guerrilla Betrayed	1980	$6
❏ YB-11786	Wondering Where the Lions Are/After the Rain	1979	$4

COCKER, JOE

A&M

Number	Title	Yr	NM
❏ 1200	Cry Me a River/Give Peace a Chance	1970	$5
❏ 1200 [PS]	Cry Me a River/Give Peace a Chance	1970	$6
❏ 1200	Cry Me a River/Please Give Peace a Chance	1970	$5
❏ 1112	Delta Lady/She's So Good to Me	1969	$5
❏ 2019	Feeling Alright/Cry Me a River	1978	$4
❏ 1063	Feeling Alright/Sandpaper Cadillac	1969	$6

— *Reissued in 1971 with the same number*

Number	Title	Yr	NM
❏ 1258	High Time We Went/Black-Eyed Blues	1971	$4
❏ 1258 [PS]	High Time We Went/Black-Eyed Blues	1971	$6
❏ 1855	I Broke Down/You Came Along	1976	$4
❏ 1626	I Can Stand a Little Rain/I Get Mad	1974	$4
❏ 1749	I Think It's Going to Rain Today/Oh Mama	1975	$4
❏ 928	Marjorine/New Age of the Lily	1968	$10
❏ 1370	Midnight Rider/Woman to Woman	1972	$4
❏ 1370 [PS]	Midnight Rider/Woman to Woman	1972	$6
❏ 1407	Pardon Me Sir/St. James Infirmary Blues	1973	$4
❏ 1407 [PS]	Pardon Me Sir/St. James Infirmary Blues	1973	$6
❏ 1539	Put Out the Light/If I Love You	1974	$4
❏ 1539 [PS]	Put Out the Light/If I Love You	1974	$6
❏ 1147	She Came In Through the Bathroom Window/Change in Louise	1969	$5
❏ 1147 [PS]	She Came In Through the Bathroom Window/Change in Louise	1969	$6
❏ 1174	The Letter/Space Captain	1970	$5
❏ 1174 [PS]	The Letter/Space Captain	1970	$6
❏ 1805	The Man in Me (Part 1)/The Man in Me (Part 2)	1976	$4
❏ 991	With a Little Help from My Friends/Something's Coming On	1968	$10

ASYLUM

Number	Title	Yr	NM
❏ 45540	Fun Time/Watching the River Flow	1978	$4
❏ 46001	Lady Put the Light Out/Wasted Years	1978	$4

CAPITOL

Number	Title	Yr	NM
❏ B-44182	A Woman Loves a Man/La Vie En Rose	1988	$3

—*B-side by Edith Piaf*

Number	Title	Yr	NM
❏ B-44182 [PS]	A Woman Loves a Man/La Vie En Rose	1988	$3
❏ B-5338	Civilized Man/A Girl Like You	1984	$3
❏ B-5338 [PS]	Civilized Man/A Girl Like You	1984	$4
❏ B-5390	Crazy in Love/Come On In	1984	$3
❏ B-5626	Don't Drink the Water/Don't You Love Me Anymore	1986	$3

Number	Title	Yr	NM
☐ B-5412	Edge of a Dream/Tempted	1984	$3
☐ B-5412 [PS]	Edge of a Dream/Tempted	1984	$4
☐ B-5557	Shelter Me/Tell Me There's a Way	1986	$3
☐ B-44101	Two Wrongs (Don't Make a Right)/Isolation	1987	$3
☐ 7PRO-79711 [DJ]	When the Night Comes (same on both sides)	1989	$5

— Vinyl is promo only

ISLAND

| ☐ 99875 | Throw It Away/Easy Rider | 1983 | $4 |

MCA

| ☐ 51177 | I'm So Glad I'm Standing Here Today/Standing Tall | 1981 | $4 |

— With the Crusaders

☐ 53077	Love Lives On/On My Way to You	1987	$4
☐ 53077 [PS]	Love Lives On/On My Way to You	1987	$4
☐ 51222	This Old World's Too Funky for Me/Standing Tall	1981	$4

— With the Crusaders

PHILIPS

| ☐ 40255 | I'll Cry Instead/Precious Words | 1965 | $50 |

— Originally by "Vance Arnold and the Avengers"

| ☐ 40255 | I'll Cry Instead/Precious Words | 1965 | $50 |

— Artist listed as "Joe Cocker

COCTEAU TWINS
CAPITOL

| ☐ B-44286 | Carolyn's Fingers/Blue Bell Knoll | 1989 | $8 |
| ☐ 7PRO-79477 | Carolyn's Fingers (same on both sides) | 1989 | $6 |

— Promo-only number

CODY, BETTY
RCA VICTOR

☐ 47-5705	A Letter I Never Should Have Mailed/The Kiss That Made a Fool of Me	1954	$30
☐ 47-5926	Always a Bridesmaid/You Want More of Me	1954	$30
☐ 47-5811	Dear Sister/Can You Live with Yourself	1954	$30
☐ 47-5869	Heart to Heart/How to Get Married	1954	$30

— With Hal Lone Pine

☐ 47-5462	I Found Out More Than You'll Ever Know/Don't Believe Everything You Read	1953	$30
☐ 47-5376	Pale Moon/I Hate Myself for Loving You So Much	1953	$30
☐ 47-5600	Please Throw Away the Glass/You Can't Feel the Way I Do	1954	$30
☐ 47-5991	Tell It Right/Butterfly Heart	1955	$30

— With Hal Lone Pine

CODY, MICHELLE
SAFARI

| ☐ 601 | Merry Christmas Elvis/All I Want For Christmas | 1978 | $8 |

COE, DAVID ALLAN
COLUMBIA

☐ 38-05876	A Country Boy (Who Rolled the Rock Away)/Take My Advice	1986	$4
☐ 3-10860	Bright Morning Light/Suicide	1978	$5
☐ 38-03997	Cheap Thrills/You Never Even Call Me by My Name	1983	$4
☐ 38-03997 [PS]	Cheap Thrills/You Never Even Call Me by My Name	1983	$6
☐ 38-04136	Crazy Old Soldier/Drinkin' to Forget	1983	$4
☐ 3-10701	Divers Do It Deeper/Million Dollar Memories	1978	$5
☐ 38-04846	Don't Cry Darlin'/You're the Only Song I Sing Today	1985	$4
☐ 3-10621	Face to Face/Play Me a Sad Song	1977	$5
☐ 1-11277	Get a Little Dirt on Your Hands/What Can I Do	1980	$5

— A-side with Bill Anderson

☐ 1-11352	Hank Williams Jr., Jr./I've Got Something to Say	1980	$5
☐ 3-10024	(If I Could Climb) The Walls of the Bottle/Another Pretty Country Song	1974	$5
☐ 3-10816	If This Is Just a Game/Tomorrow's Another Day	1978	$5
☐ 38-05631	I'm Gonna Hurt Her on the Radio/He Has to Pay (For What I Get for Free)	1985	$4
☐ 38-04553	It's Great to Be Single Again/Sweet Angeline	1984	$4
☐ 38-06227	I've Already Cheated on You/Take My Advice	1986	$4

— A-side with Willie Nelson

| ☐ 3-10475 | Lately I've Been Thinking Too Much Lately/Under Rachel's Wings | 1977 | $5 |

Number	Title	Yr	NM
☐ 3-10254	Longhaired Redneck/Family Reunion	1975	$5
☐ 38-08527	Love Is a Never Ending War/Action Speaks Louder Than Words	1989	$4
☐ 1-11167	Loving You Comes So Natural/Lost	1979	$5

— With Johnny Rodriguez

☐ 38-04396	Mona Lisa Lost Her Smile/Someone Special	1984	$4
☐ 38-05451	My Elusive Dreams/Call Me the Breeze	1985	$4
☐ 4-46012	Sad Country Song/Atlantic Song	1974	$6
☐ 38-04688	She Used to Love Me a Lot/For Lovers Only (Part IV)	1984	$4
☐ 18-02492	(Sittin' On) The Dock of the Bay/Love Robbin's Trains	1981	$4
☐ 38-06394	Son of the South/Gemini Girl	1986	$4
☐ 11-60501	Stand By Your Man/Take This Job and Shove It	1981	$4
☐ 18-02815	Take Time to Know Her/London Homesick Blues	1982	$4
☐ 38-07129	Tanya Montana/The Ten Commandments of Love	1987	$4
☐ 11-02118	Tennessee Whiskey/The Bottle (In My Hand)	1981	$4
☐ 1-11230	The Great Nashville Railroad Disaster (True Story)/Take It Easy Rider	1980	$5
☐ 18-03022	What Made You Change Your Mind/Pouring Water on a Drowning Man	1982	$4
☐ 3-10323	When She's Got Me (Where She Wants Me)/Living on the Run	1976	$5
☐ 38-03343	Whiskey, Whiskey (Take My Mind)/Those Low Down Blues	1982	$4
☐ 3-10395	Willie, Waylon and Me/Please Come to Boston	1976	$5
☐ 3-10093	Would You Be My Lady/Rock and Roll Holiday	1975	$5

PLANTATION

| ☐ 99 | How High's the Watergate, Martha/Tricky Dicky, The Only Son of King Fu | 1973 | $8 |

SSS INTERNATIONAL

| ☐ 825 | Tobacco Road/Death Row | 1971 | $10 |
| ☐ 864 | Two-Tone Brown/Funeral Parlor Blues | 1972 | $10 |

COE, JAMIE
ABC-PARAMOUNT

☐ 10120	Goodbye, My Love, Goodbye/There's Never Been a Night	1960	$30
☐ 10267	How Low Is Low/Little Darling, Little Darling	1961	$30
☐ 10203	I'm Gettin' Married/Two Dozen and a Half	1961	$30
☐ 10149	The Story of Jesse James/Say You	1960	$30

ADDISON

| ☐ 15003 | I'll Go On Loving You/School Day Blues | 1959 | $30 |
| ☐ 15001 | Summertime Symphony/There's Gonna Be a Day | 1959 | $30 |

BIG TOP

| ☐ 3107 | Cleopatra/But Yesterday | 1962 | $30 |
| ☐ 3139 | The Fool/I've Got That Feeling Again | 1963 | $30 |

CAMEO

| ☐ 424 | Greenback Dollar/But Yesterday | 1966 | $20 |

ENTERPRISE

☐ 5095	First Girl/Very Few	1966	$20
☐ 5055	Good Enough for a King/I Was the One	1965	$15
☐ 5080	Greenback Dollar/But Yesterday	1965	$30
☐ 5050	My Girl/I Cried on My Pillow	1964	$15
☐ 5005	The Dealer/Close Your Eyes	1964	$15
☐ 5070	The One Who Really Loves You/A Long Time Ago	1965	$15

REPRISE

| ☐ 0295 | Close Your Eyes/The Dealer | 1964 | $15 |

COEFIELD, BRICE
A&M

| ☐ 774 | Ain't That Right/Work for My Baby | 1965 | $600 |

MADISON

| ☐ 137 | Cha Cha Twist/Tempted | 1960 | $60 |

OMEN

| ☐ 10 | Ain't That Right/Just One More Night | 1965 | $600 |

COFFEE, RED
WARNER BROS.

| ☐ 5128 | Ducky Christmas/Jolly Jingle Bells | 1959 | $20 |

COGAN, ALMA
AMERICAN ARTS

| ☐ 4 | I Love You Much Too Much/Tennessee Waltz | 1964 | $10 |

CAPITOL

| ☐ 4547 | Cowboy Jimmy Joe/Just Couldn't Resist Her with Her Pocket Transistor | 1961 | $15 |
| ☐ F4170 | Mama Says/Last Night on the Back Porch | 1959 | $15 |

Number	Title	Yr	NM

LAURIE

| ☐ TL18 | Snakes Snails and Puppy Dog Tails/How Many Days How Many Nights | 1965 | $12 |

RCA VICTOR

☐ 47-6063	Blue Again/Paper Kisses	1955	$20
☐ 47-6236	Got N' Idea/Give a Fool a Chance	1955	$20
☐ 47-6405	Twenty Tiny Fingers/Never Do a Tango with an Eskimo	1956	$15
☐ 47-6573	Willie Can/Pickin' a Chicken	1956	$15

COHEN, LEONARD
COLUMBIA

| ☐ 44827 | Bird on the Wire/Seems So Long Ago (Nancy) | 1969 | $6 |
| ☐ 44439 | Suzanne/Hey, That's No Way to Say Goodbye | 1968 | $6 |

COHEN, MYRON
CORAL

| ☐ 61280 | Mr. and Mrs./Soup and Fish | 1954 | $15 |

COHRON, PHIL
AIR

| ☐ 182 | Across the Room from You/(B-side unknown) | 1989 | $6 |

COIN, R.C.
BGM

| ☐ 82087 | Bed of Roses/Confidential | 1987 | $6 |

COINS, THE
GEE

☐ 10	Cheatin' Baby/Blue, Can't Get No Place with You	1954	$2000
☐ 11	Look at Me Girl/S.R. Blues	1954	$2000
☐ 1007	Look at Me Girl/Two Loves Have I	1956	$600

— B-side by the Colonials

MODEL

| ☐ 2001 | Loretta/Please | 1955 | $2000 |

COLBERT, GODOY
REVUE

| ☐ 11037 | Baby I Like It/I Wanna Thank You | 1969 | $200 |

COLD BLOOD
ABC

| ☐ 12173 | I Get Off on You/We Came Down Here | 1976 | $4 |

— As "Lydia Pense and Cold Blood"

REPRISE

| ☐ 1157 | Baby I Love You/Livin' Your Dream | 1973 | $5 |
| ☐ 1092 | Down to the Bone/Valdes in the Country | 1972 | $5 |

SAN FRANCISCO

| ☐ 61 | I Wish I Knew How It Would Feel to Be Free/I'ma Good Woman | 1970 | $6 |
| ☐ 62 | Too Many People/I Can't Stay | 1970 | $6 |

COLDCUT
AHEAD OF TIME

| ☐ CCUT7 | Coldcut's Christmas Break (Radio Version)/Coldcut's Christmas Break (Club Mix) | 1989 | $6 |

— U.K. import

| ☐ CCUT7 [PS] | Coldcut's Christmas Break (Radio Version)/Coldcut's Christmas Break (Club Mix) | 1989 | $6 |

— U.K. import

COLUMBIA

| ☐ 38-07935 | Doctorin' the House/(Thief-Apella Mix) | 1988 | $5 |

— Featuring Yazz & The Plastic Population

| ☐ 38-07935 [PS] | Doctorin' the House/(Thief-Apella Mix) | 1988 | $5 |

TOMMY BOY

| ☐ 22848 | People Hold On (Radio Mix)/(Acapella) | 1989 | $4 |

— Featuring Lisa Stansfield

| ☐ 22848 [PS] | People Hold On (Radio Mix)/(Acapella) | 1989 | $4 |

COLE, ANN
BATON

☐ 218	Are You Satisfied?/Darling Don't Hurt Me	1955	$30
☐ 224	Easy Easy Baby/New Love	1956	$30
☐ 247	Give Me Love or Nothing/I've Got Nothing Working Now	1957	$30
☐ 237	Got My Mo-Jo Working/I've Got a Little Boy	1957	$50
☐ 229	I'm Waiting for You/My Tearful Heart	1956	$30
☐ 232	In the Chapel/Each Day	1956	$30
☐ 258	Love in My Heart/Summer Nights	1958	$30

Number	Title	Yr	NM
MGM			
❏ 12954	In the Chapel/Plain As the Nose on Your Face	1960	$20
ROULETTE			
❏ 4452	Don't Stop the Wedding/Have Fun	1962	$20
SIR			
❏ 275	A Love of My Own/Brand New House	1960	$20
TIMELY			
❏ 1006	Danny Boy/Smilin' Through	1954	$30
❏ 1007	I'll Find a Way/Oh Love of Mine	1954	$30
❏ 1010	So Proud of You/Down in the Valley	1955	$30

COLE, BRENDA

Number	Title	Yr	NM
MELODY DAWN			
❏ 77703	Boots (These Boots Are Made for Walkin')/Gone, Gone, Gone	1988	$5
❏ 77701	But I Never Do/Barefoot Lady	1987	$5
❏ 77701 [PS]	But I Never Do/Barefoot Lady	1987	$6
❏ 77702	Gone, Gone, Gone/ (B-side unknown)	1987	$5
❏ 77702 [PS]	Gone, Gone, Gone/ (B-side unknown)	1987	$6

COLE, COZY

Number	Title	Yr	NM
BETHLEHEM			
❏ 3067	Big Boss/Cozy and Bossa	1963	$8
COLUMBIA			
❏ 43657	Whole Lotta Shakin' Goin' On/Watch It	1966	$8
CORAL			
❏ 62339	Big Noise from Winnetka (Part 1)/ Big Noise from Winnetka (Part 2)	1962	$8
❏ 62417	Cozy Beat/Night Beach	1964	$8
❏ 62395	Ol' Man Moses/ Christopher Columbus	1964	$8
FELSTED			
❏ 8546	Caravan Part 1/Caravan Part 2	1959	$10
GRAND AWARD			
❏ 1023	Caravan Part 1/Caravan Part 2	1959	$15
KING			
❏ 5316	Blockhead/Teen-Age Ideas	1960	$10
❏ 5222	Blow-Up/Flop-Down	1959	$10
❏ 5265	Boy Meets Girl/Playtime Blues	1959	$10
—With Lee Parker			
❏ 5363	Cozy's Corner/Red Ball	1960	$12
❏ 5337	Drum Fever/Bag of Tricks	1960	$12
❏ 5390	Ha Ha Cha-Cha/The Pogo Hop	1960	$10
❏ 5254	Melody of a Dreamer/Soft	1959	$10
❏ 5303	Play, Cozy, Play/Cozy's Mambo	1960	$10
❏ 5287	Stain Glass/D'Mitri	1959	$10
❏ 5242	Strange/D Natural Rock	1959	$10
LOVE			
❏ 5003/4	Topsy I/Topsy II	1958	$20
❏ 16-5016	Topsy-Turvy (Everything Is)/Bad	1958	$15
❏ 5014	Turvy I/Turvy II	1958	$15
MERCURY			
❏ 71385	St. Louis Blues/Father Cooperates	1958	$15
MGM			
❏ 11794	Hound Dog Special/Terrible Sight	1954	$15

COLE, DON

Number	Title	Yr	NM
COED			
❏ 548	Free Flight/Squad Car	1961	$30
GUYDEN			
❏ 2059	Lie Detector Machine/Born to Be with You	1961	$125
KENT			
❏ 305	Saturday Night Party Time/Sweet Lovin' Honey	1958	$100
RPM			
❏ 502	Snake Eyed Mama/Kiss of Love	1957	$200
—With Al Casey			

COLE, FREDDIE

Number	Title	Yr	NM
SUE			
❏ 775	It's Christmas Time/Right Now	1962	$20

COLE, JERRY

Number	Title	Yr	NM
CAPITOL			
❏ 5394	Every Window in the City/Come On Over to My Place	1965	$12
❏ 5265	Meet Me on the Corner/Life Will Go On	1964	$10
❏ 5056	Midnight Mary/Land of Dreams	1963	$15
❏ 5106	Pokey/One Color Blues	1964	$10

COLE, NAT KING

Includes reissues of material by the King Cole Trio. First renowned as a piano player in The King Cole Trio, then as a male singer. The other members of the Trio were Oscar Moore (guitar) and Wesley Prince (bass).

Number	Title	Yr	NM
CAPITOL			
❏ F3095	A Blossom Fell/If I May	1955	$20
—B-side with the Four Knights			
❏ F2540	A Fool Was I/If Love Is Good to Me	1953	$10
❏ F90036	(All I Want for Christmas Is) My Two Front Teeth/The Christmas Song (Merry Christmas To You)	1949	$30
—B-side is the original King Cole Trio hit version, possibly its only U.S. release on 45			
❏ 4919	All Over the World/Nothing Goes Up (Without Coming Down)	1963	$8
❏ F1401	Always You/Destination Moon	1951	$15
❏ F3860	Angel Smile/Back in My Arms	1957	$10
❏ F2687	Answer Me, My Love/Why	1953	$10
❏ F3328	Ask Me/Nothing Ever Changes My Love for You	1956	$12
❏ F3619	Ballerina/You Are My First Love	1957	$12
❏ F1501	Because of Rain/Song of Delilah	1951	$15
❏ F2212	Because You're Mine/I'm Never Satisfied	1952	$12
❏ 54-531	Blues in My Shower/How High the Moon	1949	$30
—Part of "CCF-156"			
❏ F531	Blues in My Shower/How High the Moon	1950	$20
—Part of "CCF-156"; reissue of 54-531			
❏ F15554	Bop Kick/Laugh Cool Clown	1950	$20
❏ F2389	Can't I/Blue Gardenia	1953	$10
❏ F4004	Come Closer to Me/Nothing in the World	1958	$10
❏ F3027	Darling Je Vous Aime Beaucoup/The Sand and the Sea	1955	$12
❏ 4870	Dear Lonely Hearts/Who's Next in Line	1962	$15
❏ 4870 [PS]	Dear Lonely Hearts/Who's Next in Line	1962	$30
❏ F1565	Early American/My Brother	1951	$15
❏ F1994	Easter Sunday Morning/Summer Is a Comin' On	1952	$12
❏ F1650	Embraceable You/It's Only a Paper Moon	1951	$12
—As "The King Cole Trio"			
❏ F15566	Embraceable You/What Is This Thing Called Love	1950	$20
❏ F1036	Exactly Like You/That's What	1950	$20
❏ F2230	Faith Can Move Mountains/The Ruby and the Pearl	1952	$10
❏ F15553	For All We Know/'Tis Autumn	1950	$20
❏ F3234	Forgive My Heart/Someone You Love	1955	$10
❏ F1203	Frosty the Snow Man/A Little Christmas Tree	1950	$40
❏ F1176	Get Out and Get Under/Hey, Not Now	1950	$20
❏ F15511	(Get Your Kicks on) Route 66/Gee Baby Ain't I Been Good to You	1950	$20
❏ 4555	Goodnight, Little Leaguer/The First Baseball Game	1961	$8
❏ 4555 [PS]	Goodnight, Little Leaguer/The First Baseball Game	1961	$30
❏ F2949	Hajji Baba (Persian Lament)/Unbelievable	1954	$10
❏ F1893	Here's my Lady/Miss Me	1951	$15
❏ F1133	Home (When Shadows Fall)/Tunnel of Love	1950	$20
❏ F889	I Almost Lost My Mind/Baby Won't You Say You Love Me	1950	$20
—Nat King Cole records on Capitol before F889 are unconfirmed on 45 rpm, except as listed			
❏ F2459	I Am in Love/My Flaming Heart	1953	$10
❏ F1030	I Don't Know Why/You're the Cream in My Coffee	1950	$20
❏ 5155	I Don't Want to Be Hurt Anymore/People	1964	$8
❏ 4481	If I Knew/World in My Arms	1960	$8
❏ F1068	I'll Never Say "Never Again" Again/A Little Bit Independent	1950	$30
❏ F15729	I'll String Along with You/Too Marvelous for Words	1951	$15
❏ 4519	Illusion/When It's Summer	1961	$8
❏ F1033	(I Love You) For Sentimental Reasons/I Can't See for Lookin'	1950	$20
❏ 2451	I'm Gonna Laugh You Right Out of My Life/People	1969	$6
❏ F1032	I'm in the Mood for Love/Don't Blame Me	1950	$20
❏ 4369	Is It Better to Have Loved and Lost/That's You	1960	$8
❏ F1815	I Still See Elisa/You're OK for TV	1951	$15
❏ F2754	It Happens to Be Me/Alone Too Long	1954	$10
❏ 54-680	(It's Easy to See) The Trouble with Me Is You/Who Do You Know in Heaven	1949	$30
❏ F883	It's Only a Paper Moon/Embraceable You	1950	$30
—As "The King Cole Trio"			
❏ 54-716	Land of Love/Yes Sir, That's My Baby	1949	$30
❏ F15870	Laura/Polka Dots and Moonbeams	1952	$15
❏ 5683	Let Me Tell You, Babe/For the Want of a Kiss	1966	$8
❏ 4623	Let True Love Begin/Cappuccina	1961	$8

Number	Title	Yr	NM
❏ F606	Lillian/Lush Life	1949	$20
—Add 1/3 if "O.C." (optional center) is still in the center of the record			
❏ F1034	Little Girl/What Can I Say	1950	$20
❏ F3939	Looking Back/Do I Like It	1958	$10
❏ 4714	Look No Further/The Right Thing to Say	1962	$8
❏ F1627	Lost April/Calypso Blues	1951	$15
❏ 5261	L-O-V-E/I Don't Want to See Tomorrow	1964	$8
❏ F2610	Lover Come Back to Me/That's All	1953	$10
❏ F1672	Lush Life/I Miss You So	1951	$10
❏ F4125	Madrid/Give Me Your Love	1959	$10
❏ 4672	Magic Moment/Step Right Up	1961	$8
❏ F1747	Make Believe Land/I'll Always Remember You	1951	$15
❏ F2803	Make Her Mine/I Envy	1954	$10
❏ F15728	Makin' Whoopee/Honeysuckle Rose	1951	$15
❏ F1669	Makin' Whoopee/This Is My Night to Dream	1951	$10
❏ 5219	Marnie/More and More of the Amore	1964	$8
❏ F1673	Mona Lisa/No Moon at All	1951	$15
❏ F1010	Mona Lisa/The Greatest Inventor (Of Them All)	1950	$20
❏ F3560	Mrs. Santa Claus/Take Me Back to Toyland	1956	$20
❏ F2616	Mrs. Santa Claus/The Little Boy That Santa Claus Forgot	1953	$30
❏ 4393	My Love/Steady	1960	$8
❏ F3136	My One Sin/Blues from Kiss Me Deadly	1955	$10
❏ 5125	My True Carrie, Love/A Rag a Bone, A Hank of Hair	1964	$8
❏ 5549	One Sun/Looking Back	1965	$8
❏ F2985	Open Up the Doghouse/Long, Long Ago	1954	$20
—With Dean Martin			
❏ F1184	Orange Colored Sky/Jambo	1950	$20
❏ F15868	Penthouse Serenade/If I Should Lose You	1952	$15
❏ F1035	Portrait of Jenny/Lost April	1950	$20
❏ F2346	Pretend/Don't Let Your Eyes Go Shopping	1953	$10
❏ F1689	Pretend/Unforgettable	1954	$10
—Most of the Capitol 1600 series were reissues, some of material from 78s			
❏ F3737	Send for Me/My Personal Possession	1957	$20
—B-side with the Four Knights			
❏ F2897	Smile/It's Crazy	1954	$12
❏ F15869	Somebody Loves Me/Down by the Old Mill Stream	1952	$15
❏ F2069	Somewhere Along the Way/What Does It Take to Make You Take Me	1952	$12
❏ F15509	Straighten Up and Fly Right/Nature Boy	1950	$20
—All the Capitol 15000 series on 45s are from multi-disc box sets			
❏ F2309	Strange/How (Do I Go About It)	1952	$10
❏ F4248	Sweet Bird of Youth/Midnight Flyer	1959	$10
❏ F4248 [PS]	Sweet Bird of Youth/Midnight Flyer	1959	$40
❏ F1037	Sweet Georgia Brown/I Know That You Know	1950	$20
❏ F15564	Sweet Lorraine/It's Only a Paper Moon	1950	$20
❏ F1613	Sweet Lorraine/Kee-Mo Ky-Mo	1951	$15
❏ 4582	Take a Fool's Advice/Make It Last	1961	$8
❏ F3305	Take Me Back to Toyland/I'm Gonna Laugh You Right Out of My Life	1955	$30
—With A-side title as shown			
❏ 2088	Thank You, Pretty Baby/Brazilian Love Song	1968	$6
❏ F3456	That's All There Is to That/My Dream Sonata	1956	$12
❏ 5027	That Sunday, That Summer/Mr. Wishing Well	1963	$15
❏ 5412	The Ballad of Cat Ballou/They Can't Make Her Cry	1965	$8
—With Stubby Kay			
❏ 5412 [PS]	The Ballad of Cat Ballou/They Can't Make Her Cry	1965	$20
❏ F2955	The Christmas Song (Merry Christmas to You)/My Two Front Teeth (All I Want for Christmas)	1954	$30
❏ F3561	The Christmas Song (Merry Christmas to You)/The Little Boy That Santa Claus Forgot	1956	$20
—Original with "F" prefix, Capitol logo on top			
❏ 3561	The Christmas Song (Merry Christmas to You)/The Little Boy That Santa Claus Forgot	1960	$8
—Purple label, Capitol logo on side			
❏ 3561	The Christmas Song (Merry Christmas to You)/The Little Boy That Santa Claus Forgot	1962	$6
—Orange and yellow swirl label			
❏ 3561	The Christmas Song (Merry Christmas to You)/The Little Boy That Santa Claus Forgot	1973	$4
—Orange label with "Capitol" at bottom			
❏ 4301	The Happiest Christmas Tree/Buon Natale	1959	$15
❏ 4301 [PS]	The Happiest Christmas Tree/Buon Natale	1959	$30

Number	Title	Yr	NM
❏ F15565	The Man I Love/Body and Soul	1950	$20
❏ 54-529	These Foolish Things/Cole Capers	1949	$30
—Part of "CCF-156			
❏ F529	These Foolish Things/Cole Capers	1950	$20
—Part of "CCF-156"; reissue of 54-529			
❏ F15730	This Is My Night to Dream/ Rhumba Azul	1951	$15
❏ F1038	This Way Out/Rex Rhumba	1950	$20
❏ 4965	Those Lazy-Hazy-Crazy Days of Summer/In the Cool of Day	1963	$15
❏ 4965 [PS]	Those Lazy-Hazy-Crazy Days of Summer/In the Cool of Day	1963	$30
❏ 54-530	Three Little Words/I'll Never Be the Same	1949	$30
—Part of "CCF-156			
❏ F530	Three Little Words/I'll Never Be the Same	1950	$20
—Part of "CCF-156"; reissue of 54-530			
❏ F1270	Time Out for Tears/Get to Gettin'	1951	$15
❏ F1674	Too Young/(I Love You) For Sentimental Reasons	1952	$10
❏ F1449	Too Young/That's My Girl	1951	$15
❏ F3390	Too Young to Go Steady/ Never Let Me Go	1956	$10
❏ F3305	Toyland/I'm Gonna Laugh You Right Out of My Life	1955	$40
—With A-side title incorrect as shown			
❏ F2130	Walking My Baby Back Home/Funny (Not Much)	1952	$10
❏ F1863	Walkin'/I'm Hurtin'	1951	$15
❏ F15922	Walkin' My Baby Back Home/Kay's Lament	1952	$15
—B-side by Kay Starr			
❏ 5486	Wanderlust/You'll See	1965	$8
❏ 4325	What'cha Gonna Do/ Time and the River	1960	$8
❏ F3702	When Rock and Roll Come to Trinidad/China Gate	1957	$20
❏ F1925	Wine, Women and Song/A Weaver of My Dreams	1952	$15
❏ F3782	With You on My Mind/The Song of Raintree County	1957	$10

7-Inch Extended Plays

Number	Title	Yr	NM
❏ EAP 2-420	*A Little Street Where Old Friends Meet/This Can't Be Love/Dinner for One Please, James/There Goes My Heart	1954	$15
❏ EAP 1-1031	*Cachito/Maria Elena/ Las Mananitas/Quizas, Quizas, Quizas	1958	$15
❏ EAP 1-420	*Love Is Here to Stay/A Handful of Stars/Almost Like Being in Love/Tenderly	1954	$15
❏ EPA 1-500	*Lover Come Back/Pretend/A Fool Was I/I'm Hurtin'	1954	$15
❏ EAP 1-993	*Overture (Introducing "Love Theme" and "Hesitating Blues")/Harlem Blues/Yellow Dog Blues/St. Louis Blues	1958	$15
❏ EAP 1-782 [PS]	After Midnight, Part 1	1956	$12
❏ EAP 2-782 [PS]	After Midnight, Part 2	1956	$12
❏ EAP 3-782 [PS]	After Midnight, Part 3	1956	$12
❏ EAP 4-782 [PS]	After Midnight, Part 4	1956	$12
❏ EBF 1-782 [PS]	After Midnight, Parts 1 & 2	1956	$25
—Gatefold sleeve for some editions of EAP 1-782 and 2-782			
❏ EAP 1-813 [PS]	Around the World	1957	$15
❏ EAP 1-813	Around the World/Fascination// An Affair to Remember (Our Love Affair)/There's a Gold Mine in the Sky	1957	$15
❏ EAP 1-1031 [PS]	Cole Espanol, Part 1	1958	$15
❏ EAP 2-1031 [PS]	Cole Espanol, Part 2	1958	$15
❏ EAP 3-1031 [PS]	Cole Espanol, Part 3	1958	$15
❏ EAP 2-514	(contents unknown)	1954	$15
❏ EAP 3-824	(contents unknown)	1957	$15
❏ EAP 2-1031	(contents unknown)	1958	$15
❏ EAP 3-1031	(contents unknown)	1958	$15
❏ EAP 1-633	Darling, Je Vous Aime Beaucoup/If I May//A Blossom Fell/The Sand and the Sea	1955	$15
❏ EAP 1-514	Dream a Little Dream of Me/ There I've Said It Again// Too Soon/Rough Ridin'	1954	$15
❏ EAP 1-9120	If I Give My Heart To You/ Hold My Hand//Pappa Loves Mambo/Teach Me Tonight	1954	$15
❏ EAP 4-782	It's Only a Paper Moon/ Don't Let It Go to Your Head// Blame It On My Youth	1956	$10
❏ EAP 2-782	Lonely One/I Know That You Know//Sweet Lorraine	1956	$10
❏ EAP 1-960 [PS]	Looking Back	1958	$12
❏ EAP 1-960	Looking Back/Send for Me// Do I Like It/Angel Smile	1958	$10
❏ SXA-2195 [PS]	L-O-V-E	1965	$12
❏ EAP 1-9128	Love Is a Many-Splendored Thing/Breezin' Along with the Breeze//Autumn Leaves/ You Are My Sunshine	1955	$15

Number	Title	Yr	NM
❏ EAP 1-824 [PS]	Love Is the Thing, Part 1	1957	$15
❏ EAP 2-824 [PS]	Love Is the Thing, Part 2	1957	$15
❏ EAP 3-824 [PS]	Love Is the Thing, Part 3	1957	$15
❏ EAP 1-824	Love Is the Thing/Stay as Sweet as You Are//When I Fall in Love/ Where Can I Go Without You?	1957	$15
❏ EAP 2-824	Maybe It's Because I Love You Too Much/It's All in the Game// Stardust/When Sunny Gets Blue	1957	$15
❏ EAP 1-633	Moods in Song	1955	$15
❏ EAP 2-993 [PS]	Morning Star/Memphis Blues//Chantez Les Bas/ Friendless Blues	1958	$15
❏ EAP 4-514	Peaches/I Can't Be Bothered// Mother Nature and Father Time/ Wish I Were Somebody Else	1954	$15
❏ EAP 1-782	Sometimes I'm Happy// Just You, Just Me/When I Grow Too Old to Dream	1956	$10
❏ EPA 1-500 [PS]	Songs by Nat King Cole	1954	$15
❏ EAP 3-993 [PS]	Stay/Joe Turner's Blues//Beale Street Blues/Careless Love	1958	$15
❏ EAP 1-993 [PS]	St. Louis Blues, Part 1	1958	$15
❏ EAP 2-993 [PS]	St. Louis Blues, Part 2	1958	$15
❏ EAP 3-993 [PS]	St. Louis Blues, Part 3	1958	$15
❏ EAP 1-514 [PS]	Tenth Anniversary Album, Part 1	1954	$15
❏ EAP 2-514 [PS]	Tenth Anniversary Album, Part 2	1954	$15
❏ EAP 3-514 [PS]	Tenth Anniversary Album, Part 3	1954	$15
❏ EAP 4-514	Tenth Anniversary Album, Part 4	1954	$15
❏ EBF 1-514 [PS]	Tenth Anniversary Album, Parts 1 and 2	1954	$25
—Gatefold sleeve for some editions of EAP 1-514 and 2-514			
❏ EBF 2-514 [PS]	Tenth Anniversary Album, Parts 3 and 4	1954	$25
—Gatefold sleeve for some editions of EAP 3-514 and 4-514			
❏ EAP 3-514	The Love Nest/But All I've Got Is Me//Lovelight/Where Were You	1954	$15
❏ EAP 1-420 [PS]	Two in Love, Part 1	1954	$15
❏ EAP 2-420 [PS]	Two in Love, Part 2	1954	$15

COLE, NATALIE, AND PEABO BRYSON
CAPITOL

Number	Title	Yr	NM
❏ 4804	Gimme Some Time/ Love Will Find You	1979	$4
❏ 4826	What You Won't Do for Love/Your Lonely Heart	1980	$4

COLE, NATALIE
CAPITOL

Number	Title	Yr	NM
❏ 4572	Annie Mae/Just Can't Stay Away	1978	$4
❏ 4924	Hold On/Paradise	1980	$4
❏ 4193	Inseparable/How Come You Won't Stay Here	1975	$4
❏ 4360	I've Got Love on My Mind/ Unpredictable You	1976	$4
❏ 4623	Lucy in the Sky with Diamonds/Lovers	1978	$4
❏ 4328	Mr. Melody/Not Like Mine	1976	$4
❏ 4509	Our Love/La Costa	1977	$4
❏ 4439	Party Lights/Peaceful Living	1977	$4
❏ 4869	Someone That I Used to Love/Don't Look Back	1980	$4
❏ 4259	Sophisticated Lady (She's a Different Lady)/Good Morning Heartache	1976	$4
❏ 4722	Sorry/You're So Good	1979	$4
❏ 4690	Stand By/Who Will Carry On	1979	$4
❏ 4109	This Will Be/Joey	1975	$5

EMI

Number	Title	Yr	NM
❏ B-50231	As a Matter of Fact/ (B-side unknown)	1989	$5
❏ B-50213	I Do/Miss You Like Crazy	1989	$3
❏ B-50185	Miss You Like Crazy/ Good to Be Back	1989	$3
❏ B-50185 [PS]	Miss You Like Crazy/ Good to Be Back	1989	$5

EMI MANHATTAN

Number	Title	Yr	NM
❏ B-50117	Pink Cadillac/I Wanna Be That Woman	1988	$3
❏ B-50138	When I Fall in Love/ Pink Cadillac	1988	$3
❏ B-50138 [PS]	When I Fall in Love/ Pink Cadillac	1988	$4

EPIC

Number	Title	Yr	NM
❏ 34-04000	Too Much Mister/ Where's Your Angel	1983	$3

GEFFEN

Number	Title	Yr	NM
❏ 28152	Over You/After Midnite	1987	$3
—With Ray Parker Jr.			

MANHATTAN

Number	Title	Yr	NM
❏ B-50094	I Live for Your Love/ More Than the Stars	1987	$3

Number	Title	Yr	NM
❏ B-50094 [PS]	I Live for Your Love/ More Than the Stars	1987	$4

MODERN

Number	Title	Yr	NM
❏ 99630	A Little Bit of Heaven/When I Need It Bad, You Got It Good	1985	$3
❏ 99648	Dangerous/Love Is On the Way	1985	$3
❏ 99648 [PS]	Dangerous/Love Is On the Way	1985	$3
❏ 99589	Secrets/Nobody's Soldier	1985	$3

COLE, PATSY
TRA-STAR

Number	Title	Yr	NM
❏ 1226	Death and Taxes (And Me Lovin' You)/Lead Me On	1989	$5
❏ 1225	I Never Had a Chance with You/Morning Train	1989	$5

COLE, TONY
20TH CENTURY

Number	Title	Yr	NM
❏ 2055	Scorpio/Mermaid	1973	$10
❏ 2001	Suite: Man and Woman/ All I Meant to Do	1972	$10

COLEMAN, ALBERT, 'S ATLANTA POPS
EPIC

Number	Title	Yr	NM
❏ 34-03973	Classic Country (Part 1)/ Boots' Yakety	1983	$4
❏ 34-03362	Pop Goes the Country (Part I)/ Old Cowboys Never Die	1982	$4

RCA VICTOR

Number	Title	Yr	NM
❏ 74-0502	Foggy Mountain Breakdown/ Lonely Trumpet	1971	$8
—As "Albert Coleman and the Music City Pops"			

SOUTHERN TRACKS

Number	Title	Yr	NM
❏ 1039	Old Time Religion (Part 1)/ Old Time Religion (Part 2)	1985	$5

COLEMAN, GARY B.B.
ICHIBAN

Number	Title	Yr	NM
❏ 88-156	Merry Christmas, Baby/ Christmas Blues	1988	$5

COLEMAN, JIMMY
REVUE

Number	Title	Yr	NM
❏ 11002	Cloudy Days/Don't Seem Like You Love Me	1967	$30

COLEMAN, KING
KAREN

Number	Title	Yr	NM
❏ 1008	Blue Grey Christmas/ Holiday Season	1959	$15

COLESON, BETTY
HIT

Number	Title	Yr	NM
❏ 93	Dominique/Since I Fell for You	1963	$8
—B-side by Tom Tripp			
❏ 201	I Know a Place/I'm in a Very Romantic Mood	1965	$8
—B-side by William Randolph			
❏ 131	The Girl from Ipanema/Dang Me	1964	$8
—B-side by Harvey Frolic			
❏ 173	The Wedding/Song of Love	1965	$8
—B-side by William Randolph			
❏ 144	We'll Sing in the Sunshine/ Tottle-Dee Doodle, Dee Doo	1964	$8
—B-side by Jackie Preston			

COLLAGE, THE
SMASH

Number	Title	Yr	NM
❏ 2135	Any Day's a Sunday Afternoon/Lookin' at a Baby	1967	$8
❏ 2135 [PS]	Any Day's a Sunday Afternoon/Lookin' at a Baby	1967	$20
❏ 2150	Driftin'/Any Day's a Sunday Afternoon	1968	$8
❏ 2170	The Story of Rock & Roll/ Virginia Day's Ragtime Stories	1968	$8

COLLECTORS, THE
Early incarnation of CHILLIWACK.

VALIANT

Number	Title	Yr	NM
❏ 760	Old Man/Looking at a Baby	1967	$40

WARNER BROS.

Number	Title	Yr	NM
❏ 7300	Early Morning/My Love Delights Me	1969	$15
❏ 7059	Listen to the Words/ Fisherwoman	1967	$30
❏ 7194	Lydia Purple/I Ain't No Rich Man	1968	$15
❏ 7194	Lydia Purple/She (Will O' the Wind)	1968	$20
❏ 7159	Make It Easy/Fat Bird	1968	$30

Number	Title	Yr	NM

COLLEGIANS, THE (1)
WINLEY
| ❏ 261 | Oh I Need Your Love/Tonite, Oh Tonite | 1962 | $40 |

X-TRA
| ❏ 108 | Let's Go for a Ride/Heavenly Night | 1958 | $300 |

—Small print label (title and artist about 1/8-inch high)

| ❏ 108 | Let's Go for a Ride/Heavenly Night | 1961 | $70 |

—Large print label (title and artist about 1/4-inch high)

COLLEGIANS, THE (U)
GROOVE
| ❏ 0163 | Blue Solitude/Please Let Me Be the One | 1956 | $50 |

HILLTOP
| ❏ 1868 | Cookin'/Happy Parakeet | 1961 | $30 |
| ❏ 1867 | The Saints (Part 1)/The Saints (Part 2) | 1960 | $30 |

POST
| ❏ 10002 | I'm Ready/Grandma Told Me So | 1962 | $30 |

COLLETT, JIMMY
ARCADE
| ❏ 109 | I Don't Want To Be Alone For Christmas/What Do You Think My Heart Is Made Of | 1952 | $50 |

COLLIE, MARK
MCA
| ❏ 53778 | Something with a Ring to It/Another Old Soldier | 1989 | $4 |

COLLIE, SHIRLEY
LIBERTY
❏ 55324	Dime a Dozen/Oh Yes, Darling	1961	$20
❏ 55291	I'd Rather Hear Lies/Sad Singin' and Slow Ridin'	1960	$20
❏ 55391	If I Live Long Enough/Keeping My Fingers Crossed	1961	$20
❏ 55268	My Charlie/Didn't Work Out, Did It	1960	$20

COLLIER, MITTY
CHESS
❏ 1934	Ain't That Love/Come Back Baby	1965	$15
❏ 2050	Everybody Makes a Mistake Sometimes/Gotta Get Away from It All	1968	$20
❏ 2035	Git Out/That'll Be Good Enough for Me	1967	$20
❏ 1942	Help Me/For My Man	1965	$30
❏ 1907	I Had a Talk with My Man/Free Girl (In the Morning)	1964	$30
❏ 1871	I'm Your Part Time Love/Don't You Forget It	1963	$20
❏ 1791	I've Got Love/Got to Get Away from It All	1961	$20
❏ 1987	Like Only Yesterday/Watching and Waiting	1967	$30
❏ 1856	Miss Loneliness/My Babe	1963	$30
❏ 1964	My Party/I'm Satisfied	1966	$50
❏ 1953	Sharing You/Walk Away	1966	$30

ENTRANCE
| ❏ ZS77512 | I'd Like to Change Places/If This Is Our Last Time | 1972 | $10 |

PEACHTREE
❏ 121	I Can't Lose/You Hurt So Good	1969	$20
❏ 122	I'd Like to Change Places/Share What You Got	1969	$60
❏ 125	Lovin' on Borrowed Time/One Heck of a Lover	1970	$40
❏ 123	True Love Never Comes Easy/Fly Me to the Moon	1969	$30

COLLINS, ALBERT
20TH FOX
| ❏ 6708 | Cookin' Catfish/Taking My Time | 1968 | $8 |

GREAT SCOTT
| ❏ 07 | Albert's Alley/Defrost | 1963 | $40 |

HALLWAY
❏ 1913	Albert's Alley/Defrost	1963	$30
❏ 1925	Backstroke/Thaw Out	1964	$30
❏ 1920	Frosty/Tremble	1964	$40

IMPERIAL
❏ 66351	Ain't Got Time/Got a Good Thing Goin'	1969	$8
❏ 66412	Conversation for Collins/And Then It Started Raining	1969	$8
❏ 66391	Do the Sissy/Turnin' On	1969	$8

KANGAROO
| ❏ 104 | Collins Shuffle/(B-side unknown) | 1958 | $70 |
| ❏ 103 | Freeze/(B-side unknown) | 1958 | $70 |

LIBERTY
| ❏ 56184 | Coon 'n Collards/Do What You Want to Do | 1970 | $8 |

TCF HALL
❏ 116	Dyin' Flu/Hot 'N' Cold	1966	$12
❏ 127	Frost Bite/Don't Lose Your Cool	1966	$10
❏ 104	Sno Cone (Part 1)/Sno Cone (Part 2)	1965	$12

TUMBLEWEED
| ❏ 1007 | Eight Days on the Road/(B-side unknown) | 1972 | $8 |

COLLINS, BERT
SLEET
| ❏ 1100 | Ethelbert The Elf/Little Skidoo | 1980 | $4 |

COLLINS, BIG TOM
KING
| ❏ 4483 | Heartache Blues/Real Good Feeling | 1951 | $125 |
| ❏ 4568 | Heart Breaking Woman/Watchin' My Stuff | 1952 | $125 |

COLLINS, BOOTSY
COLUMBIA
❏ 38-08496	1st One 2 the Egg Wins (Human Race)/1st One 2 the Egg Wins (Street Legal)	1988	$3
❏ 38-07991	Party on Plastic (What's Bootsy Doin'?)/Save What's Mine for Me	1988	$3
❏ 38-07991 [PS]	Party on Plastic (What's Bootsy Doin'?)/Save What's Mine for Me	1988	$3

WARNER BROS.
❏ 29965	Shine-O-Myte (Rag Popping)/So Nice You Name Him Twice	1982	$4
❏ 8215	Stretchin' Out (In a Rubber Band)/Physical Love	1976	$6
❏ 50044	Take a Lickin' and Keep On Kickin'/Shine-O-Myte (Rag Poppin')	1982	$4

COLLINS, BRIAN
ABC DOT
❏ 17564	Faithless Love/You Won't Get Away with Mine	1975	$5
❏ 17546	I'd Still Be in Love with You/Sweet Memories	1975	$5
❏ 17694	If You Love Me (Let Me Know)/Round and Round	1977	$5
❏ 17527	That's the Way Love Should Be/Come a Little Bit Closer	1974	$5
❏ 17613	To Show You That I Love You/My Heart Would Know	1976	$5

DOT
❏ 17483	I Don't Plan on Losing You/Lonely Too Long	1973	$5
❏ 17466	I Wish (You Had Stayed)/Hand in Hand with Love	1973	$5
❏ 17499	Statue of a Fool/How Can I Tell Her	1974	$5

MEGA
❏ 0038	All I Want to Do Is Say I Love You/Time to Try My Wings	1971	$6
❏ 0078	Spread It Around/Let's Give It a Try	1972	$6
❏ 0058	There's a Kind of Hush (All Over the World)/Ain't Gonna Be Your Fool No More	1972	$6
❏ 0012	Walkin'/Your Kind of Man	1970	$6

PRIMERO
| ❏ 1001 | Before I Got to Know Her/Something Very Special | 1982 | $5 |
| ❏ 1010 | I'll Be Around/(B-side unknown) | 1983 | $5 |

RCA
❏ PB-11478	Hello Texas/Barefoot Angels	1979	$5
❏ PB-11350	Moonlight and Magnolias/Crazy You, Crazy Me	1978	$5
❏ PB-11277	Old Flames (Can't Hold a Candle to You)/Falsely Accused	1978	$5

COLLINS, DAVE AND ANSELL
BIG TREE
| ❏ 115 | Double Barrel/(Instrumental) | 1971 | $8 |

COLLINS, DOROTHY
CORAL
| ❏ 61736 | Baby's First Christmas/Christmas Comes But Once a Year | 1956 | $15 |
| ❏ 61539 | Mister Santa/The Twelve Gifts of Christmas | 1955 | $15 |

COLLINS, DUGG
CERTRON
| ❏ 10029 | I Just Want to Be Alone/Play Me Some Heart Songs | 1971 | $8 |

LITTLE DARLIN'
| ❏ 7912 | I Think I'll Wait Awhile/No Easy Way to Do | 1979 | $6 |

SCR
❏ 147	How Do You Talk to a Baby/Hurt Me One More Time	1977	$6
❏ 143	I'm the Man/If I Don't Love You	1977	$6
❏ 154	Someday I'd Like to Love You in Your Mind/Hurt Mw One More Time	1978	$6

COLLINS, EDDIE
FERNWOOD
| ❏ 104 | Patience Baby/Can't Face Life Alone | 1958 | $125 |

COLLINS, GLENDA
LAWN
| ❏ 250 | Lollipop/Everybody's Gotta Fall in Love | 1965 | $10 |

COLLINS, GWEN AND JERRY
CAPITOL
| ❏ 2710 | Get Together/We're Not Bad | 1969 | $6 |
| ❏ 2835 | One Tin Soldier/We've Gotta Give | 1970 | $6 |

COLLINS, JIM
TKM
| ❏ 111216 | The Things I've Done to Me/(B-side unknown) | 1986 | $5 |

WHITE GOLD
| ❏ 22252 | I Wanna Be a Cowboy 'Til I Die/(B-side unknown) | 1985 | $5 |
| ❏ 22251 | What a Memory You'd Make/(B-side unknown) | 1985 | $5 |

COLLINS, JUDY
ELEKTRA
❏ 45709	Amazing Grace/Nightingale II	1971	$5
❏ 45289	Angel, Spread Your Wings/The Moon Is a Harsh Mistress	1975	$4
❏ 45415	Born to the Breed/Special Delivery	1977	$4
❏ 45639	Both Sides Now/Who Knows Where the Time Goes	1968	$8

—Red, white and black label

| ❏ 45639 | Both Sides Now/Who Knows Where the Time Goes | 1968 | $6 |

—Yellow and black label

❏ 45355	Bread and Roses/Out of Control	1976	$4
❏ 45355 [PS]	Bread and Roses/Out of Control	1976	$6
❏ 46623	Bright Morning Star/Almost Free	1980	$4
❏ 45657	Chelsea Morning/Pretty Polly	1969	$6
❏ 45657 [PS]	Chelsea Morning/Pretty Polly	1969	$20
❏ 45831	Cook with Honey/So Begins the Task	1973	$4
❏ 47437 [DJ]	Drink a Round to Ireland (stereo)/(mono)	1982	$12

—Promo only on green vinyl

❏ 45372	Everything Must Change/Special Delivery	1976	$4
❏ 46020	Hard Times for Lovers/Happy End	1979	$4
❏ 46020 [PS]	Hard Times for Lovers/Happy End	1979	$6
❏ 69697	Home Again/Dream On	1984	$4

—A-side with T.G. Sheppard

❏ 45601	I'll Keep It With Mine/Thirsty Boots	1965	$8
❏ 45813	In My Life/Sunny Goodge Street	1972	$4
❏ 45610	I Think It's Going to Rain Today/Hard Lovin' Losers	1966	$8
❏ 47434	It's Gonna Be One of Those Nights/Mama Mama	1982	$4
❏ 47243	Memory/The Life You Dream	1981	$4
❏ 69662	Only You/Dream On	1985	$3
❏ 45755	Open the Door/Innisfree	1971	$5
❏ 45680	Pack Up Your Sorrows/Turn, Turn, Turn	1970	$5
❏ 45253	Send In the Clowns/Houses	1975	$5

—Large print label (original)

| ❏ 45253 | Send In the Clowns/Houses | 1977 | $4 |

—Small print label (reissue)

❏ 45649	Someday Soon/My Father	1969	$6
❏ 45849	The Hostage/Secret Gardens	1973	$4
❏ 45008	Turn, Turn, Turn/Farewell	1963	$10
❏ 46050	Where or When/Dorothy	1979	$4

COLLINS KIDS, THE
COLUMBIA
❏ 4-21470	Beetle Bug Bop/Hush Money	1955	$40
❏ 4-40921	Hop, Skip and Jump/Young Heart	1957	$40
❏ 4-41087	Hoy Hoy/Mama Worries	1958	$60
❏ 4-21543	I'm in My Teens/They're Still in Love	1956	$40
❏ 4-41149	Mercy/Sweet Talk	1958	$60
❏ 4-40824	Move a Little Closer/Go Away, Don't Bother Me	1957	$40
❏ 4-41012	Party/Heartbeat	1957	$100
❏ 4-41329	Sugar Plum/Kinda Like Love	1959	$30

COLLINS, LARRY
COLUMBIA

Number	Title	Yr	NM
❏ 4-41953	Get Along Home Cindy/What About Tomorrow	1960	$20
❏ 4-42534	Hey Mama Boom-a-Lacka/More Than a Friend	1962	$20
❏ 4-42131	One Step Down/There She Stands, The One	1961	$20
❏ 4-42394	T-Bone/Wild and Wicked Love	1962	$20

MONUMENT

Number	Title	Yr	NM
❏ 1196	The Outcast/Shake Hands with the Devil	1970	$8

COLLINS, LORRIE
COLUMBIA

Number	Title	Yr	NM
❏ 4-41673	Blues in the Night/That's Your Affair	1960	$30
❏ 4-42242	Home of the Blues/Waitin' and Watchin'	1961	$20
❏ 4-41541	The Lonesome Road/Another Man Done Gone	1959	$30

COLLINS, LYN
KING

Number	Title	Yr	NM
❏ 6373	Wheels of Life/Just Won't Do Right	1971	$60

PEOPLE

Number	Title	Yr	NM
❏ 657	Baby Don't Do It/How Long Can I Keep It Up	1975	$30
❏ 636	Give It Up or Turnit A Loose/What the World Needs Now Is Love	1974	$40
❏ 623	How Long Can I Keep It Up (Part 1)/How Long Can I Keep It Up (Part 2)	1973	$30
❏ 659	If You Don't Know Me By Now/Baby Don't Do It	1975	$30
❏ 618	Mama Feel Good/Fly Me to the Moon	1973	$30
❏ 615	Me and My Baby Got a Good Thing Goin'/I'll Never Let You Break My Heart Again	1972	$20
❏ 662	Mr. Big Stuff/Rock Me Again & Again & Again & Again & Again	1975	$30
❏ 626	Take Me As I Am/Make the World a Better Place	1973	$30
❏ 633	Take Me Just As I Am/Don't Make Me Over	1973	$15
❏ 608	Think (About It)/Ain't No Sunshine	1972	$30
❏ 630	We Want to Parrty, Parrty, Parrty/You Can't Beat Two People in Love	1973	$30
❏ 641	Wide Awake in a Dream/Rock Me Again & Again & Again & Again & Again	1974	$40

POLYDOR

Number	Title	Yr	NM
❏ 14107	Wheels of Life/Just Won't Do Right	1971	$30

—*Reissue of King 6373*

COLLINS, PHIL
Also see GENESIS; BRAND X; BRIAN ENO. Phil also drummed in ROBERT PLANT's solo band.

ATLANTIC

Number	Title	Yr	NM
❏ 89700	Against All Odds (Take a Look at Me Now)/The Search	1984	$3

—*B-side by Larry Carlton*

Number	Title	Yr	NM
❏ 89700 [PS]	Against All Odds (Take a Look at Me Now)/The Search	1984	$3
❏ 88774	Another Day in Paradise/Heat on the Street	1989	$3
❏ 88774 [PS]	Another Day in Paradise/Heat on the Street	1989	$3
❏ 89536	Don't Lose My Number/We Said Hello Goodbye	1985	$3
❏ 89536 [PS]	Don't Lose My Number/We Said Hello Goodbye	1985	$3
❏ 89017	Groovy Kind of Love/Big Noise	1988	$3
❏ 89017 [PS]	Groovy Kind of Love/Big Noise	1988	$4
❏ 89864	I Cannot Believe It's True/Thru These Walls	1983	$3
❏ 89877	I Don't Care Anymore/The West Side	1983	$3
❏ 89877 [PS]	I Don't Care Anymore/The West Side	1983	$3
❏ 3790	I Missed Again/I'm Not Moving	1981	$3
❏ 3790 [PS]	I Missed Again/I'm Not Moving	1981	$6
❏ PR655 [DJ]	In the Air Tonight (same on both sides?)	1984	$8

—*Promo-only radio reservice after the song was successfully used in the TV series "Miami Vice*

Number	Title	Yr	NM
❏ 3824	In the Air Tonight/The Roof Is Leaking	1981	$3
❏ 3824 [PS]	In the Air Tonight/The Roof Is Leaking	1981	$6
❏ 88738	I Wish It Would Rain Down/You've Been in Love (That Little Bit)	1989	$3
❏ 88738 [PS]	I Wish It Would Rain Down/You've Been in Love (That Little Bit)	1989	$3
❏ 89588	One More Night/The Man with the Horn	1985	$3
❏ 89588 [PS]	One More Night/The Man with the Horn	1985	$3
❏ 89498	Separate Lives (Love Theme from White Nights)/I Don't Wanna Know	1985	$3

—*A-side with Marilyn Martin*

Number	Title	Yr	NM
❏ 89498 [PS]	Separate Lives (Love Theme from White Nights)/I Don't Wanna Know	1985	$5

—*With promo shot from the movie on front of sleeve*

Number	Title	Yr	NM
❏ 89498 [PS]	Separate Lives (Love Theme from White Nights)/I Don't Wanna Know	1985	$4

—*With photo of Phil and Marilyn on front of sleeve*

Number	Title	Yr	NM
❏ 89560	Sussudio/I Like the Way	1985	$3
❏ 89560 [PS]	Sussudio/I Like the Way	1985	$3
❏ 89472	Take Me Home/Only You Know and I Know	1985	$3
❏ 89472 [PS]	Take Me Home/Only You Know and I Know	1985	$4
❏ 88980	Two Hearts/The Robbery	1989	$3
❏ 88980 [PS]	Two Hearts/The Robbery	1989	$4

ATLANTIC OLDIES SERIES

Number	Title	Yr	NM
❏ OS13231	In the Air Tonight/I Missed Again	1984	$3

—*Reissue*

COLLINS, SUE AND THE D.H.S. SWINGERS
VANDAN

Number	Title	Yr	NM
❏ 8156	Christmas Time Again/I Remember Christmas	1966	$10

COLLINS, TOMMY
CAPITOL

Number	Title	Yr	NM
❏ 5345	All of the Monkeys Ain't in the Zoo/Don't Let Me Stand in His Footsteps	1965	$15
❏ F3665	All of the Monkeys Ain't in the Zoo/Don't You Love Me Anymore	1957	$30
❏ F3789	A Love Is Born/I'm Nobody's Fool But Yours	1957	$30
❏ 4495	Black Cat/My Last Chance with You	1961	$60
❏ F2806	I Always Get a Souvenir/Let Me Love You	1954	$30
❏ 5051	I Can Do That/You'd Better Be Nice	1963	$20

—*As "Tommy and Wanda Collins"*

Number	Title	Yr	NM
❏ 5117	If I Could Just Go Back/I Got Mine	1964	$15
❏ F3190	I Guess I'm Crazy/You Oughta See Pickles Now	1955	$30
❏ F3289	I'll Be Gone/I Love You More and More Each Day	1955	$30
❏ F3082	It Tickles/Let Down	1955	$30
❏ F3591	I Wish I Had Died in My Cradle/I'll Never Let You Go	1956	$30
❏ F4263	Little June/A Hundred Years from Now	1959	$30
❏ 4421	Summer's Almost Gone/Keep Dreaming	1960	$20
❏ 4962	Take Me Back to the Good Old Days/When Did Right Become Wrong	1963	$20
❏ F4327	The Wreck of the Old 97/You Belong in My Arms	1959	$30
❏ F2891	Whatcha Gonna Do Now/You're for Me	1954	$30
❏ F3370	What Kind of a Sweetheart Are You/Wait a Little Longer	1956	$30

COLUMBIA

Number	Title	Yr	NM
❏ 4-44260	Big Dummy/What-Cha Gonna Do Now?	1967	$12
❏ 4-43972	Birmingham/Don't Wipe the Tears That You Cry for Him (On My Good White Shirt)	1967	$10
❏ 4-44498	He's Gonna Have to Catch Me First/Sunny Side of My Life	1968	$12
❏ 4-44664	High on a Hilltop/Woman You Have Been Told	1968	$12
❏ 4-43489	If You Can't Bite, Don't Growl/Man Machine	1965	$10
❏ 4-44386	I Made the Prison Band/No Love Have I	1967	$10
❏ 4-43628	Shindig in the Barn/Be Serious Ann	1966	$10
❏ 4-43724	There's No Girl in My Life Anymore/A Man Gotta Do What a Man Gotta Do	1966	$10

TOWER

Number	Title	Yr	NM
❏ 213	Take Me Back to the Good Old Days/Oh What a Dream	1966	$15
❏ EAP 1-607 [PS]	Tommy Collins	1955	$30

COLMAN, RONALD
DECCA

Number	Title	Yr	NM
❏ 40107	A Christmas Carol (Part 1)/A Christmas Carol (Part 6)	1950	$20

—*Sides 1 and 6 of "Album No. 9-71*

Number	Title	Yr	NM
❏ 40108	A Christmas Carol (Part 2)/A Christmas Carol (Part 5)	1950	$20

—*Sides 2 and 5 of "Album No. 9-71*

Number	Title	Yr	NM
❏ 40109	A Christmas Carol (Part 3)/A Christmas Carol (Part 4)	1950	$20

—*Sides 3 and 4 of "Album No. 9-71*

7-Inch Extended Plays

Number	Title	Yr	NM
❏ 9-71	A Christmas Carol	1950	$60

—*Includes records 40107, 40108 and 40109 (also priced separately) and box*

COLONNA, JERRY
DECCA

Number	Title	Yr	NM
❏ 28884	Too Fat For the Chimney/Sleigh Bells In The Sky	1953	$15

COLORADO
UNI

Number	Title	Yr	NM
❏ 55302	Dogwood/Moonshine	1971	$6
❏ 55280	My Babe/Country Comfort	1971	$6

COLOSSEUM
Gary Moore and Don Airey are Colosseum alumni.

ABC DUNHILL

Number	Title	Yr	NM
❏ 4200	Those Who Are About to Die Salute You/Walking in the Park	1969	$8

COLOURS
DOT

Number	Title	Yr	NM
❏ 17181	Hyannis Port Soul/Run Away from Here	1968	$8

COLTER, JESSI
CAPITOL

Number	Title	Yr	NM
❏ 5073	Holdin' On/(B-side unknown)	1981	$4
❏ 4472	I Belong to Him/There Ain't No Rain	1977	$4
❏ 4009	I'm Not Lisa/For the First Time	1974	$4
❏ 4325	I Thought I Heard You Calling My Name/You Hung the Moon (Didn't You Waylon)	1976	$4
❏ 4200	It's Morning (And I Still Love You)/Would You Walk with Me (To the Lilies)	1975	$4
❏ 4696	Love Me Back to Sleep/Don't You Think I Felt It Too	1979	$4
❏ 4641	Maybe You Should've Been Listening/My Cowboy's Last Ride	1978	$4
❏ 4087	What's Happened to Blue Eyes/You Ain't Never Been Loved (Like I'm Gonna Love You)	1975	$4
❏ 4252	Without You/All My Life I've Been Your Love	1976	$4

JAMIE

Number	Title	Yr	NM
❏ 1193	I Cried Long Enough/Making Believe	1961	$40

—*As "Mirriam Johnson"*

Number	Title	Yr	NM
❏ 1181	Lonesome Road/Young and Innocent	1961	$40

—*As "Mirriam Johnson"*

RCA VICTOR

Number	Title	Yr	NM
❏ 47-9826	Cry Softly/If She's Where You Like Livin'	1970	$5
❏ PB-10309	He Called Me Baby/Take a Message to Laura	1975	$5
❏ 74-0280	Take a Message to Laura/I Ain't the One	1969	$5
❏ 47-9962	The Golden Rocket/You Mean to Say	1971	$5

COLTON, TONY
ABC-PARAMOUNT

Number	Title	Yr	NM
❏ 10705	I Stand Accused/Further On Down the Track	1965	$20

ROULETTE

Number	Title	Yr	NM
❏ 4475	Tell the World/Goodbye Cindy, Goodbye	1963	$20

COLTRANE, CHI
CLOUDS

Number	Title	Yr	NM
❏ 10	What's Happening to Me (It's a Spell)/Changes	1978	$4

COLUMBIA

Number	Title	Yr	NM
❏ 45749	It's Really Come to This/Go Like Elijah	1972	$5
❏ 45960	Myself to You/Who Every Told You	1973	$4
❏ 45640	Thunder and Lightning/Time to Come In	1972	$5
❏ 45802	Turn Me Around/You Are My Friend	1973	$5

COLTRANE, JOHN
ATLANTIC

Number	Title	Yr	NM
❏ 5003	Cousin Mary/Naimi	1960	$12
❏ 5012	My Favorite Things (Part 1)/My Favorite Things (Part 2)	1961	$15

BLUE NOTE

Number	Title	Yr	NM
❏ 1691	Blue Train (Part 1)/Blue Train (Part 2)	1957	$20

IMPULSE!

Number	Title	Yr	NM
❏ 203	Easy to Remember/Greensleeves	1961	$12
❏ 218	Lush Life/My One and Only Love	1963	$10

—*With Johnny Hartman*

Number	Title	Yr	NM
315	Dakar/The Believer	1963	$12
249	Lush Life/I Love You	1960	$15
267	Stardust/Love Thy Neighbor	1961	$15

7-Inch Extended Plays

IMPULSE!

Number	Title	Yr	NM
EP AS-40	My One and Only/Lush Life	1963	$25

—Jukebox issue; small hole, plays at 33 1/3 rpm

COLTS, THE

ANTLER

Number	Title	Yr	NM
4007	Guiding Angel/The Shiek of Araby	1959	$50

MAMBO

112	Adorable/Lips Red as Wine	1955	$400

PLAZA

505	Hey, Pretty Baby/Sweet Sixteen	1962	$30

VITA

112	Adorable/Lips Red as Wine	1955	$200
121	Honey Bun/Sweet Sixteen	1955	$120

COLUMBUS BOYCHOIR, THE

DECCA

Number	Title	Yr	NM
34123 [PS]	Christmas Club Presents Yuletide Favorites Volume 2	1963	$15
34123	Deck The Halls/Jingle Bells/We Wish You a Merry Christmas//What Child Is This/Here We Come a-Wassailing/Joy to the World	1963	$15

—7-inch 33 1/3 rpm record

COLUMBUS PHARAOHS, THE

ESTA

290	Give Me Your Love/China Girl	1958	$1000

COLWELL-WINFIELD BLUES BAND, THE

VERVE FORECAST

5098	Cold Wind Blues/Free Will Fantasy	1968	$10

COLYER, KEN

LONDON

1674	Casey Jones/Streamline Train	1956	$15
1655	Down by the Riverside/Take This Hammer	1956	$15

COMBINATIONS, THE

KELLMAC

1007	Why/Come Back	1966	$40

COMFORTABLE CHAIR, THE

ODE

109	Be Me/Some Soon, Some Day	1968	$12
112	I'll See You/Now	1968	$10

COMMANDER CODY AND HIS LOST PLANET AIRMEN

ARISTA

Number	Title	Yr	NM
0271	Seven-Eleven/You Snooze You Lose	1977	$4
0344	Thank You Lone Ranger/My Day	1978	$4

DOT

17487	Daddy's Drinking Up Our Christmas/Honeysuckle Honey	1973	$6
17500	Diggy Liggy Lo/Outgoing Person	1974	$5

PARAMOUNT

0169	Beat Me Daddy, Eight to the Bar/Daddy's Gonna Treat You Right	1972	$6
0169 [PS]	Beat Me Daddy, Eight to the Bar/Daddy's Gonna Treat You Right	1972	$12
0146	Hot Rod Lincoln/My Home in My Hand	1972	$6
0130	Lost in the Ozone/Midnight Shift	1971	$6
0130 [PS]	Lost in the Ozone/Midnight Shift	1971	$10
0193	Semi-Truck/Watch My .38	1973	$6
0216	Smoke! Smoke! Smoke! (That Cigarette)/Rock That Boogie	1973	$6
0216 [PS]	Smoke! Smoke! Smoke! (That Cigarette)/Rock That Boogie	1973	$12
0178	Truck Stop Rock/Mama Hated Diesels	1972	$6
0178 [PS]	Truck Stop Rock/Mama Hated Diesels	1972	$10

WARNER BROS.

8073	Don't Let Go/Keep On Lovin' Her	1975	$4
8164	It's Gonna Be One of Those Nights/Roll Your Own	1975	$4

COMMODORES

MOTOWN

Number	Title	Yr	NM
1788	Animal Instinct/Lightin' Up the Sky	1985	$3
1268	Are You Happy/There's a Song in My Heart	1973	$6
1719	Been Lovin' You/Turn Off the Lights	1984	$3
1425	Brick House/Captain Quickdraw	1977	$4
1418	Easy/Can't You Let Me Tease You	1977	$4
1408	Fancy Dancer/Cebu	1977	$4
1452	Flying High/X-Rated Movie	1978	$4
1495	Heroes/Funky Situation	1980	$4
1319	I Feel Sanctified/It Is As Good As You Make It	1974	$5
1514	Lady (You Bring Me Up)/Gettin' It	1981	$4
1307 [DJ]	Machine Gun (stereo/mono)	1974	$20

—Promo only on red vinyl

1307	Machine Gun/There's a Song in My Heart	1974	$5
1527	Oh No/Lovin' You	1981	$4
1489	Old Fashion Love/Sexy Lady	1980	$4
1694	Only You/Cebu	1983	$3
1651	Painted Pictures/Reach High	1982	$3
1466	Sail On/Thumpin' Music	1979	$4
1661	Sexy Lady/Reach High	1983	$3
1338	Slippery When Wet/The Bump	1975	$5
1474	Still/Such a Woman	1979	$4
1381	Sweet Love/Better Never Than Forever	1976	$4
1381 [DJ]	Sweet Love (stereo/mono)	1976	$20

—Promo only on yellow vinyl

1361	This Is Your Life/Look What You've Done to Me	1975	$5
1443	Three Times a Lady/Look What You've Done to Me	1978	$4
1432	Too Hot Ta Trot/Funky Situation	1977	$4
1604	Why You Wanna Try Me/X-Rated Movie	1982	$4
1479	Wonderland/Lovin' You	1979	$4

MOWEST

5038	Determination/Don't You Be Worried	1973	$8
5009	I'm Looking for Love/At the Zoo	1972	$8

POLYDOR

885358-7	Goin' to the Bank/Serious Love	1986	$3
885358-7 [PS]	Goin' to the Bank/Serious Love	1986	$3
871317-7	Grrip/Ain't Giving Up	1989	$3
887939-7	Solitaire/Stretchhh	1988	$3
887939-7 [PS]	Solitaire/Stretchhh	1988	$3
885538-7	Take It from Me/I Wanna Rock You	1987	$3
885538-7 [PS]	Take It from Me/I Wanna Rock You	1987	$3

COMMODORES, THE

BRUNSWICK

Number	Title	Yr	NM
55126	Laughing with Tears/Who Dat	1959	$30

CHALLENGE

1007	Faith/I'll Be There	1957	$30
1004	Sweet Angel/Not a Day Goes By	1957	$30

DOT

15425	Cream Puff/Close to My Heart	1955	$30
15439	Speedoo/Whole Lotta Shakin' Goin' On	1956	$30
15461	Two Loves Have I/Who Said I Said That	1956	$30

COMMUNARDS

MCA

Number	Title	Yr	NM
52928	Don't Leave Me This Way/Sanctified	1986	$3
52928 [PS]	Don't Leave Me This Way/Sanctified	1986	$5

COMO, PERRY, AND THE FONTANE SISTERS

RCA VICTOR

Number	Title	Yr	NM
47-3113	Bibbidi-Bobbidi-Boo/A Dream Is a Wish Your Heart Makes	1949	$20
47-4344	Here's to My Lady/If Wishes Were Kisses	1951	$15
47-3747	Hoop-Dee-Doo/On the Outgoing Tide	1950	$15
47-3846	I Cross My Fingers/If You Were My Girl	1950	$15
47-3082	I Wanna Go Home (With You)/Hush Little Darlin'	1949	$15
47-5524	Silver Bells/Kissing Bridge	1953	$15
47-4959	To Know You (Is to Love You)/My Lady Loves to Dance	1952	$15

COMO, PERRY

RCA

Number	Title	Yr	NM
PB-13613	As My Love for You/The Second Time	1983	$3
PB-10122	Christmas Dream/Christ Is Born	1976	$3

—Reissue; black label, dog near top

PB-12028	Colors of My Life/Someone Is Waiting	1980	$3
PB-11185	Girl You Made It Happen/Where You're Concerned	1977	$3
PB-13069	Goodbye for Now (Theme from "Reds")/Jason	1982	$3
9096-7-R [DJ]	I May Never Pass This Way Again (same on both sides)	1989	$5

—Promotional record for Christmas Seals

PB-13307	I Wish It Could Be Christmas Forever/Toyland	1982	$4
PB-13453	So It Goes/Fancy Dancer	1983	$3
PB-13690	The Best of Times/Song of the Sand (La Da Da Da)	1983	$3
PB-13690 [PS]	The Best of Times/Song of the Sand (La Da Da Da)	1983	$6
PB-11434	When I Wanted You/Forever	1978	$3

RCA VICTOR

Number	Title	Yr	NM
47-5573	Abide with Me/Nearer, My God, To Thee	1953	$15
47-3930	A Bushel and a Peck/She's a Lady	1950	$15

—With Betty Hutton

47-5572	Act of Contrition/Good Night Sweet Jesus	1953	$15
47-3036	A Dreamer's Holiday/The Meadows of Heaven	1949	$20
47-6294	All at Once You Love Her/The Rose Tattoo	1955	$10
74-0906	And I Love Her So/Love Looks So Good on You	1973	$4
GB-10471	And I Love You So/Love Looks So Good on You	1975	$3

—Gold Standard Series

52-0071	Ave Maria/The Lord's Prayer	1949	$30

—Blue vinyl original

52-0071	Ave Maria/The Lord's Prayer	1949	$15

—Black vinyl reissue

447-0110	Ave Maria/The Lord's Prayer	1955	$15
47-7650	Ave Maria/The Lord's Prayer	1959	$12
47-7650 [PS]	Ave Maria/The Lord's Prayer	1959	$40
47-2899	A" You're Adorable/When Is Sometime?	1949	$20
47-2896	Bali Ha'i/Some Enchanted Evening	1949	$20
47-2728	Because/If You Had All the World and All the Gold	1949	$20
APBO-0225	Beyond Tomorrow/It All Seems to Fall Into Line	1974	$4
47-4528	Black Moonlight/Concentrate on You	1952	$15
47-3850	Bless This House/The Rosary	1950	$15
47-2844	Carolina Moon/Body and Soul	1949	$20
GB-10174	Catch a Falling Star/Dream Along with Me	1975	$3

—Gold Standard Series

47-7128	Catch a Falling Star/Magic Moments	1957	$15

—Black label, dog on top

47-7128	Catch a Falling Star/Magic Moments	1969	$8

—Orange label with original number

47-8004	Caterina/The Island of Forgotten Lovers	1962	$8
47-8004 [PS]	Caterina/The Island of Forgotten Lovers	1962	$30
47-6137	Chee Chee O-Chee (Sang the Little Bird)/Two Lost Souls	1955	$10

—With Jaye P. Morgan

47-4707	Childhood Is a Meadow/One Little Candle	1952	$15
47-9367	Christmas Bells/Love Is a Christmas Rose	1967	$8
47-9367 [PS]	Christmas Bells/Love Is a Christmas Rose	1967	$10
PB-10122	Christmas Dream/Christ Is Born	1974	$4

—Gray label

47-6991	Dancin'/Marchin' Along to the Blues	1957	$12
47-7670	Delaware/I Know What God Is	1960	$8
74-0356	Don't Leave Me/Love Is Spreading All Over the World	1970	$4
74-0436	Don't Leave Me/Love Is Spreading All Over the World	1971	$4
47-5064	Don't Let the Stars Get In Your Eyes/Lies	1952	$15
47-6059	Door of Dreams/Nobody	1955	$12
47-8533	Dream On Little Dreamer/My Own Peculiar Way	1965	$8
47-8533 [PS]	Dream On Little Dreamer/My Own Peculiar Way	1965	$30
47-3226	Easter Parade/Song of Songs	1949	$20
74-0444	El Condor Pasa/I Think of You	1971	$4
47-5574	Eli, Eli/Kol Niore	1953	$15
47-2919	Every Time I Meet You/Two Little, New Little, Blue Little Eyes	1949	$20
47-3267	Far Away Places/Missouri Waltz	1949	$20
47-2892	Forever and Ever/I Don't See Me in Your Eyes Anymore	1949	$20
47-8945	Forget Domani/One Day Is Like Another	1966	$8
47-4445	Garden in the Rain/Oh, How I Miss You Tonight	1952	$15
47-2997	Give Me Your Hand/I Wish I Had a Record	1949	$20
74-0193	Happiness Comes, Happiness Goes/That's All This Old World Needs	1969	$4
47-9533	Happy Man/One Go-Round	1968	$5
47-4112	Hello Young Lovers/We Kissed in a Shadow	1951	$15
47-5749	Hit and Run Affair/There Never Was a Night So Beautiful	1954	$15
47-6321	Home for the Holidays/God Rest Ye Merry Gentlemen	1955	$15
GB-10175	Hot Diggity (Dog Ziggity Boom)/Don't Let the Stars Get In Your Eyes	1975	$3

—Gold Standard Series

47-6427	Hot Diggity (Dog Ziggity Boom)/Juke Box Baby	1956	$10

Number	Title	Yr	NM
❑ 47-5571	I Believe/Onward Christian Soldiers	1953	$15
❑ 47-3763	If You Were Only Mine/ Let's Go to the Church	1950	$15
❑ 47-3997	If/Zing, Zing, Zoom, Zoom	1950	$15
❑ 47-7541	I Know/You Are in Love	1959	$10
❑ 47-7541 [PS]	I Know/You Are in Love	1959	$30
❑ 47-2970	I'll Be Home for Christmas/ Santa Claus Is Coming to Town	1949	$30
❑ 47-9262	I Looked Back/A World of Love (That I Found)	1967	$6
❑ 47-8186	(I Love You) Don't You Forget It/One More Mountain	1963	$8
❑ 47-8186 [PS]	(I Love You) Don't You Forget It/One More Mountain	1963	$30
❑ 47-2845	I'm Always Chasing Rainbows/ If We Can't Be the Same Old Sweethearts, We'll Just Be the Same Old Friends	1949	$20
	— The above three comprise box set WP 187, "A Sentimental Date with Perry		
❑ 47-7628	I May Never Pass This Way Again/A Still Small Voice	1959	$10
❑ PB-10045	In These Crazy Times/ Temptation	1974	$3
❑ K2NW6096/7 [DJ]	(Intro) I May Never Pass This Way Again/(Alternate Intro) I May Never Pass This Way Again	1959	$15
	— Promotional record for Christmas Seals		
❑ 47-4314	It's Beginning to Look Like Christmas/There Is No Christmas Like a Home Christmas	1951	$20
❑ 74-0387	It's Impossible/Long Life. Lots of Happiness	1970	$5
❑ 47-4034	It's Only a Paper Moon/ Me and My Shadow	1951	$15
❑ 47-2931	Let's Take an Old-Fashioned Walk/Just One Way to Say I Love You	1949	$20
❑ APBO-0096	Love Don't Care/Walk Right Back	1973	$4
❑ 47-7353	Love Makes the World Go 'Round/Mandolins in the Moonlight	1958	$10
❑ 47-7812	Make Someone Happy/ Gone Is My Love	1960	$8
❑ 47-3931	Marchita/So Long Sally	1950	$15
❑ 47-4744	Maybe/Watermelon Weather	1952	$15
	— With Eddie Fisher		
❑ 47-8722	Meet Me at the Altar/ Bye, Bye, Little Girl	1965	$8
❑ 47-6670	Moonlight Love/Chincherinchee	1956	$10
❑ 47-7274	Moon Talk/Beats There a Heart So True	1958	$10
❑ 47-6554	More/Glendora	1956	$10
❑ 47-3851	Mother Dear O Pray For Me/ Hoy God, We Praise Thy Name	1950	$15
❑ 74-0518	My Days of Loving You/ Yesterday I Heard the Rain	1971	$4
❑ 47-4529	My Heart Stood Still/ If There's Someone	1952	$15
❑ 47-4877	My Love and Devotion/ Sweethearts' Holiday	1952	$15
❑ 47-4631	One Little Candle/ It's Easter Time	1952	$15
❑ 47-8636	Oowee, Oowee/Summer Wind	1965	$8
❑ 47-5857	Papa Loves Mambo/ The Things I Didn't Do	1954	$15
❑ 47-3905	Patricia/Watchin' the Trains Go By	1950	$15
❑ 47-3211	Please Believe Me/Did Anyone Ever Tell You, Mrs. Murphy	1949	$20
❑ 47-4453	Please Mr. Sun/Tulips and Heather	1952	$15
❑ GB-10176	Prisoner of Love/ Magic Moments	1975	$3
	— Gold Standard Series		
❑ 47-2886	Prisoner of Love/Temptation	1949	$20
❑ 47-5277	Say You're Mine Again/ My One and Only Heart	1953	$15
❑ 47-9722	Seattle/Sunshine Wine	1969	$5
❑ 47-2971	Silent Night/White Christmas	1949	$30
❑ 47-6590	Somebody Up There Likes Me/Dream Along with Me	1956	$12
❑ 47-6590 [PS]	Somebody Up There Likes Me/Dream Along with Me	1956	$40
❑ 47-8823	Stay with Me/Coo Coo Roo Coo Coo Paloma	1966	$8
❑ 47-9165	Stop! And Think It Over/How Beautiful the World Can Be	1967	$6
❑ 47-4530	Summertime/While We're Young	1952	$15
❑ 47-4203	Surprising/Cara Cara Bella Bella	1951	$15
❑ 47-2969	That Christmas Feeling/ Winter Wonderland	1949	$30
❑ 47-4035	That Old Gang of Mine/I Found a Million Dollar Baby	1951	$15
❑ 47-3922	The Best Thing for You/ Marrying for Love	1950	$15
❑ 47-3933	The Christmas Symphony/ There Is No Christmas Like a Home Christmas	1950	$20
❑ 47-9448	The Father of Girls/ Somebody Makes It So	1968	$5
❑ 47-0259	The First Christmas (Part 1)/(Part 2)	1950	$30
	— Yellow vinyl		
❑ 47-0259 [PS]	The First Christmas (Part 1)/(Part 2)	1950	$40
	— Picture sleeve uses the number "WY 422		
❑ 47-6904	The Girl with the Golden Braids/My Little Baby	1957	$10

Number	Title	Yr	NM
❑ PB-10604	Then You Can Tell Me Goodbye/The Grass Keeps Right On Growing	1976	$3
❑ 47-9683	There Is No Christmas Like a Home Christmas/Christmas Eve	1968	$6
❑ 47-4158	There's No Boat Like a Rowboat/There's a Big Blue Cloud (Next to Heaven)	1951	$15
❑ SP-45-119 [DJ]	(There's No Place Like) Home For The Holidays/ I'll Be Home For Christmas	1962	$15
❑ 47-5950	(There's No Place Like) Home for the Holidays/Silk Stockings	1954	$15
❑ 47-2887	Till the End of Time/Because	1949	$20
❑ 47-6192	Tina Marie/Fooled	1955	$10
❑ 47-7464	Tomboy/Kiss Me and Kiss Me and Kiss Me	1959	$10
❑ 47-4081	Tumbling Tumbleweeds/You Don't Know What Lonesome Is	1951	$15
	— With the Sons of the Pioneers		
❑ WBY43	'Twas the Night Before Christmas/The Twelve Days of Christmas	1953	$20
❑ 47-5647	Wanted/Look Out the Window	1954	$15
❑ APBO-0274	Weave Me the Sunshine/I Don't Know What He Told You	1974	$4
❑ 47-2747	What'll I Do?/Love Me or Leave Me	1949	$20
❑ 47-9356	What Love Is Made Of/ You Made It That Way	1967	$6
❑ 47-2843	When Your Hair Has Turned to Silver/When Day Is Done	1949	$20
❑ 47-2888	When You Were Sweet Sixteen/Song of Songs	1949	$20
❑ 47-4687	Why Did You Leave Me/ Lonesome, That's All	1952	$15
❑ 47-5152	Wild Horses/I Confess	1953	$15
❑ 47-3229	With a Song in My Heart/Blue Room	1949	$20
❑ 47-4033	Without a Song/More Than You Know	1951	$15
❑ PB-10257	Wonderful Baby/ World of Dreams	1975	$3

RCA VICTOR

Number	Title	Yr	NM
❑ EPA-5012	*Don't Let the Stars Get In Your Eyes/Wanted/Papa Loves Mambo/Hot Diggity (Dog Ziggity Boom)	1958	$10
❑ EPA-451	A Bushel and a Peck/You're Just in Love//Marrying for Love/It's a Lovely Day Today	1953	$15
	— With Betty Hutton (side 1, song 1) and the Fontane Sisters (the other three)		
❑ EPA-4285 [M]	Accentuate the Positive/Red Sails in the Sunset//Birth of the Blues/It Had to Be You	1958	$10
❑ ESP-4285 [S]	Accentuate the Positive/Red Sails in the Sunset//Birth of the Blues/It Had to Be You	1958	$25
❑ 547-0454	A Hubba-Hubba-Hubba (Dig You Later)/Till the End of Time//Don't Let the Stars Get In Your Eyes/Wanted	1954	$10
	— Record 1 of 2-EP set EPB 3224		
❑ EPB3035 [PS]	A Sentimental Date with Perry	1952	$15
	— Double-pocket cover for 547-0033 and 547-0034		
❑ EPA-739 [PS]	A Sentimental Date with Perry Como	1955	$15
❑ EPB1177 [PS]	A Sentimental Date with Perry Como	1955	$15
	— Gatefold cover for 2-EP set (547-0834, 547-0835)		
❑ EPA-4326	A Still Small Voice/I May Never Pass This Way Again//He's Got the Whole World in His Hands/When You Come to the End of the Day	1958	$10
❑ EPA-410	Ave Maria/The Lord's Prayer//Mother Dear, O Pray for Me/Holy God We Praise Thy Name	1952	$15
❑ EPA-405	Blues in the Night/Wabash Blues//I Got It Bad and That Ain't Good/The Birth of the Blues	1952	$20
❑ 547-0835	Body and Soul/No Other Love//When Day Is Done/What'll I Do?	1955	$10
	— Part of 2-EP set EPB 1177		
❑ EPB3224 [PS]	Como's Golden Records	1954	$12
	— Double-pocket cover for 547-0454 and 547-0455		
❑ EPA-5012 [PS]	Como's Golden Records	1958	$12
❑ EPA-5029 [PS]	Como's Golden Records, Volume 2	1958	$12
❑ EPA-5030 [PS]	Como's Golden Records, Volume 3	1958	$12
❑ 547-1048	(contents unknown)	1955	$10
	— Part of 2-EP set EPB 1243		
❑ EPA-728	(contents unknown)	1955	$15
❑ EPA-738	(contents unknown)	1955	$15
❑ LPC-109	(contents unknown)	1961	$15
	— Compact 33 Double"; small hole, plays at 33 1/3 rpm		
❑ 599-9157	Far Away Places/Till the End of Time//Don't Let the Stars Get In Your Eyes/Bali Ha'I	1957	$8
	— Side 2 and 19 of 10-EP set SPD 27		

Number	Title	Yr	NM
❑ 599-9156	For Me and My Gal/As Time Goes By//I Believe/ When Day Is Done	1957	$8
	— Side 1 and 20 of 10-EP set SPD-27		
❑ EPA-642	For Me and My Gal/ My Funny Valentine// It Happened in Monterey/ It's the Talk of the Town	1955	$15
❑ SP-45-55	Hot Diggity/Patricia/Lazy Bones//Dream Along with Me/ Land of Dreams/Bewitched	1958	$25
	— Songs are by, in order: Perry Como/Perez Prado/Kay Starr// Perry Como/Eddie Heywood/Gogi Grant		
❑ 599-9159	If There Is Someone Lovelier Than You/Over the Rainbow// Body and Soul/Lies	1957	$8
	— Side 4 and 17 of 10-EP set SPD 27		
❑ 599-9161	If/When You Were Sweet Sixteen//I've Got the World on a String/You Do Something To Me	1957	$8
	— Side 6 and 15 of 10-EP set SPD 27		
❑ 547-0034	I'm Always Chasing Rainbows/ Love Me or Leave Me//Body and Soul/When Your Hair Has Turned to Silver (I Will Love You Just the Same)	1952	$10
	— Part of 2-EP set EPB 3035		
❑ 599-9158	It's a Good Day/My Funny Valentine//You'll Never Walk Alone/Hello Young Lovers	1957	$8
	— Side 3 and 18 of 10-EP set SPD 27		
❑ EPA-642 [PS]	P.C.	1955	$15
❑ EPA-5128 [PS]	Perry Como (Gold Standard Series)	1959	$12
❑ EPA-728 [PS]	Perry Como Sings Hits from Broadway Shows	1955	$15
❑ EPB3023 [PS]	Perry Como Sings Merry Christmas Music	1952	$15
	— Double-pocket cover for 547-0116 and 547-0117		
❑ EPB1243 [PS]	Perry Como Sings Merry Christmas Music	1955	$25
	— Cover for 2-EP set		
❑ EPA-920 [PS]	Perry Como Sings Merry Christmas Music	1956	$15
❑ EPA-409 [PS]	Perry Como Sings the Hits from Broadway Shows	1952	$15
❑ EPA-451 [PS]	Perry Como Sings the Hits from Broadway Shows	1953	$15
❑ 547-0059	Prisoner of Love/Because// When You Were Sweet Sixteen/Far Away Places	1952	$10
	— Part of 2-EP set EPB 3044		
❑ 599-9162	Prisoner of Love/Carolina Moon//One for My Baby/ In the Still of the Night	1957	$8
	— Side 7 and 14 of 10-EP set SPD 27		
❑ EPA-920	Santa Claus Is Comin' to Town/ Frosty the Snow Man/Winter Wonderland//Rudolph, the Red-Nosed Reindeer/Jingle Bells	1956	$15
❑ EPA-903 [PS]	Somebody Up There Likes Me	1956	$15
❑ EPA-903	Somebody Up There Likes Me/All at Once You Love Her//Hot Diggity (Dog Ziggity Boom)/Dream Along with Me (I'm On My Way to a Star)	1956	$15
❑ EPA-409	Some Enchanted Evening/ Bali Ha'i//Hello, Young Lovers/ We Kiss in a Shadow	1952	$15
❑ EPA-410 [PS]	Songs of Faith	1952	$15
❑ SPD-28	South of the Border/Because/ Bless This House//Breezin' Along with the Breeze/Lies/ You'll Never Walk Alone	1957	$25
❑ EPB3044 [PS]	Supper Club Favorites	1952	$12
	— Two-pocket jacket for two-EP set		
❑ EPA 1-1463	Swinging Down the Lane/South of the Border//Honey, Honey (Bless Your Heart)/Angry	1957	$10
❑ 599-9160	Temptation/Black Moonlight// All at Once You Love Her/ Look Out the Window	1957	$8
	— Side 5 and 16 of 10-EP set SPD 27		
❑ EPA-5030	Temptation/Mi Casa, Su Casa// Prisoner of Love/Because	1958	$10
❑ 547-0455	Temptation/Prisoner of Love//When You Were Sweet Sixteen/Because	1954	$10
	— Record 2 of 2-EP set EPB 3224		
❑ 547-0116	That Christmas Feeling/I'll Be Home for Christmas//Silent Night/O Come, All Ye Faithful	1952	$15
	— Record 1 of 2-EP set EPB 3023		
❑ LPC-109 [PS]	Till the End of Time	1961	$15
❑ EPA-405 [PS]	(title unknown)	1952	$20
❑ EPA-514 [PS]	(title unknown)	1954	$15
❑ EPA-4326 [PS]	(title unknown)	1958	$12
❑ EPA-4285 [PS]	(title unknown)	1958	$12
❑ ESP-4285 [PS]	(title unknown)	1958	$25
❑ EPA-5109 [PS]	(title unknown)	1959	$12
❑ EPA-563 [PS]	Wanted	1954	$15

Number	Title	Yr	NM
❑ 599-9165	Wanted/Love Me or Leave Me//Pa-Paya Mama/I Gotta Right to Sing the Blues	1957	$8

— Side 10 and 11 of 10-EP set SPD 27

Number	Title	Yr	NM
❑ EPA-563	Wanted/You Alone//Pa-Paya Mama/No Other Love	1954	$15
❑ EPA 1-1463 [PS]	We Get Letters, Vol. 1	1957	$12
❑ 599-9163	What'll I Do/Blue Moon//Hot Diggity (Dog Ziggity Boom)/It Happened in Monterey	1957	$8

— Side 8 and 13 of 10-EP set SPD 27

Number	Title	Yr	NM
❑ 547-0033	When Day Is Done/Carolina Moon//What'll I Do/If We Can't Be the Same Old Sweethearts We'll Just Be the Same Old Friends	1952	$10

— Part of 2-EP set EPB 3035

Number	Title	Yr	NM
❑ EPA-739	With a Song in My Heart/Love Me or Leave Me/Lies//Body and Soul/No Other Love	1955	$15
❑ 547-0834	With a Song in My Heart/Love Me or Leave Me/Lies//Carolina Moon/Blue Room	1955	$10

— Part of 2-EP set EPB 1177

Number	Title	Yr	NM
❑ 599-9164	With a Song in My Heart/No Other Love//Breezin' Along with the Breeze/It's the Talk of the Town	1957	$8

— Side 9 and 12 of 10-EP set SPD 27

COMPANIONS, THE

ARLEN

Number	Title	Yr	NM
❑ 722	These Foolish Things/It's Too Late	1963	$100

BROOK'S

Number	Title	Yr	NM
❑ 100	Why, Oh Why Baby/I Didn't Know (You Got Married)	1959	$70

COLUMBIA

Number	Title	Yr	NM
❑ 42279	I'll Always Love You/A Little Bit of Blue	1962	$40

DOVE

Number	Title	Yr	NM
❑ 240	Falling/Oh, What a Feeling!	1958	$120

FEDERAL

Number	Title	Yr	NM
❑ 12397	Why, Oh Why Baby/I Didn't Know (You Got Married)	1960	$40

GENERAL AMERICAN

Number	Title	Yr	NM
❑ 711	Be Yourself/Help a Lonely Guy	1962	$30

GINA

Number	Title	Yr	NM
❑ 722	These Foolish Things/It's Too Late	1963	$60

COMPETITORS, THE

DOT

Number	Title	Yr	NM
❑ 16560	Power Shift/Little Stick Nomad	1963	$50

COMPLIMENTS, THE

CONGRESS

Number	Title	Yr	NM
❑ 243	Shake It Up, Shake It Down/You Are My Sunshine	1965	$60
❑ 252	The Time of Her Life/Everybody Loves a Lover	1965	$60

MIDAS

Number	Title	Yr	NM
❑ 304	Borrow 'Til Morning/Beware, Beware	1968	$40

COMPOSERS, THE

ERA

Number	Title	Yr	NM
❑ 3118	I Had a Dream/You and Yours	1963	$30

COMPTON BROTHERS, THE

ABC DOT

Number	Title	Yr	NM
❑ 17538	Cat's in the Cradle/A Bird with Broken Wings Can't Fly	1974	$5
❑ 17563	My Music/By the Time I Get Over You	1975	$5

DOT

Number	Title	Yr	NM
❑ 17477	California Blues (Blue Yodel No. 4)/Direct Distance Dialing	1973	$6
❑ 17336	Charlie Brown/Just a Dream Away	1970	$6
❑ 17427	Claudette/It Happens All the Time	1972	$6
❑ 17454	Daddies Doin' Life/Some of Shelly's Blues	1973	$6
❑ 17231	Earthquakes/Step Up Walk with Me	1969	$8
❑ 17167	Everybody Needs Somebody/Loneliness Was Made by Man	1968	$8
❑ 17294	Haunted House/Sound of an Angel's Wings	1969	$8
❑ 17070	Honey/Poor Side of Town	1968	$8
❑ 17024	I Look a Lot Like Bill/If It's All the Same to You	1967	$8
❑ 17391	May Auld Acquaintance Be Forgot (Before I Lose My Mind)/Learning the Hard Way	1971	$6
❑ 16948	Pickin' Up the Mail/Feathers into Stone	1966	$8
❑ 17378	Pine Grove/Old Memories	1971	$6

Number	Title	Yr	NM
❑ 17511	Secret Memories/Sweet Honky Tonk Music	1974	$6
❑ 17352	That Ain't No Stuff/I Wanna Sing a Country Song	1970	$6
❑ 17110	Two Little Hearts/Money	1968	$8

COMSTOCK, BOBBY

ASCOT

Number	Title	Yr	NM
❑ 2216	Can't Judge a Book/Out of Sight	1966	$15
❑ 2175	I'm a Man/I'll Make You Glad	1965	$15
❑ 2193	This Magic Moment/Shotgun Sally	1965	$15

BLAZE

Number	Title	Yr	NM
❑ 349	Tennessee Waltz/Sweet Talk	1959	$30

FESTIVAL

Number	Title	Yr	NM
❑ 25000	Garden of Eden/Piece of Paper	1961	$30

JUBILEE

Number	Title	Yr	NM
❑ 5392	Bony Maronie/Do That Little Thing	1960	$30

LAWN

Number	Title	Yr	NM
❑ 232	Can It Be True/Ain't That Just Like Me	1964	$20
❑ 224	I Can't Help Myself/Run My Heart	1963	$20
❑ 255	I Wanna Do It/This Little Love of Mine	1965	$15
❑ 202	Let's Stomp/I Want to Do It	1963	$20
❑ 210	Susie Baby/Take a Walk	1963	$20
❑ 229	The Beatle Bounce/Since You Been Gone	1964	$30
❑ 217	The Chicken Back/Sunny	1963	$20

MOHAWK

Number	Title	Yr	NM
❑ 124	The Wayward Wind/Everyday Blues	1960	$30

CONCORDS, THE (1)

BOOM

Number	Title	Yr	NM
❑ 60021	Down the Aisle of Love/I Feel Love Comin'	1966	$50

EPIC

Number	Title	Yr	NM
❑ 9697	Should I Cry/It's Our Wedding Day	1964	$70

GRAMERCY

Number	Title	Yr	NM
❑ 304	Cross My Heart/Our Last Goodbye	1961	$60

— No candy canes on label

Number	Title	Yr	NM
❑ 304	Cross My Heart/Our Last Goodbye	1961	$200

— With candy canes on label

Number	Title	Yr	NM
❑ 305	My Dreams/Scarlet Ribbons	1961	$50

HERALD

Number	Title	Yr	NM
❑ 578	Cold and Frosty Morning/Don't Go Now	1963	$40
❑ 576	Marlene/Our Love Wasn't Meant to Be	1962	$30

POLYDOR

Number	Title	Yr	NM
❑ 14036	Down the Aisle of Love/I Feel a Love Comin' On	1970	$15

RCA VICTOR

Number	Title	Yr	NM
❑ 47-7911	Again/The Boy Most Likely	1961	$40

RUST

Number	Title	Yr	NM
❑ 5048	One Step from Heaven/Away	1962	$40

CONCORDS, THE (2)

EMBER

Number	Title	Yr	NM
❑ 1007	I'm Satisfied with Rock 'N' Roll/I'll Always Say Please	1956	$70

HARLEM

Number	Title	Yr	NM
❑ 2328	Candlelight/Monticello	1954	$600

CONCORDS, THE (U)

HIT

Number	Title	Yr	NM
❑ 121	Diane/Walk On By	1964	$8

— B-side by Mary Jones

CONCRETE BLONDE

I.R.S.

Number	Title	Yr	NM
❑ 53113	Dance Along the Edge/Only One Can Make Me Cry	1987	$5
❑ 53113 [PS]	Dance Along the Edge/Only You Can Make Me Cry	1987	$5
❑ 52982	Still in Hollywood/Cold Part of Town	1986	$5
❑ 53053	True/True II (Instrumental)	1987	$5
❑ 53053 [PS]	True/True II (Instrumental)	1987	$5

CONCRETE COWBOY BAND

EXCELSIOR

Number	Title	Yr	NM
❑ 1006	Concrete Cowboys/(B-side unknown)	1981	$6
❑ 1011	Country Is the Closest Thing to Heaven (You Can Hear)/San Antonio Rose	1981	$5

CONDELLO

SCEPTER

Number	Title	Yr	NM
❑ 12233	Crystal Clear/See What Tomorrow Brings	1968	$15

CONDORS, THE

HUNTER

Number	Title	Yr	NM
❑ 2503/4	Swetest Angel/Little Curly Top	1960	$1000

CONEY ISLAND KIDS, THE

JOSIE

Number	Title	Yr	NM
❑ 791	I Love It/Red Light, Green Light	1956	$40
❑ 809	Popcorn and Candy/Not You, Pie Face	1957	$40
❑ 802	We Want a Rock & Roll President/Thwistle Rock and Thwistle Roll	1956	$40

JUBILEE

Number	Title	Yr	NM
❑ 5215	Moonlight Beach/Baby Baby You	1955	$50

CONFESSIONS, THE

EPIC

Number	Title	Yr	NM
❑ 9474	Be-Bop Baby/Before You Change Your Mind	1961	$30

CONLEY, ARTHUR

ATCO

Number	Title	Yr	NM
❑ 6563	Funky Street/Put Our Love Together	1968	$8
❑ 6747	God Bless/(Your Love Has Brought Me A) Mighty Long Way	1970	$6
❑ 6733	Hurt/They Call the Wind Maria	1970	$6
❑ 6622	Is That You Love/Aunt Dora's Love Soul Shack	1968	$8
❑ 6640	Ob-La-Di, Ob-La-Da/Otis Sleep On	1968	$8
❑ 6588	People Sure Act Funny/Burning Fire	1968	$8
❑ 6494	Shake, Rattle and Roll/You Don't Have to See Me	1967	$8
❑ 6661	Speak Her Name/Run On	1969	$6
❑ 6706	Star Review/Love Sure Is a Powerful Thing	1969	$6
❑ 6463	Sweet Soul Music/Let's Go Steady	1967	$10
❑ 6529	Whole Lot of Woman/Love Comes and Goes	1967	$8

CAPRICORN

Number	Title	Yr	NM
❑ 0047	Bless You/It's So Nice	1973	$8
❑ 8017	I'm Living Good/I'm So Glad You're Here	1971	$10
❑ 01	More Sweet Soul Music/Walking on Eggs	1972	$10

FAME

Number	Title	Yr	NM
❑ 1007	I Can't Stop/In the Same Old Way	1966	$20
❑ 1009	Take Me (Just As I Am)/I'm Gonna Forget About You	1966	$20

JOTIS

Number	Title	Yr	NM
❑ 470	I'm a Lonely Stranger/Where Lead Me	1965	$30
❑ 472	Who's Fooling Who/There's a Place for Us	1966	$30

PHILCO-FORD

Number	Title	Yr	NM
❑ HP-15	Sweet Soul Music/You Don't Have to See Me	1968	$20

— 4-inch plastic "Hip Pocket Record" with color sleeve

CONLEY, EARL THOMAS

GRT

Number	Title	Yr	NM
❑ 041	High and Wild/The Weeds Outlived the Roses	1976	$5

— As "Earl Conley

Number	Title	Yr	NM
❑ 027	I Have Loved You Girl (But Not Like This Before)/Tryin' to Beat the Morning Home	1975	$5

— As "Earl Conley

Number	Title	Yr	NM
❑ 032	It's the Bible Against the Bottle (In the Battle for Daddy's Soul)/I Have Loved You Girl (But Not Like This Before)	1975	$5

— As "Earl Conley

Number	Title	Yr	NM
❑ 015	When I'm Under the Table/The Greenest Grass	1975	$6

— As "Earl Conley

RCA

Number	Title	Yr	NM
❑ PB-13053	After the Love Slips Away/Smokey Mountain Memories	1982	$3
❑ PB-13758	Angel in Disguise/Coward Around the Corner	1984	$3
❑ PB-13758 [PS]	Angel in Disguise/Coward Around the Corner	1984	$4
❑ JK-13758 [DJ]	Angel in Disguise (same on both sides)	1984	$10

— Promo only on red vinyl

Number	Title	Yr	NM
❑ PB-13905	Blue Christmas/White Christmas	1984	$4
❑ GB-14066	Chance of Lovin' You/Don't Make It Easy on Me	1985	$3

— Gold Standard Series" reissue

Number	Title	Yr	NM
❑ PB-13877	Chance of Lovin' You/Feels Like a Saturday Night	1984	$3

Number	Title	Yr	NM
❑ JK-13877 [DJ]	Chance of Lovin' You (same on both sides)	1984	$10
	—Promo on green vinyl		
❑ PB-13702	Don't Make It Easy for Me/You Can't Go On (Like a Rolling Stone)	1983	$3
❑ PB-13246	Heavenly Bodies/The Highway Home	1982	$3
❑ PB-13596	Holding Her and Loving You/Home So Fine	1983	$3
❑ PB-13596 [PS]	Holding Her and Loving You/Home So Fine	1983	$5
❑ GB-13787	Holding Her and Loving You/ Your Love's on the Line	1984	$3
	—Gold Standard Series" reissue		
❑ GB-14345	Honor Bound/Love Don't Care (Whose Heart It Breaks)	1986	$3
	—Gold Standard Series" reissue		
❑ JK-13960 [DJ]	Honor Bound (same on both sides)	1984	$10
	—Promo only on blue vinyl		
❑ PB-13960	Honor Bound/Too Hot to Handle	1984	$3
❑ PB-13960 [PS]	Honor Bound/Too Hot to Handle	1984	$4
❑ 5064-7-R	I Can't Win for Losing You/ Love's on the Move Again	1986	$3
❑ PB-13414	I Have Loved You, Girl (But Not Like This Before)/Bottled Up Blues	1982	$3
❑ PB-14060	Love Don't Care (Whose Heart It Breaks)/Turn This Bus Around	1985	$3
❑ 8824-7-R	Love Out Loud/No Chance, No Dance	1989	$3
❑ 8973-7-R	Love Out Loud/No Chance, No Dance	1989	$3
❑ PB-14282	Once in a Blue Moon/I Have Loved You, Girl (But Not Like This Before)	1986	$3
❑ JB-13053 [DJ]	Smokey Mountain Memories (same on both sides)	1982	$12
	—Promo only on red vinyl		
❑ PB-13320	Somewhere Between Right and Wrong/Fire and Smoke	1982	$3
❑ GB-13788	Somewhere Between Right and Wrong/Heavenly Bodies	1984	$3
	—Gold Standard Series" reissue		
❑ JB-13320 [DJ]	Somewhere Between Right and Wrong (same on both sides)	1982	$12
	—Promo only on blue vinyl		
❑ JK-12344 [DJ]	Tell Me Why (same on both sides)	1981	$10
	—Promo only on blue vinyl		
❑ PB-12344	Tell Me Why/Too Much Noise (Trucker's Waltz)	1981	$3
❑ 5129-7-R	That Was a Close One/ Right from the Start	1987	$3
❑ PB-14380	Too Many Times/Changes of Love	1986	$3
	—A-side with Anita Pointer		
❑ PB-14380 [PS]	Too Many Times/Changes of Love	1986	$4
	—A-side with Anita Pointer		
❑ 8632-7-R	We Believe in Happy Endings/ No Chance, No Dance	1988	$3
	—A-side with Emmylou Harris		
❑ 8717-7-R	What I'd Say/Carol	1988	$3
❑ 6894-7-R	What She Is (Is a Woman in Love)/Carol	1988	$3
❑ PB-13688	White Christmas/Home So Fine	1983	$4

SUNBIRD

Number	Title	Yr	NM
❑ 7561	Fire and Smoke/I Have Loved You Girl	1981	$5
	—Blue label		
❑ 7561	Fire and Smoke/I Have Loved You Girl	1981	$4
	—Multicolor label		
❑ 7556	Silent Treatment/This Time I've Hurt Her More (Than She Loves Me)	1980	$5

WARNER BROS.

Number	Title	Yr	NM
❑ 8717	Dreamin's All I Do/My Love	1978	$5
	—As "Earl Conley		
❑ 8798	Middle-Age Madness/When You Were Blue and I Was Green	1979	$4
❑ 49072	Stranded on a Dead- End Street/My Love	1979	$5
	—As "The ETC Band		

CONNIE AND CLARA

HIT

Number	Title	Yr	NM
❑ 61	I Will Follow Him/Take These Chains from My Heart	1963	$8
	—B-side by Herbert Hunter		

CONNIFF, RAY

BRUNSWICK

Number	Title	Yr	NM
❑ 55020	Beamy Boy Boogie/Super Chief	1957	$12

COLUMBIA

Number	Title	Yr	NM
❑ 44933	A Banda/La Felicidad	1969	$5
❑ 44536	A Certain Girl/Sounds of Silence	1968	$5
❑ 4-40660	Begin the Beguine/Stardust	1956	$12
❑ 42967	Blue Moon/Honeycomb	1964	$6
❑ 42967 [DJ]	Blue Moon/Honeycomb	1964	$15
	—Blue vinyl promo; white label, blue print		
❑ 45823	Charlotte's Web/Someone	1973	$4
❑ 41484	Christmas Bride/Silver Bells	1959	$15
❑ 45363	El Condor Pasa/Rosa	1971	$4
❑ 45267	Everybody Knows/Loss of Love	1970	$5
❑ 45782	Face on the Wind/A Man Without a Vision	1973	$4
❑ 42007	Golden Earrings/ The Thrill Is Gone	1961	$6
❑ S731467 [S]	Green Eyes/Lisbon Antigua	1962	$10
❑ 45137	Half and Half (A Song for Sarah)/Walk in the Spring Rain	1970	$5
❑ 43352	Happiness Is/Miss You	1965	$6
❑ 45893	Harmony/Bah, Bah, Conniff Sprach	1973	$4
❑ 44872	I Love How You Love Me/Hold Me Tight	1969	$5
❑ 10164	I Need You Baby/On the Run	1975	$4
❑ 43061	Invisible Tears/Singing the Blues	1964	$6
❑ 44724	I've Got My Eyes on You/Dear World	1968	$5
❑ 43814	Lookin' for Love/It Takes Two	1966	$6
❑ 45002	Love at First Sight/Love Made a Fool of Me	1969	$5
❑ S730447 [S]	Love Is a Many-Splendored Thing/Please	1959	$10
	—Stereo Seven" single (small hole, plays at 33 1/3 rpm)		
❑ 45333	Love Story/Out of the Darkness	1971	$4
❑ 43939	Mame/Wednesday's Child	1966	$6
❑ 43168	Melodie D'Amour/If I Knew Then	1964	$6
❑ 41800	Midnight Lace -- Part I/ Midnight Lace -- Part II	1960	$8
❑ S730911 [S]	Moments to Remember/ My Foolish Heart	1960	$10
❑ 3-10375	Moments to Remember/ Vera's Theme	1976	$4
❑ 44192	Moonlight Brings Memories/ Wonderful Season of Summer	1967	$6
❑ 41349	Oklahoma/On the Street Where You Live	1959	$8
❑ 3-10294	Paloma Blanca/Lara's Theme from "Doctor Zhivago	1976	$4
❑ 44645	People/Look Homeward Angel	1968	$5
❑ 42695	Popsy/Scarlet	1963	$8
❑ 10097	Sing Along Song/Ecstasy	1975	$4
❑ 43626	Somewhere, My Love/ Midsummer in Sweden	1966	$6
❑ 43626 [DJ]	Somewhere, My Love (same on both sides)	1966	$15
	—Promo only on red vinyl		
❑ 3-10416	Song from M*A*S*H/ Theme from "Love Story	1976	$4
❑ 45187	Songs Are For Lovers/ These Are My Flowers	1970	$5
❑ 4-42893	Sweet Sue, Just You/ How Am I to Know	1963	$8
❑ 40827	'S Wonderful/Wagon Wheels	1957	$10
❑ 41242	Tchaikovsky's First Piano Concerto/Schubert's Serenade	1958	$8
❑ 10002	The Entertainer/I Understand Just How You Feel	1974	$4
❑ 44298	The Hulilau Song/One Paddle Two Paddle	1967	$6
❑ 41040	Theme from Perry Mason/ Symphony of Love	1957	$15
❑ 41696	Theme from Perry Mason/ Walkin; and Whistlin'	1960	$8
❑ 45543	Theme from "Summer of '42"/Imagine	1972	$4
❑ 45996	The Most Beautiful Girl/ Beyond Tomorrow	1974	$4
❑ 44055	The World Will Smile Again/"17	1967	$6
❑ 41404	They Tried to Tell Me/ Early Evening	1959	$8
❑ 40862	Three Way Love/Cuddle Up a Little Closer	1957	$10
❑ 45443	Tijuana Taxi/Happy Together	1971	$4
❑ 30909 [S]	(titles unknown)	1960	$10
❑ 30910 [S]	(titles unknown)	1960	$10
❑ 30912 [S]	(titles unknown)	1960	$10
❑ 30913 [S]	(titles unknown)	1960	$10
	—The above five are "Stereo Seven" 33 1/3 rpm jukebox singles from set "JS 7-20" entitled "Memories Are Made of This"		
❑ 31119 [S]	(titles unknown)	1961	$10
❑ 31120 [S]	(titles unknown)	1961	$10
❑ 31121 [S]	(titles unknown)	1961	$10
❑ 31122 [S]	(titles unknown)	1961	$10
❑ 31123 [S]	(titles unknown)	1961	$10
❑ 31463 [S]	(titles unknown)	1962	$10
❑ 31464 [S]	(titles unknown)	1962	$10
❑ 31465 [S]	(titles unknown)	1962	$10
❑ 31466 [S]	(titles unknown)	1962	$10
❑ 31555 [S]	(titles unknown)	1962	$10
❑ 31556 [S]	(titles unknown)	1962	$10
❑ 31557 [S]	(titles unknown)	1962	$10
❑ 31558 [S]	(titles unknown)	1962	$10
❑ 31559 [S]	(titles unknown)	1962	$10
	—The above 20 all are Columbia "Stereo 7" singles		
❑ 40991	Walkin' and Whistlin'/ Melody for Two Guitars	1957	$8
❑ 45528	We Must Forget We Ever Met/Where Were You	1972	$4
❑ 45687	Where Is the Love/Because	1972	$4
❑ 45687 [PS]	Where Is the Love/Because	1972	$6
❑ 44422	Winds of Change/ We're a Home	1968	$5
❑ 45595	With Every Beat of My Heart/Sleepy Shores	1972	$4

CORAL

Number	Title	Yr	NM
❑ 61371	Beamy Boy Boogie/ Super Chief	1955	$15

7-Inch Extended Plays

COLUMBIA

Number	Title	Yr	NM
❑ B-9251	*'S Wonderful/Dancing in the Dark/Speak Low/ Begin the Beguine	1956	$10
❑ B-2578	*'S Wonderful/I Get a Kick Out of You/Begin the Beguine/ That Old Black Magic	1958	$10
❑ B-10043	Hand Around/Play a Gittar Solo//The Spinner/Honky Tonk Rock-a-Round	1956	$15
❑ B-10743	In the Still of the Night/ Someone to Watch Over Me// Be My Love/Where or When	1957	$10
❑ B-10743 [PS]	'S Marvelous	1957	$12
❑ B-9251 [PS]	'S Wonderful	1956	$12
❑ B-10043	(title unknown)	1956	$15

CONNORS, CAROL

COLUMBIA

Number	Title	Yr	NM
❑ 42155	Listen to the Beat/ My Special Boy	1961	$30
❑ 42337	That's All It Takes/What Do You See in Him	1962	$30

ERA

Number	Title	Yr	NM
❑ 3096	Tommy Go Away/I Wanna Know	1962	$40
❑ 3084	Two Rivers/Big, Big Love	1962	$40

MIRA

Number	Title	Yr	NM
❑ 219	Lonely Little Beach Girl/ My Baby Looks, But He Don't Touch	1965	$30
❑ 219 [PS]	Lonely Little Beach Girl/ My Baby Looks, But He Don't Touch	1965	$60

CONNY

CAPITOL

Number	Title	Yr	NM
❑ 4526	Midi Midnette/Little Girl	1961	$15

CONRAD, BOB

WARNER BROS.

Number	Title	Yr	NM
❑ 5242	Bye, Bye Baby/Love You	1961	$10
❑ 5242 [PS]	Bye, Bye Baby/Love You	1961	$30
❑ 5317	Cindy Is Gone/Again	1962	$10
❑ 5306	Crazy Magician/I Just Gotta Have You	1962	$12
❑ 5211	I Want You (Pretty Baby)/ Ballin' the Jack	1961	$10
❑ 5211 [PS]	I Want You (Pretty Baby)/ Ballin' the Jack	1961	$30

CONRAD, JESS

LONDON

Number	Title	Yr	NM
❑ 2005	Little Ship/Walk Away	1961	$15
❑ 1967	Mystery Girl/Just the Two of Us	1961	$15

CONRAD, JOAN

ALLEY

Number	Title	Yr	NM
❑ 1007	Christmas Day/Gee Golly, the Holly	1962	$10

CONSOLERS, THE

NASHBORO

Number	Title	Yr	NM
❑ 933	Let The Bells Ring/ No Room In The Inn	1967	$8
❑ 956	Merry Christmas/There Will Be Peace One of These Days	1970	$6

CONSORTS, THE

APT

Number	Title	Yr	NM
❑ 25066	Please Be Mine/ Time After Time	1962	$120

COUSINS

Number	Title	Yr	NM
❑ 1004	Please Be Mine/Time After Time	1961	$400

Number	Title	Yr	NM
CONTENDERS, THE			
BLUE SKY			
❏ 105	Mr. Dee Jay/Yes I Do	1959	$600
CHATTAHOOCHIE			
❏ 644	The Dune Bugy/Go Ahead	1964	$30
JACKPOT			
❏ 48002	Tequila Song/Wild Man	1959	$50
CONTI, BILL			
20TH CENTURY			
❏ 2368	Theme from "An Unmarried Woman"/An Unmarried Woman	1978	$6
— B-side by Michelle Wiley			
ARISTA			
❏ 1021	Theme from Dynasty/ Theme from Falcon Crest	1982	$5
UNITED ARTISTS			
❏ X1317	Gonna Fly Now (Theme from "Rocky")/Overture	1979	$5
❏ UA-XW940-Y	Gonna Fly Now (Theme from "Rocky")/Reflections	1976	$5
❏ XW1162	Gonna Fly Now (Theme from "Rocky")/The Final Bell	1978	$4
— Reissue			
CONTINENTAL GEMS, THE			
GUYDEN			
❏ 2091	My Love Will Follow You/Everywhere	1963	$400
CONTINENTALS, THE (1)			
ERA			
❏ 3003	Cool Penguin/Soap Sudz	1959	$30
PENGUIN			
❏ 1002	Cool Penguin/Soap Sudz	1959	$50
CONTINENTALS, THE (2)			
PORT			
❏ 70018	Dear Lord/Fine Fine Frame	1960	$40
❏ 70024	Picture of Love/Soft and Sweet	1961	$40
WHIRLIN' DISC			
❏ 101	Dear Lord/Fine Fine Frame	1956	$200
❏ 105	Picture of Love/Soft and Sweet	1957	$200
CONTINENTALS, THE (U)			
AOK			
❏ 1025	Take Me/She Wants You	1966	$30
BOLO			
❏ 720	I'm Coming Home/ The Turnaround	1960	$40
CUCA			
❏ 1063	Tic-Toc/Sue	1961	$40
DAVIS			
❏ 466	Don't Do It, Baby/ Tongue Twister	1959	$50
HUNTER			
❏ 3503	It Doesn't Matter/Whisper It	1960	$1200
KEY			
❏ 517	Take a Gamble on Me/ Meanwhile Back at the Ranch	1956	$125
LIFETIME			
❏ 1019	Cathy's Clown/Maybe Baby	1966	$10
CONTOURS, THE			
GORDY			
❏ 7029	Can You Do It/I'll Stand By You	1964	$15
❏ 7037	Can You Jerk Like Me/That Day When She Needed Me	1964	$15
❏ 7016	Don't Let Her Be Your Baby/It Must Be Love	1963	$15
❏ 7005	Do You Love Me/Move Mr. Man	1962	$30
❏ 7044	First I Look at the Purse/ Searching for a Girl	1965	$15
❏ 7059	It's So Hard Being a Loser/ Your Love Grows More Precious Every Day	1967	$15
❏ 7019	Pa I Need a Car/You Get Ugly	1963	$15
❏ 7012	Shake Sherry/You Better Get in Line	1963	$20
HOB			
❏ 116	I'm So Glad/Yours Is My Heart Alone	1961	$120
MOTOWN			
❏ 1012	The Stretch/Funny	1962	$800
❏ 1008	Whole Lotta Woman/ Come On and Be Mine	1961	$500
MOTOWN YESTERYEAR			
❏ 448	Do You Love Me/Shake Sherry	1972	$4
❏ 448 [PS]	Do You Love Me/Shake Sherry	1988	$5
— Dirty Dancing" sleeve; without cut-out hole			

Number	Title	Yr	NM
ROCKET			
❏ 41192	I'm a Winner/Makes Me Wanna Come Back	1980	$4
TAMLA			
❏ 7012	Shake Sherry/You Better Get in Line	1963	$200
— Tamla label used in error for a Gordy release			
CONWAY, DAVE			
TRUE			
❏ 105	If You're Gonna Love (You're Gonna Hurt)/Too Late for Words	1977	$6
❏ 114	I'll Go On Loving You/ Too Late for Words	1978	$6
❏ 115	Lookin' Back on Lovin' You/Please Don't Go	1978	$6
CONWAY, RUSS			
CHAPTER ONE			
❏ 2907	Polonaise/Villa D'Amour	1968	$8
COODER, RY			
MUSICOR			
❏ 1148	Life Game/1983	1966	$12
REPRISE			
❏ 0940	Alimony/Pigmeat	1970	$6
❏ 1167	Billy the Kid/Boomer's Story	1973	$6
❏ 1071	Billy the Kid/Money Honey	1972	$6
❏ 1009	Dark Is the Night/On a Monday	1971	$6
❏ 0910	Goin' to Brownsville/ Available Space	1970	$6
WARNER BROS.			
❏ 28158	All Shook Up/Get Your Lies Straight	1987	$4
❏ 28158 [PS]	All Shook Up/Get Your Lies Straight	1987	$4
❏ 49704	Crazy 'Bout an Automobile/ Borderline	1981	$4
❏ 28723	Crossroads/Feel It (Bad Blues)	1986	$4
❏ 49055	Down in Hollywood/Little Sister	1979	$5
❏ 27945	Get Rhythm/Get Back to Okinawa	1988	$4
❏ 49677	Girls from Texas/Borderline	1981	$4
❏ 8384	School Is Out/Jesus on the Mainline	1977	$5
❏ 28725	Tell Me Something Slick/ Billy and Annie	1986	$4
COOK, BILL			
OKEH			
❏ 6849	A Letter to Santa/ Christmas in Heaven	1951	$60
COOK, KEN			
PHILLIPS INT'L.			
❏ 3534	I Was a Fool/Crazy Baby	1959	$60
— Roy Orbison appears on this record (uncredited)			
COOK, PETER, AND DUDLEY MOORE			
PARROT			
❏ 3016	Bedazzled/Love Me	1967	$8
COOK, STEVEN LEE			
GRINDER'S SWITCH			
❏ 1709	Please Play More Kenny Rogers/(B-side unknown)	1979	$6
COOKE, SAM			
CHERIE			
❏ 4501	Darling I Need You Now/ Win Your Love for Me	1971	$8
KEEN			
❏ 3-2018 [M]	Everybody Likes to Cha Cha Cha/Little Things You Do	1959	$30
❏ 5-2018 [S]	Everybody Likes to Cha Cha Cha/Little Things You Do	1959	$50
❏ 34002	(I Love You) For Sentimental Reasons/Desire Me	1958	$30
— Black label			
❏ 3-2008	Love You Most of All/Blue Moon	1958	$30
❏ 2122	Mary, Mary Lou/ Eee-Yi-Ee-Yi-Oh	1960	$30
❏ 2022 [M]	Only Sixteen/Let's Go Steady Again	1959	$30
❏ 5-2022 [S]	Only Sixteen/Let's Go Steady Again	1959	$60
❏ 2118	Steal Away/So Glamorous	1960	$30
❏ 3-2005	Stealing Kisses/All of My Life	1958	$30
❏ 2101	Summertime/ Summertime (Part 2)	1959	$30
❏ 82111	'T'ain't Nobody's Bizness (If I Do)/No One	1960	$30
❏ 8-2105	There! I've Said It Again/One Hour Ahead of the Posse	1959	$30
❏ 3-2006 [M]	Win Your Love for Me/Love Song from "Houseboat" (Almost in Your Arms)	1958	$30

Number	Title	Yr	NM
❏ 5-2006 [S]	Win Your Love for Me/Love Song from "Houseboat" (Almost in Your Arms)	1959	$125
— Blue vinyl			
❏ 82117	With You/I Thank God	1960	$30
❏ 82112	Wonderful World/Along the Navajo Trail	1960	$30
RCA			
❏ PB-14146	Bring It On Home to Me/Nothing Can Change This Love	1985	$8
RCA VICTOR			
❏ SP-45-173 [DJ]	A Change Is Gonna Come (same on both sides)	1968	$60
— Promo-only number; this appears to be a radio reissue in the wake of events going on in 1968			
❏ 47-8299	Ain't That Good News/ Basin Street Blues	1963	$30
— Original A-side title (or a scarce reissue)			
❏ 47-8164	Another Saturday Night/ Love Will Find a Way	1963	$20
❏ 47-8164 [PS]	Another Saturday Night/ Love Will Find a Way	1963	$30
❏ 47-8036	Bring It On Home to Me/ Having a Party	1962	$20
❏ 47-7783	Chain Gang/I Fall in Love Every Day	1960	$20
❏ 47-7783 [PS]	Chain Gang/I Fall in Love Every Day	1960	$30
❏ 47-8426	Cousin of Mine/That's Where It's At	1964	$15
❏ 47-7883	Cupid/Farewell, My Darling	1961	$20
❏ 47-7883 [PS]	Cupid/Farewell, My Darling	1961	$30
❏ 47-7927	Feel It/It's All Right	1961	$20
❏ 47-7927 [PS]	Feel It/It's All Right	1961	$30
❏ 47-8751	Feel It/That's All	1965	$10
❏ 47-8215	Frankie and Johnny/Cool Train	1963	$15
❏ 47-8215 [PS]	Frankie and Johnny/Cool Train	1963	$30
❏ 47-8299	Good News/Basin Street Blues	1963	$15
❏ 47-8368	Good Times/Tennessee Waltz	1964	$15
❏ 47-8539	It's Got the Whole World Shakin'/Ease My Troublin' Mind	1965	$10
❏ 47-8803	Let's Go Steady Again/ Trouble Blues	1966	$12
❏ 47-8247	Little Red Rooster/ You Gotta Move	1963	$15
❏ 47-8247 [PS]	Little Red Rooster/ You Gotta Move	1963	$30
❏ 47-8934	Meet Me at Mary's Place/ If I Had a Hammer	1966	$10
❏ 47-7816	Sad Mood/Love Me	1960	$20
❏ 47-8129	Send Me Some Lovin'/ Baby, Baby, Baby	1963	$20
❏ 47-8129 [PS]	Send Me Some Lovin'/ Baby, Baby, Baby	1963	$30
❏ 47-8486	Shake/A Change Is Gonna Come	1964	$15
❏ VP-4-2555 [S]	Somebody Have Mercy/ Camptown Girl	1962	$30
— Small hole, plays at 33 1/3 rpm			
❏ 47-8631	Sugar Dumpling/Bridge of Tears	1965	$10
❏ 47-8631 [PS]	Sugar Dumpling/Bridge of Tears	1965	$30
❏ 47-7701	Teenage Sonata/If You Were the Only Girl	1960	$30
❏ 47-7853	That's It-I Quit-I'm Movin' On/What Do You Say	1961	$20
❏ 37-7853	That's It-I Quit-I'm Movin' On/What Do You Say	1961	$70
— Compact Single 33" (small hole, plays at LP speed)			
❏ VP-3-2555 [S]	The Twist/Movin' & Groovin'	1962	$30
— Small hole, plays at 33 1/3 rpm			
❏ VP-2-2555 [S]	Twistin' in the Kitchen with Dinah/A Whole Lotta Woman	1962	$30
— Small hole, plays at 33 1/3 rpm			
❏ 47-7983	Twistin' the Night Away/ One More Time	1962	$20
❏ 47-8586	When a Boy Falls in Love/The Piper	1965	$10
SPECIALTY			
❏ 596	Forever/Lovable	1957	$40
— As "Dale Cook"			
❏ 667	Happy in Love/I Need You Now	1959	$40
❏ 619	I'll Come Running Back to You/Forever	1957	$40
❏ 921	Must Jesus Bear the Cross Alone/The Last Mile of the Way	1970	$10
— With the Soul Stirrers			
❏ 627	That's All I Need to Know/I Don't Want to Cry	1958	$40
❏ 930	That's Heaven to Me/ Lord, Remember Me	1974	$12
— With the Soul Stirrers			
7-Inch Extended Plays			
KEEN			
❏ B-2006	*Mary, Mary Lou/The Gypsy/ Oh, Look at Me Now/Someday	1958	$100
❏ B-2007	*When I Fall in Love/I Cover the Waterfront/Running Wild/ Today I Sing the Blues	1958	$100
❏ B-2002	*You Send Me/The Lonesome Road/That Lucky Old Sun/ Canadian Sunset	1958	$100
❏ B-2013	(contents unknown)	1959	$100
❏ B-2006 [PS]	Encore, Volume 1	1958	$100

Number	Title	Yr	NM
❑ B-2007 [PS]	Encore, Volume 2	1958	$100
❑ B-2008 [PS]	Encore, Volume 3	1958	$100
❑ B-2008	It's the Talk of the Town/Along the Navajo Trail//My Foolish Heart/Accentuate the Positive	1958	$100
❑ B-2012	Let's Call the Whole Thing Off/God Bless the Child// Comes Love/Lover Girl	1959	$100
❑ B-2010	Love Song from Houseboat/ Lonely Island//Win Your Love for Me/All of My Life	1959	$100
❑ B-2010 [PS]	Sam Cooke Sings His Hits	1959	$100
❑ B-2014	Solitude/Lover Come Back to Me//T'Aint Nobody's Bizness (If I Do)/She's Funny That Way	1959	$100
❑ B-2001 [PS]	Songs by Sam Cooke, Volume 1	1958	$100
❑ B-2002 [PS]	Songs by Sam Cooke, Volume 2	1958	$100
❑ B-2003 [PS]	Songs by Sam Cooke, Volume 3	1958	$100
❑ B-2003	Summertime/Danny Boy// Around the World/Ol' Man River	1958	$100
❑ B-2001	The Bells of Saint Mary's/ Tammy//Moonlight in Vermont/So Long	1958	$100
❑ B-2012 [PS]	Tribute to the Lady, Volume 1	1959	$100
❑ B-2013 [PS]	Tribute to the Lady, Volume 2	1959	$100
❑ B-2014 [PS]	Tribute to the Lady, Volume 3	1959	$100

RCA VICTOR

Number	Title	Yr	NM
❑ EPA-4375 [PS]	Another Saturday Night	1963	$25
❑ EPA-4375	Another Saturday Night/ You Send Me//Only Sixteen/ Bring It On Home to Me	1963	$25
❑ LPC-126	Chain Gang/If You Were the Only Girl//Teenage Sonata/ You Understand Me	1961	$25
❑ LPC-126 [PS]	Sam Cooke Sings	1961	$25

COOKIE AND HIS CUPCAKES

CHESS

Number	Title	Yr	NM
❑ 1848	Got You On My Mind/I've Been So Lonely	1963	$20

JUDD

Number	Title	Yr	NM
❑ 1002	Mathilda/Married Life	1958	$60

—With "h" in A-side title

Number	Title	Yr	NM
❑ 1002	Matilda/Married Life	1958	$40

—Without "h" in A-side title

KHOURY'S

Number	Title	Yr	NM
❑ 703	Mathilda/Married Life	1958	$70
❑ 1004	Got You On My Mind/I've Been So Lonely	1963	$30
❑ 1003	Mathilda/I'm Twisted	1963	$30

MERCURY

Number	Title	Yr	NM
❑ 71748	Matilda Has Finally Come Back/As Part of Everything	1961	$30

PAULA

Number	Title	Yr	NM
❑ 230	Belinda/Trouble in My Life	1965	$12
❑ 221	Mathilda/I'm Twisted	1965	$15

COOKIES, THE

ATLANTIC

Number	Title	Yr	NM
❑ 1110	Down By the River/My Lover	1956	$30
❑ 1084	In Paradise/Passing Time	1956	$40
❑ 2079	Passing Time/In Paradise	1960	$30
❑ 1061	Precious Love/Later, Later	1955	$40

DIMENSION

Number	Title	Yr	NM
❑ 1002	Chains/Stranger in My Arms	1962	$30
❑ 1008	Don't Say Nothin' Bad (About My Baby)/Softly in the Night	1963	$20
❑ 1008	Don't Say Nothin' Bad/ Softly in the Night	1963	$30
❑ 1020	Girls Grow Up Faster Than Boys/Only to Other People	1963	$20
❑ 1032	I Never Dreamed/The Old Crowd	1964	$20
❑ 1012	I Want a Boy for My Birthday/Will Power	1963	$20

LAMP

Number	Title	Yr	NM
❑ 8008	Don't Let Go/All Night Mambo	1954	$50

WARNER BROS.

Number	Title	Yr	NM
❑ 7025	All My Trials/Wounded	1967	$10
❑ 7047	Mr. Cupid (Don't You Call on Me)/Hang My Head and Cry	1967	$10

—B-side by the Big Guys

COOL, CALVIN, AND THE SURF KNOBS

CHARTER

Number	Title	Yr	NM
❑ 7	Beach Bash/El Tocolote	1963	$50

COOL SOUNDS, THE

PULSAR

Number	Title	Yr	NM
❑ 2421	Comin' Home (Free)/Rag Doll	1969	$60

WARNER BROS.

Number	Title	Yr	NM
❑ 7575	A Love Like Ours Could Last a Million Years or More/ Who Can I Turn To	1972	$40
❑ 7615	Boy Wonder/Free	1972	$40
❑ 7538	I'll Take You Back/Where Do We Go from Here	1971	$40

COOLBREEZERS, THE

BALE

Number	Title	Yr	NM
❑ 102/103	Let Christmas Ring/Hello, Mister New Year	1958	$200
❑ 100/101	The Greatest Love of All/ Eda Weda Bug	1958	$70

EBONY

Number	Title	Yr	NM
❑ 1015	Won't You Come In/Pack Your Bags and Go	1956	$500

—As "The Little Coolbreezers

COOLEY, SPADE

DECCA

Number	Title	Yr	NM
❑ 9-29309	Break Up Down/You Clobbered Me	1954	$30
❑ 9-28344	Carmen's Boogie/One Sweet Letter from You	1952	$30
❑ 9-46376	Cowboy Waltz/My Heart Is Broken in Three	1951	$30
❑ 9-28253	Crazy 'Cause I Love You/ Swingin' the Devil's Dreams	1952	$30
❑ 9-46355	Down Yonder/Horse Hair Boogie	1951	$30
❑ 9-46339	Hittsitty Hottsitty/Lucky Leather Britches	1951	$30
❑ 9-29788	Seasons of My Heart/No Need to Cry Anymore	1956	$20

RCA VICTOR

Number	Title	Yr	NM
❑ 48-0032	Call Me Darlin' Do/ Four Fiddle Polka	1949	$50

—Originals on green vinyl

Number	Title	Yr	NM
❑ 47-3197	Empty Saddles/The Old Spinning Wheel	1949	$30
❑ 48-0078	Flop Eared Mule/The Eighth of January	1949	$50

—Originals on green vinyl

Number	Title	Yr	NM
❑ 48-0157	Foolish Tears/Send Ten Pretty Flowers	1950	$40

—Originals on green vinyl

Number	Title	Yr	NM
❑ 48-0330	Hillbilly Fever/Honky Tonkin'	1950	$40

—Originals on green vinyl

Number	Title	Yr	NM
❑ 48-0079	Ida Red/Six Eight to the Barn	1949	$50

—Originals on green vinyl

Number	Title	Yr	NM
❑ 47-3196	Lights Out/In the Chapel in the Moonlight	1949	$30
❑ 48-0348	Longing/Little Liza Jane	1950	$40

—Originals on green vinyl

Number	Title	Yr	NM
❑ 48-0043	Texas Playboy Rag/Lord Nottingham's War Dance	1949	$50

—Originals on green vinyl

Number	Title	Yr	NM
❑ 48-0309	Texas Star/Pretty Please Love Me	1950	$40

—Originals on green vinyl

Number	Title	Yr	NM
❑ 48-0027	The Best Deal in Town/ Spanish Fandango	1949	$50

—Originals on green vinyl

Number	Title	Yr	NM
❑ 48-0063	The Gal I Left Behind Me/ Arkansas Traveler	1949	$50

—Originals on green vinyl

Number	Title	Yr	NM
❑ 47-3195	The Last Roundup/Wagon Wheels	1949	$30
❑ 48-0077	The Wagoner/Wake Up Susan	1949	$50

—Originals on green vinyl

Number	Title	Yr	NM
❑ 48-0467	Tuesday Two-Step/ Three Fiddle Rag	1951	$30

COOLIDGE, RITA

A&M

Number	Title	Yr	NM
❑ 2551	All Time High/(Instrumental)	1983	$3
❑ 2551 [PS]	All Time High/(Instrumental)	1983	$5
❑ 1792	Am I Blue/Star	1976	$4
❑ 1256	Crazy Love/Mountains	1971	$5
❑ 1414	Donut Man/Whiskey, Whiskey	1973	$4
❑ 1398	Fever/My Crew	1972	$4
❑ 1398 [PS]	Fever/My Crew	1972	$6
❑ 2281	Fool That I Am/Can She Keep You Satisfied	1980	$4
❑ 1545	Hold an Old Friend's Hand/Mama Lou	1974	$4
❑ 2199	I'd Rather Leave While I'm in Love/Sweet Emotions	1979	$4
❑ 2541	I'll Never Let You Go/ Shadow in the Night	1983	$3
❑ 2546 [DJ]	I Will Never Let You Go (same on both sides)	1983	$4

—Stock copies do not exist

Number	Title	Yr	NM
❑ 1816	Late Again/Keep the Candle Burning	1976	$4
❑ 1324	Lay My Burden Down/Nice Feelin'	1972	$4
❑ 1642	Love Has No Pride/ Heaven's Dream	1974	$4
❑ 2090	Love Me Again/The Jealous Kind	1978	$4
❑ 1353	Most Likely You Go Your Way/Family Full of Soul	1972	$4
❑ 1271	Mud Island/I Believe in You	1971	$5
❑ 2169	One Fine Day/Sweet Emotions	1979	$4
❑ 2586	Only You/Shadow in the Night	1983	$3
❑ 2634	Something Said Love/Survivor	1984	$3
❑ 2361	The Closer You Get/Take It Home	1981	$4
❑ 2004	The Way You Do the Things You Do/I Feel the Burden (Being Lifted Off My Shoulders)	1977	$4
❑ 2004 [PS]	The Way You Do the Things You Do/I Feel the Burden (Being Lifted Off My Shoulders)	1977	$4

Number	Title	Yr	NM
❑ 1965	We're All Alone/Southern Lady	1977	$4
❑ 1965 [PS]	We're All Alone/Southern Lady	1977	$4
❑ 2385	Wishin' and Hopin'/I Did My Part	1981	$4
❑ 2318	Words/Born Under a Bad Sign	1981	$4

PEPPER

Number	Title	Yr	NM
❑ 443	Turn Around and Love You/ Walking in the Morning	1969	$8

COOPER, ALICE

ATLANTIC

Number	Title	Yr	NM
❑ 3280	Department of Youth/Some Folks	1975	$5
❑ 3254	Only Women/Cold Ethyl	1975	$5
❑ 3298	Welcome to My Nightmare/ Cold Ethyl	1975	$5

EPIC

Number	Title	Yr	NM
❑ 34-73085	House of Fire/Ballad of Dwight Fry	1989	$3
❑ 34-08114	I Got a Line on You/ Livin' on the Edge	1988	$3

—B-side by Britney Fox

Number	Title	Yr	NM
❑ 34-68958	Poison/Trash	1989	$3

MCA

Number	Title	Yr	NM
❑ 53212	Freedom/Time to Kill	1987	$3
❑ 53212 [PS]	Freedom/Time to Kill	1987	$4
❑ 52904	He's Back (The Man Behind the Mask)/Billion Dollar Baby	1986	$3
❑ 52904 [PS]	He's Back (The Man Behind the Mask)/Billion Dollar Baby	1986	$4

WARNER BROS.

Number	Title	Yr	NM
❑ 7568	Be My Lover/Yeah, Yeah, Yeah	1972	$5
❑ 7724	Billion Dollar Babies/Mary Ann	1973	$5
❑ 7490	Caught in a Dream/ Hallowed Be My Name	1971	$5
❑ 49204	Clones (We're All)/Model Citizen	1980	$4
❑ 49204 [PS]	Clones (We're All)/Model Citizen	1980	$5
❑ 49526	Dance Yourself to Death/Talk Talk	1980	$4
❑ 7449	Eighteen/Body	1971	$5
❑ GWB7141	Eighteen/Caught in a Dream	1972	$4

—Back to Back Hits" series; green label

Number	Title	Yr	NM
❑ GWB7141	Eighteen/Caught in a Dream	1973	$3

—Back to Back Hits" series; "Burbank" palm trees label

Number	Title	Yr	NM
❑ 7631	Elected/Luney Tune	1972	$5
❑ 7631 [PS]	Elected/Luney Tune	1972	$20
❑ 8760	From the Inside/Nurse Rosetta	1979	$4
❑ 49848	Generation Landslide '81/ Seven and Seven Is	1981	$4
❑ 7673	Hello Hurray/Generation Landslide	1972	$5
❑ 8695	How You Gonna See Me Now/No Tricks	1978	$5
❑ 29828	I Am the Future/Tag, You're It	1982	$4
❑ 29928	I Like Girls/Zorro's Ascent	1982	$4
❑ 8023	I'm Eighteen/Muscle of Love	1974	$5
❑ 8228	I Never Cry/Go to Hell	1976	$4
❑ 7783	Muscle of Love/Crazy Little Child	1974	$5
❑ 8607	School's Out/Eighteen	1978	$8
❑ 7596	School's Out/Gutter Cat	1972	$5
❑ 7596 [PS]	School's Out/Gutter Cat	1972	$20
❑ 7398	Shoe Salesman/Return of the Spiders	1970	$30
❑ 7762	Teenage Lament '74/ Hard Hearted Alice	1973	$5

7-Inch Extended Plays

Number	Title	Yr	NM
❑ S2748 [PS]	Muscle of Love	1973	$25

—Part of "Little LP" series (LLP #235)

Number	Title	Yr	NM
❑ S2748	Working Up a Sweat/Never Been Sold Before//Muscle of Love/Teenage Lament	1973	$25

—Jukebox issue; small hole, plays at 33 1/3 rpm

COOPER, CHRISTINE

PARKWAY

Number	Title	Yr	NM
❑ 122	I Must Have You (Or No One)/ Good Looks (They Don't Count)	1966	$20
❑ 971	S.O.S./Say What You Feel	1966	$30
❑ 983	(They Call Him) A Bad Boy/ Heartaches Away My Boy	1966	$50

COOPER, DOLLY

DOT

Number	Title	Yr	NM
❑ 15495	Big Rock Inn/I'm Looking Through Your Window	1956	$15
❑ 15535	The Confession of a Fool/ Tell Me, Tell Me	1957	$15

EBB

Number	Title	Yr	NM
❑ 109	Wild Love/Time Brings About a Change	1957	$15

MODERN

Number	Title	Yr	NM
❑ 965	My Man/Ay La Bas	1955	$50
❑ 977	Teenage Prayer/Down So Long	1956	$60
❑ 986	Teenage Wedding Bells/ Every Day and Every Night	1956	$60

COOPER, JERRY

BEAR

Number	Title	Yr	NM
❑ 187	As Long As There's Women Like You/(B-side unknown)	1988	$6
❑ 191	Code of Honor/(B-side unknown)	1988	$6
❑ 178	I'l Forget You/(B-side unknown)	1987	$6

Number	Title	Yr	NM
COOPER, JOHNNY			
ERMINE			
❑ 38	Little Bride/Dumb Dumb Bunny	1962	$40
❑ 44	Oreo/Flame of Love	1962	$30
❑ 40	While You're Young/Diggity Doggity	1962	$30
COOPER, LES, AND THE SOUL ROCKERS			
ARRAWAK			
❑ 1008	I Can Do the Soul Jerk/At the World's Fair	1965	$15
ATCO			
❑ 6644	Gonna Have a Lotta Fun/Thank God for You	1969	$8
DIMENSION			
❑ 1023	Motor City/Swobblin'	1963	$30
ENJOY			
❑ 2024	Owee Baby/Let's Do the Boston Monkey	1965	$10
EVERLAST			
❑ 5023	Garbage Can/Bossa Nova Dance	1963	$15
❑ 5016	Twistin'/Dig Yourself	1963	$15
❑ 5019	Wiggle Wobble/Dig Yourself	1963	$20
COOPER, MARTY			
MC			
❑ 5003	Like a Gypsy/$10 Room	1977	$5
COOPER, PAT			
UNITED ARTISTS			
❑ 50641	It's the Italian in Me/I Don't Wanna Go Home	1970	$6
COOPER, WILMA LEE			
DECCA			
❑ 32210	Darling, How Could You/Time Keeps Standing Still	1967	$12
❑ 32136	The Birds Are Back/Never Too Far from My Mind	1967	$12
COOPER, WILMA LEE AND STONEY			
COLUMBIA			
❑ 4-20898	All on Account of You/You Tried to Ruin My Name	1952	$30
❑ 4-21221	Bamboozled/You Can't Feel the Way I Do	1954	$30
❑ 4-21265	Brand New Baby/Can You Forget	1954	$30
❑ 4-21088	Don't Play That Song/You Belong to Someone Else	1953	$30
❑ 4-20781	Faded Love/Golden Rocket	1951	$40
❑ 4-20801	Ghost Train/Mother's Prayer	1951	$30
❑ 2-600(?)	I Ain't Gonna Work Tomorrow/The Message Came Special	1950	$50
—Microgroove 33 1/3 rpm 7-inch single, small hole			
❑ 4-21010	I Cried Again/Have Mercy on Me	1952	$30
❑ 2-434	I Dreamed About Mama Last Night/No One Now	1949	$50
—Microgroove 33 1/3 rpm 7-inch single, small hole			
❑ 4-20949	I'm Taking My Audition/Walking My Georgia Hill	1952	$30
❑ 2-310(?)	Moonlight on West Virginia/On the Banks of the River	1949	$50
—Microgroove 33 1/3 rpm 7-inch single, small hole			
❑ 4-21049	Stoney/Clinch Mountain Waltz	1952	$30
❑ 2-685	The Legend of the Dogwood Tree/White Rose	1950	$50
—Microgroove 33 1/3 rpm 7-inch single, small hole			
❑ 4-20713	The Legend of the Dogwood Tree/White Rose	1950	$40
❑ 2-370(?)	Thirty Pieces of Silver/What's the Matter with This World	1949	$50
—Microgroove 33 1/3 rpm 7-inch single, small hole			
❑ 4-20861	West Virginia Polka/Sunny Side of the Mountain	1951	$30
❑ 4-21000	Will the Lord Let You In/My Lord's Gonna Share My Hand	1952	$30
DECCA			
❑ 32482	Don't Let Your Sweet Love Die/Guide Me Home, My Georgia Moon	1969	$12
❑ 31971	Each Season Changes You/It's Easier to Say Than Do	1966	$12
❑ 31891	It's Started Again/Wedding Bells	1966	$10
❑ 32032	Three Windows/A Hero's Death	1966	$10
HICKORY			
❑ 1257	Big John's Wife/Pirate King	1964	$15
❑ 1098	Big Midnight Special/X Marks the Spot	1959	$20
❑ 1051	Cheated Too/This Crazy Crazy World	1956	$30
❑ 1085	Come Walk with Me/Is It Right	1958	$20
❑ 1070	Diamond Joe/I Tell My Heart	1957	$30
❑ 1193	Doing My Time/Singing Waterfall	1962	$15
❑ 1208	Glory Land March/Satisfied	1963	$15
❑ 1167	Have Faith in Me/Matthew 24	1962	$20
❑ 1157	Heartaches Don't Lie/The Mighty Battle Cry	1961	$20
❑ 1078	He Taught Them How/Walking My Lord Up Calvary Hill	1958	$30

Number	Title	Yr	NM
❑ 1028	How It Hurts to Cry Alone/Just for a While	1955	$30
❑ 1140	I Gotta Laugh (To Keep from Crying)/Train, You Took My Baby	1961	$20
❑ 1043	I Want to Be Loved/Row No. 2	1956	$30
❑ 1058	Loving You/Tramp on the Street	1957	$30
❑ 1179	Philadelphia Lawyer/Trouble Ahead	1962	$15
❑ 1035	Please Help Me to Be Wrong/Each Season Changes You	1955	$30
❑ 1107	There's a Big Wheel/Rachel's Guitar	1959	$20
❑ 1225	There's a Higher Power/This World Can't Stand Long	1963	$15
❑ 1126	This Ole House/Heartbreak Street	1960	$20
❑ 1064	This Thing Called Love/My Hearts Keep Crying	1957	$20
❑ 1279	This Train/I Couldn't Care Less	1964	$15
❑ 1147	Wreck on the Highway/Night After Night	1961	$20
STARDAY			
❑ 151	Sweet Fern/Hello Central, Give Me Heaven	1977	$5
COOPERETTES, THE			
ABC			
❑ 11156	Peace Maker/Trouble	1968	$15
❑ 11197	Spiral Road/Trouble	1969	$15
BRUNSWICK			
❑ 55307	Don't Trust Him/Everything's Wrong	1966	$20
❑ 55296	Goodbye School/Goodbye School (Part 2)	1966	$20
❑ 55329	(Life Has) No Meaning Now/Shing-a-Ling	1967	$30
COPAGE, MARC			
METROMEDIA			
❑ 154	Santa, Bring My Daddy Home for Christmas/Santa, Please Repair My Toys for Christmas	1969	$8
COPAS, COWBOY			
DOT			
❑ 15847	A World That's Real/Looking for an Angel	1958	$30
❑ 15668	Blue Kimono/Breeze	1957	$30
❑ 15735	Circle Rock/My Little Red Wagon	1958	$70
KING			
❑ 4865	Any Old Time/Don't Shake Hands with the Devil	1956	$30
❑ 5437	A Stranger in My Home/Old Faithful and True Love	1960	$20
❑ 1274	Blue Waltz/A Heartache Ago	1953	$30
❑ 1507	Blue Yesterday/Tell Me More	1955	$30
❑ 1064	Boomerang/It's Enough to Make Anyone Cry	1952	$40
❑ 5734	Breeze/The Road of Broken Hearts	1963	$15
❑ 1386	Carbon Copy/I'm Glad for Your Sake	1954	$30
❑ 5392	Carolina Sunshine Girl/Rose of Tennessee	1960	$20
❑ 1034	Copy Cat/Those Gone and Left Me Blues	1952	$40
❑ 1166	Doll of Clay/If Wishes Were Horses	1953	$30
❑ 1151	Feelin' Low/Love Me Now	1952	$40
❑ 1046	Four Bare Walls and a Ceiling/I Can't Stop Loving You	1952	$40
❑ 1080	Golden Moon/I Can't Remember to Forget	1952	$40
❑ 1424	Hello Darling/The Talking Mule	1955	$30
❑ 1306	He Stands By His Window/The Man Upstairs	1954	$30
❑ 5638	I Built a Fence Around My Heart/My Blues Are Gone	1962	$20
❑ 1200	I Can't Go On/A Wreath at the Door of My Heart	1953	$30
❑ 1329	I'll Be There/I'm a Stranger in My Home	1954	$30
❑ 1040	I'll Pay the Price/'Tis Sweet to Be Remembered	1951	$40
❑ 980	I'm Glad I'm On the Inside/Four Books in the Bible	1951	$40
❑ 5544	It's a Lonely World/Don't Let Them Change Your Mind	1961	$20
❑ 5479	It's a Shame/You Walked Right Out of My Dreams	1961	$20
❑ 1136	I've Grown So Used to You/It's No Sin to Love You	1952	$40
❑ 1253	Look What I Got/Will You Forget	1953	$30
❑ 1003	O Little Town of Bethlehem/It Came Upon the Midnight Clear	1951	$40
❑ 1456	Pledging My Love/Shamed of Myself	1955	$30
❑ 1139	Purple Rose/Some Fine Morning	1952	$40
❑ 5733	Signed, Sealed and Delivered/The Hopes of a Broken Heart	1963	$15
❑ 5571	Sweet Thing/Signed, Sealed, Then Forgotten	1961	$20
❑ 964	Tennessee Flat Guitar/I Love You	1951	$40
❑ 1234	Tennessee Senorita/If You Will Let Me Be Your Love	1953	$30
❑ 5270	Tennessee Waltz/Signed, Sealed and Delivered	1959	$20
—As "Lloyd Copas			
❑ 1464	The Party's Over/Summer Kisses	1955	$30

Number	Title	Yr	NM
❑ 1444	The Stone Was Rolled Away/The Silver That Nailed Him to the Cross	1955	$30
❑ 951	The Strange Little Girl/You'll Never See Me Cry	1951	$50
❑ 1000	'Tis Sweet to Be Remembered/Because of You	1951	$40
❑ 1486	Tragic Romance/Listen to My Heart	1955	$30
❑ 1407	When I Lost You/Why Should I Want Her	1954	$30
❑ 5676	When Jesus Beckons Me Home/I Saw the Light	1962	$20
❑ 1004	White Christmas/Jingle Bells	1951	$40
❑ 501	Alabam/I Can	1960	$30
❑ 658	Autobiography/The Rainbow and the Rose	1963	$15
❑ 606	Bury Me Face Down/Heart on the Run	1962	$20
❑ 750	Cowboy's Deck of Cards/Beyond the Sunset	1966	$12
❑ 612	Family Reunion/Smoke on the Water	1962	$20
❑ 542	Flat Top/True Love (Is the Greatest Thing)	1961	$20
❑ 621	Goodbye Kisses/The Gypsy Girl	1963	$15
❑ 524	I Have a Friend/The Hem of His Garment	1960	$20
❑ 641	Louisian/Break Away, Break Away	1963	$15
❑ 476	Mom and Dad's Affair/Black Cloud Risin'	1959	$20
❑ 685	Old Man's Story/Pretty Diamonds	1964	$15
❑ 573	Sal/A Thousand Miles of Ocean	1961	$20
❑ 559	Signed, Sealed and Delivered/New Filipino Baby	1961	$20
❑ 528	Sittin' Flat on Ready/Midnight in Heaven	1960	$20
❑ 595	Sold the Farm/Table in the Corner	1962	$20
❑ 493	South Pacific Shore/That's All I Can Remember	1960	$20
❑ 552	Sunny Tennessee/Dreaming	1961	$20
❑ 585	There'll Come a Time Someday/Seven Seas from You	1962	$20
❑ 729	Waltzing with Sin/Blue Kimono	1965	$10
COPASETICS, THE			
PREMIUM			
❑ 409	Believe in Me/Collegian	1956	$200
COPELAND, RUTH			
INVICTUS			
❑ IS9096 [B]	Gimme Shelter/No Commitment	1971	$20
❑ IS9088 [B]	Haré Krishna/No Commitment	1971	$12
RCA			
❑ PB10839 [B]	Heaven/Take Me to Baltimore	1976	$12
—Heaven featuring Daryl Hall			
COPELAND, KEN			
DOT			
❑ 15686	Where the Rio Rosa Flows/Locked in the Arms of Love	1958	$20
IMPERIAL			
❑ 5466	I Want to Go Steady/I Would Give My Heart	1957	$30
❑ 5432	Pledge of Love/Night Air	1957	$30
—B-side by The Mints			
❑ 5453	Teenage/Bed of Lies	1957	$30
LIN			
❑ 5017	Fanny Brown/Chaser of Hearts	1957	$50
❑ 5007	Pledge of Love/Night Air	1957	$50
—B-side by The Mints			
COPELAND, STEWART/ADAM ANT			
I.R.S.			
❑ 52885	Out of Bounds/(B-side unknown)	1986	$5
COPELAND, STEWART/STANARD RIDGWAY			
A&M			
❑ 2604	Don't Box Me In/Drama at Home	1983	$5
COPS 'N ROBBERS			
CORAL			
❑ 62466	I Could Have Danced All Night/Just Keep Right On	1965	$10
❑ 62473	It's All Over Now, Baby Blue/I Found Out	1965	$10
PARROT			
❑ 9716	St. James Infirmary/There's Got to Be a Reason	1964	$10
CORBIN, RAY			
MONUMENT			
❑ 1050	Absence/In My City	1968	$8
❑ 1002	In Baby's Eyes/Mama, Don't Cry for Me	1967	$8
❑ 1082	Mission of Loneliness/Sing the Blues to Daddy	1968	$8
❑ 1102	Passin' Through/Life Doesn't Move Me	1968	$8

Number	Title	Yr	NM
CORBIN/HANNER			
ALFA			
❏ 7022	Everyone Knows I'm Yours// Son of America/Let Her Go/ One Fine Morning	1982	$5
— As "Corbin-Hanner Band			
❏ 7007	Livin' the Good Life/ Long Gone Blues	1981	$5
— As "Corbin-Hanner Band			
❏ 7010	Oklahoma Crude/ Too Lazy for Love	1981	$5
— As "Corbin-Hanner Band			
❏ 7015	Son of America/Regular Joe	1982	$5
— As "Corbin-Hanner Band			
❏ 7001	Time Has Treated You Well/ On the Wings of My Victory	1981	$5
— As "Corbin-Hanner Band			
LIFESONG			
❏ 1783	America's Sweetheart/ Like I Used To	1978	$5
— As "Corbin and Hanner			
❏ 1773	Broken Man/Caribbean Nights	1978	$5
— As "Corbin and Hanner			
❏ 45120	One Fine Morning/Lord, I Hope This Day Is Good	1982	$5
— As "Corbin-Hanner Band			
CORDEL, PAT			
CLUB			
❏ 1011	Darling, Come Back/My My Tears	1956	$1500
— And the Crescents			
MICHELLE			
❏ 503	Darling, Come Back/My My Tears	1959	$200
— And the Elegants			
VICTORY			
❏ 1001	Darling, Come Back/My My Tears	1963	$100
— And the Elegants			
CORDELLS, THE			
BARGAIN			
❏ 5004	The Beat of My Heart/Laid Off	1962	$60
BULLSEYE			
❏ 1017	Believe in Me/Please Don't Go	1958	$125
CORDET, LOUISE			
LONDON			
❏ 9560	I'm Just a Baby/In a Matter of Moments	1963	$15
CORDIALS, THE			
7 ARTS			
❏ 707	Dawn Is Almost Here/Keep An Eye	1961	$125
BETHLEHEM			
❏ 3019	What's the Matter with Me/I'm Not Crying Anymore	1961	$30
CORDIAL			
❏ 1001	I'm Ashamed/Sentimental Jorney	1960	$125
FELSTED			
❏ 8653	Once in a Lifetime/What Kind of Fool Am I	1962	$40
LIBERTY			
❏ 55784	Oh, How I Love Her/You Can't Believe in Love	1965	$30
REVEILLE			
❏ 106	Eternal Love/The International Twist	1962	$300
WHIP			
❏ 276	Listen My Heart/My Heart's Desire	1961	$250
CORDOVANS, THE			
JOHNSON			
❏ 731	Come On Baby/My Heart	1960	$30
COREA, CHICK			
POLYDOR			
❏ 14538	Bagatelle #4/Central Park	1979	$4
COREY, JILL			
COLUMBIA			
❏ 4-41202	Big Daddy/Wherefore Art Thou, Romeo	1958	$15
❏ 4-40177	Cleo and Meo/Do You Know What Lips Are For	1954	$15
— With the Four Lads			
❏ 4-41360	Dream Boy/Love Will Find Out the Way	1959	$12
❏ 4-40410	Edward/I'm Not at All in Love	1955	$15
❏ 4-40627	First Love/Wait for Tomorrow	1955	$15

Number	Title	Yr	NM
❏ 4-41108	Give It All You've Got/ Uh Huh, Oh Yeah	1958	$15
❏ 4-41621	Have You Ever Been Lonely/I Gotta Have My Baby Back	1960	$12
❏ 4-41498	I Can't Hide My Heart/ Seems Like Old Times	1959	$10
❏ 4-41023	I Feel Pretty/How Can I Tell	1957	$15
❏ 4-41300	I Found a New Baby/My Reverie	1958	$15
❏ 4-40794	I Love My Baby (My Baby Loves Me)/Egghead	1956	$15
❏ 4-41068	I Told a Lie to My Darlin'/ Exactly Like You	1957	$15
❏ 4-40878	Let It Be Me/Make Like a Bunny, Honey	1957	$20
— With Jimmy Carroll; A-side is the first English-language recording of the song, which later was a hit for several other artists			
❏ 4-40566	Look! Look!/Ching-a-Ling	1955	$15
❏ 4-41164	Loveable/Sweet Sugar Lips	1958	$15
❏ 4-40955	Love Me to Pieces/Love	1957	$15
❏ 4-40268	One God/He Is a Man (I Am a Woman)	1954	$15
❏ 4-40188	Should I Tell/A Good Night's Work	1954	$15
❏ 4-41772	Stick 'Em Up Stuck Up/ Ten Gallon Hat	1960	$10
❏ 4-40502	That's All I Need/Come to Me for Everything	1955	$15
❏ 4-41435	The President Song/Have I Told You Lately That I Love You	1959	$15
❏ 4-40743	What Am I to Do/Let Him Know	1956	$15
❏ 4-40327	Where Are You?/Number One Boy	1954	$15
MERCURY			
❏ 71913	I Miss You Already/It's Only Me	1962	$10
COREY, JOHN			
VEE JAY			
❏ 514	Hey Little Runaround/The Prettiest Girl I've Kissed Today	1963	$12
❏ 466	Pollyanna/I'll Forget	1962	$40
— Backing group: The Four Seasons			
CORNELIUS BROTHERS AND SISTER ROSE			
PLATINUM			
❏ 105/6	Treat Her Like a Lady/ Over at My Place	1970	$15
UNITED ARTISTS			
❏ XW377	Big Time Lover/Wonderful Tune	1974	$5
❏ 50954	Don't Ever Be Lonely (A Poor Little Fool Like Me)/I'm So Glad to Be Loved by You	1972	$5
❏ XW313	I Just Can't Stop Loving You/ These Lonely Nights	1973	$5
❏ 50996	I'm Never Gonna Be Alone Anymore/Let's Stay Together	1972	$5
❏ XW208	Let Me Down Easy/Gonna Be Sweet for You	1973	$5
❏ XW534	Since I Found My Baby/I Love Music	1974	$5
❏ XW512	Too Late to Turn Back Now/ Don't Ever Be Lonely (A Poor Little Fool Like Me)	1974	$4
— Reissue			
❏ 50910	Too Late to Turn Back Now/ Lift Your Love Higher	1972	$5
❏ 50721	Treat Her Like a Lady/ Over at My Place	1970	$5
❏ 0131	Treat Her Like a Lady/ Over at My Place	1973	$4
— Silver Spotlight Series" reissue			
❏ XW533	Trouble Child/Got to Testify	1974	$5
CORNELIUS, HELEN			
AMERI-CAN			
❏ 1011	If Your Heart's a Rolling Stone/(B-side unknown)	1983	$6
COLUMBIA			
❏ 4-45921	If I Go On/Tweedle Dee Dee	1973	$6
❏ 4-45980	Little Sugar Plum/Patchwork Girl	1973	$6
ELEKTRA			
❏ 47237	Love Never Comes Easy/Losing You	1981	$5
❏ 47232 [DJ]	Oh Holy Night/Silent Night	1981	$6
— B-side by Joe Sun			
❏ 47190	Where Did Our Love Go/ Spending Time	1981	$5
— B-side by Joe Sun			
RCA			
❏ PB-11150	Everybody Everywhere Needs Somebody Sometime/ Lincoln Audrey	1977	$5
❏ PB-11753	It Started with a Smile/I'm Changing	1979	$5
❏ PB-10795	There's Always a Goodbye/ Only Road Worth Taking	1976	$5
❏ PB-11375	What Cha Doin' After Midnight, Baby/Oh What a Night for Love	1978	$5
RCA VICTOR			
❏ PB-10451	I'd Love You All Over/We Still Sing Love Songs in Missouri	1975	$5
❏ PB-10629	Only Lovers/A Mornin' Made for Lovin'	1976	$5

Number	Title	Yr	NM
CORNELL, DON; JOHNNY DESMOND; ALAN DALE			
CORAL			
❏ 61076	The Gang That Sang "Heart of My Heart"/I Think I'll Fall in Love Today	1953	$15
CORNELL, DON			
20TH CENTURY FOX			
❏ 464	Forget About Me/Lost Dreams & Lonely Tears	1964	$8
❏ 515	If You Love Her Tell Her So/ You Know You Don't Want Me	1964	$8
ABC-PARAMOUNT			
❏ 10740	Dingle Ling, Dingle Ling/ Careless Hands	1965	$6
❏ 10687	Italian Wedding Song/ Please Lie to Me	1965	$6
CORAL			
❏ 61790	Afternoon in Madrid/Let's Get Lost	1957	$10
❏ 61333	Athena/No Man Is an Island	1955	$12
❏ 61171	Believe in Me/Little Lucy	1954	$15
❏ 61631	But Love Me/Fort Knox	1956	$10
❏ 62019	But Not Your Heart/Once More	1958	$10
❏ 60900	For You/I Was Lucky	1953	$10
❏ 61659	Grazie/Could You	1956	$10
❏ 61687	Heaven Only Knows/Life Is a Song	1956	$12
❏ 61125	Hold Me/Size 12	1954	$15
❏ 61206	Hold My Hand/I'm Blessed	1954	$15
❏ 60860	I/Be Fair	1952	$15
❏ 60659	I'll Walk Alone/That's the Chance You Take	1952	$15
❏ 61068	I'm Yearning/You're On Trial	1953	$15
❏ 60690	I'm Yours/My Mother's Pearls	1952	$15
❏ 60902	It Isn't Fair/Something to Remember You By	1953	$10
❏ 61757	Let's Be Friends/Ma-Ma Pa-Pa Cha-Cha	1956	$12
❏ 60859	Let's Have an Old Fashioned Christmas/I've Got the Christmas Spirit	1952	$20
❏ 61854	Mailman, Bring Me No More Blues/No Matter What	1957	$10
❏ 61549	Make a Wish/There Once Was a Beautiful…	1955	$10
❏ 61817	Mama Guitar/A Face in the Crowd	1957	$10
❏ 61393	Most of All/The Door Is Still Open to My Heart	1955	$10
❏ 61030	Please Play Our Song (Mister Record Man)/ If I Should Love Again	1953	$15
❏ 61721	See-Saw/From the Bottom of My Heart	1956	$10
❏ 61811	Sittin' in the Balcony/My Faith, My Hope, My Love	1957	$10
❏ 60903	S'posin/If You Were Only Mine	1953	$10
❏ 60901	Stay As Sweet As You Are/ We Three (My Echo, My Shadow and Me)	1953	$10
❏ 61584	Teenage Meeting (Gonna Rock It Up Right)/I Still Have a Prayer	1956	$20
❏ 61467	The Bible Tells Me So/Love Is a Many-Splendored Thing	1955	$12
❏ 60968	There's No Escape/ Many Are the Times	1953	$15
❏ 60748	This Is the Beginning of the End/I Can't Cry Anymore	1952	$15
❏ 61367	When You Are in Love/ Give Me Your Love	1955	$10
❏ 61011	Who Loves Me/When the Hands of the Clock Pray at Midnight	1953	$15
DOT			
❏ 15938	Heart of My Heart/ This Earth Is Mine	1959	$8
❏ 16044	I/Size 12	1960	$8
RCA VICTOR			
❏ 47-3909	Au Revoir Again/A Whistle and a Prayer	1950	$20
❏ 47-2914	Baby It's Cold Outside/ Whispering Waters	1949	$20
— With Laura Leslie			
❏ 47-3239	Come Back to Me/My Baby Is Blue	1949	$20
❏ 47-4044	I'll Be Seeing You/When I Take My Sugar to Tea	1951	$15
❏ 47-3884	I Need You So/It Couldn't Happen to a Sweeter Girl	1950	$20
❏ 47-4083	My Inspiration/You Can't Tell a Lie to Your Heart	1951	$20
❏ 47-3991	Sue Me/Velvet Lips	1950	$20
❏ 47-3950	Take Me in Your Arms/The Breeze	1950	$20
❏ 47-4043	Was That the Human Thing to Do/That Old Feeling	1951	$15
❏ 47-4042	Wedding Bells/Let a Smile Be Your Umbrella	1951	$15
❏ 47-4149	Why Don't You Tell Me So/ If I Had Another Chance	1951	$20
ROULETTE			
❏ 4355	The Flying Trapeze/Wish I Was	1961	$8
SIGNATURE			
❏ 12002	Forever Couldn't Be Long Enough/Sempre Amore	1959	$8
❏ 12020	Forever/There's Still Time Brother	1959	$8
❏ 12027	Grateful/Only Time Will Tell	1960	$8
❏ EC81002 [PS]	I'm Yours	1953	$15
❏ EC81002	I'm Yours/This Is the Beginning of the End//I'll Walk Alone/(I've Cried Until) I Can't Cry Anymore	1953	$15

Number	Title	Yr	NM
❑ EC81118	Most of All/All of You//Unchained Melody/Danger Heartbreak Ahead	1955	$10

RCA VICTOR

Number	Title	Yr	NM
❑ 547-0243	Come Back to Me/Why Don't You Tell Me So//Au Revoir Again/(The Breeze) Bringin' My Honey Back to Me	1952	$15

— One record of 2-EP set EPB-3116

Number	Title	Yr	NM
❑ EPB3116 [PS]	Don Cornell Sings	1952	$20

— Fold-open cover for 2-EP set (547-0242, 547-0243)

Number	Title	Yr	NM
❑ 547-0242	It Isn't Fair/Take Me in Your Arms//I Surrender Dear/I Need You So	1952	$15

— One record of 2-EP set EPB-3116; Side 1, track 1 credited to "Swing and Sway with Sammy Kaye, vocal refrain by Don Cornell

CORNELLS, THE
GAREX

Number	Title	Yr	NM
❑ 201	Beach Bound/Lone Star Stomp	1963	$40
❑ 102	Malibu Surf/Agua Caliente	1962	$40
❑ 100	Mama's Little Baby/Wak-A-Cha	1962	$40
❑ 206	Surf Fever/Do the Slauson	1963	$40

CORNISH, GENE
DAWN

Number	Title	Yr	NM
❑ 551	I Wanna Be a Beatle/Oh Misery	1964	$50
❑ 550	Let's Do the Capri/Lonely I Will Say	1964	$40

VASSAR

Number	Title	Yr	NM
❑ 321	My Baby Ran Away from Me/Now the Story Can Be Told	1962	$30
❑ 319	Since I Lost You/Winner Take All	1962	$30

CORNOR, RANDY
ABC DOT

Number	Title	Yr	NM
❑ 17711	Free and Easy/Love Me Like the Morning	1977	$5
❑ 17625	Heart Don't Fail Me Now/Sugar Foot Rag	1976	$5
❑ 17655	I Guess You Never Loved Me Anyway/Rocky Top	1976	$5
❑ 17676	Love Doesn't Live Here Anymore/(Play That Song Again) About the Loser	1976	$5
❑ 17592	Sometimes I Talk in My Sleep/Used to Be	1975	$5

CHERRY

Number	Title	Yr	NM
❑ 783	Hurt As Big As Texas/Maybe You Should've Been Listenin	1978	$6

CORONETS, THE
CHESS

Number	Title	Yr	NM
❑ 1553	It Would Be Heavenly/Baby's Coming Home	1953	$400

— Black vinyl

Number	Title	Yr	NM
❑ 1553	It Would Be Heavenly/Baby's Coming Home	1953	$800

— Red vinyl

GROOVE

Number	Title	Yr	NM
❑ 0114	I Love You More/Crime Doesn't Pay	1955	$125
❑ 0116	The Bible Tells Me So/Hush	1955	$200

STERLING

Number	Title	Yr	NM
❑ 903	Don't Deprive Me/Little Boy	1955	$250

CORPORATION, THE
CAPITOL

Number	Title	Yr	NM
❑ 2467	Highway/I Want to Get Out of My Grave	1969	$20

CORSAIRS, THE
HY-TONE

Number	Title	Yr	NM
❑ 110	Goodbye Darling/Rock Lilly Rock	1957	$1500

SMASH

Number	Title	Yr	NM
❑ 1715	Time Waits/It Won't Be a Sin	1961	$20

TUFF

Number	Title	Yr	NM
❑ 402	On the Spanish Side/The Change in You	1964	$10
❑ 375	Save a Little Monkey/(Instrumental)	1963	$10

TUFF/CHESS

Number	Title	Yr	NM
❑ 1840	At the Stroke of Midnight/Listen to My Little Heart	1962	$15
❑ 1830	Dancing Shadows/While	1962	$15
❑ 1818	I'll Take You Home/Sittin' on Your Doorstep	1962	$15
❑ 1808	Smoky Places/Thinkin'	1961	$30
❑ 1847	Stormy/It's Almost Sunday Morning	1963	$15

CORT, BOB
LONDON

Number	Title	Yr	NM
❑ 1713	Don't You Rock Me Daddy-O/It Takes a Worried Man to Sing a Worried Blues	1957	$20
❑ 1742	Freight Train/Roll Jen Jenkins	1957	$15

Number	Title	Yr	NM
❑ 1748	Maggie Mae/Jessamine	1957	$15

— With Liz Winters

CORTEZ, DAVE "BABY
ALL PLATINUM

Number	Title	Yr	NM
❑ 2339	Funky Robot (Part 1)/Funky Robot (Part 2)	1972	$5
❑ 2345	Hell Street Junction/(Instrumental)	1973	$5
❑ 2343	Someone Has Taken Your Place/Born Funky	1973	$5
❑ 2347	Soul Walkin'/(B-side unknown)	1974	$5

ARGO

Number	Title	Yr	NM
❑ 5462	Let It Be You/I'm Gonna Stay	1964	$12

CHESS

Number	Title	Yr	NM
❑ 1874	Happy Feet/Gettin' to the Point	1963	$8
❑ 1834	Happy Weekend/Fiddle Sticks	1962	$12
❑ 1850	Hot Cakes! 1st Serving/Hot Cakes! 2nd Serving	1963	$8
❑ 1861	Organ Shout/Precious You	1963	$8
❑ 1842	Tweedle Dee/Gift of Love	1962	$10

CLOCK

Number	Title	Yr	NM
❑ 1024	Cat Nip/Talk Is Cheap	1960	$15
❑ 71875	C'mon and Stomp/Calypso Love Song	1961	$10
❑ 1016	Dave's Special/Whispers	1959	$15
❑ 1031	Hurricane/The Shift	1960	$15
❑ 1014	Piano Shuffle/It's a Sin to Tell a Lie	1959	$15
❑ 1034	Summertime/Walking with You	1961	$15
❑ 1009	The Happy Organ/Love Me As I Love You	1959	$30
❑ 71851	The Happy Organ/Piano Shuffle	1961	$10
❑ 1012	The Whistling Organ/I'm Happy	1959	$15
❑ 1036	Tootsie/Second Chance	1961	$15
❑ 71824	Tootsie/Second Chance	1961	$10

EMBER

Number	Title	Yr	NM
❑ 1011	Soft Lights/Movin' and Groovin'	1956	$50

— As "David Clowney"

EMIT

Number	Title	Yr	NM
❑ 301	Fiesta/Hey-Hey-Hey	1962	$10

EPIC

Number	Title	Yr	NM
❑ 9732	Poppin' Popcorn/The Question	1964	$12

OKEH

Number	Title	Yr	NM
❑ 7208	Popping Popcorn/The Question (Do You Love Me)	1964	$8

PARIS

Number	Title	Yr	NM
❑ 513	Shakin'/Hoot Owl	1958	$40

— As "Dave Clowney"

ROULETTE

Number	Title	Yr	NM
❑ 4717	Belly Rub (Part 1)/Belly Rub (Part 2)	1967	$8
❑ 4679	Count Down/Summertime	1966	$8
❑ 4783	Hot Chocolate/Soul Groovin'	1967	$8
❑ 4759	Hula Hoop/Come Back	1967	$8
❑ 4693	Sticks and Stones/Do Any Dance	1966	$8
❑ 4628	Tweetie Pie/Things Ain't What They Used to Be	1965	$8

T-NECK

Number	Title	Yr	NM
❑ 907	I Turned You On/I Know Who You Been Socking It To	1969	$6
❑ 913	Save Me/My Little Girl	1969	$6

WINLEY

Number	Title	Yr	NM
❑ 267	Scotty (Part 1)/Scotty (Part 2)	1962	$10
❑ 262	Skins and Sounds/Little Paris Melody	1962	$12

7-Inch Extended Plays
CLOCK

Number	Title	Yr	NM
❑ EP 1-4039-C [PS]	Dave "Baby" Cortez and His Happy Organ	1959	$30
❑ EP 1-4039-C	The Happy Organ/The Whistling Organ//Catnip/Deep in the Heart of Texas	1959	$30

RCA VICTOR

Number	Title	Yr	NM
❑ EPA-4342 [M]	*The Happy Organ/Love Me As I Love You/Dave's Special/You're the Girl	1959	$15
❑ ESP-4342 [S]	*The Happy Organ/Love Me As I Love You/Dave's Special/You're the Girl	1959	$25
❑ EPA-4342 [PS]	The Happy Organ	1959	$15
❑ ESP-4342 [PS]	The Happy Organ	1959	$25

CORVAIRS, THE
COMET

Number	Title	Yr	NM
❑ 2145	True True Love/(B-side unknown)	1962	$40

— Black label

Number	Title	Yr	NM
❑ 2145	True True Love/(B-side unknown)	1962	$30

— Yellow label

CORVELLS, THE
ABC-PARAMOUNT

Number	Title	Yr	NM
❑ 10324	Take My Love/Daisy	1962	$200

BLAST

Number	Title	Yr	NM
❑ 203	The Bells/Don't Forget	1961	$200

CUB

Number	Title	Yr	NM
❑ 9122	One (Is Such a Lonely Number)/The Joke's On Me	1963	$30

LIDO

Number	Title	Yr	NM
❑ 509	We Made a Vow/Miss Jones	1957	$200

LUPINE

Number	Title	Yr	NM
❑ 104	He's So Fine/Baby Sitting	1962	$30

TIP TOP

Number	Title	Yr	NM
❑ 509	We Made a Vow/Miss Jones	1957	$300

COSBY, BILL
CAPITOL

Number	Title	Yr	NM
❑ 4501	Boogie on Your Face/What's in a Slang	1977	$4
❑ 4299	I Luv Myself Better Than I Luv Myself/Do It To Me	1976	$4
❑ 4523	Merry Christmas Mama (Vocal)/(Instrumental)	1977	$30

TETRAGRAMMATON

Number	Title	Yr	NM
❑ 1539	Football/Golf	1969	$6

UNI

Number	Title	Yr	NM
❑ 55223	Grover Henson Feels Forgotten/(Instrumental)	1970	$6
❑ 55184	Hikky Burr/Hikky Burr	1969	$6

— A-side with the Bunions; B-side by the Bradford Band

Number	Title	Yr	NM
❑ 55247	Hybish Skybish/Martin's Funeral	1970	$5

— With Bad Foot Brown

WARNER BROS.

Number	Title	Yr	NM
❑ 7171	Funky North Philly/Stop, Look and Listen	1968	$8
❑ 7096	Hooray for the Salvation Army Band/Ursalena	1968	$8
❑ 7126	Little Ole Man (Uptight-Everything's Alright)/Funky North Philly	1969	$6

— Hall of Fame Hits (originals have green labels with "W7" logo)

Number	Title	Yr	NM
❑ 7072	Little Ole Man (Uptight-Everything's Alright)/Hush Hush	1967	$8
❑ 5499	Stand Still for My Lovin'/When I Marry	1965	$10

COSMIC RAYS, THE
SATURN

Number	Title	Yr	NM
❑ 222	Bye Bye/Someone's in Love	1960	$3000
❑ 401	Daddy's Gonna Tell You No Lies/Dreaming	1960	$2000

COSMO, TONY
FLING

Number	Title	Yr	NM
❑ 716	Wise to You/Ponytail Annie and Crewcut Joe	1960	$15
❑ 716 [PS]	Wise to You/Ponytail Annie and Crewcut Joe	1960	$30

ROULETTE

Number	Title	Yr	NM
❑ 4265	A Teenager for President/Give Me Some	1960	$10

VANN

Number	Title	Yr	NM
❑ 100	Big Party/Tiny Hands and Funny Dimples	1961	$20

COSTA, DON
ABC-PARAMOUNT

Number	Title	Yr	NM
❑ 9770	Around the World/Everybody Loves Pierre	1956	$20
❑ 9835	Bella Nunziata/Tennessee Tulip	1957	$20
❑ 9943	Bing Bang Bong/Almost in Your Arms	1958	$20
❑ 9783	By the Fireside/C'est Ca!	1957	$20
❑ 9693	Flamenco Love/Heart of Paris	1956	$20
❑ 9729	For Me and My Gal/Beer Barrel Polka	1956	$20
❑ 9717	Magic Melody/Lullaby to an Angel	1956	$20

COLUMBIA

Number	Title	Yr	NM
❑ 4-42705	Diamonds/The Harem	1963	$8
❑ 4-42307	Flamenco Guitar/Sugar Blues	1962	$10
❑ 4-42785	Losing You/Tamoure	1963	$8
❑ 4-42442	Theme from The Miracle Worker/Hully Gully	1962	$10
❑ 4-42494	Theme from The Wonderful World of the Brothers Grimm/Above the Stars	1962	$10

DCP

Number	Title	Yr	NM
❑ 1132	How to Murder Your Wife/Elise	1965	$8
❑ 1121	If I Had a Hammer/Put Your Head on My Shoulder	1964	$8
❑ 1124	I Will Wait for You/Pretty Blue Eyes	1965	$8
❑ 1100	Theme from "Golden Boy"/Main Street	1964	$8

DCP INTERNATIONAL

Number	Title	Yr	NM
❑ 1002	Love Theme from "Tom Jones"/Off Broadway	1964	$8

JAMIE

Number	Title	Yr	NM
❑ 1123	I'm in Heaven/The Main One	1959	$15

Number	Title	Yr	NM

MERCURY
❏ 72932	Love So Fine/On the South Side of Chicago	1969	$8

MGM
❏ K14201	Gemini Trip/Rosy's Theme (From Ryan's Daughter)	1970	$6
❏ K14467	Gone/Song for Anna	1972	$6
❏ 318	How in the World/That's the Way with Love	1961	$10
❏ 190	I'll Walk the Line/Cat Walk	1959	$15
❏ 349	La La La/These Things Remain	1961	$12
❏ 221	Theme from "The Unforgiven"/ Streets of Paris	1960	$10
❏ 221 [PS]	Theme from "The Unforgiven"/ Streets of Paris	1960	$60

—Promo-only sleeve with photos of Audrey Hepburn and Burt Lancaster

❏ 286	The Misfits/Chi-Chi	1961	$15
❏ 286 [PS]	The Misfits/Chi-Chi	1961	$50

—With photos of Clark Gable, Marilyn Monroe and Montgomery Clift

VERVE
❏ 10511	Illya Darling/Trini's Tune	1967	$8
❏ 10511 [PS]	Illya Darling/Trini's Tune	1967	$20

COSTELLO, ELVIS
COLUMBIA
❏ 3-33401	Accidents Will Happen/Alison	1980	$5

—Hall of Fame" reissue; red and black label

❏ AE71171 [DJ]	Accidents Will Happen/Alison/ Watching the Detectives	1979	$3

—Extra record included in first editions of LP "Armed Forces

❏ AE71171 [DJ]	Accidents Will Happen/Alison/ Watching the Detectives	1979	$3

—Small hole; extra record included in first editions of LP "Armed Forces

❏ 3-10919	Accidents Will Happen/ Sunday's Best	1979	$8
❏ 18-02629	A Good Year for the Roses/The Angel Steps Out of Heaven	1981	$5
❏ 3-10641	Alison/Miracle Man	1977	$10

—Contains a remix of "Alison" otherwise unavailable on U.S. vinyl

❏ 3-10705	Alison/Watching the Detectives	1978	$10

—Contains the same remix of "Alison" as on 10641

❏ 38-05809	Don't Let Me Be Misunderstood/ Brand New Hairdo	1986	$4

—By "The Costello Show Featuring Elvis Costello

❏ 38-04045	Everyday I Write the Book/Heathen Town	1983	$5
❏ 38-04045 [PS]	Everyday I Write the Book/Heathen Town	1983	$5
❏ 1-11389	Getting Mighty Crowded/ Radio Sweetheart	1980	$5
❏ 38-04625	I Wanna Be Loved/Love Field	1984	$5
❏ 38-04266	Let Them All Talk/Shipbuilding	1983	$5
❏ AE71171 [PS]	Live at Hollywood High	1979	$5
❏ 38-06059	Lovable/Get Yourself Another Fool	1986	$4

—By "The Costello Show Featuring Elvis Costello

❏ CNR-03269	Man Out of Time/(B-side blank)	1982	$8

—One-sided budget release

❏ 18-03202	Man Out of Time/Town Cryer	1982	$5
❏ AE71172 [DJ]	My Funny Valentine/(What's So Funny 'Bout) Peace, Love and Undestanding	1980	$15

—Promo only on red vinyl

❏ AE71172 [DJ]	My Funny Valentine/(What's So Funny 'Bout) Peace, Love and Undestanding	1980	$15

—Promo only on red vinyl

❏ 38-04502	The Only Flame in Town/ Turning the Town Red	1984	$5
❏ 38-04502 [PS]	The Only Flame in Town/ Turning the Town Red	1984	$5
❏ 3-10762	This Year's Girl/Big Tears	1978	$6
❏ 38-06326	Tokyo Storm Warning (Part 1)/(Part 2)	1986	$5
❏ 3-10696	Watching the Detectives//Blame It on Cain/Mystery Dance	1978	$10
❏ 11-60519	Watch Your Step/Luxembourg	1981	$5
❏ 11-60519 [PS]	Watch Your Step/Luxembourg	1981	$5

7-Inch Extended Plays
❏ 1-11251 [B]	I Can't Stand Up for Falling Down/Girls Talk//Secondary Modern/King Horse	1980	$10
❏ 1-11251 [PS]	I Can't Stand Up for Falling Down/Girls Talk//Secondary Modern/King Horse	1980	$12

COTTON, BILLY, ORCHESTRA
LONDON
❏ 1388	Where Did My Snowman Go/ Snow, Snow, Beautiful Snow	1953	$15

COTTON, GENE
ABC
❏ 12087	Country Spirit/Damn It All	1975	$5
❏ 12137	Let Your Love Flow/ Keepin' It on the Road	1975	$5
❏ 12282	My Love Comes Alive/ Sweet Destiny	1977	$5

ARIOLA AMERICA
❏ 7675	Before My Heart Finds Out/ Like a Sunday in Salem	1977	$5
❏ 7723	Like a Sunday in Salem (The Amos and Andy Song)/Shine On (You Got to Shine On)	1978	$4
❏ 7778	Michael/Ocean of Love	1979	$4

KNOLL
❏ 5002	If I Could Get You (Into My Life)/Rained On Before	1982	$5

MYRRH
❏ 116	American Indian Blues/ Lessons of History	1973	$6
❏ 123	Great American Noel/Mrs. Oliver	1973	$6
❏ 117	Lean On One Another/ (B-side unknown)	1973	$6
❏ 137	Sunshine Roses/Mrs. Oliver	1974	$6

(NO LABEL)
❏ 0 [DJ]	Child Of Peace (same on both sides)	1981	$8
❏ NR-16361 [DJ]	Child Of Peace (same on both sides)	1981	$8

COTTON, JAMES
BUDDAH
❏ 461	Boogie Thing/Fever	1975	$5

LOMA
❏ 2042	Laying in the Weeds/ Complete This Order	1966	$15

SUN
❏ 206	Cotton Crop Blues/Hold Me in Your Arms	1954	$1800
❏ 199	My Baby/Straighten Up, Baby	1954	$1500

VERVE FORECAST
❏ 5066	Feelin' Good/Don't Start Me Talkin'	1967	$10
❏ 5053	Good Time Charlie/Off the Wall	1967	$10
❏ 5107	The Coach's Better Days/ (B-side unknown)	1969	$8

COTTON, JOSIE
ELEKTRA
❏ 69886 [DJ]	Bye Bye Baby (same on both sides)	1982	$3

—May be promo only

❏ 69886 [DJ]	Bye Bye Baby (same on both sides)	1982	$3

—May be promo only

❏ 47481	He Could Be the One/ Systematic Way	1982	$6

—Pink vinyl

❏ 47481 [PS]	He Could Be the One/ Systematic Way	1982	$6

COUCH, ORVILLE
CUSTOM
❏ 101	Hello Trouble/Anywhere There's a Crowd	1962	$40

MERCURY
❏ 71718	Downtown/Big Jim Sandy	1960	$30

MONUMENT
❏ 915	Down Here Where the Hurt Begins/Permanent Wave	1966	$15
❏ 949	The Best Things in Life/ Farmington, New Mexico	1966	$15

STARDAY
❏ 326	Five Cent Candy/I Will If You Will	1957	$40

VEE JAY
❏ 706	Color Me Gone/You're a Little Heartache	1965	$30
❏ 528	Did I Miss You?/The Lonesomes	1963	$30
❏ 693	Greenville Diner/Big Daddy of the Bayou	1965	$30
❏ 631	Hello Doll/Uncle Red	1964	$30
❏ 470	Hello Trouble/Anywhere There's a Crowd	1962	$30
❏ 589	Strike a Match/Dance Her By Me	1964	$30

COULTERS, THE
DOLPHIN
❏ 45003 [PS]	Caroline's Still in Georgia/ Free to Love You	1983	$8

EPIC
❏ 50855	Crazy Old World/Love	1980	$5
❏ 50905	Ozark Mountain Lullaby/ For Me You're All There Is	1980	$5

COUNT FIVE, THE
DOUBLE SHOT
❏ 125	Declaration of Independence/ Revelation in Slow Motion	1968	$15
❏ 141	Mailman/Pretty Big Mouth	1969	$15
❏ 115	Merry-Go-Round/Contrast	1967	$15
❏ 106	Peace of Mind/The Morning After	1966	$15
❏ 104	Psychotic Reaction/ They're Gonna Get You	1966	$20

—First pressing, with label logo at top

❏ 104	Psychotic Reaction/ They're Gonna Get You	1966	$15

—Later pressings, with label logo at side

COUNTRY BOYS, THE
COLUMBIA
❏ 4-40810	Buddy's Boogie/ Raisin' the Dickens	1956	$40
❏ 4-21551	Country Boy Bounce/Red Wing	1956	$30

DEL-FI
❏ 4245	The Okie Surfer/Blue Surf	1964	$50

COUNTRY CAVALEERS, THE
COUNTRY SHOWCASE
❏ 156	Call Back Operator/We Were Made for Each Other	1975	$6
❏ 158	Everett the Evergreen/A Sing Along Christmas Song	1975	$6
❏ 169	If I Love You/I've Got My Mind Satisfied	1976	$6
❏ 160	Lady on the Run/We Were Made for Each Other	1976	$6
❏ 171	Te Quiero (I Love You in Many Ways)/I've Got My Mind Satisfied	1976	$6

MGM
❏ 14606	Humming Bird/Hang On to What	1973	$5

COUNTRY CHOIR, THE
COLUMBIA
❏ 4-21193	Who at My Door Is Standing/ Now the Day Is Over	1953	$30

COUNTRY GENTLEMEN, THE
BRENT
❏ 7058	For You/Saturday Night	1967	$40

RCA VICTOR
❏ 47-6764	My Heart's Desire/Right Around the Corner	1956	$30

REBEL
❏ 250	Bringing Mary Home/Northbound	1965	$20

STARDAY
❏ 628	Copper Kettle/Sunrise	1963	$30
❏ 344	Dixie/Backwoods Blues	1958	$30
❏ 367	Hey Little Girl/Hi Lonesome	1958	$30
❏ 434	I'll Never Marry/Travelin' Dobro Blues	1959	$30
❏ 347	It's the Blues/Backwoods Blues	1958	$30

COUNTRY JOE AND THE FISH
FANTASY
❏ 758	Breakfast for Two/Lost My Connection	1976	$4
❏ 822	Bring Back the Sixties, Man/ Sunshine Through My Window	1978	$4
❏ 780	Love Is a Fire/I Need You	1976	$4
❏ 876	Private Parts/Take Time Out	1979	$4
❏ 765	Save the Whales/Oh Jamaica	1976	$4
❏ 814	Southern Cross/Coyote	1978	$4

VANGUARD
❏ 35184	Chloe/Jesse James	1974	$4
❏ 35181	Doctor Hip/Satisfactorily	1973	$4
❏ 35161	Fantasy/I Seen a Rocket	1972	$5
❏ 35150	Hang On/Hand of Man	1972	$5
❏ 35090	Here I Go Again/Baby, You're Driving Me Crazy	1969	$8
❏ 35133	Hold On, It's Coming/ Playing with Fire	1971	$5

—Starting here, as "Country Joe McDonald

❏ 35112	I-Feel-Like-I'm-Fixin'- to-Die Rag/Janis	1970	$8
❏ 35061	Who Am I/Thursday	1968	$10
❏ 35061 [PS]	Who Am I/Thursday	1968	$30

7-Inch Extended Plays
RAG BABY
❏ 1001	(contents unknown)	1966	$125

COUNTRY LADS, THE
COLUMBIA
❏ 4-41062	I Won't Beg Your Pardon/ Alone in Love	1957	$20
❏ 4-41212	Lonely Lover/Anything	1958	$15

Number	Title	Yr	NM

COUNTRY SQUIRRELS, THE
METROMEDIA COUNTRY

Number	Title	Yr	NM
❑ 903	How I Love Those Christmas Songs/Country Christmas	1972	$6
❑ BMBO-0166	How I Love Those Christmas Songs/Country Christmas	1973	$5

COUNTRY STORE, THE
T-A

| ❑ 189 | To Love You/Heartache | 1969 | $30 |

COUNTRYMEN, THE
HICKORY

| ❑ 1286 | Carol of the Drum/Scarlet Ribbons | 1964 | $8 |

COUNTS, THE (1)
DOT

❑ 1226	Baby I Want You/Waitin' Around for You	1954	$50
❑ 1188	Darling Dear/I Need You Always	1954	$70
❑ 16105	Darling Dear/I Need You Always	1960	$30
❑ 1243	From This Day On/Love and Understanding	1955	$40
❑ 1199	Hot Tamales/Baby Don't You Know	1954	$60
❑ 1265	I Need You Tonight/Sally Walker	1955	$40
❑ 1210	My Dear, My Darling/She Won't Say Yes	1954	$50
❑ 1275	To Our Love/Heartbreaker	1956	$30
❑ 1235	Wailin' Little Mama/Let Me Go	1955	$40

NOTE

| ❑ 20000 | Sweet Names/I Guess I Brought It All on Myself | 1956 | $200 |

COUNTS, THE (2)
Detroit-based funk group. (45)
AWARE

❑ 049	At the Fair/I'm the Music	1975	$5
❑ 038	Funk/Too Bad	1974	$5
❑ 054	Magic Ride/Short Cut	1975	$5
❑ 046	Sacrifice/Funk Pump	1974	$5

WESTBOUND

| ❑ 191 | Thinking Single/Why Not Start All Over Again | 1972 | $5 |

COUNTS, THE (U)
MANCO

| ❑ 1060 | Surfer's Paradise/Chug-a-Lug | 1964 | $50 |

MERCURY

| ❑ 71318 | Shake the Town/Teenage Guy and Girl | 1958 | $20 |

PANORAMA

| ❑ 9 | Chitlins, Etc./Clyde, Clyde, The Cow's Outside | 1965 | $10 |
| ❑ 33 | Come Now/Since I Fell for You | 1966 | $10 |

SEA CREST

| ❑ 6004 | Doggin'/And Then I Cried | 1964 | $20 |
| ❑ 6003 | Turn On Song/Enchanted Sea | 1964 | $30 |

SHRINE

| ❑ 117 | Peaches Baby/My Only Love | 1966 | $3000 |

— VG 1000; VG+ 2000

SMASH

| ❑ 1821 | Stormy Weather/True Love's Gone | 1963 | $10 |

COURCY, JOANNE
TWIRL

| ❑ 2026 | I Got the Power/I'm Gonna Keep You | 1966 | $700 |
| ❑ 2020 | Silly Girl/My Poor Broken Heart | 1966 | $40 |

COURTNEY, LOU
BUDDAH

| ❑ 121 | Let Me Turn You On/Tryin' to Find My Woman | 1969 | $8 |

EPIC

❑ 11088	I Don't Need Nobody Else/Why	1974	$5
❑ 50046	The Best Thing a Man Can Do for His Woman/I'm Serious About Lovin' You	1974	$5
❑ 11062	What Do You Want Me to Do/Beware	1973	$5

IMPERIAL

| ❑ 66006 | Come On Home/The Man with the Cigar | 1963 | $15 |
| ❑ 66043 | Little Old Love Maker/Professional Lover | 1964 | $15 |

PHILIPS

| ❑ 40287 | I Watched You Slowly Slip Away/I'll Cry If I Want To | 1965 | $125 |

POP-SIDE

| ❑ 4594 | Hey Joyce/I'm Mad About You | 1967 | $12 |
| ❑ 4596 | If the Shoe Fits/It's Love Now | 1968 | $10 |

RIVERSIDE

| ❑ 4589 | Do the Thing/Man Is Lonely | 1967 | $12 |
| ❑ 4588 | Skate Now/I Can Always Tell | 1966 | $12 |

VERVE

| ❑ 10602 | Do the Horse/Rubber Neckin' | 1968 | $8 |
| ❑ 10631 | Please Stay/You Can Give Your Love to Me | 1968 | $8 |

COURTSHIP, THE
TAMLA

| ❑ 54217 | It's the Same Old Love/Last Row, First Balcony | 1972 | $5 |
| ❑ 54227 | Oops, It Just Slipped Out/Love Ain't Love | 1973 | $5 |

COURVALE, KEITH
DOT

| ❑ 15844 | Trapped Love/Steelworker Blues | 1958 | $125 |

COUSIN DAN
ROYAL AMERICAN

| ❑ 55 | Christmas At The White House (Dacer, Prancer and Nixon)/(B-side unknown) | 1971 | $6 |

COUSINS, THE (1)
DECCA

| ❑ 30609 | I'm in Love with You/Be Nice to Me | 1958 | $30 |

FIDELITY

| ❑ 3010 | Love Is Blind/How We'll Love | 1959 | $40 |

COUSINS, THE (2)
PARKWAY

❑ 823	St. Louis Blues/No One Knows	1961	$20
❑ 870	Sweet Georgia Brown/Outside the Wall	1963	$15
❑ 848	When My Baby Smiles at Me/Some of These Days	1962	$15

COUSINS, THE (U)
VERSATILE

| ❑ 105 | Down That Lonely Road/(B-side unknown) | 1960 | $100 |

WYNNE

| ❑ 132 | Guilty/(B-side unknown) | 1959 | $500 |

COUTURE, CHARLELIE
ZE

| ❑ WIP6763 | Christmas Fever/Christmas Wrapping | 1981 | $30 |

— B-side by the Waitresses; U.K. import

COVAY, DON
ARNOLD

| ❑ 1002 | Pony Time/Love Boat | 1961 | $30 |

— As "The Goodtimers

| ❑ 1002 | Pony Time/Love Boat | 1961 | $15 |

— As "Don Covay and the Goodtimers"

ATLANTIC

| ❑ 2407 | 40 Days -- 40 Nights/The Usual Place | 1967 | $10 |
| ❑ 1147 | Bip Bop Bip/Silver Dollar | 1957 | $100 |

— As "Pretty Boy"

❑ 2481	Chain of Fools/Prove It	1968	$10
❑ 2494	Don't Let Go/It's In the Wind	1968	$12
❑ 2725	Everything I Do Goin' Be Funky/Key to the Highway	1970	$8
❑ 2521	Gonna Send You Back to Your Mama/House on the Corner	1968	$10
❑ 2666	Ice Cream Man (The Gimmie Game)/Black Woman	1969	$10
❑ 2565	I Stole Some Love/Snake in the Grass	1968	$10
❑ 2286	Please Do Something/A Woman's Love	1965	$10
❑ 2301	See Saw/I Never Get Enough of Your Love	1965	$10
❑ 2375	Shing-Aling '67/I Was There	1967	$10
❑ 2357	Somebody's Got to Love You/Temptation Was Too Strong	1966	$12
❑ 2323	Sookie Sookie/Watching the Late Late Shoe	1966	$12
❑ 2742	Soul Stirrer/Sookie Sookie	1970	$8
❑ 2609	Sweet Pea/C.C. Rider Blues	1969	$10
❑ 2280	The Boomerang/Daddy Loves Baby	1965	$12

BIG

| ❑ 617 | Switchin' in the Kitchen/Rockin' the Mule | 1958 | $100 |

— As "Pretty Boy"

BIG TOP

| ❑ 3060 | Hey There/I'm Coming Down with the Blues | 1960 | $20 |

BLAZE

| ❑ 350 | Standing in the Doorway/(B-side unknown) | 1958 | $40 |

CAMEO

| ❑ 239 | The Popeye Waddle/One Little Bot Had Money | 1962 | $15 |

| ❑ 251 | Wiggle Wobble/Do the Bug | 1963 | $15 |

COLUMBIA

| ❑ 42058 | Hand Jive Workout/See About Me | 1961 | $30 |
| ❑ 41981 | Shake Wid the Snake/Every Which-a Way | 1961 | $30 |

EPIC

| ❑ 9484 | It's Twistin' Time/Twistin' Train | 1961 | $20 |

— As "The Goodtimers"

JANUS

| ❑ 181 | Daddy Please Don't Go Out/Shoes Under My Bed | 1972 | $6 |
| ❑ 164 | Sweet Thang/Standing in the Grits Line | 1971 | $6 |

MERCURY

❑ 71469	It's Better to Have (And Don't Need)/Leave Him (Part 1)	1974	$6
❑ 71385	I Was Checkin' Out She Was Checkin' In/Money	1973	$6
❑ 73311	Overtime Man/Dungeon #3	1972	$6
❑ 71430	Somebody's Been Enjoying My Home/Bad Mouthing	1973	$6

NEWMAN

| ❑ 500 | Badd Boy/(Instrumental) | 1980 | $5 |

PARKWAY

| ❑ 894 | Ain't That Silly/Turn It On | 1964 | $15 |
| ❑ 910 | The Froog/One Little Boy Had Money | 1964 | $15 |

PHILADELPHIA INT'L.

| ❑ 3602 | Travelin' in Heavy Traffic/Once You Have It | 1976 | $5 |

ROSEMART

| ❑ 801 | Mercy Mercy/Can't Stay Away | 1964 | $20 |
| ❑ 802 | Take This Hurt Off Me/Please Don't Let Me Know | 1964 | $15 |

SUE

| ❑ 709 | Betty Jean/Believe It or Not | 1958 | $40 |

U-VON

| ❑ 102 | Back to the Roots (Part 1)/Back to the Roots (Part 2) | 1977 | $5 |

COVEN
Jinx Dawson.
ABC

| ❑ 11377 | One Tin Soldier (The Legend of Billy Jack)/I Think You Always Knew | 1973 | $6 |

BUDDAH

| ❑ 440 | I Need a Hundred of You/(B-side unknown) | 1974 | $4 |

MERCURY

| ❑ 72973 | Wicked Woman/White Witch of Rose Hall | 1969 | $6 |
| ❑ 72973 [PS] | Wicked Woman/White Witch of Rose Hall | 1969 | $10 |

MGM

| ❑ 14308 | One Tin Soldier/I Guess It's a Beautiful Day Today | 1971 | $5 |

SGC

| ❑ 003 | I Shall Be Released/I've Come Too Far | 1968 | $6 |

WARNER BROS.

| ❑ BJS 0101 | One Tin Soldier, The Legend of Billy Jack/Johnnie | 1973 | $4 |

— B-side by Teresa Kelly

| ❑ 7509 | One Tin Soldier, The Legend of Billy Jack/Say Goodbye, 'Cause You're Leavin' | 1971 | $5 |

COWBOY CHURCH SUNDAY SCHOOL, THE
DECCA

| ❑ 9-29958 | It Is No Secret (What God Can Do)/Don't Send Those Kids to Sunday School | 1956 | $15 |
| ❑ 9-29367 | Open Up Your Heart (And Let the Sun Shine In)/The Lord Is Counting on You | 1954 | $30 |

— Black label, lines on either side of "Decca

| ❑ 9-29367 | Open Up Your Heart (And Let the Sun Shine In)/The Lord Is Counting on You | 1954 | $15 |

— Black label, star under "Decca

| ❑ 9-29530 | The Little Black Sheep/Go On By | 1955 | $15 |
| ❑ 9-29757 | Those Bad, Bad Kids/A Handful of Sunshine | 1955 | $15 |

COWBOY JUNKIES
RCA

❑ 8997-7-R	Misguided Angel/Postcard Blues	1989	$8
❑ 8879-7-R	Sweet Jane/200 More Miles	1989	$5
❑ 8879-7-R [PS]	Sweet Jane/200 More Miles	1989	$5

Number	Title	Yr	NM

COWSILL, BILL
MGM
❏ 14166	When Everybody's Here/I Wish I Could Say the Same About You	1970	$6

COWSILL, JOHN
MGM
❏ 14003	Path of Love/Captain Sad and His Ship of Fools	1968	$8

COWSILL, SUSAN
WARNER BROS.
❏ 8232	It Might As Well Rain Until September/Mohammad's Radio	1976	$5

COWSILLS, THE
JODA
❏ 103	All I Really Wanta Be Is Me/And the Next Day, Too	1965	$40

LONDON
❏ 170	Blue Road/Covered Wagon	1972	$8
❏ 149	On My Side/There Is No Child	1971	$8

MGM
❏ 14026	Hair/What Is Happy	1969	$15
❏ 13944	Indian Lake/Newspaper Blanket	1968	$10

— First pressings have black labels

❏ 13944	Indian Lake/Newspaper Blanket	1968	$8

— Second pressings have blue and gold labels

❏ 13944 [PS]	Indian Lake/Newspaper Blanket	1968	$15
❏ 13909	In Need of a Friend/Mister Flynn	1968	$8
❏ 13909 [PS]	In Need of a Friend/Mister Flynn	1968	$15
❏ 13981	Poor Baby/Meet Me at the Wishing Well	1968	$8
❏ 14084	Silver Threads and Golden Needles/Love, American Style	1969	$10
❏ 14084 [PS]	Silver Threads and Golden Needles/Love, American Style	1969	$15
❏ 14106	Start to Love/Two by Two	1970	$8
❏ 14011	The Impossible Years/Candy Kid	1968	$8
❏ 14063	The Prophecy of Daniel and John the Divine (Six-Six-Six)/Gotta Get Away from It All	1969	$8
❏ 14063 [PS]	The Prophecy of Daniel and John the Divine (Six-Six-Six)/Gotta Get Away from It All	1969	$20
❏ 13886	We Can Fly/A Time for Remembrance	1967	$8
❏ 13886 [PS]	We Can Fly/A Time for Remembrance	1967	$15

PHILIPS
❏ 40437	A Most Peculiar Man/Could It Be, Let Me Know	1967	$10
❏ 40382	Most of All/Siamese Cat	1966	$10
❏ 40382	Most of All/Siamese Cat	1966	$20
❏ 40406	Party Girl/What's It Gonna Be Like	1966	$12

7-Inch Extended Plays
MGM
❏ PEP-1 [PS]	The Cowsills Collector's Record	1969	$30

— American Dairy Association promotional item

❏ PEP-1	The Milk Song/All My Days// Nothing to Do/The Fun Song	1969	$10

— American Dairy Association promotional item

COX, DON (1)
ARC
❏ 5902	Smooth Southern Highway/The Prophet and the Saint	1979	$5

CRABBY APPLETON
ELEKTRA
❏ 45687	Go Back/Try	1970	$6
❏ 45716	Grab On/Can't Live My Life	1971	$5
❏ 45754	It's So Hard/Tomorrow Is a New Day	1971	$5
❏ 45781	Love Can Change Everything/Smokin' in the Mornin'	1972	$5
❏ 45702	Lucy/Some Madness	1970	$5

CRABTREE, RILEY
COLUMBIA
❏ 4-21073	An Orchid in My Bouquet/Tonight	1953	$30
❏ 4-20901	Between the Pages of the Bible/Information Please	1952	$30
❏ 4-20970	I Live with Memories/I Stood and Watched	1952	$30
❏ 4-21030	Love Song of the Hills/If I Had Someone to Call My Very Own	1952	$30
❏ 4-21218	When Hank Williams Met Jimmie Rodgers/I'll Make You Want Me	1954	$30
❏ 4-21268	When This World Changes Hands/Let Me Walk Through the Valley	1954	$30

CRACK THE SKY
LIFESONG
❏ 1763	Give Myself to You/A Night on the Town (With Snow White)	1978	$4
❏ 1782	I Am the Walrus/Lighten Up McGraw	1979	$4
❏ 1764	Long Nights/Give Myself to You	1978	$4
❏ 45003	She's a Dancer/Robots for Ronnie	1976	$4
❏ 45081	Techni-Generation/Suspicion	1980	$4
❏ 45016	We Want Mine (We Don't Want Your Money)/Invaders from Mars	1976	$4

CRADDOCK, BILLY "CRASH"
ABC
❏ 11342	Afraid I'll Want to Love Her One More Time/Treat Her Right	1972	$6
❏ 12335	Another Woman/The Words Still Rhyme	1978	$4
❏ 12384	Don Juan/Things Are Mostly Fine	1978	$4
❏ 11349	Don't Be Angry/I'm a White Boy	1973	$6
❏ 12104	I Love the Blues and the Boogie Woogie/No Deposit, No Return	1975	$5
❏ 11364	Slippin' and Slidin'/Living Example	1973	$6
❏ 12068	Still Thinkin' 'Bout You/Stay a Little Longer in Your Bed	1975	$5
❏ 11412	Sweet Magnolia Blossom/Home Is Such a Lonely Place to Go	1973	$6
❏ 12357	Think I'll Go Somewhere (And Cry Myself to Sleep)/It All Came Back	1978	$4
❏ 11379	'Till the Water Stops Runnin'/What Does a Loser Say	1973	$6

ABC DOT
❏ 17701	A Tear Fell/A Piece of the Rock	1977	$5
❏ 17659	Broken Down in Tiny Pieces/Shake It Easy	1976	$5
❏ 17584	Easy As Pie/She's Mine	1975	$5
❏ 17723	The First Time/Walk When Love Walks	1977	$5
❏ 17619	Walk Softly/She's About a Mover	1976	$5

CAPITOL
❏ 4624	Hubba Hubba/Let's Go Back to the Beginning	1978	$4
❏ 4545	I Cheated on a Good Woman's Love/Not a Day Goes By	1978	$4
❏ 4672	If I Could Write a Song As Beautiful As You/Never Ending	1978	$4
❏ 4838	I Just Had You on My Mind/You Just Wanta Be Mine	1980	$4
❏ 5011	I Just Need You For Tonight/Leave Your Love A-Smokin'	1981	$4
❏ 4972	It Was You/Betty Ruth	1981	$4
❏ 4575	I've Been Too Long Lonely Baby/Jailhouse Rock	1978	$4
❏ 5139	Love Busted/Darlin' Take Care of Yourself	1982	$4
❏ 4707	My Mama Never Heard Me Sing/As Long As I Live	1979	$4
❏ 4875	Sea Cruise/She's Got Legs	1980	$4
❏ 4792	Till I Stop Shaking/Sneak Out of Love with You	1979	$4

CARTWHEEL
❏ 222	Afraid I'll Want to Love Her One More Time/Treat Her Right	1972	$15

CEE CEE
❏ 5400	Tell Me When I'm Hot/When the Feeling Is Right	1983	$5

CHART
❏ 1004	Go On Home Girl/Learning to Live Without You	1967	$8
❏ 5126	Go On Home Girl/Whipping Boy	1971	$8
❏ 1415	There Ought to Be a Law/Two Arms Full of Lonely	1966	$10
❏ 1450	Whipping Boy/The Love We Live Without	1967	$10

COLONIAL
❏ 721	Bird Doggin'/Millionaire	1958	$50

COLUMBIA
❏ 41619	All I Want Is You/Letter of Love	1960	$30
❏ 41619 [PS]	All I Want Is You/Letter of Love	1960	$60
❏ 41316	Am I to Be the One/I Miss You So Much	1959	$30
❏ 41470	Don't Destroy Me/Boom Boom Baby	1959	$30
❏ 41470 [PS]	Don't Destroy Me/Boom Boom Baby	1959	$60
❏ 41822	Heavenly Love/Good Time Billy	1961	$30
❏ 41536	I Want That/Since She Turned Seventeen	1960	$40
❏ 41677	One Last Kiss/Is It True or False	1960	$30
❏ 41367	Sweetie Pie/Blabbermouth	1959	$40

DATE
❏ 1007	Lulu Lee/Ah, Poor Little Baby	1958	$50

KING
❏ 5912	Betty, Betty/Right Around the Corner	1964	$30
❏ 5924	My Baby's Got Flat Feet/One Heartache Too Many	1964	$30
❏ 5964	Teardrops on Your Letter/Love You More Everyday	1964	$30

MERCURY
❏ 71862	A Diamond Is Forever/Old King Cole	1962	$30
❏ 71811	Truly True/How Lonely He Must Be	1961	$30

CRAFT, PAUL
RCA
❏ PB-11321	Brother Juke Box/One-Track Mine	1978	$4
❏ PB-11078	Lean On Jesus "Before He Leans On You"/Daddy Please Don't Go to Vegas	1977	$5
❏ PB-11211	Teardrops in My Tequila/Rise Up	1978	$5
❏ PB-10971	We Know Better/Dropkick Me, Jesus	1977	$5

TRUTH
❏ 3205	It's Me Again, Margaret/For Linda (Child in the Cradle)	1974	$6

CRAIG AND HIS DADDY
AMY
❏ 834	Bring My Daddy An Electric Train/All Around the Christmas Tree	1961	$15

CRAIG, JIMMY
BRILL
❏ 1	All for You/Gonna Love My Baby	1959	$100

IMPERIAL
❏ 5592	Walking in Darkness/Oh Little Girl	1959	$20

WARWICK
❏ 542	Drifter/Let Me Stay	1960	$20

CRAIG, THE
FONTANA
❏ 1579	I Must Be Mad/Suspense	1967	$30

CRAMER, FLOYD
ABBOTT
❏ 146	Fancy Pants/Five Foot Two, Eyes of Blue	1953	$20

— Black vinyl

❏ 146	Fancy Pants/Five Foot Two, Eyes of Blue	1953	$30

— Red vinyl

❏ 142	Little Brown Jug/Dancin' Diane	1953	$20

MGM
❏ 12161	Battle Hymn of the Republic/Dixie	1955	$15
❏ 12619	Herman's Theme/Country Gentleman	1958	$15
❏ 12059	Piano Rag/Jealous, Cold, Cheatin' Heart	1955	$15
❏ 12306	Pretty Blue Jeans/Good Time Cakewalk	1956	$15
❏ 12242	Succotash/Tennessee Central (#9)	1956	$15
❏ 11990	Sweet Adeline/Howdy Ma'm	1955	$15
❏ 12520	Waltz with Cramer/Funny Face	1957	$15

RCA
❏ PB-11065	Coming Home/The Hurt	1977	$4
❏ PB-11916	Dallas/Lover's Minuet	1980	$3
❏ PB-11916 [PS]	Dallas/Lover's Minuet	1980	$6
❏ PB-11576	Georgia on My Mind/Boogie Woogie	1979	$4
❏ PB-12272	High Noon/Lone Ranger	1981	$3
❏ PB-10761	I'm Thinking Tonight of My Blue Eyes/Hang On Sloopy	1976	$4
❏ PB-10901	La Chicana/Four in the Morning	1977	$4

— With Chet Atkins and Danny Davis

❏ PB-11163	Looking for Mr. Goodbar/Father Time	1977	$4
❏ PB-11432	Our Winter Love/For Lovers' Sake	1978	$4
❏ PB-12195	Sleepy Shores/Help Me Make It Through the Night	1981	$3
❏ PB-11394	The Main Street Electrical Parade/Singing in the Country Rain	1978	$4

RCA VICTOR
❏ 47-7978	Chattanooga Choo Choo/Let's Go	1962	$8
❏ 74-0621	Corn Crib Symphony/Your Last Goodbye	1971	$4
❏ PB-10533	Eres Tu (Touch the Wind)/Faded Love	1975	$4
❏ 47-9874	Fancy Free/Is This Tomorrow	1970	$4
❏ 47-7156	Flip, Flop and Fly/Sophisticated Swing	1958	$10
❏ PB-10076	Forever/Flip, Flop and Fly	1974	$4
❏ 47-9940	For the Good Times/Everything Is Beautiful	1971	$4
❏ 74-0152	Games People Play/Ob-La-Di, Ob-La-Da	1969	$5
❏ 47-9396	Gentle on My Mind/By the Time I Get to Phoenix	1967	$6
❏ 74-0674	Honky Tonk (Part 2)/Detour	1972	$4
❏ 47-8041	Hot Pepper/For Those That Cry	1962	$8
❏ 47-8217	How High the Moon/Satan's Doll	1963	$8
❏ 47-8217 [PS]	How High the Moon/Satan's Doll	1963	$20
❏ VP-3-2544	I Can't Help It/Kaw-Liga	1962	$8

— Stereo jukebox issue; small hole, plays at 33 1/3 rpm

❏ 47-9157	I Wanna Be Free/Papa Gene's Blues	1967	$6
❏ 47-7775	Last Date/Sweetie Baby	1960	$15
❏ APBO-0012	Lonely Street/The Battle of New Orleans	1973	$4
❏ 47-8013	Lovesick Blues/The First Hurt	1962	$8
❏ 47-9978	Makin' Up/Theme from "Flight of the Doves"	1971	$4
❏ 47-7250	Mumble Jumble/Cryin'	1958	$10

Number	Title	Yr	NM
❏ 47-7840	On the Rebound/Mood Indigo	1961	$15
❏ 47-7840 [PS]	On the Rebound/Mood Indigo	1961	$30
❏ 47-7893	San Antonio Rose/I Can Just Imagine	1961	$10
❏ 74-0209	Seattle/Lovin' Season	1969	$5
❏ 47-9065	Stood Up/Good Vibrations	1967	$6
❏ 47-8899	Strangers in the Night/You've Lost That Lovin' Feelin'	1966	$6
❏ 47-8084	Swing Low/Losers Weepers	1962	$8
❏ 47-8084 [PS]	Swing Low/Losers Weepers	1962	$10
❏ 47-8265	The Hucklebuck/Heartless Heart	1963	$8
❏ PB-10336	The Last Farewell/My Melody of Love	1975	$4
❏ 47-9237	Theme for Sam/For No One	1967	$6
❏ 47-9841	Theme from Room 222/Leaving on a Jet Plane	1970	$4
❏ APBO-0214	Theme from "The Young and the Restless"/Boogie, Boogie, Boogie	1974	$4
❏ 47-8171	(These Are) The Young Years/Kaapsedri	1963	$8
❏ 47-8171 [PS]	(These Are) The Young Years/Kaapsedri	1963	$20
❏ 47-8414	Tomorrow's Gone/Shrum	1964	$8
❏ PB-10597	Tonight's the Night/Candy Pants	1976	$4
❏ 74-0869	Tonight's the Night/Crystal Chandelier	1973	$4
❏ 47-8541	Town Square/Long Walk Home	1965	$8
❏ 47-8325	Want Me/Naomi	1964	$8

SIMS
Number	Title	Yr	NM
❏ 121	Fancy Pants/Five Foot Two, Eyes of Blue	1961	$8

7-Inch Extended Plays

RCA VICTOR
Number	Title	Yr	NM
❏ DJEO-0272 [DJ]	Behind Closed Doors/The Most Beautiful Girl//Star Spangled Banner/Top of the World	1974	$10
❏ EPA-4377 [PS]	Last Date	1961	$12
❏ EPA-4377	Last Date/San Antonio Rose//Flip, Flop and Bop/Chattanooga Choo Choo	1961	$10
❏ VLP-2888	San Antonio Rose/Tricky/Lovesick Blues//Java/The Young Years/Flip and Fly	1964	$10

— *Stereo jukebox issue; small hole, plays at 33 1/3 rpm*

Number	Title	Yr	NM
❏ VLP-2888 [PS]	The Best of Floyd Cramer	1964	$12

CRAMPS, THE

I.R.S.
Number	Title	Yr	NM
❏ 9014	Garbage Man/Drug Train	1980	$30
❏ 9014 [PS]	Garbage Man/Drug Train	1980	$30
❏ 9021	Goo Goo Muck/She Said	1981	$20
❏ 9021 [PS]	Goo Goo Muck/She Said	1981	$20

VENGEANCE
Number	Title	Yr	NM
❏ 668	Human Fly/Domino	1978	$60
❏ 668 [PS]	Human Fly/Domino	1978	$70
❏ 666	Surfin' Bird/The Way I Walk	1978	$60
❏ 666 [PS]	Surfin' Bird/The Way I Walk	1978	$70

CRANE, BOB

EPIC
Number	Title	Yr	NM
❏ 10038	Theme from Get Smart/Happy Feet	1966	$15
❏ 10038 [PS]	Theme from Get Smart/Happy Feet	1966	$40
❏ 10108	Theme from Hogan's Heroes/Theme from "F" Troop	1966	$15

CRANE, LES

WARNER BROS.
Number	Title	Yr	NM
❏ 7582	Children Learn What They Live/The Wilderness	1972	$4
❏ 7520	Desiderata/A Different Drummer	1971	$5
❏ 7520 [PS]	Desiderata/A Different Drummer	1971	$6
❏ 7548	Desiderata (Spanish)/Desiderata (English)	1972	$6

CRANE, SHERRY

SUN
Number	Title	Yr	NM
❏ 328	Willie Willie/Winnie the Parakeet	1959	$30

CRASS

CRASS
Number	Title	Yr	NM
❏ COLD TURKEY1	Merry Crassmas (same on both sides)	1981	$30

—*U.K. import*

Number	Title	Yr	NM
❏ COLD TURKEY1 [PS]	Merry Crassmas (same on both sides)	1981	$30

—*U.K. import*

CRAWFORD, BOBBY

DEL-FI
Number	Title	Yr	NM
❏ 4236	I Want to Be a Good Guy/(B-side unknown)	1964	$20
❏ 4211	Mrs. Smith, Please Wake Up!/That Little Old Lovemaker Me	1963	$20

CRAWFORD BROTHERS, THE

DEL-FI
Number	Title	Yr	NM
❏ 4191	Good Buddies/You Gotta Wear Shoes	1963	$20
❏ 4191 [PS]	Good Buddies/You Gotta Wear Shoes	1963	$30

CRAWFORD, CAROLYN

MERCURY
Number	Title	Yr	NM
❏ 74036	Coming On Strong/Love Song for You	1978	$5

— *Mercury titles as "Caroline Crawford*

Number	Title	Yr	NM
❏ 76013	The Strut/I'll Be Here for You	1979	$5

MOTOWN
Number	Title	Yr	NM
❏ 1050	Forget About Me/Devil in His Heart	1963	$50
❏ 1070	My Heart/When Someone's Good to You	1964	$50
❏ 1064	My Smile Is Just a Frown (Turned Upside Down)/I'll Come Running	1964	$30

— *Revised version of A-side title*

Number	Title	Yr	NM
❏ 1064	My Smile Is Just a Frown Turned Upside Down/I'll Come Running	1964	$60

— *Original version of A-side title*

PHILADELPHIA INT'L.
Number	Title	Yr	NM
❏ 3580	Good & Plenty/If You Move, You Lose	1975	$5
❏ 3570	It Takes Two to Make One/No Matter How Bad Things Are, I Still Love You	1975	$5

CRAWFORD, HANK

ATLANTIC
Number	Title	Yr	NM
❏ 5030	Blueberry Hill/Any Time	1963	$10
❏ 5022	Don't Cry Baby/The Peeper	1962	$12
❏ 5049	Don't Get Around Much Anymore/Bluff City Blues	1966	$8
❏ 5016	Easy Living/Playmates	1961	$12
❏ 5042	Merry Christmas Baby/Read 'Em and Weep	1964	$10
❏ 5013	Misty (Part 1)/Misty (Part 2)	1961	$10
❏ 5039	Shake a-Plenty/Mellow Down	1964	$10
❏ 5033	Skunky Green/Whispering Grass	1963	$12
❏ 5079	Smoky City/Hush Puppies	1969	$8
❏ 5066	Soul Shoutin'/Who Can I Turn To When Nobody Needs Me	1968	$8

KUDU
Number	Title	Yr	NM
❏ 905	Brian's Song/In the Wee Small Hours of the Morning	1972	$5
❏ 944	Daytime Friends/I Don't Want No Happy Songs	1978	$5
❏ 908	Help Me Make It Through the Night/Uncle Funky	1972	$5
❏ 923	Sho Is Funky/(B-side unknown)	1975	$5
❏ 911	The Christmas Song/Winter Wonderland	1974	$5

CRAWFORD, JOHNNY

DEL-FI
Number	Title	Yr	NM
❏ 4305	Am I Too Young/Janie Please Believe It	1965	$20
❏ 4178	Cindy's Birthday/Something Special	1962	$20
❏ 4178 [PS]	Cindy's Birthday/Something Special	1962	$30
❏ 4221	Cindy's Gonna Cry/Debbie	1963	$20
❏ 4203	Cry on My Shoulder/When I Fall in Love	1963	$20
❏ 4162	Daydreams/So Goes the Story	1961	$20
❏ 4162 [PS]	Daydreams/So Goes the Story	1961	$30
❏ 4172	Patti Ann/Donna	1962	$20
❏ 4193	Proud/Lonesome Town	1963	$20
❏ 4229	Sandy/Ol' Shorty	1963	$20
❏ 4242	The Girl Next Door (Once Upon a Time)/Sittin' and Watchin'	1964	$20
❏ 4215	What Happened to Janie/Petite Chanson	1963	$20

SIDEWALK
Number	Title	Yr	NM
❏ 932	Angelica/Everybody Has Their Day	1968	$15
❏ 941	Good Guys Finish Last/Everyone Should Own a Dream	1968	$15

WYNNE
Number	Title	Yr	NM
❏ 124	Dance with the Dolly (With the Hole in Her Stocking)/Ask	1958	$30

CRAWFORD, ODESSA

HIT
Number	Title	Yr	NM
❏ 289	I Never Loved a Man the Way I Love You/Bernadette	1967	$8

— *B-side by the Fantastics*

CRAYONS, THE

COUNSEL
Number	Title	Yr	NM
❏ 122	Love at First Sight/I Saw You	1963	$40

CRAYTON, PEE WEE

ALADDIN
Number	Title	Yr	NM
❏ 3112	When It Rains It Pours/Daybreak	1952	$125

Number	Title	Yr	NM
❏ 3112	When It Rains It Pours/Daybreak	1952	$1500

— *Green vinyl*

GUYDEN
Number	Title	Yr	NM
❏ 2048	I'm Still in Love with You/Time on My Hands	1961	$20

IMPERIAL
Number	Title	Yr	NM
❏ 5288	Do Unto Others/Every Dog Has a Day	1954	$200
❏ 5345	Eyes Full of Tears/Runnin' Wild	1955	$60
❏ 5321	I Need Your Love/You Know -- Yeah	1955	$60
❏ 5338	My Idea About You/I Got News for You	1955	$60
❏ 5297	Wine-O/Hurry Hurry	1954	$500

JAMIE
Number	Title	Yr	NM
❏ 1190	'Tain't Nobody's Business If I Do/Little Bitty Things	1961	$20

MODERN
Number	Title	Yr	NM
❏ 892	Cool Evening/Have You Lost Your Love for Me	1951	$125

POST
Number	Title	Yr	NM
❏ 2007	Don't Go/I Must Go On	1955	$50

RECORDED IN HOLLYWOOD
Number	Title	Yr	NM
❏ 426	Baby Pat the Floor/I'm Your Prisoner	1954	$125
❏ 408	Pappy's Blues/Crying and Walking	1954	$125

SMASH
Number	Title	Yr	NM
❏ 1774	Sabre Twist/Hillbilly Blues	1962	$15

VEE JAY
Number	Title	Yr	NM
❏ 214	A Frosty Night/The Telephone Is Ringing	1956	$50
❏ 266	Fiddle Dee Dee/Is This the Price I Pay	1957	$50
❏ 252	I Don't Care/I Found My Peace of Mind	1957	$50

CRAZY HORSE
Also see THE ROCKETS (4); NEIL YOUNG.

M.O.C.
Number	Title	Yr	NM
❏ 671	Love/High on Lovin'	1967	$15

REPRISE
Number	Title	Yr	NM
❏ 1075	All Alone Now/One Thing I Love	1972	$5
❏ 1046	Beggars Day/Dirty, Dirty	1971	$5
❏ 1025	Dance, Dance, Dance/Carolay	1971	$5
❏ 1007	Downtown/Crow Jane Lady	1971	$5

CRAZY JOE AND THE VARIABLE SPEED BAND

CASABLANCA
Number	Title	Yr	NM
❏ 2298	Eugene/Madam Palm	1980	$8

— *Produced by Ace Frehley*

Number	Title	Yr	NM
❏ 2334	Ice Cream/Ugga Ugga Boo	1981	$5

CRAZY OTTO

DECCA
Number	Title	Yr	NM
❏ 29980	Alabamy Bound/Das Ist Musik	1956	$8
❏ 30818	Chopin's Polonaise/Sunrise Serenade	1959	$8
❏ 29503	Crazy Otto Rag/Twelfth Street Rag	1955	$12
❏ 30093	Derby Hat Medley/Swingin' Door Medley	1956	$8
❏ 29403	Glad Rag Doll/Smiles	1955	$30

— *Original pressings credited to "Happy Otto"*

Number	Title	Yr	NM
❏ 29403	Glad Rag Doll/Smiles	1955	$15

— *Later pressings credited to "Crazy Otto"*

Number	Title	Yr	NM
❏ 30377	Happy Piano Medley/Good Evening Friends Medley	1957	$8
❏ 29673	If You Knew Susie/Somebody Else Is Taking My Place	1955	$10
❏ 31185	Medley: Sleigh Ride-Winter Wonderland-White Christmas/Medley: Rudolph The Red-Nosed Reindeer-I Saw Mommy Kissing Santa Claus-Jingle Bells	1960	$15
❏ 29449	My Melancholy Baby/In the Mood	1955	$10
❏ 29571	Oh Johnny, Oh Johnny, Oh!/Palestine	1955	$10
❏ 31235	Piccadilly/Spanish Holiday	1961	$8
❏ 29658	The Marching Otto Medley (Part 1)/The Marching Otto Medley (Part 2)	1955	$15

— *As "Marching Otto"*

Number	Title	Yr	NM
❏ 29753	Tin Pan Alley Medley/Gaslight Medley	1955	$10

MGM
Number	Title	Yr	NM
❏ 13101	Alley Cat/Cheerio Choo Choo	1962	$8

7-Inch Extended Plays

DECCA
Number	Title	Yr	NM
❏ ED2260	Alabamy Bound/Indiana (Back Home Again in Indiana)//If You Knew Susie/I Know Susie/I'll Always Be in Love with You	1956	$10
❏ ED2202	Beautiful Ohio/Paddlin' Madelin' Home//S-H-I-N-E/Lights Out	1955	$10
❏ ED2569	(contents unknown)	1957	$8
❏ ED2600	(contents unknown)	1958	$8

Number	Title	Yr	NM
❏ ED2201 [PS]	Crazy Otto, Part 1	1955	$12
❏ ED2202 [PS]	Crazy Otto, Part 2	1955	$12
❏ ED2260 [PS]	Crazy Otto Rides Again, Volume 1	1956	$12
❏ ED2261 [PS]	Crazy Otto Rides Again, Volume 2	1956	$12
❏ ED2263 [PS]	Crazy Otto Rides Again, Volume 3	1956	$12
❏ ED2569 [PS]	Crazy Otto's Back in Town	1957	$8
❏ ED2600 [PS]	Honky Tonk Piano	1958	$8
❏ ED2201	Smiles/Glad Rag Doll//In the Mood/My Melancholy Baby	1955	$10
❏ ED2261	Somebody Else Is Taking My Place/Mammy o' Mine//The Darktown Strutters' Ball/Rag Mop	1956	$10
❏ ED2263	The Crazy Otto Rag/Twelfth Street Rag//Oh Johnny, Oh Johnny, Oh!/Palesteena	1956	$10

CREACH, PAPA JOHN
BUDDAH
❏ 509	I'm the Fiddle Man/Joyce	1975	$4

DJM
❏ 1102	All the World Loves a Winner/Southern Strut	1979	$4

GRUNT
❏ 65-0508	Filthy Funky (Part 1)/Filthy Funky (Part 2)	1972	$5
❏ 65-0501	Over the Rainbow/The Janitor Drives a Cadillac	1971	$5
❏ 65-0505	Papa John's Down Home Blues/String Jet Rock	1971	$5

CREAM
Also see GINGER BAKER'S AIR FORCE; JACK BRUCE; ERIC CLAPTON.
ATCO
❏ 6575 [B]	Anyone for Tennis/Pressed Rat and Warthog	1968	$25
❏ 6668	Badge/What a Bringdown	1969	$8
❏ 6646	Crossroads/Passing the Time	1969	$8
❏ 6462	I Feel Free/N.S.U.	1967	$20
❏ 6522	Spoonful/Spoonful (Part 2)	1967	$20
❏ 6488	Strange Brew/Tales of Brave Ulysses	1967	$20
❏ 6544	Sunshine of Your Love/SWLABR	1968	$8
❏ 6708	Sweet Wine/Lawdy Mama	1969	$10
❏ 6617	White Room/Those Were the Days	1968	$8

CREATION, THE
DECCA
❏ 32227	How Does It Feel to Feel/Life Is Just Beginning	1967	$15
❏ 32155	If I Stay Too Long/Nightmares	1967	$15

PLANET
❏ 116	Making Time/Try and Stop Me	1966	$20
❏ 119	Painter Man/Biff Bang Pow	1966	$20

CREATIONS, THE
GLOBE
❏ 103	I've Got to Find Her/Times Are Changing	1967	$30
❏ 1000	Oh Baby/Plenty of Love	1967	$30

JAMIE
❏ 1197	The Bells/Shang Shang	1961	$30

MERIDIAN
❏ 7550	The Wedding/I've Got a Feeling	1962	$125

PATTI-JO
❏ 1703	Seventeen/You'll Always Be Mine	1962	$200

PENNY
❏ 9022	Lady Luck/We're in Love	1962	$70

PINE CREST
❏ 101	Woke Up in the Morning/Strolling Through the Park	1961	$400

RADIANT
❏ 103	Don't Listen to What Others Say/Don't Listen to What Others Say, Part 2	1964	$30

TAKE TEN
❏ 1501	Lady Luck/We're in Love	1963	$40

TIP TOP
❏ 400	Every Night I Pray/Mommy and Daddy	1956	$200

TOP HAT
❏ 1003	Crash/Chickie Darling	1964	$50
❏ 1003 [PS]	Crash/Chickie Darling	1964	$100
❏ 1004	Don't Be Mean/41 Willies	1965	$60
❏ 1004 [PS]	Don't Be Mean/41 Willies	1965	$125

VIRTUE
❏ 2518	Don't Let Me Down/The Price I Have to Pay	1971	$6
❏ 2522	How Sweetly Simple/Lovin' Simple	1973	$6
❏ 2517	I'm So in Love with You/Save the People	1971	$6

ZODIAC
❏ 1005	A Dream/Foot Steps	1967	$8

CREATIVE SOURCE
POLYDOR
❏ 14291	Pass the Feelin' On/Turn On to Music	1975	$5

SUSSEX
❏ 632	Migration/I Just Can't See Myself Without You	1974	$5
❏ 509	Who Is He and What Is He to You (Part 1)/Who Is He and What Is He to You (Part 2)	1974	$5

CREATORS, THE (1)
DOOTO
❏ 463	I've Had You/Drafted, Volunteered, Enlisted	1961	$30

DORE
❏ 635	Too Far to Turn Around/Hello There, Mister Grave Digger	1962	$70

CREATORS, THE (2)
EPIC
❏ 9605	Crazy Love/Cross Fire	1963	$20

HI-Q
❏ 5021	Wear My Ring/Booga Bear	1961	$100
—Normal print label			
❏ 5021	Wear My Ring/Booga Bear	1961	$30
—Bold print label			

TIME
❏ 1038	Do You Remember/There's Going to Be an Angel	1961	$30

CREATORS, THE (3)
PHILIPS
❏ 40058	Boy, He's Got It/Yeah, He's Got It	1962	$30
❏ 40083	I'll Stay Home (New Year's Eve)/Shoom Ba Boom	1962	$300

T-KAY
❏ 110	I'll Never, Never Do It Again/Boy, He's Got It!	1962	$100

CREATURES, THE
COLUMBIA
❏ 43894	Looking at Tomorrow/Someone Needs You	1967	$8

CREECH, ALICE
TARGET
❏ 00313	The Hunter/Isn't It a Shame About Jeannie	1971	$8

CREEDENCE CLEARWATER REVIVAL
Also see DOUG CLIFFORD; JOHN FOGERTY; TOM FOGERTY; TOMMY FOGERTY AND THE BLUE VELVETS; THE GOLLIWOGS.
FANTASY
❏ 0 [DJ]	45 Revolutions Per Minute (Part 1)/45 Revolutions Per Minute (Part 2)	1970	$50
❏ 2832/3 [DJ]	45 Revolutions Per Minute (Part 1)/45 Revolutions Per Minute (Part 2)	1970	$50
❏ 2832/3 [PS]	45 Revolutions Per Minute (Part 1)/45 Revolutions Per Minute (Part 2)	1970	$70
❏ 622	Bad Moon Rising/Lodi	1969	$6
❏ 920	Cotton Fields/Lodi	1981	$4
❏ 634	Down on the Corner/Fortunate Son	1969	$6
❏ 634 [PS]	Down on the Corner/Fortunate Son	1969	$15
❏ 625	Green River/Commotion	1969	$6
❏ 655	Have You Ever Seen the Rain/Hey Tonight	1971	$6
❏ 759	I Heard It Through the Grapevine/Good Golly Miss Molly	1976	$4
❏ 759 [PS]	I Heard It Through the Grapevine/Good Golly Miss Molly	1976	$5
❏ 617	I Put a Spell on You/Walk on the Water	1968	$8
❏ 645	Lookin' Out My Back Door/Long As I Can See the Light	1970	$6
❏ 645 [PS]	Lookin' Out My Back Door/Long As I Can See the Light	1970	$15
❏ 957	Medley (from "I Heard It Through the Grapevine" to "Up Around the Bend")/Medley (from "Proud Mary" to "Lodi")	1985	$10
❏ 917	Medley U.S.A./Bad Moon Rising	1981	$4
❏ 619	Proud Mary/Born on the Bayou	1969	$6
❏ 676	Someday Never Comes/Tearin' Up the Country	1972	$6
❏ 616	Suzie Q (Part One)/Suzie Q (Part Two)	1968	$6
❏ 665	Sweet Hitch-Hiker/Door to Door	1971	$6
❏ 665 [PS]	Sweet Hitch-Hiker/Door to Door	1971	$15
❏ 908	Tombstone Shadow/Commotion	1981	$4
❏ 637	Travelin' Band/Who'll Stop the Rain	1970	$6
❏ 637 [PS]	Travelin' Band/Who'll Stop the Rain	1970	$15

SCORPIO
❏ 412	Porterville/Call It Pretending	1968	$100

CREEPER
ABC
❏ 12147	Santa Claus Wants Some Loving/Politicking	1975	$5

CRENSHAW, MARSHALL
WARNER BROS.
❏ 29771	Cynical Girl/Rave On/Somebody Like You	1983	$5
❏ 28865	Little Wild One (No. 5)/Like a Vague Memory	1985	$4
❏ 28865 [PS]	Little Wild One (No. 5)/Like a Vague Memory	1985	$4
❏ 29974	Someday, Someway/You're My Favorite Waste of Time	1982	$6
❏ 22878	Some Hearts/Whatever Way the Wind Blows	1989	$5
❏ 29894	There She Goes Again/Usual Thing	1982	$5
❏ 29630	Whenever You're On My Mind/Jungle Rock	1983	$4
❏ 29630 [PS]	Whenever You're On My Mind/Jungle Rock	1983	$5

CRESCENDOS, THE (1)
NASCO
❏ 6005	Oh Julie/My Little Girl	1957	$30
❏ 6009	School Girl/Crazy Hop	1958	$30
❏ 6009 [PS]	School Girl/Crazy Hop	1958	$60

NASHBORO
❏ (no #) [PS]	The Crescendos	1957	$60
—Large-hole omnibus sleeve, often found with "Oh Julie," but may have been used on other Nasco singles			

TAP
❏ 7027	Oh Julie/Angel Face	1962	$20
❏ 7027 [PS]	Oh Julie/Angel Face	1962	$30

CRESCENDOS, THE (2)
ATLANTIC
❏ 2014	I'll Be Seeing You/Sweet Dreams	1959	$20
❏ 1109	Sweet Dreams/Finders Keepers	1956	$40

CRESCENDOS, THE (U)
DOMAIN
❏ 1025	A Fellow Needs a Girl/Black Cat	1964	$20

IMPRO
❏ 5006	Tidal Wave/Crescendo Special	1962	$50

NU SOUND
❏ 1007	Count Down/Hawk Walk	1961	$40
❏ 1014	Sweet Talk/Movin' Wild	1961	$40

SCARLET
❏ 4009	Angel Face/I'm So Ashamed	1961	$60
❏ 4007	Strange Love/Let's Take a Walk	1960	$40

CRESCHENDOS, THE
GONE
❏ 5100	My Heart's Desire/Take My Heart	1961	$40

MUSIC CITY
❏ 831	My Heart's Desire/Take My Heart	1960	$400
—Green label			
❏ 831	My Heart's Desire/Take My Heart	1960	$200
—Maroon label			
❏ 831	My Heart's Desire/Take My Heart	1961	$60
—Black label			
❏ 839	Teenage Prayer/I Don't Mind	1961	$250

SATURN
❏ 404	Surfing Strip/Hanging Ten	1963	$60

CRESENTS, THE
JOYCE
❏ 102	Everybody Knew But Me/Rosemarie	1957	$250

CRESTONES, THE
MARKIE
❏ 117	She's a Bad Motorcycle/Grasshopper Dance	1963	$60

U.S.A.
❏ 835	My Girl/The Chopper	1965	$15

CRESTS, THE
COED
❏ 506	16 Candles/Beside You	1958	$40
❏ 511	Flower of Love/Molly Mae	1959	$30
❏ 543	I Remember (In the Still of the Night)/Good Golly Miss Molly	1961	$30
❏ 537	Isn't It Amazing/Molly Mae	1960	$30
❏ 561	Little Miracles/Baby I Gotta Know	1962	$40

Number	Title	Yr	NM
❑ 501	Pretty Little Angel/I Thank the Moon	1958	$200

— *Coed" in red print*

Number	Title	Yr	NM
❑ 501	Pretty Little Angel/I Thank the Moon	1958	$50

— *Coed" in red and black print*

❑ 509	Six Nights a Week/I Do	1959	$30
❑ 525	Step by Step/Gee (But I'd Give the World)	1960	$30
❑ 515	The Angels Listened In/I Thank the Moon	1959	$40
❑ 531	Trouble in Paradise/Always You	1960	$30

HARVEY

❑ 5002	Sixteen Candles/My Juanita	1981	$12

— *Red vinyl*

JOYCE

❑ 103	My Juanita/Sweetest One	1957	$300

— *Label name: "JoYce*

❑ 103	My Juanita/Sweetest One	1959	$60

— *Label name: "Joyce*

MUSICTONE

❑ 1106	My Juanita/Sweetest One	1961	$30

SCEPTER

❑ 12112	I'm Stepping Out of the Picture/Afraid of Love	1965	$20

SELMA

❑ 4000	Did I Remember/Tears Will Fall	1963	$40
❑ 311	Guilty/Number One with Me	1962	$80

— *A-side has spoken intro*

❑ 311	Guilty/Number One with Me	1962	$30

— *A-side does not have spoken intro*

TIMES SQUARE

❑ 6	Baby/I Love You So	1964	$20
❑ 97	Baby/I Love You So	1964	$15

TRANS ATLAS

❑ 696	The Actor/Three Tears in a Bucket	1962	$40

7-Inch Extended Plays

COED

❑ EPC-101 [PS]	The Angels Listened In	1959	$400
❑ EPC-101	The Angels Listened In/ Flower of Love//16 Candles/ Six Nights a Week	1959	$400

CRETONES, THE

PLANET

❑ 45926	Love Is Turning/Snap! Snap!	1981	$5

CREW CUTS, THE

4 CORNERS OF THE WORLD

❑ 120	Don't Be Angry/Earth Angel	1962	$12

ABC-PARAMOUNT

❑ 10450	Hip-Huggers/You're a Star, Donna, Donna	1963	$15

CHESS

❑ 1892	Ain't That Nice/Yeah, Yeah, She Wants Me	1964	$10

FIREBIRD

❑ 1805	My Heart Belongs to Only You/You've Been In	1970	$5

MERCURY

❑ 70490	All I Wanna Do/ The Barking Dog	1954	$20
❑ 70741	Angels in the Sky/ Mostly Martha	1955	$20
❑ 70634	A Story Untold/ Carmen's Boogie	1955	$20
❑ 70922	Bei Mir Bist Du Schoen/ Thirteen Going on Fourteen	1956	$20
❑ 70341	Crazy 'Bout You Baby/ Angela Mia	1954	$30
❑ 70491	Dance, Mr. Snowman, Dance/Twinkle Toes	1954	$20
❑ 70597	Don't Be Angry/ Chop Chop Boom	1955	$20
❑ 70668	Gum Drop/Song of the Fool	1955	$20
❑ 71223	I Like It Like That/ Be My Only Love	1957	$20
❑ 71168	I Sit in My Window/ Hey, You Face	1957	$20
❑ 70977	Love in a Home/ Keeper of the Flame	1956	$20
❑ 70443	Oop-Shoop/Do Me Good Baby	1954	$20
❑ 70840	Out of the Picture/Honey Hair, Sugar Lips, Eyes of Blue	1956	$20
❑ 70782	Seven Days/That's Your Mistake	1956	$20
❑ 70404	Sh-Boom/I Spoke Too Soon	1954	$30
❑ 70404	Sh-Boom/I Spoke Too Soon	1954	$60

— *7-inch 78 rpm on vinyl*

❑ 70404 [PS]	Sh-Boom/I Spoke Too Soon	1954	$125

— *Sleeve accompanying the 78: "PopSi Hit Record of the Month*

❑ 70710	Slam! Bam!/Are You Having Any Fun	1955	$20
❑ 71125	Suzie Q/Such a Shame	1957	$20

Number	Title	Yr	NM
❑ 70890	Tell Me Why/Rebel in Town	1956	$20
❑ 71076	The Angelus/Whatever, Whenever. Whoever	1957	$20
❑ 70494	The Whippenpoof Song/Varsity Drag	1954	$20

RCA VICTOR

❑ 47-7734	American Beauty Rose/The Shrine on Top of the Hill	1960	$15
❑ 47-7759	Aura Lee/Going to Church on Sunday	1960	$15
❑ 47-7577	Bermuda/Kin-Ni-Ki-Nic	1959	$15
❑ 47-7320	Forever My Darling/Hey Stella	1958	$15
❑ 47-7446	Fraternity Pin/Can You Hear Me	1959	$15
❑ 47-7509	Gone, Gone, Gone/ Someone in Heaven	1959	$15
❑ 47-7667	It Is No Secret/No, No, Nevermore	1960	$15
❑ 47-7359	That's My Desire/Baby Be Mine	1958	$15

VEE JAY

❑ 569	The Three Bells/Spanish Is the Loving Tongue	1963	$15

WARWICK

❑ 595	Malaguena/Why Not	1960	$15
❑ 558	Over the Mountain/Searchin'	1960	$15
❑ 623	The Legend of Gunga Din/ Number One with Me	1961	$15

WHALE

❑ 509	Hush Little Baby/Ti-Pi-Tum	1962	$15
❑ 508	Laura Love/Little Donkey	1962	$15
❑ 507	Twistin' All the World/ Electric Chair	1962	$15
❑ EP-1-3274	Down the Old Ox Road/The Whiffenpoof Song//We're Working Our Way Through College/Varsity Drag	1956	$15
❑ EP-1-3274 [PS]	The Crew Cuts On Campus	1956	$15

CREWE, BOB

20TH CENTURY

❑ 2271	Street Talk/Street Talk (Part 2)	1976	$4

ABC-PARAMOUNT

❑ 10273	Another Day/Come to Me	1961	$15
❑ 10246	One More Lie/I'm Goin' Home (On My Way)	1961	$15
❑ 10204	Swingin' Family Tree/ La La Loretta	1961	$15

BRUNSWICK

❑ 55021	I Can't Shake the Blues/ Torn and Tattered Heart	1957	$20

CORAL

❑ 61688	Melody for Lovers/Can't Get Away from It	1956	$20

CREWE

❑ 605	Dandylion/Day By Day & Prepare Ye	1971	$5

DYNO VOICE

❑ 231	After the Ball/One More Year	1967	$6
❑ 237	A Lover's Concerto/ You Only Live Twice	1967	$6
❑ 928	Angel Is Love/Black Queen's Beads	1968	$6
❑ 902	Birds of Britain/I Will Wait for You	1968	$6
❑ 233	Mini Skirts in Moscow, or … / Theme for a Lazy Girl	1967	$6
❑ 233 [PS]	Mini Skirts in Moscow, or … / Theme for a Lazy Girl	1967	$10
❑ 229	Music to Watch Girls By/ Girls on the Rocks	1966	$8
❑ 915	To Give (The Reason I Live)/ Battle Hymn of the Republic	1968	$6
❑ 906	Winter Warm/Song from Moulin Rouge	1968	$6

ELEKTRA

❑ 45404	It Took a Long Time (For the First Time in My Life)/In Another Life	1977	$4
❑ 45425	Marriage Made in Heaven/ In Another Life	1977	$4
❑ 45380	Menage a Trois/I Am Free-Keep Walkin'	1976	$4
❑ 45346	Time for You and Me/ Free (Medley)	1976	$4

JUBILEE

❑ 5148	Cash Register Heart/ Change of Heart	1954	$30
❑ 5164	Punch/It's All Over	1954	$30

MELBA

❑ 119	Guessin' Games/Don't Call Me Chicken	1957	$20

METROMEDIA

❑ 229	Mammy Blue/Better Be Gone	1972	$5
❑ 243	Takin' Care of Each Other/ (B-side unknown)	1972	$5

SPOTLIGHT

❑ 393	Penny Nickel Dime Quarter (On a Teenage Date)/How Long	1956	$30

VIK

❑ 0307	Charm Bracelet/ Do Be Do Be Do	1957	$30
❑ 0333	Of Sun, the Sea and the Sand/Sweet Talk	1958	$30

Number	Title	Yr	NM

WARWICK

❑ 534	Cool Time/Quite a Picture	1960	$15
❑ 579	Little Girl of Mine/To Ev'ry Girl, To Ev'ry Boy	1960	$15
❑ 601	Oh, How I Miss You Tonight/Ev'rytime	1960	$15
❑ 616	She's Only Wonderful/On the Street Where You Live	1961	$15
❑ 553	Silhouettes/Let's Get Serious	1960	$15
❑ 519	The Whippenpoof Song/ Let's Pretend	1959	$15

CREWS, DWAYNE

KILLER

❑ 124	Selfish Man/(B-side unknown)	1989	$8

CRIBBINS, BERNARD

CAPITOL

❑ 5933	When I'm Sixty-Four/ Oh My Word	1967	$10

CRICKETS, THE (1)

BRUNSWICK

❑ 55094	It's So Easy/Lonesome Tears	1958	$60
❑ 55124	Love's Made a Fool of You/ Someone, Someone	1959	$50
❑ 55053	Maybe Baby/Tell Me How	1958	$60
❑ 55035	Oh, Boy!/Not Fade Away	1957	$60

— *Note: Picture sleeves for this record are bootlegs*

❑ 55009	That'll Be the Day/I'm Lookin' for Someone to Love	1957	$60
❑ 55072	Think It Over/Fool's Paradise	1958	$60
❑ 55153	When You Ask About Love/Deborah	1959	$50

CORAL

❑ 62407	Maybe Baby/Not Fade Away	1964	$40
❑ 62198	More Than I Can Say/ Baby, My Heart	1960	$50
❑ 62238	Peggy Sue Got Married/ Don't Cha Know	1960	$50

EPIC

❑ 34-08028	T-Shirt/Hollywould	1988	$5
❑ 34-08028 [PS]	T-Shirt/Hollywould	1988	$5

LIBERTY

❑ 55441	Don't Ever Change/I'm Not a Bad Boy	1962	$30
❑ 55603	Don't Say You Love Me/April Avenue	1963	$30
❑ 55767	Everybody's Got a Little Problem/Now Hear This	1965	$30
❑ 55392	He's Old Enough to Know Better/I'm Feeling Better	1961	$30
❑ 55492	I Believe in You/Parisian Girl	1962	$30
❑ 55495	Little Hollywood Girl/ Parisian Girl	1962	$30
❑ 55660	Lonely Avenue/You Can't Be In-Between	1964	$30
❑ 55540	My Little Girl/Teardrops Fall Like Rain	1963	$30
❑ 55668	Please, Please Me/ From Me to You	1964	$60
❑ 55696	(They Call Her) La Bomba/All Over You	1964	$30
❑ 55742	We Gotta Get Together/I Think I've Caught the Blues	1964	$30

MGM

❑ 14541	Hayride/Wasn't It Nice	1973	$20

MUSIC FACTORY

❑ 415	Million Dollar Movie/A Million Miles Apart	1968	$30

7-Inch Extended Plays

BRUNSWICK

❑ EB71036	*I'm Looking for Someone to Love/That'll Be the Day/ Not Fade Away/Oh! Boy	1957	$300
❑ EB71038	*Maybe Baby/Rock Me My Baby/Send Me Some Lovin'/Tell Me How	1958	$250
❑ EB71036 [PS]	The Chirping Crickets	1957	$300
❑ EB71038 [PS]	The Sound of the Crickets	1958	$250

CRICKETS, THE (2)

DAVIS

❑ 459	I'm Going to Live My Life Alone/Man from the Moon	1958	$70

JAY DEE

❑ 789	Are You Looking for a Sweetheart/Never Give Up Hope	1954	$200
❑ 785	Changing Partners/Your Love	1954	$200
❑ 777	Dreams and Wishes/ When I Met You	1953	$200
❑ 781	Fine As Wine/I'm Not the Same One You Love	1953	$200
❑ 795	I'm Going to Live My Life Alone/Man from the Moon	1954	$200

MGM

❑ 11507	I'll Cry No More/For You I Have Eyes	1953	$200

Number	Title	Yr	NM

CRIME

B-SQUARE

Number	Title	Yr	NM
❏ BSQ 001	Maserati/Gangster Funk	1980	$30
❏ BSQ 001 [PS]	Maserati/Gangster Funk	1980	$30

CRIME

Number	Title	Yr	NM
❏ 0(no cat #)	Frustration/Murder by Guitar	1977	$70
❏ 0(no cat #) [PS]	Frustration/Murder by Guitar	1977	$70
❏ 0(no cat #)	Hotwire My Heart/Baby, You're So Repulsive	1976	$60
❏ 0(no cat #) [PS]	Hotwire My Heart/Baby, You're So Repulsive	1976	$60

CRISS, GARY

DIAMOND

Number	Title	Yr	NM
❏ 182	Hands of My Baby/If This Is Goodbye	1965	$8
❏ 145	Little Joe/Sweet, Warm and Soft	1963	$12
❏ 127	Long Lonely Nights/I Still Miss You So	1963	$10
❏ 190	My Baby Left Me/This Love of Mine	1965	$8
❏ 122	My Heavenly Angel/The Girl I Told You About	1962	$15
❏ 228	Welcome Home to My Heart/Hands Off Buddy	1967	$30
❏ 114	Welcome Home to My Heart/Our Favorite Melodies	1962	$15

SALSOUL

Number	Title	Yr	NM
❏ 2082	Brazilian Nights/Amazon Queen	1979	$6

STRAND

Number	Title	Yr	NM
❏ 25044	Good Golly Miss Molly/I'll Love Only You	1961	$40

CRITTERS, THE

KAPP

Number	Title	Yr	NM
❏ 793	Bad Misunderstanding/Forever or No More	1966	$12
❏ 838	Don't Let the Rain Fall Down on Me/Walk Like a Man Again	1967	$12
❏ 727	He'll Make You Cry/Children & Flowers	1965	$12
❏ 858	Little Girl/Dancing in the Streets	1967	$12
❏ 805	Marryin' Kind of Love/New York Bound	1967	$10
❏ 769	Mr. Dieingly Sad/It Just Won't Be That Way	1966	$15
❏ 769 [PS]	Mr. Dieingly Sad/It Just Won't Be That Way	1966	$30

MUSICOR

Number	Title	Yr	NM
❏ 1044	I'm Gonna Give/Georgianna	1964	$30

PROJECT 3

Number	Title	Yr	NM
❏ 1349	Cool Sunday Morning/Lisa, But Not the Same	1969	$8
❏ 1326	Good Morning Sunshine/A Moment of Being with You	1968	$8
❏ 1363	She Said She Loved Him/I Just Want to Sit Right Here and Look at You	1969	$8
❏ 1332	Touch 'N' Go/Younger Generation	1968	$8

CROCE, JIM

21 RECORDS

Number	Title	Yr	NM
❏ 94973	Bad, Bad Leroy Brown/Operator (That's Not the Way It Feels)	1987	$3
❏ 94971	I'll Have to Say I Love You in a Song/I Got a Name	1987	$3
❏ 94970	It Doesn't Have to Be That Way/Time in a Bottle	1987	$3
❏ 94969	Workin' at the Car Wash Blues/Rapid Roy (The Stock Car Boy)	1987	$3

ABC

Number	Title	Yr	NM
❏ 11359	Bad, Bad Leroy Brown/A Good Time Man Like Me Ain't Got No Business (Singin' the Blues)	1973	$5

—ABC logo in children's building blocks

Number	Title	Yr	NM
❏ 11359	Bad, Bad Leroy Brown/A Good Time Man Like Me Ain't Got No Business (Singin' the Blues)	1973	$4

—Regular ABC logo

Number	Title	Yr	NM
❏ 11389	I Got a Name/Alabama Rain	1973	$4
❏ 11424	I'll Have to Say I Love You in a Song/Salon and Saloon	1974	$4
❏ 11413	It Doesn't Have to Be That Way/Roller Derby Queen	1973	$4
❏ 11413 [PS]	It Doesn't Have to Be That Way/Roller Derby Queen	1973	$5
❏ 11346	One Less Set of Footsteps/It Doesn't Have to Be That Way	1973	$4
❏ 11335	Operator (That's Not the Way It Feels)/Rapid Roy (The Stock Car Boy)	1972	$4
❏ 11405	Time in a Bottle/Hard Time Losin' Man	1973	$4
❏ 11447	Workin' at the Car Wash Blues/Thursday	1974	$4
❏ 12015	Workin' at the Car Wash Blues/Thursday	1974	$5

LIFESONG

Number	Title	Yr	NM
❏ 45001	Chain Gang Medley/Stone Walls	1975	$4

Number	Title	Yr	NM
❏ 45018 [DJ]	It Doesn't Have to Be That Way (mono/stereo)	1976	$5

—Promo-only release; Lifesong sleeve has custom sticker (add $4)

Number	Title	Yr	NM
❏ 45018 [DJ]	It Doesn't Have to Be That Way (mono/stereo)	1976	$5

—Promo-only release; Lifesong sleeve has custom sticker (add $4)

Number	Title	Yr	NM
❏ 45005	Maybe Tomorrow/Mississippi Lady	1976	$4

7-Inch Extended Plays

ABC

Number	Title	Yr	NM
❏ PRO-769	Dreamin' Again/One Less Set of Footsteps/Next Time, This Time//Roller Derby Queen/A Good Time Man Like Me Ain't Got No Business (Singin' the Blues)/Bad, Bad Leroy Brown	1973	$10

—Jukebox issue; small hole, plays at 33 1/3 rpm

Number	Title	Yr	NM
❏ PRO- 40008 [PS]	I Got a Name	1973	$25
❏ PRO- 40008	I Got a Name/Lover's Cross/I'll Have to Say I Love You in a Song//Top Hat Bar and Grille/Thursday/Workin' at the Car Wash Blues	1973	$25

—Quadraphonic jukebox single; small hole, plays at 33 1/3 rpm

Number	Title	Yr	NM
❏ PRO-769 [PS]	Life and Times	1973	$12

—Part of "Little LP" series (LLP #232)

CROCKETT, G.L.

CHECKER

Number	Title	Yr	NM
❏ 1121	Look Out Mabel/Did You Ever Love Somebody	1965	$50

CHIEF

Number	Title	Yr	NM
❏ 7010	Look Out Mabel/Did You Ever Love Somebody	1958	$125

—As "G. Davy Crockett"

CROCKETT, HOWARD

DOT

Number	Title	Yr	NM
❏ 17482	I Feel More Like Myself Than I Did a While Ago/I'd Like to Be Everybody for Just One Day	1973	$6
❏ 15593	If You'll Let Me/You've Got Me Lyin'	1957	$60
❏ 17509	The Calling/Pictures and Memories	1974	$6
❏ 17457	The House Where Momma Lived/Last Will and Testament (Of a Drinking Man)	1973	$6

MANCO

Number	Title	Yr	NM
❏ 1002	Sluefoot the Bear/Polly Ann	1960	$60
❏ 1012	That Old Juke Box/Steamboat Bill	1961	$40

MEL-O-DY

Number	Title	Yr	NM
❏ 121	All the Good Times Are Gone/The Great Titanic	1965	$30
❏ 111	Bringing In the Gold/I've Been a Long Time Leaving	1963	$30
❏ 115	My Lil's Run Off/Spanish Lace and Memories	1964	$30
❏ 119	Put Me in Your Pocket/The Miles	1964	$30
❏ 109	The Big Wheel/That Silver-Haired Daddy of Mine	1963	$30

SMASH

Number	Title	Yr	NM
❏ 1750	Break Away Billy Boy/Out of Bounds Again	1962	$50
❏ 1721	Deep Elm Dave/Going Down to Soldiers	1961	$50

STOP

Number	Title	Yr	NM
❏ 210	Soap and Water/A Man with No Face	1969	$8
❏ 136	The Big Cat/You're Messin' Up My Mind	1968	$8
❏ 172	The Big Day/You Can't Get to All of 'Em Jack	1968	$8
❏ 250	The Law Says/Ask Little Brother	1969	$8
❏ 238	Where Were You/The Story of Bango	1969	$8

CROFT, SANDY

ANGELSONG

Number	Title	Yr	NM
❏ 1821	Easier/If I Was As Pretty As You	1982	$6
❏ 1821 [PS]	Easier/If I Was As Pretty As You	1982	$8

CAPITOL

Number	Title	Yr	NM
❏ B-5363	Easier/If I Was As Pretty As You	1984	$4

—Reissue of Angelsong 1821

Number	Title	Yr	NM
❏ B-5471	Piece of My Heart/Heart Stealer	1985	$4
❏ B-5471 [PS]	Piece of My Heart/Heart Stealer	1985	$5

CROME SYRCUS, THE

COMMAND

Number	Title	Yr	NM
❏ 4111	Cover Up/Take It Like a Man	1968	$12

CROMER, SIR HAROLD J.

CAMEO

Number	Title	Yr	NM
❏ 369	The Thing/Nick & Joe Callin'	1965	$15

CROMWELL, LINK

ORK

Number	Title	Yr	NM
❏ 81981 [B]	Crazy Like a Fox/Shock Me	1977	$40

CRONHAM, CHARLES R.

7-Inch Extended Plays

MERCURY

Number	Title	Yr	NM
❏ 3151 [PS]	Sacred Hymns	1956	$12
❏ 3151	Stand Up, Stand Up For Jesus/Love Divine, All Loves Excelling//Lead On, O King Eternal/God Of Our Fathers	1956	$10

CROPPER, STEVE

MCA

Number	Title	Yr	NM
❏ 51078	Playin' My Thang/Why Do You Say You Love Me	1981	$4
❏ 51115	Sandy Beaches/Fly	1981	$4

CROSBY, BING, AND LOUIS ARMSTRONG

DECCA

Number	Title	Yr	NM
❏ 27623	Gone Fishin'/We All Have a Song in My Heart	1951	$20

MGM

Number	Title	Yr	NM
❏ SB27 [S]	Dardanella/Brother Bill	1960	$20
❏ 12961	Dardanella/Muskrat Ramble	1960	$12
❏ SB29 [S]	Let's Sing Like a Dixieland Band/At the Jazz Band Ball	1960	$20
❏ SB26 [S]	Muskrat Ramble/Way Down in New Orleans	1960	$20
❏ SB28 [S]	Preacher/Little Ol' Tune	1960	$20

CROSBY, BING, AND PEGGY LEE

DECCA

Number	Title	Yr	NM
❏ 28238	Watermelon Weather/The Moon Came Up with a Great Idea Last Night	1952	$15

CROSBY, BING

AMOS

Number	Title	Yr	NM
❏ 111	Hey Jude/Lonely Street	1969	$6
❏ 116	It's All in the Game/More and More	1969	$5

CAPITOL

Number	Title	Yr	NM
❏ 5088	Do You Hear What I Hear/Christmas Dinner Country Style	1963	$8
❏ F3695	Man on Fire/Seven Nights a Week	1957	$15
❏ 4548	Simple Love Affair/That's How I Met Your Mother	1978	$4
❏ F3507	True Love/Well, Did You Evah?	1956	$20

—A-side with Grace Kelly; B-side with Frank Sinatra

COLUMBIA

Number	Title	Yr	NM
❏ 41387	Say One for Me/I Couldn't Care Less	1959	$15
❏ 41104	Straight Down the Middle/Tomorrow's My Lucky Day	1958	$15
❏ 41496	The Secret of Christmas/Just What I Wanted for Christmas	1959	$20

DAYBREAK

Number	Title	Yr	NM
❏ 1001	A Time to Be Jolly/And the Bells Rang	1971	$6

—Black label

Number	Title	Yr	NM
❏ 1001 [PS]	A Time to Be Jolly/And the Bells Rang	1971	$5
❏ 1001	A Time to Be Jolly/And the Bells Rang	1971	$5

—Yellow label

DECCA

Number	Title	Yr	NM
❏ 28048	2 Shillelagh O'Sullivan/That Tumbledown Shack in Athlone	1952	$10
❏ 27264	Accidents Will Happen/Milady	1950	$15

—With Dorothy Kirsten

Number	Title	Yr	NM
❏ 40181	A Crosby Christmas (Part 1)/A Crosby Christmas (Part 2)	1950	$40

—As "Gary, Phillip, Dennis, Lindsay and Bing Crosby"

Number	Title	Yr	NM
❏ 27117	All My Love/The Friendly Islands	1950	$15
❏ 27230	A Marshmallow World/Looks Like a Cold, Cold Winter	1950	$15
❏ 27241	And You'll Be Mine/Accidents Will Happen	1950	$15
❏ 27441	An Early American/My Own Bit of Land	1951	$10
❏ 29636	Angel Bells/Let's Harmonize	1955	$10
❏ 30262	Around the World/Around the World	1957	$8

—B-side by Victor Young

Number	Title	Yr	NM
❏ 30262 [PS]	Around the World/Around the World	1957	$20
❏ 30120	Around the World/Love in a Home	1956	$10
❏ 38031 [DJ]	Around the World/Mississippi Mud	1957	$10

—Green label

Number	Title	Yr	NM
❏ 38031 [PS]	Around the World/Mississippi Mud	1957	$30
❏ 27934	At Last, At Last!/The Isle of Innisfree	1952	$12

Number	Title	Yr	NM
❑ 27231	Autumn Leaves/This Is the Time	1950	$15
❑ 25643	Avalon/On the Alamo	1964	$6
❑ 27158	Ave Maria/Home Sweet Home	1950	$15
❑ 27852	A Weaver of Dreams/I Still See Alisa	1951	$10
❑ 25665	Between the Devil and the Deep Blue Sea/Georgia on My Mind	1965	$6
❑ 27631	Black Ball Ferry Line/ The Yodeling Ghost	1951	$10
—With the Andrews Sisters			
❑ 29147	Call of the South/ Cornbelt Symphony	1954	$10
—As "Bing and Gary Crosby			
❑ 25661	Chinatown, My Chinatown/I'm Confessin' (That I Love You)	1965	$6
❑ 30488	Chinatown My Chinatown/ Alabamy Bound	1957	$8
❑ 9-66	Christmas Greetings	1950	$60
—Includes records and box			
❑ 9-27831	Christmas in Killarney/ It's Beginning to Look Like Christmas	1951	$20
❑ 29790	Christmas Is A-Comin'/Is Christmas Only a Tree	1955	$15
❑ 25020	Clementine/The Old Oaken Bucket	1950	$15
—Reissue of 78; part of "Album No. 9-145			
❑ 28419	Cool Water/South Rampart Street Parade	1952	$12
—With the Andrews Sisters			
❑ 27951	Copacabana/Granada	1952	$12
❑ 27553	Country Style/Home Cookin'	1951	$12
❑ 29251	Count Your Blessings Instead of Sheep/What Can You Do with a General	1954	$12
❑ 28319	Deep in the Heart of Texas/Do You Care	1952	$12
❑ 23787	Did Your Mother Come from Ireland?/Where the River Shannon Flows	1950	$15
—Reissue of 78; part of "Album No. 9-31			
❑ 29409	Dissertation on State of Bliss/It's Mine, It's Yours	1955	$12
❑ 27830	Domino/When the World Was Young	1951	$12
❑ 28061	Don't Ever Be Afraid to Go Home/Rosaleen	1952	$12
❑ 28955	Down By the Riverside/What a Little Moonlight Can Do	1953	$12
—As "Bing and Gary Crosby			
❑ 27278	Evalina/The Eagle and Me	1950	$12
❑ 29483	Farewell/Jim, Johnny & Jonah	1955	$10
❑ 27500	Feudin' and Fightin'/Goodbye, My Lovers, Goodbye	1951	$10
❑ 28195	Galway Bay/The Isle of Innisfree	1952	$10
❑ 27589	Getting to Know You/I Whistle a Happy Tune	1951	$10
❑ 30555	Gigi/Trust Your Destiny to Your Star	1958	$8
❑ 27551	Girl of My Dreams/I'll Remember April	1951	$10
❑ 27605	Going My Way/ Swinging on a Star	1951	$10
❑ 27219	Harbor Lights/Beyond the Reef	1950	$15
❑ 27588	Hello Young Lovers/ Something Wonderful	1951	$12
❑ 27019	Home Cookin'/When the Sun Goes Down	1950	$15
❑ 29981	Honeysuckle Rose/Swanee	1956	$8
❑ 28581	Hush-a-Bye/Mother Darlin'	1953	$10
❑ 28963	Ida! Sweet as Apple Cider/I Can't Believe ThatYou're in Love	1953	$10
❑ 27018	I Didn't Slip, I Wasn't Pushed, I Fell/So Tall a Tree	1950	$15
❑ 27276	If I Loved You/Close As Pages in a Book	1950	$10
❑ 27232	If I Were a Bell/I've Never Been in Love Before	1950	$15
—A-side with Patti Andrews			
❑ 29144	If You Love Me (Really Love Me)/Liebchen	1954	$10
❑ 30126 [DJ]	I Heard the Bells on Christmas Day/Christmas Is a-Comin'	1956	$15
—Pink label, black type			
❑ 30126	I Heard the Bells on Christmas Day/Christmas Is a-Comin'	1956	$15
❑ 30126 [DJ]	I Heard the Bells on Christmas Day/Christmas Is a-Comin'	1956	$15
—Pink label, black type			
❑ 27550	I Kiss Your Hand, Madame/ The Kiss in Your Eyes	1951	$10
❑ 23779	I'll Be Home for Christmas (If Only in My Dreams)/ Faith of Our Fathers	1950	$15
—Lines label; Sides 7 and 8 of "Album No. 9-65			
❑ 28683	I Love My Baby (My Baby Loves Me)/ There's Music in You	1953	$10
❑ 27643	I Might Be Your Once in a While/Indian Summer	1951	$10
❑ 29850	In a Little Spanish Town ('Twas On a Night Like This)/Ol' Man River	1956	$8
❑ 27678	In the Cool, Cool, Cool of the Evening/Misto Christophe Columbo	1951	$10
—With Jane Wyman			

Number	Title	Yr	NM
❑ 29212	In the Good Old Summertime/ Oh Tell Me Why (The Stars Do Shine)	1954	$10
❑ 27554	I Only Want a Buddy -- Not a Sweetheart/When the White Azaleas Start Blooming	1951	$10
❑ 28743	It Had to Be You/Granada	1953	$10
❑ 27768	I Will Remember You/The Loneliness of Evening	1951	$10
❑ 27111	La Vie En Rose/I Cross My Fingers	1950	$15
❑ 27173	Life Is So Peculiar/ High on the List	1950	$15
—With the Andrews Sisters			
❑ 28814	Mademoiselle de Paris/ Embrasse -- Moi Bien	1953	$10
❑ 28805	Magic Window/ Cela Mi Est Egal	1953	$10
❑ 27536	Maria Bonita/Quizas, Quizas, Quizas	1951	$10
❑ 27404	May the Good Lord Bless and Keep You/A Perfect Day	1951	$10
❑ 23495	McNamara's Band/ Dear Old Donegal	1950	$15
—Reissue of 78; part of "Album No. 9-31			
❑ 27228	Mele Kalikimaka/ Poppa Santa Claus	1950	$15
—With the Andrews Sisters			
❑ 25520	Memories Are Made of This/My Blue Heaven	1961	$6
❑ 9-65	Merry Christmas	1950	$60
—Includes records 23281, 23777, 23778 and 23779 (also priced separately) and box			
❑ 28514	Merry Go Run Around/Hoot Mon	1952	$10
—With Peggy Lee and Bob Hope			
❑ 28210	Mine/You've Got Me Where You Want Me	1952	$15
—With Judy Garland			
❑ 25540	Moments to Remember/ Vaya Con Dios	1961	$6
❑ 27577	Moonlight Bay/When You and I Were Young Maggie Blues	1951	$10
—As "Gary and Bing Crosby			
❑ 27275	Oh! What a Beautiful Morning/ People Will Say We're in Love	1950	$10
❑ 29341	Old Man-Mandy/Gee, I Wish I Was Back in the Army	1954	$10
❑ 27606	Old Soldiers Never Die/ My Own Bit of Land	1951	$10
❑ 28254	On the 10:10 from Ten-Ten-Tennessee/Just for You	1952	$10
❑ 28470	Open Up Your Heart/You Don't Know What Lonesome Is	1952	$10
❑ 9-23484	Pistol Packin' Mama/ Don't Fence Me In	1950	$15
—With the Andrews Sisters; "lines" label			
❑ 9-23484	Pistol Packin' Mama/ Don't Fence Me In	1955	$10
—With the Andrews Sisters; star under "Decca			
❑ 27112	Play a Simple Melody/Sam's Song	1950	$15
—By "Gary Crosby and Friend" (guess who the friend is)			
❑ 28303	Poinciana/Symphony	1952	$10
❑ 29024	Secret Love/My Love, My Love	1954	$10
❑ 27483	Sentimental Music/Any Town Is Paris When You're Young	1951	$10
❑ 29568	She Is the Sunshine of Virginia/ (All She'd Say Was) Uh-Huh	1955	$10
❑ 25497	Sierra Sue/Along the Santa Fe Trail	1950	$15
—Reissue of 78; part of "Album No. 9-145			
❑ 23777	Silent Night/Adeste Fideles (O Come All Ye Faithful)	1950	$15
—Lines label; Sides 3 and 4 of "Album No. 9-65			
❑ 23777	Silent Night/Adeste Fideles (O Come All Ye Faithful)	1955	$10
—Star on label			
❑ 23777	Silent Night/Adeste Fideles (O Come All Ye Faithful)	1960	$8
—Color bars on label			
❑ 23777 [PS]	Silent Night/Adeste Fideles (O Come All Ye Faithful)	1960	$20
—Sleeve came with early 1960s pressings			
❑ 27229	Silver Bells/That Christmas Feeling	1950	$15
—A-side with Carol Richards			
❑ 27508	Silver Moon/More I Cannot Wish You	1951	$10
❑ 29493	Silver Moon/Nobody	1955	$10
❑ 28511	Sleigh Bell Serenade/ Keep It a Secret	1952	$20
❑ 28463	Sleigh Ride/Little Jack Frost Get Lost	1952	$20
❑ 27477	Sparrow in the Tree Top/ Forsaking All Others	1951	$10
—With the Andrews Sisters			
❑ 27478	St. Patrick's Day Parade/With My Shillelagh Under My Arm	1951	$10
❑ 25003	Take Me Back to My Boots and Saddle/My Little Buckaroo	1950	$15
—Reissue of 78; part of "Album No. 9-145			
❑ 28733	Tenderfoot/Walk Me By the River	1953	$10
❑ 28261	The Bells of St. Mary's/Kathleen	1952	$12
❑ 27250	The Best Thing for You/ Marrying for Love	1950	$15

Number	Title	Yr	NM
❑ 29777	The First Snowfall/The Next Time It Happens	1956	$8
❑ 29410	The Land Around Us/ The Search Is Through	1955	$10
❑ 28256	The Live Oak Tree/I'll Si-Si You in Bahia	1952	$10
—With the Andrews Sisters			
❑ 27443	The Meadows of Heaven/ The Last Mile Home	1951	$10
❑ 27461	Then You've Never Been Blue/You Gotta Show Me	1951	$10
❑ 29357	The Song from Desiree/ Who Gave You the Roses	1954	$10
❑ 27277	They Say It's Wonderful/I Love You	1950	$10
❑ 27143	This Could Be Forever/Helpless	1950	$15
—With Louanne Hogan			
❑ 28265	Till the End of the World/ Just a Little Lovin'	1952	$10
—With Grady Martin			
❑ 23789	Too-Ra-Loo-Ra-Loo-Ral/I'll Take You Home Again Kathleen	1950	$15
—Reissue of 78; part of "Album No. 9-31			
❑ 28515	To See You/Moonflowers	1952	$10
—B-side by Peggy Lee			
❑ 27555	Weddin' Day/(B-side unknown)	1951	$10
—With the Andrews Sisters			
❑ 30023	When My Baby Smiles at Me/April Showers	1956	$8
❑ 27505	When My Dreamboat Comes Home/Walking the Floor Over You	1951	$10
❑ 9-23778	White Christmas/God Rest Ye Merry Gentlemen	1950	$15
—Lines label; Sides 5 and 6 of "Album No. 9-65			
❑ 9-23778	White Christmas/God Rest Ye Merry Gentlemen	1955	$10
—Star on label			
❑ 23778	White Christmas/God Rest Ye Merry Gentlemen	1960	$8
—Color bars on label			
❑ 23778 [PS]	White Christmas/God Rest Ye Merry Gentlemen	1960	$20
—Sleeve came with early 1960s pressings			
❑ 29342	White Christmas/Snow	1954	$20
—A-side with Danny Kaye; B-side by Peggy Lee and Trudi Stevens			
❑ 23786	Who Threw the Overalls in Mrs. Murphy's Chowder?/ It's the Same Old Overalls	1950	$15
—Reissue of 78; part of "Album No. 9-31			
❑ 27653	(Why Did I Twll You I Was Going to) Shanghai/I've Got to Fall in Love Again	1951	$10
❑ 27595	With This Ring I Thee Wed/ Here Ends the Rainbow	1951	$10
❑ 27263	Wouldn't It Be Funny/One More for the Blue and White	1950	$15
KAPP			
❑ 196 [PS]	How Lovely Is Christmas/ My Own Individual Star	1957	$30
❑ 196	How Lovely Is Christmas/ My Own Individual Star	1957	$15
LONDON			
❑ 20095	There's Nothing I Haven't Sung About/The Way We Were	1977	$4
MCA			
❑ 65021	Silent Night/Adeste Fideles (O Come All Ye Faithful)	1973	$4
—Black label with rainbow			
❑ 65021	Silent Night/Adeste Fideles (O Come All Ye Faithful)	1980	$3
—Blue label with rainbow			
❑ 65022	White Christmas/God Rest Ye Merry Gentlemen	1973	$4
—Black label with rainbow			
❑ 65022	White Christmas/God Rest Ye Merry Gentlemen	1980	$3
—Blue label with rainbow			
❑ 40830	White Christmas/When the Blue of the Night Meets the Gold of the Day	1977	$5
❑ 40830 [PS]	White Christmas/When the Blue of the Night Meets the Gold of the Day	1977	$5
MGM			
❑ 12946	The Second Time Around/ Incurably Romantic	1960	$8
RCA VICTOR			
❑ 47-7695	It's a Good Day/The Music of Home	1960	$8
REPRISE			
❑ 0283	Don't Be a Do-Badder/ The Hukilau Song	1964	$6
❑ 0478	How Green Was My Valley/ Far from Home	1966	$5
❑ 0315	It's Christmas Time Again/ Christmas Candles	1964	$15
—With Fred Waring and the Pennsylvanians			
❑ 0315 [PS]	It's Christmas Time Again/ Christmas Candles	1964	$20

Number	Title	Yr	NM
❏ 0645	Step to the Rear/What Do We Do with the World	1967	$5
❏ 0424	The White World of Winter/ The Secret of Christmas	1965	$8

UNITED ARTISTS

Number	Title	Yr	NM
❏ XW700	Send In the Clowns/That's What Life Is All About	1975	$4

VERVE

Number	Title	Yr	NM
❏ 10089	Heat Wave/September in the Rain	1957	$12
❏ 2025	I've Got Five Dollars/ Mountain Greenery	1956	$10

WARNER BROS.

Number	Title	Yr	NM
❏ PRO146 [DJ]	I Wish You a Merry Christmas/ Winter Wonderland// The Littlest Angel	1962	$30
❏ PRO146 [DJ]	I Wish You a Merry Christmas/ Winter Wonderland// The Littlest Angel	1962	$30
❏ ED2427	Prisoner of Love/Ain't Misbehavin'//Paper Doll/ This Love of Mine	1956	$20
❏ ED2108	Sleepy Time Gal/Dinah//I Never Knew/I Can't Give You Anything But Love	1954	$15
❏ ED2108 [PS]	Some Fine Old Chestnuts, Vol. 2	1954	$15
❏ ED2427 [PS]	Song I Wish I Had Sung the First Time Around... Part 2	1956	$20

RCA VICTOR

Number	Title	Yr	NM
❏ EPA 3-1473 [PS]	Bing with a Beat	1957	$12
❏ EPA 3-1473	Mack the Knife/Tell Me// Down Among the Sheltering Palms/Mama Loved Papa	1957	$8

CROSBY, DAVID

ATLANTIC

Number	Title	Yr	NM
❏ 2792	Laughing/Music Is Love	1971	$5
❏ 2809	Orleans/Traction in the Rain	1971	$5

CROSBY, EDDIE

DECCA

Number	Title	Yr	NM
❏ 9-46279	Feelin' Sorry/Tears of St. Anne	1950	$40
❏ 9-46287	Poor Beggar Boy/Be Good to Your Father and Mother	1951	$30
❏ 9-46333	Six Feet Deep/Meet Me at the Station	1951	$30

CROSBY, GARY

DECCA

Number	Title	Yr	NM
❏ 9-40181	A Crosby Christmas (Part 1)/A Crosby Christmas (Part 2)	1950	$40

—As "Gary, Phillip, Dennis, Lindsay and Bing Crosby

Number	Title	Yr	NM
❏ 9-29147	Call of the South/ Cornbelt Symphony	1954	$10

—As "Bing and Gary Crosby

Number	Title	Yr	NM
❏ 9-28955	Down By the Riverside/What a Little Moonlight Can Do	1953	$12

—As "Bing and Gary Crosby

Number	Title	Yr	NM
❏ 9-29779	Get a Load o' Me/Noah Found Grace in the Eyes of the Lord	1956	$10
❏ 9-29692	Give Me a Band and My Baby/Yaller Yaller Gold	1955	$15
❏ 9-29527	His and Hers/Truly Do	1955	$30

—With the Paris Sisters

Number	Title	Yr	NM
❏ 9-29921	Lazy Bones/Easy Street	1956	$15

—With Lous Armstrong

Number	Title	Yr	NM
❏ 9-29378	Loop-de-Loop Mambo/ Palsy Walsy	1954	$15
❏ 9-29272	Mambo in the Moonlight/ Got My Eyes on You	1954	$15
❏ 9-29538	Mississippi Pecan Pie/Ayuh, Ayuh	1955	$15
❏ 9-27577	Moonlight Bay/When You and I Were Young Maggie Blues	1951	$10

—As "Gary and Bing Crosby

Number	Title	Yr	NM
❏ 9-27112	Play a Simple Melody/Sam's Song	1950	$15

— By "Gary Crosby and Friend" (guess who the friend is)

GREGMARK

Number	Title	Yr	NM
❏ 11	That's Alright Baby/Who	1962	$40

HICKORY

Number	Title	Yr	NM
❏ 1448	I'm Gonna Call My Baby/Town Girl	1967	$10

VERVE

Number	Title	Yr	NM
❏ 10163	Sentimental Journey/After the Lights Go Down Low	1959	$20
❏ 10173	The Happy Bachelor/ This Little Girl of Mine	1959	$20

WARNER BROS.

Number	Title	Yr	NM
❏ 5208	Baby Won't You Please Come Home/You're Nobody 'Till Somebody Loves You	1961	$15

CROSBY, LINDSAY

ARIOLA AMERICA

Number	Title	Yr	NM
❏ 7682	Christmas Won't Be the Same/Old Friends of Mine	1977	$4
❏ 7682 [PS]	Christmas Won't Be the Same/Old Friends of Mine	1977	$8

DECCA

Number	Title	Yr	NM
❏ 27812	That's What I Want for Christmas/ Dear Mister Santa Claus	1951	$30

ERA

Number	Title	Yr	NM
❏ 3170	Christmas Won't Be the Same/Old Friends of Mine	1966	$10

CROSBY, STILLS AND NASH

Also see DAVID CROSBY; GRAHAM NASH; STEPHEN STILLS.

ATLANTIC

Number	Title	Yr	NM
❏ 3784	Carry On/Shadow Captain	1980	$5
❏ 3432	Fair Game/Anything at All	1977	$4
❏ 3453	I Give You Give Blind/ Carried Away	1978	$4
❏ 2652	Marrakesh Express/ Helplessly Hoping	1969	$6
❏ 89969	Southern Cross/Into the Darkness	1982	$3
❏ 89969 [PS]	Southern Cross/Into the Darkness	1982	$4
❏ 2676	Suite: Judy Blue Eyes/ Long Time Gone	1969	$6
❏ 89888	Too Much Love to Hide/ Song for Susan	1983	$3
❏ 89812	War Games/Shadow Captain	1983	$3
❏ 89812 [PS]	War Games/Shadow Captain	1983	$4
❏ 4058	Wasted on the Way/Delta	1982	$3
❏ 4058 [PS]	Wasted on the Way/Delta	1982	$4

CROSBY, STILLS, NASH & YOUNG

Also see DAVID CROSBY; GRAHAM NASH; STEPHEN STILLS; NEIL YOUNG.

ATLANTIC

Number	Title	Yr	NM
❏ 89003	American Dream/Compass	1988	$3
❏ 89003 [PS]	American Dream/Compass	1988	$3
❏ 88966	Got It Made/This Old House	1989	$3
❏ 88966 [PS]	Got It Made/This Old House	1989	$3
❏ 2740	Ohio/Find the Cost of Freedom	1970	$6
❏ 2740 [PS]	Ohio/Find the Cost of Freedom	1970	$15
❏ 2760	Our House/Deja Vu	1970	$6
❏ 2735	Teach Your Children/Carry On	1970	$6
❏ 2723	Woodstock/Helpless	1970	$6

CROSS, CHRISTOPHER

ARISTA

Number	Title	Yr	NM
❏ 9530	Loving Strangers/ Seven Summers	1986	$3

—B-side by Cruzados

Number	Title	Yr	NM
❏ 9530 [PS]	Loving Strangers/ Seven Summers	1986	$3

COLUMBIA

Number	Title	Yr	NM
❏ 38-04492	A Chance for Heaven/ Talking in My Sleep	1984	$3
❏ 38-04492 [PS]	A Chance for Heaven/ Talking in My Sleep	1984	$4

REPRISE

Number	Title	Yr	NM
❏ 7-27795	I Will (Take You Forever)/ Just One Look	1988	$3

—With Frances Ruffelle

Number	Title	Yr	NM
❏ 7-27795 [PS]	I Will (Take You Forever)/ Just One Look	1988	$3
❏ 7-27673	Swept Away ("Growing Pains" Aloha Show Theme)/ (B-side unknown)	1989	$3
❏ 7-27673 [PS]	Swept Away ("Growing Pains" Aloha Show Theme)/ (B-side unknown)	1989	$4

WARNER BROS.

Number	Title	Yr	NM
❏ 29843	All Right/Long World	1983	$4
❏ 29843 [PS]	All Right/Long World	1983	$4
❏ 49787	Arthur's Theme (Best That You Can Do)/Minstrel Gigolo	1981	$4
❏ 49787 [PS]	Arthur's Theme (Best That You Can Do)/Minstrel Gigolo	1981	$5
❏ 28864	Charm the Snake/ Open Your Heart	1985	$3
❏ 28864 [PS]	Charm the Snake/ Open Your Heart	1985	$3
❏ 28804	Every Turn of the World/ Open Your Heart	1986	$3
❏ 28761	Love Is Love (In Any Language)/Love Found a Home	1986	$3
❏ 49507	Sailing/Poor Shirley	1980	$4
❏ 49705	Say You'll Be Mine/Spinning	1981	$4
❏ 29658	Think of Laura/ Words of Wisdom	1983	$4

CROSS COUNTRY

ATCO

Number	Title	Yr	NM
❏ 6934	In the Midnight Hour/ The Smile Song	1973	$8
❏ 6947	Tastes So Good to Me/A Ball Song	1973	$8

CROSS, JIMMY

CHICKEN

Number	Title	Yr	NM
❏ 101	Hey Little Girl/Hey Little Girl (Part 2)	1966	$15

RECORDO

Number	Title	Yr	NM
❏ 502	Pretty Girls Everywhere/ Suntan Sally	1961	$20

RED BIRD

Number	Title	Yr	NM
❏ Oct-0042	Hey Little Girl/Super Duper Man	1965	$20

TOLLIE

Number	Title	Yr	NM
❏ 9039	I Want My Baby Back/ Play the Other Side	1965	$30
❏ 9044	The Ballad of James Bong/ Play the Other Side Again	1965	$20

CROSSFIRES, THE (1)

CAPCO

Number	Title	Yr	NM
❏ 104	Fiberglass Jungle/Dr. Jekyll and Mr. Hyde	1963	$100

LUCKY TOKEN

Number	Title	Yr	NM
❏ 112	One Potato, Two Potato/ That'll Be the Day	1965	$60

CROSSFIRES, THE (4)

TOWER

Number	Title	Yr	NM
❏ 278	Who'll Be the Next One/ Making Love Is Fun	1966	$30

CROW

BLACK SABBATH's first single was a cover of this band's "Evil Woman."

AMARET

Number	Title	Yr	NM
❏ 106	Busy Day/Time to Make a Turn	1969	$6
❏ 119	Cottage Cheese/Busy Day	1970	$6
❏ 119	Cottage Cheese/Slow Down	1970	$6
❏ 125	Don't Try to Lay No Boogie-Woogie on the "King of Rock 'n' Roll"/Satisfied	1970	$6
❏ 145	Everything Has Got to Be Free/Mobile Blues	1972	$5
❏ 112	Evil Woman Don't Play Your Games with Me/ Gonna Leave a Mark	1969	$8
❏ 148	If It Feels Good, Do It/ Cado Queen	1972	$5
❏ 133	Something in Your Blood/Yellow Dawg	1971	$5
❏ 129	Watching Can Waste Up the Time/Yellow Dawg	1971	$5

CROWDED HOUSE

CAPITOL

Number	Title	Yr	NM
❏ B-44164	Better Be Home Soon/Kill Eye	1988	$3
❏ B-44164 [PS]	Better Be Home Soon/Kill Eye	1988	$3
❏ B-5614	Don't Dream It's Over/ That's What I Call Love	1986	$3
❏ B-5614 [PS]	Don't Dream It's Over/ That's What I Call Love	1986	$5
❏ 7PRO-79653 [DJ]	I Feel Possessed (same on both sides)	1989	$6

— Vinyl version appears to be promo-only

Number	Title	Yr	NM
❏ 7PRO-79653	I Feel Possessed (same on both sides)	1989	$6

— 7-inch vinyl is promo only

Number	Title	Yr	NM
❏ B-44226	Into Temptation/Better Be Home Soon	1988	$3
❏ B-44226 [PS]	Into Temptation/Better Be Home Soon	1988	$3
❏ 7PRO-79440	Into Temptation (Fade)/ (LP Version)	1988	$6

—Promo only number

Number	Title	Yr	NM
❏ B-5695	Something So Strong/I Walk Away	1987	$3
❏ B-5695 [PS]	Something So Strong/I Walk Away	1987	$3
❏ B-44033	World Where You Live/ Hole in the River	1987	$3
❏ B-44033 [PS]	World Where You Live/ Hole in the River	1987	$3

CROWELL, RODNEY

COLUMBIA

Number	Title	Yr	NM
❏ 38-68948	Above and Beyond/ She Loves the Jerk	1989	$3
❏ 38-68585	After All This Time/ Oh King Richard	1989	$4

—Originals were pressed on styrene (record appears translucent dark red when held to a light)

Number	Title	Yr	NM
❏ 38-07918	I Couldn't Leave You If I Tried/ The Blue Hour Comes	1988	$3
❏ 38-07693	It's Such a Small World/ Crazy Baby	1988	$3

—A-side: With Roseanne Cash

Number	Title	Yr	NM
❏ 38-06102	Let Freedom Ring/ The Best I Can	1986	$3
❏ 38-07137	Looking for You/Stay (Don't Be Cruel)	1987	$3
❏ 38-73042	Many a Long & Lonesome Highway/I Know You're Married	1989	$3
❏ 38-06584	She Loves the Jerk/ Passed Like a Mask	1987	$3

Number	Title	Yr	NM
❏ 38-08080	She's Crazy for Leavin'/Brand New Rag	1988	$3
❏ 38-06415	When I'm Free Again/The Best I Can	1986	$3

WARNER BROS.

Number	Title	Yr	NM
❏ 49535	Ain't No Money/One About England	1980	$4
❏ 49224	Ashes By Now/Blues in the Daytime	1980	$5
❏ 8637	Elvira/Ashes By Now	1978	$5
❏ 49591	Heartbroke/Here Come the 80's	1980	$4
❏ 8693	Song for the Life/Baby, Better Start Turnin' 'Em Down	1978	$5
❏ 49810	Stars on the Water/Don't Need No Other Now	1981	$4

CROWLEY, J.C.

RCA

Number	Title	Yr	NM
❏ 9012-7-R	Beneath the Texas Moon/Living for the Fire	1989	$3
❏ 8634-7-R	Boxcar 109/Living for the Fire	1988	$3
❏ 8822-7-R	I Know What I've Got/Living for the Fire	1989	$3
❏ 8747-7-R	Paint the Town and Hang the Moon Tonight/Serenade	1988	$3

CROWN, BOBBY

FELCO

Number	Title	Yr	NM
❏ 102	One Way Ticket/Your Conscience	1960	$800

MANCO

Number	Title	Yr	NM
❏ 1005	I've Never Had a Broken Heart/Wait a Minute	1960	$50

CROWN HEIGHTS AFFAIR

DE-LITE

Number	Title	Yr	NM
❏ 912	Dance Lady Dance/Come Fly with Me	1979	$4
❏ 1588	Dancin'/Love Me	1976	$4
❏ 1592	Do It the French Way/Sexy Ways	1977	$4
❏ 1592 [PS]	Do It the French Way/Sexy Ways	1977	$6
❏ 1570	Dreaming a Dream/Dreaming a Dream (Part 2)	1975	$4
❏ 915	Empty Soul of Mine/Rock Is Hot	1979	$4
❏ 1575	Every Beat of My Heart/Every Beat of My Heart (Disco Version)	1975	$4
❏ 1581	Foxy Lady/Picture Show	1976	$4
❏ 911	I Love You/Dream World	1978	$4
❏ 823	Let Me Ride on the Wave of Your Love/Wine and Dine You	1982	$4
❏ 908	Say a Prayer for Two/Galaxy of Love	1978	$4
❏ 821	Somebody Tell Me What to Do/You Gave Me Love	1982	$4
❏ 805	Sure Shot/I See the Light	1980	$4

RCA VICTOR

Number	Title	Yr	NM
❏ APBO-0243	Leave the Kids Alone/Rip-Off	1974	$5
❏ PB-10018	Special Kind of Woman/Streaking	1974	$5
❏ APBO-0023	Super Rod (Part 1)/Super Rod (Part 2)	1973	$5

CROWNS, THE (1)

CHORDETTE

Number	Title	Yr	NM
❏ 1001	Party Time/Amazon Basin Pop	1962	$30

CROWNS, THE (2)

OLD TOWN

Number	Title	Yr	NM
❏ 1171	Possibility/Watch Out	1964	$50

— *Old light blue Old Town label*

❏ 1171	Possibility/Watch Out	1964	$20

— *Black label with moon*

CROWNS, THE (4)

VEE JAY

Number	Title	Yr	NM
❏ 546	Better Luck Next Time/You Make Me Blue	1963	$20

CROWS, THE

RAMA

Number	Title	Yr	NM
❏ 50	Baby Doll/Sweet Sue (It's You)	1954	$400
❏ 29	Baby/Untrue	1954	$200
❏ 5	Gee/I Love You So	1953	$75

— *Blue label, black vinyl*

❏ 5	Gee/I Love You So	1953	$400

— *Blue label, red vinyl*

❏ 5	Gee/I Love You So	1955	$40

— *Red label, black vinyl*

❏ 10	Heartbreaker/Call a Doctor	1953	$400

— *Black vinyl*

❏ 10	Heartbreaker/Call a Doctor	1953	$800

— *Red vinyl*

❏ 10	Heartbreaker/Call a Doctor	1953	$600

— *Black vinyl, label says "The Jewels"*

Number	Title	Yr	NM
❏ 10	Heartbreaker/Call a Doctor	1953	$600

— *Black vinyl, label says "The Jewels" on one side, "The Crows" on the other*

❏ 10	Heartbreaker/Call a Doctor	1953	$1200

— *Red vinyl; label says "The Jewels*

❏ 30	Miss You/I Really, Really Love You So	1954	$400

— *Black vinyl*

❏ 30	Miss You/I Really, Really Love You So	1954	$1000

— *Red vinyl*

❏ 3	Seven Lonely Days/No Help Wanted	1953	$500

TICO

Number	Title	Yr	NM
❏ 1082	Mambo Shevitz/Mambo #5	1955	$200

— *B-side by Melino and Orchestra; black vinyl*

❏ 1082	Mambo Shevitz/Mambo #5	1955	$300

— *B-side by Melino and Orchestra; red vinyl*

CRUDUP, ARTHUR

ACE

Number	Title	Yr	NM
❏ 503	I Wonder/My Baby Boogies All the Time	1955	$200

GROOVE

Number	Title	Yr	NM
❏ 011	I Love My Baby/Fall on Your Knees and Pray	1954	$50
❏ 026	She's Got No Hair/If You Ever Been to Georgia	1954	$50

RCA VICTOR

Number	Title	Yr	NM
❏ 50-0001	Boy Friend Blues/Katie May	1949	$125

— *Gray label, orange vinyl*

❏ 50-0046	Come Back Baby/Mercy Blues	1949	$125

— *Gray label, orange vinyl*

❏ 50-0074	Dust My Broom/You Know That I Love You	1950	$125

— *Gray label, orange vinyl*

❏ 47-4572	Goin' Back to Georgia/Mr. So and So	1952	$100
❏ 50-0032	Hoodoo Lady Blues/Tired of Worry	1949	$125

— *Gray label, orange vinyl*

❏ 50-0141	I'm Gonna Dig Myself a Hole/Too Much Competition	1951	$125

— *Gray label, black vinyl*

❏ 50-0100	Lonesome World to Me/Hand Me Down My Walking Cane	1950	$125

— *Gray label, orange vinyl*

❏ 47-5070	Lookin' for My Baby/Pearly Lee	1952	$100
❏ 47-4367	Love Me Mama/Where Did You Stay Last Night	1951	$125
❏ 50-0092	Mean Old Santa Fe/Oo Wee Baby	1950	$125

— *Gray label, orange vinyl*

❏ 50-0109	My Baby Left Me/Anytime Is the Right Time	1951	$200

— *Gray label, orange vinyl*

❏ 22-0109	My Baby Left Me/Anytime Is the Right Time	1951	$100
❏ 47-4933	Second Man Blues/Do It If You Want	1952	$100
❏ 50-0105	She's Just Like Caldonia/(B-side unknown)	1951	$125

— *Gray label, orange vinyl*

❏ 50-0013	Shout Sister Shout/Crudup's Vicksburg Blues	1949	$125

— *Gray label, orange vinyl*

❏ 50-0000	That's All Right/Crudup's After Hours	1949	$400

— *Gray label, orange vinyl; the first R&B 45 rpm record!*

❏ 47-5563	War Is Over/My Wife and Woman	1953	$100
❏ 47-4753	Worried 'Bout You Baby/Late in the Evening	1952	$100

CRUSADERS, THE (1)

ABC BLUE THUMB

Number	Title	Yr	NM
❏ 270	And Then There Was the Blues/Feeling Funky	1976	$5
❏ 278	Bayou Bottoms/Covert Action	1978	$5
❏ 267	Creole/I Feel the Love	1975	$5
❏ 272	Feel It/The Way We Was	1977	$5
❏ 273	Free as the Wind/The Way We Was	1977	$5
❏ 261	Stomp and Buck Dance/A Ballad for Joe (Louis)	1975	$5

BLUE THUMB

Number	Title	Yr	NM
❏ 225	Don't Let It Get You Down/Journey from Within	1973	$5
❏ 245	Lay It On the Line/Let's Boogie	1974	$5
❏ 208	Put It Where You Want It/Mosadi	1972	$5
❏ 249	Scratch/Way Back Home	1974	$5
❏ 217	So Far Away/That's How I Feel	1972	$5
❏ 232	Take It or Leave It/That's How I Feel	1973	$5

CHISA

Number	Title	Yr	NM
❏ 8013	Pass the Plate/Greasy Spoon	1971	$6
❏ 8010	Way Back Home/Jackson	1970	$6

— *As "Jazz Crusaders"*

MCA

Number	Title	Yr	NM
❏ 53330	A.C. (Alternating Currents)/Mulholland Nights	1988	$3
❏ 52398	Dream Street/Dead End	1984	$4
❏ 52454	Gotta Lotta Shakalada/Zalal 'E Mini	1984	$4
❏ 51177	I'm So Glad I'm Standing Here Today/Standing Tall	1981	$4

— *A-side with Joe Cocker*

❏ 51029	Last Call/Honky Tonk Struttin'	1980	$4
❏ 41054	Street Life/Hustler	1979	$4
❏ 52098	Street Life/Overture	1982	$4

— *With B.B. King and the London Symphony Orchestra*

❏ 41295	Sweet Gentle Love/Soul Shadows	1980	$4
❏ 52966	The Way It Goes/Good Times	1986	$4
❏ 51222	This Old World's Too Funky for Me/Standing Tall	1981	$4

— *A-side with Joe Cocker*

❏ 51222 [PS]	This Old World's Too Funky for Me/Standing Tall	1981	$10

— *Promo-only sleeve with only the record number (neither title) and the following: "Happy Thanksgiving. If you're expecting a turkey ... this isn't it. We have a lot to be thankful for thanks to you. The Crusaders*

MOWEST

Number	Title	Yr	NM
❏ 5028	Spanish Harlem/Papa Hooper's Barrelhouse Groove	1972	$6

PACIFIC JAZZ

Number	Title	Yr	NM
❏ 88144	Eleanor Rigby/Ooga Boogaloo	1968	$6
❏ 88153	Get Back/Willie and Laura Mae Jones	1969	$6
❏ 88146	Hey Jude/Love and Peace	1969	$6
❏ 340	Sinnin' Sam/Tonight	1962	$15

WORLD PACIFIC

Number	Title	Yr	NM
❏ 77806	Aqua Dulce/Soul Bourgeoise	1966	$8
❏ 388	Boopie/Turkish Black	1963	$10

— *As "Jazz Crusaders*

❏ 401	Heat Wave/On Broadway	1964	$12
❏ 412	I Remember Tomorrow/Long John	1964	$10
❏ 77800	The Thing/Tough Talk	1965	$8

CRUSADERS, THE (U)

CAMEO

Number	Title	Yr	NM
❏ 285	Boogie Woogie/At the Club	1963	$15

DKR

Number	Title	Yr	NM
❏ 0(no cat #)	Seminole/Busted Surfboard	1962	$50

DOOTO

Number	Title	Yr	NM
❏ 472	Swinging Week-End/I Found Someone	1963	$20

TOWER

Number	Title	Yr	NM
❏ 328	Make a Joyful Noise/Praise We the Lord	1967	$10
❏ 286	The Little Drummer Boy/Battle Hymn of the Republic	1966	$10

CRYAN' SHAMES, THE

COLUMBIA

Number	Title	Yr	NM
❏ 44759	First Train to California/A Master's Fool	1969	$8
❏ 44638	Greenburg, Blickstein, Charles, David Smith & Jones/The Warm	1968	$8
❏ 44191	It Could Be We're in Love/I Was Lonely When	1967	$10
❏ 44191 [PS]	It Could Be We're in Love/I Was Lonely When	1967	$30
❏ 43836	I Wanna Meet You/We Could Be Happy	1966	$10
❏ 44037	Mr. Unreliable/Georgia	1967	$10

DESTINATION

Number	Title	Yr	NM
❏ 624	Sugar and Spice/Ben Franklin's Almanac	1966	$20

CRYIN' SHAMES, THE

LONDON

Number	Title	Yr	NM
❏ 1001	What's New Pussycat/Please Stay (Don't Go)	1966	$10

CRYSTAL, BILLY

A&M

Number	Title	Yr	NM
❏ 2774	I Hate When That Happens/(B-side unknown)	1985	$5
❏ 2774 [PS]	I Hate When That Happens/(B-side unknown)	1985	$5
❏ 2795	The Christmas Song (5:22)/(3:33)	1985	$4
❏ 2795 [PS]	The Christmas Song/(Long Version)	1985	$5

CRYSTAL, RONETTE AND CHIFFON

GEFFEN

Number	Title	Yr	NM
❏ 7-28393	Little Shop of Horrors/Grow for Me	1987	$8

— *B-side by Rick Moranis*

Number	Title	Yr	NM

CRYSTALS, THE

PHILLES
❏ 111 [DJ]	(Let's Dance) The Screw -- Part 1/ (Let's Dance) The Screw -- Part 2	1963	$4000

— White label

❏ 111 [DJ]	(Let's Dance) The Screw -- Part 1/ (Let's Dance) The Screw -- Part 2	1963	$6000

— Light blue label. Matrix numbers are stamped in dead wax. Counterfeits have numbers hand-etched.

CRYSTALS, THE (1)

GUSTO
❏ 2090	Da Doo Ron Ron/ Then He Kissed Me	1979	$4

— Re-recordings

PHILLES
❏ 122	All Grown Up/Irving (Jaggered Sixteenths)	1964	$30

— Possible Rolling Stones involvement on instrumental B-side; "Jaggered" refers to Mick

❏ 112	Da Doo Ron Ron (When He Walked Me Home)/Git' It	1963	$40
❏ 105	He Hit Me (And It Felt Like a Kiss)/No One Ever Tells You	1962	$125
❏ 106	He's a Rebel/I Love You Eddie	1962	$70

— Orange label

❏ 106	He's a Rebel/I Love You Eddie	1962	$50

— Light blue label

❏ 106	He's a Rebel/I Love You Eddie	1964	$30

— Yellow and red label

❏ 109	He's Sure the Boy I Love/ Walkin' Along (La-La-La)	1962	$40
❏ 111 [DJ]	(Let's Dance) The Screw -- Part 1/ (Let's Dance) The Screw -- Part 2	1963	$4000

— White label; copies exist with the title as "Let's Dance The Screw" (no parentheses) also, with the same value as above. VG 2000; VG+ 3000

❏ 111	(Let's Dance) The Screw -- Part 1/ (Let's Dance) The Screw -- Part 2	1963	$6000

— Light blue label; no "D.J. Only Not for Sale" on label; "Audio Matrix" stamped in dead wax (counterfeits do not have this). VG 3000; VG+ 4500

❏ 119	Little Boy/Harry (From West Virginia) and Milt	1964	$30
❏ 119X	Little Boy/Harry (From West Virginia) and Milt	1964	$30
❏ 115	Then He Kissed Me/Brother Julius	1963	$50

— Light blue label

❏ 115	Then He Kissed Me/Brother Julius	1963	$30

— Yellow and red label

❏ 100	There's No Other (Like My Baby)/Oh Yeah, Maybe Baby	1961	$50

PHILLES/COLLECTABLES
❏ 3206	Da Doo Ron Ron/All Grown Up	1985	$6

— Gold vinyl; part of box set "Phil Spector Wall of Sound Series Vol. 1

❏ 3206	Da Doo Ron Ron/All Grown Up	1986	$5

— Black vinyl

❏ 3200	He's a Rebel/He Hit Me (And It Felt Like a Kiss)	1985	$6

— Red vinyl; part of box set "Phil Spector Wall of Sound Series Vol. 2

❏ 3200	He's a Rebel/He Hit Me (And It Felt Like a Kiss)	1986	$5

— Black vinyl

❏ 3201	Then He Kissed Me/ Puddin' and Tain	1985	$6

— Red vinyl; part of box set "Phil Spector Wall of Sound Series Vol. 2"; B-side by the Alley Cats

❏ 3201	Then He Kissed Me/ Puddin' and Tain	1986	$5

— Black vinyl

❏ 3204	There's No Other (Like My Baby)/ Not Too Young to Get Married	1985	$6

— Gold vinyl; part of box set "Phil Spector Wall of Sound Series Vol. 1"; B-side by Bob B. Soxx and the Blue Jeans

❏ 3204	There's No Other (Like My Baby)/ Not Too Young to Get Married	1986	$5

— Black vinyl; B-side by Bob B. Soxx and the Blue Jeans

UNITED ARTISTS
❏ 994	I Got a Man/Are You Trying to Get Rid of Me, Baby	1966	$20

CRYSTALS, THE (2)

ALADDIN
❏ 3355	I Love My Baby/I Do Believe	1957	$70

CRYSTALS, THE (3)

BRENT
❏ 7011	Malaguena/Gypsy Ribbon	1960	$20

CUB
❏ 9064	Oh My You/Watching You	1960	$20

INDIGO
❏ 114	Dreams and Wishes/Mr. Brush	1961	$30

METRO
❏ 20026	Better Come Back to Me/ That's Where I Belong	1960	$20

REGALIA
❏ 17	Pony in Dixie/Espresso	1961	$20

CRYSTALS, THE (4)

DELUXE
❏ 6013	Four Women/My Dear	1953	$2000
❏ 6077	God Only Knows/My Girl	1955	$200
❏ 6037	Have Faith in Me/My Love	1954	$2000

LUNA
❏ 100	Squeeze Me Baby/ Come to Me, Darling	1954	$400
❏ 5001	Squeeze Me Baby/ Come to Me, Darling	1954	$200

ROCKIN'
❏ 518	My Girl/Don't You Go	1953	$250

CRYSTALS, THE (5)

FELSTED
❏ 8566	Mary Ellen/Blind Date	1959	$30

SPECIALTY
❏ 657	In the Deep/Love You So	1959	$20

CUBY AND THE BLIZZARDS

PHILIPS
❏ 40685	Thursday Night/Going Home	1970	$8

CUES, THE

CAPITOL
❏ F3245	Burn That Candle/ Oh My Darling	1955	$30
❏ F3310	Charlie Brown/You're On My Mind	1956	$30
❏ F3400	Destination 2100 and 65/ Don't Make Believe	1956	$30
❏ F3483	The Girl I Love/Crackerjack	1956	$30
❏ F3582	Why/Prince or Pauper	1956	$30

JUBILEE
❏ 5201	Only You/I Feel for Your Loving	1955	$30

LAMP
❏ 8007	Forty 'Leven Dozen Ways/ Scoochie Scoochie	1954	$30

PREP
❏ 104	I Pretend/Crazy, Crazy Party	1957	$30

CUFF LINKS, THE (1)

ATCO
❏ 6867	Sandi/The Oke-Fen-Okee Electric Harmonica Band	1972	$5

DECCA
❏ 32791	All Because of You/ Wake Up Judy	1971	$5
❏ 32687	Lay a Little Love on Me/ Robin's World	1970	$5
❏ 32732	Thank You Pretty Baby/Kiss	1970	$5
❏ 32533	Tracy/Where Do You Go	1969	$6
❏ 32533 [PS]	Tracy/Where Do You Go	1969	$30

— Three-piece gatefold sleeve

❏ 32592	When Julie Comes Around/Sally Ann	1969	$5

CUFF LINKS, THE (2)

DOOTO
❏ 474	Changing My Love/I Don't Want Nobody	1963	$30
❏ 409	Guided Missiles/My Heart	1957	$100
❏ 413	How You Lied/The Winner	1957	$50
❏ 422	It's Too Late Now/ Saxophone Rag	1957	$60
❏ 414	Twinkle/One Day Blues	1957	$50

DOOTONE
❏ 409	Guided Missiles/My Heart	1956	$200

CUGAT, XAVIER

RCA VICTOR
❏ 947-0014	Gypsy Airs/Caminito// Medias de Seda/Tina	1952	$15

— Part of 2-EP set EPBT 3022

❏ EPBT3022 [PS]	Tangos	1952	$15

— Gatefold cover for 2-EP set (947-0013, 947-0014)

CULLEY, FRANK "FLOORSHOW

BATON
❏ 226	After Hours Express (Part 1)/(Part 2)	1956	$50

CULMER, LITTLE IRIS, AND THE MAJESTICS

MARLIN
❏ 803	Frankie, My Eyes Are On You/(B-side unknown)	1957	$2500

— VG 1000; VG+ 1500

CULT, THE
Features Billy Duffy and Ian Astbury.

SIRE
❏ 22873	Edie (Ciao Baby)/Love Removal Machine	1989	$3
❏ 27543	Fire Woman/Automatic Blues	1989	$3
❏ 27543 [PS]	Fire Woman/Automatic Blues	1989	$3
❏ 28290	Lil' Devil/Memphis Hip Shake	1987	$4
❏ 28290 [PS]	Lil' Devil/Memphis Hip Shake	1987	$4
❏ 28820	She Sells Sanctuary/Little Face	1986	$5
❏ 28213	Wildflower/Love Trooper	1987	$4
❏ 28213 [PS]	Wildflower/Love Trooper	1987	$15

— Fold-open poster sleeve

CULTURE CLUB

EPIC
❏ 34-04144 [PS]	Church of the Poison Mind	1983	$8

— Demonstration -- Not for Sale" on back of sleeve

❏ 34-04144	Church of the Poison Mind/Mystery Boy	1983	$3
❏ 34-04144 [PS]	Church of the Poison Mind/Mystery Boy	1983	$3
❏ ENR-03531	Do You Really Want to Hurt Me/(B-side blank)	1983	$8

— One-sided budget release

❏ AE71591 [DJ]	Do You Really Want to Hurt Me (edited intro)/Do You Really Want to Hurt Me (no intro)	1982	$8
❏ AE71591 [DJ]	Do You Really Want to Hurt Me (edited intro)/(no intro)	1982	$12
❏ 34-03368	Do You Really Want to Hurt Me/You Know I'm Not Crazy	1982	$3
❏ 34-03912	I'll Tumble 4 Ya/Mystery Boy	1983	$3
❏ 34-03912 [PS]	I'll Tumble 4 Ya/Mystery Boy	1983	$3
❏ 34-03796	Time (Clock of the Heart)/ Romance Beyond the Alphabet	1983	$3
❏ 34-03796 [PS]	Time (Clock of the Heart)/ Romance Beyond the Alphabet	1983	$10

VIRGIN/EPIC
❏ 15-08436	Church of the Poison Mind/Do You Really Want to Hurt Me	1988	$3

— Reissue

❏ 34-06133	Gusto Blusto/From Luxury to Heartache	1986	$3
❏ 34-06133 [PS]	Gusto Blusto/From Luxury to Heartache	1986	$3
❏ 34-04457	It's a Miracle/Love Twist	1984	$3
❏ 34-04457 [PS]	It's a Miracle/Love Twist	1984	$3
❏ 34-04388	Miss Me Blind/Colour By Numbers	1984	$3
❏ 34-04388 [PS]	Miss Me Blind/Colour By Numbers	1984	$3
❏ 34-04727	Mistake No. 3/Don't Go Down That Street	1984	$3
❏ 34-05847	Move Away/Sexuality	1986	$3
❏ 34-05847 [PS]	Move Away/Sexuality	1986	$3
❏ 34-04638	The War Song/La Cancion de Guerra	1984	$3
❏ 34-04638 [PS]	The War Song/La Cancion de Guerra	1984	$3

CUMMINGS, BARBARA

LONDON
❏ 109	A Good Guy Like You/Love's on Duty (24 Hours a Day)	1967	$10
❏ 104	She's the Woman/There's Something Funny Going On	1966	$10
❏ 117	Three Little Fools/Anything She'll Do for You (I'll Do Better)	1967	$10

CUMMINGS, BURTON

ALFA
❏ 7014	Mother, Keep Your Daughters In/Someone to Lean On	1982	$5

PORTRAIT
❏ 6-70016	Break It To Them Gently/ Roll with the Punches	1978	$5
❏ 6-70016 [PS]	Break It To Them Gently/ Roll with the Punches	1978	$8
❏ 6-70002	I'm Scared/Sugartime Flashback Joys	1977	$5
❏ 6-70007	My Own Way to Rock/A Song for Him	1977	$5
❏ 6-70001	Stand Tall/Burch Magic	1976	$5
❏ 17-8100	Stand Tall/Takes a Fool to Love a Fool	1981	$4

— Reissue

❏ 6-70024	Takes a Fool to Love a Fool/I Will Play a Rhapsody	1978	$5

Number	Title	Yr	NM

CUNHA, RICK
COLUMBIA
| ❏ 3-10174 | Best Friends/Moving Picture Theme | 1975 | $4 |

GRC
| ❏ 2028 | I'm Ashamed/Jesse James (Is an Outlaw, Honey) | 1974 | $5 |
| ❏ 2016 | (I'm a) Yo Yo Man/Wild Side of Life | 1974 | $5 |

CUNNINGHAM, J.C.
CAPITOL
| ❏ 3489 | I Can Feel the Heartache Comin' On/You Take the Blame for the Roses | 1972 | $8 |

—As "Johnny Cunningham
| ❏ 3686 | Wonder What I'm Doin' in Tennessee/Over and Over Again | 1973 | $8 |

—As "Collins Cunningham
SCOTTI BROTHERS
| ❏ 601 | The Pyramid Song/I'm a Lover Not a Fighter | 1980 | $4 |

VIVA
❏ 29220	Heaven Ain't What It Used to Be/Body Talk	1984	$4
❏ 29311	Light Up/The Greatest Love	1984	$4
❏ 29168	Love Was Made to Be Made/If It Hadn't Been for Planes	1984	$4
❏ 29108	Settin' the Night on Fire/You Better Run to Him	1985	$4

CUNTS
DISTURBING
❏ 38400	Apocalyptic Breakfast/Turn of the Night	1984	$20
❏ 38400 [PS]	Apocalyptic Breakfast/Turn of the Night	1984	$20
❏ 111678	Chemicals in the Mall/Why Do You Live on My Block	1978	$40
❏ 111678 [PS]	Chemicals in the Mall/Why Do You Live on My Block	1978	$40
❏ 31783	Open Your Mind/Musician in a Bathtub	1983	$20
❏ 31783 [PS]	Open Your Mind/Musician in a Bathtub	1983	$20
❏ 112281	There Are Electrical Filaments in My Hamburger/A Date with Disaster	1982	$10

— Version 1: Green label
| ❏ 112281 [PS] | There Are Electrical Filaments in My Hamburger/A Date with Disaster | 1982 | $20 |

— Version 1: White background, three-piece photocopy art
| ❏ 112281 [PS] | There Are Electrical Filaments in My Hamburger/A Date with Disaster | 1982 | $30 |

— Version 1A: Same as above, two extra pieces of "art
| ❏ 112281 [PS] | There Are Electrical Filaments in My Hamburger/A Date with Disaster | 1982 | $10 |

— Version 2: Gray pattern background folder sleeve
| ❏ 112281 | There Are Electrical Filaments in My Hamburger/A Date with Disaster | 1982 | $10 |

— Version 2: Black labels
| ❏ 112281 | There Are Electrical Filaments in My Hamburger/A Date with Disaster | 1982 | $10 |

— Version 3: Yellow labels
| ❏ 112281 [PS] | There Are Electrical Filaments in My Hamburger/A Date with Disaster | 1982 | $10 |

— Version 3: White background, photo of band on back
| ❏ 81480 | We're Going to Crash/Penguins Addicted to Molasses | 1980 | $30 |
| ❏ 81480 [PS] | We're Going to Crash/Penguins Addicted to Molasses | 1980 | $30 |

CUPID'S INSPIRATION
BELL
| ❏ 818 | Look at Me/Sad Thing | 1969 | $8 |
DATE
| ❏ 2-1674 | Sunshine/Are You Growing Tired of My Love | 1970 | $8 |

CUPIDS, THE (1)
AANKO
| ❏ 1002 | Brenda/For You | 1963 | $125 |
KC
| ❏ 115 | Brenda/For You | 1963 | $60 |

CUPIDS, THE (3)
DECCA
| ❏ 30279 | The Answer to Your Prayer/My Dog Likes Your Dog | 1957 | $50 |

CUPIDS, THE (U)
CHAN
| ❏ 107 | I Don't Know/Troubles Not At End | 1956 | $100 |
MUSICNOTE
| ❏ 119 | Lorraine/Little Girl of Mine | 1963 | $20 |
TIMES SQUARE
| ❏ 1 | Pretty Baby/Let's Rock | 1964 | $20 |
UWR
| ❏ 4241/2 | True Love, True Love/Let's Twist | 1962 | $50 |

CURB, MIKE
BUENA VISTA
| ❏ 499 | Mickey Mouse March/Mickey Mouse Alma Mater | 1974 | $5 |

—B-side by Jimmy Dodd and the Mouseketeers
| ❏ 499 [PS] | Mickey Mouse March/Mickey Mouse Alma Mater | 1974 | $8 |
| ❏ 494 | Winnie the Pooh/Zip-a-Dee-Doo-Dah | 1973 | $5 |

CAPITOL
❏ 4166	Fools Rush In (Where Angels Fear to Tread)/Do You Wanna Dance	1975	$4
❏ 4102	Mickey Mouse March/You Were On My Mind	1975	$4
❏ 4054	Po'r Folk/You Were On My Mind	1975	$4

FORWARD
| ❏ 124 | Bandstand Theme/Oh, Calcutta | 1970 | $5 |
| ❏ 124 [PS] | Bandstand Theme/Oh, Calcutta | 1970 | $12 |

— Called "The New Bandstand Theme" on sleeve
MGM
❏ 14151	Burning Bridges/We'll Sing in the Sunshine	1970	$4
❏ 14366	I Saw the Light/Take Up the Hammer of Hope	1972	$4
❏ 14494	It's a Small, Small World/Shinin' on Me	1973	$4
❏ 14243	I Was Born in Love with You/Sweet Gingerbread Man	1971	$4
❏ 14110	Long Haired Lover from Liverpool/Sweet Gingerbread Man	1970	$4
❏ 14336	Softly Whispering I Love You/Forty Days and Forty Nights	1971	$4
❏ 14265	Sweet Gingerbread Man/Fly Me a Place for the Summer	1971	$4
❏ 14442	This Land Is Your Land/I Understand	1972	$4

REPRISE
| ❏ 0287 | Hot Dawg/Velocita | 1964 | $30 |
TOWER
| ❏ 480 | Let's Go/Eight Young Me (The Devil's Theme) | 1969 | $8 |
| ❏ 202 | Sunshine/Suzie Darling | 1966 | $10 |
WARNER BROS.
| ❏ 8463 | Cotton Fields/Dance On, Maria | 1977 | $4 |

CURE, THE
ELEKTRA
❏ 69551	Close to Me/Sinking	1986	$8
❏ 69300	Fascination Street/Babble	1989	$4
❏ 69300 [PS]	Fascination Street/Babble	1989	$4
❏ 69424	Hot Hot Hot!!!/Hey You!!!	1988	$4
❏ 69424 [PS]	Hot Hot Hot!!!/Hey You!!!	1988	$5
❏ 69604	In Between Days (Without You)/Stop Dead	1985	$5
❏ 69604 [PS]	In Between Days (Without You)/Stop Dead	1985	$6
❏ 69537	Let's Go to Bed/Boys Don't Cry	1986	$6
❏ 69280	Love Song/2 Late	1989	$3

—First pressing: Red and black label
| ❏ 69280 | Love Song/2 Late | 1989 | $5 |

— Second pressing: Gray label
❏ 69249	Lullaby/Homesick	1989	$5
❏ 69474	Why Can't I Be You?/Japanese Dream	1987	$5
❏ 69474 [PS]	Why Can't I Be You?/Japanese Dream	1987	$5

SIRE
❏ PRO02022 [DJ]	Let's Go to Bed (same on both sides)	1983	$30
❏ PRO-S-2022 [DJ]	Let's Go to Bed (stereo/mono)	1983	$30
❏ 29376	The Love Cats/Speak My Language	1984	$10
❏ 29490	The Walk/The Dream	1983	$10

CURIOSITY KILLED THE CAT
MERCURY
❏ 888167-7	Down to Earth/(Instrumental)	1986	$4
❏ 888167-7 [PS]	Down to Earth/(Instrumental)	1986	$4
❏ 888674-7	Misfit/Man	1987	$3
❏ 888674-7 [PS]	Misfit/Man	1987	$3
❏ 870101-7	Ordinary Day/Bullet	1987	$4
❏ 870101-7 [PS]	Ordinary Day/Bullet	1987	$4

CURLESS, DICK, AND KAY ADAMS
TOWER
| ❏ 226 | A Devil Like Me (Needs an Angel Like You)/No Fool Like an Old Fool | 1966 | $20 |

CURLESS, DICK
ALLAGASH
| ❏ 101 | A Tombstone Every Mile/Heart Talk | 1964 | $30 |
CAPITOL
❏ 3879	A Brand New Bed of Roses/Pinch o' Powder	1974	$6
❏ 2780	Big Wheel Cannonball/I Miss a Lot of Trains	1970	$8
❏ 3541	Chick Inspector (That's Where My Money Goes)/Travelin' Light	1973	$6
❏ 3630	China Nights (Shina No Yoru)/Old Bob Burton	1973	$6
❏ 2949	Drag 'Em Off the Interstate, Sock It to 'Em, J.P. Blues/Drop Some Silver in the Juke Box	1970	$8
❏ 2848	Hard, Hard Travelin' Man/Winter's Comin' On Again	1970	$8
❏ 3105	Loser's Cocktail/Hot Springs	1971	$8
❏ 3470	She Called Me Baby/Wait a Little Longer	1972	$8
❏ 3182	Snap Your Fingers/Bully of the Town	1971	$8
❏ 3354	Stonin' Around/For the Life of Me	1972	$8
❏ 3818	Swingin' Preacher/Get on Board My Wagon	1974	$6
❏ 3698	The Last Blues Song/Room Full of Roses	1973	$6

TOWER
❏ 444	All I Need Is You/Tears Instead of Cheers	1968	$15
❏ 306	All of Me Belongs to You/My Side of the Night	1967	$15
❏ 124	A Tombstone Every Mile/Heart Talk	1965	$20
❏ 362	Big Foot/Tornado Tillie	1967	$15
❏ 399	Bury the Bottle with Me/Bummin' on Track "E	1968	$15
❏ 219	Highway Man/Please Don't Make Me Go	1966	$20
❏ 335	House of Memories/Standing on the Outside Looking In	1967	$15
❏ 415	I Ain't Got Nobody/Shoes	1968	$15
❏ 135	Six Times a Day (The Trains Came Down)/Down by the Old River	1965	$20
❏ 161	'Tater Raisin' Man/The Friend Who Makes It Four	1965	$20
❏ 255	The Baron/A Good Job-Huntin' and Fishin'	1966	$20
❏ 255 [PS]	The Baron/A Good Job-Huntin' and Fishin'	1966	$30
❏ 193	Travelin' Man/Rocky Mountain Queen	1965	$20
❏ 471	Wild Side of Town/The Secret of Your Heart	1969	$15

CURLEY AND THE JADES
MUSIC MAKERS
| ❏ 109 | Bullfighter/Boom Stix | 1962 | $70 |
REPRISE
| ❏ 20046 | Bullfighter/Boom Stix | 1962 | $40 |

CURREY, DIANA SICILY
CONDOR
| ❏ 13 | Longneck Lone Star (And Two Step Dancin')/(B-side unknown) | 1989 | $6 |

CURRIE, CHERIE AND MARIE
Lead singer of the RUNAWAYS, plus her sister.
CAPITOL
❏ 4861	All I Want/Messin' with the Boys	1980	$5
❏ 4841	Secrets/This Time	1980	$5
❏ 4754	Since You've Been Gone/Longer Than Forever	1979	$5
❏ 4754 [PS]	Since You've Been Gone/Longer Than Forever	1979	$10

Number	Title	Yr	NM
CURTIS, EDDIE			
ABC-PARAMOUNT			
❏ 10378	Ding Bat/I Came a Long Way	1962	$12
DECCA			
❏ 31395	Gee, But I Wish You Were Home/I Was Here When You Came (And I'll Be Here When You're Gone)	1962	$10
GEE			
❏ 7	Candy Man/The Girl I Left Behind	1954	$50
—As "Eddie 'Tex' Curtis"			
❏ 9	Prayer to the Moon/Shake, Pretty Baby, Shake	1954	$50
—As "Eddie 'Tex' Curtis"			
JOSIE			
❏ 957	Those Foxes and Pussycats (Part 1)/(Part 2)	1966	$10
OKEH			
❏ 7063	Sweet Stuff/I Didn't Wanna Love You	1955	$40
—As "Eddie 'Tex' Curtis"			
PARKWAY			
❏ 825	Let It Live/How Long Will It Last	1961	$30
CURTIS, LARRY			
SCRIMSHAW			
❏ 1315	It Feels Like Love for the First Time/(B-side unknown)	1978	$8
CURTIS, MAC			
EPIC			
❏ 10438	Almost Persuaded/The Friendly City	1969	$6
❏ 10530	Don't Make Love/Us	1969	$6
❏ 10468	Happiness Lives in This House/Little Ole Wine Drinker Me	1969	$6
❏ 10574	Honey Don't/Today's Teardrops	1970	$6
❏ 10385	The Sunshine Man/It's My Way	1968	$6
❏ 10257	Too Close to Home/Too Good to Be True	1967	$6
FELSTED			
❏ 8592	Come Back Baby/No, Never Alone	1959	$30
GRT			
❏ 26	Early in the Morning/When the Hurt Moves In	1970	$5
❏ 41	Gulf Stream Line/I'd Run a Mile	1971	$5
KING			
❏ 4949	Grandaddy's Rockin'/Half Hearted Love	1956	$200
❏ 4927	If I Had Me a Woman/Just So You Call Me	1956	$200
❏ 5121	Missy Ann/Little Miss Linda	1958	$70
❏ 5059	Say So/I'll Be Gentle	1957	$50
❏ 4995	That Ain't Nothin' But Right/Don't You Love Me	1956	$200
❏ 5007	What You Want/To Protect the Innocent	1957	$125
❏ 5107	What You Want/You Are My Special Baby	1958	$70
RANWOOD			
❏ 1041	More Like I Do Now/Nine Times Out of Ten	1975	$5
❏ 1017	Pistol Packin' Mama/Asphalt Cowboy, Parking Lot Lover	1975	$5
❏ 1050	We Made It All the Way/West Texas Women	1976	$5
TOWER			
❏ 319	Ties That Bind/Stepping Out on You	1967	$6
CURTIS, SONNY			
A&M			
❏ 1359	Lights of L.A./Sunny Mornin'	1972	$40
CAPITOL			
❏ 4227	It's Only a Question of Time/When It's Just You and Me	1976	$15
❏ 4158	Lovesick Blues/It's Only a Question of Time	1975	$15
❏ 4240	Where's Patricia Now/When It's Just You and Me	1976	$15
CORAL			
❏ 60954	Someday You're Gonna Be Sorry/Forever Yours	1953	$30
DIMENSION			
❏ 1024	A Beatle I Want to Be/So Used to Loving You	1964	$30
❏ 1017	So Used to Loving You/The Last Song I'm Ever Gonna Sing	1963	$30
DOT			
❏ 15799	A Pretty Girl/Willa May Jones	1958	$40
❏ 15754	Wrong Again/Laughing Stock	1958	$50
ELEKTRA			
❏ 46568	Do You Remember Roll Over Beethoven/Walk Right Back	1979	$5
❏ 47129	Good Ol' Girls/So Used to Loving You	1981	$5

Number	Title	Yr	NM
❏ 46643	Love Is All Around/The Clone Song	1980	$5
❏ 47176	Married Woman/I Live Your Music	1981	$5
❏ 47231 [DJ]	The Christmas Song/Little Drummer Boy	1981	$8
—B-side by Hank Williams, Jr.			
❏ 47231 [DJ]	The Christmas Song/Little Drummer Boy	1981	$8
—B-side by Hank Williams, Jr.			
❏ 46526	The Cowboy Singer/Cheatin' Clouds	1979	$5
❏ 69942	Together Alone/Dream Well All of You Children	1982	$5
LIBERTY			
❏ 55710	Bo Diddley Bach/I Pledge My Love to You	1964	$30
OVATION			
❏ 1006	Love Is All Around/Here, There and Everywhere	1970	$30
VIVA			
❏ 626	Day Drinker/Atlanta, Georgia Stray	1968	$20
❏ 636	Girl of the North/Hung Up in Your Eyes	1969	$20
❏ 634	Holiday for Clowns/Day Gig	1969	$20
❏ 617	I'm a Gypsy Man/I Wanna Go Bummin' Around	1967	$20
❏ 602	My Way of Life/Last Call	1966	$20
❏ 607	The Collection/Destiny's Child	1966	$20
❏ 630	The Straight Life/How Little Men Care	1968	$20
CURTOLA, BOBBY			
KING			
❏ 6136	My Christmas Tree/Jingle Bells	1967	$8
CUSTER AND THE SURVIVORS			
ASCOT			
❏ 2207	I Saw Her Walking/Flapjacks	1965	$20
GOLDEN STATE			
❏ 1657	I Saw Her Walking/Flapjacks	1965	$15
VARDAN			
❏ 202	I Saw Her Walking/Flapjacks	1965	$30
CUTE-TEENS, THE			
ALADDIN			
❏ 3458	When My Teenage Days Are Over/From This Day Forward	1959	$250
CUTTING CREW			
VIRGIN			
❏ 7-99215	(Between a) Rock and a Hard Place/Card House	1989	$3
❏ 7-99215 [PS]	(Between a) Rock and a Hard Place/Card House	1989	$3
❏ 7-99184	Everything But My Pride/Big Noise	1989	$4
❏ 7-99481	(I Just) Died in Your Arms/For the Longest Time	1987	$3
❏ 7-99481 [PS]	(I Just) Died in Your Arms/For the Longest Time	1987	$3
❏ 7-99425	I've Been in Love Before/Life Is a Dangerous Time	1987	$3
❏ 7-99425 [PS]	I've Been in Love Before/Life Is a Dangerous Time	1987	$3
❏ 7-99464	One for the Mockingbird/Mirror and a Blade (Live)	1987	$3
❏ 7-99464 [PS]	One for the Mockingbird/Mirror and a Blade (Live)	1987	$3
CYKLE, THE			
LABEL			
❏ 101	If You Can/(B-side unknown)	1969	$40
❏ 101 [PS]	If You Can/(B-side unknown)	1969	$70
CYMANDE			
JANUS			
❏ 225	Anthracite/Fug	1973	$5
❏ 215	Bra/Ras Tafarian Folk Song	1973	$5
❏ 203	The Message/Zion I	1972	$5
CYMBAL & CLINGER			
CHELSEA			
❏ 78-0112	Dying River/Little Bit No, Little Bit Yes	1973	$5
❏ 78-0106	God Bless You Rock & Roll/Forever and Forever	1972	$5
MARINA			
❏ 502	Pool Shooter/Mookie Mookie Man	1971	$6
MGM			
❏ 14256	Pool Shooter/Mookie Mookie Man	1971	$5

Number	Title	Yr	NM
CYMBAL, JOHNNY			
AMARET			
❏ 110	Big River/Girl from Willow County	1969	$8
❏ 111	Ode to Bubblegum/Save All Your Lovin' (Hold It for Me)	1969	$8
BANG			
❏ 566	Back Door Man/Tell Your Soul	1969	$6
❏ 558	Cinnamon/This Is My Story	1968	$8
❏ 571	Inside Out-Outside In/Sell Your Soul	1969	$6
COLUMBIA			
❏ 43842	Good Morning Blues/Jessica	1966	$8
DCP			
❏ 1135	Go, VW, Go/Sorrow and Pain	1965	$40
❏ 1146	My Last Day/Summertime's Here at Last	1965	$20
KAPP			
❏ 634	Cheat, Cheat/16 Shades of Blue	1964	$20
❏ 614	Connie/Little Miss Lonely	1964	$20
❏ 556	Marshmallow/Hurdy Gurdy Man	1963	$20
❏ 503	Mr. Bass Man/Sacred Lovers' Vow	1963	$30
❏ 539	(Surfin' at) Tia Juana/Dum Dum Dee Dum	1963	$20
❏ 524	Teenage Heaven/Cinderella Baby	1963	$20
❏ 576	There Goes a Bad Girl/Refreshment Time	1964	$20
KEDLEN			
❏ 2001	Bachelor Man/Growing Up with You	1962	$30
MGM			
❏ 12935	It'll Be Me/Always, Always	1960	$30
❏ 12978	The Water Was Red/The Bunny	1961	$30
MUSICOR			
❏ 1272	Breaking Your Balloon/The Marriage of Charlotte Brown	1967	$15
❏ 1261	It Looks Like Love/May I Get to Know You	1967	$15
VEE JAY			
❏ 495	Bachelor Man/Growing Up with You	1963	$20
CYPRESS, BUDDY			
FLASH			
❏ 118	I'm in Love with You/Don't Forsake Me	1957	$60
CYRKLE, THE			
COLUMBIA			
❏ CSM-466	Camaro/SS 396	1967	$30
—B-side by Paul Revere and the Raiders			
❏ CSM-466 [PS]	Camaro/SS 396	1967	$60
—B-side by Paul Revere and the Raiders			
❏ 44426	Friends/Reading Her Papers	1968	$8
❏ 43965	I Wish You Could Be Here/The Visit (She Was Here)	1967	$8
❏ 43965 [PS]	I Wish You Could Be Here/The Visit (She Was Here)	1967	$15
❏ 44224	Penny Arcade/The Words	1967	$8
❏ 43871	Please Don't Ever Leave Me/Money to Burn	1966	$8
❏ 43729	Turn-Down Day/Big, Little Woman	1966	$10
❏ 43729 [PS]	Turn-Down Day/Big, Little Woman	1966	$20
❏ 43729 [DJ]	Turn-Down Day (same on both sides)	1966	$50
—Promo only on red vinyl			
❏ 44366	Turn of the Century/Don't Cry, No Fears, No Tears Comin'	1967	$8
❏ 44108	We Had a Good Thing Goin'/Two Rooms	1967	$8
CYRUS ERIE			
EPIC			
❏ 10451	Sparrow/Get the Message	1969	$15

D

Number	Title	Yr	NM

D.C. BLOSSOMS, THE
SHRINE
| ❏ 107 | I Know About Her/Hey Boy | 1966 | $800 |

D-MEN, THE
KAPP
| ❏ 691 | So Little Time/Every Moment of Every Day | 1965 | $15 |
VEEP
| ❏ 1206 | Don't You Know/No Hope for Me | 1965 | $20 |

DA-PREES, THE
TWIST
| ❏ 70913 | Pay Day/Sometimes | 1963 | $200 |

D'ABO, MIKE
A&M
| ❏ 1628 | Fuel to Burn/Hold On Sweet Darling | 1974 | $4 |
| ❏ 1374 | Little Miss Understood/Belinda | 1972 | $5 |
BELL
| ❏ 956 | Miss Me in the Morning/Arabella Cinderella | 1971 | $6 |

DACHE, BERTELL
DIAMOND
| ❏ 201 | Don't Stop the World for Me/Anchors Awaeigh Girl | 1966 | $20 |
UNITED ARTISTS
| ❏ 260 | All the World Loves a Lover/You Gotta Have Chicks | 1960 | $30 |

DACRONS, THE
HIT
| ❏ 38 | Don't Hang Up/Limbo Rock | 1962 | $8 |
—B-side by Bill Carmichael
| ❏ 57 | He's So Fine/Follow the Boys | 1963 | $8 |
—B-side by Connie Landers
| ❏ 56 | South Street/What Will My Mary Say | 1963 | $8 |
—B-side by Tony Christopher
| ❏ 81 | Then He Kissed Me/Surfer Girl | 1963 | $8 |
—B-side by the Jalopy Five

DADDY COOL
REPRISE
❏ 1038	Eagle Rock/Bom Bom	1971	$6
❏ 1064	Hi Honey Ho/Come Back Again	1972	$6
❏ 1090	I'll Never Smile Again/Daddy Rocks Off	1972	$6
❏ 1087	Teenage Blues/Donna Forgive Me	1972	$6

DADDY DEWDROP
CAPITOL
| ❏ 4066 | Dynamite Dyna/Goddaughter | 1975 | $4 |
INPHASION
| ❏ 7206 | If You Wanna Wanna/Turn On the Motion | 1979 | $4 |
SUNFLOWER
❏ 119	Chantilly Lace/Migraine Headaches	1972	$4
❏ 105	Chick-a-Boom (Don't Ya Jes' Love It)/John Jacob Jingleheimer Smith	1971	$5
❏ 111	Fox Huntin' (On a Weekend)/March of the White Corpuscles	1971	$4

DAFFAN, TED
COLUMBIA
| ❏ 2-750(?) | Ain't Got No Name Rag/Kiss Me Goodnight | 1950 | $50 |
—Microgroove 7-inch 33 1/3 rpm single
| ❏ 2-190(?) | Flame of Love/I'm That Kind of Guy | 1949 | $50 |
—Microgroove 7-inch 33 1/3 rpm single
| ❏ 2-560(?) | I've Got $5 And It's Saturday Night/I'm Gonna Leave This Darned Old Town | 1950 | $50 |
—Microgroove 7-inch 33 1/3 rpm single
| ❏ 2-500(?) | So Dissatisfied/Strangers Passing By | 1950 | $50 |
—Microgroove 7-inch 33 1/3 rpm single
| ❏ 2-360(?) | Take That Leash Off Me/That's a Dad Blamed Lie | 1949 | $50 |
—Microgroove 7-inch 33 1/3 rpm single
DAFFAN
| ❏ 102 | Bottom of the List/Tangled Mind | 1955 | $40 |

DAHL, STEVE
COHO
| ❏ 007 | Ayatollah/Unhappy New Year | 1980 | $6 |
OVATION
| ❏ 1132 | Do You Think I'm Disco?/Coho Lip Blues | 1979 | $4 |
| ❏ 1132 [PS] | Do You Think I'm Disco?/Coho Lip Blues | 1979 | $6 |
—Red and black print
| ❏ 1132 [PS] | Do You Think I'm Disco?/Coho Lip Blues | 1979 | $5 |
—All-black print

DAILY FLASH, THE
UNI
| ❏ 55001 | French Girl/Green Rocky Road | 1967 | $15 |

DAISIES, THE
CAPITOL
| ❏ 5667 | Cold Wave/Put Your Arms Around Me | 1966 | $30 |
ROULETTE
| ❏ 4571 | I Wanna Swim with Him/You Just Said You Loved Me | 1964 | $15 |

DAISY, PAT
RCA VICTOR
❏ 74-0743	Beautiful People/I Think I'm Falling	1972	$6
❏ 74-0637	Everybody's Reaching Out for Someone/I'll Be There	1972	$6
❏ APBO-0087	My Love Is Deep, My Love Is Wide/You've Got Everything	1973	$6
❏ 74-0932	The Lonesomest Lonesome/I Was Meant for You and You Were Meant for Me	1973	$6

DAKIL, FLOYD
EARTH
| ❏ 402 | Bad Boy/Stoppin' Traffic | 1965 | $50 |
| ❏ 404 | Stronger Than Dirt/You're the Kind of Girl | 1965 | $40 |
GUYDEN
| ❏ 2111 | Dance, Franny, Dance/Look What You've Gone and Done | 1964 | $40 |
JETSTAR
| ❏ 103 | Dance, Franny, Dance/Look What You've Gone and Done | 1964 | $125 |
POMPEII
| ❏ 66687 | Merry Christmas, Baby/One Girl | 1968 | $30 |

DAKOTAS, THE
LIBERTY
| ❏ 55618 | The Cruel Surf/The Millionaire | 1963 | $50 |

DAKUS, WES
KAPP
| ❏ 815 | Peggy Sue/See Saw | 1967 | $10 |
—As "Dennis Paul with Wes Dakus' Rebels
| ❏ 806 | Sad Souvenirs/Armful of Teddy Bears | 1967 | $10 |
—As "Barry Allen with Wes Dakus' Rebels
SWAN
| ❏ 4206 | Las Vegas Scene/Sour Biscuits | 1965 | $15 |
UNITED ARTISTS
| ❏ 722 | Pedro's Pad/Side Winder | 1964 | $30 |

DALE
PAISLEY PARK
| ❏ 28142 | Simon Simon/The Perfect Stranger | 1987 | $3 |
| ❏ 28142 [PS] | Simon Simon/The Perfect Stranger | 1987 | $4 |

DALE AND GRACE
GUYDEN
| ❏ 6002 | What's Happening to Me/Darling It's Wonderful | 1972 | $5 |
HANNA-BARBERA
| ❏ 472 | Let Them Talk/I'd Rather Be Free | 1966 | $8 |
MICHELLE
❏ 936	Cool Water/Rules of Love	1964	$20
❏ 930	Darling It's Wonderful/What's Happening to Me	1964	$20
❏ 921	I'm Leaving It Up to You/That's What I Like	1963	$30
❏ 923	Stop and Think It Over/Bad Luck	1963	$20
❏ 928	The Loneliest Night/I'm Not Free	1964	$20
MONTEL
❏ 936	Cool Water/Rules of Love	1964	$15
❏ 930	Darling It's Wonderful/What's Happening to Me	1964	$15
❏ 921	I'm Leaving It Up to You/That's What I Like About You	1963	$15
❏ 989	It Keeps Right On a-Hurtin'/So Fine	1967	$15
❏ 958	Make the World Go Away/Stranger	1965	$15
❏ 922	Stop and Think It Over/Bad Luck	1963	$15
❏ 928	The Loneliest Night/I'm Not Free	1964	$15
MONTEL/MICHELLE
❏ 942	Something Special/What Am I Living For	1964	$15

DALE, DICK, AND THE DEL-TONES
ACCENT
| ❏ 1243 | Eyes of a Child/Just a-Waitin' | 1968 | $8 |
CAPITOL
❏ 5389	Let's Go Trippin' '65/Watusi Jo	1965	$20
❏ 5290	Oh Marie/Who Can It Be	1964	$20
❏ 5010	Secret Surfin' Spot/Surfin' and a-Swingin'	1963	$30
❏ 5098	The Wedge/Night Rider	1963	$30
❏ 5187	Wild, Wild Mustang/Grunge Run	1964	$20
❏ 5048	Wild Ideas/Scavenger	1963	$30
COLUMBIA
❏ 38-07340	Pipeline/Love Struck Baby	1987	$4
—B-side by Stevie Ray Vaughan
| ❏ 38-07340 [PS] | Pipeline/Love Struck Baby | 1987 | $6 |
CONCERT ROOM
| ❏ 371 | We'll Never Hear the End of It/Fairest of Them All | 1963 | $30 |
COUGAR
| ❏ 712 | Taco Wagon/Spanish Kiss | 1967 | $20 |
CUPID
| ❏ 106 | We'll Never Hear the End of It/Fairest of Them All | 1960 | $40 |
—Black vinyl
| ❏ 106 | We'll Never Hear the End of It/Fairest of Them All | 1960 | $100 |
—Gold vinyl
DELTONE
❏ 5017	Let's Go Trippin'/Del-Tone Rock	1961	$40
❏ 5019	Misirlou/Eight Till Midnight	1962	$30
❏ 4939	Misirlou/Eight Till Midnight	1963	$30
❏ 5012	Oh Whee Marie/Breaking Heart	1959	$70
❏ 5020	Peppermint Man/Surf Beat	1962	$30
❏ 5018	Shake and Stomp/Jungle Fever	1962	$50
❏ 5013	Stop Teasin'/Without Your Love	1959	$70
❏ 4940	Surf Beat/Peppermint Man	1963	$30
—Deltone 4939 and 4940 were part of the Capitol numbering system
GNP CRESCENDO
| ❏ 804 | Let's Go Trippin'/Those Memories of You | 1975 | $6 |
SATURN
| ❏ 401 | We'll Never Hear the End of It/Fairest of Them All | 1963 | $40 |
U.S. ARMY
| ❏ 1301 [DJ] | The Enlistment Twist/Dream Girl Waltz | 1962 | $40 |
—B-side by Craig Adams and His Country Cousins; blue vinyl
| ❏ 1301 [PS] | The Enlistment Twist/Dream Girl Waltz | 1962 | $40 |
YES
| ❏ 7014 | We'll Never Hear the End of It/Fairest of Them All | 1963 | $40 |
| ❏ 7014 [PS] | We'll Never Hear the End of It/Fairest of Them All | 1963 | $50 |

DALE, JIMMY
DOOR KNOB
| ❏ 018 | Merry Christmas, Darling/Happy Anniversary, Darling | 1976 | $4 |

DALE, KENNY
AXBAR
❏ 6060	Daylight/Share All My Memories	1988	$8
❏ 6056	Perfect Angel/You Have My Heart	1987	$8
❏ 6058	Two Will Be One/I Know I Love You	1987	$8
❏ 6053	When I Be Five/(B-side unknown)	1987	$8
BGM
❏ 30186	I'm Going Crazy/Macon Georgia Love	1986	$6
CAPITOL
❏ 4389	Bluest Heartache of the Year/I'll Believe Every Word That You Lie	1977	$5
❏ 4704	Down to Earth Woman/Every Other Word Is You	1979	$5
❏ 4829	Let Me In/Rainbow Man	1980	$5
❏ 4746	Only Love Can Break a Heart/Child of the Wind	1979	$5
❏ 4457	Shame, Shame on Me (I Had Planned to Be Your Man)/Love Walked In Again	1977	$5
❏ 4788	Sharing/Child of the Wind	1979	$5
❏ 4882	Thank You, Ever-Lovin'/There Are Women (Then There's My Woman)	1980	$5
❏ 4570	The Loser/For Love	1978	$5
❏ 4619	Two Hearts Tangled in Love/Let's Make Love	1978	$5
❏ 4943	When It's Just You and Me/If the World Should Ever Run Out of Love	1980	$5
FUNDERBURG
❏ 5001	Moanin' the Blues/(B-side unknown)	1982	$8
REPUBLIC
❏ 8403	Take It Slow/(B-side unknown)	1984	$6
❏ 8301	Two Will Be One/One of a Kind	1983	$6
SABA
❏ 9214	Look What Love Did to Me/I'm In Over My Heart	1985	$6

DALEY, JIMMY, AND THE DING-A-LINGS

DECCA

Number	Title	Yr	NM
30532	Hole in the Wall/Bongo Rock	1957	$50

7-Inch Extended Plays

Number	Title	Yr	NM
ED2482	Picnic by the Sea/Young Love// Happy Is a Boy Named Me/Hot Rod/Big Band Rock and Roll	1957	$60

DALHART, VERNON

RCA VICTOR

Number	Title	Yr	NM
27-0016	The Prisoner's Song/ Wreck of the Old '97	1951	$50

DALLAS, JOHNNY

LITTLE DARLIN'

Number	Title	Yr	NM
013	Heart Full of Love/ Grey Flannel World	1966	$12
026	If You Got Problems in Your Home/Little Folks	1967	$10

DALLAS, MARIA

RCA VICTOR

Number	Title	Yr	NM
47-9279	Ambush/Lonely for You	1967	$10
47-9386	Don't Love Me Too Much/It's Such a Pretty World Today	1967	$12
47-9552	Everybody/Two Ships Passing in the Night	1968	$12

DALTON, BOB

MEGA

Number	Title	Yr	NM
0017	Blue Skies, Sunshine, My Rain/Tunnel #2	1970	$6
0003	Mama, Call Me Home/ Papa's Home	1970	$6
03 [PS]	Mama, Call Me Home/ Papa's Home	1970	$10

DALTON BOYS, THE

SKYLA

Number	Title	Yr	NM
1124	I'm Thinkin'/It's Much More Stronger	1962	$40

TEEN

Number	Title	Yr	NM
505	Who's Gonna Hold Your Hand/Walkin'	1959	$60

V.I.P.

Number	Title	Yr	NM
25025	I've Been Cheated/ Something's Bothering You	1965	$60
25025	I've Been Cheated/Take My Hand	1965	$200

DALTON, KATHY

DISCREET

Number	Title	Yr	NM
1191	At the Tropicana/Long Gone Charlie Hit & Run	1974	$5
1210	Boogie Bands and One Night Stands/Pour Your Wine All Over Me	1974	$5
1313	Midnight Creeper/Justine	1974	$5

DALTON, LACY J.

COLUMBIA

Number	Title	Yr	NM
18-03184	16th Avenue/You Can't Take the Texas Out of Me	1982	$3
11107	Crazy Blue Eyes/Late Night Kind of Lonesome	1979	$4
38-05759	Don't Fall in Love with Me/Over You	1985	$3
38-03926	Dream Baby (How Long Must I Dream)/Hold Me Again	1983	$3
18-02637	Everybody Makes Mistakes/Wild Turkey	1981	$3
11343	Hard Times/Old Soldier	1980	$4
11410	Hillbilly Girl with the Blues/Me 'n' You	1980	$4
38-04696	If That Ain't Love/Too Many Miles	1984	$3
11253	Losing Kind of Love/ Carolina Come-On	1980	$4
18-02847	Slow Down/One of the Unsatisfied	1982	$3
18-02188	Takin' It Easy/Golden Memories	1981	$3
11190	Tennessee Waltz/ Beer Drinkin' Song	1980	$4
38-06360	This Ol' Town/Up with the Wind	1986	$3
11-01036	Whisper/China Doll	1981	$3
38-04133	Windin' Down/Dixie Devil	1983	$3
38-06098	Working Class Man/Can't See Me Without You	1986	$3

UNIVERSAL

Number	Title	Yr	NM
UVL-66015	Hard Luck Ace/Turn to the One	1989	$3
UVL-66007	I'm a Survivor/Walkin' Wounded	1989	$3
53487	The Heart/Hard Luck Ace	1989	$3

DALTON, LARRY, AND THE DALTON GANG

SOUNDWAVES

Number	Title	Yr	NM
4645	Cowboy/Too Many Nights	1981	$5
4672	Tomorrow/Ain't It Funny	1982	$5

DALTREY, ROGER

Also see THE WHO.

A&M

Number	Title	Yr	NM
1779	Love's Dream/Orpheus Song	1975	$5

— With Rick Wakeman

ATLANTIC

Number	Title	Yr	NM
89491	After the Fire/Don't Satisfy Me	1985	$3
89491 [PS]	After the Fire/Don't Satisfy Me	1985	$3
89471	Let Me Down Easy/Fallen Angel	1985	$3
89471 [PS]	Let Me Down Easy/Fallen Angel	1985	$3
89667	Parting Would Be Painless/ Is There Anyone Out There?	1984	$3
89704	Walking in My Sleep/ Somebody Told Me	1984	$3
89704 [PS]	Walking in My Sleep/ Somebody Told Me	1984	$3

MCA

Number	Title	Yr	NM
40800	Avenging Annie/The Prisoner	1977	$4
40453	Come and Get Your Love/Heart's Right	1975	$5
40862	Leon/The Prisoner	1978	$4
52051	Martyrs and Madmen/ Avenging Annie	1982	$4
40512	Oceans Away/Feeling	1976	$5
40761	One of the Boys/Doing It All Again	1977	$5
40765	Satin and Lace/Say It Ain't So, Joe	1977	$4

ODE

Number	Title	Yr	NM
66040	I'm Free/Underture	1973	$5

POLYDOR

Number	Title	Yr	NM
2105	Free Me/McVicar	1980	$4
2105 [PS]	Free Me/McVicar	1980	$3
15098	See Me, Feel Me-Listening to You/Overture from Tommy	1975	$5

— B-side by Pete Townshend

Number	Title	Yr	NM
2153	Waiting for a Friend/ Bitter and Twisted	1981	$4
2153 [DJ]	Waiting for a Friend (same on both sides)	1981	$6

— One label has name misspelled as "Rodger Daltrey"

Number	Title	Yr	NM
2121	Without Your Love/ Escape (Part 1)	1980	$4

TRACK

Number	Title	Yr	NM
40053	Giving It All Away/ Way of the World	1973	$6

— B-side by Bryan Daly & the London Festival Orchestra

Number	Title	Yr	NM
40084	Thinking/There Is Love	1973	$8

DAMIAN, MICHAEL

CYPRESS

Number	Title	Yr	NM
1430	Cover of Love/(Instrumental)	1989	$3
1430 [PS]	Cover of Love/(Instrumental)	1989	$3

LEG

Number	Title	Yr	NM
007	She Did It/I Love How You Love Me	1981	$6
007 [PS]	She Did It/I Love How You Love Me	1981	$6

WEIR BROTHERS

Number	Title	Yr	NM
413	Christmas Time Without You/ What Are You Looking For	1987	$4
413 [PS]	Christmas Time Without You/ What Are You Looking For	1987	$4

DAMITA JO

ABC-PARAMOUNT

Number	Title	Yr	NM
10176	How Will I Know/ Disillusioned Lovers	1961	$10
9822	How Will I Know/I'll Never Cry	1957	$20
9849	My Heart Is Home/ Disillusioned Lovers	1957	$20

EPIC

Number	Title	Yr	NM
10235	Dinner For One/Please, James	1967	$8
9797	Gotta Travel On/ Something You Got	1965	$8
10061 [DJ]	If You Go Away (same on both sides)	1966	$30

— Promo only on yellow vinyl

Number	Title	Yr	NM
10061	If You Go Away/When the Fog Rolls In to San Francisco	1966	$8
9860	Sweet Pussycat/Who Could Ask for More	1965	$8
9887	That Special Way/ Tossin' and Turnin'	1966	$8
9766	Tomorrow Night/Silver Dollar	1965	$8

MERCURY

Number	Title	Yr	NM
71984	Another Dancing Partner/Please Send Me Someone to Love	1962	$15
72056	Dance Him By Me/Las Vegas	1962	$15
72056 [PS]	Dance Him By Me/Las Vegas	1962	$30
71871	Dance with a Dolly (With a Hole in Her Stocking)/You're Nobody 'Til Somebody Loves You	1962	$15
72121	Drama of Love/Hobo Flats	1963	$12
72121 [PS]	Drama of Love/Hobo Flats	1963	$30
71929	I Didn't Know I Was Crying/I Built My World Around a Dream	1962	$15
71840	I'll Be There/Love Laid Its Hands Me	1962	$20
71840 [PS]	I'll Be There/Love Laid Its Hands Me	1962	$30
71690	I'll Save the Last Dance for You/Forgive	1960	$20
72162	In the Dark/Melancholy Baby	1963	$10
71608	Little Things Mean a Lot/I Burned Your Letter	1960	$15
72086	Little Things/Mr. Blues (Found a Home with Me)	1963	$10
72086 [PS]	Little Things/Mr. Blues (Found a Home with Me)	1963	$30
71793	Sweet Georgia Brown/ Do What You Want	1961	$15
71493	The Dance Was Over/ Look at Yourself	1959	$15
72019	The Window Up Above/ Tennessee Waltz	1962	$15
72019 [PS]	The Window Up Above/ Tennessee Waltz	1962	$30
71568	What Would You Do/Widow Talk	1960	$15

RANWOOD

Number	Title	Yr	NM
844	Brother Love's Traveling Salvation Show/I'll Save the Last Dance for You	1969	$6
826	Grown-Up Games/Lonely Letters	1968	$6
894	Hallelujah Baby/Two Worlds	1971	$5
857	Lonely Teardrops/ Ain't Misbehavin'	1969	$6
820	Loving You/Reason to Believe	1968	$6
884	Mrs. Robinson/Two Worlds	1970	$5
869	Paint Me Loving You/ Tomorrow Is the First Day of the Rest of My Life	1970	$6

RCA VICTOR

Number	Title	Yr	NM
47-6281	Always/Freehearted	1955	$20
47-5328	Do Me a Favor/Don't You Care	1953	$20
47-5570	Face to Face/Sadie Thompson's Song	1953	$20
47-6096	Feelin' Kinda Happy/ Nuff of That Stuff	1955	$20

— B-side by Steve Gibson and His Red Caps

Number	Title	Yr	NM
47-5120	Go 'Way From My Window/ Let Me Share Your Name	1953	$20
47-5022	I'd Do It Again/I Don't Care	1952	$20
47-6185	In My Heart/Abracadabra	1955	$20
47-4685	Lonesome and Blue/I Need You	1952	$20

— By John Greer, vocals by Damita Jo

Number	Title	Yr	NM
47-5253	Missing/The Widow Walk	1953	$20
47-5987	Win or Lose/My Tzatskele	1955	$20

VEE JAY

Number	Title	Yr	NM
661	I'm Waiting for Ships That Never Come In/Hurt a Fool	1965	$8

DAMNED, THE

BIG BEAT

Number	Title	Yr	NM
NS92	There Ain't No Sanity Clause (Remix)/Looking At You (Live)	1982	$6

— U.K. import; reissue of Chiswick 139

Number	Title	Yr	NM
NS92 [PS]	There Ain't No Sanity Clause (Remix)/Looking At You (Live)	1982	$6

— U.K. import; reissue of Chiswick 139

CHISWICK

Number	Title	Yr	NM
139 [PS]	There Ain't No Sanity Clause//Hit Or Miss/Looking At You (Live)	1981	$15

— U.K. import

Number	Title	Yr	NM
139	There Ain't No Sanity Clause//Hit Or Miss/Looking At You (Live)	1981	$6

— U.K. import

I.R.S.

Number	Title	Yr	NM
9022	Dr. Jeckyl and Mr. Hyde/ Looking at You (Live)	1981	$8
9022	Dr. Jeckyl and Mr. Hyde/ Looking at You (Live)	1981	$8

MCA

Number	Title	Yr	NM
53051	Alone Again Or/In Dulce Decorum	1987	$3
53051 [PS]	Alone Again Or/In Dulce Decorum	1987	$3

DAMON, LIZ, 'S ORIENT EXPRESS

ANTHEM

Number	Title	Yr	NM
51006	All in All/Walking Backwards Down the Road	1971	$10
51005	Loneliness Remembers/ Quiet Sound	1971	$10

MAKAHA

Number	Title	Yr	NM
503	1900 Yesterday/You're Falling in Love	1970	$15

WHITE WHALE

Number	Title	Yr	NM
368	1900 Yesterday/You're Falling in Love	1970	$6
370	But For Love/You Make Me Feel Like Someone	1970	$6

DAMONE, VIC

CAPITOL

Number	Title	Yr	NM
5092	Again/Sweet Someone	1963	$8
5138	Breaking Point/Who Are You Now	1964	$8
4756	Ebb Tide/My Heart Will Tell You So	1962	$8
5191	I'm Gonna Miss You/ Where Did the Magic Go	1964	$8
4947	One Hand, One Hand/You're Just Another Pretty Face	1963	$8
5252	On the Street Where You Live/Maria	1964	$8
4645	Something You Never Had Before/Tender Is the Night	1961	$8
4827	What Kind of Fool Am I/Charmaine	1962	$8
5039	Wives and Lovers/Oooh Looka There Ain't She Pretty	1963	$8

Number	Title	Yr	NM
COLUMBIA			
❏ 42006	Adrift on a Star/The Pleasure of Her Company	1961	$8
❏ 40945	An Affair to Remember (Our Love Affair)/In the Eyes of the World	1957	$10
❏ 41185	A Toujours/The Only Man on the Island	1958	$10
❏ 41649	Christine/Never Will I Marry	1960	$8
❏ 40858	Do I Love You (Because You're Beautiful)/The Legend of the Bells	1957	$12
❏ 41245	Forever New/Oooh, My Love	1958	$10
❏ 41122	Gigi/On the Street Where You Live	1958	$10
❏ 40630	Help Me/Sure	1956	$12
❏ 40682	I Cried for You/To Love Again	1956	$10
❏ 41915	If Ever I Would Love You/I'll Be Your Lover	1961	$8
❏ 41407	My Heart Has Many Dreams/New Romance in Old Roma	1959	$10
❏ 40654	On the Street Where You Live/We All Need Love	1956	$10
❏ 41333	Save a Kiss/Penny Serenade	1959	$10
❏ 42041	Theme from "By Love Possessed"/If It's the Last Thing I Do	1961	$8
❏ 40733	War and Peace/Speak, My Love	1956	$10
❏ 41287	We Kiss in a Shadow/Separate Tables	1958	$10
❏ 40783	When My Love Smiles/One Little Boy	1956	$10
MERCURY			
❏ 70108	Afraid/Love Light	1953	$15
❏ 5909	Al-Lee-O! Al-Lee-Ay!/Roseanne	1952	$20
❏ 5496	A Marshmallow World/When the Lights Are Low	1950	$20
❏ 5865	A Message from Vic Damone to the Army Boys (Parts 1 & 2)	1952	$30
❏ 70022	April in Paris/My Love Song	1953	$15
❏ 70128	April in Portugal/I'm Walking Behind You	1953	$15
❏ 5535	Ave Maria/Our Lady of Fatima	1950	$20
❏ 70507	Ave Maria/Our Lady of Fatima	1954	$15
— With Kitty Kallen			
❏ 5698	Calla Calla/It's a Long Way	1951	$20
❏ 5477	Cincinnati Dancing Pig/Forbidden Love	1950	$20
❏ 5878	Come Hell or High Water/Girls Are Marching	1952	$20
❏ 5855	Diane/Tenderly	1952	$20
❏ 5744	Don't Blame Me/I Remember You, Love	1951	$20
❏ 70624	Don't Keep It a Secret/A Man Doesn't Know	1955	$15
❏ 5391	Don't Say Goodbye/This Is the Night	1950	$20
❏ 70216	Ebb Tide/If I Could Make You Mine	1953	$15
❏ 70186	Eternally (The Song from Limelight/Simonetta	1953	$15
❏ 70545	Foolishly/Hello, Mrs. Jones, Is Mary There	1955	$15
❏ 5374	God's Country/Where I Belong	1950	$20
—Mercury singles before 5374 are unconfirmed on 45			
❏ 5831	Goodbye for Awhile/Good Morning, Morning Glory	1952	$20
❏ 70031	Greyhound/I Don't Care	1953	$15
❏ 5858	Here in My Heart/Tomorrow Never Comes	1952	$20
❏ 5565	If/You and Your Beautiful Eyes	1951	$20
❏ 5670	In the Cool, Cool, Cool of the Evening/How D'Ya Like Your Eggs	1951	$20
❏ 5655	Longing for You/The Son of a Sailor	1951	$20
❏ 70257	Lover, Come Back to Me/I Just Love You	1953	$15
❏ 5444	Mama/Operetta	1950	$20
❏ 5563	My Heart Cries for You/Music by the Angels	1950	$20
❏ 70577	My Symphony/Meet Me Halfway	1955	$15
❏ 5646	My Truly, Truly Fair/My Life's Desire	1951	$20
❏ 70436	Once and Only Once/In My Own Quiet Way	1954	$15
❏ 70699	Por Favor/Born to Sing the Blues	1955	$15
❏ 5555	Possibilities/Use Your Imagination	1950	$20
❏ 5515	Silent Night/White Christmas	1950	$20
❏ 70384	Sleeping Beauty/Don't Take Your Lips Away	1954	$15
❏ 5638	Someday/You Gotta Show Me	1951	$20
❏ 702690	Stranger in Paradise/A Village in Peru	1953	$15
❏ 70054	Sugar/Amor	1953	$15
❏ 5486	Take Me in Your Arms/Beloved, Be Faithful	1950	$20
❏ 5572	Tell Me You Love Me/Little Café Paree	1951	$20
❏ 70179	That Old Feeling/Serenade in Blue	1953	$15
❏ 70287	The Breeze and I/To Love You	1954	$15
❏ 5454	Tzena, Tzena, Tzena/I Love That Girl	1950	$20
❏ 5402	Where Can I Go/If We Could Be A-L-O-N-E	1950	$20
❏ 70480	Wind Song/Silk Stockings	1954	$15
❏ 5669	Wonder Why/I Can See You	1951	$20
MGM			
❏ 14576	Beautiful Land/Tell Her You Love Her	1973	$4
❏ 14498	Love Me As I Love You/This Time	1973	$4
❏ 14398	Tomorrow Belongs to the Children/Come Live Your Life with Me	1972	$4

Number	Title	Yr	NM
RCA VICTOR			
❏ 47-8982	Ciao Compare/What Is a Woman	1966	$6
❏ 47-9488	Goin' Out of My Head/Nothing to Lose	1968	$5
❏ 47-9250	I'll Sleep Tonight/It Makes No Difference	1967	$6
❏ 47-9046	Love Me Longer/Pretty Butterfly	1966	$6
❏ 47-9399	The Glory of Love/Come Live with Me	1967	$6
❏ 74-0139	To Make a Big Man Cry/Take Me Walking in Your Mind	1969	$5
❏ 47-9626	When You Laughed All Your Laughter/Why Can't I Walk Away	1968	$5
REBECCA			
❏ 715	Christmas In San Francisco/(B-side unknown)	1977	$4
❏ 714	The Christmas Song/Silver Bells	1977	$4
WARNER BROS.			
❏ 5609	Bellisima/For Mama	1965	$6
❏ 5653	Lost and Found/Turn Around	1965	$6
❏ 5668	Tears/Turn Around	1965	$6
❏ 5644	The Thrill of Lovin' You/Why Don't You Believe Me	1965	$6
❏ 5801	Two of a Kind/Wonder	1966	$6
7-Inch Extended Plays			
COLUMBIA			
❏ B-2565	*On the Street Where You Live/ Smoke Gets In Your Eyes/ An Affair to Remember/You Stepped Out of a Dream	1959	$15

Number	Title	Yr	NM
DAN AND DALE			
TIFTON			
❏ 125	Batman Theme/Robin's Theme	1966	$12
❏ 125 [PS]	Batman Theme/Robin's Theme	1966	$30
DANA, VIC			
CASINO			
❏ 093	Lay Me Down (Roll Me Out to Sea)/You Never Really Know	1976	$4
COLUMBIA			
❏ 45439	Child of Mine/The Love in Your Eyes	1971	$5
❏ 45342	If You Think I Love You Now (I;ve Just Started)/Angel She Was Love	1971	$5
DOLTON			
❏ 322	A Million and One/My Baby Wouldn't Leave Me	1966	$8
❏ 305	Bring a Little Sunshine (To My Heart)/That's All	1965	$8
❏ 305 [PS]	Bring a Little Sunshine (To My Heart)/That's All	1965	$15
❏ 313	Crystal Chandelier/What Now My Love	1965	$8
❏ 73	Danger/Heart, Hand and Teardrop	1963	$8
❏ 73 [PS]	Danger/Heart, Hand and Teardrop	1963	$20
❏ 324	Distant Drums/Love Me With All of Your Heart	1966	$8
❏ 301	Frenchy/It Was Night	1964	$8
❏ 99	Garden in the Rain/Stairway to the Stars	1964	$8
❏ 99 [PS]	Garden in the Rain/Stairway to the Stars	1964	$20
❏ 42	Golden Boy/The Story Behind My Tears	1961	$8
❏ 326	Grown Up Games/So What's New	1966	$8
❏ 319	I Love You Drops/Sunny Skies	1966	$8
❏ 51	I Will/Proud	1962	$8
❏ 51 [PS]	I Will/Proud	1962	$20
❏ 48	Little Altar Boy/Hello Roomate	1961	$8
❏ 95	Love Is All We Need/I Need You Now	1964	$8
❏ 95 [PS]	Love Is All We Need/I Need You Now	1964	$20
❏ 317	Lovely Kravezit/Hello Roomate	1966	$8
❏ 309	Moonlight and Roses (Bring Mem'ries of You)/What'll I Do More/That's Why I'm Sorry	1965	$8
❏ 81	More/That's Why I'm Sorry	1963	$8
❏ 92	Shangri-La/Warm and Tender	1964	$8
❏ 89	So Wide the World/Close Your Eyes	1964	$8
❏ 34	The Girl of My Dreams/Someone New	1961	$8
❏ 87	The Prisoner's Song/Voice in the Wind	1963	$8
❏ 58	To Love and Be Loved/Time Can Change	1962	$8
LIBERTY			
❏ 55998	A Lifetime Lovin' You/Guess Who, You	1967	$6
❏ 56137	Aren't We the Lucky Ones/I Tried to Love You Today	1969	$6
❏ 56050	Didn't We/Them	1968	$5
❏ 55950	Fraulein/A Little Bit Later on Down the Line	1967	$6
❏ 56023	Glory of Love/Let the Good Times In	1968	$5
❏ 56150	If I Never Knew Your Name/Sad Day Song	1969	$6
❏ 56071	Little Arrows/Roses Are Red	1968	$5
❏ 56109	Loneliness (Is Messin' Up My Mind)/Look of Leavin'	1969	$5
MGM			
❏ 14795	The Best I Ever Had/Memories Can't Make Love to Me	1975	$4

Number	Title	Yr	NM
DANCER, PRANCER, AND NERVOUS			
CAPITOL			
❏ 4353	I Wanta Be an Easter Bunny/The Happy Birthday Song	1960	$15
—As "The Singing Reindeer			
❏ 4300	The Happy Reindeer/Dancer's Waltz	1959	$15
❏ 4300 [PS]	The Happy Reindeer/Dancer's Waltz	1959	$30
DANDERLIERS, THE			
B&F			
❏ 1344	Chop Chop Boom/My Autumn Love	1961	$30
❏ 160	My Love/She's Mine	1960	$30
❏ 150	Shu-Wop/My Loving Partner	1960	$30
STATES			
❏ 147	Chop Chop Boom/My Autumn Love	1955	$400
— Black vinyl			
❏ 147	Chop Chop Boom/My Autumn Love	1955	$1200
— Red vinyl			
❏ 152	May God Be With You/Little Man	1956	$200
❏ 160	My Love/She's Mine	1956	$250
❏ 150	Shu-Wop/My Loving Partner	1955	$200
DANDY DAN			
CAMEO			
❏ 484	(I Don't Stand a) Ghost of a Chance/If Love Is	1967	$10
DANE, BARBARA			
TREY			
❏ 3012	I'm On My Way/Go 'Way from My Window	1960	$125
DANIELS, CHARLIE, BAND			
EPIC			
❏ 34-05638	American Farmer/Runnin' with That Crowd	1985	$3
❏ 34-05638 [PS]	American Farmer/Runnin' with That Crowd	1985	$3
❏ 50806	Behind Your Eyes/Blue Star	1979	$4
❏ 50322	Billy the Kid/Slow Song	1976	$4
❏ 08002	Boogie Woogie Fiddle Country Blues/Working Man You Got It All	1988	$3
❏ 19-50955 [PS]	Carolina (I Remember You)	1980	$5
— Sleeve may have been promo only			
❏ 19 50955 [DJ]	Carolina (I Remember You) (Long Version)/(Short Version)	1980	$5
❏ 50955	Carolina (I Remember You)/South Sea Song	1980	$4
❏ 68542	Cowboy Hat in Dallas/Easy Rider	1988	$3
❏ 05835	Drinkin' My Baby Goodbye/Ever Changing Lady	1986	$3
❏ 50456	Heaven Can Be Anywhere (Twin Pines Theme)/Good Ole Boy	1977	$4
❏ 50888	In America/Blue Star	1980	$4
❏ 02154	In America/The Legend of Wooley Swamp	1981	$3
— Reissue			
❏ 50845	Long Haired Country Boy/Sweet Lousiana	1980	$4
❏ 68738	Midnight Train/Back to Dixie	1989	$3
❏ 50768	Mississippi/Passing Lane	1979	$4
❏ 73030	Simple Man/Ill Wind	1989	$3
❏ 38-05699	Still Hurtin' Me/American Rock and Roll	1985	$3
❏ 38-05699 [PS]	Still Hurtin' Me/American Rock and Roll	1985	$3
❏ 02828	Still in Saigon/Blowing Along with the Wind	1982	$4
❏ 03918	Stroker's Theme/(B-side unknown)	1983	$4
❏ 50516	Sugar Hill Saturday Night/Maria Teresa	1977	$4
❏ 02185	Sweet Home Alabama/Falling in Love for the Night	1981	$4
❏ 50278	Sweet Louisiana/Sweetwater, Texas	1976	$4
❏ 50637	Sweet Lousiana/Trudy	1978	$4
❏ 50700	The Devil Went Down to Georgia/Rainbow Ride	1979	$4
❏ 50921	The Legend of Wooley Swamp/Money	1980	$4
❏ 03251	We Had It All One Time/Makes You Want to Go Home	1982	$4
❏ 50243	Wichita Jail/It's My Life	1976	$4
KAMA SUTRA			
❏ 606	Birmingham Blues/Damn Good Cowboy	1975	$5
❏ 553	Great Big Bunches of Love/(B-side unknown)	1972	$6
❏ 595	Land of Opportunity/(B-side unknown)	1974	$5
❏ 601	Long Haired Country Boy/I've Been Down	1975	$5
❏ 607	Texas/Everything Is Kinda Alright	1975	$5
❏ 598	The South's Gonna Do It/King Size Rosewood Bed	1974	$5
❏ 593	Way Down Yonder/I've Been Down	1974	$5
❏ 590	Whiskey/(B-side unknown)	1974	$5
PAULA			
❏ 246	The Middle of a Heartache/Skip It	1966	$20
❏ 418	The Middle of a Heartache/Skip It	1976	$4

Number	Title	Yr	NM
DANIELS, DAN, AND THE SQUIRRELS			
CAMEO			
❏ 447	The First Christmas Carol/Grandma's House	1966	$20
DANIELS, JEFF			
ASTRO			
❏ 108	Foxy Dan/Someday You'll Remember	1960	$125
BIG HOWDY			
❏ 8121	Foxy Dan/Someday You'll Remember	1961	$125
❏ 777	Switch Blade Sam/You're Still on My Mind	1959	$125
MELADEE			
❏ 117	Daddy-O Rock/Hey Woman	1958	$400
DANIELS, ROLY			
COLUMBIA			
❏ 4-44793	Love Is a Symphony/Another Teardrop	1969	$10
DANKO, RICK			
Also see THE BAND.			
ARISTA			
❏ 0306	What a Town/Shake It	1978	$4
DANLEERS, THE			
AMP 3			
❏ 2115	One Summer Night/Wheelin' and Dealin'	1958	$200
— By "Dandleers			
❏ 2115	One Summer Night/Wheelin' and Dealin'	1958	$50
— Corrected group name on label			
EPIC			
❏ 9367	I Live Half a Block from an Angel/If You Don't Care	1960	$40
❏ 9421	I'll Always Be in Love with You/Little Lover	1960	$40
EVEREST			
❏ 19412	Foolish/I'm Looking Around	1961	$40
LEMANS			
❏ 08	I'm Sorry/This Thing Called Love	1963	$10
❏ 04	The Truth Hurts/Baby You've Got It	1963	$10
MERCURY			
❏ 71401	A Picture of You/Prelude to Love	1959	$30
❏ 71441	I Can't Sleep/Your Love	1959	$30
❏ 71356	I Really Love You/My Flaming Heart	1958	$30
❏ 71322	One Summer Night/Wheelin' and a-Dealin'	1958	$30
SMASH			
❏ 1872	Were You There/If	1964	$15
❏ 1895	Where Is Love/The Angels Sent You	1964	$15
DANNY AND DEANIE			
HIT			
❏ 137	Bread and Butter/House of the Rising Sun	1964	$20
— B-side by the Spartas			
DANNY AND HAROLD			
COLUMBIA			
❏ 4-21436	My Heart's Hunting a New Home/Teardrop Waltz	1955	$30
DANNY AND JERRY			
RONN			
❏ 24	I Can't See Nobody/Mo'Reen	1967	$15
❏ 12	I've Got Pride/Connection	1967	$15
❏ 5	We've Got a Groovy Thing Goin'/You Must Be Fooling	1966	$15
DANNY AND THE JUNIORS			
ABC-PARAMOUNT			
❏ 9953	A Thief/Crazy Cave	1958	$30
❏ 9871	At the Hop/Sometimes (When I'm All Alone)	1957	$40
❏ 9926	Dottie/In the Meantime	1958	$30
❏ 10004	Do You Love Me/Somehow I Can't Forget	1959	$30
❏ 10052	Playing Hard to Get/Of Love	1959	$30
❏ 9978	Sassy Fran/I Feel So Lonely	1958	$60
CRUNCH			
❏ 018001	At the Hop/Let the Good Times Roll	1973	$5
GUYDEN			
❏ 2076	Oo-La-La-Limbo/Now and Then	1962	$30
MCA			
❏ D-2411	At the Hop/Rock and Roll Is Here to Stay	1980	$4
— Reissue			
MERCURY			
❏ 72240	Sad Girl/Let's Go Ski-ing	1964	$30

Number	Title	Yr	NM
ROULETTE			
❏ GG-121	At the Hop/Rock and Roll Is Here to Stay	1973	$4
— "Golden Goodies Hit Series" issue			
SINGULAR			
❏ 711	At the Hop/Sometimes	1957	$1000
— Blue label, machine-stamped in dead wax, no mention of Artie Singer on label			
❏ 711	At the Hop/Sometimes	1957	$1000
— Blue label, machine-stamped in dead wax, with "Orchestra Directed by Artie Singer" credit. Both versions have a "count-in" before the song starts. Singular records on black labels or without the count-in are probably reproductions.			
SWAN			
❏ 4082	Back to the Hop/The Charleston Fish	1961	$30
❏ 4082 [PS]	Back to the Hop/The Charleston Fish	1961	$125
❏ 4064	Candy Cane. Sugary Plum/Oh Holy Night	1960	$30
❏ 4064 [PS]	Candy Cane. Sugary Plum/Oh Holy Night	1960	$250
❏ 4072	Cha Cha Go Go (Chicago Cha-Cha)/Mister Whisper	1961	$30
❏ 4068	Daydreamer/Pony Express	1961	$30
❏ 4100	(Do the) Mashed Potatoes/Doin' the Continental Walk	1962	$30
❏ 4092	Twistin' All Night Long/Some Kind of Nut	1962	$30
❏ 4060	Twistin' U.S.A./A Thousand Miles Away	1960	$30
❏ 4113	We Got Soul/Funny	1962	$30
7-Inch Extended Plays			
ABC-PARAMOUNT			
❏ EP-11 [PS]	At the Hop	1958	$900
❏ EP-11	At The Hop/School Boy Romance//Rock And Roll Is Here To Stay/Sometimes (When I'm All Alone)	1958	$600
DANNY AND THE MEMORIES			
VALIANT			
❏ 6049	Can't Help Lovin' That Girl of Mine/Don't Go	1964	$30
❏ 705	Can't Help Lovin' That Girl of Mine/Don't Go	1965	$30
DANTE			
A&M			
❏ 788	Speedoo/Sweet Lover	1966	$10
DARROW			
❏ 515	How Much I Care/Baby Baby	1960	$50
DECCA			
❏ 31268	Bye Bye Baby/That's Why	1961	$20
❏ 31178	If You Don't Know/Leave Your Tears Behind You	1960	$20
IMPERIAL			
❏ 5867	Magic Ring/Am I the One	1962	$20
— Imperial titles as "Dante and His Friends			
❏ 5827	Miss America/Now I've Got You	1962	$20
❏ 5798	Something Happens/Are You Just My Friend	1961	$20
MADISON			
❏ 130	Alley Oop/The Right Time	1960	$30
— As "Dante and the Evergreens			
❏ 154	Think Sweet Thoughts/Da Doo	1961	$20
❏ 135	Time Machine/Dream Land	1960	$20
❏ 143	What Are You Doing New Year's Eve/Yeah Baby	1960	$20
— As "Dante and the Evergreens			
MERCURY			
❏ 71621	How Much I Care/Baby Baby	1960	$30
TIDE			
❏ 03	My Lament/Aching Heart	1960	$30
DANTE, RON			
ALMONT			
❏ 307	Little Lollypop/Funny	1963	$20
BELL			
❏ 45610	Charmer/Yesterday Dreamin'	1974	$4
❏ 45460	Christine/Don't Call It Love	1974	$5
— As "Bo Cooper			
❏ 45619	Midnight Show/The Christian	1974	$4
COLUMBIA			
❏ 43862	I Give You Things/Janie, Janie	1966	$10
❏ 43720	Think/221 East Maple	1966	$10
DOT			
❏ 17023	Absence of Lisa/Gypsy Be Mine	1967	$10
HANDSHAKE			
❏ 02552	Letter from Zowie/God Bless Rock and Roll	1981	$4
❏ 02107	Show and Tell/God Bless Rock and Roll	1981	$4
INFINITY			
❏ 50008	Ain't Misbehavin' (One Never Knows, Do One?)/'Round About Midnight	1979	$5
❏ 50038	Brand New Key/They're Playing Our Song	1979	$5
— Infinity sides as "Dante's Inferno			

Number	Title	Yr	NM
❏ 50018	Fire Island/They're Playing Our Song	1979	$5
KIRSHNER			
❏ 63-1010	How Do You Know/Let Me Bring You Up	1970	$6
❏ 63-1010 [PS]	How Do You Know/Let Me Bring You Up	1970	$10
❏ 63-5007	Sweet Taste of Love/C'mon Girl	1970	$6
MERCURY			
❏ 72812	Follow a Dream/He's Raining in My Sunshine	1968	$10
MUSICOR			
❏ 1134	Hey Mom, Hey Pop/(Heart) Stop Calling Her Name	1965	$15
❏ 1105	If You Love Me, Laurie/Don't Stand Up in a Canoe	1965	$15
❏ 1090	In the Rain/Poor Boys	1965	$15
❏ 1058	Look at Me/There's Love	1965	$15
MUSIC VOICE			
❏ 503	If You Love Me, Laurie/Don't Stand Up in a Canoe	1964	$20
RCA			
❏ PB-10898	How Am I to Know/Sky Rider	1977	$4
RCA VICTOR			
❏ PB-10340	Sugar, Sugar/Sugar, Sugar (Disco)	1975	$5
SCEPTER			
❏ 12333 [DJ]	That's What Life Is All About (mono/stereo)	1971	$6
— Stock copy may not exist			
DANTES, THE (1)			
JAMIE			
❏ 1314	Can't Get Enough of You Love/80-96	1966	$40
MAIN LINE			
❏ 1366	Connection/Satisfied	1967	$30
DANTES, THE (2)			
ROTATE			
❏ 5008	Top Down Time/How Many Times	1965	$125
DANZIG, GLENN			
Also see THE MISFITS; SAMHAIN.			
PLAN 9			
❏ PL1015	Who Killed Marilyn?/Spook City USA	1981	$75
— Black vinyl (5,000 made)			
❏ PL1015	Who Killed Marilyn?/Spook City USA	1981	$135
— Purple vinyl (500 made)			
❏ PL1015	Who Killed Marilyn?/Spook City USA	1981	$500
— Black and purple swirl vinyl (25 made); value is conjecture			
❏ PL1015 [PS]	Who Killed Marilyn?/Spook City USA	1981	$75
DAPPERS QUINTET, THE			
FLAYR			
❏ 500	Look What I've Found/(B-side unknown)	1955	$1500
DAPPERS, THE			
EPIC			
❏ 9423	My Love Is Real/Baby You Know You're Wrong	1960	$30
FOXIE			
❏ 7005	Chicken Twist/Lonely Street	1961	$50
PEACOCK			
❏ 1651	Come Back to Me/Mambo Oongh	1955	$200
RAINBOW			
❏ 373	Bop Bop Bu/How I Need You Baby	1956	$50
STAR-X			
❏ 505	We're in Love/Spellbound	1958	$250
DAPPS, THE			
KING			
❏ 6147	Bringing Up the Guitar/Gittin' a Little Hipper	1968	$30
❏ 6201	I'll Be Sweeter Tomorrow/A Woman, a Lover, a Friend	1968	$30
❏ 6087	It's a Gas (Part 1)/It's a Gas (Part 2)	1967	$30
DAPS, THE			
MARTERRY			
❏ 5429	When You're Alone/Down and Out	1956	$70
DARBISHIRE, STEVE			
LONDON			
❏ 1011	Trains Trains/Yum Yum	1966	$8

D'ARBY, TERENCE TRENT

COLUMBIA

Number	Title	Yr	NM
❑ 38-08023	Dance Little Sister (Part One)/(Part Two)	1988	$3
❑ 38-08023 [PS]	Dance Little Sister (Part One)/(Part Two)	1988	$3
❑ 38-07398	If You Let Me Stay/Loving You Is Another Word for Lonely	1987	$3
❑ 38-07398 [PS]	If You Let Me Stay/Loving You Is Another Word for Lonely	1987	$3
❑ 38-07911	Sign Your Name/Greasy Chicken	1988	$3
❑ 38-07911 [PS]	Sign Your Name/Greasy Chicken	1988	$3
❑ 38-73074	This Side of Love/Sad Song for Sister Sarah Serenade	1989	$6
❑ 38-07675	Wishing Well/Elevators and Hearts	1988	$3
❑ 38-07675 [PS]	Wishing Well/Elevators and Hearts	1988	$3

DARIN, BOBBY

ATCO

Number	Title	Yr	NM
❑ 6179	Artificial Flowers/Somebody to Love	1960	$30
❑ 6179 [PS]	Artificial Flowers/Somebody to Love	1960	$40
❑ 6211	Ave Maria/O Come All Ye Faithful	1961	$15
❑ 6211 [PS]	Ave Maria/O Come All Ye Faithful	1961	$160
❑ 6236	Baby Face/You Know How	1962	$15
❑ 6173	Beachcomber/Autumn Blues	1960	$30
❑ 6173 [PS]	Beachcomber/Autumn Blues	1960	$40
❑ 6158	Beyond the Sea/That's the Way Love Is	1960	$30
❑ 6158 [PS]	Beyond the Sea/That's the Way Love Is	1960	$50
❑ 6183	Christmas Auld Lang Syne/Child of God	1960	$30
❑ 6183 [PS]	Christmas Auld Lang Syne/Child of God	1960	$50
❑ 6161	Clementine/Tall Story	1960	$30
❑ 6161 [PS]	Clementine/Tall Story	1960	$50
❑ 6200	Come September/Walk Back to Me	1961	$20
❑ 6200 [PS]	Come September/Walk Back to Me	1961	$60
❑ 6103	Don't Call My Name/Pretty Betty	1957	$40
❑ 6140	Dream Lover/Bullmoose	1959	$30
❑ 6140 [PS]	Dream Lover/Bullmoose	1959	$60
❑ 6121	Early in the Morning/Now We're One	1958	$30
❑ 6121	Early in the Morning/Now We're One	1958	$50

—As "The Rinky Dinks

Number	Title	Yr	NM
❑ 6244	I Found a New Baby/Keep a-Walkin'	1962	$15
❑ 6214	Irresistible You/Multiplication	1961	$15
❑ 6214 [PS]	Irresistible You/Multiplication	1961	$30
❑ 6188	Lazy River/Oo-Ee Train	1961	$15
❑ 6188 [PS]	Lazy River/Oo-Ee Train	1961	$30
❑ 6147	Mack the Knife/Was There a Call for Me	1959	$30
❑ 6147 [PS]	Mack the Knife/Was There a Call for Me	1959	$50
❑ 6128	Mighty Mighty Man/You're Gone	1958	$30
❑ 6128	Mighty Mighty Man/You're Gone	1958	$50

—As "The Rinky Dinks

Number	Title	Yr	NM
❑ 6092	Million Dollar Baby/Talk to Me	1957	$40
❑ 6297	Milord/Golden Earrings	1964	$10
❑ 6334	Minnie the Moocher/Hard Hearted Hannah	1965	$10
❑ 6133 [M]	Plain Jane/While I'm Gone	1959	$30
❑ 6133 [PS]	Plain Jane/While I'm Gone	1959	$60
❑ SD-45-6133 [S]	Plain Jane/While I'm Gone	1959	$50
❑ (no #) [DJ]	She's Tanfastic!/Moments of Love	1960	$50

—Ferrion Inc. "Special Premium Record

Number	Title	Yr	NM
❑ 6117	Splish Splash/Judy, Don't Be Moody	1958	$30
❑ 6316	Swing Low Sweet Chariot/Similau	1964	$10
❑ 6229	Things/Jalier Bring Me Water	1962	$15
❑ 6221	What'd I Say (Part 1)/What'd I Say (Part 2)	1962	$15
❑ 6221 [PS]	What'd I Say (Part 1)/What'd I Say (Part 2)	1962	$30
❑ 6167	Won't You Come Home Bill Bailey/I'll Be There	1960	$30
❑ 6167 [PS]	Won't You Come Home Bill Bailey/I'll Be There	1960	$40

ATLANTIC

Number	Title	Yr	NM
❑ 89166	Beyond the Sea/Mack the Knife	1987	$3
❑ 89166 [PS]	Beyond the Sea/Mack the Knife	1987	$3

—From the movie "Big Town

Number	Title	Yr	NM
❑ 2420	Darlin' Be Home Soon/Hello, Sunshine	1967	$8
❑ 2305	Funny What Love Can Do/We Didn't Ask to Be Brought Here	1965	$8
❑ 2350	If I Were a Carpenter/Rainin'	1966	$10
❑ 2376	Lovin' You/Amy	1967	$8
❑ 2329	Mame/Walking in the Shadow of Love	1966	$8
❑ 2317	Silver Dollar/The Breaking Point	1966	$8
❑ 2433	Talk to the Animals/After Today	1967	$8
❑ 2433	Talk to the Animals/She Knows	1967	$8
❑ 2367	The Girl That Stood Beside Me/Reason to Believe	1966	$8
❑ 2395	The Lady Came from Baltimore/I Am	1967	$8
❑ 2341	Who's Afraid of Virginia Woolf?/Merci, Cheri	1966	$8

BRUNSWICK

Number	Title	Yr	NM
❑ 55073	Early in the Morning/Now We're One	1958	$100

—As "The Ding Dongs"; also see Atco 6121

CAPITOL

Number	Title	Yr	NM
❑ 4970	18 Yellow Roses/Not for Me	1963	$12
❑ 4970 [PS]	18 Yellow Roses/Not for Me	1963	$20
❑ 5399	A World Without You/Venice Blue	1965	$10
❑ 5079	Be Mad Little Girl/Since You've Been Gone	1963	$12
❑ 5481	Gyp the Cat/That Funny Feeling	1965	$10
❑ 5359	Hello, Dolly!/Golden Earrings	1965	$12
❑ 4837	If a Man Answers/True, True Love	1962	$10
❑ 4837 [PS]	If a Man Answers/True, True Love	1962	$20
❑ 5126	I Wonder Who's Kissing Her Now/As Long As I'm Singing	1964	$10
❑ 5257	The Things in This House/Wait by the Water	1964	$10
❑ 5019	Treat My Baby Good/Down So Long	1963	$10
❑ 5443	When I Get Home/Lonely Road	1965	$10
❑ 5443 [PS]	When I Get Home/Lonely Road	1965	$30

DECCA

Number	Title	Yr	NM
❑ 30225	Dealer in Dreams/Help Me	1957	$50
❑ 29922	Silly Willy/Blue Eyed Mermaid	1956	$60
❑ 30737	Silly Willy/Dealer in Dreams	1958	$40
❑ 30031	The Greatest Builder (Of Them All)/Hear Them Bells	1956	$50

DIRECTION

Number	Title	Yr	NM
❑ 4001	Baby May/Sweet Reason	1970	$8
❑ 352	Distractions (Part 1)/Jive	1969	$8
❑ 350	Long Line Rider/Change	1968	$8
❑ 4002	Maybe We Can Get It Together/Rx Pyro (Prescription: Fire)	1970	$8
❑ 351	Song for a Dollar/Mr. and Mrs. Hohner	1969	$8
❑ 4000	Sugar Man/(9 to 5) Jive's Alive	1970	$8

MOTOWN

Number	Title	Yr	NM
❑ 1212	Average People/Something in Her Love	1972	$6
❑ 1217	Happy/Something in Her Love	1973	$6
❑ 1183	Melodie/Someday We'll Be Together	1971	$6
❑ 1203	Sail Away/Something in Her Love	1972	$6
❑ 1193	Simple Song of Freedom/I'll Be Your Baby Tonight	1971	$6

7-Inch Extended Plays

ATCO

Number	Title	Yr	NM
❑ 4502	*Splish Splash/Judy, Don't Be Moody/I Found a Million Dollar Baby/(Since You're Gone) I Can't Go On	1959	$60
❑ 4502 [PS]	Bobby Darin	1959	$60
❑ 4505 [PS]	Bobby Darin	1960	$60
❑ 4508	Clementine/My Gal Sal//Guys and Dolls/Down with Love	1960	$60
❑ 4512 [PS]	Darin at the Copa	1960	$60
❑ EP4513 #NAME? [PS]	For Teenagers Only	1960	$75

—Special promotional sleeve; has photo of LP 1001

Number	Title	Yr	NM
❑ 4512	I Got A Woman/You'd Be So Nice To Come Home To//Medley: By Myself-When Your Lover Has Gone/Love For Sale	1960	$60
❑ EP4513 #NAME?	I Want You With Me/You Know How//Hush, Somebody's Calling My Name/Keep a-Walkin'	1960	$75
❑ 4504	Mack the Knife/That's the Way Love Is//Beyond the Sea/That's All	1959	$60
❑ 4504 [PS]	That's All	1959	$60
❑ 4508 [PS]	This Is Darin	1960	$60

CAPITOL CUSTOM

Number	Title	Yr	NM
❑ TB-2262/3	18 Yellow Roses/Not for Me/The Things in This House//You're the Reason I'm Living/Treat My Baby Good/Wait by the Water, Lillian	1963	$35

—Small hole, plays at 33 1/3 rpm

Number	Title	Yr	NM
❑ TB-2262/3 [PS]	Bobby Darin Presents	1963	$50

—Manufactured by Capitol Records, Inc., Custom Services Department for Artistic Records

Number	Title	Yr	NM
❑ MB-2849/50	If a Man Answers/True, True Love//Sermon of Samson/All By Myself	1962	$25
❑ MB-2849/50 [PS]	Scripto Inc. Presents Bobby Darin	1962	$35

—Value is for sleeve alone; the pen that came with the package is very rare

DECCA

Number	Title	Yr	NM
❑ ED2676	(contents unknown)	1957	$125
❑ ED2676 [PS]	Hear Them Bells	1957	$125

MOTOWN

Number	Title	Yr	NM
❑ PR-4 [DJ]	If I Were a Carpenter/Moritat (Mack the Knife)//Blue Monday/Happy	1973	$20
❑ PR-4 [PS]	(title unknown)	1973	$25

DARLING, JOHNNY

DELUXE

Number	Title	Yr	NM
❑ 6167	I Don't Want to Wind Up in Love/Baseball Baby	1956	$200

DARNELL, BILL

X

Number	Title	Yr	NM
❑ 067	Too Fat to Be Santa/We Wanna See Santa Do the Mambo	1954	$20

DARNELL, LARRY

ANNA

Number	Title	Yr	NM
❑ 1109	With Tears in My Eyes/I'll Get Along Somehow	1960	$400

ARGO

Number	Title	Yr	NM
❑ 5372	With Tears in My Eyes/I'll Get Along Somehow	1960	$30

DELUXE

Number	Title	Yr	NM
❑ 6136	If You Go/Fing Fang Foy	1957	$40

OKEH

Number	Title	Yr	NM
❑ 6926	Christmas Blues/I Am the Sparrow	1952	$30
❑ 6869	Darlin'/Boogie-Oogie	1952	$30
❑ 6954	I'll Be Sittin', I'll Be Rockin'/Crazy She Calls Me	1953	$30
❑ 7024	I'll Carry On/What More Do You Want Me to Do	1954	$30
❑ 6919	I'll Get Along Somehow (Part 1)/I'll Get Along Somehow (Part 2)	1952	$30
❑ 7039	I'm Gonna Change/Thank You, Darlin'	1954	$30
❑ 7056	My Love for You/Feelin' Mighty Sad and Low	1955	$30
❑ 6902	What's On Your Mind/Better Be on My Way	1952	$30
❑ 6848	Work Baby Work/Left My Baby	1952	$30

REGAL

Number	Title	Yr	NM
❑ 3328	Do You Love Me Baby/Sad and Lonesome	1951	$30

—Larry Darnell records on Regal before 3328 are unconfirmed on 45 rpm

SAVOY

Number	Title	Yr	NM
❑ 1151	That's All I Want from You/Who Showed My Baby How to Love Me	1955	$40

WARWICK

Number	Title	Yr	NM
❑ 506	If I Had You/Thankful	1959	$30

7-Inch Extended Plays

EPIC

Number	Title	Yr	NM
❑ 7072	(contents unknown)	1961	$25
❑ 7072 [PS]	For You My Love	1961	$25

DARRELL, JOHNNY

CAPRICORN

Number	Title	Yr	NM
❑ 0207	Orange Blossom Special/Glendale, Arizona	1974	$4
❑ 0223	Pieces of My Life/Glendale, Arizona	1975	$4

CARTWHEEL

Number	Title	Yr	NM
❑ 203	Don't It Seem to Rain a Lot/I'll Never Get Up This Slow	1971	$5
❑ 209	Mr. Tambourine Man/Let Me Stay Awhile	1972	$5

GUSTO

Number	Title	Yr	NM
❑ 9001	Hard to Be Friends/These Days	1978	$4
❑ 9011	Was Yesterday That Long Ago/Spanish Song	1978	$4

MONUMENT

Number	Title	Yr	NM
❑ 8570	Crazy Daddy/Uncle Veneer	1973	$5
❑ 8579	Dakota the Dancing Bear/Just a Memory	1973	$5

UNITED ARTISTS

Number	Title	Yr	NM
❑ 943	As Long As the Wind Blows/Beggars Can't Be Choosers	1965	$8
❑ 50675	Brother River/Bed of Roses	1970	$6
❑ 50207	Come See What's Left of Your Man/Passin' Through	1967	$8
❑ 869	Green, Green Grass of Home/Deepening Snow	1965	$8
❑ 50442	I Ain't Buying/Little Things	1968	$6
❑ 50739	Look Out Cleveland/Winter's Comin' On	1971	$6
❑ 50629	Mama Come'n Get Your Baby Boy/These Days	1970	$6
❑ 50183	My Elusive Dreams/Pickin' with Gold	1967	$8
❑ 50610	She's Headed for the Country/Trouble Maker	1969	$6
❑ 50047	She's Mighty Gone/Baby Sitter	1966	$8
❑ 50503	The Coming of the Roads/The Other Side of the Coin	1969	$6

—With Anita Carter

Number	Title	Yr	NM
❑ 50235	The Son of Hickory Holler's Tramp/But That's Alright	1967	$8
❑ 50235 [PS]	The Son of Hickory Holler's Tramp/But That's Alright	1967	$20
❑ 50716	They'll Never Take Her Love from Me/One Love, Two Hearts, Three Lives	1970	$6
❑ 50518	Why You Been Gone So Long/You're Always the One	1969	$6
❑ 50292	With Pen in Hand/Poetry of Love	1968	$6
❑ 50481	Woman Without Love/I Fought the Law	1968	$6

Number	Title	Yr	NM

DARREN, JAMES
BUDDAH
| ❏ 177 | That's My World/Wheeling, West Virginia | 1970 | $5 |

COLPIX
❏ 765	A Married Man/Baby, Talk to Me	1964	$10
❏ 119 [M]	Angel Face/I Don't Wanna Lose Ya	1959	$20
❏ 119 [PS]	Angel Face/I Don't Wanna Lose Ya	1959	$40
❏ SCP-119 [S]	Angel Face/I Don't Wanna Lose Ya	1959	$50
❏ 142	Because They're Young/Tears in My Eyes	1960	$20
❏ 142 [PS]	Because They're Young/Tears in My Eyes	1960	$40
❏ 630	Conscience/Dream Big	1962	$15
❏ 185	Fool's Paradise/Gotta Have Love	1961	$20
❏ 696	Gegetta/Grande Luna, Italiana	1963	$15
❏ 189	Gidget Goes Hawaiian/Wild About the Girl	1961	$20
❏ 113	Gidget/You	1959	$20
❏ 609	Goodbye Cruel World/Valerie	1961	$20
❏ 609 [PS]	Goodbye Cruel World/Valerie	1961	$30
❏ 655	Hail to the Conquering Hero/Too Young to Go Steady	1962	$15
❏ 194	Hand in Hand/You Are My Dream	1961	$20
❏ 664	Hear What I Want to Hear/I'll Be Loving You	1962	$15
❏ 622	Her Royal Majesty/If I Could Only Tell You	1962	$15
❏ 155	How Sweet You Are/All the Young Men	1960	$20
❏ 128	I Ain't Sharin' Sharon/Love Among the Young	1959	$20
❏ 168	Man About Town/Come On My Love	1960	$20
❏ 644	Mary's Little Lamb/The Life of the Party	1962	$15
❏ 672	Pin a Medal on Joey/Diamond Head	1963	$15
❏ 145	P.S. I Love You/Traveling Down a Lonesome Road	1960	$20
❏ 758	Punch and Judy/Just Think of Tonight	1964	$30
❏ 130	Teenage Tears/Let There Be Love	1959	$20
❏ 102	There's No Such Thing/Mighty Pretty Territory	1959	$20
❏ 102 [PS]	There's No Such Thing/Mighty Pretty Territory	1959	$40
❏ 685	They Should Have Given You the Oscar/Blame It on My Youth	1963	$15
❏ 181	Walking My Baby Back Home/Goodbye My Lady	1960	$20

— Colpix 102-181 by "Jimmy Darren

KIRSHNER
❏ 63-5025	Brian's Song/Thnak Heaven for Little Girls	1973	$5
❏ 63-5013	Bring Me Down Slow/More and More	1971	$5
❏ 63-1012	I Think Somebody Loves Me/Ain't Been Home in a Long Time	1970	$5
❏ 63-5015	Mammy Blue/As Long As You Love Me	1971	$5

MGM
| ❏ 14558 | Let the Heartaches Begin/Sad Song | 1973 | $4 |
| ❏ 14667 | Sad-Eyed Romany Woman/Stay | 1973 | $4 |

PRIVATE STOCK
❏ 45,050	Love on the Screen/Losing You	1975	$4
❏ 45,064	One Has My Name, The Other Has My Heart/Sleepin' in a Bed of Lies	1975	$4
❏ 45,152 [DJ]	Only a Dream Away (mono/stereo)	1977	$5

— Stock copies may not exist

RCA
| ❏ PB-11316 | Let Me Take You in My Arms Again/California | 1978 | $4 |

WARNER BROS.
❏ 7206	A Little Bit of Heaven/Each and Every Part of Me	1968	$8
❏ 5874	All/Misty Morning Eyes	1966	$8
❏ 5648	Because You're Mine/Millions of Roses	1965	$8
❏ 7152	Cherie/Wait Until Dark	1967	$8
❏ 5838	Crazy Me/They Don't Know	1966	$8
❏ 7053	Didn't We/Counting the Cracks	1967	$8
❏ 7013	I Miss You So/Since I Don't Have You	1967	$8
❏ 5689	I Want to Be Lonely/Tom Hawk	1966	$8
❏ 5856	Love Is Where You Find It/(Let's Worry About) Tomorrow Tomorrow	1966	$8
❏ 7071	The House Song/They Don't Know	1967	$8
❏ 5812	Where Did We Go Wrong/Counting the Cracks	1966	$8

DARTELLS, THE
ARLEN
| ❏ 513 | Dance, Everybody, Dance/The Scoobie Song | 1963 | $30 |
| ❏ 509 | Hot Pastrami/Dartell Stomp | 1963 | $30 |

DOT
❏ 16551	Convicted/Sweet Pea	1963	$20
❏ 16502	Dance, Everybody, Dance/The Scoobie Song	1963	$30
❏ 16453	Hot Pastrami/Dartell Stomp	1963	$30
❏ 16646	Swiss Cheese/Dartell Stomp	1964	$20

HANNA-BARBERA
| ❏ 457 | Clap Your Hands/Where Do We Stand | 1965 | $20 |

SANDE
| ❏ 103 | The Girl Can't Help It/Stranger on the Shore | 1964 | $40 |

DARVELL, BARRY
ATLANTIC
| ❏ 2138 | Adam and Eve/A King for Tonight | 1962 | $30 |
| ❏ 2128 | Lost Love/Silver Dollar | 1961 | $30 |

COLT 45
❏ 110	Butterfly Baby/Send Me Some Loving	1960	$30
❏ 107	Geronimo Stomp/How Will It End	1959	$70
❏ 104	Teenage Love/(B-side unknown)	1959	$30

COLUMBIA
| ❏ 44197 | My World of Make Believe/Beggar's Paradise | 1967 | $8 |

CUB
| ❏ 9088 | Little Angel Lost/Fountain of Love | 1961 | $30 |

PROVIDENCE
| ❏ 404 | When You're Alone/It's Rainin', It's Pourin' | 1964 | $15 |

WORLD ARTISTS
| ❏ 1058 | I Found a Daisy (in the City)/Kissable Lips | 1965 | $15 |
| ❏ 1042 | I'll Remember/Where Is the Love for Me | 1965 | $15 |

DAS DAMEN
SUB POP
| ❏ 39 | Sad Mile/Making Time | 1989 | $13 |

—#9 in Sub Pop Singles Club series

| ❏ 39 [PS] | Sad Mile/Making Time | 1989 | $13 |

DASHIEL, BUD, AND THE KINSMEN
WARNER BROS.
| ❏ 5276 | In Tarrytown/Big Manuel | 1962 | $10 |
| ❏ 5231 | Pom Pa Lum/I Talk to the Trees | 1961 | $10 |

DAUGHTERS OF ALBION, THE
FONTANA
| ❏ 1619 | Well Wired/The Story of Sad | 1968 | $10 |

DAVE AND THE CARDIGANS
BAY
| ❏ 216 | My Falling Star/Cha Cha Baby | 1963 | $200 |

DAVE AND THE MARKSMEN
A&M
| ❏ 730 | Cruisin'/Kustom Kar Show | 1964 | $60 |

WARNER BROS.
| ❏ 5485 | I Wanna Cry/I Could Make You Mine | 1964 | $40 |

WESTCO
| ❏ 10 | Down the Tubes/Ooh Poo Pa Doo | 1963 | $60 |

— Black vinyl

| ❏ 10 | Down the Tubes/Ooh Poo Pa Doo | 1963 | $125 |

— Yellow vinyl

DAVE DEE, DOZY, BEAKY, MICK & TICH
ATLANTIC
| ❏ 89757 [DJ] | Staying With It (same on both sides) | 1983 | $5 |

—May be promo only

BELL
| ❏ 942 | Frisco Annie/Hey! Mr. President | 1970 | $6 |

—As "D.B.M. & T.

COTILLION
| ❏ 44061 | Bad News/Tonight-Today | 1970 | $6 |

—As "Dozy, Beaky, Mick & Tich

| ❏ 44061 [PS] | Bad News/Tonight-Today | 1970 | $12 |

—As "Dozy, Beaky, Mick & Tich

FONTANA
| ❏ 1559 | Bend It/She's So Good | 1966 | $15 |

— With "clean" lyrics that refer to a dance (starts "Bend it, bend it, show me you can move and do the dance that's really in the groove"); matrix number of "Bend It" is YW1-38890

| ❏ 1559 | Bend It/She's So Good | 1966 | $30 |

— With "dirty" lyrics that don't mention a dance (starts "Bend it, bend it, just a little bit and take it easy, show you're likin' it"); matrix number of "Bend It" is YW1-39024

❏ 1553	Hideaway/Here's a Heart	1966	$12
❏ 1545	Hold Tight/You Know What I Want	1966	$12
❏ 1591	Okay/Master Llewellyn	1967	$10
❏ 1569	Save Me/Shame	1967	$10

IMPERIAL
❏ 66309	Break Out/Mrs. Thursday	1968	$8
❏ 66325	Break Out/Mrs. Thursday	1968	$8
❏ 66287	Legend of Xanadu/Please	1968	$8
❏ 66339	Wreck of the Antoinette/Margarita Linman	1968	$8

DAVID AND DAVID
A&M
❏ 2905	Ain't So Easy/Swimming in the Ocean	1987	$3
❏ 2905 [PS]	Ain't So Easy/Swimming in the Ocean	1987	$3
❏ 2882	Swallowed by the Cracks/All Alone in the Big City	1986	$3
❏ 2857	Welcome to the Boomtown/A Rock for the Forgotten	1986	$3
❏ 2857 [PS]	Welcome to the Boomtown/A Rock for the Forgotten	1986	$3

DAVID AND JONATHAN
20TH FOX
| ❏ 6641 | Modesty/Willie Waltz | 1966 | $8 |

AMY
| ❏ 11012 | Softly Whispering I Love You/Something's Gotten Hold of My Heart | 1968 | $6 |

CAPITOL
❏ 5625	I Know/Speak Her Name	1966	$8
❏ 5625 [PS]	I Know/Speak Her Name	1966	$15
❏ 5563	Michelle/How Bitter the Taste of Love	1965	$10
❏ 5700	On My Word/Lovers of the World, Unite	1966	$8
❏ 5934	She's Leaving Home/One Born Every Minute	1967	$8
❏ 5870	Ten Stories High/Looking for My Life	1967	$8
❏ 5777	The Magic Book/Time	1966	$8

DAVID AND RUBEN
WARNER BROS.
| ❏ 7316 | (I Love Her So Much) It Hurts Me/The Girl in My Dreams | 1969 | $400 |

DAVID, THE
20TH CENTURY FOX
| ❏ 6663 | 40 Miles/Bus Token | 1966 | $40 |

V.M.C.
| ❏ 716 | I'm Not Alone/(B-side unknown) | 1968 | $30 |

DAVIDSON, JOHN
20TH CENTURY
❏ 2293	Everytime I Sing a Love Song/Love in the Shadows	1976	$4
❏ 2121	Have a Nice Day/Less Than the Sun	1974	$4
❏ 2313	I Let You Walk Away/Steal Her Away	1976	$4
❏ 2326	Patch It Up/Save the Last Dance for Me	1976	$4
❏ 2175	The Other Woman/What Will I Tell the Kids	1975	$4
❏ 2063	We Had It All/I Want to Spend My Life with You	1973	$4

COLUMBIA
❏ 44896	California Blood Lines/I Am Now	1969	$6
❏ 44005	Daydream/I'll Always Remember	1967	$6
❏ 44005 [PS]	Daydream/I'll Always Remember	1967	$8
❏ 45155	Five O'Clock Shadow/A Promise and a Lie	1970	$5
❏ 45486	Good Times/A Clown Never Cries	1971	$5
❏ 43531	I Can't Help This Feeling I Feel/I Still Send Her Flowers	1966	$6
❏ 45196	I Got Love/Politician	1970	$5
❏ 44210	In the Sunshine Days/If You Can Put That in a Bottle	1967	$6
❏ 45034	It's Such a Lovely Time of Year/What Makes a Woman Run	1969	$6
❏ 45254	Let's Get Lost In Now/What You're Doing to Me	1970	$5
❏ 45423	Say It Again/Just Magic	1971	$6
❏ 43635	Summer Love/I'll Try Lovin' You Less	1966	$6
❏ 44334	What Is a Woman/How Come You Love Me Like You Do	1967	$6
❏ 44770	Words/The Wonder of You	1969	$6

MERCURY
| ❏ 73362 | As Lonely As You/What She Left of Me | 1973 | $5 |

DAVIE, HUTCH
ATCO
❏ 6136	Begin the Beguine/The Dipsy Doodle	1959	$15
❏ 6123	In the Mood/Gwendolyn and the Werewolf	1958	$15
❏ 6149	Sweet Georgia Brown/Heartaches	1959	$15
❏ 6110	Woodchopper's Ball/Honky Tonk Train	1958	$15

CANADIAN AMERICAN
| ❏ 126 | The Glow Worm/Down Home | 1961 | $10 |

CLARIDGE
| ❏ 311 | East Is East (Part 1)/East Is East (Part 2) | 1966 | $8 |

CONGRESS
| ❏ 102 | But I Do/Time Was | 1962 | $10 |

Number	Title	Yr	NM
NEW VOICE			
❏ 823	Swingin' Shepherd Blues/Salty	1967	$6
DAVIE, ROBERT			
CONGRESS			
❏ 224	As Time Goes By/The Gypsy	1964	$8
❏ 231	Oh! What It Seemed to Be/Because of You	1964	$8
DAVIES, CYRIL			
DOT			
❏ 16515	Chicago Calling/Country Line Special	1963	$15
DAVIES, DAVE			
Also see THE KINKS.			
RCA			
❏ PB-12147	Doing the Best for You/Got No More to Lose	1981	$5
❏ PB-12089	Imagination's Real/Wild Man	1980	$5
❏ PB-12089 [PS]	Imagination's Real/Wild Man	1980	$8
REPRISE			
❏ 0614	Death of a Clown/Love Me Till the Sun Shines	1967	$50
❏ 0660	Suzannah's Still Alive/Funny Face	1968	$50
WARNER BROS.			
❏ 29509	Love Gets You/One Night with You	1983	$30
❏ 29509 [DJ]	Love Gets You (same on both sides)	1983	$8
❏ 29425	Mean Disposition/Cold Winter	1983	$30
❏ 29425 [DJ]	Mean Disposition (same on both sides)	1983	$8
DAVIS, EDDIE "LOCKJAW			
PRESTIGE			
❏ 186	Santa Claus Is Coming To Town/Christmas Song	1958	$15
DAVIS, BILLIE			
JERDEN			
❏ 758	Last One to Be Loved/You Don't Know	1965	$12
LONDON			
❏ 20049	I Can Remember/I'll Come Home	1968	$6
❏ 20041	I Want You to Be My Baby/Suffer	1968	$6
❏ 20062	There Must Be a Reason/Love	1971	$5
DAVIS, BILLY, JR.			
ABC			
❏ 12106	Three Steps from True Love/Light a Candle	1975	$5
DAVIS, BILLY			
COBBLESTONE			
❏ 731	Stanky (Get Funky)/I've Tried	1969	$6
HI			
❏ 2146	It's All Over/Once in a Lifetime	1968	$6
DAVIS, BO			
CREST			
❏ 1027	Let's Coast Awhile/Drownin' All My Sorrows	1956	$200
—Eddie Cochran plays guitar on this record.			
DAVIS, CARL			
CHART			
❏ 1075	I'm On My Way Back Home/That's What Tears Me Up	1964	$10
STOP			
❏ 176	Once in Every Lifetime/He's a Bigger Man	1968	$8
DAVIS, CARRIE			
FOUNTAIN HILLS			
❏ 130	Another Heart to Break the Fall/I'm Just Looking for the Real Thing	1989	$6
DAVIS, DANNY, AND THE NASHVILLE BRASS			
HICKORY			
❏ 1005	Can't You Feel It in Your Heart/Second Hand Dreams for Sale	1954	$15
JAROCO			
❏ 8742	Green Eyes (Cryin' Those Blue Tears)/Little Pink Cloud	1987	$5
LIBERTY			
❏ 55213	Beauty and the Beast/Glory Bugle	1959	$12
MGM			
❏ 11244	Always/Do You Ever Think of Me	1952	$20
❏ 13368	Ballad of Cat Ballou/Theme from "The Saint"	1965	$6
❏ 13270	Circus World/There Goes My Heart	1964	$6
❏ 11103	Crazy Heart/I'm Not Alone	1951	$20
❏ 11286	Forget/Love Came Out of the Night	1952	$20
❏ 11443	I Don't Want Your Kisses/Come to the Wedding	1953	$20
❏ 13374	I'm Henry VIII, I Am/The End of the World	1965	$6

Number	Title	Yr	NM
❏ 13106	Little Bandits of Juarez/Theme from "Kill Or Cure"	1962	$8
❏ 11175	Please Bring Back the Sunshine/Deep Water	1952	$20
❏ 13077	Pots 'N' Pans/Travelin' Trumpets	1962	$8
RCA			
❏ PB-11612	Ain't Misbehavin'/I'm Gonna Sit Right Down and Write Myself a Letter	1979	$4
❏ PB-12070	Cotton Eyed Joe/Colinda	1980	$4
❏ PB-10871	Country Disco/Disco Dante	1977	$4
❏ PB-11073	How I Love Them Old Songs/Tara Jeanne	1977	$4
❏ PB-11278	Old Fashioned Love Song/Falsely Accused	1978	$4
❏ PB-11466	Sugarfoot Rag/Let Your Lovelight Shine	1979	$4
RCA VICTOR			
❏ PB-10255	Branigan/Peppy Time Tune	1975	$4
❏ 47-9847	Columbus Stockade Blues/Wings of a Dove	1970	$4
❏ 47-9905	Down Yonder/May the Circle Be Unbroken	1970	$4
❏ 74-0760	From Dixie with Love/Under the Double Eagle	1972	$4
❏ 74-0506	Highland Brass/Ruby, Don't Take Your Love to Town	1971	$4
❏ 74-0439	I Can't Stop Loving You/Rose Garden	1971	$4
❏ 74-0847	I'll Fly Away/Woman	1972	$4
❏ PB-10570	Paloma Blanca/Nashville Express	1976	$4
❏ PB-10232	Singing the Blues/Stay a Little Longer	1975	$4
❏ APBO-0019	Superstar/Come See Us	1973	$4
❏ 47-9785	Wabash Cannon Ball/Sweet Dreams	1969	$4
❏ 74-0560	Wait for the Light to Shine/Blue Bayou	1971	$4
❏ 74-0858	White Christmas/Winter Wonderland	1972	$5
❏ PB-10814	Why Don't You Love Me/He'll Have to Go	1976	$4
VERVE			
❏ 10233	Theme from "Carnival"/Stardust	1961	$10
WARTRACE			
❏ 730	I Dropped Your Name/(B-side unknown)	1985	$4
DAVIS, DANNY, AND WILLIE NELSON			
RCA			
❏ PB-11999	Funny How Time Slips Away/The Local Memory	1980	$4
DAVIS, DIANNE			
16TH AVENUE			
❏ 70430	Baby Don't Go/(B-side unknown)	1989	$4
DAVIS, EUNICE			
ATLANTIC			
❏ 992	Go to Work Pretty Daddy/My Beat Is 125th Street	1953	$70
CORAL			
❏ 65075	Work Daddy Work/What Do You Want	1952	$30
DELUXE			
❏ 6068	Get Your Enjoys/24 Hours a Day	1954	$40
DERBY			
❏ 760	Evening Train/I'm a Wild West Woman	1951	$40
❏ 768	Good News for You Baby/Tell Me I'm the Baby	1951	$40
GRAND			
❏ 130	Let's Have a Party/Every Time Your Lips Meet Mine	1955	$30
DAVIS, GAIL			
COLUMBIA			
❏ 4-21469	Tomboy/I'm a Female Through and Through	1955	$30
DAVIS, GENE			
MAVERICK			
❏ 301	Oh Those Texas Women/She Says It with Love	1976	$6
DAVIS, HAL			
ALDEN			
❏ 1301	My Young Heart/(B-side unknown)	1959	$50
FEDERAL			
❏ 12429	My Only Flower/You're the Girl	1961	$15
GARDENA			
❏ 125	One More Chance/Show Me	1962	$40
GSP			
❏ 2	I Don't Know/Lover's Plan	1963	$40
VEE JAY			
❏ 387	Merchant of Love/What Do You Mean to Me	1961	$30
WIZARD			
❏ 102	I Need Someone/(B-side unknown)	1961	$40
❏ 101	Merchant of Love/What Do You Mean to Me	1961	$75

Number	Title	Yr	NM
DAVIS, JAN			
A&M			
❏ 733	Boss Machine/The Fugitive	1964	$20
❏ 744	Guitar Star/The Unwanted	1964	$20
ALJO			
❏ 104	The Surfin' Matador/Scramble	1964	$40
BEAR			
❏ 1000	Hornet's Nest/Flamenco Funk (Mosaic)	1969	$6
BIG BIRD			
❏ 128	International Love Process (Part 1)/International Love Process (Part 2)	1967	$20
COLUMBIA			
❏ 43224	More (Theme from Mondo Cane)/Mystique	1965	$20
HOLIDAY			
❏ 1213	Pooky/Watusi Zombie	1964	$20
QUAD-ETT			
❏ 10039	Hot Sauce/Soul Mate	1974	$5
RANWOOD			
❏ 1035	El Lobo/Maiden Spain	1975	$5
❏ 1023	Gypsy Fox/Child of June (Danny's Theme)	1974	$5
❏ 1015	Hot Sauce/Soulmate	1974	$5
RCA VICTOR			
❏ 47-9018	Time Tunnel/Walkin' Back	1966	$15
RENDEZVOUS			
❏ 218	Delicado/Sahara	1963	$30
❏ 205	Malaguena/Hop, Skip and Jump	1963	$30
❏ 149	Sabre Dance/Hop, Skip and Jump	1961	$30
❏ 131	Sleepless/Damascus	1960	$30
—With the Ricco-Shays			
SHAMLEY			
❏ 44016	Hornet's Nest/Flamenco Funk (Mosaic)	1969	$5
SMASH			
❏ 1863	The Snow Surfin' Matador/Scramble	1963	$30
UNI			
❏ 55029	International Love Process (Part 1)/International Love Process (Part 2)	1967	$8
❏ 55197	Walk Don't Run/Flamenco Funk	1970	$5
WHITE WHALE			
❏ 226	Lost in Space/Run for Your Life	1966	$15
DAVIS, JESSE			
ERA			
❏ 3189	Gonna Hang On In There Girl/Albuquerque	1967	$600
MULBERRY SQUARE			
❏ 3935	Benji's Theme -- I Feel Love/Benji's Theme -- Part II	1975	$30
❏ 3935 [PS]	Benji's Theme -- I Feel Love/Benji's Theme -- Part II	1975	$40
DAVIS, JESSE ED			
ATCO			
❏ 6807	Every Night Is Saturday Night/Golden Sun Goddess	1971	$5
❏ 6873	Sue Me, Sue You Blues/My Captain	1972	$8
EPIC			
❏ 11021	She's a Pain/Natural Anthem	1973	$4
DAVIS, JIMMIE			
CAPITOL			
❏ F1510	As Long As You Believe in Me/White Petals	1951	$40
❏ F1210	Cickle Cackle Song/Poodle Dog Song	1950	$40
❏ F40251	My Bucket's Got a Hole in It/Gotta Have My Baby Back	1949	$60
❏ F40281	White Lace, Red Clay and a Black Coffin/Sometimes Late at Night	1950	$50
DECCA			
❏ 9-28656	Big Mamou/Neon Love	1953	$40
❏ 32331	Bury Me Beneath the Willows/You'll Be My Last Love	1968	$10
❏ 9-46356	Cherokee Boogie/I Wish I'd Never Met Sunshine	1951	$50
❏ 9-28912	Christmas Choo Choo/I Love to Ride with Santa Claus	1953	$40
❏ 32843	Crumbs from the Table/My Boy Is Going Home	1971	$12
❏ 31602	Don't Close the Door/The Beginning of the End	1964	$20
❏ 9-30257	Do You Ever Think to Pray/I Know What He Meant	1957	$30
❏ 9-46381	Fifteen Miles from Dallas/Bayou for You	1951	$50
❏ 9-46396	Forever's a Long, Long Time/I Ain't Gonna Give	1952	$50
❏ 32062	Forgive Me Santa/Take Me Back to Babylon	1966	$15
❏ 31270	Git On Board, Little Children/Twenty-One	1961	$30
❏ 32236	Going Home for Christmas/Sniffles (Santa's Pet)	1967	$10
❏ 32677	Going Home/Three Nails	1970	$10
❏ 31686	Go Tell It on the Mountain/It's Christmas Time Again	1964	$20

Number	Title	Yr	NM
❏ 31870	(Here's My) Buryin' Ground/I'm Nearer Home (Than I Was Yesterday)	1965	$20
❏ 31797	He's Able/The Safety of His Arms	1965	$20
❏ 9-30748	How Great Thou Art/I'll Meet You in the Morning	1958	$30
❏ 9-29965	How Long Has It Been/Dear Son	1956	$30
❏ 9-28909	I Can't Stand the Pain/You Took	1953	$40
❏ 9-29082	I Don't Care What the World Might Do/Somewhere There's a Friend	1954	$40
❏ 32941	If That Isn't Love/Lord, Have You Forgotten Me	1972	$10
❏ 9-31009	If You Can Get Along with Me/Gonna Let the Good Times Roll	1959	$30
❏ 9-28259	I Heard You Talking in Your Sleep/Like the Waves Upon the River	1952	$40
❏ 9-28370	I Know Who Holds Tomorrow/The Great Milky Way	1952	$40
❏ 31739	I Wouldn't Take Nothing for My Journey/You Can Have Him	1965	$20
❏ 33020	Let's All Shine/No One to Welcome Me Home	1972	$12
❏ 9-28555	Lord, I'm Comin' Home/When Do I Remember	1953	$40
❏ 9-30899	Lost Love/My Mary	1959	$30
❏ 32559	Mary Let Your Bangs Hang Down/Today I'm Giving You Away	1969	$15
❏ 31637	My Room of Prayer/When I Lay My Burdens Down	1964	$20
❏ 32867	Put Your Hand in the Hand/Won't You Take Me Back and Try Me One More Time	1971	$10
❏ 31327	Sitting on Top of the World/Time Changes Everything	1961	$30
❏ 9-29445	Sometimes Late at Night/I Might Even Lose My Mind	1955	$30
❏ 9-30668	Sweet Mystery/I'm Bound for the Kingdom	1958	$30
❏ 9-28438	Talkin' to the Wall/Please, Please	1952	$40
❏ 32192	The Chair That Rocked Us All/Haven't Been to Church for Some Time	1967	$15
❏ 9-28799	To My Mansion in the Sky/Supper-Time	1953	$40
❏ 9-46408	Touch the Hand of the Lord/How Great Thou Art	1952	$50
❏ 9-29613	When the Savior Reached Down His Hand/I Was There When It Happened	1955	$30
❏ 9-28748	When the Train Comes Rollin' In/Lord, I'm Coming Home	1953	$40
❏ 9-46410	When the World's on Fire/You're Not Home Yet	1952	$50
❏ 9-28110	When We All Get Together/Thirty Pieces of Silver	1952	$40
❏ 9-29801	Where No One Stands Alone/My Lord Will Lead Me Home	1956	$30
❏ 31368	Where the Old Red River Flows/Lonesome Whistle (See, I Heard That Lonesome Whistle)	1962	$30
❏ 31906	Will the Circle Be Unbroken/Who Am I	1966	$15
❏ 9-14563	When They Ring Those Golden Bells/When the Morning Comes	1951	$40

MCA

Number	Title	Yr	NM
❏ 40072	Let's All Go Down to the River/God's Last Altar Call	1973	$6
❏ 53107	Over the Top/Kick the Wall	1987	$4

PAULA

❏ 416	Dating a Memory/Walking My Blues Away	1976	$6
❏ 406	Don't Let the Green Grass Fool You/Souvenirs of Yesterday	1974	$6
❏ 414	Lay It on the Line/I Can't Stand the Pain	1975	$6

PLANTATION

| ❏ 163 | Hold Me/Where the Old Red River Flows | 1977 | $5 |
| ❏ 174 | Pretending She's You/It Makes No Difference Now | 1978 | $5 |

DAVIS, JO
CUCA

| ❏ 1112 | Christmas Vacation/Jamacian Holiday | 1962 | $15 |

DAVIS, JOEY
MRC

| ❏ 1017 | Why Don't You Leave Me Alone/(B-side unknown) | 1978 | $8 |

DAVIS, LARRY
DUKE

❏ 328	Come Home/Will She Come Home	1960	$30
❏ 192	I Tried/Texas Flood	1958	$40
❏ 313	My Little Girl/Angels in Houston	1959	$30

KENT

| ❏ 507 | Driving Wheel/Sweet Little Angel | 1969 | $20 |

DAVIS, LEE
CUB

| ❏ 9026 | Three Young Men/The Flower Song | 1959 | $20 |

—B-side by the Naturals

DAVIS, LINDA
EPIC

Number	Title	Yr	NM
❏ 34-08057	All the Good Ones Are Taken/Cry Baby	1988	$3
❏ 34-68544	Back in the Swing Again/All the Good Ones Are Taken	1989	$3
❏ 34-68919	Weak Nights/All the Good Ones Are Taken	1989	$3

DAVIS, LINK
ALLSTAR

| ❏ 7185 | Ballad of Jole Blon/Visions | 1959 | $30 |
| ❏ 7203 | Little People/Tee Mamou | 1960 | $30 |

COLUMBIA

| ❏ 4-21431 | Cajun Love/Everytime I Pass Your Door | 1955 | $30 |

DAVIS, MAC
CAPITOL

| ❏ 5554 | Bad Scene/I Protest | 1965 | $8 |

CASABLANCA

❏ 818929-7	Caroline's Still in Georgia/I've Got a Dream	1984	$3
❏ 2327	Hooked On Music/Me and Fat Boy	1981	$3
❏ 2244	It's Hard to Be Humble/Greatest Gift of All	1980	$4
❏ 2286	Let's Keep It That Way/I Know You're Out There Somewhere	1980	$3
❏ 2363	Lying Here Lying/Quiet Times	1982	$3
❏ 2346	Midnight Crazy/I Got the Hots for You	1981	$3
❏ 818168-7	Most of All/Springtime Down in Dixie	1984	$3
❏ 2336	Secrets/Remember When Beverly	1981	$3
❏ 2305	Texas in My Rear View Mirror/Sad Songs	1980	$3
❏ 2355	The Beer Drinkin' Song/You Are So Lovely	1982	$3

COLUMBIA

❏ 45618	Baby Don't Get Hooked on Me/Poem for My Little Lady	1972	$4
❏ 45302	Beginning to Feel the Pain/Butterfly Girl	1971	$5
❏ 45576	Beginning to Feel the Pain/Butterfly Girl	1972	$4
❏ 10148	Burnin' Thing/A Special Place in Heaven	1975	$4
❏ 45773	Dream Me Home/Spread Your Love on Me	1973	$4
❏ 45727	Everybody Loves a Love Song/Friend, Lover, Woman, Wife	1972	$4
❏ 10418	Every Now and Then/I'm Just in Love	1976	$4
❏ 10304	Forever Lovers/The Love Lamp	1976	$4
❏ 45456	I Believe in Music/Hollywood Humpty Dumpty	1971	$5
❏ 45245	I Believe in Music/Poor Man's Gold	1970	$5
❏ 10111	(If You Add) All the Love in the World/Smiley	1975	$4
❏ 45192	I'll Paint You a Song/The Closest I Ever Came	1970	$5
❏ 10187	I Still Love You (You Still Love Me)/The Hits Just Keep On Comin'	1975	$4
❏ 45355	Lucas Was a Red-Neck/Fall in Love with Your Wife	1971	$5
❏ 10745	Music in My Life/You Are	1978	$4
❏ 46004	One Hell of a Woman/A Poor Man's Gold	1974	$4
❏ 10535	Picking Up the Pieces of My Life/Do It (With Someone You Love)	1977	$4
❏ 10018	Stop and Smell the Roses/Poor Boy Boogie	1974	$4
❏ 45404	Sweet Dreams and Sarah/Poem for My Little Lady	1971	$5
❏ 45117	Whoever Finds This, I Love You/Half and Half	1970	$5
❏ 45117 [PS]	Whoever Finds This, I Love You/Half and Half	1970	$8

JAMIE

| ❏ 1227 | I'm a Poor Loser/Let Him Try | 1962 | $10 |

MCA

❏ 52669	I Feel the Country Callin' Me/Rainy Day Lovin'	1985	$3
❏ 52573	I Never Made Love (Till I Made Love to You)/I Think I'm Gonna Make	1985	$3
❏ 52765	Sexy Young Girl/Special Place in Heaven	1986	$3
❏ 52826	Somewhere in America/I Need a Hug	1986	$3

VEE JAY

| ❏ 492 | A Little Dutch Town/Looking at Linda | 1963 | $10 |

DAVIS, MARTHA, AND SLY STONE
A&M

| ❏ 2896 | Love and Affection/Black Girls | 1986 | $3 |

—B-side by Rae Dawn Chong

DAVIS, MELVIN
GROOVESVILLE

| ❏ 1003 | I Must Love You/Still in My Heart | 1966 | $500 |

INVICTUS

| ❏ 9115 | I'm Worried/Just As Long | 1972 | $60 |

JACK POT

Number	Title	Yr	NM
❏ 3800	I Don't Want You/About Love	1963	$400

KE-KE

| ❏ 1815 | Wedding Bells/It's No News | 1964 | $600 |

MALA

| ❏ 12009 | Faith/Love Bug Got a Bear Hug | 1968 | $60 |
| ❏ 590 | Save It (Never Too Late)/This Love Was Meant to Be | 1968 | $70 |

DAVIS, MILES
COLUMBIA

❏ S731096 [S]	Bess, Oh Where's My Bess/Fishermen, Strawberries and Devil Crab	1961	$20
❏ 45946	Big Fun/Holly-Wood	1973	$8
❏ 38-04564	Code M.D./Decoy	1984	$5
❏ 30735 [S]	(contents unknown)	1960	$20
❏ 30736 [S]	(contents unknown)	1960	$20
❏ 30737 [S]	(contents unknown)	1960	$20
❏ 30738 [S]	(contents unknown)	1960	$20
❏ 30739 [S]	(contents unknown)	1960	$20
❏ 31377 [S]	(contents unknown)	1962	$20
❏ 31378 [S]	(contents unknown)	1962	$20
❏ 31379 [S]	(contents unknown)	1962	$20
❏ 31380 [S]	(contents unknown)	1962	$20
❏ 31381 [S]	(contents unknown)	1962	$20

—Anyone who can fill in these gaps -- the above all are Columbia "Stereo 7" singles -- please let us know.

❏ S731094 [S]	De Buzzard Song/Gone	1961	$20
❏ 45327	Friday Miles/Saturday Miles	1971	$8
❏ 44652	Girls of Kilimanjaro/(B-side unknown)	1969	$8
❏ S731095 [S]	Gone, Gone, Gone/Summertime	1961	$20
❏ 46074	Great Expectations/Go Ahead John	1974	$8
❏ 45090	Great Expectations/Little Blue Frog	1970	$8
❏ 42069	I Loves You, Porgy/It Ain't Necessarily So	1961	$15
❏ S731098 [S]	I Loves You Porgy/There's a Boat That's Leaving Soon for New York	1961	$20

— The above five are "Stereo Seven" 33 1/3 rpm jukebox singles from set "JS 7-26" entitled "Porgy and Bess"

❏ 42057	It Ain't Necessarily So/All Blues	1961	$15
❏ S731097 [S]	It Ain't Necessarily So/Here Comes De Honey Man	1961	$20
❏ 4-45171	Miles Runs the Voodoo Down/Spanish Key	1970	$8
❏ 45709	Molester/(B-side unknown)	1972	$8
❏ 42853	Seven Steps to Heaven/Devil May Care	1963	$15
❏ 38-02467	Shout/Fat Time	1981	$5
❏ 42583	Slow Samba/New Rhumba	1962	$15

PRESTIGE

❏ 893	Blue Haze (Part 1)/Blue Haze (Part 2)	1956	$30
❏ 777	Dig (Part 1)/Dig (Part 2)	1956	$30
❏ 165	It Never Entered My Mind (Part 1)/It Never Entered My Mind (Part 2)	1957	$20
❏ 321	It's Only a Paper Moon/Dig	1964	$15
❏ 734	Morpheus/Blue Room	1952	$30
❏ 157	Walkin' (Part 1)/Walkin' (Part 2)	1957	$20

7-Inch Extended Plays
CAPITOL

❏ EAP 1-459	*Jeru/Deception/Moon Dreams/Venus De Milo	1954	$50
❏ EAP 2-459	*Rocker/Israel/Godchild/Rouge	1954	$50
❏ EAP 1-459 [PS]	Classics in Jazz, Part 1	1954	$50
❏ EAP 2-459 [PS]	Classics in Jazz, Part 2	1954	$50

DAVIS, PAUL
ARISTA

❏ 0661	'65 Love Affair/We're Still Together	1982	$4
❏ 0645	Cool Night/One More Time for the Lonely	1981	$4
❏ 0697	Love or Let Me Be Lonely/Oriental Eyes	1982	$4

BANG

❏ 576	A Little Bit of Soap/Three Little Words	1970	$6
❏ 599	Boogie Woogie Man/Johnny Poverty	1972	$5
❏ 702	Broken Hearted and Free/Mississippi River	1973	$5
❏ 581	Can't You/Gonna Keep On Loving You	1970	$6
❏ 593	Come On Honey/Livin' On Your Love	1972	$5
❏ 4811	Cry Just a Little/Do You Believe in Love	1980	$4
❏ 736	Darlin'/You're Not Just a Rose	1978	$4
❏ 705	Daydreamer/Love Don't Come Easy	1973	$5
❏ 4808	Do Right/He Sang Our Love Songs	1980	$4
❏ 590	Got to Find My Way Back/I Can't Get Her Off My Mind	1971	$6
❏ 587	I Feel Better/When My Little Girl Is Smiling	1971	$6
❏ 568	If I Wuz a Magician/Mississippi River	1969	$6
❏ 733	I Go Crazy/Reggae Kinda Way	1977	$4
❏ 579	I Just Wanna Keep It Together/Pollyanna	1970	$8

Number	Title	Yr	NM
❑ 717	Make Her My Baby/Can't Get Back to Alabama	1975	$4
❑ 729	Medicine Woman/Hallelujah, Thank You, Jesus	1976	$4
❑ 597	Simple Man/What Would We Do Without Music	1972	$5
❑ 726	Superstar/Magnolia Blues	1976	$4
❑ 738	Sweet Life/Bad Dream	1978	$4
❑ 724	Thinking of You/Karma Baby	1976	$4
CAPITOL			
❑ B-44100	I Won't Take Less Than Your Love/Heartbreaker	1986	$3
—With Tanya Tucker and Paul Overstreet			
❑ B-44215	Sweet Life/My Home Town Boy	1988	$3
—With Marie Osmond; B-side is Marie Osmond solo			

DAVIS, PAUL (2)

Number	Title	Yr	NM
DOKE			
❑ 107	One of Her Fools/When You Fall	1960	$30

DAVIS, SAMMY, JR.

Number	Title	Yr	NM
20TH CENTURY			
❑ 2292	Baretta's Theme (Keep Your Eye on the Sparrow)/I Heard a Song	1976	$4
❑ 2282	Chico and the Man (Main Theme)/(I'd Be) A Legend in My Time	1976	$5
—May be promo only			
❑ 2236	Snap Your Fingers/Song and Dance Man	1975	$4
APPLAUSE			
❑ 100	Smoke, Smoke, Smoke (That Cigarette)/We Could Have Been the Closest of Friends	1982	$5
CAPITOL			
❑ F1050	I'm Sorry Dear/Dedicated to You	1950	$20
❑ F943	Inka Dinka Doo/Laura	1950	$30
DECCA			
❑ 29737	Ac-Cent-Tchu-Ate the Positive/Beat Me, Daddy, Eight to the Bar	1955	$15
—With Gary Crosby			
❑ 30158	All About Love/Dangerous	1956	$15
❑ 30479	All Dressed Up and No Place to Go/Moment of Madness	1957	$10
❑ 29402	All of You/Six Bridges to Cross	1955	$15
❑ 30400	Baby It's Cold Outside/Happy to Make Your Acquaintance	1957	$12
❑ 29649	Back Track/It's Bigger Than You and Me	1955	$15
❑ 29200	Because of You (Part 1)/Because of You (Part 2)	1954	$15
❑ 30371	Doncha Go 'Way Mad/'Specially for Little Girls	1957	$12
❑ 30035	Earthbound/Just One of Those Things	1956	$15
❑ 30898	Fair Warning/You'll Never Get Away from Me	1959	$10
❑ 29976	Five/You're Sensational	1956	$15
❑ 29795	Frankie and Johnny/Circus	1956	$15
❑ 29310	Glad to Be Unhappy/Red Grapes	1954	$15
❑ 30300	Good Bye, So Long, I'm Gone/French Friend Potatoes and Ketchup	1957	$10
❑ 30536	Hallelujah I Love Her So/I'm Comin' Home	1958	$10
❑ 29199	Hey There/And This Is My Beloved	1954	$15
❑ 29620	I Go for You/A Fine Romance	1955	$15
—With Carmen McRae			
❑ 31136	I Got a Woman/Mess Around	1960	$10
❑ 30915	I Got Plenty of Nothin'/There's a Boat Dat's Leaving Soon for New York	1959	$10
❑ 29672	I'll Know/Adelaide	1955	$15
❑ 29484	Love Me or Leave Me/Something's Gotta Give	1955	$15
❑ 30441	Mad Ball/Cool Credo	1957	$10
❑ 30679	Song and Dance Man/I Ain't Gonna Change	1958	$12
❑ 29541	That Old Black Magic/A Man with a Dream	1955	$15
❑ 30769	That's Anna/I Never Got Out of Paris	1958	$12
❑ 29393	The Birth of the Blues/Love	1954	$15
❑ 30189	The Golden Key/Long Before I Knew You	1957	$10
❑ 29759	The Man with the Golden Arm/In a Persian Blanket	1955	$15
❑ 31177	This Little Girl of Mine/Face to Face	1960	$10
❑ 29861	Too Close for Comfort/Jacques d'Iraque	1956	$15
❑ 29929	Without You I'm Nothing/Get Out of the Car	1956	$15
MGM			
❑ 14513	(I'd Be) A Legend in My Time/I'm Not Anyone	1973	$5
❑ 14426	Mr. Bojangles/The People Tree	1972	$5
❑ 14685	Singin' in the Rain/Chattanooga Choo Choo	1973	$5
❑ 14759	Sing/This Is the House of the People	1974	$4
❑ 14736	That's Entertainment/Singin' in the Rain	1974	$4
❑ 14320	The Candy Man/I Want to Be Happy	1971	$6
MOTOWN			
❑ 1738	Hello Detroit (Part 1)/Hello Detroit (Part 2)	1984	$4
REPRISE			
❑ 0502	All That Jazz/Ev'ry Time We Say Goodbye	1966	$6
❑ 20138	As Long As She Needs Me/Two for the Seesaw	1963	$10
❑ 0757	Break My Mind/Children, Children	1968	$6
❑ 0278	Choose/Bee Bom	1964	$8
❑ 0566	Don't Blame the Children/She Believes in Me	1967	$6
❑ 0322	Don't Shut Me Out/Disorderly Orderly	1964	$8
❑ 0321	Hello, Dolly!/Take the Moment	1964	$20
—Possibly released only outside the U.S.			
❑ 0361	Hello, Dolly!/Take the Moment	1965	$8
❑ 0(no cat #) [DJ]	Here's A Kiss For Christmas (The Christmas Seal Song)/What Kind Of Fool Am I	1963	$20
❑ 20207	If I Ruled the World/Flash, Bang, Wallop	1963	$30
—Released only in England			
❑ 0345	If I Ruled the World/Flash, Bang, Wallop	1965	$8
❑ 0425	If You Want This Love of Mine/Second-Best Secret Agent in the Whole Wide World	1965	$8
❑ 0827	I Have But One Life to Live/The Goin's Great	1969	$6
❑ 20003	I'm a Fool to Want You/Back in Your Own Back Yard	1961	$10
❑ 0779	I've Gotta Be Me/Bein' Natural Bein' Me	1968	$8
❑ 0733	I've Gotta Be Me/Lonely Is the Name	1970	$4
—Back to Back Hits" series			
❑ 0673	Lonely Is the Name/Flash, Bang, Wallop	1968	$6
❑ 0437	Lonely Weekends/More Than One Way	1965	$8
❑ 0399	Love, At Last You Have Found Me/Courage	1965	$8
❑ 20128	Me and My Shadow/Sam's Song	1962	$20
—A-side: With Frank Sinatra; B-side: With Dean Martin			
❑ 20128 [PS]	Me and My Shadow/Sam's Song	1962	$40
❑ 20087	Once in a Lifetime/Someone Nice Like You	1962	$10
❑ 20018	One More Time (A Tribute to Ray Charles)/There Was a Tavern in the Town	1961	$10
❑ 0989	She Is Today/Runaround	1971	$5
❑ 20187	Smile/This Way, My Love	1963	$30
—Released only in England			
❑ 0621	Talk to the Animals/Something in Your Smile	1967	$6
❑ 0549	The Birth of the Blues/With a Song in My Heart	1967	$6
❑ 20079	The Fool I Used to Be/Everybody Calls Me Joe	1962	$10
❑ 0521	The Good Life/We'll Be Together Again	1966	$6
❑ 20227	The Shelter of Your Arms/Falling in Love with Love	1963	$30
—Released only in England			
❑ 20216	The Shelter of Your Arms/This Was My Love	1963	$10
❑ 20212	We Kiss in a Shadow/Bye, Bye Blackbird	1963	$10
❑ 0248	What Kind of Fool Am I/Gonna Buila a Mountain	1963	$8
❑ 20048	What Kind of Fool Am I/Gonna Build a Mountain	1962	$10
❑ 0720	What Kind of Fool Am I/Gonna Build a Mountain	1968	$4
—Back to Back Hits" series			
UNITED ARTISTS			
❑ 50334	Salt and Pepper/I Like the Way You Dance	1968	$6
VERVE			
❑ 10219	Ain't That a Kick in the Head/Eee-O Eleven	1960	$8
WARNER BROS.			
❑ 49047	Showtime/That Old Black Magic	1979	$4

DAVIS SISTERS, THE

Number	Title	Yr	NM
FORTUNE			
❑ 175	Heartbreak Ahead/Steelwood	1952	$30
RCA VICTOR			
❑ 47-6291	Baby Be Mine/It's the Girl Who Gets the Blame	1955	$20
❑ 47-6409	Don't Take HIm for Granted/Blues for Company	1956	$20
❑ 47-5966	Everlovin'/Tomorrow's Just Another Day to Cry	1954	$20
❑ 47-6086	Fiddle Diddle Diddle/Come Back to Me	1955	$20
❑ 47-5345	I Forgot More Than You'll Ever Know/Rock-a-Bye Boogie	1953	$30
❑ 47-6187	I'll Get Him Back/I've Closed the Door	1955	$20
❑ 47-6490	Lonely and Blue/Lying Brown Eyes	1956	$20
❑ 47-5843	Show Me/Just Like Me	1954	$20
❑ 47-5607	Takin' Time Out for Tears/Gotta Get a-Goin'	1954	$20
❑ 47-5906	The Christmas Boogie/Tomorrow I'll Cry	1954	$20

DAVIS, SKEETER, AND DON BOWMAN

Number	Title	Yr	NM
RCA VICTOR			
❑ 47-9415	For Loving You/Baby, It's Cold Outside	1967	$8

DAVIS, SKEETER

Number	Title	Yr	NM
MERCURY			
❑ 73898	If You Loved Me Now/It's Love That I Feel	1977	$4
❑ 73818	I Love Us/It Feels So Good	1976	$4
RCA VICTOR			
❑ 47-8496 [B]	A Dear John Letter/Too Used to Being with You	1965	$12
—With Bobby Bare			
❑ 47-7671	Am I That Easy to Forget/Wishful Thinking	1960	$15
❑ 74-0148	Baby Sweet Baby/Keep Baltimore Beautiful	1969	$6
❑ 47-9896	Bridge Over Troubled Water/How in the World Do You Kill a Memory	1970	$5
❑ 47-9961	Bus Fare to Kentucky/From Her Arms Into Mine	1971	$5
❑ PB-10048	Come Mornin'/Lovin' Touch	1974	$4
❑ APBO-0188	Don't Forget to Remember/Baby Get That Leavin' Off Your Mind	1973	$4
❑ 47-9058	Fuel to the Flame/You Call This Love	1966	$8
❑ 47-8932	Goin' Down the Road/I Can't Stand the Sight of You	1966	$8
❑ 47-8347	Gonna Get Along Without You Now/Now You're Gone	1964	$10
❑ 47-7034	He Left His Heart for Me/Don't Let Your Lips Say Yes	1957	$20
❑ 47-8288	He Says the Same Things to Me/How Much Can a Lonely Heart Stand	1963	$12
❑ 74-0827	Hillbilly Song/Once	1972	$4
❑ 47-7570	Homebreaker/Give Me Death	1959	$15
❑ 47-9459	How in the World/Instinct for Survival	1968	$6
❑ 47-7401	I Ain't A-Talkin'/Slave	1958	$20
❑ 74-0968	I Can't Believe That It's All Over/Try Jesus	1973	$4
❑ 47-7767	(I Can't Help You) I'm Falling Too/No, Never	1960	$15
❑ 47-8765	I Can't See Me Without You/Don't Anybody Need My Love	1965	$8
❑ 47-8219	I Can't Stay Mad at You/It Was Only a Heart	1963	$10
❑ 47-8219 [PS]	I Can't Stay Mad at You/It Was Only a Heart	1963	$30
❑ 74-0292	I Didn't Cry Today/I'm a Lover (Not a Fighter)	1969	$6
❑ 47-8837	If I Ever Get to Heaven/If I Had Wheels	1966	$8
❑ 47-9625	I Look Up (And See You on My Mind)/Timothy	1968	$6
❑ 47-8176	I'm Saving My Love/Somebody Else on Your Mind	1963	$10
❑ 47-9818	It's Hard to Be a Woman/What a Little Girl Don't Know	1969	$6
❑ 47-8397	Let Me Get Close to You/Face of a Clown	1964	$12
❑ 47-9893	Let's Get Together/Everything Is Beautiful	1970	$6
—With George Hamilton IV			
❑ 47-7084	Lost to a Geisha Girl/I'm Going Steady with a Heartache	1957	$20
❑ 47-9997	Love Takes a Lot of Time/Love, Love, Love	1971	$5
❑ 47-7825	My Last Date (With You)/Someone I'd Like to Forget	1960	$15
❑ APBO-0277	One More Time/Stay Awhile with Me	1974	$4
❑ 74-0608	One Tin Soldier/Rachel	1971	$5
❑ 47-7928	Optimistic/Blueberry Hill	1961	$15
❑ 74-0681	Sad Situation/All I Ever Wanted Was Love	1972	$4
❑ 47-9371	Set Him Free/Is It Worth It to You	1967	$6
❑ 47-7471	Set Him Free/The Devil's Doll	1959	$15
❑ 47-8642	Sun Glasses/He Loved Me Too Little	1965	$8
❑ 74-0203	Teach Me to Love You/Bobby Blows a Blue Note	1969	$6
❑ 47-9695	The Closest Thing to Love/Mama Your Big Girl's About to Cry	1968	$6
❑ 47-8098	The End of the World/Somebody Loves You	1962	$15
❑ 47-7863	The Hand You're Holding Now/Someday Someday	1961	$15
❑ 37-7863	The Hand You're Holding Now/Someday Someday	1961	$30
—Compact Single 33" (small hole, plays at LP speed)			
❑ 47-8055	The Little Music Box/The Final Stop	1962	$10
❑ 47-9543	There's a Fool Born Every Minute/I Can't See Past the Tears	1968	$6
❑ 47-7189	Walk Softly Darling/I Need You All the Time	1958	$20
❑ 47-7293	Wave Bye Bye/I Forgot More Than You'll Ever Know	1958	$20
❑ 47-9871	We Need a Lot More Jesus/When You Gonna Bring Our Soldiers Home	1970	$5
❑ 47-8450	What Am I Going to Do with You/Don't Let Me Stand in Your Way	1964	$10
❑ 47-9242	What Does It Take (To Keep a Man Satisfied)/What I Go Through	1967	$6
❑ 47-7979	Where I Ought to Be/Something Precious	1962	$10

Number	Title	Yr	NM

DAVIS, SPENCER, GROUP
ATCO
❏ 6416	Somebody Help Me/ Stevie's Blues	1966	$20

FONTANA
| ❏ 1960 | I Can't Stand It/Midnight Train | 1964 | $20 |

UNITED ARTISTS
| ❏ 50108 | Gimme Some Lovin'/Blues in F | 1966 | $15 |
| ❏ 0115 | Gimme Some Lovin'/ Keep On Running | 1973 | $4 |

— Silver Spotlight Series" reissue
| ❏ 50144 | I'm a Man/Can't Get Enough of It | 1967 | $15 |
| ❏ 0116 | I'm a Man/Somebody Help Me | 1973 | $4 |

— Silver Spotlight Series" reissue
| ❏ 50922 | Listen to the Rhythm/ Sunday Walk in the Rain | 1972 | $6 |

— Spencer Davis solo
❏ 50286	Looking Back/After Tea	1968	$10
❏ 50162	Somebody Help Me/ On the Green Light	1967	$12
❏ 50202	Time Seller/Don't Want You No More	1967	$10
❏ 50202 [PS]	Time Seller/Don't Want You No More	1967	$30

VERTIGO
| ❏ 110 | Don't You Let It Bring You Down/Today Gluggo, Tomorrow the World | 1973 | $15 |
| ❏ 112 | Living in a Back Street/ Need a Helping Hand | 1974 | $15 |

DAVIS, TYRONE
ABC
| ❏ 11030 | Bet You Win/What If a Man | 1967 | $15 |

COLUMBIA
❏ 11035	Ain't Nothing I Can Do/ The Love I Need	1979	$4
❏ 10604	All You Got/I Got Carried Away	1977	$5
❏ 11128	Be With Me/Love You Forever	1979	$4
❏ 10773	Can't Help But Say/Bunky	1978	$4
❏ 11199	Can't You Tell It's Me/I Don't Think You Heard Me	1980	$4
❏ 10457	Close to You/Wrong Doers	1976	$5
❏ 10684	Get It Up (Disco)/ It's You, It's You	1978	$5
❏ 10388	Give It Up (Turn It Loose)/ You're Too Much	1976	$5
❏ 11344	How Sweet It Is (To Be Loved By You)/I Can't Wait	1980	$4
❏ 11415	I Just Can't Keep On Going/ We Don't Need No Music	1980	$4
❏ 10904	In the Mood/I Can't Wait	1979	$4
❏ 02634	Leave Well Enough Alone/I Won't Let Go	1981	$4
❏ 10528	This I Swear/Givin' Myself to You	1977	$5

DAKAR
❏ 609	All the Waiting Is Not in Vain/ Need Your Lovin' Everybody	1969	$8
❏ 4545	A Woman Needs to Be Loved/ Just Because of You (I Can See My Way Through)	1975	$5
❏ 1452	Can I Change My Mind/A Woman Needs to Be Loved	1968	$15
❏ 602	Can I Change My Mind/A Woman Needs to Be Loved	1968	$10
❏ 4510	Come and Get This Ring/ After All This Time	1972	$5
❏ 623	Could I Forget You/Just My Way of Loving You	1971	$6
❏ 4561	Ever Lovin' Girl/Forever	1976	$5
❏ 4536	Happiness Is Being with You/Where Lovers Meet	1974	$5
❏ 4541	Homewreckers/This Time	1975	$5
❏ 4558	I Can't Bump, Part 2/ Saving My Love for You	1976	$5
❏ 4538	I Can't Make It Without You/ You Wouldn't Believe	1974	$5
❏ 615	If I Didn't Love You/You Can't Keep a Good Man Down	1969	$8
❏ 611	If It's Love That You're After/ When I'm Not Around	1969	$8
❏ 4513	If You Had a Change in Mind/Was It Just a Feelin'	1972	$5
❏ 4501	I Had It All the Time/ You Wouldn't Believe	1972	$5
❏ 618	I'll Be Right Here/Just Because of You	1970	$6
❏ 605	Is It Something You've Got/Undying Love	1969	$8
❏ 4529	I Wish It Was Me/You Don't Have to Beg Me to Stay	1974	$5
❏ 621	Let Me Back In/Love Bones	1970	$6
❏ 624	One-Way Ticket/We Got a Love	1971	$6
❏ 4553	So Good (To Be Home with You)/I Can't Bump	1976	$5
❏ 4523	There It Is/You Wouldn't Believe	1973	$5
❏ 616	Turn Back the Hands of Time/I Keep Coming Back	1970	$8
❏ 4550	Turning Point/Don't Let It Be Too Late	1975	$5
❏ 4507	Was I Just a Fool/ After All This Time	1972	$5
❏ 4532	What Goes Up (Must Come Down)/There's Got to Be an Answer	1974	$5
❏ 4563	Where Lovers Meet (At the Dark End of the Street)/ It's All in the Game	1977	$5

| ❏ 4519 | Without You in My Life/ How Could I Forget You | 1973 | $5 |
| ❏ 4526 | Wrapped Up in Your Warm and Tender Love/True Love Is Hard to Find | 1973 | $5 |

FUTURE
❏ 103	Do You Feel It/(Instrumental)	1988	$4
❏ 204	Flashin' Back/Flashin' Back (LP Version)	1988	$4
❏ 102	I'm in Love Again/Serious Love	1987	$4
❏ 104	It's a Miracle/Wrong Doers	1988	$4
❏ 101	Sexy Thing/Save Me	1987	$5

HIGHRISE
| ❏ 2009 | A Little Bit of Loving (Goes a Long Way)/Where Did We Lose | 1983 | $4 |
| ❏ 2005 | Are You Serious/Overdrive | 1982 | $4 |

ICHIBAN
| ❏ 139 | Can I Change My Mind/ Hey There Lonely Girl | 1989 | $4 |

— B-side by Eddie Holman

OCEAN-FRONT
| ❏ 2001 | I Found Myself When I Lost You/(Instrumental) | 1983 | $4 |
| ❏ 2004 | Let Me Be Your Pacifier/ Turning Point | 1984 | $4 |

DAVIS, WILD BILL
7-Inch Extended Plays
EVEREST
| ❏ 196125 [PS] | Dis Heah | 1962 | $25 |
| ❏ 196125 | Like Young/Jo-Do// Wenkie/St. Louis Blues | 1962 | $25 |

— Jukebox issue; small hole, plays at 33 1/3 rpm

DAWN (1)
ARISTA
❏ 0105	Gimme a Good Old Mammy Song/Little Heads in Bunk Beds	1975	$4
❏ 0156	Skybird/That's the Way a Wallflower Grows	1975	$4
❏ 0301	Tie a Yellow Ribbon Round the Ole Oak Tree/Say, Has Anybody Seen My Sweet Gypsy Rose	1978	$4

BELL
❏ 903	Candida/Look At...	1970	$6
❏ 970	I Play and Sing/Get Out from Where We Are	1971	$5
❏ 45450	It Only Hurts When I Try to Smile/Sweet Summer Days of My Life	1974	$4
❏ 45620	Look in My Eyes Pretty Woman/ My Love Has No Pride	1974	$4
❏ 45374	Say, Has Anybody Seen My Sweet Gypsy Rose/The Spark of Love Is Kindlin'	1973	$4
❏ 45601	Steppin' Out (Gonna Boogie Tonight)/She Can't Hold a Candle to You	1974	$4

— As "Tony Orlando and Dawn
❏ 45107	Summer Sand/The Sweet Soft Sounds of Love	1971	$5
❏ 45318	Tie a Yellow Ribbon Round the Ole Oak Tree/I Can't Believe How Much I Love You	1973	$5
❏ 45141	What Are You Doing Sunday/ The Sweet Soft Sounds of Love	1971	$5
❏ 45424	Who's in the Strawberry Patch with Sally/Ukulele Man	1973	$4

ELEKTRA
❏ 45501	Bring It On Home to Me/Don't Let Go	1978	$4
❏ 45302	Cupid/You're Growin' on Me	1976	$4
❏ 45432	Growin' on Me/You're All I Need to Get By	1977	$4
❏ 45240	He Don't Love You (Like I Love You)/Pick It Up	1975	$4
❏ 45542	I Count the Tears/A Lover's Question	1978	$4
❏ 45542	I Count the Tears/This Is Rock and Roll	1978	$4
❏ 45319	Midnight Love Affair/ The Selfish Ones	1976	$4
❏ 45260	Mornin' Beautiful/Dance, Rosalie, Dance	1975	$4
❏ 45387	Sing/Sweet on Candy	1977	$4

DAWN (2)
ABC-PARAMOUNT
| ❏ 10791 | Baby's Gone Away/ Gotta Get Away | 1966 | $8 |

APT
| ❏ 25088 | Can't Get Him Off My Mind/Two of a Kind | 1965 | $20 |

DAWN (3)
LAURIE
| ❏ 3388 | I'm Afraid They're All Talking About Me/Lovers' Melody | 1967 | $15 |
| ❏ 3417 | Sandy/For the Love of Money | 1968 | $15 |

RUST
| ❏ 5128 | Baby I Love You/ Bring It On Home | 1968 | $15 |

DAWN, JANICE
BROOKE
| ❏ 108 | Christmas Angel/ Shine Every Day | 1959 | $15 |

DAWN (U)
CADET
| ❏ 5644 | The Fifth Day of June/ Ballad of Gene | 1969 | $6 |

GAMBLE
| ❏ 4002 | Ba Ba Ba De Ba (On the Way Through My Mind)/In Love Again | 1969 | $6 |
| ❏ 4002 [PS] | Ba Ba Ba De Ba (On the Way Through My Mind)/In Love Again | 1969 | $15 |

UNITED ARTISTS
| ❏ 50096 | Love Is a Magic Word/How Can I Get Off This Merry-Go-Round | 1966 | $15 |

DAWSON, RON
COLUMBIA
| ❏ 4-44757 | If Baby's Still on My Mind/ The Dark Side of Lovin' You | 1969 | $8 |
| ❏ 4-44978 | She Cried/Steel Rail Blues | 1969 | $8 |

DAWSON, RONNIE
BACK BEAT
| ❏ 522 | Action Packed/I Make the Love | 1958 | $125 |

— As "Ronnie Dee

MAVERICK
| ❏ 101 | My Big Desire/How Can We Tell Her | 1961 | $200 |

SWAN
| ❏ 4047 | Ain't That a Kick in the Head/Hazel | 1960 | $30 |
| ❏ 4054 | Summer's Comin'/ Decided by the Angels | 1960 | $30 |

DAY, BING
FEDERAL
| ❏ 12320 | Pony Tail Partner/ Since You Left Me | 1958 | $75 |

MERCURY
| ❏ 71494 | How Do I Do It/Mary's Place | 1959 | $30 |
| ❏ 71446 | I Can't Help It/Mama's Place | 1959 | $70 |

DAY, BOBBY
CASH
| ❏ 1031 | The Truth Hurts/Let's Live Together As One | 1956 | $125 |

— As "Bobby Byrd and the Birds

CLASS
❏ 255	Ain't Gonna Cry No More/ Love Is a One-Time Affair	1959	$20
❏ 215	Beep-Beep-Beep/ Darling, If I Had You	1957	$30
❏ 207	Come Seven/So Long Baby	1957	$30
❏ 705	Don't Leave Me Hangin' on a String/When I Started Dancin'	1965	$15
❏ 211	Little Bitty Pretty One/ When the Swallows Come Back to Capistrano	1957	$30
❏ 225	Little Turtle Dove/Saving My Life for You	1958	$30
❏ 252	Mr. and Mrs. Rock & Roll/Gotta New Girl	1959	$20
❏ 263	My Blue Heaven/I Don't Want To	1960	$20
❏ 245	That's All I Want/Say Yes	1959	$20
❏ 241	The Bluebird, the Buzzard, and the Oriole/Alone Too Long	1959	$30

CORVET
| ❏ 1017 | Why/Gotta Girl | 1958 | $70 |

— As "Bobby Byrd and the Impalas

JAMIE
| ❏ 1039 | Bippin' and Boppin' Over You/Strawberry Stomp | 1957 | $40 |

— As "Robert Byrd and His Birdies

RCA VICTOR
❏ 47-8133	Another Country, Another World/Know-It-All	1963	$10
❏ 47-8196	Buzz Buzz Buzz/Pretty Little Girl Next Door	1963	$10
❏ 47-8230	Down on My Knees/Jole Blon, Little Darling	1963	$12
❏ 47-8316	When I See My Baby Smile/ On the Street Where You Live	1964	$10

RENDEZVOUS
❏ 167	Don't Worry 'Bout Me/ Oop-E-Du-Pers Ball	1962	$15
❏ 136	Gee Whiz/Over and Over	1960	$15
❏ 146	I Need Help/Life Can Be Beautiful	1961	$15
❏ 130	Teenage Philosopher/ Undecided	1960	$15

SAGE AND SAND
| ❏ 203 | Please Don't Hurt Me/ Delicious Are Your Kisses | 1955 | $50 |

— As "Bobby Byrd

Number	Title	Yr	NM
SPARK			
❑ 501	Bippin' and Boppin' Over You/Strawberry Stomp	1957	$60
—As "Robert Byrd and His Birdies			
SURE SHOT			
❑ 5036	So Lonely/Spicks and Specks	1967	$8
ZEPHYR			
❑ 70-018	If We Should Meet Again/Looby Loo	1957	$40
—As "Bobby Byrd			

DAY, DARLENE
MUSIC MAKERS

Number	Title	Yr	NM
❑ 106	I Love You So/Will	1961	$125

DAY, DAVE DIDDLE
FEE BEE

Number	Title	Yr	NM
❑ 212	Blue Moon Baby/Suzanne My Love	1958	$30
❑ 219	Motorcycle Mike/Tired of Waiting	1958	$20
MERCURY			
❑ 71114	Blue Moon Baby/Suzanne My Love	1957	$200

DAY, DENNIS
RCA VICTOR

Number	Title	Yr	NM
❑ 47-3860	Away in a Manger/God Rest Ye Merry, Gentlemen	1950	$20
❑ 47-4321	Christmas in Killarney/Corn Keeps a-Growin'	1951	$20
❑ 47-3970	Christmas in Killarney/I'm Praying to St. Christopher	1950	$20
❑ 47-3859	O Holy Night/Jesu Bambino	1950	$20
❑ 47-3861	We Three Kings of Orient Are/Silent Night	1950	$20
—Above three with the Mitchell Boy Choir			

DAY, DORIS
COLUMBIA

Number	Title	Yr	NM
❑ 39008	A Bushel and a Peck/The Best Thing for You	1950	$30
❑ 6-838	A Bushel and a Peck/The Best Thing for You	1950	$40
❑ 1-838	A Bushel and a Peck/The Best Thing for You	1950	$50
—Microgroove 7-inch, 33 1/3 rpm single			
❑ 1-211	Again/Everywhere You Go	1949	$50
—Microgroove 7-inch, 33 1/3 rpm single			
❑ 39729	A Guy Is a Guy/What's the Use?	1952	$10
—B-side by Johnnie Ray			
❑ 39673	A Guy Is a Guy/Who, Who, Who	1952	$15
❑ 39974	Ain't We Got Fun?/If You Were the Only Girl	1953	$8
—The above five comprise a box set			
❑ 1-811	A Load of Hay/Orange Colored Sky	1950	$50
—With the Paige Cavanaugh Trio; Microgroove 33 1/3 rpm 7-inch single, small hole			
❑ 6-811	A Load of Hay/Orange Colored Sky	1950	$40
❑ 43440	Another Go-Round/Not Only Should You Love Him	1965	$8
❑ 41569	Anyway the Wind Blows/Soft As the Starlight	1960	$8
❑ 39881	April in Paris/Cherries	1952	$15
❑ 39490	Ask Me/Lonesome and Sorry	1951	$20
❑ 1-266(?)	At the Café Rendezvous/It's a Great Feeling	1949	$50
—Microgroove 7-inch, 33 1/3 rpm single			
❑ 43459	Au Revoir Is Goodbye with a Smile/Do Not Disturb	1965	$8
❑ 40096	A Woman's Touch/Higher Than the Hawk	1953	$8
❑ 1-125(?)	Beginning to Miss You/Don't Gamble with Romance	1949	$50
—Microgroove 7-inch, 33 1/3 rpm single			
❑ 41391	Be Prepared/It Happened to Jane	1959	$8
❑ 1-480	Bewitched/Imagination	1950	$50
—Microgroove 7-inch, 33 1/3 rpm single			
❑ 4-38543	Bewitched/When Your Lover Has Gone	1950	$20
—Alternate numbers are "B 189-3" and "B 189-4"			
❑ 1-353	Canadian Capers (Cuttin' Capers)/Better To Conceal Than Reveal	1949	$50
—Microgroove 7-inch, 33 1/3 rpm single			
❑ 40063	Choo Choo Train (Ch-Ch-Foo)/This Too Shall Pass Away	1953	$10
❑ 43174	Christmas Present/Be a Child at Christmas Time	1964	$8
❑ 39453	Christmas Story/I'm Forever Blowing Bubbles	1951	$15
—The above four comprise a box set			
❑ 39032	Christmas Story/Silver Bells	1950	$15
❑ 6-863	Christmas Story/Silver Bells	1950	$40
❑ 1-863	Christmas Story/Silver Bells	1950	$50
—Microgroove 7-inch, 33 1/3 rpm single, small hole			
❑ 31084 [S]	(contents unknown)	1961	$10
❑ 31085 [S]	(contents unknown)	1961	$10
❑ 31086 [S]	(contents unknown)	1961	$10

Number	Title	Yr	NM
❑ 31087 [S]	(contents unknown)	1961	$10
❑ 31088 [S]	(contents unknown)	1961	$10
—Anyone who can fill in these gaps -- the above 5 all are Columbia "Stereo 7" singles -- please let us know.			
❑ 1-708	Darn That Dream/I've Forgotten You	1950	$50
—Microgroove 7-inch, 33 1/3 rpm single			
❑ 6-708	Darn That Dream/I've Forgotten You	1950	$40
❑ 39596	Domino/If That Doesn't Do It	1951	$20
❑ 41195	Everybody Loves a Lover/Instant Love	1958	$8
❑ 41195 [PS]	Everybody Loves a Lover/Instant Love	1958	$20
❑ 39198	Fine and Dandy/I Love the Way You Say Goodnight	1951	$15
❑ 39714	Gentle Johnny/Little Kiss Goodnight	1952	$15
❑ 40374	Hold Me in Your Arms/There's a Rising Moon	1954	$8
❑ 1-591	Hoop-Dee-Doo/Marriage Ties	1950	$50
—Microgroove 7-inch, 33 1/3 rpm single			
❑ 43278	How Insensitive/Meditation	1965	$8
❑ 1-185(?)	How It Lies, How It Lies/If I Could Be with You	1949	$50
—Microgroove 7-inch, 33 1/3 rpm single			
❑ 39255	I Can't Get Over Pumpernickel/You Are My Sunshine	1951	$20
❑ 1-637	I Didn't Slip -- I Wasn't Pushed -- I Fell/Before I Loved You	1950	$50
—Microgroove 7-inch, 33 1/3 rpm single			
❑ 1-457(?)	I Don't Wanna Be Kissed/With You Anywhere You Are	1950	$50
—Microgroove 7-inch, 33 1/3 rpm single			
❑ 41307	I Enjoy Being a Girl/Kissin' My Honey	1958	$8
❑ 40300	If I Give My Heart to You/Anyone Can Fall in Love	1954	$10
❑ 6-862	If I Were a Bell/I've Never Been in Love Before	1950	$40
❑ 39031	If I Were a Bell/I've Never Been in Love Before	1950	$30
❑ 1-862	If I Were a Bell/I've Never Been in Love Before	1950	$50
—Microgroove 7-inch, 33 1/3 rpm single			
❑ 1-108(?)	If You Will Marry Me/You Was	1949	$50
❑ 39191	I'll Be Around/I Love the Way You Say Goodnight	1951	$20
❑ 40505	I'll Never Stop Loving You/Never Look Back	1955	$10
❑ 39622	I'll See You in My Dreams/Ain't We Got Fun	1951	$15
❑ 4-38544	I'm Confessin'/I Didn't Know What Time It Was	1950	$20
—Alternate numbers are "B 189-5" and "B 189-6"			
❑ 39199	In a Shanty in Old Shanty Town/You're Getting to Be a Habit with Me	1951	$15
❑ 6-893	I Only Have Eyes for You/Do Do Do	1950	$40
❑ 1-497	I Said My Pajamas (And Put On My Prayers)/Enjoy Yourself (It's Later Than You Think)	1950	$50
—Microgroove 7-inch, 33 1/3 rpm single			
❑ 40210	I Speak to the Stars/The Blue Belles of Broadway	1954	$10
❑ 39625	It Had to Be You/Nobody's Sweetheart	1951	$15
—The above four comprise a box set			
❑ 39738	It's Magic/Too Fat Polka	1952	$10
—B-side by Arthur Godfrey			
❑ 39295	It's So Laughable/Very Good Advice	1951	$20
❑ 40618	Let It Ring/Love's Little Island	1955	$12
❑ JZSP55070/1 [DJ]	Let No Walls Divide/God Rest Ye Merry, Gentlemen	1961	$15
—B-side by Andre Previn			
❑ 39971	Little Silvery Moon/King Chant	1953	$8
❑ 40168	Lost in Loveliness/What Every Girl Should Know	1954	$10
❑ 41354	Love Me in the Daytime/He's So Married	1959	$8
❑ 42295	Lover Come Back/Falling	1962	$8
❑ 39452	Love You/Cuddle Up a Little Closer	1951	$15
❑ 39197	Lullaby of Broadway/Please Don't Talk About Me When I'm Gone	1951	$15
❑ 39817	Make It Soon/My Love and Devotion	1952	$15
❑ 41944	Make Someone Happy/Bright and Shiny	1961	$8
❑ 1-454(?)	Mama, What'll I Do/Save a Little Sunbeam	1950	$50
—Microgroove 7-inch, 33 1/3 rpm single			
❑ 39906	Mister Tap Toe/Your Mother and Mine	1952	$15
❑ 39450	Moonlight Bay/Tell Me (Tell Me Why)	1951	$15
❑ 42912	Move Over Darling/Twinkle Lullaby	1963	$8
❑ 39624	My Buddy/I Wish I Had a Girl	1951	$15
❑ 40581	Ooh Bang Jiggily Bang/Jimmy Unknown	1955	$10
❑ 39637	Oops/Baby Doll	1952	$15

Number	Title	Yr	NM
❑ 41463	Pillow Talk/Inspiration	1959	$8
❑ 41463 [PS]	Pillow Talk/Inspiration	1959	$20
❑ 41630	Please Don't Eat the Daisies/Here We Go Again	1960	$8
❑ 41630 [PS]	Please Don't Eat the Daisies/Here We Go Again	1960	$20
❑ 1-113	Powder Your Face with Sunshine (Smile! Smile! Smile!)/I'll String Along with You	1949	$50
—Microgroove 7-inch, 33 1/3 rpm single			
❑ 40108	Secret Love/The Deadwood Stage (Whip Crack Away!)	1953	$10
❑ 40097	Secret Love/'Tis Harry I'm Planning to Marry	1953	$8
—The above four comprise a box set			
❑ 43153	Send Me No Flowers/Rainbow's End	1964	$8
❑ 42260	Should I Surrender/Who Knows What Might Have Been	1962	$8
❑ JZSP79171/2 [DJ]	Silver Bells/Winter Wonderland	1963	$10
—Special Album Excerpt" promo			
❑ 39200	Somebody Loves Me/Just One of Those Things	1951	$15
—The above four comprise a box set			
❑ 40234	Someone Else's Roses/Kay-Muleta	1954	$12
❑ 40375	Someone to Watch Over Me/Just One of Those Things	1954	$8
—The above four comprise a box set			
❑ 39693	Sugarbush/When I Look Into Your Eyes	1952	$15
—A-side with Frankie Laine			
❑ 43314	Summer Has Gone/Catch the Bouquet	1965	$8
❑ 41123	Teacher's Pet/A Very Precious Love	1958	$8
❑ 40095	The Black Hills of Dakota/Just Blew In from the Windy City	1953	$8
❑ 41703	The Blue Train/A Perfect Understanding	1960	$8
❑ 40094	The Deadwood Stage (Whip Crack Away!)/I Can Do Without You	1953	$8
❑ 1-406(?)	The Game of Broken Hearts/I'll Never Slip Around Again	1949	$50
—Microgroove 7-inch, 33 1/3 rpm single			
❑ 39623	The One I Love/Makin' Whoopee	1951	$15
❑ 40798	The Party's Over/What'ya Put in That Kiss	1956	$10
❑ 1-376	(There's a) Bluebird on Your Windowsill/The River Seine	1949	$50
—Microgroove 7-inch, 33 1/3 rpm single			
❑ 40408	There's a Rising Moon/Till Your Love Comes to Me	1954	$10
❑ 41542	The Sound of Music/Heart Full of Love	1959	$8
❑ 1-381(?)	The Three Rivers/Festival of Roses	1949	$50
—Microgroove 7-inch, 33 1/3 rpm single			
❑ 40372	Till My Love Comes to Me/Ready and Able	1954	$8
❑ 39451	Till We Meet Again/Every Little Movement	1951	$15
❑ 41252	Tunnel of Love/Run Away Skidaddle Skidoo	1958	$8
❑ 41252 [PS]	Tunnel of Love/Run Away Skidaddle Skidoo	1958	$20
❑ 40870	Twelve O'Clock Tonight/Today Will Be Yesterday Tomorrow	1957	$10
❑ 41993	Twinkle and Shine/Gotta Feelin'	1961	$8
❑ 40483	Two Hearts, Two Kisses/Foolishly Yours	1955	$10
❑ 41071	Walk a Chalk Line/Soft As the Starlight	1957	$8
❑ 39293	We Kissed in a Shadow/Something Wonderful	1951	$20
❑ 40673	We'll Love Again/Somebody Somewhere	1956	$10
❑ 41791	What Does a Woman Do/Daffa Down Dilly	1960	$8
❑ 40704	Whatever Will Be, Will Me (Que Sera, Sera)/I've Gotta Sing Away the Blues	1956	$10
❑ 39786	When I Fall in Love/Take Me in Your Arms	1952	$15
❑ 39970	When the Red, Red Robin Comes Bob, Bob, Bobbin' Along/Beautiful Music to Love By	1953	$8
❑ 1-251	(Where Are You) Now That I Need You/Blame My Absent-Minded Heart	1949	$50
—Microgroove 7-inch, 33 1/3 rpm single			
❑ 39423	(Why Did I Tell You I Was Going to) Shanghai/My Life's Desire	1951	$20
❑ 39159	Would I Love You (Love You, Love You)/Lullaby of Broadway	1951	$20
❑ 3-39159	Would I Love You (Love You, Love You)/Lullaby of Broadway	1951	$40
—Microgroove 7-inch, 33 1/3 rpm single			

Number	Title	Yr	NM

7-Inch Extended Plays

Number	Title	Yr	NM
❏ B-2585 [B]	*A Bushel and a Peck/ Hoop-Dee-Doo/If I Were a Bell/Lullaby of Broadway	1959	$20
❏ B-7493	*Love Me or Leave Me/Just One of Those Things/It Had to Be You/Ain't We Got Fun (contents unknown)	1956	$20
❏ B-7491	Day in Hollywood, Vol. 1	1956	$20
❏ B-7491 [PS]	Day in Hollywood, Vol. 1	1956	$20
❏ B-7493 [PS]	Day in Hollywood, Vol. 3	1956	$20
❏ B-7492 [PS]	Day in Hollywood, Vol. II	1956	$20
❏ B-2585 [PS]	Doris Day (Hall of Fame Series)	1959	$20
❏ 5-2172	Everybody Loves My Baby/ Sam the Old Accordion Man// Shaking the Blues Away// Ten Cents a Dance	1955	$10

—Alternate numbers are "B-540-3" and "B-540-4"

❏ 5-2170	It All Depends on You/You Made Me Love You//At Sundown// Love Me or Leave Me	1955	$10

—Alternate numbers are "B-540-1" and "B-540-6"

❏ B-540 [PS]	Love Me or Leave Me	1955	$12

—Gatefold sleeve for 3-EP set (5-2170, 5-2171, 5-2172)

❏ B-7492	Secret Love/Be My Little Baby Bumble Bee//Makin' Whoopie!/Till We Meet Again	1956	$20
❏ 5-2171	Stay on the Right Side Sister/ Mean to Me//I'll Never Stop Loving You//Never Look Back	1955	$10

—Alternate numbers are "B-540-2" and "B-540-5"

DAY, DORIS/JOHNNIE RAY
COLUMBIA

❏ 39898	A Full Time Job/Ma Says, Pa Says	1952	$15
❏ 40001	Candy Lips/Let's Walk That-A-Way	1953	$10

DAY, JACK
CORAL

❏ 64058	An Old Christmas Card/ Jolly Old St. Nicholas	1950	$30

DAY, JOHNNY
CAMEO

❏ 371	I've Made Up My Mind/ Something Little	1965	$30

DAY, LITTLE SUNNY, AND THE CLOUDS
TANDEM

❏ 7001	Lou Ann/Baby Doll	1961	$400

DAY, MARGIE
CAT

❏ 118	Ho Ho/Pitty Pat Bank	1955	$50

DAYBREAKERS, THE (1)
ALADDIN

❏ 3434	I Wonder Why/Up, Up and Away	1958	$50

LAMP

❏ 2016	I Wonder Why/Up, Up and Away	1958	$70

DAYBREAKERS, THE (2)
DIAL

❏ 4066	Psychedelic Siren/Afterthoughts	1967	$40

DAYE, EDDIE, AND 4 BARS
SHRINE

❏ 112	Guess Who Loves You/ What Am I Gonna Do	1966	$1000

DAYE, JOHNNY
JOMADA

❏ 603	Good Time/I've Got Soul	1966	$20
❏ 600	Marry Me/Give Me Back My Ring	1965	$10

PARKWAY

❏ 119	A Lot of Progress/You're on Top	1966	$30

STAX

❏ 238	I Need Somebody/What'll I Do for Satisfaction	1968	$50
❏ 04	Stay Baby Stay/I Love Love	1968	$50

DAYNE, TAYLOR
ARISTA

❏ 9722	Don't Rush Me/In the Darkness	1988	$3
❏ 9722 [PS]	Don't Rush Me/In the Darkness	1988	$3
❏ 9700	I'll Always Love You/Where Does That Boy Hang Out	1988	$3
❏ 9700 [PS]	I'll Always Love You/Where Does That Boy Hang Out	1988	$3
❏ 9676	Prove Your Love/Upon the Journey's End	1988	$3
❏ 9676 [PS]	Prove Your Love/Upon the Journey's End	1988	$3
❏ 9612	Tell It to My Heart/(Instrumental)	1987	$3
❏ 9612 [PS]	Tell It to My Heart/(Instrumental)	1987	$4

—All-print sleeve

❏ 9612 [PS]	Tell It to My Heart/(Instrumental)	1987	$3

—Photo sleeve

❏ 9895	With Every Beat of My Heart/All I Ever Wanted	1989	$3
❏ 9895 [PS]	With Every Beat of My Heart/All I Ever Wanted	1989	$3

DAYSPRING
CON BRIO

❏ 143	Elfie, the Littlest Elf/ Christmas, Christmas (Comes But Once a Year)	1978	$4
❏ 143 [PS]	Elfie, the Littlest Elf/ Christmas, Christmas (Comes But Once a Year)	1978	$5

DAYTONAS, THE
AMY

❏ 961	Hey Little Girl/Please Go Away	1966	$30

DAZZ BAND
20TH CENTURY

❏ 2435	Catchin' Up on Love/I Searched Around	1979	$4
❏ 2453	Dancin' Free/I Searched Around	1980	$4
❏ 2401	Get Down with the Feelin'/ Makin' Music	1979	$4
❏ 2390	I Might As Well Forget About Loving You/Dazzberry Jam	1978	$4

—20th Century sides as "Kinsman Dazz"

GEFFEN

❏ 28635	L.O.V.E. M.I.A./A Place in My Heart	1986	$3
❏ 28658	Wild and Free/Last Chance for Love	1986	$3
❏ 28658 [PS]	Wild and Free/Last Chance for Love	1986	$3

MOTOWN

❏ 1676	Cheek to Cheek/We Can Dance	1983	$4
❏ 1775	Heartbeat/Rock with Me	1985	$4
❏ 1528	Hello Girl/Let the Music Play	1981	$4
❏ 1800	Hot Spot/I've Been Waiting	1985	$4
❏ 1507	Invitation to Love/Magnetized	1981	$4
❏ 1760	Let It All Blow/Now That I Have You	1984	$4
❏ 1609	Let It Whip/Everyday Love	1982	$4
❏ 1659	On the One for Fun/ Just Believe in Love	1983	$4
❏ 1680	Party Right Here/ Gamble with My Love	1983	$4
❏ 1500	Shake It Up/Only Love	1980	$4
❏ 1725	Swoop (I'm Yours)/Bad Girl	1984	$4

RCA

❏ 7614-7-R	Anticipation/If It's Love	1988	$3
❏ 8793-7-R	Open Sesame/(Instrumental)	1989	$3
❏ 8676-7-R	Single Girls/All the Way	1988	$3

DB'S, THE
BEARSVILLE

❏ 29188	Love Is for Lovers/Darby Hall	1984	$4

CAR

❏ 0(# unknown)	If and When/I Thought (You Wanted to Know)	1978	$8
❏ 0(# unknown) [PS]	If and When/I Thought (You Wanted to Know)	1978	$8

I.R.S.

❏ 53198	I Lie (Edited)/Sharon	1987	$3
❏ 53198 [PS]	I Lie (Edited)/Sharon	1987	$3

MCA

❏ 53468	The Changing Times/21 Jump Street	1988	$3

—B-side by Holly Robinson

SHAKE

❏ 100	Black and White/Soul Kiss Part 1 & 2	1980	$4
❏ 100 [PS]	Black and White/Soul Kiss Part 1 & 2	1980	$4

DE BONAIRS
PING

❏ 1000	Lanky Linda/Mother's Son	1956	$300
❏ 1001	Say a Prayer for Me/ Cracker-Jack Daddy	1956	$400

DE-FENDERS, THE
DEL-FI

❏ 4226	Little Deuce Coupe/Hayburner	1963	$40

—B-side by the Deuce Coupes

WORLD PACIFIC

❏ 382	(Dance to the) Yakety Sax/Wild One	1963	$50

DE LA SOUL
TOMMY BOY

❏ TB7910	Plug Tunin'/Freedom of Speak	1988	$10

DE VONS, THE
KING

❏ 6226	Someone to Treat Me (The Way You Used To)/Soul Party	1969	$12

MR. G

❏ 825	Groovin' with My Thing/Wise Up	1968	$15

PARKWAY

❏ 976	Put Me Down/Freddie	1966	$40

DEAD BOYS
SIRE

❏ 1004	Sonic Reducer/Down in Flames	1977	$15
❏ 1004 [PS]	Sonic Reducer/Down in Flames	1977	$15
❏ 1029	Tell Me/Not Anymore/ Ain't Nothin' to Do	1978	$20
❏ 1029 [PS]	Tell Me/Not Anymore/ Ain't Nothin' to Do	1978	$20

DEAD KENNEDYS
Featuring Jello Biafra.
ALTERNATIVE TENTACLES

❏ VIRUS23	Bleed for Me/Life Sentence	1982	$5
❏ VIRUS23 [PS]	Bleed for Me/Life Sentence	1982	$5
❏ AT-95-41	California Uber Alles/ The Man with the Dogs	1979	$30
❏ AT-95-41 [PS]	California Uber Alles/ The Man with the Dogs	1979	$30

—Picture sleeve and lyric insert

❏ VIRUS28	Halloween/Saturday Night Holocaust	1982	$5
❏ VIRUS28 [PS]	Halloween/Saturday Night Holocaust	1982	$5
❏ VIRUS2	Too Drunk to Fuck/The Prey	1981	$8
❏ VIRUS2 [PS]	Too Drunk to Fuck/The Prey	1981	$8

—Picture sleeve and lyric insert

I.R.S./FAULTY PRODUCTS

❏ 9016	Holiday in Cambodia/ Policetruck	1980	$12
❏ 9016 [PS]	Holiday in Cambodia/ Policetruck	1980	$12

OPTIONAL MUSIC

❏ OPT-2 [PS]	California Uber Alles/ The Man with the Dogs	1979	$15
❏ OPT-2	California Uber Alles/ The Man with the Dogs	1979	$15
❏ OPT-4	Holiday in Cambodia/ Policetruck	1980	$12
❏ OPT-4 [PS]	Holiday in Cambodia/ Policetruck	1980	$12

—Picture sleeve and lyric insert

DEAD MILKMEN, THE
BEAVER/ENIGMA

❏ 775038-7	Punk Rock Girl/Dizzy in the Daylight	1988	$4

DEAD OR ALIVE
EPIC

❏ 34-06374	Brand New Lover/In Too Deep	1986	$3
❏ 34-06374 [PS]	Brand New Lover/In Too Deep	1986	$3
❏ 34-68885	Come Home With Me Baby/ (Deadhouse Dub 7" Edit)	1989	$3
❏ 34-05607	Lover Come Back to Me/Far Too Hard	1985	$3
❏ 34-05607 [PS]	Lover Come Back to Me/Far Too Hard	1985	$3
❏ 34-05832	My Heart Goes Bang (Get Me to the Doctor)/ My Cake And Eat It	1986	$4
❏ 34-07022	Something in My House/D.J. Hit That Button	1987	$3
❏ 34-07022 [PS]	Something in My House/D.J. Hit That Button	1987	$8
❏ 34-04573	That's the Way (I Like It)/Do It	1984	$8
❏ 15-08469	That's the Way (I Like It)/ My Heart Goes Bang (Get Me to the Doctor)	1988	$3

—Reissue

❏ 34-04309	What I Want/The Stranger	1984	$8

DEAL, BILL, AND THE RHONDELS
BUDDAH

❏ 330	Everybody's Got Something to Hide/I Live in the Night	1972	$6
❏ 318	It's Too Late/So What If It Rains	1972	$6

GIG/WAY

❏ 902006	Freak 'N' Freeze/(Instrumental)	1978	$5

HERITAGE

❏ 824	I'm Gonna Make You Love Me/Hey Bulldog	1970	$6
❏ 812 [PS]	I've Been Hurt/I've Got My Needs	1969	$20
❏ 812	I've Been Hurt/I've Got My Seeds	1969	$8
❏ 803	May I/Day By Day	1968	$8
	My Love Grows		
❏ 818	Swingin' Tight/Tuck's Theme	1969	$8
❏ 818 [PS]	Swingin' Tight/Tuck's Theme	1969	$20
❏ 817	What Kind of Fool Do You Think I Am/Are You Ready for This	1969	$8

Number	Title	Yr	NM

MALA
| □ 502 | Big Toe in the Wind/ Don't Put Me Down | 1965 | $40 |

—As "Bill Deal and the Big Deals

POLYDOR
□ 14061	19 Years (Everything I Do Is Wrong)/Sea of Life	1971	$6
□ 14042	Do I Love You/Won't You Set Me Free	1970	$6
□ 14103	Sea of Life/You Can Make It	1971	$6

DEAL, DON
CAPITOL
| □ 4901 | How Do You Lie to a Heart/ Ain't Gonna Try No More | 1963 | $10 |
CASH
| □ 1028 | Cryin' in One Eye/Broken Hearted Fellow | 1956 | $60 |

—Eddie Cochran plays guitar on this record

CHALLENGE
| □ 59389 | Love Touched Me/Piece at a Time | 1968 | $8 |
ERA
□ 1051	My Blind Date/Even Then	1957	$20
□ 1060	She Was Here But She's Gone/You'd Look Good with a Tear in Your Eye	1957	$20
□ 1070	Sweet Love/The First Teenager	1958	$20
MGM
| □ K13235 | Lyin' Again/After the Boy Gets the Girl | 1964 | $10 |
SAND
| □ 438 | Our Last Night/So What | 1970 | $8 |

DEAN, ALAN
MGM
□ K11187	Be Anything/All My Life	1952	$20
□ K11365	Half a Heart/Give Me Your Lips	1952	$20
□ K11683	Hold Me Close/Positively No Dancing	1954	$15
□ K12311	I'll Share Your Tears, Your Laughter and Your Dreams/A Kiss Is Forever	1956	$15
□ K11513	Love Me, Love Me/ Make Me Your Slave	1953	$15
□ K11801	Lover's Quarrel/I'm Looking for Someone	1954	$15
□ K11269	Luna Rossa (Blushing Moon)/I'll Forget You	1952	$20
□ K11393	Say You Love Me/ High on a Windy Hill	1953	$15
□ K11454	Serenade of the Mandolins/ The Moon Was Yellow	1953	$15
□ K11156	Since My Love Has Gone/ If You Go (Si Tu Partais)	1952	$20
□ K12088	So Long/You Made Me Care (When I Wasn't in Love)	1955	$15
□ K12189	Take a Bow/Without You	1956	$15
□ K11844	Tonight, My Love/The Song from Desiree	1954	$15
□ K11920	Too Much in Love to Care/Ladder of Love	1955	$15
□ K11658	What Are You Waiting For/ Call Me Any Time at All	1954	$15
□ K11747	Who's Afraid/I'm a Man	1954	$15
□ K11578	Why Do You Pretend/ Don't Make Me Love	1953	$15
RAMA
| □ 218 | The Memory Followed Me Home/ The Letter That I Never Mailed | 1956 | $15 |
ROULETTE
| □ 4028 | How Far Can Any Man Go?/ The Heart of a Fool | 1957 | $15 |

DEAN AND JEAN
EMBER
| □ 1054 | Turn It Off/Never Let Your Love Fade Away | 1959 | $15 |
| □ 1048 | We're Gonna Get Married/ Too Young to Know | 1958 | $15 |
RUST
□ 5044	Come Take a Walk with Me/Dance the Roach	1962	$10
□ 5085	Goddess of Love/The Man Who Will Never Grow Old	1964	$10
□ 5075	Hey Jean, Hey Dean/ Please Don't Tell Me Now	1964	$20
□ 5081	I Wanna Be Loved/ Thread Your Needle	1964	$10
□ 5100	Lovingly Yours/Goddess of Love	1965	$10
□ 5046	Mack the Knife/You Can't Be Happy by Yourself	1962	$10
□ 5107	She's Too Respectable/I Love the Summertime	1965	$10
□ 5089	Sticks and Stones/In My Way	1964	$10
□ 5067	Tra La La La Suzy/I Love the Summertime	1963	$10

DEAN AND MARC
BULLSEYE
| □ 1026 | Cry/The Beginning of Love | 1959 | $30 |
| □ 1025 | Tell Him No/Change of Heart | 1959 | $60 |
CHECKMATE
| □ 1008 | Boogie Woogie Twist (Parts 1 & 2) | 1962 | $20 |
HICKORY
□ 1353	In the Middle of the Night/ You'll Never Really Know	1965	$10
□ 1249	When I Stop Dreaming/ There Oughta Be a Law	1964	$10
□ 1414	When I Stop Dreaming/ With Tears in My Eyes	1966	$10

—As "The Mathis Brothers"

| □ 1227 | With Tears in My Eyes/ Kissin' Game | 1963 | $10 |

—Hickory titles as "Dean and Mark" unless noted

MAY
| □ 135 | Somebody's Smiling (While I'm Crying)/Pins and Needles (In My Heart) | 1963 | $15 |

—As "Dean and Mark"

DEAN, BOBBY
CHESS
| □ 1710 | I'm Ready/Go Mr. Dillon | 1959 | $40 |

DEAN, CHARLES
BENTON
| □ 103 | Itchy/(B-side unknown) | 1958 | $250 |

DEAN, DEBBIE
MOTOWN
□ 1007	Don't Let Him Shop Around/A New Girl	1961	$50
□ 1025	Everybody's Talking About My Baby/I Cried All Night	1962	$50
□ 1025 [PS]	Everybody's Talking About My Baby/I Cried All Night	1962	$100
□ 1014	Itty, Bitty, Pity Love/But I'm Afraid	1961	$40
V.I.P.
| □ 25044 | Why Am I Lovin' You/ Stay My Love | 1967 | $300 |

DEAN, EDDIE
CAPITOL
□ F1389	All That I'm Asking Is Sympathy/ If I Should Come Back	1951	$30
□ F1842	Beloved Enemy/ The Lord's Prayer	1951	$30
□ F1915	Blue Wedding Bells/ Tears on My Guitar	1952	$30
□ F2086	Gold, Yellow Gold/ Poor Little Swallow	1952	$30
□ F1590	I Married the Girl/ Let Me Hold You	1951	$30
□ F1729	I'm Not in Love, Just Involved/ Roses Remind Me of You	1951	$30
□ F1497	I'm the Old Friend/My Sweetheart, My Own	1951	$30
□ F1362	My Life with You/Will They Open Up That Door	1951	$30
□ F1424	Please Don't Cry/I'll Be Back	1951	$30
INTRO
| □ 6087 | I'm a Stranger in My Home/Put a Little Sweetnin' in Your Love | 1953 | $30 |
MERCURY
| □ 6282 | On the Banks of the Sunny San Juan/Cowboy | 1950 | $50 |
ODE
| □ 1710 | Bimbo/No, No, Not Grandma | 1953 | $30 |
| □ 1701 | I'm a Stranger in My Home/Put a Little Sweetnin' in Your Love | 1953 | $30 |
SAGE
□ 270	Green Grass/Your Wayward Heart	1958	$30
□ 342	I Can't Go On Alone/Saber Man	1961	$20
□ 332	If Dreams Could Come True/ Somewhere Along the Line	1960	$30
□ 249	Iowa Rose/Nothing But Echoes	1958	$30
□ 325	I Took the Blues Out of Tomorrow/Seeds of Doubt	1960	$30
□ 231	Walkin' After Midnight/ Fingerprints	1957	$30
SAGE AND SAND
| □ 180 | I Dreamed of a Hill-Billy Heaven/Stealing | 1954 | $40 |

—Whitish label, green print

□ 188	Impatient Blues/Cry of a Broken Heart	1955	$30
□ 186	Impatient Blues/Second Hand Romance	1955	$30
□ 215	Look Homeward Angel/ Downgrade	1957	$30
□ 207	Open Up the Door, Baby/ Sign on the Door	1956	$30

—With Joanie Hall

□ 200	Orphan's Prayer/Once-a-While	1956	$30
□ 208	The First Christmas Bell/ Somebody Great	1956	$30
□ 199	Walk Beside Me/ Blessed Are We	1956	$30
SAND
| □ 235 | Lonesome Guitar/Taos | 1957 | $30 |

DEAN, JIMMY
4 STAR
| □ 1613 | Bumming Around/ Picking Sweethearts | 1953 | $30 |
| □ 1732 | Bumming Around/Release Me | 1959 | $15 |
CASINO
□ 052	I.O.U./Let's Pick Up the Pieces	1976	$4
□ 074	To a Sleeping Beauty/I Didn't Have Time	1976	$4
□ 108	Where Is That Man/ (B-side unknown)	1976	$4
CHURCHILL
| □ 94024 | I.O.U./To a Sleeping Beauty | 1983 | $4 |
COLUMBIA
| □ S731550 [S] | Basin Street Blues/Please Pass the Biscuits | 1962 | $30 |
| □ 42175 | Big Bad John/I Won't Go Huntin' with You Jake (But I'll Go Chasin' Wimmin) | 1961 | $12 |

—Lyrics say: "At the bottom of this mine lies a big, big man." We think the song title was changed with the lyric, but we're not 100 percent sure. In other words, this title may exist with the "hell of a man" lyrics.

| □ 42175 [PS] | Big Bad John/I Won't Go Huntin' with You Jake (But I'll Go Chasin' Wimmin) | 1961 | $20 |
| □ 42175 | Big John/I Won't Go Huntin' with You Jake (But I'll Go Chasin' Wimmin) | 1961 | $30 |

—Lyrics say: "At the bottom of this mine lies one hell of a man.

| □ 43457 | Blue Christmas/Yes, Patricia, There Is a Santa Claus | 1965 | $8 |
| □ JZSP111915/6 [DJ] | Blue Christmas/Yes, Patricia, There Is a Santa Claus | 1965 | $30 |

—Promo only on green vinyl

□ 42259	Dear Ivan/Smoke, Smoke, Smoke That Cigarette	1962	$12
□ 42259 [PS]	Dear Ivan/Smoke, Smoke, Smoke That Cigarette	1962	$20
□ 40995	Deep Blue Sea/Love Me So I'll Know	1957	$15
□ 41956	Give Me Back My Heart/It's Been a Long, Long Time	1961	$10
□ 42600	Gonna Raise a Rukus Tonight/A Day That Changed the World	1962	$10
□ 42600 [PS]	Gonna Raise a Rukus Tonight/A Day That Changed the World	1962	$20
□ 43382	Harvest of Sunshine/ Under the Sun	1965	$6
□ S731551 [S]	Have You Ever Been Lonely/Nobody	1962	$30
□ 46039	I've Been Down Some Road/Your Sweet Love	1974	$5
□ S731552 [S]	I Was Just Walking Out the Door/The Dark Town Poker Club	1962	$30
□ S731554 [S]	Little Black Book/Old Pappy's New Banjo	1962	$30

—The above five are "Stereo Seven" 33 1/3 rpm jukebox singles from set "JS7-63" entitled "Portrait of Jimmy Dean

□ 42529	Little Black Book/Please Pass the Biscuits	1962	$12
□ 42529 [PS]	Little Black Book/Please Pass the Biscuits	1962	$20
□ 41710	Little Boy Lost/There'll Be No Teardrops Tonight	1960	$15
□ 41025	Little Sandy Sleighfoot/When They Ring the Golden Bells	1957	$20
□ 41025 [PS]	Little Sandy Sleighfoot/When They Ring the Golden Bells	1957	$30
□ 42738	Mile Long Train/This Ole House	1963	$8
□ 42934	Mind Your Own Business/I Really Don't Want to Know	1963	$8
□ 42934 [PS]	Mind Your Own Business/I Really Don't Want to Know	1963	$15
□ 41265	My Heart Is An Open Book/ Shark in the Bathtub	1958	$15
□ 42248	Oklahoma Bill/To a Sleeping Beauty	1961	$10
□ 43754	Once a Day/Let's Pretend	1966	$6
□ 42338	P.T. 109/Walk On, Boy	1962	$10
□ 42338 [PS]	P.T. 109/Walk On, Boy	1962	$20
□ 43159	Sam Hill/When I Grow Too Old to Dream	1964	$8
□ 41196	School of Love/You Should See Tennessee, Mam'selle	1958	$15
□ 43021	Shenandoah/Waitin' for the Wagon	1964	$8
□ 41395	Sing Along/Weekend Blues	1959	$15
□ 41395 [PS]	Sing Along/Weekend Blues	1959	$30
□ 41118	Starlight, Starbright/ Makin' My Mind Up	1958	$15
□ 41453	Stay a Little Longer/ Counting Tears	1959	$15
□ 42483	Steel Men/Little Bitty Big John	1962	$10
□ 42483 [PS]	Steel Men/Little Bitty Big John	1962	$20
□ 41543	Thanks for the Dream/ There's Still Time, Brother	1959	$15
□ 43263	The First Thing Ev'ry Morning (And the Last Thing Ev'ry Night)/Awkward Situation	1965	$6
□ 42861	The Funniest Thing I Ever Heard/Thumb Pick Pete	1963	$8
□ 42861 [PS]	The Funniest Thing I Ever Heard/Thumb Pick Pete	1963	$15
□ 43540	Things Have Gone to Pieces/Striker Bill	1966	$6
□ 42282	To a Sleeping Beauty/ The Cajun Queen	1962	$10

Number	Title	Yr	NM
❏ 42282 [PS]	To a Sleeping Beauty/ The Cajun Queen	1962	$20
❏ 45981	Who's Gonna Love Me Tomorrow/The Days When Jim Liked Jimmy	1973	$5

KING
❏ 5862	There Stands the Glass/ Bumming Around	1964	$8

MERCURY
❏ 71240	Bumming Around/Nothing Can Stop My Love	1957	$20
❏ 70691	False Pride/Big Blue Diamonds	1955	$20
❏ 70745	Find 'Em, Fool 'Em, and Leave 'Em Alone/My World Is You	1955	$20
❏ 70786	Freight Train Blues/Glad Rags	1956	$20
❏ 70855	Hello Mr. Blues/I Found Out	1956	$20
❏ 71172	Look on the Good Side/ Do You Love Me	1957	$20
❏ 71120	Losing Game/Happy Child	1957	$20
❏ 71313	What This Old World Needs/A Fool in Love	1958	$20

RCA VICTOR
❏ 47-9652	A Hammer and Nails/I Taught Her Everything She Knows	1968	$8
❏ 74-0600	And I'm Still Missing You/The One You Say Good Mornin' To	1971	$6
❏ 47-9454	A Thing Called Love/ One Last Time	1968	$8
❏ 47-9567	Born to Be By Your Side/ Read 'Em and Weep	1968	$8
❏ 47-9859	Down Comes the Rain/Us	1970	$6
❏ 47-9966	Everybody Knows/ Ain't Life Sweet	1971	$6
❏ 47-9350	I'm a Swinger/Your Country Boy	1967	$8
❏ 47-9947	Slowly/Sweet Thang	1971	$6

— With Dottie West
❏ 47-8971	Stand Beside Me/A Tiny Drop of Sadness	1966	$8
❏ 47-9091	Sweet Misery/When Someone Mentions Your Name	1967	$8
❏ 47-9915	Weakness in a Man/Aunt Maudie's Fun Garden	1970	$6
❏ 47-9800	When Judy Smiled/My Hometown Sweetheart	1969	$6

DEAN, LARRY
USA
❏ 620	Outside Chance/ (B-side unknown)	1989	$6
❏ 620 [PS]	Outside Chance/ (B-side unknown)	1989	$8

DEAN, RITCHIE
TOWER
❏ 183	Farewell Angelica/Time (Can't Heal This Pain of Mine)	1965	$20
❏ 102	Goodbye Girl/I'd Do Anything	1964	$30
❏ 228	It's Rainin', It's Pourin'/ The Old Cathedral	1966	$20

DEAN, TERRI
LAUREL
❏ 1003	I'm Confessin' (That I Love You)/I Blew Out the Flame	1959	$20

LAURIE
❏ 3032	Adonis/You Treat Me Like a Boy	1959	$20
❏ 3049	Friendship Ring/Oh My Papa	1960	$20

POPLAR
❏ 102	Dream Boy (Oh, Oh, Oh)/ It's Just Your Kiss	1958	$50

— As "Terry Dean"

DEANNA MARIE
LITTLE DARLIN'
❏ 021	Fight It with Love/I Dropped My Tater Chips	1967	$10

DEANS, THE
LAURIE
❏ 3114	I Don't Want to Wait/ Little White Gardenia	1961	$30

MOHAWK
❏ 119	Humpty Dumpty/La Chiam	1960	$30
❏ 126	It's You/I Don't Wanna Wait	1960	$50
❏ 114	My Heart Is Low/I'll Love You Forever	1960	$30

STAR MAKER
❏ 1931	Chills, Chills, Chills/ (Lady of the) Caravan	1962	$70
❏ 1928	Oh Little Star/You Got Me Baby	1961	$125

DEAUVILLE, RONNIE
DOT
❏ 16025	Heaven in Hawaii/Honey Hill	1959	$20

ERA
❏ 1066	Hong Kong Affair/ Crazy, Wonderful	1957	$30
❏ 1055	I Concentrate on You/ As Children Do	1957	$30
❏ 1055 [PS]	I Concentrate on You/ As Children Do	1957	$50
❏ 1056	Laura/It Wasn't Much of a Town	1957	$30
❏ 1056 [PS]	Laura/It Wasn't Much of a Town	1957	$70

DEBARGE
GORDY
Number	Title	Yr	NM
❏ 1660	All This Love/I'm in Love with You	1983	$4
❏ 7198	Dance the Night Away/ (B-side unknown)	1981	$5
❏ 1645	I Like It/Hesitated	1982	$4
❏ 1723	Love Me in a Special Way/ Dance the Night Away	1984	$4
❏ 1635	Stop! Don't Tease Me/Hesitated	1982	$5
❏ 1822	The Heart Is Not So Smart/ Share My World	1985	$3

— As "El DeBarge with DeBarge"
❏ 1822 [PS]	The Heart Is Not So Smart/ Share My World	1985	$4

— As "El DeBarge with DeBarge"
❏ 1705	Time Will Reveal/I'll Never Fall in Love Again	1983	$4
❏ 7203	What's Your Name/You're So Gentle, So Kind	1981	$5
❏ 1793	Who's Holding Donna Now/Be My Lady	1985	$3
❏ 1793 [PS]	Who's Holding Donna Now/Be My Lady	1985	$4

STRIPED HORSE
❏ 7004	Dance All Night/(Instrumental)	1987	$5
❏ 7004 [PS]	Dance All Night/(Instrumental)	1987	$6

DEBARGE, EL
GORDY
❏ 1857	Love Always/The Walls (Came Tumbling Down)	1986	$3
❏ 1857 [PS]	Love Always/The Walls (Came Tumbling Down)	1986	$3
❏ 1867	Someone/Stop! Don't Tease Me	1986	$3
❏ 1867 [PS]	Someone/Stop! Don't Tease Me	1986	$3
❏ 1842	Who's Johnny ("Short Circuit" Theme)/Love in a Special Way	1986	$3
❏ 1842 [PS]	Who's Johnny ("Short Circuit" Theme)/Love in a Special Way	1986	$3

MOTOWN
❏ 1995	Broken Dreams/(Instrumental)	1989	$4
❏ 1966	Somebody Loves You/ (Instrumental)	1989	$3

DEBBIE AND THE TEEN DREAMS
VERNON
❏ 101	Santa, Teach Me How To Dance/The Time	1962	$30

DEBERRY, JIMMY
SUN
❏ 185	Take a Little Chance/Time Has Made a Change	1953	$3000

DEBONAIRES, THE (1)
DORE
❏ 712	Everybody's Movin'/ Mama Don't Care	1964	$30
❏ 592	Every Once in a While/ Gert's Skirt	1961	$40
❏ 702	Every Once in a While/ Gert's Skirt	1964	$30
❏ 526	Every Once in a While/ Mama Don't Care	1959	$100

— As "The Debonairs
❏ 654	Hold Back the Dawn/ Mama Don't Care	1962	$30

GEE
❏ 1054	We'll Wait/Make Believe Lover	1960	$30
❏ 1008	Won't You Tell Me/I'm Gone	1956	$100

HERALD
❏ 509	Darlin'/Whispering Blues	1957	$70
❏ 509	Darlin'/Whispering Blues	1957	$200

— As "The Five Debonaires

DEBONAIRES, THE (2)
ELMONT
❏ 1004	This Must Be Paradise/I Need You Darling	1958	$200

DEBONAIRES, THE (3)
GOLDEN WORLD
❏ 17	A Little Too Long/Please Don't Say We're Through	1964	$40
❏ 38	Big Time Fun/How's Your New Love Treating You	1966	$60
❏ 44	C.O.D./How's Your New Love Treating You	1966	$40
❏ 26	Eenie Meenie Gypsaleenie/ Please Don't Say We're Through	1965	$30

SOLID HIT
❏ 104	I'm in Love Again/ Headache in My Heart	1967	$200
❏ 102	Loving You Takes All of My Time/Headache in My Heart	1967	$2000

— VG 1000; VG+ 1500

DEBONAIRES, THE (4)
MTM
❏ B-72051	I'm on Fire/Loving You's All That's On My Mind	1985	$6

DEBONAIRES, THE (U)
GALAXY
Number	Title	Yr	NM
❏ 774	Woman, Why?/Stop, Let's Be United	1971	$50

MASKE
❏ 804	Every Other Day/Jivin' Guy	1959	$50

DEBS, THE
BRUCE
❏ 129	Shoo-Doo-De-Doo/ Whadaya Want	1955	$70

CROWN
❏ 153	If You Were Here Tonight/ Look What You're Doin' to Me	1955	$50

DOUBLE L
❏ 727	Danger Ahead/Just Another Fool	1964	$15

MERCURY
❏ 72458	Give Him My Love/ Goodbye Boy	1965	$30
❏ 72566	My Best Friend/The Life and Soul of the Party	1966	$20

DEBURGH, CHRIS
A&M
❏ 7267	A Spaceman Came Travelling/Just a Poor Boy	1976	$5
❏ 7267 [PS]	A Spaceman Came Travelling/Just a Poor Boy	1976	$10

— Both sleeve and record are U.K. imports
❏ 1998 [DJ]	A Spaceman Came Travelling (mono/stereo)	1977	$6

— Stock copies do not exist
❏ 1891	A Spaceman Came Travelling/Poor Boy	1976	$6
❏ 2511	Don't Pay the Ferryman/ All the Love I Have Inside	1982	$4

DEBUTANTES, THE (1)
KAYO
❏ 928	Going Steady/Memories	1958	$250

DECARLO, YVONNE
IMPERIAL
❏ 5484	The Secret of Love/That's Love	1956	$100

DECASTRO SISTERS, THE
ABBOTT
❏ 3003	Boom Boom Boomerang/ Let Your Love Walk In	1955	$15
❏ 3007	Cuban Love Song/I Can't Escape from You	1955	$15
❏ 3004	Cuckoo in the Clock/ If I Ever Fall in Love	1955	$15
❏ 3002	I'm Bewildered/To Say You're Mine	1955	$15
❏ 3012	Snowbound for Christmas/ Christmas Is a-Comin'	1955	$20
❏ 3001	Teach Me Tonight/It's Love	1954	$20
❏ 3011	Too Late Now/Give Me Time	1955	$15
❏ 3008	Wedding Song/I'm Bewildered	1955	$15

ABC-PARAMOUNT
❏ 10007	Close to You/With My Eyes Wide Open	1959	$10
❏ 9988	Teach Me Tonight Cha Cha/ The Things I Tell My Pillow	1958	$10
❏ 9932	Who Are They to Say/ When You Look at Me	1958	$10

CAPITOL
❏ 4537	The Bells/Red Sails in the Sunset	1961	$8

RCA VICTOR
❏ 47-6661	Don't Call Me Sweetie/It's Yours	1956	$12
❏ 47-6862	Flowers on a Hillside/I Know Plenty	1957	$10
❏ 47-6774	I Never Meant to Hurt You/I Hear a Melody	1956	$10
❏ 47-7108	Old Timers' Tune/Blue and Broken Hearted	1957	$10
❏ 47-7028	Where Have You Been All My Life/That Little Word Called Love	1957	$10

ZODIAC
❏ 1016	Before the Next Teardrop Falls/Teach Me Tonight	1977	$4

DECEMBER'S CHILDREN
CAPITOL
❏ 5883	A Girl Like You/Makin' Music	1967	$15

MAINSTREAM
❏ 728	Sweet Talking Woman/ (B-side unknown)	1970	$20

WORLD PACIFIC
❏ 77887	Backwards and Forwards/ Kissin' Time	1968	$12
❏ 77910	I've Been Hurt/Good Time Boy	1969	$10
❏ 77895	Lovin' Things/Extraordinary Man	1968	$10

Number	Title	Yr	NM

DEE, CONNIE
HIT
❏ 123	Be Anything (But Be Mine)/Tell Me Why	1964	$8

— B-side by Bobby Brooks

❏ 12	Everybody Loves Me But You/Old Rivers	1962	$8

— B-side by Charlie Jarrett

❏ 85	Hello Heartache, Goodbye Love/Sugar Shack	1963	$8

— B-side by Ricky Dickens

❏ 189	Look of Love/King of the Road	1965	$8

— B-side by Charlie Bare

❏ 128	My Boy Lollipop/Tears and Roses	1964	$8

— B-side by Marty Wood

❏ 202	Once a Cheater, Always a Cheater/I Must Be Seeing Things	1965	$8

— B-side by Bobby Brooks

❏ 14	Second Hand Love/I Can't Stop Loving You	1962	$8

— B-side by Herbert Hunter

❏ 90	She's a Fool/It's All Right	1963	$8

— B-side by Leroy Jones

❏ 274	Sugar Town/Single Girl	1966	$8

— B-side by Sherry Young

❏ 114	That's the Way Boys Are/The Shoop Shoop Song	1964	$8

— B-side by Denny Dugan

❏ 197	Whisper Tell Me Sweetly/I've Got a Tiger by the Tail	1965	$8

— B-side by Jack White

DEE, DONNA
ABC-PARAMOUNT
❏ 10296	Television/Nobody's Gonna Hurt You	1962	$30

DEE, DUANE
ABC
❏ 12018	Lovin' Naturally/She Was the Woman and the Lady	1974	$5
❏ 11417	Morning Girl/She's My Woman	1974	$5

CAPITOL
❏ 5986	Before the Next Teardrop Falls/You're Not Painting the Town	1967	$12
❏ 2519	Blessed Are the Poor/Carmelita's House	1969	$8
❏ 2125	Precious/That Was My Shining Hour	1968	$8
❏ 2686	So Afraid/A Mighty Fortress Is Our Love	1969	$8
❏ 2332	True Love Travels on a Gravel Road/Have a Little Faith	1968	$8
❏ 2250	We're the Kind of People (That Make the Jukebox Play)/It Won't Matter Much	1968	$8
❏ 5887	Why Didn't I Think of That/When the Devil Rides the Wind	1967	$10

CARTWHEEL
❏ 200	How Can You Mend a Broken Heart/Georgeanna	1971	$6
❏ 192	I've Got to Sing/There Will Be an Answer	1971	$6
❏ 195	Little Garden of Love/That's How I Feel	1971	$6
❏ 215	Mary in the Morning/Cold January Morning	1972	$6
❏ 207	Sweet Apple Wine/I Can't Get Over You	1972	$6

DEE, FRANKIE
20TH FOX
❏ 146	Swingin' in a Hammock/I Had the Craziest Dream	1959	$40

RCA VICTOR
❏ 47-7276	Shake It Up Baby/After Graduation	1958	$70

DEE, GORDON
SOUTHERN TRACKS
❏ 1070	Beam Me Up Scotty/You'll Never Know How Much (I Needed You Today)	1986	$6
❏ 1035	I Forgot That I Don't Live Here Anymore/The Paradise Knife and Gun Club	1985	$5
❏ 1064	Starlite Drive-In Movie Queen/Those Old Songs	1986	$5
❏ 1002	They Just Don't Make Time Like They Used To/Happy Endings	1982	$5

— With Carol Lee

❏ 1057	Those Old Songs/(B-side unknown)	1986	$6
❏ 1047	We Don't Make Love Anymore (We Just Make Believe)/(B-side unknown)	1985	$6

DEE, JIMMY
DOT
❏ 15664	Henrietta/Don't Cry No More	1957	$50
❏ 15721	Here I Come/You're Late, Miss Kate	1958	$50

TNT
❏ 161	Feel Like Rockin'/Rock-Tick-Rock	1958	$70
❏ 148	Henrietta/Don't Cry No More	1957	$100
❏ 152	Here I Come/You're Late, Miss Kate	1958	$100

DEE, JOEY, AND THE STARLITERS
BONUS
❏ 7009	Lorraine/The Girl I Walk to School	1963	$60
❏ 7009 [PS]	Lorraine/The Girl I Walk to School	1963	$100

JUBILEE
❏ 5566	Can't Sit Down/Put Your Heart In It	1967	$20

— Stock copy may not exist

❏ 5539	Dancing on the Beach/Good Little You	1966	$20
❏ 5532	Feel Good About It Part 1/Feel Good About It Part 2	1966	$20
❏ 5554	She's So Exceptional/It's Got You	1966	$20

LITTLE
❏ 813/4	Lorraine/The Girl I Walk to School	1958	$400

ROULETTE
❏ 4467	Baby You're Driving Me Crazy/Help Me Pick Up the Pieces	1963	$15
❏ 4617	Cry a Little Sometime/Wing Ding	1965	$15
❏ 4503	Dance, Dance, Dance/Let's Have a Party	1963	$15
❏ 4539	Down by the Riverside/Getting Nearer	1963	$30
❏ 4431	Every Time (I Think About You) Part 1/Every Time (I Think About You) Part 2	1962	$15
❏ 4408	Hey, Let's Twist/Roly Poly	1962	$20
❏ 4408 [PS]	Hey, Let's Twist/Roly Poly	1962	$30
❏ 4488	Hot Pastrami with Mashed Potatoes -- Part 1/Hot Pastrami with Mashed Potatoes -- Part 2	1963	$15
❏ 4456	I Lost My Baby/Keep Your Mind on What You're Doing	1962	$15
❏ 4456 [PS]	I Lost My Baby/Keep Your Mind on What You're Doing	1962	$30
❏ 4401	Peppermint Twist -- Part 1/Peppermint Twist -- Part 2	1961	$20
❏ 4416	Shout -- Part 1/Shout -- Part 2	1962	$20
❏ 4416 [PS]	Shout -- Part 1/Shout -- Part 2	1962	$30
❏ 4438	What Kind of Love Is This/Wing Ding	1962	$15

— White label with colored "spokes

❏ 4438 [PS]	What Kind of Love Is This/Wing Ding	1962	$30
❏ 4438	What Kind of Love Is This/Wing Ding	1962	$10

— Pink label

SCEPTER
❏ 1210	Face of An Angel/Shimmy Baby	1960	$40

— Originals have "Scepter" at top of label and are credited as "Joey Dee and the Starlights

❏ 1210	Face of An Angel/Shimmy Baby	1961	$30

— Reissues have "Scepter Records" at side of label and are credited as listed

❏ 1225	Three Memories/(Bad) Bulldog	1961	$40

VASELINE HAIR TONIC
❏ 0(no cat #)	Learn to Dance the Authentic Peppermint Twist (Parts 1 & 2)	1962	$20
❏ 0(no cat #) [PS]	Learn to Dance the Authentic Peppermint Twist (Parts 1 & 2)	1962	$20

DEE, KATHY
B/W
❏ 619/20	If I Never Get to Heaven/Teardrops in My Heart	1963	$20
❏ 619/20 [PS]	If I Never Get to Heaven/Teardrops in My Heart	1963	$30
❏ 611/12	Trail of Tears/The Ways of a Heart	1963	$20

DECCA
❏ 32372	Funny How Time Slips Away/Shadow of a Girl	1968	$8

UNITED ARTISTS
❏ 687	Don't Leave Me Lonely Too Long/I Promise Not to Cry	1964	$12

DEE, KIKI
FONTANA
❏ 1649	On a Magic Carpet Ride/Now the Flowers Die	1969	$5

LIBERTY
❏ 56030	I'm Going Out/Patterns	1968	$6
❏ 56089	On a Magic Carpet Ride/Now the Flowers Die	1969	$6
❏ 55994	Stop and Think/I	1967	$6

RARE EARTH
❏ 5025	Love Makes the World Go Round/Jimmy	1970	$5

RCA
❏ PB-12347	Star/There's a Need	1981	$4

ROCKET
❏ 40157	Amoureuse/Rest My Head	1973	$4
❏ 40730	Chicago/Bad Day Child	1977	$4
❏ YB-11490	Don't Stop Loving Me/One Step Ahead of the Storm	1979	$4
❏ 40401	How Glad I Am/Peter	1975	$4
❏ 40293	I've Got the Music in Me/Simple Melody	1974	$5
❏ 40506	Once a Fool/Someone to Me	1976	$4
❏ YB-11413	One Step/Dark Side of Your Soul	1978	$4
❏ 40355	Step by Step/Amoureuse	1975	$4
❏ 40256	Super Cool/Loving and Free	1974	$4
❏ 40095	The Last Good Man in My Life/Lonnie and Josie	1973	$4

TAMLA
❏ 54193	The Day Will Come Between Sunday and Monday/My Whole World Ended (The Moment You Left Me)	1970	$5
❏ 54193 [PS]	The Day Will Come Between Sunday and Monday/My Whole World Ended (The Moment You Left Me)	1970	$20

WORLD PACIFIC
❏ 77820	I Dig You Baby/Small Town	1966	$8

DEE, LENNY
DECCA
❏ 25563	Ain't She Sweet/Alabamy Bound	1962	$6
❏ 33026	All I Ever Need Is You/Vaya Con Dios	1972	$4
❏ 25578	Baubles, Bangles and Beads/Blues in the Night	1962	$6
❏ 28413	Begin the Beguine/Peanut Vendor	1952	$15
❏ 30429	Big Boogie Dee/Cecelia	1957	$8
❏ 28109	Carolina in the Morning/Viennese Waltz Medley	1952	$15
❏ 29579	Crazy Organ Rag/Punxsutawney Boogie	1955	$12
❏ 25717	Cute/Daydream	1967	$5
❏ 25633	Devil Woman/San Antonio Rose	1964	$6
❏ 25745	Folsom Prison Blues/Turn Around, Look at Me	1969	$5
❏ 25735	Gentle on My Mind/Rossana's Theme	1968	$5
❏ 27891	Have You Ever Been Lonely/Cotton Walk	1951	$15
❏ 32804	Help Me Make It Through the Night/Remember Me	1971	$4
❏ 25750	Help Yourself/Try a Little Tenderness	1969	$5
❏ 30296	High Tide Boogie/Tara Lara	1957	$8
❏ 29689	Honeydripper/Flea Hop Boogie	1955	$12
❏ 30032	Honky Tonk Train Blues/Yodelin' Organ	1956	$8
❏ 29596	Little Brown Jug/The World Is Waiting for the Sunrise	1955	$12
❏ 28500	Midnight/Bye Bye Blues	1952	$10
❏ 25592	Moon Over Miami/Atlanta G.A.	1963	$6
❏ 31332	Mr. Santa/Auld Lang Syne	1961	$10
❏ 28639	Oh Johnny Oh/Them There Eyes	1953	$10
❏ 25531	Parade of the Wooden Soldiers/Twilight Time	1961	$6
❏ 29360	Plantation Boogie/The Birth of the Blues	1954	$10
❏ 30201	Stormy Weather/Goodnight Sweet Love	1957	$8
❏ 25678	The Gang That Sang Heart of My Heart/Down by the Old Mill Stream	1965	$6
❏ 25725	There's a Kind of Hush/Exodus	1967	$5
❏ 25613	Wagon Wheels/Hominy Grits	1963	$6

7-Inch Extended Plays
❏ ED2628 [M]	(contents unknown)	1959	$10
❏ ED 7-2628 [S]	(contents unknown)	1959	$20
❏ ED2628 [PS]	Mellow-Dee	1959	$12
❏ ED 7-2628 [PS]	Mellow-Dee	1959	$20

DEE, TOMMY

CHALLENGE

Number	Title	Yr	NM
❑ 59087	Ballad of a Drag Race/ The Story of Susie	1960	$30
❑ 59083	The Hobo and the Puppy/ There's a Star Spangled Banner Waving Somewhere	1960	$30

CREST

Number	Title	Yr	NM
❑ 1067	Merry Christmas, Mary/ Angel of Love	1959	$30

—With Carol Kay

Number	Title	Yr	NM
❑ 1061	The Chair/Hello Lonesome	1959	$30
❑ 1057 [M]	Three Stars/I'll Never Change	1959	$40

—With backing group and B-side credited to "The Teen Tones and Orchestra

Number	Title	Yr	NM
❑ 1057 [M]	Three Stars/I'll Never Change	1959	$30

—With backing group and B-side credited to "Carol Kay and the Teen-Aires

Number	Title	Yr	NM
❑ 1057 [S]	Three Stars/I'll Never Change	1959	$60

—With backing group and B-side credited to "Carol Kay and the Teen-Aires

PIKE

Number	Title	Yr	NM
❑ 5909	A Little Dog Cried/Look Homeward, Dear Angel	1961	$30
❑ 5906	Loving You (On Someone Else's Time)/Halfway to Hell	1961	$30
❑ 5917	Missing on a Mountain/Look Homeward, Dear Angel	1962	$30

SIMS

Number	Title	Yr	NM
❑ 308	How's Your Mama Em/ Goodbye High School	1966	$20
❑ 260	Missing While Surfing/ Goodbye High School	1966	$30

DEE, WILLIE

TUMBLEWEED

Number	Title	Yr	NM
❑ 100	Tear Filled Eyes/My Daddy's Not a Young Man Anymore	1968	$30

DEEP PURPLE

Also see BLACK SABBATH; TOMMY BOLIN; CAPTAIN BEYOND; GILLAN; IAN GILLAN BAND; RAINBOW; TRAPEZE; WHITESNAKE.

MERCURY

Number	Title	Yr	NM
❑ 885820-7	Bad Attitude/Black and White	1987	$3
❑ 885617-7	Call of the Wild/Dead or Alive	1987	$3
❑ 885617-7 [PS]	Call of the Wild/Dead or Alive	1987	$4

TETRAGRAMMATON

Number	Title	Yr	NM
❑ 1537	Hallelujah (I Am the Preacher)/April Part 1	1969	$10
❑ 1503	Hush/One More Rainy Day	1968	$20
❑ 1503 [PS]	Hush/One More Rainy Day	1968	$600
❑ 1519	The Bird Has Flown/Emmaretta	1969	$12

WARNER BROS.

Number	Title	Yr	NM
❑ 7405	Black Night/Into the Fire	1970	$8
❑ 7809	Burn/Coronarias Regid	1974	$5
❑ 7528	Fire Ball/I'm Alone	1971	$8
❑ 8182	Gettin' Tighter/Love Child	1976	$6
❑ 8049	High Ball Shooter/You Can't Do It Right	1974	$5
❑ 7634	Highway Star (Part 1)/ Highway Star (Part 2)	1972	$6
❑ 7654	Hush/Kentucky Woman	1972	$6
❑ 7595	Lazy/When a Blind Man Cries	1972	$6
❑ 7784	Might Just Take Your Life/ Coronorias Regid	1974	$5
❑ 7784 [DJ]	Might Just Take Your Life (Mono 3:35/Stereo 4:36)	1974	$8
❑ 7710	Smoke on the Water (Edited Version) Studio/Smoke on the Water (Edited Version) Live	1973	$5
❑ 8069	Stormbringer/Love Don't Mean a Thing	1975	$5
❑ 7493	Strange Kind of Woman/I'm Alone	1971	$8
❑ 7672	Woman from Tokyo/ Super Trouper	1972	$6
❑ 7737	Woman from Tokyo/ Super Trouper	1973	$5

7-Inch Extended Plays

Number	Title	Yr	NM
❑ S2766 [PS]	Burn	1974	$20

—Part of "Little LP" series (LLP #250)

Number	Title	Yr	NM
❑ S2766	Burn//Lay Down Stay Down/ You Fool No One	1974	$20

—Full-length versions; jukebox issue, small hole, plays at 33 1/3 rpm

Number	Title	Yr	NM
❑ S2701 [PS]	Made in Japan	1973	$20

—Part of "Little LP" series (LLP #214)

Number	Title	Yr	NM
❑ S2701	Smoke on the Water/ Highway Star	1973	$20

—Full-length versions; jukebox issue; small hole, plays at 33 1/3 rpm

DEEP SIX, THE

LIBERTY

Number	Title	Yr	NM
❑ 55926	Image of a Girl/C'mon Baby	1966	$8
❑ 55858	I Wanna Shout/Things We Say	1966	$8
❑ 55882	When Morning Breaks/Counting	1966	$8
❑ 55901	Why Say Goodbye/What Would You Wish from the Golden Fish	1966	$8

DEER, JOHN

ROYAL AMERICAN

Number	Title	Yr	NM
❑ 34	The Battle Hymn of Lt. Calley/ Sitting in Atlanta Station	1971	$8
❑ 21	Waxahachie Woman/Big Train	1970	$8

DEES, RICK

ATLANTIC

Number	Title	Yr	NM
❑ 89601	Eat My Shorts/Get Nekked	1984	$4
❑ 89601 [PS]	Eat My Shorts/Get Nekked	1984	$4
❑ 89481	I Wanna Be Elvis/(Instrumental)	1985	$8
❑ 89462	Merry Christmas (Wherever You Are)/We Are the Weird	1985	$6

FRETONE

Number	Title	Yr	NM
❑ 040	Disco Duck (Part 1)/ Disco Duck (Part 2)	1976	$30

MUSHROOM

Number	Title	Yr	NM
❑ 7048	Chantilly Lace/Disco Brief	1979	$6

NO BUDGET

Number	Title	Yr	NM
❑ 1680	Merry Christmas (Wherever You Are)/Hurt Me Baby, Make Me Write Bad Checks	1984	$10

RSO

Number	Title	Yr	NM
❑ 870	Barely White (That'll Get It Baby)/ He Ate Too Many Jelly Doughnuts	1977	$15

—B-side is an Elvis novelty; it only appears on stock copies, as "Barely White" was promoted as the hit

Number	Title	Yr	NM
❑ 8006	Disco Duck/Barely White (That'll Get It Baby)	1980	$4

—Reissue on "Top Line" series

Number	Title	Yr	NM
❑ 857	Disco Duck (Part 1)/ Disco Duck (Part 2)	1976	$4
❑ 866	Dis-Gorilla (Part 1)/ Dis-Gorilla (Part 2)	1976	$4
❑ 939	Meatballs/Run with the Pack	1979	$5

STAX

Number	Title	Yr	NM
❑ 3207	Bigfoot/Big Toe	1978	$4

DEES, SAM

ATLANTIC

Number	Title	Yr	NM
❑ 3287	Fragile, Handle with Care/ Save the Love at Any Cost	1975	$300
❑ 2991	So Tied Up/Signed Miss Heroin	1973	$30
❑ 3243	The Show Must Go On/ Child of the Streets	1975	$30
❑ 3205	Worn Out Broken Heart/ Come Back Strong	1974	$30

BIG TREE

Number	Title	Yr	NM
❑ 16054	Storybook Children/Just As Sure	1976	$125

—With Bettye Swann

CHESS

Number	Title	Yr	NM
❑ 2109	Can You Be a One Man Woman/ Put You Back in Your Place	1971	$200
❑ 2122	Love Starvation/Maryanna	1972	$70

CLINTONE

Number	Title	Yr	NM
❑ 010	Claim Jumping/I'm So Very Glad	1972	$30

LOLO

Number	Title	Yr	NM
❑ 2306	Easier to Say Than Do/Soul Sister	1969	$60

POLYDOR

Number	Title	Yr	NM
❑ 14455	Say Yeah/My World	1978	$60

SSS INTERNATIONAL

Number	Title	Yr	NM
❑ 732	Lonely for You Baby/I Need You Girl	1968	$400

DEF LEPPARD

Also see DIO.

MERCURY

Number	Title	Yr	NM
❑ 888832-7	Animal/I Wanna Be Your Hero	1987	$3
❑ 888832-7 [PS]	Animal/I Wanna Be Your Hero	1987	$3
❑ 870692-7	Armageddon It/Release Me	1988	$3

—B-side by "Stumpus Maximus and the Good Ol' Boys" (Def Leppard in disguise)

Number	Title	Yr	NM
❑ 870692-7 [PS]	Armageddon It/Release Me	1988	$3
❑ 818779-7	Bringin' On the Heartbreak/ Me and My Wine	1984	$4
❑ 818779-7 [PS]	Bringin' On the Heartbreak/ Me and My Wine	1984	$6
❑ 874444-7	Foolin'/Bringin' On the Heartbreak	1989	$4

—Timepieces" reissue

Number	Title	Yr	NM
❑ 814178-7	Foolin'/Comin' Under Fire	1983	$4
❑ 870004-7	Hysteria/Ride Into the Sun	1988	$3
❑ 870004-7 [PS]	Hysteria/Ride Into the Sun	1988	$3
❑ 76120 [DJ]	Let It Go (same on both sides)	1981	$30

—May be promo only

Number	Title	Yr	NM
❑ 870402-7	Love Bites/Billy's Got a Gun	1988	$3
❑ 870402-7 [PS]	Love Bites/Billy's Got a Gun	1988	$3
❑ 811215-7	Photograph/Action, Not Words	1983	$5

—Chicago skyline label

Number	Title	Yr	NM
❑ 811215-7	Photograph/Action, Not Words	1983	$4

—Black label

Number	Title	Yr	NM
❑ 811215-7 [PS]	Photograph/Action, Not Words	1983	$10
❑ 870298-7	Pour Some Sugar on Me/Ring of Fire	1988	$3
❑ 870298-7 [PS]	Pour Some Sugar on Me/Ring of Fire	1988	$3
❑ 888757-7	Women/Tear It Down	1987	$3
❑ 888757-7 [PS]	Women/Tear It Down	1987	$3

DEFENDERS, THE

PARKWAY

Number	Title	Yr	NM
❑ 926	Island of Love/I Laughed So Hard	1964	$10

DEFRANCO FAMILY, THE

20TH CENTURY

Number	Title	Yr	NM
❑ 2070	Abra-Ca-Dabra/Some Kind a' Love	1973	$4
❑ 2070 [PS]	Abra-Ca-Dabra/Some Kind a' Love	1973	$6
❑ 2128	Baby Blue/Write Me a Letter	1974	$4
❑ 2128 [PS]	Baby Blue/Write Me a Letter	1974	$6
❑ 2030	Heartbeat -- It's a Lovebeat/ Sweet, Sweet Loretta	1973	$4
❑ 2030 [PS]	Heartbeat -- It's a Lovebeat/ Sweet, Sweet Loretta	1973	$6
❑ 2088	Save the Last Dance for Me/ Because We Both Are Young	1974	$4
❑ 2088 [PS]	Save the Last Dance for Me/ Because We Both Are Young	1974	$6
❑ 2214	We Belong Together/ Time Enough for Love	1975	$8
❑ 2214 [PS]	We Belong Together/ Time Enough for Love	1975	$10

DEHAVEN, PENNY, AND DEL REEVES

UNITED ARTISTS

Number	Title	Yr	NM
❑ 50829	Crying in the Rain/Time	1972	$6

DEHAVEN, PENNY

BAND BOX

Number	Title	Yr	NM
❑ 372	A Grain of Salt/Thing of Pleasure	1966	$20

—As "Penny Starr

Number	Title	Yr	NM
❑ 375	One More Like You/You've Taken All the Woman Out of Me	1967	$20

—As "Penny Starr

ELEKTRA

Number	Title	Yr	NM
❑ 46645	Bayou Lullaby/How Many Teardrops	1980	$5

IMPERIAL

Number	Title	Yr	NM
❑ 66421	Down in the Boondocks/When the Sun Sets in Jackson	1969	$8
❑ 66321	I Am the Woman/ Loving You Again	1968	$8
❑ 66437	I Feel Fine/Stop & Go	1970	$8
❑ 66388	Mama Lou/That's Just the Way I Am	1969	$8
❑ 66294	Old Faithful/Big City Men	1968	$8

MAIN STREET

Number	Title	Yr	NM
❑ 93019	Friendly Game of Hearts/ (B-side unknown)	1984	$5
❑ 93015	Only the Names Have Been Changed/Waltz Me Once Again	1983	$5

MERCURY

Number	Title	Yr	NM
❑ 73504	I Gotta Stand Tall/I'll Never Stop	1974	$6
❑ 73434	I'll Be Doggone/Love Me to Sleep	1973	$6
❑ 73468	Play with Me/Shine on Me	1974	$6
❑ 73384	The Lovin' of Your Life/ When You Get Home	1973	$6

STARCREST

Number	Title	Yr	NM
❑ 080	Hit Parade of Love/ (B-side unknown)	1976	$6
❑ 080 [PS]	Hit Parade of Love/ (B-side unknown)	1976	$12
❑ 066	(The Great American) Classic Cowboy/Thank God I'm a Country Girl	1976	$6

DEJOHN SISTERS, THE

COLUMBIA

Number	Title	Yr	NM
❑ 40843	Don't Promise Me (The Can Can Song)/He's Got Time	1957	$15
❑ 40799	Mah Little Baby/Mu-Cha-Cha	1956	$20

EPIC

Number	Title	Yr	NM
❑ 9172	Big D/In My Innocence	1956	$15
❑ 9131	C'est La Vie/Uninvited Love	1955	$15
❑ 9097	D'Ja Hear What I Say/A Present for Bob	1955	$15
❑ 9108	He Loves Me/Pass the Plate of Happiness Around	1955	$15
❑ 9145	Hotta Chocolotta/The Man with the Blue Guitar	1956	$15
❑ 9031	I Took Him from You/ Juke-Box Polka	1954	$20
❑ 9080	Lover's Slang/Mandolino	1954	$20
❑ 9085	(My Baby Don't Love Me) No More/Theresa	1954	$20

Number	Title	Yr	NM
❑ 9009	Should I Run/All Present But One	1953	$20
❑ 9133	The Only Thing I Want for Christmas/That's How Santa Claus Will Look This Year	1955	$20

MERCURY

Number	Title	Yr	NM
❑ 71203	Absence Makes the Heart Grow Fonder/That's My Weakness Now	1957	$10
❑ 71131	Where Would I Be/Who Am I	1957	$10

OKEH

Number	Title	Yr	NM
❑ 6989	The Angel Passed By/Never Since Then	1953	$30

SUNBEAM

Number	Title	Yr	NM
❑ 116	Do-Die/Wedding Postponed	1958	$12
❑ 126	Hoppity Moe Joe/Don't Forget to Remember	1959	$10
❑ 106	Straighten Up and Fly Right/Wrong Guy	1958	$10
❑ 124	Watermelon Heart/Sorry for Myself	1959	$10

UNITED ARTISTS

Number	Title	Yr	NM
❑ 213	Be Anything (But Be Mine)/Yes Indeed	1960	$8

DEKKER, DESMOND, AND THE ACES

UNI

Number	Title	Yr	NM
❑ 55129	Israelites/My Precious World	1969	$6
❑ 55150	It Mek/Problems	1969	$6

DEL-AIRES, THE

CORAL

Number	Title	Yr	NM
❑ 62419	Arlene/I'm Yours Baby	1964	$75
❑ 62370	Elaine/Just Wigglin' and a-Wobblin'	1963	$50
❑ 62404	The Drag/My Funny Valentine	1964	$50

—*As "Ronnie and the Del-Aires"*

DEL AND THE ESCORTS

ROME

Number	Title	Yr	NM
❑ 103	Baby Doll/Someone to Watch Over Me	1961	$60

TAURUS

Number	Title	Yr	NM
❑ 350/1	Happy/You're for Me (And I'm for You)	1961	$40

DEL FUEGOS, THE

CZECH

Number	Title	Yr	NM
❑ 71 [PS]	I Can't Sleep/I Always Call Her Back	1983	$8
❑ 71	I Can't Sleep/I Always Call Her Back	1983	$8

SLASH

Number	Title	Yr	NM
❑ 28262	I'll Sleep with You (Cha Cha D'Amour)/I Can't Take This	1987	$3
❑ 28822	I Still Want You/Hand in Hand	1986	$3
❑ 28822 [PS]	I Still Want You/Hand in Hand	1986	$3
❑ 28822 [DJ]	I Still Want You (LP Version)/I Still Want You (Horny Mix)	1986	$4

DEL-PHIS, THE

CHECKMATE

Number	Title	Yr	NM
❑ 1005	I'll Let You Know/It Takes Two	1961	$200

DEL RAYS, THE

CORD

Number	Title	Yr	NM
❑ 1001	Our Love Is True/One Kiss, One Smile and a Dream	1958	$4000

MOON

Number	Title	Yr	NM
❑ 110	Have a Heart/Around the Corner	1959	$300

WARNER BROS.

Number	Title	Yr	NM
❑ 5022	My Darling/The One I Adore	1958	$100

DEL-RHYTHMETTES

JVB

Number	Title	Yr	NM
❑ 5000	Chic-a-Boomer/I Need Your Love	1959	$70

DEL RIO SISTERS, THE

TONE-CRAFT

Number	Title	Yr	NM
❑ 203	Beautiful Eyes/Beginning to Miss You	1955	$30
❑ 201	The Wallflower (Dance with Me, Henry)/Baby Be Sweet to Me	1955	$30

DEL RIOS, THE

BET-T

Number	Title	Yr	NM
❑ 7001	Heavenly Angel/Dangerous Lover	1962	$1200

METEOR

Number	Title	Yr	NM
❑ 5038	Lizzie/Alone on a Rainy Night	1956	$800

NEPTUNE

Number	Title	Yr	NM
❑ 108	Wait Wait Wait/I'm Crying	1959	$70

STAX

Number	Title	Yr	NM
❑ 125	There's a Love/Just Across the Street	1962	$60

DEL SATINS

B.T. PUPPY

Number	Title	Yr	NM
❑ 506	Hang Around/Candy Apple 'Vette	1965	$20
❑ 563	I'll Do My Crying Tomorrow/A Girl Named Arlene	1970	$15
❑ 509	Sweets for My Sweet/A Girl Named Arlene	1965	$40

COLUMBIA

Number	Title	Yr	NM
❑ 42802	Feelin' No Pain/Who Cares	1963	$30
❑ 42802 [PS]	Feelin' No Pain/Who Cares	1963	$125

DIAMOND

Number	Title	Yr	NM
❑ 216	A Little Rain Must Fall/Love, Hate, Revenge (If I Want You to Cry)	1967	$20

END

Number	Title	Yr	NM
❑ 1096	I'll Pray for You/I Remember the Night	1961	$200

LAURIE

Number	Title	Yr	NM
❑ 3149	Ballad of a Deejay/Does My Love Stand a Chance	1962	$30
❑ 3132	Teardrops Follow Me/Best Wishes, Good Luck, Goodbye	1962	$30

MALA

Number	Title	Yr	NM
❑ 475	Believe in Me/Two Broken Hearts	1964	$30

WIN

Number	Title	Yr	NM
❑ 702	Counting Teardrops/Remember	1961	$120

—*Black label*

Number	Title	Yr	NM
❑ 702	Counting Teardrops/Remember	1961	$70

—*Orange label*

DEL-VETTS, THE

DUNWICH

Number	Title	Yr	NM
❑ 142	I Call My Baby STP/That's the Way It Is	1966	$30
❑ 142 [PS]	I Call My Baby STP/That's the Way It Is	1966	$40

—*Some sleeves contain an STP decal.*

Number	Title	Yr	NM
❑ 125	Last Time Around/Everytime	1966	$30

SEEBERG

Number	Title	Yr	NM
❑ 3018 [S]	Little Latin Lupe Lu/Ram Charger	1965	$50

—*With "Stereo" on label*

DEL VIKINGS, THE

ABC-PARAMOUNT

Number	Title	Yr	NM
❑ 10385	An Angel Up in Heaven/Fishing Chant	1962	$60
❑ 10304	Big Silence/One More River to Cross	1962	$30
❑ 10341	Confession of Love/Kilimanjaro	1962	$30
❑ 10248	I Hear Bells (Wedding Bells)/Don't Get Slick on Me	1961	$60
❑ 10208	I'll Never Stop Crying/Bring Back Your Heart	1961	$30
❑ 10425	Too Many Miles/Sorcerer's Apprentice	1963	$30

ALPINE

Number	Title	Yr	NM
❑ 66	Pistol Packin' Mama/The Sun	1960	$100
❑ 66 [PS]	Pistol Packin' Mama/The Sun	1960	$125

BIM BAM BOOM

Number	Title	Yr	NM
❑ 111	Cold Feet/A Little Man Cried	1972	$5
❑ 115	I'm Spinning/Girl Girl	1972	$5
❑ 113	Watching the Moon/You Say You Love Me	1972	$5

DOT

Number	Title	Yr	NM
❑ 15538	Come Go with Me/How Can I Find True Love	1957	$40
❑ 16092	Come Go with Me/How Can I Find True Love	1960	$30
❑ 16236	Come Go with Me/Whispering Bells	1961	$30
❑ 16248	I Hear Bells (Wedding Bells)/Don't Get Slick on Me	1961	$30
❑ 15636	I'm Spinning/When I Come Home	1957	$40

—*As "Kripp Johnson with the Dell-Vikings*

Number	Title	Yr	NM
❑ 15571	What Made Maggie Run/Little Billy Boy	1957	$40
❑ 15592	Whispering Bells/Don't Be a Fool	1957	$40

FEE BEE

Number	Title	Yr	NM
❑ 205	Come Go with Me/How Can I Find True Love	1957	$500

—*Orange label, bee on top*

Number	Title	Yr	NM
❑ 205	Come Go with Me/How Can I Find True Love	1957	$250

—*Orange label, one side has bee, the other side doesn't*

Number	Title	Yr	NM
❑ 205	Come Go with Me/How Can I Find True Love	1961	$40

—*Orange label, no bee*

Number	Title	Yr	NM
❑ 205	Come Go with Me/Whispering Bells	1964	$30
❑ 206	Down in Bermuda/Maggie	1964	$100
❑ 218	I'm Spinning/You Say You Love Me	1957	$120

—*Bee on label*

Number	Title	Yr	NM
❑ 218	I'm Spinning/You Say You Love Me	1964	$40

—*No bee on label*

Number	Title	Yr	NM
❑ 227	Tell Me/Finger Poppin' Woman	1959	$100

Number	Title	Yr	NM
❑ 902	True Love/Baby, Let Me Know	1964	$40

—*As "The Original Dell Vikings*

Number	Title	Yr	NM
❑ 173	Welfare Blues/Hollywood and Vine	1977	$5
❑ 210	What Made Maggie Run/Down by the Stream	1964	$40
❑ 210	What Made Maggie Run/Uh Uh Baby	1957	$100
❑ 210	What Made Maggie Run/When I Come Home	1957	$120
❑ 214	Whispering Bells/Don't Be a Fool	1957	$400
❑ 221	Willette/I Want to Marry You	1958	$100
❑ 221	Willette/Woke Up This Morning	1958	$125

GATEWAY

Number	Title	Yr	NM
❑ 743	We Three/I've Got to Know	1964	$40

LUNIVERSE

Number	Title	Yr	NM
❑ 113	In the Still of the Night/The White Cliffs of Dover	1958	$30
❑ 106	Somewhere Over the Rainbow/Hey, Senorita	1957	$125
❑ 114	There I Go/Girl Girl	1958	$30

—*The above three Luniverse 45s are bootlegs, but they perversely do have collector's value!*

MERCURY

Number	Title	Yr	NM
❑ 71180	Come Along with Me/Whatcha Gonna Lose	1957	$40
❑ 71132	Cool Shake/Jitterbug Mary	1957	$40
❑ 71390	How Could You/Flat Tire	1958	$40
❑ 71198	I'm Spinning/When I Come Home	1957	$40
❑ 71241	Snowbound/Your Book of Life	1957	$40

SCEPTER

Number	Title	Yr	NM
❑ 12367	Come Go with Me/When You're Asleep	1973	$5

7-Inch Extended Plays

DOT

Number	Title	Yr	NM
❑ DEP-1058	Come Go with Me/Don't Be a Fool//Whispering Bells/What Made Maggie Run	1957	$125
❑ DEP-1058 [PS]	Come Go with Us	1957	$250

MERCURY

Number	Title	Yr	NM
❑ EP 1-3359	Come Along with Me/A Sunday Kind of Love//(There'll Be Blue Birds Over) The White Cliffs of Dover/Now Is the Hour	1957	$125
❑ EP 1-3362	Heart and Soul/My Foolish Heart//Down in Bermuda/I'm Sitting on Top of the World	1957	$125
❑ EP 1-3363	Somewhere Over the Rainbow/Is It Any Wonder//Yours/Summertime	1957	$125
❑ EP 1-3359 [PS]	They Sing -- They Swing, Vol. 1	1957	$175
❑ EP 1-3362 [PS]	They Sing -- They Swing, Vol. 2	1957	$175
❑ EP 1-3363 [PS]	They Sing -- They Swing, Vol. 3	1957	$175

DELACARDOS, THE (1)

ELGEY

Number	Title	Yr	NM
❑ 1001	A Letter to a School Girl/I'll Never Let You Down	1959	$60

SHELL

Number	Title	Yr	NM
❑ 308	Dream Girl/I Just Want to Know	1961	$30
❑ 311	Love Is the Greatest Thing/Girl-Girl	1962	$30

UNITED ARTISTS

Number	Title	Yr	NM
❑ 310	Hold Back the Tears/Mr. Dillon	1961	$30
❑ 276	I Got It/Thing-A-Ma-Jig	1960	$20

DELACARDOS, THE (2)

ATLANTIC

Number	Title	Yr	NM
❑ 2368	Got No One/She's the One I Love	1966	$10
❑ 2389	I Know I'm Not Much/You Don't Have to See Me	1967	$10
❑ 2419	They Put a Spell on You/A Fool for You	1967	$10

DELACARDOS, THE (U)

DIMENSION

Number	Title	Yr	NM
❑ 1040	Forget About the Guy/Dance, Gypsy, Dance	1964	$30

IMPERIAL

Number	Title	Yr	NM
❑ 5992	On the Beach/Everybody's Rockin'	1963	$20

DELANCEYS, THE

ABC-PARAMOUNT

Number	Title	Yr	NM
❑ 10353	High Voltage/The Scratch	1962	$30

DELANEY AND BONNIE

ATCO

Number	Title	Yr	NM
❏ 6725	Groupie (Superstar)/Comin' Home	1969	$8
❏ 6788	Miss Ann/They Call It Rock and Roll Music	1970	$8
❏ 6838	Only You Know and I Know/God Knows I Love You	1971	$6
❏ 6866	Sing My Way Home/Move 'Em Out	1972	$5
❏ 6904	Sing My Way Home/Will the Circle Be Unbroken	1972	$5
❏ 6756	Soul Shake/Free the People	1970	$8
❏ 6883	Where There's a Will There's a Way/Lonesome and a Long Way from Home	1972	$5

COLUMBIA

Number	Title	Yr	NM
❏ 45608	Country Life/Walk in the River Jordan	1972	$5

ELEKTRA

Number	Title	Yr	NM
❏ 45660	Soldiers of the Cross/Get Ourselves Together	1969	$12
❏ 45662	When the Battle Is Over/Get Ourselves Together	1969	$10

GARPAX

Number	Title	Yr	NM
❏ 44184	Cherry Pie/Hey Mr. Weatherman	1964	$20

—As "Lani & Boni

STAX

Number	Title	Yr	NM
❏ 057	Hard to Say Goodbye/Just Plain Beautiful	1969	$12
❏ 03	It's Been a Long Time Coming/We've Just Been Feeling Bad	1968	$10

DELEGATES, THE

MAINSTREAM

Number	Title	Yr	NM
❏ 5525	Convention '72/Funky Butt	1972	$10
❏ 5525	Convention '72 (same on both sides)	1972	$8

— Stock copy; "Funky Butt" deleted because of retailers' protests to the title

DELEGATES, THE

VEE JAY

Number	Title	Yr	NM
❏ 243	Mother's Son/I'm Gonna Be Glad	1957	$70
❏ 212	The Convention/Jay's Rock	1956	$70

—B-side by Big Jay McNeely

DELFONICS, THE

ARISTA

Number	Title	Yr	NM
❏ 0308	Don't Throw It All Away/I Don't Care What People Say	1978	$4

MOON SHOT

Number	Title	Yr	NM
❏ 6703	He Don't Really Love You/Without You	1967	$20

PHILLY GROOVE

Number	Title	Yr	NM
❏ 177	Alfie/Start All Over Again	1973	$8
❏ 152	Break Your Promise/Alfie	1968	$10
❏ 161	Didn't I (Blow Your Mind This Time)/Down Is Up, Up Is Down	1970	$12
❏ 156	Funny Feeling/My New Love	1969	$10
❏ 176	I Don't Want to Make You Wait/Baby I Miss You	1973	$8
❏ 151	I'm Sorry/You're Gone	1968	$10
❏ 182	I Told You So/Seventeen and In Love	1973	$8
❏ 150	La-La Means I Love You/Can't Get Over Losing You	1968	$10
❏ NS-1001/2	La-La Means I Love You/Can't Get Over Losing You	1968	$30

—Light blue label with no regular catalog number

Number	Title	Yr	NM
❏ 184	Lying to Myself/Hey Baby	1974	$8
❏ 166	Over and Over/Hey! Love	1971	$8
❏ 172	Tell Me This Is a Dream/I'm a Man	1972	$8
❏ 174	Think It Over/I'm a Man	1972	$8
❏ 162	Trying to Make a Fool of Me/Baby I Love You	1970	$10
❏ 169	Walk Right Up to the Sun/Round and Round	1971	$8
❏ 163	When You Get Right Down To It/I Gave to You	1970	$10

DELICATES, THE

CELESTE

Number	Title	Yr	NM
❏ 676	My Pillow/I Played 1,2,3,4	1961	$40

CHALLENGE

Number	Title	Yr	NM
❏ 59232	I've Been Hurt/Come On Everybody	1964	$20
❏ 59267	I Want to Get Married/Home from Camp	1965	$20
❏ 59304	Stop Shovin' Me Around/Comin' Down with Love	1965	$20

DEE DEE

Number	Title	Yr	NM
❏ 677	My Pillow/I Played 1,2,3,4	1961	$40

ROULETTE

Number	Title	Yr	NM
❏ 4387	I Don't Know Why (I Just Do)/Strange Love	1961	$30
❏ 4360	Little Boy of Mine/Dickie Went and Did It	1961	$30
❏ 4321	Little Ship/Not Tomorrow	1961	$30

UNART

Number	Title	Yr	NM
❏ 2017	Black and White Thunderbird/Ronnie Is My Lover	1959	$30

UNITED ARTISTS

Number	Title	Yr	NM
❏ 210	Flip Flip/Your Happiest Years	1960	$30

DELICATO, PAUL

ARTISTS OF AMERICA

Number	Title	Yr	NM
❏ 111	Cara Mia/Ice Cream Sodas and Lollipops and a Red Hot Spinning Top	1976	$5
❏ 110	I Can't Make It All Alone/(B-side unknown)	1976	$5
❏ 122	I'll Be There/(B-side unknown)	1976	$5
❏ 127	I Take a Lot of Pride in What I Am/Country Star	1976	$5
❏ 120	It's the Same Old Song/I Can't Make It All Alone	1976	$5
❏ 101	Lean on Me/Ice Cream Sodas and Lollipops and a Red Hot Spinning Top	1975	$5
❏ 1976	Spirit of America/Ice Cream Sodas and Lollipops and a Red Hot Spinning Top	1976	$5
❏ 105	Those Were the Days/Ice Cream Sodas and Lollipops and a Red Hot Spinning Top	1976	$5

AVI

Number	Title	Yr	NM
❏ 155	All Alone and Crying/Darling All I Need Is You	1978	$6
❏ 267	Everything Good Reminds Me of You/Hell of a Woman	1979	$6
❏ 139	I'll Show You Tomorrow/Come On Priscilla	1977	$6

DELL-COEDS, THE

DOT

Number	Title	Yr	NM
❏ 16314	Hey Mr. Banjo/Love in Return	1962	$15

DELL, DICKEY, AND THE BING BONGS

DRAGON

Number	Title	Yr	NM
❏ 10205	Ding-a-Ling-a-Ling-Ding-Dong/The Cling	1958	$200

DELL, EVELYN, AND THE VIBRATIONS

ABC-PARAMOUNT

Number	Title	Yr	NM
❏ 10218	Sincerely/Please Tell Me Why	1961	$30

DELL, RICHIE

KING

Number	Title	Yr	NM
❏ 5888	Come On Let's Sing/King Lover	1964	$30

DELL, TONY

KING

Number	Title	Yr	NM
❏ 5766	My Girl/Magic Wand	1963	$60

DELLS, THE, AND THE DRAMATICS

CADET

Number	Title	Yr	NM
❏ 5710	Love Is Missing from Our Lives/I'm in Love	1975	$6

DELLS, THE

20TH CENTURY

Number	Title	Yr	NM
❏ 2602	Ain't It a Shame/Stay in My Corner	1982	$4
❏ 2504	Happy Song/Look at Us Now	1981	$4
❏ 2463	I Touched a Dream/All About the Paper	1980	$4
❏ 2475	Passionate Breezes/Your Song	1980	$4

ABC

Number	Title	Yr	NM
❏ 12422	(I Wanna) Testify/Don't Save Me	1978	$5
❏ 12422	(I Wanna) Testify/Drowning for Your Love	1978	$5
❏ 12386	Super Woman/My Life Is So Wonderful	1978	$5

ARGO

Number	Title	Yr	NM
❏ 5456	After You/Goodbye Mary Ann	1963	$15
❏ 5415	God Bless the Child/I'm Going Home	1962	$15
❏ 5442	Hi Diddle Dee Dum Dum (It's a Good Feelin')/If It Ain't One Thing, It's Another	1963	$15
❏ 5428	The (Bossa Nova) Bird/Eternally	1962	$15

CADET

Number	Title	Yr	NM
❏ 5621	Always Together/I Want My Mama	1968	$6
❏ 5703	Bring Back the Love of Yesterday/Learning to Love You Was Easy (It's So Hard Trying to Get Over You)	1974	$6
❏ 5631	Does Anybody Know I'm Here/Make Sure (You Have Somebody to Love You)	1968	$6
❏ 5696	Give Your Baby a Standing Ovation/Closer	1973	$6
❏ 5641	I Can Sing a Rainbow-Love Is Blue/Hallelujah Baby	1969	$6
❏ 5636	I Can't Do Enough/Hallways of My Mind	1969	$6
❏ 5700	I Miss You/Don't Make Me a Storyteller	1973	$6
❏ 5689	It's All Up to You/Oh, My Dear	1972	$6
❏ 5702	I Wish It Was Me You Loved/Two Together Is Better Than One	1974	$6
❏ 5672	Long Lonely Nights/A Little Understanding	1970	$6
❏ 5698	My Pretending Days Are Over/Let's Make It Last	1973	$6
❏ 5663	Oh What a Day/The Change We Go Thru (For Love)	1970	$6
❏ 5649	Oh What a Night/Believe Me	1969	$6
❏ 5658	On the Dock of the Bay/When I'm in Your Arms	1969	$6
❏ 5574	O-O, I Love You/There Is	1967	$6
❏ 5667	Open Up My Heart/Nadine	1970	$6
❏ 5551	Over Again/Run for Cover	1967	$6
❏ 5612	Stay in My Corner/Love Is So Simple	1969	$6
❏ 5703	Sweeter as the Days Go By/Learning to Love You Was Easy (It's So Hard Trying to Get Over You)	1974	$6

—A-side is the same song with a new title

Number	Title	Yr	NM
❏ 5679	The Glory of Love/A Whiter Shade of Pale	1970	$6
❏ 5707	The Glory of Love/You're the Greatest	1975	$6
❏ 5683	The Love We Had (Stays on My Mind)/Freedom Means	1971	$6
❏ 5590	There Is/Show Me	1968	$8
❏ 5538	Thinkin' About You/The Change We Go Thru (For Love)	1966	$6
❏ 5691	Walk On By/This Guy's in Love with You	1972	$6
❏ 5599	Wear it On Our Face/Please Don't Change Me Now	1968	$6
❏ 5711	We Got to Get Our Thing Together/The Power of Love	1975	$8

CHECKER

Number	Title	Yr	NM
❏ 794	Darling I Know/Christine	1954	$1200

—As "The El Rays

MCA

Number	Title	Yr	NM
❏ 41051	Plastic People/What I Could	1979	$5

MERCURY

Number	Title	Yr	NM
❏ 73901	Betcha Never Been Loved (Like This Before)/Get On Down	1977	$5
❏ 73909	Our Love/Could It Be	1977	$5
❏ 73977	Private Property/Teaser	1977	$5
❏ 73807	Slow Motion/Ain't No Black and White in Music	1976	$5
❏ 73759	The Power of Love/Gotta Get Home to My Baby	1976	$5
❏ 73723	We Got to Get Our Thing Together/Reminiscing	1975	$5

PHILCO-FORD

Number	Title	Yr	NM
❏ HP-32	There Is/Show Me	1968	$30

—4-inch plastic "Hip Pocket Record" with color sleeve

PRIVATE I

Number	Title	Yr	NM
❏ 04343	Don't Want Nobody/You Can't Just Walk Away	1984	$4
❏ 04540	Love On/Don't Want Nobody	1984	$4
❏ 04448	One Step Closer/Come On Back to Me	1984	$4

VEE JAY

Number	Title	Yr	NM
❏ 251	A Distant Love/O-Bop She-Bop	1957	$50
❏ 166	Dreams of Contentment/Zing, Zing, Zing	1955	$200
❏ 324	Dry Your Eyes/Baby Open Up Your Heart	1959	$50
❏ 376	Hold On to What You've Got/Swingin' Teens	1961	$30
❏ 292	I'm Calling/Jeepers Creepers	1958	$40
❏ 230	Movin' On/I Wanna Go Home	1956	$50
❏ 338	Oh What a Nite/I Wanna Go Home	1960	$30
❏ 204	Oh What a Nite/Jo-Jo	1956	$120
❏ 258	Pain in My Heart/Time Makes You Change	1957	$50
❏ 712	Poor Little Boy/Hey Sugar (Don't Get Serious)	1966	$15
❏ 595	Shy Girl/What Do We Prove	1964	$15
❏ 595 [PS]	Shy Girl/What Do We Prove	1964	$60

—Promo-only sleeve

Number	Title	Yr	NM
❏ 674	Stay in My Corner/It's Not Unusual	1965	$15
❏ 134	Tell the World/Blues at Three	1955	$5000

—Red vinyl. VG 2500; VG+ 3750

Number	Title	Yr	NM
❏ 134	Tell the World/Blues at Three	1955	$2000
❏ 274	The Springer/What You Say Baby	1958	$40
❏ 615	Wait Till Tomorrow/Oh What a Good Night	1964	$15
❏ 300	Wedding Day/My Best Girl	1958	$125
❏ 236	Why Do You Have to Go/Dance, Dance, Dance	1957	$50

VETERAN

Number	Title	Yr	NM
❏ 7-101	Thought of You Just a Little Too Much/(B-side unknown)	1989	$5

Number	Title	Yr	NM
DELLTONES, THE			
BATON			
❏ 212	Don't Be Long/Baby Say You Love Me	1955	$40
❏ 223	My Special Love/Believe It	1956	$40
BRUNSWICK			
❏ 84015	My Heart's on Fire/ Yours Alone	1953	$200
RAINBOW			
❏ 244	I'm Not in Love with You/ Little Short Daddy	1954	$125
DELMIRAS, THE			
DADE			
❏ 1821	Dry Your Eyes/ The Big Sound	1961	$300
DELMONICOS, THE			
MUSICTONE			
❏ 6122	World's Biggest Fool/Until You	1963	$40
DELMORE BROTHERS, THE			
KING			
❏ 5224	Blues Stay Away from Me/Muddy Water	1959	$20
❏ 5675	Blues Stay Away from Me/Trouble Ain't Nothing But the Blues	1962	$15
❏ 570	Freight Train Boogie/ Somebody Else's Darling	1952	$50
—Reissue of 78 issued in 1946			
❏ 5866	Freight Train Boogie/ Sweet, Sweet Thing	1964	$15
❏ 1005	Heartbreak Ridge/ Kentucky Woman	1951	$40
❏ 1113	How You Gonna Get Your Lovin' Done/I Said Goodnight My Darling	1952	$40
❏ 1023	I'll Be There/Steamboat Bill Boogie	1951	$40
❏ 1053	I Won't Be Worried Long/ Good Time Saturday Night	1952	$40
❏ 946	Lonesome Day/ Everybody Loves Her	1951	$50
❏ 1084	Muddy Water/Got No Way of Knowing	1952	$40
❏ 826	Pan American Boogie/Troubles Ain't Nothin' but the Blues	1952	$50
—Reissue of 78 first issued in 1949			
❏ 5407	Silver Threads Among the Gold/Let Your Conscience Be Your Guide	1960	$20
❏ 966	Tennessee Choo Choo/Who's Gonna Be Lonesome for Me	1951	$40
❏ 1141	That Old Train/I Needed You	1952	$40
❏ 981	The Girl by the River/There's Something 'Bout Love	1951	$40
❏ 1158	What'cha Gonna Give Me/Trail of Time	1953	$30
DELPHS, JIMMY			
CARLA			
❏ 2535	Almost/I've Been Fooled Before	1967	$30
❏ 1904	Dancing a Hole in the World/ (B-side unknown)	1968	$1200
KAREN			
❏ 1550	Am I Losing You/Love, I Want You Back	1968	$15
❏ 1538	Don't Sign the Paper Baby (I Want You Back)/Almost	1968	$15
❏ 1541	Feels Like Summer's Coming On/ Mrs. Percy Please Have Mercy	1968	$15
DELRAY, MARTIN			
COMPLEAT			
❏ 125	Holding a Woman in Love/ Old Friends Over Night	1984	$5
—As "Mike Martin			
❏ 143	Sweet Nothings (Whispered in My Ear)/Break Someone Else's Heart	1985	$5
—As "Mike Martin			
❏ 139	Temptation/What My Mind's Been On All Day	1985	$5
—As "Mike Martin			
DELROYS, THE			
APOLLO			
❏ 514	Bermuda Shorts/Time	1957	$30
DELTAIRS, THE			
FELSTED			
❏ 8525	Who Would Have Thought It/ You Won't Be Satisfied	1959	$40
IVY			
❏ 101	Lullaby of the Bells/ It's Only You Dear	1957	$200
—Yellow label			
❏ 101	Lullaby of the Bells/ It's Only You Dear	1958	$40
❏ 105	Standing at the Altar/I Might Like It	1958	$40

Number	Title	Yr	NM
DELTAS, THE			
CAMBRIDGE			
❏ 124	Goodnight My Love/Give My Love a Chance	1962	$50
GONE			
❏ 5010	Let Me Share Your Dream/Lamplight	1957	$3000
—Black label			
❏ 5010	Let Me Share Your Dream/Lamplight	1957	$100
—Multi-color label			
PHILIPS			
❏ 40023	My Own True Love/Hold Me, Thrill Me, Kiss Me	1962	$20
❏ 40023	My Own True Love/Work Song	1962	$30
DELTONES, THE			
JUBILEE			
❏ 5374	La La La/Bow-Legged Annie	1959	$30
VEE JAY			
❏ 303	A Lover's Prayer/First Man to the Moon	1958	$50
❏ 288	I'm Coming Home/ Early Morning Rock	1958	$50
DELUGG, MILTON			
4 CORNERS OF THE WORLD			
❏ 114	Hooray For Santa Claus/ Lonely Beach	1963	$20
EPIC			
❏ 9728	Hooray for Santa Claus/ Ghost Meet Ghoul	1964	$20
MGM			
❏ 11099	Shake Hands With Santa Claus/Thirty-Two Feet	1951	$20
DELVETTS, THE			
END			
❏ 1106	I Want a Boy for Christmas/ Repeat After Me	1961	$40
❏ 1107	Will You Love Me in Heaven/ Repeat After Me	1962	$30
DEMARCO, RALPH			
GUARANTEED			
❏ 202	More Than Riches/Old Shep	1959	$30
❏ 202 [PS]	More Than Riches/Old Shep	1959	$50
SHELLEY			
❏ 1011	Donna/For All We Know	1960	$50
DEMARR, EDDIE			
COLUMBIA			
❏ 41969	Lie Detector/You're a Gas	1961	$15
❏ 3-41969	Lie Detector/You're a Gas	1961	$30
—Compact 33" single with small hole			
DEMATTEO, NICKY			
CAMEO			
❏ 407	I Wanna Be Lonely/ Little Red Kitten	1966	$30
—With the Sorrows			
DIAMOND			
❏ 138	The Story of My Life/ Baby, That's All	1963	$20
GUYDEN			
❏ 2042	Close to You Forever/As Big As My Love for You	1960	$20
❏ 2024	Suddenly I Couldn't Sleep a Wink Last Night	1960	$20
PARIS			
❏ 529	Secret of Love/Story of Love	1959	$20
DEMENS, THE			
TEENAGE			
❏ 1007	I'm Not in Love with You/Short Daddy	1958	$200
❏ 1006	Take Me As I Am/You Broke My Heart	1958	$200
❏ 1008	The Greatest of Them All/Hey Young Girl	1958	$200
DEMENSIONS, THE			
CORAL			
❏ 62277	Again/Count Your Blessings Instead of Sheep	1961	$30
❏ 62392	A Little White Gardenia/ Don't Cry Pretty Baby	1964	$30
❏ 65611	As Time Goes By/ My Foolish Heart	1967	$20
❏ 62293	As Time Goes By/ Seven Days a Week	1961	$30
❏ 62359	Fly Me to the Moon/ You'll Never Know	1963	$30

Number	Title	Yr	NM
❏ 62344	My Foolish Heart/Just One More Chance	1963	$40
❏ 62344 [PS]	My Foolish Heart/Just One More Chance	1963	$125
❏ 62444	Once a Day/Ting Along Ting Toy	1965	$30
—As "Lenny Dell and the Demensions			
❏ 65559	Over the Rainbow/Zing Went the Strings of My Heart	1962	$30
❏ 62432	This Time Next Year/ My Old Girlfriend	1964	$30
—As "Lenny Dell and the Demensions			
MOHAWK			
❏ 123	A Tear Fell/Theresa	1961	$70
❏ 121	God's Christmas/Ave Maria	1960	$70
❏ 116	Over the Rainbow/ Nursery Rhyme Rock	1960	$60
—Maroon label			
❏ 116	Over the Rainbow/ Nursery Rhyme Rock	1960	$40
—Brown label			
❏ 116	Over the Rainbow/ Nursery Rhyme Rock	1960	$30
—Red label			
DEMIAN			
Also see THE BUBBLE PUPPY.			
ABC			
❏ 11297	Face the Crowd/Love People	1970	$30
DEMILLES, THE			
LAURIE			
❏ 3230	Donna Lee/Um Ba Pa	1964	$40
❏ 3247	Lazy Love/Cry and Be On Your Way	1964	$60
DEMOTRONS, THE			
ATLANTIC			
❏ 2589	I Want a Home in the Country/I Don't Want to Play No More	1969	$10
CAMEO			
❏ 456	Beg, Borrow and Steal/ Midnight in New York	1967	$12
RADAR			
❏ 2615	Hombre/Swinging Soiree	1962	$30
❏ 2616	Pretzel Twist/Meet Mister Callaghan	1962	$30
❏ 2621	Sticks and Stones/Theme from "Adventures in Paradise"	1962	$30
SCEPTER			
❏ 12174	Brother Where Are You/ Take This Love I Have	1966	$15
❏ 12148	Take This Love I Have/ Sleep, Sleep, Sleep	1966	$15
DENBY, JUNIOR			
KING			
❏ 4725	This Fool Has Learned/If You Only Have Faith in Me	1954	$70
❏ 4717	With This Ring/I'm Still Lonesome	1954	$70
❏ 5217	With This Ring/I'm Still Lonesome	1959	$40
DENE, TERRY			
LONDON			
❏ 1802	Stairway of Love/Lover, Lover	1958	$15
DENNIS, BILL			
SHRINE			
❏ 113	I'll Never Let You Get Away/Poor Little Fool	1966	$1000
DENNIS, CLARK			
CAPITOL			
❏ 54-90038	O Little Town of Bethlehem and Joy to the World/ Cantique de Noel	1949	$30
DECCA			
❏ 27849	Littlest Angel's Christmas/If It Doesn't Snow on Christmas	1951	$20
—With Victor Young and His Singing Strings			
DENNIS, RICHIE			
CAMEO			
❏ 417	Dear Judy (The Summer's Gone)/Forever and a Day	1966	$30

Number	Title	Yr	NM

DENNY, MARTIN
LIBERTY
Number	Title	Yr	NM
❑ 55470	A Taste of Honey/The Brighter Side	1962	$8
❑ 55470 [PS]	A Taste of Honey/The Brighter Side	1962	$20
❑ 55230	Beyond the Reef/Forever	1959	$12
❑ 55536	Blue Carousel/Anniversary Song	1963	$8
❑ 55851	Call Me/La Paloma	1965	$8
❑ 55514	Cast Your Fate to the Wind/Pay Off	1962	$8
❑ 55384	Fandango/Bonsoir Dame	1961	$8
❑ 55236	Frankie and Johnny/Banana Choo Choo	1960	$10
❑ 55819	Hawaiian Village/Aloha Oe	1965	$8
❑ 55754	Hawaii Tattoo/White Silver Sands	1964	$8
❑ 55089	Hong Kong Blues/Ah Me Furi	1957	$12
❑ 55717	Latin Village/Angelito	1964	$8
❑ 55199	Martinique/Sake Rock	1959	$10
❑ 56126	Midnight Cowboy/Quiet Village	1969	$5
❑ 55571	More (Theme from Mondo Cane)/O Barquinho (Little Boat)	1963	$8
❑ 55301	My Tane (My Man)/Volcano	1961	$8
❑ 55426	Paradise Cove/Secu Secu	1962	$8
❑ 55331	Scimitar/My First Romance	1961	$8
❑ 55629	Something Latin/Once Is Enough	1963	$8
❑ 55655	Sugar Cane/Everything Beautiful Happens	1963	$8
❑ 55212	The Enchanted Sea/Stranger in Paradise	1959	$10
❑ 55622	Theme from The V.I.P.'s/Cousin Ray	1963	$8
❑ 55928	Tiny Bubbles/Hawaii	1967	$6

7-Inch Extended Plays
Number	Title	Yr	NM
❑ LEP-1-3034	*Quiet Village/Return to Paradise/Stone God/Jungle Fever	1959	$10
❑ LEP-2-3034	(contents unknown)	1959	$10
❑ LEP-1-3034 [PS]	Exotica Part 1	1959	$12
❑ LEP-2-3034 [PS]	Exotica Part 2	1959	$12
❑ LEP-3-3034 [PS]	Exotica Part 3	1959	$12
❑ LEP-3-3034	Lotus Land/Similau//Waipu/Love Dance	1959	$10

DENNY, SANDY
A&M
Number	Title	Yr	NM
❑ 1331	Crazy Lady Blues/Let's Jump the Broomstick	1972	$6
❑ 1410	Tomorrow Is a Long Time/Listen Listen	1973	$6

DENOBLE, TOMMY
DOT
Number	Title	Yr	NM
❑ 45-16168	Count Every Star/Anyone But You	1960	$12

SHERYL
Number	Title	Yr	NM
❑ 333	Count Every Star/Anyone But You	1960	$30
❑ 336	Teenage Dream/Young Love (Can Be a True Love)	1961	$30

STAR SATELLITE
Number	Title	Yr	NM
❑ 1003	I Wanta Go with You/Don't Procrastinate with Me Baby	1959	$20
❑ 1006	Tell Me That You Care/Deborah	1959	$20

DENSON, LEE
ENTERPRISE
Number	Title	Yr	NM
❑ 9086	A Mom and Dad for Christmas/The Miracle of the Rosary	1973	$5

KENT
Number	Title	Yr	NM
❑ 306	High School Hop/Devil Doll	1958	$70

VIK
Number	Title	Yr	NM
❑ 0251	Heart of a Fool/The Pied Piper	1957	$50

DENTON, BOB
CHANCELLOR
Number	Title	Yr	NM
❑ 1112	I Guess I'm Still in Love with You/Wrong Side of the Door	1962	$15

DOT
Number	Title	Yr	NM
❑ 15622	Love Me, So I'll Know/I'm Sending You This Record	1957	$30
❑ 15833	Playboy/Twenty-Four Hour Night	1958	$30

JUDD
Number	Title	Yr	NM
❑ 1013	I'll Always Be Yours/A Lover's Prayer	1959	$20
❑ 1001	Sweet and Innocent/Back to School Again	1958	$20

DENTON, MICKEY
AMY
Number	Title	Yr	NM
❑ 902	Top Ten/Now I'm Mr. Blue	1964	$15

BIG TOP
Number	Title	Yr	NM
❑ 3142	Dance With Me Mary/The Other Side of Betty	1963	$30
❑ 3078	Steady Kind/Now You Can't Give Them Away	1961	$30
❑ 3114	Tell Her/How Mighty Hath Fallen	1962	$30

IMPACT
Number	Title	Yr	NM
❑ 1002	Ain't Love Grand/Mi Amore	1965	$30

| ❑ 1011 | Heartache Is My Name/King Lonely the Blue | 1966 | $30 |

WORLD ARTISTS
Number	Title	Yr	NM
❑ 1043	One More Time/Don't Throw My Toys Away	1965	$15

DENVER, JOHN, AND THE MUPPETS
RCA
Number	Title	Yr	NM
❑ PB-11767	Have Yourself a Merry Little Christmas//We Wish You a Merry Christmas/A Baby Just Like You	1979	$5
❑ PB-11767 [PS]	Have Yourself a Merry Little Christmas//We Wish You a Merry Christmas/A Baby Just Like You	1979	$5

DENVER, JOHN, AND THE NITTY GRITTY DIRT BAND
UNIVERSAL
Number	Title	Yr	NM
❑ UVL-66008	And So It Goes/Amazing Grace	1989	$4

DENVER, JOHN
CHERRY MOUNTAIN
Number	Title	Yr	NM
❑ 01/02	Let Us Begin (What Are We Making Weapons For)/Flying for Me	1986	$4

COLUMBIA
Number	Title	Yr	NM
❑ 02679	Perhaps Love/Annie's Song	1982	$4

— With Placido Domingo

| ❑ 03148 | Perhaps Love/Annie's Song | 1982 | $3 |

— With Placido Domingo; reissue

RCA
Number	Title	Yr	NM
❑ PB-14406	Along for the Ride ('56 T-Bird)/Let Us Begin (What Are We Making Weapons For)	1986	$3
❑ PB-11915	Autograph/The Mountain Song	1980	$4
❑ PB-11915 [PS]	Autograph/The Mountain Song	1980	$4
❑ PB-10854	Baby, You Look Good to Me Tonight/Wrangle Mountain Song	1976	$4
❑ GB-14075	Calypso/Some Days Are Diamonds (Some Days Are Stone)	1985	$3

— Gold Standard Series

❑ PB-12017	Dancing with the Mountains/American Child	1980	$4
❑ PB-14115	Don't Close Your Eyes Tonight/A Wild Heart Looking for Home	1985	$3
❑ PB-11479	Downhill Stuff/Life Is So Good	1979	$4
❑ PB-14227	Dreamland Express/African Sunrise	1985	$3
❑ PB-14227 [PS]	Dreamland Express/African Sunrise	1985	$4
❑ PB-13642	Flight (The Higher We Fly)/Hold On Tightly	1983	$4
❑ PB-14366 [DJ]	Flying for Me (same on both sides)	1986	$4

— No stock copies were issued

❑ PB-11637	Garden Song/Berkeley Woman	1979	$4
❑ PB-11036	How Can I Leave You Again/To the Wild Country	1977	$4
❑ GB-10940	I'm Sorry/Fly Away	1977	$3

— Gold Standard Series

❑ PB-11214	It Amazes Me/Druthers	1978	$4
❑ PB-11267	I Want to Live/Tradewinds	1978	$4
❑ PB-10774	Like a Sad Song/Pegasus	1976	$4
❑ PB-13931	Love Again/It's About Time	1984	$3

— A-side: With Sylvie Vartan

| ❑ 5086-7-R | Love Again/Let Us Begin (What Are We Making Weapons For) | 1987 | $3 |
| ❑ GB-11327 | My Sweet Lady/Like a Sad Song | 1978 | $3 |

— Gold Standard Series

❑ PB-10911	My Sweet Lady/Welcome to My Morning	1977	$4
❑ PB-13371	Opposite Tables/Relatively Speaking	1982	$4
❑ PB-13270	Seasons of the Heart/Islands	1982	$4
❑ PB-13071	Shanghai Breezes/What One Man Can Do	1982	$4
❑ PB-12246	Some Days Are Diamonds (Some Days Are Stone)/Country Love	1981	$4
❑ PB-11535	Sweet Melinda/What's On Your Mind	1979	$4
❑ PB-12345	The Cowboy and the Lady/Till You Opened My Eyes	1981	$4
❑ PB-13782	The Way I Am/The Gold and Beyond	1984	$4
❑ PB-13562	Wild Montana Skies/I Remember Romance	1983	$4

— A-side with Emmylou Harris

| ❑ PB-13740 | World Games/It's About Time | 1984 | $3 |

RCA VICTOR
Number	Title	Yr	NM
❑ APBO-0295	Annie's Song/Cool An' Green An' Shady	1974	$4
❑ GB-10472	Annie's Song/Cool An' Green An' Shady	1975	$3

— Gold Standard Series

❑ 74-0305	Anthem (Revelation)/Sticky Summer Weather	1970	$10
❑ PB-10065	Back Home Again/It's Up to You	1974	$4
❑ GB-10473	Back Home Again/It's Up to You	1975	$3

— Gold Standard Series

❑ PB-10464	Christmas for Cowboys/Silent Night, Holy Night	1975	$4
❑ 74-0275	Daydream/I Wish I Knew How It Would Feel to Be Free	1969	$12
❑ 74-0647	Everyday/City of New Orleans	1972	$6
❑ APBO-0067	Farewell Andromeda (Welcome to My Morning)/Whiskey Basin Blues	1973	$4
❑ GB-10475	Farewell Andromeda (Welcome to My Morning)/Whiskey Basin Blues	1975	$3

— Gold Standard Series

❑ PB-10517	Fly Away/Two Shots	1975	$4
❑ 74-0332	Follow Me/Isabel	1970	$10
❑ 74-0567	Friends with You/Starwood in Aspen	1971	$6
❑ 74-0737	Goodbye Again/The Eagle and the Hawk	1972	$6
❑ 74-0955	I'd Rather Be a Cowboy/Sunshine on My Shoulders	1973	$4
❑ PB-10353	I'm Sorry/Calypso	1975	$4
❑ PB-10687	It Makes Me Giggle/Spirit	1976	$4
❑ 74-0801	Late Winter, Early Spring/Hard Life Hard Times	1972	$6
❑ PB-10586	Looking for Space/Windsong	1976	$4
❑ APBO-0182	Please, Daddy (Don't Get Drunk This Christmas)/Rocky Mountain High	1973	$5
❑ 74-0376	Sail Away Home/I Wish I Could Have Been There	1970	$10
❑ APBO-0213	Sunshine on My Shoulders/Around and Around	1974	$4
❑ GB-10474	Sunshine on My Shoulders/Around and Around	1975	$3

— Gold Standard Series

| ❑ PB-10148 | Sweet Surrender/Summer | 1974 | $4 |
| ❑ GB-10478 | Sweet Surrender/Summer | 1975 | $3 |

— Gold Standard Series

| ❑ 74-0445 | Take Me Home, Country Roads/Poems, Prayers and Promises | 1971 | $8 |

— With Fat City

| ❑ PB-10239 | Thank God I'm a Country Boy/My Sweet Lady | 1975 | $4 |
| ❑ GB-10476 | Thank God I'm a Country Boy/My Sweet Lady | 1975 | $3 |

— Gold Standard Series

| ❑ 74-0391 | Whose Garden Is This/Mr. Bojangles | 1970 | $10 |

WINDSTAR
Number	Title	Yr	NM
❑ 75720	Country Girl in Paris/Bread and Roses	1988	$5
❑ 75720 [PS]	Country Girl in Paris/Bread and Roses	1988	$6

7-Inch Extended Plays
RCA
Number	Title	Yr	NM
❑ DTF0-2008 [S]	Season Suite/Summer/Fall Goodbye Again//Mother Nature's Son/For Baby (For Bobbie)/Paradise	1973	$30

— Jukebox issue; small hole, plays at 33 1/3 rpm

DENVER, KARL
LONDON
Number	Title	Yr	NM
❑ 9576	Blue Weekend/Pastures of Plenty	1963	$15
❑ 2020	Marcheta/Joe Sweeney	1961	$20
❑ 9521	Wimoweh/Sleepy Lagoon	1962	$15

DEPECHE MODE
SIRE
Number	Title	Yr	NM
❑ 27991	Behind the Wheel//Route 66/Behind the Wheel	1988	$3
❑ 27991 [PS]	Behind the Wheel//Route 66/Behind the Wheel	1988	$4
❑ 28564	But Not Tonight/Stripped	1986	$5
❑ 28564 [PS]	But Not Tonight/Stripped	1986	$30
❑ 22993	Everything Counts (Live)/Nothing (Live)	1989	$3
❑ 22993 [PS]	Everything Counts (Live)/Nothing (Live)	1989	$4
❑ 29482	Everything Counts/Work Hard	1983	$6
❑ 28918	Master and Servant/(Set Me Free) Remotivate Me	1985	$3
❑ 28918 [PS]	Master and Servant/(Set Me Free) Remotivate Me	1985	$4
❑ 29221	People Are People/In Your Memory	1984	$4
❑ 29221 [PS]	People Are People/In Your Memory	1984	$4
❑ 28835	Shake the Disease/Flexible	1985	$5
❑ 28835 [PS]	Shake the Disease/Flexible	1985	$15
❑ 28366	Strangelove/FPMIP	1987	$4
❑ 28366 [PS]	Strangelove/FPMIP	1987	$4
❑ 27777	Strangelove/Nothing	1988	$3
❑ 27777 [PS]	Strangelove/Nothing	1988	$3

DEPOLIS, CHRIS
CAMEO
Number	Title	Yr	NM
❑ 310	Miss Daisy DeLite/View from My Window	1964	$15

DER RUFO

RAMA

Number	Title	Yr	NM
☐ 28	My Christmas Wish/Greetings	1954	$30

DERBY-HATVILLE

SEA ELL

Number	Title	Yr	NM
☐ 104	Instant Replay/(B-side unknown)	1967	$50

DEREK AND THE DOMINOS
Also see ERIC CLAPTON.

ATCO

Number	Title	Yr	NM
☐ 6803	Bell Bottom Blues/Keep On Growing	1971	$12
☐ 6809	Layla (2:43)/I Am Yours	1971	$12
☐ 6809	Layla (7:10)/I Am Yours	1972	$6
☐ 6780 [DJ]	Tell the Truth/Roll It Over	1970	$30

— Produced by Phil Spector; all-white label

Number	Title	Yr	NM
☐ 6780	Tell the Truth/Roll It Over	1970	$60

— Yellow and white label stock copy; withdrawn shortly after release, this is much rarer than promos

RSO

Number	Title	Yr	NM
☐ 400	Presence of the Lord/Why Does Love Got to Be So Sad	1973	$6

DERRINGER, RICK
Also see THE McCOYS; DIO, BLACK SABBATH; DUST; ALCATRAZZ; PAT BENATAR.

BLUE SKY

Number	Title	Yr	NM
☐ 2788	Don't Ever Say Godbye/Timeless	1980	$4
☐ 2757	Don't Ever Say Goodbye/Gimme More	1975	$4
☐ 2767	Don't Stop Loving Me/Let's Make It	1977	$4

— As "Derringer"

Number	Title	Yr	NM
☐ 2755	Hang On Sloopy/Skyscraper Blues	1975	$4
☐ 2753	It's Raining/Cheqap Tequila	1974	$4
☐ 2770	Lawyers, Guns and Money/Sleepless	1977	$4

— As "Derringer"

Number	Title	Yr	NM
☐ 2765	Let Me In/You Can Have Me	1976	$4

— As "Derringer"

Number	Title	Yr	NM
☐ 2794	Let the Music Play/You'll Get Yours	1980	$4
☐ 2774	Midnight Road/Rocka-Rolla	1978	$4

— As "Derringer"

Number	Title	Yr	NM
☐ 2752	Teenage Love Affair/Slide Over Slinky	1974	$4

DESARIO, TERI

CASABLANCA

Number	Title	Yr	NM
☐ 2278	Dancin' in the Streets/Moonlight Madness	1980	$4

— As "Teri DeSario with K.C."

Number	Title	Yr	NM
☐ 2256	Heart of Stone/You Got What It Takes	1980	$4
☐ 980	Stuff Dreams Are Made Of/Loving You the First Time	1979	$6

DESCENDENTS
7-Inch Extended Plays

NEW ALLIANCE

Number	Title	Yr	NM
☐ NAR-005 [PS]	Fat	1981	$50
☐ NAR-005	My Dad Sucks/Mr. Bass!/I Like Food/Hey Hey/Der Wienerschnitzel	1981	$50

DESERT ROSE BAND, THE

MCA

Number	Title	Yr	NM
☐ 53274	He's Back and I'm Blue/The One That Got Away	1988	$3
☐ 53454	I Still Believe in You/Livin' in the House	1988	$3
☐ 53048	Leave This Town/Ashes of Love	1987	$3
☐ 53142	Love Reunited/Hard Times	1987	$3
☐ 53201	One Step Forward/Glass Hearts	1987	$3
☐ 53354	Our Songs/Summer Wind	1988	$3

MCA CURB

Number	Title	Yr	NM
☐ 53671	Hello Trouble/Homeless	1989	$3
☐ 53616	She Don't Love Nobody/Step On Out	1989	$3
☐ 53746	Start All Over Again/Fooled Again	1989	$3

DESHANNON, JACKIE

AMHERST

Number	Title	Yr	NM
☐ 725	I Don't Think I Can Wait/Don't Let the Flame Burn Out	1978	$15
☐ 737	Things We Said Today/Way Above the Angels	1979	$15
☐ 728	To Love Somebody/Just to Feel This Love from You	1978	$15

ATLANTIC

Number	Title	Yr	NM
☐ 2924	Chains on My Soul/Peaceful in My Soul	1972	$10
☐ 2895	I Wanna Roo You/Paradise	1972	$10
☐ 2871	Only Love Can Break Your Heart/Vanilla Olay	1972	$10
☐ 2919	Sweet Sixteen/Speak Out to Me	1972	$10

CAPITOL

Number	Title	Yr	NM
☐ 3130	Salinas/Keep Me Warm	1971	$10
☐ 3185	Stone Cold Soul/West Virginia Mine	1971	$10

COLUMBIA

Number	Title	Yr	NM
☐ 10221	Boat to Sail/Let the Sailors Dance	1975	$20

— With Brian Wilson on backing vocal

Number	Title	Yr	NM
☐ 10340	Fire in the City/All Night Desire	1976	$10

DOT

Number	Title	Yr	NM
☐ 15928	Cajun Blues/Just Another Lie	1959	$30

— As "Jackie Shannon"

Number	Title	Yr	NM
☐ 15980	Trouble/Lies	1959	$30

— As "Jackie Shannon"

EDISON INTERNATIONAL

Number	Title	Yr	NM
☐ 416	I Wanna Go Home/So Warm	1960	$125
☐ 418	Put My Baby Down/The Foolish One	1960	$125

GONE

Number	Title	Yr	NM
☐ 5008	How Wrong I Was/I'll Be True	1957	$40

— As "Jackie Dee

IMPERIAL

Number	Title	Yr	NM
☐ 66132	A Lifetime of Loneliness/Don't Turn Your Back on Me	1965	$6
☐ 66438	Brighton Hill/You Can Come to Me	1970	$5
☐ 66171	Come and Get Me/Splendor in the Grass	1966	$6
☐ 66224	Come On Down/Find Me Love	1967	$6
☐ 66312	Didn't Want to Have to Do It/Splendor in the Grass	1968	$6
☐ 66342	Holly Would/My Heart's Been Marching	1968	$6
☐ 66202	I Can Make It with You/To Be Myself	1966	$6
☐ 66251	It's All in the Game/Changin' My Mind	1967	$6
☐ 66419	Love Will Find a Way/I Let Go Completely	1969	$5
☐ 66281	Me About You/I Keep Wanting You	1968	$6
☐ 66430	One Christmas/Do You Know How Christmas Trees Are Grown	1969	$6
☐ 66385	Put a Little Love in Your Heart/Always Together	1969	$6
☐ 66196	So Long Johnny/Windows and Doors	1966	$6
☐ 66313	The Weight/Splendor in the Grass	1968	$6
☐ 66370	What Is This/Trust Me	1969	$5
☐ 66110	What the World Needs Now Is Love/I Remember the Boy	1965	$8
☐ 66236	Where Does the Sun Go/Wishing Doll	1967	$6
☐ 66194	Will You Love Me Tomorrow/Are You Ready for This	1966	$6

LIBERTY

Number	Title	Yr	NM
☐ 55387	Baby (When You Kiss Me)/Ain't That Love	1961	$20
☐ 55148	Buddy/Strolypso Dance	1958	$30

— As "Jackie Dee"

Number	Title	Yr	NM
☐ 55526	Faded Love/Dancing Silhouettes	1962	$20
☐ 55526 [PS]	Faded Love/Dancing Silhouettes	1962	$50
☐ 55484	Guess Who/Just Like in the Movies	1962	$20
☐ 55730	He's Got the Whole World in His Hands/It's Love Baby	1964	$20
☐ 55705	Hold Your Head High/She Don't Understand Him Like I Do	1964	$20
☐ 55673	I'm Gonna Be Strong/Should I Cry	1964	$20
☐ 55358	I Won't Turn You Down/Wish I Could Find a Boy	1961	$20
☐ 55602 [DJ]	Little Yellow Roses	1963	$100

— Yellow vinyl promo

Number	Title	Yr	NM
☐ 55602	Little Yellow Roses/500 Miles	1963	$20
☐ 55602	Little Yellow Roses/Oh Sweet Chariot	1963	$20
☐ 55288	Lonely Girl/Teach Me	1960	$20
☐ 56187	Mediterranean Sky/It's So Nice	1970	$6
☐ 55678	Oh Boy/I'm Looking for Someone to Love	1964	$20
☐ 55425	The Prince/I'll Drown in My Own Tears	1962	$20
☐ 55425	The Prince/That's What Boys Are Made Of	1962	$20
☐ 55342	Think About You/Heaven Is Being with You	1961	$20
☐ 55735	When You Walk in the Room/Over You	1964	$15
☐ 55645	When You Walk in the Room/Til You Say You're Mine	1963	$20

PJ

Number	Title	Yr	NM
☐ 101	Trouble/Lies	1959	$50

— As "Jackie Shannon"

RCA

Number	Title	Yr	NM
☐ PB-11902	I Don't Need You Anymore/Find Love	1980	$5

SAGE AND SAND

Number	Title	Yr	NM
☐ 330	Trouble/Lies	1960	$30

UNITED ARTISTS

Number	Title	Yr	NM
☐ 0034	Put a Little Love in Your Heart/When You Walk in the Room	1973	$6

— Silver Spotlight Series" reissue

Number	Title	Yr	NM
☐ 0033	What the World Needs Now Is Love/Needles and Pins	1973	$6

— Silver Spotlight Series" reissue

DESIRES, THE

20TH FOX

Number	Title	Yr	NM
☐ 195	I Don't Know Why/Longing	1960	$30

DASA

Number	Title	Yr	NM
☐ 102	Phyllis Beloved/The Girl for Me	1962	$40

HERALD

Number	Title	Yr	NM
☐ 532	Bobby You/Cold Lonely Heart	1958	$30

HULL

Number	Title	Yr	NM
☐ 730	Hey Lena/Let It Please Be You	1959	$100
☐ 733	Set Me Free/Rendezvous with You	1960	$100

SEVILLE

Number	Title	Yr	NM
☐ 118	The Story of Love/I Ask You	1962	$40

SMASH

Number	Title	Yr	NM
☐ 1763	There I Go Again/I Never Loved Like This	1962	$30

DESMOND, JOHNNY

20TH CENTURY FOX

Number	Title	Yr	NM
☐ 546	Fate Is the Hunter/Rio Conchos	1964	$8

ARTISTS OF AMERICA

Number	Title	Yr	NM
☐ 119	Moonlight Serenade/(Instrumental)	1976	$4

ATCO

Number	Title	Yr	NM
☐ 6404	My Melancholy Baby/Common Touch	1966	$6
☐ 6425	The Last of the Big Time Losers/I Wanna Believe You	1966	$6

COLUMBIA

Number	Title	Yr	NM
☐ 41414	Dancin' Man/Hey Little Dolly	1959	$8
☐ 41631	Eighth Wonder of the World/Never Meant to Fall in Love	1960	$8
☐ 41343	Goodbye, My Love, Goodbye/Bye-Bye Barbara	1959	$8
☐ 41661	Hawk/Playing the Field	1960	$8
☐ 41803	Lover Come Back to Me/No One Ever Tells You	1960	$8
☐ 41525	Maria/Please	1959	$8
☐ 41302	Willingly/The Apple	1958	$10

CORAL

Number	Title	Yr	NM
☐ 61729	A Girl Named Mary/Bueno	1956	$10
☐ 61227	A Husband/A Wife	1954	$15

— B-side by Eileen Barton

Number	Title	Yr	NM
☐ 61632	A Little Love Can Go a Long, Long Way/Please Don't Forget Me Dear	1956	$10
☐ 61968	Anniversary Song/First, Last and Always	1958	$8
☐ 61835	A White Sport Coat (And a Pink Carnation)/Just Lookin'	1957	$8
☐ 61198	Backward, Turn Backward/Forever Love	1954	$20

— With Jane Russell

Number	Title	Yr	NM
☐ 60736	Battle Hymn of the Republic/How Much Will I Miss You	1952	$15
☐ 61880	Be Patient with Me/Missing	1957	$8
☐ 60862	Christmas in the Air/Christmas Is a Time	1952	$20
☐ 61768	Down Where the River Meets the Sea/18th Century Music Box	1957	$8
☐ 61934	Farewell to Naples/Temperamental You	1958	$8
☐ 60670	Festival/Confetti, I Stood and Threw	1952	$15
☐ 61255	Here I Go Walkin' Down the Road/Brooklyn Bridge	1954	$15
☐ 61797	I Just Want You to Want Me/That's Where I Shine	1957	$8
☐ 61569	In My Diary/I'll Cry Tomorrow	1956	$10
☐ 61436	It's a Sin to Tell a Lie/Learnin' the Blues	1955	$10
☐ 61031	It's So Nice to Be Your Neighbor/I'm a Love You	1953	$15
☐ 61447	Land of the Pharaohs/This Too Shall Pass	1955	$12
☐ 61505	Miss America/Gentlemen Marry Brunettes	1955	$10
☐ 61301	My Own True Love/The Song from Desiree	1954	$15
☐ 60629	Oh My Darlin'/Until	1952	$15
☐ 61747	Old Fashioned Christmas/Birthday Party of the King	1956	$15
☐ 60798	One Way Heart/I'm Meant to Be That Way	1952	$15
☐ 61379	Play Me Hearts and Flowers (I Wanna Cry)/I'm So Ashamed	1955	$10
☐ 61543	Santo Natale/Happy Holidays to You	1955	$15

Number	Title	Yr	NM
❏ 61846	Shenandoah Rose/Consideration	1957	$8
❏ 61529	Sixteen Tons/Ballo Italiano	1955	$12
❏ 60929	The Gay Caballero/Thanks for Letting Me Know	1953	$15
❏ 61232	The High and the Mighty/Got No Time	1954	$15
❏ 61204	The High and the Mighty/In God We Trust	1954	$15
❏ 61608	The Most Happy Fella/Without You	1956	$10
❏ 61663	The Proud Ones/I Only Know I Love You	1956	$10
❏ 61952	The Sands of Time/The Jealous Boyfriend	1958	$8
❏ 61410	Togetherness/A Straw Hat and a Cane	1955	$10
❏ 60823	Trying/Wild Guitars	1952	$15
❏ 61069	Woman/By the River Seine	1953	$15
❏ 61153	Would You Let Me Hold Your Heart/The Zoo	1954	$15

DIAMOND

Number	Title	Yr	NM
❏ 108	Twistin' Rose of Texas/Hello Honey	1962	$8

MGM

Number	Title	Yr	NM
❏ 10800	A Bushel and a Peck/So Long Sally	1950	$20
❏ 11005	America's Prayer/I See God	1951	$20
❏ 10947	Because of You/Andiano	1951	$20
❏ 10850	C'est La Vie/You're for Me	1950	$20
❏ K11955	Darling Je Vous Aime Beaucoup/I'll Be Yours	1955	$15
❏ 11027	I Want to Be Near You/I Will Never Change	1951	$20
❏ 11039	Mama/My Yiddishe Momme	1951	$20
❏ 10974	Mister and Mississippi/I Fall in Love	1951	$20
❏ 11122	My Lost Love/Hands Across the Table	1951	$20
❏ 10992	Out o' Breath/I'm Glad I Gave It Up for You	1951	$20
❏ 10736	Pagalle/Stars	1950	$20
❏ 10827	Sleigh Ride/Marshmallow World	1950	$20
❏ 11049	So/More Love	1951	$20
❏ 10930	The Chapel of the Roses/Forever and Always	1951	$20
❏ 10703	The Picnic Song/I've Got a Heart	1950	$20

—*Earlier Johnny Desmond singles on MGM are unconfirmed on 45 rpm*

Number	Title	Yr	NM
❏ 10920	Too Young/I Fell	1951	$20
❏ 11078	True Love/Simple, Simple, Simple	1951	$20

RCA VICTOR

Number	Title	Yr	NM
❏ 47-8233	I Can't Help Falling in Love/I Still Look at You That Way	1963	$6

RCA CAMDEN

Number	Title	Yr	NM
❏ CAE-260	Guilty/I'll Close My Eyes//Just Plain Love/If It's True	1955	$15

DESTINATIONS, THE

CAMEO

Number	Title	Yr	NM
❏ 422	Tell Her/I'd Rather Be Hurt (All at Once)	1966	$40

DESTINATION

Number	Title	Yr	NM
❏ 638	Hello Girl/With You	1967	$30

DETERGENTS, THE

KAPP

Number	Title	Yr	NM
❏ 735	I Can Never Eat Home Anymore/Igor's Cellar	1966	$20
❏ 753	Pushin' the Panic Button/Some Sunday Morning	1966	$20

ROULETTE

Number	Title	Yr	NM
❏ 4642	Bad Girl/Here She Comes	1965	$20
❏ 4603	Double-O-Seven/The Blue Kangaroo	1965	$20
❏ 4590	Leader of the Laundromat/Ulcers	1964	$30
❏ 4590 [PS]	Leader of the Laundromat/Ulcers	1964	$50
❏ 4626	Little Dum-Dum/Soldier Girl	1965	$20
❏ 4616	Tea and Trumpets/Mrs. Jones (How "Bout It)	1965	$20

DETOURS, THE

ATCO

Number	Title	Yr	NM
❏ 6448	Who Do You Love/Peace of Mind	1966	$30

MCSHERRY

Number	Title	Yr	NM
❏ 1285	Bring Back My Beatles/Money	1964	$30
❏ 1285	Bring Back My Beatles to Me/Money	1964	$30

DETROIT

PARAMOUNT

Number	Title	Yr	NM
❏ 0158	Gimmie Shelter/Oh Oh La La La La Dee Da Doo	1972	$6
❏ 0094	It Ain't Easy/Long Neck Goose	1971	$6

DETROIT CITY LIMITS, THE

OKEH

Number	Title	Yr	NM
❏ 7308	98c + Tax/Honey Chile	1968	$8

DETROIT EMERALDS

RIC TIC

Number	Title	Yr	NM
❏ 138	Shades Down/Ode to Billie Joe	1968	$15
❏ 135	Show Time/(Instrumental)	1968	$15
❏ 141	Take Me the Way I Am/I'll Keep On Coming Back	1968	$15

WESTBOUND

Number	Title	Yr	NM
❏ 203	Baby Let Me Take You (In My Arms)/I'll Never Sail the Sea Again	1972	$6
❏ 172	Do Me Right/Just Now and Then	1970	$8
❏ 209	Feel the Need in Me/There's a Love for Me Somewhere	1972	$6
❏ 55401	Feel the Need/Love Has Come to Me	1977	$5
❏ 147	Holding On/Things Are Looking Up	1969	$8
❏ 161	I Can't See Myself Doing Without You/Just Now and Then	1970	$8
❏ 156	If I Lose Your Love/I Bet You Get the One	1969	$8
❏ 226	I'm Qualified/Set It Out	1974	$6
❏ 220	Lee/Whatcha Gonna Wear Tomorrow	1973	$6
❏ 55404	Set It Out (Part 1)/Set It Out (Part 2)	1977	$5
❏ 55410	Turn On Lady/Just Don't Know About This Girl of Mine	1977	$5
❏ 181	Wear This Ring (With Love)/Bet You Got the One Who Loves You	1971	$6

DETROIT JR.

FOXY

Number	Title	Yr	NM
❏ 02	This Time Last Christmas/Christmas Day	1961	$15

DETROIT WHEELS, THE

INFERNO

Number	Title	Yr	NM
❏ 5002	Linda Sue Dixon/Tally Ho	1968	$30
❏ 5003	Think (Part 1)/Think (Part 2)	1968	$30

DEUCES OF RHYTHM AND THE TEMPO TOPPERS, THE

PEACOCK

Number	Title	Yr	NM
❏ 1616	Ain't That Good News/A Fool at the Wheel	1953	$100
❏ 1628	Always/Rice, Red Beans and Turnip Greens	1954	$100

DEVAURS, THE

D-TONE

Number	Title	Yr	NM
❏ 3	Baby Doll/Teenager	1958	$250

MOON

Number	Title	Yr	NM
❏ 105	Where Are You/Boy in Mexico	1959	$200

RED FOX

Number	Title	Yr	NM
❏ 104	Where Are You/Boy in Mexico	1965	$50

DEVILLE, WILLY

A&M

Number	Title	Yr	NM
❏ 2987	Assassin of Love/I Call Your Name	1987	$3

DEVILS, THE

MAINSTREAM

Number	Title	Yr	NM
❏ 644	Trouble with Angels/Rachel Says Goodbye	1966	$20

SARA

Number	Title	Yr	NM
❏ 1450	I'll Say Yes/I'm Leaving You	1967	$30
❏ 1449	Tell Me/Love and Understanding	1967	$30

DEVO

BACKSTREET

Number	Title	Yr	NM
❏ 52215	Theme from Doctor Detroit/King of Soul	1983	$3

—*B-side by James Brown*

BOOJI BOY

Number	Title	Yr	NM
❏ 72843/75677	Satisfaction/Sloppy	1978	$5
❏ 72843/75677 [PS]	Satisfaction/Sloppy	1978	$15

ENIGMA

Number	Title	Yr	NM
❏ 75029	Baby Doll (Ivan Ivan Mix)/Baby Doll (Devo Mix)	1988	$3
❏ 75029 [PS]	Baby Doll (Ivan Ivan Mix)/Baby Doll (Devo Mix)	1988	$6
❏ 75023	Disco Dancer/Disco Dancer	1989	$3

FULL MOON/ASYLUM

Number	Title	Yr	NM
❏ 47204	Working in the Coal Mine/Planet Earth	1981	$3
❏ 47204 [PS]	Working in the Coal Mine/Planet Earth	1981	$6

REFLEX

Number	Title	Yr	NM
❏ 5	Bush Whacked	1988	$3

—*One-sided flexi-disc given away with Reflex magazine*

WARNER BROS.

Number	Title	Yr	NM
❏ 29133	Are You Experienced/Growing Pains	1984	$3
❏ 29133 [PS]	Are You Experienced/Growing Pains	1984	$3
❏ 49834	Beautiful World/Enough Said	1981	$4
❏ 49834 [PS]	Beautiful World/Enough Said	1981	$6
❏ 8745	Come Back Jonee/Praying Hands	1979	$5
❏ 49621	Freedom of Choice/Snowball (Remix)	1980	$4
❏ 49621 [PS]	Freedom of Choice/Snowball (Remix)	1980	$3
❏ 49715	Gates of Steel (Live)/Be Still (Live)	1981	$4
❏ 49524	Girl U Want/Mr. B's Ballroom	1980	$4
❏ 8675	(I Can't Get No) Satisfaction/Uncontrollable Urge	1978	$5
❏ 29931	Peek-A-Boo/Find Out	1982	$3
❏ 29931 [PS]	Peek-A-Boo/Find Out	1982	$4
❏ 49028	Secret Agent Man/Red Eye	1979	$3
❏ 29811	That's Good/What I Must Do	1983	$3
❏ 50048	Through Being Cool/Going Under	1982	$4
❏ 49550	Whip It/Turn Around	1980	$4
❏ EP3595	Working in the Coal Mine (same on both sides)	1981	$3

—*Issued with the New Traditionalists LP*

DEVOL, FRANK

ABC-PARAMOUNT

Number	Title	Yr	NM
❏ 10628	Combat/General Hospital	1965	$10
❏ 10608	Theme from "Peyton Place"/Hush, Hush, Sweet Charlotte	1964	$8

CAPITOL

Number	Title	Yr	NM
❏ F1411	Ciribiribin on Mandolin/Chapel of Roses	1951	$15
❏ F1503	Dear John/Lonely Acres	1951	$15
❏ F1143	Dream a While/Powder and Paint	1950	$20
❏ F1560	Hopalong Cassidy March/Circus Days	1951	$15
❏ F1178	Love Letters in the Sand/This Year's Kisses	1950	$20
❏ F1359	Lullaby of Broadway/Seven Wonders of the World	1951	$15
❏ F1297	One Finger Melody/You Can Marry Me	1950	$20
❏ F835	Sing a Happy Song/Lady Play Your Mandolin	1950	$20
❏ F1340	Teardrops/It's a Lonely Town	1950	$20
❏ F1460	Theme John & Marsha/Playball	1951	$15
❏ F3457	Toy Tiger/Three Fishermen	1956	$10

COLGEMS

Number	Title	Yr	NM
❏ 66-1015	Guess Who's Coming to Dinner/The Glory of Love	1968	$6

—*As "DeVol"*

Number	Title	Yr	NM
❏ 66-1015 [PS]	Guess Who's Coming to Dinner/The Glory of Love	1968	$30

COLUMBIA

Number	Title	Yr	NM
❏ 41987	David's Dream/Columbia	1961	$8
❏ 41702	Do You Think of Me/Same Old Summer	1960	$8
❏ 41366	House on Haunted Hill/Hadies	1959	$8
❏ 41620	La Montana (If She Should Come to You)/"The Key" Theme	1960	$8
❏ 41620 [PS]	La Montana (If She Should Come to You)/"The Key" Theme	1960	$20
❏ 40953	Love in the Afternoon/Venice	1957	$10
❏ 41285	My Heart's in Portugal/How Can You Forget	1958	$8
❏ 41724	Same Old Summer/Do You Think of Me	1960	$8
❏ 42620	Whatever Happened to Baby Jane/I've Written a Letter to Daddy	1962	$8

DEVONS, THE (1)

DECCA

Number	Title	Yr	NM
❏ 31822	Are You Really Real/It's All Over Now, Baby Blue	1965	$50
❏ 31899	Come On/A Little Extra Effort	1966	$50
❏ 31777	Honda Bike/Free Fall	1965	$100

DEVONS, THE (2)

PIC ONE

Number	Title	Yr	NM
❏ 111	Wine, Wine, Wine/Joey's Guitar	1965	$100

DEVORZON, BARRY, AND PERRY BOTKIN, JR.

A&M

Number	Title	Yr	NM
❏ 1890	Bless the Beasts and Children/Down the Line	1976	$4

Number	Title	Yr	NM
DEVORZON, BARRY			
A&M			
❏ 2129	Theme from "The Warriors"/ Baseball Furies' Chase	1979	$4
COLUMBIA			
❏ 41464	Betty, Betty/Across the Street from Your House	1959	$40
❏ 41612	Hey Little Darlin'/Rosemary	1960	$30
❏ 41663	Love You Baby/Can-Can Ladies	1960	$30
❏ 42031	Penny Moved Away/Lindy Lou	1961	$30
❏ 3-42031	Penny Moved Away/Lindy Lou	1961	$50
— Compact 33" single with small hole			
RCA VICTOR			
❏ 47-7124	Barbara Jean/Baby Doll	1957	$40
❏ 47-7510	Cora Lee/Blue, Green and Gold	1959	$40
❏ 47-7226	False Love/Raindrops at My Window	1958	$40
❏ 47-7406	Honey Bunny/Too Soon	1958	$40
DEVOTIONS, THE			
KAPE			
❏ 701	(How Do You Speak?) To An Angel/Teardrops Follow Me	1966	$15
ROULETTE			
❏ 4556	A Sunday Kind of Love/ Tears from a Broken Heart	1964	$40
❏ 4580	Snow White/Zindy Lou	1964	$40
DEWITT, LEW			
COLUMBIA			
❏ 4-44160	She Went a Little Bit Farther/Brown Eyes	1967	$10
COMPLEAT			
❏ 160	Hello Houston/Don't Our Love Look	1986	$6
❏ 151	I Love Virginia/She Must Have Lovin' Eyes	1986	$6
❏ 172	Slow Dance/(B-side unknown)	1987	$6
DEWOLF, DEAN			
ARGO			
❏ 5457	The Little Drummer Boy/ As Joseph Was a-Walkin'	1963	$15
DEXTER, AL			
CAPITOL			
❏ 4724	My Little Heartache/I Won't Be Number Two	1962	$15
COLUMBIA			
❏ 2-400(?)	Always in My Heart/I'm Startin' Sweetheartin' Again	1949	$60
— Microgroove 7-inch 33 1/3 rpm single			
❏ 2-129	Calamity Jane/A Good Man Is Hard to Find	1949	$60
— Microgroove 33 1/3 rpm 7-inch single, small hole			
❏ 2-459	Each Night I Cry Over Your Picture/I Don't Suppose	1950	$50
— Microgroove 7-inch 33 1/3 rpm single			
❏ 2-280(?)	Saturday Night Boogie/ There'll Come a Time	1949	$60
— Microgroove 7-inch 33 1/3 rpm single			
DECCA			
❏ 9-28345	Counting My Teardrops/ Honeymoon Waltz	1952	$30
❏ 9-28137	Hotfoot Shuffle/ Fisherman's Boogie	1952	$30
— With Aubrey Grass			
❏ 9-28739	My Careless Heart/ Move Over Rover	1953	$30
DOT			
❏ 16977	Down at the Roadside Inn/ My Careless Heart	1966	$12
❏ 16842	Pistol Packin' Mama/Rosalita	1966	$10
EKKO			
❏ 1020	Pistol Packin' Mama/I Won't Be Number Two	1955	$30
DEXY'S MIDNIGHT RUNNERS			
MERCURY			
❏ 76189	Come On Eileen/Let's Make This Precious	1982	$5
❏ 76189 [PS]	Come On Eileen/Let's Make This Precious	1982	$10
❏ 811142-7	The Celtic Soul Brothers/ Reminisce Pt. 1	1983	$4
❏ 811142-7 [PS]	The Celtic Soul Brothers/ Reminisce Pt. 1	1983	$4

Number	Title	Yr	NM
DEY AND KNIGHT			
COLUMBIA			
❏ 43693	Sayin' Somethin'/Ooh Da La La Day	1966	$15
DEY, TRACEY			
AMY			
❏ 917	Blue Turns to Grey/Didn't Ya Me Straight Again	1964	$30
❏ 901	Gonna Get Along Without You Now/Go Away	1964	$20
❏ 908	Hangin' On to My Baby/ Ska-Doo-Dee-Yah	1964	$20
❏ 928	Hanky Panky/Shakin' the Blues Away	1965	$20
❏ 912	I Won't Tell/Any Kind of Love	1964	$20
LIBERTY			
❏ 55604	Teenage Cleopatra/Who's That	1963	$20
DEYOUNG, CLIFF			
MCA			
❏ 40239	Escaping Reality/She Bent Me Straight Again	1974	$4
❏ 40388	If I Could Put You in My Song/ You Will Never Know	1975	$4
❏ 40294	It Hurts a Little Even Now/Lives	1974	$4
❏ 40156	My Sweet Lady/Sunshine on My Shoulders	1973	$4
❏ 40156 [PS]	My Sweet Lady/Sunshine on My Shoulders	1973	$5
DEYOUNG, DENNIS			
A&M			
❏ 2816	Call Me/Please	1986	$3
❏ 2816 [PS]	Call Me/Please	1986	$3
❏ 2709	Dear Darling/Suspicious	1985	$3
❏ 2666	Desert Moon/Gravity	1984	$3
❏ 2666 [PS]	Desert Moon/Gravity	1984	$3
❏ 2692	Don't Wait for Heroes/Gravity	1984	$3
❏ 2839	This Is the Time/ Southbound Ryan	1986	$3
MCA			
❏ 53293	Beneath the Moon/Boomchild	1988	$3
❏ 53376	Outside Looking In Again/Boomchild	1988	$3
DIABLOS, THE (2)			
JUBILEE			
❏ 5553	Hombre/El Bandito	1966	$30
DIALS, THE			
HILLTOP			
❏ 2010	School Bells Are Ringing/ Ring Ting-a-Ling	1960	$300
❏ 2009	Wondering About Your Love/Sorrento	1960	$200
PHILIPS			
❏ 40040	These Foolish Things/At the Start of a New Romance	1962	$50
TIME			
❏ 1068	Monkey Dance/Monkey Walk	1963	$30
DIALTONES, THE (1)			
DIAL			
❏ 4054	Don't Let the Sun Shine on Me/You Don't Know, You Just Don't Know	1967	$30
DIALTONES, THE (2)			
GOLDISC			
❏ 3005	Till I Heard It from You/Johnny	1960	$40
❏ 3020	Till I Heard It from You/Johnny	1961	$30
DIALTONES, THE (U)			
LAWN			
❏ 203	So Young/Chicago Bird	1963	$30
DIAMOND, BRIAN, AND THE CUTTERS			
HICKORY			
❏ 1321	Big Bad Wolf/See If I Care	1965	$12
DIAMOND, GREGG			
MARLIN			
❏ 3333	Doing That (Fancy Dancer)/Holding Back	1979	$15
❏ 3329	Star Cruiser/This Side of Midnight	1979	$8
MERCURY			
❏ 74066	Shinin'/Vamp	1979	$10
— As "Hardware			
POLYDOR			
❏ 2195	Chains/Hot Butterfly	1982	$4
— As "Gregg Diamond Bionic Boogie			
❏ 14536	Chains/Paradise	1979	$10
— As "Gregg Diamond Bionic Boogie			

Number	Title	Yr	NM
❏ 14471	Dance Little Dreamer/ Feel Like Dancing	1978	$5
— As "Bionic Boogie			
❏ 14525	Hot Butterfly/When the Shit Hits the Fan	1979	$20
— As "Gregg Diamond Bionic Boogie"; A-side featuring Luther Vandross			
DIAMOND, LARRY			
ARGO			
❏ 5330	Bye Bye Doll/True Love, Come My Way	1959	$15
DIAMOND, LEO			
AMBASSADOR			
❏ 1004	Easy Melody/Off Shore	1953	$20
RCA VICTOR			
❏ 47-5765	China Nights/Hold On to Your Dreams	1954	$15
❏ 47-6600	Go See Tony/Le Refifi	1956	$15
❏ 47-6406	Lisbon Antigua/Music Box Tango	1956	$15
❏ 47-5973	Melody of Love/Phantom Gaucho	1955	$15
❏ 47-6307	Mister X/Fantasia Mexicana	1955	$15
❏ 47-6513	Polynesian/Du Bist Schoen Wie Musik	1956	$15
❏ 47-6710	Sixth Finger Tune/I Remember When	1956	$15
❏ 47-5834	The High and the Mighty/Lisbon	1954	$15
❏ 47-6194	Theme from "Female on the Beach"/Destiny	1955	$15
❏ 47-6090	The One Rose/Land of the Pharaohs	1955	$15
REPRISE			
❏ 20126	Born to Be With You/Miramor	1962	$8
❏ 20074	Harbor Lights/Theme for a New Love	1962	$8
❏ 20016	Sweet and Lovely/ Dream of Olwen	1961	$8
❏ 20036	The 400 Blows/La Dolce Vita	1961	$8
ROULETTE			
❏ 4047	Flunky/Te Amo	1957	$10
❏ 4025	Till/Sunrise in Texas	1957	$10
DIAMOND, NEIL			
BANG			
❏ 105	Cherry, Cherry/Girl, You'll Be a Woman Soon	1973	$4
— Reissue			
❏ 528	Cherry, Cherry/I'll Come Running	1966	$15
❏ 580	Do It/Hanky Panky	1970	$6
❏ 542	Girl, You'll Be a Woman Soon/You'll Forget	1967	$15
❏ 536	I Got the Feelin' (Oh No No)/ The Boat That I Row	1966	$15
❏ 586	I'm a Believer/Crooked Street	1971	$6
❏ 586	I'm a Believer/Crooked Street	1971	$20
— Rare pressing with both sides in stereo			
❏ 547	I Thank the Lord for the Night Time/The Long Way Home	1967	$20
❏ 561	Shilo/La Bamba	1968	$8
❏ 575	Shilo/La Bamba	1970	$6
❏ 519	Solitary Man/Do It	1966	$20
❏ 108	Solitary Man/I'm a Believer	1973	$4
— Reissue			
❏ 578	Solitary Man/The Time Is Now	1970	$6
❏ 547	Thank the Lord for the Night Time/The Long Way Home	1967	$10
— Title altered on second pressing			
❏ 703	The Long Way Home/ Monday, Monday	1973	$5
CAPITOL			
❏ 4994	America/Songs of Life	1981	$4
❏ 4994 [PS]	America/Songs of Life	1981	$4
❏ 4960	Hello Again/Amazed and Confused	1981	$4
❏ 4960 [PS]	Hello Again/Amazed and Confused	1981	$4
❏ 4939	Love on the Rocks/Acapulco	1980	$4
❏ 4939 [PS]	Love on the Rocks/Acapulco	1980	$4
COLUMBIA			
❏ 3-10452	Beautiful Noise/Signs	1976	$5
❏ 45942	Be/Flight of the Gull	1973	$5
❏ 18-02928	Be Mine Tonight/Right By You	1982	$3
❏ 38-07751	Cherry, Cherry/America	1988	$4
❏ 42809 [DJ]	Clown Town/At Night	1963	$250
❏ 42809	Clown Town/At Night	1963	$500
❏ 3-10657	Desiree/Once in a While	1977	$5
❏ 3-10405	Don't Think...Feel/Home Is a Wounded Heart	1976	$5
❏ 3-10897	Forever in Blue Jeans/ Remember Me	1979	$4
❏ 38-03801	Front Page Story/I'm Guilty	1983	$3
❏ 38-03801 [PS]	Front Page Story/I'm Guilty	1983	$3
❏ 38-05889	Headed for the Future/Angel	1986	$3
❏ 38-05889 [PS]	Headed for the Future/Angel	1986	$3
❏ CNR-03345	Heartlight/(B-side blank)	1982	$6
— One-sided budget release			
❏ 38-03219	Heartlight/You Don't Know Me	1982	$3

Number	Title	Yr	NM
❏ 38-03219 [PS]	Heartlight/You Don't Know Me	1982	$4
❏ 38-07614	I Dreamed a Dream/Sweet Caroline	1987	$3
❏ 38-07614 [PS]	I Dreamed a Dream/Sweet Caroline	1987	$3
❏ 3-10366	If You Know What I Mean/Street Life	1976	$5
❏ CNR-03572	I'm Alive/(B-side blank)	1983	$6
—One-sided budget release			
❏ 38-03503	I'm Alive/Lost Among the Stars	1983	$3
❏ 10084	I've Been This Way Before/Reggae Strut	1975	$5
❏ 10043	Longfellow Serenade/Rosemary's Wine	1974	$5
❏ 18-02712	On the Way to the Sky/Save Me	1982	$3
❏ 18-02712 [PS]	On the Way to the Sky/Save Me	1982	$3
❏ 3-10945	Say Maybe/Diamond Girls	1979	$4
❏ 1-11175	September Morn/I'm a Believer	1980	$4
❏ 45998	Skybird/Lonely Looking Sky	1974	$5
❏ 38-04646	Sleep with Me Tonight/One by One	1984	$4
❏ AE71115 [DJ]	Song Sung Blue (mono/stereo)	1977	$12
—Live version from "Love at the Greek"			
❏ 38-68741	The Best Years of Our Lives/Carmelita's Eyes	1989	$4
❏ 1-11232	The Good Lord Loves You/Jazz Time	1980	$4
❏ 10138	The Last Picasso/The Gift of Song	1975	$5
❏ 38-06136	The Story of My Life/Love Doesn't Live Here Anymore	1986	$3
❏ 38-06136 [PS]	The Story of My Life/Love Doesn't Live Here Anymore	1986	$3
❏ 38-08514	This Time/If I Couldn't See You Again	1988	$4
❏ 38-04541	Turn Around/Brooklyn on a Saturday Night	1984	$3
❏ 38-04541 [PS]	Turn Around/Brooklyn on a Saturday Night	1984	$3
MCA			
❏ 40017	Cherry, Cherry from Hot August Night/Morningside	1973	$5
❏ 40092	The Last Thing on My Mind/Canta Libra	1973	$5
PHILCO-FORD			
❏ HP-5	Girl, You'll Be a Woman Soon/Cherry, Cherry	1967	$20
—4-inch plastic "Hip Pocket Record" with color sleeve			
❏ HP-17	Solitary Man/You Got to Me	1967	$20
—4-inch plastic "Hip Pocket Record" with color sleeve			
UNI			
❏ 55065	Brooklyn Roads/Holiday Inn Blues	1968	$8
❏ 55109	Brother Love's Travelling Salvation Show/A Modern-Day Version of Love	1969	$6
❏ 55250	Cracklin' Rosie/Lordy	1970	$6
❏ 55264	He Ain't Heavy...He's My Brother/Free Life	1970	$6
❏ 55175	Holly Holy/Hurtin' You Don't Come Easy	1969	$6
❏ 55278	I Am...I Said/Done Too Soon	1971	$5
❏ 55346	Play Me/Porcupine Pie	1972	$5
❏ 55326	Song Sung Blue/Gitchy Goomy	1972	$5
❏ 55224	Soolaimon (African Trilogy II)/And the Grass Won't Pay No Mind	1970	$6
❏ 55224 [PS]	Soolaimon (African Trilogy II)/And the Grass Won't Pay No Mind	1970	$20
❏ 55310	Stones/Crunchy Granola Suite	1971	$5
❏ 55084	Sunday Sun/Honey-Drippin' Times	1968	$8
❏ 55136	Sweet Caroline (Good Times Never Seemed So Good)/Dig In	1969	$6
❏ 55075	Two-Bit Manchild/Broad Old Woman	1968	$8
❏ 55075 [PS]	Two-Bit Manchild/Broad Old Woman	1968	$30
❏ 55075 [DJ]	Two-Bit Manchild (same on both sides)	1968	$100
—Red vinyl			
❏ 55352	Walk on Water/High Rolling Man	1972	$5
7-Inch Extended Plays			
❏ 34818 [PS]	Gold	1970	$20
—Part of "Little LP" series (LLP #127)			
❏ 34871 [PS]	Stones	1971	$20
—Part of "Little LP" series (LLP #172)			
❏ 34871	Suzanne/Husbands and Wives//I Am... I Said and Stones/Chelsea Morning	1971	$20
—Jukebox issue; small hole, plays at 33 1/3 rpm			

Number	Title	Yr	NM
DIAMOND, RONNIE			
IMPERIAL			
❏ 5570	Candy Store/Something's Wrong with Me	1959	$20
❏ 5588	Life Begins at 4 O'Clock/Tell Me	1959	$60
❏ 5605	When We Kiss/Pretty Please	1959	$20
DIAMONDS, THE (1)			
CORAL			
❏ 61577	Be My Lovin' Baby/Smooch Me	1956	$30
❏ 61502	Black Denim Trousers and Motorcycle Boots/Nip Sip	1955	$30
GUSTO			
❏ 2019	Little Darlin'/The Stroll	1979	$4
—Re-recordings			
MERCURY			
❏ 71449	A Mother's Love/Gretchen	1959	$20
❏ 71021	A Thousand Miles Away/Ev'ry Minute of the Day	1956	$30
❏ 71291	High Sign/Chick-Lets (Don't Let Me Down)	1958	$20
❏ 71291 [PS]	High Sign/Chick-Lets (Don't Let Me Down)	1958	$125
❏ 71060	Little Darlin'/Faithful and True	1957	$50
—Maroon label, "Mercury" and logo by themselves at top			
❏ 71060	Little Darlin'/Faithful and True	1957	$50
—Black label, "Mercury" and logo in double oval at top			
❏ 71060	Little Darlin'/Faithful and True	1957	$40
—Maroon Label, "Mercury" and logo in double oval at top			
❏ 70889	Love, Love, Love/Every Night About This Time	1956	$30
❏ 70983	My Judge and My Jury/Put Your House in Order	1956	$30
❏ 71831	One Summer Night/It's a Doggone Shame	1961	$20
❏ 71404	She Say (Oom Dooby Doom)/From the Bottom of My Heart	1959	$30
❏ 71197	Silhouettes/Daddy Cool	1957	$30
❏ 71468	Sneaky Alligator/Holding Your Hand	1959	$20
❏ 70835	The Church Bells May Ring/Little Girl of Mine	1956	$30
❏ 71734	The Crumble/You'd Be Mine	1960	$20
❏ 71818	The Munch/Woomai Ling	1961	$20
❏ 71633	The Pencil Song/Slave Girl	1960	$20
❏ 71242	The Stroll/Land of Beauty	1957	$40
❏ 71366	Walking Along/Eternal Lovers	1958	$20
❏ 71534	Walking the Stroll/Batman, Wolfman, Frankenstein or Dracula	1959	$30
❏ 70790	Why Do Fools Fall in Love/You Baby You	1956	$30
❏ 71128	Words of Love/Don't Say Goodbye	1957	$30
7-Inch Extended Plays			
BRUNSWICK			
❏ EB71031	(contents unknown)	1957	$175
❏ EB71031 [PS]	The Diamonds	1957	$175
MERCURY			
❏ EP 1-3390	(contents unknown)	1958	$50
❏ EP 1-3357	Honey Bird/For You Alone//Zip Zip/Cool, Cool Baby	1957	$50
❏ EP 1-3356	Shoo Ya Blues/You Are the Limit//My Dog Likes Your Dog/Oh, How I Wish	1957	$50
❏ EP 1-3367	Silhouettes/Daddy Cool//Passion Flower/Sweet Wild Honey	1957	$50
❏ EP 1-3356 [PS]	The Diamonds	1957	$50
❏ EP 1-3357 [PS]	The Diamonds	1957	$50
❏ EP 1-3367 [PS]	The Diamonds	1957	$50
❏ EP 1-3358 [PS]	The Diamonds: America's Number One Singing Stylists	1957	$50
❏ EP 1-3390 [PS]	The Stroll	1958	$50
❏ EP 1-3358	Till My Baby Comes Home/Girl of Mine//One and Only/Honey	1957	$50
DIAMONDS, THE (2)			
ATLANTIC			
❏ 981	A Beggar for Your Kisses/Call, Baby, Call	1952	$1500
❏ 1003	I'll Live Again/Two Loves Have I	1953	$600
DIAMONDS, THE (3)			
CHURCHILL			
❏ 94102	Two Kinds of Woman/(B-side unknown)	1987	$6

Number	Title	Yr	NM
DIANA			
ADAMAS			
❏ 103	Who's Been Sleeping in My Bed/(B-side unknown)	1982	$6
❏ 103 [PS]	Who's Been Sleeping in My Bed/(B-side unknown)	1982	$8
ELEKTRA			
❏ 46539	Lonely Together/This Is the Way a Woman Wants to Feel	1979	$5
SUNBIRD			
❏ 7564	He's the Fire/What a Fool I Was (To Fall in Love with You)	1981	$5
DIANE AND THE DARLETTES			
DUNES			
❏ 2026	Here She Comes/Just You	1963	$20
—As "The Darlettes"			
DIBANGO, MANU			
ATLANTIC			
❏ 2983	Dangwa/Obaso	1973	$5
❏ 2971	Soul Makossa/Lily	1973	$5
❏ 3263	Super Kimba/Wasa N'Doto	1975	$4
❏ 3000	Weya/Moni	1974	$4
WARNER BROS.			
❏ 8680	Aloko Party/Big Blow	1978	$4
DICK AND DEEDEE			
DOT			
❏ 17305	Do I Love You/You Came Back to Haunt Me	1970	$12
❏ 17145	Escape Suite/I'm Not Gonna Get Hung-Up About It	1968	$20
❏ 17261	We'll Sing in the Sunshine/In the Season of Our Love	1969	$10
LAMA			
❏ 7780	Goodbye to Love/Swing Low	1961	$20
❏ 7783	Tell Me/Will You Always Love Me	1961	$20
❏ 7778	The Mountain's High/I Want Someone	1961	$30
LIBERTY			
❏ 55478	All I Want/Life's Just a Play	1962	$15
❏ 55382	Goodbye to Love/Swing Low	1961	$15
❏ 55412	Tell Me/Will You Always Love Me	1962	$15
❏ 55350	The Mountain's High/I Want Someone	1961	$20
UNITED ARTISTS			
❏ 0036	The Mountain's High/Tell Me	1973	$5
—Silver Spotlight Series" reissue			
WARNER BROS.			
❏ 5411	All My Trials/Don't Think Twice, It's All Right	1964	$10
❏ 5608	Be My Baby/Room 404	1965	$12
❏ 5627	Blue Turns to Grey/Some Things Just Stick in Your Mind	1965	$30
—Both sides are Mick Jagger-Keith Richards songs produced by Andrew Loog Oldham			
❏ 7017	Long Lonely Nights/I'll Always Be Around	1967	$10
❏ 5364	Love Is a Once in a Lifetime Thing/Chug-a Chug-a Choo Choo	1963	$10
❏ 5860	Make Up Before We Break Up/Can't Get Enough of Your Love	1966	$10
❏ 7069	One in a Million/Baby, I Need You	1967	$10
❏ 5671	P.S. 1402 (Your Local Charm School)/Use What You've Got	1965	$10
❏ 5830	She Didn't Even Say Goodbye/So Many Things We Didn't Know	1966	$10
❏ 5652	The World Is Waiting/Vini, Vini	1965	$10
❏ 5482	Thou Shalt Not Steal/Just 'Round the River Bend	1964	$20
—Red label with arrows			
❏ 5482	Thou Shalt Not Steal/Just 'Round the River Bend	1964	$10
—Orange label			
❏ 5482 [PS]	Thou Shalt Not Steal/Just 'Round the River Bend	1964	$30
❏ 5699	Till/Sha-Ta	1966	$10
❏ 5396	Turn Around/Don't Leave Me	1963	$10
❏ 5383	Where Did the Good Times Go/Guess Our Love Must Show	1963	$10
DICK AND RICHARD			
CAPITOL			
❏ 5097	Santa Caught a Cold on Christmas Eve/Stinky, the Little Reindeer	1963	$20

Number	Title	Yr	NM

DICKENS, CHARLES
WARNER BROS.
| ☐ 5657 | That's the Way Love Goes/In the City | 1965 | $15 |

DICKENS, JIMMY
COLUMBIA
| ☐ 4-42845 | Another Bridge to Burn/I'll Sit This One Out | 1963 | $15 |
| ☐ 2-411 | A-Sleeping at the Foot of the Bed/I'm in Love Up to My Ears | 1949 | $60 |

— Microgroove 7-inch 33 1/3 rpm single

☐ 4-20786	Bessie the Heifer/Cold Feet	1951	$40
☐ 4-20769	Bible on the Table/I'm Little But I'm Loud	1950	$40
☐ 4-21515	Big Sandy/It Scares Me	1956	$30
☐ 4-21296	Black Eyed Joes/Take Me As I Am	1954	$30
☐ 4-20905	Brother Do You Take Time to Pray/They Locked God Outside	1952	$40
☐ 4-21341	Conscience/Stinky, Pass the Hat Around	1955	$30
☐ 4-21555	Cornbread and Buttermilk/I Never Thought It Would Happen	1956	$30
☐ 2-238	Country Boy/I'm Fading Fast with the Time	1949	$60

— Microgroove 7-inch 33 1/3 rpm single

☐ 4-44025	Country Music Lover/ You've Destroyed Me	1967	$8
☐ 4-42278	Eight More Miles/ Twenty Cigarettes	1962	$15
☐ 4-41080	Family Reunion/ Whatever You Were	1957	$30
☐ 4-41916	Fire Ball Mail/John Henry	1960	$15
☐ 2-625	Foolish Me/If It Ain't One Thing	1950	$50

— Microgroove 7-inch 33 1/3 rpm single

☐ 4-41436	Hannah/Country Ways and City Ideas	1959	$20
☐ 4-43243	He Stands Real Tall/Life Turned Her That Way	1965	$12
☐ 4-41529	Hey Ma/Hot Tears	1959	$30
☐ 4-21491	Hey Worm/Where Did the Sunshine Go	1956	$30
☐ 2-550(?)	Hillbilly Fever/Then I Had to Turn Around and Get Married	1950	$50

— Microgroove 7-inch 33 1/3 rpm single

☐ 4-20930	Hot Diggety Dog/Lola Lee	1952	$40
☐ 4-41173	I Got a Hole in My Pocket/ Me and My Big Mouth	1958	$60
☐ 4-21132	I'll Dance at Your Wedding/I'm Making Love to a Stranger	1953	$40
☐ 4-43123	I'll Sit This One Out/Is Goodbye That Easy to Say	1964	$10
☐ 4-21464	I'm Braver Now/Are You Insured Beyond the Grave	1955	$30
☐ 4-40801	I'm Coming Over Tonight/Say It Now	1956	$30
☐ 4-41670	I'm Just Blue Enough (To Do Most Anything)/We Lived It Up (Now We've Got to Live It Down)	1960	$20
☐ 4-40890	I Never Had the Blues/ Happy Heartaches	1957	$30
☐ 4-20809	It May Be Silly/What About You	1951	$40
☐ 4-20866	I've Just Got to See You Once More/Poor Little Darlin'	1952	$40
☐ 4-40961	Let's Quit Before We Start/ Making the Rounds	1957	$30
☐ 2-472	Lovin' Lies/A Rose from the Bride's Bouquet	1950	$50

— Microgroove 7-inch 33 1/3 rpm single

| ☐ 4-43388 | May the Bird of Paradise Fly Up Your Nose/My Eyes Are Jealous | 1965 | $15 |
| ☐ 2-292 | My Heart's Bouquet/I'll Be Back a-Sunday | 1949 | $60 |

— Microgroove 7-inch 33 1/3 rpm single

☐ 4-21203	Old Country Preacher/Little Ole Country Churchhouse	1954	$30
☐ 4-21247	Out Behind the Barn/Closing Time	1954	$30
☐ 4-42663	Police Police/Running Into Memories of You	1963	$15
☐ 4-21384	Salty Boogie/A Ribbon and a Rose	1955	$30
☐ 4-21093	Sidemeat and Cabbage/Teardrops	1953	$40
☐ 4-20835	Sign on the Highway/ Galvanized Wash Tub	1951	$40
☐ 4-21068	Take My Hand, Precious Lord/I Shall Not Be Moved	1953	$40
☐ 4-20987	Take Up Thy Cross/ Just a Closer Walk	1952	$40
☐ 4-42013	Talking to the Wall/Farewell Party	1961	$15
☐ 3-10426	The Preacherman/ We're Gonna Make It	1976	$5
☐ 4-21159	Thick and Thin/Tomorrow Is Too Long	1953	$40
☐ 4-43040	Too Many Irons in the Fire/I Leaned Over Backwards	1964	$10
☐ 4-20976	Waitress, Waitress/They Don't Know Nothing at All	1952	$40
☐ 4-20722	Walk Chicken Walk/Just When I Needed You	1950	$40
☐ 4-21434	We Could/When They Get Too Rough	1955	$30
☐ 4-21038	Wedding Bell Waltz/You Don't Have Love at All	1952	$40
☐ 4-20744	When the Love Bug Bites You/Out of Business	1950	$40
☐ 4-43514	When the Ship Hit the Sand/ Truck Load of Starvin' Kangaroos	1966	$10
☐ 4-41340	When Your House Is Not a Home/The Honeymoon Is Over	1959	$20

| ☐ 4-43804 | Where the Buffalo Trod/ Butter Beans | 1966 | $8 |
| ☐ 4-43701 | Who Licked the Red Off Your Candy/You Don't Have Time for Me | 1966 | $10 |

STARDAY
| ☐ 979 | Dead Skunk/Alabam | 1973 | $6 |

UNITED ARTISTS
☐ 50941	Alabam/Someone to Care	1972	$6
☐ 50730	Everyday Family Man/ One More Time	1970	$6
☐ 50781	Here It Comes Again/ There'll Be Love	1971	$6
☐ 50889	Try It, You'll Like It/Helpless	1972	$6
☐ 50834	What Will I Do Then/You Only Want Me for My Baby	1971	$6

DICKENS, RICKY
HIT
| ☐ 164 | Ballad of Daniel Boone/ Legend of Daniel Boone | 1964 | $8 |

— B-side by Charlie Brown

| ☐ 102 | Daisy Petal Pickin'/ Hey Little Cobra | 1964 | $8 |

— B-side by the Roamers

| ☐ 79 | If I Had a Hammer/Hey Girl | 1963 | $8 |

— B-side by Leroy Jones

| ☐ 98 | Midnight Mary/Drip Drop | 1963 | $8 |

— B-side by Ed Hardin

| ☐ 85 | Sugar Shack/Hello Heartache, Goodbye Love | 1963 | $8 |

— B-side by Connie Dee

DICKERSON, DUB
CAPITOL
☐ F2821	Count Me In/You Started It All	1954	$30
☐ F2719	Mama Laid the Law Down/ Everything Depends on You	1954	$30
☐ F2947	My Gal Gertie/Look, Look, Look	1954	$30
☐ F2605	One Night Stand/Dear Love	1953	$30
☐ F2504	The Bells of Monterrey/ Sweet Bunch of Bitterreeds	1953	$30

DECCA
| ☐ 9-46353 | If I Had You Back/Just in Time to Be Too Late | 1951 | $30 |
| ☐ 9-46329 | Money Talks/Chinchie Hotel | 1951 | $30 |

SIMS
| ☐ 127 | It's About to Get Me Down/ Name Your Price | 1962 | $30 |
| ☐ 106 | Shot Gun Wedding/Each Time | 1956 | $30 |

TODD
| ☐ 1053 | The Bottle/Mama Laid the Law Down | 1960 | $20 |

DICKIES, THE
Famously covered BLACK SABBATH'S "Paranoid."

A&M
☐ 2241	Banana Splits (The Tra La La Song)/Sounds of Silence	1980	$12
☐ 2241 [PS]	Banana Splits (The Tra La La Song)/Sounds of Silence	1980	$12
☐ 2092	Silent Night/Sounds Of Silence	1978	$10

— All copies on white vinyl

| ☐ 2092 [PS] | Silent Night/Sounds Of Silence | 1978 | $10 |
| ☐ 2092 [DJ] | Silent Night/Sounds Of Silence | 1978 | $8 |

— All copies on white vinyl

DICKINSON, HAL
CORAL
| ☐ 9-61536 | Merry Christmas Baby/Tenderly | 1955 | $20 |

DICKS, THE
7-Inch Extended Plays
RADICAL
☐ RRR D-2	Peace?	1984	$8
☐ RRR D-2 [PS]	Peace?	1984	$8
☐ RRR D-1	The Dicks Hate the Police	1979	$60
☐ RRR D-1 [PS]	The Dicks Hate the Police	1979	$60

DICKY DOO AND THE DON'TS
ASCOT
| ☐ 2178 | Click Clack '65/Don't Count Me Out | 1965 | $10 |

SWAN
☐ 4033	Ballad of a Train/Dear Heart, Don't Cry	1959	$30
☐ 4001	Click Clack/Did You Cry	1958	$30
☐ 4014	Leave Me Alone (Let Me Cry)/Wild Party	1959	$30
☐ 4025	Teardrops Will Fall/Come with Us	1959	$30
☐ 4046	Wabash Cannonball/The Drums of Richard A. Doo	1960	$30

UNITED ARTISTS
| ☐ 238 | Teen Scene/Pity, Pity | 1960 | $30 |

DICTATORS, THE
ASYLUM
☐ 45420	Disease/Hey Boys	1977	$12
☐ 45523	I Stand Tall/Two Much Fun	1978	$10
☐ 45470	Science Has Gone Too Far/ Sleepin' with the T.V. On	1978	$10

DIDDLEY, BO
CHECKER
☐ 1123	500% More Man/Let the Kids Dance	1965	$20
☐ 1200	Another Sugardaddy/I'm High Again	1968	$20
☐ 1213	Bo Diddley 1969/Soul Train	1969	$15
☐ 814	Bo Diddley/I'm a Man	1955	$60
☐ 997	Bo Diddley/I'm a Man	1961	$30
☐ 1168	Bo-Ga-Loo Before You Go/ Wrecking My Love Life	1967	$20
☐ 907	Bo Meets the Monster/ Willie and Lillie	1958	$40
☐ 1089	Bo's Beat/Chuck's Beat	1964	$30

— B-side by Chuck Berry

☐ 850	Cops and Robbers/ Down Home Special	1956	$50
☐ 924	Crackin' Up/The Great Grandfather	1959	$30
☐ 896	Dearest Darling/Hush Your Mouth	1958	$30
☐ 819	Diddley Daddy/She's Fine, She's Mine	1955	$70

— A-side backing vocals: The Moonglows

☐ 832	Diddy Wah Diddy/I Am Looking for a Woman	1956	$60
☐ 965	Gun Slinger/Signifying	1960	$30
☐ 1098	Hey, Good Lookin'/You Ain't Bad	1965	$20
☐ 860	Hey! Bo Diddley/Mona	1957	$60

— Originals of Checker 816-860 have "Checker" over a checkerboard on top of label

☐ 914	I'm Sorry/Oh Yeah	1959	$30
☐ 1058	Memphis/Monkey Diddle	1963	$30
☐ 1158	Ooh Baby/Back to School	1966	$20
☐ 985	Pills/Call Me	1961	$40
☐ 827	Pretty Thing/Bring It to Jerome	1955	$60
☐ 878	Say! Boss Man/Before You Accuse Me	1957	$30
☐ 936	Say Man, Back Again/ She's Alright	1959	$30
☐ 931	Say Man/Clock Strikes Twelve	1959	$40
☐ 931 [PS]	Say Man/Clock Strikes Twelve	1959	$400
☐ 1045	Surfers' Love Call/Greatest Lover in the World	1963	$30
☐ 1238	The Shape I'm In/Pollution	1970	$15
☐ 951	Walkin' and Talkin'/Crawdad	1960	$30
☐ 1142	We're Gonna Get Married/Do the Frog	1966	$20
☐ 842	Who Do You Love?/I'm Bad	1956	$50

— Note altered B-side title

| ☐ 842 | Who Do You Love/In Bad | 1956 | $70 |

CHESS
☐ 2129	Bo Diddley-Itis/Infatuation	1972	$10
☐ 2134	Bo-Jam/Husband-in-Law	1972	$10
☐ 2142	I Don't Want No Lyin' Woman/ Make a Hit Record	1973	$10
☐ 2117	I Love You More Than You'll Ever Know/I Said Shut Up Woman	1971	$10

PHILCO-FORD
| ☐ HP-33 | I'm a Man/Song of Bo Diddley | 1968 | $40 |

— 4-inch plastic "Hip Pocket Record" with color sleeve

7-Inch Extended Plays
CHESS
| ☐ 5125 [PS] | Bo Diddley | 1958 | $200 |
| ☐ 5125 | Bo Diddley/I'm a Man/Willie and Lillie/Bo Meets the Monster | 1958 | $120 |

DIESEL
REGENCY
☐ 7403	Down to the Sunshine	1982	$3
☐ 7343	Goin' Back to China/The Harness	1981	$3
☐ 7339	Sausalito Summernight/Bite Back	1981	$4
☐ 96001	Sausalito Summernight/Bite Back	1981	$6

— Original issue, distributed by MCA

DIETRICH, MARLENE
DECCA
| ☐ 32076 | Candles Glowing/ This World Of Ours | 1966 | $6 |

DIFFERENT SHADES OF BROWN
TAMLA
| ☐ 54219 | Label Me Love/Life's a Ball | 1972 | $5 |

DIFFORD AND TILBROOK
A&M
| ☐ 2675 | Love's Crashing waves/ Action Speaks Faster | 1984 | $3 |
| ☐ 2648 | Picking Up the Pieces/ Within These Walls | 1984 | $3 |

Number	Title	Yr	NM
DILCHER, CHERYL			
A&M			
❏ 1378	Can't Get Enough of You (My Man)/Good Morning World	1972	$10
❏ 1464	Deep Down Inside/Rainbow Farm	1973	$12
❏ 1601	The Good Times/Together	1974	$15
BUTTERFLY			
❏ CM1202	Lovin' Woman/Follow the Love	1977	$8
❏ CM1202 [PS]	Lovin' Woman/Follow the Love	1977	$8
DILL, DANNY			
ABC-PARAMOUNT			
❏ 9734	I'm Hungry for Your Lovin'/The Stranger of Abilene	1956	$60
❏ 9681	My Girl and His Girl/Geisha Sweetheart	1956	$40
CUB			
❏ 9045	He's Biding His Time/He Ain't Gonna Study War	1959	$30
DILLARD, VARETTA			
CUB			
❏ 9083	Little Bitty Tear/Mercy Mr. Percy	1961	$15
❏ 9073	Teaser/I Know I'm Good for You	1960	$15
GROOVE			
❏ 0139	Darling, Listen to the Words of This Song/Mama Don't Want (What Poppa Don't Want)	1956	$50
❏ 0152	Gonna Tell My Daddy/Cherry Blossom	1956	$30
❏ 0159	Got You On My Mind/Skinny Jimmy	1956	$30
❏ 0167	I Miss You Jimmy/If You Want to Be My Baby	1956	$30
❏ 0177	One More Time/I Can't Help Myself	1956	$30
RCA VICTOR			
❏ 47-6869	Pray for Me Mother/Leave a Happy Fool Alone	1957	$30
❏ 47-7144	Star of Fortune/The Blues of Love	1958	$30
❏ 47-6936	Time Was/I Got a Lot of Love	1957	$30
❏ 47-7285	What'll I Do/Just Multiply	1958	$30
SAVOY			
❏ 847	Easy, Easy Baby/A Letter in Blue	1952	$50
❏ 839	Hurry Up/Please Tell Me Why	1952	$50
❏ 1118	I Ain't Gonna Tell/(That's the Way) My Mind Is Working	1953	$40
❏ 871	I Cried and Cried/Double Crossing Daddy	1952	$50
❏ 1166	I'll Never Forget You/I Can't Stop Now	1955	$40
❏ 851	I'm Yours/Here in My Heart	1952	$50
❏ 822	Love and Wine/Please Come Back to Me	1951	$60
❏ 897	Mercy, Mr. Percy/No Kinda Good No How	1953	$50
❏ 1137	Send Me Some Money/Love	1954	$40
❏ 884	Three Lies/Getting Ready for My Daddy	1953	$50
TRIUMPH			
❏ 608	Good Gravy Baby/Scorched	1959	$20
DILLARDS, THE			
ANTHEM			
❏ 51014	Billy Jack/America	1971	$5
❏ 101	It's About Time/One A.M.	1971	$5
CAPITOL			
❏ 5524	Lemon Chimes/The Last Thing on My Mind	1965	$8
ELEKTRA			
❏ 45681	Close the Door Lightly/Touch Her If You Can	1970	$8
❏ 45003	Dooley/Dong's Love	1964	$12
❏ 45006	Hootin' Banjo/Polly Vaughn	1964	$10
❏ 45661	Listen to the Sound/The Biggest Whatever	1969	$8
UNITED ARTISTS			
❏ XW382	Hot Rod Banjo/Love Has Gone Away	1974	$5
WHITE WHALE			
❏ 359	Comin' Home Again	1970	$6
❏ 351	One Too Many Mornings/Turn It Around	1970	$6
DILLINGHAM, CRAIG			
MCA CURB			
❏ 52406	1984/Neon Light Idea	1984	$4
❏ 52301	Have You Loved Your Woman Today/Every Man Should Have One	1983	$4
❏ 52352	Honky Tonk Women Make Honky Tonk Men/Slow Dancin' with Fast Women	1984	$4
DILLON, DEAN			
CAPITOL			
❏ 7PRO-79827	Back in the Swing of Things (same on both sides)	1989	$5
— Vinyl is promo only			

Number	Title	Yr	NM
❏ B-44294	Hey Heart/Appalachia Got to Have You Feelin' in My Bones	1988	$3
❏ B-44239	I Go to Pieces/Hard Time for Lovers	1988	$3
❏ B-44400	It's Love That Makes You Sexy/Appalachia Got to Have You Feelin' in My Bones	1989	$4
RCA			
❏ PB-13628	Famous Last Words of a Fool/Ten Years and Two Babies Later	1983	$4
❏ PB-11881	I'm Into the Bottle (To Get You Out of My Mind)/Tonight	1979	$4
❏ PB-13208	Play This Old Working Day Away/You Come Home To	1982	$4
❏ PB-12234	They'll Never Take Me Alive/Tonight One of Us Is Going Out of My Mind	1981	$4
❏ PB-12003	What Good Is a Heart/He's Number One	1980	$4
DILS, THE			
DANGERHOUSE			
❏ SLA268	198 Seconds of The Dils	1977	$30
❏ SLA268 [PS]	198 Seconds of The Dils	1977	$30
WHAT			
❏ 02	I Hate the Rich/You're Not Blank	1977	$18
❏ 02 [PS]	I Hate the Rich/You're Not Blank	1977	$23
—Dils" in block letters on cover			
❏ 02 [PS]	I Hate the Rich/You're Not Blank	1977	$18
—Dils" in angular letters on cover			
DIMPLES, THE			
CAMEO			
❏ 325	Dreaming of You/Please Don't Be Angry with Me	1964	$20
DORE			
❏ 517	An Invitation to a Party/My Sister's Beau	1959	$30
ERA			
❏ 1079	Gimme Jimmy/Toy Telephone	1958	$30
DINNALL, CARLTON			
BARNABY			
❏ ZS72026	A Long Way to Go/Child of the Springtime	1971	$8
❏ ZS72038	Gemini Girl/You're What's Been Missin' from My Life	1971	$8
DINNING, MARK			
CAMEO			
❏ 313	Should We Do It/Call Her Your Sweetheart	1964	$10
HICKORY			
❏ 1293	Dial AL1-4883/I'm Glad We Fell in Love	1965	$8
❏ 1368	Last Rose/There Stands a Lady	1966	$8
MGM			
❏ 12447	A Million Years Ago/Shameful Ways	1957	$30
❏ 13007	Another Lonely Girl/Can't Forget	1961	$20
❏ 12888	A Star Is Born (A Love Has Died)/You Win Again	1960	$30
❏ 12888 [PS]	A Star Is Born (A Love Has Died)/You Win Again	1960	$30
❏ 12732	Blackeyed Gypsy/Secretly in Love with You	1958	$30
❏ 12775	Cutie, Cutie/A Life of Love	1959	$30
❏ 13024	Lonely Island/Turn Me On	1961	$20
❏ 12553	School Fool/When You're Tired of Breaking Hearts	1957	$30
❏ 12958	She Cried On My Shoulder (When She Talked About You)/(Where Can You Hide Away) The World Is Getting Smaller	1960	$30
❏ 13091	She's Changed/I Catch Myself Crying	1962	$15
❏ 12845	Teen Angel/Bye Now Baby	1959	$30
❏ 12929	The Lovin' Touch/Come Back to Me (My Love)	1960	$30
❏ 12929 [PS]	The Lovin' Touch/Come Back to Me (My Love)	1960	$30
❏ 13061	The Pickup/All of This for Sally	1962	$20
❏ 13150	The Twelfth of Never/Somebody Catch Me Kissin' Mary	1963	$15
❏ 12980	Top Forty, News, Weather and Sports/Suddenly (There's Only You)	1961	$20
❏ 13048	What Will My Mary Say/In a Matter of Moments	1961	$20
UNITED ARTISTS			
❏ 50225	Hangin' On/Maggie (I Wish We'd Never Met)	1967	$8
❏ 50540	How Little Men Care/Lemon Yellow	1969	$8
❏ 50169	It's Such a Pretty World Today/Atlanta, Georgia Stray	1967	$8
❏ 50305	Throw a Little Love My Way/Dissatisfied Man	1968	$8
DINO AND SEMBELLO			
DATE			
❏ 2-1667	Imogene and Me/See the Light	1970	$8

Number	Title	Yr	NM
DINO AND THE DIPLOMATS			
LAURIE			
❏ 3103	I Can't Believe/My Dream	1961	$40
VIDA			
❏ 100/101	Hushabye My Love/Homework	1961	$40
❏ 102/103	Soft Wind/Such a Fool for You	1961	$40
DINO, DESI AND BILLY			
COLUMBIA			
❏ 4-44975	Hawley/Let's Talk It Over	1969	$15
REPRISE			
❏ 0544	If You're Thinkin' What I'm Thinkin'/Pretty Flamingo	1966	$8
❏ 0529	I Hope She's There Tonight/Josephine	1966	$8
❏ 0716	I'm a Fool/Not the Lovin' Kind	1968	$8
—Back to Back Hits" series; originals have both "W7" and "r:" logos			
❏ 0367	I'm a Fool/So Many Ways	1965	$15
❏ 0367 [PS]	I'm a Fool/So Many Ways	1965	$30
❏ 0462	It's Just the Way You Are/Tie Me Down	1966	$8
❏ 0965	Lady Love/A Certain Sound	1970	$40
—A-side is a Brian Wilson composition			
❏ 0496	Look Out Girls/She's So Far Out She's In	1966	$8
❏ 0653	My What a Shame/The Inside Outside Caspar Milquetoast Eskimo Flash	1967	$15
❏ 0653 [PS]	My What a Shame/The Inside Outside Caspar Milquetoast Eskimo Flash	1967	$30
❏ 0426	Please Don't Fight It/The Rebel Kind	1965	$10
❏ 0426 [PS]	Please Don't Fight It/The Rebel Kind	1965	$30
❏ 0444	Superman/I Can't Get Her Out of My Mind	1966	$8
❏ 0698	Tell Someone You Love Them/General Outline	1968	$15
❏ 0579	Two in the Afternoon/Good Luck, Best Wishes to You	1967	$10
❏ 0324	We Know/Since You Broke My Heart	1964	$20
UNI			
❏ 55127	Someday/Thru Spray Colored Glasses	1969	$15
DINO, KENNY			
COLUMBIA			
❏ 43062	Betty Jean/Show Me	1964	$30
MUSICOR			
❏ 1021	What Good Are Dreams/What Did I Do	1962	$20
SMASH			
❏ 1827	Time Will Tell/I Wanna Know	1963	$15
DINO, PAUL			
ENTRE			
❏ 101	I Like Your Style/Your Candy Kisses	1963	$20
PROMO			
❏ 2180	Ginnie Bell/Bye-Bye	1961	$10
UNITED ARTISTS			
❏ 481	That's How I Miss You/Tonight's the Night	1962	$100
DINOSAUR JR			
SST			
❏ 220	Freak Scene/Keep the Glove	1988	$10
—Large hole, clear vinyl			
❏ 220	Freak Scene/Keep the Glove	1988	$5
—Small hole, black vinyl			
❏ 220 [PS]	Freak Scene/Keep the Glove	1988	$5
DINU, RICHARD			
THEME			
❏ 122587	I'd Like To Be Your Santa Claus/(B-side unknown)	1987	$4
DIO, ANDY			
CRUSADE			
❏ 1023	Bonnie Jean/Rough and Bold	1961	$50
GONE			
❏ 5038	Daisy Belle/Hey Little Bluebird	1958	$60
JOY			
❏ 283	Daisy Belle/Some of These Days	1964	$50
MUSICOR			
❏ 1162	Dancing Bull/Sorrento	1966	$12
❏ 1118	Sass-Afrass/Shout	1965	$10

Number	Title	Yr	NM

DIO, RONNIE

ATLANTIC
Number	Title	Yr	NM
❏ 2145	The Ooh-Poo-Pah-Doo/Love Pains	1962	$125

KAPP
❏ 697	Say You're Mine Again/Where You Gonna Run To, Girl	1965	$60
❏ 725	Smiling by Day (Crying by Night)/Dear Darlin' (I Won't Be Comin' Home)	1965	$60
❏ 770	The Way of Love/Walking Alone	1966	$60

LAWN
| ❏ 218 | Swingin' Street/Gonna Make It Alone | 1963 | $200 |

PARKWAY
| ❏ 143 | Walking in Different Circles/Ten Days with Brenda | 1967 | $50 |

SENECA
| ❏ S 178-102 | An Angel Is Missing/What'd I Say? | 1959 | $200 |

— As "Ronnie Dio and the Red Caps

SWAN
| ❏ 4165 | Mr. Misery/Our Year | 1963 | $100 |

VALEX
| ❏ 001 | Love Potion No. 9 (same on both sides) | 1964 | $200 |

DION

ARISTA
| ❏ 9797 | And the Night Stood Still/Tower of Love | 1989 | $4 |
| ❏ 9797 [PS] | And the Night Stood Still/Tower of Love | 1989 | $4 |

BIG TREE/SPECTOR
| ❏ 16063 | Born to Be with You/Running Close Behind You | 1976 | $20 |

— Produced by Phil Spector

COLUMBIA
| ❏ 42810 | Be Careful of Stones That You Throw/I Can't Believe (That Don't Love Me Anymore) | 1963 | $20 |
| ❏ 42810 [DJ] | Be Careful of Stones That You Throw (same on both sides) | 1963 | $125 |

— Colored vinyl (some sources say blue, others red)

| ❏ (no #) [PS] | Dion Is Now on Columbia Records | 1962 | $60 |

— Promo-only sleeve issued with promos of Columbia 42662

| ❏ 42852 [DJ] | Donna the Prima Donna (same on both sides) | 1963 | $100 |

— Promo only on red vinyl

❏ 42852	Donna the Prima Donna/You're Mine	1963	$30
❏ 42917	Drip Drop/No One's Waiting for Me	1963	$20
❏ 44719	I Can't Help But Wonder Where I'm Bound/Southern Train	1968	$10
❏ 42977	I'm the Hoochie Coochie Man/The Road I'm On	1964	$20
❏ 42977 [PS]	I'm the Hoochie Coochie Man/The Road I'm On	1964	$50
❏ 43692	So Much Younger/Two-Ton Feather	1966	$20
❏ 43293	Spoonful/Kickin' Child	1965	$20
❏ 43213	Sweet Sweet Baby/Unloved, Unwanted Me	1965	$20
❏ 42776	This Little Girl/The Loneliest Man in the World	1963	$20
❏ 43483	Time in My Heart for You/Wake Up Baby	1965	$20
❏ 43423	Tomorrow Won't Bring the Rain/You Move Me Babe	1965	$20
❏ 43423 [PS]	Tomorrow Won't Bring the Rain/You Move Me Babe	1965	$200

LAURIE
❏ 3464	Abraham, Martin, and John/Daddy Rollin' (In Your Arms)	1968	$15
❏ 3225	After the Dance/Then I'll Be Tired of You	1964	$30
❏ 3171	Come Go with Me/King Without a Queen	1963	$30
❏ 3495	From Both Sides Now/Sun Fun Song	1969	$15
❏ 3081	Havin' Fun/Northeast End of the Corner	1961	$30
❏ 3081 [PS]	Havin' Fun/Northeast End of the Corner	1961	$60
❏ 3303	I Got the Blues/(I Was) Born to Cry	1965	$30
❏ 3134	Little Diane/Lost for Sure	1962	$30
❏ 3134 [PS]	Little Diane/Lost for Sure	1962	$50
❏ 3070	Lonely Teenager/Little Miss Blue	1960	$30
❏ 3070 [PS]	Lonely Teenager/Little Miss Blue	1960	$60
❏ 3187	Lonely World/Tag Along	1963	$30
❏ 3145	Love Came to Me/Little Girl	1962	$30
❏ 3123	Lovers Who Wander/(I Was) Born to Cry	1962	$30
❏ 3123 [PS]	Lovers Who Wander/(I Was) Born to Cry	1962	$50
❏ 3504	Loving You Is Sweeter Than Ever/He Looks a Lot Like Me	1969	$15
❏ 3478	Purple Haze/The Dolphins	1969	$15
❏ 3153	Sandy/Faith	1963	$30

❏ 3240	Shout/Little Girl	1964	$30
❏ 3101	Somebody Nobody Wants/Could Somebody Take My Place Tonight	1961	$30
❏ 3115 [M]	The Wanderer/The Majestic	1961	$30
❏ 3115 [PS]	The Wanderer/The Majestic	1961	$50
❏ 3115 [S]	The Wanderer/The Majestic	1961	$60

— "Stereo" in white area at right of label

| ❏ 3115 [M] | The Wanderer/The Majestic | 1979 | $10 |

— Reissue on regular Laurie label with "From the Orion Motion Picture 'The Wanderers'" on label

LIFESONG
❏ 45082	Fire in the Night/Street Mama	1980	$30
❏ 1765	Heart of Saturday Night/You've Awakened Something in Me	1978	$6
❏ 1785	(I Used to Be a) Brooklyn Dodger/Streetheart Theme	1979	$6
❏ 1770	Midtown American Main Street Gang/Guitar Queen	1978	$6

WARNER BROS.
❏ 7704	Doctor Rock and Roll/Sunshine Lady	1973	$12
❏ 8234	Hey My Love/Lover Boy Supreme	1976	$6
❏ 7469	Let It Be/Close to It All	1970	$12
❏ 8293	Oh the Night/Queen of '59	1976	$6
❏ 7537	Sanctuary/Brand New Morning	1971	$10
❏ 7537 [PS]	Sanctuary/Brand New Morning	1971	$30
❏ 7663	Seagull/Running Close Behind You	1972	$10
❏ PRO-537 [DJ]	Seagull/Soft Parade	1972	$20
❏ PRO-814 [DJ]	The Wanderer (same on both sides)	1979	$20
❏ 8258	The Way You Do the Things You Do/Lover Boy Supreme	1976	$6

WARNER/SPECTOR
| ❏ 0403 | Make the Woman Love Me/Running Close Behind You | 1975 | $20 |

— Produced by Phil Spector

DION AND THE BELMONTS

ABC
| ❏ 10896 | For Bobbie/Movin' Man | 1967 | $15 |
| ❏ 10868 | My Girl the Month of May/Berimbau | 1966 | $15 |

LAURIE
❏ 3027 [M]	A Teenager in Love/I've Cried Before	1959	$30
❏ S-3027 [S]	A Teenager in Love/I've Cried Before	1959	$60
❏ 3021	Don't Pity Me/Just You	1958	$30
❏ 3035	Every Little Thing I Do/A Lover's Prayer	1959	$30
❏ 3035 [PS]	Every Little Thing I Do/A Lover's Prayer	1959	$60
❏ 3059	In the Still of the Night/A Funny Feeling	1960	$30
❏ 3059 [PS]	In the Still of the Night/A Funny Feeling	1960	$60
❏ 3013	I Wonder Why/Teen Angel	1958	$70

— Gray label

| ❏ 3013 | I Wonder Why/Teen Angel | 1958 | $40 |

— Light blue label

| ❏ 3013 | I Wonder Why/Teen Angel | 1958 | $30 |

— Black, red and white label

❏ 3052	When You Wish Upon a Star/Wonderful Girl	1960	$30
❏ 3052 [PS]	When You Wish Upon a Star/Wonderful Girl	1960	$60
❏ 3044	Where or When/That's My Desire	1959	$30
❏ 3044 [PS]	Where or When/That's My Desire	1959	$60

MOHAWK
| ❏ 107 | Tag Along/We Went Away | 1957 | $70 |
| ❏ 106 | Teenage Clementine/Santa Margarita | 1957 | $70 |

— May be listed as "The Belmonts"

7-Inch Extended Plays

LAURIE
❏ EP-301 [PS]	Dion and the Belmonts: Their Hits	1959	$200
❏ EP-301	I Wonder Why/No One Knows//Don't Pity Me/A Teenager in Love	1959	$120
❏ 302 [PS]	Where or When	1959	$175
❏ 302	Where or When/You Better Not Do That/Wonderful Girl/That's My Desire	1959	$125

DION AND THE TIMBERLANES

JUBILEE
| ❏ 5294 | The Chosen Few/Out in Colorado | 1957 | $40 |

MOHAWK
| ❏ 105 | The Chosen Few/Out in Colorado | 1957 | $70 |

DIONNE AND FRIENDS

ARISTA
| ❏ 9422 [PS] | That's What Friends Are For/Two Ships Passing in the Night | 1985 | $3 |
| ❏ 9422 | That's What Friends Are For/Two Ships Passing in the Night | 1985 | $3 |

DIPPERS QUINTET, THE

FLAYR
| ❏ 500 | It's Almost Christmas/Look What I've Found | 1955 | $4000 |

— VG 2000; VG+ 3000

DIRE STRAITS
Also see MARK KNOPFLER.

WARNER BROS.
❏ 7-29880	Industrial Disease/Badges, Posters, Stickers, T-Shirts	1982	$8
❏ 49006	Lady Writer/Where Do You Think You're Going	1979	$6
❏ 49006 [PS]	Lady Writer/Where Do You Think You're Going	1979	$6
❏ 7-28950 [DJ]	Money for Nothing (Edit 4:05)/(Long Edit 4:38)	1985	$8
❏ 7-28950	Money for Nothing/Love Over Gold (Live)	1985	$4
❏ 7-28950 [PS]	Money for Nothing/Love Over Gold (Live)	1985	$5
❏ 49082 [DJ]	Once Upon a Time in the West (Edit 3:00)/(Long Version 5:24)	1979	$8
❏ 49082	Once Upon a Time in the West/News	1979	$30
❏ 49632	Skateaway/Solid Rock	1980	$5
❏ 49632 [PS]	Skateaway/Solid Rock	1980	$5
❏ 7-28789	So Far Away/If I Had You	1986	$3
❏ 7-28789 [PS]	So Far Away/If I Had You	1986	$3
❏ 8736RE-1 [DJ]	Sultans of Swing (Long Version 5:49)/(Edit 4:44)	1979	$8

— Contains LP version (master number "WAA 8382 S") and edit of LP version (master number "WAA 8382 V1S DJ")

| ❏ 8736 [DJ] | Sultans of Swing (Long Version 5:52)/(Edit 4:38) | 1979 | $10 |

— Contains demo version (master number "WAA 8510 S") and edit of demo version (master number is "WAA 8510 V1S"); this was quickly changed to the LP version; we know of no stock copies with the "WAA 8510 S" master number

| ❏ 8736 | Sultans of Swing/Southbound Again | 1979 | $6 |

— Burbank/palm trees label; labels we've seen don't have the "RE-1" though the disc plays the 5:49 LP version (master number is "WAA 8382 S"); erroneous "Produced by Dire Straits" credit on A-side

| ❏ 8736RE-1 | Sultans of Swing/Southbound Again | 1979 | $5 |

— White label; contains 5:49 LP version (master number on A-side is "WAA 8382 S"); "Produced by Dire Straits" on A-side label in error

| ❏ 8736RE-1 | Sultans of Swing/Southbound Again | 1979 | $4 |

— With white label; contains 5:49 LP version (master number on A-side is "WAA 8382 S"); "Produced by Muff Winwood" on A-side label

❏ 7-29706	Twisting by the Pool/Badges, Posters, Stickers, T-Shirts	1983	$8
❏ 7-28878	Walk of Life/One World	1985	$3
❏ 7-28878 [PS]	Walk of Life/One World	1985	$3
❏ 7-29013	Walk of Life/One World	1985	$10

DIRKSEN, SENATOR EVERETT MCKINLEY

CAPITOL
❏ 5805	Gallant Men/The New Colossus	1966	$6
❏ 5805 [PS]	Gallant Men/The New Colossus	1966	$8
❏ 5912	Man Is Not Alone/The Shepherd and His Flock	1967	$5
❏ 2034	The First Time the Christmas Story Was Told/I Heard the Bells on Christmas Day	1967	$8

DIRTY BLUES BAND, THE

BLUESWAY
| ❏ 61016 | Hound Dog/New Orleans Woman | 1968 | $8 |

DISCO-TEX AND THE SEX-O-LETTES

CHELSEA
❏ 3045	Dancin' Kid (Part I)/Dancin' Kid (Part II)	1976	$4
❏ 3004	Get Dancin' (Part I)/Get Dancin' (Part II)	1974	$4
❏ 3040	Hot Lava/Hot Lava 2	1976	$4
❏ 3015	I Wanna Dance Wit'choo (Part I)/I Wanna Dance Wit'choo (Part II)	1975	$4
❏ 3054	Strollin'/We're Havin' a Party (It's Gonna Be Alright)	1976	$4
❏ 3070	Wooly Bully/On Broadway	1977	$4

DISENTRI, TURNER

TOPIX
| ❏ 6001 | 10,000,000 Tears/Spanish Lace | 1961 | $125 |

DISNEYLAND BOYS' CHOIR, THE

BUENA VISTA
| ❏ 449 | Silent Night/It's a Small World | 1965 | $20 |

Number	Title	Yr	NM

DISPOTA SISTERS, THE
VERVE
❑ 10188	Whistling 'Neath the Mistletoe/Willie Claus	1959	$20

DISTANTS, THE
NORTHERN
❑ 3732	Come On/Always	1960	$600

WARWICK
❑ 577	Always/Open Up Your Heart	1960	$125
❑ 546	Come On/Always	1960	$125

DIVINYLS
CHRYSALIS
❑ VS443241	Hey Little Boy/Fighting	1988	$4
❑ VS443241 [PS]	Hey Little Boy/Fighting	1988	$4
❑ VS442673	Only Lonely/Ring Me Up	1983	$5
❑ VS442916	Pleasure and Pain/Heart Telegraph	1985	$4
❑ VS442916 [PS]	Pleasure and Pain/Heart Telegraph	1985	$5

EVATONE
❑ 15	Boys in Town/Science Fiction	1982	$8

—*Flexi-disc included with Trouser Press magazine*

DIXIANA
GRAND PRIZE
❑ 5204	Bein' Here with You/Livin' in the Country	1983	$6
❑ 5200	Dixie Anna/Livin' in the Country	1982	$6
❑ 5209	Second Fiddle in the Band/Bein' Here with You	1983	$6

SOUNDWAVES
❑ 4779	Spirit of the Land (The Hay Song)/I Surrender	1987	$6

DIXIE BLUES BOYS
FLAIR
❑ 1072	My Baby Left Town/Monte Carlo My Baby Left Town/Monte Carlo	1955	$300

DIXIE CUPS, THE
ABC
❑ 10855	Love Ain't So Bad (After All)/Daddy Said No	1966	$15

ABC-PARAMOUNT
❑ 10755	A-B-C Song/That's What the Kids Said	1965	$15
❑ 10715	I'm Not the Kind of Girl (To Marry)/What Goes Up Must Go Down	1965	$15
❑ 10692	That's Where It's At/Two-Way-Poc-A-Way	1965	$15

ANTILLES
❑ 707	Iko Iko/Hey Hey (Indian's Coming)	1987	$4

—*B-side by The Wild Tchoupitoulas*

❑ 707 [PS]	Iko Iko/Hey Hey (Indian's Coming)	1987	$4

RED BIRD
❑ Oct-001	Chapel of Love/Ain't That Nice	1964	$40
❑ Oct-0032	Gee, the Moon Is Shining Bright/I'm Gonna Get You Yet	1965	$30
❑ Oct-0024	Iko Iko/Gee, Baby, Gee	1965	$30
❑ Oct-0024	Iko Iko/I'm Gonna Get You Yet	1965	$30
❑ Oct-0017	Little Bell/Another Boy Like Me	1964	$30
❑ Oct-006	People Say/Girls Can Tell	1964	$30

DIXIEBELLES, THE
SOUND STAGE 7
❑ 2507	(Down at) Papa Joe's/Rock, Rock, Rock	1963	$12
❑ 2517	Southtown U.S.A./Why Don't You Set Me Free	1964	$10

DIXIES, THE
AUTUMN
❑ 12	He's Got You/Geisha Girl	1965	$20

DIXON, FLOYD
ALADDIN
❑ 3121	Blues for Cuba/Bad Neighborhood	1952	$200
❑ 3101	Do I Love You/Time and Place	1951	$200

—*Earlier Floyd Dixon 45s on Aladdin may exist*

❑ 3196	Lovin'/Married Woman	1953	$200
❑ 3151	Tired, Broke and Busted/Come Back Baby	1952	$200
❑ 3111	Too Much Jelly Roll/Baby, Let's Go to the Woods	1952	$200
❑ 3135	Wine, Wine, Wine!/Call Operator 210	1952	$200

CASH
❑ 1057	Oh Baby/Never Can Tell	1957	$60

CAT
❑ 114	Hey Bartender/It Is True	1955	$70

❑ 106	Moonshine/Roll Baby Roll	1954	$70

CHATTAHOOCHIE
❑ 652	Tell Me, Tell Me/There Goes My Heart	1964	$10

CHECKER
❑ 857	Alarm Clock Blues/I'm Ashamed of Myself	1957	$40

DODGE
❑ 807	Opportunity Blues/Daisy	1961	$20

EBB
❑ 105	What Is Life Without a Home/Oh-Ee Little Girl	1957	$40

IMPERIAL
❑ 5849	Tired, Broke and Busted/Call Operator 210	1962	$15

KENT
❑ 311	Change Your Mind/Dance the Thing	1958	$30

SPECIALTY
❑ 468	Hard Living Alone/Please Don't Go	1953	$100

—*Black vinyl*

❑ 468	Hard Living Alone/Please Don't Go	1953	$200

—*Red vinyl*

❑ 477	Hole in the Wall/Old Memories	1953	$100
❑ 486	Ooh-Eee Ooh-Eee/Nose Job	1954	$100

SWINGIN'
❑ 626	Tight Skirts/Wake Up and Live	1960	$30

DJINNS SINGERS
ABC PARAMOUNT
❑ 10281	Pour Noel (For Christmas)/Minuit, Chretiens (O, Holy Night)	1961	$12

DMZ
Features Jeff "Mono Man" Conolly, later of THE LYRES.

DO-RE-MI CHILDREN'S CHORUS, THE
KAPP
❑ 2071	Do You Know How Christmas Trees Are Grown?/The Wonderful Things (That He Can Do)	1969	$6
❑ 627 [PS]	Silver and Gold/Do You Hear What I Hear	1964	$10
❑ 627	Silver and Gold/Do You Hear What I Hear	1964	$8

DOBKINS, CARL, JR.
ATCO
❑ 6283	If Teardrops Were Diamonds/I'm So Sorry Little Girl	1964	$15

CHALET
❑ 1053	Days of Sand and Shovel/Linda the Motel Maid	1969	$12
❑ 1056	My Heart Is an Open Book/Pictures	1969	$10

COLPIX
❑ 762	His Loss Is My Gain/A Little Bit Later On Down the Line	1965	$15

DECCA
❑ 31353	Ask Me No Questions/Promise Me	1962	$20
❑ 31143	Different Kind of Love/Genie	1960	$20
❑ 31088	Exclusively Yours/One Little Girl	1960	$20
❑ 31088 [PS]	Exclusively Yours/One Little Girl	1960	$40
❑ 30656	Love Is Everything/If You Don't Want My Lovin'	1958	$30
❑ 31182	Lovelight/Take Time Out	1960	$20
❑ 31020	Lucky Devil/In My Heart	1959	$30
❑ 31020 [PS]	Lucky Devil/In My Heart	1959	$40
❑ 30803	My Heart Is an Open Book/My Pledge to You	1959	$30
❑ 31260	Pretty Little Girl in the Yellow Dress/That's What I Call True Love	1961	$20
❑ 31301	Sawdust Dolly/A Chance to Belong	1961	$20

FRATERNITY
❑ 794	That's Why I'm Asking/Take Hold of My Hand	1958	$40

7-Inch Extended Plays
DECCA
❑ ED2664 [PS]	My Heart Is An Open Book	1959	$50
❑ ED2664	My Heart Is An Open Book/My Pledge to You//Love Is Everything/If You Don't Want My Lovin'	1959	$50

DOBRO, LON
4 STAR
❑ 1754	I Just Like You/All the Time	1961	$70

DOBSON, ANITA
PARLOPHONE
❑ RS6172	I Dream Of Christmas/Silly Christmas	1987	$6

—*U.K. import*

❑ RS6172 [PS]	I Dream Of Christmas/Silly Christmas	1987	$6

—*U.K. import; cardboard stock sleeve*

❑ RS6172 [PS]	I Dream Of Christmas/Silly Christmas	1987	$6

—*U.K. import; paper stock sleeve*

DOC HOLLIDAY
METROMEDIA
❑ 68-0114	Whiskey Lady/Magga Blue	1973	$8

DOCKETT, JIMMY
HULL
❑ 769	Merry Christmas Mother/Season's Greetings	1964	$10

DOCTOR AND THE MEDICS
I.R.S.
❑ 52970	Burn/Barbara Can't Dance	1986	$4
❑ 52970 [PS]	Burn/Barbara Can't Dance	1986	$6
❑ 53129	Burning Love/Waterloo	1987	$6
❑ 53228	More/Stare Crazy	1987	$10
❑ 52880	Spirit in the Sky/Laughing at the Pieces	1986	$4
❑ 52880 [PS]	Spirit in the Sky/Laughing at the Pieces	1986	$6

DR. BUZZARD'S ORIGINAL SAVANNAH BAND
ELEKTRA
❑ 46607	Didn't I Love You Girl/The Seven Year Itch	1980	$4

RCA
❑ PB-10762	I'll Play the Fool/Sunshower	1976	$4
❑ PB-11239	Mister Love//Transistor Madness/Future D.J.	1978	$4
❑ GB-11325	Whispering/Cherchez La Femme/ Se Si Bon//I'll Play the Fool	1978	$3

—*Gold Standard Series reissue*

❑ PB-10827	Whispering/Cherchez La Femme/Se Si Bon//Sunshower	1976	$4

DR. FEELGOOD AND THE INTERNS
COLUMBIA
❑ 43372	Doctor of Love/Let the House Rock On	1965	$8
❑ 43615	Where Did You Go/Don't Tell Me No Dirty	1966	$8

OKEH
❑ 7153	Bald Headed Lena/What's Up Doc	1962	$15
❑ 7161	Let's Have a Good Time Tonight/The Same Old Things Keep Happening	1962	$15
❑ 7144	Mr. Moonlight/Dr. Feel-Good	1962	$15
❑ 7167	My Gal Jo/Bald Headed Lena	1963	$15
❑ 7185	The Doctor's Boogie/Blang Dong	1963	$15

DR. HOOK
CAPITOL
❑ 4280	A Little Bit More/A Couple More Years	1976	$5
❑ 4677	All the Time in the World/Dooley Jones	1979	$4
❑ 4785	Better Love Next Time/Mountain Mary	1979	$4
❑ 4615	I Don't Want to Be Alone Tonight/You Make My Pants Want to Get Up and Dance	1978	$4
❑ 4364	If Not You/Bad Eye Bill	1976	$4
❑ SPRO-8220/1 [DJ]	Interview Record for Use in Promoting the Album Release of "Bankrupt"	1975	$8
❑ 4081	Levitate/Cooky and Lila	1975	$4
❑ 4534	Making Love and Music/Who Dat	1978	$4
❑ 4171	Only Sixteen/Let Me Be Your Lover	1975	$5
❑ 4831	Sexy Eyes/Help Me Mama	1980	$4
❑ 4621	Sharing the Night Together/You Make My Pants Want to Get Up and Dance	1978	$4
❑ 4104	The Millionaire/Cooky and Lila	1975	$4
❑ SPRO-8220/1 [PS]	The Stimu Dr. Hook	1975	$15
❑ 4423	Walk Right In/Sexy Energy	1977	$4
❑ 4705	When You're in Love with a Beautiful Woman/Knowing She's There	1979	$4

CASABLANCA
❑ 2347	Baby Makes Her Blue Jeans Talk/The Turn On	1981	$4
❑ 2347 [PS]	Baby Makes Her Blue Jeans Talk/The Turn On	1981	$5
❑ 2314	Girls Can Get It/Doin' It	1980	$4
❑ 2351	Loveline/Pity the Fool	1981	$4
❑ 2325	S.O.S. For Love/99 and Me	1981	$4

Number	Title	Yr	NM
COLUMBIA			
❏ 4-45667	Carry Me, Carrie/Call That True Love	1972	$5
❏ 4-45667 [PS]	Carry Me, Carrie/Call That True Love	1972	$6
❏ 4-45392	Last Morning/One More Ride (Lucille and Bunky)	1971	$6
❏ 4-45925	Life Ain't Easy/Wonderful Stone Soup	1973	$5
❏ 3-10032	Make It Easy/Ballad of Lucy Jordan	1974	$6

— All as "Dr. Hook and the Medicine Show

❏ 4-46026	Monterey Jack/Cops and Robbers	1974	$5
❏ 4-45562	Sylvia's Mother/Makin' It Natural	1972	$6

— Orange label with "Columbia" background print

❏ 4-45562	Sylvia's Mother/Makin' It Natural	1972	$5

— Gray label

❏ 4-45732	The Cover of "Rolling Stone"/Queen of the Silver Dollar	1972	$6

— Gray label

❏ 4-45732	The Cover of "Rolling Stone"/Queen of the Silver Dollar	1972	$5

— Orange label

DR. JOHN

Number	Title	Yr	NM
ACE			
❏ 611	Good Times/Sahara	1961	$30

— As "Mac Rebennack

A.F.O.			
❏ 309	The Point/One Naughty Flat	1962	$30

— As "Mac Rebennack

ATCO			
❏ 6957	(Everybody Wanna Get Rich) Rite Away/Mos'Scocious	1974	$6
❏ 6882	Iko Iko/The Huey Smith Medley	1972	$10
❏ 6607	I Walk on Gilded Splinters (Part 1)/I Walk on Gilded Splinters (Part 2)	1968	$15
❏ 6971	Let's Make a Better World/Me Minus You Equals Loneliness	1974	$6
❏ 6900	Let the Good Times Roll/Stack-A-Lee	1972	$6
❏ 6697	Patriotic Flag Waver (Long)/Patriotic Flag Waver (Short)	1969	$8
❏ 6937	Such a Night/Cold, Cold, Cold	1973	$6
❏ 6898	Wang Dang Doodle/Big Chief	1972	$6
❏ 6755	Wash, Mama, Wash/Loup Gardo	1970	$15
HORIZON			
❏ 117	Wild Honey/Dance the Night Away with You	1979	$4
RCA			
❏ PB-11285	Take Me Higher/Sweet Rider	1978	$4
REX			
❏ 1008	Storm Warning/Foolish Little Girl	1959	$60

— As "Mac Rebennack

SCEPTER			
❏ 12393	One Night Late/She's Just a Square	1974	$5
WARNER BROS.			
❏ 22976	Makin' Whoopee!/More Than You Know	1989	$3
❏ 22976 [PS]	Makin' Whoopee!/More Than You Know	1989	$3
❏ 49703	The Sailor and the Mermaid/One Good Turn	1981	$4

— A-side with Libby Titus; B-side by Al Jarreau

DOCTOR ROSS

Number	Title	Yr	NM
HI-Q			
❏ 5033	Call the Doctor/New York Breakdown	1963	$30
❏ 5027	Cannonball/Numbers Blues	1963	$30
SUN			
❏ 193	Chicago Breakdown/Come Back Baby	1954	$600
❏ 212	The Boogie Disease/Juke Box Boogie	1954	$2000

DR. STRANGE & THE LOVERS

Number	Title	Yr	NM
JAM			
❏ 105	Santa's Brother/Doc's Resolution	1962	$15

DR. WEST'S MEDICINE SHOW AND JUG BAND
Also see NORMAN GREENBAUM.

Number	Title	Yr	NM
GO GO			
❏ 102	Gondoliers, Shakespeares, Overseers, Playboys and Bums/Daddy, I Know	1967	$10
❏ 102 [PS]	Gondoliers, Shakespeares, Overseers, Playboys and Bums/Daddy, I Know	1967	$15
❏ 100	The Eggplant That Ate Chicago/You Can't Fight City Hall Blues	1966	$15
GREGAR			
❏ 106	Bullets Laverne/Jigsaw	1968	$10

Number	Title	Yr	NM
❏ 71-0100	Gondoliers, Shakespeares, Overseers, Playboys and Bums/Daddy, I Know	1969	$10

DODD, DICK

Number	Title	Yr	NM
ATTARACK			
❏ 102	Guilty/Requiem 820	1970	$10
TOWER			
❏ 490	Fanny/Don't Be Ashamed to Call My Name	1969	$15
❏ 447	Lonely Weekends/Little Sister	1968	$15
❏ 447 [PS]	Lonely Weekends/Little Sister	1968	$40

DODD, JIMMIE

Number	Title	Yr	NM
ABC-PARAMOUNT			
❏ 9680	Mickey Mouse Mambo/Humphrey Hop-Pussy Cat	1956	$30
❏ 9665	Mouseketeer Theme/Hi to You	1956	$30

DODD, KEN

Number	Title	Yr	NM
LIBERTY			
❏ 55733	All of My Life/Happiness	1964	$15
❏ 55893	Promises/Thank You for Being You	1966	$10
❏ 55835	Tears (For Souvenirs)/You and I	1965	$10
LONDON			
❏ 1942	Love Is Like a Violin/Treasure in My Heart	1960	$15

DODDS, MALCOLM

Number	Title	Yr	NM
AURORA			
❏ 3250	Ich Bin Verry Happy (Merry, Merry Christmas)/Perfect Strangers	1962	$10
DECCA			
❏ 30857	Deep Inside/Tremble	1959	$15
❏ 30970	I Feel Peculiar/Only for You	1959	$15
❏ 30766	I'll Always Be with You/This Is Real (This Is Love)	1958	$15
❏ 30922	I've Waited So Long/Somehow	1959	$15
❏ 30653	The Swingin' Platoon/Your Voice	1958	$15
END			
❏ 1004	Fools Rush In/Can't See You	1957	$100
❏ 1000	It Took a Long Time/Beauty and the Beast	1957	$70
❏ 1010	Tonight/Unspoken Love	1958	$70
MGM			
❏ 12975	All for the Love of a Woman/Come, Oh Come	1961	$10
❏ 13029	Without a Song/Laugh My Heart	1961	$10

DODDS, NELLA

Number	Title	Yr	NM
WAND			
❏ 187	Come Back Baby/Dream Boy	1965	$15
❏ 167	Come See About Me/You Don't Love Me Anymore	1964	$20
❏ 171	Finders Keepers Losers Weepers/A Girl's Life	1964	$15
❏ 1111	Gee Whiz/Maybe Baby	1966	$20
❏ 1136	Honey Boy/I Just Gotta Have You	1966	$100

DODGERS, THE

Number	Title	Yr	NM
ALADDIN			
❏ 3271	Drip Drop/Car Hop	1954	$500

DODO, JOE, AND THE GROOVERS

Number	Title	Yr	NM
RCA VICTOR			
❏ 47-7207	Groovy/Goin' Steady	1958	$30

DODSON, DARRELL

Number	Title	Yr	NM
SCR			
❏ 135	Lone Star Cowboy/(B-side unknown)	1977	$8
❏ 139	Love Song Sing Along/One More Time	1977	$8

DODSON, HERB

Number	Title	Yr	NM
STACY			
❏ 954	A Disc Jockey's Christmas Eve/What Is a Disc Jockey	1962	$20

DOGGETT, BILL

Number	Title	Yr	NM
ABC-PARAMOUNT			
❏ 10611	Mudcat/The Kicker	1965	$6
CHUMLEY			
❏ 90001	Blue Point of View/Funky Feet	1974	$4
COLUMBIA			
❏ 42384	Buster/Ladies Choice	1962	$10
❏ 42531	Oops/Choo Choo	1962	$10
❏ 42689	Soda Pop/Ham Fat	1963	$12
❏ 42792	The Worm/Hot Fudge	1963	$10
CORAL			
❏ 61739	A Pretty Girl Is Like a Melody/If I Should Lose You	1956	$15
KING			
❏ 5227	After Hours/Big City Drag	1959	$15

Number	Title	Yr	NM
❏ 5387	A Lover's Dream/Trav'lin' Light	1960	$10
❏ 5319	Back Woods/Raw Turkey	1960	$12
❏ 5339	Big Boy/Smoochie	1960	$12
❏ 5149	Birdie/Hold It	1958	$15
❏ 5125	Boo Da Ba/Pimento	1958	$15
❏ 5482	Bugle Nose/The Doodle	1961	$10
❏ 5364	Buttered Popcorn/The Slush	1960	$10
❏ 5044	Chloe/Number Three	1957	$15
❏ 5948	Crackers/That's Enough, Lock 'Em Up	1964	$8
❏ 5058	Ding Dong/Cling to Me	1957	$15
❏ 5740	Down Home Bossa Nova/Si Si Nova	1963	$8
❏ 5642	George Washington Twist/Eleven O'Clock Twist	1962	$8
❏ 5070	Hammer Head/Shindig	1957	$15
❏ 5561	High and Wide/In the Wee Hours	1961	$12
❏ 6350	High Heels/Zee	1971	$4
❏ 5096	Hippy Dippy/Flying Home	1957	$15
❏ 5684	Hometown Shout/For All We Know	1962	$8
❏ 4838	Honey Boy/Misty Moon	1955	$20
❏ 5718	Honky Tonk Bossa Nova (Part 2)/Ocean Liner Bossa Nova	1963	$8
❏ 4950	Honky Tonk (Part 1)/Honky Tonk (Part 2)	1956	$30
❏ 5444	Honky Tonk (Part 2)/Floyd's Guitar Blues	1961	$10
❏ 6239	Honky Tonk Popcorn/Honky Tonk	1969	$5
❏ 5001	Honky Tonk (Vocal)/Peacock Alley	1956	$20

— Vocal by Tommy Brown

❏ 5080	Hot Ginger/Soft	1957	$15
❏ 5130	How Could You/Blues for Handy	1958	$15
❏ 6356	In a Sentimental Mood/Eventide	1971	$4
❏ 4888	In a Sentimental Mood/Who's Who	1956	$20
❏ 4702	It's a Dream/The Song Is Ended	1954	$30
❏ 5101	Leaps and Bounds (Part 1)/Leaps and Bounds (Part 2)	1958	$15
❏ 5176	Monster Party/Scott's Bluff	1959	$15
❏ 4769	My Reverie/King Bee	1955	$20
❏ 4795	Oof/Street Scene	1955	$20
❏ 4548	Please Don't Ever Let Me Go/Glo' Glug	1952	$30
❏ 5419	Slidin'/Afternoon Jump	1960	$12
❏ 5000	Slow Walk/Hand in Hand	1956	$20
❏ 5310	Smokie Part 2/Evening Dreams	1960	$12
❏ 5957	Snuff Box/Blood Pressure	1964	$8
❏ 4917	Squashy/We Found Love	1956	$20
❏ 4720	Sweet Lorraine/Tailor Made	1954	$30
❏ 4732	Sweet Slumber/High Heels	1954	$30
❏ 6217	Take Your Shot/Mad	1969	$5
❏ 5138	Tanya/Blip Bop	1958	$15
❏ 4759	Tara's Theme/Gumbo	1955	$20
❏ 5665	Teardrops/Moon Dust	1962	$8
❏ 6019	Teardrops/Slidin'	1966	$6
❏ 4742	The Christmas Song/Winter Wonderland	1954	$30
❏ 5599	The Doodle Twist/Gene's Dream	1962	$8
❏ 5788	The Fog/Groovy Movie	1963	$8
❏ 5281	The Goofy Organ/Zee	1959	$15
❏ 5204	The Madison/Ocean Liner	1959	$15
❏ 4711	There's No You/Easy	1954	$30
❏ 6225	Twenty-Five Miles/For Once in My Life	1969	$5
❏ 4936	What a Difference a Day Makes/Stella by Starlight	1956	$20
❏ 4784	Wild Oats/I'll Be Around	1955	$20
ROULETTE			
❏ 4749	Lovin' Mood/The Funky Wrestler	1967	$6
❏ 4732	Sapphire/Ko-Ko	1967	$6
SUE			
❏ 10-002	Fat Back/Si Si Cisco	1968	$5
WARNER BROS.			
❏ 5209	Let's Do the Continental/Pony Walk	1961	$15

7-Inch Extended Plays

Number	Title	Yr	NM
KING			
❏ EP-395	*Alone/As Time Goes By/Dedicated to You/Sweet and Lovely	1957	$25
❏ EP-399	*Caravan/Solitude/I'm Just a Lucky So and So/Prelude to a Kiss	1958	$20
❏ EP-401	*C Jam Blues/Sophisticated Lady/Perdido/Satin Doll	1958	$20
❏ EP-396	*Dream/Don't Blame Me/This Love of Mine/Fools Rush In	1957	$25
❏ EP-259	*Early Bird/Percy Speaks/Ready Mix/Moon Dust	1954	$30
❏ EP-334	*Honey/It's a Dream/High Heels/Real Gone Mambo	1955	$30
❏ EP-392	*Honky Tonk Number Three/When Your Lover Has Gone/Big Boy/Nothin' Yet	1956	$25
❏ EP-394	*I Hadn't Anyone Till You/Yesterdays/A Cottage for Sale/As You Desire Me	1957	$25
❏ EP-400	*I Let a Song Go Out of My Heart/Don't Get Around Much Anymore/I Got It Bad and That Ain't Good	1958	$20
❏ EP-382	*I'll Be Around/Street Scene/You Don't Know What Love Is/Misty Moon	1956	$30
❏ EP-391	*Leaps and Bounds/On the Sunny Side of the Street/True Blue	1956	$25

Number	Title	Yr	NM
❑ EP-404	*Marcheta/Laura/ Jeannine/Estrellita	1958	$20
❑ EP-388	*Quaker City/Oof!/ Wild Oats/Shove Off	1956	$30
❑ EP-407	*Ram-Bunk-Shus/Cling to Me/Ding Dong/Chloe	1958	$20
❑ EP-403	*Ramona/Cynthia/ Tangerine/Nancy	1958	$20
❑ EP-393	*Slow Walk/Afternoon Jump/ Peacock Alley/Honey Boy	1956	$25
❑ EP-408	*Soft/Hammer Head/ Shindig/Hot Ginger	1958	$20
❑ EP-402	*Sweet Lorraine/Diane/ Dinah/Cherry	1958	$20
❑ EP-352	*Sweet Slumber/The Nearness of You/Gumbo/Tara's Theme	1955	$30
❑ EP-325	*The Song Is Ended/ Eventide/And the Angels Sing/Tailor Made	1955	$30
❑ EP-399 [PS]	A Salute to Ellington, Vol. 1	1958	$20
❑ EP-400 [PS]	A Salute to Ellington, Vol. 2	1958	$20
❑ EP-401 [PS]	A Salute to Ellington, Vol. 3	1958	$20
❑ EP-394 [PS]	As You Desire Me, Vol. 1	1957	$25
❑ EP-395 [PS]	As You Desire Me, Vol. 2	1957	$25
❑ EP-396 [PS]	As You Desire Me, Vol. 3	1957	$25
❑ EP-259 [PS]	Bill Doggett	1954	$30
❑ EP-334 [PS]	Bill Doggett, His Organ and Combo, Vol. 4	1955	$30
❑ EP-352 [PS]	Bill Doggett, His Organ and Combo, Vol. 5	1955	$30
❑ EP-391 [PS]	Bill Doggett, Vol. 1	1956	$25
❑ EP-325 [PS]	Bill Doggett, Vol. 2	1955	$30
❑ EP-392 [PS]	Bill Doggett, Vol. 2	1956	$25
❑ EP-393 [PS]	Bill Doggett, Vol. 3	1956	$25
❑ EP-402 [PS]	Dame Dreaming, Vol. 1	1958	$20
❑ EP-403 [PS]	Dame Dreaming, Vol. 2	1958	$20
❑ EP-404 [PS]	Dame Dreaming, Vol. 3	1958	$20
❑ EP-382 [PS]	Doggett Dreams	1956	$30
❑ EP-388 [PS]	Doggett Jumps	1956	$30
❑ EP-390 [PS]	Honky Tonk	1956	$35
❑ EP-390	Honky Tonk (Part 1)/Honky Tonk (Part 2)//Squashy/Who's Who	1956	$35
❑ EP-407 [PS]	Hot Doggett	1958	$20
❑ EP-408 [PS]	Soft	1958	$20

DOGS
DETROIT
❑ 01	Slash Your Face/Fed Up/Are You a Boy or Are You a Girl	1978	$70
❑ 01 [PS]	Slash Your Face/Fed Up/Are You a Boy or Are You a Girl	1978	$70

DOHENY, NED
ASYLUM
❑ 11024	On & On/I Know Sorrow	1973	$6
COLUMBIA
❑ 3-10438	A Love of Your Own/Valentine	1976	$6
❑ 3-10476	If You Should Fall/I've Got Your Number	1977	$6

DOHERLY, SID
CAMEO
❑ 497	Lonely Sounds/When the Lights Go Out Tonight	1967	$30

DOHERTY, DENNY
ABC
❑ 11318	To Claudia on Thursday/ Tuesday Morning	1972	$6
COLUMBIA
❑ 45779	Indian Girl/Baby Catch the Moon	1973	$5
❑ 45779 [PS]	Indian Girl/Baby Catch the Moon	1973	$20
❑ 45866	My Song/Indian Girl	1973	$5
PARAMOUNT
❑ 0286	Good Night and Good Morning/You'll Never Know	1974	$5
PLAYBOY
❑ 6066	Simone (mono/stereo)	1976	$5
—May be promo only

DOLAN, RAMBLIN' JIMMIE
CAPITOL
❑ F40261	All Alone in Texas/I'm Gonna Whittle You Down to My Size	1950	$50
❑ F2977	A Sailor's Letter/I Wonder If I Can Lose the Blues This Way	1954	$30
❑ F3254	Black Denim Trousers and Motorcycle Boots/ You Don't Love Me	1955	$30
❑ F2006	Got My Heart Set on You/ There's a Blue Sky Way	1952	$30
❑ F2244	Hot Rod Mama/Nicotine Fits	1952	$30
❑ F1322	Hot Rod Race/Walking with the Blues	1950	$40
❑ F2830	I'll Never Go Sailing Again/ Looka Here Baby	1954	$30
❑ F952	I'll Sail My Ship Alone/ It Had to Come	1950	$50
❑ F1371	Many's the Time/Lost Love Blues	1951	$40
❑ F2367	Playin' Dominoes and Shootin' Dice/Memories and Heartaches	1953	$30
❑ F1970	Stingy/Trade Winds Never Lie	1952	$30
❑ F1487	The Spider and the Fly/I'm Alone Because I Love You	1951	$40

Number	Title	Yr	NM
❑ F2482	The Wheel That Does the Squeaking/I Can't Run Away	1953	$30
❑ F2713	Tool Pusher on a Rotary Rig/ If I Could Look Inside You	1954	$30
❑ F1150	Wham Bam/I'll Hate Myself Tomorrow	1950	$40
❑ F40287	Who's Kiddin' Who/I Ain't Gonna Bring My Bacon Home to You	1950	$50
❑ F1423	Wine, Women and Pink Elephants/I Always Play a Losing Hand	1951	$40

DOLBY, THOMAS
CAPITOL
❑ 5374	Dissidents/Dissidents (Dub)	1984	$3
❑ 5374 [PS]	Dissidents/Dissidents (Dub)	1984	$3
❑ 5355	Dissidents/I Scare Myself	1984	$3
❑ 5238	Europa and the Pirate Twins/Radio Silence	1983	$3
❑ 5238 [PS]	Europa and the Pirate Twins/Radio Silence	1983	$3
❑ 5321	Hyperactive/Get Out of My Mix	1984	$3
❑ 5321 [PS]	Hyperactive/Get Out of My Mix	1984	$3
❑ 5204	She Blinded Me with Science/Flying North	1983	$4
—Not issued with picture sleeve in U.S.
EMI MANHATTAN
❑ 50125	Airhead/Budapest by Blimp	1988	$3
❑ 50125 [PS]	Airhead/Budapest by Blimp	1988	$3
❑ 50148	Hot Sauce/Salsa Picante	1988	$3
❑ 50148 [PS]	Hot Sauce/Salsa Picante	1988	$3
HARVEST
❑ 5155	Europa and the Pirate Twins/Radio Silence	1982	$12
❑ 5204	She Blinded Me with Science/Flying North	1983	$10
MCA
❑ 52868	Howard the Duck/ Don't Turn Away	1986	$3
—Credited to "Dolby's Cube"
❑ 52868 [PS]	Howard the Duck/ Don't Turn Away	1986	$3
—Credited to "Dolby's Cube"

DOLENZ, JONES, BOYCE & HART
CAPITOL
❑ 4271	Savin' My Love for You/I Love You (And I'm Glad I Said It)	1976	$10

DOLENZ, JONES & TORK
CHRISTMAS
❑ 700	Christmas Is My Time of Year/White Christmas	1976	$30
—B-side by Davy Jones; green label
❑ 700 [PS]	Christmas Is My Time of Year/White Christmas	1976	$50
—Actually an insert with the lyrics that came with the first edition
❑ 702/3	Christmas Is My Time of Year/White Christmas	1986	$30
—Reissue on gold label credited on both sides to "We Three Monkees"
❑ 702/3 [PS]	Christmas Is My Time of Year/White Christmas	1986	$50
—Actual picture sleeve rather than an insert; the order as listed on the sleeve is "Davy Jones, Micky Dolenz and Peter Tork

DOLENZ, MICKEY
BELL
❑ 986	Do It in the Name of Love/Lady Jane	1971	$60
—With Davy Jones; value is for stock copy (promos worth about 50% of this)
CHALLENGE
❑ 59353	Don't Do It/Plastic Symphony III	1967	$30
❑ 59353 [PS]	Don't Do It/Plastic Symphony III	1967	$50
❑ 59372	Huff Puff/(The Obvious) Fate	1967	$30
❑ 59372 [PS]	Huff Puff/(The Obvious) Fate	1967	$70
CHRYSALIS
❑ 2297	Alicia/Love Light	1979	$6
MGM
❑ 14395	A Lover's Prayer/Unattended in the Dungeon	1972	$30
❑ 14309	Easy on You/Oh Someone	1971	$30
ROMAR
❑ 715	Buddy Holly Tribute/ Ooh, Se's So Young	1974	$30
❑ 710	Daybreak/Love War	1973	$30

DOLLAR, JOHNNY
CHART
❑ 1057	Big Rig Rollin' Man/I've Gotta Stay High	1968	$8
❑ 1070	Big Wheels Sing for Me/Wild Cherry	1969	$8
❑ 5116	Highway in the Sky/ Gold Colored Glasses	1971	$8
❑ 5019	If I Get Low/Meeting of the Bored	1969	$8
❑ 5135	If I Make the Front Door Woman/Rain Falls in Denver	1971	$8
❑ 5035	Other Seeds to Sow/ Rain Falls in Denver	1969	$8
❑ 5049	Truck Driver's Lament/ Changing Her Thinking	1969	$8
COLUMBIA
❑ 4-43537	Stop the Start (Of Tears in My Heart)/You Ain't Wrong	1966	$10
❑ 4-43343	Tear Talk/Big Red (The Hound)	1965	$10
D
❑ 1185	Crawling Back to You/ (B-side unknown)	1961	$30
❑ 1229	Lonesome Trains/West Texas	1962	$30
❑ 1011	Walking Away/No Memories	1958	$30
DATE
❑ 1600	Do-Die/Forever Is Over	1968	$8
❑ 1585	Everybody's Got to Be Somewhere/Did You Talk to Him Today	1967	$8
❑ 1566	The Wheels Fell Off the Wagon Again/Watching Me Losing You	1967	$8
DOT
❑ 16961	Crazy Eyes/Windburn	1966	$8
GEMINI
❑ 1200	Do the Reindeer/Ringo	1964	$20

DOLLS, THE
MALTESE
❑ 107	The Aeroplane Song/A Lover's Stand	1965	$1200
—As "Norma Jenkins and the Dolls
❑ 100	This Is Our Day/What Next	1965	$70
OKEH
❑ 7122	In Love/Please Come Home	1959	$15

DOLLY AND THE FASHIONS
TRI DISC
❑ 111	Absence Made My Heart Grow Fonder/Waiting for My Man	1963	$15

DOMINGO, PLACIDO
CBS
❑ AE71237 [DJ]	I Heard the Bells on Christmas Day (same on both sides)	1981	$5
❑ AE71789 [DJ]	It's Christmas Time This Year (same on both sides)	1981	$5

DOMINO, FATS
ABC
❑ 10902	I Don't Want to Set the World on Fire/I'm Living Right	1967	$10
ABC-PARAMOUNT
❑ 10596	Heartbreak Hill/Kansas City	1964	$12
❑ 10545	If You Don't Know What Love Is/Something You Got, Baby	1964	$10
❑ ABCS455-1 [S]	I Got a Right to Cry/When I'm Walking (Let Me Walk)	1963	$30
—Small hole, plays at 33 1/3 rpm
❑ 10531	Lazy Lady/I Don't Want to Set the World on Fire	1964	$12
❑ 10644	Let Me Call You Sweetheart/ Goodnight Sweetheart	1965	$12
❑ 10567	Mary, Oh Mary/Packin' Up	1964	$10
❑ 10584	Sally Was a Good Old Girl/For You	1964	$10
❑ 10444	There Goes (My Heart Again)/ Can't Go On Without You	1963	$10
❑ 10475	When I'm Walking (Let Me Walk)/I've Got a Right to Cry	1963	$10
❑ 10512	Who Cares/Just a Lonely Man	1963	$10
❑ 10631	Why Don't You Do Right/Wigs	1965	$10
BROADMOOR
❑ 105	Big Mouth/Wait 'Til It Happens to You	1968	$30
❑ 104	The Lady in Black/Work My Way Up Steady	1967	$20
IMPERIAL
❑ X5348	Ain't It a Shame/La La	1955	$50
❑ X5357	All By Myself/Troubles of My Own	1955	$100
—Red label, script logo
❑ X5357	All By Myself/Troubles of My Own	1955	$30
—Red or maroon label, block logo
❑ X5283	Baby, Please/Where Did You Stay	1954	$70
❑ X5629	Be My Guest/I've Been Around	1959	$20
❑ X5629 [PS]	Be My Guest/I've Been Around	1959	$60
❑ X5407	Blueberry Hill/Honey Chile	1956	$30
—Black vinyl, red label
❑ X5407	Blueberry Hill/Honey Chile	1956	$200

Number	Title	Yr	NM
—Red vinyl			
X5407	Blueberry Hill/Honey Chile	1957	$20
—Black vinyl, black label			
X5417	Blue Monday/What's the Reason I'm Not Pleasing You	1957	$30
X5375	Bo Weevil/Don't Blame It on Me	1956	$30
X5645	Country Boy/If You Need Me	1960	$20
5875	Did You Ever See a Dream Walking/Stop the Clock	1962	$20
X5340	Don't You Know/Helping Hand	1955	$50
45-5231	Going to the River/Mardi Gras in New Orleans	1953	$125
—Black vinyl			
45-5231	Going to the River/Mardi Gras in New Orleans	1953	$500
—Red vinyl			
45-5180	Goin' Home/Reeling and Rocking	1952	$300
45-5209	How Long/Dreaming	1952	$100
—Black vinyl			
45-5209	How Long/Dreaming	1952	$300
—Red vinyl			
5909	Hum Diddy Doo/Those Eyes	1963	$20
66005	I Can't Give You Anything But Love/Goin' Home	1963	$15
X5323	I Know/Thinking of You	1955	$60
—Black vinyl			
X5323	I Know/Thinking of You	1955	$500
—Red vinyl			
X5386	I'm in Love Again/My Blue Heaven	1956	$30
X5585	I'm Ready/Margie	1959	$20
X5428	I'm Walkin'/I'm in the Mood for Love	1957	$30
—Maroon or red label			
X5428 [PS]	I'm Walkin'/I'm in the Mood for Love	1957	$60
5959	Isle of Capri/True Confession	1963	$20
5753	It Keeps Rainin'/I Just Cry	1961	$20
X5606	I Want to Walk You Home/I'm Gonna Be a Wheel Some Day	1959	$30
5764	Let the Four Winds Blow/Good Hearted Man	1961	$20
X5526	Little Mary/The Prisoner's Song	1958	$30
X5272	Little School Girl/You Done Me Wrong	1954	$70
X5313	Love Me/Don't You Hear Me Calling You	1954	$50
X5704	My Girl Josephine/Natural Born Lover	1960	$30
5833	My Real Name/My Heart Is Bleeding	1962	$20
5980	One Night/I Can't Go On This Way	1963	$20
45-5240	Please Don't Leave Me/The Girl I Love	1953	$70
—Black vinyl			
45-5240	Please Don't Leave Me/The Girl I Love	1953	$300
—Red vinyl			
X5369	Poor Me/I Can't Go On	1955	$30
45-5197	Poor Poor Me/Trust in Me	1952	$200
5734	Shu Rah/Fell in Love on Monday	1961	$20
X5515	Sick and Tired/No, No	1958	$30
X5262	Something's Wrong/Don't Leave Me This Way	1954	$60
—Black vinyl			
X5262	Something's Wrong/Don't Leave Me This Way	1954	$250
—Red vinyl			
X5569	Telling Lies/When the Saints Go Marching In	1959	$20
X5660	Tell Me That You Love Me/Before I Grow Too Old	1960	$20
X5477	The Big Beat/I Want You to Know	1957	$30
X5477 [PS]	The Big Beat/I Want You to Know	1957	$70
45-5058	The Fat Man/Detroit City Blues	1950	$2000
—Blue-label "script" logo; pressed in 1952 or so; counterfeits exist			
X5687	Three Nights a Week/Put Your Arms Around Me Honey	1960	$20
X5467	Wait and See/I Still Love You	1957	$30
X5675	Walking to New Orleans/Don't Come Knockin'	1960	$30
5779	What a Party/Rockin' Bicycle	1961	$20
X5723	What a Price/Ain't That Just Like a Woman	1961	$20
X5454	When I See You/What Will I Tell My Heart	1957	$30
66016	When I Was Young/Your Cheatin' Heart	1964	$15
X5396	When My Dreamboat Comes Home/So-Long	1956	$30
X5553	Whole Lotta Loving/Coquette	1958	$40
—Red label			
X5553	Whole Lotta Loving/Coquette	1958	$30
—Black label			
X5553	Whole Lotta Loving/Coquette	1958	$200
—Red vinyl (translucent)			
5895	Won't You Come On Back/Hands Across the Table	1962	$20
5895	Won't You Come On Back/Your Cheatin' Heart	1962	$20

MERCURY

Number	Title	Yr	NM
72463	I Left My Heart in San Francisco/I Done Got Over You	1965	$10
72485	It's Never Too Late/What's That You Got	1965	$10
72485 [PS]	It's Never Too Late/What's That You Got	1965	$30

REPRISE

Number	Title	Yr	NM
0810	Everybody's Got Someting to Hide (Except Me and My Monkey)/So Swell When You're Well	1969	$20
0891	Have You Seen My Baby?/Make Me Belong to You	1970	$20
0763	Lady Madonna/One for the Highway	1968	$20
0775	Lovely Rita/Wait Till It Happens to You	1968	$20
0696	One for the Highway/Honest Papas Love Their Mamas Better	1968	$20

TOOT TOOT

Number	Title	Yr	NM
002	Don't Mess with My Popeye's/My Toot Toot	1985	$5
—With Doug Kershaw			
001	My Toot Toot/My Toot Toot (Rock)	1985	$5
—With Doug Kershaw			

UNITED ARTISTS

Number	Title	Yr	NM
0001	Ain't That a Shame/Goin' Home	1973	$4
0004	Blueberry Hill/Bo Weevil	1973	$4
0002	Blue Monday/I'm Gonna Be a Wheel Someday	1973	$4
0006	I Hear You Knockin'/My Blue Heaven	1973	$4
0003	I'm in Love Again/Whole Lotta Lovin'	1973	$4
0009	I'm Ready/Wait and See	1973	$4
0005	I'm Walkin'/One Night	1973	$4
0008	I Want to Walk You Home/It's You I Love	1973	$4
0010	My Girl Josephine/When My Dreamboat Comes Home	1973	$4
XW514	The Fat Man/Valley of Tears	1974	$5
—Reissue			
0011	Three Nights a Week/Let the Four Winds Blow	1973	$4
—0001 through 0011 are "Silver Spotlight Series" reissues			
0007	Walkin' to New Orleans/Country Boy	1973	$4

WARNER BROS.

Number	Title	Yr	NM
49610	Whiskey Heaven/Beers to You	1980	$4
—B-side by Texas Opera Company			

7-Inch Extended Plays

ABC-PARAMOUNT

Number	Title	Yr	NM
EP-ABCS479 [PS]	Fats on Fire	1964	$30
EP-ABCS479	I Don't Want to Set the World on Fire/Old Man Trouble/Love Me//You Know I Miss You/The Fat Man/Valley of Tears	1964	$30
—Stereo jukebox issue; small hole, plays at 33 1/3 rpm			

IMPERIAL

Number	Title	Yr	NM
IMP140	Ain't It a Shame/Poor Me//Bo Weevil/Don't Blame It on Me	1956	$125
—Maroon label, block-letter logo			
IMP140	Ain't It a Shame/Poor Me//Bo Weevil/Don't Blame It on Me	1958	$30
—Black label			
IMP143	Are Your Going My Way/If You Need Me//My Heart Is In Your Hands/Fats Frenzy	1956	$125
—Maroon label, block-letter logo			
IMP143	Are Your Going My Way/If You Need Me//My Heart Is In Your Hands/Fats Frenzy	1958	$30
—Black label			
IMP144	Blueberry Hill/Honey Chile//Troubles of My Own/You Done Me Wrong	1956	$125
—Maroon label, block-letter logo			
IMP144	Blueberry Hill/Honey Chile//Troubles of My Own/You Done Me Wrong	1958	$30
—Black label			
IMP142	Careless Love/I Love Her//I'm in Love Again/When My Dreamboat Comes Home	1956	$125
—Maroon label, block-letter logo			
IMP142	Careless Love/I Love Her//I'm in Love Again/When My Dreamboat Comes Home	1958	$30
—Black label			
IMP151 [PS]	Cookin' with Fats	1957	$60
IMP148	Detroit City Blues/Hide Away Blues//She's My Baby/New Baby	1957	$125
—Maroon label, block-letter logo			
IMP148	Detroit City Blues/Hide Away Blues//She's My Baby/New Baby	1958	$30
—Black label			
IMP138	Domino Stomp/The Girl I Love//Don't You Know/The Fat Man	1956	$125
—Maroon label, block-letter logo			
IMP138	Domino Stomp/The Girl I Love//Don't You Know/The Fat Man	1958	$30
—Black label			
IMP127 [PS]	Fats Domino	1955	$60
IMP127	Going to the River/Every Night About This Time//Going Home/Please Don't Leave Me	1955	$175
—Script" label			
IMP127	Going to the River/Every Night About This Time//Going Home/Please Don't Leave Me	1955	$125
—Maroon label, block-letter logo			
IMP127	Going to the River/Every Night About This Time//Going Home/Please Don't Leave Me	1958	$30
—Black label			
IMP147 [PS]	Here Comes Fats	1956	$60
IMP148 [PS]	Here Stands Fats Domino	1957	$60
IMP149 [PS]	Here Stands Fats Domino	1957	$60
IMP150 [PS]	Here Stands Fats Domino	1957	$60
IMP150	I'm in the Mood for Love/You Can Pack Your Suitcase//Hey! Fat Man/I'll Be Gone	1957	$125
—Maroon label, block-letter logo			
IMP150	I'm in the Mood for Love/You Can Pack Your Suitcase//Hey! Fat Man/I'll Be Gone	1958	$30
—Black label			
IMP149	Little Bee/Every Night About This Time//I'm Walkin'/Cheatin'	1957	$125
—Maroon label, block-letter logo			
IMP149	Little Bee/Every Night About This Time//I'm Walkin'/Cheatin'	1958	$30
—Black label			
IMP151	Love Me/Don't You Hear Me Calling You//It's You I Love/Valley of Tears	1957	$125
—Maroon label, block-letter logo			
IMP151	Love Me/Don't You Hear Me Calling You//It's You I Love/Valley of Tears	1958	$30
—Black label			
IMP141	My Blue Heaven/Swanee River Hop//Second Line Jump/Goodbye	1956	$125
—Maroon label, block-letter logo			
IMP141	My Blue Heaven/Swanee River Hop//Second Line Jump/Goodbye	1958	$30
—Black label			
IMP146	So Long/La La//Poor, Poor Me/Trust in Me	1956	$125
—Maroon label, block-letter logo			
IMP146	So Long/La La//Poor, Poor Me/Trust in Me	1958	$30
—Black label			
IMP152	Thinking of You/You Know I Miss You//Where Did You Stay/Baby Please	1957	$125
—Maroon label, block-letter logo			
IMP152	Thinking of You/You Know I Miss You//Where Did You Stay/Baby Please	1958	$30
—Black label			
IMP144 [PS]	This Is Fats Domino	1956	$60
IMP145 [PS]	This Is Fats Domino	1956	$60
IMP146 [PS]	This Is Fats Domino	1956	$60
IMP145	What's the Reason I'm Not Pleasing You/Blue Monday//Reeling and Rocking/The Fat Man's Hop	1956	$125
—Maroon label, block-letter logo			
IMP145	What's the Reason I'm Not Pleasing You/Blue Monday//Reeling and Rocking/The Fat Man's Hop	1958	$30
—Black label			

MERCURY

Number	Title	Yr	NM
SR-659-C [PS]	Fats Domino '65	1965	$25
SR-659-C	Introduction/Blueberry Hill/Oh, What a Price/Let the Four Winds Blow//I'm Gonna Be a Wheel Some Day/So Long/Ain't That a Shame	1965	$25
—Stereo jukebox issue; small hole, plays at 33 1/3 rpm			

Number	Title	Yr	NM
DON AND DEWEY			
❏ 659	Farmer John/Big Boy Pete	1959	$30
❏ 610	Leavin' It All Up to You/Jelly Bean	1957	$40
❏ 639	The Letter/Koko Joe	1958	$30
DON AND HIS ROSES			
DOT			
❏ 15874	Leave Those Cats Alone/ Don't Try to Change Me	1958	$200
❏ 15755	Since You Went Away to School/Right Now	1958	$60
DON AND JUAN			
BIG TOP			
❏ 3121	Magic Wand/What I Really Meant to Say	1962	$50
❏ 3145	True Love Never Runs Smooth/ Is It All Right If I Love You	1963	$60
❏ 3106	Two Fools Are We/Pot Luck	1962	$30
❏ 3079	What's Your Name/ Chicken Necks	1961	$30
MALA			
❏ 494	I Can't Help Myself/All That's Missing Is You	1964	$15
❏ 469	Lonely Man/Could This Be Love	1963	$15
❏ 479	Pledging My Love/Molinda	1964	$15
❏ 484	Sincerely/Maryana Cherie	1964	$15
❏ 509	The Heartbreaking Truth/ Thank Goodness	1965	$40
TWIRL			
❏ 2021	Because I Love You/Are You Putting Me on the Shelf	1966	$40
DON AND THE CHEVELLS			
SPEEDWAY			
❏ 1000	Inner Limits/The Only Girl	1964	$100
DON AND THE GOODTIMES			
DUNHILL			
❏ 4015	I'll Be Down Forever/Big Big Knight (On a Big White Horse)	1965	$10
❏ 4008	Little Green Thing/ Little Sally Tease	1965	$12
❏ 4022	Sweets for My Sweet/ Hey There Mary Mae	1966	$10
EPIC			
❏ 10280	Ball of Fire/May My Heart Be Cast Into Stone	1968	$12
❏ 10241	Bambi/Sally (Studio A at 6 O'Clock in the Morning)	1967	$12
❏ 10145	I Could Be So Good to You/And It's So Good	1967	$10
❏ 10145 [PS]	I Could Be So Good to You/And It's So Good	1967	$20
❏ 10199	If You Love Her, Cherish Her and Such/Happy and Me	1967	$10
WAND			
❏ 184	Straight Scepter/There's Something on Your Mind	1965	$10
❏ 165	Turn On/Make It	1964	$10
DON, DICK & JIMMY			
CROWN			
❏ 147	Baby, You!/Nobody Likes to Cry	1955	$20
❏ 158	Love Is a Many-Splendored Thing/In Madrid	1955	$20
❏ 138	Make Yourself Comfortable/ Songs from Desiree	1955	$20
❏ 116	Ol' Man River/Hawaiian War Chant	1954	$20
❏ 162	Stolen Love/Adios My Madonna	1956	$20
❏ 125	That's What I Like/You Can't Have Your Cake and Eat It, Too	1954	$20
❏ 131	The Touch of Your Lips/I Go to You	1954	$20
❏ 152	This Little Piggie/Make Me a Present	1955	$20
DOT			
❏ 15768	Too Young to Bop/ This Was My Sin	1958	$15
VERVE			
❏ 10043	A Man's Gotta Do/My Faith, My Hope, My Love	1957	$15
❏ 10062	Be Sweet to Me/ Building a Paradise	1957	$15
❏ 2020	That's the Way I Feel/ Two Voices in the Night	1956	$15
DON JUANS, THE			
ONEZY			
❏ 101	The Girl of My Dreams/Dolores	1959	$2000
DONALDSON, BO, AND THE HEYWOODS			
ABC			
❏ 11435	Billy, Don't Be a Hero/ Don't Ever Look Back	1974	$4
❏ 12011	Billy, Don't Be a Hero/ Don't Ever Look Back	1974	$5
❏ 11402	Deeper and Deeper/ Drive Me Crazy	1973	$4

Number	Title	Yr	NM
❏ 11402 [PS]	Deeper and Deeper/ Drive Me Crazy	1973	$8
❏ 12072	Make the Most of This World/ House on Telegraph Hill	1975	$4
❏ 12108	Our Last Song Together/ Make the Most of This World	1975	$4
❏ 12039	The Heartbreak Kid/Girl Don't Make Me Wait	1974	$4
❏ 12039 [PS]	The Heartbreak Kid/Girl Don't Make Me Wait	1974	$8
❏ 12006	Who Do You Think You Are/ Fool's Way of Lovin'	1974	$4
CAPITOL			
❏ 4237	Oh Boy/Tie Me Down	1976	$4
❏ 4282	Teenage Rampage/Tie Me Down	1976	$4
FAMILY PRODUCTIONS			
❏ 0918	All Over the World/Just for You	1972	$5
❏ 0918 [PS]	All Over the World/Just for You	1972	$20
— Sleeve may be promo only			
❏ 0923	Da Doo Ron Ron/Just Because	1973	$5
❏ 0917	Thank You Girl/You Don't Own Me	1972	$5
PLAYBOY			
❏ 5820	Are You Cuckoo/ Gimmie Some Time	1977	$4
DONALDSON, LOU			
ARGO			
❏ 5478	Possum Head/Laura	1964	$8
❏ 5449	Signifyin'/Time After Time	1963	$8
❏ 5494	Soul Gumbo/Cole Slaw	1965	$8
BLUE NOTE			
❏ 1934	Alligator Boogaloo/ Reverend Moses	1967	$8
❏ 1753	Be My Love/Lou's Blues	1959	$20
❏ 1662	Caravan/Old Folks	1955	$20
❏ 1970	Caterpillar/Make It with You	1971	$6
❏ 1623	Cookin'/Bellarosa	1954	$20
❏ 1624	Dedah/Carving the Rock	1954	$20
❏ 1956	Everything I Do Gohn Be Funky/Minor Bash	1970	$6
❏ 1949	Hot Dog/Who's Making Love	1969	$8
❏ 1752	Mack the Knife/The Nearness of You	1959	$20
❏ XW287	Pillow Talk/Sassy Soul Strut	1973	$5
❏ XW381	Sanford and Son/Good Morning Heartache	1974	$5
❏ 1936	Say It Loud/Snake Bone	1968	$8
❏ 1713	Sputnik (Part 1)/Sputnik (Part 2)	1957	$20
❏ 1663	That Good Old Feeling/L.D. Blues	1955	$20
CADET			
❏ 5521	Musty Rusty (Part 1)/ Musty Rusty (Part 2)	1966	$6
DONAYS, THE			
BRENT			
❏ 7033	Devil in His Heart/Bad Boy	1962	$50
DONEGAN, LONNIE			
UK skiffle king.			
APT			
❏ 25067	Pick a Bale of Cotton/ Ramblin' Round	1962	$10
ATLANTIC			
❏ 2108	Have a Drink On Me/ Beyond the Sunset	1961	$15
❏ 2081	Lorelei/Junco Partner	1960	$15
❏ 2058	My Old Man's a Dustman/ The Golden Vanity	1960	$15
❏ 2063	Take This Hammer/Nobody Understands Me	1960	$15
❏ 2123	Wreck of the John B/Sorry, But I'm Gonna Have to Pass	1961	$15
DOT			
❏ 15911	Does Your Chewing Gum Lose Its Flavor (On the Bedpost Overnight)/Aunt Rhody	1959	$30
— Reissued in 1961 with the same number			
❏ 15953	Fort Worth Jail/Whoa, Back, Back	1959	$30
❏ 15873	Sally Don't You Grieve/Times Are Getting Hard, Boys	1958	$30
❏ 15792	The Grand Coulee Dam/Nobody Loves Like an Irishman	1958	$30
❏ 16263	Whoa, Back, Back/Light from the Lighthouse	1961	$20
HICKORY			
❏ 1274	Bad News/Interstate 40	1964	$12
❏ 1345	Cajun Jo (Bully of the Bayou)/Nothing to Gain	1965	$10
❏ 1267	Fisherman's Luck/ There's a Big Wheel	1964	$10
❏ 1247	Lemon Tree/A Very Good Year	1964	$12
❏ 1299	Louisiana Man/Lovey Told Me Goodbye	1965	$10
MERCURY			
❏ 70949	Bring a Little Water, Sylvie/Dead or Alive	1956	$30
❏ 71094	Cumberland Gap/ Wabash Cannonball	1957	$30
❏ 71026	Don't You Rock Me Daddy-O/ How Long, How Long Blues	1957	$30
❏ 70872	Lost John/Stewball	1956	$30

Number	Title	Yr	NM
❏ 71248	My Dixie Darling/I'm Just a Rolling Stone	1957	$30
❏ 71181	Puttin' On the Style/Gamblin' Man	1957	$30
DONLEY, JIMMY			
CHESS			
❏ 1843	Santa, Don't Pass Me By/Think It Over	1962	$15
DECCA			
❏ 30519	Baby How Long/I Gotta Go	1957	$30
❏ 31116	My Baby's Gone/Our Love	1960	$50
❏ 30574	Please Baby Come Home/ Born to Be a Loser	1958	$30
❏ 30392	South of the Border/The Trail of the Lonesome Pine	1957	$30
❏ 30887	What Must I Do/The Shape You Left Me In	1959	$30
TEARDROP			
❏ 3009	Baby, Heaven Sent Me You/ Loving Cajun Style	1963	$15
❏ 3005	Honey Stop Twistin'/ Hello, Remember Me	1962	$20
❏ 3034	I'm So Lonesome Without the Blues/Forget the Past	1964	$10
❏ 3026	I Really Got the Blues/ Just a Game	1964	$10
❏ 3007	Santa, Don't Pass Me By/ Forever Lillie Mae	1962	$15
❏ 3021	Santa, Don't Pass Me By/Santa's Alley	1963	$15
❏ 3007	Think It Over/Forever Lillie Mae	1962	$15
DONNER, RAL			
CHICAGO FIRE			
❏ 7402	The Wedding Song/ Godfather Per Me	1974	$8
FONTANA			
❏ 1515	Good Lovin'/The Other Side of Me	1965	$30
❏ 1502	Poison Ivy League/A Tear in My Eye	1965	$30
❏ 1502	Poison Ivy League/You Finally Said Something Good	1965	$30
GONE			
❏ 5102	Girl of My Best Friend/It's Been a Long, Long Time	1961	$50
— Black label			
❏ 5102	Girl of My Best Friend/It's Been a Long, Long Time	1961	$30
— Multi-color label			
❏ 5129	Loveless Life/Bells of Love	1962	$30
❏ 5114	Please Don't Go/I Didn't Figure on Him	1961	$30
❏ 5119	School of Heartbreakers/ Because We're Young	1961	$50
❏ 5121	She's Everything (I Wanted You to Be)/Because We're Young	1961	$30
❏ 5121	She's Everything (I Wanted You to Be)/Will You Love Me in Heaven	1961	$40
— B-side sung by a girl group, not Ral Donner.			
❏ 5108	To Love/And Then	1961	$50
— Deleted shortly after release			
❏ 5125	To Love Someone/Will You Love Me in Heaven	1962	$30
— B-side sung by Ral Donner as advertised			
❏ 5133	To Love/Sweetheart	1962	$30
MID-EAGLE			
❏ 101	(If I Had My) Life to Live Over/Lost	1968	$10
❏ 275	The Wedding Song/ So Much Lovin'	1976	$6
MJ			
❏ 222	(All of a Sudden) My Heart Sings/Lovin' Place	1970	$6
❏ 222 [PS]	(All of a Sudden) My Heart Sings/Lovin' Place	1970	$6
RED BIRD			
❏ Oct-0057	Love Isn't Like That/It Will Only Make You Love	1966	$200
REPRISE			
❏ 20192	Beyond the Heartbreak/ Run Little Linda	1963	$70
❏ 20141	I Got Burned/A Tear in My Eye	1963	$50
❏ 20141 [PS]	I Got Burned/A Tear in My Eye	1963	$180
❏ 20176	I Wish This Night Would Never End/Don't Put Your Heart in His Hand	1963	$60
❏ 20135	(These Are the Things That Make Up) Christmas Day/ Second Miracle (Of Christmas)	1962	$50
SCOTTIE			
❏ 1310	Tell Me Why/That's All Right with Me	1959	$250
SMASH			
❏ 34774/5 [DJ]	Good Lovin'/The Other Side of Me	1964	$50
— A Fontana promo using Smash labels in error and omitting the Fontana number?			
STARFIRE			
❏ 100	Don't Let It Slip Away/ Wait a Minute Now	1978	$12
— Black vinyl			

Number	Title	Yr	NM
❏ 100	Don't Let It Slip Away/Wait a Minute Now	1978	$12
—White vinyl			
❏ 100 [PS]	Don't Let It Slip Away/Wait a Minute Now	1978	$12
❏ 103	(Things That Make Up) Christmas Day/Second Miracle (Of Christmas)	1978	$10
—Green vinyl			
❏ 103 [PS]	(Things That Make Up) Christmas Day/Second Miracle (Of Christmas)	1978	$10
SUNLIGHT			
❏ 1006	Don't Let It Slip Away/Wait a Minute Now	1972	$15
TAU			
❏ 105	Loneliness of a Star/And Then	1963	$60
—Blue label			
❏ 105	Loneliness of a Star/And Then	1963	$40
—Yellow label			
THUNDER			
❏ 7801	The Day the Beat Stopped/Rock on Me	1978	$6

DONNIE AND THE DARLINGTONS
ABC-PARAMOUNT
Number	Title	Yr	NM
❏ 10633	Poppin' My Clutch/Since Grandpa Got a Rail Job	1965	$30

DONNIE AND THE DELCHORDS
EPIC
Number	Title	Yr	NM
❏ 9495	So Lonely/When You're Alone	1962	$30
TAURUS			
❏ 363	Be with You/I Found Heaven	1963	$30
❏ 357	I Don't Care/I'll Be With You in Apple Blossom Time	1963	$30
❏ 364	I'm in the Mood for Love/I've Got a Woman	1964	$30
❏ 352	So Lonely/When You're Alone	1962	$50
❏ 361	Transylvania Mist/That Old Feeling	1963	$30

DONNIE AND THE DREAMERS
DECCA
Number	Title	Yr	NM
❏ 31312	Carole/Ruby My Love	1961	$60
WHALE			
❏ 500	Dorothy/Count Every Star	1961	$30
❏ 505	Teenage Love/My Memories of You	1961	$50

DONNYBROOKS, THE
CALICO
Number	Title	Yr	NM
❏ 112	Coming Home from School/Mandolins of Love	1959	$30
❏ 108	Every Time We Kiss/Break the Glass	1959	$30

DONOVAN
ALLEGIANCE
Number	Title	Yr	NM
❏ 3910	Lady of the Stars/(B-side unknown)	1983	$4
ARISTA			
❏ 0280	Dare to Be Different/International Man	1977	$4
EPIC			
❏ 10434	Atlantis/To Susan on the West Coast Waiting	1969	$8
❏ 10434 [PS]	Atlantis/To Susan on the West Coast Waiting	1969	$15
❏ 10694	Celia of the Seals/Song of the Wandering Aengus	1971	$8
❏ 10694 [PS]	Celia of the Seals/Song of the Wandering Aengus	1971	$15
❏ 50237	Dark Eyed Blue Jean Angel/Well Known Has-Been	1976	$5
❏ 10127	Epistle to Dippy/Preachin' Love	1967	$8
❏ 10127 [PS]	Epistle to Dippy/Preachin' Love	1967	$15
❏ 10510	Goo Goo Barabajagal (Love Is Hot)/Trust	1969	$8
❏ 10510 [PS]	Goo Goo Barabajagal (Love Is Hot)/Trust	1969	$15
—With the Jeff Beck Group			
❏ 10345	Hurdy Gurdy Man/Teen Angel	1968	$8
—Features John Paul Jones, Jimmy Page, and possibly John Bonham, all later of Led Zeppelin			
❏ 10345 [PS]	Hurdy Gurdy Man/Teen Angel	1968	$15
❏ 10983	I Like You/Earth Sign Man	1973	$5
❏ 10393	Lalena/Aye My Love	1968	$8
❏ 10393 [PS]	Lalena/Aye My Love	1968	$15
❏ 11023	Maria Magenta/Intergalactic Laxative	1973	$5
❏ 10098	Mellow Yellow/Sunny South Kensington	1966	$10
❏ 10098 [PS]	Mellow Yellow/Sunny South Kensington	1966	$20
❏ 10045	Sunshine Superman/The Trip	1966	$10
❏ 10045 [PS]	Sunshine Superman/The Trip	1966	$20
❏ 10045 [DJ]	Sunshine Superman/The Trip	1966	$50
—Promo only on red vinyl			

Number	Title	Yr	NM
❏ 10212	There Is a Mountain/Sand and Foam	1967	$8
❏ 10253	Wear Your Love Like Heaven/Oh Gosh	1967	$8
❏ 10253 [PS]	Wear Your Love Like Heaven/Oh Gosh	1967	$15
HICKORY			
❏ 1309	Catch the Wind/Why Do You Treat Me Like You Do	1965	$20
❏ 1324	Colours/Josie	1965	$15
❏ 1492	Do You Hear Me Now/Why Do You Treat Me Like You Do	1968	$12
❏ 1417	Hey Gyp/The War Drags On	1966	$15
❏ 1470	Sunny Goodge Street/Summer Day Reflection Song	1967	$12
❏ 1402	Turquoise/To Try for the Sun	1966	$15

DONTELS, THE
BELTONE
Number	Title	Yr	NM
❏ 2040	Lover's Reunion/Make a Chance	1963	$250

DOOBIE BROTHERS, THE
Also see MICHAEL McDONALD; PATRICK SIMMONS.

ASYLUM
Number	Title	Yr	NM
❏ 46630	Power/Cape Fear River	1980	$5
—A-side: With John Hall and James Taylor; B-side by Sweet Honey in the Rock			
CAPITOL			
❏ B-44376	The Doctor/Too High a Price	1989	$3
❏ B-44376 [PS]	The Doctor/Too High a Price	1989	$3
SESAME STREET			
❏ 49642	Wynken, Blynken and Nod/In Harmony	1980	$5
—B-side by Kate Taylor and the Simon-Taylor Family			
❏ 49642 [PS]	Wynken, Blynken and Nod/In Harmony	1980	$5
WARNER BROS.			
❏ 7795	Another Park, Another Sunday/Black Water	1974	$5
❏ 7544	Beehive State/Closer Every Day	1971	$6
❏ 8062	Black Water/Song to See You Through	1974	$4
❏ 7728	China Grove/Evil Woman	1973	$4
❏ 49029	Dependin' on You/How Do the Fools Survive	1979	$4
❏ 8471	Echoes of Love/There's a Light	1977	$4
❏ 7832	Eyes of Silver/You Just Can't Stop It	1974	$5
❏ 8011	Eyes of Silver/You Just Can't Stop It	1974	$4
❏ 50001	Here to Love You/Wynken, Bliinken and Nod	1982	$4
❏ 8161	I Cheat the Hangman/Music Man	1975	$4
❏ 8282	It Keeps You Runnin'/Turn It Loose	1976	$4
❏ 7619	Listen to the Music/Toulouse Street	1972	$5
❏ 8408	Little Darling (I Need You)/Losin' End	1977	$4
❏ 8500	Livin' on the Fault Line/Nothin' but a Heartache	1977	$4
❏ 7698	Long Train Runnin'/Without You	1973	$4
❏ 8828	Minute by Minute/Sweet Feelin'	1979	$4
❏ 49622	One Step Closer/South Bay Street	1980	$4
❏ 8126	Sweet Maxine/Double Dealin' Four Flusher	1975	$4
❏ 8092	Take Me in Your Arms (Rock Me)/Slat Key Soquel Rag	1975	$4
❏ 8196	Takin' It to the Streets/For Someone Special	1976	$4
❏ 7527	Travelin' Man/Feelin' Down Partner	1971	$6
❏ 8725	What a Fool Believes/Don't Stop to Watch the Wheels	1978	$4
❏ 8725 [PS]	What a Fool Believes/Don't Stop to Watch the Wheels	1978	$5
❏ 8233	Wheels of Fortune/Slat Key Soquel Rag	1976	$4
7-Inch Extended Plays			
❏ S2694	China Grove/Busted Down Around O'Connelly Corners/Long Train Runnin'//Without You/Natural Thing	1973	$8
—Jukebox issue, small hole, plays at 33 1/3 rpm			
❏ S2750	Eyes of Silver/Pursuit on 53rd St./Spirit//Road Angel/Tell Me What You Want	1974	$8
—Jukebox issue, small hole, plays at 33 1/3 rpm			
❏ S2694 [PS]	The Captain and Me	1973	$8
—Part of "Little LP" series (LLP #221)			
❏ S2750 [PS]	What Were Once Vices Are Now Habits	1974	$12
—Part of Little LP series (LLP #247)			

DOODLES, THE
HIT
Number	Title	Yr	NM
❏ 104	I Want to Hold Your Hand/A Fool Never Learns	1964	$15
—B-side by Fred York			

DOONE, LORNA
RCA VICTOR
Number	Title	Yr	NM
❏ 47-8532	Dangerous Town/Who Knows It?	1965	$60

DOONICAN, VAL
DECCA
Number	Title	Yr	NM
❏ 32252	I'd Rather Think of You/If the Whole World Stopped Lovin'	1968	$5
❏ 32337	The Sun Always Shines When You're Young/Now	1968	$5
LONDON			
❏ 9753	I'm Gonna Get There Somehow/How Can I Find Her	1965	$10
❏ 9735	The Special Years/Traveling Home	1965	$10
❏ 1014	Two Streets/It Must Be You	1967	$6
❏ 9717	Walk Talll/Only the Heartaches	1964	$10
PRESS			
❏ 5008	Gentle Mary/What Would I Be	1967	$6

DOORS, THE
ELEKTRA
Number	Title	Yr	NM
❏ 45611	Break On Through (To the Other Side)/End of the Night	1966	$40
—Originals have a yellow and black label with "ELEKTRA" in all capital letters and a woman's head above a white line at the top of the label			
❏ 45611 [PS]	Break On Through (To the Other Side)/End of the Night	1966	$120
❏ 45611	Break On Through (To the Other Side)/End of the Night	1967	$30
—Red, black and white label			
❏ 45611	Break On Through (To the Other Side)/End of the Night	1967	$30
—Red, black and pink label			
❏ 45793	Get Up and Dance/Treetrunk	1972	$8
❏ 69770	Gloria/Moonlight Drive	1983	$4
—Contrary to prior reports, this was not issued with a picture sleeve			
❏ 45635	Hello, I Love You, Won't You Tell Me Your Name?/Love Street	1968	$30
—Original pressings have longer title			
❏ 45635	Hello, I Love You/Love Street	1968	$15
❏ 45122	L.A. Woman/Roadhouse Blues	1983	$4
—Spun Gold" series; lighter gold label			
❏ 45051	Light My Fire/Love Me Two Times	1972	$6
—Spun Gold" series; originals have a very dark gold label			
❏ 45051	Light My Fire/Love Me Two Times	1975	$4
—Spun Gold" series; reissues have a lighter gold label			
❏ 45615	Light My Fire/The Crystal Ship	1967	$40
—Originals have a yellow and black label with "ELEKTRA" in all capital letters and a woman's head above a white line at the top of the label			
❏ 45615	Light My Fire/The Crystal Ship	1967	$15
—Second pressings have a red, black and white label			
❏ 45615	Light My Fire/The Crystal Ship	1967	$20
—Red, black and pink label			
❏ 45726	Love Her Madly/(You Need Meat) Don't Go No Further	1971	$8
❏ 45624	Love Me Two Times/Moonlight Drive	1967	$15
—Black, red and white label			
❏ 45624	Love Me Two Times/Moonlight Drive	1967	$15
—Black, red and pink label			
❏ 45123	People Are Strange/Break On Through	1983	$4
—Spun Gold" series; lighter gold label			
❏ 47097	People Are Strange/Not to Touch the Earth	1980	$4
❏ 47097 [PS]	People Are Strange/Not to Touch the Earth	1980	$8
—Also has an insert with photos of Doors albums			
❏ 45621	People Are Strange/Unhappy Girl	1967	$15
❏ 45621 [PS]	People Are Strange/Unhappy Girl	1967	$50
❏ 45768	Ships w/ Sails/In the Eye of the Sun	1972	$8
❏ 45663	Tell All the People/Easy Ride	1969	$10
❏ 45663 [PS]	Tell All the People/Easy Ride	1969	$30
❏ 45807	The Mosquito/It Slipped My Mind	1972	$8
❏ 45825	The Piano Bird/Good Rockin'	1972	$8
❏ 45757	Tightrope Ride/Variety Is the Spice of Life	1971	$8
❏ 45052	Touch Me/Hello, I Love You	1972	$6
—Spun Gold" series; originals have a very dark gold label			
❏ 45052	Touch Me/Hello, I Love You	1975	$4
—Spun Gold" series; reissues have a lighter gold label			
❏ 45646	Touch Me/Wild Child	1968	$15
❏ 45656	Wishful Sinful/Who Scared You?	1969	$10
PHILCO-FORD			
❏ HP-9	Light My Fire/Break On Through	1968	$50
—4-inch plastic "Hip Pocket Record" with color sleeve			

DOOTONES, THE

DOOTONE

Number	Title	Yr	NM
❑ 471	Sailor Boy/Down the Road	1962	$40
❑ 470	Strange Love Affair/The Day You Said Goodbye	1962	$40
❑ 366	Teller of Fortune/Ay Si Si	1955	$200

DORELLS, THE

ATLANTIC

Number	Title	Yr	NM
❑ 2244	Beating of My Heart/Maybe Baby	1964	$20

GEI

Number	Title	Yr	NM
❑ 4401	Beating of My Heart/Maybe Baby	1963	$40

DORMAN, HAROLD

RITA

Number	Title	Yr	NM
❑ 1008	I'll Come Running/River of Tears	1960	$30
❑ 1003	Mountain of Love/To Be with You	1960	$30
❑ 1012	Moved to Kansas City/ Take a Chance on Me	1960	$30

SANTO

Number	Title	Yr	NM
❑ 9051	Ain't Gonna Change/ What Comes Next	1962	$20
❑ 9005	In an Instant/There on Yonder Hill	1962	$20

SUN

Number	Title	Yr	NM
❑ 362	I'll Stick By You/There They Go	1961	$30
❑ 377	Wait 'Til Saturday Night/ In the Beginning	1962	$30

DORN, JERRY

ARWIN

Number	Title	Yr	NM
❑ 122	Brother, Can You Spare a Dime/Disappointed Lover	1959	$15

KING

Number	Title	Yr	NM
❑ 4968	I'm So in Love with You/Nightmare	1956	$20
❑ 4932	Wishing Well/ Sentimental Heaven	1956	$100

DORSAM, TOM

LOREN

Number	Title	Yr	NM
❑ 5001	Baby of Mine/(B-side unknown)	1964	$500

DORSEY, GERRY

HICKORY

Number	Title	Yr	NM
❑ 1337	Baby Turn Around/If I Could Do the Things I Want to Do	1965	$20

DORSEY, JIMMY

COLUMBIA

Number	Title	Yr	NM
❑ 4-39162	Acapulco Polka/Laugh Polka	1951	$15
❑ 4-39526	A Kiss to Build a Dream On/Cherry Pink (And Apple Blossom White)	1951	$20
❑ 1-554	Clap Hands (Here Comes Charlie)/When You Were a Tulip	1950	$50

—Microgroove 33 1/3 rpm single, small hole

Number	Title	Yr	NM
❑ 4-39161	Clarinet Polka/Julida Polka	1951	$15
❑ 4-39691	Confetti/No Other Love But Yours	1952	$20
❑ 6-865(?)	Dixieland Band from Santa Claus Land/It's The Dreamer In Me	1950	$30
❑ 1-865(?)	Dixieland Band from Santa Claus Land/It's The Dreamer In Me	1950	$50

—Microgroove 33 1/3 rpm single, small hole

Number	Title	Yr	NM
❑ 4-38656	High Society/Muskrat Ramble	1950	$20
❑ 1-449	I'll Hold You in My Arms Once More/Lost in a Dream	1950	$50

—Microgroove 33 1/3 rpm single, small hole

Number	Title	Yr	NM
❑ 1-700(?)	It's a Long, Long Way to Tipperary/You Don't Have to Be a Baby to Cry	1950	$50

—Microgroove 33 1/3 rpm single, small hole

Number	Title	Yr	NM
❑ 1-790(?)	Let a Smile Be Your Umbrella/ In a Little Spanish Town	1950	$50

—Microgroove 33 1/3 rpm single, small hole

Number	Title	Yr	NM
❑ 4-39163	Licorice Stick Polka/Helena Polka	1951	$15
❑ 4-39138	Lily of the Valley/By Heck	1950	$30
❑ 4-39896	Love Came Out of the Night/ Hump Back Honey	1952	$20
❑ 4-39477	Mine Alone/The World Your Balloon	1951	$20
❑ 4-38654	Panama/Jazz Me Blues	1950	$20
❑ 4-38657	South Rampart Street Parade/Tin Roof Blues	1950	$20

—The above four comprise a box set

Number	Title	Yr	NM
❑ 4-39558	Step by Step/Young Folks Should Get Married	1951	$20
❑ 4-38655	Struttin' with Some Barbecue/Chimes Blues	1950	$20
❑ 4-39728	Tell me True/The Night Is Filled with Echoes	1952	$20
❑ 4-39164	We're Gonna Have Some Fun Tonight/Barbara Polka	1951	$15

—The above four comprise a box set

Number	Title	Yr	NM
❑ 4-39651	Wimoweh/I'll Always Be Following You	1952	$20

CORAL

Number	Title	Yr	NM
❑ 9-60448	I Got Rhythm/Love Walked In	1951	$20
❑ 9-60450	I Was Doing Alright/They Can't Take That Away from Me	1951	$20
❑ 9-60449	Love Is Here to Stay/Let's Call the Whole Thing Off	1951	$20
❑ 9-60451	Slap That Bass/They All Laughed	1951	$20

DECCA

Number	Title	Yr	NM
❑ 9-25121	Always in My Heart/Yours (Quiereme Mucho)	1950	$20

—Black label, lines on either side of "Decca

Number	Title	Yr	NM
❑ 9-28457	Always in My Heart/Yours (Quiereme Mucho)	1952	$20

—Black label with lines on either side of "Decca"; reissue of two of his early 1940s hits on a 45

Number	Title	Yr	NM
❑ 9-25121	Always in My Heart/Yours (Quiereme Mucho)	1955	$15

—Black label, star under "Decca

Number	Title	Yr	NM
❑ 9-25120	Amapola (Pretty Little Poppy)/Maria Elena	1950	$20

—Black label, lines on either side of "Decca

Number	Title	Yr	NM
❑ 32108	Arkansas Traveler/What's the Reason (I'm Not Pleasing You)	1967	$8
❑ 9-25122	Brazil (Aquarela do Brasil)/ At the Cross-Roads	1950	$20

—Black label, lines on either side of "Decca

Number	Title	Yr	NM
❑ 9-25255	It Happened in Hawaii/Tangerine	1950	$20

—Black label, lines on either side of "Decca

Number	Title	Yr	NM
❑ 9-25119	The Breeze and I/Green Eyes (Aquellos Ojos Verdes)	1950	$20

—Black label, lines on either side of "Decca

FRATERNITY

Number	Title	Yr	NM
❑ 816	Love on the Rocks/ Under a Texas Moon	1958	$15
❑ 868	Mambo en Sax/No One Ever Lost More	1960	$10
❑ 755	So Rare/Sophisticated Swing	1957	$20
❑ 797	When You Took Your Love/ No One Ever Lost More	1958	$15

MCA

Number	Title	Yr	NM
❑ 60148	Always in My Heart/Yours (Quiereme Mucho)	1973	$5

—Black label with rainbow

Number	Title	Yr	NM
❑ 60021	Amapola (Pretty Little Poppy)/Maria Elena	1973	$5

—Black label with rainbow

Number	Title	Yr	NM
❑ 60022	It Happened in Hawaii/Tangerine	1973	$5

—Black label with rainbow

Number	Title	Yr	NM
❑ 60020	The Breeze and I/Green Eyes (Aquellos Ojos Verdes)	1973	$5

—Black label with rainbow

MGM

Number	Title	Yr	NM
❑ K11739	Angela Mia/Ballerina	1954	$20

DORSEY, LEE

ABC

Number	Title	Yr	NM
❑ 12361	God Must Have Blessed America/Say It Again	1978	$4

ABC-PARAMOUNT

Number	Title	Yr	NM
❑ 10192	Lottie Mo/Lover of Love	1961	$20

ACE

Number	Title	Yr	NM
❑ 640	Lonely Evening/Rock	1961	$20

AMY

Number	Title	Yr	NM
❑ 994	Can't Get Away/Vista Vista	1967	$6
❑ 939	Can You Hear Me/ Work, Work, Work	1965	$8
❑ 952	Confusion/The Neighbors' Daughter	1966	$8
❑ 11055	Everything I Do Gonna be Funky (From Now On)/ There Should Be a Book	1969	$6
❑ 11031	Four Corners (Part 1)/ Four Corners (Part 2)	1968	$6
❑ 945	Get Out of My Life, Woman/So Long	1965	$8
❑ 11057	Give It Up/Candy Man	1969	$6
❑ 998	Go-Go Girl/I Can Hear You Callin'	1967	$6
❑ 974	Gotta Find a Job/Rain, Rain, Go Away	1967	$6
❑ 965	Holy Cow/Operation Heartache	1966	$8
❑ 11010	I Can't Get Away/Cynthia	1968	$6
❑ 11048	I'm Gonna Sit Right Down/Little Ba-By	1968	$6
❑ 987	My Old Car/Why Wait Until Tomorrow	1967	$6
❑ 11052	What Now My Love/A Lover Was Born	1969	$6
❑ 11020	Wonder Woman/A Little Dab A Do Ya	1968	$6
❑ 958	Working in the Coal Mine/Mexico	1966	$10

BELL

Number	Title	Yr	NM
❑ 908	I Can Hear You Callin'/ What You Want	1970	$5

CONSTELLATION

Number	Title	Yr	NM
❑ 115	Organ Grinder's Swing/I Gotta Find a New Love	1964	$30

FURY

Number	Title	Yr	NM
❑ 1056	Do-Re-Mi/People Gonna' Talk	1961	$15
❑ 1061	Eenie Meenie Miny Moe/ Behind the 8-Ball	1962	$15
❑ 1074	Hoodlum Joe/When I Met My Baby	1963	$15

POLYDOR

Number	Title	Yr	NM
❑ 14106	Freedom for the Stallion/If She Won't (Find Someone Who Will)	1971	$5
❑ 14181	On Your Way Down/ Freedom for the Stallion	1973	$5
❑ 14055	Sneakin' Sally Through the Alley/ Tears, Tears and More Tears	1971	$5
❑ 14147	When Can I Come Home/Gator Tail	1972	$5

SANSU

Number	Title	Yr	NM
❑ 474	Love Lots of Lovin'/Take Care of Our Love	1967	$15

—With Betty Harris

SMASH

Number	Title	Yr	NM
❑ 1842	Hello Good Looking/Someday	1963	$12

SPRING

Number	Title	Yr	NM
❑ 114	Occapella/Tears, Tears and More Tears	1971	$5

VALIANT

Number	Title	Yr	NM
❑ 1001	Lottie Mo/Lover of Love	1958	$50

DORSEY, TOMMY

DECCA

Number	Title	Yr	NM
❑ 27429	Alone Together/ Dancing in the Dark	1951	$15
❑ 27396	As Time Goes By/ Lullaby of Broadway	1951	$15
❑ 28847	Falling in Love with Love/I Wonder Who's Kissing Her Now	1953	$15
❑ 27248	Goofus/Ev'rybody Wants to Go to Heaven	1950	$20
❑ 28057	Hambone/Come What May	1952	$15
❑ 28152	Homing Pigeon/I Got Big Eyes	1952	$15
❑ 27691	I Fall in Love with You/ Everything I Have Is Yours	1951	$15
❑ 27431	I Guess I'll Have to Change My Ways/I See Your Face Before Me	1951	$15
❑ 28978	Island Queen/You're the Cause of It All	1953	$15
❑ 29057	Liza Jane/Blue Moon	1954	$10
❑ 27430	Louisiana Hayride/Something to Remember You By	1951	$15
❑ 27890	Marcheta/Don't Take Your Love from Me	1951	$15
❑ 27973	May I/One Morning in May	1952	$15
❑ 27247	Music Maestro, Please/Strangers	1950	$20
❑ 27759	My Love/Flower of Dawn	1951	$15
❑ 27690	My Magic Heart/If You Turn Me Down	1951	$15
❑ 28684	Sentimental Me and Romantic You/I'm Getting Sentimental Over You	1953	$15
❑ 28425	Sentimental Serenade/I'm Going Home	1952	$15
❑ 27709	September in the Rain/ Black Strap Molasses	1951	$15
❑ 27733	Show Me You Love Me/ Oh! Look at Me Now	1951	$15
❑ 27843	Solitaire/With All My Heart and Soul	1951	$15
❑ 27539	Sweet Adeline/Diane	1951	$15
❑ 28766	The Most Beautiful Girl in the World/One Kiss	1953	$15
❑ 28035	There Are Such Things/ What Is Time	1952	$15
❑ 28328	They Didn't Believe Me/Nobody Knows the Trouble I've Seen	1952	$15
❑ 28366	This Is the Beginning of the End/ You Could Make Me Smile Again	1952	$15
❑ 28451	This Love of Mine/Yours Is My Heart Alone	1952	$15
❑ 28064	Trouble in Mind/The Dirty Dozens	1952	$15
❑ 47-3716	Davenport Blues/ Down Home Rag	1950	$20
❑ 47-2958	Dream of You/Pussy Willow	1949	$30
❑ 47-2900	Enjoy Yourself (It's Later Than You Think)/She's a Home Girl	1949	$30
❑ 47-3840	Happy Feet/Birmingham Bounce	1950	$20
❑ 47-3712	I Oughta Know More About You/C'est Si Bon	1950	$20
❑ 47-3910	It All Begins and Ends with You/Lullaby in Boogie	1950	$20
❑ 47-3161	It's Delovely/I Get a Kick Out of You	1949	$20

—The above three comprise a box set

Number	Title	Yr	NM
❑ 47-3869	I've Forgotten You/No Other Love	1950	$20
❑ 47-3159	Love for Sale/Just One of Those Things	1949	$20
❑ 47-2876	Marie/Song of India	1949	$20

—The above three comprise a box set

Number	Title	Yr	NM
❑ 47-3717	Milenberg Joys (Part 1)/ Milenberg Joys (Part 2)	1950	$20

—The above three comprise a box set

Number	Title	Yr	NM
❑ 47-2875	Opus No. 1/On the Sunny Side of the Street	1949	$20
❑ 47-3132	Puddle Wump/Nice to Know You Care	1949	$30
❑ 47-3087	Shake That Tree/Hollywood Hat	1949	$30
❑ 47-3002	Summertime/Dry Bones	1949	$30
❑ 47-2917	The Continental/Ain'tcha Glad I Love Youq	1949	$30
❑ 47-3028	The Huckle-Buck/Again	1949	$30
❑ 47-3791	Tiger Rag/Way Down Yonder in New Orleans	1950	$20
❑ 47-3715	Washboard Blues/Panama	1950	$20
❑ 47-3210	When/Just for Old Times	1949	$30

Number	Title	Yr	NM
RCA CAMDEN			
CAE268	Original Dixieland One-Step/Bright Eyes//But He Can Dance/The Indian on the Nickel	1954	$15
CAE268 [PS]	(title unknown)	1954	$15
RCA VICTOR			
LPC-102	Boogie Woogie/There Are Such Things//Marie/I'll Be Seeing You	1961	$10
—Compact 33 Double"; small hole, plays at 33 1/3 rpm			
EPA-5007	Chicago/Dry Bones//Mississippi Mud/There Are Such Things	1958	$10
EPAT408	Chinatown, My Chinatown/The Sheik of Araby//Twilight in Turkey/Rhythm Saved the World	1952	$25
EPAT408 [PS]	Clambake Seven	1952	$25
EPA-5045 [PS]	I'm Getting Sentimental Over You (Gold Standard Series)	1958	$12
EPA-5045	I'm Getting Sentimental Over You/Who//The Huckle-Buck/Well, Git It!	1958	$10
EPA-5007 [PS]	Tommy Dorsey (Gold Standard Series)	1958	$12
LPC-102 [PS]	Tommy Dorsey Originals	1961	$12
DOTS, THE			
CADDY			
111	Good Luck to You/Heartsick and Lonely	1957	$100
101	I Confess/I Wish I Could Meet You	1956	$100
107	I Lost You/Johnny	1957	$100
DOTTSY			
RCA			
PB-10982	(After Sweet Memories) Play Born to Lose Again/Send Me the Pillow You Dream On	1977	$5
PB-11203	Here in Love/A Good Love Is Like a Good Song	1978	$5
PB-11293	I Just Had You on My Mind/Just Remember Who Your Friends Are	1978	$5
PB-11138	It Should Have Been Easy/Everybody's Reaching Out for Someone	1977	$5
PB-10766	Love Is a Two-Way Street/Lying in My Arms	1976	$5
PB-11610	Slip Away/Love Is a Two-Way Street	1979	$5
PB-11448	Tryin' to Satisfy You/If I Only Had the Words (To Tell You)	1979	$5
PB-11743	When I'm Gone/Storms Never Last	1979	$5
RCA VICTOR			
PB-10423	I'll Be Your San Antone Rose/If You Say It's So	1975	$5
PB-10280	Storms Never Last/Follow Me	1975	$5
PB-10666	The Sweetest Thing (I've Ever Known)/We Still Sing Love Songs Here in Texas	1976	$5
TANGLEWOOD			
1910	Let the Little Bird Fly/Love in My Baby's Eyes	1981	$6
1912	Mama/Healing Hands of Time	1981	$6
1908	Somebody's Darling, Somebody's Wife/Sing Me a Love Song	1981	$6
DOTTY AND DAN			
HIT			
89	I'm Leaving It Up to You/Down at Papa Joe's	1963	$8
—B-side by the Tennessee Six and Four More			
108	Stop and Think It Over/Navy Blue	1964	$8
—B-side by Connie Dee			
DOUBLE SIX OF PARIS, THE			
CAPITOL			
4394	French Rat Race/Meet Benny Bailey	1960	$20
PHILIPS			
40220	Lonely Avenue/Sherri	1964	$30
40192	One Mint Julep/Hallelujah I Love Her So	1964	$30
DOUG AND THE SLUGS			
RCA			
PB-13513	Makin' It Work/St. Laurent Summer	1983	$4
PB-12167	Too Bad/Chinatown Calculation	1981	$4
DOUGLAS, CARL			
20TH CENTURY			
2179	Blue Eyed Soul (Part 1)/Blue Eyed Soul (Part 2)	1975	$4
2168	Dance the Kung Fu/Changing Times	1975	$4
2192	Witchfinder General/Never Had This Dream Before	1975	$4
OKEH			
7268	Crazy Feeling/Keep It to Myself	1966	$15
7287	Let the Birds Sing/Something for Nothing	1967	$15
DOUGLAS, CAROL			
20TH CENTURY			
2484	Slip Into Something Comfortable/My Simple Heart	1981	$3
MIDLAND INT'L.			
MB-10870	Dancing Queen/In the Morning	1976	$4
MB-10113	Doctor's Orders/Baby, Don't Let This Good Love Die	1974	$4
MB-10372	Headline News/Boy, You Know Just What I'm After	1975	$4
MB-10229	Hurricane Is Coming Tonight/I Fell in Love with You	1975	$4
MB-10753	Midnight Love Affair/Midnight Love Affair (Long Version)	1976	$4
MB-10979	We Do It/Lie to Me	1977	$4
MB-10304	Will We Make It Tonight/Take Me (Make Me Lose Control)	1975	$4
MIDSONG INT'L.			
1008	I Got the Answer/We're Gonna Love	1979	$4
40945	Let's Get Down to Doin' It Tonight/Burnin'	1978	$4
40912	So You Win Again/Let You Come Into My Life	1978	$4
RCA VICTOR			
GB-10479	Doctor's Orders/Baby, Don't Let This Good Love Die	1975	$3
—Gold Standard Series			
DOUGLAS, CRAIG			
BETHLEHEM			
3057	When My Little Girl Is Smiling/Ring-a-Ding	1963	$15
JARO			
77030	Heart of a Teenage Girl/New Boy	1960	$15
77016	My First Love Affair/What Do You Want	1960	$15
LONDON			
9611	Danke Schoen/Love Her While She's Young	1963	$15
TCF HALL			
107	Around the Corner/Find the Girl	1965	$10
DOUGLAS, KELLIE			
RCA VICTOR			
47-8005	My Mama Don't Like Him/Big Hunky Baby	1962	$15
DOUGLAS, KIRK			
DECCA			
29355	A Whale of a Tale/The Moon Grew Brighter and Brighter	1954	$30
DOUGLAS, LEW			
CARLTON			
533	Theme from "The Angel Wore Red"/"From the Terrace" Love Theme	1960	$10
DOUGLAS, MIKE			
ATLANTIC			
3344	Loneliness/Dancin' Again	1976	$4
3328	Philadelphia/Smile, Smile, Smile	1976	$4
DECCA			
32618	That's a Woman/Tell Me Why, Why Don't You Cry	1970	$5
32495	The Day After Forever/Someday You'll Be Sorry	1969	$5
EPIC			
10078	Cabaret/House of Love	1966	$6
10223	Father of the Bride/Hold Me	1967	$6
10132	Galway/A Little Town in Old County Down	1967	$6
10170	Here Comes My Baby Back Again/Someone Took the Sweetness Out of Sweetheart	1967	$6
10002	Here's to My Jenny/While We're Young	1966	$6
JZSP135100/1 [DJ]	Silver Bells (mono/stereo)	1967	$10
9876	The Men in My Little Girl's Life/Stranger on the Shore	1965	$6
10041	The Parents of the Kids in Love/Real Love	1966	$6
10041 [PS]	The Parents of the Kids in Love/Real Love	1966	$8
10089	Touch Hands on Christmas Morning/(The Story Of) The First Christmas Carol	1966	$15
10126	What Is a Square?/That's How Love Goes	1967	$6
MGM			
14337	For a Little While/Heaven Everyday	1971	$4
14508	High Hopes/Song for Erik	1973	$4
14453	Ole Buttermilk Sky/Wonderful World	1972	$4
PROJECT 3			
1335	Do Unto Others/Young at Heart	1968	$6
—With Pearl Bailey			
STAX			
0211	Birthday Song/Mother's Day	1974	$4
DOUGLAS, STEVE			
MGM			
13218	Snowplows Schussing (Part 1)/Snowplows Schussing (Part 2)	1964	$15
TANDEM			
7000	Magic Sound/There You Go	1961	$30
DOUGLAS, TONY			
20TH CENTURY			
2257	If I Can Make It (Through the Mornin')/Honky-Tonk Man	1975	$5
COCHISE			
121	Angola Chains/Camp Meetin' Song	1982	$6
105	Her House/The Last Time I Saw Laura	1980	$6
118	His 'n' Hers/Shrimpin'	1981	$6
119	Is Love Enough/Back to the Wind	1982	$6
110	Leanna/Layin' in the Sunshine	1980	$6
117	Let It Ride/(B-side unknown)	1981	$6
113	Meridian/I'll Fight Every Step of the Way	1981	$6
116	That's Allright/Back to the Wind	1981	$6
106	Waitin' for a Train/She Loves the Devil Out of Me	1980	$6
100	Walkin' Over Yonder/Thank You for Touching My Life	1980	$6
115	Walkin' Over Yonder/Thank You Lord for Makin' Her Mine	1981	$6
DOT			
17503	Love Her When She's Lonely/Rainbows, Wishing Wells	1974	$6
17464	My Last Day/I'll Fight Every Step of the Way	1973	$6
17443	Thank You for Touching My Life/Walkin' Over Yonder	1972	$6
PAULA			
1203	Did I Say Something Wrong/In the Time It Takes to Leave	1968	$12
268	Driven by Loneliness/The Fastest Gun Alive	1967	$12
278	Heart/Keep Your Little Eyes on Me	1967	$12
395	His and Hers/There Stands the Man	1974	$5
1220	His and Hers/Your Goodbye	1970	$8
290	I'm a One Woman Man/Mention My Name	1968	$10
304	Love Is the Reason/Me and My Lonely	1968	$10
1212	That's What I Get/Family Bouquet	1969	$12
1234	The Man/No Joy in My World	1970	$8
1225	There Stands the Man/State Trooper Sammy Young	1970	$8
SIMS			
221	Big Ache of the Year/I'm Happy	1965	$20
294	Don't Piddle 'Round the Puddle/I Can't Forget Your Memory	1966	$20
271	Empty Crowded Room/Poor Little Darling	1966	$20
160	It's Just About Time/Home Away from Home	1964	$20
255	Itsy Bitsy Heartache/It Didn't Help Much	1965	$20
236	Take the Hands Off the Clock/(B-side unknown)	1965	$20
286	Thanks a Lot/(B-side unknown)	1966	$20
VEE JAY			
481	His and Hers/Gabby Abby	1963	$30

Number	Title	Yr	NM

DOVAL, JIM, AND THE GAUCHOS
ABC-PARAMOUNT
| 10621 | Annie Ya Ya/Out of Sight | 1965 | $10 |
| 10637 | I Know You're Fooling Around/Uptown Caballero | 1965 | $10 |

DIPLOMACY
6	Beatles Rule/Pink Elephant	1964	$30
3	Donna/The Scrub	1964	$30
1000	Love Me One More Time (Part 1)/Love Me One More Time (Part 2)	1963	$30

— As "Jim SanDoval and the Gauchos"

7	She's a Very Nice Girl/Bony Moronie	1964	$125
17	She's So Fine/Mama, Keep Your Big Mouth Shut	1965	$30
5	Stranded in the Pool/Right Now	1964	$30
8	The Good and the Bad/Fireballed	1965	$30

DOT
16571	Barracuda/The Scrub	1964	$20
16468	Fire Ball/Good and Bad	1963	$20
16548	Love Me One More Time (Part 1)/Love Me One More Time (Part 2)	1963	$20

DOVE, RONNIE
DECCA
32997	It's No Sin/My World of Memories	1972	$6
33038	Lilacs in Winter/Is It Wrong	1972	$6
31288	Party Doll/Yes Darling, I'll Be Around	1961	$200

— Price is for stock copy; promos go for 20 to 25 percent of this value

DIAMOND
| 184 | A Little Bit of Heaven/If I Live to Be a Hundred | 1965 | $8 |
| 271 | Chains of Love/If I Live to Be a Hundred | 1970 | $20 |

— Promos, with "Chains of Love" on both sides, go for about half this amount

| 214 | Cry/Autumn Rhapsody | 1966 | $8 |
| 233 | Dancin' Out of My Heart/Back from Baltimore | 1967 | $30 |

— B-side written and produced by Neil Diamond, who also supplies backing vocals

205	Happy Summer Days/Long After	1966	$8
205 [PS]	Happy Summer Days/Long After	1966	$20
378	Heart/Old Time Rock and Roll	1987	$30

— The version with a B-side is much harder to find than the version with the same song on both sides; also, this version was not issued with a picture sleeve

378	Heart (same on both sides)	1987	$12
378 [PS]	Heart (same on both sides)	1987	$30
176	Hello Pretty Girl/Keep It a Secret	1965	$8
188	I'll Make All Your Dreams Come True/I Had to Lose You	1965	$8
260	I Need You Now/Bluebird	1969	$6
240	In Some Time/Livin' for Your Lovin'	1968	$8
208	I Really Don't Want to Know/Years of Tears	1966	$8
227	I Want to Love You for What You Are/I Thank You for Your Love	1967	$8
198	Let's Start All Over Again/That Empty Feeling	1966	$8
244	Mountain of Love/Never Gonna Cry	1968	$8
221	My Babe/Put My Mind at Ease	1967	$10

— A-side written and produced by Neil Diamond

179	One Kiss for Old Times' Sake/Bluebird	1965	$8
179	One Kiss for Old Times' Sake/No Greater Love	1965	$8
217	One More Mountain to Climb/All	1967	$8
167	Say You/Let Me Stay Today	1964	$10
163	Sweeter Than Sugar/I Believed in You	1964	$10
249	Tomboy/Tell Me Tomorrow	1968	$8
256	What's Wrong with My World/That Empty Feeling	1969	$6
195	When Liking Turns to Loving/I'm Learning How to Smile Again	1965	$8

DOVE
| 1021 | Lover Boy/I'll Be Around | 1959 | $4000 |

— As "Ronnie Dove and the Bell-Tones". VG 1500; VG+ 2750

HITSVILLE
| 6045 | The Morning After the Night Before/Why Daddy | 1976 | $5 |
| 6038 | Tragedy/Songs We Sang As Children | 1976 | $5 |

M.C.
| 5013 | The Angel in Your Eyes (Brings Out the Devil in Me)/Songs We Sang As Children | 1978 | $6 |

MCA
| 40106 | So Long Dixie/Take My Love | 1973 | $5 |

MELODYLAND
| 6021 | Drina (Take Your Lady Off for Me)/Your Sweet Love | 1975 | $5 |

| 6004 | Please Come to Nashville/Pictures on Paper | 1975 | $5 |
| 6011 | Things/Here We Go Again | 1975 | $5 |

DOVELLS, THE
ABKCO
4029	Baby Workout/Hully Gully Baby	1973	$12
4011	Bristol Stomp/You Can't Sit Down	1972	$4
4032	Bristol Twistin' Annie/Betty in Bermudas	1973	$4

EVENT
| 216 | Dancing in the Street/Back on the Road Again | 1974 | $5 |

JAMIE
| 1369 | Our Winter Love/Blue | 1969 | $10 |

MGM
| 14568 | Don't Vote for Luke McCabe/Mary's Magic Show | 1973 | $5 |
| 13628 | There's a Girl/Love Is Everywhere | 1966 | $10 |

PARAMOUNT
| 0134 | L-O-V-E Love/We're All In This Together | 1971 | $5 |

PARKWAY
901	Be My Girl/Dragster on the Prowl	1964	$30
882	Betty in Bermudas/Dance the Froog	1963	$15
882 [PS]	Betty in Bermudas/Dance the Froog	1963	$40
827	Bristol Stomp/Letters of Love	1961	$20
827	Bristol Stomp/Out in the Cold Again	1961	$40
838	Bristol Twistin' Annie/The Actor	1962	$20
838 [PS]	Bristol Twistin' Annie/The Actor	1962	$40
833	Do the New Continental/Mope-Itty Mope Stomp	1962	$20
833 [PS]	Do the New Continental/Mope-Itty Mope Stomp	1962	$40
845	Hully Gully Baby/Your Last Chance	1962	$20
845 [PS]	Hully Gully Baby/Your Last Chance	1962	$40
911	One Potato/Happy Birthday Just the Same	1964	$20
861	Save Me Baby/You Can't Run Away from Yourself	1963	$30
861 [PS]	Save Me Baby/You Can't Run Away from Yourself	1963	$40
889	Stop Monkeyin' Aroun'/No, No, No	1963	$15
889 [PS]	Stop Monkeyin' Aroun'/No, No, No	1963	$40
925	Watusi with Lucy/What in the World's Come Over You	1964	$15
925 [PS]	Watusi with Lucy/What in the World's Come Over You	1964	$40

SWAN
| 4231 | Happy/(Hey, Hey, Hey) Alright | 1965 | $30 |

VERVE
| 10701 | Far Away/Sometimes | 1973 | $5 |

DOVER, NEAL
DIAMOND
| 270 | Mr. Bus Driver/Paper Man | 1970 | $30 |

DOVERS, THE
DAVIS
| 465 | Sweet as a Flower/(B-side unknown) | 1959 | $50 |

NEW HORIZON
| 501 | Devil You May Be/(B-side unknown) | 1961 | $40 |

DOWD, LARRY
SPINNING
| 6009 | Blue Swinging Mama/Pink Cadillac | 1959 | $200 |
| 6004 | Why, Oh Why/Forbidden Love | 1958 | $30 |

DOWELL, JOE
JOURNEY
| 1238 [DJ] | Homeward on the Wind (mono/stereo) | 1973 | $6 |

— Stock copy not known to exist

| 1238 [PS] | Homeward on the Wind (mono/stereo) | 1973 | $6 |

MONUMENT
| 952 | If I Could Find Out What Is Wrong/Indian Summer Days | 1966 | $8 |

SMASH
1816	Bobby Blue Loves Linda Lou/My Darling Wears White Today	1963	$15
1816 [PS]	Bobby Blue Loves Linda Lou/My Darling Wears White Today	1963	$20
1728	(I Wonder) Who's Spending Christmas with You/A Kiss for Christmas	1961	$20
1759	Little Red Rented Rowboat/The One I Left for You	1962	$15

1759 [PS]	Little Red Rented Rowboat/The One I Left for You	1962	$15
1799	Our School Days/Bringa-Branga-Brought	1963	$15
1799 [PS]	Our School Days/Bringa-Branga-Brought	1963	$20
1786	Poor Little Cupid/No Secrets	1962	$15
1786 [PS]	Poor Little Cupid/No Secrets	1962	$20
1717	The Bridge of Love/Just Love Me	1961	$15
1717 [PS]	The Bridge of Love/Just Love Me	1961	$20
1730	The Sound of Sadness/The Thorn on the Rose	1962	$15
1708	Wooden Heart/Little Bo Peep	1961	$20
1708 [PS]	Wooden Heart/Little Bo Peep	1961	$30

DOWLANDS, THE
TOLLIE
| 9002 | All My Loving/Hey Sally | 1964 | $20 |

DOWLING, CHET & BILL MINKIN
COLUMBIA
| ZLP135464/5 [DJ] | Christmas Eve With The Senator//The Opening and the Gift List/The Christmas Haircut/What to Get the Kids/The Christmas Cards | 1967 | $15 |

— Small hole, 33 1/3 rpm; promo for "Senator Bobby's Christmas Party"

DOWNBEATS, THE (1)
GEE
| 1019 | My Girl/China Girl | 1956 | $800 |

— Red label

| 1019 | My Girl/China Girl | 1958 | $40 |

— Gray label

DOWNBEATS, THE (2)
SARG
| 168 | Darling of Mine/Come On Over | 1959 | $50 |
| 197 | Falling Stars/I Just Can't Understand | 1960 | $50 |

— As "O.S. Grant and the Downbeats"

DOWNBEATS, THE (4)
WILCO
| 9 | Alfalfa/Red X | 1960 | $30 |
| 16 | Playin' Possum/One at a Time | 1960 | $30 |

DOWNEY, MORTON, JR.
ARTISTS OF AMERICA
| 109 | He Played a Yo-Yo in Nashville/You'll Never Have to Ask Me If I Love You | 1976 | $5 |

— As "Sean Morton Downey"

| 123 | He Played a Yo-Yo in Nashville/You'll Never Have to Ask Me If I Love You | 1976 | $4 |

— As "Sean Morton Downey"

BULLDOG
| 105 | A Tear Fell in the Chapel/Tender Years | 1959 | $20 |

— As "Sean Downey"

CADENCE
| 1407 | The Ballad of Billy Brown/Flattery | 1961 | $12 |

CONTENDER
| 1317 | Love Bug/Rags to Riches | 1959 | $20 |

ESO
| 932 | Green Eyed Girl/(B-side unknown) | 1981 | $8 |

— As "Sean Morton Downey"

IMPERIAL
| 5556 | Boulevard of Broken Dreams/Proud Possession | 1958 | $10 |

MAGIC LAMP
| 517 | The Ballad of Billy Brown/Flattery | 1964 | $8 |

PERSONALITY
| 3506 | Little Miss U.S.A./Football Freddy | 1959 | $15 |

PRIVATE STOCK
| 45,168 | Family Tree/Spanish Harlem | 1977 | $4 |

SCEPTER
| 12360 | Break the Habit of Hate/Second Chance Lord | 1972 | $6 |

— As "Sean Downey"

| 12316 | Love Theme from Christine/Christine's a Lady | 1971 | $6 |

— As "Sean Morton Downey, Jr."

Number	Title	Yr	NM

STAX
- ❏ 0195 — I Believe in America/My Last Day on Earth — 1974 — $4

—As "Sean Downey

WYE
- ❏ 1010 — I Beg Your Pardon/Three Steps to the Phone — 1961 — $15

DOWNING, BIG AL

CARLTON
- ❏ 507 — It Must Be Love/When My Blue Moon Turns to Gold Again — 1959 — $50
- ❏ 489 — Miss Lucy/Just Around the Corner — 1959 — $60

CHALLENGE
- ❏ 59006 — Down on the Farm/Oh Babe — 1958 — $60

CHESS
- ❏ 2158 — I'll Be Holding On/Baby Let's Talk It Over — 1974 — $5
- ❏ 1817 — The Story of My Life/I'd Love to Be Loved — 1962 — $15

COLUMBIA
- ❏ 43185 — I Feel Good/Georgia Slop — 1964 — $10
- ❏ 43028 — I'm Just Nobody/All I Want Is You — 1964 — $10

DOOR KNOB
- ❏ 340 — Bound for Baltimore/(B-side unknown) — 1989 — $5
- ❏ 345 — Father #1/(B-side unknown) — 1989 — $5
- ❏ 328 — I Guess By Now/(B-side unknown) — 1989 — $5

JANUS
- ❏ 234 — I'll Be Holding On/Hands — 1974 — $6
- ❏ 211 — Thank You Baby/(B-side unknown) — 1974 — $6

LENOX
- ❏ 5572 — Mr. Hurt Walked In/If I Had Our Love to Live Over — 1963 — $15

POLYDOR
- ❏ 14311 — I Love to Love/I'm Just Nobody — 1976 — $5

SILVER FOX
- ❏ 3 — Cornbread Row/The Saints — 1969 — $8
- ❏ 11 — Medley of Soul/These Arms You Push Away — 1969 — $8

TEAM
- ❏ 1002 — Darlene/(B-side unknown) — 1982 — $5
- ❏ 1001 — I'll Be Loving You/Don't Mess with an Angel — 1982 — $5
- ❏ 1004 — It Takes Love/If You're Leaving — 1983 — $5
- ❏ 1003 — Let's Sing About Love/We Can Only Say Goodbye — 1983 — $5
- ❏ 1007 — The Best of Families/Fool of the Year — 1983 — $5
- ❏ 1008 — There'll Never Be a Better Night for Bein' Wrong/(B-side unknown) — 1984 — $5

VINE ST.
- ❏ 103 — How Beautiful You Are (To Me)/The Only Thing Missing Is You — 1986 — $6
- ❏ 106 — How Ya Gonna Do It/The Only Thing Missing Is You — 1987 — $6

V-TONE
- ❏ 220 — If I Had Our Love to Live Over/Words of Love — 1961 — $15
- ❏ 230 — So Many Memories/There'll Come a Time — 1961 — $15

WARNER BROS.
- ❏ 49270 — Bring It On Home/Beer Drinking People — 1980 — $4
- ❏ 49141 — I Ain't No Fool/Mr. Jones — 1979 — $4
- ❏ 49034 — Midnight Lace/Counting Highway Signs — 1979 — $4
- ❏ 8716 — Mr. Jones/I Don't Cry (The Onion Song) — 1978 — $5
- ❏ 49161 — The Story Behind the Story/Daddy Played the Banjo — 1980 — $4
- ❏ 8787 — Touch Me (I'll Be Your Fool Once More)/I Ain't No Fool — 1979 — $5

WHITE ROCK
- ❏ 1111 — Down on the Farm/Oh Babe — 1958 — $200
- ❏ 1113 — Miss Lucy/Just Around the Corner — 1958 — $200

DOWNLINERS SECT, THE

SMASH
- ❏ 1954 — Little Egypt/I Feel Good — 1965 — $15

DOWNS, LAVERNE

PEACH
- ❏ 735 — But You Used To/What Have I Done — 1960 — $30

DOZIER, GENE, AND THE BROTHERHOOD

MINIT
- ❏ 32041 — Funky Broadway/Soul Stroll — 1968 — $10
- ❏ 32026 — House of Funk/One for Bess — 1967 — $10
- ❏ 32031 — I Wanna Testify/Mustang Sally — 1967 — $10

DOZIER, LAMONT

ABC
- ❏ 12076 — All Cried Out/Rose — 1975 — $4
- ❏ 11438 — Fish Ain't Bitin'/Breaking Out All Over — 1974 — $4
- ❏ 12012 — Fish Ain't Bitin'/Breaking Out All Over — 1974 — $4
- ❏ 12044 — Let Me Start Tonite/I Wanna Be with You — 1974 — $4
- ❏ 12234 — Out Here on My Own/Take Off Your Make-Up — 1976 — $4
- ❏ 11407 — Trying to Hold On to My Woman/We Don't Want Nobody to Come Between Us — 1973 — $4

—Also see "Holland-Dozier

ANNA
- ❏ 1125 — Let's Talk It Over/Benny the Skinny Man — 1960 — $30

—As "Lamont Anthony
- ❏ 1125 — Let's Talk It Over/Popeye — 1960 — $250

—As "Lamont Anthony

COLUMBIA
- ❏ 02035 — Cool Me Out/Starting Over (We've Made the Necessary Changes) — 1981 — $4
- ❏ 02238 — Too Little Too Long/Chained (To Your Love) — 1981 — $4

M&M
- ❏ 502 — Shout About It/(Instrumental) — 1982 — $5

MEL-O-DY
- ❏ 102 — Dearest One/Fortune Teller Please Tell Me — 1962 — $125

WARNER BROS.
- ❏ 8792 — Boogie Business/True Love Is Bittersweet — 1979 — $4
- ❏ 8432 — Sight for Sore Eyes/Tear Down the Walls — 1977 — $4

DRAG KINGS, THE

UNITED ARTISTS
- ❏ 676 — Bearing Burners/Nitro — 1963 — $40

DRAGON, PAUL

STARFIRE
- ❏ 503 — My Heart Is Achin' for You/You're My Baby — 1984 — $4

DRAGONS, THE

CAPITOL
- ❏ 5278 — Elephant Stomp/Troll — 1964 — $30

DRAKE, CHARLIE

UNITED ARTISTS
- ❏ 398 — My Boomerang Won't Come Back/She's My Girl — 1961 — $40

—With A-side lyric "Practiced 'til I was black in the face.
- ❏ 398 — My Boomerang Won't Come Back/She's My Girl — 1961 — $20

—With A-side lyric "Practiced 'til I was blue in the face.
- ❏ 477 — Sweet Freddie Green/Zulu Drake — 1962 — $15
- ❏ 437 — Tanglefoot/Drake's Progress — 1962 — $15

DRAKE, PETE

SMASH
- ❏ 1978 — Dream/Am I That Easy to Forget — 1965 — $8
- ❏ 1867 — Forever/Sleepwalk — 1964 — $8
- ❏ 2046 — I'm a Fool to Care/Mystic Dream — 1966 — $8
- ❏ 1910 — I'm Sorry/I'm Just a Guitar (Everybody Picks On Me) — 1964 — $8
- ❏ 1935 — I'm Walkin'/Are You Sincere — 1964 — $8
- ❏ 1888 — Midnight in Amarillo/Forever — 1964 — $8

STARDAY
- ❏ 751 — My Abilene/Y'All Come — 1966 — $8

STOP
- ❏ 349 — Lay Lady Lay/For Pete's Sake — 1970 — $6

DRAKES, THE

CONQUEST
- ❏ 1001 — Oo Wee So Good/Kitty — 1958 — $600

OLIMPIC
- ❏ 252 — I Made a Wish/Ole King Cole — 1965 — $120

DRAMATICS, THE

ABC
- ❏ 12235 — Be My Girl/The Nicest Man Alive — 1976 — $5
- ❏ 12400 — Do What You Want to Do/Jane — 1978 — $5
- ❏ 12220 — Finger Fever/Say the Word — 1976 — $5
- ❏ 12258 — I Can't Get Over You/Sundown Is Coming (Hold Back the Night) — 1977 — $5
- ❏ 12460 — I Just Wanna Dance with You/I've Got a Schoolboy Crush on You — 1979 — $5
- ❏ 12125 — (I'm Going By) The Stars in Your Eyes/Trying to Get Over You — 1975 — $5
- ❏ 12090 — Mr. and Mrs. Jones/I Cried All the Way Home — 1975 — $5
- ❏ 12331 — Ocean of Thoughts and Dreams/Come Inside — 1978 — $5
- ❏ 12299 — Shake It Well/That Heaven Kind of Feeling — 1977 — $5
- ❏ 12372 — Stop Your Weeping/California Sunrise — 1978 — $5
- ❏ 12180 — Treat Me Like a Man/I Was the Life of the Party — 1976 — $5
- ❏ 12429 — Why Do You Wanna Do Me Wrong/Yo' Love (Can Only Bring Me Happiness) — 1978 — $5

CADET
- ❏ 5706 — Don't Make Me No Promises/Tune Up — 1974 — $6
- ❏ 5704 — Door to Your Heart/Choosing Up on You — 1974 — $6
- ❏ 5710 — Love Is Missing from Our Lives/I'm in Love — 1975 — $6

—With the Dells

CAPITOL
- ❏ B-5103 — Live It Up/She's My Kind of Girl — 1982 — $4
- ❏ B-5140 — Treat Me Right/Night Life — 1982 — $4

CRACKERJACK
- ❏ 4015 — Toy Soldier/Hello Summer — 1968 — $70

FANTASY
- ❏ 966 — Luv's Calling/Dream Lady — 1985 — $3
- ❏ 967 — One Love Ago/Dream Lady — 1986 — $3

MCA
- ❏ 41241 — Be With the One You Love/If You Feel Like You Wanna Dance, Dance — 1980 — $4
- ❏ 12460 — I Just Wanna Dance with You/I've Got a Schoolboy Crush on You — 1979 — $4
- ❏ 41017 — I Just Wanta Dance With You/I've Got a Schoolboy Crush on You — 1979 — $4
- ❏ 51004 — Share Your Love with Me/Get It — 1980 — $4
- ❏ 41056 — That's My Favorite Song/Bottom Line Woman — 1979 — $4
- ❏ 41178 — Welcome Back Home/Marriage on Paper Only — 1980 — $4
- ❏ 51041 — (We Need More) Lovin' Time/You're the Best Thing in My Life — 1980 — $4

SPORT
- ❏ 101 — All Because of You/If You Haven't Got Love — 1967 — $70

VOLT
- ❏ 4105 — And I Panicked/Beware of the Man — 1974 — $8
- ❏ 302 — Bridge Over Troubled Water/(B-side unknown) — 1989 — $4
- ❏ 4099 — Fell for You/Now You Got Me Loving You — 1973 — $8
- ❏ 4071 — Get Up and Get Down/Fall in Love, Lady Love — 1971 — $8
- ❏ 4090 — Hey You! Get Off My Mountain/The Devil Is Dope — 1973 — $8
- ❏ 4108 — I Made Myself Lonely/Highway to Heaven — 1974 — $8
- ❏ 4075 — In the Rain/Good Soul Music — 1972 — $8
- ❏ 4029 — Since I've Been in Love/Your Love Was Strange — 1969 — $8
- ❏ 4082 — Toast to the Fool/Your Love Was Strange — 1972 — $8
- ❏ 4058 — Whatcha See Is Whatcha Get/Thankful for Your Love — 1971 — $8

WINGATE
- ❏ 22 — Baby I Need You/Inky Dinky Wang Dang Doo — 1966 — $60

—As "The Dynamics
- ❏ 18 — Somewhere/Bingo! — 1966 — $60

—As "The Dynamics

Number	Title	Yr	NM

DRAPER, RUSTY

KL

❑ 001	Harbor Lights/ (B-side unknown)	1979	$4

MERCURY

❑ 70004	Angry/Blue Tears	1952	$15
❑ 71784	Another/The Meadow	1961	$8
❑ 70757	Are You Satisfied/ Wabash Cannonball	1955	$10
❑ 71976	Beggar to a King/Deep Roots	1962	$8
❑ 71221	Buzz Buzz Buzz/I Get the Blues When It Rains	1957	$10
❑ 5851	Devil of a Woman/ Bouncing on the Bayou	1952	$20
❑ 70619	Eating Goober Peas/ That's All I Need	1955	$15
❑ 71102	Freight Train/Seven Come Eleven	1957	$10
❑ 70167	Gambler's Guitar/Free Home Demonstration	1953	$15
❑ 71298	Gamblin' Gal/That's My Doll	1958	$10
❑ 70938	Giant/Old Buttermilk Sky	1956	$20
❑ 70818	Held for Questioning/Forty-Two	1956	$12
❑ 71418	Hey Li Lee Li Lee Li/The Sun Will Always Shine	1959	$12
❑ 71351	Hip Monkey/Can You Depend on Me	1958	$12
❑ 71545	I Get So Jealous/But For the Flow of Flo	1959	$10
❑ 70921	In the Middle of the House/Pink Cadillac	1956	$10
❑ 70365	It Ain't Me Baby/Knock on Wood	1954	$15
❑ 71664	It's a Little More Like Heaven/Luck of the Irish	1960	$8
❑ 70178	Lazy River/Bummin' Around	1953	$15
❑ 71039	Let's Go Calypso/Should I Ever Love Again	1957	$12
❑ 70188	Lighthouse/I Love to Jump	1953	$15
❑ 70526	Lookin' Back to See/ Shame on You	1955	$15
❑ 70446	Muskrat Ramble/ The Magic Circle	1954	$15
❑ 70300	Peter Rabbit/Easter Morning	1954	$15
❑ 70415	Please, Please/ Workshop of the Lord	1954	$15
❑ 71634	Please Help Me, I'm Falling/ Mule Skinner Blues	1960	$8
❑ 70651	Seventeen/Can't Live Without Them Anymore	1955	$15
❑ 71854	Signed, Sealed and Delivered/ Scared to Go Home	1961	$8
❑ 5894	Sing Baby Sing/I Gotta Have My Baby Back	1952	$20
❑ 70853	Sometimes You Win, Sometimes You Lose/The Gun of Billy the Kid	1956	$12
❑ 71581	That Lucky Old Sun/Any Time	1960	$8
❑ 70555	The Ballad of Davy Crockett/I've Been Thinkin'	1955	$20
❑ 70696	The Shifting, Whispering Sands/Time	1955	$10
❑ 70327	The Train with a Rhumba Beat/Melancholy Baby	1954	$15
❑ 71564	Two of a Kind/If My Mother'd Only Let Me Cross the Street	1960	$8
❑ 71914	Well I've Learned/Tongue Tied Over You	1961	$8
❑ 71388	With This Ring/Shopping Around	1958	$10

MONUMENT

❑ 1074	Buffalo Nickel/Make Believe I'm Him	1968	$6
❑ 1044	California Sunshine/The Gypsy	1968	$6
❑ 1137	Don't Build No Fences for Me/ Am I That Easy to Forget	1969	$6
❑ 1202	Every Man Has a Prison/Tie Me to Your Apron Strings Again	1970	$5
❑ 1157	I Walk Alone/Sunshine Man	1969	$6
❑ 969	Love Is Gone for Good/You Call Everybody Darling	1966	$6
❑ 1116	Love Is Just a Game/Something Old, Something New	1968	$6
❑ 1019	My Elusive Dreams/ Memory Lane	1967	$6
❑ 944	Mystery Train/The Shifting, Whispering Sands	1966	$6
❑ 1223	There She Goes/Travelling Song	1970	$5
❑ 1188	Two Little Boys/It Don't Mean a Thing to Me	1970	$5
❑ 8628	Walking on New Grass/ You Were Right	1974	$4

DRAWDY, BOBBY

DOOR KNOB

❑ 239	Elmo and the Time Machine/ The Rooster and the Cockroach	1985	$6

I.E.

❑ 0010	Football Withdrawal (same on both sides)	1982	$6

DREAD ZEPPELIN

LED ZEPPELIN tribute band with a reggae beat.

BIRDCAGE

❑ 45-2690	Whole Lotta Love/Tour-Telvis: A Bad Trip	1989	$10
— Pink vinyl			
❑ 45-2690 [PS]	Whole Lotta Love/Tour-Telvis: A Bad Trip	1989	$10

DREAM ACADEMY, THE

REPRISE

❑ 27889	Everybody's Got to Learn Sometime/In Exile (For Rodrigo Rojas)	1988	$5
❑ 28199DJ [DJ]	Indian Summer (Edit)/ (LP Version)	1987	$4
❑ 28199	Indian Summer/Heaven Part 1	1987	$4
❑ 28199 [PS]	Indian Summer/Heaven Part 1	1987	$5
❑ 28118	The Lesson of Love/Here	1988	$4
❑ 28118 [PS]	The Lesson of Love/Here	1988	$4
❑ 28750	The Love Parade/A Girl in a Million (For E. Sedgwick)	1986	$4
❑ 28750 [PS]	The Love Parade/A Girl in a Million (For E. Sedgwick)	1986	$4

WARNER BROS.

❑ 28841	Life in a Northern Town/ Test Tape No. 3	1985	$3
❑ 28841 [PS]	Life in a Northern Town/ Test Tape No. 3	1985	$3

DREAM GIRLS, THE

BIG TOP

❑ 3059	Don't Break My Heart/I Could Write a Book	1960	$30
❑ 3100	Duchess of Earl/Mine All Mine	1962	$30
❑ 3111	Here Comes Baby/I Got a Feeling My Love	1962	$30
❑ 3085	Wanted/Mr. Fine	1961	$30

— The rest of the Big Top singles as "Bobbie Smith and the Dream Girls"

CAMEO

❑ 165	Don't Break My Heart/ Oh This Is Why	1959	$30

METRO

❑ 20034	Heartaches/Love Hen	1961	$30
❑ 20029	I'm in Love with You/ Cryin' in the Night	1960	$40

TWIRL

❑ 1002	Don't Break My Heart/ Oh This Is Why	1959	$60

DREAM KINGS, THE

CHECKER

❑ 858	M.T.Y.L.T.T./Oh What a Baby	1957	$200

DREAM SYNDICATE, THE

FORCED EXPOSURE

❑ 04	Ballad of Dwight Frye/Low Rider	1986	$40
❑ 04 [PS]	Ballad of Dwight Frye/Low Rider	1986	$40

DREAM TEAM, THE

EPIC

❑ 9701	I'm Not Afraid/Inka Dinka Doo	1964	$15

DREAM WEAVERS, THE

DECCA

❑ 29905	A Little Love Can Go a Long, Long Way/Is There Somebody Else	1956	$15
❑ 30276	Fool's Gold/I'll Try, I'll Try	1957	$15
❑ 29990	Give Us This Day/ Why I Chose You	1956	$15
❑ 29683	It's Almost Tomorrow/You've Got Me Wondering	1955	$20
❑ 30156	Till We Meet Again/ All This Is Home	1956	$15

DREAMERS, THE

ABC-PARAMOUNT

❑ 9746	The Girl Down the Street/ The Right Time for Love	1956	$30

ALADDIN

❑ 3303	My Plea/Charles My Darling	1955	$200

APT

❑ 25053	Mary's Little Lamb/I Sing This Song	1960	$30

BLUE STAR

❑ 8001	I Really Love You/You Made Me Darling	1960	$30

COUSINS

❑ 1005	Because of You/Little Girl	1961	$125

FAIRMOUNT

❑ 612	Daydreamin' of You/The Promise	1963	$30

FLIP

❑ 319	Since You've Been Gone/ Do Not Forget	1956	$50
❑ 354	Since You've Been Gone/ Do Not Forget	1961	$30

GOLDISC

❑ 3015	Teenage Vows of Love/Natalie	1961	$40

GRAND

❑ 131	Tears in My Eyes/535	1955	$300

GUARANTEED

❑ 219	Mary, Mary/Canadian Sunset	1961	$20

JUBILEE

❑ 5053	These Things I Miss/Can't Get You Off My Mind	1951	$300

MANHATTAN

❑ 503	Lips Were Meant for Kissing/No Obligation	1956	$125

MAY

❑ 133	Because of You/Little Girl	1963	$50

MERCURY

❑ 5843	I'm Gonna Hate Myself in the Morning/Ain't Gonna Worry No More	1952	$200
❑ 70019	Please Don't Leave Me/ Walkin' My Blues	1953	$200

NUGGET

❑ 1000	Don't Cry/It's Gonna Be Alright	1959	$40

UNITED ARTISTS

❑ 841	Henry, Henry, Henry/ Love, Love, Love	1965	$15

DREAMETTES, THE

UNITED ARTISTS

❑ 921	Gonna Make That Little Boy Mine/Run, Steven, Run	1965	$30

DREAMLOVERS, THE

CAMEO

❑ 326	These Will Be the Good Old Days/Oh Baby Mine (I Get So Lonely)	1964	$20

CASINO

❑ 1308	Amazons and Coyotes/Together	1963	$20

COLUMBIA

❑ 42842	Pretty Little Girl/I'm Through with You	1963	$60
❑ 42752	Sad, Sad Boy/Black Bottom	1963	$15
❑ 42698	Sad, Sad Boy/If I Were a Magician	1963	$30

END

❑ 1114	If I Should Lose You/I Miss You	1962	$30

HERITAGE

❑ 104	Welcome Home/Let Them Love (And Be Loved)	1961	$20
❑ 102	When We Get Married/ Just Because	1961	$30

LEN

❑ 1006	Take It from a Fool/ For the First Time	1958	$200

MERCURY

❑ 72595	Bless Your Soul/Bad Time Make the Good Times	1966	$10
❑ 72630	Calling Jo-Ann/You Gave Me Someone to Love	1966	$10

SWAN

❑ 4167	Amazons and Coyotes/Together	1963	$30
— White label			
❑ 4167	Amazons and Coyotes/Together	1963	$15
— Black label			

V-TONE

❑ 211	Annabelle Lee/Home Is Where the Heart Is	1960	$30
❑ 229	May I Kiss the Bride/Time	1961	$30

DREAMS, THE

SAVOY

❑ 1130	Darlene/A Letter to My Girl	1954	$200
❑ 1157	I'll Be Faithful/My Little Honeybun	1955	$125

DREW-VELS, THE

CAPITOL

❑ 5244	Creepin'/I've Known	1964	$12
❑ 5145	It's My Time/Everybody Knows	1964	$10
❑ 5055	Tell Him/Just Because	1963	$15

QUILL

❑ 100	True Enough/Chilly Kisses	1966	$10

DREW, PATTI

CAPITOL

❑ 2339	Hard to Handle/Just Can't Forget About You	1968	$8
❑ 2575	He's the One/Which One Should I Choose	1969	$8
❑ 2989	I'm Calling/It's Just a Dream	1970	$8
❑ 2389	I've Been Here All the Time/Welcome Back	1969	$8
❑ 5969	Stop and Listen/Tired of Falling In and Out of Love	1967	$8
❑ 5861	Tell Him/Turn Away from Me	1967	$8
❑ 2473	The Love That a Woman Should Give to a Man/Save the Last Dance for Me	1969	$8
❑ 2713	The Pick-Up/Hundreds and Thousands of Guys	1970	$8
❑ 2042	Where Is Daddy/Sufferer	1967	$8
❑ 2712	Wild Is Love/World of No Return	1969	$8
— B-side by John Stewart			

Number	Title	Yr	NM
❑ 2197	Workin' on a Groovy Thing/Without a Doubt	1968	$8

QUILL

Number	Title	Yr	NM
❑ 101	Where Is Daddy/Sufferer	1966	$10

DRIFTERS, THE

ATLANTIC

Number	Title	Yr	NM
❑ 1078	Adorable/Steamboat	1955	$50
❑ 2366	Aretha/Baby What I Mean	1966	$8
❑ 2268	At the Club/Answer the Phone	1965	$12
❑ 1043	Bip Bam/Someday You'll Want Me to Want You	1954	$50
❑ 2285	Come On Over to My Place/Chains of Love	1965	$10
❑ 2040	Dance with Me/(If You Cry) True Love, True Love	1959	$30
❑ 1187	Drip Drop/Moonlight Bay	1958	$40

—Last record by the "old" Drifters. The below Atlantic 45s are by a completely different group, although personnel changes resulted in at least one "old" Drifter (Johnny Moore) spending time with the "new" Drifters.

Number	Title	Yr	NM
❑ 2292	Follow Me/The Outside World	1965	$10
❑ 1123	Fools Fall in Love/It Was a Tear	1957	$40
❑ 1029	Honey Love/Warm Your Heart	1954	$60
❑ 1141	Hypnotized/Drifting Away from You	1957	$40
❑ 2087	I Count the Tears/Suddenly There's a Valley	1960	$20
❑ 1161	I Know/Yodee Yakee	1957	$40
❑ 2201	I'll Take You Home/I Feel Good All Over	1963	$20
❑ 2298	I'll Take You Where the Music's Playing/Far from the Maddening Crowd	1965	$10
❑ 2471	I Need You Now/Still Burning in My Heart	1968	$8
❑ 2253	I've Got Sand in My Shoes/He's Just a Playboy	1964	$15
❑ 2062	Lonely Winds/Hey Senorita	1960	$30
❑ 2325	Memories Are Made of This/My Islands in the Sun	1966	$8
❑ 1006	Money Honey/The Way I Feel	1953	$100
❑ 2182	On Broadway/Let the Music Play	1963	$20
❑ 2225	One Way Love/Didn't It	1964	$20
❑ 2105	Please Stay/No Sweet Lovin'	1961	$20
❑ 2260	Saturday Night at the Movies/Spanish Lace	1964	$15
❑ 2260 [PS]	Saturday Night at the Movies/Spanish Lace	1964	$50
❑ 2071	Save the Last Dance for Me/Nobody But Me	1960	$30
❑ 1101	Soldier of Fortune/I Got to Get Myself a Woman	1956	$40
❑ 2096	Some Kind of Wonderful/Honey Bee	1961	$20
❑ 2151	Sometimes I Wonder/Jackpot	1962	$20
❑ 2143	Stranger on the Shore/What to Do	1962	$20
❑ 1019	Such a Night/Lucille	1954	$75
❑ 2117	Sweets for My Sweet/Loneliness or Happiness	1961	$20
❑ 2261	The Christmas Song/I Remember Christmas	1964	$15
❑ 2261 [PS]	The Christmas Song/I Remember Christmas	1964	$40
❑ 2025	There Goes My Baby/Oh My Love	1959	$30
❑ 2050	This Magic Moment/Baltimore	1960	$30
❑ 1055	What'Cha Gonna Do/Gone	1955	$60
❑ 2134	When My Little Girl Is Smiling/Mexican Divorce	1962	$20
❑ 1048	White Christmas/The Bells of St. Mary's	1954	$70

—Yellow label, no spinner (original)

Number	Title	Yr	NM
❑ 1048	White Christmas/The Bells of St. Mary's	1956	$30

—Red label, no "fan" logo at lower left

Number	Title	Yr	NM
❑ 1048	White Christmas/The Bells of St. Mary's	1962	$8

—Red label with "fan" logo at lower left

BELL

Number	Title	Yr	NM
❑ 45387	The Songs We Used to Sing/Like Sister and Brother	1973	$5

CROWN

Number	Title	Yr	NM
❑ 108	The World Is Changing/Sacroiliac Swing	1954	$200

MUSICOR

Number	Title	Yr	NM
❑ 1498	Midsummer Night in Harlem/Lonely Drifter, Don't Cry	1974	$5

—As "Charlie Thomas and the Drifters

7-Inch Extended Plays

ATLANTIC

Number	Title	Yr	NM
❑ 534 [PS]	Clyde McPhatter and the Drifters	1954	$300
❑ 534	(contents unknown)	1954	$250
❑ 592	Fools Fall in Love/Adorable//Steamboat/Ruby Baby	1957	$125
❑ 592 [PS]	The Drifters	1957	$250

DRIFTERS, THE (3)

CORAL

Number	Title	Yr	NM
❑ 65040	And I Shook/I Had to Find Out for Myself	1951	$300
❑ 65037	Wine Head Woman/I'm the Caring Kind	1950	$300

DRIFTERS, THE (4)

RAMA

Number	Title	Yr	NM
❑ 22	Besame Mucho/Summertime	1953	$200

DRIFTERS, THE (U)

STEELTOWN

Number	Title	Yr	NM
❑ 671	Peace of Mind/The Struggler	1973	$5

DRIFTING COWBOYS, THE

MGM

Number	Title	Yr	NM
❑ K11590	Canal Street Parade/Swing Shift Boogie	1953	$30
❑ K11691	Fish Tail/Rock Point	1954	$30
❑ K11497	Mud Hut/Corn Crib	1953	$30

DRIFTWOOD, JIMMIE

MONUMENT

Number	Title	Yr	NM
❑ 825	Lonesome Ape/What Is the Color of the Soul of Man	1963	$15

RCA VICTOR

Number	Title	Yr	NM
❑ 47-7571	The Answer to The Battle of New Orleans/Sal's Got a Sugar Lip	1959	$20
❑ 47-7534	The Battle of New Orleans/Damyankee Lad	1959	$20

DRIVERS, THE

COMET

Number	Title	Yr	NM
❑ 2142	High Gear/Low Gear	1961	$30

DELUXE

Number	Title	Yr	NM
❑ 6117	Dangerous Lips/Oh Miss Nellie	1957	$100
❑ 6104	My Lonely Prayer/Midnight Hours	1957	$200
❑ 6094	Women/Smooth, Slow and Easy	1956	$125

KING

Number	Title	Yr	NM
❑ 5645	Mr. Astronaut/Dry Bones Twist	1962	$15

LIN

Number	Title	Yr	NM
❑ 1002	A Man's Glory/Teeter Totter	1954	$400

RCA VICTOR

Number	Title	Yr	NM
❑ 47-7023	Blue Moon/I Get Weak	1957	$70

D'RONE, FRANK

CADET

Number	Title	Yr	NM
❑ 5619	Brand New Morning/Bluesette	1968	$10
❑ 5585	The Copla Song/I Wouldn't Know Where to Begin	1967	$12
❑ 5595	Think I Will/Make Me Rainbows	1968	$10

CAMEO

Number	Title	Yr	NM
❑ 282	Mr. Blue/Have a Good Time	1963	$20

COLUMBIA

Number	Title	Yr	NM
❑ 4-43460	Falling in Love in the Fall/Names in a Heart	1965	$10
❑ 4-43733	Too Good to Be Forgotten/Who's Afraid	1966	$10

MERCURY

Number	Title	Yr	NM
❑ 71626	After the Ball/Warm All Over	1960	$15
❑ 71846	Again/If You Were the Only Girl in the World	1961	$15
❑ 71429	Fascinating Rhythm/Yesterdays	1959	$20
❑ 71544	I Love You/Serenade in Blue	1959	$15
❑ 71980	I'm in Love/Show Me the Way to Go Home	1962	$15
❑ 71193	My Special Angel/Once in a Million Years	1957	$20
❑ 71329	Our Summer Love/Little Pixie	1958	$20
❑ 71720	Strawberry Blonde/Time Hurries By	1960	$15
❑ 71939	Twist Li'l Liza/What's In It for Me	1962	$15
❑ 71775	(When You're Young and) Only Seventeen/Yea, Yea, Baby	1961	$15

DRUIDS OF STONEHENGE, THE

UNI

Number	Title	Yr	NM
❑ 55021	A Garden Where Nothing Grows/Painted Woman	1967	$30

DRUMM, DON

CASINO

Number	Title	Yr	NM
❑ 106	Lonely Hours Lady/(B-side unknown)	1976	$5

CHART

Number	Title	Yr	NM
❑ 5223	In at Eight and Out at Ten/Baby's Gone	1974	$6

CHURCHILL

Number	Title	Yr	NM
❑ 7704	Bedroom Eyes/Stormy	1977	$5
❑ 7717	Something to Believe In/Sad Songs	1978	$5

DRUMS, DONALD

CHALLENGE

Number	Title	Yr	NM
❑ 59099	Merry Christmas Window/(There's Something About a) Home Town Band	1960	$15

DRUNKS WITH GUNS

CHEAP BEER

Number	Title	Yr	NM
❑ 0(# unknown)	Blood Bath/Punched in the Head-I Got the Gun	1985	$60
❑ 0(# unknown) [PS]	Blood Bath/Punched in the Head-I Got the Gun	1985	$60

—300 copies were pressed; beware of bootlegs

7-Inch Extended Plays

CHEAP BEER

Number	Title	Yr	NM
❑ 0(# unknown)	Thirst for Knowledge	1986	$60
❑ 0(# unknown) [PS]	Thirst for Knowledge	1986	$60

—300 copies were pressed; beware of bootlegs

DRUSKY, ROY, AND PRISCILLA MITCHELL

MERCURY

Number	Title	Yr	NM
❑ 72650	I'll Never Tell on You/Bed of Roses	1967	$8
❑ 72497	Slippin' Around/Trouble on Our Line	1965	$8

DRUSKY, ROY

CAPITOL

Number	Title	Yr	NM
❑ 4281	Battle for Daddy's Soul/Never Before	1976	$6
❑ 3859	Close to Home/One Day at a Time	1974	$6
❑ 3942	Dixie Lily/If I Could Paint the World	1974	$6
❑ 4028	I'm Knee Deep in Loving You/The Baptism of Jesse Taylor	1975	$6
❑ 4132	Sunrise/Warm, Warm Bed	1975	$6
❑ 4232	When My Room Gets Dark Again/This Life of Mine	1976	$6

COLUMBIA

Number	Title	Yr	NM
❑ 4-21478	Come On Back and Love Me/What Am I Worth	1955	$30
❑ 4-21516	I Just Can't Help Me Lovin' You/So in Love Again	1956	$30
❑ 4-40830	That's When My Heartaches Began/God Planned It That Way	1957	$30
❑ 4-21537	Three Blind Mice/I'll Make Amends	1956	$30
❑ 4-40964	Walkin'/I Walk to Heaven	1957	$30

DECCA

Number	Title	Yr	NM
❑ 31411	After You Turn Out Your Light/I'm Not Getting Over You	1962	$15
❑ 31024	Another/The Same Corner	1959	$20
❑ 31109	Anymore/I'm So Helpless	1960	$20
❑ 31486	Divided Love/She Never Cried When She Was Mine	1963	$12
❑ 31297	I Went Out of My Way (To Make You Happy)/I've Got Some	1961	$15
❑ 31443	Second Hand Rose/It Worries Me	1962	$15
❑ 30943	Such a Fool/Our Church -- Your Wedding	1959	$20
❑ 31717	Summer, Winter, Spring and Fall/Almost Can't	1964	$10
❑ 31366	There's Always One (Who Loves a Lot)/Marking Time	1962	$15
❑ 31193	Three Hearts in a Tangle/I'd Rather Loan You Out	1961	$15
❑ 30793	Wait and See/Just About That Time	1958	$20

MERCURY

Number	Title	Yr	NM
❑ 72325	All for the Love of a Girl/So Much Got Lost	1964	$10
❑ 72376	(From Now On All My Friends Are Gonna Be) Strangers/Birmingham Jail	1964	$10
❑ 72627	If the Whole World Stopped Lovin'/Too Many Fingerprints	1966	$8
❑ 72865	I Wouldn't Be Alone/Memphis Morning	1968	$8
❑ 72928	My Grass Is Green/Alone with You	1969	$8
❑ 72204	Peel Me a Nanner/The Room Across the Hall	1963	$10
❑ 72204 [PS]	Peel Me a Nanner/The Room Across the Hall	1963	$30
❑ 72265	Pick of the Week/Yesterday	1964	$10
❑ 72964	Such a Fool/All Over My Mind	1969	$8
❑ 72586	The World Is Round/Unless You Make Him Set You Free	1966	$8
❑ 72742	Weakness in a Man/I've Got a Right to the Blues	1967	$8
❑ 72886	Where the Blue and Lonely Go/I'm Gonna Get You Off My Mind	1969	$8
❑ 72471	White Lightnin' Express/Lonely Thing Called Me	1965	$8

PLANTATION

Number	Title	Yr	NM
❑ 183	Beautiful Sunday/You've Got Your Troubles	1979	$5
❑ 187	The Last Farewell/Welcome Home	1979	$5
❑ 194	What a Difference a Day Makes/(B-side unknown)	1980	$5

SCORPION

Number	Title	Yr	NM
❑ 0540	Betty's Song/Naked Truth	1977	$5
❑ 0515	Deep in the Heart of Dixie/Last Call for Alcohol	1976	$5
❑ 154	I Used to Be a Cowboy/Don't Touch Me	1978	$4
❑ 0527	Lovers, Friends and Strangers/Five String Hero	1977	$5

STARDAY

Number	Title	Yr	NM
❑ 185	Such a Fool/Mumbling to Myself	1955	$50

Number	Title	Yr	NM

DRYSDALE, DON
REPRISE
❏ 20162	Give Her Love/One Love	1963	$10
❏ 20162 [PS]	Give Her Love/One Love	1963	$30

DU DROPPERS, THE
GROOVE
❏ 036	Boot 'Em Up/Let Nature Take Its Course	1955	$60
❏ 0120	I Wanna Love You/ You're Mine Already	1955	$60
❏ 01	Speed King/Dead Broke	1954	$100
❏ 0104	Talk That Talk/Give Me Some Consideration	1955	$60

RCA VICTOR
❏ 47-5504	Don't Pass Me By/Get Lost	1953	$50
❏ 47-5321	I Found Out/Little Girl, Little Girl	1953	$50
❏ 47-5229	I Wanna Know/Laughing Blues	1953	$50
❏ 47-5425	Whatever You're Doin'/Somebody Work on My Baby's Mind	1953	$50

RED ROBIN
❏ 108	Can't Do Sixty No More/Chain Me Baby (Blues of Desire)	1952	$500

—Red vinyl
❏ 108	Can't Do Sixty No More/Chain Me Baby (Blues of Desire)	1952	$200
❏ 116	Come On and Love Me Baby/Go Back	1953	$200

7-Inch Extended Plays
GROOVE
❏ 2	(contents unknown)	1955	$250
❏ 5	(contents unknown)	1955	$250
❏ 2 [PS]	Talk That Talk	1955	$250
❏ 5 [PS]	Tops in Rhythm and Blues	1955	$250

DUALS, THE
FURY
❏ 1013	Wait Up Baby/Forever and Ever	1958	$50

INFINITY
❏ 032	Oozy Groove/The Big Race	1964	$30

JUGGY
❏ 321	Oozy Groove/The Big Race	1964	$60

STAR REVUE
❏ 1031	Stick Shift/Cruising	1961	$800

SUE
❏ 745	Stick Shift/Cruising	1961	$40
❏ 758	Travelin' Guitar/Cha Cha Guitar	1962	$30

UNITED ARTISTS
❏ 0128	Stick Shift/Keem-O-Sabe	1973	$4

— Silver Spotlight Series" reissue; B-side by The Electric Indian

DU'AMBRA, JOEY
ABC-PARAMOUNT
❏ 9917	Baby Sue/Come Back-A Little Mama	1958	$40

DUANE, DICK
ABC-PARAMOUNT
❏ 9709	Fame and Fortune/ Mean Don't Cry	1956	$40
❏ 9656	Sobony/Now	1955	$40
❏ 9677	To Make a Mistake/Blue Prelude	1956	$40

GNP
❏ 130	Eternally/I'll Never Make You Cry Again	1957	$30
❏ 127	What Good Does It Do/Savannah	1957	$30

DUBS, THE
ABC-PARAMOUNT
❏ 10100	Don't Laugh at Me/You Never Belong to Me	1960	$60
❏ 10150	For the First Time/Ain't That So	1960	$30
❏ 10198	If I Only Had Magic/ Joogie Boogie	1961	$40
❏ 10269	Lullaby/Down, Down, Down I Go	1961	$40

CLIFTON
❏ 2	Where Do We Go from Here/I Only Have Eyes for You	1973	$6

GONE
❏ 5020	Beside My Love/Gonna Make a Change	1957	$70
❏ 5046	Chapel of Dreams/Is There a Love for Me	1958	$70
❏ 5069	Chapel of Dreams/Is There a Love for Me	1959	$60
❏ 5011	Could This Be Magic/Such Lovin'	1957	$60

—Black label
❏ 5011	Could This Be Magic/Such Lovin'	1957	$30

—Multi-color label
❏ 5002	Don't Ask Me (To Be Lonely)/Darling	1957	$125

—Black label, "shadow" logo
❏ 5002	Don't Ask Me (To Be Lonely)/Darling	1957	$70

— Black label, clown-face logo
❏ 5002	Don't Ask Me (To Be Lonely)/Darling	1957	$30

—Multi-color label
❏ 5034	Song in My Heart/ Be Sure (My Love)	1958	$70

JOHNSON
❏ 097	Connie/Home Under My Hat	1973	$6
❏ 102	Don't Ask Me (To Be Lonely)/Darling	1957	$1500
❏ 098	Somebody Goofed/I Won't Have You Breaking My Heart	1973	$6

JOSIE
❏ 911	Wisdom of a Fool/This I Swear	1963	$30

LANA
❏ 115	Could This Be Magic/Blue Velvet	1964	$8

—A-side is an alternate take of the hit version
❏ 116	Don't Ask Me (To Be Lonely)/ Your Very First Love	1964	$8

—A-side is an alternate take of the hit version

MARK-X
❏ 8008	Be Sure My Love/ Song in My Heart	1960	$30

VICKIE
❏ 229	I'm Downtown/Lost in the Wilderness	1971	$10

— As "Richard Blandon and the Dubs"

DUCKS DELUXE
MOTORS related.
RCA VICTOR
❏ APBO-0297	Daddy Put the Bomp/ Please, Please, Please	1974	$8

DUDLEY, DAVE
GOLDEN RING
❏ 3030	Cowboy Boots/I Think I'll Cheat (A Little Tonight)	1963	$20

— Golden Ring" straight across top of label
❏ 3030	Cowboy Boots/I Think I'll Cheat (A Little Tonight)	1963	$15

— Golden Ring" on two lines, curved at top of label

GOLDEN WING
❏ 3020	Six Days on the Road/I Feel a Cry Coming On	1963	$15

—Black vinyl
❏ 3020	Six Days on the Road/I Feel a Cry Coming On	1963	$40

— Blue vinyl

KING
❏ 1508	Cry Baby Cry/This Is the Last Time	1955	$50
❏ 4866	Ink Dries Quicker Than Tears/I'll Be Waiting for You	1956	$50
❏ 5792	Ink Dries Quicker Than Tears/I'll Be Waiting for You	1963	$30

MERCURY
❏ 72741	Anything Leaving Town Today/I'd Rather Be Forgotten	1967	$8
❏ 72254	Big Ole House/If I Had One	1964	$12
❏ 72952	George (And the North Woods)/It's Not a Very Pleasant Day Today	1969	$8
❏ 72818	I Keep Coming Back for More/ Where Does a Little Boy Go	1968	$8
❏ 72212	Last Day in the Mines/ Last Year's Heartaches	1963	$12
❏ 72585	Lonelyville/Time and Place	1966	$8
❏ 72618	Long Time Gone/I Feel a Cry Comin' On	1966	$8
❏ 72308	Mad/Don't Be Surprised	1964	$10
❏ 72655	My Kind of Love/ Subject to Change	1967	$8
❏ 72902	One More Mile/Angel	1969	$8
❏ 72856	Please Let Me Prove (My Love for You)/I'll Be Moving Along	1968	$8
❏ 73142	Six Tons of Toys/Old Time Merry Christmas	1970	$8
❏ 73029	The Pool Shark/The Bigger They Come, The Harder They Fall	1970	$8
❏ 72779	There Ain't No Easy Run/Why I Can't Be With You (Is a Shame)	1968	$8
❏ 72442	Truck Drivin' Son-of-a-Gun/I Got Lost	1965	$10
❏ 72697	Trucker's Prayer/Don't Come Cryin' to Me	1967	$8
❏ 72384	Two Six Packs Away/Hiding Behind the Curtain	1965	$10
❏ 72500	What We're Fighting For/ Coffee, Coffee, Coffee	1965	$10

NRC
❏ 024	Where There's a Will There's a Way/I Won't Be Just Your Friend	1959	$30

RICE
❏ 5069	Counterfeit Cowboy/ That's How Cold	1974	$8
❏ 5070	Devils in Heaven Bound Machines/Farewell to Arms	1974	$8
❏ 5067	Have It Your Way/Blue Bedroom Eyes	1974	$8

STARDAY
❏ 364	Cry Baby/Careless Fool	1958	$50
❏ 499	It's Gotta Be That Way/ Where Do I Go from Here	1960	$30

SUN
❏ 1155	Big Fanny/Where's the Truck	1980	$6

— With Charlie Douglas
❏ 1158	Cowboy, You're America/ The Driver	1980	$6
❏ 1180	I Wish I Had a Nickel/ Fools Rush In	1982	$6
❏ 1140	Moonlight in Vermont/Moritat	1979	$6
❏ 1150	White Line Fever/The Last Run	1980	$6

UNITED ARTISTS
❏ XW836	38 and Lonely/Texas Ruby	1976	$6
❏ XW630	Fireball Rolled a Seven/ Blue Bedroom Eyes	1975	$6
❏ XW585	How Come It Took So Long (To Say Goodbye)/I've Lived Like a Piece of Grass	1974	$6
❏ XW722	Me and Ole C.B./I Can't Remember You	1975	$6
❏ XW766	Sentimental Journey/The Night You Broke the News	1976	$6
❏ XW773	Seventeen Seventy-Six (1776)/I Don't See the Rain	1976	$6
❏ XW693	Where Did All the Cowboys Go/Wave At 'Em Billy Boy	1975	$6
❏ XW882	Where Does a Little Boy Go/Rooster Hill	1977	$6

VEE
❏ 7003	Maybe I Do/Your Only One	1961	$40

DUFF, ARLIE
DECCA
❏ 9-29987	Alligator Came Across/So Close and Yet So Far	1956	$30
❏ 9-29243	Courtin' in the Rain/ She's a Housewife	1954	$30
❏ 9-29866	Home Boy/Oh, How I Cried	1956	$30
❏ 9-29428	I Dreamed of a Hill-Billy Heaven/Lie Detector	1955	$30
❏ 9-29589	Pass the Plate of Happiness Around/Take It Easy on Me	1955	$30

STARDAY
❏ 176	Courtin's Here to Stay/ Fifteen Cents a Pop	1955	$40
❏ 132	Let Me Be Your Salty Dog/ Back to the Country	1954	$70
❏ 105	Stuck-in-a-Mud Hole/A Million Tears	1953	$40
❏ 302	What a Way to Die/ You've Done It Right	1957	$125

DUFFILL, TAM
GROOVE
❏ 58-0004	Cooly Dooly/You Put the Hurt on Me	1963	$70

DUGAN, DENNY
HIT
❏ 114	The Shoop Shoop Song/ That's the Way Boys Are	1964	$8

—B-side by Connie Dee

DUKAYS, THE
NAT
❏ 4001	The Big Lie/The Girl's a Devil	1961	$30

VEE JAY
❏ 491	Combination/Every Step	1963	$20
❏ 460	I Feel Good All Over/I Never Knew	1962	$20
❏ 442	I'm Gonna Love You So/Please Help	1962	$20

DUKE, BILLY
20TH FOX
❏ 296	Amen/Walking Cane	1962	$15
❏ 276	Be a Dreamer/Where Is That Feeling	1961	$15
❏ 301	(Oooh Looka There) Ain't She Pretty/Timbuctu	1962	$15
❏ 301 [PS]	(Oooh Looka There) Ain't She Pretty/Timbuctu	1962	$60

ABC-PARAMOUNT
❏ 9816	Chalypso/Fork in the Road	1957	$30

CAPITOL
❏ 5012	Echoes/The Best Man	1963	$15
❏ 4907	Goodbye Stranger/Millionaire	1963	$15
❏ 4831	Summer at the Shore/ Good Old Days	1962	$15

CASINO
❏ 138	Flip, Flop and Fly/ Fun Lovin' Mama	1956	$70

CORAL
❏ 9-61203	I Cried/Love Ya, Love Ya, Love Ya	1954	$30

PEAK
❏ 104	Chalypso/Fork in the Road	1957	$40

Number	Title	Yr	NM
SEVILLE			
❏ 132	I'm the Lonesomest Guy in Town/ While the Bloom Is on the Roses	1964	$15
❏ 136	Prisoner of Love/Sugar and Spice	1965	$15
❏ 134	Six-O-Nine/Ciumachella (Tender Flower)	1964	$15
TEEN			
❏ 110	Paradise Princess/I Know I Was Wrong	1955	$50

DUKE, DENVER, AND JEFFERY NULL

Number	Title	Yr	NM
MERCURY			
❏ 70970	Hank Williams Isn't Dead/ Rock and Roll Blues	1956	$70

DUKE, GEORGE

Number	Title	Yr	NM
ELEKTRA			
❏ 69524	Broken Glass/Island Girl	1986	$3
❏ 69504	Good Friend/African Violet	1986	$3
❏ 69504 [PS]	Good Friend/African Violet	1986	$3
❏ 69315	Guilty/(Instrumental)	1989	$3
❏ 69296	Love Ballad/560SL	1989	$3
❏ 69649	Thief in the Night/La La	1985	$3
EPIC			
❏ 50531	Dukey Stick (Part One)/ Dukey Stick(Part Two)	1978	$4
❏ 50853	Every Little Step I Take/Games	1980	$4
❏ 50792	I Want You for Myself/Party Down	1979	$4
❏ 50593	Movin' On/The Way I Feel	1978	$4
❏ 50660	Say That You Will/I Am for Real (May the Funk Be With You)	1979	$4
❏ 02701	Shine On/Positive Energy	1982	$4
❏ 50719	Straight from the Heart/Pluck	1979	$4

DUKE, PATTY

Number	Title	Yr	NM
UNITED ARTISTS			
❏ 50216	Come Live with Me/ My Own Little Place	1967	$6
❏ 50299	Dona, Dona/And We Were Strangers	1968	$6
❏ 875	Don't Just Stand There/ Everything But Love	1965	$12
❏ 875 [PS]	Don't Just Stand There/ Everything But Love	1965	$30
❏ 0127	Don't Just Stand There/ Say Something Funny	1973	$4
—Silver Spotlight Series" reissue			
❏ 915	Funny Little Butterflies/ Say Something Funny	1965	$8
❏ 915 [PS]	Funny Little Butterflies/ Say Something Funny	1965	$30
❏ 50034	Little Things Mean a Lot/ The World Is Watching Us	1966	$8
❏ 50034 [PS]	Little Things Mean a Lot/ The World Is Watching Us	1966	$30
❏ 50057	The Wall Came Tumbling Down/ What Makes You Special	1966	$8
❏ 978	Whenever She Holds You/Nothing But Me	1966	$8
❏ 50073	Why Don't They Understand/ Danke Schoen	1966	$8

DUKES, THE

Number	Title	Yr	NM
FLIP			
❏ 345	I Love You/Leap Year Cha Cha	1959	$50
❏ 343	Looking for You/Groceries Sir	1959	$40
IMPERIAL			
❏ 5401	Teardrop Eyes/Shimmies and Shakes	1956	$250
❏ 5415	Wini Brown/Cotton Pickin' Hands	1956	$120
SPECIALTY			
❏ 543	Ooh Bop She Bop/Oh-Kay	1954	$80

DUMAURIERS, THE

Number	Title	Yr	NM
FURY			
❏ 1011	Baby I Love You/All Night Long	1957	$125

DUNCAN, HERBIE

Number	Title	Yr	NM
GLENN			
❏ 1400	Hot Lips Baby/Little Angel	1961	$400
❏ 1402	That's All/End of the Rainbow	1961	$100
MAR-VEL			
❏ 1400	Hot Lips Baby/Little Angel	1960	$125

DUNCAN, JOHNNY

Number	Title	Yr	NM
ABC-PARAMOUNT			
❏ 10775	Forgive Me and Forget Me/ Who Do They Think They Are	1966	$20
CAPITOL			
❏ F3814	Last Train to San Fernando/ Jig Along Home	1957	$60
COLUMBIA			
❏ 1-11385	Acapulco/Am I That Easy to Forget	1980	$4
❏ 18-02570	All Night Long/My Heart's Not In It	1981	$4
❏ 3-10554	A Song in the Night/Use My Love	1977	$5
❏ 4-44383	Baby Me Baby/Mystery	1967	$8
❏ 3-10085	Charley Is My Name/Gentle Fire	1975	$5
❏ 3-10634	Come a Little Bit Closer/ Loneliness (Can Break a Good Man Down)	1977	$5
❏ 3-10262	Gentle Fire/Good Morning Love	1975	$5
❏ 4-44196	Hard Luck Joe/Gotta Get Back (On the Right Track)	1967	$8
❏ 3-10783	Hello Mexico (And Adios Baby to You)/I Watched an Angel (Going Through Hell)	1978	$5
❏ 4-44693	I Live to Love You/Louisville Nashville Southbound Train	1968	$8
❏ 1-11280	I'm Gonna Love You Tonight (In My Dreams)/Wine Oh Wine	1980	$4
❏ 4-44484	I'm the One/Solo Soul	1968	$8
❏ 3-10474	It Couldn't Have Been Any Better/Denver Woman	1977	$5
❏ 4-43988	Looking for Someone Lonely/Rainbow Road	1967	$10
❏ 1-11185	Play Another Slow Song/ My Woman's Good to Me	1979	$4
❏ 3-10007	Scarlet Water/We're Not Fooling Our Hearts	1974	$5
❏ 3-10694	She Can Put Her Shoes Under My Bed (Anytime)/Maybe I Just Crossed Your Mind	1978	$5
❏ 3-10915	Slow Dancing/One Night of Love	1979	$5
❏ 3-10302	Stranger/Flashing, Screaming, Silent Neon Sign	1976	$5
❏ 4-45818	Sweet Country Woman/ The Look in Baby's Eyes	1973	$6
❏ 4-45917	Talkin' with My Lady/ You're My Woman	1973	$6
❏ 1-11097	The Lady in the Blue Mercedes/Too Far Gone	1979	$4
❏ 4-46018	The Pillow/Ain't No Way That I Can Forget You	1974	$6
❏ 3-10417	Thinkin' of a Rendezvous/ Love Should Be Easy	1976	$5
❏ 4-44580	To My Sorrow/I'm in This Town for Good	1968	$8
❏ 4-44864	When She Touches Me/ Shreveport to L.A.	1969	$8
❏ 4-45006	Window Number Five/ Day Drinker	1969	$8
LEADER			
❏ 807	Bring Your Heart/Hot Sunshine	1960	$50
❏ 812	Hello Mary Lou, Goodbye Heart/ Freddie and His Go-Cart	1960	$40
PHAROAH			
❏ 2503	Texas Moon/(B-side unknown)	1986	$5
❏ 2502	The Look of a Lady in Love/ (B-side unknown)	1986	$5

DUNCAN, TOMMY

Number	Title	Yr	NM
CAPITOL			
❏ F40282	Chattanoogie Shoe Shine Boy/Never No Mo' Blues	1950	$50
❏ F895	In the Jailhouse Now/I Don't Believe	1950	$40
CORAL			
❏ 9-64182	I Just Can't Take It Anymore/ Walkin' in the Shadow of the Blues	1954	$30
❏ 9-61391	San Antonio Rose/Time Changes Everything	1955	$30
❏ 9-61474	Somebody's Pushin'/I'll Never Worry You	1955	$30
❏ 9-64173	The Parting of the Wa/ Wastin' Your Life Away	1954	$30
SMASH			
❏ 2073	I Brought It On Myself/ Let Me Take You Out	1967	$10

DUNGAREE DARLINGS, THE

Number	Title	Yr	NM
KAREN			
❏ 1005	Boy of My Dreams/ Little Wallflower	1959	$125
REGO			
❏ 1003	Boy of My Dreams/ Little Wallflower	1958	$250
—As "The Dungaree Dolls			

DUNN, HOLLY

Number	Title	Yr	NM
MTM			
❏ B-72075	Daddy's Hands/Hideaway	1986	$8
❏ B-72116	(It's Always Gonna Be) Someday/ On the Wings of an Angel	1988	$5
❏ B-72057	My Heart Holds On/ Shot in the Dark	1985	$5
❏ B-72091	Only When I Love/ Little Prairie House	1987	$5
❏ B-72052	Playing for Keeps/I'm Not Through Loving You Yet	1985	$5
❏ B-72093	Strangers Again/Wrap Me Up	1987	$5
❏ B-72108	That's What Your Love Does to Me/Lonesome Highway	1988	$5
❏ B-72064	Two Too Many/You	1986	$5
WARNER BROS.			
❏ 22957	Are You Ever Gonna Love Me/If I'd Never Loved You	1989	$3
❏ 22796	There Goes My Heart Again/ Blue Rose of Texas	1989	$3

DUNN, JOHN

Number	Title	Yr	NM
HIT			
❏ 22	Ahab the Arab/Dancin' Party	1962	$8
— B-side by Herbert Hunter			

DUNN, RONNIE

Number	Title	Yr	NM
CHURCHILL			
❏ 94018	It's Written All Over Your Face/ You Never Crossed My Mind	1983	$8
❏ 94018 [PS]	It's Written All Over Your Face/ You Never Crossed My Mind	1983	$15
❏ 94008	She Put the Sad in All His Songs/Change of Attitude	1983	$8
❏ 52383	She Put the Sad in All His Songs/Change of Attitude	1984	$6

DUPONTS, THE

Number	Title	Yr	NM
ROULETTE			
❏ 4060	Half Past Nothing/A Screamin' Ball (At Dracula Hall)	1958	$30
ROYAL ROOST			
❏ 627	Somebody/Prove It Tonight	1957	$60
SAVOY			
❏ 1552	Must Be Falling in Love/You	1958	$30
—As "Little Anthony Guardine and the Duponts			
WINLEY			
❏ 212	Must Be Falling in Love/You	1957	$100

DUPREE, CHAMPION JACK

Number	Title	Yr	NM
ATLANTIC			
❏ 2032	Frankie and Johnny/Strollin'	1959	$15
—As "Champion Jack			
❏ 2095	My Mother-in-Law/Evil Woman	1961	$10
EVERLAST			
❏ 5032	Highway Blues/Shake Baby Shake	1964	$8
❏ 5025	Shake Baby Shake/Walking Down the Highway	1963	$10
FEDERAL			
❏ 12408	Two Below Zero/Sharp Harp	1961	$15
GROOVE			
❏ 0171	Lonely Road Blues/ When I Get Married	1956	$50
— With Mr. Bear			
KING			
❏ 4938	Big Leg Woman/Mail Order Woman	1956	$40
❏ 6299	Blues for Everybody/ Tongue-Tied Blues	1970	$6
❏ 4779	Blues for Everybody/ Two Below Zero	1955	$40
❏ 4706	Camille/Rub a Little Boogie	1954	$40
❏ 4695	Hard Feeling/Walking Upside Your Head	1954	$40
❏ 4797	Let the Doorbell Ring/ Harelip Blues	1955	$40
❏ 4876	Me and My Mule/ Failing Health Blues	1956	$40
❏ 4859	Silent Partner/She Cooks Me Cabbage	1955	$40
❏ 4906	So Sorry, So Sorry/Overhead	1956	$40
❏ 4827	That's My Pa/Stumbling Block	1955	$40
❏ 4812	Walking the Blues/ Daybreak Rock	1955	$40
—B-side by Mr. Bear and the Bearcats			
RED ROBIN			
❏ 130	Drunk Again/Shim Sham Shimmy	1954	$200
❏ 112	Shake Baby Shake/ Highway Blues	1952	$200
❏ 109	Stumblin' Block Blues/ Number Nine Blues	1952	$400
VIK			
❏ 0279	Old Time Rock and Roll/ Rocky Mountain	1957	$50
❏ 0304	Shake Baby Shake/Lollipop Baby	1957	$50

DUPREE, SIMON, AND THE BIG SOUND

Number	Title	Yr	NM
TOWER			
❏ 427	Daytime, Night Time/I've Seen It All Before	1968	$8

Number	Title	Yr	NM

DUPREES, THE

COED

❏ 576	Gone with the Wind/ Let's Make Love Again	1963	$20
❏ 585	Have You Heard/Love Eyes	1963	$20
❏ 574	I'd Rather Be Here in Your Arms/I Wish I Could Believe You	1963	$20
❏ 580	I Gotta Tell Her Now/ Take Me As I Am	1963	$20
❏ 596	I'm Yours/Wishing Ring	1964	$20
❏ 587	(It's No) Sin/The Sand and the Sea	1964	$20
❏ 571	My Own True Love/Ginny	1962	$30
❏ 591	Please Let Her Know/ Where Are You	1964	$20
❏ 595	So Little Time/It Isn't Fair	1964	$20
❏ 584	Why Don't You Believe Me/My Dearest One	1963	$20
❏ 584	Why Don't You Believe Me/ The Things I Love	1963	$40

COLOSSUS

❏ 110	Check Yourself/The Sky's the Limit	1970	$6

—As "The Italian Asphalt and Pavement Company" or "The I.A.P. Co." for short

❏ 110 [PS]	Check Yourself/The Sky's the Limit	1970	$6

—As "The Italian Asphalt and Pavement Company" or "The I.A.P. Co." for short

COLUMBIA

❏ 43336	Around the Corner/They Said It Couldn't Be Done	1965	$15
❏ 44078	Be My Love/I Understand	1967	$12
❏ 43802	It's Not Time Now/Don't Want to Have to Do It	1966	$10
❏ 43577	The Exodus Song/ Let Them Talk	1966	$15

HERITAGE

❏ 805	Goodnight My Love/ Ring of Love	1968	$10
❏ 805 [PS]	Goodnight My Love/ Ring of Love	1968	$30
❏ 826	Have You Heard/My Love, My Love	1970	$12
❏ 808	My Love, My Love/ The Sky's the Limit	1968	$10
❏ 808 [PS]	My Love, My Love/ The Sky's the Limit	1968	$30
❏ 804	My Special Angel/Ring of Love	1968	$10
❏ 811	Two Different Worlds/Hope	1969	$10
❏ 811 [PS]	Two Different Worlds/Hope	1969	$30

RCA VICTOR

❏ PB-10407	The Sky's the Limit/Delicious	1975	$10

DURAN DURAN

CAPITOL

❏ B-44287	All She Wants Is//I Believe-All I Need to Know (Medley)	1988	$3
❏ B-44287 [PS]	All She Wants Is//I Believe-All I Need to Know (Medley)	1988	$3
❏ B-44337	Do You Believe in Shame?/ The Krush Brothers LSD Edit	1989	$3
❏ B-44337 [PS]	Do You Believe in Shame?/ The Krush Brothers LSD Edit	1989	$3
❏ B-5195	Hungry Like the Wolf (4:11)/ Hungry Like the Wolf (5:14)	1983	$5

—Reissue of Harvest 5195 on purple label; much scarcer than the Harvest edition

❏ B-44237 [PS]	I Don't Want Your Love/ (instrumental)	1988	$3
❏ B-44237	I Don't Want Your Love/ (LP Version)	1988	$3
❏ B-5233	Is There Something I Should Know?/Careless Memories	1983	$3
❏ B-5233 [PS]	Is There Something I Should Know?/Careless Memories	1983	$4
❏ P-B-44001 [DJ]	Meet El Presidente (same on both sides)	1987	$30

—White vinyl in heavy clear plastic sleeve

❏ B-44001	Meet El Presidente/Vertigo (Do the Demolition)	1987	$3
❏ B-44001 [PS]	Meet El Presidente/Vertigo (Do the Demolition)	1987	$6

—Fold-open poster sleeve

❏ 7-PRO-9330 [DJ]	Save a Prayer (Rio Edit)/(Arena Edit)	1985	$8
❏ 7-PRO-9330 [PS]	Save a Prayer (Rio Edit)/(Arena Edit)	1985	$15
❏ B-5438	Save a Prayer/Save a Prayer (From the Arena)	1985	$3
❏ B-5438 [PS]	Save a Prayer/Save a Prayer (From the Arena)	1985	$3
❏ PB-5670 [DJ]	Skin Trade (same on both sides)	1987	$30

—Red vinyl in heavy clear plastic sleeve

❏ B-5670	Skin Trade/We Need You	1987	$3
❏ B-5670 [PS]	Skin Trade/We Need You	1987	$3

—American all-red sleeve

❏ B-5670 [PS]	Skin Trade/We Need You	1987	$30

—Canada-only nude butt sleeve

❏ B-5417	The Wild Boys/((I'm Looking for) Cracks in the Pavement	1984	$3
❏ B-5417 [PS]	The Wild Boys/((I'm Looking for) Cracks in the Pavement	1984	$3

HARVEST

❏ A-5070	Girls on Film/Faster Than Light	1981	$30
❏ P-A-5070 [DJ]	Girls on Film (same on both sides)	1981	$15
❏ B-5134	Hungry Like the Wolf (3:23)/ Careless Memories	1982	$30
❏ P-B-5134 [DJ]	Hungry Like the Wolf (3:23) (same on both sides)	1982	$20
❏ B-5195	Hungry Like the Wolf (4:11)/ Hungry Like the Wolf (5:14)	1982	$3
❏ B-5195 [PS]	Hungry Like the Wolf (4:11)/ Hungry Like the Wolf (5:14)	1982	$10
❏ P-A-5017 [DJ]	Planet Earth (same on both sides)	1981	$20
❏ A-5017	Planet Earth/To the Shore	1981	$40

DURANTE, JIMMY

MGM

❏ 30257	Frosty The Snowman/ Christmas Comes But Once A Year	1950	$20

WARNER BROS.

❏ 5843	Bill Bailey (Won't You Please Come Home)/Margie	1966	$8
❏ 7367	He Ain't Heavy, He's My Brother/Look Ahead Little Girl	1970	$6
❏ 5410	Hello Young Lovers/ This Is All I Ask	1964	$8
❏ 7024	Hellzapoppin'/M.F. O'Brien	1967	$6
❏ 7253	He Touched Me/Amen	1968	$6
❏ 5686	(I Wonder) What Became of Life/One of Those Songs	1965	$8
❏ 5823	Mame/We're Going UFO'ing	1966	$15
❏ 5483	Old Man Time/I Came Here to Swim	1964	$8
❏ 5382	September Song/ Young at Heart	1963	$8
❏ 5456	This Train/When Love Flies Out the Window	1964	$8

DURHAM, BOBBY

CAPITOL

❏ 5511	Let the Sad Times Roll On/Let That Be a Lesson to You, Heartache	1965	$15
❏ 5202	My Past Is Present/ Queen of Snob Hill	1964	$15
❏ 5616	Why Don't You Just Be You/Home Is Where I Hang My Head	1966	$10

HIGHTONE

❏ 502	Let's Start a Rumor Today/ (B-side unknown)	1988	$6
❏ 501	Where I Grew Up/ (B-side unknown)	1988	$6

DURY, IAN, AND THE BLOCKHEADS

STIFF

❏ SS1000	Wake Up and Make Love to Me/Billericay Dickie	1978	$15

STIFF/EPIC

❏ 50726	Hit Me With Your Rhythm Stick/There Ain't Half Been Some Clever Bastards	1979	$12
❏ 50726 [PS]	Hit Me With Your Rhythm Stick/There Ain't Half Been Some Clever Bastards	1979	$15

DUSK

BELL

❏ 961	Angel Baby/If We Just Leave Today	1971	$6
❏ 961	Angel Baby/Reach Out and Speak My Name	1971	$6
❏ 990	I Hear Those Church Bells Ringing/I Cannot See to See You	1971	$6
❏ 45207	Point of No Return/ (B-side unknown)	1972	$6
❏ 45148	Suburbia U.S.A./Treat Me Like a Good Piece of Candy	1971	$6

DUST

Also see RAMONES, RICK DERRINGER.

KAMA SUTRA

❏ 541	Love Me Hard/(B-side unknown)	1972	$6
❏ 534	Stone Woman/ (B-side unknown)	1971	$6

DUSTERS, THE (1)

ABC-PARAMOUNT

❏ 9887	Pretty Girl/Coolation	1958	$40

GLORY

❏ 287	Darling Love/Teen-Age Jamboree	1958	$60

DUSTERS, THE (2)

ARC

❏ 3000	Give Me Time/Sallie Mae	1956	$300

DUVALL, HUELYN

CHALLENGE

❏ 59025	Friday Night on a Dollar Bill/Juliette	1958	$40
❏ 59002	Hum-Dinger/You Knock Me Out	1958	$40
❏ 59014	Little Boy Blue/Three Months to Kill	1958	$50
❏ 59069	Pucker Paint/Boom Boom Baby	1960	$40
❏ 1012	Teen Queen/Comin' or Goin'	1957	$125

—Blue label

❏ 1012	Teen Queen/Comin' or Goin'	1957	$40

—Maroon label

DYESS, DAVID WAYNE

ACE

❏ 578	Hi Ho Merry Christmas/ Christmas Morn	1959	$20

DYKE AND THE BLAZERS

ARTCO

❏ 45-101	Funky Broadway -- Part 1/ Funky Broadway -- Part 2	1966	$125

ORIGINAL SOUND

❏ 64	Funky Broadway -- Part 1/ Funky Broadway -- Part 2	1966	$10
❏ 83	Funky Bull -- Part 1/ Funky Bull -- Part 2	1968	$8
❏ 79	Funky Walk Part 1 -- East/ Funky Walk Part 2 -- West	1967	$8
❏ 89	Let a Woman Be a Woman -- Let a Man Be a Man/Uhh	1969	$8
❏ 69	So Sharp/Don't Bug Me	1967	$8
❏ 86	We Got More Soul/ Shotgun Slim	1969	$8

DYKE, MIKE

SOUTHERN TRACKS

❏ 1073 [DJ]	A Christmas Card (same on both sides)	1986	$4

DYLAN, BOB

ASYLUM

❏ 45212	All Along the Watchtower/ It Ain't Me Babe	1974	$15
❏ 11043	Most Likely You Go Your Way (And I'll Go Mine)/Stage Fright	1974	$6

—With The Band

❏ 11033	On a Night Like This/ You Angel You	1974	$6
❏ 11035	Something There Is About You/Going, Going, Gone	1974	$6

COLUMBIA

❏ 45982	A Fool Such As I/Lily of the West	1973	$6
❏ AE25 [DJ]	All the Tired Horses (mono/stereo)	1970	$50
❏ 10805	Baby Stop Crying/New Pony	1978	$5
❏ 42856	Blowin' in the Wind/Don't Think Twice, It's All Right	1963	$500
❏ JZSP75606/7 [DJ]	Blowin' in the Wind/Don't Think Twice, It's All Right	1963	$300

—Special Album Excerpt" promo

❏ 42856 [DJ]	Blowin' in the Wind/Don't Think Twice, It's All Right	1963	$300

—Regular promo

❏ 42856 [PS]	Blowin' in the Wind/Don't Think Twice, It's All Right	1963	$800

—Rebel with a Cause" promotional flyer

❏ 43477	Can You Please Crawl Out Your Window?/ Highway 61 Revisited	1965	$30
❏ 10851	Changing of the Guards/Senor (Tales of Yankee Power)	1978	$4
❏ 10851 [DJ]	Changing of the Guards (Short 3:39)/(Long 6:36)	1978	$8
❏ 05697	Emotionaly Yours/ When the Night Comes Falling from the Sky	1985	$4
❏ 73042	Everything Is Broken/ Dead Man, Dead Man	1989	$8
❏ 45516	George Jackson (Acoustic Version)/George Jackson (Big Band Version)	1971	$10
❏ 11072	Gotta Serve Somebody/ Trouble in Mind	1979	$4
❏ 02510	Heart of Mine/The Groom's Still Waiting at the Altar	1981	$4
❏ 02510 [PS]	Heart of Mine/The Groom's Still Waiting at the Altar	1981	$5
❏ 10245 [DJ]	Hurricane (mono/stereo)	1975	$30

—Plays at 33 1/3 rpm; does not have "Special Rush Reservice" on label

❏ 10245 [DJ]	Hurricane (mono/stereo)	1975	$20

—Plays at 33 1/3 rpm; has "Special Rush Reservice" on label

❏ 10245 [PS]	Hurricane (mono/stereo)	1975	$20

—Special sleeve for above record

❏ 10245	Hurricane (Part 1)/ Hurricane (Part 2)	1975	$6
❏ 10245 [PS]	Hurricane (Part 1)/ Hurricane (Part 2)	1975	$15
❏ AE71039 [DJ]	If Not for You/Tomorrow Is a Long Time	1971	$50

Number	Title	Yr	NM
❏ 44826	I Threw It All Away/Drifter's Escape	1969	$8
❏ 43683	I Want You/Just Like Tom Thumb's Blues (Live)	1966	$20
❏ 43683 [PS]	I Want You/Just Like Tom Thumb's Blues (Live)	1966	$100
❏ 43683 [DJ]	I Want You (same on both sides)	1966	$200

— *Promo only on red vinyl*

❏ 4-33178	Lay Lady Lay/I Threw It All Away	1970	$5

— *"Hall of Fame" reissue; red and black label*

❏ 44926	Lay Lady Lay/Peggy Day	1969	$8
❏ 44069	Leopard-Skin Pill-Box Hat/Most Likely You'll Go Your Way and I'll Go Mine	1967	$30
❏ 43346	Like a Rolling Stone/Gates of Eden	1965	$30
❏ JZSP110939/40 [DJ]	Like a Rolling Stone (Part 1)/Like a Rolling Stone (Part 2)	1965	$70
❏ 43346 [DJ]	Like a Rolling Stone (same on both sides)	1965	$200

— *Promo only on red vinyl*

❏ 11168	Man Gave Names to All the Animals/When You Gonna Wake Up	1979	$4
❏ 10217	Million Dollar Bash/Tears of Rage	1975	$10
❏ 42656	Mixed-Up Confusion/Corrina, Corrina	1962	$1500

— *Orange label*

❏ 42656 [DJ]	Mixed-Up Confusion/Corrina, Corrina	1962	$500

— *White label*

❏ 10298	Mozambique/Oh, Sister	1976	$6
❏ JZSP113096/147 [DJ]	One Of Us Must Know (Sooner or Later) (4:49)/(3:07)	1966	$125

— *Promo only, long and short versions*

❏ 43541	One of Us Must Know (Sooner or Later)/Queen Jane Approximately	1966	$30
❏ 43389	Positively 4th Street/From a Buick 6	1965	$30

— *Standard version*

❏ 43389 [PS]	Positively 4th Street/From a Buick 6	1965	$75
❏ 43389 [DJ]	Positively 4th Street/From a Buick 6	1965	$120

— *A-side contains alternate version of "Can You Please Crawl Out Your Window." Evidently must be heard to identify.*

❏ 43389	Positively 4th Street/From a Buick 6	1965	$200

— *A-side contains alternate version of "Can You Please Crawl Out Your Window." Evidently must be heard to identify.*

❏ 43389	Positively 4th Street/From a Buick 6	1965	$40

— *Odd version, possibly pressed for export, that plays at 45 but has a small center hole*

❏ 43389	Positively 4th Street/From a Buick 6	1972	$30

— *Briefly issued on gray label, which was used for about six months in 1972*

❏ 43389 [DJ]	Positively 4th Street (same on both sides)	1965	$200

— *Promo only on red vinyl*

❏ 11370	Saved/Are You Ready	1980	$30

— *Scarce on stock copy (promos worth about 20%)*

❏ 07970	Silvio/Too Far from Home	1988	$5
❏ 11235	Slow Train/Do Right to Me Baby (Do Unto Others)	1980	$4
❏ 11235 [PS]	Slow Train/Do Right to Me Baby (Do Unto Others)	1980	$5
❏ 11318	Solid Rock/Covenant Woman	1980	$4
❏ 10454	Stuck Inside of Mobile with the Memphis Blues Again/Rita Mae	1976	$5
❏ 10454 [PS]	Stuck Inside of Mobile with the Memphis Blues Again/Rita Mae	1976	$6
❏ 43242 [DJ]	Subterranean Homesick Blues (same on both sides)	1965	$250

— *Promo only on red vinyl*

❏ 43242	Subterranean Homesick Blues/She Belongs to Me	1965	$30
❏ 43242 [PS]	Subterranean Homesick Blues/She Belongs to Me	1965	$1500

— *Only issued with some promos*

❏ 43242	Subterranean Homesick Blues/She Belongs to Me	1972	$40

— *Briefly issued on gray label, which was used for about six months in 1972*

❏ 04301	Sweetheart Like You/Union Sundown	1983	$4
❏ 04301 [PS]	Sweetheart Like You/Union Sundown	1983	$5
❏ 10106	Tangled Up in Blue/If You See Her Say Hello	1975	$6
❏ 04933	Tight Connection to My Heart (Has Anybody Seen My Love)/We Better Talk This Over	1985	$4
❏ 04933 [PS]	Tight Connection to My Heart (Has Anybody Seen My Love)/We Better Talk This Over	1985	$4
❏ 45004	Tonight I'll Be Staying Here with You/Country Pie	1969	$10
❏ 45409	Watching the River Flow/Spanish Is the Loving Tongue	1971	$6

Number	Title	Yr	NM
❏ 45199	Wigwam/Copper Kettle (The Pale Moonlight)	1970	$6

— *Red label, black print*

❏ 45199	Wigwam/Copper Kettle (The Pale Moonlight)	1970	$6

— *Red label, "Columbia" repeated around outside of label*

❏ 45199	Wigwam/Copper Kettle (The Pale Moonlight)	1970	$6

— *Orange label with "Columbia" background print*

MCA

❏ 52811	Band of the Hand/Theme from Joe's Death	1986	$3

— *By "Bob Dylan and the Heartbreakers*

❏ 52811 [PS]	Band of the Hand/Theme from Joe's Death	1986	$3

DYNA-SORES, THE
RENDEZVOUS

❏ 120	Alley-Oop/Jungle Walk	1960	$30

DYNAMIC TINTS, THE
TWINIGHT

❏ 133	Be My Lady/(B-side unknown)	1970	$30
❏ 145	Falling in Love/(B-side unknown)	1970	$30

DYNAMICS, THE (1)
BIG TOP

❏ 516	And That's a Natural Fact/I Wanna Know	1964	$20
❏ 3161	Misery/I'm the Man	1963	$20

BLACK GOLD

❏ 9	Funkey Key/Count Your Chips	1973	$6
❏ 11	She's for Real (Bless You)/(B-side unknown)	1974	$6
❏ 8	What a Shame/Shucks, I Love You	1973	$6

COTILLION

❏ 44004	Ain't No Sun/Murder in the First Degree	1968	$10
❏ 44045	Dum-De-Dum/I Want to Thank You	1969	$12
❏ 44021	Ice Cream Song/The Love That I Need	1969	$10
❏ 44038	What Would I Do/Ain't No Love at All	1969	$10

DYNAMICS, THE (2)
BOLO

❏ 730	At the Mardi Gras/J.A.J.	1962	$12
❏ 740	Tennessee Boy/Tough Talk	1963	$10
❏ 735	Wild Child/Spongy	1962	$10

GUARANTEED

❏ 201	Aces Up/Baby	1959	$30

PENGUIN

❏ 1006	Aces Up/Baby	1959	$60

SEAFAIR

❏ 107	At the Mardi Gras/J.A.J.	1961	$30
❏ 100	Onion Salad/Lonesome Llama	1960	$30

DYNAMICS, THE (3)
HERALD

❏ 569	Forever Love/Betty My Own	1962	$500

DYNAMICS, THE (4)
U.S.A.

❏ 769	Summertime in the U.S.A./Coast to Coast	1964	$30

DYNAMICS, THE (6)
CINDY

❏ 3005	When the Saints Come Marching In/Gone Is My Love	1957	$100

IMPALA

❏ 501	Moonlight/Someone	1959	$120

SEECO

❏ 6008	Moonlight/Someone	1959	$50

DYNAMICS, THE (U)
ARC

❏ 4450	Enchanted Love/Happiness and Love	1959	$50

COLUMBIA

❏ 3-10666	We Found Love/You Can Make It If You Try	1978	$5

DECCA

❏ 31129	At the End of Each Day/Girl by the Gate	1960	$40
❏ 31046	How Should I Feel/Seems Like Only Yesterday	1960	$40
❏ 31450	How Should I Feel/Seems Like Only Yesterday	1962	$20

DELTA

❏ 1002	Blue Moon/Pigeon-Toed	1959	$40

Number	Title	Yr	NM
DO-KAY-LO			
❏ 101	I Guess You Don't Love Me (No More)/Oh Night of Nights	1963	$40
DOUGLAS			
❏ 200	I Love to Be Loved/You Don't Seem to Realize	1961	$40
DYNAMIC			
❏ 578/9	Christmas Plea/Dream Girl	1962	$75
❏ 109	Don't Be Late/Eenie Meenie	1959	$50
❏ 1001	Don't Leave Me/Wasted	1959	$60
❏ 1008	If She Should Call/Dream Girl	1961	$50
❏ 1002	So Fine/Delsinia	1963	$50
❏ 504	The Girl I Met Last Night/Nobody's Going Out with Me	1959	$50
JERDEN			
❏ 800	I'll Be Standing There/All She Said	1966	$10
LAVERE			
❏ 186	Wrap Your Troubles in Dreams/I Can't Give You Anything But Love	1961	$30
LIBAN			
❏ 1006	If I Give My Heart to You/Blind Date	1962	$100
LIBERTY			
❏ 55628	Chapel on a Hill/Conquistador	1963	$50
PANORAMA			
❏ 51	Stop and Take a Look Around/(B-side unknown)	1967	$10
RCA VICTOR			
❏ 47-9278	Lights Out/You Make Me Feel So Good	1967	$70

— *As "Zerben R. Hicks and the Dynamics*

❏ 47-9084	Love Me/I Need Your Love	1967	$50
REPRISE			
❏ 20183	So Fine/Delsinia	1963	$20
WARNER			
❏ 1016	A Hundred Million Les/Ka Joom	1957	$100

DYNAMO, SKINNY
EXCELLO

❏ 2097	So Long, So Long/Jingle Bell	1956	$40

DYNATONES, THE (1)
HANNA-BARBERA

❏ 494	The Fife Piper/And I Always Will	1966	$10

ST. CLAIR

❏ 117	The Fife Piper/And I Always Will	1966	$40

DYNELLS, THE
ATCO

❏ 6638	Call On Me/Let Me Prove That I Love You	1968	$800

DYSON, RONNIE
COLUMBIA

❏ 10667	Ain't Nothing Wrong/Just As You Are	1978	$5
❏ 4-45025	Are We Ready for Love/God Bless the Children	1969	$6
❏ 10071	Captain of Your Soul/Life and Breath	1974	$5
❏ 10599	Don't Be Afraid/I Just Want to Be There	1977	$5
❏ 4-45240	I Don't Wanna Cry/She's Gone	1970	$5
❏ 4-45110	(If You Let Me Make Love to You Then) Why Can't I Touch You?/Girl Don't Care	1970	$5
❏ 10441	(I Like Being) Close to You/Lovin' Feelin'	1976	$5
❏ 10211	Lady in Red/Cup (Runneth Over)	1975	$5
❏ 4-45776	One Man Band (Plays All Alone)/I Think I'll Tell Her	1973	$5
❏ 4-45776 [PS]	One Man Band (Plays All Alone)/I Think I'll Tell Her	1973	$8
❏ 10716	Sara Smile/No Way	1978	$4
❏ 10356	The More You Do It (The More I Like It Done to Me)/You and Me	1976	$5
❏ 4-46021	We Can Make It Last Forever/Just a Little Love from Me	1974	$5
❏ 4-45974	Wednesday in Your Garden/I Think I'll Tell Her	1973	$6
❏ 4-45387	When You Get Right Down To It…/Sleeping Sun	1971	$5
COTILLION			
❏ 99841	All Over Your Face/Don't Need You Now	1983	$3
❏ 47005	Heart to Heart/Bring It On Home	1982	$3
RCA VICTOR			
❏ 74-0128	Aquarius/Hair	1969	$10

— *By "Ronald Dyson & Co.*

❏ GB-10658	Aquarius/Hair	1976	$5

— *Gold Standard Series" reissue*

E

E-TYPES, THE

Number	Title	Yr	NM
DOT			
❑ 16864	I Can't Do It/Long Before	1966	$15
LINK			
❑ 1	I Can't Do It/Long Before	1966	$40
❑ 1 [PS]	I Can't Do It/Long Before	1966	$40
SUNBURST			
❑ 01	Love of the Loved/She Moves Me	1966	$30
TOWER			
❑ 325	Put the Clock Back On the Wall/14th Street	1967	$30
UPTOWN			
❑ 754	Big City/Back to Me	1967	$30

EADY, ERNESTINE

Number	Title	Yr	NM
JUNIOR			
❑ 1007	The Change/That's the Way It Goes	1963	$40
SCEPTER			
❑ 12102	The Change/That's the Way It Goes	1965	$15

EAGER, BRENDA LEE

Number	Title	Yr	NM
MERCURY			
❑ 73607	Ah, Sweet Mystery of Life/There Ain't No Way	1974	$5
❑ 73292	I'm a Lonely Woman/In My World	1972	$6
❑ 73450	Let Me Be/When I'm With You	1974	$5
PLAYBOY			
❑ 6047	Good Old Fashioned Lovin'/I'll Get By	1975	$5
PRIVATE I			
❑ ZS4 04621	Watch My Body Talk/(Instrumental)	1984	$4

EAGER, JIMMY

Number	Title	Yr	NM
SABRE			
❑ 100	Please Mr. Doctor/I Should Have Loved Her More	1953	$200

EAGER, VINCE

Number	Title	Yr	NM
LONDON INT'L.			
❑ 10527	It's Only Make Believe/I Shall Not Be Moved	1964	$15

EAGLE

Number	Title	Yr	NM
JANUS			
❑ 135	Brown Hair/Working Man	1970	$8

EAGLES

Popular 1970s California band. Few of its records used the article "The" before the name. Its members had previously been in THE JAMES GANG; LONGBRANCH PENNYWHISTLE; POCO; and SHILOH, among others. Also see JOE WALSH.

Number	Title	Yr	NM
ASYLUM			
❑ 11036	Already Gone/Is It True	1974	$4
❑ 45218	Best of My Love/Ol' 55	1974	$4
❑ 46545	Heartache Tonight/Teenage Jail	1979	$4
❑ 45386	Hotel California/Pretty Maids All in a Row	1977	$4
❑ 46608	I Can't Tell You Why/The Greeks Don't Want No Freaks	1980	$4
❑ 45403	Life in the Fast Lane/The Last Resort	1977	$4
❑ 45279	Lyin' Eyes/Too Many Hands	1975	$4
❑ 45257	One of These Nights/Visions	1975	$4
❑ 11025	Outlaw Man/Certain Kind of Fool	1973	$4
❑ 11013	Peaceful Easy Feeling/Trying	1973	$4
❑ 45555	Please Come Home for Christmas/Funky New Year	1978	$4
—Original with "clouds" label			
❑ 45555 [PS]	Please Come Home for Christmas/Funky New Year	1978	$4
—Sleeve was available with both original and reissue			
❑ 45555	Please Come Home for Christmas/Funky New Year	1984	$3
—Reissue with black and yellow label			
❑ 47100	Seven Bridges Road/The Long Run	1980	$4
❑ 11005	Take It Easy/Get You in the Mood	1972	$5
❑ 45293	Take It to the Limit/After the Thrill Is Gone	1975	$4
❑ 11017	Tequila Sunrise/21	1973	$4
❑ 46569	The Long Run/The Disco Strangler	1979	$4
❑ 11008	Witchy Woman/Early Bird	1972	$4
FULL MOON			
❑ 49654	I Can't Tell You Why/Outside	1981	$5
—B-side by Ambrosia			
FULL MOON/ASYLUM			
❑ 47073	Lyin' Eyes/Hello Texas	1980	$5
—B-side by Jimmy Buffett			
❑ 47004	Lyin' Eyes/Looking for Love	1980	$4
—B-side by Johnny Lee; contains the full-length version of "Lyin' Eyes"			
❑ 47004 [PS]	Lyin' Eyes/Looking for Love	1980	$5

EAGLES, THE (2)

Number	Title	Yr	NM
MERCURY			
❑ 70524	I Told Myself/What a Crazy Feeling	1955	$40
❑ 70464	Such a Fool/Don't You Wanna Be Mine	1954	$40
❑ 70391	Tryin' to Get to You/Please, Please	1954	$40

EAGLES, THE (3)

Number	Title	Yr	NM
SMASH			
❑ 1837	Christine/Stalactite	1963	$15

EAGLES, THE (U)

Number	Title	Yr	NM
WARNER BROS.			
❑ 5654	Ballad to a Lady/Eagle	1965	$15

EANES, JIM

Number	Title	Yr	NM
BLUE RIDGE			
❑ 510	Long Journey Home/Lady of Spain	1960	$20
DECCA			
❑ 9-29536	Cotton Pickers Stomp/There's No Place Like Home	1955	$30
❑ 9-29841	Don't Go Lookin' for Trouble/It's a Shame	1956	$20
❑ 9-28140	I Cried Again/Between the Lines	1952	$30
❑ 9-46403	I Cried Again/They Locked God Outside the Iron Curtain	1952	$30
❑ 9-28825	I'd Love to Be Your Darling/The Beginning of the End	1953	$30
❑ 9-28949	Plunkin' Rag/Riding the Waves	1953	$30
—Credited to "Shenandoah Valley Boys			
❑ 9-29446	Possum Hollow/The Things I Love About You	1955	$30
❑ 9-28387	Prisoner of War/Tomorrow May Be Different	1952	$30
❑ 9-29201	Shopworn Heart/Just Suppose	1954	$30
❑ 9-28609	When the One That You Love Is in Love with You/Gloomy Tomorrow	1953	$30
❑ 9-29112	Wiggle Worm Wiggle/In a Spanish Restaurant	1954	$40
MERCURY			
❑ 71229x45	Settle Down/Two Hearts Are Better Than One	1957	$20
SALEM			
❑ 503	Tears the World Can't See/Riding the Roads	1964	$15
❑ 545	These Memories/She Took the Bus (And Left the Crying to Me)	1965	$20
❑ 512	Wide, Wide Road/Throw Me Together	1964	$15
STARDAY			
❑ 535	Borderline/Mark of Cain	1961	$20
❑ 456	Budded Roses/Log Cabin in the Lane	1959	$30
❑ 482	Celebration/Road of No Return	1960	$20
❑ 414	Christmas Doll/It Won't Seem Like Christmas	1958	$30
❑ 407	Don't Make Me Ashamed/Blue Sunday	1958	$30
❑ 504	I Gotta Know/There'll Come a Time	1960	$200
❑ 426	Orchids of Love/Road Walked by Fools	1959	$30
TOWER			
❑ 129	These Memories/She Took the Bus (And Left the Crying to Me)	1965	$8

EARL-JEAN

Number	Title	Yr	NM
COLPIX			
❑ 729	I'm Into Somethin' Good/We Love and Learn	1964	$15

EARL, KENNY

Number	Title	Yr	NM
CINNAMON			
❑ 751	Once More/North of Sally	1973	$6
KARI			
❑ 124	Wasn't It Supposed to Be Me/Raindrops	1981	$6
KIK			
❑ 904	We Have to Start Meeting Like This/Raindrops	1981	$6

EARLE, STEVE

Number	Title	Yr	NM
EPIC			
❑ 34-04784 [PS]	A Little Bit in Love	1985	$8
—Demonstration -- Not for Sale" on back			
❑ 34-04784	A Little Bit in Love/The Crush	1985	$4
❑ 34-04784 [PS]	A Little Bit in Love/The Crush	1985	$4
❑ 34-04307	Squeeze Me In/The Devil's Right Hand	1984	$5
❑ 34-04666	What'll You Do About Me/Cry Myself to Sleep	1984	$5
MCA			
❑ 53011	Goodbye's All We Got Left/Good Ol' Boy (Gettin' Tough)	1987	$3
❑ 53532	Guitar Town/Hillbilly Highway	1988	$3
—Double Hit" reissue			
❑ 52856	Guitar Town/Little Rock 'N' Roller	1986	$3
❑ 52785	Hillbilly Highway/Down the Road	1986	$3
❑ 53249	Six Days on the Road/The Week of Living Dangerously	1988	$3

Number	Title	Yr	NM
❑ 53608	Someday/Goodbye's All We Got Left to Say	1988	$3
—Double Hit" reissue			
❑ 52920	Someday/Hillbilly Highway	1986	$3
❑ 53182	Sweet Little '66/Angry Young Man	1987	$3
UNI			
❑ 55018	Back to the Wall/Little Sister (Live)	1988	$4
7-Inch Extended Plays			
LSI			
❑ 8209	*Nothin' But You/Continental Trailways Blues/Squeeze Me In/My Baby Worships Me	1982	$30
❑ 8209 [PS]	Pink and Black	1982	$30

EARLS, JACK, AND THE JIMBOS

Number	Title	Yr	NM
SUN			
❑ 240	Slow Down/A Fool for Loving You	1956	$70

EARLS, THE (1)

Number	Title	Yr	NM
ABC			
❑ 11109	It's Been a Long Time Coming/My Lonely, Lonely Room	1968	$20
BARRY			
❑ 1021	I Believe/Don't Forget	1963	$50
CLIFTON			
❑ 47	Dreams Come True/My Heart's Desire	1974	$5
❑ 39	Lookin' for My Baby/Cross My Heart	1974	$5
❑ 43	Lost Love/My Heart's Desire	1974	$5
COLUMBIA			
❑ 3-10225	Goin' Uptown/Mrs. Woman	1975	$8
GONE			
❑ 5117	I'll Never Cry/My Heart's Desire	1961	$70
HARVEY			
❑ 100	A Sunday Kind of Love/Teenage Dreams	1975	$8
MR. G			
❑ 801	If I Could Do It Over Again/Papa	1967	$20
OLD TOWN			
❑ 1145	Cry, Cry, Cry/Kissin'	1963	$30
❑ 1141	Eyes/Look My Way	1963	$30
❑ 1149	I Believe/Don't Forget	1963	$50
—Blue label			
❑ 1149	I Believe/Don't Forget	1963	$30
—Mostly black label with moon			
❑ 1169	Oh What a Time/Ask Anybody	1964	$40
POWER MARTIN			
❑ 1005	Stormy Weather/Could This Be Magic	1975	$5
—B-side by the Pretenders			
ROME			
❑ 114/5	All Through Our Teens/Whoever You Are	1976	$8
—Black vinyl			
❑ 114/5	All Through Our Teens/Whoever You Are	1976	$15
—Colored vinyl			
❑ 101	Life Is But a Dream/It's You	1961	$120
❑ 101	Life Is But a Dream/Without You	1961	$50
❑ 112/3	Little Boy and Girl/Lost Love	1976	$4
❑ 102	Lookin' for My Baby/Cross My Heart	1961	$50
❑ 111	Stormy Weather/Could This Be Magic	1976	$5
—B-side by the Pretenders			
WOODBURY			
❑ 101	Tonight (Could Be the Night)/Meditation	1977	$8

EARLS, THE (2)

Number	Title	Yr	NM
GEM			
❑ 221	Believe Me My Love/Spinnin'	1954	$400

EARLY, SAM

Number	Title	Yr	NM
APT			
❑ 25041	Do You Love Me/You Are the Greatest of Them All	1960	$30

EARTH AND FIRE

Number	Title	Yr	NM
ATCO			
❑ 6744	Seasons/Hazy Paradise	1970	$10

EARTH ISLAND

Number	Title	Yr	NM
PHILIPS			
❑ 40673	Doomsday Afternoon/Tuesday Afternoon	1970	$8

EARTH OPERA

Number	Title	Yr	NM
ELEKTRA			
❑ 45636	American Eagle Tragedy/When You Were Full of Wonder	1968	$8
❑ 45650	Home to You/Alfie Finney	1969	$8

EARTH QUAKE

A&M

Number	Title	Yr	NM
❑ 1365	Bright Lights/Live and Let Live	1972	$8
❑ 1338	I Get the Sweetest Feeling/Live and Let Live	1972	$8
❑ 1338 [PS]	I Get the Sweetest Feeling/Live and Let Live	1972	$20
❑ 1301	Tickler/Guarding You	1971	$8

BESERKLEY

Number	Title	Yr	NM
❑ 5701	Friday on My Mind/Roadrunner	1975	$10

—B-side by Jonathan Richman and the Modern Lovers

Number	Title	Yr	NM
❑ 5701 [PS]	Friday on My Mind/Roadrunner	1975	$10
❑ 5736/7	Friday on My Mind/Tall Order for a Short Guy	1975	$5
❑ 5742	Hit the Floor/Don't Want to Go Back	1976	$5
❑ 5734/5	Mr. Security/Madness	1975	$5

EARTH, WIND, AND FIRE

ARC

Number	Title	Yr	NM
❑ 11033	After the Love Has Gone/Rock That!	1979	$5
❑ 11434	And Love Goes On/Win or Lose	1981	$4
❑ 11093	In the Stone/You and I	1979	$4
❑ 11366	Let Me Talk/(Instrumental)	1980	$4
❑ 11366 [PS]	Let Me Talk/(Instrumental)	1980	$5
❑ 02536	Let's Groove/(Instrumental)	1981	$4
❑ 10854	September/Love's Holiday	1978	$5
❑ 11165	Star/You and I	1979	$4
❑ 02688	Wanna Be with You/Kalimba Tree	1982	$4

COLUMBIA

Number	Title	Yr	NM
❑ 3-10309	Can't Hide Love/Gratitude	1976	$5
❑ 3-10026	Devotion/Fair But So Uncool	1974	$6
❑ 4-45888	Evil/Clover	1973	$5
❑ 4-45888 [PS]	Evil/Clover	1973	$10
❑ 38-07687	Evil Roy/(Instrumental)	1988	$3
❑ 38-07687 [PS]	Evil Roy/(Instrumental)	1988	$4
❑ CNR-03566	Fall in Love with Me	1983	$6

—One-sided budget release

Number	Title	Yr	NM
❑ 38-03375	Fall in Love with Me/(Instrumental)	1982	$4
❑ 38-03375 [PS]	Fall in Love with Me/(Instrumental)	1982	$4
❑ 3-10688	Fantasy/Runnin'	1978	$5
❑ 3-10373	Getaway/(Instrumental)	1976	$5
❑ 3-10373 [PS]	Getaway/(Instrumental)	1976	$10
❑ 3-10796	Got to Get You Into My Life/I'll Write a Song for You	1978	$5
❑ 3-10056	Hot Dawgit/R.L. Tambura	1974	$5

—With Ramsey Lewis

Number	Title	Yr	NM
❑ 13-03136	Let's Groove/Sing a Song	1982	$3

—Reissue

Number	Title	Yr	NM
❑ 38-04210	Magnetic/Speed of Love	1983	$4
❑ 38-04210 [PS]	Magnetic/Speed of Love	1983	$4
❑ 4-46007	Mighty Mighty/Drum Song	1974	$5
❑ 4-46007 [PS]	Mighty Mighty/Drum Song	1974	$10
❑ 38-04427	Moonwalk/We're Living in Our Own Time	1984	$4
❑ 3-10492	On Your Face/Biyo	1977	$5
❑ 4-45747	Power/M-O-M	1972	$6
❑ 3-10439	Saturday Nite/Departure	1976	$5
❑ 3-10625	Serpentine Fire/(Instrumental)	1977	$5
❑ 3-10090	Shining Star/Yearnin', Learnin'	1975	$5
❑ 3-10090 [PS]	Shining Star/Yearnin', Learnin'	1975	$10
❑ 38-03814	Side by Side/Something Special	1983	$4
❑ 3-10251	Sing a Song/(Instrumental)	1975	$5

—Later pressings have title as three words

Number	Title	Yr	NM
❑ 3-10251	Singasong/(Instrumental)	1975	$6

—Original pressings have title as one word

Number	Title	Yr	NM
❑ 38-04002	Spread Your Love/Freedom of Choice	1983	$4
❑ 3-10103	Sun Goddess/Jungle Strut	1975	$5

—With Ramsey Lewis

Number	Title	Yr	NM
❑ 38-07608	System of Survival/Writing on the Wall	1987	$3
❑ 38-07608 [PS]	System of Survival/Writing on the Wall	1987	$3
❑ 3-10172	That's the Way of the World/Africano	1975	$5
❑ 38-07695	Thinking of You/Money Tight	1988	$3
❑ 38-07695 [PS]	Thinking of You/Money Tight	1988	$3
❑ 4-45800	Tims Is On Your Side/Where Have All the Flowers Gone	1973	$6
❑ 38-04329	Touch/Sweet Sassy Lady	1984	$4
❑ 38-04329 [PS]	Touch/Sweet Sassy Lady	1984	$4
❑ 38-08107	Turn On (The Beat Box)/(Instrumental)	1988	$3

WARNER BROS.

Number	Title	Yr	NM
❑ 7480	Fan the Fire/This World Today	1971	$6
❑ 7549	I Think About Lovin' You/C'mon Children	1972	$6
❑ 7492	Love Is Life/This World Today	1971	$6

EARTH, WIND, AND FIRE WITH THE EMOTIONS

ARC

Number	Title	Yr	NM
❑ 10956	Boogie Wonderland/(Instrumental)	1979	$5

EAST OF EDEN

DERAM

Number	Title	Yr	NM
❑ 85042	Southern Hemisphere/Communion	1969	$8

EASTON, SHEENA

EMI AMERICA

Number	Title	Yr	NM
❑ B-8186	Almost Over You/I Don't Need Your Word	1983	$4
❑ B-8201	Devil in a Fast Car/Sweet Talk	1984	$3
❑ B-8201 [PS]	Devil in a Fast Car/Sweet Talk	1984	$4
❑ B-8295	Do It for Love/Can't Wait Till Tomorrow	1985	$3
❑ B-8295 [PS]	Do It for Love/Can't Wait Till Tomorrow	1985	$3
❑ 7PRO-79036 [DJ]	Eternity (Edit)/(LP Version)	1987	$4
❑ B-43011	Eternity/Shockwave	1987	$3
❑ B-43011 [PS]	Eternity/Shockwave	1987	$6

—Fold-open poster sleeve

Number	Title	Yr	NM
❑ B-8150	I Don't Need Your Work/You Do It	1983	$10
❑ B-8142	I Wouldn't Beg for Water/Some of Us Will	1982	$5
❑ B-8131	Machinery/So We Say Goodbye	1982	$4
❑ B-8131 [PS]	Machinery/So We Say Goodbye	1982	$4
❑ B-8305	Magic of Love/When the Lightning Strikes	1985	$3
❑ B-8305 [PS]	Magic of Love/When the Lightning Strikes	1985	$3
❑ 8080	Modern Girl/Summer's Over	1981	$4
❑ 8080 [PS]	Modern Girl/Summer's Over	1981	$5
❑ 8071	Morning Train (Nine to Five)/Calm Before the Storm	1981	$4
❑ 8071 [PS]	Morning Train (Nine to Five)/Calm Before the Storm	1981	$5
❑ B-8332	So Far So Good/Magic of Love	1986	$3
❑ B-8332 [PS]	So Far So Good/Magic of Love	1986	$3
❑ B-8227	Strut/Letters from the Road	1984	$3
❑ B-8227 [PS]	Strut/Letters from the Road	1984	$4
❑ B-8253	Sugar Walls/Straight Talking	1984	$3
❑ B-8253 [PS]	Sugar Walls/Straight Talking	1984	$6
❑ B-8263	Swear/Double Standard	1985	$3
❑ B-8263 [PS]	Swear/Double Standard	1985	$3
❑ B-8172	Telefone (Long Distance Love Affair)/Wish You Were Here Tonight	1983	$4
❑ B-8172 [PS]	Telefone (Long Distance Love Affair)/Wish You Were Here Tonight	1983	$4
❑ B-8113	When He Shines/Family of One	1982	$4

LIBERTY

Number	Title	Yr	NM
❑ A-1418	For Your Eyes Only/(Instrumental)	1981	$5

—First pressing credited to "Original Motion Picture Soundtrack" with Sheena Easton's name in fine print

Number	Title	Yr	NM
❑ A-1418	For Your Eyes Only/(Instrumental)	1981	$4

—Second pressing has Sheena Easton's name in bold print

Number	Title	Yr	NM
❑ B-1492	We've Got Tonight/You Are So Beautiful	1983	$3

—A-side: With Kenny Rogers; B-side: Kenny Rogers solo

Number	Title	Yr	NM
❑ B-1492 [PS]	We've Got Tonight/You Are So Beautiful	1983	$4

MCA

Number	Title	Yr	NM
❑ 53629	101/(Instrumental)	1989	$5
❑ 53499	Days Like This/(Instrumental)	1989	$4
❑ 53416	The Lover in Me/(Instrumental)	1988	$3
❑ 53416 [PS]	The Lover in Me/(Instrumental)	1988	$3

ODEON

Number	Title	Yr	NM
❑ OSK5058	La Noche Y Tu/Todo Me Recuerda A Ti	1984	$30

—Spanish versions of "We've Got Tonight" and "Almost Over You"; this was indeed pressed in the United States

Number	Title	Yr	NM
❑ OSK9027	Me Gustas Tal Como Eres/(B-side unknown)	1984	$30

—With Luis Miguel

Number	Title	Yr	NM
❑ OSK9027 [PS]	Me Gustas Tal Como Eres/(B-side unknown)	1984	$40

EASTWOOD, CLINT

CERTRON

Number	Title	Yr	NM
❑ 10010	Burning Bridges/When I Loved Her	1970	$10
❑ 10010 [PS]	Burning Bridges/When I Loved Her	1970	$30

GNP CRESCENDO

Number	Title	Yr	NM
❑ 177	Get Yourself Another Fool/For You, For Me, Forevermore	1962	$50
❑ 177 [PS]	Get Yourself Another Fool/For You, For Me, Forevermore	1962	$125

PARAMOUNT

Number	Title	Yr	NM
❑ 010	Best Things/Wand'rin' Star	1969	$15

—B-side by Lee Marvin

WARNER BROS.

Number	Title	Yr	NM
❑ 49760	Cowboy in a Three-Piece Business Suit/Dark Blue Feeling	1981	$5

EASYBEATS, THE

ASCOT

Number	Title	Yr	NM
❑ 2214	In My Book/Make You Feel Alright (Women)	1966	$20
❑ 2214 [PS]	In My Book/Make You Feel Alright (Women)	1966	$50

RARE EARTH

Number	Title	Yr	NM
❑ 5009	St. Louis/Can't Find Love	1969	$20

UNITED ARTISTS

Number	Title	Yr	NM
❑ 50289	Come In, You'll Get Pneumonia/Hello, How Are You	1968	$10
❑ 50206	Falling Off the Edge of the World/Remember Sam	1967	$10
❑ 0114	Friday on My Mind/Gonna Have a Good Time	1973	$4

—Silver Spotlight Series" reissue

Number	Title	Yr	NM
❑ 50106	Friday on My Mind/Made My Bed; Gonna Lie in It	1966	$20
❑ 50488	Gonna Have a Good Time/Lay Me Down and Die	1969	$10
❑ 50187	Pretty Girl/Heaven and Hell	1967	$10

EAT, THE

GIGGLING HITLER

Number	Title	Yr	NM
❑ 0(# unknown)	Communist Radio/Catholic Love (Live)	1979	$250
❑ 0(# unknown) [PS]	Communist Radio/Catholic Love (Live)	1979	$250

7-Inch Extended Plays

Number	Title	Yr	NM
❑ 0(# unknown)	God Punishes The Eat	1980	$60
❑ 0(# unknown) [PS]	God Punishes The Eat	1980	$60

—Sleeve with baseball card and lyrics insert; other inserts include a 45 adaptor, photos, a sticker and (in some) a $1 rebate offer (each adds another 10% to value)

EATON, HERB

HIT

Number	Title	Yr	NM
❑ 242	Ballad of the Green Berets/Listen People	1966	$8

—B-side by the Chords (2)

EBBTIDES, THE

DUANE

Number	Title	Yr	NM
❑ 1022	Star of Love/First Love	1964	$4000

—VG 2000; VG+ 3000

JAN-LAR

Number	Title	Yr	NM
❑ 101	Love Doctor/Lonesome	1959	$300

MONUMENTAL

Number	Title	Yr	NM
❑ 520	Come On and Cry/Straightaway	1960	$50

TEEN

Number	Title	Yr	NM
❑ 121	What Is Your Name Dear/Only Be Mine	1957	$4000

—VG 2000; VG+ 3000

EBBTONES, THE

EBB

Number	Title	Yr	NM
❑ 100	I've Got a Feeling/Danny's Blues	1957	$200

EBON-KNIGHTS, THE

STEPHENY

Number	Title	Yr	NM
❑ 1822	First Date/Only Only You	1958	$30
❑ 1817	Poor Butterfly/The Way the Ball Bounces	1958	$30

EBONAIRES, THE

ALADDIN

Number	Title	Yr	NM
❑ 3211	3 O'Clock in the Morning/Baby, You're the One	1953	$500

COLONIAL

Number	Title	Yr	NM
❑ 117	We're in Love/Thinkin' and Thinkin'	1959	$120

HOLLYWOOD

Number	Title	Yr	NM
❑ 1062	Let's Kiss and Say Hello Again/Jivarama Hop	1956	$400
❑ 1046	Love For Christmas/Jingle Bell Hop	1955	$400

LENA

Number	Title	Yr	NM
❑ 101	Love Call/Somewhere in My Heart	1959	$200

STARFIRE

Number	Title	Yr	NM
❑ 116	Ooh Baby Baby/Most of the Pretty Young Girls	1979	$5
❑ 116 [PS]	Ooh Baby Baby/Most of the Pretty Young Girls	1979	$5

EBONYS, THE

BUDDAH

Number	Title	Yr	NM
❑ 537	Makin' Love Ain't No Fun (Without the One You Love) Part 1/Part 2	1976	$6

PHILADELPHIA INT'L.

Number	Title	Yr	NM
❑ 3513 [DJ]	(Christmas Ain't Christmas, New Year's Ain't New Year's) Without The One You Love (mono/stereo)	1971	$8
❑ 3510	Determination/Do It	1971	$8
❑ 3514	Do You Like the Way I Love/I'm So Glad I'm Me	1972	$8

SOUL CLOCK

Number	Title	Yr	NM
❑ 108	Don't Knock Me/Can't Get Enough	1969	$20

EBSEN, BUDDY

MGM

Number	Title	Yr	NM
❑ K13210	Mail Order Bride/Ballad of Jed Clampett	1964	$30

REPRISE

Number	Title	Yr	NM
❑ 0389	Howdy/Bonaparte's Retreat	1965	$20

ECHELONS, THE

BAB

Number	Title	Yr	NM
❏ 129	A Christmas Long Ago (Jingle Jingle)/Mystery	1987	$20

ECHO AND THE BUNNYMEN

Number	Title	Yr	NM
❏ 28260	Lips Like Sugar/Rollercoaster	1987	$3
❏ 28260 [PS]	Lips Like Sugar/Rollercoaster	1987	$3
❏ 29288	Seven Seas/Angels and Devils	1984	$3
❏ 29664	The Cutter/Gods Will Be Gods	1983	$3

ECHOES, THE (1)

SEG-WAY

Number	Title	Yr	NM
❏ 1002	Angel of My Heart/Gee Oh Gee	1962	$50
❏ 103	Baby Blue/Boomerang	1961	$30
❏ 106	Sad Eyes (Don't You Cry)/It's Raining	1961	$30

SMASH

Number	Title	Yr	NM
❏ 1850	Annabelle Lee/If Love Is	1963	$20
❏ 1766	Bluebirds Over the Mountain/A Chicken Ain't Nothin' But a Bird	1962	$20

SRG

Number	Title	Yr	NM
❏ 101	Baby Blue/Boomerang	1960	$200

ECHOES, THE (2)

ANDEX

Number	Title	Yr	NM
❏ 22102	Time/Dee Dee Di Oh	1958	$40

ECHOES, THE (3)

COLUMBIA

Number	Title	Yr	NM
❏ 4-41549	Bye-Bye My Baby/Do I Love You?	1960	$20
❏ 4-41709	Loving and Losing/Ecstasy	1960	$20

ECHOES, THE (4)

COMBO

Number	Title	Yr	NM
❏ 128	My Little Honey/Aye Senorita	1957	$50

ECHOES, THE (5)

DOLTON

Number	Title	Yr	NM
❏ 18	Born to Be With You/My Guiding Light	1960	$30

ECHOES, THE (6)

ROCKIN'

Number	Title	Yr	NM
❏ 523	All That Wine Is Gone/Please Say You're Mine	1953	$400

ECHOES, THE (U)

ASCOT

Number	Title	Yr	NM
❏ 2188	I Love Candy/Paper Roses	1965	$60

FELSTED

Number	Title	Yr	NM
❏ 8614	Angel of Love/Twistin' Town	1961	$60

GEE

Number	Title	Yr	NM
❏ 1028	Ding Dong/My Heart Beats for You	1957	$70

HI TIDE

Number	Title	Yr	NM
❏ 106	Angel of Love/Twistin' Town	1961	$200

—Black vinyl

Number	Title	Yr	NM
❏ 106	Angel of Love/Twistin' Town	1961	$400

—Colored vinyl

SPECIALTY

Number	Title	Yr	NM
❏ 601	Over the Rainbow/Someone	1957	$40

SWAN

Number	Title	Yr	NM
❏ 4013	Scratch My Back/The Little Green Man	1959	$15

ECKSTINE, BILLY

A&M

Number	Title	Yr	NM
❏ 1858	The Best Thing/Love Theme from "The Getaway"	1976	$4
❏ 1858 [PS]	The Best Thing/Love Theme from "The Getaway"	1976	$6

ENTERPRISE

Number	Title	Yr	NM
❏ 9076	I Didn't Mean to Love You/I Wanna Be Your Man	1973	$5
❏ 9093	If She Walked Into My Life/Remembering	1974	$5
❏ 9025	I Wanna Be Your Baby/The Name of My Sorrow	1970	$6
❏ 9009	Stormy/When You Look in the Mirror	1970	$6
❏ 9046	When Something Is Wrong with My Baby/Today Was Tomorrow Yesterday	1972	$6

MERCURY

Number	Title	Yr	NM
❏ 71161	All of My Life/Poor Little Heart	1957	$10
❏ 71217	Boulevard of Broken Dreams/If I Can Help Somebody	1957	$10
❏ 72128	Everything I Have Is Yours/Darling, Why Did You	1963	$8
❏ 71250	Gigi/Trust in Me	1957	$10
❏ 71967	Guilty/I Want to Talk About You	1962	$8
❏ 72264	People/Sweet Georgia Brown	1963	$8
❏ 71372	Prisoner of Love/Funny	1958	$10
❏ 71861	Theme from Exodus/It Isn't Fair	1961	$8
❏ 72302	Wanted/What Are You Afraid Of	1964	$8
❏ 72022	What Kind of Fool Am I/Till There Was You	1962	$8

MGM

Number	Title	Yr	NM
❏ K11439	A Fool in Love/Until Today	1953	$20
❏ K12617	Bali Ha'i/Younger Than Springtime	1958	$12
❏ K11351	Be Fair/Come to the Mardi Gras	1952	$20
❏ K11744	Beloved/Temporarily Blue	1954	$20
❏ K10799	Be My Love/Only a Moment Ago	1950	$30
❏ K10796	Blue Christmas/The Lonely Shepherd	1950	$30
❏ K11998	Careless Lips/A Man Doesn't Know	1955	$15
❏ K11177	Carnival/Room with a View	1952	$20
❏ K11694	Don't Get Around Much Anymore/Lost in Loveliness	1954	$20
❏ K11301	Early Autumn/Because You're Mine	1952	$20
❏ K11028	Enchanted Land/I've Got My Mind on You	1951	$20
❏ K11144	Every Day/I Love You	1952	$20
❏ K10643	Free/Baby Won't You Say You Love Me	1950	$30
❏ K11948	Give Me Another Chance/More Than You'll Ever Know	1955	$15
❏ K12180	Good-Bye/The Show Must Go On	1956	$15
❏ K11291	Have a Good Time/Strange Sensation	1952	$20
❏ K10903	I Apologize/Bring Back the Thrill	1951	$20
❏ K11217	If They Ask Me/Hold Me Close to You	1952	$20
❏ K10896	If/When You Return	1951	$20
❏ K10916	I Left My Hat/Here Come the Blues	1951	$20
❏ K10825	I'll Know/I've Never Been in Love Before	1951	$20
❏ K10982	I'm a Fool/Lose Me	1951	$20
❏ K11587	I'm Saving Dreams/Fortune Telling Cards	1953	$20
❏ K10856	I'm So Crazy for Love/Guess I'll Have to Dream	1951	$20
❏ K10944	I'm Yours to Command/What Will I Tell My Heart	1951	$20
❏ K11550	It Can't Be Wrong/I Can Read Between the Lines	1953	$20
❏ K12400	I Thought I'd Seen Everything/I Let a Song Go to My Heart	1956	$15
❏ K10716	I Wanna Be Loved/Stardust	1950	$30
❏ K12105	La De Do De Do (The Honey Bug Song)/Farewell to Romance	1955	$15
❏ K11855	Love Me/One Sweet Kiss	1954	$20
❏ K11984	Love Me or Leave Me/Only You	1955	$15
❏ K11845	Mood Indigo/Do Nothing 'Till You Hear from Me	1954	$20
❏ K10684	My Destiny/Roses	1950	$30
❏ K10623	My Foolish Heart/Sure Thing	1950	$30
❏ K10525	O Come, All Ye Faithful/O, Holy Night	1949	$20
❏ K11803	Olay, Olay/You Leave Me Breathless	1954	$20
❏ K11073	Once/Out in the Cold	1951	$20
❏ K12237	Out of My Mind/My Fickle Heart	1956	$15
❏ K10996	Pandora/Wonder Why	1951	$20
❏ K11511	Send My Baby Back to Me/Laugh to Keep From Crying	1953	$20
❏ K12055	September Song/Pass the Word Around	1955	$15
❏ K11573	St. Louis Blues (Part 1)/St. Louis Blues (Part 2)	1953	$20
❏ K11125	Take Me Back/Weaver of Dreams	1952	$20
❏ K11101	Taking a Chance/You're Driving Me Crazy	1951	$20
❏ K10778	The Show Must Go On/You've Got Me Cryin' Again	1950	$30
❏ K11623	What Are You Doing New Year's Eve/Christmas Eve	1953	$30
❏ K11915	What More Is There to Say/Touching Shoulders	1955	$15

MOTOWN

Number	Title	Yr	NM
❏ 1100	A Warmer World/And There You Were	1966	$15
❏ 1131	For Love of Ivy/A Woman	1968	$10
❏ 1077	Had You Been Around/Down to Earth	1965	$15
❏ 1120	Is Anyone Here Going My Way/Thank You Love	1968	$10
❏ 1105	I Wonder Why (Nobody Loves Me)/I've Been Blessed	1967	$15
❏ 1143	My Cup Runneth Over/Ask the Lonely	1969	$10
❏ 1091	Wish You Were Here/Slender Thread	1966	$15

RCA VICTOR

Number	Title	Yr	NM
❏ 47-6827	Blue Illusion/Oh My Pretty Pretty	1957	$15
❏ 47-6488	My Heart Says No/Joey, Joey, Joey	1956	$15
❏ 47-6524	Tennessee Rock 'n' Roll/Condemned for Life	1956	$30
❏ 47-6436	The Bitter with the Sweet/Grapevine	1956	$15
❏ 47-6691	The Chosen Few/Just Call Me Crazy	1956	$15

ROULETTE

Number	Title	Yr	NM
❏ 4199	Anything You Wanna Do/Like Wow	1959	$15
❏ 4239	I Love You/I Apologize	1960	$15
❏ X1052 [PS]	Billy Eckstine Sings "Tenderly	1953	$20
❏ X-1110	(contents unknown)	1955	$20
❏ X-1111	(contents unknown)	1955	$20
❏ X-1152 [PS]	Early Autumn	1955	$15
❏ X-1152	Early Autumn/September Song// Blue Moon/Oh! You Crazy Moon	1955	$15
❏ X-1110 [PS]	I Let a Song Go Out of My Heart, Vol. 1	1955	$20
❏ X-1111 [PS]	I Let a Song Go Out of My Heart, Vol. 2	1955	$20
❏ X1052	Tenderly/If You Could See Me Now//Laura/One for My Baby (And One More for the Road)	1953	$20

ECSTASIES, THE

AMY

Number	Title	Yr	NM
❏ 853	That Lucky Old Sun/Time for Love	1962	$60

ECSTASY, PASSION AND PAIN

ROULETTE

Number	Title	Yr	NM
❏ 7159	Ask Me/I'll Take the Blame	1974	$8
❏ 7209	Dance the Night Away/There's So Much Love All Around Me	1977	$8
❏ 7156	Good Things Don't Last Forever/Born to Lose You	1974	$8
❏ 7151	I Wouldn't Give You Up/Don't Burn Your Bridges Behind You	1973	$8
❏ 7163	One Beautiful Day/Try to Believe Me	1975	$8
❏ 7203	Passion/There's So Much Love All Around Me	1976	$8
❏ 7178	There's So Much Love All Around Me/(Long Version)	1975	$8
❏ 7182	Touch and Go/I'll Do Anything for You	1976	$6

—As "Ecstasy, Passion and Pain Featuring Barbara Roy

EDDIE AND BETTY

LARK

Number	Title	Yr	NM
❏ 4512	Sweet Someone/Saturday Night Fish Fry	1959	$30

SIX THOUSAND

Number	Title	Yr	NM
❏ 601	Sweet Someone/Saturday Night Fish Fry	1957	$30

WARNER BROS.

Number	Title	Yr	NM
❏ 5079	Embarcadeno Boogie/Give Up Your Twin Pipe Mother	1959	$20
❏ 5054	Sweet Someone/Saturday Night Fish Fry	1959	$20

EDDIE AND DUTCH

IVANHOE

Number	Title	Yr	NM
❏ 507	Ah-Choo, Gesundheit/Rignt in My Own Back Yard	1970	$10
❏ 505	My Mother-in-Law Came Out of Retirement/Bambino	1970	$6
❏ 502	My Wife, the Dancer/Can't Help Lovin' That Girl	1970	$6

EDDIE AND ERNIE

BUDDAH

Number	Title	Yr	NM
❏ 250	Hiding in the Shadows/Standing at the Crossroads	1971	$40

CHECKER

Number	Title	Yr	NM
❏ 1086	Time Waits for No One/That's the Way It Is	1964	$30
❏ 1057	Who's That Knocking at My Door/It's a Weak Man That Cries	1963	$30

—As "Ernie and Eddie"

CHESS

Number	Title	Yr	NM
❏ 1984	We Try Harder/I Believe She Will	1967	$30

COLUMBIA

Number	Title	Yr	NM
❏ 4-44276	Doggone It/Falling Tears (Indian Drums)	1967	$30

EASTERN

Number	Title	Yr	NM
❏ E609	I Can't Do It (I Just Can't Leave You)/Lost Friends	1966	$30
❏ 45-606	I'm Goin' for Myself/The Cat	1965	$20
❏ E608	Outcast/I'm Gonna Always Love You	1966	$30
❏ 45-602	Time Waits for No One/That's the Way It Is	1965	$20
❏ 45-603	Turn Here/I'm a Young Man	1965	$20

REVUE

Number	Title	Yr	NM
❏ R11049	Thanks for Yesterday/Woman, What Do You Be Doing	1969	$20

SHAZAM

Number	Title	Yr	NM
❏ 1004	We Try Harder/I Believe She Will	1967	$200

EDDIE AND THE DE HAVELONS

PEACOCK

Number	Title	Yr	NM
❏ 1920	Christmas Party/Baby Dumplings	1963	$10

EDDIE AND THE SHOWMEN

LIBERTY

Number	Title	Yr	NM
❏ 55695	Faw Away Places/Lanky Bones	1964	$40
❏ 55659	Movin'/Mr. Rebel	1963	$40
❏ 55608	Squad Car/Scratch	1963	$40
❏ 55566	Toes on the Nose/Border Town	1963	$40
❏ 55720	We Are the Young/Young and Lonely	1964	$40

EDDIE AND THE STARLITES

ALJON

Number	Title	Yr	NM
❏ 1260	Come On Home/(B-side unknown)	1963	$40

SCEPTER

Number	Title	Yr	NM
❏ 1202	To Make a Long Story Short/Pretty Little Girl	1958	$70

—White label

Number	Title	Yr	NM
❏ 1202	To Make a Long Story Short/Pretty Little Girl	1958	$40

—Red label

Number	Title	Yr	NM

EDDIE AND THE SUBTITLES
(NO LABEL)

☐ (No number)	Louie, Louie/American Society	1980	$40
☐ (No number) [PS]	Louie, Louie/American Society	1980	$40

— *Folder sleeve in plastic bag*

EDDY, DUANE
CAPITOL

☐ B-44018	Spies/Rockabilly Holiday	1987	$5
☐ B-44018 [PS]	Spies/Rockabilly Holiday	1987	$5

CHINA

☐ 42986 [PS]	Peter Gunn/Something Always Happens	1986	$3
☐ 42986	Peter Gunn/Something Always Happens	1986	$3

— *With Art of Noise; B-side does not feature Eddy*

COLPIX

☐ 788	Don't Think Twice, It's All Right/House of the Rising Sun	1965	$20
☐ 788 [PS]	Don't Think Twice, It's All Right/House of the Rising Sun	1965	$60
☐ 795	El Rancho Grande/Poppa's Movin' On	1966	$20
☐ 779	Trash/South Phoenix	1965	$20

CONGRESS

☐ 6010	Freight Train/Put a Little Love in Your Heart	1970	$20

GREGMARK

☐ 5	Caravan (Part 1)/Caravan (Part 2)	1961	$20

— *Credited to Duane Eddy, but is actually Al Casey*

JAMIE

☐ 1156	Because They're Young/Rebel Walk	1960	$20
☐ 1156 [PS]	Because They're Young/Rebel Walk	1960	$40
☐ 1144	Bonnie Came Back/Lost Island	1959	$30
☐ 1144 [PS]	Bonnie Came Back/Lost Island	1959	$50
☐ 1111	Cannonball/Mason Dixon Lion	1958	$30
☐ 1195	Drivin' Home/Tammy	1961	$20
☐ 1195 [PS]	Drivin' Home/Tammy	1961	$40
☐ 1126 [M]	Forty Miles of Bad Road/The Quiet Three	1959	$30
☐ 1126 [PS]	Forty Miles of Bad Road/The Quiet Three	1959	$60
☐ 1126 [S]	Forty Miles of Bad Road/The Quiet Three	1959	$60
☐ JLP-74 [S]	Hard Times/Along Came Linda	1960	$30
☐ JLP-71 [S]	Lonesome Road/I Almost Lost My Mind	1960	$30
☐ JLP-72 [S]	Loving You/Anything	1960	$30
☐ 1101	Moovin N' Groovin'/Up and Down	1958	$60

— *Originals have pink labels*

☐ 1101	Moovin N' Groovin'/Up and Down	1958	$30

— *All-yellow label, "Jamie" at top*

☐ 1200	My Blue Heaven/Along Came Linda	1961	$20
☐ 1200 [PS]	My Blue Heaven/Along Came Linda	1961	$40
☐ 1175	Pepe"/Lost Friend	1960	$20
☐ 1175 [PS]	Pepe"/Lost Friend	1960	$50

— *Red sleeve*

☐ 1175 [PS]	Pepe"/Lost Friend	1960	$40

— *Yellow sleeve*

☐ 1168	Peter Gunn/Along the Navaho Trail	1960	$20
☐ 1168 [PS]	Peter Gunn/Along the Navaho Trail	1960	$40
☐ JLP-73 [S]	Peter Gunn/Along the Navaho Trail	1960	$30
☐ 1151	Shazam!/The Secret Seven	1960	$20
☐ 1151 [PS]	Shazam!/The Secret Seven	1960	$40
☐ 1130 [M]	Some Kind-a Earthquake/First Love, First Tears	1959	$30
☐ 1130 [PS]	Some Kind-a Earthquake/First Love, First Tears	1959	$50
☐ 1130 [S]	Some Kind-a Earthquake/First Love, First Tears	1959	$60
☐ 1206	The Avenger/Londonderry Air	1961	$20
☐ 1209	The Battle/Trambone	1962	$20
☐ JLP-75 [S]	The Battle/You Are My Sunshine	1960	$30

— *The above five are 33 1/3 rpm singles with small holes*

☐ 1117 [M]	The Lonely One/Detour	1959	$30
☐ 1117 [S]	The Lonely One/Detour	1959	$60
☐ 1183	Theme from Dixie/Gidget Goes Hawaiian	1961	$20
☐ 1183 [PS]	Theme from Dixie/Gidget Goes Hawaiian	1961	$40

RCA VICTOR

☐ 47-8131	Boss Guitar/Desert Rat	1963	$15
☐ 47-8131 [PS]	Boss Guitar/Desert Rat	1963	$40
☐ 47-8087	(Dance with the) Guitar Man/Stretchin' Out	1962	$20
☐ 47-8087 [PS]	(Dance with the) Guitar Man/Stretchin' Out	1962	$40
☐ 47-7999	Deep in the Heart of Texas/Saints and Sinners	1962	$15
☐ 47-7999 [PS]	Deep in the Heart of Texas/Saints and Sinners	1962	$30
☐ 47-8335	Guitar Child/Jerky Jalopy	1964	$15
☐ 47-8335 [PS]	Guitar Child/Jerky Jalopy	1964	$40
☐ 47-8442	Guitar Star/The Iguana	1964	$15
☐ 47-8442 [PS]	Guitar Star/The Iguana	1964	$40

Number	Title	Yr	NM
☐ 47-8180	Lonely Boy, Lonely Guitar/Joshin'	1963	$15
☐ 47-8180 [PS]	Lonely Boy, Lonely Guitar/Joshin'	1963	$30
☐ 47-8507	Moonshot/Roughneck	1965	$15
☐ 47-8507 [PS]	Moonshot/Roughneck	1965	$120
☐ 47-8047	The Ballad of Paladin/The WIld Westerner	1962	$15
☐ 47-8047 [PS]	The Ballad of Paladin/The WIld Westerner	1962	$30
☐ 47-8276	The Son of Rebel Rouser/The Story of Three Loves	1963	$15
☐ 47-8276 [PS]	The Son of Rebel Rouser/The Story of Three Loves	1963	$30
☐ 47-8376	Water Skiing/Theme from A Summer Place	1964	$15
☐ 47-8376 [PS]	Water Skiing/Theme from A Summer Place	1964	$70

REPRISE

☐ 0504	Daydream/This Guitar Was Made for Twangin'	1966	$12
☐ 0662	There Is a Mountain/This Town	1968	$10

UNI

☐ 55237	The Five-Seventeen/Something	1970	$20

7-Inch Extended Plays
JAMIE

☐ JEP-304 [PS]	Because They're Young	1960	$60
☐ JEP-304	Because They're Young/Easy//Rebel Walk/The Battle	1960	$60
☐ JEP-100	Cannonball/Moovin' N' Groovin'//Mason-Dixon Lion/The Lonely One	1958	$60
☐ JEP-301 [PS]	Detour	1959	$60
☐ JEP-100 [PS]	Duane Eddy	1958	$60
☐ JEP-301	Lonesome Road/I Almost Lost My Mind//Detour/Loving You	1959	$60
☐ JEP-303 [PS]	Shazam!	1960	$60
☐ JEP-303	Shazam/Tiger Love//My Blue Heaven/Night Train To Memphis	1960	$60

EDDY, DUANE AND MIRRIAM
REPRISE

☐ 0622	Guitar on My Mind/Wicked Women from Wickenborg	1967	$10

EDELMAN, RANDY
20TH CENTURY

☐ 2274	Concrete and Clay/Weekend in New England	1976	$8
☐ 2155	Everybody Wants to Find a Bluebird/Pistol Packin' Melody	1974	$6
☐ 2245	Fresh Out-a Love/Bring the Baby In with the Bacon	1975	$8
☐ 2196	Isn't It a Shame/Everybody Wants to Call You Sweetheart	1975	$6
☐ 2134	What Are You Going to Do When the Plumbing Goes/Pistol Packin' Melody	1974	$6

ARISTA

☐ 0347	Autumn Days with You/(B-side unknown)	1978	$6
☐ 0268	Can't It All Be Love/Sentimental Fools	1977	$6
☐ 0309	Take My Hand/Today (June Song)	1978	$6

LION

☐ 144	Mexico/(B-side unknown)	1972	$8
☐ 153	The Laughter and the Tears/Lost	1973	$8

MGM

☐ 14599	Everybody Wants to Call You Sweetheart/Ball-Buster Circus	1973	$8

SUNFLOWER

☐ 108	Give a Little Laughter/Just Somebody	1971	$8
☐ 121	My Cabin/T-Shirt 'n' Jeans	1972	$8

EDEN, BARBARA
DOT

☐ 16999	Bend It/I Wouldn't Be a Fool	1967	$8
☐ 17032	Pledge of Love/I'm a Fool to Care	1967	$8

PLANTATION

☐ 178	Widow Jones/We Tried	1978	$5

EDEN, CHANCE
ROULETTE

☐ 4698	Barefoot Through the Grass/I Could Have Loved You So Well	1966	$20
☐ 4602	Here I Am Broken Hearted/String Along	1965	$20
☐ 4664	I'm Looking Through You/Another Love	1966	$30
☐ 4592	Things I Love/You'd Better Go	1965	$20

EDEN'S CHILDREN
ABC

☐ 11053	Goodbye Girl/Just Let Go	1968	$15

EDISON, HARRY "SWEETS"
SUE

☐ 117	Blues for Christmas/Green Dolphin Christmas	1964	$20

Number	Title	Yr	NM

EDISON ELECTRIC BAND, THE
COTILLION

☐ 44071	Ship of the Future/West Wind	1970	$10

EDISON LIGHTHOUSE
BELL

☐ 960	It's Up to You Petula/Let's Make It Up	1971	$5
☐ 858	Love Grows (Where My Rosemary Goes)/Every Lonely Day	1970	$6
☐ 907	She Works in a Woman's Way/It's Gonna Be a Lonely Summer	1970	$5
☐ 989	Take a Little Time/What's Happening	1971	$5

EDMUNDS, DAVE, AND NICK LOWE
COLUMBIA

☐ AE7-1219	Take a Message to Mary/Crying in the Rain//Poor Jenny/When Will I Be Loved	1980	$6

— *Bonus EP included in the Rockpile LP "Seconds of Pleasure*

EDMUNDS, DAVE
Also see LOVE SCULPTURE; ROCKPILE.

COLUMBIA

☐ 04700	Breaking Out/How Could I Be So Wrong	1984	$3
☐ 04923	Do You Want to Dance/Don't Call Me Tonight	1985	$3
☐ 02960	From Small Things (Big Things One Day Come)/Warmed Over Kisses (Left Over Love)	1982	$4

— *A-side is a Bruce Springsteen composition.*

☐ 04080	Information/What Have I Got to Do to Win	1983	$3
☐ 07040	Paralyzed/Here Comes the Weekend	1987	$3
☐ 03877	Slipping Away/Don't Call Me Tonight	1983	$3
☐ 04585	Something About You/Can't Get Enough	1984	$3
☐ 06599	The Wanderer/Here Comes the Weekend	1987	$3
☐ 06599	The Wanderer/Information	1987	$3

MAM

☐ 3611	Blue Monday/I'll Get Along	1971	$6
☐ 3601	I Hear You Knocking/Black Bill	1970	$8
☐ 3608	I'm Coming Home/Country Roll	1971	$6

RCA VICTOR

☐ 74-0882	Baby I Love You/Maybe	1973	$6
☐ LPBO-5000	Born to Be with You/Pick Axe Rag	1973	$6
☐ PB-10118	Let It Be Me/Need a Shot of Rhythm and Blues	1974	$5

SWAN SONG

☐ 72000	Almost Saturday Night/You'll Never Get Me Up	1981	$3
☐ 72000 [PS]	Almost Saturday Night/You'll Never Get Me Up	1981	$3
☐ 71002	Crawling from the Wreckage/Queen of Hearts	1979	$5
☐ 70116	Get Out of Denver/Work Out Suits	1978	$4
☐ 71001	Girls Talk/Creature from the Black Lagoon	1979	$5
☐ 70113	I Knew the Bride/Little Darlin'	1978	$4
☐ 70118	Trouble Boys/What Looks Best on You	1978	$4

EDSELS, THE
CAPITOL

☐ 4588	Bone Shaker Joe/My Jealous One	1961	$30
☐ 4675	If Your Pillow Could Talk/Shake Shake Sherry	1961	$30
☐ 4836	Shaddy Daddy Dip Dip/Don't You Feel	1962	$30

DOT

☐ 16311	My Whispering Heart/Could It Be	1962	$30

DUB

☐ 2843	Lama Rama Ding Dong/Bells	1958	$75

— *Originals have the wrong title and the same recording as on Twin 700*

EMBER

☐ 1078	Three Precious Words/Let's Go	1961	$30

ROULETTE

☐ 4151	Do You Love Me/Rink-a-Dink-a-Doo	1959	$30

TAMMY

☐ 1027	Count the Tears/Twenty-Four Hours	1961	$50
☐ 1023	The Girl I Love/Got to FInd Out About Love	1961	$50
☐ 1014	Three Precious Words/Let's Go	1960	$60
☐ 1010	What Brought Us Together/Don't Know What to Do	1960	$60

EDWARD BEAR

CAPITOL

Number	Title	Yr	NM
❑ 3581	Close Your Eyes/Cachet County	1973	$4
❑ 3581 [PS]	Close Your Eyes/Cachet County	1973	$10
❑ 3780	Coming Home Christmas/ Does Your Mother Know	1973	$8
❑ 3978	Freedom for the Stallion/ Why Don't You Marry Me	1974	$4
❑ 3869	I Had Dreams/You, Me and Mexico	1974	$4
❑ 3683	I Love Her (You Love Me)/ Walking On Back	1973	$4
❑ 3683 [PS]	I Love Her (You Love Me)/ Walking On Back	1973	$10
❑ 3452	Last Song/Best Friend	1972	$5
❑ 3452 [PS]	Last Song/Best Friend	1972	$8
❑ 3351	Masquerade/The Pirate King	1972	$4
❑ 3804	Same Old Feeling/Fool	1973	$4

EDWARDS, BOBBY

CAPITOL

Number	Title	Yr	NM
❑ 5006	Don't Pretend/Help Me	1963	$8
❑ 4726	Singing the Blues/What'll I Do Without You	1962	$8
❑ 4789	Someone New/Here's My Heart	1962	$8
❑ 4674	What's the Reason/ Walk Away Slowly	1961	$8

CHART

Number	Title	Yr	NM
❑ 5016	Bring My Baby Home/ Loving You Is Killing Me	1969	$5
❑ 1045	Each Time You Cross My Mind/Just Ain't My Day	1968	$5
❑ 1020	I'm Sorry to See You Go/ Once a Fool (Always a Fool)	1968	$5

MUSICOR

Number	Title	Yr	NM
❑ 1101	A Little Less Heartache/ Within Your Arms	1965	$6

EDWARDS, DEWEY

CAMEO

Number	Title	Yr	NM
❑ 364	Come On Over to My Place/I Let a Good Thing Go By	1965	$30

EDWARDS, J.D.

IMPERIAL

Number	Title	Yr	NM
❑ 5245	Crying/Hobo	1953	$120

EDWARDS, JIMMY

MERCURY

Number	Title	Yr	NM
❑ 71348	Do That Again/Wedding Band	1958	$40
❑ 71209	Love Bug Crawl/Honey Lovin'	1957	$40
❑ 71272	My Honey/Golden Ruby Blue	1958	$40

RCA VICTOR

Number	Title	Yr	NM
❑ 47-7597	A Favor for a Friend/Your Love Is a Good Love	1959	$30
❑ 47-7773	Silver Slippers/What Do You Want from Me	1960	$30

EDWARDS, JOEY

COLUMBIA

Number	Title	Yr	NM
❑ 4-43620	Trapped/How Big Is Big	1966	$15
❑ 4-43620 [PS]	Trapped/How Big Is Big	1966	$30

LILLY

Number	Title	Yr	NM
❑ 501	This Little Girl/Shirley, Shirley	1960	$200

EDWARDS, JONATHAN

ATCO

Number	Title	Yr	NM
❑ 6920	Honky-Tonk Stardust Cowboy/ (B-side unknown)	1973	$5
❑ 6911	That's What Our Life Is/ Stop and Start It All Again	1972	$5
❑ 6881	Train of Glory/Everybody Knows Her	1972	$5

CAPRICORN

Number	Title	Yr	NM
❑ 8021	Sunshine/Emma	1971	$5

MCA CURB

Number	Title	Yr	NM
❑ 53467	Look What We Made (When We Made Love)/Fewer Threads Than These	1988	$3
❑ 53613	My Baby's a Country Song/ It's a Natural Thing	1989	$3
❑ 53390	We Need to Be Locked Away/Back Up Grinnin'	1988	$3

REPRISE

Number	Title	Yr	NM
❑ 1358	White Line/Favorite Song	1976	$4

WARNER BROS.

Number	Title	Yr	NM
❑ 8364	Carolina Caroline/Never Together (But Close Sometimes)	1977	$4

EDWARDS, JONATHAN AND DARLENE

Actually JO STAFFORD and PAUL WESTON as a comedy team.

DOT

Number	Title	Yr	NM
❑ 17012	Carioca/Who	1967	$8

EDWARDS, SHIRLEY

SHRINE

Number	Title	Yr	NM
❑ 110	Dream My Heart/It Is Your Love	1966	$800

EDWARDS, STONEY

CAPITOL

Number	Title	Yr	NM
❑ 3005	A Two Dollar Toy/ An Old Mule's Hip	1970	$6
❑ 4188	Blackbird (Hold Your Head High)/Pickin' Wildflowers	1975	$5
❑ 4015	Clean Your Own Tables/ Do You Know the Man	1974	$5
❑ 3766	Daddy Bluegrass/It's Rainin' on My Sunny Day	1973	$5
❑ 3270	Daddy Did His Best/I Bought the Shoes That Just Walked Out on Me	1972	$6
❑ 4337	Don't Give Up on Me/ July 12, 1939	1976	$5
❑ 3671	Hank and Lefty Raised My Country Soul/A Few of the Reasons	1973	$5
❑ 3878	I Will Never Get Over You/Honey	1974	$5
❑ 4246	Love Still Makes the World Go 'Round/(I Want) The Real Thing	1976	$5
❑ 4051	Mississippi You're on My Mind/A Two Dollar Toy	1975	$5
❑ 4124	Moon Over Morocco/ Partners on the Road	1975	$5
❑ 3191	Odd-Job Dollar-Bill Man/ The Fishin' Song	1971	$6
❑ 3949	Our Garden of Love/ Talk About a Woman	1974	$5
❑ 3061	Poor Folks Stick Together/ Mama's Love	1971	$6
❑ 3462	She's My Rock/I Won't Make It Through the Day	1972	$5
❑ 3131	The Cute Little Waitress/ Please Bring a Bottle	1971	$6

JMI

Number	Title	Yr	NM
❑ 47	If I Had to Do It All Over Again/I Feel Chained	1978	$5
❑ 49	My Olkahome/Someone Like You	1979	$5

MUSIC AMERICA

Number	Title	Yr	NM
❑ 109	One Bar at a Time/ Stranger in My Arms	1980	$5

EDWARDS, TOM

CORAL

Number	Title	Yr	NM
❑ 61938	Goodnight Rock 'n' Roll/ The Spirit of Seventeen	1958	$10
❑ 61826	The Story of Elvis Presley/ What Is Rock 'n' Roll	1957	$30
❑ 61773	What Is a Teen Age Boy/ What Is a Teen Age Girl	1957	$15

DOT

Number	Title	Yr	NM
❑ 15811	What Is a Boyfriend/All About Girls and Women	1958	$10

EDWARDS, TOMMY

MGM

Number	Title	Yr	NM
❑ 11465	Au Revoir/I Lived When I Met You	1953	$30
❑ 12095	Baby, Let Me Take You Dreaming/My Sweetheart	1955	$30
❑ 11097	Christmas Is for Children/ Kris Kringle	1951	$30
❑ 13172	Country Boy/Love Is Best of All	1963	$12
❑ 12871	Don't Fence Me In/I'm Building Castles Again	1960	$15
❑ 11268	Easy to Say/The Greatest Sinner of Them All	1952	$30
❑ 11624	Every Day Is Christmas/ It's Christmas Once Again	1953	$30
❑ 11170	Forgive Me/The Bridge	1952	$30
❑ 10921	Gypsy Heart/Operetta	1951	$30
❑ 12837	Honestly and Truly/(New In) The Ways of Love	1959	$20
❑ 13057	I'll Cry You Out of My Heart/ Tables Are Turning	1962	$15
❑ 10973	I'll Never Know Why/A Beggar in Love	1951	$30
❑ 13032	I'm So Lonesome I Could Cry/ My Heart Would Know	1961	$15
❑ 12890	I Really Don't Want to Know/Unloved	1960	$15
❑ 12890 [PS]	I Really Don't Want to Know/Unloved	1960	$40
❑ 11035	It's All in the Game/All Over Again	1951	$30
❑ SK50104 [S]	It's All in the Game/ Love Is All We Need	1958	$40
❑ 12688	It's All in the Game/Please Love Me Forever	1958	$20
❑ 12916	It's Not the End of Everything/ Blue Heartaches	1960	$15
❑ 12814 [M]	I've Been There/I Looked at Heaven	1959	$20
❑ SK-50126 [S]	I've Been There/I Looked at Heaven	1959	$30
❑ 11763	Linger in My Arms/If You Would Love Me Again	1954	$30
❑ 12248	Love Is a Child/There Must Be a Way to Your Heart	1956	$30
❑ 12722	Love Is All We Need/ Mr. Music Man	1958	$20
❑ 11541	Lover's Waltz/Baby, Baby, Baby	1953	$30
❑ 13128	May I/Sometimes You Win, Sometimes You Lose	1963	$10
❑ 11209	My Girl/Piano, Bass and Drums	1952	$30
❑ 12794	My Melancholy Baby/It's Only the Good Times	1959	$20
❑ 10884	Once There Lived a Fool/A Friend of Johnny's	1951	$30
❑ 13100	Please Don't Tell Me/ Tonight I Won't Be There	1962	$15
❑ 11134	Please Mr. Sun/I May Live with You	1952	$30
❑ 12757 [M]	Please Mr. Sun/The Morning Side of the Mountain	1959	$20
❑ SK50112 [S]	Please Mr. Sun/The Morning Side of the Mountain	1959	$30
❑ 11932	Serenade to a Fool/It Could Have Been Me	1955	$30
❑ 11077	Solitaire/My Concerto	1951	$30
❑ 11582	So Little Time/Blue Bird	1953	$30
❑ 12959	Suzie Wong/As You Desire Me	1960	$15
❑ 11485	Take These Chains from My Heart/Paging Mr. Jackson	1953	$30
❑ 13317	Take These Chains from My Heart/You WIn Again	1965	$10
❑ 12054	Teardrop on a Rose/ To Those Who Wait	1955	$30
❑ 11604	That's All/Secret Love	1953	$30
❑ 12342	The Day That I Lost You/My Ship	1956	$30
❑ 13002	The Golden Chain/That's the Way with Love	1961	$15
❑ 10989	The Morning Side of the Mountain/For Instance	1951	$30
❑ 11668	There Was a Time/Wall of Ice	1954	$30
❑ 11993	Welcome to My Heart/Spring Never Came Around This Year	1955	$30
❑ 12514	We're Not Children Anymore/ Any Place, Any Time	1957	$30

MUSICOR

Number	Title	Yr	NM
❑ 1159	I Must Be Doing Something Wrong/I Cried, I Cried	1966	$10
❑ 1046	Left-Over Dreams/9 Chances Out of 10	1964	$12

7-Inch Extended Plays

MGM

Number	Title	Yr	NM
❑ X-1614	*It's All in the Game/My Sugar, My Sweet/I'll Always Be with You/That's All	1958	$25
❑ X-1666 [PS]	For Young Lovers, Vol. 1	1959	$25
❑ SX-1666 [PS]	For Young Lovers, Vol. 1	1959	$30
❑ X-1667 [PS]	For Young Lovers, Vol. 2	1959	$25
❑ SX-1667 [PS]	For Young Lovers, Vol. 2	1959	$30
❑ X-1668 [PS]	For Young Lovers, Vol. 3	1959	$25
❑ SX-1668 [PS]	For Young Lovers, Vol. 3	1959	$30
❑ X-1003 [PS]	It's All in the Game	1952	$50
❑ X-1614 [PS]	It's All in the Game, Vol. 1	1958	$25
❑ X1618 [PS]	It's All in the Game, Vol. 2	1958	$25
❑ X1619 [PS]	It's All in the Game, Vol. 3	1958	$25
❑ X-1003	It's All in the Game/Forgive Me//You Win Again/Solitaire	1952	$50
❑ X-1666 [M]	My Melancholy Baby/A Teardrop on a Rose//Paradise/I Looked at Heaven	1959	$25
❑ SX-1666 [S]	My Melancholy Baby/A Teardrop on a Rose//Paradise/I Looked at Heaven	1959	$30
❑ X-1668 [M]	Once There Lived a Fool/Up in a Cloud//It's Only the Good Times I Remember/Welcome Me	1959	$25
❑ SX-1668 [S]	Once There Lived a Fool/Up in a Cloud//It's Only the Good Times I Remember/Welcome Me	1959	$30
❑ X1619	Please Love Me Forever/ Love Is a Sacred Thing//Now and Then There's a Fool Such as I/Love Is All We Need	1958	$25
❑ X-1667 [M]	She Sends Her Regards/ It All Belongs to You//Music, Maestro, Please/Take These Chains From My Heart	1959	$25
❑ SX-1667 [S]	She Sends Her Regards/ It All Belongs to You//Music, Maestro, Please/Take These Chains From My Heart	1959	$30
❑ X1618	The Morning Side of the Mountain/You Win Again//Mr. Music Man/Please, Mr. Sun	1958	$25

EDWARDS, TYRONE

INVICTUS

Number	Title	Yr	NM
❑ ZS71269	Can't Get Enough of You/You Took Me from a World Outside	1974	$30

EDWARDS, VERN

PROBE

Number	Title	Yr	NM
❑ 100	Cool Baby, Cool/Glenda	1959	$200

EDWARDS, VINCENT

CAPITOL

Number	Title	Yr	NM
❑ 4819	Lollipop/As You Desire Me	1962	$10
❑ F3836	Lollipop/Wiget	1957	$20

—As "Vince Edwards

DECCA

Number	Title	Yr	NM
❑ 31563	Does Goodnight Mean Goodbye/Per Te Per Me	1963	$8
❑ 31413	Don't Worry 'Bout Me/And Now	1962	$8
❑ 31413 [PS]	Don't Worry 'Bout Me/And Now	1962	$30
❑ 31426	I Got It Bad (And That Ain't Good)/Say It Isn't So	1962	$8
❑ 31426 [PS]	I Got It Bad (And That Ain't Good)/Say It Isn't So	1962	$15
❑ 31534	This Train/Looking for Someone	1963	$8
❑ 31460	To Kill a Mockingbird/ You'll Still Have Me	1963	$8

MAGIC LAMP

Number	Title	Yr	NM
❑ 701	I'm Not the Marrying Kind/ What Colors Are You	1964	$8
❑ 7001	Why Did You Leave Me/ Squealin' Parrot Twist	1962	$10

Number	Title	Yr	NM

EELY, JACK
BANG
| ❏ 534 | Louie Go Home/Ride Ride Baby | 1966 | $20 |
| ❏ 520 | Louie Louie '66/David's Mood | 1966 | $20 |

EGAN, WALTER
BACKSTREET
❏ 52200	Fool Moon Fire/Tammy Ann	1983	$3
❏ 52200 [PS]	Fool Moon Fire/Tammy Ann	1983	$3
❏ 52249	Star of My Heart/Joyce	1983	$3
COLUMBIA
❏ 10824	Hot Summer Nights/She's So Tough	1978	$4
❏ 11297	Let's Run Away/Johnny Z (Is a Real Cool Guy)	1980	$4
❏ 10719	Magnet and Steel/Tunnel O' Love	1978	$5
❏ 10531	Only the Lucky/I'd Rather Have Fun	1977	$5
❏ 11116	That's That/Hi-Fi Love	1979	$4
❏ 10591	Waitin'/When I Get My Wheels	1977	$5

EHRET, BOB
ALADDIN
| ❏ 3377 | Stop the Clock/So Lonely | 1957 | $200 |

EIGHT MINUTES, THE
PERCEPTION
| ❏ 533 | Looking for a Brand New Game/Find the One Who Loves You | 1973 | $20 |

8TH DAY, THE
A&M
| ❏ 2539 | Call Me Up/I've Got My Heart in the Right Place | 1983 | $4 |
| ❏ 2595 [DJ] | In the Valley (same on both sides) | 1983 | $4 |
CADET
| ❏ 5660 | Hear the Grass Grow/Bring Your Love Back | 1969 | $12 |
INVICTUS
❏ 9117	Eeny-Meeny-Miny-Mo (Three's a Crowd)/Rocks in My Head	1972	$5
❏ 9124	Good Book/I Gotta Get Home	1972	$5
❏ 9107	If I Could See the Light/If I Could See the Light (Part 2)	1971	$5
❏ 9087	She's Not Just Another Woman/I Can't Fool Myself	1971	$5
KAPP
❏ 916	Glory/Building with a Steeple	1968	$8
❏ 862	Hey Boy (The Girl's in Love with You)/Million Lights	1967	$8
❏ 862 [PS]	Hey Boy (The Girl's in Love with You)/Million Lights	1967	$15

EL CAPRIS
ARGYLE
| ❏ 1010 | Ooh But She Did/(Shimmy, Shimmy) Ko Ko Wop | 1961 | $40 |
BULLSEYE
| ❏ 102 | Oh But She Did/(Shimmy Shimmy) Ko Ko Wop | 1956 | $200 |
—Note slight difference in A-side title
| ❏ 102 | Ooh But She Did/(Shimmy Shimmy) Ko Ko Wop | 1956 | $200 |
HI-Q
| ❏ 5006 | Girl of Mine/These Lonely Nights | 1958 | $125 |
—Blue label
| ❏ 5006 | Girl of Mine/These Lonely Nights | 1958 | $50 |
—Yellow label
PARIS
| ❏ 525 | They're Always Laughing at Me/Ivy League Clean | 1958 | $50 |
RING-O
| ❏ 308 | Safari/Quit Pulling My Woman | 1960 | $40 |

EL CLOD
CHALLENGE
| ❏ 9159 | Tijuana Border (Wolverton Mountain)/Pedro's Piano Roll Twist | 1962 | $30 |
MERCURY
| ❏ 72082 | He's Not a Rebel/Holiday in Havana | 1963 | $20 |
VEE JAY
| ❏ 647 | Tijuana Watusi/Gringo | 1965 | $20 |

EL DOMINGOS
CANDLELITE
| ❏ 418 | Made in Heaven/Lucky Me, I'm in Love | 1963 | $30 |
CHELSEA
| ❏ 1009 | Made in Heaven/Lucky Me, I'm in Love | 1962 | $200 |
KARMIN
| ❏ 1001 | Are You Ready to Say "I Do"/I Want to Know | 1964 | $300 |

EL DORADOS
OLDIES 45
| ❏ 68 | Baby, I Need You/Lovers Never Say Goodbye | 1964 | $8 |
—B-side by the Flamingos
PAULA
| ❏ 347 | Looking In from the Outside/Since You Came Into My Life | 1971 | $10 |
| ❏ 369 | Loose Booty (Part 1)/Loose Booty (Part 2) | 1971 | $10 |
TORRID
| ❏ 100 | In Over My Head/You Make My Heart Sing | 1970 | $20 |
VEE JAY
| ❏ 118 | Annie's Answer/Living with Vivian | 1954 | $300 |
—Red vinyl
❏ 118	Annie's Answer/Living with Vivian	1954	$100
❏ 147	At My Front Door/What's Buggin' You Baby	1955	$75
❏ 115	Baby I Need You/My Loving Baby	1954	$400
—Red vinyl
❏ 115	Baby I Need You/My Loving Baby	1954	$100
❏ 211	Bim Bam Boom/There in the Night	1956	$100
❏ 197	Fallen Tear/Chop Ling Soon	1956	$60
❏ 165	I'll Be Forever Lovin' You/I Began to Realize	1955	$70
❏ 302	Oh What a Girl/The Lights Are Low	1958	$200
❏ 127	One More Chance/Little Miss Love	1954	$200
❏ 250	Tears on My Pillow/A Rose for My Darling	1957	$40
❏ 263	Three Reasons Why/Boom Diddle Boom	1958	$200

EL VENOS, THE
RCA VICTOR
| ❏ 47-8303 | My Heart Beats Faster/You Won't Be There | 1963 | $30 |
VIK
| ❏ 0305 | My Heart Beats Faster/You Must Be True | 1957 | $100 |

ELAINE AND DEREK
VEE JAY
| ❏ 415 | The Christmas Story/It's Christmas | 1961 | $20 |

ELBERT, DONNIE
ALL PLATINUM
❏ 2336	If I Can't Have You/Can't Get Over Losing You	1972	$6
❏ 2337	Little Piece of Leather/Sweet Baby	1972	$6
❏ 2351	Love Is Strange/(Instrumental)	1973	$6
❏ 2333	Sweet Baby/Can't Get Over Losing You	1971	$6
❏ 2338	That's If You Love Me/Can't Get Over Losing You	1972	$6
❏ 2346	This Feeling of Losing You/Can't Stand These Lonely Nights	1973	$6
❏ 2367	What Do You Do/Will You Love Me Tomorrow	1974	$5
❏ 2330	Where Did Our Love Go/That's If You Love Me	1971	$6
ATCO
❏ 6550	Too Far Gone/In Between the Heartaches	1968	$8
AVCO
❏ 4587	I Can't Help Myself/Love Is Here and Now You're Gone	1972	$6
❏ 4598	Ooh, Baby Baby/Tell Her for Me	1972	$6
CUB
❏ 9125	Don't Cry My Love/Love Stew	1963	$15
DELUXE
❏ 6143	Believe It or Not/Tell Me So	1957	$30
❏ 6168	I Want to Be Near You/Come On Sugar	1958	$30
❏ 6148	Leona/Have I Sinned	1957	$30
❏ 6161	My Confession of Love/Peek-a-Boo	1958	$30
❏ 6125	What Can I Do/Hear My Plea	1957	$30
❏ 6156	Wild Child/Let's Do the Stroll	1958	$30
DERAM
❏ 7526	Without You/Baby Please Come Home	1969	$8
PARKWAY
❏ 844	Set My Heart at Ease/Baby Cares	1962	$20
RARE BULLET
❏ 101	Can't Get Over Losing You/Got to Get Myself Together	1970	$6
VEE JAY
❏ 353	Baby Let Me Love You Tonight/Half as Old	1960	$20
❏ 336	Hey Baby/Will You Ever Be Mine	1960	$20
❏ 370	I've Loved You Baby/I Beg of You	1960	$20

ELCHORDS, THE
GOOD
| ❏ 544 | Peppermint Stick/Gee, I'm in Love | 1958 | $100 |
—Straight lines on label
| ❏ 544 | Peppermint Stick/Gee, I'm in Love | 1962 | $70 |
—Red vinyl
| ❏ 544 | Peppermint Stick/Gee, I'm in Love | 1962 | $30 |
—Sawtooth lines on label
| ❏ 544 | Peppermint Stick/Gee, I'm in Love | 1962 | $20 |
—No lines on label

ELECTRIC ELVES, THE
MGM
| ❏ K13839 [DJ] | Hey, Look Me Over/It Pays to Advertise | 1967 | $60 |
—Stock copy not known to exist; it would probably go for at least twice this amount

ELECTRIC EXPRESS, THE
AVCO
| ❏ 4607 | I Can't Believe We Did (The Whole Thing)/Bee Pee | 1972 | $20 |
LINCO
❏ 1003	I Can't Believe We Did (The Whole Thing)/Bee Pee	1972	$30
❏ 1001	It's the Real Thing - Pt. 1/Pt. 2	1971	$10
❏ 1002	Where You Coming From - Pt. 1/Pt. 2	1972	$30

ELECTRIC FLAG, THE
ATLANTIC
| ❏ 3237 | Doctor Oh Doctor/The Band Kept Playing | 1975 | $4 |
| ❏ 3222 | Sweet Soul Music/Every Now and Then | 1974 | $4 |
COLUMBIA
❏ 44307	Groovin' Is Easy/Over-Lovin' You	1967	$8
❏ 44307 [PS]	Groovin' Is Easy/Over-Lovin' You	1967	$30
❏ 44376	Soul Searchin'/Sunny	1967	$8
❏ 44765	Soul Searchin'/Sunny	1969	$6
SIDEWALK
❏ 929	Green and Gold/Peter's Trip	1967	$20

ELECTRIC LIGHT ORCHESTRA
Evolved from THE MOVE. Also see JEFF LYNNE; ROY WOOD.
CBS ASSOCIATED
❏ 05766	Calling America/Caught in a Trap	1986	$3
❏ 05766 [PS]	Calling America/Caught in a Trap	1986	$3
❏ 05892	So Serious/Endless Lies	1986	$3
❏ 05892 [PS]	So Serious/Endless Lies	1986	$3
JET
❏ 5064	Confusion/Poker	1979	$4
❏ 5060	Don't Bring Me Down/Dreaming of 4000	1979	$4
❏ 04130	Four Little Diamonds/Letter from Spain	1983	$4
❏ 03086	Hold On Tight/Mr. Blue Sky	1982	$3
—Reissue
❏ 02408	Hold On Tight/When Time Stood Still	1981	$4
❏ 5052	It's Over/The Whale	1978	$4
❏ 5067	Last Train to London/Down Home Town	1979	$4
❏ 5050	Mr. Blue Sky/One Summer Dream	1978	$4
❏ 5057	Shine a Little Love/Jungle	1979	$4
❏ 5057 [PS]	Shine a Little Love/Jungle	1979	$8
❏ 04208	Stranger/Train of Gold	1983	$4
❏ XW1145	Sweet Talkin' Woman/Fire on High	1978	$5
—Purple vinyl
❏ XW1145	Sweet Talkin' Woman/Fire on High	1978	$4
❏ XW1145 [PS]	Sweet Talkin' Woman/Fire on High	1978	$5
❏ XW1099	Turn to Stone/Mister Kingdom	1977	$4
❏ XW1099 [PS]	Turn to Stone/Mister Kingdom	1977	$8
❏ 02559	Twilight/Julie Don't Live Here	1981	$4
MCA
❏ 41289	All Over the World/Drum Dreams	1980	$4
❏ 41289 [PS]	All Over the World/Drum Dreams	1980	$5
❏ 41246	I'm Alive/Drum Dreams	1980	$4
❏ 41246 [PS]	I'm Alive/Drum Dreams	1980	$5
UNITED ARTISTS
❏ 50914	10538 Overture/(Battle of) Marston Moor	1972	$8
❏ XW634	Boy Blue/Eldorado	1975	$5
❏ XW1179	Boy Blue/Telephone Line	1978	$4
❏ XW573	Can't Get It Out of My Head/Illusions in G Major	1974	$4
❏ XW573 [PS]	Can't Get It Out of My Head/Illusions in G Major	1974	$6
❏ XW1176	Can't Get It Out of My Head/Strange Magic	1978	$4
❏ XW405	Daybreaker/Ma-Ma-Ma-Belle	1974	$6
❏ XW939	Do Ya/Nightrider	1977	$4
❏ XW1178	Do Ya/Nightrider	1978	$4

Number	Title	Yr	NM
❏ XW729	Evil Woman/10538 Overture (Live)	1975	$4
❏ XW1177	Evil Woman/Livin' Thing	1978	$4
❏ XW888	Livin' Thing/Ma-Ma-Ma-Belle	1976	$4
❏ XW1180	Ma-Ma-Ma-Belle/10538 Overture	1978	$4

—1176 through 1180 were available for a very short time just before ELO's rights transfered from UA to CBS.

❏ XW842	Showdown/Daybreaker (Live)	1976	$5
❏ XW337	Showdown/In Old England Town	1973	$6
❏ XW770	Strange Magic/New World Rising	1976	$4
❏ XW770 [PS]	Strange Magic/New World Rising	1976	$6
❏ XW1000	Telephone Line/Poorboy (The Greenwood)	1977	$5

—Green vinyl

| ❏ XW1000 [PS] | Telephone Line/Poorboy (The Greenwood) | 1977 | $5 |

—Picture sleeves can be found with either green or black vinyl versions, but few black vinyl copies were issued with the picture sleeve

| ❏ XW1000 | Telephone Line/Poorboy (The Greenwood) | 1977 | $4 |

ELECTRIC PRUNES, THE
REPRISE
❏ 0473	Ain't It Hard/Little Olive	1966	$50
❏ 0564	Get Me to the World on Time/Are You Lovin' Me	1967	$30
❏ PRO305 [DJ]	Help Us (Our Father, Our King)/The Adoration	1968	$50
❏ 0805	Hey, Mr. President/Flowing Smoothly	1969	$30
❏ 0594	Hideaway/Dr. Do-Good	1967	$30
❏ 0704	I Had Too Much to Dream (Last Night)/Get Me to the World On Time	1968	$5

—"Back to Back Hits" series -- originals have "W7" and "r:" logos

❏ 0532	I Had Too Much to Dream (Last Night)/Lovin	1966	$30
❏ 0858	Love Grows/Finders Keepers, Losers Weepers	1969	$30
❏ PRO277 [DJ]	Sanctus/Credo	1968	$60
❏ 0607	The Great Banana Hoax/Wind-Up Toys	1967	$30

ELEGANTS, THE
ABC-PARAMOUNT
| ❏ 10219 | I've Seen Everything/Tiny Cloud | 1961 | $50 |
APT
| ❏ 25017 | Goodnight/Please Believe Me | 1958 | $40 |
| ❏ 25005 | Little Star/Getting Dizzy | 1958 | $60 |

—All-black label

| ❏ 25005 | Little Star/Getting Dizzy | 1958 | $50 |

—Black label with rainbow

| ❏ 25029 | Pay Day/True Love Affair | 1959 | $40 |
BANGAR
| ❏ 613 | Minor Chaos/Lost Souls | 1964 | $40 |
BIM BAM BOOM
| ❏ 121 | It's Just a Matter of Time/Lonesome Weekends | 1974 | $6 |

—Colored vinyl

| ❏ 121 | It's Just a Matter of Time/Lonesome Weekends | 1974 | $4 |

—Black vinyl

HULL
| ❏ 732 | Little Boy Blue/Get Well Soon | 1960 | $125 |
LAURIE
| ❏ 3283 | A Letter from Viet Nam/Barbara Beware | 1965 | $40 |
| ❏ 3324 | Belinda/Lazy Love | 1965 | $30 |

—As "Vito and the Elegants"

| ❏ 3298 | Wake Up/Bring Back Wendy | 1965 | $60 |
PHOTO
| ❏ 2662 | Dressin' Up/A Dream Can Come True | 1963 | $60 |
| ❏ 2662 [PS] | Dressin' Up/A Dream Can Come True | 1963 | $200 |
UNITED ARTISTS
| ❏ 295 | Happiness/Spiritual | 1961 | $60 |
| ❏ 230 | Speak Low/Let My Prayers Be With You | 1960 | $50 |

ELENA
ROULETTE
| ❏ 4605 | Evening Time/Road of Love | 1965 | $20 |

ELEPHANTS MEMORY
APPLE
❏ 1854	Liberation Special/Madness	1972	$8
❏ 1854 [PS]	Liberation Special/Madness	1972	$12
❏ 1854	Liberation Special/Power Boogie	1972	$400
ATLANTIC
| ❏ 3257 | Shakedown/Brother Can You Spare Me a Dime | 1975 | $5 |

Number	Title	Yr	NM
BUDDAH			
❏ 98	Cross Roads of the Stepping Stones/Jungle Gym at the Zoo	1969	$8
❏ 209	Don't Put Me on Trial No More/Hot Dog	1971	$8
METROMEDIA			
❏ 182	Mongoose/I Couldn't Dream	1970	$6
❏ 182 [PS]	Mongoose/I Couldn't Dream	1970	$6
❏ 210	Skyscraper Commando/Power	1971	$6

ELEVENTH HOUR, THE
20TH CENTURY
❏ 2114	Far As We Felt Like Goin'/Volcano	1974	$8
❏ 2278	Get On or Get Off/You'll Never Know Until You Try	1976	$8
❏ 2215	Hollywood Hot/Hollywood Hotter	1975	$6
❏ 2076	So Good/My Bed	1974	$6

ELEVENTH HOUSE, THE (WITH LARRY CORYELL)
ARISTA
| ❏ 0154 | Some Greasy Stuff/ (B-side unknown) | 1975 | $4 |
VANGUARD
| ❏ 35176 | The Funky Waltz/Low-Lee-Tah | 1974 | $5 |

ELF
EASTERN ARTISTS
| ❏ 5015 | Sit Down Honey (Everything Will Be Alright)/Gambler, Gambler | 1972 | $60 |
EPIC
| ❏ 5-10933 | Hoochie Koochie Lady/First Avenue | 1972 | $30 |
MGM
| ❏ M14752 | L.A. 59/(B-side unknown) | 1974 | $20 |

—Stock copy may not exist

ELFMAN, DANNY
MCA
| ❏ 52560 | Gratitude/Tough as Nails | 1985 | $3 |
| ❏ 52560 [PS] | Gratitude/Tough as Nails | 1985 | $3 |
WARNER BROS.
| ❏ 22756 | The Batman Theme (Edit)/The Batman Theme (Action Mix) | 1989 | $3 |
| ❏ 22756 [PS] | The Batman Theme (Edit)/The Batman Theme (Action Mix) | 1989 | $3 |

ELGART, LARRY
DECCA
| ❏ 9-29043 | More Than You Know/You're Driving Me Crazy (What Did I Do) | 1954 | $15 |
| ❏ 9-29666 | Spanish Lace/What the Thunder Said | 1955 | $10 |
MGM
❏ K12979	Arkansas Holler/This Heart of Mine	1961	$8
❏ K13063	Elgart Twist/Cornelia	1962	$8
❏ K13012	For the Soul/Green Valley	1961	$8
RCA
❏ PB-13733	Caravan/The Best of Times	1984	$6
❏ PB-13342	Hooked on Astaire/Hooked on the Blues	1982	$5
❏ PB-13411	Hooked on Dixie/Swingin' the Classics	1982	$5
❏ GB-14071	Hooked on Swing/Caravan	1985	$3

—Gold Standard Series" reissue

| ❏ PB-13219 | Hooked on Swing/Hooked on the Big Bands | 1982 | $5 |
| ❏ PB-13626 | La Cage Aux Folles/The Best of Times | 1983 | $5 |
RCA VICTOR
❏ 47-7651	Have You Heard/Duet from Saratoga-Game of Poker	1959	$8
❏ 47-7575 [M]	Honeysuckle Rose/Mountain Greenery	1959	$8
❏ 61-7575 [S]	Honeysuckle Rose/Mountain Greenery	1959	$20

—Living Stereo" on label

ELGART, LES
COLUMBIA
❏ 4-40500	At the Boppin' Stop/I Didn't Even Know Her Name	1955	$8
❏ 4-40180	Bandstand Boogie/When Yuba Plays the Rhumba on the Tuba	1954	$30
❏ ZSP56767/8 [DJ]	Bandstand Twist/Hawaiian War Chant	1962	$20

—Special Album Excerpt" promotional item

❏ ZSP56767/8 [PS]	Bandstand Twist/Hawaiian War Chant	1962	$30
❏ 4-40388	Bazoom (I Need Your Lovin')/Charlie's Dream	1954	$12
❏ S7-31150 [S]	Beat Junction/Sidewinder	1961	$8
❏ 4-40214	Charleston/Meet Me Tonight in Dreamland	1954	$10
❏ 4-40458	Come to the Mardi Gras/Chattanooga Legion Band	1955	$8
❏ 4-40202	Flat Foot Floogie/Roo Roo (Kangaroo)	1954	$10

Number	Title	Yr	NM
❏ 4-40571	Honky Tonk Train Blues/Ain't She Sweet	1955	$8
❏ S7-31153 [S]	I'll Remember April/Together	1961	$8

—The above five are 33 1/3 rpm "Stereo Seven" jukebox singles from set "JS 7-33"entitled "Half Satin - Half Latin

❏ 4-40353	It Ain't Necessarily So Pt. 1/Pt. 2	1954	$10
❏ 4-40822	It Must Be True/I Ain't Foolin'	1957	$8
❏ 4-40294	Little White Duck/Zing Went the Strings of My Heart	1954	$10
❏ S7-31151 [S]	Love for Sale/When You Were Sweet Sixteen	1961	$8
❏ 4-40525	Love Me or Leave Me/When Yuba Plays the Rhumba on the Tuba	1955	$8
❏ 4-40664	Main Title -- Golden Arm/D.J. Jamboree	1956	$10
❏ 4-40215	Mango/East Is East	1954	$10
❏ 4-41394	Moonlight Shuffle/When I Take My Sugar to Tea	1959	$8
❏ 4-40383	Mr. Sandman/Don't Let the Kiddy Geddin	1954	$10
❏ 4-40326	One O'Clock Jump Mambo/I Don't Want to Set the World on Fire	1954	$10
❏ 4-40671	Saddle Shoe Boogie/La Chnouf	1956	$8
❏ 4-40545	Start Dancin' with a Smile No. 1/No. 2	1955	$8
❏ 4-41363	Strike Up the Band/Indian Summer	1959	$8
❏ 4-40137	The Gang That Sang "Heart of My Heart"/Geronimo	1953	$10
❏ 4-40703	The Left Bank/The Poor Pianist of Paris	1956	$8
❏ S7-31152 [S]	The Touch of Your Lips/Let Me Call You Sweetheart	1961	$8
❏ 4-40617	The Trouble with Harry/Devil May Care	1955	$8
❏ S7-30838 [S]	(titles unknown)	1960	$8
❏ S7-30839 [S]	(titles unknown)	1960	$8
❏ S7-30840 [S]	(titles unknown)	1960	$8
❏ S7-30841 [S]	(titles unknown)	1960	$8
❏ S7-30842 [S]	(titles unknown)	1960	$8

—The above five are 33 1/3 rpm "Stereo Seven" jukebox singles with small center holes

❏ S7-31267 [S]	(titles unknown)	1962	$8
❏ S7-31268 [S]	(titles unknown)	1962	$8
❏ S7-31269 [S]	(titles unknown)	1962	$8
❏ S7-31270 [S]	(titles unknown)	1962	$8
❏ S7-31271 [S]	(titles unknown)	1962	$8

—The above five are 33 1/3 rpm "Stereo Seven" jukebox singles with small center holes

| ❏ 4-40249 | Wedding Bells (Are Breaking Up That Old Gang of Mine)/Spending the Summer in Love | 1954 | $10 |
| ❏ 4-40716 | What'd Ya Know/While the City Sleeps | 1956 | $8 |

7-Inch Extended Plays
❏ B-8752	*Stompin' at the Savoy/Street of Dreams/I Had the Craziest Dream/Three to Get Ready (contents unknown)	1956	$10
❏ B-8751	(contents unknown)	1956	$10
❏ B-8753	(contents unknown)	1956	$10
❏ B-8751 [PS]	The Elgart Touch, Vol. 1	1956	$12
❏ B-8752 [PS]	The Elgart Touch, Vol. 2	1956	$12
❏ B-8753 [PS]	The Elgart Touch, Vol. 3	1956	$12

ELGINS, THE (1)
V.I.P.
| ❏ 25029 | Darling Baby/Put Yourself in My Place | 1965 | $200 |

—First pressings credited "The Downbeats

❏ 25029	Darling Baby/Put Yourself in My Place	1965	$30
❏ 25037	Heaven Must Have Sent You/Stay in My Lonely Arms	1965	$30
❏ 25065	Heaven Must Have Sent You/Stay in My Lonely Arms	1970	$12
❏ 25043	It's Been a Long, Long Time/I Understand My Man	1966	$30

ELGINS, THE (2)
A.B.S.
| ❏ 113 | Pretending/Lonesome | 1961 | $400 |

ELGINS, THE (3)
CONGRESS
| ❏ 225 | Here in Your Arms/We're Gonna Have a Good Time | 1964 | $40 |
| ❏ 214 | The Times We've Wasted/Ritha Mae | 1964 | $30 |

ELGINS, THE (4)
LUMMTONE
| ❏ 109 | A Winner Never Quits/Johnny I'm Sorry | 1962 | $30 |
| ❏ 112 | Finally/I Lost My Love in the Big City | 1963 | $30 |

ELGINS, THE (U)
DOT
| ❏ 16563 | Cheryl/Tell Gina | 1963 | $70 |
JOED
| ❏ 716 | Once Upon a Time/The Huddle | 1964 | $700 |

Number	Title	Yr	NM
MGM			
❑ 12670	A Picture of You/Mademoiselle	1958	$70
TITAN			
❑ 1724	My Illness/Extra, Extra	1962	$250
❑ 1724	My Illness/Heartache Heartbreak	1962	$200
VALIANT			
❑ 712	Street Scene/You Found Yourself Another Fool	1965	$30

ELIGIBLES, THE
CAPITOL

Number	Title	Yr	NM
❑ 4203	Car Trouble/I Wrote a Song	1959	$15
❑ 4409	East of West Berlin/Young Is My Lover	1960	$15
❑ 4265	Faker, Faker/24 Hours	1959	$15
❑ 4304	My First Christmas with You/Little Engine	1959	$20
MERCURY			
❑ 72000	That Carmen Twist/Come Back, Music	1962	$10
WARNER BROS.			
❑ 5344	Gabie/See What You Can Do For Me	1963	$10

ELIZABETH
VANGUARD

Number	Title	Yr	NM
❑ 35070	Mary Anne/The World's For Free	1968	$20

ELLEDGE, JIMMY
4 STAR

Number	Title	Yr	NM
❑ 1015	Lady Lover/(B-side unknown)	1976	$4
❑ 1003	One By One/After You	1975	$4
HICKORY			
❑ 1341	A Good Woman's Love (Not Easy to Find)/World of Lavender Lace	1965	$8
❑ 1363	A Legend in My Time/Pink Dally Rue	1966	$8
❑ 1313	Follow Every Rainbow/I Just Walked In (Your Heart Last Night)	1965	$8
❑ 1420	Let Me Love You a Little (So I Can Love You a Lot)/She Should Save Some Loving (For a Rainy Day)	1966	$8
❑ 1452	The Darkest Part of Night (Is Dawn)/She Should Save Some Loving (For a Rainy Day)	1967	$8
❑ 1393	Time Is a Thief/I Just Walked In (Your Heart Last Night)	1966	$8
LITTLE DARLIN'			
❑ 0047	Florence Jean/No One Ever Lost More	1968	$6
RCA VICTOR			
❑ 47-8081	A Golden Tear/I'll Get By (Don't Worry)	1962	$8
❑ 47-8081 [PS]	A Golden Tear/I'll Get By (Don't Worry)	1962	$30
❑ 47-8042	Bo Diddley/Diamonds	1962	$8
❑ 47-8012	Can't You See It in My Eyes/What a Laugh	1962	$30
❑ 47-8355	Dream of the Year/Gonna Turn My Voodoo On	1964	$8
❑ 47-7946	Funny How Time Slips Away/Hey Jimmy Joe Jim Jack	1961	$10
❑ 47-8241	I Had to Run Away/There's Nothing There for Me	1963	$8
❑ 47-8191	Please Love Me Forever/A Penny's Worth of Happiness	1963	$8
❑ 47-8191 [PS]	Please Love Me Forever/A Penny's Worth of Happiness	1963	$30
❑ 47-7910	Send Me a Letter/Swanee River Rocket	1961	$15
SIMS			
❑ 204	I Gotta Live Here/Hold My Heart for Awhile	1964	$8

ELLEN, IVY, & FAMILY
FELSTED

Number	Title	Yr	NM
❑ 8609	Go Tell Santa/(Instrumental)	1960	$20
—B-side by the Reindeers			
❑ 8609 [PS]	Go Tell Santa/(Instrumental)	1960	$30

ELLEY, MICKEY, AND THE ARISTOCRACY
WARNER BROS.

Number	Title	Yr	NM
❑ 7083	Someone Like Me/Yesterday's Rain	1967	$60

ELLIE POP
MAINSTREAM

Number	Title	Yr	NM
❑ 686	Can't Be Love/Seven North Frederick	1968	$30

ELLIMAN, YVONNE
DECCA

Number	Title	Yr	NM
❑ 32949	Can't Find My Way Home/I Would Have Had a Good Time	1972	$4
❑ 33018	Could We Start Again, Please/Heaven on Their Minds	1972	$5
—B-side by Ben Vereen			
❑ 32870	Everything's Alright/Heaven on Their Minds	1971	$5

Number	Title	Yr	NM
❑ 32785	I Don't Know How to Love Him/Overture	1971	$5
MCA			
❑ 40235	Casserole Me Over/Come On Back Where You Belong	1974	$4
❑ 40121	Hawaii/I Can't Explain	1973	$4
RSO			
❑ 871	Hello Stranger/She'll Be the Home	1977	$4
❑ 884	If I Can't Have You/Good Sign	1977	$4
❑ 877	I Knew/I Can't Get You Out of My Mind	1977	$4
❑ 858	Love Me/I Keep Hangin' On (I Don't Know Why)	1976	$4
❑ 1007	Love Pains/Rock Me Slowly	1979	$4
❑ 915	Moment by Moment/Sailing Ships	1978	$4
❑ 915 [PS]	Moment by Moment/Sailing Ships	1978	$4
❑ 905	Savannah/Up to the Man in You	1978	$4
❑ 514	Somewhere in the Night/Who's Gonna Save the World	1975	$4
❑ 517	Walk Right In/Small Town Talk	1975	$4

ELLINGTON, DUKE
BETHLEHEM

Number	Title	Yr	NM
❑ 11066	In a Mellow Tone/Jack the Bear	1960	$10
❑ 11007	Indian Summer/The Jeep Is Jumpin'	1958	$10
❑ 11016	The Blues (Part 1)/The Blues (Part 2)	1959	$12
CAPITOL			
❑ F2980	12th Street Rag Mambo/Chile Bowl	1954	$15
❑ F2503	Ballin' the Blues/Nothin' Nothin' Baby	1953	$15
❑ F2546	Blue Jean Beguine/Warm Vallen	1953	$15
❑ F2723	Blue Moon/Ultra Deluxe	1954	$15
❑ F2598	Boo-Dar/Give Me the Right	1953	$15
❑ F2875	Bunny Hop Mambo/Is It a Sin	1954	$15
❑ F3049	Echo Tango/All Day Long	1955	$15
❑ F2817	Isle of Capri/Band Call	1954	$15
❑ F2458	Satin Doll/Without a Song	1953	$15
❑ F2930	Smile/If I Give My Heart to You	1954	$15
COLUMBIA			
❑ 41421	Anatomy of a Murder/Flirtbird	1959	$10
❑ 42144	Asphalt Jungle Theme (Part 1)/Asphalt Jungle Theme (Part 2)	1961	$12
❑ S731479 [S]	B D B/Wild Man	1962	$15
❑ 39712	Blues at Sundown/Bensonality	1952	$20
❑ 41689	Blues in Orbit/Villes, Ville Is the Place, Man	1960	$10
❑ 39110	Build That Railroad/Love You Madly	1950	$20
❑ 40903	Cop-Out/Rock City Rock	1957	$12
❑ 39545	Deep Night/Please Be Kind	1951	$20
❑ 41180	Duke's Place/Jones	1958	$12
❑ S731433 [S]	I've Just Seen Her/Back to School	1962	$15
❑ 39496	Monologue/8th Veil	1951	$20
❑ 41098	My Heart, My Mind, My Everything/Nightfall	1958	$10
❑ S731435 [S]	Once Upon a Time/Nightlife	1962	$15
❑ 42237	Paris Blues (Part 1)/Paris Blues (Part 2)	1962	$12
❑ 31100 [S]	Pie Eye's Blues/Sweet and Pungent	1961	$15
❑ S731482 [S]	Segue in C (Part I)/(Part II)	1962	$15
—The above five are "Stereo Seven" 33 1/3 rpm jukebox singles from set "JS 7-59" and the album "First Time!			
❑ 50014	Solitude/Mood Indigo	1954	$15
—Hall of Fame Series			
❑ 41362	Spank No. 1/Spank No. 2	1959	$10
❑ S731481 [S]	Take the "A" Train/Until I Met You	1962	$15
❑ 31099 [S]	Three J's Blues/Smada	1961	$15
❑ 31101 [S]	(titles unknown)	1961	$15
❑ 31102 [S]	(titles unknown)	1961	$15
❑ 31103 [S]	(titles unknown)	1961	$15
❑ S731436 [S]	(titles unknown)	1962	$15
❑ S731478 [S]	(titles unknown)	1962	$15
❑ S731480 [S]	To You/Jumpin' at the Woodside	1962	$15
❑ 41401	Walkin' and Singin' the Blues/Hand Me Down Love	1959	$10
❑ S731437 [S]	What a Country!/We Speak the Same Language	1962	$15
—The above five are "Stereo Seven" 33 1/3 rpm jukebox singles from set "JS 7-54" and the album "All American in Jazz			
❑ S731434 [S]	Which Way?/If I Were You	1962	$15
RCA VICTOR			
❑ 47-4711	Balcony Serenade/Strange Feeling	1952	$20
❑ 47-3035	Beale Street Blues/Pretty Woman	1949	$15
❑ 47-4712	Dancers in Love/Coloratura	1952	$20
❑ 47-3034	Drawing Room Blues/St. Louis Blues	1949	$15
❑ 47-3033	Frankie & Johnny/Royal Garden Blues	1949	$15
❑ 47-2955	The Sidewalks of New York/Don't Get Around Much Anymore	1949	$30
REPRISE			
❑ 0545	Satin Doll/Don't Get Around Much Anymore	1967	$6
❑ EAP 1-477	(contents unknown)	1954	$20
❑ EAP 1-521 [PS]	Ellington '55, Part 1	1955	$20
❑ EAP 2-521 [PS]	Ellington '55, Part 2	1955	$20

Number	Title	Yr	NM
❑ EAP 3-521 [PS]	Ellington '55, Part 3	1955	$20
❑ EAP 4-521 [PS]	Ellington '55, Part 4	1955	$20
❑ EAP 4-521	Happy Go Lucky Local/Flying Home	1955	$20
❑ EAP 3-521	One O'Clock Jump/Honeysuckle Rose	1955	$20
❑ EAP 2-521	Stompin' at the Savoy/In the Mood	1955	$20
❑ EAP 1-477 [PS]	The Duke Plays Ellington	1954	$20
❑ B-8301	(contents unknown)	1956	$15
❑ B-8303	(contents unknown)	1956	$15
❑ B-8301 [PS]	Hi-Fi Ellington Uptown, Vol. 1	1956	$15
❑ B-8302 [PS]	Hi-Fi Ellington Uptown, Vol. 2	1956	$15
❑ B-8303 [PS]	Hi-Fi Ellington Uptown, Vol. 3	1956	$15
❑ B-8302	Skin Deep/The Mooche	1956	$15
RCA VICTOR			
❑ EPA-5054 [PS]	Caravan (Gold Standard Series)	1958	$20
❑ EPA-5054	Caravan/Sophisticated Lady//Perdido/Mood Indigo	1958	$20

ELLIOT, CASS
Also see THE BIG THREE; THE MAMAS AND THE PAPAS; DAVE MASON; THE MUGWUMPS.

ABC DUNHILL

Number	Title	Yr	NM
❑ 4244	A Song That Never Comes/I Can Dream, Can't I?	1970	$6
❑ 4166	California Earthquake/Talkin' to Your Toothbrush	1968	$6
❑ 4264	Don't Let the Good Times Pass You By/A Song That Never Comes	1971	$6
—The above five as "Mama Cass Elliot			
❑ 4145	Dream a Little Dream of Me/Midnight Voyage	1968	$6
—Label credit: "Featuring Mama Cass with the Mamas and the Papas			
❑ 4253	Good Times Are Coming/Welcome to the World	1970	$6
❑ 4195	It's Getting Better/Who's to Blame	1969	$6
—The above three as "Mama Cass			
❑ 4214	Make Your Own Kind of Music/Ladylove	1969	$6
❑ 4184	Move In a Little Closer, Baby/All for Me	1969	$6
DUNHILL			
❑ 4145	Dream a Little Dream of Me/Midnight Voyage	1968	$30
—Label credit: "Featuring Mama Cass with the Mamas and the Papas"; no "ABC" at top of label			
RCA VICTOR			
❑ 74-0644	Baby, I'm Yours/Cherries Jubilee	1972	$6
❑ 74-0764	Disney Girls/Break Another Heart	1972	$6
❑ 74-0957	I Think a Lot About You/Listen to the World	1973	$6
❑ 74-0693	That Song/When It Doesn't Work Out	1972	$6

7-Inch Extended Plays
ABC DUNHILL

Number	Title	Yr	NM
❑ SP-DS-50040	California Earthquake/Talkin' to Your Toothbrush/Blues for Breakfast//Long Time Loving You/Jane the Insane Dog Lady/Burn Your Hatred	1968	$15
—As "Mama Cass"; jukebox issue; small hole, plays at 33 1/3 rpm			
❑ SP-DS-50040 [PS]	Dream a Little Dream	1968	$15

ELLIOTT, BERN, AND THE FENMEN
LONDON

Number	Title	Yr	NM
❑ 9733	Money/Nobody But Me	1965	$15

ELLIOTT, BILL, AND THE ELASTIC OZ BAND
APPLE

Number	Title	Yr	NM
❑ 1835	God Save Us/Do the Oz	1971	$8
❑ 1835 [PS]	God Save Us/Do the Oz	1971	$10
❑ P-1835 [DJ]	God Save Us/Do the Oz	1971	$30
—Has black star on A-side and unsliced apple on both sides			

ELLIOTT, WALTER & BENNETT
PAID

Number	Title	Yr	NM
❑ ATL3	The Twelve Days of a Atlanta Falcon Christmas/It	1980	$8
—Label is ungrammatical as above			
❑ BBS6	The Twelve Days of a Buffalo Bill Christmas/It	1980	$8
❑ COB9	The Twelve Days of a Cleveland Brown Christmas/It	1980	$8
❑ DAL1	The Twelve Days of a Dallas Cowboy Christmas/It	1980	$8
❑ LAX8	The Twelve Days of a Los Angeles Ram Christmas/It	1980	$8
❑ NEP5	The Twelve Days of a New England Patriot Christmas/It	1980	$8
❑ OAK2	The Twelve Days of an Oakland Raider Christmas/It	1980	$8
❑ PES7	The Twelve Days of a Philadelphia Eagle Christmas/It	1980	$8

Number	Title	Yr	NM
❏ PIT4	The Twelve Days of a Pittsburg Steelers Christmas/It	1980	$8

—*The label misspells "Pittsburg"*

❏ SDC10	The Twelve Days of a San Diego Charger Christmas/It	1980	$8
❏ 120	We Love the Atlanta Falcons/The Race Is On	1981	$10
❏ 123	We Love the Dallas Cowboys/ The Race Is On	1981	$10
❏ 127	We Love the Minnesota Vikings/The Race Is On	1981	$10

—*We know of at least eight in this series. The contents of Paid 119, 128 and 129 are not known, so there may be even more that eight in the series. Any help in filling in the gaps would be appreciated.*

❏ 124	We Love the Oakland Raiders/The Race Is On	1981	$10
❏ 122	We Love the San Diego Chargers/The Race Is On	1981	$10
❏ 121	We Love the (team unknown)/ The Race Is On	1981	$10
❏ 125	We Love the (team unknown)/ The Race Is On	1981	$10
❏ 126	We Love the (team unknown)/ The Race Is On	1981	$10

ELLIS, BOBBY
CAMEO

❏ 354	It's the Talk of the Town/ She's Got a Heart of Stone	1965	$30

CHELTENHAM

❏ 1007	It's the Talk of the Town/ She's Got a Heart of Stone	1965	$200

ELLIS, JIMMY
BOBLO

❏ 536	I'm Not Trying to Be Like Elvis/ Games You've Been Playing	1978	$4
❏ 536 [PS]	I'm Not Trying to Be Like Elvis/ Games You've Been Playing	1978	$10
❏ 532	Movin' On/My Baby's Out of Sight	1977	$4
❏ 531	There You Go/Here Comes That Wonderful Feeling	1977	$4
❏ 526	Tupelo Woman/The Closer He Gets	1976	$4

DRADCO

❏ 1892	Don't Count Your Chickens/ Love Is But Love	1964	$20

MCA

❏ 40060	There Ya Go/Here Comes That Feeling Again	1973	$4

SOUTHERN TRACKS

❏ 1069	I Make the Livin' (You Make the Livin' Worthwhile)/ Thank God for America	1986	$4
❏ 1080	Sunday Fathers/Thank God for America	1987	$4

SUN

❏ 1136	D.O.A./Misty/That's All Right/ Blue Moon of Kentucky	1977	$4
❏ 1131	I Use Her to Remind Me of You/Changing	1974	$4
❏ 1129	That's All Right/Blue Moon of Kentucky	1973	$5

—*Originals have no artist on label in an attempt to make people believe these were lost Elvis Presley outtakes*

❏ 1129	That's All Right/Blue Moon of Kentucky	1973	$4

—*Second pressings credit Jimmy Ellis*

ELLIS, JIMMY (2)
ATLANTIC

❏ 2572	I Don't Mind/Take the Lord With You	1968	$8

ELLIS, LARRY
DALE

❏ 107	Buzz Goes the Bee/ Nothing You Can Do	1958	$20

DART

❏ 112	I Know the Place/Love That Used to Be	1959	$20

ROULETTE

❏ 4195	Hide and Seek/Really and Truly	1959	$15
❏ 4243	Look, My Love/Nothing You Can Do	1960	$15

SWAN

❏ 4007	My Heart Understood/Tennessee	1958	$15

ELLIS, LLOYD
MERCURY

❏ 70520X45	Boogie Blues/Blue Champagne	1954	$40
❏ 70590X45	Cottontail Rag/Sweet and Lovely	1955	$40

Number	Title	Yr	NM

ELLIS, LORRAINE
BULLSEYE

❏ 100	Perfidia/Piano Player Play a Tune	1955	$70

GEE

❏ 1	Perfidia/Piano Player Play a Tune	1953	$300

ELLIS, RAY
20TH CENTURY FOX

❏ 593	Theme from "Von Ryan's Express"/Theme from "Morituri"	1965	$8

ASCOT

❏ 2203	A Thousand Clowns/ We'll Say Goodbye	1966	$8

ATCO

❏ 6396	I Got You Babe/King of the Road	1966	$8
❏ 6389	I'll Never Be Lonely Again/ Wait Till We're 65	1965	$8

COLUMBIA

❏ 4-41094	36-26-36/Come to Me	1958	$15
❏ 4-40982	Fascination/Soft Sands	1957	$15
❏ 4-41056	Like Jingle Bells/Snow, Snow, Beautiful Snow	1957	$15

MGM

❏ K12874	Fallout/U.S. Marshal	1960	$10
❏ K12942	Midnight Lace/Theme from "Grand Jury"	1960	$10
❏ K12770	Sweet Kentucky Belle/Lauralee	1959	$10
❏ K12797	The Love That Used to Be/I Know the Place	1959	$10

RCA VICTOR

❏ 47-8150	Anything, Anywhere/Rubia	1963	$10
❏ 47-7888	La Dolce Vita (The Sweet Life)/ Parlami Di Me (Speak to Me)	1961	$12
❏ 47-7888 [PS]	La Dolce Vita (The Sweet Life)/ Parlami Di Me (Speak to Me)	1961	$15
❏ 37-7888	La Dolce Vita (The Sweet Life)/ Parlami Di Me (Speak to Me)	1961	$30

—*Compact Single 33" (small hole, plays at LP speed)*

❏ 37-7888 [PS]	La Dolce Vita (The Sweet Life)/ Parlami Di Me (Speak to Me)	1961	$30

—*Special picture sleeve for "Compact Single 33*

❏ 47-7953	Portofino/Shalom	1961	$12
❏ 47-8023	The Sheik/Dumpy	1962	$10

ELLIS, SHIRLEY
COLUMBIA

❏ 44021	Soul Time/Waitin'	1967	$8
❏ 44137	Sugar Let's Shing-a-Ling/ How Lonely Is Lonely	1967	$8
❏ 43829	Truly, Truly, Truly/Birds, Bees, Cupids and Bows	1966	$8

CONGRESS

❏ 260	Ever See a Diver Kiss His Wife While the Bubbles Bounce About Above the Water/Stardust	1965	$12
❏ 246	I Never Will Forget/I Told You So	1965	$10
❏ 251	One Sour Note/You Better Be Good, World	1965	$10
❏ 210	Shy One/Takin' Care of Business	1964	$10
❏ 221	Such a Night/Bring It On Home to Me	1964	$10
❏ 208	(That's) What the Nitty Gritty Is/Get Out	1964	$12
❏ 234	The Clapping Song (Clap Pat Clap Slap)/This Is Beautiful	1965	$10
❏ 234 [PS]	The Clapping Song (Clap Pat Clap Slap)/This Is Beautiful	1965	$30
❏ 238	The Puzzle Song (A Puzzle in Song)/I See It, I Like It, I Want It	1965	$10

ELLISON, LORRAINE
LOMA

❏ 2074	Heart Be Still/Cry Me a River	1967	$12
❏ 2094	Try (Just a Little Bit Harder)/ In My Tomorrow	1968	$10
❏ 2083	When Love Flies Away/I Want to Be Loved	1967	$10

MERCURY

❏ 72534	Call Me Anytime You Need Some Lovin'/Please Don't Teach Me to Love You	1966	$20
❏ 72472	Don't Let It Go to Your Head/I Dig You Baby	1965	$20

SHARP

❏ 635	Open Up Your Heart/ This Is the Day	1963	$30

WARNER BROS.

❏ 5879	Good Love/I'm Over You	1966	$15
❏ 7042	He's My Guy/No Matter How It All Turns Out	1967	$12
❏ 5895	If I Had a Hammer/Heart and Soul	1967	$15
❏ 7700	Many Rivers to Cross/ Stormy Weather	1973	$8
❏ 7302	Only Your Love/What Is a Woman	1969	$8
❏ GWB 0324	Stay with Me/Heart Be Still	1975	$6

—*Back to Back Hits" series; "Burbank" palm trees label*

❏ 5850	Stay with Me/I Got My Baby Back	1966	$15
❏ 7361	Stay with Me/Try (Just a Little Bit Harder)	1970	$8

Number	Title	Yr	NM

ELLWANGER, SANDY
DOOR KNOB

❏ 326	I Just Came In Here (To Let a Little Love Out)/(B-side unknown)	1989	$5
❏ 334	What Kind of Girl Do You Think I Am/(B-side unknown)	1989	$5

ELMO AND ALMO
DADDY BEAT

❏ 2501	When the Good Sun Shines/Part II	1967	$8

ELMO AND PATSY
ELMO 'N' PATSY

❏ KP-2984	Grandma Got Run Over by a Reindeer/Christmas	1978	$30

—*Original pressing of this Christmas classic; cream label, brown print*

EPIC

❏ 34-04703	Grandma Got Run Over by a Reindeer/Percy, the Puny Poinsettia	1984	$4

—*First issue of new recording*

❏ 34-04703 [PS]	Grandma Got Run Over by a Reindeer/Percy, the Puny Poinsettia	1984	$4

—*Picture sleeve known to exist with either 04703 or 05479 records inside*

❏ 34-05479	Grandma Got Run Over by a Reindeer/Percy, the Puny Poinsettia	1985	$3

—*Gray label reissue*

OINK

❏ 2984	Grandma Got Run Over by a Reindeer/Christmas	1979	$8

—*Second issue of original recording; white label, red print*

SOUNDWAVES

❏ 4658	Grandma Got Run Over by a Reindeer/Christmas	1981	$6

—*Third issue of original recording; white label, red print*

ELMORE, RUSS AND RUSSANNE
DOLTON

❏ 14	What Does Santa Claus Want for Christmas/Big Words	1959	$20

ELVES, THE
DECCA

❏ 732617	Amber Velvet/West Virginia	1970	$30
❏ 732507	Walking in Different Circles/ She's Not the Same	1969	$30

ELY, JOE
MCA

❏ 40666	All My Love/Mardi Gras Waltz	1976	$4
❏ 40956	Cornbread Moon/She Never Spoke Spanish to Me	1978	$4
❏ 40870	Fingernails/Because of the Wind	1978	$4
❏ 40709	Gambler's Bride/Tennessee's Not the State I'm In	1977	$4
❏ 40906	Honky Tonk Masquerade/ Johnny Blues	1978	$4

SOUTH COAST

❏ 51102	Musta Notta Gotta Lotta/ Rock Me My Baby	1981	$4

EMANONS, THE
ABC-PARAMOUNT

❏ 9913	Dear One/We Teenagers (Know What We Want)	1958	$30

GEE

❏ 1005	Change of Time/Hindu Baby	1956	$120

JOSIE

❏ 801	Blue Moon/Wish I Had My Baby	1956	$125

WINLEY

❏ 226	Dear One/We Teenagers (Know What We Want)	1958	$50

EMBERS, THE
ATLANTIC

❏ 2627	Where Did I Go Wrong/ You Got What You Want	1969	$10

BELL

❏ 664	It Ain't No Big Thing/ It Ain't Necessary	1967	$30

COLUMBIA

❏ 40287	Sweet Lips/There'll Be No One Else But You	1954	$50

DOT

❏ 16162	Please Mr. Sun/My Dearest Darling	1960	$20
❏ 16101	Wait for Me/Couldn't Wait Any Longer	1960	$20

EMBER

❏ 101	Sound of Love/Paradise Hill	1953	$800

EMPRESS

❏ 107	Abigail/I Was Too Careful	1962	$40
❏ 104	I Won't Cry Anymore/I Was Too Careful	1961	$40
❏ 101	Solitaire/I'm Feeling All Right Again	1961	$40
❏ 108	What a Surprise/I Was Too Careful	1962	$50

Number	Title	Yr	NM
HERALD			
❑ 410	Sound of Love/Paradise Hill	1953	$200
— Black label			
❑ 410	Sound of Love/Paradise Hill	1953	$100
— Yellow label			
❑ 410	Sound of Love/Paradise Hill	1953	$200
— Red vinyl			
JCP			
❑ 1008	In My Lonely Room/Good Good Lovin'	1964	$70
LIBERTY			
❑ 55944	Evelyn/And Now I'm Blue	1967	$12
MGM			
❑ 14167	Watch Out Girl/Far Away Places	1970	$40
WYNNE			
❑ 101	Peter Gunn Cha Cha/Chinny Chin Cha Cha	1958	$20

EMBLEMS, THE

Number	Title	Yr	NM
BAYFRONT			
❑ 108	Bang, Bang, Shoot 'Em Daddy/Too Young	1962	$125
— Black vinyl			
❑ 107	Would You Still Be Mine/Poor Humpty Dumpty	1962	$125
— Label has parallel horizontal lines			
❑ 107	Would You Still Be Mine/Poor Humpty Dumpty	1962	$50
— Label has wavy lines or no lines			
CAMEO			
❑ 293	(It Still Would Be a) Cruel World/Whenever I'm Feelin' Low	1964	$20

EMERALDS, THE

Number	Title	Yr	NM
ABC-PARAMOUNT			
❑ 9948	I'm Dreaming/Confess	1958	$30
ALLIED			
❑ 10002	Sally Lou/Why Must I Wonder	1958	$50
BOBBIN			
❑ 121	Lover's Cry/Rumblin' Tumblin' Baby	1960	$50
❑ 107	That's the Way It's Got to Be/Maria's Cha-Cha	1959	$60
JUBILEE			
❑ 5474	Dancing Alone/Wanna Make Him Mine	1964	$15
❑ 5489	Did You Ever Love a Guy/I'm Gonna Ask That Boy to Dance	1964	$15
KICKS			
❑ 3	Sally Lou/Why Must I Wonder	1954	$700
KING			
❑ 6078	Baby You've Got Me/Promises	1967	$30
MOONGLOW			
❑ 232	Moonlight Surf/Little D Special	1964	$40
— Black vinyl			
❑ 232	Moonlight Surf/Little D Special	1964	$100
— Green vinyl			
❑ 230	Ooh Poo Pah Doo/Sally's Snake	1964	$40
REX			
❑ 1004	All the Time/Gotta Be on Time	1959	$40
❑ 1013	I Kneel at Your Throne/Custer's Last Stand	1960	$40
TOY			
❑ 7734	Silver/Roadrunner	1961	$30
VENUS			
❑ 1002	Mademoiselle/The Lover	1959	$125
❑ 1003	Marsha/You're Driving Me Crazy	1959	$200
YALE			
❑ 232	The Web/Trapped	1960	$30

EMERALS, THE

Number	Title	Yr	NM
TRIPLE X			
❑ 100/101	Please Don't Crush My Dreams/Jukebox Rock	1960	$600

EMERSON, BILLY

Number	Title	Yr	NM
CHESS			
❑ 1711	Give Me a Little Love/Woodchuck	1959	$30
❑ 1728	Holy Mackerel Baby/Believe Me	1959	$30
CONSTELLATION			
❑ 148	Aunt Molly (Part 1)/Aunt Molly (Part 2)	1965	$20
SUN			
❑ 203	I'm Not Going Home/The Woodchuck	1954	$600
❑ 214	Move, Baby, Move/When It Rains, It Pours	1955	$60
❑ 233	Something for Nothing/Little Fine Healthy Thing	1956	$60
VEE JAY			
❑ 219	Every Woman I Know/Tomorrow Never Comes	1956	$40
❑ 247	Somebody Show Me/The Pleasure Is All Mine	1957	$40

EMERSON, LAKE AND PALMER
Also see GREG LAKE; ASIA.

Number	Title	Yr	NM
ATLANTIC			
❑ 3555	All I Want Is You/Tiger in a Spotlight	1979	$5
❑ 3398	Fanfare for the Common Man/Brain Salad Surgery	1977	$5
❑ 3641	Peter Gunn Theme/Tiger in a Spotlight	1980	$5
COTILLION			
❑ 44131	A Time and a Place/Stone of Years	1971	$5
❑ 44158	From the Beginning/Living Sin	1972	$5
❑ 44106	Lucky Man/Knife's Edge	1971	$6
MANTICORE			
❑ 2003	Still...You Turn Me On/Brain Salad Surgery	1973	$5
❑ 2003 [PS]	Still...You Turn Me On/Brain Salad Surgery	1973	$10

EMERSON, LEE

Number	Title	Yr	NM
COLUMBIA			
❑ 4-40868	I Cried Like a Baby/Where D'Ja Go	1957	$30
— With Marty Robbins			
❑ 4-21525	I'll Know You're Gone/How Long Will It Be	1956	$30
— With Marty Robbins			
❑ 4-21570	I Thought I Heard You Callin' My Name/It's So Easy for You to Be Mean	1956	$30
❑ 4-21487	So Little Time/Thank You My Darling	1956	$30
❑ 4-40985	Start All Over/Do You Think	1957	$30
❑ 4-41046	What a Night/Catch That Train	1957	$30

EMERY, RALPH

Number	Title	Yr	NM
ABC			
❑ 10920	In the Misty Moonlight/Last Night Morning Sidewalks	1967	$10
❑ 11001	One More for the Road/Yodelin' Jim	1967	$10
ELEKTRA			
❑ 46010	Daddy, Is She Pretty As Mama/Wrestling Matches	1979	$5
LIBERTY			
❑ 55524	Christmas Dinner/Christmas Can't Be Far Away	1962	$20
❑ 55352	Hello Fool/It's Not a Lot	1961	$20
❑ 55383	I'll Take Good Care of Your Baby/Legend of Sleepy Hollow	1961	$20
❑ 55546	Poor Boy/The Touch of the Master's Hand	1963	$20
❑ 55429	Tough Top Cat/Two Minutes to Live	1962	$20
MERCURY			
❑ 72295	Sit Down and Write a Letter to Me, Won'tcha Baby/I Cry at Ball Games	1964	$15
ORLANDO			
❑ 101	Daddy, Is She Pretty As Mama/Wrestling Matches	1979	$12

EMMONS, BUDDY

Number	Title	Yr	NM
COLUMBIA			
❑ 40922	Silver Bells/Border Serenade	1957	$15

EMOTIONS, THE (1)

Number	Title	Yr	NM
ARC			
❑ 18-02239	Turn It Out/When You Gonna Wake Up	1981	$4
❑ 11134	What's the Name of Your Love?/Layed Back	1979	$5
❑ 11205	Where Is Your Love?/Layed Back	1980	$5
COLUMBIA			
❑ 3-10544	Best of My Love/A Feeling Is	1977	$5
❑ 3-10622	Don't Ask My Neighbors/Love's What's Happenin'	1977	$5
❑ 3-10347	Flowers/I Don't Wanna Lose Your Love	1976	$5
❑ 3-10791	Smile/Changes	1978	$5
❑ 3-10874	Walking the Line/Ain't No Doubt About It	1978	$5
❑ 3-10828	Whole Lotta Shakin'/Time Is Passing By	1978	$5
MOTOWN			
❑ 1784	I Can't Wait to Make You Mine/I'm Gonna Miss Your Love	1985	$4
❑ 1792	If I Only Knew Then (What I Know Now)/Eternally	1985	$4
RED LABEL			
❑ 001-3	Are You Through with My Heart/(B-side unknown)	1984	$5
STAX			
❑ 3205	Baby, I'm Through/Any Way You Look at It	1978	$5
❑ 3200	Shouting Out Love/Baby, I'm Through	1977	$5
❑ 3215	What Do the Lonely Do at Christmas/(Instrumental)	1978	$5

Number	Title	Yr	NM
TWIN STACKS			
❑ 130	I Love You But I'll Leave You/Brushfire	1968	$10
❑ 126	Somebody New/Brushfire	1968	$12
VOLT			
❑ 4053	Black Christmas/(Instrumental)	1970	$10
❑ 4045	Heart Association/The Touch of Your Lips	1970	$8
❑ 4010	So I Can Love You/Got to Be the Man	1969	$8
❑ 4031	Stealing Love/When Tomorrow Comes	1970	$8
❑ 4021	The Best Part of a Love Affair/I Like It	1969	$8
❑ 4104	What Do the Lonely Do at Christmas/(Instrumental)	1973	$8

EMOTIONS, THE (2)

Number	Title	Yr	NM
20TH FOX			
❑ 430	A Story Untold/One Life. One Love, One You	1963	$30
❑ 478	Boomerang/I Love You Madly	1964	$30
❑ 6623	Heart Strings/Every Time	1966	$20
CALLA			
❑ 122	Baby I Need Your Lovin'/She's My Baby (I Just Can't Let Her Go)	1966	$20
KAPP			
❑ 490	Echo/Come Dance Baby	1962	$30
❑ 513	L-O-V-E/A Million Reasons	1963	$30

EMOTIONS, THE (U)

Number	Title	Yr	NM
BRAINSTORM			
❑ 125	Can't Stand No More Heartaches/You'd Better Get Used to It	1968	$8
CARD			
❑ 600	(By the Light of the) Silvery Moon/Do You Love Me	1962	$200
FLIP			
❑ 356	I Ran to You/Keep Lookin' Your Way	1961	$40
FURY			
❑ 1010	Candlelight/It's Love	1958	$50
KARATE			
❑ 506	Hey Baby/I Wonder	1964	$30
LAURIE			
❑ 3167	Fool's Paradise/Starlit Night	1963	$30
VARDAN			
❑ 201	Love of a Girl/Do This for Me	1965	$30

EMPERORS, THE (1)

Number	Title	Yr	NM
MALA			
❑ 554	My Baby Likes to Boogaloo/You Got Me Where You Want Me	1967	$15
❑ 561	Searchin'/Lookin' for My Baby	1967	$15

EMPERORS, THE (2)

Number	Title	Yr	NM
HAVEN			
❑ 511	I May Be Wrong/Come Back, Come Back	1954	$4000
— VG 2000; VG+ 3000			

EMPERORS, THE (3)

Number	Title	Yr	NM
OLIMPIC			
❑ 245	Darlin' in the Moonlight/Steve Allen	1964	$50

EMPIRES, THE (1)

Number	Title	Yr	NM
AMP 3			
❑ 132	If I'm a Fool/Zippety Zip	1957	$125
HARLEM			
❑ 2325	Corn Whiskey/My Baby, My Baby	1954	$400
❑ 2333	Magic Mirror/Make Me or Break Me	1955	$400
WHIRLIN' DISC			
❑ 104	Linda/Whispering Heart	1957	$75
WING			
❑ 90050	By the Riverside/Tell Me Pretty Baby	1956	$50
❑ 90080	Don't Touch My Gal/My First Discovery	1956	$50
❑ 90023	I Want to Know/Shirley	1955	$60

EMPIRES, THE (2)

Number	Title	Yr	NM
CALICO			
❑ 121	Definition of Love/Only in My Dreams	1960	$30
CANDI			
❑ 1026	Love You So Bad/Come Back Girl	1962	$30
CHAVIS			
❑ 1026	Love You So Bad/Come Back Girl	1962	$20
COLPIX			
❑ 680	Everyone Knew But Me/Three Little Fishes	1963	$30
DCP			
❑ 1116	Have Mercy/Love Is Strange	1964	$15
LAKE			
❑ 711	Over the Summer Vacation/You're So Popular	1961	$30

Number	Title	Yr	NM

EMPIRES, THE (3)
EPIC
| ❏ 5-9527 | A Time and a Place/Punch Your Nose | 1962 | $50 |

ENALOUISE AND THE HEARTS
ARGYLE
| ❏ 1635 | From a Cap and a Gown/A Prisoner to You | 1959 | $60 |

ENCHANTERS, THE (1)
BALD EAGLE
| ❏ 3001 | Come On Baby, Let's Do the Stroll/Rock Around | 1958 | $40 |
BAMBOO
| ❏ 513 | Touch of Love/Cafe Bohemian | 1961 | $30 |
CANDELITE
| ❏ 432 | Oh Rose Marie/Bewildered | 1964 | $15 |
EP-SOM
| ❏ 103 | I Need Your Love/Goddess of Love | 1962 | $400 |
J.J. & M.
| ❏ 1562 | Oh Rose Marie/Bewildered | 1962 | $200 |
MUSITRON
| ❏ 1072 | I Lied to My Heart/Talk While You Walk | 1961 | $50 |
ORBIT
| ❏ 532 | Touch of Love/Cafe Bohemian | 1959 | $60 |
SHARP
| ❏ 105 | We Make Mistakes/The Decision | 1960 | $30 |
STARDUST
| ❏ 102 | Spellbound by the Moon/Know It All | 1956 | $1500 |

ENCHANTERS, THE (2)
LOMA
| ❏ 2012 | I Want to Be Loved/I Paid for the Party | 1965 | $10 |
| ❏ 2054 | We Got Love/I've Lost All Communications | 1966 | $10 |
WARNER BROS.
| ❏ 5460 | I Wanna Thank You/I'm a Good Man | 1964 | $20 |

ENCHANTERS, THE (3)
CORAL
| ❏ 61916 | Mambo Santa Mambo/Bottle Up and Go | 1957 | $50 |
| ❏ 61832 | There Goes (A Pretty Girl)/Fan Me Baby | 1957 | $100 |
—Full-length version of A-side; matrix number is "100,974"
| ❏ 61832 | There Goes (A Pretty Girl)/Fan Me Baby | 1957 | $30 |
—Edited version of A-side; matrix number is "102,966"
❏ 62373	True Love Gone/The Day	1963	$30
❏ 65610	True Love Gone/Today Is Your Birthday	1963	$15
❏ 61756	True Love Gone/Wait a Minute Baby	1956	$70
MERCER
| ❏ 992 | True Love Gone/Wait a Minute Baby | 1956 | $2000 |

ENCHANTERS, THE (4)
JUBILEE
| ❏ 5080 | I've Lost/Housewife Blues | 1952 | $200 |
| ❏ 5072 | Today Is Your Birthday/How Could You | 1952 | $250 |

ENCHANTERS, THE (U)
TOM TOM
| ❏ 301 | Surf Blast/Tom Tiki | 1963 | $60 |

ENCHANTMENTS, THE
FARO
| ❏ 620 | I'm in Love with Your Daughter/(B-side unknown) | 1964 | $125 |
GONE
| ❏ 5130 | (I Love You) Sherry/Come On Home | 1962 | $40 |
RITZ
| ❏ 17003 | I Love You Baby/Pains in My Heart | 1963 | $125 |

ENCORES, THE
BOW
| ❏ 302 | Barbara/Thank You | 1958 | $125 |
CHECKER
| ❏ 760 | When I Look at You/Young Girls, Young Girls | 1952 | $4000 |
— VG 2000; VG+ 3000
HOLLYWOOD
| ❏ 1034 | Time Is Moving On/Ha-Chi-Bi-Ri-Bi-Ri | 1955 | $100 |

LOOK
| ❏ 105 | Time Is Moving On/Ha-Chi-Bi-Ri-Bi-Ri | 1955 | $400 |
MGM
| ❏ 11947 | Chloe/Wa Va Ga Dot | 1955 | $15 |

ENCOUNTERS, THE
SWAN
| ❏ 4206 | Don't Stop Now/Place in Your Heart | 1964 | $200 |

END, THE
LONDON
| ❏ 1016 | Shades of Orange/Loving, Sacred Loving | 1968 | $30 |
PHILIPS
| ❏ 40323 | Hey Little Girl/I Can't Get Any Joy | 1965 | $12 |

ENDEAVORS, THE (1)
J&S
| ❏ 254 | Suffering with My Heart/I Got the Feeling | 1960 | $1200 |

ENDEAVORS, THE (2)
STOP
| ❏ 372 | Shattered Dreams/I Know You Don't Want Me | 1971 | $10 |

ENDORSERS, THE
MOON
| ❏ 109 | Crying/Hold My Hand | 1959 | $2000 |

ENEMYS, THE
MGM
❏ 13485	Glitter and Gold/Too Much Monkey Business	1966	$20
❏ 13525	Hey Joe/My Dues Have Been Paid	1966	$20
❏ 13573	Mo-Jo Woman/My Dues Have Been Paid	1966	$20
VALIANT
| ❏ 714 | Say Goodbye to Donna/Sinner Man | 1965 | $30 |
—As "Corey Wells and the Enemys"

ENGEL, SCOTT
CHALLENGE
| ❏ 9206 | Devil Surfer/Your Guess | 1963 | $30 |
LIBERTY
| ❏ 55428 | Anything Will Do/Forever More | 1962 | $30 |
| ❏ 55312 | Mr. Jones/Anything Will Do | 1961 | $30 |
MARTAY
| ❏ 2004 | Devil Surfer/Your Guess | 1963 | $50 |
ORBIT
❏ 512	Blue Bell/Paper Doll	1958	$30
❏ 512 [PS]	Blue Bell/Paper Doll	1958	$60
❏ 511	Charley Bop/All I Do Is Dream	1958	$40
❏ 511 [PS]	Charley Bop/All I Do Is Dream	1958	$70
❏ 545	Comin' Home/I Don't Wanna Know	1959	$30
❏ 537	The Golden Rule/Sunday	1959	$30
❏ 537 [PS]	The Golden Rule/Sunday	1959	$60
❏ 506	The Livin' End/Good for Nothin'	1958	$30
❏ 506 [PS]	The Livin' End/Good for Nothin'	1958	$60
RKO UNIQUE
| ❏ 386 | Steady As a Rock/When Is a Boy a Man | 1957 | $30 |

ENGLAND, BENNY
SNAP
| ❏ 400 | Eloping/Some How | 1958 | $300 |

ENGLAND DAN AND JOHN FORD COLEY
A&M
❏ 1369	Carolina/Free the People	1972	$5
❏ 1354	Casey/Simone	1972	$5
❏ 1465	I Hear the Music/Miss You Song	1973	$5
❏ 1871	I Hear the Music/Simone	1976	$4
BIG TREE
❏ 16102	Gone Too Far/Where Do I Go from Here	1977	$4
❏ 16135	Hollywood Heckle and Jive/Rolling Fever	1979	$4
❏ 16069	I'd Really Love to See You Tonight/It's Not the Same	1976	$4
❏ 16125	If the World Ran Out of Love Tonight/Lovin' Somebody on a Rainy Night	1978	$4
❏ 17002	In It for Love/Who's Lonely Now	1980	$4
❏ 16088	It's Sad to Belong/The Time Has Come	1977	$4
❏ 16131	Love Is the Answer/Running After You	1979	$4
❏ 16110	We'll Never Have to Say Goodbye Again/Calling for You Again	1978	$4
❏ 16130	Westward Wind/Some Things Don't Come Easy	1979	$4

| ❏ 17000 | What Can I Do with My Broken Heart/Caught Up in the Middle | 1979 | $4 |
MCA
| ❏ 51027 | Part of Me, Part of You/Just Tell Me You Love Me | 1980 | $4 |

ENGLER, JERRY, AND THE FOUR EKKOS
BRUNSWICK
| ❏ 55037 | Sputnik (Satellite Girl)/Unfaithful One | 1957 | $100 |
—BUDDY HOLLY appears on this record

ENGLISH, BARBARA
ALITHIA
❏ 6046	Baby I'm-a Want You/Don't Make Me Over	1973	$6
❏ 6064	Breakin' Up a Happy Home/Guess Who	1974	$6
❏ 6059	Comin' or Goin'/Love's Arrangement	1973	$6
❏ 6040	I'm Living a Lie/All This	1972	$6
❏ 6042	I'm Sorry/Lil' Baby	1972	$6
❏ 6041	So Many Ways to Die/(B-side unknown)	1972	$6
AURORA
| ❏ 155 | Standin' on Tip-Toe/(You Got Me) Sittin' in the Corner | 1965 | $100 |
MALA
| ❏ 488 | Easy Come, Easy Go/I Don't Deserve a Boy Like You | 1964 | $30 |
REPRISE
| ❏ 0290 | I've Gotta Date/Shoo Fly | 1964 | $30 |
| ❏ 0349 | Small Town Girl/Tell It Like It Is | 1965 | $30 |
ROULETTE
| ❏ 4450 | Fever/Bad News | 1962 | $40 |
| ❏ 4428 | We Need Them/La-Ta-Tee-Ta-Ta | 1962 | $40 |
WARNER BROS.
| ❏ 5685 | All Because I Love Somebody/All the Good Times Are Gone | 1965 | $30 |

ENGLISH BEAT, THE
I.R.S.
❏ 9913	I Confess/March of the Swivel Heads	1983	$4
❏ 9909	Save It for Later/Jeanette	1982	$4
❏ 9909 [PS]	Save It for Later/Jeanette	1982	$4
SIRE
| ❏ 49265 | Tears of a Clown/Twist and Crawl | 1980 | $8 |

ENGLISH MUFFINS, THE (2)
GAMA
| ❏ 702 | Leave or Stay/It's My Pride | 1967 | $50 |

ENGLISH, SCOTT
DOT
| ❏ 16099 | White Cliffs of Dover/4000 Miles Away | 1960 | $40 |
JANUS
| ❏ 171 | Brandy/Lead Me Back | 1971 | $15 |
—A-side later recorded by Barry Manilow as "Mandy"
| ❏ 192 | Woman in My Life/Ballad of the Unloved | 1972 | $5 |
SPOKANE
| ❏ 4007 | Here Comes the Pain/All I Want Is You | 1964 | $50 |
| ❏ 4003 | High on a Hill/When | 1964 | $30 |
SULTAN
| ❏ 1003 | High on a Hill/When | 1963 | $60 |

ENJOYABLES, THE
CAPITOL
| ❏ 5321 | Push a Little Harder/We'll Make Our Way | 1964 | $40 |
SHRINE
| ❏ 118 | Shame/I'll Take You Back | 1966 | $600 |

ENNIS, ETHEL
JUBILEE
| ❏ 5236 | I've Got You Under My Skin/You Better Go Now | 1956 | $15 |
RCA VICTOR
❏ 47-8491	For a Short While/San Juan	1964	$8
❏ 47-8448	Matchmaker, Matchmaker/Now I Have Everything	1964	$8
❏ 47-8379	The Boy from Ipanema/When Will the Hurt Be Over	1964	$8

ENO, BRIAN
Also see ROXY MUSIC.
ISLAND
| ❏ 036 | The Lion Sleeps Tonight/I'll Come Running (To Tie Your Shoes) | 1975 | $30 |
| ❏ 036 [DJ] | The Lion Sleeps Tonight (mono/stereo) | 1975 | $20 |

Number	Title	Yr	NM
ENTWISTLE, JOHN			
Also see THE WHO.			
ATCO			
❑ 7344	Talk Dirty/Try Me	1982	$4
❑ 7337	Too Late the Hero/Dancin' Master	1981	$4
DECCA			
❑ 32896	I Believe in Everything/My Size	1971	$6
❑ 33052	I Wonder/Who Cares	1973	$6
TRACK			
❑ 40066	Made in Japan/Roller Skate Kate	1973	$5
ENYA			
GEFFEN			
❑ 27633	Orinoco Flow (Sail Away)/Out of the Blue	1988	$3
❑ 27633 [PS]	Orinoco Flow (Sail Away)/Out of the Blue	1988	$3
EPIC SPLENDOR, THE			
HOT BISCUIT			
❑ 1450	A Little Rain Must Fall/Cowboys and Indians	1967	$8
❑ 1452	It Could Be Wonderful/She's High on Life	1968	$8
❑ 1452 [PS]	It Could Be Wonderful/She's High on Life	1968	$30
EPICS, THE			
HANNA-BARBERA			
❑ 480	Blue Turns to Grey/Goes to Show	1966	$20
EPISODE SIX			
CHAPTER ONE			
❑ 2902	Lucky Sunday/Mr. Universe	1968	$15
COMPASS			
❑ 7007	Morning Dew/Sunshine Girl	1967	$20
ELEKTRA			
❑ 45617	Baby, Baby, Baby/Love-Hate-Revenge	1967	$20
WARNER BROS.			
❑ 5851	Here, There and Everywhere/Mighty Morris Ten	1966	$20
EPISODES, THE			
FOUR SEASONS			
❑ 1014	The Christmas Tree/Where Is My Love	1965	$200
EPPS, PRESTON			
ADMIRAL			
❑ 901	Bongo Express/Flamenco Bongo	1963	$20
DONNA			
❑ 1367	Mister Bongo/B'Wana Bongo	1962	$20
JO JO			
❑ 106	Afro Mania/Love Is the Only Good Thing	1969	$6
MAJESTY			
❑ 1300	Bongo Boogie/Flamenco Bongo	1962	$20
ORIGINAL SOUND			
❑ 9	Bongo, Bongo, Bongo/Hully Gully Bongo	1960	$30
❑ 4 [M]	Bongo Rock/Bongo Party	1959	$30
❑ 4 [S]	Bongo Rock/Bongo Party	1959	$60
❑ 17	Bongo Rocket/Jungle Drums	1961	$20
❑ 14	Bongo Shuffle/Bongo in the Congo	1960	$20
POLO			
❑ 218	Bongo Rock 1965/Bongo Waltz	1965	$15
TOP RANK			
❑ 2067	Blue Bongo/Bongola	1960	$20
❑ 2091	Bongo Hop/Caravan	1960	$20
7-Inch Extended Plays			
ORIGINAL SOUND			
❑ EP1001 [PS]	Bongo Rock	1959	$50
❑ EP1001	Bongo Rock/Doin' the Cha Cha Cha//Bongos in Pastel/Bongo Party	1959	$50
EPSILONS, THE			
SHRINE			
❑ 106	Mad at the World/I'm So Devoted	1966	$250
STAX			
❑ 021	The Echo/Really Rockin'	1969	$70
EQUADORS, THE			
ARGO			
❑ 5353	Say You'll Be Mine/Let Me Sleep, Woman	1959	$70
EQUALLOS, THE			
M&M			
❑ 1296	Beneath the Sun/In Between Tears	1962	$1500

Number	Title	Yr	NM
EQUALS, THE			
BANG			
❑ 582	Ain't Got Nothing to Give You/Black Skin, Blue Eyed Boys	1971	$10
PRESIDENT			
❑ 103	Fire/I Won't Be There	1967	$15
❑ 108	Giddy Up a Ding-Dong/I Get So Excited	1968	$15
❑ 110	Honey Gun/Michael and the Slipper Tree	1968	$15
❑ 111	I Can't Let You Go/Viva Bobby Joe	1969	$15
❑ 109	Lovely Rita/Softly, Softly	1968	$15
❑ 105	My Life Ain't Easy/You Got Too Many Boyfriends	1967	$15
RCA VICTOR			
❑ 47-9186	Baby Come Back/Hold Me Closer	1967	$20
❑ 47-9583	Baby Come Back/Hold Me Closer	1968	$12
SHOUT			
❑ 247	Ain't Got Nothing to Give You/Black Skin, Blue Eyed Boys	1970	$15
EQUIPE 84			
IMPERIAL			
❑ 66266	The Twenty-Ninth of September/Auschwitz	1967	$30
ERASURE			
SIRE			
❑ 27738	A Little Respect/Like Zsa Zsa Gabor	1988	$3
❑ 27738 [PS]	A Little Respect/Like Zsa Zsa Gabor	1988	$3
❑ 27738DJ [DJ]	A Little Respect (LP Version)/(Remix Edit)	1988	$6
❑ 27844DJ [DJ]	Chains of Love (7" Remix) (Shep Pettibone Radio Remix Edit)	1988	$6
❑ 27844	Chains of Love/Don't Suppose	1988	$3
❑ 27844 [PS]	Chains of Love/Don't Suppose	1988	$3
❑ 28614	Oh L'Amour/Gimme! Gimme! Gimme!	1986	$20
❑ 28614 [DJ]	Oh L'Amour (same on both sides)	1986	$5
❑ PRO-S-3409 [DJ]	She Won't Be Home (Lonely Christmas)/God Rest Ye Merry Gentlemen	1988	$20
❑ PRO-S-3409 [PS]	She Won't Be Home (Lonely Christmas)/God Rest Ye Merry Gentlemen	1988	$20
— Not a picture sleeve, but an insert contained in the generic sleeve			
❑ 28362	Sometimes/It Doesn't Have to Be	1987	$8
❑ 28362 [PS]	Sometimes/It Doesn't Have to Be	1987	$8
❑ 28362DJ [DJ]	Sometimes (Original Single Edit)/(Shiver Mix)	1987	$6
❑ 22879	Stop!/Ship of Fools	1989	$3
❑ 28728	Who Needs Love Like That/Push Me Shove Me	1986	$20
❑ 28728 [DJ]	Who Needs Love Like That (same on both sides)	1986	$5
ERLENE AND HER GIRLFRIENDS			
OLD TOWN			
❑ 1150	A Guy Is a Guy/My Dada Say	1963	$30
❑ 1152	Because of You/Casanova	1963	$30
ERNIE AND THE EMPERORS			
REPRISE			
❑ 0414	Got a Lot I Want to Say/Meet Me at the Corner	1965	$40
ERVIN, FRANKIE			
HOLLYWOOD			
❑ 1045	Christmas Eve Baby/Christmas Everyday	1955	$50
— With Johnny Moore's Blazers			
PUNCHLINE			
❑ 9923	It's Christmas Time/Decorate My Christmas Tree	1985	$3
7-Inch Extended Plays			
HOLLYWOOD			
❑ 1044	Christmas Everyday/Christmas Letter//Christmas Eve Baby/Christmas Dreams	1955	$125
— With Johnny Moore's Blazers			
ERVIN, SENATOR SAM			
COLUMBIA			
❑ 4-45956	Bridge Over Troubled Water/Zeke and the Snake	1973	$6
ERVIN SISTERS, THE			
TRI PHI			
❑ 1014	Changing Baby/Do It Right	1962	$70
❑ 1022	Every Day's a Holiday/Why I Love Him	1963	$100
ESCAPE CLUB, THE			
ATLANTIC			
❑ 7-88983	Shake for the Sheik/Working for the Fatman	1988	$3

Number	Title	Yr	NM
❑ 7-88983 [PS]	Shake for the Sheik/Working for the Fatman	1988	$3
❑ 7-88802	Twentieth Century Fox/When a Man Loves a Woman	1989	$10
— B-side by Percy Sledge			
❑ 7-88951	Walking Through Walls/Standing on a Bridge	1989	$3
❑ 7-88951 [PS]	Walking Through Walls/Standing on a Bridge	1989	$3
❑ 7-89048	Wild, Wild West/We Can Run	1988	$3
❑ 7-89048 [PS]	Wild, Wild West/We Can Run	1988	$6
ESCORTS, THE (1)			
ALITHIA			
❑ 6048	All We Need (Is Another Chance) (Short)/All We Need (Is Another Chance) (Long)	1973	$6
❑ 6062	Disrespect Can Wreck/All We Need	1974	$5
❑ 6055	I'll Be Sweeter Tomorrow/I'm So Glad I Found You	1973	$5
❑ 6066	Let's Make Love (At Home Sometime)/Within Without	1974	$5
❑ 6052	Look Over Your Shoulder/By the Time I Get to Phoenix	1973	$5
ESCORTS, THE (2)			
CORAL			
❑ 62317	As I Love You/Gaudeamus	1962	$50
❑ 62372	Back Home Again/Something Has Changed Him	1963	$30
— As "Goldie and the Escorts			
❑ 62385	Give Me Tomorrow/My Heart Cries for You	1963	$30
❑ 62302	Gloria/Seven Wonders of the World	1961	$50
❑ 62349	One Hand. One Heart/I Can't Be Free	1963	$30
❑ 62336	Somewhere/Submarine Race Watching	1962	$30
ESCORTS, THE (3)			
FONTANA			
❑ 1512	Come On Home Baby/She Gets No Loving	1965	$20
❑ 1912	Dizzy Miss Lizzy/All I Want Is You	1964	$20
ESCORTS, THE (U)			
BOOMERANG			
❑ 621	Little Big Horn/Wiped Out	1962	$50
JUDD			
❑ 1014	My First Year/Clap Happy	1959	$20
RCA VICTOR			
❑ 47-6834	Bad Boy/Tore Up Over You	1957	$20
❑ 47-6963	So Hard to Laugh, So Easy to Cry/Lonely Man	1957	$20
❑ 47-8327	The Hurt/No City Folks Allowed	1964	$15
SCARLET			
❑ 4005	I Will Be Home Again/Leaky Heart and His Red Go-Kart	1960	$70
SCEPTER			
❑ 1201	Why Why Why/Ugly Duckling	1958	$50
— With Don Crawford			
SOMA			
❑ 1144	Main Drag/Judy or Jo Ann	1961	$30
ESMERELDY			
MGM			
❑ K10739	Whoopin' in the Holler/Good Man in Memphis	1950	$40
ESQUERITA			
CAPITOL			
❑ F4145	Laid Off/Just Another Lie	1959	$40
❑ F4007	Please Come On Home/Oh Baby	1958	$40
ESQUIRE BOYS, THE			
20TH FOX			
❑ 110	Taboo/Have You Got Good Religion	1958	$30
DOT			
❑ 15433	Dance with a Rock/At the Balalaika	1955	$30
❑ 15380	Guitar Mambo/Dark Eyes	1955	$30
❑ 15	Summertime/Sorrento Cha Cha	1961	$20
MEDIA			
❑ 1004	Play Me Boogie/Bye Bye Blues	1955	$30
RAINBOW			
❑ 188	Caravan/We Drifted Apart	1952	$40
— Red vinyl			
❑ 188	Caravan/We Drifted Apart	1952	$30
— Black vinyl			
❑ 178	Forgetting You/I Don't Want Everything	1952	$30
— Black vinyl			
❑ 178	Forgetting You/I Don't Want Everything	1952	$40
— Red vinyl			

Number	Title	Yr	NM

ESQUIRES, THE (1)

BUNKY

Number	Title	Yr	NM
❑ 7752	And Get Away/Everybody's Laughin'	1967	$10
❑ 7750	Get On Up/Listen to Me	1967	$10
❑ 7756	How Could It Be/I Know I Can	1968	$10
❑ 7755	Why Can't I Stop/The Feeling's Gone	1968	$10

CIGAR MAN

❑ 79880	The Show Ain't Over/What Good Is Music?	1980	$6

JU-PAR

❑ 104	Get On Up '76/Feeling's Gone (Also Known As Disco Dancing)	1976	$6

LAMARR

❑ 1001	Girls in the City/Ain't Gonna Give It Up	1971	$8

WAND

❑ 1195	I Don't Know/Part Angel	1969	$8
❑ 11201	Whip It On Me/It Was Yesterday	1969	$8

ESQUIRES, THE (2)

ARGO

❑ 5435	Boat of Love/With a Feeling	1963	$30

ESQUIRES, THE (3)

EPIC

❑ 5-9024	If You Only Knew What a Three-Cent Stamp Can Do/Now, Now, Now	1954	$1500

— This does exist on 45

HI-PO

❑ 1003	Only the Angels Know/One Word for This	1955	$2000

ESQUIRES, THE (U)

COLUMBIA

❑ 4-43815	It's a Dirty Shame/Love Hides a Multitude of Sins	1966	$30

DOT

❑ 16954	Misfortune/She's My Woman	1966	$20

DURCO

❑ 1001	Flashin' Red/What a Burn	1964	$50

TOWER

❑ 174	Love's Made a Fool of You/Summertime	1965	$20

ESQUIVEL

RCA VICTOR

❑ 47-5969	Beasme Mucho/Vereda Tropical	1954	$30

— As "Juan Garcia Esquivel"

❑ 47-7462	I Feel Merely Marvelous/Whatchamacallit	1959	$20
❑ 47-7360	It Had to Be You/Begin the Beguine	1958	$20
❑ 47-6514	Port Au Prince/To Love Again	1956	$20
❑ 47-7316	That Old Black Magic/Cielito Lindo	1958	$20

ESSEX, DAVID

COLUMBIA

❑ 10005	America/Dance Little Girl	1974	$5
❑ 10005 [PS]	America/Dance Little Girl	1974	$8
❑ 10039	Gonna Make You a Star/Window	1974	$5
❑ 10256	Good Ol' Rock 'N' Roll/Hold Me Close	1975	$5
❑ 46041	Lamplight/We're All Insane	1974	$5
❑ 46041 [PS]	Lamplight/We're All Insane	1974	$12

RSO

❑ 1006	Oh What a Circus (From Evita)/Ships That Pass in the Night	1979	$4

UNI

❑ 55020	She's Leaving Home/He's a Better Man Than Me	1967	$10

ESSEX, THE

BANG

❑ 537	The Eagle/Moonlight, Music, and You	1966	$8

ROULETTE

❑ 4515	A Walkin' Miracle/What I Don't Know Won't Hurt Me	1963	$20
❑ 4494	Easier Said Than Done/Are You Going My Way	1963	$20
❑ 4530	She's Got Everything/Out of Sight, Out of Mind	1964	$10
❑ 4542	What Did I Do/Curfew Lover	1964	$10

ESTEFAN, GLORIA

EPIC

❑ 34-07921	1-2-3/(Instrumental)	1988	$3
❑ 34-07921 [PS]	1-2-3/(Instrumental)	1988	$3

— Gloria Estefan and Miami Sound Machine

❑ 34-07759	Anything for You/(Spanish Version)	1988	$3

❑ 34-07759 [PS]	Anything for You/(Spanish Version)	1988	$3

— Gloria Estefan and Miami Sound Machine

❑ 34-07371	Betcha Say That/Love Toy	1987	$3
❑ 34-07371 [PS]	Betcha Say That/Love Toy	1987	$3

— Gloria Estefan and Miami Sound Machine

❑ 34-07641	Can't Stay Away from You/Let It Loose	1987	$3
❑ 34-07641 [PS]	Can't Stay Away from You/Let It Loose	1987	$3

— Gloria Estefan and Miami Sound Machine

❑ 34-68959	Don't Wanna Lose You/Si Voy A Prederte	1989	$4
❑ 34-69064	Get On Your Feet/Words Get In The Way	1989	$4
❑ 34-73084	Here We Are!/1-2-3 (Live)	1989	$3

ESTHER AND MEL

SAVOY

❑ 1146	My Christmas Blues/Love for Christmas	1954	$50

ETERNALS, THE (1)

HOLLYWOOD

❑ 70	Babalu's Wedding Day/My Girl	1959	$60

— Red label

❑ 70	Babalu's Wedding Day/My Girl	1959	$30

— Blue label

WARWICK

❑ 611	Blind Date/Today	1961	$30

ETERNALS, THE (2)

QUALITY

❑ 1902	Falling Tears/Sticks and Stones	1968	$30

ETERNITY'S CHILDREN

LIBERTY

❑ 56162	Alone Again/From You Unto Us	1970	$8

TOWER

❑ 498	Blue Horizon/Lifetime Day	1969	$10
❑ 416	Mrs. Bluebird/Little Boy	1968	$10
❑ 416 [PS]	Mrs. Bluebird/Little Boy	1968	$30
❑ 476	Sidewalks of the Ghetto/Look Away	1969	$10
❑ 449	Till I Hear from You/I Wanna Be with You	1968	$10

ETHERIDGE, MELISSA

ISLAND

❑ 99287	Bring Me Some Water/Occasionally	1988	$4
❑ 99287 [PS]	Bring Me Some Water/Occasionally	1988	$4
❑ 99251	Similar Features/Bring Me Some Water	1989	$3
❑ 99251 [PS]	Similar Features/Bring Me Some Water	1989	$3

ETHICS, THE (1)

GOLDEN FLEECE

❑ 3252	Good Luck/Who in the World	1974	$20

VENT

❑ 1006	Farewell/I Want My Baby Back	1969	$40
❑ 1004	Sad, Sad Story/Searching	1968	$30
❑ 1008	Standing in the Darkness/That's the Way Love Goes	1970	$60
❑ 1007	Tell Me/There'll Still Be a Sweet Tomorrow	1969	$40
❑ 0 (no cat #)	Think About Tomorrow/Look at Me Now	1968	$70

— First pressings have no catalog number

❑ 1001	Think About Tomorrow/Look at Me Now	1968	$30

ETHICS, THE (U)

DYNAMIC SOUND

❑ 2001	Confusion/Out of My Mind	1966	$50

ETTA AND HARVEY

CHESS

❑ 1760	If I Can't Have You/My Heart Cries	1960	$30
❑ 1771	Spoonful/It's a Crying Shame	1960	$30

ETZEL, ROY

HICKORY

❑ 1197	I Can't Stop Loving You/I Hate to Love You	1963	$8

MGM

❑ 13381	Melancholy/The Silence	1965	$8
❑ 13801	Mexican Holiday/Vaya Con Dios	1967	$8

PRESIDENT

❑ 820	Tell Laura I Love Her/Reach for the Stars	1961	$10

EUBANKS, JACK

MONUMENT

❑ 862	Action/Pickin' White Gold	1964	$8
❑ 462	After the Rain/Since I Met You Baby	1962	$10
❑ 809	Casino/Te Juana	1963	$8
❑ 434	Chiricahua/What'd I Say	1961	$10
❑ 451	Searching/Take a Message to Mary	1961	$10

EUPHORIA (1)

MAINSTREAM

❑ 655	Hungry Women/No Me Tomorrow	1967	$30

EURYTHMICS

ARISTA

❑ 9917	Angel/Precious	1989	$4
❑ 9917 [PS]	Angel/Precious	1989	$4
❑ 9880	Don't Ask Me Why/Rich Girl	1989	$3
❑ 9880 [PS]	Don't Ask Me Why/Rich Girl	1989	$3

RCA

❑ JB-13725 [DJ]	Here Comes the Rain Again (Long Version 5:05)/(Short Version 3:50)	1984	$6
❑ PB-13725	Here Comes the Rain Again/Paint a Rumour	1984	$3

— All stock copies have a 5:05 version of A-side

❑ PB-13725 [PS]	Here Comes the Rain Again/Paint a Rumour	1984	$3
❑ GB-14063	Here Comes the Rain Again/Right By Your Side	1985	$3

— Gold Standard Series reissue

❑ 5361-7-R	I Need a Man/Heaven	1987	$3
❑ 5361-7-R [PS]	I Need a Man/Heaven	1987	$3
❑ PB-14284	It's Alright (Baby's Coming Back)/Conditioned Soul	1986	$3
❑ PB-14284 [PS]	It's Alright (Baby's Coming Back)/Conditioned Soul	1986	$3
❑ PB-13618	Love Is a Stranger/Monkey, Monkey	1983	$3
❑ PB-13618 [PS]	Love Is a Stranger/Monkey, Monkey	1983	$20

— Sleeve claims the B-side is "I've Got an Angel," though this song was not released as the B-side of the single in the U.S.; this may explain the scarcity of this sleeve

❑ PB-14414	Missionary Man/Take Your Pain Away	1986	$3
❑ PB-14414 [PS]	Missionary Man/Take Your Pain Away	1986	$3
❑ 5177-1-RG	Missionary Man/Thorn in My Side	1987	$3

— Gold Standard Series reissue

❑ PB-13956	Sexcrime (Nineteen Eighty-Four)/I Did It Just the Same	1984	$3
❑ PB-13956 [PS]	Sexcrime (Nineteen Eighty-Four)/I Did It Just the Same	1984	$3
❑ PB-13533	Sweet Dreams (Are Made of This)/I Could Give You (A Mirror)	1983	$3
❑ PB-13533 [PS]	Sweet Dreams (Are Made of This)/I Could Give You (A Mirror)	1983	$5
❑ GB-13790	Sweet Dreams (Are Made of This)/Love Is a Stranger	1984	$3

— Gold Standard Series reissue

❑ PB-14160	There Must Be An Angel (Playing with My Heart)/Grown Up Girls	1985	$3
❑ PB-14160 [PS]	There Must Be An Angel (Playing with My Heart)/Grown Up Girls	1985	$3
❑ 5058-7-R	Thorn in My Side/In This Town	1986	$3
❑ 5058-7-R [PS]	Thorn in My Side/In This Town	1986	$3
❑ PB-13800	Who's That Girl?/Aqua	1984	$3
❑ PB-13800 [PS]	Who's That Girl?/Aqua	1984	$3
❑ PB-14078	Would I Lie to You?/Here Comes That Sinking Feeling	1985	$3
❑ PB-14078 [PS]	Would I Lie to You?/Here Comes That Sinking Feeling	1985	$4
❑ GB-14338	Would I Lie to You/There Must Be An Angel (Playing with My Heart)	1986	$3

— Gold Standard Series reissue

EURYTHMICS AND ARETHA FRANKLIN

RCA

❑ PB-14214	Sisters Are Doin' It for Themselves/I Love You Like a Ball and Chain	1985	$3

— B-side by Eurythmics

❑ PB-14214 [PS]	Sisters Are Doin' It for Themselves/I Love You Like a Ball and Chain	1985	$3

EVANS, BARBARA

RCA VICTOR

❑ 47-7634	Beatnik Daddy/A Game of Poker	1959	$30
❑ 47-7576	Oo La La La/The Little Girl Cried	1959	$30
❑ 47-7519	Souvenirs/Play for Me, Mother	1959	$30

EVANS, DALE

RCA VICTOR

❑ 48-0360	A Two Seated Saddle/Hawaii No	1950	$50

— Originals on green vinyl

Number	Title	Yr	NM
☐ 48-0395	Cowgirl Polka/San Angelo	1950	$50
— Originals on green vinyl			
☐ 48-0073	Don't Ever Fall in Love with a Cowboy/Nothin' in My Letter Box	1949	$60
— Originals on green vinyl			
☐ 47-4242	I'm Gonna Lock You Out/Put All Your Kisses in an Envelope	1951	$30
☐ 48-0148	It's Saturday Night/Saddle on My Heart	1950	$50
— Originals on green vinyl			
☐ 48-0310	Lock, Stock and Barrel/A Heart of Stone	1950	$50
— Originals on green vinyl			
☐ 48-0465	Please Send Me Someone to Love/Last Night My Heart Crossed the Ocean	1951	$40
☐ 47-4308	Thirty-Two Feet and Eight Little Tails/Fuzzy Wuzzy	1951	$30

EVANS, MAUREEN
COLUMBIA
Number	Title	Yr	NM
☐ 43189	Get Away/I've Often Wondered	1964	$10

DOT
| ☐ 16678 | Time and Time Again/Tomorrow Is Another Day | 1964 | $10 |

LITTLE DARLIN'
| ☐ 019 | Touch My Heart/(B-side unknown) | 1967 | $10 |

LONDON INT'L.
| ☐ 10407 | Like I Do/Starlight, Starbright | 1963 | $15 |
| ☐ 10409 | Melancholy Me/Pick the Petals | 1963 | $15 |

EVANS, PAUL
ATCO
| ☐ 6138 | At My Party/Beat Generation | 1959 | $20 |
| ☐ 6170 | Long Gone/Mickey, My Love | 1960 | $20 |

BIG TREE
| ☐ 16050 | Happy Birthday, America/You Made Me Over | 1975 | $5 |

CARLTON
☐ 543	After the Hurricane/Not Me	1961	$20
☐ ST130-4 [S]	Mister Hangman/British Grenadiers	1961	$30
—Jukebox issue; small hole, plays at 33 1/3 rpm			
☐ 558	Over the Mountain, Across the Sea/Sisal Twine	1961	$20
☐ 539	Show Folk/I Love to Make Love to You	1961	$20

CINNAMON
| ☐ 604 | One Night Led to Two/Hangin' Out and Hangin' In | 1980 | $5 |

COLUMBIA
| ☐ 44472 | One Red Rose/Bound to Silence | 1968 | $6 |

DECCA
| ☐ 30680 | I Think About You All the Time/Oh No | 1958 | $30 |

DOT
| ☐ 17463 | That's What Loving You Is All About/Do You Remember | 1973 | $5 |

EPIC
☐ 9726	Bewitched/I Think I'm Gonna Kill Myself	1964	$12
— By Paul & Mimi Evans			
☐ 9842	I Wonder What to Do/Always Thinking of the Roses	1965	$10
☐ 9751	Little Miss Tease/Gina Marina Petunia	1964	$12

GUARANTEED
☐ 208	Happy-Go-Lucky Me/Fish in the Ocean	1960	$20
☐ 213	Hushabye Little Guitar/Blind Boy	1960	$20
☐ 205	Midnite Special/Since I Met You Baby	1960	$20
☐ 200	Seven Little Girls Sitting in the Back Seat/Worshipping an Idol	1959	$30
☐ 210	The Brigade of Broken Hearts/Twins	1960	$20

KAPP
☐ 473	A Picture of You/Feelin' No Pain	1962	$15
☐ 486	D-Darling/Gonna Build a Mountain	1962	$15
☐ 520	(Mama and Papa) We've Got Something On You/What Are the Lips of Janet	1963	$15
☐ 527	Ten Thousand Years/Evan Tan	1963	$15
☐ 499	The Bell That Couldn't Jingle/Gilding the Lily	1962	$15

LAURIE
| ☐ 3581 | The Man in a Row Boat/Here We Go Around Again | 1971 | $6 |
| ☐ 3571 | Think Summer/For Old Times Sake | 1971 | $6 |

MERCURY
| ☐ 73650 | All My Children/Move In with Me | 1975 | $5 |
| ☐ 73499 | But I Was Born in New York City!/Just As Long As You Are There | 1974 | $5 |

RANWOOD
| ☐ 928 | Try It, You'll Like It/We Liked It | 1972 | $6 |

RCA VICTOR
| ☐ 47-6992 | Caught/Poor Broken Heart | 1957 | $30 |

Number	Title	Yr	NM
☐ 47-6924	Looking for a Sweetie/Any Little Thing	1957	$30
☐ 47-6806	What Do You Know/Dorothy	1957	$30
SPRING			
☐ 193	Disneyland Daddy/Build An Ark	1979	$4
☐ 187	Down at the Bluebird/I'm Givin' Up My Baby	1978	$4
☐ 183	Hello, This Is Joanie (The Telephone Answering Machine Song)/Lullabye Tissue Paper Company	1978	$4

EVANS, REVEREND CLAY
JEWEL
| ☐ 283 | Go Tell It On The Mountain/Angels Sing | 1981 | $4 |

EVELS, THE
TRA-X
| ☐ 14 | The Magic of Love/Wonderful Guy | 1960 | $70 |

EVENTUALS, THE
OKEH
| ☐ 4-7142 | Charlie Chan/Just the Things That You Do | 1961 | $20 |
| ☐ 4-7142 [PS] | Charlie Chan/Just the Things That You Do | 1961 | $40 |

EVER-READY SINGERS, THE
CAPITOL
☐ F2984	I Don't Care What the World May Do/Oh Mary Don't You Weep	1954	$50
☐ F2763	I'm a Pilgrim and a Stranger/One Day While I Was Walking	1954	$40
☐ F2867	This Heart of Mine/Two Wings	1954	$40

EVERETT, BETTY, AND JERRY BUTLER
VEE JAY
☐ 691	Fever/The Way You Do the Things You Do	1965	$15
☐ 613	Let It Be Me/Ain't That Loving You Baby	1964	$15
☐ 676	Since I Don't Have You/Just Be True	1965	$15
☐ 633	Smile/Love Is Strange	1964	$15

EVERETT, BETTY
ABC
☐ 10861	Bye, Bye Baby/Your Love Is Important to Me	1966	$8
☐ 10978	I Can't Say/My Baby Loving My Best Friend	1967	$8
☐ 10829	In Your Arms/Nothing I Wouldn't Do	1966	$8
☐ 10919	Love Comes Tumbling Down/People Around Me	1967	$8

CJ
☐ 674	Days Gone By/Her New Love	1964	$20
☐ 611	Why Did You Have to Go/Please Come Back	1961	$30
— As "Bettie Everett & Daylighters"			

COBRA
☐ 5024	Ain't Gonna Cry/Killer Diller	1958	$30
☐ 5019	My Love/My Life Depends on You	1957	$40
☐ 5031	Weep No More/Tell Me Darling	1959	$30

FANTASY
☐ 658	Ain't Nothing Gonna Change Me/What Is It?	1971	$5
☐ 687	Black Girl/Innocent Bystanders	1972	$5
☐ 687	Black Girl/What Is It?	1972	$5
☐ 696	Danger/Just a Matter of Time Till You're Gone	1973	$5
☐ 738	Happy Endings/Keep It Up	1974	$5
☐ 652	I Got to Tell Somebody/Why Are You Leaving Me	1970	$5
☐ 667	I'm a Woman/Prove It	1971	$5
☐ 714	Sweet Dan/Who Will Your Next Fool Be	1973	$5
☐ 725	Try It, You'll Like It/Wondering	1974	$5

ONE-DERFUL
| ☐ 4823 | I'll Be There/Please Love Me | 1964 | $15 |
| ☐ 4806 | I've Got a Claim on You/Your Love Is Important to Me | 1962 | $20 |

UNI
☐ 55122	I Can't Say No to You/Better Tomorrow Than Today	1969	$6
☐ 55189	Sugar/Just Another Winter	1969	$6
☐ 55100	Take Me/There'll Come a Time	1968	$6

UNITED ARTISTS
| ☐ XW1200 | True Love (You Took My Heart)/You Can Do It | 1978 | $4 |

VEE JAY
☐ 513	By My Side/Prince of Players	1963	$20
☐ 628	Getting Mighty Crowded/Chained to a Memory	1964	$20
☐ 599	I Can't Hear You/Can I Get to Know You	1964	$20
☐ 699	I Don't Hurt Anymore/Too Hot to Hold	1965	$20
☐ 610	It Hurts to Be in Love/Until You Were Gone	1964	$20
☐ 585	The Shoop Shoop Song (It's In His Kiss)/Hands Off	1964	$30

Number	Title	Yr	NM
☐ 716	Trouble Over the Weekend/My Shoe Won't Fly	1966	$20

EVERETT, VINCE
ABC-PARAMOUNT
☐ 10472	Baby, Let's Play House/Livin' High	1963	$100
☐ 10624	Big Brother/To Have, to Hold and Let Go	1965	$50
☐ 10360	I Ain't Gonna Be Your Low Down Dog No More/Sugaree	1962	$60
☐ 10313	Such a Night/Don't Go	1962	$70
☐ 10538	Sweet Flavors/Box Candy	1964	$50

TOWN
| ☐ 1964 | Buttercup/Land of No Return | 1960 | $50 |

EVERETTE, LEON
MERCURY
☐ 880829-7	A Good Love Died Tonight/(You're Never Guilty) When Love Is Your Alibi	1985	$4
☐ 884040-7	'Til a Tear Becomes a Rose/It Never Felt Like This Before	1985	$4
☐ 880611-7	Too Good to Say No To/It Never Felt Like This Before	1985	$4

ORLANDO
☐ 112	Danger List (Give Me Someone I Can Love)/Over	1986	$5
☐ 103	Don't Feel Like the Lone Ranger/We Let Love Fade Away	1979	$5
☐ 103 [PS]	Don't Feel Like the Lone Ranger/We Let Love Fade Away	1979	$8
☐ 102	Giving Up Easy/Mama Rocked Us to Sleep (With Country Music)	1979	$5
☐ 106	I Don't Want to Lose/Mama Rocked Us to Sleep	1980	$5
☐ 105	I Love That Woman (Like the Devil Loves Sin)/Never Ending Crowded Circle	1979	$5
☐ 107	Over/Let Me Apologize	1980	$5
☐ 114	Sad State of Affairs/Danger List (Give Me Someone I Can Love)	1986	$5
☐ 115	Still in the Picture/Danger List (Give Me Someone I Can Love)	1986	$5
☐ 104	The Sun Went Down in My World Tonight/Cheater's Trap	1979	$5
☐ 100	We Let Love Fade Away/Never Ending Crowded Circle	1979	$5

RCA
☐ PB-12111	Giving Up Easy/Setting Me Up	1980	$4
☐ PB-12270	Hurricane/Make Me Stop Loving Her	1981	$4
☐ PB-13717	I Could'a Had You/I Wanna Know Your Name	1984	$4
☐ JK-13717 [DJ]	I Could'a Had You (same on both sides)	1984	$10
— Promo only on green vinyl			
☐ PB-12177	If I Keep On Going Crazy/The Sun Went Down in My World Tonight	1981	$4
☐ PB-12355	Midnight Rodeo/Don't Be Angry	1981	$4
☐ JK-13466 [DJ]	My Lady Loves Me (Just As I Am) (same on both sides)	1983	$10
— Promo only on yellow vinyl			
☐ PB-13466	My Lady Loves Me (Just As I Am)/Somebody Killed Dewey Jones' Daughter	1983	$4
☐ PB-13391	Shadows of My Mind/I Keep On Going Crazy	1982	$4
☐ JK-13391 [DJ]	Shadows of My Mind (same on both sides)	1982	$10
— Promo only on blue vinyl			
☐ PB-13834	Shot in the Dark/I Want to Be in Pictures	1984	$4
☐ PB-13282	Soul Searchin'/Misery	1982	$4
☐ JK-13282 [DJ]	Soul Searchin' (same on both sides)	1982	$12
— Promo only on red vinyl			
☐ PB-13584	The Lady, She's Right/Knocking on Her Door	1983	$4
☐ JK-13584 [DJ]	The Lady, She's Right (same on both sides)	1983	$10
— Promo only on blue vinyl			

TRUE
☐ 107	Goodbye King of Rock 'n' Roll/Where the Daisies Grow Wild	1977	$20
☐ 110	I Love That Woman (Like the Devil Loves Sin)/Still Loving You	1977	$6
☐ 112	Put It Out of Your Mind Babe/Still Loving You	1978	$6

EVERGREEN BLUES, THE
ABC
| ☐ 11198 | Funky Woman/Don't Mess Up My Mind | 1969 | $6 |
| ☐ 11216 | The Moon Is High/Girl I Got Wise | 1969 | $6 |

MERCURY
☐ 72826	Feelin' Your Love/Three's a Crowd	1968	$10
☐ 72780	Laura (Keep Hangin' On)/Yesterday's Coming	1968	$12
☐ 72780 [PS]	Laura (Keep Hangin' On)/Yesterday's Coming	1968	$30
☐ 72756	Midnight Confessions/That's My Baby (Yes)	1967	$10
☐ 72756 [PS]	Midnight Confessions/That's My Baby (Yes)	1967	$30

EVERLY BROTHERS, THE

CADENCE

Number	Title	Yr	NM
❑ 1348	All I Have to Do Is Dream/Claudette	1958	$30
❑ 1348	All I Have to Do Is Dream/Claudette	1961	$30

—Reissue with red and black label; scarcer than original

Number	Title	Yr	NM
❑ 1350	Bird Dog/Devoted to You	1958	$30
❑ 1315	Bye, Bye Love/I Wonder If I Care As Much	1957	$30
❑ 1429	I'm Here to Get My Baby Out of Jail/Lightning Express	1962	$30
❑ 1429 [PS]	I'm Here to Get My Baby Out of Jail/Lightning Express	1962	$50
❑ 1376	Let It Be Me/Since You Broke My Heart	1959	$30
❑ 1376 [PS]	Let It Be Me/Since You Broke My Heart	1959	$60
❑ 1388	Like Strangers/Brand New Heartache	1960	$30
❑ 1355	Problems/Love of My Life	1958	$30
❑ 1355 [PS]	Problems/Love of My Life	1958	$60
❑ 1364	Take a Message to Mary/Poor Jenny	1959	$30
❑ 1342	This Little Girl of Mine/Should We Tell Him?	1958	$30
❑ 1369	('Til) I Kissed You/Oh, What a Feeling	1959	$30
❑ 1369 [PS]	('Til) I Kissed You/Oh, What a Feeling	1959	$60
❑ 1337	Wake Up Little Susie/Maybe Tomorrow	1957	$40
❑ 1337 [PS]	Wake Up Little Susie/Maybe Tomorrow	1957	$250
❑ 1380	When Will I Be Loved/Be Bop A-Lula	1960	$30

CAPITOL

Number	Title	Yr	NM
❑ B-44297	Don't Worry Baby/Tequila Dreams	1989	$4

—A-side with the Beach Boys; B-side by Dave Grusin

Number	Title	Yr	NM
❑ B-44297 [PS]	Don't Worry Baby/Tequila Dreams	1989	$12

MERCURY

Number	Title	Yr	NM
❑ 872420-7	Ballad of a Teenage Queen/Get Rhythm	1988	$3

—With Johnny Cash and Roseanne Cash

Number	Title	Yr	NM
❑ 884428-7	Don't Say Goodnight/Born Yesterday	1986	$4
❑ 884694-7	I Know Love/These Shoes	1986	$4
❑ 884694-7 [PS]	I Know Love/These Shoes	1986	$4
❑ 880213-7	On the Wings of a Nightingale/Asleep	1984	$5

—A-side written and produced by Paul McCartney

Number	Title	Yr	NM
❑ 880423-7	The Story of Me/First in Line	1984	$4

RCA VICTOR

Number	Title	Yr	NM
❑ 74-0849	Lay It Down/Paradise	1972	$12
❑ SP-45-409 [DJ]	Pass the Chicken and Listen	1971	$40

—Promo-only interview record

Number	Title	Yr	NM
❑ 74-0717	Stories We Could Tell/Ridin' High	1972	$10

WARNER BROS.

Number	Title	Yr	NM
❑ 7020	Bowling Green/I Don't Want to Love You	1967	$15
❑ 7121	Bye Bye Love/All I Have to Do Is Dream	1969	$8

—Back to Back Hits" series; originals have green "W7" label; re-recordings

Number	Title	Yr	NM
❑ 7326	Carolina on My Mind/My Little Yellow Bird	1969	$20
❑ 5151 [DJ]	Cathy's Clown/Always It's You	1960	$125

—Promo-only gold vinyl pressing

Number	Title	Yr	NM
❑ 5151 [M]	Cathy's Clown/Always It's You	1960	$30

—Original stock copies have pink labels

Number	Title	Yr	NM
❑ 5151 [M]	Cathy's Clown/Always It's You	1960	$20

—Second-pressing stock copies have red labels with arrows

Number	Title	Yr	NM
❑ 5151 [PS]	Cathy's Clown/Always It's You	1960	$60
❑ S-5151 [S]	Cathy's Clown/Always It's You	1960	$60
❑ 7110	Cathy's Clown/So Sad	1968	$8

—Back to Back Hits" series; originals have green "W7" label

Number	Title	Yr	NM
❑ 5250	Crying in the Rain/I'm Not Angry	1961	$20
❑ 5250 [PS]	Crying in the Rain/I'm Not Angry	1961	$30
❑ 7111	Crying in the Rain/Lucille	1968	$8

—Back to Back Hits" series; originals have green "W7" label

Number	Title	Yr	NM
❑ 5297	Don't Ask Me to Be Friends/No One Can Make My Sunshine Smile	1962	$30
❑ 5297 [PS]	Don't Ask Me to Be Friends/No One Can Make My Sunshine Smile	1962	$40
❑ 5501	Don't Blame Me/Walk Right Back//Muskrat/Lucille	1961	$30
❑ 5501 [PS]	Don't Blame Me/Walk Right Back//Muskrat/Lucille	1961	$50

—Part of Warner Bros. "+2" series, with two new songs and excerpts of two prior hits

Number	Title	Yr	NM
❑ 5199 [DJ]	Ebony Eyes/Walk Right Back	1961	$125

—Promo-only gold vinyl pressing

Number	Title	Yr	NM
❑ 5199	Ebony Eyes/Walk Right Back	1961	$20
❑ 5199 [PS]	Ebony Eyes/Walk Right Back	1961	$30
❑ 7192	Empty Boxes/It's My Time	1968	$15
❑ 5857	Fifi the Flea/Like Every Time Before	1966	$30

—A-side listed as "Don Everly Brother," B-side as "Phil Everly Brother

Number	Title	Yr	NM
❑ 5478	Gone, Gone, Gone/Torture	1964	$20
❑ 5422	Hello, Amy/Ain't That Loving You, Baby	1964	$20
❑ 5639	I'll Never Get Over You/Follow Me	1965	$15
❑ 5362	I'm Afraid/It's Been Nice	1963	$20
❑ 7290	I'm On My Way Home Again/Cuckoo Bird	1969	$15
❑ 5682	It's All Over/I Used to Love You	1965	$15
❑ 7226	Lord of the Manor/Milk Train	1968	$15
❑ 5389	Love Her/The Girl Sang the Blues	1963	$20
❑ 5649	Love Is Strange/A Man with Money	1965	$15
❑ 5649 [PS]	Love Is Strange/A Man with Money	1965	$200
❑ 7088	Love of the Common People/The Voice Within	1967	$15
❑ 7062	Mary Jane/Talking to the Flowers	1967	$15
❑ 5901	She Never Smiles Anymore/Devil Child	1967	$15
❑ 5346	(So It Was...So It Is...) So It Always Will Be/Nancy's Minuet	1963	$20
❑ 5833	Somebody Help Me/Hard, Hard Year	1966	$15
❑ 5163 [DJ]	So Sad (To Watch Good Love Go Bad)/Lucille	1960	$125

—Promo-only gold vinyl pressing

Number	Title	Yr	NM
❑ 5163	So Sad (To Watch Good Love Go Bad)/Lucille	1960	$20
❑ 5163 [PS]	So Sad (To Watch Good Love Go Bad)/Lucille	1960	$60
❑ 5220	Temptation/Stick With Me, Baby	1961	$20
❑ 5220 [PS]	Temptation/Stick With Me, Baby	1961	$40
❑ 7262	T for Texas/I Wonder If I Care As Much	1969	$15
❑ 5611	That'll Be the Day/Give Me a Sweetheart	1965	$15
❑ 5273	That's Old Fashioned (That's the Way Love Should Be)/How Can I Meet Her?	1962	$20
❑ 5273 [PS]	That's Old Fashioned (That's the Way Love Should Be)/How Can I Meet Her?	1962	$40
❑ 5698	The Doll House Is Empty/Lovey Kravezit	1966	$15
❑ 5441	The Ferris Wheel/Don't Forget to Cry	1964	$20
❑ 5808	The Power of Love/Leave My Girl Alone	1966	$15
❑ 5628	The Price of Love/It Only Costs a Dime	1965	$15
❑ 7120	Wake Up Little Susie/Bird Dog	1969	$8

—Back to Back Hits" series; originals have green "W7" label; re-recordings

7-Inch Extended Plays

CADENCE

Number	Title	Yr	NM
❑ CEP-110	*Down in the Willow Garden/Kentucky/I'm Here to Get My Baby Out of Jail/Rockin' Alone in My Old Rockin' Chair	1958	$60
❑ CLLP 33-4	All I Have to Do Is Dream/I Wonder If I Care As Much/Take a Message to Mary//Let It Be Me/Devoted to You/Maybe Tomorrow	1961	$50

—Jukebox issue; small hole, plays at 33 1/3 rpm

Number	Title	Yr	NM
❑ CEP-109	Barbara Allen/Long Time Gone//Lightning Express/Who's Gonna Shoe Your Pretty Little Feet	1958	$60
❑ CEP-111	Bird Dog/Devoted to You//All I Have to Do Is Dream/Claudette	1959	$60
❑ CEP-107	Brand New Heartache/Keep a Knockin'//Rip It Up/Hey Doll Baby	1957	$60
❑ CLLP 33-3	Bye Bye Love/('Til) I Kissed You/Bird Dog//Wake Up Little Susie/When Will I Be Loved/Problems	1961	$50

—Jukebox issue; small hole, plays at 33 1/3 rpm

Number	Title	Yr	NM
❑ CEP-118	(contents unknown)	1959	$60
❑ CLLP 33-4 [PS]	Dream with the Everly Brothers	1961	$70

—Cardboard insert in heavy vinyl envelope

Number	Title	Yr	NM
❑ CEP-121	Let It Be Me/Since You Broke My Heart//'Til I Kissed You/Oh, What a Feeling	1960	$30
❑ CEP-108 [PS]	Songs Our Daddy Taught Us, Vol. 1	1958	$60
❑ CEP-109 [PS]	Songs Our Daddy Taught Us, Vol. 2	1958	$60
❑ CEP-110 [PS]	Songs Our Daddy Taught Us, Vol. 3	1958	$60
❑ CEP-104 [PS]	The Everly Brothers	1957	$60
❑ CEP-105 [PS]	The Everly Brothers	1957	$60
❑ CEP-107 [PS]	The Everly Brothers	1957	$60
❑ CEP-111 [PS]	The Everly Brothers	1959	$60
❑ CEP-118 [PS]	The Everly Brothers	1959	$60
❑ CEP-105	This Little Girl of Mine/Leave My Woman Alone//Should We Tell Him/Be-Bop-a-Lula	1957	$60
❑ CEP-104	Wake Up Little Susie/Maybe Tomorrow//Bye Bye Love/I Wonder If I Care As Much	1957	$60

WARNER BROS.

Number	Title	Yr	NM
❑ EB1381 [PS]	Especially for You	1960	$50
❑ EA1381 [PS]	Foreverly Yours	1960	$50
❑ PRO135 [DJ]	My Gal Sal/Grandfather's Clock/Bully of the Town/The Wayward Wind/Chlo-E//Hi-Lili, Hi-Lo/Don't Blame Me/Now Is the Hour/When I Grow Too Old to Dream/Love Is Where You Find It	1961	$75

—7-inch record, large hole, with excerpts from each of the above songs

Number	Title	Yr	NM
❑ EB1381	Sleepless Nights/Carol Jane//Nashville Blues/That's What You Do to Me	1960	$50
❑ EA1381	So Sad (To Watch Good Love Go Bad)/You Thrill Me (Through and Through)//Memories Are Made of This/Oh, True Love	1960	$50
❑ PRO135 [PS]	Souvenir Sampler	1961	$125

—Back cover of sleeve has a coupon for LP W/WS 1418

Number	Title	Yr	NM
❑ S1471	That's Old Fashioned (That's the Way Love Should Be)/Crying in the Rain/Lucille//Cathy's Clown/Walk Right Back/So Sad (To Watch Good Love Go Bad)	1963	$30

—Stereo jukebox issue; small hole, plays at 33 1/3 rpm

Number	Title	Yr	NM
❑ 2S1858 [PS]	The Everly Brothers Show	1970	$20

—Part of "Little LP" series (#120)

Number	Title	Yr	NM
❑ S1471 [PS]	The Golden Hits of the Everly Brothers	1963	$30
❑ 2S1858	('Til) I Kissed You/Wake Up Little Susie/Cathy's Clown//Mama Tried/Bowling Green/Walk Right Back	1970	$20

—Stereo jukebox issue; small hole, plays at 33 1/3 rpm

EVERLY, DON

ABC HICKORY

Number	Title	Yr	NM
❑ 54012	Brother Juke-Box/Oh, What a Feeling	1977	$6
❑ 54002	Love at Last Sight/Oh I'd Like to Go Away	1976	$6
❑ 54005	Since You Broke My Heart/Deep Water	1977	$6

ODE

Number	Title	Yr	NM
❑ 66009	Only Me/Tumbling Tumbleweeds	1970	$8
❑ 66046	Warming Up the Band/Evelyn Swing	1974	$8

EVERLY, PHIL

CAPITOL

Number	Title	Yr	NM
❑ B-5197	One Way Love/Who's Gonna Keep Me Warm	1983	$10

CURB

Number	Title	Yr	NM
❑ 5401	Dare to Dream Again/Lonely Days, Lonely Nights	1980	$12
❑ 02116	Sweet Southern Love/In Your Eyes	1981	$10

ELEKTRA

Number	Title	Yr	NM
❑ 46556	Buy Me a Beer/You Broke It	1979	$5
❑ 46007	Don't Say You Don't Love Me No More/I Seek the Night	1979	$5

—A-side: With Sondra Locke; B-side: Sondra Locke solo

Number	Title	Yr	NM
❑ 46519	Living Alone/I Just Don't Feel Like Dancing	1979	$5

PYE

Number	Title	Yr	NM
❑ 71056	God Bless Older Ladies/Sweet Grass Country	1976	$6
❑ 71014	Old Kentucky River/Summershine	1975	$8
❑ 71055	Words in Your Eyes/Back When the Bands Played in Rag Time	1976	$8

RCA VICTOR

Number	Title	Yr	NM
❑ APBO-0064	God Bless Older Ladies/Sweet Grass Country	1973	$8

EVERPRESENT FULLNESS, THE

WHITE WHALE

Number	Title	Yr	NM
❑ 248	Darlin' You Can Count On Me/Yeah	1967	$20
❑ 233	Wild About My Lovin'/Doin' a Number	1966	$20
❑ 233	Wild About My Lovin'/Fine and Dandy	1966	$20

EVERYTHING BUT THE GIRL

SIRE

Number	Title	Yr	NM
❑ 7-28526	Don't Leave Me Behind/Draining the Bar	1986	$4
❑ 7-27892	I Always Was Your Girl/Hang Out the Flags	1988	$4
❑ 7-27892 [PS]	I Always Was Your Girl/Hang Out the Flags	1988	$4

EVERYTHING IS EVERYTHING

VANGUARD APOSTOLIC

Number	Title	Yr	NM
❑ 35082	Witchi Tai To/Ooh Baby	1969	$8

EVIL ENCORPORATED

SCENE

Number	Title	Yr	NM
❑ 102	Baby It's You/All I Really Want to Do	1967	$40
❑ 101	Hey You/The Thing Is...	1967	$40

Number	Title	Yr	NM

EVIL, THE
CAPITOL
| ❑ 2038 | Whatcha Gonna Do About It/Always Runnin' Around | 1967 | $30 |

LIVING LEGEND
| ❑ 108 | Whatcha Gonna Do About It/Always Runnin' Around | 1967 | $50 |

EXCELLENTS, THE
BLAST
| ❑ 205 | Coney Island Baby/You Baby You | 1962 | $40 |

—All-red label
| ❑ 205 | Coney Island Baby/You Baby You | 1962 | $30 |

—Red and white label
| ❑ 205 | Coney Island Baby/You Baby You | 1965 | $30 |

—Purple label
| ❑ 207 | I Hear a Rhapsody/Why Did You Laugh | 1963 | $70 |

MERMAID
| ❑ 106 | Love No One But You/Red Red Robin | 1961 | $200 |

— With mermaid on label
| ❑ 106 | Love No One But You/Red Red Robin | 1961 | $60 |

— No mermaid on label

EXCELS, THE (1)
GONE
| ❑ 5094 | My Foolish Heart/Just You and I Together | 1960 | $30 |

RSVP
| ❑ 111 | Can't Help Lovin' That Girl of Mine/Till You | 1961 | $60 |

EXCELS, THE (2)
CARLA
❑ 2536	California on My Mind/Arrival of Mary	1967	$30
❑ 2529	Gonna Make You Mine Girl/Goodbye Poor Boy	1966	$30
❑ 2534	I Wanna Be Free/Too Much Too Soon	1967	$30
❑ 1901	Little Innocent Girl/Some Kind of Fun	1968	$30

EXCEPTIONS, THE (1)
CAPITOL
| ❑ 2046 | Business As Usual/My Mind Goes Traveling | 1967 | $15 |

—As "The Exception
| ❑ 5982 | The Girl from New York City/As Far As I Can See | 1967 | $15 |

—As "The Exception
MERCURY
| ❑ 72562 | Ask Me If I Care/Do-Do-Do Bah | 1966 | $50 |

QUILL
| ❑ 114 | As Far As I Can See/Girl from New York | 1966 | $40 |

TOLLIE
| ❑ 9043 | Come On Home/Dancing Danny | 1965 | $30 |

—As "Kal David and the Exceptions
| ❑ 9007 | Searchin'/Daydreaming of You | 1964 | $30 |

—As "Kal David and the Exceptions

7-Inch Extended Plays
FLAIR
| ❑ 6444 | Lord Have Mercy/Glory to God//Holy, Holy, Holy/Our Father/Lamb of God | 1966 | $60 |

—7-inch 33 1/3 rpm single with small hole

EXCEPTIONS, THE (2)
CAMEO
| ❑ 378 | Down by the Ocean/Pancho's Villa | 1965 | $30 |

EXCITERS, THE
BANG
| ❑ 515 | A Little Bit of Soap/I'm Gonna Get Him Someday | 1966 | $15 |

FARGO
| ❑ 1400 | Alone Again, Naturally/(B-side unknown) | 1972 | $8 |

RCA VICTOR
| ❑ 47-9633 | Take One Step (I'll Take Two)/If You Want My Love | 1968 | $40 |

ROULETTE
❑ 4594	Are You Satisfied/Just Not Ready	1965	$15
❑ 4632	I Knew You Would/There They Go	1965	$15
❑ 4591	I Want You to Be My Boy/Tonight, Tonight	1965	$15
❑ 4591 [PS]	I Want You to Be My Boy/Tonight, Tonight	1965	$60
❑ 4614	My Father/Run Mascara	1965	$15

SHOUT
| ❑ 214 | Soulmotion/You Know It Ain't Right | 1967 | $12 |

TODAY
| ❑ 1002 | Learning How to Fly/Life, Love and Peace | 1970 | $8 |

UNITED ARTISTS
❑ 662	Do-Wah-Diddy/If Love Came Your Way	1963	$15
❑ 572	Drama of Love/He's Got the Power	1963	$15
❑ 604	Get Him/It's So Exciting	1963	$15
❑ 721	Having My Fun/We Were Lovers (When the Party Began)	1964	$15
❑ 830	Having My Fun/We Were Lovers (When the Party Began)	1965	$12
❑ 0029	Tell Him/Do Wah Diddy	1973	$4

— Silver Spotlight Series" reissue
| ❑ 544 | Tell Him/Hard Way to Go | 1963 | $20 |

EXILE
ATCO
| ❑ 7072 | Try It On/Show Me What You Got | 1977 | $5 |

COLUMBIA
| ❑ 4-44972 | Church Street Soul Revival/Your Day Is Comin' | 1969 | $8 |

—As "The Exiles
| ❑ 4-45210 | Put Your Hands Together/Your Day Is Comin' | 1970 | $8 |

—As "The Exiles
EPIC
❑ 34-04722	Crazy for Your Love/Just in Case	1984	$3
❑ 34-07710	Feel Like Foolin' Around/Showdown	1988	$3
❑ 34-04567	Give Me One More Chance/Ain't That a Pity	1984	$3
❑ 34-04567 [PS]	Give Me One More Chance/Ain't That a Pity	1984	$4
❑ 34-05580	Hang On to Your Heart/She Loves Her Lovin'	1985	$3
❑ 34-04041	High Cost of Leaving/Like a Fool's Supposed to Do	1983	$3
❑ 34-07597	I Can't Get Close Enough/As Long As I Have Your Memory	1987	$3
❑ 34-05723	I Could Get Used to You/Practice Makes Perfect	1985	$3
❑ 34-04421	I Don't Want to Be a Memory/After All These Years (I'm Still Chasing You)	1984	$3
❑ 34-06229	It'll Be Me/Music	1986	$3
❑ 34-08020	It's You Again/The Girl Can't Help It	1988	$3
❑ 34-04864	She's a Miracle/I've Never Seen Anything	1985	$3
❑ 34-07135	She's Too Good to Be True/Promises, Promises	1987	$3
❑ 34-05860	Super Love/Proud to Be Your Man	1986	$3
❑ 34-04247	Woke Up in Love/First Things First	1983	$4

MCA CURB
| ❑ 52596 | Dixie Girl/Someone Like You | 1985 | $3 |
| ❑ 52551 | Stay with Me/Kiss You All Over | 1985 | $3 |

WARNER BROS.
❑ 49794	Heart and Soul/Your Love Is Everything	1981	$4
❑ 8796	How Could This Go Wrong/Being in Love with You Is Easy	1979	$4
❑ 8848	Part of Me That Needs You Most/Let's Do It All Over Again	1979	$4
❑ 49548	Take Me Down/It Takes Love to Make Love	1980	$6

—A-side was later a hit for Alabama
| ❑ 49863 | Till the Very End/What Kind of Love Is This | 1981 | $4 |
| ❑ 49048 | Too Proud to Cry/Destiny | 1979 | $4 |

EXITS, THE
GEMINI
| ❑ 1006 | I Don't Want to Hear It/(Instrumental) | 1967 | $60 |

KAPP
| ❑ 2028 | Another Sundown in Watts/I'm So Bad | 1969 | $500 |

EXODUS
JAMIE
| ❑ 1442 | Four Seasons Medley (mono/stereo) | 1981 | $5 |

—As "Exodus II
WAND
| ❑ 11248 | M&M/Silhouettes-You Cheated | 1972 | $125 |

— Black and white label
| ❑ 11248 | M&M/Silhouettes-You Cheated | 1972 | $40 |

— Multi-colored label

EXOTICS, THE
BOLO
| ❑ 722 | Oasis/Chattanooga Choo Choo | 1962 | $15 |

CORAL
❑ 62310	Fortune Hunter/Manpower	1962	$30
❑ 62399	Let's Get Together/Sad, Sad Song	1964	$20
❑ 62439	Like You Hurt Me/Big Time Charlie	1964	$30
❑ 62343	My Life's Desire (Part 1)/My Life's Desire (Part 2)	1963	$20
❑ 62268	That's My Desire/Darking, I Want to Get Married	1961	$30
❑ 62289	The Gang That Sang (Heart of My Heart)/Hotcha Mighty Knows	1961	$30

EXCELLO
| ❑ 2284 | Boogaloo Investigator/I Won't Ever Stop Loving You | 1967 | $8 |
| ❑ 2292 | Let Me Be a Part of You/Let's Try to Build a Love Affair | 1968 | $8 |

JERDEN
| ❑ 106 | Four Banger/Cat Hairs | 1960 | $20 |

MONUMENT
| ❑ 984 | Fire Engine Red/Morning Sun | 1966 | $15 |

SEAFAIR
| ❑ 108 | Ginger Snap/(B-side unknown) | 1962 | $10 |

SPRINGBOARD
| ❑ 101 | Gee/Lorraine | 1963 | $30 |
| ❑ 101 [PS] | Gee/Lorraine | 1963 | $50 |

EXPLORERS, THE
CORAL
| ❑ 62175 | Don't Be a Fool/In the Wee Small Hours of the Morning | 1960 | $125 |

EXPORTS, THE
KING
| ❑ 5917 | Car Hop/Seat Belts Please | 1964 | $30 |
| ❑ 5985 | Mustang '65/Always It's You | 1965 | $30 |

EXPOSE
ARISTA
❑ 9555	Come Go with Me/December	1987	$3
❑ 9555 [PS]	Come Go with Me/December	1987	$3
❑ 9440	Exposed to Love/(B-side unknown)	1986	$8
❑ 9617	Let Me Be the One/Love Is Our Destiny	1987	$3
❑ 9617 [PS]	Let Me Be the One/Love Is Our Destiny	1987	$3
❑ 9325	Point of No Return/(B-side unknown)	1985	$10
❑ 9579	Point of No Return/Extra Extra	1987	$3
❑ 9579 [PS]	Point of No Return/Extra Extra	1987	$3
❑ 9640	Seasons Change/December	1987	$3
❑ 9640 [PS]	Seasons Change/December	1987	$3
❑ 9916	Tell Me Why/Let Me Down Easy	1989	$3
❑ 9916 [PS]	Tell Me Why/Let Me Down Easy	1989	$3
❑ 9836	What You Don't Know/Walk Along with Me	1989	$3
❑ 9836 [PS]	What You Don't Know/Walk Along with Me	1989	$3
❑ 9868	When I Looked at Him/(Suave Mix)	1989	$3
❑ 9868 [PS]	When I Looked at Him/(Suave Mix)	1989	$3

EXPRESSIONS, THE
ARLISS
| ❑ 1012 | My Love, My Love/The Sign of Happiness | 1962 | $60 |

GUYDEN
| ❑ 2122 | Be-Bop-a-Lula/Skinnie Minnie | 1965 | $20 |

—As "J-D and the Expressions
PARKWAY
| ❑ 892 | On the Corner/To Cry | 1963 | $20 |

REPRISE
| ❑ 0360 | Playboy/One Plus One | 1965 | $30 |

EXTERMINATORS, THE
CHANCELLOR
| ❑ 1148 | Beatle Stomp/Stomp 'Em Out | 1964 | $20 |

—A-sides are the same song with different titles
| ❑ 1143 | The Beetle Bomb/Stomp 'Em Out | 1963 | $30 |

GOLDEN WEST
| ❑ 1002 | Beatle Stomp/Stomp 'Em Out | 1964 | $30 |

EXTREMES, THE
EVERLAST
| ❑ 5013 | Come Next Spring/Let's Elope | 1958 | $200 |

PARO
| ❑ 733 | The Bells/That's All I Want | 1962 | $300 |

F

Number	Title	Yr	NM

FABARES, SHELLEY
COLPIX
Number	Title	Yr	NM
❏ 667	Big Star/Telephone (Don't You Ring)	1962	$30
❏ 721	Football Season's Over/ He Don't Love Me	1963	$125

—Produced by Jan Berry of Jan and Dean

❏ 654	The Things We Did Last Summer/Breaking Up Is Hard to Do	1962	$30
❏ 705	Welcome Home/Billy Boy	1963	$30
❏ 631	What Did They Do Before Rock and Roll/Very Unlikely	1962	$30

—With Paul Petersen

❏ 631 [PS]	What Did They Do Before Rock and Roll/Very Unlikely	1962	$400

DUNHILL
❏ 4001	My Prayer/Pretty Please	1965	$40
❏ 4041	See Ya 'Round on the Rebound/Pretty Please	1966	$40

VEE JAY
❏ 632	I Know You'll Be There/ Lost Summer Love	1964	$50

FABIAN
CHANCELLOR
❏ 1047 [M]	About This Thing Called Love/String Along	1960	$15
❏ 1047 [PS]	About This Thing Called Love/String Along	1960	$40
❏ S-1047 [S]	About This Thing Called Love/String Along	1960	$60
❏ 1084	A Girl Like You/ Dream Factory	1961	$15
❏ 1084 [PS]	A Girl Like You/ Dream Factory	1961	$40
❏ 1024	Be My Steady Date/Lilly Lou	1958	$30
❏ 1041 [M]	Come On and Get Me/ Got the Feeling	1959	$30
❏ 1041 [PS]	Come On and Get Me/ Got the Feeling	1959	$50
❏ S-1041 [S]	Come On and Get Me/ Got the Feeling	1959	$60
❏ 1072	Grapevine/David and Goliath	1961	$15
❏ 1044	Hound Dog Man/ Friendly World	1959	$30
❏ 1044 [M]	Hound Dog Man/ This Friendly World	1959	$30

—Note difference in B-side title

❏ 1044 [PS]	Hound Dog Man/ This Friendly World	1959	$50
❏ S-1044 [S]	Hound Dog Man/ This Friendly World	1959	$60
❏ 1029 [PS]	I Am a Man/Hypnotized	1959	$60

—Incorrect title on A-side of sleeve

❏ 1029 [M]	I'm a Man/Hypnotized	1959	$30
❏ 1029 [PS]	I'm a Man/Hypnotized	1959	$50
❏ S-1029 [S]	I'm a Man/Hypnotized	1959	$60
❏ 1051	I'm Gonna Sit Right Down and Write Myself a Letter/ Strollin' in the Springtime	1960	$15
❏ 1051 [PS]	I'm Gonna Sit Right Down and Write Myself a Letter/ Strollin' in the Springtime	1960	$40
❏ 1020	I'm in Love/Shivers	1958	$30
❏ 1079	The Love That I'm Giving to You/You're Only Young Once	1961	$20
❏ 1079 [PS]	The Love That I'm Giving to You/You're Only Young Once	1961	$50
❏ 1037 [M]	Tiger/Mighty Cold (To a Warm, Warm Heart)	1959	$30
❏ 1037 [PS]	Tiger/Mighty Cold (To a Warm, Warm Heart)	1959	$50
❏ S-1037 [S]	Tiger/Mighty Cold (To a Warm, Warm Heart)	1959	$60
❏ 1055	Tomorrow/King of Love	1960	$15
❏ 1055 [PS]	Tomorrow/King of Love	1960	$40
❏ 1086	Tongue-Tied/Kansas City	1961	$30
❏ 1033 [M]	Turn Me Loose/Stop Thief!	1959	$30
❏ 1033 [PS]	Turn Me Loose/Stop Thief!	1959	$50
❏ S-1033 [S]	Turn Me Loose/Stop Thief!	1959	$60
❏ 1092	Wild Party/Made You	1961	$30
❏ 1092 [PS]	Wild Party/Made You	1961	$50
❏ 1092	Wild Party/The Gospel Truth	1961	$30

CREAM
❏ 7717	Ease On (Into My Life)/ The American East	1977	$5
❏ 7717 [PS]	Ease On (Into My Life)/ The American East	1977	$5

DOT
❏ 16413	Break Down and Cry/She's Staying Inside with Me	1963	$10

7-Inch Extended Plays
CHANCELLOR
❏ A-5003	*Hold Me (In Your Arms)/ Just One More Time/ Please Don't Stop/ Ooh, What You Do!	1959	$75
❏ A-301	*Hound Dog Man/This Friendly World/Pretty Little Girl/I'm Growin' Up/Single	1960	$60

Number	Title	Yr	NM
❏ A-301 [PS]	5 Songs from Hound Dog Man	1960	$60
❏ B-5003	(contents unknown)	1959	$75
❏ B-5005	(contents unknown)	1959	$75
❏ C-5005	(contents unknown)	1959	$75
❏ A-5003 [PS]	Hold That Tiger! Volume 1	1959	$70
❏ B-5003 [PS]	Hold That Tiger! Volume 2	1959	$70
❏ C-5003 [PS]	Hold That Tiger! Volume 3	1959	$70
❏ A-5005 [PS]	The Fabulous Fabian, Volume 1	1959	$75
❏ B-5005 [PS]	The Fabulous Fabian, Volume 2	1959	$75
❏ C-5005 [PS]	The Fabulous Fabian, Volume 3	1959	$75
❏ C-5003	Turn Me Loose/Steady Date//Don't You Think It's Time?/Cuddle Up a Little Closer	1959	$75

FABRIC, BENT
ATCO
❏ 6226	Alley Cat/Marking Time	1962	$8
❏ 6245	Chicken Feed/That Certain Party	1962	$8
❏ 6401	Sweet Charity Theme/ Can't You See	1966	$8
❏ 6363	The Drunken Penguin/ Alley Cat	1965	$8
❏ 6271	The Happy Puppy/ Sermonette	1963	$8
❏ 6333	The Old Piano Roll Blues/Titena	1964	$8
❏ 6304	The Organ Grinder's Swing/Goofus	1964	$8

FABS, THE
COTTON BALL
❏ 1005	That's the Bag I'm In/ Dinah Wants Religion	1966	$200

FABULAIRES, THE
EASTWEST
❏ 103	While Walking/No No	1957	$300

MAIN LINE
❏ 103	While Walking/No No	1958	$200

FABULONS, THE (1)
EMBER
❏ 1069	Smoke From Your Cigarette/ Give Me Back My Ring	1960	$60

—White label

❏ 1069	Smoke From Your Cigarette/ Give Me Back My Ring	1960	$30

—Black label

FABULONS, THE (2)
TOWER
❏ 259	Since You've Been Gone/Don't Ask Me	1966	$20

FABULOUS CONTINENTALS
CB
❏ 5007	Let's Get Goin'/ New York Walk	1964	$20

FABULOUS COUNTS, THE
MOIRA
❏ 105	Dirty Red/Scrambled Eggs	1970	$20
❏ 108	Get Down People/ Lunar Funk	1970	$10

FABULOUS FLAMES, THE (1)
BAY-TONE
❏ 102	Do You Remember/ Get to Stepping	1961	$50
❏ 105	Lover/I'm So All Alone	1961	$60

FABULOUS FLIPPERS, THE
CAMEO
❏ 439	Harlem Shuffle/I Don't Want to Cry	1966	$40
❏ 454	Shout/Turn On Your Love Light	1967	$30

QUILL
❏ 110	Dry My Eyes/Women Ain't Good for Me	1966	$50
❏ 111	Harlem Shuffle/I Don't Want to Cry	1966	$50

FABULOUS FOUR, THE
BRASS
❏ 316	I'm Always Doing Something Wrong/Young Blood	1964	$30
❏ 314	Who Could It Be/Happy	1964	$30

CHANCELLOR
❏ 1090	Everybody Knows/I'm Coming Home	1961	$30
❏ 1102	Forever/((It's No) Sin	1962	$30
❏ 1062	In the Chapel in the Moonlight/Mr. Twist	1960	$30

Number	Title	Yr	NM
❏ 1068	Let's Try Again/ Precious Moments	1961	$30
❏ 1098	Mr. Twist/Everybody Knows	1961	$30
❏ 1085	Prisoner of Love/Betty Ann	1961	$100
❏ 1078	Why Do Fools Fall in Love/ Sounds of Summer	1961	$50

MELIC
❏ 4114	Welcome Me Home/ Oop Shoobee Doop	1962	$60

FABULOUS PEPS, THE
D-TOWN
❏ 1065	My Love Looks Good on You/Speak Your Peace	1966	$60
❏ 1060	Thinking About You/ This I Pray	1965	$50

—As "The Peps

GE GE
❏ 503	This Love I Have for You/ She's Going to Leave You	1965	$50

PREMIUM STUFF
❏ 7	Gypsy Woman/Why Are You Blowing My Mind	1967	$50
❏ 3	So Fine/I'll Never Be the Same Again	1967	$50
❏ 1	Why Are You Blowing My Mind/I Can't Get Right	1967	$50

WEE-3
❏ 233	With These Eyes/I've Been Trying	1967	$40

WHEELSVILLE
❏ 109	With These Eyes/ Light of My Life	1968	$15

FABULOUS POODLES
EPIC
❏ 9-50835	Bionic Man/Suicide Bridge	1980	$5
❏ 9-50823	Man with Money/B Movies	1980	$5
❏ 8-50666	Mirror Star/Tit Photographer Blues	1979	$5
❏ 8-50720	Work Shy/Toytown People	1979	$5

FABULOUS RHINESTONES, THE
JUST SUNSHINE
❏ 501	Free/Live It Out to the End	1972	$5
❏ 509	Freewheelin'/Whitecaps	1973	$5
❏ 500	What a Wonderful Thing We Have/Nothing New	1972	$5
❏ 500 [PS]	What a Wonderful Thing We Have/Nothing New	1972	$6

FABULOUS THUNDERBIRDS, THE
CBS ASSOCIATED
❏ ZS4 07602	How Do You Spell Love/ Love in Common	1987	$3
❏ ZS4 07230	Stand Back/It Takes a Big Man to Cry	1987	$3
❏ ZS4 07230 [PS]	Stand Back/It Takes a Big Man to Cry	1987	$3
❏ ZS4 05838	Tuff Enuff/Look at That, Look at That	1986	$3
❏ ZS4 05838 [PS]	Tuff Enuff/Look at That, Look at That	1986	$3
❏ ZS4 07649	Wasted Tears/It Comes to Me Naturally	1987	$3
❏ ZS4 06396	Why Get Up/I Don't Care	1986	$3
❏ ZS4 06270	Wrap It Up/True Love	1986	$3
❏ ZS4 06270 [PS]	Wrap It Up/True Love	1986	$3

ELEKTRA
❏ 69384	Powerful Stuff/Tutti Frutti	1988	$3

—B-side by Little Richard

EPIC
❏ ES72594 [DJ]	Merry Christmas Darling/ (Rockin') Winter Wonderland	1983	$5

FACENDA, TOMMY
ATLANTIC
❏ 2057	Bubba Ditty/I Don't Know	1960	$30
❏ 45-61	High School U.S.A.- Boston/Plea of Love	1959	$50
❏ 45-63	High School U.S.A.- Buffalo/Plea of Love	1959	$50
❏ 45-67	High School U.S.A.- Chicago/Plea of Love	1959	$50
❏ 45-71	High School U.S.A.- Cincinnati/Plea of Love	1959	$50
❏ 45-62	High School U.S.A.- Cleveland/Plea of Love	1959	$50
❏ 45-77	High School U.S.A.- Denver/Plea of Love	1959	$50
❏ 45-56	High School U.S.A.- Detroit/Plea of Love	1959	$50
❏ 45-59	High School U.S.A.- Florida/Plea of Love	1959	$50
❏ 45-70	High School U.S.A.-Georgia, Alabama/Plea of Love	1959	$50
❏ 45-64	High School U.S.A.-Hartford, Conn./Plea of Love	1959	$50
❏ 45-66	High School U.S.A.- Indianapolis/Plea of Love	1959	$50
❏ 45-73	High School U.S.A.-Los Angeles/Plea of Love	1959	$50
❏ 45-72	High School U.S.A.- Memphis/Plea of Love	1959	$50

Number	Title	Yr	NM
❏ 45-58	High School U.S.A.-Minneapolis-St. Paul/Plea of Love	1959	$50
❏ 45-65	High School U.S.A.-Nashville/Plea of Love	1959	$50
❏ 45-60	High School U.S.A.-Newark, N.J./Plea of Love	1959	$50
❏ 45-68	High School U.S.A.-New Orleans/Plea of Love	1959	$50
❏ 45-52	High School U.S.A.-New York City/Plea of Love	1959	$50
❏ 45-53	High School U.S.A.-North & South Carolina/Plea of Love	1959	$50
❏ 45-78	High School U.S.A.-Oklahoma/Plea of Love	1959	$50
❏ 45-55	High School U.S.A.-Philadelphia/Plea of Love	1959	$50
❏ 45-57	High School U.S.A.-Pittsburgh/Plea of Love	1959	$50
❏ 45-74	High School U.S.A.-San Francisco/Plea of Love	1959	$50
❏ 45-76	High School U.S.A.-Seattle, Portland/Plea of Love	1959	$50
❏ 45-69	High School U.S.A.-St. Louis & Kansas City/Plea of Love	1959	$50
❏ 45-75	High School U.S.A.-Texas/Plea of Love	1959	$50
❏ 45-51	High School U.S.A.-Virginia/Plea of Love	1959	$50
❏ 45-54	High School U.S.A.-Washington, D.C./Plea of Love	1959	$50

LEGRAND
Number	Title	Yr	NM
❏ 1001	High School U.S.A./Give Me Another Chance	1959	$30

— Original pressings have purple labels

NASCO
Number	Title	Yr	NM
❏ 6018	Little Baby/You Are My Everything	1958	$30

FACES
Also see SMALL FACES; ROD STEWART; RONNIE WOOD.

WARNER BROS.
Number	Title	Yr	NM
❏ 7393	Around the Phynth/Wicked Messenger	1970	$10

— As "Small Faces"

Number	Title	Yr	NM
❏ 7681 [PS]	Cindy Incidentally/Skewiff (Mend the Fuse)	1973	$6
❏ 7681	Cindy Incidentally/Skewiff (Mend the Fuse)	1973	$5
❏ 7483	Maybe I'm Amazed/Oh Lord I'm Browned Off	1971	$8
❏ 7711	Ooh-La-La/Borstal Boys	1973	$5
❏ 7545	Stay with Me/You're So Rude	1971	$6

FACES, THE
IGUANA
Number	Title	Yr	NM
❏ 601	Christmas/New Year's Resolution	1965	$125

REGINA
Number	Title	Yr	NM
❏ 328	I'll Walk Alone/I Didn't Want Her	1965	$30
❏ 326	Skier Jones/What Is This Dream (I Have)	1965	$30

FACTORY, THE
UNI
Number	Title	Yr	NM
❏ 55005	Smile, Let Your Life Begin/When I Was An Apple	1967	$15

FACTS OF LIFE
KAYVETTE
Number	Title	Yr	NM
❏ 5126	Caught in the Act (Of Gettin' It On)/L-O-V-E	1976	$6
❏ 5137	Did He Make Love to You (Part 1)/(Part 2)	1978	$6
❏ 5131	Givin' Me Your Love/A Hundred Pounds of Pain	1977	$6
❏ 5134	Lost Inside You/Looks Like We Made It	1977	$6
❏ 5128	Sometimes/Love Is the Final Truth	1976	$6
❏ 5136	We Can't Hide It Anymore/Dr. Feel Good	1977	$6

FAGAN, SCOTT
BANG
Number	Title	Yr	NM
❏ 530	Give Love a Chance/Tutsie	1966	$15

BOURNEFIELD
Number	Title	Yr	NM
❏ 800	Sandy the Blue-Nosed Reindeer/The Story of Sandy the Blue-Nosed Reindeer	1979	$6

EPIC
Number	Title	Yr	NM
❏ 5-10619	I Am/Where My Lover Has Gone	1970	$10

RCA VICTOR
Number	Title	Yr	NM
❏ PB-10678	Surrender to the Sun/Many Sunny Places	1976	$6

FAGEN, DONALD
Also see STEELY DAN. (SC2)
Also see STEELY DAN.
Also see STEELY DAN. (45)

FULL MOON/ASYLUM
Number	Title	Yr	NM
❏ 47244	True Companion/All of You	1981	$5

— B-side by Don Felder

WARNER BROS.
Number	Title	Yr	NM
❏ 27972	Century's End/Shanghai Confidential	1988	$5
❏ 27972 [PS]	Century's End/Shanghai Confidential	1988	$5
❏ 29900	I.G.Y. (What a Beautiful World)/Walk Between Raindrops	1982	$4
❏ 29900 [PS]	I.G.Y. (What a Beautiful World)/Walk Between Raindrops	1982	$5

FAHEY, JOHN
VANGUARD
Number	Title	Yr	NM
❏ 35076	A March for Martin Luther King/Singing Bridge	1968	$20

FAIR, YVONNE
DADE
Number	Title	Yr	NM
❏ 1851	Straighten Up/Say Yeah Yeah	1963	$15
❏ 5006	Straighten Up/Say Yeah Yeah	1963	$30

KING
Number	Title	Yr	NM
❏ 5594	I Found You/If I Knew	1962	$20

— With the James Brown Band

Number	Title	Yr	NM
❏ 5687	It Hurts to Be in Love/You Can Make It If You Try	1962	$20

— With James Brown

Number	Title	Yr	NM
❏ 5654	Tell Me Why/Say So Long	1962	$20

— With James Brown

Number	Title	Yr	NM
❏ 6017	Tell Me Why/You Can Make It If You Try	1966	$8

MOTOWN
Number	Title	Yr	NM
❏ 1384	It Should Have Been Me/Tell Me Something Good	1976	$6
❏ 1323 [PS]	Walk Out the Door If You Wanna/It Should Have Been Me	1974	$10

SOUL
Number	Title	Yr	NM
❏ 35075	Stay a Little Longer/We Should Never Be Lonely My Love	1970	$8

FAIRBURN, WERLY
CAPITOL
Number	Title	Yr	NM
❏ F2770	Good Deal Lucille/Baby He's a Wolf	1954	$40
❏ F3101	It's a Cold, Weary World/Spiteful Heart	1955	$40
❏ F2844	Love Spelled Backwards Is Evol/Nothing But Lovin'	1954	$40
❏ F2963	Prison Cell of Love/I Feel Like Cryin'	1954	$40

COLUMBIA
Number	Title	Yr	NM
❏ 4-21483	Broken Hearted Me/Stay Close to Me	1956	$40
❏ 4-21528	Everybody's Rockin'/It's Heaven	1956	$125
❏ 4-21432	I Guess I'm Crazy/That Sweet Love of Mine	1955	$40

SAVOY
Number	Title	Yr	NM
❏ 1503	All the Time/I'm a Fool About Your Love	1956	$30
❏ 1509	My Heart's on Fire/Speak to Me Baby	1957	$30
❏ 1521	Telephone Baby/No Blues Tomorrow	1957	$30

FAIRCHILD, BARBARA
AUDIOGRAPH
Number	Title	Yr	NM
❏ 443	The Biggest Hurt/Every Flower Has to Have a Seed	1982	$6

CAPITOL
Number	Title	Yr	NM
❏ B-5607	All My Cloudy Days Are Gone/You Burned Me So Bad	1986	$4
❏ B-5688	Too Much Love/Bluebird	1987	$4

COLUMBIA
Number	Title	Yr	NM
❏ 4-45063	A Girl Who'll Satisfy Her Man/Chains of Love	1970	$6
❏ 4-45690	A Sweeter Love (I'll Never Know)/That's Loving You	1972	$6
❏ 4-45988	Baby Doll/Color Them with Love	1974	$5
❏ 3-10423	Cheatin' Is/Touch of My Heart	1976	$5
❏ 4-45522	Color My World/Tell Me Again	1972	$6
❏ 4-45173	Find Out What's Happenin'/(When You Close Your Eyes) I'll Make You See	1970	$6
❏ 3-10607	For All the Right Reasons/The Other Side of the Morning	1977	$5

Number	Title	Yr	NM
❏ 3-10261	I Just Love Being a Woman/Your Good Girl's Gonna Go Bad	1975	$5
❏ 3-10825	It's Sad to Go to the Funeral (Of a Good Love That Has Died)/Good Time Days	1978	$5
❏ 3-10485	Let Me Love You Once Before You Go/You Are Always There	1977	$5
❏ 3-10128	Let's Love While We Can/Tara	1975	$5
❏ 3-10047	Little Girl Feeling/His Green Eyes	1974	$5
❏ 4-45422	Love's Old Song/Back Then	1971	$6
❏ 4-45272	(Loving You Is) Sunshine/Whatever Happened to Happiness	1970	$6
❏ 3-10378	Mississippi/Over the Rainbow	1976	$5
❏ 3-10686	She Can't Give It Away/Painted Faces	1978	$5
❏ 4-46053	Standing in Your Line/You're the One I'm Living For	1974	$5
❏ 4-45589	Thanks for the Mem'ries/Let Me Be Your Queen	1972	$6
❏ 4-45344	What Do You Do/Break Away	1971	$6

KAPP
Number	Title	Yr	NM
❏ 943	Lonely Old Man/Breakin' In a Brand New Man	1968	$8
❏ 925	Something Different/Remember the Alamo	1968	$8

FAIRLANES, THE
ARGO
Number	Title	Yr	NM
❏ 5357	Little Girl, Little Girl/Comin' After You	1960	$40

CONTINENTAL
Number	Title	Yr	NM
❏ 1001	Writing This Letter/Playboy	1961	$300

LUCKY SEVEN
Number	Title	Yr	NM
❏ 102	Seventeen Steps/Johnny Rhythm	1959	$70

MINARET
Number	Title	Yr	NM
❏ 103	The Dagwood/I'm Not the Kind of Guy	1962	$30

RADIANT
Number	Title	Yr	NM
❏ 101	Baby Baby/Tell Me	1964	$250

REPRISE
Number	Title	Yr	NM
❏ 20213	Surf Train/Lonely Weekends	1963	$40

FAIRPORT CONVENTION
A&M
Number	Title	Yr	NM
❏ 1108	Fotheringay/I'll Keep It with Mine	1969	$15
❏ 1155	Genesis Hall/Si Tu Dois Partie	1969	$15

FAITH, ADAM
AMY
Number	Title	Yr	NM
❏ 936	Don't You Know/Someone's Taken Marie Away	1965	$20
❏ 913	It's Alright/I Just Don't Know	1964	$20
❏ 922	Talk About Love/Stop Feeling Sorry for Yourself	1965	$20
❏ 895	The First Time/So Long Baby	1964	$20
❏ 899	We Are in Love/What Now	1964	$20

CAPITOL
Number	Title	Yr	NM
❏ 5543	I'm Used to Losing You/I Don't Need That Kind of Lovin'	1965	$10
❏ 5699	To Make a Big Man Cry/Here's Another Day	1966	$10

CUB
Number	Title	Yr	NM
❏ 9074	I Did What You Told Me/When Johnny Comes Marching Home	1960	$30
❏ 9068	Poor Me/The Reason	1960	$30
❏ 9061	What Do You Want/From Now Until September	1960	$30

DOT
Number	Title	Yr	NM
❏ 16405	Don't That Beat All/Mix Me a Person	1962	$20

EMI
Number	Title	Yr	NM
❏ 2691	What Do You Want/Lonely Pup (In A Christmas Shop)//How About That/Someone Else's Baby	1977	$8

— U.K. import

LAURIE
Number	Title	Yr	NM
❏ 3455	Daddy, What'll Happen to Me/Cowman, Milk Your Cow	1968	$8

FAITH BAND
MERCURY
Number	Title	Yr	NM
❏ 74090	Big City Lights/Touchy Situation	1979	$5
❏ 74037	Dancin' Shoes/Desire	1978	$5
❏ 76024	Paradise/Is It for Real	1979	$5

VILLAGE
Number	Title	Yr	NM
❏ 202	Dancin' Shoes/Desire	1978	$12

Number	Title	Yr	NM

FAITH HOPE & CHARITY

20TH CENTURY

Number	Title	Yr	NM
☐ 2370	Don't Pity Me/Find What You Need	1978	$4
☐ 2391	How Can I Help But Love You/Keep Me Baby	1978	$4

MAXWELL

☐ 808	Baby Don't Take Your Love/Make Love to Me	1970	$6
☐ 805	So Much Love/Let's Try It Over	1970	$6

RCA

☐ PB-10865	Life Goes On/You've Gotta Tell Her	1976	$5

RCA VICTOR

☐ PB-10542	Don't Go Looking for Love/Disco Dan	1976	$5
☐ PB-10343	To Each His Own/Find a Way	1975	$5

SUSSEX

☐ 216	Come Back and Finish What You Started/I Worship the Very Ground You Walk On	1971	$5
☐ 243	I Was There/Who Could Love You More Than I	1972	$5
☐ 231	We Can Change the World/God Bless the World	1972	$5
☐ 252	Who Made You Go/Heavy Love	1973	$5

FAITH NO MORE

SLASH

☐ 28287	We Care a Lot/Spirit	1987	$6

FAITH, PERCY

COLUMBIA

☐ 42423	Advise and Consent/Jacqueline's Journey	1962	$6
☐ 45114	Airport Love Theme/Theme for Young Lovers	1970	$4
☐ 1-752	All My Love/This Is the Time	1950	$20

—Microgroove 33 1/3 rpm 7-inch single

☐ 6-752	All My Love/This Is the Time	1950	$20
☐ 44086	A Man and a Woman/This Hotel	1967	$5
☐ 39874	Amorada/Funny Fellow	1952	$15
☐ 45374	Anytime of the Year/I Can Hear the Music	1971	$4
☐ 42011	At Last-Angel Face/Tammy Tell Me True	1961	$8
☐ JZSP111903/4 [DJ]	Away In A Manger/We Three Kings Of Orient Are	1965	$15

—Promo only on green vinyl

☐ 40764	Baby Doll/Vagabond Waltz King	1956	$12
☐ 40174	Baubles, Bangles and Beads/And This Is My Beloved	1954	$12
☐ 39643	Beautiful Love/Nightingale	1952	$12

—The above four comprise a box set

☐ 39426	Black Ball Perry Line/Wondrous Word	1951	$20
☐ 1-812(?)	Brazilian Sleighride/What Is This Thing Called Love	1950	$30

—Microgroove 33 1/3 rpm 7-inch single

☐ 6-812(?)	Brazilian Sleighride/What Is This Thing Called Love	1950	$20
☐ 39642	Brazilian Sleighride/What Is This Thing Called Love	1952	$10
☐ 44319	Can't Take My Eyes Off You/Windy	1967	$5
☐ 39664	Carefree/Invitation	1952	$15
☐ 39782	Caribbean Night/Cu-Tu-Gu-Ru	1952	$10
☐ 39356	Carousel Waltz/When I'm Not Near the Girl I Love	1951	$15
☐ 43642	Cheryl/Swingin' Village	1966	$6
☐ 40390	Ching-Ching-a-Ling/Petite	1954	$10
☐ 1-899	Christmas In Killarney/Norah	1950	$30

—Microgroove 33 1/3 rpm 7-inch single

☐ 6-899	Christmas In Killarney/Norah	1950	$20
☐ 1-841(?)	Christmas in My Heart/Sleigh Ride	1950	$30

—Microgroove 33 1/3 rpm 7-inch single

☐ 6-841(?)	Christmas in My Heart/Sleigh Ride	1950	$20
☐ JZSP119961/2 [DJ]	Christmas Is . . ./Happy Holiday	1966	$10

— Yellow label

☐ JZSP119961/2 [DJ]	Christmas Is . . ./Happy Holiday	1967	$10

— White label

☐ JZSP119961/2 [PS]	Christmas Is . . ./Happy Holiday	1967	$20

— Sleeve announces this as the 1967 Christmas Seals Record

☐ 43846	Christmas Is.../Silver Bells	1966	$6
☐ 31536 [S]	(contents unknown)	1962	$8
☐ 31537 [S]	(contents unknown)	1962	$8
☐ 31538 [S]	(contents unknown)	1962	$8
☐ 31540 [S]	(contents unknown)	1962	$8

— The above 10 are Columbia "Stereo 7" singles

Number	Title	Yr	NM
☐ 45945	Corazon/Crunchy Granola Suite	1973	$4
☐ 39708	Delicado/Festival	1952	$15
☐ 39732	Delicado/The Gandy Dancers' Ball	1952	$12

—B-side by Frankie Laine; this is part of a various-artists box set

☐ 45525	Diamonds Are Forever/Love Theme from "Mary Queen of Scots"	1972	$4
☐ 10165	El Bimbo/Cherry Cherry	1975	$4
☐ 40185	Eleanora/Dream, Dream, Dream	1954	$12
☐ 10301	Emmanuelle-The Joys of a Woman/Ding Dong	1976	$4
☐ 39781	Enlloro/Jungle Fantasy	1952	$12
☐ 46013	Euterpe/Hill Where the Lord Hides	1974	$4
☐ 40115	Ev'rybody Loves Saturday Night/True or What	1953	$10
☐ 39491	Fiddle Derby/March of the Siamese Children	1951	$20
☐ 39640	Flight 33 1/3/Ba-Tu-Ca-Da	1952	$10
☐ 44446	For Those in Love/There Was a Time	1968	$5
☐ 40124	Genevieve/Suddenly	1953	$10
☐ 41328	Goin' Home Train/Isle of Paradise	1959	$8
☐ 1-835	Green Grass/I'm in the Middle of a Riddle	1950	$20

—Microgroove 33 1/3 rpm 7-inch single

☐ 6-835	Green Grass/I'm in the Middle of a Riddle	1950	$20
☐ 40949	Hey Jose/What's It Like in Paree?	1957	$12
☐ 1-607	I Cross My Fingers/Valencia	1950	$30

—Microgroove 33 1/3 rpm 7-inch single

☐ 45297	I Don't Know How to Love Him/Everything's Alright	1971	$4
☐ 40428	If Hearts Could Talk/Blue Mirage	1955	$10
☐ 39613	If I Loved You/Dizzy Fingers	1951	$20
☐ 40900	Italiano!/Bahama Lullaby	1957	$10
☐ 1-699(?)	I Was Dancing with Someone/Friendly Star	1950	$30

—Microgroove 33 1/3 rpm 7-inch single

☐ JZSP75661/2 [DJ]	I Will Follow You/Theme for Young Lovers	1963	$15

—Promo-only "Special Album Excerpt"

☐ 40482	Land of the Pharaohs/The World Is Mine	1955	$12
☐ 43326	Love Me/We're Gonna Be Alright	1965	$6
☐ 42333	Love Theme from "The Four Horsemen of the Apocalypse"/Theme from "Light in the Piazza	1962	$6
☐ 45563	Love Theme from "The Godfather"/Godfather Waltz	1972	$5
☐ 44585	MacArthur Park/Elvira Madigan Theme	1968	$5
☐ 40076	Many Times/In Love	1953	$10
☐ 41095	Maria/The Stars	1958	$8
☐ 31539 [S]	Maxine/The Minute Samba	1962	$8
☐ 39783	Minute Samba/The Girl with the Spanish Drawl	1952	$10
☐ 39641	One Night of Love/My Shawl	1952	$10
☐ 10098	Orange Blossom Special/1,2,3,4	1975	$4
☐ 39907	Over the Mountain/Caress	1952	$15
☐ 39784	Oye Negra/Jamaican Rhumba	1952	$10

— The above four comprise a box set

☐ 45051	Peppermint Hill and Strawberry Lane/The Time for Love Is Anytime	1969	$4
☐ 41181	Same Old Moon/Indiscreet	1958	$8
☐ 39559	Sleigh Ride/Christmas in Killarney	1951	$20
☐ 42991	Sloop John B/This Train	1964	$6
☐ 4-40277	Song for Sweethearts/Bubbling Over	1954	$12
☐ 43555	Song from "The Oscar"/Glass Mountain	1966	$6
☐ 41731	Sons and Lovers/Hawaiian Lullaby	1960	$8
☐ 44987	Spinning Wheel/April Fools	1969	$4
☐ 10233	Summer Place '76/Chompin'	1975	$4
☐ 31504 [S]	Swedish Rhapsody/All My Love	1962	$8
☐ 41978	The Bilbao Song/Lover's Prelude	1961	$8
☐ 3-42239	The Brass Ring/I Just Can't Wait	1961	$15

— Columbia Single 33" with small hole; orange label

☐ 4-42239	The Brass Ring/I Just Can't Wait	1961	$8
☐ 40512	The Fiddling Bullfighter/Not As a Stranger	1955	$10
☐ 41126	The Impala Theme/Pizzicato Polka	1958	$8
☐ 39192	The Loveliest Night of the Year/You Are the One	1951	$20
☐ 41655	Theme for Young Lovers/Bimini Goombay	1960	$8
☐ 41490	Theme from "A Summer Place"/Go-Go-Po-Go	1959	$8
☐ 41490 [PS]	Theme from "A Summer Place"/Go-Go-Po-Go	1959	$20
☐ 44932	Theme from "A Summer Place"/Hello Tomorrow	1969	$5

Number	Title	Yr	NM
☐ 10010	Theme from "Chinatown"/Tubular Bells	1974	$4
☐ 45619	Theme from "Kotch"/Back's Lunch	1972	$4
☐ 45401	Theme from "Summer of '42"/Tres	1971	$4
☐ 41796	Theme from "The Dark at the Top of the Stairs"/Our Language of Love	1960	$8
☐ 44412	Theme from "The Dark at the Top of the Stairs"/Tara's Theme (From "Gone with the Wind")	1967	$5
☐ 41271	The Pyramid Dance/Quia Quia	1958	$8
☐ 39944	The Song from Moulin Rouge (Where Is Your Heart)/Swedish Rhapsody	1953	$10

— Vocal on A-side by Felicia Sanders

☐ 42844	The Sound of Surf/Our Love	1963	$6
☐ 31501 [S]	The Syncopated Clock/Delicado	1962	$8
☐ 42979	The Virginian/Melody from "Mahogany	1964	$6
☐ 44876	The Windmills of Your Mind/Theme from "The Fox	1969	$4
☐ 1-681(?)	They Can't Take That Away from Me/If I Had a Magic Carpet	1950	$30

— Microgroove 33 1/3 rpm 7-inch single

☐ 40826	Till/The Last Dance	1957	$10
☐ 40543	Tropical Merengue/We Won't Say Goodbye	1955	$10
☐ 40029	Tropic Holiday/Gaviotta	1953	$10
☐ 43746	Tropic Holiday/Reza	1966	$6
☐ 39359	Waltz in Swingtown/I'll Take Romance	1951	$15

— The above four comprise a box set

☐ 40644	We All Need Love/Carmelita	1956	$10
☐ 39528	When the Saints Go Marching In/I Want to Be Near You	1951	$20
☐ 39357	While We're Young/The Girl That I Marry	1951	$15
☐ 40696	With a Little Bit of Luck/The Rain in Spain	1956	$10
☐ 40719	Wouldn't It Be Loverly/Sierra Madre	1956	$10
☐ 39638	Would You/I Talk to the Trees	1952	$15

DECCA

☐ 27544	Amor/Spring Will Be a Little Late This Year	1951	$15
☐ 27543	I'll Close My Eyes/There's No Holding Me	1951	$15

— With Hildegarde

☐ 27542	I Love You/Long Ago (and Far Away)	1951	$15

RCA VICTOR

☐ 47-4003	Beyond the Sea/El Cumbanchero	1950	$20
☐ 47-4002	Body and Soul/Cumana	1950	$20
☐ 47-3004	Deep Purple/Oodles of Noodles	1949	$20
☐ 47-4001	Perpetual Motion/Solitude	1950	$20
☐ 47-3063	Whirlwind/My Dream Concerto	1949	$20

7-Inch Extended Plays

COLUMBIA

☐ B-2529	*The Song from Moulin Rouge/Swedish Rhapsody/Delicado/Invitation	1958	$10
☐ B-2529 [PS]	Percy Faith (Hall of Fame Series)	1958	$12

FAITHFULL, MARIANNE

ISLAND

☐ 49121	Broken English/Brain Drain	1979	$5
☐ 49873	Sweetheart/For Beauty's Sake	1981	$4

LONDON

☐ 9697	As Tears Go By/Greensleeves	1964	$15
☐ 9731	Come and Stay with Me/What Have I Done Wrong	1965	$10
☐ 20012	Counting/Tomorrow's Calling	1966	$12
☐ 20012 [PS]	Counting/Tomorrow's Calling	1966	$30
☐ 9802	Go Away from My World/Oh Look Around You	1965	$10
☐ 9802 [PS]	Go Away from My World/Oh Look Around You	1965	$30
☐ 20020	Is This What I Get for Loving You/Tomorrow's Calling	1966	$10
☐ 1022	Sister Morphine/Something Better	1969	$125

— Promo worth about 50% of these values.

☐ 9780	Summer Nights/The Sha-La-La Song	1965	$10
☐ 9759	This Little Bird/Morning Sun	1965	$10

Number	Title	Yr	NM
FALCO			
A&M			
❑ 2532	Der Kommissar (The Commissoner)/Helden Von Heute (Alles Wartele Auf)	1983	$6
SIRE			
❑ 28590	The Sound of Musik (The Single Edit)/(The 7 Inch Edit)	1986	$4
❑ 28590 [PS]	The Sound of Musik (The Single Edit)/(The 7 Inch Edit)	1986	$4
FALCON, BILLY			
MANHATTAN			
❑ XY1105	Friday Night/Reachin'	1977	$6
❑ X1232	Sail Away/Reachin'	1978	$6
MCA			
❑ 41256	Business Man's Lunch/I Never Did It with Him	1980	$6
UNITED ARTISTS			
❑ X1322	Girls/Goodnight	1979	$6
FALCONS, THE (1)			
ATLANTIC			
❑ 2153	Darling/Lah-Tee-Lah-Tah	1962	$30
❑ 2179	Let's Kiss and Make Up/Take This Love I've Got	1963	$30
❑ 2207	Oh Baby/Fine, Fine, Fine	1963	$30
BIG WHEEL			
❑ 1972	Good Good Feeling/You Like You Never Been Loved	1966	$30
❑ 323/4	I Can't Help It/Standing on Guard	1966	$30
❑ 321	I Must Love You/Love, Love, Love	1966	$30
❑ 1967	Standing On Guard/I Can't Help It	1966	$30
KUDO			
❑ 661	This Heart of Mine/Romanita	1958	$400
LUPINE			
❑ 103	I Found a Love/Swim	1962	$60
❑ 1003	I Found a Love/Swim	1962	$60
❑ 124	Lonely Nights/Has It Happened to You	1962	$125
❑ 1024	Lonely Nights/Has It Happened to You	1962	$50
UNITED ARTISTS			
❑ 255	I Plus Love Plus You/Wonderful Love	1960	$30
❑ 289	Pow! You're in Love/Workin' Man's Song	1961	$30
❑ 229	The Teacher/Waiting for You	1960	$30
7-Inch Extended Plays			
❑ UAE10010	*The Teacher/Waiting for You/You're So Fine/Goddess of Angels	1960	$300
❑ UAE10010 [PS]	The Falcons	1960	$300
FALCONS, THE (2)			
CASH			
❑ 1002	Tell Me Why/I Miss You Darling	1955	$500
FLIP			
❑ 301	Stay Mine/Du-Bi-A-Do	1954	$200
FALCONS, THE (U)			
MERCURY			
❑ 70940	Baby That's It/This Day	1956	$70
SILHOUETTE			
❑ 522	Can This Be Christmas/Sent Up	1957	$300
FALLEN ANGELS, THE			
LAURIE			
❑ 3343	Eveytime I Fall in Love/I Have Found	1966	$30
❑ 3369	Have You Ever Lost a Love/A Little Love from You Will Do	1966	$30
ROULETTE			
❑ 4785	Most Children Do/Hello Girl	1967	$30
FALLENROCK			
CAPRICORN			
❑ 0227	Mary Anne/My World Begins and Ends with You	1975	$5
❑ 0211	Sayin' It's So Don't Make It So/She's a Mystery	1974	$5
FALLING PEBBLES, THE			
ALLEY CAT			
❑ 201	Lawdy Miss Clawdy/Virginia Wolf	1964	$30
FALLOWS, SCOTT, AND THE EBBTONES			
DOT			
❑ 16577	Surfing Boop-Boop-A-Do/King of Lovers	1964	$30

Number	Title	Yr	NM
FALLS, RUBY			
50 STATES			
❑ 43	Beware of the Woman (Before She Gets to Your Man)/Jump in a River of Tears	1976	$5
❑ 77	Bringing Home That Feeling/(B-side unknown)	1980	$5
❑ 50	Do the Buck Dance/Too Many Hurts, Too Many Heartaches	1977	$5
❑ 71	Empty Arms and Teardrops (Sure Go Together)/Rainy Rainy Day	1979	$5
❑ 33	He Loves Me All to Pieces/Let's Spend Summer in the Country	1975	$5
❑ 63	If That's Not Loving You (You Can't Say I Didn't Try)/Nobody's Baby But Mine	1978	$5
❑ 70	I'm Gettin' Into Your Love/Midnight Rendezvous	1979	$5
❑ 39	Show Me Where/Somewhere There's a Rainbow Over Texas	1976	$5
❑ 67	Song of the Season/There's a Holiday Feeling in the Air	1978	$6
❑ 31	Sweet Country Music/Love Away the Wrong I'm About to Do	1975	$5
❑ 60	Three Nights a Week/Give Me Some Lovin'	1978	$5
FALTERMEYER, HAROLD			
COLUMBIA			
❑ 38-06282	Top Gun Anthem/Memories	1986	$4
— With Steve Stevenson on A-side			
❑ 13-68719	Top Gun Anthem/Memories	1989	$3
— A-side with Steve Stevenson; reissue			
MCA			
❑ 52536	Axel F/Shoot Out	1985	$3
❑ 52536 [PS]	Axel F/Shoot Out	1985	$3
❑ 52641	Fletch Theme/Exotic Skates	1985	$4
❑ 52641 [PS]	Fletch Theme/Exotic Skates	1985	$4
❑ 53432	Must Be Paradise/Bad Guys	1988	$4
FAME, GEORGIE			
EPIC			
❑ 10166	Because I Love You/Bidin' My Time ('Cos I Love You)	1967	$8
❑ 10640	Fire and Rain/The Movie Star Song	1970	$6
❑ 10347	Hideaway/Runaway Child	1968	$6
❑ 10477	I'll Be Your Baby Tonight/Down Along the Cove	1969	$6
❑ 10546	Peaceful/Hideaway	1969	$6
❑ 10402	Someone to Watch Over Me/For Your Pleasure	1968	$6
❑ 10283	The Ballad of Bonnie and Clyde/Beware of the Dog	1968	$12
IMPERIAL			
❑ 66125	Blue Monday/Like We Used to Be	1965	$10
❑ 66189	El Bandido/Get Away	1966	$12
❑ 66299	Funny How Time Slips Away/Last Night	1968	$8
❑ 66220	Last Night/Sitting in the Park	1966	$12
❑ 66104	Let the Sunshine In/In the Meantime	1965	$12
ISLAND			
❑ 035	Everlovin' Woman/Ozone	1975	$5
7-Inch Extended Plays			
EPIC			
❑ 5-26368 [PS]	The Ballad of Bonnie & Clyde	1968	$25
❑ 5-26368	The Ballad of Bonnie & Clyde/Ask Me Nice/Exactly Like You//Someone to Watch Over Me/Blue Prelude/Side by Side	1968	$25
— Jukebox issue; small hole, plays at 33 1/3 rpm			
FAMILY			
REPRISE			
❑ 0881	Good Friend of Mine/No Mule Fool	1969	$8
❑ 0786	Hey Mr. Policeman/Old Songs, New Songs	1968	$8
❑ 0809	Second Generation Woman/Hometown	1969	$8
UNITED ARTISTS			
❑ 50882	Between Blue and Me/Laff and Sing	1972	$5
❑ XW171	My Friend the Sun/Glove	1973	$5
❑ 50832	Seasons/In My Own Time	1971	$6
❑ XW416	Suspicion/It's Only a Movie	1974	$5
FAMILY BROWN			
OVATION			
❑ 1174	It's Really Love This Time/Nothing Really Changes	1981	$5

Number	Title	Yr	NM
RCA			
❑ PB-13015	But It's Cheating/No One's Gonna Love Me (Like You Do)	1981	$4
❑ PB-50837	Feel the Fire/Comin' from a Blue Place	1985	$5
— Canadian number issued in U.S.			
❑ PB-13285	Some Never Stand a Chance/Arkansas Traveler	1982	$4
❑ PB-13565	We Really Got a Hold on Love/Mister and Misbehavin'	1983	$4
❑ PB-50851	What If It's Right/Guess Who	1986	$5
— Canadian number issued in U.S.			
UNITED ARTISTS			
❑ XW1090	Crossing Over/I Can't Get Used to Being Alone	1977	$6
FAMILY DOGG			
BELL			
❑ 848	Arizona/The House and the Heather	1969	$6
❑ 863	Moonshine Mary/Sympathy	1970	$6
❑ 939	This Unhappy Heart of Mine/(B-side unknown)	1970	$5
❑ 885	This Unhappy Heart of Mine/When Tomorrow Becomes Tomorrow	1970	$6
FAMILY TREE, THE			
MIRA			
❑ 228	Prince of Dreams/Live Your Own Life	1966	$10
PAULA			
❑ 329	Electric Kangaroo/Terry Tommy	1970	$6
RCA VICTOR			
❑ 47-9184	Do You Have the Time/Keepin' a Secret	1967	$8
FANNY			
CASABLANCA			
❑ 814	Butter Boy/Beggar Man	1974	$5
❑ 0009	I've Had It/First Time	1974	$5
REPRISE			
❑ 1080	Ain't That Peculiar/Think About the Children	1972	$6
❑ 1148	All Mine/I Need You Need Me	1972	$6
❑ 0963	Changing Horses/Conversation with a Copy	1970	$6
❑ 1033	Charity Ball/Place in the Country	1971	$6
❑ 0901	Ladies' Choice/New Day	1970	$6
❑ 1162	Last Night I Had a Dream/Beside Myself	1973	$6
❑ 0938	One Step at a Time/Nowhere to Run	1970	$6
FANS, THE			
DOT			
❑ 16688	I Want a Beatle for Christmas/How Far Should I Let My Heart Go Tonight	1964	$20
FANTASIES, THE			
HIT			
❑ 84	Mickey's Monkey/Cry Baby	1963	$8
FANTASTIC BAGGYS, THE			
IMPERIAL			
❑ 66092	Alone on the Beach/It Was I	1965	$60
❑ 66072	Anywhere the Girls Are/Debbie Be True	1964	$60
❑ 66047	Tell 'Em I'm Surfin'/Surfer Boy's Dream	1964	$75
FANTASTIC FOUR, THE			
EASTBOUND			
❑ 609	I Had the Whole World to Choose From/If You Need Me	1973	$8
❑ 620	I'm Falling in Love (I Feel Good All Over)/I Believe in Miracles	1974	$10
RIC-TIC			
❑ 113	Can't Stop Looking for My Baby/Can't Stop Looking for My Baby (Part 2)	1966	$200
❑ 121	Can't Stop Looking for My Baby/Just the Lonely	1967	$125
❑ 119	Girl Have Pity/Live Up to What She Thinks	1967	$30
❑ 134	Goddess of Love/As Long As the Feeling Is There	1968	$20
❑ 144	I Love You Madly/(Instrumental)	1968	$30
❑ 139	I've Got to Have You/Win or Lose	1968	$20
❑ 136	Love Is a Many-Splendored Thing/Goddess of Love	1968	$20
❑ 122	The Whole World Is a Stage/Ain't Love Wonderful	1967	$20

Number	Title	Yr	NM
❑ 130	To Share Your Love/As Long As I Live (I Live for You)	1967	$20

SOUL

Number	Title	Yr	NM
❑ 35058	I Feel Like I'm Falling in Love/Pin Point It Out	1969	$20
❑ 35052	I Love You Madly/ (Instrumental)	1968	$15
❑ 35072	On the Brighter Side of a Blue World/I'm Gonna Hurry On	1970	$15

WESTBOUND

Number	Title	Yr	NM
❑ 55419	BYOF (Bring Your Own Funk)/If This Is Love	1979	$5
❑ 5030	Don't Risk Your Happiness On Foolish Things/They Took the Show on the Road	1976	$5
❑ 5017	Have a Little Mercy/County Line	1975	$5
❑ 5032	Hideaway/They Took the Show on the Road	1976	$5
❑ 55403	I Got to Have Your Love/Ain't I Been Good to You	1977	$5
❑ 55408	Mixed Up Moods and Attitudes/Disco Fool Blues	1978	$5
❑ 55417	Sexy Lady/If This Is Love	1979	$5

FANTASTIC JOHNNY C, THE

KAMA SUTRA

Number	Title	Yr	NM
❑ 515	Good Love/You Got Your Hooks in Me	1970	$5
❑ 511	Let's Do It Together/Peace Treaty	1970	$5

PHILCO-FORD

Number	Title	Yr	NM
❑ HP-39	Boogaloo Down Broadway/Got What You Need	1969	$30

—*4-inch plastic "Hip Pocket Record" with color sleeve*

PHIL.-LA OF SOUL

Number	Title	Yr	NM
❑ 320	Baby I Need You/Some Kind of Wonderful	1968	$6
❑ 305	Boogaloo Down Broadway/Look What Love Can Make You Do	1967	$8
❑ 361	Don't Depend on Me/Waitin' for the Rain	1973	$4
❑ 309	Got What You Need/New Love	1968	$6
❑ 315	Hitch It to the Horse/Cool Broadway	1968	$6
❑ 327	Is There Anything Better Than Making Love/New Love	1969	$6

FANTASTIC ZOO, THE

DOUBLE SHOT

Number	Title	Yr	NM
❑ 109	Light Show/Silent Movies	1967	$30
❑ 105	Midnight Snack/This Calls for a Celebration	1966	$30

FANTASTICS, THE (1)

BELL

Number	Title	Yr	NM
❑ 45157	(Love Me) Love the Life I Lead/Old Rags and Tatters	1971	$20
❑ 977	Something Old, Something New/High and Dry	1971	$30

DERAM

Number	Title	Yr	NM
❑ 7528	Face to Face with Heartache/This Must Be My Rainy Day	1970	$20

FANTASTICS, THE (2)

RCA VICTOR

Number	Title	Yr	NM
❑ 47-7572	There Goes My Love/I Wanna Be a Millionaire Hobo	1965	$20

—*Evidently, a reissue with the same number, but the dog on side of label rather than on top, exists*

Number	Title	Yr	NM
❑ 47-7572	There Goes My Love/Millionaire Hobo	1959	$50

—*Black label, dog on top*

Number	Title	Yr	NM
❑ 47-7664	This Is My Wedding Day/I Got a Zero	1960	$50

UNITED ARTISTS

Number	Title	Yr	NM
❑ 309	Dancing Doll/I Told You Once	1961	$60

FANTASTICS, THE (3)

HIT

Number	Title	Yr	NM
❑ 340	1-2-3, Red Light/The House That Jack Built	1968	$8

—*B-side by Kathy Shannon*

Number	Title	Yr	NM
❑ 297	A Whiter Shade of Pale/San Francisco (Be Sure to Wear Flowers in Your Hair)	1967	$8

—*B-side by Bobby Sims*

Number	Title	Yr	NM
❑ 289	Bernadette/I Never Loved a Man the Way I Love You	1967	$8

—*B-side by Odessa Crawford*

Number	Title	Yr	NM
❑ 324	Cowboys to Girls/Tighten Up	1968	$8

—*B-side by the Classmates*

Number	Title	Yr	NM
❑ 293	Here Comes My Baby/I Got Rhythm	1967	$8

—*B-side by the Jalopy Five*

Number	Title	Yr	NM
❑ 302	Light My Fire./Mercy, Mercy, Mercy	1967	$8

—*B-side by the Chords (2)*

Number	Title	Yr	NM
❑ 329	Mony Mony/I Wanna Live	1968	$8

—*B-side by Ed Hardin*

Number	Title	Yr	NM
❑ 344	Over You/My Special Angel	1968	$8

—*B-side by the Chords (2)*

Number	Title	Yr	NM
❑ 314	Pata Pata/Massachusetts	1967	$8

—*B-side by the Chords (2)*

Number	Title	Yr	NM
❑ 309	People Are Strange/Please Love Me Forever	1967	$8

—*B-side by Bobby Sims*

Number	Title	Yr	NM
❑ 336	Stoned Soul Picnic/Hurdy Gurdy Man	1968	$8

—*B-side by the Jalopy Five*

Number	Title	Yr	NM
❑ 352	Touch Me/Everyday People	1969	$8

—*B-side by the Jalopy Five*

Number	Title	Yr	NM
❑ 348	White Room/Who's Making Love	1968	$8

—*B-side by Bobby Sims*

FANTASTICS, THE (U)

SCORPIO

Number	Title	Yr	NM
❑ 407	Malaguena/Dance for an Unnamed Gypsy Queen	1966	$30

SOUND STAGE 7

Number	Title	Yr	NM
❑ 2565	Have a Little You/Me and You	1966	$15

FANTASY

IMPERIAL

Number	Title	Yr	NM
❑ 66394	Painted Horse/I Got the Fever	1969	$10

LIBERTY

Number	Title	Yr	NM
❑ 56190	Stoned Cowboy/Understand	1970	$8

FAR CRY

VANGUARD

Number	Title	Yr	NM
❑ 35085	Shapes/Hellhound	1969	$10

FARAGHER BROTHERS, THE

ABC

Number	Title	Yr	NM
❑ 12277	Follow My Heart/I'm Wakin' Up	1977	$5
❑ 12191	It's All Right/Give It Up	1976	$5
❑ 12259	Thanx a Lot/You Know That	1977	$5

POLYDOR

Number	Title	Yr	NM
❑ 2057	Mystic Eyes/Those Days Are Gone	1980	$5
❑ 14563	Open Your Eyes/Long Hot Climb	1979	$5
❑ 2038	Say When/Had to Leave	1980	$5
❑ 14533	Stay the Night/That's a Start	1979	$5

FARDON, DON

CAPITOL

Number	Title	Yr	NM
❑ 3929	St. Matthew, St. Mark, St. Luke and St. John/Lola	1974	$5

CHELSEA

Number	Title	Yr	NM
❑ 78-0115	Delta Queen/Home Town Baby	1973	$6

DECCA

Number	Title	Yr	NM
❑ 32696	Belfast Boy/Echoes of the Cheers	1970	$6

GNP CRESCENDO

Number	Title	Yr	NM
❑ 421	Sally Goes 'Round the Moon/How Do You Break a Broken Heart	1969	$6
❑ 418	Take a Heart/How Do You Break a Broken Heart	1968	$6
❑ 405	Indian Reservation (The Lament of the Cherokee)/Dreaming Room	1968	$8

ROXBURY

Number	Title	Yr	NM
❑ BRBO-0159	Louisiana/Lady Zelda	1973	$5

FARGO, DONNA

ABC/DOT

Number	Title	Yr	NM
❑ 17660	Don't Be Angry/You Don't Mess Around with Jim	1976	$4
❑ 17557	Hello Little Bluebird/2 Sweet 2 Be 4 Gotten	1975	$5
❑ 17692	I'd Love You to Want Me/How Close You Came (To Being Gone)	1977	$4
❑ 17541	If Do Feel Good/Only the Strong	1974	$5
❑ 17579	Whatever I Say/Rain Song	1975	$5
❑ 17586	What Will the New Year Bring/A Woman's Prayer	1975	$5

CHALLENGE

Number	Title	Yr	NM
❑ 59387	Daddy/Sticks and Stones	1968	$12
❑ 59391	Wishful Thinking/All That's Keeping Me Alive	1968	$10

CLEVELAND INTERNATIONAL

Number	Title	Yr	NM
❑ 1	My Heart Will Always Belong to You/Reasons to Be	1984	$4

COLUMBIA

Number	Title	Yr	NM
❑ 04097	The Sign of the Times/Reasons to Be	1983	$4

COUNTRY HEARTS

Number	Title	Yr	NM
❑ CH-001 [DJ]	My Side of the Bed/Country Singer's Wife	1970	$40

—*Promo-only release*

DECCA

Number	Title	Yr	NM
❑ 33001	Daddy/Sticks and Stones	1972	$8

DOT

Number	Title	Yr	NM
❑ 17429	Funny Face/How Close You Came (To Being Gone)	1972	$6
❑ 17491	I'll Try a Little Bit Harder/All About a Feeling	1973	$5
❑ 17476	Little Girl Gone/Just Call Me	1973	$5
❑ 17476 [PS]	Little Girl Gone/Just Call Me	1973	$8
❑ 17444	Superman/Forever Is As Far As I Could Go	1973	$5
❑ 17409	The Happiest Girl in the Whole U.S.A./The Awareness of Nothing	1972	$6
❑ 17409 [PS]	The Happiest Girl in the Whole U.S.A./The Awareness of Nothing	1972	$8

MCA

Number	Title	Yr	NM
❑ 51209	Say "I Do"/All About a Feeling	1981	$4

MERCURY

Number	Title	Yr	NM
❑ 888093-7	Me and You/I've Laid Too Many Eggs	1986	$3
❑ 888680-7	Members Only/Funny Face	1987	$3

—*A-side: With Billy Joe Royal*

Number	Title	Yr	NM
❑ 888043-7	Winners/I've Laid Too Many Eggs	1986	$3
❑ 884712-7	Woman of the 80's/You Were Always There	1986	$3

RAMCO

Number	Title	Yr	NM
❑ 1988	Who's Been Playin' House/You Reach for the Bottle	1967	$20

RCA

Number	Title	Yr	NM
❑ PB-13329	Did We Have to Go This Far (To Say Goodbye)/All I Need to Know	1982	$4
❑ PB-13264	It's Hard to Be the Dreamer/I Just Saw My Reflection in You	1982	$4

WARNER BROS.

Number	Title	Yr	NM
❑ 8643	Another Goodbye/Changes in My Life	1978	$4
❑ 8867	Daddy/For the Rest of My Life	1979	$4
❑ 8509	Do I Love You (Yes in Every Way)/Dee Dee	1977	$5
❑ 8227	I've Loved You All the Way/One of God's Children	1976	$5
❑ 49514	Land of Cotton/I Still Believe in You	1980	$4
❑ 49757	Lonestar Cowboy/Utah Song	1981	$4
❑ 49757 [PS]	Lonestar Cowboy/Utah Song	1981	$6
❑ 8305	Mockingbird Hill/Second Chance	1976	$5
❑ 8186	Mr. Doodles/If You Can't Love All of Me	1976	$5
❑ 49093	Preacher Berry/I Don't Know What to Do	1979	$4
❑ 49575	Seeing Is Believing/Look What You've Done	1980	$4
❑ 8431	Shame on Me/Hey, Mister Music Man	1977	$5
❑ 8722	Somebody Special/Changes in My Life	1978	$4
❑ 8375	That Was Yesterday/Cricket Song	1977	$5
❑ 49183	Walk On By/I Wrote This Song Just for You	1980	$4

7-Inch Extended Plays

DOT

Number	Title	Yr	NM
❑ JBA26000 [PS]	The Happiest Girl in the Whole U.S.A	1972	$12
❑ JBA26000	Would Have Been Just Perfect/Daddy Dumplin'/Manhattan, Kansas!/Johnny B. Goode/A Little Somethin' (To Hang On To)/Society's Got Us	1972	$10

—*Jukebox issue; small hole, plays at 33 1/3 rpm*

FARLOWE, CHRIS

GENERAL AMERICAN

Number	Title	Yr	NM
❑ 718	What You Gonna Do/Just a Dream	1964	$20

IMMEDIATE

Number	Title	Yr	NM
❑ 5005	Handbags and Gladrags/Everyone Makes a Mistake	1968	$12
❑ 5002	Paint It Black/You're So Good to Me	1967	$10
❑ 5011	What Have I Been Doing/Paint It Black	1968	$10

Number	Title	Yr	NM
MGM			
❏ 13567	Out of Time/Baby Make It Soon	1966	$30

—A-side is a Mick Jagger-Keith Richards composition only later recorded by the Rolling Stones.

Number	Title	Yr	NM
POLYDOR			
❏ 14008	Circles 'Round the Sun/ Save Your Tears	1969	$8
❏ 14013	Medicated Goo/Betty Lou	1970	$8

FARMER BOYS, THE

Number	Title	Yr	NM
CAPITOL			
❏ F3569	Cool Down Mame/ Oh How It Hurts	1956	$30
❏ F3732	Flash, Crash and Thunder/ Someone to Love	1957	$30
❏ F3322	Flip Flop/Charming Betsy	1956	$30
❏ F3162	Lend a Helping Hand/ Onions, Onions	1955	$30
❏ F3476	My Baby Done Left Me/Somehow, Someway, Someday	1956	$30

FARNER, MARK, AND DON BREWER
Both later of GRAND FUNK RAILROAD.

Number	Title	Yr	NM
LUCKY ELEVEN			
❏ 366	Does It Matter to You Girl/ We Gotta Have Love	1968	$15
❏ 366 [PS]	Does It Matter to You Girl/ We Gotta Have Love	1968	$50

FARNER, MARK

Number	Title	Yr	NM
ATLANTIC			
❏ 3510	When a Man Loves a Woman/If It Took All Day	1978	$4
LUCKY ELEVEN			
❏ 352	Down in the Valley/I Got News for You	1968	$12

FARNHAM, JOHN

Number	Title	Yr	NM
CAPITOL			
❏ 3522	Don't You Know It's Magic/ Sweet Cherry Wine	1973	$12

—As "Johnny Farnham"

Number	Title	Yr	NM
❏ 2128	Sadie the Cleaning Lady/In My Room	1968	$10

—As "Johnny Farnham"

Number	Title	Yr	NM
MCA			
❏ 52798	Break the Ice/Thunder in Your Heart	1986	$4
MCA CURB			
❏ 52580	Love (It's Just the Way It Goes)/Ragtop Day	1984	$5

—A-side with Sarah M. Taylor

Number	Title	Yr	NM
RCA			
❏ 5264-7-R	Pressure Down/Trouble	1986	$4
❏ 8915-7-R	Two Strong Hearts/ Some Do, Some Don't	1988	$4

FARON'S FLAMINGOS

Number	Title	Yr	NM
COLUMBIA			
❏ 43018	Let's Stomp/I Can Tell	1964	$30

—B-side by Rory Storm and the Hurricanes

FARQUAHR

Number	Title	Yr	NM
ELEKTRA			
❏ 45735	Holy Moses/My Island	1971	$6
VERVE FORECAST			
❏ 5077	My Eggs Don't Taste the Same Without You/ Sister Theresa's East River Orphanage	1968	$8

FARR, GARY, AND THE T-BONES

Number	Title	Yr	NM
EPIC			
❏ 9832	Don't Stop and Stare/ Give All She's Got	1965	$15

FARRELL AND THE FLAMES

Number	Title	Yr	NM
FRANSIL			
❏ 14	Dreams and Memories/ You'll Be Sorry	1961	$400

FARREN, MICK

Number	Title	Yr	NM
ORK			
❏ 81980 [B]	Play With Fire/Lost Johnny	1977	$40

FASCINATIONS, THE (1)

Number	Title	Yr	NM
ABC-PARAMOUNT			
❏ 10387	Mama Didn't Lie/ Someone Like You	1962	$30

—Some of the ABC-Paramount pressings are misspelled "Fasinations

Number	Title	Yr	NM
❏ 10443	Tears In My Eyes/You're Gonna Be Sorry	1963	$30

Number	Title	Yr	NM
MAYFIELD			
❏ 7714	Girls Are Out to Get You/You'll Be Sorry	1966	$10
❏ 7716	I Can't Stay Away from You/(B-side unknown)	1967	$10
❏ 7711	(Say It Isn't So) Say You'd Never Go/I'm So Lucky	1966	$10

FASCINATIONS, THE (2)

Number	Title	Yr	NM
DORE			
❏ 593	If I Had Your Love/Why	1961	$60
PAXLEY			
❏ 750	If I Had Your Love/Why	1960	$200

FASCINATIONS, THE (U)

Number	Title	Yr	NM
A&G			
❏ 101	I'm Gonna Cry/Since You Went Away	1972	$30
SURE			
❏ 106	It's Midnight/Boom Bada Boom	1960	$100
❏ 106	Midnight/Boom Bada Boom	1960	$120

FASCINATORS, THE (1)

Number	Title	Yr	NM
BIM BAM BOOM			
❏ 110	Oh, Rose Marie/Forgive Me, My Darling	1974	$10
CAPITOL			
❏ F-4053	Chapel Bells/I Wonder Who	1958	$200
❏ 4544	Chapel Bells/I Wonder Who	1961	$100
❏ F-4137	Come to Paradise/Who Do You Think You Are	1959	$200
❏ F-4247	Oh Rose Marie/Fried Chicken and Macaroni	1959	$200

FASCINATORS, THE (2)

Number	Title	Yr	NM
BLUE LAKE			
❏ 112	Can't Stop/Don't Give My Love Away	1953	$2000

FASCINATORS, THE (3)

Number	Title	Yr	NM
BURN			
❏ 845	I'll Be Gone/Can't You See I'm Lonely	1965	$30

FASCINATORS, THE (4)

Number	Title	Yr	NM
DOOTO			
❏ 441	Teardrop Eyes/ Shivers and Shakes	1958	$70

FASCINATORS, THE (5)

Number	Title	Yr	NM
YOUR COPY			
❏ 1136	My Beauty, My Own/ Don't Give It Away	1954	$1000
❏ 1135	The Bells of My Heart/ Sweet Baby	1954	$1000

—Black vinyl

Number	Title	Yr	NM
❏ 1135	The Bells of My Heart/ Sweet Baby	1954	$2000

—Red vinyl

FASCINATORS, THE (U)

Number	Title	Yr	NM
KING			
❏ 5119	Cuddle Up with Carolyn/Tee Hee	1958	$60

FASHIONS, THE (1)

Number	Title	Yr	NM
CAMEO			
❏ 331	Baby That's Me/Nick and Joe Callin'	1964	$12
ELMOR			
❏ 301	Please Let It Be Me/ Fairy Tales	1961	$30
EMBER			
❏ 1084	I Just Got a Letter/ Try My Love	1962	$15
V-TONE			
❏ 202	I'm Dreaming of You/I Love You So	1959	$40

—Orange label

Number	Title	Yr	NM
❏ 202	I'm Dreaming of You/I Love You So	1959	$30

—Blue label

Number	Title	Yr	NM
❏ 202	I'm Dreaming of You/ Lonesome Road	1959	$60
WARWICK			
❏ 646	All I Want/Dearest One	1961	$30

FASHIONS, THE (2)

Number	Title	Yr	NM
FELSTED			
❏ 8689	Surfer's Memories/ Surfin' Back to School	1964	$40

FASHIONS, THE (3)

Number	Title	Yr	NM
PHIL-L.A. OF SOUL			
❏ 354	I Don't Mind Doin' It/ What Goes Up (Must Come Down)	1972	$6

FASHIONS, THE (4)

Number	Title	Yr	NM
20TH CENTURY FOX			
❏ 6710	Lover's Stand/Only Those in Love	1968	$8

FASTBACKS, THE

Number	Title	Yr	NM
NO THREES			
❏ 05	It's Your Birthday/You Can't Be Happy	1981	$40

— With drummer Duff McKagan, pre-Guns N' Roses

Number	Title	Yr	NM
❏ 05 [PS]	It's Your Birthday/You Can't Be Happy	1981	$40
7-Inch Extended Plays			
❏ 009	In the Summer/You Can't Be Happy/Everything That I Don't Need/Queen of Eyes	1989	$8
❏ 009 [PS]	In the Summer/You Can't Be Happy/Everything That I Don't Need/Queen of Eyes	1989	$8

FASTER PUSSYCAT

Number	Title	Yr	NM
ELEKTRA			
❏ 69413	Babylon/Smash House	1988	$4
❏ 69413 [PS]	Babylon/Smash House	1988	$4
❏ 69437	Bathroom Wall/Cathouse	1987	$6
❏ 69274	Poison Ivy/Tattoo	1989	$4

FASTEST GROUP ALIVE, THE

Number	Title	Yr	NM
TEEN			
❏ 100	The Bears/Beside	1966	$40
VALIANT			
❏ 759	Lullabye/5:15 Sports	1967	$30
❏ 754	The Bears/Beside	1966	$30

FAT BOYS

Number	Title	Yr	NM
SUTRA			
❏ 139	Can You Feel It/Stick 'Em	1984	$6
❏ 149	Chillin' with the Refrigerator/ (B-side unknown)	1985	$8
❏ 148	Don't Be Stupid/ (B-side unknown)	1985	$8
❏ 147	Hard Core Reggae/ Human Beat Box #2	1985	$8
❏ 156	In the House/Breakdown	1986	$6
❏ 152	Sex Machine/Human Beat Box Part III	1986	$8
❏ 144	The Fat Boys Are Back/ (Instrumental)	1985	$6
TIN PAN APPLE			
❏ 887894-7	Are You Ready for Freddy/Back and Forth	1988	$3
❏ 887894-7 [PS]	Are You Ready for Freddy/Back and Forth	1988	$3
❏ 885766-7	Falling in Love//Protect Yourself/My Nuts	1987	$4
❏ 885766-7 [PS]	Falling in Love//Protect Yourself/My Nuts	1987	$4
❏ 889746-7	Lie-Z/On and On	1989	$4
❏ 871010-7	Louie, Louie/All Day Lover	1988	$3
❏ 871010-7 [PS]	Louie, Louie/All Day Lover	1988	$3
❏ 887571-7	The Twist (Yo, Twist!)/ (Buffapella)	1988	$3

—With Chubby Checker

Number	Title	Yr	NM
❏ 887571-7 [PS]	The Twist (Yo, Twist!)/ (Buffapella)	1988	$3
❏ 885960-7	Wipeout/Crushin'	1987	$4

—A-side with the Beach Boys

Number	Title	Yr	NM
❏ 885960-7 [PS]	Wipeout/Crushin'	1987	$4
❏ PRO525-7 [DJ]	Wipeout (same on both sides?)	1987	$10

—Possibly does not give credit to the Beach Boys on label

Number	Title	Yr	NM
WARNER BROS.			
❏ 28829	All You Can Eat/ Pick Up the Pace	1985	$8

—B-side by U.T.F.O.

FAT CITY

Number	Title	Yr	NM
ABC PROBE			
❏ 469	Wall Street/City Cat	1969	$6
PARAMOUNT			
❏ 0162	I Guess He'd Rather Be in Colorado/Morning Go Away	1972	$6
❏ 0176	Workingman's Day/ Hey, Loretta	1972	$5

FATBACK

Number	Title	Yr	NM
COTILLION			
99749	Call Out My Name/I Love You So	1984	$3
99665	Girls on My Mind/Osiris (There's a Party Goin' On)	1985	$3
99642	Lover Undercover/ (B-side unknown)	1985	$3
EVENT			
227	(Are You Ready) Do the Bus Stop/Gotta Learn to Dance	1975	$5
224	(Hey I) Feel Real Good (Part 1)/(Hey I) Feel Real Good (Part 2)	1975	$5
229	Spanish Hustle/Put Your Love (In My Tender Care)	1976	$5
219	Wicki-Wacky/Can't Fight the Flame	1974	$5
PERCEPTION			
520	Soul March/To Be with You	1973	$5
526	Street Dance/Goin' to See My Baby	1973	$5
SPRING			
3016	Angel/Concrete Jungle	1981	$4
3012	Backstrokin'/Love Spell	1980	$4
188	Boogie Freak/I'm Fired Up	1978	$5
195	(Do the) Boogie Woogie/Hesitation	1979	$5
171	Double Dutch/ Spank the Baby	1977	$5
191	Freak the Freak the Funk (Rock)/Wild Dreams	1979	$5
3008	Gotta Get My Hands on Some (Money)/Street Band	1980	$4
181	I Like Girls/Get Out on the Dance Floor	1978	$5
3032	Is This the Future?/ Double Love Affair	1983	$4
3037	I Wanna Be Your Lover/ (B-side unknown)	1984	$4
3015	Let's Do It Again/Come and Get the Love	1980	$4
3005	Love in Perfect Harmony/ Disco Bass	1979	$4
177	Master Booty/Zodiac Man	1977	$5
180	Mile High/Midnight Freak	1978	$5
3025	On the Floor/Chillin' Out	1982	$4
165	Party Time/Groovy Kind of Day	1976	$5
3026	She's My Shining Star/UFO (Unidentified Funk Object)	1982	$4
3018	Take It Any Way You Want It/Lady Groove	1981	$4
168	The Booty/If That's the Way You Want It	1976	$5
3030	The Girl Is Fine (So Fine)/ (B-side unknown)	1983	$4

FAUN

Members of JOURNEY.

Number	Title	Yr	NM
GREGAR			
7000	Better Dig What You Find/I Asked My Mother	1969	$30
7001	Son of a Literate Man/ Yes I'm Really Lonely	1969	$30

FAWNS, THE

Number	Title	Yr	NM
APT			
25015	Come On/Until I Die	1958	$30

FAYE, LITTLE RITA

Number	Title	Yr	NM
CAPITOL			
4823	Salt and Pepper/Don't You Come Back at All	1962	$30

— As "Rita Faye"

5998	Thinking About Hurting You/Nothing Else to Lose	1967	$15

— As "Rita Faye"

MGM			
K11565	Alabama/Johnny's Got a Sweetheart	1953	$30
K12483	Bonaparte's Retreat/ Out at the Pool	1957	$20

— As "Rita Faye"

K12203	E-A-S-T-E-R/Eldo, the Easter Bunny	1956	$20
K11867	I Want Santa Claus for Christmas/There Really Is a Santa Claus	1954	$30
K12047	I Wonder When We'll Ever Know/Wait for the Light to Shine	1955	$20
K12024	Little Painted Horse/ Something Teacher Never Taught Me	1955	$20
K11757	Mama's Little Helper/ Don't You Play with Billy	1954	$30
K11923	Mommie's Real Peculiar/I Love You More and More	1955	$20
K11664	Mr. Lightnin' Bug/I'm a Problem Child	1954	$30
K11625	The Miracle of Christmas/I Fell Out of a Christmas Tree	1953	$30
K12104	The Santa Claus Parade/Sleigh Bells, Reindeer and Snow	1955	$20

Number	Title	Yr	NM
K12163	Why Don't You Love Me/Lovesick Blues	1955	$20
STOP			
353	Follow It/I Think I'll Be Going	1969	$20

— As "Rita Faye"

FEAR

Number	Title	Yr	NM
CRIMINAL RECORDS			
0(no cat #)	I Love Livin' in the City/ Now Your Dead	1978	$250
0(no cat #) [PS]	I Love Livin' in the City/ Now Your Dead	1978	$250
SLASH			
900	Fuck Christmas/*Uck Christmas	1979	$50

— Not issued with picture sleeve; add 20% for plain white sleeve rubber-stamped with Christmas tree

FEAR ITSELF

Number	Title	Yr	NM
DOT			
17278	The Letter/Born Under a Bad Sign	1969	$8

FEATHER

Number	Title	Yr	NM
COLUMBIA			
4-45405	Choo Choo Nairobi/ Down to the Wire	1971	$8
4-45231	The Fifth Stone/No Time for Sorrow	1970	$8
WHITE WHALE			
353	Friends/Salli	1970	$6

FEATHERBED

Number	Title	Yr	NM
BELL			
971	Amy/Morning	1971	$70

— Stock copies are much scarcer than promo copies

45133 [DJ]	Could It Be Magic (mono/stereo)	1971	$125

— Stock copy may not exist

FEATHERS, CHARLIE

Number	Title	Yr	NM
FLIP			
503	I've Been Deceived/ Peeping Eyes	1955	$500
HOLIDAY INN			
114	Deep Elm Blues/ Nobody's Darling	1962	$200
KING			
4971	Can't Hardly Stand It/ Everybody's Lovin' My Baby	1956	$600
4997	One Hand Loose/ Bottle to the Baby	1956	$500
5043	When You Come Around/ Too Much Alike	1957	$400
MEMPHIS			
103	Wild, Wild Party/Today and Tomorrow	1961	$125
METEOR			
5032	Tongue-Tied Jill/Get With It	1956	$1500

— Maroon label

5032	Tongue-Tied Jill/Get With It	1956	$400

— Blue label

ROLLIN' ROCK			
45-025	That Certain Female/ She Set Me Free	1978	$8
SUN			
231	Defrost Your Heart/ Wedding Gown of White	1956	$600
503	I've Been Deceived/ Peeping Eyes	1956	$600
WAL-MAY			
101	Dinky John/South of Chicago	1960	$200

FEATHERS, THE (1)

Number	Title	Yr	NM
ALADDIN			
3277	I Need a Girl/Standing Right There	1955	$200
CLASSIC ARTISTS			
109	Charlene/Irene My Darling	1989	$6

— Black vinyl

109	Charlene/Irene My Darling	1989	$30

— Blue vinyl

HOLLYWOOD			
1051	Dear One/Lonesome Tonight	1956	$3000

— VG 1000; VG+ 2000

SHOW TIME			
1106	Love Only You/ Crashing the Party	1955	$200
1105	Why Don't You Write Me/Busy as a Bee	1954	$200
1105	Why Don't You Write Me/ Where Did Caledonia Go	1954	$200

FEATHERS, THE (2)

Number	Title	Yr	NM
KAPP			
887	Give Him Love/To Be Loved by You	1968	$200

FEATHERS, THE (U)

Number	Title	Yr	NM
VEEP			
1200	The Dummy/Them Onions	1964	$8

FEDERALS, THE (1)

Number	Title	Yr	NM
CAPITOL			
5526	Bucketful of Love/Leah	1965	$10

FEDERALS, THE (2)

Number	Title	Yr	NM
DELUXE			
6112	Come Go with Me/Cold Cash	1957	$100
FURY			
1009	Dear Lorraine/She's My Girl	1958	$125
1005	While Our Hearts are Young/ You're the One I Love	1957	$125

FELDER, DON

Also see EAGLES.

Number	Title	Yr	NM
ASYLUM			
69784	Bad Girls/Night Owl	1983	$4
69743	Who Tonight/Winners	1984	$3
69673	Winters/(B-side unknown)	1984	$3
FULL MOON/ASYLUM			
47244	All of You/True Companion	1981	$4

— B-side by Donald Fagen

47175	Heavy Metal (Takin' a Ride)/All of You	1981	$4
47175 [PS]	Heavy Metal (Takin' a Ride)/All of You	1981	$4

FELDERS ORIOLES

Number	Title	Yr	NM
MERCURY			
72480	Down Home Girl/Misty	1965	$12

FELDMAN, VICTOR

Number	Title	Yr	NM
AVA			
123	Theme from "Lawrence of Arabia"/Theme from "David & Lisa"	1963	$10
INFINITY			
020	A Taste of Honey/Valerie	1962	$10
030	Moon River/Theme from 9073	1963	$10
PACIFIC JAZZ			
88127	Do the Jake/Have a Heart	1966	$8
VEE JAY			
662	Green Dolphin Street/ Overfat Cat	1965	$10
630	Hard to Find/Make Me a Present of You	1964	$12

FELICIANO, JOSE

Number	Title	Yr	NM
MOTOWN			
1673 [DJ]	Balada Del Pianista (same on both sides)	1983	$4

— May be promo only

1618	Free Me from My Freedom/I Second That Emotion	1982	$4
1524	I Second That Emotion/Let's Make Love Over the Telephone	1981	$4
1530	I Wanna Be Where You Are/Let's Make Love Over the Telephone	1981	$4
1674	Let's Find Each Other Tonight/Cuidado	1983	$4
1679	Lonely Teardrops/Cuidado	1983	$4
1647	Samba Pa Ti (Long)/ Samba Pa Ti (Short)	1982	$4
1517	The Drought Is Over/ Everybody Loves Me	1981	$4
PRIVATE STOCK			
45,085	Angela (Spanish)/ (B-side unknown)	1976	$4
45,062	Angela/Willful Strut	1975	$4
45,143	Marguerita/(B-side unknown)	1977	$4
45,151	The Air That I Breathe/I Love Making Love to You	1977	$4
45,103	Why/(B-side unknown)	1976	$4
RCA VICTOR			
47-9085	A Man and a Woman/And We Were Lovers (Theme from The Sand Pebbles)	1967	$8
PB-10145	Chico and the Man/Hard Times in El Barrio	1974	$4
74-0545	Come Down Jesus/Only Once	1971	$5
74-0586	Daytime Dreams/Fireworks	1971	$5
47-8425	Everybody Do the Click/ Ginny's Garden	1964	$8
74-0404	Feliz Navidad/The Little Drummer Boy	1970	$10
74-0341	Girl (You'll Never Get Away from Me)/Younger Generation	1970	$6
PB-10094	Golden Lady/Virgo	1974	$4
47-9714	Hey Baby/My World Is Empty Without You	1969	$6

Number	Title	Yr	NM
❏ 74-0975	Hey Look at the Sun/ Compartments	1973	$5
❏ 47-9641	Hi-Heel Sneakers/ Hitchcock Railway	1968	$6
❏ 47-8884	(I Love You) For Sentimental Reasons/ Quit While You're Ahead	1966	$8
❏ 74-0476	I Only Want to Say/ Watch It With My Heart	1971	$5
❏ APBO-0140	I Want to Learn a Love Song/Find Somebody	1973	$5
❏ 47-9550	Light My Fire/ California Dreamin'	1968	$8
❏ 74-0768	Magnolia/It Doesn't Matter Anyhow	1972	$5
❏ 47-9739	Marley Purt Drive/The Old Turkey Buzzard	1969	$6
❏ 47-9912	Pegao/Life Is That Way	1970	$6
❏ 74-0452	Shake a Hand/There's No One About	1971	$5
❏ 74-0290	So Long, Paul/Here Comes Werbley	1969	$12
—As "Werbley Finster"			
❏ 74-0358	Susie Q/Destiny	1970	$6
❏ APBO-0206	The Gypsy/I Like What You Give	1974	$4
❏ 47-9665	The Star Spangled Banner/ And I Love Her	1968	$10
❏ PB-10306	Twilight Time/Stay with Me	1975	$4
❏ 47-8683	Where I'm Goin'/A Woman, a Lover, a Friend	1965	$8
❏ 74-0841	Where Is My Woman/ One More Mile	1972	$5
❏ 47-9807	Wichita Lineman/Point of View	1969	$6

FELICITY
WILSON
Number	Title	Yr	NM
❏ 101	Hurtin'/I'll Try It	1965	$40

FELIX AND THE ESCORTS
JAG
Number	Title	Yr	NM
❏ 685	The Syracuse/Save	1964	$200

FELL, TERRY
GILT EDGE
Number	Title	Yr	NM
❏ 5071	Dreamer's Paradise/Yesterday	1953	$40
❏ 5076	Fireball Boogie/I Can Hear You Clucking	1953	$40
❏ 5084	Smoking Cornsilks/ Hillbilly Impersonations	1954	$40
LODE
| ❏ 2004 | Child Bride/Paper Kite | 1959 | $30 |
RCA VICTOR
❏ 47-6707	Caveman/Play the Music Louder	1956	$30
❏ 47-9719	I Are a Millionaire/I've Never Been Sober	1969	$8
❏ 47-6621	I Can Hear You Cluckin'/ Don't Do It, Joe	1956	$30
❏ 47-6444	Over and Over/If I Didn't Have You	1956	$30
❏ 47-6353	That's the Way the Big Ball Bounces/What Am I Worth	1955	$30
❏ 47-6256	That's What I Like/I Really Go Crazy	1955	$30
❏ 47-6515	Wham Bam! Hot Ziggity Zam/Consolation Prize	1956	$30
SCORPION
| ❏ 0508 | Coffee Jim the Trucker/ Big Truck Stop in the Sky | 1976 | $6 |
SIMS
| ❏ 192 | If I Could Learn to Love You Less/Music City U.S.A. | 1964 | $15 |
X
❏ 010	Don't Drop It/Truck Driving Man	1954	$40
❏ 078	Get Aboard My Wagon/You Don't Give a Hang About Me	1955	$30
❏ 0149	I'm Hot to Trot/Fa-So-La	1955	$30
❏ 0114	Mississippi River Shuffle/ He's in Love with You	1955	$30
❏ 069	We Wanna See Santa Do the Mambo/Let's Stay Together Till After Christmas	1954	$40
❏ 2315	Give Me the Light/First Kiss	1981	$6
❏ 2242	Love on the Phone/Bad Boy	1980	$5
❏ 2263	Permanent Damage/Bad Boy	1980	$5

FELONY
CBX
Number	Title	Yr	NM
❏ DR1004	The Fanatic/Positively Negative	1982	$20
❏ DR1004 [PS]	The Fanatic/Positively Negative	1982	$20
ROCK 'N' ROLL
| ❏ ZS4 04220 | Pied Piper/Positively Negative | 1983 | $5 |
| ❏ ZS4 03497 | The Fanatic/The Girl Ain't Straight | 1983 | $4 |

FELTS, NARVEL
ABC
Number	Title	Yr	NM
❏ 12441	Everlasting Love/Small Enough to Crawl	1978	$5
❏ 12414	One Run for the Roses/ Lie to Me (Darling)	1978	$5
ABC DOT
| ❏ 17569 | Funny How Time Slips Away/No One Knows | 1975 | $5 |

Number	Title	Yr	NM
❏ 17700	I Don't Hurt Anymore/ When We Were Together	1977	$5
❏ 17620	Lonely Teardrops/ Remember You	1976	$5
❏ 17664	My Good Thing's Gone/I'm Afraid to Be Alone	1976	$5
❏ 17643	My Prayer/If Ever Two Were One (Then Surely We Are)	1976	$5
❏ 17731	Please/Blue Darlin'	1977	$5
❏ 17598	Somebody Hold Me (Until She Passes By)/Away	1975	$5
❏ 17680	The Feeling's Right/ Another Crazy Dream	1977	$5
❏ 17715	To Love Somebody/Remember	1977	$5
ARA
| ❏ 203 | Four Seasons of Life/ All That Heaven Sent | 1964 | $30 |
| ❏ 213 | Welcome Home Mr. Blues/Your True Love | 1965 | $30 |
CELEBRITY CIRCLE
| ❏ 6903 | Welcome Home Mr. Blues/Back Street | 1965 | $15 |
| ❏ 6905 | What's Wrong with Me/It All Depends | 1965 | $15 |
CINNAMON
❏ 771	All in the Name of Love/ Before You Have to Go	1973	$6
❏ 763	Drift Away/Foggy Misty Morning	1973	$6
❏ 798	I Want to Stay/Wrap My Arms Around the World	1974	$6
❏ 779	When Your Good Love Was Mine/Fraulein	1973	$6
COLLAGE
| ❏ 101 | Because of Losing You/After You | 1979 | $6 |
COMPLEAT
| ❏ 104 | Cry Baby/Now I Don't Have to Love You | 1983 | $5 |
| ❏ 101 | Smoke Gets in Your Eyes/ You're the Reason | 1982 | $5 |
EVERGREEN
❏ 1011	Anytime You're Ready/ Nobody's Fool	1983	$5
❏ 1014	Fool/Anytime You're Ready	1983	$5
❏ 1027	Hey Lady/Anytime You're Ready	1984	$5
❏ 1030	If It Was Any Better (I Couldn't Stand It)/ Nobody's Fool	1985	$5
❏ 1025	I'm Glad You Couldn't Sleep Last Night/It Amazes Me	1984	$5
❏ 1083	I Need Somebody Bad/ (B-side unknown)	1988	$6
❏ 1022	Let's Live This Dream Together/Nobody's Fool	1984	$5
❏ 1034	Out of Sight Out of Mind/It Amazes Me	1985	$5
❏ 1054	When a Man Loves a Woman/Hey Lady	1987	$5
GMC
| ❏ 115 | Fire in the Night/Look What Love Has Done | 1981 | $5 |
| ❏ 114 | Louisiana Lonely/Look What Love Has Done | 1981 | $5 |
GROOVE
| ❏ 58-0029 | Mountain of Love/The End of My World Is Near | 1963 | $30 |
HI
❏ 2118	Bells/86 Miles	1967	$15
❏ 2126	Don't Let Me Cross Over/Like Magic	1967	$15
❏ 2141	Since I Met You Baby/I Had to Cry Again	1968	$15
❏ 2137	Starry Eyes/Dee-Dee	1968	$15
❏ 2110	The Greatest Gift/I'll Trade All My Tomorrows	1966	$20
❏ 2305	This Time/I Had to Cry Again	1976	$5
HI COUNTRY
❏ 8002	A Little Bit of Soap/You're Out of My Reach	1972	$8
❏ 8003	Butterfly/Closed by a Dream	1973	$8
❏ 8001	Endless Love/Walkin' to the Pearly Gates	1972	$8
KARI
| ❏ 110 | Love the One You're With/When There's a Will (There's a Way) | 1980 | $6 |
LOBO
| ❏ III | I'd Love You to Want Me/The First Time We Made Love | 1982 | $6 |
| ❏ VIII | Sweet Southern Moonlight/The First Time We Made Love | 1982 | $6 |
MCA
| ❏ 41011 | Moment by Moment/ Never Again | 1979 | $5 |
| ❏ 41055 | Tower of Strength/ You're a Heartbreaker | 1979 | $5 |
MERCURY
| ❏ 71190 | Cry, Cry, Cry/ Lonesome Feeling | 1957 | $40 |
| ❏ 71347 | Little Girl Step This Way/Vadalou | 1958 | $40 |

PINK
Number	Title	Yr	NM
❏ 706	Darling Sue/Tony	1960	$50
❏ 702	Honey Love/Genavee	1959	$50
❏ 701	Three Thousand Miles/Cutie Baby	1959	$50

FEMALE BEATLES, THE
20TH FOX
| ❏ 531 | I Don't Want to Cry/I Want You | 1964 | $30 |

FEMININE COMPLEX, THE
ATHENA
❏ 5008	Are You Lonesome Like Me/ Run That Through Your Mind	1969	$15
❏ 5006	I Won't Run/Forgetting	1969	$15
❏ 5003	Six O'Clock in the Morning/ I've Been Workin' on You	1969	$15

FENDER, FREDDY
ABC
❏ 12415	I'm Leaving It All Up to You/ Whe It Rains It Really Pours	1978	$4
❏ 12339	Louisiana Woman/If You're Looking for a Fool	1978	$4
❏ 12453	Sweet Summer Day/ Walking Piece of Heaven	1979	$4
❏ 12370	Talk to Me/Please Mr. Sun	1978	$4
ABC/DOT
❏ 17540	Before the Next Teardrop Falls/Waiting for Your Love	1974	$5
❏ 17734	Christmas Time in the Valley/Please Come Home for Christmas	1977	$5
❏ 17713	If You Don't Love Me (Why Don't You Just Leave Me Alone)/Thank You, My Love	1977	$4
❏ 17652	Living It Down/Take Her a Message, I'm Lonely	1976	$4
❏ 17585	Secret Love/Loving Cajun Style	1975	$4
❏ 17730	Think About Me/If That's the Way You Want It	1977	$4
❏ 17558	Wasted Days and Wasted Nights/I Love My Rancho Grande	1975	$5
ARGO
| ❏ 5375 | A Man Can Cry/You're Something Else for Me | 1960 | $20 |
DUNCAN
❏ 1000	Mean Woman/Holy One	1959	$50
❏ 1004	Since I Met You Baby/ Little Mama	1959	$30
❏ 1001	Wasted Days and Wasted Nights/San Antonio Walk	1959	$30
❏ 1002	Wild Side of Life/Crazy Baby	1959	$30
GOLDBAND
| ❏ 1264 | Bye, Bye, Little Angel/ Oh My Love | 1975 | $5 |
| ❏ 1272 | Three Wishes/Me and My Bottle of Rum | 1975 | $5 |
GRT
| ❏ 031 | Since I Met You Baby/ Little Mama | 1975 | $5 |
| ❏ 039 | Wild Side of Life/ Go On Baby | 1975 | $5 |
IMPERIAL
| ❏ 5659 | Mean Woman/Holy One | 1960 | $30 |
| ❏ 5670 | Wasted Days and Wasted Nights/I Can't Remember When I Didn't Love You | 1960 | $30 |
INSTANT
| ❏ 3332 | Some People Say/Today's Your Wedding Day | 1972 | $8 |
MCA
| ❏ 52003 | Across the Borderline/Before the Next Teardrop Falls | 1982 | $4 |
| ❏ 12453 | Sweet Summer Day/ Walking Piece of Heaven | 1979 | $4 |
NORCO
❏ 103	Coming Home Soon/ Going Out with the Tide	1964	$10
❏ 111	Donna/Lover's Quarrel	1965	$12
❏ 108	In the Still of the Night/ You Don't Have to Go	1965	$10
❏ 100	Love's Light Is an Ember/ The New Stroll	1963	$10
❏ 107	Magic of Love/Bony Moronie	1965	$10
—With Noel Vill			
❏ 106	Ooh Poo Pah Doo/ Three Wishes	1964	$10
PA GO GO
| ❏ 115 | Cool Mary Lou/You Are My Sunshine | 1967 | $12 |
STARFLITE
❏ 4906	My Special Prayer/ (B-side unknown)	1979	$4
❏ 4908	Please Talk to My Heart/ (B-side unknown)	1980	$4
❏ 4904	Squeeze Box/Turn Around	1979	$4
WARNER BROS.
| ❏ 29794 | Chokin' Kind/I Might As Well Forget You | 1983 | $4 |

Number	Title	Yr	NM
FENDER IV			
IMPERIAL			
❑ 66098	Malibu Run/Everybody Up	1965	$60
❑ 66061	Mar-Gaya/You Better Tell Me Now	1964	$60
FENDERMEN, THE			
CUCA			
❑ 1003	Mule Skinner Blues/Torture	1960	$200
SOMA			
❑ 1142	Don't You Just Know It/Beach Party	1960	$30
❑ 1155	Heartbreakin' Special/Can't You Wait	1960	$30
❑ 1137	Mule Skinner Blues/Torture	1960	$30
FENNELL, FREDERICK			
MERCURY			
❑ 71238	A Christmas Festival/Sleigh Ride	1957	$15
FENTON, SHANE, AND THE FENTONES			
20TH FOX			
❑ 439	Don't Do That/I'll Know	1963	$20
LAURIE			
❑ 3287	Don't Do That/I'll Know	1965	$12
FENWAYS, THE			
BEVMAR			
❑ 402	Be Careful Little Girl/(Instrumental)	1964	$50
❑ 401	Humpty Dumpty/Nothing to Offer You	1964	$30
BLUE CAT			
❑ 116	The Fight/Hard Road Ahead	1965	$100
CHESS			
❑ 1901	Humpty Dumpty/Nothing to Offer You	1964	$30
CO & CE			
❑ 243	I'm Your Toy/Theme for Pammy	1967	$20
❑ 237	Love Me for Myself/Satisfied	1966	$30
❑ 233	Satisfied/I'm a Mover	1966	$30
IMPERIAL			
❑ 66082	The Walk/Whip and Jerk	1964	$30
ROULETTE			
❑ 4573	Be Careful Little Girl/(Instrumental)	1964	$40
FERG, JOHNNY			
DECCA			
❑ 30572	Candy Love/Sad, Sad Day	1958	$40
FERGUSON, DAVIS AND JONES			
EPIC			
❑ 5-10661	Canterbury Road/Happy and Free (Out in the Country)	1970	$40
❑ 5-10592	I Think I'm Gonna Cry/Up Grade	1970	$40
FERGUSON, DAVIS AND LEE			
CHESS			
❑ 2138	She's Gone/She's Not an Ordinary Girl	1973	$30
GRT			
❑ 51	Must Be Going Out of My Head/Please Don'tcha Mention	1974	$30
FERGUSON, HELEN			
20TH CENTURY-FOX			
❑ 485	One Last Chance/Forgetfulness	1964	$8
FERGUSON, HELENA			
COMPASS			
❑ 7017	Don't Spoil Our Good Thing/The Loneliness	1968	$30
❑ 7009	Where Is the Party/My Terms	1967	$30
CONGRESS			
❑ 6009	I'm So Glad/I'd Rather Go Blind	1970	$70
FERGUSON, JAY			
ASYLUM			
❑ 45480	Losing Control/Happy Birthday Baby	1978	$4
❑ 46508	Paying Time/Too Late to Save Your Heart	1979	$4
❑ 46041	Shakedown Cruise/City of Angels	1979	$4
❑ 45444	Thunder Island/Magic Moment	1977	$4
CAPITOL			
❑ B-5111	Empty Sky/Tonite	1982	$4

Number	Title	Yr	NM
❑ B-5130	I Come Alive/Inside Out	1982	$4
❑ 4923	Modern Girl/My Baby's Eyes	1980	$4
FERGUSON, JOHNNY			
DECCA			
❑ 30731	Last Date/'Til School Starts Again	1959	$30
MGM			
❑ 12789	Afterglow/Waitin' for the Sandman	1959	$40
❑ 12855	Angela Jones/Blue Serge and White Lace	1959	$30
❑ 12905	I Understand Just How You Feel/Flutter Flutter	1960	$40
FERGUSON, MAYNARD			
CAMEO			
❑ 261	Antony & Cleopatr/Theme from Naked City	1963	$8
❑ 275	Blues for a Four-String Guitar/Groove	1963	$8
CAPITOL			
❑ F1713	Hot Canary/What's New	1951	$20
❑ F1269	Love Locked Out/Band Ain't Draggin'	1950	$20
COLUMBIA			
❑ 11411	An Offering of Love Pt. 1/Dance to Your Heart	1980	$4
❑ 45352	Eli's Coming/MacArthur Park	1971	$5
❑ 10468	Gonna Fly Now (Theme from "Rocky")/The Fly	1977	$4
❑ 11183	Main Theme from Star Trek The Motion Picture)/Naima	1980	$4
❑ 10595	Main Title (From the 20th Century Fox Film Star Wars)/Oasis	1977	$4
❑ 10678	Maria/Oasis	1978	$4
❑ 10823	Theme from "Battlestar Galactica"/M.F. Carnival	1978	$4
❑ 11151	Theme from Star Trek/Topa-Topa Woman	1979	$4
MAINSTREAM			
❑ 604	Marcarena (Part 1)/Marcarena (Part 2)	1965	$8
❑ 603	People/Marcarena	1965	$8
MERCURY			
❑ 70686	Autumn Leaves/Finger-Snappin'	1955	$15
❑ 70355	The Way You Look Tonight/Lonely Town	1954	$15
ROULETTE			
❑ 4317	Christmas for Moderns (Part 1)/Christmas for Moderns (Part 2)	1960	$15
❑ 4250	Doin' the Madison (Part 1)/Doin' the Madison (Part 2)	1960	$12
❑ 4207	Hey There/Let's Fall in Love	1959	$12
❑ 4421	Hip Twist/Maria	1962	$12
FERGUSON, SHEILA			
LANDA			
❑ 706	How Did That Happen/Little Red Riding Hood	1965	$40
SWAN			
❑ 4225	And In Return/Are You Satisfied	1965	$40
❑ 4217	I Weep for You/Don't (Leave Me Lover)	1965	$50
❑ 4234	Signs of Love/Heartbroken Memories	1965	$50
FERGUSON, TOMMY, TRIO			
ARCADE			
❑ 119	Christmas Is On Its Way/Just an Old-Fashioned Christmas	1953	$30
FERKO STRING BAND			
ARGO			
❑ 5451	Ferko's Monkey/Golden Slipper Strut	1963	$10
MEDIA			
❑ 1010	Alabama Jubilee/Sing a Little Melody	1955	$10
—Orange label			
❑ 1010	Alabama Jubilee/Sing a Little Melody	1955	$20
—Maroon label			
❑ 1016	Happy Days Are Here Again/Deep in the Heart of Texas	1955	$12
SAVOY			
❑ 1169	Smiles/There Are Two "I"s in Dixie	1955	$20
FERRANTE AND TEICHER			
ABC-PARAMOUNT			
❑ 9975	Aflame/How High the Moon	1958	$15
❑ 9957	Che Si Dice/How High the Moon	1958	$15
❑ 10017	Prairie Blues/Side Saddle	1959	$15
❑ 10165	Take Me Along/Lida Rose	1960	$15

Number	Title	Yr	NM
❑ 10347	Till There Was You/Lida Rose	1962	$15
COLUMBIA			
❑ 40088	Taboo/Semper Fideles	1953	$20
UNITED ARTISTS			
❑ XW1034	A Bridge Too Far/Theme from "New York, New York	1977	$4
❑ 50101	A Man and a Woman/Dark Eyes	1966	$6
❑ XW1272	Can You Read My Mind/Ski Fever	1979	$4
❑ 50501	Chitty Chitty Bang Bang/Buona Sera, Mrs. Campbell	1969	$5
❑ 903	Country Boy/The Knack	1965	$6
❑ 660	Crystal Fingers/Greensleeves	1963	$8
❑ 50869	Diamonds Are Forever/There's a New Day Coming	1971	$4
❑ 50963	Everything You Always Wanted to Ask/Tranquillo	1972	$4
❑ 0111	Exodus/Tonight	1973	$4
❑ 274	Exodus/Twilight	1960	$15
❑ 274 [PS]	Exodus/Twilight	1960	$20
❑ XW433	Freedom/Early Morning	1974	$4
❑ XW915	Gonna Fly Now (Theme from "Rocky")/You Take My Heart Away	1976	$4
❑ XW448	I'm Stone in Love with You/Cristo Redentor	1974	$4
❑ 50257	In the Heat of the Night/You Only Live Twice	1968	$5
❑ 700	It's Alright/Corn Pone	1964	$8
❑ XW205 [DJ]	Last Tango in Paris (mono/stereo)	1973	$4
❑ 563	Lawrence of Arabia/Paris Joy Ride	1963	$8
❑ 50646	Lay Lady Lay/Theme from "Z	1970	$4
❑ 470	Lisa/Negligee	1962	$12
❑ 50228	Live for Life/Pavanne	1967	$6
❑ 196	Lover's Symphony/Dream Concerto	1960	$10
❑ 607	(Love Theme from) Cleopatra/Caesar and Cleopatra Theme	1963	$8
❑ XW295	Love Theme from "Lady Sings the Blues"/Summer Is Coming	1973	$4
❑ 300	Love Theme from One-Eyed Jacks/Tara's Theme	1961	$10
❑ 300 [PS]	Love Theme from One-Eyed Jacks/Tara's Theme	1961	$20
❑ 50895	Love Theme from "The Godfather"/There's a New Day Coming	1972	$4
❑ 50554	Midnight Cowboy/Rock-a-Bye Baby	1969	$5
❑ 0112	Midnight Cowboy/Theme from "The Apartment	1973	$4
❑ 50747	Music Lovers/Love Is Now	1971	$4
❑ 977	Ol' Man River/Judith	1966	$6
❑ 50711	Pieces of Dreams/Magical Connection	1970	$4
❑ 50468	Prelude to Love/A Boy and a Girl	1969	$5
❑ 631	Sands of Time/Devotion	1963	$8
❑ 431	Smile/Streets of Paris	1962	$12
❑ XW168	Song Sung Blue/American Pie	1973	$4
❑ 816	The Greatest Story Ever Told/Isn't Spring	1965	$6
❑ XW759	Theme from "Breakheart Pass"/Mandy	1976	$4
❑ 319	Theme from "Goodbye Again"/Possessed	1961	$10
❑ 50038	Theme from "Khartoum"/Firebird	1966	$6
❑ 50038 [PS]	Theme from "Khartoum"/Firebird	1966	$10
❑ XW779	Theme from "Mahogany"/Theme from "Breakheart Pass	1976	$4
❑ XW1173	Theme from "Star Trek"/Swinging on a Star	1978	$4
❑ 231	Theme from "The Apartment"/Lonely Room	1960	$10
❑ 231 [PS]	Theme from "The Apartment"/Lonely Room	1960	$20
❑ 50084	Theme from "The Bible"/Three Over Four	1966	$6
❑ 537	Theme from "The Eleventh Hour"/Wishing Star	1963	$8
❑ XW1224	Theme from "The Last Waltz"/Finger Painting	1978	$4
❑ XW821	Theme from "The Missouri Breaks"/Serendipity	1976	$4
❑ 735	The Seventh Dawn/You're Too Much	1964	$8
❑ 735 [PS]	The Seventh Dawn/You're Too Much	1964	$15
❑ 373	Tonight/Dream of Love	1961	$10
❑ 770	What More Can I Say/I've Grown Accustomed to Her Face	1964	$8
❑ XW367	When Heaven Smiles/I Want to Spend My Life with You	1973	$4
7-Inch Extended Plays			
❑ UALP 9-6526	The More I See You/Three Over Four/Work Song//You Don't Have to Say You Love Me/Lara's Theme from "Dr. Zhivago"	1966	$10

—Jukebox issue; small hole, plays at 33 1/3 rpm

Number	Title	Yr	NM
FERRIS AND THE WHEELS			
BAMBI			
❑ 801	I Want to Dance (Every Night)/Chop Chop	1961	$30
UNITED ARTISTS			
❑ 458	Moments Like This/He Was a Fortune Teller	1962	$125
FERRY AID			
PROFILE			
❑ 5147	Let It Be/Let It Be (Gospel Jam Mix)	1987	$12
❑ 5147 [PS]	Let It Be/Let It Be (Gospel Jam Mix)	1987	$12
FERRY, BRYAN			
Also see ROXY MUSIC.			
ATLANTIC			
❑ 3017	A Hard Rain's Gonna Fall/2 HB	1974	$5
❑ 3364	Heart on My Sleeve/Re-Make, Re-Model	1976	$4
❑ 3351	Let's Stick Together (Let's Work Together)/Sea Breezes	1976	$4
❑ 3539	Sign of the Times/Can't Let Go	1978	$4
❑ 3399	Tokyo Joe/As the World Turns	1977	$4
MCA			
❑ 52788	Is Your Love Strong Enough/Windswept	1986	$3
❑ 52788 [PS]	Is Your Love Strong Enough/Windswept	1986	$3
REPRISE			
❑ 28116	Limbo (Brooklyn Version)/Limbo (Latin Version)	1988	$3
❑ 28116 [PS]	Limbo (Brooklyn Version)/Limbo (Latin Version)	1988	$3
WARNER BROS.			
❑ 28887	Don't Stop the Dance/Nocturne	1985	$3
❑ 28887 [PS]	Don't Stop the Dance/Nocturne	1985	$3
❑ 28582	Help Me/Broken Wings	1986	$3
❑ 28582 [PS]	Help Me/Broken Wings	1986	$3
❑ 28990	Slave to Love/Valentine	1985	$3
❑ 28990 [PS]	Slave to Love/Valentine	1985	$3
FESTIVALS, THE			
BLUE ROCK			
❑ 4076	Hey Girl/Checkin' Out	1969	$8
GORDY			
❑ 7120	Green Grows the Lilacs/So in Love	1972	$6
SMASH			
❑ 2196	Hey Girl/Not Gonna Let Her	1968	$8
❑ 2056	I'll Always Love You/Music	1966	$8
FEVER TREE			
AMPEX			
❑ 11028	I Put a Spell on You/Hey Joe, Where You Gonna Go	1970	$20
❑ 11013	She Comes in Colors/You're Not the Same Baby	1970	$20
MAINSTREAM			
❑ 665	Girl, Oh Girl (Don't Push Me)/Steve Lenore	1967	$15
❑ 661	Hey Mister/I Can Beat Your Drum	1967	$15
UNI			
❑ 55202	Catcher in the Rye/What Time Did You Say It Is in Salt Lake City?	1970	$30
❑ 55228	I Am/Grand Candy Young Sweet	1970	$30
❑ 55146	Love Makes the Sun Rise/Filigree and Shadow	1969	$20
❑ 55060	San Fransisco Girls (Return of the Native)/Come with Me	1968	$15
❑ 55060 [DJ]	San Fransisco Girls (Return of the Native) (same on both sides)	1968	$50
—Promo only on blue vinyl			
❑ 55172	The Sun Also Rises/Clancey	1969	$20
❑ 55095	What Time Did You Say It Is in Salt Lake City/Where Do You Go	1968	$20
FI-TONES, THE			
ANGLE TONE			
❑ 536	Deep In My Heart/Minnie	1959	$70
❑ 530	It Wasn't a Lie/What Am I Goin' to Do	1958	$100
ATLAS			
❑ 1050	Foolish Dreams/Let's Fall in Love	1955	$400
—Originals identify label as "Atlas Record Company" and have Atlas logo at far upper left			
❑ 1050	Foolish Dreams/Let's Fall in Love	1955	$125
—Second pressings identify label as "Atlas Records" and have Atlas logo at left side			
❑ 1055	I Belong to You/Silly and Happy	1956	$125
❑ 1052	I Call to You/Love You Baby	1955	$125
❑ 1051	It Wasn't a Lie/Lots and Lots of Love	1955	$125
❑ 1056	Waiting for Your Call/My Tired Feet	1956	$125

Number	Title	Yr	NM
OLD TOWN			
❑ 1042	My Faith/My Heart	1957	$400
FIDELITY'S, THE			
BATON			
❑ 261	Captain of My Ship/My Greatest Thrill	1958	$30
❑ 256	Memories of You/Can't You Come Out	1958	$30
❑ 252	The Things I Love/Hold On to Whatcha Got	1958	$30
SIR			
❑ 271	Marie/The Invitation	1959	$30
❑ 274	Walk with the Wind/Only to You	1959	$30
❑ 276	Where in the World/This Girl of Mine	1960	$30
❑ 277	Wishing Star/Broken Love	1960	$40
FIELD, JERRY, AND THE LAWYERS			
PARKWAY			
❑ 801	The Trial/Easy Steppin'	1958	$40
—Blue label			
❑ 801	The Trial/Easy Steppin'	1958	$30
—White label. This is actually a cover of a break-in record (for the original, see HERB B. LOU AND THE LEGAL EAGLES).			
FIELD, SALLY			
COLGEMS			
❑ 66-1008	Felicidad/Find Yourself a Rainbow	1967	$10
❑ 66-1008 [PS]	Felicidad/Find Yourself a Rainbow	1967	$20
❑ 66-1014	Golden Days/You're a Grand Old Flag	1967	$8
FIELDS, BOBBY			
ACE			
❑ 504	Pity Poor Me/Give Me a Helping Hand	1955	$70
FIELDS, ERNIE			
CAPITOL			
❑ 5161	St. Louis Blues/Lilies of the Field	1964	$8
❑ 5326	Swanne River/Chloe	1964	$8
RENDEZVOUS			
❑ 161	A String of Pearls/Castle Rock	1961	$10
❑ 148	Be Anything (But Be Mine)/Fallin'	1961	$12
❑ 122	Begin the Beguine/Things Ain't What They Used to Be	1960	$12
❑ 117	Chattanooga Choo Choo/Workin' Out	1960	$10
❑ 170	Hucklebuck (Twist)/Ernie's Tune	1962	$8
❑ 110	In the Mood/Christopher Columbus	1959	$15
❑ 129	Teen Flip/Sweet Slumber	1960	$10
❑ 150	The Charleston/12th Street Rag	1961	$12
❑ 142	The Happy Whistler/Honky Tonk	1961	$10
❑ 138	The Honeydripper/Monkey	1960	$10
❑ 181	Theme from Perry Mason/Me and My Shadow	1962	$10
FIELDS, SHEP			
MGM			
❑ 10841	Silver Bells/Christmas Symphony	1950	$20
FIELDS, THE			
UNI			
❑ 55106	Bide My Time/Take You Home	1969	$12
FIESTAS, THE			
CHIMNEYVILLE			
❑ 10221	Is That Long Enough for You/I'm Gonna Make Myself	1977	$15
❑ 10216	Tina, the Disco Queen/I'm No Better Than You	1977	$15
COTILLION			
❑ 44117	So Fine/Broken Heart	1971	$30
OLD TOWN			
❑ 1189	Ain't She Sweet/I Gotta Have Your Lovin'	1965	$20
❑ 1166	All That's Good/Rock-a-By Baby	1964	$30
❑ 1122	Broken Heart/Railroad Song	1962	$30
❑ 1080	Dollar Bill/It Don't Make Sense	1960	$30
❑ 1148	Foolish Dreamer/Rock-a-By Baby	1963	$30
❑ 1074	Good News/That Was Me	1959	$30
❑ 1067	Grandma Gave a Party/I'm Your Slave	1959	$30
❑ 1111	Hobo's Prayer/She's Mine	1961	$50
❑ 1127	I Feel Good All Over/Look at That Girl	1962	$30
❑ 1104	Look at That Girl/Mr. Dillon, Mr. Dillon	1961	$30
❑ 1187	Love Is Strange/Love Is Good to Me	1965	$20
❑ 1069	Our Anniversary/I'm Your Slave	1959	$30

Number	Title	Yr	NM
❑ 1062	So Fine/Last Night I Dreamed	1958	$60
—Versions pressed by Columbia have a piano intro not available elsewhere. Look for "ZTSP" on label			
❑ 1062	So Fine/Last Night I Dreamed	1958	$40
—Standard version; no "ZTSP" on label			
❑ 1090	So Nice/You Could Be My Girlfriend	1960	$30
❑ 1134	The Gypsy Said/Mama Put the Law Down	1963	$30
❑ 1140	The Party's Over/Try It One More Time	1963	$30
❑ 1178	Think Smart/Anna	1965	$100
RESPECT			
❑ 2509	I Can't Shake Your Love (Can't Shake You Loose)/A Sometimes Storm	1972	$8
STRAND			
❑ 25046	Come On Everybody/Julia	1961	$50
VIGOR			
❑ 712	So Fine/Darling You've Changed	1974	$8
FIFTH DIMENSION, THE			
ABC			
❑ 12181	Love Hangover/Will You Be There	1976	$4
❑ 12136	Magic in My Life/Lean On Me Always	1975	$4
❑ 12168	Walk Your Feet in the Sunshine/Speaking with My Heart	1976	$4
BELL			
❑ 45380	Ashes to Ashes/The Singer	1973	$4
❑ 45338	Everything's Been Changed/There Never Was a Day	1973	$4
❑ 45425	Flashback/Diggin' for a Livin'	1973	$4
❑ 45612	Harlem/My Song	1974	$4
❑ 45261	If I Could Reach You/Tomorrow Belongs to the Children	1972	$5
❑ 45195	(Last Night) I Didn't Get to Sleep at All/The River Witch	1972	$5
❑ 999	Light Sings/Viva Tirado	1971	$5
❑ 45310	Living Together, Growing Together/What Do I Need to Be Me	1973	$4
❑ 965	Love's Lines, Angles and Rhymes/The Singer	1971	$5
❑ 860	Medley: A Change Is Gonna Come & People Gotta Be Free/The Declaration	1970	$5
❑ 940	One Less Bell to Answer/Feelin' Alright?	1970	$5
❑ 913	On the Beach (In the Summertime)/This Is Your Life	1970	$5
❑ 880	Puppet Man/A Love Like Ours	1970	$5
❑ 895	Save the Country/Dimension 5	1970	$5
❑ 45170	Together Let's Find Love/I Just Wanta Be Your Friend	1972	$5
MOTOWN			
❑ 1453	Everybody's Got to Give It Up/You're My Star	1978	$4
SOUL CITY			
❑ 755	Another Day, Another Heartache/Rosecrans Blvd.	1967	$10
❑ 755 [PS]	Another Day, Another Heartache/Rosecrans Blvd.	1967	$30
❑ 772	Aquarius/Let the Sunshine In (The Flesh Failures)//Don'tcha Hear Me Callin' To Ya	1969	$8
❑ 772 [PS]	Aquarius/Let the Sunshine In (The Flesh Failures)//Don'tcha Hear Me Callin' To Ya	1969	$20
❑ 772 [DJ]	Aquarius/Let the Sunshine In (The Flesh Failures) (same on both sides?)	1969	$20
—Promo only on yellow vinyl			
❑ 780	Blowing Away/Skinny Man	1970	$6
❑ 770	California Soul/It'll Never Be the Same	1968	$8
❑ 762	Carpet Man/Magic Garden	1968	$8
❑ 753	Go Where You Wanna Go/Too Poor to Die	1967	$8
❑ 753 [PS]	Go Where You Wanna Go/Too Poor to Die	1967	$30
❑ 752	I'll Be Loving You Forever/Train, Keep On Movin'	1966	$70
❑ 760	Paper Cup/Poor Side of Town	1967	$8
❑ 766	Stoned Soul Picnic/The Sailboat Song	1968	$8
❑ 766 [PS]	Stoned Soul Picnic/The Sailboat Song	1968	$20
❑ 768	Sweet Blindness/Bobby's Blues	1968	$8
❑ 768 [PS]	Sweet Blindness/Bobby's Blues	1968	$20
❑ 781	The Girls' Song/It'll Never Be the Same Again	1970	$6
❑ 779	Wedding Bell Blues/Lovin' Stew	1969	$8
❑ 776	Workin' on a Groovy Thing/Broken Wing Bird	1969	$8
SUTRA			
❑ 122	Surrender/Fantasy	1983	$4

Number	Title	Yr	NM
FIFTH ESTATE, THE			
JUBILEE			
❑ 5627	Coney Island Sally/ Tomorrow Is My Turn	1968	$8
❑ 5573	Ding! Dong! The Witch Is Dead/The Rub-a-Dub	1967	$15
❑ 5617	Do Drop Inn/That's Love	1968	$8
❑ 5595	Heigh-Ho/It's Waiting There for You	1967	$8
❑ 5588	Lost Generation/ The Goofin' Song	1967	$8
❑ 5655	Mickey Mouse Club March/I Knew You Before I Met You	1969	$8
❑ 5607	Morning, Morning/ Tomorrow Is My Turn	1967	$8
❑ 5683	Parade of the Wooden Soldiers/I Knew You Before I Met You	1969	$30
❑ 5683 [DJ]	Parade of the Wooden Soldiers (mono/stereo)	1969	$10
RED BIRD			
❑ Oct-0064	Love Is All a Game/ Like I Love You	1966	$20
FIGURES ON A BEACH			
SIRE			
❑ 22870	Accidentally 4th Street (Gloria)/Get Serious	1989	$5
FILETS OF SOUL			
SAVOY			
❑ 1630	Since I Fell for You/C'mon Let's Dance	1968	$30
FILLET OF SOUL			
MERCURY			
❑ 73096	Don't Touch the Sun/ Wake Up Now	1970	$15
❑ 73044	Swingin' on a Love Vine/High-High	1970	$10
FINDERS KEEPERS			
CHALLENGE			
❑ 59364	Don't Give In to Him/I've Done All I Can	1967	$20
❑ 59338	Lavender Blue/Raggedy Ann	1966	$20
FONTANA			
❑ 1609	Friday Kind of Monday/ On the Beach	1968	$15
FINE YOUNG CANNIBALS			
I.R.S.			
❑ 53695	Don't Look Back/ As Hard As It Is	1989	$3
❑ 53695 [DJ]	Don't Look Back (Short 3:36)/(Long 3:50)	1989	$4
❑ 52981	Ever Fallen in Love/ Move to Work	1986	$3
❑ 52981 [PS]	Ever Fallen in Love/ Move to Work	1986	$3
❑ 53639	Good Thing/Social Security	1989	$5
—Slight premium because B-side is a doo-wop-style non-LP track			
❑ 53686	I'm Not the Man I Used to Be/Don't Let It Get You Down	1989	$4
❑ 53483	She Drives Me Crazy/ Pull the Sucker Off	1988	$3
❑ 53483 [PS]	She Drives Me Crazy/ Pull the Sucker Off	1988	$4
❑ 52836	Suspicious Minds/ Prick Up Your Ears	1986	$5
❑ 52836 [PS]	Suspicious Minds/ Prick Up Your Ears	1986	$5
FINN, MICKY			
CHATTAHOOCHIE			
❑ 663	I Still Want You/ Reelin' and Rockin'	1965	$15
FINNEGAN, LARRY			
CORAL			
❑ 62313	I'll Be Back, Jack/There Ain't Nothin' in This World	1962	$10
OLD TOWN			
❑ 1113	Dear One/Candy Lips	1961	$15
❑ 1120	Pretty Susie Sunshine/ It's Walkin' Talkin' Time	1962	$10
RIC			
❑ 146	The Other Ringo (A Tribute to Ringo Starr)/When My Love Passes By	1964	$20
FINNEGAN, MIKE, AND THE SERFS			
PARKWAY			
❑ 113	Help Me Somebody/ Bread and Water	1966	$30

Number	Title	Yr	NM
FIRE & ICE LTD.			
CAPITOL			
❑ 2587	Music Man/For the Money	1969	$8
—As "Fire & Ice"			
FIRE AND RAIN			
20TH CENTURY			
❑ 2280	Dance for Me/Make Love to Me	1976	$6
❑ 2240	Don't Throw It All Away/ Layin' in Your Arms (Before Daybreak)	1975	$6
MERCURY			
❑ 73358	Alright Tonight/Home to You	1973	$10
❑ 73373	Hello Stranger/ Somebody to Love	1973	$50
❑ 73420	Take Me for a Little While/Touch Me	1973	$10
FIRE ESCAPE, THE			
GNP CRESCENDO			
❑ 384	Blood Beat/Love Special Delivery	1967	$15
FIRE INC.			
MCA			
❑ 52377	Tonight Is What It Means to Be Young/Hold That Snake	1984	$4
—B-side by Ry Cooder			
❑ 52377 [PS]	Tonight Is What It Means to Be Young/Hold That Snake	1984	$4
FIREBALLET			
PASSPORT			
❑ 7908	Desiree/Carrollon	1975	$5
FIREBALLS, THE			
7 ARTS			
❑ 714 [PS]	Callin' the Sheriff/Don't Stop	1961	$60
ASTRA			
❑ 1021	Torquay/Sweet Walk	1966	$10
ATCO			
❑ 6491	Bottle of Wine/Can't You See I'm Tryin'	1967	$10
❑ 6595	Chicken Little/Three Minutes' Time	1968	$8
❑ 6614	Come On, React!/ Woman Help Me	1968	$8
❑ 6569	Goin' Away/Groovy Motions	1968	$8
❑ 6651	Long Green/Light in the Window	1969	$8
❑ 6678	Watch Her Walk/Good Morning Shame	1969	$8
DOT			
❑ 16745	Ahhh, Soul/Campusology	1965	$20
❑ 16583	Ain't Gonna Tell Anybody/Young Am I	1964	$15
—Jimmy Gilmer and the Fireballs			
❑ 16881	All I Do Is Dream of You/Ain't That Rain	1966	$10
—Jimmy Gilmer and the Fireballs			
❑ 16714	Born to Be with You/ Lonesome Tears	1965	$10
—Jimmy Gilmer and the Fireballs			
❑ 16687	Break His Heart for Me/ Cinnamon Cindy	1965	$10
—Jimmy Gilmer and the Fireballs			
❑ 16768	Codine/Come to Me	1965	$10
—Jimmy Gilmer and the Fireballs			
❑ 16666	Cry Baby/Thunder 'N' Lightnin'	1964	$12
—Jimmy Gilmer and the Fireballs			
❑ 16539	Daisy Petal Pickin'/When My Tears Have Dried	1963	$15
—Jimmy Gilmer and the Fireballs			
❑ 16591	Daytona Drag/Gently, Gently	1964	$20
❑ 16661	Dumbo/Mr. Reed	1964	$20
❑ 16833	Hungry, Hungry, Hungry/Wild Roses	1966	$10
—Jimmy Gilmer and the Fireballs			
❑ 16609	I'll Send for You/Look at Me	1964	$10
—Jimmy Gilmer and the Fireballs			
❑ 16715	More Than I Can Say/ Beating of My Heart	1965	$20
❑ 16786	She Belongs to Me/ Rambler's Blues	1965	$10
❑ 16992	Shy Girl/I Think I'll Catch a Bus	1967	$10
—Jimmy Gilmer and the Fireballs			
❑ 16979	Sugar Shack/Daisy Petal Pickin'	1966	$10
—Jimmy Gilmer and the Fireballs			
❑ 16487	Sugar Shack/My Heart Is Free	1963	$20
—Jimmy Gilmer and the Fireballs			

Number	Title	Yr	NM
❑ 16743	The Fool/Somebody Stole My Watermelon	1965	$10
—Jimmy Gilmer and the Fireballs			
❑ 16493	Torquay Two/Peg Leg	1963	$20
❑ 16918	Torquay Two/Say I Am	1966	$20
❑ 16642	Wishing/What Kinda Love	1964	$10
—Jimmy Gilmer and the Fireballs			
HAMILTON			
❑ 50036	Blacksmith Blues/Tuff-a-Nuff	1960	$30
JARO			
❑ 77029	Long, Long Ponytail/ Let There Be Love	1960	$100
—Chuck Tharp and the Fireballs			
KAPP			
❑ 248	Fireball/I Don't Know	1958	$125
—Chuck Tharp and the Fireballs			
TOP RANK			
❑ 2081	Almost Paradise/Sweet Talk	1960	$30
❑ 2026 [M]	Bulldog/Nearly Sunrise	1959	$30
❑ 2026ST [S]	Bulldog/Nearly Sunrise	1959	$60
❑ 2038 [M]	Foot Patter/Kissin'	1959	$30
❑ 2038ST [S]	Foot Patter/Kissin'	1959	$60
❑ 2008	Torquay/Cry Baby	1959	$30
FIREFALL			
ATLANTIC			
❑ 89916	Always/In the Dead of the Night	1982	$4
❑ 89963	Body and Soul/ It's Not Too Late	1982	$4
❑ PR473 [DJ]	Christmas in Love/Always	1982	$6
❑ PR473 [DJ]	Christmas in Love (same on both sides)	1982	$5
❑ 3392	Cinderella/Dolphin's Lullaby	1977	$4
❑ 89702 [DJ]	Every Little Word (same on both sides)	1984	$4
—May be promo only			
❑ 89833 [DJ]	Falling in Love (same on both sides)	1983	$4
—May be promo only			
❑ 3544 [PS]	Goodbye, I Love You/Baby	1978	$5
❑ 3544	Goodbye, I Love You/Baby	1978	$4
❑ 3657	Headed for a Fall/Just What You Need	1980	$4
❑ 3333	Livin' Ain't Livin'/Love Isn't All	1976	$4
❑ 3670	Love That Got Away/ Business Is Business	1980	$4
❑ 3763 [DJ]	Only Time Will Tell (same on both sides)	1980	$4
—May be promo only			
❑ 3452	So Long/You and Me Baby	1978	$4
❑ 3791	Staying With It/Dreamers	1981	$4
❑ 3518	Strange Way/Anymore	1978	$4
❑ 3518 [PS]	Strange Way/Anymore	1978	$6
❑ 3566	Sweet and Sour/ Wrong Side of Town	1979	$4
FIREFLIES, THE			
CANADIAN AMERICAN			
❑ 117	Marianne/Give All Your Love to Me	1960	$30
RIBBON			
❑ 6904	I Can't Say Goodbye/ What Did I Do Wrong	1959	$30
❑ 6906	My Girl/Because of My Pride	1960	$30
TAURUS			
❑ 366	Good Friends/My Prayer for You	1964	$30
❑ 355	One O'Clock Twist/You Were Mine for Awhile	1962	$30
❑ 380	Tonight/A Time for Us	1965	$30
FIREFLY (1)			
A&M			
❑ 1736	Hey There Little Firefly Part I/Part II	1975	$5
❑ 1798	If You Ever Stopped Callin' Me Baby Part I/Part II	1976	$6
POLYDOR			
❑ 14496	My Jole Part I/Part II	1978	$10
FIREFLY (2)			
EMERGENCY			
❑ 4509	Love (Is Gonna Be on Your Side)/Forget It	1981	$6
FIREHOSE			
Also see MINUTEMEN.			
CO & CE			
❑ 241	A-Go-Go/I Move Around	1966	$30
SST			
❑ PSST-079 [DJ]	Brave Captain/Perfect Pairs	1986	$10
—Not issued with picture sleeve			

FIRESIDERS, THE

SWAN

Number	Title	Yr	NM
❑ 4074	(I'll Remember) One and All/ No One Cares for Me	1961	$30

FIRESIGN THEATRE, THE

COLUMBIA

Number	Title	Yr	NM
❑ 45052	Forward Into the Past/ Station Break	1969	$10
❑ 45052 [PS]	Forward Into the Past/ Station Break	1969	$50

FIRM, THE

Supergroup featuring Jimmy Page of LED ZEPPELIN and Paul Rodgers of BAD COMPANY.

ATLANTIC

Number	Title	Yr	NM
❑ 89458	All the King's Horses/ Fortune Hunter	1986	$3
❑ 89458 [PS]	All the King's Horses/ Fortune Hunter	1986	$4
❑ 89421	Live in Peace/Free to Live	1986	$3
❑ 89561	Satisfaction Guaranteed/Closer	1985	$3
❑ 89561 [PS]	Satisfaction Guaranteed/Closer	1985	$4

FIRST CHOICE

GOLD MIND

Number	Title	Yr	NM
❑ 4023	Breakaway/House for Sale	1980	$5
❑ 4004	Doctor Love/I Love You More Than Before	1977	$5
❑ 4019	Double Cross/Game of Love	1979	$5
❑ 4017	Hold Your Horses/Now I've Thrown It All Away	1978	$5
❑ 4009	Love Having You Around/ Indian Giver	1977	$5
❑ 4022	Love Thang/Great Expectations	1980	$5

PHILLY GROOVE

Number	Title	Yr	NM
❑ 175	Armed and Extremely Dangerous/Gonna Keep On Lovin' Him	1973	$5
❑ 202	Guilty/Wake Up to Me	1974	$6
❑ 204	Love Freeze/A Boy Named Junior	1975	$10
❑ 179	Smarty Pants/One Step Away	1973	$6
❑ 200	The Player -- Part 1/ The Player -- Part 2	1974	$6

SCEPTER

Number	Title	Yr	NM
❑ 12347	This Is the House (Where Love Died)/One Step Away	1972	$60

WARNER BROS.

Number	Title	Yr	NM
❑ 8251	First Choice Theme/Let Him Go	1976	$8
❑ 8214	Gotta Get Away (From You Baby)/Yes, Maybe Not	1976	$8

FIRST CLASS (1)

UK

Number	Title	Yr	NM
❑ 49022	Beach Baby/Both Sides of the Story	1974	$5

— Most stock copies have the full-length (4:59) version of the A-side

Number	Title	Yr	NM
❑ 49022	Beach Baby/Both Sides of the Story	1974	$6

— Some stock copies have a short version of the A-side

Number	Title	Yr	NM
❑ 49028	Dreams Are Ten a Penny/ Lavender Man	1974	$4
❑ 49033	Funny How Love Can Be/Surfer Queen	1975	$4

FIRST CLASS (2)

ALL PLATINUM

Number	Title	Yr	NM
❑ 2372	Coming Back to You/This Is It	1977	$5
❑ 2365	Me and My Gemini/Me and My Gemini (Part 2)	1976	$5
❑ 2368	This Is It/Filled with Desire	1977	$5

EBONY SOUNDS

Number	Title	Yr	NM
❑ 187	The Beginning of My End/ (B-side unknown)	1975	$5

TODAY

Number	Title	Yr	NM
❑ 1528	What About Me/ Outside Your World	1974	$5

FIRST CLASS (U)

PRIVATE STOCK

Number	Title	Yr	NM
❑ 45,093	Ain't No Love/Long Time Gone	1976	$4

FIRST CROW TO THE MOON

ROULETTE

Number	Title	Yr	NM
❑ 4774	The Sun Lights Up the Shadows of Your Mind/Spend Your Life	1967	$40

FIRST EDITION, THE

JOLLY ROGERS

Number	Title	Yr	NM
❑ 1007	A Stranger in My Place/ Makin' Music for Money	1974	$5

— All of the above as "Kenny Rogers and the First Edition

Number	Title	Yr	NM
❑ 1003	(Do You Remember) The First Time/Indian Joe	1973	$5
❑ 1001	Lady, Play Your Symphony/ There's An Old Man in Our Town	1973	$5
❑ 1004	Today I Started Loving You Again/She Thinks I Still Care	1973	$5
❑ 1006	Whatcha Gonna Do/ Something About Your Song	1973	$5

REPRISE

Number	Title	Yr	NM
❑ 0799	But You Know I Love You/ Homemade Lies	1968	$6
❑ 0683	Dream On/Only Me	1968	$6
❑ 0822	Good Time Liberator/Once Again She's All Alone	1969	$5

— Starting above, by "Kenny Rogers and the First Edition

Number	Title	Yr	NM
❑ 0953	Heed the Call/A Stranger in My Place	1970	$5
❑ 0773	If I Could Only Change Your Mind/Are My Thoughts With You	1968	$6
❑ 0693	Look Around, I'll Be There/ Charlie the Fer-De-Lance	1968	$6
❑ 1069	School Teacher/ Trigger Happy Kid	1972	$5
❑ 0999	Someone Who Cares/ Mission of San Mohera	1971	$5
❑ 0888	Something's Burning/ Mama's Waiting	1970	$5
❑ 0747	Something's Burning/ Someone Who Cares	1972	$4

— As "Kenny Rogers and the First Edition"; "Back to Back Hits" series

Number	Title	Yr	NM
❑ 1018	Take My Hand/All God's Lonely Children	1971	$5
❑ 0748	Tell It All Brother/Heed the Call	1972	$4

— As "Kenny Rogers and the First Edition"; "Back to Back Hits" series

Number	Title	Yr	NM
❑ 0923	Tell It All Brother/Just Remember You're My Sunshine	1970	$5
❑ 0628	Ticket to Nowhere/I Found a Reason	1967	$8
❑ 1053	Where Does Rosie Go/ What Am I Gonna Do	1971	$5

FISCHER, WILD MAN

REPRISE

Number	Title	Yr	NM
❑ 0781	Merry-Go-Round/The Circle	1968	$30

FISCHOFF, GEORGE

AVALANCHE

Number	Title	Yr	NM
❑ XW231	That Summer Night/For Gladys	1973	$6

DRIVE

Number	Title	Yr	NM
❑ 6273	The Piano Picker/Love Dust	1979	$5

GNP CRESCENDO

Number	Title	Yr	NM
❑ 491	That Great Old Song/Blue Night	1975	$5

RANWOOD

Number	Title	Yr	NM
❑ 1053	Funky Doodle/Quiet Time	1976	$5

REWARD

Number	Title	Yr	NM
❑ WS4-04354	Boogie Piano Man/Blues for the Boogie Man	1984	$4

UNITED ARTISTS

Number	Title	Yr	NM
❑ XW410	Georgia Porcupine/I'll Never Forget You	1974	$6

FISHBONE

COLUMBIA

Number	Title	Yr	NM
❑ 38-08500	Freddie's Dead/Question of Life	1988	$4
❑ 38-04922	? (Modern Industry)/ V.T.T.L.O.T.S.D.G.F.	1985	$4

WTG

Number	Title	Yr	NM
❑ 31-68936	Skankin' to the Beat/ In Your Eyes	1989	$4

— B-side by Peter Gabriel

FISHBONE AND CURTIS MAYFIELD

Number	Title	Yr	NM
❑ 9806 [PS]	He's a Flyguy/(Instrumental)	1989	$3

FISHER, CHIP

RCA VICTOR

Number	Title	Yr	NM
❑ 47-7213	I Love Your Poni-Tail/I Want You to Be My Own	1958	$30
❑ 47-7308	Sugar Bowl Rock/Did You Ever See a Dream Walking	1958	$40

FISHER, EDDIE, AND DEBBIE REYNOLDS

RCA VICTOR

Number	Title	Yr	NM
❑ 47-6820	Lullaby in Love/I Never Felt This Way Before	1957	$10

FISHER, EDDIE

7 ARTS

Number	Title	Yr	NM
❑ 719	Tonight/Breezin' Along with the Breeze	1961	$8

ABC-PARAMOUNT

Number	Title	Yr	NM
❑ 10326	Arrividerci, Roma/A Camminare	1962	$8
❑ 10371	Back in Your Back Yard/ The Sweetest Sounds	1962	$8
❑ 10264	Milk and Honey/Shalom	1961	$8

DOT

Number	Title	Yr	NM
❑ 16753	Any Time/When I Was Wrong	1965	$6
❑ 16779	I Don't Care If the Sun Don't Shine/Young and Foolish	1965	$6
❑ 16732	Sunrise, Sunset/Walking in the Footsteps of a Fool	1965	$6
❑ 16824	They Call the Wind Maria/Great Day	1966	$6
❑ 16792	White Christmas/ Mary Christmas	1965	$30

MUSICOR

Number	Title	Yr	NM
❑ 1354	I'll Pick a Rose for My Rose/Lady Mae	1969	$5

RAMROD

Number	Title	Yr	NM
❑ 0(# unknown)	Scent of Mystery/The Chase	1960	$8
❑ 0(# unknown) [PS]	Scent of Mystery/The Chase	1960	$10
❑ 100	This Nearly Was Mine/ Don't Let It Get You Down	1960	$8
❑ 100 [PS]	This Nearly Was Mine/ Don't Let It Get You Down	1960	$10

RCA VICTOR

Number	Title	Yr	NM
❑ 47-5675	A Girl, A Girl (Zoom-Ba Di Alli Nella)/Anema E Core (With All My Heart and Soul)	1954	$15
❑ 47-4617	A Little Bit Independent/ If You Should Love Me	1952	$15
❑ 47-6015	A Man Chases a Girl (Until She Catches Him)/(I'm Always Hearing) Wedding Bells	1955	$15
❑ 47-6015 [PS]	A Man Chases a Girl (Until She Catches Him)/(I'm Always Hearing) Wedding Bells	1955	$30

— This Is His Life" picture sleeve (possibly promo only)

Number	Title	Yr	NM
❑ 47-4359	Any Time/Never Before	1951	$20
❑ 47-6947	Around the World/ Slow Burning Love	1957	$10
❑ 47-4016	Bring Back the Thrill/If It Hadn't Been for You	1951	$20
❑ 47-4911	Christmas Baby/You're All I Want for Christmas	1952	$20
❑ 47-5038	Christmas Day/That's What Christmas Means to Me	1952	$20
❑ 47-6677	Cindy, Oh Cindy/ Around the World	1956	$10
❑ 47-5871	Count Your Blessings/Fanny	1954	$20

— Some pressings do not list the subtitle

Number	Title	Yr	NM
❑ 47-5871	Count Your Blessings (Instead of Sheep)/Fanny	1954	$20
❑ 47-5137	Downhearted/How Do You Speak to an Angel	1953	$15
❑ AMAO-0121	Dungaree Doll/Anytime	1973	$4

— Gold Standard Series

Number	Title	Yr	NM
❑ 47-6337	Dungaree Doll/Everybody's Got a Home But Me	1955	$12
❑ 47-5106	Even Now/If It Were Up to Me	1952	$15
❑ 47-5106 [PS]	Even Now/If It Were Up to Me	1952	$30
❑ 47-9430	Fool on the Hill/Sunny	1968	$6
❑ 47-4574	Forgive Me/That's the Chance You Take	1952	$20
❑ 47-8956	Games That Lovers Play/Mame	1966	$6
❑ 47-4100	Goodbye, G.I. Al/Get Your Paper	1951	$20
❑ 47-5748	Green Years/My Friend	1954	$15
❑ 47-6097	Heart/Near to You	1955	$15
❑ 47-4912	Here Comes Santa/ Christmas Means	1952	$20
❑ 47-4841	Hold Me/Everything I Have Is Yours	1952	$15
❑ 47-7135	I Don't Hurt Anymore/ What's the Use of Cryin'	1958	$10
❑ 47-4191	I'll Hold You in My Heart ('Til I Can Hold You in My Arms)/I Heard a Song	1951	$20
❑ 47-4619	I Love You Because/ Thinking of You	1952	$15

— The above four comprise a box set

Number	Title	Yr	NM
❑ 47-4840	I'm in the Mood for Love/ You'll Never Know	1952	$15
❑ 47-5293	I'm Walking Behind You/ Just Another Polka	1953	$15
❑ 47-4680	I'm Yours/Just a Little Lovin' (Will Go a Long Way)	1952	$20
❑ 47-5830	I Need You Now/Heaven Was Never Like This	1954	$15
❑ 47-4618	I Remember When/Am I Wasting My Time on You	1952	$15
❑ 47-4953	Lady of Spain/Outside of Heaven	1952	$15
❑ 47-6264	Magic Fingers/I Wanna Go Where You Go, Do What You Do (Then I'll Be Happy)	1955	$15
❑ 47-5453	Many Times/Just to Be with You	1953	$15
❑ 47-4744	Maybe/Watermelon Weather	1952	$15

— With Perry Como

Number	Title	Yr	NM
❑ 47-4038	My Buddy/At Sundown	1951	$20

— The above three comprise a box set

Number	Title	Yr	NM
❑ 47-4036	My Mammy/My Blue Heaven	1951	$20
❑ 47-6615	Oh My Maria/If I'm Elected	1956	$10
❑ 47-5552	Oh My Papa (O Mein Papa)/ Until You Said Goodbye	1953	$15

— The above exists with both punctuated and unpuctuated A-side

Number	Title	Yr	NM
❑ 47-5552 [PS]	Oh My Papa (O Mein Papa)/ Until You Said Goodbye	1953	$30
❑ 47-5552	Oh! My Pa-Pa (O Mein Papa)/ Until You Said Goodbye	1953	$15
❑ 47-6529	On the Street Where You Live/Sweet Heartaches	1956	$10
❑ 47-4843	Paradise/I've Got You Under My Skin	1952	$15

— The above four comprise a box set

Number	Title	Yr	NM
❑ 47-9070	People Like You/Come Love	1967	$6
❑ 47-7230	Pick a Partner/Kari Waits for Me	1958	$10
❑ 47-7051	Sayonara/That's the Way It Goes	1957	$10
❑ 47-4910	Silent Night/White Christmas	1952	$20

Number	Title	Yr	NM
❏ 47-6746	Some Day Soon/All About Love	1956	$12
❏ 47-6196	Song of the Dreamer/Don't Stay Away Too Long	1955	$15
❏ 47-6913	Sunshine Girl/Did You Close Your Eyes	1957	$10
❏ 47-7352	Take Me/The Best Thing for You	1958	$10
❏ 47-4444	Tell Me Why/Trust in Me	1951	$20
❏ 47-4842	That Old Feeling/Full Moon and Empty Arms	1952	$15
❏ 47-3901	Thinking of You/If You Should Leave Me	1950	$20
❏ 47-6849	Tonight My Heart Will Be Crying/Blues for Me	1957	$10
❏ 47-4257	Turn Back the Hands of Time/I Can't Go On Without You	1951	$20
❏ 47-4037	What Can I Say After I Say I'm Sorry/My Mom	1951	$20
❏ 47-3955	When You Kiss a Stranger/ You Love Me	1950	$20
❏ 47-3764	Where in the World/A Little Bit Independent	1950	$30
❏ 47-4830	Wish You Were Here!/ The Hand of Fate	1952	$15
❏ 47-6470	Without You/No Other One	1956	$10
❏ 47-5365	With These Hands/ When I Was Young	1953	$15
❏ 47-5365 [PS]	With These Hands/ When I Was Young	1953	$30
❏ 547-0326	April Showers/I'm Just a Vagabond Lover//You Call It Madness But I Call It Love/ Where the Blue of the Night Meets the Gold of the Day	1953	$15

— *Record 2 of 2-EP set EPB 3185*

Number	Title	Yr	NM
❏ EPA-4018 [PS]	Bundle of Joy	1957	$20
❏ EPA-426 [PS]	Cheek to Cheek: Irving Berlin Songs	1953	$20
❏ EPA-426	Cheek to Cheek/They Say It's Wonderful/All By Myself/Remember (contents unknown)	1953	$20
❏ EPA-742	Dungaree Doll	1956	$20
❏ EPA-718 [PS]	Dungaree Doll	1956	$20
❏ EPA-718	Dungaree Doll/Everybody Has a Home But Me/Magic Fingers/I Wanna Go Where You Go	1956	$20
❏ EPA-720 [PS]	Eddie Fisher Sings Academy Award Winning Songs Volume 1	1956	$20
❏ EPB-3058 [PS]	I'm in the Mood for Love	1952	$15

— *Two-pocket jacket for two-EP set (547-0009, 547-0010)*

Number	Title	Yr	NM
❏ EPA-742 [PS]	I'm in the Mood for Love	1956	$20
❏ 547-0009	I'm in the Mood for Love/ You'll Never Know//Hold Me/ Everything I Have Is Yours	1952	$15

— *Record 1 of 2-EP set EPB 3058*

Number	Title	Yr	NM
❏ EPB-3185 [PS]	May I Sing to You	1953	$15

— *Two-pocket jacket for two-EP set (547-0325, 547-0326)*

Number	Title	Yr	NM
❏ CEP-6144X [PS]	Souvenir Record from Coke Time with Eddie Fisher	1956	$25
❏ 547-0010	That Old Feeling/Full Moon and Empty Arms//Paradise/I've Got You Under My Skin	1952	$15

— *Record 2 of 2-EP set EPB 3058*

Number	Title	Yr	NM
❏ EPA-720	The Continental/Lullaby of Broadway/The Way You Look Tonight//Sweet Leilani/ Thanks for the Memory/ Over the Rainbow/When You Wish Upon a Star	1956	$20
❏ EPA-4047 [PS]	Thinking of You	1957	$15
❏ EPA-4047	Thinking of You/Wish You Were Here!/My Blue Heaven/I Need You Now	1957	$15
❏ CEP-6144X	Wish You Were Here!/I'll Hold You in My Heart (Till I Can Hold You in My Arms)/ Lady of Spain//I'm Walking Behind You/Downhearted/ Outside of Heaven	1956	$15

— *Coca-Cola logo on label*

Number	Title	Yr	NM
❏ EPA-4018	Worry About Tomorrow - Tomorrow/What's So Good About Good Morning; Worry About Tomorrow - Tomorrow (reprise)/Lullaby in Blue//I Never Felt This Way Before/Bundle of Joy and All About Love	1957	$20

FISHER, JERRY
NEW DESIGN

Number	Title	Yr	NM
❏ ZS71007	I Never Had It So Good/ Yonder Stands Little Maggie	1972	$8

FISHER, MARY ANN
FIRE

Number	Title	Yr	NM
❏ 1010	Only Yesterday/Wild As You Can Be	1960	$30
❏ 1002	Put On My Shoes/Wild As You Can Be	1959	$30

IMPERIAL

Number	Title	Yr	NM
❏ 5853	I Keep Comin' Back for More/It's a Man's World	1962	$30

SEG-WAY

Number	Title	Yr	NM
❏ 1007	Can't Take the Heartbreak/Give	1961	$30
❏ 1001	I Can't Take It/Forever More	1961	$30

FISHER, SONNY
PEACOCK

Number	Title	Yr	NM
❏ 1947	Hurtin'/I'm Goin' All the Way	1966	$30

STARDAY

Number	Title	Yr	NM
❏ 244	Pink and Black/ Little Red Wagon	1956	$400
❏ 190	Sneaky Pete/Hey Mama	1955	$500

FISHER, TONI
BIG TOP

Number	Title	Yr	NM
❏ 3124	The Music from the House Next Door/Quickly My Love	1962	$15
❏ 3097	West of the Wall/ What Did I Do	1962	$15

CAPITOL

Number	Title	Yr	NM
❏ 5901	Train of Love/A Million Heartbeats from Now	1967	$8

COLUMBIA

Number	Title	Yr	NM
❏ 42066	If I Loved You/Love Big	1961	$15
❏ 279	Everlasting Love/The Red Sea of Mars	1960	$15
❏ 276	How Deep Is the Ocean/ Blue, Blue, Blue	1960	$15
❏ 664	Springtime of Love/ Train of Love	1964	$8
❏ 275	The Big Hurt/Memphis Belle	1959	$20

SMASH

Number	Title	Yr	NM
❏ 1820	Cry a Little for Me/365 Disappointments	1963	$12
❏ 1797	Hold Me/Laugh or Cry	1963	$12
❏ 1832	Lovers, Dreamers, Fools/ You Won't Forget Me	1963	$10

FITE, BUDDY
CYCLONE

Number	Title	Yr	NM
❏ 75017	Evil Ways/El Jepe (The Chief)	1972	$30
❏ 75004	For Once in My Life/ Glad Rag Rag	1971	$10
❏ 75009	So Rare/They Can't Take That Away from Me	1971	$12

FITZGERALD, ELLA, AND LOUIS ARMSTRONG

DECCA

Number	Title	Yr	NM
❏ 27209	Can Anyone Explain? (No, No, No)/Dream a Little Dream of Me	1950	$30
❏ 28552	Who Walks In When I Walk Out/Would You Like to Take a Walk	1953	$20

VERVE

Number	Title	Yr	NM
❏ 10079	Goody Goody/A-Tisket, A-Tasket	1957	$30
❏ 2023	Stars Fell on Alabama/ Can't We Be Friends	1956	$15

FITZGERALD, ELLA
CAPITOL

Number	Title	Yr	NM
❏ 2099	Born to Lose/I Taught Him Everything He Knows	1968	$8
❏ 2212	Brighten the Corner/ It's Up to Me and You	1968	$8
❏ 2267	Hawaiian War Chant/ It's Only Love	1968	$8

DECCA

Number	Title	Yr	NM
❏ 28049	A Guy Is a Guy/ That Old Feeling	1952	$20
❏ 27200	Ain't Nobody's Business If I Do/I'll Never Be Free	1950	$30

— *With Louis Jordan*

Number	Title	Yr	NM
❏ 28707	Angel Eyes/Nowhere Guy	1953	$20
❏ 28993	A Sunday Kind of Love/ That's My Desire	1954	$20
❏ 27900	Baby Doll/Lady Bug	1951	$30
❏ 29108	Baby/I Need	1954	$20
❏ 27369	But Not for Me/ Looking for a Boy	1951	$20
❏ 28671	Careless/Blue Lou	1953	$20
❏ 27680	Come On-a My House/ Mixed Emotions	1951	$30
❏ 28762	Crying in the Chapel/ When the Hands of the Clock Pray at Midnite	1953	$20
❏ 28321	Ding-Dong Boogie/Preview	1952	$20
❏ 27634	Do You Really Love Me/ Even As You and I	1951	$30
❏ 29810	Early Autumn/Ella's Contribution to the Blues	1956	$15
❏ 29259	Empty Ballroom/If You Don't, I Know Who Will	1954	$20
❏ 27724	Give a Little -- Get a Little/There Never Was a Baby (Like My Baby)	1951	$30
❏ 28126	Goody Goody/ Air Mail Special	1952	$20
❏ 30405	Goody Goody/It's Too Soon to Know	1957	$30

— *Reissued to compete with Frankie Lymon's remake, this is scarcer than the original on 28126*

Number	Title	Yr	NM
❏ 31142	How High the Moon/ Smooth Sailing	1960	$10
❏ 28589	I Can't Lie to Myself/ Don't Wake Me Up	1953	$20
❏ 27948	I Don't Want to Take a Chance/Rough Ridin'	1952	$20
❏ 28181	I Hadn't Anyone Till You/ Gee, But I'm Glad to Know You Love Me	1952	$20
❏ 29136	(I Love You) For Sentimental Reasons/ It's Only a Paper Moon	1954	$20

— *With the Delta Rhythm Boys*

Number	Title	Yr	NM
❏ 27370	I've Got a Crush on You/ How Long Has This Been Going On	1951	$20
❏ 27120	I've Got the World on a String/Peas and Rice	1950	$30
❏ 28034	Lazy Day/What Does It Take	1952	$20
❏ 27419	Little Small Town/I Still Feel the Same About You	1951	$30

— *With the Ink Spots*

Number	Title	Yr	NM
❏ 29746	(Love Is) The Tender Trap/ My One and Only Love	1955	$15
❏ 29198	Lullaby of Birdland/Later	1954	$20
❏ 27061	Mississippi/I Don't Want the World (With a Fence Around It)	1950	$30
❏ 29475	Moanin' Low/Take a Chance on Love	1955	$15
❏ 28433	My Favorite Song/ Walkin' by the River	1952	$20
❏ 27368	My One and Only/Someone to Watch Over Me	1951	$20
❏ 29580	Old Devil Moon/Lover, Come Back to Me	1955	$15
❏ 27901	Oops!/Necessary Evil	1951	$30
❏ 29609	Pete Kelly's Blues/Hard Hearted Hannah	1955	$15
❏ 27255	Santa Claus Got Stuck (In My Chimney)/ Molasses, Molasses (It's Icky Sticky Goo)	1950	$30
❏ 27693	Smooth Sailing/ Love You Madly	1951	$30
❏ 29648	Soldier Boy/A Satisfied Mind	1955	$15
❏ 29008	Somebody Bad Stole De Wedding Bell/ Melancholy Me	1954	$20
❏ 27371	Soon/Maybe	1951	$20

— *The above four comprise a box set*

Number	Title	Yr	NM
❏ 30222	Stone Cold Dead in the Market/Peas and Rice	1957	$15
❏ 27453	The Beanbag Song/ Lonesome Gal	1951	$30
❏ 27602	The Chesapeke and Ohio/Because of Rain	1951	$30
❏ 28930	The Greatest There Is/I Wonder What Kind of Guy You'd Be	1953	$20
❏ 27578	The Hot Canary/ Two Little Men	1951	$30
❏ 29665	The Impatient Years/ But Not Like Mine	1955	$15
❏ 28375	Trying/My Bonnie Lies Over the Ocean	1952	$20
❏ 29137	Who's Afraid/I Wished on the Moon	1954	$20

PRESTIGE

Number	Title	Yr	NM
❏ 715	Hey Jude/Sunshine of Your Love	1969	$8

REPRISE

Number	Title	Yr	NM
❏ 0850	Get Ready/Open Your Window	1969	$6
❏ 0875	I'll Never Fall in Love Again/Savoy Truffle	1969	$6
❏ 0995	I Wonder Why/ Ooo Baby Baby	1971	$6

VERVE

Number	Title	Yr	NM
❏ 2012	A Beautiful Friendship/ Stay There	1956	$15
❏ 10368	A Hard Day's Night/ And the Angels Sing	1965	$10
❏ 10077	All of Me/It's All Right with Me	1957	$15
❏ 10341	All the Livelong Day/ (B-side unknown)	1965	$8
❏ 10130	Beale Street Blues/ St. Louis Blues	1958	$12
❏ 10288	Bill Bailey, Won't You Please Come Home/Ol' Man Mose	1963	$8
❏ 10180	But Not for Me/You Make Me Feel So Young	1959	$10
❏ 10324	Can't Buy Me Love/ Hello, Dolly!	1964	$10
❏ 10241	Clap Hands (Here Come Charlie!)/Cry Me a River	1961	$10
❏ 10241 [PS]	Clap Hands (Here Come Charlie!)/Cry Me a River	1961	$30
❏ 10274	Desafinado (Slightly Out of Tune)/Stardust Bossa Nova	1962	$8
❏ 10031	Hotta Chocolatta/ Hear My Heart	1957	$15
❏ 10220	How High the Moon (Part 1)/ How High the Moon (Part 2)	1960	$10
❏ 10222	I Can't Give You Anything But Love/ Reach for Tomorrow	1960	$10
❏ 10379	Imagine My Frustration (Part 1)/Imagine My Frustration (Part 2)	1966	$8

Number	Title	Yr	NM
❏ 2002	It's Only a Man/Too Young for the Blues	1956	$15
❏ 10337	I've Grown Accustomed to Your Face/I Could Have Danced All Night	1964	$8
❏ 10050	Let's Do It (Let's Fall in Love)/Manhattan	1957	$15
❏ 10189	Like Young/Beat Me Daddy, Eight to the Bar	1959	$12
❏ 10408	Love Theme from "The Sandpiper"/Duke's Place	1966	$8
❏ 10209	Mack the Knife/Lorelei	1960	$10
❏ 10359	Mae (She's Just a Quiet Girl)/We Three	1965	$8
❏ 10158	Oh What a Night for Love/Dreams Are Made for Children	1959	$10
❏ 10319	See See Rider/Trouble in Mind	1964	$8
❏ 10305	Shiny Stockings/Into Each Love Some Rain Must Fall	1963	$8
❏ 10171	Stairway to the Stars/I'm Through with Love	1959	$10
❏ 10132	Swingin' Shepherd Blues/Teach Me How to Cry	1958	$10
❏ 10166	Teardrops from My Eyes/A Little Jazz	1959	$10
❏ 10186	The Christmas Song/The Secret of Christmas	1959	$20
❏ 2021	The Silent Treatment/The Sun Forgot to Shine This Morning	1956	$15
❏ 10143	Trav'lin' Light/Your Red Wagon	1958	$10
❏ 10248	What Is This Thing Called Love/Call Me Darling	1962	$8
❏ 10111	What Will I Tell My Heart/Midnight Sun	1958	$10

7-Inch Extended Plays

DECCA

Number	Title	Yr	NM
❏ ED2269	(contents unknown)	1955	$25
❏ ED2269 [PS]	Pete Kelly's Blues	1955	$25

FI-DELLS, THE
IMPERIAL

Number	Title	Yr	NM
❏ 5780	What Is Love/Don't Let Me Love You	1961	$30

FIVE AMERICANS, THE
ABC-PARAMOUNT

Number	Title	Yr	NM
❏ 10686	Show Me/Love, Love, Love	1965	$20

ABNAK

Number	Title	Yr	NM
❏ 126	7:30 Guided Tour/See Saw Baby	1967	$8
❏ 126 [DJ]	7:30 Guided Tour/See Saw Baby	1967	$30

—*Promo only on yellow vinyl*

❏ 126 [PS]	7:30 Guided Tour/See Saw Baby	1967	$20
❏ 131	Con Man/Lovin' Is Lovin'	1968	$8
❏ 131 [DJ]	Con Man/Lovin' Is Lovin'	1968	$30

—*Promo only on yellow vinyl*

| ❏ 132 | Generation Gap/The Source | 1968 | $8 |
| ❏ 132 [DJ] | Generation Gap/The Source | 1968 | $30 |

—*Promo only on yellow vinyl*

| ❏ 116 | If I Could/Now That It's Over | 1966 | $10 |
| ❏ 116 [DJ] | If I Could/Now That It's Over | 1966 | $30 |

—*Promo only on yellow vinyl*

| ❏ 139 | I See the Light '69/Red Cape | 1969 | $8 |

—*As "Michael Rabon and the Five Americans*

| ❏ 139 [DJ] | I See the Light '69/Red Cape | 1969 | $30 |

—*As "Michael Rabon and the Five Americans"; promo only on yellow vinyl*

| ❏ 109 | I See the Light/The Outcast | 1965 | $30 |
| ❏ 109 [DJ] | I See the Light/The Outcast | 1965 | $30 |

—*Promo only on yellow vinyl*

| ❏ 106 | Say That You Love Me/Without You | 1965 | $10 |
| ❏ 106 [DJ] | Say That You Love Me/Without You | 1965 | $30 |

—*Promo only on yellow vinyl*

| ❏ 137 | Scrooge/Ignert Woman | 1969 | $8 |
| ❏ 137 [DJ] | Scrooge/Ignert Woman | 1969 | $30 |

—*Promo only on yellow vinyl*

| ❏ 142 | She's Too Good to Me/Molly Black | 1969 | $8 |
| ❏ 142 [DJ] | She's Too Good to Me/Molly Black | 1969 | $30 |

—*Promo only on yellow vinyl*

| ❏ 120 | Sound of Love/Sympathy | 1967 | $8 |
| ❏ 120 [DJ] | Sound of Love/Sympathy | 1967 | $30 |

—*Promo only on yellow vinyl*

| ❏ 125 | Stop Light/Tell Ann I Love Her | 1967 | $8 |
| ❏ 125 [DJ] | Stop Light/Tell Ann I Love Her | 1967 | $30 |

—*Promo only on yellow vinyl*

| ❏ 125 [PS] | Stop Light/Tell Ann I Love Her | 1967 | $20 |
| ❏ 118 | Western Union/Now That It's Over | 1967 | $15 |

Number	Title	Yr	NM
❏ 118 [DJ]	Western Union/Now That It's Over	1967	$30

—*Promo only on yellow vinyl*

HANNA-BARBERA

❏ 468	Evol-Not Love/Don't Blame Me	1966	$15
❏ 468 [PS]	Evol-Not Love/Don't Blame Me	1966	$20
❏ 483	Good Times/The Losing Game	1966	$15
❏ 454	I See the Light/The Outcast	1965	$15

JETSTAR

| ❏ 105 | I'm Feeling OK/Slippin' and Slidin' | 1966 | $40 |
| ❏ 104 | It's You Girl/I'm Gonna Leave You | 1966 | $30 |

PHILCO-FORD

| ❏ HP-10 | Western Union/Sounds of Love | 1968 | $30 |

—*4-inch plastic "Hip Pocket Record" with color sleeve*

FIVE BARS, THE
MONEY

Number	Title	Yr	NM
❏ 224	Stormy Weather/Somebody Else's Fool	1957	$70

FIVE BELLS, THE
BRUNSWICK

| ❏ 84004 | Till Dawn and Tomorrow/Waiting, Waiting | 1952 | $500 |
| ❏ 84002 | Till I Waltz Again with You/Can't Wait for Tomorrow | 1952 | $500 |

FIVE BLIND BOYS, THE
VEE JAY

| ❏ 872 | Waiting at the River/Where There's a Will | 1959 | $30 |

FIVE BLOBS, THE
COLUMBIA

| ❏ 4-41250 | The Blob/Saturday Night in Tiajuana | 1958 | $30 |

FIVE BLUE NOTES, THE
SABRE

| ❏ 103 | My Gal Is Gone/Ooh Baby | 1953 | $1000 |
| ❏ 108 | The Beat of Our Hearts/You Gotta Go Baby | 1954 | $2500 |

FIVE BUDDS, THE
RAMA

| ❏ 2 | I Guess It's All Over Now/I Want Her Back | 1953 | $500 |
| ❏ 1 | I Was Such a Fool (To Fall in Love with You)/Midnight | 1953 | $500 |

FIVE BY FIVE
PAULA

❏ 326	15 Going on 20/Penthouse Pauper	1970	$12
❏ 311	Ain't Gonna Be Your Fool No More/She Digs My Love	1968	$15
❏ 319	Apple Cider/Fruitstand Man	1970	$10
❏ 302	Fire/Hang Up	1968	$20
❏ 283	Harlem Shuffle/You Really Got a Hold on Me	1967	$15
❏ 261	Shake a Tail Feather/Tell Me What to Do	1967	$15
❏ 322	Too Much Tomorrow/Ain't Gonna Be Your Fool No More	1970	$10

FIVE CAMPBELLS, THE
MUSIC CITY

| ❏ 794 | Hey Baby/Morrine | 1956 | $500 |

FIVE CARD STUD
RED BIRD

| ❏ Oct-0082 | Be-Bop-A-Lula/Everybody Needs Somebody | 1967 | $20 |

SMASH

| ❏ 2080 | Bag Me/Once | 1967 | $20 |

FIVE CATS, THE
RCA VICTOR

| ❏ 47-5885 | He Follows She/Santa Lucia | 1954 | $30 |
| ❏ 47-6181 | I Was So Wrong/Someone's Gonna Cry | 1955 | $50 |

FIVE CHANCES, THE
ATOMIC

| ❏ 2494 | Make Love to Me/California | 1977 | $15 |

BLUE LAKE

| ❏ 115 | All I Want/Shake-a-Link | 1955 | $800 |

CHANCE

| ❏ 1157 | I May Be Small/Nagasaki | 1954 | $1000 |

Number	Title	Yr	NM
FEDERAL			
❏ 12303	My Days Are Blue/Tell Me Why	1957	$500
P.S.			
❏ 1510	Is This Love/Need Your Love	1960	$300
STATES			
❏ 156	Gloria/Sugar Lips	1956	$800

—*Black vinyl*

| ❏ 156 | Gloria/Sugar Lips | 1956 | $1200 |

—*Red vinyl*

FIVE CROWNS, THE
CARAVAN

| ❏ 15609 | I Can't Pretend/Popcorn Willie | 1955 | $60 |

DE'BESTH

| ❏ 1121/2 | A Surprise from Outer Space/Memories of Yesterday | 1959 | $400 |
| ❏ 1123 | I Want You/Hillum Boy | 1959 | $400 |

GEE

| ❏ 1001 | Do You Remember/God Bless You | 1956 | $200 |

OLD TOWN

| ❏ 790 | Good Luck Darling/You Could Be My Love | 1952 | $500 |

—*Black vinyl*

| ❏ 790 | Good Luck Darling/You Could Be My Love | 1952 | $3000 |

—*Red vinyl*

RAINBOW

| ❏ 179 | A Star/You're My Inspiration | 1952 | $300 |

—*Black vinyl*

| ❏ 179 | A Star/You're My Inspiration | 1952 | $800 |

—*Red vinyl*

| ❏ 281 | I Was Wrong/Hug Me Baby | 1954 | $500 |

TRANS WORLD

| ❏ 717 | I Can't Pretend/Popcorn Willie | 1956 | $100 |

FIVE DELIGHTS, THE
ABEL

| ❏ 228 | The Thought of Losing You/That Love Affair | 1959 | $300 |

NEWPORT

| ❏ 7002 | There'll Be No Goodbye/Okey Dokey Mama | 1958 | $200 |

UNART

| ❏ 2003 | There'll Be No Goodbye/Okey Dokey Mama | 1958 | $40 |

FIVE DEMARCO SISTERS, THE
DECCA

❏ 9-29470	Dreamboat/Two Hearts, Two Kisses	1955	$15
❏ 9-30181	Five Little Misses/I'm Through with Love	1957	$10
❏ 9-29299	Love Me/Just a Girl That Men Forget	1954	$15
❏ 9-29388	Mumbo Is the Word/This Love of Mine	1954	$15
❏ 9-29470	Sailor Boys Have to Talk to Me in English/The Hot Barcarolle	1955	$15

FIVE DISCS, THE
CALO

| ❏ 202 | Adios/My Baby Loves Me | 1961 | $200 |

—*Green label*

| ❏ 202 | Adios/My Baby Loves Me | 1962 | $125 |

—*White label*

CRYSTAL BALL

❏ 114	Mirror Mirror/Most of All I Wonder Why	1978	$10
❏ 136	Playing a Game of Love/Bells	1979	$8
❏ 141	This Love of Ours/To the Fair	1979	$8

DWAIN

| ❏ 6072 | My Chinese Girl/Roses | 1959 | $2000 |
| ❏ 803 | My Chinese Girl/Roses | 1959 | $200 |

—*As "Mario and the Five Discs*

| ❏ 803 | My Chinese Girl/Roses | 1959 | $200 |

EMGE

| ❏ 1004 | I Remember/The World Is a Beautiful Place | 1958 | $400 |

MELLO MOOD

| ❏ 1002 | My Chinese Girl/Roses | 1964 | $20 |

RUST

| ❏ 5027 | I Remember/The World Is a Beautiful Place | 1961 | $30 |

VIK

| ❏ 0327 | I Remember/The World Is a Beautiful Place | 1958 | $100 |

YALE

| ❏ 243/4 | Come On Baby/I Don't Know What to Do | 1961 | $400 |
| ❏ 240 | When Love Comes Knocking/Go-Go | 1961 | $400 |

Number	Title	Yr	NM

FIVE DOLLARS, THE
FORTUNE
Number	Title	Yr	NM
❑ 821	Harmony of Love/Doctor Baby	1955	$125
❑ 830	I Will Wait/Hard Working Mama	1956	$125
❑ 826	So Strange/You Know I Can't Refuse	1956	$125
❑ 854	That's the Way It Goes/My Baby-O	1960	$60

FRATERNITY
| ❑ 821 | Harmony of Love/Doctor Baby | 1958 | $50 |

FIVE DU-TONES, THE
ONE-DERFUL
❑ 4814	Dry Your Eyes/Come Back Baby	1963	$20
❑ 4836	Mountain of Love/Outside the Record Hop	1965	$20
❑ 4815	Shake a Tail Feather/Divorce Court	1963	$20
❑ 4828	Sweet Lips/Let Me Love You	1964	$40
❑ 4824	The Cool Bird/The Chicken Astronaut	1964	$20
❑ 4811	The Flea/Please Change Your Mind	1963	$20
❑ 4818	The Gouster/Monkey See-Monkey Do	1963	$20
❑ 4831	We Want More/The Woodbine Twine	1965	$20

FIVE ECHOES, THE
SABRE
| ❑ 102 | Baby Come Back to Me/Lonely Mood | 1953 | $600 |

— *Black vinyl*

| ❑ 102 | Baby Come Back to Me/Lonely Mood | 1953 | $1500 |

— *Red vinyl*

| ❑ 105 | So Lonesome/Broke | 1954 | $600 |

— *Black vinyl*

| ❑ 105 | So Lonesome/Broke | 1954 | $1500 |

— *Red vinyl*

VEE JAY
❑ 156	Fool's Prayer/Tastee Freeze	1955	$1000
❑ 129	I Really Do/Tell Me Baby	1954	$300
❑ 190	Soldier Boy/Pledging to You	1956	$200

FIVE EMBERS, THE
GEM
| ❑ 224 | Please Come Home/(B-side unknown) | 1954 | $800 |

FIVE EMERALDS, THE
S.R.C.
| ❑ 107 | Darling/Pleasure Me | 1954 | $1200 |
| ❑ 106 | I'll Beg/Let Me Take You Out Tonight | 1953 | $1000 |

— *Label uses numeral "5" in group name, and "S.R.C." has periods in it*

| ❑ 106 | I'll Beg/Let Me Take You Out Tonight | 1953 | $1000 |

— *Label spells out "Five" in group name, and "S-R-C" has hyphens in it*

FIVE EMPREES, THE
FREEPORT
❑ 1002	Hey Baby/Why	1965	$15
❑ 1007	Little Miss Happiness/Over the Mountain	1966	$15
❑ 1001	Little Miss Sad/Hey Lover	1965	$15
❑ 1001	Little Miss Sad/Hey Lover	1965	$30

— *Originally released as "The Five Empressions*

| ❑ 1009 | Pretty Face (Part 1)/Pretty Face (Part 2) | 1966 | $15 |

SMASH
| ❑ 2065 | Gone from My Mind/Hey Diddle Diddle | 1966 | $10 |

FIVE FLIGHTS UP
T-A
❑ 207	After the Feeling Is Gone/Where Are You Going, Girl?	1970	$8
❑ 202	Do What You Wanna Do/Black Cat	1970	$8
❑ 212	Like Monday Follows Sunday/California Girl	1971	$8

FIVE JETS, THE
DELUXE
❑ 6064	Crazy Chicken/Everybody Do the Chicken	1954	$70
❑ 6071	Down Slow/Please Love Me Baby	1955	$120
❑ 6018	I Am in Love/Not a Hand to Shake	1953	$200
❑ 6053	I'm Stuck/I Want a Woman	1954	$200
❑ 6058	Tell Me You're Mine/Give In	1954	$200

KING
| ❑ 6058 | Tell Me You're Mine/Give In | 1966 | $30 |

FIVE KEYS, THE
ALADDIN
Number	Title	Yr	NM
❑ 3167	Can't Keep From Crying/Come Go My Bail, Louise	1953	$800
❑ 3119	Darling/Goin' Downtown	1952	$1000
❑ 3245	Deep in My Heart/How Do You Expect Me to Get It	1954	$800
❑ 3136	Hold Me/I Hadn't Anyone Till You	1952	$800
❑ 3131	How Long/Mistakes	1952	$1200
❑ 3158	I Cried for You/Serve Another Round	1953	$900
❑ 3182	I'll Always Be in Love with You/Rocking and Crying Blues	1953	$800
❑ 3113	It's Christmas Time/Old Mac Donald	1951	$1000
❑ 3263	My Love/Why, Oh Why	1954	$300
❑ 3214	My Saddest Hour/Oh! Babe!	1953	$800
❑ 3228	Someday Sweetheart/Love My Loving	1954	$800
❑ 3312	Story of Love/Serve Another Round	1956	$300
❑ 3204	Teardrops in Your Eyes/I'm So High	1953	$800
❑ 3099	The Glory of Love/Hucklebuck with Jimmy	1951	$1000
❑ 3175	There Ought to Be a Law/Mama (Your Daughter Told a Lie on Me)	1953	$800
❑ 3190	These Foolish Things/Lonesome Old Story	1953	$4000

CAPITOL
❑ F-3786	Boom Boom/Face of An Angel	1957	$30
❑ F-3267	'Cause You're My Lover/Gee Whittakers	1955	$50
❑ F-3032	Close Your Eyes/Doggone It, You Did It	1955	$50
❑ F-3830	Do Anything/It's a Cryin' Shame	1957	$30
❑ F-3185	Don't You Know I Love You/I Wish I'd Never Learned to Read	1955	$50
❑ F-4009	Emily Please/Handy Andy	1958	$30
❑ F-3710	Four Walls/It's a Groove	1957	$30
❑ F-3861	From Me to You/Whippety Whirl	1957	$30
❑ F-2945	Ling, Ting, Tong/I'm Alone	1954	$50
❑ F-3455	My Pigeon's Gone/Peace and Love	1956	$50
❑ F-4092	One Great Love/Really-O, Truly-O	1958	$30
❑ 4828	Out of Sight/Out of Mind/From the Bottom of My Heart	1962	$30
❑ F-3502	Out of Sight, Out of Mind/That's Right	1956	$40
❑ F-3392	She's the Most/I Dreamt I Dwelt in Heaven	1956	$50

— *Regular large hole*

| ❑ F-3392 | She's the Most/I Dreamt I Dwelt in Heaven | 1956 | $75 |

— *Small hole*

❑ F-3738	This I Promise You/The Blues Don't Care	1957	$30
❑ F-3660	Tiger Lily/Let There Be You	1957	$30
❑ F-3597	Wisdom of a Fool/Now Don't That Prove I Love You	1956	$40

CLASSIC ARTISTS
| ❑ 115 | I Want You For Christmas/Express Yourself Back Home | 1989 | $5 |

— *As "Rudy West and the Five Keys*

GROOVE
| ❑ 0031 | I'll Follow You/Lawdy Miss Mary | 1954 | $4000 |

— *There is some debate about whether this record actually exists on 45.. VG 2000; VG+ 3000*

INFERNO
| ❑ 4500 | Hey Girl/No Matter | 1967 | $30 |

KING
❑ 5398	Bimbo/Valley of Love	1960	$30
❑ 5273	Dancing Senorita/Dream On	1959	$30
❑ 5496	Do Something for Me/Stop Your Crying	1961	$30
❑ 5330	Gonna Be Too Late/Rosetta	1960	$30
❑ 5302	How Can I Forget You/I Burned Your Letter	1960	$30
❑ 5358	I Didn't Know/No, Says My Heart	1960	$30
❑ 5877	I'll Never Stop Loving You/I Can't Escape from You	1964	$15
❑ 5251	I Took Your Love for a Toy/Ziggus	1959	$40

LIBERTY
| ❑ 1394 | It's Christmas Time/It's Christmas | 1980 | $8 |

— *B-side by Marvin and Johnny*

OWL
| ❑ 321 | A Dreamer/Your Teeth and Your Tongue | 1973 | $8 |

SEG-WAY
| ❑ 1008 | Out of Sight, Out of Mind/You're the One | 1962 | $20 |

UNITED ARTISTS
Number	Title	Yr	NM
❑ 0150	The Glory of Love/My Saddest Hour	1973	$4

— *Silver Spotlight Series" reissue*

7-Inch Extended Plays
CAPITOL
❑ EAP 3-828	C'est La Vie/Dream//Let There Be You/All I Need Is You	1957	$125
❑ EAP 1-828	(contents unknown)	1957	$125
❑ EAP 2-828	(contents unknown)	1957	$125
❑ EAP 1-572	Ling Ting Tong/I'm Alone//Close Your Eyes/Doggone It, You Did It	1955	$125
❑ EAP 1-572 [PS]	The Five Keys	1955	$125
❑ EAP 1-828 [PS]	The Five Keys On Stage! Volume 1	1957	$175

— *On cover, the far left singer has his thumb sticking out (inadvertently?) in a phallic way*

| ❑ EAP 1-828 [PS] | The Five Keys On Stage! Volume 1 | 1957 | $125 |

— *On cover, the far left singer's "offending" thumb is airbrushed out*

| ❑ EAP 2-828 [PS] | The Five Keys On Stage! Volume 2 | 1957 | $175 |

— *On cover, the far left singer has his thumb sticking out (inadvertently?) in a phallic way*

| ❑ EAP 2-828 [PS] | The Five Keys On Stage! Volume 2 | 1957 | $125 |

— *On cover, the far left singer's "offending" thumb is airbrushed out*

| ❑ EAP 3-828 [PS] | The Five Keys On Stage! Volume 3 | 1957 | $175 |

— *On cover, the far left singer has his thumb sticking out (inadvertently?) in a phallic way*

| ❑ EAP 3-828 [PS] | The Five Keys On Stage! Volume 3 | 1957 | $125 |

— *On cover, the far left singer's "offending" thumb is airbrushed out*

FIVE KIDS, THE
MAXWELL
| ❑ 101 | Carolyn/Oh Baby | 1955 | $3000 |

— *VG 1000; VG+ 2000*

FIVE LYRICS, THE
MUSIC CITY
| ❑ 799 | I'm Traveling Light/My Honeysweet Pea | 1956 | $1500 |

FIVE MAN ELECTRICAL BAND
CAPITOL
❑ 2517	Baby/Lovin' Look	1969	$6
❑ 2368	It Never Rains on Maple Lane/Private Train	1968	$6
❑ 2562	Sunrise to Sunset/Little Bit of Love	1969	$6

LION
❑ 112	Coming of Age/The Devil and Miss Lucy	1972	$5
❑ 149	I'm a Stranger Here/Doin' The Best We Can Rag	1973	$5
❑ 127	Money Back Guarantee/Find the One	1972	$5
❑ 160	Sweet Paradise/Baby Wanna Boogie	1973	$5

LIONEL
❑ 3220	Absolutely Right/Butterfly	1971	$5
❑ 3224	Friends and Family/Julianna	1971	$5
❑ 3213	Signs/Hello Melinda Goodbye	1971	$8

— *Lists "Hello Melinda Goodbye" as the A-side and contains the full-length version of "Signs*

| ❑ 3213 | Signs/Hello Melinda Goodbye | 1971 | $6 |

— *Lists no A and B sides and contains an edited version (3:20) of "Signs*

MGM
| ❑ 14182 [DJ] | Hello Melinda Goodbye/Signs | 1970 | $12 |

— *Evidently only exists as a promo*

| ❑ 14149 | Moonshine/Forever Together | 1970 | $6 |

POLYDOR
| ❑ 14221 | Werewolf/Country Angel | 1974 | $4 |

FIVE NOTES, THE
CHESS
| ❑ 1614 | Show Me the Way/Park Your Lover | 1955 | $200 |

FIVE PLAYBOYS, THE
DOT
| ❑ 15605 | When We Were Young/Pages of My Scrapbook | 1957 | $30 |

FEE BEE
| ❑ 232 | Angel Mine/She's My Baby | 1959 | $125 |

Number	Title	Yr	NM
❏ 213	When We Were Young/Pages of My Scrapbook	1958	$60

MERCURY

Number	Title	Yr	NM
❏ 71269	Time Will Allow/Why Be a Fool	1958	$30

PETITE

Number	Title	Yr	NM
❏ 504	She's My Baby/Mr. Echo	1959	$50

FIVE ROVERS, THE

MUSIC CITY

Number	Title	Yr	NM
❏ 798	Down to the Sea/Change Your Mind	1956	$120

FIVE ROYALES, THE

ABC-PARAMOUNT

Number	Title	Yr	NM
❏ 10348	Catch That Teardrop/Goof Ball	1962	$10
❏ 10368	What's In Your Heart/I Want It Like That	1962	$10

APOLLO

Number	Title	Yr	NM
❏ 443	Baby Don't Do It/Take All of Me	1952	$125
— Black vinyl			
❏ 443	Baby Don't Do It/Take All of Me	1952	$400
— Red vinyl			
❏ 441	Courage to Love/You Know I Know	1952	$125
— Black vinyl			
❏ 441	Courage to Love/You Know I Know	1952	$400
— Red vinyl			
❏ 454	Cry Some More/I Like It Like That	1954	$100
❏ 446	Help Me, Somebody/Crazy, Crazy, Crazy	1953	$125
❏ 452	I Do/Good Things	1954	$100
❏ 449	I Want to Thank You/All Righty	1953	$100
❏ 448	Too Much Lovin' (Much Too Much)/Laundromat Blues	1953	$120
❏ 458	What's That/Let Me Come Back Home	1954	$75
❏ 467	With All Your Heart/6 O'Clock in the Morning	1955	$75

HOME OF THE BLUES

Number	Title	Yr	NM
❏ 243	Catch That Teardrop/Goof Ball	1962	$700
❏ 218	If You Don't Need Me/I'm Gonna Tell Them	1961	$20
❏ 112	Please, Please, Please/I Got to Know	1960	$20
❏ 232	Take Me With You Baby/Not Going to Cry	1961	$20

KING

Number	Title	Yr	NM
❏ 5098	Dedicated to the One I Love/Don't Be Ashamed	1958	$50
❏ 5453	Dedicated to the One I Love/Miracle of Love	1961	$20
❏ 5756	Dedicated to the One I Love/Tears of Joy	1963	$20
❏ 5329	Don't Give No More Than You Can Take/I'm with You	1960	$30
❏ 5131	Do the Cha Cha Cherry/The Feeling Is Real	1958	$30
❏ 4770	Every Dog Has His Day/You Didn't Learn It at Home	1955	$100
❏ 4952	Get Something Out of It/Come On and Save Me	1956	$60
❏ 4785	How I Wonder/Mohawk Squaw	1955	$100
❏ 4830	I Ain't Gettin' Caught/Someone Made You for Me	1955	$60
❏ 4901	I Could Love You/My Wants for Love	1956	$60
❏ 4740	I'm Gonna Run It Down/Behave Yourself	1954	$100
❏ 4806	I Need Your Lovin'/When I Get Like This	1955	$60
❏ 5892	I Wonder Where Your Love Has Gone/I Need Your Lovin' Baby	1964	$20
— The Five Royals			
❏ 5082	Messin' Up/Say It	1957	$50
❏ 5191	Miracle of Love/I Know It's Hard, But It's Fair	1959	$30
❏ 4744	Monkey Hips and Rice/Devil with the Rest	1954	$100
❏ 5266	My Sugar Sugar/It Hurts Inside	1959	$30
❏ 4762	School Girl/One Mistake	1955	$100
❏ 5032	Tears of Joy/Thirty Second Lover	1957	$50
❏ 5237	Tell Me You Care/Wonder Where Your Love Has Gone	1959	$30
❏ 5141	Tell the Truth/Double or Nothing	1958	$30
❏ 5153	The Slummer the Slum/Don't Let It Be in Vain	1958	$30
❏ 5053	Think/I'd Better Make a Move	1957	$50
❏ 4869	When You Walked Through the Door/Right Around the Corner	1956	$60
❏ 5357	Why/Within My Heart	1960	$30
❏ 4819	Women About to Make Me Go Crazy/Do Unto You	1955	$60

SMASH

Number	Title	Yr	NM
❏ 1936	Baby Don't Do It/I Like It Like That	1964	$12

TODD

Number	Title	Yr	NM
❏ 1088	Baby Don't Do It/There's Somebody Over There	1963	$12
❏ 1086	I'm Standing in the Shadows/Doin' Everything	1963	$10

VEE JAY

Number	Title	Yr	NM
❏ 431	Help Me Somebody/Talk About My Woman	1962	$20
❏ 412	Much in Need/They Don't Know	1961	$20

FIVE SATINS, THE

BUDDAH

Number	Title	Yr	NM
❏ 477	Everybody Stand and Clap Your Hands/Hey There Pretty Lady	1975	$5
— As "Black Satin"			

CANDELITE

Number	Title	Yr	NM
❏ 411	She's Gone (With the Wind)/Somewhere a Voice Is Calling	1974	$6

CHANCELLOR

Number	Title	Yr	NM
❏ 1121	Do You Remember/Downtown	1962	$30
❏ 1110	The Masquerade Is Over/Raining in My Heart	1962	$30

CUB

Number	Title	Yr	NM
❏ 9090	Golden Earrings/Can I Come Over Tonight	1961	$30
❏ 9077	These Foolish Things/A Beggar with a Dream	1960	$30

ELEKTRA

Number	Title	Yr	NM
❏ 69938	Breaking Up/Loving You (Would Be the Sweetest Thing)	1982	$5
❏ 69888	Didn't I (Blow Your Mind)/Loving You (Would Be the Sweetest Thing)	1982	$5
❏ 69984	I'll Be Seeing You/Loving You (Would Be the Sweetest Thing)	1982	$5
❏ 47411	Memories of Days Gone By Medley/Loving You (Would Be the Sweetest Thing)	1982	$30
— As "Fred Parris and the Five Satins"			

EMBER

Number	Title	Yr	NM
❏ 1028	A Million to One/Love with No Love in Return	1957	$50
❏ 1066	Candlelight/The Time	1960	$30
❏ 1061	I'll Be Seeing You/A Night Like This	1960	$40
❏ 1005	I'll Remember (In the Still of the Nite)/The Jones Girl	1956	$40
— Red label			
❏ 1005	I'll Remember (In the Still of the Nite)/The Jones Girl	1959	$60
— Multi-color "logs" label; reads "Special Demand Release			
❏ 1005	I'll Remember (In the Still of the Nite)/The Jones Girl	1959	$40
— Multi-color "logs" label; no "Special Demand Release			
❏ 1005	In the Still of the Night "I'll Remember"/The Jones Girl	1961	$40
— Black label, white logo and red flames at left; A-side title revised yet again			
❏ 1005	In the Still of the Nite/The Jones Girl	1956	$200
— Red label; has "6106A" in the trail-off vinyl			
❏ 1005	In the Still of the Nite/The Jones Girl	1956	$60
— Red label; has "E-2105-45" in the trail-off vinyl			
❏ 1005	In the Still of the Nite/The Jones Girl	1956	$40
— Red label; has "E-1005" in the trail-off vinyl			
❏ 1005	In the Still of the Nite/The Jones Girl	1959	$50
— Multi-color "logs" label with original A-side title			
❏ 1025	Our Anniversary/Pretty Baby	1957	$50
— Red label			
❏ 1025	Our Anniversary/Pretty Baby	1957	$30
— Black label			
❏ 1014	Our Love Is Forever/Oh Happy Day	1957	$50
❏ 1056	Shadows/Toni My Love	1959	$40
❏ 1019	To the Aisle/Wish I Had My Baby	1957	$50
— Red label			
❏ 1019	To the Aisle/Wish I Had My Baby	1960	$40
— Multi-color "logs" label			
❏ 1019	To the Aisle/Wish I Had My Baby	1961	$30
— Black label			
❏ 1008	Weeping Willow/Wonderful Girl	1956	$50
❏ 1070	Wishing Ring/Tell Me Dear	1961	$30

FIRST

Number	Title	Yr	NM
❏ 104	When Your Love Comes Along/Skippity Doo	1959	$50
— Orange label			
❏ 104	When Your Love Comes Along/Skippity Doo	1959	$30
— Green label			

KIRSHNER

Number	Title	Yr	NM
❏ 4252	Two Different Worlds/Love Is Such a Beautiful Thing	1974	$10

KLIK

Number	Title	Yr	NM
❏ 1020	I Love You So/Story to You	1973	$10

MAMA SADIE

Number	Title	Yr	NM
❏ 1001	In the Still of the Night "67"/Heck No (Instrumental)	1967	$15

MUSICTONE

Number	Title	Yr	NM
❏ 1108	To the Aisle/Just to Be Near You	1961	$30

NIGHTRAIN

Number	Title	Yr	NM
❏ 901	All Mine/The Voice	1970	$10

RCA

Number	Title	Yr	NM
❏ 6989-7-R	In the Still of the Night/Yes	1988	$3
— B-side by Merry Clayton			

RCA VICTOR

Number	Title	Yr	NM
❏ 74-0478	Summer in New York/Dark at the Top of My Heart	1971	$10

ROULETTE

Number	Title	Yr	NM
❏ 4563	Ain't Gonna Cry/You Can Count on Me	1964	$10

STANDORD

Number	Title	Yr	NM
❏ 100	All Mine/Rose Mary	1956	$700
— Red label			
❏ 100	All Mine/Rose Mary	1962	$200
— Maroon label			
❏ 200	In the Still of the Nite/The Jones Girl	1956	$900
❏ 200	In the Still of the Nite/The Jones Girl	1956	$2000
— With "Produced by Martin Kuegell" credit. VG 1000; VG+ 1500			

TIME MACHINE

Number	Title	Yr	NM
❏ 571	The Masquerade Is Over/Lonely Hearts	1962	$8
❏ 570	Wonder Why/No One Knows	1962	$8

TIMES SQUARE

Number	Title	Yr	NM
❏ 4	All Mine/Rose Mary	1962	$30
— Blue vinyl			
❏ 21	Paradise on Earth/Monkey Business	1963	$30
❏ 94	Paradise on Earth/Monkey Business	1964	$20

UNITED ARTISTS

Number	Title	Yr	NM
❏ 368	On a Lover's Island/Till the End	1961	$30

7-Inch Extended Plays

EMBER

Number	Title	Yr	NM
❏ EEP-100	I'll Remember/The Jones Girl//Wonderful Girl/Pretty Baby	1957	$250
❏ EEP-102	Our Anniversary/I'll Get Along/Wish I Had My Baby/Moonlight and I	1957	$250
❏ EEP-100 [PS]	The Five Satins Sing (Vol. 1)	1957	$250
❏ EEP-101 [PS]	The Five Satins Sing (Vol. 2)	1957	$250
❏ EEP-102 [PS]	The Five Satins Sing (Vol. 3)	1957	$250
❏ EEP-101	To the Aisle/Sugar//Our Love Is Forever/Weeping Willow	1957	$250

FIVE SCALDERS, THE

DRUMMOND

Number	Title	Yr	NM
❏ 3001	Girl Friend/Willow Blues	1956	$1500
— Blue label			
❏ 3001	Girl Friend/Willow Blues	1956	$1000
— Maroon label			
❏ 3000	If Only You Were Mine/There Will Come a Time	1956	$1000

SUGAR HILL

Number	Title	Yr	NM
❏ 3000	If Only You Were Mine/There Will Come a Time	1956	$2000

FIVE SECRETS, THE

DECCA

Number	Title	Yr	NM
❏ 30350	See You Next Year/Queen Bee	1957	$100
❏ 30350	See You Next Year/Queen Bee	1957	$50
— As "The Secrets"			

Number	Title	Yr	NM

FIVE SHARKS, THE

AMBER

❏ 852	The Lion Sleeps Tonight/ Land of 1000 Dances	1966	$10

OLD TIMER

❏ 604	Gloria/Flames	1964	$30
❏ 611	Gloria/Flames	1965	$30

—*Red vinyl*

❏ 611	Gloria/Flames	1965	$20

—*Black vinyl*

❏ 605	Stand By Me/I'll Never Let You Go	1964	$30

—*Gold vinyl*

❏ 605	Stand By Me/I'll Never Let You Go	1964	$20

—*Blue vinyl*

RELIC

❏ 525	Stormy Weather (2:45)/ If You Love Me	1965	$10

SIAMESE

❏ 404	Gloria/Flames	1965	$15

TIMES SQUARE

❏ 35	Stormy Weather (2:45)/ If You Love Me	1964	$40
❏ 35	Stormy Weather (3:45)/ If You Love Me	1964	$70

—*Blue vinyl*

❏ 35	Stormy Weather (3:45)/ If You Love Me	1964	$50

—*Black vinyl*

FIVE SHARPS, THE (1)

BIM BAM BOOM

❏ 103	Stormy Weather/ Sleepy Cowboy	1972	$8

—*Reissue mastered off the cracked Jubilee 78 (see below); the original master has long since disappeared*

FIVE SHARPS, THE (2)

JUBILEE

❏ 5478	Stormy Weather/ Mammy Jammy	1964	$15

FIVE SHITS

CHANCE

❏ 1163	My Pretty Little Girl/ Stormy Weather	1974	$30

—*This was not released in the 1950s; this used the classic 1950s label, either as a lark or an attempt to fool gullible collectors. (Come on; would a group called the Five Shits ever made it onto record in the 1950s?)*

LOST-CAUSE

❏ 100	Dreaming of You/ Let Me Tell You	1974	$30

—*Blue vinyl*

FIVE SOUNDS, THE

EPIC

❏ 9856	Baby, Please Don't Cry/Loadin' Coal	1965	$30
❏ 10016	Miss Ann/Peanut Butter	1966	$30

FIVE SPECIAL

ELEKTRA

❏ 46572	Do It Baby/It's a Wonderful Day	1979	$6
❏ 47023	Do Something Special (For Your Lady)/Be Mine for a While	1980	$6
❏ 47119	Heaven (You Are to Me)/ Had You a Lover (But You Let Her Go)	1981	$6
❏ 46032	Why Leave Us Alone/ (Instrumental)	1979	$6

MERCURY

❏ 73849	The More I Get to Know You/(Part II)	1976	$30

FIVE STAIRSTEPS, THE

BUDDAH

❏ 26	A Million to One/You Make Me So Mad	1968	$8

—*As "Five Stairsteps and Cubie"*

❏ 26 [PS]	A Million to One/You Make Me So Mad	1968	$20
❏ 188	Because I Love You/ America Standing	1970	$5
❏ 165	Dear Prudence/O-o-h Child	1970	$8
❏ 213	Didn't It Look So Easy/ Peace Is Gonna Come	1971	$5

—*Starting with the above, as "Stairsteps"*

❏ 320	Every Single Way/ Two Weeks' Notice	1972	$5
❏ 291	Hush Child/The Easy Way	1972	$5
❏ 277	I Love You-Stop/I Feel a Song (In My Heart Again)	1972	$5

❏ 165	O-o-h Child/Who Do You Belong To	1970	$6
❏ 222	Snow/Look Out	1971	$5
❏ 20	Something's Missing/ Tell Me Who	1967	$8

—*As "Five Stairsteps and Cubie*

❏ 20 [PS]	Something's Missing/ Tell Me Who	1967	$20
❏ 35	The Shadow of Your Love/Bad News	1968	$8

CURTOM

❏ 1936	Baby Make Me Feel So Good/Little Young Lover	1969	$6
❏ 1931	Don't Change Your Love/ New Dance Craze	1968	$6

—*Curtom releases as "Five Stairsteps and Cubie"*

❏ 1933	I Made a Mistake/ Stay Close to Me	1968	$6
❏ 1944	Madame Mary/ Little Boy Blue	1969	$6
❏ 1945	We Must Be in Love/ Little Young Lover	1969	$6

DARK HORSE

❏ 10005	From Us to You/Time	1975	$5
❏ 10005 [PS]	From Us to You/Time	1975	$6
❏ 10009	Tell Me Why/Salaam	1976	$5

WINDY "C"

❏ 605	Ain't Gonna Rest (Till I Get You)/You Can't See	1967	$10
❏ 603	Come Back/You Don't Love Me	1966	$10
❏ 604	Danger, She's a Stranger/ Behind Curtains	1967	$12
❏ 607	Oooh, Baby Baby/ The Girl I Love	1967	$10
❏ 608	The Touch of You/ Change of Face	1967	$10
❏ 602	World of Fantasy/ Playgirl's Love	1966	$10

FIVE STAR

RCA

❏ PB-14108	All Fall Down/First Avenue	1985	$4
❏ 8853-7-R	Another Weekend/U	1989	$5
❏ 5149-7-R	Are You Man Enough?/ Summer Groove	1987	$4
❏ PB-14421	Can't Wait Another Minute/ Don't You Know I Love It	1986	$4
❏ PB-14421 [PS]	Can't Wait Another Minute/ Don't You Know I Love It	1986	$4
❏ 5179-7-RG	Can't Wait Another Minute/ Let Me Be the One	1987	$3

—*Gold Standard Series" reissue*

❏ PB-13818	Hide and Seek/I'm Gonna Make This a Night You'll Never Forget	1984	$12
❏ 5083-7-R	If I Say Yes/Let Me Down Easy	1986	$4
❏ 5083-7-R [PS]	If I Say Yes/Let Me Down Easy	1986	$4
❏ PB-14229	Let Me Be the One (Edit)/ (Edited Philadelphia Remix)	1985	$4
❏ PB-14229 [PS]	Let Me Be the One (Edit)/ (Edited Philadelphia Remix)	1985	$4
❏ PB-14323	Love Take Over/ Keep in Touch	1986	$4
❏ 8711-7-R	Someone's in Love/ Rare Groove	1988	$5
❏ 5365-7-R	Strong as Steel/The Man	1987	$5
❏ 5292-7-R	Whenever You're Ready/ Forever Yours	1987	$4
❏ 5292-7-R [PS]	Whenever You're Ready/ Forever Yours	1987	$4

FIVE STARS, THE (1)

ABC-PARAMOUNT

❏ 9911	Pickin' on the Wrong Chicken/Dreaming	1958	$30

HUNT

❏ 318	Pickin' on the Wrong Chicken/Dreaming	1959	$30

NOTE

❏ 10031	Am I Wasting My Time/ Gamblin' Man	1959	$40
❏ 10016	My Paradise/Friction	1958	$50
❏ 10011	Pickin' on the Wrong Chicken/Dreaming	1958	$40

FIVE STARS, THE (2)

SHOW TIME

❏ 1102	Where Did Caledonia Go?/Walkin' An' Talkin'	1954	$250

FIVE STARS, THE (U)

ATCO

❏ 6065	Take Five/Humpty Dump	1956	$40

BLUES BOYS KINGDOM

❏ 106	So Lonely, Baby/Hey Juanita	1957	$200

COLUMBIA

❏ 4-42056	Baby Baby/Blabber Mouth	1961	$70

DOT

❏ 15579	Atom Bomb Baby/You Sweet Little Thing	1957	$30

END

❏ 1028	Baby Baby/Blabber Mouth	1958	$100

KERNEL

❏ 3195	Atom Bomb Baby/You Sweet Little Thing	1957	$125

MARK-X

❏ 7006	Dead Wrong/Ooh Shucks	1957	$125

TREAT

❏ 505	Let's Fall in Love/We Danced in the Moonlight	1955	$2000

FIVE SUPERIORS, THE

GARPAX

❏ 44170	There's a Fool Born Every Day/Big Shot	1962	$200

FIVE SWANS, THE

MUSIC CITY

❏ 795	Little Girl of My Dreams/ Little Tipa Tins	1956	$300

5000 VOLTS

PHILIPS

❏ 40804	Bye Love/Look Out I'm Coming	1976	$6
❏ 40801	I'm on Fire/Still on Fire	1975	$6

PRIVATE STOCK

❏ 45,114	Doctor Kiss-Kiss/Thunderfire	1976	$8

FIVE THRILLS, THE

PARROT

❏ 800	Gloria/Wee Wee Baby	1954	$2000

—*Black vinyl. VG 1000; VG+ 1500*

❏ 800	Gloria/Wee Wee Baby	1954	$4000

—*Red vinyl*

❏ 796	My Baby's Gone/ Feel So Good	1954	$800

FIVE TINOS, THE

SUN

❏ 222	Sitting By My Window/ Don't Do That	1955	$1200

FIVE TRUMPETS, THE

GOTHAM

❏ 693	My Chains Fell Off/The Lord Knows What I Need	1952	$70
❏ 681	Stand By Me/Jesus Is Here Today	1951	$70

RCA VICTOR

❏ 50-0014	Oh Lord/Don't Let Nobody Turn You Around	1949	$75

—*Orange vinyl*

❏ 50-0034	Swing Low Sweet Chariot/ Sign of the Judgment	1949	$75

—*Orange vinyl*

❏ 50-0080	When the Saints Go Marching In/ Preach My Word	1950	$75

—*Orange vinyl*

SAVOY

❏ 4060	Amazing Grace/Lord I Want to Be a Christian	1955	$30
❏ 4072	I've Got Jesus/I Shall Not Be Moved	1956	$30

FIVE WHISPERS, THE

DOLTON

❏ 69	Awake of Asleep/ Especially for You	1963	$20
❏ 90	Can't Face the Crowd/ Sleep Walker	1964	$20
❏ 61	Midnight Sun/Moon in the Afternoon	1962	$20

FIVE WILLOWS, THE

ALLEN

❏ 1002	Delores/All Night Long	1953	$600
❏ 1000	My Dear, Dearest Darling/ Rock, Little Francis	1953	$300
❏ 1003	The White Cliffs of Dover/ With These Hands	1953	$700

HERALD

❏ 433	Baby Come a Little Closer/Lay Your Head on My Shoulder	1954	$300
❏ 442	Look Me in the Eyes/ So Help Me	1954	$400

PEE DEE

❏ 290	Love Bells/Please, Baby	1953	$1500

FIVE WINGS, THE

KING

❏ 4781	Teardrops Are Falling/ Rock-A-Locka	1955	$400

—*Later released on King 5199 as The Checkers.*

Number	Title	Yr	NM

FIXX, THE
MCA
52444	Are We Ourselves?/Deeper and Deeper	1984	$3
52444 [PS]	Are We Ourselves?/Deeper and Deeper	1984	$3
52902	Built for the Future/Camphor	1986	$4
52902 [PS]	Built for the Future/Camphor	1986	$8
52529	Less Cities, More Moving People/Woman on a Train	1984	$4
52529 [PS]	Less Cities, More Moving People/Woman on a Train	1984	$4
52264	One Thing Leads to Another/Opinions	1983	$4
52264 [PS]	One Thing Leads to Another/Opinions	1983	$4
52213	Saved by Zero/Going Overboard	1983	$4
52213 [PS]	Saved by Zero/Going Overboard	1983	$4
52832	Secret Separation/Sense of Adventure	1986	$4
52106	Stand or Fall/Sinking Island	1982	$4
52498	Sunshine in the Shade/Question	1984	$4
52498 [PS]	Sunshine in the Shade/Question	1984	$4
52498 [DJ]	Sunshine in the Shade (same on both sides)	1984	$10

— Promo only on yellow vinyl (black vinyl promos are about the same as a stock copy in value)

52316 [PS]	The Sign of Fire	1983	$4

— Most copies of this sleeve had a "Sealed for Your Protection" sticker that kept the record from being removed; the same sleeve was used for both variations of the record

52316	The Sign of Fire/One Thing Leads to Another (Live)	1983	$5
52316	The Sign of Fire/Saved by Zero (Live)	1983	$4

RCA
8837-7-R	Driven Out/Shred of Evidence	1988	$3
8837-7-R [PS]	Driven Out/Shred of Evidence	1988	$3

FLACK, ROBERTA, AND DONNY HATHAWAY
ATLANTIC
3661	Back Together Again/God Don't Like Ugly	1980	$4
3463	The Closer I Get to You/Love Is the Healing	1978	$4

— B-side by Flack alone

2879	Where Is the Love/Mood	1972	$5

FLACK, ROBERTA
ATLANTIC
2665	Compared to What/That's No Way to Say Goodbye	1969	$8
3753	Don't Make Me Wait Too Long/Only Heaven Can Wait (For Love)	1980	$4
3271	Feelin' That Glow/Some Gospel According to Matthew	1975	$4
3025	Feel Like Makin' Love/When You Smile	1974	$5
3203	Feel Like Makin' Love/When You Smile	1974	$4
2730	How Many Broken Wings/Baby Baby	1970	$6

— With Les McCann

3483	If Ever I See You Again/I'd Like to Be a Baby to You	1978	$4
4068	I'm the One/'Til the Morning Comes	1982	$4
89932	In the Name of Love/Happiness	1982	$4
2785	Let It Be Me/Do What Cha Gotta Do	1971	$6
89440	Let Me Be a Light to Shine/We Shall Overcome	1986	$3

— With Howard Hewett

4005	Making Love/Jesse	1982	$4
4005 [PS]	Making Love/Jesse	1982	$6
88996	Oasis/You Know What It's Like	1988	$3
88996 [PS]	Oasis/You Know What It's Like	1988	$3
89931	Our Love Will Stop the World/Only Heaven Can Wait (For Love)	1982	$4

— A-side: With Eric Mercury

88898	Shock to My System/You Know What It's Like	1989	$3
3441	The 25th of Last December/Move In with Me	1977	$4
2864	The First Time Ever I Saw Your Face/Trade Winds	1972	$5
89295	We Shall Overcome/We Shall Overcome	1987	$3
3521	When It's Over/Come Share My Love	1978	$4
2851	Will You Still Love Me Tomorrow/Go Up Moses	1972	$5

COLUMBIA
44448	Cold, Cold Winter/If You Ever Leave Me Now	1968	$10

44050	Si, Si, Senor/This Year	1967	$10

MCA
51173	Lovin' You/Hittin' Me Where It Hurts	1981	$4

VIVA
29401	This Side of Forever/Robbery Suspects	1983	$4

— B-side by The Enforcers

7-Inch Extended Plays
ATLANTIC
SD 7-7271	I'm the Girl/Conversation Love//River/When You Smile	1973	$8

— Jukebox issue; small hole, plays at 33 1/3 rpm

FLAGG, BILL
MGM
12637	Doin' My Time/I Will Always Love You	1958	$125

TETRA
4445	Go Cat, Go/A Good Woman's Leaving	1956	$200
4448	Guitar Rock/I'm So Lonely	1957	$200

FLAIRS, THE (1)
ABC-PARAMOUNT
9740	Aladdin's Lamp/Steppin' Out	1956	$50

FLAIR
1041	Baby Wants/You Were Untrue	1954	$400
1012	I Had a Love/She Wants to Rock	1953	$400
1056	I'll Never Let You Go/Hold Me, Thrill Me, Chill Me	1955	$400
1051	Love Me, Love Me, Love Me/My Heart's Crying for You	1954	$400

— As "The Chimes"

1028	Love Me Girl/Gettin' High	1954	$400
1067	She Loves to Dance/My Darling, My Sweet	1955	$400
1019	Tell Me You Love Me/You Should Care for Me	1953	$400
1044	This Is the Night for Love/Let's Make with Some Love	1954	$400

FLAME, THE
BROTHER
3502	Another Day Like Heaven/I'm So Happy	1970	$20
3501	See the Light/Got Your Mind Made Up	1970	$20

FLAMES, THE
7-11
2107	Together/Baby, Pretty Baby	1953	$500

BERTRAM
203	I'll Never Let You Go/Crazy	1958	$30

DOT
15813	The Scramble (Part 1)/The Scramble (Part 2)	1958	$20

FARGO
1018	Making Time/Letti Lu	1961	$30

HARLEM
114	So Long My Darling/I'm Going to Try to Live My Life All Over	1960	$3000

— As "The Fabulous Flames." VG 1500; VG+ 2250

114	So Long My Darling/I'm Going to Try to Live My Life All Over	1960	$800

— As "The Flames"

SPIN
101	Cryin' for My Baby/Starnge Land Blues	1952	$500

FLAMIN' GROOVIES, THE
EPIC
10564	Somethin' Else/Laurie Did It	1969	$12

KAMA SUTRA
527	Have You Seen My Baby/Yesterday's Numbers	1971	$12

RCA
PB-11266	Too Many Cooks/Watch Me Run	1978	$6

SIRE
731	I Can't Hide/Teenage Confidential	1976	$6

FLAMING EMBER, THE
FORTUNE
869	Gone, Gone, Gone/You Can Count on Me	1965	$70

HOT WAX
7109	If It's Good to You (Part 1)/If It's Good to You (Part 2)	1971	$6
7006	I'm Not My Brothers Keeper/Deserted Village	1970	$6
6902	Mind, Body and Soul/Filet de Soul	1969	$6
6907	Shades of Green/Don't You Wanna Wanna	1969	$6
7010	Stop the World and Let Me Off/Robot in a Robot's World	1970	$6
7103	Sunshine/1200 Miles	1971	$6
7003	Westbound #9/Why Don't You Stay	1970	$6

RIC-TIC
140	Bless You (My Love) (Instrumental)/Bless You (My Love) (Vocal)	1968	$20

— B-side by Al Kent

143	Children (Vocal)/Children (Instrumental)	1968	$20
132	Hey Mama/Let's Have a Love-In	1967	$30
129	Let's Have a Love-In (Vocal)/Let's Have a Love-In (Instrumental)	1967	$30

— B-side credited to Wingate's Love-In Strings

131	She's a Real Live Wire/Let's Have a Love-In (Instrumental)	1967	$30

— B-side credited to Wingate's Love-In Strings

145	Tell It Like It Is/Just Like Children	1968	$20

FLAMING LIPS, THE
SUB POP
SP28	Drug Machine//Strychnine/What's So Funny 'Bout Peace, Love and Understanding	1989	$30

— 1500 copies, all on black vinyl

SP28 [PS]	Drug Machine//Strychnine/What's So Funny 'Bout Peace, Love and Understanding	1989	$30

— Sub Pop Singles Club release for January 1989 (#3)

FLAMINGOS, THE
CHANCE
1154	Cross Over the Bridge/Listen to My Plea	1954	$1000
1145	Golden Teardrops/Carried Away	1953	$1000

— Black vinyl

1145	Golden Teardrops/Carried Away	1953	$3000

— Red vinyl

1133	If I Can't Have You/Someday, Somehow	1953	$800

— Black vinyl

1133	If I Can't Have You/Someday, Somehow	1953	$2000

— Red vinyl. VG 1000; VG+ 1500

1149	Plan for Love/You Ain't Ready	1953	$2000

— Yellow and black label

1149	Plan for Love/You Ain't Ready	1953	$800

— Blue and silver label

1140	That's My Desire/Hurry Home Baby	1953	$600

— Black vinyl

1140	That's My Desire/Hurry Home Baby	1953	$1500

— Red vinyl

CHECKER
1091	Goodnight Sweetheart/Does It Really Matter	1964	$20
830	I'll Be Home/Need Your Love	1956	$100
821	I Want to Love You/Please Come Back Home	1955	$100
1084	Lover Come Back to Me/Your Little Guy	1964	$20
815	That's My Baby (Chick-a-Boom)/When	1955	$100
915	Whispering Stars/Dream of a Lifetime	1959	$60

DECCA
30454	Helpless/My Faith in You	1957	$40
30335	The Ladder of Love/Let's Make Up	1957	$40

END
1044	At the Prom/Love Walked In	1959	$50
1070	Besame Mucho/You, Me and the Sea	1960	$30
1079	Beside You/When I Fall in Love	1960	$30
1116	For All We Know/Near You	1962	$30
1121	I Know Better/Flame of Love	1963	$30
1046 [M]	I Only Have Eyes for You/At the Prom	1959	$30
1046 [S]	I Only Have Eyes for You/At the Prom	1959	$60

— This B-side has been confirmed for the stereo version; others are not yet known

Number	Title	Yr	NM
❑ 1046 [M]	I Only Have Eyes for You/Goodnight Sweetheart	1959	$40
❑ 1046 [M]	I Only Have Eyes for You/Love Walked In	1959	$30
❑ 1040	I Shed a Tear at Your Wedding/But Not for Me	1959	$40
❑ 1111	It Must Be Love/I'm No Fool Anymore	1962	$30
❑ 1062	I Was Such a Fool/Heavenly Angel	1959	$30
❑ 1035	Lovers Never Say Goodbye/That Love Is You	1958	$50

—A-sides of End 1035 are the same song, the titles were changed

❑ 1073	Mio Amore/At Night	1960	$30
❑ 1065	Mio Amore/You, Me and the Sea	1960	$30
❑ 1099	My Memories of You/I Want to Love You	1961	$30
❑ 1035	Please Wait for Me/That Love Is You	1958	$70
❑ 1124	(Talk About) True Love/Come to My Party	1963	$30
❑ 1085	Thatr's Why I Love You/Ko Ko Mo	1961	$30
❑ 1092	Time Was/Dream Girl	1961	$30

JULMAR
❑ 506	Dealin' All the Way/Dealin' (Groovin' with Feelin')	1969	$12

OLDIES 45
❑ 35	Golden Teardrops/Carried Away	1963	$8
❑ 43	I Only Have Eyes for You/At the Prom	1963	$8
❑ 68	Lovers Never Say Goodbye/Baby, I Need You	1964	$8

—B-side by the El Dorados

PARROT
❑ 808	Dream of a Lifetime/On My Merry Way	1954	$800

—Black vinyl

❑ 808	Dream of a Lifetime/On My Merry Way	1954	$1600

—Red vinyl

❑ 812	I'm Yours/Ko Ko Mo	1955	$800

—Black vinyl

❑ 812	I'm Yours/Ko Ko Mo	1955	$1600

—Red vinyl

❑ 811	I Really Don't Want to Know/Get With It	1955	$8000

—Red vinyl. VG 4000; VG+ 6000

❑ 811	I Really Don't Want to Know/Get With It	1955	$5000

—Black vinyl. VG 2500; VG+ 2750

PHILIPS
❑ 40378	Brooklyn Boogaloo/Since My Baby Put Me Down	1966	$20
❑ 40413	Itty Bitty Baby/She Shook My World	1966	$20
❑ 40496	Oh Mary Don't You Worry/Do It, Do It	1967	$20
❑ 40308	Temptation/Call Her on the Phone	1965	$20
❑ 40347	The Boogaloo Party/The Nearness of You	1965	$20

POLYDOR
❑ 14019	Buffalo Soldier (Long)/Buffalo Soldier (Short)	1970	$10
❑ 14044	Straighten It Up (Get It Together)/Lover Come Back to Me	1970	$10

RONZE
❑ 116	Love Keeps the Doctor Away (Long)/Love Keeps the Doctor Away (Short)	1972	$5
❑ 115	Someone to Watch Over Me/Heavy Hips	1972	$5
❑ 111	Welcome Home/Gotta Have All Your Lovin'	1971	$5

ROULETTE
❑ 4524	Ol' Man River (Part 1)/Ol' Man River (Part 2)	1963	$30

TIMES SQUARE
❑ 102	A Lovely Way to Spend an Evening/Walking My Baby Back Home	1964	$20

VEE JAY
❑ 384	Golden Teardrops/Carried Away	1961	$30

WORLDS
❑ 103	Think About Me/(Instrumental)	1974	$5

7-Inch Extended Plays

END
❑ 205	Goodnight Sweetheart/Music Maestro Please//I Only Have Eyes for You/I'm in the Mood for Love	1959	$250
❑ 205 [PS]	The Flamingos	1959	$250

FLANAGAN, RALPH
RCA VICTOR
Number	Title	Yr	NM
❑ 54-0004	White Christmas/She Wore A Yellow Ribbon	1949	$20

FLARES, THE
FELSTED
❑ 8624	Foot Stomping -- Part 1/Foot Stomping -- Part 2	1961	$30
❑ 8604	Loving You/Hotcha Cha-Cha Brown	1960	$30
❑ 8607	What Do You Want If You Don't Want Love/Jump and Hump	1960	$30

PRESS
❑ 2802	Doing the Hully Gully/Truck and Trailer	1962	$20
❑ 2807	Do It with Me/Yon He Go	1963	$20
❑ 2808	Hand Clappin'/Shimmy and Stomp	1963	$20
❑ 2814	I Didn't Lose a Doggone Thing/Write a Song About Me	1964	$20
❑ 2803	Madhouse/Make It Be Me	1962	$20
❑ 2810	Monkey Walk/Do It If You Wanna	1963	$20

FLASH AND THE PAN
EPIC
❑ 9-50761 [DJ]	Down Among the Dead Men (Long Version)/(Short Version)	1979	$5
❑ 9-50761	Down Among the Dead Men/The Man Who Knew the Answer	1979	$6
❑ 8-50715	Hey, St. Peter/Walking in the Rain	1979	$6
❑ 9-50882	Media Man/Captain Beware	1980	$6
❑ 9-50920	Welcome to the Universe/Lights in the Night	1980	$6
❑ 34-03316	Where Were You/Hey Jimmy	1982	$6

MIDLAND INT'L.
❑ JB-10934 [DJ]	Hey, St. Peter (Short)/(Long)	1977	$12
❑ MB-10934	Hey, St. Peter/Walking in the Rain	1977	$20

FLASH CADILLAC AND THE CONTINENTAL KIDS
EPIC
❑ 11043	At the Hop/She's So Fine	1973	$5
❑ 10930	Muleskinner Blues/Teenage Eyes	1972	$5
❑ 11102	The Way I Feel Tonight/Dancin'	1974	$5

PRIVATE STOCK
❑ 45,079	Did You Boogie (With Your Baby)/Maybe It's All in My Mind	1976	$4
❑ 45,006	Good Times, Rock and Roll/It's Hard	1974	$4
❑ 45,026	Hot Summer Girls/Time Will Tell	1975	$4
❑ 45,134	See My Baby Jive/Brown Water	1977	$4

FLATT AND SCRUGGS
COLUMBIA
❑ 41064	A Hundred Years from Now/I Won't Be Hanging Around	1957	$20
❑ 41336	A Million Years in Glory/Jesus Savior, Pilot Me	1959	$20
❑ 21209	Be Ready/Mother Prays Loud	1954	$30
❑ 41125	Big Black Train/Crying Alone	1958	$20
❑ 20915	Brother I'm Getting Ready to Go/Get in Line Brother	1952	$30
❑ S730908 [S]	Bugle Call Rag/Cumberland Gap	1960	$20

—The above five are "Stereo Seven" 33 1/3 rpm jukebox singles from "JS7-19

❑ 41184	Building on Sand/Heaven	1958	$20
❑ 41389	Cabin in the Hills/Someone You Have Forgotten	1959	$20
❑ 44194	California Up Tight Band/Last Train to Clarksville	1967	$10
❑ 44194 [PS]	California Up Tight Band/Last Train to Clarksville	1967	$20
❑ 20777	Come Back Darling/I'm Waiting to Hear You Call My Darling	1951	$30
❑ S730906 [S]	Cripple Creek/Lonesome Road Blues	1960	$20
❑ 41518	Crying My Heart Out Over You/Foggy Mountain Rock	1959	$20
❑ 21125	Dear Old Dixie/If I Should Wander Back	1953	$30
❑ 21054	Dim Lights Thick Smoke/Flint Hill Special	1952	$30
❑ 20854	Don't Get Above Your Raisin'/I've Lost You	1951	$30
❑ 40990	Don't Let Your Deal Go Down/Let Those Brown Eyes Smile at Me	1957	$30
❑ 44380	Foggy Mountain Breakdown/Down in the Flood	1967	$15
❑ 44380 [PS]	Foggy Mountain Breakdown/Down in the Flood	1967	$15

❑ 21295	Foggy Mountain Breakdown/You're Not a Drop in the Bucket	1954	$30
❑ 21179	Foggy Mountain Chimes/I'll Go Steppin' Too	1953	$30
❑ 43627	For Lovin' Me/Colours	1966	$10
❑ 40928	Give Me Flowers While I'm Living/Is There Room for Me?	1957	$20
❑ 42141	Go Home/Where Will I Shelter My Sheep	1961	$15
❑ 21460	Gone Home/Bubbling in My Soul	1955	$30
❑ 43497	Green Acres/I Had a Dream	1965	$20

—With June Carter

❑ S730904 [S]	Ground Speed/Home Sweet Home	1960	$20
❑ 41983	I Ain't Going to Work Tomorrow/I Should Wander Back Tonight	1961	$20
❑ 44731	I'll Be Your Baby Tonight/Universal Soldier	1969	$10
❑ 20957	I'll Stay Around/Old Home Town	1952	$30
❑ 21043	I'm Gonna Settle Down/I'm Lonesome and Blue	1952	$30
❑ 21412	I'm Gonna Sleep with One Eye Open/Before I Met You	1955	$30
❑ 21147	I'm Workin' on a Road/He Took Your Place	1953	$30
❑ 43204	I Still Miss Someone/Father's Table Grace	1964	$10
❑ 43973	It Was Only the Wind/Why Can't I Find Myself with You	1967	$10
❑ 44623	Like a Rolling Stone/I'd Like to Say a Word About Texas	1968	$12
❑ 45030	Maggie's Farm/Tonight We'll Be Fine	1969	$10
❑ 41244	Mama's and Daddy's Little Girl/I Don't Care Anymore	1958	$20
❑ 43412	Memphis/Foggy Mountain Breakdown	1965	$10
❑ 21002	Over the Hills to the Poorhouse/My Darling's Last Goodbye	1952	$30
❑ 42755	Pearl Pearl Pearl/Hard Travelin'	1963	$15
❑ 42755 [PS]	Pearl Pearl Pearl/Hard Travelin'	1963	$20
❑ 42982	Petticoat Junction/Have You Seen My Dear Companion	1964	$20
❑ 41786	Polka on a Banjo/Shuckin' the Corn	1960	$20
❑ S730905 [S]	Sally Ann/Reuben	1960	$20
❑ 43135	Sally Don't You Grieve/Little Birdie	1964	$10
❑ 40853	Shuckin' the Corn/Six White Horses	1957	$20
❑ 21248	Somebody Took My Place with You/I'd Rather Be Alone	1954	$30
❑ 42606	The Ballad of Jed Clampett/Coal Loadin' Johnny	1962	$20
❑ 42606 [PS]	The Ballad of Jed Clampett/Coal Loadin' Johnny	1962	$30
❑ 4-42606 [DJ]	The Ballad of Jed Clampett (same on both sides)	1962	$40

—Promo only on red vinyl

❑ 41708	The Great Historical Bum/All I Want Is You	1960	$20
❑ 43803	The Last Thing on My Mind/Mama You Been on My Mind	1966	$10
❑ 42413	The Legend of the Johnson Boys/Hear the Whistle Blow a Hundred Miles	1962	$15
❑ 21334	Till the End of the World Rolls Around/Don't This Road Look Rough	1954	$30
❑ 20886	'Tis Sweet to Be Remembered/Earl's Breakdown	1952	$30
❑ 20805	We Can't Be Darlings/I'm Head Over Heels in Love	1951	$30
❑ 21091	Why Did You Wander/Thinking About You	1953	$30
❑ 43080	Workin' It Out/Fireball	1964	$10

MERCURY
❑ 6333	Doin' My Time/Farewell Blues	1951	$30
❑ 6211	Down the Road/Why Don't You Tell Me So	1950	$40
❑ 70064	God Loves His Children/Back to the Cross	1953	$30
❑ 6161	God Loves His Children/I'm Going to Make Heaven My Home	1950	$40

—Note: Earlier Mercury 45s by Flatt and Scruggs may exist

❑ 6287	I'll Never Love Another/My Little Girl in Tennessee	1950	$40
❑ 6268	Is It Too Late Now/So Happy I'll Be	1950	$40
❑ 6317	Pain in My Heart/Take Me in a Lifeboat	1951	$30
❑ 6396	Pike County Breakdown/Old Salty Dog Blues	1952	$30
❑ 70016	Preachin', Prayin', Singin'/Will Roses Bloom	1952	$30
❑ 6302	That Little Old Country Church House/Cora Is Gone	1951	$30
❑ 72739	Theme from Bonnie & Clyde (Foggy Mountain Breakdown)/My Cabin in Caroline	1967	$10

Number	Title	Yr	NM
❏ 72739 [PS]	Theme from Bonnie & Clyde (Foggy Mountain Breakdown)/ My Cabin in Caroline	1967	$20

FLATT, LESTER, AND MAC WISEMAN
RCA VICTOR
Number	Title	Yr	NM
❏ 47-9989	Will You Be Loving Another Man/Jimmie Brown the Newsboy	1971	$8

FLATT, LESTER
COLUMBIA
| ❏ 4-45050 | Great Big Woman/ Life of Reilly | 1969 | $8 |

NUGGET
| ❏ 1056 | Drink That Mash and Talk That Trash/ Sunny Side of Me | 1971 | $12 |

RCA VICTOR
❏ 74-0680	Backin' to Birmingham/ You're Still Mine Tonight	1972	$8
❏ 74-0541	Don't Take It So Hard, Mr. Webster/Father's Table Grace	1971	$8
❏ 47-9953	Everybody Has One (But You)/I Can't Tell the Boys from the Girls	1971	$8

FLAVOR
BUNKY
| ❏ 711 | Don't Freeze Up/ (Instrumental) | 1976 | $12 |

COLUMBIA
❏ 4-44881	Comin' On Home/ Dancing in the Streets	1969	$15
❏ 4-44673	Heart Teaser/Yeah, I'm Hip	1968	$8
❏ 4-44521	Sally Had a Party/ Shop Around	1968	$8

JU-PAR
| ❏ 8001 | Don't Freeze Up/ (Instrumental) | 1976 | $8 |

FLAX, FOGWELL, AND THE ANKLE BITERS FROM FREEHOLD JUNIOR SCHOOL
EMI
| ❏ 5255 | One-Nine For Santa/Cheers To You At Christmas | 1981 | $6 |

— U.K. import

FLEAS, THE
CHALLENGE
| ❏ 9115 | Scratchin'/Tears | 1961 | $50 |

FLEETWOOD MAC
Also see LINDSEY BUCKINGHAM; BUCKINGHAM NICKS; BILLY BURNETTE; MICK FLEETWOOD; DANNY KIRWAN; DAVE MASON; CHRISTINE McVIE; STEVIE NICKS; JEREMY SPENCER; BOB WELCH.
BLUE HORIZON
| ❏ 304 | Hungry Country Woman/Walkin' | 1970 | $15 |

— A-side by Otis Spann with Fleetwood Mac; B-side by Otis Spann

DJM
| ❏ 1007 | Man of the World/Best Girl in the World | 1976 | $10 |

— B-side by Danny Kirwan

EPIC
❏ 5-11029	Albatross/Black Magic Woman	1973	$8
❏ 5-10436	Albatross/Jigsaw Puzzle Blues	1969	$15
❏ 5-10351	Black Magic Woman/ Long Grey Mare	1968	$20
❏ 5-10368	Stop Messin' Around/ Need Your Love So Bad	1968	$15

REPRISE
❏ 1172	Did You Ever Love Me/Revelation	1973	$15
❏ 1172 [DJ]	Did You Ever Love Me (stereo/mono)	1973	$8
❏ 1188	For Your Love/Hypnotized	1973	$20
❏ 1188 [DJ]	For Your Love (stereo/mono)	1973	$10
❏ 1317	Heroes Are Hard to Find/Born Enchanter	1974	$8
❏ 0883 [DJ]	Oh Well, Part 1/Part 2	1970	$10
❏ 0883	Oh Well, Part 1/Part 2	1970	$30
❏ 1077	Oh Well, Part 1/The Green Manalishi (With the Two-Prong Crown)	1971	$8

— Back to Back Hits" reissue
| ❏ GRE 0108 | Oh Well, Part 1/The Green Manalishi (With the Two-Prong Crown) | 1972 | $5 |

— Back to Back Hits" reissue
| ❏ 1339 | Over My Head/I'm So Afraid | 1975 | $5 |
| ❏ 1057 | Sands of Time/ Lay It All Down | 1971 | $10 |

Number	Title	Yr	NM
❏ 1356	Say You Love Me (Edited)/ Monday Morning	1976	$5

— The A-sides of Reprise 1339, 1345 and 1356 feature significantly different mixes than those on their parent album, "Fleetwood Mac.

❏ 1093	Sentimental Lady/ Sunny Side of Heaven	1972	$30
❏ 1093 [DJ]	Sentimental Lady/ Sunny Side of Heaven	1972	$15
❏ 0925 [DJ]	The Green Manalishi (With the Two-Prong Crown)/ World In Harmony	1970	$10
❏ 0925	The Green Manalishi (With the Two-Prong Crown)/ World In Harmony	1970	$30

WARNER BROS.
❏ 27644	As Long As You Follow/ Oh Well (Live)	1988	$3
❏ 27644 [PS]	As Long As You Follow/ Oh Well (Live)	1988	$3
❏ 21943	Big Love/Seven Wonders	1988	$3

— Back to Back Hits" series
❏ 28398	Big Love/You and I, Part 1	1987	$3
❏ 28398 [PS]	Big Love/You and I, Part 1	1987	$3
❏ 8413	Don't Stop/Never Going Back Again	1977	$4
❏ 8413 [PS]	Don't Stop/Never Going Back Again	1977	$5
❏ 21990	Don't Stop/Silver Springs	1988	$3

— Back to Back Hits" series
❏ 8371	Dreams/Songbird	1977	$4
❏ 28143	Everywhere/When I See You Again	1987	$3
❏ 28143 [PS]	Everywhere/When I See You Again	1987	$3
❏ 28114	Family Man/Down Endless Street	1988	$3
❏ 28114 [PS]	Family Man/Down Endless Street	1988	$3
❏ 49660	Fireflies/Over My Head (Live)	1981	$4
❏ 49660 [PS]	Fireflies/Over My Head (Live)	1981	$4
❏ GWB 0348	Go Your Own Way/Dreams	1979	$3

— Back to Back Hits" series
| ❏ 8304 | Go Your Own Way/ Silver Springs | 1976 | $8 |

— Sought-after because of its non-LP B-side
❏ 29918	Gypsy/Cool Water	1982	$3
❏ 29918 [PS]	Gypsy/Cool Water	1982	$3
❏ 29966	Hold Me/Eyes of the World	1982	$3
❏ 29966 [PS]	Hold Me/Eyes of the World	1982	$3
❏ GWB 0439	Hold Me/Gypsy	1984	$3

— Back to Back Hits" series
| ❏ 21888 | Little Lies/Everywhere | 1989 | $3 |

— Back to Back Hits" series
❏ 28291	Little Lies/Ricky	1987	$3
❏ 28291 [PS]	Little Lies/Ricky	1987	$3
❏ 29848	Love in Store/Can't Go Back	1983	$3
❏ 29698	Oh Diane/That's Alright	1983	$3
❏ 49150	Sara/That's Enough for Me	1979	$4
❏ 49150 [PS]	Sara/That's Enough for Me	1979	$6
❏ 28317	Seven Wonders/ Book of Miracles	1987	$3
❏ 28317 [PS]	Seven Wonders/ Book of Miracles	1987	$3
❏ 49500	Sisters of the Moon/ Walk a Thin Line	1980	$10

— Scarce on stock copy; A-side is a different mix than the LP version
❏ 49700	The Farmer's Daughter/ Monday Morning (Live)	1982	$6
❏ 49700 [PS]	The Farmer's Daughter/ Monday Morning (Live)	1982	$6
❏ 49196	Think About Me/ Save Me a Place	1980	$4
❏ 49196 [PS]	Think About Me/ Save Me a Place	1980	$6
❏ 49077	Tusk/Never Make Me Cry	1979	$4
❏ 49077 [PS]	Tusk/Never Make Me Cry	1979	$5

— Version 1: Brown print, small dog photo
| ❏ 49077 [PS] | Tusk/Never Make Me Cry | 1979 | $4 |

— Version 2: Black print, large dog photo
| ❏ GWB 0388 | Tusk/Sara | 1981 | $3 |

— Back to Back Hits" series

FLEETWOOD, MICK
RCA
❏ PB-13739	Angel Come Home/I Give	1984	$4
❏ PB-13621	I Want You Back/ Put Me Right	1983	$4
❏ PB-13621 [PS]	I Want You Back/ Put Me Right	1983	$4

FLEETWOODS, THE
DOLPHIN
| ❏ 1 | Come Softly to Me/I Care So Much | 1959 | $30 |

DOLTON
| ❏ 86 | Baby Bye-O/What'll I Do | 1963 | $12 |
| ❏ 302 | Before and After (Losing You)/Lonely Is As Lonely Does | 1964 | $12 |

Number	Title	Yr	NM
❏ 49	Billy Old Buddy/Trouble	1962	$20
❏ 307	Come Softly to Me/I'm Not Jimmy	1965	$10
❏ 30	Confidential/I Love You So	1960	$20
❏ 315	For Lovin' Me/This Is Where I See Her	1965	$10
❏ 75	Goodnight My Love/ Jimmy Beware	1963	$20
❏ 3	Graduation's Here/ Oh Lord, Let It Be	1959	$30
❏ S-3 [S]	Graduation's Here/ Oh Lord, Let It Be	1959	$60
❏ 45	(He's) The Great Impostor/ Poor Little Girl	1961	$20
❏ 93	Lonesome Town/Ruby Red Baby Blue	1964	$10
❏ 5	Mr. Blue/You Mean Everything to Me	1959	$30
❏ 98	Mr. Sandman/This Is My Prayer	1964	$10
❏ 15	Outside My Window/ Magic Star	1960	$30
❏ 97	Ten Times Blue/Ska Light Ska Bright	1964	$10
❏ 27	The Last One to Know/Dormilona	1960	$20
❏ 62	They Tell Me It's Summer/ Lovers by Night, Strangers by Day	1962	$20
❏ 40	Tragedy/Little Miss Sad One	1961	$20

LIBERTY
❏ 55188 [M]	Come Softly to Me/I Care So Much	1959	$30
❏ 77188 [S]	Come Softly to Me/I Care So Much	1959	$60
❏ 62	They Tell Me It's Summer/ Lovers by Night, Strangers by Day	1970	$20

— Odd reissue keeping the Dolton number

UNITED ARTISTS
| ❏ 0038 | Come Softly to Me/ Runaround | 1973 | $4 |
| ❏ 0040 | He's the Great Impostor/ Goodnight My Love | 1973 | $4 |

— 0038, 0039 and 0040 are "Silver Spotlight Series" reissues
| ❏ XW515 | (He's) The Great Impostor/ Goodnight My Love | 1974 | $4 |

— Reissue
| ❏ 0039 | Mr. Blue/Tragedy | 1973 | $4 |

7-Inch Extended Plays
DOLTON
| ❏ BEP-502 [PS] | The Fleetwoods | 1960 | $100 |

FLEMONS, WADE
VEE JAY
❏ 368	Ain't That Lovin' You Baby/I'll Come Runnin'	1960	$40
❏ 471	Ain't These Tears/I Hope, I Think, I Wish	1962	$30
❏ 377	At the Party/Devil in Your Soul	1961	$40
❏ 344	Easy Lovin'/Woops Now	1960	$40
❏ 335	Goodnite, It's Time To Go/What's Happening	1959	$40
❏ 427	Half a Love/Welcome Stranger	1962	$30
❏ 295	Here I Stand/My Baby Likes to Rock	1958	$40
❏ 309	Hold Me Close/You'll Remain Forever	1959	$40
❏ 614	I Knew You When/ That Other Place	1964	$300
❏ 389	Please Send Me Someone to Love/Keep On Loving Me	1961	$40
❏ 321	Slow Motion/Wailing by the River	1959	$40
❏ 533	That Time of the Year/I Came Running	1963	$60
❏ 578	When It Rains, It Pours/ Watch Over Her	1964	$50

— The Four Seasons sing backup on this record
| ❏ 668 | Where Did You Go Last Night/Empty Balcony | 1965 | $30 |

FLESH GORDON AND THE NUDE HOLLYWOOD ARGYLES
PARAMOUNT
| ❏ 0289 | Superstreaker/Naked | 1974 | $15 |

FLESHEATERS
7-Inch Extended Plays
UPSETTER
| ❏ 0(no cat #) | Flesheaters | 1978 | $35 |
| ❏ 0(no cat #) [PS] | Flesheaters | 1978 | $35 |

Number	Title	Yr	NM

FLETCHER, DARROW

ATCO
❏ 7083	Improve/Let's Get Together	1977	$30

CONGRESS
❏ 6011	I Think I'm Gonna Write a Song/Sitting There That Night	1970	$20

CROSSOVER
❏ 980	It's No Mistake/Try Something New	1975	$50
❏ 983	We've Got to Get an Understanding/This Time (I'll Be the Fool)	1976	$10

GROOVY
❏ 3007	Gotta Draw the Line/I've Gotta Know Why	1966	$30
❏ 3004	My Young Misery/I've Gotta Know Why	1966	$30
❏ 3009	That Certain Little Something/My Judgement Day	1966	$30
❏ 3001	The Pain Gets a Little Deeper/My Judgement Day	1965	$30

JACKLYN
❏ 1003	Infatuation/Little Girl	1966	$30
❏ 1006	What Good Am I Without You/Little Girl	1967	$30
❏ 1002	What Have I Got Now/Sitting There That Night	1966	$60

REVUE
❏ 11023	Gonna Keep Loving You/We Can't Go On This Way	1967	$20
❏ 11008	I Like the Way I Feel/The Way of a Man	1967	$20
❏ 11035	Those Hanging Heartaches/Sitting There That Night	1968	$30

UNI
❏ 55244	Changing by the Minute/When Love Calls	1970	$15
❏ 55270	Dolly Baby/What Is This	1971	$15

FLETCHER, LOIS

COLUMBIA
❏ 4-43633	Winken, Blinken and Nod/Until I Get Over You	1966	$10

PLAYBOY
❏ 6003	Ever Lovin' Sunshine/Man Smart, Woman Smarter	1974	$6
❏ 50049	I Am What I Am/One More Time	1974	$6

FLETCHER, SAM

CUB
❏ 9048	Only Heaven Knows/Beyond My Wildest Dreams	1959	$40

METRO
❏ 20013	Before/Torn Between Two Loves	1959	$30
❏ 20022	Out in the Cold Again/If You Love Me	1959	$30

RCA VICTOR
❏ 47-7872	Hold Me/You Did It	1961	$20
❏ 47-7972	I Believe in You/Sweet Slumber	1961	$20
❏ 47-8027	My Girl/This One Night	1962	$30
❏ 47-7676	Take Me in Your Arms/I Just Had to Tell Someone	1960	$30
❏ 47-7817	Tall Hope/Far Away from Home	1960	$30
❏ 47-8076	The Answer to Everything/Me and the One I Love	1962	$30

TOLLIE
❏ 9012	I'd Think It Over/Friday Night	1964	$200
❏ 934	The Look of Love/You Better Come Home	1967	$20

VEE JAY
❏ 623	Guess Who/The Sinner	1964	$15

WARNER BROS.
❏ 5384	As Time Goes By/My Wish	1963	$20

FLETCHER, VICKY

COLUMBIA
❏ 3-10040	Little Boy Blue/That's the Way We Fall in Love	1974	$5
❏ 4-46043	Touching Me, Touching You/That's the Way We Fall in Love	1974	$5

MUSIC ROW
❏ 213	Ain't It Good to Be in Love Again/Countin' Charlie's Ribs	1976	$6

FLINT, SHELBY

CADENCE
❏ 1352	Oh, I Miss Him So/I Will Love You	1958	$20

VALIANT
❏ 6014	A Broken Vow/Magic Wand	1961	$10
❏ 701	Angel on My Shoulder/I Will Love You	1965	$8

❏ 6001	Angel on My Shoulder/Someday	1960	$15
❏ 743	Cast Your Fate to the Wind/The Lily	1966	$8
❏ 6060	I've Grown Accustomed to Her (Your) Face/Our Town	1964	$10
❏ 6010	I Will Love You/Every Night	1961	$10
❏ 6031	Little Dancing Doll/It Really Wouldn't Matter	1963	$12
❏ 6022	The Boy I Love/Ugly Duckling	1962	$12
❏ 6052	Wonderland/Pipes of Keith	1964	$10

FLINTSTONE, FRED

EPIC
❏ 9475	Bedrock Beat/Stone Age Roll	1961	$30

FLIPPER

SUBTERRANEAN
❏ SUB35	Get Away/The Old Lady That Swallowed the Fly	1982	$6
❏ SUB35 [PS]	Get Away/The Old Lady That Swallowed the Fly	1982	$6
❏ SUB23	Sexbomb/Brainwash	1981	$6
❏ SUB23 [PS]	Sexbomb/Brainwash	1981	$6

THERMIDOR/SUBTERRANEAN
❏ T 1/SUB7	Love Canal/Ha Ha Ha	1980	$6
❏ T 1/SUB7 [PS]	Love Canal/Ha Ha Ha	1980	$6

FLIRTATIONS, THE (1)

DERAM
❏ 85062	Can't Stop Lovin' You/Everybody Needs Somebody	1970	$6
❏ 85036	Christmas Time Is Here Again/Nothing But a Heartache	1968	$8
❏ 7531	Give Me Love, Love, Love/This Must Be the End	1970	$8
❏ 85057	I Wanna Be There/Keep On Searching	1970	$6

PARROT
❏ 40028	Somewhere Out There/How Can You Tell Me	1968	$15

FLIRTATIONS, THE (2)

FESTIVAL
❏ 705	Stronger Than Her Love/Settle Down	1967	$70

FLO AND EDDIE
Also see THE TURTLES.

COLUMBIA
❏ 10028	Come to My Rescue, Webelos/Let Me Make Love to You	1974	$6
❏ 10204	Come to My Rescue, Webelos/Let Me Make Love to You	1975	$5
❏ 10425	Elenore/The Love You Gave Away	1976	$5
❏ 10264	Illegal, Immoral and Fattening/Rebecca	1975	$5

REPRISE
❏ 1142	Afterglow/Original Soundtract from "Carlos & De Bull	1972	$5
❏ 1160	If We Only Had the Time/You're a Lady	1973	$5

FLOATERS, THE

ABC
❏ 12284	Float On/Everything Happens for a Reason	1977	$4
❏ 12284 [PS]	Float On/Everything Happens for a Reason	1977	$6
❏ 12237	I Am So Glad I Took My Time/Take One Step at a Time	1976	$4
❏ 12364	I Just Want to Be with You/Whatever Your Sign	1978	$4
❏ 12399	Let's Try Love/The Time Is Now	1978	$4

FEE
❏ 2080	For Your Love/Glass House	1980	$10
❏ 2661	Get Ready/For Your Love	1981	$10
❏ 311	I Am So Glad I Took My Time/Take One Step at a Time	1976	$8

MCA
❏ 41063	Levitation/Best of Our Love	1979	$4
❏ 41063 [PS]	Levitation/Best of Our Love	1979	$8

FLOATING BRIDGE, THE

VAULT
❏ 953	Don't Mean a Thing/Mr. Jaybird	1969	$12
❏ 947	Watch Your Step/Brought Up Wrong	1969	$10

FLOCK OF SEAGULLS, A

JIVE
❏ VS102	I Ran (So Far Away)/Pick Me Up	1982	$5
❏ 9069	(It's Not Me) Talking/I Ran (Live)	1983	$4
❏ 9069 [PS]	(It's Not Me) Talking/I Ran (Live)	1983	$5
❏ VS2003	Space Age Love Song/Windows	1982	$4
❏ VS2003 [PS]	Space Age Love Song/Windows	1982	$4
❏ 9220	The More You Live, The More You Love/Lost Control	1984	$3
❏ 9220 [PS]	The More You Live, The More You Love/Lost Control	1984	$3
❏ 9018	Wishing (If I Had a Photograph of You)/Committed	1983	$3
❏ 9018 [PS]	Wishing (If I Had a Photograph of You)/Committed	1983	$3
❏ VS2006	Wishing (If I Had a Photograph of You)/Committed	1983	$4
❏ VS2006 [PS]	Wishing (If I Had a Photograph of You)/Committed	1983	$4

FLOCK, THE

COLUMBIA
❏ 45295	Mermaid/Crabfoot	1971	$8
❏ 45021	Tired of Waiting/Store Bought Store Thought	1969	$8

DESTINATION
❏ 631	Are You the Kind/I Like You	1966	$10
❏ 628	Can't You See/Hold On to My Mind	1966	$10
❏ 635	Take Me Back/Each Day Is a Lonely Night	1967	$10

U.S.A.
❏ 910	Magical Winds/What Would You Do If the Sun Died?	1968	$8

FLOOD, DICK

EPIC
❏ 5-9556	Another Stretch of Track/Outside Your Door (Someone Was Standing)	1962	$15
❏ 5-9479	Hellbound Train/Judy Lynn	1961	$15

KAPP
❏ 681	Between Two Worlds/From Warm to Cool to Cold	1965	$12
❏ 754	Don't Sweetheart Me/Trouble's Back in Town	1966	$12
❏ 640	These Things Make a Heartache/I Need All the Friends	1965	$10

MONUMENT
❏ 45-427	Carita/Cowpoke	1960	$20
❏ 45-414	It's My Way/It Only Costs a Dime	1960	$20
❏ 45-408	The Three Bells (The Jimmy Brown Story)/Far Away	1959	$20

NASCO
❏ 025	Slow It Down/Speak My Name	1971	$8

NUGGET
❏ 1026	Home Was Never Like This/Woman Leave Me Alone	1968	$8

TOTEM
❏ 7	Sure Gets Dark/(B-side unknown)	1967	$8

FLORIDIANS, THE

ABC-PARAMOUNT
❏ 10185	That Lucky Old Sun/I Love Marie	1961	$60

FLOW

CTI
❏ 503	Mr. Invisible/Daddy	1970	$6

FLOWER SISTERS, THE

HIT
❏ 120	Chapel of Love/A World Without Love	1964	$8
—B-side by Bobby Brooks
| ❏ 136 | People Say/C'Mon and Swim | 1964 | $8 |
—B-side by Leroy Jones

FLOWERPOT MEN, THE

DERAM
❏ 7516	Am I Losing You/A Walk in the Sky	1968	$20
❏ 85051	A Moment of Madness/Young Birds Fly	1969	$15
❏ 7513	Let's Go to San Francisco/Let's Go to San Francisco, Part 2	1967	$20
—As "The Flower Pots

Number	Title	Yr	NM
FLOYD, EDDIE			
ATLANTIC			
❏ 2275	Hush Hush/Drive On	1965	$15
LUPINE			
❏ 115	Set My Soul on Fire/ Will I Be the One	1963	$20
MALACO			
❏ 1035	Chi-Town Hustler/ In Paradise	1976	$5
❏ 1032	Somebody Touch Me/ Never Too Old	1976	$5
❏ 1039	Special Christmas Day/ Mother, My Dear Mother	1976	$5
❏ 1040	We Should Really Be in Love/I'll Never Be Loved	1977	$5
— With Dorothy Moore			
MERCURY			
❏ 74003	Disco Summer/Do It in the Water	1978	$4
❏ 73964	If You Really Love Me/It's Me	1977	$4
SAFICE			
❏ 336	Can This Be Christmas/I'll Be Home For Christmas	1964	$15
STAX			
❏ 0171	Baby Lay Your Head Down (Gently on My Bed)/Check Me Out	1973	$6
❏ 0095	Blood Is Thicker Than Water/Have You Heard the Word	1971	$6
❏ 0012	Bring It On Home to Me/ The Sweet Things You Do	1968	$6
❏ 0060	California Girl/ The Woodman	1970	$6
❏ 219	Don't Rock the Boat/ This House	1967	$12
❏ 0036	Don't Tell Your Mama (Where You've Been)/ Consider Me	1969	$6
❏ 0209	Guess Who/Something to Write Home About	1974	$6
❏ 246	Holding On with Both Hands/Big Bird	1968	$12
❏ 0251	I'm So Glad I Met You/I'm So Grateful	1975	$6
❏ 0025	I've Got to Have Your Love/Girl I Love You	1969	$6
❏ 0002	I've Never Found a Girl (To Love Me Like You Do)/I'm Just the Kind of Fool	1968	$6
❏ 0188	I Wanna Do Things for You/We've Been Through Too Much Together	1973	$6
❏ 223	Love Is a Doggone Good Thing/Hey Now	1967	$10
❏ 0072	My Girl/Laurie	1970	$6
❏ 0087	Oh How It Rained/When My Baby Said Goodbye	1971	$6
❏ 233	On a Saturday Night/ Under My Nose	1967	$10
❏ 0216	Soul Street/Highway Man	1974	$6
❏ 0232	Stealing Love/I Got a Reason to Smile	1974	$6
❏ 0239	Talk to the Man/I Got a Reason to Smile	1975	$6
❏ 0077	The Best Years of My Life/My Little Girl	1970	$6
❏ 187	Things Get Better/ Good Love, Bad Love	1966	$15
❏ 0051	Why Is the Wine Sweeter (On the Other Side)/ People Get It Together	1969	$6
FLOYD, KING			
CHIMNEYVILLE			
❏ 437	Baby Let Me Kiss You/Please Don't Leave Me Lonely	1971	$5
❏ 437 [PS]	Baby Let Me Kiss You/Please Don't Leave Me Lonely	1971	$8
❏ 10212	Body English/I Really Love You	1976	$5
❏ 10206	Can't Give It Up/I'm Gonna Fall in Love with You	1975	$5
❏ 10205	Don't Cry No More/I'm Missing You	1974	$5
❏ 439	Got to Have Your Lovin'/Let Us Be	1971	$5
❏ 435	Groove Me/What Our Love Needs	1970	$6
❏ 10209	Hey Baby/I Really Love You	1976	$5
❏ 10202	I Feel Like Dynamite/ Handle with Care	1974	$5
❏ 442	It's Wonderful/Let Me See You Do That Thing	1971	$5
❏ 1779	So Much Confusion/So Much Confusion (Part 2)	1973	$5
❏ 10218	Stop, Look and Listen/Trouble	1977	$5
❏ 446	Think About It/Here It Is	1973	$5
❏ 10207	We Can Love/Making Love	1975	$6
— With Dorothy Moore			
❏ 443	Woman Don't Go Astray/Everybody Needs Somebody	1972	$5
DIAL			
❏ 1027	Can You Dig It/Learning to Forget You	1974	$6

Number	Title	Yr	NM
ORIGINAL SOUND			
❏ 52	Why Did She Leave Me/ Walkin' and Thinkin'	1964	$20
PULSAR			
❏ 2401	Times Have Changed/ Groov-a-Ling	1969	$10
— With the Three Queens			
❏ 2406	Together We Can Do It/ You Got the Love I Need	1969	$10
UPTOWN			
❏ 733	Come On Home (Where You Belong)/I Don't Care (No More)	1966	$15
❏ 719	Love Makes the World Go Round/Walkin' and Thinkin'	1965	$15
V.I.P.			
❏ 25061	Heartaches/Together We Can Do Anything	1970	$30
FLYERS, THE			
ATCO			
❏ 6088	On Bended Knee/ My Only Desire	1957	$50
FLYING BURRITO BROTHERS, THE			
A&M			
❏ 1189	Down in the Churchyard/ Older Guys	1970	$8
❏ 1166	If You Gotta Go, Go Now/Cody, Cody	1970	$8
❏ 1067	Train Song/Hot Burrito #1	1969	$8
❏ 1277	White Line Fever/Colorado	1971	$8
❏ 1277 [PS]	White Line Fever/Colorado	1971	$20
COLUMBIA			
❏ 10389	Big Bayou/Waiting for Love to Begin	1976	$5
❏ 10287	Bon Soir Blues/ Hot Burrito No. 3	1976	$5
❏ 10229	Building Fires/Hot Burrito No. 3	1975	$5
CURB			
❏ 03314	Blue and Broken Hearted Me/Our Roots Are Country Music	1982	$4
— As "Burrito Brothers			
❏ 02835	Closer to You/Coast to Coast	1982	$4
— As "Burrito Brothers			
❏ 01011	Does She Wish She Was Single Again/ Oh Lonesome Me	1981	$4
— As "Burrito Brothers			
❏ 02667	If Something Should Come Between Us	1982	$4
— As "Burrito Brothers			
❏ 02641	If Something Should Come Between Us/Damned If I'll Be Lonely Tonight	1981	$4
— As "Burrito Brothers			
❏ 03023	I'm Drinkin' Canada Dry/How'd We Ever Get This Way	1982	$4
— As "Burrito Brothers			
❏ 02243	She Belongs to Everyone But Me/Why Must the Ending Always Be So Sad	1981	$4
— As "Burrito Brothers			
❏ 5402	She's a Friend of a Friend/ (B-side unknown)	1981	$4
— As "Burrito Brothers			
MCA CURB			
❏ 52329	Almost Saturday Night/ Juke Box Kind of Night	1983	$3
— As "Burrito Brothers			
❏ 52379	My Kind of Lady/ Dream Chaser	1984	$3
— As "Burrito Brothers			
REGENCY			
❏ 45001	White Line Fever/ (B-side unknown)	1980	$6
FLYING LIZARDS, THE			
VIRGIN			
❏ 67003	Money/Money B	1979	$4
❏ 67003 [PS]	Money/Money B	1979	$4
❏ 67006	TV/Tube	1980	$4
❏ 67006 [PS]	TV/Tube	1980	$4
FLYING MACHINE, THE			
CONGRESS			
❏ 6000	Smile a Little Smile for Me/Maybe We've Been Loving Too Long	1969	$8
❏ 6012	There She Goes/ Baby Make It Soon	1970	$6
JANUS			
❏ 121	Hanging on the Edge of Sadness/My Baby's Coming Home	1970	$6

Number	Title	Yr	NM
❏ 137	Hey Little Girl/The Devil Has Possession of My Mind	1971	$6
FOCUS			
ATCO			
❏ 7002	Harem Scarem/Birth	1974	$6
SIRE			
❏ 704	Hocus Pocus/ Hocus Pocus II	1973	$6
❏ 352	House of the King/ Black Beauty	1971	$8
❏ 708	Sylvia/Love Remembered	1973	$5
FOGELBERG, DAN, AND TIM WEISBERG			
FULL MOON/EPIC			
❏ 8-50605	Tell Me to My Face/ Hurtwood Alley	1978	$6
❏ 8-50606	The Power of Gold/ Lahaina Luna	1978	$4
FOGELBERG, DAN			
COLUMBIA			
❏ 4-45764	Anyway I Love You/ Looking for a Lady	1973	$8
FULL MOON/EPIC			
❏ 34-04447	Believe in Me/ Windows and Walls	1984	$4
❏ 8-50189	Below the Surface/ Comes and Goes	1976	$4
❏ 8-50165	Captured Angel/Next Time	1975	$6
❏ 8-50108	Changing Horses/ Morning Sky	1975	$6
❏ 34-05446	Down the Road-Mountain Pass/High Country Snows	1985	$4
❏ 34-04835	Go Down Easy/High Country Snows	1985	$4
❏ 14-02488	Hard to Say/The Innocent Age	1981	$4
❏ 9-50862	Heart Hotels/Beggar's Game	1980	$5
❏ ES72142 [DJ]	High Country Snows (same on both sides)	1985	$5
❏ 15-03843	Leader of the Band/ Run for the Roses	1983	$3
— Reissue			
❏ 14-02647	Leader of the Band/ Times Like These	1981	$4
❏ 34-07275	Lonely in Love/ Beyond the Edge	1987	$4
❏ 34-07275 [PS]	Lonely in Love/ Beyond the Edge	1987	$4
❏ 9-50824	Longer/Along the Road	1980	$4
❏ 15-02155	Longer/Heart Hotels	1981	$4
— Reissue			
❏ 8-50412	Love Gone By/ Scarecrow's Dream	1977	$6
❏ ENR-03570	Make Love Stay/ (B-side blank)	1983	$6
— One-sided budget release			
❏ 34-03525	Make Love Stay/ Hearts and Crafts	1983	$4
❏ ENR-03323	Missing You/(B-side blank)	1982	$8
— One-sided budget release			
❏ 34-03289	Missing You/Hearts and Crafts	1982	$4
❏ 15-05498	Missing You/Make Love Stay	1985	$3
— Reissue			
❏ 8-50234	Old Tennessee/The Crow	1976	$6
❏ 8-50055	Part of the Plan/Song from Half Mountain	1974	$5
❏ 15-03087	Same Old Lang Syne/ Hard to Say	1982	$3
— Reissue			
❏ 19-50961	Same Old Lang Syne/ Hearts and Crafts	1980	$4
❏ 19-50961 [PS]	Same Old Lang Syne/ Hearts and Crafts	1980	$6
❏ 34-07640	Seeing You Again/ Hearts in Decline	1987	$4
❏ 34-07044	She Don't Look Back/ It Doesn't Matter	1987	$3
❏ 34-07044 [PS]	She Don't Look Back/ It Doesn't Matter	1987	$3
❏ 8-50536	Sketches/Promises Made	1978	$6
❏ 34-04660	Sweet Magnolia and the Traveling Salesman/ The Loving Cup	1984	$4
❏ 34-04314	The Language of Love/ Windows and Walls	1984	$3
❏ 34-04314 [PS]	The Language of Love/ Windows and Walls	1984	$3
❏ 8-50577	There's a Place in the World for a Gambler/Souvenirs	1978	$6
❏ 34-07756	The Way It Must Be/ What You're Doing	1988	$4

Number	Title	Yr	NM

FOGERTY, JOHN

Also see CREEDENCE CLEARWATER REVIVAL; TOMMY FOGERTY AND THE BLUE VELVETS; THE GOLLIWOGS.

ASYLUM
| ❏ 45293 | Almost Saturday Night/Sea Cruise | 1975 | $6 |

FANTASY
| ❏ 710 | Back in the Hills/You Don't Own Me | 1973 | $5 |

— As "The Blue Ridge Rangers

| ❏ 683 | Blue Ridge Mountain Blues/ Have Thine Own Way, Lord | 1972 | $5 |

— As "The Blue Ridge Rangers

| ❏ 683 [PS] | Blue Ridge Mountain Blues/ Have Thine Own Way, Lord | 1972 | $20 |

— As "The Blue Ridge Rangers

| ❏ 717 | Coming Down the Road/Ricochet | 1973 | $5 |
| ❏ 700 | Hearts of Stone/ Somewhere Listening | 1973 | $5 |

— As "The Blue Ridge Rangers

WARNER BROS.
❏ 28535	Change in the Weather/ My Toot Toot	1986	$4
❏ 28535 [PS]	Change in the Weather/ My Toot Toot	1986	$5
❏ 28657	Eye of the Zombie/I Confess	1986	$4
❏ 28657 [PS]	Eye of the Zombie/I Confess	1986	$5
❏ 29100	The Old Man Down the Road/Big Train (From Memphis)	1985	$4
❏ 29100 [PS]	The Old Man Down the Road/Big Train (From Memphis)	1985	$5

FOGERTY, TOM

Also see CREEDENCE CLEARWATER REVIVAL; TOMMY FOGERTY AND THE BLUE VELVETS; THE GOLLIWOGS.

FANTASY
❏ 680	Cast the First Stone/ Lady of Fatima	1972	$5
❏ 691	Forty Years/Faces, Places, People	1972	$5
❏ 661	Goodbye, Media Man/ Goodbye, Media Man (Part 2)	1971	$5
❏ 661 [PS]	Goodbye, Media Man/ Goodbye, Media Man (Part 2)	1971	$10
❏ 702	Heartbeat/Joyful Resurrection	1973	$5
❏ 726	It's Been a Good Day/Money	1974	$5
❏ 715	Mystic Island Avalon/Reggie	1973	$5
❏ 737	Sweet Things to Come/ There Was a Time	1974	$5

FOGERTY, TOMMY, AND THE BLUE VELVETS

ORCHESTRA
| ❏ 6177 | Come On Baby/Oh! My Love | 1961 | $100 |
| ❏ 1010 | Have You Ever Been Lonely/Bonita | 1961 | $100 |

FOGHAT

Also see SAVOY BROWN.

BEARSVILLE
❏ PRO-S-1002 [DJ]	All I Want for Christmas Is You (same on both sides)	1981	$10
❏ 0313	Drivin' Wheel/Night Shift	1976	$4
❏ 0307	Fool for the City/ Take It or Leave It	1976	$5
❏ 0329	High on Love/Sweet Home Chicago	1978	$4
❏ 0008	I Just Want to Make Love to You/Hole to Hide In	1973	$5
❏ 0319	I Just Want to Make Love to You (Live)/Fool for the City (Live)	1977	$4
❏ 0315	I'll Be Standing By/ Take Me to the River	1977	$4
❏ 0021	Maybelline/Step Outside	1974	$5
❏ 29612	Seven Day Weekend/ That's What Love Can Do	1983	$4
❏ 29860	Slipped, Tripped, Fell in Love/And I Do Just What I Want	1982	$4
❏ 0306	Slow Ride/Save Your Loving	1975	$5
❏ 0325	Stone Blue/Chevrolet	1978	$4
❏ 49510	Stranger in My Home Town/Be My Woman	1980	$4
❏ 0019	That'll Be the Day/ Wild Cherry	1974	$5
❏ 49125	Third Time Lucky (First Time I Was a Fool)/Love in Motion	1979	$4
❏ 49125 [PS]	Third Time Lucky (First Time I Was a Fool)/Love in Motion	1979	$5
❏ 0014	What a Shame/ Helping Hand	1973	$5
❏ 49779	Wide Boy/Love Zone	1981	$4

FOGHAT
| ❏ 1069 | Goin' Home For Christmas/ Santa Claus Is Back In Town | 1986 | $6 |

FOLEY, BETTY

BANDERA
| ❏ 1308 | Do You Wonder at All/I'm Not Surprised | 1959 | $30 |
| ❏ 1304 | Old Moon/Magic Love | 1959 | $30 |

FOLEY, BRIAN

DOT
| ❏ 16889 | Where Are We Going in Such a Hurry/Time and Tide | 1966 | $10 |

KAPP
❏ 924	Elvira Madigan Theme/Let's Go	1968	$8
❏ 885	Love Never Changes/ Once There Was a Time	1968	$8
❏ 861	Love Was Here Before the Stars/Love Me, Please Love Me	1967	$8
❏ 861 [PS]	Love Was Here Before the Stars/Love Me, Please Love Me	1967	$15

FOLEY, RED, AND GRADY MARTIN

DECCA
| ❏ 9-29059 | My Window Faces South/ Pork Chop Stomp | 1954 | $30 |

FOLEY, RED, AND ERNEST TUBB

DECCA
❏ 9-29195	Double-Datin'/It's the Mileage That's Slowin' Us Down	1954	$30
❏ 9-46255	Goodnight Irene/ Hillbilly Fever No. 2	1950	$50
❏ 9-46278	The Lovebug Itch/ Texas vs. Kentucky	1950	$40
❏ 9-46311	The Strange Little Girl/ Kentucky Waltz	1951	$30
❏ 9-46387	Too Old to Cut the Mustard/ I'm in Love with Molly	1952	$30
❏ 9-28911	Too Old to Tango/ Doctor Ketchum	1953	$30

FOLEY, RED

DECCA
❏ 9-27810	Alabama Jubilee/Dixie	1951	$30
❏ 31254	Another Heartache (For Me)/Just Before Dawn	1961	$20
❏ 9-28288	Are You Trying to Tell Me Goodbye/Kisses on Paper	1952	$30
❏ 31369	A Wasted Year/Happy Song	1962	$20
❏ 9-46293	Back to Tennessee/Sunday Down in Tennessee	1951	$30
❏ 9-46234	Birmingham Bounce/ Choc'late Ice Cream Cone	1950	$40
❏ 31727	Chained to a Memory/ Shame on You	1965	$10
❏ 9-46205	Chattanoogie Shoe Shine Boy/Sugarfoot Rag	1950	$50

— The 45 was released later than the 78 by a few months

❏ 9-46261	Cincinnati Dancing Pig/ Somebody's Cryin'	1950	$40
❏ 9-46349	Cock-a-Doodle-Doo/Sugar Foot Rag Square Dance	1951	$30
❏ 9-30249	Come a Little Closer/ One Life, Two Loves	1957	$30
❏ 9-30975	Crazy 'Bout Banjos/Living Is a Lonesome Thing	1959	$20
❏ 9-30674	Crazy Little Guitar Man/Fate	1958	$40
❏ 9-28460	Don't Let the Stars Get In Your Eyes/Sally	1952	$30
❏ 31194	End of the World/ Georgia Town Blues	1961	$20
❏ 9-46267	Frosty the Snowman/ Rudolph the Red- Nosed Reindeer	1950	$40
❏ 9-88060	Frosty the Snowman/ Rudolph the Red- Nosed Reindeer	1950	$50

— Yellow label "Childrens Series" issue

❏ 9-30924	God Walks These Hills with Me/God Forgive Me When I Whine	1959	$30
❏ 9-28944	Goodbye, Bobby Boy/ Peace of Mind	1953	$30
❏ 9-30710	Good Night, Irene/ If I Can Help Somebody	1958	$30
❏ 31530	Goodnight Mama, Goodnight Papa/Poor Jack	1963	$15
❏ 31437	Hang Your Head in Shame/That's What's Wrong with Me	1962	$20
❏ 9-29505	Have a Little Talk with Jesus/ Strange Things Happen	1955	$30

— With Sister Rosetta Tharpe

❏ 9-29375	Hearts of Stone/Never	1954	$30
❏ 9-46304	Hobo Boogie/Heska Holka	1951	$30
❏ 9-28759	Hot Dog Rag/That Old River Line	1953	$30
❏ 9-46286	Hot Rod Race/Smoke on the Water No. 2	1951	$40
❏ 9-28587	Hot Toddy/Playin' Dominoes and Shootin' Dice	1953	$30
❏ 9-28694	I Believe/Mansion Over the Hilltop	1953	$30
❏ 9-28147	I'm Bound For Christmas/I'd Rather Have Jesus	1952	$30

❏ 9-28695	I'm Sorry We Met/ Treasure Untold	1953	$30
❏ 9-29775	I See God/Someone to Care	1956	$30
❏ 32063	Is There Really a Santa Claus/From Our House to Your House	1966	$15
❏ 9-46277	I Won't Be Home/ Dear Little Girls	1950	$40
❏ 9-46235	Let's Go to Church/ Remember Me	1950	$40
❏ 31482	Lights Across the Bay/ One True Love	1963	$15
❏ 9-29339	Lookin' Glass/Walkin' in the Cold, Cold Rain	1954	$30
❏ 9-30802	Love Is Love/Smiles	1959	$30
❏ 9-28420	Midnight/Deep Blues	1952	$30
❏ 9-27981	Milk Bucket Boogie/ Salty Dog Rag	1952	$30
❏ 9-46241	Mississippi/Old Kentucky Fox Chase	1950	$40
❏ 31408	Mountain Dew/ Polka on a Banjo	1962	$20
❏ 9-29159	My Friend/Lady of Guadaloupe	1954	$30
❏ 32044	My Gal Country Style/How's the World Treating You	1966	$10
❏ 9-28447	My God Is Real/ The Mocking Bird	1952	$30
❏ 9-27378	My Heart Cries for You/'Tater Pie	1951	$30

— With Evelyn Knight

| ❏ 9-46052 | Old Shep/Honey Be My Honey Bee | 1950 | $50 |

— Lines on either side of "Decca

| ❏ 9-46052 | Old Shep/Honey Be My Honey Bee | 1955 | $30 |

— Star under "Decca

| ❏ 9-46291 | Old Shep/Just a Man and His Dog | 1951 | $30 |
| ❏ 9-46185 | Our Christmas Waltz/Here Comes Santa Claus | 1950 | $50 |

— With Judy Martin

❏ 25634	Pack Up Your Troubles/ When You're Smiling	1964	$15
❏ 9-30177	Passing By (Just Passing By)/His Arms	1957	$30
❏ 9-29517	Plantation Boogie/ You Little So-and-So	1955	$30
❏ 9-28940	Put Christ Back in Christmas/The Gentle Carpenter of Bethlehem	1953	$30
❏ 9-27856	Say a Little Prayer/ Peace in the Valley	1951	$30
❏ 9-28839	Shake a Hand/Stranded in Deep Water	1953	$30
❏ 9-29222	She'll Never Know/Bury Me Beneath the Willow	1954	$30

— With the Andrews Sisters

❏ 9-28567	Slaves of a Hopeless Love Affair/Blue Letter	1953	$30
❏ 9-28252	Somebody Bigger Than You and I/God's Little Candle	1952	$30
❏ 9-46285	Someone Else Not Me/ Music by the Angels (Lyrics by the Lord)	1951	$40
❏ 9-30470	Steal Away/Just a Closer Walk with Thee	1957	$30
❏ 9-30639	Strolling the Blues/ With You Beside Me	1958	$30
❏ 9-30334	Sweet Innocence/Why Ask for the Moon	1957	$30
❏ 9-30010	Take My Hand, Precious Lord/Someday, Somewhere	1956	$30
❏ 9-46317	Tennessee Hillbilly Ghost/Giles County Pulaski Post Office	1951	$30
❏ 9-46292	Tennessee Polka/ Tennessee Saturday Night	1951	$30
❏ 9-46136	Tennessee Saturday Night/Blues in My Heart	1950	$50

— Reissue of 78 originally issued in 1948; lines on either side of "Decca

| ❏ 9-46294 | That Little Boy of Mine/ Don't Make Me Go to Bed | 1951 | $30 |

— The above four comprise a box set

❏ 9-46297	The Chicken Song/So Long	1951	$30
❏ 9-29894	The Hoot Owl Boogie/A Handful of Love	1956	$30
❏ 9-88030	The Prettiest Song in the World/(B-side unknown)	1950	$50

— Yellow label "Childrens Series" issue

❏ 9-30080	(There'll Be) Peace in the Valley/A Servant	1956	$30
❏ 9-46319	There'll Be Peace in the Valley for Me/Old Soldiers Never Die	1951	$30
❏ 31302	The South/Dear Young Lovers	1961	$30
❏ 9-30452	This Could Very Well Be It/ Strike While the Iron Is Hot	1957	$30
❏ 9-30882	Travelin' Man/Just This Side of Memphis	1959	$30
❏ 9-46411	When the Saints Go Marching In/Lonely Mile	1952	$30
❏ 9-29667	When You Come to the End of the Day/The Night Watch	1955	$30
❏ 9-27929	Whistle While You Work/Who's Afraid of the Big Bad Wolf	1952	$40

Number	Title	Yr	NM
DECCA FAITH SERIES			
❏ 9-14566	He Bought My Soul at Calvary/It Is No Secret (What God Can Do)	1951	$40
❏ 9-14553	He'll Understand and Say Well Done/Milky White Way	1951	$40
❏ 9-14537	I Hear a Choir/The Place Where I Worship	1951	$40
❏ 9-14526	Our Lady of Fatima/The Rosary	1950	$50
❏ 9-14573	Peace in the Valley/Where Could I Go But to the Lord	1951	$40
❏ 9-14505	Steal Away/Just a Closer Walk with Thee	1950	$50
❏ ED2207 [PS]	Beyond the Sunset	1955	$30
❏ ED2207	Beyond the Sunset-Should You Go First/(There'll Be) Peace in the Valley (For Me)/Old Pappy's New Banjo/Someone to Care	1955	$30

FOLEY, RED AND BETTY
DECCA

Number	Title	Yr	NM
❏ 9-29000	As Far As I'm Concerned/Tennessee Whistling Man	1954	$30
❏ 9-29704	Croce di Oro (Cross of Gold)/Sweet Kentucky Rose	1955	$30
❏ 9-29526	Satisfied Mind/How About Me	1955	$30

FOLEY, WEBB
EMERALD

Number	Title	Yr	NM
❏ 2013	Bee Bop Baby/You Oughta Make Records	1956	$600
❏ 2011	Little Town/It Wasn't Faith	1956	$400

7-Inch Extended Plays
EMERALD

Number	Title	Yr	NM
❏ 750	Makin' a Plan/Pinkey//They Never Should'a Done It/Little Bitty Mama	1957	$300
❏ 750 [PS]	Webb Foley Sings	1957	$300

FOLKSWINGERS, THE
WORLD PACIFIC

Number	Title	Yr	NM
❏ 396	12 String Special/Amor A Todos	1963	$10
❏ 391	This Train/Black Mountain Rag	1963	$10

FONTAINE, EDDIE
CHANCELLOR

Number	Title	Yr	NM
❏ 1018	Goodness, It's Gladys/Middle of the Road	1958	$30

DECCA

Number	Title	Yr	NM
❏ 30121	As Far As I'm Concerned/'Til Tonight	1956	$30

— With Karen Chandler

Number	Title	Yr	NM
❏ 30042	Cool It Baby/Into Each Life Some Rain Must Fall	1956	$30
❏ 30446	Fun Lovin'/Honky Tonk Man	1957	$30
❏ 30338	Hey Marie, Rock with Me/The One and Only	1957	$30
❏ 30202	I'll Be There/East of Mississippi	1957	$30
❏ 30256	Money/Homesick Blues	1957	$30

JALO

Number	Title	Yr	NM
❏ 102	Where Is Da Woman/It Ain't Gonna Happen No More	1956	$100

LIBERTY

Number	Title	Yr	NM
❏ 55776	Blue Roses/Way Down Home	1965	$10
❏ 55823	I Need You/It Can Happen to You	1965	$10

SUNBEAM

Number	Title	Yr	NM
❏ 118	Love Eyes/Something Cha Cha	1958	$30

VIK

Number	Title	Yr	NM
❏ 0193	Here 'Tis/I Look at You	1956	$30
❏ 0203	Stand On That Rock/Baby You Did This to Me	1956	$30
❏ 0184	Turn the Light On/Boom-De-De-Boom	1955	$30

WARNER BROS.

Number	Title	Yr	NM
❏ 5345	(It's No) Sin/All I Want Is You	1963	$20
❏ 5313	My Heart Belongs to You/I'm Gonna Settle Down	1962	$20

X

Number	Title	Yr	NM
❏ 0193	Here 'Tis/I Look at You	1956	$40
❏ 0108	On Bended Knees/I Miss You So	1955	$40
❏ 0151	Poor Little Monday/The Rain Song	1955	$40
❏ 0203	Stand On That Rock/Baby You Did This to Me	1956	$40
❏ 0184	Turn the Light On/Boom-De-De-Boom	1955	$40

FONTAINE, FRANK
ABC-PARAMOUNT

Number	Title	Yr	NM
❏ 10574	Any Man Who Loves His Mother/When Your Old Wedding Ring Was New	1964	$8

Number	Title	Yr	NM
❏ 10491	Daddy's Little Girl/Oh How I Miss You Tonight	1963	$8
❏ 10430	Easter Parade/Always	1963	$8
❏ 10662	I Ain't Got Nobody/Someday	1965	$8
❏ 10618	Mexicali Rose/I'm Counting on You	1965	$8
❏ 10384	When Your Hair Has Turned to Silver/Here in My Heart	1962	$8
❏ 10384 [PS]	When Your Hair Has Turned to Silver/Here in My Heart	1962	$15

MGM

Number	Title	Yr	NM
❏ 12129	Everybody Rocks/Livin' It Up	1955	$70

FONTANA, WAYNE, AND THE MINDBENDERS
Also see WAYNE FONTANA; THE MINDBENDERS.
A&M

Number	Title	Yr	NM
❏ 3010	Game of Love/What a Wonderful World	1988	$4

— B-side by Louis Armstrong

Number	Title	Yr	NM
❏ 3010 [PS]	Game of Love/What a Wonderful World	1988	$4

— Good Morning Vietnam" sleeve

FONTANA

Number	Title	Yr	NM
❏ 1509	Game of Love/One More Time	1965	$15
❏ 1503	Game of Love/Since You've Been Gone	1965	$20
❏ 1514	It's Just a Little Bit Too Late/Long Time Comin'	1965	$10
❏ 1524	She Needs Love/Like I Do	1965	$10
❏ 1917	Stop, Look, Listen/Road Runner	1964	$15

FONTANA, WAYNE
Also see WAYNE FONTANA AND THE MINDBENDERS.
BRUT

Number	Title	Yr	NM
❏ 812	Sweet America/Interested	1973	$5

METROMEDIA

Number	Title	Yr	NM
❏ 133	Say Goodbye to Yesterday/Dayton, Ohio	1969	$6

MGM

Number	Title	Yr	NM
❏ 13516	Come On Home/My Eyes	1966	$8
❏ 13762	From a Boy to a Girl/24 Sycamore	1967	$6
❏ 13456	It Was Easier to Hurt Her/You Made Me What I Am Today	1966	$8
❏ 13661	Pamela, Pamela/Something Keeps Calling Me Back	1967	$6

FONTANE SISTERS, THE
DOT

Number	Title	Yr	NM
❏ 15682	Ain't It the Truth/Love Like a Fool	1957	$10
❏ 15908	Billy Boy/Third Man Theme	1959	$10
❏ 15782	Buttermilk/Take a Step	1958	$10
❏ 15736	Chanson D'Amour/Coconut Grove	1958	$10
❏ 16086	Come Home Eddie/Lover's Leap	1960	$8
❏ 15428	Daddy-O/Adorable	1955	$15
❏ 15547	Dancing to the Rock and Roll/I'm the One Who Loves You	1957	$12
❏ 15450	Eddie My Love/Yum, Yum	1956	$15
❏ 15853	Encore D'Amour/Jealous Heart	1958	$12
❏ 15581	Fool Around/Which Way to Your Heart	1957	$10
❏ 15171	Happy Days and Lonely Nights/If I Didn't Have You	1954	$15
❏ 15265	Hearts of Stone/Bless Your Heart	1954	$20
❏ 16027	Hearts of Stone/Seventeen	1960	$8
❏ 15462	I'm in Love Again/You Always Hurt the One You Love	1956	$15
❏ 15555	I'm Stickin' with You/Let the Rest of the World Go By	1957	$10
❏ 16014	Listen to Your Heart/Please Be Kind	1959	$12
❏ 15352	Most of All/Put Me in the Mood	1955	$15
❏ 15501	Please Don't Leave Me/Still	1956	$15
❏ 15386	Seventeen/If I Could Be with You	1955	$15
❏ 15527	The Banana Boat Song/Honolulu Moon	1957	$12
❏ 16059	Theme from "A Summer Place"/Darling, It's Wonderful	1960	$8
❏ 16499	The Tip of My Fingers/Summertime Love	1963	$6
❏ 15248	Willow Weep for Me/A Love Like You	1954	$15

RCA VICTOR

Number	Title	Yr	NM
❏ 47-4322	A Howdy Doody Christmas/The Popcorn Song	1951	$30

— With Howdy Doody

Number	Title	Yr	NM
❏ 47-4387	Alabama Jubilee/Grand Central Station	1951	$15
❏ 47-4009	Bouncy Bouncy Bally/What Did I Do	1950	$15
❏ 47-4233	Castle Rock/Makin' Like a Train	1951	$15

Number	Title	Yr	NM
❏ 47-4274	Cold, Cold Heart/I Get the Blues When It Rains	1951	$15
❏ 47-3127	Fairy Tales/The Cinderella Work Song	1949	$15
❏ 47-3713	(If I Knew You Were Comin') I'd've Baked a Cake/Mississippi Mud	1950	$15
❏ 47-4776	If You Would Only Be Mine/There's Doubt in My Mind	1952	$15
❏ 47-2926	I'm a Little Cuckoo/Turtle Song	1949	$15

— With the Cavanaugh Trio

Number	Title	Yr	NM
❏ 47-3772	I Wanna Be Loved/I Didn't Know What Time It Was	1950	$15
❏ 47-4077	Let Me In/Hurry Home to Me	1951	$20

— With Texas Jim Robertson

Number	Title	Yr	NM
❏ 47-5266	Mexican Joe/He Who Has Love	1953	$15
❏ 47-5383	Please Play Our Song/Falling	1953	$15
❏ 47-3940	Sleigh Bells/Jing-a-Ling, Jing-a-Ling	1950	$15

— With Dick Contino

Number	Title	Yr	NM
❏ 47-4449	Snowflakes/River in Moonlight	1952	$15

— With Merv Griffin and Freddie Martin

Number	Title	Yr	NM
❏ 47-3979	Tennessee Waltz/I Guess I'll Have to Dream the Rest	1950	$15
❏ 47-2976	The Bumpity Bus/24 Hours of Sunshine	1949	$15
❏ 47-4106	The Fortune Teller Song/The Fifth Wheel on the Wagon	1951	$15
❏ 47-3814	Three Little Rings/Down Home Rag	1950	$15
❏ 47-5612	Till Then/Baion	1954	$15
❏ 47-5162	Walkin' the Floor Over You/The Price I Paid for Loving You	1953	$15
❏ 47-4667	When I Dream/I Grabbed for the Ending	1952	$15
❏ 47-5049	Winter's Here Again/Lonesome Road	1952	$15

FOOL, THE
MERCURY

Number	Title	Yr	NM
❏ 72896	Lay It Down/Rainbow Man	1969	$8
❏ 72918	We Are One/Shining Light	1969	$8

FOOLS GOLD
COLUMBIA

Number	Title	Yr	NM
❏ 3-10635	Wouldn't I Love to Love You/Where Did Our Love Go Wrong	1977	$5

MORNING SKY

Number	Title	Yr	NM
❏ 701	One By One/Choices	1976	$8
❏ 701	One By One/I Will Run	1976	$6

FOOLS, THE
EMI AMERICA

Number	Title	Yr	NM
❏ 8046	Easy for You/I Won't Grow Up	1980	$6
❏ 8036	It's a Night for Beautiful Girls/Sold Out	1980	$5
❏ SPRO-9324 [DJ]	It's a Night for Beautiful Girls/Sold Out	1980	$8

— Promo-only picture disc in plastic sleeve

Number	Title	Yr	NM
❏ 8081	Lost Number/Local Talent	1981	$6
❏ SPRO-9330/1 [DJ]	Psycho Chicken (Beeped)/(Clucked)	1980	$10

— Promo only on yellow vinyl

FORBERT, STEVE
GEFFEN

Number	Title	Yr	NM
❏ 27548	On the Streets of This Town/Search Your Heart	1989	$5

NEMPEROR

Number	Title	Yr	NM
❏ 7535	Get Well Soon/Planet Earth Song	1981	$5
❏ 7520	Goin' Down to Laurel/Steve Forbert's Moon River	1978	$6
❏ 7519	It Isn't Gonna Be That Way/Big City Cat	1978	$6
❏ 7536	Lonely Girl/Planet Earth Song	1981	$5
❏ ZS97529	Say Goodbye to Little Jo/You're Darn Right	1980	$5
❏ ZS670066	Song for Katrina/Rain	1981	$5
❏ AE71184 [DJ]	The Oil Song/(B-side blank)	1979	$6

— Promo only, small hole

Number	Title	Yr	NM
❏ 7532	The Sweet Love That You Give (Sure Goes a Long, Long Way)/Sadly Sorta Like a Soap	1980	$5
❏ ZS5 02990	When You Walk in the Room/I Don't Know	1982	$5

FORCE FIVE, THE
ASCOT

Number	Title	Yr	NM
❏ 2206	Gee Too Tiger/I Want You Babe	1966	$60

Number	Title	Yr	NM

FORD, BILLY
JOSIE
Number	Title	Yr	NM
❑ 775	String of Pearls/ Stop Lyin' on Me	1955	$50

REPRISE
| ❑ 0265 | This Is Worth Fighting For/My Girl | 1964 | $15 |

UNITED
| ❑ 167 | Confessing/Old Age | 1955 | $40 |
| ❑ 142 | Smooth Rocking/ You Foxie Thing | 1954 | $40 |

VIK
| ❑ 0263 | How Can I Be Sure/ Billy Boy Blow | 1957 | $30 |

FORD, CAROL
KING
| ❑ 6188 | Christmas Letters/Please Come Home For Christmas | 1968 | $15 |

FORD, DEE DEE
BRIAR
| ❑ 142 | Good Morning Blues/I Just Can't Believe | 1962 | $15 |

TODD
| ❑ 1049 | Good Morning Blues/I Just Can't Believe | 1959 | $20 |

FORD, EMILE, AND THE CHECKMATES
ANDIE
| ❑ 5018 | Don't Tell Me Your Troubles/ What Do You Want to Make Those Eyes at Me For | 1960 | $20 |

FORD, FRANKIE
ABC
| ❑ 11431 | All Alone Am I/Blue Monday | 1974 | $5 |

ACE
❑ 566	Alimony/Can't Tell My Heart (What to Do)	1959	$30
❑ 592	Chinatown/What's Goin' On	1960	$30
❑ 592 [PS]	Chinatown/What's Goin' On	1960	$60
❑ 8009	Ocean Full of Tears/ Hour of Need	1963	$20
❑ 554	Sea Cruise/Roberta	1959	$40
❑ 549	The Last One to Cry/ Cheatin' Woman	1958	$30
❑ 580	Time After Time/Want to Be Your Man	1960	$30

BRIARMEADE
❑ 7701	Desperado/Mardi Gras in New Orleans	1977	$5
❑ 7901	Halfway to Paradise/I'm Proud of What I Am	1979	$5
❑ 7600	I've Found Someone of My Own/Battle Hymn of the Republic	1976	$5

CINNAMON
| ❑ 767 | Talk to a Carpenter/ When I Stop Dreamin' | 1973 | $5 |
| ❑ 752 | When I Stop Dreamin'/I'm Proud of What I Am | 1972 | $5 |

CONSTELLATION
| ❑ 101 | Chinatown/Ocean Full of Tears | 1963 | $20 |

DOUBLOON
| ❑ 101 | Half a Crown/I Can't Face Tomorrow | 1967 | $10 |

IMPERIAL
❑ 5776	Let 'Em Talk/What Happened to You	1961	$20
❑ 5706	My Southern Belle/ The Groom	1960	$20
❑ 5749	Saturday Night Fish Fry/ Love Don't Love Nobody	1961	$20
❑ 5735	Seventeen/Doghouse	1961	$20
❑ 5819	They Said It Couldn't Be Done/A Man Only Does	1962	$20

PAULA
| ❑ 351 | Peace of Mind/I'm Proud of What I Am | 1971 | $8 |

STARFIRE
| ❑ 119 | Time After Time/ Cheatin' Woman | 1979 | $5 |

SYC
| ❑ 1227 | Growing Pains/ Ups and Downs | 1982 | $4 |
| ❑ 1228 | My Prayer/Gospel Ship | 1983 | $4 |

7-Inch Extended Plays

ACE
| ❑ 105 | Chinatown My Chinatown/ Time After Time//Sea Cruise/Roberta | 1959 | $175 |
| ❑ 105 [PS] | The Best of Frankie Ford | 1959 | $175 |

FORD, JOY
COUNTRY INT'L.
Number	Title	Yr	NM
❑ 222	Always in My Heart/ Can I Believe	1989	$6
❑ 195	Baby Have a Baby with Me/(B-side unknown)	1983	$5
❑ 197	Big City Turn Me Loose/ (B-side unknown)	1984	$5
❑ 207	Blues, Stay Away from Me/Carousel	1985	$5
❑ 113	Breaker, Breaker, Breaker, Lies and Kisses/ (B-side unknown)	1976	$6
❑ 179	Carousel/Luziana River	1982	$5
❑ 176	Christmas Card/ (B-side unknown)	1982	$5

— With John Krondes
❑ 212	Crazy Arms/(B-side unknown)	1987	$5
❑ 224	Crystal Chandelier/ (B-side unknown)	1989	$6
❑ 200	Deeper in Love/ (B-side unknown)	1984	$5
❑ 144	Give Me Something to Hold On To/I Love the Way You Love on Me	1980	$5
❑ 198	Heartaches/Big City Turn Me Loose	1984	$5
❑ 107	Her Bridal Bouquet/ White Gardenia	1976	$6
❑ 138	I Love the Way You Love on Me/(B-side unknown)	1979	$5
❑ 100	It's Your Turn to Cry/Just Listen to Your Heart	1975	$5
❑ 133	Listening for the Wind/Thirty Days Hath September	1978	$5

— With Herb Oscar Anderson
❑ 134	Love Isn't Love (Till You Give It Away)/Another Favour	1978	$5
❑ 211	Love Makes the Livin' Worthwhile/ (B-side unknown)	1986	$5
❑ 163	Love Me Again/ Luziana River	1982	$5
❑ 209	Lovin' Dangerously/ (B-side unknown)	1986	$5
❑ 153	Luziana River/ (B-side unknown)	1981	$5
❑ 206	Melted Down Memories/ Big City Turn Me Loose	1985	$5
❑ 119	My Heart Is an Open Book/(B-side unknown)	1977	$6
❑ 102	One Foot in Alabama/ You'll Get Over It	1975	$6
❑ 213	Only Six Feet Away/Look What Love Can Do	1987	$5
❑ 150	Pretend/(B-side unknown)	1981	$5
❑ 203	String Around My Finger/ (B-side unknown)	1985	$5
❑ 142	Take My Love/I Love the Way You Love on Me	1979	$5
❑ 105	Tears on My Pillow/Till the End of the World	1976	$6
❑ 193	The Hand That Rocks the Cradle Rules the World/ (B-side unknown)	1983	$5
❑ 218	There's a Fire in Our Bedroom/(B-side unknown)	1988	$6

— With Eddie Moore
| ❑ 117 | Walking After Midnight/ You'll Get Over It | 1977 | $6 |

FORD, LITA
Also see THE RUNAWAYS.
RCA
❑ 8640-7-R	Back to the Cave/ Under the Gun	1988	$3
❑ 8640-7-R [PS]	Back to the Cave/ Under the Gun	1988	$4
❑ 8899-7-R	Close My Eyes Forever/ Under the Gun	1989	$3

—A-side with Ozzy Osbourne
❑ 8899-7-R [PS]	Close My Eyes Forever/ Under the Gun	1989	$3
❑ 9008-7-R	Falling In and Out of Love/Fatal Passion	1989	$3
❑ 9008-7-R [PS]	Falling In and Out of Love/Fatal Passion	1989	$3

FORD, MARILYN
TOWER
| ❑ LO8W2629/30 | Please, Dear God, Help Santa Claus/I'm A Little Elf | 1960 | $15 |

FORD, NEAL, AND THE FANATICS
HICKORY
❑ 1468	Get Together with Me/Pain	1967	$30
❑ 1433	Gonna Be My Girl/ Shame on You	1967	$30
❑ 1490	I Have Thoughts of You/ That Girl of Mine	1967	$30
❑ 1516	I'll Put My Boots On Backwards/Buttercup	1968	$30
❑ 1500	Movin' Along/Little World Girl	1968	$30

TANTARA
Number	Title	Yr	NM
❑ 1101	Don't Tie Me Down/ Bitter Bells	1966	$40
❑ 1107	I Will If You Want/ (B-side unknown)	1966	$40
❑ 1104	Searchin'/All I Have to Do Is Dream	1966	$40

FORD, TENNESSEE ERNIE, AND MOLLY BEE
CAPITOL
| ❑ F2473 | Don't Start Courtin' in a Hot Rod/We're a-Growin' Up | 1953 | $30 |

FORD, TENNESSEE ERNIE
CAPITOL
| ❑ 4044 | Baby/I'd Like to Be | 1975 | $4 |

— With Andra Willis
❑ F3058	Ballad of Davy Crockett/Farewell	1955	$20
❑ F2170	Blackberry Boogie/ Tennessee Local	1952	$30
❑ 4468	Bless This Land/ Lord of All Creation	1960	$8
❑ F3868	Bless Your Pea Pickin' Heart/Down Deep	1957	$15
❑ F3343	Bright Lights and Blonde Haired Women/That's All	1956	$30
❑ F1174	Bright Lights/The Cincinnati Dancing Pig	1950	$20
❑ F1275	Bryant's Boogie/ Little Juan Pedro	1950	$30
❑ F2602	Catfish Boogie/Kiss Me Big	1953	$30
❑ F4173	Code of the Mountains/ Black-Eyed Susie	1959	$10
❑ 3704	Colorado Country Morning/ Daddy Usta Say	1973	$4
❑ 3916	Come On Down/Bits and Pieces of Life	1974	$4
❑ 4531	Dark As a Dungeon/ His Love (Makes the World Go Round)	1961	$8
❑ 3631	Farther Down the River (Where the Fishin's Good)/You've Still Got Love All Over You	1973	$4
❑ F3553	First Born/Have You Seen Her	1956	$15
❑ 5520	Girl Don't You Know/ Now It's All Over	1965	$6
❑ 5757	God Lives/How Great Thou Art	1966	$6
❑ F2017	Hambone/Candy Dancers' Ball	1952	$20
❑ 3079	Happy Songs of Love/ Don't Let the Good Life Pass You By	1971	$5
❑ F1809	Hey, Good Lookin'/ Cool, Cool Kisses	1951	$20
❑ F2443	Hey, Mr. Cotton Picker/Three Things (A Man Must Do)	1953	$20
❑ 2522	Honey-Eyed Girl (That's You That's You)/Good Morning, Dear	1969	$6
❑ 4838	How Great Thou Art/ Eternal Life	1962	$8
❑ F3135	I Am a Pilgrim/His Hands	1955	$15
❑ 4285	I Been to Georgia on a Fast Train/Baby's Home	1976	$4
❑ F1124	I'll Never Be Free/Ain't Nobody's Business But My Own	1950	$20

— With Kay Starr
| ❑ F1623 | I'll Never Be Free/Ain't Nobody's Business But My Own | 1951 | $15 |

— With Kay Starr; reissue
| ❑ F2215 | I'm Hog Tied Over You/ False Hearted Girl | 1952 | $20 |

— With Ella Mae Morse
❑ F3762	In the Middle of An Island/Ivy League	1957	$15
❑ 3848	I've Got Confidence/I'd Like to Be	1974	$4
❑ F985	I've Got to Feed 'Em in the Morning/My Hobby	1950	$20
❑ 4446	Little Klinker/Jingle-O-The-Brownie	1960	$15
❑ 4446 [PS]	Little Klinker/Jingle-O-The-Brownie	1960	$30
❑ 4577	Litttle Red Rockin' Hood/I Gotta Have My Baby Back	1961	$8
❑ F3700	Lonely Man/False Hearted Girl	1957	$15
❑ F2876	Losing You/Eins, Zwei, Drei	1954	$15
❑ 4302	Love Is the Only Thing/ Sunny Side of Heaven	1959	$8
❑ F3997	Love Makes the World Go Round/Sunday Barbecue	1958	$10
❑ F1205	Mama Goes Everywhere Papa Goes/Please Love Me	1950	$20

— With Kay Starr
❑ F1521	Mr. and Mississippi/ She's My Baby	1951	$20
❑ F1695	Mule Train/The Cry of the Wild Goose	1951	$15
❑ F1567	Oceans of Tears/ You're My Sugar	1951	$20

— With Kay Starr
| ❑ 3422 | Pea-Pickin' Cook/The Song | 1972 | $5 |
| ❑ 5900 | Pearly Shells/Lahaina Luna | 1967 | $6 |

Number	Title	Yr	NM
❏ 3556	Printers' Alley Stars/Baby	1973	$4
❏ F2042	Put Your Arms Around Me/Everybody's Got a Girl But Me	1952	$20
❏ 3783	She Picked Up the Pieces/ Sweet Child of Sunshine	1973	$4
❏ 5534	Sing We Now of Christmas/ The Little Drummer Boy	1965	$8
❏ 5425	Sixteen Tons/Hicktown	1965	$6
❏ F3262	Sixteen Tons/You Don't Have to Be a Baby to Cry	1955	$20
❏ F4107	Sleepin' at the Foot of the Bed/Glad Rags	1958	$12
❏ F2179	Smokey Mountain Boogie/ Country Junction	1952	$30
❏ F2066	Snowshoe Thompson/ Fatback Louisiana USA	1952	$20
❏ F2939	Somebody Bigger Than You and I/There Is Beauty in Everything	1954	$15
❏ 4333	Sweet Feelin's/Dogs and Sheriff John	1976	$4
❏ F2338	Sweet Temptation/I Don't Know	1953	$20
❏ F1349	Tailor Made Woman/ Stack-O-Lee	1951	$20
❏ 4734	Take Your Girlie to the Movies/There'll Be No New Tunes	1962	$8
❏ 2145	Talk to the Animals/What a Wonderful World	1968	$6
❏ F40280	The Cry of the Wild Goose/ The Donkey Serenade	1950	$30
❏ 4160	The Devil Ain't a Lonely Woman's Friend/Smokey Taverns, Bar Room Girls	1975	$4
❏ F2809	The Honeymoon's Over/ This Must Be the Place	1954	$15

— With Betty Hutton

Number	Title	Yr	NM
❏ 2334	The Little Boy King/Bring a Torch, Jeanette, Isabella	1968	$6
❏ F1626	The Shot Gun Boogie/ Anticipation Blues	1951	$15
❏ F1295	The Shot Gun Boogie/I Ain't Gonna Let It Happen No More	1950	$30
❏ F3649	The Watermelon Song/One Suit	1957	$15
❏ 4793	The Work Song/ Rags and Old Iron	1962	$8
❏ F1159	What This Country Needs/ The Lord's Lariat	1950	$20

7-Inch Extended Plays

Number	Title	Yr	NM
❏ EAP 3-1332	*Bring In the Sheaves/ Jesus Loves Me/All Hail the Power/The Home Over There/Count Your Blessings	1960	$15
❏ EAP 1-1071	*Joy to the World/O Little Town of Bethlehem/The Star Carol/Hark! The Herald Angels Sing	1958	$15
❏ EAP 1-413	*Shot Gun Boogie/Smokey Mountain Boogie/Blackberry Boogie/Anticipation Blues	1953	$25
❏ EAP 2-1071	*Some Children See Him/God Rest Ye Merry Gentlemen/O Hearken Ye/Adeste Fideles	1958	$15
❏ EAP 1-1332	*There Is Power in the Blood/When the Roll Is Called Up Yonder/Shall We Gather at the River/ Brighten The Corner Where You Are/What a Friend	1960	$15
❏ EAP 1-693 [PS]	16 Tons	1956	$20
❏ EAP 1-1272 [PS]	A Friend We Have, Part 1	1959	$15
❏ EAP 2-1272 [PS]	A Friend We Have, Part 2	1959	$15
❏ EAP 3-1272 [PS]	A Friend We Have, Part 3	1959	$15
❏ EAP 1-413 [PS]	Backwoods Boogie and Blues	1953	$25
❏ EAP 1-1227	Brown's Ferry Blues/Black Is the Color of My True Love's Hair//Old Blue/ Freight Train Blues	1959	$15
❏ EAP 3-700	Chicken Road/Who Will Shoe Your Pretty Little Foot//The Rovin' Gambler/In the Pines	1956	$20
❏ EAP 3-1071	(contents unknown)	1958	$15
❏ EAP 1-888	Country Junction/Milk 'Em in the Mornin' Blues// Anticipation Blues/ Catfish Boogie	1956	$20
❏ EAP 2-700	Dark as a Dungeon/ False Hearted Girl//I Gave My Love a Cherry/ Nine Pound Hammer	1956	$20
❏ EAP 1-1227 [PS]	Gather 'Round, Part 1	1959	$15
❏ EAP 2-1227 [PS]	Gather 'Round, Part 2	1959	$15
❏ EAP 3-1227 [PS]	Gather 'Round, Part 3	1959	$15
❏ EAP 1-756 [PS]	Hymns, Part 1	1956	$20
❏ EAP 2-756 [PS]	Hymns, Part 2	1956	$20
❏ EAP 3-756 [PS]	Hymns, Part 3	1956	$20
❏ EAP 3-756	Let the Lower Lights Be Burning/Others//My Task/Ivory Palaces	1956	$20
❏ EAP 3-1272	Life's Railway to Heaven/ Good Night And Good Morning//Drifting Too Far from the Shore/My Jesus As Thou Wilt	1959	$15

Number	Title	Yr	NM
❏ EAP 3-1227	Look Down/My Grandfather's Clock// Twenty-One Years/Left My Gal in the Mountains	1959	$15
❏ EAP 3-1005	Lord, I'm Coming Home/I Need Thee Every Hour// Take Time to Be Holy/ God Be With You	1958	$10
❏ EAP 1-888 [PS]	Ol' Rockin' Ern, Part 1	1956	$20
❏ EAP 2-888 [PS]	Ol' Rockin' Ern, Part 2	1956	$20
❏ EAP 3-888 [PS]	Ol' Rockin' Ern, Part 3	1956	$20
❏ EAP 2-1332	Onward Christian Soldiers/ Oh How I Love Jesus//I Love to Tell the Story/The Church in the Wilderness	1960	$15
❏ EAP 2-888	Shot-Gun Boogie/She's My Baby//Blackberry Boogie/Kiss Me Big	1956	$20
❏ EAP 1-1332 [PS]	Sing a Hymn with Me, Part 1	1960	$15
❏ EAP 2-1332 [PS]	Sing a Hymn with Me, Part 2	1960	$15
❏ EAP 3-1332 [PS]	Sing a Hymn with Me, Part 3	1960	$15
❏ EAP 1-693	Sixteen Tons/River of No Return//You Don't Have to Be a Baby to Cry/ Give Me Your Word	1956	$20
❏ EAP 3-888	Smokey Mountain Boogie/ Ain't Nobody's Business But My Own//I Ain't a-Gonna Let It Happen No More/ The Lord's Lariat	1956	$20
❏ EAP 1-1071 [PS]	The Star Carol, Part 1	1958	$15
❏ EAP 2-1071 [PS]	The Star Carol, Part 2	1958	$15
❏ EAP 3-1071 [PS]	The Star Carol, Part 3	1958	$15
❏ EAP 1-700 [PS]	This Lusty Land! Part 1	1956	$20
❏ EAP 2-700 [PS]	This Lusty Land! Part 2	1956	$20
❏ EAP 3-700 [PS]	This Lusty Land! Part 3	1956	$20
❏ EAP 1-1005	What a Friend We Have in Jesus/Jesus, Savior, Pilot Me//His Eye Is on the Sparrow/Beautiful Isle of Somewhere	1958	$10
❏ EAP 2-756	When They Ring the Golden Bells/In the Garden// Sweet Hour of Prayer/ The Old Rugged Cross	1956	$20
❏ EAP 2-1272	Where Could I Go/O Come Angel Band//Hold To God's Unchanging Hand/Wondrous Love	1959	$15

GREEN GIANT

Number	Title	Yr	NM
❏ PB-2565 [DJ]	Down in the Valley/Medley: The More We Get Together-Dear Evalina-Keep on the Sunny Side of Life-How Many Biscuits Can We Eat-For He's a Jolly Green Giant/ How the Green Giant Found His Song (And Almost Lost His Ho-Ho-Ho)/Good Things from the Garden	1963	$10

— Promotional item for the Green Giant Company/Le Sueur Peas

Number	Title	Yr	NM
❏ PB-2565 [PS]	When Pea-Pickers Get Together	1963	$12

— Promotional item for the Green Giant Company/Le Sueur Peas

FORD THEATRE, THE
ABC

Number	Title	Yr	NM
❏ 11227	I've Got the Fever/ Jefferson Airplane	1969	$10
❏ 11118	Theme for the Masses/I Can't Help It Baby	1968	$10

FOREHAND, EDDIE "BUSTER
JOSIE

Number	Title	Yr	NM
❏ 981	I'm So Lonely/But I Do	1967	$40

MINIT

Number	Title	Yr	NM
❏ 32076	City of Blues/Cry Me a River	1969	$30

FOREIGNER
Also see BLACK SHEEP; SPOOKY TOOTH; MICK JONES; LOU GRAMM. (45)

ATLANTIC

Number	Title	Yr	NM
❏ 3543	Blue Morning, Blue Day/I Have Waited So Long	1978	$4
❏ 3543 [DJ]	Blue Morning, Blue Day (same on both sides)	1978	$10

— Promo only on blue vinyl

Number	Title	Yr	NM
❏ 4044 [DJ]	Break It Up (Edit)/ (LP Version)	1982	$6
❏ 4044	Break It Up/Head Games (Live)	1982	$4
❏ 4044 [PS]	Break It Up/Head Games (Live)	1982	$4
❏ 3410	Cold As Ice/I Need You	1977	$4

— Has a different mix (with strings) than the LP version

Number	Title	Yr	NM
❏ 3618	Dirty White Boy/Rev on the Red Line	1979	$4
❏ 3618 [PS]	Dirty White Boy/Rev on the Red Line	1979	$5
❏ 3514	Double Vision/ Lonely Children	1978	$4
❏ 3514 [PS]	Double Vision/ Lonely Children	1978	$5

Number	Title	Yr	NM
❏ 89493	Down on Love/Growing Up the Hard Way	1985	$3
❏ 3394	Feels Like the First Time/ Woman, Oh Woman	1977	$4
❏ 3633	Head Games/Do What You Like	1979	$4
❏ 3633 [PS]	Head Games/Do What You Like	1979	$5
❏ 89046	Heart Turns to Stone/ Counting Every Minute	1988	$3
❏ 89046 [PS]	Heart Turns to Stone/ Counting Every Minute	1988	$3
❏ 3488	Hot Blooded/Tramontane	1978	$4
❏ 89101	I Don't Want to Live Without You/Face to Face	1988	$3
❏ 89101 [PS]	I Don't Want to Live Without You/Face to Face	1988	$3
❏ 89596	I Want to Know What Love Is/Street Thunder	1984	$4

— Generic red and black Atlantic label

Number	Title	Yr	NM
❏ 89596	I Want to Know What Love Is/Street Thunder	1984	$3

— Custom black and colorblocked label

Number	Title	Yr	NM
❏ 89596 [PS]	I Want to Know What Love Is/Street Thunder	1984	$4
❏ 3439	Long, Long Way from Home/ The Damage Is Done	1977	$4

— Has a different vocal with slightly altered lyrics from the LP version

Number	Title	Yr	NM
❏ 4072	Luanne/Fool For You Anyway	1982	$4
❏ 89169	Say You Will/A Night to Remember	1987	$3
❏ 89169 [PS]	Say You Will/A Night to Remember	1987	$3
❏ 89571	That Was Yesterday/ Two Different Worlds	1985	$3
❏ 89571 [PS]	That Was Yesterday/ Two Different Worlds	1985	$3
❏ 3868	Waiting for a Girl Like You/I'm Gonna Win	1981	$3
❏ 3868 [PS]	Waiting for a Girl Like You/I'm Gonna Win	1981	$5
❏ 3651	Women/The Modern Day	1980	$4

ATLANTIC OLDIES SERIES

Number	Title	Yr	NM
❏ OS13218	Dirty White Boy/ Head Games	1981	$3

— Reissue

Number	Title	Yr	NM
❏ OS13208	Feels Like the First Time/Cold As Ice	1980	$3

— Reissue

Number	Title	Yr	NM
❏ OS13209	Hot Blooded/Double Vision	1980	$3

— Reissue

Number	Title	Yr	NM
❏ 84973	I Want to Know What Love Is/That Was Yesterday	1987	$3

— Reissue

Number	Title	Yr	NM
❏ 84924	Say You Will/I Don't Want to Live Without You	1989	$3

— Reissue

FOREVER MORE
RCA VICTOR

Number	Title	Yr	NM
❏ 74-0335	Beautiful Afternoon/One O'Clock and All's Well	1970	$8
❏ 74-0277	Home Country Blues/ Back in the States Again	1969	$8

FORMATIONS, THE
BANK

Number	Title	Yr	NM
❏ 1007	At the Top of the Stairs/ Magic Melody	1968	$40

MGM

Number	Title	Yr	NM
❏ 13899	At the Top of the Stairs/ Magic Melody	1968	$12
❏ 14009	Don't Get Close/ There's No Room	1968	$15
❏ 13963	Love's Not Only for the Heart/Lonely Voice of Love	1968	$30

FORREST, SONNY
ATCO

Number	Title	Yr	NM
❏ 6157	Diddy Bop/Knockdown	1960	$50

RED TOP

Number	Title	Yr	NM
❏ 128	Mama, Keep My Wife at Home/Madame Bootie Green	1960	$50

VERVE

Number	Title	Yr	NM
❏ 10306	Travelin'/Now That I'm Lonely	1963	$40

— As "Sonny Forest

Number	Title	Yr	NM

FORTUNE, JOHNNY
ARENA
| ❏ 102 | I'm a Fool for You/Gee But I Miss You | 1963 | $30 |

ARHAVEN
| ❏ 1001 | I'm a Fool for You/Gee But I Miss You | 1962 | $30 |

BEAVER
| ❏ 111 | I'm Requesting a Love Song/Stay Just One More Day | 1966 | $20 |

CRUSADER
| ❏ 104 | If You Love Me/Gee But I Miss You | 1964 | $20 |

CURRENT
❏ 104	Dan Stole My Girl/You Want Me to Be Your Baby	1965	$20
❏ 105	I Am Lonely for You/I'll Never Let You Go	1965	$20
❏ 101	Say You Will/Come On and Love Me	1965	$20

EMMY
| ❏ 1001 | If You Love Me/Alone and Crying | 1960 | $40 |
| ❏ 1002 | I'm in Heaven (When You Kiss Me)/Gee But I Miss You | 1960 | $40 |

PARK AVENUE
❏ 130	Dragster/Siboney	1963	$20
❏ 4905	I'm Talkin' About You/My Wandering Love	1963	$20
❏ 110	Midnight Surf/Soul Surfer	1963	$20
❏ 126	Surfer's Trip/Soul Traveler	1963	$20

UNITED ARTISTS
| ❏ 780 | Don't You Lie to Me/Don't Stay Out After Midnight | 1964 | $20 |

FORTUNES, THE (1)
CAPITOL
❏ 3179	Freedom Comes, Freedom Goes/There's a Man	1971	$5
❏ 3626	Give Me Some Room/Whenever It's a Sunday	1973	$5
❏ 3086	Here Comes That Rainy Day Feeling Again/Bad Side of Town	1971	$12
❏ 3086	Here Comes That Rainy Day Feeling Again/I Gotta Dream	1971	$6
❏ 3514	I Can't Remember When the Sun Went In/Secret Love	1973	$5
❏ 3248	Storm in a Teacup/I'm Not Following You	1971	$5
❏ 3445	Wait Until September/Don't Sing to Me	1972	$5

PRESS
❏ 60001	Gone from My Mind/Silent Street	1966	$10
❏ 9798	Here It Comes Again/Things I Should Have Known	1965	$20
—White label stock copy			
❏ 9798	Here It Comes Again/Things I Should Have Known	1965	$12
—Purple label			
❏ 9811	This Golden Ring/Someone to Care	1966	$10

UNITED ARTISTS
| ❏ 50280 | Painting a Shadow/Fire Brigade | 1968 | $10 |
| ❏ 50211 | The Idol/His Smile Was a Lie | 1967 | $10 |

WORLD PACIFIC
| ❏ 77937 | That Same Old Feeling/Lifetime of Love | 1970 | $8 |

FORTUNES, THE (U)
ARGO
| ❏ 5364 | Congratulations/Look at Me, Look at You | 1960 | $70 |

CHECKER
| ❏ 818 | Believe in Me/My Baby Is Fine | 1955 | $70 |

CUB
| ❏ 9123 | The Ghoul in School/You Don't Know (What I've Been Through) | 1963 | $20 |

DECCA
| ❏ 30688 | How Clever of You/Trees | 1958 | $60 |
| ❏ 30541 | Tarnished Angel/Who Cares? | 1958 | $70 |

DRA
| ❏ 320 | Tell Me/Running Away from Love | 1962 | $300 |

TOP RANK
| ❏ 2019 | Steady Vows/In the Night | 1959 | $50 |

YUCCA
| ❏ 168 | Laugh of the Train/Chi Wawa | 1964 | $40 |
| ❏ 170 | Lonely Teardrops/This Is Love | 1964 | $50 |

49TH PARALLEL, THE
MAVERICK
| ❏ 1004 | Close the Barn Door/Twilight Woman | 1968 | $30 |
| ❏ 1011 | (Come On Little Child and) Talk to Me/Now That I'm a Man | 1968 | $30 |

FORUM, THE
MIRA
| ❏ 248 | A Girl Without a Boy/Go Try to Put Out the Sun | 1968 | $15 |
| ❏ 243 | Trip on Me/It's Sunday | 1967 | $15 |

FOSTER AND LLOYD
RCA
❏ 8942-7-R	Before the Heartache Rolls In/Happy for a While	1989	$3
❏ 5210-7-R	Crazy Over You/The Part I Know by Heart	1987	$4
❏ 5210-7-R [PS]	Crazy Over You/The Part I Know by Heart	1987	$6
—Sleeve is promo only			
❏ 8795-7-R	Fair Shake/After I'm Gone	1989	$3
❏ 5281-7-R	Sure Thing/Hard to Say No	1987	$3
❏ 5281-7-R [PS]	Sure Thing/Hard to Say No	1987	$4
❏ 9028-7-R	Suzette/I'll Always Be Here Loving You	1989	$3
❏ 6900-7-R	Texas in 1880/Token of Love	1988	$3
❏ 8633-7-R	What Do You Want from Me This Time/Don't Go Out with Him	1988	$3

FOSTER, BRUCE
MILLENNIUM
❏ 600	Born to Break My Heart/Baby It's Gone	1977	$6
❏ 602 [PS]	Platinum Heroes	1977	$10
—Sleeve is promo only			
❏ 602 [DJ]	Platinum Heroes (3:45)/(5:45)	1977	$6

FOSTER, CELL, AND THE AUDIOS
ULTRA
❏ 105	Honest I Do/I Prayed for You	1956	$400
—Yellow label			
❏ 105	Honest I Do/I Prayed for You	1956	$250
—Maroon label			

FOSTER, DAVID
ATLANTIC
❏ 89528	Love Theme from St. Elmo's Fire/Georgetown	1985	$3
❏ 89528 [PS]	Love Theme from St. Elmo's Fire/Georgetown	1985	$5
—With "Georgetown" listed on front of sleeve			
❏ 89528 [PS]	Love Theme from St. Elmo's Fire/Georgetown	1985	$3
—With David Foster's name on front of sleeve in place of "Georgetown"			
❏ 89420	The Best of Me/Saje	1986	$3
—A-side with Olivia Newton-John			
❏ 89420 [PS]	The Best of Me/Saje	1986	$3
❏ 89376	Who's Gonna Love You Tonight/Playing with Fire	1986	$3
❏ 89140	Winter Games/Piano Concerto in G	1988	$3
❏ 89140 [PS]	Winter Games/Piano Concerto in G	1988	$3

FOSTER, JERRY
BACK BEAT
❏ 534	Lonely One/Romeo	1961	$15
❏ 529	My First Love/I'm Here to Tell You	1959	$15
❏ 520	What Would I Do/Your Love	1958	$20

CINNAMON
❏ 764	Copperhead/Ain't It Sad	1973	$6
❏ 757	I Won't Ever Love Again/Turn It Over in Your Mind	1973	$6
❏ 774	Looking Back/Hard to Handle	1973	$6

HITSVILLE
| ❏ 6052 | Family Man/Just Another Song Away | 1977 | $5 |
| ❏ 6043 | I Knew You When/One | 1976 | $5 |

KARI
❏ 106	Giving Up Easy/I Wonder If You'll Ever Learn to Cry	1980	$5
❏ 109	Matchbox/Don't Let Go	1980	$5
❏ 112	That's Alright/Hard to Handle	1980	$5
❏ 116	When My Blue Moon Turns to Gold Again/Looking Back	1981	$5

MONUMENT
| ❏ 45-242 | Don't Take Your Sunshine From My Life/The Fifties | 1978 | $5 |
| ❏ 45-256 | I Want to Love You/My Baby Left Me | 1978 | $5 |

SUN
| ❏ 1176 [DJ] | The 50's (same on both sides) | 1982 | $6 |
| —Promo only | | | |

TCF HALL
| ❏ 115 | The Fight/Here Comes the Loser | 1966 | $8 |

FOSTER, JOHN, AND SONS BLACK DYKE MILLS BAND
APPLE
❏ 1800	Thingumybob/Yellow Submarine	1968	$125
—With "Thingumybob" on uncut apple side			
❏ 1800	Thingumybob/Yellow Submarine	1968	$125
—With "Yellow Submarine" on uncut apple side			
❏ 1800	Thingumybob/Yellow Submarine	1968	$120
—With black star on uncut apple side			

FOSTER, LARRY
20TH CENTURY FOX
| ❏ 325 | My Christmas Message to the World/My Son, the Folk Monster | 1962 | $20 |

FOTHERINGAY
A&M
| ❏ 1223 | Ballad of Ned Kelly/The Sea | 1970 | $8 |

FOTINE, LARRY
DECCA
| ❏ 27331 | Christmas In Killarney/Jumpin' Jiminey | 1950 | $20 |

FOTO-FI FOUR, THE
FOTO-FI
❏ 107	Stand Up and Holler!/Ismael	1964	$30
❏ 107 [PS]	Stand Up and Holler!/Ismael	1964	$60
—Sleeve states: "The Beatles arrive in America! Have fun running the film with this specially scored recording." Price does not include film.			

FOUNDATIONS, THE
UNI
❏ 55038	Baby, Now That I've Found You/Come On Back to Me	1967	$8
❏ 55058	Back on My Feet Again/I Can Take or Leave Your Loving	1968	$6
❏ 55101	Build Me Up Buttercup/New Direction	1968	$8
❏ 55315	I'll Give You Love/Stoney Ground	1972	$6
❏ 55117	In the Bad, Bad Old Days (Before You Loved Me)/Give Me Love	1969	$6
❏ 55137	My Little Chickadee/Solomon Grundy	1969	$6
❏ 55210	Take a Girl Like You/I'm Gonna Be a Rich Man	1970	$6
❏ 55073	We Are Happy People/Any Old Time	1968	$6
❏ 55162	Why Did You Cry/Born to Live, Born to Die	1969	$6

FOUNTAIN, CAPT. JESSE
CAMEO
| ❏ 457 | When It Rains Love (It Pours)/I'm Marchin' | 1967 | $30 |

FOUNTAIN OF YOUTH
COLGEMS
❏ 66-1020	Livin' Too Fast/(Angie, Love Me) Make the Hurt Go Away	1968	$30
❏ 66-5003	Liza Jane/Mistress People	1969	$20
❏ 66-1024	Take a Giant Step/Don't Blame Me (For Trying)	1968	$30
❏ 66-1032	The Day Don't Come/Sunshine on a Cold Morning	1969	$20

FOUNTAIN, PETE, AND AL HIRT
CORAL
| ❏ 65544 | March of the Bob Cats/Farewell Blues | 1962 | $8 |

FOUNTAIN, PETE
CORAL
❏ 62154	A Closer Walk/Do You Know What It Means to Miss New Orleans	1959	$8
❏ 62243	Alone Together/Forbidden Love	1961	$8
❏ 62561	Aquarius/The Flesh Failures	1969	$5
❏ 62365	Casablanca/Lost Love	1963	$6
❏ 62376	China Nights/Theme from "Women of the World"	1963	$6
❏ 62545	For Pete's Sake/Danke Schoen	1967	$5

Number	Title	Yr	NM
❏ 65586	Hello, Dolly!/Tippin' In	1964	$6
❏ 62557	Les Bicyclettes De Belsize/Puddin	1969	$5
❏ 62413	Licorice Stick/Estrellita	1964	$6
❏ 62454	Mae/Gotta Travel On	1965	$6
❏ 65619	Make Your Own Kind of Music/Early in the Morning	1970	$4
❏ 62496	Mood Indigo/Sleepy Serenade	1966	$5
❏ 62441	Mr. Stick Man/Amazon	1965	$6
❏ 62527	Music to Turn You On/(Carol's Theme) The Eyes of Love	1967	$5
❏ 62107	My Inspiration/Japansy	1959	$8
❏ 62266	Oh, Didn't He Ramble/Allison's Theme from Parrish	1962	$8
❏ 65545	San Antonio Rose/Dixie	1961	$8
❏ 62211	Sentimental Journey/Columbus Stockade Blues	1960	$8
❏ 62564	Sunday in the Country/Applause	1970	$4
❏ 65605	The Christmas Song (Merry Christmas To You)/Santa Claus Medley	1966	$8
❏ 62350	The Grasshopper/Lonely Little Tune	1963	$6
❏ 62427	The Horny Wind Blows/Humbug	1964	$6
❏ 62516	Thoroughly Modern Millie/Jimmy	1967	$5
❏ 62446	Whipped Cream/Midnight Pete	1965	$6

FOUR ACES

ABC-PARAMOUNT

Number	Title	Yr	NM
❏ 10183	Me Without You/The Ballad of Patrick Henry	1961	$10
❏ 10166	Searching/Dolce Par Niente	1960	$10

DECCA

Number	Title	Yr	NM
❏ 29036	Amor/So Long	1954	$20
❏ 29725	A Woman in Love/Of This I'm Sure	1955	$15
❏ 30242	Bahama Mama/You're Mine	1957	$15
❏ 28979	Bandera (Texas Polka)/What More Is There	1954	$20
❏ 30874	Ciao, Ciao Bambino/Paradise Island	1959	$10
❏ 28744	Don't Forget Me/False Love	1953	$20
❏ 29217	Dream/It Shall Come to Pass	1954	$20
❏ 30041	Friendly Persuasion (Thee I Love)/You Can't Run Away from It	1956	$15
❏ 30384	Half of My Heart/When My Sugar Walks Down the Street	1957	$15
❏ 28390	Heart and Soul/Just Squeeze Me	1952	$30
❏ 29476	Heart/Sluefoot	1955	$15
❏ 30466	How Do You Say Goodbye?/I Would Love You Still	1957	$15
❏ 29809	If You Can Dream/The Gal with the Yaller Shoes	1956	$15
❏ 28391	I'll Never Smile Again/My Devotion	1952	$30
❏ 31027	I Love Paris/Till Tomorrow	1959	$10
❏ 28162	I'm Yours/I Understand	1952	$30
❏ 29989	I Only Know I Love You/Dreamer	1956	$15
❏ 29269	It's a Woman's World/The Cuckoo Bird in the Pickle Tree	1954	$20
❏ 28393	La Rosita/Take Me in Your Arms	1952	$30
❏ 28843	Laughing on the Outisde (Crying on the Inside)/I've Been Waiting a Lifetime	1953	$20
❏ 29625	Love is a Many-Splendored Thing/Shine On Harvest Moon	1955	$15
❏ 29395	Melody of Love/There Is a Tavern in the Town	1954	$20
❏ 29344	Mister Sandman/(I'll Be With You) In Apple Blossom Time	1954	$20
❏ 28073	My Hero/Spring Is a Wonderful Thing	1952	$30
❏ 29712	O Holy Night/Silent Night	1955	$15
❏ 30775	Ol' Fatso/Christmas Tree	1958	$15
❏ 28691	Organ Grinder's Swing/Honey in the Horn	1953	$20
❏ 27937	Perfidia/You Brought Me Love	1952	$30
❏ 31081	Poor Butterfly/You Are Music	1960	$12
❏ 30649	Saturday Swing-Out/Take My Heart	1958	$15
❏ 28323	Should I/There's Only Tonight	1952	$30
❏ 30123	Someone to Love/Written on the Wind	1956	$15
❏ 27860	Tell Me Why/A Garden in the Rain	1951	$30
❏ 29702	The Christmas Song (Merry Christmas to You)/Jingle Bells	1955	$15
❏ 30897	The Five Pennies/Anyone Would Love You	1959	$10
❏ 28927	The Gang That Sang "Heart of My Heart"/Stranger in Paradise	1953	$20
❏ 29435	There Goes My Heart/You'll Always Be the One	1955	$15
❏ 30764	The World Outside/How Can You Forget	1958	$15

Number	Title	Yr	NM
❏ 29123	Three Coins in the Fountain/ Wedding Bells (Are Breaking Up That Old Gang of Mine)	1954	$20
❏ 30348	Three Sheets to the Wind/Yes Sir, That's My Baby	1957	$15
❏ 28392	Tip-Pi-Tin/Heaven Can Wait	1952	$30
❏ 29889	To Love Again/Charlie Was a Boxer	1956	$15
❏ 30695	Two Arms, Two Lips, One Heart/Heartache in Costume	1958	$15
❏ 30989	Waltzing Matilda/The Wonder of It All	1959	$10

FLASH

Number	Title	Yr	NM
❏ 103	Who's to Blame/Two Little Kisses	1950	$40

JUBILEE

Number	Title	Yr	NM
❏ 5416	It's All Over But the Crying/Lonely Hill	1962	$8

RADNOR

Number	Title	Yr	NM
❏ 301	Always Keep Me in Your Heart/Didn't We	1968	$5
❏ 302	I Started a Joke/Summer Won't Be Summer	1969	$5

VICTORIA

Number	Title	Yr	NM
❏ 101	Sin/Arizona Moon	1951	$70
— Red vinyl			
❏ 101	Sin/Arizona Moon	1951	$30
— Black vinyl			
❏ 102	There's a Christmas Tree in Heaven/There's a Small Hotel	1951	$40
❏ ED2309 [PS]	A Merry Christmas with the Four Aces, Part 1	1956	$15
❏ ED2310 [PS]	A Merry Christmas with the Four Aces, Part 2	1956	$15
❏ ED2311 [PS]	A Merry Christmas with the Four Aces, Part 3	1956	$15
❏ ED2675 [PS]	Beyond the Blue Horizon	1959	$15
❏ ED2675	(contents unknown)	1959	$15
❏ ED2311	Santa Claus Is Comin' to Town/Rudolph the Red-Nosed Reindeer//O Holy Night (Cantique de Noel)/The First Nowell/Deck the Hall	1956	$15
❏ ED2310	Silver Bells/Jingle Bells//O Come All Ye Faithful/Hark! The Herald Angels Sing/We Three Kings of Orient Are	1956	$15
❏ ED2309	White Christmas/The Christmas Song//Silent Night/O Little Town of Bethlehem/Joy to the World	1956	$15

FOUR BARS, THE

JOSIE

Number	Title	Yr	NM
❏ 762	Grief by Day, Grief by Night/Hey Baby	1954	$300
❏ 768	If I Give My Heart to You/Stop It! Quit It!	1954	$300
❏ 783	Let Me Live/Why Do You Treat Me This Way	1955	$600

REPUBLIC

Number	Title	Yr	NM
❏ 7101	Memories of You/When Did You Leave Heaven	1954	$600

FOUR BELLS, THE

GEM

Number	Title	Yr	NM
❏ 220	Only a Miracle/My Tree	1954	$800
❏ 207	Please Tell It to Me/Long Way to Go	1953	$800

FOUR BROTHERS AND A COUSIN

JAGUAR

Number	Title	Yr	NM
❏ 3003	Trust in Me/Whistle Stop Blues	1954	$400
❏ 3005	Whispeing Wind/Can It Be	1954	$500

FOUR BUDDIES, THE (1)

SAVOY

Number	Title	Yr	NM
❏ 779	Don't Leave Me Now/Sweet Slumber	1951	$400
❏ 817	Heart and Soul/Sin	1951	$300
❏ 891	I'd Climb the Highest Mountain/I Wanna Know	1953	$300
— B-side by Dolly Cooper			
❏ 769	I Will Wait/Just to See You Smile Again	1951	$400
❏ 769	I Will Wait/Just to See You Smile Again	1951	$500
— As "The Four Buds"			
❏ 888	My Mother's Eyes/Ooh Ow	1953	$300
❏ 789	My Summer's Gone/Why at a Time Like This	1951	$300
❏ 866	What's the Matter with Me/Sweet Tooth for My Baby	1952	$300
❏ 823	Window Eyes/Simply Say Goodbye	1951	$300

FOUR BUDDIES, THE (2)

CLUB 51

Number	Title	Yr	NM
❏ 105	Delores/Look Out	1956	$200
— Black vinyl			
❏ 105	Delores/Look Out	1956	$4000
— Red vinyl			

FOUR BUDDIES, THE (3)

CORAL

Number	Title	Yr	NM
❏ 62217	Hurt/Moonglow & Theme from Picnic	1960	$30
❏ 62325	The Light/Cin Cin (Che Bell)	1962	$30

IMPERIAL

Number	Title	Yr	NM
❏ 66018	I Want to Be the Boy You Love/Just Enough of Your Love	1964	$70

PHILIPS

Number	Title	Yr	NM
❏ 40122	Lonely Summer/Slow Locomotion	1963	$30

FOUR CAL-QUETTES, THE

CAPITOL

Number	Title	Yr	NM
❏ 4574	Billy, My Billy/Star Bright	1961	$40
❏ 4725	I'll Never Come Back (Silly Boy)/Again	1962	$40
❏ 4657	Most of All/I'm Gonna Love Him Anyway	1961	$40
❏ 4534	Sparkle and Shine/In This World	1961	$40
— As "The Four Coquettes"			

LIBERTY

Number	Title	Yr	NM
❏ 55549	I Cried/Movie Magazines	1963	$20

FOUR CASTS, THE

ATLANTIC

Number	Title	Yr	NM
❏ 2228	Stormy Weather/Workin' at the Factory	1964	$15

FOUR CHEERS, THE

END

Number	Title	Yr	NM
❏ 1034	Fatal Charms of Love/Periwinkle Blue	1958	$200

FOUR CHEVELLES, THE

BAND BOX

Number	Title	Yr	NM
❏ 358	I Can't Believe/I Know	1957	$30
❏ 357	This Is Our Wedding Day/Darling Forever	1957	$30

DELFT

Number	Title	Yr	NM
❏ 357	This Is Our Wedding Day/Darling Forever	1957	$600

FOUR CHICADEES, THE

CHECKER

Number	Title	Yr	NM
❏ 849	Ding Dong/Teenage Blues	1956	$70

FOUR CLEFS, THE

RCA VICTOR

Number	Title	Yr	NM
❏ 47-4507	Dig These Blues/Four Clefs Woogie	1952	$60

FOUR COINS, THE

COLUMBIA

Number	Title	Yr	NM
❏ 44006	If You Love Me (Really Love Me)/Learning to Live Without Your Love	1967	$6

EPIC

Number	Title	Yr	NM
❏ 9337	Angel in the Rain/First Signs of Love	1959	$10
❏ 9306	Angel of Love/Who Are You	1959	$10
❏ 9107	A Story Untold/Magnolia	1955	$20
❏ 9348	Buon Natale/Serenade of the Bells	1959	$10
❏ 9164	Cherry Lips/All My Tomorrows	1956	$15
❏ 9192	Destination Love/The Time of the Year	1956	$15
❏ 9276	Dream World/One Life, One Love	1958	$12
❏ 9200	Falling Star/My Love Is a Little Kitten	1957	$15
❏ 9253	Follow Your Heart/A Broken Promise	1957	$15
❏ 9082	I Love You Madly/Maybe	1954	$20
❏ 9183	Manhattan Serenade/Too Late	1956	$15
❏ 9129	Memories of You/Tear Down the Fence	1955	$20
❏ 9091	My Anxious Heart/Oh Mother Dear	1955	$20
❏ 9314	My First Love/One Love, One Heart	1959	$10
❏ 9258	My Love Loves Me/New World	1957	$15
❏ 9229	My One Sin/This Life	1957	$15
❏ 9383	My Only Love/You're Breaking My Heart	1960	$10
❏ 9074	Once More/We'll Be Married...	1954	$20

Number	Title	Yr	NM
❏ 9104	Promises, Promises/ That's the Way	1955	$20
❏ 9213	Shangri-La/First in Line	1957	$15
❏ 9116	The Song That Brought Us Together/Need You	1955	$20
❏ 9148	The Song That God Sings/ The Old Professor	1956	$15
❏ 9295	The World Outside/Roselle	1958	$10
❏ 9171	This I Offer You/One Kiss (Is Worth a Thousand Words)	1956	$15
❏ 9286	Wendy, Wendy/ Be Still My Heart	1958	$10

JOY

❏ 287	Answer Me, My Love/Joanna	1964	$8
❏ 284	Love Me with All Your Heart (Cuando Calienta El Sol)/Boys Cry	1964	$8

JUBILEE

❏ 5419	Come a Little Closer/ Windows of Heaven	1962	$8
❏ 5411	Gee, Officer Krupki/The Miracle of St. Marie	1961	$8
❏ 5429	One Red Rose/I Wish You Were Here	1962	$8

LAURIE

❏ 3331	I'll Never Love Again/ Try Your Luck	1966	$6
❏ 3360	Shout Shout (Knock Yourself Out)/People Get Jealous	1966	$6

MGM

❏ 12977	Love Is Where You Find It/Beat on Your Drum Little Susan	1961	$8
❏ 12951	Pledging My Love/I Want a Little Girl	1960	$8
❏ 13031	Pretty Nina/Moon of Manakoora	1961	$8
❏ 13003	To Love/From Your Very Own Lips	1961	$8

VEE JAY

❏ 551	Take a Bow (Little Darlin')/Nina	1963	$8
❏ 474	They Say/Jimmy San	1962	$8

FOUR DATES, THE

CHANCELLOR

❏ 1027	Feel Good/Teenage Neighbor	1958	$30
❏ 1014	I'm Happy/Eloise	1958	$30
❏ 1019	I say babe/Hey Roly Poly	1958	$30

FOUR DEALS, THE

CAPITOL

❏ F1313	It's Too Late Now/ There Ain't No Bears	1950	$125

FOUR DEUCES, THE

EVEREST

❏ 19311	Polly/Yella Shoes	1959	$40

MUSIC CITY

❏ 796	Down It Went/ Goose Is Gone	1955	$70
❏ 790	W-P-L-J/Here Lies My Love	1955	$200
—Maroon label			
❏ 790	W-P-L-J/Here Lies My Love	1955	$50
—Black label			

FOUR DIRECTIONS, THE

CORAL

❏ 62456	(Doin' the) Arthur/ Tonight We Love	1965	$40

FOUR DOTS, THE

FREEDOM

❏ 44005	Pleading for Your Love/ Don't Wake Up the Kids	1958	$125

FOUR DUKES, THE (1)

DUKE

❏ 116	Crying in the Chapel/I Done Done It	1953	$800

FOUR DUKES, THE (2)

IMPERIAL

❏ 5653	Baby Won't You Please Come Home/John Henry	1960	$40

FOUR EPICS, THE

HERITAGE

❏ 109	I'm On My Way to Love/ When the Music Ends	1962	$125

LAURIE

❏ 3155	Again/I Love You Diane	1963	$30
❏ 3183	How I Wish I Was Single Again/Dance Joanne	1963	$30

FOUR ESQUIRES, THE

CADENCE

Number	Title	Yr	NM
❏ 1277	Adorable/Thunderbolt	1955	$30
❏ 1260	Three Things/The Sphinx Won't Tell	1955	$30

LONDON

❏ 1652	Look Homeward Angel/ Santo Domingo	1956	$30

PARIS

❏ 535	Act Your Age/So Ends the Night	1959	$30
❏ 515	All Around the Clock/ The Big Dance	1958	$30
❏ 512	Always and Forever/I Walk Down the Street	1958	$30
❏ 526	Follow Me/The Land of You and Me	1958	$30
❏ 520	Hideaway/Repeat After Me	1958	$30
—With Rosemary June			
❏ 509	Love Me Forever/I Ain't Been Right Since You Left	1957	$30
❏ 531	Lucky Old Sun/Non E Cosi	1959	$30
❏ 544	Make Them Mine/ Peg O' My Heart	1960	$30
❏ 501	Song of April/Everyone's Sweet on My Sugar	1957	$30
❏ 549	Sweet Sixteen She'll Never Be/The Chopstick Rock	1960	$30
❏ 505	The Chopstick Rock/ Never Look for Love	1957	$30
❏ 539	Wonderful One/Wouldn't It Be Wonderful	1959	$30

PILGRIM

❏ 717	Follow Me/Summer Vacation	1956	$30

TERRACE

❏ 7502	Can't Help Falling in Love/ Merry-Go-Round of Love	1961	$20

FOUR-EVERS, THE

CHATTAHOOCHIE

❏ 630	Colors/Come Up in the World	1963	$20

COLUMBIA

❏ 43886	A Lovely Way to Say Goodnight/The Girl I Wanna Bring Home	1966	$30

CONSTELLATION

❏ 151	Stormy/Out of the Crowd	1965	$40

JAMIE

❏ 1247	Everybody South Street/ One More Time	1963	$20

SMASH

❏ 1887	Be My Girl/If I Were a Magician	1964	$20
—Same A-side, different title			
❏ 1853	Lover Come Back to Me/It's Love	1963	$20
❏ 1887	Please Be Mine/If I Were a Magician	1964	$40
❏ 1921	(Say I Love You) Doo Bee Dum/Everlasting	1964	$20

FOUR FELLOWS, THE

DERBY

❏ 862	I Tried/Bend of the River	1954	$400

GLORY

❏ 236	Angels Say/In the Rain	1955	$70
❏ 242	Darling You/Please Don't Deprive Me of My Love	1956	$100
❏ 238	Fallen Angel/Hold 'Em Joe	1956	$70
❏ 244	I Sit in My Window/ Please Play My Song	1956	$70
❏ 231	I Wish I Didn't Know You/I Know Love	1955	$100
❏ 250	Loving You, Darling/Give Me Back My Broken Heart	1957	$70
❏ 234	Soldier Boy/Take Me Back Baby	1955	$70

FOUR FIFTHS, THE

COLUMBIA

❏ 43913	If You Still Want Me/Have You Ever Loved a Girl	1966	$15

HUDSON

❏ 8101	After Graduation/ Come On Girl	1963	$400
—Blue vinyl			
❏ 8101	After Graduation/ Come On Girl	1963	$200
—Black vinyl			

FOUR FRESHMEN, THE

CAPITOL

Number	Title	Yr	NM
❏ F3359	Angel Eyes/Love Is Just Around the Corner	1956	$10
❏ F2398	Baltimore Oriole/Poinciana	1953	$15
❏ 4341	Candy/Route 66	1960	$8
❏ 5083	Charade/Funny How Time Slips Away	1963	$8
❏ F3292	Charmaine/In This Whole Wide World	1955	$10
❏ F3154	Day by Day/How Can I Tell Her	1955	$12
❏ 5151	Don't Make Me Sorry/ My Baby's Gone	1964	$8
❏ F3410	Graduation Day/ Lonely Night in Paris	1956	$20
❏ F3832	Grenada/How Can I Begin to Tell	1957	$10
❏ F2564	Holiday/It Happened Once Before	1953	$15
❏ F2832	I'll Be Seeing You/ Please Remember	1954	$15
❏ 4824	I'm Gonna Go Fishin'/ Taps Miller	1962	$8
❏ F3070	It Never Occurred to Me/Malaya	1955	$10
❏ F2152	It's a Blue World/ Tuxedo Junction	1952	$15
❏ F2961	Mood Indigo/Love Turns Winter to Spring	1954	$15
❏ F1293	Mr. B's Blues/Then I'll Be Happy	1950	$20
❏ F2745	Seems Like Old Times/ Crazy Bones	1954	$15
❏ 4749	Shangri-La/Teach Me Tonight	1962	$8
❏ F2286	Stormy Weather/The Day Isn't Long Enough	1952	$15
❏ 5007	Summertime/Baby Won't You Please Come Home	1963	$8
❏ 5007 [PS]	Summertime/Baby Won't You Please Come Home	1963	$20
❏ F3652	That's the Way I Feel/ What's It Gonna Be	1957	$12
❏ 5471	Those Magnificent Men in Their Flying Machines/ Old Cape Cod	1965	$10
❏ F2898	We'll Be Together Again/ My Heart Stood Still	1954	$15
❏ 5401	When I Stop Lovin' You/ Nights Are Long	1965	$8
❏ F3930	Whistle Me Some Blues/ Nights Are Longer	1958	$10

DECCA

❏ 32070	Cry/Nowhere to Go	1966	$6

LIBERTY

❏ 56099	By the Time I Get to Phoenix-My Special Angel/It's a Blue World	1969	$6
❏ 56047	Cherish-Windy/Come Fly with Me-Up Up and Away	1968	$6

7-Inch Extended Plays

CAPITOL

❏ EAP 1-844	*Liza/You've Got Me Cryin' Again/This Love of Mine/I Get Along Without You Very Well	1957	$10
❏ EAP 1-763 [PS]	4 Freshmen and 5 Trumpets, Part 1	1957	$12
❏ EAP 2-763 [PS]	4 Freshmen and 5 Trumpets, Part 2	1957	$12
❏ EAP 3-763 [PS]	4 Freshmen and 5 Trumpets, Part 3	1957	$12
❏ EAP 1-763	After You've Gone/ Ev'ry Time We Say Goodbye//Easy Street/ Good Night Sweetheart	1957	$10
❏ EAP 1-683	(contents unknown)	1956	$15
❏ EAP 3-683	(contents unknown)	1956	$15
❏ EAP 2-763	(contents unknown)	1957	$10
❏ EAP 3-763	(contents unknown)	1957	$10
❏ EAP 2-844	(contents unknown)	1957	$10
❏ EAP 3-844	(contents unknown)	1957	$10
❏ EAP 1-743	(contents unknown)	1957	$10
❏ EAP 3-743	(contents unknown)	1957	$10
❏ EAP 1-922	(contents unknown)	1958	$10
❏ EAP 2-922	(contents unknown)	1958	$10
❏ EAP 1-1255	(contents unknown)	1959	$10
❏ EAP 2-1255	(contents unknown)	1959	$10
❏ EAP 3-1255	(contents unknown)	1959	$10
❏ EAP 1-844 [PS]	Four Freshmen and Five Saxes, Part 1	1957	$12
❏ EAP 2-844 [PS]	Four Freshmen and Five Saxes, Part 2	1957	$12
❏ EAP 3-844 [PS]	Four Freshmen and Five Saxes, Part 3	1957	$12
❏ EAP 1-683 [PS]	Four Freshmen and Five Trombones, Part 1	1956	$15
❏ EAP 2-683 [PS]	Four Freshmen and Five Trombones, Part 2	1956	$15
❏ EAP 3-683 [PS]	Four Freshmen and Five Trombones, Part 3	1956	$15
❏ EAP 1-743 [PS]	Freshmen Favorites, Part 1	1957	$12
❏ EAP 2-743 [PS]	Freshmen Favorites, Part 2	1957	$12
❏ EAP 3-743 [PS]	Freshmen Favorites, Part 3	1957	$12
❏ EAP 2-743	Graduation Day/Poinciana// Lonely Night in Paris/ Seems Like Old Times	1957	$10
❏ EAP 2-683	Mam'selle/Speak Low// Love/Love Is Here to Stay	1956	$15
❏ EAP 1-1255 [PS]	The Four Freshmen and Five Guitars, Part 1	1959	$12

Number	Title	Yr	NM
❏ EAP 2-1255 [PS]	The Four Freshmen and Five Guitars, Part 2	1959	$12
❏ EAP 3-1255 [PS]	The Four Freshmen and Five Guitars, Part 3	1959	$12
❏ EAP 3-922	What's New/Chelsea Bridge//Tangerine/Brazil	1958	$10

FOUR GRADUATES, THE
CRYSTAL BALL
| ❏ 116 | May I Have This Dance/Caught in a Lie | 1978 | $4 |

RUST
| ❏ 5084 | Candy Queen/A Girl in Love | 1964 | $180 |
| ❏ 5062 | Picture of An Angel/A Lovely Way to Spend An Evening | 1963 | $125 |

FOUR GUYS, THE
AUDIOGRAPH
| ❏ 478 | Fanny Mae/If You Don't Lose It | 1984 | $5 |
| ❏ 463 | Whiskey and Water/(B-side unknown) | 1983 | $5 |

CINNAMON
| ❏ 791 | Streakin' with My Baby/Girl of Mine | 1974 | $6 |

COLLAGE
| ❏ 102 | Mama Rocked Us to Sleep (With Country Music)/Forever in Blue Jeans | 1979 | $6 |

GARPAX/GRT
| ❏ 139 | I Remember (Edit)/I Remember (Complete) | 1978 | $5 |
| ❏ 143 | Mother Country/The Only Fool Is Me | 1978 | $5 |

J&B
| ❏ 1001 | Made in the U.S.A./Pretty Lady | 1982 | $6 |

MERCURY
| ❏ 70908 | Drive-In Rock/Do Unto Others | 1956 | $30 |
| ❏ 70452 | Tonight's the Night/Not As a Stranger | 1955 | $30 |

MYRTLE
| ❏ 1001 | Stealing the Feeling/(B-side unknown) | 1982 | $6 |

RCA VICTOR
| ❏ PB-10055 | Too Late to Turn Back Now/Gatherin' Dust | 1974 | $5 |

STOP
| ❏ 202 | Half a Man/Labor of Love | 1968 | $10 |

WING
| ❏ 90036 | Bye Bye for Just a While/May This Be Your Life | 1956 | $30 |

FOUR HAVEN KNIGHTS, THE
ANGLETONE
| ❏ 1066 | In My Lonely Room/I'm Just a Dreamer | 1958 | $60 |

ATLAS
| ❏ 1066 | In My Lonely Room/I'm Just a Dreamer | 1957 | $200 |

JOSIE
| ❏ 824 | In My Lonely Room/I'm Just a Dreamer | 1957 | $40 |

FOUR HOLIDAYS, THE
UNITED ARTISTS
| ❏ 163 | Who Can Say/Nobody Loves You Like-a Me | 1959 | $40 |

VERVE
| ❏ 10204 | I Don't Wanna Go to School/Love Ya' Baby | 1960 | $20 |

FOUR HORSEMEN, THE
MGM
❏ 11566	A Dear John Letter/No Stone Unturned	1953	$20
❏ 11300	Indian Love Call/San Antonio Rose	1952	$20
❏ 11345	Memories/By the Waters of the Minnetonka	1952	$20
❏ 12159	The Iron Horse/Go On with the Wedding	1955	$20

UNITED ARTISTS
| ❏ 134 | A Long Long Time/My Heartbeat | 1958 | $200 |

FOUR HUES, THE
CORAL
| ❏ 61617 | Ivory Tower/Sister Jenny | 1956 | $40 |

FOUR IMPERIALS, THE
CHANT
| ❏ 10067 | My Girl/Teen Age Fool | 1958 | $60 |

DOT
| ❏ 15737 | Lazy Bonnie/Let's Make a Scene | 1958 | $30 |

FOX
| ❏ 102 | Give Me One More Chance/Look Up and Live | 1958 | $100 |

LORELEI
| ❏ 4444 | Lazy Bonnie/Let's Make a Scene | 1958 | $125 |

TWIRL
| ❏ 2005 | Santa's Got a Coupe de Ville/Seven Lonely Days | 1960 | $30 |

FOUR JACKS AND A JILL (1)
RCA VICTOR
❏ 47-9655	Hey Mister/Sad Little Pigeon	1968	$6
❏ 47-9473	Master Jack/I Looked Back	1968	$8
❏ 47-9572	Mister Nico/Hamba Liliwam	1968	$6
❏ 47-9728	Stone in My Shoe/Grandfather Dugan	1969	$6

FOUR JACKS AND A JILL (2)
FORTUNE
| ❏ 507 | Love's Not Love Without You/I'm in Love with Someone | 1955 | $40 |

FOUR JACKS, THE
FEDERAL
| ❏ 12087 | The Last of the Good Rockin' Men/I'll Be Home Again | 1952 | $500 |

FOUR JEWELS, THE
CHECKER
| ❏ 1039 | Dapper Dan/Loaded with Goodies | 1963 | $30 |
| ❏ 1069 | Time for Love/That's What They Put Erasers on Pencils For | 1964 | $30 |

START
| ❏ 641 | All That's Good/I Love Me Some You | 1963 | $40 |
| ❏ 638 | Loaded with Goodies/Fire | 1963 | $50 |

TEC
| ❏ 3007 | Baby It's You/She's Wrong for You Baby | 1964 | $30 |

FOUR JOKERS, THE (1)
AMY
| ❏ 832 | She's a Flirt/Uggaboo | 1961 | $30 |

FOUR JOKERS, THE (2)
CRYSTALLETTE
| ❏ 733 | Beyond the Reef/That's the Way | 1959 | $20 |

FOUR JOKERS, THE (3)
DIAMOND
| ❏ 3004 | Transfusion/You Dig | 1956 | $40 |

FOUR JOKERS, THE (4)
MGM
| ❏ 11815 | Tell Me Now/Caring | 1954 | $40 |

FOUR JOKERS, THE (5)
SUE
| ❏ 703 | Written in the Stars/The Run-Around | 1958 | $70 |

FOUR J'S, THE, AND THE FABULOUS IMPERIALS
MGM
| ❏ 12687 | Class Ring/Weird | 1958 | $100 |

FOUR J'S, THE
4-J
| ❏ 506 | Will You Be My Love/Nursery | 1963 | $20 |

CONGRESS
| ❏ 6003 | Dreamin'/Love My Life | 1969 | $12 |

JAMIE
| ❏ 1274 | By Love Possessed/My Love, My Love | 1964 | $30 |
| ❏ 1267 | Here I Am Broken-Hearted/She Said That She Loved Me | 1964 | $30 |

FOUR JUST MEN
TOWER
| ❏ 118 | That's My Baby/Things Will Never Be the Same | 1965 | $15 |

FOUR KINGS, THE
CANADIAN AMERICAN
| ❏ 173 | One Night/Lonely Lovers | 1964 | $30 |
— The Four Seasons sing backup
| ❏ 173 [DJ] | One Night (no B-side) | 1964 | $50 |
— White label promo with blank B-side

FOUR KNIGHTS, THE
CAPITOL
❏ F2403	Anniversary Song/A Few Kind Words	1953	$30
❏ F2517	Baby Doll/Tennessee Train	1953	$30
❏ F3386	Bottle Up the Moonlight/Mistaken	1956	$20
❏ F1875	Cry/Charmaine	1951	$50
❏ F3494	Don't Depend on Me/You're a Honey	1956	$20
❏ F3192	Don't Sit Under the Apple Tree/Believing You	1955	$30
❏ F15896	Easy Street/Ida, Sweet As Apple Cider	1952	$40
❏ F3093	Foolishly Yours/Inside You	1955	$30
❏ F15897	Georgia on My Mind/Sentimental Journey	1952	$40
❏ F3155	Gratefully Yours/Me	1955	$30
❏ F3279	Guilty/You	1955	$30
❏ F2847	How Wrong Can You Be/Period	1954	$30
❏ F15895	I Ain't Got Nobody/When My Baby Smiles at Me	1952	$40
❏ F2938	I Don't Wanna See You Cryin'/Saw Your Eyes	1954	$30
❏ F2654	I Get So Lonely (When I Dream About You)/I Couldn't Stay Away from You	1953	$30
❏ F1787	I Go Crazy/Get Her Off My Hands	1951	$50
❏ F1587	I Love the Sunshine of Your Smile/Sentimental Fool	1951	$60
❏ F3339	I Love You Still/Happy Birthday Baby	1956	$20
❏ F2087	I'm the World's Biggest Fool/It's a Sin to Tell a Lie	1952	$40
❏ F2894	In the Chapel in the Moonlight/Easy Street	1954	$30
❏ F3689	It Doesn't Cost Money/How Can You Not Believe	1957	$20
❏ F1806	It's No Sin/The Glory of Love	1951	$50
❏ F2782	I Was Meant for You/They Tell Me	1954	$30
❏ F2234	Lies/One Way Kisses	1952	$40
❏ F1914	Marshmallow Moon/Five Foot Two, Eyes of Blue	1951	$40
❏ F2654	Oh Baby Mine/I Couldn't Stay Away from You	1953	$50
❏ F2315	Oh Happy Day/A Million Tears	1953	$30
❏ F3250	Perdido/After	1955	$30
❏ F2195	Say No More/That's the Way It's Gonna Be	1952	$40
❏ F1998	The More I Go Out with Somebody Else/The Doll with the Sawdust Heart	1952	$40
❏ F1971	There Are Two Sides to Every Heartache/Walkin' in Sunshine	1952	$40
❏ F1930	The Way I Feel/I Wish I Had a Girl	1952	$40
❏ F3730	Walkin' and Whistlin' Blues/I Love That Song	1957	$20
❏ F1707	Walkin' and Whistlin' Blues/Who Am I	1951	$50
❏ F2127	Win or Lose/Do-Wacka-Do	1952	$40
❏ F3024	Write Me Baby/Honey Bunch	1955	$30

CORAL
❏ 62045	O Falling Star/Foolish Tears	1959	$15
❏ 61936	The Four Minute Mile/When Your Lover Has Gone	1958	$15
❏ 62110	Where Is the Love/Things to Do Today	1959	$15

DECCA
| ❏ 9-48018 | He'll Understand and Say Well Done/Lead Me to That Rock | 1952 | $125 |
— Reissue of original 78 from 1947 (Decca 48014 and 48026 are known to exist only on 78s)

DECCA FAITH SERIES
| ❏ 9-14524 | He'll Understand and Say Well Done/Lead Me to That Rock | 1950 | $120 |
— Purple label

7-Inch Extended Plays
CAPITOL
❏ EAP 1-414	*(It's No) Sin/The Glory of Love/Cry/Charmaine	1953	$50
❏ EAP 1-506 [PS]	I Get So Lonely	1954	$50
❏ EAP 1-506	I Get So Lonely/Tennessee Train//Till Then/Anniversary Song	1954	$50
❏ EAP 1-414 [PS]	The Four Knights Sing	1953	$50

Number	Title	Yr	NM

FOUR LADS, THE

COLUMBIA

Number	Title	Yr	NM
❏ 39902	Blackberry Boogie/ Girl on the Shore	1952	$20
❏ 40005	Down By the Riverside/ Take Me Back	1953	$20
❏ 41194	Enchanted Island/Guess What the Neighbors'll Say	1958	$12
❏ 41194 [PS]	Enchanted Island/Guess What the Neighbors'll Say	1958	$20
❏ 40236	Gilly Gilly Ossenfeffer Katzenelle Bogen by the Sea/I Hear It Everywhere	1954	$20
❏ 41443	Got a Locket in My Pocket/Real Thing	1959	$10
❏ 41497	Happy Anniversary/Who Do You Think You Are	1959	$12
❏ 41497 [PS]	Happy Anniversary/Who Do You Think You Are	1959	$20
❏ 40140	Harmony Brown/Gotta Go to the Fais Do Do	1953	$20
❏ 39958	He Who Has Love/I Wonder, I Wonder, I Wonder	1953	$20
❏ 40914	I Just Don't Know/Golly	1957	$15
❏ 40082	Istanbul (Not Constantinople)/I Should Have Told You Long Ago	1953	$20
❏ 40204	Long John/The Place Where I Worship	1954	$20
❏ 40788	Mary's Little Boy Child/The Stingiest Man in Town	1956	$15
❏ 40539	Moments to Remember/ Dream On, My Love, Dream On	1955	$15
❏ 41682	Our Lady of Fatima (Vocal)/Our Lady of Fatima (Recitation)	1960	$10
❏ 40436	Pledging My Love/I've Been Thinking	1955	$15
❏ 41058	Put a Light in the Window/The Things We Did Last Summer	1957	$10
❏ 40306	Skokiaan (South African Song)/Why Should I Love You So	1954	$20
❏ 39865	Somebody Loves Me/ Thanks to You	1952	$20
❏ 40674	Standing on the Corner/ My Little Angel	1956	$15
❏ 40736	The Bus Stop Song (A Paper of Pins)/A House with Love In It	1956	$15
❏ 41409	The Chosen Few/Together Wherever We Go	1959	$12
❏ 40974	The Eyes of God/ His Invisible Hand	1957	$15
❏ 41365	The Fountain of Youth/Meet Me Tonight in Dreamland	1959	$10
❏ 41310	The Girl on Page 44/Sunday	1958	$10
❏ 41266	The Mocking Bird/I May Hate Myself in the Morning	1958	$10
❏ 41136	There's Only One of You/Blue Tattoo	1958	$10
❏ 40490	Too Much! Baby, Baby/ The Average Giraffe	1955	$15
❏ 40402	Two Ladies in De Shade of De Banana Tree/ Dance Calinda	1954	$20
❏ 41733	Two Other People/The Sheik of Chicago (Mustafa)	1960	$10
❏ 40220	What Can I Lose by Letting You Know/ Oh That'll Be Joyful	1954	$20
❏ 40811	Who Needs You/It's So Easy to Forget	1956	$15
❏ 40811 [PS]	Who Needs You/It's So Easy to Forget	1956	$30

DOT

Number	Title	Yr	NM
❏ 16412	Beyond My Heart/ Not That I Care	1962	$8
❏ 16328	Don't Fly Away, Flamingo/ Winter Snow	1962	$8
❏ 16390	That's What I Like/Sweet Mama Tree-Top Tall	1962	$8
❏ 16373	The Exodus Song/ Never on Sunday	1962	$8

EPIC

Number	Title	Yr	NM
❏ 9150	The Mocking Bird/I May Hate Myself in the Morning	1956	$15

FONA

Number	Title	Yr	NM
❏ 1001	Moments to Remember/ Skokiaan	1977	$4

KAPP

Number	Title	Yr	NM
❏ 404	555 Times/I Should Know Better	1961	$8
❏ 412	Giuggiola/Oceans of Love	1961	$8

OKEH

Number	Title	Yr	NM
❏ 6885	The Mocking Bird/I May Hate Myself in the Morning	1952	$30

REPRISE

Number	Title	Yr	NM
❏ 20163	My Home Town/ Cornflower Blue	1963	$8

UNITED ARTISTS

Number	Title	Yr	NM
❏ 962	Give Her My Love/ All the Winds	1965	$6
❏ 653	It's a Mad, Mad, Mad, Mad World/Stolen Hours	1963	$6
❏ 702	Love Theme from "Tom Jones"/Theme from "Lilies of the Field	1964	$6

Number	Title	Yr	NM
❏ 760	Memories of You/Always Thinking of the Roses	1964	$6
❏ 50585	Moments to Remember/ Free Again	1969	$5
❏ 50517	My Heart's Symphony/ Pardon Me Kiss	1969	$5
❏ 852	Thanks, Mr. Florist/ Barabanchik	1965	$6
❏ 50339	Where Do I Go/A Woman	1968	$5
❏ 893	With My Eyes Wide Open/I'm Not a Run-Around	1965	$6
❏ B-2557	*Standing on the Corner/ Take Me Back/Skokiaan/ Who Needs You	1958	$20
❏ B-9122	(contents unknown)	1956	$15
❏ B-9123	(contents unknown)	1956	$15
❏ B-9121 [PS]	On the Sunny Side, Vol. 1	1956	$15
❏ B-9122 [PS]	On the Sunny Side, Vol. 2	1956	$15
❏ B-9123 [PS]	On the Sunny Side, Vol. 3	1956	$15
❏ B-9121	On the Sunny Side of the Street/The Things We Did Last Summer// Taking a Chance on Love/Bidin' My Time	1956	$15
❏ B-2557 [PS]	The Four Lads (Hall of Fame Series)	1958	$20

FOUR LARKS, THE

TOWER

Number	Title	Yr	NM
❏ 450	Can I Have Another Helping, Please/I've Got Plenty	1968	$10
❏ 402	I Still Love You (From the Bottom of My Heart)/ Groovin' at the Go-Go	1968	$50

FOUR LOVERS, THE

EPIC

Number	Title	Yr	NM
❏ 9255	My Life for Your Love/ Pucker Up	1957	$2000

RCA VICTOR

Number	Title	Yr	NM
❏ 47-6646	Be Lovey Dovey/Jambalaya	1956	$40
❏ 47-6768	Happy Am I/Never Never	1956	$40
❏ 47-6519	Honey Love/Please Don't Leave Me	1956	$50
❏ 47-6812	Shake a Hand/The Stranger	1957	$50

7-Inch Extended Plays

Number	Title	Yr	NM
❏ EPA-869	Diddley Diddley Babe/ Shake a Hand/The Stranger/Night Train	1956	$175
❏ EPA-871	I Want a Girl Just Like the Girl That Married Dear Old Dad/(I Love You) For Sentimental Reasons//This Is My Story/Memories of You	1956	$175
❏ EPA-869 [PS]	The Four Lovers	1956	$175

FOUR NATURALS, THE

RED TOP

Number	Title	Yr	NM
❏ 113	How Strange/Blue Moon	1958	$60

— As "The Naturals"

Number	Title	Yr	NM
❏ 119	I Hear a Rhapsody/ When I'm In Your Arms	1959	$60
❏ 125	The Thought of You Darling/Long Long Ago	1959	$100

FOUR OF A KIND

BOMARC

Number	Title	Yr	NM
❏ 302	It's Better That Way/I Care for You	1959	$30

LAURIE

Number	Title	Yr	NM
❏ 3309	Chippies' Playground/ Prance Around	1965	$10

MELBA

Number	Title	Yr	NM
❏ 117	Dreamy Eyes/Fools Fall in Love	1957	$30
❏ 110	I'm Gonna Rock My Heart/ Our Song Dedicated to You	1957	$30

FOUR PEARLS, THE

DOLTON

Number	Title	Yr	NM
❏ 26	Look at Me/It's Almost Tomorrow	1960	$200

FOUR PENNIES, THE (U)

BRUNSWICK

Number	Title	Yr	NM
❏ 55324	Shake a Hand/'Tis the Season	1967	$30

FOUR PREPS, THE

CAPITOL

Number	Title	Yr	NM
❏ F3845	26 Miles (Santa Catalina)/It's You	1957	$30
❏ 5236	A Girl Without a Top/Two Wrongs Don't Make a Right	1964	$8
❏ 5143	A Letter to the Beatles/ College Cannonball	1964	$30
❏ 4792	Alice/Goodnight Sweetheart	1962	$10
❏ 5609	Annie in Her Granny/ Something to Remember You By	1966	$8
❏ 4478	Balboa/I've Already Started In	1960	$15
❏ F3775	Band of Angels/ How About That	1957	$30

Number	Title	Yr	NM
❏ F3960	Big Man/Stop Baby	1958	$30
❏ F4218	Big Surprise/Try My Arms	1959	$30
❏ 4508	Calcutta/Gone Are the Days	1961	$15
❏ 4974	Charmaine/Hi-Ho Anybody Home	1963	$10
❏ F4078	Cinderella/Gidget	1958	$30
❏ 4312	Down by the Station/ Listen Honey	1959	$15
❏ 5921	Draft Dodger Rag/ The Hitchhiker	1967	$8
❏ 4568	Dream, Boy, Dream/ Grounded	1961	$40
❏ F3576	Dreamy Eyes/Fools Will Be Fools	1956	$30
❏ 5351	Everlasting/I'll Set My Love to Music	1965	$8
❏ F3699	Falling Star/Where Wuzz You	1957	$30
❏ 4362	Got a Girl/Wait Till You Hear It from Me	1960	$15
❏ 5274	How to Succeed in Love/ My Love, My Love	1964	$8
❏ F4256	I Ain't Never/Memories, Memories	1959	$30
❏ 5178	I've Known You All My Life/ What Kind of Bird Is That	1964	$8
❏ F4023	Lazy Summer Night/ Summertime Lies	1958	$30
❏ 5687	Let's Call It a Day, Girl/ The Girl in the Shade of a Striped Umbrella	1966	$8
❏ 5819	Love of the Common People/What I Don't Know Won't Hurt Me	1967	$8
❏ F3621	Moonstruck in Madrid/I Cried a Million Tears	1957	$30
❏ 4599	More Money for You and Me/Swing Down Chariot	1961	$20

— With full-length version of A-side

Number	Title	Yr	NM
❏ 4599 [PS]	More Money for You and Me/Swing Down Chariot	1961	$30
❏ 4599	More Money for You and Me/Swing Down Chariot	1961	$15

— With edited version of A-side

Number	Title	Yr	NM
❏ 5020	Oh Where, Oh Where/ Demons and Witches	1963	$10
❏ 4659	Once Around the Block/The Seine	1961	$15
❏ F3761	Promise Me Baby/Again 'N Again 'N Again	1957	$30
❏ 4400	Sentimental Kid/Madelina	1960	$15
❏ F4126	She Was Five and He Was Ten/Riddle of Love	1959	$30
❏ 4641	Smoke Gets In Your Eyes/ Swing Down Chariot	1961	$15
❏ 4716	The Big Draft/Suzy Cockroach	1962	$12
❏ 4716 [PS]	The Big Draft/Suzy Cockroach	1962	$12
❏ 5074	The Greatest Surfer Couple/ I'm Falling in Love with a Girl	1963	$10
❏ 4435	The Sand and the Sea/Kaw-Liga	1960	$15

7-Inch Extended Plays

Number	Title	Yr	NM
❏ EAP 1-1015	26 Miles/It's You// Moonstruck in Madrid/ How About That	1958	$30
❏ EAP 1-1064 [PS]	Big Man	1958	$30
❏ EAP 1-1064	Big Man/Too Young for Love//Stop, Baby/ Humble Pie	1958	$30
❏ EAP 1-1090	(contents unknown)	1959	$30
❏ EAP 1-1139	(contents unknown)	1959	$30
❏ EAP 1-1139 [PS]	Lazy Summer Night	1959	$30
❏ EAP 1-1090 [PS]	Things We Did Last Summer	1959	$30
❏ EAP 1-1015 [PS]	Twenty-Six Miles	1958	$30

FOUR SEASONS, THE

COLUMBIA

Number	Title	Yr	NM
❏ 0(# unknown)	Big Man's World	1964	$40

— One-sided cardboard soundsheet, a promo for the Columbia Record Club. Number has been reported as both 6675 and 6724.

CREWE

Number	Title	Yr	NM
❏ 333	And That Reminds Me (My Heart Reminds Me)/ The Singles Game	1969	$8
❏ 333 [PS]	And That Reminds Me (My Heart Reminds Me)/ The Singles Game	1969	$10

— No shadow behind Frankie Valli's and Joe Long's heads

Number	Title	Yr	NM
❏ 333 [PS]	And That Reminds Me (My Heart Reminds Me)/ The Singles Game	1969	$15

— With shadow behind Frankie Valli's and Joe Long's heads

FBI

Number	Title	Yr	NM
❏ 7701	East Meets West/Rhapsody	1986	$30

— With the Beach Boys

GONE

Number	Title	Yr	NM
❏ 5122 [DJ]	Bermuda/Spanish Lace	1961	$70
❏ 5122	Bermuda/Spanish Lace	1961	$100

MCA/CURB

Number	Title	Yr	NM
❏ 53440	Big Girls Don't Cry (Enhanced Original Mix)/Big Girls Don't Cry (Dirty Dancing Rap)	1988	$4

Number	Title	Yr	NM
❏ 52871	Book of Love/What About Tomorrow	1986	$4
❏ 52724	Moonlight Memories/What About Tomorrow	1985	$4
❏ 52618	Streetfighter/Deep Inside Your Love	1985	$4

MOTOWN

❏ 1288	Hickory/Charisma	1973	$12
❏ 1255	How Come/Life and Breath	1973	$10

MOWEST

❏ 5026	Walk On, Don't Look Back/Sun Country	1972	$10

OLDIES 45

❏ 47	Big Girls Don't Cry/Connie-O	1964	$8
❏ 116	Candy Girl/Marlena	1964	$8
❏ 18	Sherry/I've Cried Before	1964	$8
❏ 319	Stay/Goodnight My Love	1965	$8
❏ 60	Walk Like a Man/Lucky Ladybug	1964	$8

PHILIPS

❏ 40433	Beggin'/Dody	1967	$12
— Black label			
❏ 40433 [PS]	Beggin'/Dody	1967	$30
❏ 40433	Beggin'/Dody	1967	$8
— Light blue label			
❏ 40238	Big Man in Town/Little Angel	1964	$12
❏ 40238 [PS]	Big Man in Town/Little Angel	1964	$30
❏ 40260	Bye, Bye Baby (Baby Goodbye)/Searching Wind	1965	$10
❏ 40260 [PS]	Bye, Bye Baby (Baby Goodbye)/Searching Wind	1965	$30
❏ 40460	C'mon Marianne/Let's Ride Again	1967	$10
— Black label			
❏ 40460	C'mon Marianne/Let's Ride Again	1967	$15
— Blue label; contains a noticeably different, slowed-down mix of A-side			
❏ 40460 [PS]	C'mon Marianne/Let's Ride Again	1967	$30
❏ 40166	Dawn (Go Away)/No Surfin' Today	1964	$20
— Black label			
❏ 40166	Dawn (Go Away)/No Surfin' Today	1967	$8
— Light blue label with "S" stamp			
❏ 40500	Donneybrook/Around and Around	1968	$30
— Only released in Canada			
❏ 40324	Don't Think Twice/Sassy	1965	$12
❏ 40324 [PS]	Don't Think Twice/Sassy	1965	$30
— Philips 40324 by "The Wonder Who?"			
❏ 40577	Electric Stories/Pity	1968	$6
❏ 40305	Girl Come Running/Cry Myself to Sleep	1965	$10
❏ 40305 [PS]	Girl Come Running/Cry Myself to Sleep	1965	$30
❏ 40393	I've Got You Under My Skin/Huggin' My Pillow	1966	$10
❏ 40393 [PS]	I've Got You Under My Skin/Huggin' My Pillow	1966	$30
❏ 40688	Lay Me Down (Wake Me Up)/Heartaches and Rainbows	1970	$30
❏ 40688 [DJ]	Lay Me Down (Wake Me Up) (mono/stereo)	1970	$20
❏ 40317	Let's Hang On!/On Broadway Tonight	1965	$12
— Black label			
❏ 40317	Let's Hang On!/On Broadway Tonight	1967	$8
— Light blue label with "S" stamp			
❏ 40471	Lonesome Road/Around and Around	1967	$10
❏ 40471 [PS]	Lonesome Road/Around and Around	1967	$30
— Philips 40471 by "The Wonder Who?"; B-side listed as The Four Seasons			
❏ 40380	On the Good Ship Lollipop/You're Nobody Until Somebody Loves You	1966	$10
❏ 40380 [PS]	On the Good Ship Lollipop/You're Nobody Until Somebody Loves You	1966	$30
— Philips 40380 by "The Wonder Who?			
❏ 40370	Opus 17 (Don't You Worry 'Bout Me)/Beggar's Paradise	1966	$10
❏ 40370 [PS]	Opus 17 (Don't You Worry 'Bout Me)/Beggar's Paradise	1966	$30
❏ 40662	Patch of Blue/She Gives Me Light	1970	$8
— As "Frankie Valli & THE 4 SEASONS			
❏ 40662 [PS]	Patch of Blue/She Gives Me Light	1970	$10
❏ 40542	Saturday's Father/Good-Bye Girl	1968	$6
❏ 40542 [PS]	Saturday's Father/Good-Bye Girl	1968	$10
— Standard sleeve			
❏ 40542 [PS]	Saturday's Father/Good-Bye Girl	1968	$20
— Fold-open sleeve			

Number	Title	Yr	NM
❏ 40225	Save It for Me/Funny Face	1964	$10
❏ 40597	Something's On Her Mind/Idaho	1969	$6
❏ 40597 [PS]	Something's On Her Mind/Idaho	1969	$12
❏ 40412	Tell It to the Rain/Show Girl	1966	$10
❏ 40412 [PS]	Tell It to the Rain/Show Girl	1966	$30
❏ 40278	Toy Soldier/Betrayed	1965	$10
❏ 40278 [PS]	Toy Soldier/Betrayed	1965	$30
❏ 40490	Watch the Flowers Grow/Raven	1967	$10
❏ 40490 [PS]	Watch the Flowers Grow/Raven	1967	$30
❏ 40694	Where Are My Dreams?/Any Day Now-Oh Happy Day	1971	$30
❏ 40694 [DJ]	Where Are My Dreams? (mono/stereo)	1971	$20
❏ 40523	Will You Love Me Tomorrow/Around and Around	1968	$15
— Black label			
❏ 40523	Will You Love Me Tomorrow/Around and Around	1968	$10
— Blue label			
❏ 40350	Working My Way Back to You/Too Many Memories	1966	$10

SEASONS 4-EVER

❏ 777	Trance/I Am All Alone	1971	$20
— As "Billy Dixon and the Topics"; blue vinyl			
❏ 777	Trance/I Am All Alone	1971	$8
— As "Billy Dixon and the Topics"; green vinyl			

TOPIX

❏ 6002	I Am All Alone/Trance	1961	$200
— As "Billy Dixon and the Topics			
❏ 6008	Lost Lullaby/Trance	1961	$200
— As "Billy Dixon and the Topics			
❏ 6000	Too Young to Start/Red Lips	1960	$200
— As "The Village Voices"; yellow and black label			
❏ 6000	Too Young to Start/Red Lips	1960	$125
— As "The Village Voices"; yellow, black and white label			

VEE JAY

❏ 512	Ain't That a Shame!/Soon (I'll Be Home Again)	1963	$30
❏ 597	Alone/Long, Lonely Nights	1964	$20
— Black rainbow label			
❏ 597	Alone/Long, Lonely Nights	1964	$30
— Plain black label			
❏ 597	Alone/Long, Lonely Nights	1964	$40
— Yellow label			
❏ 597 [PS]	Alone/Long, Lonely Nights	1964	$60
❏ 465	Big Girls Don't Cry/Connie-O	1962	$30
— First pressings have black rainbow labels with oval logo			
❏ 465	Big Girls Don't Cry/Connie-O	1962	$30
— A later pressing has an all-black label			
❏ 539	Candy Girl/Marlena	1963	$20
❏ 618	Happy, Happy Birthday Baby/You're the Apple of My Eye	1964	$30
❏ 626	I Saw Mommy Kissing Santa Claus/Christmas Tears	1964	$30
❏ 626 [PS]	I Saw Mommy Kissing Santa Claus/Christmas Tears	1964	$60
❏ 713	Little Boy (In Grown Up Clothes)/Silver Wings	1965	$30
— Maroon label			
❏ 713	Little Boy (In Grown Up Clothes)/Silver Wings	1965	$40
— Black label			
❏ 719	My Mother's Eyes/Stay	1966	$20
❏ 901 [DJ]	Peanuts	1963	$125
— One-sided promo from EP 901			
❏ 717	Peanuts/My Sugar	1966	$40
— As "The Wonder Who			
❏ 576 [DJ]	Peanuts/Stay	1963	$70
❏ 576	Peanuts/Stay	1963	$125
❏ 478	Santa Claus Is Coming to Town/Christmas Tears	1962	$30
❏ 456	Sherry/I've Cried Before	1962	$30
— First pressings have black rainbow labels with oval logo			
❏ 456	Sherry/I've Cried Before	1962	$30
— A later pressing has an all-black label			
❏ 664	Since I Don't Have You/Tonite, Tonite	1965	$40
❏ 608	Sincerely/One Song	1964	$30
❏ 582	Stay/Goodnight My Love	1964	$20
❏ 485	Walk Like a Man/Lucky Ladybug	1963	$20

WABC RADIO

❏ 77	Cousin Brucie Go Go	1964	$200
— One-sided yellow vinyl; theme song for Cousin Brucie's radio show			

WARNER BROS.

❏ 8168	December, 1963 (Oh, What a Night)/Slip Away	1975	$5
❏ 8407	Down the Hall/I Believe in You	1977	$8

Number	Title	Yr	NM
❏ 49585	Heaven Must Have Sent You (Here in the Night)/Silver Star	1981	$8
❏ 8203	Silver Star/Mystic Mr. Sam	1976	$5
❏ 49597	Spend the Night in Love/Slip Away	1980	$8
❏ 8122	Who Loves You/Who Loves You (Disco Version)	1975	$5

7-Inch Extended Plays

PHILIPS

❏ PHS810-C	Dawn/Rag Doll/Bye Bye Baby//Let's Hang On!/Big Man in Town/Save It for Me	1966	$20
— Jukebox issue; small hole, plays at 33 1/3 rpm			
❏ PL-2705 [PS]	Edizione D'Oro	1968	$20
❏ PL-2704 [PS]	Genuine Imitation Life Gazette	1968	$20
❏ PL-2705	Sherry/Big Girls Don't Cry/Will You Still Love Me Tomorrow///I've Got You Under My Skin/Silence Is Golden/Walk Like a Man	1968	$20
— Stereo jukebox issue; small hole, plays at 33 1/3 rpm			
❏ PHS810-C [PS]	The 4 Seasons' Gold Vault of Hits	1966	$20
❏ PL-2704	Wall Street Village Day/Mrs. Stately's Garden//Idaho/Something's On Her Mind/Wonder What You'll Be	1968	$20
— Stereo jukebox issue; small hole, plays at 33 1/3 rpm			

VEE JAY

❏ EP 1-901 [PS]	The Four Seasons Sing	1962	$30
❏ EP 1-902 [PS]	The Four Seasons Sing	1963	$30
❏ EP 1-902	Why Do Fools Fall in Love/Silhouettes//Since I Don't Have You/Alone	1963	$30

FOUR SEASONS, THE (2)

ALANNA

❏ 555	Don't Sweat It Baby/That's the Way the Ball Bounces	1959	$50
❏ 555	I'm Still in Love with You, Baby/That's the Way the Ball Bounces	1959	$70
❏ 558	Love Knows No Season/Hot Water Bottle	1959	$40

ROBBEE

❏ 106	Mirage/Nancy's Trampoline	1960	$200

FOUR SHARPS, THE

CAMEO

❏ 426	The Fife Piper/Happiness Is	1966	$30

FOUR SONICS, THE

SPORT

❏ 111	Easier Said Than Done/The Greatest Love	1968	$30

FOUR SPARKS, THE

ABC-PARAMOUNT

❏ 9906	My Sweet Juanita/Out of This World	1958	$30

FOUR SPEEDS, THE

CHALLENGE

❏ 9202	Four on the Floor/Cheater Slicks	1963	$50

FEDERAL

❏ 6070	I Need You Baby/The Girls Back Home	1954	$100

FOUR SPORTSMEN, THE

SUNNYBROOK

❏ 6	If Your Heart Can Take It!/Records, Records, Records	1961	$50
❏ 2	Lucille/Mother-in-Law	1961	$40
❏ 4	Pitter-Patter/Git Up Paint	1961	$40
❏ 5	Sixty Minute Man/Jellyroll Brown	1961	$40
❏ 1	Surrender/Franklin Delano Brown	1960	$70

FOUR STUDENTS, THE

GROOVE

❏ 0110	So Near and Yet So Far/Hot Rotten Soda Pop	1955	$60

FOUR TEENS, THE

CHALLENGE

❏ 59021	Go Little Go Cat/Spark Plug	1958	$70

FOUR TEMPTATIONS, THE

ABC-PARAMOUNT

❏ 9920	Cathy/Rock and Roll Baby	1958	$40

Number	Title	Yr	NM

FOUR TOPS, THE

ABC

Number	Title	Yr	NM
❏ 12214	Catfish/Look at My Baby	1976	$4
❏ 12236	Feel Free/I Know You Like It	1976	$4
❏ 12155	I'm Glad You Walked Into My Life/Mama, You're All Right with Me	1975	$4
❏ 12427	Inside a Brokenhearted Man/H.E.L.P.	1978	$4
❏ 12223	Look at My Baby/Catfish	1976	$4
❏ 12096	Seven Lonely Nights/I Can't Hold Out Much Longer	1975	$4
❏ 12267	Strung Out for Your Love/You Can't Hold Back on Love	1977	$4
❏ 12123	We All Gotta Stick Together/ (It Would Almost) Drive Me Out of My Mind	1975	$4

ABC DUNHILL

Number	Title	Yr	NM
❏ 4339	Ain't No Woman (Like the One I've Got)/The Good Lord Knows	1973	$5
❏ 4354	Are You Man Enough/ Peace of Mind	1973	$5
❏ 4334	Guardian De Tu Castle/ Jubilee with Soul	1972	$5
❏ 4377	I Just Can't Get You Out of My Mind/Am I My Brother's Keeper?	1973	$5
❏ 15005	Midnight Flower/All My Love	1974	$5
❏ 4386	One Chain Don't Make No Prison/Light of Your Love	1974	$5
❏ 4366	Sweet Understanding Love/Main Street People	1973	$5

ARISTA

Number	Title	Yr	NM
❏ 9801	Change of Heart/ Loco in Acapulco	1989	$3
❏ 9766	If Ever a Love There Was/Indestructible	1988	$3

—A-side with Aretha Franklin

Number	Title	Yr	NM
❏ 9766 [PS]	If Ever a Love There Was/Indestructible	1988	$3
❏ 9706	Indestructible/Are You With Me	1988	$3
❏ 9706 [PS]	Indestructible/Are You With Me	1988	$3

CASABLANCA

Number	Title	Yr	NM
❏ 2344	Let Me Set You Free/ From a Distance	1981	$4
❏ 2353	Sad Hearts/I Believe in You and Me	1982	$4
❏ 2345	Tonight I'm Gonna Love You All Over/I'll Never Leave Again	1981	$4
❏ 2338	When She Was My Girl/ Something to Remember	1981	$4

CHESS

Number	Title	Yr	NM
❏ 1623	Could It Be You?/ Kiss Me, Baby	1956	$200

COLUMBIA

Number	Title	Yr	NM
❏ 41755	Ain't That Love/ Lonely Summer	1960	$70
❏ 43356	Ain't That Love/ Lonely Summer	1965	$30

GRADY

Number	Title	Yr	NM
❏ 012	If Only I Had Known/ (B-side unknown)	1956	$600

—As "The Four Aims"

MOTOWN

Number	Title	Yr	NM
❏ 1110	7-Rooms of Gloom/I'll Turn to Stone	1967	$15
❏ 1196	A Simple Game/L.A. My Town	1972	$6
❏ 1073	Ask the Lonely/ Where Did You Go	1965	$20
❏ 1073 [PS]	Ask the Lonely/ Where Did You Go	1965	$100
❏ 1062	Baby I Need Your Loving/Call On Me	1964	$20
❏ 1104	Bernadette/I Got a Feeling	1967	$15
❏ 1159	Don't Let Him Take Your Love from Me/The Key	1969	$8
❏ 1811	Don't Tell Me That It's Over/I'm Ready for Love	1985	$3
❏ 1854	Hot Nights/Again	1986	$3
❏ 1076	I Can't Help Myself/ Sad Souvenirs	1965	$20
❏ 1198	I Can't Quit Your Love/ Happy (Is a Bumpy Road)	1972	$6
❏ 1124	If I Were a Carpenter/ Wonderful Baby	1968	$15
❏ 1706	I Just Can't Walk Away/Hang	1983	$3
❏ 1132	I'm in a Different World/ Remember When	1968	$8
❏ 1185	In These Changing Times/ Right Before My Eyes	1971	$6
❏ 1164	It's All in the Game/ Love (Is the Answer)	1970	$8
❏ 1164 [PS]	It's All in the Game/ Love (Is the Answer)	1970	$30
❏ 1081	It's the Same Old Song/ Your Love Is Amazing	1965	$20
❏ 1210	(It's the Way) Nature Planned It/I'll Never Change	1972	$6
❏ 1096	Loving You Is Sweeter Than Ever/I Like Everything About You	1966	$20
❏ 1189	MacArthur Park (Part 2)/ MacArthur Park (Part 1)	1971	$6
❏ 1718	Make Yourself Right at Home/Sing a Song of Yesterday	1984	$3
❏ 1790	Sexy Ways/Body and Soul	1985	$3
❏ 1090	Shake Me, Wake Me (When It's Over)/Just As Long As You Need Me	1966	$20
❏ 1084	Something About You/ Darling, I Hum Our Song	1965	$20
❏ 1102	Standing in the Shadows of Love/Since You've Been Gone	1966	$20
❏ 1170	Still Water (Love)/ Still Water (Peace)	1970	$6
❏ 1119	Walk Away Renee/Your Love Is Wonderful	1968	$15
❏ 1147	What Is a Man/Don't Bring Back Memories	1969	$8
❏ 1069	Without the One You Love (Life's Not Worth While)/Love Has Gone	1964	$15

RELIANT

Number	Title	Yr	NM
❏ 1691	I'm Here Again/ (Instrumental)	1983	$4

RIVERSIDE

Number	Title	Yr	NM
❏ 4534	Pennies from Heaven/ Where Are You?	1962	$80

RSO

Number	Title	Yr	NM
❏ 1069	Back to School Again/ Rock-a-Hula Luau	1982	$3
❏ 1069 [PS]	Back to School Again/ Rock-a-Hula Luau	1982	$3

—B-side: by The Cast (from the movie Grease 2)

TOPPS/MOTOWN

Number	Title	Yr	NM
❏ 9	Baby I Need Your Loving	1967	$80

— These are cardboard discs

Number	Title	Yr	NM
❏ 5	I Can't Help Myself	1967	$80

FOUR TUNES, THE

JUBILEE

Number	Title	Yr	NM
❏ 5212	Brooklyn Bridge/Three Little Chickens	1955	$30
❏ 5276	Cool Water/A Little on the Lonely Side	1957	$30
❏ 5165	Don't Cry Darling/L'Amour Toujours, L'Amour	1954	$40
❏ 5245	Far Away Places/Dancing with Tears in My Eyes	1956	$30
❏ 5239	I Gotta Go/Hold Me Closer	1956	$30
❏ 5183	I Hope/I Close My Eyes	1955	$30
❏ 5174	I Sold My Heart to the Junkman/Good News	1954	$40
❏ 5174	I Sold My Heart to the Junkman/Let Me Go Lover	1954	$40
❏ 5132	I Understand Just How You Feel/Sugar Lump	1953	$40
❏ 5152	Lonesome/The Greatest Feeling in the World	1954	$40
❏ 5128	Marie/I Gambled with Love	1953	$50
❏ 5135	My Wild Irish Rose/ Do-Do-Do It Again	1954	$40
❏ 5255	The Ballad of James Dean/ Japanses Farewell	1956	$30
❏ 5200	Tired of Waitin'/Time Out for Texas	1955	$30

KAY-RON

Number	Title	Yr	NM
❏ 1005	I Understand/Just in Case You Change Your Mind	1953	$50
❏ 1000	I Want to Be Loved/ Savannah Sings the Blues	1953	$50

RCA VICTOR

Number	Title	Yr	NM
❏ 47-4198	Cool Water/Carry Me Back to the Lone Prairie	1951	$50
❏ 47-5532	Don't Get Around Much Anymore/Water Boy	1953	$40
❏ 47-4489	Greatest Song I Ever Heard/Come What May	1952	$30
❏ 47-3967	How Can You Say That I Don't Care/Cool Water	1950	$50
❏ 47-4968	I Don't Want to Set the World On Fire/Let's Give Love Another Chance	1952	$50
❏ 50-0042	I'm Just a Fool in Love/ The Lonesome Road	1949	$200

— Gray label, orange vinyl

Number	Title	Yr	NM
❏ 47-4663	I Wonder/Can I Say Any More?	1952	$30
❏ 50-0131	May That Day Never Come/Carry Me Back to the Lone Prairie	1951	$200

— Gray label, orange vinyl

Number	Title	Yr	NM
❏ 47-4305	My Buddy/Early in the Morning	1951	$40
❏ 50-0016	My Last Affair/I'm the Guy	1949	$200

— Gray label, orange vinyl

Number	Title	Yr	NM
❏ 50-0085	Old Fashioned Love/ Kentucky Babe	1950	$200

— Gray label, orange vinyl

Number	Title	Yr	NM
❏ 47-3881	Say When/Do I Worry?	1950	$60
❏ 47-4427	Tell Me Why/I'll See You in My Dreams	1951	$50
❏ 47-4241	The Prisoner's Song/I Married An Angel	1951	$40
❏ 50-0072	There Goes My Heart/Am I Blue	1950	$200

— Gray label, orange vinyl

Number	Title	Yr	NM
❏ 47-4828	They Don't Understand/ Why Did You Do This	1952	$30
❏ 47-4102	Wishing You Were Here Tonight/The Last Roundup	1951	$50

7-Inch Extended Plays

Number	Title	Yr	NM
❏ EPA-586	(contents unknown)	1954	$50
❏ EPA-586 [PS]	The Four Tunes	1954	$50

FOUR UPSETTERS, THE

SUN

Number	Title	Yr	NM
❏ 381	Crazy Arms/Midnight Soiree	1962	$30
❏ 386	Surfin' Calliope/ Wabash Cannonball	1963	$40

FOUR WINDS, THE (1)

B.T. PUPPY

Number	Title	Yr	NM
❏ 555	Let It Ride/One Face in the Crowd	1970	$12

CRYSTAL BALL

Number	Title	Yr	NM
❏ 105	Arlene/Goodbye, Maureen	1978	$10

—Red vinyl

Number	Title	Yr	NM
❏ 105	Arlene/Goodbye, Maureen	1978	$5

—Black vinyl

Number	Title	Yr	NM
❏ 102	Come Softly to Me/Judy	1978	$5

FOUR WINDS, THE (U)

CHATTAHOOCHIE

Number	Title	Yr	NM
❏ 655	Down and Out/To Love or Not to Love	1964	$20

DECOR

Number	Title	Yr	NM
❏ 175	Short Shorts/Five Minutes More	1961	$30

DERBY

Number	Title	Yr	NM
❏ 10022	Playgirl/Jennifer	1964	$40

DIAL

Number	Title	Yr	NM
❏ 3006	Woe Is Me/Promised Land	1962	$20

FELSTED

Number	Title	Yr	NM
❏ 8703	Playgirl/Jennifer	1964	$30

HIDE-A-WAY

Number	Title	Yr	NM
❏ 101	Mission by the Sea/These Hearts Were Mine	1958	$30

VIK

Number	Title	Yr	NM
❏ 0221	Colorado Moon/Find Someone New	1956	$30

WARWICK

Number	Title	Yr	NM
❏ 633	Daddy's Home/Bull-Moose Stomp	1961	$50

FOURMOST, THE

ATCO

Number	Title	Yr	NM
❏ 6280	Hello Little Girl/Just in Case	1963	$30
❏ 6317	How Can I Tell Her/ You Got That Way	1964	$20
❏ 6307	If You Cry/Little Bit of Loving	1964	$20
❏ 6285	I'm in Love/Respectable	1964	$20

CAPITOL

Number	Title	Yr	NM
❏ 5591	Girls, Girls, Girls/Why Do Fools Fall in Love	1966	$15
❏ 5738	Here, There and Everywhere/You've Changed	1966	$30

FOURTH WAY, THE

CAPITOL

Number	Title	Yr	NM
❏ 2619	Bucklehuggin'/Clouds	1969	$8

SOUL CITY

Number	Title	Yr	NM
❏ 765	Far Side of Your Moon/Pink Cloud	1968	$8

FOWLER, RAY

HIT

Number	Title	Yr	NM
❏ 09	What'd I Say/Soul Twist	1962	$8

—B-side by the Hit Combo

FOWLEY, KIM

Instrumental in the career of THE RUNAWAYS.

CAPITOL

Number	Title	Yr	NM
❏ 3662	A Born Dancer/ Something New	1973	$6
❏ 3403	Forbidden Love/I'm Bad	1972	$6
❏ 3534	International Heroes/ E.S.P. Reader	1973	$6

IMPERIAL

Number	Title	Yr	NM
❏ 66326	Born to Be Wild/ Space Odyssey	1968	$10
❏ 66349	Bubble Gum/Wildfire	1969	$10

LIVING LEGEND

Number	Title	Yr	NM
❏ 721	Mr. Responsibility/ My Foolish Heart	1965	$20

LOMA

Number	Title	Yr	NM
❏ 2064	Lights/Something New and Different	1966	$12

MIRA

Number	Title	Yr	NM
❏ 209	American Dream/The Statue	1965	$10

Number	Title	Yr	NM
ORIGINAL SOUND			
❑ 98	Thunder Road/Born to Make You Cry	1970	$10
REPRISE			
❑ 0569	Don't Be Cruel/Strangers from the Sky	1967	$12
TOWER			
❑ 342	Love Is Alive and Well/Reincarnation	1967	$10

FOX
ARIOLA AMERICA

Number	Title	Yr	NM
❑ 7608	Imagine Me Imagine You/If I Point at the Moon	1975	$6
❑ 7601	Only You Can/Out of My Body	1975	$6
GTO			
❑ 1003	Only You Can/Out of My Body	1975	$10

— Original issue

FOX, BARNEY
HIT

Number	Title	Yr	NM
❑ 30	Teenage Idol/Sherry	1962	$8

— B-side by the Four Chellows

FOX, NORMAN, AND THE ROB ROYS
BACK BEAT

Number	Title	Yr	NM
❑ 508	Dance Girl Dance/My Dearest One	1958	$100
❑ 501	Tell Me Why/Audry	1957	$100

— White label

Number	Title	Yr	NM
❑ 501	Tell Me Why/Audry	1957	$50

— Red label

CAPITOL

Number	Title	Yr	NM
❑ F4128	Dream Girl/Pizza Pie	1959	$700
HAMMER			
❑ 544	Dream Girl/Pizza Pie	1958	$40

FOX, SAMANTHA
JIVE

Number	Title	Yr	NM
❑ 1031-7-J	Do Ya Do Ya (Wanna Please Me)/Want You to Want Me	1987	$3
❑ 1031-7-J [PS]	Do Ya Do Ya (Wanna Please Me)/Want You to Want Me	1987	$4
❑ 1192-7-J	I Only Wanna Be with You/Confession	1989	$3
❑ 1192-7-J [PS]	I Only Wanna Be with You/Confession	1989	$4
❑ 1154-7-J	I Wanna Have Some Fun/Don't Cheat on Me	1988	$3
❑ 1154-7-J [PS]	I Wanna Have Some Fun/Don't Cheat on Me	1988	$4
❑ 1233-7-J	Love House/Don't Cheat on Me	1989	$3
❑ 1233-7-J [PS]	Love House/Don't Cheat on Me	1989	$4
❑ 1006-7-J	Touch Me (I Want Your Body)/Drop Me a Line	1986	$4
❑ 1006#NAME? [PS]	Touch Me (I Want Your Body)/Drop Me a Line	1986	$10

— Fold-out poster sleeve

Number	Title	Yr	NM
❑ 1006-7-J RE [PS]	Touch Me (I Want Your Body)/Drop Me a Line	1986	$4

— Regular sleeve

FOX, SAMMY
HIT

Number	Title	Yr	NM
❑ 80	The Monkey Time/My Boyfriend's Back	1963	$8

— B-side by Dot Hester

FOX, VIRGIL
7-Inch Extended Plays

RCA VICTOR RED SEAL

Number	Title	Yr	NM
❑ ERB-42 [PS]	Christmas Carols on the Organ	1954	$8

— Fold-open cover for 2-EP set (549-5129, 549-5130)

Number	Title	Yr	NM
❑ ERA-1-1845 [PS]	Christmas Carols on the Organ	1958	$15
❑ ERA-1-1845	Hark the Herald Angels Sing/We Three Kings/It Came Upon a Midnight Clear//Joy to the World/Gesu Bambino/God Rest Ye Merry Gentlemen	1958	$15
❑ 549-5129	Hark! the Herald Angels Sing/We Three Kings/It Came Upon a Midnight Clear//O Little Town of Bethlehem/Away in a Manger/Christmas	1954	$8

— "Side 1" and "Side 4" of "ERB 42"

FOXFIRE
ELEKTRA

Number	Title	Yr	NM
❑ 46625	I Can See Forever Loving You/Dreaming Won't Take Me That Far	1980	$4
❑ 47070	Whatever Happened to Those Drinking Songs/Do That to Me Again	1980	$4
❑ 47021	What's a Nice Girl Like You (Doin' in a Love Like This)/Do That To Me Again	1980	$4
NSD			
❑ 24	Fell Into Love/Head Over Heels in Love with You	1979	$5

FOXTON, KELLY
COMPLEAT

Number	Title	Yr	NM
❑ 117	Backfield in Motion/Sixteen Tons	1983	$5

FOXX, INEZ (AND CHARLIE)
DYNAMO

Number	Title	Yr	NM
❑ 112	(1-2-3-4-5-6-7) Count the Days/A Stranger I Don't Know	1967	$8
❑ 127	Baby Give It to Me/You Fixed My Heartache	1968	$8
❑ 102	Baby Take It All/Tightrope	1967	$8
❑ 126	Come On In/Baby Drop a Dime	1968	$8
❑ 104	I Stand Accused/Guilty	1967	$8
❑ 134	We Got a Chance to Be Free/Speed Ticket	1969	$8
SYMBOL			
❑ 926	Ask Me/I See You My Love	1963	$20
❑ 922	Broken Hearted Fool/He's the One You Love	1963	$20
❑ 204	Don't Do It No More/I Fancy You	1964	$15
❑ 924	Hi Diddle Diddle/Talk with Me	1963	$20
❑ 213	Hummingbird/If I Need Anyone	1966	$15
❑ 20-001	Hurt by Love/Confusion	1964	$15
❑ 206	I Feel Alright/My Mama Told Me	1965	$15
❑ 208	I've Come to One Conclusion/Down by the Seashore	1965	$15
❑ 201	La De Da, I Love You/Yankee Doodle Dandy	1964	$15
❑ 919	Mockingbird/Jaybirds	1963	$30
UNITED ARTISTS			
❑ XW516	Mockingbird/I Know (You Don't Love Me No More)	1974	$4

— Reissue; B-side by Barbara George

VOLT

Number	Title	Yr	NM
❑ 4107	Circuit's Overloaded/There's a Hand That's Reading Out	1974	$6
❑ 4096	Crossing Over That Bridge/You're Saving Me for a Rainy Day	1973	$6
❑ 4101	I Had a Talk with My Man/The Lady, The Doctor and the Prescription	1973	$6
❑ 4093	One Woman's Man/The Time	1973	$6
❑ 4087	Watch the Dog/You Hurt Me for the Last Time	1972	$6

FOXX, REDD
DOOTO

Number	Title	Yr	NM
❑ 464	Christmas Hard Times/Jaw Resting	1961	$15

FOXY
DASH

Number	Title	Yr	NM
❑ 5058	Fantazy/Girls	1980	$8
❑ 5046	Get Off/You Make Me Hot	1978	$8

— Originals on greenish label

Number	Title	Yr	NM
❑ 5046	Get Off/You Make Me Hot	1978	$6

— Second pressings on multicolor "flying geese" label

Number	Title	Yr	NM
❑ 5022	Get Off Your Aahh! And Dance (Part 1)/(Part 2)	1976	$8
❑ 5053	Headhunter/Lady of the Streets	1979	$6
❑ 5050	Hot Number/Call It Love	1979	$6
❑ 5063	Party Boys/(B-side unknown)	1980	$8
❑ 5061	Sex Symbol/Girls	1980	$8
❑ 5036	The Way You Do the Things You Do/(Instrumental)	1976	$8

FOXY (1)
DOUBLE SHOT

Number	Title	Yr	NM
❑ 145	Call Me Later/I Like the Way You Love Me	1969	$10
❑ 153	Trouble/I Like the Way You Love Me	1970	$10

FRACTION
ANGELUS

Number	Title	Yr	NM
❑ 5005	Sanc Divided/(B-side unknown)	1971	$125

FRADY, GARLAND
COUNTRYSIDE

Number	Title	Yr	NM
❑ 45104	The Barrooms Have Found You/Silver Moon	1973	$8
GNP CRESCENDO			
❑ 500	The Way the World Is Going Now (You Need Country Music)/I Think of Her	1975	$6

FRAGGIES, THE
CAMEO

Number	Title	Yr	NM
❑ 410	Stick with You/I Wanna Love You	1966	$20

FRAMPTON, PETER
Also see THE HERD; HUMBLE PIE.

A&M

Number	Title	Yr	NM
❑ 1456	All Night Long/Don't Fade Away	1973	$6

— As "Frampton's Camel"

Number	Title	Yr	NM
❑ 1832	Baby, I Love Your Way/It's a Plain Shame	1976	$4
❑ 1832 [PS]	Baby, I Love Your Way/It's a Plain Shame	1976	$6
❑ 1738	Baby I Love Your Way/(I'll Give You) Money	1975	$8
❑ 2350	Breaking All the Rules/Night Town	1981	$4
❑ 2350 [PS]	Breaking All the Rules/Night Town	1981	$6
❑ 1867	Do You Feel Like We Do/Penny for Your Thoughts	1976	$4
❑ 1470	I Believe (When I Fall in Love It Will Be Forever)/Which Way the Wind Blows	1973	$8

— As "Frampton's Camel"

Number	Title	Yr	NM
❑ 2148	I Can't Stand It No More/Where Should I Be	1979	$4
❑ 2148 [PS]	I Can't Stand It No More/Where Should I Be	1979	$5
❑ 1763	(I'll Give You) Money/Nowhere's Too Far (For My Baby)	1975	$6
❑ 8604	I'm in You/Do You Feel Like We Do	1978	$4

— Forget Me Nots" reissue; green and gold label

Number	Title	Yr	NM
❑ 1941	I'm in You/St. Thomas (Don't You Know How I Feel)	1977	$4
❑ 1941 [PS]	I'm in You/St. Thomas (Don't You Know How I Feel)	1977	$6
❑ 1941	I'm in You/St. Thomas (Know How I Feel)	1977	$5
❑ 2174	She Don't Reply/St. Thomas (Don't You Know How I Feel)	1979	$4
❑ 8595	Show Me the Way/Baby, I Love Your Way	1977	$4

— Forget Me Nots" reissue; green and gold label

Number	Title	Yr	NM
❑ 8595 [PS]	Show Me the Way/Baby, I Love Your Way	1977	$10
❑ 1693	Show Me the Way/Crying Clown	1975	$8
❑ 1795	Show Me the Way/Shine On	1976	$4
❑ 1795 [PS]	Show Me the Way/Shine On	1976	$6
❑ 1972	Signed, Sealed, Delivered (I'm Yours)/Rocky's Hot Club	1977	$4
❑ 1972 [PS]	Signed, Sealed, Delivered (I'm Yours)/Rocky's Hot Club	1977	$6
❑ 2442	Sleepwalk/Theme from Nivram	1982	$8
❑ 1506	Somethin's Happening/I Wanna Go to the Sun	1974	$6
❑ 2070	The Long and Winding Road/Tried to Love	1978	$6
❑ 1988	Tried to Love/You Don't Have to Worry	1977	$4
❑ 1988 [PS]	Tried to Love/You Don't Have to Worry	1977	$6

ATLANTIC

Number	Title	Yr	NM
❑ 89426	All Eyes on You/So Far Away	1986	$3
❑ 89426 [PS]	All Eyes on You/So Far Away	1986	$3
❑ 89395	Hiding from a Heartache/Into View	1986	$3
❑ 89463	Lying/Into View	1985	$3
❑ 89463 [PS]	Lying/Into View	1985	$3

Number	Title	Yr	NM

FRANCHI, SERGIO

LAX
Number	Title	Yr	NM
❏ 41164	Laugh You Silly Clown/ (B-side unknown)	1979	$4

METROMEDIA
❏ 238	If/Somehow	1971	$4

RCA VICTOR
❏ 47-8686	Ciao, Ciao (So Long for Now)/Moon Over Naples	1965	$6
❏ 47-8315	Cuando Caliente El Sol/Chicago	1964	$6
❏ 47-8103	I Mustn't Say I Love Her/Once	1962	$10

— Some copies of the record have this incorrect title

❏ 47-8103	I Mustn't Say I Love You/Once	1962	$8
❏ 47-8103 [PS]	I Mustn't Say I Love You/Once	1962	$20
❏ 47-9277	I Should Care/No One Else	1967	$6
❏ 47-8552	Someone Like You/ Take the Moment	1965	$6
❏ 47-8149	The Good Life/Bella Nina	1963	$8
❏ 47-9471	Time Alone Will Tell/I'm a Fool to Want You	1968	$6
❏ 47-9124	What Will Tomorrow Bring/ Maybe It's Time for Me	1967	$6

UNITED ARTISTS
❏ 50630	Granada/Within Me	1970	$5
❏ 50681	Here We Go Again/ Love Is All	1970	$5
❏ 50612	Hold Me/Song of Santa Vittoria	1969	$5
❏ 50664	More Than Strangers/Buona Fortuna, Addio Bambino	1970	$5

FRANCIS, CLEVE

PLAYBACK
❏ 1334	Lovelight/(B-side unknown)	1989	$6

SOUTHERN TRACKS
❏ 1050	Martin (same on both sides)	1985	$10

FRANCIS, CONNIE

GSF
❏ 6901	The Answer (Should I Tie a Yellow Ribbon Round the Ole Oak Tree?)/Paint the Rain	1973	$5

MGM
❏ 13545	A Letter from a Soldier (Dear Mama)/ Somewhere, My Love	1966	$10
❏ 13578	All the Love in the World/So Nice	1966	$10
❏ 12841 [M]	Among My Souvenirs/ God Bless America	1959	$40

— First pressing has a yellow label

❏ 12841 [M]	Among My Souvenirs/ God Bless America	1959	$30

— Second pressing has a black label

❏ SK-50133 [S]	Among My Souvenirs/ God Bless America	1959	$60
❏ 13665	Another Page/ Souvenir d'Italie	1967	$10
❏ 12122	Are You Satisfied/ My Treasure	1956	$30
❏ 13005	Atashi-No/Swanee	1961	$40
❏ 13237	Be Anything (But Be Mine)/Tommy	1964	$15
❏ 13237 [PS]	Be Anything (But Be Mine)/Tommy	1964	$20
❏ 13214	Blue Winter/You Know You Don't Want Me (So Why Don't You Leave Me Alone)	1964	$15
❏ 13214 [PS]	Blue Winter/You Know You Don't Want Me (So Why Don't You Leave Me Alone)	1964	$20
❏ 12995	Breakin' In a Brand New Broken Heart/ Someone Else's Boy	1961	$20
❏ 12995 [PS]	Breakin' In a Brand New Broken Heart/ Someone Else's Boy	1961	$30
❏ CS6-5	Celebrity Scene: Connie Francis	1967	$70

— Box set of five singles (13708-13712). Price includes box, all 5 singles, jukebox title strips, bio. Records are sometimes found by themselves, so they are also listed separately.

❏ 13059	Don't Break the Heart That Loves You/Drop It, Joe	1962	$20
❏ 13059 [PS]	Don't Break the Heart That Loves You/Drop It, Joe	1962	$30
❏ 13287	Don't Ever Leave Me/We Have Something More (Than a Summer Love)	1964	$15
❏ 13287 [PS]	Don't Ever Leave Me/We Have Something More (Than a Summer Love)	1964	$20
❏ 13160	Drownin' My Sorrows/ Mala Femmena	1963	$15
❏ 13160 [PS]	Drownin' My Sorrows/ Mala Femmena	1963	$20
❏ 12490	Eighteen/Faded Orchid	1957	$30
❏ 12899	Everybody's Somebody's Fool/Jealous of You	1960	$20
❏ 12899 [PS]	Everybody's Somebody's Fool/Jealous of You	1960	$30

Number	Title	Yr	NM
❏ 12713	Fallin'/Happy Days and Lonely Nights	1958	$30
❏ 13127	Follow the Boys/ Waiting for Billy	1962	$15
❏ 13127 [PS]	Follow the Boys/ Waiting for Billy	1962	$20
❏ 13363	Forget Domani/No One Sends Me Roses	1965	$10
❏ 13325	For Mama (La Mamma)/ She'll Be Coming 'Round the Mountain	1965	$15
❏ 12015	Freddy/Didn't I Love You Enough	1955	$60
❏ 14058	Gone Like the Wind/ Am I Blue?	1969	$8
❏ 14058 [PS]	Gone Like the Wind/ Am I Blue?	1969	$30
❏ 12669	Heartaches/I Miss You So	1958	$60
❏ 13039	(He's My) Dreamboat/ Hollywood	1961	$20
❏ 13039 [PS]	(He's My) Dreamboat/ Hollywood	1961	$30
❏ SB-10 [S]	I Almost Lost My Mind/ Come Back to Sorrento	1960	$60
❏ 14004	I Don't Wanna Play House/ The Welfare Check	1968	$8
❏ 12769	If I Didn't Care/Toward the End of the Day	1959	$30
❏ 12769 [PS]	If I Didn't Care/Toward the End of the Day	1959	$40
❏ 13143	If My Pillow Could Talk/You're the Only One Can Hurt Me	1963	$15
❏ 13143 [PS]	If My Pillow Could Talk/You're the Only One Can Hurt Me	1963	$20
❏ 13116	I'm Gonna' Be Warm This Winter/Al Di La	1962	$15
❏ 13116 [PS]	I'm Gonna' Be Warm This Winter/Al Di La	1962	$20
❏ 14853	I'm Me Again/Comme Si, Comme Sa	1976	$6
❏ 12647	I'm Sorry I Made You Cry/ Lock Up Your Heart	1958	$30
❏ 12375	I Never Had a Sweetheart/ Little Blue Wren	1957	$30
❏ 13203	In the Summer of His Years/My Buddy	1963	$15
❏ 13203 [PS]	In the Summer of His Years/My Buddy	1963	$50
❏ 13505	It's a Different World/ Empty Chapel	1966	$10
❏ 13505 [PS]	It's a Different World/ Empty Chapel	1966	$30
❏ 13096	I Was Such a Fool (To Fall in Love with You)/ He Thinks I Still Care	1962	$15
❏ 13096 [PS]	I Was Such a Fool (To Fall in Love with You)/ He Thinks I Still Care	1962	$20
❏ 12793 [M]	Lipstick on Your Collar/Frankie	1959	$30
❏ SK-50121 [S]	Lipstick on Your Collar/Frankie	1959	$70
❏ 13814	Lonely Again/When You Care a Lot for Someone	1967	$10
❏ 13256	Looking for Love/This Is My Happiest Moment	1964	$15
❏ 13256 [PS]	Looking for Love/This Is My Happiest Moment	1964	$20
❏ 13470	Love Is Me, Love Is You/I'd Let You Break My Heart All Over Again	1966	$10
❏ 13470 [PS]	Love Is Me, Love Is You/I'd Let You Break My Heart All Over Again	1966	$15
❏ 13710	Malaguena/I Love You Much Too Much	1967	$10

— Part of Celebrity Series CS-5

❏ 13708	Mama/Never on Sunday	1967	$10

— Part of Celebrity Series CS-5

❏ 12878	Mama/Teddy	1960	$20
❏ 12964	Many Tears Ago/Senza Mama (With No One)	1960	$20
❏ 12964 [PS]	Many Tears Ago/Senza Mama (With No One)	1960	$30
❏ 14091	Mr. Love/Zingara	1969	$8
❏ 14091 [PS]	Mr. Love/Zingara	1969	$30
❏ 12191	My First Real Love/ Believe in Me	1956	$70
❏ 13709	My Happiness/Al Di La	1967	$10

— Part of Celebrity Series CS-5

❏ 12738 [M]	My Happiness/Never Before	1958	$30
❏ 12738 [PS]	My Happiness/Never Before	1958	$40

— Pink sleeve

❏ 12738 [PS]	My Happiness/Never Before	1958	$50

— White sleeve

❏ SK-50117 [S]	My Happiness/Never Before	1958	$60
❏ 13773	My Heart Cries for You/Someone Took the Sweetness Out of Sweetheart	1967	$10
❏ 13773 [PS]	My Heart Cries for You/Someone Took the Sweetness Out of Sweetheart	1967	$30
❏ 12923	My Heart Has a Mind of Its Own/Malaguena	1960	$20
❏ 12923 [PS]	My Heart Has a Mind of Its Own/Malaguena	1960	$30
❏ 12335	My Sailor Boy/Everyone Needs Someone	1956	$30

Number	Title	Yr	NM
❏ 13876	My World Is Slipping Away/ Till We're Together	1967	$10
❏ 12056	Oh Please Make Him Jealous/Goody Goodbye	1955	$60
❏ 13711	Once in a Lifetime/ Oh Lonesome Me	1967	$10

— Part of Celebrity Series CS-5

❏ 13074	Second Hand Love/ Gonna Git That Man	1962	$30

— A-side is said to have been produced by Phil Spector, though Connie Francis disputes this; regardless, Spector did co-write the song

❏ 13074 [PS]	Second Hand Love/ Gonna Git That Man	1962	$30
❏ 12251	Send for My Baby/Forgetting	1956	$30
❏ 13948	Somebody Else Is Taking My Place/Brother, Can You Spare a Dime?	1968	$8
❏ 13610	Spanish Nights and You/ Games That Lovers Play	1966	$10
❏ 13610 [PS]	Spanish Nights and You/ Games That Lovers Play	1966	$30
❏ 12683	Stupid Cupid/Carolina Moon	1958	$30
❏ 14034	The Wedding Cake/Over Hill, Under Ground	1969	$8
❏ 13718	Time Alone Will Tell/ Born Free	1967	$10
❏ 13019	Together/Too Many Rules	1961	$20
❏ 13019 [PS]	Together/Too Many Rules	1961	$30
❏ 13051	When the Boy in Your Arms (Is the Boy in Your Heart)/ Baby's First Christmas	1961	$20
❏ 13051 [PS]	When the Boy in Your Arms (Is the Boy in Your Heart)/ Baby's First Christmas	1961	$30
❏ 12971	Where the Boys Are/No One	1961	$20
❏ 12971 [PS]	Where the Boys Are/No One	1961	$30
❏ 13303	Whose Heart Are You Breaking Tonight/ Come On Jerry	1965	$10
❏ 13303 [PS]	Whose Heart Are You Breaking Tonight/ Come On Jerry	1965	$15
❏ 12588	Who's Sorry Now?/You Were Only Fooling	1958	$30
❏ 13923	Why Say Goodbye/ Adios, Me Amore	1968	$8
❏ 13331	Wishing It Was You/ You're Mine (Just When You're Lonely)	1965	$10
❏ 13331 [PS]	Wishing It Was You/ You're Mine (Just When You're Lonely)	1965	$15

POLYDOR
❏ 2143	I'm Me Again/Comme Si, Comme Sa	1981	$5
❏ 810087-7	There's Still a Few Good Love Songs Left in Me/ Let's Make It Love Tonight	1983	$5

7-Inch Extended Plays

MGM
❏ X-1663	*Come Rain or Come Shine/Time After Time/ Hallelujah, I Love Him So/How Did He Look	1959	$50
❏ SX-1663 [S]	*Come Rain or Come Shine/Time After Time/ Hallelujah, I Love Him So/How Did He Look	1959	$100
❏ X-1605	*You Always Hurt the One You Love/If I Had You/How Deep Is the Ocean?/I'll Get By	1958	$50
❏ X-1599 [PS]	Connie Francis	1958	$50
❏ X-1687 [PS]	Connie Francis	1959	$35
❏ X-1703 [PS]	Connie Francis	1961	$35

— Has paper sleeve rather than a cardboard sleeve

❏ X-1706 [PS]	Connie Francis	1962	$50

— Paper sleeve rather than the typical cardboard EP sleeve

❏ X-1688 [PS]	Connie's Greatest Hits (Part 1)	1960	$35
❏ X-1689 [PS]	Connie's Greatest Hits (Part 2)	1960	$35
❏ X-1690 [PS]	Connie's Greatest Hits (Part 3)	1960	$35
❏ X-1603	(contents unknown)	1958	$50
❏ X-1604	(contents unknown)	1958	$50
❏ X-1664	(contents unknown)	1959	$50
❏ X-1665	(contents unknown)	1959	$50
❏ X-1689	(contents unknown)	1960	$35
❏ X-1690	(contents unknown)	1960	$35
❏ X-1691	(contents unknown)	1960	$35
❏ X-1692	(contents unknown)	1960	$35
❏ X-1693	(contents unknown)	1960	$35
❏ X-1694	(contents unknown)	1960	$35
❏ X-1695	(contents unknown)	1960	$35
❏ X-1696	(contents unknown)	1960	$35
❏ X-1694 [PS]	Country & Western Golden Hits (Part 1)	1960	$35
❏ X-1695 [PS]	Country & Western Golden Hits (Part 2)	1960	$35
❏ X-1696 [PS]	Country & Western Golden Hits (Part 3)	1960	$35
❏ X-1706	Don't Break the Heart That Loves You/It Happened Last Night/Too Many Rules/Kiss 'N' Twist	1962	$50
❏ HC5-6 [DJ]	Heart Circuit Interview	1959	$125
❏ X-1662 [PS]	If I Didn't Care	1959	$50

Number	Title	Yr	NM
❑ X-1662	If I Didn't Care/Toward the End of the Day// Don't Speak of Love/If You Loved Me Tonight	1959	$50
❑ X-1655 [PS]	My Happiness	1958	$50
❑ X-1655	My Happiness/No Other One//You're My Everything/Never Before	1958	$50
❑ X-1663 [PS]	The Exciting Connie Francis Vol. 1	1959	$50
❑ SX-1663 [PS]	The Exciting Connie Francis Vol. 1	1959	$100

—A stereo copy of the above has recently emerged. We presume that Vol. 2 and Vol. 3 of the same title also were made in stereo, but we don't have concrete proof, so we don't list them yet.

Number	Title	Yr	NM
❑ X-1664 [PS]	The Exciting Connie Francis Vol. 2	1959	$50
❑ X-1665 [PS]	The Exciting Connie Francis Vol. 3	1959	$50
❑ X-1688	Who's Sorry Now/Fallin'// Happy Days and Lonely Nights/Stupid Cupid	1960	$35
❑ X-1603 [PS]	Who's Sorry Now Vol. I	1958	$50
❑ X-1604 [PS]	Who's Sorry Now Vol. II	1958	$50
❑ X-1605 [PS]	Who's Sorry Now Vol. III	1958	$50
❑ X-1599	Who's Sorry Now/You Were Only Fooling (While I Was Falling in Love)// Eighteen/Faded Orchid	1958	$50

FRANCISCUS, JAMES

MGM

Number	Title	Yr	NM
❑ K13319	Droppity Dropouts/ On Friday Day	1965	$12

—B-side by Vince Howard

Number	Title	Yr	NM
❑ K13319 [PS]	Droppity Dropouts/ On Friday Day	1965	$30

FRANK AND JACK

BERGEN

Number	Title	Yr	NM
❑ 100	'Twas The Night Before Christmas/Jingle Bells	1957	$30

JOSIE

Number	Title	Yr	NM
❑ 827	Twas the Night Before Christmas (Breaking Thru the Sound Barrier)/ Jingle Bells (From the Sound Track)	1957	$20

FRANK, JOE, AND THE KNIGHTS

ABC-PARAMOUNT

Number	Title	Yr	NM
❑ 10782	Can't Find a Way/Won't You Come Home	1966	$30

FRANKE AND THE KNOCKOUTS

MCA

Number	Title	Yr	NM
❑ 52370	Outrageous/So Cool (Nobody's Fool)	1984	$4

MILLENNIUM

Number	Title	Yr	NM
❑ YB-13108	Morning Sun (Dream On)/ Never Had It Better	1982	$4
❑ YB-11801	Sweetheart/Don't Stop	1981	$4
❑ JH-11801 [DJ]	Sweetheart (stereo/mono)	1981	$20

—Promo only on red vinyl (black vinyl promos go for about the same as stock copies)

Number	Title	Yr	NM
❑ YB-13105	Without You (Not Another Lonely Night)/Shakedown	1982	$4

FRANKIE AND JOHNNY

EPIC

Number	Title	Yr	NM
❑ 5-10010	Over the Rainbow/ Two's Company	1966	$15

HICKORY

Number	Title	Yr	NM
❑ 1391	I'll Hold You/(I'm) Never Gonna Leave You	1966	$120

INTERNATIONAL ARTISTS

Number	Title	Yr	NM
❑ 117	A Present of the Past/ Right String Baby	1968	$30
❑ 112	Sweet Thang/ Times Gone By	1968	$50

LIBERTY

Number	Title	Yr	NM
❑ 55271	Do You Love Me/ My First Love	1960	$20

LIDO

Number	Title	Yr	NM
❑ 604	Big Clem/Together Tonight	1959	$50

MERCURY

Number	Title	Yr	NM
❑ 72955	Hometown, U.S.A./ Lucille-Slippin' and Slidin'	1969	$15

SABRINA

Number	Title	Yr	NM
❑ 331	Do You Love Me/ My First Love	1959	$30

WARNER BROS.

Number	Title	Yr	NM
❑ 7684	Life Line/Mr. R.M.	1973	$8

FRANKIE AND THE C-NOTES

RICHIE

Number	Title	Yr	NM
❑ 2	Forever and Ever/Fade Out	1959	$400

FRANKIE GOES TO HOLLYWOOD

ISLAND

Number	Title	Yr	NM
❑ 99695	Two Tribes/One February Friday	1984	$3
❑ 99695 [PS]	Two Tribes/One February Friday	1984	$3
❑ 99486	Warriors of the Wasteland (Edited Mix)/(Extended Mix)	1986	$4
❑ 99486 [PS]	Warriors of the Wasteland (Edited Mix)/(Extended Mix)	1986	$4
❑ 99653	Welcome to the Pleasuredome/Relax International (Live)	1985	$3
❑ 99653 [PS]	Welcome to the Pleasuredome/Relax International (Live)	1985	$3

FRANKLIN, ARETHA

ARISTA

Number	Title	Yr	NM
❑ 9474	Ain't Nobody Ever Loved You/Push	1986	$3

—B-side with Peter Wolf

Number	Title	Yr	NM
❑ 9453	Another Night/Kind of Man	1986	$3
❑ 0600	Come to Me/School Days	1981	$4
❑ 9095	Every Girl (Wants My Guy)/I Got Your Love	1983	$4
❑ 9354 [DJ]	Freeway of Love (Short) (Long)	1985	$30

—Promo only on pink vinyl

Number	Title	Yr	NM
❑ 9354	Freeway of Love/Until You Say You Love Me	1985	$3
❑ 9354 [PS]	Freeway of Love/Until You Say You Love Me	1985	$3
❑ 9034	Get It Right/Giving In	1983	$4
❑ 9884	Gimme Your Love/Think	1989	$3

—With James Brown

Number	Title	Yr	NM
❑ 9884 [PS]	Gimme Your Love/Think	1989	$3

—With James Brown

Number	Title	Yr	NM
❑ 9623	If You Need My Love Tonight/He'll Come Along	1987	$3

—A-side with Larry Graham

Number	Title	Yr	NM
❑ 9559	I Knew You Were Waiting (For Me)/(Instrumental)	1987	$3

—With George Michael

Number	Title	Yr	NM
❑ 9559 [PS]	I Knew You Were Waiting (For Me)/(Instrumental)	1987	$3

—With George Michael

Number	Title	Yr	NM
❑ 9850	It Isn't, It Wasn't, It Ain't Never Gonna Be/If Ever a Love There Was	1989	$3

—A-side with Whitney Houston; B-side with the Four Tops

Number	Title	Yr	NM
❑ 9850 [PS]	It Isn't, It Wasn't, It Ain't Never Gonna Be/If Ever a Love There Was	1989	$3

—A-side with Whitney Houston; B-side with the Four Tops

Number	Title	Yr	NM
❑ 0646	It's My Turn/Kind of Man	1981	$4
❑ 0665	Livin' in the Streets/There's a Star for Everyone	1982	$4
❑ 0624	Love All the Hurt Away/ Whole Lotta Me	1981	$4

—Aretha Franklin and George Benson

Number	Title	Yr	NM
❑ 1023	Love Me Right/(It's Just) Your Love	1982	$4
❑ 9672	Oh Happy Day/The Lord's Prayer	1988	$5
❑ 9672 [PS]	Oh Happy Day/The Lord's Prayer	1988	$5
❑ 1043	This Is for Real/I Just Want to Make It Up to You	1983	$4
❑ 9809	Through the Storm/ Come to Me	1989	$3

—A-side with Elton John

Number	Title	Yr	NM
❑ 9809 [PS]	Through the Storm/ Come to Me	1989	$3
❑ 0591	What a Fool Believes/ Love Me Forever	1980	$4
❑ 9410	Who's Zoomin' Who/ Sweet Bitter Love	1985	$3
❑ 9410 [PS]	Who's Zoomin' Who/ Sweet Bitter Love	1985	$3

ATLANTIC

Number	Title	Yr	NM
❑ 3200	Ain't Nothing Like the Real Thing/Eight Days on the Road	1974	$8
❑ 2883	All the King's Horses/ April Fools	1972	$8
❑ 3468	Almighty Fire (Woman of the Future)/I'm Your Speed	1978	$8
❑ 2969	Angel/Hey Hey Now (Sister from Texas)	1973	$8
❑ 2427	Baby I Love You/ Going Down Now	1967	$15
❑ 2772	Border Song (Holy Moses)/You and Me	1970	$10
❑ 3393	Break It To Me Gently/ Meadows of Springtime	1977	$8
❑ 2796	Bridge Over Troubled Water/Brand New Me	1971	$8
❑ 2706	Call Me/Son of a Preacher Man	1970	$10
❑ 2464	Chain of Fools/Prove It	1967	$15
❑ 2866	Day Dreaming/I've Been Loving You Too Long	1972	$8
❑ 2751	Don't Play That Song/Let It Be	1970	$12
❑ 2683	Eleanor Rigby/It Ain't Fair	1969	$12
❑ 3632	Half a Love/Only Star	1979	$6
❑ 2619	I Can't See Myself Leaving You/Gentle On My Mind	1969	$10
❑ 2999	I'm in Love/Oh Baby	1974	$8
❑ 2386	I Never Loved a Man (The Way I Love You)/Do Right Woman, Do Right Man	1967	$15
❑ 2546	I Say a Little Prayer/The House That Jack Built	1968	$15
❑ 3605	Ladies Only/What If I Should Ever Need You	1979	$6
❑ 3373	Look Into Your Heart/ Rock with Me	1977	$8
❑ 2941	Master of Eyes (The Deepness of Your Eyes)/ Moody's Mood for You	1973	$8
❑ 3495	More Than Just a Joy/ This You Can Believe	1979	$8
❑ 3289	Mr. D.J. (5 for the D.J.)/As Long As You Are There	1975	$8
❑ 2574	See Saw/My Song	1968	$10
❑ 2650	Share Your Love with Me/ Pledging My Love-The Clock	1969	$10
❑ 3326	Something He Can Feel/ Loving You, Baby	1976	$8
❑ 2817	Spanish Harlem/ Lean On Me	1971	$8
❑ 2731	Spirit in the Dark/ The Thrill Is Gone	1970	$10
❑ 2486	(Sweet Sweet Baby) Since You've Been Gone/Ain't No Way	1968	$15
❑ 2603	The Weight/Tracks of My Tears	1969	$10
❑ 2518	Think/You Send Me	1968	$15
❑ 3418	When I Think About You/Touch Me Up	1978	$8
❑ 2901	Wholy Holy/Give Yourself to Jesus	1972	$8
❑ 3249	With Everything I Feel in Me/ Sing It Again, Say It Again	1975	$8
❑ 3224	Without Love/Don't Go Breaking My Heart	1974	$8

CHECKER

Number	Title	Yr	NM
❑ 941	Precious Lord, Part 1/ Precious Lord, Part 2	1960	$20

COLUMBIA

Number	Title	Yr	NM
❑ 41965	Are You Sure/ Maybe I'm a Fool	1961	$15
❑ S731206 [S]	(Blue) By Myself/Today I Sing the Blues	1961	$15

—The above five are "Stereo Seven" 33 1/3 rpm jukebox singles from set "JS 7-38" entitled "Aretha (with the Ray Bryant Combo)

Number	Title	Yr	NM
❑ 43203	Can't You Just See Me/ Little Miss Raggedy Ann	1965	$10
❑ 43827	Cry Like a Baby/Swanee	1966	$12
❑ 42456	Don't Cry, Baby/Without the One You Love	1962	$12
❑ 42456 [PS]	Don't Cry, Baby/Without the One You Love	1962	$40
❑ 44851	Friendly Persuasion/Jim	1969	$8
❑ 43515	Hands Off/Tighten Up Your Tie, Button Up Your Jacket	1966	$12
❑ 42796	Here's Where I Came In/Say It Isn't So	1963	$12
❑ 42796 [PS]	Here's Where I Came In/Say It Isn't So	1963	$40
❑ 42266	I Surrender, Dear/ Rough Lover	1962	$10
❑ 42266 [PS]	I Surrender, Dear/ Rough Lover	1962	$40
❑ S731205 [S]	Maybe I'm a Fool/It Ain't Necessarily So	1961	$15
❑ 44381	Mockingbird/A Mother's Love	1967	$8
❑ 43241	One Step Ahead/I Can't Wait Until I See My Baby's Face	1965	$10
❑ 42874	Skylark/You've Got Her	1963	$12
❑ 43009	Soulville/Evil Gal Blues	1964	$12
❑ 44441	Soulville/If Ever I Would Leave You	1968	$8
❑ S731203 [S]	Sweet Lover/All Night Long	1961	$15
❑ 44270	Take a Look/Follow Your Heart	1967	$10
❑ 41793	Today I Sing the Blues/ Love Is the Only Thing	1960	$15
❑ 44951	Today I Sing the Blues/People	1969	$8
❑ 42625	Trouble in Mind/God Bless the Child	1962	$10
❑ 42520	Try a Little Tenderness/ Just for a Thrill	1962	$10
❑ 42520 [PS]	Try a Little Tenderness/ Just for a Thrill	1962	$30
❑ S731204 [S]	Who Needs You?/Right Now	1961	$15
❑ 43177	Winter Wonderland/The Christmas Song (Chestnuts Roasting on an Open Fire)	1964	$10
❑ S731202 [S]	Won't Be Long/Love Is the Only Thing	1961	$15
❑ 41923	Won't Be Long/Right Now	1961	$15

JVB

Number	Title	Yr	NM
❑ 75	Precious Lord, Part 1/ Precious Lord, Part 2	1959	$40

7-Inch Extended Plays

ATLANTIC

Number	Title	Yr	NM
❑ A1025 [PS]	Amazing Grace	1972	$25
❑ SD77205 [PS]	Aretha Live at Fillmore West	1971	$15
❑ SD 7-7265 [PS]	Hey Now Hey	1973	$12

Number	Title	Yr	NM
❏ SD 7-8248	Let It Be/The Weight/ Eleanor Rigby//This Girl's in Love with You/Share Your Love with Me	1970	$15

—Jukebox issue; small hole, plays at 33 1/3 rpm

❏ A1025 [DJ]	Precious Lord, Take My Hand/You've Got a Friend/ Precious Memories//Wholy Holy/Mary, Don't You Weep	1972	$20

—Mono; white label promo sampler

❏ SD 7-7265	Somewhere/Moody's Mood//Hey Now Hey/So Swell When You're Well	1973	$10

—Jukebox issue; small hole, plays at 33 1/3 rpm

❏ SD77205	Spirit in the Dark (with Ray Charles)//Respect/ Love the One You're With	1971	$15

—Stereo jukebox issue; small hole, plays at 33 1/3 rpm

❏ SD 7-8248 [PS]	This Girl's in Love with You	1970	$15

FRANKLIN, CAROLYN
RCA VICTOR

Number	Title	Yr	NM
❏ 74-0289	Ain't That Groovy/All I Want Is to Be Your Woman	1969	$6
❏ 74-0783	As Long As You're There/I Want to Be With You	1972	$5
❏ 74-0314	Everybody's Talkin'/ Chain Reaction	1970	$5
❏ PB-10688	I Can't Help My Feeling So Blue/If You Want Me	1976	$4
❏ 47-9734	The Boxer/I Don't Want to Lose You	1969	$6

FRANKLIN, DOUG, AND THE BLUENOTES
COLONIAL

Number	Title	Yr	NM
❏ 7779	Christmas Chimes/ Let Her Know	1958	$30
❏ 9999	Darling of Mine/ Never Never Land	1959	$30
❏ 8888	I Used to Wonder/I Wonder Who's Kissing Her Now	1959	$30
❏ 7777	My Lucky Love/Drizzlin' Rain	1958	$30

FRANKLIN, ERMA
BRUNSWICK

Number	Title	Yr	NM
❏ 55403	Change My Thoughts from You/Gotta Find Me a Lover	1969	$8
❏ 55424	I Just Don't Need You (At All)/It Could've Been Me	1969	$8
❏ 55415	Saving My Love/You've Been Cancelled	1969	$8
❏ 55430	Whispers (Gettin' Louder)/ (I Get the) Sweetest Feeling	1970	$8

EPIC

Number	Title	Yr	NM
❏ 5-9610	Abracadabra/Love Is Blind	1963	$20
❏ 5-9516	Dear Mama/Never Again	1962	$30
❏ 5-9468	Don't Blame Me/What Kind of Girl (Do You Think I Am)	1961	$30
❏ 5-9559	Don't Wait Too Long/ Time After Time	1962	$30
❏ 5-9511	Each Night I Cry/ Time After Time	1962	$30
❏ 5-9594	Have You Ever Had the Blues/I Don't Want No Mama's Boy	1963	$20
❏ 5-9488	Hello Again/It's Over	1962	$30

SHOUT

Number	Title	Yr	NM
❏ 218	Big Boss Man/Didn't Catch the Dog's Bone	1967	$12
❏ 230	Open Up Your Soul/I'm Just Not Ready for Love	1967	$10
❏ 221	Piece of My Heart/Baby What You Want Me to Do	1967	$15

FRANKS, MICHAEL
BRUT

Number	Title	Yr	NM
❏ 809	Can't Seem to Shake This Rock 'n' Roll/ King of Oklahoma	1973	$20

JOHN HAMMOND

Number	Title	Yr	NM
❏ WS4 03794	Can't Seem to Shake This Rock 'n' Roll/ Just Like Key Largo	1983	$5
❏ WS4 03794 [PS]	Can't Seem to Shake This Rock 'n' Roll/ Just Like Key Largo	1983	$5

REPRISE

Number	Title	Yr	NM
❏ 1360	Popsicle Toes/I Don't Know Why I'm So Happy I'm Sad	1976	$5

WARNER BROS.

Number	Title	Yr	NM
❏ 49556	Baseball/Loving You More and More	1980	$4
❏ 28184	Face to Face/Innuendo	1987	$5
❏ 28285	Island Life/Innuendo	1987	$5
❏ 50025	Love Duet/No One But You	1982	$5

—With S. Renee Diggs

❏ 49271	One Bad Habit/Still Lifes	1980	$5
❏ 27997	The Camera Never Lies/Innuendo	1988	$5
❏ 28819	When I Give My Love to You/When She Is Mine	1986	$4

—With Brenda Russell

Number	Title	Yr	NM
❏ 28819 [PS]	When I Give My Love to You/When She Is Mine	1986	$4
❏ 8811	When It's Over/ (B-side unknown)	1979	$5
❏ 29400	When Sly Calls/ Never Satisfied	1983	$8
❏ 8583	When the Cookie Jar Is Empty/Burchfield Nines	1978	$5

FRANKS, TILLMAN
STARDAY

Number	Title	Yr	NM
❏ 651	Tadpole/Pretty Little Girls	1963	$20
❏ 670	When the World's on Fire/Uncle Eph	1964	$20

FRANLKIN, DOUG, WITH THE BLUENOTES
COLONIAL

Number	Title	Yr	NM
❏ 7777	My Lucky Love/Drizzin' Rain	1958	$30

FRANTIC
LIZARD

Number	Title	Yr	NM
❏ 21002	Midnight to Six Man/ Shady Sam	1970	$20

FRANTICS, THE
BOLO

Number	Title	Yr	NM
❏ 736	Oh Yeah/Let Our Love Roll On	1962	$10
❏ 728	Pony Moronie/Meet Me in Seattle Twist	1962	$12

DOLTON

Number	Title	Yr	NM
❏ 13	Checkerboard/Werewolf	1959	$30
❏ 6	Fog Cutter/Black Sapphire	1959	$30
❏ 33	San Antonio Rose/Trees	1961	$20
❏ 2	Straight Flush/Young Blues	1959	$30
❏ 24	The Whip/Delilah	1960	$20
❏ 16	Werewolf/No Werewolf	1960	$20

SEAFAIR

Number	Title	Yr	NM
❏ 111	San Francisco Swim/ Blue Day	1964	$10

FRATERNITY OF MAN, THE
ABC

Number	Title	Yr	NM
❏ 11106	Don't Bogart Me/ Wispy Paisley Skies	1968	$8

FRAZIER, BRENDA
TYRO

Number	Title	Yr	NM
❏ 1004	I've Given Up Giving In to the Blues/ Steppin' Out Tonight	1980	$8

FRAZIER, DALLAS
20TH CENTURY

Number	Title	Yr	NM
❏ 2171	Cash on Delivery/Watching My World Walk Away	1975	$6
❏ 2233	I'm Sorry If My Love Got In Your Way/Harvey, Where'd You Get That Yellow Yo-Yo	1975	$6
❏ 2199	Liberal Acres/Heaven Hangin' Over My Head	1975	$6

CAPITOL

Number	Title	Yr	NM
❏ 5560	Elvira/That Ain't No Stuff	1966	$20
❏ 2011	Everybody Oughta Sing a Song/Only a Fool	1967	$12
❏ 2257	I Hope I Like Mexico Blues/I Just Thought That I Love Her ('Till I Lost You)	1968	$10
❏ F2895	Love Life at 14/I'm Gonna Move Over Yonder	1954	$30
❏ F2956	My Birthday Comes on Christmas/Jingle o' the Brownie	1954	$30

—With Joe "Fingers" Carr

❏ 5862	My Woman Up't and Gone/ Clawhammer Clyde	1967	$15
❏ F2813	Space Command/Ain't You Had No Bringin' Up at All	1954	$30
❏ 5728	Tennessee Sue/ Especially for You	1966	$15
❏ 2402	The Conspiracy of Homer Jones/Sundown of My Mind	1969	$12
❏ 2133	The Sunshine of My World/ Lonelier and More in Love	1968	$10
❏ 5670	Walkin' Wonder/Just a Little Bit of You	1966	$15

JAMIE

Number	Title	Yr	NM
❏ 1135	Can't Go On/Without Your Love	1959	$30

MERCURY

Number	Title	Yr	NM
❏ 72279	My Little Swing Broke Down/ Money Greases the Wheels	1964	$15

RCA VICTOR

Number	Title	Yr	NM
❏ 47-9950	Big Mable Murphy/ White Fences and Evergreen Trees	1971	$8
❏ 74-0259	California Cotton Fields/ Sweetheart Don't Throw Yourself Away	1969	$8
❏ 74-0569	Common, Broke Elastic, Rotten Cotton, Hound Dog Snoopin', Ankle Droopin', Funky Fuzzy, White Sock Blues No. 2/ High Steppin' Mama	1971	$8
❏ 47-9991	My Baby Packed Up My Mind and Left Me/I'm Finally Over You	1971	$8
❏ 47-9881	The Birthmark Henry Thompson Talks About/If My Heart Had Windows	1970	$8
❏ 74-0903	This Time the Hurtin's on Me/Lonesome Fiddle Man	1973	$8

FREAK SCENE, THE
COLUMBIA

Number	Title	Yr	NM
❏ 4-44056	A Million Grains of Sand/ Behind the Mind	1967	$30

FREBERG, STAN
CAPITOL

Number	Title	Yr	NM
❏ F2125	Abe Snake for President/ Ba Ba Ball and Chain	1952	$60
❏ F3687	Banana Boat (Day-O)/ Tele-Vee-Shun	1957	$30
❏ F2677	C'est Si Bon (It's So Good)/A Dear John & Marsha Letter	1953	$30
❏ F2671	Christmas Dragnet Part 1/ Christmas Dragnet Part 2	1953	$40
❏ 4433	Comments for Our Time Part 1/Comments for Our Time Part 2	1960	$30
❏ 5726	Flackman and Reagan Part 1/Flackman and Reagan Part 2	1966	$30
❏ 5726 [PS]	Flackman and Reagan Part 1/Flackman and Reagan Part 2	1966	$40
❏ 3503	Green Chritma (Part 1)/ Green Chritma (Part 2)	1972	$10
❏ F4097	Green Chritma/The Meaning of Christmas	1958	$30
❏ F4097 [PS]	Green Chritma/The Meaning of Christmas	1958	$40
❏ F3480	Heartbreak Hotel/ Rock Island Line	1956	$30
❏ F1962	Maggie/Tele-Vee-Shun	1951	$40
❏ F2838	Point of Order/ Person to Pearson	1954	$30
❏ F2929	Sh-Boom/Widescreen Mama Blues	1954	$30
❏ F2596	St. George and the Dragonet/Little Blue Riding Hood	1953	$40
❏ F1697	St. George and the Dragonet/Little Blue Riding Hood	1954	$30

—Reissue (despite the lower number)

❏ F1711	That's My Boy/I've Got You Under My Skin	1951	$40
❏ F3396	The Great Pretender/ The Quest for Bridey Hammerschlaugen	1956	$30
❏ F3138	The Honey Earthers/ The Lone Psychiatrist	1955	$40

—With Daws Butler

❏ 4329	The Old Payola Roll Blues Part 1/The Old Payola Roll Blues Part 2	1960	$30
❏ 4329 [PS]	The Old Payola Roll Blues Part 1/The Old Payola Roll Blues Part 2	1960	$40
❏ F2279	The World Is Waiting for the Sunrise/Boogie Woogie Banjo Man from Birmingham	1952	$30
❏ 3355	Try/John and Marsha	1972	$10
❏ F2029	Try/Pass the Udder Udder	1952	$40
❏ F3815	Wun'erful, Wun'erful! (Part uh-one)/Wun'erful, Wun'erful! (Part uh-two)	1957	$30

7-Inch Extended Plays

Number	Title	Yr	NM
❏ EAP 1-496 [PS]	Any Requests?	1954	$35
❏ EAP 1-628	St. George and the Dragonet/C'est Si Bon (It's So Good)//Sh-Boom/That's My Boy	1955	$35

FRED, JOHN, AND HIS PLAYBOY BAND
BELL

Number	Title	Yr	NM
❏ 45382	I'm in Love Again/ In the Mood	1973	$5

—As "John Fred and the Creepers

JEWEL

Number	Title	Yr	NM
❏ 737	Boogie Children/ My First Love	1964	$10

—As "The Playboys"

❏ 736	Lenne/You're Mad at Me	1964	$12
❏ 730	The Fool/There'll Be No Teardrops Tonight	1964	$10
❏ 743	Wrong to Me/How Can I Prove	1965	$10

MONTEL

Number	Title	Yr	NM
❏ 904	Down in New Orleans/I Love You	1959	$20
❏ 1007	Good Lovin'/You Know You Made Me Cry	1961	$10

Number	Title	Yr	NM
❏ 2001	Mirror Mirror (On the Wall)/To Have and to Hold	1962	$10
❏ 1002	Shirley/My Love for You	1959	$20

N-JOY

Number	Title	Yr	NM
❏ 1005	Boogie Children/My First Love	1965	$10

PAULA

Number	Title	Yr	NM
❏ 273	Agnes English/Sad Story	1967	$8
❏ 234	Can't I Get a Word In/Sun City	1966	$8
❏ 244	Doin' the Best I Can/Leave Her Never	1966	$8
❏ 225	Fortune Teller/Making Love to You	1965	$8
❏ 294	Hey Hey Bunny/No Letter Today	1968	$8
❏ 303	Lonely Are the Lonely/We Played Games	1968	$8
❏ 247	Outta My Head/Love Comes in Time	1966	$8
❏ 310	Tissue Paper/Little Dum Dum	1968	$8
❏ 315	What Is Happiness/Sometimes You Just Can't Win	1968	$8

UNI

Number	Title	Yr	NM
❏ 55135	Back in the U.S.S.R./Silly Sarah Carter	1969	$6
❏ 55220	Come with Me/Where's Everybody Going	1970	$6
❏ 55187	Love My Soul/Julia Julia	1969	$6
❏ 55160	Open Doors/Three Deep Is a Feeling	1969	$6

FREDDIE AND THE DREAMERS

CAPITOL

Number	Title	Yr	NM
❏ 5053	I'm Telling You Now/What Have I Done to You	1963	$30

MERCURY

Number	Title	Yr	NM
❏ 72462	A Little You/Things I'd Like to Say	1965	$10
❏ 72327	Don't Do That to Me/Just for You	1965	$12
❏ 72428	Do the Freddie/A Love Like You	1965	$15
❏ 72428	Do the Freddie/Tell Me When	1965	$12
❏ 72487	I Don't Know/Windmill in Old Amsterdam	1965	$10
❏ 72487 [PS]	I Don't Know/Windmill in Old Amsterdam	1965	$30
❏ 72285	I Love You Baby/Don't Make Me Cry	1965	$10
❏ 72285 [PS]	I Love You Baby/Don't Make Me Cry	1965	$30
❏ 72377	I Understand (Just How You Feel)/I Will	1965	$10
❏ 72604	Some Day/Short Shorts	1966	$12
❏ 72548	When I'm Home with You/If You Got a Minute Baby	1966	$10

SUPER K

Number	Title	Yr	NM
❏ 146	She Needs Me/Susan's Tuba	1970	$8

TOWER

Number	Title	Yr	NM
❏ 125	I'm Telling You Now/What Have I Done to You	1964	$20
❏ 163	Send a Letter to Me/There's Not One Thing	1965	$20

—B-side by 4 Just Men

7-Inch Extended Plays

MERCURY

Number	Title	Yr	NM
❏ SRC661-C [PS]	Fun Lovin' Freddie	1965	$25
❏ SRC661-C	Thou Shalt Not Steal/Funny Over You/He Got What He Wanted//I Fell in Love with Your Picture/I Think of You/Some Other Guy	1965	$25

—Jukebox mini-LP

FREDDIE AND THE PARLIAMENTS

TWIRL

Number	Title	Yr	NM
❏ 1003	Darlene/That Girl	1959	$125

FREDRIC

EVOLUTION

Number	Title	Yr	NM
❏ 1001	Five O'Clock Traffic/Red Pier	1968	$30

FORTE

Number	Title	Yr	NM
❏ 3001	Five O'Clock Traffic/Red Pier	1968	$50

FREE

Also see PAUL KOSSOFF; BAD COMPANY; THE FIRM.

A&M

Number	Title	Yr	NM
❏ 1206	All Right Now/Mouthful of Grass	1970	$5
❏ 1720	All Right Now/Stealer	1975	$4
❏ 1248	Highway Song/Love You So	1971	$4
❏ 1172	I'll Be Creepin'/Mouthful of Grass	1970	$4
❏ 1099	I'm a Mover/Worry	1969	$4
❏ 1352	Little Bit of Love/Sail On	1972	$4
❏ 1266	Mr. Big/I'll Be Creepin'	1971	$4
❏ 1276	My Brother Jake/Only My Soul	1971	$4

Number	Title	Yr	NM
❏ 1230	Stealer/Broad Daylight	1970	$4
❏ 1230 [PS]	Stealer/Lying in the Sunshine	1970	$10

—Picture sleeve lists a different B-side than is on the record

ISLAND

Number	Title	Yr	NM
❏ 1212	Wishing Well/Let Me Show You	1972	$4

FREE DESIGN, THE

PROJECT 3

Number	Title	Yr	NM
❏ 1366	2002: A Hit Song/Hurry Sundown	1969	$8
❏ 1370	Butterflies Are Free/(B-side unknown)	1970	$8
❏ 1347 [DJ]	Close Your Mouth (It's Christmas)/Christmas Is The Day	1968	$10

— Stock copy may not exist

Number	Title	Yr	NM
❏ 1345	Eleanor Rigby/Make the Madness Stop	1968	$8
❏ 1393	Felt So Good/You Are My Sunshine	1971	$8
❏ 1360	If I Were a Carpenter/Now Is the Time	1969	$8
❏ 1336	I Found Love/Umbrellas	1968	$8
❏ 1375	I'm a Yogi/Bubbles	1970	$8
❏ 1404	Stay Off of Your Frown/Friendly Man	1971	$8
❏ 1358	Summertime/Dorian Benediction	1969	$8
❏ 1383	Tomorrow Is the First Day of the Rest of My Life/Kije's Ouija	1970	$8
❏ 1356	Where Do I Go/Girls Alone	1969	$8

FREE, JOHNNY

SABRE

Number	Title	Yr	NM
❏ 4509	Borrowed Time/(B-side unknown)	1979	$8

FREE MOVEMENT, THE

COLUMBIA

Number	Title	Yr	NM
❏ 45567	Could You Believe in a Dream/Love the One You're With	1972	$5
❏ 45778	Every Step of the Way/I Can't Move No Mountains	1973	$5
❏ 45512	The Harder I Try (The Bluer I Get)/Comin' Home	1972	$5

DECCA

Number	Title	Yr	NM
❏ 32818	I've Found Someone of My Own/I Can't Convince My Heart	1971	$6

FREE SPEECH CAROLS

FSM

Number	Title	Yr	NM
❏ 1	Oski Dolls/We Three Deans/UC Administration/Hail to IBM/It Belongs to the University//Silent Night/Call Out the Deans/Masters of Sproul Hall/God Rest Ye Free Speech/Come All Ye Mindless/Joy to UC	1964	$30
❏ 1 [PS]	Oski Dolls/We Three Deans/UC Administration/Hail to IBM/It Belongs to the University//Silent Night/Call Out the Deans/Masters of Sproul Hall/God Rest Ye Free Speech/Come All Ye Mindless/Joy to UC	1964	$50

FREED, ALAN

CORAL

Number	Title	Yr	NM
❏ 61818	Sentimental Journey/Stop! Look! and Run!	1957	$50
❏ 61660	THe Camel Rock/I Don't Need Lotsa Money	1956	$40
❏ 61693	The Space Man/Jazzbo's Theory	1956	$40

— With Al "Jazzbo" Collins and the Modernaires

FREEMAN, ART

FAME

Number	Title	Yr	NM
❏ 1012	A Piece of My Heart/Everybody's Got to Cry Sometime	1966	$40
❏ 1008	I Can't Get You Out of My Mind/Slippin' Around with You	1966	$60

FREEMAN, ARTHUR

EXCELLO

Number	Title	Yr	NM
❏ 2322	Here I Am/Played Out Play Girl	1971	$30

FREEMAN, BOBBY

AUTUMN

Number	Title	Yr	NM
❏ 2	C'mon and Swim/C'mon and Swim -- Part 2	1964	$15

— White label, red print

Number	Title	Yr	NM
❏ 2	C'mon and Swim/C'mon and Swim -- Part 2	1964	$10

— Tan label

Number	Title	Yr	NM
❏ 1	Come to Me/Let's Surf Again	1964	$30
❏ 25	Cross My Heart/The Duck	1965	$12
❏ 9	I'll Never Fall in Love Again/Friends	1965	$10

Number	Title	Yr	NM
❏ 5	S-W-I-M/That Little Old Heartbreaker	1964	$10

DOUBLE SHOT

Number	Title	Yr	NM
❏ 148	Can You Stand the Pressure/Put Another Dime in the Parking Meter	1970	$6
❏ 152	Do You Wanna Dance 1970/Society for the Prevention of Cruelty to People	1970	$6
❏ 144	Susie Sunshine/Four Piece Funky Nitty Gritty Junky Band	1969	$6
❏ 139	There Oughta Be a Law/Everybody's Got a Hang-Up	1969	$6

JOSIE

Number	Title	Yr	NM
❏ 855	A Love to Last a Lifetime/When You're Smiling	1959	$20
❏ 841	Betty Lou Got a New Pair of Shoes/Starlight	1958	$30
❏ 835	Do You Want to Dance/Big Fat Woman	1958	$30
❏ 872	Ebb Tide/Sinbad	1959	$20
❏ 879	I Need Someone/First Day of Spring	1960	$15
❏ 896	Love Me/Little Girl Don't You Understand	1962	$15
❏ 863	Love Me/Mary Ann Thomas	1959	$20
❏ 886	Miss You So/Baby What Would You Do	1961	$15
❏ 867	My Guardian Angel/Where Did My Baby Go	1959	$20
❏ 889	Put You Down/She Said She Wants to Dance	1961	$15
❏ 928	The Mess Around/Little Girl Don't You Understand	1965	$10
❏ 887	The Mess Around/So Much to Do	1961	$15

KING

Number	Title	Yr	NM
❏ 5975	Come to Me/There's Gonna Be a Change	1965	$10
❏ 5953	Fever/What Can I Do	1964	$10
❏ 5373	(I Do the) Shimmy Shimmy/You Don't Understand Me	1960	$15
❏ 5962	Somebody, Somewhere/Be My Little Chick-A-Dee	1964	$12

LOMA

Number	Title	Yr	NM
❏ 2080	I Got a Good Thing/Lies	1967	$8
❏ 2056	Shadow of Your Love/Soulful Sound of Music	1966	$8

PARKWAY

Number	Title	Yr	NM
❏ 875	She's a Hippy/Whip It Up Baby	1963	$15

FREEMAN BROTHERS, THE

MALA

Number	Title	Yr	NM
❏ 553	I'm Counting on You/Everyday It's You	1966	$30

SOUL

Number	Title	Yr	NM
❏ 35011	My Baby/Beautiful Brown Eyes	1965	$50

FREEMAN, CHARLIE C.

SUN

Number	Title	Yr	NM
❏ 1112	From Saigon to Little Rock/You're More Than...	1970	$5

FREEMAN, ERNIE

IMPERIAL

Number	Title	Yr	NM
❏ 5612	A Summer Love/Always with You	1959	$10
❏ 5677	Autumn and Eve/Prayer	1960	$8
❏ 5633	Big River/Night Sounds	1959	$12
❏ 5769	Conquest/Swingin' Preacher	1961	$8
❏ 5461	Dumplin's/Beautiful Weekend	1957	$20
❏ 5716	Hawaiian Eye/Heartbreak Hotel	1960	$8
❏ 5518	Indian Love Call/Summer Serenade	1958	$15
❏ 5566	Live It Up/Whispering Hope (Freedom and Land)	1959	$10
❏ 5621	Lost Dreams/One More Time Around	1959	$10
❏ 5574	Marshmallows, Popcorn & Soda Pop/Honey Dripper	1959	$10
❏ 5551	School Room Rock/Blues After Hours	1958	$15
❏ 5403	Spring Fever/Walking the Beat	1956	$20
❏ 5732	Swamp Meeting/That's All	1961	$8
❏ 5444	Swing It/River Boat	1957	$20
❏ 5883	The Freeloader/Say It Isn't So	1962	$8
❏ 5752	Theme from "Return to Peyton Place"/Warsaw Concerto	1961	$8
❏ 5693	Theme from "The Dark at the Top of the Stairs"/Come On Home	1960	$8
❏ 5841	The Stripper/I Hear You Knocking	1962	$8
❏ 5486	The Tuttle/Leaps and Bounds	1958	$15
❏ 5793	The Twist/Shine On Harvest Moon	1961	$8
❏ 5815	What Am I Living For/I Didn't Want to Do It	1962	$8
❏ 5430	Without Love/Night Life	1957	$20

LIBERTY

Number	Title	Yr	NM
❏ 55515	Half as Much/I'm Sorry for You My Friend	1962	$8

Number	Title	Yr	NM

FREEMAN, GEORGE
EPIC
❏ 5-10668	I'll Be Long Gone (Make My Life Shine)/Stop Now (There's Still Time)	1971	$15

GARDENA
| ❏ 129 | Sugar Lips/If I Told You | 1962 | $30 |

OKEH
| ❏ 4-7333 | All Right Now/You Lied, I Cried, Love Died | 1969 | $30 |

SHOUT
| ❏ 201 | Why Are You Doing This to Me/I'm Like a Fish | 1966 | $30 |

VALIANT
❏ 6035	Come to Me/You Guessed It	1963	$30
❏ 6039	Down and Out/The Quiver	1963	$250
❏ 6057	One Last Dance/You're Guilty	1964	$30

FREEMAN, PAUL
COLUMBIA
| ❏ 06576 | Carol of the Birds/Adeste Fideles | 1985 | $3 |

FREEPORT
MAINSTREAM
| ❏ 730 | I Need Your Lovin'/(B-side unknown) | 1970 | $10 |

FREEWHEELERS, THE
EPIC
❏ 9725	Beach Boy/Annie	1964	$20
❏ 9700	San Francisco Bay Blues/Susu	1964	$30
❏ 9664	Walk, Walk/The Best of It	1964	$30

FREHLEY, ACE
Also see KISS
ATLANTIC
| ❏ 89072 | Insane/The Acorn Is Spinning | 1988 | $3 |

—As "Frehley's Comet
| ❏ 89072 [PS] | Insane/The Acorn Is Spinning | 1988 | $4 |

—As "Frehley's Comet
| ❏ 89255 [PS] | Into the Night/Fractured Too | 1987 | $4 |

FRENCH, DON
LANCER
| ❏ 105 | Little Blonde Girl/I Look Into My Heart | 1959 | $40 |
| ❏ 104 | Lonely Saturday Night/Goldilocks | 1959 | $30 |

FREY, GLENN
Also see EAGLES; LONGBRANCH PENNYWHISTLE.

ASYLUM
❏ 69857	All Those Lies/That Girl	1982	$4
❏ 47466	I Found Somebody/She Can't Let Go	1982	$4
❏ 47466 [PS]	I Found Somebody/She Can't Let Go	1982	$5
❏ 69974	The One You Love/All Those Lies	1982	$4

MCA
❏ 53497	Livin' Right/Soul Searchin'	1989	$3
❏ 52413	Sexy Girl/Better in the U.S.A.	1984	$3
❏ 52413 [PS]	Sexy Girl/Better in the U.S.A.	1984	$3
❏ 52546	Smuggler's Blues/New Love	1985	$3
❏ 52546 [PS]	Smuggler's Blues/New Love	1985	$3
❏ 53452	Soul Searchin'/It's Cold in Here	1988	$3
❏ 52461	The Allnighter/Smuggler's Blues	1984	$3
❏ 52461 [PS]	The Allnighter/Smuggler's Blues	1984	$3
❏ 52512	The Heat Is On/Shoot Out	1984	$3
❏ 52512 [PS]	The Heat Is On/Shoot Out	1984	$3

—B-side by Harold Faltermeyer
❏ 53363	True Love/Working Man	1988	$3
❏ 53363 [PS]	True Love/Working Man	1988	$3
❏ 53684	Two Hearts/Some Kind of Blue	1989	$3

FRIAR TUCK
MERCURY
| ❏ 72684 | Alley-Oop/Sweet Pea | 1967 | $10 |

FRIEDMAN, KINKY
ABC
| ❏ 12073 | Lover Please/Autograph | 1975 | $6 |
| ❏ 12107 | Wild Man from Borneo/Popeye the Sailor Man | 1975 | $6 |

EPIC
| ❏ 50299 | Catfish/Dear Abby | 1976 | $5 |

Number	Title	Yr	NM

SUNRISE
| ❏ 41932 | Twirl/Hello, Good Mornin' | 1983 | $6 |

—B-side with Ronee Blakely

VANGUARD
| ❏ 35173 | Sold American/Western Union Wire | 1973 | $8 |

FRIEND AND LOVER
ABC
| ❏ 10910 | Town Called Love/If Tomorrow | 1967 | $15 |

CADET CONCEPT
| ❏ 7019 | Hard Lovin'/Colorado Exile | 1970 | $6 |
| ❏ 7019 [PS] | Hard Lovin'/Colorado Exile | 1970 | $20 |

VERVE FORECAST
❏ 5091	If Love Is In Your Heart/Zig Zag	1968	$8
❏ 5100	I Want to Be Free/Circus	1968	$8
❏ 5106	Ode to a Dandelion/A Wise Man Changes His Mind	1969	$6

FRIENDS OF DISTINCTION, THE
RCA VICTOR
❏ 74-0888	Ain't No Woman (Like the One I've Got)/Easy Evil	1973	$5
❏ 74-0416	Check It Out/I Need You	1971	$5
❏ 74-0956	Check It Out/Love Can Make It Easier	1973	$5
❏ 74-0204	Going in Circles/Let Yourself Go	1969	$6
❏ 74-0107	Grazing in the Grass/I Really Hope You Do	1969	$6
❏ PB-10197	Honey Baby Theme Part 1/Honey Baby Theme Part 2	1975	$4
❏ 74-0516	It Don't Matter to Me/Down I Go	1971	$5
❏ 74-0562	Let Me Be/Long Time Comin' My Way	1971	$5
❏ 74-0679	Love Is the Way of Life/Jenny Wants to Know	1972	$5
❏ 74-0319	Love Or Let Me Be Lonely/This Generation	1970	$6
❏ PB-10220	Love Shack Part 1/Love Shack Part 2	1975	$4
❏ 74-0385	Time Waits for No One/Mother Nature	1970	$5

FRIENDS, THE
MGM
| ❏ 14646 | Gonna Have a Good Time/Would You Laugh | 1973 | $6 |
| ❏ 14646 [PS] | Gonna Have a Good Time/Would You Laugh | 1973 | $15 |

FRIJID PINK
LION
❏ 158	Big Betty/Shady Lady	1973	$6
❏ 115	Earth Omen/Lazy Day	1972	$8
❏ 136	Go Now/Lazy Day	1972	$8

PARROT
❏ 340	God Gave Me You/Drivin' Blues	1970	$6
❏ 352	Heartbreak Hotel/Bye Bye Blues	1970	$6
❏ 341	House of the Rising Sun/Drivin' Blues	1970	$6
❏ 360	Lost Son/I Love Her	1971	$6
❏ 355	Music for the People/Sloony	1971	$6
❏ 349	Sing a Song for Freedom/End of the Line	1970	$6
❏ 334	Tell Me Why/Cryin' Shame	1969	$6
❏ 358	We're Gonna Be There/Shorty Kline	1971	$6

FRIZZELL, DAVID
CAPITOL
❏ 3983	I Gave Her Mine/She's Loved Me Away from You	1974	$6
❏ 3934	I'm the Bartender's Best Friend/You Won't Be Happy 'Til I'm Sad	1974	$6
❏ 3787	I've Been Satisfied/Jesus and Joe	1973	$6
❏ 3537	Last Night Was the First Night/Get Out of Town Before Sundown	1973	$6
❏ 3684	Take Me One More Ride/The Bottle, Me, and Joann	1973	$6
❏ 3589	Words Don't Come Easy/It's Too Late to Keep from Losing You	1973	$6

CARTWHEEL
❏ 197	Country Pride/Kicking Sand	1971	$8
❏ 202	Goodbye/500 Times	1971	$8
❏ 211	Shake Hands with the Devil/(B-side unknown)	1972	$8

COLUMBIA
❏ 4-45238	I Just Can't Help Believing/Carmen Jones	1970	$8
❏ 4-45325	In the Arms of Love/Hungry Row	1971	$8
❏ 4-45139	L.A. International Airport/Just Passing Through	1970	$8
❏ 4-41460	Love Baby/My Kind of Love	1959	$30

Number	Title	Yr	NM

| ❏ 4-44995 | Marley Purt Drive/Little Toy Trains | 1969 | $10 |
| ❏ 4-41425 | Tag Along/I Hang My Head and Cry | 1959 | $30 |

COMPLEAT
| ❏ 168 | Beautiful Body/All That I Am | 1987 | $5 |

MCA
❏ 40877	Brand New Tennessee Waltz/Red, Red Wine	1978	$5
❏ 40736	The Oleander/Lifetime Woman	1977	$5
❏ 40786	Why You Been Gone So Long/Lifetime Woman	1977	$5

NASHVILLE AMERICA
| ❏ 1001 | She Ain't Whistlin' Dixie/(B-side unknown) | 1985 | $6 |

RSO
| ❏ 856 | A Case of You/Forever (And Always) | 1976 | $5 |

VIVA
❏ 29498	A Million Light Beers Ago/Sweet Sweet Sin	1983	$3
❏ 29388	Black and White/All the King's Memories	1983	$3
❏ 29066	Country Music Love Affair/Maybe There's Love After All	1985	$3
❏ 29232	When We Get Back to the Farm (That's When We Really Go to Town)/Settin' the Night on Fire	1984	$3
❏ 29617	Where Are You Spending Your Nights These Days/We're Back in Love Again	1983	$3
❏ 29332	Who Dat/Honest Man	1984	$3

WARNER BROS.
| ❏ 50063 | I'm Gonna Hire a Wino to Decorate Our Home/She's Up to All Her Old Tricks Again | 1982 | $4 |
| ❏ 49778 | Lefty/Three Blind Hearts | 1981 | $4 |

—A-side with Merle Haggard; B-side with Shelly West
| ❏ 29901 | Lost My Baby Blues/Single and Alone | 1982 | $4 |

FRIZZELL, LEFTY
ABC
| ❏ 11350 | I Buy the Wine/Let Me Give Her the Flowers | 1973 | $8 |

COLUMBIA
❏ 4-43364	A Little Unfair/Love Looks Good on You	1965	$10
❏ 4-20837	Always Late (With Your Kisses)/Mom and Dad's Waltz	1951	$30
❏ 4-20960	Always Late (With Your Kisses)/Mom and Dad's Waltz	1952	$30
❏ 4-44738	An Article from Life/Only Way to Fly	1969	$10
❏ 4-44390	Anything You Can Spare/A Prayer on Your Lips	1967	$10
❏ 4-20840	Blue Yodel #2/Treasures Untold	1951	$30
❏ 4-20841	Brakeman's Blues/My Old Pal	1951	$30
❏ 4-21102	California Blues/I'm Lonely and Blue	1953	$30
❏ 4-41268	Cigarettes and Coffee Blues/You're Humbuggin' Me	1958	$30
❏ 4-42839	Don't Let Her See Me Cry/James River	1963	$15
❏ 4-20961	Don't Stay Away (Till Love Grows Cold)/If You Can Spare the Time	1952	$30

—The above four comprise a box set
| ❏ 4-20941 | Don't Stay Away (Till Love Grows Cold)/Sad Singin', Slow Ridin' | 1952 | $30 |

—B-side by Polly Possum; part of a 4-record various-artists box set
❏ 4-20911	Don't Stay Away (Till Love Grows Cold)/You're Here, So Everything's All Right	1952	$30
❏ 4-41455	Farther Than My Eyes Can See/Ballad of the Blue and Gray	1959	$30
❏ 4-21488	First to Have a Second Chance/These Hands	1956	$30
❏ 4-42676	Forbidden Lovers/A Few Steps Away	1963	$15
❏ 4-20997	Forever (And Always)/I Know You're Lonesome While Waiting for Me	1952	$30
❏ 4-40867	From an Angel to a Devil/Now That You Are Gone	1957	$30
❏ 4-43169	'Gator Hollow/Make That One for the Road a Cup of Coffee	1964	$15
❏ 4-44205	Get This Stranger Out of Me/Hobo's Pride	1967	$10
❏ 38-04264	Get This Stranger Out of Me/This Just Ain't No Good Day for Leaving	1983	$5
❏ 4-20885	Give Her More, More, More (Of Your Kisses)/How Long Will It Take (To Stop Loving You)	1951	$30

Number	Title	Yr	NM
❏ 4-40818	Glad I Found You/Lullaby Waltz	1957	$30
❏ 4-21554	Heart's Highway/I'm a Boy Left Alone	1956	$30
❏ 4-21084	(Honey, Baby, Hurry) Bring Your Sweet Self Back to Me/Time Changes Things	1953	$30
❏ 4-44984	Honky Tonk Hill/Wasted Way of Life	1969	$12
❏ 4-45347	Honky Tonk Stardust Cowboy/What Am I Gonna Do	1971	$10
❏ 4-21169	Hopeless Love/Then I'll Come Back to You	1953	$30
❏ 4-42253	I Feel Sorry for Me/So What, Let It Rain	1961	$20
❏ 4-20950	If You Can Spare the Time/It's Just You	1952	$30
❏ 4-20739	If You've Got the Money, I've Got the Time/I Love You a Thousand Ways	1950	$50
❏ 4-20958	If You've Got the Money, I've Got the Time/Look What Thoughts Will Do	1952	$30
❏ 4-43747	I Just Couldn't See the Forest (For the Trees)/Everything Keeps Coming Back (But You)	1966	$10
❏ 4-21393	I'll Sit Alone and Cry/Moonlight Darling and You	1955	$30
❏ 4-20959	I Love You a Thousand Ways/I Want to Be with You Always	1952	$30
❏ 4-21328	I Love You Mostly/Mama	1954	$30
❏ 4-21034	I'm an Old, Old Man (Tryin' to Live While I Can)/You're Just Mine (Only in My Dreams)	1952	$30
❏ 4-40938	Is It Only That You're Lonely/No One to Talk To	1957	$30
❏ 4-21458	It Gets Late So Early/Your Tomorrows Will Never Come	1955	$30
❏ 4-20799	I Want to Be With You Always/My Baby's Just Like Money	1951	$30
❏ 4-41984	Looking for You/Heaven's Plan	1961	$20
❏ 4-20772	Look What Thoughts Will Do/Shine, Shave, Shower (It's Saturday)	1951	$30
❏ 4-21366	Making Believe/A Forest Fire	1955	$30
❏ 4-45145	My Baby Is a Tramp/She Brought Love, Sweet Love	1970	$10
❏ 4-21208	My Little Her and Him/I've Been Away Way Too Long	1954	$30
❏ 4-20843	My Rough and Rowdy Ways/Lullaby Yodel	1951	$30
—The above four comprise a box set (20842 was also available separately)			
❏ 4-21506	Promises Promises/Today Is That Tomorrow	1956	$30
❏ 4-42924 [DJ]	Saginaw, Michigan (same on both sides)	1963	$40
—Promo only on blue vinyl			
❏ 4-42924	Saginaw, Michigan/When It Rains the Blues	1963	$15
❏ 4-43256	She's Gone Gone Gone/Confused	1965	$10
❏ 4-41635	She's Gone/My Blues Will Pass	1960	$20
❏ 4-41161	Silence/The Torch Within My Heart	1958	$30
❏ 4-42521	Stranger/Just Passing Through	1962	$20
❏ 4-21433	Sweet Lies/I'm Lost Between Right and Wrong	1955	$30
❏ 4-41384	The Long Black Veil/Knock Again, True Love	1959	$30
❏ 4-44563	The Marriage Bit/When the Grass Grows Green Again	1968	$10
❏ 4-45310	Three Cheers for the Good Guys/I Must Be Getting Over You	1971	$10
❏ 4-41080	Time Out for the Blues/Tell Me Dear	1957	$30
❏ 4-20842	Travellin' Blues/Blue Yodel #6	1951	$30
❏ 4-21142	Two Friends of Mine/Before You Go	1953	$30
❏ 4-44692	Wasted Way of Life/Keep the Flowers Watered When I'm Gone	1968	$10
❏ 38-04480	Watermelon Time in Georgia/Everything Keeps Coming Back to You	1984	$5
❏ 4-45197	Watermelon Time in Georgia/Out of You	1970	$10
❏ 4-21118	We Crucified Our Jesus/When It Comes to Measuring Love	1953	$30
❏ 4-41751	What You Gonna Do Leroy/That's All I Can Remember	1960	$20
❏ 4-43590	Writing on the Wall/Mama	1966	$10

7-Inch Extended Plays

Number	Title	Yr	NM
❏ B-2802 [B]	*Always Late (With Your Kisses)/Mom and Dad's Waltz/If You've Got the Money, I've Got the Time/I Love You a Thousand Ways	1957	$25

FROGMEN, THE

CANDIX
| ❏ 326 | Beware Below/Tioga | 1961 | $30 |

SCOTT
| ❏ 101 | Seahorse Flats/Tioga | 1961 | $60 |

TEE JAY
| ❏ 131 | Sea Haunt/Diamond Back | 1964 | $100 |
| —Blue vinyl | | | |

FROGS, THE

MUMS
| ❏ 6025 | Alfie, the Christmas Tree/Tweedlee Dee | 1973 | $5 |

FROLIC, HARVEY

HIT
❏ 148	Chug-a-Lug/Lonesome Fool	1964	$8
—B-side by Joanne Kay			
❏ 131	Dang Me/The Girl from Ipanema	1964	$8
—B-side by Betty Coleson			
❏ 181	Midnight Special/Sha La La	1965	$15
—B-side by the Spartas			
❏ 105	Talking About My Baby/You Don't Know Me	1964	$8
—B-side by Bill Austin			
❏ 91	The Matador/Maria Elena	1963	$8
—B-side by the Music City Five			
❏ 23	Things/Heart in Hand	1962	$8
—B-side by Connie Landers			

FROLIC, ROGER

HIT
| ❏ 267 | My Uncle Used to Love Me But She Died/Almost Persuaded | 1966 | $8 |
| —B-side by Leroy Jones | | | |

FRONT PAGE NEWS

DIAL
| ❏ 4052 | Thoughts/You Better Behave | 1967 | $30 |

FROST, DAVID, AND BILLY TAYLOR

BELL
| ❏ 950 | House of Christmas/Away in a Manger | 1970 | $6 |

FROST, FRANK

JEWEL
❏ 765	My Back Scratcher/Harp and Soul	1966	$20
❏ 778	Pocketful of Money/Ride with Your Daddy Tonight	1967	$30
❏ 771	Things You Do/Harpin' On It	1966	$20

FROST, MAX, AND THE TROOPERS

SIDEWALK
| ❏ 938 | There Is a Party Going On/Stomper's Ride | 1968 | $20 |

TOWER
❏ 452	52%/Max Frost Theme	1968	$20
❏ 452 [PS]	52%/Max Frost Theme	1968	$30
❏ 478	Paxton Quigley's Had the Course/Sittin' in Circles	1969	$20
❏ 478 [PS]	Paxton Quigley's Had the Course/Sittin' in Circles	1969	$30
❏ 419	Shape of Things to Come/Free Lovin'	1968	$20
❏ 419 [PS]	Shape of Things to Come/Free Lovin'	1968	$60
—Promo-only sleeve with message to DJs on back			

FROST, THE

DATE
❏ 1577	Bad Girl/Rainy Day	1967	$15
—As "Dick Wagner and the Frosts			
❏ 1596	Little Girl/Sunshine	1968	$15
—As "Dick Wagner and the Frosts			

VANGUARD
| ❏ 35115 | A Long Way from Home/Black As Night | 1970 | $8 |
| ❏ 35099 | Linda/Sweet Lady Love | 1969 | $8 |

FROST, THOMAS AND RICHARD

IMPERIAL
❏ 66451	Hello Stranger/Fairy Tale Affair	1970	$12
❏ 66405	She's Got Love/The Word Is Love	1969	$8
❏ 66426	With Me My Love/Gotta Find a New Place to Stay	1969	$10

UNI
| ❏ 55320 | Got to Find the Light/St. Petersburg | 1972 | $10 |
| ❏ 55320 | Mona Lisas and Mad Hatters/Kentucky Moon | 1972 | $10 |

FRUMIOUS BANDERSNATCH
7-Inch Extended Plays

MUGGLES GRAMOPHONE WORKS
❏ 0(no cat #) [PS]	Frumious Bandersnatch	1967	$250
❏ 0(no cat #)	Hearts to Cry/Misty Cloudy//Cheshire	1967	$250
—Legitimate copies show purple vinyl when held to a light; all others are counterfeits			

FRUMMOX

PROBE
| ❏ 470 | Mary Martin/There You Go | 1970 | $8 |

FRUSHAY, RAY

PARAMOUNT
| ❏ 0069 | Let the Heartaches Begin/(B-side unknown) | 1970 | $8 |
| ❏ 0030 | Santa Ana Winds/(B-side unknown) | 1970 | $8 |

FRUT

WESTBOUND
| ❏ 189 | Prison of Love/Send Me Down | 1972 | $10 |

FRYE, DAVID

ELEKTRA
| ❏ 45722 | My Way/Farm Report | 1971 | $10 |

FUGS, THE

ESP-DISK'
| ❏ 4507 | Frenzy/I Want to Know | 1966 | $40 |

FULL FORCE

COLUMBIA
❏ 38-68975	Ain't My Type of Hype/The Man Upstairs	1989	$3
❏ 38-05623	Alice, I Want You Just for Me!/Alice (Ecrof's Favorite Mix)	1985	$4
❏ 38-07705	All in My Mind/The Mind (F.F. Mellow Mix)	1988	$3
❏ 38-07705 [PS]	All in My Mind/The Mind (F.F. Mellow Mix)	1988	$3
❏ 38-73025	Friends B-4 Lovers/Make Love to My Mind	1989	$5
❏ 38-05395	Girl If You Take Me Home/Let's Dance Against the Wall	1985	$4
❏ 38-07594	Love Is for Suckers (Like Me and You)/Sucker Punch!	1987	$3
❏ 38-07594 [PS]	Love Is for Suckers (Like Me and You)/Sucker Punch!	1987	$3
❏ 38-06600	Old Flames Never Die/Body Heavenly	1987	$3
❏ 38-06600 [PS]	Old Flames Never Die/Body Heavenly	1987	$3
❏ 38-08086	Take Care of Homework/3 O'Clock ... School's Out	1988	$4
❏ 38-06116	Temporary Love Thing/Temporary Bow-Legged Theater	1986	$4

FULL MOON

DOUGLAS
| ❏ ZS76506 | To Know/(B-side unknown) | 1972 | $8 |

FULLER, BOBBY, FOUR

CAPITOL
| ❏ 3038 | The Only God I Know/A Name Like Watermelon | 1971 | $30 |

DONNA
| ❏ 1403 | Those Memories of You/Our Favorite Martian | 1965 | $200 |
| —As "Bobby Fuller and the Fantastics | | | |

EXETER
| ❏ 126 | Fool of Love/Shakedown | 1964 | $120 |
| ❏ 124 | I Fought the Law/She's My Girl | 1964 | $350 |

LIBERTY
| ❏ 55812 | Let Her Dance/Another Sad and Lonely Night | 1965 | $40 |

MUSTANG
❏ 3014	I Fought the Law/Little Annie Lou	1966	$20
❏ 3006	Let Her Dance/Another Sad and Lonely Night	1965	$20
❏ 3012	Let Her Dance/Another Sad and Lonely Night	1965	$20
❏ 3016	Love's Made a Fool of You/Don't Ever Let Me Know	1966	$20
❏ 3018	Magic Touch/My True Love	1966	$15
❏ 3004	She's My Girl/Take My Hand	1965	$30

TODD
| ❏ 1090 | Saturday Night/The Stinger | 1963 | $125 |

YUCCA
| ❏ 144 | My Heart Jumped/Gently My Love | 1961 | $100 |

Number	Title	Yr	NM

FULLER BROTHERS, THE

CHALLENGE
❏ 9145	Ballad of the Midnight Special/The Gallows Tree	1962	$30
❏ 9119	Moon River/Framed, Convicted and Condemned	1961	$30

FULLER, JERRY
Also see THE FLEAS; THE FULLER BROTHERS.

ABC
❏ 12436	Salt on the Wound/No Time	1978	$4

BELL
❏ 45433	Arianne/(B-side unknown)	1974	$5
❏ 45295	Bookends/(B-side unknown)	1972	$5
❏ 45349	Lazy Susan/How Do We Stand	1973	$5

CHALLENGE
❏ 59074	Above and Beyond/One Heart	1960	$30

— With Diane Maxwell
❏ 59052	Betty My Angel/Memories of You	1959	$40
❏ 59252	Don't Let Go/Roses Love Sunshine	1964	$20
❏ 59307	Don't Look at Me Like That/What Happened to the Music	1965	$20
❏ 59329	Double Life/Turn to Me	1966	$30
❏ 59235	Footprints in the Snow/Hollywood Star	1964	$20
❏ 9184	Give My Love to Christy/Dear Teresa	1963	$30
❏ 59085	Gone for the Summer/Anna from Louisiana	1960	$30
❏ 9114	Guilty of Loving You/First Love Never Dies	1961	$30
❏ 59279	I Get Carried Away/Am I That Easy to Forget	1965	$40
❏ 59217	I Only Came to Dance with You/Young Land	1963	$30
❏ 59315	Man in Black/Master Plan	1965	$20
❏ 59104	Shy Away/Heavenly	1961	$30
❏ 59057	Tennessee Waltz/Charlene	1959	$30
❏ 9128	The Place Where I Cry/Poor Little Heart	1961	$30
❏ 9148	Too Many People/Willingly, I'll Let You Go	1962	$30
❏ 59068	Two Loves Have I/I Dreamed About My Lover	1960	$30
❏ 9132	Wake Up Sleeping Beauty/Trust Me	1962	$30
❏ 9161	Why Do They Say Goodbye/Let Me Be with You	1962	$30

COLUMBIA
❏ 4-45131	Could It Be/I Know We Can Make It	1970	$8
❏ 4-45209	Go/If I Had a Mind To	1970	$8

LIN
❏ 5015	A Certain Smile/Angel from Above	1958	$40
❏ 5011	Blue Memories/I Found a New Love	1958	$40
❏ 5012	Do You Love Me/Teenage Love	1958	$40
❏ 5019	Lipstick and Rouge/Mother Goose at the Bandstand	1959	$40
❏ 5016	The Door Is Open/Through Eternity	1958	$40

MCA
❏ 41114	Don't Do Anything/Don't Tell Me	1979	$4
❏ 41022	Lines/Over You	1979	$4

FULLER, JOHNNY

ALADDIN
❏ 3286	Cruel, Cruel World/My Heart Beats for You	1955	$70

FLAIR
❏ 1054	Buddy/Hard Times	1955	$200

HOLLYWOOD
❏ 1063	Comin' Round the Corner/Roughest Place in Town	1956	$100
❏ 1057	Mean Old World/How Long	1956	$100
❏ 1077	My Mama Told Me/Too Late to Change My Mind	1956	$100
❏ 1084	Sunny Road/I Can't Succeed	1957	$100
❏ 1043	Train Train Blues/Bad Luck Overtook Me	1955	$100

IMPERIAL
❏ 5580	Heavenly Love/Whispering Wind	1959	$30
❏ 5697	Miss You/Stop, Look and Listen	1960	$30

IRMA
❏ 110	First Stage of the Blues/No More, No More	1958	$100
❏ 106	Weeping and Mourning/Strange Land	1958	$100

MONEY
❏ 206	I Walk All Night/These Young Girls	1955	$70

SPECIALTY
❏ 655	Haunted House/The Mighty Hand	1959	$30

❏ 671	Swingin' at the Creek/Many Rivers, Mighty Seas	1959	$30

FULSON, LOWELL

ALADDIN
❏ 3233	Blues Never Fail/You've Gotta Reap	1954	$100
❏ 3217	Don't Leave Me Baby/Check with the Boys	1954	$100
❏ 3088	Double Trouble/Good Woman Blues	1951	$200

CASH
❏ 1051	Love Society Blues/Blue Shadows	1957	$50

CHECKER
❏ 854	Blues Rhumba/Please Don't Go	1957	$30
❏ 952	Comin' Home/Have You Changed Your Mind	1960	$30
❏ 865	Don't Drive Me, Baby/You're Gonna Miss Me	1957	$30
❏ 959	I'm Glad You Reconsidered/Blue Shadows	1960	$30
❏ 841	It's Your Fault, Baby/Tollin' Bells	1956	$40
❏ 937	It Took a Long Time/That's Alright	1960	$30
❏ 972	I Want to Know (Part 1)/I Want to Know (Part 2)	1961	$20
❏ 882	I Want to Make Love to You/Rock This Morning	1958	$30
❏ 820	Lonely Hours/Do Me Right	1955	$40
❏ 812	Loving You (Is All I Crave)/Check Yourself	1955	$50
❏ 1027	Shed No Tears/Can She	1962	$20
❏ 992	So Many Tears/Hung Down Head	1961	$20
❏ 829	Trouble, Trouble/I Still Love You Baby	1955	$40
❏ 1046	Trouble with the Blues/Love Grows Cold	1963	$20

GRANITE
❏ 533	Do You Love Me/A Step at a Time	1975	$5
❏ 538	The Old Blues Singer/Monday Morning Blues	1976	$5

HOLLYWOOD
❏ 1029	Everyday I Have the Blues/Guitar Shuffle	1955	$60
❏ 1103	Everyday I Have the Blues/Guitar Shuffle	1962	$20
❏ 1022	The Original Lonesome Christmas Part 1/The Original Lonesome Christmas Part 2	1955	$30

JEWEL
❏ 827	Change of Heart/Every Second a Fool Is Born	1972	$6
❏ 808	Don't Leave Me/Thug	1970	$8
❏ 811	Do You Feel It/Don't Destroy Me	1970	$8
❏ 805	How Do You Want Your Man/Sleeper	1969	$8
❏ 801	Letter Home/Lady in the Rain	1969	$8
❏ 813	Lonesome Christmas (Part 1)/Lonesome Christmas (Part 2)	1970	$6
❏ 832	Look at You Baby/Fed Up	1972	$6
❏ 818	My Baby/Bluesway	1971	$6
❏ 820	Teach Me/Man of Motion	1971	$6
❏ 802	Why Don't We Do It in the Road/Too Soon	1969	$10

KENT
❏ 431	Black Nights/Little Angel	1965	$10
❏ 443	Blues Around Midnight/Talkin' Woman	1966	$10
❏ 489	Blues Pain/Mellow Together	1968	$10
❏ 448	Change Your Ways/My Aching Back	1966	$10
❏ 466	Everyday I Have the Blues/No Hard Feelings	1967	$12
❏ 395	Every Time It Rains/Just One More Time	1964	$15
❏ 395	Every Time It Rains/My Heart Belongs to You	1964	$15
❏ 471	I Cried/The Well	1967	$10
❏ 474	I'm a Drifter/Hobo Meetin'	1967	$10
❏ 477	I Wanna Spend Christmas with You Part 1/I Wanna Spend Christmas with You Part 2	1967	$15
❏ 4535	Let's Go Get Stoned/Funky Broadway	1970	$8
❏ 505	Lovin' Touch/Price for Love	1969	$10
❏ 463	Make a Little Love/I'm Sinking	1967	$10
❏ 463 [PS]	Make a Little Love/I'm Sinking	1967	$30
❏ 440	Sittin' Here Thinkin'/Shattered Dreams	1966	$10
❏ 410	Strange Feeling/What's Gonna Be	1965	$15
❏ 497	Sweetest Thing/What the Heck	1968	$10
❏ 486	The Letter/Let's Go Get Stoned	1968	$10
❏ 452	The Trouble I'm In/Ask at Any Door in Town	1966	$10
❏ 479	Tomorrow/Push Me	1968	$10

❏ 456	Tramp/Pico	1966	$10

MOVIN'
❏ 128	Stop and Think/Baby	1964	$15

PARROT
❏ 787	I've Been Mistreated/Juke Box Shuffle	1953	$125

— Black vinyl
❏ 787	I've Been Mistreated/Juke Box Shuffle	1953	$200

— Red vinyl

SWING TIME
❏ 308	Black Widow Spider/Midnight Showers of Rain	1953	$60
❏ 335	Cash Box Boogie/My Daily Prayer	1954	$60
❏ 295	Guitar Shuffle/Mean Old Lonesome Song	1952	$60
❏ 243	I'm a Night Owl (Part 1)/I'm a Night Owl (Part 2)	1951	$125
❏ 338	I've Been Mistreated/Juke Box Shuffle	1954	$60
❏ 289	Let's Live Right/Best Wishes	1952	$60
❏ 242	Lonesome Christmas (Part 1)/Lonesome Christmas (Part 2)	1951	$70

— 78 released in 1950; 45 released in 1951
❏ 330	The Blues Come Rollin' In/I Love My Baby	1954	$60
❏ 272	Why Can't You Cry for Me/Blues with a Feeling	1951	$200

— This has been confirmed to exist on 45

FUN AND GAMES

UNI
❏ 55086	Elephant Candy/The Way She Smiles	1968	$15
❏ 55128	Gotta Say Goodbye/We	1969	$15
❏ 55098	The Grooviest Girl in the World/It Must Have Been the Wind	1968	$15

FUN SONS, THE

CAMEO
❏ 478	Hang Ten/Don't Hold It Against Me	1967	$30

FUNK INC.
❏ 754	The Thrill Is Gone/Bowlegs	1973	$6
❏ 752	Whipper (Part 1)/Whipper (Part 2)	1972	$6

FUNKADELIC
Also see PARLIAMENT.

MCA
❏ 53654	By Way of the Drum/(Instrumental)	1989	$3

WARNER BROS.
❏ 8735	Cholly (Funk Getting Ready to Roll)/Into You	1979	$5
❏ 8618	One Nation Under a Groove (Part 1)/One Nation Under a Groove (Part 2)	1978	$5
❏ 8618 [PS]	One Nation Under a Groove (Part 1)/One Nation Under a Groove (Part 2)	1978	$5
❏ 49807	Shockwaves/Bullino's Bounce	1981	$4
❏ 49667	The Electric Spanking of War Babies/The Electric Spanking of War Babies (Part 2)	1981	$4
❏ 49667 [PS]	The Electric Spanking of War Babies/The Electric Spanking of War Babies (Part 2)	1981	$5

WESTBOUND
❏ 5014	Better by the Pound/Stuffs and Things	1975	$8
❏ 185	Can You Get to That/Back in Our Minds	1971	$10
❏ 218	Cosmic Slop/If You Don't Like the Effects, Don't Produce the Cause	1973	$12
❏ 198	Hit It and Quit It/A Whole Lot of B.S.	1972	$12
❏ 158	I Got a Thing, You Got a Thing, Everybody's Got a Thing/Fish, Chips and Sweat	1970	$10
❏ 150	I'll Bet You/Open Your Eyes	1969	$10
❏ 197	I Miss My Baby/Baby I Owe You Something Good	1972	$10

— As "U.S. Music with Funkadelic
❏ 167	I Wanna Know If It's Good to You?/I Wanna Know If It's Good to You? (Part 2)	1970	$10
❏ 5026	Let's Take It to the Stage/Bilogical Speculation	1976	$8
❏ 148	Music for My Mother/(Instrumental)	1969	$10
❏ 224	Standing on the Verge of Getting It On/Jimmy's Got a Little Bit of Bitch in Him	1974	$10

Number	Title	Yr	NM
FUNKADELIC (2)			
LAX			
❏ 70055	Connections and Disconnections/The Witch	1981	$4
FUNKY COMMUNICATIONS COMMITTEE			
FREE FLIGHT			
❏ PB-11595	Baby I Want You/That Didn't Hurt Too Bad	1979	$6
❏ PB-11744	It Took a Woman Like You/Woman	1979	$6
—As "FCC			
RCA			
❏ PB-12054	Do You Believe in Magic/Changes	1980	$6
—As "FCC			
FUNKY KINGS			
ARISTA			
❏ 0209	Slow Dancing/Nothing Was Exchanged	1976	$5
—A-side was remade by Johnny Rivers as "Swayin' to the Music			
FUNT, ALLEN			
CAMEO			
❏ 294	Cee Cee's Theme/Theme from The Young Ones	1964	$10
FURAY, RICHIE			
ASYLUM			
❏ 45520	Dance a Little Light/Ooh Dreamer	1978	$5
❏ 46534	I Still Have Dreams/Headin' South	1979	$5
❏ 46534 [DJ]	Lonely Too Long (stereo/mono)	1979	$8
—Promo only; appears to have been the originally planned first single from the "I Still Have Dreams" LP but was changed in favor of the title song			
❏ 46599	Oooh Child/Come On	1980	$5
❏ 45351	Still Rolling Stones/Starlight	1976	$6
❏ 45487	This Magic Moment/Bittersweet Love	1978	$5
FURY, BILLY			
LONDON			
❏ 9594	Because of Love/Like I've Never Loved Before	1963	$20
❏ 1925	Colette/Baby How I Cried	1960	$30
❏ 9615	Don't Walk Away/When Will I Say I Love You	1963	$20
❏ 1991	Halfway to Paradise/Cross My Heart	1961	$30
❏ 9662	Hippy Hippy Shake/Glad All Over	1964	$20
❏ 9515	I'll Never Find Another You/Don't Jump	1962	$20
❏ 9740	I'm Lost Without You/Go Ahead and Ask Her	1965	$20
❏ 9675	I Will/What Am I Living For	1964	$20
❏ 1857	Maybe Tomorrow/Gonna Type a Letter	1959	$30
❏ 9548	Once Upon a Dream/Running Around	1962	$20
❏ 2004	Stick Around/Coming Up in the World	1961	$30
MALA			
❏ 595	Beyond the Shadow of a Doubt/Baby Do You Love Me	1968	$12
❏ 569	Loving You/I'll Go Along With It	1967	$10
❏ 12018	Silly Boy Blue/One Minute Woman	1968	$10
❏ 583	Suzanne in the Mirror/It Just Don't Matter Now	1968	$10
PARROT			
❏ 9692	Baby What You Want Me to Do/It's Only Make Believe	1964	$20
UNITED ARTISTS			
❏ 968	In Thoughts of You/Away from You	1966	$15
❏ 50061	She's So Far Out She's In/Give Me Your Word	1966	$15
FURYS, THE (1)			
EDSEL			
❏ 786	So Tough/I've Got a Pain in My Head (Over You)	1961	$70
LIBERTY			
❏ 55692	Baby You Can Bet Your Boots/The Man Who Has Everything	1964	$60
❏ 55719	If I Didn't Have a Dime/Dream	1964	$60
MACK IV			
❏ 114	If There's a Next Time/Another Fella	1963	$40
❏ 115	I Really Feel So Good/Always	1963	$50
❏ 118	What Is Soul/I Lost My Baby	1963	$50
WORLD PACIFIC			
❏ 386	Cat 'n Mouse/Anything for You	1964	$40

Number	Title	Yr	NM
FURYS, THE (2)			
CUCA			
❏ 1010	This Way Out/St. Louis Blues	1960	$40
FURYS, THE (3)			
FLEETWOOD			
❏ 4569	I Walk Away/Gone in the Night	1966	$40
LAURIE			
❏ 3382	I Walk Away/Gone in the Night	1967	$15
FURYS, THE (4)			
LAVENDER			
❏ 1926	Merryman/Sand Flea	1963	$30
❏ 1806	Parchman Farm/Beachin'	1962	$30
FURYS, THE (5)			
STUDIO CITY			
❏ 1026	Baby What's Wrong/Little Queenie	1965	$40
FURYS, THE (6)			
BEAT			
❏ 02	Moving Target/We Talk, We Dance	1979	$30
❏ 02 [PS]	Moving Target/We Talk, We Dance	1979	$30
DOUBLE R			
❏ 1010	Hey Ma/Jim Stark Dark	1977	$12
❏ 1010 [PS]	Hey Ma/Jim Stark Dark	1977	$12
❏ 1011	Say Goodbye to the Black Sheep/Suburbia Suburbia	1978	$6
❏ 1011 [PS]	Say Goodbye to the Black Sheep/Suburbia Suburbia	1978	$6
FURYS, THE (U)			
DIAMOND			
❏ 242	That's All Right You're in Love/You're My Little Baby	1968	$15
FUSE			
Early version of Cheap Trick.			
EPIC			
❏ 10514	Cruisin' for Burgers/Hound Dog	1969	$30
FUT, THE			
BEACON			
❏ 160	Have You Heard the Word/Futting	1970	$12
FUT			
❏ 160	Have You Heard the Word/Futting	1976	$5
FUTURE, FREDDY			
PARKWAY			
❏ 832	Don't Forget Me/Like Soiree	1961	$15
FUTURE, THE			
UNI			
❏ 55082	The Shape of Things to Come/52%	1968	$8
FUTURES, THE			
AMJO			
❏ 3033	Breaking Up/Our Thing	1971	$40
AVALANCHE			
❏ 36000	Breaking Up/Our Thing	1971	$30
BUDDAH			
❏ 462	Castles/(I Feel the) Ice Breaking	1975	$20
GAMBLE			
❏ ZS72502	Love Is Here/Stay with Me	1972	$30
PHILADELPHIA INT'L.			
❏ ZS83674	Ain't No Time Fa Nothin'/Someone Special (You're the One)	1979	$50
❏ 3747	In Answer to Your Question/Let's Dance Together	1980	$60
❏ ZS83661	Party Time Man/You Got It (The Love That I Need)	1978	$70
❏ 3119	Silhouettes/We're Gonna Make It Somehow	1980	$30
FUZZ, THE			
CALLA			
❏ 174	I Love You for All Seasons/I Love You for All Seasons (Part 2)	1970	$6
❏ 179	I'm So Glad/All About Love	1971	$6
❏ 177	Like an Open Door/Leave It All Behind Me	1971	$6
❏ 183	Mr. Heartache and Miss Tears/Do Just What You Can	1971	$6

Number	Title	Yr	NM
G			
G-CLEFS, THE			
LOMA			
❏ 2048	I Can't Stand It/Whirlwind	1966	$10
❏ 2034	Party '66/Little Lonely Boy	1966	$12
PARIS			
❏ 502	Symbol of Love/Love Her in the Mornin'	1957	$40
PILGRIM			
❏ 720	'Cause You're Mine/Please Write While I'm Away	1956	$40
REGINA			
❏ 1319	Angel Listen to Me/Nobody But Betty	1964	$30
❏ 1314	To the Winner Goes the Prize/I Believe in All I Feel	1964	$40
TERRACE			
❏ 7514	All My Trials/Big Train	1963	$30
❏ 7510	A Lover's Prayer/Sitting in the Moonlight	1962	$30
❏ 7503	Girl Has to Know/Lad (There Never Was a Dog Like You)	1962	$30
❏ 7500	I Understand (Just How You Feel)/Little Girl I Love You	1961	$30
❏ 7507	Make Up Your Mind/They'll Call Me Away	1962	$30
VEEP			
❏ 1218	I Have/On the Other Side of Town	1965	$20
❏ 1226	This Time/On the Other Side of Town	1965	$20
G.T.O.'S, THE (1)			
CLARIDGE			
❏ 312	She Rides with Me/Rudy Vahoo	1966	$30
—Reissue of Claridge 304 by "Joey and the Continentals			
PARKWAY			
❏ 108	Girl from New York City/Missing Out on the Fun	1966	$20
GABRIEL AND THE ANGELS			
AMY			
❏ 802	Chumba/Hey	1960	$30
APRIL			
❏ 1102	Chumba/Hey	1960	$60
NORMAN			
❏ 510	Gabriel, Blow Your Horn (Part 1)/Gabriel, Blow Your Horn (Part 2)	1961	$20
❏ 506	I'm Gabriel/Ginza	1961	$20
❏ 514	Miss You So/See See Rider	1962	$20
—As "Gabriel and His Trumpet			
SWAN			
❏ 4118	That's Life/Don't Wanna Twist No More	1962	$20
—No subtitle on A-side			
❏ 4118	That's Life (That's Tough)/Don't Wanna Twist No More	1962	$15
❏ 4133	The Peanut Butter Song/All Work and No Play	1963	$15
GABRIEL, PETER			
Also see GENESIS.			
ATCO			
❏ 7079	Solsbury Hill/Moribund the Burgermeister	1977	$12
ATLANTIC			
❏ 3479	D.I.Y. (Do It Yourself)/Mother of Violence	1978	$12
❏ 7-89668	Walk Through the Fire/Making a Big Mistake	1984	$4
❏ 7-89668 [PS]	Walk Through the Fire/Making a Big Mistake	1984	$4
GEFFEN			
❏ 28503	Big Time/We Do What We're Told (milgram's 37)	1986	$3
❏ 28503 [PS]	Big Time/We Do What We're Told (milgram's 37)	1986	$3
❏ 28463	Don't Give Up/Curtains	1987	$3
—A-side: Peter Gabriel/Kate Bush			
❏ 28463 [PS]	Don't Give Up/Curtains	1987	$3
❏ 28622	In Your Eyes/In Your Eyes (Special Mix)	1986	$3
❏ 28622 [PS]	In Your Eyes/In Your Eyes (Special Mix)	1986	$3
❏ PRO-S-2602 [DJ]	In Your Eyes (LP Version) (same on both sides)	1986	$10
❏ 29883	Shock the Monkey/Soft Dog	1982	$5
❏ 28718	Sledgehammer/Don't Break This Rhythm	1986	$3
❏ 28718 [PS]	Sledgehammer/Don't Break This Rhythm	1986	$3
❏ 29542	Solsbury Hill (Live)/I Go Swimming	1983	$5
MERCURY			
❏ 76063	Games Without Frontiers/Lead a Normal Life	1980	$4

Number	Title	Yr	NM
❑ 76063 [PS]	Games Without Frontiers/Lead a Normal Life	1980	$15
❑ 76086 [DJ]	I Don't Remember (same on both sides)	1980	$8

— Promos are much more common than stock copies

Number	Title	Yr	NM
❑ 76086	I Don't Remember/Shosholoza	1980	$20

WTG

| ❑ 68977 | In Your Eyes/In Your Eyes (Live Version) | 1989 | $3 |
| ❑ 68936 | In Your Eyes/Skankin' to the Beat | 1989 | $4 |

— B-side by Fishbone

GADABOUTS, THE

JARO

| ❑ 77022 | Caress Me/Deep Are the Roots of a Happy Home | 1960 | $20 |

MERCURY

❑ 70823	Busy Body Rock/All My Love Belongs to You	1956	$30
❑ 70495	By the Waters of the Minnetonka/Giuseppe Mandolino	1954	$30
❑ 70581	Go Boom Boom/Oochi Pachi	1955	$30
❑ 70898	Stranded in the Jungle/Blues Train	1956	$30
❑ 70978	Too Much Monkey Business/To Be with You	1956	$30

WING

❑ 90062	Busy Body Rock/All My Love Belongs to You	1956	$30
❑ 90043	Teenage Rock/If You Only Had a Heart	1955	$30
❑ 90008	Two Things I Love/Glass Heart	1955	$30

GADDY, BOB

DOT

| ❑ 1185 | Honey Stealin' Blues/Hold That Train, Conductor | 1954 | $125 |

— As "Doctor Gaddy and His Orchestra"

HARLEM

| ❑ 2330 | The Blues Has Walked in My Room/Slow Down Baby | 1954 | $200 |

OLD TOWN

❑ 1085	Don't Tell Her/Could I	1960	$30
❑ 1077	Early One Morning/What Wrong Did I Do	1960	$30
❑ 1031	I Love My Baby/Operator	1956	$30
❑ 1162	I Love My Baby/Operator	1964	$15
❑ 1039	Paper Lady/Out of My Name	1957	$30
❑ 1070	Till the Day I Die/I'll Go My Way	1959	$30
❑ 1064	What Would I Do/Paper Lady	1959	$30
❑ 1050	Woe, Woe Is Me/Rip and Run	1958	$30

GADSON, MEL

BIG TOP

| ❑ 3034 | Comin' Down with Love/I'm Getting Sentimental Over You | 1959 | $30 |

GAILTONES, THE

DECCA

| ❑ 30726 | Lover Boy/Please Don't Go | 1958 | $50 |

GAINES, ROY

CHART

| ❑ 606 | Loud Mouth Lucy/I'm Setting You Free | 1955 | $70 |

DEL-FI

| ❑ 4169 | What Is This Thing Called Love/Lizzie | 1961 | $20 |

DELUXE

| ❑ 6147 | Annabelle/Night Beat | 1957 | $30 |
| ❑ 6119 | Isabella/Gainesville | 1957 | $30 |

GROOVE

| ❑ 0161 | Worried 'Bout You Baby/All My Life | 1956 | $40 |

RCA VICTOR

| ❑ 47-7243 | Skippy Is a Sissy/Weeping Willow | 1958 | $70 |

GALAXIES, THE

CAPITOL

| ❑ 4427 | Big Triangle/Until the Next Time | 1960 | $20 |

CHESS

| ❑ 1757 | This Rock and Roll/6:15 | 1960 | $30 |

DOT

| ❑ 16212 | My Blue Heaven/Tremble | 1961 | $30 |

ETIQUETTE

❑ 17	I'm a Worker/Make Love to Me Baby	1965	$30
❑ 25	I (Who Have Nothing)/I Am Yours	1966	$30
❑ 20	On the Beach/She Said I Do	1965	$30

GUARANTEED

| ❑ 216 | My Tattle Tale/Love Has Its Way | 1960 | $60 |

— Eddie Cochran plays guitar on this record

PANORAMA

| ❑ 54 | Along Comes the Man/She Said I Do | 1966 | $10 |

RICHIE

| ❑ 458 | Dear Someone/The Leopard | 1961 | $80 |

SEAFAIR

| ❑ 110 | Shaken/Tacoma | 1964 | $20 |

GALAXYS, THE

CARTHAY

| ❑ 103 | A Lover's Prayer/Jelly Bean | 1959 | $1500 |

GALE, BARBARA

LLOYDS

❑ 107	Lonely Weather/So Long, Good-Bye Joe	1953	$120
❑ 109	Once Again/Fool Fool Me	1953	$120
❑ 111	When You're Near/Who Walks In	1954	$300

— With the Larks

GALE, SUNNY

BLAINE

| ❑ 4003 | March of the Angels/Let the Rest of the World Go By | 1965 | $6 |
| ❑ 4002 | Stay/Once in Every Lifetime | 1965 | $6 |

CANADIAN AMERICAN

❑ 176	I Really Loved Him So/I'm Telling My Heart	1964	$8
❑ 171	I Wish I Didn't Love You So/I'm Not Sorry	1964	$8
❑ 163	Too Bad for You/I'm Telling My Heart	1963	$8

DECCA

❑ 9-30670	A Certain Smile/Just Friends	1958	$10
❑ 9-30518	A Meeting of the Eyes/Who Are We to Say?	1957	$10
❑ 9-30231	Come Go with Me/Please Go	1957	$10
❑ 9-30597	For Crying Out Loud/I Don't Want Your Greenback Dollars	1958	$10
❑ 9-30125	Hot Dog! That Made Him Mad/Welcome to My Heart	1956	$10
❑ 9-30157	I Have You/Maybe You'll Be There	1956	$10
❑ 9-30319	Let's Be Friendly/Mirror	1957	$12
❑ 9-30391	My Arms Are a House/Don't Worry 'Bout Me	1957	$10
❑ 9-30063	One Kiss Led to Another/Two Hearts	1956	$10
❑ 9-30837	The Gypsy Told Me So/Oh What It Seemed to Be	1959	$10
❑ 9-30791	Wheel of Fortune/Three O'Clock	1958	$10

RCA VICTOR

❑ 47-6286	C'est La Vie/Looking Glass	1955	$10
❑ 47-5609	Close to Me/Just in Case You Change Your Mind	1954	$15
❑ 47-6160	Constantly/A Little You	1955	$10
❑ 47-5677	Dream, Dream, Dream/Don't Cry Mama	1954	$15
❑ 47-5746	Goodnight, Sweetheart, Goodnight/Call Off the Wedding	1954	$15
❑ 47-5216	How Could You/I Feel Like I'm Gonna Live Forever	1953	$15
❑ 47-6588	If You Really Want to Know/Try a Little Prayer	1956	$10
❑ 47-4789	I Laughed at Love/Father Time	1952	$15
❑ 47-5952	Let Me Go, Lover!/Unsuspecting Heart	1954	$15
❑ 47-5424	Love Me Again/Before It's Too Late	1953	$15
❑ 47-6398	On the Way to Your Heart/Devotion	1956	$10
❑ 47-5306	Send My Baby Back to Me/Meanwhile	1953	$15
❑ 47-5836	Smile/An Old Familiar Love Song	1954	$15
❑ 47-6227	Soldier Boy/Certainly Baby	1955	$12
❑ 47-5103	Teardrops on My Pillow/A Stolen Waltz	1952	$15
❑ 47-4901	Tossin' and Turnin'/You Could Make Me Smile Again	1952	$15

TERRACE

| ❑ 7505 | Crying in the Chapel/Love Me Again | 1962 | $8 |

THIMBLE

| ❑ THS 009 | Birningham Rag/Sunshine State | 1974 | $6 |

WARWICK

❑ 540	Church Bells May Ring/My Foolish Heart	1960	$8
❑ 526	Falling Star/What Do You Want to Make Those Eyes at Me For	1960	$8
❑ 578	It's Your Turn/Where Have You Been All My Life	1960	$8
❑ 626	Please Love Me Forever/Sunny	1961	$10

GALES, THE

DEBRA

| ❑ 1002 | Tommy/Around the Clock with You | 1963 | $50 |

J.O.B.

| ❑ 3001 | Darling Patricia/All Is Well, All Is Well | 1956 | $200 |

JVB

| ❑ 35 | Darling Patricia/All Is Well, All Is Well | 1955 | $500 |
| ❑ 34 | His Eyes Keep Me in Trouble/Don't Let the Sun Catch You Cryin' | 1955 | $3000 |

— VG 1000; VG+ 2000

MEL-O

| ❑ 111 | Guiding Angel/Boy Come Home | 1958 | $250 |

WINN

| ❑ 916 | I Love You/Squeeze Me | 1960 | $500 |

GALLAGHER, JAMES

DECCA

| ❑ 29984 | Crazy Chicken/Just for You | 1956 | $120 |

GALLAHADS, THE (1)

CAPITOL

| ❑ F-3175 | Do You Believe Me/If It Wasn't for You | 1955 | $30 |
| ❑ F-3060 | Ooh Ah/Careless | 1955 | $30 |

JUBILEE

| ❑ 5259 | Take My Love/I Give You My Word | 1956 | $30 |
| ❑ 5252 | The Fool/The Morning Mail | 1956 | $40 |

GALLAHADS, THE (2)

DEL-FI

| ❑ 4148 | Be Fair/I'm Without a Girl Friend | 1960 | $50 |

— Green label

| ❑ 4148 | Be Fair/I'm Without a Girl Friend | 1960 | $30 |

— Black label

| ❑ 4137 | Lonely Guy/Jo Jo the Big Wheel | 1960 | $50 |

— Green label

| ❑ 4137 | Lonely Guy/Jo Jo the Big Wheel | 1960 | $30 |

— Black label

DONNA

| ❑ 1322 | Lonely Guy/Jo Jo the Big Wheel | 1960 | $50 |
| ❑ 1361 | This Letter to You/The Answer to Love | 1962 | $60 |

GALLAHADS, THE (U)

NITE OWL

| ❑ 20 | Gone/So Long | 1961 | $70 |

RENDEZVOUS

| ❑ 153 | Gone/Why Do Fools Fall in Love | 1961 | $50 |

SEA CREST

| ❑ 6005 | Have Love, Will Travel/My Offering | 1964 | $50 |

GALLALADS, THE

VIK

❑ 4X-0316	Best Wishes/Steady Man	1958	$30
❑ 4X-0332	Silently/Barracuda	1958	$30
❑ 4X-0291	Take Back My Ring/One Love Alone	1957	$30

GALT, JAMES

AURORA

| ❑ 158 | With My Baby/Most Unusual Feeling | 1966 | $40 |

GAMBLE, KENNY

ARCTIC

| ❑ 114 | Ain't It Baby (Part 1)/Ain't It Baby (Part 2) | 1965 | $200 |
| ❑ 107 | Down by the Seashore (Part 1)/Down by the Seashore (Part 2) | 1965 | $60 |

COLUMBIA

| ❑ 43132 | Our Love/You Don't Know What You Got Until You Lose It | 1964 | $80 |

EPIC

| ❑ 9636 | Standing in the Shadows/No Mail on Monday | 1963 | $300 |

Number	Title	Yr	NM

GAMBLERS, THE (1)
LAST CHANCE
| ❏ 2 | Teen Machine/Tonky | 1961 | $50 |
| ❏ 108 | Teen Machine/Tonky | 1962 | $30 |

WORLD PACIFIC
| ❏ 815 | Moon Dawg/LSD-25 | 1960 | $70 |

GAMBLERS, THE (2)
CORAL
| ❏ 62525 | Cry Me a River/Who Will Buy | 1967 | $8 |

GAME
EVOLUTION
| ❏ 1042 | Fat Mama/The Girl Next Door | 1970 | $6 |
| ❏ 1053 | Two Songs for the Senorita/ (B-side unknown) | 1971 | $6 |

GAMMA GOOCHEE
COLPIX
| ❏ 786 | I'm Gonna Buy Me a Dog/(You Got the) Gamma Goochee | 1965 | $50 |
| ❏ 804 | I'm So Glad/Sweet Violets | 1966 | $50 |

MGM
| ❏ 13874 | Booga-Loo/Everybody's Somebody's Fool | 1967 | $40 |

GANDALF
CAPITOL
| ❏ 2400 | Golden Earrings/Never Too Far | 1969 | $30 |

GANEY, JERRY
MGM
| ❏ 13697 | Hi-Heel Sneakers/You Don't Love Me | 1967 | $200 |

VERVE
| ❏ 10454 | Who Am I/Just a Fool | 1966 | $200 |

GANG OF FOUR
WARNER BROS.
| ❏ 29921 | I Love a Man in a Uniform/I Will Be a Good Boy | 1982 | $4 |
| ❏ 29449 | Is It Love/Arabic | 1983 | $4 |

GANT, CECIL
DECCA
❏ 9-48212	Don't You Worry/My Little Baby	1951	$50
❏ 9-48249	God Bless My Daddy/The Grass Is Gettin' Greener	1951	$50
❏ 9-48167	Goodnight Irene/My House Fell Down	1950	$60

—As "Gunter Lee Carr"
❏ 9-48185	It's Christmas Time Again/Hello Santa Claus	1950	$50
❏ 9-30320	I Wonder/Cecil's Boogie	1957	$40
❏ 9-48231	Owl Stew/Playin' Myself the Blues	1951	$50
❏ 9-48200	Shot Gun Boogie/Rock Little Baby	1951	$60
❏ 9-48171	Someday You'll Be Sorry (Part 1)/Someday You'll Be Sorry (Part 2)	1950	$50
❏ 9-48191	Train Time Blues No. 2/It Ain't Gonna Be Like That	1951	$50
❏ 9-48170	We're Gonna Rock/Yesterday	1950	$60

—As "Gunter Lee Carr"

DOT
| ❏ 1112 | All By Myself/It Hurts Me Too | 1952 | $50 |
—Earlier singles on Dot may not exist on 45s
| ❏ 1121 | Sloppy Joes/Train Time Blues | 1952 | $50 |

GILT EDGE
| ❏ 5090 | I Wonder/Cecil's Boogie | 1955 | $50 |
—Reissue of 78 first released in 1944

GANTS, THE
ALADDIN
| ❏ 3387 | My Unfaithful Love/Happening After School | 1957 | $70 |

LIBERTY
❏ 55884	Dr. Feelgood/Crackin' Up	1966	$12
❏ 55965	Drifter's Sunrise/Just a Good Show	1967	$12
❏ 55940	Greener Days/I Wonder	1967	$10
❏ 55903	I Want Your Lovin'/A Spoonful of Sugar	1966	$10
❏ 55853	Smoke Rings/Little Boy Sad	1966	$12

STATUE
| ❏ 608 | What's Happening/Careless Hands | 1965 | $30 |
—B-side by the Niteliters

GAP BAND, THE
A&M
| ❏ 1788 | Hard Time Charlie/This Place Called Heaven | 1976 | $5 |

ARISTA
| ❏ 9788 | I'm Gonna Git Ya Sucka/Clean Up Your Act | 1988 | $3 |
—B-side by Jermaine Jackson
| ❏ 9788 [PS] | I'm Gonna Git Ya Sucka/Clean Up Your Act | 1988 | $3 |

CAPITOL
| ❏ B-44418 | All of My Love (7" Version)/(Radio Mix) | 1989 | $4 |

MERCURY
| ❏ 76091 | Burn Rubber (Why You Wanna Hurt Me)/Nothin' Comes to a Sleeper | 1980 | $4 |
| ❏ 811357-7 | Burn Rubber/Yearning for Your Love | 1983 | $4 |
—Reissue
❏ 76114	Humpin'/No Hiding Place	1981	$4
❏ 76037	I Don't Believe You Want to Get Up and Dance (Oops, Up Side Your Head)/Who Do You Call	1980	$4
❏ 74080	Open Up Your Mind (Wide)/I Can Sing	1979	$4
❏ 76062	Party Lights/The Boys Are Back in Town	1980	$4
❏ 74053	Shake/Got to Get Away	1979	$4
❏ 76021	Steppin' (Out)/You Are My High	1979	$4
❏ DJ-568 [DJ]	The Boys Are Back in Town (stereo/mono?)	1980	$8

RCA
| ❏ 5035-7-R | Sweeter Than Candy (Penitentiary III)/(Instrumental) | 1986 | $4 |

SHELTER
| ❏ 40228 | Backbone/Loving You Is Everything | 1974 | $6 |
| ❏ 40295 | I-Yike-It/Tommy's Groove | 1974 | $6 |

TATTOO
| ❏ TB-10990 | Little Bit of Love/Knucklehead Sunckin' | 1977 | $5 |
| ❏ TB-10884 | Out of the Blue (Can You Feel It)/Silly Grin | 1977 | $5 |

TOTAL EXPERIENCE
❏ 2428	Automatic Brain/(Instrumental)	1986	$4
❏ 2440	Automatic Brain/(With Rap)	1986	$3
❏ 2405	Beep a Freak/(Dub Version)	1984	$3
❏ 2405 [PS]	Beep a Freak/(Dub Version)	1984	$4
❏ 2700	Big Fun/(Ooh Ah Dub)	1986	$3
❏ 2427	Desire/(Album Version)	1985	$3
❏ 2418	Disrespect/(Instrumental)	1985	$3
❏ 8201	Early in the Morning/I'm in Love	1982	$3
❏ 8201 [PS]	Early in the Morning/I'm in Love	1982	$5
❏ 2436	Going in Circles/I Believe	1986	$3
❏ 2436 [DJ]	Going in Circles (Remix 3:59)/(Remix Instrumental with Harmonica 5:15)	1986	$6
❏ 2412	I Found My Baby/(Instrumental)	1985	$3
❏ 8211	I'm Ready (If You're Ready)/Shake a Leg	1984	$4
❏ 8205	Outstanding/The Blues Are Back in Town	1982	$4
❏ 8209	Party Train/The Special Party Train Dance Mix	1983	$4
❏ 101	Straight from the Heart/(Dub Mix)	1988	$3
❏ 101 [PS]	Straight from the Heart/(Dub Mix)	1988	$4
❏ 2435	The Christmas Song (Chestnuts Roasting on an Open Fire)/Joy to the World	1985	$5
—B-side by Oliver Scott

GARCIA, JERRY
Also see THE GRATEFUL DEAD; NEW RIDERS OF THE PURPLE SAGE; OLD & IN THE WAY.
ROUND
| ❏ 4504 | Let It Rock/Midnight Town | 1974 | $10 |

WARNER BROS.
| ❏ 7551 | Deal/The Wheel | 1972 | $10 |
| ❏ PRO514 [DJ] | Deal/The Wheel | 1972 | $20 |
—White label, small hole, plays at 33 1/3 rpm
| ❏ PRO514 [PS] | Deal/The Wheel | 1972 | $40 |
—Title sleeve with the above promo
| ❏ 7569 | Deep Hour/Sugaree | 1972 | $10 |

GARDENIAS, THE (1)
FEDERAL
| ❏ 12284 | Flaming Love/My Baby's Tops | 1956 | $120 |

GARDENIAS, THE (2)
FAIRLANE
| ❏ 21019 | Darling It's You, You, You/What's the Matter with Me | 1962 | $30 |

GARDNER, BROTHER DAVE
DECCA
| ❏ 30548 | Hop Along Rock/All By Myself | 1958 | $30 |
| ❏ 30627 | Slick Slacks/Wild Streak | 1958 | $50 |

OJ
| ❏ 1006 | Love Is My Business/Mad Witch | 1958 | $20 |
| ❏ 1002 | White Silver Sands/Fat Charlie | 1957 | $20 |

RCA VICTOR
| ❏ 47-7876 | Coward at the Alamo/You Are My Love | 1961 | $12 |

GARDNER, DON
BRUCE
❏ 105	How Do You Speak to an Angel/Sonotone Bounce	1954	$70
❏ 108	I'll Walk Alone/Going Down Mary	1954	$60
❏ 127	It's a Sin to Tell a Lie/I Hear a Rhapsody	1955	$60

CAMEO
| ❏ 102 | Love Only Brings Happiness/Sneakin' In | 1957 | $50 |

DELUXE
| ❏ 6155 | There! I've Said It Again/I Don't Want to Go Home | 1958 | $30 |
| ❏ 6133 | This Nearly Was Mine/A Dagger in My Chest | 1957 | $30 |

JUBILEE
❏ 5482	I Really Love You Baby/Talking About You	1964	$30
❏ 5493	Little Girl Blue/I'm In Such Misery	1964	$30
❏ 5484	The Bitter with the Sweet/I Don't Know What I'm Gonna Do	1964	$30

JUNIOR
| ❏ 394 | Dark Alley/Up the Street | 1957 | $40 |
| ❏ 393 | High School Baby/Crying All Alone | 1957 | $50 |

KAISER
| ❏ 399 | Ask Anything/Humility | 1958 | $30 |
| ❏ 402 | At Last/The Hump | 1959 | $30 |

GARFUNKEL, ART
Also see SIMON AND GARFUNKEL.
COLUMBIA
❏ 02307	A Heart in New York/Is This Love	1981	$4
❏ 02307 [PS]	A Heart in New York/Is This Love	1981	$4
❏ 45926	All I Know/Mary Was An Only Child	1973	$5
—As "Garfunkel"
| ❏ 45926 | All I Know/Mary Was An Only Child | 1973 | $5 |
—As "Art Garfunkel"
| ❏ 45926 [Q] | All I Know/Mary Was An Only Child | 1973 | $25 |
—As "Garfunkel"; promo-only quadraphonic pressing
| ❏ 45926 [DJ] | All I Know (mono/stereo) | 1973 | $8 |
—As "Garfunkel"; mono version is about 10 seconds longer than any other version of this song (longer piano fade at the end)
❏ 10274	Breakaway/Disney Girls	1975	$5
❏ 11050	Bright Eyes/Sail on a Rainbow	1979	$4
❏ 02627	Bright Eyes/The Romance	1981	$4
❏ 06590	Carol of the Birds/The Decree	1986	$3
—With Amy Grant
❏ 06590 [PS]	Carol of the Birds/The Decree	1986	$3
❏ 10608	Crying in My Sleep/Mr. Shuck 'N' Jive	1977	$5
❏ 10933	In a Little While (I'll Be On My Way)/And I Know	1979	$4
❏ 10190	I Only Have Eyes for You/Looking for the Right One	1975	$5
❏ 45983	I Shall Sing/Feuilles-Oh: Do Space Men Pass Dead Souls on Their Way to the Moon	1973	$5
—As "Garfunkel"
| ❏ 10020 | Second Avenue/Woyaya | 1974 | $5 |
—As "Garfunkel"
❏ 10999	Since I Don't Have You/When Someone Doesn't Want You	1979	$4
❏ 07711	So Much in Love/King of Tonga	1988	$3
❏ 07949	This Is the Moment/Slow Breakup	1988	$3

Number	Title	Yr	NM
❏ 46030	Traveling Boy/Old Men	1974	$5
— As "Garfunkel			
❏ 10676	(What a) Wonderful World/Wooden Planes	1978	$6
— A-side: Art Garfunkel with Paul Simon and James Taylor			
❏ 08511	When a Man Loves a Woman/I Have a Love	1988	$3

OCTAVIA

Number	Title	Yr	NM
❏ 8002	Forgive Me/Private World	1960	$50
— As "Artie Garr			

WARWICK

Number	Title	Yr	NM
❏ 515	Beat Love/Dream Alone	1959	$50
— As "Artie Garr			

GARI AND THE PRISTINES
CAMEO

Number	Title	Yr	NM
❏ 408	Losers Club/Let Me Go Lover	1966	$50

GARLAND, JUDY, AND LIZA MINNELLI
CAPITOL

Number	Title	Yr	NM
❏ 5497	Hello Dolly/He's Got the Whole World In His Hands	1965	$8

GARLAND, JUDY
ABC

Number	Title	Yr	NM
❏ 10973	I Feel a Song Coming On/What Now My Love	1967	$8
❏ 4938	Hello Bluebird/I Could Go On Singing	1963	$12
❏ 4656	Sweet Danger/Comes Once in a Lifetime	1961	$10

CAPITOL STARLINE

Number	Title	Yr	NM
❏ 6128	Over the Rainbow/Maybe I'll Come Back	1968	$8
— Originals have red and white "target" labels			
❏ 6125	San Francisco/Chicago	1968	$8
— Originals have red and white "target" labels			
❏ 6129	That's Entertainment/Swanee	1968	$8
— Originals have red and white "target" labels			
❏ 6126	The Man That Got Away/April Showers	1968	$8
— Originals have red and white "target" labels			

COLUMBIA

Number	Title	Yr	NM
❏ 40023	Go Home Joe/Heartbroken	1953	$20
❏ 40010	Send My Baby Back to Me/Without a Memory	1953	$20
❏ 40270	The Man That Got Away/Here's What I'm Here For	1954	$20

DECCA

Number	Title	Yr	NM
❏ 29295	Have Yourself a Merry Little Christmas/You'll Never Walk Alone	1954	$20

MGM

Number	Title	Yr	NM
❏ 505	Over the Rainbow/You Made Me Love You	1969	$8

WARNER BROS.

Number	Title	Yr	NM
❏ 5310	Little Drops of Rain/Paris Is a Lonely Town	1962	$12

MGM

Number	Title	Yr	NM
❏ X1038 [PS]	Get Happy	1953	$30
❏ X1038	Get Happy/Love of My Life//Johnny One Note/Who?	1953	$30

GARNER, ERROLL
ABC-PARAMOUNT

Number	Title	Yr	NM
❏ 10260	Dreamstreet/When You're Smiling	1961	$8

COLUMBIA

Number	Title	Yr	NM
❏ 39681	Ain't She Sweet/Please Don't Talk About Me When I'm Gone	1952	$15
❏ 39918	Am I Blue/I Never Knew	1953	$15
❏ 39748	Chopin Impressions/How Come You Do	1952	$10
❏ 39746	Cocktails for Two/Dancing in the Dark	1952	$10
❏ 40074	Frenesi/Mean to Me	1953	$15
❏ 39249	Honeysuckle Rose/My Heart Stood Still	1951	$20
❏ 39145	How High the Moon/Poor Butterfly	1951	$20
❏ 41231	I Can't Get Started/Just Blues	1958	$10
❏ 39273	I Cover the Waterfront/Laura	1951	$15
❏ 39274	I'm in the Mood for Love/Body and Soul	1951	$15
❏ 39168	It Could Happen to You/I Don't Know Why	1951	$15
— The above four comprise a box set			
❏ 39580	It's the Talk of the Town/Robbins' Nest	1951	$20
❏ 39996	Lullaby of Birdland/Easy to Love	1953	$15
❏ 41067	Misty/Moment's Delight	1957	$15
❏ 41482	Misty/Solitude	1959	$10

Number	Title	Yr	NM
❏ 40766	On the Street Where You Live/Dreamy	1956	$10
❏ 39734	Out of Nowhere/Music, Maestro, Please	1952	$15
❏ 39276	Penthouse Serenade/Play, Piano, Play	1951	$15
— The above four comprise a box set			
❏ 39100	People Will Say We're in Love/Lover	1950	$20
❏ 6-874	Petite Waltz Bounce/Petite Waltz	1950	$20
❏ 1-874	Petite Waltz Bounce/Petite Waltz	1950	$30
— Microgroove 33 1/3 rpm 7-inch single			
❏ 39166	Poor Butterfly/Long Ago and Far Away	1951	$15
❏ 39615	Sophisticated Lady/Fine and Dandy	1951	$20
❏ 40043	St. Louis Blues/My Ideal	1953	$15
❏ 39888	Summertime/What's New	1952	$15
❏ 39275	The Way You Look Tonight/Indiana	1951	$15
❏ 40899	Way Back Blues (Part 1)/Way Back Blues (Part 2)	1957	$10
❏ 6-869	When Johnny Comes Marching Home/I Don't Know Why	1950	$20
❏ 1-869	When Johnny Comes Marching Home/I Don't Know Why	1950	$30
— Microgroove 33 1/3 rpm 7-inch single			
❏ 39165	When Johnny Comes Marching Home/My Heart Stood Still	1951	$15
❏ 39167	When You're Smiling/Spring Is Here	1951	$15
❏ 39747	Willow Weep for Me/I Don't Hear a Thing	1952	$10
❏ 39749	With Every Breath I Take/Love Me or Leave Me	1952	$10
— The above four comprise a box set			
❏ 73177	For Once in My Life/Mood Island	1971	$4
❏ 72192	Mimi/Theme from "A New Kind of Love	1963	$8
❏ 70442	Misty/Exactly Like You	1954	$20
❏ 70649	That Old Black Magic/Night and Day	1955	$15

MGM

Number	Title	Yr	NM
❏ 13547	Affinidad/That's My Kick	1966	$6
❏ 13471	As Time Goes By/You Made Me Love You	1966	$6
❏ 13870	Blue Moon/Like It Is	1967	$6
❏ 14043	Cheek to Cheek/It's the Talk of the Town	1969	$5
❏ 13988	Coffee Song/Up in Erroll's Room	1968	$5
❏ 13677	More/It Ain't Necessarily So	1967	$6
❏ 13677 [PS]	More/It Ain't Necessarily So	1967	$20
❏ 13916	Watermelon Man/Gaslight	1968	$5

OKEH

Number	Title	Yr	NM
❏ 6898	Laura/Penthouse Serenade	1952	$30

RCA VICTOR

Number	Title	Yr	NM
❏ 47-4723	Stariway to the Stars/I Can't Escape from You	1952	$20

REPRISE

Number	Title	Yr	NM
❏ 20179	Moritat/Sweet and Lovely	1963	$8
❏ B-2586	*Penthouse Serenade/The Way You Look Tonight/I'm in the Mood for Love/Indiana	1959	$15
❏ B-2586 [PS]	Erroll Garner (Hall of Fame Series)	1959	$15

GARNER, JOHNNY
IMPERIAL

Number	Title	Yr	NM
❏ 5548	Didi Didi/The Fool	1958	$60

GARNETT, GALE
COLUMBIA

Number	Title	Yr	NM
❏ 44479	Breaking Through/Fall in Love Again	1968	$40

RCA VICTOR

Number	Title	Yr	NM
❏ 47-8549	I'll Cry Alone/Where Do You Go to Go Away	1965	$60
❏ 47-8668	I'm Gonna Sit Right Down and Write Myself a Letter/Why Am I Standing in the Window	1965	$8
❏ 47-8961	It's Been a Lonely Summer/You've Got to Fall in Love Again	1966	$20
❏ 47-8472	Lovin' Place/I Used to Live Here	1964	$8
❏ 47-8472 [PS]	Lovin' Place/I Used to Live Here	1964	$8
❏ 47-9196	Over the Rainbow/The Cats I Know	1967	$6
❏ 47-9020	The Sun Is Gray/I Make Him Fly	1966	$6
❏ 47-8824	This Kind of Love/Oh There'll Be Laughter	1966	$6
❏ 47-8388	We'll Sing in the Sunshine/Prism Song	1964	$10

GARRETT, LEIF
20TH CENTURY

Number	Title	Yr	NM
❏ 2320	Come Back When You Grow Up/Young World	1977	$6

ATLANTIC

Number	Title	Yr	NM
❏ 3466	Put Your Head on My Shoulder/Kari	1978	$3
❏ 3423	Surfin' USA/A Special Kind of Girl	1977	$3
❏ 3423 [PS]	Surfin' USA/A Special Kind of Girl	1977	$5
❏ 3476	The Wanderer/Love on the Run	1978	$3
❏ 3476 [PS]	The Wanderer/Love on the Run	1978	$5

SCOTTI BROS.

Number	Title	Yr	NM
❏ 407	Feel the Need/New York City Nights	1979	$3
❏ 407 [PS]	Feel the Need/New York City Nights	1979	$4
❏ 516	I Was Looking for Someone to Love/The Little Things You Do	1980	$3
❏ 403	I Was Made for Dancin'/Living Without Your Love	1978	$3
❏ 403 [PS]	I Was Made for Dancin'/Living Without Your Love	1978	$4
❏ 510	Memorize Your Number/Moonlight Dancin'	1979	$3
❏ 502	When I Think of You/New York City Nights	1979	$3

GARRETT, PAT
GOLD DUST

Number	Title	Yr	NM
❏ 104	Everlovin' Woman/(B-side unknown)	1981	$6
❏ 101	Sexy Ole Lady/Humpty Dumpty	1980	$6

MDJ

Number	Title	Yr	NM
❏ 73087	Suck It In/(B-side unknown)	1987	$6

GARRETT, SCOTT
LAURIE

Number	Title	Yr	NM
❏ 3023	House of Love/So Far So Good	1959	$30
❏ 3029	Love Story/Graduation Souvenir	1959	$60
— With vocal backing by the Mystics			
❏ 3034	Where Are You/Jumpin' Blue Blazes	1959	$30

OKEH

Number	Title	Yr	NM
❏ 7104	In My Heart/The Day I Died	1960	$30

GARRETT, TOMMY, 50 GUITARS OF
LIBERTY

Number	Title	Yr	NM
❏ 55797	Corcovado/La Violetra	1965	$6
❏ 56129	Flamenco Funk/Mexican Standoff	1969	$5
❏ 56046	Hang 'Em High/Spanish Pearls	1968	$5
❏ 55888	La Cucaracha/Spanish Lights	1966	$6
❏ 55868	Our Man Flint/Tender Moments	1966	$6
❏ 55731	Stranger from Durango/Juarez	1964	$6
❏ 55969	Theme for Someone in Love/Courtin'	1967	$6

GARRIGAN, EDDIE
FONTANA

Number	Title	Yr	NM
❏ 1575	I Wish I Was/Mail Call	1966	$125

GARRISON, AL
MOTION

Number	Title	Yr	NM
❏ 1032	Where Do I Go from Here/(B-side unknown)	1987	$6

GARRISON, GLEN
CREST

Number	Title	Yr	NM
❏ 1047	Lovin' Lorene/You're My Darling	1958	$70

IMPERIAL

Number	Title	Yr	NM
❏ 66257	Goodbye Swingers/Hello Mama	1967	$10
❏ 66401	Goodnight Irene/Change Me	1969	$8
❏ 66191	Green to Blue/You Can't Win 'Em All	1966	$10
❏ 66300	I'll Be Your Baby Tonight/You Know I Love You	1968	$8
❏ 66230	Listen, They're Playing My Song/My New Creation	1967	$12
❏ 66333	That Lucky Old Sun/She Thinks I Still Care	1968	$8
❏ 66215	Where Do I Go from Here/Strong and Handsome, Sweet and Simple Side	1966	$10

LODE

Number	Title	Yr	NM
❏ 106	Pony Tail Girl/Ballad of Hank Gordon	1959	$70

Number	Title	Yr	NM

GARRON, JESS
CHARTA

Number	Title	Yr	NM
❏ 158	Get Down Country Music/ Weary Lonesome Song	1981	$6
❏ 136	It's Summer Time/You Can't Love a Woman (Who Doesn't Want to Be Loved)	1979	$6
❏ 131	Lo Que Sea (What Ever May the Future Be)/Those Good Times Are Over	1979	$6
❏ 146	Sunshine Girl/Weary Lonesome Song	1980	$6
❏ 140	That Old Piano Man/Tomorrow's a Brand New Day	1979	$6
❏ 152	Why Did You Do It to Me/ You'll Never Do It Again	1980	$6

GARY AND DAVE
LONDON

Number	Title	Yr	NM
❏ 200	Could You Ever Love Me Again/Where Do We Go from Here	1973	$6
❏ 204	I Fell in Love with You Sometime/For You	1974	$6
❏ 207	It Might As Well Rain Until September/ (B-side unknown)	1974	$30

GARY AND THE CASUALS
VANDAN

Number	Title	Yr	NM
❏ 609	My Own Desire/ Someone Like You	1959	$70

GARY AND THE HORNETS
SMASH

Number	Title	Yr	NM
❏ 2090	Baby It's You/Tell Tale	1967	$15
❏ 2061	Hi, Hi, Hazel/Patty Girl	1966	$20
❏ 2061 [PS]	Hi, Hi, Hazel/Patty Girl	1966	$30
❏ 2145	Turn the World On/ Holdin' Back	1968	$15

GARY AND THE KNIGHT-LITES
BELL

Number	Title	Yr	NM
❏ 643	Lonely Soldier's Pledge/ So Far Away from Home	1966	$20

NIKE

Number	Title	Yr	NM
❏ 1020	I'm Glad She's Mine/ How Can I Forget Her	1963	$50

PRIMA

Number	Title	Yr	NM
❏ 1016	I Can't Love You Anymore/ Will You Go Steady	1963	$125

SEEBURG

Number	Title	Yr	NM
❏ 3017	Bony Moronie/Glad You're Mine	1965	$30
❏ 3016	Sweet Little Sixteen/ Take Me Back	1965	$30

U.S.A.

Number	Title	Yr	NM
❏ 833	Bid Bad Wolf/I Don't Need Your Help	1966	$50

GARY, JOHN
ACE

Number	Title	Yr	NM
❏ 861	First Lady Waltz/A River of Silver	1962	$15

FRATERNITY

Number	Title	Yr	NM
❏ 799	How Many Tear Drops/ Little People	1958	$20
❏ 844	Let Them Talk/Tell My Love	1959	$20
❏ 958	Let Them Talk/Tell My Love	1966	$6
❏ 858	Little Things Mean a Lot/ Ever Since I Met Lucy	1959	$20
❏ 860	Thank the Lord (For This Thanksgiving Day)/ The Rest of My Days	1959	$20
❏ 870	The Bell Rings/Forget It	1960	$15
❏ 864	The Shrine of St. Cecelia/ When I'm Alone	1960	$15

RCA VICTOR

Number	Title	Yr	NM
❏ 47-9456	A Certain Girl/The End of Time	1968	$5
❏ 47-8731	Ashamed/She Wasn't You	1965	$6
❏ 47-9361	Cold/Imagine	1967	$6
❏ 47-8526	Color of Love/My First Love Song	1965	$6
❏ 47-8677	Don't Throw Those Roses Away/Give Me This Moment	1965	$6
❏ 47-8475	Do You Hear What I Hear/Little Snow Girl	1964	$15
❏ 47-9213	Everybody Say Peace/ Spanish Moonlight	1967	$6
❏ 47-9119	Hang On to Me/ Sleeping Beauty	1967	$6
❏ 47-9868	In the Morning/In the Wind	1970	$5
❏ 47-9540	Let There Be Peace on Earth/Give Some Time to Be Happy	1968	$5
❏ 47-8993	Mine/You've Never Kissed Her	1966	$6
❏ 47-8413	Soon I'll Wed My Love/ The Young Lovers	1964	$8
❏ 47-8479	Sunrise, Sunset/ The Bell Rings	1964	$8
❏ 47-8890	Sunrise, Sunset/ The Bell Rings	1966	$6

Number	Title	Yr	NM
❏ 47-8292	That's Life/Ciumanchella	1963	$8
❏ 74-0149	The Windmills of Your Mind/Then She's a Lover	1969	$5
❏ 47-8386	Warm and Willing/ Friend and Lover	1964	$8

GAS AND FUNK FACTORY, THE
BRUNSWICK

Number	Title	Yr	NM
❏ 55434	Goodnight Song/Everybody Get Some Love	1970	$40

GATEMEN, THE
COLPIX

Number	Title	Yr	NM
❏ 671	Silent Night/White Christmas	1962	$30

MAY

Number	Title	Yr	NM
❏ 141	Goodnight Irene/The Klan	1963	$30

GATES, DAVID
ARISTA

Number	Title	Yr	NM
❏ 0653	Come Home for Christmas/ Lady Valentine	1981	$8
❏ 0615	Take Me Now/It's What You Say	1981	$4

EASTWEST

Number	Title	Yr	NM
❏ 123	Walkin' and Talkin'/ Swingin' Baby Doll	1959	$200

ELEKTRA

Number	Title	Yr	NM
❏ 46646	Can I Call You/Chingo	1980	$4
❏ 45857	Clouds/I Use the Soap	1973	$4
❏ 45857 [PS]	Clouds/I Use the Soap	1973	$6
❏ 47011	Falling in Love Again/ Sweet Desire	1980	$4
❏ 45450	Goodbye Girl/Sunday Rider	1977	$4
❏ 45450 [PS]	Goodbye Girl/Sunday Rider	1977	$5

— Version 1: Titles on both sides, no photo

Number	Title	Yr	NM
❏ 45450 [PS]	Goodbye Girl/Sunday Rider	1977	$5

— Version 2: Titles on one side, photo on other side

Number	Title	Yr	NM
❏ 45245	Part-Time Love/Chain Me	1975	$4
❏ 45868	Sail Around the World/ Help Is On the Way	1973	$4
❏ 45500	Took the Last Train/Ann	1978	$4
❏ 46588	Where Does the Lovin' Go/Starship Ride	1980	$4

MALA

Number	Title	Yr	NM
❏ 418	The Happiest Man Alive/A Road That Leads to Love	1960	$60

MANCHESTER

Number	Title	Yr	NM
❏ 101	There's a Heaven/ She Don't Cry	1964	$50

— As "Del Ashley"

PLANETARY

Number	Title	Yr	NM
❏ 108	Let You Go/Once Upon a Time	1965	$30
❏ 103	Little Miss Stuck-Up/ The Brighter Side	1965	$30

— As "Del Ashley"

GATES, WALTER
SWAN

Number	Title	Yr	NM
❏ 4190	Ace in the Hole/ Never Before	1964	$8
❏ 4160	I Remember Papa/ That's My Boy	1963	$8
❏ 4180	My Man/Rose of Washington Square	1964	$8

GATEWAY SINGERS, THE
DECCA

Number	Title	Yr	NM
❏ 30088	Bury Me in My Overalls/Monaco	1956	$15
❏ 30630	Hey Li Lee/Come to the Dance	1958	$12
❏ 29972	The Midnight Special/ Puttin' On the Style	1956	$15

MGM

Number	Title	Yr	NM
❏ 12927	Billy Boy/Goin' Down the Road	1960	$8
❏ 12939	Wait for the Wagon/ Kingston Market	1960	$8

WARNER BROS.

Number	Title	Yr	NM
❏ 5073	The M.T.A./Keep a-Movin'	1959	$10

GATEWAY TRIO, THE
CAPITOL

Number	Title	Yr	NM
❏ 5286	Coney Island/All the Good Times	1964	$20
❏ 5045	Soldiers Who Want to Be Heroes/Poor Man's Travellin' Blues	1963	$20

GATLIN, LARRY, AND THE GATLIN BROTHERS BAND
COLUMBIA

Number	Title	Yr	NM
❏ 07998	Alive and Well/One on One	1988	$3
❏ 11066	All the Gold in California/ How Much Is Man Supposed to Take	1979	$4

Number	Title	Yr	NM
❏ 03517	Almost Called Her Baby By Mistake/Somethin' Like Each Other's Arms	1983	$3
❏ 07320	Changin' Partners/Got a Lot of Women on His Hands	1987	$3
❏ 04395	Denver/A Dream That Got Out of Hand	1984	$3
❏ 03885	Easy on the Eye/ Anything But Leavin'	1983	$3
❏ 07088	From Time to Time (It Feels Like Love Again)/Texas (Is What Life Is All About)	1987	$3

— With Janie Frickie

Number	Title	Yr	NM
❏ 04105	Houston (Means I'm One Day Closer to You)/The Whole Wide World Stood Still	1983	$3
❏ 02698	In Like With Each Other/ Hard Workin' Hands	1982	$3
❏ 11438	It Don't Get No Better Than This/Straight to My Heart	1981	$4
❏ 07747	Love of a Lifetime/Don't Blame Me for Colorado	1988	$3
❏ 06252	She Used to Be Somebody's Baby/Being Alone	1986	$3
❏ 02910	She Used to Sing on Sunday/Can't Take It With You	1982	$3
❏ 03356	Steps/Sweet Baby Jesus	1982	$4
❏ CNR-03364	Sure Feels Like Love	1982	$5

— One-sided budget release

Number	Title	Yr	NM
❏ 03159	Sure Feels Like Love/Home Is Where the Healin' Is	1982	$3
❏ 11369	Take Me to Your Lovin' Place/Straight to My Heart	1980	$4
❏ 11219	Taking Somebody With Me When I Fall/Piece by Piece	1980	$4
❏ 06592	Talkin' to the Moon/ Give Me a Chance	1986	$3
❏ 04533	The Lady Takes the Cowboy Everytime/It's Me	1984	$3
❏ 11169	The Midnight Choir/ Hold Me Closer	1980	$4
❏ 11282	We're Number One/ Can't Cry Anymore	1980	$4
❏ 02522	What Are We Doin' Lonesome/You Wouldn't Know Love	1981	$3
❏ 02123	Wind Is Bound to Change/ Help Yourself to Me	1981	$3

MONUMENT

Number	Title	Yr	NM
❏ 45-212	Anything But Leavin'/ Take Back "It's Over	1977	$4
❏ 8602	Bitter They Are Harder They Fall/Silver Threads and Golden Needles	1974	$5
❏ 8680	Broken Lady/Heart	1975	$5
❏ 8568	Come On In/The Way I Did Before	1973	$6

— As "The Gatlins"

Number	Title	Yr	NM
❏ 8622	Delta Dirt/Those Also Love	1974	$5
❏ 45-259	Do It Again Tonight/ Cold Day in Hell	1978	$4
❏ 45-221	I Don't Wanna Cry/ Mercy River	1977	$4
❏ 45-234	I Just Wish You Were Someone I Love/ Kiss It All Goodbye	1977	$4
❏ 45-270	I've Done Enough Dyin' Today/Nothin' You Do	1978	$4
❏ 8657	Let's Turn the Lights On/ Takin' a Chance on You	1975	$5
❏ 45-226	Love Is Just a Game/ Everytime a Plane Flies Over Our House	1977	$4
❏ 8569	My Mind's Gone to Memphis/Try to Win a Friend	1973	$5
❏ 45-201	Statues Without Hearts/ What Will I Do Now	1976	$4
❏ 8584	Sweet Becky Walker/You've Been Handed Down to Me	1973	$5
❏ 8696	Warm and Tender/The Heart Is Quicker Than the Eye	1976	$5

UNIVERSAL

Number	Title	Yr	NM
❏ UVL-66005	I Might Be What You're Looking For/Rain	1989	$3
❏ 53501	When She Holds Me/Go or Stay	1989	$3

7-Inch Extended Plays

SWORD AND SHIELD

Number	Title	Yr	NM
❏ EP601	I'm Feeling Fine/He's Already Done//He's Everywhere/I Wonder What My New Address Will Be	1959	$125

— As "The Gatlin Family: La Donna - age 5, Rudy - age 7, Stevie - age 8, Larry - age 11

Number	Title	Yr	NM
❏ EP601 [PS]	(title unknown)	1959	$125

GAUDET, JOHN, AND THE LAURELS
MARY GLEN

Number	Title	Yr	NM
❏ 1001/2	Christmas Will Soon Be Here/Your Name Shall Be Remembered	1961	$60

Number	Title	Yr	NM

GAULT, JONNA, AND HER SYMPHONOPOP SCENE
RCA VICTOR
❏ 47-9704	Watch Me/The Answer Has to Come from Within	1968	$8
❏ 47-9440	Wonder Why, I Guess/What If They Gave a War and No One Came?	1968	$15

GAULT, LENNY
KING COAL
❏ 03	The Honky-Tonks Are Calling Me Again/I'm Gonna Leave	1979	$6

MRC
❏ 1024	I Just Need a Coke (To Get the Whiskey Down)/Steppin' Aside Just Ain't My Style	1978	$6
❏ 1020	Turn On the Bright Lights/When a Woman Cries	1978	$6

GAVIN, TONY
20TH FOX
❏ 228	Ever Lovin' Baby/I Just Don't Know	1960	$50

GAY KNIGHTS, THE
PET
❏ 801	The Loudness of My Heart/Angel	1958	$50

GAY NOTES, THE
DREXEL
❏ 905	For Only a Moment/Pu-Pu-Pa-Doo	1955	$600

POST
❏ 2006	Crossroads/Hear My Plea	1955	$70

VIM
❏ 501	Something Special/Cherie	1959	$70

GAYE, ELLIE
RCA VICTOR
❏ 47-7231	Silly Isn't It/Cha Cha Charming	1958	$50

GAYE, MARVIN, AND TAMMI TERRELL
TAMLA
❏ 54149	Ain't No Mountain High Enough/Give a Little Love	1967	$8
❏ 54163	Ain't Nothing Like the Real Thing/Little Ole Boy, Little Ole Girl	1968	$8
❏ 54179	Good Lovin' Ain't Easy to Come By/Satisfied Feelin'	1969	$6
❏ 54179 [PS]	Good Lovin' Ain't Easy to Come By/Satisfied Feelin'	1969	$30
❏ 54161	If I Could Build My Whole World Around You/If This World Were Mine	1967	$8
❏ 54192	The Onion Song/California Soul	1970	$6
❏ 54187	What You Gave Me/How You Gonna Keep It	1969	$6

GAYE, MARVIN, AND MARY WELLS
MOTOWN
❏ 1057	Once Upon a Time/What's the Matter with You Baby	1964	$20
❏ 1057 [PS]	Once Upon a Time/What's the Matter with You Baby	1964	$70

GAYE, MARVIN, AND KIM WESTON
TAMLA
❏ 54141	It Takes Two/It's Got to Be a Miracle	1966	$15
❏ 54104	What Good Am I Without You/I Want You 'Round	1964	$20

GAYE, MARVIN
COLUMBIA
❏ 38-05442	It's Madness/Ain't It Funny (How Things Turn Around)	1985	$4
❏ 38-04861	Sanctified Lady/(Instrumental)	1985	$4
❏ CNR-03344	Sexual Healing/(B-side blank)	1982	$6
— One-sided budget release			
❏ 38-03302	Sexual Healing/(Instrumental)	1982	$4
❏ 13-03585	Sexual Healing/(Instrumental)	1983	$3
— Reissue			
❏ 38-03589	'Til Tomorrow/Rockin' After Midnight	1983	$4

DETROIT FREE PRESS
❏ 0(no cat #) [DJ]	The Teen Beat Song/Loraine Alterman Interviews Marvin Gaye	1966	$200

TAMLA
❏ 54273	After the Dance/Feel All My Love Inside	1976	$4
❏ 54122	Ain't That Peculiar/She's Got to Be Real	1965	$20
❏ 54101	Baby Don't You Do It/Walk on the Wild Side	1964	$20
❏ 54101 [PS]	Baby Don't You Do It/Walk on the Wild Side	1964	$70
❏ 54087	Can I Get a Witness/I'm Crazy 'Bout My Baby	1963	$30
❏ 54170	Chained/At Last I Found a Love	1968	$10
❏ 54241	Come Get to This/Distant Lover	1973	$4
❏ 54253	Distant Lover/Trouble Man	1974	$4
❏ 54305	Ego Tripping Out/(Instrumental)	1979	$4
❏ 54322	Funk Me/Praise	1981	$4
❏ 54298	Funky Space Reincarnation -- Pt. 1/Funky Space Reincarnation -- Pt. 2	1979	$4
❏ 54190	Gonna Give Her All the Love I've Got/How Can I Forget You	1970	$8
❏ 54280	Got to Give It Up -- Pt. 1/Got to Give It Up -- Pt. 2	1977	$4
❏ 54280 [PS]	Got to Give It Up -- Pt. 1/Got to Give It Up -- Pt. 2	1977	$10
❏ 54326	Heavy Love Affair/Far Cry	1981	$4
❏ 54075	Hitch Hike/Hello There Angel	1963	$30
❏ 54107	How Sweet It Is To Be Loved By You/Forever	1964	$20
❏ 54176	I Heard It Through the Grapevine/You're What's Happening (In the World Today)	1968	$10
❏ 54112	I'll Be Doggone/You've Been a Long Time Coming	1965	$20
❏ 54209	Inner City Blues (Make Me Wanna Holler)/Wholly Holy	1971	$6
❏ 54264	I Want You/I Want You (Instrumental)	1975	$4
❏ 54234	Let's Get It On/I Wish It Would Rain	1973	$4
❏ 54041	Let Your Conscience Be Your Guide/Never Let You Go	1961	$200
❏ 54138	Little Darling, I Need You/Hey Diddle Diddle	1966	$15
❏ 0(no cat #) [DJ]	Masquerade (Is Over)/Witchcraft	1962	$600
— As "Marvin Gay"; label states "Single Not Available extracted from Album (TM-221)			
❏ 54207	Mercy Mercy Me (The Ecology)/Sad Tomorrows	1971	$6
❏ 54129	One More Heartache/When I Had Your Love	1966	$15
❏ 54117	Pretty Little Baby/Now That You've Won Me	1965	$20
❏ 54079	Pride and Joy/One of These Days	1963	$30
❏ 54055	Sandman/I'm Yours, You're Mine	1962	$70
❏ 54063	Soldier's Plea/Taking My Time	1962	$50
— With label credit "Marvin Gaye Love Tones"			
❏ 54063	Soldier's Plea/Taking My Time	1962	$60
— With label credit "Marvin Gaye"			
❏ 54068	Stubborn Kind of Fellow/It Hurts Me Too	1962	$40
❏ 54132	Take This Heart of Mine/Need Your Lovin' (Want You Back)	1966	$15
❏ 54185	That's the Way Love Is/Gonna Keep On Tryin' Till I Win Your Love	1969	$8
❏ 54195	The End of Our Road/Me and My Lonely Room	1970	$8
❏ 1836	The World Is Rated X/No Greater Love	1986	$5
❏ 1836 [PS]	The World Is Rated X/No Greater Love	1986	$5
❏ S4KM 0741/2 [DJ]	This Is the Life/My Way	1965	$60
❏ 54300	Time to Get It Together/Anger	1979	$10
— Only released in Canada			
❏ 54181	Too Busy Thinking About My Baby/Wherever I Lay My Hat (That's My Home)	1969	$8
❏ 54228	Trouble Man/Don't Mess With Mister "T	1972	$6
❏ 54095	Try It Baby/If My Heart Could Sing	1964	$20
❏ 54095 [PS]	Try It Baby/If My Heart Could Sing	1964	$70
❏ 54201	What's Going On/God Is Love	1971	$6

TOPPS/MOTOWN
❏ 6	How Sweet It Is	1967	$80
— Cardboard record			

GAYLARKS, THE
MUSIC CITY
❏ 809	Church on the Hill/Mr. Rock-n-Roll	1957	$120
❏ 819	Ivy League Clothes/Rockin' Satellite	1958	$60
❏ 805	My Greatest Sin/Teenage Mambo	1957	$125
❏ 792	Tell Me Darling/Whole Lot of Love	1956	$120
— B-side by the Rovers			

GAYLE, CRYSTAL, AND GARY MORRIS
WARNER BROS.
❏ 28106	All of This And More/Makin' Up for Lost Time	1988	$3
❏ 28373	Another World/Makin' Up for Lost Time	1987	$3
❏ 28856	Makin' Up for Lost Time (The Dallas Lovers' Song)/A Few Good Men	1985	$3
❏ 28856 [PS]	Makin' Up for Lost Time (The Dallas Lovers' Song)/A Few Good Men	1985	$3

GAYLE, CRYSTAL
COLUMBIA
❏ 11087	Half the Way/Room for One More	1979	$4
❏ 11359	If You Ever Change Your Mind/I Just Can't Leave Your Love Alone	1980	$4
❏ 11198	It's Like We Never Said Goodbye/Don't Go My Love	1980	$4
❏ 03048	Livin' in These Troubled Times/Ain't No Sunshine	1982	$4
❏ 11436	Take It Easy/Ain't No Love in the Heart of the City	1981	$4
❏ 11270	The Blue Side/The Danger Zone	1980	$4
❏ 02523	The Woman in Me/Crying in the Rain	1981	$4
❏ 02078	Too Many Lovers/Help Yourself to Each Other	1981	$4

DECCA
❏ 32925	Everybody Oughta Cry/MRS Degree	1972	$8
❏ 32969	I Hope You're Havin' Better Luck Than Me/Too Far	1972	$8
❏ 32721	I've Cried (The Blue Right Out of My Eyes)/Sparkling Look of Love	1970	$8

ELEKTRA
❏ 69893	'Til I Gain Control Again/Easier Said Than Done	1982	$4
❏ 69893 [PS]	'Til I Gain Control Again/Easier Said Than Done	1982	$4

MCA
❏ 40016	Clock on the Wall/Show Me How	1973	$6
❏ 40837	I've Cried (The Blue Right Out of My Eyes)/Sparklin' Look of Love	1977	$6

UNITED ARTISTS
❏ XW600	Beyond You/Loving You So Long Now	1975	$5
❏ 1347	Come Home Daddy/River Road	1980	$4
❏ XW1016	Don't It Make My Brown Eyes Blue/It's All Right with Me	1977	$4
❏ XW1148	Don't It Make My Brown Eyes Blue/The Green Door	1978	$4
— Reissue			
❏ 1362	Heart Mender/This Is My Year for Mexico	1980	$4
❏ XW948	I'll Do It All Over Again/I'm Not So Far Away	1977	$5
❏ XW1150	I'll Do It All Over Again/This Is My Year for Mexico	1978	$4
— Reissue			
❏ XW781	I'll Get Over You/High Time	1976	$5
❏ XW1146	I'll Get Over You/The Wrong Road Again	1978	$4
— Reissue			
❏ XW1149	I Wanna Come Back to You/One More Time	1978	$4
— Reissue			
❏ XW838	One More Time/Oh My Soul	1976	$5
❏ XW740	Somebody Loves You/Coming Closer	1975	$5
❏ XW1147	Somebody Loves You/You Never Miss a Real Good Thing (Till He Says Goodbye)	1978	$4
— Reissue			
❏ XW1214	Talking in Your Sleep/Paintin' This Old Town Blue	1978	$4
❏ XW680	This Is My Year for Mexico/When I Dream	1975	$5
❏ XW1288	When I Dream/Hello I Love You	1979	$4
❏ XW1259	Why Have You Left the One You Left Me For/Cry Me a River	1978	$4
❏ XW555	Wrong Road Again/They Come Out at Night	1974	$5

Number	Title	Yr	NM
WARNER BROS.			
❏ 28963	A Long and Lasting Love/ Someone Like You	1985	$3
❏ 29582	Baby, What About You/ He Is Beautiful to Me	1983	$4
❏ 28689	Cry/Crazy in the Heart	1986	$3
❏ 28555	Have Yourself a Merry Little Christmas/Silver Bells	1986	$4
❏ 29356	I Don't Wanna Lose Your Love/Victim or a Fool	1984	$4
❏ 28499	I Still Hear the Music of Nashville/I Still Hear the Music of Nashville (Part 2)	1987	$3
❏ 29151	Me Against the Night/ You Made a Fool of Me	1984	$4
❏ 28210	Oh Holy Night/I'll Be Home for Christmas	1987	$4
❏ 28209	Only Love Can Save Me Now/Till I Gain Control Again	1987	$3
❏ 29719	Our Love Is On the Faultline/ Deeper in the Fire	1983	$4
❏ 28518	Straight to the Heart/Do I Have to Say Goodbye	1986	$3
❏ 27682	Tennessee Nights/ When Love Is New	1988	$3
❏ 29452	The Sound of Goodbye/ Take Me Home	1983	$4
❏ 29254	Turning Away/On Our Way to Love	1984	$4
GAYLES, BILLY, WITH IKE TURNER'S RHYTHM ROCKERS			
FEDERAL			
❏ 12265	I'm Tore Up/If I Had Never Known You	1956	$50
❏ 12272	Let's Call It a Day/Take Your Fine Frame Home	1956	$50
GAYLES, THE			
ABC-PARAMOUNT			
❏ 9707	Shortnin' Bread Rock/You Fool	1956	$30
KING			
❏ 4860	I Had to Love You/ Too Late I Learned	1955	$30
❏ 4846	My Boy, Flat Top/I Get So Happy	1955	$30
GAYLORD, RONNIE			
MERCURY			
❏ 70504	Santo Natale/My Vow	1954	$20
GAYLORDS, THE			
MERCURY			
❏ 71399	Again/How About Me	1959	$8
❏ 70979	A Little Love, A Little Kiss/ The Mountain Climber	1956	$10
❏ 70834	Bella Bambinella/Who's Gonna Take You to the Prom	1956	$12
❏ 70630	Chee Chee O-Chee/ Who's Got the Pain	1955	$10
❏ 70543	Chow Mein/Poppa Poppadopolis	1955	$10
❏ 71762	Daisy, You're Driving Me Crazy/Born to Be Loved	1961	$8
❏ 70891	First Row Balcony/ One Night Only	1956	$10
❏ 71369	Flamingo L'Amore/I'm Longing for Love	1958	$8
❏ 70308	From the Vine Came the Grape/Patzo for Pizza	1954	$10
❏ 70296	From the Vine Came the Grape/Stolen Moments	1954	$15
❏ 70660	Happy Time Medley (1. Minnie the Mermaid; 2. The Man Who Broke the Bank at Monte Carlo; 3. Goodbye My Coney Island Baby; 4. If You Knew Susie)/Madalaina	1955	$12
❏ 71970	How About Me/ Two-Ton Tessie	1962	$8
❏ 70350	Isle of Capri/Love I You	1954	$15
❏ 71902	It Hurts Me More (The Second Time Around)/ American 100%	1961	$8
❏ 71265	Love/Each Time I Love You More	1958	$8
❏ 71601	Love Me Now and Forever/ Whip of the Wind	1960	$8
❏ 71337	Ma Ma Ma Marie/ Buona Sera	1958	$8
❏ 70589	Mambo Rock/ Plantation Boogie	1955	$10
❏ 70778	Molly-O/Vino Vino	1956	$10
❏ 71832	Oh Lonesome Me/ Yakety Yak	1961	$8
❏ 71236	O Mari/Magic Song	1957	$10
❏ 71186	Satin Doll/Wandering Heart	1957	$10
❏ 71625	Sensation/Carina	1960	$8
❏ 71569	She's Gone/Please Consider	1960	$8
❏ 70286	Stolen Moments/ Patzo for Pizza	1954	$15
❏ 71450	Sweeter Than You/ Homin' Pigeon	1959	$8
❏ 70170	Tell Me That You Love Me/Coquette	1953	$15
❏ 70067	Tell Me You're Mine/ Aye Aye Aye	1952	$15
❏ 70030	Tell Me You're Mine/ Cuban Love Song	1952	$20

Number	Title	Yr	NM
❏ 71051	The Dum-De-Dum Song/ Open the Letter	1957	$10
❏ 70403	The Little Shoemaker/ Masque, Masque	1954	$15
❏ 70258	The Strings of My Heart/ Mama Papa Polka	1953	$15
❏ 70586	The Woodpecker Song/My Babe	1955	$10
❏ 70479	Wonderful Lips/Pupalina	1954	$15
❏ 70235	Wonderin'/Sweet Sue	1953	$15
GAYNOR, GLORIA			
ATLANTIC			
❏ 89824 [DJ]	America (same on both sides)	1983	$4
—May be promo only			
❏ 89887	Stop in the Name of Love/ For You, My Love	1982	$4
❏ 89947	Tease Me/Mack Side	1982	$4
COLUMBIA			
❏ 45909	Honey Bee/All It Took, Boy, Was Losing You	1973	$6
MGM			
❏ 14706	Honey Bee/Come Tonight	1974	$5
❏ 14838	How High the Moon/ My Man's Gone	1975	$4
❏ 14823	(If You Want It) Do It Yourself/I'm Still Yours	1975	$4
❏ 14808	Walk On By/Real Good People	1975	$4
POLYDOR			
❏ 14443	After the Lovin'/You're All I Need to Get By	1977	$4
❏ 14558	Anybody Wanna Party?/ Please Be There	1979	$4
❏ 14342	Do It Right/Touch of Lightning	1976	$4
❏ 2179	I Kinda Like Me/ Fingers in the Rain	1981	$4
❏ 14508	I Will Survive/Substitute	1978	$4
❏ 2021	Let Me Know (I Have a Right)/One Plus One	1979	$4
❏ 14357	Let's Make a Deal/ Let's Make Love	1976	$4
❏ 2173	Let's Mend What's Been Broken/I Love You Because	1981	$4
❏ 2056	Midnight Rocker/Can't Fight This Feelin'	1980	$4
❏ 14391	Most of All/So Much Love	1977	$4
❏ 2089	The Luckiest Girl in the World/Ain't No Bigger Fool	1980	$4
❏ 14472	This Love Affair/For the First Time in My Life	1978	$4
SILVER BLUE			
❏ 04294	I Am What I Am/More Than Enough	1983	$4
❏ 720	I Am What I Am/More Than Enough	1983	$5
❏ 04422	Strive/I've Been Watching You	1984	$4
GAYTEN, PAUL			
ANNA			
❏ 1112	Beatnick Beat/Scratch Back	1960	$30
❏ 1106	The Hunch/Hot Cross Buns	1959	$30
ARGO			
❏ 5263	Driving Home Part 1/ Driving Home Part 2	1957	$30
❏ 5267	Old Buttermilk Sky/ The Sweeper	1957	$30
❏ 5257	The Music Goes Round and Round/Be My Baby	1956	$30
❏ 5300	Windy/Tickle Toe	1958	$30
CHECKER			
❏ 801	I'm Tired/Get It	1954	$30
OKEH			
❏ 6982	Cow Cow Blues/Ooh-Boo	1953	$40
❏ 6870	Give Me Liberty or Give Me Death/Happy Days	1952	$40
❏ 7003	Hurry Home/Sugar Baby	1953	$40
❏ 6847	Lonesome for My Baby/ All Alone and Lonely	1952	$40
❏ 7019	Mule Face/It's Over	1954	$40
❏ 6972	Time Is a-Passin'/Ain't Nothin' Happenin'	1953	$40
❏ 7068	True (You Don't Love Me)/Cow Cow Blues	1956	$30
❏ 6908	True (You Don't Love Me)/ They All Ask for You	1952	$40
GAYTUNES, THE			
JOYCE			
❏ 101	I Love You/You Left Me	1957	$200
GAZELLES, THE			
GOTHAM			
❏ 315	Honest/Pretty Baby, Baby	1956	$300
GEARS, THE			
FOUR SPEED			
❏ 0(# unknown)	Let's Go to the Beach/ Hard Rock/Don't Be Afraid to Pogo	1979	$125

Number	Title	Yr	NM
❏ 0(# unknown) [PS]	Let's Go to the Beach/ Hard Rock/Don't Be Afraid to Pogo	1979	$125
GEE CEES, THE			
CREST			
❏ 1088	Buzz Saw/Annie Had a Party	1961	$50
— Glen Campbell is on A-side; Eddie Cochran is on B-side			
❏ 1088	Buzz Saw Twist/ Annie Had a Party	1962	$40
GEE, JOEY			
ABC-PARAMOUNT			
❏ 10781	Don't Blow Your Cool/It's More Than I Deserve	1966	$400
SARA			
❏ 6599	She's Mean/You Know Till the End of Time	1965	$30
GEEZINSLAW BROTHERS, THE			
CAPITOL			
❏ 2184	Boney and Claude/Sugar	1968	$10
❏ 5918	Change of Wife/ Brooklyn Bridge	1967	$10
❏ 2002	Chubby (Please Take Your Love to Town)/ Tender-Hearted Me	1967	$10
❏ 2356	Don't Blow Your Horn/ My Bluebird Flew Away	1968	$12
❏ 2086	I Couldn't Spell Ywuk/ We Split the Blanket	1968	$10
COLUMBIA			
❏ 4-42829	Cool It in Outer Space/ My Old Buddy	1963	$20
LONE STAR			
❏ 709	The Diet Song/If You Think I'm Crazy Now	1979	$6
GEILS, J., BAND			
Featuring Peter Wolf.			
ATLANTIC			
❏ 3350	(Ain't Nothing But a) House Party/Give It To Me	1976	$5
❏ 2802	Cruisin' for a Love/Wait	1971	$6
❏ 2843	Dead Presidents/I Don't Need You No More	1971	$6
❏ 3007	Did You No Wrong/That's Why I'm Thinking of You	1974	$5
❏ 2784	First I Look at the Purse/Homework	1971	$8
❏ 2953	Give It To Me/Hold Your Loving	1973	$5
❏ 3251	Givin' It All Up/Gettin' Out	1975	$5
❏ 2929	Hard Drivin' Man/ Whammer Jammer	1972	$6
❏ 3454	I Do/Trying to Live My Life Without You	1978	$5
—As "Geils			
❏ 3454 [PS]	I Do/Trying to Live My Life Without You	1978	$8
—As "Geils			
❏ 2844	Looking for a Love/What's Your Whammer Jammer	1971	$6
❏ 2974	Make Up Your Mind/ Southside Shuffle	1973	$5
❏ 2974 [PS]	Make Up Your Mind/ Southside Shuffle	1973	$10
❏ 3438	Monkey Island (Part 1)/Surrender	1977	$5
—As "Geils			
❏ 3214	Must of Got Lost/ Funky Judge	1974	$5
❏ 3378	Peanut Buuter/Magic's Mood	1976	$5
❏ 3301	Think It Over/Love-Itis	1975	$5
❏ 3320	Where Did Our Love Go/ What's Your Hurry	1976	$5
EMI AMERICA			
❏ 8100	Angel in Blue/Rage in the Cage	1982	$3
❏ 8100 [PS]	Angel in Blue/Rage in the Cage	1982	$4
❏ 8102	Centerfold/Rage in the Cage	1981	$5
—Regular gray EMI America label			
❏ 8102	Centerfold/Rage in the Cage	1981	$3
—Custom pink label			
❏ 8102 [PS]	Centerfold/Rage in the Cage	1981	$10
❏ 8032 [DJ]	Come Back (Long)/ Come Back (Edit)	1980	$5
❏ 8032	Come Back/Takin' You Down	1980	$4
❏ 8242	Concealed Weapons/ Tell 'Em Jonsey	1984	$3
❏ 8242 [PS]	Concealed Weapons/ Tell 'Em Jonsey	1984	$4
❏ 8260	Eenie Meenie Miney Mo/I Will Carry You Home	1985	$3
❏ 8108	Freeze-Frame/Flamethrower	1982	$3
❏ 8108 [PS]	Freeze-Frame/Flamethrower	1982	$6
❏ 8148	I Do/Sanctuary	1982	$3
❏ 8148 [PS]	I Do/Sanctuary	1982	$4
❏ 8156	Land of 1000 Dances/ Jus' Can't Stop Me	1983	$3
❏ 8039	Love Stinks/Till the Walls Come Tumblin' Down	1980	$4

Number	Title	Yr	NM
❏ 8039 [PS]	Love Stinks/Till the Walls Come Tumblin' Down	1980	$5
❏ 8007	One Last Kiss/Revenge	1978	$4
❏ 8007 [PS]	One Last Kiss/Revenge	1978	$6
❏ 8012	Take It Back/I Can't Believe You	1979	$4
❏ 8016	Wild Man/Just Can't Stop Me	1979	$4
❏ 8016 [PS]	Wild Man/Just Can't Stop Me	1979	$10

PRIVATE I
| ❏ 05462 | Fright Night/Boppin' Tonight | 1985 | $3 |

— B-side by The Fabulous Fontaines
| ❏ 05462 [PS] | Fright Night/Boppin' Tonight | 1985 | $4 |

SILVER SPOTLIGHT SERIES
| ❏ X-7106 | Centerfold/I Do (Live Version) | 1983 | $5 |

— Unusual reissue

7-Inch Extended Plays

ATLANTIC
| ❏ SD 7-7260 [PS] | Bloodshot | 1973 | $20 |

— Part of "Little LP" series (LLP #219)
| ❏ SD 7-7260 | House Party/Give It to Me//Start All Over Again/ Make Up Your Mind | 1973 | $20 |

— Jukebox issue; small hole, plays at 33 1/3 rpm

GELDOF, BOB

ATLANTIC
❏ 89261	Heartless Heart/Pulled Apart by Horses	1987	$3
❏ 89309	Love Is Like a Rocket/ Pulled Apart by Horses	1986	$3
❏ 89309 [PS]	Love Is Like a Rocket/ Pulled Apart by Horses	1986	$3
❏ 89341	This Is the World Calling/Talk Me Up	1986	$3
❏ 89341 [PS]	This Is the World Calling/Talk Me Up	1986	$3

GEMS, THE (1)

CHESS
❏ 1882	A Love of Mine/That's Why They Put Erasers On	1964	$50
❏ 2104	Girls Can Do It/Ain't That Loving You	1971	$30
❏ 1930	He Makes Me Feel So Good/Happy New Love	1965	$50
❏ 1908	I Can't Help Myself/ Can't You Take a Hint	1964	$50
❏ 1875	If It's the Last Thing I Do/A Girl's Impression	1963	$15
❏ 1917	Love For Christmas/All Of It	1964	$20
❏ 1863	One More Year/Let Your Hair Down	1963	$15

GEMS, THE (2)

DREXEL
| ❏ 901 | Deed I Do/Talk About the Weather | 1954 | $400 |

— Black vinyl
| ❏ 901 | Deed I Do/Talk About the Weather | 1954 | $2500 |

— Red vinyl
| ❏ 903 | I Thought You'd Care/ Kitty from New York City | 1954 | $300 |

— Black vinyl
| ❏ 903 | I Thought You'd Care/ Kitty from New York City | 1954 | $600 |

— Red vinyl
| ❏ 909 | One Woman Man/ The Darkest Night | 1955 | $400 |
| ❏ 915 | Till the Day I Die/ Monkey Face Baby | 1956 | $400 |

GEMS, THE (U)

MERCURY
| ❏ 71819 | Crazy Chicken/Hippy Dippy | 1961 | $12 |

PAT
| ❏ 101 | There's No One Like My Love/School Rock | 1961 | $40 |

RECORTE
| ❏ 407 | Waiting/Please Change Your Mind | 1959 | $60 |

RIVERSIDE
| ❏ 4590 | I'll Be There/I Miss Him | 1967 | $40 |

GENE AND DEBBE

SAN
| ❏ 1519 | Go with Me/The Torch I Carry | 1967 | $30 |

TRX
❏ 5002	Go with Me/The Torch I Carry	1967	$8
❏ 5021	I'm Only Human/Loan Some	1969	$8
❏ 5010	Lovin' Season/Love Will Give Us Wings	1968	$8

Number	Title	Yr	NM
❏ 5017	Memories Are Made of This/ The Sun Won't Shine Again	1969	$8
❏ 5006	Playboy/I'll Come Running	1967	$10

GENE AND EUNICE

ALADDIN
❏ 3351	Bom Bom Lulu/ Hi Diddle Diddle	1956	$30
❏ 3376	Doodle Doodle Doo/Don't Treat Me This Way	1957	$30
❏ 3292	Flim Flam/Can We Forget It	1954	$30
❏ 3315	Hootchy Kootchy/I'll Never Believe in You	1955	$30
❏ 3305	I Gotta Go Home/Have You Changed Your Mind	1954	$30
❏ 3414	I Mean Love/The Angels Gave You to Me	1958	$30
❏ 3321	Let's Get Together/I'm So in Love with You	1955	$30
❏ 3282	This Is My Story/ Move It Over Baby	1954	$30

CASE
❏ 1002	Ah! Ah!/You Think I'm Not Thinking	1959	$40
❏ 1001	Poco-Loco/Go-On Kokomo	1959	$40
❏ 1007	Sugar Babe/Let's Play the Game	1960	$30
❏ 1005	Without Love/ (B-side unknown)	1959	$30

LILLY
| ❏ 512 | Everlovin' Baby/Got a Right to Know | 1962 | $20 |

GENE AND JERRY

ROULETTE
| ❏ 4537 | Hootenanny Christmas/ Carousel | 1963 | $15 |

GENE LOVES JEZEBEL

GEFFEN
❏ 28104	Suspicion/Drowning Crazy	1988	$4
❏ 28104 [PS]	Suspicion/Drowning Crazy	1988	$4
❏ 28183	The Motion of Love/ Bugg's Bruises	1987	$4
❏ 28183 [PS]	The Motion of Love/ Bugg's Bruises	1987	$4

GENERAL PUBLIC

I.R.S.
❏ 53016	Come Again/Cheque in the Post	1987	$3
❏ 9937	Hot Your Cool/Day-to-Day	1985	$3
❏ 9934	Tenderness/Limited Balance	1984	$3
❏ 9934 [PS]	Tenderness/Limited Balance	1984	$3
❏ 52941	Too Much or Nothing/ Taking the Day Off	1986	$3
❏ 52941 [PS]	Too Much or Nothing/ Taking the Day Off	1986	$3

GENESIS

Also see PHIL COLLINS; PETER GABRIEL; STEVE HACKETT; MIKE RUTHERFORD; PETER BANKS.

ATCO
❏ 7050	Entangled/Ripples	1976	$40
❏ 7013	The Lamb Lies Down on Broadway/ Counting Out Time	1975	$60
❏ 7013 [DJ]	The Lamb Lies Down on Broadway (stereo/mono)	1975	$40

ATLANTIC
❏ 3891	Abacab/Who Dunnit?	1982	$4
❏ 3891 [PS]	Abacab/Who Dunnit?	1982	$5
❏ 3474	Follow You Follow Me/ Inside and Out	1978	$5

— A radically different mix than the LP version of A-side
❏ 3511	Go West Young Man (In the Motherlode)/Scene from a Night's Dream	1978	$30
❏ 3511 [DJ]	Go West Young Man (In the Motherlode)/Scene from a Night's Dream (stereo/mono)	1978	$6
❏ 7-89698 [DJ]	Illegal Alien (Edit)/ (LP Version)	1984	$6
❏ 7-89698	Illegal Alien/Turn It On Again (Live in Philadelphia)	1984	$4
❏ 7-89698 [PS]	Illegal Alien/Turn It On Again (Live in Philadelphia)	1984	$4
❏ 7-89316	In Too Deep/I'd Rather Be You	1987	$3
❏ 7-89316 [PS]	In Too Deep/I'd Rather Be You	1987	$4
❏ 7-89407	Invisible Touch/ The Last Domino	1986	$3
❏ 7-89407 [PS]	Invisible Touch/ The Last Domino	1986	$3
❏ 7-89336	Land of Confusion/ Feeding the Fire	1986	$3

— Regular Atlantic red and black label
| ❏ 7-89336 | Land of Confusion/ Feeding the Fire | 1986 | $12 |

— Black label with different Atlantic logo
| ❏ 7-89336 [PS] | Land of Confusion/ Feeding the Fire | 1986 | $12 |

— Sleeve came only with black-label versions

Number	Title	Yr	NM
❏ 7-89770	Mama/It's Gonna Get Better	1983	$3
❏ 7-89770 [PS]	Mama/It's Gonna Get Better	1983	$4
❏ 4025	Man on the Corner/ Submarine	1982	$4
❏ 4025 [PS]	Man on the Corner/ Submarine	1982	$5
❏ 3662	Misunderstanding/ Behind the Lines	1980	$4
❏ 3662 [PS]	Misunderstanding/ Behind the Lines	1980	$6
❏ PR453 [DJ]	Paperlate/Turn It On Again (Live)	1982	$8
❏ 4053	Paperlate/You Might Recall	1982	$4
❏ 4053 [PS]	Paperlate/You Might Recall	1982	$6
❏ 7-89656	Taking It All Too Hard/ Silver Rainbow	1984	$3
❏ 7-89656 [PS]	Taking It All Too Hard/ Silver Rainbow	1984	$6
❏ 7-89724	That's All/Second Home by the Sea	1983	$3

— With custom labels
| ❏ 7-89724 [PS] | That's All/Second Home by the Sea | 1983 | $5 |

— Brown title sleeve with no center cut-out
| ❏ 7-89724 [PS] | That's All/Second Home by the Sea | 1983 | $4 |

— Brown title sleeve with center cut-out
❏ 7-89372	Throwing It All Away/ Do the Neurotic	1986	$3
❏ 7-89372 [PS]	Throwing It All Away/ Do the Neurotic	1986	$3
❏ 7-89290	Tonight, Tonight, Tonight/ In the Glow of the Night	1987	$3
❏ 7-89290 [PS]	Tonight, Tonight, Tonight/ In the Glow of the Night	1987	$5

— Color sleeve
| ❏ 7-89290 [PS] | Tonight, Tonight, Tonight/ In the Glow of the Night | 1987 | $6 |

— Black and white sleeve
| ❏ 3751 | Turn It On Again/ Evidence of Autumn | 1980 | $4 |

ATLANTIC OLDIES SERIES
| ❏ 7-84957 | Follow You Follow Me/Illegal Alien | 1987 | $3 |

— Reissue
| ❏ OS13239 | I Know What I Like (In Your Wardrobe)/The Lamb Lies Down on Broadway | 1984 | $10 |

— Reissue
| ❏ 7-84956 | In Too Deep/Mama | 1987 | $3 |

— Reissue
| ❏ 7-84959 | Invisible Touch/ Throwing It All Away | 1987 | $3 |

— Reissue
| ❏ 7-84958 | Land of Confusion/ Tonight, Tonight, Tonight | 1987 | $3 |

— Reissue
| ❏ OS13252 | Misunderstanding/ Turn It On Again | 1984 | $5 |

— Reissue; black and gold label
| ❏ OS13254 | Paperlate/Man on the Corner | 1984 | $5 |

— Reissue; black and gold label
| ❏ 7-84996 | That's All/Taking It All Too Hard | 1987 | $3 |

— Reissue

CHARISMA
| ❏ 26002 [DJ] | I Know What I Like (In Your Wardrobe) (stereo/mono) | 1973 | $40 |
| ❏ 26002 | I Know What I Like (In Your Wardrobe)/ Twilight Ale House | 1973 | $60 |

PARROT
| ❏ 3018 [DJ] | Silent Sun/That's Me | 1968 | $125 |

— May be promo only
| ❏ 3018 [DJ] | Silent Sun/That's Me | 1968 | $125 |

— Promotional copy; orangeish label with black bird
| ❏ 3018 | Silent Sun/That's Me | 1968 | $400 |

— Stock copy with black label and green and yellow bird

GENESIS (3)

MERCURY
| ❏ 72806 | Angeline/Suzanne | 1968 | $15 |
| ❏ 72869 | Gloomy Sunday/ What's It All About | 1968 | $10 |

GENESIS (4)

RIPCHORD
| ❏ 04 | Window of Sand/ Would You Like To | 1967 | $30 |

GENESIS (5)

SCEPTER
| ❏ 12341 | Second Coming/ Double Bubble | 1972 | $5 |

Number	Title	Yr	NM
GENIES, THE (1)			
SHAD			
❏ 5002	Who's That Knocking/ The First Time	1959	$30
—Pink label			
❏ 5002	Who's That Knocking/ The First Time	1959	$20
—Blue label			
WARWICK			
❏ 573	Crazy Love/There Goes That Rain	1960	$20
❏ 643	Little Young Girl/ Crazy Feeling	1961	$20
GENIES, THE (2)			
RONN			
❏ 50	Anybody Here Know How to Pray/Take Me There	1971	$6
GENTEELS, THE			
CAPITOL			
❏ 4798	Take It Off/Hitchhiker	1962	$30
STAG			
❏ 2930/1	Take It Off/Hitch Hiker	1962	$60
❏ 4949/50	The Force of Gravity/ Springboard	1962	$60
GENTLE GIANT			
CAPITOL			
❏ 4484	Cogs in Cogs/I'm Turning Around	1977	$5
❏ 4652	Spooky Boogie/Words from the Wise	1978	$5
GENTLE SOUL, THE			
COLUMBIA			
❏ 4-44152	Song for Three/Our National Anthem	1967	$30
❏ 4-43952	Tell Me Love/You Move Me	1966	$30
❏ 4-43952 [PS]	Tell Me Love/You Move Me	1966	$50
GENTLEMEN FOUR, THE			
WAND			
❏ 1184	It Won't Hurt Baby/You Can't Keep a Good Man Down	1968	$600
GENTLEMEN, THE			
APOLLO			
❏ 470	Don't Leave Me Baby/ Baby Don't Go	1955	$125
❏ 464	Something to Remember Me By/Tired of You	1954	$200
CAMEO			
❏ 419	Come On (If You Can)/Only Me	1966	$30
GENTONES, THE			
CASINO			
❏ 52261	City Lights/Counting Stars	1961	$500
GENTRY, BOBBIE			
BRUNSWICK			
❏ 55517	Another Place -- Another Time/I Think I'll Cry Out Loud	1975	$6
CAPITOL			
❏ 2849	Apartment 21/Seasons Come, Seasons Go	1970	$6
❏ 3071	But I Can't Get Back/ Marigolds and Tangerines	1971	$6
❏ 2675	Fancy/Courtyard	1969	$6
❏ 3413	Girl from Cincinnati/ You and Me Together	1972	$6
❏ 3413 [PS]	Girl from Cincinnati/ You and Me Together	1972	$8
❏ 2788	He Made a Woman Out of Me/Billy the Kid	1970	$6
❏ 2295	Hushabye Mountain/ Sweet Peony	1968	$8
❏ 5992	I Saw An Angel Die/ Poppa, Won'tcha Let Me Go to Town with You	1967	$8
❏ 2147	Louisiana Man/Courtyard	1968	$8
❏ 5950	Ode to Billie Joe/ Mississippi Delta	1967	$10
❏ 4294	Ode to Billie Joe/ Mississippi Delta	1976	$5
❏ 2044	Okolona River Bottom Band/Penduli Pendulum	1967	$8
❏ 2044 [PS]	Okolona River Bottom Band/Penduli Pendulum	1967	$20
❏ 2501	Touch 'Em With Love/ Casket Vignette	1969	$6
WARNER BROS.			
❏ 8210	Ode to Billie Joe/ There'll Be a Time	1976	$5
—B-side by Michel Legrand			
❏ 8210 [PS]	Ode to Billie Joe/ There'll Be a Time	1976	$10
❏ 8532	Steal Away/He Did Me Wrong But He Did It Right	1978	$4
GENTRY, GARY			
ELEKTRA			
❏ 47122	I Sold All of Tom T.'s Songs Last Night/Because of You	1981	$4
❏ 47238	(S.O.B.) Same Old Boy/ The Devil Offered More	1981	$4
GENTRY, RAY			
MAVERICK			
❏ 614	Willie Was a Bad Boy/Do the Fly	1958	$400
GENTRYS, THE			
BELL			
❏ 753	Midnight Train/You Tell Me You Love Me	1968	$6
❏ 740	Thinking Like a Child/Silky	1968	$6
CAPITOL			
❏ 3459	Changin'/Let Me Put This Ring Upon Your Finger	1972	$5
MGM			
❏ 13495	Everyday I Have to Cry/ Don't Let It Be (This Time)	1966	$15
❏ 13749	I Can See/90 Pound Weakling	1967	$10
❏ 13432	Spread It On Thick/ Brown Paper Sack	1965	$15
❏ 13432 [PS]	Spread It On Thick/ Brown Paper Sack	1965	$20
❏ 13561	There Are Two Sides to Every Story/Woman of the World	1966	$15
❏ 13690	There's a Love/You Make Me Feel So Good	1967	$30
STAX			
❏ 0223	All Hung Up on You/ Little Gold Band	1974	$4
❏ 0242	High Flyer/Little Gold Band	1975	$4
SUN			
❏ 1114	Cinnamon Girl/I Just Got the News	1970	$5
❏ 1114 [DJ]	Cinnamon Girl/I Just Got the News	1970	$10
—Promo only on blue vinyl			
❏ 1120	Friends/Goddess of Love	1970	$40
❏ 1126	God Save Our Country/ Love You All My Life	1971	$5
❏ 1118	I Hate to See You Go/ He'll Never Love Me	1970	$5
❏ 1108	I Need Love/Why Should I Cry	1969	$5
❏ 1122	Wild World/Sunshine	1971	$5
YOUNGSTOWN			
❏ 600	Sometimes/Little Drops of Water	1965	$30
GEORGE AND EARL			
MERCURY			
❏ 70773	Cry, Baby, Cry/Take a Look at My Darlin'	1956	$30
❏ 70852	Done Gone/Better Stop, Look and Listen	1956	$70
❏ 70935	Eleven Roses/ Remember and Regret	1956	$30
❏ 70632	Goin' Steady with the Blues/ Sweet Little Miss Blue Eyes	1955	$30
❏ 70605	Got Anything Good/Can I?	1955	$30
❏ 70683	Heartaches/Don't, Don't, Don't	1955	$30
GEORGE, BARBARA			
A.F.O.			
❏ 302	I Know (You Don't Love Me No More)/Love	1961	$15
—Orange and black label			
❏ 302	I Know (You Don't Love Me No More)/Love	1961	$20
—All-orange label			
SUE			
❏ 763	If You Think/If When You've Done the Best You Can	1962	$8
❏ 766	Send for Me (If You Need Some Lovin')/Bless You	1962	$8
❏ 796	Something's Definitely Wrong/I Need Something Different	1963	$12
UNITED ARTISTS			
❏ XW516	I Know (You Don't Love Me No More)/Mockingbird	1974	$4
—Reissue; B-side by Charles and Inez Foxx			
GEORGE, LLOYD			
IMPERIAL			
❏ 5896	Come On Train/Frog Hunt	1962	$20
❏ 5837	Twistville/Young Date	1962	$20
GEORGIA SATELLITES, THE			
ELEKTRA			
❏ 7-69267	Another Chance/Saddle Up	1989	$3
❏ 7-69497	Battleship Chains/ Golden Light	1987	$3
❏ 7-69497 [PS]	Battleship Chains/ Golden Light	1987	$3
❏ 7-69366	Hippy Hippy Shake/ Hand to Mouth	1988	$3
❏ 7-69393	Open All Night/Dunk 'N' Dine	1988	$3
❏ 7-69393 [PS]	Open All Night/Dunk 'N' Dine	1988	$3
❏ 7-69328	Sheila/Hippy Hippy Shake	1988	$3
❏ 7-69328 [PS]	Sheila/Hippy Hippy Shake	1988	$3
GERARD, DANYEL			
COLUMBIA			
❏ 4-45468	Butterfly/One White Rose	1971	$8
MGM VERVE			
❏ 10670	Butterfly/Let's Love	1972	$6
❏ 10670 [PS]	Butterfly/Let's Love	1972	$10
❏ 10685	Elie Lama Sabacthani/ The Gun	1972	$6
GERMS, THE			
SLASH			
❏ 101	Lexicon Devil/Circle One/No God	1978	$30
❏ 101 [PS]	Lexicon Devil/Circle One/No God	1978	$30
WHAT			
❏ 01	Forming/Sex Boy	1977	$30
❏ 01 [PS]	Forming/Sex Boy	1977	$30
—With lyric insert			
GERMZ, THE			
VERTIGO			
❏ 8001	Boy-Girl Love/No Easy Way Down	1967	$20
GERONIMO BLACK			
Also see FRANK ZAPPA, as this band included members of the Mothers of Invention.			
UNI			
❏ 55339	Let Us Live/'59 Chevy	1972	$12
GERRARD, DONNY			
GREEDY			
❏ 114	Darlin'/He's Always Somewhere Around	1977	$6
❏ 107	He's Always Somewhere Around/Greedy (For Your Love)	1976	$12
❏ 109	Peace for Us All/Stay Awhile with Me	1976	$10
❏ 101	Words (Are Impossible)/ Stand Up	1976	$6
ROCKET			
❏ 40405	(Baby) Don't Let It Mess Your Mind/A Woman, a Lover, a Friend	1975	$8
GERRY AND THE GEORGETTES			
HIT			
❏ 83	Be My Baby/Sally Go 'Round the Roses	1963	$8
—As "The Georgettes"; B-side by the Belles			
GERRY AND THE PACEMAKERS			
LAURIE			
❏ 3251	Don't Let the Sun Catch You Crying/Away from You	1964	$20
❏ 3323	Dreams/Walk Hand in Hand	1965	$12
❏ 3284	Ferry Across the Mersey/Pretend	1965	$15
❏ 3354	Girl on a Swing/The Way You Look Tonight	1966	$10
❏ 3313	Give All Your Love to Me/ You're the Reason	1965	$10
❏ 3162	How Do You Do It/ Away From You	1963	$30
❏ 3261	How Do You Do It/You'll Never Walk Alone	1964	$15
❏ 3196	I Like It/It Happened to Me	1963	$30
❏ 3271	I Like It/Jambalaya	1964	$15
❏ 3279	I'll Be There/You, You, You	1964	$15
❏ 3233	I'm the One/How Do You Do It	1964	$20
❏ 3233	I'm the One/It's All Right	1964	$20
❏ 3233	I'm the One/You've Got What I Like	1964	$30
❏ 3293	It's Gonna Be Alright/ Skinny Minnie	1965	$10
❏ 3337	La La La/Without You	1966	$12
❏ 3370	The Big Bright Green Pleasure Machine/ Looking for My Life	1966	$15
GESTURES, THE			
SOMA			
❏ 1426	Don't Mess Around/ Candlelight	1965	$30

Number	Title	Yr	NM

GETZ, STAN, AND LAURINDO ALMEIDA
VERVE

| ❏ 10468 | Winter Moon/Menina Moca | 1966 | $6 |

GETZ, STAN, AND CHARLIE BYRD
VERVE

| ❏ 10260 | Desafinado/Theme from Dr. Kildare | 1962 | $8 |

GETZ, STAN, AND JOAO GILBERTO
VERVE

❏ 10336	Only Trust Your Heart/Telephone Song	1964	$8
❏ 10323	The Girl from Ipanema/Blowin' in the Wind	1964	$8
❏ 10322	The Girl from Ipanema/Corcovado	1964	$10

GETZ, STAN
COLUMBIA

| ❏ 10132 | La Fiesta/(B-side unknown) | 1975 | $5 |

DAWN

| ❏ 204 | Pennies from Heaven/It's the Talk of the Town | 1954 | $20 |

MERCURY

| ❏ 89059 | Erudition/Have You Met Miss Jones | 1953 | $20 |
| ❏ 89042 | 'Tis Autumn/Lover Come Back to Me | 1953 | $20 |

MGM

❏ 13430	Once Upon a Time/Taste of Living	1965	$6
❏ 13430 [PS]	Once Upon a Time/Taste of Living	1965	$20
❏ 240	My Old Flame/The Lady in Red	1962	$10

—*Reissue of 712*

VERVE

❏ 10279	Balanco No Samba/Mahna de Carnaval	1963	$8
❏ 10676	Communication '72/Back to Bach	1972	$5
❏ 10251	I Remember When/I'm Late-I'm Late	1962	$8
❏ 10557	Midnight Samba/Once	1967	$6
❏ 10571	My Own True Love/A Tribute to Stan	1967	$6
❏ 10291	O Morro/Sambalero	1963	$8

GIANT CRAB, THE
UNI

❏ 55103	Believe It or Not/The Color Purple	1968	$8
❏ 55134	Cool It/Intensify My Soul	1969	$8
❏ 55155	ESP/Hot Line Conversation	1969	$8
❏ 55094	Hi Ho Silver Lining/Hot Line Conversation	1968	$8

GIBB, ANDY
RSO

| ❏ 1065 | All I Have to Do Is Dream/Good Feeling | 1981 | $4 |

—*With Victoria Principal*

❏ 1065 [PS]	All I Have to Do Is Dream/Good Feeling	1981	$5
❏ 904	An Everlasting Love/Flowing Rivers	1978	$4
❏ 1019	Desire/Waiting for You	1980	$4

—*A picture sleeve is rumored to exist, but we haven't seen it*

| ❏ 1026 | I Can't Help It/Someone I Ain't | 1980 | $4 |

—*A-side: With Olivia Newton-John*

❏ 872	I Just Want to Be Your Everything/In the End	1977	$4
❏ 872 [PS]	I Just Want to Be Your Everything/In the End	1977	$5
❏ 883	(Love Is) Thicker Than Water/Words and Music	1977	$4
❏ 1056	Me (Without You)/Melody	1980	$4
❏ 911	(Our Love) Don't Throw It All Away/One More Look at the Night	1978	$4
❏ 911 [PS]	(Our Love) Don't Throw It All Away/One More Look at the Night	1978	$5
❏ 893	Shadow Dancing/Let It Be Me	1978	$4
❏ 1059	Time Is Time/I Go for You	1980	$4

GIBB, BARRY
MCA

❏ 52501	Fine Line/Stay Alone	1984	$3
❏ 52501 [PS]	Fine Line/Stay Alone	1984	$4
❏ 52443	Shine Shine/She Says	1984	$3
❏ 52443 [PS]	Shine Shine/She Says	1984	$3

GIBB, ROBIN
ATCO

| ❏ 6737 | August October/Give Me a Smile | 1970 | $15 |
| ❏ 6727 | One Million Years/Weekend | 1969 | $15 |

Number	Title	Yr	NM
❏ 6698	Saved by the Bell/Mother and Jack	1969	$10

EMI AMERICA

❏ B-8291	Like a Fool/Possession	1985	$3
❏ B-8291 [PS]	Like a Fool/Possession	1985	$4
❏ B-8304	Toys/Do You Love Her	1986	$3
❏ B-8304 [PS]	Toys/Do You Love Her	1986	$4

MIRAGE

❏ 99743	Boys Do Fall in Love/Diamonds	1984	$3
❏ 99743 [PS]	Boys Do Fall in Love/Diamonds	1984	$3
❏ 99688 [DJ]	In Your Diary (same on both sides)	1984	$8

—*Stock copy unknown*

| ❏ 99712 | Secret Agent/Robot | 1984 | $3 |

RSO

| ❏ 1047 | Help Me/(Instrumental) | 1980 | $4 |

—*With Marcy Levy*

| ❏ 1047 [PS] | Help Me/(Instrumental) | 1980 | $4 |
| ❏ 907 | Oh Darling/She's Leaving Home | 1978 | $4 |

—*B-side by The Bee Gees*

SESAME STREET

| ❏ 99070 | Sesame Street Fever/Trash | 1978 | $5 |
| ❏ 99070 [PS] | Sesame Street Fever/Trash | 1978 | $6 |

GIBBS, GEORGIA
BELL

❏ 626	Call Me/Don't Cry Joe	1965	$6
❏ 635	In Time/Let Me Dream	1965	$6
❏ 608	I Wouldn't Have It Any Other Way/You Can Never Get Away from Me	1965	$6
❏ 615	Let Me Cry on Your Shoulder/Venice Blue	1965	$6

CORAL

❏ 60315	Ballin' the Jack/Looks Like a Cold Cold Winter	1950	$20
❏ 60462	Ballin' the Jack/Then I'll Be Happy	1951	$20
❏ 60463	Get Out Those Old Records/I'll Get Myself a Choo-Choo Train (And Go Far, Far Away)	1951	$20
❏ 60210	I Don't Care If the Sun Don't Shine/I'll Get Myself a Choo-Choo Train (And Go Far, Far Away)	1950	$20
❏ 60310	If I Were a Bell/I'll Know	1950	$20
❏ 61525	If I Were a Bell/I'll Know	1955	$10
❏ 60353	I Still Feel the Same About You/Get Out Those Old Records	1951	$20
❏ 60255	I Was Dancing with Someone/Then I'll Be Happy	1950	$20
❏ 60406	Shoo Shoo Baby/Once Upon a Nickel	1951	$20
❏ 60227	Simple Melody/A Little Bit Independent	1950	$20

—*With Bob Crosby*

EPIC

| ❏ 9585 | I Will Follow Him (You)/Candy Kisses | 1963 | $8 |
| ❏ 9606 | Tater Poon/Nine Girls Out of Ten Girls | 1963 | $30 |

IMPERIAL

| ❏ 5652 | Seven Lonely Days/The Stroll That Stole My Heart | 1960 | $10 |
| ❏ 5688 | So in Love/Loch Lomond | 1960 | $12 |

KAPP

| ❏ 286 | Pretend/Hamburgers, Frankfurters and Potato Chips | 1959 | $10 |

MERCURY

❏ 70034	A Moth and a Flame/Photograph on the Piano	1953	$15
❏ 5758	Be My Life's Companion/The Oklahoma Polka	1951	$20
❏ 70238	Bridge of Sighs/Hard Lovin' Man	1953	$15
❏ 5749	Cry/My Old Man	1951	$20
❏ 70572	Dance with Me Henry (Wallflower)/Every Road Must Have a Turning	1955	$20
❏ 70172	For Me, For Me/Thunder and Lightning	1953	$15
❏ 70743	Goodbye to Rome (Arrivederci Roma)/24 Hours a Day (365 a Year)	1955	$15
❏ 5662	Good Morning Mister Echo/Be Doggone Sure You Call	1951	$20
❏ 5687	Got Him Offa My Hands/Cherry Pink	1951	$20
❏ 70920	Happiness Street/Happiness Is a Thing Called Joe	1956	$15
❏ 70274	I Love Paris/Under Paris Skies	1953	$15
❏ 70685	I Want You to Be My Baby/Come Rain or Come Shine	1955	$15
❏ 70473	Mambo Baby/Love Me	1954	$15
❏ 5912	My Favorite Song/Sinner or Saint	1952	$15
❏ 70339	My Sin/I'll Always Be Happy with You	1954	$15

Number	Title	Yr	NM
❏ 70218	Say It Isn't So/He's Funny That Way	1953	$15
❏ 70095	Seven Lonely Days/If You Take My Heart Away	1953	$15
❏ 71058	Silent Lips/Pretty Pretty	1957	$15
❏ 5874	So Madly in Love/Make Me Love You	1952	$15
❏ 70298	Somebody Bad Stole De Wedding Bell (Who's Got de Ding Dong)/Baubles, Bangles and Beads	1954	$15
❏ 70647	Sweet and Gentle/Blueberries	1955	$15
❏ 70430	The Man That Got Away/More Than Ever	1954	$15
❏ 71103	The Sheik of Araby/I Am a Heart, a Heart, a Heart	1957	$15
❏ 5644	Tom's Tune/I Wish, I Wish	1951	$20
❏ 70998	Tra La La/Morning, Noon and Night	1956	$15
❏ 70517	Tweedle Dee/You're Wrong, All Wrong	1954	$20
❏ 70386	Wait for Me Darling/Whistle and I'll Wait	1954	$15
❏ 70057	What Does It Mean/Winter's Here Again	1953	$15
❏ 5718	What You Do to Me/While We Danced	1951	$20
❏ 5681	While You Danced, Danced, Danced/While We're Young	1951	$20

RCA VICTOR

❏ 47-7047	Fun Lovin' Baby/I Never Had the Blues	1957	$15
❏ 47-7098	Great Balls of Fire/I Miss You	1957	$15
❏ 47-7239	Hello Happiness, Goodbye Blues/It's My Pleasure	1958	$15
❏ 47-6922	I'm Walking the Floor Over You/Sugar Candy	1957	$15
❏ 47-9173	Time Will Tell/Where's the Music Coming From	1967	$6

ROULETTE

| ❏ 4106 | The Hula Hoop Song/Keep in Touch | 1958 | $10 |
| ❏ 4126 | Ther Hucklebuck/Better Loved You'll Never Be | 1959 | $10 |

GIBBS, TERRI
HORIZON

| ❏ 2963 | Turn Around/(B-side unknown) | 1987 | $4 |

MCA

❏ 52252	Anybody Else's Heart But Mine/What a Night	1983	$4
❏ 52040	Ashes to Ashes/Plans	1982	$4
❏ 52134	Baby I'm Gone/I Don't Need You	1982	$4
❏ 51180	I Wanna Be Around/Rocky Top	1981	$4
❏ 52440	I Wanna Be Around/Rocky Top	1984	$4
❏ 51225	Mis'ry River/Too Long	1982	$4
❏ 41309	Somebody's Knockin'/Some Days It Rains All Night Long	1980	$4
❏ 52088	Some Days It Rains All Night Long/All I Wanna Do in Life	1982	$4
❏ 52308	Tell Mama/Bells	1983	$4

WARNER BROS.

| ❏ 29056 | A Few Good Men/Ain't Nobody | 1985 | $3 |
| ❏ 28895 | Somebody Must Be Missing You Tonight/Here I Go Again | 1985 | $3 |

GIBSON, ALTHEA
DOT

| ❏ 15758 | Around the World/So Much to Live For | 1958 | $20 |

GIBSON, BOBBY, AND THE VOYAGERS
GIBSON

| ❏ 6003 | B-52/Samoa | 1959 | $60 |

GIBSON, DAVE
HIT

| ❏ 50 | I Saw Linda Yesterday/Hey Paula | 1963 | $8 |

—*B-side by Bob and Bobbie*

GIBSON, DON, AND SUE THOMPSON
HICKORY

❏ 1654	Cause I Love You/My Tears Don't Show	1972	$8
❏ 1629	Did You Ever Think/Love Garden	1972	$8
❏ 1665	Go with Me/Two of Us Together	1973	$8
❏ 1646	I Think They Call It Love/Over There's the Door	1972	$8
❏ 1607	The Two of Us Together/Oh Yes, I Love You	1971	$8

HICKORY/MGM

| ❏ 367 | Get Ready, Here I Come/Once More | 1976 | $6 |
| ❏ 324 | Good Old Fashioned Country Love/Ages and Ages Ago | 1974 | $6 |

Number	Title	Yr	NM
❑ 360	Maybe Tomorrow/I Can't Tell My Heart That	1975	$6
❑ 350	Oh, How Love Changes/ Sweet and Tender Times	1975	$6
❑ 303	Warm Love/Fly the Friendly Skies with Jesus	1973	$6

GIBSON, DON
ABC HICKORY
Number	Title	Yr	NM
❑ 54039	Any Day Now/ Baby's Not Home	1978	$5
❑ 54010	Fan the Flame, Feed the Fire/Bringin' In the Georgia Mail	1977	$5
❑ 54014	If You Ever Get to Houston (Look Me Down)/It's All Over	1977	$5
❑ 54001	I'm All Wrapped Up in You/We Live in Two Different Worlds	1976	$5
❑ 54036	Oh, Such a Stranger/I Love You Because	1978	$5
❑ 54024	Starting All Over Again/I'd Rather Die Young (Than Grow Old Without You)	1978	$5
❑ 54029	The Fool/Every Song I Sang Would Be Blue	1978	$5
❑ 54019	When Do We Stop Starting Over/Love Is Not the Way (You Told Me)	1977	$5

COLUMBIA
Number	Title	Yr	NM
❑ 21060	Sample Kisses/Let Me Stay in Your Arms	1952	$30
❑ 21281	Selfish with Your Kisses/ Ice Cold Heart	1954	$30
❑ 21231	Symptoms of Love/Many Times I've Waited	1954	$30

HICKORY
Number	Title	Yr	NM
❑ 1571	A Perfect Mountain/ Would You Believe	1970	$5
❑ 1614	Country Green/ Move It On Over	1971	$8
❑ 1559	Don't Take All Your Loving/ Pretending Every Day	1970	$5
❑ 1623	Far, Far Away/What's Happened to Me	1972	$8
❑ 1588	Guess Away the Blues/I Wanna Live	1970	$5
❑ 1661	If You're Goin' Girl/ Lonesome Number One	1973	$8
❑ 1598	(I Heard That) Lonesome Whistle/Window Shopping	1971	$8
❑ 1651	Is This the Best I'm Gonna Feel/Watching It Go	1972	$8
❑ 1579	Someway/Comfort for Your Mind	1970	$5
❑ 1671	Touch the Morning/ Too Much to Know	1973	$8
❑ 1638	Woman (Sensuous Woman)/If You Want Me To I'll Go	1972	$8

HICKORY/MGM
Number	Title	Yr	NM
❑ 327	Bring Back Your Love to Me/Drinking Champagne	1974	$6
❑ 372	Doing My Time/The World Is Waiting for the Sunrise	1976	$6
❑ 353	Don't Stop Loving Me/ Somebody's Words	1975	$6
❑ 361	I Don't Think I'll Ever (Get Over You)/It Can't Last Always	1975	$6
❑ 338	I'll Sing for You/Pocatello	1974	$6
❑ 318	One Day at a Time/ Rainbow Love	1974	$6
❑ 312	Snap Your Fingers/Love Is a Lonesome Thing	1973	$6
❑ 306	That's What I'll Do/ Sweet Dreams	1973	$6
❑ 345	(There She Goes) I Wish Her Well/Funny Familiar Forgotten Feelings	1975	$6
❑ 301	Touch the Morning/ Too Much to Know	1973	$6

MCA
Number	Title	Yr	NM
❑ 41031	Forever One Day at a Time/Look Who's Blue	1979	$4

MGM
Number	Title	Yr	NM
❑ 12494	I Ain't a-Studying You Baby/It's Hoppin'	1957	$50
❑ 12290	I Ain't Gonna Waste My Time/Ah-Ha	1956	$50
❑ 12331	I Believed in You/What a Fool I Was to Fall	1956	$40
❑ 12194	Sweet Dreams/The Road of Life Alone	1956	$40

RCA VICTOR
Number	Title	Yr	NM
❑ 47-8732	A Born Loser/All the World Is Lonely Now	1965	$8
❑ 47-8589	Again/You're Going Away	1965	$8
❑ 47-9266	All My Love/No Doubt About It	1967	$8
❑ 47-8192	Anything New Gets Old (Except My Love for You)/ After the Heartache	1963	$10
❑ 47-8192 [PS]	Anything New Gets Old (Except My Love for You)/ After the Heartache	1963	$20
❑ 47-9460	Ashes of Love/Good Morning, Dear	1968	$6
❑ 47-7010	Blue Blue Day/Too Soon to Know	1957	$20
❑ 47-8456	Cause I Believe in You/A Love That Can't Be	1964	$10
❑ 47-4473	Dark Future/Blue Million Tears	1952	$30
❑ 47-7566	Don't Tell Me Your Troubles/ Heartbreak Avenue	1959	$20
❑ 47-9663	Ever Changing Mind/Thoughts	1968	$6
❑ 47-6942	Everything Turns Out for the Best/Sittin' Here Cryin'	1957	$30
❑ 47-7762	Far, Far Away/A Legend in My Time	1960	$15
❑ 61-7762 [S]	Far, Far Away/A Legend in My Time	1960	$30

—Living Stereo" (large hole, plays at 45 rpm)

Number	Title	Yr	NM
❑ 47-8367	Fireball Mail/Oh, Such a Stranger	1964	$10
❑ 47-8975	Funny, Familiar, Forgotten, Feelings/Forget Me	1966	$8
❑ 47-7330	Give Myself a Party/ Look Who's Blue	1958	$20
❑ 47-8144	Head Over Heels in Love with You/It Was Worth It All	1963	$12
❑ 47-8144 [PS]	Head Over Heels in Love with You/It Was Worth It All	1963	$20
❑ 47-8017	I Can Mend Your Broken Heart/I Let Her Get Lonely	1962	$10
❑ 47-6860	I Can't Leave/I Love You Still	1957	$30
❑ 48-0424	I Love No One But You/ Carolina Breakdown	1951	$30
❑ 47-7629	I'm Movin' On/Big Hearted Man	1959	$20
❑ 47-9563	It's a Long, Long Way to Georgia/Low and Lonely	1968	$6
❑ 74-0219	I Will Always/And As Much	1969	$6
❑ 47-7959	Lonesome Number One/ Same Old Trouble	1961	$15
❑ 47-7505	Lonesome Old House/I Couldn't Care Less	1959	$20
❑ 47-9177	Lost Highway/ Around the Town	1967	$8
❑ 47-9906	Montego Bay/If My Heart Had Windows	1970	$6
❑ 47-7133	Oh Lonesome Me/I Can't Stop Lovin' You	1958	$20
❑ 47-9395	Satisfied/Where No Man Stands Alone	1967	$8
❑ 47-7890	Sea of Heartbreak/I Think It's Best (To Forget Me)	1961	$15
❑ 47-8085	So How Come (No One Loves Me)/Baby We're Really in Love	1962	$12
❑ 47-8085 [PS]	So How Come (No One Loves Me)/Baby We're Really in Love	1962	$20
❑ 74-0143	Solitary/I Just Said Goodbye to My Dreams	1969	$6
❑ 47-7805	Sweet Dreams/ The Same Street	1960	$15
❑ 47-8678	Watch Where You're Going/ There's a Big Wheel	1965	$8
❑ 47-7841	What About Me/The World Is Waiting for the Sunrise	1961	$15
❑ 37-7841	What About Me/The World Is Waiting for the Sunrise	1961	$30

—Compact Single 33" (small hole, plays at LP speed)

Number	Title	Yr	NM
❑ 47-7437	Who Cares/A Stranger to Me	1959	$20

WARNER BROS.
Number	Title	Yr	NM
❑ 49504	I'd Be Crazy Over You/Somewhere Between Yesterday	1980	$4
❑ 49602	Love Fires/Come Back and Love Me	1980	$4
❑ 49193	Sweet Sensuous Sensations/Stranger to Me	1980	$4

7-Inch Extended Plays
COLUMBIA
Number	Title	Yr	NM
❑ B-2146	(contents unknown)	1957	$25
❑ B-2146 [PS]	Don Gibson	1957	$25

RCA VICTOR
Number	Title	Yr	NM
❑ EPA-4323 [PS]	Blue, Blue Day	1958	$20
❑ EPA-5114 [PS]	Blue and Lonesome	1959	$20
❑ EPA-4323	(contents unknown)	1958	$20
❑ EPA-4335	(contents unknown)	1958	$20
❑ EPA-5114	Oh Lonesome Me/ Look Who's Blue//Who Cares/Blue, Blue Day	1959	$20
❑ EPA-4335 [PS]	That Lonesome Valley	1958	$20

GIBSON, GINNY
ABC-PARAMOUNT
Number	Title	Yr	NM
❑ 9872	Homing Pigeon/ September Till June	1957	$20
❑ 9786	I Pledge Allegiance to Your Heart/Pair of Fools	1957	$20
❑ 9739	Miracle of Love/Two Innocent Hearts	1956	$20

DAVIS
Number	Title	Yr	NM
❑ 442	Mommy's Little Angel/ Wanting You	1955	$20

MGM
Number	Title	Yr	NM
❑ K12019	Am I Asking Too Much/ Chihuahua Choo-Choo	1955	$30
❑ K11736	Aye, Aye, Aye/ Serenade to Spring	1954	$30
❑ K11672	Baton Rouge/Don't Stop Kissing Me Goodnight	1954	$30
❑ K11435	Condemned Without a Trial/Kiss	1953	$30
❑ K11571	Dansero/No More Tears	1953	$30
❑ K11913	Like M-A-D/Once There Was a Little Girl	1955	$30
❑ K11499	Lonely Lover/Unless You're Really Mine	1953	$30
❑ K12113	Ooh (How I Love Ya)/If You Want to Make Me Happy	1955	$30
❑ K11814	There's a Small Hotel/The Song That Broke My Heart	1954	$30
❑ K11961	Whatever Lola Wants/ If Anything Should Happen to You	1955	$30
❑ K10661	Where in the World/ You're Finding Out How Much I Love You	1950	$30

GIBSON, JILL
IMPERIAL
Number	Title	Yr	NM
❑ 66068	It's as Easy as 1,2,3/ Jilly's Flip Side	1964	$70

—Produced by Jan Berry

GIBSON, JOHNNY
BIG TOP
Number	Title	Yr	NM
❑ 3118	After Midnight/ Walking On Down	1962	$30
❑ 3088	Midnight/Chuck-a-Luck	1961	$30
❑ 3149	Summer Holiday/ Ooh Poo Pa Doo	1963	$30

LAURIE
Number	Title	Yr	NM
❑ 3256	Beachcomber/Swanky	1964	$30

—As "The Johnny Gibson Trio

TWIRL
Number	Title	Yr	NM
❑ 2012	Beachcomber/Swanky	1964	$50

—As "The Johnny Gibson Trio

GIBSON, STEVE, AND THE RED CAPS
ABC-PARAMOUNT
Number	Title	Yr	NM
❑ 10105	I Went to Your Wedding/Together	1960	$20
❑ 9702	Love Me Tenderly/ Rock and Roll Stomp	1956	$30
❑ 9856	Silhouettes/Flamingo	1957	$30
❑ 9750	Write to Me/Cuacho Serenade	1956	$30

HUNT
Number	Title	Yr	NM
❑ 326	Bless You/Cheryl Lee	1959	$20
❑ 330	Where Are You/San Antonio Rose	1959	$20

JAY DEE
Number	Title	Yr	NM
❑ 796	It Hurts Me But I Like It/Ouch!	1954	$50

MERCURY
Number	Title	Yr	NM
❑ 8146	Blueberry Hill/I Love You	1951	$100

—78 released in 1949

Number	Title	Yr	NM
❑ 5380	I'll Never Love Anyone Else/(B-side unknown)	1950	$200
❑ 70389	Wedding Bells (Are Breaking Up That Old Gang of Mine)/ Second Hand Romance	1954	$60

RCA VICTOR
Number	Title	Yr	NM
❑ 47-5130	Big Game Hunter/ Do I, Do I, Do I	1953	$50
❑ 47-4076	Did Ya Eat Yet, Joe/$3.98	1951	$60
❑ 47-6345	How I Cry/Bobbin'	1955	$30
❑ 50-0127	I'm to Blame/ Sidewalk Shuffle	1951	$70
❑ 47-4835	I Went to Your Wedding/Wait	1952	$50
❑ 47-4294	Shame/Boogie Woogie on Saturday Night	1951	$60
❑ 47-3986	The Thing/Am I To Blame?	1950	$70
❑ 47-4670	Two Little Kisses/I May Hate Myself in the Morning	1952	$50
❑ 47-5013	Why Don't You Love Me/Truthfully	1952	$50
❑ 50-0138	Would I Mind/When You Come Back to Me	1951	$70

7-Inch Extended Plays
MERCURY
Number	Title	Yr	NM
❑ EP1-3215 [PS]	Blueberry Hill	1952	$250
❑ EP1-3215	(contents unknown)	1952	$250

GIESE, JIMMY
DECCA
Number	Title	Yr	NM
❑ 9-46334	Heading for Glory Land/ There's Gonna Be a Jubilee	1951	$30

GIGI
COLPIX
Number	Title	Yr	NM
❑ 668	Peace for Christmas/ The Sound of Angels	1962	$15

Number	Title	Yr	NM

GIGOLOS, THE
BROADWAY
❏ 1000	Movin' Out/Black and Blue	1961	$40

CHESS
| ❏ 1715 | Luna Rock/La Companola | 1959 | $40 |

DAYNITE
| ❏ 1 | Swingin' Saints/
Night Crawlers | 1960 | $60 |

ENTERPRISE
| ❏ 5000 | Don't You Just Know
It/Movin' Out | 1965 | $20 |

GILBERTO, ASTRUD
PERCEPTION
| ❏ 524 | Make Love to Me/
General Da Banda | 1973 | $5 |

VERVE
| ❏ 10554 | A Banda/You Didn't
Have to Be So Nice | 1967 | $6 |
| ❏ 10480 | A Certain Smile/A
Certain Sadness | 1967 | $6 |

— With Walter Wanderley

| ❏ 10532 [DJ] | Aruanda/Dindi | 1967 | $8 |
| ❏ CS?-5 | Celebrity Scene:
Astrud Gilberto | 1967 | $60 |

— Box set of five singles (10531-10535). Price includes box, all 5 singles, jukebox title strips, bio. Records are sometimes found by themselves, so they are also listed separately.

❏ 10580	Come Softly to Me- Hushabye/Lilies by Monet	1968	$6
❏ 10347	Day by Day/Ecco Homo	1965	$8
❏ 10414	Don't Go Breaking My Heart/Wish Me a Rainbow	1966	$6
❏ 10651	Holiday/Let's Have the Morning After	1970	$5
❏ 10638	I Haven't Got Anything Better to Do/The Sea Is My Soul	1969	$5
❏ 10534 [DJ]	Look to the Rainbow/ Lugar Bonita	1967	$8
❏ 10534 [DJ]	Look to the Rainbow/ Lugar Bonita	1967	$8
❏ 10643	Love Theme from "Romeo and Juliet"/The Thought of Loving You	1969	$5
❏ 10533 [DJ]	Manha De Carnival/ Berimbau	1967	$8
❏ 10531 [DJ]	Once Upon a Summertime/ Once I Loved	1967	$8
❏ 10535 [DJ]	So Nice/Wish Me a Rainbow	1967	$8
❏ 10535 [DJ]	So Nice/Wish Me a Rainbow	1967	$8
❏ 10548	Stay/I Had the Craziest Dream	1967	$6
❏ 10358	The Shadow of Your Smile/O Gauso	1965	$8
❏ 10339	Who Can I Turn To/ Funny World	1965	$8
❏ 10457	Who Needs Forever/Main Theme "The Deadly Affair"	1966	$6

GILDER, NICK
CHRYSALIS
❏ 2357	Electric Love/Worlds Collide	1979	$4
❏ 2264	Here Comes the Night/Rockaway	1978	$5
❏ 2216	Hot Child in the City/ Backstreet Noise	1978	$5
❏ 2382	Metro Jets/(B-side unknown)	1979	$4

RCA
| ❏ PB-14177 | Let Me In/Don't Forget | 1985 | $4 |

GILKYSON, TERRY
COLUMBIA
❏ 41088	Blue Mountain/Shorty Joe	1958	$10
❏ 40817	Marianne/Goodbye Chiquita	1957	$15
❏ 40817 [PS]	Marianne/Goodbye Chiquita	1957	$20
❏ 40189	Tall Timber/Come Home Zelda	1954	$15
❏ 40742	The Sky Is High/ Yearmo's Nightmare and Yearmo's Red	1956	$15
❏ 41016	The Times/South Coast	1957	$10
❏ 40910	Tina/Strollin' Blues	1957	$10
❏ 40860	True Love and Tender Care/ Don't Hurry Worry Me	1957	$10
❏ 41284	Wanderin' Blues/ Sweet Sugar Cane	1958	$10
❏ 41147	Windjammer/Kari Waits for Me	1958	$10

DECCA
| ❏ 27337 | A Solitary Singer/
Runnin' Away | 1950 | $20 |
| ❏ 27071 | Black Eyed Susie/
Boll Weevil | 1950 | $20 |

— The above four comprise a box set

❏ 27338	Fast Freight/The Secret	1950	$20
❏ 28258	Fond Affection/The Man You Don't Meet Everyday	1952	$20
❏ 27586	Hoofbeat Serenade/ Fast Freight	1951	$20
❏ 27068	I Know Where I'm Going/ Black Is the Color (Of My True Love's Hair)	1950	$20

| ❏ 27340 | Mr. Buzzard/Everyone's
Crazy 'Ceptin' Me | 1950 | $20 |

— The above four comprise a box set

❏ 27793	Stay Awhile/Rollin' Stone	1951	$20
❏ 27708	The Girl in the Wood/ Mr. Buzzard	1951	$20
❏ 27070	The Story of the Creation// Cotton Eyed Joe/Billy Boy	1950	$20

KAPP
| ❏ 355 | Ballad of the Alamo/The
Green Leaves of Summer | 1960 | $8 |
| ❏ 350 | Saturday's Child/
Young In Love | 1960 | $8 |

GILL, JOHNNY
COTILLION
❏ 99646	Can't Wait Till Tomorrow/ One Small Light	1985	$4
❏ 99671	Half Crazy/Chemistry	1985	$4
❏ 99671 [PS]	Half Crazy/Chemistry	1985	$4
❏ 99859	Super Love/I'm Sorry	1983	$4
❏ 99840	When Something Is Wrong with My Baby/Half Steppin'	1983	$4

GILL, VINCE
MCA
| ❏ 53780 | Oklahoma Swing/We
Could Have Been | 1989 | $4 |

RCA
| ❏ 5131-7-R | Cinderella/Something's
Missing | 1987 | $4 |
| ❏ 5131-7-R [PS] | Cinderella/Something's
Missing | 1987 | $8 |

— Sleeve is promo only

❏ 5331-7-R	Everybody's Sweetheart/ The Way Back Home	1987	$4
❏ PB-14140	If It Weren't for Him/ Savannah (Do You Ever Think of Me)	1985	$4
❏ 5257-7-R	Let's Do Something/It Doesn't Matter Anymore	1987	$4
❏ PB-13809	Oh Carolina/Half a Chance	1984	$4
❏ PB-14216	Oklahoma Borderline/ She Don't Know	1985	$4
❏ PB-14020	True Love/Livin' the Way I Do	1985	$4
❏ PB-14020	True Love/Livin' the Way I Do	1985	$4
❏ PB-13860	Turn Me Loose/'Til the Best Comes Along	1984	$4
❏ PB-14371	With You/Colder Than Winter	1986	$4

GILLESPIE, DANA
JERDEN
| ❏ 764 | Donna Donna/It's
No Use Saying If | 1965 | $15 |

GILLESPIE, DARLENE
CORAL
| ❏ 62178 | I Loved, I Laughed, I Cried/
Ring the Bell, Beat the Drum | 1960 | $20 |

DISNEYLAND
| ❏ F-061 | Break of Day/Perri | 1957 | $30 |

— With Jimmie Dodd

❏ F-051	Butterfly/Seven Days	1957	$40
❏ F-052	I've Never Been in Love/Rock-a-Billy	1957	$40
❏ F-050	Sittin' in the Balcony/ Too Much	1957	$40
❏ F-060	Together Time/Now to Sleep	1957	$30

— A-side with Jimmie Dodd

GILLESPIE, DIZZY
7-Inch Extended Plays
RCA VICTOR
| ❏ EJC1009 [PS] | Dizzier and Dizzier | 1954 | $20 |

— Triple-pocket sleeve for 3-EP set (947-0210, 947-0211, 947-0212)

| ❏ 947-0211 | St. Louis Blues/Dizzier
and Dizzier//Swedish
Suite/I'll Be Boppin' Too | 1954 | $20 |

— Side 2 and Side 5 of 3-EP set EJC 1009

| ❏ 947-0210 | Woodyn't You/Duff Capers//
Two Bass Hit/Ow | 1954 | $15 |

— Side 1 and Side 6 of 3-EP set EJC 1009

GILLETTE, STEVE
REGENCY
| ❏ 45002 | Lost the Good Thing/
Three Lines | 1980 | $5 |

— A-side with Jennifer Warnes

GILLEY, MICKEY
ACT 1
| ❏ 101 | Say No More/Make
Me Believe | 1966 | $10 |

AIRBORNE
❏ 10002	I'm Your Puppet/Don't Show Me Your Memories (And I Won't Show You Mine)	1988	$4
❏ 10008	She Reminded Me of You/Easy Climb	1988	$4
❏ 75740	There I've Said It Again/It's Killing Me to Watch Love Die	1989	$4
❏ 5002	Everything Is Yours That Once Was Mine/Don't Throw a Good Love Away	1971	$8

DARYL
| ❏ 101 | What Have I Done/
Three's a Crowd | 1963 | $10 |

DOT
| ❏ 15706 | Call Me Shorty/
Come On Baby | 1958 | $200 |

EPIC
❏ 50973	A Headache Tomorrow (Or a Heartache Tonight)/ Million Dollar Memories	1981	$4
❏ 50801	A Little Getting Used To/ Can't Nobody Love You	1979	$4
❏ 03332	Blue Christmas/ Jingle Bell Rock	1982	$4
❏ 06184	Doo-Wah Days/ After She's Gone	1986	$3
❏ 03783	Fool for Your Love/ Shakin' a Heartache	1983	$3
❏ 07009	Full Grown Fool/To My One and Only	1987	$3
❏ 50580	Here Comes the Hurt Again/I Hate It, But I Drink It Anyway	1978	$4
❏ AE71774	Home to Texas for Christmas/I'm Spending Christmas with You	1982	$5
❏ 04746	I'm the One Mama Warned You About/You Can Lie to Me Tonight	1985	$3
❏ 02578	Lonely Nights/We've Watched Another Evening Waste Away	1981	$3
❏ 51003	Mamas Don't Let Your Babies Grow Up to Be Cowboys/Cotton-Eyed Joe	1981	$4

— A-side with Johnny Lee; B-side by Bayou City Beats

❏ AE71356 [DJ]	Mickey Gilley's Christmas Medley (2:51)/Mickey Gilley's Christmas Medley (3:34)	1981	$10
❏ AE71356 [DJ]	Mickey Gilley's Christmas Medley (2:51)/Mickey Gilley's Christmas Medley (3:34)	1981	$10
❏ 50740	My Silver Lining/ Picture of Our Love	1979	$4
❏ 05895	Play, Ruby, Play/ After She's Gone	1986	$3
❏ 03055	Put Your Dreams Away/If I Can't Hold Her on the Outside	1982	$3
❏ 03326	Talk to Me/Honky Tonkin' (I Guess I Done Some)	1982	$3
❏ 02774	Tears of the Lonely/ Ladies Night	1982	$3
❏ 50940	That's All That Matters/ The Blues Don't Care Who's Got 'Em	1980	$4
❏ 50631	The Song We Made Love To/Memphis Memories	1978	$4
❏ 04563	Too Good to Stop Now/A Shoulder to Cry On	1984	$3
❏ 50876	True Love Ways/The More I Turn the Bottle	1980	$4

ERIC
| ❏ 7021 | Whole Lot of Twistin'
Going On/Fraulein | 1962 | $30 |

FULL MOON/ASYLUM
| ❏ 46640 | Stand By Me/
Cotton Eyed Joe | 1980 | $4 |

— B-side by the Unstrung Heroes

| ❏ 46640 [PS] | Stand By Me/
Cotton Eyed Joe | 1980 | $5 |

— Urban Cowboy" sleeve (John Travolta pictured)

GOLDBAND
| ❏ 1223 | I Ain't Goin' Home/
No Greater Love | 1964 | $10 |

GRT
| ❏ 27 | I'm Nobody Today (But I
Was Somebody Last Night)/
She's Not Yours Anymore | 1970 | $8 |
| ❏ 45 | Time to Tell Another Lie/
Because I Love You | 1970 | $8 |

KHOURY'S
| ❏ 712 | Drive In Movie/Give
Me a Chance | 1959 | $300 |

LYNN
❏ 515	Long Lonely Nights/My Babe	1961	$30
❏ 508	My Baby's Been Cheating Again/Turn Around	1960	$30
❏ 512	Slippin' and Slidin'/ End of the Line	1961	$30

MINOR
| ❏ 106 | Oo-Ee Baby/Tell Me Why | 1957 | $600 |

Number	Title	Yr	NM

PAULA
❑ 269	A World of My Own/Love in the Want Ads	1967	$8
❑ 280	Blame It on the Moon/Sounds Like Trouble	1967	$8
❑ 256	Make Me Believe/Say No to You	1966	$10
❑ 281	One Way Street/Tears in My Eyes	1967	$8
❑ 441	She Cheats on Me/You Can Count Me Missing	1983	$4
❑ 1208	She's Still Got a Hold on You/There's No One Like You	1969	$8
❑ 1215	Watching the Way/It's Just a Matter of Making Up My Mind	1969	$8

PLAYBOY
❑ 6041	Bouquet of Roses/If You Were Mine to Lose	1975	$5
❑ 6075	Bring It On Home to Me/How's My Ex Treating You	1976	$5
❑ 5818	Chains of Love/No. 1 Rock 'n Roll C & W Boogie Blues Man	1977	$4
❑ 6015	City Lights/Fraulein	1974	$5
❑ 6063	Don't All the Girls Get Prettier at Closing Time/Where Do You Go to Lose a Heartache	1976	$5
❑ 5807	Honky Tonk Memories/Five Foot Two, Eyes of Blue	1977	$4
❑ 6004	I Overlooked an Orchid/Swinging Doors	1974	$5
❑ 6089	Lawdy Miss Clawdy/What Is It	1976	$5
❑ 6055	Overnight Sensation/I'll Sail My Ship Alone	1975	$5
❑ 6095	Pretty Paper/Lonely Christmas Call	1976	$5
❑ 6100	She's Pulling Me Back Again/Sweet Mama Goodtime	1977	$5
❑ 5826	The Power of Positive Drinkin'/Playing My Old Piano	1978	$4
❑ 6031	Window Up Above/I'm Movin' On	1975	$5

POTOMAC
❑ 901	Is It Wrong/No Greater Love	1960	$20
❑ 4004	Drive-In Movie/Your First Time	1962	$50
❑ 4006	Wild Side of Life/Caught in the Middle	1962	$50

RESCO
| ❑ 622 | She Gives Me Love/Quittin' Time | 1974 | $6 |

REX
| ❑ 1007 | Grapevine/That's How It's Got to Be | 1959 | $40 |

SAN
| ❑ 1513 | I Ain't No Bo Diddley/I'm to Blame | 1966 | $10 |

SUPREME
| ❑ 102 | Everything Turned to Love/No One Will Ever Know | 1962 | $20 |

TCF HALL
| ❑ 126 | When Two Worlds Collide/Let's Hurt Together | 1965 | $8 |

GILLIS, RICHARD
20TH CENTURY
| ❑ 2316 | C. B. Santa Claus/Come Love Me Long | 1976 | $4 |

GILMER, JIMMY
ATCO
| ❑ 6716 | Sugar in the Woods/Model Child | 1969 | $8 |
| ❑ 6583 | Three Squares (And a Place to Lay Your Head)/Baby | 1968 | $8 |

DECCA
| ❑ 30942 | Look Alive/Because I Need You | 1959 | $30 |

HAMILTON
| ❑ 50037 | Won't Be Long/I'm Gonna Go Walkin' | 1960 | $20 |

WARWICK
| ❑ 592 | Good Good Lovin'/Do You Think | 1960 | $30 |

GILMORE, JIMMIE DALE
HIGHTONE
| ❑ 510 | Honky Tonk Song/(B-side unknown) | 1989 | $5 |
| ❑ 504 | White Freight Liner Blues/Trying to Get to You | 1988 | $5 |

GILMOUR, DAVID
COLUMBIA
❑ 04378	Blue Light/Cruise	1984	$4
❑ 04490	Love on the Air/Near the End	1984	$4
❑ 10803	There's No Way Out of Here/Deafinitely	1978	$5

Number	Title	Yr	NM

GILREATH, JAMES
JOY
❑ 286	Blue Is My Color/Keep Her Out of Sight	1964	$10
❑ 274	Little Band of Gold/I'll Walk with You	1963	$15
❑ 278	Lollipops, Lace and Lipstick/Mean Ole River	1963	$20

GILSON, PATTI
GOLDEN WORLD
| ❑ 6 | Don't You Tell a Lie/Pulling Petals from a Daisy | 1964 | $300 |

GILSTRAP, JIM
BELL
| ❑ 45435 | Airport/(B-side unknown) | 1974 | $5 |
| ❑ 45474 | When You Come Back Down/(B-side unknown) | 1974 | $5 |

ROXBURY
❑ 2032	Hello It's Me/Never Stop Your Loving Me	1976	$4
❑ 2013	House of Strangers/Take Your Daddy for a Ride	1975	$4
❑ 2016	I'm on Fire/I'm on Fire (Part 2)	1975	$4
❑ 2029	Love Talk/Love Talk (Part 2)	1976	$4
❑ 2026	Move Me/Move Me (Part 2)	1976	$4
❑ 2006	Swing Your Daddy/Swing Your Daddy (Part 2)	1975	$4

GINGER
TITAN
| ❑ 1717 | Dry Tears/Spare Time | 1961 | $125 |

GINGER AND THE CHIFFONS
GROOVE
| ❑ 58-0003 | She/Where Were You Last Night | 1963 | $40 |

GINGER AND THE SNAPS
MGM
| ❑ 13413 | Growing Up Is Hard to Do/Seven Days in September | 1965 | $200 |

TORE
| ❑ 1008 | Love Me the Way That I Love You/Truly | 1961 | $80 |

GINGER-SNAPS, THE
DUNHILL
| ❑ 4003 | The Sh-Down-Down Song/I've Got Faith in Him | 1965 | $30 |

GINGOLD, HERMIONE
CAMEO
| ❑ 462 | Does the Chewing Gum Lose Its Flavor on the Bed Post Over Night?/I've Got the Rudy Vallee Blues | 1967 | $20 |
| ❑ 492 | Somethin' Stupid/Millions of Hearts | 1967 | $20 |

GINNY AND THE GALLIONS
DOWNEY
| ❑ 110 | Hava Nagila/Hava Nagila Part 2 | 1963 | $15 |
| ❑ 112 | Wheel of Fortune/Hava Nagila | 1963 | $15 |

GINO AND GINA
BRUNSWICK
| ❑ 55215 | I Hope You're Satisfied/Why Do You Make Believe | 1961 | $30 |

MERCURY
❑ 71370X45	Brand New Penny/I Don't Love You	1958	$30
❑ 71483X45	I Don't Need a Ring Around Your Finger/Charlie	1959	$30
❑ 71283X45	(It's Been a Long Time) Pretty Baby/Love's a Carousel	1958	$30
❑ 71283X45	Pretty Baby/Love's a Carousel	1958	$20
❑ 71346X45	She Belongs to Me/Rainin' and Rainin'	1958	$30

WARWICK
| ❑ 554 | I'm Bugged Over You/Come On Legs | 1960 | $30 |

GINO AND THE DELLS
GOLDEN CREST
❑ 567	Altar of Dreams/Baby Don't Go Now	1962	$50
❑ 581	It's Only a Paper Moon/Home Sweet Home	1963	$200
❑ 576	We'll Make It Someday/I'm a Boy in Love	1963	$50

Number	Title	Yr	NM

GIORDANO, LOU
BRUNSWICK
| ❑ 55115 | Stay Close to Me/Don'Cha Know | 1959 | $1200 |

— *With Buddy Holly on guitar*

GIRLFRIENDS, THE
COLPIX
| ❑ 744 | Baby Don't Cry/I Don't Believe in You | 1964 | $30 |
| ❑ 712 | My One and Only Jimmy Boy/For My Sake | 1963 | $30 |

PIONEER
| ❑ 71833 | Four Shy Girls (In Their Itsy Bitsy Teeny Weeny Yellow Polka Dot Bikinis)/Jackie | 1961 | $30 |

GIRLS NEXT DOOR
ATLANTIC
| ❑ 88791 | He's Gotta Have Me/Wasn't It You | 1989 | $4 |

MTM
❑ B-72078	Baby I Want It/(Sing-Along Version)	1986	$4
❑ B-72095	Easy to Find/Message from My Heart	1987	$4
❑ B-72106	Love and Other Fairy Tales/I Can Hear My Heart Begin to Cry	1988	$4
❑ B-72059	Love Will Get You Through Times with No Money/Ruins of Love	1985	$4
❑ B-72068	Slow Boat to China/Pretty Boy's Cadillac	1986	$4
❑ B-72084	Walk Me in the Rain/The Fool in Me	1987	$4
❑ B-72088	What a Girl Next Door Could Do/I Think I'm Gonna Fall (In Love with You)	1987	$4

GIRLS OF THE GOLDEN WEST, THE
MANCO
| ❑ 1059 | Christmas Secret/Christmas | 1964 | $10 |

GIRLS, THE
20TH CENTURY FOX
| ❑ 6651 | Way, Way Out/Modesty Blaise | 1966 | $30 |

CAPITOL
| ❑ 5675 | Chico's Girl/The Dumb Song | 1966 | $30 |
| ❑ 5528 | My Baby/My Love | 1965 | $40 |

SCEPTER
| ❑ 12242 | Perfect Love/Mr. Poster | 1969 | $8 |

GIVENS, VAN
PAULA
| ❑ 286 | Droopy Christmas Tree/Daddy's Baby Boy | 1967 | $12 |

GLAD SINGERS, THE
COLUMBIA
| ❑ JZSP0 [DJ] | Deck The Halls/Happy New Year | 1965 | $15 |

— *Promo only on green vinyl*

| ❑ JZSP111919/20 [DJ] | Deck The Halls/Happy New Year | 1965 | $15 |

— *Promo only on green vinyl*

GLAD, THE
EQUINOX
| ❑ 70004 | See What You Mean/Bedtime Story | 1968 | $30 |

GLADIATORS, THE
DIG
| ❑ 135 | Girl of My Heart/My Baby Doll | 1957 | $300 |

GLADIOLAS, THE
EXCELLO
❑ 2120	Hey Little Girl/I Wanta Know	1957	$60
❑ 2101	Little Darlin'/Sweetheart, Please Don't Go	1957	$80
❑ 2136	Shoop Shoop/Say You'll Be Mine	1958	$60

GLAHE, WILL
LONDON
❑ 1693	Beer Barrel Polka/Hearts and Heartaches	1957	$12
❑ 1523	Came the Morning/Rose of the Wildwood	1954	$10
❑ 1818	Duschka/The Pretzel Waltz	1958	$12
❑ 1859	In Einen Weindorf/The 30th of May	1959	$10
❑ 1755	Liechtensteiner Polka/Schweizer Kanton Polka	1957	$12
❑ 1788	Sweet Elizabeth/Tavern in the Town	1958	$10
❑ 1673	The March Hare/The Peanut Polka	1956	$10

Number	Title	Yr	NM

GLASER, CHUCK
MGM

Number	Title	Yr	NM
❏ 14663	Gypsy Queen/That's When I Love You the Most	1973	$5

GLASER, JIM
MCA

Number	Title	Yr	NM
❏ 40742	Chasin' My Tail/Sleeping Beauty	1977	$4
❏ 40813	Don't Let My Love Stand in Your Way/Honky Tonk Lady	1977	$4
❏ 52748	If I Don't Love You/It's Not Easy	1985	$3
❏ 52619	I'll Be Your Fool Tonight/Tough Act to Follow	1985	$3
❏ 52672	In Another Minute/Merry-Go-Round	1985	$3
❏ 40636	She's Free But She's Not Easy/Lonely Bein' Free	1976	$4
❏ 52808	The Lights of Albuquerque/Waltzing Through a Rock and Roll Life	1986	$3

MGM

Number	Title	Yr	NM
❏ 14713	Fool Passin' Through/If It Pleases You	1974	$5
❏ 14758	Forgettin' 'Bout You/If It Pleases You	1974	$5
❏ 14590	I See His Love All Over You/It's Still a Long Way	1973	$5
❏ 14798	One, Two, Three (Never Gonna Fall in Love Again)/One Night Man	1975	$5
❏ 14834	Woman, Woman/Turn to Me	1975	$5

MONUMENT

Number	Title	Yr	NM
❏ 985	A Pair of Loaded Dice/Thanks a Lot for Trying Anyway	1966	$15
❏ 909	I'd Rather Not Know/The Outcast	1965	$15
❏ 924	My Mind and Me/Wonderful World of Love	1966	$15

NOBLE VISION

Number	Title	Yr	NM
❏ 104	If I Could Only Dance with You/Woman, Woman	1984	$4
❏ 107	Let Me Down Easy/I'd Love to See You Again	1984	$4
❏ 103	The Man in the Mirror/Pretend	1983	$4
❏ 101	When You're Not a Lady/I Don't Wanna Make Love	1982	$4

RCA VICTOR

Number	Title	Yr	NM
❏ 47-9587	God Help You Woman/She Was Too Good to Me	1968	$8
❏ 47-9696	Please Take Me Back/Kiss Her Once for Me	1968	$8

GLASER, TOMPALL
ABC

Number	Title	Yr	NM
❏ 12366	Bad Times/Carry Me On	1978	$4
❏ 12329	Drinking Them Beers/Duncan and Brady	1978	$4
❏ 12261	It'll Be Her/Sweethearts or Strangers/I Will Always Love You	1977	$4
❏ 12309	It Never Crossed My Mind/Easy on My Mind	1977	$4

MGM

Number	Title	Yr	NM
❏ 14622	Bad, Bad, Bad Cowboy/Let It Be Pretty	1973	$6
❏ 14740	Musical Chairs/Grab a Hold	1974	$6
❏ 14800	Put Another Log on the Fire (Male Chauvinist National Anthem)/Mendocino	1975	$6

—As "Tompall"

Number	Title	Yr	NM
❏ 14701	Texas Law Sez/Pass Me On By	1974	$6
❏ 14843	The Hunger/Wild Side of Life	1976	$6

—As "Tompall"

POLYDOR

Number	Title	Yr	NM
❏ 14314	T for Texas/Broken Down Momma	1976	$5

ROBBINS

Number	Title	Yr	NM
❏ 1003	Baby Be Good/I Want You	1957	$40
❏ 1001	Five Penny Nickel/You're in My Heart	1957	$40

GLASS BOTTLE, THE
AVCO

Number	Title	Yr	NM
❏ 4592	Don't It Make You Feel So Good/(B-side unknown)	1972	$5
❏ 4597	Pretty Thing/(B-side unknown)	1972	$5

—Both of the above credit lead singer Gary Criss

Number	Title	Yr	NM
❏ 4584	The Girl Who Loved Me When/Because She's Mine Again	1971	$6

AVCO EMBASSY

Number	Title	Yr	NM
❏ 4575	I Ain't Got Time Anymore/The First Time	1971	$6

GLASS HARP
DECCA

Number	Title	Yr	NM
❏ 32830	Children's Fantasy/Village Queen	1971	$10
❏ 32995	La De Da/(B-side unknown)	1972	$12
❏ 32915	The Answer/Just Always	1972	$12

GLASS HOUSE, THE
INVICTUS

Number	Title	Yr	NM
❏ 9071	Crumbs Off the Table/Bad Bill of Goods	1969	$6
❏ 9076	I Can't Be You (You Can't Be Me)/He's In My Life	1970	$6
❏ 9111	Let It Flow/Playing Games	1972	$6
❏ 9097	Look What We've Done to Love/Heaven's There to Guide Us	1971	$6
❏ 9082	Stealing Moments From Another Woman's Life/If It Ain't Love, It Don't Matter	1970	$6
❏ 9129	Thanks I Needed That/I Don't See Me in Your Eyes Anymore	1972	$6
❏ 9090	Touch Me Jesus/If It Ain't Love, It Don't Matter	1971	$6

GLASS TIGER
EMI MANHATTAN

Number	Title	Yr	NM
❏ B-50144	Far Away from Here/This Island Earth	1988	$3
❏ B-50144 [PS]	Far Away from Here/This Island Earth	1988	$4
❏ B-50116	I'm Still Searching/Suffer in Silence	1988	$3
❏ B-50116 [PS]	I'm Still Searching/Suffer in Silence	1988	$5
❏ B-50172	My Song/It's Love You Feel	1988	$4

MANHATTAN

Number	Title	Yr	NM
❏ B-50037	Don't Forget Me (When I'm Gone)/Ancient Evenings	1986	$3
❏ B-50037 [PS]	Don't Forget Me (When I'm Gone)/Ancient Evenings	1986	$3
❏ B-50066	I Will Be There/Do You Wanna Dance with Me	1987	$3
❏ B-50066 [PS]	I Will Be There/Do You Wanna Dance with Me	1987	$3
❏ B-50048	Someday/Vanishing Tribe	1986	$3
❏ B-50048 [PS]	Someday/Vanishing Tribe	1986	$6

GLEAMS, THE
HIT

Number	Title	Yr	NM
❏ 36	He's a Rebel/Next Door to an Angel	1962	$12

—B-side by Ward Oliver

J-V

Number	Title	Yr	NM
❏ 101	Bad Boy/Give Me a Chance	1961	$300

GLEASON, JACKIE
CAPITOL

Number	Title	Yr	NM
❏ 4800	'Allo 'Allo 'Allo/Joi De Vivre	1962	$8
❏ F2437	Alone Together/Body & Soul	1953	$10
❏ F3223	Autumn Leaves/Oo! What You Do to Me	1955	$15
❏ 5131	Bird Brain/Soldier in the Rain	1964	$8
❏ F2439	But Not for Me/Love	1953	$10
❏ F2440	I'm in the Mood for Love/I Only Have Eyes for You	1953	$10

— The above four comprise a box set

Number	Title	Yr	NM
❏ 4933	It's Such a Happy Day/La La La La La La La	1963	$8
❏ 4704	Melancholy Serenade/Apology at Bedtime	1962	$8
❏ F2361	Melancholy Serenade/You're Getting to Be a Habit	1953	$20
❏ F2438	My Funny Valentine/Love Is Here to Stay	1953	$10
❏ F2659	Mystery Street/Golden Violins	1954	$20
❏ F2507	Terry's Theme from "Limelight"/Peg o' My Heart	1953	$20
❏ F3144	The Band Played On/In the Good Old Summertime	1955	$15
❏ F4062	Where Is She Now/Just One Yesterday	1958	$10
❏ F2515	White House Serenade/The President's Lady	1953	$20

DECCA

Number	Title	Yr	NM
❏ 27684	What Is a Girl?/What Is a Boy?	1951	$20

7-Inch Extended Plays
CAPITOL

Number	Title	Yr	NM
❏ EAP 4-627	*Mad About the Boy/Dancing on the Ceiling/How Deep Is the Ocean/Someday I'll Find You	1955	$10
❏ EAP 2-627	*Remember/Speak Low/The Thrill Is Gone/I Wished on the Moon	1955	$10
❏ SU-106	All By Myself/The Song Is Ended/How About Me/How Deep Is the Ocean/Say It Isn't So	1969	$10

—Jukebox issue; small hole, plays at 33 1/3 rpm

Number	Title	Yr	NM
❏ SXA-1830 [PS]	Champagne, Candlelight and Kisses	1963	$12

Number	Title	Yr	NM
❏ EAP 1-758	(contents unknown)	1956	$10
❏ EAP 3-627	Deep Purple/I Still Get a Thrill//I Don't Know Why/A Garden in the Rain	1955	$10
❏ EAP 1-568	Don't Blame Me/You Can't Pull the Wool Over My Eyes//Soon/My Blue Heaven	1955	$10
❏ EAP 1-627 [PS]	Lonesome Echo, Part 1	1955	$15
❏ EAP 2-627 [PS]	Lonesome Echo, Part 2	1955	$15
❏ EAP 3-627 [PS]	Lonesome Echo, Part 3	1955	$15
❏ EAP 4-627 [PS]	Lonesome Echo, Part 4	1955	$15
❏ EBF 1-627 [PS]	Lonesome Echo, Parts 1 & 2	1955	$30

— Gatefold sleeve with some editions of 1-627 and 2-627

Number	Title	Yr	NM
❏ EBF 2-627 [PS]	Lonesome Echo, Parts 3 & 4	1955	$30

— Gatefold sleeve with some editions of 3-627 and 4-627

Number	Title	Yr	NM
❏ EAP 1-758 [PS]	Merry Christmas	1956	$15
❏ SU-2471 [PS]	Music Around the World -- For Lovers Only	1966	$12
❏ SU-106 [PS]	Music for Lovers	1969	$12
❏ SXA-2144	People/Softly As I Leave You/I Wish You Love//On the Street Where You Live/Lazy Afternoon/The Last Dance	1964	$10

—Jukebox issue; small hole, plays at 33 1/3 rpm

Number	Title	Yr	NM
❏ SU-2409 [PS]	Silk 'N' Brass	1966	$12
❏ SU-2471	Swedish Rhapsody/I Love Paris/On Miami Shore//Hawaiian Wedding Song/Brazil/On a Slow Boat to China	1966	$10

—Jukebox issue; small hole, plays at 33 1/3 rpm

Number	Title	Yr	NM
❏ SU-2409	The Girl from Ipanema/Everything's Coming Up Roses/Real Live Girl//You're Nobody Until Somebody Loves You/Shangri-La/Somebody Else Is Taking My Place	1966	$10

—Jukebox issue; small hole, plays at 33 1/3 rpm

Number	Title	Yr	NM
❏ SXA-2144 [PS]	The Last Dance ... For Lovers Only	1964	$12
❏ SXA-1830	Theme from "Bus Stop"/Everything Happens to Me//Keepin' Out of Mischief Now/I Double Dare You/Fascinating Rhythm	1963	$10

—Jukebox issue; small hole, plays at 33 1/3 rpm

Number	Title	Yr	NM
❏ EAP 2-568	There'll Be Some Changes Made/How About You//The World Is Waiting for the Sunrise/The Love Nest	1955	$10
❏ EAP 1-627	There Must Be a Way/Come Rain or Come Shine//Darling, Je Vous Aime Beaucoup/I'm Always Chasing Rainbows	1955	$10
❏ EAP 1-871 [PS]	To a Sleeping Beauty	1957	$20
❏ EAP 1-871	To a Sleeping Beauty//Apology at Bedtime	1957	$20
❏ SXA-1978 [PS]	Today's Romantic Hits/For Lovers Only	1963	$12
❏ SXA-1978	What Kind of Fool Am I/I Left My Heart in San Francisco/As Long As He Needs Me//Misty/Make Someone Happy/More	1963	$10

—Jukebox issue; small hole, plays at 33 1/3 rpm

GLEEMS, THE
PARKWAY

Number	Title	Yr	NM
❏ 893	Sandra Baby/You Are the One	1964	$30

GLENCOVES, THE
SELECT

Number	Title	Yr	NM
❏ 727	Devil's Waitin'/Better Think Twice	1963	$12
❏ 726	Don't Knock/Ginny's Come Home	1963	$12
❏ 724	Hootenanny/It's Sister Ginny's Turn to Throw the Bomb	1963	$10

GLENN, DARRELL
COLUMBIA

Number	Title	Yr	NM
❏ 4-44146	But She's Untrue/The Meaning of Blue	1967	$10
❏ 4-44291	Everybody's Wishin' Sometime/You Only Used Me	1967	$12
❏ 4-43643	I Believe/Once in a While	1966	$10
❏ 4-43775	I Can't Say Goodbye/I Waited a Long Time	1966	$10

DOT

Number	Title	Yr	NM
❏ 15471	Send This Wanderer Home/Your Little Red Wagon	1956	$30

LONGHORN

Number	Title	Yr	NM
❏ 539	A Matter of Fact/Bonnie Sue	1964	$15
❏ 546	I Know I've Lost You/The Ways of the World	1965	$15

NRC

Number	Title	Yr	NM
❏ 04	Congratulations to Me/Make Me Smile Again	1958	$30
❏ 07	Mr. Moonlight/So I've Been Told	1958	$30

Number	Title	Yr	NM

POMPEII
❑ 66680 — The Message/I've Been Too Long — 1968 — $10

RCA VICTOR
❑ 47-6107 — Banjo Mambo/Run Little Echo — 1955 — $30
❑ 47-6031 — Bye Bye Young Girls/No Tears, No Regrets — 1955 — $30
❑ 47-5798 — In the Chapel in the Moonlight/Once and Only Once — 1954 — $30
❑ 47-5859 — We'll Be Married/Then and Only Then — 1954 — $30

ROBBEE
❑ 101 — Hoo Doo the Voo Doo/(B-side unknown) — 1960 — $20

VALLEY
❑ 119 — Christmas Is Just Around the Corner/(B-side unknown) — 1954 — $40
❑ 105 — Crying in the Chapel/Hang Up That Telephone — 1953 — $50

— *Original version of this classic, which was written by his father, Artie Glenn*

❑ 109 — Only a Pastime/I Think I'm Falling in Love with You — 1953 — $40

GLENN, GLEN

DORE
❑ 523 — Goofin' Around/Susie Green from Abilene — 1959 — $20

ERA
❑ 1061 — Everybody's Movin'/I'm Glad My Baby's Gone — 1957 — $70
❑ 1074 — One Cup of Coffee/Laurie Ann — 1958 — $60

GLENN, HOWDY

WARNER BROS.
❑ 8546 — Don't Take Pretty to the City/That Lucky Old Sun — 1978 — $4
❑ 8402 — Don't Take Pretty to the City/White Line Fever — 1977 — $4
❑ 8447 — Touch Me/White Line Fever — 1977 — $4
❑ 8704 — When You Were Blue and I Was Green/Don't Take Pretty to the City — 1978 — $4

GLENN, LLOYD

ALADDIN
❑ 3346 — After Hours (Part 1)/After Hours (Part 2) — 1956 — $30
❑ 3353 — Chica-Boo/Old Time Shuffle — 1957 — $30
❑ 3407 — Cute-Tee/Black Fantasy — 1958 — $30
❑ 3288 — Footloose/Glen's Glide — 1955 — $30
❑ 3400 — Hyde Park/Love for Sale — 1957 — $30
❑ 3459 — Long Gone (Part 1)/Long Gone (Part 2) — 1959 — $20
❑ 3446 — Petite Fleur/Honky Tonk Train — 1959 — $20
❑ 3327 — Southbound Special/Blue Ivories — 1956 — $30
❑ 3307 — Sunrise/Tiddly Winks — 1955 — $30

HOLLYWOOD
❑ 1028 — Chica-Boo/Old Time Shuffle — 1954 — $30
❑ 1021 — Merry Christmas Baby/Sleigh Ride — 1954 — $30

— *B-side by Charles Brown; red label*

❑ 1033 — Sleigh Ride/China Doll — 1954 — $30

IMPERIAL
❑ 5839 — Twistville/Young Date — 1962 — $15

SWING TIME
❑ 292 — After Hours/Yancey Special — 1952 — $40
❑ 296 — Angora/Cuba Doll — 1952 — $40
❑ 311 — Boogie Woogie on St. Louis Blues/Ugh — 1953 — $40
❑ 254 — Chica-Boo/Jungle Town Jubilee — 1951 — $40
❑ 278 — Cute-Tee/Rhumba — 1952 — $40
❑ 277 — Day Break Stomp/Jungle Twilight — 1952 — $40
❑ 293 — Honky Tonk Train/Pine Top Boogie Woogie — 1952 — $40
❑ 271 — Sleigh Ride/Savage Boy — 1951 — $40

GLITTER, GARY

ARISTA
❑ 592 — Another Rock and Roll Christmas/(Instrumental Re-Mix) — 1984 — $5

— *U.K. import*

❑ ARISD592 — Another Rock and Roll Christmas/(Instrumental Re-Mix) — 1984 — $15

— *U.K. import; shaped picture disc with plinth*

❑ 592 [PS] — Another Rock and Roll Christmas/(Instrumental Re-Mix) — 1984 — $5

— *U.K. import*

❑ 0173 — I Love You Love Me Love/Hands Up! It's a Stick-Up — 1976 — $5

BELL
❑ 45345 — Baby Please Don't Go/I.O.U. — 1973 — $5
❑ 45375 — Come On, Come In/Happy Birthday — 1973 — $5
❑ 45326 — Do You Wanna Touch Me (Oh Yeah)/I Would If I Could But I Can't — 1973 — $5
❑ 45276 — I Didn't Know I Loved You (Till I Saw You Rock and Roll)/Shakey Sue — 1972 — $5
❑ 45438 — I Love You Love Me Love/(B-side unknown) — 1974 — $5
❑ 45398 — (I'm the) Leader of the Gang (I Am)/(B-side unknown) — 1973 — $5

DECCA
❑ 32714 — Goodbye Seattle/Wait for Me — 1970 — $20

— *As "Paul Raven"*

GLITTERHOUSE

DYNOVOICE
❑ 927 — Barbarella/Love Drags Me Down — 1968 — $15
❑ 925 — I Lost Me a Friend/Tinkerbell's Mind — 1968 — $10

GLOBETROTTERS, THE

BUDDAH
❑ 309 — Don't Rock the Boat/Hatfield Small — 1972 — $12

KIRSHNER
❑ 63-5006 — Cheer Me Up/Gravy — 1970 — $15
❑ 63-5006 [PS] — Cheer Me Up/Gravy — 1970 — $20
❑ 63-5012 — Duke of Earl/Everybody's Got Hot Pants — 1971 — $15
❑ 63-5016 — Everybody Needs Love/ESP — 1971 — $15

GLORIES, THE

DATE
❑ 1647 — Don't Make the Good Girls Go Bad/The Dark End of the Street — 1969 — $30
❑ 1571 — Give Me My Freedom/Security — 1967 — $30
❑ 1553 — I Stand Accused (Of Loving You)/Wish They Could Write a Song — 1967 — $10
❑ 1615 — I Worship You Baby/Don't Dial My Number — 1968 — $200
❑ 1579 — Sing Me a Love Song/Ooh, That's Love, Baby — 1967 — $30
❑ 1593 — Stand By (I'm Coming Home)/My Sweet, Sweet Baby — 1968 — $30
❑ 1593 [PS] — Stand By (I'm Coming Home)/My Sweet, Sweet Baby — 1968 — $60
❑ 1636 — Try a Little Tenderness/There He Is — 1969 — $30

GLORY (1)

AVALANCHE
❑ XW-289 — Find Out Lover/Mrs. Walter — 1973 — $6

GLOSSON, LONNIE

DECCA
❑ 9-46361 — I Want You to Know That I Love You/Till the Cows Come Home — 1951 — $30

GLOWTONES, THE

EASTWEST
❑ 101 — The Girl I Love/Ping Pong — 1957 — $40

GO-GO'S

I.R.S.
❑ 9910 — Get Up and Go/Speeding — 1982 — $3
❑ 9910 [PS] — Get Up and Go/Speeding — 1982 — $3
❑ 9926 — Head Over Heels/Good for Gone — 1984 — $3
❑ 9926 [PS] — Head Over Heels/Good for Gone — 1984 — $3
❑ 9901 — Our Lips Are Sealed/Surfing and Spying — 1981 — $3
❑ 9901 [PS] — Our Lips Are Sealed/Surfing and Spying — 1981 — $6
❑ 9911 — This Old Feeling/It's Everything But Partytime — 1982 — $3
❑ 9911 [PS] — This Old Feeling/It's Everything But Partytime — 1982 — $3

— *Die-cut "Go-Go's" sleeve (yellow)*

❑ 9928 — Turn to You/I'm With You — 1984 — $3
❑ 9928 [PS] — Turn to You/I'm With You — 1984 — $3
❑ 9903 — We Got the Beat/Can't Stop the World — 1982 — $3
❑ 9903 [PS] — We Got the Beat/Can't Stop the World — 1982 — $3
❑ 8001 [PD] — We Got the Beat/Our Lips Are Sealed — 1982 — $10

— *7-inch picture disc*

GO-GO'S, THE

RCA VICTOR
❑ 47-8370 — Lonely Girl/Chicken of the Sea — 1964 — $20
❑ 47-8435 — The Wild One/Saturday's Hero — 1964 — $40

GO GO JOES, THE

JOSIE
❑ 770 — Cool Yule/No Dough Blues — 1954 — $30

GO WEST

CHRYSALIS
❑ VS442865 — Call Me/Haunted — 1985 — $3
❑ VS442865 [PS] — Call Me/Haunted — 1985 — $3
❑ VS443141 — Don't Look Down -- The Sequel/Let's Build a Boat — 1987 — $3
❑ VS443141 [PS] — Don't Look Down -- The Sequel/Let's Build a Boat — 1987 — $3
❑ VS442903 — Eye to Eye/Man in My Mirror — 1985 — $3
❑ VS442903 [PS] — Eye to Eye/Man in My Mirror — 1985 — $3
❑ VS443191 — From Baltimore to Paris/Little Caesar — 1987 — $4
❑ VS443191 [PS] — From Baltimore to Paris/Little Caesar — 1987 — $4
❑ VS442850 — We Close Our Eyes/Missing Persons — 1985 — $3
❑ VS442850 [PS] — We Close Our Eyes/Missing Persons — 1985 — $3

GODDARD, GEOFF

LAWN
❑ 235 — Walk With My Angel/Sky Men — 1964 — $15

GODFREY, ARTHUR

CONTEMPO
❑ 905 — Every Christmas Morning/Pine Cones & Holly Berries — 1963 — $8

GODFREY, RAY

ABC
❑ 10999 — I Can't Go On Living Like This/Right Straight in the Eye — 1967 — $10

COLUMBIA
❑ 4-43618 — I Can Live It Down/Keep Your Chin Up, Soldier — 1966 — $10
❑ 4-43618 [PS] — I Can Live It Down/Keep Your Chin Up, Soldier — 1966 — $15
❑ 4-43398 — Old Love/There's Always Room (For One More Fool Like Me) — 1965 — $10
❑ 4-44071 — Three Little Words from You/The Difference in Me — 1967 — $10
❑ 4-43785 — Winner Take All/Please Don't Mention My Name — 1966 — $10

J&J
❑ 01 — The Picture/The Overall Song — 1960 — $50

PEACH
❑ 757 — Let's Move to the City/Wait, Weep and Wonder — 1961 — $30

SAVOY
❑ 3021 — The Picture/The Overall Song — 1960 — $30

SIMS
❑ 130 — Better Times a-Comin'/Ten Silver Dollars — 1962 — $30

SPRING
❑ 135 — Candy Clown/I Want to Be Your Only Love — 1973 — $6
❑ 104 — I Gotta Get Away/Sherry Washington — 1970 — $8

TOLLIE
❑ 9030 — Count Me Out/If the Good Lord's Willing — 1964 — $20

GODSPELL

BELL
❑ 45351 — Beautiful City/Bless the Lord — 1973 — $5
❑ 45275 — By My Side/(B-side unknown) — 1972 — $5
❑ 45147 — By My Side/Crucifixion, Resurrection — 1971 — $5
❑ 45210 — Day By Day/Bless the Lord — 1972 — $4
❑ 45240 — We Beseech Thee/On the Willows — 1972 — $5

GODZ, THE

ESP-DISK'
❑ 4503 — Lay in the Sun/I Want a Word with You — 1966 — $12

GOGGLES, THE

AUDIO FIDELITY
❑ 168 — Don't Say You Don't Remember/We All Live on a Rainbow — 1971 — $5

Number	Title	Yr	NM

GOINS, HERBIE, AND THE NIGHT-RIDERS
CAPITOL

❑ 5978	Coming Home to You/The Incredible Miss Brown	1967	$50

GOLD, ANDREW
ASYLUM

❑ 45378	Angel Woman/ Do Wah Diddy	1976	$4
❑ 45439	Go Back Home Again/Firefly	1977	$4
❑ 45522	I'm On My Way/ Always for You	1978	$4
❑ 45384	Lonely Boy/Must Be Crazy	1977	$4
❑ 45384 [PS]	Lonely Boy/Must Be Crazy	1977	$5
❑ 45521	Looking for My Love/ How Can This Be Love	1978	$4
❑ 45417	One of Them Is Me/ Passing Thing	1977	$4
❑ 45339	Stay/Firefly	1976	$4
❑ 45456	Thank You for Being a Friend/Still You Linger On	1978	$4
❑ 45286	That's Why I Love You/A Note from You	1975	$4

GOLD BUGS, THE
CORAL

❑ 62453	Stop That Wedding/ It's So Nice	1965	$50

GOLD, MARTY
KAPP

❑ 244	Hey! Paesano Cha Cha Cha/I'm Not Afraid Anymore	1958	$12

RCA VICTOR

❑ 47-7856	Carnival in Rome/ My Romance	1961	$8
❑ 47-7696	Lissabon/Music of Home	1960	$8
❑ 47-7722	Lonely Guitar/Home from the Hill	1960	$8
❑ 47-7822	The Breeze and I/ Cry Like the Wind	1960	$8

GOLD, SANDY
HIT

❑ 27	Sheila/She's Not You	1962	$8

—*B-side by George Killebrew*

GOLDBERG-MILLER BLUES BAND
EPIC

❑ 9865	More Soul Than Soulful/ Mother Song	1965	$20
❑ 9865 [DJ]	More Soul Than Soulful/ Mother Song	1965	$30

—*Promo only on blue vinyl*

❑ 9865 [PS]	More Soul Than Soulful/ Mother Song	1965	$60

—*Promo only*

GOLDBERG, BARRY
ATCO

❑ 6946	(I've Got to Use My) Imagination/Dusty Country	1973	$10

—*A-side co-produced by Bob Dylan*

BUDDAH

❑ 59	Sittin' in Circles/ Hole in My Pocket	1968	$10

EPIC

❑ 10007	Blowing My Mind/Think	1966	$20
❑ 10033	Ginger Man/Whole Lotta Shakin' Goin' On	1966	$20

GOLDDIGGERS, THE
METROMEDIA

❑ 141	I Wanna Be Loved/ It's Fun to Be Young	1969	$5
❑ 156	We Need A Little Christmas/I Just Want You For Christmas	1969	$6

RCA VICTOR

❑ 74-0670	A-Flat Cricket and B-Flat Frog/Nobody Else But You	1972	$5

GOLDEBRIARS, THE
EPIC

❑ 9806	Don't Want Your Love/ Give Me Lovin'	1965	$15
❑ 9673	Pretty Girls and Rolling Stones/Shenandoah	1964	$15
❑ 9719	The Castle in the Corner/I've Got to Love Somebody	1964	$15

GOLDEN EARRING
21 RECORDS

❑ 113	Fist in Glove/One Night Moonlight	1984	$3
❑ 99515	Love in Motion/Why Do I	1986	$3
❑ 881415-7	Something Heavy Going Down/Enough Is Enough	1984	$3
❑ 108	The Devil Made Me Do It/Chargin' Batteries	1983	$4

❑ 103	Twilight Zone/King Dark	1982	$4
❑ 112	When the Lady Smiles/ Orwell's Ear	1984	$3
❑ 112 [PS]	When the Lady Smiles/ Orwell's Ear	1984	$5

ATLANTIC

❑ 2710	Eight Miles High/ One Huge Road	1970	$6

DWARF

❑ 2001	Back Home/As Long As the Wind Blows	1969	$12
❑ 2001 [PS]	Back Home/As Long As the Wind Blows	1969	$30

MCA

❑ 40513	Babylon/Sleep Walkin'	1976	$4

POLYDOR

❑ 14001	It's Alright, But I Admit It Could Be Better/Song of a Devil's Servant	1969	$10
❑ 2004	Weekend Love/Tiger Bay	1979	$4

TRACK

❑ 40309	Candy's Going Bad/She Flies on Strange Wings	1974	$5
❑ 40369	Ce Soir/Lucky Numbers	1975	$5
❑ 40412	The Switch/Lonesome D.J.	1975	$5

GOLDEN NUGGETS, THE
FUTURA

❑ 1691	I Was a Fool/Teenage Josephine	1959	$600

HAWK

❑ 107/8	Surf Everybody/ Everybody Bird	1963	$50

GOLDEN TRUMPETS
NASHBORO

❑ 835	So Called Christmas/ Sweeter Life	1964	$12

GOLDENRODS, THE
VEE JAY

❑ 307	Wish I Was Back in School/Color Cartoons	1959	$250

GOLDENTONES, THE
BEACON

❑ 560	Meaning of Love/ (B-side unknown)	1961	$30

JAY-DEE

❑ 806	Meaning of Love/ (B-side unknown)	1955	$100

GOLDIE, DAN
TEARDROP

❑ 3070	Take Our Last Walk Tonight/ Walking the Streets	1966	$30

—*The Sir Douglas Quintet is the backing band*

GOLDSBORO, BOBBY
BUENA VISTA

❑ 561	These Are the Best Times/ (B-side unknown)	1979	$5

CURB

❑ 70052	Alice Doesn't Love Here Anymore/Green-Eyed Woman, Nashville Blues	1981	$4
❑ 5400	Goodbye Marie/Love Has Made a Woman Out of You	1980	$4
❑ 02117	Love Ain't Never Hurt Nobody/Wings of an Angel	1981	$4
❑ 02726	Lucy and the Stranger/ Outrun the Sun	1982	$4

EPIC

❑ 50480	He'll Have to Go/ Too Hot to Handle	1977	$4
❑ 50535	Life Gets Hard on Easy Street/Black Fool's Gold	1978	$4
❑ 50342	Me and the Elephants/I Love Music	1977	$4
❑ 50413	The Cowboy and the Lady/Me and Millie	1977	$4

LAURIE

❑ 3168	Light the Candles/That's What Love Will Do	1963	$20
❑ 3130	Lonely Traveler/You Better Go Home	1962	$20
❑ 3148	Molly/Honey Babe	1962	$20
❑ 3159	The Letter/The Runaround	1963	$20

UNITED ARTISTS

❑ XW793	A Butterfly for Bucky/ Another Night Alone	1976	$4
❑ 50470	A Christmas Wish/ Look Around You (It's Christmas Time)	1968	$10
❑ 50776	And I Love You So/ Gentle of a Man	1971	$5
❑ XW451	And Then There Was Gina/Quicksand	1974	$4

❑ XW633	And Then There Was Gina/ You Pull Me Down (Into Sweet, Sweet Love)	1975	$4
❑ 50318	Autumn of My Life/ She Chased Me	1968	$6
❑ 50318 [PS]	Autumn of My Life/ She Chased Me	1968	$20
❑ 50087	Blue Autumn/I Just Don't Love You Anymore	1966	$8
❑ 952	Broomstick Cowboy/Ain't Got Time for Happy	1965	$8
❑ 50891	California Wine/ To Be with You	1972	$5
❑ 50650	Can You Feel It/Time Good, Time Bad	1970	$5
❑ 51107	Country Feelin's/Brand New Kind of Love	1973	$5
❑ 50696	Down on the Bayou/ It's Gonna Change	1970	$5
❑ 50497	Glad She's a Woman/ Letter to Emily	1969	$6
❑ XW529	Hello Summertime/And Then There Was Gina	1974	$4
❑ 0046	Honey/Autumn of My Life	1973	$4
❑ 50283	Honey/Danny	1968	$12

—*Black label*

❑ 50283	Honey/Danny	1968	$8

—*Orange and pink label*

❑ XW422	I Believe the South Is Gonna Rise Again/She	1974	$4
❑ 781	I Don't Know You Anymore/ Little Drops of Water	1964	$8
❑ 908	If You Wait for Love/ If You've Got a Heart	1965	$8
❑ 50018	I Know You Better Than That/When Your Love Has Gone	1966	$8
❑ 50018 [PS]	I Know You Better Than That/When Your Love Has Gone	1966	$20
❑ 50807	I'll Remember You/ Come Back Home	1971	$5
❑ 50525	I'm a Drifter/Hobos and Kings	1969	$6
❑ 50056	It Hurts Me/Pity the Fool	1966	$8
❑ 980	It's Too Late/I'm Goin' Home	1966	$8
❑ 0045	It's Too Late/Voodoo Woman	1973	$4
❑ XW681	I Wrote a Song (Sing Along)/You Pull Me Down (Into Sweet, Sweet Love)	1975	$4
❑ 810	Little Things/I Can't Go On Pretending	1965	$10
❑ 50044	Longer Than Forever/ Take Your Love	1966	$8
❑ 50138	Love Is/Goodbye to All You Women	1967	$8
❑ XW371	Marlena/Sing Me a Smile	1973	$5
❑ 742	Me Japanese Boy, I Love You/Everyone But Me	1964	$8
❑ 50614	Mornin' Mornin'/Requiem	1969	$6
❑ 50565	Muddy Mississippi Line/A Richer Man Than I	1969	$6
❑ 50715	My God and I/The World Beyond	1970	$5
❑ 50224	Pledge of Love/Jo-Jo's Place	1967	$8
❑ 50846	Poem for the Little Lady/ Danny Is a Mirror to Me	1971	$5
❑ 672	See the Funny Little Clown/Hello Loser	1963	$10
❑ 0044	See the Funny Little Clown/Little Things	1973	$4
❑ XW866	She Taught Me How to Live Again/Reunion	1976	$4
❑ XW251	Summer (The First Time)/ Childhood 1949	1973	$5
❑ XW251 [PS]	Summer (The First Time)/ Childhood 1949	1973	$6
❑ XW517	Summer (The First Time)/Marlena	1974	$4

—*Reissue*

❑ 50461	The Straight Life/ Tomorrow Is Forgotten	1968	$6
❑ 50186	Three in the Morning/ Trusty Little Herbert	1967	$8
❑ 0047	Watching Scotty Grow/I'm a Drifter	1973	$4

—*0044 through 0047 are "Silver Spotlight Series" reissues*

❑ 50727	Watching Scotty Grow/ Water Color Days	1970	$5
❑ 710	Whenever He Holds You/If She Was Mine	1964	$8
❑ 710 [PS]	Whenever He Holds You/If She Was Mine	1964	$20
❑ 50938	With Pen in Hand/Southern Fried Singin' Sunday Mornin'	1972	$5

GOLDTONES, THE
A&R

❑ 714	Strike/Gutterball	1963	$40
❑ 714 [PS]	Strike/Gutterball	1963	$60

GOLLIWOGS, THE
Early CREEDENCE CLEARWATER REVIVAL. Also see TOMMY FOGERTY AND THE BLUE VELVETS.

FANTASY

❑ 590	Don't Tell Me No Lies/Little Girl, Does Your Mama Know	1964	$70
❑ 597	Where You Been/ You Came Walking	1965	$70

Number	Title	Yr	NM
SCORPIO			
❑ 404	Brown Eyed Girl/You Better Be Careful	1967	$60
❑ 405	Fragile Child/Fight Fire	1967	$60
❑ 412 [DJ]	Porterville/Call It Pretending	1968	$70

— Only promos credit the Golliwogs; all known stock copies credit Creedence Clearwater Revival.

Number	Title	Yr	NM
❑ 408	Walking on the Water/You Better Get It Before It Gets You	1967	$60
GOMM, IAN			
STIFF/EPIC			
❑ 50747	Hold On/Another Year	1979	$15
❑ 50802	Hooked on Love/Chicken Run	1979	$15
GONE ALL STARS			
GONE			
❑ 5016	7-11/Down Yonder Rock	1957	$30
GONKS, THE			
LONDON			
❑ 9696	The Gonk Song/Take Care	1964	$15
GONN			
EMIR			
❑ SS-9217-01	Blackout of Gretley/Pain in My Heart	1966	$800
EMIR/MCCM			
❑ 88-9217	Blackout of Gretley/Pain in My Heart	1988	$5

— Black vinyl

Number	Title	Yr	NM
❑ 88-9217	Blackout of Gretley/Pain in My Heart	1988	$20

— Red vinyl

Number	Title	Yr	NM
❑ 88-9217 [PS]	Blackout of Gretley/Pain in My Heart	1988	$10
MERRY JAINE			
❑ IT-2316	Come with Me (To the Stars)/You're Looking Fine	1967	$125
GONNEAU, PIERRE			
LAURIE			
❑ 3280	The Little Boy That Santa Forgot/Chanson du Soir	1964	$15
GONZALES-GONZALES, JOSE			
LIBERTY			
❑ 55770	Pancho Claus/Tacos for Two	1964	$15
GONZALES, BABS			
ATLAS			
❑ 1206	Teenage Santa Claus/Pay Dem Dues	1959	$15
BRUCE			
❑ 122	The Be-Bop Santa Claus/Manhattan Fable	1955	$30
ESSEX			
❑ 377	The Be-Bop Santa Claus/Manhattan Fable	1954	$30
KING			
❑ 4836 [DJ]	Be-Bop Santa Claus/Watch Them Resolutions	1955	$20
GONZALES, FRANK			
F-G			
❑ 1001	Sweet Surfing Little Girl/Let's Make Up	1961	$250
GOOBERS, THE			
SURF			
❑ 1001	Hawaiian Holiday/Buyer Beware	1963	$60
GOOD AND PLENTY			
SENATE			
❑ 2105	Living in a World of Make Believe/I Played My Part Well	1967	$10
❑ 2106	Sunny and Me/Children Dreamin'	1967	$10
GOOD GUYS, THE			
GNP CRESCENDO			
❑ 326	Asphalt Wipe Out/Scratch	1964	$30
GOOD RATS, THE			
KAPP			
❑ 946	The Hobo/Truth Is Gone	1968	$15
GOOD ROCKIN' SAM			
EXCELLO			
❑ 2059	Baby I'm Fool Proof/Thing-a-Ma-Jig	1955	$60

Number	Title	Yr	NM
GOOD TIMES, THE			
KAMA SUTRA			
❑ 215	That's When Your Heartaches Begin/Good Life	1966	$8
GOOD, TOMMY			
GORDY			
❑ 7034	Baby I Miss You/Leaving Here	1964	$125
GOODEES, THE			
HIP			
❑ 8005	Condition Red/Didn't Know Love Was So Good	1968	$10
❑ 109	For a Little While/Would You, Could You	1968	$8
❑ 8016	He's a Rebel/Goodies	1969	$8
GOODLEY, GERRI			
DOOTONE			
❑ 316	Santa Claus Walks Just Like Daddy/You're My Christmas	1953	$40

— B-side by Buell Thomas

Number	Title	Yr	NM
GOODMAN, AL			
RCA VICTOR			
❑ 47-3833	Adeste Fideles/Because You're You	1950	$20
GOODMAN, BENNY			
CAPITOL			
❑ F1646	Chicago/Back in Your Own Backyard	1951	$15

— Reissue

Number	Title	Yr	NM
❑ F3331	Goody Goody/Sometimes I'm Happy	1956	$15
❑ F860	It Isn't Fair/You're Always There	1950	$30
❑ F3043	Let's Dance/Jumpin' at the Woodside	1954	$15
❑ F828	Spin a Record/Little Girl Don't Cry	1950	$30
CHESS			
❑ 1742	Mission to Moscow/You Do Something to Me	1959	$10
COLUMBIA			
❑ 40625	A Fine Romance/Goodbye	1955	$15

— With Rosemary Clooney

Number	Title	Yr	NM
❑ 39314	Avalon/Blue Skies	1951	$15
❑ 39287	Bei Mir Bist Du Schoen/Stompin' at the Savoy (Conclusion)-Dizzy Spells (Beginning)	1951	$15
❑ 39312	Blue Moon/Swingtime in the Rockies	1951	$15
❑ 39284	Blue Skies/Sing, Sing, Sing (Conclusion)	1951	$15
❑ 39313	Body and Soul/Loch Lomond	1951	$15
❑ 39288	China Boy/Stompin' at the Savoy	1951	$15
❑ 39307	Dixieland One Step-I'm Coming Virginia-When My Baby Smiles at Me/Dizzy Spells (Conclusion)-Big John's Special	1951	$15
❑ 39280	Dixieland One Step/Jam Session	1951	$15
❑ 39304	Don't Be That Way/Sing, Sing, Sing (Conclusion)	1951	$15
❑ 39277	Don't Be That Way/The Man I Love	1951	$15
❑ 39564	Farewell Blues/King Porter Stomp	1951	$20
❑ 39976	I'll Never Say "Never Again" Again/What a Little Moonlight Can Do	1952	$20
❑ 39309	Life Goes to a Parrty/Stompin' at the Savoy (Beginning)	1951	$15
❑ 39282	Life Goes to a Party (Beginning)/Life Goes to a Party (Conclusion)	1951	$15
❑ 39285	Loch Lomond/Sing, Sing, Sing (Beginning)	1951	$15
❑ 39121	Lullaby of the Leaves/Temptation Rag	1950	$30
❑ 3-39121	Lullaby of the Leaves/Temptation Rag	1950	$40

— Microgroove 7-inch, 33 1/3 rpm, small hole single

Number	Title	Yr	NM
❑ 40616	Memories of You/It's Bad for Me	1955	$15

— With Rosemary Clooney

Number	Title	Yr	NM
❑ 1-889	Oh Babe/Walkin' with the Blues	1950	$40

— Microgroove 33 1/3 rpm 7-inch small hole single

Number	Title	Yr	NM
❑ 6-889	Oh Babe/Walkin' with the Blues	1950	$30
❑ 39278	One O'Clock Jump/Avalon	1951	$15
❑ 39305	One O'Clock Jump (Beginning)/Sing, Sing, Sing (Continuation)	1951	$15
❑ 39279	One O'Clock Jump/Body and Soul	1951	$15

Number	Title	Yr	NM
❑ 39306	One O'Clock Jump (Conclusion)/Sing, Sing, Sing (Beginning)	1951	$15
❑ 39281	Shine/Blue Reverie	1951	$15
❑ 39308	Shine-Blue Reverie/Stompin' at the Savoy (Conclusion)-Dizzy Spells (Beginning)	1951	$15
❑ 39416	South of the Border/Down South CampMeeting'	1951	$20
❑ 39286	Swingtime in the Rockies/Dizzy Spells (Conclusion)	1951	$15
❑ 39315	The Man I Love/I Got Rhythm	1951	$15
❑ 39478	The Wang-Wang Blues/It Never Entered My Mind	1951	$20
COMMAND			
❑ 4108	Mimi/Petite Fleur	1967	$6
❑ 4104	Peace/Hava Nagila	1967	$6
DECCA			
❑ 25548	Don't Be That Way/Jersey Bounce	1962	$12
❑ 47-2953	Don't Be That Way/My Melancholy Baby	1949	$20
❑ 47-2954	Tiger Rag/Alexander's Ragtime Band	1949	$20
❑ EAP 1-479	Classics in Jazz, Part 1	1954	$20
❑ EAP 1-479	Classics in Jazz, Part 2	1954	$20
❑ EAP 1-479	(contents unknown)	1954	$20
❑ EAP 2-479	Love Is Just Around the Corner/I'll Never Be the Same//Cherokee/Music, Maestro, Please	1954	$20
❑ ZTEP27372/3 [PS]	Swing Into Spring	1956	$25

— Texaco premium

Number	Title	Yr	NM
❑ ZTEP27372/3	Swing Into Spring/Blue Skies//Have You Met Miss Jones/Swingtime in the Rockies	1956	$20

— Purple label; has Texaco star at right and "Prepared Expressly for Texaco" at left

Number	Title	Yr	NM
RCA VICTOR			
❑ 947-0135	Camel Hop/Riffin' at the Ritz//Wrappin' It Up/Life Goes to a Party	1954	$20

— Record 2 of 2-EP set EPBT 3056

Number	Title	Yr	NM
❑ 947-0134	Swingtime in the Rockies/Sugarfoot Stomp//Changes/Big John Special	1954	$20

— Record 1 of 2-EP set EPBT 3056

Number	Title	Yr	NM
❑ EPBT3056 [PS]	This Is Benny Goodman	1954	$20

— Two-pocket jacket for 2-EP set (947-0134 and 947-0135)

Number	Title	Yr	NM
GOODMAN, DICKIE			
20TH FOX			
❑ 443	Senate Hearing/Lock-Up	1963	$20
AUDIO SPECTRUM			
❑ 75	Presidential Interview (Flying Saucer '64)/Paul Revere	1964	$50
CASH			
❑ 451	Mr. Jaws/Irv's Theme	1975	$5
❑ 451	Mr. Jaws/Irv's Theme	1975	$60

— Clear purple vinyl, possibly an "after-hours" edition; at least two, and probably more, exist

Number	Title	Yr	NM
COTIQUE			
❑ 173	Luna Trip/My Victrola	1969	$6

— B-side by Joey Pastrana

Number	Title	Yr	NM
❑ 158	On Campus/Mombo Suzie	1969	$6

— B-side by Johnny Colo

Number	Title	Yr	NM
DAVY JONES			
❑ 663	White House Happening/President Johnson	1967	$30
❑ 663 [PS]	White House Happening/President Johnson	1967	$50
DIAMOND			
❑ 119	Ben Crazy/Flip Side	1962	$20
EXTRAN			
❑ 601	Hey, E.T./Get a Job	1982	$5
GOODNAME			
❑ 7100	Safe Sex Report/Safety First	1987	$20

— His last record

Number	Title	Yr	NM
HOT LINE			
❑ 1017	Energy Crisis '79/Pain	1979	$6

— Common version has a light green label and "Hot Line" as two words

Number	Title	Yr	NM
❑ 1017	Energy Crisis '79/Pain	1979	$8

— Less common version has a reddish label and the label as "Hotline" (one word)

Number	Title	Yr	NM
JANUS			
❑ 271	Star Warts/The Boys Tune	1977	$5
J.M.D.			
❑ 01	Ben Crazy/Flip Side	1962	$30
MARK-X			
❑ 8010	The Touchables in Brooklyn/Mystery	1961	$30

Number	Title	Yr	NM
❑ 8009	The Touchables/Martian Melody	1961	$40
— Yellow label			
❑ 8009	The Touchables/Martian Melody	1961	$30
—Black label			
M.D.			
❑ 101	Schmonanza/Backwards Theme	1961	$30
MONTAGE			
❑ 1220 [DJ]	Hey, E.T. (same on both sides)	1982	$5
❑ 1220	Hey, E.T./The Ride of Paul Revere	1982	$20
ORON			
❑ 101	Washington Uptight/The Cat	1967	$30
—As "The Pennsylvania Players			
PRELUDE			
❑ 8018	Election '80 (same on both sides)	1980	$5
RAINY WEDNESDAY			
❑ 206	Energy Crisis '74/Ruthie's Theme	1974	$8
❑ 206	Energy Crisis '74/The Mistake	1974	$6
❑ 208	Gerry Ford, A Special Report/Robert	1974	$6
❑ 209	Inflation in the Nation/Jon and Jed's Theme	1975	$6
❑ 207	Mr. President/Popularity	1974	$6
❑ 204	Purple People Eater/Ruthie's Theme	1973	$6
❑ 205	The Constitution/The End	1973	$6
❑ 202	Watergrate/Friends	1973	$30
RAMGO			
❑ 501	Speaking of Ecology/Dayton's Theme	1970	$30
RED BIRD			
❑ Oct-0058	Batman & His Grandmother/Suspense	1966	$30
RORI			
❑ 601	Horror Movies/Whoa, Mule	1961	$30
❑ 701	Santa and the Touchables/North Pole Rock	1961	$30
❑ 602	The Berlin Top Ten/Little Tiger	1961	$30
SCEPTER			
❑ 12339	Speaking of Ecology/Dayton's Theme	1971	$15
SHARK			
❑ 1001	Mrs. Jaws/(B-side unknown)	1979	$30
❑ 1002	Super Superman/Chomp Chomp	1979	$20
SHELL			
❑ 711	Election '84/Herb's Theme	1984	$4
WACKO			
❑ 1381	America '81 (two different versions)	1981	$8
❑ 1001	Mr. President/Dancin' U.S.A.	1981	$5
❑ 1002	Super-Duper Man/Robert's Tune	1981	$5
Z-100			
❑ 100 [DJ]	Attack of the Z Monster/Mystery	1984	$12
— Promo item for New York radio station			

GOODMAN, SHIRLEY

IMPERIAL

Number	Title	Yr	NM
❑ 5944	When a Boy Meets a Girl/Don't Marry Too Soon	1963	$15

GOODMAN, STEVE, AND PHOEBE SNOW

ASYLUM

Number	Title	Yr	NM
❑ 47069	Sometimes Love Forgets/Can't Find My Heart	1980	$5

GOODMAN, STEVE

ASYLUM

Number	Title	Yr	NM
❑ 45331	Between the Lines/Can't Go Back	1976	$6
❑ 47107	Bobby Don't Stop/Trust Me	1981	$5
❑ 46012	Men Who Love Women Who Love Men/The One That Got Away	1979	$6
❑ 46522	Men Who Love Women Who Love Men/The One That Got Away	1979	$5

BUDDAH

Number	Title	Yr	NM
❑ 270	City of New Orleans/(B-side unknown)	1971	$15
❑ 326	Election Year Rag/Someone Else's Troubles	1972	$12
❑ 348	The Dutchman/Song for David	1973	$10

RED PAJAMA

Number	Title	Yr	NM
❑ 1001	A Dying Cub Fan's Last Request/Take Me Out to the Ball Game	1981	$20

WGN

Number	Title	Yr	NM
❑ 784	Go Cubs Go (WGN Radio Cubs Theme) (same on both sides)	1984	$15

GOODNIGHT, GARY

AWESOME

Number	Title	Yr	NM
❑ 102	I Got a Thing About You Baby/(B-side unknown)	1984	$6

DOOR KNOB

Number	Title	Yr	NM
❑ 149	Get Me High, Off This Low/(B-side unknown)	1981	$5
❑ 138	I Have to Break the Chains That Bind Me/(B-side unknown)	1980	$5
❑ 169	Lady Lay Down (Lay Down on My Pillow)/(B-side unknown)	1981	$5
❑ 159	Let Me Fill for You a Fantasy/(B-side unknown)	1981	$5
❑ 166	Losin' Myself in You/Vagabond Cowboy	1981	$5
❑ 141	Make Me Believe/Back Door Slam	1981	$5
❑ 155	Tell Me So/There'll Be a Blue Moon Tonight	1981	$5
❑ 133	Texas Let Me In/Ladies Don't Marry Cowboys	1980	$5

SOUNDWAVES

Number	Title	Yr	NM
❑ 4675	Bringing Out the Fool in Me/Texas Let Me In	1982	$5
❑ 4689	Goodnight My Love/These Magic Feelings	1982	$5
❑ 4703	My Baby's Gone/Goodnight My Love	1983	$5

GOODTIME WASHBOARD THREE, THE

FANTASY

Number	Title	Yr	NM
❑ 609	Santa Charges Through Your Bank Account/(B-side unknown)	1966	$10

GOODWIN, BILL

VEE JAY

Number	Title	Yr	NM
❑ 564	I Won't Wait Up Tonight/The Stand-In	1963	$20
❑ 501	Shoes of a Fool/It Keeps Right On a-Hrtin'	1963	$20
❑ 602	The Saddest Eyes/The House at 103	1964	$20

GOODWIN, RON

CAPITOL

Number	Title	Yr	NM
❑ F3834	Lingering Lovers/Swedish Polka	1957	$12
❑ F3748	Swinging Sweethearts/I'll Find You	1957	$10
❑ F3708	The Headless Horseman/When I Fall in Love	1957	$10
❑ F4139	Wagon Train/Latin Lovers	1959	$10

GOONS, THE

DECCA

Number	Title	Yr	NM
❑ F10756	I'm Walking Backwards for Christmas/Bluebottle Blues	1956	$30
—U.K. import (original)			
❑ F13414	I'm Walking Backwards for Christmas/Ying Tong Song	1973	$20
—U.K. import (reissue)			

LONDON

Number	Title	Yr	NM
❑ 1684	I'm Walking Backwards for Christmas/Bluebottle Blues	1956	$30

GOOSE CREEK SYMPHONY

CAPITOL

Number	Title	Yr	NM
❑ 2729	Big Time Saturday Nite/Beautiful Bertha	1970	$6
❑ 2853	Charlie's Tune/No News Is Good News	1970	$6
❑ 3371	Guitars Pickin', Fiddles Playin'/Broken Creek Goose Down	1972	$5
❑ 3246	(Oh Lord Won't You Buy Me a) Mercedes Benz/Rich on Love	1971	$5

COLUMBIA

Number	Title	Yr	NM
❑ 10062	Hot Dog Daddy/Plans of the Lord	1974	$5

GORDIAN KNOT, THE

VERVE

Number	Title	Yr	NM
❑ 10612	Broken Down Old Merry-Go-Round/We Must Be Doin' Something Right	1968	$10

GORDON, BARRY

ABC

Number	Title	Yr	NM
❑ 11113	The Girl I Left Behind/A House Built on Sand	1968	$8

ABC DUNHILL

Number	Title	Yr	NM
❑ 4126	Days of Pearly Spencer/Ramshackle Guy	1968	$8

Number	Title	Yr	NM
❑ 4141	The Girl I Left Behind/A House Built on Sand	1968	$8
DUNHILL			
❑ 4110	Angelica/Take Off the Veil	1967	$8
❑ 4126	Days of Pearly Spencer/Ramshackle Guy	1968	$20
— No "ABC" logo next to "Dunhill" at top of label			
ERA			
❑ 1092	Bluebird Song/Rabbit Habit	1959	$15
MERCURY			
❑ 71878	Sad Little Girl/She's Got Soul	1961	$15
MGM			
❑ K12276	How Do We Look to the Monkeys/Ten Years to Go	1956	$30
❑ K12222	I Can't Whistle/The Milkman's Polka	1956	$30
❑ K12468	The Thief/Yes, We Have No Bananas	1957	$20
UNITED ARTISTS			
❑ 730	Go Back Little Tear/Susan	1964	$10
❑ 950	Let Me Try/The World Is Mine	1965	$12
❑ 876	Sealed with a Kiss/Talk, Talk, Talk	1965	$10
❑ 795	True Love Can Never Die/The Two of Them	1964	$10

GORDON, LUKE

ISLAND

Number	Title	Yr	NM
❑ 0640	Dark Hollow/You May Be Someone (Where You Came From)	1958	$30

GORDON, MIKE, AND THE AGATES

DORE

Number	Title	Yr	NM
❑ 780	Curfew on the Strip/Last Call for Dinner	1966	$20

GORDON, MIKE, AND THE EL TEMPOS

CAT

Number	Title	Yr	NM
❑ 101	Why Don't You Do Right/You Got to Give	1954	$60

GORDON, ROBERT

PRIVATE STOCK

Number	Title	Yr	NM
❑ 45,203	Fire/If This Is Wrong	1979	$6
❑ 45,203 [PS]	Fire/If This Is Wrong	1979	$15
❑ 45,191	Sea Cruise/If This Is Wrong	1978	$6
— With Link Wray			
RCA			
❑ PB-11452	Blue Christmas/Fire	1978	$5
— With Link Wray			
❑ JH-11452 [DJ]	Blue Christmas (mono/stereo)	1978	$6
❑ PB-11919	Born to Lose/Need You	1980	$5
❑ PB-11471	It's Only Make Believe/Rock Billy Boogie	1979	$5
❑ PB-12239	Someday, Someway/Drivin' Wheel	1981	$5
❑ PB-13399	Something's Gonna Happen/Flying Saucers Rock and Roll	1982	$5
❑ PB-11608	Walk On By/Black Slacks	1979	$5

GORDON, ROSCOE

ABC-PARAMOUNT

Number	Title	Yr	NM
❑ 10351	A Girl to Love/As You Walk Away	1962	$80
❑ 10407	A Little Bit of Magic/I Want Revenge	1963	$50
❑ 10501	I Don't Stand a Chance/That's What You Did	1963	$50
— As "Barbara & Roscoe Gordon			
CHESS			
❑ 1487	Booted/I Love You Till the Day I Die	1951	$1500
DUKE			
❑ 114	Ain't No Use/Roscoe's Mambo	1953	$60
❑ 320	Dilly Bop/You'll Never Know	1960	$20
❑ 173	I've Loved and Lost/Tummer Tee	1957	$40
❑ 101	Tell Daddy/Hey Fat Girl	1952	$125
❑ 129	Three Can't Love/You Figure It Out	1954	$60
❑ 106	T-Model Boogie/New Orleans Woman	1953	$60
❑ 109	Too Many Women/Wise to You, Baby	1953	$60
FLIP			
❑ 237	The Chicken (Dance with You)/Love for You Baby	1956	$60
❑ 227	Weeping Blues/Just Love Me, Baby	1956	$300
OLD TOWN			
❑ 1167	Gotta Keep Rollin'/Just a Little at a Time	1964	$30

Number	Title	Yr	NM
❑ 1175	It Ain't Right/Could This Be Love	1965	$10

—As "Roscoe and Barbara"

RPM

Number	Title	Yr	NM
❑ 344	Booted/Cold, Cold Winter	1952	$200
❑ 336	Dime a Dozen/A New Remedy for Love	1951	$250
❑ 379	I'm in Love/Just In from Texas	1953	$70
❑ 373	Lucille/Blues for My Baby	1953	$70
❑ 324	Saddled the Cow/Ouch, Pretty Baby	1951	$400
❑ 369	Trying/Dream Baby	1952	$70
❑ 384	We're All Loaded/Tomorrow May Be Too Late	1953	$70
❑ 365	What You Got on Your Mind/Two Kinds of Women	1952	$125

SUN

Number	Title	Yr	NM
❑ 305	Sally Jo/Torro	1958	$30
❑ 257	Shoobie Oobie/Cheese and Crackers	1956	$60
❑ 237	The Chicken (Dance with You)/Love for You Baby	1956	$200
❑ 227	Weeping Blues/Just Love Me, Baby	1956	$500

VEE JAY

Number	Title	Yr	NM
❑ 316	A Fool in Love/No More Doggin'	1959	$20
❑ 348	Surely I Love You/What You Do to Me	1960	$20
❑ 385	What I Wouldn't Do/Let 'Em Try	1961	$15

GORDY, POPPA JOHN

RCA VICTOR

Number	Title	Yr	NM
❑ 47-5902	Santa Plays the Trombone (In the North Pole Band)/Oh Didn't He Ramble	1954	$20

GORE, LESLEY

A&M

Number	Title	Yr	NM
❑ 1710	Give It to Me, Sweet Thing/Immortality	1975	$5
❑ 1710 [PS]	Give It to Me, Sweet Thing/Immortality	1975	$6
❑ 1830	Sometimes/Give It To Me, Sweet Thing	1976	$5

CREWE

Number	Title	Yr	NM
❑ 601	Back Together/Quiet Love	1971	$12
❑ 344	When Yesterday Was Tomorrow/Why Me, Why You	1970	$10
❑ 338	Why Doesn't Love Make Me Happy/Tomorrow's Children	1970	$10

MANHATTAN

Number	Title	Yr	NM
❑ 50039	Since I Don't Have You-It's Only Make Believe/Our Love Was Meant to Be	1986	$8

—With Lou Christie

MERCURY

Number	Title	Yr	NM
❑ 72412	All of My Life/I Cannot Hope for Anything	1965	$10
❑ 72412 [PS]	All of My Life/I Cannot Hope for Anything	1965	$30
❑ 72726	Brink of Disaster/On a Day Like This	1967	$10
❑ 72649	California Nights/I'm Goin' Out	1967	$10
❑ 72819	He Gives Me Love (La, La, La)/Brand New Me	1968	$15
❑ 72352	Hey Now/Sometimes I Wish I Were a Boy	1964	$12
❑ 72352 [PS]	Hey Now/Sometimes I Wish I Were a Boy	1964	$30
❑ 72270	I Don't Wanna Be a Loser/It's Gotta Be You	1964	$10
❑ 72270 [PS]	I Don't Wanna Be a Loser/It's Gotta Be You	1964	$30
❑ 72759	It's a Happening/Magic Colors	1967	$10
❑ 72119	It's My Party/Danny	1963	$20
❑ 72119 [PS]	It's My Party/Danny	1963	$40
❑ 72513	I Won't Love You Anymore (Sorry)/No Matter What You Do	1966	$10
❑ 72513 [PS]	I Won't Love You Anymore (Sorry)/No Matter What You Do	1966	$30
❑ 72372	Look of Love/Little Girl Gone Home	1964	$10
❑ 72372 [PS]	Look of Love/Little Girl Gone Home	1964	$30
❑ 72867	Look the Other Way/I'll Be Standing By	1968	$15
❑ 72309	Maybe I Know/Wonder Boy	1964	$10
❑ 72309 [PS]	Maybe I Know/Wonder Boy	1964	$30
❑ 72611	Maybe Now/Treat Me Like a Lady	1966	$10
❑ 72475	My Town, My Guy and Me/Girl in Love	1965	$10
❑ 72475 [PS]	My Town, My Guy and Me/Girl in Love	1965	$30
❑ 72580	Off and Running/I Don't Care	1966	$10
❑ 72180	She's a Fool/The Old Crowd	1963	$20
❑ 72180 [PS]	She's a Fool/The Old Crowd	1963	$30
❑ 72787	Small Talk/Say What You See	1968	$15

Number	Title	Yr	NM
❑ 72683	Summer and Sandy/I'm Fallin' Down	1967	$10
❑ 72683 [PS]	Summer and Sandy/I'm Fallin' Down	1967	$30
❑ 72931	Summer Symphony/98.6-Lazy Day	1969	$20
❑ 72433	Sunshine, Lollipops and Rainbows/You've Come Back	1965	$10
❑ 72433 [PS]	Sunshine, Lollipops and Rainbows/You've Come Back	1965	$30
❑ 72892	Take Good Care (Of My Heart)/I Can't Make It Without You	1969	$15
❑ 72892	Take Good Care (Of My Heart)/You Sent Me Silver Bells	1969	$15
❑ 72259	That's the Way Boys Are/That's the Way the Ball Bounces	1964	$12
❑ 72259 [PS]	That's the Way Boys Are/That's the Way the Ball Bounces	1964	$30
❑ 72969	Wedding Bell Blues/One by One	1969	$20
❑ 72530	We Know We're in Love/That's What We'll Do	1966	$10
❑ 72842	Where Can I Go/I Can't Make It Without You	1968	$15

GORMAN, FREDDIE

MIRACLE

Number	Title	Yr	NM
❑ 11	The Day Will Come/Just for You	1962	$125

RIC-TIC

Number	Title	Yr	NM
❑ 101	In a Bad Way/There Can Be Too Much	1964	$40
❑ 102	Take Me Back/Can't Get It Out of My Mind	1965	$60

GORMAN SISTERS, THE

JOY

Number	Title	Yr	NM
❑ 224	Daddy Is My Santa Claus/Chickery Check	1958	$20

GORME, EYDIE

ABC-PARAMOUNT

Number	Title	Yr	NM
❑ 10155	Be Sure My Love/I Will Follow You	1960	$12
❑ 10383	Fly Me to the Moon/I'm Yours	1962	$10
❑ 9944	Gotta Have Rain/To You From Me	1958	$10
❑ 10061	Happiness/Fool Around	1959	$12
❑ 9773	I'll Come Back/It's a Pity to Say Goodnight	1956	$10
❑ 9780	I'll Take Romance/First Impression	1957	$10
❑ 10006	I'm Yours/Don't Take Your Love from Me	1959	$10
❑ 9863	Love Me Forever/Let Me Be Loved	1957	$10
❑ 9722	Mama, Teach Me to Dance/You Bring Out the Lover in Me	1956	$10
❑ 9655	Sincerely Yours/Come Home	1955	$20

—The first 45 (numerically) on ABC-Paramount

Number	Title	Yr	NM
❑ 9758	Soda Pop Hop/I've Got a Right to Cry	1956	$12
❑ 10041	Taking a Chance on Love/The Years Between	1959	$10
❑ 10111	The Dance Is Over/Too Young to Know	1960	$12
❑ 9684	Too Close for Comfort/That's How	1956	$10
❑ 9852	When Your Lover Has Gone/Until They Sail	1957	$10

CALENDAR

Number	Title	Yr	NM
❑ 63-1002	He Needs Me/How Could I Be So Wrong	1968	$5
❑ 63-1004	This Guy's (Girl's) in Love with You/It's You Again	1968	$5

COLUMBIA

Number	Title	Yr	NM
❑ JZSP116419/20 [DJ]	Alegre Navidad/Blanca Navidad	1966	$10

—With Trio Los Panchos

Number	Title	Yr	NM
❑ 43856	Allegre Navidad/Navidad Y Ano Nuevo	1966	$8
❑ 42661	Blame It on the Bossa Nova/Guess I Should Have Loved Him More	1963	$8
❑ 42661 [PS]	Blame It on the Bossa Nova/Guess I Should Have Loved Him More	1963	$10
❑ 43225	Do I Hear a Waltz/After You've Gone	1965	$6
❑ 43444	Don't Go to Strangers/Mas Amor (More Love)	1965	$6
❑ 42790	Don't Try to Fight It, Baby/Theme from Light Fantastic (My Secret World)	1963	$6
❑ 42854	Everybody Go Home/The Message	1963	$6
❑ 43906	Guess I Should Have Loved Him More/What Is a Woman	1966	$6
❑ 43660	If He Walked Into My Life/Tell Him I Said Hello	1966	$6

Number	Title	Yr	NM
❑ 4-43082	I Want You to Meet My Baby/Can't Get Over (The Bossa Nova)	1964	$6
❑ 4-43082 [DJ]	I Want You to Meet My Baby (same on both sides)	1964	$20

—Promo only on red vinyl

Number	Title	Yr	NM
❑ 44299	Life Is But a Moment/What Makes Me Love Him	1967	$6
❑ 43971	Softly, As I Leave You/What's Good About Goodbye	1967	$6
❑ 42953	The Friendliest Thing/Something to Live For	1963	$6
❑ 43191	The Moon and the Stars and a Little Bit of Wine/Piel Canela	1964	$6
❑ 43542	What Did I Have That I Didn't Have/Tell Him I Said Hello	1966	$6
❑ 42607	Where Is Love/Before Your Time	1962	$8

CORAL

Number	Title	Yr	NM
❑ 61138	Crocodile Tears/Fallen Apples	1954	$15
❑ 60921	Don't Tell Lies/Love Me Not Just a Little	1953	$15
❑ 60977	Frenesi/All Night Long	1953	$15
❑ 61093	Gimme Gimme John/Fini	1953	$15
❑ 61347	Give a Fool a Chance/A Girl Can't Say	1955	$15
❑ 61036	I Danced with My Darling/I'd Be Forgotten	1953	$15
❑ 61481	Soldier Boy/What Is the Secret to Success	1955	$15
❑ 61189	Tea for Two/Climb Up the Wall	1954	$15
❑ 60879	That Night of Heaven/Tell Me More	1952	$20

MGM

Number	Title	Yr	NM
❑ 14213	Mem'ries and Souvenirs/Rosy's Theme	1971	$5
❑ 14397	Mr. Number One/Butterfly	1972	$5
❑ 14276	Sal and Sally/Somebody Waiting	1971	$5
❑ 14563	Take One Step/The Garden	1973	$5
❑ 14681	Touch the Wind (Eres Tu)/It Takes Too Long to Learn to Live Alone	1973	$5

RCA VICTOR

Number	Title	Yr	NM
❑ 74-0360	Ladies Who Lunch/My World Keeps Getting Smaller Every Day	1970	$5
❑ 74-0250	Wild One/Tonight I'll Say a Prayer	1969	$5

UNITED ARTISTS

Number	Title	Yr	NM
❑ 414	Frenesi/Granada	1962	$8
❑ 283	Let Me Be the First to Wish You a Merry Christmas/I Love to Dance (But Never on Sunday)	1960	$15
❑ 325	Mem'ries and Souvenirs/My Heart	1961	$8
❑ 292	What Happened to Our Love/Yours Tonight	1961	$8
❑ XW852	What I Did for Love/Can It Ever Be the Same	1976	$4
❑ A-246 [PS]	Eydie in Love, Volume 1	1958	$12
❑ C-246 [PS]	Eydie in Love, Volume 3	1958	$12
❑ A-246	When the World Was Young/In Love In Vain//Here I Am in Love Again/Why Shouldn't I?	1958	$10
❑ C-246	Why Try to Change Me Now/Idle Conversation//It Could Happen to You/In the Wee Small Hours of the Morning	1958	$10

GOSDIN BROTHERS, THE

BAKERSFIELD INT'L.

Number	Title	Yr	NM
❑ 1002	Hangin' On/Multiple Heartache	1967	$20
❑ 1006	She Still Wishes I Was You/There Must Be Someone	1968	$20

CAPITOL

Number	Title	Yr	NM
❑ 3074	I Remember/Just Like the Wind	1971	$8
❑ 2412	Louisiana Man/Till the End	1969	$10
❑ 2265	Sounds of Goodbye/The Victim	1968	$12
❑ 2553	The Day the Rains Came/My Love Keeps Reaching Out for You	1969	$12

WORLD PACIFIC

Number	Title	Yr	NM
❑ 77835	Love at First Sight/To Ramona	1966	$15

GOSDIN, REX

GRC

Number	Title	Yr	NM
❑ 2074	How Can Anything That Sounds So Good (Make Me Feel So Bad)/Things I Remember	1975	$6

METROMEDIA COUNTRY

Number	Title	Yr	NM
❑ 904	Sarah Lee/(B-side unknown)	1973	$8

Number	Title	Yr	NM

GOSDIN, VERN
AMI
Number	Title	Yr	NM
❏ 1302	Don't Ever Leave Me Again/ Love Is All We Had to Share	1982	$5
❏ 1312	Friday Night Feelin'/Lovin' You Is Music to My Mind	1983	$5
❏ 1310	Today My World Slipped Away/Ain't It Been Love	1982	$5

COLUMBIA
Number	Title	Yr	NM
❏ 38-08003	Chiseled in Stone/ Tight as Twin Fiddles	1988	$3
❏ 38-07627	Do You Believe Me Now/ Nobody Calls from Vegas Just to Say Hello	1987	$3
❏ 38-68888	I'm Still Crazy/Paradise '83	1989	$3
❏ 38-07762	Set 'Em Up Joe/There Ain't Nothing Wrong (Just Ain't Nothing Right)	1988	$4
❏ 38-69084	That Just About Does It/Set 'Em Up Joe	1989	$3
❏ 38-08528	Who You Gonna Blame It On This Time/ It's Not Over Yet	1988	$3

COMPLEAT
Number	Title	Yr	NM
❏ 142	Dim Lights, Thick Smoke (And Loud, Loud Music)/ For a Minute There	1985	$5
❏ 122	I Can Tell by the Way You Dance (You're Gonna Love Me Tonight)/My Heart Is a Good Hands	1984	$5
❏ 102	If You're Gonna Do Me Wrong (Do It Right)/ Favorite Fool of All	1983	$5
❏ 145	I Know the Way to You By Heart/Rainbows and Roses	1985	$5
❏ 153	It's Only Love Again/Today My World Slipped Away	1986	$5
❏ 149	It's Only Love Again/ What a Price I've Paid	1985	$5
❏ 115	I Wonder Where We'd Be Tonight/I Feel Love Closin' In	1983	$5
❏ 135	Slow Burning Memory/I've Got a Heart Full of You	1984	$5
❏ 158	Time Stood Still/Slow Burning Memory	1986	$5
❏ 155	Was It Just the Wine/ Way Down Deep	1986	$5
❏ 108	Way Down Deep/Today My World Slipped Away	1983	$5
❏ 126	What Would Your Memories Do/Lovely Right to the End	1984	$5

ELEKTRA
Number	Title	Yr	NM
❏ 46052	All I Want and Need Forever/Fifteen Hundred Times a Day	1979	$5
❏ 45532	Break My Mind/ Without You There's a Sadness in My Song	1978	$5
❏ 45353	Hangin' On/ Yesterday's Gone	1976	$5
❏ 45436	Mother Country Music/ We Make Beautiful Music Together	1977	$5
❏ 46550	Sarah's Eyes/She's Gone	1979	$5
❏ 45411	Till the End/It Started All Over Again	1977	$5

OVATION
Number	Title	Yr	NM
❏ 1171	Dream of Me/Ain't It Been Love	1981	$5
❏ 1163	Too Long Gone/She's Just a Place to Fall	1981	$5

GOSPEL STARS, THE
TAMLA
Number	Title	Yr	NM
❏ 54037	He Lifted Me/Behold the Saints of God	1961	$200

—*Horizontal lines logo*

Number	Title	Yr	NM
❏ 54037	He Lifted Me/Behold the Saints of God	1961	$70

—*Globe logo*

GOTHAM CITY CRIME FIGHTERS, THE
BATWING
Number	Title	Yr	NM
❏ 1001	Who Stole the Batmobile/That's Life	1966	$40

GOULDMAN, GRAHAM
A&M
Number	Title	Yr	NM
❏ 2251	Away from It All/Bionic Boar	1980	$4

RCA VICTOR
Number	Title	Yr	NM
❏ 47-9584	For Your Love/ Pamela, Pamela	1968	$15
❏ 47-9453	Impossible Years/ No Milk Today	1968	$15

GOULET, ROBERT
ABC
Number	Title	Yr	NM
❏ 12049	The Little Prince: Title/ Mack and Mable: I Won't Send Roses	1974	$4
❏ 12049 [PS]	The Little Prince: Title/ Mack and Mable: I Won't Send Roses	1974	$5

ARTISTS OF AMERICA
Number	Title	Yr	NM
❏ 118	After All Is Said and Done/ (B-side unknown)	1976	$4
❏ 103	Someone to Give My Love To/Something to Believe In	1975	$4

COLUMBIA
Number	Title	Yr	NM
❏ 42835	Believe in Me/How Very Special You Are	1963	$6
❏ 44019	Ciao Compare/World of Clowns	1967	$5
❏ 43481	Crazy Heart of Love/Everlasting	1965	$5
❏ 43668	Daydreamer/My Best Girl	1966	$5
❏ JZSP76415/6 [DJ]	December Time/Silver Bells	1963	$12
❏ 44847	Didn't We/Bon Soir Dame	1969	$5
❏ 44368	Follow Me/If Ever I Would Leave You	1967	$5
❏ 44466	Happy Time/I Don't Remember You	1968	$5
❏ 45250	Heaing River/One at a Time	1970	$5
❏ 44710	Hurry Home for Christmas/ Wonderful World of Christmas	1968	$8
❏ 44710 [PS]	Hurry Home for Christmas/ Wonderful World of Christmas	1968	$15
❏ 43224	I Never Got to Paris/ Begin to Love	1965	$5
❏ 44305	Mon Amour, Mon Amour/This Year	1967	$5
❏ 43131	My Love, Forgive Me (Amore, Scusami)/I'd Rather Be Rich	1964	$6
❏ 45165	My Woman, My Woman, My Wife/Come Saturday	1970	$5
❏ 43394	On a Clear Day You Can See Forever/Come Back to Me, My Love	1965	$5
❏ 43760	Once I Had a Heart/I Heard a Different Drummer	1966	$5
❏ 44100	One Life, One Dream/ If There's a Way	1967	$5
❏ 42249	One Life/I'mJust Taking My Time	1961	$8
❏ 44935	One Life to Live/Only Yesterday	1969	$5
❏ 45054	One Night/I Can't Live Without You	1969	$5
❏ JZSP58877/ 59227 [PS]	Opening Night Souvenir: The Fabulous Flamingo Prsents Columbia Record Star Robert Goulet, February 11th, 1963, Las Vegas, Nevada	1963	$30

—*Sleeve for above promotional record*

Number	Title	Yr	NM
❏ 4-43063	Seventh Dawn/Too Good	1964	$6
❏ 43301	Summer Sounds/The More I See of Mimi	1965	$5
❏ 43865	There But for You Go I/Fortissimo	1966	$5
❏ 42740	These Are the Closing Credits/Two of Us	1963	$6
❏ 42740 [PS]	These Are the Closing Credits/Two of Us	1963	$8
❏ 44186	The Sinner/How Can I Leave You	1967	$5
❏ 44618	Thirty Days Hath September/A Chance to Live in Camelot	1968	$5
❏ JZSP0 [DJ]	This Christmas I Spend With You/White Christmas	1965	$10

—*Promotional record for Christmas Seals*

Number	Title	Yr	NM
❏ JZSP111805/6 [PS]	This Christmas I Spend With You/White Christmas	1965	$15
❏ JZSP111805/6 [DJ]	This Christmas I Spend With You/White Christmas	1965	$10

—*Promotional record for Christmas Seals*

Number	Title	Yr	NM
❏ 42369	Too Soon/Two Different Worlds	1962	$6
❏ 42369 [PS]	Too Soon/Two Different Worlds	1962	$8
❏ 44754	Wait for Me/I'll Catch the Sun	1969	$5
❏ 44548	What a Wonderful World/I Don't Want to Hurt You Anymore	1968	$5
❏ 42519	What Kind of Fool Am I/ Where Do I Go from Here	1962	$6
❏ 42519 [PS]	What Kind of Fool Am I/ Where Do I Go from Here	1962	$8
❏ JZSP58174/203 [DJ]	What Kind of Fool Am I?/ Where Do I Go from Here?	1962	$10

—*Custom silver label with portrait of Goulet; promo only on yellow vinyl*

Number	Title	Yr	NM
❏ JZSP58174/203 [PS]	What Kind of Fool Am I?/ Where Do I Go from Here?	1962	$20

—*Special Presentation Record" on full-color sleeve*

MGM
Number	Title	Yr	NM
❏ 14487	God Is at Work Within You/One Solitary Life	1973	$4

PARAMOUNT
Number	Title	Yr	NM
❏ 0271	Pages of Life/Summer Green, Autumn Gold	1974	$4

7-Inch Extended Plays
COLUMBIA
Number	Title	Yr	NM
❏ 7-9096 [PS]	My Love, Forgive Me	1964	$12
❏ 7-9096	My Love, Forgive Me/ Softly, As I Leave You/What Kind of Fool Am I//Just Say I Love Her/Welcome Home Angelina/Too Good	1964	$10

—*33 1/3 rpm, small hole, "Special Coin Operator Release"*

GOVERNMENT ISSUE
7-Inch Extended Plays
DISCHORD
Number	Title	Yr	NM
❏ 4	Legless Bull	1981	$40
❏ 4 [PS]	Legless Bull	1981	$40

—*1,000 copies were pressed*

GRACIE, CHARLIE
20TH CENTURY
Number	Title	Yr	NM
❏ 5033	Head Home, Honey/ My Baby Loves Me	1955	$60
❏ 5035	Honey Honey/ Wildwood Boogie	1955	$70

CADILLAC
Number	Title	Yr	NM
❏ 141	Boogie Boogie Blues/I'm Gonna Sit Right Down and Write Myself a Letter	1953	$200

CAMEO
Number	Title	Yr	NM
❏ 105	Butterfly/Ninety-Nine Ways	1957	$30
❏ 118	Cool Baby/You've Got a Heart Like a Rock	1957	$30
❏ 127	Crazy Girl/Dressin' Up	1958	$30
❏ 107	Fabulous/Just Lookin'	1957	$30
❏ 111	I Love You So Much It Hurts/Wandering Eyes	1957	$30
❏ 141	Love Bird/Trying	1958	$30

CORAL
Number	Title	Yr	NM
❏ 62115	Angel of Love/I'm a Fool, That's Why	1959	$20
❏ 62073	Hurry Up Buttercup/ Doodlebug	1959	$20
❏ 62141	Oh-Well-a/Because I Love You So	1959	$20

DIAMOND
Number	Title	Yr	NM
❏ 178	He'll Never Love You Like I Do/Keep My Love Next to Your Heart	1965	$125

FELSTED
Number	Title	Yr	NM
❏ 8629	W-Wow/Makin' Whoopee	1961	$20

PRESIDENT
Number	Title	Yr	NM
❏ 828	Count to Three/Just Like Us	1963	$20
❏ 825	Pretty Baby/Night and Day U.S.A.	1962	$20

ROULETTE
Number	Title	Yr	NM
❏ 4255	I Look for You/The Race	1960	$20
❏ 4312	Sorry for You/Scenery	1960	$20

GRADS, THE
A&M
Number	Title	Yr	NM
❏ 797	Everything in the Garden/Stage Door	1966	$12

MERCURY
Number	Title	Yr	NM
❏ 72346	Cool One/Wild One	1964	$30

MGM
Number	Title	Yr	NM
❏ 13216	Their Hearts Were Full of Spring/It Happened Once Before	1964	$10

VALIANT
Number	Title	Yr	NM
❏ 6023	Once Again/White Steeple	1962	$20

GRADUATES, THE (1)
CORSICAN
Number	Title	Yr	NM
❏ 058	What Good Is Graduation/Lonely	1959	$50

LAWN
Number	Title	Yr	NM
❏ 208	Ballad of a Girl and Boy/ Goodbye My Love	1963	$30

SHAN-TODD
Number	Title	Yr	NM
❏ 055	Ballad of a Girl and Boy/Care	1959	$40

GRADUATES, THE (2)
GNP CRESCENDO
Number	Title	Yr	NM
❏ 404	(The Shape of) Things to Come/Listen to the Music	1968	$10

GRADUATES, THE (U)
RISING SONS
Number	Title	Yr	NM
❏ 712	If Ever I Get Out of This Mess I'm In/Seventh Generation Breakthrough	1968	$50

GRADY, DON
CANTERBURY
Number	Title	Yr	NM
❏ 507	Impressions with Syvonne/ Leaving It Up to You	1967	$15
❏ 501	The Children of St. Monica/A Good Man to Have Around the House	1967	$15
❏ 501 [PS]	The Children of St. Monica/A Good Man to Have Around the House	1967	$20

CAPITOL
Number	Title	Yr	NM
❏ 5181	I Think You're Through/A Broken Heart Knows Better	1964	$15

Number	Title	Yr	NM
❏ 5362	It's Better This Way/ One Good Turn Deserves Another	1965	$15

CHALLENGE
| ❏ 59328 | Don't Let It Happen/Out | 1966 | $15 |

ELEKTRA
| ❏ 45860 | Bloodstream/Two-
Bit Afternoon | 1973 | $6 |

—As "Don Agrati"
| ❏ 45846 | One Man Woman/Story | 1973 | $6 |

—As "Don Agrati"

ORANGE EMPIRE
| ❏ 91647 | Summertime Game/
Little People | 1965 | $30 |

GRAFFITI
ABC
| ❏ 11123 | He's Got the Knack/
Love In Spite | 1968 | $40 |

GRAHAM CENTRAL STATION
WARNER BROS.
❏ 7782	Can You Handle It/Ghetto	1974	$5
❏ 8464	Crazy Chicken/Saving My Love for You	1977	$4
❏ 8288	Do Yah/I Got a Reason	1976	$4
❏ 8235	Entrow -- Part 1/ Entrow -- Part 2	1976	$4
❏ 8061	Feel the Need/We Be's Gettin' Down	1974	$5
❏ 8665	Is It Love?/Are You Happy?	1978	$4
❏ 8148	It's Alright/Luckiest People	1975	$4
❏ 8205	Love/Why	1976	$4
❏ 8602	My Radio Sure Sounds Good to Me/Turn It Out	1978	$4
❏ 49067	Sneaky Freak/Boogie Baby	1979	$4
❏ 49011	Star Walk/Boogie Baby	1979	$4
❏ 8417	Stomped Beat-Up and Whooped/Ole Smokey	1977	$4

GRAHAM, DON
WARNER BROS.
| ❏ 5131 | I Saw Mommy Kissing
Santa Claus/And It
Ain't Paid For Yet | 1959 | $20 |

GRAHAM, JIMMY
REVUE
| ❏ 11065 | Love Can't Be Modernized/
We Shall Overcome | 1970 | $50 |
| ❏ 11044 | Soul Walk In/Soul Walk | 1969 | $40 |

GRAHAM, LARRY
WARNER BROS.
❏ 50068	Don't Stop When You're Hot/I Love Loving You	1982	$4
❏ 50068 [PS]	Don't Stop When You're Hot/I Love Loving You	1982	$5
❏ 49833	Guess Who/Sweetheart	1981	$4
❏ 29529	I'm Sick and Tired/I'd Rather Be Loving You	1983	$4
❏ 29620	I Never Forgot Your Eyes/ Movin' Inside Your Love	1983	$4
❏ 29884	Let Me Come Into Your Life/What You Are Inside	1982	$4
❏ 49221	One in a Million You/ The Entertainer	1980	$4
❏ 49221 [PS]	One in a Million You/ The Entertainer	1980	$5
❏ 29956	Sooner or Later/I Feel Good	1982	$4
❏ 29956 [PS]	Sooner or Later/I Feel Good	1982	$5
❏ 29003	What We All Need Is More Love/Tearing Out My Heart	1985	$3
❏ 49581	When We Get Married/Tonight	1980	$4

GRAHAM, LOU
CLYMAX
| ❏ 318 | Wee Willie Brown/You
Were Mean Baby | 1957 | $300 |

CORAL
| ❏ 61931 | Wee Willie Brown/You
Were Mean Baby | 1958 | $125 |

GRAMM, LOU
ATLANTIC
❏ 89236	Lost in the Shadows (The Lost Boys)/Power Play	1987	$3
❏ 89236 [PS]	Lost in the Shadows (The Lost Boys)/Power Play	1987	$3
❏ 89304	Midnight Blue/ Chains of Love	1987	$3
—			
—			
❏ 89304 [PS]	Midnight Blue/ Chains of Love	1987	$3

GRAMMER, BILLY
DECCA
❏ 31892	Brown's Ferry Blues/ Souvenirs of Sorrow	1966	$8
❏ 31226	Columbus Stockade Blues/There's a Rainbow 'Round My Shoulder	1961	$10
❏ 31618	Don't Drop It/I Saw Your Face in the Moon	1964	$8
❏ 31274	Have a Drink on Me/Finger	1961	$12
❏ 31396	He Ain't My Buddy No More/Blue Roller Rink	1962	$12
❏ 31449	I Wanna Go Home (Detroit City)/Bottom of the Glass	1962	$10
❏ 31757	Little Bit of Happiness/I'm Letting You Go (Goodbye)	1965	$8
❏ 31514	Love Gets Better with Time/Lonesome Life	1963	$10
❏ 31562	Old Foolish Me/I'll Leave the Porch Lights a-Burning	1963	$10
❏ 31321	Save Your Tears/I'd Like to Know You	1961	$10
❏ 31669	Wabash Cannonball/Gonna Lay Down My Old Guitar	1964	$8

EPIC
❏ 10052	Bottles/Temporarily	1966	$8
❏ 10103	Heaven Help This Heart of Mine/The Real Thing	1966	$8
❏ 10169	I've Seen That Look on Me (A Thousand Times)/ Written on a Jailhouse	1967	$8

EVEREST
| ❏ 19384 | Big Big Dream/
River of Regret | 1960 | $12 |

MERCURY
❏ 72785	Money, Love and War/ Last of My Future	1968	$8
❏ 72836	The Ballad of John Dillinger/ Do You Still Believe	1968	$8
❏ 72893	The Hour of Separation/ The Changing Scene	1969	$6

MONUMENT
❏ 403	Bonaparte's Retreat/ The Kissing Tree	1959	$15
❏ 8653	Family Man/What We Have in Common Is Love	1975	$4
❏ 400	Gotta Travel On/ Chasing a Dream	1958	$20
❏ 407	It Takes You/Willie, Quit Your Playing	1959	$15
❏ 413	Loveland/On the Job Too Long	1960	$15
❏ 8665	Steppin' Out/Mom and Dad's Waltz	1975	$4
❏ 8685	That's Life/Who's Gonna Buy You the Ribbons	1976	$4

RICE
| ❏ 5025 | Mabel (You Have
Been a Friend to Me)/
Papa and Mama | 1967 | $8 |

GRANAHAN, GERRY
20TH CENTURY FOX
| ❏ 425 | Hang Up the Phone/
Too Weak to Win | 1963 | $20 |

ATCO
| ❏ 6122 | Sweet Affection/Confess
It to Your Heart | 1958 | $40 |

CANADIAN AMERICAN
| ❏ 121 | Short Skirts/I'm Afraid
You'll Never Know | 1960 | $30 |
| ❏ 116 | When Irish Eyes Are
Smiling/In My Heart | 1960 | $30 |

CAPRICE
| ❏ 108 | Too Big for Her Bikini/
Dance, Girl, Dance | 1961 | $125 |

—With backing by the Belmonts or the Five Satins (sources disagree)

GONE
❏ 5081	It Hurts/Look for Me	1959	$30
❏ 5081 [PS]	It Hurts/Look for Me	1959	$70
❏ 5065	Let the Rumors Fly/ Put Me Anywhere	1959	$30

MARK
| ❏ 121 | Love's Young Dream/Oh
Well-A Watch-A Gonna Do | 1957 | $40 |

SUNBEAM
| ❏ 108 | Baby Wait/Completely | 1958 | $30 |
| ❏ 112 | I'm Ready As I'll Ever
Be/Nobody Can
Handle This Job | 1958 | $30 |

—B-side by Eddie Fontaine

VEEP
| ❏ 1205 | All the Live-Long
Day/Sophia | 1965 | $15 |

GRANATA, ROCCO
EPIC
| ❏ 5-9401 | E Primavera/Oh Oh Rose | 1960 | $12 |

LAURIE
❏ 3048	Lo Bella/Torna A Sorriento	1960	$15
❏ 3041	Marina/Manuela	1959	$15
❏ 3041 [PS]	Marina/Manuela	1959	$20

—All black and white sleeve
| ❏ 3041 [PS] | Marina/Manuela | 1959 | $30 |

—Pink title strip on otherwise black and white sleeve

GRAND CANYON
BANG
| ❏ 713 | Evil Boll-Weevil/Got to
Find My Way Back | 1974 | $8 |

GRAND FUNK RAILROAD
Includes records as "Grand Funk." Also see MARK FARNER; MARK FARNER AND DON BREWER; TERRY KNIGHT AND THE PACK.

CAPITOL
❏ 4046	Bad Time/Good and Evil	1975	$4
❏ 2877	Closer to Home/ Aimless Lady	1970	$6
❏ 3095	Feelin' Alright/I Want Freedom	1971	$6
❏ 3255	Footstompin' Music/I Come Tumblin'	1972	$6
❏ 3160	Gimme Shelter/I Can Feel Him in the Morning	1971	$6
❏ 3160 [PS]	Gimme Shelter/I Can Feel Him in the Morning	1971	$10
❏ 2732	Heartbreaker/Please Don't Worry	1970	$6
❏ 2996	Mean Mistreater/ Mark Says Alright	1970	$6
❏ 2691	Mr. Limousine Driver/ High Falootin' Woman	1969	$6
❏ 3217	People, Let's Stop the War/Save the Land	1971	$6
❏ 4235	Sally/Love Is Dyin'	1976	$4
❏ 4235 [PS]	Sally/Love Is Dyin'	1976	$5
❏ 3917	Shinin' On/Mr. Pretty Boy	1974	$4
❏ 3917 [PS]	Shinin' On/Mr. Pretty Boy	1974	$5
❏ 4002	Some Kind of Wonderful/Wild	1974	$4
❏ 4002 [PS]	Some Kind of Wonderful/Wild	1974	$5
❏ 4199	Take Me/Genevieve	1975	$4
❏ 4199 [PS]	Take Me/Genevieve	1975	$5
❏ 3840	The Loco-Motion/ Destitute and Losin'	1974	$4
❏ 3840 [PS]	The Loco-Motion/ Destitute and Losin'	1974	$5
❏ 2567	Time Machine/ High on a Horse	1969	$6
❏ 3760	Walk Like a Man/ The Railroad	1973	$4
❏ 3760 [PS]	Walk Like a Man/ The Railroad	1973	$5
❏ 3660	We're An American Band/Creepin'	1973	$6

—Originals on gold vinyl
| ❏ 3660 | We're An American
Band/Creepin' | 1973 | $4 |
| ❏ 3660 [PS] | We're An American
Band/Creepin' | 1973 | $5 |

MCA
❏ 40590	Can You Do It/1976	1976	$5
❏ 40590 [PS]	Can You Do It/1976	1976	$6
❏ 40641	Out to Get You/Just Couldn't Wait	1976	$5

—The MCA sides were produced by Frank Zappa

GRANDMASTER FLASH
ELEKTRA
❏ 69459	All Wrapped Up/ Kid Named Flash	1987	$3
❏ 69617	Alternate Groove/ Who's That Lady?	1985	$5
❏ 69530	Behind Closed Doors/Lies	1986	$5
❏ 69400	Fly Girl/Gold In Effect	1988	$6
❏ 69643	Girls Love the Way He Spins/Larry's Dance Theme	1985	$6
❏ 69416	Gold/Back in the Old Days of Hip-Hop	1988	$5
❏ 69380	Magic Carpet Ride/ On the Strength	1988	$6
❏ 69677	Sign of the Times/ Larry's Dance Theme	1984	$6
❏ 69552	Style (Peter Gunn Theme)/(Instrumental)	1986	$6

SUGAR HILL
❏ 756	Freedom/(Instrumental)	1980	$20
❏ 775	It's Nasty (Genius of Love)/(Instrumental)	1982	$20
❏ 759	The Birthday Party/ (Instrumental)	1981	$20

GRANDMASTER MELLE MEL
ATLANTIC
| ❏ 89659 [PS] | Beat Street Breakdown/
Beat Street Breakdown | 1984 | $4 |
| ❏ 89659 | Beat Street Breakdown
- Part I/Part II | 1984 | $4 |

SUGAR HILL
| ❏ 92011 | We Don't Work for
Free/(Instrumental) | 1984 | $10 |

GRANT, AMY

Number	Title	Yr	NM

A&M

Number	Title	Yr	NM
❏ 2920	Angels/Love Can Do	1987	$6
❏ 2785	Everywhere I Go/Where Do You Hide Your Heart	1985	$6
❏ 2734	Find a Way/Angels	1985	$4
❏ 2734 [PS]	Find a Way/Angels	1985	$5
❏ 1243	If You Have to Go Away/1974	1988	$3
❏ 1218	Lead Me On/Sure Enough	1988	$4
❏ 1218 [PS]	Lead Me On/Sure Enough	1988	$4
❏ 1260	Saved by Love/Say Once More	1989	$4
❏ 2864	Stay for Awhile/Love of Another Kind	1986	$4
❏ 2864 [PS]	Stay for Awhile/Love of Another Kind	1986	$5
❏ 2777	Tennessee Christmas/Little Town	1985	$5
❏ 2777 [PS]	Tennessee Christmas/Little Town	1985	$6
❏ 2762	Wise Up/Straight Ahead	1985	$4
❏ 2762 [PS]	Wise Up/Straight Ahead	1985	$5

MYRRH

Number	Title	Yr	NM
❏ M-001 [DJ]	Ageless Medley/(B-side unknown)	1986	$10

— Promo-only 7-inch 33 1/3 rpm record of song snippets

Number	Title	Yr	NM
❏ 198	On and On/What a Difference You've Made	1978	$15

GRANT, BARRY

COUNTRYSTOCK

Number	Title	Yr	NM
❏ 1602	We're In for Hard Times/Most Wanted Outlaw	1979	$6

— As "Breakfast Barry"

CSI

Number	Title	Yr	NM
❏ 001	Out with the Boys/Pretty Poison	1979	$6

NSD

Number	Title	Yr	NM
❏ 104	A Little Bit Crazy/Out with the Boys	1981	$5

— As "Amarillo"

Number	Title	Yr	NM
❏ 81	How Long Has This Been Going On/Somehow, Someway and Someday	1981	$5

— As "Amarillo"

Number	Title	Yr	NM
❏ 72	That's the Way My Woman Loves/Pretty Poison	1980	$5

— As "Amarillo"

GRANT, CARY

COLUMBIA

Number	Title	Yr	NM
❏ 4-44377	Christmas Lullaby/Here's to You	1967	$40

GRANT, EARL

DECCA

Number	Title	Yr	NM
❏ 30983	All for the Best/Not One Minute More	1959	$10
❏ 30719	(At) The End (Of a Rainbow)/Hunky Dunky Doo	1958	$15

— Same song, altered title on A-side

Number	Title	Yr	NM
❏ 25743	Bewitched/In Motion	1968	$6
❏ 25626	Black Coffee/I'm Just a Lucky So-and-So	1964	$8
❏ 25697	Blue Velvet/The Sweetest Sounds	1966	$6
❏ 25601	Caravan/I'll Build a Stairway to Paradise	1963	$8
❏ 31022	Christmas Card/Swingin' Christmas	1959	$10
❏ 31110	Dreamy/Building Castles	1960	$12
❏ 25526	Ebb Tide/Deep Purple	1962	$8
❏ 31222	Ebb Tide/Next Time	1961	$8
❏ 30819	Evening Rain/Evening Rain (Instrumental)	1959	$12
❏ 30475	Fever/Malaguena	1957	$20
❏ 30150	Goodnight My Love, Pleasant Dreams/My Consolation	1956	$20
❏ 32667	Grant's Pass/Elizabethan Reggae	1970	$5
❏ 31328	Honey/Tender Is the Night	1961	$8
❏ 30561	Honky Tonk/The Next Time You See Me	1958	$15
❏ 31044	House of Bamboo/Two Loves Have I	1960	$30
❏ 31902	I'll Drown in My Own Tears/I Can't Stop Loving You	1966	$6
❏ 32093	I Love You, Yes I Do/Hide Nor Hair	1967	$60
❏ 25730	I Miss You So/Stormy Weather	1967	$6
❏ 32443	It Was a Very Good Year/If I Only Had Time	1969	$5
❏ 32499	I Wonder/The Importance of the Rose	1969	$5
❏ 30856	Last Night/Imitation of Life	1959	$12
❏ 25607	More (Theme from "Mondo Cane")/Sukiyaki	1963	$8
❏ 25737	My Foolish Heart/One Note Samba	1968	$6
❏ 31263	My Foolish Heart/Sermonette	1961	$8
❏ 30640	Ol' Man River/Kathy-O	1958	$15
❏ 25638	Satin Doll/Just One More Time	1964	$8
❏ 25674	Stand By Me/After Hours	1965	$8
❏ 31468	Steve's Theme (From "Forty Pounds of Trouble")/Yes Sirree	1963	$8
❏ 25713	Summertime/September in the Rain	1967	$6
❏ 25574	Sweet Sixteen Bars/Learnin' the Blues	1962	$8
❏ 25560	Swingin' Gently/Beyond the Roof	1962	$8
❏ 30244	Thanks for You/Through the Eyes of a Boy and Girl	1956	$20
❏ 30719	The End/Hunky Dunky Doo	1958	$20
❏ 25704	The Lonesome Road/When I Grow Too Old to Dream	1966	$6
❏ 30908	The Wish/Don't Point Your Finger at Anyone Else	1959	$10
❏ 31716	This Little Girl of Mine/Come to Me (Pretty Baby)	1964	$8
❏ 25721	Without a Song/I'm in the Mood for Love	1967	$6
❏ 25659	Without a Song/Meditation	1965	$8

MCA

Number	Title	Yr	NM
❏ 65023	Silver Bells/Jingle Bells	1973	$4

— Black label with rainbow

Number	Title	Yr	NM
❏ 65023	Silver Bells/Jingle Bells	1980	$3

— Blue label with rainbow

PRINCE

Number	Title	Yr	NM
❏ 1201	One Way Street/(B-side unknown)	1956	$20

— Black vinyl

Number	Title	Yr	NM
❏ 1201	One Way Street/(B-side unknown)	1956	$30

— Colored vinyl

7-Inch Extended Plays

DECCA

Number	Title	Yr	NM
❏ ED2639 [M]	(contents unknown)	1959	$10
❏ ED 7-2639 [S]	(contents unknown)	1959	$20
❏ ED2639 [PS]	The End	1959	$12
❏ ED 7-2639 [PS]	The End	1959	$20

GRANT, EDDY

CAPITOL

Number	Title	Yr	NM
❏ B-44212	Gimme Hope Jo'Anna/Don't Talk to Strangers	1988	$6

EPIC

Number	Title	Yr	NM
❏ 9-50929	Everybody Dance/Feel the Rhythm (Of You and I)	1980	$8
❏ 9-50834	Living on the Front Line/Front Line Symphony	1980	$8
❏ 9-50878	My Turn to Love You/Use It or Lose It	1980	$6
❏ 9-50766	Walking on Sunshine/Sunshine Jam	1979	$8

PORTRAIT

Number	Title	Yr	NM
❏ 37-04620	Boys in the Street/Time to Let Go	1984	$4
❏ 37-06238	Dance Party/Rock You Good	1986	$4
❏ 37-03793	Electric Avenue/Time Warp	1983	$4
❏ 37-04039	I Don't Wanna Dance/I Don't Wanna Dance (Acapella)	1983	$5

GRANT, GOGI

20TH FOX

Number	Title	Yr	NM
❏ 297	Magic Music/Tender Is the Night	1962	$10
❏ 403	Magic Music/Tender Is the Night	1963	$8

ERA

Number	Title	Yr	NM
❏ 1062	I Gave You My Heart/I Don't Want to Walk Without You	1957	$15
❏ 1003	Suddenly There's a Valley/Love Is	1955	$20
❏ 1053	The Golden Ladder/All of Me	1957	$15
❏ 1013	The Wayward Wind/No More Than Forever	1956	$20
❏ 3205	The Wayward Wind/Suddenly There's a Valley	1969	$5
❏ 3046	The Wayward Wind/The Tide Is High	1961	$8
❏ 1008	Who Are We/We Believe in Love	1955	$20

LIBERTY

Number	Title	Yr	NM
❏ 55229	Goin' Home/All God's Children Got Shoes	1959	$10
❏ 55214	If and When/I'll Never Smile Again	1959	$10
❏ 55252	I Never Meant to Fall in Love/Stay Here with Me	1960	$10
❏ 55316	That One Kiss/Adrift on a Star	1961	$12
❏ 55286	Two Lovers by the Sea/In a Sentimental Mood	1960	$10

MONUMENT

Number	Title	Yr	NM
❏ 986	Don't Touch Me/Pathfinder	1966	$6
❏ 1005	The Sea/How Much Will I Love You	1967	$6

PETE

Number	Title	Yr	NM
❏ 708	Buy Me Penny Candy/Paradise	1968	$5
❏ 701	Down Here on the Ground/The Magic of People	1968	$5
❏ 718	On the Mountain/Faure	1969	$5

RCA VICTOR

Number	Title	Yr	NM
❏ 47-7146	Chinese Nightingale/Bonjour Tristesse	1958	$10
❏ 47-5436	Everyone Knows I Love You/Ricochet	1953	$30
❏ 47-4994	Forget Me Not/Where There's Smoke, There's Fire	1952	$30
❏ 47-5053	Mommy's Little Angel/My Tormented Heart	1952	$30
❏ 47-7215	My Secret Prayer/How Do We Know We're in Love	1958	$10
❏ 47-5512	Secret Love/Ricochet	1953	$30
❏ 47-7294	Strange Are the Ways of Love/Marjolaino	1958	$10
❏ 47-6996	That's the Love for Me/It's a Wonderful Thing to Be Loved	1957	$12
❏ 47-7438	Two Dreams/(Kiss Me) Honey Honey (Kiss Me)	1959	$10

GRANT, JANIE

CAPRICE

Number	Title	Yr	NM
❏ 111	I Wonder Who's Kissing You Now/Unhappy	1961	$20
❏ 113	Oh Johnny/Oh My Love	1962	$20
❏ 119	Peggy Got Engaged/Two Is Company and Three's a Crowd	1962	$20
❏ 115	That Greasy Kid Stuff/Trying to Forget You	1962	$20
❏ 104	Triangle/She's Going Steady with You	1961	$20

PARKWAY

Number	Title	Yr	NM
❏ 982	My Heart, Your Heart/And That Reminds Me of You	1966	$200

UNITED ARTISTS

Number	Title	Yr	NM
❏ 775	After Last Night/All I Did Was Fall in Love	1964	$15
❏ 843	I Shouldn't Care (If You're Using Me)/There Ain't No Party Tonight	1965	$15
❏ 616	Tell Me Mama/Whose Heart Are You Breaking Now	1963	$15
❏ 649	That Kind of Boy/Priceless Persuasion	1963	$15

GRANT, JERRY

ATCO

Number	Title	Yr	NM
❏ 6100	Talkin' About Love/Some Day, Maybe Tonight	1957	$50

GRANT, JULIE

HICKORY

Number	Title	Yr	NM
❏ 1260	Every Day I Have to Cry/Watch What You Do with Your Baby	1964	$15

GRANT, TOM (2)

ELEKTRA

Number	Title	Yr	NM
❏ 69961	I'm Gonna Love You Right Out of This World/Sundown Lady	1982	$5

REPUBLIC

Number	Title	Yr	NM
❏ 036	If You Could See Me Through My Eyes/You're Easy to Love	1979	$6
❏ 045	Sail On/Meet You in Paradise	1979	$6
❏ 043	We've Gotta Get Away From It All/Catching Up on Love	1979	$6

GRAPEFRUIT

ABC DUNHILL

Number	Title	Yr	NM
❏ 4178	This Little Man/Round Going Round	1968	$10

EQUINOX

Number	Title	Yr	NM
❏ 70008	C'mon Marianne/Ain't It Good	1968	$20
❏ 70000	Dear Delilah/Dead Boot	1967	$20
❏ 70005	Elevator/Yes	1968	$20

RCA VICTOR

Number	Title	Yr	NM
❏ 74-0241	Thunder and Lightning/Blues in Your Head	1969	$20

GRASS ROOTS, THE

ABC DUNHILL

Number	Title	Yr	NM
❏ 4325	Any Way the Wind Blows/Monday Love	1972	$5
❏ 4237	Baby Hold On/Get It Together	1970	$6
❏ 4237 [PS]	Baby Hold On/Get It Together	1970	$12
❏ 4162	Bella Linda/Hot Bright Blues	1968	$8
❏ 4249	Come On and Say It/Something's Comin' Over Me	1970	$6
❏ 4249 [PS]	Come On and Say It/Something's Comin' Over Me	1970	$10
❏ 4162	Della Linda/Hot Bright Blues	1968	$15

— Some labels have A-side typographical error as shown

Number	Title	Yr	NM
❏ 4302	Glory Bound/The Only One	1972	$5
❏ 4217	Heaven Knows/Don't Remind Me	1969	$6
❏ 4198	I'd Wait a Million Years/Fly Me to Havana	1969	$6
❏ 4335	Love Is What You Make It/Someone to Love	1973	$6
❏ 4180	Lovin' Things/You and Love Are the Same	1969	$8
❏ 4144	Midnight Confessions/Who Will You Be Tomorrow	1968	$8
❏ 4279	Sooner or Later/I Can Turn Off the Rain	1971	$5
❏ 15006	Stealin' Love (In the Night)/We Almost Made It Together	1974	$20
❏ 4263	Temptation Eyes/Keepin' Me Down	1971	$5
❏ 4289	Two Divided by Love/Let It Go	1971	$5
❏ 4227	Walking Through the Country/Truck Drivin' Man	1970	$6
❏ 4371	We Can't Dance to Your Music/Look but Don't Touch	1973	$10
❏ 4345	Where There's Smoke There's Fire/Look but Don't Touch	1973	$10

DUNHILL

Number	Title	Yr	NM
❏ 4122	A Melody for You/Hey Friend	1968	$10
❏ 4129	Feelings/Here's Where You Belong	1968	$10
❏ 4084	Let's Live for Today/Depressed Feeling	1967	$15
❏ 4144	Midnight Confessions/Who Will You Be Tomorrow	1968	$40

—Original label has no "ABC" logo next to "Dunhill

Number	Title	Yr	NM
❏ 4013	Mr. Jones (A Ballad of a Thin Man)/You're a Lonely Girl	1965	$30
❏ 4043	Only When You're Lonely/This Is What I Was Made For	1966	$30
❏ 4094	Things I Should Have Said/Tip of My Tongue	1967	$10
❏ 4094 [PS]	Things I Should Have Said/Tip of My Tongue	1967	$20
❏ 4053	Tip of My Tongue/Look Out, Girl	1966	$30
❏ 4105	Wake Up, Wake Up/No Exit	1967	$10
❏ 4029	Where Were You When I Needed You/(These Are) Bad Times	1966	$30

HAVEN

Number	Title	Yr	NM
❏ 7015	Mamacita/Last Time Around	1975	$5
❏ 802	Out in the Open/Optical Illusion	1976	$8

MCA

Number	Title	Yr	NM
❏ 52058	Here Comes That Feeling Again/Temptation Eyes	1982	$12
❏ 52104	She Don't Know Me/Keep On Burning	1982	$10

7-Inch Extended Plays

ABC

Number	Title	Yr	NM
❏ PRO-40013	Midnight Confessions/Sooner or Later/Where Were You When I Needed You//Temptation Eyes/Wait a Million Years/Heaven Knows	1974	$25

—Quadraphonic jukebox issue; small hole, plays at 33 1/3 rpm

Number	Title	Yr	NM
❏ PRO-40013 [PS]	Their 16 Greatest Hits	1974	$25

—Has the same sleeve as ABC-Dunhill PRO-50107, except for a sticker "4 Channel - Quadraphonic" on front

ABC DUNHILL

Number	Title	Yr	NM
❏ PRO-50107	Midnight Confessions/Sooner or Later/Where Were You When I Needed You//Temptation Eyes/Wait a Million Years/Heaven Knows	1971	$20

—Jukebox issue; small hole, plays at 33 1/3 rpm

Number	Title	Yr	NM
❏ PRO-50107 [PS]	Their 16 Greatest Hits	1971	$20

—Part of "Little LP" series (LLP #165)

GRATEFUL DEAD, THE

Also see JERRY GARCIA; MICKEY HART; KEITH AND DONNA; BOB WEIR.

ARISTA

Number	Title	Yr	NM
❏ 0519	Alabama Getaway/Far from Me	1980	$5
❏ 0519 [PS]	Alabama Getaway/Far from Me	1980	$8
❏ 0276	Dancin' in the Streets/Terrapin Station	1977	$6
❏ 0546	Don't Ease Me In/Far from Me	1980	$5
❏ 9899	Foolish Heart/We Can Run	1989	$4
❏ 9899 [PS]	Foolish Heart/We Can Run	1989	$4
❏ 0410	France/Shakedown Street	1979	$6
❏ 0383	Good Lovin'/Stagger Lee	1978	$6
❏ 0383 [PS]	Good Lovin'/Stagger Lee	1978	$600
❏ 0291	Passenger/Terrapin Station	1977	$6
❏ 9643	Throwing Stones (Ashes Ashes) Edit/Throwing Stones (Ashes Ashes) LP Version	1987	$3
❏ 9606	Touch of Grey/My Brother Esau	1987	$5

—Grey vinyl

Number	Title	Yr	NM
❏ 9606	Touch of Grey/My Brother Esau	1987	$3

—Black vinyl (not issued with picture sleeve)

GRATEFUL DEAD

Number	Title	Yr	NM
❏ 02	Eyes of the World/Weather Report (Part 1)	1974	$15
❏ XW-762	Franklin's Tower/Help on the Way	1976	$30
❏ 01	Here Comes Sunshine/Let Me Sing Your Blues Away	1973	$15
❏ XW-718	The Music Never Stopped/Help on the Way	1975	$20

SCORPIO

Number	Title	Yr	NM
❏ 201 [B]	Stealin'/Don't Ease Me In	1966	$4000

WARNER BROS.

Number	Title	Yr	NM
❏ 7186	Dark Star/Born Cross-Eyed	1968	$30
❏ 7186 [PS]	Dark Star/Born Cross-Eyed	1968	$500
❏ 7324	Dupree's Diamond Blues/Cosmic Charlie	1969	$30
❏ 7667	Sugar Magnolia/Mr. Charlie	1972	$20
❏ 7016	The Golden Road (To Unlimited Devotion)/Cream Puff War	1967	$30
❏ 7653	Truckin'/Johnny B. Goode	1973	$8

—Back to Back Hits" series

Number	Title	Yr	NM
❏ 7464	Truckin'/Ripple	1971	$20

7-Inch Extended Plays

Number	Title	Yr	NM
❏ S1893 [PS]	American Beauty	1973	$35

—Part of Little LP series (LLP #226)

Number	Title	Yr	NM
❏ S1893	Sugar Magnolia/Operator/Till the Morning Comes//Truckin'/Friend of the Devil	1973	$25

—Jukebox issue, small hole, plays at 33 1/3 rpm

GRAVES, BILLY

MONUMENT

Number	Title	Yr	NM
❏ 404	Long Journey Home/Midnight Bus	1959	$20
❏ 992	The Lonesome Ape/I've Got a Feeling	1966	$8
❏ 401	The Shag (Is Totally Cool)/Uncertain	1958	$30

GRAVES, CARL

A&M

Number	Title	Yr	NM
❏ 1620	Baby, Hang Up the Phone/Walk Softly	1974	$12
❏ 1757	Heart Be Still/Breaking Up Is Hard to Do	1975	$12
❏ 1716	Hey Radio/Something's Telling Me	1975	$12
❏ 1799	My Whole World Ended (The Moment You Left Me)/Baby Don't Knock	1976	$10

ARIOLA AMERICA

Number	Title	Yr	NM
❏ 7660	Sad Girl/Walk in Love	1977	$10

GRAVES, JOE

PARKWAY

Number	Title	Yr	NM
❏ 103	Debbie/A Boy and a Girl Fall in Love	1966	$60
❏ 964	See Saw/Beautiful Girl	1965	$40

GRAY, BARRY, AND THE SPACEMAKERS

ABC-PARAMOUNT

Number	Title	Yr	NM
❏ 10424	Fireball/XL 5	1963	$15

GRAY, BILLY

DECCA

Number	Title	Yr	NM
❏ 29678	Harbor of Love/Girls, Girls, Girls	1955	$40
❏ 29489	Okie Blondie/I've Had At My Heart	1955	$40
❏ 29800	Tennessee Toddy/It Could Have Been Me	1956	$50

LIBERTY

Number	Title	Yr	NM
❏ 55599	I'll Never Live Long Enough/I Left My Heart in San Francisco	1963	$15
❏ 55712	Last Call for Alcohol/Late Last Night	1964	$12

GRAY, CLAUDE

COLUMBIA

Number	Title	Yr	NM
❏ 4-43443	For Losing You/Thank You for the Ride	1965	$10
❏ 4-43614	Mean Old Woman/Then Cry You Away	1966	$10
❏ 4-43294	Thank You Neighbor/Kinderhook Bill	1965	$10
❏ 4-43150	Too Many Rivers/House of Tears	1964	$10

COUNTRY INT'L.

Number	Title	Yr	NM
❏ 158	Every Night Sensation/(B-side unknown)	1980	$6
❏ 169	He's Just an Illusion/Every Night Sensation	1981	$6
❏ 164	Pride Goes Before a Fall/Every Night Sensation	1980	$6
❏ 208	Sweet Caroline/Half a Mind	1986	$6

D

Number	Title	Yr	NM
❏ 1093	Best Part of Me/Loneliness	1959	$30
❏ 1118	Family Bible/Crying in the Night	1960	$30
❏ 1059	Letter Overdue/I'm Not Supposed	1959	$30
❏ 1144	My Party's Over/Leave Alone	1960	$30
❏ 1154	When the Light Shines in the Valley/Homecoming in Heaven	1960	$30

DECCA

Number	Title	Yr	NM
❏ 32786	Angel/Save My Mind	1971	$6
❏ 32852	Baton Rouge/Your Devil Memory	1971	$6
❏ 32456	Don't Give Me a Chance/Once in Every Lifetime	1969	$6
❏ 32266	Easy Way Out/Your Devil Memory	1968	$6
❏ 32697	Everything Will Be Alright/Apartment No. 9	1970	$6
❏ 32039	I Never Had the One I Wanted/Effects Your Leaving Had on Me	1966	$8
❏ 32566	Take Off Time/Sherry Ann	1969	$6
❏ 32648	The Cleanest Man in Cincinnati/Crazy Arms	1970	$6
❏ 32393	The Love of a Woman/The Kind You Find Tonight Forget Tomorrow	1968	$6

MERCURY

Number	Title	Yr	NM
❏ 72001	Daddy Stopped In/Three Times	1962	$15
❏ 72236	Eight Years (And Two Children Later)/Lonesome	1964	$15
❏ 72088	First Love Never Dies/Heartbreak Eve	1963	$15
❏ 72156	Go Home Cheater/I'm Gonna Lie Again	1963	$15
❏ 71732	I'll Just Have a Cup of Coffee (Then I'll Go)/I Just Want to Be Alone	1960	$15
❏ 71898	Let's End It Before It Begins/Talk to Me Old Lonesome Heart	1961	$15
❏ 71826	My Ears Should Burn (When Fools Are Talked About)/Crying in the Night	1961	$15

MILLION

Number	Title	Yr	NM
❏ 36	Loving You Is a Habit I Can't Break/We Could	1973	$8
❏ 3	Straight Down to Heaven/Jeannie	1972	$8
❏ 18	What Every Woman Wants to Hear/There's You	1972	$8
❏ 31	Woman Ease My Mind/Don't Fight the Feeling	1972	$8

GRAY, DOBIE

ANTHEM

Number	Title	Yr	NM
❏ 200	Guess Who?/Bits and Pieces	1972	$5

ARISTA

Number	Title	Yr	NM
❏ 1047	One Can Fake It/(B-side unknown)	1983	$4

CAPITOL

Number	Title	Yr	NM
❏ B-5647	From Where I Stand/So Far So Good	1986	$3
❏ B-5562	Gonna Be a Long Night/That's One to Grown On	1986	$3
❏ B-44126	Love Letters/Steady As She Goes	1988	$3
❏ B-44087	Take It Real Easy/You Must Have Been Reading My Heart	1987	$3
❏ B-5596	The Dark Side of Life/A Night in the Life of a Country Boy	1986	$3
❏ 2241	We the People/Funny and Groovy	1968	$10

CAPRICORN

Number	Title	Yr	NM
❏ 0259	Find 'Em, Fool 'Em and Forget 'Em/Mellow Man	1976	$4
❏ 0249	If Love Must Go/Lover's Sweat	1975	$4
❏ 0267	Let Go/Mellow Man	1976	$4

CHARGER

Number	Title	Yr	NM
❏ 109	In Hollywood/Mr. Engineer	1965	$10
❏ 113	Monkey Jerk/My Baby	1965	$10
❏ 107	See You at the "Go-Go"/Walk with Love	1965	$10
❏ 105	The "In" Crowd/Be a Man	1964	$20

CORDAK

Number	Title	Yr	NM
❏ 1602	Look at Me/Walkin' and Whistlin'	1962	$30

DECCA

Number	Title	Yr	NM
❏ 33057	Drift Away/City Stars	1973	$5

INFINITY

Number	Title	Yr	NM
❏ 50020	Spending Time, Making Love, and Going Crazy/Let This Man Take Hold of Your Life	1979	$4
❏ 50043	The In Crowd/Let This Man Take Hold of Your Life	1979	$4
❏ 50010	Who's Lovin' You/Thank You for Tonight	1979	$4

Number	Title	Yr	NM

MCA

Number	Title	Yr	NM
❏ 40153	Good Old Song/ Reachin' for the Feelin'	1973	$4
❏ 40100	Loving Arms/Now That I'm Without You	1973	$4
❏ 40315	The Music's Real/Roll On Sweet Mississippi	1974	$4
❏ 40201	There's a Honky Tonk Angel (Who'll Take Me Back In)/ Lovin' the Easy Way	1974	$4
❏ 40268	Watch Out for Lucy/ Turning On You	1974	$4

ROBOX

Number	Title	Yr	NM
❏ RRS-117	Decorate the Night (same on both sides)	1979	$5

WHITE WHALE

Number	Title	Yr	NM
❏ 342	Honey, You Can't Take It Back	1970	$200
❏ 330	What a Way to Go/Do You Really Have a Heart	1969	$500

GRAY, DOLORES

CAPITOL

Number	Title	Yr	NM
❏ F3774	I'm Innocent/My Mama Likes You	1957	$10

DECCA

Number	Title	Yr	NM
❏ 9-28032	Beware/Frankie	1952	$15
❏ 9-28676	Big Mamou/Say You're Mine Again	1953	$15
❏ 9-28755	Call of the Far-Away Hills/Darling, the Moon Is So Bright	1953	$15
❏ 9-28218	Dancing on the Grapes/A Diamond Mine in Madagascar	1952	$15
❏ 9-28968	Face to Face/ Poppa Piccolino	1954	$15
❏ 9-29064	Happy Habit/Hang Up	1954	$15
❏ 9-29380	Heat Wave/After You Get What You Want	1954	$15
❏ 9-27942	I Got a Feelin' You're Foolin'/Did Anybody Call	1952	$15
❏ 9-29109	In Paris and In Love/ Lost in Loneliness	1954	$15
❏ 9-28783	L-O-V-E/That's Love I Guess	1953	$20
❏ 9-27832	Shrimp Boats/More, More, More	1951	$20
❏ 9-29031	Sweet Cheat/Flowers for the Lady	1954	$15
❏ 9-28051	To Be Loved by You/If Someone Had Told Me	1952	$15
❏ 9-29205	Too Bad/One	1954	$15
❏ 9-28469	Two Other People/I Don't Care	1952	$15
❏ 9-29353	Without Love/The Finger of Suspicion Points at You	1954	$15

GRAY, GENE, AND THE STINGRAYS

DOT

Number	Title	Yr	NM
❏ 16478	Surf Bunny/Surfer's Mood	1963	$30

LINDA

Number	Title	Yr	NM
❏ 110	Surf Bunny/Surfer's Mood	1963	$50

GRAY, GLEN

Number	Title	Yr	NM
❏ EAP 1-747 [PS]	Casa Loma in Hi-Fi! Part 1	1956	$12
❏ EAP 2-747 [PS]	Casa Loma in Hi-Fi! Part 2	1956	$12
❏ EAP 3-747 [PS]	Casa Loma in Hi-Fi! Part 3	1956	$12
❏ EAP 4-747 [PS]	Casa Loma in Hi-Fi! Part 4	1956	$12
❏ EAP 3-747	(contents unknown)	1956	$10

— Sides 3 and 6 of "Album 747

Number	Title	Yr	NM
❏ EAP 2-747	Memories of You/White Jazz//Dance of the Lame Duck/For You	1956	$10

— Sides 2 and 7 of "Album 747

Number	Title	Yr	NM
❏ EAP 4-747	Sunrise Serenade/Maniac's Ball//Casa Loma Stomp/ Just an Old Manuscript	1956	$10

— Sides 4 and 5 of "Album 747

DECCA

Number	Title	Yr	NM
❏ 7-34556 [PS]	Glen Gray and the Original Casa Loma Orchestra's Greatest Hits	1968	$12
❏ 7-34556	Smoke Rings/Casa Loma Stomp/It's the Talk of the Town//No Name Jive (Part 1 & 2)	1968	$10

— Jukebox issue; small hole, plays at 33 1/3 rpm

GRAY, MAUREEN

CHANCELLOR

Number	Title	Yr	NM
❏ 1091	Come On and Dance/I Don't Want to Cry	1961	$30
❏ 1082	Crazy Over You/ Today's the Day	1961	$30
❏ 1100	I'm So Young/There's a Boy	1962	$30

LANDA

Number	Title	Yr	NM
❏ 689	Dancin' the Strand/Oh My	1962	$20
❏ 692	People Are Talking/Oh My	1962	$20

MERCURY

Number	Title	Yr	NM
❏ 72227	I'm a Happy Girl (Tra La La)/Goodbye Baby	1964	$15

Number	Title	Yr	NM
❏ 72131	Story of My Love/ Summertime Is Near	1963	$15

GRAYGHOST

COMPLEAT

Number	Title	Yr	NM
❏ 166	As Long As I've Been Loving You/Out of Control	1987	$5

— As "Razorback

Number	Title	Yr	NM
❏ 174	Make a Living Out of Loving You/(B-side unknown)	1987	$5
❏ 184	This Ole House/ (B-side unknown)	1987	$5

— As "Razorback

ICR

Number	Title	Yr	NM
❏ 184	This Ole House/ (B-side unknown)	1987	$6

— As "Razorback

MERCURY

Number	Title	Yr	NM
❏ 874770-7	If This Ain't Love (There Ain't No Such Thing)/ Take a Little Time	1989	$3
❏ 874194-7	Let's Sleep on It/ (B-side unknown)	1989	$3
❏ 870633-7	Where Were You When I Was Blue/Something So Hot	1988	$4

— As "Razorback

GRAYSON, JACK

ABC DOT

Number	Title	Yr	NM
❏ 17699	Mind Over Matter/ Waiting Room	1977	$6

— As "Jack Lebsock

AMI

Number	Title	Yr	NM
❏ 1318	Lean on Me/(B-side unknown)	1983	$5

CAPITOL

Number	Title	Yr	NM
❏ 3665	For Lovers Only/World That Cannot See	1973	$6

— As "Jack Lebsock

Number	Title	Yr	NM
❏ 3579	For the Love of a Woman Like That/Heavy on My Mind	1973	$6

— As "Jack Lebsock

Number	Title	Yr	NM
❏ 3751	Lovin' Comes Easy/I'll Be Damned If I Do (Damned If I Don't)	1973	$6

— As "Jack Lebsock

CHURCHILL

Number	Title	Yr	NM
❏ 7729	I Ain't Never Been to Heaven (But I've Spent the Night with You)/Tonight I'm Feeling You (All Over Again)	1979	$5

HITBOUND

Number	Title	Yr	NM
❏ 4504	The Devil Stands Only Five Foot Five/Free to Love	1980	$5
❏ 4503	The Stores Are Full of Roses/(B-side unknown)	1980	$5
❏ 4501	Tonight I'm Feelin' You (All Over Again)/Free to Love	1979	$5

JOE-WES

Number	Title	Yr	NM
❏ 81006	I Ain't Giving Up on Her Yet/Mama's Secret	1982	$5
❏ 81000	Tonight I'm Feeling You (All Over Again)/ Let's Hold Hands	1982	$5

KOALA

Number	Title	Yr	NM
❏ 328	A Loser's Night Out/Devil Stands Only 5 Foot 5	1980	$5
❏ 328 [PS]	A Loser's Night Out/Devil Stands Only 5 Foot 5	1980	$8
❏ 331	Magic Eyes/The Stores Are Full of Roses	1981	$5
❏ 334	My Beginning Was You/ Hanging On by a Heartstring	1981	$5
❏ 346	Tonight I'm Feeling You (All Over Again)/ (B-side unknown)	1982	$6
❏ 340	When a Man Loves a Woman/A Little Tear	1981	$5

MONUMENT

Number	Title	Yr	NM
❏ 8693	She Took My Words Away/ Country Music Is a Lady	1976	$6

— As "Jack Lebsock

GRAYSON, KIM

SOUNDWAVES

Number	Title	Yr	NM
❏ 4795	If You Only Knew/Love's Slippin' Up on Me	1987	$5
❏ 4795 [PS]	If You Only Knew/Love's Slippin' Up on Me	1987	$6
❏ 4787	Love's Slippin' Up on Me/(B-side unknown)	1987	$5
❏ 4787 [PS]	Love's Slippin' Up on Me/(B-side unknown)	1987	$6
❏ 4800	Missin' Texas/ (B-side unknown)	1988	$5
❏ 4800 [PS]	Missin' Texas/ (B-side unknown)	1988	$6

GRAYZELL, RUDY

ABBOTT

Number	Title	Yr	NM
❏ 147	Bonita Chiquita/I'm Gone Again	1953	$100
❏ 157	Ocean Paradise/ It Ain't My Baby	1954	$100

CAPITOL

Number	Title	Yr	NM
❏ F2946	Hearts Made of Stone/ There's Gonna Be a Ball	1954	$50
❏ F3149	Please Big Mama/ My Heart Is Willing	1955	$50

— Capitol titles as "Rudy Gray

MERCURY

Number	Title	Yr	NM
❏ 71138	Let's Get Wild/I Love You So	1957	$100

STARDAY

Number	Title	Yr	NM
❏ 241	Duck Dail/You're Gone	1956	$100
❏ 321	Let's Get Wild/I Love You So	1957	$125
❏ 229	The Moon Is Up/Day by Day	1956	$100

GREAN, CHARLES RANDOLPH

RANWOOD

Number	Title	Yr	NM
❏ 901	Any Time of the Year/ Although You Make Me Cry	1971	$5
❏ 891	Bullfrog/Singalong Junk	1970	$5
❏ 918	Concerto for Knives, Forks, Spoons and Soup Ladle/Gymnopedie	1971	$5
❏ 872	Marcus Welby, M.D. Theme/ Come Touch the Sun	1970	$6
❏ 864	Peter and the Wolf/Georgy	1970	$5
❏ 1044	Star Trek/Love Theme from "Hustle	1975	$4
❏ 1064	The $128,000 Question/ Sentimentale	1976	$4
❏ 938	Theme from Star Trek/Rayo de Sol	1972	$5
❏ 880	The Odd Couple/Theme from "Borsalino	1970	$6
❏ 952	The Old Piano Roll Blues/Rag-a-Muffin	1972	$5

GREASE BAND

SHELTER

Number	Title	Yr	NM
❏ 7310	All I Wanna Do/Jesse James	1971	$6
❏ 7304	Let It Be Gone/Laughed at the Judge	1971	$6

GREAT BUILDINGS

COLUMBIA

Number	Title	Yr	NM
❏ 02008	Combat Zone/Hold On Something	1981	$6

GREAT LOVE TRIP, THE

UNI

Number	Title	Yr	NM
❏ 55163	Why Can't We Be/Noah	1969	$10

GREAT SCOTTS, THE

EPIC

Number	Title	Yr	NM
❏ 9805	Don't Want Your Love/ Give Me Lovin'	1965	$30
❏ 9866	That's My Girl (Rotten to the Core)/Lost in Conversation	1965	$50

TRIUMPH

Number	Title	Yr	NM
❏ 66	Ball and Chain/Run, Run for Your Life	1966	$40
❏ 67	Light Hurts My Eyes/You Know What You Can Do	1966	$40

GREAT SOCIETY, THE

COLUMBIA

Number	Title	Yr	NM
❏ 44583	Sally Go 'Round the Roses/Didn't Think So	1968	$30

NORTH BEACH

Number	Title	Yr	NM
❏ 1001	Someone to Love/ Free Advice	1966	$250

— As "The Great!! Society!!

GREAT SPECKLED BIRD

AMPEX

Number	Title	Yr	NM
❏ 11006	Trucker's Café/Smiling Wine	1970	$8
❏ 11003	We Sail/Disappearing Woman	1970	$8

GREATS, THE

EBB

Number	Title	Yr	NM
❏ 145	Marching Elvis/ Fiddler's Rock	1958	$60

GREAVES, R.B.

20TH CENTURY

Number	Title	Yr	NM
❏ 2203	Let's Try It Again/ My Place or Yours	1975	$4

ATCO

Number	Title	Yr	NM
❏ 6726	Always Something There to Remind Me/ Oh, When I Was a Boy	1969	$6
❏ 6745	Fire and Rain/The Ballad of Leroy	1970	$6

Number	Title	Yr	NM
6778	Oh When I Was a Boy/Georgia Took Her Back	1970	$6
6839	Paperback Writer/Over You Now	1971	$5
6714	Take a Letter Maria/Big Bad City	1969	$8
6789	Whiter Shade of Pale/Show Me the Way to Go	1970	$6

BAREBACK

Number	Title	Yr	NM
523	Margie, Who's Watching the Baby/(B-side unknown)	1977	$6

MGM

Number	Title	Yr	NM
14567	All I Want to Do/Long Live the King	1973	$5
14483	Margie, Who's Watching the Baby/Area Code 213	1973	$5

MIDSONG INT'L.

Number	Title	Yr	NM
72006	Let Me Be the One Tonight/Please Mister Mailman	1980	$4

SUNFLOWER

Number	Title	Yr	NM
128	Margie, Who's Watching the Baby/Area Code 213	1972	$6

GREBEL, DEBBIE
CON BRIO

Number	Title	Yr	NM
111	Grandma Was the Motor (But She Let My Grandpa Drive)/You Won't Remember Her Name	1976	$6
123	He Always Writes Me (When He's Done Me Wrong)/If You Wanna Love Me	1977	$6
128	Please Take Me With You!/If You Wanna Love Me	1977	$6

GRECO, BUDDY
CORAL

Number	Title	Yr	NM
9-61038	Don't Say Goodbye/How Do You Think I Feel	1953	$15
9-61236	If I Give My Heart to You/Cold Glass of Water	1954	$15
9-60904	I'll Always Love You Some/And So Goodbye	1953	$15
9-60573	I Ran All the Way Home/The Glory of Love	1951	$20
9-60672	It's a Sin to Tell a Lie/Never Leave Your Sugar	1952	$15
9-61265	Paris Loves Lovers/Ain't No In-Between	1954	$15
9-60623	Take Me Back/'Til the Stars Fall	1952	$15
9-61409	Tonight/Truly	1955	$10
9-61190	What Word Is Sweeter Than Sweetheart/Lulu's Back in Town	1954	$15
9-61483	Why Don't You Write Me/Pennies from Heaven	1955	$15

EPIC

Number	Title	Yr	NM
5-9451	Around the World/Hey There	1961	$8
5-9379	Cheek to Cheek/How About You	1960	$8
5-9657	Ciumachella (Tender Flower)/I'll Be a Fool	1964	$8
5-9817	I Can't Begin to Tell You/When the Subject Was Roses	1965	$8
5-9750	I Can't Help It (If I'm Still in Love with You)/Jambalaya	1965	$8
5-9439	I Could Write a Book/They Took John Away	1961	$8
5-9380	(I Don't Care) Only Love Me/Misty	1960	$8
5-9713	It's Such a Happy Day/Zip-a-Dee Do-Dah	1964	$8
5-9499	Let Me Love You/Twistin' to the Blues	1962	$8
5-9499 [PS]	Let Me Love You/Twistin' to the Blues	1962	$12
5-9378	Like Young/Something's Gotta Give	1960	$8
5-9588	Make Up Your Mind/What Now My Love	1963	$8
5-9588 [PS]	Make Up Your Mind/What Now My Love	1963	$10
5-9666	More/It Had Better Be Tonight	1964	$8
5-9536	Mr. Lonely/Sentimental Fool	1962	$8

—A-side has the same backing track as Bobby Vinton's 1964 hit version of the song

Number	Title	Yr	NM
5-9404	Oooh Look-a-There, Ain't She Pretty/This Could Be the Start of Something	1960	$8
5-9404 [PS]	Oooh Look-a-There, Ain't She Pretty/This Could Be the Start of Something	1960	$10
5-9563	Stranger/Just Walk Away	1962	$8
5-9563 [PS]	Stranger/Just Walk Away	1962	$10
5-9864	That Darn Cat/I'm Gonna Laugh You Out of My Life	1965	$8
5-9864 [PS]	That Darn Cat/I'm Gonna Laugh You Out of My Life	1965	$12
5-9834	The Best Is Yet to Come/Time's a-Wastin' While You're Gone	1965	$8
5-9387	The Lady Is a Tramp/Like Young	1960	$8
5-9387 [PS]	The Lady Is a Tramp/Like Young	1960	$10
5-9377	The Lady Is a Tramp/The More I See You	1960	$8
5-9627	The Magic of a Girl/Miss Kiss and Run	1963	$8
5-9786	The Most Beautiful Girl in the World/You Win Again	1965	$8
5-9408	(titles unknown)	1960	$8
5-9409	(titles unknown)	1960	$8
5-9410	(titles unknown)	1960	$8
5-9411	(titles unknown)	1960	$8
5-9412	(titles unknown)	1960	$8

— The above five presumably are stereo jukebox singles from the album "Songs for Swinging Losers"

Number	Title	Yr	NM
5-9455	(titles unknown)	1961	$8
5-9456	(titles unknown)	1961	$8
5-9457	(titles unknown)	1961	$8
5-9458	(titles unknown)	1961	$8
5-9459	(titles unknown)	1961	$8

— The above five presumably are stereo jukebox singles from the album "I Like It Swinging"

HERALD

Number	Title	Yr	NM
545	Ooh Baby/Ask Her	1959	$15

KAPP

Number	Title	Yr	NM
183	Game of Love/With All My Heart	1957	$10
165	Holiday Romance/You're the Love of My Love	1956	$12
155	In Time to Come/Love Don't Be a Stranger	1956	$10
170	Wow/Pink Flamingo and Dancing Crane	1957	$10

MGM

Number	Title	Yr	NM
14269	Days of Icy Fingers/You Can Close Your Eyes	1971	$5
14235	How Can I Live Without Your Love/Mountain Girl	1971	$5

REPRISE

Number	Title	Yr	NM
0551	Dani/Where's the Girl	1967	$6
0657	Girl Talk/This Is Your Life	1968	$6
0638	Good Times/Is All That Bright and Beautiful	1967	$6
0605	I Will Wait for You/She's a Cariocia	1967	$6
0584	Love's Gonna Live Here Again/Bonita	1967	$6
0562	There She Goes/Your Name	1967	$6

SCEPTER

Number	Title	Yr	NM
12270	Distant Carolina/Double Life	1970	$6
12260	From Atlanta to Goodbye/Love Is a Hurtin' Thing	1969	$6
12278	Let It Be/Walking Backwards Down the Road	1970	$6
12287	My God and I/Walking Backwards Down the Road	1970	$6

GREELEY, GEORGE
REPRISE

Number	Title	Yr	NM
0490	Who's Afraid/Jungle Fantasy	1966	$6

WARNER BROS.

Number	Title	Yr	NM
5188	Come Back to Sorrento/Guinevere	1960	$8
5175	Love Music from Tristan & Isolde/My Love	1960	$8
5175 [PS]	Love Music from Tristan & Isolde/My Love	1960	$15
5218	Lucy's Theme from Parrish/Allison's Theme from Parrish	1961	$8
5218 [PS]	Lucy's Theme from Parrish/Allison's Theme from Parrish	1961	$15
5207	Main Theme from "Gone with the Wind"/Tara's Theme	1961	$8
5100	Malaguena/My Love	1959	$10
5311	Theme from Mutiny on the Bounty/Love Song from Mutiny on the Bounty	1962	$8
5239	Tonight/Tender Is the Night	1961	$8
5511	Tonight/Tender Is The Night//Polonaise/Mattinata	1961	$15
5511 [PS]	Tonight/Tender Is The Night//Polonaise/Mattinata	1961	$15

—Part of Warner Bros. "+2" series, with two new songs and excerpts of two prior hits

Number	Title	Yr	NM
5264	What Now My Love/11th Hour Melody	1962	$8

GREEN, JANICE (THE "OH JULIE" GIRL)
NASCO

Number	Title	Yr	NM
6013	With All My Heart/Jackie	1958	$30

GREEN
ATCO

Number	Title	Yr	NM
6833	Big Dipper/All My Bells	1971	$5

GREEN, AL
A&M

Number	Title	Yr	NM
1427	As Long As We're Together/Blessed	1989	$3
2919	Everything's Gonna Be Alright/So Real to Me	1987	$3
2786	Going Away/Building Up	1985	$4
2962	Soul Survivor/Jesus Will Fix It	1987	$3
2807	True Love/He Is the Light	1986	$4

BELL

Number	Title	Yr	NM
45258	Guilty/Let Me Help You	1972	$30
45305	Hot Wire/Don't Leave Me	1973	$30

HI

Number	Title	Yr	NM
77505	Belle/Chariots of Fire	1977	$4
77505 [PS]	Belle/Chariots of Fire	1977	$6
2235	Call Me (Come Back Home)/What a Wonderful Thing Love Is	1973	$5
2188	Driving Wheel/True Love	1971	$6
2300	Full of Fire/Could I Be the One	1975	$5
2247	Here I Am (Come and Take Me)/I'm Glad You're Mine	1973	$5
2182	I Can't Get Next to You/Ride Sally Ride	1970	$6
78511	I Feel Good/Feels Like Summer	1978	$4
2216	I'm Still in Love with You/Old Time Lovin'	1972	$5
2322	I Tried to Tell Myself/Something	1977	$10
2159	I Want to Hold Your Hand/What Am I Gonna Do with Myself	1969	$8
2306	Let It Shine/There's No Way	1976	$5
2262	Let's Get Married/So Good to Be Here	1974	$5
2202	Let's Stay Together/Tomorrow's Dream	1971	$5
2257	Livin' for You/It Ain't No Fun to Me	1973	$5
2211	Look What You Done for Me/La La for You	1972	$5
2324	Love and Happiness/Glory Glory	1977	$5
2282	L-O-V-E (Love)/I Wish You Were Here	1975	$5
2288	Oh Me, Oh My (Dreams in My Arms)/Strong As Death (Sweet As Love)	1975	$5
2164	One Woman/Tomorrow's Dream	1969	$8
2274	Sha-La-La (Make Me Happy)/School Days	1974	$5
2194	Tired of Being Alone/Get Back Baby	1971	$5
78522	Wait Here/To Sir with Love	1978	$4
78522 [PS]	Wait Here/To Sir with Love	1978	$6

HOT LINE JOURNAL

Number	Title	Yr	NM
15000	Back Up Train/Don't Leave Me	1967	$40
15001	Don't Hurt Me No More/Get Yourself Together	1967	$30
15002	I'll Be Good to You/Lover's Hideaway	1967	$30

7-Inch Extended Plays

HI

Number	Title	Yr	NM
SBG87 [PS]	Call Me	1973	$12
SBG87	Funny How Time Slips Away/Love Is Like the Morning Sun//Have You Been Making Out O.K./Stand Up	1973	$10

—Jukebox issue; small hole, plays at 33 1/3 rpm

Number	Title	Yr	NM
SBG81	How Can You Mend a Broken Heart/So You're Leaving//I've Never Found a Girl/What Is This Feeling/It Ain't No Fun to Me	1972	$10

—Jukebox issue; small hole, plays at 33 1/3 rpm

Number	Title	Yr	NM
SBG81 [PS]	Let's Stay Together	1972	$12

GREEN, BILL
NSD

Number	Title	Yr	NM
39	Big Fat Mama/Rainy Day Song	1980	$5
11	Fool Such As I/Let's Cheat Again	1978	$5
15	Free Born Man/Texas Greats	1979	$5
30	I Hang Around/I Don't Know Why I Keep Loving You	1979	$5

PHONO

Number	Title	Yr	NM
2629	Texas on a Saturday Night/Let's Cheat Again	1976	$8

GREEN DAY
7-Inch Extended Plays

LOOKOUT!

Number	Title	Yr	NM
17 [PS]	1,000 Hours	1989	$3

GREEN, FRED, AND THE MELLARDS
BALLAD

Number	Title	Yr	NM
1016	Love Me Crazy/That's Life	1955	$200
1012	My Sweetheart/You Can't Keep Love in a Broken Heart	1955	$300

GREEN, FRED
BOBBIN

Number	Title	Yr	NM
123	Don't Make a Fool Out of Me/If You Ever Try to Leave Me	1960	$125
111	Wham Slam Baby/It's Funny	1959	$125

GREEN, GARLAND

CASINO
Number	Title	Yr	NM
056	I.O.U./It's a Backdoor World	1976	$5

COTILLION
Number	Title	Yr	NM
44098	Plain and Simple Girl/Hey Cloud	1971	$6

OCEAN-FRONT
Number	Title	Yr	NM
2000	Tryin' to Hold On/(B-side unknown)	1983	$4

RCA
Number	Title	Yr	NM
PB-10889	Don't Let Love Walk Out on Us/Ask Me for What You Want	1977	$6
PB-11126	Let's Celebrate/Let Me Be Your Pacifier	1977	$5
PB-11023	Shake Your Shaker/Lovin' You Baby	1977	$5

REVUE
Number	Title	Yr	NM
11001	Girl I Love You/It Rained Forty Days and Nights	1967	$100

SPRING
Number	Title	Yr	NM
158	Bumpin' and Stompin'/Nothing Can Take You from Me	1975	$5
142	He Didn't Know (He Kept On Talkin')/Please Come Home	1973	$5
151	Let the Good Times Roll/You and I Go Good Together	1974	$5
146	Sweet Loving Woman/Sending My Best Friend	1974	$5

UNI
Number	Title	Yr	NM
55213	Angel Baby/You Played on a Player	1970	$8
55188	Don't Think That I Am a Violent Guy/All She Said (Was Goodbye to Me)	1969	$8

GREEN, GRANT

BLUE NOTE
Number	Title	Yr	NM
1983	Afro Party/Father's Lament	1972	$5
1960	Ain't It Funky Now (Part 1)/Ain't It Funky Now (Part 2)	1970	$5
1969	Does Anybody Really Know What Time It Is?/Never Can Say Goodbye	1971	$5
1965	Sookie, Sookie/Time to Remember	1971	$5
1972	The Battle (Part 1)/The Battle (Part 2)	1972	$5

VERVE
Number	Title	Yr	NM
10361	Cantaloupe Woman/Daddy Grapes	1965	$8

GREEN, JERRY

CONCORDE
Number	Title	Yr	NM
154	Genuine Texas Good Guy/(B-side unknown)	1977	$6
152	I Know the Feeling/How Sweet It Is	1977	$6

GREEN, JESSE

UNITED ARTISTS
Number	Title	Yr	NM
XW955	Flip/Highwaves of the Sea	1977	$8

GREEN, KEITH

DECCA
Number	Title	Yr	NM
31799	A Go-Go Letter/The Way I Used to Be	1965	$30
31859	Girl Don't Tell Me/How to Be Your Guy	1965	$30
31973	Home Town Girls/Hear What's Happening, Baby	1966	$30

ERA
Number	Title	Yr	NM
3210	Fantastic/L.A. City Smog Blues	1969	$10
108	Sgt. Pepper's Epitaph/Country Store	1970	$10

GREEN, LARRY

RCA VICTOR
Number	Title	Yr	NM
47-3074	Our Christmas Waltz/Follow The Swallow To Hide-A-Way Hollow	1949	$20

GREEN, LIL

ATLANTIC
Number	Title	Yr	NM
951	Every Time/I've Got That Feeling	1952	$125

GREEN, LLOYD

CHART
Number	Title	Yr	NM
1071	Bar Hoppin'/Greenblue	1969	$8
5014	Orbit/Robin	1969	$8
5043	Tell Ya What/Steel Blue	1969	$8
1029	Woman, Woman/Mr. Nashville Sound	1968	$8

LITTLE DARLIN'
Number	Title	Yr	NM
023	Pedal Pattle/Little Darlin'	1967	$30
07	Skillet Lickin'/Green Strings	1966	$30
050	Sweet Cheeks/Green Strings	1968	$10

MONUMENT
Number	Title	Yr	NM
8608	Atlantis/San Antonio Rose	1974	$6
8624	Canadian Sunset/Spirit of '49	1974	$6
8574	Here Comes the Sun/Peace	1973	$6
8648	I Can Help/Theme from A Summer Place	1975	$5

—With Charlie McCoy

Number	Title	Yr	NM
8562	I Can See Clearly Now/Steelin' Away	1973	$6
8549	Morning Has Broken/Phase Phive	1972	$6
8635	Sally G/Lucretia	1974	$6
8615	Seaside/Summer Clouds	1974	$6
8592	Sleep Walk/Dixie Drive-In	1973	$6

OCTOBER
Number	Title	Yr	NM
1009	Feelings/Stainless Steel	1977	$6

SOUNDWAVES
Number	Title	Yr	NM
4560	The Whistler/Afterglow	1977	$5

GREEN RIVER

Members of this band later joined MOTHER LOVE BONE, MUDHONEY and PEARL JAM.

TASQUE FORCE
Number	Title	Yr	NM
ICP 01	Together We'll Never/Ain't Nothing to Do	1984	$130

—500 pressed on green vinyl; no picture sleeve

GREEN SLIME, THE

MGM
Number	Title	Yr	NM
K14052	The Green Slime/Far Beyond the Stars	1969	$10
K14052 [PS]	The Green Slime/Far Beyond the Stars	1969	$60

GREENBAUM, NORMAN

Also see DR. WEST'S MEDICINE SHOW AND JUG BAND.

REPRISE
Number	Title	Yr	NM
1008	California Earthquake/Rhode Island Red	1971	$6
0919	Canned Ham/Junior Cadillac	1970	$6
0752	Children of Paradise/School for Sweet Talk	1968	$10
1134	Dairy Queen/Petaluma	1972	$6
0818	Marcy/Children of Paradise	1969	$10
0739	Spirit in the Sky/Canned Ham	1971	$4

—Back to Back Hits" series

Number	Title	Yr	NM
0885	Spirit in the Sky/Milk Cow	1969	$8

GREENBEATS, THE

JERDEN
Number	Title	Yr	NM
763	So Sad/I'm on Fire	1965	$15

GREENBERG, STEVE

TRIP
Number	Title	Yr	NM
3000	Big Bruce/Run to You	1969	$12

GREENE, BARBARA

ATCO
Number	Title	Yr	NM
6250	Long Tall Sally/Slippin' and Slidin'	1963	$40

RENEE
Number	Title	Yr	NM
5004	A Lover's Plea/Our Love Is No Secret Now	1968	$60

GREENE, JACK, AND JEANNIE SEELY

DECCA
Number	Title	Yr	NM
32991	What in the World Has Gone Wrong with Our Love/Willingly	1972	$6

GREENE, JACK

DECCA
Number	Title	Yr	NM
32123	All the Time/Wanting You But Never Having You	1967	$8
32558	Back in the Arms of Love/The Key That Fits Her Door	1969	$8
31768	Don't You Ever Get Tired/The Hurt's On Me	1965	$12
31856	Ever Since My Baby Went Away/Room for One More Heartache	1965	$8
32352	Love Takes Care of Me/Your Favorite Fool	1968	$8
32490	Statue of a Fool/There's More to Love	1969	$8
32023	There Goes My Everything/The Hardest Easy Thing	1966	$8
32190	What Locks the Door/Left Over Feelings	1967	$8

EMH
Number	Title	Yr	NM
0031	Dying to Believe/There Goes My Everything	1984	$5
0019	From Cotton to Satin/I'd Be Home on Christmas Day	1983	$5
0015	I'd Be Home On Christmas Day/(B-side unknown)	1982	$6
0028	I'd Do As Much for You/Singing My Heart Out for You	1984	$5
0035	If It's Love (Then Bet It All)/Statue of a Fool	1984	$5
0025	Midnight Tennessee Woman/Goin' Through Hell for an Angel	1983	$5

FIRSTLINE
Number	Title	Yr	NM
709	Devil's Den/It's Not the End of the World	1980	$5

MCA
Number	Title	Yr	NM
40526	Birmingham/My Long Gone Reason	1976	$5
40415	Cheatin' River/On the Way Home	1975	$5
40481	He Little Thing'd Her Out of His Arms/Let Me Love You Back Together Again	1975	$5
40108	I Need Somebody Bad/Joyride	1973	$5
40179	It's Time to Cross That Bridge/Half That Much	1974	$5
40263	Sing for the Good Times/Something Seems to Fall Apart Inside	1974	$5
40035	The Fool I've Been Today/You Left Me	1973	$5
40354	This Time The Hurtin's On Me/Sawmill Depot	1974	$5

GREENE, LORNE

COLUMBIA
Number	Title	Yr	NM
4-44971	The Perfect Woman/It's All in the Game	1969	$6

GRT
Number	Title	Yr	NM
32	Daddy (I'm Proud to Be Your Son)/I Love a Rainbow	1969	$6
37	The First Word/I Love a Rainbow	1970	$6

RCA VICTOR
Number	Title	Yr	NM
47-8554	An Ol' Tin Cup/Sand	1965	$8
47-8554 [PS]	An Ol' Tin Cup/Sand	1965	$20
47-8819	Daddy's Little Girl/I Love a Rainbow	1966	$8
47-8757	Five Card Stud/Shadow of the Cactus	1965	$8
47-8229	I'm the Same Old Me/Love Finds a Way	1963	$10
47-9037	Must Be Santa/One Solitary Life	1966	$10
47-8113	My Sons, My Sons/The Place Where I Worship	1962	$10
47-8490	The Man/Pop Goes the Hammer	1964	$8
47-8901	Waco/All But the Remembering	1966	$8

GREENE, RUDY

CHANCE
Number	Title	Yr	NM
1151	I Had a Feeling/Meet Me Baby	1954	$200

—Black vinyl

Number	Title	Yr	NM
1151	I Had a Feeling/Meet Me Baby	1954	$400

—Red vinyl

Number	Title	Yr	NM
1139	Love Is a Pain/No Need of Your Crying	1953	$200
1146	The Letter/It's You I Love	1953	$200

CLUB 51
Number	Title	Yr	NM
103	Highway No. 1/You Mean Everything to Me	1956	$200

—With the Four Buddies

EMBER
Number	Title	Yr	NM
1020	Lonesome/Wild Life	1957	$50

EXCELLO
Number	Title	Yr	NM
2074	Cool Lovin' Mama/My Mumblin' Baby	1955	$60
2090	Teeny Weeny Baby/Queer Feeling	1956	$60

GREENWICH, ELLIE

Also see THE RAINDROPS.

BELL
Number	Title	Yr	NM
855	Ain't That Peculiar/I Don't Want to Be Left Outside	1970	$10
933	That Certain Someone/It's Like a Sad Old Kind of Movie	1970	$10

UNITED ARTISTS
Number	Title	Yr	NM
50278	A Long Time Comin'/Niki-Hoeky	1968	$20
50151	I Want You to Be My Baby/Goodnight, Goodnight	1967	$40

VERVE
Number	Title	Yr	NM
10724	Chapel of Love/River Deep, Mountain High	1973	$10
10719	Today I Met the Boy I'm Gonna Marry/Maybe I Know	1973	$10

Number	Title	Yr	NM

GREENWOOD COUNTY SINGERS, THE
KAPP
❑ 623	Anne/Cake Walking Babies from Home	1964	$8
❑ 688	Ballad of Cat Ballou/ Blue Is the Wind	1965	$8
❑ 660	Easter Rebellion/ Trombone Cholly	1965	$8
❑ 591	Frankie and Johnny/Climb Up Sunshine Mountain	1964	$8
❑ 742	Please Don't Sell My Daddy No More Wine/Southbound	1966	$8

— As "The Greenwoods
❑ KJB-47	Seven Daffodils/ Old Home Place	1965	$8
❑ 760	Tear Down the Walls/ Friends I Used to Know	1966	$8

— As "The Greenwood Singers
❑ 675	The Bridge Washed Out/ Nobody Waved Goodbye	1965	$8
❑ 774	The Eagle and Me/Eternal Love, Eternal Spring	1966	$8

— As "The Greenwood Singers

GREENWOOD, LEE
DOT
❑ 17271	Love Is Not Enough/ Someone to Watch Over Me	1969	$20
❑ 17312	Maria/Turn It Over	1969	$15

MCA
❑ 52150	Ain't No Trick (It Takes Magic)/Broken Pieces of My Heart	1982	$4
❑ 52733	Christmas to Christmas (Loving You)/Lone Star Christmas	1987	$4
❑ 52733 [PS]	Christmas to Christmas (Loving You)/Lone Star Christmas	1987	$5
❑ S45-17739 [DJ]	Christmas to Christmas (Loving You) (same on both sides)	1987	$5
❑ 52896	Didn't We/Heartbreak Radio	1986	$3
❑ 52564	Dixie Road/(I Found) Love in Time	1985	$3
❑ 52564 [PS]	Dixie Road/(I Found) Love in Time	1985	$4
❑ 52741	Don't Underestimate My Love for You/Leave My Heart the Way You Found It	1985	$3
❑ 52741 [PS]	Don't Underestimate My Love for You/Leave My Heart the Way You Found It	1985	$4
❑ 52426	Fool's Gold/Worth It for the Ride	1984	$4
❑ 52386	God Bless the USA/ This Old Bed	1984	$4

— Reissued in 1991 with the same catalog number, but without a picture sleeve
❑ 52386 [PS]	God Bless the USA/ This Old Bed	1984	$5
❑ 52322	Going, Going, Gone/ Come On Back and Love Me Some More	1983	$4
❑ 52807	Hearts Aren't Made to Break (They're Made to Love)/The Will to Love	1986	$3
❑ 52656	I Don't Mind the Thorns (If You're the Rose)/ Same Old Song	1985	$3
❑ 53156	If There's Any Justice/ We Could Have Been	1987	$3
❑ 53716	I Go Crazy/Any Way the Law Allows	1989	$3
❑ 53475	I'll Be Lovin' You/Do That to Me One More Time	1988	$3
❑ 53655	I Love the Way He Left You/Home to Alaska	1989	$3
❑ 52199	I.O.U./Another You	1983	$4
❑ 52199 [PS]	I.O.U./Another You	1983	$5
❑ 53312	I Still Believe/I'll Be Lovin' You	1988	$3
❑ 51159	It Turns Me Inside Out/Thank You for Changing My Life	1981	$4
❑ 52984	Mornin' Ride/Little Red Caboose	1986	$3
❑ 52087	She's Lying/Home Away from Home	1982	$4
❑ 52257	Somebody's Gonna Love You/You're the Woman I Love	1983	$4
❑ 53096	Someone/Let's Make the Most of Love	1987	$3
❑ 53234	Touch and Go Crazy/ Silver Dollar	1987	$3

PARAMOUNT
❑ 0102	Touch and Go/My First Night Alone Without You	1971	$10

GREENWOODS, THE
DECCA
❑ 31953	Silver Dagger/Harlan Breakdown	1965	$8

GREER, BIG JOHN
GROOVE
❑ 0131	A Man and a Woman/Blam	1955	$70

— With the Four Students
❑ 02	Bottle It Up and Go/ You'll Never Be Mine	1954	$50
❑ 0119	Come Back Mambellene/ Night Crawlin'	1955	$60
❑ 0108	Soon, Soon, Soon/I'm Glad for Your Sake	1955	$50
❑ 038	We Wanna See Santa Do the Mambo/Wait Till After Christmas	1954	$50
❑ 016	When the Roses Bloom in Lover's Lane/Too Long	1954	$50

KING
❑ 5057	Duck Walk/I Still Love You So	1957	$30
❑ 4941	Let Me Come Home/ Come Back, Uncle John	1956	$30
❑ 5006	Midnight Ramble/ Sweet Slumber	1957	$30

RCA VICTOR
❑ 50-0137	Big Rock/How Can You Forget?	1951	$60
❑ 50-0096	Cheatin'/It's Better to Have Been Taken for Granted	1950	$70

— Orange vinyl
❑ 50-0125	Clambake Boogie/ When You Love	1951	$60
❑ 47-5531	Drinkin' Fool/Gettin' Mighty Lonesome for You	1953	$50
❑ 50-0007	Drinkin' Wine Spo-Dee-O-Dee/Long Tall Gal	1949	$75

— Orange vinyl
❑ 47-4348	Got You on My Mind/Woman Is a Five-Letter Word	1951	$50
❑ 47-4293	Have Another Drink/I'm Savin' All My Lovin'	1951	$50
❑ 50-0029	If I Told You Once/I Found a Dream	1949	$75

— Orange vinyl
❑ 50-0076	I'll Never Do That Again/A Fool Hasn't Got a Chance	1950	$70

— Orange vinyl
❑ 47-5170	I'll Never Let You Go/You Played on My Piano	1953	$50
❑ 47-5037	I'm the Fat Man/Since You Went Away from Me	1952	$50
❑ 50-0108	Once There Lived a Fool/I Want Ya, I Need Ya	1951	$60
❑ 47-4484	Strong Red Whiskey/ If You Let Me	1952	$50
❑ 50-0113	Why Did You Go/ Our Wedding Time	1951	$60

GREER, DAN
MGM
❑ 14653	Hell Paso (Part I)/(Part II)	1973	$12
❑ 14653 [PS]	Hell Paso (Part I)/(Part II)	1973	$20

ODE
❑ 66002	Curiosity Killed the Cat/I Remember Mama	1970	$60

SOUNDS OF MEMPHIS
❑ 702	Masquerade/Thanks to You	1972	$15

GREGG, BOBBY
COTTON
❑ 1006	Potato Peeler/Sweet Georgia Brown	1962	$20

EPIC
❑ 5-9579	Drummer Man/Walk On	1963	$15
❑ 5-9541	Let's Jam Again Part 1/Part 2	1962	$15
❑ 5-9601	Scarlet O'Hara/Take Me Out to the Ball Game	1963	$15

LAURIE
❑ 3358	Theme from The Other Side/ If You Wanna Be Happy	1966	$10

VEEP
❑ 1207	Hullabaloo/Charly Ba-Ba	1965	$10

GREGORY, DICK
B-SHARP
❑ 272	Did You Need to Know/ (B-side unknown)	1966	$300

— Probably a different performer than the comedian/activist

VEE JAY
❑ 469	They Won't Hire Me/Benefit	1962	$15

GREGORY, IVAN, AND THE BLUE NOTES
G&G
❑ 110	Elvis Presley Blues/Kathy	1956	$250

GREGORY, TERRY
HANDSHAKE
❑ WS9-02442	Cinderella/We Better Talk It Over	1981	$4
❑ WS9-02563	I Can't Say Goodbye to You/We Had All It Takes to Fall in Love	1981	$4
❑ WS9-02959	I'm Takin' a Heart Break/After You've Shopped Around	1982	$4
❑ WS9-02736	I Never Knew the Devil's Eyes Were Blue/I Need Another Lover (Like a Hole in the Heart)	1982	$4

SCOTTI BROTHERS
❑ ZS4-04410	Cowgirl in a Coupe de Ville/The Old Songs	1984	$3
❑ ZS4-04735	Pardon Me, But This Heart's Taken/Fallin'	1985	$3

GREY, JOEL
COLUMBIA
❑ 4-44907	Don't Remind Me Now of Time/1941	1969	$6

GRIER, FRANKIE, QUARTET
SWAN
❑ 4019	Oh, Gloria/Lonesome for You	1958	$400

GRIER, ROOSEVELT
20TH CENTURY
❑ 2212	Take the Time to Love Somebody/Your Love Is Right Up My Alley	1975	$8

A&M
❑ 1457	Beautiful People/I'll Be Back Tomorrow	1973	$200
❑ 1500	If You Hit a Good Lick, Lay On It/You're the Violin	1974	$5

A
❑ 110	Moonlight in Vermont/ Smoky Morning	1960	$30
❑ 105	Sincerely/Why Don't You Do Me Right	1959	$30

AGP
❑ 109	Bad News/Ring Around the World	1969	$8

AMY
❑ 11029	Hard to Forget/People Make the World	1968	$20
❑ 11015	High Society Woman/ C'mon Cupid	1968	$40
❑ 11004	Who's Got the Ball (Y'All)/Halftime	1967	$40

BATTLE
❑ 45911	Why/Lover Set Me Free	1963	$50

BELL
❑ 45459	It's All Right to Cry/ (B-side unknown)	1974	$8

D-TOWN
❑ 1058	Pizza Pie Man/ Welcome to the Club	1965	$200

LIBERTY
❑ 55413	Struttin' 'n Twistin'/Let the Cool Wind Blow	1962	$20
❑ 55453	The Mail Must Go Thru/ Your Has Been	1962	$20

MGM
❑ 13698	Slow Drag/Yesterday	1967	$40
❑ 13840	Spanish Harlem/I'm Living Good	1967	$15

RIC
❑ 112	Down So Long/ In My Tenement	1964	$300
❑ 102	Fool, Fool, Fool/Since You've Been Gone	1964	$30

SPINDLE TOP
❑ 102	I'm Going Home/Jinny	1961	$30

UNITED ARTISTS
❑ 50893	Bring Back the Time/Oh How I Miss You Baby	1972	$50

YOUNGSTOWN
❑ 609	Deputy Dog/(B-side unknown)	1966	$40

Number	Title	Yr	NM

GRIFF, RAY

ABC DOT
❏ 17542	If That's What It Takes/ Adam's Child	1974	$6

CAPITOL
❏ 4446	A Cold Day in July/Rusty	1977	$5
❏ 4415	A Passing Thing/Piano Man	1977	$5
❏ 4208	If I Let Her Come In/Runnin'	1976	$5
❏ 4266	I Love the Way That You Love Me/Wrapped Around Your Finger	1976	$5
❏ 4320	That's What I Get (For Doin' My Own Thinkin')/Falling	1976	$5
❏ 4368	The Last of the Winfield Amateurs/You Put the Bounce Back Into My Step	1976	$5

DOT
❏ 17456	A Song for Everyone/ Another Sad Affair	1973	$6
❏ 17440	It Rains Just the Same in Missouri/Somewhere Between Atlanta and Mobile	1972	$6
❏ 17252	Miracles Do Happen/ Pebbles on the Beach	1969	$8
❏ 17206	Move a Little Farther Along/Wanderin' Through the Valley	1969	$8
❏ 17171	Sweet Bird of Youth/A Lean Horse	1968	$8
❏ 17501	That Doesn't Mean (I Don't Love My God)/ Lost Love of Mine	1974	$6
❏ 17288	The Entertainer/ Caution to the Wind	1969	$8
❏ 17519	The Hill/All Loved Out	1974	$6
❏ 17082	The Sugar from My Candy/Till the Right One Comes Along	1968	$8
❏ 17471	What Got to You (Before It Got to Me)/Darlin'	1973	$6

RCA
❏ JB-50807	Christmas Isn't Christmas Without You (same on both sides)	1984	$6

— Canadian number issued in U.S.

❏ PB-50722	If Tomorrow Never Comes/ Draw Me a Line	1983	$5

— Canadian number issued in U.S.

❏ PB-50846	What My Woman Does to Me/(B-side unknown)	1986	$5

— Canadian number issued in U.S.

ROYAL AMERICAN
❏ 30	Don't Look at Me/ (B-side unknown)	1971	$8
❏ 56	It's the First Day/ Waxamachie Woman	1972	$8
❏ 16	My Everlasting Love/ Ain't Nowhere to Go	1970	$8
❏ 19	Patches/Dixie	1970	$8
❏ 46	The Mornin' After Baby Let Me Down/I'll Love You Enough for Both of Us	1971	$8
❏ 38	What Can I Say/Wait a Little Longer	1971	$8

VISION
❏ 440	Draw Me a Line/Heaven	1981	$5
❏ 442	Things That Songs Are Made Of/Light as a Feather	1982	$5
❏ 442 [PS]	Things That Songs Are Made Of/Light as a Feather	1982	$8

GRIFFIN, BUCK

HOLIDAY INN
❏ 109	Pretty Lou/The Girl in Room 1209	1963	$50

LIN
❏ 1015	Bawlin' and Squallin'/ Let's Elope, Baby	1955	$80
❏ 1008	Going Home, All Alone/ Lookin' for the Green	1955	$70
❏ 1016	Go-Stop-O/Cochise	1955	$125
❏ 1018	Little Dan/Neither Do I	1956	$70
❏ 1005	Meadowlark Boogie/It Don't Make No Never Mind	1954	$70

METRO
❏ 20007	The Party/Every Night	1958	$40

MGM
❏ 12439	Bow My Back/Old Bee Tree	1957	$100
❏ 12284	Stutterin' Papa/Watchin' the 7:10 Roll By	1956	$125

GRIFFIN, JIMMY

IMPERIAL
❏ 66152	He Will Break Your Heart/ Hard Row to Hoe	1965	$15
❏ 66108	These Are the Times/ Walking to New Orleans	1965	$15

POLYDOR
❏ 14213	Breakin' Up Is Easy/ Melody Maker	1973	$5
❏ 14236	She Knows/ Beachwood Band	1974	$5
❏ 14282	Treat Her Right/How Do You Say Goodbye	1975	$5

REPRISE
❏ 0268	All My Loving/My Baby Made Me Cry	1964	$20
❏ 20114	Girls Grow Up Faster Than Boys/It's a Free Country	1962	$30
❏ 0280	Gotta Lotta Love/ Running to You	1964	$20
❏ 20221	Little Miss Cool/ Marie Is Moving	1963	$30
❏ 20178	Love Letters in the Sand/ Summer Holiday	1963	$30
❏ 20161	What Kind of Girl Are You/A Little Like Lovin' You	1963	$30

VIVA
❏ 611	Miracle Worker/Looking So Much Better	1967	$10
❏ 642	Miracle Worker/ Thank You Love	1970	$10
❏ 627	Thank You Love/ Light of Your Mind	1968	$10

GRIFFIN, KEN

COLUMBIA
❏ 38910	Away In A Manger/O, Little Town Of Bethlehem	1951	$15
❏ 38911	I'll Be Home For Christmas/ White Christmas	1951	$15
❏ 38909	Silent Night/Adeste Fideles	1951	$15

GRIFFIN, MERV

CAMEO
❏ 266	Always/Hey Pretty Baby	1963	$10
❏ 298	Have I Told You Lately That I Love You/I'm Sorry I Made You Cry	1964	$12

CARLTON
❏ 540	Banned in Boston/The World We Love In	1961	$20
❏ 562	Screamin' Memories from Planet X/I've Got a Lovely Bunch of Coconuts	1961	$10
❏ 545	The Charanga/ Along Came Joe	1961	$12
❏ 552	Would You/You Came a Long Way from St. Louis	1961	$10

COLUMBIA
❏ 4-40624	Call Out the Engines/A Handful of Dreams	1955	$15
❏ 4-40328	Do You Remember Me?/ The Story of Tina	1954	$15
❏ 4-40557	Five Cups of Coffee (Five Cups of Tea)/(I Couldn't Get the Hang of) The Merengue	1955	$15
❏ 4-40685	Ginny/Joey, Joey, Joey	1956	$15
❏ 4-40141	Hey Garcon!/All the Live Long Day	1953	$20
❏ 4-40026	I'll Be There/I Kiss Your Hand, Madame	1953	$20
❏ 4-40424	I Never Has Seen Snow/Hot-Cha-Cha	1955	$15
❏ 4-40274	Much Too Young to Die/A Girl with a Figure Like an Hour Glass	1954	$15
❏ 4-40765	Prunes/We Ain't Goin' Nowhere	1956	$15

— With Rita Farrell

❏ 4-40530	Sweet and Gentle/That's Hot-Cha-Cha with Me	1955	$15

CORAL
❏ 62480	I Keep Running Away from You/Think of All the Nice Things He's Done	1966	$10

DECCA
❏ 9-30525	Homing Bird/Think of All the Nice Things He's Done	1957	$15
❏ 9-30380	I Keep Running Away from You/Will I Find My Love Today	1957	$15
❏ 9-30562	Introduce Me to the Gal/ You're the Prettiest Thing	1958	$15
❏ 9-30240	Love Story/I'll Be Thinking of You	1957	$15
❏ 9-30131	Wringle, Wrangle/It Was My Father's Habit	1957	$15

DOT
❏ 17184	And I'll Forget You/ Have a Nice Trip	1968	$8

MERCURY
❏ 72069	Count Your Blessings (Every Day)/Casanova Bossa Nova	1962	$8
❏ 71993	House of Horrors/Pretty Girl	1962	$8

METROMEDIA
❏ 167	Theme from Minnie's Boys/Time for Tony	1970	$6

MGM
❏ K13638	Santa Claus Is Coming to Town/Sleep My Little Child	1966	$10

RCA VICTOR
❏ 47-4217	Belle, Belle, My Liberty Belle/I Fall in Love with You Ev'ry Day	1951	$30
❏ 47-4748	Galway Bay/The Kerry Dance	1952	$20
❏ 47-4644	Heart of a Clown/With No One to Love Tonight	1952	$20

❏ 47-4778	Mama's Gone, Goodbye/ Love Me, Love Me	1952	$20
❏ 47-4747	Mush-Mush-Mush-Tural-I-Addy/The Humour Is On Me Now	1952	$20
❏ 47-4512	The Hills of County Clare/ The Isle of Innisfree	1952	$20
❏ 47-4181	The Morningside of the Mountain/I Love the Sunshine of Your Smile	1951	$30
❏ 47-4749	The Wild Colonial Boy/I'll Take You Home Again, Kathleen	1952	$20

— The above four comprise a box set

❏ 47-4270	Twenty Three Starlets (And Me)/The Lord's Ridin' with Me Tonight	1951	$30

ZOO YORK
❏ WS4 03949	Changing Keys/Nightwalk	1983	$6

— As "The Merv Griffin Orchestra"; "Changing Keys" is the second (and most familiar) theme song to the game show "Wheel of Fortune"

GRIFFINS, THE

MERCURY
❏ 70650	Bad Little Girl/Scheming	1955	$120
❏ 70558	I Swear By All the Stars Above/Sing to Me	1955	$120
❏ 70913	My Baby's Gone/ Why Must You Go	1956	$50

WING
❏ 90067	Forever More/Leave It to Me	1956	$200

GRIFFITH, ANDY

CAPITOL
❏ 5073	Andy and Cleopatra (Part 1)/ Andy and Cleopatra (Part 2)	1963	$20
❏ F3938	Andy's Lament/Thank Heaven for Little Girls	1958	$30
❏ 4684	Flop Eared Mule/A Good Man Is Hard to Find	1962	$20
❏ F3706	Free Man in the Morning/Just a Closer Walk with Thee	1957	$30
❏ F4157	Hamlet (Part 1)/ Hamlet (Part 2)	1959	$30
❏ 4236	Look at the Son-Shine/ My Dog Underdog	1976	$6
❏ F3990	Love Poems: To the Lovely Juanita Beasley/ Togetherness	1958	$30
❏ F3057	Make Yourself Comfortable/ Ko Ko Mo (I Love You So)	1955	$30
❏ F3705	Mama Guitar/A Face in the Crowd	1957	$30
❏ F4052	Midnight Special/She's Bad, Bad Business	1958	$30
❏ F4204	Once Knew a Fella/ Don't Look Back	1959	$20
❏ F3402	Opera Carmen (Part 1)/ Opera Carmen (Part 2)	1956	$30
❏ F3872	Silhouettes/Conversation with a Mule	1958	$30
❏ F3498	Standing on the Corner/ No Time for Sergeants	1956	$30
❏ F2855	Swan Lake (Part 1)/ Swan Lake (Part 2)	1954	$30
❏ 4848	The Pool Table/Whistling Ping Pong Game	1962	$20
❏ F2693	What It Was, Was Football (Part 1)/What It Was, Was Football (Part 2)	1953	$40

— Original pressings as "Deacon Andy Griffith"

COLONIAL
❏ E3	What It Was, Was Football (Part 1)/What It Was, Was Football (Part 2)	1953	$70

COLUMBIA
❏ 4-45711	Lead Me to That Rock/ Somebody Bigger Than You and I	1972	$8

7-Inch Extended Plays

CAPITOL
❏ EAP 1-630 [PS]	Make Yourself Comfortable	1955	$35
❏ EAP 1-630	Make Yourself Comfortable/ Ko Ko Mo/I Love You So	1955	$35
❏ EAP 1-498 [PS]	What It Was, Was Football!	1954	$50
❏ EAP 1-498	What It Was, Was Football/ Romeo and Juliet	1954	$50

GRIFFITH, GLENDA

ARIOLA AMERICA
❏ 7695	Angel, Spread Your Wings/Heavenly Island	1978	$4
❏ 7680	Don't Worry ('Bout Me)/ Heavenly Island	1977	$4
❏ 7698	Oh, Boy!/Angel, Spread Your Wings	1978	$4

Number	Title	Yr	NM

GRIFFITH, NANCI
MCA
Number	Title	Yr	NM
❏ 53374	Anyone Can Be Someone's Fool/Love Wore a Halo (Back Before the War)	1988	$4
❏ 53147	Cold Heart, Closed Minds/Ford Econoline	1987	$4
❏ 53761	I Don't Want to Talk About Love/Drive-In Movies and Dashboard Lights	1989	$4
❏ 53306	I Knew Love/So Long Ago	1988	$4
❏ 53700	It's a Hard Life Wherever You Go/From a Distance	1989	$4
❏ 53009	Lone Star State of Mind/There's a Light Beyond the Woods (Mary Margaret)	1987	$4
❏ 53082	Trouble in the Fields/Love in a Memory	1987	$4

PHILO
Number	Title	Yr	NM
❏ 1096	Once in a Very Blue Moon/(B-side unknown)	1986	$6

GRIFFITH, PEGGI
DOLTON
Number	Title	Yr	NM
❏ 35	Lovely Girl/You're In My Dreams to Stay	1961	$30

GRILL, ROB
MERCURY
Number	Title	Yr	NM
❏ 76068	Where Were You When I Needed You/Rockin' on the Road Again	1979	$5

GRIMES, SCOTT
JAMEX
Number	Title	Yr	NM
❏ 017	We Believe In Christmas/I Saw Christmas	1984	$6
❏ 017 [PS]	We Believe In Christmas/I Saw Christmas	1984	$10

GRIN
Features NILS LOFGREN.
A&M
Number	Title	Yr	NM
❏ 1502	Beggar's Day/You're the Weight	1974	$4

SPINDIZZY
Number	Title	Yr	NM
❏ ZS74006	End Unkind/Slippery Fingers	1972	$6
❏ ZS74002	Everybody's Missing the Sun/Eighteen-Faced Lover	1971	$6
❏ ZS74001	If I Were a Song/See What a Love Can Do	1971	$6
❏ ZS74005	White Lies/Just to Have You	1972	$6

THUNDER
Number	Title	Yr	NM
❏ 4000	We All Sung Together/See What a Love Can Do	1970	$8

GRINER, LINDA
MOTOWN
Number	Title	Yr	NM
❏ 1037	Good-By Cruel Love/Envious	1963	$400
— With corrected A-side title			
❏ 1037	Good-By Cruel World/Envious	1963	$600
— With incorrect A-side title			

GROCE, LARRY
DISNEYLAND
Number	Title	Yr	NM
❏ 564	Winnie the Pooh for President (Campaign Song)/(B-side unknown)	1976	$30

MGM
Number	Title	Yr	NM
❏ 14621	Muddy Boggy Banjo Man/Sweet Sweet Love	1973	$5

WARNER BROS.
Number	Title	Yr	NM
❏ 8327	The Ballad of Billy Don Rice/Big White House in Indiana	1977	$4
❏ 8442	Turn On Your TV/Hog and Dog Factory	1977	$4
❏ 8221	We've Been Malled/Old Fashioned Girl	1976	$4

GROGAN, TOBY
VEE JAY
Number	Title	Yr	NM
❏ 560	Angel/Just a Friend	1963	$40
— The Four Seasons sing on this record.			

GROOMS, SHERRY
ABC
Number	Title	Yr	NM
❏ 10987	Forever Is a Long Time/That Same Old Song	1967	$30
❏ 10812	The Girls' Song/Call of the Wild One	1966	$30

PARACHUTE
Number	Title	Yr	NM
❏ 514	Me/Mama's Boys	1978	$5

GROOTNA
COLUMBIA
Number	Title	Yr	NM
❏ 45461	Full Time Woman/Is It All Over	1971	$8
❏ 45538	Waitin' for My Ship/That's What You Get	1972	$8

GROSS, HENRY
A&M
Number	Title	Yr	NM
❏ 1534	Come On Say It/Ever Lovin' Days	1974	$4
❏ 1494	Fly Away/Simone	1974	$4
❏ 1613	Meet Me on the Corner/With the Sleep in My Eyes	1974	$4
❏ 1682	One More Tomorrow/Evergreen	1975	$4
❏ 1701	Travelin' Time/All My Love	1975	$4

ABC
Number	Title	Yr	NM
❏ 11334	Close My Eyes/Prayer for All	1972	$6

CAPITOL
Number	Title	Yr	NM
❏ 4946	Better Now We're Friends/You're My Ride Home	1980	$4
❏ 4980	How Long Is Forever/I Love You Now	1981	$4

LIFESONG
Number	Title	Yr	NM
❏ 1769	Love Is the Stuff/Shake Down Your Love	1978	$4
❏ 1761	Only the Beautiful/Creepin' Jenny	1978	$4
❏ 45002	Shannon/Pokey	1976	$5
❏ 45014	Someday (I Didn't Want to Have to Be the One)/Lincoln Road	1976	$4
❏ 45008	Springtime Mama/Overton Square	1976	$4
❏ 45023	String of Hearts/Painting My Love Song	1977	$4
❏ 45024	What a Sound/Painting My Love Song	1977	$4

GROSS SISTERS, THE
CHECKER
Number	Title	Yr	NM
❏ 932	Oom Baby!/My Baby Ain't Nothin' But Bad	1959	$50

GROUNDHOGS, THE
Featuring Tony McPhee.
LIBERTY
Number	Title	Yr	NM
❏ 56205	Ship on the Ocean/Sailor	1970	$8

GROUNDSPEED
DECCA
Number	Title	Yr	NM
❏ 32344	In a Dream/L-12 East	1968	$30

GROUP "B
SCORPIO
Number	Title	Yr	NM
❏ 406	I Know Your Name Girl/I Never Really Knew	1967	$30
❏ 402	Stop Calling Me/She's Gone	1967	$30

GROUP, THE
WARNER BROS.
Number	Title	Yr	NM
❏ 5840	Baby, Baby It's You/Can't Get Enough of Your Love	1966	$15

GROUP THERAPY
CANTERBURY
Number	Title	Yr	NM
❏ 517	Magic in the Air/Bad News	1967	$15

MERCURY
Number	Title	Yr	NM
❏ 72702	Thoughts/Come On	1967	$15

PHILIPS
Number	Title	Yr	NM
❏ 40598	Can't Stop Lovin' You Baby/I Must Go	1969	$8

RCA VICTOR
Number	Title	Yr	NM
❏ 47-9527	People Get Ready/Who'll Be Next	1968	$8

GROUPIES, THE
ATCO
Number	Title	Yr	NM
❏ 6393	I'm a Hog for You/Primitive	1966	$40

GROWING CONCERN, THE
MAINSTREAM
Number	Title	Yr	NM
❏ 685	Tomorrow Has Been Canceled/A Boy I Once Knew Well	1968	$40

GRUNDY, DAVE, COMBO
HIT
Number	Title	Yr	NM
❏ 32	Green Onions/I Remember You	1962	$8
— B-side by Ed Mendel			

GRUNION HUNTERS, THE
HIGHLAND
Number	Title	Yr	NM
❏ 1035	The Four-Eyed, Tongue-Tied, Swimmin' Surfer Biter/Sing Along to the Swimmin' Surfer Biter	1963	$50

GRUNIONS, THE
JOCKO
Number	Title	Yr	NM
❏ 505	Surfin' Psycho/Big Noise from Winnetka	1963	$60

GTR
Also see YES; GENESIS.
ARISTA
Number	Title	Yr	NM
❏ 9512	The Hunter/Sketches in the Sun	1986	$3
❏ 9512 [PS]	The Hunter/Sketches in the Sun	1986	$3
❏ 9470	When the Heart Rules the Mind/Reach Out (Never Say No)	1986	$3
❏ 9470 [PS]	When the Heart Rules the Mind/Reach Out (Never Say No)	1986	$3

GUADALCANAL DIARY
ELEKTRA
Number	Title	Yr	NM
❏ 69316	Always Saturday/Kiss of Fire	1989	$4
❏ 69316 [PS]	Always Saturday/Kiss of Fire	1989	$6

GUARALDI, VINCE
FANTASY
Number	Title	Yr	NM
❏ 563	Cast Your Fate to the Wind/Samba de Orpheus	1962	$10
❏ 608	Christmas Time Is Here/What Child Is This	1966	$30
❏ 580	Days of Wine and Roses/(B-side unknown)	1963	$12
❏ 606	Humbly I Adore Thee/Theme to Grace	1965	$10
❏ 613	I'm a Loser/Favela	1966	$10
❏ 593	Linus & Lucy/Oh, Good Grief	1964	$30
❏ 571	Mr. Lucky/Treat Street	1963	$10

ORIGINAL JAZZ CLASSICS
Number	Title	Yr	NM
❏ 18001	Cast Your Fate to the Wind/Mr. Lucky	1984	$5
— Stereo reissue			

GUARD, DAVE, AND THE WHISKEYHILL SINGERS
CAPITOL
Number	Title	Yr	NM
❏ 4787	Plane Wreck at Los Gatos/Ride On, Railroad Bill	1962	$10

GUERRERO, LALO
L&M
Number	Title	Yr	NM
❏ 1004	Pancho Claus/Christmas In Mexico	1956	$30
❏ 1000	Pancho Claus/Pound Dog (Hound Dog)	1956	$50

GUESS WHO, THE
Also see CHAD ALLAN; RANDY BACHMAN; BURTON CUMMINGS.
AMY
Number	Title	Yr	NM
❏ 967	And She's Mine/All Right	1966	$30
— The existence of stock copies of this record has been questioned			
❏ 976	His Girl/It's My Pride	1967	$40
— Price is for stock copy; promos go for less			

FONTANA
Number	Title	Yr	NM
❏ 1597	This Time Long Ago/There's No Getting Away from It	1967	$40

HILLTAK
Number	Title	Yr	NM
❏ 7803	C'mon Little Mama/Moon Wave Maker	1979	$6
❏ 7807	Sweet Young Thing/It's Getting Pretty Bad	1979	$6

RCA VICTOR
Number	Title	Yr	NM
❏ 74-0458	Albert Flasher/Broken	1971	$5
❏ 74-0325	American Woman/No Sugar Tonight	1970	$5
❏ APBO-0324	Clap for the Wolfman/Road Food	1974	$5
❏ GB-10161	Clap for the Wolfman/Star Baby	1975	$4
— Gold Standard Series			
❏ PB-10075	Dancin' Fool/Seems Like I Can't Live With You, But I Can't Live Without You	1974	$5
❏ PB-10360	Dreams/Rosanne	1975	$5
❏ 74-0880	Follow Your Daughter Home/Bye Bye Babe	1973	$5
❏ SPS-45-223 [DJ]	Friends of Mine (Part 1)/Friends of Mine (Part 2)	1969	$15
❏ 74-0708	Guns, Guns, Guns/Heaven Only Moved Once Yesterday	1972	$5
❏ 74-0367	Hand Me Down World/Runnin' Down the Street	1970	$5
❏ 74-0414	Hang On to Your Life/Do You Miss Me, Darlin'?	1970	$5

Number	Title	Yr	NM
❑ 74-0414 [PS]	Hang On to Your Life/Do You Miss Me, Darlin'?	1970	$30
❑ 74-0659	Heartbroken Bopper/ Arrividerci Girl	1972	$5
❑ 74-0195	Laughing/Undun	1969	$6
❑ 74-0977	Lie Down/Glamour Boy	1973	$5
❑ PB-10216	Loves Me Like a Brother/ Hoe Down Time	1975	$5
❑ 74-0388	Share the Land/Bus Rider	1970	$5
❑ 74-0388 [PS]	Share the Land/Bus Rider	1970	$10
❑ PB-10716	Silver Bird/Runnin' Down the Street	1976	$15
❑ 74-0578	Sour Suite/Life in the Bloodstream	1971	$5
❑ APBO-0217	Star Baby/Musicione	1974	$5
❑ 74-0102	These Eyes/Lightfoot	1969	$6
❑ 74-0926	The Watcher/Orly	1973	$5
❑ PB-10410	When the Band Was Singin' (Shakin' All Over)/Women	1975	$6

SCEPTER

Number	Title	Yr	NM
❑ 12131	Believe Me/Baby Feelin'	1966	$30
❑ 12108	Hey Ho What You Do to Me/Goodnight Goodnight	1965	$20
❑ 12118	Hurting Each Other/ Baby's Birthday	1965	$30
❑ 12144	One Day/Clock on the Wall	1966	$30
❑ 1295	Shakin' All Over/ Monkey in a Cage	1965	$40

—B-side by the Discotays

| ❑ 1295 | Shakin' All Over/ Till We Kissed | 1965 | $20 |

GUIDES, THE

GUYDEN

Number	Title	Yr	NM
❑ 2023	How Long Must a Fool Go On/You Must Try	1959	$40

—Originally released under the name "The Swallows

GUILLOTEENS, THE

COLUMBIA

Number	Title	Yr	NM
❑ 44089	I Love That Girl/Dear Mrs. Applebee	1967	$15
❑ 43852	Wild Child/You Think You're Happy	1966	$20
❑ 43852 [PS]	Wild Child/You Think You're Happy	1966	$50

—Sleeve is promo only

HANNA-BARBERA

Number	Title	Yr	NM
❑ 451	Don't Let the Rain Get You Down/For My Own	1965	$20
❑ 451 [PS]	Don't Let the Rain Get You Down/For My Own	1965	$40
❑ 446	I Don't Believe/Hey You	1965	$20
❑ 486	I Sit and Cry/Crying All Over My Time	1966	$30

GUITAR, BILLY

DECCA

Number	Title	Yr	NM
❑ 30634	Here Comes the Night/ You Should Have Loved Her More	1958	$75

GUITAR, BONNIE

4 STAR

Number	Title	Yr	NM
❑ 1041	Honey on the Moon/ Lonely Eyes	1980	$5

—Number also listed as 1003. Which is correct? Or are both?

| ❑ 1006 | I Wanna Spend My Life with You/Maggie | 1975 | $5 |

DOLTON

Number	Title	Yr	NM
❑ 10	Candy Apple Red/Come to Me, I Love You	1959	$15
❑ 19	Candy Apple Red/Come to Me, I Love You	1960	$10

DOT

Number	Title	Yr	NM
❑ 17150	Almost Like Being with You/Leaves Are the Tears of Autumn	1968	$5
❑ 16919	Are You Sincere/ The Tallest Tree	1966	$6
❑ 15894	Baby Moon/Solitude	1959	$15
❑ 15550	Dark Moon/Big Mile	1957	$20
❑ 17097	Faded Love/I Believe in Love	1968	$5
❑ 15587	Half Your Heart/If You See My Love Dancing	1957	$15
❑ 15776	I Found You Out/If You'll Be the Teacher	1958	$15
❑ 16968	I'll Be Missing You (Under the Mistletoe)/ Blue Christmas	1966	$30
❑ 17276	I'll Pick Up My Heart/ That See Me Later Look	1969	$5
❑ 16811	I'm Living in Two Worlds/ Goodtime Charlie	1965	$6
❑ 17029	I Want My Baby/ Woman in Love	1967	$6
❑ 15678	Making Believe/I Saw Your Face in the Moon	1957	$15
❑ 17249	Perfect Strangers/I'll Meet You in Denver	1969	$5
❑ 15612	There's a New Moon Over My Shoulder/ Mister Fire Eyes	1957	$15

Number	Title	Yr	NM
❑ 17057	Wings of a Dove/ Stop the Sun	1967	$6
❑ 16872	Would You Believe/Get Your Life the Way You Want It	1966	$6

FABOR

Number	Title	Yr	NM
❑ 4017	Clinging Vine/ Dream Dreamers	1956	$30
❑ 4018	Dark Moon/Big Mile	1957	$50
❑ 4013	If You See My Love Dancing/ Hello, Hello, Please Answer	1956	$30

JERDEN

Number	Title	Yr	NM
❑ 707	There'll Be No Teardrops Tonight/The Fool	1963	$10

MCA

Number	Title	Yr	NM
❑ 40306	From This Moment On/Shine	1974	$4
❑ 40192	The Bed I Love In/ Wishing Star	1974	$4

PLAYBACK

Number	Title	Yr	NM
❑ 1341	Lonely Eyes/Honey on the Moon	1989	$6
❑ 1309	Paradise/Wine from My Table	1988	$6
❑ 75714	Still the Same/If You Were Here	1989	$5
❑ 1304	Things Songs Are Made Of/Here We Lie	1988	$6
❑ 1326	What Can I Say/ What's In It for Me	1989	$6

RADIO

Number	Title	Yr	NM
❑ 101	Please, My Love/Love Is Over, Love Is Done	1958	$15
❑ 110	Shanty Boat/Only the Moon Man Knows	1958	$15

RCA VICTOR

Number	Title	Yr	NM
❑ 47-8063	Broken Hearted Girl/ Who Is She	1962	$10
❑ 47-7951	I'll Step Down/Tell Her Bye	1961	$10
❑ 37-7951	I'll Step Down/Tell Her Bye	1961	$30

—Compact Single 33"; small hole, plays at 33 1/3 rpm

GUITAR SLIM

ATCO

Number	Title	Yr	NM
❑ 6120	If I Had My Life to Live Over/ When There's No Way Out	1958	$40
❑ 6097	It Hurts to Love Someone/ If I Should Lose You	1957	$40
❑ 6108	I Won't Mind at All/Hello, How Ya' Been, Goodbye	1958	$40
❑ 6072	Oh Yeah/Down Through the Years	1956	$50

IMPERIAL

Number	Title	Yr	NM
❑ 5278	Woman Troubles/ Cryin' in the Mornin'	1954	$70

SPECIALTY

Number	Title	Yr	NM
❑ 527	Later for You Baby/ Troubles Don't Last	1954	$30
❑ 542	Stand By Me/Our Only Child	1955	$30
❑ 490	Story of My Life/A Letter to My Girl Friend	1954	$50
❑ 536	Sufferin' Mind/ Twenty-Five Lies	1955	$30
❑ 569	Sumthin' to Remember Me By/You Give Me Nothin' But the Blues	1956	$30
❑ 482	The Things That I Used to Do/Well, I Done Get Over It	1954	$60
❑ 557	Think It Over/Quicksand	1955	$30

GUITARS, INC.

HAMILTON

Number	Title	Yr	NM
❑ 50035	Little Toy/Holiday Love	1960	$30

GULLIVER

With DARYL HALL. John Oates joined later, but is not on these records.

ELEKTRA

Number	Title	Yr	NM
❑ 45689	Angelina/Every Day's a Lovely Day	1970	$8
❑ 45698	A Truly Good Song/Every Day's a Lovely Day	1970	$8

GUM DROPS, THE

CORAL

Number	Title	Yr	NM
❑ 62102	I Spoke Too Soon/Sie Tu (It's You, It's You)	1959	$20
❑ 62138	It Happens Every Day/ They Wake Me	1959	$20
❑ 62003	My Own True Love/On the Wings of the Wind	1958	$20

KING

Number	Title	Yr	NM
❑ 5051	Ba-Bee Da Boat Is Leaving/Pigeon	1957	$30
❑ 1496	Gum Drop/Don't Take It So Hard	1955	$30
❑ 1499	I'll Wait for One More Train/ Don't Take It So Hard	1955	$30
❑ 4913	I Wonder and Wonder/I'll Follow You	1956	$30

GUN

EPIC

Number	Title	Yr	NM
❑ 10537	Don't Look Back/Hobo	1969	$12
❑ 10593	Drown Yourself in the River/Long Hair Wildman	1970	$12

GUNHILL ROAD

KAMA SUTRA

Number	Title	Yr	NM
❑ 569	Back When My Hair Was Short/We Can't Ride the Roller Coaster Anymore	1973	$6
❑ 562	Ford, De Soto, Cadillac/ (B-side unknown)	1972	$5
❑ 582	Ford, De Soto, Cadillac/Sailing	1973	$5
❑ 591	She Made a Man Out of Me/(B-side unknown)	1974	$5

MERCURY

Number	Title	Yr	NM
❑ 73232	42nd Street/(B-side unknown)	1971	$6

GUNN, J.W.

PRIMERO

Number	Title	Yr	NM
❑ 1013	Love Me Today, Love Me Forever/Bessie, Jane & I	1982	$6

GUNS N' ROSES

Also see VELVET REVOLVER.

GEFFEN

Number	Title	Yr	NM
❑ 7-27570	Paradise City/ Move to the City	1989	$4
❑ 7-27570 [PS]	Paradise City/ Move to the City	1989	$4
❑ 7-22996	Patience/Rocket Queen	1989	$4
❑ 7-22996 [PS]	Patience/Rocket Queen	1989	$4
❑ 7-27963	Sweet Child O' Mine/ It's So Easy	1988	$4
❑ 7-27963 [PS]	Sweet Child O' Mine/ It's So Easy	1988	$4
❑ 7-21901	Sweet Child O' Mine/ Welcome to the Jungle	1989	$3

—Back to Back Hits" series

❑ 7-27759	Welcome to the Jungle/ Mr. Brownstone	1988	$4
❑ 7-27759 [PS]	Welcome to the Jungle/ Mr. Brownstone	1988	$4
❑ PRO-S-3094 [DJ]	Welcome to the Jungle (same on both sides)	1987	$10
❑ PRO-S-3094 [PS]	Welcome to the Jungle (same on both sides)	1987	$30

—Promo-only "Don't Report This Record" sleeve

GUNTER, ARTHUR

EXCELLO

Number	Title	Yr	NM
❑ 2125	Baby Can't You See/You're Always on My Mind	1958	$30
❑ 2047	Baby Let's Play House/ Blues After Hours	1954	$120
❑ 2073	Baby You Better Listen/ Trouble with My Baby	1955	$40
❑ 2147	Crazy Me/Don't Leave Me Now	1959	$30
❑ 2084	Hear My Plea Baby/ Love Has Got Me	1956	$40
❑ 2058	Honey Babe/No Happy Home	1955	$70
❑ 2191	Little Blue Jeans/Mind Your Own Business Babe	1960	$30
❑ 2137	Ludella/We're Gonna Shake	1959	$30
❑ 2201	My Heart's Always Lonesome/I'm Fallin', Love's Got Me	1961	$30
❑ 2053	She's Mine, All Mine/You Are Doin' Me Wrong	1955	$70

GUNTER, CORNEL

ABC-PARAMOUNT

Number	Title	Yr	NM
❑ 9698	She Loves to Rock/ In Self Defense	1956	$50

—As "Cornel Gunter and the Flairs

CHALLENGE

Number	Title	Yr	NM
❑ 59281	If I Had the Key to Your Heart/Wishful	1965	$10

EAGLE

Number	Title	Yr	NM
❑ 301	Baby Come Home/I Want You Madly	1957	$40

LIBERTY

Number	Title	Yr	NM
❑ 55096	If We Should Meet Again/ Neighborhood Dance	1957	$30

LOMA

Number	Title	Yr	NM
❑ 705	I'm Sad/One Thing	1956	$125

—The Loma singles credit "The Ermines," and may or may not mention Gunter.

| ❑ 701 | True Love/Peek, Peek-a-Boo | 1955 | $125 |

WARNER BROS.

Number	Title	Yr	NM
❑ 5292	It Ain't No Use/In a Dream of Love	1962	$15
❑ 5266	Lieft Me Up Angel/ Hope of Sand	1962	$15

Number	Title	Yr	NM

GUNTER, HARDROCK
DECCA

Number	Title	Yr	NM
❑ 9-46300	Boogie Woogie on a Saturday Night/Honky Tonk	1951	$50
❑ 9-46367	Dixieland Boogie/If I Could Only Live My Dreams	1951	$30
❑ 9-46383	Hesitation Boogie/ Don't You Agree	1951	$30
❑ 9-46350	I've Done Gone Hog Wild/I Believe That Mountain Music	1951	$30
❑ 9-46401	Silver and Gold/Senator from Tennessee	1952	$30
❑ 9-46363	Sixty Minute Man/ Tennessee Blues	1951	$30

KING

❑ 4858	Turn the Other Cheek/ Before My Time	1955	$30

MGM

❑ K-11520	Like the Lovers Do/ Naptown, Indiana	1953	$30
❑ K-11596	Sunday Angel/Where Have You Been	1953	$30

SUN

❑ 201	Fallen Angel/Gonna Dance All Night	1954	$2000

GUNTER, SHIRLEY
FLAIR

❑ 1027	Found Some Good Lovin'/ Strange Romance	1954	$40
❑ 1076	How Can I Tell You/ Ipsy Gypsy Ooh	1955	$70
— With the Flairs			
❑ 1050	Oop Shoop/It's You	1955	$40
❑ 1020	Send Him Back/ Since I Fell for You	1953	$50
❑ 1070	That's the Way I Like It/ Gimme, Gimme, Gimme	1955	$40
❑ 1065	What Difference Does It Make/Baby I Love You So	1955	$40

MODERN

❑ 1001	Fortune in Love/Just Got Rid of a Heartache	1956	$30
— With the Flairs			
❑ 1011	I'm So Sorry/I've Been Searching	1956	$30
❑ 979	Please Tell Me/Come On	1956	$30

TANGERINE

❑ 949	Stuck Up/You Let My Love Grow Cold	1965	$60

TENDER

❑ 503	Believe Me/Crazy Little Baby	1958	$50

GURLEY, RANDY
ABC

❑ 12392	True Love Ways/I'll Never Get Over Loving You	1978	$4

ABC DOT

❑ 17728	Heartbreaker/Louisville	1977	$5

RCA

❑ PB-11611	Don't Treat Me Like a Stranger/Every Night	1979	$4
❑ PB-11726	If I Ever/How Long	1979	$4

GURUS, THE
UNITED ARTISTS

❑ 50089	Come Girl/Blue Snow Night	1966	$15
❑ 50089 [PS]	Come Girl/Blue Snow Night	1966	$30
❑ 50140	It Just Won't Be That Way/Everybody's Got to Be Alone Sometime	1967	$15

GUTHRIE, ARLO
REPRISE

❑ 0877	Alice's Rock & Roll Restaurant/Coming Into Los Angeles	1969	$15
❑ 1158	A Week on the Rag/ Gypsy Dave	1973	$5
❑ 0951	Gabriel's Mother's Hiway/ Ballad #16 Blues	1970	$8
❑ 1376	Grocery Blues/Guabi, Guabi	1976	$4
❑ 1388	Massachusetts/My Love	1977	$4
❑ 0644	Motorcycle Song/ Now and Then	1967	$15
❑ 0793	Motorcycle Song (Part 1)/ Motorcycle Song (Part 2)	1968	$15
❑ PRO304 [DJ]	Motorcycle Song/The Pause of Mr. Claus	1970	$30
❑ 1363	Patriot's Dream/ Ocean Crossing	1976	$4
❑ 0994	The Ballad of Tricky Fred/ Shackles and Chains	1971	$6
❑ 1103	The City of New Orleans/ Days Are Short	1972	$6

WARNER BROS.

Number	Title	Yr	NM
❑ 49889	Oklahoma Nights/ Power of Love	1981	$4
❑ 49796	Slow Boat/If I Could Only Touch Your Life	1981	$4
❑ 49037	Wedding Song/Prologue	1979	$4

GUTHRIE, JACK
CAPITOL

❑ F2128	Oklahoma Hills/ Oakie Boogie	1952	$50

CAPITOL STARLINE

❑ 6085	Oklahoma Hills/ Oakie Boogie	1966	$10
— Originals on green swirl label			

GUY, ART
VALIANT

❑ 762	Where You Gonna Go/ Teenage Millionaire	1967	$40

GUY, BOB
DONNA

❑ 1380	Letter from Jeepers/ Dear Jeepers	1963	$125

GUY, BROWLEY, AND THE SKYSCRAPERS
CHECKER

❑ 779	Watermelon Man/You Look Good to Me	1954	$300
— Black vinyl			
❑ 779	Watermelon Man/You Look Good to Me	1954	$750
— Red vinyl			

GUY, BUDDY
ARTISTIC

❑ 1501	Sit and Cry/Try to Quit You Baby	1958	$50

CHESS

❑ 2022	Gonna Keep It to Myself/Suffer	1967	$20
❑ 1753	I Got My Eyes on You/The First Time I Met the Blues	1960	$40
❑ 1936	Leave My Girl Alone/ Crazy Music	1965	$30
❑ 1784	Let Me Love You Baby/ Ten Years Ago	1961	$30
❑ 1974	My Mother/Mother-in-Law Blues	1966	$30
❑ 1899	My Time After a While/I Dig Your Wig	1964	$30
❑ 2067	She Suits Me to a Tee/ Buddy's Groove	1969	$20
❑ 1812	Stone Crazy/Skippin'	1962	$30
❑ 1759	Stop Around/Broken Hearted Blues	1960	$30
❑ 1838	When My Left Eye Jumps/ My Treasure Untold	1962	$30

VANGUARD

❑ 35060	Sweet Little Angel/Mary Had a Little Lamb	1968	$15

GUYTON, HOWARD
VERVE

❑ 10386	I Watched You Slowly Slip Away/I Got My Own Thing Going	1966	$125

GUYTONES, THE
DELUXE

❑ 6163	Baby, I Don't Care/ Young Dreamer	1958	$70
❑ 6159	Hunky Dory/This Is Love	1958	$100
❑ 6152	She's Mine/Not Wanted	1957	$100
❑ 6169	Tell Me (How Was I to Know)/Your Heart's Bigger Than Mine	1958	$70

GYPSIES, THE
ATLAS

❑ 1073	Why/Young Girl to Calypso	1957	$100

GROOVE

❑ 0117	One, Two, Three, Go/I'm Good to You Baby	1955	$30

OLD TOWN

❑ 1168	Blue Bird/Hey There Hey There	1964	$60
❑ 1184	It's a Woman's World/ They're Having a Party	1965	$300
❑ 1193	Oh I Wonder Why/ Diamonds, Rubies, Gold and Fame	1966	$50

H

H.P. LOVECRAFT
MERCURY

Number	Title	Yr	NM
❑ 73698	Flight/I Feel Better	1975	$6
—As "Lovecraft			
❑ 73707	We Love You (Whoever You Are)/Ain't Gettin' Home	1975	$6
—As "Lovecraft			

PHILIPS

❑ 40464	Anyway That You Want Me/It's All Over for You	1967	$15
❑ 40578	Blue Jack of Diamonds/ Keeper of the Keys	1968	$15
❑ 40506	The White Ship (Part 1)/ The White Ship (Part 2)	1967	$15
❑ 40491	Wayfaring Stranger/ The Time Machine	1967	$15
❑ 40491 [PS]	Wayfaring Stranger/ The Time Machine	1967	$30

REPRISE

❑ 0996	We Can All Have It Together/Will I Know When My Time Comes	1971	$8
—As "Lovecraft			

HACKAMORE BRICK
KAMA SUTRA

❑ 521	Searchin'/Radio	1971	$6

HACKBERRY RAMBLERS, THE
ARHOOLIE

❑ 503	Turtle Tail/Madame Sustin	1963	$30

HACKERT, VALINE
BRUNSWICK

❑ 55151	Billy Boy/Show Me How	1959	$200

HACKETT, BOBBY
EPIC

❑ 5-26061 [PS]	The Great Music of Henry Mancini	1963	$12
❑ 5-26061 [S]	Theme from "Mr. Lucky"/ Baby Elephant Walk/Days of Wine and Roses//Theme from "Peter Gunn"/Moon River/Song About Love	1963	$10
—33 1/3 rpm, small hole. "For Jukebox Use Only			

HACKETT, BUDDY
CORAL

❑ 61921	Dear Santa Claus/Funny Li'l Duck (That Just Says Moo)	1957	$20

HADAWAY, HENRY, ORCHESTRA AND CHORUS
RCA

❑ JH-13378 [DJ]	Turned On Winter Medley (same on both sides)	1982	$4

HADDOCK, DURWOOD
CAPRICE

❑ 2004	Angel in an Apron/ Truck Driver's Turn	1974	$6
❑ 2008	It Sure Looks Good on You/(B-side unknown)	1975	$6

COUNTRY INT'L.

❑ 140	Low Down Time/ Everynight Sensation	1979	$5
❑ 132	The Perfect Love Song/You Loved Me So Good (That's Why I Miss You So Bad)	1978	$5

D

❑ 1228	Start All Over/How Lonesome Can I Get	1961	$30

EAGLE INT'L.

❑ 1162	Baby One More Time/ (B-side unknown)	1981	$5
❑ 1148	Everynight Sensation/ Low Down Time	1978	$5
❑ 1161	It Sure Looks Good on You/(B-side unknown)	1980	$5
❑ 1137	Low Down Time/She Gave Me Good Love	1977	$5
❑ 1144	The Perfect Love Song/You Loved Me So Good (That's Why I Miss You So Bad)	1978	$5

METROMEDIA

❑ 136	California Hillbilly Bar/When the Swelling Goes Down	1969	$8
❑ 200	East Bourbon Street/ Odds and Ends	1970	$8
❑ 179	The Thought of Losing You/I Gotta Get Drunk (And I Sure Do Dread It)	1970	$8

MONUMENT

❑ 1080	I'm Gonna Quit Drinking/Wait Till I Get My Hands on You	1968	$8
❑ 1112	Mac the Merchant/The Newest Thing in Night Life	1968	$8

UNITED ARTISTS

❑ 506	Big Night at My House/ Funny Fair	1962	$20

Number	Title	Yr	NM

HADLEY, JIM
BUDDY
❏ 125	Blues of a Truck Driving Man/Adorable Baby	1960	$40
❏ 119	Everybody's Somebody's Fool/Just Dreaming	1959	$50
❏ 115	Honky Tonk Girl/Foolish Ways	1958	$50
❏ 117	Midnight Train/I Remember	1959	$120
❏ 126	Out of a Blue Clear Sky/Night Bird	1960	$40
❏ 114	Wanted/My Broken Heart	1958	$50

HAGAN, SAMMY, AND THE VISCOUNTS
CAPITOL
❏ F-3772	Out of Your Heart/Shoochie Poochie	1957	$50
❏ F-3885	Tail Light/Snuggle Bunny	1958	$40
❏ F-3818	Wild Bird/Don't Cry	1957	$50

HAGAR, SAMMY
Also see MONTROSE; VAN HALEN; CHICKENFOOT.
CAPITOL
❏ 4388	Catch the Wind/Red	1977	$5
❏ 4411	Cruisin' and Boozin'/Love Has Found Me	1977	$5
❏ 4825	Growing Pains/Straight to the Top	1980	$4
❏ 4893	Heartbeat/Miles from Boredom	1980	$4
❏ 4596	I've Done Everything for You/Someone Out There	1978	$5
❏ 4757	Plain Jane/Wounded in Love	1979	$5
❏ 4699	(Sittin' On) The Dock of the Bay/I've Done Everything for You	1979	$5
❏ 4550	Turn Up the Music/Hey Boys	1978	$5

COLUMBIA
❏ 06647	Winner Takes It All/The Fight	1987	$3

— B-side by Giorgio Moroder

❏ 06647 [PS]	Winner Takes It All/The Fight	1987	$4

GEFFEN
❏ 28185	Eagles Fly/Hands and Knees	1987	$3
❏ 28185 [PS]	Eagles Fly/Hands and Knees	1987	$4
❏ 29718	Fast Times At Ridgemont High/Never Give Up	1983	$3
❏ 28314	Give to Live/When the Hammer Falls	1987	$3
❏ 28314 [PS]	Give to Live/When the Hammer Falls	1987	$3
❏ 29173	I Can't Drive 55/Dick in the Dirt	1984	$3
❏ 29173 [PS]	I Can't Drive 55/Dick in the Dirt	1984	$4
❏ 49881	I'll Fall in Love Again/Satisfied	1981	$3
❏ 29090	I'll Only Fall in Love Again/Only the Young	1985	$4

— B-side by Journey

❏ 50059	Piece of My Heart/Sweet Hitchhiker	1982	$3
❏ 29246	Two Sides of Love/Burnin' Down the City	1984	$5

— Red vinyl

❏ 29246 [PS]	Two Sides of Love/Burnin' Down the City	1984	$5

HAGER, CHARLIE
KILLER
❏ 114	Men with Broken Hearts/(B-side unknown)	1988	$6

HAGERS, THE
BARNABY
❏ 5016	A Fool Such As I/Summer Only Needs Its Autumn	1973	$6
❏ 2056	Ain't No Sunshine/Mammy Blue	1972	$6
❏ 5002	I Just Don't Feel at Home/Summer Only Needs Its Autumn	1972	$6
❏ 2062	The Cost of Love Is Getting Higher/Cynthia Daye	1972	$6

ELEKTRA
❏ 45219	Cherry Pie/All Your Love	1974	$4
❏ 45239	Heartaches by the Number/Take Me	1975	$4
❏ 45266	Hot Lips/Old Fashioned Girl	1975	$4
❏ 45209	Love My Life Away/You Can't Get There from Here	1974	$4

HAGGARD, MERLE, AND JANIE FRICKE
EPIC
❏ 04663	A Place to Fall Apart/All I Want to Do Is Sing My Song	1984	$3

HAGGARD, MERLE, AND GEORGE JONES
EPIC
❏ 03405	C.C. Waterback/After I Sing All My Songs	1982	$3

HAGGARD, MERLE, AND WILLIE NELSON
EPIC
❏ 34-07400	If I Could Only Fly/Without You on My Side	1987	$3
❏ 03842	Pancho and Lefty/Opportunity to Cry	1983	$4

— As "Willie Nelson and Merle Haggard"

HAGGARD, MERLE, AND LEONA WILLIAMS
MCA
❏ 40962	The Bull and the Beaver/I'm Gettin' High	1978	$4

MERCURY
❏ 880139-7	Don't Ever Let Your Lover Sleep Alone/It's Cold in California	1984	$4
❏ 814359-7	Waltz Across Texas/Waitin' on the Good Life to Come	1983	$3
❏ 812214-7	We're Strangers Again/Sally Let Your Bangs Hang Down	1983	$3

HAGGARD, MERLE
CAPITOL
❏ 4027	Always Wanting You/I've Got a Yearning	1975	$5
❏ 4477	A Workin' Man Can't Get Nowhere Today/Blues Stay Away from Me	1977	$5
❏ 5931	Branded Man/You Don't Have Very Far to Go	1967	$8
❏ 5931 [PS]	Branded Man/You Don't Have Very Far to Go	1967	$8
❏ 3222	Carolyn/When the Feelin' Goes Away	1971	$6
❏ 4326	Cherokee Maiden/What Have You Got Planned Tonight Diana	1976	$5
❏ 3198	Daddy Frank (The Guitar Man)/My Heart Would Know	1971	$6
❏ 3641	Everybody's Had the Blues/Nobody Knows I'm Hurtin'	1973	$5
❏ 3294	Grandma Harp/Turnin' Off a Memory	1972	$6
❏ 4267	Here Comes the Freedom Train/I Won't Give Up My Train	1976	$5
❏ 2383	Hungry Eyes/California Blues	1969	$8
❏ 2383 [PS]	Hungry Eyes/California Blues	1969	$8
❏ 2891	I Can't Be Myself/Sidewalks of Chicago	1970	$8
❏ 2891 [PS]	I Can't Be Myself/Sidewalks of Chicago	1970	$8
❏ 3746	If We Make It Through December/Bobby Wants a Puppy Dog for Christmas	1973	$5
❏ 5803	I'm a Lonesome Fugitive/Someone Told My Story	1967	$8

— Retitled A-side

❏ 5460	I'm Gonna Break Every Heart I Can/Falling for You	1965	$10
❏ 2289	I Take a Lot of Pride in What I Am/Keep Me from Cryin' Today	1968	$8
❏ 2289 [PS]	I Take a Lot of Pride in What I Am/Keep Me from Cryin' Today	1968	$8
❏ 5844 [PS]	I Threw Away the Rose/Loneliness Is Eating Me Alive	1967	$8
❏ 5844	I Threw Away the Rose/Loneliness Is Eating Me Alive	1967	$8
❏ 4141	It's All in the Movies/Living with the Shades Pulled Down	1975	$5
❏ 3419	It's Not Love (But It's Not Bad)/My Woman Keeps Lovin' Her Man	1972	$6
❏ 3488	I Wonder If They Ever Think of Me/I Forget You Every Day	1972	$6
❏ 2219 [PS]	Mama Tried/You'll Never Love Me Now	1968	$8
❏ 2219	Mama Tried/You'll Never Love Me Now	1968	$8
❏ 4085	Movin' On/Here in Frisco	1975	$5
❏ 2626	Okie from Muskogee/If I Had Left It Up to You	1969	$8
❏ 2626 [PS]	Okie from Muskogee/If I Had Left It Up to You	1969	$8
❏ 3900	Old Man from the Mountain/Holding Things Together	1974	$5
❏ 3989	Santa Claus and Popcorn/If We Make It Through December	1974	$5
❏ 2017 [PS]	Sing Me Back Home/Good Times	1967	$8

Number	Title	Yr	NM
❏ 2017	Sing Me Back Home/Good Times	1967	$8
❏ 3024	Soldier's Last Letter/The Farmer's Daughter	1971	$6
❏ 3024 [PS]	Soldier's Last Letter/The Farmer's Daughter	1971	$8
❏ 3112	Someday We'll Look Back/It's Great to Be Alive	1971	$6
❏ 2778	Street Singer/Mexican Rose	1970	$8
❏ 5600	Swinging Doors/The Girl Turned Ripe	1966	$10
❏ 5704	The Bottle Let Me Down/The Longer You Wait	1966	$12
❏ 3552	The Emptiest Arms in the World/Radiator Man from Waco	1973	$5
❏ 2719	The Fightin' Side of Me/Every Fool Has a Rainbow	1970	$8
❏ 2719 [PS]	The Fightin' Side of Me/Every Fool Has a Rainbow	1970	$8
❏ 5803	The Fugitive/Someone Told My Story	1966	$15
❏ 2123	The Legend of Bonnie and Clyde/I Started Loving You Again	1968	$8
❏ 4636	The Way It Was in '51/Moanin' the Blues	1978	$5
❏ 3830	Things Aren't Funny Anymore/Honky Tonk Night Time Man	1974	$5
❏ 5523	This Town's Not Big Enough/Shade Tree	1965	$10
❏ 2503	Workin' Man Blues/Silver Wings	1969	$8
❏ 2503 [PS]	Workin' Man Blues/Silver Wings	1969	$8

ELEKTRA
❏ 46634	Bar Room Buddies/The Not So Great Train Robbery	1980	$4

— With Clint Eastwood

❏ 46634 [PS]	Bar Room Buddies/The Not So Great Train Robbery	1980	$5

EPIC
❏ 68598	5:01 Blues/Man from Another Time	1989	$3
❏ 68979	A Better Love Next Time/Losin' in Las Vegas	1989	$3
❏ 06097	A Friend in California/Mama's Prayers	1986	$3
❏ 07036	Almost Persuaded/Love Don't Hurt Everytime	1987	$3
❏ 05659	Amber Waves of Grain/I Wish Things Were Simple Again	1985	$3
❏ 05734	American Waltz/The Farmer's Daughter	1985	$3
❏ 02894	Are the Good Times Really Over (I Wish a Buck Was Still Silver)/I Always Get Lucky with You	1982	$3
❏ 02686	Big City/I Think I'm Gonna Live Forever	1981	$3
❏ 07754	Chill Factor/Thanking the Good Lord	1988	$3
❏ 03365	Going Where the Lonely Go	1982	$8

— One-sided budget release

❏ 03315	Going Where the Lonely Go/Someday You're Gonna Need Your Friends Again	1982	$3
❏ 03406	Goin' Home for Christmas/If We Make It Through December	1982	$4
❏ 73076	If You Want to Be My Woman/Someday We'll Know	1989	$3
❏ 05782	I Had a Beautiful Time/This Time I Really Do	1986	$3
❏ 04512	Let's Chase Each Other Around the Room/All I Want to Do Is Sing My Song	1984	$3
❏ 02504	My Favorite Memory/Texas Fiddle Song	1981	$3
❏ 06344	Out Among the Stars/Suzie	1986	$3
❏ AE71777 [DJ]	Santa Claus and Popcorn/Grandma's Homemade Christmas Card	1982	$5
❏ 04402	Someday When Things Are Good/If You Hated Me	1984	$3
❏ 04226	That's the Way Love Goes/Don't Seem Like We've Been Together All Our Lives	1983	$3
❏ 07631	Twinkle, Twinkle, Lucky Star/I Don't Have Any Love Around	1987	$3
❏ 07944	We Never Touch at All/Man from Another Time	1988	$3
❏ 04006	What Am I Gonna Do (With the Rest of My Life)/I Think I'll Stay	1983	$3

MCA
❏ 52020	Dealing with the Devil/Fiddle Breakdown	1982	$4
❏ 40804	From Graceland to the Promised Land/Are You Lonesome Tonight	1977	$6
❏ 41168	If We Make It Through December/The Fightin' Side of Me	1979	$5
❏ 40700	If We're Not Back in Love By Monday/I Think It's Gone Forever	1977	$4

Number	Title	Yr	NM
❏ 40869	I'm Always on a Mountain When I Fall/The Life of a Rodeo Cowboy	1978	$4
❏ 51014	I Think I'll Just Stay Here and Drink/Back to the Barrooms	1980	$4
❏ 52276	It's All in the Game/New Cocaine Blues	1983	$3
❏ 40936	It's Been a Great Afternoon/Love Me When You Can	1978	$4
❏ 51048	Leonard/Our Paths May Never Cross	1981	$4
❏ 52595	Make-Up and Faded Blue Jeans/Love Me When You Can	1985	$3
❏ 41255	Misery and Gin/No One to Sing For	1980	$4
❏ 41255 [PS]	Misery and Gin/No One to Sing For	1980	$5
❏ 41112	My Own Kind of Hat/Heaven Was a Drink of Wine	1979	$4
❏ 41200	The Way I Am/Wake Up	1980	$4

TALLY

Number	Title	Yr	NM
❏ 179	(My Friends Are Gonna Be) Strangers/Please Mr. D.J.	1964	$20
❏ 178	Sam Hill/You Don't Have Far to Go	1964	$20
❏ 155	Sing a Sad Song/You Don't Even Try	1963	$20
❏ 152	Singin' My Heart Out/Skid Row	1963	$30

7-Inch Extended Plays

CAPITOL

Number	Title	Yr	NM
❏ SU-384	Hobo Bill's Last Ride/No Hard Times/Silver Wings//Billy Overcame His Size/Blue Rock/White Line Fever	1970	$20

— Jukebox issue; small hole, plays at 33 1/3 rpm

Number	Title	Yr	NM
❏ SU-2702 [PS]	I'm a Lonesome Fugitive/	1967	$25
❏ SU-2702	I'm a Lonesome Fugitive/Skid Row/If You Want to Be My Woman//Someone Told My Story/My Rough and Rowdy Ways/Mixed Up Mess of a Heart	1967	$25

— Jukebox issue; small hole, plays at 33 1/3 rpm

Number	Title	Yr	NM
❏ SU-384 [PS]	Okie from Muskogee	1970	$20

HAGGETT, JIMMY

CAPROCK

Number	Title	Yr	NM
❏ 107	All I Have Is You/Without You	1958	$50

METEOR

Number	Title	Yr	NM
❏ 5043	Gonna Shut You Off Baby/Tell Her True	1957	$200

HAIG, RONNIE

ABC-PARAMOUNT

Number	Title	Yr	NM
❏ 9912	Don't You Hear Me Calling, Baby/Traveler of Love	1958	$40
❏ 10209	Don't You Hear Me Calling, Baby/Traveler of Love	1961	$100

NOTE

Number	Title	Yr	NM
❏ 10010	Don't You Hear Me Calling, Baby/Traveler of Love	1958	$40

HAINES, CONNIE

MOTOWN

Number	Title	Yr	NM
❏ 1092	What's Easy for Two Is Hard for One/Walk in Silence	1966	$50

HAIRCUT ONE HUNDRED

ARISTA

Number	Title	Yr	NM
❏ 0708 [DJ]	Favourite Shirts (Boy Meets Girl) (same on both sides)	1982	$4

— Stock copy may not exist

Number	Title	Yr	NM
❏ 0672	Love Plus One/Favourite Shirts (Boy Meets Girl)	1982	$4

HAIRCUTS, THE

PARKWAY

Number	Title	Yr	NM
❏ 899	She Loves You/Love Me Do	1964	$30
❏ 899 [PS]	She Loves You/Love Me Do	1964	$50

HAIRSTON, BROTHER WILL

JVB

Number	Title	Yr	NM
❏ 44	The Alabama Bus (Part 1)/The Alabama Bus (Part 2)	1956	$300

HAIRSTON, JACKIE

ATCO

Number	Title	Yr	NM
❏ 6464	Monkey on My Back/Hijack	1967	$30

HALEY, AMBROSE

MERCURY

Number	Title	Yr	NM
❏ 6346	Mammy o' Mine/Sweet Adeline	1951	$40

MGM

Number	Title	Yr	NM
❏ K11897	I Hurried Back/New Flame	1954	$30

Number	Title	Yr	NM
❏ K11678	Let's Take Our Troubles to Church/Why Can't You See Things My Way	1954	$30

HALEY, BILL, AND HIS COMETS

APT

Number	Title	Yr	NM
❏ 25087	Haley A-Go-Go/Tongue Tied Tony	1965	$30
❏ 25081	Stop, Look, and Listen/Burn That Candle	1965	$30

DECCA

Number	Title	Yr	NM
❏ 29713	Burn That Candle/Rock-a-Beatin' Boogie	1955	$30
❏ 30926	Caldonia/Shakey	1959	$30
❏ 30844	Charmaine/I Got a Woman	1959	$30
❏ 30741	Chiquita Linda/Whoa Mabel	1958	$30
❏ 30781	Corrine, Corrina/B.B. Betty	1958	$30
❏ 29317	Dim, Dim the Lights (I Want Some Atmosphere)/Happy Baby	1954	$50

— With lines on either side of "Decca"

Number	Title	Yr	NM
❏ 29317	Dim, Dim the Lights (I Want Some Atmosphere)/Happy Baby	1954	$30

— With star under "Decca"

Number	Title	Yr	NM
❏ 30148	Don't Knock the Rock/Choo Choo Ch'Boogie	1956	$30
❏ 30214	Forty Cups of Coffeee/Hook, Line and Sinker	1957	$30
❏ 29948	Hot Dog Buddy Buddy/Rockin' Through the Rye	1956	$30
❏ 30530	It's a Sin/Mary, Mary Lou	1957	$30
❏ 30530 [PS]	It's a Sin/Mary, Mary Lou	1957	$100
❏ 30681	Lean Jean/Don't Nobody Move	1958	$30
❏ 29418	Mambo Rock/Birth of the Boogie	1955	$30
❏ 31080	Music, Music, Music/Strictly Instrumental	1960	$30
❏ 29791	See You Later, Alligator/The Paper Boy (On Main Street, U.S.A.)	1956	$30
❏ 29204	Shake, Rattle and Roll/A.B.C. Boogie	1954	$50

— With lines on either side of "Decca"

Number	Title	Yr	NM
❏ 29204	Shake, Rattle and Roll/A.B.C. Boogie	1954	$30

— With star under "Decca"

Number	Title	Yr	NM
❏ 30592	Skinny Minnie/Sway with Me	1958	$40
❏ 31030	Skokiaan (South African Song)/Puerto Rican Peddler	1959	$30
❏ 30394	The Dipsy Doodle/Miss You	1957	$30
❏ 31649	The Green Door/Yeah, She's Evil	1964	$15
❏ 9-29124	(We're Gonna) Rock Around the Clock/Thirteen Women (And Only One Man in Town)	1954	$70

— With lines on either side of "Decca"

Number	Title	Yr	NM
❏ 9-29124	(We're Gonna) Rock Around the Clock/Thirteen Women (And Only One Man in Town)	1955	$30

— With star under "Decca"

ESSEX

Number	Title	Yr	NM
❏ 348	Chattanooga Choo Choo/Straight Jacket	1954	$50
❏ 321	Crazy Man, Crazy/Whatcha Gonna Do	1953	$70
❏ 332	Live It Up/Farewell, So Long, Goodbye	1953	$50
❏ 327	Pat-a-Cake/Fractured	1953	$50
❏ 374	Sundown Boogie/Jukebox Cannonball	1954	$80
❏ 340	Ten Little Indians/I'll Be True	1953	$50

GNP CRESCENDO

Number	Title	Yr	NM
❏ 475	I'm Walkin'/Crazy Man, Crazy	1974	$15

GONE

Number	Title	Yr	NM
❏ 5111	Spanish Twist/My Kind of Woman	1961	$30

HOLIDAY

Number	Title	Yr	NM
❏ 113	Sundown Boogie/Jukebox Cannonball	1951	$500

— As "Bill Haley and the Saddlemen"; the only Holiday single known to exist on a 45. Earlier Holiday singles only exist on 78s.

JANUS

Number	Title	Yr	NM
❏ 162	Travelin' Band/A Little Piece at a Time	1971	$15

KASEY

Number	Title	Yr	NM
❏ 7006	A.B.C. Boogie/Rock Around the Clock	1961	$30

— B-side by Phil Flowers

MCA

Number	Title	Yr	NM
❏ 60025	(We're Gonna) Rock Around the Clock/Thirteen Women (And Only One Man in Town)	1973	$5

— Reissue on black label with rainbow; made the Top 40 in 1974

NEWTOWN

Number	Title	Yr	NM
❏ 5024	Dance Around the Clock/What Can I Say After I Say I'm Sorry	1963	$30

Number	Title	Yr	NM
❏ 5013	Tenor Man/Up Goes My Love	1962	$30

UNITED ARTISTS

Number	Title	Yr	NM
❏ 50483	Ain't Love Funny, Ha Ha Ha/That's How I Got to Memphis	1969	$15

WARNER BROS.

Number	Title	Yr	NM
❏ 5145	Candy Kisses/Tamiami	1960	$30
❏ 5145 [DJ]	Candy Kisses/Tamiami	1960	$60

— Promo only on yellow vinyl

Number	Title	Yr	NM
❏ 5228	Flip, Flop and Fly/Honky Tonk	1961	$30
❏ 5154	Hawk/Chick Safari	1960	$30
❏ 5171	Let the Good Times Roll, Creole/So Right Tonight	1960	$30

7-Inch Extended Plays

CLAIRE

Number	Title	Yr	NM
❏ 4779	*All I Need Is Some More Lovin'/Trouble in Mind/Life of the Party/I Should Write a Song About You	1978	$20
❏ 4779 [PS]	Bill Haley and the Comets	1978	$20

DECCA

Number	Title	Yr	NM
❏ ED2564	*Me Rock-a-Hula/Wooden Shoe Rock/Oriental Rock/Rockin' Matilda	1957	$60
❏ ED2534	*Moon Over Miami/Ain't Misbehavin'/You Can't Stop Me from Dreaming/I'm Gonna Sit Right Down and Write Myself a Letter	1957	$60
❏ ED2533	*One Sweet Letter from You/Please Don't Talk About Me When I'm Gone/Apple Blossom Time/Somebody Else Is Taking My Place	1957	$60
❏ ED2576	*Piccadilly Rock/Vive La Rock & Roll/Rockin' Rollin' Schnitzlebank/Come Rock with Me	1957	$60
❏ ED2577	*Pretty Alouette/El Rocko/Rockin' Rita/Jamaican DJ	1957	$60
❏ ED2638 [M]	*Whoa Mabel!/Ida Sweet as Apple Cider/Eloise/Dinah	1958	$50
❏ ED 7-2638 [S]	*Whoa Mabel!/Ida Sweet as Apple Cider/Eloise/Dinah	1959	$100
❏ ED2670 [PS]	Bill Haley and His Comets	1959	$50
❏ ED 7-2670 [PS]	Bill Haley and His Comets	1959	$100
❏ ED2638 [PS]	Bill Haley's Chicks	1958	$50
❏ ED 7-2638 [PS]	Bill Haley's Chicks	1959	$100
❏ ED2416	Calling All Comets/Rockin' Through the Rye//Hook, Line and Sinker/Rudy's Rock	1956	$60
❏ ED2209 [PS]	Dim, Dim the Lights	1955	$75
❏ ED2209	Dim, Dim the Lights/Happy Baby//Birth of the Boogie/Mambo Rock	1955	$75
❏ ED2398 [PS]	He Digs RnR (Music for the Boyfriend)	1956	$60
❏ ED2418	Hey Then, There Now/Goofin' Around//Hot Dog Buddy Buddy/Tonight's the Night	1956	$60
❏ ED2398	See You Later Alligator/R-O-C-K//The Saints Rock 'n Roll/Burn That Candle	1956	$60
❏ ED2168 [PS]	Shake, Rattle and Roll	1954	$75
❏ ED2168	Shake, Rattle and Roll/A.B.C. Boogie//(We're Gonna) Rock Around the Clock/Thirteen Women (And Only One Man in Town)	1954	$75
❏ ED2671 [PS]	Strictly Instrumental	1959	$50
❏ ED 7-2671 [PS]	Strictly Instrumental	1959	$100
❏ ED2671 [M]	Strictly Instrumental/South Africa Song/Mack the Knife/In a Little Spanish Town	1959	$50
❏ ED 7-2671 [S]	Strictly Instrumental/South Africa Song/Mack the Knife/In a Little Spanish Town	1959	$100
❏ ED2532	The Dipsy Doodle/Miss You//Is It True What They Say About Dixie?/Carolina in the Morning	1957	$60

ESSEX

Number	Title	Yr	NM
❏ EP-117	*Live It Up/Farewell, So Long, Goodbye/Real Rock Drive/Fractured	1954	$125
❏ EP-118	*Stop Beatin' Round the Mulberry Bush/Watcha Gonna Do/I'll Be True/Juke Box Cannon Ball	1954	$125
❏ EP-119	(contents unknown)	1954	$125
❏ TWEP-102 [PS]	For Your Dance Party	1954	$120

SOMERSET

Number	Title	Yr	NM
❏ 460	(contents unknown)	1955	$100

TRANS WORLD

Number	Title	Yr	NM
❏ TWEP-117	(contents unknown)	1955	$100
❏ TWEP-118	(contents unknown)	1955	$100
❏ TWEP-119	(contents unknown)	1955	$100

HALL, DARYL, AND JOHN OATES

ARISTA

Number	Title	Yr	NM
9753	Downtown Life (LP Version)/Downtown Life (Urban Mix)	1988	$3
9753 [PS]	Downtown Life (LP Version)/Downtown Life (Urban Mix)	1988	$3
9684	Everything Your Heart Desires/Real Love	1988	$3
9684 [PS]	Everything Your Heart Desires/Real Love	1988	$3
9727	Missed Opportunity/Soul Love	1988	$3
9727 [PS]	Missed Opportunity/Soul Love	1988	$3

ATLANTIC

Number	Title	Yr	NM
3239	Can't Stop the Music/70's Scenario	1975	$5
2922	Goodnight & Good Morning/All Our Love	1972	$10

— As "Whole Oats

Number	Title	Yr	NM
3397	It's Uncanny/Lilly (Are You Happy)	1977	$4
3026	Lady Rain/When the Morning Comes	1974	$5
2939	Lilly (Are You Happy/I'm Sorry	1973	$8
2993	She's Gone/I'm Just a Kid (Don't Make Me Feel Like a Man)	1973	$8
3332	She's Gone/I'm Just a Kid (Don't Make Me Feel Like a Man)	1976	$4
3332 [DJ]	She's Gone (Long Version)/She's Gone	1976	$6

CHELSEA

Number	Title	Yr	NM
3063	If That's What Makes You Happy/The Reason Why	1977	$5

— B-side by "Daryl Hall and Gulliver

Number	Title	Yr	NM
3069	Perkiomen/The Provider	1977	$5

RCA

Number	Title	Yr	NM
PB-13714	Adult Education/Maneater	1984	$3
PB-13714 [PS]	Adult Education/Maneater	1984	$4
PB-11920	All You Want Is Heaven/Who Said the World Was Fair	1980	$4
PB-10970	Back Together Again/Room to Breathe	1977	$4
PB-13065	Did It in a Minute/Head Above Water	1982	$4
PB-11181	Don't Change/The Emptiness	1977	$4
PB-10808	Do What You Want, Be What You Are/You'll Never Learn	1976	$4
PB-13507	Family Man/Open All Night	1983	$3
GB-13797	Family Man/Say It Isn't So	1984	$3

— Gold Standard Series

Number	Title	Yr	NM
PB-12048	How Does It Feel to Be Back/United State	1980	$4
JB-12361 [DJ]	I Can't Go for That (No Can Do)/(Club Mix)	1981	$10

— Promo only

Number	Title	Yr	NM
PB-12357	I Can't Go for That (No Can Do)/Unguarded Minute	1981	$4
PB-11424	I Don't Wanna Lose You/August Day	1978	$4
GB-11970	It's a Laugh/I Don't Wanna Lose You	1980	$3

— Gold Standard Series

Number	Title	Yr	NM
PB-11371	It's a Laugh/Serious Music	1978	$4
PB-13354	Maneater/Delayed Reaction	1982	$3
PB-13354 [PS]	Maneater/Delayed Reaction	1982	$4
GB-13796	Maneater/One on One	1984	$3

— Gold Standard Series

Number	Title	Yr	NM
GB-14340	Method of Modern Love/Possession Obsession	1986	$3

— Gold Standard Series

Number	Title	Yr	NM
PB-13970	Method of Modern Love (Remix Edit)/Method of Modern Love	1984	$3
PB-13970 [PS]	Method of Modern Love (Remix Edit)/Method of Modern Love	1984	$3
PB-13421	One on One/Art of Heartbreak	1983	$3
PB-13421 [PS]	One on One/Art of Heartbreak	1983	$4
GB-14064	Out of Touch/Adult Education	1985	$3

— Gold Standard Series

Number	Title	Yr	NM
PB-13916	Out of Touch/Cold, Dark, and Yesterday	1984	$3
PB-13916 [PS]	Out of Touch/Cold, Dark, and Yesterday	1984	$3
PB-14098	Possession Obsession/Dance on Your Knees	1985	$3
PB-14098 [PS]	Possession Obsession/Dance on Your Knees	1985	$3
GB-13480	Private Eyes/I Can't Go for That (No Can Do)	1983	$3

— Gold Standard Series

Number	Title	Yr	NM
PB-12296	Private Eyes/Tell Me What You Want	1981	$4
GB-10942	Sara Smile/Do What You Want, Be What You Are	1977	$3

— Gold Standard Series

Number	Title	Yr	NM
PB-13654	Say It Isn't So/Kiss on My List	1983	$3

(continued)

Number	Title	Yr	NM
PB-13654 [PS]	Say It Isn't So/Kiss on My List	1983	$4
PB-14035	Some Things Are Better Left Unsaid/All American Girl	1985	$3
PB-14035 [PS]	Some Things Are Better Left Unsaid/All American Girl	1985	$3
GB-14341	Some Things Are Better Left Unsaid/A Nite at the Apollo Live! The Way You Do the Things You Do-My Girl	1986	$3

— Gold Standard Series

Number	Title	Yr	NM
PB-11747	Wait for Me/No Brain No Pain	1979	$4
PB-11132	Why Do Lovers (Break Each Other's Heart?)/A Girl Who Used to Be	1977	$4

RCA VICTOR

Number	Title	Yr	NM
PB-10373	Camellia/Ennui on the Mountain	1975	$5
PB-10530	Sara Smile/Soldering	1975	$5

SIRE

Number	Title	Yr	NM
22967	Love Train/"Earth Girls Are Easy" Theme	1989	$3
22967 [PS]	Love Train/"Earth Girls Are Easy" Theme	1989	$3

HALL, DARYL

AMY

Number	Title	Yr	NM
11049	The Princess and the Soldier (Part 1)/The Princess and the Soldier (Part 2)	1969	$6

RCA

Number	Title	Yr	NM
PB-14387	Dreamtime/Let It Out	1986	$3
PB-14387 [PS]	Dreamtime/Let It Out	1986	$3
5038-7-R	Foolish Pride/What's Gonna Happen to Us	1986	$3
5038-7-R [PS]	Foolish Pride/What's Gonna Happen to Us	1986	$3
5105-7-R	Someone Like You (The Guitar Solo)/Someone Like You (The Sax Solo)	1987	$3
5105-7-R [PS]	Someone Like You (The Guitar Solo)/Someone Like You (The Sax Solo)	1987	$3
PB-12001	Something in 4/4 Time/Sacred Songs	1980	$4
PB-12001 [PS]	Something in 4/4 Time/Sacred Songs	1980	$5

HALL, FRANCES

SURF

Number	Title	Yr	NM
5031	Christmas Lullaby/Jack in the Box	1958	$30

HALL, LARRY

HOT

Number	Title	Yr	NM
1	Sandy/Lovin' Tree	1959	$60

STRAND

Number	Title	Yr	NM
25013	A Girl Like You/Rosemary	1960	$30
25016	For Every Boy/I'll Stay Single	1960	$30
25048	Ladder of Love/The One You Left Behind	1961	$30
25029	Lips of Wine/Rebel Heart	1961	$30
25007	Sandy/Lovin' Tree	1959	$30
25025	The Girl I Left Behind/Kool Love	1961	$30

HALL, ROY (1)

DECCA

Number	Title	Yr	NM
29880	Blue Suede Shoes/Luscious	1956	$60
29786	See You Later, Alligator/Don't Stop Now	1956	$60
30060	Three Alley Cats/Diggin' the Boogie	1956	$60
29697	Whole Lotta Shakin' Goin' On/All By Myself	1955	$100

FORTUNE

Number	Title	Yr	NM
521	Corrine, Corrina/Don't Ask Me No Questions	1956	$60
170	Going Down the Road/Jealous Love	1952	$50

— B-side by the Davis Sisters

HALL, SIDNEY

SHRINE

Number	Title	Yr	NM
109	The Weekend/I'm a Lover	1966	$1000

HALL, TOM T., AND EARL SCRUGGS

COLUMBIA

Number	Title	Yr	NM
18-03033	Song of the South/Shackles and Chains	1982	$4
18-02858	There Ain't No Country Music on This Jukebox/Don't This Road Look Rough and Rocky	1982	$4

HALL, TOM T.

MERCURY

Number	Title	Yr	NM
880690-7	A Bar with No Beer/Red Sails in the Sunset	1985	$3
72835	Ain't Got the Time/Hope	1968	$8
72998	A Week in a Country Jail/Flat-Footin' It	1969	$6
72863	Ballad of Forty Dollars/Highways	1968	$6
DJ-111 [DJ]	Ballad of Forty Dollars//Memphis Morning/Since They Fired the Band Director (At Murphy High)/Please Let Me Prove (My Love for You)	1968	$20

—Promo only; the B-side contains 60-second excerpts of the three songs performed by Roy Drusky, Linda Manning and Dave Dudley, respectively

Number	Title	Yr	NM
72749	Beauty Is a Fading Flower/Your Love Is Mine Again	1967	$8
73617	Country Is/God Came Through Bellville, Ga.	1974	$4
73686	Deal/It Rained in Every Town Except Paducah	1975	$4
888155-7	Down at the Mall/We're All Through Dancing	1986	$3
884017-7	Down in the Florida Keys/Song in a Seashell	1985	$3
812835-7	Everything from Jesus to Jack Daniels/(Old Dogs-Children and) Watermelon Wine	1983	$3
880030-7	Famous in Missouri/I Only Think About You When I'm Drunk	1984	$3
73755	Faster Horses (The Cowboy and the Poet)/No New Friends Please	1975	$4
73850	Fox on the Run/Bluegrass Festival in the Sky	1976	$4
72951	Homecoming/Myra	1969	$6
814560-7	How'd You Get Home So Soon/The Year That Clayton Delaney Died	1983	$3
73641	I Care/Sneaky Snake	1974	$4
73704	I Like Beer/From a Mansion to a Honky Tonk	1975	$4
73436	I Love/Back When We Were Young	1973	$4
55001	It's All in the Game/The Little Green Flower with the Yellow on Top	1977	$4
72700	I Washed My Face in the Morning Dew/A Picture of Your Mother	1967	$8
870669-7	Let's Play Remember/Fox Hollow's Animal Train	1988	$3
872180-7	Let's Spend Christmas at My House/Let's Go Shopping Today	1988	$3
76147	Little Lady Preacher/Ramona's Revenge	1982	$4
73278	Me and Jesus/Coot Marseilles Blues	1972	$5
73327	More About John Henry/Windy City Anne	1972	$5
73189	Ode to a Half Pound of Ground Round/Pinto the Wonder Horse Is Dead	1971	$6
73346	(Old Dogs-Children and) Watermelon Wine/Grandma Whistled	1972	$5
73140	One Hundred Children/I Took a Memory to Lunch	1970	$6
880216-7	P.S. I Love You/My Heroes Have Always Been Cowboys	1984	$3
73078	Salute to a Switchblade/That'll Be Alright with Me	1970	$6
73039	Shoeshine Man/Kentucky in the Morning	1970	$6
72913	Strawberry Farms/3	1969	$6
884850-7	Susie's Beauty Shop/Love Letters in the Sand	1986	$3
73488	That Song Is Driving Me Crazy/Forget It	1974	$4
73297	The Monkey That Became President/She Gave Her Heart to Jethro	1972	$5
72786	The World the Way I Want It/Shame on the Rain	1968	$8
73394	Watergate Blues/Spokane Motel Blues	1973	$5

RCA

Number	Title	Yr	NM
PB-12066	Back When Gas Was Thirty Cents a Gallon/Texas Never Fell in Love with Me	1980	$3
PB-11765	Christmas Is/Thanksgiving Is	1979	$4
PB-11253	I Wish I Loved Somebody Else/Whiskey	1978	$4
PB-11158	May the Force Be With You Always/No One Feels My Heart	1977	$5
PB-12005	Soldier of Fortune/The World According to Raymond	1980	$3
PB-11453	Son of Clayton Delaney/The Great East Broadway Onion Championship of 1978	1978	$4
PB-12219	The All New Me/Pour Me (Pour Me Another Drink)	1981	$3
PB-11888	The Old Side of Town/Jesus on the Radio (Daddy on the Phone)	1979	$4
PB-11568	There Is a Miracle in You/Saturday Morning Show	1979	$4
PB-11376	What Have You Got to Lose/The Three Sofa Story	1978	$4

Number	Title	Yr	NM
HALLMAN, VICKI			
BRIAR			
❏ 123	Merry Christmas Time/ Send My Daddy Home	1961	$10
HALLMARKS, THE			
DOT			
❏ 16418	My Little Sailor Boy/ Congratulations	1963	$30
EPIC			
❏ 9681	Let There Be You/Royal King	1964	$15
SMASH			
❏ 2115	Soul Shakin' Psychedelic Sally/Girl of My Dreams	1967	$40
HALLORAN, JACK, SINGERS			
DOT			
❏ 16275	Mary's Little Boy Chile/ Little Girl and Boy	1961	$10
❏ 16410	The Little Drummer Boy/ Mary's Little Boy Chile	1962	$10
REPRISE			
❏ 245	The Christmas Star/ What Can I Give Him	1963	$12
HALLOWAY, LARRY			
PARKWAY			
❏ 903	Beatle Teen Beat/Going Up	1964	$30
HALLYDAY, JOHNNY			
PHILIPS			
❏ 40043	Hey Little Girl/Caravan of Lonely Men	1962	$30
❏ 40024	I Got a Woman/ Be-Bop-a-Lula	1962	$30
HALO OF FLIES			
AMPHETAMINE REPTILE			
❏ Scale19	Death of a Fly/Sit It Out/ There Ain't No Hell	1988	$20
❏ Scale19 [PS]	Death of a Fly/Sit It Out/ There Ain't No Hell	1988	$20
❏ Scale3	M.D. 20-20/Pipebomb/ Sinner Sings	1986	$80
— Yellow vinyl (300 made)			
❏ Scale3	M.D. 20-20/Pipebomb/ Sinner Sings	1986	$30
— Black vinyl (1,700 made)			
❏ Scale3 [PS]	M.D. 20-20/Pipebomb/ Sinner Sings	1986	$30
❏ Scale2	Snapping Back Roscoe Bottles: DDT Fin 13-PCP/ Can't Touch Her	1985	$125
— Numbered edition of 400			
❏ Scale2 [PS]	Snapping Back Roscoe Bottles: DDT Fin 13-PCP/ Can't Touch Her	1985	$125
— With lyrics			
FORCED EXPOSURE			
❏ FE-019	Human Fly/I'ma Big	1989	$30
❏ FE-019 [PS]	Human Fly/I'ma Big	1989	$30
HALOS, THE			
7 ARTS			
❏ 720	Come On/What'd I Say	1962	$30
CONGRESS			
❏ 253	Baby What You Want Me to Do/Hey, Hey, Love Me	1965	$15
❏ 262 [DJ]	Come Softly to Me/ (B-side unknown)	1966	$15
— May be promo-only			
❏ 244	Do I/Just Keep On Loving Me	1965	$15
❏ 249	Since I Fell for You/You're Never Gonna Find	1965	$15
HAMBLEN, STUART			
COLUMBIA			
❏ 4-42363	Across the Great Divide/My Home	1962	$10
❏ 4-21061	A Million Wild Horses/ My Mary	1953	$30
❏ 4-21277	Beyond the Sun/ Please Tell Me	1954	$30
❏ 4-20938	Black Diamond/ This Ship of Mine	1952	$30
❏ 2-541	Condemnation/ Sheepskin Corn and a Wrinkle on a Horn	1950	$50
— Microgroove 33 1/3 rpm 7-inch record, small hole			
❏ 4-21116	Daddy's Cutie Pie/ The Hidden You	1953	$30
❏ 4-21079	Friends I Know/Old Pappy's New Banjo	1953	$30
❏ 2-741	Good Mornin' Y'all/I Whisper Your Name	1950	$50
— Microgroove 33 1/3 rpm 7-inch record, small hole			
❏ 4-20733	Good Mornin' Y'all/I Whisper Your Name	1950	$40

Number	Title	Yr	NM
❏ 4-42198	Good Old Days/What Can I Do for My Country	1961	$15
❏ 4-20988	Got So Many Million Years (I Can't Count 'Em)/Lord, I Pray	1952	$30
❏ 4-21014	Grasshopper MacClain/ Oklahoma Bill	1952	$30
❏ 4-21124	I Believe/Teach Me Lord to Wait	1953	$30
❏ 4-20848	I Believe/These Things Shall Pass	1951	$30
❏ 4-21013	I Get Lonesome/ Our Love Affair	1952	$30
❏ 4-21012	Is He Satisfied/ Known Only to Him	1952	$30
❏ 4-20724	It Is No Secret (What God Can Do)/Blood on Your Hands	1950	$40
❏ 4-21428	I've Got So Many Million Years (I Can't Count 'Em)/Lord, I Pray	1955	$30
❏ 2-351	(I Won't Go Huntin', Jake) But I'll Go Chasin' Women/ Let's See You Fix It	1949	$50
— Microgroove 33 1/3 rpm 7-inch record, small hole			
❏ 4-21190	My Religion's Not Old Fashioned/He Made a Way	1953	$30
❏ 4-20779	Old Glory/My Life with You	1951	$30
❏ 4-20827	Our Old Captain/Don't Fool Around with Calico	1951	$30
❏ 4-21158	Partners with God/You Must Be Born Again	1953	$30
❏ 2-430(?)	Pony Express/Blue Bonnets in Her Golden Hair	1950	$50
— Microgroove 33 1/3 rpm 7-inch record, small hole			
❏ 4-41780	The Foreman/Golden River	1960	$15
KAPP			
❏ 733	This Old House Has Got to Go/Tho' Autumn's Comin' On	1965	$8
RCA VICTOR			
❏ 47-6333	A Handful of Sunshine/ You'll Always Be Mine	1955	$20
❏ 47-6759	Beyond the Sun/Dear Lord, Be My Shepherd	1956	$20
❏ 47-6714	Desert Sunrise/ Whistler's Dream	1956	$20
❏ 47-6736	God Is a Good God/The Sweetest Story Ever Told	1956	$20
❏ 47-6465	Hell Train/A Few Things to Remember	1956	$20
❏ 47-5810	I Am Persuaded/ Heavenly Cannonball	1954	$30
❏ 47-5990	If We All Said a Prayer/ My Brother	1955	$30
❏ 47-6250	I've Got So Many Million Years (I Can't Count 'Em)/ Lord, I Can't Come Now	1955	$20
— With Martha Carson			
❏ 47-6152	Lord, I'll Try/ Lonesome Valley	1955	$20
❏ 47-5918	Old Pappy Time Is a-Pickin' Pockets/Toy Violin	1954	$30
❏ 47-6911	The Lonesome Cowboy's Prayer/My Father	1957	$20
❏ 47-7052	The Old Rugged Cross/ Old Time Religion	1957	$20
❏ 47-6581	This Book/The Rock	1956	$20
❏ 47-5739	This Ole House/When My Lord Picks Up the 'Phone	1954	$30
❏ 47-7111	This Ole World/Don't Mess Around with Calico	1957	$20
HAMILTON, LITTLE JOHNNY			
DORE			
❏ 754	Oh How I Love You/Go	1966	$500
HAMILTON, ROY			
AGP			
❏ 116	Angelica/Hang Ups	1969	$40
❏ 125	It's Only Make Believe/100 Years	1969	$30
❏ 113	The Dark End of the Street/100 Years	1969	$30
CAPITOL			
❏ 2057	Let This World Be Free/ Wait Until Dark	1967	$30
EPIC			
❏ 9118	A Little Voice/All This Is Mine	1955	$30
❏ 9232	(All of a Sudden) My Heart Sings/I'm Gonna Lock You in My Heart	1957	$30
❏ 9398	A Lover's Prayer/ Never Let Me Go	1960	$20
❏ 9520	Climb Ev'ry Mountain/I'll Come Running Back to You	1962	$30
❏ 9268	Crazy Feelin'/In a Dream	1958	$40
❏ 9492	Don't Come Cryin' to Me/ If Only I Had Known	1962	$40
❏ 9257	Don't Let Go/The Night to Love	1957	$30
❏ 9372	Down by the Riverside/ Nobody Knows the Trouble I've Seen	1960	$20
❏ 9068	Ebb Tide/Beware	1954	$30
❏ 9132	Everybody's Got a Home/ Take Me with You	1955	$30

Number	Title	Yr	NM
❏ 9460	Excerpts from "You Can Have Her	1961	$20
❏ 9461	Excerpts from "You Can Have Her	1961	$20
❏ 9462	Excerpts from "You Can Have Her	1961	$20
❏ 9463	Excerpts from "You Can Have Her	1961	$20
❏ 9464	Excerpts from "You Can Have Her	1961	$20
❏ 9111	Forgive This Fool/You Wanted to Change Me	1955	$30
❏ 9342	Great Romance/On My Way Back Home	1959	$20
❏ 9386	Having Myself a Ball/Slowly	1960	$20
—B-side by Bobby Sykes			
❏ 9086	Hurt/Star of Love	1954	$30
❏ 9538	I Am/Earthquake	1962	$200
❏ 9092	I Believe/If You Are But a Dream	1955	$30
❏ 9373	I Let a Song Go Out of My Heart/I Get the Blues When It Rains	1960	$20
❏ 9307	I Need Your Lovin'/ Blue Prelude	1959	$30
❏ 9180	I Took My Grief to Him/Chained	1956	$30
❏ 9301	It's Never Too Late/ Somewhere Along the Way	1959	$20
❏ 9274	Lips/Jungle Fever	1958	$20
❏ 9407	Lonely Hands/Your Love	1960	$20
❏ 9212	My Faith, My Hope, My Love/So Long	1957	$30
❏ 9374	My Story/Please Send Me Someone to Love	1960	$20
❏ 9294	Pledging My Love/My One and Only Love	1958	$20
❏ 9376	Sing You Sinners/ Blow, Gabriel, Blow	1960	$20
❏ 9047	So Let There Be Love/ If You Loved Me	1954	$30
❏ 9160	Somebody, Somewhere/ Since I Fell for You	1956	$30
❏ 9224	The Aisle/That Old Feeling	1957	$30
❏ 9390	The Clock/I Get the Blues When It Rains	1960	$40
❏ 9147	There Goes My Heart/ Walk Along with Kings	1956	$30
❏ 9466	There We Were/If	1961	$15
❏ 9203	The Simple Prayer/A Mother's Love	1957	$30
❏ 9354	The Ten Commandments/ Dowm by the Riverside	1959	$20
❏ 9354	The Ten Commandments/ Nobody Knows the Trouble I've Seen	1959	$20
❏ 9323	Time Marches On/ Take It Easy, Joe	1959	$20
❏ 9282	Wait for Me/Everything	1958	$20
❏ 9125	Without a Song/ Cuban Love Song	1955	$30
MGM			
❏ 13247	Answer Me, My Love/ Unchained Melody	1964	$10
❏ 13138	Let Go/You Still Love Him	1963	$40
❏ 13157	Midnight Town-Daybreak City/Intermezzo	1963	$20
❏ 13315	Sweet Violets/A Thousand Years Ago	1965	$10
❏ 13175	Theme from "The V.I.P.'s" (The Willow)/The Sinner	1963	$50
❏ 13217	The Panic Is On/ There She Is	1964	$200
RCA VICTOR			
❏ 47-8705	And I Love Her/ Tore Up Over You	1965	$30
❏ 47-8641	Heartache/Ain't It the Truth	1965	$80
❏ 47-9061	I Taught Her Everything She Knows/Lament	1967	$40
❏ 47-9171	So High My Love/ You Shook Me Up	1967	$400
❏ 47-8813	The Impossible Dream/ She's Got a Heart	1966	$70
❏ 47-8960	Walk Hand in Hand/ Crackin' Up Over You	1966	$300
❏ 48-1034	Walk Hand in Hand/ Crackin' Up Over You	1972	$60
7-Inch Extended Plays			
EPIC			
❏ EG-7200	(contents unknown)	1958	$20
❏ EG-7205	(contents unknown)	1958	$20
❏ EG-7200 [PS]	Don't Let Go	1958	$20
❏ EG-7205 [PS]	Lips	1958	$20
HAMILTON, RUSS			
KAPP			
❏ 250	All Alone/The Things I Didn't Say	1958	$15
❏ 219	Drifting and Dreaming/Tip Toe Through the Tulips	1958	$15
❏ 281	I Found Out/My Unbreakable Heart	1959	$15
❏ 204	My Mother's Eyes/I Had a Dream	1957	$15
❏ 194	Wedding Ring/I Still Belong to You	1957	$15
MGM			
❏ 12947	Gonna Find Me a Bluebird/Choir Girl	1960	$15

Number	Title	Yr	NM

HAMILTON STREETCAR
DOT
❏ 17279	Brother Speed/Wasn't It You	1969	$15
❏ 17306	Honey and Wine/Now I Taste the Tears	1969	$15
❏ 17253	Silver Wings/I See I Am	1969	$15

LHI
❏ 1206	Confusion/Your Own Come Down	1968	$20
❏ 17016	Invisible People/Flash	1967	$20

HAMLISCH, MARVIN
A&M
❏ 1775	All I Needed Was the Laughter/If You Hadn't Left Me Crying	1975	$4

ARISTA
❏ 0392	Theme from "Ice Castles"/Touch	1979	$4

MCA
❏ 40307	Maple Leaf Rag/ Mexican Dreams	1974	$4
❏ 52175	The Entertainer/ Heliotrope Bouquet	1983	$4

—B-side by Lalo Schifrin

❏ 40174	The Entertainer/Solace	1974	$5

PLANET
❏ 45922 [DJ]	Theme from "Ordinary People" (same on both sides)	1980	$4

UNITED ARTISTS
❏ 50798	Bananas/'Cause I Believe in Loving	1971	$5
❏ XW1082	Bond '77 -- James Bond Theme (Part 1)/Bond '77 -- James Bond Theme (Part 2)	1977	$4

HAMMER, JAN
ASYLUM
❏ 46548	Oh Pretty Woman/Goodbye	1979	$10

MCA
❏ 53239	Crockett's Theme/ Through the Storm	1988	$3
❏ 53239 [PS]	Crockett's Theme/ Through the Storm	1988	$4
❏ 52666	Miami Vice Theme// Evan/The Original Miami Vice Theme	1985	$3
❏ 52666 [PS]	Miami Vice Theme// Evan/The Original Miami Vice Theme	1985	$4

—Original sleeves have a black sticker on the front saying "The Original Version As Heard on 'Miami Vice'"

❏ 52666 [PS]	Miami Vice Theme// Evan/The Original Miami Vice Theme	1985	$3

—Later sleeves have "The Original Version As Heard on 'Miami Vice'" added to the front above Jan Hammer's name

❏ 52666 [PS]	Miami Vice Theme// Evan/The Original Miami Vice Theme	1985	$6

—With no reference to "The Original Version As Heard on 'Miami Vice'" on the front of the sleeve, either by sticker or as part of the type

NEMPEROR
❏ 7515	Don't You Know/ Window of Love	1977	$15
❏ 06	Oh, Yeah?/Let the Children Grow	1976	$10
❏ 7516	Too Much to Lose/What It Is	1977	$15

HAMMER, MC
BUSTIN'
❏ 1987-7	Let's Get It Started/ (Instrumental)	1987	$30

CAPITOL
❏ 7PRO-79667 [DJ]	(Hammer Hammer) They Put Me in the Mix (same on both sides)	1989	$6
❏ B-44497	Help the Children/ (Instrumental)	1989	$3
❏ B-44229	Let's Get It Started/ (Instrumental)	1988	$3
❏ B-44266	Pump It Up/(Instrumental)	1988	$3
❏ B-44290	Turn This Mutha Out/Ring 'Em	1989	$3

HAMMOND-HAZLEWOOD
CAPITOL
❏ 2616	Wendy, Wendy/Broken Hearts Brigade	1969	$10

HAMMOND, ALBERT
COLUMBIA
❏ 03412	Before You Change the World/Somewhere in America	1982	$4
❏ 02470	Memories/I Want You Back with Me	1981	$4

❏ 60510	When I'm Gone/ World of Love	1981	$4

EPIC
❏ 50277	Moonlight Lady/Cry Baby	1976	$4

MUMS
❏ 6037	99 Miles from L.A./ Rivers Are for Boats	1975	$4
❏ 6030	Air Disaster/Candlelight, Sweet Candlelight	1974	$4
❏ 6009	Down by the River/The Last One to Know	1972	$4
❏ 6032	Fountain Avenue/Names, Tags, Numbers, Labels	1974	$4
❏ 6024	Half a Million Miles from Home/I Think I'll Go That Way	1973	$4
❏ 6015	If You Gotta Break Another Heart/That Old American Dream	1973	$4
❏ 6026	I'm a Train/Brand New Day	1974	$4
❏ 6011	It Never Rains in Southern California/Anyone Here in the Audience	1972	$5

—Bizarrely, the stock copy is in rechanneled stereo

❏ 6018	The Free Electric Band/You Taught Me to Sing the Blues	1973	$4
❏ 6021	The Peacemaker/Who's for Lunch Today	1973	$4

HAMMOND, JOHN
ATLANTIC
❏ 2696	I'm Tore Down/Shake for Me	1969	$8

COLUMBIA
❏ 45372	As the Years Go Passing By/Mellow Down Easy	1971	$6

RED BIRD
❏ Oct-0047	I Wish You Would/I Can Tell	1966	$30

HAMMOND, JOHNNY
KUDU
❏ 900	It's Too Late/Workin' on a Groovy Thing	1971	$6
❏ 914	Thunder and Lightning (Part 1)/Thunder and Lightning (Part 2)	1973	$6

MILESTONE
❏ 302	Los Conquistadores Chocolates/Shifting Gears	1975	$5
❏ 725	Soul Talk (Part 1)/ Soul Talk (Part 2)	1970	$6

HAMPTON, JOHN
UNITED
❏ 210	Honey Hush/Shadow Blues	1958	$120

HAMPTON, LIONEL
DECCA
❏ 27325	Boogie Woogie Santa Claus/Merry Christmas	1950	$30

HANCOCK, HERBIE
❏ 1863	Driftin'/Alone Am I	1962	$8
❏ 1862	Watermelon Man/ Three Bags Full	1962	$8

COLUMBIA
❏ 04268	Autodrive/Chameleon	1983	$4
❏ 07987	Beat Wise/Chemical Residue	1988	$3
❏ 46002	Chameleon/Vein Melter	1974	$5
❏ 11122	Doin' It/Honey from the Jar	1979	$4
❏ 10408	Doin' It/People Music	1976	$5
❏ 02404	Everybody's Broke/ Help Yourself	1981	$4
❏ 03004	Gettin' to the Good Part/ The Fun Tracks	1982	$4
❏ 04565	Hardrock (2 versions)	1984	$4
❏ 04565 [PS]	Hardrock (2 versions)	1984	$4
❏ 10781	I Thought It Was You/ No Means Yes	1978	$5
❏ 02824	Lite Me Up/Satisfied with Love	1982	$4
❏ 02615	Magic Number/Help Yourself	1981	$4
❏ 10563	Maiden Voyage/Spider	1977	$5
❏ 11323	Making Love/It All Comes Around	1980	$4
❏ 04473	Mega-Mix/TFS	1984	$4
❏ 04633	Metal Beat/Karabali	1984	$4
❏ 10050	Palm Grease/Butterfly	1974	$5
❏ 03318	Paradise/The Fun Tracks	1982	$4
❏ 10094	Spank-a-Lee/Actual Proof	1975	$5
❏ 11236	Stars in Your Eyes/Go For It	1980	$4
❏ 10835	Sunlight/Come Running to Me	1978	$5
❏ 10239	Suntouch/Hang Up Your Hang-Ups	1975	$5
❏ 11021	Tell Everybody/ Honey from the Jar	1979	$5
❏ 46073	Watermelon Man/Sly	1974	$5

WARNER BROS.
❏ 7358	Fat Mama/Wiggle-Waggle	1969	$6
❏ 7598	Water Torture/Crossings	1972	$6

HANDS OF TIME, THE
SIDEWALK
❏ 903	Got to Get You Into My Life/Midnight Rider	1966	$40

HANDY, WAYNE
DIAL
❏ 3002	Conscience Let Me Go/Pain Reliever	1961	$15

PARKWAY
❏ 812	So Much to Remember/ You'll Never Be Mine	1960	$30

HANEY, JACK, AND NIKITER ARMSTRONG
MEL-O-DY
❏ 107	The Interview/Peaceful	1963	$30

HANEY, RAY
MGM
❏ 12106 [DJ]	The Picture On The Christmas Card/Story Of A Christmas Tree	1955	$15
❏ 12106 [DJ]	The Picture On The Christmas Card/Story Of A Christmas Tree	1955	$15

HANGMEN, THE
MONUMENT
❏ 951	Faces/Bad Goodbye	1966	$30
❏ 910	What a Girl Can't Do/The Girl Who Faded Away	1965	$30

HANK AND CAROLEE
MALA
❏ 424	Go On and Go/I've Never Known	1960	$50

HANKS, KAMRYN
COUNTRY PRIDE
❏ 0025	Eyes Never Lie/ (B-side unknown)	1989	$6

HANNAN, JIMMY
ATLANTIC
❏ 2247	Beach Ball/You Gotta Have Love	1964	$200

—Backing Hannan on this record are THE BEE GEES, three years before their first American release!

HAPPENINGS, THE
BIG TREE
❏ 153	Me Without You/ God Bless Joanna	1972	$4
❏ 146	Strawberry Morning/Workin' My Way Back to You	1972	$4

B.T. PUPPY
❏ 543	Breaking Up Is Hard to Do/Anyway	1968	$8
❏ 545	Crazy Rhythm/Love Song of Mommy and Daddy	1968	$8
❏ 517	Girls on the Go-Go-Go	1966	$10
❏ 522	Go Away Little Girl/Tea Time	1966	$8
❏ 523	Goodnight My Love/ Lillies By Money	1966	$8
❏ 181 [DJ]	Have Yourself a Merry Little Christmas (same on both sides)	1966	$40

—Stock copies do not exist

❏ 181 [DJ]	Have Yourself a Merry Little Christmas (same on both sides)	1966	$40

—Stock copies do not exist

❏ 527	I Got Rhythm/You're in a Bad Way	1967	$8
❏ 538	Music, Music, Music/ When I Lock My Door	1968	$8
❏ 538 [PS]	Music, Music, Music/ When I Lock My Door	1968	$20
❏ 530	My Mammy/I Believe in Nothing	1967	$8
❏ 530 [PS]	My Mammy/I Believe in Nothing	1967	$20
❏ 542	Sealed with a Kiss/Anyway	1968	$8
❏ 520	See You in September/ He Thinks He's a Hero	1966	$10
❏ 549	That's All I Want from You/ He Thinks He's a Hero	1968	$8
❏ 532	Why Do Fools Fall in Love/When the Summer Is Through	1967	$8
❏ 532 [PS]	Why Do Fools Fall in Love/When the Summer Is Through	1967	$20

JUBILEE
❏ 5686	Answer Me, My Love/I Need a Woman	1970	$6
❏ 5703	Condition Red/ Sweet September	1970	$10

—As "The Honor Society"

❏ 5702	Crazy Love/Chain of Hands	1970	$6

Number	Title	Yr	NM
❏ 5677	El Paso County Jail/Won't Anybody Listen	1969	$6
❏ 5712	Lullaby in the Rain/I Wish You Could Know Me (Naomi)	1971	$6
❏ 5721 [DJ]	Make Your Own Kind of Music (mono/stereo)	1971	$6

—Stock copies may not exist

Number	Title	Yr	NM
❏ 5721 [DJ]	Make Your Own Kind of Music (mono/stereo)	1971	$6

—Stock copies may not exist

Number	Title	Yr	NM
❏ 5698	Tomorrow, Today Will Be Yesterday/Chain of Hands	1970	$6
❏ 5666	Where Do I Go and Be In/New Day Comin'	1969	$6

MIDLAND INT'L.

Number	Title	Yr	NM
❏ MB-11127	Let Me Stay/Someone Special	1977	$4
❏ MB-10897	That's Why I Love You/Beyond the Hurt	1977	$4

PHILCO-FORD

Number	Title	Yr	NM
❏ HP-7	Go Away Little Girl/See You in September	1967	$30

—4-inch plastic "Hip Pocket Record" with color sleeve

HAPPY CONTINENTALS, THE
MGM

Number	Title	Yr	NM
❏ 13402	Sleigh Ride Kisses/Hello Mr. Strauss	1965	$8

HAPPY ELVES, THE
GARLIN

Number	Title	Yr	NM
❏ 101	Santa Got Stuck In The Chimney/(B-side unknown)	1960	$15

HAPPY HARTS, THE
KAPP

Number	Title	Yr	NM
❏ 314	Let's All Sing a Song for Christmas/I Want the South to Win the War for Christmas	1959	$30

—B-side by Spike Jones and the City Slickers

HARBOR LIGHTS, THE
JARO

Number	Title	Yr	NM
❏ 77020	Is That Too Much to Ask/What Would I Do Without You	1960	$50

MALA

Number	Title	Yr	NM
❏ 422	Angel of Love/Tick-a-Tick-a-Tock	1960	$60

HARD, RANDY
NRC

Number	Title	Yr	NM
❏ 013	Honey Doll/May It Be My Fortune	1959	$70
❏ 044	Let Her Go/Make Me a Dreamer	1959	$60

HARD TIMES, THE
WORLD PACIFIC

Number	Title	Yr	NM
❏ 77873	Blew Mind/Colours	1967	$10
❏ 77826	Come To Your Window/That's All I'll Do	1966	$10
❏ 77851	Fortune Teller/Good-By	1966	$10
❏ 77816	There'll Be a Time/You're Bound to Cry	1966	$10

HARDIN, ED
HIT

Number	Title	Yr	NM
❏ 157	Ask Me/Pay It No Mind	1964	$8

—B-side by Fred York

Number	Title	Yr	NM
❏ 282	Baby I Need Your Lovin'/Pretty Ballerina	1967	$8

—B-side by the Chords (2)

Number	Title	Yr	NM
❏ 315	By the Time I Get to Phoenix/Daydream Believer	1967	$8

—B-side by the Jalopy Five

Number	Title	Yr	NM
❏ 285	Detroit City/A Little Bit Me, A Little Bit You	1967	$8

—B-side by the Jalopy Five

Number	Title	Yr	NM
❏ 87	Donna the Prima Donna/Washington Square	1963	$8

—B-side by the Music City Five & Ten

Number	Title	Yr	NM
❏ 219	Down in the Boondocks/What's New Pussycat?	1965	$8

—B-side by Bobby Brooks

Number	Title	Yr	NM
❏ 98	Drip Drop/Midnight Mary	1963	$8

—B-side by Ricky Dickens

Number	Title	Yr	NM
❏ 13	Follow That Dream/Lovers Who Wander	1962	$8
❏ 103	For You/Um, Um, Um, Um, Um, Um	1964	$8

—B-side by Thomas Henry

Number	Title	Yr	NM
❏ 211	Game of Love/One Fine Day	1965	$8
❏ 02	Good Luck Charm/Slow Twistin'	1962	$8

—B-side by Herbert Hunter

Number	Title	Yr	NM
❏ 199	Goodnight/Hearts Are Funny Things	1965	$8

—B-side by Bobby Brooks

Number	Title	Yr	NM
❏ 279	Good Thing/Tell It Like It Is	1967	$8

—As "Ed Hardin and the Cadets"; B-side by Leroy Jones

Number	Title	Yr	NM
❏ 280	Green, Green Grass of Home/Mercy, Mercy, Mercy	1967	$8

—B-side by the New Society Group

Number	Title	Yr	NM
❏ 256	Green Grass/A Groovy Kind of Love	1966	$8

—B-side by the Chords (2)

Number	Title	Yr	NM
❏ 349	Hold Me Tight/Abraham, Martin and John	1968	$8

—B-side by Joe Smith

Number	Title	Yr	NM
❏ 245	It's Too Late/Nowhere Man	1966	$15

—B-side by the Jalopy Five

Number	Title	Yr	NM
❏ 329	I Wanna Live/Mony Mony	1968	$8

—B-side by the Fantastics

Number	Title	Yr	NM
❏ 117	Little Children/My Guy	1964	$8

—B-side by Clara Wilson

Number	Title	Yr	NM
❏ 44	Love Came to Me/Everybody Loves a Lover	1962	$8

—B-side by Alpha Zoe

Number	Title	Yr	NM
❏ 261	Love Letters/Sweet Pea	1966	$8
❏ 130	Memphis/Bad to Me	1964	$8
❏ 175	My World's a Blue World/Don't Forget I Still Love You	1965	$8

—B-side by Shari Baker

Number	Title	Yr	NM
❏ 142	Oh Pretty Woman/Broken Hearted, Sad and Blue	1964	$8
❏ 54	One Broken Heart for Sale/Let's Turkey Trot	1963	$8

—B-side by Alpha Zoe

Number	Title	Yr	NM
❏ 33	Only Love Can Break a Heart/Do You Love Me	1962	$8

—B-side by Leroy Jones

Number	Title	Yr	NM
❏ 268	See See Rider/Psychotic Reaction	1966	$8

—As "Ed Hardin and the Cadets"; B-side by the Jalopy Five

Number	Title	Yr	NM
❏ 138	Such a Night/And I Love Her	1964	$10

—B-side by the Jalopy Five

Number	Title	Yr	NM
❏ 247	Sure Gonna Miss Her/The Cheater	1966	$8

—B-side by the Chellows

Number	Title	Yr	NM
❏ 112	Suspicion/Don't Let the Rain Come Down	1964	$8

—B-side by the Music City Singers

Number	Title	Yr	NM
❏ 149	That's All That's Important Now/From a Window	1964	$8
❏ 320	The Ballad of Bonnie and Clyde/Honey	1968	$8

—B-side by Bobby Sims

Number	Title	Yr	NM
❏ 190	True Love You Can't Buy/You've Lost That Lovin' Feelin'	1965	$8

—B-side by Wayne Harris

HARDY BOYS, THE
RCA VICTOR

Number	Title	Yr	NM
❏ 47-9831	Good, Good Lovin'/Love Train	1970	$8
❏ 74-0228	Love and Let Love/Sink or Swim	1969	$8
❏ 47-9795	Wheels/Sha-La-La	1969	$8

HARDY, FRANCOISE
REPRISE

Number	Title	Yr	NM
❏ 0808	Loving You/Hang On to a Dream	1969	$8

HARDY, JOHNNY
ACE

Number	Title	Yr	NM
❏ 624	In Memory of Johnny Horton/Wasting My Time	1961	$30

J&J

Number	Title	Yr	NM
❏ 03	In Memory of Johnny Horton/Wasting My Time	1961	$30

HARGRAVE, RON
CUB

Number	Title	Yr	NM
❏ 9025	Drive-In Movie/Buttercup	1959	$15

MGM

Number	Title	Yr	NM
❏ 12344	A Fool Am I/Too Late	1956	$30
❏ 12475	Hold Me/Song of the Moonlight	1957	$30
❏ 12571	If You Should Go/Heartbreaker	1957	$30
❏ 12422	Latch On/Only a Daydream	1957	$50

HARLAN, BILLY
BRUNSWICK

Number	Title	Yr	NM
❏ 55066	I Wanna Bop/School House Rock	1958	$200

HARLEM CHILDREN'S CHOIR, THE
COMMONWEALTH UNITED

Number	Title	Yr	NM
❏ 3003 [PS]	Black Christmas/Do You Hear What I Hear	1969	$20
❏ 3003	Black Christmas/Do You Hear What I Hear	1969	$10

HARLESS, OGDEN
DOOR KNOB

Number	Title	Yr	NM
❏ 297	Down on the Bayou/(B-side unknown)	1988	$5
❏ 272	How Many More Like Me/(B-side unknown)	1987	$5
❏ 293	I Wish We Were Strangers/(B-side unknown)	1988	$5
❏ 283	Somebody Ought to Tell Him That She's Gone/(B-side unknown)	1987	$5
❏ 287	Walk On Boy/(B-side unknown)	1987	$5

MSC

Number	Title	Yr	NM
❏ 188	Together Alone/(B-side unknown)	1988	$5

HARMON, BOB
REPUBLIC

Number	Title	Yr	NM
❏ 7030	Bob's Boogie/Boogie Woogie Jubilee	1953	$60
❏ 7089	Sad Blues Boogie/Bye Bye Blues Boogie	1954	$60
❏ 7114	Shake Rag Shuffle/Begin the Beguine Boogie	1955	$60

HARMONAIRES, THE
HOLIDAY

Number	Title	Yr	NM
❏ 2602	Come Back/Lorraine	1957	$300

—Black label

Number	Title	Yr	NM
❏ 2602	Come Back/Lorraine	1960	$70

—Red label, double horizontal lines

HARMONY GRITS, THE
END

Number	Title	Yr	NM
❏ 1051	Am I to Be the One/I Could Have Told You	1959	$30
❏ 1063	Gee/I Could Have Told You	1959	$30
❏ 1063	Gee/Santa Claus Is Coming to Town	1959	$50

HARMS, DALLAS
CON BRIO

Number	Title	Yr	NM
❏ 157	Legend of the Duke/In the Loving Arms of Marie	1979	$6

HARMS, JONI
UNIVERSAL

Number	Title	Yr	NM
❏ 53492	I Need a Wife/The Only Thing Bluer Than His Eyes	1989	$3
❏ UVL-66012	The Only Thing Bluer Than His Eyes/A Woman Knows	1989	$4

HARNER, BILLY
ATLANTIC

Number	Title	Yr	NM
❏ 2351	A Message to My Babe/Everything's Hunky-Dory	1966	$15

KAMA SUTRA

Number	Title	Yr	NM
❏ 238	Homicide Dresser/Lavender Room	1967	$15
❏ 226	Sally Sayin' Somethin'/Don't Want My Lovin'	1967	$15
❏ 242	What About the Music/Please Spare Me This Time	1968	$15

KENT

Number	Title	Yr	NM
❏ 493	Irresistible You/Honky Dory	1968	$15

LAWN

Number	Title	Yr	NM
❏ 239	Anymore/Whatcha Gonna Do	1964	$50
❏ 244	Coney Island Wild Child/Feel Good	1964	$75

MIDLAND INT'L.

Number	Title	Yr	NM
❏ MB-10783	Two Lonely People/Whenever I'm Away from You	1976	$10

OPEN

Number	Title	Yr	NM
❏ 1253	She's Almost You/Fool Me	1969	$20

OR

Number	Title	Yr	NM
❏ 1255	I Struck It Rich/Watch Your Step	1969	$30
❏ 1253	She's Almost You/Fool Me	1969	$15

PARKWAY

Number	Title	Yr	NM
❏ 950	Let's Get in Line/All Through the Night	1965	$30

HAROLD AND THE CASUALS
SCOTTY

Number	Title	Yr	NM
❏ 628	Darling Do You Love Me/You Can Shake a Tail Feather	1959	$300

Number	Title	Yr	NM

HARPER, CHUCK
FELSTED
| ❏ 8658 | Summer Is Thru/Call on Me | 1962 | $40 |

HARPER, HERMAN H., II
LOADSTONE
| ❏ 3960 | Waiting Up For Santa Claus/ Headed For The Streets | 1967 | $15 |

HARPER, ROY
EPIC
| ❏ 10268 | Midspring Dithering/Zengfm | 1967 | $20 |

HARPER, TONI
COLUMBIA
| ❏ 39571 | That's All I Want for Christmas/Mom and Dad's Waltz | 1951 | $20 |

HARPERS BIZARRE
WARNER BROS.
| ❏ 7123 | Anything Goes/ Chattanooga Choo Choo | 1969 | $6 |

—Back to Back Hits" series -- originals have green labels with "W7" logo

❏ 7063	Anything Goes/Malibu U.	1967	$8
❏ 7388	Anything Goes/Virginia City	1970	$5
❏ 7223	Battle of New Orleans/ Green Apple Tree	1968	$6
❏ 7200	Both Sides Now/Small Talk	1968	$6
❏ 7090	Chattanooga Choo Choo/ Hey, You in the Crowd	1967	$8
❏ 7028	Come to the Sunshine/ Debutante's Ball	1967	$8
❏ 7399	If We Ever Needed the Lord Before/Mad	1970	$5
❏ 7238	I Love You, Alice B. Toklas/ Look to the Rainbow	1968	$6
❏ 7377	Poly High/Soft Soundin' Music	1970	$5
❏ 7106	The 59th Street Bridge Song (Feelin' Groovy)/ Come to the Sunshine	1968	$6

—Back to Back Hits" series -- originals have green labels with "W7" logo

| ❏ 5890 | The 59th Street Bridge Song (Feelin' Groovy)/ Lost My Love Today | 1967 | $12 |

7-Inch Extended Plays
| ❏ S1739 | Battle of New Orleans/Las Mananitas/Sentimental Journey/I'll Build a Stairway to Paradise/Sit Down, You're Rocking the Boat/ Green Apple Tree | 1968 | $20 |

—Jukebox issue; small hole, plays at 33 1/3 rpm

| ❏ S1739 [PS] | The Secret Life of Harpers Bizarre | 1968 | $20 |

HARPO, SLIM
EXCELLO
❏ 2273	Baby Scratch My Back/I'm Gonna Miss You (Like the Devil)	1965	$15
❏ 2184	Blues Hangover/ What a Dream	1960	$40
❏ 2239	Buzzin'/I Love the Life I'm Livin'	1963	$20
❏ 2171	Buzz Me Babe/ Late Last Night	1960	$40
❏ 2306	Folsom Prison Blues/ Mututal Friend	1969	$20
❏ 2276	Goin' Away Blues/Just a Lonely Stranger	1966	$10
❏ 2113	I'm a King Bee/I Got Love If You Want It	1957	$70
❏ 2289	I'm Gonna Keep What I've Got/I've Got to Be with You Tonight	1967	$10
❏ 2282	I'm Your Bread-Maker, Baby/ Loving You (The Way I Do)	1966	$10
❏ 2309	I've Got My Finger on Your Trigger/The Price Is Too High	1969	$30
❏ 2246	Little Queen Bee (Got a Brand New King)/I Need Money (Keep Your Alibis)	1964	$15
❏ 2278	Midnight Blues/ Shake Your Hips	1966	$10
❏ 2301	Mohair Sam/I Just Can't Leave You	1969	$30
❏ 2162	One More Day/You'll Be Sorry One Day	1959	$40
❏ 2265	Please Don't Turn Me Down/Harpo's Blues	1965	$15
❏ 2261	Sittin' Here Wondering/ What's Goin' On Baby	1964	$15
❏ 2253	Still Rainin' in My Heart/ We're Two of a Kind	1964	$15
❏ 2294	Te-Ni-Lee-Ni-Nu/ Mailbox Blues	1968	$40
❏ 2285	Tip On In (Part 1)/ Tip On In (Part 2)	1967	$10
❏ 2138	Wonderin' and Worryin'/ Strange Love	1958	$40

HARPTONES, THE
AMBIENT SOUND
| ❏ 02807 | Love Needs a Heart/It's You | 1982 | $6 |
ANDREA
| ❏ 100 | What Is Your Decision/ Gimme Some | 1956 | $50 |
BRUCE
| ❏ 101 | A Sunday Kind of Love/I'll Never Tell | 1953 | $3000 |

—Bruce" in script lettering. VG 1000; VG+ 2000

| ❏ 101 | A Sunday Kind of Love/I'll Never Tell | 1953 | $100 |

—Bruce" in block lettering

❏ 109	Forever Mine/Why Should I Love You	1954	$100
❏ 123	High Flying Baby/ Loving a Girl Like You	1955	$70
❏ 128	I Almost Lost My Mind/ Oh Wee Baby	1955	$70
❏ 104	I Depended on You/ Mambo Boogie	1954	$100
❏ 102	My Memories of You/ It Was Just for Laughs	1954	$200
❏ 102	My Memories of You/ The Laughs on You	1954	$120

—Same B-side with different title (and missing the apostrophe)

| ❏ 113 | Since I Fell for You/ Oobidee-Oobidee-Oo | 1954 | $100 |
COED
| ❏ 540 | Answer Me My Love/ Rain Down Kisses | 1960 | $30 |
COMPANION
| ❏ 102 | All in Your Mind/ The Last Dance | 1961 | $40 |
| ❏ 103 | What Will I Tell My Heart/Foolish Me | 1961 | $100 |
CUB
| ❏ 9097 | Devil in Velvet/Your Love Is a Good Love | 1961 | $30 |
GEE
| ❏ 1045 | Cry Like I Cried/So Good, So Fine, You're Mine | 1957 | $70 |

—Red label

KT
| ❏ 201 | Sunset/I Gotta Have Your Love | 1963 | $60 |
PARADISE
| ❏ 105 | It All Depends on You/ Guitar Shuffle | 1955 | $200 |

—Maroon label

| ❏ 105 | It All Depends on You/ Guitar Shuffle | 1955 | $70 |

—Purple label

| ❏ 101 | Life Is But a Dream/ You Know You're Doing Me Wrong | 1954 | $200 |

—Maroon label

| ❏ 101 | Life Is But a Dream/ You Know You're Doing Me Wrong | 1954 | $70 |

—Purple label

| ❏ 103 | My Success/I've Got a Notion | 1955 | $300 |
RAMA
❏ 214	The Masquerade Is Over/ On Sunday Afternoon	1956	$100
❏ 221	The Shrine of St. Cecelia/ Oo Wee Baby	1957	$100
❏ 203	Three Wishes/That's the Way It Goes	1956	$100
RAVEN
| ❏ 8001 | A Sunday Kind of Love/ Mambo Boogie | 1962 | $20 |
TIP TOP
| ❏ 401 | My Memories of You/ High Flyin' Baby | 1956 | $50 |
WARWICK
| ❏ 500 | I Remember/Laughing on the Outside | 1959 | $30 |
| ❏ 512 | Love Me Completely/ Hep Teenager | 1959 | $30 |

7-Inch Extended Plays
BRUCE
| ❏ BEP201 | A Sunday Kind of Love/Ou Wee Baby//Forever Mine/I Almost Lost My Mind | 1954 | $5000 |

—VG 2500; VG+ 3750

| ❏ BEP201 [PS] | The Sensational Harptones | 1954 | $5000 |

—VG 2500; VG+ 3750

HARRIS, ANITA
COLUMBIA
| ❏ 44438 | Anniversary Waltz/ Comes the Night | 1968 | $8 |
LONDON
| ❏ 9720 | Lies/Don't Think About Love | 1964 | $15 |
WARNER BROS.
| ❏ 5638 | Trains and Boats and Planes/Upside Down | 1965 | $10 |

HARRIS BROTHERS, THE
HIT
| ❏ 258 | The Sun Ain't Gonna Shine Anymore/Paint It Black | 1966 | $15 |

—B-side by the Jalopy Five

HARRIS, DONNA
ABC
❏ 10839	He Was Almost Persuaded/ I'm Sending Hin Back to You	1966	$12
❏ 10921	I Just Now Remembered I Forgot/My Hi-Fi to Cry By	1967	$8
❏ 10886	Masquerade Party/ If You Think You've Reached the Bottom	1966	$8

HARRIS, EDDIE
ATLANTIC
❏ 2607	1974 Blues/Free at Last	1969	$20
❏ 5117	Baby/I've Tried Everything	1973	$6
❏ 5106	Boogie Woogie Bossa Nova/Wait Please	1971	$6
❏ 5112	Carry On Brother/ Children's Song	1972	$6
❏ 5118	Drunk Man/Here Goes Funky	1973	$12
❏ 5101	Foolish/Why Don't You Quit	1971	$6
❏ 3256	Get On Down/Time to Do Your Thing	1975	$8
❏ 3288	Get Up and Dance/ Why Must We Part	1975	$8
❏ 3245	I Don't Want Nobody/I Need Some Money	1975	$8
❏ 5115	Instant Death/Was	1972	$6
❏ 5120	Is It In/Funkaroma	1974	$6
❏ 3216	Is It In/Funkaroma	1974	$20
❏ 2487	Listen Here/A Theme in Search of a Movie	1968	$30
❏ 5072	Listen Here/Mean Greens	1968	$6
❏ 2561	Live Right Now/It's Crazy	1968	$20
❏ 5052	Love Theme from "The Sandpiper"/Cryin' Blues	1966	$8
❏ 2667	Movin' On Out/Funky Doo	1969	$20
❏ 2447	Sham Time (Part 1)/ Sham Time (Part 2)	1967	$8
❏ 5116	Ten Minutes to Four/ Please Let Me Go	1973	$6
❏ 3347	That Is Why You're Overweight/It's All Right Now	1976	$8
❏ 2404	When a Man Loves a Woman/The Tender Storm	1967	$8
COLUMBIA
| ❏ 43075 | Chicago Serenade/More Soul Than Soulful | 1964 | $8 |
| ❏ 43188 | People/Groovy Movies | 1964 | $8 |
VEE JAY
❏ 378	Exodus/Alicia	1961	$10
❏ 407	God Bless the Child/ My Buddy	1961	$8
❏ 543	Half and Half/K.C. Blues	1963	$8
❏ 496	Mima/Lolita Marie	1963	$8
❏ 420	Moon River/Mr. Yunioshi	1962	$8
❏ 410	Spartacus/Willow Weep for Me	1961	$8
❏ 518	Theme from Lawrence of Arabia/Yea! Yea! Yea!	1963	$8
❏ 464	Tonight/Be My Love	1962	$8
WARNER BROS.
| ❏ 49890 | Sharkey's Theme/Theme from "Sharkey's Machine" | 1980 | $4 |

—B-side by Sarah Vaughan

HARRIS, EMMYLOU
JUBILEE
| ❏ 5679 | I'll Be Your Baby Tonight/I'll Never Fall in Love Again | 1969 | $30 |
| ❏ 5697 | Paddy/Fugue for the Ox | 1970 | $30 |
MCA
| ❏ 53236 | I Still Dream of You/ Back in Baby's Arms | 1988 | $3 |
REPRISE
❏ 27635	Heartbreak Hill/ Icy Blue Heart	1989	$3
❏ 22999	Heaven Only Knows/A River for Him	1989	$3
❏ 1332	If I Could Only Win Your Love/Boulder to Birmingham	1975	$5
❏ 22850	I Still Miss Someone/ No Regrets	1989	$3
❏ 1341	Light of the Stable/ Bluebird Wine	1975	$12

—A-side is a longer version than later releases

Number | Title | Yr | NM

(continued)

Number	Title	Yr	NM
1341 [PS]	Light of the Stable/Bluebird Wine	1975	$15
1379	Light of the Stable/Boulder to Birmingham	1976	$5
1371	Sweet Dreams/Amarillo	1976	$5
1353	Till I Gain Control Again/One of These Days	1976	$5
1346	Together Again/Here, There and Everywhere	1976	$5
1326	Too Far Gone/Boulder to Birmingham	1975	$5

WARNER BROS.

Number	Title	Yr	NM
49633	Beautiful Star of Bethlehem/The Little Drummer Boy	1980	$4
49164	Beneath Still Waters/'Til I Gain Control Again	1980	$4
49056	Blue Kentucky Girl/Leaving Louisiana in the Broad Daylight	1979	$4
29993	Born to Run/Colors of My Heart	1982	$4
8329	C'est La Vie (You Never Can Tell)/You're Supposed to Be Feeling Good	1977	$5
29443	Drivin' Wheel/Good News	1983	$4
8623	Easy from Now On/You're Supposed to Be Feeling Good	1978	$5
49739	I Don't Have to Crawl/Colors of Your Heart	1981	$4
49809	If I Needed You/Ashes By Now	1981	$4

— A-side with Don Williams

Number	Title	Yr	NM
28770	I Had My Heart Set on You/Your Long Journey	1986	$3
29729	I'm Movin' On/Maybe Tonight	1983	$4
29329	In My Dreams/Like an Old Fashioned World	1984	$4
PRO02872 [DJ]	Light of the Stable/It Came Upon a Midnight Clear	1987	$12

— B-side by Highway 101

Number	Title	Yr	NM
PRO-S-2872 [DJ]	Light of the Stable/It Came Upon a Midnight Clear	1987	$12

— B-side by Highway 101

Number	Title	Yr	NM
49645	Little Drummer Boy/Light of the Stable	1980	$4
29898	(Lost His Love) On Our Last Date/Another Pot O' Tea	1982	$4
8388	Making Believe/I'll Be Your San Antone Rose	1977	$5
49684	Mister Sandman/Fools' Thin Air	1981	$4
29218	Pledging My Love/Baby, Better Start Turnin' 'Em Down	1984	$4
8815	Save the Last Dance for Me/Even Cowgirls Get the Blues	1979	$5
28302	Someday My Ship Will Sail/When He Calls	1987	$3
29138	Someone Like You/Light of the Stable	1984	$4
29583	So Sad (To Watch Good Love Go Bad)/Amarillo	1983	$4
49892	Tennessee Rose/Mama Help	1982	$4
49262	That Lovin' You Feeling Again/Lola	1980	$5

— A-side with Roy Orbison; B-side by Craig Hundley

Number	Title	Yr	NM
49551	The Boxer/Precious Love	1980	$4
28852	Timberline/Sweet Chariot	1985	$4
8498	To Daddy/Tulsa Queen	1977	$5
28714	Today I Started Loving You Again/When I Was Young	1986	$3
8732	Too Far Gone/Tulsa Queen	1979	$4
8553	Two More Bottles of Wine/I Ain't Living Long Like This	1978	$5
49239	Wayfaring Stranger/Green Pastures	1980	$4
29041	White Line/Long Tall Sally Rose	1985	$4

HARRIS, GENEE

ABC-PARAMOUNT

Number	Title	Yr	NM
9900	Bye Bye Elvis/You're Like a Jumping Jack	1958	$60

HARRIS, GEORGIA, AND THE LYRICS

HY-TONE

Number	Title	Yr	NM
111	Let's Exchange Hearts for Christmas/It's Time to Rock	1958	$500
117	Let's Exchange Hearts for Christmas/Kiss, Kiss, Kiss	1958	$500

HARRIS, JET, AND TONY MEECHAN

LONDON

Number	Title	Yr	NM
9622	Applejack/Tall Texan	1963	$20
9589	Diamonds/Footstomp	1963	$20
9608	Scarlet O'Hara/(Doin' the) Hully Gully	1963	$20

HARRIS, JUDY

SUN

Number	Title	Yr	NM
1117	Glory Train/You Touched Me	1970	$5

HARRIS, KURT

DIAMOND

Number	Title	Yr	NM
158	Go On/Emperor of My Baby's Heart	1964	$500

JOSIE

Number	Title	Yr	NM
898	Let Her Dance/I Can't Love Nobody Else	1962	$30

HARRIS, MAJOR

ATLANTIC

Number	Title	Yr	NM
3217	Each Morning I Wake Up/Just a Thing I Do	1974	$5
3303	I Got Over Love/Loving You Is Mellow	1975	$40
3336	It's Got to Be Magic/Just a Thing That I Do	1976	$4
3248	Love Won't Let Me Wait/After Loving You	1975	$20
3299 [DJ]	Loving You Is Mellow (mono/stereo)	1975	$5

— May be promo-only

Number	Title	Yr	NM
3299 [DJ]	Loving You Is Mellow (mono/stereo)	1975	$5

— May be promo-only

OKEH

Number	Title	Yr	NM
7327	Like a Rolling Stone/Call Me Tomorrow	1969	$500

WMOT

Number	Title	Yr	NM
02091	Here We Are/Living's Easy Now	1981	$4
4002	Laid Back Love/This Is What You Mean to Me	1976	$4

HARRIS, PEPPERMINT

ALADDIN

Number	Title	Yr	NM
3183	Don't Leave Me Alone/Wet Rat	1953	$100
3107	Have Another Drink and Talk to Me/Middle of Winter	1951	$100
3141	I Cry for My Baby/There's a Dead Cat on the Line	1952	$100
3097	I Got Loaded/It's You, Yes It's You	1951	$125

— Black vinyl

Number	Title	Yr	NM
3097	I Got Loaded/It's You, Yes It's You	1951	$250

— Green vinyl

Number	Title	Yr	NM
3206	I Never Get Enough of You/Three Sheets in the Wind	1953	$100
3154	I Sure Do Miss My Baby/Hey Little Schoolgirl	1952	$100
3108	Let the Back Door Hit You/P.H. Blues	1951	$100
3177	Wasted Love/Goodbye Blues	1953	$100

CASH

Number	Title	Yr	NM
1003	Cadillac Funeral/Treat Me Like I Treat You	1954	$200

COMBO

Number	Title	Yr	NM
114	Love at First Sight/I Don't Care	1956	$70

DUKE

Number	Title	Yr	NM
319	Ain't No Business/Angel Child	1960	$40

JEWEL

Number	Title	Yr	NM
795	24 Hours/Little Girl	1968	$40
772	Anytime Is the Right Time/Wait Until It Happens to You	1966	$200
789	Bad Bad Whiskey/Lonesome As Can Be	1967	$12
747	Ma Ma/Anything You Can Do	1965	$10
742	Marking Time/Bad, Mad Woman	1965	$50

MODERN

Number	Title	Yr	NM
936	Bye Bye, Fare Thee Well/Black Cat Bone	1951	$125

HARRIS, PHIL

BUENA VISTA

Number	Title	Yr	NM
F-478	Everybody Wants to Be a Cat/Thomas O'Malley Cat	1970	$20
F-461	The Bare Necessities/I Wanna Be Like You	1967	$20

— B-side by Louis Prima

Number	Title	Yr	NM
F-464	The Bare Necessities/The Bare Necessities	1968	$20

— B-side by the Jungle V.I.P.'s

Number	Title	Yr	NM
F-477	What! No Mickey Mouse (What Kind of Party Is This)/Minnie's Yoo Hoo	1970	$8
F-477 [PS]	What! No Mickey Mouse (What Kind of Party Is This)/Minnie's Yoo Hoo	1970	$15

COLISEUM

Number	Title	Yr	NM
2711	But I Loved You/This Is All I Ask	1968	$8

MEGA

Number	Title	Yr	NM
0111	Dark Town Poker Club/That's What I Like About the South	1973	$8

RCA VICTOR

Number	Title	Yr	NM
47-2847	44 Sycamore/Darktown Poker Club	1949	$20
47-3216	Chattanoogie Shoe Shine Boy/That's a Plenty	1950	$30
47-3825	Dig-Dig-Dig for Your Dinner/I've Been Floating Down Green River	1950	$30
47-4224	Golden Train/Tennessee Hillbilly Ghost	1951	$30
47-4584	Hambone/Mama's on the Warpath	1952	$30
47-3064	I Ain't Gonna Give Nobody None of This Jelly Roll/Row, Row, Row	1949	$30
47-5615	I Know an Old Lady/Take Your Girlie to the Movies	1954	$20
47-3066	Is It True What They Say About Dixie?/After You've Gone	1949	$30
47-5945	I Wouldn't Touch You with a Ten-Foot Pole/There's a Lot More Layin' Down	1954	$20
47-2846	Look Out Stranger, I'm a Texas Ranger/That's What I Like About the South	1949	$20
47-5873	Muskrat Ramble/Stars Fell on Alabama	1954	$20
47-3723	Muskrat Ramble/Walk with a Wiggle	1950	$30
47-4070	Oh What a Face/Southern Fried Boogie	1951	$30
WP199 [PS]	On the Record by Phil Harris	1949	$20

— Box for three 45s (47-2846, 47-2847, 47-2848)

Number	Title	Yr	NM
47-2848	Pappy's Little Jug/Minnie the Mermaid	1949	$20

— The above three comprise box set WP 199

Number	Title	Yr	NM
47-5730	Persian Kitty/I Guess I'll Have to Change My Plan	1954	$20
47-2909	Shadrach/The General's House	1949	$30
47-3003	Silas Lee/Is It True What They Say About Dixie?	1949	$30
47-3781	Simple Melody/Down the Mississippi	1950	$30
47-3260	Smoke, Smoke, Smoke (That Cigarette)/Crawdad Song	1950	$30

— 78 originally released in 1947 with a different number

Number	Title	Yr	NM
47-2938	Thank the Man Upstairs/I Wish I Were a Goldfish	1949	$30
47-4124	The Letter/Possibilities	1951	$30

— With Alice Faye

Number	Title	Yr	NM
47-4225	The Musicians/How D'Ya Do and Shake Hands	1951	$30

— With Dinah Shore, Betty Hutton and Tony Martin

Number	Title	Yr	NM
47-3114	The Old Master Painter/St. James Infirmary	1949	$30
47-3968	The Thing/Goofus	1950	$30
47-4342	Where the Blues Were Born in New Orleans/Ragged But Right	1951	$30
47-4450	Wine, Women, Song/8th Street Association	1952	$30
47-2770	Woodman, Spare That Tree/Ain't Nobody Here But Us Chickens	1949	$30

7-Inch Extended Plays

Number	Title	Yr	NM
EPA-5127	(contents unknown)	1958	$15
547-0189	Minnie the Mermaid (A Love Song in Fish Time)/Woodman, Spare That Tree/44 Sycamore/Look Out Stranger I'm a Texas Ranger	1952	$25

— Part of 2-EP set EPB 3037

Number	Title	Yr	NM
EPB3037 [PS]	On the Record by Phil Harris	1952	$25

— Cover for 2-EP set (547-0188, 547-0189)

Number	Title	Yr	NM
EPA-5127 [PS]	That's What I Like About the South	1958	$15
547-0188	That's What I Like About the South/The Dark Town Poker Club//Ain't Nobody Here But Us Chickens/Pappy's Little Jug	1952	$25

— Part of 2-EP set EPB 3037

HARRIS, RAY

SUN

Number	Title	Yr	NM
254	Come On Little Mama/Where'd You Stay Last Night	1956	$200
272	Greenback Dollar Watch and Chain/Foolish Hearts	1957	$125

HARRIS, RICHARD

ABC DUNHILL

Number	Title	Yr	NM
4241	Ballad of a Man Called Horse/Morning of the Mourning for Another	1970	$5
4194	Didn't We?/Paper Chase	1969	$5
4218	Fill the World with Love/What a Lot of Flowers	1969	$5
4218 [PS]	Fill the World with Love/What a Lot of Flowers	1969	$6
4310	Half of Every Dream/Turning Back the Pages	1972	$5
4336	How I Spent My Summer/I Don't Have to Tell You	1973	$5
4134	MacArthur Park/Didn't We	1968	$6

— With both ABC and Dunhill logos at top of label

Number	Title	Yr	NM
4134 [PS]	MacArthur Park/Didn't We	1968	$8

— Regular stock sleeve

Number	Title	Yr	NM
4293	My Boy/Why Did You Leave Me	1971	$5
4322	There Are Too Many Saviours on My Cross/All the Broken Children	1972	$5
4322 [PS]	There Are Too Many Saviours on My Cross/All the Broken Children	1972	$6
4185	Watermark/One of the Nicer Things	1969	$5

ATLANTIC

Number	Title	Yr	NM
3238	On Crime and Punishment/Theme from "The Prophet	1975	$4
3238 [PS]	On Crime and Punishment/Theme from "The Prophet	1975	$5

DUNHILL

Number	Title	Yr	NM
4134	MacArthur Park/Didn't We	1968	$8

— First pressings have Dunhill standing alone at top of label

Number	Title	Yr	NM
4134 [PS]	MacArthur Park/Didn't We	1968	$20

— Special promotional issue, so marked on sleeve

7-Inch Extended Plays

ABC DUNHILL

Number	Title	Yr	NM
LP-DS-50032 [PS]	A Tramp Shining	1968	$20
LP-DS-50032	MacArthur Park//Didn't We/If You Must Leave My Life	1968	$20

— Stereo jukebox issue; small hole, plays at 33 1/3 rpm

HARRIS, ROLF

20TH FOX

Number	Title	Yr	NM
230	Lost Little Boy/The Big Black Hat	1960	$20
414	Lost Little Boy/The Big Black Hat	1963	$15
295	Six White Boomers/Tame Eagle	1962	$20
207	Tie Me Kangaroo Down, Sport/Nick Teen & Al K. Hall	1960	$30

— Different versions than the Epic recordings

EPIC

Number	Title	Yr	NM
9641	Lost Little Boy/Six White Boomers	1963	$10
9641 [PS]	Lost Little Boy/Six White Boomers	1963	$30
9567	Sun Arise/Someone's Pinched My Winkles	1963	$15
9682	The Court of King Caractacus/Two Buffalos	1964	$12
9756	The Thing/Wild Colonial Boy	1965	$10
9596	Tie Me Kangaroo Down, Sport/The Big Black Hat	1963	$20
9596 [PS]	Tie Me Kangaroo Down, Sport/The Big Black Hat	1963	$30
9780	Tie My Hunting Dog Down, Jed/Five Young Apprentices	1965	$10

MGM

Number	Title	Yr	NM
14103	Two Little Boys/I Love My Love	1970	$10

HARRIS, THURSTON

ALADDIN

Number	Title	Yr	NM
3415	Be Baby Leba/I'm Out to Getcha	1958	$40
3448	Don't You Know/From the Bottom of My Heart	1959	$30
3399	Do What You Did/I'm Asking Forgiveness	1957	$40
3447	From the Bottom of My Heart/You Don't Know How Much I Love You	1959	$30
3450	Hey Little Girl/My Love Will Last	1959	$30
3398	Little Bitty Pretty One/I Hope You Won't Hold It Against Me	1957	$50
3462	Moonlight Cocktail/Recess in Heaven	1960	$30
3468	One Scotch, One Bourbon, One Beer/Send Me Some Loving	1960	$30
3428	Only One Love Is Blessed/Smokey Joe's	1958	$40
3430	Over and Over/You're Gonna Miss Me	1958	$30
3435	Over Someone Else's Shoulder/Tears from My Heart	1958	$30

Number	Title	Yr	NM
3440	Purple Stew/I Heard a Rhapsody	1958	$30
3456	Slip Slop/Paradise Hill	1959	$30

CUB

Number	Title	Yr	NM
9108	I'd Like to Start Over Again/Mr. Satan	1962	$15

DOT

Number	Title	Yr	NM
16427	Poop-A-Loop/She's the One	1963	$12

IMPERIAL

Number	Title	Yr	NM
5928	Got You on My Mind/Tears from My Heart	1963	$10

REPRISE

Number	Title	Yr	NM
0255	Dance On Little Girl/Dancing Silhouettes	1964	$40

UNITED ARTISTS

Number	Title	Yr	NM
0152	Little Bitty Pretty One/Over and Over	1973	$4

— Silver Spotlight Series" reissue

HARRIS, TONY

DEE GEE

Number	Title	Yr	NM
3014	Super Man/How Much Do I Love You	1966	$20

EBB

Number	Title	Yr	NM
104	Chicken Baby Chicken/I'll Forever Love You	1957	$60
120	Try This Little Ol' Heart/When I Get You Back	1957	$40

TRIUMPH

Number	Title	Yr	NM
60	Go, Go, Little Scrambler/Poor Boy	1964	$40

HARRIS, WYNONIE

ATCO

Number	Title	Yr	NM
6081	Destination Love/Tell a Whale of a Tale	1956	$40

KING

Number	Title	Yr	NM
4763	All She Wants to Do Is Mambo/Christina	1955	$70
4593	Bad News Baby (There'll Be Rockin' Tonight)/Bring It Back	1953	$125
6011	Big Old Country Fool/Bloodshot Eyes	1965	$12
5050	Big Ole Country Fool/That's Me Right Now	1957	$40
4461	Bloodshot Eyes/Confessin' the Blues	1951	$120
4555	Do it Again Please/Night Train	1952	$125
4685	Down Boy Down/Quiet Whiskey	1953	$100
4565	Drinking Blues/Adam Come and Get Your Rib	1952	$125
4814	Drinkin' Sherry Wine/Get With the Guts	1955	$60
4789	Fishtail Blues/Mr. Dollar	1955	$70
4774	Good Mambo Tonight/Git to Gittin' Baby	1955	$70
4852	Good Morning Judge/Bloodshot Eyes	1955	$60
5416	Good Rockin' Tonight/Bloodshot Eyes	1960	$20
6304	Good Rockin' Tonight/Good Morning Judge	1970	$6
4210	Good Rockin' Tonight/Good Morning Mister Blues	1952	$200

— 78 originally released in 1948; the only known Wynonie Harris 45 on King before 4461

Number	Title	Yr	NM
4592	Greyhound/Rot Gut	1953	$125
4724	I Get a Thrill/Don't Take My Whiskey Away from Me	1954	$100
4468	I'll Never Give Up/Man Have I Got Troubles	1951	$120
4485	Lovin' Machine/Luscious Woman	1951	$120

— Black vinyl

Number	Title	Yr	NM
4485	Lovin' Machine/Luscious Woman	1951	$400

— Blue vinyl

Number	Title	Yr	NM
4620	Mama Your Daughter Done Lied on Me/Wasn't That Good	1953	$125
4507	My Playful Baby's Gone/Here Comes the Night	1952	$125
4668	Please Louise/Nearer My Love to Thee	1953	$100
4716	Shake That Thing/Keep A-Talking	1954	$100
4839	Shot Gun Wedding/I Don't Know Where to Go	1955	$60
4635	Song of the Bayou/The Deacon Doesn't Like It	1953	$125
5073	There's No Substitute for Love/A Tale of Woe	1957	$40
4662	Tremblin'/Rot Gut	1953	$100
4826	Wine, Wine, Sweet Wine/Man's Best Friend	1955	$60

ROULETTE

Number	Title	Yr	NM
4291	Bloodshot Eyes/Sweet Lucy Brown	1960	$15

7-Inch Extended Plays

KING

Number	Title	Yr	NM
EP-260	*Good Rockin' Tonight/Bloodshot Eyes/All She Wants to Do Is Rock/Good Morning Judge	1954	$500
EP-260 [PS]	Wynonie Harris	1954	$500

HARRISON, GEORGE
Also see THE BEATLES.

APPLE

Number	Title	Yr	NM
1836	Bangla-Desh/Deep Blue	1971	$30

— With star on A-side label

Number	Title	Yr	NM
1836	Bangla-Desh/Deep Blue	1971	$8

— Without star on A-side label

Number	Title	Yr	NM
1836 [PS]	Bangla-Desh/Deep Blue	1971	$30
P-1877 [DJ]	Dark Horse (edited mono/stereo)	1974	$70
P-1877 [DJ]	Dark Horse (edited mono/stereo)	1974	$70
P-1877 [DJ]	Dark Horse (full length mono/stereo)	1974	$50
P-1877 [DJ]	Dark Horse (full length mono/stereo)	1974	$50
1877	Dark Horse/I Don't Care Anymore	1974	$8

— Light blue and white custom photo label

Number	Title	Yr	NM
1877	Dark Horse/I Don't Care Anymore	1974	$12

— White label; NOT a promo

Number	Title	Yr	NM
1877 [PS]	Dark Horse/I Don't Care Anymore	1974	$100
1879	Ding Dong, Ding Dong/Hari's on Tour (Express)	1974	$30

— Black and white custom photo label

Number	Title	Yr	NM
1879	Ding Dong, Ding Dong/Hari's on Tour (Express)	1974	$250

— Blue and white custon photo label

Number	Title	Yr	NM
1879 [PS]	Ding Dong, Ding Dong/Hari's on Tour (Express)	1974	$30
P-1879 [DJ]	Ding Dong, Ding Dong (remixed mono/edited stereo)	1974	$50
P-1879 [DJ]	Ding Dong, Ding Dong (remixed mono/edited stereo)	1974	$50
1862	Give Me Love (Give Me Peace on Earth)/Miss O'Dell (2:20)	1973	$8

— B-side playing time corrected

Number	Title	Yr	NM
1862	Give Me Love (Give Me Peace on Earth)/Miss O'Dell (2:30)	1973	$8

— With incorrect time for B-side listed

Number	Title	Yr	NM
P-1862 [DJ]	Give Me Love (Give Me Peace on Earth) (mono/stereo)	1973	$60
P-1862 [DJ]	Give Me Love (Give Me Peace on Earth) (mono/stereo)	1973	$60
2995	My Sweet Lord/Isn't It a Pity	1970	$50

— With black star on label

Number	Title	Yr	NM
2995	My Sweet Lord/Isn't It a Pity	1970	$8

— With "Mfd. by Apple" on label

Number	Title	Yr	NM
2995 [PS]	My Sweet Lord/Isn't It a Pity	1970	$50
2995	My Sweet Lord/Isn't It a Pity	1975	$30

— With "All Rights Reserved" disclaimer

Number	Title	Yr	NM
1885	This Guitar (Can't Keep from Crying)/Maya Love	1975	$30

— The last Apple 45 until 1995

Number	Title	Yr	NM
P-1885 [DJ]	This Guitar (Can't Keep from Crying) (mono/stereo)	1975	$60
P-1885 [DJ]	This Guitar (Can't Keep from Crying) (mono/stereo)	1975	$60
1828	What Is Life/Apple Scruffs	1971	$20

— With star on A-side label

Number	Title	Yr	NM
1828	What Is Life/Apple Scruffs	1971	$8

— Without star on A-side label

Number	Title	Yr	NM
1828 [PS]	What Is Life/Apple Scruffs	1971	$50

CAPITOL

Number	Title	Yr	NM
1836	Bangla-Desh/Deep Blue	1976	$40

— Orange label

Number	Title	Yr	NM
1836	Bangla-Desh/Deep Blue	1978	$6

— Purple late-1970s label

Number	Title	Yr	NM
1836	Bangla-Desh/Deep Blue	1983	$20

— Black colorband label

Number	Title	Yr	NM
1879	Ding Dong, Ding Dong/Hari's on Tour (Express)	1978	$8

— Purple late-1970s label

Number	Title	Yr	NM
1862	Give Me Love (Give Me Peace on Earth)/Miss O'Dell	1978	$8

— Purple late-1970s label

Number	Title	Yr	NM
1862	Give Me Love (Give Me Peace on Earth)/Miss O'Dell	1978	$20

— Black colorband label

Number	Title	Yr	NM
2995	My Sweet Lord/Isn't It a Pity	1976	$30

— Orange label with "Capitol" at bottom

Number	Title	Yr	NM
2995	My Sweet Lord/Isn't It a Pity	1978	$6

— Purple label; label has reeded edge

Number	Title	Yr	NM
❏ 2995	My Sweet Lord/Isn't It a Pity	1983	$6
—Black label with colorband			
❏ 2995	My Sweet Lord/Isn't It a Pity	1988	$5
—Purple label; label has smooth edge			
❏ 1828	What Is Life/Apple Scruffs	1976	$40
—Orange label			
❏ 1828	What Is Life/Apple Scruffs	1978	$6
—Purple late-1970s label			

COLUMBIA

Number	Title	Yr	NM
❏ 04887	I Don't Want to Do It/ Queen of the Hop	1985	$30
—B-side by Dave Edmunds			

DARK HORSE

Number	Title	Yr	NM
❏ 49725	All Those Years Ago/ Writing's on the Wall	1981	$5
❏ 49725 [PS]	All Those Years Ago/ Writing's on the Wall	1981	$5
❏ 8763	Blow Away/Soft-Hearted Hana	1979	$5
— With "RE-1" on label			
❏ 8763	Blow Away/Soft-Hearted Hana	1979	$30
— Without "RE-1" on label (no "Loka Productions S.A." on label)			
❏ 8763 [PS]	Blow Away/Soft-Hearted Hana	1979	$5
❏ 8313	Crackerbox Palace/ Learning How to Love You	1977	$5
❏ 28178	Got My Mind Set on You/Lay His Head	1987	$4
❏ 28178 [PS]	Got My Mind Set on You/Lay His Head	1987	$4
❏ 29744	I Really Love You/Circles	1983	$30
❏ 8844	Love Comes to Everyone/Soft Touch	1979	$10
❏ 8844 [PS]	Love Comes to Everyone/Soft Touch	1979	$750
❏ 49785	Teardrops/Save the World	1981	$10
❏ 27913	This Is Love/Breath Away from Heaven	1988	$5
❏ 27913 [PS]	This Is Love/Breath Away from Heaven	1988	$5
❏ 8294	This Song/Learning How to Love You	1976	$10
— Tan label			
❏ 8294	This Song/Learning How to Love You	1976	$8
— White label, NOT a promo			
❏ 8294 [PS]	This Song/Learning How to Love You	1976	$40
❏ 8294 [DJ]	This Song (mono/stereo)	1976	$30
❏ 8294 [DJ]	This Song (mono/stereo)	1976	$30
❏ 8294 [PS]	This Song (mono/stereo)	1976	$50
— Promotional only sleeve, different from stock sleeve			
❏ 8294 [PS]	This Song (mono/stereo)	1976	$50
— Flyer with "The Story Behind This Song"			
❏ 29864	Wake Up My Love/Greece	1982	$10
❏ 28131	When We Was Fab/Zig Zag	1988	$5
❏ 28131 [PS]	When We Was Fab/Zig Zag	1988	$5

WARNER BROS.

Number	Title	Yr	NM
❏ 22807 [DJ]	Cheer Down (same on both sides)	1989	$200
❏ 22807 [DJ]	Cheer Down (same on both sides)	1989	$200
❏ 22807	Cheer Down/That's What It Takes	1989	$20
❏ 22807 [PS]	Cheer Down/That's What It Takes	1989	$20

HARRISON, HARRY

AMY

Number	Title	Yr	NM
❏ 944	Auld Lang Syne/ May You Always	1965	$12

HARRISON, NOEL

LONDON

Number	Title	Yr	NM
❏ 20017	Cheryl's Going Home/ In a Dusty Old Room	1966	$8
❏ 20017 [PS]	Cheryl's Going Home/ In a Dusty Old Room	1966	$15
❏ 9815	It's All Over Now, Baby Blue/Much As I Love You	1966	$8
❏ 9755	One Too Many Mornings/ Barbara Allen	1965	$8
❏ 20021	Out for the Day/ Fly Sing Song	1967	$8
❏ 20011	The Man Behind the Red Balloon/Marlene	1966	$8

REPRISE

Number	Title	Yr	NM
❏ 0914	Another Virgin Spring/ Tin Wedding	1970	$6
❏ 0795	I'll Be Your Baby Tonight/The Greatest Experiment Is Over	1968	$6
❏ 0615	Life Is a Dream/Suzanne	1967	$6
❏ 0682	Santa Monica Pier/ In Your Chidren	1968	$6
❏ 0599	Sign of the Queen/ Mrs. Williams' Rose	1967	$6
❏ 0758	The Windmills of Your Mind/Leitch on the Beach	1968	$8

HARRISON, WES

LIN

Number	Title	Yr	NM
❏ 5002	There Y'Are/Uncle Winnie's Sound Stories	1956	$40

PHILIPS

Number	Title	Yr	NM
❏ DJP-4 [DJ]	Wes' Car/Better Late Than Never	1963	$15
— Promo only			

HARRISON, WILBERT

BELL

Number	Title	Yr	NM
❏ 869	C.C. Rider/Since I Fell for You	1970	$6

BRUNSWICK

Number	Title	Yr	NM
❏ 55519	I'm Going to the River/I Need Some (Honey Honey)	1975	$6
❏ 55511	Lovin' Operator/Love You	1974	$6

CHART

Number	Title	Yr	NM
❏ 626	Cool Water/Calypso Man	1956	$30

DELUXE

Number	Title	Yr	NM
❏ 6002	This Woman of Mine/ The Letter	1953	$70

FURY

Number	Title	Yr	NM
❏ 1031	C.C. Rider/Why Did You Leave	1960	$20
❏ 1027	Cheating Baby/Don't Wreck My Life	1959	$30
❏ 1055	Drafted/My Heart Is Yours	1961	$30
❏ 1028	Goodbye Kansas City/1960	1960	$20
❏ 1047	Happy in Love/ Calypso Dance	1961	$20
❏ 1059	Let's Stick Together/ Kansas City Twist	1962	$12
❏ 1063	Let's Stick Together/ My Heart Is Yours	1962	$20
❏ 1037	Since I Fell for You/ Little School Girl	1960	$20
❏ 1041	The Horse/Da-De-Ya-Da (I'd Do Anything for You)	1961	$40

GLADES

Number	Title	Yr	NM
❏ 603	Gonna Tell You a Story/ Letter Edged in Black	1959	$15

PORT

Number	Title	Yr	NM
❏ 3003	Baby Move On/You're Still My Baby	1965	$40
❏ 3009	Don't Take It So Hard/ Sugar Lump	1965	$40

ROCKIN'

Number	Title	Yr	NM
❏ 526	This Woman of Mine/ The Letter	1952	$125

SAVOY

Number	Title	Yr	NM
❏ 1531	Baby Don't You Know/My Love for You Lingers On	1958	$30
❏ 1198	Confessin' My Dream/ The Way I Feel	1956	$40
❏ 1571	Don't Drop It/Baby Don't You Know	1959	$20
❏ 1138	Don't Drop It/The Ways of a Woman	1954	$50
❏ 1164	Florida Special/Darling, Listen to This Song	1955	$40
❏ 1517	My Love Is True/I Know My Baby Loves Me	1957	$30
❏ 1149	Women and Whiskey/ Da-De-Ya-Da (I'd Do Anything for You)	1955	$40

SEA HORN

Number	Title	Yr	NM
❏ 502	Say It Again/Near to You	1963	$30

SSS INTERNATIONAL

Number	Title	Yr	NM
❏ 830 [DJ]	My Heart Is Yours (mono/stereo)	1971	$10
— Promo only on blue vinyl			
❏ 830	My Heart Is Yours/ Pretty Little Woman	1971	$6

SUE

Number	Title	Yr	NM
❏ 11	Let's Work Together (Part 1)/ Let's Work Together (Part 2)	1969	$30

WET SOUL

Number	Title	Yr	NM
❏ 4	My Heart Is Yours/ Pretty Little Woman	1970	$30

HARRY, DEBBIE

CHRYSALIS

Number	Title	Yr	NM
❏ 2526	Backfired/Military Rap	1981	$3
❏ 2526 [PS]	Backfired/Military Rap	1981	$3
❏ VS443328	Denis (The '88 Remix)/ Rapture (Teddy Riley Remix)	1988	$3
❏ VS443328 [PS]	Denis (The '88 Remix)/ Rapture (Teddy Riley Remix)	1988	$3

GEFFEN

Number	Title	Yr	NM
❏ 7-28546	French Kissin'/Rockbird	1986	$3
❏ 7-28546 [PS]	French Kissin'/Rockbird	1986	$3
❏ 7-28476	In Love with Love/Secret Life	1987	$3
❏ 7-28476 [PS]	In Love with Love/Secret Life	1987	$3

REPRISE

Number	Title	Yr	NM
❏ 7-27792	Liar, Liar/Queen of Voodoo	1988	$3
— B-side by Voodooist Corporation			
❏ 7-27792 [PS]	Liar, Liar/Queen of Voodoo	1988	$3

SIRE

Number	Title	Yr	NM
❏ 7-22816	I Want That Man/Bike Boy	1989	$3
❏ 7-22816 [PS]	I Want That Man/Bike Boy	1989	$4

HART, BILLY AND DON

ROULETTE

Number	Title	Yr	NM
❏ 4172	Check-Mated and Bingooed/Blabbermouth	1959	$40

HART, BOBBY

ARIOLA AMERICA

Number	Title	Yr	NM
❏ 809	Lovers for the Night/You Get Smoke in Your Eyes	1980	$5

BAMBOO

Number	Title	Yr	NM
❏ 507	The Girl I Used to Know/ The Spider and the Fly	1961	$40

CHELSEA

Number	Title	Yr	NM
❏ BCBO-0026	Easy Evil/California	1973	$5

DCP

Number	Title	Yr	NM
❏ 1152	Around the Corner/ Cry My Eyes Out	1966	$50
❏ 1142	Baby Let Your Hair Down/ Jealous Feeling	1965	$40
❏ 1113	That'll Be the Day/Turn On Your Lovelight	1964	$20

ERA

Number	Title	Yr	NM
❏ 3039	Girl in the Window/ Journey of Love	1961	$30

GUYDEN

Number	Title	Yr	NM
❏ 2022	Is You Is Or Is You Ain't My Baby/Girl of My Dreams	1959	$40
— As "Robert Luke Harshman"			

INFINITY

Number	Title	Yr	NM
❏ 022	Lovesick Blues/I Think It's Called a Heartache	1963	$30
❏ 017	Too Many Teardrops/ The People Next Door	1963	$30

RADIO

Number	Title	Yr	NM
❏ 122	Stop Talkin', Start Lovin'/ Love Whatcha Doin' to Me	1959	$50
— As "Robert Luke Harshman"			

REEL

Number	Title	Yr	NM
❏ 100	Girl in the Window/ Journey of Love	1961	$50

WARNER BROS.

Number	Title	Yr	NM
❏ 8058	Hard Core Man/To Keep from Crying	1974	$5
❏ 8058 [PS]	Hard Core Man/To Keep from Crying	1974	$8
❏ 49079	The Loneliest Night/ Sometimes Love	1979	$5

HART, COREY

EMI AMERICA

Number	Title	Yr	NM
❏ B-8385 [PS]	Dancin' with My Mirror/ (Instrumental)	1988	$15
❏ B-8385	Dancin' with My Mirror/ (Instrumental)	1988	$3

HART, FREDDIE

CAPITOL

Number	Title	Yr	NM
❏ 3353	Bless Your Heart/ Conscience Makes Cowards (Of Us All)	1972	$6
❏ F2524	Butterfly Love/My Heart Is a Playground	1953	$30
❏ 2933	California Grapevine/What's Wrong with Your Head, Fred	1970	$8
❏ F3203	Canada to Tennessee/ No Thanks to You	1955	$30
❏ F2873	Caught at Last/It Just Don't Seem Like Home	1954	$30
❏ 3115	Easy Loving/ Brother Bluebird	1971	$6
❏ 2839	Fingerprints/I Can't Keep My Hands Off of You	1970	$8
❏ 3453	Got the All Overs for You (All Over Me)/Just Another Girl	1972	$6
❏ 3827	Hang In There Girl/ You Belong to Me	1974	$6
❏ F3299	Hiding in Darkness/That's What You Gave to Me	1955	$30
❏ 4031	I'd Like to Sleep Til I Get Over You/Nothing's Better Than That	1975	$6
❏ 3730	If You Can't Feel It (It Ain't There)/Skid Row Street	1973	$6
❏ F2991	I'm Going Out on the Front Porch and Cry/ Please Don't Tell Her	1954	$30
❏ F2726	Loose Talk/The Curtain Never Falls	1954	$30
❏ F3090	Miss Lonely Heart/Oh Heart Let Her Go	1955	$30
❏ 3261	My Hang-Up Is You/ Big Bad Wolf	1972	$6
❏ 4684	My Lady/Guilty	1979	$5
❏ 3970	My Woman's Man/Let's Clean Up the Country	1974	$6
❏ 2768	One More Mountain to Climb/Just Another Girl	1970	$8
❏ 4561	Only You/I Love You, I Just Don't Like You	1978	$5

Number	Title	Yr	NM
❏ F2588	Secret Kisses/Whole Hog or None	1953	$30
❏ 4251	She'll Throw Stones at You/ Love Makes It Alright	1976	$6
❏ 4530	So Good, So Rare, So Fine/There's an Angel Living There	1978	$5
❏ 3524	Super Kind of Woman/ Mother Nature Made a Believer Out of Me	1973	$6
❏ 4409	Thank God She's Mine/ Falling All Over Me	1977	$4
❏ 4313	That Look in Her Eyes/ Try My Love for Size	1976	$6
❏ 4099	The First Time/Sexy	1975	$6
❏ 4448	The Pleasure's Been All Mine/It's Heaven Loving You	1977	$4
❏ 4498	The Search/Honky Tonk Toys	1977	$5
❏ 3898	The Want-To's/Phenix City, Alabama	1974	$6
❏ 2692	The Whole World Holding Hands/Without You	1969	$8
❏ 4609	Toe to Toe/And Then Some	1978	$5
❏ 3612	Trip to Heaven/Look-a Here	1973	$6
❏ 4152	Warm Side of You/I Love You, I Just Don't Like You	1975	$6
❏ 4720	Wasn't It Easy Baby/ My Lady Loves	1979	$5
❏ 4363	Why Lovers Turn to Strangers/Paper Sack Full of Memories	1976	$6

COLUMBIA

Number	Title	Yr	NM
❏ 42769	Angels Like You/Mary Ann	1963	$15
❏ 41456	Chain Gang/Rock Bottom	1959	$15
❏ 21512	Dig Boy Dig/Two of a Kind	1956	$60
❏ 21558	Drink Up and Go Home/Blue	1956	$20
❏ 40896	Fraulein/Baby Don't Leave	1957	$20
❏ 42679	I'll Hit It with a Stick/ Stranger Drive Away	1963	$15
❏ 41269	I'm No Angel/Midnight Date	1958	$20
❏ 41144	I Won't Be Home Tonight/ Love, Come to Me	1958	$20
❏ 41805	Lying Again/Do My Heart a Favor	1960	$15
❏ 40821	On the Prowl/Extra	1957	$20
❏ 41005	Say No More/The Outside World	1957	$20
❏ 21550	Snatch It and Grab It/ Human Thing to Do	1956	$20
❏ 42285	Some Do, Some Don't, Some Will, Some Won't/Like You Are	1962	$15
❏ 42491	Stand Up/Ugly Duckling	1962	$15
❏ 41345	The Wall/Davy Jones	1959	$15
❏ 42146	What a Laugh!/Heart Attack	1961	$15

FIFTH ST.

Number	Title	Yr	NM
❏ 1091	Best Love I Never Had/I'm Not Going Hungry	1987	$6

KAPP

Number	Title	Yr	NM
❏ 841	Anna Maria/Leon and the Rain	1967	$10
❏ 910	Born a Fool/Hands of a Man	1968	$10
❏ 944	Don't Cry Baby/ Here Lies a Heart	1968	$12
❏ 694	Hank Williams' Guitar/I Created a Monster	1965	$12
❏ 820	I'll Hold You in My Heart/Too Much of You (Left of Me)	1967	$10
❏ 993	I Lost All My Tomorrows/ That's How High a Man Can Go	1969	$10
❏ 632	Love Can Make or Break a Heart/Hurts Feel So Good	1964	$10
❏ 794	Misty Blue/Elm Street Pawn Shop	1966	$10
❏ 661	Moon Gal/You've Got It Coming To Ya	1965	$10
❏ 765	Together Again/ Waiting for a Train	1966	$10
❏ 879	Togetherness/Portrait of a Lonely Man	1967	$10
❏ 879 [PS]	Togetherness/Portrait of a Lonely Man	1967	$20
❏ 976	Why Leave Something I Can't Use/Hang On to Her	1969	$10
❏ 743	Why Should I Cry Over You/Keys in the Mailbox	1966	$10

MCA

Number	Title	Yr	NM
❏ 40011	Born a Fool/My Anna Maria	1973	$6

MONUMENT

Number	Title	Yr	NM
❏ 838	First You Go Through Me/Valentino	1964	$15
❏ 826	For a Second There/ The Almighty Dollar	1963	$15

SUNBIRD

Number	Title	Yr	NM
❏ 110	Sure Thing/Makin' Love to a Memory	1980	$6
❏ 7550	Sure Thing/Makin' Love to a Memory	1980	$5

HART, MICKEY
Also see THE GRATEFUL DEAD.

WARNER BROS.

Number	Title	Yr	NM
❏ 7644	Blind John/Pump Man	1972	$10

HART, RITCHIE
FELSTED

Number	Title	Yr	NM
❏ 8593	The Great Duane/I'm Hypnotized	1959	$125

MCI

Number	Title	Yr	NM
❏ 1025	Choo Choo Train/I Want You	1960	$30

HART, ROCKY
BIG TOP

Number	Title	Yr	NM
❏ 3069	Crying/Baby You've Got It Made	1961	$40

CUB

Number	Title	Yr	NM
❏ 9052	Every Day/Come with Me	1959	$40

GLO

Number	Title	Yr	NM
❏ 216	I Play the Part of a Fool/ Someone Stole My Baby While Doing the Twist	1961	$200

HARUMI
VERVE FORECAST

Number	Title	Yr	NM
❏ 5086	First Impressions/ Talk About It	1968	$15

HARVELL, NATE
REPUBLIC

Number	Title	Yr	NM
❏ 019	Another Worn Out Rhinestone/(B-side unknown)	1978	$5
❏ 033	One in a Million/Silver Rails	1978	$5
❏ 025	Three Times a Lady/ Happy Ending	1978	$5
❏ 265	Wine and Weakness/ (B-side unknown)	1976	$5

HARVESTERS, THE
COLUMBIA

Number	Title	Yr	NM
❏ 4-41074	I Shall Not Be Moved/ Closer Than a Brother	1957	$30
❏ 4-21495	I Want You to Be More Like Jesus/When I'm Alone	1956	$30
❏ 4-21457	Let God Abide/I Just Telephone Upstairs	1955	$30
❏ 4-40897	These Are the Things That Matter/That Will Be a Great Day	1957	$30

HARVEY
CHESS

Number	Title	Yr	NM
❏ 1749	Blue Skies/Ooh, Ouch, Stop!	1960	$30
❏ 1760	If I Can't Have You/ My Heart Cries	1960	$30

—*As "Etta and Harvey" (Etta is Etta James)*

Number	Title	Yr	NM
❏ 1713	I Want Somebody/ Da Da Goo Goo	1959	$50
❏ 1771	Spoonful/It's a Crying Shame	1960	$30

—*As "Etta and Harvey" (Etta is Etta James)*

Number	Title	Yr	NM
❏ 1781	The First Time/Mama	1961	$30

—*As "Harvey Fuqua"*

Number	Title	Yr	NM
❏ 1725	Twelve Months of the Year/ Don't Be Afraid of Love	1959	$50

HARVEY

Number	Title	Yr	NM
❏ 121	What Can You Do Now/Will I Do	1962	$50

—*As "Harvey and Ann"*

TRI-PHI

Number	Title	Yr	NM
❏ 1024	Memories of You/Come On and Answer Me	1963	$40
❏ 1017	She Loves Me So/ Any Way You Wanta	1962	$125

HARVEY, ALEX (1)
ATLANTIC

Number	Title	Yr	NM
❏ 3293	Delilah/Soul in Chains	1975	$5

VERTIGO

Number	Title	Yr	NM
❏ 113	Swamp Snake/Gang Bang	1974	$25
❏ 200	Tomahawk Kid/ Sergeant Fury	1974	$45

HARVEY, ALEX (2)
CAPITOL

Number	Title	Yr	NM
❏ 3469	Angeline/Devil on My Shoulder	1972	$4
❏ 3336	Delta Dawn/ Momma's Waiting	1972	$4
❏ 3493	Good Time Christmas/ Someone Who Cares	1972	$4

—*With Son Lex*

Number	Title	Yr	NM
❏ 3847	Tangerine/Jody's Face	1974	$4
❏ 3172	To Make My Life Beautiful/Lady	1971	$4

METROMEDIA

Number	Title	Yr	NM
❏ 143	Louisiana River Bay/ King of New Orleans	1969	$6
❏ 173	Tell It All Brother/Mama Tried	1970	$6

UNITED ARTISTS

Number	Title	Yr	NM
❏ 50494	It Takes a Lot of Tenderness/ I'll Be Your Tomorrow	1969	$8

HARVEY AND DOC WITH THE DWELLERS
ANNETTE

Number	Title	Yr	NM
❏ 1002	Oh, Baby/Uncle Kev	1964	$250

—*Phil Spector appeared on and produced this*

HARVEY, PHIL
IMPERIAL

Number	Title	Yr	NM
❏ 5583	Willy Boy/Bumbershoot	1959	$200

HASLAM, ANNIE
SIRE

Number	Title	Yr	NM
❏ 1016	I Never Believed in Love/Inside My Life	1978	$6

HASSAN, ALI
PHILLES

Number	Title	Yr	NM
❏ 103	Malaguena/Chop Sticks	1962	$40

HASSLES, THE
BILLY JOEL was in this group. (45)

UNITED ARTISTS

Number	Title	Yr	NM
❏ 50450	4 O'Clock in the Morning/ Let Me Bring You to the Sunshine	1968	$15
❏ 50258	I Hear Voices/Every Step I Take	1968	$15
❏ 50586	Traveling Band/ Great Balls of Fire	1969	$15

HATCH, TONY
LONDON

Number	Title	Yr	NM
❏ 10523	Cyril's Tune/Out of This World	1963	$15
❏ 10505	Ghost Squad/What's All That About	1962	$15
❏ 10524	Theme from Dick Powell Theatre/Sharon	1963	$15

REPRISE

Number	Title	Yr	NM
❏ 0356	Crossroads/The Marie Celeste	1965	$12

WARNER BROS.

Number	Title	Yr	NM
❏ 7023	Beautiful Rain/While the City Sleeps	1967	$8
❏ 5887	I Didn't Know What Time It Was/Working in the Coal Mine	1967	$8

HATCHER, ROGER
BROWN DOG

Number	Title	Yr	NM
❏ 9009	We Gonna Make It/ High Blood Pressure	1976	$30

COLUMBIA

Number	Title	Yr	NM
❏ 4-45993	Caught Making Love (mono/stereo)	1974	$50

EXCELLO

Number	Title	Yr	NM
❏ 2297	Sweetest Girl in the World/I'm Gonna Dedicate My Song to You	1968	$500

VOLT

Number	Title	Yr	NM
❏ 4084	I'm Gonna Make Love to Someone's Old Lady/I Dedicate My Love to You	1972	$30

HATCHER, WILLIE
COLUMBIA

Number	Title	Yr	NM
❏ 44259	Good Things Come to Those Who Wait/Searching	1968	$200

COTILLION

Number	Title	Yr	NM
❏ 44014	Have a Heart, Girl/ You Got Quality	1968	$70

EXCELLO

Number	Title	Yr	NM
❏ 2310	Tell Me So/Who's Got a Woman Like Mine	1970	$50

KING

Number	Title	Yr	NM
❏ 6360	Head Over Heels/Who's Gotta Woman Like Mine	1971	$80

HATFIELD, BOBBY
MOONGLOW

Number	Title	Yr	NM
❏ 220	I Need a Girl/Hot Tamale	1963	$40

VERVE

Number	Title	Yr	NM
❏ 10641	Answer Me My Love/I Only Have Eyes for You	1969	$8
❏ 10621	Brothers/What's the Matter Baby	1968	$8
❏ 10598	Hang-Ups/Soul Cafe	1968	$8
❏ 10639	My Prayer/I Wish I Didn't Love You So	1969	$8
❏ 10634	Only You/The Wonder of You	1969	$8

WARNER BROS.

Number	Title	Yr	NM
❏ 7649	Stay with Me/Rock 'N Roll Woman	1972	$5

Number	Title	Yr	NM
HATFIELD, JEANNE			
ATCO			
❏ 6653	Stop/Busy Signal	1969	$50
CAMEO			
❏ 386	Time/Unprejudice Girl	1965	$30
JOX			
❏ 047	Time/Wonderin'	1965	$30
—Black vinyl			
❏ 047 [DJ]	Time/Wonderin'	1965	$50
—Promo only on green vinyl			
HATHAWAY, DONNY			
ATCO			
❏ 6828	A Song for You/Put Your Hand in the Hand	1971	$10
❏ 6899	Bossa Nova/Come Back Charleston Blue	1972	$5
—With Margie Joseph			
❏ 6951	Come Little Children/The Slums	1973	$5
❏ 6884	Giving Up/Jealous Love	1972	$5
❏ 6903	I Love You More Than You'll Ever Know/Lord Help Me	1972	$5
❏ 6880	Little Ghetto Boy/We're Still Friends	1972	$5
❏ 6928	Love, Love, Love/Someday We'll All Be Free	1973	$5
❏ 6817	Take a Love Song/Magnificent Sanctuary Band	1971	$5
❏ 6759	Thank You Master/Je Vous Aime	1970	$5
❏ 6719	The Ghetto (Part 1)/The Ghetto (Part 2)	1969	$20
❏ 6799	This Christmas/Be There	1970	$8
❏ 7066	This Christmas/Be There	1975	$5
❏ 7320	This Christmas/Be There	1980	$4
❏ 99956	This Christmas/Be There	1982	$4
❏ 6768	Tryin' Times/Voices Inside	1970	$5
CURTOM			
❏ 1935	I Thank You Baby/What's This I See	1969	$40
—By "June and Donnie"			
❏ 1971	I Thank You/Just Another Reason	1972	$5
—By "June Conquest and Donnie Hathaway"; same A-side as 1935 but with revised title			
7-Inch Extended Plays			
ATCO			
❏ SD 7-7029 [PS]	Extension of a Man	1973	$8
❏ SD 7-7029	I Know It's You/Flying Easy/The Slums/Valdez in the Country	1973	$8
—Jukebox issue; small hole, plays at 33 1/3 rpm			
HAVEN, SHIRLEY			
FEDERAL			
❏ 12092	Troubles of My Own/Stop Foolin' Around	1952	$300
—With the Four Jacks			
HAVENS, RICHIE			
A&M			
❏ 1882	I'm Not in Love/Dreaming as One	1976	$4
❏ 1984	We All Wanna Boogie/Nobody Left to Crown	1977	$4
❏ 1869	We Can't Hide It Anymore/Dreaming as One	1976	$4
ELEKTRA			
❏ 46619	Every Night/Here's a Song	1980	$4
❏ 46657	The Girl, the Gold Watch and Everything/Two Hearts in Perfect Time	1980	$4
MGM			
❏ 14141	Sandy/Handsome Johnny	1970	$5
ODE			
❏ 66032	Eyesight to the Blind/Underture	1973	$8
STORMY FOREST			
❏ 660	Fire and Rain/Think About the Children	1971	$5
❏ 666	Freedom/Handsome Johnny	1972	$5
❏ 653	Give All My Love Away/Nobody Knows	1970	$5
❏ 656	Here Comes the Sun/Younger Men Get Older	1971	$8
—First pressing has an edited version of A-side			
❏ 656	Here Comes the Sun/Younger Men Get Older	1971	$6
—Second (hit) pressing has full-length version of A-side and "REV" on label			
❏ 671	It Was a Very Good Year/I Know I Won't Be There	1973	$5
❏ 651	Minstrel from Gault/There's a Hole in My Future	1970	$5
❏ 658	Missing Train/I've Got to Get to Know Myself	1971	$5
❏ 672	Tight Rope/Woman	1973	$5

Number	Title	Yr	NM
❏ 664	Where You Gonna Run To/I've Got to Get to Know Myself	1972	$5
VERVE FOLKWAYS			
❏ 5022	I Can't Make It Anymore/Morning Morning	1966	$8
❏ 5039	I've Gotta Go/Morning Morning	1967	$20
VERVE FORECAST			
❏ 5092	Indian Rope Man/Just Above My Hobby Horse's Head	1968	$40
❏ 5068	Three Day Eternity/No Opportunity Necessary, No Experience Needed	1968	$10
HAWKETTS, THE			
CHESS			
❏ 1591	Mardi Gras Mambo/Your Time Is Up	1955	$125
HAWKINS, DALE			
ABC-PARAMOUNT			
❏ 10668	I'll Fly High/La La Song	1965	$10
ABNAK			
❏ 110	The Flag/And I Believed You	1965	$15
ATLANTIC			
❏ 2126	Stay at Home, Lulu/I Can't Erase You	1961	$30
❏ 2150	What a Feeling/Women, That's What's Happening	1962	$30
BELL			
❏ 807	Back Street/Little Rain Cloud	1969	$8
❏ 827	Heavy on My Mind/Joe	1969	$8
CHECKER			
❏ 923	Ain't That Lovin' You Baby/My Dream	1959	$30
❏ 876	Baby, Baby/Mrs. Merguitory's Daughter	1957	$40
❏ 916	Class Cutter (Yeah Yeah)/Lonely Nights	1959	$30
❏ 970	Grandma's House/I Want to Love You	1961	$30
❏ 940	Hot Dog/Don't Break Your Promise to Me	1960	$30
❏ 900	La-Do-Dada/Cross Ties	1958	$30
❏ 962	Linda/Who	1960	$30
❏ 892	Little Pig/Tornado	1958	$30
❏ 934	Liza Jane/Back to School Blues	1959	$30
❏ 906	My Babe/A House, a Car, and a Wedding Ring	1958	$30
❏ 929	Our Turn/Lifeguard Man	1959	$30
❏ 944	Poor Little Rhode Island/Every Little Girl	1960	$30
❏ 944 [PS]	Poor Little Rhode Island/Every Little Girl	1960	$300
❏ 843	See You Soon, Baboon/Four Letter Word	1956	$40
❏ 913	Someday, One Day/Take My Heart	1959	$30
❏ 863	Susie-Q/Don't Treat Me This Way	1957	$60
PAULA			
❏ 424	First Cut Is the Deepest/Nothing Left to Do But Say Goodbye	1977	$5
TILT			
❏ 783	Forbidden Love/Wish I Hadn't Called Home	1962	$30
❏ 785	Hawk Blows, Band Plays (Part 1)/Hawk Blows, Band Plays (Part 2)	1962	$30
❏ 781	Money Honey/The Same Old Way	1962	$30
ZONK			
❏ 1002	Gotta Dance/Peaches	1973	$5
HAWKINS, HAWKSHAW			
COLUMBIA			
❏ 4-41574	Alaska Lil and Texas Bill/Patanio	1960	$30
❏ 4-42441	I Can't Seem to Say Goodbye/Darkness on the Face of the Earth	1962	$20
❏ 4-41714	Put a Nickel in the Jukebox/Your Conscience	1960	$30
❏ 4-41419	Soldier's Joy/Big Red Benson	1959	$30
❏ 4-42223	Twenty Miles from Shore/Big Ole Heartache	1961	$20
KING			
❏ 5695	Bad News Travels Fast/Let Them Talk	1962	$20
❏ 1190	Barbara Allen/The Life Story of Hank Williams	1953	$40
❏ 1039	Be My Life's Companion/Everybody's Got a Girl But Me	1952	$40
❏ 5810	Caught in the Middle of Two Hearts/If I Ever Get Rich Mom	1963	$20
❏ 1133	Heavenly Road/An Empty Mansion	1952	$40
❏ 1134	I'm a Lone Wolf/I Hope You're Cryin' Too	1952	$40

Number	Title	Yr	NM
❏ 5871	I'm Beginning to Forget/Teardrops on Your Letter	1964	$20
❏ 969	I'm Waiting Just for You/A Heartache to Recall	1951	$50
❏ 1081	Loaded with Love/I Love the Way You Say Goodnight	1952	$40
❏ 5712	Lonesome 7-7203/Everything Has Changed	1963	$20
❏ 5765	Love Died Tonight/Sunny Side of the Mountain	1963	$20
❏ 1047	Over the Hill/I Am Slowly Dying of a Broken Heart	1952	$40
❏ 5692	Silver Threads and Golden Needles/Girl Without a Name	1962	$20
❏ 998	Slow Poke/Two Roads	1951	$50
❏ 997	Sunny Side of the Mountain/Blue Skies in Your Eyes	1951	$50
❏ 1154	Tangled Heart/Betty Lorraine	1953	$40
❏ 6047	The Last Letter/Never Mind the Tears	1967	$15
❏ 1174	The Life Story of Hank Williams/Picking Sweethearts	1953	$50
❏ 5909	This Particular Baby/The Shadows	1964	$20
RCA VICTOR			
❏ 47-6794	Action/Oh How I Cried	1957	$30
❏ 47-5444	A Heap of Lovin'/Mark Round My Finger	1953	$30
❏ 47-7486	Are You Happy/She Was Here	1959	$30
❏ 47-6211	Car Hoppin' Mama/The Love You Steal	1955	$30
❏ 47-6910	Dark Moon/With This Pen	1957	$30
❏ 47-5623	Flashing Lights/Waitin' for My Baby	1954	$30
❏ 47-7145	Guilty of Dreaming/It's Easier Said Than Done	1958	$30
❏ 47-6103	How Can Anything So Pretty Be So Doggone Mean/Pedro Gonzalez Tennessee Lopez	1955	$30
❏ 47-7222	I Don't Apologize/I'll Get Even with You	1958	$30
❏ 47-6396	If It Ain't on the Menu/Borrowing	1956	$30
❏ 47-6298	I Gotta Have You/Standing at the End of My World	1955	$30
❏ 47-6716	I'll Be Gone/My Fate Is In Your Hands	1956	$30
❏ 47-5549	I'll Never Close My Heart to You/When You Say Yes	1953	$30
❏ 47-5890	I'll Take a Chance with You/Why Don't You Leave This Town	1954	$30
❏ 47-5333	I'll Trade Yours for Mine/Long Long Way	1953	$30
❏ 47-7054	Is My Ring on Your Finger/Sensation	1957	$30
❏ 47-6509	It Would Be a Doggone Lie/Sunny Side of the Mountain	1956	$30
❏ 47-7389	I've Got It Again/Freedom	1958	$30
❏ 47-6022	Ling Ting Tong/Ko Ko Mo, I Love You So	1955	$30
—With Rita Robbins			
❏ 47-5808	One White Rose/I Wanna Be Hugged to Death	1954	$30
HAWKINS, RONNIE			
COTILLION			
❏ 44067	Forty Days/Bitter Green	1970	$6
❏ 44076	Little Bird/One More Night	1970	$6
❏ 44060	Matchbox/Down in the Alley	1970	$6
MONUMENT			
❏ 8583	Bo Diddley/Lonely Hours	1973	$5
❏ 8573	Diddley Daddy/Cora Mae	1973	$5
❏ 8548	Lawdy Miss Clawdy/Cora Mae	1972	$5
❏ 8561	Lonesome Town/Kinky	1973	$5
ROULETTE			
❏ 4483	Bo Diddley/Who Do You Love	1963	$30
❏ 4311	Cold, Cold Heart/Nobody's Lonesome for Me	1960	$30
❏ 4400	Come Love/I Feel Good	1961	$30
❏ 4154 [M]	Forty Days/One of These Days	1959	$30
❏ SSR-4154 [S]	Forty Days/One of These Days	1959	$60
❏ 4502	High Blood Pressure/There's a Screw Loose	1963	$30
❏ 4228	Lonely Hours/Clara	1960	$30
❏ 4177 [M]	Mary Lou/Need Your Lovin'	1959	$40
❏ SSR-4177 [S]	Mary Lou/Need Your Lovin'	1959	$60
❏ 4209	Southern Love/Love Me Like You Can	1959	$80
❏ 4267	Summertime/Mister and Mississippi	1960	$30
❏ 4231	The Ballad of Caryl Chessman/The Tale of Floyd Collins	1960	$30

HAWKINS, SCREAMIN' JAY

Number	Title	Yr	NM
APOLLO			
❏ 528	Baptize Me in Wine/Not Anymore	1958	$30
❏ 506	Please Try to Understand/Not Anymore	1957	$30
CHANCELLOR			
❏ 1117	Ashes/Nitty Gritty	1962	$20
DECCA			
❏ 32019	All Night/I'm Not Made of Clay	1966	$20
❏ 32100	I Put a Spell on You/You're an Exception to the Rule	1967	$125
ENRICA			
❏ 1010	I Hear Voices/I Just Don't Care	1962	$30
GRAND			
❏ 135	Take Me Back/I Is	1957	$30
MERCURY			
❏ 70549	This Is All/She Put the Whammee on Me	1955	$100
OKEH			
❏ 7101	Alligator Wine/There's Something Wrong with You	1958	$40
❏ 7072	I Put a Spell on You/Little Demon	1956	$60
❏ 7087	Person to Person/Frenzy	1957	$40
PHILIPS			
❏ 40645	Constipation Blues/Do You Really Love Me	1969	$6
❏ 40668	Moanin'/Do You Really Love Me	1970	$40
❏ 40674	Our Love Is Not for Three/Take Me Back	1970	$6
❏ 40606	Stone Crazy/I'm Lonely	1969	$6
❏ 40636	Too Many Teardrops/Makaka Ways	1969	$6
PROVIDENCE			
❏ 411	My Kind of Love/Po' Folks	1965	$15
QUEEN BEE			
❏ 1314	Monkberry Moon Delight/Sweet Ginny	1973	$6
ROULETTE			
❏ 4579	The Whammy/Strange	1964	$20
TIMELY			
❏ 1004	Baptize Me in Wine/Not Anymore	1954	$100
❏ 1005	I Found My Way to Wine/Please Try to Understand	1954	$100
WING			
❏ 90055	Even Though/Talk About Me	1956	$40
❏ 90005	Well, I Tried/You're All of Life to Me	1955	$50

HAWKS, COLBY

Number	Title	Yr	NM
CAMEO			
❏ 411	I'm Gonna Jump Right Off (The Brooklyn Bridge)/A Little Love Goes a Long, Long Way	1966	$20

HAWKS, EDDIE

Number	Title	Yr	NM
MERCURY			
❏ 6367	Santa Claus Is Coming To Town/Jingle Bells	1951	$20

HAWKS, MICKEY

Number	Title	Yr	NM
C-HORSE			
❏ 589	Me and My Harley-Davidson/The Good Old Days	1989	$10
HUNCH			
❏ 347	Hidi Hidi Hidi/(B-side unknown)	1961	$125
PROFILE			
❏ 4002	Bip Bop Boom/Rock 'n' Roll Rhythm	1958	$800
❏ 4007	Hidi Hidi Hidi/Cottonpickin'	1959	$800
❏ 4010	Screamin' Mini Jeanie/I'm Lost	1959	$1000

HAWKS, THE (1)

Number	Title	Yr	NM
IMPERIAL			
❏ 5317	All Women Are the Same/That's What You Are	1954	$125
❏ 5292	It Ain't That Way/I-Yi	1954	$125
❏ 5332	It's Too Late Now/I Can't See for Lookin'	1955	$125
❏ 5281	She's All Right/Good News	1954	$200
MODERN			
❏ 990	It's All Over/Ever Since You Been Gone	1956	$250
POST			
❏ 2004	These Blues/Why Oh Why	1955	$300

HAWKS, THE (U)

Number	Title	Yr	NM
ABC-PARAMOUNT			
❏ 10116	Grasshopper/The Grissle	1960	$30
DEL-FI			
❏ 4108	A Little More Wine, My Dear?/Fussy	1958	$50
MALA			
❏ 401	Cupcake/Lupp!!	1959	$30

HAWKWIND

Also see HIGH TIDE; MOTORHEAD.

Number	Title	Yr	NM
UNITED ARTISTS			
❏ 50949	Seven by Seven/Silver Necklace	1972	$50

HAWLEY, DEANE

Number	Title	Yr	NM
DORE			
❏ 536	Good Morning, Mr. Sun/Bossman	1959	$20
❏ 577	Hey There/Rainbow	1960	$20
❏ 569	Like a Fool/Stay at Home Blues	1960	$20
❏ 554	Look for a Star/Bossman	1960	$20
❏ 543	Where Is My Angel/I'll Never Be a Fool Again	1960	$20
LIBERTY			
❏ 55359	Pocketful of Rainbows/That Dream Could Never Be	1961	$30
VALOR			
❏ 2003	Mummy's Bracelet/Don't Keep Me Guessin'	1961	$40
WARNER BROS.			
❏ 5484	I Know She'll Be There/You'll Never Have to Cry Again	1964	$15

HAWN, GOLDIE

Number	Title	Yr	NM
REPRISE			
❏ 1089	Butterfly/Uncle Pen	1972	$8
❏ 1126	Pitta Patta/(Instrumental)	1972	$8
❏ 1126 [PS]	Pitta Patta/(Instrumental)	1972	$10

HAYES, BILL

Number	Title	Yr	NM
ABC-PARAMOUNT			
❏ 9895	Bop Boy/Uh Huh Oh Yeah	1958	$70
❏ 9785	Wringle, Wrangle/Westward Ho the Wagons	1957	$15
❏ 9785 [PS]	Wringle, Wrangle/Westward Ho the Wagons	1957	$30
CADENCE			
❏ 1301	A Message from James Dean/The Trail's End	1956	$20
❏ 1245	I Knew an Old Lady/(B-side unknown)	1954	$15
❏ 1294	I Knew an Old Lady/Das Ist Music	1956	$15
❏ 1274	That Do Make It Nice/Kwela Kwela	1955	$15
❏ 1256	The Ballad of Davy Crockett/Farewell	1955	$20
❏ 1261	The Berry Tree/Blue Back Hair	1955	$15
❏ 1275	The Legend of Wyatt Earp/White Buffalo	1955	$20
KAPP			
❏ 298	Choppin' Mountains/Tall Teller of Tall Tales	1959	$10
❏ 258	Wimoweh/Goin' Down the Road Feelin' Bad	1959	$10
MGM			
❏ 11556	A Little Kiss Each Morning/Love You	1953	$20
— With Judy Johnson			
❏ 11205	April Sings/Golden Haired Boy	1952	$20
❏ 11112	Charmaine/For All We Know	1951	$20
❏ 11266	High Noon/Padam Padam	1952	$20
❏ 11394	How Do You Speak to An Angel/The Donkey Song	1953	$20
❏ 11064	I Love You/Never	1951	$20
❏ 11492	I'm So Lonesome/There's Music in You	1953	$20
❏ 11384	My Ever Lovin'/As Long As You Care	1952	$20
❏ 11296	Say You'll Wait for Me/My Search for You	1952	$20
❏ 11042	The Love of a Gypsy/I've Got an Idea for a Song	1951	$20
❏ 11006	Waltz of the Wind/Mine	1951	$20
❏ 12004	Wanderin'/You're Nearer	1955	$15
❏ 11142	We Won't Live in A.../Tulips and Heather	1952	$20
❏ 11210	When I Dream/Don't Send Me Home	1952	$20
— With Judy Johnson			

7-Inch Extended Plays

Number	Title	Yr	NM
ABC-PARAMOUNT			
❏ B-194 [PS]	Bill Hayes Sings the Best of Disney, Vol. 2	1957	$20
❏ B-194	Lavender Blue/Zip-a-Dee Do-Dah//'Twas Brillig/A Whale of a Tale	1957	$20

HAYES, ISAAC, AND DIONNE WARWICK

Number	Title	Yr	NM
ABC/HBS			
❏ 12253	By the Time I Get to Phoenix--I Say a Little Prayer/That's the Way I Like It--Cry Down	1977	$4

HAYES, ISAAC

Number	Title	Yr	NM
ABC/HBS			
❏ 12118	Chocolate Chip/(Instrumental)	1975	$4
❏ 12138	Come Live with Me/Body Language	1975	$4
❏ 12171	Disco Connection/St. Thomas Square	1976	$4
— By the "Isaac Hayes Movement			
BRUNSWICK			
❏ 55258	Sweet Temptation/Laura	1964	$10
COLUMBIA			
❏ 07104	If You Want My Lovin' (Do Me Right)/(Instrumental)	1987	$3
❏ 06363	Ike's Rap/Hey Girl (Edited)	1986	$3
❏ 06363 [PS]	Ike's Rap/Hey Girl (Edited)	1986	$4
❏ 08116	Let Me Be Your Everything/Curious	1988	$3
❏ 07978	Showdown/(Instrumental)	1988	$3
❏ 06655	Thing for You/Thank God for Love	1987	$3
ENTERPRISE			
❏ 9049	Ain't That Loving You (For More Reasons Than One)/Baby I'm-a Want You	1972	$5
— With David Porter			
❏ 9003	By the Time I Get to Phoenix/Walk On By	1969	$6
❏ 9042	Do Your Thing/Ellie's Love Theme	1972	$5
❏ 9065	(If Loving You Is Wrong) I Don't Want to Be Right/Rolling Down a Mountainside	1973	$40
❏ 9017	I Stand Accused/I Just Don't Know What to Do with Myself	1970	$5
❏ 9045	Let's Stay Together/Soulville	1972	$5
❏ 002	Precious Precious/Going to Chicago Blues	1969	$8
❏ 9028	The Look of Love/Ike's Mood	1970	$5
❏ 9038	Theme from Shaft/Cafe Regio's	1971	$5
❏ 9058	Theme from The Men/Type Thang	1972	$5
❏ 9006	The Mistletoe and Me/Winter Snow	1969	$6
❏ 9104	Title Theme/Hung Up on My Baby	1974	$5
❏ 9095	Wonderful/Someone Made You for Me	1974	$40
POLYDOR			
❏ 2068	A Few More Kisses to Go/What Does It Take	1980	$4
❏ 2011	Don't Let Go/You Can't Hold Your Woman	1979	$4
❏ 2192	Fugitive/Lifetime Thing	1981	$4
❏ 2090	I Ain't Never/Love Has Been Good to Us	1980	$4
❏ 2182	I'm So Proud/I'm Gonna Make Me Love You	1981	$4
❏ 2102	It's All in the Game/Wherever You Are	1980	$4
❏ 14464	Moonlight Lovin' (Menage a Trois)/It's Heaven to Me	1978	$4
❏ 14446	Out of the Ghetto/It's Heaven to Me	1977	$4
STAX			
❏ 3209	Feel Like Makin' Love (Part 1)/Feel Like Makin' Love (Part 2)	1978	$5

HAYES, JIMMY, AND THE SOUL SURFERS

Number	Title	Yr	NM
IMPERIAL			
❏ 5986	Summer Surfin'/Down on the Beach	1963	$30

HAYES, LINDA

Number	Title	Yr	NM
ANTLER			
❏ 4000	I Had a Dream/You Ain't Movin' Me	1956	$40
DECCA			
❏ 29644	Our Love's Forever Blessed/You're the Only One for Me	1955	$40
HOLLYWOOD			
❏ 1027	Change of Heart/Darling Angel	1954	$50
❏ 1032	Our Love's Forever Blessed/You're the Only One for Me	1955	$70
❏ 1016	Play It Right/Your Back's Out	1954	$50
❏ 1003	Take Me Back/Yours for the Asking	1953	$60
KING			
❏ 4752	My Name Ain't Annie/Let's Babalu	1954	$80
❏ 4773	Please Have Mercy/Oochi Poochi	1955	$60

Number	Title	Yr	NM
RECORDED IN HOLLYWOOD			
❑ 246	Big City (Part 1)/ Big City (Part 2)	1953	$60

HAYES, RICHARD, AND KITTY KALLEN
MERCURY

Number	Title	Yr	NM
❑ 5661	Everyone Is Welcome (In the House of the Lord)/Good Luck	1951	$20
❑ 5499	Halls of Ivy/Dream	1950	$20
❑ 5564	It Is No Secret (What God Can Do)/Get Out the Old Records	1950	$20
❑ 5466	Our Lady of Fatima/ Honestly I Love You	1950	$20
❑ 5501	Silver Bells/A Bushel and a Peck	1950	$20
❑ 5532	Silver Bells/Jing-a-Ling	1950	$20
❑ 5586	The Aba Daba Honeymoon/I Don't Want to Love	1951	$20

HAYES, RICHARD, AND ROBERTA QUINLAN
MERCURY

Number	Title	Yr	NM
❑ 5639X45	I'm Late/The Unbirthday Song	1951	$30
❑ 5615X45	I Whistle a Happy Tune/ When You and I Were Young Maggie Blues	1951	$30

HAYES, RICHARD
ABC-PARAMOUNT

Number	Title	Yr	NM
❑ 9706	Blue Bolero/My Girl and His Girl	1956	$30
❑ 9754	If'n/Chaperone	1956	$30
❑ 9777	Let Your Lips Run Away with Your Heart/Where Are You	1956	$30
❑ 9670	Please Say Hello for Me/ Street of 33 Steps	1956	$30

COLUMBIA

Number	Title	Yr	NM
❑ 4-41802	Come On-a My House/ Italian Style	1960	$10
❑ 4-42159	Familiar/Cora Belle	1961	$10
❑ 4-41952	Seventeen Come Sunday/ Blacksmith Blues	1961	$10
❑ 4-42220	Somewhere in the Night/ To Look Upon My Love	1961	$12

CONTEMPO

Number	Title	Yr	NM
❑ 910	Let There Be You/ Top of the World	1964	$12

DECCA

Number	Title	Yr	NM
❑ 9-30888	Ballad of a Gun/ Love Is a Carousel	1959	$12
❑ 9-30376	Missing You/Misery's Child	1957	$10
❑ 9-30232	My Only Love/Bringing the Blues to My Door	1957	$10
❑ 9-30788	Oh Shenandoah/There's a Leak in the Boat	1958	$10
❑ 9-30436	Swinging Sweethearts/ Hangin' Around	1957	$10
❑ 9-30469	The First Time I Spoke of You/Red Letter Day	1957	$10
❑ 9-30285	The Power of Prayer/ And So Am I	1957	$10
❑ 9-30696	Tulips from Amsterdam/ So Happy in Love	1958	$10

MERCURY

Number	Title	Yr	NM
❑ 70103x45	And the Bull Walked Along Olay/Changeable	1953	$20
❑ 5780x45	Babalu/More Than Love	1952	$20
— With Xavier Cugat			
❑ 5671x45	Come On-a My House/ Go Go Go Go	1951	$20
❑ 5910x45	Forgetting You/ Forgive and Forget	1952	$20
❑ 70110x45	Hot Dog Rag/Let Me Know	1953	$20
❑ 5821x45	I'll Walk Alone/Tattletale	1952	$20
❑ 5699x45	Lonely Little Robin/ Go Go Go Go	1951	$20
❑ 70239x45	Long Black Rifle/ All Is Forgiven	1953	$20
❑ 5834x45	Lost Love/No Strings Attached	1952	$20
❑ 70169x45	Matilda, Matilda/ Midnight in Paris	1953	$20
❑ 70215x45	Moonlight/Lovely	1953	$20
❑ 5603x45	My Prayer/Fast Freight	1951	$20
❑ 70068x45	Once in a Lifetime/Can't I	1953	$20
❑ 5724x45	Out in the Cold Again/Once	1951	$20
❑ 5558x45	Tambourine/This and No More	1950	$20
❑ 70363x45	The Continental/ Move It On Over	1954	$15
❑ 5763x45	The Lady Drinks Champagne/River Stay 'Way from My Door	1951	$20
❑ 5872x45	The Mask Is Off/ Never Leave Me	1952	$20
❑ 5599x45	Too Young/ Shenandoah Waltz	1951	$30
❑ 5409x45	Truly/Thunder in My Heart	1950	$30
— Earlier Richard Hayes 45s on Mercury may exist			
❑ 70147x45	Trust Me/It's Just Another Polka	1953	$20
❑ 5456x45	Why Fight the Feeling/ Iron Horse	1950	$30

HAYES, TOMMY
PHILIPS

Number	Title	Yr	NM
❑ 40259	Trance/Glistening Lights	1965	$125
— The Four Seasons sing backup			

HAYMES, DICK
CAPITOL

Number	Title	Yr	NM
❑ F3662	C'est La Vie/Now at Last	1957	$15
❑ F3531	Love Is a Great Big Nothin'/I Never Get Enough of You	1956	$15
❑ F3565	Two Different Worlds/ Never Leave Me	1956	$15

CONGRESS

Number	Title	Yr	NM
❑ 105	Down the Road/A Woman Knows	1962	$12

DECCA

Number	Title	Yr	NM
❑ 9-28540	All I Need to Know/ Let's Fall in Love	1953	$20
— With Gordon Jenkins and His Orchestra			
❑ 9-27731	And So to Sleep Again/Long Ago	1951	$20
❑ 9-27885	Anytime/Bouquet of Roses	1951	$20
❑ 9-24121	Ave Maria/It Came Upon a Midnight Clear	1950	$20
— Sides 3 and 4 of "Album No. 9-70"; 78 originally issued in 1947			
❑ 9-27076	Blind Date/Say When	1950	$30
— With Evelyn Knight			
❑ 9-27195	Boulevard of Broken Dreams/Your Eyes Have Told Me So	1950	$30
❑ 9-27161	Can Anyone Explain? (No, No, No!)/If I Had a Magic Carpet	1950	$30
❑ 9-24169	Christmas Dreaming/ The Christmas Song	1950	$20
— Sides 5 and 6 of "Album No. 9-70"; 78 originally issued in 1947			
❑ 9-70 [PS]	Christmas Songs	1950	$20
— Box for records 9-24120, 24121 and 24169			
❑ 9-27042	Count Every Star/If You Were Only Mine	1950	$30
— With Artie Shaw			
❑ 9-27980	Darlene/Dreamer's Cloth	1952	$20
❑ 9-27217	Home/Could Be	1950	$30
❑ 9-28087	I Am a Heart/And So I Waited Around	1952	$20
❑ 9-27682	I Believe/When the Lights Are Low	1951	$20
❑ 9-27312	I Guess I'll Have to Dream the Rest/Everything Happens to Me	1951	$20
— With Tommy Dorsey and His Orchestra			
❑ 9-27545	I'll Never Know Why/ How Thoughtful of You	1951	$20
❑ 9-28213	I'm Sorry/Here in My Heart	1952	$20
— With the Andrews Sisters			
❑ 9-27020	Is There Anything Wrong with That/A Little Bit Independent	1950	$30
❑ 9-27497	It Might as Well Be Spring/ It's a Grand Night for Singing	1951	$20
❑ 9-27498	It's Magic/Searching Wind	1951	$20
— With Gordon Jenkins and His Orchestra			
❑ 9-27518	Laura/The Girl That I Marry	1951	$20
❑ 9-23753	Let the Rest of the World Go By/Indiana	1950	$20
— 78 originally issued in 1947			
❑ 9-24480	Little White Lies/I'll Never Smile Again	1950	$30
— 78 originally issued in 1948			
❑ 9-27565	My Prayer/Too Late Now	1951	$20
❑ 9-27175	My Silent Love/ Don't Be Afraid	1950	$30
❑ 9-24120	Oh, Little Town Of Bethlehem/Joy To The World	1950	$20
— Sides 1 and 2 of "Album No. 9-70"; 78 originally issued in 1947			
❑ 9-27318	Once Upon a Time Today/ It's a Lovely Day Today	1951	$20
❑ 9-27473	Operetta/Little Angel	1951	$20
❑ 9-24305	Serenade of the Bells/ Some Hearts Sing	1950	$30
— 78 originally issued in 1948			
❑ 9-27811	Such Is My Love/ My Beloved	1951	$20
❑ 9-27598	Tahiti, My Island/At the Bay of Rainbows	1951	$20
❑ 9-28361	That's the Last Tear/ Tinsel and Gold	1952	$20
❑ 9-27644	There's a Big Blue Cloud/ These Things I Offer You	1951	$20
❑ 9-27472	There's More Pretty Girls Than One/No One But You	1951	$20
❑ 9-23751	They Didn't Believe Me/ Where or When	1950	$20
— 78 originally issued in 1947			
❑ 9-27234	Till the End of Time/ Iron Horse	1950	$30
— Originally issued on 78 on Decca 18699 in 1945			
❑ 9-27448	What'll I Do/Our Waltz	1951	$20

Number	Title	Yr	NM
❑ 9-27499	When I'm Not Near the Girl I Love/My Future Just Passed	1951	$20
❑ 9-27737	Who Can I Turn To/Just One of Those Things	1951	$20
❑ 9-27646	Who'll Take My Place/Tell Me	1951	$20

GNP CRESCENDO

Number	Title	Yr	NM
❑ 494	Bein' Green/Feel Like Makin' Love	1975	$6

JUBILEE

Number	Title	Yr	NM
❑ 5299	Lonesome and Sorry/I'll Still Be True	1957	$20

SUNBEAM

Number	Title	Yr	NM
❑ 113	As Young As You Feel/Suffer	1958	$15
❑ 120	She Is Beautiful/C'est Fini	1958	$15

WARWICK

Number	Title	Yr	NM
❑ 571	Anything Goes/ Pick Yourself Up	1960	$10
❑ 568	Blue Champagne/ Playboy's Theme	1960	$10

HAYWARD, JUSTIN, AND JOHN LODGE
Also see each artist's individual listings; THE MOODY BLUES.
THRESHOLD

Number	Title	Yr	NM
❑ 67021	Blue Guitar/When You Wake Up	1975	$4
❑ 67021 [PS]	Blue Guitar/When You Wake Up	1975	$5
❑ 67019	I Dreamed Last Night/ Remember Me, My Friend	1975	$4

HAYWARD, JUSTIN
COLUMBIA

Number	Title	Yr	NM
❑ 10799	Forever Autumn/The Fighting Machine	1978	$8

DERAM

Number	Title	Yr	NM
❑ 402	A Face in the Crowd/ It's Not On	1980	$4
❑ 7542	Country Girl/ Songwriter Part 2	1977	$4
❑ 7541	Lay It On Me/ Songwriter Part 2	1977	$4

RED BIRD

Number	Title	Yr	NM
❑ Oct-0049	London Is Behind Me/ Day Must Come	1966	$30

HAYWOOD, LEON
20TH CENTURY

Number	Title	Yr	NM
❑ 2146	Believe Half of What You See (And None of What You Hear)/The Day I Laid Eyes on You	1974	$20
❑ 2191	Come an' Get Yourself Some/B.M.F. Beautiful	1975	$6
❑ 2191	Come an' Get Yourself Some/Who You Been Givin' It Up To	1975	$5
❑ 2469	Daydream/Love Is What We Came Here For	1980	$4
❑ 2443	Don't Push It Don't Force It/Who You Been Givin' It Up To	1980	$4
❑ 2454	If You're Lookin' for a Night of Fun (Look Past Me, I'm Not the One)/ That's What Time It Is	1980	$4
❑ 2228	I Want'a Do Something Freaky to You/I Know What Love Is	1975	$5
❑ 2022	La La Song/Sweet Loving Fair	1973	$6
❑ 2003	One Way Ticket to Loveland/There Ain't Enough Love Around	1972	$6
❑ 2285	Strokin' (Part 1)/ Strokin' (Part 2)	1976	$5
❑ 2103	Sugar Lump/That Sweet Woman of Mine	1974	$5

ATLANTIC

Number	Title	Yr	NM
❑ 2858	Clean Up Your Own Back Yard/String Bean	1972	$6

CAPITOL

Number	Title	Yr	NM
❑ 2752	I Wanna Thank You/I Was Sent to Love You	1970	$40

CASABLANCA

Number	Title	Yr	NM
❑ 812164-7	I'm Out to Catch/Keep It in the Family	1983	$3
— With Karen Roberts			
❑ 814217-7	T.V. Mama/Steppin' Out	1983	$3

COLUMBIA

Number	Title	Yr	NM
❑ 10477	Dream Dream/Let Me Make It Good	1977	$4
❑ 10413	The Streets Will Love You to Death - Part 1/ The Streets Will Love You to Death - Part 2	1976	$4

DECCA

Number	Title	Yr	NM
❑ 32414	Blues Get Off My Shoulder/Everyday Will Be Like a Holiday	1968	$20
❑ 32164	It's Got to Be Mellow/ Cornbread & Buttermilk	1967	$40

Number	Title	Yr	NM
❏ 32348	I Want to Talk About My Baby/You Don't Have to See Me Cry	1968	$30
❏ 32230	Mellow Moonlight/Tennessee Waltz	1967	$30
❏ 32310	Mercy, Mercy, Mercy/It's the Last Time	1968	$30

FANTASY

Number	Title	Yr	NM
❏ 581	The Truth About Money/Would I	1964	$80

FAT FISH

Number	Title	Yr	NM
❏ 8005	Soul Cargo/Spice of the Blues	1966	$40

IMPERIAL

Number	Title	Yr	NM
❏ 66123	She's With Her Other Love/Pain in My Heart	1965	$40

—As "Leon Hayward"

Number	Title	Yr	NM
❏ 66149	Soul-On/1-2-3	1965	$40

MCA

Number	Title	Yr	NM
❏ 40989	Disco Fever/Self Respect	1979	$4
❏ 40849	Double My Pleasure/It's Gonna Be Alright	1978	$4
❏ 41035	Energy/You Bring Out the Freak in Me	1979	$4
❏ 40889	Fine and Healthy Thing/She's Built, She's Stacked	1978	$4
❏ 40941	Party/Life Goes On	1978	$4
❏ 40793	Super Sexy/Life Goes On	1977	$4

MODERN

Number	Title	Yr	NM
❏ 99708	Tenderoni/(Instrumental)	1984	$3

HAZLEWOOD, LEE
Also see ANN-MARGRET; NANCY SINATRA.

CAPITOL

Number	Title	Yr	NM
❏ 3737	Feathers/The Performer	1973	$8

JAMIE

Number	Title	Yr	NM
❏ 1158	The Girl on Death Row/Words Mean Nothing	1960	$20

—With Duane Eddy

LHI

Number	Title	Yr	NM
❏ 7	Greyhound Bus Depot/No Regrets	1969	$10
❏ 17	The Bed/(B-side unknown)	1969	$12
❏ 20	Trouble Maker/Greyhound Bus Depot	1970	$10

MCA

Number	Title	Yr	NM
❏ 41003	Dolly Parton's Guitar/A Taste of You	1979	$5
❏ 41188	Hollywood (Just Ain't No Place)/Willie John	1980	$4

MGM

Number	Title	Yr	NM
❏ K13716	Girls in Paris/Them Girls	1967	$8
❏ K13434	I Move Around/Bugles in the Afternoon	1965	$20
❏ K13490	My Autumn's Done Come/Sand	1966	$20
❏ K13664	Summer Wine/After Six	1967	$10
❏ K13605	The Old Man and His Guitar/Suzie Jane Is Back in Town	1966	$10

REPRISE

Number	Title	Yr	NM
❏ 0613	Charlie BIII Nelson/Ode to Billie Joe	1967	$10
❏ 0699	The House Song/Morning Dew	1968	$10

SMASH

Number	Title	Yr	NM
❏ 1734	Don't Cry No More/Della	1961	$20

HEAD EAST
A&M

Number	Title	Yr	NM
❏ 1930	Gettin' Lucky/Sands of Time	1977	$4
❏ 2208	Got to Be Real/Morning	1979	$4
❏ 2278	I Surrender/Out of the Blue	1980	$4
❏ 1784	Love Me Tonight/Brother Jacob	1976	$4
❏ 2026	Since You Been Gone/Pictures	1978	$4
❏ 2026 [PS]	Since You Been Gone/Pictures	1978	$8
❏ 2222	Specialty/Morning	1980	$4

HEAD, ROY
ABC

Number	Title	Yr	NM
❏ 12418	Dixie/Love Survived	1978	$4
❏ 12346	How You See 'Em, Now You Don't/Smooth Whiskey	1978	$4
❏ 12383	Tonight's the Night/A Lady in My Room	1978	$4

ABC DOT

Number	Title	Yr	NM
❏ 17629	Ain't It Funny (How Times Haven't Changed)/A Bridge for Crawling Back	1976	$4
❏ 17722	Come to Me/Georgia on My Mind	1977	$4
❏ 17608	Lady Luck and Mother Nature/The Door I Used to Close	1976	$4
❏ 17650	One Night/Deep Elem Blues	1976	$4

ABC DUNHILL

Number	Title	Yr	NM
❏ 4240	I'm Not a Fool Anymore/Mama Mama	1970	$6

ATLANTIC AMERICA

Number	Title	Yr	NM
❏ 99529	There's Something on Your Mind/Everything A Man Can Do (And I Love You)	1986	$3

BACK BEAT

Number	Title	Yr	NM
❏ 555	Apple of My Eye/I Pass the Day	1965	$30
❏ 571	Don't Cry No More/To Make a Big Man Cry	1966	$30
❏ 563	Driving Wheel/Wigglin' and Gigglin'	1966	$30
❏ 560	My Babe/Pain	1966	$10
❏ 543	Teenage Letter/Pain	1965	$30
❏ 546	Treat Her Right/So Long, My Love	1965	$30

CHURCHILL

Number	Title	Yr	NM
❏ 7778	After Texas/California Day	1981	$5

ELEKTRA

Number	Title	Yr	NM
❏ 47029	Drinking Them Long Necks/Baby's Found Another Way to Love Me	1980	$4
❏ 46549	In Our Room/Things I Never Could Have Left Behind	1979	$4
❏ 47081	I've Never Gone to Bed With an Ugly Woman/All Night Long Is Gone	1981	$4
❏ 46653	Long Drop/Gonna Save It for My Baby	1980	$4
❏ 46582	The Fire of Two Old Flames/Under Suspicion	1980	$4

MEGA

Number	Title	Yr	NM
❏ 1219	Baby's Not Home/Do What You Can Do	1974	$5

MERCURY

Number	Title	Yr	NM
❏ 72848	Ain't Goin' Down Right/Lovin' Man on Your Hands	1968	$8
❏ 72799	Broadway Walk/Turn Out the Lights	1968	$30
❏ 72750	Got Down on Saturday (Sunday in the Rain)/The Grass Was Green	1967	$8
❏ 72922	I Miss You Baby/I Want Some Action	1969	$30

NSD

Number	Title	Yr	NM
❏ 129	Play Another Gettin' Drunk and Take Somebody Home Song/Your Next One and Only	1982	$5
❏ 146	The Trouble with Hearts/Naughty Smile	1982	$5

SCEPTER

Number	Title	Yr	NM
❏ 12138	Convicted/One More Time	1966	$10
❏ 12124	Get Back -- Part 1/Get Back -- Part 2	1965	$20
❏ 12117	Won't Be Blue/One More Time	1965	$10

SHANNON

Number	Title	Yr	NM
❏ 833	Help Yourself to Me/To Make a Big Man Cry	1975	$5
❏ 838	I'll Take It/The One That Got Away	1975	$5
❏ 829	The Most Wanted Woman in Town/Gingerbread Man	1975	$5

TEXAS CRUDE

Number	Title	Yr	NM
❏ 614	Break Out the Good Stuff/She Needs Time	1985	$8

TMI

Number	Title	Yr	NM
❏ 9010	Bit By Bit/Wait Till I Arrive	1972	$6
❏ 75-0113	Carol/Clyde O'Riley	1973	$5
❏ 9000	Puff of Smoke/Lord Take a Bow	1971	$6
❏ BTBO-0111	Small Town Girl/Chug All Night	1973	$5
❏ 75-0106	Why Don't We Go Somewhere and Love/Smell-A-Woman	1972	$5

TNT

Number	Title	Yr	NM
❏ 194	Don't Be Blue/One More Time	1965	$20

HEADHUNTERS
ARISTA

Number	Title	Yr	NM
❏ 0115	God Made Me Funky/Daffy's Dance	1975	$4
❏ 0137	If You've Got It, You'll Get It/(B-side unknown)	1975	$4

HEADROOM, MAX
CHRYSALIS

Number	Title	Yr	NM
❏ 44000	Merry Christmas Santa Claus (You're a Lovely Guy)/Gimme Shades	1985	$8
❏ 44000 [PS]	Merry Christmas Santa Claus (You're a Lovely Guy)/Gimme Shades	1985	$10
❏ 44000 [DJ]	Merry Christmas Santa Claus (You're a Lovely Guy) (same on both sides)	1985	$4
❏ 44000 [DJ]	Merry Christmas Santa Claus (You're a Lovely Guy) (same on both sides)	1985	$4

HEADS, HANDS AND FEET
ATCO

Number	Title	Yr	NM
❏ 6923	One Woman/Dirty, Heavy Weather Road	1973	$6

HEADS, THE
LIBERTY

Number	Title	Yr	NM
❏ 56025	Are You Lonely for Me, Baby/You	1968	$10

HEAP, JIMMY
CAPITOL

Number	Title	Yr	NM
❏ F3434	A Heap o' Boogie/Conscience, I'm Guilty	1956	$30
❏ F3333	Butternut/It Takes a Heap of Lovin'	1956	$30
❏ F2636	Cat'n Around/Make Me Live Again	1953	$30
❏ F2767	Cry, Cry Darling/Then I'll Be Happy	1954	$30
❏ F2866	Ethyl in My Gas Tank/You Oughta Know	1954	$30
❏ F3156	Go Ahead On/Love Can Move Mountains	1955	$30
❏ F2294	Heartbreaker/You Didn't Have Time	1952	$40
❏ F2425	Let's Do It Just Once/This Night Won't Last Forever	1953	$30
❏ F3071	Seven Come Eleven/That's All I Want from You	1955	$30
❏ F2990	Sharp Shooter/I Told You So	1954	$30
❏ F3543	This Song Is Just for You/Mingling	1956	$30
❏ F1958	True or False/A Lifetime of Shame	1952	$40

D

Number	Title	Yr	NM
❏ 1050	Someone Else Is Filling Your Shoes/Born to Love You	1959	$30

DART

Number	Title	Yr	NM
❏ 119	Gismo/Meanwhile	1959	$20

IMPERIAL

Number	Title	Yr	NM
❏ 8325	Wild Side of Life/When They Operated on Papa	1960	$20

HEART
Well-known Pacific Northwest-based group featuring the Wilson sisters, Ann and Nancy. Also see BORDERSONG; ANN WILSON; ANN AND NANCY WILSON.

CAPITOL

Number	Title	Yr	NM
❏ B-44002	Alone/Barracuda (Live)	1987	$3
❏ B-44002 [PS]	Alone/Barracuda (Live)	1987	$3
❏ B-5605	If Looks Could Kill/What He Don't Know	1986	$3
❏ B-5605 [PS]	If Looks Could Kill/What He Don't Know	1986	$3
❏ 7PRO-79311 [DJ]	I Want You So Bad (7" Remix) (same on both sides)	1988	$8
❏ B-44116	I Want You So Bad/Easy Target	1988	$3
❏ B-44089	There's the Girl/Bad Animals	1987	$3
❏ B-44089 [PS]	There's the Girl/Bad Animals	1987	$3
❏ B-5541	These Dreams/Shell Shock	1985	$3
❏ B-5541 [PS]	These Dreams/Shell Shock	1985	$3
❏ B-5481	What About Love/Heart of Darkness	1985	$3
❏ B-5481 [PS]	What About Love/Heart of Darkness	1985	$3
❏ B-44040	Who Will You Run To/Magic Man (Live)	1987	$3
❏ B-44040 [PS]	Who Will You Run To/Magic Man (Live)	1987	$3

CAPITOL STARLINE

Number	Title	Yr	NM
❏ X-6342	What About Love/Never	1986	$3

—Reissue

EPIC

Number	Title	Yr	NM
❏ 34-04184	Allies/Together Now	1983	$5
❏ 34-04184 [PS]	Allies/Together Now	1983	$5
❏ 15-08101	Barracuda/Straight On	1988	$3

—Reissue

Number	Title	Yr	NM
❏ 9-50892	Bebe Le Strange/Silver Wheels	1980	$4
❏ 9-50847	Even It Up/Pilot	1980	$4
❏ 34-04047	How Can I Refuse/Johnny Moon	1983	$3
❏ 34-04047 [PS]	How Can I Refuse/Johnny Moon	1983	$3
❏ 14-03071	Private Audition/Bright Light Girl	1982	$3
❏ 19-50950	Tell It Like It Is/Strange Euphoria	1980	$4
❏ 14-02925	This Man Is Mine/America	1982	$3
❏ 14-02925 [PS]	This Man Is Mine/America	1982	$3

MUSHROOM

Number	Title	Yr	NM
❏ 7021	Crazy on You/Dreamboat Annie	1976	$6
❏ 7023	Dreamboat Annie/Sing Child	1976	$5

—Bizarre version of A-side with part of the intro to "Crazy on You" grafted on.

Number	Title	Yr	NM
❏ 7031	Heartless/Just the Wine	1978	$4
❏ 7043	Magazine/Devil Delight	1978	$4
❏ 7011 [DJ]	Magic Man (2:45) (5:35)	1976	$10
❏ 7011	Magic Man/How Deep It Goes	1976	$5
❏ 7035	Without You/Here Song	1978	$4

Number	Title	Yr	NM
PORTRAIT			
❏ 6-70004	Barracuda/Cry to Me	1977	$4
❏ 17-8101	Barracuda/Straight On	1981	$4
— Reissue			
❏ 6-70025	Dog and Butterfly/Mistral Wind	1979	$5
❏ 6-70008	Little Queen/Treat Me Well	1977	$5
❏ AE71168 [DJ]	Straight On (Edit) (same on both sides)	1978	$8
❏ 6-70020	Straight On/Lighter Touch	1978	$4
— Custom label			

HEART (2)
EMI

Number	Title	Yr	NM
❏ 4008	Beautiful Woman/Lovemaker	1974	$4

HEART (3)
LOOK

Number	Title	Yr	NM
❏ 5023	Give Me a Happy Heart/Now	1969	$6
❏ 5029	I Love You/Love	1970	$6

HEART-THROBS, THE
ALADDIN

Number	Title	Yr	NM
❏ 3394	So Glad/All the Way Home	1957	$50

LAMP

Number	Title	Yr	NM
❏ 2010	So Glad/All the Way Home	1957	$50

HEART (U)
REPRISE

Number	Title	Yr	NM
❏ 0772	Heartbeat/The Train	1968	$6

HEARTBEATS, THE
GEE

Number	Title	Yr	NM
❏ 1047	500 Miles to Go/After New Year's Eve	1958	$50
— Red label			
❏ 1047	500 Miles to Go/After New Year's Eve	1958	$30
— Gray label			
❏ 1062	Darling How Long/Hurry Home Baby	1960	$30
❏ 1061	People Are Talking/Your Way	1960	$30
❏ 1043	When I Found You/Hands Off My Baby	1957	$60

GUYDEN

Number	Title	Yr	NM
❏ 2011	One Million Years/Darling, I Want to Get Married	1959	$50
— Yellow label			
❏ 2011	One Million Years/Darling, I Want to Get Married	1959	$40
— Purple label			

HULL

Number	Title	Yr	NM
❏ 720	A Thousand Miles Away/Oh Baby Don't	1957	$250
— Black label			
❏ 720	A Thousand Miles Away/Oh Baby Don't	1957	$100
— Red label			
❏ 711 [DJ]	Crazy for You/Rockin-N-Rollin-N-Rhythm-N-Blues-N	1955	$600
— White label			
❏ 711	Crazy for You/Rockin-N-Rollin-N-Rhythm-N-Blues-N	1955	$300
— Pink label, "Sheppard-Miller" as A-side composers			
❏ 711	Crazy for You/Rockin-N-Rollin-N-Rhythm-N-Blues-N	1955	$200
— Pink label, "Miller" as A-side composer			
❏ 711	Crazy for You/Rockin-N-Rollin-N-Rhythm-N-Blues-N	1955	$125
— Black label			
❏ 711 [DJ]	Crazy for You/Rockin-N-Rollin-N-Rhythm-N-Blues-N	1955	$600
— White label			
❏ 713	Darling How Long/Hurry Home Baby	1956	$200
❏ 716	People Are Talking/Your Way	1956	$200

JUBILEE

Number	Title	Yr	NM
❏ 5202	Finally/Boil and Bubble	1955	$40

NETWORK

Number	Title	Yr	NM
❏ 71200	Tormented/After Everybody's Gone	1955	$300
— Cream label, black vinyl			

RAMA

Number	Title	Yr	NM
❏ 216	A Thousand Miles Away/Oh Baby Don't	1956	$100
❏ 231	I Want to Know/Everybody's Somebody's Fool	1957	$125
❏ 222	Wedding Bells/I Won't Be the Fool Anymore	1957	$125

ROULETTE

Number	Title	Yr	NM
❏ 4194	Crazy for You/Down on My Knees	1959	$40
❏ 4054	I Found a Job/Down on My Knees	1958	$40
❏ 4091	One Day Next Year/Sometimes I Wonder	1958	$40

HEARTBREAKERS, THE
ATCO

Number	Title	Yr	NM
❏ 6258	The Willow Wept/You Had Time	1963	$70

BRENT

Number	Title	Yr	NM
❏ 7037	I'm Leaving It All Up to You/Corrido Mash	1962	$40

DONNA

Number	Title	Yr	NM
❏ 1381	Everytime I See You/Cradle Rock	1963	$120
— Frank Zappa plays guitar on this record			

LINDA

Number	Title	Yr	NM
❏ 114	Please Answer/She Is My Baby	1964	$20

MARKAY

Number	Title	Yr	NM
❏ 106	Since You've Been Gone/John Law	1962	$100

MAX'S KANSAS CITY

Number	Title	Yr	NM
❏ 213	All By Myself/Milk Me	1979	$30

MGM

Number	Title	Yr	NM
❏ 13129	It's Hard Being a Girl/Special Occasions	1963	$20

RCA VICTOR

Number	Title	Yr	NM
❏ 47-4327	Heartbreaker/Wanda	1951	$600
❏ 47-4849	There Is Time/It's OK With Me	1952	$500
❏ 47-4662	Why Don't I/Rockin' Daddy-O	1952	$500

SWAN

Number	Title	Yr	NM
❏ 4242	Baby Baby/I Told You So	1966	$20

VIK

Number	Title	Yr	NM
❏ 0299	My Love/Love You Till the Day I Die	1957	$250
❏ 0261	Without a Cause/One, Two, I Love You	1957	$200

HEARTS, THE
BATON

Number	Title	Yr	NM
❏ 211	All My Love Belongs to You/Talk About Him Girlie	1955	$60
❏ 222	Disappointed Bride/Going Home to Stay	1956	$40
❏ 215	Gone, Gone, Gone/Until the Real Thing Comes Along	1955	$60
❏ 228	He Drives Me Crazy/I Had a Guy	1956	$30
❏ 208	Lonely Nights/Oo-Wee	1955	$60

J&S

Number	Title	Yr	NM
❏ 995	A Thousand Years from Today/I Feel So Good	1960	$50
❏ 1657	Dancing in a Dream World/You Needn't Tell, I Know	1957	$70
❏ 4571/2	Goodbye Baby/There Is No Love at All	1959	$50
❏ 10002/3	If I Had Known/There Are So Many Ways	1958	$60
❏ 1626/7	I Want Your Love Tonight/Like Later Baby	1958	$60
❏ 425/6	My Love Has Gone/You or Me Have Got to Go	1959	$60
❏ 1660	So Long, Baby/You Say You Love Me	1957	$70

TUFF

Number	Title	Yr	NM
❏ 370	Dear Abby/(Instrumental)	1963	$20

HEARTSFIELD
MERCURY

Number	Title	Yr	NM
❏ 73742	Magic Mood/Rocking Chair	1975	$5
❏ 73449	Music Eyes/Gypsy Rider	1974	$5
❏ 73600	Shine On/Eight Hours at a Time	1974	$5

HEATH, TED
LONDON

Number	Title	Yr	NM
❏ 1344	Alouette/Yours Is My Heart	1953	$15
❏ 1290	Alpine Boogie/Floreintine	1952	$15
❏ 1531	Asia Minor/Dig Deep	1955	$10
❏ 1690	Autumn Concerto/Lost	1956	$12
— B-side by Bobbie Britton			
❏ 1305	Beyond the Sea/On the Bridge	1953	$15
❏ 1836	Bullfighters Patrol/Strolling Along with the Blues	1958	$10
❏ 1057	Button Up Your Overcoat/You're Nearer	1951	$15
❏ 1692	Canadian Sunset/Oriental Holiday	1956	$10
❏ 1184	Casey Jones/I Want to Be Happy	1952	$15
❏ 1809	Cha Cha Baby/Tom Hark	1958	$10
❏ 9503	Charmaine Cha Cha/Sucu Sucu	1962	$6
❏ 1647	Cloudburst/The Trouble with Harry	1956	$10
❏ 1379	Dragnet/Sloppy Joe	1953	$15
❏ 1867	Frogmarch/9:20 Special	1959	$8
❏ 1887	Honky Tonk Train Blues/Bluest Kind of Blue	1959	$8
❏ 1182	L'Heure Bleu/A Kiss in the Dark	1952	$15
❏ 1800	Little Serenade/I've Got the World on a String	1958	$10

Number	Title	Yr	NM
❏ 1183	Live House Blues/The Black Bottom	1952	$15
❏ 1026	London Fog/Romanian Roundabout	1951	$15
❏ 1390	Lullaby of Birdland/Seven-Eleven	1953	$15
❏ 1712	Madagascar/Jungle Drums	1957	$10
❏ 1644	Main Title -- The Man with the Golden Arm/Siboney	1956	$10
❏ 1621	Malaguena/Barber Shop Jump	1955	$10
❏ 1975	Man from Madrid/Theme from "Dangerman"	1961	$8
❏ 1198	Obsession/Hawaiian Mambo	1952	$15
❏ 2014	Peanut Vendor/Daddy	1961	$8
❏ 1534	Peg o' My Heart Mambo/In the Mood	1955	$10
❏ 1324	Phantom Regiment/Strike Up the Band	1953	$15
❏ 1014	Saxophone Mambo/Take a Letter Miss Smith	1951	$15
❏ 1006	Sixty Seconds/The Girl in the Little Green Hat	1951	$15
❏ 1500	Skokiaan/Skokiaan	1954	$15
— B-side by the Johnston Brothers			
❏ 1920	Slaughter on Tenth Avenue/Sleepy Lagoon	1960	$8
❏ 1404	Slim Jim/The Original Creep	1954	$15
❏ 1495	Stomp and Whistle/Bernie's Tune	1954	$15
❏ 1893	Swinging Ghosts/Indian Love Call	1959	$8
❏ 1421	The Champ/Pick Yourself Up	1954	$15
❏ 1675	The Faithful Hussar/Have You Met Miss Jones	1956	$10
❏ 9602	Theme from Cleopatra/Mirage	1963	$6
❏ 9629	Theme from "Lord of the Flies"/Paris Mist	1963	$6
❏ 9680	Theme from "The Carpetbaggers"/Wigwam	1964	$6
❏ 1015	This Is the Time/In a Little Spanish Town	1951	$15
❏ 1181	Turkey in the Straw/Entry of the Gladiators	1952	$15
❏ 1762	Witch Doctor/Headin' North	1957	$10

HEATHERTON, JOEY
CORAL

Number	Title	Yr	NM
❏ 62451	Hullaballoo/My Blood Runs Cold	1965	$125
❏ 62422	That's How It Goes/I'll Be Seeing You	1964	$40
❏ 62422 [PS]	That's How It Goes/I'll Be Seeing You	1964	$50
❏ 62459	Tomorrow Is Another Day/But He's Not Mine	1965	$30

DECCA

Number	Title	Yr	NM
❏ 31962	Live and Learn/When You Call Me Baby	1966	$300
❏ 31962 [PS]	Live and Learn/When You Call Me Baby	1966	$100

MGM

Number	Title	Yr	NM
❏ 14499	Crazy/God Only Knows	1973	$5
❏ 14387	Gone/The Road I Took to You	1972	$5
❏ 14387 [PS]	Gone/The Road I Took to You	1972	$10
❏ 14434	I'm Sorry/Crazy	1972	$6
❏ 14434	I'm Sorry/Someone to Watch Over Me	1972	$5

HEBB, BOBBY
BOOM

Number	Title	Yr	NM
❏ 60017	Betty Jo from Ohio/Sam Hall Jr.	1966	$8

CADET

Number	Title	Yr	NM
❏ 5690	I Was a Boy When You Needed a Man/Woman in the Window	1972	$30

LAURIE

Number	Title	Yr	NM
❏ 3638	Sunny '76/Sunny Disco	1976	$10
❏ 3632	True, I Love You/Proud Soul Heritage	1975	$50

PHILIPS

Number	Title	Yr	NM
❏ 40400	A Satisfied Mind/Love, Love, Love	1966	$8
❏ 40400 [PS]	A Satisfied Mind/Love, Love, Love	1966	$15
❏ 40551	Dreamy/You Want to Change Me	1968	$70
❏ 40482	Everything Is Coming Up Roses/Bound by Love	1967	$30
❏ 40448	I Love Everything About You/Some Kind of Magic	1967	$20
❏ 40421	Love Me/Crazy Baby	1966	$20
❏ 40431	My Pretty Sunshine/Ooh La La	1967	$8
❏ 40365	Sunny/Bread	1966	$10

RICH

Number	Title	Yr	NM
❏ 1006	Cherry/Feel So Good	1960	$20

SCEPTER

Number	Title	Yr	NM
❏ 12166	I Love Mary (Part 1)/I Love Mary (Part 2)	1966	$8

Number	Title	Yr	NM

HEDGEHOPPERS ANONYMOUS
PARROT

Number	Title	Yr	NM
❏ 9817	Don't Push Me/Please Don't Hurt Your Heart for Me	1966	$12
❏ 9800	It's Good News Week/Afraid of Love	1965	$15

HEIGHT, RONNIE
BAMBOO

❏ 500	Dolores/I'm Confessin'	1961	$15

DORE

❏ 516	Come Softly to Me/So Young, So Wise	1959	$30

ERA

❏ 3009	Maybe Tomorrow/A Kiss to Build a Dream On	1959	$20
❏ 3017	Mem'ries and Habits/One Finger Symphony	1960	$20
❏ 3005	Mr. Blue, I Presume/Juvenile	1959	$20
❏ 3000	Portrait of Linda/It's Not That Easy	1959	$20

HEINZ
TOWER

❏ 172	Digging My Potatoes/Don't Think Twice, It's All Right	1965	$30
❏ 195	Don't Worry Baby/Heart Full of Sorrow	1966	$40
❏ 253	I'm Not a Bad Boy/Movin' In	1966	$30

HELL, RICHARD, AND THE VOIDOIDS
Early member of TELEVISION.

ORK

❏ 81976	I Could Live With You in Another World/Blank Generation/You Gotta Lose	1977	$50
❏ 81976 [PS]	I Could Live With You in Another World/Blank Generation/You Gotta Lose	1977	$60

SIRE

❏ 1003	Blank Generation/Love Comes in Spurts	1977	$10
❏ 1003 [PS]	Blank Generation/Love Comes in Spurts	1977	$10

7-Inch Extended Plays
SHAKE

❏ SHK101	Don't Die/Time//That's All I Know (Right Now)/Love Comes in Spurts	1980	$14

—B-side tracks by Neon Boys

HELLO PEOPLE, THE
ABC

❏ 12160	Book of Love/How High Is the Moon	1976	$5

ABC DUNHILL

❏ 15023	Future Shock/Destiny	1974	$5

MEDIARTS

❏ 109	Pass Me By/Maybe We Should Have Had Rain	1971	$10

PHILIPS

❏ 40585	Anthem/Jelly Jam	1969	$8
❏ 40531	(As I Went Down to) Jerusalem/It's a Monday Kind of Tuesday	1968	$8
❏ 40522	A Stranger at Her Door/Paisley Teddy Bear	1968	$8
❏ 40572	If I Should Sing Too Softly/Pray for Rain	1968	$8
❏ 40481	Let's Go Hide in the Forest/Disparity Waterfront Blues	1967	$8

UNITED ARTISTS

❏ 50797	Pass Me By/Maybe We Should Have Had Rain	1971	$6

HELM, LEVON
A&M

❏ 2291	The Death of Me/One More Shot	1980	$4

—With Johnny Cash

ABC

❏ 12416	Ain't No Way to Forget You/Standing on a Mountaintop	1978	$4
❏ 12336	Milk Cow Boogie/Blues So Bad	1978	$4

MCA

❏ 41242	America's Farm/Blue Moon of Kentucky	1980	$4
❏ 41202	Working in the Coal Mine/Blue Moon of Kentucky	1980	$4

HELMET
AMPHETAMINE REPTILE

❏ Scale22	Born Annoying/Rumble	1989	$30
❏ Scale22 [PS]	Born Annoying/Rumble	1989	$30

HELMS, BOBBY
CERTRON

Number	Title	Yr	NM
❏ 10023	I Wouldn't Take the World for You/Look What You've Done	1970	$8
❏ 10002	Mary Goes 'Round/Cold Winds Blow on Me	1970	$8

COLUMBIA

❏ 4-42801	Fraulein/My Special Angel	1963	$10
❏ 4-43031	It's a Girl/Put Your Arms Around Him	1964	$10

DECCA

❏ 9-30749	A Hundred Hearts/The Fool and the Angel	1958	$30
❏ 9-30194	Fraulein/(Got a) Heartsick Feeling	1957	$30
❏ 9-30194 [PS]	Fraulein/(Got a) Heartsick Feeling	1957	$60
❏ 31287	How Can You Divide a Little Child/My Greatest Weakness	1961	$15
❏ 31103	Let Me Be the One/I Wanna Be with You	1960	$20
❏ 31148	Lonely River Rhine/Guess We Thought the World Would End	1960	$20
❏ 9-30976	My Lucky Day/Hurry Baby	1959	$20
❏ 9-30423	My Special Angel/Standing at the End of My World	1957	$30
❏ 31356	One Deep Love/Once in a Lifetime	1962	$15
❏ 31230	Sad-Eyed Baby/You're the One	1961	$15
❏ 9-30682	Schoolboy Crush/Borrowed Dreams	1958	$30
❏ 9-30886	Soon It Can Be Told/I Guess I'll Miss the Prom	1959	$20
❏ 9-29947	Tennessee Rock 'N' Roll/I Don't Owe You Nothing	1956	$60
❏ 31403	Then Came You!/Yesterday's Champagne	1962	$15
❏ 9-31041	To My Sorrow/Someone Was Already There	1960	$20

GUSTO

❏ 116	That Heart Belongs to Me/With Jenny on My Mind	1974	$6
❏ 119	Work Things Out with Annie/With Jenny on My Mind	1974	$6

KAPP

❏ 876	I Miss My Fraulein/Where Does a Shadow Go	1967	$8
❏ 708	I'm the Man/Have This Love on Me	1965	$10
❏ 777	The Things I Remember Most/Sorry, My Name Isn't Fred	1966	$10
❏ 732	Those Snowy Glowy Blowy Days of Winter/Sailor	1965	$10

LITTLE DARLIN'

❏ 073	Echoes and Shadows/Step Into My Soul	1969	$12
❏ 030	He Thought He'd Die Laughing/You'd Better Make Up Your Mind	1967	$12
❏ 041	I Feel You, I Love You/The Day You Stop Loving Me	1968	$10
❏ 7801	I'm Gonna Love the Devil Out of You/I Can't Promise You	1978	$6
❏ 054	My Special Angel/Expressing My Love	1968	$10
❏ 7916	One More Dollar for the Band/Touch My Heart	1979	$6
❏ 049	Or Is It Love/Touch My Heart	1968	$10
❏ 062	So Long/Just Do the Best You Can	1969	$12
❏ 034	The Day You Stop Loving Me/You Can Tell the World	1967	$12
❏ 7807	The Things I Remember Most/I'm Not Sorry	1978	$6

PLAYBACK

❏ 1305	Lay Me Down Look/Dance with Me	1988	$6
❏ 1322	Somebody Wrong Is Looking Right/This Song for You	1988	$6
❏ 1328	Southern Belle/Troubles Wall to Wall	1989	$6
❏ 75709	Southern Belle/Troubles Wall to Wall	1989	$5

SPEED

❏ 45-117	Freedom Lovin' Guy/I've Never Seen Anyone	1957	$40

7-Inch Extended Plays
DECCA

❏ ED2629 [PS]	Bobby Helms	1957	$25
❏ ED2555	If Only I Knew/Far Away Heart/My Shoes Keep Walking Back to You/Sugar Moon	1957	$25
❏ ED2586	Plaything/Magic Song//Tonight's the Night/Just a Little Lonesome (title unknown)	1957	$25
❏ ED2555 [PS]	(title unknown)	1957	$25
❏ ED2586 [PS]	Tonight's the Night	1957	$25

HELMS, DON
SMASH

Number	Title	Yr	NM
❏ 1781	Fire Ball Mail/I Can't Help It (If I'm Still in Love with You)	1962	$30

HELMS, JIMMY
CAPITOL

❏ 3003	The Only Thing That Matters/Just Hold My Hand and Sing	1970	$30

HELP
DECCA

❏ 32879	Good Time Music/Hold On Child	1971	$15

HEMLOCKS, THE
FURY

❏ 1004	Cora Lee/Joys of Love	1957	$125

HENCHMEN, THE
PUNCH

❏ 1009	Please Tell Me/Livin'	1966	$60

HENDERSON, JOE
FONTANA

❏ 1658	Don't Forget to Catch Me/Please Don't Go	1969	$6
❏ 1638	Help Yourself/A Man Without Love	1969	$6

KAPP

❏ 590	If We Could Start All Over/You Take One Step, I'll Take Two	1964	$10

RIC

❏ 149	Honey on My Lips/Like a Child	1965	$8
❏ 141	I Ain't Never/The River or the Railroad Track	1964	$20
❏ 181	Sweet Lovin' Baby/Too Much to Lose	1966	$8

TODD

❏ 1066	Baby Don't Leave Me/Right Now	1961	$20
❏ 1077	Big Love/After Loving You	1962	$15
❏ 1082	Cause We're in Love/Sad Teardrops at Dawn	1963	$15
❏ 1096	If We Could Start All Over/You Take One Step, I'll Take Two	1964	$15
❏ 1085	Love Me Sweet/My Hands Are Tied	1963	$15
❏ 1091	Lovin' Part Time/Blues for a Four-String Guitar	1963	$15
❏ 1072	Snap Your Fingers/If You See Me Cry	1962	$20
❏ 1079	Three Steps/The Searching Is Over	1962	$30

HENDRICKS, BOBBY
MERCURY

❏ 71810	Good Lovin'/Honey Crisp	1961	$15
❏ 71788	Happy Hearts/Pleasing You	1961	$15
❏ 71881	I'm Comin' Home/Every Other Night	1961	$15

MGM

❏ 13179	Let's Get It Over/Love in My Heart	1963	$125

SUE

❏ 710	Cast Your Vote/It's Misery	1959	$30
❏ 727	City of Angels/If I Just Had Your Love	1960	$30
❏ 708	Dreamy Eyes/Molly Be Good	1958	$30
❏ 712	I'm a Big Boy Now/Good Things Will Come	1959	$30
❏ 706	Itchy Twitchy Feeling/A Thousand Dreams	1958	$40
❏ 717	Little John Green/Sincerely, Your Lover	1959	$30
❏ 732	Psycho/Too Good to Be True	1960	$30

UNITED ARTISTS

❏ 0142	Itchy Twitchy Feeling/Psycho	1973	$4

—Silver Spotlight Series" reissue

HENDRIX, JIMI, AND LITTLE RICHARD
ALA

❏ 1175	Goodnight Irene/Why Don't You Love Me	1972	$8

HENDRIX, JIMI
REPRISE

❏ 0767	All Along the Watchtower/Burning of the Midnight Lamp	1968	$40
❏ 0742	All Along the Watchtower/Crosstown Traffic	1971	$6

—Back to Back Hits" series

❏ PRO595 [PS]	...And a Happy New Year	1974	$100

Number	Title	Yr	NM
❑ 0792	Crosstown Traffic/ Gypsy Eyes	1968	$40
❑ 1044	Dolly Dagger/Star Spangled Banner	1971	$20
❑ 29845	Fire/Little Wing	1982	$6
❑ 0641	Foxey Lady/Hey Joe	1967	$30
❑ 1000	Freedom/Angel	1971	$20
❑ EP2239	Gloria (B-side blank)	1979	$5
❑ EP2239 [PS]	Gloria (B-side blank)	1979	$5

— Above was a bonus record in "The Essential Jimi Hendrix, Volume 2

Number	Title	Yr	NM
❑ 0572	Hey Joe/51st Anniversary	1967	$125
❑ 0572 [PS]	Hey Joe/51st Anniversary	1967	$1000
❑ 0853	If 6 Was 9/Stone Free	1969	$50
❑ PRO595 [DJ]	Medley: The Little Drummer Boy-Silent Night/Auld Lang Syne	1974	$180
❑ PRO595 [DJ]	Medley: The Little Drummer Boy-Silent Night/Auld Lang Syne	1974	$200
❑ 0728	Purple Haze/Foxey Lady	1968	$20

— Back to Back Hits" series -- originals have both "r:" and "W7" logos

Number	Title	Yr	NM
❑ 0597	Purple Haze/The Wind Cries Mary	1967	$30
❑ 0905	Stepping Stone/Izabella	1970	$125

— As "Hendrix Band of Gypsys

Number	Title	Yr	NM
❑ 1118	The Wind Cries Mary/Little Wing	1972	$20

TRIP

Number	Title	Yr	NM
❑ 3002	Hot Trigger/Suspicious	1972	$5

HENDRIX SINGERS, THE
EXCELLO

Number	Title	Yr	NM
❑ 2001	Away in the Manger/O Come All Ye Faithful	1952	$30

HENLEY, DON
Also see EAGLES; STEVIE NICKS; SHILOH.

ASYLUM

Number	Title	Yr	NM
❑ 69894	Dirty Laundry/Lilah	1982	$4
❑ 69894 [PS]	Dirty Laundry/Lilah	1982	$6
❑ 69931	I Can't Stand Still/ Them and Us	1982	$4

GEFFEN

Number	Title	Yr	NM
❑ 29065	All She Wants to Do Is Dance/Building the Perfect Beast	1985	$3
❑ 29065 [PS]	All She Wants to Do Is Dance/Building the Perfect Beast	1985	$3
❑ 28906	Sunset Grill/Man with a Mission	1985	$4
❑ 29141	The Boys of Summer/A Month of Sundays	1984	$3
❑ 29141 [PS]	The Boys of Summer/A Month of Sundays	1984	$3
❑ 22925	The End of the Innocence/ If Dirt Were Dollars	1989	$3
❑ 22925 [PS]	The End of the Innocence/ If Dirt Were Dollars	1989	$3
❑ 22771	The Last Worthless Evening/ Gimme What You Got	1989	$3
❑ 22771 [PS]	The Last Worthless Evening/ Gimme What You Got	1989	$3

HENRY, CLARENCE
ARGO

Number	Title	Yr	NM
❑ 5259	Ain't Got No Home/ Troubles, Troubles	1956	$30
❑ 5408	A Little Too Much/I Wish I Could Stay the Same	1962	$15
❑ 5378	But I Do/Just My Baby and Me	1960	$20

— A-side: Same song, new title

Number	Title	Yr	NM
❑ 5414	Dream Myself a Sweetheart/ Lost Without You	1962	$15
❑ 5378	I Don't Know Why/Just My Baby and Me	1960	$30
❑ 5448	If I Didn't Care/It Takes Two to Tango	1963	$15
❑ 5273	I Found a Home/ It Won't Be Long	1957	$20
❑ 5266	I'm a Country Boy/ Lonely Tramp	1957	$20
❑ 5305	I'm in Love/Baby Baby Please	1958	$20
❑ 5395	Lonely Street/Why Can't You	1961	$20
❑ 5480	Looking Back/Long Lost and Worried	1964	$10
❑ 5401	On Bended Knees/Standing in the Need of Love	1961	$20

CADET

Number	Title	Yr	NM
❑ 5259	Ain't Got No Home/ Troubles, Troubles	1966	$8

DIAL

Number	Title	Yr	NM
❑ 4072	Shake Your Money Maker/ That's When I Guessed	1968	$6
❑ 4057	This Time/Hummin' a Heartache	1967	$6

PARROT

Number	Title	Yr	NM
❑ 45004	Have You Ever Been Lonely/Little Green Frog	1964	$12
❑ 45015	I Might As Well/Tore Up Over You	1965	$10

Number	Title	Yr	NM
❑ 45009	I Told My Pillow/ Can't Hide My Tear	1964	$10

HENRY, EARL
DOT

Number	Title	Yr	NM
❑ 15875	My Suzanne/Believe a Traveler	1958	$40
❑ 15756	Whatcha Gonna Do?/I Am the Man	1958	$60

HENRY, THOMAS
HIT

Number	Title	Yr	NM
❑ 73	So Much in Love/No One	1963	$8

— B-side by Leroy Jones

HENRY TREE
MAINSTREAM

Number	Title	Yr	NM
❑ 729	Penfield Town/ (B-side unknown)	1970	$15

HENSLEE, GENE
IMPERIAL

Number	Title	Yr	NM
❑ 8227	Diggin' and Datin'/A Girl Named Haertbreak	1954	$75

MEL-O-DY

Number	Title	Yr	NM
❑ 110	Beautiful Women/Shambles	1963	$30

UNITED ARTISTS

Number	Title	Yr	NM
❑ 946	I Don't Wanna Go Home/Shambles	1964	$20

HENSON, JIM
ATLANTIC

Number	Title	Yr	NM
❑ 3642	Movin' Right Along/Never Before, Never Again	1980	$6

— As "Kermit and Fozzie Bear (Jim Henson)

SIGNATURE

Number	Title	Yr	NM
❑ 12023	Tick-Tock Sick/ The Countryside	1960	$60

HEP STARS, THE
CAMEO

Number	Title	Yr	NM
❑ 376	Cadillac/Farmer John	1965	$50

CHARTMAKER

Number	Title	Yr	NM
❑ 414	It's Now Winter's Day/ Musty Dusty	1969	$50

DUNHILL

Number	Title	Yr	NM
❑ 4040	Sunny Girl/No Response	1966	$50

HEPSTERS, THE
RONEL

Number	Title	Yr	NM
❑ 110	I Gotta Sing the Blues/ This-a-Way	1956	$300

HERALDS, THE
HERALD

Number	Title	Yr	NM
❑ 435	Eternal Love/ Gonna Love You	1954	$250

HERMAN, PEE-WEE
COLUMBIA

Number	Title	Yr	NM
❑ 07301	Surfin' Bird/My Beach	1987	$3

— B-side by Surf Punks

Number	Title	Yr	NM
❑ 07301 [PS]	Surfin' Bird/My Beach	1987	$3

HERMAN, WOODY
CADET

Number	Title	Yr	NM
❑ 5659	I Can't Get Next to You/It's Your Thing	1969	$5
❑ 5635	Light My Fire/Hush	1969	$5
❑ 5669	My Cherie Amour/The Hut	1970	$5
❑ 5643	Pontico/Keep On Keeping On	1969	$5

CAPITOL

Number	Title	Yr	NM
❑ F3042	Have It Your Way/ My Sin Is You	1955	$15
❑ F3488	I Don't Want Nobody (To Have My Love But You)/To Love Again	1956	$15
❑ F1637	Lemon Drop/Early Autumn	1951	$15
❑ F3202	Love Is a Many-Splendored Thing/House of Bamboo	1955	$15
❑ F2960	Mexican Hat Trick/ Sleepy Serenade	1954	$15
❑ F1126	Music to Dance To/I Want a Little Girl	1950	$30
❑ F2942	Muskrat Ramble/ Woodchopper Mambo	1954	$15
❑ F3269	Skinned/Skinned Again	1955	$15
❑ F1170	Sonny Speaks/Pennies from Heaven	1950	$30
❑ F1215	When It Rains It Pours/ Starlight Souvenirs	1950	$20

COLUMBIA

Number	Title	Yr	NM
❑ 39411	Apple Honey/Wild Root	1951	$15
❑ 39409	Caldonia/(B-side unknown)	1951	$15
❑ 39410	Happiness Is a Thing Called Joe/Bijou	1951	$15

Number	Title	Yr	NM
❑ 43449	Mardi Gras/Sting Ray	1965	$6
❑ 43262	My Favorite Things/Do Anything You Wanna	1965	$6
❑ 43750	Sidewinder/Greasy Sack Blues	1966	$6
❑ 44124	The Duck/Hallelujah, Baby!	1967	$6

FANTASY

Number	Title	Yr	NM
❑ 672	After Hours/(B-side unknown)	1972	$4
❑ 723	Corazon/America Drinks and Goes Home	1974	$4
❑ 695	Fat Mama/The Raven Speaks	1973	$4
❑ 699	The First Thing I Do/ Freedom Jazz Dance	1973	$4

MGM

Number	Title	Yr	NM
❑ 11661	Prelude to a Kiss/ Cuban Holiday	1954	$20

PHILIPS

Number	Title	Yr	NM
❑ 40213	C'mon and Ska/Theme from Golden Boy	1964	$8
❑ 40125	Days of Wine and Roses/ Jazz Me Blues	1963	$8
❑ 40003	Swing Low, Sweet Chariot/Rose Room	1962	$8
❑ 40187	Taste of Honey/ Hallelujah Time	1964	$8

VERVE

Number	Title	Yr	NM
❑ 10053	I Wonder/Like a House Built on a Strong Foundation	1957	$10
❑ 10069	Makin' Whoopee/ Comes Love	1957	$10

HERMAN'S HERMITS
ABKCO

Number	Title	Yr	NM
❑ 4043	A Must to Avoid/Leaning on the Lamp Post	1973	$5
❑ 4022	I'm Into Something Good/Can't You Hear My Heartbeat	1972	$5
❑ 4024	Listen People/Dandy	1972	$5
❑ 4021	Mrs. Brown You've Got a Lovely Daughter/I'm Henry VIII, I Am	1972	$5
❑ 4042	Silhouettes/Just a Little Bit Better	1973	$5
❑ 4023	There's a Kind of Hush (All Over the World)/ Wonderful World	1972	$5

BUDDAH

Number	Title	Yr	NM
❑ 516	Lonely Situation (Love Is All I Need)/Blond Haired Blue Eyed Boy	1976	$8

MGM

Number	Title	Yr	NM
❑ 13437	A Must to Avoid/The Man with the Cigar	1966	$8
❑ 13310	Can't You Hear My Heartbeat/I Know Why	1964	$10
❑ 13310 [PS]	Can't You Hear My Heartbeat/I Know Why	1964	$20
❑ 13603	Dandy/My Reservation's Been Confirmed	1966	$8
❑ 13603 [PS]	Dandy/My Reservation's Been Confirmed	1966	$20
❑ 13761	Don't Go Out Into the Rain (You're Going to Melt)/Moonshine Man	1967	$8
❑ 13761 [PS]	Don't Go Out Into the Rain (You're Going to Melt)/Moonshine Man	1967	$20
❑ 13639	East West/What Is Wrong What Is Right	1966	$8
❑ 0(no cat #) [PS]	Hold On	1966	$250

— Promo-only sleeve similar to the LP cover of the same name; rear of sleeve has "The Mod Shirts Are Here" advertisement; this may have come with some promos of MGM 13500

Number	Title	Yr	NM
❑ 13885	I Can Take or Leave Your Loving/Marcel's	1967	$8
❑ 13367	I'm Henry VIII, I Am/ The End of the World	1965	$10
❑ 13367 [PS]	I'm Henry VIII, I Am/ The End of the World	1965	$30
❑ 13280	I'm Into Something Good/ Your Hand in Mine	1964	$10
❑ 14100	It's Alright Now/(Here Comes) The Star	1969	$10
❑ 13500	Leaning on the Lamp Post/Hold On	1966	$8
❑ 13462	Listen People/Got a Feeling	1966	$8
❑ 13341	Mrs. Brown You've Got a Lovely Daughter/I Gotta Dream On	1965	$10
❑ 13341 [PS]	Mrs. Brown You've Got a Lovely Daughter/I Gotta Dream On	1965	$20
❑ 13787	Museum/Last Bus Home	1967	$8
❑ 13787 [PS]	Museum/Last Bus Home	1967	$20
❑ 14060	My Lady/My Sentimental Friend	1969	$10
❑ 13994	Ooh, She's Done It Again/ The Most Beautiful Thing in My Life	1968	$10
❑ 13332	Silhouettes/Walkin' With My Angel	1965	$10
❑ 13934	Sleepy Joe/Just One Girl	1968	$12

— Black label

Number	Title	Yr	NM
❑ 13934	Sleepy Joe/Just One Girl	1968	$8

Number	Title	Yr	NM
—Blue and gold label			
❑ 14035	Something's Happening/ Little Miss Sorrow, Child of Tomorrow	1969	$12
❑ 13973	Sunshine Girl/Nobody Needs to Know	1968	$10
❑ 13681	There's a Kind of Hush (All Over the World)/ No Milk Today	1967	$10
❑ 13681	There's a Kind of Hush/ No Milk Today	1967	$8
❑ 13681 [PS]	There's a Kind of Hush/ No Milk Today	1967	$20
❑ 13548	This Door Swings Both Ways/For Love	1966	$8
❑ 13354	Wonderful World/ Traveling Light	1965	$10
❑ 13354 [PS]	Wonderful World/ Traveling Light	1965	$20

PRIVATE STOCK

Number	Title	Yr	NM
❑ 45,019	Ginny Go Softly/Blond Haired, Blue Eyed Boy	1975	$8

ROULETTE

Number	Title	Yr	NM
❑ 7213	Truck Stop Mama/Heart Get Ready for Love	1977	$20

HERRING, RED
COUNTRY JUBILEE

Number	Title	Yr	NM
❑ 533	Wasted Love/ (B-side unknown)	1960	$30

HERROLD, DENNIS
IMPERIAL

Number	Title	Yr	NM
❑ 5482	Hip Hip Baby/Make with the Lovin'	1957	$100

HESITATIONS, THE
GWP

Number	Title	Yr	NM
❑ 504	Is This the Way to Treat a Girl/Yes I'm Ready	1969	$60

KAPP

Number	Title	Yr	NM
❑ 948	A Whiter Shade of Pale/ With Pen in Hand	1968	$10
❑ 878	Born Free/Love Is Everywhere	1967	$30
❑ 911	Climb Every Mountain/ My World	1968	$20
❑ 822	I'll Be Right There/She Won't Come Back	1967	$125
❑ 810	Soul Kind of Love/ Wait a Minute	1967	$125
❑ 790	Soul Superman/I'm Not Built That Way	1966	$200
❑ 899	The Impossible Dream/ Nobody Knows You When You're Down and Out	1968	$10
❑ 926	Who Will Answer/If You Ever Need a Hand	1968	$30

HEWITT, BEN
MERCURY

Number	Title	Yr	NM
❑ 71577	My Search/I Want a New Girl Now	1960	$50
❑ 71472	Patricia June/For Quite a While	1959	$60

HEWITT, DOLPH
JANIE

Number	Title	Yr	NM
❑ 461	Half a Chance/Look Into Your Heart	1960	$30
❑ 460	If You Are Present at Christmas/Look Into Your Heart	1959	$30
❑ 455	Last Night Was the End of My World/Autumn Love	1959	$30
❑ 459	The Door to Your Love/ Soap and Water	1959	$30

RCA VICTOR

Number	Title	Yr	NM
❑ 48-0462	Don't Tell Me Goodbye/ Tear Drops on the Roses	1951	$40
❑ 48-0369	I Hurt Inside/For Every Kiss	1950	$40
—Originals on green vinyl			
❑ 48-0107	I Wish I Knew/I Would Send You Roses	1949	$50
—Originals on green vinyl			
❑ 48-0162	Waltzing My Blues Away/ Check My Heart	1950	$50
—Originals on green vinyl			
❑ 48-0311	When a Dream Is Broken Into/An Empty Promise	1950	$40
—Originals on green vinyl			

HEYWOOD, EDDIE
20TH CENTURY FOX

Number	Title	Yr	NM
❑ 453	Theme from "The Prize"/Li'l Darlin'	1963	$8

COLUMBIA

Number	Title	Yr	NM
❑ 39317	All the Things You Are/ St. Louis Blues	1951	$10
❑ 39318	Mighty Like a Rose/When Your Lover Has Gone	1951	$10
❑ 39319	Try a Little Tenderness/ The Birth of the Blues	1951	$10
—The above four comprise a box set			
❑ 39316	Without a Song/A Pretty Girl Is Like a Melody	1951	$10

DECCA

Number	Title	Yr	NM
❑ 28549	Begin the Beguine/On the Sunny Side of the Street	1953	$15
❑ 28893	The Moon Was Yellow/ You Too, You Too	1953	$15

LIBERTY

Number	Title	Yr	NM
❑ 55575	Canadian Sunset Bossa Nova/The Good Life	1963	$8
❑ 55539	Harlem Blues/The Sidewalks of New York	1963	$8
❑ 55396	The Good Earth/ Dream of Olwen	1961	$8

MERCURY

Number	Title	Yr	NM
❑ 71504	High on a Windy Hill/ Wings in Autumn	1959	$8
❑ 70645	Land of Dreams/ Summer Holiday	1955	$12
❑ 70677	Love for Love/ Sunny Sunday	1955	$10
❑ 71014	Lover/If It's Sunny Sunday	1956	$10
❑ 71650	(Love Theme) Rat Race/ Everything in Manhattan	1960	$8
❑ 71603	Out of Bounds/ There You Are	1960	$8
❑ 70950	Secret Love/Let's Fall in Love	1956	$10
❑ 71462	Soft Summer Breeze/ Castillian Rhapsody	1959	$8
❑ 70863	Soft Summer Breeze/ Heywood's Bounce	1956	$12

RCA VICTOR

Number	Title	Yr	NM
❑ 47-6816	Begin the Beguine/ No Miracle Needed	1957	$12
❑ 47-7262	Haiti Lady/It's Really Nothing	1957	$10
❑ 47-7058	Lies/All About You	1957	$12
❑ 47-6674	Lost Love/Mozambique	1956	$15
❑ 47-6956	Love Is All/Virgin Isle Vamp	1957	$10
❑ 47-7385	St. Louis Blues/Rendezvous	1958	$10

HI-FI-DELS, THE
ATLANTIC

Number	Title	Yr	NM
❑ 2121	Did I Cry/Tricky Tricky	1961	$20

HI-FI'S, THE
CAMEO

Number	Title	Yr	NM
❑ 349	I Keep Forgettin'/Why Can't I Stop Loving You	1965	$15

INTERPHON

Number	Title	Yr	NM
❑ 7701	Will Yer or Won't Yer/ She's the One	1964	$15

UNITED ARTISTS

Number	Title	Yr	NM
❑ 50160	I'm a Box/No Two Ways	1967	$8

HI-FIVES, THE (1)
JERDEN

Number	Title	Yr	NM
❑ 730	Goin' Away/Tort	1964	$20

HI-FIVES, THE (2)
BINGO

Number	Title	Yr	NM
❑ 1006	Felicia/Windy City Special	1960	$40

DECCA

Number	Title	Yr	NM
❑ 30657	Dorothy/Just a Shoulder to Cry On	1958	$60
❑ 30744	Lonely/What's New	1958	$50
❑ 30576	My Friend/How Can I Win?	1958	$50

HI-LITERS, THE (1)
HICO

Number	Title	Yr	NM
❑ 2432	Let Me Be True to You/In the Night	1958	$125
❑ 2433	Over the Rainbow/ (B-side unknown)	1958	$200

HI-LITERS, THE (U)
VEE JAY

Number	Title	Yr	NM
❑ 184	Bobby Sox Baby/Hello Dear	1956	$1000

WEN-DEE

Number	Title	Yr	NM
❑ 1927	Baby Don't Treat Me This Way/Route 66	1955	$70

HI-LITES, THE (2)
JULIA

Number	Title	Yr	NM
❑ 1105	Gloria/For Your Precious Love	1962	$120

MONOGRAM

Number	Title	Yr	NM
❑ 119	Everybody's Somebody's Fool/Moonlight	1976	$8
❑ 121	Pretty Face/Maybe You'll Be There	1976	$8

RECORD FAIR

Number	Title	Yr	NM
❑ 501	For Sentimental Reasons/ For Your Precious Love	1962	$60
❑ 500	I'm Falling in Love/Walking My Baby Back Home	1961	$60

HI-LITES, THE (U)
BRUNSWICK

Number	Title	Yr	NM
❑ 55102	Friday Night Go Go/ Chicka-Rocka-Chee- Chi-Cho (Cha Cha)	1958	$30

JET

Number	Title	Yr	NM
❑ 502	4000 Miles Away/Woke Up This Morning	1961	$40
❑ 501	The Pony (Part 1)/ The Pony (Part 2)	1961	$30

KING

Number	Title	Yr	NM
❑ 5730	Death of an Angel/ Our Winter Love	1963	$30

OKEH

Number	Title	Yr	NM
❑ 7046	I Found a Love/Zanzee	1954	$500

RENO

Number	Title	Yr	NM
❑ 1030	Please Believe Me I Love You/Sweet and Lovely	1958	$250

TWIST TIME

Number	Title	Yr	NM
❑ 12	Twistin' Time/Twistin' Pony	1962	$20

WASSEL

Number	Title	Yr	NM
❑ 701	Groovy/Hey Baby	1965	$10

HI-LO'S, THE
COLUMBIA

Number	Title	Yr	NM
❑ 40915	A Face in the Crowd/ Autumn Rain	1957	$10
❑ 41647	Cindy's Prayer/A Lot of Livin' to Do	1960	$10
❑ 41465	Goody Goody/Indiana	1959	$10
❑ 41867	The Trolley Song/Five Foot Two, Eyes of Blue	1960	$10
❑ 41197	Whistlin' Down the Lane/ When I Remember	1958	$10

HIATT, JOHN
A&M

Number	Title	Yr	NM
❑ 2970	Have a Little Faith in Me/Thank You Girl	1987	$3
❑ 2950	Lipstick Sunset/ Thank You Girl	1987	$3
❑ 1245	Slow Turning/Your Dad Did (Live)	1988	$3

ATLANTIC

Number	Title	Yr	NM
❑ 89461	Snakecharmer/ This Is Your Day	1985	$4

EPIC

Number	Title	Yr	NM
❑ 50115	Down Home (Keep On Fallin')/Motorboat to Heaven	1975	$5
❑ 50022	Hangin' Around the Observatory/Full Moon	1974	$5
❑ 11095	Sure As I'm Sittin' Here/Ocean	1974	$5
❑ 10990	The Boulevard Ain't So Bad/We Make Spirit	1973	$6

GEFFEN

Number	Title	Yr	NM
❑ 29945	I Look for Love/Take Time to Know Her	1982	$4
❑ 29045	Living a Little, Laughing a Little/I'm a Real Man	1985	$4

MCA

Number	Title	Yr	NM
❑ 41300	I Spy (For the FBI)/It Hasn't Happened Yet	1980	$4
❑ 41132	Madonna Road/Slug Line	1979	$4

HICKEY, ERSEL
EPIC

Number	Title	Yr	NM
❑ 9395	Another Wasted Day/ Money Brought Me You	1960	$30
❑ 9263	Bluebirds Over the Mountain/Hangin' Around	1958	$40
❑ 9309	Don't Be Afraid of Love/ You Threw a Dart	1959	$30
❑ 9278	Goin' Down That Road/ Lovers' Land	1958	$30
❑ 9320	I Can't Love Another/ People Gotta Talk	1959	$30
❑ 9357	Love in Bloom/What Do You Want	1960	$30

JANUS

Number	Title	Yr	NM
❑ 151	Bluebirds Over the Mountain/Self Made Man	1971	$5

KAPP

Number	Title	Yr	NM
❑ 372	Teardrops at Dawn/I Guess You Can Call It Love	1961	$30

LAURIE

Number	Title	Yr	NM
❑ 3165	Some Enchanted Evening/ Put Your Mind at Ease	1963	$30

RAMESES II

Number	Title	Yr	NM
❑ 2003	Waitin' for Baby/In Spite of the Fool That I Am	1976	$6

UNIFAX

Number	Title	Yr	NM
❑ 100	How Unlucky Can You Get/Put It to Your Heart	1972	$8

7-Inch Extended Plays

EPIC

Number	Title	Yr	NM
❑ EG-7206	(contents unknown)	1958	$125
❑ EG-7206 [PS]	Ersel Hickey in Lover's Land	1958	$125

HILL, GOLDIE • 343

Number	Title	Yr	NM
HICKMAN, DWAYNE			
ABC-PARAMOUNT			
❏ 9908	School Dance/Pretty Baby	1958	$30
❏ 9908 [PS]	School Dance/Pretty Baby	1958	$50
CAPITOL			
❏ 4445	I'm a Lover, Not a Fighter/I Pass Your House	1960	$30
HICKS, JOHNNY			
COLUMBIA			
❏ 4-21098	A Good Man Is Hard to Find/I Care No More	1953	$40
❏ 4-20954	An Angel in Disguise/Ho Dee Ree Dee Ah	1952	$40
❏ 4-20900	Are You Sorry/Rainy Night Blues	1952	$40
❏ 4-20990	Brush the Dust Off Your Bible/Take My Hand	1952	$40
❏ 4-20761	Butane Blues/I Need a Good Woman Bad	1950	$50
❏ 4-20826	Crossroads/Get Your Kicks	1951	$40
❏ 4-20737	Heart After Heart/Hamburger Hop	1950	$50
❏ 2-780(?)	Heart After Heart/Hamburger Hop	1950	$50
—Microgroove 33 1/3 rpm 7-inch single, small hole			
❏ 2-701	Honky Tonk Heart/Get a Ring for Her Finger	1950	$50
—Microgroove 33 1/3 rpm 7-inch single, small hole			
❏ 4-20716	Honky Tonk Heart/Get a Ring for Her Finger	1950	$50
❏ 2-610(?)	I Can't Get Enough of That Ah Ha/Curb Service	1950	$50
—Microgroove 33 1/3 rpm 7-inch single, small hole			
❏ 4-21135	I Swear/Too Late To	1953	$30
❏ 4-20743	I Thought I Was Home to Stay/Mended One Broken Heart	1950	$50
❏ 2-787	I Thought I Was Home to Stay/Mended One Broken Heart	1950	$60
—Microgroove 33 1/3 rpm 7-inch single, small hole			
❏ 4-20791	So Long/All My Life	1951	$40
❏ 4-20975	The Man on the Corner/My Next Gal	1952	$40
❏ 4-20859	The Sweetheart Waltz/Gotta Get a Guitar	1951	$40
HIDE-A-WAYS, THE			
MGM			
❏ 55004	Cherie/Me Make Em Powwow	1955	$500
RONNI			
❏ 1000	Can't Help Lovin' That Girl of Mine/I'm Coming Home	1954	$6000
—VG 2000; VG+ 4000			
HIGH MOUNTAIN HOEDOWN			
ET CETERA			
❏ 45-200	Pickin' Berries/My Thoughts	1970	$8
HIGH SOCIETY			
CAMEO			
❏ 452	People Passing By/Star of Eastern Street	1967	$100
—Red and black label with white cameo figure at left			
❏ 452	People Passing By/Star of Eastern Street	1967	$70
—Red and orange label with "CP" logo at top			
HIGHLIGHTS, THE			
BALLY			
❏ 1016	City of Angels/Listen, My Love	1956	$40
❏ 1044	Indian Style/Turn Around Shoes	1957	$30
❏ 1027	To Be with You/Will I Ever Know	1957	$40
HIGHTOWER, WILLIE			
CAPITOL			
❏ 5916	Because I Love You/For Sentimental Reasons-You Send Me	1967	$200
❏ 2651	If I Had a Hammer/It's Too Late	1969	$20
❏ 2226	It's a Miracle/Nobody But You	1968	$50
❏ 2547	Ooh Baby How I Love You/It's Wonderful to Be in Love with You	1969	$30
FAME			
❏ 1477	Back Road Into Town/Poor Man	1971	$50
❏ 1474	I Can't Love Without You/Time Has Brought About a Change	1970	$40
❏ 1465	Walk a Mile in My Shoes/You Used Me Baby	1970	$40

Number	Title	Yr	NM
MERCURY			
❏ 73390	Don't Blame Me/Hungry for Your Love	1973	$40
❏ 73338	I Love You So/Easy Lovin'	1972	$20
SOUND STAGE 7			
❏ 2503	Chicago, Send Her Home/Ain't Nothing Wrong	1977	$80
HIGHWAY 101			
WARNER BROS.			
❏ 7-27735	All the Reasons Why/Higher Ground	1988	$3
❏ 7-28105	Cry, Cry, Cry/One Step Closer	1988	$3
❏ 7-28105 [PS]	Cry, Cry, Cry/One Step Closer	1988	$4
❏ 7-27867	(Do You Love Me) Just Say Yes/I'll Be Missing You	1988	$3
❏ 7-27867 [PS]	(Do You Love Me) Just Say Yes/I'll Be Missing You	1988	$4
❏ 7-22955	Honky Tonk Heart/Desperate Road	1989	$3
❏ PRO-S-2872 [DJ]	It Came Upon a Midnight Clear/Light of the Stable	1987	$10
—B-side by Emmylou Harris			
❏ 7-27581	Setting Me Up/Long Way Down	1989	$3
❏ 7-28646	Some Find Love/What a Lonely Night Can Be	1986	$4
❏ 7-28223	Somewhere Tonight/Are You Still Mine	1987	$3
❏ 7-28223 [PS]	Somewhere Tonight/Are You Still Mine	1987	$4
❏ 7-28483	The Bed You Made for Me/I'm Gonna Run Through the Wind	1986	$3
❏ 7-28372	Whiskey, If You Were a Woman/I'll Take You (Heartache and All)	1987	$3
❏ 7-22779	Who's Lonely Now/Don't It Make Your Mama Cry	1989	$3
HIGHWAYMEN, THE			
ABC			
❏ 10824 [B]	Flame/My Foolish Pride	1966	$8
❏ 10801	She's Not There/Little Bird, Little Bird	1966	$8
ABC-PARAMOUNT			
❏ 10716	I'll Show You the Way/Never a Thought for Tomorrow	1965	$8
❏ 10688	Should I Go, Should I Stay/Permit to Be a Hermit	1965	$8
UNITED ARTISTS			
❏ 602	All My Trials/Midnight Train	1963	$15
❏ 475	Cindy, Oh Cindy/The Birdman	1962	$15
❏ 370	Cotton Fields/Gypsy Rover	1961	$15
❏ 540	I Know Where I'm Going/Well, Well, Well	1963	$15
❏ 568	I Never Will Marry/Pretoria	1963	$15
❏ 801	Michael '65/Puttin' On the Style	1964	$10
❏ 258	Michael/Santiano	1960	$20
❏ 788	Puttin' On the Style/Michael	1964	$10
❏ 695	The Sinking of the Reuben James/Bon Soir	1964	$10
❏ 439	Whiskey in the Jar/I'm On My Way	1962	$15
HILDEBRAND, RAY			
PHILIPS			
❏ 40339	Hello Viet Nam (Goodbye My Love)/You, Wonderful You	1965	$8
❏ 40318	Hey Little Julie/The Way of the DJ	1965	$8
❏ 40174	It's All Over, Paula/Snow Girl	1964	$10
—As "Paul"			
TOWER			
❏ 304	Paper Clown/Patsy	1966	$8
—As "Paul (Paul and Paula)"			
HILL, BUNKER			
MALA			
❏ 451	Hide and Go Seek (Part 1)/Hide and Go Seek (Part 2)	1962	$30
❏ 464	The Girl Can't Dance/You Can't Make Me Doubt My Baby	1963	$30
HILL, EDDIE			
COLUMBIA			
❏ 4-40829	I'm Gonna Be a Loser Again/I Cried in My Dream Last Night	1957	$30
❏ 4-21556	I'm Worried/Unredeemed Diamonds	1956	$30
❏ 4-41093	Wild Cat/The Magic of Your Sweet Love	1958	$40
MERCURY			
❏ 6392	Baby My Heart/Mountain Jam	1952	$40
❏ 6375	Cold, Cold Woman/Educated Fool	1952	$40

Number	Title	Yr	NM
❏ 6410	Fire Ball Eight/A Full Time Job	1952	$40
❏ 70195	Hit and Run Lover/High, Wide and Handsome	1953	$30
❏ 70142	Live While You're Young, Dream When You're Old/Buckshot	1953	$30
❏ 6383	Stolen Love/Salty Dog Rag	1952	$40
❏ 6347	The Hot Guitar/Steamboat Stomp	1951	$40
RCA VICTOR			
❏ 47-6279	Black Denim Trousers and Motorcycle Boots/Someday You'll Call My Name	1955	$30
❏ 47-5641	I Changed My Mind/Presswood the Giant Killer	1954	$30
❏ 47-5893	I Did, It Does and I Do/Knock It Off	1954	$30
❏ 47-5706	My Sugar Booger/Slender, Tender and Sweet	1954	$30
❏ 47-5809	Same Old Dream (About You)/Whittlin' on a Piece of Wood	1954	$30
❏ 47-6136	Smack Dab in the Middle/'Cause I Have You	1955	$30
❏ 47-5978	The Gottalotta Song/I Don't Think I'm Gonna Like It	1955	$30
❏ 47-5642	Who Wrote That Letter to Old John/Lovin' Spree	1954	$30
STARDAY			
❏ 435	Move Over/Too Weak (To Go Home)	1959	$30
—With Billie Morgan			
UNIVERSITY			
❏ 206	Daddy, You Know What/Monkey Business	1959	$30
HILL, GOLDIE			
DECCA			
❏ 9-29602	Ain't Gonna Wash My Face/Why Don't You Let Me Go	1955	$30
❏ 9-30290	A Wasted Love Affair/Cleanin' House	1957	$20
❏ 31172	Baby Blue/Your Love Came Into My Heart	1960	$20
❏ 31466	Baby Go Slow/Pretending I'm a Fool	1963	$15
❏ 31535	Closer/Still Wanting You	1963	$15
❏ 9-29161	Cry, Cry Darling/Call Off the Wedding	1954	$30
❏ 9-28355	Don't Send No More Roses/Why Talk to My Heart	1952	$30
❏ 9-30142	Footsteps/New Names, New Faces	1956	$30
❏ 9-30918	Honky Tonk Music/It's Here to Stay	1959	$20
❏ 31496	If I Could Hold Back the Dawn/I'm Gonna Bring You Down	1963	$15
❏ 9-28473	I Let the Stars Get In My Eyes/Waiting for a Letter	1952	$30
❏ 31389	I'm Afraid/Door Step to Heaven	1962	$15
❏ 9-28769	I'm the Loneliest Gal in Town/My Love Is Aflame	1953	$30
❏ 9-28898	I'm Yesterday's Girl/Let Me Be the One	1953	$30
❏ 9-28685	I'm Yvonne (On the Bayou)/Say Big Boy	1953	$30
❏ 31221	It's a Lovely, Lovely World/Loved and Lost	1961	$20
❏ 9-30460	It's Only a Matter of Time/Till I Said It to You	1957	$20
❏ 9-29045	Liquor and Women/Am I Still Your Baby	1954	$30
❏ 31434	Little Boy Blue/Come Back to Me	1962	$15
❏ 9-31083	Living Alone/Twice As Blue	1960	$20
❏ 31261	Lonely Heartaches/I'm the One Who Loves You	1961	$20
❏ 9-29069	Make Love to Me/Young at Heart	1954	$30
❏ 31342	Many Lies Ago/Live for Tomorrow	1961	$20
❏ 9-29224	Please Don't Betray Me/Treat Me Kind	1954	$30
❏ 31620	Put Yourself in My Place/Don't Let Him	1964	$15
❏ 9-29955	Sample My Kissin'/I'm Beginning to Feel Mistreated	1956	$30
❏ 9-29771	Second Chance/Steel Guitar	1956	$30
❏ 31675	Three's a Crowd/You're Free to Go	1964	$15
EPIC			
❏ 5-10423	Got Me Sumpin' Goin'/Tell It to Your Lonely Walls	1968	$10
—As "Goldie Hill Smith			
❏ 5-10296	Lovable Fool/Making Plans	1968	$10
—As "Goldie Hill Smith			
❏ 5-10245	There's Gotta Be More to Life (Than Loving a Man)/Almost Enough	1967	$10
—As "Goldie Hill Smith			

Number	Title	Yr	NM

HILL, JESSIE
DOWNEY
Number	Title	Yr	NM
❏ 115	Chip Chop/Woodshed	1964	$20

MINIT
Number	Title	Yr	NM
❏ 646	Can't Get Enough of That Ooh Pah Doo/Pot's on a Strike	1962	$20
❏ 622	Oh My Oh My/I Got Mine	1961	$15
❏ 628	Oogsey Moo/My Love	1961	$15
❏ 607	Ooh Poo Pah Doo -- Part 1/Ooh Poo Pah Doo -- Part 2	1960	$20
❏ 616	Scoop Scoobie Doobie/Highland Blues	1960	$15
❏ 638	Sweet Jelly Roll/It's My Fault	1961	$20
❏ 611	Whip It On Me/I Need Your Love	1960	$15

UNITED ARTISTS
Number	Title	Yr	NM
❏ 0081	Ooh Poo Pah Doo -- Part 1/Ooh Poo Pah Doo -- Part 2	1973	$4

— Silver Spotlight Series" reissue

HILL, LAINIE
NEW VOICE
Number	Title	Yr	NM
❏ 809	Time Marches On/Ain't I Worth a Dime	1966	$400

HILL, RAYMOND
SUN
Number	Title	Yr	NM
❏ 204	Bourbon Street Jump/The Snuggle	1954	$750

HILL SISTERS, THE
ANNA
Number	Title	Yr	NM
❏ 103	Hit and Run Away Love/Advertising for Love	1959	$500
❏ 1103	Hit and Run Away Love/Advertising for Love	1959	$60

HILL, TINY
MERCURY
Number	Title	Yr	NM
❏ 5726	Battle with the Bottle/Something I Et	1951	$30
❏ 5840	Busybody/Diesel Smoke, Dangerous Curves	1952	$30
❏ 5557	Country Wedding Day/Melanae in "F	1950	$40
❏ 5691	Dancing My Fanny Around/How'm I Doin'	1951	$30
❏ 70079	Dew Dew Dewy Day/I'm Alone Because I Love You	1953	$30
❏ 70395	Don't Do It Darling/On the Uppermost Branch	1954	$30
❏ 5543	Don't Make Love to Me/Everybody Loves That Hadocol	1950	$40
❏ 5765	Find 'Em -- Fool 'Em/Cryin'	1951	$30
❏ 5546	Handcuffed to Love/(B-side unknown)	1950	$40
❏ 5598	Hot Rod Race #2/Let's Live a Little	1951	$40
❏ 5547	Hot Rod Race/Lovebug Itch	1950	$40
❏ 70448	I Get the Blues/Someday You'll Be Sorry	1954	$30
❏ 5508	I'll Sail My Ship Alone/Back in Your Own Back Yard	1950	$40
❏ 5524	I'm Moving On/Just a Girl That Men Forget	1950	$40
❏ 70005	It's Enough to Make a Preacher Cuss/That's Where I Came In	1952	$30
❏ 5789	Milk Bucket Boogie/Silver and Gold	1952	$30
❏ 5552	Mocking Bird Hill/If You've Got the Money (I've Got the Time)	1950	$40
❏ 70029	Move It On Over/Five Foot Two	1953	$30
❏ 5582	Old Fashioned Love/Stingy	1951	$30
❏ 5876	Omaha/After I Say I'm Sorry	1952	$30
❏ 5635	Pick Up Truck/Two Letters	1951	$30
❏ 5605	Please Don't Talk About Me When I'm Gone/You're a Sweetheart	1951	$30
❏ 5740	Slow Poke/Don't Put a Tax on Love	1951	$30
❏ 5664	Take Back Your Paper Heart/Three Handed Woman	1951	$30
❏ 5830	The Wild Side of Life/Just Lookin'	1952	$30
❏ 70249	Two Ton Tessie/Don't Bring Lulu	1953	$30

HILL, Z.Z.
ATLANTIC
Number	Title	Yr	NM
❏ 2659	It's a Hang-Up Baby/(Home Just Ain't Home at) Suppertime	1969	$8

COLUMBIA
Number	Title	Yr	NM
❏ 10552	Love Is So Good When You're Stealing It/Need You By My Side	1977	$5
❏ 10680	This Time They Told the Truth/Near But Yet So Far	1978	$5

HILL
Number	Title	Yr	NM
❏ 222	Don't Make Me Pay for His Mistakes/Think People	1971	$6

KENT
Number	Title	Yr	NM
❏ 464	Baby I'm Sorry/Where She At	1967	$12
❏ 502	Don't Make Promises (You Can't Keep)/Set Your Sights Higher	1968	$12
❏ 439	Everybody Has to Cry/Happiness Is All I Need	1965	$12
❏ 427	Hey Little Girl/Oh Darlin'	1965	$12
❏ 404	I Could Do It All Over/You Don't Love Me	1964	$10
❏ 4560	If I Could Do It All Over/You Won't Hurt No More	1971	$8
❏ 449	I Found Love/Set Your Sights Higher	1966	$10
❏ 416	I Need Someone (To Love Me)/Have Mercy Someone	1965	$10
❏ 4547	I Need Someone (To Love Me)/Oh Darling	1971	$8
❏ 460	Oh Darling/Greatest Love	1967	$10
❏ 481	Steal Away/Nothing Can Change the Love I Have for You	1967	$10
❏ 432	That's It/What's More	1965	$12
❏ 478	What Am I Living For/You're Gonna Need My Lovin'	1967	$10

MALACO
Number	Title	Yr	NM
❏ 2076	Bump and Grind/Somethin' Goin' On	1981	$4
❏ 2079	Cheating in the Next Room/Right Arm for Your Love	1982	$4
❏ 2141	Down Home Blues/Please Don't Let Our Good Thing End	1988	$4
❏ 2094	Get a Little, Give a Little/Blind Side	1983	$4
❏ 2109	I'm Gonna Stop You from Givin' Me the Blues/Personally	1984	$4
❏ 2090	Open House at My House/Who You Been Givin' It To	1983	$4
❏ 2069	Please Don't Make Me (Do Something Bad to You)/Blue Monday	1981	$4
❏ 2074	Separate Ways/Chained to Your Love	1981	$4
❏ 2103	Someone Else Is Steppin' In/Shade Tree Mechanic	1984	$4
❏ 2097	Steal Away/Three Into Two Won't Go	1984	$4
❏ 2085	What Am I Gonna Tell Her/Get You Some Business	1982	$4
❏ 2082	When It Rains It Pours/When Can We Do This Again	1982	$4

MANKIND
Number	Title	Yr	NM
❏ 12003	Faithful and True/I Think I'd Do It	1971	$8
❏ 12007	The Chokin' Kind/Hold Back	1971	$8

UNITED ARTISTS
Number	Title	Yr	NM
❏ XW225	Ain't Nothing You Can Do/Love in the Street	1973	$6
❏ XW412	Am I Groovin' You/Bad Mouth and Gossip	1974	$6
❏ XW631	I Created a Monster/Steppin' in the Shoes of a Fool	1975	$6
❏ XW307	I Don't Need Half a Love/Friendship Only Goes So Far	1973	$6
❏ XW536	I Keep On Lovin' You/Whatever's Thrilling You Is Killing Me	1974	$6
❏ XW365	Let Them Talk/Red Rooster	1973	$6

HILLMAN, CHRIS
ASYLUM
Number	Title	Yr	NM
❏ 45350	Falling Again/Love Is the Sweetest Amnesty	1976	$4
❏ 45428	Heartbreaker/Lucky in Love	1977	$4
❏ 45330	Step On Out/Take It on the Run	1976	$4

SUGAR HILL
Number	Title	Yr	NM
❏ 4105	Somebody's Back in Town/Desert Rose	1984	$5

HILLTOPPERS, THE
DOT
Number	Title	Yr	NM
❏ 15594	A Fallen Star/Footsteps	1957	$15
❏ 15318	D-A-R-L-I-N/Frivolette	1955	$20
❏ 15451	Do the Bop/When You're Alone	1956	$20
❏ 16024	From the Vine Came the Grape/Love Walked In	1960	$10
❏ 15127	From the Vine Came the Grape/Time Will Tell	1954	$20
❏ 15889	I'd Rather Die Young/Welcome to My Heart	1959	$10
❏ 15220	If I Didn't Care/Bertha	1954	$20
❏ 15055	If I Were King/I Can't Lie to Myself	1953	$20
❏ 15560	I Love My Girl/I'm Serious	1957	$15
❏ 15468	I'm Walking Thru Heaven/Eyes of Fire, Lips of Wine	1956	$20
❏ 15958	Lots of Luck/Lizzie Darlin'	1959	$10
❏ 15105	Love Walked In/To Be Alone	1953	$20
❏ 16039	Marianne/To Be Alone	1960	$10
❏ 15537	Marianne/You're Wasting Your Time	1957	$15
❏ 15034	Must I Cry Again/I Keep Telling Myself	1952	$20
❏ 15626	My Cabin of Dreams/Dedicated to You	1957	$15
❏ 15437	My Treasure/The Last Word in Love	1955	$20
❏ 16025	Only You (And You Alone)/Till Then	1960	$10
❏ 15423	Only You (And You Alone)/Until the Real Thing Comes Along	1955	$20
❏ 16556	Only You/No Longer Lonely	1963	$8
❏ 15085	P.S. I Love You/I'd Rather Die Young	1953	$20
❏ 15415	Searching/All I Need Is You	1955	$20
❏ 15814	Signorina/Peggy's Sister	1958	$15
❏ 15459	So Tired/Faded Rose	1956	$20
❏ 15712	Starry Eyes/You Sure Look Good to Me	1958	$15
❏ 15201	Sweetheart/Old Cabaret	1954	$20
❏ 15351	The Door Is Still Open/Tears from My Eyes	1955	$20
❏ 16010	The Prisoner's Song/Phone	1959	$10
❏ 15132	Till Then/I Found Your Letter	1954	$20
❏ 16054	To Be Alone/P.S. I Love You	1960	$10
❏ 16022	Trying/P.S. I Love You	1960	$10
❏ 15018	Trying/You Made Up My Mind	1952	$30

— As "The Hill Toppers"

Number	Title	Yr	NM
❏ 15156	Wrapped in a Dream/Poor Butterfly	1954	$20

MGM
Number	Title	Yr	NM
❏ 14603	Little Things You Do/Sunshine and Love	1973	$5

— As "Jimmy Sacca and the Hilltoppers"

7-Inch Extended Plays
DOT
Number	Title	Yr	NM
❏ DEP-1-1006	*You Made Up My Mind/Trying/Must I Cry Again/I Keep Telling Myself	1953	$20
❏ DEP-113	I Can't Lie to Myself/If I Were King//I'd Rather Die Young (Than Grow Old Without You)/P.S. I Love You	1953	$20

— Maroon label

Number	Title	Yr	NM
❏ DEP-1-1006 [PS]	The Hilltoppers	1953	$20
❏ DEP-113 [PS]	(title unknown)	1953	$20

HINES, MIMI
RCA VICTOR
Number	Title	Yr	NM
❏ 47-7646	Santa Baby/I Saw Mommy Kissing Santa Claus	1959	$15

HINTON, JOE
ARVEE
Number	Title	Yr	NM
❏ 5028	My Love Is Real/I Won't Be Your Fool	1961	$70

— Arvee titles as "Little Joe Hinton

BACK BEAT
Number	Title	Yr	NM
❏ 539	Better to Give Than to Receive/There Is No In Between	1963	$20
❏ 581	Close to My Heart/You've Been Good to Me	1967	$30
❏ 547	Darling Come and Talk to Me/Everything	1965	$12
❏ 541	Funny/You Gotta Have Love	1964	$30
❏ 594	Got You on My Mind/Please	1968	$80
❏ 574	If I Had Only Known/Lots of Love	1966	$30
❏ 532	If You Love Me/A Thousand Cups of Happiness	1960	$30
❏ 519	I Know/Ladder of Prayer	1958	$20
❏ 589	I'm Satisfied/Be Ever Wonderful	1968	$40
❏ 565	I'm Waiting/How Long Can I Last	1966	$10
❏ 545	I Want a Little Girl/True Love	1965	$20
❏ 550	Pledging My Love/Just a Kid Named Joe	1965	$20
❏ 526	Pretty Little Mama/Will You	1959	$30
❏ 526 [PS]	Pretty Little Mama/Will You	1959	$40
❏ 535	The Girls in My Life/Come On Baby	1961	$30
❏ 540	There Oughta Be a Law/You're My Girl	1964	$30

SOUL
Number	Title	Yr	NM
❏ 35080	Let's Save the Children/You Are Blue	1971	$30

HIPPIES, THE
PARKWAY
Number	Title	Yr	NM
❏ 863	Memory Lane/A Lonely Piano	1963	$30

— Originally released as "The Tams"; B-side by Reggie Harrison

HIPPY DIPPYS, THE
UNI
Number	Title	Yr	NM
❏ 55004	Thoroughly Modern Millie/Jimmy	1967	$15

Number	Title	Yr	NM

HIRT, AL

GWP

Number	Title	Yr	NM
529	Glory of Love/I Can Dream, Can't I	1970	$6
516	I Still See Elisa/The Gospel of No-Name City	1969	$6
519	Louisiana Man/Break My Mind	1969	$6
522	Orange Blossom Special/I Really Don't Want to Know	1970	$6

MONUMENT

Number	Title	Yr	NM
8652	Feudin' Pipers (Dueling Banjos)/Southern Scramble	1975	$4
8619	Melody for Michele/Sweet Sauce	1974	$4
8671	The Sound of Jazz and the Scent of Jasmine/Monkey Farm	1975	$4

RCA VICTOR

Number	Title	Yr	NM
47-8016	Al Di La/Talkin' About That River	1962	$10
47-8542	Al's Place/Mister Sandman	1965	$8
47-9198	Big Honey/Puppet on a String	1967	$8
47-9106	Boywatchers Theme/Yo Yo (Puppet Song)	1967	$8
47-9285	Calypsoul/Honey Pot	1967	$8
47-8346	Cotton Candy/Walkin'	1964	$8
47-8487	Fancy Pants/Star Dust	1964	$8
47-8684	Feelin' Fruggy/Louisiana Lullaby	1965	$8
47-8925	Green Hornet Theme/Strawberry Jam	1966	$15
47-8478	Hooray for Santa Claus/White Christmas	1964	$15
47-8478 [PS]	Hooray for Santa Claus/White Christmas	1964	$20
47-9381	Ludwig/Long Gone	1967	$8
47-8774	Mame/Seven Days to Tahiti	1966	$8
47-8774 [PS]	Mame/Seven Days to Tahiti	1966	$10
47-9060	Music to Watch Girls By/His Girl	1967	$8
47-9717	Penny Arcade/If	1969	$8
47-7903	Perky/I'm On My Way	1961	$10
47-8128	Pickin' Cotton/Roman Nocturne	1963	$10
47-8128 [PS]	Pickin' Cotton/Roman Nocturne	1963	$15
47-8854	Skillet Lickin'/Trumpet Pickin'	1966	$8
47-8391	Sugar Lips/Poupee Brisee	1964	$8
47-8104	Theme from "The Eleventh Hour"/Song from "Two for the See-Saw"	1962	$10
47-9023	Theme from The Monkees/The Evil One	1966	$10
47-9539	The Odd Couple/Do You Know the Way to San Jose	1968	$10
47-8653	The Silence (Il Silenzio)/Love Theme from "The Sandpiper"	1965	$8
47-9664	Those Were the Days/The Garbage	1968	$8
47-9500	We Can Fly-Up, Up and Away/The Glory of Love	1968	$8

7-Inch Extended Plays

Number	Title	Yr	NM
VLP3337	Alley Cat/Over the Rainbow/Butterball//You Took Advantage of Me/Flowers and Candy/Danny Boy	1965	$10

—Jukebox issue; small hole, plays at 33 1/3 rpm

Number	Title	Yr	NM
VLP2607	Clarinet Marmalade/Ja-Da/Muskrat Ramble//When It's Sleepy Time Down South/The Birth of the Blues	1963	$10

—Jukebox issue; small hole, plays at 33 1/3 rpm

Number	Title	Yr	NM
TLP2917 [PS]	Cotton Candy	1964	$12

—Sleeve came with two records, TLP-A 2917 and TLP-B 2917; one record was included in the sleeve, the other was packaged in a company sleeve, and the entire package was enclosed in a plastic bag with jukebox strips; add 100 percent if the strips and plastic bag are included

Number	Title	Yr	NM
TLP-A2917	Cotton Candy/Hello, Dolly!/Django's Castle//Moo Moo/Last Date/Big Man	1964	$10

—Jukebox issue; small hole, plays at 33 1/3 rpm; Part 1 of two-record set

Number	Title	Yr	NM
VLP3492	I Had the Craziest Dream/Deep Purple/I'll Get By//There! I've Said It Again/It's Been a Long, Long Time/I'll Be Seeing You	1966	$10

—Jukebox issue; small hole, plays at 33 1/3 rpm

Number	Title	Yr	NM
VLP2607 [PS]	Our Man in New Orleans	1963	$12
VLP2965 [PS]	Sugar Lips	1964	$12
VLP2965	Sugar Lips/Lookin' for the Blues/New Orleans, My Home Town/Pink Confetti//Back Home Again in Indiana/Up Above My Head	1964	$10

—Jukebox issue; small hole, plays at 33 1/3 rpm

Number	Title	Yr	NM
VLP3337 [PS]	That Honey Horn Sound	1965	$12
VLP3309 [PS]	The Best of Al Hirt	1965	$12
VLP3579	The Fox/Syncopated Clock/Mardi Gras//The Happy Trumpet/What the World Needs Now Is Love/Skokiaan	1966	$10

—Jukebox issue; small hole, plays at 33 1/3 rpm

Number	Title	Yr	NM
VLP3579 [PS]	The Happy Trumpet	1966	$12
VLP3492 [PS]	They're Playing Our Song	1966	$12
TLP-B2917	Walkin'/Too Late/Rumpus//Melissa/Walkin' with Mr. Lee/12th Street Rag	1964	$10

—Jukebox issue; small hole, plays at 33 1/3 rpm; Part 2 of two-record set

HITCHCOCK, ROBYN, AND THE EGYPTIANS

A&M

Number	Title	Yr	NM
3023	Balloon Man/A Globe of Frogs (Electric)	1988	$5
3023 [PS]	Balloon Man/A Globe of Frogs (Electric)	1988	$5
1409	Madonna of the Wasps/Ruling Class	1989	$30

RELATIVITY

Number	Title	Yr	NM
8076 [DJ]	Heaven/Listening to the Higsons	1985	$30

HITCHCOCK, STAN

CINNAMON

Number	Title	Yr	NM
770	Half-Empty Bed/When Love Was At Its Best	1973	$6
750	I Did It All for You/Love Don't Live Here	1973	$6
782	I'm Free/Oklahoma Wind	1974	$6
754	Let Me Roll/The Shadow of Your Smile	1973	$6
759	The Same Old Way/Lonely Wine	1973	$6

EPIC

Number	Title	Yr	NM
5-10586	Call Me Gone/Your Kind of Man	1970	$8
5-10464	Golden Slipper Rose/I Don't Know When That Will Be	1969	$8
5-10022	Hello World/Hush-a-Bye	1966	$12
5-10525	Honey, I'm Home/Slip-Up And She'll Slip Away	1969	$8
5-9581	I Had Heaven in My Arms/Somebody Had to Lose	1963	$15
5-10307	I'm Easy to Love/Don't Do Like I've Done (Do What I Say)	1968	$8
5-9854	Imitation of a Man/Swiss-Made Heart	1965	$10
5-9733	Lonely Wine/Candy Apple Red	1964	$15
5-9699	Ole Bad/Looking Through a Teardrop	1964	$15
5-10182	She's Looking Good/Have I Stayed Away Too Long	1967	$8
5-10432	Test of Time/Someday You'll Call My Name	1969	$8
5-10388	The Phoenix Flash/My Memory	1968	$8
5-9634	This Town (Just Ain't Big Enough)/Someone to Be Lonesome For	1963	$15
5-9802	Thumbing My Way Back Home/Back in My Baby's Arms	1965	$10
5-10081	To Tell the Truth/He Took My Place	1966	$10

MMI

Number	Title	Yr	NM
1024	Falling/Only One	1978	$6
1028	Finders Keepers, Losers Weepers/(B-side unknown)	1979	$6

—A-side with Sue Richards

Number	Title	Yr	NM
1023	Slowly Turning to Love/Kiss Away	1978	$6

RAMBLIN'

Number	Title	Yr	NM
1711	She Sings Amazing Grace/(B-side unknown)	1981	$5

HJERPE, BILL

EPIC

Number	Title	Yr	NM
5-10026	Behind the Times/Mrs. Frost	1966	$40

HO-DADS, THE

IMPERIAL

Number	Title	Yr	NM
66023	After Dark/Space Race	1964	$40
66001	Legends/Honey	1963	$40

HO, DON

HEL

Number	Title	Yr	NM
149	Christmas Is for Everyone/Christmas Is You and Me	1977	$4
149 [PS]	Christmas Is for Everyone/Christmas Is You and Me	1977	$4

MEGA

Number	Title	Yr	NM
1225	Today I Started Loving You Again/Take a Walk in the Country	1975	$4
1215	Watch Out Woman/A New Love Song	1974	$4

REPRISE

Number	Title	Yr	NM
0609	Forbidden Fruit/Sleepy Summer Days	1967	$8
0800	Galveston/Has Anybody Lost a Love	1968	$6
0950	Gotta Move Along/Home	1970	$5
0871	Honey Come Back/Sands of Waikiki	1969	$6
0388	I'll Remember You/E Lei Ka Lei Lei	1965	$8
0573	I Love You/All That's Left Is the Lemon Tree	1967	$8
0669	Instant Happy/White Silver Sands	1968	$6
0896	It Must Have Been the Wine/Questions	1970	$5
0936	Melody Fair/Only Foolish People	1970	$5
1016	My God and I/What Do I Need to Be Free	1971	$4
0441	Suck 'Em Up/La Haina Luna	1965	$8
0451	Sweet Someone/La Haina Luna	1966	$8
0643	The Windward Side (Of the Island)/Tu Tu Kane	1967	$8
0960	This Is America/United We Stand	1970	$5
0507	Tiny Bubbles/Born Free	1966	$8
0705	Tiny Bubbles/Do I Love You	1968	$4

—Back to Back Hits" series

Number	Title	Yr	NM
0590	Tiny Bubbles/Macao	1967	$10
0600	Tomorrow/This Sacred Hour	1967	$8
1059	Waikiki/Chotto Matte Kidasi	1971	$4
0591	What Now My Love/One Paddle, Two Paddle	1967	$8

HOBBITS, THE

DECCA

Number	Title	Yr	NM
32270	Pretty Young Thing/Strawberry Children	1968	$15
32226	Sunny Day Girl/Daffodil Days	1967	$15

ZAR

Number	Title	Yr	NM
25	Frodo Lives/Jolly Good Fellow	1967	$30

HOBBS, BUD

MGM

Number	Title	Yr	NM
11579	Goose Rock/Rightfully Yours	1953	$100

HOBBS, LOU

CINNAMON

Number	Title	Yr	NM
792	What's Wrong with Me/Mission Bell	1974	$8

—As "Louis Hobbs

KIK

Number	Title	Yr	NM
902	Loving You Was All I Ever Needed/It's All Your Fault	1981	$8
911	We're Building Our Love on a Rock/Run Right Back	1981	$8

LOBO

Number	Title	Yr	NM
XIII	Somebody Shot the Jukebox/(B-side unknown)	1982	$6
X	There Ain't No Way/A Simple Man	1982	$6

HODGES, EDDIE

AURORA

Number	Title	Yr	NM
150	Across the Street (Is a Million Miles Away)/She Doesn't Love Me	1965	$10
161	Hitch Hike/Old Man Rag	1966	$12
156	Love Minus Zero (No Limit)/The Water Is Over My Head	1965	$10

CADENCE

Number	Title	Yr	NM
1410	Bandit of My Dreams/Mugmates	1962	$30
1421	(Girls, Girls, Girls) Made to Love/I Make Believe It's You	1962	$20
1397	I'm Gonna Knock on Your Door/Ain't Gonna Wash for a Week	1961	$20

—Red and black label with "Cadence Records" along edge three times

Number	Title	Yr	NM
1397 [PS]	I'm Gonna Knock on Your Door/Ain't Gonna Wash for a Week	1961	$30
1397	I'm Gonna Knock on Your Door/Ain't Gonna Wash for a Week	1961	$30

—Maroon and silver label with metronome at top

COLUMBIA

Number	Title	Yr	NM
42649	Seein' Is Believin'/Secret	1962	$15
42649 [PS]	Seein' Is Believin'/Secret	1962	$20
42697	Would You Come Back?/Too Soon to Know	1962	$15

DECCA

Number	Title	Yr	NM
30903	High Hopes/Don't Dance on Momma's Rug	1959	$20
30675	That Funny Little Dog/What Would It Be Like in Heaven	1958	$20

MGM

Number	Title	Yr	NM
13219	Avalanche/Just a Kid in Love	1964	$12

Number	Title	Yr	NM

HOFNER, ADOLPH
COLUMBIA
Number	Title	Yr	NM
❏ 4-20749	In My Heart and On My Mind/Please Don't Take That Bottle from Me	1950	$40

SARG
❏ 152	Bandera Waltz/Dance the Paul Jones and Old Joe Clark	1957	$20
❏ 183	Dude Ranch/ Westphalia Waltz	1959	$20
❏ 249	Fast Women, Slow Horses and Wine/Kansas City	1966	$8
❏ 195	Mexico/The Three Caballeros	1960	$15
❏ 207	Milk Cow Blues/Put Your Little Foot Out	1961	$30
❏ 202	Pipeliner Blues/ Over the Waves	1960	$15

HOG HEAVEN
The Shondells after Tommy James went solo.
ROULETTE
❏ 7101	Happy/Prayer	1971	$8
❏ 7106	If It Feels Good/ (B-side unknown)	1971	$8
❏ 7091	Theme from a Thought/ (B-side unknown)	1970	$8

HOGG, SMOKEY
COMBO
❏ 11	Where Have You Been/Believe I'll Change My Towns	1952	$200

—Also had releases on Combo 4 and 9, but these are unknown on 45

EBB
❏ 127	Good Morning Baby/ Sure 'Nuff	1958	$30

FEDERAL
❏ 12127	Gone, Gone, Gone/I Ain't Got Over It Yet	1953	$125

IMPERIAL
❏ 5290	My Baby's Gone/ Train Whistle	1954	$125
❏ 5269	When I've Been Drinkin'/ Tear Me Down	1954	$125

METEOR
❏ 5021	I Declare/Dark Clouds	1955	$125

HOGS, THE
HANNA-BARBERA
❏ 511	Loose Lip Sync Ships/ Blues Theme	1967	$200

—Contrary to previous reports, Frank Zappa was NOT involved with this record in any way

HOGSED, ROY
CAPITOL
❏ F40274	Cocaine Blues/ Fishtail Boogie	1950	$50
❏ F1721	Free Samples/I Wish I Wuz	1951	$30
❏ F3007	I'm Hurtin' Again/Do You Call That a Sweetheart	1955	$30
❏ F1987	Mean, Mean Woman/Let Your Pendulum Swing	1952	$30
❏ F1529	Shuffleboard Shuffle/ Poco Tempo	1951	$30
❏ F1854	Snake Dance Boogie/I'm Gonna Get Along Without Ya	1951	$30
❏ F2083	Stretchin' a Point or Two/Put Some Sugar in Your Shoes	1952	$30
❏ F2720	Who Wrote That Letter to John/Babies and Bacon	1954	$30

HOLDEN, RON
CHALLENGE
❏ 59360	I Tried/I'll Forgive and Forget	1967	$300

DONNA
❏ 1324	Gee, But I'm Lonesome/ Susie Jane	1960	$30
❏ 1315	Love You So/My Babe	1959	$40
❏ 1335	The Big Shoe/Rock and Roll Call	1961	$30
❏ 1328	True Love Can Be/ Everything's Gonna Be Alright	1960	$30
❏ 1331	Who Says There Ain't No Santa Claus/ Your Line Is Busy	1960	$30

ELDO
❏ 117	I'll Be Happy/I'll Always Have You	1961	$30

NITE OWL
❏ 10	Love You So/My Babe	1959	$800

NOW
❏ 6	Can You Talk?/I Need Ya	1974	$30

RAMPART
❏ 645	Girl I Love You/Nothing I Wouldn't Do	1965	$50

HOLIDAY, BILLIE
ATLANTIC
Number	Title	Yr	NM
❏ 2923	Strange Fruit/I Love My Man	1973	$6

CLEF
❏ 89132	How Deep Is the Ocean/What a Little Moonlight Can Do	1955	$20
❏ 89108	If the Moon Turns Green/ Autumn in New York	1954	$20
❏ 89150	Love Me or Leave Me/I Thought About You	1955	$20
❏ 89089	My Man/He's Funny That Way	1954	$20

COLUMBIA
❏ 1-613	Am I Blue?/God Bless the Child	1950	$60

—Microgroove 33 1/3 rpm 7-inch record, small hole

❏ S731710 [S]	But Beautiful/I'll Be Around	1963	$20

— The above five are "Stereo Seven" 33 1/3 rpm jukebox singles from set "JS 7-71" entitled "Lady in Satin"

❏ S731706 [S]	(titles unknown)	1963	$20
❏ S731707 [S]	(titles unknown)	1963	$20
❏ S731708 [S]	(titles unknown)	1963	$20

DECCA
❏ 48259	Do Your Duty/The Blues Are Brewin'	1951	$30
❏ 27145	Them There Eyes/ Keeps On Rainin'	1950	$30

MAINSTREAM
❏ 614	Strange Fruit/Fine and Mellow	1964	$8

MERCURY
❏ 89005	East o' the Sun/Solitude	1952	$30
❏ 89037	Lover Come Back to Me/Yesterdays	1953	$30
❏ 89064	Stormy Weather/Tenderly	1953	$30
❏ 89002	These Foolish Things/I Only Have Eyes for You	1952	$30

MGM
❏ 12813	Don't Worry 'Bout Me/ Just One More Chance	1959	$15

UNITED ARTISTS
❏ 50999	My Man/Them There Eyes	1973	$6
❏ 50999 [PS]	My Man/Them There Eyes	1973	$10

VERVE
❏ 10181	Strange Fruit/The Foolish Things	1959	$15
❏ 7-00021 [PS]	The Golden Years	1972	$20
❏ 7-00021	When a Woman Loves a Man/The Man I Love/I'll Never Be the Same//Back in Your Own Backyard/God Bless the Child/All of Me	1972	$20

—Jukebox issue; small hole, plays at 33 1/3 rpm

HOLIDAY, GEORGIE
DATE
❏ 1541	Have a Gluey Christmas/ Clarence the Cross-Eyed Bear	1966	$15

—As " 'Little' Georgie Holiday

MAP CITY
❏ 302	Have a Gluey Christmas/A Little Boy's Christmas Prayer	1969	$12

HOLIDAYS, THE (1)
GOLDEN WORLD
❏ 36	Makin' Up Time/I'll Love You Forever	1966	$30

REVILOT
❏ 210	I Know She Cares/I Keep Holding On	1967	$30
❏ 226	I'll Keep Coming Back/All That Is Required of You	1968	$60
❏ 205	Love's Creeping Up on Me/Never Alone	1967	$50

HOLIDAYS, THE (U)
ANDIE
❏ 5019	The Stars Will Remember/ Who Knows, Who Cares	1960	$70

BRENT
❏ 7018	Come Back to Me/ No Other Love	1961	$30

BRUNSWICK
❏ 55084	Sands of Gold/ French Riviera	1958	$20

CORAL
❏ 62430	Love and Learn/I Want You to Love Me	1964	$30

GALAXY
❏ 714	Send Back My Love/ Deacon Brown	1962	$30
❏ 714 [DJ]	Send Back My Love/ Deacon Brown	1962	$40

—Promo on colored vinyl

KING
Number	Title	Yr	NM
❏ 1217	I'm a-Like a-You (Pizza Pie)/Rolling River	1953	$40

MONUMENT
❏ 431	Merry Christmas Song/A Very Merry Christmas	1960	$20

NIX
❏ 537	One Little Kiss/My Girl	1961	$40

ROBBEE
❏ 107	Lonely Summer/Then I'll Be Tired of You	1960	$60
❏ 103	Them There Eyes/ The Kiss Cha Cha	1960	$70

SPECIALTY
❏ 533	Irene/Aw-Aw Baby	1954	$50

TRACK
❏ 101	Patty Ann/Big Brown Eyes	1962	$20

HOLLAND-DOZIER
INVICTUS
❏ 9110	Don't Leave Me (Part 1)/ Don't Leave Me (Part 2)	1972	$20
❏ 9133	Don't Leave Me Starvin' for Your Love (Part 1)/ Don't Leave Me Starvin' for Your Love (Part 2)	1972	$8
❏ 1254	If You Don't Wanta Be in My Life/New Breed Kinda Woman	1973	$125
❏ 1253	Slipping Away/Can't Get Enough	1973	$20
❏ 9125	Why Can't We Be Lovers/ Don't Leave Me	1972	$8

MOTOWN
❏ 1045	What Goes Up Must Come Down/Come On Home	1963	$60

HOLLAND, BRIAN
INVICTUS
❏ 1265	I'm So Glad (Part 1)/I'm So Glad (Part 2)	1974	$5
❏ 1272	Super Woman/Let's Get Together	1974	$5

KUDO
❏ 667	(Where's the Joy?) In Nature Boy/Shock	1958	$600

—First name as "Briant

HOLLAND, EDDIE
MOTOWN
❏ 1043	Brenda/Baby Shake	1963	$50
❏ 1063	Candy to Me/If You Don't Want My Love	1964	$40
❏ 1036	Darling I Hum Our Song/ Just a Few Memories	1963	$70
❏ 1030	If Cleopatra Took a Chance/What About Me	1962	$30
❏ 1030 [PS]	If Cleopatra Took a Chance/What About Me	1962	$125
❏ 1031	If It's Love (It's All Right)/It's Not Too Late	1962	$50
❏ 1049	I'm On the Outside Looking In/I Couldn't Cry If I Wanted To	1963	$300
❏ 1052	Leaving Here/Brenda	1964	$70

TAMLA
❏ 102	Merry-Go-Round/ It Moves Me	1959	$400

UNITED ARTISTS
❏ 191	Because I Love Her/ Everybody's Going	1959	$40
❏ 207	Magic Mirror/Will You Love Me	1960	$40
❏ 172	Merry-Go-Round/ It Moves Me	1959	$40
❏ 280	The Last Laugh/Why Do You Want to Let Me Go	1960	$60

HOLLIDAY, MICHAEL
CAPITOL
❏ F3720	Good Luck, Good Health, God Bless You/ John and Julie	1957	$15

HOLLIES, THE
ATLANTIC
❏ 89768 [DJ]	Casualty (same on both sides)	1983	$5

—May be promo only

❏ 89784	If the Lights Go Out/ Someone Else's Eyes	1983	$3
❏ 89819	Stop in the Name of Love/Musical Pictures	1983	$3
❏ 89819 [PS]	Stop in the Name of Love/Musical Pictures	1983	$5

EPIC
❏ 50110	Another Night/Time Machine Jive	1975	$4
❏ 50522	Burn Out/Writing on the Wall	1978	$4
❏ 10180	Carrie-Anne/Signs That Will Never Change	1967	$8

Number	Title	Yr	NM
❏ 10180 [PS]	Carrie-Anne/Signs That Will Never Change	1967	$20
❏ 50204	Crocodile Woman (She Bites)/Write On	1976	$4
❏ 10251	Dear Eloise/When Your Light's Turned On	1967	$8
❏ 10251 [PS]	Dear Eloise/When Your Light's Turned On	1967	$20
❏ 50029	Don't Let Me Down/Layin' to the Music	1974	$5
❏ 10361	Do the Best You Can/Elevated Observations	1968	$8
❏ 50422	Draggin' My Heels/I Won't Move Over	1977	$4
❏ 10677	Gasoline Alley Bred/Dandelion Wine	1970	$10
❏ 10532	He Ain't Heavy, He's My Brother/Cos You Like to Love Me	1969	$6

— A-side: Elton John on piano

❏ 10754	Hey Willy/Row the Boat Together	1971	$12
❏ 10613	I Can't Tell the Bottom from the Top/Mad Professor Blythe	1970	$6
❏ 10400	Listen to Me/Everything Is Sunshine	1968	$8
❏ 10871	Long Cool Woman (In a Black Dress)/Look What We've Got	1972	$5
❏ 10920	Long Dark Road/Indian Girl	1972	$5
❏ 50144	Look Out Johnny/I'm Down	1975	$4
❏ 10951	Magic Woman Touch/Blue in the Morning	1973	$5
❏ 50086	Sandy/Second Hand Hangups	1975	$5
❏ 50359	Sandy/Second Hand Hangups	1977	$4
❏ 10454	Sorry Suzanne/Not That Way at All	1969	$8
❏ 10716	Survival of the Fittest/Man Without a Heart	1971	$15
❏ 11100	The Air That I Breathe/No More Riders	1974	$5
❏ 10842	The Baby/Oh Granny	1972	$12
❏ 10842 [PS]	The Baby/Oh Granny	1972	$125
❏ 11051	The Day That Curley Billy Shot Down Crazy Sam McGee/Born a Man	1973	$5
❏ 11025	Won't We Feel Good/Slow Down	1973	$5

IMPERIAL

❏ 66186	Bus Stop/Don't Run and Hide	1966	$15
❏ 66070	Come On Back/We're Through	1964	$20
❏ 66044	Here I Go Again/Lucille	1964	$20
❏ 66158	I Can't Let Go/I've Got a Way of My Own	1966	$20
❏ 66271	If I Needed Someone/I'll Be True to You (Yes I Will)	1968	$50
❏ 66119	I'm Alive/You Know He Did	1965	$20
❏ 66134	Look Through Any Window/So Lonely	1965	$15
❏ 66231	On a Carousel/All the World Is Love	1967	$15
❏ 66231 [PS]	On a Carousel/All the World Is Love	1967	$40
❏ 66240	Pay You Back With Interest/Whatcha Gonna Do 'Bout It	1967	$15
❏ 66214	Stop Stop Stop/It's You	1966	$15

LIBERTY

❏ 55674	Stay/Now's the Time	1964	$70

UNITED ARTISTS

❏ 50079	After the Fox/The Fox Trot	1966	$30

— With Peter Sellers

HOLLOWAY, BRENDA
DONNA

❏ 1358	Echo/Hey Fool	1962	$50
❏ 1366	Game of Love/Echo-Echo-Echo	1962	$60
❏ 1370	I'll Give My Life/More Echo	1962	$60

TAMLA

❏ 54094	Every Little Bit Hurts/Land of 1,000 Boys	1964	$15
❏ 54137	Hurt a Little Every Day/Where Were You	1966	$40
❏ 54099	I'll Always Love You/Sad Song	1964	$20
❏ 54115	Operator/I'll Be Available	1965	$20
❏ 206312 [DJ]	Play It Cool, Stay in School	1966	$1000

— Promo for Women's Ad Club of Detroit

❏ 54125	Sad Song/Together 'Til the End of Time	1965	$30
❏ 54144	'Til Johnny Comes/Where Were You	1967	$200
❏ 54111	When I'm Gone/I've Been Good to You	1965	$20
❏ 54111 [PS]	When I'm Gone/I've Been Good to You	1965	$125

HOLLOWAY, PATRICE
CAPITOL

❏ 3265	Black Mother Goose/That's the Chance You Gotta Take	1972	$40
❏ 3176	Evidence/That's the Chance You Gotta Take	1971	$50
❏ 5778	Love and Desire/Ecstasy	1967	$300
❏ 5985	Stay with Your Own Kind/That's All You Got to Do	1967	$50
❏ 5680	Stolen Hours/Lucky My Boy	1966	$500

TASTE

❏ 125	Do the Del Viking (Pt. 1)/Do the Del Viking (Pt. 2)	1963	$100

V.I.P.

❏ 25001	(He Is) The Boy of My Dreams/Stevie	1964	$5000

— VG 2500; VG+ 3750

HOLLOWELL, TERRI
CON BRIO

❏ 134	Happy Go Lucky Morning/Say What I Feel Tonight	1978	$6
❏ 156	It's Too Soon to Say Goodbye/Holding It Back	1979	$6
❏ 150	May I/I Wasn't There	1979	$6
❏ 139	Strawberry Fields Forever/If You Wanna	1978	$6

HOLLY, BUDDY
CORAL

❏ 62369	Brown Eyed Handsome Man/Wishing	1963	$50
❏ 62006	Early in the Morning/Now We're One	1958	$60
❏ 62051	Heartbeat/Well...All Right	1958	$60
❏ 61947	I'm Gonna Love You Too/Listen to Me	1958	$60
❏ 62074	It Doesn't Matter Anymore/Raining in My Heart	1959	$50
❏ 62558	Love Is Strange/You're the One	1969	$30
❏ 62558 [PS]	Love Is Strange/You're the One	1969	$40
❏ 61885	Peggy Sue/Everyday	1957	$60

— Orange label

❏ 62134	Peggy Sue Got Married/Crying, Waiting, Hoping	1959	$70
❏ 62448	Slippin' and Slidin'/What to Do	1965	$125
❏ 62352	True Love Ways/Bo Diddley	1963	$70
❏ 62210	True Love Ways/That Makes It Tough	1960	$60
❏ 61852	Words of Love/Mailman, Bring Me No More Blues	1957	$400

— Promos for any Coral title valued at $50 or under Near Mint are worth 2-4 times the stock copy value.

DECCA

❏ 29854	Blue Days, Black Nights/Love Me	1956	$600

— With lines on either side of "Decca

❏ 29854	Blue Days, Black Nights/Love Me	1956	$300

— With star under "Decca

❏ 29854 [DJ]	Blue Days, Black Nights/Love Me	1956	$400

— Promos have pink labels

❏ 30543	Love Me/You Are My One Desire	1958	$300
❏ 30543 [DJ]	Love Me/You Are My One Desire	1958	$300

— Green label promos

❏ 30543 [DJ]	Love Me/You Are My One Desire	1958	$200

— Pink label promos

❏ 30166	Modern Don Juan/You Are My One Desire	1956	$500

— With lines on either side of "Decca

❏ 30166	Modern Don Juan/You Are My One Desire	1956	$250

— With star under "Decca

❏ 30166 [DJ]	Modern Don Juan/You Are My One Desire	1956	$300

— Promos have pink labels

❏ 30434 [DJ]	That'll Be the Day/Rock Around with Ollie Vee	1957	$300

— Green label promo

❏ 30434	That'll Be the Day/Rock Around with Ollie Vee	1957	$250

— With star under "Decca

❏ 30434 [DJ]	That'll Be the Day/Rock Around with Ollie Vee	1957	$250

— Pink label promo

❏ 30434	That'll Be the Day/Rock Around with Ollie Vee	1957	$400

— With lines on either side of "Decca

❏ 30650	Ting-a-Ling/Girl on My Mind	1958	$300
❏ 30650 [DJ]	Ting-a-Ling/Girl on My Mind	1958	$200

— Promos have pink labels

MCA

Number	Title	Yr	NM
❏ 40905	It Doesn't Matter Anymore/Peggy Sue	1978	$5
❏ 40905 [PS]	It Doesn't Matter Anymore/Peggy Sue	1978	$5

7-Inch Extended Plays
CORAL

❏ EC81193 [PS]	Brown Eyed Handsome Man	1961	$250
❏ EC81193	Brown Eyed Handsome Man/Wishing//Bo Diddley/True Love Ways	1961	$250
❏ EC81191 [PS]	Buddy Holly	1961	$250
❏ EC81182	It Doesn't Matter Anymore/Heartbeat//Raining in My Heart/Early in the Morning	1959	$300
❏ EC81169 [PS]	Listen to Me	1958	$300
❏ EC81169	Listen to Me/Peggy Sue/I'm Gonna Love You Too/Everyday	1958	$300
❏ EC81191	Peggy Sue Got Married/Crying, Waiting, Hoping//Learning the Game/That Makes It Tough	1961	$250
❏ EC81182 [PS]	The Buddy Holly Story	1959	$300

DECCA

❏ ED2575	*That'll Be the Day/Blue Days -- Black Nights/Ting-a-Ling/You Are My One Desire	1958	$600
❏ ED2575 [PS]	That'll Be the Day	1958	$2000

— Sleeve has liner notes on back

❏ ED2575 [PS]	That'll Be the Day	1958	$600

— Sleeve has other EP ads on back

HOLLY, DOYLE
50 STATES

❏ 46	Senorita Del Noche/Hey Ginny	1976	$6
❏ 48	Somebody to Love/Heaven Help the Poor Man	1977	$6
❏ 55	Takin' a Chance/Goodbye Rose	1977	$6

BARNABY

❏ 612	Funky Water/Watch Out Woman	1975	$5
❏ 5010	Headed for the Country/Slow Poke	1973	$5
❏ 5027	Lila/Darling, Are You Ever Coming Home	1973	$5
❏ 5030	Lord How Long Has This Been Going On/January Bittersweet Jones	1974	$5
❏ 5004	My Heart Cries for You/All the Way from Alabama	1972	$5

CAPITOL

❏ 2756	Cinderella/I'll Be Alright Tomorrow	1970	$8
❏ 2637	I'm a Natural Loser/The Biggest Storm of All	1969	$8

HOLLY TWINS, THE
LIBERTY

❏ 55048	I Want Elvis for Christmas/The Tender Age	1956	$60
❏ 55015	Take Me Back/It's Easy	1956	$30

RENDEZVOUS

❏ 180	Okee-Feenokee/Potato Chips	1962	$15
❏ 180 [PS]	Okee-Feenokee/Potato Chips	1962	$40

HOLLYHAWKS, THE
JUBILEE

❏ 5441	I Cry All the Time/When Came the Fall	1962	$100

HOLLYWOOD ARGYLES, THE
CHATTAHOOCHIE

❏ 691	Long Hair, Unsquare Dude Called Jack/Ole	1965	$20

FELSTED

❏ 8674	Bossy Nover/Find Another Way	1963	$30

FINER ARTS

❏ 1002	The Morning After/See You in the Morning	1961	$30

KAMMY

❏ 105	Alley-Oop '65/Do the Funky Foot	1965	$30

— As "The New Hollywood Argyles

LUTE

❏ 5905	Alley Oop/Sho' Know a Lot About Love	1960	$30
❏ 5908	Gun Totin' Critter Called Jack/Bug-Eye	1960	$30
❏ 6002	Hully Gully/So Fine	1960	$30

Number	Title	Yr	NM

HOLLYWOOD FLAMES, THE

ATCO
❏ 6164	Ball and Chain/I Found a Boy	1960	$20
❏ 6171	Devil or Angel/Do You Ever Think of Me	1960	$20
❏ 6155	Every Day, Every Way/If I Thought I Needed You	1959	$20
❏ 6180	Money Honey/My Heart's On Fire	1960	$20

CHESS
❏ 1787	Gee/Yes They Do	1961	$15

DECCA
❏ 48331	Let's Talk It Over/I Know	1955	$80
❏ 29285	Peggy/Ooh La La	1954	$80

EBB
❏ 149	A Star Fell/I'll Get By	1958	$30
❏ 119	Buzz-Buzz-Buzz/Crazy	1957	$40
❏ 146	Chains of Love/Let's Talk It Over	1958	$30
❏ 144	Frankenstein's Den/Strollin' on the Beach	1958	$30
❏ 131	Give Me Back My Heart/A Little Bird	1958	$30
❏ 153	I'll Be Seeing You/Just for You	1959	$40
❏ 163	Much Too Much/In the Dark	1959	$30
❏ 158	So Good/There Is Something on Your Mind	1959	$30

LUCKY
❏ 009	Let's Talk It Over/I Know	1954	$400
❏ 001	One Night with a Fool/Ride, Helen, Ride	1954	$600
❏ 006	Peggy/Ooh-La-La	1954	$600

MONA-LEE
❏ 135	Buzz-Buzz-Buzz/Crazy	1958	$30

MONEY
❏ 202	Fare Thee Well/I'm Leaving	1954	$400

SWING TIME
❏ 346	Go and Get Some More/Another Soldier Gone	1953	$500

—B-side by the Question Marks

❏ 345	Let's Talk It Over/I Know	1953	$500

SYMBOL
❏ 211	Dance Senorita/Annie Don't Love Me Anymore	1965	$200
❏ 215	I'm Coming Home/I'm Gonna Stand By You	1966	$60

VEE JAY
❏ 515	Drop Me a Line/Letter to My Love	1963	$80

HOLLYWOOD PERSUADERS, THE

ORIGINAL SOUND
❏ 50	Drums-A-Go-Go/Agua Caliente	1965	$30
❏ 58	Hollywood A-Go-Go/Eve of Destruction	1965	$60
❏ 44	Persuasion/Juarez	1964	$30
❏ 39	Tijuana/Grunion Run	1964	$60
❏ 39	Tijuana Surf/Grunion Run	1964	$60

HOLLYWOOD PLAYBOYS, THE

SURE
❏ 105	Ding Dong School Is Out/Talk to Audrey	1960	$40

HOLLYWOOD PRODUCERS, THE

PARKWAY
❏ 993	Whits Silk Glove/You're Not Welcome	1966	$40

HOLLYWOOD SQUARES, THE

SQUARE
❏ 0(no cat #)	Hillside Strangler/Hollywood Square	1978	$75
❏ 0(no cat #) [PS]	Hillside Strangler/Hollywood Square	1978	$75

—Plain sleeve with rubber-stamp on it

HOLMAN, EDDIE

ABC
❏ 11276	Cathy Called/I Need Somebody	1970	$40
❏ 11261	Don't Stop Now/Since I Don't Have You	1970	$6
❏ 11240	Hey There Lonely Girl/It's All in the Game	1969	$20
❏ 11265	I'll Be There/Cause You're Mine Little Girl	1970	$6
❏ 11149	I Love You/I Surrender	1968	$60
❏ 11292	Love Story/Four Walls	1971	$6

ASCOT
❏ 2142	Go Get Your Own/Laughing at Me	1963	$200

BELL
❏ 712	I'm Not Gonna Give Up/I'll Cry 1,000 Tears	1968	$40

GSF
❏ 6873	My Mind Keeps Telling Me (That I Really Love You, Girl)/Stranded in a Dream	1972	$10

PARKWAY
❏ 106	Am I a Loser/You Know That I Will	1966	$30
❏ 981	Don't Stop Now/Eddie's My Name	1966	$80
❏ 133	Somewhere Waits a Lonely Girl/Stay Mine for Heaven's Sake	1967	$50
❏ 960	This Can't Be True/A Free Country	1965	$30
❏ 157	Why Do Fools Fall in Love/Never Let Me Go	1967	$60

SALSOUL
❏ 2026	This Will Be a Night to Remember/Time Will Tell	1977	$40

HOLMES, CARL, AND THE COMMANDERS

ATLANTIC
❏ 2140	Mashed Potatoes (Part 1)/(Part 2)	1962	$30

PARKWAY
❏ 900	I Want My Ya Ya/I'm At My Best (When I'm Down)	1964	$30

VERVE
❏ 10510	Telegram/My Lonely Sad Eyes	1967	$20

HOLMES, LEROY

UNITED ARTISTS
❏ 867	Theme from "Zorba the Greek"/Theme from "The Amorous Adventures of Moll Flanders	1965	$8
❏ 867 [PS]	Theme from "Zorba the Greek"/Theme from "The Amorous Adventures of Moll Flanders	1965	$15

HOLMES, MARVIN

UNI
❏ 55111	Ooh, Ooh, The Dragon (Part 1)/Ooh, Ooh, The Dragon (Part 2)	1969	$30
❏ 55233	Sweet Talk/Thang	1970	$30

HOLMES, MONTY

ASHLEY
❏ 1001	A Way to Survive/(B-side unknown)	1989	$6

HOLMES, RUPERT

EPIC
❏ 50096 [PS]	I Don't Wanna Hold Your Hand	1975	$10

—Promo-only sleeve

❏ 50096	I Don't Wanna Hold Your Hand/The Man Behind the Woman	1975	$6
❏ 11117	Our National Pastime/Phantom of the Opera	1974	$6
❏ 11014	Philly/Talk	1973	$6
❏ 50013	Terminal/Bagdad	1974	$6
❏ 50161	Terminal/Deco Lady	1975	$6
❏ 50161 [PS]	Terminal/Deco Lady	1975	$10
❏ 50223	Weekend Lover/Weekend Lover	1976	$5

INFINITY
❏ 50035	Escape (The Pina Colada Song)/Drop It	1979	$5

MCA
❏ 41235	Answering Machine/Lunch Hour	1980	$4
❏ 51045	Blackjack/Crowd Pleaser	1981	$4
❏ 50035	Escape (The Pina Colada Song)/Drop It	1980	$4
❏ 41173	Him/Get Outta Yourself	1980	$4
❏ 51092	I Don't Need You/Cold	1981	$4
❏ 51019	Morning Man/The Mask	1980	$4

PRIVATE STOCK
❏ 45,183	Bedside Companions/So Beautiful It Hurts	1978	$5
❏ 45,199	Let's Get Crazy Tonight/The Long Way Home	1978	$5

HOLMES, SALTY

DECCA
❏ 9-46313	Harmonica Boogie/Blue Eyes Crying in the Rain	1951	$30

HOLY MODAL ROUNDERS, THE

ELEKTRA
❏ 45644	Bird Song/Dame Fortune	1968	$20

METROMEDIA
❏ 223	Boobs a Lot/Love Is the Closest Thing	1971	$10

HOMBRES, THE

SUN
❏ 1104	If This Ain't Loving You Baby/You Made Me What I Am	1969	$10

VERVE FORECAST
❏ 5076	It's a Gas/Am I High	1967	$10
❏ 5058	Let It All Hang Out/Go Girl, Go	1967	$20
❏ 5058	Let It Out (Let It All Hang Out)/Go Girl, Go	1967	$15
❏ 5093	Take My Overwhelming Love (And Cram It Up Your Heart)/Pumpkin Man	1968	$10
❏ 5083	The Prodigal/Mau, Mau, Mau	1968	$10

HOMEMADE THEATER

A&M
❏ 1887	C.B. Santa/Soup of the Day	1976	$20
❏ 1776	Santa Jaws (Part 1)/Santa Jaws (Part 2)	1975	$20

HOMER

UNITED
❏ 123-10	Dandelion Wine/(B-side unknown)	1970	$30
❏ 123-6/7	I Never Cared for You/Dandilion Wine	1969	$30
❏ 123-8	Texas Lights/(B-side unknown)	1970	$30

HOMER AND JETHRO

KING
❏ 1216	Don't Let Your Sweet Love Die/Long Handle Line	1953	$40
❏ 5747	Five Minutes More/Tell a Woman	1963	$15

RCA VICTOR
❏ 47-8874	Act Naturally/Finished Musicians	1966	$10
❏ 47-7852	Are You Lonesome Tonight/I Love Your Pizza	1961	$20
❏ 47-5099	A Screwball's Love Song/Settin' the Woods on Fire No. 2	1952	$30
❏ 47-7162	At the Flop/My Special Angel	1958	$20
❏ 48-0075	Baby, It's Cold Outside/Country Girl	1949	$60

— With June Carter; originals on green vinyl

❏ 47-4397	Cold, Cold Heart #2/Alabama Jubilee	1951	$30
❏ 47-5708	Crazy Mixed Up Song/That Tired Run Down Feeling	1954	$30
❏ 47-9866	Daddy Played First Base/You Smell Like Turtles	1970	$8
❏ 47-5214	Don't Let the Stars Get In Your Eyeballs/Unhappy Day	1953	$30
❏ 47-7493	Don't Sing Along (On Top of Old Smoky)/Middle Aged Teenager	1959	$20
❏ 47-7704	El Paso (Numero Dos)/That's Good, That's Bad	1960	$20
❏ 47-6954	Gone/Ramblin' Rose	1957	$20
❏ 47-9922	Hello Darlin' No. 2/Funny Farm	1970	$8
❏ 47-5788	Hernando's Hideaway/Wanted	1954	$30
❏ 47-9581	Hill Billy Boogie/I Crept Into the Crypt and Cried	1968	$12
❏ 47-6706	Houn' Dawg/Screen Door (Green Door)	1956	$30
❏ 47-5280	(How Much Is) That Hound Dog in the Window/Pore Ol' Koo-Liger	1953	$40
❏ 47-6765	I'm My Own Grand Paw/Mama from the Train	1956	$30
❏ 47-5372	I'm Walking Behind You-All/Mexican Joe #6 7/8	1953	$30
❏ 48-0181	I Said My Nightshirt (And Put On My Prayers)/Music, Music, Music	1950	$50

— Originals on green vinyl

❏ 47-5456	I Saw Mommy Smoochin' Santa Claus/(All I Want for Christmas Is) My Upper Plate	1953	$30
❏ 47-5456 [PS]	I Saw Mommy Smoochin' Santa Claus/(All I Want for Christmas Is) My Upper Plate	1953	$40
❏ 47-7790	Itsy Bitsy Teenie Weenie Yellow Polka Dot Bikini/Please Help Me, I'm Falling	1960	$20
❏ 47-8345	I Want to Hold Your Hand/She Loves You	1964	$20
❏ 47-8345 [PS]	I Want to Hold Your Hand/She Loves You	1964	$40
❏ 47-6053	Let Me Go, Blubber/Over the Rainbow	1955	$30
❏ 47-4770	Li'l Ole Kiss of Fire/I'm Torn	1952	$30
❏ 47-6374	Love and Marriage/This Is a Wife?	1955	$30
❏ 47-7342	Lullaby of Bird Dog/I Guess Things Happen That Way	1958	$20
❏ 47-6029	Mister Sandman/The Nutty Lady of Shady Lane	1955	$30
❏ 47-8604	Misty/Tenderly	1965	$15
❏ 47-7030	My Dog Likes Your Dog/Kentucky	1957	$20

Number	Title	Yr	NM
❏ 48-0404	Oh Babe/Disc Jockey Nightmare	1951	$40
❏ 47-5633	Oh My Pappy/ Swappin' Partners	1954	$30
❏ 48-0349	Pistol Pete/Put That Knife Away Nellie	1950	$50
— Originals on green vinyl			
❏ 48-0170	She Made Toothpicks Out of the Timber of My Heart/I've Got Tears in My Ears	1950	$50
— Originals on green vinyl			
❏ 47-8075	She Thinks I Don't Care/ Are You Kissing More Now (But Enjoying It Less)	1962	$15
❏ 47-7744	Sink the Bismarck/ He'll Have to Go	1960	$20
❏ 47-4557	Slow Poke #2/When It's Tooth Pickin' Time in False Teeth Valley	1952	$30
❏ 48-0446	So Long -- No. 2/I'm Movin' On -- No. 2	1951	$40
❏ 47-9299	Somethin' Stupid/The Ballad of Roger Miller	1967	$12
❏ 47-4239	Sound Off #2/I Love You 1,000 Ways	1951	$30
❏ 48-0113	Tennessee Border -- No. 2/I'm Gettin' Older Every Day	1949	$50
— Originals on green vinyl			
❏ 47-6178	The Ballad of Davy Crew-Cut/Pickin' and Singin' (Medley)	1955	$30
❏ 47-7585	The Battle of Kookamonga/Waterloo	1959	$20
❏ 47-4936	The Billboard Song/ Child Psychology	1952	$30
❏ 47-9674	The Gal from Possum Holler/There Ain't a Chicken Safe in Tennessee	1968	$10
❏ 47-6342	The Sifting, Whimpering Sands They Laid Him in the Ground	1955	$30
❏ 48-0144	The Wedding of Hillbilly Lilli Marlene/The Hucklebuck	1950	$50
— With June Carter; originals on green vinyl			
❏ 47-4290	Too Young/Too Old to Cut the Mustard	1951	$40
❏ 47-6542	Two Tone Shoes/ Hart Brake Motel	1956	$30
❏ 48-0086	Waltz with Me/Roll Along Kentucky Moon	1949	$50
— Originals on green vinyl			
❏ 74-0566	We Didn't Make It Through the Night/ Fer the Good Times	1971	$8
❏ 47-6651	Where Is That Doggone Gal of Mine/Just Be Here	1956	$30

7-Inch Extended Plays

Number	Title	Yr	NM
❏ EPA 1-1412 [PS]	Barefoot Ballads, Vol. I	1956	$25
❏ EPA 1-1412	Cigareetes, Whusky and Wild Wild Women/The West Virginny Hills//Keep Them Cold Icy Fingers Off of Me/Ground Hog	1956	$25
❏ EPA424 [PS]	Homer & Jethro Kid the Top Pops	1952	$25

HOMESTEADERS, THE
LITTLE DARLIN'

Number	Title	Yr	NM
❏ 045	Gonna Miss Me/ Homewrecker	1968	$10
❏ 033	Homesteadin'/If You Should Come Back Today	1967	$12
❏ 018	Love, Love, Love (Makes the World Go Round)/It's a Woman	1967	$10
❏ 036	Lovin' Time/Making Believe	1967	$10
❏ 010	Show Me the Way to the Circus/The Country Joined the Country Club	1966	$10
❏ 053	Sleep/In Magnolia Blossoms	1968	$12

HONDELLS, THE
AMOS

Number	Title	Yr	NM
❏ 131	Follow the Bouncing Ball/The Legend of Frankie and Johnny	1969	$15
❏ 150	Shine On Ruby Mountain/ The Legend of Frankie and Johnny	1970	$15

COLUMBIA
| ❏ 44557 | Another Woman/ Atlanta Georgia Stray | 1968 | $30 |

MERCURY
❏ 72626	Cheryl's Goin' Home/ Show Me	1966	$20
❏ 72605	Country Love/Kissin' My Life Away	1966	$20
❏ 72523	Endless Sleep/ Follow Your Heart	1966	$20
❏ 72324	Little Honda/Hot Rod High	1964	$30
❏ 72405	Little Sidewalk Surfer Girl/ Come On Baby (Pack It In)	1965	$30
❏ 72366	My Buddy Seat/You're Gonna Ride with Me	1964	$30
❏ 72366 [PS]	My Buddy Seat/You're Gonna Ride with Me	1964	$30
❏ 72443	Sea of Love/Do As I Say	1965	$30

HONEY AND THE BEES
ACADEMY
Number	Title	Yr	NM
❏ 114	Inside o' Me/Two Can Play the Same Game	1965	$15

HONEY BEES, THE (1)
FONTANA
| ❏ 1939 | One Wonderful Night/ She Don't Deserve You | 1964 | $70 |

VEE JAY
| ❏ 611 | One Girl, One Boy/No Guy | 1964 | $30 |

HONEY BEES, THE (2)
IMPERIAL
| ❏ 5400 | Endless/Let's See What's Happening | 1956 | $50 |

HONEY CONE, THE
HOT WAX
Number	Title	Yr	NM
❏ 7212	Ace in the Hole/ Ooo Baby Baby	1972	$6
❏ 6903	Girls It Ain't Easy/ The Feeling's Gone	1969	$30
❏ 7301	If I Can't Fly/Woman Can't Live by Bread Alone	1973	$40
❏ 7208	Innocent Till Proven Guilty/ Don't Send Me an Invitation	1972	$30
❏ 7110	One Monkey Don't Stop No Show Part I/One Monkey Don't Stop No Show Part II	1971	$20
❏ 7205	Sittin' on a Time Bomb (Waitin' for the Hurt to Come)/It's Better to Have Loved and Lost	1972	$6
❏ 7106	Stick-Up/V.I.P.	1971	$6
❏ 7001	Take Me With You/ Take My Love	1970	$6
❏ 7113	The Day I Found Myself/ When Will It End	1971	$6
❏ 9255	The Truth Will Come Out/ Somebody Is Always Messing Up a Good Thing	1974	$50
❏ 7011	Want Ads/We Belong Together	1970	$6
— Mostly white label			
❏ 7011	Want Ads/We Belong Together	1970	$5
— Mostly orange label			
❏ 7005	When Will It End/ Take Me With You	1970	$6
❏ 6901	While You're Out Looking for Sugar?/The Feeling's Gone	1969	$20

HONEY DREAMERS, THE
CAPITOL
| ❏ F2857 | Perdido/Sometimes I'm Happy | 1954 | $15 |

COLUMBIA
| ❏ 40564 | The Little Bell (That Just Went Ding)/ Rootie Tootie Tootie (The Kewtee Bear Song) | 1955 | $10 |

HONEYCOMBS, THE
INTERPHON
Number	Title	Yr	NM
❏ 7716	Color Slide/That's the Way	1965	$10
❏ 7716 [PS]	Colour Slide/That's the Way	1965	$30
— Yes, the American sleeve spells the A-side the British way			
❏ 7707	Have I the Right?/Please Don't Pretend Again	1964	$15
❏ 7713	I Can't Stop/I'll Cry Tomorrow	1964	$10
❏ 7713 [PS]	I Can't Stop/I'll Cry Tomorrow	1964	$30

WARNER BROS.
❏ 5803	How Will I Know/ Who Is Sylvia	1966	$10
❏ 5655	I Can't Get Through to You/That's the Way	1965	$10
❏ 5634	I'll See You Tomorrow/ Something Better Beginning	1965	$10

HONEYCONES, THE
EMBER
Number	Title	Yr	NM
❏ 1033	Betty Moretti/Cool It Baby	1958	$30
❏ 1042	Gee Whiz/Rockin' in the Knees	1958	$30
❏ 1036	Op/Vision of You	1958	$30
❏ 1049	Tell Me Baby/Your Face	1959	$30

HONEYCUTT, GLENN
FERNWOOD
| ❏ 142 | Campus Love/ Tombigbee Queen | 1964 | $125 |

SUN
| ❏ 264 | I'll Be Around/I'll Wait Forever | 1957 | $40 |

HONEYDRIPPERS, THE
ES PARANZA
Number	Title	Yr	NM
❏ 99701	Sea of Love/I Get a Thrill	1984	$3
❏ 99701 [PS]	Sea of Love/I Get a Thrill	1984	$4
❏ 99701	Sea of Love/Rockin' at Midnight	1984	$5
❏ 99701 [PS]	Sea of Love/Rockin' at Midnight	1984	$6

HONEYMOON KILLERS
SUB POP
❏ 51	Get It Hot/Gettin' Hot	1989	$50
— Red vinyl pressing of 1,200			
❏ 51	Get It Hot/Gettin' Hot	1989	$30
— Black vinyl pressing of 800			
❏ 51 [PS]	Get It Hot/Gettin' Hot	1989	$30
— #13 in Sub Pop Singles Club series			

HONEYS, THE
CAPITOL
Number	Title	Yr	NM
❏ 2454	Goodnight My Love/ Tonight You Belong to Me	1969	$100
❏ 5034	Hide Go Seek/Pray for Surf	1963	$200
❏ 4952	Surfin' Down the Swanee River/Shoot the Curl	1963	$200
❏ 4952 [PS]	Surfin' Down the Swanee River/Shoot the Curl	1963	$800
❏ 5093	The One You Can't Have/ From Jimmy With Tears	1963	$200

WARNER BROS.
❏ 5430	He's a Doll/The Love of a Boy and Girl	1964	$600
— Stock copy; red label			
❏ 5430 [DJ]	He's a Doll/The Love of a Boy and Girl	1964	$200
— Promotional copy; white label			

HONEYTONES, THE
BIG TOP
| ❏ 3002 | Don't Look Now, But/I Know, I Know | 1958 | $30 |

MERCURY
| ❏ 70557 | Too Bad/Somewhere, Sometime, Someday | 1955 | $30 |

WING
| ❏ 90013 | False Alarm/Honeybun Cha Cha | 1955 | $40 |

HONK
20TH CENTURY
Number	Title	Yr	NM
❏ 2029	I Wanna Do for You/ Another Light	1973	$6
❏ 2007	Made My Statement/ Pipeline Sequence	1973	$6

AMARET
| ❏ 123 | Don't Take Anything/ Love Machine | 1970 | $8 |

EPIC
| ❏ 8-50056 | Hesitation/Dog at Your Dog | 1974 | $5 |

GRANITE
| ❏ 101 | Made My Statement/ Pipeline Sequence | 1972 | $8 |

HOODOO GURUS
A&M
| ❏ 2670 | I Want You Back/Death Ship | 1984 | $6 |

BIG TIME
❏ BTS1503	Bittersweet/Mars Needs Guitars	1985	$5
❏ BTS1503 [PS]	Bittersweet/Mars Needs Guitars	1985	$5
❏ BTS1588	Like Wow -- Wipeout/ Bring the Hoodoo Down	1985	$5
❏ BTS1588 [PS]	Like Wow -- Wipeout/ Bring the Hoodoo Down	1985	$5

ELEKTRA
❏ 69544	Bittersweet/Bring the Hoodoo Down	1986	$3
❏ 69536	Death Defying (Ooh-Wee)/Turkey Dinner	1986	$3
❏ 69481	Good Times/Heart of Darkness	1987	$3
❏ 69481 [PS]	Good Times/Heart of Darkness	1987	$3
❏ 69440	What's My Scene/ Heart of Darkness	1987	$3

HOOK, THE
UNI
Number	Title	Yr	NM
❏ 55149	In the Beginning/ Show You the Way	1969	$10
❏ 55077	Love Theme in E Major/Homes	1968	$10
❏ 55057	Son of Fantasy/Plug Your Head In	1968	$12

HOOKER, EARL

Number	Title	Yr	NM
AGE			
❑ 29106	Blue Guitar/Swear to Tell the Truth	1962	$50
❑ 29114	That Man/Win the Dance	1963	$50
❑ 29111	These Cotton Picking Blues/How Long Can This Go On	1962	$50
ARGO			
❑ 5265	Guitar Rhumba/Frog Hop	1957	$50
ARHOOLIE			
❑ 521	Wah Wah Blues/(B-side unknown)	1970	$30
BEA & BABY			
❑ 106	Dynamite/Trying to Make a Living	1960	$30
BLUE THUMB			
❑ 103	Boogie, Don't Blot/Funky Blues	1969	$20
CHECKER			
❑ 1025	Tanya/Put Your Shoes On, Willie	1962	$30
CHIEF			
❑ 7106	Blues in D Natural/(B-side unknown)	1960	$30
❑ 7039	Messing with the Kid/(B-side unknown)	1961	$30
❑ 7021	Messing with the Kid/Universal Rock	1960	$30
— With Junior Wells			
CJ			
❑ 613	Do the Chicken/Yea Yea	1961	$40
❑ 643	Wild Moments/Chicken	1965	$20
CUCA			
❑ 1194	Bertha/Walkin' the Floor	1964	$60
❑ 1445	Dust My Broom/You Took All My Love	1969	$30
MEL			
❑ 1005	Messing with the Kid/(B-side unknown)	1964	$30
MEL-LON			
❑ 1001	The Leading Brand/(B-side unknown)	1964	$30
❑ 1000	Want You to Rock/(B-side unknown)	1964	$30
ROCKIN'			
❑ 513	Sweet Angel/On the Hook	1952	$400

HOOKER, JOHN LEE, AND CANNED HEAT

Number	Title	Yr	NM
UNITED ARTISTS			
❑ 50779	Whiskey and Wimmen/Let's Make It	1971	$5

HOOKER, JOHN LEE

Number	Title	Yr	NM
ABC			
❑ 11298	Doin' the Shout/Kick Hit 4 Hit Kix U	1971	$6
BLUESWAY			
❑ 61017	Back Biters and Syndicators/Think Twice Before You Go	1968	$6
❑ 61023	I Don't Wanna Go to Vietnam/Simply the Truth	1969	$6
❑ 61010	Motor City Is Burning/Want Ad Blues	1967	$8
❑ 61014	Mr. Lucky/Cry Before I Go	1968	$6
CHANCE			
❑ 1122	609 Boogie/Road Trouble	1952	$2000
— As "John L. Booker			
❑ 1110	Graveyard Blues/I Love to Boogie	1952	$3000
— As "John Lee Booker			
❑ 1108	Miss Lorraine/Talkin' Boogie	1951	$3000
— As "John Lee Booker			
CHART			
❑ 614	Blue Monday/My Baby Put Me Down	1955	$60
❑ 609	Going South/Wobbling Baby	1955	$60
CHESS			
❑ 1505	High Priced Woman/Union Station Blues	1952	$1200
❑ 1562	It's My Own Fault/Women and Money	1954	$250
❑ 1965	Let's Go Out Tonight/In the Mood	1966	$12
❑ 1513	Sugar Mama/Walkin' the Boogie	1952	$1000
DELUXE			
❑ 6004	Blue Monday/Lovin' Guitar Man	1953	$500
— As "John Lee Booker			
❑ 6009	I Came to See You Baby/I'm a Boogie Man	1953	$800
— As "Johnny Lee			
❑ 6046	My Baby Don't Love Me/Real, Real Gone	1954	$400
— As "John Lee Booker			

Number	Title	Yr	NM
❑ 6032	Stuttering Blues/Pouring Down Rain	1954	$400
— As "John Lee Booker			
ELMOR			
❑ 303	Blues for Christmas/Big Fine Woman	1959	$30
FEDERAL			
❑ 12377	Late Last Night/Don't You Remember Me	1960	$20
FORTUNE			
❑ 846	609 Boogie/Curl My Baby's Hair	1959	$30
❑ 855	Crazy About That Walk/We're All God's Chillun	1960	$30
❑ 853	Cry Baby/Love You Baby	1960	$30
GALAXY			
❑ 716	I Lost My Job/You Gotta Shake It Up and Go	1963	$10
HI-Q			
❑ 5018X	609 Blues/Blues for Christmas	1961	$30
❑ 5018	Blues for Christmas/Big Fine Woman	1960	$30
IMPULSE			
❑ 242	Honey/Bottle Up and Go	1966	$50
JEWEL			
❑ 824	I Feel Good (Part 1)/I Feel Good (Part 2)	1971	$5
❑ 852	Stand By (Part 1)/Stand By (Part 2)	1977	$4
JVB			
❑ 30	Boogie Rambler/No More Doggin'	1953	$1500
KENT			
❑ 332	Boogie Chillen/I'm in the Mood	1960	$30
KING			
❑ 6298	Don't Go Baby/Moanin' and Stompin' Blues	1970	$6
❑ 45-4504	Moaning Blues/Stomp Boogie	1952	$1000
— As "John Lee Cooker			
LAUREN			
❑ 361	Ballad to Abraham Lincoln (He Got Assassinated)/Mojo Hand (Louisiana Voodoo)	1961	$30
❑ 362	I Lost My Job/You Gotta Shake It Up and Go	1961	$30
MODERN			
❑ 45x847	Anybody Seen My Baby? (Johnny Says Come Back)/Turn Over a New Leaf	1951	$300
❑ 45x862	Cold Chills All Over Me/Rock Me, Mama	1952	$100
❑ 45x942	Cool Little Car/Bad Boy	1954	$60
❑ 45x923	Gotta Boogie/Down Child	1953	$70
❑ 45x852	Ground Hog Blues/Louise	1951	$120
❑ 45x948	Half a Stranger/Shake, Holler and Run	1954	$60
❑ 45x835	How Can You Do It/I'm in the Mood	1951	$400
❑ 45x966	Hug and Squeeze/The Syndicator	1955	$60
❑ 45x876	It Hurts Me So/I Got Eyes for You	1952	$100
— With Little Eddie Kirkland			
❑ 45x935	I Tried Hard/Let's Talk It Over	1954	$60
❑ 45x897	It's Been a Long Time Baby/Rock House Boogie	1952	$100
❑ 45x978	Looking for a Woman/I'm Ready	1955	$70
❑ 45x908	Please Take Me Back/Love Money Can't Buy	1953	$70
❑ 45x958	Taxi Driver/You Receive Me	1955	$60
❑ 45x916	Too Much Boogie/Need Somebody	1953	$70
RIVERSIDE			
❑ 438	I Need Some Money/No More Diggin'	1960	$30
ROCKIN'			
❑ 524	Blue Monday/Lovin' Guitar Man	1953	$1000
— As "John Lee Booker			
❑ 525	Stuttering Blues/Pouring Down Rain	1953	$1000
— As "John Lee Booker			
SPECIALTY			
❑ 528	Everybody's Blues/I'm Mad	1954	$50
STAX			
❑ 0053	Slow and Easy/Grinder Man	1969	$6
VEE JAY			
❑ 670	Big Legs, Tight Skirt/Your Baby Ain't Sweet Like Mine	1965	$15
❑ 438	Boom Boom/Drug Store Woman	1962	$30
❑ 205	Dimples/Baby Lee	1956	$40
❑ 366	Dusty Road/Tupelo	1960	$30
❑ 188	Every Night/Trouble Blues	1956	$40
❑ 331	Hobo Blues/Crawlin' King Snake	1959	$30

Number	Title	Yr	NM
❑ 293	I Love You Honey/You've Taken My Woman	1958	$30
❑ 538	I'm Leaving/Birmingham Blues	1963	$20
❑ 379	I'm Mad Again/I'm Going Upstairs	1961	$30
❑ 245	I'm So Excited/I See You When You're Weak	1957	$30
❑ 708	It Serves Me Right/Flowers on the Hour	1966	$10
❑ 255	Little Wheel/Rosie Mae	1957	$30
❑ 164	Mambo Chillen/Time Is Marching	1955	$40
❑ 308	Maudie/I'm In the Mood	1959	$30
❑ 575	Send Me Your Pillow/Don't Look Back	1964	$20
❑ 453	She's Mine/A New Leaf	1962	$30
❑ 493	Take a Look at Yourself/Frisco Blues	1963	$30
❑ 493	Take a Look at Yourself/I Love Her	1963	$60
❑ 319	Tennessee Blues/Boogie Chillun	1959	$30
❑ 397	Want Ad Blues/Take Me As I Am	1961	$30

HOOSIER HOT SHOTS
7-Inch Extended Plays

Number	Title	Yr	NM
TOPS			
❑ 45-R261-49	Humming Bird/The Man from Laramie/The Kentuckian/Daniel Boone	1955	$25
— We're not sure about the existence of a cover; if it does, add another $20			

HOOTERS

Number	Title	Yr	NM
ANTENNA			
❑ HOO84	Hangin' on a Heartbeat/Concubine	1984	$12
❑ HOO84 [PS]	Hangin' on a Heartbeat/Concubine	1984	$12
COLUMBIA			
❑ 73013	500 Miles/The House of Wolfgang	1989	$3
— Backing vocals on A-side: Peter, Paul and Mary			
❑ 04854	All You Zombies/Nervous Night	1985	$4
— Not issued with picture sleeve in U.S.			
❑ 08384	And We Danced/All You Zombies	1988	$3
— Reissue			
❑ 05568	And We Danced/Blood from a Stone	1985	$3
❑ 05568 [PS]	And We Danced/Blood from a Stone	1985	$3
❑ 05730	Day By Day/South Ferry Road	1985	$3
❑ 05730 [PS]	Day By Day/South Ferry Road	1985	$3
❑ 07607	Satellite/One Way Home	1987	$3
❑ 07607 [PS]	Satellite/One Way Home	1987	$3
❑ 05854	Where Do the Children Go/Nervous Night	1986	$3
❑ 05854 [PS]	Where Do the Children Go/Nervous Night	1986	$3
EIGHTY PERCENT			
❑ HOO82	All You Zombies (Live)/Rescue Me	1982	$10
❑ HOO82 [PS]	All You Zombies (Live)/Rescue Me	1982	$10
❑ HOO80	Fightin' on the Same Side/Wireless	1980	$10
❑ HOO80 [PS]	Fightin' on the Same Side/Wireless	1980	$10

HOPE, BOB

Number	Title	Yr	NM
CAPITOL			
❑ F2109	Am I in Love/Wing Ding	1952	$30
❑ F2161	Four Legged Friend/There's a Cloud in My Valley of Sunshine	1952	$30
— B-side by Jimmy Wakely			
DECCA			
❑ 34117 [DJ]	Bob Hope Accepts 1962 Patriot's Award from University of Notre Dame/Bob Hope in Moscow	1962	$20
RCA VICTOR			
❑ 47-7517	Ain't a-Hankerin'/Protection	1959	$15
— With Rosemary Clooney			
❑ 47-6577	That Certain Feeling/Zing! Went the Strings of My Heart	1956	$20
UNITED ARTISTS			
❑ 603	Call Me Bwana/The Flip Side	1963	$15
— B-side by Edie Adams			
❑ 603 [PS]	Call Me Bwana/The Flip Side	1963	$40

Number	Title	Yr	NM

HOPE, EDDIE
MARLIN
Number	Title	Yr	NM
❏ 804	A Fool No More/Lost Child	1956	$200

HOPE, LYNN
ALADDIN
Number	Title	Yr	NM
❏ 3297	All of Me/Summertime	1955	$30
❏ 3095	Blue Moon/Blow, Lynn, Blow	1951	$50
❏ 3229	Brazil/C. Jam Blues	1954	$30
❏ 3178	Broken Heart/Morocco	1953	$30
❏ 3322	Cherry/Blues in F	1956	$30
❏ 3134	Driftin'/Sentimental Journey	1952	$40
❏ 3155	Move It/Don't Worry 'Bout Me	1952	$40
❏ 3165	September Song/Blues for Anna Bocoa	1953	$30
❏ 3109	She's Funny That Way/Eleven Till Two	1951	$50
❏ 3208	Swing Train/Rose Room	1953	$30
❏ 3103	Too Young/Free and Easy	1951	$50

KING
Number	Title	Yr	NM
❏ 5378	A Ghost of a Chance/Little Landslide	1960	$15
❏ 5352	Body and Soul/Sands of Sahara	1960	$15
❏ 5431	Shockin'/Blue and Sentimental	1960	$15
❏ 5336	Tenderly/Full Moon	1960	$15

HOPEFUL, THE
MERCURY
Number	Title	Yr	NM
❏ 72637	7 O'Clock News (Silent Night)/6 O'Clock News (America The Beautiful)	1966	$15

HOPKIN, MARY
APPLE
Number	Title	Yr	NM
❏ 1806	Goodbye/Sparrow	1969	$8
❏ 1806 [PS]	Goodbye/Sparrow	1969	$15
❏ 1816	Temma Harbour/Lantano Dagli Occhi	1970	$8
❏ 1816 [PS]	Temma Harbour/Lantano Dagli Occhi	1970	$15
❏ 1825	Think About Your Children/Heritage	1970	$8
❏ 1825	Think About Your Children/Heritage	1970	$15

— With star on A-side label

Number	Title	Yr	NM
❏ 1825 [PS]	Think About Your Children/Heritage	1970	$15
❏ 1801	Those Were the Days/Turn, Turn, Turn	1968	$10
❏ 1843	Water, Paper and Clay/Streets of London	1972	$8
❏ 1843	Water, Paper and Clay/Streets of London	1972	$15

— With star on A-side label

APPLE/AMERICOM
Number	Title	Yr	NM
❏ 1801P/M-238	Those Were the Days/Turn, Turn, Turn	1969	$600

— Four-inch flexi-disc sold from vending machines

RCA VICTOR
Number	Title	Yr	NM
❏ PB-10694	Tell Me Now/If You Love Me	1976	$4

HOPKINS, LIGHTNIN'
ACE
Number	Title	Yr	NM
❏ 516	Bad Boogie/Wonder What Is Wrong with Me	1956	$50

ALADDIN
Number	Title	Yr	NM
❏ 3096	Miss Me Blues/Abilene	1951	$200
❏ 3077	Moonrise Blues/Honey, Honey Blues	1951	$200
❏ 3063	Shotgun Blues/Rolling Blues	1950	$700
❏ 3262	So Long/My California	1954	$125

ARHOOLIE
Number	Title	Yr	NM
❏ 513	Come On Baby/Money Taker	1965	$15
❏ 508	My Woman/Lousiana Blues	1965	$15

BLUESVILLE
Number	Title	Yr	NM
❏ 817	Back to New Orleans/Hard to Love a Woman	1961	$30
❏ 814	Death Bells/Sail On	1961	$30
❏ 824	Going Away/Better Stop Her	1963	$30
❏ 820	Happy Blues for John Glenn (Part 1)/Happy Blues for John Glenn (Part 2)	1962	$30
❏ 821	Last Night Blues/Walkin' Blues	1962	$30
❏ 822	Sinner's Prayer/Angel Child	1962	$30
❏ 813	So Sorry to Leave You/Got to Move Your Baby	1960	$30
❏ 823	The Business You're Doing/Wake Up Old Lady	1963	$30

CHART
Number	Title	Yr	NM
❏ 636	Walkin' the Streets/Mussy Haired Woman	1957	$40

DART
Number	Title	Yr	NM
❏ 123	Grievance Blues/Unsuccessful Blues	1959	$30

Number	Title	Yr	NM
❏ 152	Mary Lou/Wait to Go Home	1960	$30

DECCA
Number	Title	Yr	NM
❏ 9-48312	Highway Blues/Cemetery Blues	1954	$100
❏ 9-48321	I'm Wild About You Baby/Bad Things on My Mind	1954	$125
❏ 9-48306	Merry Christmas/Happy New Year	1953	$100
❏ 9-28841	The War Is Over/Policy Game	1953	$100

FIRE
Number	Title	Yr	NM
❏ 1034	Mojo Hand/Glory Be	1961	$30

HARLEM
Number	Title	Yr	NM
❏ 2321	Contrary Mary/I'm Begging You	1954	$200
❏ 2331	Fast Life/The Jackstropper	1955	$200
❏ 2336	Good Old Woman/Untrue	1955	$200
❏ 2324	Mad Man's Boogie/Nobody Cares for Me	1954	$200

HERALD
Number	Title	Yr	NM
❏ 504	Boogie Woogie Dance/The Blues Is a Mighty Bad Feeling	1957	$30
❏ 449	Evil Hearted Woman/They Wonder Who I Am	1955	$40
❏ 483	Finally Met My Baby/That's Alright Baby	1956	$30
❏ 547	Flash Lightning/Gonna Change My Ways	1960	$30
❏ 476	Grandma's Boogie/I Love You Baby	1956	$30
❏ 531	Hear Me Talkin'/Lightnin's Stomp	1958	$30
❏ 471	Hopkins Sky Hop/Lonesome in Your Home	1956	$30
❏ 465	I Had a Gal Named Sal/Blues for My Cookie	1955	$30
❏ 542	Let's Move/I'm Achin'	1959	$30
❏ 425	Lightnin's Boogie/Don't Think 'Cause You're Pretty	1954	$40
❏ 428	Lightnin's Special/Life Is Used to Live	1954	$40
❏ 520	Little Kewpie Doll/Lightnin' Don't Feel Well	1958	$30
❏ 436	Movin' On Out Boogie/Sick Feelin' Blues	1954	$40
❏ 456	My Baby's Gone/Don't Need No Job	1955	$30
❏ 490	Shine On Moon/Sitting and Thinking	1956	$30
❏ 490	Shine On Moon/Sitting and Thinking	1956	$30

IMPERIAL
Number	Title	Yr	NM
❏ 5834	Feel So Bad/Shotgun	1962	$20
❏ 5852	Picture on the Wall/Lightnin's Boogie	1962	$20

JAX
Number	Title	Yr	NM
❏ 318	Automobile/Organ Blues	1953	$300

— Red vinyl

Number	Title	Yr	NM
❏ 635	Coffee Blues/New Short Haired Woman	1954	$250

— Reissue of Sittin' In With 635

Number	Title	Yr	NM
❏ 321	Contrary Mary/I'm Begging You	1953	$300

— Red vinyl

Number	Title	Yr	NM
❏ 661	Gone Again/Down to the River	1954	$250

— Reissue of Sittin' In With 661

Number	Title	Yr	NM
❏ 660	Mad Blues/I've Been a Bad Man	1954	$250

— Reissue of Sittin' In With 660

JEWEL
Number	Title	Yr	NM
❏ 788	Back Door Friends/Fishing Clothes	1968	$6
❏ 809	I'm Comin' Home/You're Too Fast	1970	$40
❏ 803	Lovin' Arms/Ride in Your New Auto	1969	$6
❏ 816	My Charlie (Part 1)/My Charlie (Part 2)	1970	$6
❏ 807	Play with Your Poodle/Breakfast Blues	1970	$40
❏ 796	Wig Wearin' Woman/Move On Out, Part 2	1968	$6

MERCURY
Number	Title	Yr	NM
❏ 70081x45	Ain't It a Shame/Crazy About My Baby	1953	$125
❏ 8252x45	Everybody's Down on Me/You Do Too	1952	$120
❏ 8293x45	Gone with the Wind/She's Almost Dead	1952	$125
❏ 70191x45	My Mama Told Me/What's the Matter Now	1953	$125
❏ 8274x45	Sad News from Korea/Let Me Fly Your Kite	1952	$125
❏ 8274	Sad News from Korea/Let Me Fly Your Kite	1952	$30

PRESTIGE
Number	Title	Yr	NM
❏ 326	I Like to Boogie/Let's Go Sit on the Lawn	1964	$10
❏ 405	I'm Gonna Build Me a Heaven (Part 1)/I'm Gonna Build Me a Heaven (Part 2)	1966	$10

Number	Title	Yr	NM
❏ 452	Mama Blues/Pneumonia Blues	1968	$8
❏ 343	Mojo Hand/Automobile Blues	1964	$10
❏ 391	Sinner's Prayer/Got to Move Your Baby	1965	$10
❏ 374	T Model Blues/You Cook Alright	1965	$10

RPM
Number	Title	Yr	NM
❏ 45x378	Another Fool in Town/Candy Kitchen	1953	$300
❏ 45x337	Beggin' You to Stay/Bad Luck and Trouble	1951	$600
❏ 45x388	Black Cat/Mistreated Blues	1953	$300
❏ 45x351	Don't Keep My Baby Long/Last Affair	1952	$400
❏ 45x346	Lonesome Dog Blues/Jake Head	1952	$800
❏ 45x398	Santa Fe Blues/Some Day Baby	1954	$200

SHAD
Number	Title	Yr	NM
❏ 5011	Hello Central/Mad As I Can Be	1959	$20

SITTIN' IN WITH
Number	Title	Yr	NM
❏ 647	Bald Headed Woman/Dirty House	1952	$500
❏ 635	Coffee Blues/New Short Haired Woman	1952	$500
❏ 658	Freight Train Blues (When I Started Hoboing)/Broken Hearted Blues	1953	$500
❏ 621	Give Me Central 209/New York Boogie	1951	$500
❏ 661	Gone Again/Down to the River	1953	$500
❏ 621	Hello Central/New York Boogie	1952	$400
❏ 660	Mad Blues/I've Been a Bad Man	1953	$500
❏ 652	Papa Bones Boogie/Everything Happens to Me	1953	$500

TNT
Number	Title	Yr	NM
❏ 8002	Lightnin' Jump/Late in the Evening	1954	$700
❏ 8003	Moanin' Blues/Leavin' Blues	1954	$700

VAULT
Number	Title	Yr	NM
❏ 965	Easy on Your Heels/No Education	1970	$50

HOPSON, JOYCE
REVUE
Number	Title	Yr	NM
❏ 11034	I Surrender to You/This Time	1969	$200

HORNE, JIMMY "BO"
ALSTON
Number	Title	Yr	NM
❏ 4606	Clean Up Man/Down the Road of Love	1972	$40

— Reissue of Dade 2031

Number	Title	Yr	NM
❏ 3712	Don't Worry About It/Music to Make Love By	1975	$12
❏ 3729	Get Happy/It's Your Sweet Love	1977	$6
❏ 3714	Gimme Some (Part 1)/(Part 2)	1975	$6
❏ 4618	If We Were Still Together/Two People in Love	1973	$40
❏ 3724	It's Your Sweet Love/Don't Worry About It	1976	$10
❏ 4612	On the Street Corner/If You Want My Love	1972	$40

DADE
Number	Title	Yr	NM
❏ 2031	Clean Up Man/Down the Road of Love	1972	$125

— Original issue

Number	Title	Yr	NM
❏ 2025	I Can't Speak/Street Corners	1969	$2000

— Reproductions exist as double A-sides on Dade JBH-001; these usually sell in the $20-$25 range

EDGE
Number	Title	Yr	NM
❏ 7011	Show Me How Much (You Want My Love)/(Extended Version)	1987	$8

SUNSHINE SOUND
Number	Title	Yr	NM
❏ 1003	Dance Across the Floor/It's Your Sweet Love	1978	$8
❏ 1005	Let Me (Let Me Be Your Lover)/Ask the Birds and the Bees	1978	$8
❏ 1007	Spank/I Wanna Go Home with You	1978	$8
❏ 1016	They Long to Be Close to You/(B-side unknown)	1980	$8

HORNE, LENA

Number	Title	Yr	NM
20TH CENTURY FOX			
❏ 460	Blowin' in the Wind/ The Eagle and Me	1964	$10
BUDDAH			
❏ 233	Feels So Good/ Nature's Baby	1971	$6
❏ 215	Watch What Happens/ Rocky Raccoon	1971	$6
MCA			
❏ 40979	Believe in Yourself/Main Title Overture (Part 1)	1978	$5
MGM			
❏ K30396	Can't Help Lovin' Dat Man/Where or When	1951	$15
❏ K30397	Is It Always Like This/ Love of My Life	1951	$15
—One record of box set K-72			
RCA VICTOR			
❏ 47-6431	If You Can Dream/ What's Right for You	1956	$15
❏ 47-6175	It's All Right with Me/It's Love	1955	$15
❏ 47-6073	Love Me or Leave Me/I Love to Love	1955	$15
❏ 47-7037	Push De Button/ Coconut Street	1957	$15
❏ 47-7332	When Johnny Comes Marching Home/You'd Better	1957	$15
❏ 47-8092	Where Is Love/ Come On Strong	1962	$10
❏ 47-8092 [PS]	Where Is Love/ Come On Strong	1962	$20
SKYE			
❏ 4523	Watch What Happens/ Rocky Raccoon	1970	$8
THREE CHERRIES			
❏ 7301	I Wish I'd Met You/ When I Fall in Love	1989	$4
—A-side with Sammy Davis Jr.			
❏ 7301 [PS]	I Wish I'd Met You/ When I Fall in Love	1989	$4
UNITED ARTISTS			
❏ 1661 [DJ]	Let It Snow! Let It Snow! Let It Snow! (same on both sides)	1966	$8
—Silver Spotlight Series promo			
❏ 1661 [DJ]	Let It Snow! Let It Snow! Let It Snow! (same on both sides)	1966	$8
—Silver Spotlight Series promo			
❏ 1661	Let It Snow! Let It Snow! Let It Snow!/What Are You Doing New Year's Eve	1966	$12
—Silver Spotlight Series			
❏ 50051	Love Bug/Wonder What I'm Gonna Do	1966	$8
❏ 851	Pleasures and Palaces/ Feeling Good	1965	$8
❏ 911	The Sand and the Sea/ Softly, As I Leave You	1965	$8

7-Inch Extended Plays

Number	Title	Yr	NM
RCA CAMDEN			
❏ CAE380 [PS]	Lena Horne Sings the Blues	1956	$15
❏ CAE380	St. Louis Blues/Beale Street Blues//Aunt Hagar's Blues/ Careless Love Blues	1956	$15
RCA VICTOR			
❏ EPA-4038	Ain't It De Truth?/Take It Slow, Joe//Cocoanut Sweet/Push De Button	1957	$20
❏ VLP2587	I've Grown Accustomed to His Face/I Concentrate on You/I Found a New Baby//I Surrender, Dear/I Let a Song Go Out of My Heart/I Want to Be Happy	1963	$15
—Jukebox issue; small hole, plays at 33 1/3 rpm			
❏ EPBT-3061 [PS]	Lena Horne Sings	1954	$25
—Gatefold cover for 2-EP set (947-0164, 947-0165)			
❏ VLP2587 [PS]	Lena...Lovely and Alive	1963	$15
❏ 947-0164	Moanin' Low/I Gotta Right to Sing the Blues/The Man I Love/Where or When	1954	$25
—Silver label, red print; part of 2-EP set EPBT-3061			
❏ 947-0165	Stormy Weather/Ill Wind// Mad About the Boy/What Is This Thing Called Love?	1954	$25
—Silver label, red print; part of 2-EP set EPBT-3061			

HORNETS, THE

Number	Title	Yr	NM
COLUMBIA			
❏ 42999	Fruit Cake/Seven Days to Tahiti	1964	$70
FLASH			
❏ 125	Crying Over You/ Tango Moon	1957	$250
LIBERTY			
❏ 55688	Motorcycle U.S.A./ On the Track	1964	$40

Number	Title	Yr	NM
REV			
❏ 3515	Slow Dance/Strollin'	1958	$30
STATES			
❏ 127	I Can't Believe/ Lonesome Baby	1953	$8000
—Black vinyl. VG 4000; VG+ 6000			
❏ 127	I Can't Believe/ Lonesome Baby	1953	$15000
—Red vinyl. VG 7500; VG+ 10000			
V.I.P.			
❏ 25004	She's My Baby/ Give Me a Kiss	1964	$70

HORNSBY, BRUCE, AND THE RANGE

Number	Title	Yr	NM
RCA			
❏ 8776-7-R	Defenders of the Flag/ On the Western Skyline	1988	$4
❏ 5165-7-R	Every Little Kiss (Remix)/ Mandolin Rain (Live)	1987	$3
❏ PB-14361	Every Little Kiss/ The Red Plains	1986	$5
❏ 8678-7-R	Look Out Any Window/ The Way It Is	1988	$3
❏ 8678-7-R [PS]	Look Out Any Window/ The Way It Is	1988	$3
❏ 5087-7-R	Mandolin Rain/The Red Plains	1987	$3
❏ 5087-7-R [PS]	Mandolin Rain/The Red Plains (Live)	1987	$3
❏ 8340-7-R	The Way It Is/Mandolin Rain	1988	$3
—Gold Standard Series			
❏ 5023-7-R	The Way It Is/The Wild Frontier	1986	$3

HORSE FEATHERS
7-Inch Extended Plays

Number	Title	Yr	NM
ROWENA			
❏ 1287	Get Your Reindeer Off My Roof/How Ya Do That, Santa Claus?//Do You Remember Me, Santa?/Me, My Dog 'N My Cat 'N My Bird	1987	$4
—7-inch 33 1/3 rpm			
❏ 1287 [PS]	Get Your Reindeer Off My Roof/How Ya Do That, Santa Claus?//Do You Remember Me, Santa?/Me, My Dog 'N My Cat 'N My Bird	1987	$4

HORTON, BILLIE JEAN

Number	Title	Yr	NM
20TH FOX			
❏ 291	Devoted to You/Octopus	1961	$20
❏ 238	I'd Give the World (To Have You Back Again)/Angel Eyes	1961	$20
❏ 266	Ocean of Tears/Don't Take His Love	1961	$20
ABC-PARAMOUNT			
❏ 10332	Tell Him I Can't See Him Anymore/I'd Rather You Didn't Love Me	1962	$20
ATLANTIC			
❏ 2249	I Know I'll Never See Him Again/Johnny Come Lately	1964	$20

HORTON, JAY

Number	Title	Yr	NM
MUSTANG			
❏ 3010	I Trip on You Girl/ (B-side unknown)	1965	$40
❏ 3021	It's Love/Come What May	1966	$40

HORTON, JOHNNY

Number	Title	Yr	NM
ABBOTT			
❏ 103	Birds and Butterflies/Coal Smoke, Valve Oil and Steam	1951	$50
❏ 100	Candy Jones/ Devilish Lovelight	1951	$50
❏ 104	Go and Wash (Those Dirty Feet)/In My Home in Shelby County	1951	$50
❏ 101	Happy Millionaire/Mean Mean Son of a Gun	1951	$50
❏ 107	Long Rocky Road/On the Banks of the Beautiful Nile	1952	$50
❏ 102	Plaid and Calico/ Done Roving	1951	$50
—B-side by Bill Thompson's Westerners			
❏ 135	Plaid and Calico/Shadows on the Old Bayou	1953	$40
❏ 105	Shadows on the Old Bayou/Talk Gobbler Talk	1951	$50
❏ 106	Smokey Joe's Barbeque/Words	1951	$50
❏ 108	Somebody Rocking in My Broken Chair/Betty Lorraine	1952	$50
—With Hillbilly Barton			
COLUMBIA			
❏ S731107 [S]	All for the Love of a Girl/ Sink the Bismarck	1961	$30
❏ 41210	All Grown Up/ Counterfeit Love	1958	$30
❏ 42653	All Grown Up/I'm a One Woman Man	1962	$15

Number	Title	Yr	NM
❏ 42653 [PS]	All Grown Up/I'm a One Woman Man	1962	$30
❏ S731108 [S]	Comanche (The Brave Horse)/Jim Bridger	1961	$30
—The above five are "Stereo Seven" 33 1/3 rpm jukebox singles from "JS7-28" entitled "Johnny Horton's Greatest Hits"			
❏ 41110	Honky Tonk Hardwood Floor/The Wild One	1958	$70
❏ 21504	Honky Tonk Man/I'm Ready If You're Willing	1956	$40
❏ 42302	Honky Tonk Man/Words	1962	$20
❏ 42302 [PS]	Honky Tonk Man/Words	1962	$30
❏ 42993	Hooray for That Little Difference/Tell My Baby I Love Her	1964	$10
❏ 42993 [PS]	Hooray for That Little Difference/Tell My Baby I Love Her	1964	$30
❏ 40986	I'll Do It Every Time/Let's Take the Long Way Home	1957	$30
❏ 21538	I'm a One Woman Man/I Don't Like I Did	1956	$30
❏ 40813	I'm Coming Home/I Got a Hole in My Picture	1957	$40
❏ 41502	I'm Ready If You're Willing/ Take Me Like I Am	1959	$20
❏ 43143	Lost Highway/The Same Old Tale the Crow Told Me	1964	$10
❏ 42063	Ole Slewfoot/Miss Marcy	1961	$15
❏ 42063 [PS]	Ole Slewfoot/Miss Marcy	1961	$30
❏ 43719	Sam Magee/All for the Love of a Girl	1966	$8
❏ 40919	She Knows Why/The Woman I Need	1957	$30
❏ 41568	Sink the Bismarck/ The Same Old Tale the Crow Told Me	1960	$15
❏ 41568 [PS]	Sink the Bismarck/ The Same Old Tale the Crow Told Me	1960	$30
❏ 30568 [S]	Sink the Bismarck/ The Same Old Tale the Crow Told Me	1960	$30
—Stereo Single 33"; small hole, plays at 33 1/3 rpm			
❏ 41963	Sleepy Eyed John/ They'll Never Take Her Love from Me	1961	$15
❏ 41963 [PS]	Sleepy Eyed John/ They'll Never Take Her Love from Me	1961	$30
❏ 42774	Sugar Coated Baby/ When It's Springtime in Alaska (It's Forty Below)	1963	$10
❏ 41339	The Battle of New Orleans/ All for the Love of a Girl	1959	$20
❏ 41339 [PS]	The Battle of New Orleans/ All for the Love of a Girl	1959	$30
—Red and black print sleeve with lyrics			
❏ 41339 [PS]	The Battle of New Orleans/ All for the Love of a Girl	1959	$70
—Promo-only four-page booklet sleeve			
❏ 44156	The Battle of New Orleans/ All for the Love of a Girl	1967	$6
❏ 41522	They Shined Up Rudolph's Nose/The Electrified Donkey	1959	$20
❏ 41522 [PS]	They Shined Up Rudolph's Nose/The Electrified Donkey	1959	$125
❏ 41308	When It's Springtime in Alaska (It's Forty Below)/ Whispering Pines	1958	$20
❏ 41308 [PS]	When It's Springtime in Alaska (It's Forty Below)/ Whispering Pines	1958	$40
—Promo-only black and white sleeve			
❏ S731106 [S]	When It's Springtime in Alaska/The Battle of New Orleans	1961	$30
CORMAC			
❏ 1197	Birds and Butterflies/Coal Smoke, Valve Oil and Steam	1951	$120
❏ 1193	Plaid and Calico and Done Roving	1951	$120
DOT			
❏ 15966	Plaid and Calico/Shadows on the Old Bayou	1959	$15
MERCURY			
❏ 70227	All for the Love of a Girl/ Broken Hearted	1953	$40
❏ 70707	Big Wheels Rollin'/Hey Sweet, Sweet Thing	1955	$40
❏ 70014	I Won't Forget/The Child's Side of Life	1952	$40
❏ 70325	Move On Down the Line/ Train with the Rhumba Beat	1954	$40
❏ 70156	S.S. Loveline/I Won't Get Dreamy-Eyed	1953	$40
❏ 70100	Tennessee Jive/The Mansion You Stole	1953	$40
❏ 6412	The Devil Sent Me You/ First Train Headin' South	1952	$40
❏ 70399	The Door of Your Mansion/ Ha Ha and Moonface	1954	$40

7-Inch Extended Plays

Number	Title	Yr	NM
COLUMBIA			
❏ B-13623	All for the Love of a Girl/ The Golden Rocket// Mr. Moonlight/Got the Bull by the Horns	1960	$15

Number	Title	Yr	NM
❏ B-13621	The Battle of New Orleans/ Whispering Pines// The First Train Heading South/Lost Highway	1960	$15

HOSEA, DON
SUN

Number	Title	Yr	NM
❏ 368	Since I Met You/Uh Huh Unh	1961	$30

HOSFORD, LARRY
SHELTER

| ❏ 40381 | Everything's Broken Down/ Long Line to Chicago | 1975 | $5 |
| ❏ 40312 | Long Distance Kisses/ Long Line to Chicago | 1974 | $5 |

WARNER BROS.

| ❏ 8445 | Home Run Willie/Salinas | 1977 | $5 |

HOT BUTTER
MUSICOR

❏ 1466	Apache/Hot Butter	1972	$5
❏ 1473	Percolator/Tristana	1973	$5
❏ 1491	Pipeline/Apache	1974	$5
❏ 1458	Popcorn/At the Movies	1972	$6
❏ 1481	Slay Solution/Kappi Maki	1973	$5
❏ 1468	Tequila/Hot Butter	1972	$5

HOT CHOCOLATE
APPLE

| ❏ 1812 | Give Peace a Chance/ Living Without Tomorrow | 1969 | $10 |
| *—As "Hot Chocolate Band"* | | | |

BIG TREE

❏ 16038	Disco Queen/Makin' Music	1975	$5
❏ 16060	Don't Stop It Now/ Beautiful Lady	1976	$5
❏ 16031	Emma/A Love Like Yours	1975	$5
❏ 16078	Heaven Is in the Back Seat of My Cadillac/ (B-side unknown)	1976	$5
❏ 16101	Man to Man/Brother Louie	1977	$5
❏ 16096	So You Win Again/Part of Being with You	1977	$5

EMI AMERICA

| ❏ 8143 | Are You Getting Enough Happiness/One Night's Not Enough | 1982 | $4 |
| ❏ 8157 | Bed Games/It Started with a Kiss | 1983 | $4 |

INFINITY

❏ 50002	Every 1's a Winner/ Power of Love	1978	$4
❏ 50016	Going Through the Motions/Don't Turn It Off	1979	$4
❏ 50033	I Just Love What You're Doing/Congas Man	1979	$4
❏ 50048	Mindless Boogie/Dance (Get Down To It)	1979	$4

RAK

❏ 4515	Brother Louie/I Want to Be Free	1973	$6
❏ 4506	I Believe in Love/ Caveman Billy	1972	$6
❏ 4508	Mary Anne/Ruth	1972	$6

HOT TUNA
Offshoot of JEFFERSON AIRPLANE.
GRUNT

❏ PB-10443	Hot Jellyroll Blues/ Surphase Tension	1975	$5
❏ PB-10776	It's So Easy/I Can't Be Satisfied	1976	$5
❏ 65-0502	Water Song/Keep On Truckin'	1972	$6
❏ 65-0502 [PS]	Water Song/Keep On Truckin'	1972	$15

RCA VICTOR

| ❏ 74-0528 | Candy Man/Been So Long | 1971 | $6 |
| ❏ 74-0528 [PS] | Candy Man/Been So Long | 1971 | $30 |

HOUND DOG CLOWNS
UNI

| ❏ 55047 | Superfox/Wicked Witch | 1968 | $30 |

HOUR GLASS, THE
LIBERTY

❏ 56053	D-I-V-O-R-C-E/Changing of the Guard	1968	$15
❏ 56002	Heartbeat/Nothing But Tears	1967	$15
❏ 56091	I've Been Trying/Silently	1969	$15
❏ 56029	Power of Love/I Still Want Your Love	1968	$15
❏ 56065	She Is My Woman/ Going Nowhere	1968	$15

HOUSEKEEPERS, THE
CLONE

| ❏ CS13 [B] | I Gotta Know/ Down the Road | 1981 | $20 |

HOUSEMARTINS, THE
ELEKTRA

Number	Title	Yr	NM
❏ 69436	Caravan of Love/When I First Met Jesus	1987	$3
❏ 69436 [PS]	Caravan of Love/When I First Met Jesus	1987	$3
❏ 69491	Flag Day/The Mighty Ship	1987	$5
❏ 69491 [PS]	Flag Day/The Mighty Ship	1987	$5
❏ 69515	Happy Hour/The Mighty Ship	1986	$5
❏ 69515 [PS]	Happy Hour/The Mighty Ship	1986	$5

HOUSTON, DAVID, AND JOY FORD
COUNTRY INT'L.

| ❏ 146 | (Making the Best of) A Bad Situation/(B-side unknown) | 1980 | $5 |

HOUSTON, DAVID, AND BARBARA MANDRELL
EPIC

❏ 10656	After Closing Time/ My Song of Love	1970	$8
❏ 10908	A Perfect Match/ Almost Persuaded	1972	$8
❏ 11068	I Love You, I Love You/ Let's Go Down Together	1973	$6
❏ 11120	Lovin' You Is Worth It/ How Can It Be Wrong	1974	$6
❏ 20005	Ten Commandments of Love/Try a Little Harder	1974	$6
❏ 10779	We've Got Everything But Love/Try a Little Harder	1971	$8

HOUSTON, DAVID, AND TAMMY WYNETTE
EPIC

| ❏ 10274 | It's All Over/Together We Stand | 1967 | $10 |
| ❏ 10194 | My Elusive Dreams/ Marriage on the Rocks | 1967 | $10 |

HOUSTON, DAVID
COLONIAL

| ❏ 101 | Waltz of the Angels/ (B-side unknown) | 1978 | $8 |

COUNTRY INT'L.

❏ 220	A Penny for Your Thoughts Tonight Virginia/ (B-side unknown)	1989	$6
❏ 155	Bandera Waltz/ (B-side unknown)	1981	$6
❏ 148	Sad Love Song Lady/Thanks for Being You and Loving Me	1980	$6
❏ 149	The Bottom Line/We Couldn't Make It Love	1980	$6

DERRICK

| ❏ 127 | Here's to All the Hard Working Husbands (In the World)/Next Sunday I'm Gonna Be Saved | 1979 | $6 |
| ❏ 126 | Let Your Love Fall Back on Me/Take Me to Your Heart | 1979 | $6 |

ELEKTRA

❏ 45552	Best Friends Make the Worst Enemies/There Won't Be a Wedding	1978	$4
❏ 46028	Faded Love and Winter Roses/ Beyond the Blue Horizon	1979	$4
❏ 45513	Sunday I'm Gonna Be Saved/Waltz of the Angels	1978	$4

EPIC

❏ 10025	Almost Persuaded/We Got Love	1966	$8
❏ 10102	A Loser's Cathedral/Where Could I Go? (But to Her)	1966	$6
❏ 10102 [PS]	A Loser's Cathedral/Where Could I Go? (But to Her)	1966	$10
❏ 10338	Already It's Heaven/ Lighter Shade of Pale	1968	$6
❏ 10338 [PS]	Already It's Heaven/ Lighter Shade of Pale	1968	$10
❏ 50066	A Man Needs Love/ Flower of Love	1975	$5
❏ 10696	A Woman Always Knows/ The Rest of My Life	1970	$6
❏ 10539	Baby, Baby (I Know You're a Lady)/True Love's a Lasting Thing	1969	$6
❏ 50009	Can't You Feel It/I Walk and I Walk and I Walk	1974	$5
❏ 9658	Chickashay/Passing Through	1964	$8
❏ 50275	Come On Down (To Our Favorite Forget-About-Her Place)/Me and Susan Wright	1976	$5
❏ 10939	Good Things/The Love She Gives	1973	$6
❏ 10291	Have a Little Faith/Too Far Gone	1968	$6
❏ 10291 [PS]	Have a Little Faith/Too Far Gone	1968	$12
❏ 10596	I Do My Swinging at Home/ Then I'll Know You Care	1970	$6
❏ 50113	I'll Be Your Steppin' Stone/ Then I'll Know You Care	1975	$5
❏ 10488	I'm Down to My Last "I Love You"/Watching My World Walk Away	1969	$6
❏ 10911	I Wonder How John Felt (When He Baptized Jesus)/ Will the Circle Be Unbroken	1972	$8
❏ 9831	Livin' in a House Full of Love/Cowpoke	1965	$8
❏ 9720	Love Looks Good on You/My Little Lady	1964	$8
❏ 50241	Lullaby Song/White Circle	1976	$5

Number	Title	Yr	NM
❏ 10778	Maiden's Prayer/ Home Sweet Home	1971	$6
❏ 9625	Mountain of Love/Angeline	1963	$8
❏ 10430	My Woman's Good to Me/ Lullaby to a Little Girl	1968	$6
❏ 9690	One If For Him, Two If For Me/Your Memories	1964	$8
❏ 9884	Sammy/I'll Take You Home Again, Kathleen	1966	$8
❏ 9884 [PS]	Sammy/I'll Take You Home Again, Kathleen	1966	$10
❏ 10995	She's All Woman/Sweet Lovin'	1973	$5
❏ 10870	Soft, Sweet and Warm/ The Rest of My Life	1972	$6
❏ 9746	Sweet, Sweet Judy/Too Many Times (Away from You)	1964	$8
❏ 50134	Sweet Molly/Old Blind Fiddler	1975	$5
— With Calvin Crawford			
❏ 11096	That Same Ol' Look of Love/Clinging Vine	1974	$5
❏ 10830	The Day That Love Walked In/Sweet Lovin'	1972	$6
❏ 11048	The Lady of the Night/ Thank You Teardrop	1973	$5
❏ 50156	The Woman on My Mind/I Can't Sit Still	1975	$5
❏ 50186	What a Night/From the Bottom of My Heart	1976	$5
❏ 10394	Where Love Used to Live/I Love a Rainbow	1968	$6
❏ 10154	With One Exception/ Sweet, Sweet Judy	1967	$6
❏ 10154 [PS]	With One Exception/ Sweet, Sweet Judy	1967	$10
❏ 10643	Wonders of the Wine/ If God Can Forgive Me	1970	$6

EXCELSIOR

❏ 1015	After All/(B-side unknown)	1981	$4
❏ 1007	My Lady/Something You've Never Heard	1981	$5
❏ 1012	Texas Ida Red/(B-side unknown)	1981	$6

GUSTO

❏ 162	Ain't That Lovin' You Baby/ Love Is a Mystery	1977	$6
❏ 172	It Started All Over Again/ Touch My World	1977	$6
❏ 156	So Many Ways/Touch My World	1977	$6
❏ 168	The Twelfth of Never/ Barroom Champagne	1977	$6

IMPERIAL

| ❏ 8291 | I'm Sorry I Made You Cry/Blue Prelude | 1955 | $50 |

NRC

| ❏ 047 | It's Been So Long/Kalua | 1959 | $30 |
| ❏ 05 | Waited So Long/All I Do Is Dream of You | 1958 | $30 |

PHILLIPS INTERNATIONAL

| ❏ 3583 | Sherry's Lips/Miss Brown | 1961 | $40 |

RCA VICTOR

❏ 47-6696	Blue Prelude/I'll Always Have It on My Mind	1956	$40
❏ 47-6927	One and Only/Hackin' Around	1957	$60
❏ 47-6837	Someone Else's Arms/Ain't Going There No More	1957	$40
❏ 47-6611	Sugar Sweet/Hasta Luego	1956	$40
❏ 47-7001	The Teenage Frankie and Johnny/I'll Follow	1957	$40

SOUNDWAVES

| ❏ 4712 | E.T. Still Means Ernest Tubb to Me/One Good Cry Away from Happiness | 1982 | $4 |

SUN

| ❏ 403 | Sherry's Lips/Miss Brown | 1966 | $30 |
| ❏ 1127 | Sherry's Lips/Miss Brown | 1972 | $8 |

7-Inch Extended Plays
EPIC

❏ 5-26213 [PS]	Almost Persuaded	1966	$15
❏ 5-26342	Almost Persuaded/A Loser's Cathedral/With One Exception// You Mean the World to Me/I'll Take You Home Again, Kathleen/Where Could I Go	1968	$10
—Jukebox issue; small hole, plays at 33 1/3 rpm			
❏ 5-26213	Almost Persuaded/Ramblin' Rose/From a Jack to a King// Tonight You Belong to Me/Don't Mention Tomorrow/Little Pedro	1966	$15
—Jukebox issue; small hole, plays at 33 1/3 rpm			
❏ 5-26391 [PS]	Already It's Heaven	1968	$12
❏ 5-26391	Already It's Heaven/Release Me/I Love You So Much It Hurts//Have a Little Faith/ Gentle on My Mind/Just A Little Lovin' (Will Go a Long Way)	1968	$10
—Jukebox issue; small hole, plays at 33 1/3 rpm			
❏ 5-26432	Before You Travel On/The One Rose That's Left My Heart//Lullaby to a Little Girl// My Woman's Good to Me/I Walk Alone/Sweet Lovin'	1969	$10
—Jukebox issue; small hole, plays at 33 1/3 rpm			
❏ 5-26342 [PS]	David Houston's Greatest Hits	1968	$12
❏ 5-26432 [PS]	Where Love Used to Live/ My Woman's Good to Me	1969	$12

Number	Title	Yr	NM

HOUSTON, JOHNNY
EVENT
| ❏ 4277 | Slick Chick/Playboy | 1959 | $40 |
| ❏ 4280 | Torrid Tessie Lee/ Our Very First Kiss | 1959 | $40 |

HOUSTON, SOLDIER BOY
ATLANTIC
| ❏ 971 | Western Rider Blues/ Hug Me Baby | 1952 | $250 |

HOUSTON, THELMA
ABC DUNHILL
| ❏ 11 [DJ] | Everybody Gets to Go to the Moon (same on both sides) | 1969 | $20 |

— Special Apollo 11 promotional item

| ❏ 11 [DJ] | Everybody Gets to Go to the Moon (same on both sides) | 1969 | $20 |

— Special Apollo 11 promotional item

| ❏ 11 [PS] | Everybody Gets to Go to the Moon (same on both sides) | 1969 | $30 |

— Special Apollo 11 promotional item

❏ 4222	Save the Country/I Just Can't Stay Away	1970	$8
❏ 4197	Sunshower/If This Was the Last Song	1969	$10
❏ 4260	The Good Earth/ Ride, Louie, Ride	1970	$8

CAPITOL
| ❏ 5767 | Baby Mine/Woman Behind Her Man | 1966 | $200 |
| ❏ 5882 | Don't Cry, My Soldier Boy/ Let's Try to Make It | 1967 | $60 |

MCA
❏ 52489	(I Guess) It Must Be Love/ Running in Circles	1984	$3
❏ 52491	Love Is a Dangerous Game/ You Used to Hold Me So Tight	1984	$3
❏ 52239	Make It Last/Just Like All the Rest	1983	$3
❏ 52582	What a Woman Feels Inside/ Fantasy and Heartbreak	1985	$3
❏ 52196	Working Girl/Running in Circles	1983	$3

MOTOWN
❏ 1260	Do You Know Where You're Going/Together	1973	$5
❏ 1245	I'm Just a Part of Yesterday/Piano Man	1973	$5
❏ 1385	The Bingo Long Song/ Razzle Dazzle	1976	$5

— B-side by William Goldstein

| ❏ 1385 [PS] | The Bingo Long Song/ Razzle Dazzle | 1976 | $15 |

— B-side by William Goldstein

MOWEST
❏ 5050	I'm Just a Part of Yesterday/Piano Man	1973	$6
❏ 5008	I Want to Go Back There Again/Pick Up the Week	1972	$6
❏ 5013	Me and Bobby McGee/No One's Gonna Be a Fool Forever	1972	$6
❏ 5023	Piano Man/Me and Bobby McGee	1972	$6
❏ 5027	What If/There Is a Fool	1972	$6

RCA
❏ PB-12285	96 Tears/There's No Runnin' Away from Love	1981	$4
❏ PB-12215	If You Feel It/Hollywood	1981	$4
❏ PB-11913	Suspicious Minds/Gone	1980	$5

TAMLA
❏ 54278 [DJ]	Don't Leave Me This Way (Long Version)/Don't Leave Me This Way (Short Version)	1977	$6
❏ 54278 [DJ]	Don't Leave Me This Way (Long Version)/Don't Leave Me This Way (Short Version)	1977	$6
❏ 54278	Don't Leave Me This Way (Short Version)/Today Will Soon Be Yesterday	1977	$4
❏ 54292	I Can't Go On Living Without Your Love/Any Way You Like It	1978	$4
❏ 54283	If It's the Last Thing I Do/If You Won't Let Me Walk on the Water	1977	$4
❏ 54287	I'm Here Again/Sharin' Something Perfect	1977	$4
❏ 54295	I'm Not Strong Enough to Love You/Triplin'	1978	$4
❏ 54275	One Out of Every Six (Censored)/Pick of the Week	1976	$10
❏ 54297	Saturday Night, Sunday Morning/Come to Me	1979	$30

HOUSTON, WHITNEY
ARISTA
❏ 9616	Didn't We Almost Have It All/Shock Me	1987	$3
❏ 9616 [PS]	Didn't We Almost Have It All/Shock Me	1987	$3
❏ 9466	Greatest Love of All/ Thinking About You	1986	$3
❏ 9466 [PS]	Greatest Love of All/ Thinking About You	1986	$3
❏ 9434	How Will I Know/ Someone for Me	1985	$3
❏ 9434 [PS]	How Will I Know/ Someone for Me	1985	$3
❏ 9598	I Wanna Dance with Somebody (Who Loves Me)/Moment of Truth	1987	$3
❏ 9598 [PS]	I Wanna Dance with Somebody (Who Loves Me)/Moment of Truth	1987	$3
❏ 9720	Love Will Save the Day/ How Will I Know	1988	$3
❏ 9720 [PS]	Love Will Save the Day/ How Will I Know	1988	$3
❏ 9743	One Moment in Time/ Love Is a Contact Sport	1988	$3
❏ 9743 [PS]	One Moment in Time/ Love Is a Contact Sport	1988	$3
❏ 9381	Saving All My Love for You/All at Once	1985	$3
❏ 9381 [PS]	Saving All My Love for You/All at Once	1985	$3
❏ 9642	So Emotional/For the Love of You	1987	$3
❏ 9642 [PS]	So Emotional/For the Love of You	1987	$3
❏ 9412	Thinking About You/ Someone for Me	1985	$4
❏ 9412 [PS]	Thinking About You/ Someone for Me	1985	$4
❏ 9674	Where Do Broken Hearts Go/Where Are You	1988	$3
❏ 9674 [PS]	Where Do Broken Hearts Go/Where Are You	1988	$3

HOWARD, CHUCK
ABC
| ❏ 11105 | Great Dreams/What the Robin Gonna Do | 1968 | $10 |

BOONE
| ❏ 1057 | Anywhere the Wind Blows/ Please Stay with Me | 1967 | $20 |
| ❏ 1049 | Easy to Say, Hard to Do/You Don't Have Time for Me | 1966 | $20 |

COLUMBIA
| ❏ 4-43194 | After My Laughter Came Tears/I Hope You Hear Sad Songs | 1964 | $20 |
| ❏ 4-43329 | I Want to Hear It from You/ Searching for Baby | 1965 | $20 |

FLAME
| ❏ 1020 | Gossip/(B-side unknown) | 1959 | $200 |

FRATERNITY
| ❏ 923 | Don't Let Them Move/ Thing Called Sadness | 1964 | $15 |

JOY
| ❏ 238 | Let Me Walk You Home, Jeanette/Congratulations to You | 1960 | $20 |

MONUMENT
| ❏ 916 | Someone Please Cry/ What Does He Do | 1966 | $30 |

NEW STAR
| ❏ 120 | Don't Let Them Move/ Thing Called Sadness | 1964 | $30 |

PORT
| ❏ 70002 | Crazy Crazy Baby/Can't You Tell | 1958 | $70 |

SAND
| ❏ 266 | Crazy Crazy Baby/Can't You Tell | 1958 | $125 |

VIVA
| ❏ 29499 | Suddenly Single/ Wedding Prayer | 1983 | $4 |

WARNER BROS.
❏ 49625	Easy to Say, Hard to Do/ Love Won't Work	1980	$4
❏ 49509	I've Come Back (To Say I Love You One More Time)/ Everyone But Me	1980	$4
❏ 49719	Thing Called Sadness/ Beginnings	1981	$4

HOWARD, EDDY
MERCURY
| ❏ 70513 | All of You/I'll Wrap You in My Arms | 1954 | $15 |
| ❏ 5433 | American Beauty Rose/ Seems Like Only Yesterday | 1950 | $20 |

—Note: Earlier Eddy Howard releases on Mercury may exist on 45.

❏ 70135	Am I Loving You/Almost Always	1953	$15
❏ 5567	A Penny a Kiss -- A Penny a Hug/I Still Feel the Same About You	1951	$20
❏ 5590	Around the World/ That's All That's Left	1951	$20
❏ 5871	Auf Wiederseh'n Sweetheart/I Don't Want to Take a Chance	1952	$20
❏ 5663	(A Woman Is a) Deadly Weapon/I'm in Love Again	1951	$20
❏ 5815	Be Anything (But Be Mine)/She Took	1952	$20
❏ 70301	Bimbo/Call Me Darling	1954	$15
❏ 70989	Confidential/Tiger Lily	1956	$10
❏ 5475	Daddy's Little Boy/They Put the Lights Out	1950	$20
❏ 5578	Daddy's Little Girl/ Daddy's Little Boy	1951	$20
❏ 71072	Delia's Gone/Love Me a Little Bit	1957	$12
❏ 71008	Driftwood/The Hour of Love	1956	$12
❏ 70272	Ebenezer Scrooge/Bimbo	1953	$20
❏ 70107	Gomen Nasai (Forgive Me)/Someone to Kiss Your Tears Away	1953	$15
❏ 70475	Happy Birthday/ Anniversary Waltz	1954	$20
❏ 5678	Hello Young Lovers/ We Kiss in a Shadow	1951	$20
❏ 5516	I'll Be Home for Christmas/ Dearest Santa	1950	$20
❏ 5697	I'm Cryin'/Put All Your Kisses in an Envelope	1951	$20
❏ 5490	I'm Forever Blowing Bubbles/Red We Want	1950	$20
❏ 5748	It's All Over But the Memories/Chances Are	1951	$20
❏ 5711	It's No Sin/My Wife and I	1951	$30
❏ 70015	It's Worth Any Price You Pay/Kentucky Babe	1952	$15
❏ 71773	I Want You to Want Me to Want You/Just a Year Ago Tonight	1961	$10
❏ 70293	Little Miss One/Till We Two Are One	1954	$15
❏ 70176	Love Every Moment That You Live/The Right Way	1953	$15
❏ 70467	Love Me Tonight/You're Always Welcome Home	1954	$15
❏ 5898	Mademoiselle/I Don't Know Any Better	1952	$20
❏ 70304	Melancholy Me/I Wonder What's Become of Sally	1954	$15
❏ 5791	My Adobe Hacienda/Wishin'	1952	$20
❏ 5453	My Heart Isn't In It/I Do Better in the Mountains	1950	$20
❏ 70533	Old Memories/Finger of Suspicion	1955	$15
❏ 5623	One Kind Word/How Thoughtful of You	1951	$20
❏ 5491	Patricia/So Long, Sally	1950	$20
❏ 5439	Put Your Arms Around Me Honey/Lassus Trombone	1950	$20
❏ 70134	Say You're Mine Again/ Broken Wings	1953	$15
❏ 5832	Singing in the Rain/All I Do Is Dream of You	1952	$20
❏ 5711	Sin/My Wife and I	1951	$20

— Revised A-side title

❏ 5771	Stolen Love/I'll See You in My Dreams	1952	$20
❏ 70225	That's the Price I Paid for You/Skirts	1953	$15
❏ 5837	The Family That Prays Together/(B-side unknown)	1952	$20
❏ 70639	The Man from Laramie/ The Three of Us	1955	$15
❏ 5752	There's a Christmas Tree/ Auld Lang Syne	1951	$20
❏ 70700	The Teen-Agers' Waltz/ Choo Choo Cha Cha	1955	$15
❏ 5517	To Think You've Chosen Me/The One Rose	1950	$20
❏ 70881	Whatever Will Be, Will Be/ You Can't Keep Running	1956	$10
❏ 5630	What Will I Tell My Heart/ The Strange Little Girl	1951	$20
❏ 5576	When You Return/Little Small Town Girl	1951	$20
❏ 70800	Why Is Your Dog Following Me/Rustic Old Cathedral	1956	$10
❏ 70566	Words of Love/Forevermore	1955	$15

HOWARD, HARLAN
CAPITOL
❏ 4813	I Ain't Got Nobody/ Ramblin' Son of a Gun	1962	$30
❏ 4612	Legion of the Lost/We're Proud to Call Him Son	1961	$30
❏ 4928	My Baby's His Baby Now/ Someday Sweetheart	1963	$30
❏ 4682	She Called Me Baby/ Wishin' She Was Here	1962	$30

MONUMENT
❏ 919	Another Bridge to Burn/Baby, That Would Sure Go Good	1966	$15
❏ 907	Busted/The Everglades	1965	$15
❏ 864	Hobo Jungle/The Deepening Snow	1964	$20
❏ 883	How Slow Time Goes/ What's Left of Me	1965	$15
❏ 833	I Can't Stand It/It's All in Your Mind	1964	$20
❏ 1207	Look Behind You/ Too Many Rivers	1970	$10
❏ 849	Time to Bum Again/Previews of Coming Attractions	1964	$20

NUGGET
| ❏ 1058 | Sunday Morning Christian/That Little Boy Who Follows Me | 1971 | $10 |

RCA VICTOR
❏ 47-9252	I'd Rather Be a Fool/ Take It and Go	1967	$10
❏ 47-9352	It's Nothin' to Me/Home from the Forest	1967	$10
❏ 47-9535	Where Were You When I Was Young/Old Podner	1968	$10

HOWARD, JAN
CAPITOL
| ❏ 4987 | Dime a Dozen/I Can't Stop Crying | 1963 | $15 |

Number	Title	Yr	NM
❑ 5122	I Walked a Hundred Miles/I'm Here to Get My Baby Out of Jail	1964	$15
❑ 5035	I Wish I Was a Single Girl Again/The Saddest Part of All	1963	$15
❑ 4869	Looking Back/See One Broken Heart	1962	$15
❑ 4744	Please Pass the Kisses/Tomorrow You Won't Even Know My Name	1962	$15
❑ 4918	Wind Me Up (I Cry)/You've Got Me Where You Want Me	1963	$15

CHALLENGE

Number	Title	Yr	NM
❑ 59106	All Alone Again/Too Many Teardrops Too Late	1961	$20
❑ 59094	A World I Can't Live In/I've Got My Pride	1960	$20
❑ 9125	Bring It On Back to Me/My Baby's in Berlin	1961	$20
❑ 9112	Careless Hands/Let Me Know	1961	$20
❑ 59080	If Your Conscience Can't Stop You/Many Dreams Ago	1960	$20
❑ 59059	The One You Slip Around With/I Wish I Could Fall in Love Again	1959	$20
❑ 59361	The One You Slip Around With/Jealous Love	1967	$10

CON BRIO

Number	Title	Yr	NM
❑ 125	Better Off Alone/My Coloring Book	1977	$6
❑ 118	I'll Hold You in My Heart (Till I Can Hold You in My Arms)/Thought I Had Her	1977	$6
❑ 132	To Love a Rolling Stone/Thought I Had Him	1978	$6

DECCA

Number	Title	Yr	NM
❑ 32096	Any Old Way You Do/Your Ole Handy Man	1967	$10
❑ 32778	Baby Without You/Marriage Has Ruined More Good Love Affairs	1971	$8
❑ 32016	Bad Seed/You Go Your Way (I'll Go Crazy)	1966	$12
❑ 32269	Count Your Blessings, Woman/But Not for Love My Dear	1968	$8
❑ 32822	Dallas You've Won/Love Is a Sometimes Thing	1971	$8
❑ 31933	Evil on Your Mind/Crying for Love	1966	$10
❑ 31858	I Don't Mind/You Don't Find a Good Man Every Day	1965	$10
❑ 32357	I Still Believe in Love/Life's That Way	1968	$8
❑ 31791	I've Got Feelings Too!/What Do You Want Now	1965	$10
❑ 32955	Let Him Have It/Remember the Good	1972	$8
❑ 32905	Love Is Like a Spinning Wheel/I Never Once Stopped Loving You	1971	$8
❑ 32407	My Son/The Tip of My Fingers	1968	$8
❑ 32743	The Soul You Never Had/I Have Your Love	1970	$8
❑ 32543	We Had All the Good Things Going/I'll Go Where You Go	1969	$8
❑ 31701	What Makes a Man Wander?/Slipping Back to You	1964	$10
❑ 32447	When We Tried/I Hurt All Over	1969	$8

GRT

Number	Title	Yr	NM
❑ 019	Get It While the Gettin's Good/I'm All Right 'Til I See You	1975	$6
❑ 010	Seein' Is Believin'/My Kind of People	1974	$6
❑ 024	Wedding Song/You'll Never Know	1975	$6

MCA

Number	Title	Yr	NM
❑ 40020	Too Many Ties That Bind/Everybody Knows I Love You	1973	$6

HOWARD, JIM

DEL-MAR

Number	Title	Yr	NM
❑ 1013	Meet Me Tonight Outside of Town/Too Much Taking -- Not Enough Giving	1964	$20

HOWARD, RONNIE

BIG TOP

Number	Title	Yr	NM
❑ 3093	If Santa Fell/Give My Toy to the Boy Next Door	1961	$20

HOWELL, REUBEN

MOTOWN

Number	Title	Yr	NM
❑ 1325	Constant Disappointment/I Believe	1974	$10
❑ 1274	When You Take Another Chance on Love/You Can't Stop a Man in Love	1973	$30
❑ 1274 [PS]	When You Take Another Chance on Love/You Can't Stop a Man in Love	1973	$40

HOWL THE GOOD

RARE EARTH

Number	Title	Yr	NM
❑ 5045	Long Way from Home/Why Do You Cry	1972	$8

HOWLIN' WOLF

CADET CONCEPT

Number	Title	Yr	NM
❑ 7013	Evil/Tail Dragger	1969	$8

CHESS

Number	Title	Yr	NM
❑ 1870	300 Pounds of Joy/Built for Comfort	1963	$30
❑ 1557	All Night Boogie/I Love My Baby	1953	$300
❑ 2145	Back Door Wolf/Coon on the Moon	1973	$8
❑ 1607	Come to Me Baby/Don't Mess with My Baby	1955	$50
❑ 1844	Do the Do/Mama's Baby	1962	$30
❑ 2118	Do the Do/Red Rooster	1971	$8
❑ 1648	Goin' Back Home/My Life	1957	$50
❑ 1726	Howlin' Blues/I Better Go Now	1959	$50
❑ 1575	How Long/Evil Is Going On	1954	$125
❑ 1632	I Asked for Water/So Glad	1956	$50
❑ 2009	I Had a Dream/Pop It to Me	1967	$20
❑ 1584	I'll Be Around/Forty Four	1955	$60
❑ 1712	I'm Leaving You/Change My Way	1959	$50
❑ 2108	I Smell a Rat/Just As Long	1971	$8
❑ 1945	I Walked from Dallas/Don't Laugh at Me	1965	$20
❑ 1793	Little Baby/Down in the Bottom	1961	$40
❑ 1911	Love Me Darlin'/My Country Sugar Mama	1964	$30
❑ 2081	Mary Sue/Hard Luck	1970	$8
❑ 1695	Moaning for My Baby/I Didn't Know	1958	$50
❑ 1735	Mr. Airplane Man/I've Been Abused	1959	$50
❑ 1528	Oh! Red/My Last Affair	1952	$700

— Note: Howlin' Wolf releases on Chess before 1528 are unknown on 45 rpm

Number	Title	Yr	NM
❑ 1679	Sittin' On Top of the World/Poor Boy	1958	$50
❑ 1618	Smoke Stack Lightning/You Can't Be Beat	1956	$50
❑ 1668	Somebody in My Home/Nature	1957	$50
❑ 1762	Spoonful/Howlin' for My Baby	1960	$40
❑ 1890	Tail Dragger/Hidden Charms	1964	$30
❑ 1928	Tell Me What I've Done/Ooh Baby	1965	$20
❑ 1777	Wang Dang Doodle/Back Door Man	1961	$40
❑ 1593	Who Will Be Next/I Have a Little Girl	1955	$50

RPM

Number	Title	Yr	NM
❑ 347	My Baby Stole Off/I Want Your Picture	1952	$2400

— VG 800; VG+ 1600

Number	Title	Yr	NM
❑ 340	Passing By Blues/Crying at Daybreak	1952	$3000

— Note: Howlin' Wolf releases on RPM before 340 are unknown on 45 rpm. VG 1000; VG+ 2000

7-Inch Extended Plays

CHESS

Number	Title	Yr	NM
❑ 7-LPS-1469 [PS]	Howlin' Wolf	1963	$250
❑ 7-LPS-1469	Tell Me/Who's Been Talkin'/Spoonfull//Shake for Me/Goin' Down Slow/Down in the Bottom	1963	$125

— Stereo jukebox issue; small hole, plays at 33 1/3 rpm; we don't know if these tracks are true stereo or rechanneled stereo

HUBCAPS, THE

LAURIE

Number	Title	Yr	NM
❑ 3219	Hot Rod City (Vocal)/Hot Rod City (Instrumental)	1964	$20

HUDDLE, JACK

KAPP

Number	Title	Yr	NM
❑ 207	Starlight/Believe Me	1959	$200

— Buddy Holly plays guitar on these tracks

PETSY

Number	Title	Yr	NM
❑ 1002	Starlight/Believe Me	1958	$500

HUDSON AND LANDRY

DORE

Number	Title	Yr	NM
❑ 868	Ajax Airlines/Bruiser La Rue	1972	$10
❑ 855	Ajax Liquor Store/The Hippie and the Redneck	1971	$10
❑ 881	Ajax Mortuary/Ajax Pet Store	1973	$10
❑ 880	Frontier Christmas (Harlowe and The Mrs.)/The Soul Bowl	1972	$10
❑ 874	Obscene Phone Bust/The Prospectors	1972	$10
❑ 879	Soul Bowl/Friar Shuck	1972	$12
❑ 891	The Chocolate Freak/The Fate of the Mightiest Nation	1973	$12
❑ 895	The Gas Man/Sir Basil	1974	$10
❑ 852	The Hippie and the Redneck/Top 40 DJ's	1971	$10
❑ 898	The Weird Kingdom/Montague for President	1974	$10

HUDSON BROTHERS, THE

ARISTA

Number	Title	Yr	NM
❑ 0208	Help Wanted/Last Time I Looked	1976	$5
❑ 0286	I Don't Wanna Be Lonely/Pauline	1977	$5

CASABLANCA

Number	Title	Yr	NM
❑ 816	Me and My Guitar/Coochie Coochie Coo	1975	$5

Number	Title	Yr	NM
❑ 0108	So You Are a Star/Ma Ma Ma Baby	1974	$6

— With long version of A-side

Number	Title	Yr	NM
❑ 801	So You Are a Star/Ma Ma Ma Baby	1974	$5

— With short version of A-side

COLUMBIA

Number	Title	Yr	NM
❑ 03976	Don't Try to Fight It/You Keep Me Up	1983	$4

— As "The Hudsons

DECCA

Number	Title	Yr	NM
❑ 32634	Love Is a Word/Laugh, Funny, Funny	1970	$6

— As "Everyday Hudson

ELEKTRA

Number	Title	Yr	NM
❑ 47049	Afraid to Love/Sidewalk	1980	$4

— As "Hudson

Number	Title	Yr	NM
❑ 46648	Annie/Joni	1980	$4

— As "Hudson

LIONEL

Number	Title	Yr	NM
❑ 3211	Love Nobody/The World Would Be a Little Bit Better	1971	$6

— As "Hudson

PLAYBOY

Number	Title	Yr	NM
❑ 50001	Someday/Leavin' It's Over	1972	$6

ROCKET

Number	Title	Yr	NM
❑ 40141	America -- Fight Back/If You Really Need Me	1973	$6

— As "Hudson

Number	Title	Yr	NM
❑ 40141 [PS]	America -- Fight Back/If You Really Need Me	1973	$10
❑ 40464	Lonely School Year/If You Really Need Me	1975	$5
❑ 40464 [PS]	Lonely School Year/If You Really Need Me	1975	$8
❑ 40508	Spinning the Wheel (With the Girl You Love)/Bernie Was a Friend of Ours	1976	$5
❑ 40317	Sunday Driver/Be a Man	1974	$6

HUDSON, POOKIE

DOUBLE L

Number	Title	Yr	NM
❑ 720	I Love You For Sentimental Reasons/Miracles	1963	$30

JAMIE

Number	Title	Yr	NM
❑ 1319	This Gets To Me/All the Places I've Been	1966	$70

HUDSON, ROCK

DECCA

Number	Title	Yr	NM
❑ 30966	Pillow Talk/Roly Poly	1959	$20
❑ 30966 [PS]	Pillow Talk/Roly Poly	1959	$30

HUES CORPORATION, THE

LIBERTY

Number	Title	Yr	NM
❑ 56204	Goodfootin'/We're Keepin' Our Business Together	1970	$6

— As "The Hughes Corporation

RCA VICTOR

Number	Title	Yr	NM
❑ 74-0900	Freedom for the Stallion/Off My Cloud	1973	$5
❑ APBO-0139	Go to the Poet/Miracle Maker	1973	$5
❑ PB-10200	Love Corporation/He's My Home	1975	$5
❑ PB-10311	One Good Night Together/When You Look Down the Road	1975	$5
❑ 74-0813	There He Is Again/Main Chance	1972	$5

WARNER BROS.

Number	Title	Yr	NM
❑ 8559	Give Me Everything/Needed	1978	$4
❑ 8400	I Caught Your Act/Natural Find	1977	$4
❑ 8638	Love Dance/With All My Love and Affection	1978	$4
❑ 8454	Telegram of Love/Dancing Together Again	1977	$4
❑ 8454 [PS]	Telegram of Love/Dancing Together Again	1977	$8

HUGHES, CAROL

CARLTON

Number	Title	Yr	NM
❑ 571	Hello Heartbreak/If She's Right for You	1962	$12

DOT

Number	Title	Yr	NM
❑ 15923	Bobby/Sholem Aleichem	1959	$15
❑ 15863	Don't Forget I Love You/The Bass	1958	$15

MERCURY

Number	Title	Yr	NM
❑ 70986	Mine All Mine/Fancy Dance	1956	$20
❑ 71095x45	My Big Brother's Friend/Lover Boy	1957	$20

RCA VICTOR

Number	Title	Yr	NM
❑ 47-7763	Congratulations/I Can Tell	1960	$15
❑ 47-7726	Creation/Love, Kisses and Heartaches	1960	$15
❑ 47-7605	Goin' to the Dogs/Staying Young	1959	$30
❑ 47-7617	It's Me, It's Me, It's Me/I Must Have Done Something Wonderful	1959	$30

Number	Title	Yr	NM
❏ 47-7665	Let Me Go Lover/When Did I Fall in Love	1960	$15

ROULETTE

Number	Title	Yr	NM
❏ 4041	Lend Me Your Comb/First Date	1958	$20
❏ 4032	Pick Another Baby/ Never Go 'Way	1957	$20

HUGHES, JIMMY

FAME

Number	Title	Yr	NM
❏ 1014	Don't Lose Your Good Thing/You Can't Believe Everything That You Hear	1967	$12
❏ 6407	Goodbye My Lover, Goodbye/It Was Nice	1965	$30
❏ 1015	Hi-Heel Sneakers/Time Will Bring You Back	1967	$30
❏ 6404	I Want Justice/I'm Getting Better	1964	$10
❏ 1006	I Worship the Ground You Walk On/A Shot of Rhythm and Blues	1966	$30
❏ 1000	Midnight Affair/When It Comes to Dancing	1965	$30
❏ 6401	Steal Away/Lollipops, Lace and Lipstick	1964	$10

— Black label

Number	Title	Yr	NM
❏ 6401	Steal Away/Lollipops, Lace and Lipstick	1964	$15

— Red label

Number	Title	Yr	NM
❏ 6403	Try Me/Lovely Ladies	1964	$10
❏ 1011	Why Not Tonight/I'm a Man of Action	1967	$30

GUYDEN

Number	Title	Yr	NM
❏ 2075	I'm Qualified/My Loving Time	1962	$50

JAMIE

Number	Title	Yr	NM
❏ 1280	I'm Qualified/My Loving Time	1964	$30

VOLT

Number	Title	Yr	NM
❏ 4017	Chains of Love/I'm Not Ashamed to Beg or Plead	1969	$20
❏ 4002	I Like Everything About You/ What Side of the Door	1968	$8
❏ 4024	I'm So Glad/Lay It on the Line	1969	$8
❏ 4008	Let 'Em Down Baby/The Sweet Things You Do	1969	$8

HUGHES, MARJORIE

COLUMBIA

Number	Title	Yr	NM
❏ 1-571	Over the Mountain, Under the Moon/Let's Stay Home Tonight	1950	$40

— Microgroove 7-inch 33 1/3 rpm single, small hole

HULLABALLOOS, THE

ROULETTE

Number	Title	Yr	NM
❏ 4593	Beware/Did You Ever	1965	$30
❏ 4593 [PS]	Beware/Did You Ever	1965	$50
❏ 4587	I'm Gonna Love You Too/Party Doll	1964	$30
❏ 4587 [PS]	I'm Gonna Love You Too/Party Doll	1964	$50
❏ 4622	I Won't Turn Around Now/ My Heart Keeps Telling Me	1965	$30
❏ 4622 [PS]	I Won't Turn Around Now/ My Heart Keeps Telling Me	1965	$50
❏ 4612	Learning the Game/Don't Stop	1965	$30
❏ 4612 [PS]	Learning the Game/Don't Stop	1965	$50

HUMAN BEINZ, THE

CAPITOL

Number	Title	Yr	NM
❏ 2198	Every Time Woman/The Face	1968	$12
❏ 2431	I've Got to Keep On Pushin'/ This Little Girl of Mine	1969	$10
❏ 2119	Turn On Your Love Light/ It's Fun to Be Clean	1968	$10
❏ 2119 [PS]	Turn On Your Love Light/ It's Fun to Be Clean	1968	$30

GATEWAY

Number	Title	Yr	NM
❏ 828	Gloria/The Times They Are a-Changin'	1967	$20

HUMAN EXPRESSION, THE

ACCENT

Number	Title	Yr	NM
❏ 1226	Calm Me Down/Optical Sound	1967	$125
❏ 1214	Every Night/Love at Psychedelic Velocity	1967	$200
❏ 1252	I Don't Need Nobody/Sweet Child of Nothingness	1967	$125

HUMAN LEAGUE

A&M

Number	Title	Yr	NM
❏ 2934	Are You Ever Coming Back?/Jam	1987	$6
❏ 2650	Don't You Know I Want You/Thirteen	1984	$6
❏ 2508	Don't You Want Me/ (Instrumental)	1982	$6

— B-side by "League Unlimited Orchestra

Number	Title	Yr	NM
❏ 2397	Don't You Want Me/Seconds	1982	$3
❏ 2397 [PS]	Don't You Want Me/Seconds	1982	$5
❏ 2861	Human/(Instrumental)	1986	$3
❏ 2861 [PS]	Human/(Instrumental)	1986	$3
❏ 2893	I Need Your Loving/Are You Ever Coming Back?	1986	$3

Number	Title	Yr	NM
❏ 2893 [PS]	I Need Your Loving/Are You Ever Coming Back?	1986	$15
❏ 2661 [DJ]	Life on Your Own (same on both sides)	1984	$12

— No stock copies issued

Number	Title	Yr	NM
❏ 2657	Louise/The World Tonight	1984	$5
❏ 2425	Love Action (I Believe in Love)/Hard Times	1982	$4
❏ 2425 [PS]	Love Action (I Believe in Love)/Hard Times	1982	$5
❏ 2918	Love Is All That Matters/ (Instrumental)	1987	$5
❏ 2587	Mirror Man/Non-Stop	1983	$3
❏ 2587 [PS]	Mirror Man/Non-Stop	1983	$4
❏ 2641	The Lebanon/Thirteen	1984	$3
❏ 2641 [PS]	The Lebanon/Thirteen	1984	$4
❏ 2449	Things That Dreams Are Made Of/(Instrumental)	1982	$6

— B-side by "League Unlimited Orchestra

HUMBLE PIE

Also see PETER FRAMPTON; STEVE MARRIOTT.

A&M

Number	Title	Yr	NM
❏ 1406	Black Coffee/Say No More	1973	$4
❏ 1406 [PS]	Black Coffee/Say No More	1973	$15
❏ 1440	Honky Tonk Woman/ Get Down to It	1973	$4
❏ 1349	Hot and Nasty/You're So Good for Me	1972	$4
❏ 1349 [PS]	Hot and Nasty/You're So Good for Me	1972	$6
❏ 1282	I Don't Need No Doctor/ Song for Jenny	1971	$4
❏ 1282 [PS]	I Don't Need No Doctor/ Song for Jenny	1971	$6
❏ 1484	Oh La De Da/The Out Crowd	1974	$4
❏ 1366	Sweet Peace and Time/30 Days in the Hole	1972	$4

ATCO

Number	Title	Yr	NM
❏ 7216	Fool for a Pretty Face/ You Soppy Pratt	1980	$5

HUMOROUS DIAN

VELTONE

Number	Title	Yr	NM
❏ 712	Interview with Mr-K/The Three Hep Piggies	1961	$40

HUMPERDINCK, ENGELBERT

EPIC

Number	Title	Yr	NM
❏ 50899	A Chance to Be a Hero/ Any Kind of Love at All	1980	$3
❏ 50270	After the Lovin'/Let's Remember the Good Times	1976	$5
❏ 50447	A Lover's Holiday/Look at Me	1977	$4
❏ 50692	Can't Help Falling in Love/You Know Me	1979	$4
❏ AE71170 [DJ]	Christmas Song/Silent Night	1978	$4
❏ AE71170 [PS]	Christmas Song/Silent Night	1978	$4
❏ 50933	Don't Cry Out Loud/ Don't Touch That Dial	1980	$3
❏ 02060	Don't You Love Me Anymore/ Till I Get It Right	1981	$3
❏ 50365	I Believe in Miracles/ Goodbye My Friend	1977	$4
❏ 50958	It's Not Easy to Live Together/Royal Affair	1980	$3
❏ 50566	Love Me Tender/This Time One Year Ago	1978	$4
❏ 50579	Love's In Need of Love Today/Sweet Marjorene	1978	$4
❏ 50844	Love's Only Love/ Burning Ember	1980	$3
❏ 50732	Lovin' Too Well/Much, Much Greater Love	1979	$4
❏ 02245	Maybe This Time/When the Night Ends	1981	$3
❏ 50526	The Last of the Romantics/I Have Paid the Toll	1978	$4
❏ 50632	This Moment in Time/ And the Day Begins	1978	$4
❏ 03817	Till You and Your Lover Are Lovers Again/What Will I Write	1983	$3

HICKORY

Number	Title	Yr	NM
❏ 1337	Baby Turn Around/If I Could Do the Things I Want to Do	1965	$20

— As "Gerry Dorsey

PARROT

Number	Title	Yr	NM
❏ 40027	A Man Without Love/Call on Me	1968	$8
❏ 40065	Another Time, Another Place/ You're the Window of My World	1971	$6
❏ 40079	Catch Me I'm Falling/ Love, Oh Precious Love	1974	$4
❏ 40082	Forever and Ever/ Precious Love	1974	$4
❏ 40077	Free as the Wind/My Friend the Wind	1974	$4
❏ 40040	I'm a Better Man/Cafe	1969	$6
❏ 40073	I'm Leavin' You/My Summer Song	1973	$4
❏ 40072	I Never Said Goodbye/ Time After Time	1972	$5
❏ 40071	In Time/How Does It Feel	1972	$5
❏ 40032	Les Bicyclettes De Belsize/ Three Little Words	1968	$8
❏ 40032 [PS]	Les Bicyclettes De Belsize/ Three Little Words	1968	$15
❏ 40076	Love Is All/Lady of the Night	1973	$4

Number	Title	Yr	NM
❏ 40049	My Marie/Our Song (La Paloma)	1970	$6
❏ 40049 [PS]	My Marie/Our Song (La Paloma)	1970	$8
❏ 40054	Sweetheart/Born to Be Wanted	1970	$6
❏ 40054 [PS]	Sweetheart/Born to Be Wanted	1970	$8
❏ 40019	The Last Waltz/That Promise	1967	$8
❏ 40019 [PS]	The Last Waltz/That Promise	1967	$15
❏ 40015	There Goes My Everything/You Love	1967	$8
❏ 40036	The Way It Used to Be/A Good Thing Going	1969	$6
❏ 40036 [PS]	The Way It Used to Be/A Good Thing Going	1969	$10
❏ 40085	This Is What You Mean to Me/A World Without Music	1975	$4
❏ 40069	Too Beautiful to Last/A Hundred Times a Day	1972	$5
❏ 40059	When There's No You/ Stranger, Step In My World	1971	$6
❏ 40059 [PS]	When There's No You/ Stranger, Step In My World	1971	$8
❏ 40044	Winter World of Love/ Take My Heart	1969	$6
❏ 40044 [PS]	Winter World of Love/ Take My Heart	1969	$10

7-Inch Extended Plays

Number	Title	Yr	NM
❏ SBG77	Café/A Time for Us/Didn't We// Aquarius-Let the Sunshine In/ The Signs of Love/Love Letters	1969	$8

— Stereo jukebox issue; small hole, plays at 33 1/3 rpm

Number	Title	Yr	NM
❏ SBG73 [PS]	Engelbert	1969	$8
❏ SBG77 [PS]	Engelbert Humperdinck	1969	$8
❏ SBG82	Help Me Make It Through the Night/My Prayer/You'll Never Walk Alone/My Wife the Dancer/Just a Little Bit of You/It's Impossible	1971	$8

— Jukebox issue; small hole, plays at 33 1/3 rpm

Number	Title	Yr	NM
❏ SBG82 [PS]	Live at the Riviera, Las Vegas	1971	$8
❏ SBG73	Love Can Fly/Let Me Into Your Life/Through the Eyes of Love//Marry Me/To Get to You/You're Easy to Love	1969	$8

— Stereo jukebox issue; small hole, plays at 33 1/3 rpm

Number	Title	Yr	NM
❏ SBG80 [PS]	We Made It Happen	1970	$8

HUNGER

PUBLIC

Number	Title	Yr	NM
❏ 1001	Colors/(B-side unknown)	1969	$40
❏ 101	Mind Machine/(B-side unknown)	1968	$30

HUNS, THE

GOD

Number	Title	Yr	NM
❏ 01	Busy Kids/Glad He's Dead	1979	$125
❏ 01 [PS]	Busy Kids/Glad He's Dead	1979	$125

— Oversized sleeve with insert

HUNT, DANNY

DYNAMITE

Number	Title	Yr	NM
❏ 8663	What's Happening to Our Love Affair/(B-side unknown)	1974	$30

HUNT, GERALDINE

ABC

Number	Title	Yr	NM
❏ 10859	Winner Take All/For Lovers Only	1966	$500

BOMBAY

Number	Title	Yr	NM
❏ 4501	(Two Can Live) Cheaper Than One/He's for Real	1964	$300

— Yellow label

Number	Title	Yr	NM
❏ 4501	(Two Can Live) Cheaper Than One/He's for Real	1964	$200

— Black label

CHECKER

Number	Title	Yr	NM
❏ 1028	I Let Myself Go/I Wished I Had Listened	1962	$50

PRISM

Number	Title	Yr	NM
❏ 315	Can't Fake the Feeling/ (B-side unknown)	1980	$4
❏ 323	Heart Heart/(B-side unknown)	1981	$4

ROULETTE

Number	Title	Yr	NM
❏ 7129	Baby, I Need Your Loving/ (B-side unknown)	1972	$12
❏ 7132	Cold Blood/Just Believe in Me	1972	$40

U.S.A.

Number	Title	Yr	NM
❏ 732	Sneak Around/It Never Happened Before	1962	$40
❏ 737	Sneak Around/It Never Happened Before	1963	$30

HUNTER, IAN

Also see MOTT THE HOOPLE.

CHRYSALIS

Number	Title	Yr	NM
❏ 2569	Central Park 'N' West/ (B-side unknown)	1981	$4
❏ 2352	Cleveland Rocks/ Just Another Night	1979	$5
❏ 2542	I Need Your Love/ (B-side unknown)	1981	$4

Number	Title	Yr	NM
❏ 2405	We Gotta Get Out of Here/ Sons and Daughters	1980	$4
❏ 2324	When the Daylight Comes/ Life After Death	1979	$5

COLUMBIA

❏ 03929	All of the Good Ones Are Taken/Death 'N' Glory Boys	1983	$4
❏ 10161	Once Bitten Twice Shy/3000 Miles from Here	1975	$6
❏ 04166	Seeing Double/That Girl Is Rock 'N' Roll	1983	$4

HUNTER, IVORY JOE

4 STAR

❏ 1634	Foolish Pride/Did You Mean It	1953	$50

ATLANTIC

❏ 1164	All About the Blues/If Only You Were Here with Me	1957	$30
❏ 1086	A Tear Fell/I Need You By My Side	1956	$30
❏ 1128	Empty Arms/Love's a Hurting Game	1957	$30
❏ 2020	I Just Want to Love You/ Now I Don't Worry No More	1959	$20
❏ 1183	I'm So Glad I Found You/Shooty Booty	1958	$20
❏ 1049	It May Sound Silly/I Got to Learn to Do the Mambo	1954	$30
❏ 1066	I Want Somebody/Heven Came Down to Earth	1955	$30
❏ 1151	She's Gone/Everytime I Hear That Song	1957	$30
❏ 1111	Since I Met You Baby/You Can't Stop This Rocking and Rolling	1956	$40

CAPITOL

❏ 4587	I'm Hooked/Because I Love You	1961	$15
❏ 4648	May the Best Man Win/You Better Believe It Baby	1961	$15
❏ 4688	The Life I Live/A Great Big Heart Full of Love	1962	$15

DOT

❏ 15880	City Lights/Stolen Moments	1958	$20
❏ 15957	I Love You So Much/ Welcome Home Baby	1959	$20
❏ 15986	My Search Was Ended/ Did You Mean It	1959	$20
❏ 15930	Old Fashioned Love/ Cottage for Sale	1959	$20

EPIC

❏ 10725	Heartbreak and Misery/I'm Coming Down with the Blues	1971	$6
❏ 10725	Heartbreak and Misery/We All Like That Groovy Feeling	1971	$6

GOLDISC

❏ 3010	It's Love, It's Love, It's Love/ You Satisfy Me Baby	1960	$20

GOLDWAX

❏ 307	Every Little Bit Helped Me/I Can Make You Happy	1966	$30

KING

❏ 4424	False Friend Blues/ Send Me Pretty Mama	1951	$50

—*Ivory Joe Hunter records on King before 4422 are unconfirmed on 45 rpm*

❏ 5280	Guess Who/Don't Fall in Love with Me	1959	$20
❏ 4455	Old Gal and New Gal Blues/Woo Wee Blues	1951	$50
❏ 4443	She's Gone Blues/Stop Rockin' That Train	1951	$50

MGM

❏ K11325	Big Bounce/Tell Her for Me	1952	$40
❏ K11132	Blue Moon/U Name It	1952	$40
❏ K11818	Do You Miss Me/Whose Arms Are You Missing	1954	$30
❏ K10578	I Almost Lost My Mind/ If I Give You My Love	1949	$50
❏ 8011	I Almost Lost My Mind/ If I Give You My Love	1949	$60

—*Original 45 issue of this record*

❏ K10951	I Can't Get You Off My Mind/I Can't Resist You	1951	$40
❏ K10899	I Found My Baby/I Ain't Got No Gal	1951	$40
❏ K11263	I Get That Lonesome Feeling/I Thought I Had Loved	1952	$40
❏ K11459	I Had a Girl/If You See My Baby	1953	$40
❏ K11702	I Have a Secret/I Feel So Good	1954	$30
❏ K11549	I'm Afraid/Don't Make Me Cry	1953	$40
❏ K11195	I'm Sorry for You My Friend/I Will Be	1952	$40
❏ K11599	I Must Be Talking to Myself/ My Best Wishes	1953	$40
❏ K11052	I'm Yours/Wrong Woman Blues	1951	$40
❏ K10663	I Need You So/Leave Her Alone	1950	$40
❏ K10818	It's A Sin/Don't You Believe Me	1950	$40
❏ K11165	Laugh/Where Shall I Go	1952	$40
❏ K10733	Let Me Dream/Gimme a Pound of Round Ground	1950	$40
❏ K10761	Old Man's Boogie/Living a Lie	1950	$40
❏ K10618	S.P. Blues/Why Fool Yourself	1950	$40

PARAMOUNT

❏ 0253	He'll Never Love You/ San Antonio Rose	1973	$6

Number	Title	Yr	NM

SMASH

❏ 1825	My Arms Are Waiting/ Congratulations	1963	$15
❏ 1860	There's No Forgetting You/ My Lover's Prayer	1963	$15

SOUND STAGE 7

❏ 2623	Ivory Tower/I'll Give You All Night to Stop	1968	$8
❏ 2643	Straighten Up Baby/ Baby Me Baby	1969	$8

STAX

❏ 155	This Kind of Woman/Can't Explain Why It Happened	1964	$15

VEE JAY

❏ 452	Somebody's Stealing My Love/You Only Want Me When You Need Me	1962	$15

VEEP

❏ 1270	Did She Ask About Me/From the First Time We Met	1967	$8
❏ 1258	What's the Matter Baby/ Don't You Believe Me	1967	$8

7-Inch Extended Plays

ATLANTIC

❏ EP608	*Empty Arms/Love's a Hurting Game/She's Gone/ Everytime I Hear That Song	1958	$75
❏ EP589	*Since I Met You Baby/I Got to Learn to Do the Mambo/It May Sound Silly/A Tear Fell	1958	$60
❏ EP589 [PS]	Ivory Joe Hunter (Since I Met You Baby)	1958	$60

KING

❏ 265	(contents unknown)	1954	$100
❏ 265 [PS]	Ivory Joe Hunter	1954	$100

MGM

❏ X-1376	(contents unknown)	1957	$60
❏ X-1378	(contents unknown)	1957	$60
❏ X-1376 [PS]	I Get That Lonesome Feeling, Volume 1	1957	$60
❏ X-1377 [PS]	I Get That Lonesome Feeling, Volume 2	1957	$60
❏ X-1378 [PS]	I Get That Lonesome Feeling, Volume 3	1957	$60
❏ X-1377	I Get That Lonesome Feeling/I Found a New Baby/I Need You So/If You See My Baby	1957	$60

HUNTER, TAB

DOT

❏ 15657	Don't Let It Get Around/I'm Alone Because I Love You	1957	$30
❏ 16355	I Can't Stop Loving You/Born to Lose	1962	$20
❏ 15767	I'm a Runaway/It's All Over Town	1958	$30
❏ 16187	My Devotion/You Cheated	1961	$20
❏ 16264	The Way You Look Tonight/You Cheated	1961	$20
❏ 16205	Wild Side of Life/My Devotion	1961	$20

WARNER BROS.

❏ 5160	Again/Love Is Just Around the Corner	1960	$30
❏ 5160 [PS]	Again/Love Is Just Around the Corner	1960	$30
❏ 5021	Candy/My Baby Just Cares for Me	1958	$30
❏ 5032 [M]	I'll Be With You in Apple Blossom Time/What Can I Give My Only Love	1959	$30
❏ S-5032 [S]	I'll Be With You in Apple Blossom Time/What Can I Give My Only Love	1959	$30
❏ 5093	Our Love/Waitin' for Fall	1959	$30
❏ 5093 [PS]	Our Love/Waitin' for Fall	1959	$30
❏ 5051 [M]	There's No Fool Like a Young Fool/I'll Never Smile Again	1959	$30
❏ S-5051 [S]	There's No Fool Like a Young Fool/I'll Never Smile Again	1959	$30
❏ 5051 [PS]	There's No Fool Like a Young Fool/I'll Never Smile Again	1959	$30

7-Inch Extended Plays

❏ EA1221 [M]	(contents unknown)	1958	$25
❏ ESB1221 [S]	(contents unknown)	1959	$30
❏ EA1221 [PS]	Tab Hunter	1958	$25
❏ ESB1221 [PS]	Tab Hunter	1959	$30

HUNTER, TOMMY

COLUMBIA

❏ 4-44104	In a Way/Cup of Disgrace	1967	$8
❏ 4-44234	Mary in the Morning/The Battle of the Little Big Horn	1967	$8

HUNTER, TY

ANNA

❏ 1114	Everything About You/ Orphan Boy	1960	$30
❏ 1123	Every Time/I'm Free	1960	$40

CHECK MATE

❏ 1015	Gladness to Sadness/ Lonely Baby	1961	$30
❏ 1002	Memories/The Envy of Every Man	1961	$30

Number	Title	Yr	NM

CHESS

❏ 1881	Am I Losing You/Love Walked Right Out on Me	1964	$20
❏ 1893	Bad Loser/Something Like a Storm	1964	$20
❏ 1857	Darling, My Babe/In Time	1963	$30

INVICTUS

❏ 9120	Hey There Lonely Girl/I Don't See Me in Your Eyes Anymore	1972	$20

HURRICANES, THE

KING

❏ 4947	Dear Mother/You May Not Know	1956	$120
❏ 5018	Fallen Angel/I'll Always Be in Love with You	1957	$125
❏ 4926	Little Girl of Mine/Your Promise to Me	1956	$200
❏ 4867	Maybe It's All for the Best/Yours	1956	$200
❏ 4817	Poor Little Dancin' Girl/ Pistol Packin' Mama	1955	$200
❏ 5042	Priceless/Now That I Need You	1957	$125

HUSKER DU

Also see BOB MOULD; SUGAR.

NEW ALLIANCE

❏ 010	In a Free Land/What Do I Want/M.I.C.	1982	$75
❏ 010 [PS]	In a Free Land/What Do I Want/M.I.C.	1982	$60

REFLEX

❏ 0A	Statues/Amusement (Live)	1980	$50
❏ 0A [PS]	Statues/Amusement (Live)	1980	$70

SST

❏ PSST 031 [DJ]	Celebrated Summer/ New Day Rising	1984	$20
❏ PSST 031 [PS]	Celebrated Summer/ New Day Rising	1984	$20

—*Rubber-stamped sleeve with sticker and enclosed press release*

HUSKY, FERLIN

4 STAR

❏ 1572	Crying Heart Blues/If You Don't Believe I'm Leaving (Just Count the Days I'm Gone)	1951	$50
❏ 1516	Guilty Feeling/Road to Heaven	1950	$60

—*All 4 Star records as "Terry Preston"; it's possible that not all these exist on 45s*

❏ 1542	Irma/Put Me in Your Pocket	1950	$60
❏ 1518	Let's Keep the Communists Out/The Sabbath	1950	$60
❏ 1566	Wise Guy/Cross Eyed Gal from the Ozarks	1951	$50

ABC

❏ 11381	Baby's Blue/One	1973	$6
❏ 11360	Between Me and Blue/ My Special Angel	1973	$6
❏ 12085	Burning/A Touch of Yesterday	1975	$5
❏ 12048	Champagne Ladies and Blue Ribbon Babies/I Feel Better All Over	1974	$5
❏ 12020	Drinkin' Man/Cuzz Yore So Sweet	1974	$6

—*As "Simon Crum*

❏ 11432	Freckles and Polliwog Days/Everything Is Nothing Without You	1974	$6
❏ 11345	True True Lovin'/A Legend in My Time	1973	$6

ABC DOT

❏ 17574	An Old Memory (Got in My Eye)/She's Not Yours Anymore	1975	$5

CAPITOL

❏ F3742	A Fallen Star/Prize Possession	1957	$15
❏ F3270	A Hillbilly Deck of Cards/ Ooh I Want You	1955	$30

—*As "Simon Crum*

❏ F3428	Aladdin's Lamp/That Big Old Moon	1956	$20
❏ F3316	A Sinful Secret/Slow Down Brother	1956	$20
❏ 4548	Before I Lose My Mind/ What Good Will I Ever Be	1961	$15
❏ F4278	Black Sheep/I'll Always Return	1959	$15
❏ F3460	Bop Cat Bop/Muki Ruki	1956	$30

—*As "Simon Crum*

❏ F1861	China Doll/Tennessee Central #9	1951	$30
❏ 2023	Christmas Dream/ Christmas Is Holy	1967	$8
❏ F2105	Counting My Heartaches/I Love You	1952	$30

—*As "Terry Preston*

❏ 4464	Country Music Fiddler/I Feel Better All Over	1960	$20

—*As "Simon Crum*

❏ F4073	Country Music Is Here to Stay/Stand Up, Sit Down, Shut Your Mouth	1958	$30

—*As "Simon Crum*

❏ F3063	Cuzz Yore So Sweet/My Gallina	1955	$30

—*As "Simon Crum*

Number	Title	Yr	NM
❑ F3233	Dear Mr. Brown/I'll Be Here for a Lifetime	1955	$20
❑ 4966	Don't Be Mad/Little Red Webb	1963	$15
—As "Simon Crum			
❑ F3183	Don't Blame the Children/ Saith the Lord	1955	$20
❑ F4186	Draggin' the River/Sea Sand	1959	$15
❑ F2814	Each Time You Leave/Deceived	1954	$30
—As "Terry Preston			
❑ F2746	Eli the Camel/Somebody Lied	1954	$30
❑ 4499	Enormity in Motion/ Cuzz Yore So Sweet	1961	$20
—As "Simon Crum			
❑ 2666	Every Step of the Way/ That's What I'd Do	1969	$8
❑ 5067	Face of a Clown/Love Looks Good on You	1963	$10
❑ 2411	Flat River, Mo./One Life to Live	1969	$8
❑ F3628	Gone/Missing Persons	1957	$20
❑ F2298	Gone/Out of Reach	1952	$40
—As "Terry Preston			
❑ F2397	Hank's Song/I'll Never Have You	1953	$30
❑ 2793	Heavenly Sunshine/All My Little Loving Ways	1970	$6
❑ 3415	How Could You Be Anything But Love/I'd Walk a Mile for a Smile	1972	$6
❑ F2558	How Much Are You Mine/ You'll Die a Thousand Deaths	1953	$30
❑ 5615	I Could Sing All Night/ What Does Your Conscience Say to You	1966	$10
❑ F3001	I Feel Better All Over (More Than Anywhere's Else)/Little Tom	1954	$20
❑ 5679	I Hear Little Rock Calling/ Stand Beside Me	1966	$10
❑ F3097	I'll Baby Sit with You/ She's Always There	1955	$20
❑ F2211	I'm Only Wishing/Are You Afraid	1952	$30
—As "Terry Preston			
❑ 2154	I Promised You the World/ You Should Live My Life	1968	$8
❑ F4000	I Saw God/I Feel That Old Heartache Again	1958	$15
❑ 4853	It Was You/Near You	1962	$10
❑ F2467	I've Got a Woman's Love/ Watch the Company You Keep	1953	$30
—As "Terry Preston			
❑ F1947	I Want You So/Time	1952	$30
—As "Terry Preston			
❑ F4046	I Will/All of the Time	1958	$15
❑ F3790	Make Me Live Again/ This Moment of Love	1957	$15
❑ F2495	Mini Ha Cha/I Lost My Love Today	1953	$30
❑ 5522	Money Greases the Wheels/Lasting Love	1965	$10
❑ F4252	Morgan Poisoned the Water Hole/I Fell Out of Love with You	1959	$20
—As "Simon Crum			
❑ F2391	My Foolish Heart/Undesired	1953	$30
—As "Terry Preston			
❑ 4343	My Love for You/Asi Es La Vida	1960	$15
❑ F4123	My Reason for Living/Wrong	1959	$15
❑ 5775	Once/Why Do I Put Up with You	1966	$10
❑ 3069	One More Time/Don't Let the Good Life Pass You By	1971	$6
❑ 3165	Open Up the Book (And Take a Look)/Even If It's True	1971	$6
❑ 4721	Somebody Save Me/Just Another Lonely Night	1962	$12
❑ 4779	Stand Up/It Scares Me	1962	$10
❑ 2999	Sweet Misery/Because You're Mine	1970	$6
❑ 2512	That's Why I Love You So Much/Forever Yours	1969	$8
❑ F2835	The Drunken Driver/Homesick	1954	$30
❑ 4650	The Waltz You Saved for Me/ Out of a Clear Blue Sky	1961	$15
❑ 4650 [PS]	The Waltz You Saved for Me/ Out of a Clear Blue Sky	1961	$30
❑ 5111	Timber I'm Falling/Don't Count the Diamonds	1964	$10
❑ 5355	True, True Lovin'/Love Built the House	1965	$10
❑ F2627	Walkin' and Hummin'/I Wouldn't Treat a Dog Like You're Treating Me	1953	$30
❑ 5852	What Am I Gonna Do Now/General G	1967	$8
❑ F3862	What'cha Doin' After School/ Wang Dang Doo	1957	$15
❑ 2288	White Fences and Evergreen Trees/Love's Been Good to Me	1968	$8
❑ 4977	Who's Next/As Close As We'll Ever Be	1963	$10
❑ 5438	Willie Was a Gamblin' Man/ Picking Up the Pieces	1965	$10
❑ 4594	Willow Tree/Take a Look	1961	$15
❑ 4406	Wings of a Dove/Next to Jimmy	1960	$15
❑ F2024	Words/I'm Missin' Lots of Lovin'	1952	$30
—As "Terry Preston			

KING

Number	Title	Yr	NM
❑ 5476	Electrified Donkey/ Guilty Feeling	1961	$15
❑ 5434	Irma/Cotton Pickin' Heart	1960	$15

7-Inch Extended Plays

CAPITOL

Number	Title	Yr	NM
❑ EAP 1-837	A Fallen Star/Prize Possession//I Feel Better All Over/Pick-a-Nickin'	1957	$25
❑ EAP 1-880 [PS]	Boulevard of Broken Dreams, Part 1	1957	$20
❑ EAP 2-880 [PS]	Boulevard of Broken Dreams, Part 2	1957	$20
❑ EAP 3-880 [PS]	Boulevard of Broken Dreams, Part 3	1957	$20
❑ EAP 1-880	Boulevard of Broken Dreams/I'll Walk Alone//But Where Are You/ It All Comes Back to Me Now	1957	$20
❑ EAP 1-609	(contents unknown)	1955	$25
❑ EAP 3-880	(contents unknown)	1957	$20
❑ EAP 1-1280	(contents unknown)	1960	$15
❑ EAP 2-1280	(contents unknown)	1960	$15
❑ EAP 1-921 [PS]	Country Music Holiday	1958	$15
❑ EAP 3-1280	Deep Water/Sioux City Sue// Keeper of My Heart/Detour	1960	$15
❑ EAP 1-921	Don't Walk Away/Somewhere There's Sunshine//My Home Town/This Whole Wide World	1958	$15
❑ EAP 3-718	Farther and Farther Apart/ Never Have, Never Will//I Dreamed of an Old Love Affair/Daddy's Little Girl	1956	$20
❑ EAP 1-1280 [PS]	Ferlin Favorites, Part 1	1960	$15
❑ EAP 2-1280 [PS]	Ferlin Favorites, Part 2	1960	$15
❑ EAP 3-1280 [PS]	Ferlin Favorites, Part 3	1960	$15
❑ EAP 1-609 [PS]	Ferlin Husky	1955	$25
❑ EAP 1-1516	Gone/Black Sheep//Wings of a Dove/My Love for You	1961	$15
❑ EAP 1-718	Hang Your Head in Shame/ That Silver Haired Daddy of Mine//Honky-Tonkin' Party Girl/Useless	1956	$20
❑ EAP 1-837 [PS]	Husky Hits	1957	$25
❑ EAP 2-718	I Can't Go On This Way/That Little Girl of Mine//You Make Me Feel Funny, Honey/Rockin' Alone in an Old Rockin' Chair	1956	$20
❑ EAP 1-718 [PS]	Songs of the Home and Heart, Part 1	1956	$20
❑ EAP 2-718 [PS]	Songs of the Home and Heart, Part 2	1956	$20
❑ EAP 3-718 [PS]	Songs of the Home and Heart, Part 3	1956	$20
❑ EAP 2-880	Stormy Weather/It's the Talk of the Town//(Here Am I) Broken Hearted/Out in the Cold Again	1957	$20
❑ EAP 1-1516 [PS]	Wings of a Dove	1961	$15

HUTCH, WILLIE

DUNHILL

Number	Title	Yr	NM
❑ 4012	The Duck/Love Runs Out	1965	$1500

MODERN

Number	Title	Yr	NM
❑ 1021	I Can't Get Enough/Your Love Has Made Me a Man	1966	$80

MOTOWN

Number	Title	Yr	NM
❑ 1222	Brother's Gonna Work It Out/I Choose You	1973	$20
❑ 1339	Get Ready for the Get Down/ Don't Let Nobody Tell You How to Do Your Thing	1975	$5
❑ 1287	If You Ain't Got No Money (You Can't Get No Honey) Pt. 1/Pt. 2	1974	$5
❑ 1331	I'm Gonna Stay/Woman You Touched Me	1975	$5
❑ 1637	In and Out/Girl	1982	$4
❑ 1406	Let Me Be the One, Baby/ She's Just Doing Her Thing	1976	$4
❑ 1360	Love Power/Talk to Me	1975	$20
❑ 1371	Party Down/Just Another Day	1976	$20
❑ 1411	Shake It, Shake It/I Feel Like We Can Make It	1976	$4
❑ 1252	Slick/Mother's Theme	1973	$5
❑ 1252 [PS]	Slick/Mother's Theme	1973	$6
❑ 1282	Sunshine Lady/I Just Wanted to Make Her Happy	1973	$5
❑ 1292	Theme of Foxy Brown/Give Me Some of That Good Old Love	1974	$5
❑ 1416	We Gonna Have a House Party/Never Had It So Good	1977	$4
❑ 1424	We Gonna Party Tonight/ Precious Pearl	1977	$4
❑ 1433	What You Gonna Do After the Party/I Feel Like We Can Make It	1977	$4

RCA VICTOR

Number	Title	Yr	NM
❑ 74-0189	Ain't Gonna Stop/Do What You Wanna Do	1969	$40
❑ 74-0327	Magic of Love/Walking on My Love	1970	$40
❑ 74-0294	When a Boy Falls in Love (Part 1)/When a Boy Falls in Love (Part 2)	1969	$70

WHITFIELD

Number	Title	Yr	NM
❑ 8615	All American Funkathon/ And All Hell Broke Loose	1978	$4
❑ 49015	Deep in Your Love/ Everybody Needs Money	1979	$30
❑ 49102	Down Here on Disco Street/Kelly Green	1979	$4
❑ 8689	Paradise/Hip Shakin' Sexy Lady	1978	$4

HYLAND, BRIAN

ABC-PARAMOUNT

Number	Title	Yr	NM
❑ 10549	Act Naturally/Out of Sight, Out of Mind	1964	$10
❑ 10294	Ginny Come Lately/I Should Be Gettin' Better	1962	$10
❑ 10294 [PS]	Ginny Come Lately/I Should Be Gettin' Better	1962	$30
❑ 10400	If Mary's There/Remember Me	1963	$10
❑ 10400 [PS]	If Mary's There/Remember Me	1963	$30
❑ 10262	I'll Never Stop Wanting You/The Night I Cried	1961	$10
❑ 10262 [PS]	I'll Never Stop Wanting You/The Night I Cried	1961	$30
❑ 10452	I'm Afraid to Go Home/ Save Your Heart for Me	1963	$10
❑ 10374	I May Not Live to See Tomorrow/It Ain't That Way at All	1962	$10
❑ 10374 [PS]	I May Not Live to See Tomorrow/It Ain't That Way at All	1962	$30
❑ 10236	Let Me Belong to You/Let It Die	1961	$12
❑ 10336	Sealed with a Kiss/Summer Job	1962	$15
❑ 10336 [PS]	Sealed with a Kiss/Summer Job	1962	$30
❑ 10427	Somewhere in the Night/I Wish Today Was Yesterday	1963	$12
❑ 10359	Warmed Over Kisses (Left Over Love)/Walk a Lonely Mile	1962	$10
❑ 10359 [PS]	Warmed Over Kisses (Left Over Love)/Walk a Lonely Mile	1962	$30

DOT

Number	Title	Yr	NM
❑ 17222	A Million to One/It Could All Begin Again	1969	$6
❑ 17050	Apologize/Words on Paper	1967	$6
❑ 17078	Come with Me/Delilah	1968	$6
❑ 17291	Dreamy Eyes/Gonna Make a Woman Out of You	1970	$6
❑ 17258	Early April Morning/Stay and Love Me All Summer	1969	$6
❑ 17061	It's Christmas Time Once Again/Words on Paper	1967	$15
❑ 17109	The Lover/Springfield, Illinois	1968	$6
❑ 17176	Tragedy/You'd Better Stop and Think It Over	1968	$6

KAPP

Number	Title	Yr	NM
❑ 352	Four Little Heels (The Clickety Clack Song)/That's How Much	1960	$15
❑ 352 [PS]	Four Little Heels (The Clickety Clack Song)/That's How Much	1960	$30
❑ 363	I Gotta Go/Lopsided, Over Loaded	1960	$15
❑ 363 [PS]	I Gotta Go/Lopsided, Over Loaded	1960	$30
❑ 342	Itsy Bitsy Teeny Weeny Yellow Polka Dot Bikini/ Don't Dilly Dally, Sally	1960	$20
❑ 342 [PS]	Itsy Bitsy Teeny Weeny Yellow Polka Dot Bikini/ Don't Dilly Dally, Sally	1960	$40
❑ 401	Lipstick on Your Lips/ When Will I Know	1961	$15

LEADER

Number	Title	Yr	NM
❑ 805	Itsy Bitsy Teeny Weeny Yellow Polka Dot Bikini/ Don't Dilly Dally, Sally	1960	$40
❑ 801	Library Love Affair/Rosemary	1960	$30

PHILIPS

Number	Title	Yr	NM
❑ 40354	3000 Miles/Sometimes They Do, Sometimes They Don't	1966	$8
❑ 40203	Devoted to You/ Pledging My Love	1964	$8
❑ 40203 [PS]	Devoted to You/ Pledging My Love	1964	$15
❑ 40472	Get the Message/Kinda Groovy	1967	$6
❑ 40263	He Don't Understand You/ Love Will Find a Way	1965	$8
❑ 40263 [PS]	He Don't Understand You/ Love Will Find a Way	1965	$15
❑ 40179	Here's to Our Love/ Two Kinds of Girls	1964	$8
❑ 40179 [PS]	Here's to Our Love/ Two Kinds of Girls	1964	$15
❑ 40444	Holiday for Clowns/ Yesterday I Had a Girl	1967	$8
❑ 40424	Hung Up in Your Eyes/Why Mine	1967	$8
❑ 40424 [PS]	Hung Up in Your Eyes/Why Mine	1967	$15
❑ 40306	Stay Away from Her/I Can't Keep a Secret	1965	$8
❑ 40405	Why Did You Do It/Run, Run, Look and See	1966	$8

UNI

Number	Title	Yr	NM
❑ 55240	Gypsy Woman/You and Me (#2)	1970	$20
❑ 55323	I Love Every Little Thing About You/With My Eyes Wide Open	1972	$5
❑ 55272	Lonely Teardrops/Lorraine	1971	$20
❑ 55334	Only Wanna Make You Happy/ When You're Lovin' Me	1972	$5
❑ 55306	Out of the Blue/If You Came Back	1971	$5
❑ 55287	So Long, Marianne/ No Place to Run	1971	$5

Number	Title	Yr	NM

I

I KADEZ
HIT
Number	Title	Yr	NM
❏ 95	Louie Louie/Popsicles and Icicles	1963	$8

— B-side by the Scotties

I.V. LEAGUERS, THE
NAU-VOO
Number	Title	Yr	NM
❏ 803	Told by the Stars/Jim Jam	1959	$400

IAN AND THE ZODIACS
PHILIPS
Number	Title	Yr	NM
❏ 40277	Good Morning Little Schoolgirl/ Message to Martha	1965	$10
❏ 40291	So Much in Love with You/ This Empty Place	1965	$12
❏ 40291 [PS]	So Much in Love with You/ This Empty Place	1965	$30
❏ 40244	The Cryin' Game/ Livin' Lovin' Wreck	1964	$12
❏ 40343	Why Can't It Be Me/ Leave It to Me	1965	$10

7-Inch Extended Plays
Number	Title	Yr	NM
❏ PHS-807-C	Good Morning, Little Schoolgirl/The Crying Game/ Jump Back//So Much in Love with You/Clarabella/ Baby, I Need Your Loving	1965	$50

— Jukebox issue; small hole, plays at 33 1/3 rpm

Number	Title	Yr	NM
❏ PHS-807-C [PS]	Ian and the Zodiacs	1965	$50

IAN, JANIS
CAPITOL
Number	Title	Yr	NM
❏ 3107	He's a Rainbow/Here in Spain	1971	$8
COLUMBIA
Number	Title	Yr	NM
❏ 10297	Aftertones/Boy, I Really Tied One On	1976	$5
❏ 10154	At Seventeen/Stars	1975	$5
❏ 10154 [PS]	At Seventeen/Stars	1975	$8
❏ 10526	Candlelight/I Want to Make You Love Me	1977	$5
❏ 10979	Here Comes the Night/ Tonight Will Last Forever	1979	$4
❏ 10228	In the Winter/Thankyouse	1975	$5
❏ 10331	I Would Like to Dance/ Goodbye to Morning	1976	$5
❏ 10484	Miracle Row/Take It to the Sky	1977	$5
❏ 02176	Sugar Mountain/ Under the Covers	1981	$4
❏ 10813	That Grand Illusion/ Hopper Paining	1978	$5
❏ 10864	The Bridge/Do You Wanna Dance	1978	$5
❏ 11327	The Other Side of the Sun/Memories	1980	$4
❏ 10119	When the Party's Over/ Bright Lights and Promises	1975	$5
POLYDOR
Number	Title	Yr	NM
❏ 14299	Society's Child (Baby I've Been Thinking)/I'll Give You a Stone If You Throw It	1975	$6
VERVE
Number	Title	Yr	NM
❏ 5027	Society's Child (Baby I've Been Thinking)/Letter to Jon	1967	$12
VERVE FOLKWAYS
Number	Title	Yr	NM
❏ 5027	Society's Child (Baby I've Been Thinking)/Letter to Jon	1966	$15
VERVE FORECAST
Number	Title	Yr	NM
❏ 5099	Everybody Knows/ Janey's Blues	1968	$8
❏ 5041	I'll Give You a Stone If You'll Throw It/Younger Generation Blues	1967	$8
❏ 5072	Insanity Comes Quietly to the Structured Mind/Snowflakes Fall, Snowrays Call	1967	$8
❏ 5090	Lady of the Night/Friends Again	1968	$8
❏ 5113	Month of May/Calling Your Name	1969	$8
❏ 5027	Society's Child (Baby I've Been Thinking)/Letter to Jon	1967	$8
❏ 5079	Somg for All the Seasons of Your Mind/Lonely One	1968	$8

ICE-T
SIRE
Number	Title	Yr	NM
❏ 27902	Colors/Squeeze the Trigger	1988	$5
❏ 27902 [PS]	Colors/Squeeze the Trigger	1988	$5
❏ 27574	High Rollers/The Hunted Child	1989	$4
❏ 27768	I'm Your Pusher/ Girls L.G.B.N.A.F.	1988	$4
❏ 27768 [PS]	I'm Your Pusher/ Girls L.G.B.N.A.F.	1988	$4
❏ 22810	Lethal Weapon/Heartbeat	1989	$4
❏ PRO-S-2751 [DJ]	Make It Funky (same on both sides)	1987	$6
❏ 28126	Somebody Gotta Do It/Our Most Requested Record	1988	$5

ICEHOUSE
CHRYSALIS
Number	Title	Yr	NM
❏ 2568 [DJ]	Can't Help Myself (same on both sides)	1981	$8

— Stock copy not known to exist

Number	Title	Yr	NM
❏ VS443156	Crazy/No Promises (Live)	1987	$3
❏ VS443156 [PS]	Crazy/No Promises (Live)	1987	$4
❏ VS443057	Cross the Border/The Flame	1986	$5
❏ VS443201	Electric Blue/Over My Head	1988	$3
❏ VS443201 [PS]	Electric Blue/Over My Head	1988	$3
❏ VS442670	Hey Little Girl/Goodnight Mr. Mathews	1983	$20
❏ VS442670 [DJ]	Hey Little Girl (same on both sides)	1983	$8
❏ VS443240	My Obsession/Your Confession	1988	$3
❏ VS443240 [PS]	My Obsession/Your Confession	1988	$3
❏ VS443041	Paradise/Baby, You're So Strange	1986	$8
❏ VS443041 [PS]	Paradise/Baby, You're So Strange	1986	$10
❏ B-23414	Touch the Fire/Great Southern Land	1989	$8
❏ 2556 [DJ]	Walls (same on both sides)	1981	$8

— Stock copy not known to exist

Number	Title	Yr	NM
❏ 2530	We Can Get Together/ Not My Kind	1981	$5
❏ 2530 [PS]	We Can Get Together/ Not My Kind	1981	$5

ICICLE WORKS
ARISTA
Number	Title	Yr	NM
❏ 9155	Whisper to a Scream (Birds Fly)/ In the Dance the Shaman Led	1984	$3

ID, THE
RCA VICTOR
Number	Title	Yr	NM
❏ 47-9136	Short Circuit/Boil the Kettle, Mother	1967	$15
❏ 47-9195	Wild Times/The Take	1967	$15

IDEALS, THE (1)
PASO
Number	Title	Yr	NM
❏ 6402	Magic/Teens	1961	$60
❏ 6401	Together/What's the Matter with You Sam	1961	$60
SATELLITE
Number	Title	Yr	NM
❏ 2011	Go Go Gorilla/Kissing Won't Go Out of Style	1966	$200

IDEALS, THE (U)
COOL
Number	Title	Yr	NM
❏ 108	Do I Have the Right/ You Won't Like It	1958	$300
CORTLAND
Number	Title	Yr	NM
❏ 110	Don Juan/Gorilla	1963	$70
❏ 115	Feeling of a Kiss/You Came a Long Way from St. Louis	1964	$50
❏ 117	Local Boy/L.A.	1964	$20
❏ 113	Mo Joe Hanna/Simple Simon	1964	$20
DECCA
Number	Title	Yr	NM
❏ 30720	Annie Has a Stroller/My Girl	1959	$50
❏ 30800	Ivy League Lover/Don't Be a Baby, Baby	1959	$30
FARGO
Number	Title	Yr	NM
❏ 1024	The Duchess/Trans Zizstor	1962	$30
STARS OF HOLLYWOOD
Number	Title	Yr	NM
❏ 1001	Please, Jan/Always Yours	1959	$50
ST. LAWRENCE
Number	Title	Yr	NM
❏ 1001	Cathy's Clown/Go Get a Wig	1965	$15
❏ 1020	I Got Lucky (When I Found You)/Tell Her I Apologize	1966	$40

IDENTITIES, THE
HOUSE OF THE FOX
Number	Title	Yr	NM
❏ HOF-6	Hey Brother/When Love Slips Away	1971	$50
TOGETHERNESS
Number	Title	Yr	NM
❏ 300	When You Find Love Slipping Away/(B-side unknown)	1971	$50

IDES OF MARCH, THE
PARROT
Number	Title	Yr	NM
❏ 326	Hole in My Soul/Girls Don't Grow on Trees	1967	$12
❏ 304	I'll Keep Searching/ You Wouldn't Listen	1966	$10
❏ 321	My Foolish Pride/Give Your Mind Wings	1967	$10
RCA VICTOR
Number	Title	Yr	NM
❏ APBO-0052	Hot Water/Heavy on the Country	1973	$5
❏ 74-0850	Mother America/Ladyland	1972	$5
WARNER BROS.
Number	Title	Yr	NM
❏ 7526	Giddy-Up, Ride Me/ Freedom Sweet	1971	$6
❏ 7334	High on a Hillside/ One Woman Man	1969	$6
❏ 7466	L.A. Goodbye/Mrs. Grayson's Farm	1971	$6
❏ 7426	Melody/The Sky Is Falling	1970	$6
❏ 7403	Superman/Home	1970	$6
❏ 7507	Tie-Dye Princess/ Friends of Feeling	1971	$6

IDLE RACE, THE
JEFF LYNNE, later of THE MOVE and ELECTRIC LIGHT ORCHESTRA, was in this group.
LIBERTY
Number	Title	Yr	NM
❏ 55997 [DJ]	Here We Go 'Round the Lemon Tree/My Father's Son	1967	$30

— Audition Copy" on cream label

Number	Title	Yr	NM
❏ 55997	Here We Go 'Round the Lemon Tree/My Father's Son	1967	$100

— Stock copy on black label

IDOL, BILLY
Also see GENERATION X.
CHRYSALIS
Number	Title	Yr	NM
❏ VS442840	Catch My Fall/Daytime Drama	1984	$5
❏ 2488	Dancing with Myself/ Happy People	1981	$20

— Label credit: "Billy Idol and Gen X

Number	Title	Yr	NM
❏ VS442723	Dancing with Myself/Love Calling (Rub a Dub Mix)	1983	$5

— Label credit: "Billy Idol and Gen X

Number	Title	Yr	NM
❏ VS442723 [PS]	Dancing with Myself/Love Calling (Rub a Dub Mix)	1983	$5
❏ VS443087	Don't Need a Gun/Fatal Charm	1986	$3
❏ VS443087 [PS]	Don't Need a Gun/Fatal Charm	1986	$3
❏ VS442786	Eyes Without a Face/ Blue Highway	1984	$3
❏ VS442786 [PS]	Eyes Without a Face/ Blue Highway	1984	$3
❏ VS842956	Eyes Without a Face/ Flesh for Fantasy	1985	$3

— Silver label reissue

Number	Title	Yr	NM
❏ VS442809	Flesh for Fantasy/The Dead Next Door	1984	$3
❏ VS442809 [PS]	Flesh for Fantasy/The Dead Next Door	1984	$3
❏ VS443203	Hot in the City/Catch My Fall (Remix Fix)	1988	$3
❏ VS443203 [PS]	Hot in the City/Catch My Fall (Remix Fix)	1988	$3
❏ 2605	Hot in the City/Hole in the Wall	1982	$5
❏ 2605 [PS]	Hot in the City/Hole in the Wall	1982	$5
❏ VS842953	Hot in the City/Mony Mony	1985	$3

— Silver label reissue

Number	Title	Yr	NM
❏ 2543	Mony Mony/Baby Talk	1981	$15
❏ VS443161	Mony Mony "Live"/ Shakin' All Over "Live	1987	$4
❏ VS443161 [PS]	Mony Mony "Live"/ Shakin' All Over "Live	1987	$4

— Non-LP tracks (both sides!)

Number	Title	Yr	NM
❏ VS443114	Sweet Sixteen/Beyond Belief	1987	$3
❏ VS443114 [PS]	Sweet Sixteen/Beyond Belief	1987	$3
❏ VS443024	To Be a Lover/All Summer Single	1986	$3
❏ VS443024 [PS]	To Be a Lover/All Summer Single	1986	$3
❏ VS842954	White Wedding/ Dancing with Myself	1985	$3

— Silver-label reissue

Number	Title	Yr	NM
❏ 2648	White Wedding/Dead on Arrival	1982	$5
❏ VS442697	White Wedding/Dead on Arrival	1983	$4

IDOLS, THE
RCA VICTOR
Number	Title	Yr	NM
❏ 47-7339	30 Days/The Prowler	1958	$30
❏ 47-7417	Here in My Heart/ The Counterfeiter	1958	$30

IF
CAPITOL
Number	Title	Yr	NM
❏ 3932	I Believe in Rock and Roll/Still Alive	1974	$6
❏ 2909	The Promised Land/I'm Reaching Out on All Sides	1970	$8
METROMEDIA
Number	Title	Yr	NM
❏ 258	Waterfall/(B-side unknown)	1972	$6

IFIELD, FRANK
CAPITOL
Number	Title	Yr	NM
❏ 5134	Don't Blame Me/Say It Isn't So	1964	$12
❏ 5032	I'm Confessin' (That I Love You)/Waltzing Matilda	1963	$10
❏ 5089	Please/Mule Train	1963	$10
❏ 5170	Sweet Lorraine/You Came a Long Way from St. Louis	1964	$10
❏ 5275	True Love Ways/I Should Care	1964	$10
❏ 5349	Without You/Don't Make Me Laugh	1965	$10
HICKORY
Number	Title	Yr	NM
❏ 1499	Adios Matador/Movin' Lover	1968	$8
❏ 1411	Call Her Your Sweetheart/ Give Myself a Party	1966	$8

Number	Title	Yr	NM
❏ 1507	Don't Forget to Cry/Morning in Your Eyes	1968	$8
❏ 1514	Good Morning Dear/Innocent Years	1968	$8
❏ 1550	I Love You Because/It's My Time	1969	$6
❏ 1435	I Remember You/Stranger to You	1967	$8
❏ 1540	Let Me Into Your Life/Mary in the Morning	1969	$6
❏ 1556	Lights of Home/Love Hurts	1969	$6
❏ 1525	Maurie/I'm Learning Child	1968	$8
❏ 1486	Oh, Such a Stranger/Then You Can Tell Me Goodbye	1967	$8
❏ 1595	Someone/One More Mile, One More Town (One More Time)	1971	$6
❏ 1574	Sweet Memories/You've Still Got a Place in My Heart	1970	$6

MAM

❏ 3612	Lonesome Jubilee/Teach Me Little Children	1971	$5

VEE JAY

❏ 553	I'm Confessin' (That I Love You)/Heart and Soul	1963	$15
❏ 457	I Remember You/I Listen to My Heart	1962	$20

— With Frank Ifield's name spelled correctly on label

❏ 457	I Remember You/I Listen to My Heart	1962	$30

— With both labels misspelled "Farnk Ifield

❏ 477	Lovesick Blues/Anytime	1962	$15
❏ 499	The Wayward Wind/I'm Smiling Now	1963	$15

WARNER BROS.

❏ 8853	Crystal/Touch the Morning	1979	$4
❏ 49095	Play Born to Lose Again/Yesterday Just Passed My Way Again	1979	$4
❏ 8730	Why Don't We Leave Together/Crawling Back	1979	$4

IGGY AND THE STOOGES

Includes records as "The Stooges." Also see IGGY POP.

COLUMBIA

❏ 45877	Search and Destroy/Penetration	1973	$20

SIAMESE

❏ 01	I Got a Right/Gimme Some Skin	1977	$30
❏ 001 [PS]	I Got a Right/Gimme Some Skin	1977	$8

— Only issued with Bomp!-distributed copies; has "Iggy && The Stooges" on cover

❏ 01	I Got a Right/Gimme Some Skin	1977	$10

— Second pressing: "Siamese" in fake Asian lettering with iguana logo

IGGY POP

Also see IGGY AND THE STOOGES.

A&M

❏ 2874	Cry for Love/Winners and Losers	1986	$4

ARISTA

❏ 0438	I'm Bored/African Man	1979	$6

RCA

❏ PB-10989 [B]	Sister Midnight/Baby	1977	$15

IKETTES, THE

ATCO

❏ 6243	I Do Love You/I Had a Dream the Other Night	1962	$20
❏ 6212	I'm Blue (The Gong-Gong Song)/Find My Baby	1961	$30
❏ 6223	Troubles on My Mind/Come On and Truck	1962	$20

MODERN

❏ 1024	Da Doo Ron Ron/Not That I Recall	1966	$8
❏ 1008	(He's Gonna Be) Fine, Fine, Fine/How Come	1965	$12
❏ 1011	I'm So Thankful/Don't Feel Sorry for Me	1965	$8
❏ 1005	Peaches 'N' Cream/The Biggest Players	1965	$10
❏ 1015	Sally Go Round the Roses/Lonely for You	1965	$8

PHI-DAN

❏ 5009	Down Down/What'cha Gonna Do	1966	$12

POMPEII

❏ 66683	Beauty Is Just Skin Deep/Make Them Wait	1968	$6

TEENA

❏ 1702	Prisoner in Love/Those Words	1963	$30

UNITED ARTISTS

❏ 50866	If You Take a Close Look/Got What It Takes	1971	$5
❏ 51103	I'm Just Not Ready for Love/Two Timin' Double Dealin'	1973	$5

ILL WIND, THE

ABC

❏ 11107	In My Dark World/Walkin' and Singin'	1968	$30

ILL WINDS, THE

REPRISE

❏ 0492	I Idolize You/A Letter	1966	$20
❏ 0423	So Be On Your Way (I Won't Cry)/Fear of the Rain	1965	$20

ILLUSION, THE

DYNO VOICE

❏ 914	It's Groovy Time/My Party	1968	$10

STEED

❏ 732	Collection/Wait a Minute	1970	$6
❏ 712	Did You See Her Eyes/Falling in Love	1969	$12
❏ 718	Did You See Her Eyes/Falling in Love	1969	$6
❏ 721	How Does It Feel/Once in a Lifetime	1969	$6
❏ 726	Let's Make Each Other Happy/Beside You	1970	$6
❏ 722	Together/Don't Push It	1969	$6

ILLUSIONS, THE

COLUMBIA

❏ 43700	I Know/Take My Heart	1966	$10

CORAL

❏ 62173	The Letter/Henry and Henrietta	1960	$50

DIAL

❏ 4004	I Don't Believe It/The World Outside	1965	$10

DOT

❏ 16752	Secrets of Love/Don't Put Me Down	1965	$30

EMBER

❏ 1071	How High Is the Mountain/Can't We Fall in Love	1961	$50

LAURIE

❏ 3245	Maybe/In the Beginning	1964	$30

LITTLE DEBBIE

❏ 105	Story of My Life/Walking Boy	1964	$600

MALI

❏ 104	Hey Boy/Lonely Soldier	1962	$60

NORTHEAST

❏ 801	Hey Boy/Lonely Soldier	1962	$20

RELIC

❏ 512	Hey Boy/Lonely Soldier	1964	$12

SHERATON

❏ 104	Hey Boy/Lonely Soldier	1962	$30

IMAGINATIONS, THE (1)

BALLAD

❏ 500	Wait a Little Longer Son/Mama's Little Baby	1962	$200

BO MARC

❏ 301	Guardian Angel/Hey You	1961	$50

DUEL

❏ 507	Guardian Angel/Hey You	1961	$30

MUSIC MAKERS

❏ 103	Goodnight Baby/The Search Is Over	1961	$60
❏ 108	Guardian Angel/Hey You	1961	$60

IMAGINATIONS, THE (2)

DUNHILL

❏ 4092	I Love You When You're Mad/Summer in New York	1967	$30

IMAGINATIONS, THE (3)

FRATERNITY

❏ 1001	I Just Can't Get Over Losing You/Strange Neighborhood	1967	$600

IMPACT, THE

MGM

❏ 13726	Could You Love Me/My World Fell Down	1967	$12

IMPACTS, THE

ANDERSON

❏ 104	Summer/Linda	1964	$60

CARLTON

❏ 548	Darling, Now You're Mine/Help Me Somebody	1961	$40
❏ 548	Darling, No You're Mine/Help Me Somebody	1961	$60

— With incorrect A-side title

DCP

❏ 1147	Wishing Well/Heartaches	1965	$60

— As "Kenny and the Impacts"

KIP

❏ 1890	Burnt Valves/Chrome Reverse	1963	$60

RCA VICTOR

❏ 47-7583	Bobby Sox Squaw/Croc-O-Doll	1959	$30
❏ 47-7609	Canadian Sunset/They Say	1959	$60

IMPALAS, THE

20TH FOX

❏ 428	Last Night I Saw a Girl/There Is Nothin' Like a Dame	1963	$15

BUNKY

❏ 7760	Whay Should He Do/I Still Love You	1969	$20
❏ 7762	Whip it On Me/I Still Love You	1969	$30

CAPITOL

❏ 2709	Speed Up/Soul	1969	$80

CHECKER

❏ 999	For the Love of Mike/I Need You So Much	1961	$15

CUB

❏ 9066	All Alone/When My Heart Does All the Talking	1960	$30

— As "Speedo and the Impalas

❏ 9022	I Ran All the Way Home/Fool, Fool, Fool	1959	$70

— Original A-side title

❏ 9033	Oh What a Fool/Sandy Went Away	1959	$30
❏ 9053	Peggy Darling/Bye Everybody	1959	$30
❏ 9022	Sorry (I Ran All the Way Home)/Fool, Fool, Fool	1959	$30

HAMILTON

❏ 50026	I Was a Fool/First Date	1960	$30

RED BOY

❏ 113	When You Dance/I Can't See Me Without You	1966	$30

STEADY

❏ 044	When You Dance/I Can't See Me Without You	1967	$30

SUNDOWN

❏ 115	The Lonely One/Lost Boogie	1959	$20

7-Inch Extended Plays

CUB

❏ 5000	(contents unknown)	1959	$400
❏ 5000 [PS]	Sorry (I Ran All the Way Home)	1959	$400

IMPERIALITES, THE

IMPERIAL

❏ 66015	Have Love, Will Travel/Let's Get One	1964	$30

IMPERIALS MINUS TWO, THE

IMPERIAL

❏ 5787	A Swingin' Dream/In Any Language	1961	$30

IMPERIALS, THE (2)

BUZZY

❏ 1	My Darling/You Should Have Told Me	1962	$30

— Red vinyl

SAVOY

❏ 1104	My Darling/You Should Have Told Me	1954	$200

IMPERIALS, THE (3)

NEWTIME

❏ 503	A Short Prayer/Where Will You Be	1962	$20
❏ 505	The Letter/Go and Get Your Heart Broken	1962	$200

IMPERIALS, THE (4)

OMNI

❏ 5501	Who's Gonna Love Me/You Better Take Time to Love	1978	$5

IMPERIALS, THE (U)

CAPITOL

❏ 4921	I'm Still Dancing/Bermuda Wonderful	1963	$50

CARLTON

❏ 566	Faithfully Yours/Vut Vut	1961	$30

IMPOSSIBLES, THE

BLANCHE

❏ 029	Chapel Bells/Little by Little	1960	$400

REPRISE

❏ 0305	Lonely Bluebird/Paint Me a Pretty Picture	1964	$30

RMP

❏ 501	Everywhere I Go/Well, It's Alright	1966	$30
❏ 1030	Mr. Maestro/Well, It's Alright	1964	$30

ROULETTE

❏ 4745	I Wanna Know/It's All Right	1967	$125

IMPRESSIONS, THE
Also see JERRY BUTLER; CURTIS MAYFIELD.

20TH FOX

Number	Title	Yr	NM
❑ 172	All Through the Night/ Meanwhile, Back in My Heart	1959	$50

ABC

Number	Title	Yr	NM
❑ 10831	Can't Satisfy/This Must End	1966	$8
❑ 11135	Don't Cry My Love/ Sometimes I Wonder	1968	$8
❑ 11188	East of Java/Just Before Sunrise	1969	$8
❑ 10964	I Can't Stay Away from You/ You Ought to Be in Heaven	1967	$8
❑ 11103	I Loved and I Lost/ Up, Up and Away	1968	$8
❑ 10932	It's Hard to Believe/ You've Got Me Runnin'	1967	$8
❑ 10869	Love's a-Comin'/ Wade in the Water	1966	$8
❑ 11022	We're a Winner/It's All Over	1967	$8
❑ 11071	We're Rolling On (Part 1)/ We're Rolling On (Part 2)	1968	$8

ABC-PARAMOUNT

Number	Title	Yr	NM
❑ 10602	Amen/Long, Long Winter	1964	$20
❑ 10537	Girl You Don't Know Me/A Woman Who Loves Me	1964	$20
❑ 10289	Grow Closer Together/ Can't You See	1962	$20
❑ 10241	Gypsy Woman/As Long As You Love Me	1961	$20
❑ 10544	I'm So Proud/I Made a Mistake	1964	$20
❑ 10386	I'm the One Who Loves You/I Need Your Love	1962	$60
❑ 10710	I Need You/Never Could You Be	1965	$15
❑ 10487	It's All Right/You'll Want Me Back	1963	$20
❑ 10328	Little Young Lover/ Never Let Me Go	1962	$20
❑ 10670	Meeting Over Yonder/I've Found That I've Lost	1965	$15
❑ 10622	People Get Ready/I've Been Trying	1965	$20
❑ 10431	Sad, Sad Girl and Boy/ Twist and Limbo	1963	$20
❑ 10761	Since I Lost the One I Love/ Falling in Love with You	1966	$10
❑ 10511	Talking About My Baby/ Never Too Much Love	1963	$20
❑ 10789	Too Slow/No One Else	1966	$10
❑ 10647	Woman's Got Soul/ Get Up and Move	1965	$15

ABNER

Number	Title	Yr	NM
❑ 1017	Come Back My Love/Love Me	1958	$40
❑ 1013	For Your Precious Love/ Sweet Was the Wine	1958	$50

— As "Jerry Butler and the Impressions

Number	Title	Yr	NM
❑ 1025	Lonely One/Senorita I Love You	1959	$40
❑ 1034	Say That You Love Me/A New Love	1960	$40
❑ 1023	The Gift of Love/At the County Fair	1959	$40

BANDERA

Number	Title	Yr	NM
❑ 2504	Listen/Shorty's Got to Go	1959	$40

CHI-SOUND

Number	Title	Yr	NM
❑ 2491	For Your Precious Love/You're Mine	1981	$5
❑ 2499	Love, Love, Love/Fan the Fire	1981	$5
❑ 2438	Maybe I'm Mistaken/All I Wanna Do Is Make Love to You	1980	$5
❑ 2418	Sorry/All I Wanna Do Is Make Love to You	1979	$5

COTILLION

Number	Title	Yr	NM
❑ 44222	Can't Get Along/You're So Right for Me	1977	$5
❑ 44211	Silent Night/I Saw Mommy Kissing Santa Claus	1976	$6
❑ 44210	This Time/I'm a Fool for Love	1976	$5

CURTOM

Number	Title	Yr	NM
❑ 1957	Ain't Got Time/I'm So Proud	1971	$6
❑ 1954	(Baby) Turn On to Me/ Soulful Love	1970	$6
❑ 1951	Check Out Your Mind/ Can't You See	1970	$6
❑ 1943	Choice of Colors/Mighty Mighty Spade and Whitey	1969	$6
❑ 1997	Finally Got Myself Together (I'm a Changed Man)/I'll Always Be Here	1974	$6
❑ 1932	Fool for You/I'm Loving Nothing	1968	$6
❑ 1932 [PS]	Fool for You/I'm Loving Nothing	1968	$20
❑ 1994	If It's In You to Do Wrong/ Times Have Changed	1973	$6
❑ 1973	I Need to Belong to Someone/Love Me	1972	$6
❑ 1966	Inner City Blues/We Must Be in Love	1971	$6
❑ 1959	Love Me/Do You Wanna Win	1971	$6
❑ 0110	Loving Power/First Impressions	1975	$5
❑ 1937	My Deceiving Heart/You Want Somebody Else	1969	$6
❑ 1982	Preacher Man/Times Have Changed	1973	$6
❑ 0106	Same Thing It Took/I'm So Glad	1975	$5
❑ 1946	Say You Love Me/You'll Be Always Mine	1969	$6
❑ 1940	Seven Years/The Girl I Find	1969	$6
❑ 2003	Something's Mighty, Mighty Wrong/Three the Hard Way	1974	$6
❑ 0103	Sooner or Later/ Miracle Woman	1975	$5

Number	Title	Yr	NM
❑ 0116	Sunshine/I Wish I'd Stayed in Bed	1976	$5
❑ 1985	Thin Line/I'm Loving You	1973	$6
❑ 1934	This Is My Country/ My Woman's Love	1968	$6
❑ 1970	This Loves for Real/ Times Have Changed	1972	$6
❑ 1948	Wherever She Leadeth Me/Amen (1970)	1970	$6

FALCON

Number	Title	Yr	NM
❑ 1013	For Your Precious Love/ Sweet Was the Wine	1958	$70

— As "Jerry Butler and the Impressions

MCA

Number	Title	Yr	NM
❑ 52995	Can't Wait 'Til Tomorrow/ Love Workin' On Me	1987	$10

PORT

Number	Title	Yr	NM
❑ 70031	Listen/Shorty's Got to Go	1962	$20

SWIRL

Number	Title	Yr	NM
❑ 107	I Need Your Love/ Don't Leave Me	1962	$50

VEE JAY

Number	Title	Yr	NM
❑ 280	For Your Precious Love/ Sweet Was the Wine	1958	$8000

— As "Jerry Butler and the Impressions." VG 4000; VG+ 6000

Number	Title	Yr	NM
❑ 424	Say That You Love Me/ Senorita I Love You	1962	$30
❑ 621	Say That You Love Me/ Senorita I Love You	1964	$20
❑ 574	The Gift of Love/At the County Fair	1963	$20

7-Inch Extended Plays

ABC-PARAMOUNT

Number	Title	Yr	NM
❑ LP-ABCS-505[PS]	People Get Ready	1965	$35
❑ LP-ABCS-505	Woman's Got Soul/ Emotions/We're in Love// People Get Ready/ See the Real Me/You Must Believe Me	1965	$35

— Stereo jukebox issue; small hole, plays at 33 1/3 rpm

IN-BETWEENS, THE

HIGHLAND

Number	Title	Yr	NM
❑ 1173	Girl Child, I Am An Evil Witchman/Security	1966	$300

IN CROWD, THE (1)

ABNAK

Number	Title	Yr	NM
❑ 121	Inside Out/Big Cities	1967	$8
❑ 121 [DJ]	Inside Out/Big Cities	1967	$15

— Promo only on yellow vinyl

Number	Title	Yr	NM
❑ 129	Let's Take a Walk/Hangin' From Your Lovin' Tree	1968	$8
❑ 129 [DJ]	Let's Take a Walk/Hangin' From Your Lovin' Tree	1968	$15

— Promo only on yellow vinyl

IN CROWD, THE (2)

VIVA

Number	Title	Yr	NM
❑ 610	If I Knew a Magic Word/ Never Ending Symphony	1967	$20

IN CROWD, THE (3)

TOWER

Number	Title	Yr	NM
❑ 147	That's How Strong My Love Is/Things She Says	1965	$30
❑ 196	Why Must They Criticize/I Don't Mind	1966	$30

IN CROWD, THE (U)

BRENT

Number	Title	Yr	NM
❑ 7046	Grapevine/Cat Dance	1965	$50

HICKORY

Number	Title	Yr	NM
❑ 1413	In the Midnight Hour/ Just Give Me Time	1966	$15
❑ 1378	Speed Queen/Cry, Boy, Cry	1966	$20

MUSICOR

Number	Title	Yr	NM
❑ 1111	Do the Surfer Jerk/Girl in the Black Bikini	1965	$30

RONN

Number	Title	Yr	NM
❑ 1	In the Midnight Hour/ Nothing You Do	1967	$10

SWAN

Number	Title	Yr	NM
❑ 4204	Let's Shindig/Klink	1965	$20

INCREDIBLE BONGO BAND, THE

MGM

Number	Title	Yr	NM
❑ 14588	Bongo Rock/Bongolia	1973	$6
❑ 14635	Let There Be Drums/ Dueling Bongos	1973	$8

PRIDE

Number	Title	Yr	NM
❑ 1015	Bongo Rock/Bongolia	1972	$15

INCREDIBLE STRING BAND, THE

ELEKTRA

Number	Title	Yr	NM
❑ 45696	This Moment/Big Ted	1970	$8

INCREDIBLES, THE

AUDIO ARTS

Number	Title	Yr	NM
❑ 60014	Fool, Fool, Fool/ Lost Without You	1968	$10
❑ 60010	For Sentimental Reasons/Can't Get Over Losing Your Love	1968	$10
❑ 60007	Heart and Soul/I Found Another Love	1967	$12
❑ 60001	I'll Make It Easy (If You Come On Home)/Crying Heart	1966	$15
❑ 60016	Miss Treatment/All of a Sudden	1968	$10
❑ 60017	Standing Here Crying/ All of a Sudden	1968	$10
❑ 60018	Stop the Raindrops/ Fool, Fool, Fool	1968	$10
❑ 60006	There's Nothing Else to Say/Another Dirty Deal	1967	$10
❑ 60009	Without a Word/ Standing Here Crying	1967	$10

TETRAGRAMMATON

Number	Title	Yr	NM
❑ 1515	All of a Sudden/Standing Here Crying	1969	$8

INDIGO GIRLS

EPIC

Number	Title	Yr	NM
❑ 34-68912	Closer to Fine/Cold As Ice	1989	$20
❑ 73003	Land of Canaan/Never Stop	1989	$12

J ELLIS

Number	Title	Yr	NM
❑ A1264 [PS]	Crazy Game/Everybody's Waiting (For Someone to Come Home)	1985	$200
❑ A1264	Crazy Game/Everybody's Waiting (For Someone to Come Home)	1985	$120

— A-side is credited to Emily Saliers; B-side credited to Amy Ray

INGLE, RED

CAPITOL

Number	Title	Yr	NM
❑ 54-713	A" Yore A-Dopey-Gal/ Two Dollar Pistol	1949	$30
❑ F1431	Chew Tobacco Rag/Let Me In	1951	$30
❑ F1599	People Are Funny/Pool	1951	$30
❑ 54-686	Temptation (Tim-Tayshun)/ Cigareetes, Whuskey and Wild, Wild Women	1949	$40

MERCURY

Number	Title	Yr	NM
❑ 70085	Don't Let the Stars Get In Your Eyes/Why Don't You Believe Me	1953	$30

INGMANN, JORGEN

ATCO

Number	Title	Yr	NM
❑ 6235	Africa/Johnny's Tune	1962	$10
❑ 6195	Anna/Cherokee	1961	$15
❑ 6184	Apache/Echo Boogie	1960	$20
❑ 6403	Corfu/Seven Roses	1966	$8
❑ 6277	Fourth Man Theme/Drina	1963	$8
❑ 6265	I Loved You/My Little Boy	1963	$8

— As "Grethe and Jorgen Ingmann

Number	Title	Yr	NM
❑ 6205	Milord/Oceans of Love	1961	$10
❑ 6370	Theme from "Zorba the Greek"/Gorilla	1965	$8
❑ 6305	Tovarisch/Desert March	1964	$8

PARROT

Number	Title	Yr	NM
❑ 45006	Sunrise Serenade/Tokyo Melody	1964	$10

INGRAM, JAMES

MCA

Number	Title	Yr	NM
❑ 53125	Better Way/Bad Guys	1987	$3

— B-side by The Heat

Number	Title	Yr	NM
❑ 53125 [PS]	Better Way/Bad Guys	1987	$3

QWEST

Number	Title	Yr	NM
❑ 28669	Always/(Instrumental)	1986	$3
❑ 28669 [PS]	Always/(Instrumental)	1986	$3
❑ 29493	Party Animal/Come A Da Machine (To Take A My Place)	1983	$4
❑ 29235	She Loves Me (The Best That I Can Be)/Come A Da Machine (To Take A My Place)	1984	$4
❑ 29316	There's No Easy Way/ Come A Da Machine (To Take A My Place)	1984	$4
❑ 29316 [PS]	There's No Easy Way/ Come A Da Machine (To Take A My Place)	1984	$4
❑ 29132	Whatever We Imagine/ It's Your Night	1984	$4

WARNER BROS.

Number	Title	Yr	NM
❑ 22975	It's Real/Aren't You Tired	1989	$3
❑ 22975 [PS]	It's Real/Aren't You Tired	1989	$5
❑ 22863	I Wanna Come Back/Ooo	1989	$3

INGRAM, LUTHER

DECCA

Number	Title	Yr	NM
❑ 31794	Ain't That Nice/You Never Miss Your Water	1965	$300

HIB

Number	Title	Yr	NM
❑ 698	If It's All the Same To You Babe/Exus Trek	1967	$750

— Light green label

Number	Title	Yr	NM
❑ 698	If It's All the Same To You Babe/Exus Trek	1967	$1000

—Orange label (with "Wylie" credit)

Number	Title	Yr	NM
❑ 698	If It's All the Same To You Babe/Exus Trek	1967	$80

—Orange label (with "Wylia" credit)

KOKO

Number	Title	Yr	NM
❑ 721	Ain't Good for Nothing/ These Are the Things	1976	$6
❑ 2105	Ain't That Loving You (For More Reasons Than One)/ Home Don't Seem Like Home	1970	$8
❑ 2115	Always/Help Me Love	1973	$8
❑ 2107	Be Good to Me Baby/ Since You Don't Want Me	1971	$8
❑ 728	Do You Love Somebody/ How I Miss My Baby	1977	$6
❑ 731	Get to Me/Trying to Find My Love	1978	$50
❑ 101	I Can't Stop/You Got to Give Love to Get Love	1968	$40
❑ 2111	(If Loving You Is Wrong) I Don't Want to Be Right/ Puttin' Game Down	1972	$8
❑ 725	I Like the Feeling/Gonna Be the Next Time	1977	$6
❑ 2113	I'll Be Your Shelter (In Time of Storm)/I Can't Stop	1972	$8
❑ 2108	I'll Love You Until the End/Ghetto Train	1971	$8
❑ 724	Let's Steal Away to the Hideaway/I've Got Your Love in My Life	1977	$6
❑ 2116	Love Ain't Gonna Run Me Away/To the Other Man	1973	$8
❑ 103	Missing You/Since You Don't Want Me	1968	$60
❑ 2104	My Honey and Me/I Can't Stop	1969	$20
❑ 2102	Pity for the Lonely/ Looking for a New Love	1969	$8
❑ 2103	Puttin' Game Down/Since You Don't Want Me	1969	$8
❑ 2106	To the Other Man/I'll Just Call You Honey	1970	$20

PROFILE

Number	Title	Yr	NM
❑ 5125	Baby Don't Go Too Far/ How Sweet It Would Be	1986	$3
❑ 5132	Don't Turn Around/ (B-side unknown)	1987	$3
❑ 5143	Gotta Serve Somebody/ All in the Name of Love	1987	$3

SMASH

Number	Title	Yr	NM
❑ 2019	(I Spy) For the F.B.I./Foxey Devil	1966	$60

INJECTIONS, THE

RADIO ACTIVE

Number	Title	Yr	NM
❑ 04	Prison Walls/Lies	1980	$200

—Not issued with picture sleeve

INK SPOTS

DECCA

Number	Title	Yr	NM
❑ 25533	All My Life/You Were Only Fooling	1961	$15
❑ 9-25240	Coquette/When the Swallows Come Back to Capistrano	1950	$30

—From "Album No. 9-5

Number	Title	Yr	NM
❑ 9-27493	Do Something for Me/A Fool Grows Wise	1951	$30
❑ 9-27259	Dream Awhile/Time Out for Tears	1950	$30
❑ 9-27996	Honest and Truly/All My Life	1952	$30
❑ 9-25239	I'd Climb the Highest Mountain/ I'm Gettin' Sentimental Over You	1950	$30

—From "Album No. 9-5

Number	Title	Yr	NM
❑ 9-27742	I Don't Stand a Ghost of a Chance/I'm Lucky I Have You	1951	$30
❑ 9-27391	If/A Friend of Johnny's	1951	$30
❑ 9-23632	If I Didn't Care/Whispering Grass (Don't Tell the Trees)	1950	$30

—Black label, lines on either side of "Decca

Number	Title	Yr	NM
❑ 9-23632	If I Didn't Care/Whispering Grass (Don't Tell the Trees)	1955	$15

—Black label, star under "Decca

Number	Title	Yr	NM
❑ 23632	If I Didn't Care/Whispering Grass (Don't Tell the Trees)	1961	$10

—Black label, color bars at right

Number	Title	Yr	NM
❑ 9-25238	I'll Get By (As Long As I Have You)/Just for a Thrill	1950	$30

—Side 1 and 6 of "Album No. 9-5

Number	Title	Yr	NM
❑ 9-5 [PS]	Ink Spots, Volume 2	1950	$20

—Box for 25238, 25239 and 25240

Number	Title	Yr	NM
❑ 25505	It's a Sin to Tell a Lie/That's When Your Heartaches Begin	1961	$10
❑ 9-29750	Memories of You/It's Funny to Everyone But Me	1955	$30
❑ 9-27632	More of the Same Sweet You/What Can You Do	1951	$30
❑ 9-29991	My Prayer/Bewildered	1956	$30
❑ 9-27256	Our Lady of Fatima/ Stranger in the City	1950	$30
❑ 9-27102	Sometime/I Was Dancing with Someone	1950	$30
❑ 9-27464	Tell Me You Love Me/ Castles in the Sand	1951	$30
❑ 9-30058	The Best Things in Life Are Free/I Don't Stand a Ghost of a Chance	1956	$20
❑ 9-27214	The Way It Used to Be/ Right About Now	1950	$30
❑ 9-23615	To Each His Own/I Never Had a Dream Come True	1950	$30

—Black label, lines on either side of "Decca"; reissue of 78 from 1946

Number	Title	Yr	NM
❑ 9-23615	To Each His Own/I Never Had a Dream Come True	1955	$15

—Black label, star under "Decca

Number	Title	Yr	NM
❑ 23615	To Each His Own/I Never Had a Dream Come True	1960	$8

—Black label, color bars at right

KING

Number	Title	Yr	NM
❑ 1304	Changing Partners/ Stranger in Paradise	1954	$75
❑ 4857	Command Me/I'll Walk a Country Mile	1955	$50
❑ 1512	Don't Laugh at Me/ Keep It Movin'	1955	$50
❑ 1297	Ebb Tide/If You Should Say Goodbye	1953	$70
❑ 4670	Here in My Lonely Room/A Fool in Love	1953	$200
❑ 1336	Melody of Love/Am I Too Late	1954	$75
❑ 1429	Melody of Love/There Is Something Missing	1955	$50
❑ 1425	When You Come to the End of the Day/Someone's Rocking My Dreamboat	1955	$60

VERVE

Number	Title	Yr	NM
❑ 10198	Secret Love/A Little Bird Told Me	1960	$15

INMAN, AUTRY

DECCA

Number	Title	Yr	NM
❑ 28798	A Dear John Letter/ Brown Eyed Baby	1953	$30
❑ 29936	Be-Bop Baby/It Would Be a Doggone Lie	1956	$125
❑ 29690	Blue Monday/Look Over Your Shoulder	1955	$30
❑ 28495	Does Your Sweetheart Seem Different Lately/All of a Sudden	1952	$30
❑ 29362	Finally I'm Free/Don't Put It Off	1954	$30
❑ 28592	I'll Miss My Heart/Stop Stallin'	1953	$30
❑ 28960	It Hurts Too Much to Cry/ Happy Go Lucky	1953	$30
❑ 46407	Let's Take the Long Way Home Tonight/I Hope Tomorrow Never Comes	1952	$30
❑ 29170	Little One/Once More	1954	$30
❑ 28778	Pucker Up/That's When I Need You the Most	1953	$30
❑ 29635	Tell Me Now/A Friend	1955	$30
❑ 28629	That's All Right/Uh Huh Honey	1953	$30
❑ 28290	Who Do You Love/Just Smile As You Go By	1952	$30

EPIC

Number	Title	Yr	NM
❑ 10389	Ballad of Two Brothers/ Don't Call Me (I'll Call You)	1968	$8
❑ 10232	Don't Call Me (I'll Call You)/ Love Has to Die (All By Itself)	1967	$8
❑ 10452	Home Is Heavy on My Mind/ You're the Only One in My Heart	1969	$8
❑ 10327	I Can See an Angel/Wish in One Hand (Cry in the Other)	1968	$8
❑ 10494	I'll Be Waiting/Traveling Salesman	1969	$8
❑ 10276	There Stands the Glass/This Heart Was Made for Lovin'	1968	$8

GLAD

Number	Title	Yr	NM
❑ 1002	I'm Still in Love with Mary/ Please Cut Me Down	1960	$20

JUBILEE

Number	Title	Yr	NM
❑ 9016	Hurtache/Mr. Love Passed Away	1965	$8
❑ 9001	The Drinks Are On Me/You Don't Live There Anymore	1964	$8

KOALA

Number	Title	Yr	NM
❑ 325	That's Why You're Being Paid/(B-side unknown)	1980	$5

MERCURY

Number	Title	Yr	NM
❑ 71983	Living with One and Loving Two/I Guess I'm Crazy	1962	$15

MILLION

Number	Title	Yr	NM
❑ 24	If You Were Mine/Please Let Me Love You	1972	$6
❑ 4	Please Let Me Love You/ Maybe This Is the Day	1972	$6

RCA VICTOR

Number	Title	Yr	NM
❑ 47-7173	Dream Boat/Remember the Night	1958	$40
❑ 47-7260	Mary Nell/The Hard Way	1958	$40

SIMS

Number	Title	Yr	NM
❑ 140	Big Sam/My Word	1963	$12
❑ 219	Give Me 40 Acres (To Turn This Rig Around)/Six Rounds of Love and Hate	1964	$10
❑ 188	My Past/You're Welcome Dear	1964	$10
❑ 170	The Ballad of John F. Kennedy/ The World's Worst Lover	1964	$12

UNITED ARTISTS

Number	Title	Yr	NM
❑ 303	Let's Take the Long Way Home/Too Blue to Cry	1961	$20
❑ 278	That's All Right/Farther to Go Than I've Been	1960	$20

78s

BULLET

Number	Title	Yr	NM
❑ 687	Double Cross/In My Imagination	1949	$40

INMAN, JERRY

COLUMBIA

Number	Title	Yr	NM
❑ 4-44453	From Me to You/Help!	1968	$8
❑ 4-44774	Mississippi Woman/One If for Him, Two If for Her	1969	$8
❑ 4-44894	Spanish Eyes/Talk	1969	$8
❑ 4-44619	Train of Thought/Leaves Are the Tears of Autumn	1968	$8

ELEKTRA

Number	Title	Yr	NM
❑ 45333	She's Lying Next to Me/ Woman with a Gun	1976	$5
❑ 45352	Single Again/Six Weeks in Alaska	1976	$5
❑ 45414	Smoke on the Far Horizon/ J.C.'s Country Band	1977	$4
❑ 45508	Why, Baby, Why/Gonna Save It for My Baby	1978	$4
❑ 46006	Why Don't We Lie Down and Talk It Over/Gonna Save It for My Baby	1979	$4

HILLSIDE

Number	Title	Yr	NM
❑ 8004	Make Room for the Blues/What She Don't Know Won't Hurt Me	1980	$6
❑ 8102	Take These Chains/ Tulsa Turnaround	1981	$6

INNER CIRCLE, THE

DUNHILL

Number	Title	Yr	NM
❑ 4128	So Long Mary Ann/ Goes to Show	1968	$30

IMPACT

Number	Title	Yr	NM
❑ 1019	Sally Go Round the Roses/Sugar	1967	$50

INNOCENCE, THE

KAMA SUTRA

Number	Title	Yr	NM
❑ 228	All I Do Is Think About You/ Whence, I Make Thee Mine	1967	$8
❑ 237	Day Turns Me On (The Bufferin Song)/It's Not Gonna Take Too Long	1967	$8
❑ 222	Mairzy Doats/Lifetime Lovin' You	1967	$10
❑ 232	Someone Got Caught in My Eye/Your Show Is Over	1967	$8
❑ 214	There's Got to Be a Word!/I Don't Wanna Be Around You	1966	$8

INNOCENTS, THE

DECCA

Number	Title	Yr	NM
❑ 31519	Don't Cry/Come On Lover	1963	$30

INDIGO

Number	Title	Yr	NM
❑ 124	Beware/Because I Love You	1961	$30
❑ 128	Donna/You Got Me Goin'	1961	$30
❑ 111	Gee Whiz/Please Mr. Sun	1960	$30
❑ 105	Honest I Do/My Baby Hully Gullys	1960	$30
❑ 132	Pains in My Heart/When I Become a Man	1961	$30

REPRISE

Number	Title	Yr	NM
❑ 20112	Be Mine/Oh How I Miss My Baby	1962	$30

WARNER BROS.

Number	Title	Yr	NM
❑ 5450	My Heart Stood Still/Don't Call Me Lonely Anymore	1964	$40

INSECT TRUST, THE

CAPITOL

Number	Title	Yr	NM
❑ 2386	Miss Fun City/Special Rider Blues	1969	$20

INSECTS, THE

APPLAUSE

Number	Title	Yr	NM
❑ 1002	Let's Bug the Beatles/ Dear Beatles	1964	$30

—B-side by the Little Lady Beatles

INSIDE OUT (CALIFORNIA BAND)

7-Inch Extended Plays

REVELATION

Number	Title	Yr	NM
❑ 19 [PS]	Burning Fight	1988	$8
❑ 19	Burning Fight	1988	$23

—Blue vinyl

Number	Title	Yr	NM
❑ 19	Burning Fight	1988	$8

—Black vinyl

INSIDE OUT (NEW YORK BAND)

NOISEVILLE

Number	Title	Yr	NM
❑ 3	Above All/Beat Life/Cracking Up	1989	$38

—Blue vinyl

Number	Title	Yr	NM
❑ 3	Above All/Beat Life/Cracking Up	1989	$13

Number	Title	Yr	NM
—Black vinyl			
❑ 3	Above All/Beat Life/Cracking Up	1989	$23
—Red vinyl			
❑ 3	Above All/Beat Life/Cracking Up	1989	$5
—Reissue as "Inside Out NY			
❑ 3 [PS]	Above All/Beat Life/Cracking Up	1989	$5
—Reissue as "Inside Out NY			
❑ 3 [PS]	Above All/Beat Life/Cracking Up	1989	$13

INSIDERS, THE
RCA VICTOR

Number	Title	Yr	NM
❑ 47-9325	If You Had a Heart/Movin' On	1967	$80
❑ 47-9225	I'm Just a Man/I'm Better Off Without You	1967	$125

RED BIRD

Number	Title	Yr	NM
❑ Oct-0055	Chapel Bells Are Calling/I'm Stuck on You	1966	$80

INSIGHT, THE
CASCADE

Number	Title	Yr	NM
❑ 364	Please Come Home For Christmas/Out Of Sight	1964	$40

INSPIRATIONS, THE
AL-BRITE

Number	Title	Yr	NM
❑ 1651	Angel in Disguise/Stool Pigeon	1960	$100

BELTONE

Number	Title	Yr	NM
❑ 2037	The Girl By My Side/Neckin'	1963	$70

FEATURE

Number	Title	Yr	NM
❑ 110	Baby Please Come Back/That Girl	1966	$60

GONE

Number	Title	Yr	NM
❑ 5097	Angel in Disguise/Stool Pigeon	1961	$30

JAMIE

Number	Title	Yr	NM
❑ 1034	Dry Your Eyes/Good-Bye	1956	$80
❑ 1212	Dry Your Eyes/Good-Bye	1962	$30

LAMP

Number	Title	Yr	NM
❑ 2019	Don't Cry/Indian Jane	1958	$200

SPARKLE

Number	Title	Yr	NM
❑ 102	Angel in Disguise/Stool Pigeon	1960	$200

SULTAN

Number	Title	Yr	NM
❑ 1	The Genie/The Feeling of Her Kiss	1959	$40
❑ 1 [PS]	The Genie/The Feeling of Her Kiss	1959	$60

INSULTS, THE
RIC-MER

Number	Title	Yr	NM
❑ 0(# unknown)	Population Zero/Zombie Lover	1979	$50
❑ 0(# unknown) [PS]	Population Zero/Zombie Lover	1979	$50

SICK SOUND

Number	Title	Yr	NM
❑ 0(# unknown)	Stiff Love/Tax War/I'm a Doper	1979	$10
❑ 0(# unknown) [PS]	Stiff Love/Tax War/I'm a Doper	1979	$12

7-Inch Extended Plays

INSULTS

Number	Title	Yr	NM
❑ 01	Thrasher Go Home	1982	$25
❑ 01 [PS]	Thrasher Go Home	1982	$25

INTENTIONS, THE
JAMIE

Number	Title	Yr	NM
❑ 1253	Summertime Angel/Mr. Misery	1963	$1500

KENT

Number	Title	Yr	NM
❑ 455	Dancing Fast, Dancing Slow/My Love She's Gone	1966	$60

MELRON

Number	Title	Yr	NM
❑ 5014	I'm in Love with a Go-Go Girl/Wonderful Girl	1965	$200

PHILIPS

Number	Title	Yr	NM
❑ 40428	Don't Forget That I Love You/Night Rider	1967	$30

UPTOWN

Number	Title	Yr	NM
❑ 710	Time/Cool Summer Night	1965	$200

INTERLUDES, THE
KING

Number	Title	Yr	NM
❑ 5633	Darling I'll Be True/Wilted Rose Bud	1962	$40

RCA VICTOR

Number	Title	Yr	NM
❑ 47-7281	I Shed a Million Tears/Oo-Wee	1958	$30

STAR-HI

Number	Title	Yr	NM
❑ 103	I Want You to Know/Split a Kiss	1959	$20

VALLEY

Number	Title	Yr	NM
❑ 105	Heartbreaker/Scandalous	1959	$20
❑ 107	White Sailor Hat/Evil	1960	$20

INTERNATIONAL SUBMARINE BAND, THE
Also see GRAM PARSONS.

COLUMBIA

Number	Title	Yr	NM
❑ 43935	Sum Up Broke/One Day Week	1966	$40

LHI

Number	Title	Yr	NM
❑ 1205	Luxury Liner/Blue Eyes	1968	$20
❑ 1217	Miller's Cave/I Must Be Somebody Else	1968	$20

INTERNS, THE
CAPITOL

Number	Title	Yr	NM
❑ 5747	Is It Really What You Want/Just Like Me	1966	$15

UPTOWN

Number	Title	Yr	NM
❑ 730	Hard to Get/And I'm Glad	1966	$15

INTIMATES, THE
EPIC

Number	Title	Yr	NM
❑ 9743	I've Got a Tiger in My Tank/Smart, Too Late	1964	$20

INTRIGUES, THE
TOOT

Number	Title	Yr	NM
❑ 609	Soul Brother (Part 1)/Soul Brother (Part 2)	1968	$12

YEW

Number	Title	Yr	NM
❑ 1002	I'm Gonna Love You/I Gotta Find Out for Myself	1969	$10
❑ 1001	In a Moment/Scotchman Rock	1969	$15
❑ 1013	Mojo Hannah/To Make a World	1971	$10
❑ 1012	The Language of Love/I Got Love	1971	$10
❑ 1010	Tuck a Little Love Away/I Know There's Love	1970	$10

INTRUDERS, THE (1)
GAMBLE

Number	Title	Yr	NM
❑ 209	Baby I'm Lonely/A Love That's Real	1967	$12
❑ 214	Cowboys to Girls/Turn the Hands of Time	1968	$12
❑ 203	Devil with an Angel's Smile/A Book for the Broken Hearted	1966	$12
❑ 203 [PS]	Devil with an Angel's Smile/A Book for the Broken Hearted	1966	$20
❑ 223	Give Her a Transplant/Girls, Girls, Girls	1969	$10
❑ 4016	I Bet He Don't Love You (Like I Love You)/Do You Remember Yesterday	1971	$30
❑ 2506	I'll Always Love My Mama (Part 1)/I'll Always Love My Mama (Part 2)	1973	$8
❑ 4009	I'm Girl Scoutin'/Wonder What Kind of Bag She's In	1971	$8
❑ 204	It Must Be Love/Check Yourself	1966	$10
❑ 2508	I Wanna Know Your Name/Hang On In There	1973	$8
❑ 231	Lollipop (I Like You)/Don't Give It Away	1969	$10
❑ 217	(Love Is Like a) Baseball Game/Friends No More	1968	$10
❑ 225	Me Tarzan You Jane/Favorite Candidate	1969	$10
❑ 240	Old Love/Every Day Is a Holiday	1969	$10
❑ 4014	Pray for Me/Best Days of My Life	1971	$20
❑ 235	Sad Girl/Let's Go Downtown	1969	$10
❑ 221	Slow Drag/So Glad I'm Yours	1968	$12
❑ 4001	Tender (Was the Love We Knew)/By the Time I Get to Phoenix	1970	$8
❑ 4007	This Is My Love Song/Let Me in Your Mind	1970	$8
❑ 205	Together/Up and Down the Ladder	1967	$10
❑ 201	(We'll Be) United/Up and Down the Ladder	1966	$10
❑ 4004	When We Get Married/Doctor Doctor	1970	$8
❑ 4019	(Win, Place or Show) She's a Winner/Memories Are Here to Stay	1972	$10
❑ 2501	(Win, Place or Show) She's a Winner/Memories Are Here to Stay	1972	$8

GOWEN

Number	Title	Yr	NM
❑ 1401	I'm Sold on You/Come Home Soon	1961	$50

PHILADELPHIA INT'L.

Number	Title	Yr	NM
❑ 3624	I'll Always Love My Mama (Part 1)/I'll Always Love My Mama (Part 2)	1977	$5
❑ 3689	I'll Always Love My Mama/Save the Children	1979	$5

TSOP

Number	Title	Yr	NM
❑ 4771	Plain Old Fashioned Girl/Energy of Love	1975	$6

INTRUDERS, THE (2)
BELTONE

Number	Title	Yr	NM
❑ 1009	Camptown Rock/Morse Code	1961	$20

FAME

Number	Title	Yr	NM
❑ 313	Creepin'/Frankfurters and Sauerkraut	1959	$30
❑ 101	Fried Eggs/Jeffrie's Rock	1959	$30

INVITATIONS, THE
DIAMOND

Number	Title	Yr	NM
❑ 253	Got to Have It Now/Swingin' on the Love Vine	1968	$40

DYNO VOICE

Number	Title	Yr	NM
❑ 215	Skiing in the Snow/Why Did My Baby Turn Bad	1966	$400
❑ 210	What's Wrong with Me Baby/Why Did My Baby Turn Bad	1965	$300
❑ 206	Written on the Wall/Hallelujah	1965	$70

MGM

Number	Title	Yr	NM
❑ 13574	The Skate/Girl I'm Leavin' You	1966	$50
❑ 13666	Watch Out Little Girl/You're Like a Mystery	1967	$125

SILVER BLUE

Number	Title	Yr	NM
❑ 804	Let's Love/Love Has to Grow	1973	$70
❑ 809	Living Together Is Keeping Us Apart/I Didn't Know	1974	$40
❑ 818	Look on the Good Side/Look on the Good Side (Part 2)	1974	$50
❑ 801	They Say the Girl's Crazy/For Your Precious Love	1973	$50

INXS
ATCO

Number	Title	Yr	NM
❑ 99703	Burn for You/Johnson's Aeroplane	1984	$4
❑ 99703 [PS]	Burn for You/Johnson's Aeroplane	1984	$4
❑ 99874	Don't Change/Long in Tooth	1983	$4
❑ 99874 [PS]	Don't Change/Long in Tooth	1983	$4
❑ 99731	I Send a Message/Mechanical	1984	$4
❑ 99731 [PS]	I Send a Message/Mechanical	1984	$4
❑ 99766	Original Sin/Stay Young	1984	$4
❑ 99766 [PS]	Original Sin/Stay Young	1984	$4
❑ 99905	The One Thing/Phantim of the Opera	1983	$4
❑ 99905 [PS]	The One Thing/Phantim of the Opera	1983	$4
❑ 99833	To Look at You/Sax Thing	1983	$4
❑ 99833 [PS]	To Look at You/Sax Thing	1983	$4

ATLANTIC

Number	Title	Yr	NM
❑ 89144	Devil Inside/On the Rocks	1988	$3
❑ 89144 [PS]	Devil Inside/On the Rocks	1988	$3
❑ 89237	Good Times/Laying Down the Law	1987	$3
—With Jimmy Barnes			
❑ 89237 [PS]	Good Times/Laying Down the Law	1987	$3
—With Jimmy Barnes			
❑ 89429	Listen Like Thieves/Begotten	1986	$3
❑ 89429 [PS]	Listen Like Thieves/Begotten	1986	$3
❑ 89497	This Time/I'm Over You	1985	$3
❑ 89497 [PS]	This Time/I'm Over You	1985	$3
❑ 89460	What You Need/Sweet as Sin	1986	$3
❑ 89460 [PS]	What You Need/Sweet as Sin	1986	$3

IRBY, JERRY
4 STAR

Number	Title	Yr	NM
❑ 1578	Buy Me a Bottle of Beer/Rose	1951	$30
❑ 1591	Standing on the Corner/The First Time I Saw That Gal	1952	$30

DAFFAN

Number	Title	Yr	NM
❑ 106	Call for Me Darling/It's Time You Started Loving	1956	$60
❑ 108	Clickety Clack/A Man Is a Slave	1956	$125
❑ 111	That's Too Bad/I'd Give Anything in This World	1957	$70

JER-RAY

Number	Title	Yr	NM
❑ 222	Chantilly Lace/(B-side unknown)	1959	$40

MGM

Number	Title	Yr	NM
❑ 10475	By the Rio Grande/You Just Can't Be Trusted Anymore	1949	$50
❑ 10771	Cuddling Baby/I'm So Disgusted	1950	$40
❑ 10809	Hillbilly Boogie/Ball and Chain	1950	$40
❑ 10580	Mama Don't Allow It/Memory of a Rose	1949	$50
❑ 10595	One Way Blues/Don't Know Where I'm Goin'	1950	$40
❑ 11109	There's a Moon to Love By/I've Got the Blues	1951	$40

IRIDESCENTS, THE
HUDSON

Number	Title	Yr	NM
❑ 8102	Three Coins in the Fountain/Strong Love	1963	$125
—Blue vinyl			
❑ 8102	Three Coins in the Fountain/Strong Love	1963	$30

ULTRASONIC

Number	Title	Yr	NM
❑ 109	I Know/The Angels Sang	1960	$400

IRIS, DONNIE
HME

Number	Title	Yr	NM
❑ 04734	Injured in the Game of Love/I Want You Back	1985	$3
❑ 04734 [PS]	Injured in the Game of Love/I Want You Back	1985	$4
❑ 04885	State of the Heart/You're My Serenity	1985	$3

MCA

Number	Title	Yr	NM
❑ 51025	Ah! Leah!/Joking	1980	$5
❑ 52230	Do You Compute?/I Belong	1983	$3

Number	Title	Yr	NM
❑ 52230 [PS]	Do You Compute?/I Belong	1983	$4
❑ 51223	Love Is Like a Rock/Agnes	1981	$5
❑ 52031	My Girl/The Last to Know	1982	$3
❑ 51093	She's So Wild/You're Only Dreaming	1981	$5
❑ 51198	Sweet Merilee/Back on the Streets	1981	$5
❑ 52169	This Time It Must Be Love/ You're Gonna Miss Me	1983	$3
❑ 52127	Tough World/You're Gonna Miss Me	1982	$3
❑ 52127 [PS]	Tough World/You're Gonna Miss Me	1982	$5

MIDWEST NATIONAL

Number	Title	Yr	NM
❑ 6006	Ah! Leah!/Joking	1980	$15

IRISH ROVERS, THE

DECCA

Number	Title	Yr	NM
❑ 32575	Fifi O'Toole/Winkin', Blinkin', and Nod	1969	$8
❑ 32444	Lily the Pink/Mrs. Crandall's Boardinghouse	1969	$8
❑ 32371	Liverpool Lou/The Bi-Plane, Ever More	1968	$8
❑ 32529	Peter Knight/Did She Mention My Name	1969	$8
❑ 32775	The Marvelous Toy/ Marika's Lullaby	1970	$6
❑ 32333	(The Puppet Song) Whiskey on a Sunday/The Orange and the Green	1968	$8
❑ 32723	Two Little Boys/Years May Come, Years May Go	1970	$6

IRMA AND THE LARKS

FAIRMOUNT

Number	Title	Yr	NM
❑ 1003	Without You Baby/Don't Cry	1966	$125

PRIORITY

Number	Title	Yr	NM
❑ 322	Without You Baby/Don't Cry	1966	$200

IRON BUTTERFLY

Also see CAPTAIN BEYOND.

ATCO

Number	Title	Yr	NM
❑ 6782	Easy Rider (Let the Wind Pay the Way)/Soldier in Town	1970	$8
❑ 6606	In-A-Gadda-Da-Vida/ Iron Butterfly Theme	1968	$10
❑ 6676	In the Times of Our Lives/ It Must Be Love	1969	$8
❑ 6573	Possession/Unconscious Power	1968	$8
❑ 6818	Silly Sally/Stone Believer	1971	$6
❑ 6647	Soul Experience/In the Crowds	1969	$8
❑ 6712	To Be Alone/I Can't Help But Deceive You Little Girl	1969	$8

MCA

Number	Title	Yr	NM
❑ 40493	Beyond the Milky Way/Get It Out	1975	$4
❑ 40379	Pearly Gates/Searchin' Circles	1975	$4

IRON CROSS

7-Inch Extended Plays

SKINFLINT

Number	Title	Yr	NM
❑ 2	Hated and Proud	1983	$25
❑ 2 [PS]	Hated and Proud	1983	$25

SKINFLINT/DISCHORD

Number	Title	Yr	NM
❑ 1-8 1/2	Skinhead Glory	1982	$75

—Green vinyl

Number	Title	Yr	NM
❑ 1-8 1/2	Skinhead Glory	1982	$25

—Black vinyl

Number	Title	Yr	NM
❑ 1-8 1/2 [PS]	Skinhead Glory	1982	$25

IRON MAIDEN

CAPITOL

Number	Title	Yr	NM
❑ B-44154	Can I Play with Madness/ Black Bart Blues	1988	$8
❑ B-5248	Flight of Icarus/I've the Fire	1983	$10
❑ B-5248 [PS]	Flight of Icarus/I've the Fire	1983	$20

IRONSTRINGS, IRA

WARNER BROS.

Number	Title	Yr	NM
❑ 5117	Christmas Is for the Birds/ Deck Them Halls	1959	$20

IRRIDESCENTS, THE

HAWK

Number	Title	Yr	NM
❑ 4001	Bali Ha'i/Swamp Surfer	1963	$60

INFINITY

Number	Title	Yr	NM
❑ 037	Bali Ha'i/Swamp Surfer	1963	$30

OLDIES 45

Number	Title	Yr	NM
❑ 183	Bali Ha'i/Swamp Surfer	1964	$15

IRVING, LONNIE

LONNIE IRVING

Number	Title	Yr	NM
❑ (# unknown)	Pinball Machine/I Got Blues on My Mind	1959	$60

STARDAY

Number	Title	Yr	NM
❑ 505	Gooseball Brown/An Old Fashioned Love	1960	$30
❑ 520	I Wish I Had My Heart Back/Trucker's Vitus	1960	$30
❑ 486	Pinball Machine/I Got Blues on My Mind	1960	$30

IRWIN, BIG DEE

CUB

Number	Title	Yr	NM
❑ 9155	I Only Get This Feeling/ Wrong Direction	1968	$8

—As "Dee Erwin

DIMENSION

Number	Title	Yr	NM
❑ 1001	Everybody's Gotta Dance But Me/And Heaven Was There	1962	$70
❑ 1028	Heigh Ho/I Want So Much to Know You	1964	$60
❑ 1015	Soul Waltzin'/Happy Being Fat	1963	$20
❑ 1010	Swinging on a Star/Another Night with the Boys	1963	$30
❑ 1021	The Christmas Song/I Wish You a Merry Christmas	1963	$20

—With Little Eva

IMPERIAL

Number	Title	Yr	NM
❑ 66420	Ain't No Way/Cherish	1969	$30
❑ 66334	All I Want for Christmas Is Your Love//By the Time I Get to Phoenix/I Say a Little Prayer	1968	$15

—With Mamie Galore

Number	Title	Yr	NM
❑ 66359	Day Tripper/I Didn't Wanna Do It, But I Did	1969	$8

—With Mamie Galore

Number	Title	Yr	NM
❑ 66320	I Can't Stand the Pain/ My Hope to Die Girl	1968	$30
❑ 66295	Wrong Direction/I Only Get This Feeling	1968	$50

—As "Dee Irwin

PHIL-LA OF SOUL

Number	Title	Yr	NM
❑ 303	Better to Have Loved and Lost/Linda	1967	$50

—As "Dee Erwin

ROULETTE

Number	Title	Yr	NM
❑ 4596	Discotheque/The Sun's Gonna Shine Tomorrow	1965	$12

—As "Big Dee Erwin

ISAAK, CHRIS

WARNER BROS.

Number	Title	Yr	NM
❑ 7-28374 [DJ]	Blue Hotel (same on both sides)	1987	$4
❑ 7-28374	Blue Hotel/Waiting for the Rain to Fall	1987	$8
❑ 7-28374 [PS]	Blue Hotel/Waiting for the Rain to Fall	1987	$8
❑ 7-29073 [DJ]	Dancin' (same on both sides)	1985	$3
❑ 7-29073	Dancin'/Unhappiness	1985	$6
❑ 7-29073 [PS]	Dancin'/Unhappiness	1985	$6
❑ 7-28907 [DJ]	Gone Ridin' (Theme from American Flyers) (same on both sides)	1985	$3
❑ 7-28907	Gone Ridin' (Theme from American Flyers)/Tears	1985	$6
❑ 7-28907 [PS]	Gone Ridin' (Theme from American Flyers)/Tears	1985	$6
❑ 7-28971 [DJ]	Livin' for Your Lover (same on both sides)	1985	$3
❑ 7-28971	Livin' for Your Lover/Talk to Me	1985	$6
❑ 7-28971 [PS]	Livin' for Your Lover/Talk to Me	1985	$6

ISABEL, DAVE

SARG

Number	Title	Yr	NM
❑ 109	Make Believe It's Christmas/ Let's Down It Up Brown	1957	$20

ISLE, JIMMY

BALLY

Number	Title	Yr	NM
❑ 1034	Baby-O/Hssle	1957	$30

EVEREST

Number	Title	Yr	NM
❑ 19320	Oh Judy/Billy Boy	1959	$30

MALA

Number	Title	Yr	NM
❑ 459	Our Town/Everybody Gotta Little Girl But Me	1963	$30

ROULETTE

Number	Title	Yr	NM
❑ 4065	Goin' Wild/You and Johnny Smith	1958	$40

SUN

Number	Title	Yr	NM
❑ 306	Diamond Ring/I've Been Waiting	1958	$30
❑ 318	Time Will Tell/Without a Love	1959	$30
❑ 332	What a Life/Together	1959	$30

ISLEY BROTHERS, THE

ATLANTIC

Number	Title	Yr	NM
❑ 2122	A Fool for You/Just One More Time	1961	$20
❑ 2263	Looking for a Love/The Last Girl	1964	$40
❑ 2303	Move Over and Let Me Dance/Have You Ever Been Disappointed	1965	$30
❑ 2100	Shine On Harvest Moon/ Standing on the Dance Floor	1961	$20
❑ 2277	Simon Says/Wild As a Tiger	1965	$40

CINDY

Number	Title	Yr	NM
❑ 3009	Don't Be Jealous/This Is the End	1958	$200

—Cindy" in shadow print

Number	Title	Yr	NM
❑ 3009	Don't Be Jealous/This Is the End	1958	$80

—Cindy" in regular print

GONE

Number	Title	Yr	NM
❑ 5022	I Wanna Know/Everybody's Gonna Rock and Roll	1958	$100
❑ 5048	My Love/The Drag	1958	$100

MARK-X

Number	Title	Yr	NM
❑ 7003	The Drag/Rockin' MacDonald	1957	$125
❑ 8000	The Drag/Rockin' MacDonald	1959	$40

PHILCO-FORD

Number	Title	Yr	NM
❑ HP-41	Twist and Shout/Rubberleg Twist	1969	$30

—4-inch plastic "Hip Pocket Record" with color sleeve

RCA

Number	Title	Yr	NM
❑ 447-0589	Shout (Part 1)/Shout (Part 2)	1976	$4

—Gold Standard Series; black label, dog near top

RCA VICTOR

Number	Title	Yr	NM
❑ 47-7746	Gypsy Love Song/ Open Up Your Heart	1960	$30
❑ 47-7718	He's Got the Whole World in His Hands/How Deep Is the Ocean	1960	$30
❑ 47-7537	I'm Gonna Knock on Your Door/Turn to Me	1959	$30
❑ 47-7787	Say You Love Me Too/ Tell Me Who	1960	$30
❑ 47-7588	Shout (Part 1)/Shout (Part 2)	1959	$40
❑ 61-7588 [S]	Shout (Part 1)/Shout (Part 2)	1959	$70

—Living Stereo" (large hole, plays at 45 rpm)

Number	Title	Yr	NM
❑ 447-0589	Shout (Part 1)/Shout (Part 2)	1962	$15

—Gold Standard Series; black label, dog on top (this charted with this number in 1962)

Number	Title	Yr	NM
❑ 447-0589	Shout (Part 1)/Shout (Part 2)	1965	$8

—Gold Standard Series; black label, dog on side

Number	Title	Yr	NM
❑ 447-0589	Shout (Part 1)/Shout (Part 2)	1969	$5

—Gold Standard Series; red label

TAMLA

Number	Title	Yr	NM
❑ 54175	Behind a Painted Smile/ All Because I Love You	1968	$30
❑ 54146	Got to Have You Back/ Just Ain't Enough Love	1967	$20
❑ 54135	I Guess I'll Always Love You/I Hear a Symphony	1966	$30
❑ 54154	One Too Many Heartaches/ That's the Way Love Is	1967	$20
❑ 54164	Take Me in Your Arms (Rock Me a Little While)/ Why When Love Is Gone	1968	$20
❑ 54182	Take Some Time Out for Love/ Just Ain't Enough Love	1969	$30
❑ 54133	Take Some Time Out for Love/ Who Could Ever Doubt My Love	1966	$20
❑ 54128	This Old Heart of Mine (Is Weak for You)/There's No Love Left	1966	$20

TEENAGE

Number	Title	Yr	NM
❑ 1004	Angels Cried/The Cow Jumped Over the Moon	1957	$800

T-NECK

Number	Title	Yr	NM
❑ 03797	Between the Sheets/ (Instrumental)	1983	$5
❑ 906	Black Berries -- Pt. 1/ Black Berries -- Pt. 2	1969	$6
❑ 912	Bless Your Heart/Give the Women What They Want	1969	$6
❑ 03994	Choosey Lover/(Instrumental)	1983	$5
❑ 2290	Don't Say Goodnight (It's Time for Love) (Part 1)/ Don't Say Goodnight (It's Time for Love) (Part 2)	1980	$5
❑ 02151	Don't Say Goodnight (It's Time for Love) (Parts 1 & 2)	1981	$4

—Reissue

Number	Title	Yr	NM
❑ 2256	Fight the Power Part 1/ Fight the Power Part 2	1975	$5
❑ 2259	For the Love of You (Part 1&2)/You Walk Your Way	1975	$5
❑ 927	Freedom/I Need You So	1970	$6
❑ 924	Get Into Something/Get Into Something (Part 2)	1970	$20
❑ 921	Girls Will Be Girls, Boys Will Be Boys/Get Down Off of the Train	1970	$6
❑ 2277	Groove with You/ Footsteps in the Dark	1978	$5
❑ 2261	Harvest for the World/Harvest for the World (Part 2)	1976	$5
❑ 2291	Here We Go Again (Part 1)/ Here We Go Again (Part 2)	1980	$5
❑ 02033	Hurry Up and Wait/(Instrumental)	1981	$5
❑ 919	If He Can, You Can/Holdin' On	1970	$6
❑ 02531	Inside You (Part 1)/ Inside You (Part 2)	1981	$5
❑ 02179	I Once Had Your Love (And I Can't Let Go)/(Instrumental)	1981	$5
❑ 2287	It's a Disco Night (Rock Don't Stop)/Ain't Givin' Up on Love	1979	$5
❑ 03281	It's Alright with Me/(Instrumental)	1982	$5
❑ 937	It's Too Late/Nothing to Do But Today	1973	$6
❑ 901	It's Your Thing/Don't Give It Away	1969	$6
❑ 902	I Turned You On/I Know Who You Been Socking It To	1969	$6
❑ 2279	I Wanna Be with You (Part 1)/I Wanna Be with You (Part 2)	1979	$5
❑ 934	Lay-Away/Feel Like the World	1972	$6
❑ 933	Lay Lady Lay/Vacuum Cleaner	1971	$20
❑ 04320	Let's Make Love Tonight/ (Instrumental)	1984	$5
❑ 2254	Live It Up (Part 1)/ Live It Up (Part 2)	1974	$5
❑ 2264	Livin' in the Life/Go for Your Guns	1977	$5
❑ 930	Love the One You're With/ He's Got Your Love	1971	$6
❑ 2255	Midnight Sky (Part 1)/ Midnight Sky (Part 2)	1974	$5
❑ 02705	Party Night/Welcome Into My Night	1982	$5

Number	Title	Yr	NM
❏ 935	Pop That Thang/I Got to Find Me One	1972	$6
❏ 2292	Say You Will (Part 1)/Say You Will (Part 2)	1980	$5
❏ 2278	Showdown (Part 1)/Showdown (Part 2)	1978	$5
❏ 932	Spill the Wine/Take Inventory	1971	$20
❏ 2253	Summer Breeze (Part 1)/Summer Breeze (Part 2)	1974	$5
❏ 2272	Take Me to the Next Phase (Part 1)/Take Me to the Next Phase (Part 2)	1978	$5
❏ 501	Testify (Part 1)/Testify (Part 2)	1964	$40
❏ 2251	That Lady (Part 1)/That Lady (Part 2)	1973	$5
❏ 2262	The Pride (Part 1)/The Pride (Part 2)	1977	$5
❏ 929	Warpath/I Got to Find Me One	1971	$6
❏ 908	Was It Good to You/I Got to Get Myself Together	1969	$6
❏ 2252	What It Comes Down To/Highways of My Life	1973	$5
❏ 2260	Who Loves You Better-Part 1/Who Loves You Better-Part 2	1976	$5
❏ 02293	Who Said?/(Can't You See) What You Do to Me	1981	$4

— Reissue

Number	Title	Yr	NM
❏ 2293	Who Said?/(Can't You See) What You've Done to Me	1980	$5
❏ 2284	Winner Takes All/Fun and Games	1979	$5
❏ 936	Work to Do/Beautiful	1972	$30

UNITED ARTISTS

❏ 659	Please, Please, Please/You'll Never Leave Him	1963	$30
❏ 605	She's Gone/Tango	1963	$30
❏ 638	Surf and Shout/Whatcha Gonna Do	1963	$30
❏ 714	Who's That Lady/My Little Girl	1964	$60

VEEP

| ❏ 1230 | Love Is a Wonderful Thing/Open Up Her Eyes | 1966 | $10 |

V.I.P.

| ❏ 25020 | I Hear a Symphony/Who Could Ever Doubt My Love | 1965 | $400 |

WAND

❏ 137	I Say Love/Hold On Baby	1963	$20
❏ 124	Twist and Shout/Spanish Twist	1962	$10
❏ 127	Twistin' with Linda/You Better Come Home	1962	$20

WARNER BROS.

❏ 28860	Colder Are My Nights/(Instrumental)	1985	$4
❏ 28241	Come My Way/(Instrumental)	1987	$4
❏ 27954	It Takes a Good Woman/(Instrumental)	1988	$4
❏ 28129	I Wish/(Instrumental)	1988	$4
❏ 28129 [PS]	I Wish/(Instrumental)	1988	$4
❏ 28764	May I?/(Instrumental)	1986	$4
❏ 22748	One of a Kind/You'll Never Walk Alone	1989	$3
❏ 28385	Smooth Sailin' Tonight/(Instrumental)	1987	$4
❏ 28385 [PS]	Smooth Sailin' Tonight/(Instrumental)	1987	$4
❏ 22900	Spend the Night (Ce Soir)/(Instrumental)	1989	$3
❏ 22900 [PS]	Spend the Night (Ce Soir)/(Instrumental)	1989	$3

ISM

S.I.N.

| ❏ 716 | Attack/Queen Jap | 1980 | $13 |

— B-side is "King Tut" with new lyrics

❏ 716 [PS]	Attack/Queen Jap	1980	$13
❏ 03	I Think I Love You/A7	1983	$30
❏ 03 [PS]	I Think I Love You/A7	1983	$30

— With mail-order insert

IVAN

CORAL

| ❏ 62081 | That'll Be Alright/Frankie Frankenstein | 1959 | $400 |

IVES, BURL

BELL

| ❏ 943 | Time/Galisteo | 1970 | $5 |

BIG TREE

| ❏ 130 | Gingerbread House/Tumbleweed Snowman | 1971 | $5 |

BUENA VISTA

| ❏ 419 | On the Front Porch/Ugly Bug Ball | 1963 | $8 |
| ❏ 419 [PS] | On the Front Porch/Ugly Bug Ball | 1963 | $15 |

COLUMBIA

| ❏ 1-630(?) | Got the World by the Tail/My Momma Told Me | 1950 | $40 |

— Microgroove 33 1/3 rpm 7-inch single

| ❏ 4-124 [PS] | Grandfather Kringle/The 12 Days Of Christmas | 1951 | $20 |
| ❏ 4-124 | Grandfather Kringle/The 12 Days Of Christmas | 1951 | $15 |

— Yellow-label "Chidren's Series" record; alternate number is 90138

| ❏ 44508 | I'll Be Your Baby Tonight/Maria | 1968 | $6 |

Number	Title	Yr	NM
❏ 44606	Little Green Apples/One Too Many Mornings	1968	$6
❏ 44974	Montego Bay/Tessie's Bar Mystery	1969	$6
❏ 1-418	Mule Train/Greer County Bachelor	1950	$40

— Microgroove 33 1/3 rpm 7-inch single

| ❏ 39328 | On Top of Old Smoky/The Syncopated Clock | 1951 | $20 |

— With Percy Faith co-credited

| ❏ 6-780(?) | Pig Pig/Last Night the Nightingale Woke Me | 1950 | $30 |
| ❏ 1-780(?) | Pig Pig/Last Night the Nightingale Woke Me | 1950 | $40 |

— Microgroove 33 1/3 rpm 7-inch single

❏ 44711 [PS]	Santa Mouse/Oh What a Lucky Boy Am I	1968	$10
❏ 44711	Santa Mouse/Oh What a Lucky Boy Am I	1968	$6
❏ 1-580(?)	The Doughnut Song/I Got a Fever in My Bones	1950	$40

— Microgroove 33 1/3 rpm 7-inch single

| ❏ 6-910(?) | There's a Little White House/Little White Duck | 1950 | $30 |
| ❏ 1-910(?) | There's a Little White House/Little White Duck | 1950 | $40 |

— Microgroove 33 1/3 rpm 7-inch single

DECCA

❏ 31695	A Holly Jolly Christmas/Snow for Johnny	1964	$10
❏ 31330	A Little Bitty Tear/Shanghaid	1961	$10
❏ 29549	Be Sure You're Right (Then Go Ahead)/Ol' Betsy	1955	$20
❏ 32282	Bury the Bottle/That's Where My Baby Used to Be	1968	$8
❏ 31405	Call Me Mr. In-Between/What You Gonna Do, Leroy	1962	$10
❏ 31729	Call My Name/My Gal Sal	1965	$8
❏ 28708	Close the Door Richard/Left My Gal in the Mountains	1953	$20
❏ 28161	Diesel Smoke, Dangerous Curves/The Little Green Valley	1952	$20

— With Grady Martin

❏ 31997	Evil Off My Mind/Taste of Heaven	1966	$8
❏ 31610	Four Initials on a Tree/This Is Your Day	1964	$8
❏ 31857	Frangipani/A Girl Sittin' Up in a Tree	1965	$8
❏ 32165	Funny Little Show/Holding Hands for Joe	1967	$8
❏ 31371	Funny Way of Laughin'/Mother Wouldn't Do That	1962	$10
❏ 28849	Great White Bird/Brighten the Corner Where You Are	1953	$20
❏ 31981	Here She Comes (There She Goes)/Atlantic Coastal Line	1966	$8
❏ 31504	I'm the Boss/The Moon Is High	1963	$10
❏ 25754	I Talk to the Trees/They Call the Wind Maria	1970	$6
❏ 31543	It Comes and Goes/I Found My Best Friend in the Dog Pound	1963	$10
❏ 29533	I Wonder What's Become of Sally/Wabash Cannonball	1955	$15
❏ 32078	Lonesome 7-7203/Hollow Words	1967	$8
❏ 31248	Long Black Veil/Forty Hour Week	1961	$10
❏ 30217	Marianne/Pretty Girl	1957	$15
❏ 31433	Mary Ann Regrets/How Do You Fall Out of Love	1962	$10
❏ 33049	Miss Johnson's Happiness Emporium/Anytime You Say	1972	$6
❏ 31772	On the Beach at Waikiki/Some Hangin' Round You All the Time	1965	$8
❏ 31659	Pearly Shells/What Little Tears Are Made Of	1964	$8
❏ 31811	Salt Water Guitar/The Story of Bobby Lee Trent	1965	$8
❏ 32990	Stayin' Song/The Best Is Yet to Come	1972	$6
❏ 29423	The Ballad of Davy Crockett/Goober Peas	1955	$20
❏ 30046	The Bus Stop Song/That's My Heart Strings	1956	$15
❏ 28935	The Crawdad Song/Hound Dog	1953	$20
❏ 28347	The Friendly Beasts/There Were Three Ships	1952	$15
❏ 29282	The Mission San Miguel/Tangled Web	1954	$20
❏ 28299	There's a Mule Up in Tombstone, Arizona/Lonesome, So Lonesome	1952	$20
❏ 29039	There's Plenty of Fish in the Ocean/The Old Red Barn	1954	$20
❏ 31453	The Same Old Hurt/Curry Road	1963	$10
❏ 28349	The Seven Joys of Mary (Part 1)/The Seven Joys of Mary (Part 2)	1952	$15
❏ 31918	The Sixties/Don't Forget Your Paddle	1966	$8
❏ 31518	This Is All I Ask/There Goes Another Pal of Mine	1963	$10
❏ 27079	This Time Tomorrow/One Hour Ahead of the Posse	1950	$30
❏ 28079	This Time Tomorrow/One Hour Ahead of the Posse	1952	$20
❏ 29088	True Love Goes On and On/Brave Man	1954	$20
❏ 31571	True Love Goes On and On/I Wonder What's Become of Sally	1963	$10
❏ 25585	Twelve Days of Christmas/The Indian Christmas Carol	1962	$10

Number	Title	Yr	NM
❏ 29129	Wait for Me Darling/Casey Jones	1954	$15
❏ 30855	We Love Ye, Jimmy/I Never See Maggie Alone	1959	$15
❏ 28055	Wild Side of Life/It's So Long and Goodbye to You	1952	$20

DISNEYLAND

| ❏ F-130 | Chim Chim Chiree/Lavender Blue | 1964 | $8 |
| ❏ F-130 [PS] | Chim Chim Chiree/Lavender Blue | 1964 | $15 |

MCA

| ❏ 31695 | A Holly Jolly Christmas/Snow for Johnny | 1989 | $5 |

— Double the NM value if insert is enclosed

| ❏ 40082 | Payin' My Dues Again/All Around | 1973 | $5 |
| ❏ 40175 | Tale of the Comet Kohoutek/A Very Fine Lady | 1974 | $5 |

MONKEY JOE

| ❏ MJ-1 [DJ] | The Christmas Legend of Monkey Joe/It's Gonna Be A Mixed Up Xmas | 1978 | $12 |

UNITED ARTISTS

❏ 293	Alexander's Ragtime Band/Say It Isn't So	1961	$8
❏ 429	All Alone/Always	1962	$8
❏ ED2714 [PS]	Burl Ives	1961	$12
❏ ED2726 [PS]	Call Me Mr. In-Between	1962	$12
❏ ED2726	Call Me Mr. In-Between/Poor Little Jimmie//In Foggy Old London/Thumbin' Johnny Brown	1962	$10
❏ ED2714	(contents unknown)	1961	$10
❏ ED2741	(contents unknown)	1962	$10
❏ ED2720	Funny Way of Laughin'/Mother Wouldn't Do That//What You Gonna Do Leroy/I Ain't Comin' Home Tonight	1962	$10
❏ ED2720 [PS]	It's Just My Funny Way of Laughin'	1962	$12
❏ ED2741 [PS]	Mary Ann Regrets	1962	$12
❏ ED2771 [PS]	True Love Goes On and On	1963	$12
❏ ED2771	True Love Goes On and On/This Is All I Ask/It Comes and Goes/I'm the Boss	1963	$10

IVIES, THE

BRUNSWICK

| ❏ 9-55112 | Sunshine/Come On | 1959 | $40 |

IVY

| ❏ 110 | Sunshine/Come On | 1958 | $125 |

ROULETTE

| ❏ 4183 | I Really Want You to Know/Voodoo | 1959 | $15 |

IVOLEERS, THE

BUZZ

| ❏ 101 | Lover's Quarrel/Come with Me | 1959 | $400 |

IVORYS, THE

DARLA

| ❏ 1000 | Wishing Well/Deep Freeze | 1962 | $400 |

SPARTA

| ❏ 01 | Why Don't You Write Me/Deep Freeze | 1962 | $100 |

IVY LEAGUE, THE

CAMEO

❏ 365	A Girl Like You/That's Why I'm Crying	1965	$20
❏ 356	Lonely Room/Funny How Love Can Be	1965	$20
❏ 388	Our Love Is Slipping Away/I Could Make You Fall in Love	1966	$20
❏ 388 [PS]	Our Love Is Slipping Away/I Could Make You Fall in Love	1966	$30
❏ 377	Tossing & Turning/Graduation Day	1965	$20
❏ 377 [PS]	Tossing & Turning/Graduation Day	1965	$40
❏ 343	Wait a Minute/What More Do You Want	1965	$20
❏ 449	When You're Young/My World Fell Down	1966	$20

J

JACK AND DANIEL
DECCA
Number	Title	Yr	NM
❏ 9-28467	Don't Make Love in a Buggy/ Tennessee Tango	1952	$30

JACK AND JILL
CADDY
Number	Title	Yr	NM
❏ 110	Party Time/No One to Talk To (But the Blues)	1957	$50
JOSIE
| ❏ 943 | Something Special/The Chase | 1965 | $30 |
MAXX
| ❏ 330 | Two of a Kind/Just As You Are | 1964 | $40 |

JACK AND TRINK
NSD
Number	Title	Yr	NM
❏ 12	After the Roses/I Can't See Me Without You	1978	$6
❏ 48	Get Back to the Basics/I've Got a Brand New Love Song	1980	$6
❏ 61	I'm Not Really Drinking, I'm Just Holding the Can/I Can't See Me Without Her	1980	$6
❏ 4	I'm Tired of Being Me/Ain't No Way of Gettin'...	1978	$6

JACKIE AND JILL
U.S.A.
Number	Title	Yr	NM
❏ 791	I Want a Beatle for Christmas/Jingle Bells	1964	$30

JACKIE AND THE GIANTS
HIT
Number	Title	Yr	NM
❏ 185	I Go to Pieces/Ford G.T.	1965	$10
❏ 209	I'm Telling You Now/Come On In	1965	$10
❏ 230	Turn! Turn! Turn!/May the Bird of Paradise Fly Up Your Nose	1965	$10

— B-side by Buddy Scott

JACKIE AND THE RAINDROPS
COLPIX
Number	Title	Yr	NM
❏ 738	Down Our Street/My Heart Is Your Heart	1964	$12

JACKIE AND THE STARLITES
FIRE & FURY
Number	Title	Yr	NM
❏ 1000	They Laughed at Me/You Put One Over on Me	1959	$2000
FURY
| ❏ 1057 | I Found Out Too Late/I'm Coming Home | 1962 | $40 |
| ❏ 1045 | Silver Lining/Ain't Cha' Ever Coming Home | 1961 | $60 |

— As "The Starlites

HULL
| ❏ 760 | I Cried My Heart Out/I Still Remember | 1964 | $60 |
MASCOT
| ❏ 128 | For All We Know/I Heard You | 1962 | $70 |

— No horseshoe on label

| ❏ 128 | For All We Know/I Heard You | 1962 | $50 |

— With horseshoe on label

| ❏ 131 | I'll Burn Your Letter/Walking from School | 1963 | $60 |
SPHERE SOUND
| ❏ 705 | Seven Day Fool/Don't Be Afraid | 1966 | $100 |

— As "The Starlites

JACKS, TERRY
BELL
Number	Title	Yr	NM
❏ 45467	If You Go Away/Me and You	1974	$4
❏ 45606	Love Game/Rock and Roll	1974	$4
❏ 45432	Seasons in the Sun/Put the Bone In	1974	$5
LONDON
| ❏ 181 | Concrete Sea/She Even Took the Cat | 1972 | $5 |
| ❏ 188 | I'm Gonna Love You, Too/Something Good Was Over Before It Ever Got to Start | 1972 | $5 |
PARROT
| ❏ 347 | A Good Thing Lost/I'm Gonna Capture You | 1970 | $6 |

PRIVATE STOCK
Number	Title	Yr	NM
❏ 45,023	Christina/The Feeling That We've Lost	1975	$4
❏ 45,094	In My Father's Footsteps/ Until You're Down	1976	$4

JACKS, THE
KENT
Number	Title	Yr	NM
❏ 344	Why Don't You Write Me/ This Empty Heart	1960	$20
RPM
❏ 433	I'm Confessin'/Since My Baby's Been Gone	1955	$70
❏ 467	Let's Make Up/Dream a Little Longer	1956	$70
❏ 454	So Wrong/How Soon	1956	$60
❏ 458	Sugar Baby/Why Did I Fall in Love	1956	$70
❏ 444	This Empty Heart/My Clumsy Heart	1955	$60
❏ 428	Why Don't You Write Me/ My Darling	1955	$70
❏ 428	Why Don't You Write Me/ Smack Dab in the Middle	1955	$200

JACKSON, ALAN
ARISTA
Number	Title	Yr	NM
❏ 9892	Blue Blooded Woman/Home	1989	$10

— Issued on blue vinyl

| ❏ 9922 | Here in the Real World/Blue Blooded Woman | 1989 | $4 |

JACKSON, BULL MOOSE
BOGUS
Number	Title	Yr	NM
❏ 12-042684	Get Off the Table, Mable (The Two Dollars Is For the Beer)/I've Got a Gal Who Lives Up on a Hill	1984	$5
❏ 12-042684 [PS]	Get Off the Table, Mable (The Two Dollars Is For the Beer)/I've Got a Gal Who Lives Up on a Hill	1984	$5
KING
❏ 4551	Bearcat Blues/There Is No Greater Love	1952	$70
❏ 4580	Big Ten Inch Record/I Needed You	1952	$200
❏ 4472	Cherokee Boogie/I'm Lucky I Have You	1951	$70
❏ 4775	If You Ain't Lovin'/I Wanna Hug Ya, Kiss Ya	1955	$30
❏ 4655	If You'll Let Me/Hodge Podge	1953	$50
❏ 4493	I'll Be Home for Christmas/I Never Loved Anyone But You	1951	$70
❏ 4181	I Love You Yes I Do/Sneaky Pete	1951	$70

— 78 originally released in 1947

| ❏ 4802 | I'm Glad for Your Sake/Must You Keep On Pretending | 1955 | $30 |
| ❏ 4189 | I Want a Bowlegged Woman/All My Love Belongs to You | 1951 | $100 |

— 78 originally released in 1948 -- 5191 and 5198 are the only legitimate 45s known before 4451

❏ 4535	(Let Me Love You) All Night Long/Bootsie	1952	$70
❏ 4634	Meet Me with Your Black Dress On/Try to Forget Him	1953	$50
❏ 4451	Trust in Me/Wonder When My Baby's Coming Home	1951	$70
SEVEN ARTS
| ❏ 705 | I Love You Yes I Do/Aw Shucks Baby | 1961 | $30 |
WARWICK
| ❏ 575 | I Found My Love/More of the Same | 1960 | $30 |

7-Inch Extended Plays
KING
| ❏ EP-211 | *I Love You, Yes I Do/I Want a Bowlegged Woman/All My Love Belongs to You/Little Girl Don't Cry | 1953 | $175 |
| ❏ EP-211 [PS] | Bull Moose Jackson Sings His All Time Hits | 1953 | $175 |

JACKSON, CHUCK, AND MAXINE BROWN
WAND
Number	Title	Yr	NM
❏ 1155	Daddy's Home/Don't Go	1967	$20
❏ 191	Don't Go/Can't Let You Out of My Sight	1965	$20
❏ 1148	Hold On I'm Comin'/Never Had It So Good	1967	$20
❏ 198	I Need You So/Cause We're in Love	1965	$20
❏ 1109	Please Don't Hurt Me/I'm Satisfied	1966	$20
❏ 1162	See See Rider/Tennessee Waltz	1967	$20
❏ 181	Something You Got/Baby Take Me	1965	$20

JACKSON, CHUCK
ABC
Number	Title	Yr	NM
❏ 11398	I Can't Break Away/Just a Little Tear	1973	$60
❏ 11423	If Only You Believe/Maybe This Will Be the Morning	1974	$30
❏ 11368	I Only Get This Feeling/ Slowly But Surely	1973	$30
❏ 12024	Take Off Your Make-Up/Talk a Little Less	1974	$30
ALL PLATINUM
❏ 2373	I Fell Asleep/One of Those Yesterdays	1976	$5
❏ 2363	If You Were My Woman (Part 1)/If You Were My Woman (Part 2)	1976	$5
❏ 2360	I'm Needing You, Wanting You/We Can't Hide It Anymore	1975	$5
❏ 2357	Love Lights/(Instrumental)	1975	$5
❏ 2370	One of Those Yesterdays/ Love Lights	1976	$20
AMY
| ❏ 849 | Come On and Love Me/ Ooh Baby | 1962 | $30 |
| ❏ 868 | I'm Yours/Hula Lula | 1962 | $20 |
BELTONE
| ❏ 1005 | Mr. Price/Hula Lula | 1961 | $30 |
CLOCK
| ❏ 1015 | Come On and Love Me/ Ooh Baby | 1959 | $30 |

— Clock sides as "Charles Jackson

| ❏ 1022 | Hula Lula/I'm Yours | 1960 | $30 |
| ❏ 1027 | This Is It/Mr. Pride | 1960 | $30 |
DAKAR
| ❏ 4512 | I Forgot to Tell You/The Man and the Woman | 1972 | $30 |
DOT
| ❏ 15673 | Woke Up This Morning/ Wilette | 1957 | $40 |

— With Kripp Johnson

EMI AMERICA
| ❏ 8056 | After You/Let's Get Together | 1980 | $4 |
| ❏ 8042 | I Wanna Give You Some Love/Waiting in Vain | 1980 | $4 |
MOTOWN
❏ 1144	Are You Lonely for Me Baby/ Your Wonderful Love	1969	$20
❏ 1118	(Don't Let the Boy Overpower) The Man in You/ Girls, Girls, Girls	1968	$30
❏ 1152	Honey Come Back/What Am I Gonna Do Without You	1969	$30
❏ 1160	The Day My World Stood Still/Baby, I'll Get It	1970	$500
SUGARHILL
| ❏ 764 | Sometimes When We Touch/(B-side unknown) | 1981 | $4 |
VIBRATION
| ❏ 569 | We Can't Hide It Anymore/I'm Needing You, Wanting You | 1977 | $5 |

— With Sylvia

V.I.P.
❏ 25059	Is There Anything Love Can't Do/Pet Names	1971	$40
❏ 25056	Let Somebody Love Me/Two Feet from Happiness	1970	$30
❏ 25052	The Day My World Stood Still/Baby, I'll Get It	1970	$30
❏ 25067	Who You Gonna Run To/ Forgive My Jealousy	1971	$400
WAND
❏ 1119	All in My Mind/And That's Saying a Lot	1966	$30
❏ 122	Any Day Now (My Wild Beautiful Bird)/The Prophet	1962	$30
❏ 141	Any Other Way/Big New York	1963	$30
❏ 154	Beg Me/This Broken Heart	1964	$30
❏ 1151	Every Man Needs a Down Home Girl/Need You There	1967	$8
❏ 128	Gettin' Ready for the Heartbreak/In Between Tears	1962	$40
❏ 1105	Good Things Come to Those Who Wait/Yah	1965	$30
❏ 149	Hand It Over/Look Over Your Shoulder	1964	$60
❏ 1159	Hound Dog/Love Me Tender	1967	$8
❏ 106	I Don't Want to Cry/Just Once	1961	$20
❏ 188	If I Didn't Love You/Just a Little Bit of Your Soul	1965	$30
❏ 126	I Keep Forgetting/Who's Gonna Pick Up the Pieces	1962	$30
❏ 179	I Need You/Soul Brother Twist	1965	$30
❏ 108	(It Never Happens) In Real Life/The Same Old Story	1961	$40
❏ 1142	I've Got to Be Strong/Where Did She Stay	1967	$30
❏ 110	I Wake Up Crying/ Everybody Needs Love	1961	$30

Number	Title	Yr	NM
❏ 138	I Will Never Turn My Back on You/Tears of Joy	1963	$10
❏ 1178	My Child's Child/Theme to the Blues	1968	$8
❏ 1166	Shame on Me/Candy	1967	$20
❏ 169	Since I Don't Have You/Hand It Over	1964	$50
❏ 161	Somebody New/Stand By Me	1964	$30
❏ 132	Tell Him I'm Not Home/Lonely Am I	1963	$30
❏ 132 [PS]	Tell Him I'm Not Home/Lonely Am I	1963	$50
❏ 115	The Breaking Point/My Willow Tree	1961	$20
❏ 1129	These Chains of Love/Theme to the Blues	1966	$8
❏ 119	What'cha Gonna Say Tomorrow/Angel of Angels	1962	$30

JACKSON, DEE D.
AVI
| ❏ 211 | Automatic Lover/Didn't Think You'd Do It | 1978 | $12 |

JACKSON, DEON
ATLANTIC
| ❏ 2252 | Come Back Home/Nursery Rhymes | 1964 | $10 |
| ❏ 2213 | Hush Little Baby/You Said You Loved Me | 1963 | $10 |
CARLA
❏ 2530	I Can't Do Without You/That's What You Do to Me	1966	$8
❏ 1900	I Can't Go On/I Need a Love Like Yours	1968	$8
❏ 2526	Love Makes the World Go Round/You Said You Loved Me	1966	$10
❏ 2527	Love Takes a Long Time Growing/Hush Little Baby	1966	$8
❏ 2537	Ooh Baby/All on a Sunny Day	1967	$8
❏ 2533	When Your Love Has Gone/Hard to Get Thing Called Love	1967	$8
SHOUT
❏ 254	I'll Always Love You/Life Can Be That Way	1969	$30

JACKSON, EARL
ABC
| ❏ 11142 | Self Soul Satisfaction/Looking Through the Eyes of Love | 1968 | $40 |

JACKSON FIVE, THE
MOTOWN
| ❏ 1174 | Santa Claus Is Coming to Town/Christmas Won't Be the Same This Year | 1970 | $15 |

JACKSON, FREDDIE
CAPITOL
❏ B-44354	Crazy (For Me)/(Radio Edit)	1989	$3
❏ B-5661	Have You Ever Loved Somebody/Tasty Love	1986	$3
❏ B-5661 [PS]	Have You Ever Loved Somebody/Tasty Love	1986	$3
❏ B-5535	He'll Never Love You (Like I Do)/I Wanna Say I Love You	1985	$3
❏ B-5535 [PS]	He'll Never Love You (Like I Do)/I Wanna Say I Love You	1985	$3
❏ B-44208	Hey Lover/Look Around	1988	$3
❏ B-44208 [PS]	Hey Lover/Look Around	1988	$3
❏ B-5680	I Don't Want to Lose Your Love/Love Is Just a Touch Away	1987	$3
❏ B-5680 [PS]	I Don't Want to Lose Your Love/Love Is Just a Touch Away	1987	$3
❏ B-44075	Look Around/I Can't Let You Go	1987	$3
❏ B-5565	Love Is Just a Touch Away/(Sonata)	1986	$3
❏ B-5565 [PS]	Love Is Just a Touch Away/(Sonata)	1986	$3
❏ B-5616	Tasty Love/I Wanna Say I Love You	1986	$3
❏ B-5616 [PS]	Tasty Love/I Wanna Say I Love You	1986	$3

JACKSON, GEORGE
CAMEO
| ❏ 460 | When I Stop Lovin' You/That Lonely Night | 1967 | $70 |
CHESS
| ❏ 2167 | Things Are Gettin' Better/Mackin' on You | 1975 | $200 |
DOT
| ❏ 16724 | Blinkety Blink/There Goes My Pride | 1965 | $125 |

FAME
| ❏ 1457 | Find 'Em, Fool 'Em, and Forget 'Em/My Desires Are Getting the Best of Me | 1969 | $30 |
| ❏ 1468 | That's How Much You Mean to Me/I'm Gonna Hold On | 1970 | $30 |
HI
❏ 2212	Aretha, Sing One for Me/I'm Gonna Wait	1972	$20
❏ 2130	I'm Gonna Wait/So Good to Me	1967	$50
❏ 2236	Let Them Know You Care/Patricia	1973	$40
MERCURY
❏ 72782	I Don't Have the Time to Love You/Don't Use Me	1968	$400
MGM
❏ 14767	Soul Train/Smoking and Drinking	1974	$6
❏ 14680	We've Only Just Begun/You Can't Run Away from Love	1973	$6
❏ 14732	Willie Lump Lump/How Can I Get Next to You	1974	$30
RPM
❏ 441	Hold Me Up/Heaven on Earth	1955	$30
VERVE
❏ 10658	Love Highjacker/I Found What I Wanted	1970	$125

JACKSON HEIGHTS
VERVE
| ❏ 10706 | Long Time Dying/Maureen | 1973 | $8 |

JACKSON, J.J.
CALLA
❏ 119	But It's Alright/Boogaloo Baby	1966	$50
❏ 133	Four Walls (Three Windows and Two Doors)/Here We Go Again	1967	$30
❏ 125	I Dig Girls/That Ain't Right	1966	$20
❏ 130	Til Love Goes Out of Style/Seems Like I've Been Here Before	1967	$60
CONGRESS
❏ 6008	Fat, Black and Together/That Woman Loving	1969	$8
EVEREST
❏ 2012	False Face/Ring Telephone	1963	$60
LOMA
❏ 2096	Come See Me (I'm Your Man)/I Don't Want to Live My Life Alone	1968	$30
❏ 2090	Down But Not Out/Why Does It Take So Long	1968	$30
❏ 2104	That Ain't Right/Courage Ain't Strength	1968	$20
❏ 2102	Too Late/You Do It Cause You Wanna	1968	$20
❏ 2082	Try Me/Sho Nuff (Gotta Good Thing Goin')	1967	$30
MAGNA GLIDE
❏ 5N-325	Let Me Try Again/(B-side unknown)	1975	$20
WARNER BROS.
❏ 7278	But It's Alright/Ain't Too Proud to Beg	1969	$8
❏ 7130	But It's Alright/Four Walls (Three Windows and Two Doors)	1970	$6
—Back to Back Hits" series
| ❏ 7321 | Four Walls (Three Windows and Two Doors)/That Ain't Right | 1969 | $8 |

JACKSON, JANET
❏ 2522	Come Give Your Love to Me/Forever Yours	1983	$5
❏ 2522 [PS]	Come Give Your Love to Me/Forever Yours	1983	$5
❏ 2877	Control/Fast Girls	1986	$3
❏ 2877 [PS]	Control/Fast Girls	1986	$3
❏ 2660	Don't Stand Another Chance/Rock 'N' Roll	1984	$5
❏ 2660 [PS]	Don't Stand Another Chance/Rock 'N' Roll	1984	$5
❏ 2682	Dream Street/Love and My Best Friend	1984	$6
❏ 2693	Fast Girls/Love and My Best Friend	1984	$5
❏ 2906	Let's Wait Awhile/Pretty Boy	1987	$3
❏ 2906 [PS]	Let's Wait Awhile/Pretty Boy	1987	$3
❏ AM-1445	Miss You Much/You Need Me	1989	$6
❏ 2545	Say You Do/You'll Never Find (A Love Like Mine)	1983	$5
❏ 2927	The Pleasure Principle/Fast Girls	1987	$3
❏ 2927 [PS]	The Pleasure Principle/Fast Girls	1987	$3
❏ 2812	What Have You Done for Me Lately/He Doesn't Know I'm Alive	1986	$3
❏ 2812 [PS]	What Have You Done for Me Lately/He Doesn't Know I'm Alive	1986	$3
❏ 2855	When I Think of You/Pretty Boy	1986	$3
❏ 2855 [PS]	When I Think of You/Pretty Boy	1986	$3

JACKSON, JERMAINE
ARISTA
| ❏ 9788 | Clean Up Your Act/I'm Gonna Git Ya Sucka | 1988 | $3 |
—B-side by the Gap Band
❏ 9788 [PS]	Clean Up Your Act/I'm Gonna Git Ya Sucka	1988	$3
❏ 9356	(Closest Thing to) Perfect/(Instrumental)	1985	$3
❏ 9356 [PS]	(Closest Thing to) Perfect/(Instrumental)	1985	$3
❏ 9875	Don't Take It Personal/Clean Up Your Act	1989	$3
❏ 9875 [PS]	Don't Take It Personal/Clean Up Your Act	1989	$3
❏ 9279	Do What You Do/Tell Me I'm Not Dreaming (Too Good to Be True)	1984	$3
❏ 9502	Do You Remember Me/Whatcha Doin'	1986	$3
❏ 9502 [PS]	Do You Remember Me/Whatcha Doin'	1986	$3
❏ 9190 [DJ]	Dynamite (same on both sides)	1984	$8
—Promo only on red vinyl
❏ 9190	Dynamite/Tell Me I'm Not Dreaming (Too Good to Be True) (Instrumental)	1984	$3
❏ 9190 [PS]	Dynamite/Tell Me I'm Not Dreaming (Too Good to Be True) (Instrumental)	1984	$3
❏ 9444	I Think It's Love/Voices in the Dark	1985	$3
❏ 9444 [PS]	I Think It's Love/Voices in the Dark	1985	$3
❏ 9275	Take Good Care of My Heart/Tell Me I'm Not Dreaming (Too Good to Be True)	1984	$5
—A-side with Whitney Houston
| ❏ 9495 | Words Into Action/Our Love Story | 1986 | $3 |
| ❏ 9495 [PS] | Words Into Action/Our Love Story | 1986 | $3 |
MOTOWN
❏ 1441	Castles of Sand/I Love Every Little Thing About You	1978	$5
❏ 1216	Daddy's Home/Take Me in Your Arms (Rock Me for a Little While)	1972	$5
❏ 1525	I'm Just Too Shy/All Because of You	1981	$4
❏ 1628	Let Me Tickle Your Fancy/Maybe Next Time	1982	$4
—Devo is the backing group
❏ 1401	Let's Be Young Tonight/Boss Odyssey	1976	$5
❏ 1469	Let's Get Serious/Je Vous Aime Beaucoups	1980	$4
❏ 1499	Little Girl Don't You Worry/We Can Put It Back Together	1980	$4
❏ 1600	Paradise in Your Eyes/I'm My Brother's Keeper	1982	$4
❏ 1201	That's How Love Goes/I Lost My Love in the Big City	1972	$5

JACKSON, JERRY
CAPITOL
| ❏ 2112 | Miss You/Take Over Now | 1968 | $50 |
COLUMBIA
| ❏ 43056 | Shrimp Boats/Always | 1964 | $15 |
| ❏ 43158 | Tell Her Johnny Said Goodbye/Are You Glad When We're Apart | 1964 | $70 |
KAPP
❏ 543	Blowin' in the Wind (Part 1)/Blowin' in the Wind (Part 2)	1963	$30
❏ 511	Gypsy Eyes/Turn Back	1963	$125
❏ 420	I Don't Play Games/You Might Be There With Him	1961	$40
❏ 438	If I Only Had Known How to Keep Her (She Would Never Have Gone to You)/Till the End of Time	1961	$30
❏ 448	La-Dee-Dah (Ha-Ha-Ha)/You Don't Wanna Hurt Me	1962	$20
❏ 496	She Lied/Wide Awake in a Dream	1962	$300
❏ 464	They Really Don't Know You/Blues in the Night	1962	$20
❏ 387	Time/Se Habla Espanol	1961	$30
PARKWAY
❏ 100	It's Rough Out There/I'm Gonna Paint a Picture	1966	$300
TOP RANK
❏ 2042	A Chance to Prove My Love/For Every One There's Someone	1960	$30
❏ 2072	Every Time You Kiss Me/Meaning of My Love	1960	$30

Number	Title	Yr	NM

JACKSON, JILL
REPRISE

Number	Title	Yr	NM
❏ 0362	Born Too Late/Here Comes the Night	1965	$20
❏ 0297	Hey Handsome Boy/All Over Again	1964	$20
❏ 0323	Pixie Girl/I Just Don't Know What to Do With Myself	1964	$20
❏ 0411	Treasure of Love/I'll Love You for a While	1965	$20

JACKSON JILLS, THE
DOT

❏ 16541	Mommie's Little Baby/Pretty Little Dutch Girl	1963	$20

JACKSON, JOE
A&M

❏ 2548	Another World/Otro Mundo	1983	$5
❏ 2673	Be My Number Two/Heart of Ice	1984	$5
❏ 2510 [DJ]	Breaking Us in Two (3:48)/(4:57)	1982	$6

— The shorter version does not appear on the stock copy

❏ 2510	Breaking Us in Two/Target	1982	$3
❏ 2510 [PS]	Breaking Us in Two/Target	1982	$3
❏ 2635	Happy Ending/Loisaida	1984	$4
❏ 2635 [PS]	Happy Ending/Loisaida	1984	$4
❏ 1228	(He's a) Shape in a Drape/ Speedway	1988	$4
❏ 2847	Home Town/I'm the Man (Live)	1986	$5
❏ SP-18000	I'm the Man	1979	$30

— Boxed set of five 7" singles with small holes and picture sleeves, comprising the album of the same name

❏ 2209	I'm the Man/Come On	1979	$5
❏ 2132	Is She Really Going Out with Him?/(Do the) Instant Mash	1979	$4
❏ 2132 [PS]	Is She Really Going Out with Him?/(Do the) Instant Mash	1979	$5
❏ 2186	It's Different for Girls/ Come On	1979	$5
❏ 2186 [PS]	It's Different for Girls/ Come On	1979	$5
❏ 1207	Look Sharp (Live)/Memphis (Live)	1988	$5
❏ 2601	Memphis/Breakdown	1983	$4
❏ 2601 [PS]	Memphis/Breakdown	1983	$5
❏ 2276	One to One/Enough Is Not Enough	1980	$5
❏ 2428	Steppin' Out/Chinatown	1982	$3
❏ 2428 [PS]	Steppin' Out/Chinatown	1982	$5

JACKSON, JUNE
BELL

❏ 45173	Little Dog Heaven/Tenderly with Feeling	1972	$50

IMPERIAL

❏ 66185	It's What's Up Front That Counts/Fifty Per Cent Won't Do	1966	$200

JACKSON, LA TOYA
LARC

❏ 81025	Bet'cha Gonna Need My Lovin'/(Instrumental)	1983	$4

POLYDOR

❏ 2188	I Don't Want You to Go/ Love Song	1981	$4
❏ 2137	If You Feel the Funk/Lonely Is She	1980	$4
❏ 2177	Stay the Night/Camp Kuchi Kalai	1981	$4

PRIVATE I

❏ 04439	Heart Don't Lie/Without You	1984	$4
❏ 04439 [PS]	Heart Don't Lie/Without You	1984	$4
❏ 05783	He's a Pretender/How Do I Tell Them	1986	$4
❏ 05783 [PS]	He's a Pretender/How Do I Tell Them	1986	$4
❏ 04572	Hot Potato/Think Twice	1984	$4
❏ 06040	Love Talk/Imagination	1986	$4

RCA

❏ 8873-7-R	Such a Wicked Love/Does It Really Matter	1989	$3

JACKSON, LEE, AND THE CADILLAC BABY SPECIALS
BEA & BABY

❏ 121	Christmas Song/Santa Came Home Drunk	1960	$40

— B-side by Clyde Lasley

❏ 119	The Christmas Song/The Christmas Song	1960	$40

— B-side by Clyde Lasley

JACKSON, LIL' SON
IMPERIAL

❏ 5276	Big Rat/Piggly Wiggly	1954	$100
❏ 5218	Black and Brown/Sad Letter Blues	1953	$125
❏ 5259	Dirty Work/Little Girl	1953	$125
❏ 5851	Everybody's Blues/Travelin' Woman	1962	$20
❏ 5300	Get High Everybody/Let Me Down Easy	1954	$100
❏ 5312	How Long/Good Ole Wagon	1954	$100
❏ 5229	Lonely Blues/Freight Train Blues	1953	$125
❏ 5248	Movin' to the Country/ Confession	1953	$125
❏ 5319	My Younger Days/I Wish to Go Home	1954	$100
❏ 5963	Prison Bound/Rolling Mill	1963	$15
❏ 5237	Spending Money Blues/ All Alone	1953	$125
❏ 5339	Sugar Mama/Messin' Up	1955	$100
❏ 5267	Thrill Me, Baby/Doctor, Doctor	1954	$100
❏ 5286	Trouble Don't Last Always/ Blues by the Hour	1954	$100

JACKSON, MAHALIA
APOLLO

❏ 245	Bless This House/The Lord's Prayer	1951	$30
❏ 313	Didn't It Rain/Nobody Knows	1956	$20
❏ 240	Get Away Jordan/I Gave Up Everything	1951	$30
❏ 282	Hands of God/It's Real	1954	$30
❏ 269	He Said He Would/God Spoke to Me	1953	$30
❏ 304	He's My Light/If You Just Keep Still	1956	$30
❏ 258	He's the One/I'm Getting Nearer My Home	1952	$30
❏ 311	His Eyes Are On the Sparrow/I Can Put My Trust in Jesus	1956	$20
❏ 246	His Eyes Are On the Sparrow/It Is No Secret (What God Can Do)	1951	$30
❏ 248	How I Got Over/Just As I Am	1951	$30
❏ 273	I'm Going Down the River/ Do You Know Him	1953	$30
❏ 286	I'm On My Way/My Story	1954	$30
❏ 314	I'm On My Way/My Story	1956	$20
❏ 262	In the Upper Room (Part 1)/ In the Upper Room (Part 2)	1952	$30
❏ 291	I Walked Into the Garden/I'm Going to Tell God	1955	$30
❏ 278	I Wonder If I Will Ever Rest/ Coming to Jesus	1953	$30
❏ 235	Silent Night, Holy Night/Go Tell It On The Mountain	1951	$30

— Note: Earlier Mahalia Jackson 45s on Apollo may exist

❏ 539	Silent Night/The Lord's Prayer	1959	$20
❏ 750	Silent Night/The Lord's Prayer	1962	$15
❏ 750 [PS]	Silent Night/The Lord's Prayer	1962	$30
❏ 289	Walking to Jerusalem/What Then	1954	$30

COLUMBIA

❏ 45068	Abraham, Martin and John/ Day Is Done	1970	$6
❏ 41322	Elijah Rock/Hold Me	1959	$15
❏ 41258	For My Good Fortune/Have You Any Rivers	1958	$15
❏ 40854	God Is So Good/I Complained	1957	$20
❏ JZSP137705/6 [DJ]	Happy Birthday To You, Our Lord/Silver Bells	1968	$5
❏ 41150	He's Got the Whole World In His Hands/Didn't It Rain	1958	$15
❏ 40529	His Hands/I See God	1955	$20
❏ 40721	I Ask the Lord/I'm Going to Live	1956	$20
❏ 42946	In the Summer of His Years/ Song for My Brother	1964	$10
❏ 41779	My Country 'Tis of Thee (America)/Onward, Christian Soldiers	1960	$15
❏ 40777	Silent Night, Holy Night/ Mary's Little Boy Chile	1956	$20
❏ 43474	Sunrise, Sunset/Like the Breeze Blows	1965	$10
❏ 41055	Sweet Little Jesus Boy/A Star Stood Still	1957	$15
❏ 44529	Take My Hand, Precious Lord/We Shall Overcome	1968	$8
❏ 41382	Tell the World About This/ Trouble of the World	1959	$15
❏ 40554	The Bible Tells Me So/ Satisfied Mind	1955	$20
❏ 40610	The Lord Is a Busy Man/ You're Not Living in Vain	1955	$20
❏ 40753	The Lord's Prayer/Precious Lord	1956	$20
❏ 41000	Trouble/He's a Light Unto My Pathway	1957	$20
❏ 40412	Walk Over God's Heaven/ Jesus Met the Woman	1955	$20
❏ 42910	We Shall Overcome/Let's Pray Together	1963	$10

GRAND AWARD

❏ 1025	Dig a Little Deeper/I'm On My Way	1959	$20
❏ 300	In the Upper Room (Part 1)/ In the Upper Room (Part 2)	1964	$8
❏ 750	Silent Night/The Lord's Prayer	1964	$10

Albums
HARMONY

❏ KH31111	Lord Don't Let Me Fall	1972	$12

JACKSON, MARLON
CAPITOL

❏ B-44092	Baby Tonight (Radio Edit)/ Baby Tonight (Video Version)	1987	$3
❏ B-44092 [PS]	Baby Tonight (Radio Edit)/ Baby Tonight (Video Version)	1987	$3
❏ B-44047	Don't Go/(Instrumental)	1987	$3
❏ B-44047 [PS]	Don't Go/(Instrumental)	1987	$3
❏ B-5675	(Let Your Love Find) The Chosen One/Sardo and the Child	1987	$4
❏ B-44122	Lovely Eyes/(Instrumental)	1988	$3

JACKSON, MICHAEL, AND PAUL McCARTNEY
COLUMBIA

❏ 38-04168	Say, Say, Say/Ode to a Koala Bear	1983	$5

— As "Paul McCartney and Michael Jackson"; B-side by Paul McCartney

❏ 38-04168 [PS]	Say, Say, Say/Ode to a Koala Bear	1983	$4

EPIC

❏ ENR-03372	The Girl Is Mine/(B-side blank)	1982	$15

— One-sided budget release

❏ 34-03288	The Girl Is Mine/Can't Get Outta the Rain	1982	$5

— B-side by Michael Jackson

JACKSON, MICHAEL
EPIC

❏ 34-07962	Another Part of Me/ (Instrumental)	1988	$3
❏ 34-07962 [PS]	Another Part of Me/ (Instrumental)	1988	$3
❏ 34-07418	Bad/I Can't Help It	1987	$3
❏ 34-07418 [PS]	Bad/I Can't Help It	1987	$3
❏ 34-03759	Beat It/Get On the Floor	1983	$6
❏ ENR-03575	Billie Jean/(B-side blank)	1983	$20

— One-sided budget release

❏ 34-03509	Billie Jean/Can't Get Outta the Rain	1983	$6
❏ 34-07739	Dirty Diana/(Instrumental)	1988	$3
❏ 34-07739 [PS]	Dirty Diana/(Instrumental)	1988	$3
❏ 9-50742	Don't Stop 'Til You Get Enough/I Can't Help It	1979	$4
❏ 34-04026 [PS]	Human Nature	1983	$10

— Demonstration -- Not for Sale" on sleeve

❏ 34-04026	Human Nature/Baby Be Mine	1983	$6
❏ 34-04026 [PS]	Human Nature/Baby Be Mine	1983	$5
❏ 34-07253	I Just Can't Stop Loving You/ Baby Be Mine	1987	$3
❏ 34-07253 [PS]	I Just Can't Stop Loving You/ Baby Be Mine	1987	$3
❏ 34-07668	Man in the Mirror/ (Instrumental)	1988	$3
❏ 34-07668 [PS]	Man in the Mirror/ (Instrumental)	1988	$3
❏ 9-50838	Off the Wall/Get On the Floor	1980	$4
❏ 34-04165	P.Y.T. (Pretty Young Thing)/ Working Day and Night	1983	$6
❏ 34-04165 [PS]	P.Y.T. (Pretty Young Thing)/ Working Day and Night	1983	$5
❏ 9-50871	She's Out of My Life/Get On the Floor	1980	$4
❏ 15-02157	She's Out of My Life/Lovely One	1981	$6

— Memory Lane" reissue; B-side by The Jacksons

❏ 34-08044	Smooth Criminal/ (Instrumental)	1988	$3
❏ 34-08044 [PS]	Smooth Criminal/ (Instrumental)	1988	$3
❏ 34-07645	The Way You Make Me Feel/(Instrumental)	1987	$5
❏ 34-07645 [PS]	The Way You Make Me Feel/(Instrumental)	1987	$3
❏ 34-04364	Thriller/Can't Get Outta the Rain	1984	$6
❏ 34-03914	Wanna Be Startin' Somethin'/(Instrumental)	1983	$8
❏ 34-03914 [PS]	Wanna Be Startin' Somethin'/(Instrumental)	1983	$5

MCA

❏ 40947	Ease On Down the Road/ Poppy Girls	1978	$5

— With Diana Ross

❏ 40947 [PS]	Ease On Down the Road/ Poppy Girls	1978	$8
❏ S45-1786 [DJ]	Someone in the Dark (same on both sides)	1982	$60
❏ S45-1786 [PS]	Someone in the Dark (same on both sides)	1982	$60

MOTOWN

Number	Title	Yr	NM
☐ 1207	Ben/You Can Cry on My Shoulder	1972	$5
☐ 1739	Farewell My Summer Love/Call On Me	1984	$5
☐ 1739 [PS]	Farewell My Summer Love/Call On Me	1984	$5
☐ 1757	Girl You're So Together/Touch the One You Love	1984	$5
☐ 1202 [PS]	I Wanna Be Where You Are!/We Got a Good Thing Going	1972	$10
☐ 1512	One Day in Your Life/Take Me Back	1981	$5
☐ 1914	Twenty-Five Miles/Up on the House Top	1987	$8
☐ 1914 [PS]	Twenty-Five Miles/Up on the House Top	1987	$8
☐ 1341	We're Almost There/Take Me Back	1975	$5

JACKSON, RANDY

A&M

Number	Title	Yr	NM
☐ 1449	Perpetrators/(Instrumental)	1989	$4

—As "Randy and the Gypsys"

EPIC

Number	Title	Yr	NM
☐ 8-50576	How Can I Be Sure/Love Song for Kids	1978	$6

JACKSON, RUDY

IMPERIAL

Number	Title	Yr	NM
☐ 5945	Go On Lover, Go On/Who Do You Think You Are	1963	$15
☐ 5425	Teasing Me/Give Me Your Hand	1957	$50

R & B

Number	Title	Yr	NM
☐ 1310	I'm Crying/Enfold Me	1955	$100

JACKSON, SHIRLEY

METRO

Number	Title	Yr	NM
☐ 20031	The Wedding/Wait for Me	1960	$15

JACKSON, STONEWALL

COLUMBIA

Number	Title	Yr	NM
☐ 4-41785	A Little Guy Called Joe/I'm Gonna Find You	1960	$20
☐ 4-44625	Angry Words/Red Roses Blooming Back Home	1968	$10
☐ 4-42229	A Wound Time Can't Erase/Second Choice	1961	$20
☐ 4-45075	Better Days for Mama/The Harm You've Done	1970	$8
☐ 4-42889	B.J. the D.J./Big House on the Corner	1963	$15
☐ 4-43718	Blues Plus Booze (Means I Lose)/Still Awake	1966	$10
☐ 4-45151	Born That Way/Blue Field	1970	$8
☐ 4-42628	Can't Hang Up the Phone/Slowly	1962	$15
☐ 4-43076	Don't Be Angry/It's Not Me	1964	$15
☐ 4-40883	Don't Be Angry/Knock Off Your Naggin'	1957	$30
☐ 4-41932	Greener Pastures/Wedding Bells for You and Me	1961	$20
☐ 4-41199	Grieving in My Heart/I Can't Go On Living This Way	1958	$30
☐ 4-42028	Hungry for Love/For the Last Time	1961	$20
☐ 4-44501	I Believe in Love/Drinking and Driving	1968	$10
☐ 4-44501 [PS]	I Believe in Love/Drinking and Driving	1968	$20
☐ 4-43411	If This House Could Talk/Poor Red Georgia Dirt	1965	$10
☐ 4-41488	Igmoo (The Pride of South Central High)/Uncle Sam and Big John Bull	1959	$20
☐ 4-45738	I'm Not Strong Enough (To Build Another Dream)/I've Run Out of Reasons	1972	$8
☐ 4-40997	I Need You Real Bad/A Broken Heart, A Wedding Band	1957	$30
☐ 4-43197	I Washed My Hands in Muddy Water/I've Got to Change	1964	$15
☐ 4-42426	Leona/One Look at Heaven	1962	$15
☐ 4-41257	Life to Go/Misery Known As Heartache	1958	$30
☐ 4-43304	Lost in the Shuffle/Trouble and Me	1965	$10
☐ 4-41533	Mary Don't You Weep/Run	1959	$20
☐ 4-45381	Me and You and a Dog Named Boo/Here's to Hank	1971	$8
☐ 4-43917	Mommy Look, Santa Is Crying/Blue Christmas	1966	$15
☐ 4-45217	Oh, Lonesome Me/When He Was Nine	1970	$8
☐ 4-42765	Old Showboat/A Toast to the Bride	1963	$15
☐ 4-44121	Promises and Hearts (Were Made to Break)/While the Daisies Go Free	1967	$10
☐ 4-45465	Push the Panic Button/Waitin' for Dawn 'Til Dawn	1971	$8
☐ 4-45291	Save a Little Place for Me/Wings of a Dove	1970	$8
☐ 4-44976	Ship in a Bottle/Thoughts of a Lonely Man	1969	$10

Number	Title	Yr	NM
☐ 4-44726	Somebody's Always Leaving/Recess Time	1969	$12
☐ 4-43966	Stamp Out Loneliness/Road to Recovery	1967	$10
☐ 4-41114	Tears on Her Brodal Bouquet/Gettin' Older	1958	$30
☐ 4-45546	That's All This Old World Needs/Big Busy World	1972	$8
☐ 4-43552	The Minute Men (Are Turning in Their Graves)/I Wish I Had a Girl	1966	$10
☐ 4-43552 [PS]	The Minute Men (Are Turning in Their Graves)/I Wish I Had a Girl	1966	$30
☐ 4-41695	Thirty Links of Chain/Sixteen Fathoms	1960	$20
☐ 4-44283	This World Means Nothing (Since You're Gone)/Almsot Hear the Blues	1967	$10
☐ 4-45632	Torn from the Pages of Life/Waterloo	1972	$8
☐ 4-45831	True Love Is the Thing/House of Bottles and Cans	1973	$8
☐ 4-41393	Waterloo/Smoke Along the Track	1959	$20
☐ 4-41393 [PS]	Waterloo/Smoke Along the Track	1959	$40
☐ 4-41591	Why I'm Walkin'/Life of a Poor Boy	1960	$20
☐ 4-42846	Wild Wind Wind/The Water's So Cold	1963	$15

GRT

Number	Title	Yr	NM
☐ 023	Waterloo/I Washed My Hands in Muddy Water	1975	$6

LITTLE DARLIN'

Number	Title	Yr	NM
☐ 7915	Come On Home/Point of No Return	1979	$6
☐ 7806	I Can't Sing a Love Song/My Favorite Sin	1978	$6
☐ 7927	Listening to Johnny Paycheck/Here's to the Ripoff	1979	$6
☐ 7800	Spirits of St. Louis/Alcohol of Fame	1978	$6
☐ 7802	Walk Out on Me Before I Walk Out on You/Burned On Low	1978	$6

JACKSON, TONY, AND THE VIBRATIONS

KAPP

Number	Title	Yr	NM
☐ 639	This Little Girl of Mine/You Beat Me to the Punch	1965	$20

RED BIRD

Number	Title	Yr	NM
☐ Oct-0038	That's What I Want/Stage Door	1965	$20

JACKSON, WALTER

BRUNSWICK

Number	Title	Yr	NM
☐ 55502	It Doesn't Take Much/Let Me Come Back	1973	$200

CHI-SOUND

Number	Title	Yr	NM
☐ XW964	Baby, I Love Your Way/What Would You Do	1977	$5
☐ XW908	Feelings/Words (Are Impossible)	1976	$5
☐ XW1140	If I Had My Way/We Could Fly	1978	$20
☐ XW1044	It's All Over/Gonna Find Me an Angel	1977	$5
☐ 2426	Magic Man/Golden Rays	1979	$4
☐ XW1216	Manhattan Skyline/I Won't Remember Ever Loving You	1978	$5

COLUMBIA

Number	Title	Yr	NM
☐ 42823	Opportunity/It Will Be the Last Time	1963	$125
☐ 42659	Starting Tomorrow/Then, Only Then	1963	$200
☐ 02037	Tell Me Where It Hurts/When I See You	1981	$4
☐ 42528	This World of Mine/I Don't Want to Suffer	1962	$125
☐ 02294	What If I Walked Out on You/I Come to Me	1981	$4

COTILLION

Number	Title	Yr	NM
☐ 44053	Anyway That You Want Me/Life Has Its Ups and Downs	1969	$20

EPIC

Number	Title	Yr	NM
☐ 10408	Ad Lib/No Butterflies	1968	$8

KELLI-ARTS

Number	Title	Yr	NM
☐ 1006	If I Had a Chance/(B-side unknown)	1982	$30

OKEH

Number	Title	Yr	NM
☐ 7260	A Corner in the Sun/Not You	1966	$30
☐ 7256	After You There Can Be Nothing/My Funny Valentine	1966	$40
☐ 7295	Cold, Cold Winter/My Ship Is Comin' In	1967	$40
☐ 7285	Deep in the Heart of Harlem/My One Chance to Make It	1967	$30
☐ 7285 [PS]	Deep in the Heart of Harlem/My One Chance to Make It	1967	$60
☐ 7305	Everything/Road to Ruin	1968	$30
☐ 7236	Funny (Not Much)/One Heart Lonely	1965	$60
☐ 7229	I'll Keep On Trying/Where Have All the Flowers Gone	1965	$50
☐ 7204	It's All Over/Lee Cross	1964	$30

Number	Title	Yr	NM
☐ 7247	It's an Uphill Climb to the Bottom/Tear for Tear	1966	$70
☐ 7247 [PS]	It's an Uphill Climb to the Bottom/Tear for Tear	1966	$125
☐ 7272	Speak Her Name/They Don't Give Medals (To Yesterday's Heroes)	1967	$30
☐ 7272 [PS]	Speak Her Name/They Don't Give Medals (To Yesterday's Heroes)	1967	$60
☐ 7215	Suddenly I'm All Alone/Special Love	1965	$30
☐ 7189	That's What Mama Say/What Would You Do	1964	$50
☐ 7219	Welcome Home/Blowin' in the Wind	1965	$40

JACKSON, WANDA

ABC

Number	Title	Yr	NM
☐ 12116	Take a Look/I Can't Stand to Hear You Say Goodbye	1975	$5

CAPITOL

Number	Title	Yr	NM
☐ F4207	A Date with Jerry/You're the One for Me	1959	$30
☐ 2021	A Girl Don't Have to Drink to Have Fun/My Days Are Darker Than Your Nights	1967	$10
☐ 4681	A Little Bitty Tear/I Don't Wanta Go	1962	$30
☐ 2761	A Woman Lives for Love/What Have We Done	1970	$6
☐ 3143	Back Then/I'm Gonna Walk Out of Your Life	1971	$6
☐ 5645	Because It's You/Long As I Have You	1966	$12
☐ 5863	Both Sides of the Line/Famous Last Words	1967	$10
☐ 4917	But I Was Lying/Sympathy	1963	$20
☐ 2085	By the Time You Get to Phoenix/Wishing Well	1968	$8
☐ 5287	Candy Man/Weary Blues From Waitin'	1964	$15
☐ F3764	Cool Love/Did You Miss Me	1957	$40
☐ F3637	Cryin' Through the Night/Baby Loves Him	1957	$60
☐ F3683	Don'a Wan'a/Let Me Explain	1957	$40
☐ 2524	Everything's Leaving/You Cheated Me	1969	$8
☐ F4026	(Every Time They Play) Our Song/Mean, Mean Man	1958	$40
☐ 2986	Fancy Satin Pillows/Why Don't We Love Like That Anymore	1970	$6
☐ F3843	Fujiyama Mama/No Wedding Bells for Joe	1957	$40
☐ 5433	Have I Grown Used to Missing You/Take Me Home	1965	$15
☐ F3575	Hot Dog! That Made Him Mad/Silver Threads and Golden Needles	1956	$50
☐ 3218	I Already Know (What I'm Gettin' for My Birthday)/The Man You Could Have Been	1971	$6
☐ 3599	I Don't Know How to Tell Him/Your Memory Comes and Gets Me	1973	$6
☐ 4723	If I Cried Every Time You Hurt Me/Let My Love Walk In	1962	$30
☐ 4723 [PS]	If I Cried Every Time You Hurt Me/Let My Love Walk In	1962	$40
☐ 2379	If I Had a Hammer/The Pain of It All	1969	$8
☐ F3485	I Gotta Know/Half As Good a Girl	1956	$50
☐ 3293	I'll Be Whatever You Say/The More You See Me Less	1972	$6
☐ 4785	I Misunderstood/Between the Window and the Phone	1962	$20
☐ 4635	In the Middle of a Heartache/I'd Be Ashamed	1961	$30
☐ 2315	I Wish I Was Your Friend/Poor Old Me	1968	$8
☐ 3385	I Wouldn't Want You Any Other Way/Song of the Wind	1972	$6
☐ 5228	Leave My Baby Alone/I'm Mad at Me	1964	$15
☐ 4397	Let's Have a Party/Cool Love	1960	$50
☐ 2245	Little Boy Soldier/I Talk a Pretty Story	1968	$8
☐ 4469	Mean, Mean Man/Happy, Happy Birthday	1960	$30
☐ 5015	Memory Mountain/Let Me Talk to You	1963	$20
☐ 5364	My Baby's Gone/If I Were You	1965	$15
☐ 2151	My Baby Walked Right Out on Me/No Place to Go but Home	1968	$8
☐ 2614	My Big Iron Skillet/The Hunter	1969	$8
☐ 4354	My Destiny/Please Call Today	1960	$30
☐ 5491	My First Day Without You/Send Me No Roses	1965	$15
☐ 5960	My Heart Gets All the Breaks/You'll Always Have My Love	1967	$10
☐ 3070	People Gotta Be Loving/Glory Hallelujah	1971	$6
☐ F4142	Savin' My Love/I Wanna Waltz	1959	$30
☐ F4081	Sinful Heart/Rock Your Baby	1958	$40

Number	Title	Yr	NM
❏ 5072	Slippin'/Just for You	1963	$20
❏ 5789	Tears Will Be the Chaser for Your Wine/Reckless Love Affair	1967	$10
❏ 5559	The Box It Came In/Look Out Heart	1965	$15
❏ 4833	The Greatest Actor/You Bug Me Bad	1962	$20
❏ 5712	This Gun Don't Care/I Wonder If She Knows	1966	$10
❏ 4973	This Should Go On Forever/ We Haven't a Moment to Lose	1963	$20
❏ 2693	Two Separate Bar Stools/ Two Wrongs Don't Make a Right	1969	$8
❏ 4884	Whirlpool/One Teardrop at a Time	1962	$125
❏ 2872	Who Shot John/Stop the World	1970	$6

DECCA

Number	Title	Yr	NM
❏ 29677	Don't Do the Things He'd Do/It's the Same World	1955	$40
❏ 29267	If You Don't, Somebody Else Will/You'd Be the First One to Know	1954	$60

—With Billy Gray

Number	Title	Yr	NM
❏ 29514	Tears at the Grand Ole Opry/Nobody's Darlin' But Mine	1955	$60
❏ 29803	Wasted/I Cried Again	1956	$60

MYRRH

Number	Title	Yr	NM
❏ 126	Come On Home (To This Lonely Heart)/It's a Long, Long Time to Cry	1973	$5
❏ 122	When It's Time to Fall in Love Again/Say "I Do"	1973	$5
❏ 152	Where Do I Put His Memory/ Take a Look	1975	$5

JACKSON, WILLIS

ATCO

Number	Title	Yr	NM
❏ 6089	Later 'Gator/Back Door	1957	$60

ATLANTIC

Number	Title	Yr	NM
❏ 3294	Brown Eyed Girl/The Way We Were	1975	$8
❏ 975	Gator's Groove/Estralita	1952	$100
❏ 946	Harlem Nocturne/Street Scene	1951	$200
❏ 967	Here in My Heart/Rock, Rock, Rock	1952	$125
❏ 998	Walkin' Home/Shake Dance	1953	$100
❏ 957	Wine-O-Wine/Good Gliding	1952	$200

CADET

Number	Title	Yr	NM
❏ 5529	Goose Pimples/Who Can I Turn To (When Nobody Wants Me)	1966	$30

COTILLION

Number	Title	Yr	NM
❏ 44204	Feelings/Do It, Do It	1976	$6

DELUXE

Number	Title	Yr	NM
❏ 6073	Howling at Midnight/We'll Be Together Again	1955	$40
❏ 6060	The Cracker Jack/Try a Little Tenderness	1954	$50

FIRE

Number	Title	Yr	NM
❏ 1003	Good to the Bone/Making It	1959	$20

PRESTIGE

Number	Title	Yr	NM
❏ 277	Arrividerci Roma/Y'All	1963	$10
❏ 303	As Long As She Needs Me/ Troubled Times	1963	$10
❏ 207	Cookin' Sherry (Part 1)/ (Part 2)	1961	$15
❏ 293	Gra-a-avy/Brother Elijah	1963	$10
❏ 234	I Left My Heart in San Francisco/What Kind of Fool Am I	1962	$15
❏ 258	Secret Love (Part 1)/(Part 2)	1963	$10
❏ 457	Song of Ossanha/Soul Grabber	1968	$15
❏ 719	Swivel Hips (Part 1)/(Part 2)	1969	$8
❏ 221	Thunderbird/Jambalaya	1962	$15
❏ 410	That Twistin' Train/Without a Song	1962	$15

—A-side is the same recording as "Backtrack" with a new title

VERVE

Number	Title	Yr	NM
❏ 10332	I Almost Lost My Mind/ Swimmin' Home Babe	1964	$10

JACKSONS, THE
Includes records as "The Jackson Five." Also see JACKIE JACKSON; JERMAINE JACKSON; MARLON JACKSON; MICHAEL JACKSON.

EPIC

Number	Title	Yr	NM
❏ 34-69022	2300 Jackson Street/When I Look at You	1989	$3
❏ 8-50595	Blame It on the Boogie/Do What You Wanna	1978	$4
❏ 34-04673	Body/(Instrumental)	1984	$4
❏ 34-04673 [PS]	Body/(Instrumental)	1984	$4
❏ 19-01032	Can You Feel It/Everybody	1981	$4
❏ 19-50959	Heartbreak Hotel/The Things I Do for You	1980	$4
❏ 9-50938	Lovely One/Bless His Soul	1980	$4

Number	Title	Yr	NM
❏ 15-02157	Lovely One/She's Out of My Life	1981	$3

—Reissue; B-side by Michael Jackson

Number	Title	Yr	NM
❏ 8-50656	Shake Your Body (Down to the Ground)/That's What You Get (For Being Polite)	1979	$5

—Original issue has orange label

Number	Title	Yr	NM
❏ 8-50656	Shake Your Body (Down to the Ground)/That's What You Get (For Being Polite)	1979	$4

—Second issue has dark blue label

Number	Title	Yr	NM
❏ 34-04503	State of Shock/Your Ways	1984	$4

—A-side with Mick Jagger

Number	Title	Yr	NM
❏ 34-04503 [PS]	State of Shock/Your Ways	1984	$4
❏ 14-02720	The Things I Do for You/ Working Day and Night	1982	$4
❏ 34-04575	Torture/(Instrumental)	1984	$4
❏ 34-04575 [PS]	Torture/(Instrumental)	1984	$4
❏ 19-02132	Walk Right Now/Your Ways	1981	$4

EPIC/PHILADELPHIA INT'L.

Number	Title	Yr	NM
❏ 8-50289	Enjoy Yourself/Style of Life	1976	$5
❏ 8-50496	Find Me a Girl/Different Kind of Lady	1977	$5
❏ 8-50454	Goin' Places/Do What You Wanna	1977	$5
❏ 8-50350	Show You the Way to Go/ Blues Away	1977	$5

MCA

Number	Title	Yr	NM
❏ 53032	Time Out for the Burglar/ News at Eleven	1987	$3

—B-side by the Distants

Number	Title	Yr	NM
❏ 53032 [PS]	Time Out for the Burglar/ News at Eleven	1987	$3

MOTOWN

Number	Title	Yr	NM
❏ 1163	ABC/The Young Folks	1970	$8
❏ 1214	Corner of the Sky/To Know	1972	$6
❏ 1286	Dancing Machine/It's Too Late to Change the Time	1974	$6
❏ 1356	Forever Came Today/All I Do Is Think of You	1975	$6
❏ 1277 [DJ]	Get It Together (same on both sides)	1973	$30

—Promo only on red vinyl

Number	Title	Yr	NM
❏ 1277	Get It Together/Touch	1973	$6
❏ 1224	Hallelujah Day/You Made Me What I Am	1973	$6
❏ 1310	I Am Love (Part 1)/I Am Love (Part 2)	1975	$8
❏ 1310	I Am Love (Parts 1 & 2)/I Am Love (Part 2)	1975	$6
❏ 1166 [DJ]	I Found That Girl (same on both sides)	1970	$30

—Red vinyl

Number	Title	Yr	NM
❏ 1171	I'll Be There/One More Chance	1970	$8
❏ 1157	I Want You Back/Who's Lovin' You	1969	$8
❏ 1199	Little Bitty Pretty One/If I Had to Move a Mountain	1972	$6
❏ 1205	Looking Through the Windows/Love Song	1972	$6
❏ 1177	Mama's Pearl/Darling Dear	1971	$6
❏ 1177 [PS]	Mama's Pearl/Darling Dear	1971	$20
❏ 1186	Maybe Tomorrow/I Will Find a Way	1971	$6
❏ 1174	Santa Claus Is Coming to Town/Christmas Won't Be the Same This Year	1970	$15
❏ 1194	Sugar Daddy/I'm So Happy	1971	$6
❏ 1166 [DJ]	The Love You Save	1970	$40

—Blank back promo

Number	Title	Yr	NM
❏ 1166	The Love You Save/I Found That Girl	1970	$8
❏ 1308	Whatever You Got, I Want/I Can't Quit Your Love	1974	$6

STEELTOWN

Number	Title	Yr	NM
❏ 681	Big Boy/You've Changed	1968	$60

7-Inch Extended Plays

MOTOWN

Number	Title	Yr	NM
❏ M60718 [PS]	Third Album	1970	$20

—Part of "Little LP" series (LLP #132)

JACOBS, HANK

IMPERIAL

Number	Title	Yr	NM
❏ 5894	Sting Ray/Sheryl Ann	1962	$20

SUE

Number	Title	Yr	NM
❏ 102	Bacon Fat/Out of Sight	1964	$12
❏ 113	Heide/Playboy's Penthouse	1964	$12
❏ 795	So Far Away/Monkey Hips & Rice	1963	$15

JACOBY BROTHERS, THE

COLUMBIA

Number	Title	Yr	NM
❏ 4-21359	Who Ye Primpin' Fer/One Man's Opinion	1955	$30

JACQUET, RUSSELL

IMPERIAL

Number	Title	Yr	NM
❏ 5722	Sail On/You're Gonna Be Paid	1961	$40

JADE, FAINE

RSVP

Number	Title	Yr	NM
❏ 1130	Introspection/(B-side unknown)	1968	$30

JADE WARRIOR

VERTIGO

Number	Title	Yr	NM
❏ 108	A Winter's Tale/The Demon Trucker	1972	$20
❏ 106	We Have Reason to Believe/ Barazinbar	1972	$25

JADES, THE

ADONA

Number	Title	Yr	NM
❏ 1445	Hey Senorita/(B-side unknown)	1962	$40

CAPITOL

Number	Title	Yr	NM
❏ 2281	Ain't It Funny What Love Can Do/Baby I Need Your Love	1968	$40

CHRISTY

Number	Title	Yr	NM
❏ 113	Don't Be a Fool/Friday Night with My Baby	1959	$500
❏ 114	Look for a Lie/Blue Memories	1959	$1500
❏ 110	Oh Why/Big Beach Party	1959	$500
❏ 111	Tell Me Pretty Baby/ Applesauce	1959	$250

DORE

Number	Title	Yr	NM
❏ 687	Hold Back the Dawn/When They Ask About You	1963	$30

DOT

Number	Title	Yr	NM
❏ 15822	I'm Pretending/Beverly	1958	$100

GAITY

Number	Title	Yr	NM
❏ 2-23-64	Surfin' Crow/Blue Black Hair	1964	$180

IMPERIAL

Number	Title	Yr	NM
❏ 66425	L-O-V-E I Love You/Don't Give What's Mine Away	1969	$80
❏ 66383	Wheel of Fortune/Gotta Find Somebody to Love	1969	$6

LIBERTY

Number	Title	Yr	NM
❏ 56192	All's Quiet on West 23rd/ Love of a Woman	1970	$5

MGM

Number	Title	Yr	NM
❏ 13399	There's a Kinder Way to Say Goodbye/You're So Right for Me	1965	$40

NAU VOO

Number	Title	Yr	NM
❏ 807	Walking All Alone/Hey Little Girl	1959	$200

OXBORO

Number	Title	Yr	NM
❏ 2005	Little Marlene/Shake Baby Shake	1965	$120
❏ 2002	Surfin' Crow/Blue Black Hair	1964	$120

PORT

Number	Title	Yr	NM
❏ 70042	He's My Guy/There Will Come a Day	1964	$30

TIME

Number	Title	Yr	NM
❏ 1002	Leave Her For Me/So Blue	1957	$200

—Lou Reed is alleged to have been in this group, but he would have been 15 at the time.

UNI

Number	Title	Yr	NM
❏ 55032 [DJ]	Privilege (same on both sides)	1967	$8
❏ 55019	The Glide/Flower Power	1967	$20

VERVE

Number	Title	Yr	NM
❏ 10385	For Just Another Day/I'm By Your Side (Baby)	1966	$40

JAGGED EDGE, THE

RCA VICTOR

Number	Title	Yr	NM
❏ 47-8880	Baby You Don't Know/Deep Inside	1966	$50

TWIRL

Number	Title	Yr	NM
❏ 2024	How Many Times/Midnight to Six Man	1966	$40

JAGGER, MICK

COLUMBIA

Number	Title	Yr	NM
❏ 38-07306	Let's Work/Catch as Catch Can	1987	$3
❏ 38-07306 [PS]	Let's Work/Catch as Catch Can	1987	$3
❏ 38-04893	Lucky in Love/Running Out of Luck	1985	$3
❏ 38-04893 [PS]	Lucky in Love/Running Out of Luck	1985	$4
❏ 38-07703	Say You Will/Shoot Off Your Mouth	1988	$3
❏ 38-07703 [PS]	Say You Will/Shoot Off Your Mouth	1988	$5
❏ 38-07653	Throwaway/Peace for the Wicked	1987	$3
❏ 38-07653 [PS]	Throwaway/Peace for the Wicked	1987	$3

Number	Title	Yr	NM

JAGGERZ, THE
GAMBLE
❏ 226 — Gotta Find My Way Back Home/Forever Together, Together Forever — 1968 — $50
❏ 4008 — Higher and Higher/Ain't No Sun — 1970 — $40
❏ 218 — (That's Why) Baby I Love You/Bring It Back — 1968 — $30
❏ 238 — Together/Let Me Be the One — 1969 — $40
KAMA SUTRA
❏ 509 — I Call My Baby Candy/Will She Believe Me — 1970 — $6
❏ 583 — Let's Talk About Love/Ain't That Sad — 1973 — $4
❏ 517 — Let's Talk About Love/I'll Never Forget You — 1971 — $5
❏ 513 — What a Bummer/Memories of the Traveller — 1970 — $6
WOODEN NICKEL
❏ PB-10194 — Don't It Make You Want to Dance/2 Plus 2 — 1975 — $4

JAGUARS, THE (1)
AARDELL
❏ 06 — Be My Sweetie/Why Don't You Believe Me — 1956 — $60
BARONET
❏ 1 — The Way You Look Tonight/Baby, Baby, Baby — 1962 — $30
CLASSIC ARTISTS
❏ 117 — Happy Holiday/More Than Enough for Me — 1989 — $6
—B-side by Johnny Staton and the Feathers
ORIGINAL SOUND
❏ 59 — The Way You Look Tonight/Baby, Baby, Baby — 1966 — $30
❏ 6 — Thinking of You/Look Into My Eyes — 1959 — $100
❏ 20 — Thinking of You/Look Into My Eyes — 1962 — $50
R-DELL
❏ 117 — Girl of My Dreams/Don't Go Home — 1960 — $70
❏ 16 — I Love You Baby/Baby, Baby, Baby — 1957 — $120
❏ 11 — The Way You Look Tonight/Baby, Baby, Baby — 1956 — $60
❏ 11 — The Way You Look Tonight/Moonlight and You — 1956 — $250
—Black vinyl
❏ 11 — The Way You Look Tonight/Moonlight and You — 1956 — $600
—Red vinyl

JAGUARS, THE (2)
DOT
❏ 16723 — Dead Sea/Supersonic — 1965 — $12
❏ 16931 — The Gorilla/He'll Turn Away — 1966 — $10

JAGUARS, THE (3)
EPIC
❏ 9325 — Drive-In/Exit 6 — 1959 — $30

JAGUARS, THE (4)
FARO
❏ 618 — Where Lovers Go/Discover a Lover — 1965 — $15

JAGUARS, THE (U)
EBB
❏ 129 — Hold Me Tight/Piccadilly — 1958 — $125
RENDEZVOUS
❏ 159 — Fine, Fine, Fine/It Finally Happened — 1961 — $30
❏ 216 — Fine, Fine, Fine/It Finally Happened — 1963 — $15
SKOOP
❏ 1067 — It's Gonna Be Alright/(B-side unknown) — 1966 — $30

JALOPY FIVE, THE
HIT
❏ 277 — 98.6/Kind of a Drag — 1967 — $8
—B-side by the Buchanans
❏ 134 — A Hard Day's Night/Rag Doll — 1964 — $8
—B-side by the Chellows
❏ 285 — A Little Bit Me, A Little Bit You/Detroit City — 1967 — $8
—B-side by Ed Hardin
❏ 138 — And I Love Her/Such a Night — 1964 — $10
—B-side by Ed Hardin
❏ 156 — Be Yourself/Mountain of Love — 1964 — $12
—B-side by Bobby Brooks
❏ 240 — California Dreamin'/Uptight (Everything's Alright) — 1966 — $10
—B-side by Ritchie Brown
❏ 132 — Can't You See That She's Mine/The Little Old Lady from Pasadena — 1964 — $10
—B-side by the Roamers
❏ 223 — Catch Us If You Can/Just a Little Bit Better — 1965 — $15
—B-side by Hank's Hounds
❏ 327 — Cry Like a Baby/Do You Know the Way to San Jose — 1968 — $8
—B-side by Kathy Shannon
❏ 307 — Dandelion/The Letter — 1967 — $12
—B-side by the Chords (2)
❏ 315 — Daydream Believer/By the Time I Get to Phoenix — 1967 — $8
—B-side by Ed Hardin
❏ 259 — Did You Ever Have to Make Up Your Mind/I Am a Rock — 1966 — $8
—B-side by Sammy and Theodore
❏ 100 — Drag City/Forget Him — 1964 — $8
—B-side by Wayne Harris
❏ 332 — D.W. Washburn/Reach Out of the Darkness — 1968 — $8
—B-side by the Chords (2)
❏ 192 — Eight Days a Week/She's Come of Age — 1965 — $15
—B-side by Bobby Brooks
❏ 347 — Elenore/Little Green Apples — 1968 — $8
—B-side by Leroy Jones
❏ 311 — Even the Bad Times Are Good/To Sir with Love — 1967 — $8
—B-side by the Jalopy Five
❏ 352 — Everyday People/Touch Me — 1969 — $8
—B-side by the Fantastics
❏ 110 — Fun, Fun, Fun/Glad All Over — 1964 — $8
❏ 228 — Get Off of My Cloud/One, Two, Three — 1965 — $15
—B-side by Henry Bary
❏ 295 — Groovin'/Somebody to Love — 1967 — $8
—B-side by the Chellows
❏ 220 — Help!/California Girls — 1965 — $15
—B-side by the Chellows
❏ 343 — Hey Jude/Harper Valley P.T.A. — 1968 — $8
—B-side by Kathy Shannon
❏ 336 — Hurdy Gurdy Man/Stoned Soul Picnic — 1968 — $8
—B-side by the Fantastics
❏ 217 — (I Can't Get No) Satisfaction/I Want Candy — 1965 — $15
—B-side by the Roamers
❏ 171 — I Feel Fine/She's a Woman — 1965 — $15
❏ 293 — I Got Rhythm/Here Comes My Baby — 1967 — $8
—B-side by the Fantastics
❏ 218 — I Like It Like That/I Want Candy — 1965 — $15
—B-side by the Roamers
❏ 273 — I'm a Believer/Mellow Yellow — 1966 — $8
—B-side by Joe King
❏ 145 — (I've Got a) Tiger in My Tank/Dancing in the Street — 1964 — $10
—B-side by Mary Sue and the Trams
❏ 266 — Last Train to Clarksville/Yellow Submarine — 1966 — $12
❏ 183 — Let's Lock the Door/California Street — 1965 — $12
—As "Johnny and the Jalopy Five"
❏ 150 — Little Honda/Making a Fool of Myself — 1964 — $8
❏ 147 — Matchbox/When I Grow Up (To Be a Man) — 1964 — $10
—B-side by the Roamers
❏ 345 — Midnight Confessions/Suzie-Q — 1968 — $8
—B-side by the Classmates
❏ 252 — Monday, Monday/Gloria — 1966 — $15
—B-side by the Chellows
❏ 263 — Mother's Little Helper/This Door Swings Both Ways — 1966 — $10
—B-side by the Chords (2)
❏ 276 — Music to Watch Girls By/Wild Thing — 1967 — $8
—B-side by Bobby Sims
❏ 258 — Paint It Black/The Sun Ain't Gonna Shine Anymore — 1966 — $15
—B-side by the Harris Brothers
❏ 287 — Penny Lane/I Think We're Alone Now — 1967 — $10
—B-side by Bobby Sims
❏ 300 — Pleasant Valley Sunday/Carrie-Anne — 1967 — $8
—B-side by the Chords (2)
❏ 268 — Psychotic Reaction/See See Rider — 1966 — $8
—B-side by Ed Hardin and the Cadets
❏ 161 — Sidewalk Surfin'/Any Way You Want It — 1964 — $15
—B-side by the Bugs
❏ 253 — Sloop John B/Rhapsody in the Rain — 1966 — $15
—B-side by Fred York
❏ 281 — Sock It To Me Baby/The Beat Goes On — 1967 — $8
—B-side by Bobby and Connie
❏ 81 — Surfer Girl/Then He Kissed Me — 1963 — $8
—B-side by the Dacrons
❏ 271 — The Hair on My Chinny Chin Chin/Have You Seen Your Mother, Baby — 1966 — $10
—B-side by the Chords (2)
❏ 283 — Then You Can Tell Me Goodbye/Ruby Tuesday — 1967 — $8
—B-side by the Chellows
❏ 317 — We Can Fly/Judy in Disguise (With Glasses) — 1967 — $8
—B-side by Jack Jones and the Jet Set Band
❏ 232 — We Can Work It Out/Over and Over — 1965 — $15
—B-side by the Chords (2)
❏ 262 — Wild Thing/Little Red Riding Hood — 1966 — $8
—B-side by the Chellows
❏ 299 — Windy/Up, Up and Away — 1967 — $8
—B-side by the Chords (2)
❏ 215 — Wooly Bully/First Impressions — 1965 — $10

JAM FACTORY
EPIC
❏ 5-10766 — Talk Is Cheap/Together — 1971 — $15

JAM, THE
POLYDOR
❏ 14566 — Down in the Tube Station at Midnight/Mr. Clean — 1979 — $6
❏ 2051 — Eton Rifles/Smithers-Jones — 1980 — $6
❏ PRO145 [DJ] — Going Underground/Dreams of Children — 1980 — $8
❏ 14462 — I Need You (For Someone)/In the City — 1978 — $8
❏ 14442 — In the City/Takin' My Love — 1977 — $10
❏ 2074 — (Love Is Like a) Heat Wave/Saturday's Kids — 1980 — $6
❏ 2155 — Start/When You're Young — 1980 — $6
❏ 2155 [PS] — Start/When You're Young — 1980 — $8
❏ 14553 [DJ] — The Butterfly Collector (same on both sides) — 1979 — $8
— Yellow vinyl promo
❏ 14553 — The Butterfly Collector/Strange Town — 1979 — $12
— Yellow vinyl stock copy
❏ 2206 — Town Called Malice/Precious — 1982 — $6

JAMAL, AHMAD
20TH CENTURY
❏ 2448 — Don't Ask My Neighbors/Chaser — 1980 — $5
❏ 2053 — M*A*S*H Theme/Keep On Trucking — 1973 — $8
❏ 2260 — Pablo Sierra/(B-side unknown) — 1975 — $5
❏ 2026 — Peace at Last/The World Is a Ghetto — 1973 — $5
ARGO
❏ 5416 — All of You/You're Blase — 1962 — $8
❏ 5419 — April in Paris/Like Someone in Love — 1962 — $8
❏ 5370 — Billy Boy/Poor Butterfly — 1960 — $10
❏ 5441 — Bossa Nova Do Marilia (Part 1)/Bossa Nova Do Marilia (Part 2) — 1963 — $8
❏ 5294 — But Not for Me/Music, Music, Music — 1958 — $10
❏ 5513 — Extensions (Part 1)/Extensions (Part 2) — 1965 — $8
❏ 5504 — Feeling Good/A Wonderful Day Like Today — 1965 — $8
❏ 5434 — Haitian Market Place/Montevidas Has Macanudo — 1963 — $8
❏ 5379 — It's a Wonderful World/Valentina — 1960 — $10
❏ 5306 — Poinciana/Soft Winds — 1958 — $10
❏ 5317 — Secret Love/Taking a Chance on Love — 1958 — $10
❏ 5354 — Should I/I Like to Recognize the Tune — 1959 — $10
❏ 5337 — Tangerine/Seleritus — 1959 — $10
❏ 5397 — The Breeze and I/We Kiss in a Shadow — 1961 — $8
❏ 5512 — This Terrible Planet/Dance to the Lady — 1965 — $8
❏ 5508 — Who Can I Turn To/Look at the Face — 1965 — $8

Number	Title	Yr	NM
ATLANTIC			
❏ 89476 [DJ]	It's That Time Of Year Again (same on both sides)	1985	$5
— With Larry Goshorn; may be promo only			
CADET			
❏ 5527	Love Theme from "The Sandpiper"/This Could Be the Start of Something Big	1966	$6
❏ 5581	Minor Moods/Beautiful Friendship	1967	$6
❏ 5605	Wild Is the Wind/I Wish I Knew (How It Would Feel to Be Free)	1968	$6
OKEH			
❏ 6921	A Gal in Calico/Aki And Ukthay	1952	$30
❏ 6889	Billy Boy/Perfidia	1952	$30
❏ 6855	The Surrey with the Fringe on Top/Rica Pulpa	1952	$30
❏ 6945	Will You Still Be Mine/Ahmad's Blues	1953	$30
PARROT			
❏ 810	But Not for Me/Seleritus	1955	$30
❏ 818	It Could Happen to You/Excerpts from the Blues	1955	$30

JAMES, BOB

Number	Title	Yr	NM
CTI			
❏ 24	Feel Like Makin' Love/Soulero	1974	$5
❏ 26	I Feel a Song (In My Heart)/Golden Apple	1975	$5
❏ 22	In the Garden/Soulero	1974	$5
❏ 31	Westchester Lady (Part 1)/Westchester Lady (Part 2)	1976	$5
❏ 37	Where the Wind Blows Free/El Verano	1977	$5
TAPPAN ZEE			
❏ 3-10896	Angela (Theme from "Taxi")/Caribbean Nights	1979	$6
❏ 04532	Courtship (Basketball Theme)/Marco Polo	1984	$4
❏ 11096	Friends/Blue Lick	1979	$4
❏ 1-11171	Main Theme from Star Trek -- The Motion Picture/I Want to Thank You (Very Much)	1980	$6
❏ 1-11171 [PS]	Main Theme from Star Trek -- The Motion Picture/I Want to Thank You (Very Much)	1980	$8
❏ 02530	Sign of the Times/Enchanted Forest	1981	$4
❏ 02672	Steamin' Feelin'/Enchanted Forest	1982	$4
❏ 10969	Touchdown/Sun Runner	1979	$4
❏ 10668	We're All Alone/Heads	1978	$4

JAMES, BOBBY

Number	Title	Yr	NM
INDIGO			
❏ 145	Memories Linger/5000 Years Ago	1962	$20
LANOR			
❏ 530	Fortune Teller/Get Out of My Life Woman	1967	$10
❏ 533	Going Back to Philly/That's What People Say	1967	$10

JAMES, CHARLES

Number	Title	Yr	NM
ZAB			
❏ 103	One Mint Julep/Please Wait	1961	$20

JAMES, DENNIS, AND HIS BOYS AND GIRLS

Number	Title	Yr	NM
KAPP			
❏ 126	Let's All Sing a Song for Christmas/Jingle Bells	1955	$20

JAMES, DICK

Number	Title	Yr	NM
LONDON			
❏ 1002	Eleanor/Mary Rose	1950	$20
❏ 1050	Happy Valley/My Truly Truly Fair	1951	$20
❏ 1162	Pretending/It Would Break My Heart	1951	$20
❏ 1053	Tell Me Again/With All My Heart and Soul	1951	$20
❏ 1013	Theater/My Life's Desire	1950	$20
❏ 1044	We'll Keep a Welcome/The Minute Waltz	1951	$20

JAMES, ELMORE

Number	Title	Yr	NM
ACE			
❏ 508	I Believe My Time Ain't Long/I Wish I Was a Catfish	1955	$250
CHECKER			
❏ 777	Country Boogie/She Just Won't Do Right	1953	$1000
CHESS			
❏ 1756	I Can't Hold Out/The Sun Is Shining	1960	$20
CHIEF			
❏ 7006	Cry for Me Baby/Take Me Where You Go	1957	$70

Number	Title	Yr	NM
❏ 7004	It Hurts Me Too/Elmore's Contribution to Jazz	1957	$100
❏ 7001	The Twelve Year Old Boy/Coming Home	1957	$100
ENJOY			
❏ 2027	Dust My Broom/Everyday I Have the Blues	1965	$20
❏ 2015	It Hurts Me Too/Bleeding Heart	1965	$30
❏ 2015	It Hurts Me Too/Pickin' the Blues	1965	$20
❏ 2020	Mean Mistreatin' Mama/Bleeding	1965	$30
FIRE			
❏ 1031	Fine Little Mama/Done Somebody Wrong	1961	$30
❏ 1024	I'm Worried/Rollin' and Tumblin'	1960	$30
❏ 1011	Make My Dreams Come True/Bobby's Rock	1960	$40
❏ 504	Shake Your Moneymaker/Look on Yonder Wall	1962	$50
❏ 1503	Stranger Blues/Anna Lee	1963	$20
❏ 1016	The Sky Is Crying/Held My Baby Last Night	1960	$50
FLAIR			
❏ 1079	Blues Before Sunrise/Goodbye Baby	1955	$200
❏ 1014	Can't Stop Lovin'/Make a Little Love	1953	$200
❏ 1048	Dark and Dreary/Rock My Baby Right	1954	$300
❏ 1074	Dust My Blues/I Was a Fool	1955	$250
❏ 1011	Early in the Morning/Hawaiian Boogie	1953	$500
❏ 1069	Happy Home/No Love in My Heart	1955	$200
❏ 1062	Late Hours at Midnight/The Way You Treat Me	1955	$200
❏ 1031	Make My Dreams Come True/Hand in Hand	1954	$300
❏ 1039	Sho'nuff, I Do/1839 Blues	1954	$300
❏ 1057	Standing at the Cross Roads/Sunny Land	1955	$250
❏ 1022	Strange Kinda Feeling/Please Find My Baby	1953	$200
JEWEL			
❏ 783	Catfish Blues/Make a Little Love	1967	$10
❏ 764	Dust My Broom/Gotta Find My Baby	1966	$12
KENT			
❏ 331	Dust My Blues/Happy Home	1960	$15
❏ 394	Dust My Blues/Happy Home	1964	$40
❏ 508	I Believe/1839 Blues	1969	$6
❏ 465	Sunnyland/Goodbye Baby	1967	$8
METEOR			
❏ 5003	Baby What's Wrong/Sinful Woman	1953	$500
❏ 5000	I Believe/I Held My Baby Last Night	1953	$800
❏ 5024	San Symphonic Boogie/Flaming Blues	1955	$250
❏ 5016	Saxony Boogie/Dumb Woman Blues	1954	$300
MODERN			
❏ 983	Wild About You/Long Tall Woman	1956	$300
M-PAC			
❏ 7231	Cry for Me/Take Me Where You Go	1966	$12
VEE JAY			
❏ 249	Coming Home/The 12-Year-Old Boy	1957	$30
❏ 269	Cry for Me Baby/Take Me Where You Go	1958	$30
❏ 259	It Hurts Me Too/Elmore's Contribution to Jazz	1957	$30

JAMES, ETTA

Number	Title	Yr	NM
ARGO			
❏ 5359	All I Could Do Was Cry/Girl of My Dreams	1960	$15
❏ 5380	At Last/I Just Want to Make Love to You	1961	$20
❏ 5459	Baby What You Want Me to Do/What I Say	1964	$20
❏ 5445	Be Honest with Me/Pay Back	1963	$30
❏ 5477	Breaking Point/That Man Belongs Back Here with Me	1964	$30
❏ 5390	Dream/Fool That I Am	1961	$12
❏ 5430	How Do You Speak to An Angel/Would It Make Any Difference to You	1962	$10
❏ 5402	It's Too Soon to Know/Seven Day Fool	1961	$125
— Black label			
❏ 5402	It's Too Soon to Know/Seven Day Fool	1961	$80
— Brown label			
❏ 5465	Look Who's Blue/Loving You More Every Day	1964	$10
❏ 5485	Mellow Fellow/Bobby Is His Name	1964	$125
— Black label			

Number	Title	Yr	NM
❏ 5485	Mellow Fellow/Bobby Is His Name	1964	$80
— Brown label			
❏ 5368	My Dearest Darling/Tough Mary	1960	$15
❏ 5437	Pushover/I Can't Hold It In Anymore	1963	$30
❏ 5409	Something's Got a Hold on Me/Waiting for Charlie to Come Home	1962	$30
❏ 5418	Stop the Wedding/Street of Tears	1962	$30
❏ 5393	Sunday Kind of Love/Don't Cry, Baby	1961	$10
❏ 5385	Trust in Me/Anything to Say You're Mine	1961	$10
❏ 5452	Two Sides (To Every Story)/I Worry Bout You	1963	$30
CADET			
❏ 5630	Almost Persuaded/Steal Away	1968	$8
❏ 5564	Don't Take Me for Your Fool/It Must Be Your Love	1967	$20
❏ 5620	Fire/You Got It	1968	$20
❏ 5568	Happiness/842-3089 (Call My Name)	1967	$8
❏ 5606	I Got You Babe/I Worship the Ground You Walk On	1968	$8
❏ 5539	In the Basement -- Part 1/In the Basement -- Part 2	1966	$8
— With Sugar Pie DeSanto			
❏ 5552	I Prefer You/I'm So Glad	1966	$20
❏ 5676	Losers Weepers -- Part I/Weepers	1970	$8
❏ 5655	Miss Pitiful/Bobby Is His Name	1969	$20
❏ 5526	Only Time Will Tell/I'm Sorry for You	1966	$8
❏ 5594	Security/I'm Gonna Take What He's Got	1968	$30
❏ 5519	Somewhere Down the Line/Do I Make Myself Clear	1966	$8
— With Sugar Pie DeSanto			
❏ 5578	Tell Mama/I'd Rather Go Blind	1967	$20
❏ 5671	The Sound of Love/When I Stop Dreaming	1970	$20
❏ 5664	Tighten Up Your Own Thing/What Fools We Mortals Be	1970	$30
CAPITOL			
❏ B-44333	Avenue D/My Head Is a City	1989	$4
— With David A. Stewart			
CHESS			
❏ 2144	All the Way Down/Lay Back Daddy	1973	$6
❏ 2125	I Found a Love/Nothing from Nothing Leaves Nothing	1972	$6
❏ 2112	I Think It's You/Take Out Some Insurance	1971	$6
❏ 2148	Leave Your Hat On/Only a Fool	1974	$6
❏ 2171	Lovin' Arms/Take Out Some Insurance	1975	$6
❏ 2153	Out on the Street Again/Feeling Uneasy	1974	$6
❏ 2100	The Love of My Man/Nothing from Nothing Leaves Nothing	1971	$6
EPIC			
❏ 68593	Baby What You Want Me to Do/Max's Theme (Instrumental)	1989	$4
KENT			
❏ 304	Baby, Baby, Every Night/Sunshine of Love	1958	$40
❏ 370	Do Something Crazy/Good Rockin' Daddy	1962	$30
❏ 352	How Big a Fool/Good Rockin' Daddy	1961	$30
MODERN			
❏ 1022	By the Light of the Silvery Moon/Come What May	1957	$30
❏ 998	Fools We Mortals Be/Tough Lover	1956	$40
❏ 1007	Good Lookin'/Then I'll Care	1957	$30
❏ 962	Good Rockin' Daddy/Crazy Feeling	1955	$40
❏ 957	Hey Henry (Doin' Fine, Henry)/Be Mine	1955	$30
❏ 984	I'm a Fool/Number One (My One and Only)	1956	$30
❏ 988	Shortnin' Bread Rock/Tears of Joy	1956	$30
❏ 972	That's All/W-O-M-A-N	1955	$30
❏ 1016	The Pick-Up/Market Place	1957	$30
❏ 947	The Wallflower (Dance With Me Henry)/Hold Me, Squeeze Me	1955	$30
❏ 947	The Wallflower (Roll With Me Henry)/Hold Me, Squeeze Me	1955	$50
PHILCO-FORD			
❏ HP-31	Tell Mama/Security	1968	$30
— 4-inch plastic "Hip Pocket Record" with color sleeve			
T-ELECTRIC			
❏ 41264	It Takes Love to Keep a Woman/Mean Mother	1980	$5

Number	Title	Yr	NM
WARNER BROS.			
8545	Piece of My Heart/Lovesick Blues	1978	$5
8611	Sugar on the Floor/Lovesick Blues	1978	$5

JAMES GANG, THE (1)
Also see TOMMY BOLIN; JOE WALSH; THE EAGLES.

Number	Title	Yr	NM
ABC			
11272	Funk #49/Thanks	1970	$6
11336	Had Enough/Kick Back Man	1972	$6
11325	Looking for My Lady/Hairy Hypochondriac	1972	$6
11301	Walk Away/Yadig?	1971	$6
11312	White Man--Black Man/Midnight	1971	$6
ATCO			
7006	Cruisin' Down the Highway/Miami Two-Step	1974	$5
7067	I Need Love/Feelin' Alright	1975	$5
7021	Merry Go Round/Red Satin Lover	1975	$5
6953	Must Be Love/Got No Time for Trouble	1974	$5
6966	Standing in the Rain/From Another Time	1974	$5
BLUESWAY			
61030	Funk #48/Collage	1969	$10
61027	I Don't Have the Time/Fred	1969	$8
61033	Take a Look Around/Stop	1970	$8

JAMES GANG, THE (2)

Number	Title	Yr	NM
ASCOT			
2168	Everybody Knows/Ladies' Man	1965	$15
2196	Georgia Pines/Baby Take Me Back	1965	$15

JAMES, GEORGE

Number	Title	Yr	NM
JANC			
10417	It's Gonna Be Magic/I'm Takin' a Heartbreak	1979	$8
103	When Our Love Began (Cowboys and Indians)/Break My Mind	1979	$8

JAMES, JESSE

Number	Title	Yr	NM
20TH CENTURY			
2201	If You Want a Love Affair/I Never Meant to Love Her	1975	$200
20TH CENTURY FOX			
6684	Believe in Me Baby - Part I/Part II	1967	$20
6704	If You're Lonely (Take My Hand)/Green Power	1968	$40
6700	Thank You Darlin'/Bring My Baby Back	1967	$20
HIT			
6120	Believe in Me Baby - Part I/Part II	1967	$60
MIDTOWN			
08	At Last/I Can Feel Your Love Vibes	1984	$12
MUSICOR			
1008	Dreams Never Hurt Nobody/Somebody Really Mine	1961	$30
T.T.E.D.			
3026	I Can Do Bad by Myself/(Dub Version)	1987	$6
3031	I'm Gonna Be Rich and Famous/Don't Get Amnesia on Me Baby	1987	$6
UNI			
55171	Ain't Much of a Home/Don't Fight It	1969	$20
ZAY			
30002	At Last/I Know I'll Never Find Another One	1971	$60
30003	I Know I'll Never Find Another One/I Need Your Love So Bad	1971	$50
ZEA			
50000	Don't Nobody Want to Get Married (Part I)/(Part II)	1970	$30
50003	I Need You, Baby/Home at Last	1971	$20

JAMES, JONI

Number	Title	Yr	NM
MGM			
11696	Am I in Love/Maybe Next Time	1954	$30
13117	Anyone But Her/Forgive a Fool	1962	$20
12828	Are You Sorry/What I Don't Know Won't Hurt Me	1959	$20
12639	Arrivederci Roma/Non Dimenticar	1958	$20
12948	Be My Love/Tall As a Tree	1960	$15
12948 [PS]	Be My Love/Tall As a Tree	1960	$30

Number	Title	Yr	NM
13243	Break, My Heart, Break/Don't Let the Neighbors Know	1964	$30
11637	Christmas and You/Nina-Non	1953	$30
12660	Coming from You/Junior Prom	1958	$20
12531	Crying in the Shadows/Day Dreaming	1957	$20
12369	Danny Boy/To You I Give My Heart	1956	$20
12607	Dansero/Love Works Miracles	1958	$20
13304	Dondi/Once I Loved	1964	$30
12175	Don't Tell Me Not to Love You/Somewhere Someone Is Lonely	1956	$20
11865	Everytime You Tell Me You Love Me/When We Come of Age	1954	$30
12288	Give Us This Day/How Lucky You Are	1956	$20
13016	Go Away (Bother Me No More)/I Gave My Love	1961	$15
11390	Have You Heard/Wishing Ring	1953	$30
13159	Hey, Good Lookin'/He Says the Same Things to Me	1963	$20
11919	How Important Can It Be?/This Is My Confession	1955	$30
K13060	I'll Be Around/I Almost Lost My Mind	1962	$15
11606	I'll Never Stand in Your Way/Why Can't I	1953	$30
11753	In a Garden of Roses/Every Day	1954	$30
12885	I Need You Now/You Belong to Me	1960	$15
12450	I Need You So/Only Trust Your Heart	1957	$20
11470	Is It Any Wonder/Almost Always	1953	$30
12779	I Still Get a Thrill (Thinking of You)/Perhaps	1959	$20
12779 [PS]	I Still Get a Thrill (Thinking of You)/Perhaps	1959	$30
12807	I Still Get Jealous/My Prayer of Love	1959	$20
13080	It's Magic/Tender and True	1962	$15
12213	I Woke Up Crying/The Maverick Queen	1956	$20
11223	Let There Be Love/My Baby Just Cares for Me	1952	$30
12849	Little Things Mean a Lot/I Laughed at Love	1959	$20
12353	Love Letters/Don't Take Your Love from Me	1956	$20
11802	Mama, Don't Cry at My Wedding/Pa Pa Pa	1954	$30
12126	My Believing Heart/You Never Fall in Love Again	1955	$30
12933	My Last Date (With You)/I Can't Give You Anything But Love	1960	$15
12933 [PS]	My Last Date (With You)/I Can't Give You Anything But Love	1960	$30
11543	My Love, My Love/You're Fooling Someone	1953	$30
13267	Pearly Shells/Hawaiian War Chant	1964	$30
13288	Sentimental Me/You're Nearer	1964	$100
13037	Somebody Else Is Taking My Place/You Were Wrong	1961	$15
13037 [PS]	Somebody Else Is Taking My Place/You Were Wrong	1961	$30
12480	Summer Love/I'm Sorry for You, My Friend	1957	$20
13206	Teach Me to Forget You/Un Cafe	1964	$30
12091	The Christmas Song/Have Yourself a Merry Little Christmas	1955	$30
12990	Theme from "Carnival"/Can You Imagine That	1961	$15
12020	The Moment I Saw You/Where Is That Someone for Me	1955	$30
12706	There Goes My Heart/Funny	1958	$20
12706 [PS]	There Goes My Heart/Funny	1958	$60
SK-12706 [S]	There Goes My Heart/Funny	1958	$50

— Note different prefix. Also, label will say "Stereo."

Number	Title	Yr	NM
13365	There Goes My Heart/I Still Get Jealous	1965	$30
12746	There Must Be a Way/Sorry for Myself	1959	$20
SK-50111 [S]	There Must Be a Way/Sorry for Myself	1959	$40
12895	They Really Don't Know You/We Know	1960	$15
11960	When You Wish Upon a Star/Is This the End of the Line	1955	$30
12368	White Christmas/I'll Be Home for Christmas	1956	$30
11333	Why Don't You Believe Me/Purple Shades	1952	$40
SHARP			
46	Let There Be Love/My Baby Just Cares for Me	1952	$300

7-Inch Extended Plays

Number	Title	Yr	NM
MGM			
X-1656 [B]	*All Through the Day/Too Young/My Heart Tells Me/Imagination	1959	$50
X-1222	*Little Girl Blue/I'm Through with Love/These Foolish Things (Remind Me of You)/It's the Talk of the Town	1956	$50
X-1656 [PS]	100 Strings and Joni, Part 1	1959	$50
X-1657 [PS]	100 Strings and Joni, Part 2	1959	$50
X-1658 [PS]	100 Strings and Joni, Part 3	1959	$50
X-1545	Always/When You Were Sweet Sixteen//Let Me Call You Sweetheart/Alice Blue Gown	1957	$50
X-1545 [PS]	Among My Souvenirs, Vol. I	1957	$50
X-1546 [PS]	Among My Souvenirs, Vol. II	1957	$50
X-1547 [PS]	Among My Souvenirs, Vol. III	1957	$50
X-1219 [PS]	Award Winning Album, Part 1	1956	$50
X-1221 [PS]	Award Winning Album, Part 3	1956	$50
X-1220 [PS]	Award Winning Album, Volume 2	1956	$50
X-1658	But Beautiful/Wait and See//It Could Happen to You/Maybe You'll Be There	1959	$50
X-1212	(contents unknown)	1956	$50
X-1221	(contents unknown)	1956	$50
X-1389	(contents unknown)	1957	$50
X-1399	(contents unknown)	1957	$75
X-1401	(contents unknown)	1957	$75
X-1546	(contents unknown)	1957	$50
X-1547	(contents unknown)	1957	$50
X1615	(contents unknown)	1958	$50
X1617	(contents unknown)	1958	$50
X-1657	(contents unknown)	1959	$50
X-1652	(contents unknown)	1959	$50
X-1653	(contents unknown)	1959	$50
X-1654	(contents unknown)	1959	$50
X-1391	Count Your Blessings/Ave Maria (Gounod)//Abide with Me/May the Good Lord Bles and Keep You	1957	$50
X-1389 [PS]	Give Us This Day, Vol. 1	1957	$50
X-1390 [PS]	Give Us This Day, Vol. 2	1957	$50
X-1391 [PS]	Give Us This Day, Vol. 3	1957	$50
X-4090	Have You Heard/Almost Always//Purple Shades/Your Cheatin' Heart	1954	$60

— One record of "X234

Number	Title	Yr	NM
X-1219	Have You Heard/Almost Always//Purple Shades/Your Cheatin' Heart	1956	$50
X-1172 [PS]	Have Yourself a Merry Little Christmas	1955	$70
X-1172	Have Yourself a Merry Little Christmas/Christmas and You//The Christmas Song (Merry Christmas to You)/Nina-Non	1955	$70
X-4296	I Could Write a Book/Don't Blame Me//My One and Only Love/As Time Goes By	1955	$50

— One record of "X326

Number	Title	Yr	NM
X-1160	I'm in the Mood for Love/Where Can I Go Without You//People Will Say We're in Love/Love Letters	1955	$70
X-1227	I Need You Now/This Is My Confession/The Moment I Saw You/Am I in Love	1956	$50
X-1223	In Love in Vain/Too Late Now//Autumn Leaves/That Old Feeling	1956	$50
X-1211 [PS]	In the Still of the Night, Part 1	1956	$50
X-1212 [PS]	In the Still of the Night, Part 2	1956	$50
X-1213 [PS]	In the Still of the Night, Vol. 3	1956	$50
X-1213	In the Still of the Night/What's New//Deep Purple/You'd Be So Nice to Come Home To	1956	$50
X-222 [PS]	Let There Be Love	1953	$60

— Cover for X-4047 and X-4048

Number	Title	Yr	NM
X-1226 [PS]	Let There Be Love, Vol. 2	1956	$50
X-1227 [PS]	Let There Be Love, Vol. 3	1956	$50
X-4047	Let There Be Love/My Romance//The Nearness of You/You're Mine You	1953	$60

— One record of "X222

Number	Title	Yr	NM
X-1226	Let There Be Love/My Romance//The Nearness of You/You're Mine You	1956	$50
X-1222 [PS]	Little Girl Blue, Vol. 1	1956	$50
X-1223 [PS]	Little Girl Blue, Vol. 2	1956	$50
X-1390	Look for the Silver Lining/Panis Angelicus//I Believe/The Rosary	1957	$50
X-1399 [PS]	Merry Christmas from Joni, Part 1	1957	$75
X-1400 [PS]	Merry Christmas from Joni, Part 2	1957	$75
X-1401 [PS]	Merry Christmas from Joni, Part 3	1957	$75

Number	Title	Yr	NM
❏ X-1343	My Foolish Heart/I Don't Stand a Ghost of a Chance with You//Stella by Starlight/A Hundred Years from Today	1956	$50
❏ X-1345	On a Slow Boat to China/I'll Know//Spring Will Be a Little Late This Year/Anywhere I Wander	1956	$50
❏ X1615 [PS]	Second Award Winning Album, Vol. 1	1958	$50
❏ X1616 [PS]	Second Award Winning Album, Vol. 2	1958	$50
❏ X1617 [PS]	Second Award Winning Album, Vol. 3	1958	$50
❏ X-1344	Song of Surrender/Everything I Do//If I Were a Bell.My Darling, My Darling	1956	$50
❏ X-1652 [PS]	Songs of Hank Williams, Part 1	1959	$50
❏ X-1653 [PS]	Songs of Hank Williams, Part 2	1959	$50
❏ X-1654 [PS]	Songs of Hank Williams, Part 3	1959	$50
❏ X-1211	Star Dust/But Not for Me//Someone to Watch Over Me/My Heart Stood Still	1956	$50
❏ X-1400	The Christmas Song/It Came Upon the Midnight Clear//O Come All Ye Faithful/Nina-Non	1957	$75
❏ X-326 [PS]	When I Fall in Love	1955	$50
—Cover with X-4295 and X-4296			
❏ X-4295	When I Fall in Love/To Each His Own//I've Never Been in Love Before/Embraceable You	1955	$50
—One record of "X326			
❏ X-4091	Why Don't You Believe Me/Is It Any Wonder//Wishing Ring/My Love, My Love	1954	$60
—One record of "X234			
❏ X-1220	Why Don't You Believe Me/Is It Any Wonder//Wishing Ring/My Love, My Love	1956	$50

JAMES, MARK

BELL

Number	Title	Yr	NM
❏ 45323	Flyin' to Memphis/(B-side unknown)	1973	$6

LIBERTY

| ❏ 55953 | I Can't Let You Go/Bimbo Knows | 1967 | $8 |

MERCURY

| ❏ 73718 | Moody Blue/Wrong Kind of Love | 1975 | $8 |

PRIVATE STOCK

| ❏ 45,190 | Who's Loving You/(B-side unknown) | 1978 | $5 |

SCEPTER

| ❏ 12221 | Suspicious Minds/Taste of Heaven | 1968 | $10 |

JAMES, MILTON

DORE

| ❏ 767 | My Lonely Feeling/(B-side unknown) | 1966 | $1500 |

JAMES, RICK

A&M

| ❏ 1615 | Funkin' Around/My Mama | 1974 | $30 |

GORDY

❏ 1730	17/(Instrumental)	1984	$4
❏ 7185	Big Time/Island Lady	1980	$5
❏ 7167	Bustin' Out/Sexy Lady	1979	$5
❏ 1776	Can't Stop/Oh What a Night	1985	$4
❏ 1776 [PS]	Can't Stop/Oh What a Night	1985	$5
❏ 1687	Cold Blooded/(Instrumental)	1983	$4
❏ 7177	Come Into My Life (Part 1)/Come Into My Life (Part 2)	1980	$5
❏ 1619	Dance Wit' Me -- Part 1/Dance Wit' Me -- Part 2	1982	$4
❏ 1619 [PS]	Dance Wit' Me -- Part 1/Dance Wit' Me -- Part 2	1982	$5
❏ 1714	Ebony Eyes/1,2,3	1983	$5
—As "Rick James and Friend			
❏ 1714	Ebony Eyes/1,2,3	1983	$4
—As "Rick James and Smokey Robinson			
❏ 7171	Fool on the Street/Jefferson Hall	1979	$5
❏ 1862	Forever and a Day/(Instrumental)	1986	$3
❏ 7191	Gettin' it On (In the Summertime)/Summer Love	1980	$5
❏ 7215	Ghetto Life/Below the Funk (Pass the J)	1981	$4
❏ 7197	Give It to Me Baby/Don't Give Up on Love	1981	$4
❏ 1796	Glow/(Instrumental)	1985	$4
❏ 1634	Hard to Get/My Love	1982	$4
❏ 7164	High on Your Love Suite/Stone City Band High	1979	$5
❏ 7164 [PS]	High on Your Love Suite/Stone City Band High	1979	$6

Number	Title	Yr	NM
❏ 7176	Love Gun/Stormy Love	1979	$5
❏ 7162	Mary Jane/Dream Maker	1978	$5
❏ 1646	She Blew My Mind (69 Times)/(B-side unknown)	1982	$4
❏ 1806	Spend the Night with Me/(Instrumental)	1985	$4
❏ 7205	Super Freak (Part 1)/Super Freak (Part 2)	1981	$4
❏ 1844	Sweet and Sexy Thing/(Instrumental)	1986	$3
❏ 1844 [PS]	Sweet and Sexy Thing/(Instrumental)	1986	$8
—Sleeve may be promo only			
❏ 1658	Teardrops/Throwdown	1983	$4

REPRISE

❏ 27885	Loosey's Rap/(Instrumental)	1988	$3
—With Roxanne Shante			
❏ 27885 [PS]	Loosey's Rap/(Instrumental)	1988	$3
❏ 27764	Sexual Love Affair/In the Girls' Room	1988	$3
❏ 27828	Wonderful/(Instrumental)	1988	$3
❏ 27828 [PS]	Wonderful/(Instrumental)	1988	$3

WARNER BROS.

| ❏ 27763 | This Magic Moment-Dance with Me/(Instrumental) | 1989 | $3 |
| ❏ 27763 [PS] | This Magic Moment-Dance with Me/(Instrumental) | 1989 | $3 |

JAMES, SONNY

CAPITOL

Number	Title	Yr	NM
❏ 3931	All the Way Together/Clinging Vine	1974	$6
❏ F3962	Are You Mine/Let's Play Love	1958	$30
❏ 5197	Ask Marie/Sugar Lump	1964	$15
❏ 2067	A World of Our Own/An Old Sweetheart of Mine	1967	$10
❏ 2067 [PS]	A World of Our Own/An Old Sweetheart of Mine	1967	$20
❏ 5129	Baltimore/Least of All You	1964	$15
❏ 5454	Behind the Tear/Runnin'	1965	$15
❏ 5454 [PS]	Behind the Tear/Runnin'	1965	$30
❏ 2271	Born to Be With You/In Waikiki	1968	$10
❏ 2271 [PS]	Born to Be With You/In Waikiki	1968	$15
❏ 3114	Bright Lights, Big City/True Love Lasts Forever	1971	$8
❏ 3114 [PS]	Bright Lights, Big City/True Love Lasts Forever	1971	$10
❏ F3281	Careless with My Heart/Pigtails and Ribbons	1955	$30
❏ F2958	Christmas in My Home Town/I Forgot to Remember Santa Claus	1954	$40
❏ F3112	Deceive Me Once Again/Ain't Gonna Take No Chance	1955	$30
❏ 2834	Don't Keep Me Hangin' On/Woodbine Valley	1970	$8
❏ 2834 [PS]	Don't Keep Me Hangin' On/Woodbine Valley	1970	$12
❏ 3015	Empty Arms/Everything Begins and Ends with You	1971	$8
❏ 3015 [PS]	Empty Arms/Everything Begins and Ends with You	1971	$12
❏ 2914	Endlessly/Happy Memories	1970	$8
❏ 2914 [PS]	Endlessly/Happy Memories	1970	$12
❏ F3674	First Date, First Kiss, First Love/Speak to Me	1957	$30
❏ F3357	For Rent (One Empty Heart)/My Stolen Love	1956	$30
❏ 5057	Going Through the Motions (Of Living)/Bad Times a-Comin'	1963	$15
❏ 2155	Heaven Says Hello/Fairy Tales	1968	$12
❏ 2155 [PS]	Heaven Says Hello/Fairy Tales	1968	$20
❏ 3174	Here Comes Honey Again/The Only Ones We Truly Hurt	1971	$8
❏ 3174 [PS]	Here Comes Honey Again/The Only Ones We Truly Hurt	1971	$12
❏ F2508	I Forgot More Than You'll Ever Know/Poor Boy, Rich Lovin'	1953	$30
❏ 5375	I'll Keep Holding On (Just to Your Love)/I'm Getting Gray from Being Blue	1965	$15
❏ 5375 [PS]	I'll Keep Holding On (Just to Your Love)/I'm Getting Gray from Being Blue	1965	$30
❏ 5914	I'll Never Find Another You/Goodbye, Maggie, Goodbye	1967	$15
❏ 5914 [PS]	I'll Never Find Another You/Goodbye, Maggie, Goodbye	1967	$20
❏ 2700	It's Just a Matter of Time/This World of Ours	1969	$10
❏ 2700 [PS]	It's Just a Matter of Time/This World of Ours	1969	$15
❏ 5987	It's the Little Things/Don't Cut Timber on a Windy Day	1967	$15
❏ 5987 [PS]	It's the Little Things/Don't Cut Timber on a Windy Day	1967	$20
❏ F2734	I've Always Wanted You/That's How I Need You	1954	$30
❏ F4066	Let Me Be the One to Love You/I Can't Stay Away from You	1958	$30

Number	Title	Yr	NM
❏ F3792	Love Conquered/Mighty Loveable Man	1957	$30
❏ F3734	Lovesick Blues/Dear Love	1957	$30
❏ F3025	Lovin' Season/This Kiss Must Last Forever	1955	$30
❏ 5733	My Christmas Dream/Barefoot Santa Claus	1966	$15
❏ 5733 [PS]	My Christmas Dream/Barefoot Santa Claus	1966	$30
❏ 2782	My Love/Blue for You	1970	$8
❏ 2782 [PS]	My Love/Blue for You	1970	$10
❏ 3232	Only Love Can Break a Heart/He Has Walked This Way Before	1971	$8
❏ 3232 [PS]	Only Love Can Break a Heart/He Has Walked This Way Before	1971	$10
❏ 2370	Only the Lonely/The Journey	1968	$10
❏ 2370 [PS]	Only the Lonely/The Journey	1968	$15
❏ F4229	Pure Love/This Love of Mine	1959	$30
❏ F2906	She Done Give Her Heart to Me/Oceans of Tears	1954	$30
❏ F2164	Short Cut/It's So Nice to Make Up	1952	$30
❏ 2595	Since I Met You, Baby/Clinging to a Hope	1969	$10
❏ 2595 [PS]	Since I Met You, Baby/Clinging to a Hope	1969	$15
❏ F2829	Table Next to Mine/Believe Another's Lips	1954	$30
❏ 5612	Take Good Care of Her/On the Fingers of One Hand	1966	$15
❏ 5612 [PS]	Take Good Care of Her/On the Fingers of One Hand	1966	$30
❏ F4178	Talk of the School/The Table	1959	$30
❏ F2259	That's Me Without You/Cool, Cold and Colder	1952	$30
❏ 3322	That's Why I Love You Like I Do/Still Water Runs Deep	1972	$8
❏ F3542	The Cat Came Back/Hello, Old Broken Heart	1956	$30
❏ 4969	The Minute You're Gone/Gold and Silver	1963	$15
❏ F2399	The One I Can't Forget/Somebody's Heartache	1953	$30
❏ 4307	Till Tomorrow/I Forgot More Than You'll Ever Know	1959	$30
❏ F3163	Til the Last Leaf Shall Fall/You Don't Have to Walk Alone	1955	$30
❏ F3198	Too Much/Let's Go Bunny Huggin'	1955	$30
❏ 5536	True Love's a Blessing/Just Ask Your Heart	1965	$15
❏ 5536 [PS]	True Love's a Blessing/Just Ask Your Heart	1965	$30
❏ F3441	Twenty Feet of Muddy Water/All Mixed Up	1956	$30
❏ F4268	Who's Next in Line/Red Mud	1959	$30
❏ F4268 [PS]	Who's Next in Line/Red Mud	1959	$50
❏ F2641	Won't Somebody Tell Me/My Greatest Thrill	1953	$30

COLUMBIA

❏ 3-10628	Abilene/Pistol Packin' Mama	1977	$5
❏ 3-10072	A Little Bit South of Saskatoon/Home Style Lovin'	1974	$5
❏ 3-10072 [PS]	A Little Bit South of Saskatoon/Home Style Lovin'	1974	$8
❏ 3-10001	A Mi Esposa Con Amor (To My Wife with Love)/Just Don't Stop Lovin' Me	1974	$5
❏ 3-10001 [PS]	A Mi Esposa Con Amor (To My Wife with Love)/Just Don't Stop Lovin' Me	1974	$8
❏ 3-10852	Building Memories/Little Band of Gold	1978	$5
❏ 3-10764	Caribbean/Each Time I Look at You	1978	$5
❏ 3-10392	Come On In/Baby's Eyes	1976	$5
❏ 3-10249	Eres Tu (Touch the Wind)/Apache	1975	$5
❏ 4-45871	If She Just Helps Me Get Over You/I Won't Think About It Now	1973	$6
❏ 4-45770 [PS]	I Love You More and More Everyday/I'll Think About That Tomorrow	1973	$10
❏ 3-10139	Indian Love Call/Maria Elena	1975	$5
—As "The Guitars of Sonny James			
❏ 3-10551	In the Jailhouse Now/Amazing Grace	1977	$5
❏ 3-10551 [PS]	In the Jailhouse Now/Amazing Grace	1977	$5
❏ 4-46003	Is It Wrong (For Loving You)/Suddenly There's a Valley	1974	$6
❏ 3-10121	Little Band of Gold/Pop and Me	1975	$5
❏ 3-10121 [PS]	Little Band of Gold/Pop and Me	1975	$8
❏ 3-10276	The Prisoner's Song/Back in the Saddle Again	1975	$5
❏ 3-10276 [PS]	The Prisoner's Song/Back in the Saddle Again	1975	$5
❏ 3-10703	This Is the Love/It'll Still Be Worth It All	1978	$5
❏ 3-10703 [PS]	This Is the Love/It'll Still Be Worth It All	1978	$6
❏ 3-10184	What in the World's Come Over You/Walking the Railroad Trestle	1975	$5
❏ 3-10184 [PS]	What in the World's Come Over You/Walking the Railroad Trestle	1975	$6

Number	Title	Yr	NM
❏ 3-10335	When Something Is Wrong with My Baby/Big Silver Bird	1976	$5
❏ 4-45644 [PS]	When the Snow Is On the Roses/Love is a Rainbow	1972	$10

DIMENSION

Number	Title	Yr	NM
❏ 1045	A Free Roamin' Mind/Don't Let the Stars Get In Your Eyes	1983	$5
❏ 1033	A Place in the Sun/Lean On Me Girl	1982	$5
❏ 1033 [PS]	A Place in the Sun/Lean On Me Girl	1982	$8
❏ 1036	I'm Looking Over the Rainbow/Something's Got a Hold on Me	1982	$5
❏ 1036 [PS]	I'm Looking Over the Rainbow/Something's Got a Hold on Me	1982	$8
❏ 1026	Innocent Lies/Don't Let the Stars Get in Your Eyes	1981	$5
❏ 1026 [PS]	Innocent Lies/Don't Let the Stars Get in Your Eyes	1981	$8
❏ 1040	The Fool in Me/Little Rainbow	1982	$5

DOT

Number	Title	Yr	NM
❏ 16381	A Mile and a Quarter/Just One More Lie	1962	$20
❏ 16419	On the Longest Day/The Only Cure	1963	$20

MONUMENT

Number	Title	Yr	NM
❏ 45-280	Hold What You've Got/Hanging On to Yesterday	1979	$5
❏ 45-280 [PS]	Hold What You've Got/Hanging On to Yesterday	1979	$6
❏ 45-288	Lorelei/If I Ever Wanted You	1979	$5

NRC

Number	Title	Yr	NM
❏ 061	Bimbo/I Wish This Night Would Never End	1960	$30
❏ 056	Cold in the Morning/Wondering	1960	$30

RCA VICTOR

Number	Title	Yr	NM
❏ 47-7858	Apache/Magnetism	1961	$20
❏ 47-7919	Innocent Angel/Hey Little Ducky	1961	$20
❏ 47-7998	The Day's Not Over Yet/The Legend of Brown Mountain Light	1962	$20
❏ SU-111 [PS]	Born to Be with You	1969	$20

— Above "For Coin Operated Phonographs Only"

Number	Title	Yr	NM
❏ EAP 1-779	Can't Get Over Missin' You/Cold, Cold Heart//Only One Heart to Give/I Got the Feeling	1957	$25
❏ EAP 1-988	(contents unknown)	1958	$25
❏ EAP 2-988	(contents unknown)	1958	$25
❏ SU-111	(contents unknown)	1969	$25

— Jukebox issue; small hole, plays at 33 1/3 rpm

Number	Title	Yr	NM
❏ EAP 1-988 [PS]	Honey, Part 1	1958	$25
❏ EAP 1-988 [PS]	Honey, Part 2	1958	$25
❏ EAP 1-988 [PS]	Honey, Part 3	1958	$25
❏ EAP 2-779	I Wish I Knew/Forgive Me/I'll Always Wonder (But I'll Never Know)/Lonesome	1957	$25
❏ EAP 1-779 [PS]	Southern Gentleman, Part 1	1957	$25
❏ EAP 2-779 [PS]	Southern Gentleman, Part 2	1957	$25
❏ EAP 3-779 [PS]	Southern Gentleman, Part 3	1957	$25
❏ EAP 3-779	'Til the Last Leaf Shall Fall/Only a Shadow Between//May God Be With You/My God and I	1957	$25

JAMES, TOMMY, AND THE SHONDELLS

PHILCO-FORD

Number	Title	Yr	NM
❏ HP-2	Hanky Panky/Gettin' Together	1967	$20

— 4-inch plastic "Hip Pocket Record" with color sleeve

Number	Title	Yr	NM
❏ HP-1	Mirage/I Think We're Alone Now	1967	$20

— 4-inch plastic "Hip Pocket Record" with color sleeve

RED FOX

Number	Title	Yr	NM
❏ 110	Hanky Panky/Thunderbolt	1966	$50

— As "The Shondells

ROULETTE

Number	Title	Yr	NM
❏ 7060	Ball of Fire/Makin' Good Time	1969	$8
❏ 7076	Come to Me/Talkin' and Signifyin'	1970	$8
❏ 7028	Crimson and Clover/(I'm) Taken	1968	$20
❏ 7028	Crimson and Clover/Some Kind of Love	1968	$12
❏ 7050	Crystal Blue Persuasion/I'm Alive	1969	$12
❏ 7024	Do Something to Me/Ginger Bread Man	1968	$8
❏ 7000	Get Out Now/Wish It Were True	1968	$8
❏ 4762	Gettin' Together/Real Girl	1967	$8
❏ 4762 [PS]	Gettin' Together/Real Girl	1967	$20
❏ 7071	Gotta Get Back to You/Red Rover	1970	$8
❏ 4686	Hanky Panky/Thunderbolt	1966	$12
❏ 4756	I Like the Way/(Baby) Baby I Can't Take It No More	1967	$8
❏ 4720	I Think We're Alone Now/Gone, Gone, Gone	1967	$10

Number	Title	Yr	NM
❏ 4720 [PS]	I Think We're Alone Now/Gone, Gone, Gone	1967	$20
❏ 4710	It's Only Love/Don't Let My Love Pass You By	1966	$8
❏ 4710	It's Only Love/Ya Ya	1966	$15
❏ 4736	Mirage/Run, Run, Baby, Run	1967	$8
❏ 4736 [PS]	Mirage/Run, Run, Baby, Run	1967	$20
❏ 7008	Mony Mony/One Two Three and I Fell	1968	$10
❏ 4775	Out of the Blue/Love's Closin' In on Me	1967	$8
❏ 4695	Say I Am (What I Am)/Lots of Pretty Girls	1966	$8
❏ 4695 [PS]	Say I Am (What I Am)/Lots of Pretty Girls	1966	$20
❏ 7066	She/Loved One	1969	$8
❏ 7016	Somebody Cares/Do Unto Me	1968	$8
❏ 7039	Sweet Cherry Wine/Breakaway	1969	$8

SNAP

Number	Title	Yr	NM
❏ 102	Hanky Panky/Thunderbolt	1966	$30

— As "The Shondells"; with "Dist. by Red Fox Records, Pgh, Pa." on label

Number	Title	Yr	NM
❏ 102	Hanky Panky/Thunderbolt	1966	$50

— As "The Shondells"; with A-side title NOT hyphenated; no mention of Red Fox on the label

Number	Title	Yr	NM
❏ 102	Hanky-Panky/Thunderbolt	1964	$200

— As "The Shondells"; A-side title is hyphenated, which is true only on the 1964 pressings

JAMES, TOMMY

21 RECORDS

Number	Title	Yr	NM
❏ 105	Two-Time Lover/Say Please	1983	$3
❏ 105 [PS]	Two-Time Lover/Say Please	1983	$4

FANTASY

Number	Title	Yr	NM
❏ 761	I Love You Love Me Love/Devil Gate Drive	1976	$4
❏ 761 [PS]	I Love You Love Me Love/Devil Gate Drive	1976	$5
❏ 811	Love Is Gonna Find a Way/I Don't Love You Anymore	1977	$5
❏ 776	Tighter, Tighter/Comin' Down	1976	$5
❏ 886	Tighter, Tighter/Comin' Down	1980	$4

MCA

Number	Title	Yr	NM
❏ 40289	Glory, Glory/Comin' Down	1974	$5

MILLENNIUM

Number	Title	Yr	NM
❏ YB-11788	It's Alright (For Now)/You Got Me	1980	$4
❏ YB-11814	The Lady in White/Payin' for My Lover's Mistake	1981	$4
❏ YB-11785	Three Times in Love/I Just Wanna Play the Music	1980	$4

ROULETTE

Number	Title	Yr	NM
❏ 7100	Adrienne/Light of Day	1971	$6
❏ 7084	Ball and Chain/Candy Maker	1970	$6
❏ 7140	Boo, Boo, Don't Cha Be Blue/Rings and Things	1973	$5
❏ 7147	Calico/Hey, My Lady	1973	$5
❏ 7126	Cat's Eye in the Window/Dark Is the Night	1972	$5
❏ 7135	Celebration/The Last One to Know	1972	$5
❏ 7093	Church Street Soul Revival/Draggin' the Line	1970	$8
❏ 7103	Draggin' the Line/Bits & Pieces	1971	$6
❏ 7110	I'm Coming Home/Sing, Sing, Sing	1971	$5
❏ 7130	Love Song/Kingston Highway	1972	$5
❏ 7119	Tell 'Em Willie Boy's A-Comin'/Forty Days and Dorty Nights	1972	$5

JAMESON, BOBBY

CURRENT

Number	Title	Yr	NM
❏ 103	All Alone/Your Sweet Lovin'	1964	$15

LONDON

Number	Title	Yr	NM
❏ 9730	All I Want Is My Baby/Each and Everyday	1965	$50

TALAMO

Number	Title	Yr	NM
❏ 1934	I'm So Lonely/I Wanna Love You	1964	$10

JAMESTOWN MASSACRE

DESTINATION

Number	Title	Yr	NM
❏ 0 (no cat #)	Comin' Home to You/The Next Road	1971	$20

LUV

Number	Title	Yr	NM
❏ 104	Summer Sun/Words and Rhymes	1972	$20

WARNER BROS.

Number	Title	Yr	NM
❏ 7787	Saturday Night/Valley	1974	$8
❏ 7603	Summer Sun/Words and Rhymes	1972	$8

JAMIE AND JANE

DECCA

Number	Title	Yr	NM
❏ 30934	Faithful Our Love/Classical Rock and Roll	1959	$40

Number	Title	Yr	NM
❏ 30862	Snuggle Up Baby/Strollin' Thru the Park	1959	$40

JAMIES, THE

EPIC

Number	Title	Yr	NM
❏ 9281	Summertime, Summertime/Searching for You	1958	$15

— Reissued in 1962 with the same catalog number and label design

Number	Title	Yr	NM
❏ 9281 [PS]	Summertime, Summertime/Searching for You	1958	$30
❏ 11129	Summertime, Summertime/Searching for You	1974	$5
❏ 9299	When the Sun Goes Down/Snow Train	1958	$30
❏ 9565	When the Sun Goes Down/Snow Train	1963	$15

UNITED ARTISTS

Number	Title	Yr	NM
❏ 193	The Evening Star/Don't Darken My Door	1959	$30

JAN AND ARNIE

ARWIN

Number	Title	Yr	NM
❏ 111	Gas Money/Bonnie Lou	1958	$50
❏ 113	I Love Linda/The Beat That Can't Be Beat	1958	$70

DORE

Number	Title	Yr	NM
❏ 522	Baby Talk/Jeannette Get Your Hair Done	1959	$600

— Actually by Jan and Dean, but incorrectly credited

DOT

Number	Title	Yr	NM
❏ 16116	Gas Money/Gotta Getta Date	1960	$60

JAN AND DEAN

CHALLENGE

Number	Title	Yr	NM
❏ 9111	Heart and Soul/A Midsummer Night's Dream	1961	$30
❏ 9111	Heart and Soul/Those Words	1961	$50
❏ 9120	Wanted: One Girl/Something a Little Bit Different	1961	$40

DORE

Number	Title	Yr	NM
❏ 522	Baby Talk/Jeannette Get Your Hair Done	1959	$40
❏ 583	Baggy Pants/Judy's an Angel	1961	$40
❏ 548	Cindy/Whiter Tennis Sneakers	1960	$30
❏ 539	Clementine/You're On My Mind	1960	$30
❏ 576	Gee/Such a Good Night to Be Together	1960	$30
❏ 576 [PS]	Gee/Such a Good Night to Be Together	1960	$300
❏ 531	There's a Girl/My Heart Sings	1959	$30
❏ 555	We Go Together/Rosie Lane	1960	$30

— B-side title was altered after the record no longer was issued with picture sleeve

Number	Title	Yr	NM
❏ 555	We Go Together/Rosilane	1960	$30
❏ 555 [PS]	We Go Together/Rosilane	1960	$120

EVATONE

Number	Title	Yr	NM
❏ 7801X	Surf Bunkey	1980	$8

— 6-inch red flexi-disc; Dutch version of "Surf City"

J&D

Number	Title	Yr	NM
❏ 01	California Lullabye/Summertime	1966	$40
❏ 402	Like a Summer Rain/Louisiana Man	1966	$40
❏ 1271 [DJ]	Ocean Park Angel/Wipe Out	1981	$10

— B-side by the Surfaris

JAN & DEAN

Number	Title	Yr	NM
❏ 11	Fan Tan/Love and Hate	1966	$120
❏ 10	Hawaii/Tijuana	1966	$80

LIBERTY

Number	Title	Yr	NM
❏ 55397	A Sunday Kind of Love/Poor Little Puppet	1961	$30
❏ 55860	Batman/Bucket "T"	1966	$30
❏ 55672	Dead Man's Curve/The New Girl in School	1964	$20
❏ 55672 [PS]	Dead Man's Curve/The New Girl in School	1964	$50
❏ 55641	Drag City/Schlock Rod (Part 1)	1963	$20
❏ 55641 [PS]	Drag City/Schlock Rod (Part 1)	1963	$50
❏ 55905	Fiddle Around/Surfer's Dream	1966	$15
❏ 55849	Folk City/A Beginning from an End	1965	$15
❏ 55849 [PS]	Folk City/A Beginning from an End	1965	$40
❏ 55522	Frosty (The Snow Man)/(She's Still Talking) Baby Talk	1962	$200

— Promos worth about half this value

Number	Title	Yr	NM
❏ 55766	(Here They Come) From All Over the World/Freeway Flyer	1965	$15

Number	Title	Yr	NM
❏ 55766 [PS]	(Here They Come) From All Over the World/Freeway Flyer	1965	$200
❏ 55613	Honolulu Lulu/Someday	1963	$20
❏ 55613 [PS]	Honolulu Lulu/Someday	1963	$50
❏ 55833	I Found a Girl/It's a Shame to Say Goodbye	1965	$15
❏ 55531	Linda/When I Learn How to Cry	1963	$30
❏ 55886	Popsicle/Norwegian Wood	1966	$15
❏ 55727	Sidewalk Surfin'/When It's Over	1964	$20
❏ 55727 [PS]	Sidewalk Surfin'/When It's Over	1964	$50
❏ 55580	Surf City/She's My Summer Girl	1963	$20
❏ 55580 [PS]	Surf City/She's My Summer Girl	1963	$50
❏ 55454	Tennessee/Your Heart Has Changed Its Mind	1962	$30
❏ 55704	The Little Old Lady (From Pasadena)/My Mighty G.T.O.	1964	$20
❏ 55704 [PS]	The Little Old Lady (From Pasadena)/My Mighty G.T.O.	1964	$50
❏ 55496	Who Put the Bomp/My Favorite Dream	1962	$60

MAGIC LAMP

Number	Title	Yr	NM
❏ 401	California Lullaby/Summertime	1966	$40

ODE

Number	Title	Yr	NM
❏ 66111	Fun City/Totally Wild	1975	$30

UNITED ARTISTS

Number	Title	Yr	NM
❏ 092	Dead Man's Curve/Drag City	1973	$20
❏ 093	Honolulu Lulu/Sidewalk Surfin'	1973	$20
❏ 090	Linda/The New Girl in School	1973	$20
❏ XW670	Sidewalk Surfin'/Gonna Hustle You	1975	$20
❏ 091	Surf City/Ride the Wild Surf	1973	$20
❏ 094	The Little Old Lady (From Pasadena)/Popsicle	1973	$20

—0089 through 0094 are "Silver Spotlight Series" reissues

WARNER BROS.

Number	Title	Yr	NM
❏ 7240 [DJ]	In the Still of the Night/Girl, You're Blowing My Mind	1968	$100

—Stock copy may not exist

Number	Title	Yr	NM
❏ 7219	Laurel and Hardy/I Know My Mind	1968	$60
❏ 7151	Only a Boy/Love and Hate	1967	$50

JAN AND KJELD

IMPERIAL

Number	Title	Yr	NM
❏ 5568	Tiger Rag/Buona Sera	1959	$10

JARO

Number	Title	Yr	NM
❏ 77032	Ting-a-Ling My Banjo Sings/Penny Melody	1960	$10

KAPP

Number	Title	Yr	NM
❏ 335	Banjo Boy/Don't Raise a Storm	1960	$12
❏ 373	Carry Me Back to Old Virginny/Oh, Mein Papa	1961	$20

JANE'S ADDICTION

WARNER BROS.

Number	Title	Yr	NM
❏ 27520	Mountain Song/Standing in the Shower...Thinking	1989	$10
❏ 27520 [PS]	Mountain Song/Standing in the Shower...Thinking	1989	$10

JANIS, JOHNNY

ABC-PARAMOUNT

Number	Title	Yr	NM
❏ 45-9840	All the Time/Later Baby	1957	$30
❏ 45-9800	Pledge of Love/I Played the Field	1957	$30

BOMARC

Number	Title	Yr	NM
❏ 304	I Never Believed/Willing to Learn	1959	$20
❏ 307	Living in a Candy Store/I Said You	1960	$20

CARLTON

Number	Title	Yr	NM
❏ 463	The Better to Love You/Can This Be Love	1958	$30

COLUMBIA

Number	Title	Yr	NM
❏ 4-41933	Catch a Falling Star/As I Was Walkin'	1961	$15
❏ 4-41797	Gina/If the Lord's Willin'	1960	$20
❏ 4-42040	I Get Ideas/Save a Thought for Me	1961	$15

CORAL

Number	Title	Yr	NM
❏ 9-61552	Move It or Lose It/I'm Throwing Rice (At the Girl That I Love)	1956	$30

MONUMENT

Number	Title	Yr	NM
❏ 1117	Anything's the Part of You/One of These Days	1968	$10
❏ 1205	Distant Dreams/Ride Me Donkey	1970	$8

Number	Title	Yr	NM
❏ 1042	I Hear It Now/A Rose Is a Rose	1967	$10
❏ 1177	Walk Through This World with Me/All This World and the Seven Seas	1969	$8

JANSEN, GUSS

ARVEE

Number	Title	Yr	NM
❏ 5085	Mr. Snowman Goes To Town/Rudolph, The Red-Nose Reindeer	1963	$15

JANSKY, CLIFTON

AXBAR

Number	Title	Yr	NM
❏ 6033	Will You Love Me in the Morning/Just Can't Help Believing	1985	$8

JANSSEN, DANNY

STEPHENY

Number	Title	Yr	NM
❏ 1843	Christmas All Alone/Winter Wonderland	1960	$20

JAPAN

ARIOLA AMERICA

Number	Title	Yr	NM
❏ 7756	Life in Tokyo/Love Is Infectious	1979	$8
❏ 7727	Sometimes I Feel So Low/Love Is Infectious	1979	$8

JAPANESE BEATLES, THE

GOLDEN CREST

Number	Title	Yr	NM
❏ 584	The Beatle Song (Japanese Style) (Part 1)/The Beatle Song (Japanese Style) (Part 2)	1964	$30

JARMELS, THE

LAURIE

Number	Title	Yr	NM
❏ 3098	A Little Bit of Soap/The Way You Look Tonight	1961	$30
❏ 3174	Come On Girl/Keep Your Mind on Me	1963	$20
❏ 3116	I'll Follow You/Gee Oh Gosh	1962	$20
❏ 3142	Little Bug/One By One	1962	$20
❏ 3085	Little Lonely One/She Loves to Dance	1961	$20

JARREAU, AL

MCA

Number	Title	Yr	NM
❏ 53124	Moonlighting (Theme)/(Dub Version)	1987	$3
❏ 53124 [PS]	Moonlighting (Theme)/(Dub Version)	1987	$3

POLYDOR

Number	Title	Yr	NM
❏ 883513-7	Day by Day/Don't Push Me	1985	$4

—With Shakatak

RAYNARD

Number	Title	Yr	NM
❏ 1022	I Am Not Afraid/Ska-Bobbi	1964	$200

REPRISE

Number	Title	Yr	NM
❏ 22929	All of My Love/Killer Love	1989	$3
❏ 27550	All or Nothing at All/Heart's Horizon	1989	$3
❏ 27664	So Good/Pleasure Over Pain	1988	$3
❏ 27664 [PS]	So Good/Pleasure Over Pain	1988	$3

SESAME STREET

Number	Title	Yr	NM
❏ 49703	One Good Turn/The Sailor and the Mermaid	1981	$4

—B-side by Dr. John with Libby Titus

WARNER BROS.

Number	Title	Yr	NM
❏ 29262	After All/I Keep Callin'	1984	$3
❏ 29262 [PS]	After All/I Keep Callin'	1984	$3
❏ 29624	Boogie Down/Our Love	1983	$3
❏ 49842	Breakin' Away/(Round, Round, Round) Blue Ronda A La Turk	1981	$4
❏ 49588	Distracted/Alonzo	1980	$4
❏ 49538	Gimme What You Got/Spain	1980	$4
❏ 28400	Give a Little More Lovin'/Says	1987	$3
❏ 28686	L Is for Lover/No Ordinary Romance	1986	$3
❏ 28686 [PS]	L Is for Lover/No Ordinary Romance	1986	$3
❏ 29720	Mornin'/Not Like This	1983	$3
❏ 29720 [PS]	Mornin'/Not Like This	1983	$5
❏ 28925	Pretend/Black and Blues	1985	$3
❏ 8751	She's Leaving Home/All	1979	$4
❏ 8443	Take Five/Loving You	1977	$4
❏ 50032	Teach Me Tonight/Easy	1982	$4
❏ 28538	Tell Me What I Gotta Do/Across the Midnight Sky	1986	$3
❏ 0PRA [DJ]	The Christmas Song/Al's Greeting/The Christmas Song	1983	$5
❏ 0PRA [PS]	The Christmas Song/Al's Greeting/The Christmas Song	1983	$6

—Promo sleeve has blank green back

Number	Title	Yr	NM
❏ 29446	The Christmas Song/Our Love	1983	$4
❏ 29446 [PS]	The Christmas Song/Our Love	1983	$5
❏ 8677	Thinkin' About It Too/Fly	1978	$4
❏ 29501	Trouble in Paradise/Step by Step	1983	$3
❏ 29501 [PS]	Trouble in Paradise/Step by Step	1983	$3
❏ 8481	We Got By/So Long Girl	1977	$4
❏ 49746	We're In This Love Together/Alonzo	1981	$4

JARRETT, KEITH

ABC IMPULSE!

Number	Title	Yr	NM
❏ 31001	Treasure Island/Sister Fortune	1975	$5

ATLANTIC

Number	Title	Yr	NM
❏ 5110	All I Want/Standing Outside	1971	$6

ECM

Number	Title	Yr	NM
❏ 29483	God Bless the Child/Meaning of the Blues	1983	$4

JAXON, BOB

20TH CENTURY FOX

Number	Title	Yr	NM
❏ 441	Weep, Mary, Weep/Do the People	1963	$10

ABC-PARAMOUNT

Number	Title	Yr	NM
❏ 10364	It's a Cruel, Cruel Thing/One Way to Love Me	1962	$15

CADENCE

Number	Title	Yr	NM
❏ 1264	Ali Baba/Why Does a Woman Cry	1955	$20

RCA VICTOR

Number	Title	Yr	NM
❏ 47-6945	Beach Party/I'm Hangin' Around	1957	$20
❏ 47-7106	Declaration of Love/I'm Hurtin' Inside	1957	$20
❏ 47-7232	For the Love of You/(Well It's) No Lie	1958	$20
❏ 47-7006	(Gotta Have Something in the) Bank Frank/Come On Down	1957	$30
❏ 47-7168	Me! Please! Me!/All About Me	1958	$20

JAY AND THE AMERICANS

EEOC

Number	Title	Yr	NM
❏ 1140	Things Are Changing/Things Are Changing	1965	$200
❏ 1140 [PS]	Things Are Changing/Things Are Changing	1965	$200

—Promotional item for the Equal Employment Opportunity Commission

UNITED ARTISTS

Number	Title	Yr	NM
❏ 50086	Baby Come Home/Stop the Clock	1966	$8
❏ 0027	Cara Mia/Let's Lock the Door (And Throw Away the Key)	1973	$5
❏ 881	Cara Mia/When It's All Over	1965	$10
❏ 759	Come a Little Bit Closer/Goodbye Boys, Goodbye	1964	$10
❏ 669	Come Dance with Me/Look in My Eyes Maria	1963	$10
❏ 50016	Crying/I Don't Need a Friend	1966	$8
❏ 50016 [PS]	Crying/I Don't Need a Friend	1966	$15
❏ 50683	Do I Love You?/Tricia (Tell Your Daddy)	1970	$6
❏ 50654	Do You Ever Think of Me/Capture the Moment	1970	$6
❏ 50094	(He's) Raining in My Sunshine/The Reason for Living (For You My Darling)	1966	$8
❏ 50535	Hushabye/Gypsy Woman	1969	$6
❏ 50567	(I'd Kill) For the Love of a Lady/Learnin' How to Fly	1969	$6
❏ 479	It's My Turn to Cry/This Is It	1962	$15
❏ 805	Let's Lock the Door (And Throw Away the Key)/I'll Remember You	1965	$12
❏ 50046	Livin' Above Your Head/Look at Me, What Do You See	1966	$8
❏ 50046 [PS]	Livin' Above Your Head/Look at Me, What Do You See	1966	$50
❏ 626	Only in America/My Clair De Lune	1963	$10
❏ 50222	Shanghai Noodle Factory/French Provincial	1967	$8
❏ 0026	She Cried/Come a Little Bit Closer	1973	$5
❏ 415	She Cried/Dawning	1962	$20
❏ 919	Some Enchanted Evening/Girl	1965	$12
❏ 919 [PS]	Some Enchanted Evening/Girl	1965	$20
❏ 948	Sunday and Me/Through This Doorway	1965	$10
❏ 948 [PS]	Sunday and Me/Through This Doorway	1965	$60
❏ 50858	There Goes My Baby/Solitary Man	1971	$6
❏ 845	Think of the Good Times/If You Were Mine, Girl	1965	$10
❏ 50475	This Magic Moment/Since I Don't Have You	1969	$15

Number	Title	Yr	NM
❏ 0028	This Magic Moment/Walking in the Rain	1973	$5

—0026, 0027, 0028 are "Silver Spotlight Series" reissues

Number	Title	Yr	NM
❏ 504	Tomorrow/Yes	1962	$15
❏ 353	Tonight/The Other Girls	1961	$15
❏ 693	To Wait for Love/Friday	1964	$10
❏ 50605	Walkin' in the Rain/(I'll Kill) For the Love of a Lady	1969	$8
❏ 50196	(We'll Meet in the) Yellow Forest/Got Hung Up Along the Way	1967	$60
❏ 566	What's the Use/Strangers Tomorrow	1963	$10
❏ 50510	When You Dance/No, I Don't Know Her	1969	$6
❏ 992	Why Can't You Bring Me Home/Baby Stop Your Cryin'	1966	$8

JAY AND THE DELTAS
WARNER BROS.

Number	Title	Yr	NM
❏ 5404	Bells Are Ringing/Super Hawk	1964	$60

JAY AND THE TECHNIQUES
EVENT

Number	Title	Yr	NM
❏ 222	I Feel Love Coming On/World of Mine	1975	$5

GORDY

Number	Title	Yr	NM
❏ 7123	I'll Be Here/Robot Man	1973	$50

PHILCO-FORD

Number	Title	Yr	NM
❏ HP-22	Apples Peaches Pumpkin Pie/Loving for Money	1968	$20

—4-inch plastic "Hip Pocket Record" with color sleeve

SMASH

Number	Title	Yr	NM
❏ 2086	Apples, Peaches, Pumpkin Pie/Stronger Than Dirt	1967	$20
❏ 2154	Baby Make Your Own Sweet Music/Help Yourself to All My Lovin'	1968	$20
❏ 2154 [PS]	Baby Make Your Own Sweet Music/Help Yourself to All My Lovin'	1968	$30
❏ 2217	Change Your Mind/Are You Ready for This	1969	$40
❏ 2237	Dancin' Mood/If I Should Lose You	1969	$30
❏ 2185	Hey Diddle Diddle/If I Should Lose You	1968	$20
❏ 2142	Strawberry Shortcake/Still (In Love with You)	1967	$20
❏ 2142 [PS]	Strawberry Shortcake/Still (In Love with You)	1967	$30
❏ 2171	The Singles Game/Baby How Easy Your Heart Forgets Me	1968	$20
❏ 2171 [PS]	The Singles Game/Baby How Easy Your Heart Forgets Me	1968	$30

JAY, ERIC
BULLSEYE

Number	Title	Yr	NM
❏ 1021	Little Drummer Boy/Silent Night	1959	$15

JAY FIVE, THE
RCA VICTOR

Number	Title	Yr	NM
❏ 47-9449	My Angel/Platform Ticket	1968	$15

JAY, MORTY
20TH CENTURY FOX

Number	Title	Yr	NM
❏ 402	The Longest Day/(B-side unknown)	1963	$10

—With a severely truncated version of the A-side

LEGEND

Number	Title	Yr	NM
❏ 124	Saltwater Taffy/What Is Surfin' All About	1963	$30

—B-side by Jerry Norell and the Beach Girls

JAY, PETER, AND THE JAYWALKERS
WAND

Number	Title	Yr	NM
❏ 180	What's Easy/Parchment Farm	1965	$10

JAY WALKERS, THE
LAURIE

Number	Title	Yr	NM
❏ 3363	Oh Babe/Love at First Sight	1966	$50

JAYBEES, THE
RCA VICTOR

Number	Title	Yr	NM
❏ 47-8904	Do You Think I'm in Love/I'm a Lover	1966	$30

JAYE, JERRY
COLUMBIA

Number	Title	Yr	NM
❏ 10170	It's All in the Game/Love Me 'Til the Morning Comes	1975	$4
❏ 10269	Maybellene/Because It's Love	1975	$4

HI

Number	Title	Yr	NM
❏ 2139	Brown-Eyed Handsome Man/In the Middle of Nowhere	1968	$6
❏ 2310	Honky Tonk Women Love Redneck Men/What's Left	1976	$4
❏ 2318	Hot and Still Heatin'/Crazy	1976	$4
❏ 2128	Let the Four Winds Blow/Singin' the Blues	1967	$8
❏ 2150	Long Black Veil/(Today) I Started Loving You Again	1968	$6
❏ 2120	My Girl Josephine/Five Miles from Home	1967	$8
❏ 2323	When Morning Comes to Memphis//(B-side unknown)	1977	$4

MEGA

Number	Title	Yr	NM
❏ 0045	Don't Bring the Rain Back Again/Tiny Praying Hands	1971	$5
❏ 0116	Honky Tonk Livin'/I'm Gonna Spend My Whole Life Lovin' You	1973	$5
❏ 0033	I Didn't Hear a Thing/Love Is a Job	1971	$5
❏ 1218	Poor Side of Town/Lay Down	1974	$4
❏ 0066	Share Your Love with Me/When My Ship Comes In	1972	$5
❏ 209	Walkin' My Baby Back Home/I Slipped But I Didn't Fall	1974	$4

STEPHENY

Number	Title	Yr	NM
❏ 1820	Sugar Dumplin'/How Could You Lose Your Trust in Me	1958	$50

JAYHAWKS, THE (1)
ALADDIN

Number	Title	Yr	NM
❏ 3393	Everyone Should Know/The Creature	1957	$100

ARGYLE

Number	Title	Yr	NM
❏ 1005	Lonely Highway/La Macerena	1961	$30

EASTMAN

Number	Title	Yr	NM
❏ 792	Start the Fire/I Wish the World Owed Me a Living	1958	$200

FLASH

Number	Title	Yr	NM
❏ 105	Counting Teardrops/The Devil's Cousin	1955	$200
❏ 111	Love Train/Don't Mind Dyin'	1956	$40
❏ 109	Stranded in the Jungle/My Only Darling	1956	$60

JAYNELLS, THE
CAMEO

Number	Title	Yr	NM
❏ 286	I'll Stay Home New Year's Eve/Down Home	1963	$30

DIAMOND

Number	Title	Yr	NM
❏ 153	I'll Stay Home (New Year's Eve)/Down Home	1963	$50

JAYNETTS, THE

Number	Title	Yr	NM
❏ 1686	Looking for Wonderland, My Lover/Make It an Extra	1965	$8

TUFF

Number	Title	Yr	NM
❏ 369	Sally, Go 'Round the Roses/(Instrumental)	1963	$20
❏ 374	Snowman, Snowman, Sweet Potato Nose/(Instrumental)	1963	$20

JAYTONES, THE
BRUNSWICK

Number	Title	Yr	NM
❏ 55087	The Clock/Gasoline	1958	$120

CUB

Number	Title	Yr	NM
❏ 9057	My Only Love/Absolutely Right	1960	$70

TIMELY

Number	Title	Yr	NM
❏ 1003/4	My Darling/The Bells	1958	$1500

JAZZY JEFF AND FRESH PRINCE
JIVE

Number	Title	Yr	NM
❏ 1042-7	A Touch of Jazz/(Instrumental)	1987	$4
❏ 9428	Fire/We Just Want to Have Fun	1985	$4

—Label credit: "DJ Jazzy Jeff

Number	Title	Yr	NM
❏ 1147-7	Girls Ain't Nothin' But Trouble/Brand New Funk	1988	$3
❏ 1147-7 [PS]	Girls Ain't Nothin' But Trouble/Brand New Funk	1988	$3
❏ 1282-7	I Think I Can Beat Mike Tyson/(Instrumental)	1989	$3
❏ 1282-7 [PS]	I Think I Can Beat Mike Tyson/(Instrumental)	1989	$3
❏ 9377	Mix So I Can Go Crazy	1985	$4

—Label credit: "DJ Jazzy Jeff

Number	Title	Yr	NM
❏ 1099-7	Parents Just Don't Understand/(Instrumental)	1988	$3
❏ 1099-7 [PS]	Parents Just Don't Understand/(Instrumental)	1988	$3
❏ 1029-7	The Magnificent Jazzy Jeff/(Instrumental)	1987	$4

JEANETTE, JOAN & KAY
TEEN-ED

Number	Title	Yr	NM
❏ 5	Christmas Time (Part 1)/Christmas Time (Part 2)	1961	$20

JEFFERSON
DECCA

Number	Title	Yr	NM
❏ 32501	The Colour of My Love/Look No Further	1969	$8

JANUS

Number	Title	Yr	NM
❏ 106	Baby Take Me in Your Arms/I Fell Flat on My Face	1969	$8

JEFFERSON AIRPLANE
Also see MARTY BALIN; PAPA JOHN CREACH; HOT TUNA; JEFFERSON STARSHIP; PAUL KANTNER; GRACE SLICK; STARSHIP.

EPIC

Number	Title	Yr	NM
❏ 73044	Summer of Love/Panda	1989	$5

GRUNT

Number	Title	Yr	NM
❏ 65-0506	Long John Silver/Milk Train	1972	$5
❏ 65-0506 [PS]	Long John Silver/Milk Train	1972	$20
❏ 65-0500	Pretty As You Feel/Wild Turkey	1971	$5
❏ 65-0500 [PS]	Pretty As You Feel/Wild Turkey	1971	$10
❏ 65-0511	Trial by Fire/Twilight Double Leader	1972	$5
❏ JB-10988 [DJ]	White Rabbit (mono/stereo)	1978	$40

— White vinyl

RCA

Number	Title	Yr	NM
❏ 5156-7-R	White Rabbit/Plastic Fantastic Lover	1987	$5

— White vinyl

Number	Title	Yr	NM
❏ 5156-7-R [PS]	White Rabbit/Plastic Fantastic Lover	1987	$5

RCA VICTOR

Number	Title	Yr	NM
❏ 47-9297	Ballad of You & Me & Pooneil/Two Heads	1967	$12
❏ 47-8967	Bringing Me Down/Let Me In	1966	$20
❏ 47-8848	Come Up the Years/Blues from an Airplane	1966	$20
❏ 47-9644	Crown of Creation/Lather	1968	$8
❏ 47-9644 [PS]	Crown of Creation/Lather	1968	$30
❏ 47-9496	Greasy Heart/Share a Little Joke (With the World)	1968	$8
❏ 74-0343	Have You Seen the Saucers/Mexico	1970	$6
❏ 74-0343 [PS]	Have You Seen the Saucers/Mexico	1970	$20
❏ 47-8769	It's No Secret/Runnin' 'Round This World	1966	$20
❏ 47-9063	My Best Friend/How Do You Feel	1967	$20
❏ 74-0150	Plastic Fantastic Lover/Other Side of This Life	1969	$6
❏ 74-0150 [PS]	Plastic Fantastic Lover/Other Side of This Life	1969	$30
❏ 47-9140	Somebody to Love/She Has Funny Cars	1967	$20
❏ 47-9389	Watch Her Ride/Martha	1967	$10
❏ 47-9248	White Rabbit/Plastic Fantastic Lover	1967	$20

JEFFERSON STARSHIP
See cross-references under JEFFERSON AIRPLANE.

GRUNT

Number	Title	Yr	NM
❏ FB-13350	Be My Lady/Out of Control	1982	$3
❏ FB-13531	Can't Find Love/I Will Stay	1983	$3
❏ FB-10206	Caroline/Be Young You	1975	$4
❏ GB-11506	Count on Me/Runaway	1979	$3

— Gold Standard Series

Number	Title	Yr	NM
❏ FB-11196	Count on Me/Show Yourself	1978	$4
❏ FB-11196 [PS]	Count on Me/Show Yourself	1978	$5
❏ FB-11374	Crazy Feelin'/Love Too Good	1978	$4
❏ FB-11374 [PS]	Crazy Feelin'/Love Too Good	1978	$5
❏ FB-12211	Find Your Way Back/Modern Times	1981	$3
❏ FB-11921	Girl with the Hungry Eyes/Just the Same	1980	$4
❏ FB-11921 [PS]	Girl with the Hungry Eyes/Just the Same	1980	$5
❏ FB-13872	Layin' It on the Line/Showdown	1984	$3
❏ FB-13872 [PS]	Layin' It on the Line/Showdown	1984	$4
❏ FB-11426	Light the Sky On Fire/Hyperdrive	1978	$4
❏ FB-11426 [PS]	Light the Sky On Fire/Hyperdrive	1978	$5
❏ FB-10367	Miracles/Al Garimaso (There Is Love)	1975	$5
❏ GB-10941	Miracles/With Your Love	1977	$3

— Gold Standard Series

Number	Title	Yr	NM
❏ FB-10456	Play on Love/I Want to See Another World	1975	$4
❏ FB-12332	Save Your Love/Wild Eyes	1981	$3
❏ FB-10791	St. Charles/Love Lovely Day	1976	$4
❏ FB-12275	Stranger/Free	1981	$3
❏ FB-13439	Winds of Change/Black Widow	1983	$3
❏ FB-10746	With Your Love/Switchblade	1976	$5

JEFFREY, JOE, GROUP

WAND

Number	Title	Yr	NM
11235	A Hundred Pounds of Clay/Power of Love	1971	$6
11213	Chance of Loving You/Hey Hey Woman	1969	$6
11219	My Baby Loves Lovin'/Chance of Loving You	1970	$6
11200	My Pledge of Love/Margie	1969	$8
11207	The Train/Dreamin' Till Then	1969	$6

JEFFREYS, GARLAND

A&M

Number	Title	Yr	NM
2178	American Boy and Girl/Livin' for Me	1979	$4
2244	American Boy and Girl/Matador	1980	$4
2030	One-Eyed Jack/Reelin'	1978	$4
2074	She Didn't Lie/Scream in the Night	1979	$4
1934	Wild in the Streets/Ghost Writer	1977	$4

ARISTA

Number	Title	Yr	NM
0119	The Disco Kid Part 1/The Disco Kid Part 2	1975	$5

ATLANTIC

Number	Title	Yr	NM
2948	She Didn't Lie/Lon Chaney	1973	$5
2981	Wild in the Streets/Lon Chaney	1973	$5

EPIC

Number	Title	Yr	NM
51008	96 Tears/Escape Goat Dab	1981	$3
AE71225 [DJ]	Interview with Garland Jeffreys	1981	$8
AE71225 [PS]	Interview with Garland Jeffreys	1981	$8
02073	Modern Lovers/Spanish Manners	1981	$3
03189	Surrender/Rebel Love	1982	$3

7-Inch Extended Plays

Number	Title	Yr	NM
AE71223 [DJ]	(contents unknown)	1981	$8
AE71223 [PS]	Escapades	1981	$8

JEFFRIES, HERB

ALGER

Number	Title	Yr	NM
85	Los Angeles 1/Los Angeles 2	1983	$5
85 [PS]	Los Angeles 1/Los Angeles 2	1983	$5

COLUMBIA

Number	Title	Yr	NM
1-399(?)	A Man Wrote a Song/The Shepherd	1949	$40

— Microgroove 33 1/3 rpm 7-inch single, small hole

1-555(?)	Count Every Star/Our Love Story	1950	$40

— Microgroove 33 1/3 rpm 7-inch single, small hole

1-138(?)	Girls Were Made to Take Care of Boys/Bewildered	1949	$40

— Microgroove 33 1/3 rpm 7-inch single, small hole

1-748(?)	If I Should Lose You/Love Me Long	1950	$40

— Microgroove 33 1/3 rpm 7-inch single, small hole

1-140(?)	It's Easy to Remember/A Dreamer with a Penny	1949	$40

— Microgroove 33 1/3 rpm 7-inch single, small hole

1-672(?)	My Mother Singing/Dancing with You	1950	$40

— Microgroove 33 1/3 rpm 7-inch single, small hole

1-287	Pagan Love Song/Twilight	1949	$50

— Microgroove 33 1/3 rpm 7-inch single, small hole

1-430	Sunday Isn't Sunday Anymore/Flamingo Sand	1950	$40

— Microgroove 33 1/3 rpm 7-inch single, small hole

1-561(?)	The Flying Dutchman/Baby, Won't You Say You Love Me	1950	$40

— Microgroove 33 1/3 rpm 7-inch single, small hole

1-256	The Four Winds and the Seven Seas/Never Be It Said	1949	$40

— Microgroove 33 1/3 rpm 7-inch single, small hole

1-589(?)	There Goes My Heart/Swamp Girl	1950	$40

— Microgroove 33 1/3 rpm 7-inch single, small hole

1-820(?)	Wanderlust/Manon	1950	$40

— Microgroove 33 1/3 rpm 7-inch single, small hole

6-820(?)	Wanderlust/Manon	1950	$30

CORAL

Number	Title	Yr	NM
9-60456	A Beggar in Love/I'll Never Know Why	1951	$20
9-60552	A Fool Grows Wise/Love Comes Along	1951	$20
9-60527	All Alone/Time on My Hands	1951	$15
9-60528	All By Myself/I Didn't Know What Time It Was	1951	$15
9-60530	As Time Goes By/Once In Awhile	1951	$15

— The above four comprise a box set

9-60425	I'm Yours to Command/Love Me	1951	$20
9-60478	Old Soldiers Never Die/Unless	1951	$20
9-60403	Was It a Dream/You Know You Belong to Somebody Else	1951	$20
9-60505	Wonder Why/Dark Is the Night	1951	$20

MGM

Number	Title	Yr	NM
K12767	A Picture No Artist Can Paint/Buenas Noches, Mi Amor	1959	$10

RCA VICTOR

Number	Title	Yr	NM
47-6950	Mailman, Bring Me No More Blues/So Shy	1957	$20
47-7008	Sing to Me/Sweet Leilani	1957	$15

JELLY BEAN BANDITS, THE

MAINSTREAM

Number	Title	Yr	NM
674	Country Woman/Generation	1967	$40

JELLY BEANS, THE

ESKEE

Number	Title	Yr	NM
001	I'm Hip to You/You Don't Mean No Good to Me	1965	$200

RED BIRD

Number	Title	Yr	NM
Oct-003	I Wanna Love Him So Bad/So Long	1964	$30

JEMISON, MIKE

COTILLION

Number	Title	Yr	NM
7-99721	Break On Down/(B-side unknown)	1984	$10

GENEVA

Number	Title	Yr	NM
512	Geritol Funk/Bright Light Lady	1979	$40
510	When You're Around/Let's Bring Back the Good Times	1979	$40

JENKINS, GORDON

CAPITOL

Number	Title	Yr	NM
F3556	Married I Can Always Get/Repeat After Me	1956	$15
F3751	Theme from Saint Joan/Fire Down Below	1957	$15
F1263	White Christmas/I'm Always Chasing Rainbows	1950	$20

COLUMBIA

Number	Title	Yr	NM
4-42981	Blues for Beverly/I'm Forever Blowing Bubbles	1963	$10
4-42608	I Left My Heart in San Francisco/This Is All I Ask	1962	$10

DECCA

Number	Title	Yr	NM
9-24602	Again/Skip to My Lou	1950	$30

— 78 originally issued in 1949

9-27168	All the Things You Are/The Touch of Your Hand	1950	$20
9-29879	Angel's Lullaby — Mama Darling/Through the Night	1956	$15
9-27912	Anna Maria/Somebody	1951	$20
9-28580	Are You Teasing Me?/Midnight	1953	$20
9-24983	Bewitched/Where in the World	1950	$30
9-27172	Blue Evening/Goodbye	1950	$20
9-27169	Blue Prelude/You Have Taken My Heart	1950	$20
9-27859	Charmaine/When a Man Is Free	1951	$20
9-27886	Charmaine/When I Grow Too Old to Dream	1951	$20
9-28632	Daniel in the Lions' Den/The Masquerade Is Over	1953	$20
9-24478	For You/On the Painted Desert	1950	$30
9-28148	If They Ask Me/It Only Takes a Moment	1952	$20
9-27490	I Love You Much Too Much/Would I Love You	1951	$30
9-29562	I Love You So/My Love Came Back to Me	1955	$15
9-29244	In an Indiana/Slowly But Surely	1954	$15
9-27319	It's a Lovely Day/Just in Love/The Ocarina	1950	$30
9-28450	Leave Me Just a Little Bit of Love/I'll Know My Love	1952	$20
9-24403	Maybe You'll Be There/Dark Eyes	1950	$30

— 78 originally issued in 1948 with the same number

9-27394	More Than I Care to Remember/I Wish Someone Knew	1951	$30
9-27933	Mother, Mother/Every Hour	1952	$20
9-24830	My Foolish Heart/Don't Do Something to Someone Else (That You Wouldn't Want Done to You)	1950	$30
9-29365	My Own True Love (Tara's Theme)/Vera Cruz	1954	$15
9-28657	One Wild Oat/When They Speak of You	1953	$20
9-27171	P.S. I Love You/Homesick, That's All	1950	$20
9-28750	P.S. I Love You/I Thought About Marie	1953	$20
9-27433	Sally Doesn't Care/More Than I Care to Remember	1951	$30
9-27031	Santa Catalina/Blue Sails	1950	$30
9-28876	Secret Love/Theme from "Seven Dreams	1953	$20
9-27166	Smoke Gets In Your Eyes/Yesterdays	1950	$20
9-27681	Tell the Truth/I Wish Someone Knew I Was Lonesome	1951	$30
9-24523	Temptation/My Funny Valentine	1950	$30

— 78 originally issued in 1948

9-28612	The Ties That Bind/Gomen Nasai	1953	$20
9-27165	The Way You Look Tonight/Long Ago (And Far Away)	1950	$20
9-27167	They Didn't Believe Me/Till the Clouds Roll By	1950	$20
9-27358	They Like Ike/Lichtenburg	1951	$30
9-27585	Whsipering/Song of the Bayou	1951	$30
9-27170	With You So Far Away/When a Woman Loves a Man	1950	$20

KAPP

Number	Title	Yr	NM
339	April Moon-Lover's Moon/If She Should Come to You	1960	$10
572	Ciumachella (Tender Flower)/What Can I Say Afer I Say I'm Sorry	1964	$8
326	Clock Song/Romantica	1960	$10

TIME

Number	Title	Yr	NM
1051	I Wish You Love/Fascination	1962	$10
1049	Theme from Lolita/Hava Nagila	1962	$10

VIK

Number	Title	Yr	NM
0190	How Do I Love You?/You're Not Alone	1956	$15

X

Number	Title	Yr	NM
0175	Follow Me, Baby/Wish I Could Say the Same	1955	$15
0159	Goodnight, Sweet Dreams/Young Ideas	1955	$15
097	My Own/Tired of Waiting	1955	$15
0127	Theme for Lovers/Last Love	1955	$15

JENNINGS, WAYLON, AND JERRY REED

RCA

Number	Title	Yr	NM
GB-13789	Hold On, I'm Comin'/The Conversation	1984	$3

— Gold Standard Series; B-side by Waylon and Hank Williams, Jr.

PB-13580	Hold On, I'm Comin'/Waiting On Down the Line	1983	$4

JENNINGS, WAYLON

A&M

Number	Title	Yr	NM
739	Four Strong Winds/Just to Satisfy You	1964	$20

BAT

Number	Title	Yr	NM
121639	Dream Baby/Crying	1962	$50
121636	White Lightning/(B-side unknown)	1962	$60

COLUMBIA

Number	Title	Yr	NM
05594	Desperadoes Waiting for a Train/The Twentieth Century Is Almost Over	1985	$3

— A-side: Willie Nelson/Waylon Jennings/Johnny Cash/Kris Kristofferson; B-side: Nelson, Cash

08406	Highwayman/Desperadoes Waiting for a Train	1988	$3

— Waylon Jennings/Willie Nelson/Johnny Cash/Kris Kristofferson; reissue

04881 [PS]	Highwayman/The Human Condition	1985	$4

— A-side: Willie Nelson/Waylon Jennings/Johnny Cash/Kris Kristofferson; B-side: Nelson, Cash

04881	Highwayman/The Human Condition	1985	$3

— A-side: Willie Nelson/Waylon Jennings/Johnny Cash/Kris Kristofferson; B-side: Nelson, Cash

MCA

Number	Title	Yr	NM
53088	Fallin' Out/Deep in the West	1987	$3
53314	How Much Is It Worth to Live in L.A./G.I. Joe	1988	$3
53243	If Ole Hank Could Only See Us Now (Chapter Five… Nashville)/You Went Out with Rock 'n' Roll	1988	$3
53158	My Rough and Rowdy Days/Love Song (I Can't Sing Anymore)	1987	$3
53634	Trouble Man/Yoyos, Bozos, Bimbos and Heroes	1989	$3
52915	What You'll Do When I'm Gone/That Dog Won't Hurt	1986	$3
53476	Which Way Do I Go (Now That I'm Gone)/Hey Willie	1988	$3
52830	Will the Wolf Survive/I've Got Me a Woman	1986	$3
52776	Working Without a Net/They Ain't Got 'Em All	1986	$3

RAMCO

Number	Title	Yr	NM
1997	My World/Another Blue Day	1968	$15

Number	Title	Yr	NM
RCA			
❏ GB-12313	Amanda/I Ain't Living Long Like This	1981	$3
— Gold Standard Series" reissue			
❏ PB-11596	Amanda/Lonesome, On'ry and Mean	1979	$4
❏ PB-11596 [PS]	Amanda/Lonesome, On'ry and Mean	1979	$5
❏ PB-13908	America/People Up in Texas	1984	$4
❏ PB-10842	Are You Ready for the Country/So Good Woman	1976	$5
❏ GB-11500	Are You Ready for the Country/The Wurlitzer Prize (I Don't Want to Get Over You)	1978	$3
— Gold Standard Series			
❏ PB-13543	Breakin' Down/Livin' Legends (A Dyin' Breed)	1983	$4
❏ PB-12007	Clyde/I Came Here to Party	1980	$4
❏ PB-11723	Come with Me/Mes'kin	1979	$4
❏ PB-11390	Don't You Think This Outlaw Bit's Done Got Out of Hand/Girl I Can Tell (You're Trying to Work It Out)	1978	$4
❏ GB-10927	Dreaming My Dreams with You/Can't You See	1977	$3
— Gold Standard Series			
❏ PB-14094	Drinkin' and Dreamin'/Prophets Show Up in Strange Places	1985	$4
❏ PB-11898	I Ain't Living Long Like This/The World's Crazy	1979	$4
❏ PB-13729	I May Be Used (But Baby I Ain't Used Up)/So You Want to Be a Cowboy Singer	1984	$4
❏ GB-11991	I've Always Been Crazy/Don't You Think This Outlaw Bit's Done Got Out of Hand	1980	$3
— Gold Standard Series			
❏ PB-11344	I've Always Been Crazy/I Never Said It Would Be Easy	1978	$4
❏ PB-13465	Lucille (You Won't Do Your Daddy's Will)/Medley of Hits	1983	$4
❏ PB-10924	Luckenbach, Texas (Back to the Basics of Love)/Belle of the Ball	1977	$5
❏ GB-11757	Luckenbach, Texas (Back to the Basics of Love)/Belle of the Ball	1979	$3
— Gold Standard Series			
❏ PB-12367	Shine/White Water	1981	$4
❏ PB-13903	Silent Night, Holy Night/Precious Memories	1984	$4
—A-side with Jessi Colter			
❏ PB-14291	Sweet Mother Texas/Hanging On	1985	$4
❏ 5034-7-R	The Broken Promise Land/I Don't Have Any More Love Songs	1986	$4
❏ PB-13631	The Conversation/Fancy Free	1983	$4
—A-side with Hank Williams, Jr.			
❏ PB-14215	The Devil's on the Loose/Good Morning John	1985	$4
❏ GB-12187	Theme from "The Dukes of Hazzard" (Good Ol' Boys)/Come with Me	1981	$3
— Gold Standard Series			
❏ PB-12067	Theme from "The Dukes of Hazzard" (Good Ol' Boys)/It's Alright	1980	$4
❏ PB-12067 [PS]	Theme from "The Dukes of Hazzard" (Good Ol' Boys)/It's Alright	1980	$5
❏ PB-11118	The Wurlitzer Prize (I Don't Want to Get Over You)/Lookin' for a Feeling	1977	$5
❏ PB-13984	Waltz Me to Heaven/Dream On	1984	$4
❏ PB-13257	Women Do Know How to Carry On/Honky Tonk Blues	1982	$4
RCA VICTOR			
❏ 47-8729	Anita, You're Dreaming/Look Into My Teardrops	1965	$10
❏ PB-10379	Are You Sure Hank Done It This Way/Bob Wills Is Still the King	1975	$6
❏ GB-10673	Are You Sure Hank Done It This Way/Bob Wills Is Still the King	1976	$4
— Gold Standard Series			
❏ 74-0281	Brown Eyed Handsome Man/Sorrow (Breaks a Good Man Down)	1969	$8
❏ PB-10721	Can't You See/I'll Go Back to Her	1976	$5
❏ 48-1003	Cedartown, Georgia/I Think It's Time She Learned	1971	$8
❏ 47-9925	(Don't Let the Sun Set on You) Tulsa/You'll Look for Me	1970	$8
❏ PB-10270	Dreaming My Dreams with You/Waymore's Blues	1975	$6
❏ 74-0615	Good Hearted Woman/It's All Over Now	1971	$8
❏ 47-9025	Green River/Silver Ribbons	1966	$10
❏ 47-9480	I Got You/No One's Gonna Miss Me	1968	$10
—A-side with Anita Carter			

Number	Title	Yr	NM
❏ PB-10020	I'm a Ramblin' Man/Got a Lot Going for Me	1974	$6
❏ GB-10498	I'm a Ramblin' Man/Got a Lot Going for Me	1975	$4
— Gold Standard Series			
❏ 74-0210	MacArthur Park/But You Know I Love You	1969	$8
❏ AMAO-0122	MacArthur Park/The Taker	1973	$5
❏ 47-9146	Mental Revenge/Born to Love You	1967	$10
❏ 47-9967	Mississippi Woman/Life Goes On	1971	$8
❏ 47-9561	Only Daddy That'll Walk the Line/Right Before My Eyes	1968	$10
❏ 74-0808	Pretend I Never Happened/Nothin' Worth Takin' or Leavin'	1972	$8
❏ 47-9819	Singer of Sad Songs/Lila	1970	$8
❏ 74-0105	Something's Wrong in California/Farewell Party	1969	$8
❏ 47-8652	Stop the World (And Let Me Off)/The Dark Side of Fame	1965	$10
❏ 74-0716	Sweet Dream Woman/Sure Didn't Take Him Long	1972	$8
❏ 47-8572	That's the Chance I'll Have to Take/I Wonder Just Where I Went Wrong	1965	$12
❏ 47-8917	(That's What You Get) For Lovin' Me/Time Will Tell the Story	1966	$12
❏ 47-9259	The Chokin' Kind/Love of the Common People	1967	$12
❏ 74-0157	The Days of Sand and Shovels/Delia's Gone	1969	$8
❏ 47-9885	The Taker/Shadows of the Gallows	1970	$8
❏ APBO-0251	This Time/Mona	1974	$6
❏ GB-10169	This Time/You Asked Me To	1975	$4
— Gold Standard Series			
❏ 47-8822	Time to Bum Again/Norwegian Wood	1966	$10
❏ 47-9414	Walk On Out of My Mind/Julie	1967	$10
❏ 74-0961	We Had It All/Do No Good Woman	1973	$8
TREND			
❏ 102	Another Blue Day/Never Again	1962	$40
❏ 106	The Stage/My Baby Walks All Over Me	1963	$125
JENSEN, KRIS			
A&M			
❏ 1204	Dead End Street/Me and Bobby McGee	1970	$5
COLPIX			
❏ 118	Bonnie Baby/Staying Up Late	1959	$15
HICKORY			
❏ 1224	Big As I Can Dream/Donna, Donna	1963	$8
❏ 1224 [PS]	Big As I Can Dream/Donna, Donna	1963	$30
❏ 1195	Claudette/Don't Take Her from Me	1962	$8
❏ 1256	Come Back to Me (My Love)/You've Only Got Me to Lose	1964	$8
❏ 1243	In Time/Lookin' for Love	1964	$8
❏ 1285	Little Wind-Up Doll/Somebody's Smilin'	1964	$8
❏ 1203	Poor Unlucky Me/Cut Me Down (From Your Whipping Post)	1963	$8
❏ 1311	That's a Whole Lotta Love/What Should I Do	1965	$8
❏ 1173	Torture/Let's Sit Down	1962	$15
KAPP			
❏ 433	Busy Signal/Mary, Mary	1961	$10
❏ 493	Busy Signal/Mary, Mary	1962	$8
❏ 410	Danny'd Dream/3 Vanilla, 2 Chocolate, 1 Pistachio Ice Cream Cones	1961	$12
LEADER			
❏ 808	Perfect Love/School Bus	1960	$15
❏ 813	Please Let Me Love You Tonight/Your Daddy Don't Like Me	1961	$15
WHITE WHALE			
❏ 229	I Got You/I Can't Get Nowhere with You	1966	$6
❏ 240	I Love to Call You Sweetheart/Good Pop Music	1966	$6
JENSON, JIMMY			
BANGAR			
❏ 0651	I Yust Go Nuts At Christmas/Yingle Bells	1964	$20
❏ 0650	Walkin' in My Vinter Underwear/Copenhagen	1964	$20
JEREMY AND THE SATYRS			
REPRISE			
❏ 0664	Let's Go to the Movie Show/Lonely Child of Tears	1968	$12

Number	Title	Yr	NM
JERICHO			
BEARSVILLE			
❏ 31003	Cheater Man/Make It Better	1971	$8
JERRY AND WAYNE			
ABC-PARAMOUNT			
❏ 9808	Baby Baby Baby, Be Mine/I'm Sad, Blue and Lonesome	1957	$30
❏ 9806	Baby Baby Baby/I'm Sad, Blue and Lonesome	1957	$30
JESSE AND MARVIN			
SPECIALTY			
❏ 447	Dream Girl/Daddy Loves Baby	1952	$200
— Red vinyl			
❏ 447	Dream Girl/Daddy Loves Baby	1952	$80
— Black vinyl			
JESSIE MAE			
DRA			
❏ 319	Don't Freeze on Me/It Might As Well Be Spring	1962	$15
JESTERS, THE			
AMY			
❏ 859	Alexander Graham Bell/Buffalo	1962	$8
CYCLONE			
❏ 5011	I Laughed/Now That You're Gone	1958	$60
FEATURE			
❏ 101	Panther Pounce/Tiger Tail	1964	$60
SIDEWALK			
❏ 916	Hands of Time/If You Love Her, Tell Her So	1967	$12
❏ 910	Leave Me Alone/Don't Try to Crawl Back	1967	$12
SUN			
❏ 400	Cadillac Man/My Babe	1966	$40
ULTIMA			
❏ 705	Drag Like Boogie/A-Rab	1964	$40
WINLEY			
❏ 252	Come Let Me Show You/Uncle Henry's Basement	1961	$40
❏ 221	I'm Falling in Love/Please Let Me Love You	1957	$60
❏ 218	So Strange/Love No One But You	1957	$60
❏ 248	That's How It Goes/Tutti Frutti	1961	$60
— Red vinyl			
❏ 248	That's How It Goes/Tutti Frutti	1961	$40
— Black vinyl			
❏ 225	The Plea/Oh Baby	1958	$50
❏ 242	The Wind/Sally Green	1959	$50
JESUS AND MARY CHAIN, THE			
WARNER BROS.			
❏ 27754	Surfin' USA (Summer Mix)/Kill Surf City	1988	$4
JET SET, THE			
CAPITOL			
❏ 5421	How Can I Know/Dancing Yet	1965	$30
— As "Liza and the Jet Set"			
❏ 5358	True to You/You Got Me Hooked	1965	$30
JETHRO TULL			
Featuring flutist Ian Anderson.			
CHRYSALIS			
❏ TULL5 [PS]	Another Christmas Song/Intro - A Christmas Song	1989	$8
— U.K. import			
❏ TULL5	Another Christmas Song/Intro - A Christmas Song	1989	$8
— U.K. import			
❏ 2017	A Passion Play (Edit #6)/A Passion Play (Edit #10)	1973	$5
❏ 2012	A Passion Play (Edit #9)/A Passion Play (Edit #8)	1973	$6
❏ 2101	Bungle in the Jungle/Back Door Angels	1974	$5
❏ 2101 [PS]	Bungle in the Jungle/Back Door Angels	1974	$10
❏ 2613	Fallen on Hard Times/Pussy Willow	1982	$4
❏ 2387	Home/Warm Sporran	1979	$5
❏ 2006	Living in the Past/Christmas Song	1972	$6
❏ 2110	Locomotive Breath/Fat Man	1975	$5

Number	Title	Yr	NM
❏ 2106	Minstrel in the Gallery/ Sumer Day Sand	1975	$5
❏ 2103	Skating Away (On the Thin Ice of a New Day)/Sealion	1975	$5
❏ 43172	Steel Monkey/Down at the End of Your Road	1987	$4
❏ 2135	The Whistler/Strip Cartoon	1977	$5
❏ 2114	Too Old to Rock and Roll, Too Young to Die/Bad Eyed and Loveless	1976	$5

REPRISE

❏ 1024	Hymn 43/Mother Goose	1971	$5
❏ 0927	Inside/Time for Everything	1970	$5
❏ 0845 [DJ]	Living in the Past/Driving Song	1969	$30

— May be promo-only

❏ 1054	Locomotive Breath/Wind-Up	1971	$5
❏ 0815 [DJ]	Love Story/Song for Jeffrey	1969	$20

— May be promo-only

❏ 0899	Teacher/Witch's Promise	1970	$20
❏ 1153	Thick as a Brick (Edit)/ Hymn 43	1972	$5

— Back to Back Hits" series

JETS, THE
GEE

❏ 1020	Heaven Above Me/(B-side unknown)	1956	$2000

MCA

❏ 53446	Anytime/Christmas in My Heart	1988	$3

—A-side is not a Christmas song

JETT, JOAN, AND THE BLACKHEARTS
Also see THE RUNAWAYS.

BLACKHEART

❏ 06336	Good Music/Fantasy	1986	$3
❏ 06336 [PS]	Good Music/Fantasy	1986	$3
❏ 07919	I Hate Myself for Loving You/ Love Is Pain (Live)	1988	$3
❏ 07919 [PS]	I Hate Myself for Loving You/ Love Is Pain (Live)	1988	$3
❏ 06692	Light of Day/Roadrunner (Radio On)	1987	$3

— As "The Barbusters

❏ 06692 [PS]	Light of Day/Roadrunner (Radio On)	1987	$3

— As "The Barbusters

❏ 08095	Little Liar/What Can I Do for You	1988	$3
❏ 08095 [PS]	Little Liar/What Can I Do for You	1988	$3

BOARDWALK

❏ NB7-11-144	Crimson and Clover/Oh Woe Is Me	1982	$3
❏ NB7-11-144 [PS]	Crimson and Clover/Oh Woe Is Me	1982	$3
❏ NB 11-150-7	Do You Wanna Touch Me (Oh Yeah)/Victim of Circumstance	1982	$3
❏ NB 11-150-7 [PS]	Do You Wanna Touch Me (Oh Yeah)/Victim of Circumstance	1982	$3
❏ NB7-11-135	I Love Rock 'N Roll/You Don't Know What You've Got	1982	$3
❏ NB7-11-135 [PS]	I Love Rock 'N Roll/You Don't Know What You've Got	1982	$10
❏ NBS-7-006 [DJ]	Little Drummer Boy (same on both sides)	1981	$20

DEF JAM

❏ 07630	She's Lost You/Hazy Shade of Winter	1987	$3

— B-side by Bangles

❏ 07630 [PS]	She's Lost You/Hazy Shade of Winter	1987	$3

— B-side by Bangles

MCA

❏ 52272	Everyday People/Why Can't We Be Happy	1983	$3
❏ 52272 [PS]	Everyday People/Why Can't We Be Happy	1983	$3
❏ 52254	Fake Friends/Handy Man	1983	$4

—Evidently a jukebox single with a different flip side so the needle wouldn't get stuck!

❏ 52240	Fake Friends/Nite Time	1983	$3
❏ 52240 [PS]	Fake Friends/Nite Time	1983	$3

— Nite Time" has a locked groove. In other words, if left on an automatic turntable, it'll just keep playing...

❏ 52472	I Love You Love/Talkin' 'Bout My Baby	1984	$3
❏ 52472 [PS]	I Love You Love/Talkin' 'Bout My Baby	1984	$3

JEWEL AND EDDIE
SILVER

❏ 1008	My Eyes Are Cryin' for You/ Sixteen Tons	1960	$40
❏ 1004	Opportunity/Doin' the Hully Gully	1960	$50
❏ 1004	Opportunity/Strollin' Guitar	1960	$40

JEWELS, THE (1)
DIMENSION

❏ 1034	Opportunity/Gotta Find a Way	1964	$30
❏ 1048	Smokey Joe/But I Do	1965	$20

JEWELS, THE (2)
ANTLER

❏ 1102	The Wind/Pearlie Mae	1959	$50

IMPERIAL

❏ 5351	Angel in My Life/Hearts Can Be Broken	1955	$125
❏ 5377	How/Rickety Rock	1956	$125
❏ 5387	My Baby/Goin', Goin', Goin'	1956	$125

ORIGINAL SOUND

❏ 38	Hearts of Stone/Oh Yes I Know	1964	$30

R&B

❏ 1301	Hearts of Stone/Runnin'	1954	$200
❏ 1303	Oh Yes I Know/A Fool in Paradise	1954	$300

RPM

❏ 474	She's a Flirt/Be-Bomp Baby	1956	$75

JEWELS, THE (3)
DYNAMITE

❏ 2000	Papa Left Mama Holdin' the Bag/This Is My Story	1966	$20

FEDERAL

❏ 12541	My Song/This Is My Story	1966	$30

KING

❏ 6068	Smokie Joe's/Lookie Lookie	1967	$15

JEWELS, THE (U)
MGM

❏ 13577	We Got Togetherness/I'm Forever Blowing Bubbles	1966	$30

SHASTA

❏ 115	I Worry 'Bout You/Are You Coming to the Party	1959	$30

JIANTS, THE
CLAUDRA

❏ 112	Tornado/She's My Woman	1959	$200

JIM & JESSE
CAPITOL

❏ F2233	Are You Missing Me/I'll Wash You Love From My Heart	1952	$40
❏ 3921	Billy, Don't Be a Hero/Ain't No Place for a Country Boy	1974	$6
❏ 3969	Bring Back Your Sweet Love/Love Is a Fading Rose	1974	$6
❏ 3026	Freight Train/Just Wondering Why	1971	$6
❏ 3099	I'll Always Be Waiting for You/San Quentin Quail	1971	$6
❏ F3505	I'll Wear the Banner/My Garden of Love	1956	$30
❏ F2578	Is It True/My Darling's in Heaven	1953	$30
❏ F2798	Look for Me/Are You Lost in Sin	1954	$30
❏ F3141	Memory of You/Too Many Tears	1955	$30
❏ F2683	My Little Honeysuckle Rose/ Just Wondering Why	1953	$30
❏ F2365	Purple Heart/I Will Always Be Waiting for You	1953	$30

COLUMBIA

❏ 4-42180	Beautiful Moon of Kentucky/ Diesel Train	1961	$15

EPIC

❏ 5-9729	Better Times a-Coming/Wild Georgia Boys	1964	$8
❏ 5-9676	Cotton Mill Man/(It's a Long, Long Way) To the Top of the World	1964	$8
❏ 5-10040	Don't Let Nobody Tie You Down/If You've Seen One You've Seen Them All	1966	$8
❏ 5-9635	Drifting and Dreaming of You/Lascassas, Tennessee	1963	$12
❏ 5-9851	Memphis/Maybellene	1965	$8
❏ 5-9508	My Empty Arms/Stormy Horizons	1962	$10
❏ 5-9528	Pickin' and a Grinnin'/Sweet Little Miss Blue Eyes	1962	$10
❏ 5-9716	The Old Country Church/ Swing Low, Sweet Chariot	1964	$8
❏ 5-10429	When the Snow Is on the Roses/(B-side unknown)	1969	$8

MSR

❏ 198310	Oh Louisiana/(B-side unknown)	1986	$6

STARDAY

❏ 412	Hard Hearted/Pardon Me	1958	$20
❏ 433	Let Me Whisper/Border Ride	1959	$20

JIMENEZ, JOSE
A&M

❏ 779	All I Need Is You/Make Nice	1965	$8

—As "Bill Dana

KAPP

❏ 434	Christmas Sing Along with Jose: Jingle Bells/Sing Along with Jose: Shine On Harvest Moon	1961	$20
❏ 409	The Astronaut (Part 1)/The Astronaut (Part 2)	1961	$8
❏ 409 [PS]	The Astronaut (Part 1)/The Astronaut (Part 2)	1961	$15

SIGNATURE

❏ 12046	Bob Sled Racer/U.S. Senator	1960	$15

—As "Bill Dana

❏ 12041	My Name – Jose Jimenez/In the Wee Small Hours	1960	$15

JIMMIE DALE AND THE FLATLANDERS
PLANTATION

❏ 92	Dallas/Tonight I'm Gonna Go Downtown	1972	$60

JIMMY, JOE AND BETTY
HIT

❏ 59	Puff the Magic Dragon/Don't Be Afraid Little Darling	1963	$8

—B-side by Fred York

JIMMY AND DUANE
EB X. PRESTON

❏ 212	I Want Some Lovin' Baby/ Soda Fountain Girl	1955	$300

JIMMY AND JOHNNY
CHESS

❏ 4862	Can't You, Won't You/The Fun Is Over	1955	$40
❏ 4859	If You Don't Somebody Else Will/I'm Beginning to Remember	1954	$40

—As "Jimmy Lee and Johnny Mathis

D

❏ 1004	I Can't Find the Door Knob/ Keep Telling Me	1958	$30
❏ 1089	My Little Baby/All I Need Is Time	1959	$30

DECCA

❏ 9-29954	Another Man's Name/Til the End of the World	1956	$30
❏ 9-30278	Don't Give Me That Look/ Here Comes My Baby	1957	$30
❏ 9-30061	Sweet Love on My Mind/ Imagination	1956	$30
❏ 9-29772	Sweet Swinging Daddy/ Take Me	1956	$30
❏ 9-30410	What'cha Doin' to Me/I'll Do It Every Time	1957	$30

FEATURE

❏ 1092	If You Don't Somebody Else Will/I'm Beginning to Remember	1954	$125

—As "Jimmy Lee and Johnny Mathis

TNT

❏ 184	Two Empty Arms/Call You	1960	$20

JIMMY AND WALTER
SUN

❏ 180	Easy/Before Long	1953	$2000

—The earliest known 45 on Sun

JINGOLEERS, THE
BRUNSWICK

❏ 55108	Christmas Morn/Jingle Bell Rock	1958	$20

JIV-A-TONES, THE
FELSTED

❏ 8506	Flirty Gertie/Fire Engine Baby	1958	$70

JIVE BOMBERS, THE
SAVOY

❏ 1508	Bad Boy/When Your Hair Has Turned to Silver	1957	$30
❏ 1513	If I Had a Talking Picture of You/The Blues Don't Mean a Thing	1957	$30
❏ 1560	Star Dust/You Give Your Love to Me	1959	$30

Number	Title	Yr	NM

JIVE FIVE, THE
AMBIENT SOUND
452	Are You Lonesome Tonight/ Happier Than Before	1985	$6
03053	Hey Sam/Don't Believe Him Donna	1982	$5
02742	Magic Maker, Music Maker/ Oh Baby	1982	$5

AVCO
4568	Come Down in Time/Love Is Pain	1971	$6
4589	Follow the Lamb/Lay Lady Lay	1972	$6
4589	Follow the Lamb/Let the Feeling Belong	1972	$6

BELTONE
2019	Hully Gully Calling Time/No, Not Again	1962	$30
2030	Lily Marlene/Johnny Never Knew	1963	$30
1006	My True Story/When I Was Single	1961	$40
2034	She's My Girl/Rain	1963	$30
2029	These Golden Rings/Do You Hear Wedding Bells	1962	$30
2024	What Time Is It?/Beggin' You Please	1962	$30

BRUT
| 814 | All I Ever Do Is Dream About You/Super Woman (Part 2) | 1973 | $6 |

DECCA
| 32671 | (If You Let Me Make Love to You) Why Can't I Touch You/You Showed Me the Light of Love | 1970 | $8 |
| 32736 | I Want You to Be My Baby/ Give Me Just a Chance | 1970 | $8 |

MUSICOR
| 1250 | Crying Like a Baby/You'll Fall in Love | 1967 | $50 |
| 1305 | Sugar (Don't Take Away My Candy)/Blues in the Ghetto | 1968 | $15 |

UNITED ARTISTS
| 50004 | Goin' Wild/Main Street | 1966 | $30 |
| 0100 | I'm a Happy Man/It Will Stand | 1973 | $5 |
— Silver Spotlight Series" reissue; B-side by The Showmen
853	I'm a Happy Man/Kiss Kiss Kiss	1965	$30
50033	In My Neighborhood/Then Came Heartbreak	1966	$60
936	Please Baby Please/A Bench in the Park	1965	$30

JIVERS, THE
ALADDIN
| 3329 | Cherie/Little Mama | 1956 | $160 |

JO ANN AND TROY
ATLANTIC
| 2293 | Same Old Feeling/Just Because | 1965 | $20 |
| 2256 | Who Do You Love/I Found a Love, Oh What a Love | 1964 | $20 |

JODIMARS, THE
CAPITOL
F3588	Clarabella/Midnight	1956	$30
F3633	Cloud 99/Later	1957	$30
F3360	Dancin' the Bop/Boom Boom My Bayou Baby	1956	$30
F3436	Lotsa Love/Rattle My Bones	1956	$30
F3285	Well Now -- Dig This/Let's All Rock Together	1955	$30

PRESIDENT
| 1017 | Shoo-Sue/Story-Telling Baby | 1957 | $30 |

JOE & EDDIE
CAPITOL
F4209	Green Grass/And I Believe	1959	$10
F4288	Take My Hand/Remember Me	1959	$10
F4149	The Fox/Lonesome Road	1959	$10

GNP CRESCENDO
305	Children Go/I Laid Around	1963	$8
344	Depend On Yourself/With You in Mind	1965	$6
321	Frankie and Johnny Blues/ Gonna Build a Mountain	1964	$6
324	Goodnight Irene/Pearly Shells	1964	$6
338	He's Got the Whole World in His Hands/Gabrielle	1965	$6
185	I Got Shoes/Water Boy	1962	$8
355	I Got You (I've Got Everything)/Petticoat White (Summer Blue Sky)	1965	$6
353	It Ain't Me Babe/Walkin' Down the Line	1965	$6
333	Lonesome Road/Tear Down the Walls	1964	$6
195	Lonesome Traveler/There's a Meetin' Here Tonight	1963	$8

366	Michael, Row the Boat Ashore/That Was the Last Thing on My Mind	1965	$6
306	What's That I Hear/Farewell My Cindy Jane	1963	$8
316	Wild Is the Wind/Swing Down Chariot	1964	$6

JOEL, BILLY
COLUMBIA
| CNR-03426 | Allentown/(B-side blank) | 1982 | $8 |
— One-sided budget release
38-03413	Allentown/Elvis Presley Blvd.	1982	$4
38-03413 [PS]	Allentown/Elvis Presley Blvd.	1982	$4
38-06108	A Matter of Trust/Getting Closer	1986	$3
38-04259	An Innocent Man/I'll Cry Instead	1983	$3
38-04259 [PS]	An Innocent Man/I'll Cry Instead	1983	$4
13-08416	An Innocent Man/I'll Cry Instead	1988	$3
— Reissue
| 38-06994 | Baby Grand/Big Man on Mulberry Street | 1987 | $3 |
— A-side with Ray Charles
| 38-06994 [PS] | Baby Grand/Big Man on Mulberry Street | 1987 | $3 |
| 38-07626 [DJ] | Back in the U.S.S.R.//Back in the U.S.S.R./The Times They Are a-Changin' | 1987 | $12 |
— Promo-only coupling; white label
| 38-07626 [PS] | Back in the U.S.S.R.//Back in the U.S.S.R./The Times They Are a-Changin' | 1987 | $20 |
— Promo-only picture sleeve for promo-only coupling; "Demonstration--Not for Sale" on upper right rear corner of sleeve
38-07626	Back in the U.S.S.R./Big Shot	1987	$3
38-07626 [PS]	Back in the U.S.S.R./Big Shot	1987	$4
3-10913	Big Shot/Root Beer Rag	1979	$4
1-11331	Don't Ask Me Why/C'etait Toi (You Were the One)	1980	$3
1-11331 [PS]	Don't Ask Me Why/C'etait Toi (You Were the One)	1980	$6
38-03780	Goodnight Saigon/A Room of Our Own	1983	$4
38-03780 [PS]	Goodnight Saigon/A Room of Our Own	1983	$4
13-03241	Honesty/Sometimes a Fantasy	1982	$3
— Reissue
3-10959	Honesty/The Mexican Connection	1979	$4
38-73091	I Go to Extremes/When in Rome	1989	$3
13-03238	It's Still Rock and Roll to Me/ Don't Ask Me Why	1982	$3
— Reissue
1-11276	It's Still Rock and Roll to Me/ Through the Long Night	1980	$4
1-11276 [PS]	It's Still Rock and Roll to Me/ Through the Long Night	1980	$6
38-04514	Leave a Tender Moment Alone/This Night	1984	$3
38-04514 [PS]	Leave a Tender Moment Alone/This Night	1984	$4
13-08418	Leave a Tender Moment Alone/This Night	1988	$3
— Reissue
3-10708	Movin' Out (Anthony's Song)/Everybody Has a Dream	1978	$4
3-10624	Movin' Out (Anthony's Song)/She's Always a Woman	1977	$15
3-10853	My Life/52nd Street	1978	$4
3-10750	Only the Good Die Young/ Get It Right the First Time	1978	$5
4-45963	Piano Man/You're My Home	1973	$8
CNR-03321	Pressure/(B-side blank)	1982	$8
— One-sided budget release (large hole)
38-03244	Pressure/Laura	1982	$4
38-03244 [PS]	Pressure/Laura	1982	$4
3-10562	Say Goodbye to Hollywood/ I've Loved These Days	1977	$10
18-02518	Say Goodbye to Hollywood/ Summer, Highland Falls	1981	$4
18-02518 [PS]	Say Goodbye to Hollywood/ Summer, Highland Falls	1981	$4
3-10788	She's Always a Woman/ Vienna	1978	$4
18-02628	She's Got a Way/The Ballad of Billy the Kid	1981	$4
18-02628 [PS]	She's Got a Way/The Ballad of Billy the Kid	1981	$4
1-11379	Sometimes a Fantasy/All for Leyna	1980	$5
1-11379 [PS]	Sometimes a Fantasy/All for Leyna	1980	$8
38-04012 [PS]	Tell Her About It	1983	
— Demonstration -- Not for Sale" on sleeve
| 38-04012 | Tell Her About It/Easy Money | 1983 | $3 |
| 38-04012 [PS] | Tell Her About It/Easy Money | 1983 | $4 |

| 13-08415 | Tell Her About It/Easy Money | 1988 | $3 |
— Reissue
3-10064	The Entertainer/The Mexican Connection	1974	$8
38-04400	The Longest Time/Christie Lee	1984	$3
38-04400 [PS]	The Longest Time/Christie Lee	1984	$4
13-08417	The Longest Time/Christie Lee	1988	$3
— Reissue
38-07664	The Times They Are a-Changin'/Back in the U.S.S.R.	1987	$4
38-06526	This Is the Time/Code of Silence	1986	$3
38-06526 [PS]	This Is the Time/Code of Silence	1986	$3
3-10015	Travelin' Prayer/Ain't No Crime	1974	$10
38-73021	We Didn't Start the Fire/ House of Blue Light	1989	$3
4-46055	Worse Comes to Worst/ Somewhere Along the Line	1974	$10

EPIC
| 34-06118 | Modern Woman/Sleeping with the Television On | 1986 | $3 |
| 34-06118 [PS] | Modern Woman/Sleeping with the Television On | 1986 | $4 |

FAMILY PRODUCTIONS
| 0900 | She's Got a Way/Everybody Loves You Now | 1971 | $40 |
| 0906 | Tomorrow Is Today/ Everybody Loves You Now | 1971 | $40 |

JOEY AND DANNY
SWAN
| 4276 | Santa's Got a Brand New Bag/Rats in My Room | 1967 | $30 |

JOEY AND THE CONTINENTALS
CLARIDGE
| 304 | She Rides with Me/Rudy Vahoo | 1966 | $30 |
— Reissued on Claridge 312 as "The G.T.O.'s

LAURIE
| 3294 | Sad Girl/Baby | 1965 | $30 |

JOEY AND THE LEXINGTONS
COMET
| 2154 | Heaven/The Girl I Love | 1962 | $200 |
DUNES
| 2029 | Bobbie/Tears from My Eyes | 1963 | $125 |

JOEY AND THE TEENAGERS
COLUMBIA
| 42054 | What's On Your Mind/The Draw | 1961 | $100 |

JOHN, ELTON, AND KIKI DEE
ROCKET
| 40585 | Don't Go Breakin' My Heart/ Snow Queen | 1976 | $4 |
| 40585 [PS] | Don't Go Breakin' My Heart/ Snow Queen | 1976 | $5 |

JOHN, ELTON, AND MILLIE JACKSON
GEFFEN
| 28956 | Act of War, Part 1/Act of War, Part 2 | 1985 | $4 |
| 28956 [PS] | Act of War, Part 1/Act of War, Part 2 | 1985 | $4 |

JOHN, ELTON
CONGRESS
6022 [DJ]	Border Song/Bad Side of the Moon	1970	$40
6022	Border Song/Bad Side of the Moon	1970	$60
6017 [DJ]	Lady Samantha/It's Me That You Need	1970	$40
6017	Lady Samantha/It's Me That You Need	1970	$60

DJM
| 70008 [DJ] | Lady Samantha/All Across the Havens | 1969 | $125 |
| 70008 | Lady Samantha/All Across the Havens | 1969 | $300 |

GEFFEN
29846	Ball & Chain/Where Have All the Good Times Gone?	1982	$4
29954	Blue Eyes/Hey Papa Legba	1982	$4
29954 [PS]	Blue Eyes/Hey Papa Legba	1982	$5
49788 [DJ]	Chloe//Fanfare/Chloe	1981	$8
— B-side of this promo-only single is full-length version
| 49788 | Chloe/Tortured | 1981 | $4 |
| 50049 | Empty Garden (Hey Hey Johnny)/Take Me Down to the Ocean | 1982 | $4 |

Number	Title	Yr	NM
❑ 50049 [PS]	Empty Garden (Hey Hey Johnny)/Take Me Down to the Ocean	1982	$5
❑ 50049 [DJ]	Empty Garden (LP version)/ Empty Garden (Edit)	1982	$8
❑ 28578	Heartache All Over the World/Highlander	1986	$3
❑ 28578 [PS]	Heartache All Over the World/Highlander	1986	$3
❑ 29460	I Guess That's Why They Call It the Blues/The Retreat	1983	$3
❑ 29460 [PS]	I Guess That's Why They Call It the Blues/The Retreat	1983	$3
❑ 29639	I'm Still Standing/Love So Cold	1983	$3
❑ 29639 [PS]	I'm Still Standing/Love So Cold	1983	$3
❑ 29111	In Neon/Tactics	1984	$3
❑ 29292	Sad Songs (Say So Much)/A Simple Man	1984	$3
❑ 7-29292 [DJ]	Sad Songs (Say So Much) (Special Radio Mix) (same on both sides)	1984	$10

—Contains a 4:05 mix unavailable elsewhere; label has "RE-1" on both sides

❑ 29189	Who Wears These Shoes?/ Lonely Boy	1984	$3
❑ 29189 [PS]	Who Wears These Shoes?/ Lonely Boy	1984	$3
❑ 28873	Wrap Her Up/The Man Who Never Died	1985	$3
❑ 28873 [PS]	Wrap Her Up/The Man Who Never Died	1985	$3

MCA

❑ 53408	A Word in Spanish/Heavy Traffic	1988	$3
❑ 53408 [PS]	A Word in Spanish/Heavy Traffic	1988	$3
❑ 40198	Bennie and the Jets/ Harmony	1974	$5
❑ 53196	Candle in the Wind/Sorry Seems to Be the Hardest Word	1987	$3
❑ 53196 [PS]	Candle in the Wind/Sorry Seems to Be the Hardest Word	1987	$4

—White sleeve

❑ 53196 [PS]	Candle in the Wind/Sorry Seems to Be the Hardest Word	1987	$3

—Yellow sleeve with album jackets pictured on back

❑ 40000	Crocodile Rock/Elderberry Wine	1972	$6

—Original pressings have a solid black label

❑ 40046	Daniel/Skyline Pigeon	1973	$5
❑ 40259	Don't Let the Sun Go Down on Me/Sick City	1974	$5
❑ 40892	Ego/Flinstone Boy	1978	$4
❑ 40892 [PS]	Ego/Flinstone Boy	1978	$12
❑ 40148	Goodbye Yellow Brick Road/ Young Man's Blues	1973	$5
❑ 40505	Grow Some Funk of Your Own/I Feel Like a Bullet (in the Gun of Robert Ford)	1976	$4
❑ 53692	Healing Hands/Dancing in the End Zone	1989	$3
❑ 53345	I Don't Wanna Go On with You Like That/Rope Around a Fool	1988	$3
❑ 53345 [PS]	I Don't Wanna Go On with You Like That/Rope Around a Fool	1988	$3
❑ 40461	Island Girl/Sugar on the Floor	1975	$4
❑ 41236	Little Jeannie/Conquer the Sun	1980	$4

—Originals have a colorful custom label

❑ 41236 [PS]	Little Jeannie/Conquer the Sun	1980	$5
❑ S45-1938 [DJ]	Love Song (Long)/(Short)	1976	$30

—Promo-only release from the Here And There live album

❑ 40344	Lucy in the Sky with Diamonds/One Day at a Time	1974	$5

—Both sides feature "Dr. Winston O'Boogie" (John Lennon)

❑ 40344 [PS]	Lucy in the Sky with Diamonds/One Day at a Time	1974	$10
❑ 41042	Mama Can't Buy You Love/ Three Way Love Affair	1979	$4
❑ 41042 [PS]	Mama Can't Buy You Love/ Three Way Love Affair	1979	$4
❑ 40973	Part-Time Love/I Cry at Night	1978	$4
❑ 40973 [PS]	Part-Time Love/I Cry at Night	1978	$4
❑ 40364	Philadelphia Freedom/I Saw Her Standing There	1975	$5

—B-side features John Lennon

❑ 40364 [PS]	Philadelphia Freedom/I Saw Her Standing There	1975	$6
❑ 40364 [PS]	Philadelphia Freedom/I Saw Her Standing There	1975	$50

—Promo-only sleeve for radio in Philadelphia

❑ 53750	Sacrifice/Love Is a Cannibal	1989	$3
❑ 41293	(Sartorial Eloquence) Don't Ya Wanna Play This Game No More?//Cartier/White Man Danger	1980	$4

Number	Title	Yr	NM
❑ 40105	Saturday Night's Alright for Fighting//Jack Rabbit/ Whenever You're Ready	1973	$5
❑ 40421	Someone Saved My Life Tonight/House of Cards	1975	$5

—Original copies have "Captain Fantastic" label

❑ 40421	Someone Saved My Life Tonight/House of Cards	1975	$4

—With MCA black/rainbow label

❑ 40993 [DJ]	Song for Guy/Lovesick	1979	$5
❑ 40993 [PS]	Song for Guy/Lovesick	1979	$5
❑ 40993	Song for Guy/Lovesick	1979	$12

—The stock copy is much scarcer than the promo, the only Elton John MCA single where this is the case.

❑ 65018	Step Into Christmas/Ho! Ho! Ho! (Who'd Be a Turkey at Christmas)	1973	$5

—Originals have black labels with rainbow

❑ 65018	Step Into Christmas/Ho! Ho! Ho! (Who'd Be a Turkey at Christmas)	1978	$4

—Second edition: Tan label

❑ 65018	Step Into Christmas/Ho! Ho! Ho! (Who'd Be a Turkey at Christmas)	1980	$3

—Third edition: Blue label with rainbow

❑ 53260	Take Me to the Pilot/Tonight	1988	$4
❑ 53260 [PS]	Take Me to the Pilot/Tonight	1988	$4
❑ 40297	The Bitch Is Back/Cold Highway	1974	$5

POLYDOR

❑ PRO-002	Pinball Wizard/Acid Queen	1975	$50

—Promo-only release; B-side by Tina Turner

ROCKET

❑ 40677	Bite Your Lip (Get up and dance!)/Chameleon	1977	$4
❑ EJS3 [PS]	Cold As Christmas (In the Middle of the Year)/Crystal	1983	$5

—U.K. import; also came in a "double pack" with the Elton John/Kiki Dee single Don't Go Breakin' My Heart/Snow Queen (add $5 NM)

❑ EJS3	Cold As Christmas (In the Middle of the Year)/Crystal	1983	$5

—U.K. import

❑ 40645	Sorry Seems to Be the Hardest Word/Shoulder Holster	1976	$4

UNI

❑ 55246	Border Song/Bad Side of the Moon	1970	$6
❑ 55277	Friends/Honey Roll	1971	$6
❑ 55343	Honky Cat/Slave	1972	$6
❑ 55314	Levon/Goodbye	1971	$6
❑ 55318 [DJ]	Tiny Dancer/Razor Face	1971	$10

—With a severely truncated version of the A-side

❑ 55318	Tiny Dancer/Razor Face	1971	$6

—Stock copies have full-length version of A-side

VIKING

❑ 1010 [DJ]	From Denver to L.A. (same on both sides)	1970	$30

—Credited to "Elton Johns"; B-side by The Barbara Moore Singers; the promo version of this has been counterfeited

❑ 1010	From Denver to L.A./Warm Summer Rain	1970	$70

—Credited to "Elton Johns"; B-side by The Barbara Moore Singers

7-Inch Extended Plays

MCA

❑ 34961	Daniel/Teacher I Need You//High Flying Bird/Crocodile Rock	1973	$20

—Jukebox issue; small hole, plays at 33 1/3 rpm

❑ 34961 [PS]	Don't Shoot Me I'm Only the Piano Player	1973	$20

—Part of "Little LP" series (LLP #207)

UNI

❑ 1903 [DJ]	Come Down in Time/ Country Comfort//Amoreena/Love Song	1971	$20

—Jukebox issue; small hole, plays at 33 1/3 rpm

❑ 1903 [PS]	Tumbleweed Connection	1971	$20

—Part of Little LP series (LLP 143)

JOHN, LITTLE WILLIE

ATLANTIC

❑ 89189	Fever/Ruby Baby	1987	$3

—B-side by the Drifters

❑ 89189 [PS]	Fever/Ruby Baby	1987	$3

—From the movie "Big Town"

KING

❑ 5886	All Around the World/All My Love Belongs to You	1964	$15
❑ 4818	All Around the World/Don't Leave Me Dear	1955	$30

Number	Title	Yr	NM
❑ 6302	All Around the World/Need Your Love So Bad	1970	$8
❑ 5154	All My Love Belongs to You/ Why Don't You Haul Off and Love Me	1958	$30
❑ 4893	Are You Ever Coming Back/I'm Stickin' with You Baby	1956	$30
❑ 5850	Bill Bailey/My Love Will Never Change	1964	$15
❑ 5681	Doll Face/Big Blue Diamonds	1962	$20
❑ 5717	Don't Play with Love/Heaven All Around Me	1963	$15
❑ 5949	Do Something for Me/Don't You Know I'm in Love	1964	$15
❑ 4960	Do Something for Me/My Nerves	1956	$30
❑ 5641	Every Beat of My Heart/I Wish I Could Cry	1962	$20
❑ 5591	Fever/Bo-Da-Ley Dino-Ley	1962	$20
❑ 4935	Fever/Letter from My Darling	1956	$40
❑ 6170	Fever/Let Them Talk	1968	$10
❑ 5356	Heartbreak (It's Hurtin' Me)/Do You Love Me	1960	$30
❑ 5342	I'm Shakin'/Cottage for Sale	1960	$125
❑ 5458	I'm Sorry/The Very Thought of You	1961	$20
❑ 4989	I've Been Around/Suffering with the Blues	1956	$30
❑ 5503	(I've Got) Spring Fever/ Flamingo	1961	$20
❑ 5045	I've Got to Go Cry/Look What You've Done to Me	1957	$30
❑ 5452	Leave My Kitten Alone/I'll Never Go Back on My Word	1961	$30
❑ 5219	Leave My Kitten Alone/Let Nobody Love You	1959	$30
❑ 5142	Let's Rock While the Rockin's Good/You're a Sweetheart	1958	$30
❑ 5274	Let Them Talk/Right There	1959	$30
❑ 5799	Let Them Talk/Talk to Me	1963	$15
❑ 5023	Love, Life and Money/You Got to Get Up Early in the Morning	1957	$30
❑ 5318	Loving Care/My Love Is	1960	$30
❑ 5179	Made for Me/Do More in Life	1959	$30
❑ 5744	My Baby's in Love with Another Guy/Come On Sugar	1963	$15
❑ 5823	Person to Person/I'm Shakin'	1963	$50
❑ 5091	Person to Person/Until You Do	1957	$30
❑ 5667	She Thinks I Still Care/Come Back to Me	1962	$20
❑ 5394	Sleep/There's a Difference	1960	$30
❑ 5818	So Lovely/Inside Information	1963	$15
❑ 5516	Take My Love (I Want to Give It All to You)/Now You Know	1961	$20
❑ 5108	Talk to Me, Talk to Me/Spasms	1958	$30
❑ 6003	Talk to Me/Take My Love	1965	$10
❑ 5147	Tell It Like It Is/Don't Be Ashamed to Call My Name	1958	$30
❑ 5602	The Masquerade Is Over/ Katanga	1962	$20
❑ 5577	There Is Someone in This World for Me/Autumn Leaves	1961	$20
❑ 5428/30 [DJ]	Walk Slow/The Hoochi Coochi	1960	$30

—White label; B-side by Hank Ballard and the Midnighters

❑ 5428	Walk Slow/You Hurt Me	1960	$20
❑ 5003	Will the Sun Shine Tomorrow/A Little Bit of Loving	1956	$30
❑ 5694	Without a Friend/Half a Love	1962	$20

7-Inch Extended Plays

❑ EP-423	*Talk to Me, Talk to Me/You're a Sweetheart/Fever/Tell It Like It Is	1958	$250
❑ EP-423 [PS]	Talk to Me	1958	$250

JOHN, MABLE

MOTOWN

❑ 54031	Who Wouldn't Love a Man Like That/You Made a Fool Out of Me	1960	$500

—Mispress with wrong label; may have been promo only

STAX

❑ 249	Don't Get Caught/Able Mable	1968	$30
❑ 234	Don't Hit Me No More/Left Over Love	1967	$30
❑ 205	If You Give Up What You Got/ You're Taking Up Another Man's Place	1967	$30
❑ 225	I'm a Big Girl Now/Wait You Dog	1967	$30
❑ 215	Same Time, Same Place/ Bigger and Better	1967	$30

TAMLA

❑ 54050	Take Me/Action Speaks Louder Than Words	1962	$500
❑ 54081	Who Wouldn't Love a Man Like That/Say You'll Never Let Me Go	1963	$200
❑ 54031	Who Wouldn't Love a Man Like That/You Made a Fool Out of Me	1960	$200

JOHN, ROBERT

A&M

❑ 1341	I'm Gonna Be Strong/I Don't Want to Make You Love Me	1972	$5
❑ 1210	When the Party Is Over/ Raindrops, Love and Sunshine	1970	$5

Number	Title	Yr	NM

ARIOLA AMERICA

Number	Title	Yr	NM
❑ 7693	Poor Side of Town/Give a Little More	1978	$4

ATLANTIC

Number	Title	Yr	NM
❑ 2884	Hushabye/To Touch, To Feel	1972	$5
❑ 2846	The Lion Sleeps Tonight (Wimoweh) (Mbube)/Janet	1971	$6
❑ 2906	The Way You Do the Things You Do/To Touch, To Feel	1972	$5

BIG TOP

Number	Title	Yr	NM
❑ 3008	Betty Blue Eyes/Pajama Party	1958	$50

— As "Bobby Pedrick, Jr."

Number	Title	Yr	NM
❑ 3024	My Private Joy/Summer Nights	1959	$50

— As "Bobby Pedrick, Jr."

Number	Title	Yr	NM
❑ 3004	White Bucks and Saddle Shoes/Stranded	1958	$60

— As "Bobby Pedrick, Jr."

COLUMBIA

Number	Title	Yr	NM
❑ 44697	Can't Stop Loving You/Thirteen Times	1968	$15
❑ 44639	Don't Leave Me/Children	1968	$8
❑ 44435	If You Don't Want My Love/Don't Go	1968	$8
❑ 44706	Ooh Baby Baby/Children	1968	$8
❑ 44950	Who Could Ever Believe It/Children in the Making	1969	$8

DUEL

Number	Title	Yr	NM
❑ 516	Dining and Dancing/Two Ton Tessie	1962	$30

— As "Bobby Pedrick, Jr."

Number	Title	Yr	NM
❑ 525	If I Had My Life to Live Over/If Mary Only Knew	1963	$30

— As "Bobby Pedrick, Jr."

Number	Title	Yr	NM
❑ 504	That Girl Is You/I'm Scared	1962	$30

— As "Bobby Pedrick, Jr."

EMI AMERICA

Number	Title	Yr	NM
❑ 8049	Hey There Lonely Girl/You Could Have Told Me	1980	$4
❑ 8030	Lonely Eyes/Dance the Night Away	1979	$4
❑ 8013	Only Time/That's What Keeps Us Together	1979	$4
❑ 8015	Sad Eyes/Am I Ever Gonna Hold You	1979	$4
❑ 8061	Sherry/On My Own	1980	$4
❑ 8023	Stay a Little Longer/Only Time	1979	$4

MGM

Number	Title	Yr	NM
❑ 13384	Don't Try to Change My Ways/(I Have to) Teach Myself How to Cry	1965	$20

— As "Bobby Pedrick"

MOSAIC

Number	Title	Yr	NM
❑ 04445	Greased Lightning/(Instrumental)	1984	$3

MOTOWN

Number	Title	Yr	NM
❑ 1664	Bread and Butter/If You Don't Want My Love	1983	$3

SHELL

Number	Title	Yr	NM
❑ 722	School Crush/Come Out, Come Out	1960	$30

— As "Bobby Pedrick"

VERVE

Number	Title	Yr	NM
❑ 10402	Maybe/Karine	1966	$60

— As "Bobby Pedrick"

JOHN'S CHILDREN

WHITE WHALE

Number	Title	Yr	NM
❑ 239	Strange Affair/Smashed, Blocked	1966	$30

JOHNNIE AND JACK

DECCA

Number	Title	Yr	NM
❑ 31423	36-22-36/What Do You Think of Her Now	1962	$15
❑ 31472	Bye, Bye Love/I Overlooked an Orchid	1963	$15
❑ 31255	I'm Always By Myself/When I'm Alone	1961	$15
❑ 31289	Let My Heart Be Broken/Uncle John's Bongos	1961	$15
❑ 31517	Love Problems/Smiles and Tears	1963	$15
❑ 31397	Slow Poison/You'll Never Get a Better Chance Than This	1962	$15
❑ 31361	The Moon Is High and So Am I/Sweet Baby	1962	$15

RCA VICTOR

Number	Title	Yr	NM
❑ 47-6857	All the Time/Pleasure Not a Habit in Mexico	1957	$30
❑ 47-5427	Angels Rock Me to Sleep/When the Saviour Reached Down	1953	$30
❑ 47-4389	Ashes of Love/You Tried to Ruin My Name	1951	$30
❑ 47-5649	Borrowed Diamonds/But I Love You Just the Same	1954	$30
❑ 47-5581	Cheated Out of Love/Love Trap	1954	$30
❑ 47-7799	Country Music Has Gone to Town/Talkin' Eyes	1960	$20
❑ 48-0478	Cryin' Heart Blues/How Can I Believe You	1951	$30
❑ 47-5040	Don't Let the Stars Get in Your Eyes/The Only One I Ever Loved, I Lost	1952	$30
❑ 48-0160	For Old Time's Sake/I Heard My Saviour Call	1950	$50

— Originals on green vinyl

Number	Title	Yr	NM
❑ 47-5517	From the Manger to the Cross/God Put a Rainbow in the Clouds	1953	$30
❑ 47-5775	Goodnight, Sweetheart, Goodnight/Honey, I Need You	1954	$30
❑ 47-5164	Hank Williams Will Live Forever/Just for Tonight	1953	$40
❑ 47-4251	Hummingbird/Let Your Conscience Be Your Guide	1951	$30
❑ 48-0415	I Can't Tell My Heart That/A Smile on My Lips	1951	$30
❑ 47-5098	I'll Live with God/The Eastern Gate	1952	$30
❑ 47-6594	I Loved You Better Than You Know/Love, Love, Love	1956	$30
❑ 47-7246	I've Seen This Movie Before/Yeah!	1958	$20
❑ 47-6395	I Want to Be Loved/Feet of Clay	1956	$30

— With Ruby Wells

Number	Title	Yr	NM
❑ 47-7324	Lonely Island Pearl/Leave Our Moon Alone	1958	$20
❑ 47-6203	Look Out/So Lovely, Baby	1955	$30
❑ 47-7018	Move It On Over/Love Fever	1957	$30
❑ 47-5681	(Oh Baby Mine) I Get So Lonely/You're Just What the Doctor Ordered	1954	$30
❑ 47-6932	Oh Boy, I Love Her/That's Why I'm Leavin'	1957	$30
❑ 47-5483	Pig Latin Serenade/You're My Downfall	1953	$30
❑ 48-0377	Poison Love/Lonesome	1950	$40

— Originals on green vinyl

Number	Title	Yr	NM
❑ 47-5375	Private Property/Don't Say Goodbye If You Love Me	1953	$30
❑ 47-7545	Sailor Man/Wild and Wicked World	1959	$20
❑ 48-0055	She Went with a Smile/Trials and Tribulations	1949	$50

— Originals on green vinyl

Number	Title	Yr	NM
❑ 48-0323	Shout/Too Far from God	1950	$40

— Originals on green vinyl

Number	Title	Yr	NM
❑ 47-6014	Sincerely/Carry On	1955	$30
❑ 47-4765	Slow Poison/Heart Trouble	1952	$30
❑ 47-6295	S.O.S./Weary Moments	1955	$30
❑ 47-5290	South in New Orleans/Winner of Your Heart	1953	$30
❑ 47-7137	Stop the World (And Let Me Off)/Camel Walk Stroll	1958	$20
❑ 47-7698	Sweetie Pie/Happy Lucky Love	1960	$20
❑ 48-0448	Take My Ring from Your Finger/I'm Gonna Love You One More Time	1951	$30
❑ 47-7402	That's the Way the Cookie Crumbles/Poison Love	1958	$20
❑ 47-6777	The Banana Boat Song/Mr. Clock	1956	$30
❑ 47-4555	Three Ways of Knowing/When You Want a Little Lovin'	1952	$30
❑ 47-6680	Tom Cat's Kittens/Live and Let Live	1956	$30
❑ 47-4949	Two Timing Blues/Gone and Done It Again	1952	$30
❑ 48-0215	What About You/Pray Together	1950	$50

— Originals on green vinyl

Number	Title	Yr	NM
❑ 47-7478	What Do You Know About Heartaches/I Wonder If I Know?	1959	$20

JOHNNIE AND JOE

ABC-PARAMOUNT

Number	Title	Yr	NM
❑ 10079	I Adore You/I Want You Here Beside Me	1960	$20

CHESS

Number	Title	Yr	NM
❑ 1769	Across the Sea/You Said It, And Don't Forget It	1960	$20
❑ 1641	I'll Be Spinning/Feel Alright	1956	$30
❑ 1677	I Was So Lonely/If You Tell Me You're Mine	1957	$30
❑ 1706	My Baby's Gone/Darling	1958	$30
❑ 1654	Over the Mountain; Across the Sea/My Baby's Gone, On, On	1957	$30

— Originals with blue and silver "chess pieces" label

Number	Title	Yr	NM
❑ 1654	Over the Mountain; Across the Sea/My Baby's Gone, On, On	1958	$15

— Reissues on blue labels with vertical "CHESS

Number	Title	Yr	NM
❑ 1654	Over the Mountain; Across the Sea/My Baby's Gone, On, On	1963	$10

— Reissues on other labels (multicolor, black)

Number	Title	Yr	NM
❑ 1693	Why Oh Why/Why Did She Go	1958	$30

GONE

Number	Title	Yr	NM
❑ 5024	Who Do You Love/Trust in Me	1958	$40
❑ 1659	It Was There/There Goes My Heart	1957	$30
❑ 1603	I Was So Lonely/If You Tell Me You're Mine	1957	$30
❑ 1654	Over the Mountain; Across the Sea/My Baby's Gone, On, On	1957	$200

— With horizontal lines on label

Number	Title	Yr	NM
❑ 1654	Over the Mountain; Across the Sea/My Baby's Gone, On, On	1962	$30

— Without horizontal lines on label

Number	Title	Yr	NM
❑ 1008	Over the Mountain (Part 2)/Won't You Come Back to Me	1959	$30
❑ 1630/1	Warm, Soft and Lovely/False Love Has Got to Go	1958	$30
❑ 1701	Where Did She Go/Red Sails in the Sunset	1959	$30
❑ 1605/6	Who Do You Love/Trust in Me	1958	$30

TUFF

Number	Title	Yr	NM
❑ 379	Here We Go Baby/That's the Way You Go	1964	$15

JOHNNY AND JACKEY

ANNA

Number	Title	Yr	NM
❑ 1120	Hoy Boy/No One Else But You	1960	$30
❑ 1108	Let's Go to a Movie Baby/Lonely and Blue	1960	$30

TRI-PHI

Number	Title	Yr	NM
❑ 1019	Baby Don'tcha Worry/Stop What You're Saying	1963	$30
❑ 1002	Carry Your Own Load/So Disappointing	1961	$30
❑ 1016	Do You See My Love for You Growing/Carry Your Own Load	1962	$30
❑ 1005	Someday We'll Be Together/She Don't Play	1961	$40

JOHNNY AND JON

JEWEL

Number	Title	Yr	NM
❑ 776	Christmas in Viet Nam/Why Did You Leave Me Crawl	1966	$40

JOHNNY AND THE HURRICANES

ATILA

Number	Title	Yr	NM
❑ 215	Because I Love You/Wisdom's 5th Take	1967	$12
❑ 211	Saga of the Beatles/Rene	1967	$10

BIG TOP

Number	Title	Yr	NM
❑ 3036	Down Yonder/Sheba	1960	$30
❑ 3036 [PS]	Down Yonder/Sheba	1960	$50
❑ 3103	Misirlou/Salvation	1962	$30
❑ 3076	Old Smokie/High Voltage	1961	$30
❑ 3076 [PS]	Old Smokie/High Voltage	1961	$50
❑ 3113	San Antonio Rose/Come On Train	1962	$30
❑ 3125	Shiek of Araby/Minnesota Fats	1962	$30
❑ 3090	Traffic Jam/Farewell, Farewell	1961	$30
❑ 3132	Whatever Happened to Baby Jane/Greens and Beans	1963	$30

JEFF

Number	Title	Yr	NM
❑ 211	Saga of the Beatles/Rene	1964	$20

MALA

Number	Title	Yr	NM
❑ 470	It's a Mad, Mad, Mad, Mad World/Shadows	1963	$10
❑ 483	That's All/Honey, Honey	1964	$12

TWIRL

Number	Title	Yr	NM
❑ 1001	Crossfire/Lazy	1958	$60

WARWICK

Number	Title	Yr	NM
❑ 520	Beatnik Fly/Sand Storm	1960	$30
❑ 520 [PS]	Beatnik Fly/Sand Storm	1960	$70
❑ 502	Crossfire/Lazy	1959	$30

JOHNNY AND THE JAMMERS

DART

Number	Title	Yr	NM
❑ 131	School Day Blues/You Know I Love You	1959	$300

JOHNNY AND THE TOKENS

WARWICK

Number	Title	Yr	NM
❑ 658	The Taste of a Tear/Never Till Now	1961	$30

Number	Title	Yr	NM

JOHNNY HATES JAZZ
VIRGIN
Number	Title	Yr	NM
☐ 7-99304	I Don't Want to Be a Hero/The Cage	1988	$3
☐ 7-99304 [PS]	I Don't Want to Be a Hero/The Cage	1988	$10
☐ 7-99383	Shattered Dreams/My Secret Garden	1988	$3
☐ 7-99383 [PS]	Shattered Dreams/My Secret Garden	1988	$3
☐ 7-99308	Turn Back the Clock/Cracking Up	1988	$4
☐ 7-99308 [PS]	Turn Back the Clock/Cracking Up	1988	$4

JOHNS, PORTER
DECCA
Number	Title	Yr	NM
☐ 9-46341	Angel of Peace/Each Day I Live I Love You More	1951	$30
☐ 9-46379	This Lonely World/Just a Few	1951	$30

JOHNSON, BETTY
ATLANTIC
Number	Title	Yr	NM
☐ 2019	Does Your Heart Beat for Me?/You and Only You	1959	$15
☐ 1186	Dream/How Much	1958	$15
☐ 2056	Fantastic/You Don't Care a Rowboat	1960	$15
☐ 2002	Hoopa Hoola/One More Time	1958	$15
☐ 1169	The Little Blue Man/Winter in Miami	1958	$20
☐ 2039	The Lonely Willow Tree/Waltz Me Around	1959	$15

BALLY
Number	Title	Yr	NM
☐ 1013	Clay Idol/Why Do You Cry?	1956	$15
☐ 1005	Honky Tonk Rock/Say It Ain't So, Joe	1956	$20
☐ 1020	I Dreamed/If It's Wrong to Love You	1956	$15
☐ 1000	I'll Wait/Please Tell Me Why	1956	$15
☐ 1033	Little White Lies/1492	1957	$15
☐ 1041	The Song You Heard When You Fell in Love/I'm Beginning to Wonder	1957	$15

BELL
Number	Title	Yr	NM
☐ 1074	Make Yourself Comfortable/All of You	1955	$20

— May or may not be the same Betty Johnson as the others

COED
Number	Title	Yr	NM
☐ 532	There's a Star Spangled Banner Waving Somewhere/Take a Little Look (In the Good Book)	1960	$10

DOT
Number	Title	Yr	NM
☐ 16127	Slipping Around/One Has My Name, The Other Has My Heart	1960	$12

NEW-DISC
Number	Title	Yr	NM
☐ 10013	I Want Eddie Fisher For Christmas/Show Me	1954	$30

RCA VICTOR
Number	Title	Yr	NM
☐ 47-8143	Betty's Bossa Nova/Ginny's Got a Phone	1963	$8
☐ 47-6268	I'm a Sinner/Beginner's Luck	1955	$15
☐ 47-6034	Seven Pretty Dreams/Be a Lover	1955	$15
☐ 47-6158	That's Happiness/Give Me Something I Can Dream About	1955	$15

REPUBLIC
Number	Title	Yr	NM
☐ 2011	Depend on Me/I Don't Want to Go to Sleep Tonight	1961	$12
☐ 2025	How Do You Tell Your Heart/Why, Why	1961	$10
☐ 2026	I Dreamed/Luna Caprese	1962	$10
☐ 2017	Let Me Be the One/Only When I Dream	1961	$12
☐ 2021	My Kind of Guy/A Gal's Best Friend Is Her Makeup	1961	$10

WORLD ARTISTS
Number	Title	Yr	NM
☐ 1014	Wednesday's Child/What's the Matter	1963	$8

JOHNSON, BILL
SUN
Number	Title	Yr	NM
☐ 340	Bobaloo/Bad Times Ahead	1960	$30

JOHNSON BROTHERS, THE
IMPERIAL
Number	Title	Yr	NM
☐ 5550	Love Ain't Got a Thing/Find Another Heart	1958	$30

JOHNSON, BUBBER
KING
Number	Title	Yr	NM
☐ 5014	Butterfly/Too Many Hearts	1957	$30
☐ 4822	Come Home/There'll Be No One	1955	$30
☐ 4988	Confidential/Let's Take a Walk	1956	$30
☐ 5068	Crazy Afternoon/So Much Tonight	1957	$30

Number	Title	Yr	NM
☐ 5117	Dedicated to the One I Love/Prince of Players	1958	$20
☐ 4793	Drop Me a Line/Ding Dang Doo	1955	$30
☐ 5132	Finger Tips/I'm Confessin'	1958	$20
☐ 5193	House of Love/Until Sunrise	1959	$20
☐ 5148	I Can't See Why/As Long As I Live	1958	$20
☐ 5232	I Do (Love You)/Come On	1959	$20
☐ 5143	I Surrender Dear/Everybody's With You When You're Winning	1959	$20
☐ 4855	It's Christmas Time/Let's Make Everyday a Christmas Day	1955	$30
☐ 5034	Little Girls Don't Cry/The Search	1957	$30
☐ 5089	Muddy Water/The Whisperers	1957	$30
☐ 4939	My Lonely Heart/Have a Little Faith in Me	1956	$30
☐ 4924	My One Desire/I Lost Track of Everything	1956	$30
☐ 5174	One Good Reason/Time Was	1959	$20
☐ 5267	Tell Me Who/I Know My Way	1959	$20
☐ 5298	Those Who Dream/Atlanta	1959	$20
☐ 4872	Wonderful Things Happen/Keep a Light in the Window	1956	$30

MERCURY
Number	Title	Yr	NM
☐ 8285	I've Got an Invitation/Forget It If You Can	1952	$70

JOHNSON, BUDDY & ELLA
MERCURY
Number	Title	Yr	NM
☐ 70377	Ain't Cha Got Me/Let's Start All Over Again	1954	$30
☐ 70421	Any Day Now/A Pretty Girl, a Cadillac and Money	1954	$30
☐ 70912	Bring It Home to Me/You Got It Made	1956	$15
☐ 70523	Crazy 'Bout a Saxophone/Gotta Go Upside Your Head	1955	$20
☐ 70775	Doot Doot Dow/I Don't Want Nobody	1956	$15
☐ 71723	I Don't Want Nobody (To Have My Love But You)/I'm Just Your Fool	1960	$10
☐ 70251	I'm Just Your Fool/A-12	1953	$30
☐ 70321	One More Time/Mush Mouth	1954	$30
☐ 70459	We'll Do It/It Used to Hurt Me	1954	$30

ROULETTE
Number	Title	Yr	NM
☐ 4134	Tune No. 1/Don't Fail Me Baby	1959	$15

JOHNSON, BUDDY
ATLANTIC
Number	Title	Yr	NM
☐ 1013	Don't Take Your Love from Me/Off Shore	1953	$30

DECCA
Number	Title	Yr	NM
☐ 29058	A Handful of Stars/Two Cigarettes in the Dark	1954	$30
☐ 28907	Talkin' About Another Man's Wife/Jeannette	1953	$30

MERCURY
Number	Title	Yr	NM
☐ 70488	I Never Had It So Good/There's No One Like You	1954	$20
☐ 70695	It's Obdacious/Save Your Love for Me	1955	$20
☐ 71159	I've Surrendered/Slide's Mambo	1957	$15
☐ 71262	Minglin'/I Wonder Where Our Love Has Gone	1958	$15
☐ 70656	Send Out for a Bottle of Beer/Bitter Sweet	1955	$20
☐ 71799	The Last Laugh's on You (Ha, Ha, Baby)/Good Time Man	1961	$10
☐ 71017	Why Don't Cha Stop It/Kool Kitty	1956	$15

WING
Number	Title	Yr	NM
☐ 90074	Buddy's Boogie/I'll Dearly Love You	1956	$20
☐ 90064	Doot Doot Dow/I Don't Want Nobody	1956	$20
☐ 90084	Goodbye Baby/I Still Love You	1956	$20

JOHNSON, CHARLES
ALSTON
Number	Title	Yr	NM
☐ 3751	Baby I Cried, Cried, Cried/Never Had a Love So Good	1980	$700
☐ 3751 [DJ]	Baby I Cried, Cried, Cried (stereo/mono)	1980	$60

DASH
Number	Title	Yr	NM
☐ 5065	Good Good Lovin'/Don't Lose That Groove	1980	$125

JOHNSON, CLIFF
COLUMBIA
Number	Title	Yr	NM
☐ 40865	Go 'Way Hound Dog/Twenty Four Hours a Day	1957	$100

JOHNSON, ERNIE
ARTCO
Number	Title	Yr	NM
☐ 45-104	I Can't Stand the Pain/These Very Tender Moments	1967	$1500

ASNES
Number	Title	Yr	NM
☐ 104	Tell Her For Me/You Need Love	1961	$30

RONN
Number	Title	Yr	NM
☐ 109	Cold Woman/Party All Night	1984	$10
☐ 102	Mouth to Mouth Resuscitation/You're Gonna Miss Me	1984	$6

JOHNSON FAMILY, THE
COLUMBIA
Number	Title	Yr	NM
☐ 4-21308	His Love Is Mine/My Home Sweet Home	1954	$30
☐ 4-21251	The Old Family Circle/I'd Like to Feel at Home	1954	$30

JOHNSON, HERB
LEN
Number	Title	Yr	NM
☐ 1007	Have You Heard/Guilty	1960	$40

PALM
Number	Title	Yr	NM
☐ 301	Help/(B-side unknown)	1959	$300

JOHNSON, HOYT
ERWIN
Number	Title	Yr	NM
☐ 555	Eeny Meany Minie Mo/(B-side unknown)	1957	$200

RCA VICTOR
Number	Title	Yr	NM
☐ 47-7607	Little Boy Blue/My Special Girl	1959	$200
☐ 47-7522	Sylvia/Bella Renee	1959	$50
☐ 47-7731	Too Shy/Eca-La	1960	$50

SATELLITE
Number	Title	Yr	NM
☐ 110	Cindy/I Just Can't Learn	1961	$30

JOHNSON, JIMMY
ALLIGATOR
Number	Title	Yr	NM
☐ 792	Serves Me Right to Suffer/Your Turn to Cry	1979	$4

CLASS
Number	Title	Yr	NM
☐ 237	Cool, Cool School/Lone Ranger Gonna Get Married	1958	$70

RENDEZVOUS
Number	Title	Yr	NM
☐ 145	Cool, Cool School/Lone Ranger Gonna Get Married	1961	$30

VIV
Number	Title	Yr	NM
☐ 3001	How About Me? Pretty Baby/Cat Daddy	1956	$200

JOHNSON, JOE
ABET
Number	Title	Yr	NM
☐ 9417	Santa, Bring My Baby Back/Dirty Woman Blues	1966	$10

JOHNSON, LEN
RAY-CO
Number	Title	Yr	NM
☐ 503	Sweet Thing/One Day	1963	$20

JOHNSON, LOIS
20TH CENTURY
Number	Title	Yr	NM
☐ 2106	Come On In and Let Me Love You/If I Throw Away My Pride	1974	$6
☐ 2223	Hope for the Flowers/Merrily We Love Along	1975	$6
☐ 2151	Loving You Will Never Grow Old/Lonesome Number One	1974	$6
☐ 2242	The Door's Always Open/Bring It On Home	1975	$6

COLUMBIA
Number	Title	Yr	NM
☐ 4-44646	One Drink Farther Away/Paying Dues	1968	$8
☐ 4-44725	Softly and Tenderly/Goin' Down	1968	$8

EMH
Number	Title	Yr	NM
☐ 0030	It Won't Be Easy/You Are the Melody	1984	$5
☐ 0036	Loveshine/Angel in My Arms	1984	$5
☐ 0034	Middle of the Road/Angel in My Arms	1984	$5

EPIC
Number	Title	Yr	NM
☐ 5-10043	Daddy, Don't Hang Up the Pgone/Letters Have No Arms	1966	$8
☐ 5-9898	G.I. Joe/Heaven in My Arms	1966	$10
☐ 5-10238	How Will You Hurt Me Then/To Chicago with Love	1967	$8
☐ 5-10143	Mr. John/Your Second Wedding Day	1967	$8
☐ 5-10316	Tell Me a Lie/Turn On Your Love Light	1968	$8

Number	Title	Yr	NM
POLYDOR			
❏ 14435	All the Love We Threw Away/We Can't Make It Anymore	1977	$5
— With Bill Rice			
❏ 14392	I Hate Goodbyes/I'm Your Friend	1977	$5
❏ 14355	Midnight/I'm Not That Good at Goodbye	1976	$5
❏ 14328	Weep No More My Baby/Birthday Wish	1976	$5
❏ 14476	When I Need You/A Dreamer of Dreams	1978	$5

JOHNSON, LONNIE

Number	Title	Yr	NM
FEDERAL			
❏ 12376	Friendless Blues/What a Real Woman	1960	$20
KING			
❏ 4492	Happy New Year, Darling/Christmas Blues	1951	$60
— B-side by Gatemouth Moore			
❏ 4553	I'm Guilty/Can't Sleep Anymore	1952	$50
❏ 4473	It Was All in Vain/You Only Want Me When You're Lonely	1951	$50
❏ 5907	Love Me Tonight/Brenda	1964	$10
❏ 4510	My Mother's Eyes/My Crazy Self	1951	$50
❏ 4503	Seven Long Days/Darlin'	1951	$50
❏ 4459	Take Me I'm Yours/Why Should I Cry	1951	$50
❏ 6303	Tomorrow Night/Blues Stay Away from Me	1970	$6
❏ 4758	Tomorrow Night/Pleasing You	1954	$50
❏ 5293	Tomorrow Night/Pleasing You	1959	$20
❏ 4201	Tomorrow Night/What a Woman	1951	$70
— 78 released in 1948			
PRESTIGE			
❏ 310	Mr. Jelly Roll Baker/I'll Get Along Somehow	1964	$10
RAMA			
❏ 19	It's Been So Long/Vaya Con Dios	1953	$70
❏ 9	My Woman Is Gone/Don't Make Me Cry Baby	1953	$70
— Black vinyl			
❏ 9	My Woman Is Gone/Don't Make Me Cry Baby	1953	$200
— Red vinyl			
❏ 14	Stick With It Baby/Will You Remember	1953	$70
❏ 20	This Love of Mine/I Love a Dream	1953	$70

JOHNSON, MARV

Number	Title	Yr	NM
GORDY			
❏ 7077	I'll Pick a Rose for My Rose/You Got the Love I Love	1968	$20
❏ 7042	Why Do You Want to Let Me Go/I'm Not a Plaything	1965	$20
KUDO			
❏ 663	My Baby-O/Once Upon a Time	1958	$600
TAMLA			
❏ 101	Come to Me/Whisper	1959	$200
— No address on label			
❏ 101	Come to Me/Whisper	1959	$200
— With Gladstone St., Detroit, address on label			
UNITED ARTISTS			
❏ 226	Ain't Gonna Be That Way/All the Love I've Got	1960	$30
❏ 617	Come On and Stop/Not Available	1963	$200
❏ 160	Come to Me/Whisper	1959	$30
❏ 643	Congratulations, You've Hurt Me Again/Crying on My Pillow	1963	$30
❏ 386	Easier Said Than Done/Johnny One Stop	1961	$30
❏ 273	Happy Days/Baby, Baby	1960	$20
❏ 454	He Gave Me You/That's How Bad	1962	$30
❏ 590	He's Got the Whole World In His Hands/Another Tear Falls	1963	$30
❏ 322	How Can We Tell Him/I've Got a Notion	1961	$30
❏ 208	I Love the Way You Love/Let Me Love You	1960	$30
❏ 483	Let Yourself Go/That's Where I Lost My Baby	1962	$30
❏ 423	Magic Mirror/With All That's In Me	1962	$30
❏ 294	Merry-Go-Round/Tell Me That You Love Me	1961	$20
❏ 0031	Move Two Mountains/Come to Me	1973	$5
— Silver Spotlight Series" reissue			
❏ 359	Show Me/Oh Mary	1961	$30

7-Inch Extended Plays

Number	Title	Yr	NM
❏ 10,009	Ain't Gonna Be That Way/All the Love I've Got//Come to Me/Whisper	1960	$125
❏ 10,007	I Love the Way You Love/Let Me Love You//You Got What It Takes/Don't Leave Me	1960	$125
❏ 10,007 [PS]	Marv Johnson	1960	$125
❏ 10,009 [PS]	Marv Johnson	1960	$125

JOHNSON, ROLAND

Number	Title	Yr	NM
BRUNSWICK			
❏ 9-55110	I Traded Her Love (For Deep Purple Wine)/I'll Be With You	1958	$30
DECCA			
❏ 9-28302	Deep South Rhythm/The Almanse Song	1952	$30
❏ 9-46405	Warmed Over Love/Honest and Truly	1952	$30

JOHNSON, ROZETTA

Number	Title	Yr	NM
ATLANTIC			
❏ 2297	That Hurts/It's Nice to Know	1965	$200
— As "Rosetta Johnson			
CLINTONE			
❏ 01	A Woman's Way/Mine Was Real	1970	$60
❏ 06	Chained and Bound/Holding the Losing Hand	1971	$70
❏ 008	How Can You Lose Something You Never Had/Personal Woman	1971	$300
❏ 07	To Love Somebody/Can't You Just See Me	1971	$15
❏ 03	Who Are You Gonna Love (Your Woman or Your Wife)/I Can Feel My Love Comin' Down	1971	$40

JOHNSON, TERRY

Number	Title	Yr	NM
GORDY			
❏ 7091	My Springtime/Suzie	1969	$120
❏ 7095	Whatcha Gonna Do/Suzie	1970	$30

JOHNSTON, BRUCE

Number	Title	Yr	NM
COLUMBIA			
❏ 10568	Pipeline/Disney Girls	1977	$10
— Promos (with "Pipeline" on both sides) worth 50% less			
DEL-FI			
❏ 4202	The Original Surfer Stomp/Pajama Party	1963	$70
— Originals credit "The Surf Stompers			
❏ 4202	The Original Surfer Stomp/Pajama Party	1963	$40
DONNA			
❏ 1354	Do the Surfer Stomp (Part 1)/Do the Surfer Stomp (Part 2)	1962	$60
— Originals credit "The Surf Stompers			
❏ 1354	Do the Surfer Stomp (Part 1)/Do the Surfer Stomp (Part 2)	1962	$40
❏ 1354 [PS]	Do the Surfer Stomp (Part 1)/Do the Surfer Stomp (Part 2)	1962	$125
❏ 1364	Soupy Shuffle Stomp (SSS)/Moon Shot	1962	$40
❏ 1374	The Original Surfer Stomp (Part 1)/The Original Surfer Stomp (Part 2)	1962	$40
RONDA			
❏ 1003	Do the Surfer Stomp (Part 1)/Do the Surfer Stomp (Part 2)	1962	$50

JOLLY JESTERS, THE

Number	Title	Yr	NM
CRYSTALETTE			
❏ 735	On This Silent Night/A Hundred Dollars Worth of Mistletoe	1959	$15

JOLSON, AL

Number	Title	Yr	NM
DECCA			
❏ 9-24683	After You've Gone/Chinatown, My Chinatown	1950	$30
— Side 5 and Side 6 of "Album No. 9-4"; reissue of 78 rpm material			
❏ 9-27043	Are You Lonesome Tonight/No Sad Songs for Me	1950	$30
❏ 9-23714	Avalon/Anniversary Song	1950	$30
— Reissue of 78 from 1947			
❏ 9-27363	Beautiful Dreamer/Old Folks at Home	1951	$20
❏ 9-24109	Carolina in the Morning/Liza	1950	$30
— Side 7 and Side 8 of "Album No. 9-8"; reissue of 78 rpm material			
❏ 9-27181	De Camptown Races/Oh Susannah	1950	$30

Number	Title	Yr	NM
❏ 9-24682	Give My Regards to Broadway/I'm Just Wild About Harry	1950	$30
— Side 3 and Side 4 of "Album No. 9-4"; reissue of 78 rpm material			
❏ 9-24107	Golden Gate/I'm Sitting on Top of the World (Just Rolling Along -- Just Rolling Along)	1950	$30
— Side 3 and Side 4 of "Album No. 9-8"; reissue of 78 rpm material			
❏ 9-27364	I Dream of Jeannie with the Light Brown Hair/Old Black Joe	1951	$20
❏ 9-28697	I'm Sitting on Top of the World/When the Red, Red Robin Comes Bob, Bob, Bobbin' Along	1953	$15
❏ 9-27410	In Our House/I'm Crying Just for You	1951	$20
❏ 9-24684	I Only Have Eyes for You/Is It True What They Say About Dixie?	1950	$30
— Side 7 and Side 8 of "Album No. 9-4"; reissue of 78 rpm material			
❏ 9-27365	Massa's in De Cold, Cold Ground/My Old Kentucky Home	1951	$20
— The above four comprise a box set			
❏ 9-24681	Pretty Baby//I'm Looking Over a Four Leaf Clover/Baby Face	1950	$30
— Side 1 and Side 2 of "Album No. 9-4"; reissue of 78 rpm material			
❏ 9-23614	Sonny Boy/My Mammy	1950	$30
❏ 9-8 [PS]	Souvenir Album, Vol. 2	1950	$30
— Box for set of four records (24106, 24107, 24108, 24109)			
❏ 9-27024	The Old Piano Roll Blues/Way Down Yonder in New Orleans	1950	$30
❏ 9-24108	Toot, Toot, Tootsie! (Goo'Bye)/Back in Your Own Back Yard	1950	$30
— Side 5 and Side 6 of "Album No. 9-8"; reissue of 78 rpm material			
❏ 9-24106	Waiting for the Robert E. Lee/When You Were Sweet Sixteen	1950	$30
— Side 1 and Side 2 of "Album No. 9-8"; reissue of 78 rpm material			
MCA			
❏ 60038	Avalon/Anniversary Song	1973	$5
— Black label with rainbow			
❏ 60037	Swanee/April Showers	1973	$5
— Black label with rainbow			

JON AND LYNN

Number	Title	Yr	NM
SOUNDWAVES			
❏ 4656	Let the Good Times Roll/I Want To (Do Everything for You)	1981	$5
❏ 4677	(What a Day for a) Day Dream/I Never Do Get Tired of Telling You	1982	$5

JON AND ROBIN AND THE IN CROWD

Number	Title	Yr	NM
ABNAK			
❏ 113	Can't Make It With You/If I Need Someone	1966	$10
❏ 113 [DJ]	Can't Make It With You/If I Need Someone	1966	$20
— Promo only on yellow vinyl			
❏ 119	Do It Again A Little Bit Slower/If I Need Someone -- It's You	1967	$15
❏ 119 [DJ]	Do It Again A Little Bit Slower/If I Need Someone -- It's You	1967	$20
— Promo only on yellow vinyl			
❏ 127	Dr. Jon (The Medicine Man)/Love Me Baby	1968	$8
❏ 127 [DJ]	Dr. Jon (The Medicine Man)/Love Me Baby	1968	$15
— Promo only on yellow vinyl			
❏ 122	Drums/You Don't Care	1967	$12
❏ 122 [DJ]	Drums/You Don't Care	1967	$20
— Promo only on yellow vinyl			
❏ 135	Gift of Love/Gift of Love (Country Style)	1969	$8
❏ 135 [DJ]	Gift of Love/Gift of Love (Country Style)	1969	$15
— Promo only on yellow vinyl			
❏ 138	Give Me Your Love/Lonely One	1969	$8
❏ 138 [DJ]	Give Me Your Love/Lonely One	1969	$15
— Promo only on yellow vinyl			
❏ 115	Hey Girl/If I Need Someone	1966	$12
❏ 115 [DJ]	Hey Girl/If I Need Someone	1966	$20
— Promo only on yellow vinyl			

Number	Title	Yr	NM
❏ 141	If You Got It, Flaunt It/I'll Come Running to You	1969	$8
❏ 141 [DJ]	If You Got It, Flaunt It/I'll Come Running to You	1969	$15

— Promo only on yellow vinyl

Number	Title	Yr	NM
❏ 124	I Want Some More/Love Me Baby	1967	$10
❏ 124 [DJ]	I Want Some More/Love Me Baby	1967	$20

— Promo only on yellow vinyl

Number	Title	Yr	NM
❏ 111	Lonely One/How Come	1965	$10
❏ 111 [DJ]	Lonely One/How Come	1965	$20

— Promo only on yellow vinyl

Number	Title	Yr	NM
❏ 133	Save Me, Save Me/Thursday Morning	1968	$8

— As "Jon and the In Crowd

Number	Title	Yr	NM
❏ 133 [DJ]	Save Me, Save Me/Thursday Morning	1968	$15

— Promo only on yellow vinyl

Number	Title	Yr	NM
❏ 140	There's an American Flag on the Moon (Part 1)/There's An American Flag on the Moon (Part 2)	1969	$8
❏ 140 [DJ]	There's an American Flag on the Moon (Part 1)/There's An American Flag on the Moon (Part 2)	1969	$15

— Promo only on yellow vinyl

JONES, GLORIA
CAPITOL
Number	Title	Yr	NM
❏ 72301 [B]	Heartbeat part one/part two	1965	$20

CHAMPION
Number	Title	Yr	NM
❏ 14003 [B]	My Bad Boy's Comin' Home / Tainted Love	1965	$20

MINIT
Number	Title	Yr	NM
❏ 32046 [B]	I Know / What You Want	1968	$25
❏ 32051 [B]	When He Touches Me / Look What You Started	1968	$20

UPTOWN
Number	Title	Yr	NM
❏ 732 [B]	Come Go With Me / How Do You Tell An Angel	1966	$30
❏ 724 [B]	Finders Keepers / Run One Flight Of Stairs	1966	$100

JONES, ANN
CAPITOL
Number	Title	Yr	NM
❏ F1059	I Wish We Could Try All Over Again/You've Got to See Mama Ev'ry Night	1950	$40

DECCA
Number	Title	Yr	NM
❏ 9-30523	Mountain Dew/Old Rattler's Pup	1957	$30

KING
Number	Title	Yr	NM
❏ 1264	A Big Fat Gal Like You/Lonesome with You	1953	$30
❏ 1285	A Little Bit of Nylon/How Many Times	1953	$30
❏ 1028	Be Safe, Be Sure/You Won't Find Me Singing	1952	$40
❏ 961	Hi-Ballin' Daddy/God Gave Me You	1951	$50
❏ 5502	Hit and Run/Pieces of My Heart	1961	$15
❏ 1232	I've Had It/Love Is a Losing Game	1953	$30
❏ 1148	Love Bird/If I Could Buy You	1952	$40
❏ 1123	Monkey Business/I Love You As Time Goes By	1952	$40
❏ 1307	Our Kind of Love/You Ain't Got It Anymore	1954	$30
❏ 972	Secret Love/Knockin' Blues	1951	$50
❏ 1094	Smart Alec/Out of Sight	1952	$40
❏ 1017	Too Old to Cut the Mustard/I Carry Your Picture	1951	$50

SIMS
Number	Title	Yr	NM
❏ 102	Get Up and Go/What Do They Know About Being So Good	1955	$60

JONES BROTHERS, THE
SUN
Number	Title	Yr	NM
❏ 213	Every Night/Look to Jesus	1954	$800

JONES, DAVY
Also see DOLENZ, JONES & TORK; DOLENZ, JONES, BOYCE & HART; THE MONKEES.

BELL
Number	Title	Yr	NM
❏ 45159	Girl/Take My Love	1971	$60
❏ 45178	I'll Believe in You/The Road to Love	1972	$30
❏ 45136	I Really Love You/Sitting in the Apple Tree	1971	$10

COLPIX
Number	Title	Yr	NM
❏ 764	Dream Girl/Take Me to Paradise	1965	$30

— Colpix sides as "David Jones

Number	Title	Yr	NM
❏ 764 [PS]	Dream Girl/Take Me to Paradise	1965	$40

Number	Title	Yr	NM
❏ 789	The Girl from Chelsea/Theme for a New Love	1965	$30
❏ 789 [PS]	The Girl from Chelsea/Theme for a New Love	1965	$50
❏ 784	What Are We Going to Do/This Bouquet	1965	$30
❏ 784 [PS]	What Are We Going to Do/This Bouquet	1965	$40

MGM
Number	Title	Yr	NM
❏ 14458	Who Was It/You're a Lady	1972	$40

JONES, EDDIE
FAIRMOUNT
Number	Title	Yr	NM
❏ 1009	Let's Stop Fooling Ourselves/Give Me Good Lovin'	1966	$125

JONES, GEORGE, AND BRENDA CARTER
MUSICOR
Number	Title	Yr	NM
❏ 1375	Lonesome End of the Line/Just Your Average Couple	1969	$8
❏ 1325	Milwaukee, Here I Come/Great Big Spirit of Love	1968	$8

JONES, GEORGE, AND JEANETTE HICKS
MERCURY
Number	Title	Yr	NM
❏ 71029	Don't Stop the Music/Uh, Huh, No	1957	$30
❏ 71339	I'm with the Wrong One/Nothing Can Stop Me	1958	$30

JONES, GEORGE, AND BRENDA LEE
EPIC
Number	Title	Yr	NM
❏ 04723	Hallelujah I Love Her So/(What Love Can Do) The Second Time Around	1984	$4

JONES, GEORGE, AND MELBA MONTGOMERY
MUSICOR
Number	Title	Yr	NM
❏ 1204	Close Together (As You and Me)/Long As We're Dreaming	1966	$8
❏ 1238	Party Pickin'/Simply Divine	1967	$8

UNITED ARTISTS
Number	Title	Yr	NM
❏ 50015	Afraid/Now Tell Me	1966	$10
❏ 941	Blue Moon of Kentucky/I Can't Get Over You	1965	$10
❏ 899	Don't Go/I Let You Go	1965	$12
❏ 828	House of Gold/I Dreamed My Baby Came Home	1965	$10
❏ 635	Let's Invite Them Over/What's In Our Hearts	1963	$12
❏ 784	Multiply the Heartaches/Once More	1964	$10
❏ 732	Please Be My Love/Will There Ever Be Another	1964	$10
❏ 704	There's a Friend in the Way/Suppose Tonight Would Be Our Last	1964	$10
❏ 575	We Must Have Been Out of Our Minds/Until Then	1963	$10

JONES, GEORGE, AND JOHNNY PAYCHECK
EPIC
Number	Title	Yr	NM
❏ 50647	Mabellene/Don't Want No Stranger Sleepin' in My Bed	1978	$4
❏ 50891	When You're Ugly Like Us (You Just Naturally Got to Be Cool)/Kansas City	1980	$4

JONES, GEORGE, AND MARGIE SINGLETON
MERCURY
Number	Title	Yr	NM
❏ 72159	Are You Mine/I Didn't Hear You	1963	$15
❏ 71856	Did I Ever Tell You/Not Even Friends	1961	$15
❏ 71955	Waltz of the Angels/Talk About Lovin'	1962	$15

JONES, GEORGE, AND TAMMY WYNETTE
EPIC
Number	Title	Yr	NM
❏ 50930	A Pair of Old Sneakers/We'll Talk About It Later	1980	$4
❏ 50099	God's Gonna Getcha (For That)/Those Were the Good Times	1975	$5
❏ 50235	Golden Ring/We're Putting It Back Together	1976	$5
❏ 10963	Let's Build a World Together/Touching Shoulders	1973	$5
❏ 11077	Mr. and Mrs. Santa Claus/The Greatest Christmas Gift	1973	$5
❏ 10923	Old Fashioned Singing/We Love to Sing About Jesus	1972	$5
❏ 50418	Southern California/Keep the Change	1977	$4
❏ 10815	Take Me/We Go Together	1971	$5
❏ 10881	The Ceremony/The Great Divide	1972	$5
❏ 50849	Two Story House/It Sure Was Good	1980	$4
❏ 11151	We Loved It Away/Ain't It Been Good	1974	$5
❏ 11031	We're Gonna Hold On/My Elusive Dreams	1973	$5

Number	Title	Yr	NM
❏ 11083	(We're Not) The Jet Set/The Crawdad Song	1974	$5

JONES, GEORGE
EPIC
Number	Title	Yr	NM
❏ 10917	A Picture of Me (Without You)/The Man Worth Loving You	1972	$5
❏ 50495	Bartender's Blues/Rest in Peace	1977	$4
❏ 50271	Her Name Is…/Diary of My Mind	1976	$5
❏ 50867	He Stopped Loving Her Today/A Hard Act to Follow	1980	$6
❏ 03883	I Always Get Lucky with You/I'd Rather Have What We Had	1983	$3
❏ 50968	If Drinkin' Don't Kill Me (Her Memory Will)/Brother to the Blues	1980	$4
❏ 08011	If I Could Bottle This Up/I Always Get It Right with You	1988	$3

— With Shelby Lynne

Number	Title	Yr	NM
❏ 50423	If I Could Put Them All Together (I'd Have You)/You've Got the Best of Me Again	1977	$4
❏ 50564	I'll Just Take It Out in Love/Leaving Love All Over the Place	1978	$4
❏ 08509	I'm a One Woman Man/Pretty Little Lady from Beaumont, Texas	1988	$3
❏ 07748	I'm a Survivor/The Real McCoy	1988	$3
❏ 50922	I'm Not Ready Yet/Garage Sale Today	1980	$4
❏ 07107	I Turn to You/Don't Leave Without Taking Your Silver	1987	$3
❏ 10858	Loving You Could Never Be Better/Try It, You'll Like It	1972	$5
❏ 50127	Memories of Us/I Just Don't Give a Damn	1975	$5
❏ 50385	Old King Kong/It's a 10-33 (Let's Get Jesus on the Line)	1977	$4
❏ 11053	Once You've Had the Best/Mary Don't Go Round	1973	$5
❏ 02696	Same Ol' Me/Together Alone	1982	$3
❏ 04609	She's My Rock/(What Love Can Do) The Second Time Around	1984	$3
❏ 03489	Shine On (Shine All Your Sweet Love on Me)/Memories of Mama	1982	$3
❏ 04876	Size Seven Round (Made of Gold)/All I Want to Do in Life	1985	$3

— A-side with Lacy J. Dalton; B-side with Janie Frickie

Number	Title	Yr	NM
❏ 05862	Somebody Wants Me Out of the Way/Call the Wrecker for My Heart	1986	$3
❏ 50684	Someday My Day Will Come/We Oughta Be Ashamed	1979	$4
❏ 02526	Still Doin' Time/Good Ones and Bad Ones	1981	$3
❏ 04082	Tennessee Whiskey/Almost Persuaded	1983	$3
❏ 50187	The Battle/I'll Come Back	1976	$5
❏ 07655	The Bird/I'm Goin' Home Like I Never Did Before	1987	$3
❏ 50038	The Door/Wean Me	1974	$5
❏ 11122	The Grand Tour/Our Private Life	1974	$5
❏ 07913	The Old Man No One Loves/One Hell of a Song	1988	$3
❏ 05698	The One I Loved Back Then (The Corvette Song)/If Only You'd Love Me Again	1985	$3
❏ 50088	These Days (I Barely Get By)/Baby, There's Nothing Like You	1975	$5
❏ 10831	We Can Make It/One of These Days	1972	$5
❏ 10959	What My Woman Can't Do/My Loving Wife	1973	$5
❏ 05439	Who's Gonna Fill Their Shoes/A Whole Lot of Trouble for You	1985	$3
❏ 06296	Wine Colored Roses/These Old Eyes Have Seen It All	1986	$3
❏ 68991	Writing on the Wall/Burning Bridges	1989	$3

MERCURY
Number	Title	Yr	NM
❏ 71583	Accidently on Purpose/Sparkling Blue Eyes	1960	$20
❏ 71910	Aching, Breaking Heart/When My Heart Hurts No More	1962	$15
❏ 71910 [PS]	Aching, Breaking Heart/When My Heart Hurts No More	1962	$20
❏ 71257	Color of the Blues/Eskimo Pie	1958	$30
❏ 71721	Family Bible/Taggin' Along	1961	$20
❏ 71636	Family Bible/Your Old Standby	1960	$30
❏ 71615	Have Mercy on Me/If You Believe	1960	$30
❏ 72087	I Love You Because/Revenoor Man	1963	$15
❏ 72087 [PS]	I Love You Because/Revenoor Man	1963	$20

Number	Title	Yr	NM
❏ 72362	I Wouldn't Know About That/ You Better Treat Your Man Right	1964	$15
❏ 71514	Money to Burn/Big Harlan Taylor	1959	$20
❏ 72200	Mr. Fool/One Is a Lonely Number	1963	$15
❏ 71506	My Lord Has Called Me/If You Want to Wear a Crown	1959	$30
❏ 72293	Oh Lonesome Me/Life to Go	1964	$15
❏ 72293 [PS]	Oh Lonesome Me/Life to Go	1964	$20
❏ 71641	Out of Control/Just Little Boy Blue	1960	$20
❏ 71224	Take the Devil Out of Me/A Cup of Loneliness	1957	$30
❏ 71176	Tall, Tall Trees/Hearts in My Dream	1957	$30
❏ 71804	Tender Years/Battle of Love	1961	$15
❏ 71804 [PS]	Tender Years/Battle of Love	1961	$20
❏ 72233	The Last Town I Painted/ Tarnished Angel	1964	$15
❏ 72233 [PS]	The Last Town I Painted/ Tarnished Angel	1964	$20
❏ 71700	The Window Up Above/ Candy Hearts	1960	$20
❏ 71096	Too Much Water/All I Want to Do	1957	$30
❏ 71373	Treasure of Love/If I Don't Love You (Grits Ain't Groceries)	1958	$30
❏ 71340	Wandering Soul/Jesus Wants Me	1958	$30
❏ 71406	White Lightning/Long Time to Forget	1959	$20
❏ 71464	Who Shot Sam/Into My Arms Again	1959	$20

MUSICOR

Number	Title	Yr	NM
❏ 1244	A Cup of Loneliness/That the World But Give Me Jesus	1967	$15
❏ 1425	A Good Year for the Roses/ Let a Little Loving Come In	1970	$8
❏ 1298	As Long As I Live/Your Angel Steps Out of Heaven	1968	$8
❏ 1181	Four-O-Thirty Three/Don't Think I Don't	1966	$8
❏ 1404	Going Life's Way/Uncloudy Day	1970	$6
❏ 1243	I Can't Get There from Here/A Poor Man's Riches	1967	$8
❏ 1267	If My Heart Had Windows/ Honky Tonk Downstairs	1967	$8
❏ 1366	If Not for You/When the Wife Runs Off	1969	$8
❏ 1446	I'll Follow You (Up to Our Cloud)/Getting Over the Storm	1971	$6
❏ 1351	I'll Share My World with You/I'll See You a While Ago	1969	$8
❏ 1143	I'm a People/I Woke Up from Dreaming	1966	$8
❏ 1339	Lonely Christmas Call/My Mom and Santa Claus	1968	$8
❏ 1098	Love Bug/I Can't Get Used to Being Lonely	1965	$8
❏ 1174	Old Brush Arbors/Flowers for Mama	1966	$8
❏ 1289	Say It's Not You/Poor Chinee	1968	$8
❏ 1381	She's Mine/No Blues Is Good News	1969	$8
❏ 1297	Small Time Laboring Man/ Well It's Alright	1968	$8
❏ 1432	Sometimes You Just Can't Win/Brothers of a Bottle	1971	$6
❏ 1117	Take Me/Ship of Love	1965	$8
❏ 1408	Tell Me My Lying Eyes Are Wrong/You've Become My Everything	1970	$6
❏ 1067	Things Have Gone to Pieces/Wearing My Heart Away	1965	$8
❏ 1067 [PS]	Things Have Gone to Pieces/Wearing My Heart Away	1965	$20
❏ 1226	Walk Through This World with Me/Developing My Pictures	1967	$8
❏ 1333	When the Grass Grows Over Me/Heartaches and Hangovers	1968	$8
❏ 1392	Where Grass Won't Grow/ Shoulder to Shoulder	1970	$6

RCA VICTOR

Number	Title	Yr	NM
❏ 74-0625	A Day in the Life of a Fool/ Old, Old House	1971	$6
❏ PB-10052	I Can Love You Enough/Talk to Me Lonesome Heart	1974	$5
❏ 74-0878	I Can Still See Him in Your Eyes/She's Mine	1973	$6
❏ 74-0700	I Made Leaving (Easy for You)/How Proud I Would Have Been	1972	$6
❏ APBO-0218	My Favorite Lies/You Gotta Be My Baby	1974	$5
❏ AMBO-0123	Tender Years/White Lightnin'	1973	$5
❏ 74-0792	Wrapped Around Her Finger/ With Half a Heart	1972	$6

STARDAY

Number	Title	Yr	NM
❏ 256	Boat of Life/Taggin' Along	1956	$50
❏ 188	Hold Everything/What's Wrong with You	1955	$60
❏ 234	I'm Ragged But I'm Right/ Your Heart	1956	$50

Number	Title	Yr	NM
❏ 160	Let Him Know/Let Me Catch My Breath	1954	$70
❏ 146	Play It Cool, Man/Wrong About You	1954	$70
—B-side with Sonny Burns			
❏ 165	Tell Her/Heartbroken Me	1954	$70
—B-side with Sonny Burns			
❏ 216	What Am I Worth/Still Hurtin'	1955	$50
❏ 202	Why Baby Why/Season of My Heart	1955	$60

UNITED ARTISTS

Number	Title	Yr	NM
❏ 500	A Girl I Used to Know/Big Fool of the Year	1962	$10
❏ 442	Beacon in the Night/He Made Me Free	1962	$15
❏ 50014	Best Guitar Picker/A Good Old Fashioned Cry	1966	$12
❏ 463	He Is So Good to Me/Magic Valley	1962	$15
❏ 804	Least of All/Brown to Blue	1965	$12
❏ 530	Lonely Christmas Call/My Mom and Santa Claus	1962	$20
❏ 462	Open Pit Mine/Geronimo	1962	$10
❏ 424	She Thinks I Still Care/ Sometimes You Just Can't Win	1962	$10
❏ 424 [PS]	She Thinks I Still Care/ Sometimes You Just Can't Win	1962	$20
❏ 901	What's Money/I Get Lonely in a Hurry	1965	$10
❏ 724	Where Does a Little Tear Come From/Something I Dreamed	1964	$10
❏ 965	World's Worse Loser/I Can't Change Overnight	1965	$10
❏ 858	Wrong Number/Old Old House	1965	$10

JONES, GRANDPA, AND MINNIE PEARL

RCA VICTOR

Number	Title	Yr	NM
❏ 47-6088	Matrimony Ridge/Spring Fever	1955	$30
❏ 47-5891	Papa Loves Mambo/Gotta Marry Off Our Daughter	1954	$30

JONES, GRANDPA

DECCA

Number	Title	Yr	NM
❏ 9-30655	Daylight Saving Time/Don't Look Back	1958	$30
❏ 9-30904	Don't Bring Your Banjo Home/It Takes a Lot of Livin'	1959	$30
❏ 9-30264	Eight More Miles to Louisville/Dark As a Dungeon	1957	$30
❏ 9-30523	Mountain Dew/Old Rattler's Tip	1957	$30
❏ 9-30823	The All American Boy/Pickin' Time	1959	$30

KING

Number	Title	Yr	NM
❏ 1097	A Light in His Soul/There's a Hole in the Ground	1952	$40
❏ 5321	Are You from Dixie/Fast Moving Night Train	1960	$20
❏ 1301	Come Be My Rainbow/You Done Me Mean and Dirty	1954	$30
❏ 1061	Down in Dixie/Time, Time, Time, Time	1952	$40
❏ 1069	Fix Me a Pallet/Fifteen Cents Is All I Got	1952	$40
❏ 5397	Grandpa's Banjo Boogie/ Uncle Eph's Got the Coon	1960	$20
❏ 5489	It's Raining Here This Morning/And So You Have Come Back to Me	1961	$20
❏ 5867	Old Rattler/Mountain Dew	1964	$15
❏ 1029	That Memphis Train/You Done Me Mean and Hateful	1952	$40
❏ 976	What'll I Do with the Baby-O/ Chicken Don't Roost Too High	1951	$50

MONUMENT

Number	Title	Yr	NM
❏ 903	Are You from Dixie/My Darlin's Not My Darlin' Anymore	1965	$15
❏ 820	Away Out on the Mountain/ My Little Lady	1963	$20
❏ 454	Banjo Sam/Count Your Blessings	1962	$20
❏ 1069	Bill's Gonna Be Home Soon/ These Hills	1968	$10
❏ 440	Billy Yank and Johnny Reb/ These Hills	1961	$20
❏ 1179	Christmas Guest/Christmas Roses	1969	$15
❏ 8556	Christmas Guest/Christmas Roses	1972	$8
❏ 8677	Christmas Guest/Christmas Roses	1975	$6
❏ 1939	Christmas Guest/Christmas Roses	1976	$4
—Golden Series" reissue			
❏ 1043	Don't Look Back/That's All This Old World Needs	1967	$12
❏ 973	Eight More Miles to Louisville/As Long As We're Dreaming	1966	$15
❏ 866	Falling Leaves/Here Comes the Champion	1964	$15

Number	Title	Yr	NM
❏ 844	Going from the Cotton Field/ Root Hog Root	1964	$15
❏ 8539	Here I Am Makin' Plans/ Coal Camp	1972	$8
❏ 430	Hip Cats' Wedding/I Don't Love Nobody	1960	$20
❏ 1000	Moon of Arizona/Everything I Had Going for Me Is Gone	1967	$10
❏ 8577	Mountain Dew/Four Winds a-Blowin'	1973	$8
❏ 1143	Mountain Laurel/Old Troupe Dog	1969	$10
❏ 811	My Carolina Sunshine/Night Train to Memphis	1963	$20
❏ 1108	Smoke, Smoke, Smoke (But Not Around Me)/I'll Just Keep Living Alone	1968	$12
❏ 801	T for Texas/Tritzem Yodel	1962	$20
❏ 422	The Thing/Ladies Man	1960	$20
❏ 1203	Trouble in Mind/I've Learned to Leave That to the Lord	1970	$10

RCA VICTOR

Number	Title	Yr	NM
❏ 47-5770	Back Up Buddy If You Don't Want a Whipping/Lookin' Back to See	1954	$30
—With Ruby Wells			
❏ 47-6179	Herd o' Turtles/In the Future	1955	$30
❏ 47-4771	I'm No Communist/Pickin' on Me	1952	$40
❏ 47-5475	My Heart Is Like a Train/ That New Vitamine	1953	$30
❏ 47-6006	Old Dan Tucker/Gooseberry Pie	1955	$30
❏ 47-5113	Old Rattler's Son/Deal Old Sunny South by the Sea	1953	$30
❏ 47-5234	Papa's Corn Likker Still/ Bread and Gravy	1953	$30
❏ 47-4956	Sassafrass/Closer to the Bone	1952	$40
❏ 47-5685	Some More Mountain Dew/ Old Blue	1954	$30
❏ 47-5789	Standing in the Depot/High Silk Hat and a Gold Top Walkin' Cane	1954	$30
❏ 47-5576	The Trader/Y'All Come	1954	$30
❏ 47-4660	T.V. Blues/Stop That Ticklin' Me	1952	$40
❏ 47-6263	What Has She Got/The Champion	1955	$30

JONES, HOWARD

ELEKTRA

Number	Title	Yr	NM
❏ 69494	All I Want/Dig This Well Deep	1987	$3
❏ 69494 [PS]	All I Want/Dig This Well Deep	1987	$3
❏ 69308	Everlasting Love/The Brutality of Fact	1989	$3
❏ 69308 [PS]	Everlasting Love/The Brutality of Fact	1989	$3
❏ 69631	Life in One Day/Learning How to Love	1985	$3
❏ 69631 [PS]	Life in One Day/Learning How to Love	1985	$3
❏ 69598	Like to Get to Know You Well/Equality	1985	$3
❏ 69705	Pearl in the Shell/Don't Always Look at the Rain	1984	$4
❏ 69288	The Prisoner/Rubber Morals	1989	$3
❏ 69651	Things Can Only Get Better/ Why Look for the Key	1985	$3
❏ 69651 [PS]	Things Can Only Get Better/ Why Look for the Key	1985	$3
❏ 69737	What Is Love/It Just Doesn't Matter	1984	$3
❏ 69737 [PS]	What Is Love/It Just Doesn't Matter	1984	$3
❏ 69479	Will You Still Be There/ (Acoustic)	1987	$5
❏ 69479 [PS]	Will You Still Be There/ (Acoustic)	1987	$5

JONES, JACK

CAPITOL

Number	Title	Yr	NM
❏ F3991	Come On Baby Let's Go/ You Laugh	1958	$10
❏ F3844	For Crying Out Loud/Born to Be Lucky	1957	$15
❏ F3808	Good Luck Good Buddy/ Baby Come Home	1957	$15
❏ F4089	Laffin' at Me/Deeply Devoted	1958	$12
❏ F4161	Make Room for the Joy/ When I Love I'll Love Forever	1959	$10
❏ F4161 [PS]	Make Room for the Joy/ When I Love I'll Love Forever	1959	$20

KAPP

Number	Title	Yr	NM
❏ 781	A Day in the Life of a Fool/ Shining Sea	1966	$6
❏ 380	Big Time/She's My Darling, She's My Heart	1961	$10
❏ 2143	Breathe Deep/Trippin' on a Country Road	1971	$5
❏ 900	Brother, Where Are You/ Gypsies, Jugglers and Clowns	1968	$6
❏ 516	Call Me Irresponsible/Mutiny on the Bounty	1963	$8
❏ 635	Dear Heart/Emily	1964	$6
❏ 635 [PS]	Dear Heart/Emily	1964	$8

Number	Title	Yr	NM
❏ 880	Don't Give Your Love Away/Oh How Much I Love You	1967	$6
❏ 964	Far Away/Meditation	1968	$6
❏ 461	Gift of Love/Pick Up the Pieces	1962	$8
❏ 2154	I'll See You Through/No Concern	1971	$5
❏ 818	I'm Indestructible/Afterthoughts	1967	$6
❏ 2063	It Only Takes a Moment/Once Upon a Time	1969	$5
❏ 341	It's a Lonesome Town/A Lot of Livin' to Do	1960	$10
❏ 495	I've Got My Pride/That's Her Little Way	1962	$8
❏ 800	Lady/Afraid to Love	1966	$6
❏ 507	La Paloma/The Lonely Bull	1963	$8
❏ 435	Lollipops and Roses/This Was My Love	1961	$8
❏ 722	Love Bug/And I Love Her	1965	$6
❏ 722 [PS]	Love Bug/And I Love Her	1965	$8
❏ 534	Love Is a Ticklish Affair/That's the Way I Come to You	1963	$8
❏ 571	Love with the Proper Stranger/The Mood I'm In	1964	$6
❏ 571 [PS]	Love with the Proper Stranger/The Mood I'm In	1964	$8
❏ 629	Lullaby for Christmas Eve/The Village of St. Bernadette	1964	$8
❏ 2022	Mathilda/Far Away	1969	$5
❏ 2138	Mirrored Door/Feather Bed	1971	$5
❏ 860	Open for Business As Usual/The Mood I'm In	1967	$6
❏ 847	Our Song/Michelle	1967	$6
❏ 937	People/Don't Rain on My Parade	1968	$6
❏ 477	Poetry/Dreamin' All the Time	1962	$8
❏ 672	Seein' the Right Love Go Wrong/Travelin' On	1965	$6
❏ 589	The First Night of the Full Moon/Far Away	1964	$6
❏ 589 [PS]	The First Night of the Full Moon/Far Away	1964	$8
❏ 755	The Impossible Dream (The Quest)/Strangers in the Night	1966	$6
❏ 699	The True Picture/Just Yesterday	1965	$6
❏ 736	The Weekend/Wildflower	1966	$6
❏ 608	Where Love Has Gone/The Lorelei	1964	$6
❏ 608 [PS]	Where Love Has Gone/The Lorelei	1964	$8
❏ 551	Wives and Lovers/Toys in the Attic	1963	$6
❏ 551 [PS]	Wives and Lovers/Toys in the Attic	1963	$8

POLYDOR
| ❏ 815096-7 | The Love Boat Theme/The Rockford Files | 1983 | $4 |

— Reissue; B-side by Mike Post

RCA VICTOR
❏ 74-0734	Coming Apart/A Game of Magic	1972	$5
❏ PB-11076	Dixie Chicken/Perfect Strangers	1977	$4
❏ APBO-0220	Do Me Wrong, But Do Me/Fools in Love	1974	$4
❏ 47-9441	If You Ever Leave Me/Pretty	1968	$5
❏ 47-9564	I Really Want You to Know!/This World Is Yours	1968	$5
❏ 74-0475	Let Me Be the One/Talk It Over in the Morning	1971	$5
❏ 74-0278	Little Altar Boy/What's Out There for Me	1969	$5
❏ 47-9365	Live for Life/That Tiny World	1967	$5
❏ 47-9687	Love Story/L.A. Breakdown (And Take Me In)	1968	$5
❏ 74-0425	Pieces of Dreams/Years of My Youth	1971	$5
❏ PB-10845	Send In the Clowns/You Need a Man	1976	$4
❏ PB-10025	She Doesn't Live Here Anymore/Write Me a Love Song Charlie	1974	$4
❏ 74-0350	Sweet Changes/I Wish We'd All Been Ready	1970	$5
❏ 74-0185	Sweet Child/The Last Seven Days	1969	$5
❏ 74-0683	The Mountain/How Can We Run Away	1972	$5
❏ 47-9639	The Way That I Live/Dirty Word	1968	$5
❏ PB-10955	Try It Again/With One More Look at You	1977	$4
❏ PB-10317	What I Did for Love/Don't Mention Love	1975	$4
❏ 47-9510	Without Her/Follow Me	1968	$5

JONES, JAN
DAY-WOOD
| ❏ 101 | Independent Woman/(Part 2) | 1980 | $500 |

JONES, JIMMY
ABC-PARAMOUNT
| ❏ 10094 | Blue and Lonely/Daddy Needs Baby | 1960 | $200 |

— As "Jimmy Jones and the Pretenders

ARROW
| ❏ 717 | Heaven in Your Eyes/The Whistlin' Man | 1957 | $180 |

— As "Jimmy Jones and the Jones Boys

BELL
| ❏ 682 | Personal Property/39-21-40 | 1967 | $8 |
| ❏ 689 | True Love Ways/Snap My Fingers | 1967 | $8 |

CAPITOL
| ❏ 3849 | If I Knew Then (What I Know Now)/Everything's Gonna Be All Right | 1974 | $5 |

CONCHILLO
| ❏ 1 | Ain't Nothing Wrong Makin' Love the First Night/Time and Changes | 1976 | $6 |

CUB
❏ 9093	Dear One/I Say Love	1961	$20
❏ 9067	Good Timin'/My Precious Angel	1960	$30
❏ 9049	Handy Man/The Search Is Over	1959	$30
❏ 9076	Itchin'/Ee-I-Ee-I-Oh	1960	$30
❏ 9085	I Told You So/You Got It	1961	$20
❏ 9102	Mr. Music Man/Holler Hey	1961	$20
❏ 9072	That's When I Cried/I Just Go for You	1960	$30
❏ 9072 [PS]	That's When I Cried/I Just Go for You	1960	$60

EPIC
| ❏ 9339 | Whenever You Need Me/You for Me to Love | 1959 | $120 |

PARKWAY
| ❏ 988 | Don't You Just Know It/Dynamite | 1966 | $12 |

RAMA
| ❏ 210 | Lover/Plain Old Love | 1956 | $120 |

— As "Jimmy Jones and the Pretenders

ROULETTE
| ❏ 4232 | Lover/Plain Old Love | 1960 | $40 |

— As "Jimmy 'Handyman' Jones"

JONES, JOE
CAPITOL
| ❏ F2951 | Adam Bit the Apple/Will Call | 1954 | $50 |

ROULETTE
❏ 4344	California Sun/Please Don't Talk About Me When I'm Gone	1961	$15
❏ 4316	One Big Mouth/Here's What You Gotta Do	1960	$15
❏ 4377	The Big Mule/I've Got a Uh Uh Wife	1961	$15

JONES, JOHN PAUL
Also see LED ZEPPELIN.

COTILLION
| ❏ 44102 [B] | Man from Nazareth/Got To Get Together Now | 1971 | $30 |

JERDEN
| ❏ 761 | Sound City/Broken Promises | 1965 | $40 |

— B-side by Rosemary and Howard

PARKWAY
| ❏ 915 | Baja/A Foggy Day in Vietnam | 1964 | $50 |

JONES, JONAH
CAPITOL
❏ F3893	76 Trombones/Baubles, Bangles and Beads	1958	$10
❏ F3999	Ballin' the Jack/Slowly But Surely	1958	$12
❏ 4375	Blueberry Hill/Shanghai	1960	$10
❏ F4199	Cherry/I Dig Chicks	1959	$10
❏ 4993	Doodles/Pink Shutters	1963	$8
❏ F4238	High Hopes/Hit Me Again	1959	$12
❏ 4497	I Ain't Down Yet/Blue Champagne	1961	$8
❏ F3747	On the Street Where You Live/Rose Room	1957	$10
❏ 4878	The Bells of St. Mary's/Brotherhood of Man	1962	$8
❏ 4944	The Work Song/Jonah's Sermon	1963	$8
❏ F4297	Where Did We Go? Out/Gentleman Jimmy	1959	$10

Number	Title	Yr	NM
❏ 31765	Think Beautiful/Don't Forget 127th Street (127th Street March)	1965	$6

GROOVE
| ❏ 0140 | Come Sit By Me/God Loves You Child | 1956 | $20 |

MOTOWN
| ❏ 1145 | For Better or Worse/Don't Mess with Bill | 1969 | $120 |

7-Inch Extended Plays
CAPITOL
❏ EAP 1-963	*Baubles, Bangles and Beads/The Party's Over/Till There Was You/Seventy Six Trombones	1958	$15
❏ EAP 3-963	(contents unknown)	1958	$15
❏ EAP 2-839	(contents unknown)	1958	$15
❏ EAP 3-839	(contents unknown)	1958	$15
❏ EAP 1-839 [PS]	Muted Jazz, Part 1	1958	$15
❏ EAP 2-839 [PS]	Muted Jazz, Part 2	1958	$15
❏ EAP 3-839 [PS]	Muted Jazz, Part 3	1958	$15
❏ EAP 1-963 [PS]	Swingin' on Broadway, Part 1	1958	$15
❏ EAP 3-963 [PS]	Swingin' on Broadway, Part 3	1958	$15

JONES, LEROY
HIT
| ❏ 267 | Almost Persuaded/My Uncle Used to Love Me But She Died | 1966 | $8 |

— B-side by Roger Frolic
| ❏ 68 | Another Saturday Night/It's My Party | 1963 | $8 |

— B-side by Connie Landers
| ❏ 153 | Baby Don't You Do It/Baby Love | 1964 | $8 |

— B-side by Jenny and the Jewels
| ❏ 60 | Baby Workout/Can't Get Used to Losing You | 1963 | $8 |

— B-side by Fred Brown
| ❏ 136 | C'Mon and Swim/People Say | 1964 | $8 |

— B-side by the Flower Sisters
| ❏ 239 | Crying Time/Lightnin' Strikes | 1966 | $8 |

— B-side by Fred York
| ❏ 33 | Do You Love Me/Only Love Can Break a Heart | 1962 | $8 |

— B-side by Ed Hardin
| ❏ 79 | Hey Girl/If I Had a Hammer | 1963 | $8 |

— B-side by Ricky Dickens
| ❏ 176 | Hold What You've Got/Wise Like Solomon | 1965 | $8 |

— B-side by Bobby Brooks
| ❏ 122 | I Don't Want to Be Hurt Anymore/People | 1964 | $8 |

— B-side by Morti Webb
| ❏ 249 | I'm So Lonesome I Could Cry/A Sign of the Times | 1966 | $8 |

— B-side by Fred York
| ❏ 90 | It's All Right/She's a Fool | 1963 | $8 |

— B-side by Connie Dee
| ❏ 257 | It's a Man's Man's Man's World/Love Is Like an Itching in My Heart | 1966 | $8 |

— B-side by Jenny and the Jewels
| ❏ 53 | Let's Limbo Some More/Blame It on the Bossa Nova | 1963 | $8 |

— B-side by Sylvia Richards
| ❏ 347 | Little Green Apples/Elenore | 1968 | $8 |

— B-side by the Jalopy Five
| ❏ 97 | Loddy Lo/Quicksand | 1963 | $8 |

— B-side by Gerry and the Georgettes
| ❏ 270 | Satisfied Mind/Reach Out I'll Be There | 1966 | $8 |

— B-side by the Chellows
| ❏ 51 | Send Me Some Lovin'/Walk Like a Man | 1963 | $8 |

— B-side by the Chellows
| ❏ 184 | Someday/Shake | 1965 | $8 |
| ❏ 133 | Steal Away/Where Did Our Love Go | 1964 | $8 |

— B-side by the Houstons
| ❏ 279 | Tell It Like It Is/Good Thing | 1967 | $8 |

— B-side by Ed Hardin and the Cadets
| ❏ 255 | When a Man Loves a Woman/Rainy Day Women #12 and 35 | 1966 | $8 |

— B-side by Bobby Brooks

JONES, LITTLE ANTHONY
EMBER
| ❏ 1090 | Dear Gesu Bambino (Part 1)/Dear Gesu Bambino (Part 2) | 1962 | $20 |

Number	Title	Yr	NM

JONES, LITTLE JOHNNY
ATLANTIC
| ❏ 1045 | Hoy, Hoy/Doin' the Best I Can | 1954 | $100 |

FLAIR
| ❏ 1010 | Sweet Little Woman/I May Be Wrong | 1953 | $800 |

JONES, LITTLE SONNY
IMPERIAL
| ❏ 5275 | I Got Booted/Tend to Your Business Blues | 1954 | $125 |
| ❏ 5287 | Winehead Baby/Going to the Country | 1954 | $125 |

SPECIALTY
| ❏ 443 | Is Everything All Right/Do You Really Love Me | 1952 | $100 |

JONES, NEAL
COLUMBIA
❏ 4-21292	Foolin' Women/Maybe Next Week Sometime	1954	$30
❏ 4-21356	Hot Jing Jolly/Down Boy	1955	$40
❏ 4-21415	I'm Playin' It Cool/High Steppin' Baby	1955	$40
❏ 4-21475	Two Wrongs/What This World Needs	1955	$30
❏ 4-21236	Walkin', Plowin', Talkin', Cryin'/Who-R-O-Ee, My Life Has Just Begun	1954	$40

JONES, PAUL
Original lead singer for MANFRED MANN.

BELL
| ❏ 805 | It's Getting Better/Not Before Time | 1969 | $8 |

CAPITOL
❏ 5800	High Time/It Is Coming Closer	1966	$8
❏ 5745	I Can't Hold On Much Longer/Baby Tomorrow	1966	$8
❏ 5970	Privilege/Free Me	1967	$8
❏ 5857	Sonny Boy Williamson/I've Been a Bad, Bad Boy	1967	$8

LONDON
| ❏ 168 | Mighty Ship/Who Are the Masters | 1972 | $5 |
| ❏ 178 | The Pod That Came Back/Construction Worker's Song | 1972 | $5 |

PRIVATE STOCK
| ❏ 45,004 | Love Enough | 1974 | $5 |

JONES, QUINCY
A&M
❏ 2309	Ai No Corrida/Lenta Letina	1981	$4
❏ 1663	Body Heat/One Track Mind	1975	$4
❏ 1184	Bridge Over Troubled Water (Part 1)/Bridge Over Troubled Water (Part 2)	1970	$5
❏ 1606	If I Ever Lose This Heaven/Along Came Betty	1974	$4
❏ 1606 [PS]	If I Ever Lose This Heaven/Along Came Betty	1974	$6
❏ 1323	Ironside/Cast Your Fate to the Wind	1972	$5
❏ 1743	Is It Love That We're Missing/Cry Baby	1975	$4
❏ 1743 [PS]	Is It Love That We're Missing/Cry Baby	1975	$6
❏ 2080	Love, I Never Had It So Good/I Heard That	1978	$4
❏ 1404	Love Theme from "The Getaway" (Part 1)/Love Theme from "The Getaway" (Part 2)	1973	$4
❏ 1791	Mellow Madness/Paranoid	1976	$4
❏ 1878	Midnight Soul Patrol/Brown Soft Shoe	1976	$4
❏ 1115	Oh Happy Day/Love and Peace	1969	$6
❏ 1139	Oh Happy Day/Love and Peace	1969	$5
❏ 2387	One Hundred Ways/Velas	1981	$4
—Featuring James Ingram
❏ 1455	Sanford & Son Theme/Summer in the City	1973	$4
❏ 1638	Soul Saga/Boogie Joe, The Grinder	1974	$4
❏ 2043	Stuff Like That/There's a Train Leavin'	1978	$4
❏ 2043 [PS]	Stuff Like That/There's a Train Leavin'	1978	$6
❏ 2417	There's a Train Leavin'/Something Special	1981	$4
—Featuring Patti Austin
| ❏ 1316 | What's Going On (Part 1)/What's Going On (Part 2) | 1971 | $5 |
| ❏ 1923 | What Shall I Do (Hush, Hush, Somebody's Calling My Name)/Oh, Lord, Come By Here | 1977 | $4 |

ABC
| ❏ 11086 | For Love of Ivy/The Pussyfoot | 1968 | $8 |

BELL
❏ 838	Bob & Carol & Ted & Alice/Giggle Grass	1969	$6
❏ 833	Cactus Flower Theme/The Time for Love Is Anytime	1969	$6
❏ 832	I'm a Believer/The Time for Love Is Anytime	1969	$6

COLGEMS
| ❏ 66-1016 | Hangin' Paper/Lonely Bottles | 1968 | $8 |

MERCURY
❏ 72348	A Hard Day's Night/Soul Serenade	1964	$10
❏ 72012	A Taste of Honey/Shagnasty	1962	$15
❏ 72533	Baby Cakes/Mohair Sam	1966	$12
❏ 72289	Baby Elephant Walk/Mr. Lucky	1964	$12
❏ 71546	Birth of a Band/Change of Pace	1959	$15
❏ 72105	Boogie Bossa Nova/Morning of the Carnival	1963	$10
❏ 71460	Choo Choo Ch-Boogie/Marchin' the Blues	1959	$15
❏ 71737	G-Man Train/Pleasingly Plump	1960	$15
❏ 72496	(I Can't Get No) Satisfaction/What's New Pussycat	1965	$10
❏ 71665	Love Is Here to Stay/Moonglow	1960	$15
❏ 71825	Mack the Knife/Hot Saki	1961	$15
❏ 72460	Mirage/Pack It Up	1965	$10
❏ 71489	Moanin'/The Preacher	1959	$15
❏ 71940	St. Louis Blues/Twistin' Chicken	1962	$15
❏ 72306	Theme from "Golden Boy"/Sea Weed	1964	$10
❏ 72436	The Pawnbroker/Harlem Drive	1965	$10
❏ 71425	The Syncopated Clock/Tuxedo Junction	1959	$15

RCA VICTOR
| ❏ 74-0221 | Ole Turkey Buzzard/Soul Full of Gold | 1969 | $6 |

REPRISE
| ❏ 1072 | Passin' the Buck/Money Runner | 1972 | $5 |

UNI
| ❏ 55142 | The Lost Man/Main Squeeze | 1969 | $6 |

UNITED ARTISTS
| ❏ 50706 | Call Me Mister Tibbs/Soul Flower | 1970 | $5 |

JONES, RICKIE LEE
WARNER BROS.
❏ 8825	Chuck E.'s in Love/On Saturday Afternoons in 1963	1979	$5
❏ 29059	It Must Be Love/Magazine	1985	$4
❏ 49100	Last Chance Texaco/Danny's All-Star Joint	1979	$4
❏ 49816	Lucky Girl/Skeletons	1981	$4
❏ 49871	We Belong Together/The Returns	1981	$4

JONES, RONNIE, AND THE CLASSMATES
END
❏ 1014	Lonely Boy/Baby Cries	1958	$120
❏ 1002	Teenage Rock/Little Girl Next Door	1957	$120
❏ 1125	Teenage Rock/Little Girl Next Door	1963	$30

JONES, SPIKE, AND THE CITY SLICKERS
KAPP
| ❏ 314 | I Want the South to Win the War for Christmas/Let's All Sing a Song for Christmas | 1959 | $50 |
—B-side by the Happy Harts
| ❏ 314 [PS] | I Want the South to Win the War for Christmas/Let's All Sing a Song for Christmas | 1959 | $70 |

LIBERTY
❏ 55253	Ah-1, Ah-2, Ah-Sunset Strip (Part 1)/Ah-1, Ah-2, Ah-Sunset Strip (Part 2)	1960	$15
❏ 55684	Dominique/Sweet and Lovely	1964	$12
❏ 55718	I'm in the Mood for Love/Paradise	1964	$10
❏ 55788	Let's Kiss, Kiss, Kiss/Star Jenka	1965	$12
❏ 55649	The Ballad of Jed Clampett/Green, Green	1963	$12
❏ 55191	The Late Late Late Movies (Part 1)/The Late Late Late Movies (Part 2)	1959	$15

RCA VICTOR
❏ 47-2963	(All I Want for Christmas Is) My Two Front Teeth/Happy New Year	1949	$40
❏ 47-4831	(All of a Sudden) My Heart Sings/I'll Never Work Here Anymore	1952	$30
❏ 47-5015	Barnyard Christmas/Socko the Smallest Snowball	1952	$30
—With the Bell Sisters
| ❏ WY-461 | Barnyard Christmas/Socko the Smallest Snowball | 1952 | $30 |
—With the Bell Sisters; "Little Nipper" children's series
❏ 47-3199	Black Bottom/Doin' the New Raccoon	1949	$30
❏ 47-3741	Chinese Mule Train/Riders in the Sky	1950	$30
❏ 47-2992	Dance of the Hours/None But the Lonely Heart	1949	$30
❏ 47-4546	Deep Purple/It Never Rains in Sunny California	1952	$30
❏ 47-4568	Down South/I've Turned a Gadabout	1952	$30
❏ 47-4875	Hotter Than a Pistol/Hot Lips	1952	$30
❏ 47-5413	I Just Love My Mommy/God Bless Us All	1953	$30
❏ 47-3827	I Know a Secret/Charlestone-Mio	1950	$30
❏ 47-5067	I Saw Mommy Kissing Santa Claus/Winter	1952	$30
❏ 47-5067 [PS]	I Saw Mommy Kissing Santa Claus/Winter	1952	$50
❏ 47-5920	I Want Eddie Fisher for Christmas/Japanese Skokiaan	1954	$30
❏ 47-5107	I Went to Your Wedding/I'll Never Work There Anymore	1952	$30
❏ 47-3200	I Wonder Where My Baby Is Tonight/The Varsity Drag	1949	$30
— The above three comprise a box set
❏ 47-3288	Love in Bloom/My Old Flame	1949	$30
❏ 47-4125	My Daddy Is a General to Me/Ill Barkio	1951	$30
❏ 47-5472	Pal-Yat-Chee/Dragnet	1953	$30
❏ 47-4055	Peter Cottontail/Rhapsody from Hungary	1951	$30
❏ 47-5742	Secret Love/I'm in the Mood for Love	1954	$30
❏ 47-4011	Tennessee Waltz/I Haven't Been Home for Three Whole Nights	1950	$30
❏ 47-3287	That Old Black Magic/Liebestraum	1949	$30
❏ 47-3198	The Charleston/Charlestone-Mio	1949	$30
❏ 47-4669	There's a Blue Sky Way Out Yonder/Stop Your Gamblin'	1952	$30
❏ 47-6064	This Song Is For the Birds/Hi Mister	1955	$30
❏ 47-5320	Three Little Fishes/A Din Skal, A Min Skal (Swedish Polka)	1953	$30
❏ 47-4209	Too Young/So 'Elp Me	1951	$30
❏ 47-5497	Where Did My Snowman Go/Santa Brought Me Choo Choo Trains	1953	$30
❏ 47-3126	Wild Bill Hiccup/Morpheus	1949	$30
❏ 47-3289	William Tell Overture/I Kiss Your Hand Madame	1949	$30
— The above three comprise a box set

VERVE
| ❏ 10037 | I'm Popeye the Sailor Man/My Heart Went Boom Boom | 1957 | $20 |
| ❏ 2026 | My Birthday Comes on Christmas/Wouldn't It Be Fun | 1956 | $20 |

WARNER BROS.
| ❏ 5116 | Monster Movie Babe/Teenage Brain Surgeon | 1959 | $20 |

7-Inch Extended Plays
RCA VICTOR
❏ EPA-5058	*Cocktails for Two/Chloe/William Tell Overture/Hawaiian War Chant	1958	$35
❏ EPA288 [PS]	Spike Jones Favorites	1952	$35
❏ EPA-5058 [PS]	Spike Jones (Gold Standard Series)	1958	$35
❏ EPA288	That Old Black Magic/Liebestraum//Love in Bloom/My Old Flame	1952	$35

VERVE
| ❏ 2003 | Love and Marriage/Memories Are Made of This//16 Tacos/The Trouble with Pascual | 1956 | $20 |

JONES, TAMIKO
A&M
| ❏ 1016 | Please Return Your Love to Me/Goodnight My Love | 1969 | $15 |

ARISTA
| ❏ 0110 | Touch Me Baby (Reaching Out for Your Love)/Creepin' (In My Dreams) | 1975 | $6 |

ATLANTIC
❏ 2362	A Man and a Woman/Sidewinder	1966	$30
❏ 716	Cloudy/Let It Flow	1977	$8
❏ 715	Touch Me Baby (Reaching Out for Your Love)/Creepin' (In My Dreams)	1974	$8

CONTEMPO
| ❏ 7001 | Let It Flow/(Instrumental) | 1976 | $8 |

Number	Title	Yr	NM

DECEMBER

Number	Title	Yr	NM
881	Pearl/Don't Go Breaking My Heart	1968	$60
882	Someone to Light Up My Life/Where Do I Go from Here	1968	$12

GOLDEN WORLD

| 40 | I'm Spellbound/Am I Glad Now | 1966 | $300 |

— Yellow label stock copy

| 40 [DJ] | I'm Spellbound/Am I Glad Now | 1966 | $125 |

— White label promo

METROMEDIA

| 205 | Cross My Heart/Since I Don't Have You | 1970 | $50 |
| 197 | Please Don't Tell Me/Blossom | 1970 | $10 |

POLYDOR

| 14580 | Can't Live Without Your Love/Let It Flow | 1979 | $5 |

JONES, TOM

EPIC

50636	Hey Love/Baby, As You Turn Away	1978	$4
50308	Say You'll Stay Until Tomorrow/Lady Lay	1976	$4
50382	Take Me Tonight/I Hope You'll Understand	1977	$4
50506	There's Nothing Stronger Than Our Love/No One Gave Me Love	1978	$4
50468	What a Night/That's Where I Belong	1977	$4

MCA

| 41127 | Dancing Endlessly/Never Had a Lady Before | 1979 | $4 |

MERCURY

880173-7	All the Love Is On the Radio/ (B-side unknown)	1984	$3
76172	A Woman's Touch/I'll Never Get Over You	1982	$4
76100	Darlin'/I Don't Want to Know You That Way	1981	$4
880569-7	Give Her All the Roses (Don't Wait Until Tomorrow)/A Picture of You	1985	$3
880402-7	I'm an Old Rock and Roller (Dancin' to a Different Beat)/My Kind of Girl	1984	$3
812631-7	It'll Be Me/If I Ever Had to Say Goodbye to You	1983	$3
884252-7	It's Four in the Morning/I'll Never Get Over You	1985	$3
814820-7	I've Been Rained On Too/That Old Piano	1983	$3
76125	Lady Lay Down/A Daughter's Question	1981	$4
888911-7	Lover to Lover/A Daughter's Question	1987	$3
870233-7	Things That Matter Most to Me/Green, Green Grass of Home	1988	$3
818801-7	This Time/Memphis, Tennessee	1984	$3
810445-7	Touch Me (I'll Be Your Fool Once More)/We're Wasting Our Time	1983	$3
76115	What in the World's Come Over You/The Things That Matter Most to Me	1981	$4

PARROT

40083	Ain't No Love/When the Band Goes Home	1974	$5
40035	A Minute of Your Time/Looking Out My Window	1968	$8
40056	Can't Stop Loving You/Never Give Away Love	1970	$6
40056 [PS]	Can't Stop Loving You/Never Give Away Love	1970	$8
40008	City Girl/What a Party	1966	$8
40048	Daughter of Darkness/Tupelo Mississippi Flash	1970	$6
40048 [PS]	Daughter of Darkness/Tupelo Mississippi Flash	1970	$8
40025	Delilah/Smile Away Your Blues	1968	$8
40012	Detroit City/Ten Guitars	1967	$8
40014	Funny Familiar Forgotten Feelings/I'll Never Let You Go	1967	$8
40009	Green, Green Grass of Home/If I Had You	1966	$8
40029	Help Yourself/Day by Day	1968	$8
40084	I Got Your Number/The Pain of Love	1974	$5
40018	I'll Never Fall in Love Again/Once Upon a Time	1967	$15

— First pressings contain the full-length version of the A-side; time is listed at over four minutes

| 40018 | I'll Never Fall in Love Again/Once Upon a Time | 1967 | $8 |

— Later pressings delete a verse from the A-side; time is listed at 2:55

| 40024 | I'm Coming Home/Lonely One | 1967 | $8 |

Number	Title	Yr	NM
9737	It's Not Unusual/To Wait for Love (Is to Waste Your Life Away)	1965	$10
40051	I (Who Have Nothing)/Stop Breaking My Heart	1970	$6
40051 [PS]	I (Who Have Nothing)/Stop Breaking My Heart	1970	$8
40078	La, La, La (Just Having You Here)/Love, Love, Love	1973	$5
40020	Land of a Thousand Dances/I Can't Stop Loving You	1967	$30

— May be promo only

40074	Letter to Lucille/Thank the Lord	1973	$5
40038	Love Me Tonight/Hide and Seek	1969	$6
40038 [PS]	Love Me Tonight/Hide and Seek	1969	$8
40086	Memories Don't Leave Like People Do/Wake Up	1975	$5
40081	Pledging My Love/I'm Too Far Gone	1974	$5
9809	Promise Her Anything/Little You	1966	$8
40062	Puppet Man/Every Mile	1971	$6
40062 [PS]	Puppet Man/Every Mile	1971	$20
40064	Puppet Man/Resurrection Shuffle	1971	$5
40058	She's a Lady/My Way	1971	$6
40058 [PS]	She's a Lady/My Way	1971	$8
40016	Sixteen Tons/Things I Wanna Do	1967	$8
40080	Somethin' 'Bout You Baby I Like/Keep a-Talkin' 'Bout Love	1973	$5
9801	Thunderball/Key to My Heart	1965	$8
9801 [PS]	Thunderball/Key to My Heart	1965	$30

— Version 1: with a dead female and a spear gun

| 9801 [PS] | Thunderball/Key to My Heart | 1965 | $15 |

— Version 2: without the above elements on sleeve

40067	Till/One Day Soon	1971	$5
9765	What's New Pussycat/Once Upon a Time	1965	$10
9765 [PS]	What's New Pussycat/Once Upon a Time	1965	$20
40045	Without Love (There Is Nothing)/The Man Who Knows Too Much	1969	$6
40045 [PS]	Without Love (There Is Nothing)/The Man Who Knows Too Much	1969	$8
9787	With These Hands/Some Other Guy	1965	$8
9787 [PS]	With These Hands/Some Other Guy	1965	$15

TOWER

190	Baby I'm in Love/Chills and Fever	1966	$12
126	Little Lonely One/That's What We'll All Do	1965	$15
126 [PS]	Little Lonely One/That's What We'll All Do	1965	$30
176	Lonely One/I Was a Fool	1965	$15
176 [PS]	Lonely One/I Was a Fool	1965	$30

7-Inch Extended Plays

PARROT

| SBG83 | Bridge Over Troubled Water/My Way//Dance of Love/Cabaret/Soul Man | 1971 | $10 |

— Jukebox issue; small hole, plays at 33 1/3 rpm

| SBG62 | Delilah/I Wake Up Crying/It's a Man's Man's World//Danny Boy/Don't Fight It/Get Ready | 1968 | $10 |

— Jukebox issue; small hole, plays at 33 1/3 rpm

| SBG70 [PS] | Help Yourself | 1969 | $12 |
| SBG70 | Help Yourself/I Can't Break the News to Myself/The Bed//I Get Carried Away/If I Promise/All I Can Say Is Goodbye | 1969 | $10 |

— Jukebox issue; small hole, plays at 33 1/3 rpm

| SBG35 [PS] | It's Not Unusual | 1965 | $15 |
| SBG35 | It's Not Unusual/I Need Your Loving/Watcha Gonna Do//Memphis, Tennessee/Skye Boat Song/Worried Man | 1965 | $15 |

— Jukebox issue; small hole, plays at 33 1/3 rpm

SBG83 [PS]	Live at Caesar's Palace	1971	$12
SBG76 [PS]	Live in Las Vegas	1969	$12
SBG62 [PS]	The Tom Jones Fever Zone	1968	$12
SBG75 [PS]	This Is Tom Jones	1969	$12
SBG78 [PS]	Tom	1970	$12
SBG76	Turn On Your Love Light/Bright Lights and You Girl/I Can't Stop Loving You/Help Yourself//Hard to Handle/Twist and Shout	1969	$10

— Jukebox issue; small hole, plays at 33 1/3 rpm

| SBG75 | Wichita Lineman/Fly Me to the Moon/Dance of Love//Hey Jude/I'm a Fool to Want You/Let It Be Me | 1969 | $10 |

— Jukebox issue; small hole, plays at 33 1/3 rpm

Number	Title	Yr	NM

JOPLIN, JANIS
Also see BIG BROTHER AND THE HOLDING COMPANY.

COLUMBIA

45630	Bye Bye Baby/Down on Me	1972	$5
45433	Get It While You Can/Move Over	1971	$5
45314	Me and Bobby McGee/Half Moon	1971	$5
45379	Mercedez Benz/Cry Baby	1971	$5
45080	One Good Man/Try (Just a Little Bit Harder)	1970	$6
45128	Wake Me, Lord/Maybe	1970	$6

JORDAN BROTHERS, THE

CAMEO

| 370 | Good Love Goes Bad/Break Down and Cry | 1965 | $20 |

JAMIE

1133	Be Mine/Dream Romance	1959	$30
1390	It's You Girl/Dream Romance	1970	$70
1205	Love's Made a Fool of You/Whispering Wind	1961	$30
1112	Send Me Your Picture/Oh Lolly	1958	$40
1169	Things I Didn't Say/Polly Plays Her Kettle Drum	1960	$30

JORDAN

| J-100/101 | Send Me Your Picture/Oh Lolly | 1958 | $60 |
| J-102/103 | Sloe Gin/Basin Street Rumble | 1963 | $40 |

PARKWAY

| 945 | What's Wrong With You Baby/The Jordan Theme | 1965 | $20 |

PHILIPS

| 40415 | Gimme Some Lovin'/When I'm With Her | 1966 | $10 |

SSS INTERNATIONAL

| 723 | Good Time/I Want to Be Hers | 1967 | $20 |

TURBO

| 02 | We'll Make It/Charlotte | 1968 | $15 |

JORDAN, LOUIS

ALADDIN

45-3270	Fat Back and Corn Liquor/The Dripper	1955	$40
45-3279	Gal, You Need a Whippin'/Time Is a-Passin'	1955	$40
45-3243	Hurry Home/A Dollar Down	1954	$50
45-3295	It's Hard to Be Good Without You/Gotta Go	1955	$40
45-3249	Louis' Blues/If I Had Any Sense I'd Go Back Home	1954	$40
45-3246	Messy Bessie/I Seen Watcha Done	1954	$40
45-3227	Ooh Wee!/I'll Die Happy	1954	$40
45-3264	Put Some Money in the Pot Boy/Yeah, Yeah, Baby	1954	$40
45-3223	Whiskey, Do Your Stuff/Dad Gum Yo' Hide Boy	1954	$40

DECCA

9-28335	All of Me/There Goes My Heart	1952	$30
9-28543	A Man's Best Friend Is a Bed/You Didn't Want Me Baby	1953	$30
9-28211	Azure-Te (Paris Blues)/Junco Partner	1952	$30
9-27114	Blue Light Boogie -- Part 1/Part 2	1950	$30
9-27784	Cock-a-Doodle-Doo/Trust in Me	1951	$30
9-28983	Fat Sam from Birmingham/The Soona Baby	1954	$20
9-28756	House Party/Hog Wash	1953	$30
9-27620	I Can't Give You Anything But Love, Baby/You Will Always Have a Friend	1951	$30
9-27648	If You're So Smart, How Come You Ain't Rich?/How Blue Can You Get	1951	$30
9-29860	I Gotta Move/Everything That's Made of Wood	1956	$20
9-28664	It's Better to Love/Just Like a Butterfly	1953	$30
9-27898	Lay Somethin' on the Bar/No Sale	1951	$30
9-27324	Lemonade/(You Dyed Your Hair) Chartreuse	1950	$30
9-29018	Lollypop/Nobody Knows You When You're Down and Out	1954	$20
9-27969	Louisville Lodge Meeting/Work Baby Work	1952	$30
9-27806	May Every Day Be Christmas/Bone Dry	1951	$30
9-27058	Onion/Psych-Loco	1950	$40
9-29166	Only Yesterday/I Didn't Know What Time It Was	1954	$20
9-29424	Perdido/Locked Up	1955	$20
9-27129	Show Me How/I Want a Roof Over My Head	1950	$30
9-27203	Tamburitza Boogie/Trouble Then Satisfaction	1950	$30
9-27428	Teardrops from My Eyes/It's a Great, Great Pleasure	1951	$30

Number	Title	Yr	NM
❏ 9-27694	Three Handed Woman/Please Don't Leave Me	1951	$30
❏ 9-28820	Time Marches On/There Must Be A Way	1953	$30
❏ 9-29263	Wake Up Jacob/If It's True	1954	$20
❏ 9-27547	Weak Minded Blues/Is My Pop In There?	1951	$30

MERCURY

❏ 71023x45	Ain't Nobody Here But Us Chickens/Choo Choo Ch'Boogie	1956	$20
❏ 70993x45	Cat Scratchin'/Big Bess	1956	$20
❏ 71106x45	Fire/Ella Mae	1957	$20
❏ 71052x45	Morning Light/Rock Dock	1957	$30
❏ 71206x45	Peace of Mind/I Never Had a Chance	1957	$20
❏ 71319x45	Sweet Hunk of Junk/Wish I Could Make Some Money	1958	$20

PZAZZ

❏ 015	Santa Claus, Santa Claus/Sakatumi	1968	$8
❏ 924	Texarkana Twist/You're My Mule	1962	$10
❏ 926	Workin' Man/The Meeting	1962	$10

WARWICK

❏ 583	Bills/Fifty Cents	1960	$15
❏ 621	I See a Million People/I'm Going Home	1961	$15

X

❏ 4X-0148	Bananas/Baby Let's Do It	1955	$20
❏ 4X-0116	Whatever Lola Wants/It's Been Said	1955	$20

JORDANAIRES, THE

CAPITOL

❏ F3356	A House of Gold/Blow, Whistle, Blow	1956	$30
❏ F3807	Any Which-a-Way/Mood for the Blues	1957	$30
❏ F2815	Bugle Call from Heaven/Oh Lord Stand By Me	1954	$30
❏ F1363	David and Goliath/Journey to the Sky	1951	$30
❏ F3492	Hands of God/Fighting for the Lord	1956	$30
❏ F1499	He Bought My Soul/Read That Book	1951	$30
❏ F3158	Let's Make a Joyful Noise/Will You Be Ready	1955	$30
❏ F3940	Little Miss Ruby/All I Need Is You	1958	$20
❏ F1407	One Day/Something Within	1951	$30
❏ F3265	Shaking Bridges/What Will the Verdict Be	1955	$30
❏ 4431	Sit Down/Girl in the Valley	1960	$15
❏ F3610	Sugaree/Baby Won't You Please Come Home	1957	$30
❏ F3750	Summer Vacation/Each Day	1957	$30
❏ F2725	Tattler's Wagon/In My Saviour's Loving Arms	1954	$30
❏ F2915	This Ole House/Be Prepared	1954	$30
❏ F3684	Walk Away/Ridin' for a Fall	1957	$30
❏ F4025	Wella Wella Honey/Where Many Go	1958	$20
❏ F3022	When the Saints Go Marching In/All the Way	1955	$30
❏ F1254	Working on the Building/I Want to Rest	1950	$40

COLUMBIA

❏ 4-43283	Malibu Run/Who Does He Think He Is	1965	$10

— Said to be a different group than the rest.

DECCA

❏ 9-46242	Dig a Little Deeper/I'm Free Again	1950	$50
❏ 9-46366	Loafin' on a Lazy River/Sweet Roses of Morn	1951	$30

DECCA FAITH SERIES

❏ 9-14530	Peace in the Valley/(B-side unknown)	1950	$40

RCA VICTOR

❏ 47-5076	Beautiful City/Stand by Me	1952	$30
❏ 47-5077	By the River of Life/Noah	1952	$30
❏ 47-4645	Goodbye Pharaoh/Roll, Jordan, Roll	1952	$30
❏ 47-5021	He'll Understand and Say Well Done/I'm Moving On to Glory	1952	$30
❏ 47-5458	Is He Satisfied/I Am So Glad Jesus Lifted Me	1953	$30
❏ 47-4948	My Rock/I'll Tell It Wherever I Go	1952	$30
❏ 47-5373	On the Jericho Road/The Lord Will Make a Way Somehow	1953	$30
❏ 47-4378	The Four Horsemen (Of the Apocalypse)/Mansion Over the Hilltop	1951	$30
❏ 47-5079	When Dey Ring Dem Golden Bells/Didn't They Crucify My Lord	1952	$30
❏ 47-4607	Who Can He Be/Gonna Walk Those Golden Stairs	1952	$30

X

❏ 034	Say It Again/I Can't Smoke You Out of My Heart	1954	$30

JOSEPH, MARGIE

ATLANTIC

❏ 2907	Born to Wander/Let's Go Somewhere and Love	1972	$10
❏ 2988	Come Lay Some Lovin' on Me/Ridin' High	1973	$40
❏ 3445	Come On Back to Me Lover/He Came Into My Life	1978	$60
❏ 3269	I Can't Move No Mountains/Just As Soon As the Feeling's Over	1975	$10
❏ 3509	I Feel His Love Getting Stronger/How Will I Know	1978	$20
❏ 2954	Let's Stay Together/I'd Rather Go Blind	1973	$12
❏ 3525	Love Takes Tears/I Don't Want to Get Over You	1978	$30
❏ 3032	My Love/Sweet Surrender	1974	$8
❏ 3290	Stay Still/Just As Soon As the Feeling's Over	1975	$10
❏ 2933	Touch Your Woman/I'm So Glad I'm Your Woman	1973	$6
❏ 3220	Words (Are Impossible)/I Still Love You	1974	$8

COTILLION

❏ 99737	Big Strong Man/(B-side unknown)	1984	$5
❏ 44207	Don't Turn the Lights Off/All Cried Out	1976	$8
❏ 44201	Hear the Words, Feel the Feeling/I Get Carried Away	1976	$12

H.C.R.C.

❏ HC7-31500	Move to the Groove/(Instrumental)	1983	$6

OKEH

❏ 4-7313	A Matter of Life or Death/Show Me	1968	$70
❏ 4-7304	Why Does a Man Have to Lie/Show Me	1967	$60

VOLT

❏ 4012	One More Chance/Never Can You Be	1969	$15
❏ 4046	Punish Me/A Sweeter Tomorrow	1970	$50
❏ 4056	Stop! In the Name of Love/Make Me Believe You'll Stay	1971	$10
❏ 4061	The Other Woman Got My Man and Gone/I'll Always Love You	1971	$100
❏ 4023	What You Gonna Do/Nobody	1969	$125

JOSEPHINE XIII

CAMEO

❏ 427	Down on the Funny Farm (Oy Vey)/Break the Drums	1966	$30

JOSHUA FOX

TETRAGRAMMATON

❏ 1532	Don't Tell Me a Story/It's Just Meant to Be	1969	$15
❏ 1527	Goin' Down for Big Numbers/Moontime Bore	1969	$15

JOSIE AND THE PUSSYCATS

CAPITOL

❏ 2967	Every Beat of My Heart/It's All Right with Me	1970	$30

— Same song as CP 59, but a slightly different title and a mono mix

❏ CP61-4	I Wanna Make You Happy/It's Gotta Be Him	1970	$30
❏ CP61-4 [PS]	I Wanna Make You Happy/It's Gotta Be Him	1970	$40
❏ CP58-1	Letter to Mama/Inside, Outside, Upside Down	1970	$30
❏ CP58-1 [PS]	Letter to Mama/Inside, Outside, Upside Down	1970	$40
❏ 3045	Stop, Look and Listen/You've Come a Long Way, Baby	1971	$30
❏ CP59-2	With Every Beat of My Heart/Josie	1970	$30
❏ CP59-2 [PS]	With Every Beat of My Heart/Josie	1970	$40

JOURNEY

Original lead singer Gregg Rolie was also the original lead singer of SANTANA.

COLUMBIA

❏ 38-04004	After the Fall/Only Solutions	1983	$3
❏ 3-10757	Anytime/Can Do	1978	$4
❏ 1-11213	Any Way You Want It/When You're Alone (It Ain't Easy)	1980	$3
❏ 38-05869	Be Good to Yourself/Only the Young	1986	$3
❏ 38-05869 [PS]	Be Good to Yourself/Only the Young	1986	$3
❏ 18-02567	Don't Stop Believin'/Natural Thing	1981	$3
❏ 18-02567 [PS]	Don't Stop Believin'/Natural Thing	1981	$4
❏ 38-03840	Faithfully/Frontiers	1983	$3
❏ 38-06302	Girl Can't Help It/It Could Have Been You	1986	$3
❏ 38-06302 [PS]	Girl Can't Help It/It Could Have Been You	1986	$3
❏ 1-11339	Good Morning Girl//Stay Awhile/Line of Fire	1980	$3
❏ 38-06301 [DJ]	I'll Be Alright Without You (Hot Mix)/(Album Version)	1986	$5
❏ 38-06301	I'll Be Alright Without You/The Eyes of a Woman	1986	$3
❏ 38-06301 [PS]	I'll Be Alright Without You/The Eyes of a Woman	1986	$3
❏ 3-10800	Lights/Somethin' to Hide	1978	$4
❏ 3-11036	Lovin', Touchin', Squeezin'/Daydream	1979	$3
❏ 3-10324	On a Saturday Night/To Play Some Music	1976	$6
❏ 18-02687	Open Arms/Little Girl	1982	$3
❏ 18-02687 [PS]	Open Arms/Little Girl	1982	$4
❏ 13-03133	Open Arms/The Party's Over	1982	$3

— Reissue

❏ 38-04151	Send Her My Love/Chain Reaction	1983	$3
❏ CNR-03568	Separate Ways (Worlds Apart)/(B-side blank)	1983	$5

— One-sided budget release

❏ 38-03513	Separate Ways (Worlds Apart)/Frontiers	1983	$3
❏ 38-03513 [PS]	Separate Ways (Worlds Apart)/Frontiers	1983	$4
❏ 3-10370	She Makes Me (Feel Alright)/It's All Too Much	1976	$6
❏ 3-10522	Spaceman/Nickel and Dime	1977	$6
❏ 18-02883	Still They Ride/La Raza Del Sol	1982	$3
❏ 18-02883 [PS]	Still They Ride/La Raza Del Sol	1982	$4
❏ 38-06134	Suzanne/Ask the Lonely	1986	$3
❏ 38-06134 [PS]	Suzanne/Ask the Lonely	1986	$3
❏ 11-60505	The Party's Over (Hopelessly in Love)/Just the Same Way	1981	$3
❏ 1-11143	Too Late/Do You Recall	1979	$3
❏ 3-10137	To Play Some Music/Topaz	1975	$6
❏ 1-11275	Walks Like a Lady/People and Places	1980	$3
❏ 3-10700	Wheel in the Sky/Can Do	1978	$4
❏ 13-03134	Who's Crying Now/Don't Stop Believin'	1982	$3

— Reissue

❏ 18-02241	Who's Crying Now/Mother, Father	1981	$3
❏ 18-02241 [PS]	Who's Crying Now/Mother, Father	1981	$4
❏ 38-07043	Why Can't This Night Go On Forever/Positive Touch	1987	$3
❏ 38-07043 [PS]	Why Can't This Night Go On Forever/Positive Touch	1987	$3

GEFFEN

❏ 7-29090	Only the Young/I'll Only Fall in Love Again	1985	$4

— B-side by Sammy Hagar

❏ 7-29090 [PS]	Only the Young/I'll Only Fall in Love Again	1985	$4

JOURNEYMEN, THE (1)

AMY

❏ 821	Cup-E-Co/Hush Storm	1961	$15

CAPITOL

❏ 4625	500 Miles/The River She Comes Down	1961	$10
❏ 4737	Don't Turn Around/Hush Now Sally	1962	$12
❏ 4678	Soft Blow the Summer Winds/Kumbaya	1962	$12
❏ 4829	What'll I Do/Loadin' Coal	1962	$10

JOURNEYMEN, THE (2)

IONA

❏ 1115	Surfer's Blues/Surfer's Rule	1963	$60
❏ 1115	Surfer's Blues/Surfer's Rule	1963	$50

— Rerelease as "The Baylanders"

❏ 1111	Work Out/Bag's Groove	1961	$60

JOY, BENNY

ANTLER

❏ 4011	Crash the Party/Little Red Book	1959	$500

DECCA

❏ 31280	Birds of a Feather Fly Together/You Go Your Way (And I'll Go Mine)	1961	$20

DIXIE

❏ 2001	Steady with Betty/Spin the Bottle	1958	$500

DOT

❏ 16445	I'm of No More Use to You Old Earth/Harry's Harem	1963	$20

RAM

❏ 1107	Ittie Bittie Everything/(B-side unknown)	1959	$500

TRI-DEC

❏ 8667	Steady with Betty/Spin the Bottle	1958	$600

Number	Title	Yr	NM

JOY DIVISION
Also see NEW ORDER.

FACTORY
Number	Title	Yr	NM
❑ FACTUS23	Love Will Tear Us Apart/ These Days	1980	$20
❑ FACTUS23 [PS]	Love Will Tear Us Apart/ These Days	1980	$20
❑ FACUS23 [DJ]	Love Will Tear Us Apart/ These Days	1980	$125

— White label promo

JOY, RODDIE

PARKWAY
Number	Title	Yr	NM
❑ 991	A Boy Is Just a Toy/Stop	1966	$20
❑ 134	Every Breath I Take/Walkin' Back	1967	$15
❑ 151	I Want You Back/Let's Start All Over	1967	$15
❑ 101	Something Strange Is Going On/Stop	1966	$15

RED BIRD
Number	Title	Yr	NM
❑ Oct-0037	If There's Anything Else You Want (Let Me Know)/Stop	1965	$50
❑ Oct-0021	Love Hit Me with a Wallop/ Come Back Baby	1965	$30
❑ Oct-0031	The La La Song/He's So Easy to Love	1965	$30

JOY TONES, THE

COED
Number	Title	Yr	NM
❑ 600	This Love (That I'm Giving You)/I Wanna Party Some More	1965	$15

JOYETTES, THE

ONYX
Number	Title	Yr	NM
❑ 502	Story of Love/The Boy Next Door	1956	$125

JOYTONES, THE

RAMA
Number	Title	Yr	NM
❑ 191	All My Love Belongs to You/You Just Won't Treat Me Right	1956	$200
❑ 202	Gee What a Boy/Is This Really the End	1956	$300
❑ 215	My Foolish Heart/Jimbo Jango	1956	$500

J'S WITH JAMIE, THE

COLUMBIA
Number	Title	Yr	NM
❑ 4-43017	Everybody Says Don't/ Yoshiko	1984	$12
❑ 4-42903	Here's Love/Au Revoir	1963	$12
❑ 4-42595	Laugh It Up/Nowhere to Go But Up	1962	$12
❑ 4-42635	Little Me/Come On Strong	1962	$12
❑ 4-42939	London (Is a Little Bit of All Right)/This Ole House	1964	$10
❑ 4-42422	Momma, Momma, Momma/ The Sound of Money	1962	$10
❑ 4-42488	One Little World Apart/Let's Not Be Sensible	1962	$10
❑ 4-43068	Theme from "A Summer Place"/Popsicles in Paris	1964	$10

JUDAS PRIEST
FIGHT, TWO, HALFORD, TRAPEZE, RACER X, WINTERS BANE related.

COLUMBIA
Number	Title	Yr	NM
❑ 11135	Diamonds and Rust/ Starbreaker	1979	$4
❑ 03168	Diamonds and Rust/You've Got Another Thing Comin'	1982	$4
❑ 02083	Heading Out to the Highway/ Rock Forever	1981	$4
❑ 11308	Living After Midnight/Metal Gods	1980	$4
❑ 05856	Locked In/Hot for Love	1986	$3
❑ 04436	Love Bites/Jawbreaker	1984	$3
❑ 06281	Parental Guidance/Rock You All Around the World	1986	$3
❑ 04371	Some Heads Are Gona Roll/ Breaking the Law (Live)	1984	$3
❑ 06142	Turbo Lover/Reckless	1986	$3

JUDDS, THE

RCA
Number	Title	Yr	NM
❑ 8715-7-R	Change of Heart/I Wish She Wouldn't Treat You That Way	1988	$3
❑ 5000-7-R	Cry Myself to Sleep/Dream Chaser	1986	$3
❑ 5094-7-R	Don't Be Cruel/The Sweetest Gift	1987	$3
❑ 5094-7-R [PS]	Don't Be Cruel/The Sweetest Gift	1987	$6

— Sleeve may be promo only

Number	Title	Yr	NM
❑ GB-14348	Girls Night Out/Love Is Alive	1986	$3

— Gold Standard Series

Number	Title	Yr	NM
❑ PB-13991	Girls Night Out/Sleeping Heart	1985	$4
❑ 8300-7-R	Give a Little Love/Why Don't You Believe Me	1988	$3
❑ PB-14290	Grandpa (Tell Me 'Bout the Good Old Days)/Drops of Water	1986	$4
❑ PB-13673	Had a Dream (For the Heart)/Don't You Hear Jerusalem Moan	1983	$5
❑ PB-13673 [DJ]	Had a Dream (For the Heart) (same on both sides)	1983	$30

— Promo only on red vinyl

Number	Title	Yr	NM
❑ PB-14193	Have Mercy/Bye Bye Blues	1985	$4
❑ 5164-7-R	I Know Where I'm Going/If I Were You	1987	$3
❑ 8947-7-R	Let Me Tell You About Love/ Water of Love	1989	$3
❑ PB-13906	Light of the Stable/Change of Heart	1984	$4
❑ PB-14093	Love Is Alive/Mr. Pain	1985	$4
❑ PB-13772	Mama He's Crazy/Down Home	1984	$4
❑ GB-14068	Mama He's Crazy/Why Not Me	1985	$3

— Gold Standard Series

Number	Title	Yr	NM
❑ 5255-7-R	Maybe Your Baby's Got the Blues/My Baby's Gone	1987	$3
❑ 9077-7-R	One Man Woman/Sleepless Nights	1989	$3
❑ 5350-7-R	Silver Bells/Away in a Manger	1987	$3
❑ 9069-7-R	Silver Bells/Oh Holy Night	1989	$4
❑ 5329-7-R	Turn It Loose/Cow Cow Boogie	1987	$3
❑ 8383-7-R	Turn It Loose/Maybe Your Baby's Got the Blues	1988	$3

— Gold Standard Series

Number	Title	Yr	NM
❑ PB-14240	Who Is This Babe/Change of Heart	1985	$4
❑ 5048-7-R	Who Is This Babe/Light of the Stable	1986	$3
❑ GB-14352	Why Not Me/Have Mercy	1986	$3

— Gold Standard Series

Number	Title	Yr	NM
❑ PB-13923	Why Not Me/Lazy Country Evening	1984	$4

JUDY AND THE DUETS

WARE
Number	Title	Yr	NM
❑ 6000	Christmas With The Beatles/ The Blind Boy	1964	$30

JULIAN, DON, AND THE MEADOWLARKS

CLASSIC ARTISTS
Number	Title	Yr	NM
❑ 105	White Christmas/Marry Christmas, Baby	1988	$6

DOOTO
Number	Title	Yr	NM
❑ 424	Blue Moon/Big Mama Wants to Rock	1957	$60

DOOTONE
Number	Title	Yr	NM
❑ 367	Always and Always/I Got Tore Up	1955	$80

— Red label

Number	Title	Yr	NM
❑ 367	Always and Always/I Got Tore Up	1955	$60

— Maroon label

Number	Title	Yr	NM
❑ 359	Heaven and Paradise/ Embarrassing Moments	1955	$300
❑ 405	I Am a Believer/Boogie Woogie Teenager	1956	$100
❑ 394	Please Love a Fool/Oop Boopy Oop	1956	$60
❑ 372	This Must Be Paradise/Mine All Mine	1955	$70

DYNAMITE
Number	Title	Yr	NM
❑ 1112	Heaven Only Knows/Popeye	1962	$40

ORIGINAL SOUND
Number	Title	Yr	NM
❑ 3	Please Say You Want Me/ Doin' the Cha Cha Cha	1959	$50
❑ 12	There's a Girl/Blue Moon	1960	$40

RPM
Number	Title	Yr	NM
❑ 399	Love Only You/Real Pretty Mama	1954	$300

— As "The Meadow Larks"

Number	Title	Yr	NM
❑ 406	LSMFT Blues (Lord Find My Sweet Theresa)/Pass the Gin	1954	$3000

— As "The Meadow Larks"

7-Inch Extended Plays

DOOTO
Number	Title	Yr	NM
❑ 203	(contents unknown)	1958	$250
❑ 203 [PS]	Don Julian and the Meadowlarks	1958	$250

— Reissue of Dootone 203

DOOTONE
Number	Title	Yr	NM
❑ 203	(contents unknown)	1956	$400
❑ 203 [PS]	Don Julian and the Meadowlarks	1956	$400

JULY FOUR, THE

CAMEO
Number	Title	Yr	NM
❑ 480	Mr. Miff/Frightened Little Girl	1967	$30

JUNIOR AND HIS FRIENDS

ABC-PARAMOUNT
Number	Title	Yr	NM
❑ 10089	Who's Our Pet, Annette!/ A.B.C. Love	1960	$40

JUST THREE

HIT
Number	Title	Yr	NM
❑ 222	The "In" Crowd/Hang On Sloopy	1965	$15

— B-side by the Roamers

JUSTICE, JIMMY

BLUE CAT
Number	Title	Yr	NM
❑ 101	Don't Let the Stars Get In Your Eyes/Guitar Player (Her and Him)	1964	$12

KAPP
Number	Title	Yr	NM
❑ 469	Ain't That Funny/One	1962	$15
❑ 514	I Wake Up Crying/World of Lonely People	1963	$15
❑ 482	When My Little Girl Is Smiling/If I Lost Your Love	1962	$15

JUSTIS, BILL

BELL
Number	Title	Yr	NM
❑ 921	Electric Dreams/Dark Continent Contribution	1970	$5

MCA
Number	Title	Yr	NM
❑ 40810	Foxy Lady/Orange Blossom Special	1977	$4

MONUMENT
Number	Title	Yr	NM
❑ 8699	Sea Dream/Touching, Feeling, Dreaming	1976	$5

NRC
Number	Title	Yr	NM
❑ 1119	Boogie Woogie Rock/ Blowing Rock	1959	$30

PHILLIPS INTERNATIONAL
Number	Title	Yr	NM
❑ 3535	Bop Train/String of Pearls	1958	$30
❑ 3529	Cattywampus/Summer Holiday	1958	$30
❑ 3522	College Man/The Stranger	1958	$30
❑ 3544	Flea Circus/Cloud Nine	1959	$30
❑ 3525	Wild Rice/Scroungie	1958	$30

PLAY ME
Number	Title	Yr	NM
❑ 1119	Boogie Woogie Rock/ Blowing Rock	1959	$50

— As "The Jury"; contains a different version of the A-side than those that give Bill Justis credit

Number	Title	Yr	NM
❑ 1119	Boogie Woogie Rock/ Blowing Rock	1959	$40

— As "Bill Justis and the Jury"; second pressing

SMASH
Number	Title	Yr	NM
❑ 1955	How Soon/Ska-Ha	1964	$10
❑ 1812	I'm Gonna Learn to Dance/ Tamoure	1963	$10
❑ 1812 [PS]	I'm Gonna Learn to Dance/ Tamoure	1963	$20
❑ 1977	Late Game/Last Farewell	1965	$12
❑ 1902	Lavender Sax/Fia, Fia	1964	$12
❑ 1851	Sunday in Madrid/Satin and Velvet	1963	$10

K

K.C. AND THE SUNSHINE BAND

CASABLANCA

Number	Title	Yr	NM
❏ 2278	Dancin' in the Streets/ Moonlight Madness	1980	$4

—As "Teri DeSario with K.C.

EPIC

Number	Title	Yr	NM
❏ 34-03556	Don't Run (Come Back to Me)/On the One	1983	$4
❏ 14-02652	It Happens Every Night/ Stand Up	1981	$4
❏ 14-02545	Love Me/Don't Say No	1981	$4

MECA

Number	Title	Yr	NM
❏ 1001	Give It Up/Uptight	1983	$4

—K.C. solo

Number	Title	Yr	NM
❏ 1003	On the Top/(B-side unknown)	1984	$6

T.K.

Number	Title	Yr	NM
❏ 1026	Black Water Gold (Part 1)/ Black Water Gold (Part 2)	1978	$4

—As "The Sunshine Band

Number	Title	Yr	NM
❏ 1001	Blow Your Whistle/I'm Going to Do Something Good to You	1973	$5

—As "K.C. and the Sunshine Junkanoo Band

Number	Title	Yr	NM
❏ 1025	Boogie Shoes/I Get Lifted	1978	$4
❏ 1025 [PS]	Boogie Shoes/I Get Lifted	1978	$8
❏ 1030	Do You Feel All Right/I Will Love You Tomorrow	1978	$4
❏ 1030 [PS]	Do You Feel All Right/I Will Love You Tomorrow	1978	$4
❏ 1033	Do You Wanna Go Party/ Come to My Island	1979	$4
❏ 1009	Get Down Tonight/You Don't Know	1975	$4
❏ 1020	I Like to Do It/Come On In	1976	$4
❏ 1008	I'm a Pushover/You Don't Know	1974	$5
❏ 1022	I'm Your Boogie Man/Wrap Your Arms Around Me	1977	$4
❏ 1028	It's the Same Old Song/Let's Go Party	1978	$4
❏ 1028 [PS]	It's the Same Old Song/Let's Go Party	1978	$4
❏ 1036	Let's Go Rock and Roll/I've Got the Feeling	1980	$4
❏ 1038	Make Me a Star/Do Me	1980	$4

—K.C. solo

Number	Title	Yr	NM
❏ 1035	Please Don't Go/I Betcha Didn't Know That	1979	$4
❏ 1019	(Shake, Shake, Shake) Shake Your Booty/Boogie Shoes	1976	$4
❏ 1010	Shotgun Shuffle/Hey J	1975	$4

—As "The Sunshine Band

Number	Title	Yr	NM
❏ 1003	Sound Your Funky Horn/ Why Don't We Get Together	1974	$5
❏ 1044	Space Cadet/Do Me	1981	$4

—K.C. solo

Number	Title	Yr	NM
❏ 1015	That's the Way (I Like It)/ What Makes You Happy	1975	$4
❏ 1031	Who Do Ya Love/Sho-Nuff	1978	$4
❏ 1031 [PS]	Who Do Ya Love/Sho-Nuff	1978	$4

K-DOE, ERNIE

DUKE

Number	Title	Yr	NM
❏ 437	Gotta Pack My Bag/How Sweet You Are	1968	$8
❏ 456	I'll Make Everything Be Alright/Wishing in Vain	1969	$8
❏ 450	I'm Sorry/Trying to Make You Love Me	1969	$8
❏ 423	(It Will Have to Do) Until the Real Thing Comes Along/ Little Marie	1967	$8
❏ 411	Later for Tomorrow/Dancin' Man	1966	$8
❏ 387	Little Bit of Everything/ Someone	1965	$8
❏ 404	Little Marie/Somebody Told Me	1966	$8
❏ 420	Love Me Like I Wanna/Don't Kill My Groove	1967	$8
❏ 378	My Mother-in-Law (Is In My Hair Again)/Looking Into the Future	1964	$8
❏ 400	Please Don't Stop/ Boomerang	1966	$8

EMBER

Number	Title	Yr	NM
❏ 1075	My Love for You/Shirley's Tuff	1961	$20
❏ 1050	My Love for You/Tuff-Enuff	1959	$30

INSTANT

Number	Title	Yr	NM
❏ 3260	Baby, SInce I Met You/ Sufferin' So	1963	$12

ISLAND

Number	Title	Yr	NM
❏ 031	Let Me Love You/So Good	1975	$6

JANUS

Number	Title	Yr	NM
❏ 167	Here Come the Girls/Long Way Home	1971	$6

MINIT

Number	Title	Yr	NM
❏ 634	A Certain Girl/I Cried My Last Tear	1961	$20
❏ 651	Beating Like a Tom-Tom/I Got to Find Somebody	1962	$20
❏ 661	Easier Said Than Done/ Be Sweet	1963	$20
❏ 645	Hey Hey Hey/Love You the Best	1962	$20
❏ 665	I'm the Boss/Pennies Worth o' Happiness	1963	$20
❏ 656	Loving You/Get Out of My House	1962	$20
❏ 604	Make You Love Me/There's a Will, There's a Way	1959	$40
❏ 623	Mother-in-Law/Wanted, $10,000 Reward	1961	$30

—Side 1 is at the correct speed. Trail-off number is "SO-738-2

Number	Title	Yr	NM
❏ 623	Mother-in-Law/Wanted, $10,000 Reward	1961	$200

—Side 1 was accidentally mis-mastered at 33 1/3 rpm. Trail-off number is "45-SO-738

Number	Title	Yr	NM
❏ 641	Popeye Joe/Come On Home	1962	$20
❏ 614	'Tain't It the Truth/Hello My Lover	1960	$30
❏ 627	Te-Ta-Te-Ta-Ta/Real Man	1961	$20

SPECIALTY

Number	Title	Yr	NM
❏ 563	Eternity/Do Baby Do	1955	$50

—As "Ernest Kador

UNITED ARTISTS

Number	Title	Yr	NM
❏ 0110	Mother-in-Law/A Wonderful Dream	1973	$5

—Silver Spotlight Series" reissue; B-side by the Majors

KACT-TIES, THE

ATCO

Number	Title	Yr	NM
❏ 6299	Oh What a Night/Let Me In Your Life	1964	$20

—As "The Kac-Ties

KAPE

Number	Title	Yr	NM
❏ 501	Happy Birthday/Girl in My Heart	1965	$20

—As "The Kac-Ties

Number	Title	Yr	NM
❏ 503	Let Your Love Light Shine/ Were-Wolf	1965	$20

—As "The Kac-Ties

Number	Title	Yr	NM
❏ 502	Walkin' in the Rain/Smile	1965	$20

—As "The Kac-Ties

SHELLEY

Number	Title	Yr	NM
❏ 163	Let Your Love Light Shine/ Were-Wolf	1963	$30
❏ 165	Oh What a Night/Let Me In Your Life	1963	$30

TRANS ATLAS

Number	Title	Yr	NM
❏ 695	Walkin' in the Rain/Smile	1962	$300

—With thunderstorm sound effects

Number	Title	Yr	NM
❏ 695	Walkin' in the Rain/Smile	1962	$200

—Without thunderstorm sound effects

KAEMPFERT, BERT

DECCA

Number	Title	Yr	NM
❏ 31350	Afrikaan Beat/Echo in the Night	1961	$8
❏ 31666	Almost There/Treat for Trumpet	1964	$6
❏ 31882	Bye Bye Blues/Remember When	1965	$6
❏ 32241	Caravan/Milina	1967	$6
❏ 30866	Cerveza/Catalina	1959	$8
❏ 31611	Dancing in a Dream/Big Build Up	1964	$6
❏ 31498	Danke Schoen/Give and Take	1963	$6
❏ 32518	Games People Play/Here's My Life (Here's My Love)	1969	$5
❏ 31463	Gentleman Jim/Tipsy Gypsy	1963	$6
❏ 31420	Goden Wings in the Sun/ Cinderella After Midnight	1962	$8
❏ 31439	Happy Trumpeter/Tootsie Flutie	1962	$8
❏ 31873	Holiday for Bells/Jumpin' Jiminy Christmas	1965	$8
❏ 32008	I Can't Give You Anything But Love/Milica	1966	$6
❏ 32809	(I'll Be With You) In Apple Blossom Time/My Life	1971	$5
❏ 32935	Lonely Is the Name/Only a Fool	1972	$5
❏ 31638	Love/Blue Midnight	1964	$6
❏ 32204	Love for Love/You Are My Sunshine	1967	$6
❏ 30616	Midnight Blues/Ducky	1958	$10
❏ 32329	Mister Sandman/Lonely Is the Name	1968	$5
❏ 31812	Moon Over Naples/The Moon Is Making Eyes	1965	$6
❏ 32379	My Way of Life/Malaysian Melody	1968	$5
❏ 732471	One Lonely Night/The Maltese Melody	1969	$5
❏ 32875	Proud Mary/In Our Time	1971	$5
❏ 32094	Pussy Footin'/Hold Me	1967	$6

Number	Title	Yr	NM
❏ 32647	Someday We'll Be Together/ We Can Make It Girl	1970	$5
❏ 32772	Something/Sweet Caroline	1971	$5
❏ 32051	So What's New/Hold Back the Dawn	1966	$6
❏ 31945	Strangers in the Night/But Not Today	1966	$6
❏ 32159	Talk/Night Dreams	1967	$6
❏ 31236	Tenderly/Without Your Love	1961	$8
❏ 31388	That Happy Feeling/Take Me	1962	$8
❏ 31532	The Bass Walks/Don't Talk to Me	1963	$6
❏ 32283	The First Waltz/Somebody Loves You	1968	$5
❏ 32715	Theme from "You Can't Win Them All"/Flight to Mecca	1970	$5
❏ 31778	Three O'Clock in the Morning/Nothing's New	1965	$6
❏ 31141	Wonderland by Night/ Dreaming the Blues	1960	$8

MCA

Number	Title	Yr	NM
❏ 40221	The Most Beautiful Girl/ Moon Over Baja	1974	$4

7-Inch Extended Plays

DECCA

Number	Title	Yr	NM
❏ 7-34390 [PS]	Bert Kaempfert's Greatest Hits	1966	$12
❏ ED2697 [PS]	Wonderland by Night	1961	$12
❏ 7-34390	Wonderland by Night/ Afrikaan Beat/Red Roses for a Blue Lady//Strangers in the Night/That Happy Feeling/Wiedershe'n	1966	$10

—Jukebox issue; small hole, plays at 33 1/3 rpm; "Wiedershe'n" is the spelling on the label

Number	Title	Yr	NM
❏ ED2697	Wonderland by Night/ Dreaming the Blues//As I Love You/Tammy	1961	$10

KAINAPAU, GEORGE

DECCA

Number	Title	Yr	NM
❏ 27220	Silent Night/Mele Kalikimaka	1950	$20

KAK

EPIC

Number	Title	Yr	NM
❏ 10383 [DJ]	Everything's Changing (Long Version)/Everything's Changing (Edited Version)	1968	$30

—May be promo only

Number	Title	Yr	NM
❏ 10446	I've Got Time/Disbelievin'	1969	$30

KALEIDOSCOPE, THE

EPIC

Number	Title	Yr	NM
❏ 10117	Elevator Man/Please	1967	$40
❏ 10239	I Found Out/Rampe Rampe	1967	$40
❏ 10481	Lie to Me/Let the Good Love Flow	1969	$40
❏ 10219	Little Orphan Annie/Why Try	1967	$40

KALIN TWINS, THE

AMY

Number	Title	Yr	NM
❏ 969	Thinkin' About You Baby/ Sometimes It Comes	1966	$8

DECCA

Number	Title	Yr	NM
❏ 31286	Bubbles (I'm Forever Blowing Bubbles)/One More Time	1961	$20
❏ 30868	Cool/When I Look in the Mirror	1959	$30
❏ 30745	Forget Me Not/Dream of Me	1958	$30
❏ 30807	It's Only the Beginning/Oh My Goodness	1959	$30
❏ 31064	Loneliness/Chicken Thief	1960	$20
❏ 31220	Momma-Poppa/You Mean the World to Me	1961	$20
❏ 30911	Sweet Sugar Lips/Moody	1959	$30
❏ 31410	Trouble/A Picture of You	1962	$20
❏ 31111	True to You/Blue, Blue Town	1960	$20
❏ 30642	When/Three O'Clock Thrill	1958	$30
❏ 30977	Why Don't You Believe Me/ The Meaning of the Blues	1959	$30
❏ 30977 [PS]	Why Don't You Believe Me/ The Meaning of the Blues	1959	$40

7-Inch Extended Plays

Number	Title	Yr	NM
❏ ED2641 [PS]	Forget Me Not	1958	$70
❏ ED2641	Forget Me Not/Cool//Clickety Clack/Tag-A-Long	1958	$60
❏ ED2623 [PS]	When	1958	$100
❏ ED2623	When/Three O'Clock Thrill// Jumpin' Jack/Walkin' to School	1958	$75

KALLEN, KITTY, AND GEORGIE SHAW

DECCA

Number	Title	Yr	NM
❏ 29776	Go On with the Wedding/ The Second Greatest Sex	1955	$15

Number	Title	Yr	NM

KALLEN, KITTY

20TH CENTURY FOX
Number	Title	Yr	NM
❏ 471	Make Somebody Love You/ Lies and More Lies	1964	$8

BELL
| ❏ 673 | Summer, Summer Wind/ Oba, Oba | 1967 | $8 |

COLUMBIA
❏ 41622	Always in My Heart/Got a Date with an Angel	1960	$15
❏ 41769	Come Live with Me/Be True to Me	1960	$15
❏ 41934	Hey Good Lookin'/Raining in My Heart	1961	$15
❏ 41857	I Believe in You/The Things You Left in My Heart	1960	$15
❏ 41473	If I Give My Heart to You/The Door That Won't Open	1959	$15
❏ 42247	It Wasn't God Who Made Honky Tonk Angels/You Are My Sunshine	1961	$15
❏ 41671	Make Love to Me/Heaven Help Me	1960	$15
❏ 42038	Summertime Lies/Yassu	1961	$15
❏ 41546	That Old Feeling/Need Me	1959	$15
❏ 40298	The High and the Mighty/Still You'd Break My Heart	1954	$20

— With Harry James
| ❏ 41236 | When Will I Know/Love Is a Sacred Thing | 1958 | $15 |

DECCA
❏ 28904	A Little Lie/Are You Looking for a Sweetheart	1953	$20
❏ 29473	By Bayou Bay/Kitty Who?	1955	$15
❏ 30516	Crying Roses/I Never Was the One	1957	$15
❏ 30049	How About Me/The Lonely One	1956	$15
❏ 29417	I'd Never Forgive Myself/ Honestly	1955	$15
❏ 29548	If It's a Dream/Forgive Me	1955	$15
❏ 29130	In the Chapel in the Moonlight/Take Everything But You	1954	$20
❏ 29268	I Want You All to Myself (Just You)/Don't Let the Kitty Geddin	1954	$20
❏ 30404	Lasting Love/Long Lonely Nights	1957	$15
❏ 29593	Let's Make the Most of Tonight/Just Between Friends	1955	$15
❏ 29037	Little Things Mean a Lot/I Don't Think You Love Me Anymore	1954	$20
❏ 28813	Lonely/Heartless Heart	1953	$20
❏ 29663	Only Forever/Come Spring	1955	$15
❏ 30144	Saturday Blues/Ah, Ah, Ah (The Song That Haunts)	1956	$15
❏ 30267	Star Bright/Gently, Johnny	1957	$15
❏ 29708	Sweet Kentucky Rose/How Lonely Can I Get?	1955	$15
❏ 30346	Teen-Age Heart/Hideaway Heart	1957	$15
❏ 88181	The Spirit of Christmas/Baby Brother (Santa Claus, Dear Santa Claus)	1954	$15

— Children's Series issue
| ❏ 88181 [PS] | The Spirit of Christmas/Baby Brother (Santa Claus, Dear Santa Claus) | 1954 | $30 |

— Children's Series issue
| ❏ 29315 | The Spirit of Christmas/Baby Brother (Santa Claus, Dear Santa Claus) | 1954 | $15 |
| ❏ 29959 | True Love/Will I Always Be Your Sweetheart | 1956 | $15 |

MERCURY
❏ 5727	Another Human Being of the Opposite Sex/More, More, More	1951	$20
❏ 5587	If You Want Some Lovin'/ Last Night	1951	$20
❏ 5452	I Got Tookn'/If You Smile at the Sun	1950	$30
❏ 5700	I Wish I Had a Daddy in the White House/The Old Soft Shoe	1951	$20

PHILIPS
| ❏ 40375 | One Grain of Sand/From Your Lips to the Arms of an Angel | 1966 | $8 |

RCA VICTOR
| ❏ 47-8202 | I'll Teach You How to Cry/ We'll Cross That Bridge | 1963 | $10 |
| ❏ 47-8124 | My Coloring Book/Here's to Us | 1962 | $10 |

7-Inch Extended Plays

DECCA
❏ ED2467	(contents unknown)	1956	$30
❏ ED2468	(contents unknown)	1956	$30
❏ ED2469	(contents unknown)	1956	$30
❏ ED2467 [PS]	It's a Lonesome Old Town, Part 1	1956	$30
❏ ED2468 [PS]	It's a Lonesome Old Town, Part 2	1956	$30
❏ ED2469 [PS]	It's a Lonesome Old Town, Part 3	1956	$30

Number	Title	Yr	NM
❏ ED2164	Little Things Mean a Lot/I Don't Think You Love Me Anymore//In the Chapel in the Moonlight/Take Everything But You	1954	$50

MERCURY
❏ EP 1-3293	(contents unknown)	1955	$50
❏ EP 1-3294	(contents unknown)	1955	$50
❏ EP 1-3293 [PS]	Pretty Kitty Kallen Sings, Vol. 1	1955	$50
❏ EP 1-3294 [PS]	Pretty Kitty Kallen Sings, Vol. 2	1955	$50

KANDY, JIM

K-ARK
❏ 672	Cheaters Never Win/Flip a Coin	1966	$20
❏ 637	Cocaine Blues/Only Girl for Me	1965	$20
❏ 673	Everybody But Me Wants to Go Home/Which One	1966	$20
❏ 709	From Your House to Hers/ Wake Up in the Morning	1967	$20
❏ 664	How Great Thou Art/Where No One Stands Alone	1966	$20
❏ 647	I'm the Man/Angelville + Sky	1965	$20
❏ 635	Strangers/Looking Through a Teardrop	1965	$20

KANE, EDEN

FONTANA
| ❏ 1891 | Boys Cry/Don't Come Crying to Me | 1964 | $15 |
| ❏ 1961 | Hangin' Around/Do Something About You | 1964 | $15 |

LONDON
❏ 9516	Forget Me Not/New Kind of Lovin'	1962	$20
❏ 9508	Get Lost/I'm Telling You	1961	$20
❏ 9532	I Don't Know Why/Music for Strings	1962	$20
❏ 1993	Well, I Ask You/Before I Lose My Mind	1961	$20

KANGAROO

MGM
| ❏ 13961 | Daydream Stallion/The Only Thing I Had | 1968 | $15 |

— As "Barbara Keith and Kangaroo"
| ❏ 13962 | Frogg Giggin'/Maybe Tomorrow | 1968 | $15 |

— As "N.D. Smart and Kangaroo"
| ❏ 13960 | I Never Tell Me Twice/Such a Long Long Time | 1968 | $15 |

KANSAS
Vocalist Steve Walsh was also in STREETS. Chief writer Kerry Livgren's solo album included a Ronnie James Dio cameo.

CBS ASSOCIATED
| ❏ ZS4-04213 [PS] | Everybody's My Friend | 1983 | $8 |

—Demonstration Only -- Not for Sale" on sleeve
❏ ZS4-04213	Everybody's My Friend/End of the Age	1983	$3
❏ ZS4-04213 [PS]	Everybody's My Friend/End of the Age	1983	$4
❏ ZS4-04057	Fight Fire with Fire/Incident on a Bridge	1983	$3
❏ ZS4-04057 [PS]	Fight Fire with Fire/Incident on a Bridge	1983	$4
❏ ZS4-04057 [PS]	Fight Fire with Fire/Incident on a Bridge	1983	$8

—Demonstration Only -- Not for Sale" on sleeve (sleeve lists both tracks, though the enclosed promo record only has the A-side on both sides)

KIRSHNER
❏ ZS74253	Can I Tell You/The Pilgrimage	1974	$6
❏ ZS84267	Carry On Wayward Son/ Questions of My Childhood	1976	$5
❏ ZS84274	Dust in the Wind/Paradox	1978	$5
❏ ZS64292	Got to Rock On/No Room for a Stranger	1980	$4
❏ ZS94291	Hold On/Don't Open Your Eyes	1980	$4
❏ ZS84259	It's You/It Takes a Woman's Love to Make a Man	1975	$6
❏ ZS84256	Lonely Wind/Bringing It Back	1974	$6
❏ ZS84280	Lonely Wind/Song for America	1979	$4
❏ ZS84284	People of the South Wind/ Stay Out of Trouble	1979	$4
❏ ZS5-02903	Play the Game Tonight/ Play On	1982	$4
❏ ZS84273	Point of Know Return/Closet Chronicles	1977	$4
❏ ZS84276	Portrait (He Knew)/ Lightning's Hand	1978	$4
❏ ZS84258	Song for America (Part 1)/ (Part 2)	1975	$6
❏ ZS84270	What's On My Mind/Lonely Street	1977	$4

MCA
| ❏ 52958 | All I Wanted/We're Not Alone Anymore | 1986 | $3 |

Number	Title	Yr	NM
❏ 52958 [PS]	All I Wanted/We're Not Alone Anymore	1986	$3
❏ 53070	Can't Cry Anymore/Three Pretenders	1987	$3
❏ 53070 [PS]	Can't Cry Anymore/Three Pretenders	1987	$3
❏ S45-17290 [DJ]	Power (same on both sides)	1987	$4
❏ S45-17290 [PS]	Power (same on both sides)	1987	$4
❏ 53027	Power/Tomb 19	1987	$3
❏ 53027 [PS]	Power/Tomb 19	1987	$3
❏ 53425	Stand Beside Me/House on Fire	1988	$3
❏ 53425 [PS]	Stand Beside Me/House on Fire	1988	$4

KANTNER, PAUL/JEFFERSON STARSHIP

RCA VICTOR
| ❏ 74-0426 | Let's Go Together/A Child Is Coming | 1971 | $5 |
| ❏ 74-0426 [PS] | Let's Go Together/A Child Is Coming | 1971 | $8 |

KARAS, ANTON

LONDON
| ❏ 30005 | The Third Man" Theme/The Cafe Mozart Waltz | 1950 | $30 |

KAREN, KENNY

ABC
| ❏ 11171 | M'Lady/Sans Toi | 1969 | $20 |

BIG TREE
| ❏ 16007 | That's Why You Remember/A Nice Place to Live | 1973 | $15 |

COLUMBIA
❏ 4-42264	Oh Susie Forgive Me/The Light in Your Window	1962	$40
❏ 4-42638	Sixteen Years Ago Tonight/ Take Me Back	1962	$40
❏ 4-42452	To Sandy with Love/A Face in the Crowd	1962	$40

STRAND
| ❏ 25017 | Broken Dreams/You're the Only One I Love | 1960 | $30 |
| ❏ 25008 | Little Boy/Nature Boy | 1959 | $30 |

KARIM, TY

ROMARK
| ❏ 73-104 | Lightin' Up/Don't Let Me Be Lonely Tonight | 1973 | $1200 |

KARL, FRANKIE

DC
| ❏ 180 | Don't Be Afraid (Do As I Say)/I'm So Glad | 1968 | $30 |

LIBERTY
| ❏ 56164 | Don't Sleep Too Long/Put a Little Love in Your Heart | 1970 | $40 |

KARMEN, STEVE

AUDIO FIDELITY
| ❏ 179 | Everybody Likes It/The Easy Way | 1971 | $15 |
| ❏ 190 | I've Never Had the Time/37-21 | 1972 | $10 |

CUB
| ❏ 9059 | Free Passes/Lost | 1960 | $50 |

EL DORADO
| ❏ 510 | Freight Train/Mama Look a Boo Boo | 1957 | $40 |

MERCURY
❏ 71208X45	Didja Mean Watcha Said?/ How Soon	1957	$30
❏ 71386X45	Watchin' and Waitin'/Oh! Oh!	1958	$30
❏ 71164X45	We Belong Together/Wild Eyes and Tender Lips	1957	$30

STRUTTIN'
| ❏ 103 | I Love New York/(B-side unknown) | 1977 | $15 |

UNITED ARTISTS
| ❏ 50451 | Breakaway Part 1/Part 2 | 1968 | $60 |

— Featuring Jimmy Radcliffe
| ❏ 50534 | Moments (Vocal)/ (Instrumental) | 1969 | $40 |
| ❏ 50636 | What Do You Say to a Naked Lady?/Too Bad You Can't Read My Mind | 1970 | $15 |

KARTUNES, THE

MGM
| ❏ 12680 | Dedicated to Love/Willie the Weeper | 1958 | $30 |

KAT MANDU

MARLIN
| ❏ 3338 | The Break (Short Version)/ (Long Version) | 1979 | $12 |

Number	Title	Yr	NM
KATRINA AND THE WAVES			
CAPITOL			
❏ B-5450	Do You Want Crying/The Sun Won't Shine Without You	1985	$3
❏ B-5450 [PS]	Do You Want Crying/The Sun Won't Shine Without You	1985	$3
❏ B-5566	Is That It?/I Really Taught Me to Watusi	1986	$3
❏ B-5566 [PS]	Is That It?/I Really Taught Me to Watusi	1986	$3
❏ B-5593	Sun Street/(A Man Only Needs) One Woman	1986	$3
❏ B-5593 [PS]	Sun Street/(A Man Only Needs) One Woman	1986	$3
❏ B-5466	Walking on Sunshine/Going Down to Liverpool	1985	$3
❏ B-5466 [PS]	Walking on Sunshine/Going Down to Liverpool	1985	$3
SBK			
❏ B-07303	That's the Way/Love Calculator	1989	$3
❏ B-07303 [PS]	That's the Way/Love Calculator	1989	$3
KAYAK			
JANUS			
❏ 274	I Want You to Be Mine/Irene	1978	$5
MERCURY			
❏ 76059	Periscope Life/Stop That Song	1980	$4
KAYE, ANGELA			
YATAHEY			
❏ 804	Catching Fire/(B-side unknown)	1981	$6
KAYE, DANNY			
DECCA			
❏ 27829	Santa Claus Looks Like My Daddy/Eat, Eat, Eat!	1951	$20
KAYE, JOHNNY			
LEGEND			
❏ 127	A Christmas Love/Christmas In Paree	1963	$30
KAYE, MARY, TRIO			
20TH CENTURY FOX			
❏ 457	Man's Favourite Sport/What's Yours?	1964	$8
CAMELOT			
❏ 132	Can't Get You Off My Mind/Writing on the Wall	1967	$8
COLUMBIA			
❏ 1-340(?)	All I Want for Christmas/Down Christmas Tree Lane	1949	$50
— Microgroove 33 1/3 rpm 7-inch single			
❏ 1-230(?)	I'm in the Mood for Love/The Monkey Song	1949	$50
— Microgroove 33 1/3 rpm 7-inch single, small hole			
DECCA			
❏ 9-30241	Almost Like Being in Love/Spring Reunion	1957	$15
❏ 9-30596	Another Time, Another Place/With a Love That's True	1958	$15
❏ 9-30344	Calypso Rock/Boy on a Dolphin	1957	$20
❏ 9-30145	Fools Rush In/Add Another Leaf	1956	$15
❏ 9-29761	Lonesome Road/Get Out of Town	1955	$15
❏ 9-29622	Mad About the Boy/My Funny Valentine	1955	$15
RCA VICTOR			
❏ 47-5751	Almost/Don't Laugh at Me	1954	$20
❏ 47-5784	Anyone Can Dream/The Cuddlin' Song	1954	$20
❏ 47-5586	Do You Believe in Dreams?/Toreador	1954	$20
WARNER BROS.			
❏ 5041	Believe in Me/Wonder Why	1959	$12
❏ 5020	Home Before Dark/Belong to Me	1958	$12
❏ 5015	Mad Passionate Love/The Hawaiian Wedding Song	1958	$10
❏ 5095	My Isle of Golden Dreams/That Wasn't Me	1959	$10
KAYE, SAMMY			
COLUMBIA			
❏ 39894	All Around the Christmas Tree/Santa, Santa, Santa Claus	1952	$20
❏ 39772	All the Things You Are/Who	1952	$15
❏ 40151	Bella Bella Donna Mis/Y (That's Why)	1954	$15
❏ 40966	Charleston/Posin'	1957	$10
❏ 41656	Chopsticks Boogie/Harvey's Melody	1960	$10

Number	Title	Yr	NM
❏ 39376	Come Back to Angueleme/Please Don't Talk About Me	1951	$20
❏ 39583	Daddy/Bouquet of Roses	1951	$20
❏ 41508	Deep Purple/Till Tomorrow	1959	$12
❏ 39421	Del Rio/Would Mind	1951	$20
❏ 39492	Dixie/Tennessee Tears	1951	$20
❏ 40248	Dream for Sale/Sittin' 'n' Waitin'	1954	$15
❏ 40795	Faded Roses/I'm Through with Love	1956	$15
❏ 39883	Forget Me Not/Sailin' Along the Ohio	1952	$20
❏ 40269	Friends and Neighbors/Through	1954	$15
❏ 39575	Frosty the Snow Man/Santa Claus Is Coming to Town	1951	$15
— The above four comprise a box set			
❏ 41084	Garden of Allah/Well, Anyway	1957	$10
❏ 39771	Girl of My Dreams/My Extraorinary Girl	1952	$15
❏ 40205	Godspeed to You/Till You Kiss Me at the Altar	1954	$15
❏ 39957	Gomen-Sasai (Forgive Me)/Until Tomorrow	1953	$15
❏ 6-740(?)	Guilty/Checky-Checky Hoopla	1950	$30
❏ 1-740(?)	Guilty/Checky-Checky Hoopla	1950	$40
— Microgroove 33 1/3 rpm 7-inch single			
❏ 41028	Ha, Ha, Ha/You'd Be Surprised	1957	$10
❏ 38963	Harbor Lights/Sugar Sweet	1950	$20
❏ 40621	Hey Pretty Girl/In the Valley of the Moon	1955	$15
❏ 40431	Hindustan/She Went That-a-Way	1955	$15
❏ 39917	Hurry, Hurry, Hurry/Dance of Mexico	1953	$15
❏ 40707	I Could Have Danced All Night/I've Grown Accustomed to Your Face	1956	$15
❏ 39816	I Don't Know Any Better/God's Little Candles	1952	$20
❏ 39270	I Love You Because/Pretty Little Bells	1951	$20
❏ 3-39270	I Love You Because/Pretty Little Bells	1951	$30
— Microgroove 33 1/3 rpm 7-inch single (note prefix)			
❏ 40839	I Met a Girl/Mountain of Kisses	1957	$10
❏ 40485	Impossible/Jim, Johnny and Jonas	1955	$15
❏ 39325	I'm Yours to Command/Shenandoah Waltz	1951	$20
❏ 40061	In the Mission of St. Augustine/No Stone Unturned	1953	$15
❏ 39531	It's All in the Game/Be Mine Tonight	1951	$20
❏ 39567	(It's No) Sin/Jealous Eyes	1951	$20
❏ 39856	It Wasn't God Who Made Honky Tonk Angels/I Went to Your Wedding	1952	$15
❏ 41348	Leave the Door Wide Open/Dah Dee (Daddy)	1959	$12
❏ 39936	Lighthouse in the Harbor/Angel Made of Ice	1953	$15
❏ 39774	Little Girl/We'll Meet Again	1952	$15
— The above four comprise a box set			
❏ 39499	Longing for You/Mary Rose	1951	$20
❏ 40988	Mary Lou/Moonlight Swim	1957	$10
❏ 40417	Melody of Love/You Are the One	1955	$15
❏ 40869	Money/The Ship That Never Sailed	1957	$10
❏ 41552	My Happiness/Melody of Love	1960	$10
❏ 39360	My Prayer/Down the Trail of Aching Hearts	1951	$20
❏ 40698	Once Again/Every Sunday Morning	1956	$15
❏ 39999	Orange Blossom Serenade/The Tattle-Tale Duck	1953	$15
❏ 40936	Past My Prime/Charm Bracelet	1957	$10
❏ 39030	Patricia/Petite Waltz	1950	$20
❏ 39186	Peter Cottontail/Easter Parade	1951	$20
❏ 40299	Sentimental/If We Should Ever Meet Again	1954	$15
❏ 39572	Silent Night-O Little Town Of Bethlehem/Joy To The World-Hark the Herald Angels Sing-O Come All Ye Faithful	1951	$15
❏ 40518	Sweet and Lovely/Yearning	1955	$15
❏ 41293	Sweet Leilani/How Good Can a Good Girl Be	1958	$10
❏ 39977	Sweet Sue-Just You/I Couldn't Keep from Crying	1953	$15
❏ 39140	Tell Me You Love Me/Dear Little Girl of Theta Chi	1950	$20
❏ 39113	Tennessee Waltz/Get Out Those Old Records	1950	$20
❏ 41178	That Daffodil Feelin'/Spain	1958	$12
❏ 41140	That Girl Next Door/Our First Formal Dance	1958	$12
❏ 40517	The Banjo's Back in Town/Joe, Joe, Joe	1955	$15
❏ 40574	The Lucky Little Bell/Don't Cry Baby	1955	$15
❏ 40025	The Midnight Ride/The One in Your Heart	1953	$15
❏ 39602	The Three Bells/I Only Have One Life	1951	$20
❏ 39036	To Think You've Chosen Me/You Oughta Be in Pictures	1950	$20
❏ 39769	Walkin' to Missouri/One for the Wonder	1952	$20
❏ 40645	We All Need Love/Try Another Cherry Tree	1956	$15
❏ 40909	What a Saturday Night/A Young Lover's Dream	1957	$10
❏ 39667	Wheel of Fortune/Goodbye Sweetheart	1952	$20

Number	Title	Yr	NM
❏ 39573	White Christmas/Jingle Bells	1951	$15
❏ 41206	Why Can't This Night Go On Forever/Yearning	1958	$10
❏ 39688	Winnipesaukee/I Ain't Lazy	1952	$20
❏ 39574	Winter Wonderland/Rudolph the Red-Nosed Reindeer	1951	$15
DECCA			
❏ 25555	After You've Gone/Who's Sorry Now	1962	$8
❏ 31448	Big Deal/Shoot the Piano Player	1962	$8
❏ 31589	Charade/Maria Elena	1964	$6
❏ 25752	Charley, My Boy/Hot Lips	1969	$5
❏ 31175	Christmas Child (Loo, Loo, Loo)/Let It Snow, Let It Snow, Let It Snow	1960	$10
❏ 31773	Goldfinger/Blue Prelude	1965	$6
❏ 31700	House of the Rising Sun/Theme from Golden Boy	1964	$6
❏ 31854	Hush…Hush, Sweet Charlotte/The Hucklebuck	1965	$6
❏ 32442	I Love to Cry at Weddings/I'm a Brass Band	1969	$5
❏ 31264	I'm a Big Girl Now/Strange Interlude	1961	$8
❏ 31935	Lara's Theme (from Dr. Zhivago)/Swedish Rhapsody (Madame X Love Theme)	1966	$6
❏ 31294	Lydia, the Tattooed Lady/I'm Married to a Strip Tease Dancer	1961	$8
❏ 31174	Merry Merry Christmas (To You)/Silver Bells	1960	$10
❏ 32071	Oh, How I Miss You Tonight/Gambit	1966	$6
❏ 25511	Oh Johnny, Oh Johnny, Oh!/Got a Date with an Angel	1962	$8
❏ 32034	Smile/In the Arms of Love	1966	$6
❏ 32624	Something/Juanita (Love Theme from "Topaz")	1970	$5
❏ 31336	Swing and Sway Twist/Mama and Papa Twist	1961	$15
❏ 32258	Talk to the Animals/Glory of Love	1968	$5
❏ 25722	The Whiffenpoof Song/There Is a Tavern in the Town	1967	$6
❏ 31204	Welcome Home/What's New at the Zoo	1961	$8
PROJECT 3			
❏ 1421	For the Good Times/If You've Got the Time	1972	$4
RCA VICTOR			
❏ 47-3170	Alexander's Ragtime Band/A Pretty Girl Is Like a Melody	1950	$20
❏ 47-3168	Always/Blue Skies	1950	$20
❏ 47-2862	April Showers/June Is Bustin' Out All Over	1949	$20
❏ 47-2936	Belmont Boogie/Hollywood Square Dance	1949	$20
❏ 47-2901	Careless Hands/Powder Your Face with Sunshine	1949	$20
❏ 47-3101	Careless Kisses/Echoes	1949	$20
❏ 47-2810	Cuddle Up a Little Closer, Lovey Mine/I Want a Girl (Just Like the Girl That Married Dear Old Dad)	1949	$20
❏ 47-3010	Dime a Dozen/Everything They Said Came True	1949	$20
❏ 47-2811	Down Among the Sheltering Palms/The World Is Waiting for the Sunrise	1949	$20
❏ 47-2942	Fiddle Dee Dee/It's a Great Feeling	1949	$20
❏ 47-3067	Funny Face/Toot Toot Tootsie	1949	$20
❏ 47-3077	Hawaiian War Chant/Hawaiian Sunset	1949	$20
❏ 47-3071	Here Comes Santa Claus/I Want to Wish You a Merry Christmas	1949	$20
❏ 47-3169	How Deep Is the Ocean/Say It Isn't So	1950	$20
❏ 47-2863	Indian Summer/September Song	1949	$20
❏ 47-2813	I Still Love You/We Just Couldn't Say Goodbye	1949	$20
❏ 47-3115	It Isn't Fair/My Lily and My Rose	1950	$20
❏ 47-3048	Let's Harmonize/Makin' Love Ukulele Style	1949	$20
❏ 47-3891	Miss You/There's No Use	1950	$20
❏ 47-3076	My Isle of Golden Dreams/Sweet Leilani	1949	$20
❏ 47-3075	My Little Grass Shack in Kaelakekua, Hawaii/My Tan	1949	$20
❏ 47-2923	The Four Winds and the Seven Seas/Out of Love	1949	$20
❏ 47-3038	The Last Mile Home/Hawaiian Sunset	1949	$20
❏ 47-3828	The Object of My Affection/I Thought She Was a Local	1950	$20
❏ 47-2812	There But For You Go I/My Son	1949	$20
❏ 47-3203	Wanderin'/The Bicycle Song	1950	$20
❏ 47-2864	White Christmas/Winter Wonderland	1949	$20
RCA VICTOR			
❏ EPA258	Sweet Leilani/My Isle of Golden Dreams//Hawaiian War Chant/Hawaiian Sunset	1952	$15
❏ EPA258 [PS]	The Heart of the Islands in Song	1952	$15

Number	Title	Yr	NM

KAYLI, BOB
CARLTON
| ❏ 482 | Everyone Was There/I Took a Dare | 1958 | $30 |

GORDY
| ❏ 7004 | Toodle Loo/Everyone Was There | 1962 | $400 |
| ❏ 7008 | Toodle Loo/Hold On Pearl | 1962 | $80 |

TAMLA
| ❏ 54051 | Small Sad Sam/Tie Me Tight | 1962 | $80 |

KEANE BROTHERS, THE
20TH CENTURY
❏ 2330	Amy (Show the World You're There)/I Wanna Get Back on the Floor and Boogie	1977	$6
❏ 2357	Goodbye Summer/Sherry	1977	$6
❏ 2337	Help! Help!/Goodbye Momma and Poppa	1977	$6
❏ 2302	Sherry/God Loves Little Girls	1976	$6

ABC
| ❏ 12445 | Dancin' in the Moonlight/Rain or Shine | 1979 | $6 |

REGENCY
| ❏ 99948 | Tryin' to Kill a Saturday Night/(B-side unknown) | 1982 | $6 |

KEARNEY, RAMSEY
CHALLENGE
| ❏ 59346 | Soft Lips and Sweet Perfume/Night to Away | 1966 | $15 |

HICKORY
❏ 1233	El Diablo/Move Over	1963	$15
❏ 1251	Google Eyes/Take a Walk (In My Shoes)	1964	$15
❏ 1192	I'll Cry Myself to Sleep (Again Tonight)/But Whatcha Gonna Do	1962	$15
❏ 1176	I Never Let You Cross My Mind/Nine Little Teardrops	1962	$15
❏ 1211	The Blues Keep Hangin' On/Put Away That Gun Boy	1963	$15

NASHCO
| ❏ 51686 | A School Teacher's Dream/Hell Yes, I'm Country | 1986 | $8 |

SAFARI
❏ 1001	Cattle Call/Jack Benny's Fiddle	1977	$10
❏ 108	I Found Love (When I Found You)/Emotions	1984	$8
❏ 111	It's Time to Go/From One Lover to Another	1984	$8
❏ 117	One Time Thing/(B-side unknown)	1988	$8
❏ 107	Put On Your Love Tonight (same on both sides)	1983	$8
❏ 104	That's How Much I Love You/My Love for You	1982	$8
❏ 101	White Man's Blues/Evergreen Love	1981	$8

KEEN, BILL, AND THE TRADEWINDS
LESLEY
| ❏ 1922 | Don't Call Me/Summer in the Lowlands | 1961 | $40 |

KEGGS, THE
ORBIT
| ❏ 20959 | To Find Out/(B-side unknown) | 1967 | $4000 |

—Counterfeit identification: The producer's first name, "Yolanda," is misspelled "Yalanda" on fakes.

KEITH
COLUMBIA
| ❏ 43268 | Dream/Caravan of Lonely Men | 1965 | $20 |

—As "Keith and the Admirations"

DISCREET
| ❏ 1193 | What Did You Do in the Revolution, Dad/In and Out of Love | 1974 | $5 |

MERCURY
❏ 72639	98.6/The Teenie Bopper Song	1966	$12
❏ 72639 [PS]	98.6/The Teenie Bopper Song	1966	$20
❏ 72596	Ain't Gonna Lie/Our Love Started All Over Again	1966	$8
❏ 72824	Always Tomorrow/I Can't Go Wrong	1968	$8
❏ 72695	Daylight Savin' Time/Happy Walking Around	1967	$8
❏ 72695 [PS]	Daylight Savin' Time/Happy Walking Around	1967	$15
❏ 72715	Easy-As-Pie/Sugar Man	1967	$8
❏ 72715 [PS]	Easy-As-Pie/Sugar Man	1967	$15
❏ 72794	Hurry/Pleasure of Your Company	1968	$8
❏ 72746	I'm So Proud/Candy Candy	1967	$8
❏ 72746 [PS]	I'm So Proud/Candy Candy	1967	$30
❏ 72652	Tell Me To My Face/Pretty Little Shy One	1967	$8
❏ 72652 [PS]	Tell Me To My Face/Pretty Little Shy One	1967	$20

RCA VICTOR
| ❏ 74-0140 | Marstrand/The Problem | 1969 | $6 |
| ❏ 74-0222 | Trixin's Election/A Fairy Tale or Two | 1969 | $6 |

KELLER, JERRY
CAPITOL
| ❏ 4668 | I'll Get By/My Year of Love | 1961 | $15 |

CORAL
❏ 62348	It's Too Late/What Will I Tell My Darling	1963	$10
❏ 62378	Sea Shell Sherry/What Happens When He Comes Home	1963	$10
❏ 62409	Small Wonder/The Tears Keep Falling Down	1964	$12
❏ 62361	Sume Summer/Goodnight Pretty Girl	1963	$10

KAPP
❏ 322	American Beauty Rose/Lonesome Lullaby	1960	$15
❏ 277 [M]	Here Comes Summer/Time Has a Way	1959	$20
❏ KS-277 [S]	Here Comes Summer/Time Has a Way	1959	$40
❏ 277 [PS]	Here Comes Summer/Time Has a Way	1959	$30
❏ 295	If I Had a Girl/Lovable	1959	$15
❏ 295 [PS]	If I Had a Girl/Lovable	1959	$30
❏ 337	My Name Ain't Joe/White for You and Bless for Me	1960	$15
❏ 353	What More Can I Say/Whole-Heartedly	1960	$15

REPRISE
| ❏ 0351 | Fickle Finger of Fate/Glory of Love | 1965 | $8 |
| ❏ 0397 | Ma (She's Such a Quiet Girl)/The Mack | 1965 | $8 |

KELLEY, JOHN
COMSTAR
| ❏ 8201 | This Morning I Woke Up in New York City/(B-side unknown) | 1982 | $8 |

KELLUM, MURRY
CINNAMON
❏ 794	Girl of My Life/Since You've Been Gone	1974	$5
❏ 777	Lovely Lady/Alive and Doing Well	1973	$5
❏ 765	Walking Tall/Huckleberry's Ferry Boat Building Blues	1973	$5

EPIC
| ❏ 10832 | Love You to Sleep Tonight/You Do the Callin' (I'll Do the Crawlin') | 1972 | $5 |
| ❏ 10784 | Train Train (Carry Me Away)/What's Made Milwaukee Famous | 1971 | $5 |

M.O.C.
| ❏ 658 | I Dreamed I Was a Beatle/Oh How Sweet It Could Be | 1964 | $30 |
| ❏ 653 | Long, Tall Texan/I Gotta Leave This Town | 1963 | $15 |

—B-side by Glenn Sutton

PLANTATION
| ❏ 176 [DJ] | Memphis Sun (mono/stereo) | 1978 | $5 |

—Released only as a promo

RANWOOD
| ❏ 1047 | Shoot Low Sheriff/How Long Has It Been (Since They Played Something You Could Dance To) | 1976 | $5 |

KELLY, AL
RCA THESAURUS
| ❏ HO7H-0934 [DJ] | An Exclusive Interview with Santa Claus//O Come, All Ye Faithful/Lo! How A Rose E'er Blooming/Silent Night | 1957 | $20 |

—B-side by Domenico Savino and His Orchestra

KELLY FOUR, THE
CANDIX
| ❏ 325 | Annie Had a Party/Sweet Angelina | 1961 | $30 |

—A-side is an alternate take of Silver 1006

| ❏ 325 | Annie Had a Party/Sweet Angelina | 1961 | $30 |

—As "Big Daddy Greenfield"; same recordings as above

SILVER
| ❏ 1006 | Annie Had a Party/So Fine, Be Mine | 1960 | $50 |

—A-side was reissued on Crest 1088 by "The Gee Cees"

| ❏ 1001 | Strollin' Guitar/Guybo | 1959 | $50 |

—A-side was reissued on Silver 1004 by "Jewel and Eddie

KELLY, IRENE
MCA
| ❏ 53756 | Love Is a Hard Road/Too Late (To Turn Back Now) | 1989 | $4 |

KELLY, J., AND THE PREMIERS
ROADSHOW
| ❏ 7005 | She Calls Me Baby/Signed Sealed Delivered (My Heart) | 1973 | $10 |

KELLY, MONTY
CARLTON
❏ 517	I Loves You Porgy/Tango Bongo	1959	$10
❏ 527	Summer Set/Amalia	1960	$10
❏ 495	Willingly/The Blue Cha Cha	1959	$10

ESSEX
❏ 404	Bali Ha'i/To You with Love	1955	$15
❏ 386	Blue Mirage/That Sweetheart of Mine	1955	$15
❏ 351	Cubamba/Cross Winds	1954	$15
❏ 341	Granada/Snow, Snow	1953	$15
❏ 373	Shangri-La/Monte Carlo	1954	$15
❏ 328	Three O'Clock in the Morning/Doreen	1953	$15
❏ 325 [S]	Tropicana/Life in New York	1953	$15

KELLY, NORVIN
COLUMBIA
| ❏ 4-21381 | I'm Back in Your Arms Again/You Can't Make Me Live with the Blues | 1955 | $30 |
| ❏ 4-21279 | Without You/You Didn't Want a Home | 1954 | $30 |

KELLY, PAT
CHIC
| ❏ 1009 | She's a Devil/The Stranger Dressed in Black | 1957 | $40 |

JUBILEE
| ❏ 5315 | Hey Doll Baby/Cloud 13 | 1958 | $70 |
| ❏ 5333 | Patsy/That Is Where My Money Goes | 1958 | $30 |

KELLY, PAUL
DIAL
❏ 4088	Call Another Doctor/We're Gonna Make It	1968	$10
❏ 4021	Chills and Fever/Only Your Love	1965	$50
❏ 4025	Since I Found You/Can't Help It	1966	$70

HAPPY TIGER
❏ 573	Hangin' On In There/Soul Flow	1971	$20
❏ 568	Poor But Proud/Hot Runnin' Soul	1971	$6
❏ 555	Sailing/509	1970	$6
❏ 541	Stealing in the Name of the Lord/Day After Forever	1970	$30

PHILIPS
❏ 40457	Cryin' for My Baby/Sweet Sweet Lovin'	1967	$40
❏ 40513	Glad to Be Sad/My Love Is Growing Stronger	1968	$30
❏ 40480	If This Old House Could Talk/You Don't Know, You Just Don't Know	1967	$80
❏ 40409	I Need Your Love So Bad/Nine Times Out of Ten	1966	$40

WARNER BROS.
❏ 7707	Come Lay Some Lovin' on Me/Come By Here	1973	$5
❏ 7657	Don't Burn Me/Love Me Now	1972	$5
❏ 8120	Get Sexy/I Believe I Can	1975	$5
❏ 7823	Hooked, Hogtied & Collared/I Wanna Be Close to You	1974	$5
❏ 7765	I'm Into Something I Can't Shake Loose/Joy	1974	$5
❏ 8040	Let Your Love Come Down (Let It Fall on Me)/I Wanna Be Close to You	1974	$5
❏ 8187	Play Me a Love Song/Stealin' Love on the Side	1976	$5
❏ 8067	Take It Away from Him (Put It On Me)/Try My Love	1975	$5
❏ 7614	Travelin' Man/Here Comes Old Jezebel	1972	$5

KEMP, WAYNE, AND BOBBY G. RICE
DOOR KNOB
| ❏ 250 | One More Time Around/From Housewife to Everyone's Girl | 1986 | $5 |

KEMP, WAYNE

DECCA

Number	Title	Yr	NM
❏ 32824	Award to an Angel/Darling Who's the Stranger	1971	$6
❏ 32534	Bar Room Habits/Here We Go Again	1969	$6
❏ 32946	Darlin'/Just to Know She'd Let Me Leave Her	1972	$6
❏ 32891	Did We Have to Come This Far to Say Goodbye/Play Me a Cheatin' Song	1971	$6
❏ 32653	Too Close to the End/She Won't Live It Down	1970	$6
❏ 32767	Who'll Turn Out the Lights/Burn Another Honky Tonk Down	1971	$6
❏ 32422	Won't You Come Home (And Talk to a Stranger)/I Turn My Mind on You	1968	$6

DOOR KNOB

Number	Title	Yr	NM
❏ 200	Don't Send Me No Angels/Living Off the Memories	1983	$5
❏ 211	I've Always Wanted To/Happy Anniversary Darling	1984	$5
❏ 206	Merry Christmas, Darling/Happy Birthday, Darling	1983	$5

JAB

Number	Title	Yr	NM
❏ 9005	Babblin' Incoherently/An Image of Me	1967	$8

MCA

Number	Title	Yr	NM
❏ 40249	Harlan County/I'll Leave This World Loving You	1974	$5
❏ 40019	Honky Tonk Wine/Pretty Mansions	1973	$5
❏ 40176	Listen/She Knows When You're On My Mind Again	1974	$5

MERCURY

Number	Title	Yr	NM
❏ 57035	I'll Leave This World Loving You/Who Left the Door to Heaven Open	1980	$4
❏ 57023	Love Goes to Hell When It Dies/She Won't Close the Book on Me	1980	$4
❏ 76165	She Only Meant to Use Him/I Know Just How She Feels	1982	$4
❏ 76139	Sloe Gin and Fast Women/I'm the Man	1982	$4
❏ 57060	Why Am I Doing Without/Wrecked Up Frame of Mind	1981	$4

UNITED ARTISTS

Number	Title	Yr	NM
❏ XW678	I Can't Wait to Dream That Dream/We're Waking a Sleeping Prayer	1975	$5
❏ XW1031	I Love It (When You Love All Over Me)/Love's Already Been Here and Gone	1977	$5
❏ XW850	I Should Have Watched That First Step/Tell Ole I Ain't Here to Get On Home	1976	$5
❏ XW980	Leona Doesn't Live Here Anymore/Baby This and Baby That	1977	$5
❏ XW805	Waiting for the Tables to Turn/I Can't Wait to Dream That Dream Again	1976	$5

KEMPER, JIMMY, AND THE TIERS

LE MANS

Number	Title	Yr	NM
❏ 02	Lonely for Kathy/I'm Free to Choose	1964	$200

KENDALL, JEANNIE

DOT

Number	Title	Yr	NM
❏ 17497	Baby Went Bye Bye/Come Back Home	1974	$8
❏ 17513	Birmingham/(B-side unknown)	1974	$8

KENDALL SISTERS, THE

ARGO

Number	Title	Yr	NM
❏ 5310	Billy, Billy, Billy/Let's Wait	1958	$20
❏ 5278	I'm Available/Don't Bother Me	1957	$20

CHECKER

Number	Title	Yr	NM
❏ 884	Make It Soon/Three Wishes	1958	$20

KENDALLS, THE

DOT

Number	Title	Yr	NM
❏ 17422	Everything I Own/Big Silver Jet	1972	$8
❏ 17473	I Wanna Live Here in Your Love/Part of My Life	1973	$8
❏ 17405	Two Divided by Love/Easy to Love	1972	$8

EPIC

Number	Title	Yr	NM
❏ 34-68933	Blue Blue Day/Temporarily Out of Order	1989	$3

MCA CURB

Number	Title	Yr	NM
❏ 52933	Fire at First Sight/You Can't Fool Love	1986	$3
❏ 52983	Little Doll/He Can't Make Your Kind of Love	1986	$3
❏ 52850	Too Late/Party Line	1986	$3

MERCURY

Number	Title	Yr	NM
❏ 76155	Cheater's Prayer/Borrowing Lovin'	1982	$4
❏ 880588-7	Four Wheel Drive/This Ain't the First Time I've Fallen	1985	$3
❏ 880306-7	I'd Dance Every Dance with You/Dark End of the Street	1984	$3
❏ 880828-7	If You Break My Heart/One Good-Bye from Gone	1985	$3
❏ 76131	If You're Waiting on Me (You're Backing Up)/I'm Lettin' You In (On a Feelin')	1981	$4
❏ 814195-7	Movin' Train/Say the Word	1983	$3
❏ 822203-7	My Baby's Gone/I'll Be Faithful to You	1984	$3
❏ 812300-7	Precious Love/Take Me to Heaven (Before You Take Me Home)	1983	$3
❏ 57055	Teach Me to Cheat/Summer Melodies	1981	$4
❏ 818056-7	Thank God for the Radio/Flaming Eyes	1984	$3
❏ 76178	That's What I Get for Thinking/Honey Dew	1982	$4
❏ 884140-7	Two Heart Harmony/I Don't Know Any Better	1985	$3

OVATION

Number	Title	Yr	NM
❏ 1170	Heart of the Matter/Mandolin Man	1981	$5
❏ 1103	Heaven's Just a Sin Away/Live and Let Live	1977	$6
❏ 1129	I Don't Do Like That No More/Never My Love	1979	$5
❏ 1119	I Had a Lovely Time/Love Is a Hurting Thing	1978	$5
❏ 1143	I'm Already Blue/I Don't Drink from the River	1980	$5
❏ 1106	It Don't Feel Like Sinnin' to Me/Try Me Again	1978	$5
❏ 1101	Makin' Believe/Let the Music Play	1977	$8
❏ 1109	Pittsburgh Stealers/When Can We Do This Again	1978	$5
❏ 1154	Put It Off Until Tomorrow/Gone Away	1980	$5
❏ 1112	Sweet Desire/Old Fashioned Love	1978	$5

STEP ONE

Number	Title	Yr	NM
❏ 374	Dancin' with Myself Tonight/A Whole Lot to Lose	1987	$4
❏ 379	Still Pickin' Up After You/Country Music Station	1987	$4

STOP

Number	Title	Yr	NM
❏ 394	Behind That Locked Door/Love, Love, Love	1971	$12
❏ 373	Leaving on a Jet Plane/She Thinks I Still Care	1970	$12
❏ 379	Please Tell Me Why/You've Lost That Lovin' Feeling	1970	$10

UNITED ARTISTS

Number	Title	Yr	NM
❏ XW721	I Can't Believe I'm Loving You Again/Diesel Gypsy	1975	$8
❏ XW645	I'd Have to Lie/Love Do or Die	1975	$8
❏ XW782	Imaginary Harmony/Miss Lucy's on the Juice Again	1976	$8

KENDRICK, NAT, AND THE SWANS

DADE

Number	Title	Yr	NM
❏ 1808	Dish Rag (Part 1)/Dish Rag (Part 2)	1960	$20
❏ 1804	(Do the) Mashed Potatoes (Part 1)/(Do the) Mashed Potatoes (Part 2)	1959	$20
❏ 5004	(Do the) Mashed Potatoes (Part 1)/(Do the) Mashed Potatoes (Part 2)	1961	$15
❏ 1812	Hot Chili/Slow Down	1960	$20
❏ 5003	Wobble Wobble (Part 1)/Wobble Wobble (Part 2)	1961	$20

KENDRICK, WILLIE

GOLDEN WORLD

Number	Title	Yr	NM
❏ 1	Fine As Wine/Stop This Train	1963	$80

RCA VICTOR

Number	Title	Yr	NM
❏ 47-8947	Give Me Lots of Lovin'/You Can't Bypass Love	1966	$200
❏ 47-9212	What's That on Your Finger/Change Your Ways	1967	$1000

KENDRICKS, EDDIE

ARISTA

Number	Title	Yr	NM
❏ 0325	Ain't No Smoke Without Fire/Love, Love, Love	1978	$4
❏ 0466	I Just Want to Be the One in Your Life/I Can't Let You Walk Away	1979	$4
❏ 0346	The Best of Strangers Now/Don't Underestimate the Power of Love	1978	$4

ATLANTIC

Number	Title	Yr	NM
❏ 3874 [DJ]	I Don't Need Nobody Else (same on both sides)	1981	$5
—May be promo only			
❏ 3796	Looking for Love/Need Your Lovin'	1981	$4

CORNER STONE

Number	Title	Yr	NM
❏ 1001	Surprise Attack/(B-side unknown)	1984	$4

TAMLA

Number	Title	Yr	NM
❏ 54290	Baby/Intimate Friends	1977	$5
❏ 54243	Boogie Down/Can't Help What I Am	1974	$5
❏ 54210	Can I/I Did It All for You	1971	$5
❏ 54236	Darling Come Back Home/Loving You the Second Time Around	1973	$5
❏ 54285	Date with the Rain/Born Again	1977	$70
❏ 54218	Eddie's Love/Let Me Run Into Your Lonely Heart	1972	$5
❏ 54270	Get It While It's Hot/Never Gonna Leave You	1976	$5
❏ 54260	Get the Cream Off the Top/Honey Brown	1975	$5
❏ 54230	Girl You Need a Change of Mind (Part 1)/Girl You Need a Change of Mind (Part 2)	1973	$5
❏ 54277	Goin' Up in Smoke/Thanks for the Memories	1976	$30
❏ 54263	Happy/Deep and Quiet Love	1975	$5
❏ 54266	He's a Friend/All of My Life	1976	$5
❏ 54266 [DJ]	He's a Friend (stereo/mono)	1976	$20
—Promo only on red vinyl			
❏ 54222	If You Let Me/Just Memories	1972	$5
❏ 54203	It's So Hard for Me to Say Good-Bye/I Tried to Be the Home of Johnnie Mae	1971	$5
❏ 54255	One Tear/The Thin Man	1974	$5
❏ 54257	Shoeshine Boy/Hooked on Your Love	1975	$5
❏ 54247	Son of Sagittarius/Trust Your Heart	1974	$5
❏ 54249	Tell Her Love Has Felt the Need/Loving You the Second Time Around	1974	$5

KENNEDY, GENE, AND KAREN JEGLUM

DOOR KNOB

Number	Title	Yr	NM
❏ 192	Be Happy for Me/What About Tonight	1983	$5
❏ 173	Easier to Go/A Thing or Two on My Mind	1981	$5
❏ 151	I'd Rather Be the Stranger in Your Eyes/(B-side unknown)	1981	$5
❏ 145	I Want to See Me in Your Eyes/Nothing Left to Lose	1981	$5
❏ 181	What About Tonight (We Might Find Something Beautiful Tonight)/You're Still the One (Who Makes My Life Complete)	1982	$5
❏ 199	Will You Still Love Me Tomorrow/Today We're Gonna Get Married	1983	$5

KENNEDY, GENE

DOOR KNOB

Number	Title	Yr	NM
❏ 205	In the Misty Moonlight/(B-side unknown)	1983	$5
❏ 003	She Took Me Where I've Never Been Before/High Flies the Eagle	1976	$6

SOCIETY

Number	Title	Yr	NM
❏ 110	My Wife's House/(B-side unknown)	1986	$5

KENNEDY, JOYCE

A&M

Number	Title	Yr	NM
❏ 2727	Didn't I Tell You/Different Now	1985	$4
❏ 2809	Do Me Right/Too Much Smoke (Not Enough Fire)	1986	$4
❏ 2790	Hold On (For Love's Sake)/Oh	1985	$4
❏ 2685	Stronger Than Before/Chain Reaction	1984	$4
❏ 2685 [PS]	Stronger Than Before/Chain Reaction	1984	$4
❏ 2665 [DJ]	Tailor Made (same on both sides?)	1984	$8
—45 is promo only			
❏ 2710	Tailor Made/Watch My Body	1985	$8
❏ 2656	The Last Time I Made Love/Different Now	1984	$4
—A-side with Jeffrey Osborne			

BLUE ROCK

Number	Title	Yr	NM
❏ 4023	Does Anybody Love Me/Hi Fi Albums and I	1965	$40
❏ 4016	I'm a Good Girl/Does Anybody Love Me	1965	$125

FONTANA

Number	Title	Yr	NM
❏ 1924	Paddle My Own Canoe/Could This Be Love	1964	$30

RAN-DEE

Number	Title	Yr	NM
❏ 118	Can't Take a Chance/How Old Is Old	1963	$50
❏ 110	I Still Love You (Darling)/Misunderstood	1963	$40

Number	Title	Yr	NM

KENNER, CHRIS
BATON
| ❏ 220 | Grandma's House/Don't Let Her Pin That Charge | 1956 | $50 |

IMPERIAL
❏ 5448	Sick and Tired/Nothing Will Keep Me from You	1957	$30
❏ 5767	Sick and Tired/Nothing Will Keep Me from You	1961	$15
❏ 5488	Will You Be Mine/I Have News for You	1958	$30

INSTANT
❏ 3280	All Night Rambler, Part 1/All Night Rambler, Part 2	1966	$10
❏ 3257	Come Back and See/Go Thru Life	1963	$15
❏ 3286	Fumigate Funky Broadway/Wind the Clock	1967	$10
❏ 3244	How Far/Time	1962	$15
❏ 3229	I Like It Like That, Part 1/I Like It Like That, Part 2	1961	$20
❏ 3277	I'm Lonely, Take Me/Cinderella	1966	$10
❏ 3252	Land of 1000 Dances/That's My Girl	1962	$15
❏ 3247	Let Me Show You How (To Twist)/Johnny Little	1962	$15
❏ 3290	Memories of a King (Let Freedom Ring), Part 1/Memories of a King (Let Freedom Ring), Part 2	1968	$15
❏ 3293	Mini-Skirts and Soul/Sad Mistake	1968	$10
❏ 3265	She Can Dance/Anybody Here See My Baby	1964	$15
❏ 3283	Shoo Rah/Stretch My Hands to You	1967	$10
❏ 3237	Something You Got/Come See About Me	1961	$15
❏ 3263	What's Wrong with Life/Never Reach Perfection	1963	$15

UPTOWN
| ❏ 716 | I'm the Greatest/Get On This Train | 1965 | $10 |
| ❏ 708 | Life of My Baby/They Took My Money | 1965 | $12 |

VALIANT
| ❏ 3229 | I Like It Like That, Part 1/I Like It Like That, Part 2 | 1960 | $50 |

KENNY AND THE CADETS
RANDY
| ❏ 422 | Barbie/What Is a Young Man Made Of | 1962 | $400 |

—Pink label original (white labels are counterfeits)

| ❏ 422 | Barbie/What Is a Young Man Made Of | 1962 | $1000 |

—Red and gold vinyl

KENNY AND THE FIENDS
DOT
| ❏ 16568 | House on Haunted Hill (Part 1)/House on Haunted Hill (Part 2) | 1963 | $30 |
| ❏ 16596 | Moon Shot/One-Two-Three-Four | 1964 | $30 |

POSEA
| ❏ 87 | House on Haunted Hill/Green Door | 1963 | $50 |

—As "Kenny and the Beach Fiends

PRINCESS
| ❏ 51 | House on Haunted Hill (Part 1)/House on Haunted Hill (Part 2) | 1963 | $40 |

KENNY AND THE KASUALS
MARK IV
❏ 1002	Don't Let Your Baby Go/(B-side unknown)	1966	$40
❏ 1006	I'm Gonna Make It/Journey to Tyme	1966	$50
❏ 1003	It's All Right/You Make Me Feel So Good	1966	$40
❏ 1008	See-Saw Ride/As I Knew	1967	$40
❏ 1004	Strings of Time/(B-side unknown)	1966	$40

UNITED ARTISTS
| ❏ 50085 | I'm Gonna Make It/Journey to Tyme | 1966 | $30 |

KENNY AND THE SOCIALITES
CROSSTOWN
| ❏ 01 | I'll Have to Decide/King Tut Rock | 1958 | $200 |

KENNY, BILL
DECCA
| ❏ 9-27326 | It Is No Secret/I Hear a Choir | 1950 | $30 |

—As "Bill Kenny of The Ink Spots"

Number	Title	Yr	NM

KENNY G
ARISTA
❏ 9830	Against Doctor's Orders/Tradewinds	1989	$3
❏ 9830 [PS]	Against Doctor's Orders/Tradewinds	1989	$3
❏ 9544	Don't Make Me Wait for Love/Esther	1986	$4
❏ 9544 [PS]	Don't Make Me Wait for Love/Esther	1986	$4
❏ 9625	Don't Make Me Wait for Love/Midnight Motion	1987	$3
❏ 9625 [PS]	Don't Make Me Wait for Love/Midnight Motion	1987	$3
❏ 1027 [DJ]	Here We Are (stereo/mono)	1982	$5

—May be promo only

| ❏ 9105 | Hi, How Ya Doin'?/(Instrumental) | 1984 | $4 |
| ❏ 1001 [DJ] | I Can't Tell You Why (stereo/mono) | 1982 | $5 |

—May be promo only

❏ 9105	I've Been Missin' You/I Wanna Be Yours	1984	$4
❏ 9336	Love on the Rise/Virgin Island	1985	$4
❏ 9336 [PS]	Love on the Rise/Virgin Island	1985	$4
❏ 9385	One Night Stand/Japan	1985	$5
❏ 9751	Silhouette/Home	1988	$3
❏ 9751 [PS]	Silhouette/Home	1988	$3
❏ 9588	Songbird/Midnight Motion	1987	$3
❏ 9588 [PS]	Songbird/Midnight Motion	1987	$3
❏ 9573 [DJ]	Songbird (same on both sides)	1987	$6

—May be promo only

❏ 9573 [PS]	Songbird (same on both sides)	1987	$6
❏ 9785	We've Saved the Best for Last/Silhouette	1989	$3
❏ 9785 [PS]	We've Saved the Best for Last/Silhouette	1989	$3
❏ 9516	What Does It Take (To Win Your Love)/Songbird	1986	$5

KENT, AL
BARITONE
| ❏ 942 | Hold Me/Tell Me Why | 1960 | $80 |

CHECKER
| ❏ 881 | Dat's Why (I Love You So)/Am I the Man | 1958 | $200 |

RIC-TIC
❏ 140	Bless You (My Love)/(Instrumental)	1968	$20
❏ 133	Finders Keepers/Ooh! Pretty Lady	1967	$30
❏ 123	The Way You Been Acting Lately/(Instrumental)	1967	$50

WIZARD
| ❏ 100 | Hold Me/You Know Me | 1959 | $125 |

KENT, GEORGE
MERCURY
❏ 73066	Doogie Ray/The Great South Side Truck Stop Disaster	1970	$6
❏ 73182	Hitting the Bottle/I'm in a Bad Mood Tonight	1971	$6
❏ 73127	Mama Bake a Pie (Daddy Kill a Chicken)/Let's Just Pretend	1970	$6

RICE
❏ 5040	Falling Apart/You Wouldn't Want Me Now	1971	$8
❏ 5054	Hardscuffle Road/Doggie Ray	1972	$8
❏ 5027	Hitting the Bottle/Missing You	1967	$12
❏ 5050	I Can't Leave Now ('Cause Someone Moved the Door)/I'm Not Gonna Fly	1972	$8
❏ 5044	It Takes a Drinking Man/Running with the Wind	1972	$8

SHANNON
❏ 830	Honky Tonkin' Soul/Just Because You Understand Your Woman	1975	$5
❏ 815	It Takes a Fool a Time or Two/(B-side unknown)	1973	$5
❏ 840	Shake 'Em Up and Let 'Em Roll/Singin' Lonesome Cowboy Songs	1976	$5
❏ 834	She'll Wear It Out Leaving Town/Don't Tell It to Me	1975	$5
❏ 811	Sweet Lovin' Woman/I Can't Say I Love You	1973	$5
❏ 818	Take My Life and Shape It with Your Love/Sunshine Light	1974	$5
❏ 824	Whole Lotta Difference in Love/Coming Back on My Mind	1974	$5

SOUNDWAVES
| ❏ 4542 | Low Class Reunion/(How Can I Write on Paper) What I Feel in My Heart | 1977 | $5 |

Number	Title	Yr	NM

KENTON, STAN
CAPITOL
| ❏ F3134 | 23 Degrees N -- 82 Degrees W/Falling | 1955 | $15 |
| ❏ F1661 | Across the Alley from the Alamo/After You | 1951 | $15 |

—Reissue of 78 rpm material

❏ F2789	Alone Too Long/Don't Take Your Love from Me	1954	$15
❏ F15530	Artistry in Bolero/Come Back to Sorrento	1950	$20
❏ F900	Artistry in Boogie/Machito	1950	$30
❏ F15533	Artistry in Percussion/Ain't No Misery in Me	1950	$20

—The above four comprise a box set

| ❏ F1636 | Artistry in Rhythm/Artistry Jumps | 1951 | $15 |

—Reissue of 78 rpm material

❏ F3046	A-Ting-a-Ling/Malaguena	1955	$15
❏ F3345	Baa Too Kee/Winter in Madrid	1956	$15
❏ F2511	Baja/All About Ronnie	1953	$15
❏ F1874	Blues in Burlesque (Part 1)/Blues in Burlesque (Part 2)	1951	$20
❏ 4500	Carnival/Malibu Moonlight	1961	$8
❏ F3110	Casanova/Dark Eyes	1955	$15
❏ 4764	Come On Back/Warm Blue Stream	1962	$8
❏ F901	Concerto to End All Concertos, Part 1/Part 2	1950	$30
❏ F2064	Cool Eyes/She's a Comely Wench	1952	$20
❏ F2415	Curiosity/Theme to the West	1953	$15
❏ F1823	Daddy/Street of Dreams	1951	$20

—A-side with June Christy, vocals

❏ F2040	Delicado/Bag and Baggage	1952	$20
❏ F2409	Do Nothing Till You Hear from Me/How Many Hearts Have You Broken	1953	$15
❏ F2411	Don't Let Me Dream/It's Been a Long, Long Time	1953	$15
❏ 5828	Dragnet/Spanish Days	1967	$12
❏ F903	Eager Beaver/Harlem Folk Dance	1950	$30
❏ F1191	Easy Go/But Then You Kissed Me	1950	$30
❏ F1043	Evening in Pakistan/Jolly Rogers	1950	$30
❏ F2412	Every Time We Say Goodbye/Four Months, Three Weeks, Two Days	1953	$15
❏ F2449	Fascinating Rhythm/Over the Rainbow	1953	$15
❏ F1774	Francesca/Night Watch	1951	$20
❏ F3151	Freddy/Handwriting on the Wall	1955	$15
❏ F2418	Harlem Holiday/Don't Want That Man Around	1953	$15
❏ F906	Harlem Holiday/Ricka Jicka Jack	1950	$30
❏ F913	His Feets Too Big for De Bed/Down in Chihuahua	1950	$30
❏ F2419	How Am I to Know/He Was a Good Man	1953	$15
❏ F2373	Hushabye/Harlem Nocturne	1953	$20
❏ F908	Interlude/Thermopolae	1950	$30
❏ F899	Intermission Riff/Minor Riff	1950	$30

—Note: Earlier Stan Kenton 45s on Capitol may exist

❏ F2414	It's a Pity to Say Goodnight/There Is No Greater Love	1953	$15
❏ F1704	Laura/Jump for Joe	1951	$20
❏ F3836	Lemon Twist/Baby You're Through	1957	$12
❏ F1236	Love for Sale/Be Easy, Be Tender	1950	$30
❏ F1625	Love for Sale/Opus in Pastels	1951	$15
❏ 4707	Magic Moment/Waltz of the Prophet	1962	$8
❏ 4847	Mama Sang a Song/Whispering Hope	1962	$8
❏ 4666	Maria/Tonight	1961	$8
❏ F2871	More Love Than Your Love/Skoot	1954	$15
❏ 4370	Opus in Chartreuse Cha Cha Cha/Chocolate Caliente	1960	$10
❏ 5085	O Tannenbaum/What Is a Santa Claus	1963	$10
❏ F1306	Pagliacci/Santa Lucia	1950	$20
❏ F902	Painted Rhythm/Southern Scandal	1950	$30
❏ 5572	Patch of Blue/Make Me Love You	1966	$8
❏ F909	Peg o' My Heart/How Am I to Know	1950	$30
❏ 5480	Peyton Place Theme/007	1965	$8
❏ F15532	Safranski (Artistry in Bass)/Opus in Pastels	1950	$20
❏ F2879	Sambo Mambo/Mambo Riff	1954	$15
❏ F1480	September Song/Artistry in Tango	1951	$20
❏ F2413	Shoo Fly Pie and Apple Pie Down/I Been Down in Texas	1953	$15
❏ F2446	Sophisticated Lady/Begin the Beguine	1953	$15
❏ F2214	Stardust/Beehive	1952	$20
❏ F3243	Sunset Tower/Opus in Chartreuse	1955	$15
❏ F2410	Sweet Dreams Sweetheart/Gotta Be Gettin'	1953	$15
❏ F2250	Taboo/Lonesome Train	1952	$20

Number	Title	Yr	NM
❏ F910	Tampico/And Her Tears Flowed Like Wine	1950	$30
❏ F2685	Tenderly/The Creep	1953	$15
❏ F3928	Tequila/Cuban Mumble	1958	$10
❏ F2822	The Lady in Red/Under a Blanket of Blue	1954	$15
❏ 4629	Theme from "Splendor in the Grass"/Officer Krupke	1961	$8
❏ F905	Theme to the West/Collaboration	1950	$30
❏ 2278	The Odd Couple/MacArthur Park	1968	$10
❏ F904	The Peanut Vendor/Lover	1950	$30
❏ F2447	There's a Small Hotel/Shadow Waltz	1953	$15
❏ F1616	The Spider and the Fly/Are You Livin' Old Man	1951	$15

— Reissue of 78 rpm material

Number	Title	Yr	NM
❏ F1535	Tortillas and Beans/Dynaflow	1951	$20
❏ F4196	Whistle Walk/Tamer Lane	1959	$10
❏ F15531	Willow Weep for Me/Fantasy	1950	$20
❏ F911	Willow Weep for Me/How High the Moon	1950	$30
❏ EBF358 [PS]	A Collection of Stan Kenton Classics	1954	$25

— Gatefold sleeve for some editions of 1-358 and 2-358

Number	Title	Yr	NM
❏ EAP 1-358 [PS]	A Collection of Stan Kenton Classics, Part 1	1954	$20
❏ EAP 2-358 [PS]	A Collection of Stan Kenton Classics, Part 2	1954	$20
❏ EAP 2-358	Southern Scandal/Machito//And Her Tears Flowed Like Wine/Minor Riff	1954	$20
❏ EAP 1-358	Tampico/Artistry in Boogie//Across the Valley from the Alamo/Unison Riff	1954	$20

KENTS, THE

ARGO

Number	Title	Yr	NM
❏ 5299	I Found My Girl/With All My Heart and Soul	1958	$40

DOME

Number	Title	Yr	NM
❏ 501	I Love You So/Happy Beat	1958	$500

KENTUCKY HEADHUNTERS, THE

MERCURY

Number	Title	Yr	NM
❏ 874744-7	Walk Softly on This Heart of Mine/Skip a Rope	1989	$4

KERR, ANITA, SINGERS

AMPEX

Number	Title	Yr	NM
❏ 11042	Eli's Comin'/Something in the Way She Moves	1971	$5
❏ 11051	Oh Holy Night/Medley: Angels We Have Heard on High-What Child Is This?-Joy to the World	1970	$6
❏ 11050	Shine, Shine//Medley: O Come All Ye Faithful-Noel	1970	$6

DECCA

Number	Title	Yr	NM
❏ 28996	After You/Not Mine	1954	$10
❏ 28260	A Promise and a Prayer/Mt Grandmother's Place	1952	$10
❏ 27767	Borrowed Angel/My Evening	1951	$15
❏ 30756	Give In, Give In/Keep Your Belt Buttoned Up, Baby	1958	$8
❏ 27872	Have Faith/Pray	1951	$15
❏ 30417	In the Middle of an Island/For You	1957	$10
❏ 33032	Mary Kaye's Theme/Where Do I Go from Here	1972	$6
❏ 9-31002	My Love Is a Kitten/Strange Little Melody	1959	$8

— As "Anita Kerr Quartet

DOT

Number	Title	Yr	NM
❏ 17210	Alfie/A House Is Not a Home	1969	$5
❏ 17334	Coco/Money Rings Out Like Freedom	1969	$5
❏ 17270	Lalena/Suppose	1969	$5
❏ 17315	Ob-La-Di, Ob-La-Da/You and I	1969	$5
❏ 16602	Sails/For Just a Little While Tonight	1964	$8

— As "The Little Dippers

RCA VICTOR

Number	Title	Yr	NM
❏ 47-8332	Copper Kettle/Summer Green and Winter White	1964	$6
❏ 47-8246	Guitar Country/Waitin' for the Evening Train	1963	$15

— With Chet Atkins

Number	Title	Yr	NM
❏ PB-10388	The Masterpiece/At Seventeen	1975	$4
❏ 47-8050	To Each His Own/Tell Tale	1962	$15

— As "Anita and th' So-and-So's

UNIVERSITY

Number	Title	Yr	NM
❏ 210	Forever/Two by Four	1959	$10

— As "The Little Dippers

Number	Title	Yr	NM
❏ 608	Lonely/I Wonder, I Wonder, I Wonder	1960	$10

— As "The Little Dippers

Number	Title	Yr	NM
❏ 603	Tonight/Be Sincere	1960	$10

— As "The Little Dippers

WARNER BROS.

Number	Title	Yr	NM
❏ 7161	All This (She Does to Me)/No Salt on Her Tail	1967	$6
❏ 5866	A Man and a Woman/Just Say Goodbye	1966	$6
❏ 7065	For Bert/I Can't Help Remembering You	1967	$6
❏ 7211	Happiness/Wine in the Wind	1968	$5
❏ 7085	In the Morning/The Smile You Save for Strangers	1967	$6
❏ 7185	One Day/One Up on Me	1968	$5
❏ 7010	One in a Row/The Ever Constant Sea	1967	$6

KERSHAW, DOUG

BGM

Number	Title	Yr	NM
❏ 12989	Boogie Queen/Jambalaya	1989	$5
❏ 81588	Cajun Baby/I Wanna Hold You	1988	$5

K-ARK

Number	Title	Yr	NM
❏ 754	Fa-Do-Do/Ain't Gonna Get Me Down	1967	$10

SCOTTI BROTHERS

Number	Title	Yr	NM
❏ ZS5-02957	Flash/Ballad of the General Lee	1982	$4
❏ ZS6-02137	Hello Woman/Sing Along	1981	$4
❏ ZS5-02508	Instant Hero/Don't We Make Music	1981	$4

WARNER BROS.

Number	Title	Yr	NM
❏ 8033	All You Want to Do Is Make Kids/Whatcha Gonna Do When You Can't	1974	$5
❏ 7648	Devil's Elbow/Jamestown Ferry	1972	$6
❏ 7329	Diggy Diggy Lo/Papa and Mama Had Love	1969	$6
❏ 7304	Feed It to the Fish/You Fight Your Fight (I'll Fight Mine)	1969	$6
❏ 8257	House Husband/I'm Just a Nobody	1976	$5
❏ 8374	I'm Walkin'/Kershaw's Two Step	1977	$5
❏ 8195	It Takes All Day to Get Over Night/Mon Cheaux	1976	$5
❏ 7494	Mama Said Yeah/Natural Man	1971	$6
❏ 7763	Mama's Got the Know How!/Hippy Ti Yo	1973	$5
❏ 8594	Marie/Louisiana Sun	1978	$5
❏ 7413	Orange Blossom Special/Swamp Rat	1970	$6
❏ 7463	Play, Fiddle, Play/They Don't Make You No Better Than Me	1971	$6
❏ 7590	Sally Jo/Swamp Grass	1972	$6

KERSHAW, NIK

MCA

Number	Title	Yr	NM
❏ 52466	Dancing Girls/Bogart	1984	$12

— May only exist as a Canadian pressing

Number	Title	Yr	NM
❏ 52687	Don Quixote/Don't Lie	1985	$12

— May only exist as a Canadian pressing

Number	Title	Yr	NM
❏ 52427	I Won't Let the Sun Go Down on Me/Dark Glasses	1984	$10

— May only exist as a Canadian pressing

Number	Title	Yr	NM
❏ 52601	Wide Boy/So Quiet	1985	$4
❏ 52371	Wouldn't It Be Good/Monkey Business	1984	$4
❏ 52371 [PS]	Wouldn't It Be Good/Monkey Business	1984	$4
❏ 52690	Wouldn't It Be Good/Monkey Business	1985	$4

KERSHAW, RUSTY AND DOUG

FEATURE

Number	Title	Yr	NM
❏ 2003	It's Better to Be a Has Been (Than Be a Never Was)/No, No, It's Not So	1954	$125

HICKORY

Number	Title	Yr	NM
❏ 1177	Cajun Joe (Bully of the Bayou)/Sweet Sweet to Me	1962	$40
❏ 1036	Can I Be Dreaming/Look Around	1955	$40
❏ 1163	Cheated Too/So Lovely Baby	1961	$40
❏ 1101	Dancing Shoes/I Love You Like This	1959	$70
❏ 1151	Diggy Liggy Lo/Hey Mae	1961	$70
❏ 1072	Dream Queen/Take My Love	1957	$40
❏ 1063	Going Down the Road/You'll See	1957	$50
❏ 1077	Hey Mae/Why Don't You Love Me	1958	$40
❏ 1083	Hey Sheriff/Sweet Thing	1958	$40
❏ 1048	Hey You There/Your Crazy, Crazy Heart	1956	$40
❏ 1042	Honey Honey/Let's Stay Together	1956	$40
❏ 1061	If I Win, I Win/Money	1957	$40

— B-side by Al Terry

Number	Title	Yr	NM
❏ 1055	I'll Understand/Mister Love	1956	$40
❏ 1091	It's Too Late/We'll Do It Anyway	1958	$40
❏ 1137	Louisiana Man/Make Me Realize	1960	$60

Number	Title	Yr	NM
❏ 1575	Louisiana Man/(Our Own) Jole Blon	1970	$10
❏ 1068	Love Me to Pieces/I Never Had the Blues	1957	$50
❏ 1027	So Lovely, Baby/Why Cry for You	1955	$40
❏ 1110	The Love I Want/Oh Love	1959	$40

RCA VICTOR

Number	Title	Yr	NM
❏ 47-8266	Cajun Stripper/Half the Time	1963	$20
❏ 47-8362	Cleopatra/Malinda	1964	$20
❏ 47-8415	St. Louis Blues/I Can't See Myself	1964	$20

KESNER, DICK

7-Inch Extended Plays

BRUNSWICK

Number	Title	Yr	NM
❏ EB-771044 [PS]	Lawrence Welk Presents Dick Kesner	1959	$15

— Stereo

Number	Title	Yr	NM
❏ EB-771044	Silver Moon/I Love You Truly//Melody of Love/Play Fiddle Play	1959	$15

— Stereo

KESTRELS, THE

LAURIE

Number	Title	Yr	NM
❏ 3053	There Comes a Time/In the Chapel in the Moonlight	1960	$30

KEYES, TROY

ABC

Number	Title	Yr	NM
❏ 11116	A Good Love Gone Bad/I Can Wait My Turn	1968	$30

— With Norma Jenkins

Number	Title	Yr	NM
❏ 11027	Love Explosion/I'm Crying (Inside)	1967	$10

KEYMEN, THE

ABC-PARAMOUNT

Number	Title	Yr	NM
❏ 10039	Camilia/Cha Cha Marcha Congo	1959	$15
❏ 10016	Dream/Nancy Lee	1959	$15
❏ 9991 [M]	Gazachstahagen/Miss You	1959	$20
❏ S-9991 [S]	Gazachstahagen/Miss You	1959	$30
❏ 9977 [M]	Miss You/Isle of Capri	1958	$20
❏ S-9977 [S]	Miss You/Isle of Capri	1958	$30
❏ 9976	Sentimental Journey/Like Help, Man	1958	$20

KEYNOTES, THE

APOLLO

Number	Title	Yr	NM
❏ 484	I Don't Know/A Star	1955	$100
❏ 503	In the Evening/O Yeah Hm-m-m	1956	$100
❏ 513	One Little Kiss/Now I Know	1957	$100
❏ 478	Suddenly/Zenda	1955	$200

DOT

Number	Title	Yr	NM
❏ 15225	Who/They Say	1954	$40

INDEX

Number	Title	Yr	NM
❏ 101	Open the Door (To Your Heart)/Dum-De, Dum-Dum	1958	$125

POP

Number	Title	Yr	NM
❏ 111	Carelessly/Congratulations Baby	1957	$100

TOP RANK

Number	Title	Yr	NM
❏ 2005	With These Rings/We're Not Getting Along	1959	$20

KEYSTONERS, THE

EPIC

Number	Title	Yr	NM
❏ 9187	The Magic Kiss/After I Propose	1956	$70

G&M

Number	Title	Yr	NM
❏ 102	The Magic Kiss/I'd Write About the Blues	1956	$300

OKEH

Number	Title	Yr	NM
❏ 7210	The Magic Kiss/After I Propose	1964	$30

RIFF

Number	Title	Yr	NM
❏ 202	Sleep and Dream/T.V. Gal	1961	$200

KEYTONES, THE

CHELSEA

Number	Title	Yr	NM
❏ 101	I Don't Care/La-Do-Da Da	1962	$40
❏ 1013	Sweet Chariot/One, Two, Three	1963	$20

OLD TOWN

Number	Title	Yr	NM
❏ 1041	Seven Wonders of the World/A Fool in Love	1957	$125
❏ 1041	Wonders of the World/A Fool in Love	1957	$300

Number	Title	Yr	NM

KHAN, CHAKA
ATLANTIC
Number	Title	Yr	NM
❏ 89449	The Other Side of the World/ (Instrumental)	1986	$3

MCA
| ❏ 52730 | Own the Night/(Instrumental) | 1985 | $3 |
| ❏ 52730 [PS] | Own the Night/(Instrumental) | 1985 | $3 |

WARNER BROS.
❏ 49847	And the Melody Still Lingers On/I Know You, I Live You	1981	$4
❏ 49804	Any Old Sunday/Heed the Warning	1981	$4
❏ 27541	Baby Me/Everybody Needs Some Love	1989	$3
❏ 49216	Clouds/What You Did	1980	$4
❏ 28459	Earth to Mickey/My Destiny	1987	$3
❏ 49571	Get Ready, Get Set/So Naughty	1980	$4
❏ 29881	Got to Be There/Pass It On, A Sure Thing	1982	$4
❏ 29195	I Feel for You/Chinatown	1984	$4
❏ 29195 [PS]	I Feel for You/Chinatown	1984	$4
❏ 8683	I'm Every Woman/Woman in a Man's World	1978	$5
—Tan label			
❏ 8683	I'm Every Woman/Woman in a Man's World	1978	$8
—Burbank" palm trees label			
❏ 8683 [PS]	I'm Every Woman/Woman in a Man's World	1978	$5
❏ 27678	It's My Party/Where Are You Tonite	1988	$3
❏ 27678 [PS]	It's My Party/Where Are You Tonite	1988	$3
❏ 8740	Life Is a Dance/Some Love	1979	$4
❏ 28671	Love of a Lifetime/Coltrane Dreams	1986	$3
❏ 28671 [PS]	Love of a Lifetime/Coltrane Dreams	1986	$3
❏ 49256	Papillon (AKA Hot Butterfly)/ Too Much Love	1980	$4
❏ 22913	Soul Talkin'/I'm Every Woman	1989	$3
❏ 29745	Tearin' It Up/So Not to Worry	1983	$4
❏ 29097	This Is My Night/Caught in the Act	1985	$3
❏ 29097 [PS]	This Is My Night/Caught in the Act	1985	$3
❏ 29025	Through the Fire/La Flamme	1985	$3
❏ 28576	Tight Fit/Who's It Gonna Be	1986	$3
❏ 28576 [PS]	Tight Fit/Who's It Gonna Be	1986	$3
❏ 49759	We Can Work It Out/Only Once	1981	$4
❏ 49692	What Cha' Gonna Do for Me/Lover's Touch	1981	$4

KID CREOLE AND THE COCONUTS
ANTILLES
| ❏ 103 | There But for the Grace of God Go I/He's Not Such a Bad Guy After All | 1980 | $5 |
| ❏ 103 [PS] | There But for the Grace of God Go I/He's Not Such a Bad Guy After All | 1980 | $6 |

ATLANTIC
| ❏ 86927 [DJ] | My Male Curiosity/The Race | 1984 | $8 |
| ❏ 89664 | My Male Curiosity/The Race | 1984 | $5 |

ELEKTRA MUSICIAN
| ❏ 69306 | People Will Talk/Another Tribe | 1989 | $3 |
| ❏ 69306 [PS] | People Will Talk/Another Tribe | 1989 | $4 |

SIRE
❏ 29738	Annie, I'm Not Your Daddy/ Imitation	1983	$5
❏ 29738 [PS]	Annie, I'm Not Your Daddy/ Imitation	1983	$5
❏ 28959	Endicott/ Dowopsalsaboprock	1985	$4
❏ 49811	Going Places/In the Jungle	1981	$5
❏ 29468	If You Wanna Be Happy/The Seven Year Itch	1983	$5
❏ 50069	I'm a Wonderful Thing, Baby/No Fish Today	1982	$4
❏ 29909	Stool Pigeon/Love We Have	1982	$5

ZE/ISLAND
| ❏ PWIP6840 [PD] | Dear Addy//No Fish Today/ Christmas on Riverside Drive | 1982 | $12 |
| —U.K. import picture disc | | | |

KID, THE
RUMBLE
| ❏ 1347 | Sleep Tight/True Love | 1959 | $180 |

KIDD, JOHNNY, AND THE PIRATES
APT
| ❏ 25040 | Shakin' All Over/Yes Sir, That's My Baby | 1960 | $30 |

CAPITOL
| ❏ 5065 | I'll Never Get Over You/Then I Got Everything | 1963 | $20 |

KIDDS, THE
IMPERIAL
Number	Title	Yr	NM
❏ 5335	Are You Forgetting Me/ Drunk, Drunk, Drunk	1955	$500

KIDS NEXT DOOR, THE
4 CORNERS OF THE WORLD
| ❏ 129 | Inky Dinky Spider (The Spider Song)/Goodbye, Don't Cry (Fare Thee Well) | 1965 | $8 |
| ❏ 129 [PS] | Inky Dinky Spider (The Spider Song)/Goodbye, Don't Cry (Fare Thee Well) | 1965 | $15 |

DECCA
| ❏ 32157 | The Devil Rides in Jericho/ Hold Me, Now and Forever | 1967 | $8 |

KIHN, GREG, BAND
BESERKLEY
❏ B-5740	Any Other Woman/What Goes On	1976	$6
❏ 46517	Beside Myself/Getting Away with Murder	1979	$5
❏ 47441	Every Love Song/Trouble in Paradise	1982	$4
❏ 47463	Happy Man/Trouble in Paradise	1982	$4
❏ 47463 [PS]	Happy Man/Trouble in Paradise	1982	$5
❏ 47058	I Can't Stop Hurting Myself/ Serenade Her	1980	$5
❏ 69820	Love Never Fails/Talkin' to Myself	1983	$4
❏ B-5744	Love's Made a Fool of You/ Sorry	1977	$6
❏ B-5744 [PS]	Love's Made a Fool of You/ Sorry	1977	$10
❏ 47131	Sheila/When the Music Starts	1981	$5
❏ 46629	Small Change/Anna Belle Lee	1980	$5
❏ 47149	The Breakup Song (They Don't Write 'Em)/When the Music Starts	1981	$4
❏ 47149 [PS]	The Breakup Song (They Don't Write 'Em)/When the Music Starts	1981	$6
❏ 47206	The Girl Most Likely/True Confessions	1981	$4

EMI AMERICA
❏ B-8272	Boys Won't (Leave the Girls Alone)/Good Life	1985	$4
❏ B-8272 [PS]	Boys Won't (Leave the Girls Alone)/Good Life	1985	$4
❏ B-8306	Love and Rock and Roll/ Paint Me a Picture	1986	$4
❏ B-8255	Lucky/Sad Situation	1985	$4
❏ B-8255 [PS]	Lucky/Sad Situation	1985	$4

KILGORE, MERLE
ASHLEY
| ❏ 6000 | Packing an Unpacking/ Beyond My Conscience and the Door | 1968 | $10 |

COLUMBIA
| ❏ 4-44279 | Fast Talking Louisiana Man/ Avenue of Tears | 1967 | $10 |
| ❏ 4-44463 | Patches (Made the Change)/ Wild Rose | 1968 | $10 |

D
| ❏ 1042 | It'll Be My First Time/I Take a Trip to the Moon | 1959 | $30 |

ELEKTRA
| ❏ 47252 | Mister Garfield/I'm a One Woman Man | 1981 | $5 |

EPIC
❏ 5-9873	Baby, I Got It/Mama's Killing Daddy	1965	$15
❏ 5-9816	Dig, Dig, Dig, Dig (There's No More)/Help Me Up Darling (All Fools Fall Down)	1965	$15
❏ 5-9762	Every Day's a Holiday/It's All Over Now	1965	$15
❏ 5-10146	I Just Don't Care Anymore/ I'd Cry Like a Baby	1967	$15

IMPERIAL
❏ 5409	Ernie/Trying to Find (Someone Like You)	1956	$70
❏ 8300	Everybody Needs a Little Lovin'/Funny Feelin'	1955	$60
❏ 8256	More and More/What Makes Me Love You	1954	$50
❏ 5379	Please, Please, Please/ Teen-Ager's Holiday	1956	$40
❏ 8266	Seeing Double, Feeling Single/It Can't Rain	1954	$50
❏ 5584	Start All Over Again/Static	1959	$30
❏ 5555	Tom Dooley, Jr./Hang Doll	1958	$30

MERCURY
❏ 71918	42 in Chicago/Lover's Hell	1962	$30
❏ 71978	A Girl Named Liz/Trouble at the Towers	1962	$30
❏ 72048	Ain't Nothin' but a Man/ Somethin' Goin' On	1962	$30
❏ 71839	Wicked City/I'll Take Ginger and Run Away	1961	$30

MGM
Number	Title	Yr	NM
❏ 13209	Always an Apple/Johnny Zero	1964	$20
❏ 13168	Five Miles Down the Road/ Whiskey Road	1963	$20
❏ 13277	The Bell Witch/Slow Hard Way	1964	$20

PARKWAY
| ❏ 864 | I Am/When It Rains the Blues on You | 1963 | $20 |

STARDAY
❏ 533	Daddy's Place/Just Another Song Now	1961	$30
❏ 469	Dear Mama/Jimmie Brings Sunshine	1959	$30
❏ 964	Different Kind of Pretty/My Side of Life	1973	$8
❏ 497	Love Has Made You Beautiful/Gettin' Old Before My Time	1960	$30
❏ 644	Pinball Machine/Old Smokey	1963	$20

WARNER BROS.
❏ 29062	Guilty/When You Leave That Way You Can Never Go Back	1985	$4
❏ 8081	I'm Not Responsible/Tied	1975	$5
❏ 8039	Love o' Love/Baby's Comin' Home to Stay	1974	$5
❏ 7831	Montgomery Mable/Old Home Filler-Up An' Keep On-a Truckin' Cafe	1974	$5

KILGORE, THEOLA
CANDIX
| ❏ 311 | The Sound of My Man/Later I'll Cry | 1960 | $30 |

KT
| ❏ 501 | I'll Keep Trying/He's Coming Back to Me | 1964 | $20 |

MERCURY
| ❏ 72564 | I Can't Stand It/It's Gonna Be Alright | 1966 | $15 |

SCEPTER
| ❏ 12170 | The Love of My Man/As Long As You Need Me | 1966 | $15 |

SEROCK
| ❏ 2004 | The Love of My Man/I Know That He Loves Me | 1963 | $20 |
| ❏ 2006 | This Is My Prayer/As Long As You Need Me (Want Me, Love Me) | 1963 | $20 |

KIM, ANDY
20TH CENTURY FOX
| ❏ 6709 | Give Me Your Love/That Girl | 1968 | $8 |

CAPITOL
❏ 3962	Fire, Baby, I'm on Fire/Here Comes the Mornin'	1974	$4
❏ 3962 [PS]	Fire, Baby, I'm on Fire/Here Comes the Mornin'	1974	$6
❏ 4032	Hang Up Those Rock 'N' Roll Shoes/Essence of Joan	1975	$4
❏ 4086	Mary Ann/You Are My Everything	1975	$4
❏ 4234	Oh, Pretty Woman/Baby You're All I Got	1976	$4
❏ 4130	(She Got Me) Dancin'/Baby, You're All I Got	1975	$4

RED BIRD
| ❏ Oct-0040 | I Hear You Say (I Love You Baby)/Falling in Love | 1965 | $20 |

STEED
❏ 723	A Friend in the City/You	1970	$6
❏ 723 [PS]	A Friend in the City/You	1970	$15
❏ 716	Baby I Love You/Gee Girl	1969	$8
❏ 729	Be My Baby/Love That Little Woman	1970	$6
❏ 715	Foundation of My Soul/Tricia Tell Your Daddy	1969	$8
❏ 707	How'd We Ever Get This Way/Are You Ever Coming Home	1968	$8
❏ 734	I Been Moved/If I Had You Here	1971	$6
❏ 734 [PS]	I Been Moved/If I Had You Here	1971	$15
❏ 727	It's Your Life/To Be Continued	1970	$6
❏ 731	I Wish I Were/Walking My La De La	1971	$6
❏ 710	Shoot 'Em Up Baby/ Ordinary Kind of Girl	1968	$8
❏ 720	So Good Together/I Got to Know	1969	$6
❏ 720 [PS]	So Good Together/I Got to Know	1969	$15

TCF
| ❏ 5 | Give Me Your Love/Li'l Liz (I Love You) | 1964 | $20 |

UNI
❏ 55353	Love Song/Love the Poor Boy	1972	$5
❏ 55356	Oh What a Day/Sunshine	1972	$5
❏ 55332	Who Has the Answers?/ Shady Hollow Dreamers	1972	$5

Number	Title	Yr	NM
UNITED ARTISTS			
591	Love Me, Love Me/I Loved You Once	1963	$20
KIMBERLY, ADRIAN			
CALLIOPE			
6503	Greensleeves/God Bless America	1961	$50
6501	The Graduation Song... Pomp and Circumstance/Black Mountain Stomp	1961	$50
6504	When You Wish Upon a Star/Draggin' Dragon	1961	$50
KIMBERLYS, THE			
CANADIAN AMERICAN			
160	Forever/I Won't Be Back This Year	1963	$10
147	Save Me a Kiss at Your Wedding/You Just Smiled	1962	$10
154	Since the Word Got Around/One Room Flat	1963	$10
COLUMBIA			
4-43399	Denver/Pretty Little Children	1965	$12
4-44403	I Never Will Marry/Early Morning Sun	1967	$8
4-43601	Soldiers and Lilies/Don't Send Me Away	1965	$12
RCA VICTOR			
47-9782	Drivin' Nails in the Wall/These New Changing Times	1969	$8
KING, EVELYN "CHAMPAGNE"			
EMI MANHATTAN			
B-50101	Flirt/(Instrumental)	1988	$3
—As "Evelyn King			
B-50101 [PS]	Flirt/(Instrumental)	1988	$4
—As "Evelyn King			
B-50142	Hold On to What You've Got/(Set It Off Dub)	1988	$3
PRIVATE I			
ZS4-05627	Give It Up/Armies of the Night	1985	$4
—B-side by Sparks			
RCA			
PB-13682	Action/Let's Get Crazy	1983	$4
PB-13380	Betcha She Don't Love You/Get Up Off Your Love	1982	$4
—As "Evelyn King			
JB-13398 [DJ]	Betcha She Don't Love You (Long)/(Short)	1982	$8
—As "Evelyn King"; promo-only number			
PB-11025	Dancin', Dancin', Dancin'/Till I Come Off the Road	1977	$12
PB-12322	Don't Hide Our Love/The Best Is Yet to Come	1981	$4
—As "Evelyn King			
PB-13461	Get Loose/Spirit of the Dancer	1983	$4
—As "Evelyn King			
PB-14308	High Horse/Take a Chance	1986	$3
PB-11386	I Don't Know If It's Right/We're Going to a Party	1978	$4
PB-11386 [PS]	I Don't Know If It's Right/We're Going to a Party	1978	$5
PB-12243	I'm in Love/The Other Side of Love	1981	$4
—As "Evelyn King			
PB-12243 [PS]	I'm in Love/The Other Side of Love	1981	$5
—As "Evelyn King			
PB-12156	I Need Your Love/Bedroom Eyes	1981	$4
PB-12075	Let's Get Funky Tonight/Just a Little Bit of Love	1980	$4
GB-13493	Love Come Down/I'm in Love	1983	$3
—As "Evelyn King"; Gold Standard Series			
PB-13273	Love Come Down/(Instrumental)	1982	$4
—As "Evelyn King			
PB-11586	Music Box/It's Okay	1979	$4
PB-13980	Out of Control/Show Me (Don't Tell Me)	1984	$3
PB-13980 [PS]	Out of Control/Show Me (Don't Tell Me)	1984	$4
PB-11680	Out There/Make Up Your Mind	1979	$4
PD-11681	Out There/Make Up Your Mind	1979	$15
PB-13748	Shake Down/Tell Me Something Good	1984	$4
PB-11122	Shame/Dancin', Dancin', Dancin'	1977	$5
GB-11969	Shame/I Don't Know If It's Right	1980	$3
—Gold Standard Series			
PB-14373	Slow Down/Better Deal	1986	$3
PB-13017	Spirit of the Dancer/I Can't Take It	1981	$4
—As "Evelyn King			
PB-13825	Teenager/Don't It Feel Good	1984	$4
PB-14048	Till Midnight/I'm So Romantic	1985	$3
PW-14049	Till Midnight (Remixed Version) (Dub Version) (Instrumental) (Acappella)	1985	$8
KING, ALBERT/STEVE CROPPER/POP STAPLES			
STAX			
0047	Tupelo (Part 1)/Tupelo (Part 2)	1969	$8
0048	Water/Opus de Soul	1969	$8
KING, ALBERT			
ATLANTIC			
2604	The Hunter/As the Years Go Passing By	1969	$8
BOBBIN			
126	Blues at Sunrise/Let's Have a Natural Ball	1960	$30
131	Don't Thow Your Love on Me So Strong/This Morning	1961	$30
135	I Get Evil/What Can I Do to Change Your Mind	1962	$30
141	I'll Do Anything for You/Got to Be Some Changes Made	1963	$30
129	I Walked All Night Long/I've Made Nights By Myself	1961	$30
143	Old Blue Ribbon/I've Made Nights By Myself	1963	$30
130	Travelin' to California/Dyna-Flow	1961	$30
114	Why Are You So Mean to Me/Ooh-Ee Baby	1959	$30
KING			
5575	Don't Throw Your Love on Me So Strong/This Morning	1961	$15
5751	This Funny Feeling/Had You Told It Like It Was	1963	$15
6265	Travelin' to California/Don't Throw Your Love on Me So Strong	1969	$8
5588	Travelin' to California/Dyna-Flow	1961	$15
PARROT			
798	Bad Luck Blues/Be On Your Merry Way	1954	$1200
STAX			
217	Born Under a Bad Sign/Personal Manager	1967	$10
0069	Can't You See What You're Doing to Me/Cold Sweat	1970	$8
241	Cold Feet/Drive a Hard Bargain	1967	$10
201	Crosscut Saw/Down Don't Bother Me	1966	$12
0034	Drowning on Dry Land (Vocal)/(Instrumental)	1969	$8
197	Funk-Shun/Pretty Woman (Can't Make You Love Me)	1966	$10
252	(I Love) Lucy/You're Gonna Need Me	1968	$10
190	Laundromat Blues/Overall Junction	1966	$12
3225	Santa Claus Wants Some Lovin'/Don't Burn Down the Bridges	1979	$6
3203	The Pinch Paid Off (Part 1)/The Pinch Paid Off (Part 2)	1978	$5
0058	Wrapped Up in Love Again/Cockroach	1969	$8
TOMATO			
10012	Born Under a Bad Sign/I've Got the Blues	1979	$5
10001	Call My Job/Love Shack	1978	$5
10002	Chump Change/Good Time Charlie	1978	$5
UTOPIA			
PB-10879	Ain't Nothing You Can Do/I Don't Care What My Baby Do	1977	$5
PB-10544	Cadillac Assembly Line/Nobody Wants a Loser	1976	$5
PB-10770	Guitar Man/Rub My Back	1976	$5
PB-10682	Sensation, Communication Together/Gonna Make It Somehow	1976	$5
KING, ANNA			
END			
1126	Mama's Got a Bag of Her Own/Sally	1963	$40
SMASH			
1884	Baby, Baby, Baby/(Instrumental)	1964	$30
—With Bobby Byrd			
1942	Come On Home/Sittin' in the Dark	1964	$30
1858	If Somebody Told You/Come and Get These Memories	1963	$30
1904	If You Don't Think/Make Up Your Mind	1964	$30
1970	That's When I Cry/Tennessee Waltz	1965	$20
KING, B.B.			
ABC			
11316	Ain't Nobody Home/Alexi's Boogie	1971	$8
11290	Ask Me No Questions/Nobody Loves Me But My Mother	1971	$8
11280	Chains and Things/King's Special	1970	$8
10856	Don't Answer the Door (Part 1)/Don't Answer the Door (Part 2)	1966	$20
12053	Friends/My Song	1974	$6
11310	Ghetto Woman/Seven Minutes	1971	$8
11330	Guess Who/Better Lovin' Man	1972	$6
11302	Help the Poor/Lucille's Granny	1971	$8
11268	Hummingbird/Ask Me No Questions	1970	$8
11321	I Got Some Help I Don't Need/Lucille's Granny	1972	$6
12412	I Just Can't Leave Your Love Alone/Midnight Believer	1978	$6
11406	I Like to Live the Love/Love	1973	$6
12029	Philadelphia/Up at 5 A.M.	1974	$6
12247	Slow and Easy/I Wonder Why	1977	$6
11339	Summer in the City/Five Long Years	1972	$6
11319	Sweet Sixteen/I've Been Blue Too Long	1972	$6
11373	To Know You Is to Love You/I Can't Leave	1973	$6
10889	Waitin' on You/Night Life	1966	$20
12158	When I'm Wrong/Have Faith	1976	$6
11433	Who Are You/On to Me	1974	$6
ABC-PARAMOUNT			
10724	All Over Again/The Things You Put Me Through	1965	$20
10334	Blues at Midnight/My Baby's Coming Home	1962	$20
10361	Chains of Love/Sneakin' Around	1962	$20
10634	Everyday I Have the Blues/It's My Own Fault	1965	$20
10754	Goin' to Chicago Blues/I'd Rather Drink Muddy Water	1965	$20
10390	Guess Who/By Myself	1962	$20
10552	Help the Poor/I Wouldn't Have It Any Other Way	1964	$20
10486	How Do I Love You/Slowly Losing My Mind	1963	$20
10316	I'm Gonna Sit In Till You Give In/You Ask Me	1962	$20
10455	On My Word of Honor/Young Dreamers	1963	$20
10616	Please Send Me Someone to Love/The Worst Thing in My Life	1965	$20
10675	Tired of Your Jive/Night Owl	1965	$20
10367	Tomorrow Night/Mother's Love	1962	$20
10766	Tormented/You're Still a Square	1966	$20
10576	Whole Lotta Lovin'/The Hurt	1964	$20
BLUESWAY			
61021	Dance with Me/Please Send Me Someone to Love	1968	$12
61022	Don't Waste My Time/Get Myself Somebody	1969	$12
61026	Get Off My Back Woman/I Want You So Bad	1969	$10
61018	I'm Gonna Do What They Do to Me/Losing Faith in You	1968	$10
61015	Paying the Cost to Be the Boss/Having My Say	1968	$10
61035	So Excited/Confessin' the Blues	1970	$8
61012	Sweet Sixteen (Part 1)/Sweet Sixteen (Part 2)	1968	$10
61032	The Thrill Is Gone/You're Mean	1969	$15
61032 [PS]	The Thrill Is Gone/You're Mean	1969	$30
61004	Think It Over/I Don't Want You Cutting Off Your Hair	1967	$10
61024	Why I Sing the Blues/Friends	1969	$10
61007	Worried Dream/That's Wrong, Little Mama	1967	$10
KENT			
373	3 O'Clock Stomp/Mashed Potato Twist	1962	$15
447	Ain't Nobody's Business/I Wonder Why	1966	$15
325	A Lonely Lover's Plea/Woman in Love	1959	$30
392	Army of the Lord/Precious Lord	1964	$20
470	Bad Breaks/Growing Old	1967	$8
353	Bad Luck Soul/Get Out of Here	1961	$20
403	Beautician Blues/I Can Hear My Name	1964	$12
337	Blind Love/You Upset Me Baby	1960	$20
426	Blue Shadows/And Like That	1965	$15
387	Christmas Celebration/Easy Listening	1962	$15

Number	Title	Yr	NM
❏ 412	Christmas Celebration/Easy Listening	1964	$15
❏ 307	Days of Old/Don't Look Now, But You Got the Blues	1958	$30
❏ 339	Did You Ever Love a Woman/Three O'Clock Blues	1960	$20
❏ 4566	Don't Get Around Much Anymore/Poontanging	1972	$8
❏ 4515	Dreams/House Rocker	1970	$12
❏ 327	Everyday I Have the Blues/Time to Say Goodbye	1959	$30
❏ 441	Eyesight to the Blind/Just Like a Woman	1966	$15
❏ 445	Five Long Years/Love, Honor and Obey	1966	$15
❏ 383	Going Down Slow/When My Heart Beats Like a Hammer	1962	$15
❏ 372	Gonna Miss You Around Here/Hully Gully Twist	1962	$15
❏ 333	Got a Right to Love My Baby/My Own Fault	1960	$20
❏ 415	Got 'Em Bad/The Worst Thing in My Life	1965	$15
❏ 358	Hold That Train/Understand	1961	$20
❏ 4549	I'll Survive/Long Nights	1971	$8
❏ 4513	I'm Cracking Up Over You/Powerhouse	1969	$10
❏ 450	I Stay in the Mood/Early Every Morning	1966	$15
❏ 458	It's a Mean World/Blues Stay Away	1966	$8
❏ 396	Let Me Love You/You're Gonna Miss Me	1964	$12
❏ 435	Mercy, Mercy, Mercy/Broken Promise	1965	$15
❏ 390	My Reward/The Road I Travel	1963	$10
❏ 365	My Sometime Baby/Lonely	1962	$15
❏ 346	Partin' Time/Good Man Gone Bad	1960	$20
❏ 360	Peace of Mind/Someday	1961	$20
❏ 421	Please Love Me/Baby Look at You	1965	$15
❏ 336	Please Love Me/Crying Won't Help You	1960	$20
❏ 4562	Precious Lord/Swing Low, Sweet Chariot	1972	$8
❏ 499	Slow Burn/3 O'Clock Blues	1968	$6
❏ 329	Sugar Mama/Mean Old Friend	1959	$30
❏ 340	Sweet Little Angel/You Done Lost Your Good Thing Now	1960	$20
❏ 330	Sweet Sixteen, Pt. 1/Sweet Sixteen, Pt. 2	1960	$30
❏ 475	Sweet Thing/Soul Beat	1967	$8
❏ 381	Tell Me Baby/Mashing the Popeye	1962	$15
❏ 338	Ten Long Years/Everyday I Have the Blues	1960	$20
❏ 4542	That Evil Child/Tell Me Baby	1971	$8
❏ 319	The Fool/Come By Here	1959	$30
❏ 391	The Letter/You Never Know	1963	$10
❏ 492	The Woman I Love/Blues for Me	1968	$6
❏ 351	Things Are Not the Same/Fishin' After Me	1961	$20
❏ 467	Treat Me Right/Who Can Your Good Man Be	1967	$8
❏ 389	Trouble in Mind/Long Nights	1963	$10
❏ 350	Waking Dr. Bill/You Done Lost Your Good Thing Now	1960	$20
❏ 388	Whole Lot of Loving/Down Now	1963	$10
❏ 4526	Worried Life/Walkin' Dr. Bill	1970	$10
❏ 484	Worry, Worry, Worry/Why Do Everything Happen to Me	1968	$6
❏ 317	Worry Worry/I Am	1959	$30

MCA

Number	Title	Yr	NM
❏ 52675	Big Boss Man/My Guitar Sings the Blues	1985	$3
❏ 41062	Happy Birthday Blues/Better Not Look Down	1979	$4
❏ 52530	Into the Night/Century City Chase of J.B. in Teheran	1985	$3
❏ 52530 [PS]	Into the Night/Century City Chase of J.B. in Teheran	1985	$3
❏ 53644	Lay Another Log on the Fire/Go On	1989	$3
❏ 52125	Love Me Tender/The World I Never Made	1982	$3
❏ 52751	Memory Lane/Six Silver Strings	1985	$3
❏ 52574	My Lucille/Keep It Light	1985	$3

—B-side by Thelma Houston

Number	Title	Yr	NM
❏ 52218	Sell My Monkey/Inflation Blues	1983	$3
❏ 52057	Since I Met You Baby/One of Those Nights	1982	$3
❏ 52098	Street Life/Overture	1982	$3

—With the Crusaders and the London Symphony Orchestra

Number	Title	Yr	NM
❏ 51101	There Must Be a Better World Somewhere/You're Going with Me	1981	$4

RPM

Number	Title	Yr	NM
❏ 339	3 O'Clock Blues/That Ain't the Way to Do It	1951	$900

—B.B. King singles on RPM before 339 are unconfirmed on 45 rpm

Number	Title	Yr	NM
❏ 468	Bad Luck/Sweet Little Angel	1956	$30
❏ 451	Crying Won't Help You/Can't We Talk It Over	1956	$30

Number	Title	Yr	NM
❏ 451	Crying Won't Help You/Sixteen Tons	1956	$30
❏ 459	Dark Is the Night (Part 1)/Dark Is the Night (Part 2)	1956	$30
❏ 457	Did You Ever Love a Woman/Let's Do the Boogie	1956	$30
❏ 421	Every Day I Have the Blues/Sneakin' Around	1955	$40
❏ 411	Everything I Do Is Wrong/Don't You Want a Man Like Me	1954	$40
❏ 348	Fine Lookin' Woman/She Don't Move Me No More	1952	$300
❏ 360	Gotta Find My Baby/Someday Somewhere	1952	$125
❏ 490	How Do I Love You/You Can't Fool My Heart	1957	$30
❏ 450	I'm Cracking Up Over You/Ruby Lee	1956	$30
❏ 430	I'm in Love/Shut Your Mouth	1955	$40
❏ 498	I Wonder/I Need You So Bad	1957	$30
❏ 425	Lonely and Blue/Jump with You Baby	1955	$40
❏ 408	Love Me Baby/The Woman I Love	1954	$40
❏ 479	On My Word of Honor/Bim Bam	1956	$30
❏ 391	Please Hurry Home/Neighborhood Affair	1953	$100
❏ 386	Please Love Me/Highway Bound	1953	$200
❏ 403	Praying to the Lord/Please Help Me	1954	$40
❏ 355	Shake It Up and Go/My Own Fault, Darling	1952	$200
❏ 374	Story from My Heart and Soul/Boogie Woogie Woman	1952	$200
❏ 435	Talkin' the Blues/Boogie Rock	1955	$40
❏ 437	Ten Long Years/What Can I Do	1955	$40
❏ 492	Troubles, Troubles, Troubles/I Want to Get Married	1957	$30
❏ 412	When My Heart Beats Like a Hammer/Bye Bye Baby	1954	$40
❏ 395	Why Did You Leave Me/Blind Love	1953	$100
❏ 380	Woke Up This Morning (My Baby She Was Gone)/Don't Have to Cry	1953	$125

7-Inch Extended Plays

ABC

Number	Title	Yr	NM
❏ LP-ABCS-528 [PS]	Confessin' the Blues	1966	$30
❏ LP-ABCS-528	See See Rider/I'd Rather Drink Muddy Water/Confessin' the Blues//Goin' to Chicago Blues/I'm Gonna Move to the Outskirts of Town/How Long, How Long Blues	1966	$30

—Jukebox issue; small hole, plays at 33 1/3 rpm

ABC-PARAMOUNT

Number	Title	Yr	NM
❏ LP-ABCS-456 [PS]	Mr. Blues	1963	$30

BLUESWAY

Number	Title	Yr	NM
❏ LP-BLS-6016 [PS]	Lucille	1968	$30

KING BEES, THE

CHECKER

Number	Title	Yr	NM
❏ 909	Buzzin'/Good Rockin' Tonight	1958	$100

FLIP

Number	Title	Yr	NM
❏ 323	Puppy Love/Give Me Your Number	1957	$50

KRC

Number	Title	Yr	NM
❏ 302	Lovely Love/Can't You Understand?	1957	$50

NOBLE

Number	Title	Yr	NM
❏ 715	Tender Love/What Could Have Been Can't Be	1959	$250

RCA VICTOR

Number	Title	Yr	NM
❏ 47-8979	Lost in the Shuffle/Hardly (Part 3)	1966	$15
❏ 47-8787	On Your Way Down the Drain/Rhythm and Blues	1966	$15
❏ 47-8688	What She Does to Me/That Ain't Love	1965	$15

KING, BEN E.
Also see AVERAGE WHITE BAND; THE DRIFTERS.

ATCO

Number	Title	Yr	NM
❏ 6472	A Man Without a Dream/Tears, Tears, Tears	1967	$8
❏ 6203	Amor/Souvenir of Mexico	1961	$20
❏ 6371	Cry No More/There's No Place to Hide	1965	$12
❏ 6222	Don't Play That Song (You Lied)/Hermit of Misty Mountain	1962	$20
❏ 6571	Don't Take Your Love from Me/Forgive This Soul	1968	$8

Number	Title	Yr	NM
❏ 6527	Don't Take Your Sweet Love Away/She Knows What to Do for Me	1967	$12
❏ 6215	Ecstasy/Yes	1962	$20
❏ 6431	Get in a Hurry/I Swear by Stars Above	1966	$8
❏ 6390	Goodnight My Love/I Can't Break the News to Myself	1965	$10
❏ 6666	Hey Little One/When You Love Someone	1969	$12
❏ 6256	How Can I Forget/Gloria Gloria	1963	$15
❏ 6275	I Could Have Danced All Night/Gypsy	1963	$15
❏ 6237	I'm Standing By/Walking in the Footsteps of a Fool	1962	$15
❏ 6637	It Ain't Fair/Till I Can't Take It Anymore	1968	$8
❏ 6315	It's All Over/Let the Water Run Down	1964	$10
❏ 6267	I (Who Have Nothing)/The Beginning of Time	1963	$15
❏ 6328	Seven Letters/River of Tears	1964	$10
❏ 6357	She's Gone Again/Not Now (I'll Tell You When)	1965	$10
❏ 6166	Show Me the Way/Brace Yourself	1960	$20
❏ 6413	So Much Love/Don't Drive Me Away	1966	$8
❏ 6185	Spanish Harlem/First Taste of Love	1960	$30
❏ 6194	Stand By Me/On the Horizon	1961	$30
❏ 6246	Tell Daddy/Auf Weidersehn, My Dear	1962	$15
❏ 6288	That's When It Hurts/Around the Corner	1964	$12
❏ 6454	They Don't Give Medals to Yesterday's Heroes/What Is Soul	1966	$8
❏ 6231	Too Bad/My Heart Cries for You	1962	$15
❏ 6557	We Got a Thing Goin' On!/What 'Cha Gonna Do About It	1968	$8

—With Dee Dee Sharp

Number	Title	Yr	NM
❏ 6303	What Can a Man Do/Si, Senor	1964	$10
❏ 6284	What Now My Love/Groovin'	1964	$10
❏ 6596	Where's the Girl/It's Amazing	1968	$8

ATLANTIC

Number	Title	Yr	NM
❏ 3427	A Star in the Ghetto/What Is Soul?	1977	$5

—With the Average White Band

Number	Title	Yr	NM
❏ 3274	Do It in the Name of Love/Imagination	1975	$5
❏ 3535	Fly Away to My Wonderland/Spoiled	1978	$5
❏ 3444	Fool for You Anyway/The Message	1977	$5

—With the Average White Band

Number	Title	Yr	NM
❏ 3402	Get It Up/Keepin' It To Myself	1977	$5

—With the Average White Band

Number	Title	Yr	NM
❏ 3337	I Betch'a You Didn't Know/Smooth Sailing	1976	$5
❏ 3494	I See the Light/Tippin'	1978	$5
❏ 3635	Music Trance/And This Is Love	1979	$4
❏ 3359	One More Time/Somebody's Knocking	1976	$5
❏ 89234	Spanish Harlem/First Taste of Love	1987	$3
❏ 89361 [PS]	Stand By Me Medley	1986	$8

—Promo-only sleeve accompanying above medley. Stock and promo sleeves are identical in front but different on back.

Number	Title	Yr	NM
❏ 89361 [DJ]	Stand By Me Medley (same on both sides)	1986	$8

—Contains excerpts from all 10 songs on the "Stand By Me" soundtrack album. It is listed here because it uses the same number as the stock release of "Stand By Me.

Number	Title	Yr	NM
❏ 89361	Stand By Me/Yakety Yak	1986	$3

—B-side by the Coasters

Number	Title	Yr	NM
❏ 89361 [PS]	Stand By Me/Yakety Yak	1986	$3
❏ 3808	Street Tough/Why Is the Question	1981	$4
❏ 3241	Supernatural Thing -- Part 1/Supernatural Thing -- Part 2	1975	$5
❏ 3308	We Got Love/I Had a Love	1975	$5

MANDALA

Number	Title	Yr	NM
❏ 2513	Into the Mystic/White Moon	1972	$5
❏ 2518	Spread Myself Around/Travellin' Woman	1973	$5
❏ 2512	Take Me to the Pilot/I Guess It's Goodbye	1972	$5

MANHATTAN

Number	Title	Yr	NM
❏ 50078	Save the Last Dance for Me/Wheel of Love	1987	$3
❏ 50078 [PS]	Save the Last Dance for Me/Wheel of Love	1987	$3

MAXWELL

Number	Title	Yr	NM
❏ 800	I Can't Take It Like a Man/(B-side unknown)	1969	$8

Number	Title	Yr	NM

KING, CAROLE

ABC-PARAMOUNT
Number	Title	Yr	NM
❏ 9986	Baby Sittin'/Under the Stars	1958	$200
❏ 9921	Goin' Wild/The Right Girl	1958	$200

ALPINE
| ❏ 57 | Oh, Neil/A Very Special Boy | 1959 | $700 |

ATLANTIC
❏ 89756	Crying in the Rain/Sacred Heart of Stone	1983	$4
❏ 4026	One to One/Goat Annie	1982	$4
❏ 4026 [PS]	One to One/Goat Annie	1982	$5
❏ 89694 [DJ]	Speeding Time (same on both sides)	1984	$4

—May be promo only

CAPITOL
❏ 4941	Chains/Bad Girl	1980	$4
❏ 7PRO-79520 [DJ]	City Streets (same on both sides)	1989	$4
❏ 7PRO-79520 [PS]	City Streets (same on both sides)	1989	$4
❏ B-44336	City Streets/Time Heals All Wounds	1989	$3
❏ B-44336 [PS]	City Streets/Time Heals All Wounds	1989	$3
❏ 4455	Hard Rock Cafe/To Know That I Love You	1977	$4
❏ 4455 [PS]	Hard Rock Cafe/To Know That I Love You	1977	$5
❏ 7PRO-79873 [DJ]	Lovelight (same on both sides)	1989	$5

—Vinyl is promo only

❏ 4593	Main Street Saturday Night/Changes	1978	$4
❏ 4718	Move Lightly/Whiskey	1979	$4
❏ 4718 [PS]	Move Lightly/Whiskey	1979	$5
❏ 4864 [PS]	One Fine Day/Recipients of History	1980	$8

—First pressing sleeves list the wrong title for the B-side (no records are known to exist with this title)

| ❏ 4864 | One Fine Day/Rulers of This World | 1980 | $4 |
| ❏ 4864 [PS] | One Fine Day/Rulers of This World | 1980 | $4 |

—Second pressing sleeves don't list a B-side at all

❏ 4497	Simple Things/Hold On	1977	$4
❏ 4649	Sunbird/Morning Sun	1978	$4
❏ 4911	The Locomotion/Oh No Not My Baby	1980	$4
❏ 4766	Time Gone By/Dreamlike I Wander	1979	$4

COMPANION
| ❏ 2000 | It Might As Well Rain Until September/Nobody's Perfect | 1962 | $300 |

DIMENSION
| ❏ 1009 | He's a Bad Boy/We Grew Up Together | 1963 | $30 |
| ❏ 2000 | It Might As Well Rain Until September/Nobody's Perfect | 1962 | $20 |

—Purple label

| ❏ 2000 | It Might As Well Rain Until September/Nobody's Perfect | 1962 | $15 |

—Blue label

| ❏ 1004 | School Bells Are Ringing/I Didn't Have Any Summer Romance | 1962 | $30 |

ODE
❏ 66031	Been to Canaan/Bitter with the Sweet	1972	$4
❏ 66031 [PS]	Been to Canaan/Bitter with the Sweet	1972	$5
❏ 66035	Believe in Humanity/You Light Up My Life	1973	$4
❏ 66035 [PS]	Believe in Humanity/You Light Up My Life	1973	$5
❏ 66112SP	Chicken Soup with Rice/Pierre	1975	$8

—33 1/3 rpm 7-inch record

❏ 66112SP [PS]	Chicken Soup with Rice/Pierre	1975	$10
❏ 66039	Corazon/That's How Things Go Down	1973	$4
❏ 66006	Eventually/Up On the Roof	1970	$8
❏ 66123	High Out of Time/I'd Like to Know You Better	1976	$4
❏ 66026	It's Going to Take Some Time/Brother Brother	1972	$6
❏ 66015	It's Too Late/I Feel the Earth Move	1971	$4
❏ 66015 [PS]	It's Too Late/I Feel the Earth Move	1971	$5
❏ 66119	Only Love Is Real/Still Here Thinking of You	1976	$4
❏ 66019	So Far Away/Smackwater Jack	1971	$4
❏ 66019 [PS]	So Far Away/Smackwater Jack	1971	$5
❏ 66022	Sweet Seasons/Pocket Money	1971	$4
❏ 66022 [PS]	Sweet Seasons/Pocket Money	1971	$5

RCA VICTOR
| ❏ 47-7560 | Short Mort/Queen of the Beach | 1959 | $125 |

7-Inch Extended Plays

ODE
| ❏ LLP77013 | Brother, Brother/Song of Long Ago/Brighter//Some Kind of Wonderful/Sweet Seasons | 1971 | $8 |

—Jukebox issue; small hole, plays at 33 1/3 rpm

| ❏ LLP77013 [PS] | Music | 1971 | $8 |

—Part of "Little LP" series (LLP #180)

KING, CLAUDE

CINNAMON
Number	Title	Yr	NM
❏ 808	Don't Do Me Mad/It's Such a Perfect Day for Making Love	1974	$5

COLUMBIA
❏ 44833	All for the Love of a Girl/I Remember Johnny	1969	$8
❏ 44833 [PS]	All for the Love of a Girl/I Remember Johnny	1969	$15
❏ 42043	Big River, Big Man/Sweet Lovin'	1961	$12
❏ 42782	Building a Bridge/What Will I Do	1963	$10
❏ 42782 [PS]	Building a Bridge/What Will I Do	1963	$20
❏ 43510	Catch a Little Raindrop/Hold That Tiger	1966	$8
❏ 45340	Chip 'n' Dale's Place/Highway Lonely	1971	$6
❏ 45515	Darlin' Raise the Shade (Let the Sun Shine In)/Sweet Mary Ann	1971	$6
❏ 45015	Friend, Lover, Woman, Wife/The House of the Rising Sun	1969	$8
❏ 45704	He Ain't Country/This Time I'm Through	1972	$6
❏ 42833	Hey Lucille!/Scarlet O'Hara	1963	$12
❏ 42833 [PS]	Hey Lucille!/Scarlet O'Hara	1963	$20
❏ 45142	I'll Be Your Baby Tonight/It's Good to Have My Baby Home	1970	$6
❏ 42630	I've Got the World by the Tail/Shopping Center	1962	$10
❏ 42630 [PS]	I've Got the World by the Tail/Shopping Center	1962	$20
❏ 44237	Laura (What's He Got That I Ain't Got)/Good-By My Love	1967	$8
❏ 43416	Little Buddy/Come On Home	1965	$8
❏ 43867	Little Things That Every Girl Should Know/The Right Place	1966	$8
❏ 45248	Mary's Vineyard/Johnny Valentine	1970	$6
❏ 44504	Parchman Farm Blues/Birmingham Bus Station	1968	$8
❏ 43083	Sam Hill/Big Ole Shoulder	1964	$8
❏ 42688	Sheepskin Valley/I Backed Out	1963	$10
❏ 42688 [PS]	Sheepskin Valley/I Backed Out	1963	$20
❏ 44749	Sweet Love on My Mind/Four Roses	1969	$8
❏ 42959	That's What Makes the World Go Around/A Lace Mantilla and a Rose of Red	1964	$8
❏ 42581	The Burning of Atlanta/Don't That Moon Look Lonesome	1962	$12
❏ 42581 [PS]	The Burning of Atlanta/Don't That Moon Look Lonesome	1962	$20
❏ 42196	The Comancheros/I Can't Get Over the Way You Got Over Me	1961	$12
❏ 42196 [PS]	The Comancheros/I Can't Get Over the Way You Got Over Me	1961	$20
❏ 45614	The Lady of Our Town/Just As Soon As I Get Over Loving You	1972	$6
❏ 44642	The Power of Your Sweet Love/Beertops and Teardrops	1968	$8
❏ 44035	The Watchman/That's the Way the Wind Blows	1967	$8
❏ 43298	Tiger Woman/When You Gotta Go	1965	$8
❏ 45441	When You're Twenty-One/Heart	1971	$6
❏ 43157	Whirlpool (Of Your Love)/This Land of Yours and Mine	1964	$8
❏ 42352	Wolverton Mountain/Little Bitty Heart	1962	$15
❏ 42352 [PS]	Wolverton Mountain/Little Bitty Heart	1962	$20

TRUE
| ❏ 103 | Cotton Dan/I'll Spend My Lifetime Loving You | 1977 | $6 |
| ❏ 106 | Sugar Baby, Candy Girl/(B-side unknown) | 1977 | $6 |

KING, CLYDIE

IMPERIAL
Number	Title	Yr	NM
❏ 66172	He Always Comes Back to Me/Soft and Gentle Ways	1966	$30
❏ 66139	My Love Grows Deeper/Missin' My Baby	1965	$30
❏ 66109	The Thrill Is Gone/If You Were a Man	1965	$30

LIZARD
| ❏ 21007 | 'Bout Love/(B-side unknown) | 1971 | $6 |

Number	Title	Yr	NM

MINIT
| ❏ 32025 | Good for Cryin' Over You Days/Mistakes of Yesterday | 1967 | $15 |
| ❏ 32054 | Love Now, Pay Later/One Part, Two Part | 1969 | $8 |

PHILIPS
❏ 40001	Boys in My Life/Promises	1962	$30
❏ 40107	Only the Guilty Cry/By Noro	1963	$30
❏ 40051	Turn Around/Don't Hang Up the Phone	1962	$30

SPECIALTY
| ❏ 605 | Our Romance/Written on the Wall | 1957 | $40 |

KING CRIMSON
Also see YES; ADRIAN BELEW; PETER GABRIEL; URIAH HEEP.

ATLANTIC
| ❏ 2702 | The Court of the Crimson King - Part 1/Part 2 | 1970 | $15 |

WARNER BROS.
| ❏ 29964 | Heartbeat/Requiem | 1982 | $5 |
| ❏ 29309 | Sleepless/Nuages (That Which Passes, Passes Like Clouds) | 1984 | $5 |

KING CROONERS, THE

EXCELLO
| ❏ 2187 | Memoirs/School Daze | 1960 | $70 |
| ❏ 2168 | Won't You Let Me Know/Now That She's Gone | 1959 | $50 |

HART
| ❏ 1002 | She's Mine All Mine/Lonely Nights | 1959 | $400 |

KING CURTIS

ABC-PARAMOUNT
| ❏ 10133 | Beatnick Hoedown/King Neptune's Guitar | 1960 | $20 |

ATCO
❏ 6135	Castle Rock/Chili	1959	$30
❏ 6711	C.C. Rider/Rocky Roll	1969	$8
❏ 6785	Changes (Part 1)/Changes (Part 2)	1970	$6
❏ 6834	Changes (Part 1)/Changes (Part 2)	1971	$6
❏ 6429	Dancing in the Streets/He'll Have to Go	1966	$8
❏ 6534	For What It's Worth/Cook Out	1968	$8
❏ 6664	Games People Play/Foot Pattin' (Part 2)	1969	$8
❏ 6762	Get Ready/Bridge Over Troubled Water	1970	$6
❏ 6613	Harper Valley P.T.A./Makin' Hey	1968	$8
❏ 6152	Heavenly Blues/Restless Guitar	1959	$30
❏ 6143	Honey Dripper (Part 1)/Honey Dripper (Part 2)	1959	$30
❏ 6598	I Heard It Through the Grapevine/Whiter Shade of Pale	1968	$8
❏ 6547	I Never Loved a Man (The Way I Love You)/I Was Made to Love Her	1968	$8
❏ 6680	Instant Groove/Sweet Inspiration	1969	$8
❏ 6695	Little Green Apples/La Jeanne	1969	$8
❏ 6419	Make the World Go Away/You've Lost That Lovin' Feeling	1966	$8
❏ 6511	Memphis Soul Stew/Blue Nocturne	1967	$8
❏ 6516	Ode to Billie Joe/In the Pocket	1967	$8

—As "The Kingpins

❏ 6406	On Broadway/Quicksand	1966	$8
❏ 6720	Pop Corn Willie/Patty Cake	1969	$8
❏ 6447	Pots and Pans (Part 1)/Pots and Pans (Part 2)	1966	$8
❏ 6562	(Sittin' On) The Dock of the Bay/This Is Soul	1968	$8
❏ 6457	Something on Your Mind/Soul Theme	1966	$8
❏ 6738	Soulin'/Teasin'	1970	$6
❏ 6387	Spanish Harlem/The Boss	1965	$10
❏ 6114	The Birth of the Blues/Just Smoochin'	1958	$30
❏ 6630	The Christmas Song/What Are You Doing New Year's Eve?	1968	$15
❏ 6582	(Theme from) Valley of the Dolls/Eighth Wonder	1968	$8
❏ 6779	Whole Lotta Love/Floatin'	1970	$6

CAPITOL
❏ 4788	Beach Party/Turn 'Em On	1962	$12
❏ 4841	Beautiful Brown Eyes/Your Cheatin' Heart	1962	$12
❏ 5377	Bill Bailey/Soul Twine	1965	$10
❏ 4998	Do the Monkey/Feel All Right	1963	$12
❏ 5324	Sister Sadie/Tanya	1964	$10
❏ 5109	Soul Serenade/More Soul	1964	$12

Number	Title	Yr	NM
❑ 5270	Stranger on the Shore/Hide Away	1964	$10
❑ 4891	Strollin' Home/Mess Around	1962	$10
❑ 5212	Summer Dream/Melancholy Serenade	1964	$10
❑ 5061	Theme from "Lilies of the Field" (Part 1)/Theme from "Lilies of the Field" (Part 2)	1963	$10
❑ 5490	The Prance/Slow Drag	1965	$10

DELUXE

❑ 6142	The Stranger/Steel Guitar Rag	1957	$30
❑ 6157	Wicky Wacky (Part 1)/Wicky Wacky (Part 2)	1958	$30

ENJOY

❑ 1000	Soul Twist/Twisting Time	1962	$20
❑ 1001	Twisting with the King/Wobble Twist	1962	$20

EVERLAST

❑ 5030	Soul Twist/Twisting Time	1965	$12

GEM

❑ 208	Tenor in the Sky/No More Crying on My Pillow	1954	$50

GROOVE

❑ 1060	Movin' On/Rockabye Baby	1956	$30

MONARCH

❑ 702	Wine Head/I've Got News for You Baby	1953	$70

NEW JAZZ

❑ 45-510	Soul Meeting/All the Way	1961	$20

SEG-WAY

❑ 1006	Hot Rod/Bonaparte's Retreat	1962	$20

SKY ROCKET

❑ 106	Madisonville (Part 1)/Madisonville (Part 2)	1960	$30

TRU SOUND

❑ 415	Free for All/When the Saints Go Marching In	1962	$20
❑ 422	Low Down/I'll Wait for You	1962	$20
❑ 412	So Rare/Hucklebuck Twist	1961	$20
❑ 401	Trouble in Mind/But That's Alright	1961	$20
❑ 406	Twistin' and Jivin'/I Have to Worry	1961	$20

7-Inch Extended Plays

ATCO

❑ SD 37-266	Harper Valley P.T.A./Ode to Billy Joe/I Was Made to Love Her//Soul Serenade/The Dock of the Bay/Jump Back	1968	$25

—*Jukebox issue; small hole, plays at 33 1/3 rpm*

❑ SD 37-189	Spanish Harlem/I Left My Heart in San Francisco/Cryin' Time//You've Lost That Lovin' Feeling/And I Love Her/Make the World Go Away	1966	$25

—*Jukebox issue; small hole, plays at 33 1/3 rpm*

❑ SD 37-189 [PS]	That Lovin' Feeling	1966	$25
❑ SD 37-266 [PS]	The Best of King Curtis	1968	$25

CAPITOL

❑ SXA-1756 [PS]	Country Soul	1963	$35
❑ SXA-1756	Home on the Range/Wagon Wheels/Walkin' the Floor Over You/Brown Eyes/Tennessee Waltz/Night Train to Memphis	1963	$35

—*Jukebox issue; small hole, plays at 33 1/3 rpm*

EVEREST

❑ 196121 [PS]	Azure	1961	$60
❑ 196121	Close Your Eyes/Unchained Melody/Off Shore//It Ain't Necessarily So/Our Love Is Here to Stay/My Love Is Your Love	1961	$60

—*Jukebox issue; small hole, plays at 33 1/3 rpm*

KING, CURTIS

COLUMBIA

❑ 44096	Bad Habits/So Nice While It Lasted	1967	$30

KING, DON

615

❑ 1015	Can't Stop the Music/(B-side unknown)	1988	$5

BENCH MARK

❑ 8601	All We Had Was One Another/(B-side unknown)	1986	$5

CON BRIO

❑ 112	Cabin High (In the Blue Ridge Mountains)/Leavin' Talk	1976	$5
❑ 108	Dancing Across My Memory/I Can See Forever in Your Eyes	1976	$6

Number	Title	Yr	NM
❑ 106	Days of You and Me/Diamond Red Cowboy	1976	$6
❑ 133	Don't Make No Promises (You Can't Keep)/Cabin High (In the Blue Ridge Mountains)	1978	$5
❑ 126	I Must Be Dreaming/Truck Drivin' Lash LaRue	1977	$5
❑ 153	I've Got Country Music in My Soul/She's the Girl of My Dreams	1979	$5
❑ 116	I've Got You (To Come Home To)/Diamond Red Cowboy	1977	$5
❑ 149	Live Entertainment/I Must Be Dreaming	1979	$5
❑ 129	Music Is My Woman/Drinkin' in Texas	1977	$5
❑ 120	She's the Girl of My Dreams/Dancing Across My Memory	1977	$5
❑ 137	The Feeling's So Right Tonight/Where Were You	1978	$5

EPIC

❑ 50877	Here Comes That Feeling Again/My Happiness Is You	1980	$4
❑ 19-02046	I Still Miss Someone/More Than a Memory	1981	$4
❑ 50840	Lonely Hotel/Same Old Feeling	1980	$4
❑ 14-03155	Maximum Security (To Minimum Wage)/The Shadow of My Love	1982	$4
❑ 50928	Take This Heart/Saddle the Stallion	1980	$4
❑ 14-02468	The Closer You Get/The Time of Our Lives	1981	$4

KING, EARL

ACE

❑ 598	Don't You Know You're Wrong/Buddy It's Time to Go	1960	$50
❑ 543	I'll Never Get Tired/Well'o, Well'o, Well'o Baby	1958	$60
❑ 520	Is Everything Alright/Mother Told Me Not to Go	1956	$60
❑ 517	It Must Have Been Love/I'll Take You Back Home	1956	$60
❑ 514	My Love Is Strong/Little Girl	1956	$60
❑ 529	Those Lonely, Lonely Feelings/You Can Fly High	1957	$60
❑ 509	Those Lonely, Lonely Nights/Baby You Can Get Your Gun	1955	$70
❑ 564	Weary Silent Night/Everybody's Carried Away	1959	$50

IMPERIAL

❑ 5891	Come Along with Me/Case of Love	1962	$30
❑ 5750	Come Along with Me/You're More to Me Than Gold	1961	$30
❑ 5713	Come On -- Part 1/Come On -- Part 2	1960	$30
❑ 5730	Love Me Now/The Things That I Used to Do	1961	$30
❑ 5811	Trick Bag/Always a First Time	1962	$30
❑ 5858	We Are Just Friends/You're More to Me That Gold	1962	$30

REX

❑ 1015	I Can't Help Myself/Darling Honey, Angel Child	1961	$30

SPECIALTY

❑ 495	A Mother's Love/I'm Your Best Bet Baby	1954	$70
❑ 558	Funny Face/Sittin' and Wonderin'	1955	$70

KING FAMILY, THE

WARNER BROS.

❑ PRO216 [DJ]	Go Tell It on the Mountain/Here the Sledges with the Bells	1965	$10
❑ 5869	The Men in My Little Girl's Life/Bill Bailey (Won't You Please Come Home)	1966	$6
❑ 5647	The Sweetheart Tree/Amen	1965	$6

KING, FREDDIE

COTILLION

❑ 44015	Funky/Play It Cool	1968	$8
❑ 44058	I Wonder Why/Yonder Wall	1970	$8

EL-BEE

❑ 157	Country Boy/That's What You Think	1956	$400

FEDERAL

❑ 12439	Christmas Tears/I Hear Jingle Bells	1961	$40
❑ 12470	Come On/Just Pickin'	1962	$30
❑ 12518	Driving Sideways/Someday After Awhile (You'll Be Gone)	1964	$15
❑ 12537	Full Time Love/She's the One	1965	$15
❑ 12384	Have You Ever Loved a Woman/You've Got to Love Her with a Feeling	1960	$50
❑ 12401	Hideaway/I Love the Woman	1961	$40

Number	Title	Yr	NM
❑ 12491	(I'd Love To) Make Love to You/One Hundred Years	1963	$20
❑ 12443	If You Believe in What You Do/Heads Up	1961	$30
❑ 12535	If You Have It/I Love You More Every Day	1965	$15
❑ 12432	I'm Tore Down/Sen-Say-Shun	1961	$40
❑ 12475	In the Open/I'm On My Way to Atlanta	1962	$30
❑ 12415	Lonesome Whistle Blues/It's Too Bad Things Are Going So Tough	1961	$40
❑ 12515	Meet Me at the Station/Ting-a-Ling	1964	$20
❑ 12428	San-Ho-Zay/See See Baby	1961	$40
❑ 12521	She Put the Whammy on Me/High Rise	1964	$15
❑ 12456	Side Tracked/Sittin' on the Boat Dock	1962	$30
❑ 12532	Some Other Day, Some Other Time/Manhole	1965	$15
❑ 12509	Surf Monkey/Monkey Donkey	1963	$30
❑ 12450	Takin' Care of Business/The Stumble	1962	$30
❑ 12482	The Bossa Nova Watusi Twist/Look Ma, I'm Crying	1963	$20
❑ 12499	(The Welfare) Turns Its Back on You/You're Barkin' Up the Wrong Tree	1963	$20
❑ 12462	What About Love/Texas Oil	1962	$30

KING

❑ 6264	Have You Ever Loved a Woman/Hideaway	1969	$8

RSO

❑ 516	Boogie Bump/It's Your Love	1975	$5
❑ 505	My Credit Didn't Go Through/Texas Flyer	1975	$5

SHELTER

❑ 40410	Going Down/Me and My Guitar	1975	$5
❑ 7303	Going Down/Toke Down	1971	$6
❑ 7320	Me and My Guitar/Downtown in Lodi	1972	$6
❑ 7333	Woman Across the River/Help Me Through the Day	1973	$6

KING, JEAN

HANNA-BARBERA

❑ 497	Don't Say Goodbye/It's Good Enough for Me	1966	$12

KING, JO ANN

FAIRMOUNT

❑ 1008	Let Them Love and Be Loved/Don't Play with Fire	1966	$250

PHIL-L.A. OF SOUL

❑ 344	Hey Lancelot/This Lovin' Way (Let's Leave It)	1970	$50

KING, JOE

HIT

❑ 273	Mellow Yellow/I'm a Believer	1966	$8

—*B-side by the Jalopy Five*

❑ 265	Sunshine Superman/Dandy	1966	$8

—*B-side by the Chords (2)*

KING, JONATHAN

PARROT

❑ 3021	1968 (Message to the Presidential Candidates)/Colloquial Sex	1968	$8
❑ 40055	Cherry Cherry/Gay Girl	1970	$6
❑ 9774	Everyone's Gone to the Moon/Summer's Coming	1965	$12
❑ 3030	Flirt/Hey Jim	1969	$6
❑ 9804	Green Is the Grass/Where the Sun Has Never Shown	1965	$8
❑ 3029	Hooked on a Feeling/I Don't Want to Be Gay	1969	$6
❑ 3008	Icicles (Fell from the Heart of a Bluebird)/In a Hundred Years from Now	1966	$6
❑ 3027	Lazy Bones/Just Want to Say Thank You	1968	$8
❑ 40047	Let It All Hang Out/Colloquial Sex	1970	$6

UK

❑ 49002	It's a Tall Order for a Short Guy/Learned Tax Counsel	1972	$5
❑ 49014	Mary, My Love/A Little Bit Left of Right	1973	$5
❑ 49034	The Way You Look Tonight/The True Story of Molly Malone	1974	$5

Number	Title	Yr	NM

KING, MORGANA
20TH FOX
| ❏ 142 | Give Me Love/Lost, Lonely and Looking for Love | 1959 | $15 |

MAINSTREAM
❏ 600	A Taste of Honey/Corcavado	1964	$10
❏ 623	Try to Remember/Cuore di Mama	1964	$10
❏ 602	When the World Was Young/Lazy Afternoon	1964	$10

MERCURY
| ❏ 70967 | Four Walls, Two Windows, One Broken Heart/Mine for the Taking | 1956 | $20 |
| ❏ 70927 | Homesick in Paris/For You and Me | 1956 | $20 |

PARAMOUNT
| ❏ 0245 | A Song for You/You Are the Sunshine of My Life | 1973 | $5 |

REPRISE
| ❏ 0481 | If You Should Leave Me (E Se Domani)/Mountain High, Valley Low | 1966 | $8 |
| ❏ 0604 | The Look of Love/I Have Loved Me a Man | 1967 | $8 |

VERVE
| ❏ 10630 | Didn't We/Eleanor Rigby | 1968 | $6 |
| ❏ 10615 | I Know How It Feels to Be Lonely/I Only Know I Loved You | 1968 | $6 |

WING
| ❏ 90073 | In the Wee Small Hours of the Morning/It's De-Lovely | 1956 | $20 |

KING, PEE WEE
CUCA
❏ 1247	Danny Boy/I Am Praying for the Day Peace Will Come	1965	$12
❏ 1207	Guitar Polka/Wings of a Dove	1965	$10
❏ 1275	History Repeats Itself/Hope, Faith and Love	1966	$12
❏ 1420	I'm in Love with the Bridesmaid/(No One) Unless It's You	1966	$10
❏ 1315	Too Many Years/I Want to Light a Candle	1966	$10

JARO
| ❏ 77025 | Hi Diddle Diddle/Vagabond Waltz | 1960 | $15 |

LANDA
| ❏ 673 | Bumming Around/When, When, When | 1961 | $15 |
| ❏ 668 | Looking Back to Sea/Slow Poke | 1961 | $15 |

RCA VICTOR
❏ 47-5694	Backward, Turn Backward/Indian Giver	1954	$30
❏ 47-6666	Ballroom Baby/Absolutely Positive	1956	$20
❏ 48-0124	Billy in the Low Ground/Whistling Rufus	1950	$30
— Green vinyl original; the above three comprise a box set
| ❏ 48-0332 | Birmingham Bounce/What, Where and When | 1950 | $30 |
— Green vinyl original
| ❏ 48-0307 | Blame It All on Nashville/The Kissing Dance | 1950 | $30 |
— Green vinyl original
| ❏ 48-0354 | Blue Grass Waltz/Get Together Polka | 1950 | $30 |
— Green vinyl original
| ❏ 47-6450 | Blue Suede Shoes/Tennessee Dancin' Doll | 1956 | $30 |
| ❏ 48-0114 | Bonaparte's Retreat/The Waltz of Regret | 1949 | $40 |
— Green vinyl original
| ❏ 48-0037 | Bull Fiddle Boogie/Chattanooga Bus | 1949 | $40 |
— Green vinyl original
❏ 47-4655	Busybody/I Don't Mind	1952	$30
❏ 47-5537	Changing Partners/Bimbo	1953	$30
❏ 48-0379	Cincinnati Dancing Pig/We're Gonna Go Fishin'	1950	$30
— Green vinyl original
| ❏ 47-7090 | Congratulations Joe/Prelude to a Broken Heart | 1957 | $20 |
| ❏ 48-0120 | Cornbread, Lasses and Sassafras Tea/Fire on the Mountain | 1950 | $30 |
— Green vinyl original; the above three comprise a box set
| ❏ 48-0122 | Fisher's Hornpipe/Devil's Dream | 1950 | $30 |
— Green vinyl original
| ❏ 47-5782 | In a Garden of Roses/How Long | 1954 | $30 |
| ❏ 48-0393 | Mop Rag Boogie/River Road Two-Step | 1950 | $40 |
— Green vinyl original
❏ 47-4969	My Adobe Hacienda/Spanish Two-Step	1952	$20
❏ 47-5889	Peaches and Cream/I Can't Tell a Waltz from a Tango	1954	$30
❏ 47-6302	Peek-a-Boo Waltz/You Won't Need My Love Anymore	1955	$20
❏ 47-6070	Plantation Boogie/Jim, Johnny and Jonas	1955	$20
❏ 48-0123	Sally Goodin/Arkansas Traveler	1950	$30
— Green vinyl original
❏ 47-4971	San Antonio Rose/Varsouviana	1952	$20
❏ 47-5260	Screwball/Last Night on the Back Porch	1953	$30
❏ 47-6233	Seven Come Eleven/Farewell Blues	1955	$20
❏ 47-4458	Silver and Gold/Ragtime Annie Lee	1952	$30
❏ 47-4602	Silver and Gold/Texas Toni Lee	1952	$20
❏ 47-4603	Slow Poke/Ten Gallon Boogie	1952	$20
❏ 48-0489	Slow Poke/Whisper Waltz	1951	$30
❏ 47-4970	Steel Guitar Rag/Over the Waves	1952	$20
❏ 47-6793	Sugar Beet/I'll Be Walking Alone in a Crowd	1957	$20
❏ 48-0085	Tennessee Polka/The Nashville Waltz	1949	$40
— Green vinyl original
❏ 47-5009	Tennessee Tango/Crazy Waltz	1952	$30
❏ 47-4601	Tennessee Waltz/Bullfiddle Boogie	1952	$20
❏ 48-0407	Tennessee Waltz/Hilegged, Hilegged	1951	$30
❏ 48-0003	Tennessee Waltz/Rootie Tootie	1949	$40
— Green vinyl original
| ❏ 48-0119 | The Battle Hymn of the Republic/Blackeyed Susie | 1950 | $30 |
— Green vinyl original
| ❏ 47-4972 | The One Rose/Under the Double Eagle | 1952 | $20 |
— The above four comprise a box set
❏ 48-0451	The Strange Little Girl/Chew Tobacco Rag	1951	$30
❏ 47-6005	Tweedlee Dee/You Can't Hardly Get Them No More	1955	$20
❏ 47-4883	Two Faced Clock/Mighty Pretty Waltz	1952	$30
❏ 47-4238	Two Roads/Makin' Like a Train	1951	$30
❏ 47-5632	Why Don't Y'All Go Home/Huggin' My Pillow	1954	$30

STARDAY
❏ 668	Goodbye New Orleans/Waitin'	1964	$10
❏ 698	Ten Thousand Crying Towels/The Urge	1964	$10
❏ 682	When the Lights Go Dim Downtown/Stay Away from Me	1964	$10

TODD
| ❏ 1009 | Slow Poke Cha Cha/I Got a Wife | 1959 | $15 |
| ❏ 1020 | Too Tall/Slow Poke Cha Cha | 1959 | $15 |

TOP RANK
| ❏ 2087 | Do You Remember/(B-side unknown) | 1960 | $15 |

7-Inch Extended Plays
RCA VICTOR
| ❏ EPA797 | Flying Home/Over the Waves//Tippin' In/San Antonio Rose | 1956 | $20 |
| ❏ EPA797 [PS] | Swing West | 1956 | $20 |

KING, PEGGY
BUENA VISTA
| ❏ 397 | Bon Voyage/I Get a Kick Out of Kissin' | 1962 | $10 |

BULLET
| ❏ 77 | I Can't Make It on My Own/I Can't Get Over Gettin' | 1971 | $6 |

COLUMBIA
❏ 4-40437	Any Questions/You Never Gave It a Try	1955	$15
❏ 4-40273	Burn 'Em Up/The Hottentot	1954	$20
❏ 4-40996	If You Don't Love Me/C'mon Over	1957	$15
❏ 4-40362	I'm Gonna Put Some Glue 'Round The Christmas Tree/Counting Sheep	1954	$20
❏ 4-40562	Learning to Love/Song of Seventeen	1955	$15
❏ 4-40773	Love Sick/He Never Looks My Way	1956	$15
❏ 4-40363	Make Yourself Comfortable/The Gentleman in the Next Apartment	1954	$15
❏ 4-40863	Mircle Man/In My Own Little Corner	1957	$15
❏ 4-40524	Please Wait for Me/You Did, You Did	1955	$15
❏ 4-40744	Tall Boy/The Test of Time	1956	$15

MGM
| ❏ K11260 | There's Doubt in My Mind/I Cried for You | 1952 | $20 |

ROULETTE
| ❏ 4327 | I'll Be Around/Up, Up, Up (Flying High) | 1961 | $10 |

KING, PETE, CHORALE
KAPP
| ❏ 360 | Little Shepherd Boy/My Favorite Things | 1960 | $10 |

KING PINS, THE (1)
FEDERAL
❏ 12480	Believe in Me/Don't Wait Pretty Baby	1963	$30
❏ 12512	Hop Scotch/Wonderful One	1964	$20
❏ 12519	I Got the Monkey Off My Back/You're Using Me	1964	$20
❏ 12484	It Won't Be This Way (Always)/How Long Will It Last	1963	$30
❏ 12505	The Monkey One More Time/With the Other Guy	1963	$20
❏ 12517	Two Hearts/I Won't Have It	1964	$20

KING PINS, THE (2)
LARSE
| ❏ 101 | 94 Second Turf/Rod Hot Rod | 1966 | $50 |

KING, RANDY
BANDBOX
| ❏ 340 | Legend Of Little Orphan Joe/Merry Christmas | 1963 | $15 |

KING, REV. MARTIN LUTHER
The 1968 releases are posthumous tributes.

GORDY
| ❏ 7023 | I Have a Dream/We Shall Overcome | 1963 | $40 |
| ❏ 7023 | I Have a Dream/We Shall Overcome | 1968 | $8 |
—B-side by Liz Lands; "Gordy" on side of label

MERCURY
| ❏ 72814 | I Have a Dream/I've Been to the Mountain Top-Eulogy | 1968 | $8 |

KING, SID
COLUMBIA
| ❏ 4-21505 | Blue Suede Shoes/Let 'Er Roll | 1956 | $70 |
| ❏ 4-21403 | Drinkin' Wine Spoli-Oli/Crazy Little Heart | 1955 | $70 |
—As "The Five Strings"
| ❏ 4-21564 | Good Rockin' Baby/Gonna Shake This | 1956 | $70 |
| ❏ 4-21361 | I Like It/Put Something in the Pot Now | 1955 | $60 |
—As "The Five Strings"
❏ 4-40833	It's True, I'm Blue/When My Baby Left Me	1957	$60
❏ 4-41019	I've Got the Blues/What Have Ya Got to Lose	1957	$60
❏ 4-21489	Mama I Want You/Purr, Kitty, Purr	1956	$60
❏ 4-40680	Oobie Doobie/Boozer Red	1956	$60
❏ 4-21449	Sag, Drag and Fall/But I Don't Care	1955	$60

DOT
| ❏ 16293 | Hello There Rockin' Chair/Once Upon a Time | 1961 | $40 |

SOUNDWAVES
| ❏ 4612 | Back Door Man/I'd Rather Hear Willie | 1980 | $8 |

KING SISTERS, THE
CAPITOL
| ❏ 4310 | Chree-See-Mus/Girls and Boys | 1959 | $15 |
| ❏ 4099 [DJ] | Holiday of Love/Over The River | 1958 | $15 |

KING, SLEEPY
JOY
❏ 261	It's Written All Over Your Face/Happy Music	1962	$20
❏ 263	Lovin' Time/Slowly But Surely	1962	$20
❏ 257	Pushin' Your Luck/The King Steps Out	1961	$20

SYMBOL
| ❏ 904 | Begging/My Time Ain't Long | 1959 | $40 |

VEEP
| ❏ 1236 | Hello Martha/Please Let a Fool In Out of the Rain | 1966 | $15 |

Number	Title	Yr	NM
KING, TEDDI			
CORAL			
❏ 9-62094	BLue Tango/River of Regret	1959	$10
RCA VICTOR			
❏ 47-7074	Every Woman/A Lot in Common	1957	$15
❏ 47-6575	Impossible/I Can Honestly Say It's a Lie	1956	$15
❏ 47-7026	I Was a Child Till Tonight/ Then It Starts Again	1956	$15
❏ 47-6660	Married I Can Always Get/ Traveling Down a Lonely Road	1956	$15
❏ 47-6392	Mr. Wonderful/Are You Slipping Through My Fingers	1956	$15
❏ 47-6392 [PS]	Mr. Wonderful/Are You Slipping Through My Fingers	1956	$30
— Promo-only "This Is Her Life" cartoon sleeve			
❏ 47-7297	Say a Prayer/Baisez-Moi (Kiss Me)	1958	$15
❏ 47-6866	Say It Isn't So/There's So Much More	1956	$15
KING, WAYNE			
DECCA			
❏ 25616	Winter Wonderland/Jing-a-Ling-a-Ling	1963	$10
RCA VICTOR			
❏ EPA70	The Waltz You Saved for Me/I'm Forever Blowing Bubbles//I Love You Truly/La Golondrina	1952	$10
❏ EPA70 [PS]	Waltzes You Saved for Me	1952	$12
KINGDOM			
SPECIALTY			
❏ 722	Seven Fathoms Deep/If I Never Was to See Her Again	1970	$15
KINGS, THE			
BATON			
❏ 245	Long Lonely Nights/Let Me Know	1957	$50
ELEKTRA			
❏ 47213	All the Way/Loading Zone	1981	$3
❏ 47110	Don't Let Me Know/Partyitis	1981	$3
❏ 47006	Switchin' to Glide/My Habit	1980	$5
❏ 47052	Switchin' to Glide/This Beat Goes On	1980	$3
EPIC			
❏ 9370	I Want to Know/Bomp-I-Ty Bump	1960	$40
GONE			
❏ 5013	Don't Go/Love Is Something from Within	1957	$125
GOTHAM			
❏ 316	God Made You Mine/The Good Book	1956	$125
HARLEM			
❏ 2322	Fire in My Heart/You Never Know	1954	$200
JALO			
❏ 203	Angel/Come On Little Baby	1958	$50
JAY-WING			
❏ 5805	Surrender/Hold Me	1959	$200
JOX			
❏ 052	I've Got a License/Just a Little Bit of You	1965	$50
LOOKIE			
❏ 18	I Want to Know/Bomp-I-Ty Bump	1960	$50
RCA VICTOR			
❏ 47-7419	Till You/Elephant Walk	1958	$30
❏ 47-7544	Troubles Don't Last/Your Sweet Love	1959	$30
SPECIALTY			
❏ 497	What Can I Do/Till I Say Well Done	1954	$120
KINGSMEN, THE (1)			
JERDEN			
❏ 712	Louie Louie/Haunted Castle	1963	$70
WAND			
❏ 189	Annie Fanny/Give Her Lovin'	1965	$10
❏ 1164	Bo Diddley Bach/Just Before the Break of Day	1968	$8
❏ 164	Death of an Angel/Searching for Love	1964	$12
❏ 1174	Get Out of My Life Woman/ Since You've Been Gone	1968	$8
❏ 1137	If I Need Someone/The Grass Is Green	1966	$10
❏ 1180	I Guess I Was Dreamin'/ Oh Love	1968	$8
❏ 1157	(I Have Found) Another Girl/ Don't Say No	1967	$8
❏ 157	Little Latin Lupe Lu/David's Mood	1964	$12
❏ 143	Louie, Louie/Haunted Castle	1963	$30

Number	Title	Yr	NM
❏ 143	Louie Louie 64-65-66.../ Haunted Castle	1966	$20
❏ 150	Money/Bent Scepter	1964	$15
❏ 1127	My Wife Can't Dance/Little Sally Tease	1966	$10
❏ 183	The Climb/I'm Waiting	1965	$12
❏ 1154	The Wolf of Manhattan/ Children's Caretaker	1967	$8
❏ 1147	Trouble/Daytime Shadows	1967	$8
KINGSMEN, THE (2)			
EASTWEST			
❏ 120	Conga Rock/The Cat Walk	1958	$50
❏ 115	Week End/Better Believe It	1958	$50
KINGSMEN, THE (3)			
ALL STAR			
❏ 500	Guardian Angel/I'm Your Lover Man	1957	$100
KINGSMEN, THE (U)			
JALYNNE			
❏ 108	Ladies Choice/Dig This	1960	$30
NEIL			
❏ 102	One Foolish Mistake/ Stranded Love	1956	$70
KINGSTON TRIO, THE			
Also see DAVE GUARD AND THE WHISKEYHILL SINGERS; BOB SHANE; JOHN STEWART.			
CAPITOL			
❏ 5078	Ally Ally Oxen Free/Marcelle Vanine	1963	$10
❏ F4271	A Worried Man/San Miguel	1959	$30
❏ 4379	Bad Man Blunder/Escape of Old John Webb	1960	$20
❏ 4379 [PS]	Bad Man Blunder/Escape of Old John Webb	1960	$60
❏ SM-1705 [S]	Billy Goat Hill/Take Her Out of Pity	1962	$20
— Small hole, plays at 33 1/3 rpm			
❏ X3-1407 [S]	Buddy Better Get On Down the Line/South Wind	1960	$30
— 33 1/3 rpm, small hole jukebox pressing			
❏ XE5-1446 [S]	Bye Bye Thou Little Tiny Child/Mary Mild	1960	$20
— 33 1/3 rpm, small hole jukebox pressing			
❏ X5-1407 [S]	Colorado Trail/The Tattooed Lady	1960	$30
— 33 1/3 rpm, small hole jukebox pressing			
❏ 4642	Coming from the Mountains/ Nothing More to Look Forward To	1961	$20
❏ 4303	Coo Coo-U/Green Grasses	1959	$20
❏ 5005	Desert Pete/Ballad of the Thresher	1963	$12
❏ 4338	El Matador/Home from the Hill	1960	$20
❏ 4338 [PS]	El Matador/Home from the Hill	1960	$50
— This sleeve's existence has been confirmed			
❏ 4441	Everglades/This Mornin', This Evenin', So Soon	1960	$20
❏ 2006/7 [DJ]	Farewell Adelita/Corey, Corey	1960	$20
❏ 2006/7 [PS]	Farewell Adelita/Corey, Corey	1960	$30
— Promo item for Welgrume Sportswear			
❏ XE4-1446 [S]	Follow Now, Oh Shepherd/ Somerset Gloucestershire Wassail	1960	$20
— 33 1/3 rpm, small hole jukebox pressing			
❏ 4898	Greenback Dollar/New Frontier	1963	$10
❏ SXE2-1809 [S]	Honey, Are You Mad at Your Man/Adios Farewell	1963	$20
— 33 1/3 rpm, small hole jukebox pressing			
❏ 5132	Last Night I Had the Strangest Dream/Patriot Game	1964	$12
❏ SXE4-1809 [S]	Long Black Veil/Genny Glen	1963	$20
— 33 1/3 rpm, small hole jukebox pressing			
❏ 2782/3 [DJ]	Molly Dee/Haul Away	1959	$20
❏ 2782/3 [PS]	Molly Dee/Haul Away	1959	$30
— Promo item for "The New March of Dimes"			
❏ F4221	M.T.A./All My Sorrows	1959	$30
❏ 4808	Old Joe Clark/C'mon Betty Home	1962	$10
❏ 4842	One More Town/She Was Too Good to Me	1962	$10
❏ 4842 [PS]	One More Town/She Was Too Good to Me	1962	$40
❏ SXE3-1809 [S]	Poor Ellie Smith/My Lord What a Mornin'	1963	$20
— 33 1/3 rpm, small hole jukebox pressing			
❏ F3970	Scarlet Ribbons (For Her Hair)/Three Jolly Coachmen	1958	$30
❏ 4740	Scotch and Soda/Jane, Jane, Jane	1962	$10
❏ 4740 [PS]	Scotch and Soda/Jane, Jane, Jane	1962	$40

Number	Title	Yr	NM
❏ 5166	Seasons in the Sun/If You Don't Look Around	1964	$10
❏ XE2-1446 [S]	Sing We Noel/Go Where I Send Thee	1960	$20
— 33 1/3 rpm, small hole jukebox pressing			
❏ SXE1-1809 [S]	Some Fool Made a Soldier Out of Me/To Be Redeemed	1963	$20
— 33 1/3 rpm, small hole jukebox pressing			
❏ 4475	Somerset Gloucestershire Wassail/Goodnight My Baby	1960	$20
❏ 4475 [PS]	Somerset Gloucestershire Wassail/Goodnight My Baby	1960	$70
❏ 3149	Tell the Riverboat Captain/ Windy Wakefield	1971	$10
— As "The New Kingston Trio"			
❏ SXE5-1809 [S]	The First Time/Dogie's Lament	1963	$20
— 33 1/3 rpm, small hole jukebox pressing			
❏ PRO856 [DJ]	The Merry Minuet/Tick, Tick, Tick	1959	$50
❏ F4167 [M]	The Tijuana Jail/Oh Cindy	1959	$30
❏ SF4167 [S]	The Tijuana Jail/Oh Cindy	1959	$60
❏ XE3-1446 [S]	The White Snows of Winter/ All Through the Night	1960	$20
— 33 1/3 rpm, small hole jukebox pressing			
❏ X2-1407 [S]	This Mornin', This Evenin', So Soon/Everglades	1960	$30
— 33 1/3 rpm, small hole jukebox pressing			
❏ F4049	Tom Dooley/Ruby Red	1958	$30
❏ XE1-1446 [S]	We Wish You a Merry Christmas/The Last Month of the Year	1960	$20
— 33 1/3 rpm, small hole jukebox pressing			
❏ X1-1407 [S]	When I Was Young/Leave My Woman Alone	1960	$30
— 33 1/3 rpm, small hole jukebox pressing			
❏ 4671	Where Have All the Flowers Gone/O Ken Karanga	1961	$20
❏ X4-1407 [S]	Who's Gonna Hold Her Hand/To Morrow	1960	$30
— 33 1/3 rpm, small hole jukebox pressing			
CAPITOL CUSTOM			
❏ NKB-2670/1 [PS]	Cool Cargo	1960	$40
— Promotional item for 7-Up			
❏ NKB-2670/1	Tom Dooley/A Worried Man// The Hunter/With You My Johnny	1960	$40
CAPITOL STARLINE			
❏ 6046	A Worried Man/Scotch and Soda	1964	$8
— Originals have two-tone green swirl labels			
❏ 6071	Greenback Dollar/Reverend Mr. Black	1965	$8
— Originals have two-tone green swirl labels; "Greenback Dollar" does NOT have the word "damn" obliterated by a guitar chord, as the original 45 does			
❏ 6002	Tom Dooley/M.T.A.	1962	$8
— Originals have two-tone green swirl labels			
DECCA			
❏ 32040	Babe, You've Been On My Mind/Texas Across the River	1966	$12
❏ 31730	Little Play Soldiers/I'm Going Home	1965	$10
❏ 32010	Lock All the Windows/Hit and Run	1966	$10
❏ 31702	My Ramblin' Boy/Hope You Understand	1964	$20
❏ 31702 [PS]	My Ramblin' Boy/Hope You Understand	1964	$30
❏ 31790	Stay Awhile/Yes I Can Feel It	1965	$10
❏ 31790 [PS]	Stay Awhile/Yes I Can Feel It	1965	$30
❏ 31961	The Spinnin' of the World/A Little Soul Is Born	1966	$10
MOUNTAIN CREEK			
❏ 301/2	Big Ship Glory/Johnson Party of Four	1977	$30
NAUTILUS			
❏ NR2-45	Aspen Gold/Longest Beer of the Night	1979	$5
TETRAGRAMMATON			
❏ 1526	One Too Many Mornings/ Scotch and Soda	1969	$10
XERES			
❏ 10004	Looking for the Sunshine/ Reverend Mr. Black	1982	$4
❏ 10004 [PS]	Looking for the Sunshine/ Reverend Mr. Black	1982	$4
7-Inch Extended Plays			
CAPITOL			
❏ EAP 1-1322 [PS]	A Worried Man	1959	$30
❏ EAP 1-1322	A Worried Man/Molly Dee// San Miguel/Oleanna	1959	$30
❏ EAP 1-1407	Bad Man Blunder/The Escape of Old John Webb// Colorado Trail/The Tattooed Lady	1960	$30
❏ EAP 2-1199	Blow Ye Winds/Corey Corey//The Long Black Rifle/ Early in the Mornin'	1959	$30

Number	Title	Yr	NM
❏ EAP 1-1446	Bye Bye Thou Little Tiny Child/The Snows of Winter//Sing We Noel/The Last Month of the Year	1960	$30
❏ EAP 1-1642 [PS]	Close Up, Part 1	1961	$30
❏ EAP 2-1642 [PS]	Close Up, Part 2	1961	$30
❏ EAP 3-1642 [PS]	Close Up, Part 3	1961	$30
❏ EAP 1-1642	Coming from the Mountains/Oh Sail Away//Weeping Willow/Reuben James	1961	$30
❏ EAP 2-1352	Don't Cry Katie/Medley: Tanga Tiki-Toerau//Mangwani Mpulele/With You My Johnny	1960	$30
❏ EAP 1-1352	El Matador/The Mountains o' Mourne//The Hunter/Farewell Adelita	1960	$30
❏ EAP 1-1474	En El Agua/Come All You Fair and Tender Ladies//Blow the Candle Out/Blue Eyed Gal	1961	$30
❏ EAP 3-1446	Goodnight My Baby Goodnight/Go Where I Send Thee//Follow Now, Oh Shepherds/Somerset Gloucestershire Wassail	1960	$30
❏ EAP 2-1258	Haul Away/The Wanderer//E Inu Tatou E/A Rollin' Stone	1959	$30
❏ EAP 1-1258 [PS]	Here We Go Again! Part 1	1959	$30
❏ EAP 2-1258 [PS]	Here We Go Again! Part 2	1959	$30
❏ EAP 3-1258 [PS]	Here We Go Again! Part 3	1959	$30
❏ EAP 1-1474 [PS]	Make Way, Part 1	1961	$30
❏ EAP 2-1474 [PS]	Make Way, Part 2	1961	$30
❏ EAP 3-1474 [PS]	Make Way, Part 3	1961	$30
❏ EAP 1-1258	Molly Dee/Across the Wide Missouri//Goober Peas/A Worried Man	1959	$30
❏ EAP 1-1119	M.T.A.	1959	$35
❏ EAP 1-1199	M.T.A./All My Sorrows//Scarlet Ribbons/Remember the Alamo	1959	$30
❏ EAP 1-1119	M.T.A./Como Se Viene, Se Va//All My Sorrows/Sail Away Ladies	1959	$35
❏ EAP 1-1352 [PS]	Sold Out, Part 1	1960	$30
❏ EAP 2-1352 [PS]	Sold Out, Part 2	1960	$30
❏ EAP 3-1352 [PS]	Sold Out, Part 3	1960	$30
❏ EAP 1-1407 [PS]	String Along, Part 1	1960	$30
❏ EAP 2-1407 [PS]	String Along, Part 2	1960	$30
❏ EAP 3-1407 [PS]	String Along, Part 3	1960	$30
❏ EAP 2-1642	Take Her Out of Pity/Don't You Weep, Mary//When My Love Was Here/Karu	1961	$30
❏ EAP 1-1446 [PS]	The Last Month of the Year, Part 1	1960	$30
❏ EAP 2-1446 [PS]	The Last Month of the Year, Part 2	1960	$30
❏ EAP 3-1446 [PS]	The Last Month of the Year, Part 3	1960	$30
❏ EAP 3-1199	The Seine/I Bawled//Good News/Getaway John	1959	$30
❏ EAP 1-1129	The Tijuana Jail/Oh Cindy//Coplas/Tom Dooley	1959	$35
❏ EAP 3-1642	The Whistling Gypsy/O Ken Karanga//Jessie James/Glorious Kingdom	1961	$30
❏ EAP 3-1407	This Mornin', This Evenin', So Soon/Everglades//Buddy Better Get On Down the Line/South Wind	1960	$30
❏ EAP 1-996	Three Jolly Coachmen/Sloop John B//Bay of Mexico/Saro Jane	1958	$35
❏ EAP 1-1129 [PS]	Tijuana Jail	1959	$35
❏ MA1-1577	Tijuana Jail/A Worried Man//Bad Man's Blunder/Raspberries, Strawberries	1961	$30

— Small hole, plays at 33 1/3 rpm

Number	Title	Yr	NM
❏ EAP 1-1136 [PS]	Tom Dooley	1959	$35
❏ EAP 1-1136	Tom Dooley/Coplas//Banua/Santy Anno	1959	$35
❏ EAP 2-1446	We Wish You a Merry Christmas/All Through the Night//Mary Mild/A Round About Christmas	1960	$30
❏ EAP 2-1407	When I Was Young/Leave My Woman Alone//Who's Gonna Hold Her Hand/To Morrow	1960	$30
❏ EAP 3-1352	With Her Head Tucked Underneath Her Arm/Carrier Pigeon//Bimini/Raspberries, Strawberries	1960	$30

KINKS, THE
Also see DAVE DAVIES.

ARISTA

Number	Title	Yr	NM
❏ 0649	Better Things/Yo-Yo	1981	$4
❏ 0372	Black Messiah/Live Life	1978	$4
❏ 0458	Catch Me Now I'm Falling/Low Budget	1979	$4
❏ 1054	Come Dancing/Noise	1983	$4
❏ 1054 [PS]	Come Dancing/Noise	1983	$4
❏ 9016	Come Dancing/Noise	1983	$3
❏ 9016 [PS]	Come Dancing/Noise	1983	$3
❏ 0619	Destroyer/Back to Back	1981	$4
❏ 9309	Do It Again/Guilty	1984	$3
❏ 9309 [PS]	Do It Again/Guilty	1984	$3
❏ 9075	Don't Forget to Dance/Young Conservatives	1983	$3
❏ 0296	Father Christmas/Prince of the Punks	1977	$5

Number	Title	Yr	NM
❏ 0296 [PS]	Father Christmas/Prince of the Punks	1977	$5
❏ 0247	Life Goes On/Juke Box Music	1977	$4
❏ 0541	Lola/Celluloid Heroes	1980	$4
❏ 0541 [PS]	Lola/Celluloid Heroes	1980	$5
❏ 0448	Low Budget/A Gallon of Gas	1979	$4
❏ SP-5 [DJ]	Sleepwalker/All the Kids on the Street	1977	$12

— Gold vinyl; B-side by the Hollywood Stars

Number	Title	Yr	NM
❏ SP-5 [PS]	Sleepwalker/All the Kids on the Street	1977	$12
❏ 0240	Sleepwalker/Full Moon	1977	$4
❏ 9334	Summer's Gone/Going Solo	1985	$3
❏ 0409	Superman/Low Budget	1979	$5
❏ 0409	(Wish I Could Fly Like) Superman/Party Line	1979	$4

CAMEO

Number	Title	Yr	NM
❏ 308	Long Tall Sally/I Took My Baby Home	1964	$600
❏ 345	Long Tall Sally/I Took My Baby Home	1965	$300

MCA

Number	Title	Yr	NM
❏ 53699	How Do I Get Close/War Is Over	1989	$10
❏ 53015	Lost and Found/Killing Time	1987	$3
❏ 53015 [PS]	Lost and Found/Killing Time	1987	$3
❏ 53093	Working at the Factory/How Are You	1987	$10

RCA VICTOR

Number	Title	Yr	NM
❏ 74-0620	20th Century Man/Skin and Bones	1971	$8
❏ 74-0852	Celluloid Heroes/Hot Potatoes	1972	$8
❏ PB-10251	Everybody's a Star (Starmaker)/Ordinary People	1975	$6
❏ PB-10551	I'm in Disgrace/The Hard Way	1976	$6
❏ PB-10019	Mirror of Love/It's Evil	1974	$6
❏ APBO-0275	Money Talks/Here Comes Flash	1974	$10
❏ DJBO-0275 [DJ]	Money Talks (short/long versions)	1974	$8
❏ 74-0940	One of the Survivors/Scrap Heap City	1973	$200

— Released with acoustic versions of the two songs rather than the LP versions and quickly deleted

Number	Title	Yr	NM
❏ PB-10121	Preservation/Salvation Road	1974	$6
❏ LPBO-5001	Sitting in the Midday Sun/Sweet Lady Genevieve	1973	$12
❏ 74-0807	Supersonic Rocket Ship/You Don't Know My Name	1972	$8

REPRISE

Number	Title	Yr	NM
❏ 0334	All Day and All of the Night/I Gotta Move	1964	$30
❏ 0979	Apeman/Rats	1970	$10
❏ 0647	Autumn Almanac/David Watts	1967	$50
❏ 0420	A Well Repected Man/Such a Shame	1965	$20
❏ 0715	A Well Respected Man/Set Me Free	1968	$10
❏ 0762	Days/She's Got Everything	1968	$50
❏ 0540	Dead End Street/Big Black Smoke	1966	$50
❏ 0471	Dedicated Follower of Fashion/Sittin' on My Sofa	1966	$20
❏ 0712	Dedicated Follower of Fashion/Who'll Be the Next in Line	1968	$12
❏ 1017	God's Children/The Way Love Used to Be	1971	$30
❏ 0743	Lola/Apeman	1972	$5

— Back to Back Hits" series

Number	Title	Yr	NM
❏ 0930	Lola/Mindless Child of Motherhood	1970	$10
❏ 0587	Mr. Pleasant/Harry Rag	1967	$50
❏ 0409	See My Friends/Never Met a Girl Like You Before	1965	$20
❏ 0379	Set Me Free/I Need You	1965	$30
❏ 0806	Starstruck/Picture Book	1969	$50
❏ 0708	Sunny Afternoon/Dead End Street	1968	$10
❏ 0497	Sunny Afternoon/I'm Not Like Everybody Else	1966	$30
❏ 0454	Till the End of the Day/Where Have All the Good Times Gone	1966	$20
❏ 0719	Tired of Waiting for You/All Day and All of the Night	1968	$10
❏ 0347	Tired of Waiting for You/Come On Now	1965	$30
❏ 0612	Waterloo Sunset/Two Sisters	1967	$50
❏ 0366	Who'll Be the Next in Line/Everybody's Gonna Be Happy	1965	$30
❏ 0691	Wonderboy/Polly	1968	$50

KIPPINGTON LODGE

CAPITOL

Number	Title	Yr	NM
❏ 2236	And She Cried/Rumors	1968	$40

KIRBY, DAVE

BOONE

Number	Title	Yr	NM
❏ 1083	A Walk on the Outside/Mary and Jane	1969	$8
❏ 1078	Marie St. John/My Faults Will Fade Away	1969	$8

CAPITOL

Number	Title	Yr	NM
❏ 4119	Colorado/Good to Be Back on the Road	1975	$6

DIMENSION

Number	Title	Yr	NM
❏ 1013	Great All American Good Timin' Honky Tonk Man/Ain't Nothing Older Than That	1980	$5
❏ 1022	Moccasin Man/When Will Forgetting Begin	1981	$5
❏ 1030	Something New to Love/Cowboy Connection	1982	$5

DOT

Number	Title	Yr	NM
❏ 17461	Charleston Cotton Mill/Is Anybody Goin' to San Antone	1973	$6
❏ 17437	Lila Is My Kind of Woman/So Long Train Whistle	1972	$6

MONUMENT

Number	Title	Yr	NM
❏ 1168	Her and the Car and the Mobile Home/Don't It Make You Want to Go Home	1969	$6
❏ 1215	I Came Out Smelling Like a Rose/The Hobo	1970	$6

SOMA

Number	Title	Yr	NM
❏ 1416	The Old, Old House/Cantalope Jones	1964	$15

ZODIAC

Number	Title	Yr	NM
❏ 1007	What Kind of Bird Is That/Gonna Ride the Santa Fe to Santa Fe	1976	$6

KIRBY, GEORGE

ARGO

Number	Title	Yr	NM
❏ 5498 [PS]	Feeling Good/No More	1965	$30
❏ 5498	Feeling Good/No More	1965	$20

CADET

Number	Title	Yr	NM
❏ 5523	What Can I Do/Goodnight Irene	1966	$500

CAMEO

Number	Title	Yr	NM
❏ 317	(I Want Some) Meat on My Tomatoes/No Communication	1964	$60

KIRBY, KATHY

ASCOT

Number	Title	Yr	NM
❏ 2232	In All the World/Time	1967	$8

LONDON

Number	Title	Yr	NM
❏ 9621	Dance On/Playboy	1963	$20
❏ 9572	(He's a) Big Man/Slowly	1963	$20
❏ 9750	I Belong/I'll Try Not to Cry	1965	$20
❏ 9645	Let Me Go Lover/Sweetest Sounds	1964	$20
❏ 9677	Love Me Baby/You're the One	1964	$20
❏ 9628	Secret Love/Too Bad for Johnny	1964	$20

PARROT

Number	Title	Yr	NM
❏ 9767	Secret Love/Soon I'll Wed My Love	1965	$15
❏ 9775	The Way of Love/Oh Darling How I Miss You	1965	$15
❏ 9827	Till the End of Time/Spanish Flea	1966	$10
❏ 9805	Where in the World/Wonderful Feeling of Love	1965	$15

KIRK, DAVE

HI-Q

Number	Title	Yr	NM
❏ 5024	Oh! Baby/Those Lonely Blue Nights	1962	$60

KIRK, EDDIE

CAPITOL

Number	Title	Yr	NM
❏ F1591	Alone in a Tavern/Drifting Texas Sand	1951	$30
❏ F1287	Blue Bonnet Blues/In the Shambles of My Heart	1950	$40
❏ F40260	Dear Hearts and Gentle People/Careless Kisses	1949	$50
❏ F974	Four Hearts/Saturday Night Blues	1950	$40
❏ F1445	Honey Costs Money/Sowing Teardrops	1951	$30
❏ F1790	I'll Save My Heart/Freight Train Breakdown	1951	$30
❏ F1175	Puppy Love/Somebody's Cryin'	1950	$40
❏ F1048	Sugar Baby/An Armful of Great Heartaches	1950	$40
❏ F877	Two Years We Were Married/Unfaithful One	1950	$40

RCA VICTOR

Number	Title	Yr	NM
❏ 47-5412	Caribbean/As God Is My Witness	1953	$30
❏ 47-5149	Five Star President/Hit and Run Lover	1953	$30
❏ 47-5287	Wanderin' Eyes/The Country Way	1953	$30

Number	Title	Yr	NM

KIRK, RAHSAAN ROLAND
ATLANTIC
❏ 5111	Ain't No Sunshine/Black Boot	1971	$8
❏ 5080	Here Comes the Whistleman/Making Love After Hours	1969	$20

LIMELIGHT
❏ 3070	Mystical Dream/Once in a While	1966	$15

MERCURY
❏ 72325	Berkshire Blues/Dirty Money Blues	1964	$15
❏ 72075	Domino/3-in-1 Without the Oil	1963	$20
❏ 72144	Limbo Boat/Hey No	1963	$15
❏ 71924	Three for the Festival/You Did It, You Did It	1962	$20

PRESTIGE
❏ 420	Funk Underneath (Part 1)/(Part 2)	1967	$20

KIRK, RED
MERCURY
❏ 6288	Can't Understand a Woman/Teardrops from My Eyes	1950	$40
❏ 6409	Careless Mind/Knock Out the Lights and Call the Law	1952	$30
❏ 6309	Cold Steel Blues/Three's a Crowd	1951	$30
❏ 6363	Gentle Hands/Only One Step More	1951	$30
❏ 6358	Sentimental Journey/Train Track Shuffle	1951	$30
❏ 6332	Sugar Coated Love/Mad at My Heart	1951	$30

KISS
Also see PETER CRISS; ACE FREHLEY; GENE SIMMONS; PAUL STANLEY (and their simultaneously released solo albums from 1978).

CASABLANCA
❏ 2343	A World Without Heroes/Dark Light	1981	$5
❏ 863	Beth/Detroit Rock City	1976	$6
—With "Beth" listed as "Side A"; brown label with camel			
❏ 863	Beth/Detroit Rock City	1977	$5
—With "Beth" listed as "Side A"; "Casablanca Record and FilmWorks" label			
❏ 880	Calling Dr. Love/Take Me	1977	$6
—Brown label with camel			
❏ 880	Calling Dr. Love/Take Me	1977	$5
—Casablanca Record and FilmWorks" label			
❏ 889	Christine Sixteen/Shock Me	1977	$6
—A-side listed as 2:52, B-side time listed as 4:17; brown label with camel			
❏ 889	Christine Sixteen/Shock Me	1977	$5
—A-side listed as 2:52, B-side time listed as 4:17; "Casablanca Record and FilmWorks" label			
❏ 889	Christine Sixteen/Shock Me	1977	$6
—A-side time listed as 3:10, B-side time listed as 3:45; brown label with camel			
❏ 889	Christine Sixteen/Shock Me	1977	$5
—A-side time listed as 3:10, B-side time listed as 3:45; "Casablanca Record and FilmWorks" label			
❏ 841	C'mon and Love Me/Getaway	1975	$30
—Blue label			
❏ 841	C'mon and Love Me/Getaway	1977	$15
—Casablanca Record and FilmWorks" label			
❏ 863	Detroit Rock City/Beth	1976	$12
—With "Detroit Rock City" listed as "Side A			
❏ 858	Flaming Youth/God of Thunder	1976	$10
❏ 858 [PS]	Flaming Youth/God of Thunder	1976	$70
❏ 873	Hard Luck Woman/Mr. Speed	1976	$6
❏ 2365	I Love It Loud/Danger	1982	$5
❏ 2365 [PS]	I Love It Loud/Danger	1982	$30
❏ 983	I Was Made for Lovin' You/Hard Times	1979	$5
❏ 823	Let Me Go, Rock and Roll/Hotter Than Hell	1975	$30
—Blue label			
❏ 823	Let Me Go, Rock and Roll/Hotter Than Hell	1977	$15
—Casablanca Record and FilmWorks" label			
❏ 895	Love Gun/Hooligan	1977	$6
❏ 04	Love Theme from Kiss/Nothin' to Lose	1974	$20
❏ 2282	Shandi/She's So European	1980	$5
❏ 906	Shout It Out Loud (Live)/Nothin' to Lose	1977	$6
❏ 854	Shout It Out Loud/Sweet Pain	1976	$10
—Blue label			

❏ 854	Shout It Out Loud/Sweet Pain	1977	$8
—Casablanca Record and FilmWorks" label			
❏ 928	Strutter '78/Shock Me	1978	$6
❏ 015	Strutter/100,000 Years	1974	$20
❏ 2205	Sure Know Something/Dirty Livin'	1979	$5
❏ 2299	Tomorrow/Naked City	1980	$5

MERCURY
❏ 818216-7	All Hell's Breaking Loose/Young and Wasted	1984	$4
❏ 888796-7	Crazy Crazy Nights/No, No, No	1987	$4
❏ 888796-7 [PS]	Crazy Crazy Nights/No, No, No	1987	$4
❏ 880205-7	Heaven's on Fire/Lonely Is the Hunter	1984	$4
❏ 876146-7	Hide Your Heart/Betrayed	1989	$5
❏ 872244-7	Let's Put the X in Sex/Calling Dr. Love	1989	$5
❏ 872244-7 [PS]	Let's Put the X in Sex/Calling Dr. Love	1989	$6
❏ PRO694-7 [DJ]	Let's Put the X in Sex (Hot Urban Mix)/(Hot Rock Mix)	1989	$30
❏ 814671-7	Lick It Up/Dance All Over Your Face	1983	$4
❏ 884141-7	Tears Are Falling/Any Way You Slice It	1985	$4
❏ 884141-7 [PS]	Tears Are Falling/Any Way You Slice It	1985	$5
❏ 880535-7	Thrills in the Night/Burn Bitch Burn	1985	$4
❏ 870215-7	Turn On the Night/Hell or High Water	1988	$4
❏ 870215-7 [PS]	Turn On the Night/Hell or High Water	1988	$5

KIT AND THE OUTLAWS
BLACK KNIGHT
❏ 902	Midnight Hour/Don't Tread on Me	1966	$40

PHILIPS
❏ 40420	Midnight Hour/Don't Tread on Me	1966	$15

KIT KATS, THE
JAMIE
❏ 1337	Breezy/Won't Find Better Than Me	1967	$15
❏ 1345	Distance/Find Someone	1968	$12
❏ 1422	Find Someone/Breezy	1974	$6
—As "New Hope			
❏ 1362	Hey Saturday Noon/That's the Way	1968	$12
❏ 1346	I Got the Feeling/That's the Way	1968	$10
❏ 1353	I Want to Be/Need You	1968	$10
❏ 1326	Let's Get Lost on a Country Road/Find Someone (Who'll Make You Happy)	1966	$15
❏ 1388	Look Away/The Money Game	1970	$8
—As "New Hope			
❏ 1343	Sea of Love/Cold Walls	1967	$15
❏ 1321	That's the Way/Won't Find Better Than Me	1966	$15
❏ 1381	Won't Find Better (Than Me)/(They Call It) Love	1969	$8
—As "New Hope			

LAURIE
❏ 3186	Good Luck Charlie/Aba Daba Honeymoon	1963	$30

PARAMOUNT
❏ 0110	That You Love/Taking My Time	1971	$8

KITCHEN CINQ, THE
DECCA
❏ 32262	Good Lovin'/For Never We Met	1968	$10
❏ 32374	She's So Fine/The Minstrel	1968	$10

LHI
❏ 17005	If You Think/Ride the Wind	1967	$15
❏ 17010	Still in Love with You Baby/Ride the Wind	1967	$15
❏ 17015	Street Song/When the Rain Disappears	1967	$15

KITT, EARTHA
DECCA
❏ 31807	The Art of Love/Nikki	1965	$30

KAPP
❏ 333	I Wantcha Around/Johnny with the Gentle Hands	1960	$15
❏ 294	Love Is a Gamble/Sholem	1959	$15

MUSICOR
❏ 1203	Anyway You Want It Baby/The Little Gold Screw	1966	$60
❏ 1220	There Comes a Time/Anyway You Want It, Baby	1966	$200

RCA VICTOR
❏ 47-6928	A Woman Wouldn't Be a Woman/Toujour Gai	1957	$15
❏ 47-5358	C'est Si Bon (It's So Good)/African Lullaby	1953	$30
❏ 47-6197	Do You Remember/Mambo de Paree	1955	$20
❏ 47-6138	Fredy/Sweet and Gentle	1955	$20
❏ 47-6521	Honolulu Rock and Roll/There Is No Cure for L'Amour	1956	$20
❏ 47-7118	If I Can't Take It With Me/Proceed with Caution	1957	$15
❏ 47-5882	If I Was a Boy/Tea in Chicago	1954	$20
❏ 47-6727	I'm a Funny Dame/Put More Wood on the Fire	1956	$20
❏ 47-5447	I Want to Be Evil/Annie Doesn't Live Here Anymore	1953	$30
❏ 47-5737	Let's Do It/Senor	1954	$20
❏ 47-5756	Mink Schmink/Easy Does It	1954	$20
❏ 47-4952	Monotonous/Boston Beguine	1952	$30
❏ 47-5502	Santa Baby/Under the Bridges of Paris	1953	$30
❏ 47-5502 [PS]	Santa Baby/Under the Bridges of Paris	1953	$50
❏ 47-5610	Somebody Bad Stole De Wedding Bell/Lovin' Spree	1954	$20
❏ 47-7013	Take My Love, Take My Love/Yomme Yomme	1957	$15
❏ 47-6009	The Heel/My Heart's Delight (This Year's)	1955	$20
❏ 47-5914	Santa Baby/Hey Jacque	1954	$30

STREETWISE
❏ 1117	Where Is My Man/(Instrumental)	1983	$6

KITTENS, THE
ABC
❏ 10835	The Masquerade Is Over/It's Gotta Be Love	1966	$10

ABC-PARAMOUNT
❏ 10783	Is It Our Baby/Undecided You	1966	$200
❏ 10730	Lookie Lookie/We Find Him Guilty	1965	$125
❏ 10619	Shindig/I Got to Know Him	1965	$80

ALPINE
❏ 67	A Letter on His Sweater/Broken Dreams	1960	$40
❏ 64	Dark, Dark Sunglasses/Itsy Bitsy Teeny Weeny Yellow Polka Dot Bikini	1960	$40

CHESS
❏ 2027	Hey Operator/Ain't No More Room	1967	$50
❏ 2055	How Long Can I Go On/I've Got to Get Over You	1968	$50

CHESTNUT
❏ 203	Count Every Star/I'm Worried	1963	$60

DON-EL
❏ 205	I Need Your Love Tonight/Johnny's Place	1963	$20
❏ 122	Walter/Lite Bulb	1963	$20

UNART
❏ 2010	It's All Over Now/Letter to Donna	1959	$60

KLAATU
Subject of extensive BEATLES hoax. (45)

CAPITOL
❏ 4516	Around the Universe in 80 Days/We're Off You Know	1977	$5
❏ 4377	Calling Occupants/Doctor Marvello	1976	$8
❏ 4412	Calling Occupants/Sub-Rosa Subway	1977	$5
❏ 4627	Dear Christine/Older	1978	$5

ISLAND
❏ 011	California Jam/Doctor Marvello	1975	$10

KLARK KENT
Stewart Copeland of THE POLICE in disguise.

KRYPTONE/I.R.S.
❏ 9012	Away from Home/Office Talk	1980	$5
—Green vinyl, custom label, small hole			
❏ 9012 [PS]	Away from Home/Office Talk	1980	$6

KLINT, PETE, QUINTET
MERCURY
❏ 72709	Walkin' Proud/Shake	1967	$10

KNACK, THE
ATCO
❏ 7051	Pick It Up/Always	1976	$8
—Probably not the same as The "My Sharona" Knack; also probably not The Knack that were on Capitol in the 1960s			

Number	Title	Yr	NM
CAPITOL			
❏ 4822	Baby Talks Dirty/End of the Game	1980	$4
❏ 4822 [PS]	Baby Talks Dirty/End of the Game	1980	$12
❏ 5940	Banana Man/Pretty Daisy	1967	$12
❏ A-5078	Boys Go Crazy/We Are Waiting	1981	$6
❏ 4853	Can't Put a Price on Love/Rave Up	1980	$4
❏ 2075	Freedom Now/Lady in the Window	1968	$10
❏ 4771	Good Girls Don't/Frustrated	1979	$4

—A-side contains different lyrics from LP version in three places

Number	Title	Yr	NM
❏ 4771 [PS]	Good Girls Don't/Frustrated	1979	$6
❏ 4731	My Sharona/Let Me Out	1979	$4
❏ 4731 [PS]	My Sharona/Let Me Out	1979	$6
❏ A-5054	Pay the Devil (Ooo, Baby, Ooo)/Lil' Cal's Big Mistake	1981	$4
❏ A-5054 [PS]	Pay the Devil (Ooo, Baby, Ooo)/Lil' Cal's Big Mistake	1981	$4
❏ 5889	The Spell/Softly, Softly	1967	$10
❏ 5774	Time Waits for No One/I'm Aware	1966	$10

KNICKERBOCKERS, THE
CHALLENGE

Number	Title	Yr	NM
❏ 59268	All I Need Is You/Bite, Bite Barracuda	1965	$60
❏ 59384	As a Matter of Fact/They Ran for Their Lives	1968	$30
❏ 59348	Can You Help Me/Please Don't Love Him	1966	$30
❏ 59366	Come and Get It/Wishful Thinking	1967	$80
❏ 59332	High on Love/Stick with Me	1966	$30
❏ 59321	Lies/The Coming Generation	1965	$20
❏ 59341	Love Is a Bird/Rumors, Gossip, Words Untrue	1966	$25
❏ 59326	One Track Mind/I Must Be Doing Something Right	1966	$25
❏ 59359	What Does That Make You/Sweet Green Fields	1967	$25

KNIGHT, BOB
LAUREL

Number	Title	Yr	NM
❏ 1020	Good, Goodby/(B-side unknown)	1961	$30

TAURUS

Number	Title	Yr	NM
❏ 100	Good, Goodby/So Long	1961	$30

KNIGHT BROS., THE
CHECKER

Number	Title	Yr	NM
❏ 1146	All I Have to Do Is Dream/Hand of Faith	1966	$30
❏ 1076	Come On Girl/City Life	1964	$30
❏ 1124	I Owe Her My Life/I'm Never Gonna Live It Down	1965	$30
❏ 1064	I Really Love You/Second Hand Lover	1963	$30
❏ 1107	Temptation 'Bout to Get Me/Sinking Low	1965	$30
❏ 1153	That'll Get It/She's A-1	1966	$30

MERCURY

Number	Title	Yr	NM
❏ 72829	Ghetto Joe/Tried So Hard to Please Her	1968	$30

KNIGHT, CHRIS, AND MAUREEN McCORMICK
Also see each artist's individual listings; THE BRADY BUNCH.

PARAMOUNT

Number	Title	Yr	NM
❏ 0246	Little Bird/Just a-Singin' Along	1973	$20

KNIGHT, CHRIS
PARAMOUNT

Number	Title	Yr	NM
❏ 0177	Good for Each Other/Over and Over	1972	$20
❏ 0177 [PS]	Good for Each Other/Over and Over	1972	$20

KNIGHT, EVELYN
DECCA

Number	Title	Yr	NM
❏ 9-27182	He Can Come Back Anytime He Wants To/Lucky Lucky Lucky Me	1950	$30
❏ 9-27281	I Am Loved/Nobody's Chasing Me	1950	$30

KNIGHT, FREDERICK
1-2-3

Number	Title	Yr	NM
❏ 1724	Have a Little Mercy/Sauerkraut	1970	$20

JUANA

Number	Title	Yr	NM
❏ 3408	High Society/(Instrumental)	1976	$5
❏ 3402	I'm Falling in Love Again/Done Got Over Lover	1976	$5
❏ 1948	Let Me Ring Your Bell Again/When It Ain't Right	1980	$5
❏ 3420	My Music Makes Me Feel Good/When It Ain't Right with My Baby	1978	$5
❏ 3415	Sit Down on Your Love/Staying Power	1977	$5

Number	Title	Yr	NM
❏ 3411	Staying Power/Wrapped in Your Love	1977	$5
❏ 3404	Sugar/I'm Falling in Love	1976	$5
❏ 3700	The Old Songs/Bundle of Love	1981	$5
STAX			
❏ 0117	I've Been Lonely for So Long/Lean on Me	1972	$8
TRUTH			
❏ 3216	I Betcha Didn't Know That/Let's Make a Deal	1974	$6
❏ 3228	I Wanna Play with You/I Miss You	1975	$6
❏ 3202	Passing Through/Sometimes Storm	1974	$6

KNIGHT, GLADYS, AND THE PIPS
BRUNSWICK

Number	Title	Yr	NM
❏ 55048	Whistle My Love/Ching Ching	1958	$120

BUDDAH

Number	Title	Yr	NM
❏ 569	Baby Don't Change Your Mind/I Love to Feel That Feeling	1977	$5
❏ 403	Best Thing That Ever Happened to Me/Once in a Lifetime	1974	$5
❏ 1974 [DJ]	Do You Hear What I Hear/Silent Night	1974	$6
❏ 1974 [PS]	Do You Hear What I Hear/Silent Night	1974	$6
❏ 433	I Feel a Song (In My Heart)/Don't Burn Down the Bridge	1974	$5
❏ 601	I'm Coming Home Again/Love Gives You the Power	1978	$5
❏ 598	It's a Better Than Good Time/Everybody's Got to Find a Way	1978	$5
❏ 393	I've Got to Use My Imagination/I Can See Clearly Now	1973	$5
❏ 453-N	Love FInds Its Own Way/Better You Go Your Way	1975	$6

— Some copies have the grammatically correct A-side title as above

Number	Title	Yr	NM
❏ 453	Love FInds It's Own Way/Better You Go Your Way	1975	$5

— Some copies have a grammatically incorrect A-side title as above

Number	Title	Yr	NM
❏ 523	Make Yours a Happy Home/The Going Up and the Coming Down	1976	$5
❏ 383	Midnight Train to Georgia/(Instrumental)	1973	$6
❏ 383	Midnight Train to Georgia/Window Raising Granny	1973	$5
❏ 487	Money/Street Brothers	1975	$5
❏ 423	On and On/The Makings of You	1974	$5
❏ 423 [PS]	On and On/The Makings of You	1974	$8
❏ 513	Part Time Love/Where Did I Put His Memory	1975	$5
❏ 605	Sail Away/I'm Still Caught Up with You	1979	$5
❏ 584	Sorry Doesn't Always Make It Right/You Put a New Life in My Body	1977	$5
❏ 544	So Sad the Song/(Instrumental)	1976	$5
❏ 592	The One and Only/Pipe Dreams	1978	$5
❏ 463	The Way We Were-Try to Remember/The Need to Be	1975	$5
❏ 363	Where Peaceful Waters Flow/Perfect Love	1973	$5
❏ 363 [PS]	Where Peaceful Waters Flow/Perfect Love	1973	$8

CASABLANCA

Number	Title	Yr	NM
❏ 949	Baby I'm Your Fool/Lights of the City	1978	$4

—As "The Pips"

Number	Title	Yr	NM
❏ 912	If I Could Bring Back Yesterday/Since I Found Love	1978	$4

—As "The Pips"

COLUMBIA

Number	Title	Yr	NM
❏ 3-10922	Am I Too Late/It's the Same Old Song	1979	$4
❏ 1-11375	Bourgie', Bourgie'/Get the Love	1980	$4
❏ 11-02113	Forever Yesterday (For the Children)/(Instrumental)	1981	$4
❏ 11-02113 [PS]	Forever Yesterday (For the Children)/(Instrumental)	1981	$5
❏ 18-02706	Friend of Mine/Reach High	1982	$4
❏ 38-04333	Here's That Sunny Day/Oh La De Da	1984	$4
❏ 38-04219	Hero (The Wind Beneath My Wings)/Seconds	1983	$5
❏ 18-02413	If That'll Make You Happy/Love Was Made for Two	1981	$4
❏ 18-02549	I Will Fight/God Is	1981	$4
❏ 1-11239	Landlord/We Need Hearts	1980	$4
❏ 38-04761	My Time/(Instrumental)	1985	$4
❏ 38-04761 [PS]	My Time/(Instrumental)	1985	$5
❏ 38-03761	Save the Overtime (For Me)/Ain't No Greater Love	1983	$4

Number	Title	Yr	NM
❏ 1-11330	Taste of Bitter Love/Add It Up	1980	$4
❏ 38-03418	That Special Time of Year/Santa Claus Is Comin' to Town	1982	$5
❏ 3-11088	The Best Thing We Can Do Is Say Goodbye/You Don't Have to Say I Love You	1979	$4
❏ 38-05679	Till I See You Again/Strivin'	1985	$4
❏ 11-11409	When a Child Is Born/The Lord's Prayer	1980	$5

— With Johnny Mathis

Number	Title	Yr	NM
❏ 38-04369	When You're Far Away/Seconds	1984	$4

ENJOY

Number	Title	Yr	NM
❏ 2012	What Shall I Do/Love Call	1964	$20

EVERLAST

Number	Title	Yr	NM
❏ 5025	Happiness/I Had a Dream Last Night	1963	$30

—As "The Pips"

FURY

Number	Title	Yr	NM
❏ 1073	Come See About Me/I Want That Kind of Love	1963	$40
❏ 1067	Darling/Linda	1962	$30

—As "The Pips"

Number	Title	Yr	NM
❏ 1050	Every Beat of My Heart/Room in Your Heart	1961	$30

— Re-recordings of the same songs on Huntom and Vee Jay

Number	Title	Yr	NM
❏ 1052	Guess Who/Stop Running Around	1961	$20
❏ 1054	Letter Full of Tears/You Broke Your Promise	1961	$20
❏ 1064	Operator/I'll Trust in You	1962	$20

HUNTOM

Number	Title	Yr	NM
❏ 2510	Every Beat of My Heart/Room in Your Heart	1961	$500

—As "The Pips"

MAXX

Number	Title	Yr	NM
❏ 331	Either Way I Lose/Go Away, Stay Away	1964	$20
❏ 326	Giving Up/Maybe, Maybe Baby	1964	$20
❏ 329	Lovers Always Forget/Another Love	1964	$20
❏ 335	Tell Her You're Mine/If I Should Ever Be in Love	1965	$20
❏ 334	Who Knows/Stop and Get a Hold of Myself	1965	$20

MCA

Number	Title	Yr	NM
❏ 53351	It's Gonna Take All Our Love/(Instrumental)	1988	$3
❏ 53676	Licence to Kill/Pam	1989	$3

— B-side by National Philharmonic Orchestra

Number	Title	Yr	NM
❏ 53657	Licence to Kill/You	1989	$3
❏ 53210	Love Overboard/(Instrumental)	1987	$3
❏ 53210 [PS]	Love Overboard/(Instrumental)	1987	$3
❏ 53211	Lovin' on Next to Nothin'/(Instrumental)	1988	$3
❏ 53211 [PS]	Lovin' on Next to Nothin'/(Instrumental)	1988	$3
❏ 53002	Send It to Me/When You Love Somebody (It's Christmas Every Day)	1987	$3
❏ 53002 [PS]	Send It to Me/When You Love Somebody (It's Christmas Every Day)	1987	$3

SCOTTI BROS.

Number	Title	Yr	NM
❏ ZS4-06267	Loving on Borrowed Time (Love Theme from Cobra)/Angel of the City	1986	$3

—A-side: Gladys Knight and Bill Medley; B-side: Robert Tepper

SOUL

Number	Title	Yr	NM
❏ 35107	All I Need Is Time/The Only Time You Love Me (Is When You're Losing Me)	1973	$6
❏ 35111	Betwen Her Goodbye and My Hello/This Child Needs Its Father	1974	$6
❏ 35105	Daddy Could Swear I Declare/For Once in My Life	1973	$6
❏ 35057	Didn't You Know (You'd Have to Cry Sometime)/Keep an Eye	1969	$8
❏ 35034	Everybody Needs Love/Since I've Lost You	1967	$8
❏ 35068	Friendship Train/Cloud Nine	1969	$8
❏ 35094	Help Me Make It Through the Night/If You're Gonna Leave (Just Leave)	1972	$6
❏ 35083	I Don't Want to Do Wrong/Is There a Place In His Heart for Me	1971	$6
❏ 35039	I Heard It Through the Grapevine/It's Time to Go Now	1967	$10
❏ 35045	It Should Have Been Me/You Don't Love Me No More	1968	$8
❏ 35047	I Wish It Would Rain/It's Summer	1968	$8
❏ 35091	Make Me the Woman You Come Home To/If You're Gonna Leave (Just Leave)	1972	$6

Number	Title	Yr	NM
❏ 35033	Take Me in Your Arms and Love Me/Do You Love Me Just a Little More?	1967	$8
❏ 35042	The End of Our Road/Don't Let Her Take Your Love from Me	1968	$8

TRIP
Number	Title	Yr	NM
❏ 3004	It Hurt Me So Bad/What Will Become of Me	1973	$6
❏ 3004 [PS]	It Hurt Me So Bad/What Will Become of Me	1973	$15

VEE JAY
Number	Title	Yr	NM
❏ 545	A Love Like Mine/Queen of Tears	1963	$30
❏ 386	Every Beat of My Heart/ Ain'tcha Got Some Room (In Your Heart for Me)	1961	$30

— By "The Pips"; same B-side, different title

Number	Title	Yr	NM
❏ 386	Every Beat of My Heart/ Room in Your Heart	1961	$30

— By "The Pips"

KNIGHT, JEAN
CHELSEA
Number	Title	Yr	NM
❏ 3020	Don't Ask for 24 Hours/Hold Back the Night	1975	$5

DIAL
Number	Title	Yr	NM
❏ 1026	Dirt/Jesse Joe	1974	$5

JETSTREAM
Number	Title	Yr	NM
❏ 706	Doggin' Around/The Man That Left Me	1965	$12

MIRAGE
Number	Title	Yr	NM
❏ 99606	Let the Good Times Roll/ Magic	1985	$3
❏ 99643	My Toot Toot/My Heart Is Willing (And My Body Is Too)	1985	$3
❏ 99643 [PS]	My Toot Toot/My Heart Is Willing (And My Body Is Too)	1985	$3

STAX
Number	Title	Yr	NM
❏ 0116	Carry On/Call Me Your Fool	1972	$5
❏ 0150	Do Me/Save the Last Kiss for Me	1972	$5
❏ 0136	Helping Man/Pick Up the Pieces	1972	$5
❏ 0088	Mr. Big Stuff/Why I Keep Living These Memories	1971	$6

TRIBE
Number	Title	Yr	NM
❏ 8313	Anyone Can Love Him/A Tear	1966	$15
❏ 8304	Lonesome Tonight/Love	1964	$15
❏ 8306	T'Ain't It the Truth/I'm So Glad for Your Sake	1965	$15

KNIGHT, LARRY, AND THE UPSETTERS
GOLDEN WORLD
Number	Title	Yr	NM
❏ 37	Hurt Me/Everything's Gone Wrong	1966	$50

KNIGHT, MARIE
DECCA
Number	Title	Yr	NM
❏ 48262	Adeste Fideles/It Came Upon A Midnight Clear	1951	$30

KNIGHT OWLS, THE
CAMEO
Number	Title	Yr	NM
❏ 379	Goody Galum-Shus/What	1965	$20

KNIGHT RIDERS, THE
UNITED ARTISTS
Number	Title	Yr	NM
❏ 366	Annie's Place/Unchained Melody	1961	$30

KNIGHT, ROBERT
DOT
Number	Title	Yr	NM
❏ 16256	Because/Dance Only with Me	1961	$40
❏ 16303	Free Me/The Other Half of Man	1962	$50

ELF
Number	Title	Yr	NM
❏ 90037	I Only Have Eyes for You/I'm Sticking with You	1969	$40
❏ 90019	Isn't It Lonely Together/We'd Better Stop	1968	$6
❏ 90030	Smokey/If I Had My Way	1969	$6

MONUMENT
Number	Title	Yr	NM
❏ 8612	Better Get Ready for Love/ Somebody's Baby	1974	$20
❏ 8629	Dynamite/The Outsider	1974	$20

PRIVATE STOCK
Number	Title	Yr	NM
❏ 45,038	I'm Coming Home to You/ (B-side unknown)	1975	$10
❏ 45,118	I've Got News for You/ (B-side unknown)	1976	$5
❏ 45,069	Second Chance/Glitter Lady	1976	$5

RISING SONS
Number	Title	Yr	NM
❏ 707	Blessed Are the Lonely/It's Been Worth It All	1967	$30
❏ 705	Everlasting Love/ Somebody's Baby	1967	$20

Number	Title	Yr	NM
❏ 708	Power of Love/Love on a Mountain Top	1968	$20

KNIGHT, SONNY
A&M
Number	Title	Yr	NM
❏ 728	Be True to Your Dog/State Street	1964	$12
❏ 718	Evil Minded Woman/Georgia Town	1963	$10

ALADDIN
Number	Title	Yr	NM
❏ 3357	But Officer/Dear Wonderful God	1957	$40

AURA
Number	Title	Yr	NM
❏ 403	If You Want This Love/I Just Called to Say Hello	1964	$8
❏ 4505	Love Me As Though There Were No Tomorrow/Fool Like Me	1964	$8
❏ 4505 [PS]	Love Me As Though There Were No Tomorrow/Fool Like Me	1964	$30

DOT
Number	Title	Yr	NM
❏ 15507	Confidential/Jailbird	1956	$30

— Originals have maroon labels

Number	Title	Yr	NM
❏ 15507	Confidential/Jailbird	1956	$20

— Second pressings have black labels

Number	Title	Yr	NM
❏ 15635	Dedicated to You/Short Walk	1957	$20
❏ 15542	End of a Dream/Worthless and Lowdown	1957	$20
❏ 15597	Lovesick Blues/Insha Allot	1957	$20

EASTMAN
Number	Title	Yr	NM
❏ 787	Lipstick Kisses/East Your Mush and Hush	1959	$60

FIFO
Number	Title	Yr	NM
❏ 105	A Swingin' Door/(B-side unknown)	1961	$20
❏ 102	Cold, Cold Night/Saving My Love	1961	$20

ORIGINAL SOUND
Number	Title	Yr	NM
❏ 2	Once in Awhile/School's Out	1959	$30
❏ 18	Those Oldies But Goodies Are Dedicated to You/She Had Me Reelin'	1961	$20

STARLA
Number	Title	Yr	NM
❏ 1	Dedicated to You/Short Walk	1957	$40
❏ 10	Once in a While/School's Out	1958	$20

VITA
Number	Title	Yr	NM
❏ 137	Confidential/Jailbird	1956	$50

WORLD PACIFIC
Number	Title	Yr	NM
❏ 77832	Angel Love/If I Ruled the World	1966	$8
❏ 77811	If I May/Need Your Love So Bad	1966	$8
❏ 403	If You Want This Love/I Just Called to Say Hello	1964	$15

KNIGHT, TERRY, AND THE PACK
Group evloved into GRAND FUNK RAILROAD.

CAMEO
Number	Title	Yr	NM
❏ 495	Come Home Baby/Dirty Lady	1967	$10
❏ 482	Forever and a Day/Lizbeth Peach	1967	$10

CAPITOL
Number	Title	Yr	NM
❏ 2737	I'll Keep Waiting Patiently/ Lullaby	1970	$10
❏ 2506	St. Paul/(Legend of) William and Mary	1969	$10
❏ 2409	Such a Lonely Life/Lullaby	1969	$10
❏ 2174	Without a Woman/Let Me Stand Next to Your Fire	1968	$15

— As "The Pack

LUCKY ELEVEN
Number	Title	Yr	NM
❏ 07	Does It Matter to You Girl/ Wide Trackin'	1965	$20

— As "The Fabulous Pack

Number	Title	Yr	NM
❏ 07 [PS]	Does It Matter to You Girl/ Wide Trackin'	1965	$30

— As "The Fabulous Pack

Number	Title	Yr	NM
❏ 03	Harlem Shuffle/I've Got News for You	1965	$20

— As "The Pack

Number	Title	Yr	NM
❏ 225	How Much More/I've Been Told	1966	$20
❏ 226	I Got Love/Better Man Than I	1966	$20
❏ 230	I (Who Have Nothing)/ Numbers	1966	$20
❏ 228	Lady Jane/Lovin' Kind	1966	$20
❏ 236	One Monkey Don't Stop No Show/The Train	1967	$20
❏ 235	This Precious Time/Love, Love, Love, Love, Love	1967	$20
❏ 229	What's On Your Mind/A Change on the Way	1966	$20

WINGATE
Number	Title	Yr	NM
❏ 07	The Tears Come Rollin'/The Colour of My Love	1965	$30

— As "The Pack

KNIGHTS, THE
Both are probably by different groups.

CAPITOL
Number	Title	Yr	NM
❏ 5302	Hot Rod High/Theme for Teen Love	1964	$60

FELSTED
Number	Title	Yr	NM
❏ 8640	White Fang/Night Train	1962	$15

KNOCKOUTS, THE (1)
SCEPTER
Number	Title	Yr	NM
❏ 1269	Got My Mojo Workin'/Every Day of the Week	1964	$15

SHAD
Number	Title	Yr	NM
❏ 5013	Darling Lorraine/Riot in Room 3C	1959	$60

— With long ending on A-side

Number	Title	Yr	NM
❏ 5013	Darling Lorraine/Riot in Room 3C	1959	$30

— With short ending on A-side

Number	Title	Yr	NM
❏ 5018	Please Be Mine/Rich Boy, Poor Boy	1960	$30

TRIBUTE
Number	Title	Yr	NM
❏ 199	Got My Mojo Working (Part 1)/ Got My Mojo Working (Part 2)	1964	$20
❏ 201	Tweet-Tweet/What's On Your Mind	1964	$20

KNOCKOUTS, THE (U)
MGM
Number	Title	Yr	NM
❏ 13010	Fever/You Can Take My Girl	1961	$30

KNOX, BUDDY
LIBERTY
Number	Title	Yr	NM
❏ 55366	All By Myself/Three Eyed Man	1961	$15
❏ 55411	Cha-Hua-Hua/Open	1962	$15
❏ 55503	Dear Abby/Three Way Love Affair	1962	$15
❏ 55694	Good Lovin'/All Time Loser	1964	$10
❏ 55305	Ling, Ting, Tong/The Kisses	1961	$15
❏ 55305 [PS]	Ling, Ting, Tong/The Kisses	1961	$40
❏ 55290	Lovey Dovey/I Got You	1960	$15
❏ 55592	Shadaroom/Tomorrow Is a-Comin'	1963	$10
❏ 55473	She's Gone/There's Only Me	1962	$15
❏ 55650	Thanks a Lot/Hitchhike Back to Georgia	1963	$10

REPRISE
Number	Title	Yr	NM
❏ 0431	A Lover's Question/You Said Goodbye	1965	$10
❏ 0463	A White Sport Coat/That Don't Do Me No Good	1966	$10
❏ 0395	Livin' in a House Full of Love/ Good Time Girl	1965	$10
❏ 0501	Love Has Many Ways/Sixteen Feet of Patio	1966	$10

ROULETTE
Number	Title	Yr	NM
❏ 4018	Hula Love/Devil Woman	1957	$30
❏ 4140	I Think I'm Gonna Kill Myself/To Be with You	1959	$30
❏ 4262	Long Lonely Nights/Storm Clouds	1960	$30
❏ 4002	Party Doll/My Baby's Gone	1957	$60

— Maroon label, silver print, with roulette wheel around outside

Number	Title	Yr	NM
❏ 4002	Party Doll/My Baby's Gone	1957	$40

— Red label, roulette wheel on top half of label

Number	Title	Yr	NM
❏ 4002	Party Doll/My Baby's Gone	1957	$30

— Red label, no roulette wheel

Number	Title	Yr	NM
❏ 4002	Party Doll/My Baby's Gone	1957	$50

— Red label, black print, with roulette wheel around outside

Number	Title	Yr	NM
❏ 4002	Party Doll/My Baby's Gone	1958	$20

— White label with color spokes

Number	Title	Yr	NM
❏ 4082	Somebody Touched Me/C'mon Baby	1958	$30
❏ 4042	Swingin' Daddy/Whenever I'm Lonely	1958	$30
❏ 4179	Taste of the Blues/I Ain't Sharin' Sharon	1959	$30
❏ 4120	That's Why I Cry/Teaseable, Pleaseable You	1958	$30

TRIPLE D
Number	Title	Yr	NM
❏ 798	Party Doll/I'm Stickin' With You	1956	$1000

— B-side by Jimmy Bowen

UNITED ARTISTS
Number	Title	Yr	NM
❏ 50789	Come Softly to Me/Travelin' Light	1971	$6
❏ 50526	God Knows I Love You/Night Runners	1969	$8
❏ 50596	Salt Lake City/I'm Only Rockin'	1969	$8
❏ 50301	This Time Tomorrow/Gypsy Man	1968	$8
❏ 50463	Today My Sleepless Nights Came Back to Town/A Million Years or So	1968	$8
❏ 50722	White Dove/Glory Train	1970	$6

7-Inch Extended Plays

ROULETTE
Number	Title	Yr	NM
❏ EPR-1-301 [PS]	Buddy Knox	1957	$100

Number	Title	Yr	NM
❑ EPR-1-301	Party Doll/Rock Your Little Baby to Sleep//Hula Love/Rock Around the Clock	1957	$100

KOALA, THE
CAPITOL
Number	Title	Yr	NM
❑ 2365	Don't You Know What I Mean/Scattered Children's Toys	1968	$20

KODAKS, THE
FURY
Number	Title	Yr	NM
❑ 1015	Oh Gee Oh Gosh/Make Believe World	1957	$70

—As "The Kodoks"

Number	Title	Yr	NM
❑ 1007	Teenager's Dream/Little Boy and Girl	1957	$100

KOFFMAN, MOE
ASCOT
Number	Title	Yr	NM
❑ 2111	Bumpin'/The Pretzel	1962	$8
❑ 2118	Growing Up/Jazz Merengue	1963	$8
❑ 2100	Swingin' Shepherd Blues Twist/Train Whistle Twist	1962	$8

ATCO
Number	Title	Yr	NM
❑ 6382	Bulldog Walk/Big Bad Irving	1965	$8

JUBILEE
Number	Title	Yr	NM
❑ 5471	Coffee House/Flootenanny	1964	$8
❑ 5485	I Want to Hold Your Hand/Soul Brothers	1964	$10
❑ 5324	Little Pixie/Koko-Mamey	1958	$10
❑ 5352	Shepherd's Cha Cha/The Great Healer	1958	$10
❑ 5367	Shepherd's Hoedown/Stroll Along with the Blues	1959	$10
❑ 5311	The Swingin' Shepherd Blues/Hamburg Bound	1958	$10

PALETTE
Number	Title	Yr	NM
❑ 5045	Black Eyed Peas/Sapphire	1959	$10
❑ 5106	Cool Ghoul/Sapphire	1963	$8

KOKOMO (1)
FELSTED
Number	Title	Yr	NM
❑ 8612	Asia Minor/Roy's Tune	1961	$12
❑ 8612 [PS]	Asia Minor/Roy's Tune	1961	$20
❑ 8622	Humorous/Theme from a Silent Movie	1961	$8
❑ 8628	Piano Rhapsody/Sweet Memories	1961	$8
❑ 8641	Poinciana/The Good Earth	1962	$8

KOKOMOS, THE
GONE
Number	Title	Yr	NM
❑ 5134	Mama's Boy/Yours Truly	1962	$20

JOSIE
Number	Title	Yr	NM
❑ 906	Open House Party/No Lies	1963	$15

KONGOS, JOHN
ELEKTRA
Number	Title	Yr	NM
❑ 45729	He's Gonna Step on You Again/Sometimes It's Not Enough	1971	$6
❑ 45809	He's Gonna Step on You Again/Tokoloshe Man	1972	$5
❑ 45760	Tokoloshe Man/Can Someone Please Direct Me Back to Earth	1972	$5

KAPP
Number	Title	Yr	NM
❑ 799	I Love Mary/Good Time Party Companion	1966	$10

RCA VICTOR
Number	Title	Yr	NM
❑ 47-8226	The Enchanted Sea/Tulips for 'Toinette	1963	$15

KOOBAS, THE
CAPITOL
Number	Title	Yr	NM
❑ 2416	First Cut Is the Deepest/Walking Out	1969	$8

KAPP
Number	Title	Yr	NM
❑ 737	Take Me for a Little While/Give a Little Bit	1965	$20
❑ 737 [PS]	Take Me for a Little While/Give a Little Bit	1965	$30

KOOL AND THE GANG
DE-LITE
Number	Title	Yr	NM
❑ 905	A Place in Space/The Force	1978	$5
❑ 822	Big Fun/No Show	1982	$4
❑ 1573	Caribbean Festival/Caribbean Festival (Disco Version)	1975	$5
❑ 807	Celebration/Morning Star	1980	$4
❑ 880869-7	Cherish/(Instrumental)	1985	$3
❑ 880869-7 [PS]	Cherish/(Instrumental)	1985	$4
❑ 555	Country Junkie/I Remember John W. Coltrane	1973	$6
❑ 884199-7	Emergency/You Are the One	1985	$3

Number	Title	Yr	NM
❑ 910	Everybody's Dancin'/Stay Awhile	1978	$5
❑ 880623-7	Fresh/In the Heart	1985	$3
❑ 880623-7 [PS]	Fresh/In the Heart	1985	$4
❑ 553	Funky Granny/Blowing with the Wind	1973	$6
❑ 534	Funky Man/1,2,3,4,5,6,7,8	1970	$6
❑ 557	Funky Stuff/More Funky Stuff	1973	$6
❑ 818	Get Down On It/Steppin' Out	1982	$4
❑ 552	Good Times/The Frog	1972	$6
❑ 804	Hangin' Out/Got You Into My Life	1980	$4
❑ 1562	Higher Plane/Wild Is Love	1974	$5
❑ 561	Hollywood Swinging/Dujii	1974	$5
❑ 909	I Like Music/It's All You Need	1978	$5
❑ 540	I Want to Take You Higher/Pneumonia	1971	$6
❑ 801	Ladies Night/If You Feel Like Dancin'	1979	$4
❑ 824	Let's Go Dancin' (Ooh, La, La, La)/Be My Lady	1982	$4
❑ 529	Let the Music Take Your Mind/Chocolate Buttermilk	1970	$6
❑ 1579	Love and Understanding (Come Together)/Sunshine and Love	1976	$5
❑ 546	Love the Life You Live, Part I/Love the Life You Live, Part II	1972	$6
❑ 880431-7	Misled/Rollin'	1984	$3
❑ 550	Music Is the Messenger, Part I/Music Is the Messenger, Part II	1972	$6
❑ 1586	Open Sesame -- Part 1/Open Sesame -- Part 2	1976	$5
❑ 901	Slick Superchick/Life's a Song	1978	$5
❑ 1567	Spirit of the Boogie/Summer Madness	1975	$5
❑ 816	Steppin' Out/Love Festival	1982	$4
❑ 831	Straight Ahead/September Love	1984	$3
❑ 825	Street Kids/As One	1983	$4
❑ 1590	Super Band/Sunshine	1977	$5
❑ 810	Take It to the Top/Love Affair	1981	$4
❑ 815	Take My Heart/Just Friends	1981	$5

—First pressings have no subtitle

Number	Title	Yr	NM
❑ 815	Take My Heart (You Can Have It If You Want It)/Just Friends	1981	$4
❑ 523	The Gangs Back Again!/Kools Back Again	1969	$6
❑ 543	The Penguin/Lucky for Me	1971	$6
❑ 830	Tonight/Home Is Where the Heart Is	1984	$3
❑ 802	Too Hot/Tonight's the Night	1979	$4
❑ 538	Who's Gonna Take the Weight (Part One)/Who's Gonna Take the Weight (Part Two)	1970	$6
❑ 1577	Winter Sadness/Father, Father	1975	$5

MERCURY
Number	Title	Yr	NM
❑ 888712-7	Holiday/(Jam Mix)	1987	$3
❑ 888712-7 [PS]	Holiday/(Jam Mix)	1987	$3
❑ 888867-7	In a Special Way/God's Country	1987	$3
❑ 888867-7 [PS]	In a Special Way/God's Country	1987	$3
❑ 888292-7	Stone Love/Dance Champion	1987	$3
❑ 888292-7 [PS]	Stone Love/Dance Champion	1987	$3
❑ 872038-7	Strong/Funky Stuff	1988	$3

KOOL, D.,, AND THE KASUALS
CAMEO
Number	Title	Yr	NM
❑ 360	She's Good to Me/Broken Glass	1965	$20

KOOL GENTS
VEE JAY
Number	Title	Yr	NM
❑ 173	This Is the Night/Do Ya Do	1956	$200

KOOPER, AL
Also see BLOOD, SWEAT AND TEARS; THE BLUES PROJECT.
COLUMBIA
Number	Title	Yr	NM
❑ 4-45243	I Got a Woman/Easy Does It	1970	$5
❑ 44811	I Stand Alone/Hey, Western Union Man	1969	$5
❑ 45179	Love Theme from "The Landlord"/Brand New Day	1970	$5
❑ 45093	One Room Country Shack/Bury My Body	1970	$5
❑ 45691	Sam Stone/Be Real	1972	$5
❑ 45148	She Gets Me Where I Live/God Sheds His Grace on Thee	1970	$5
❑ 45566	The Monkey Time/Bended Knees (Please Don't Let Me Down)	1972	$5
❑ 03312	Two Sides (To Every Situation)/Snowblind	1982	$4

UNITED ARTISTS
Number	Title	Yr	NM
❑ XW879	This Diamond Ring/Hollywood Vampire	1976	$4

VERVE FOLKWAYS
Number	Title	Yr	NM
❑ 5026	Changes/Pack Up Your Sorrows	1966	$15

KORNER, ALEXIS
COLUMBIA
Number	Title	Yr	NM
❑ 10166	Get Off My Cloud/Strange N' Deranged	1975	$8

KOSTELANETZ, ANDRE
COLUMBIA
Number	Title	Yr	NM
❑ 43034	Bluesette/Fall in Love	1964	$6
❑ 45061	Come Saturday Morning/Leaving on a Jet Plane	1970	$5
❑ JZSP116040/1 [DJ]	Galop from "Moscow, Cheremushki"/Galop from "Ballet Suite No. 2	1966	$8

—White label promo only

Number	Title	Yr	NM
❑ JZSP116040/1 [PS]	Galop from "Moscow, Cheremushki"/Galop from "Ballet Suite No. 2	1966	$15

—Title on sleeve: "Kosty Plays Shosty

Number	Title	Yr	NM
❑ JZSP76389/90 [DJ]	Medley: Santa Claus Is Coming To Town & Have Yourself A Merry Little Christmas/Christmas Chopsticks	1963	$10
❑ JZSP111905/6 [DJ]	O Come All Ye Faithful/Oh Tannenbaum	1965	$15

—Green vinyl

Number	Title	Yr	NM
❑ JZSP111905/6 [DJ]	O Come All Ye Faithful/Oh Tannenbaum	1965	$8

—Black vinyl

Number	Title	Yr	NM
❑ 40044	Playing Around/Time on My Hands	1953	$10
❑ 41534	Sabre Dance/Gypsy Fiddler	1959	$8
❑ 40350	Sweet Surrender/April in Paradise	1954	$10
❑ 44147	The Impossible Dream/Born Free	1967	$6
❑ 45357	Theme from "Love Story"/Mr. Bojangles	1971	$4
❑ 45244	Things of Life/Valse de Rothschild	1970	$5
❑ 42604	Washington Twist/Secret Service	1962	$8

KOTTKE, LEO
CAPITOL
Number	Title	Yr	NM
❑ 4177	Can't Quite Put It Into Words/Power Failure	1975	$5
❑ 3854	Pamela Brown/A Child Should Be a Fish	1974	$6

KRAFTWERK
CAPITOL
Number	Title	Yr	NM
❑ 4460	Trans-Europe Express/Franz Schubert	1977	$5

VERTIGO
Number	Title	Yr	NM
❑ 203	Autobahn/Morgan Spaziergance	1975	$25
❑ 204	Mitternacht (Midnight)/Kometen Melodie (Comet Melody 2)	1975	$25
❑ 28532 [PS]	Musique Non-Stop (Long)/Musique Non-Stop (Short)	1986	$6
❑ 49723	Pocket Calculator/Dentaku	1981	$4
❑ 49723	Pocket Calculator/Dentaku	1981	$5

—Yellow vinyl

Number	Title	Yr	NM
❑ 28441	The Telephone Call/Der Telefon Anruf	1987	$3
❑ 28441 [PS]	The Telephone Call/Der Telefon Anruf	1987	$6
❑ 29342	Tour de France (Remix)/Tour de France (French)	1984	$3

KRAMER, BILLY J., AND THE DAKOTAS
EPIC
Number	Title	Yr	NM
❑ 10331	1941/His Love Is Just a Lie	1968	$12

IMPERIAL
Number	Title	Yr	NM
❑ 66051	From a Window/I'll Be On My Way	1964	$15
❑ 66051 [PS]	From a Window/I'll Be On My Way	1964	$30
❑ 66143	I'll Be Doggone/Neon City	1965	$10
❑ 66048	I'll Keep You Satisfied/I Know	1964	$15
❑ 66135	Irresistible You/Twilight Time	1965	$10
❑ 66085	It's Gotta Last Forever/They Remind Me of You	1965	$15
❑ 66027	Little Children/Bad to Me	1964	$15
❑ 66115	Trains and Boats and Planes/I'll Be On My Way	1965	$15
❑ 66115	Trains and Boats and Planes/That's the Way I Feel	1965	$10

LIBERTY
Number	Title	Yr	NM
❑ 55667	Bad to Me/Do You Want to Know a Secret	1964	$30
❑ 55626	Bad to Me/I Call Your Name	1963	$40
❑ 55586	Do You Want to Know a Secret/I'll Be On My Way	1963	$40
❑ 55643	I'll Keep You Satisfied/I Know	1963	$40
❑ 55618	The Cruel Surf/The Millionaire	1963	$50

Number	Title	Yr	NM

KRISTOFFERSON, KRIS, AND RITA COOLIDGE
A&M

Number	Title	Yr	NM
❏ 1475	A Song I'd Like to Sing/From the Bottle to the Bottom	1973	$4
❏ 1475 [PS]	A Song I'd Like to Sing/From the Bottle to the Bottom	1973	$6
❏ 1498	Loving Arms/I'm Down	1974	$4

MONUMENT
❏ 8636	Lover Please/Slow Down	1975	$4
❏ 8646	We Must Have Been Out of Our Minds/Sweet Susannah	1975	$4

KRISTOFFERSON, KRIS
COLUMBIA
❏ 05594	Desperadoes Waiting for a Train/The Twentieth Century Is Almost Over	1985	$3

— *A-side: Willie Nelson/Waylon Jennings/Johnny Cash/Kris Kristofferson; B-side: Nelson, Cash*

❏ 08406	Highwayman/Desperadoes Waiting for a Train	1988	$3

— *Waylon Jennings/Willie Nelson/Johnny Cash/Kris Kristofferson; reissue*

❏ 04881 [PS]	Highwayman/The Human Condition	1985	$4

— *A-side: Willie Nelson/Waylon Jennings/Johnny Cash/Kris Kristofferson; B-side: Nelson, Cash*

❏ 04881	Highwayman/The Human Condition	1985	$3

— *A-side: Willie Nelson/Waylon Jennings/Johnny Cash/Kris Kristofferson; B-side: Nelson, Cash*

❏ 11383	I'll Take Any Chance I Can with You/Maybe You Heard	1980	$4
❏ 11160	Prove It to You One More Time Again/Fallen Angel	1979	$4
❏ 10731	The Fighter/Forever in Your Love	1978	$4
❏ 10525	Watch Closely Now/Crippled Crow	1977	$4

EPIC
❏ 10225	Golden Idol/Killing Time	1967	$20

MERCURY
❏ 888723-7	El Coyote/They Killed Him	1987	$3
❏ 888554-7	Love Is the Way/This Old Road	1987	$3
❏ 888345-7	They Killed Him/Anthem '84	1987	$3

MONUMENT
❏ 8658	Easy, Come On/Rocket to Star	1975	$4
❏ 21000	Here Comes That Rainbow Again/(B-side unknown)	1981	$4
❏ 8679	If It's All the Same to You/The Year 2000 Minus 25	1975	$4
❏ 8618	I May Smoke Too Much/Lights of Magdala	1974	$5
❏ 8525	Loving Her Was Easier (Than Anything I'll Ever Do Again)/Epitaph	1971	$6
❏ 1210	Sunday Morning Comin' Down/To Beat the Devil	1970	$8
❏ 8707	The Prisoner/It's Never Gonna Be the Same Again	1976	$4
❏ 8531	The Taker/Pilgrim: Chapter 33	1971	$6
❏ 8571	Why Me/Help Me	1973	$5

7-Inch Extended Plays
❏ SSP-532	To Beat the Devil/Blame It on the Stones//Casey's Last Ride/Sunday Morning Coming Down	1971	$15

— *Stereo jukebox issue; small hole, plays at 33 1/3 rpm*

KUBAN, BOB, AND THE IN-MEN
MUSICLAND U.S.A.
❏ 20017	Batman Theme/You Better Run You Better Hide	1967	$8
❏ 20007	Drive My Car/The Pretzel	1966	$12
❏ 20013	Harlem Shuffle/Theme from "Virginia Wolff"	1967	$8
❏ 20001	The Cheater/Try Me Baby	1966	$30

— *With "Vocal by Walter Scott" on both sides' labels*

❏ 20001	The Cheater/Try Me Baby	1966	$15

— *With "Vocal by Walter Scott" on only B-side label*

❏ 20001	The Cheater/Try Me Baby	1966	$12

— *With no mention of "Vocal by Walter Scott"*

❏ 20006	The Teaser/All I Want	1966	$10

NORMAN
❏ 567	Little Girl/I Don't Want to Know	1965	$15

REPRISE
❏ 0937	Soul Man/Hard to Handle	1970	$8

KUF-LINX, THE
CHALLENGE
❏ 59015	Climb Love Mountain/All That's Good	1958	$20
❏ 59004	Eyeballin'/Service with a Smile	1958	$20
❏ 1013	So Tough/What'cha Gonna Do	1957	$50
❏ 1013	So Tough/What'cha Gonna Do	1958	$30
❏ 59102	So Tough/What'cha Gonna Do	1961	$15

KUSTOM KINGS, THE
SMASH
❏ 1883	In My '40 Ford/Clutch Rider	1964	$60

L

L.L. COOL J
DEF JAM

Number	Title	Yr	NM
❏ 38-69056	Big Ole Butt/One Shot at Love	1989	$4
❏ 38-07620	Go Cut Creator Go/Kanday	1987	$3
❏ 38-07620 [PS]	Go Cut Creator Go/Kanday	1987	$5
❏ 38-07679	Going Back to Cali/Jack the Ripper	1988	$3
❏ 38-07679 [PS]	Going Back to Cali/Jack the Ripper	1988	$4
❏ 38-05665	I Can't Live Without My Radio/I Can Give You More	1985	$3
❏ 13-08380	I Can't Live Without My Radio/Rock the Bells	1988	$3

— *Reissue*

❏ 38-07120	I'm Bad/Get Down	1987	$4
❏ 38-68902	I'm That Type of Guy/It Gets No Rougher	1989	$3
❏ CS71604 [DJ]	I'm That Type of Guy (Radio Edit) (same on both sides)	1989	$6
❏ 13-08381	I Need Love/I'm Bad	1988	$3

— *Reissue*

❏ 38-07350	I Need Love/My Rhyme Ain't Done	1987	$3

L.T.D.
A&M
❏ 2395	April Love/Stay on the One	1982	$5
❏ 2414	Cuttin' It Up/Love Magic	1982	$4
❏ 2142	Dance "N" Sing "N"/Give It All	1979	$5
❏ 2142 [PS]	Dance "N" Sing "N"/Give It All	1979	$6
❏ 1665	Don't Lose Your Cool/Thank You Mother	1975	$5
❏ 1514	Elegant Love/Success	1974	$5
❏ 1974	(Every Time I Turn Around) Back in Love Again/Material Things	1977	$5
❏ 1974 [PS]	(Every Time I Turn Around) Back in Love Again/Material Things	1977	$8
❏ 2057	Holding On (When Love Is Gone)/Together Forever	1978	$5
❏ 1847	Love Ballad/Let the Music Keep Playing	1976	$5
❏ 1847 [PS]	Love Ballad/Let the Music Keep Playing	1976	$6
❏ 1897	Love to the World/Get Your It Together	1976	$5
❏ 2176	Share My Love/Sometimes	1979	$5
❏ 2283	Shine On/Love Is What You Need	1980	$5
❏ 2346	Shine On (Spanish Version)/Where Did We Go Wrong	1981	$5
❏ 2192	Stranger/Sometimes	1979	$5
❏ 1681	Trying to Find a Way/I Told You I'd Be Back	1975	$5
❏ 2095	We Both Deserve Each Other's Love/It's Time to Be Real	1978	$5
❏ 1537	What Goes Around/To the Bone	1974	$5
❏ 2250	Where Did We Go Wrong/Stand Up L.T.D.	1980	$5

MONTAGE
❏ 908	For You/Party with You (All Night)	1983	$4

LABEEF, SLEEPY
COLUMBIA
❏ 44261	Completely Destroyed/Go Ahead On Baby	1967	$10
❏ 43452	Everybody's Got to Have Somebody (To Love)/You Can't Catch Me	1965	$15
❏ 44455	Every Day/If I'm Right I'm Wrong	1968	$12
❏ 43875	I Feel a Lot More Like I Do Now/I'm Too Broke	1966	$15
❏ 44068	Sure Beats the Heck Out of Settlin' Down/Schneider	1967	$10

MERCURY
❏ 71179	All the Time/Lonely	1957	$125
❏ 71112	I'm Through/All Alone	1957	$125

PLANTATION
❏ 66	Asphalt Cowboy/Got You on My Mind	1971	$12
❏ 74	Blackland Farmer/Got You on My Mind	1971	$10
❏ 74 [DJ]	Blackland Farmer (mono/stereo)	1971	$15

— *Promo only on green vinyl*

❏ 55	Too Much Monkey Business/Got You on My Mind	1970	$30

STARDAY
❏ 292	I'm Through/All Alone	1957	$200

SUN
❏ 1145	Flying Saucers Rock and Roll/Boogie Woogie Country Girl	1979	$4

Number	Title	Yr	NM
❏ 1133 [DJ]	Ghost Riders in the Sky (same on both sides)	1975	$4

— *Promo only*

❏ 1137	Good Rockin' Boogie (Part 1)/Good rockin' Boogie (Part 2)	1978	$4
❏ 1134	There Ain't Much After Taxes/A Hundred Pounds of Lovin'	1976	$4
❏ 1132	Thunder Road/A Hundred Pounds of Lovin'	1974	$4

WAYSIDE
❏ 1654	Tore Up/Lonely	1959	$300
❏ 1652	Walkin' Slowly/(B-side unknown)	1959	$250

LABELLE
EPIC
❏ 8-50262	Get You Somebody New/Who's Watching the Watcher	1976	$8
❏ 50315	Isn't It a Shame/Gypsy Moths	1976	$6
❏ 50048	Lady Marmalade/Space Children	1974	$6
❏ 50140	Messin' My Mind/Take the Night Off	1975	$6
❏ 50168	Slow Burn/Far As We Felt Like Going	1975	$6

RCA VICTOR
❏ APBO-0157	Mr. Sunshine Man/Sunshine	1973	$8
❏ 74-0965	Open Up Your Heart/Going Up a Holiday	1973	$8

WARNER BROS.
❏ 7579	Moonshadow/If I Can't Have You	1972	$8
❏ 7512	Morning Much Better/Shades of Difference	1971	$8
❏ 7624	Touch Me All Over/Ain't It Sad It's All Over	1972	$8

LABELLE, PATTI, AND THE BLUE BELLES
ATLANTIC
❏ 2318	A Groovy Kind of Love/Over the Rainbow	1966	$10
❏ 2311	All or Nothing/You Forgot How to Love	1965	$15
❏ 2610	Dance to the Rhythm of Love/He's Gone	1969	$12
❏ 2333	Ebb Tide/Patti's Prayer	1966	$12
❏ 2548	He's My Man/Wonderful	1968	$12
❏ 2347	I'm Still Waiting/Family Man	1966	$10
❏ 2629	Loving Blues/Pride's No Match for Love	1969	$80
❏ 2446	Oh My Love/I Need Your Love	1967	$10
❏ 2712	Suffer/Trustin' in You	1970	$70
❏ 2373	Take Me for a Little While/I Don't Want to Go On Without You	1967	$10
❏ 2390	(There's) Always Something There to Remind Me/Tender Words	1967	$10

KING
❏ 5777	Down the Aisle (Wedding Song)/C'est La Vie	1963	$20

NEWTIME
❏ 510	Love Me Just a Little/The Joke's On You	1962	$30

NEWTOWN
❏ 5019	Academy Award/Decatur Street	1963	$30
❏ 5009	Cool Water/When Johnny Comes Marching Home	1962	$30
❏ 5777	Down the Aisle (Wedding Song)/C'est La Vie	1963	$20
❏ 5006	I Found a New Love/Pitter Patter	1962	$30

— *Most of the Newtown sides credit "The Blue-Belles"*

❏ 5000	I Sold My Heart to the Junkman/Itty Bitty Twist	1962	$30

— *Credited to "The Blue-Belles" but actually recorded by The Starlets*

❏ 5007	Tear After Tear/Go On, This Is Goodbye	1962	$30

PARKWAY
❏ 935	Danny Boy/I Believe	1964	$15
❏ 913	One Phone Call/You Will Fill My Eyes No More	1964	$15

PEAK
❏ 7042	I've Got to Let Him Know/I Sold My Heart to the Junkman	1962	$30

— *Credited to "The Blue-Belles" but actually recorded by The Starlets*

❏ 7042 [PS]	I've Got to Let Him Know/I Sold My Heart to the Junkman	1962	$100

LABELLE, PATTI
BEVERLY GLEN
❏ 2018	It Takes a Lot of Strength to Say Goodbye/Who's Foolin' Who	1984	$4

Number	Title	Yr	NM

— With Bobby Womack

Number	Title	Yr	NM
❏ 2012	Love Has Finally Come at Last/American Dream	1984	$4

— With Bobby Womack

ELEKTRA

| ❏ 69887 | The Best Is Yet to Come/Bye Bye Love | 1982 | $4 |

— With Grover Washington Jr.

EPIC

❏ 8-50510	Dan Swit Me/Since I Don't Have You	1978	$8
❏ 9-50910	Don't Make Your Angel Cry/Ain't That Enough	1980	$6
❏ 9-50872	I Don't Go Shopping/Come and Dance with Me	1980	$6
❏ 8-50659	It's Alright with Me/Music Is My Way of Life	1979	$15
❏ 8-50583	Little Girls/You Make It So Hard (To Say No)	1978	$6
❏ 9-50763	Love and Learn/Love Is Just a Touch Away	1979	$8
❏ 8-50550	Teach Me Tonight (Me Gusta Tu Baile)/Quiet Time	1978	$6

MCA

❏ 53774	I Can't Complain/I Can Fly	1989	$4
❏ 53358	If You Asked Me To/(Instrumental)	1988	$4
❏ 52877	Oh, People/Love Attack	1986	$3
❏ 52877 [PS]	Oh, People/Love Attack	1986	$4
❏ 52770	On My Own/Stir It Up	1986	$3

— A-side with Michael McDonald

❏ 52770 [PS]	On My Own/Stir It Up	1986	$4
❏ 52876	Something Special (Is Gonna Happen Tonight)/(Instrumental)	1986	$4
❏ 52610	Stir It Up/The Discovery	1985	$4

— B-side by Harold Faltermeyer

| ❏ 52610 [PS] | Stir It Up/The Discovery | 1985 | $4 |
| ❏ 53064 | The Last Unbroken Heart/Miami Vice: New York Theme | 1987 | $3 |

— A-side with Bill Champlin; B-side by Harold Faltermeyer

| ❏ 53064 [PS] | The Last Unbroken Heart/Miami Vice: New York Theme | 1987 | $3 |

PHILADELPHIA INT'L.

❏ ZS4 05436	I Can't Forget You/Living Double	1985	$5
❏ ZS4 04248	If Only You Knew/I'll Never, Never Give Up	1983	$5
❏ AE71816 [DJ]	If Only You Knew (same on both sides?)	1983	$8
❏ ZS4 05755	If You Don't Know Me By Now - Part 1/Part 2	1986	$5
❏ ZS4 05877	Look to the Rainbow/What Can I Do for You	1986	$6
❏ ZS4 04399	Love, Need and Want You/I'm in Love Again	1984	$5
❏ ZS4 05658	Shy/Love Symphony	1985	$5
❏ ZS5 02655	The Spirit's In It/The Family	1981	$6

LACEWING

MAINSTREAM

| ❏ 731 | Paradox/(B-side unknown) | 1971 | $15 |

LADDERS, THE

HOLIDAY

| ❏ 2611 | Counting the Stars/I Want to Know | 1957 | $300 |

— Red label, double lines

VEST

| ❏ 826 | My Love Is Gone/Hey, Pretty Baby | 1959 | $200 |

— No stars around "Vest" logo

| ❏ 826 | My Love Is Gone/Hey, Pretty Baby | 1960 | $60 |

— With stars around "Vest" logo

LADDIN, HILARY

WHAT

| ❏ 101 | The Sell/City of Fame | 1980 | $30 |
| ❏ 101 [PS] | The Sell/City of Fame | 1980 | $30 |

LADY BUGS, THE

CHATTAHOOCHIE

| ❏ 637 | How Do You Do It/Liverpool | 1964 | $20 |

DEL-FI

| ❏ 4233 | Sooner or Later/It's the Last Time | 1964 | $30 |

LEGRAND

| ❏ 1033 | Who Sends the Love Note/Fraternity U.S.A. | 1964 | $30 |

LADY FLASH

RSO

| ❏ 852 | Street Singin'/Hypnotizin' | 1976 | $5 |

LADYBIRDS, THE

ATCO

| ❏ 6329 | Memories/Lady Bird | 1964 | $15 |

LAWN

| ❏ 231 | Handsome Boy/Yes I Know | 1964 | $12 |

LAFITS AND KITTY

APOLLO

| ❏ 520 | Christmas Letters/Can Can Rock and Roll | 1957 | $20 |

LAGUNA, KENNY

SIRE

| ❏ 49142 | Home for Christmas/Carianne and Meryl's Song | 1979 | $5 |
| ❏ 4030 | Home for Christmas/Carianne and Meryl's Song | 1979 | $12 |

— U.K. import

| ❏ 4030 [PS] | Home for Christmas/Carianne and Meryl's Song | 1979 | $6 |

— U.K. import

LAI, FRANCIS

PARAMOUNT

| ❏ 0086 | Holiday For Jenny (The Christmas Tree)/Snow Frolic | 1971 | $6 |

LAINE, DENNY
Also see THE MOODY BLUES; WINGS.

CAPITOL

| ❏ 4425 | Heartbeat/Moondreams | 1977 | $6 |
| ❏ 4340 | It's So Easy-Listen to Me/I'm Lookin' for Someone to Love | 1976 | $6 |

DERAM

| ❏ 7509 | Ask the People/Say You Don't Mind | 1967 | $20 |

LAINE, FRANKIE, AND JIMMY BOYD

COLUMBIA

❏ 40069	Let's Go Fishin'/Poor Little Piggy Bank	1953	$20
❏ 40650	Little Child/Let's Go Fishin'	1956	$15
❏ 39945	Tell Me a Story/The Little Boy and the Old Man	1953	$20

LAINE, FRANKIE, AND PATTI PAGE

MERCURY

| ❏ 5442 | I Love You for That/If I Were You Baby, I'd Love Me | 1950 | $30 |

LAINE, FRANKIE, AND JO STAFFORD

COLUMBIA

❏ 39893	Christmas Roses/Chow Willy	1952	$20
❏ 39672	Hambone/Let's Have a Party	1952	$20
❏ 39570	Hey, Good Lookin'/Gambella (The Gamblin' Lady)	1951	$20
❏ 40401	High Society/Back Where I Belong	1954	$20
❏ 39466	In the Cool of the Evening/That's Good, That's Bad	1951	$20
❏ 39388	Pretty Eyed Baby/That's One for Me	1951	$20
❏ 39867	Settin' the Woods on Fire/Piece a-Puddin'	1952	$20
❏ 40116	Way Down Yonder in New Orleans/Floatin' Down to Cotton Town	1953	$20

LAINE, FRANKIE

ABC

❏ 11224	Dammit Isn't God's Last Name/Fresh Out of Tears	1969	$6
❏ 11097	Forsaking All Others/Take Me Back	1968	$6
❏ 11057	I Don't Want to Set the World On Fire/I Found You	1968	$6
❏ 11231	If I Didn't Believe in You/Allegra	1969	$6
❏ 10891	I'll Take Care of Your Cares/Every Street's a Boulevard	1966	$6
❏ 10967	Laura, What's He Got That I Ain't Got/Sometimes (I Just Can't Stand You)	1967	$6
❏ 10924	Making Memories/Moment of Truth	1967	$6
❏ 11129	Please Forgive Me/Pretty Little Princess	1968	$6
❏ 11032	To Each His Own/I'm Happy to Hear You're Sorry	1967	$6

AMOS

❏ 161	Don't Blame the Child/My God and I	1971	$5
❏ 138	I Believe/On the Sunny Side of the Street	1970	$5
❏ 153	Put Your Hand in the Hand/Going to Newport	1971	$5

CAPITOL

| ❏ 5299 | Go On With Your Dancing/Halfway | 1964 | $8 |
| ❏ 5472 | House of Laughter/A Girl | 1965 | $8 |

| ❏ 5525 | Seven Days of Love/Heartaches Can Be Fun | 1965 | $8 |
| ❏ 5569 | The Meaning of It All/Pray and He Will Answer You | 1966 | $8 |

COLUMBIA

❏ 41283	A Cottage for Sale/When I Speak Your Name	1958	$15
❏ 41106	Annabelle Lee/All of These…And More	1958	$15
❏ 40079	Another Me/Blowing Wild	1953	$20
❏ 42383	A Wedded Man/We'll Be Together Again	1962	$10
❏ 40583	A Woman in Love/Walking the Night Away	1955	$15
❏ 40457	Cool Water/Strange Lady in Town	1955	$15
❏ 40693	Don't Cry/Ticky Ticky Tick (I'm Gonna Tell on You)	1956	$15

— With Paul Weston

| ❏ 42767 [PS] | Don't Make My Baby Blue | 1963 | $40 |

— Promo-only custom "This Sleeve Contains One Broken Record

| ❏ 42767 [DJ] | Don't Make My Baby Blue (same on both sides) | 1963 | $30 |

— Promo only on red vinyl

❏ 42767	Don't Make My Baby Blue/The Moment of Truth	1963	$12
❏ 41036	East Is East/The Greater Sin	1957	$15
❏ 41430	El Diablo/The Valley of a Hundred Hills	1959	$12
❏ 40136	Granada/I'd Give My Life	1953	$20
❏ 40916	Gunfight at the O.K. Corral/Without Him	1957	$15
❏ 41974	Gunslinger/Wanted Man	1961	$10
❏ 40558	Hawk-Eye/Your Love	1955	$15
❏ 40663	Hell Hath No Fury/The Most Happy Fella	1956	$15
❏ 40036	Hey Joe!/Sittin' in the Sun	1953	$20
❏ 39770	High Noon (Do Not Forsake Me)/Rock of Gibraltar	1952	$20
❏ 40526	Humming Bird/My Little One	1955	$15
❏ 39938	I Believe/Your Cheatin' Heart	1953	$20
❏ 41187	I Have to Cry/Choombala Bay	1958	$15
❏ 40600	I Heard the Angels Singing/Ain't It a Pity and a Shame	1955	$15

— With the Four Lads

❏ 42843	I'm Gonna Be Strong/And Doesn't She Roll	1963	$10
❏ 39903	I'm Just a Poor Bachelor/Tonight You Belong to Me	1952	$20
❏ 40378	In the Beginning/Old Shoes	1954	$20
❏ 42966	Lonely Days of Winter/Up Among the Stars	1964	$10
❏ 40856	Love Is a Golden Ring/There's Not a Moment to Spare	1957	$15
❏ 41163	Lovin' Up a Storm/A Kiss Can Change the World	1958	$15
❏ 40720	Make Me a Child Again/The Thief	1956	$15
❏ 42233	Miss Satan/Ride Through the Night	1961	$10
❏ 40669	Moby Dick/A Capitol Ship	1956	$15
❏ 40780	Moonlight Gambler/Lotus Land	1956	$15
❏ 40780 [PS]	Moonlight Gambler/Lotus Land	1956	$30
❏ 41139	My Gal and a Prayer/Lonesome Road	1958	$15
❏ 41376	My Little Love/Journey's End	1959	$10
❏ 39597	One for My Baby/Tomorrow Mountain	1951	$15
❏ 40741	On the Road to Mandalay/Only If We Love	1956	$15
❏ 41700	Seven Women/And Doesn't She Roll	1960	$10
❏ 39599	She Reminds Me of You/Love Is Such a Cheat	1951	$15
❏ 39600	Sleepy Time Down South/To Be Worthy	1951	$15

— The above four comprise a box set

❏ 40235	Some Day/There Must Be a Reason	1954	$20
❏ 39598	Song of the Islands/Necessary Evil	1951	$15
❏ 41613	St. James Infirmary/Et Voila	1960	$10
❏ 42884	Take Her/I'm Gonna Be Strong	1963	$10
❏ 39716	That's How It Goes/Snow in Lover's Lane	1952	$20
❏ 41331	That's My Desire/In My Wildest Dreams	1959	$12
❏ 40962	The 3:10 to Yuma/You Know How It Is	1957	$15
❏ 39665	The Gandy Dancers' Ball/When You're in Love	1952	$20
❏ 39862	The Mermaid/The Ruby and the Pearl	1952	$20
❏ 39798	There's a Rainbow 'Round My Shoulder/She's Funny That Way	1952	$15
❏ 40433	The Tarrier Song/Bubbles	1955	$15
❏ 41299	When I Speak Your Name/Midnight on a Rainy Monday	1958	$15
❏ 40022	When the Wind Blows/Te Amo	1953	$20
❏ 39489	Wonderful, Wasn't It?/The Girl in the Wood	1951	$20
❏ 39799	Wonderful, Wasn't It?/The Girl in the Wood	1952	$15

Number	Title	Yr	NM

MAINSTREAM
❏ 5579	Tell Me 'Bout the Hard Times/(B-side unknown)	1975	$4

MERCURY
❏ 70099	Ain't Misbehavin'/How Rhythm Was Born	1953	$20
❏ 58920	All of Me/South of the Border	1952	$30
❏ 57680	Baby I Need You/Yes My Darling Daughter	1951	$30
❏ 55800	Dear, Dear, Dear/May the Good Lord Bless and Keep You	1951	$30
❏ 57330	Get Happy/I Would Do Most Anything for You	1951	$30
❏ 55000	If I Were a Bell/Sleepy Ol' River	1950	$30
❏ 55440	I'm Gonna Live 'Til I Die/A Man Gets Awfully Lonesome	1950	$30
❏ 56850	Isle of Capri/The Day Isn't Long Enough	1951	$30
❏ 55530	Merry Christmas Everywhere/What Am I Gonna Do This Christmas	1950	$30
❏ 55810	Metro Polka/The Jalopy Song	1951	$30
❏ 53450	Mule Train/Carry Me Back to Old Virginny	1950	$40

—Turquoise label

❏ 54580	Music, Maestro, Please/Dream a Little Dream of Me	1950	$30
❏ 1027	On the Sunny Side of the Street/Blue Turning Grey Over You	1950	$30
❏ 53580	Satan Wears a Satin Gown/Baby Just for Me	1950	$30
❏ C-30056X45	September in the Rain/Georgia on My Mind	1958	$10

—Pink label; early "Celebrity Series" reissue

❏ 54210	Stars and Stripes Forever/Thanks for the Kisses	1950	$30
❏ 50280	Stay As Sweet As You Are/I May Be Wrong	1950	$30

—Reissue of 78 rpm

❏ 53900	Swamp Girl/A Kiss for Tomorrow	1950	$30
❏ 53160	That Lucky Old Sun/I Get Sentimental Over Nothing	1950	$30

—Reissue of 78 rpm; black vinyl

❏ 53160	That Lucky Old Sun/I Get Sentimental Over Nothing	1950	$50

—Reissue of 78 rpm; red vinyl

❏ 53630	The Cry of the Wild Goose/Black Lace	1950	$30

—Maroon label

❏ 53630	The Cry of the Wild Goose/Black Lace	1950	$40

—Turquoise label

❏ 56560	The Gang That Sang Heart of My Heart/Out in the Rain	1951	$30
❏ 70262	(The Gang That Sang) Heart of My Heart/South of the Border	1953	$20
❏ 70275	West End Blues/I Can't Believe That You're in Love with Me	1953	$20

SUNFLOWER
❏ 125	My Own True Love/Time to Ride	1972	$5

WARNER BROS.
❏ 7774	Blazing Saddles/I'm Tired	1974	$6

—B-side by Madeline Kahn

7-Inch Extended Plays

COLUMBIA
❏ B-2590	*Shine/That's My Desire/That Lucky Old Sun/Moonlight Gambler	1960	$20
❏ B-2086 [PS]	Bring Your Smile Along	1956	$25
❏ B-2086	(contents unknown)	1956	$25
❏ B-2121	(contents unknown)	1957	$25
❏ B-2590 [PS]	Frankie Laine (Hall of Fame Series)	1960	$20
❏ B-2132 [PS]	Love Is a Golden Ring and Other Hits	1957	$25
❏ B-2132	Love Is a Golden Ring/There's Not a Moment to Spare//After You've Gone/Lullaby in Rhythm	1957	$25
❏ B-2121 [PS]	Moonlight Gambler	1957	$25

LAINE, LINDA, AND THE SINNERS
TOWER
❏ 108	Low Grades and High Fever/After Today	1964	$15

LAKE, GREG
ATLANTIC
❏ 3405	C'est La Vie/Jeremy Bender	1977	$5
❏ 3305	I Believe in Father Christmas/Humbug	1975	$6
❏ 3305 [PS]	I Believe in Father Christmas/Humbug	1975	$10

CHRYSALIS
❏ 2517	Let Me Love You Once/(B-side unknown)	1981	$4

LAKE, KAREN
BIG TOP
❏ 3077	Air Mail Special Delivery/I'd Like to Miss My Graduation	1961	$40

—Produced by Phil Spector

LALA AND THE LALARETTES
ELPECO
❏ 2922	This Day of Ours/Getting Ready for Freddy	1963	$70

LAMARR, GENE
SPRY
❏ 115	Close to Me/Moon Eyes	1959	$125
❏ 113	Crazy Little House on the Hill/You Don't Love Me Anymore	1959	$200

LAMB, BECKY
WARNER BROS.
❏ 7154	Little Becky's Christmas Wish/Go to Sleep, Little Lambs	1967	$15

—B-side by Bill Lamb

LAMM, ROBERT
COLUMBIA
❏ 10068	Skinny Boy/Temporary Jones	1974	$5

LAMONT, BILLY
KING
❏ 5403	Come On Right Now/Hear Me Now	1960	$15

OKEH
❏ 7125	Country Boy/Can't Make It By Myself	1959	$30
❏ 7131	I'm Gonna Try/Now Darling	1960	$30

SAVOY
❏ 1522	I'm So Lonely/I Got a Rock 'n' Roll Gal	1957	$20

THREE-D
❏ 850	Country Boy/Can't Make It By Myself	1959	$200

LAMONT, CHARLES
REVUE
❏ 11047	Before It's Over/Hog Blues	1969	$15
❏ 11061	Two Thousand Years Ago/Lefty	1970	$15

LAMP, BUDDY
ABC-PARAMOUNT
❏ 10398	I'm Comin' Home/Promised Land	1963	$200

DOUBLE L
❏ 716	Thank You Love/My Tears	1963	$80

DUKE
❏ 461	Devil's Gonna Get You/Wall Around Your Heart	1970	$30
❏ 468	Hen Pecked/If You See Kate	1971	$30
❏ 438	I'm Coming Home/Where Have You Been	1968	$30

GONE
❏ 5104	Good News/What Here Can I Do	1961	$20

LAMPLIGHTERS, THE
FEDERAL
❏ 12242	Don't Make It So Good/Hug a Little, Kiss a Little	1955	$200
❏ 12192	Five Minutes Longer/You Hear	1954	$200
❏ 12152	Give Me/Be-Bop Wino	1953	$200
❏ 12261	It Ain't Right/Everything's All Right	1956	$125
❏ 12206	I Wanna Know/Believe in Me	1955	$200
❏ 12149	Part of Me/Turn Me Loose	1953	$300
❏ 12182	Salty Dog/Ride, Jockey, Ride	1954	$200
❏ 12166	Smoothie/I Can't Stand It	1954	$200
❏ 12176	Tell Me You Came/I Used to Cry Mercy, Mercy	1954	$200

KING
❏ 5890	Be-Bop Wino/Thunderbird	1964	$20

—B-side by Dossie Terry

LANCASTRIANS, THE
JERDEN
❏ 798	The World Keeps Going Round/Not the Same Anymore	1966	$10

LANCE, HERB
MALA
❏ 426	Deep in My Heart/Prayer in My Heart	1961	$30
❏ 404	Like a Baby/My Good Mind	1959	$30
❏ 405	Some Love/Until the Real Thing	1959	$30

LANCE, LYNDA K.
ABC
❏ 10942	It Just Can't Be/King of Sorrow	1967	$10

GARPAX
❏ 081	Say You Love Me/Pretend My Eyes Are Brown	1976	$6

NSD
❏ 64	Backslidin' Again/Morning Sky	1980	$5

ROYAL AMERICAN
❏ 287	Ain't Had No Lovin'/That's All That Matters	1969	$8
❏ 290	A Woman's Side of Love/That's All I Want from You	1969	$8
❏ 281	Loving Kind/The World I Used to Know	1969	$8

SUNBIRD
❏ 7567	All I Really Need Is You/(B-side unknown)	1981	$6

TRIUNE
❏ 7202	God's Gift to Me/I've Just Gotta Feel Like a Woman Tonight	1973	$6

WARNER BROS.
❏ 7827	It's No Laughing Matter/Long Distance Kissing	1974	$5
❏ 8068	Let's Let Our Hearts Talk It Over/Love and Golden Rings	1975	$5

WAYSIDE
❏ 1015	Fool of the Year/Now That It's Over	1968	$10

LANCE, MAJOR
COLUMBIA
❏ 10488	Come On, Have Yourself a Good Time/Come What May	1977	$5

CURTOM
❏ 1956	Must Be Love Coming Down/Little Young Lover	1970	$6
❏ 1953	Stay Away from Me (I Love You Too Much)/Gypsy Woman	1970	$6

DAKAR
❏ 608	Follow the Leader/Since You've Been Gone	1969	$8
❏ 612	Shadows of a Memory/Sweeter As the Days Go By	1969	$8

KAT FAMILY
❏ 04185	Are You Leaving Me/I Wanna Go Home	1983	$4
❏ 03024	I Wanna Go Home/(Instrumental)	1982	$4

MERCURY
❏ 71582	I've Got a Girl/Phyllis	1960	$200

OKEH
❏ 7223	Ain't It a Shame/Gotta Get Away	1965	$10
❏ 7266	Ain't No Soul (In These Shoes)/I	1966	$20
❏ 7216	Come See/You Belong to Me My Love	1965	$10
❏ 7216 [PS]	Come See/You Belong to Me My Love	1965	$20
❏ 7233	Everybody Loves a Good Time/I Just Can't Help It	1965	$20
❏ 7181	Hey Little Girl/Crying in the Rain	1963	$15
❏ 7197	It Ain't No Use/Girls	1964	$10
❏ 7255	It's the Beat/You'll Want Me Back	1966	$10
❏ 7250	Little Young Lover/Investigate	1966	$20
❏ 7250 [PS]	Little Young Lover/Investigate	1966	$60
❏ 7209	Sometimes I Wonder/I'm So Lost	1965	$12
❏ 7191	The Matador/Gonna Get Married	1964	$10
❏ 7175	The Monkey Time/Mama Didn't Know	1963	$20
❏ 7200	Think Nothing About It/It's Alright	1964	$60
❏ 7226	Too Hot to Hold/Dark and Lovely	1965	$80
❏ 7298	Without a Doubt/Forever	1967	$10

PLAYBOY
❏ 6020	Sweeter/Wild and Free	1975	$30

SOUL
❏ 35123	I Never Thought I'd Be Losing You/Chicago Disco	1977	$5

Number	Title	Yr	NM

VOLT
❏ 4085	Ain't No Sweat/Since I Lost My Baby's Love	1972	$30
❏ 4079	I Wanna Make Up/That's the Story of My Life	1972	$40

LANCELOT LINK AND THE EVOLUTION REVOLUTION
ABC
❏ 11285	Daydreams/Magic Feelings	1970	$12
❏ 11278	Sha La Love You/Blind Date	1970	$10

LANCERS, THE
CLOUD
❏ 500	Baja/When Johnny Comes Draggin' Home	1965	$30

CORAL
❏ 61527	Alphabet Rock/How Lonely Can I Get	1955	$15
❏ 61831	Charm Bracelets/And I Don't Feel Bad	1957	$15
❏ 61899	Don't Go Near the Water/A Hundred Heartbeats	1957	$15
❏ 61769	Freckle Face Sara Jane/It Happened in Monterey	1957	$15
❏ 61712	I Came Back to Say I'm Sorry/Never Leave Me	1956	$15
❏ 61887	I'm Awfully Strong for You/I'd Move Heaven and Earth	1957	$15
❏ 61468	It Shouldn't Hurt to Love You/It Takes a Heap of Livin'	1955	$15
❏ 61998	It Was Great While It Lasted/The Lord Is a Generous Man	1958	$15
❏ 61416	Leave the Door Partly Open/The Lucky Black Cat	1955	$15
❏ 61616	Little Fool/A Man Is As Good As His Word	1956	$15
❏ 61866	Lover's Rendezvous/Follow the River	1957	$15
❏ 61288	Mr. Sandman/Little White Light	1954	$15
❏ 61374	Somebody Else Is Taking My Place/Cherry	1955	$15
❏ 61611	Sorry/A Man Is As Good As His Word	1956	$15
❏ 61966	Sorry/The Sound	1958	$15
❏ 61686	The Bonnie Banks of Loch Lomon'/Maybe Now	1956	$15
❏ 61665	The First Traveling Saleslady/Free	1956	$15
❏ 61930	The Stroll/Jo-Ann	1958	$15
❏ 61343	Timberjack/Crazy Music	1955	$15
— With Lawrence Welk and His Orchestra			
❏ 61314	'Twas the Night Before Christmas/I Wanna Do More Than Whistle (Under the Mistletoe)	1954	$15
❏ 61332	Tweedlee Dee/Open Up Your Heart (And Let the Sun Shine In)	1955	$15
❏ 61382	Two Hearts, Two Kisses/Afraid	1955	$15

OLD TIMER
❏ 604	Baja/When Johnny Comes Draggin' Home	1965	$50
—Black vinyl			
❏ 604	Baja/When Johnny Comes Draggin' Home	1965	$12
—Red vinyl (reissue)			

VEE JAY
❏ 654	The Warmth of the Sun/Hush-A-Bye	1965	$10

LANDERS, CONNIE
HIT
❏ 40	Bobby's Girl/Ride!	1962	$8
—B-side by Peggy Gaines			
❏ 57	Follow the Boys/He's So Fine	1963	$8
—B-side by the Dacrons			
❏ 23	Heart in Hand/Things	1962	$8
—B-side by Harvey Frolic			
❏ 34	He Thinks I Still Care/All Alone Am I	1962	$8
—B-side by Katy Richards			
❏ 46	I'm Gonna Be Warm This Winter/Half Heaven Half Heartache	1962	$8
—B-side by George Killebrew			
❏ 68	It's My Party/Another Saturday Night	1963	$8
—B-side by Leroy Jones			
❏ 43	My Coloring Book/Go Away Little Girl	1962	$8
—B-side by Fred York			
❏ 48	Shake Me I Rattle/My Dad	1962	$8
—B-side by Woody Martin			

LANDERS, DAVE
MGM
❏ K10933	Don't Do Anything/What's the Use to Take You Back Again	1951	$30
❏ K10682	Draw Up the Papers, Lawyer/How Many Hearts Do You Have	1950	$40
❏ K10872	Everything That's Good/Clomp, Click, Click	1951	$30
❏ K11050	I Got a Cinder in My Eye/Bumble Bee	1951	$30

LANDS, HOAGY
ABC-PARAMOUNT
❏ 10171	(I'm Gonna) Cry Some Tears/Lighted Windows	1960	$30
❏ 10392	Tender Years/I'm Yours	1963	$20

ATLANTIC
❏ 2217	Baby Come On Home/Baby Let Me Hold Your Hand	1964	$20

JUDI
❏ 054	(I'm Gonna) Cry Some Tears/Lighted Windows	1960	$100

LAURIE
❏ 3349	Theme from The Other Side/Friends and Lovers Don't Go Together	1966	$30

MGM
❏ K-13062	Goodnight Irene/It Ain't As Easy As That	1962	$30
❏ K-13041	My Tears Are Dry/It's Gonna Be Morning	1961	$30

LANDS, LIZ
GORDY
❏ 7026	May What He Lived For Live/He's Got the Whole World in His Hands	1963	$40
❏ 7030	Midnight Journey/Keep Me	1964	$200
— The Temptations sing backup			
❏ 7023	We Shall Overcome/I Have a Dream	1963	$30
— B-side by Rev. Martin Luther King			

ONE-DERFUL
❏ 4847	One Man's Poison/Don't Shut Me Out	1967	$50

LANE, JERRY "MAX
ABC
❏ 12091	I've Got a Lotta Missin' You to Do/Back on My Feet Again	1975	$5
❏ 11444	Tearjoint/Walk Off the World	1974	$5
❏ 11410	The Snake/Don't Take the You Out of Us	1973	$5

CHART
❏ 1335	Anywhere But Gone/I Miss You Every Chance I Get	1966	$10
❏ 5025	Crawling Back to You/The More I Think of You	1969	$8
❏ 1185	Gonna Live It Up/(B-side unknown)	1965	$10
❏ 1056	It's Also New to Me/Ten Years of Life	1968	$8
❏ 1395	I've Done Wrong/The Things I Do Best	1966	$10
❏ 1012	Lover's Lane/My Mind Won't Mind Me	1967	$8
❏ 1034	She Lives in Your World/Quietly Losing My Mind	1968	$8

STOCKYARD
❏ 1003	I've Got a Lot of Missin' You to Do/(B-side unknown)	1983	$6
❏ 1000	When the Music Stops/(B-side unknown)	1983	$6

LANE BROTHERS, THE
FXL
❏ 0026	Marianne/(You've Gotta) Believe in America	1981	$8

LEADER
❏ 804	Mimi/Two Dozen and a Half	1960	$10

RCA VICTOR
❏ 47-7220	Boppin' in a Sack/Somebody Sweet	1958	$15
❏ 47-6900	Ding Dang Dinglin'/Uh Uh Honey	1957	$15
❏ 47-7107	Don't Tempt Me Baby/Lover's Heart	1957	$15
❏ 47-7304	Little Brother/So Satisfied	1958	$15
❏ 47-6810	Marianne/Sogni D'Oro	1957	$20

LANE, CRISTY
K-ARK
❏ 717	Let's Pretend/Subtract His Love	1966	$15
❏ 686	Stop Foolin' with Me/Janie Took My Place	1966	$15

LIBERTY
❏ 1432	Cheatin' Is Still on My Mind/Just a Mile from Nowhere	1981	$4
❏ 1508	Footprints in the Sand/Miracle Maker	1983	$4
❏ 1461	Fragile -- Handle with Care/Tangerine	1982	$4
❏ 1396	I Have a Dream/Rio Grande	1981	$4
❏ 1396 [PS]	I Have a Dream/Rio Grande	1981	$6
❏ 1501	I've Come Back (To Say I Love You One More Time)/Now the Day Is Over	1983	$4
❏ 1443	Lies on Your Lips/I Really Got the Blues	1981	$4
❏ 1406	Love to Love You/Everything I Own	1981	$4
❏ 1521	Midnight Blue/Simple Little Words	1984	$4
❏ 1483	The Good Old Days/Do I Dare	1982	$4

LS
❏ 169	I Just Can't Stay Married to You/Rain Song	1978	$5
❏ 156	I'm Gonna Love You Anyway/I Can't Tell You	1978	$5
❏ 1987	I Wanna Wake Up with You/He's Got the Whole World in His Hands	1987	$5
❏ 131	Let Me Down Easy/This Is the First Time (I've Seen the Last Time on Your Face)	1977	$5
❏ 9146	Man from Galilee/Shake Me I Rattle (Squeeze Me I Cry)	1984	$6
❏ 167	Penny Arcade/Somebody's Baby	1978	$5
❏ 148	Shake Me I Rattle/I Can't Tell You	1978	$5
❏ 148	Shake Me I Rattle/Pretty Paper	1977	$6
❏ 172	Simple Little Words/He Believes in Me	1979	$6
❏ 121	Sweet Deceiver/Walk On Baby	1977	$5
❏ 110	Tryin' to Forget About You/By the Way	1977	$5

UNITED ARTISTS
❏ X1328	Come to My Love/Love Lies	1979	$4
❏ X1342	One Day at a Time/I Knew the Mason	1980	$4
❏ X1304	Simple Little Words/He Believes in Me	1979	$4
❏ X1314	Slippin' Up, Slippin' Around/He's Back in Town	1979	$4
❏ X1369	Sweet Sexy Eyes/Maybe I'm Thinkin'	1980	$4

LANE, MICKEY
BRUNSWICK
❏ 55098	Daddy's Little Baby/Toasted Love	1958	$30

LAURIE
❏ 3071	Dum Dee Dee Dum/Night Cap	1960	$30

LANE, MICKEY LEE
MALA
❏ 12032	Tutti Frutti/With Your Love	1968	$8

SWAN
❏ 4222	Hey Sah-Lo-Ney/Of Yesterday	1965	$12
❏ 4210	Little Girl (I Was Wrong)/When You're in Love	1965	$12
❏ 4183	Shaggy Dog/Oo-Oo	1964	$15
❏ 4252	The Only Thing to Do/She Don't Want To	1966	$10

LANE, ROBIN, AND THE CHARTBUSTERS
DELI PLATTERS
❏ RLC1	When Things Go Wrong/Why Do You Tell Lies/The Letter	1979	$10
❏ RLC1 [PS]	When Things Go Wrong/Why Do You Tell Lies/The Letter	1979	$10

WARNER BROS.
❏ 49546	Don't Cry/Waitin' in Line	1980	$4
❏ 49742	Solid Rock/Say Goodbye	1981	$4
❏ 49246	When Things Go Wrong/Many Years Ago	1980	$4
❏ 49246 [PS]	When Things Go Wrong/Many Years Ago	1980	$4

LANE, ROCKI, AND THE GROSS GROUP
EPIC
❏ 10556	Happy Hairy Hippy Harry Claus/Santa Soul	1969	$30

LANG, K.D.
SIRE
❏ 7-22932	Full Moon Full of Love/Wallflower Waltz	1989	$5
❏ 7-22932 [PS]	Full Moon Full of Love/Wallflower Waltz	1989	$8
❏ 7-27919	I'm Down to My Last Cigarette/Western Stars	1988	$4

Number	Title	Yr	NM
❑ 7-27919 [PS]	I'm Down to My Last Cigarette/Western Stars	1988	$5
❑ 7-27813	Lock, Stock and Teardrops/ Don't Let the Stars Get In Your Eyes	1988	$8
❑ 7-27813 [PS]	Lock, Stock and Teardrops/ Don't Let the Stars Get In Your Eyes	1988	$8
❑ 7-22734	Three Days/Trail of Broken Hearts	1989	$6
❑ 7-22734 [PS]	Three Days/Trail of Broken Hearts	1989	$10
❑ 7-28338	Turn Me Round/Diet of Strange Places	1987	$6
❑ 7-28338 [PS]	Turn Me Round/Diet of Strange Places	1987	$30

LANIN, LESTER
AUDIO FIDELITY

Number	Title	Yr	NM
❑ 134	All You Need Is Love/The Windows of the World	1968	$5
❑ 135	Mame/Cabaret	1968	$5

EPIC

Number	Title	Yr	NM
❑ 9571	Ballad of the Red River Valley/ Tumbling Tumbleweeds	1963	$8
❑ 9426	Blue Tango Rock/This Could Be the Start of Something Big	1960	$8
❑ JZSP123259/60 [DJ]	Christmas Medley/Jingle Bells	1967	$8
❑ JZSP123257/8 [DJ]	Dance of the Sugar-Plum Fairies/Ring In the New	1967	$8
❑ 9514	Give Me a Song/You Can't Be True, Dear	1962	$8
❑ 9396	Glow-Worm Cha Cha/Yellow Rose of Texas Meringue	1960	$8
❑ 9279	Lester Lanin Cha-Cha-Cha (And Medley)/Toreador Song	1958	$12
❑ 9482	Organ Twist/Sweet Georgia Brown	1961	$8
❑ 9296	Over the Rainbow Cha-Cha-Cha/I Want My Mama	1958	$10
❑ 9350	Sleigh Ride/Christmas Carol Medley	1959	$15
❑ 9624	Tamoure Shake/Theme from "The Seven Capital Sins"	1963	$8
❑ 9444	The Bells/Bow and Arrow	1961	$8
❑ 9618	Theme from "The Seven Capital Sins"/Hora (Happiness)	1963	$8
❑ 9349	Winter Wonderland/Dance of the Sugar-Plum Fairies	1959	$15
❑ JZSP123255/6 [DJ]	Winter Wonderland/Sleigh Ride	1967	$8

METROMEDIA

Number	Title	Yr	NM
❑ 118	Love Theme from Romeo and Juliet/Aquarius	1969	$4
❑ 135	Ob-La-Di, Ob-La-Da/Dizzy	1969	$4

PHILIPS

Number	Title	Yr	NM
❑ 40217	Down by the Riverside/West Indies Ska	1964	$6
❑ 40344	Theme from "The Yearling"/ Dancing Tambourines	1965	$6

LANSDOWNE, JERRY
STEP ONE

Number	Title	Yr	NM
❑ 400	She Had Every Right to Do You Wrong/I Will Carry You	1989	$4
❑ 404	Who'll Give This Heart a Home/I Will Carry You	1989	$4

LANZA, MARIO
RCA VICTOR

Number	Title	Yr	NM
❑ 47-7164	Arrivederci Roma/Younger Than Springtime	1958	$15
❑ 47-6334	Ave Maria/I'll Walk with God	1955	$20
❑ 47-7119	Come Dance with Me/Never Till Now	1957	$15
❑ 47-6664	Do You Wonder/Love in a Home	1956	$15
❑ 47-6644	Earthbound/This Land	1956	$15
❑ 47-7439	For the First Time/O Sole Mio	1959	$15
❑ 47-7622	I'll Walk with God/Guardian Angels	1959	$15
❑ 49-3207	Because/For You Alone	1951	$30
— Red vinyl			
❑ 49-3914	Because You're Mine/The Song Angels Sing	1952	$20
— Red vinyl			
❑ 49-1353	Be My Love/I'll Never Love You	1950	$30
— Red vinyl			
❑ 49-1353	Be My Love/I'll Never Love You	1951	$30
— Black vinyl			
❑ 49-4218	Deep in My Heart, Dear/ Serenade	1954	$20
❑ 49-4220	Drink, Drink, Drink/(B-side unknown)	1954	$20
❑ 49-1169	Granada/Lolita	1950	$30
— Red vinyl			
❑ 49-4216	I'll Walk with God/Beloved	1954	$20
❑ 49-3208	My Song, My Love/I Love Thee	1951	$30
— Red vinyl			
❑ 49-0902	O Sole Mio/Mattinata	1950	$30

Number	Title	Yr	NM
— Red vinyl			
❑ 49-3209	O Tu Che in Seno Agli Angeli/Addio Alla Madre	1951	$30
— Red vinyl			
❑ 49-3155	Serenade (Toselli)/Serenade (Drigo)	1951	$30
— Red vinyl			
❑ 49-4209	Song of India/If You Were Mine	1953	$20
❑ 49-3300	The Loveliest Night of the Year/La Donna E Mobile	1951	$30
— Red vinyl			

7-Inch Extended Plays
RCA VICTOR

Number	Title	Yr	NM
❑ EPA-4344	*Come Prima/Pineapple Pickers/O, Mon Amour/O Sole Mio/Hofbrauhaus Song	1959	$15
❑ EPA-4222	*Seven Hills of Rome/ Arrividerci Roman/Come Dance with Me/Lolita	1958	$15
❑ LPC-117	Deep in My Heart, Dear/ Gaudeamus Igitur// Serenade/Drink, Drink, Drink	1961	$20
— 33 1/3 rpm, small hole			
❑ EPA-4344 [PS]	For the First Time	1959	$15
❑ EPA-4222 [PS]	Seven Hills of Rome	1958	$15
❑ LPC-117 [PS]	The Student Prince	1961	$20

RCA VICTOR RED SEAL

Number	Title	Yr	NM
❑ ERA51	Addio Alla Madre (Turiddu's Farewell)/Granada//Mama Mia Che Vo Sape?/The Lord's Prayer	1952	$15
— Red vinyl			
❑ ERA-288	Away in a Manger/Deck the Halls/Joy to the World//O Little Town of Bethlehem/ It Came Upon a Midnight Clear	1956	$15
❑ ERA222	Because/Vesta La Giubba// Core 'Ingrato/Toselli's Serenade	1954	$15
❑ ERA130	I Know, I Know, I Know/ Be My Love//The Loveliest Night of the Year/Because You're Mine	1953	$15
❑ ERA130 [PS]	Mario Lanza In Movie Hits	1953	$15
❑ ERA222 [PS]	Mario Lanza Sings Because	1954	$15
❑ ERA-288 [PS]	Mario Lanza Sings Christmas Carols	1956	$15
❑ ERA51 [PS]	Selections from "Because You're Mine"	1952	$15

LAPELS, THE
DOT

Number	Title	Yr	NM
❑ 16129	Sneakin' Around/Sneakin' Blues	1960	$15

MELKER

Number	Title	Yr	NM
❑ 103	Sneakin' Around/Sneakin' Blues	1960	$50

LARADOS, THE
MADOG

Number	Title	Yr	NM
❑ 801	Will You Love Me Tomorrow/ You Didn't Care	1980	$20

LARCHMONT SINGERS, THE
CRUSADER

Number	Title	Yr	NM
❑ 112	A Christmas Wish/Welcome, Little Stranger	1964	$10

LARGE, BILLY
COLUMBIA

Number	Title	Yr	NM
❑ 4-44002	My $3.98 Plaster Mail Order Guitar/New Street to Walk On	1967	$10
❑ 4-43741	The Goodie Wagon/Big Yellow Peaches	1966	$10
❑ 4-43741 [PS]	The Goodie Wagon/Big Yellow Peaches	1966	$20

LARKIN, BILLY
AURA

Number	Title	Yr	NM
❑ 4504	Pigmy (Part 1)/Pigmy (Part 2)	1965	$20
— As "The Delegates			
❑ 4508	The Peeper/Hainty	1965	$20
— As "The Delegates			

BRYAN

Number	Title	Yr	NM
❑ 1026	Indian Giver/Dig a Little Deeper	1975	$6
❑ 1010	Leave It Up to Me/When You Left	1974	$6
❑ 1018	The Devil in Mrs. Jones/No Reason Why	1975	$6

CASINO

Number	Title	Yr	NM
❑ 097	Here's to the Next Time/ Lonely Woman	1976	$5

MERCURY

Number	Title	Yr	NM
❑ 55065	Every Night/Haven't I Loved You Somewhere Before	1979	$4

Number	Title	Yr	NM
❑ 55040	My Side of Town/Ring in My Pocket	1978	$4

SUNBIRD

Number	Title	Yr	NM
❑ 7557	20-20 Hindsight/Lonely Woman	1981	$4
❑ 107	I Can't Stop Now/Lovin' a Lie	1980	$4
❑ 7562	Longing for the High/Is There Nothing Left to Say	1981	$4

WORLD PACIFIC

Number	Title	Yr	NM
❑ 77844	Hold On! I'm a-Comin'/Dirty Water	1966	$8
❑ 4504	Pigmy (Part 1)/Pigmy (Part 2)	1965	$15
— As "The Delegates			
❑ 88120	Pigmy (Part 1)/The Peeper	1966	$10
— As "The Delegates			

LARKS, THE (1)
MONEY

Number	Title	Yr	NM
❑ 115	Can You Do the Duck/Sad Sad Boy	1965	$15
❑ 601	I Love You/I Want You Back	1973	$6
❑ 119	Lost My Love Yesterday/The Answer Came Too Late	1966	$15
❑ 109	Mickey's East Coast Jerk/ Soul Jerk	1965	$15
❑ 604	My Favorite Beer Joint/ (Instrumental)	1973	$6
❑ 122	Philly Dog/Heaven Only Knows	1966	$15
❑ 607	Shorty the Pimp (Part 1)/ Shorty the Pimp (Part 2)	1974	$6
— Money 604 and 607 as "Don Julian and the Larks			
❑ 127	The Skate/Come Back Baby	1967	$15
❑ 110	The Slauson Shuffle/Soul Jerk	1965	$15

LARKS, THE (2)
SHERYL

Number	Title	Yr	NM
❑ 334	It's Unbelievable/I Can't Believe It	1961	$40
❑ 338	There Is a Girl/Let's Drink a Toast	1961	$30

LARKS, THE (3)
APOLLO

Number	Title	Yr	NM
❑ 437	Darlin'/Lucy Brown	1952	$1000
❑ 1180	Hopefully Yours/When I Leave These Prison Walls	1951	$4000
❑ 1194	I Live True to You/Hold Me	1952	$1000
❑ 429	Little Side Car/Hey Little Girl	1951	$4000
❑ 435	My Lost Love/How Long Must I Wait for You	1952	$1000
❑ 1184	My Reverie/Let's Say a Prayer	1951	$2000
— Black vinyl			
❑ 1184	My Reverie/Let's Say a Prayer	1951	$8000
— Red vinyl. VG 4000; VG+ 6000			
❑ 430	Ooh, It Feels So Good/I Don't Believe in Tomorrow	1951	$4000
❑ 1189	Shadrack/Honey in the Rock	1952	$2000
❑ 1190	Stolen Love/In My Lonely Room	1952	$2500
— Black vinyl			
❑ 1190	Stolen Love/In My Lonely Room	1952	$5000
— Red vinyl. VG 2500; VG+ 3750			

LLOYDS

Number	Title	Yr	NM
❑ 114	Forget It/I Live True to You	1954	$600
❑ 108	Margie/Rockin' in the Rockin' Room	1954	$800
❑ 110	Tippin' In/If It's a Crime	1954	$800

LARKS, THE (U)
CROSS FIRE

Number	Title	Yr	NM
❑ 74-0.98	Fabulous Cars and Diamond Rings/Life Is Sweeter Now	1961	$30

GUYDEN

Number	Title	Yr	NM
❑ 2103	Fabulous Cars and Diamond Rings/Life Is Sweeter Now	1964	$15
❑ 2098	I Want Her to Love Me/ (Instrumental)	1963	$15

JETT

Number	Title	Yr	NM
❑ 3001	Love You So/Love Me True	1965	$70

NASCO

Number	Title	Yr	NM
❑ 028	I Love You/I Want You Back	1972	$8

STACY

Number	Title	Yr	NM
❑ 969	Food Sticks/Scavenger	1963	$15

VIOLET

Number	Title	Yr	NM
❑ 1051	I Want Her to Love Me/ (Instrumental)	1962	$30

LARKTONES, THE
ABC-PARAMOUNT

Number	Title	Yr	NM
❑ 9909	The Letter/Rockin' Swingin' Man	1958	$40

Number	Title	Yr	NM

RIKI
| ❏ 140 | Why Are You Tearing Us Apart/Nosy Neighbor | 1960 | $70 |

LAROSA, JULIUS
ABC
| ❏ 10959 | For Once in My Life/Summer Love | 1967 | $6 |

CADENCE
❏ 1230	Anywhere I Wander/This Is Heaven	1953	$20
❏ 1252	Campanelle (Jingle Bells)/I Hope You'll Be Very Happy	1954	$15
❏ 1440	David and Lisa's Love Song/Suddenly There's a Valley	1963	$8
❏ 1265	Domani (Tomorrow)/Mama Rosa	1955	$15
❏ 1232	Eh, Cumpari/Till They've All Gone Home	1953	$20
❏ 1444	Gonna Build a Mountain/JE	1964	$8
❏ 1258	Let's Stay Home Tonight/Pass It On	1955	$15
❏ 1251	Mobile/I Hate to Say Hello	1954	$15
❏ 1236	My Funny Valentine/Roseanne	1954	$15
❏ 1244	My Heart's on a Fast Express/In My Own Quiet Way	1954	$15
❏ 1231	My Lady Loves to Dance/Let's Make Up Before We Say Goodnight	1953	$20
❏ 1270	Suddenly There's a Valley/Everytime That I Kiss Carrie	1955	$15
❏ 1235	The Big Bell and the Little Bell/I Couldn't Believe My Eyes	1954	$15
❏ 1240	Three Coins in the Fountain/Me Gotta Have You	1954	$15
❏ 1237	When You're in Love/Have a Heart	1954	$15

CREWE
| ❏ 335 | Where Do I Go/This Is All I Had | 1969 | $6 |

— With the Bob Crewe Generation

GP
| ❏ 592 | A Christmas Gift/To Find Our Children | 1981 | $6 |

KAPP
❏ 348	Bewitched/It's Alright with Me	1960	$8
❏ 323	Green Fields/Your Hand in Mine	1960	$8
❏ 371	Let Your Lips Tell Me/Seventeen	1961	$8
❏ 417	There's No Other Love/Caress Me	1961	$8

METROMEDIA
| ❏ 186 | Brooklyn Roads/Being Alive | 1970 | $5 |

MGM
| ❏ CS5-5 | Celebtrity Scene: Julius LaRosa | 1967 | $60 |

— Box set of five singles (13671-13675). Price includes box, all 5 singles, jukebox title strips, bio. Records are sometimes found by themselves, so they are also listed separately.

❏ 13575	I Think It's Going to Rain Today/You Only See Her	1966	$6
❏ 13497	Lonely As I Leave You/You're Gonna Hear from Me	1966	$6
❏ 13454	Small, Small World/Unless	1966	$6
❏ 13672	Somethin' Special/You're Gonna Hear from Me	1967	$8
❏ 13671	(titles unknown)	1967	$8
❏ 13673	(titles unknown)	1967	$8
❏ 13651	We Need A Little Christmas/Our Venetian Affair	1966	$8
❏ 13674	What Did I Have That I Don't Have/Spring	1967	$8
❏ 13675	Who Am I/What'll I Do	1967	$8

RCA VICTOR
❏ 47-6700	All I Want/Priscilla	1956	$10
❏ 47-6923	Crying My Heart Out for You/When You're With the One You Love	1957	$12
❏ 47-6567	Get Me to the Church On Time/I've Grown Accustomed to Her Face	1956	$10
❏ 47-6499	I've Got Love/Augustine	1956	$10
❏ 47-6416	Lipstick and Candy and Rubber Sole Shoes/Winter in New England	1956	$12
❏ 47-7186	Lover, Lover/A Heart for a Heart	1958	$10
❏ 47-6878	Mama Guitar/Man to Man	1957	$10
❏ 74-0938	The Good Life/Sing Me a Song	1973	$5
❏ 47-6648	The Opposite Sex/Namely You	1956	$10
❏ 47-7227	Torero/Milano	1958	$10
❏ 47-6998	Worlds Apart/Famous Last Words	1957	$10

ROULETTE
| ❏ 4162 | Honey Bunch/Port of Love | 1959 | $12 |
| ❏ 4135 | Where's the Girl/Protect Me | 1959 | $10 |

7-Inch Extended Plays
CADENCE
| ❏ EP1234 | Ave Maria/Adeste Fideles//Silent Night/Oh Holy Night | 1953 | $20 |

RCA VICTOR
| ❏ 547-1026 | But Not for Me/I Love My Bed//Our Love Is Here to Stay/Ev'ry Time | 1956 | $10 |

— One record of EPB 1299

| ❏ 547-1025 | Candy/Don't You Know I Care//No Love, No Nothin'/Wait 'Till You See Her | 1956 | $10 |

— One record of EPB 1299

| ❏ EPA841 | (contents unknown) | 1956 | $20 |
| ❏ SPA-7-38 [PS] | Pajama Party | 1956 | $15 |

LARRY AND THE CROSSFIRES
SEARCY
| ❏ 711 | Torquay '65/Wee Wee Hours | 1965 | $60 |

LARRY AND THE LEGENDS
ATLANTIC
| ❏ 2220 | Don't Pick On My Baby/The Creep | 1964 | $30 |

— With the Four Seasons

LARSON, NICOLETTE
MCA
❏ 52653	Building Bridges/You Were the One	1985	$4
❏ 52797	Let Me Be the First/If I Didn't Love You	1986	$4
❏ 52528	Only Love Will Make It Right/Blow on Chilly Wind	1985	$4
❏ 52839	That's How You Know When Love's Right/As an Eagle Stirreth Her Nest	1986	$4
❏ 52937	That's More About Love (Than I Wanted to Know)/Captured by Love	1986	$4
❏ 52571	When You Get a Little Lonely/I Just Keep Falling in Love	1985	$4

WARNER BROS.
❏ 49520	Back in My Arms/Just in the Nick of Time	1980	$4
❏ 49820	Fool Me Again/Arthur's Theme (Instrumental)	1981	$4
❏ 29948	I Only Want to Be with You/Now We Can Go Home	1982	$4
❏ 49130	Let Me Go, Love/Trouble	1979	$4
❏ 49130 [PS]	Let Me Go, Love/Trouble	1979	$6
❏ 8664	Lotta Love/Angels Rejoiced	1978	$5
❏ 8851	Mexican Divorce/Give a Little	1979	$5
❏ 49666	Ooo-Eee/Straight from the Heart	1981	$4
❏ 49710	When You Come Around/How Can We Go On	1981	$4

LASALLE, DENISE
ABC
❏ 12238	Freedom to Express Yourself/Second Breath	1977	$4
❏ 12225	Hellfire Loving/I Get What I Want	1976	$30
❏ 12312	Love Me Right/Fool Me Good	1977	$4
❏ 12353	One Life to Live/Before You Take It to the Streets	1978	$4
❏ 12443	P.A.R.T.Y. (Where It Is)/Under the Influence	1979	$4
❏ 12419	Workin' Overtime/No Matter What They Say	1978	$40

CHESS
❏ 2005	A Love Reputation/One Little Thing	1967	$125
❏ 2058	Count Down (And Fly Me to the Moon)/A Promise Is a Promise	1968	$30
❏ 2044	Private Property/I've Been Waiting	1968	$10

MALACO
❏ 2152	Bring It On Home to Me/Write This One Off (As Actors)	1987	$4
❏ 2156	Caught in Your Mess/I Forgot to Remember	1987	$4
❏ 2167	Drop That Zero/Chain Letter	1988	$4
❏ 2138	Hold What You Got/Footsteps of a Fool	1986	$4
❏ 2112	My Tu-Tu/Give Me Yo' Strongest Whiskey	1985	$4
❏ 2124	Santa Claus Got the Blues/Love Is a Five Letter Word	1985	$5
❏ 2105	Treat Your Man Like a Baby/Come to Bed	1985	$4
❏ 2131	What's Going On in My House/He's That Way Sometime	1986	$4

MCA
❏ 41222	I'm So Hot/Miracle, You and Me	1980	$4
❏ 51046	I'm Trippin' on You/I'll Get You Some Help	1981	$4
❏ 51098	Sharing Your Love/I'll Get You Some Help	1981	$4

TARPEN
| ❏ 6603 | A Love Reputation/One Little Thing | 1967 | $30 |

WESTBOUND
❏ 221	Don't Nobody Live Here (By the Name of Fool)/Goody Goody Getter	1973	$6
❏ 223	Get Up Off My Mind/The Best Thing I Ever Had	1974	$6
❏ 162	Heartbreaker of the Year/Hung Up, Strung Out	1971	$30
❏ 5008	Here I Am Again/Hung Up, Strung Out	1975	$70
❏ 206	Man Sized Job/I'm Over You	1972	$6
❏ 5019	Married, But Not to Each Other/Who's the Fool	1976	$5
❏ 5004	My Brand on You/Anytime Is the Right Time	1975	$5
❏ 182	Trapped by a Thing Called Love/Keep It Coming	1971	$20
❏ 229	Trying to Forget/We've Got Love	1974	$6
❏ 215	What It Takes to Get a Good Woman (That's What It's Gonna Take to Keep Her)/Making a Good Thing Better	1973	$6

LAST, JAMES
MGM
| ❏ 13599 | Lara's Theme/Games That Lovers Play | 1966 | $12 |

POLYDOR
❏ 2108	Fantasy/Last Glow	1980	$3
❏ 15024	Girl of the North Country/The Party Is Over	1971	$4
❏ 15004	Happy Heart/A Man and a Woman	1969	$4
❏ 15050	Heart of Gold/It's Going to Take Some Time	1972	$4
❏ 15028	Music from Across the Way/Endless Journey	1971	$4
❏ 15017	Proud Mary/Washington Square	1970	$4
❏ 2119	So Excited/Last Glow	1980	$3
❏ 15108	Summertime/Love for Sale	1975	$4
❏ 2071	The Seduction (Love Theme)/Night Drive	1980	$3
❏ 15045	Wedding Song (There Is Love)/Love Must Be the Reason	1972	$4

LAST POETS, THE
BLUE THUMB
| ❏ 216 | Tribute to Orabi/Bird's Word | 1972 | $15 |

DOUGLAS
❏ ADS8	O.D./Black Thighs	1971	$20
❏ ADS8 [PS]	O.D./Black Thighs	1971	$40
❏ ZS76500	True Blues/Black Is	1971	$15

LAST RIGHTS
TAANG!
| ❏ 2 | Chunks/So Ends Our Night | 1984 | $20 |
| ❏ 2 [PS] | Chunks/So Ends Our Night | 1984 | $20 |

— White cardboard with band member "Choke" swinging the mike stand

| ❏ 2 [PS] | Chunks/So Ends Our Night | 1984 | $27 |

— Mike stand edition with four inserts with a different photo

| ❏ 2 [PS] | Chunks/So Ends Our Night | 1984 | $20 |

— Shirtless "Choke" edition, another live shot

| ❏ 2 [PS] | Chunks/So Ends Our Night | 1984 | $75 |

— Hitler" version: two-piece white outersleeve over regular white sleeve

| ❏ 2 [PS] | Chunks/So Ends Our Night | 1984 | $75 |

— Hitler" version on green paper

LAST, THE
BACKLASH
❏ 003	L.A. Explosion/Hitler's Brother	1978	$8
❏ 003 [PS]	L.A. Explosion/Hitler's Brother	1978	$8
❏ 01	She Don't Know Why I'm Here/Bombing of London	1978	$40
❏ 01 [PS]	She Don't Know Why I'm Here/Bombing of London	1978	$40

BOMP!
❏ 126	Every Summer's Day/Slavedriver	1979	$6
❏ 126 [PS]	Every Summer's Day/Slavedriver	1979	$6
❏ 119	She Don't Know Why I'm Here/Bombing of London	1978	$3
❏ 119 [PS]	She Don't Know Why I'm Here/Bombing of London	1978	$3

LATEEF, YUSEF
ARGO
| ❏ 5292 | Cookin'/Marching Piper Blues | 1958 | $15 |

Number	Title	Yr	NM

ATLANTIC

Number	Title	Yr	NM
❏ 5104	Buddy and Lou/Russel and Eliot	1971	$5
❏ 2562	Othelia/Stay with Me	1968	$6
❏ 2997	Superfine/Down in Atlanta	1973	$5
❏ 223	Theme from "The Prize"/Megeve	1963	$8

PRESTIGE

Number	Title	Yr	NM
❏ 332	Blues for the Orient/I'll Remember April	1964	$8
❏ 127	Love and Humor/Meditation	1957	$15
❏ 254	Love Theme from "Spartacus"/Snafu	1960	$10

RIVERSIDE

Number	Title	Yr	NM
❏ 445	Goin' Home/Salt Water Blues	1960	$10

LATIMORE

ATLANTIC

Number	Title	Yr	NM
❏ 2639	I Pity the Fool/I'm Just an Ordinary Man	1969	$8

DADE

Number	Title	Yr	NM
❏ 2013	Girl, I Got News for You/Ain't Gonna Cry No More	1967	$10
❏ 2020	Have a Little Faith/I'm a Believer	1968	$12
❏ 2026	I'll Be Good to You/Life's Little Ups and Downs	1969	$10
❏ 2022	I Pity the Fool/I'm Just an Ordinary Man	1968	$10
❏ 2015	It's Just a Matter of Time/Let's Move and Groove Together	1967	$10
❏ 2017	The Power and the Glory/Love Don't Love Me	1968	$10
❏ 2014	There She Is/It Was So Nice While It Lasted	1967	$10

GLADES

Number	Title	Yr	NM
❏ 1750	Dig a Little Deeper/Let Me Go	1978	$6
❏ 1756	Discoed to Death/Just One Step	1979	$6
❏ 1755	Goodbye Heartache/We Got to Hit It Off	1979	$6
❏ 1720	If You Were My Woman/Put Pride Aside	1974	$6
❏ 1742	I Get Lifted/All the Way Lover	1977	$6
❏ 1744	Let Me Live the Life I Love/It Ain't Where You Been	1977	$6
❏ 1722	Let's Straighten It Out/Ain't Nobody Gonna Make Me Change My Mind	1974	$6
❏ 1752	Long Distance Love/Out to Get 'Cha	1979	$6
❏ 1739	Somethin' 'Bout 'Cha/Sweet Vibrations	1976	$6
❏ 1716	Stormy Monday/There's No End	1973	$6
❏ 1761	Take Me to the Mountaintop/Joy	1980	$6
❏ 1729	There's a Red-Neck in the Soul Band/Just One Step	1975	$6
❏ 2083	Let the Doorknob Hit'cha/Do That To Me One More Time	1982	$4
❏ 2099	One Shirt, Soulless Shoes/You	1984	$4
❏ 2130	Sunshine Lady/There's No Limit to My Love	1986	$4

LATIN SOULS, THE

KAPP

Number	Title	Yr	NM
❏ 898	I've Got You/Look But Don't Touch	1968	$8
❏ 844	La Bamba/The Party Is Over	1967	$8

LATTIMORE, ALMETA

MAINSTREAM

Number	Title	Yr	NM
❏ 5575	These Memories/Oh My Love	1974	$500
❏ 5575 [DJ]	These Memories/Oh My Love	1974	$400

LATTIMORE, BENNY

HIT

Number	Title	Yr	NM
❏ 15	Snap Your Fingers/I Sold My Heart to the Junkman	1962	$8

—B-side by Peggy Thompson

LATTISAW, STACY, AND JOHNNY GILL

COTILLION

Number	Title	Yr	NM
❏ 99750	Baby It's You/50-50 Love	1984	$4
❏ 99725	Block Party/Come Out of the Shadows	1984	$4
❏ 99785	Perfect Combination/Heartbreak Look	1984	$4

MOTOWN

Number	Title	Yr	NM
❏ 2026	Where Do We Go from Here/(Instrumental)	1989	$5

LATTISAW, STACY

COTILLION

Number	Title	Yr	NM
❏ 99968	Attack of the Name Game/I Could Love You So Divine	1982	$5

Number	Title	Yr	NM
❏ 47011	Don't Throw It All Away/Down for You	1982	$5
❏ 45015	Dynamite!/Dreaming	1982	$5
❏ 46026	Feel My Love Tonight/Young Girl	1981	$5
❏ 99614	He's Just Not You/Coming Alive	1985	$4
❏ 99943	Hey There Lonely Boy/Tonight I'm Gonna Make You Mine	1982	$5
❏ 99635	I'm Not the Same Girl/Toughen Up	1985	$4
❏ 99635 [PS]	I'm Not the Same Girl/Toughen Up	1985	$4
❏ 46024	It Was So Easy/Screaming Off the Top	1981	$5
❏ 46001	Let Me Be Your Angel/You Don't Love Me Anymore	1980	$5
❏ 46015	Love On a Two-Way Street/Baby I Love You	1981	$5
❏ 99819	Million Dollar Babe/The Ways of Love	1983	$5
❏ 99855	Miracles/Black Pumps and Pink Lipstick	1983	$5
❏ 44250	When You're Young and In Love/Three Wishes	1979	$6
❏ 44250 [PS]	When You're Young and In Love/Three Wishes	1979	$6

MOTOWN

Number	Title	Yr	NM
❏ 1945	Call Me/Call Me (With Rap)	1988	$3
❏ 1945 [PS]	Call Me/Call Me (With Rap)	1988	$4
❏ 1912	Every Drop of Your Love/Long Shot	1987	$3
❏ 1912 [PS]	Every Drop of Your Love/Long Shot	1987	$4
❏ 1934	Let Me Take You Down/The Hard Way	1988	$3
❏ 1891	Take Me All the Way/Little Bit of Heaven	1987	$3
❏ 1978	What You Need/(Instrumental)	1989	$3

LAUGHNER, PETER

FORCED EXPOSURE

Number	Title	Yr	NM
❏ FE-018 [PS]	Cinderella Backstreet/White Light White Heat	1987	$10
❏ FE-018	Cinderella Backstreet/White Light White Heat	1987	$10

— Pre-Pere Ubu recordings from 1973-75, not issued until '87

LAUGHTON, CHARLES

DECCA

Number	Title	Yr	NM
❏ 23365	The Oldest Christmas Story/The Story of the Three Wise Men	1950	$20

— 78 rpm released in 1944

LAUPER, CYNDI

EPIC

Number	Title	Yr	NM
❏ 34-07940	Hole in My Heart (All the Way to China)/Boy Blue (Live)	1988	$3
❏ 34-07940 [PS]	Hole in My Heart (All the Way to China)/Boy Blue (Live)	1988	$3
❏ 34-68759	I Drove All Night/Maybe He'll Know	1989	$3
❏ 34-68945	My First Night Without You/Unabbreviated Love	1989	$4
❏ 15-08443	True Colors/What's Going On	1988	$3

—Reissue

PORTRAIT

Number	Title	Yr	NM
❏ 37-04639	All Through the Night/Witness	1984	$3
❏ 37-04639 [PS]	All Through the Night/Witness	1984	$3
❏ 37-07181	Boy Blue/The Faraway Nearby	1987	$3
❏ 37-07181 [PS]	Boy Blue/The Faraway Nearby	1987	$20
❏ 37-06431 [DJ]	Change of Heart (3:58)/(4:24)	1986	$6
❏ 37-06431	Change of Heart/Witness	1986	$3
❏ 37-06431 [PS]	Change of Heart/Witness	1986	$3
❏ 37-04120 [PS]	Girls Just Want to Have Fun	1983	$8

—Demonstration -- Not for Sale" on back

Number	Title	Yr	NM
❏ 37-04120	Girls Just Want to Have Fun/Right Track Wrong Train	1983	$3
❏ 37-04120 [PS]	Girls Just Want to Have Fun/Right Track Wrong Train	1983	$8
❏ 37-04737	Money Changes Everything (Studio)/(Live)	1984	$3
❏ 37-04737 [PS]	Money Changes Everything (Studio)/(Live)	1984	$3
❏ 37-04516	She Bop/Witness	1984	$3
❏ 37-04516 [PS]	She Bop/Witness	1984	$3
❏ 34-04918	The Goonies 'R' Good Enough/What a Thrill	1985	$3
❏ 34-04918 [PS]	The Goonies 'R' Good Enough/What a Thrill	1985	$3

— Picture sleeve claims to be on "Epic" but the record is on Portrait

Number	Title	Yr	NM
❏ 37-04432	Time After Time/I'll Kiss You	1984	$3
❏ 37-06247	True Colors/Heading for the Moon	1986	$3
❏ 37-06247 [PS]	True Colors/Heading for the Moon	1986	$3
❏ 37-06970	What's Going On/One Track Mind	1987	$3
❏ 37-06970 [PS]	What's Going On/One Track Mind	1987	$3

LAURELS, THE (1)

ABC-PARAMOUNT

Number	Title	Yr	NM
❏ 10048	Hand in Hand/Picture of Love	1959	$60

LAURELS, THE (2)

X

Number	Title	Yr	NM
❏ 0143	Truly, Truly/'Tis Night	1955	$250

LAURELS, THE (U)

SPRING

Number	Title	Yr	NM
❏ 1112	Baby Talk/You Left Me	1959	$70

LAUREN, ROD

CHANCELLOR

Number	Title	Yr	NM
❏ 1126	I Ain't Got You/Mexicali Rose	1962	$15
❏ 1141	I Wanna Know/Searcher for Love	1963	$15
❏ 1146	Let Me Tell You 'Bout My Baby/I can't Get You Out of My Heart	1963	$15
❏ 1132	Oh How I Miss You Tonight/Blame Your Friends	1963	$15

RCA VICTOR

Number	Title	Yr	NM
❏ 47-7786	A Wild Imagination/The One Finger Symphony	1960	$20
❏ 47-8020	I Dreamed/A Wondrous Place	1962	$15
❏ 47-7645	If I Had a Girl/No Wonder	1959	$20
❏ 47-7645 [PS]	If I Had a Girl/No Wonder	1959	$30
❏ 47-7720	Listen My Love/This I Know	1960	$20

LAURIE, ANNIE

DELUXE

Number	Title	Yr	NM
❏ 6189	If You're Lonely/It's Gonna Come Out in the Wash Someday	1960	$20
❏ 6107	It Hurts to Be in Love/Hand in Hand	1957	$30
❏ 6135	It Must Be You/Please Honey Don't Go	1957	$20
❏ 6151	Love Is a Funny Thing/Nobody's Gonna Hurt You Baby	1957	$20
❏ 6182	Since I Fell for You/Lost Love	1959	$20
❏ 6173	Someday Someway/Hold On to What You Got	1958	$20

OKEH

Number	Title	Yr	NM
❏ 7025	I'm in the Mood for You/Feeling the Need	1954	$30
❏ 6973	It's Been a Long, Long Time/I Ain't Got It Bad No More	1953	$30
❏ 6933	Stop Talkin' and Start Walkin'/Give Me Half a Chance	1953	$30

LAURIE, LINDA

ANDIE

Number	Title	Yr	NM
❏ 5015	All Winter Long/Stay with Me	1960	$15

GLORY

Number	Title	Yr	NM
❏ 290	Ambrose (Part Five)/Ooh! What a Lover	1958	$20
❏ 294	Forever Ambrose/Wherever He Goes, I Go	1959	$15

MCA

Number	Title	Yr	NM
❏ 40119	Leave Me Alone (Ruby Red Dress)/Sweet Deceiver	1973	$6

RUST

Number	Title	Yr	NM
❏ 5022	Prince Charming/Soupin' Up Your Motor	1960	$10
❏ 5042	Stay at Home Sue/Lazy Love	1961	$10

LAVELLE, RONNIE

PARKWAY

Number	Title	Yr	NM
❏ 831	Cartoons/The Crazy Way of Love	1961	$15
❏ 837	Let Her Go/A Dog's Life	1962	$15

LAVETTE, BETTY

ATCO

Number	Title	Yr	NM
❏ 6891	Heart of Gold/You'll Wake Up Wisely	1972	$50

ATLANTIC

Number	Title	Yr	NM
❏ 2160	My Man -- He's a Lovin' Man/Shut Your Mouth	1962	$40

—As "Betty LaVett"

CALLA

Number	Title	Yr	NM
❏ 104	I Feel Good (All Over)/Only Your Love Can Save Me	1965	$80

Number	Title	Yr	NM
102	Let Me Down Easy/What I Don't Know (Won't Hurt Me)	1965	$40
106	Stand Up Like a Man/I'm Just a Fool for You	1965	$50

KAREN

Number	Title	Yr	NM
1544	Get Away/What Condition My Condition Is In	1968	$200
1540	Love Makes the World Go Round/Almost	1968	$50
1548	Ticket to the Moon/Let Me Down Easy	1969	$8
1545	With a Little Help from My Friends/Hey Love	1969	$30

LUPINE

Number	Title	Yr	NM
123	Witch Craft in the Air/You Killed the Love	1964	$50

—As "Betty LaVett"

Number	Title	Yr	NM
1021	Witch Craft in the Air/You Killed the Love	1964	$30

—As "Betty LaVett"

MOTOWN

Number	Title	Yr	NM
1614	Either Way, We Lose/I Can't Stop	1982	$5

—As "Bettye LaVette"

SILVER FOX

Number	Title	Yr	NM
21	Do Your Duty/Love's Made a Fool Out of Me	1970	$6
24	Games People Play/My Train's Comin' In	1970	$6
17	He Made a Woman Out of Me/Nearer to You	1969	$6

SSS INTERNATIONAL

Number	Title	Yr	NM
839	Take Another Piece of My Heart/At the Mercy of a Man	1971	$6

WEST END

Number	Title	Yr	NM
1213	Doin' the Best That I Can/(Instrumental)	1983	$20

—As "Bettye LaVette"

LAWRENCE, BILL

BERTRAM INT'L.

Number	Title	Yr	NM
207	Hey Baby!/Caribbean	1959	$125
227	Please Don't Leave Me/Billy Boy	1960	$70

FREEDOM

Number	Title	Yr	NM
44004	Hey Baby!/Caribbean	1958	$200

LAWRENCE, EDDIE

CORAL

Number	Title	Yr	NM
61821	Abner the Baseball (Part 1)/Abner the Baseball (Part 2)	1957	$15
61799	German Baseball/Golden Baskos	1957	$15
61168	Old, Old Vienna (Part 1)/Old, Old Vienna (Part 2)	1954	$15
62005	The Good Old Days/Hi-Fi Blues	1958	$15
61915	The Merry Old Philosopher/That Holiday Spirit	1957	$30
62367	The Mets' Philosopher/We Love the Mets	1963	$20
62070	The Mother Philosopher/The Salesman's Philosopher	1959	$10
61671	The Old Philosopher/King Arthur's Mine	1956	$20
61863	The Old Philosopher on the Range/Memories of Louise	1957	$15
61978	The Philosopher Strikes Back/Frankensteiner Polka	1958	$15
62298	The Philosopher Twist/The D.J. Philosopher Returns	1961	$10
62049	The Space Philosopher/Outta This World	1958	$15
62267	The Suburban Philosopher/We Sure Had Fun	1961	$10

EPIC

Number	Title	Yr	NM
9804	The World's Fair Philosopher/The Old Philosopher and the Single Girl	1965	$15

SIGNATURE

Number	Title	Yr	NM
12031	Anyone for President/Unequal	1960	$10
12010	The Doctor's Philosopher/Blackouts of 1984	1960	$12

LAWRENCE, STEVE, AND EYDIE GORME

ABC-PARAMOUNT

Number	Title	Yr	NM
10104	This Could Be the Start of Something Big/Darn It, Baby, That's Love	1960	$10

CALENDAR

Number	Title	Yr	NM
63-1003	Two of Us/Mr. Spoons	1968	$6

COLUMBIA

Number	Title	Yr	NM
44123	Cabaret/Mame	1967	$6
43179	Happy Holiday/That Holiday Feeling	1964	$12
42932	I Can't Stop Talking About You/To the Movies We Go	1963	$8
42815	I Want to Stay Here/Ain't Love	1963	$8
4-42815 [DJ]	I Want to Stay Here (same on both sides)	1963	$30

—Promo only on red vinyl

Number	Title	Yr	NM
44228	Summer Wind/Be Still	1967	$6

CORAL

Number	Title	Yr	NM
61411	Besame Mucho/Close Your Eyes, Take a Deep Breath	1955	$15
61313	Make Yourself Comfortable/I've Gotta Crow	1954	$15

MGM

Number	Title	Yr	NM
14493	Feelin'/Lead Me On	1973	$4
14340	Lead Me On/Tea for Two	1971	$4
14383	We Can Make It Together/E Fini	1972	$4

—With the Osmonds

RCA VICTOR

Number	Title	Yr	NM
74-0123	Chapter One/Real True Lovin'	1969	$5
47-9656	Dear World/A Break at Love	1968	$5
74-0386	For All We Know/Did You Give the World My Love Today, Babe	1970	$5
47-9694	Hurry Home for Christmas/Dedicated to Love	1968	$8
74-0420	Love Is Blue-Autumn Leaves/Hi Sweetie	1971	$5

UNITED ARTISTS

Number	Title	Yr	NM
282	The Facts of Life/I'm a Girl, You're a Boy	1960	$10

LAWRENCE, STEVE

ABC-PARAMOUNT

Number	Title	Yr	NM
10146	Come Back Silly Girl/Going Steady	1960	$10
10085	Footsteps/You Don't Know	1960	$10
10005	(I Don't Care) Only Love Me/Loving Is a Way of Living	1959	$10
10058	Pretty Blue Eyes/You're Nearer	1959	$10
10031	There'll Be Some Changes Made/You're Everything Wonderful	1959	$10

CALENDAR

Number	Title	Yr	NM
63-1001	I've Gotta Be Me/Love's a Game	1968	$6

COLUMBIA

Number	Title	Yr	NM
42455	A House Without Windows/The Endless Night	1962	$10
44022	Did I Ever Really Live/Girl in the White Glove	1967	$6
42699	Don't Be Afraid, Little Darlin'/Don't Come Runnin' Back	1963	$8
42699 [PS]	Don't Be Afraid, Little Darlin'/Don't Come Runnin' Back	1963	$15
43047	Everybody Knows/One Love Too Late	1964	$8
42601	Go Away Little Girl/If You Love Her Tell Her So	1962	$8
42601 [PS]	Go Away Little Girl/If You Love Her Tell Her So	1962	$15
S731547 [S]	It's a Sin to Tell a Lie/I'll Always Be in Love with You	1962	$15
44514	I Want to Be with You/Dulcinea	1968	$6
43192	I Will Wait for You/Bewitched	1964	$8
42952	My Home Town/A Room Without Windows	1964	$8
42795	Poor Little Rich Girl/(Theme from Mondo Cane)	1963	$8
44084	The Impossible Dream/Sweet Maria	1967	$6
42396	The Lady Wants to Twist/Tell Her I Said Hello	1962	$10
S731546 [S]	(titles unknown)	1962	$15
S731548 [S]	(titles unknown)	1962	$15
S731549 [S]	(titles unknown)	1962	$15

—The above five are "Stereo Seven" 33 1/3 rpm jukebox singles from "JS 7-62"

Number	Title	Yr	NM
42865	Walking Proud/All the Way Home	1963	$8
42865 [PS]	Walking Proud/All the Way Home	1963	$15

CORAL

Number	Title	Yr	NM
61537	Adelaide/The Lord Is a Busy Man	1955	$15
61904	A Long Last Look/At a Time Like This	1957	$15
62080	Blah, Blah, Blah/Lover in the House	1959	$10
61834	Can't Wait for Summer/Fabulous	1957	$15
61667	Ethel Baby/Never My Love	1956	$15
61876	Fraulein/Blue Rememberin' You	1957	$15
61925	Geisha Girl/I Don't Know	1958	$15
62052	I Only Have Eyes for You/These Things Are Free	1958	$10
62025	Many a Time/All About Love	1958	$10
61486	Open Up the Gates of Mercy/My Impression of Jamie	1955	$15
61792	Party Doll/(The Bad Donkey) Pum-Pa-Lum	1957	$20
61563	Speedoo/The Chicken and the Hawk	1956	$15
61992	Stranger in Mexico/Those Nights at the Round Table	1958	$10
61279	Tell Me What to Do (To Make You Mine)/Willow	1954	$15
61761	The Banana Boat Song/Long Before I Knew You	1956	$15

KING

Number	Title	Yr	NM
15208	How Many Stars Have to Shine/Tango	1952	$30
15190	Poinciana/All My Love Belongs to You	1952	$30
5360	Poinciana/Mine and Mine Alone	1960	$10
15199	Sudden Fear/Always Love Me	1952	$30
15218	Tomorrow/If Not for You	1953	$30
1223	To the Birds/With Every Breath I Take	1953	$30

MGM

Number	Title	Yr	NM
14368	Ain't No Sunshine-You Are My Sunshine/In My Own Lifetime	1972	$4
14257	Lookin' Good/Frosty Morning	1971	$4
14531	The Best Thing That Ever Happened (To Me)/Hello, Los Angeles	1973	$4
14631	The End/You Light Up My Life	1973	$4
14288	The Last Run/Frosty Morning	1971	$4

RCA VICTOR

Number	Title	Yr	NM
74-0303	Cry for Us All/Mama, a Rainbow	1969	$5
74-0357	Groovin'/Being Alone	1970	$5
74-0169	Pickin' Up the Pieces/I've Got My Eyes on You	1969	$5
74-0237	The Drifter/To Say Goodbye	1969	$5

UNITED ARTISTS

Number	Title	Yr	NM
XW1050	Everytime I Sing a Love Song/I Wasn't Man Enough	1977	$4
233	Girls, Girls, Girls/Little Boy Blue	1960	$10
233 [PS]	Girls, Girls, Girls/Little Boy Blue	1960	$30
335	My Clair de Lune/In Time	1961	$8
403	Our Concerto/Send Someone to Love Me	1962	$8
291	Portrait of My Love/Oh How You Lied	1961	$8
364	Somewhere Along the Way/While There's Still Time	1961	$8
240	Tears from Heaven/Hold Back the Dike	1960	$10

WARNER BROS.

Number	Title	Yr	NM
8584	Take My Hand/Don't Wish Too Hard	1978	$4

7-Inch Extended Plays

COLUMBIA

Number	Title	Yr	NM
7-9565 [DJ]	Go Away Little Girl/More/Millions of Roses//The Impossible Dream (The Quest)/Sweet Maria/Love Me with All Your Heart	1967	$10

—Stereo Seven" jukebox issue, small hole

Number	Title	Yr	NM
7-9565 [PS]	Steve Lawrence's Greatest Hits	1967	$12

LAWRENCE, SYD

COSMIC

Number	Title	Yr	NM
1001	The Answer to the Flying Saucer/Haunted Guitar	1956	$50

—B-side by Billy Mure

LAWRENCE, VICKI

BELL

Number	Title	Yr	NM
45362	He Did with Me/Mr. Allison	1973	$4
45437	Mama's Gonna Make It Better/Cameo	1974	$4
45409	Sensual Man/Ships in the Night	1973	$4

ELF

Number	Title	Yr	NM
90035	And I'll Go/The Whole State of Alabama	1970	$6

PRIVATE STOCK

Number	Title	Yr	NM
45,121	Love in the Hot Afternoon/(B-side unknown)	1976	$4
45,036	The Other Woman/Cameo	1975	$4
45,067	There's a Gun Still Smokin' in Nashville	1976	$4

LAWS, HUBERT

ATLANTIC

Number	Title	Yr	NM
5046	Miss Thing/Blue Eyed Peas and Rice	1965	$8

COLUMBIA

Number	Title	Yr	NM
10736	False Faces/The Baron	1978	$4
02694	Goodbye for Now (Theme from "Reds")/(Instrumental)	1982	$4
10811	It Happens Every Day/Love Gets Better	1978	$4
11022	Land of Passion/Heartbeats	1979	$4
11368	Wildfire/Family	1980	$4

CTI

Number	Title	Yr	NM
13	Amazing Grace (Part 1)/Amazing Grace (Part 2)	1973	$5

Number	Title	Yr	NM
❏ 3	Fire and Rain/Theme from Love Story	1971	$5
❏ 21	Mean Lene/Come All Ye Disconsolate	1974	$5
❏ 27	The Chicago Theme (Love Loop)/I Had a Dream	1975	$5

LAZY COWGIRLS
BOMP!
❏ 137	Sock It To Me Santa/Goddamn Bottle	1986	$12
❏ 137 [PS]	Sock It To Me Santa/Goddamn Bottle	1986	$12

SUB POP
❏ 43	Loretta/Hybrid Moments	1989	$30

—1,000 copies on clear vinyl
❏ 43	Loretta/Hybrid Moments	1989	$5

—Black vinyl
❏ 43 [PS]	Loretta/Hybrid Moments	1989	$5

—#11 in Sub Pop Singles Club series

LEADBELLY
7-Inch Extended Plays
CAPITOL
❏ EAP 1-369	Back Water Blues/Take This Hammer//On a Christmas Day/Irene	1954	$125
❏ EAP 1-369 [PS]	Classics in Jazz, Part 1	1954	$125
❏ EAP 2-369 [PS]	Classics in Jazz, Part 2	1954	$125
❏ EAP 2-369	Sweet Mary Blues/Ella Speed//Tell Me Baby/Western Plain	1954	$125

LEADERS, THE
GLORY
❏ 243	Can't Help Lovin' That Girl of Mine/Lovers	1956	$100
❏ 235	Stormy Weather/A Lover of the Time	1955	$70

LEAPER, BOB
REPRISE
❏ 0274	Sunday Morning/Come and Join Us	1964	$10

LEAPING FERNS, THE
X-PANDED SOUND
❏ 103	It Never Works Out for Me/Maybe Baby	1964	$40

LEAPY LEE
DECCA
❏ 32808	Best to Forget/I'll Be Your Baby Tonight	1971	$6
❏ 32380	Little Arrows/Time Will Tell	1968	$8
❏ 32692	Tupelo Mississippi Flash/Green Green Trees	1970	$6

MAM
❏ 3622	Summer Rain/No Full Moon	1972	$6

MCA
❏ 40470	Every Road Leads Back to You/Honey Go Drift Away	1975	$5

LEARY, DR. TIMOTHY
MERCURY
❏ 72713	Turn On, Tune In, Drop Out (Part 1)/Turn On, Tune In, Drop Out (Part 2)	1967	$40

LEATHER BOY
FLOWER
❏ 100	My Prayer/You Gotta Have Soul	1968	$40

MGM
❏ 13724	I'm a Leather Boy/Shadows	1967	$40
❏ 13724 [PS]	I'm a Leather Boy/Shadows	1967	$70
❏ 13790	On the Go/Soulin'	1967	$40

LEATHERWOOD, BILL
COUNTRY JUBILEE
❏ 539	The Long Walk/(B-side unknown)	1960	$20

LEAVES, THE
CAPITOL
❏ 5799	Lemon Princess/Twilight Sanctuary	1966	$15

MIRA
❏ 220	Be with You/Funny Little World	1966	$60
❏ 234	Be with You/You Better Move On	1966	$50
❏ 231	Get Out of My Life Woman/Girl from the East	1966	$50
❏ 207	Hey Joe, Where You Gonna Go/Be with You	1965	$125
❏ 222	Hey Joe/Funny Little World	1966	$60
❏ 222	Hey Joe/Girl from the East	1966	$50
❏ 202	Love Minus Zero-No Limit/Too Many People	1965	$60
❏ 227	Too Many People/Girl from the East	1966	$50

LED ZEPPELIN
Also see JOHN PAUL JONES; JIMMY PAGE; ROBERT PLANT; THE FIRM.
ATLANTIC
❏ 2849	Black Dog/Misty Mountain Hop	1971	$10
❏ 2613	Communication Breakdown/Good Times Bad Times	1969	$30
❏ 2986	D'yer Mak'er/The Crunge	1973	$6

—Defective pressing -- the left channel starts to fade out midway through the A-side, making it sound like rechanneled stereo. The number "3" follows the matrix number in the trail-off wax of those copies we've encountered.
❏ 2986	D'yer Mak'er/The Crunge	1973	$12

—Normal pressing in true stereo throughout
❏ PR157 [DJ]	Gallows Pole (mono/stereo)	1971	$200
❏ 2777 [DJ]	Immigrant Song	1970	$120

—One-sided promo
❏ 2777	Immigrant Song/Hey, Hey, What Can I Do	1970	$30

—First pressings with "Do What Thou Wilt Shalt Be the Whole of the Law" in trail-off
❏ 2777	Immigrant Song/Hey, Hey, What Can I Do	1971	$20

—Second pressings without "Do What Thou Wilt Shalt Be the Whole of the Law" in trail-off; no Warner Commuications logo in perimeter print
❏ 2777	Immigrant Song/Hey, Hey, What Can I Do	1977	$8

—Third pressings with smaller, bolder type and Warner Communications logo in perimeter print; available well into the late 1980s
❏ 2970	Over the Hills & Far Away/Dancing Days	1973	$10
❏ PR175 [DJ]	Stairway to Heaven (mono/stereo)	1972	$125
❏ PR175 [PS]	Stairway to Heaven (mono/stereo)	1972	$250
❏ PR269 [DJ]	Stairway to Heaven (stereo/stereo)	1973	$60
❏ 2690	Whole Lotta Love/Living Loving Maid (She's Just a Woman)	1969	$20

—With A-side time of 3:12
❏ 2690	Whole Lotta Love/Living Loving Maid (She's Just a Woman)	1969	$30

—With A-side time of 5:33; no Warner Communications logo in perimeter print

SWAN SONG
❏ 70110	Candy Store Rock/Royal Orleans	1976	$6
❏ 71003	Fool in the Rain/Hot Dog	1979	$6
❏ 71003 [DJ]	Fool in the Rain (Short 3:20)/(Long 6:08)	1979	$20
❏ 70102	Trampled Under Foot/Black Country Woman	1975	$6

7-Inch Extended Plays
ATLANTIC
❏ SD 7-7208	Black Dog/Rock and Roll//Stairway to Heaven	1972	$125

—Jukebox issue; small hole, plays at 33 1/3 rpm
❏ SD 7-7255	Dancing Days/D'yer Mak'er//The Song Remains the Same/The Crunge	1973	$100

—Jukebox issue; small hole, plays at 33 1/3 rpm
❏ SD 7-7255 [PS]	Houses of the Holy	1973	$125
❏ SD 7-7208 [PS]	Led Zeppelin (IV)	1972	$175

LEE, ALVIN
Also see TEN YEARS AFTER.
21 RECORDS
❏ 99527	Detroit Diesel/Let's Go	1986	$3
❏ 99501	Heart of Stone/She's So Cute	1986	$3

ATLANTIC
❏ 4004 [DJ]	Can't Stop (same on both sides)	1982	$4

—May be promo only
COLUMBIA
❏ 45987	So Sad/Riffin'	1974	$4

—With Mylon LeFevre

LEE AND THE LEOPARDS
FORTUNE
❏ 867	What About Me/Don't Press Your Luck	1964	$60

GORDY
❏ 7002	Come Into My Palace/Trying to Make It	1962	$70

LAURIE
❏ 3197	Come Into My Palace/Trying to Make It	1963	$30

LEE, BILLY, AND THE RIVIERAS
HYLAND
❏ 3016	Won't You Dance with Me/You Know	1964	$30

LEE, BRENDA
DECCA
❏ 31970	Ain't Gonna Cry No More/It Takes One to Know One	1966	$8
❏ 30411	Ain't That Love/One Teenager to Another	1957	$30
❏ 31424 [PS]	All Alone Am I/Save All Your Lovin' for Me	1962	$30
❏ 31424	All Alone Am I/Save All Your Lovin' for Me	1962	$20
❏ 31628	Alone with You/My Dreams	1964	$10
❏ 31628 [PS]	Alone with You/My Dreams	1964	$20
❏ 32975	Always on My Mind/That Ain't Right	1972	$6
❏ 31570	As Usual/Lonely Lonely Lonely Me	1963	$20
❏ 30806	Bill Bailey Won't You Please Come Home/Hummin' the Blues	1959	$30
❏ 32119	Born to Be By Your Side/Take Me	1967	$8
❏ 31348 [PS]	Break It To Me Gently/So Deep	1962	$30
❏ 31348	Break It To Me Gently/So Deep	1962	$20
❏ 32299	Cabaret/Mood Indigo	1968	$8

—With Pete Fountain
❏ 88215	Christy Christmas/I'm Gonna Lasso Santa Claus	1956	$60

—As "Little Brenda Lee" on Decca's Children's Series
❏ 88215 [PS]	Christy Christmas/I'm Gonna Lasso Santa Claus	1956	$100
❏ 30107	Christy Christmas/I'm Gonna Lasso Santa Claus	1956	$30
❏ 32018	Coming On Strong/You Keep Coming Back to Me	1966	$8
❏ 32734	Do Right Woman, Do Right Man/Sisters in Sorrow	1970	$6
❏ 31272	Dum Dum/Eventually	1961	$20
❏ 30333	Dynamite/Love You 'Til I Die	1957	$30
❏ 31195 [PS]	Emotions/I'm Learning About Love	1961	$40
❏ 31195	Emotions/I'm Learning About Love	1961	$20
❏ 31379	Everybody Loves Me But You/Here Comes That Feelin'	1962	$20
❏ 31309 [PS]	Fool #1/Anybody But Me	1961	$40
❏ 31309	Fool #1/Anybody But Me	1961	$20
❏ 7-34063 [S]	Fools Rush In (Where Angels Fear to Tread)/I'll Always Be in Love with You	1962	$30
❏ 31407	Heart in Hand/It Started All Over Again	1962	$20
❏ 7-34062 [S]	How Deep Is the Ocean (How High Is the Sky)/Send Me Some Lovin'	1962	$30
❏ 32848	If This Is Our Last Time/Everybody's Reaching Out for Someone	1971	$6
❏ 38275 [S]	If You Love Me (Really Love Me)/Just Another Lie	1961	$30
❏ 7-34064 [S]	I'll Be Seeing You/Hold Me	1962	$30

—The above five are 7-inch 33 1/3 rpm singles with small holes
❏ 32918	I'm a Memory/Misty Memories	1972	$6
❏ 38279 [S]	I'm in the Mood for Love/Cry	1961	$30

—The above five are 7-inch 33 1/3 rpm singles with small holes
❏ 31093 [PS]	I'm Sorry/That's All You Gotta Do	1960	$60
❏ 31093	I'm Sorry/That's All You Gotta Do	1960	$30
❏ 31690	Is It True/Just Behind the Rainbow	1964	$10
❏ 31690 [PS]	Is It True/Just Behind the Rainbow	1964	$20
❏ 32675	I Think I Love You Again/Hello Love	1970	$6
❏ 7-34061 [S]	It's the Talk of the Town/You've Got Me Crying Again	1962	$30
❏ 31149 [PS]	I Want to Be Wanted/Just a Little	1960	$50
❏ 31149	I Want to Be Wanted/Just a Little	1960	$20
❏ 7-34060 [S]	Lazy River/You Always Hurt the One You Love	1962	$30
❏ 32560	Let It Be Me/You Better Move On	1969	$6
❏ 30885	Let's Jump the Broomstick/One of These Days	1959	$40
❏ 31478 [PS]	Losing You/He's So Heavenly	1963	$30
❏ 31478	Losing You/He's So Heavenly	1963	$20
❏ 32161	My Heart Keeps Hangin' On/Where Love Is	1967	$8
❏ 31510	My Whole World Is Falling Down/I Wonder	1963	$20
❏ 31510 [PS]	My Whole World Is Falling Down/I Wonder	1963	$30

Number	Title	Yr	NM
30198	One Step at a Time/Fairyland	1957	$30
38277 [S]	Swanee River Rock/Around the World	1961	$30
30967 [PS]	Sweet Nothin's/Weep No More My Baby	1959	$120
30967	Sweet Nothin's/Weep No More My Baby	1959	$30
31728	Thanks a Lot/The Crying Game	1965	$10
32248	That's All Right/Fantasy	1967	$8
31539	The Grass Is Greener/Sweet Impossible You	1963	$20
31539 [PS]	The Grass Is Greener/Sweet Impossible You	1963	$30
31599	Think/The Waiting Game	1964	$10
31599 [PS]	Think/The Waiting Game	1964	$20
31688	This Time of the Year/Christmas Will Be Just Another Lonely Day	1964	$15
31688 [PS]	This Time of the Year/Christmas Will Be Just Another Lonely Day	1964	$20
31917	Too Little Time/Time and Time Again	1966	$8
31792	Too Many Rivers/No One	1965	$10
31762	Truly, Truly, True/I Still Miss Someone	1965	$10
31762 [PS]	Truly, Truly, True/I Still Miss Someone	1965	$20
38276 [S]	When I Fall in Love/Crazy Talk	1961	$30
31654	When You Loved Me/He's Sure to Remember Me	1964	$10
31654 [PS]	When You Loved Me/He's Sure to Remember Me	1964	$20
34494 [DJ]	Where's the Melody? (same on both sides)	1967	$20

— Promo-only number, pink label

Number	Title	Yr	NM
32213	Where's the Melody/Save Me for a Rainy Day	1967	$8
38278 [S]	Will You Love Me Tomorrow/Georgia on My Mind	1961	$30

ELEKTRA

Number	Title	Yr	NM
45492	Left-Over Love/Could It Be I Found Love Tonight	1978	$5

MCA

Number	Title	Yr	NM
52394	A Sweeter Love (I'll Never Know)/A Woman's Mind	1984	$4
40262	Big Four Poster Bed/Castles In The Sand	1974	$5
40442	Bringing It Back/Papa's Knee	1975	$5
41322	Broken Trust/Right Behind The Rain	1980	$5

— With the Oak Ridge Boys

Number	Title	Yr	NM
40584	Brother Shelton/Now He's Coming Home	1976	$5
52268	Didn't We Do It Good/We're So Close	1983	$4
41270	Don't Promise Me Anything (Do It)/You Only Broke My Heart	1980	$5
51154	Enough For You/What Am I Gonna Do	1981	$4
51047	Every Now And Then/He'll Play The Music	1981	$4
40511	Find Yourself Another Puppet/What I Had With You	1976	$5
51113	Fool, Fool/Right Behind The Rain	1981	$4
51230	From Levis to Calvin Klein Jeans/I Know A Lot About Love	1982	$4
40385	He's My Rock/Feel Free	1975	$5
52654	I'm Takin' My Time/That's The Way It Was Then	1985	$4
51195	Only When I Laugh/Too Many Nights Alone	1981	$4
40107	Sunday Sunrise/Must I Believe	1973	$5
40640	Takin' What I Can Get/Your Favorite Wornout Nightmare's Coming Home	1976	$5
41130	Tell Me What It's Like/Let Your Love Fall Back On Me	1979	$5
41187	The Cowgirl And The Dandy/Do You Wanna Spend The Night	1980	$5
52804	Two Hearts/Loving Arms	1986	$4
52804 [DJ]	Two Hearts (same on both sides)	1986	$10

— Promo only on red vinyl

Number	Title	Yr	NM
52720	Why You Been Gone So Long/He Can't Make Your Kind of Love	1985	$4
52720 [PS]	Why You Been Gone So Long/He Can't Make Your Kind of Love	1985	$4
52720 [DJ]	Why You Been Gone So Long (same on both sides)	1985	$10

— Promo only on gold vinyl

Number	Title	Yr	NM
40171	Wrong Ideas/Something For A Rainy Day	1973	$5

7-Inch Extended Plays

DECCA

Number	Title	Yr	NM
ED2738 [PS]	All Alone Am I	1962	$25
7-34107 [PS]	All Alone Am I, Vol. I	1962	$30
7-34108 [PS]	All Alone Am I; Vol. II	1962	$30
7-34108	All Alone Am I/By Myself/I Left My Heart in San Francisco//It's All Right with Me/My Coloring Book/My Prayer	1962	$30

— Jukebox issue; small hole, plays at 33 1/3 rpm

Number	Title	Yr	NM
ED2738	All Alone Am I/It's a Lonely Old Town/Save All Your Loving for Me	1962	$25
7-34107	All By Myself/Lover/What Kind of Fool Am I//Come Rain or Come Shine/I Hadn't Anybody Till You/Fly Me to the Moon	1962	$30

— Jukebox issue; small hole, plays at 33 1/3 rpm

Number	Title	Yr	NM
ED2775 [PS]	As Usual	1963	$25
ED2775	As Usual/The End of the World//There Goes My Heart/Out in the Cold Again	1963	$25
ED2682	Be My Love Again/Just Let Me Dream//Jambalaya/Wee Wee Willie	1960	$25
ED2716 [PS]	Break It to Me Gently	1962	$25
ED2716	Break It to Me Gently/Will You Love Me Tomorrow//Tragedy/So Deep	1962	$25
7-34363 [PS]	Bye Bye Blues	1966	$25
7-34363	Bye Bye Blues/September in the Rain/What a Difference a Day Makes//The Good Life/Shadow of Your Smile/Softly As I Leave You	1966	$25

— Jukebox EP, stereo, small hole, plays at 33 1/3 rpm

Number	Title	Yr	NM
7-34242/3 [PS]	By Request	1964	$25

— Sleeve came with two records, 7-34242 and 7-34243; one record was included in the sleeve, the other was packaged in a company sleeve, and the entire package was enclosed in a plastic bag with jukebox strips; add 100 percent if the strips and plastic bag are included

Number	Title	Yr	NM
DL 734528	Cabaret/Night and Day//One of Those Songs//Anything Goes/There's a Kind of Hush/Can't Take My Eyes Off You	1968	$20

— With Pete Fountain; jukebox issue; small hole, plays at 33 1/3 rpm

Number	Title	Yr	NM
7-4825 [PS]	Coming On Strong	1966	$25
7-34422 [PS]	Coming On Strong	1966	$25
7-34422	Coming On Strong/You Don't Have to Say You Love Me (Io Che Non Vivo) (Senza Te)/What Now My Love (Et Maintenant)//Crying Time/Sweet Dreams/You've Got Your Troubles	1966	$25

— Stereo jukebox issue; small hole, plays at 33 1/3 rpm

Number	Title	Yr	NM
ED2678	(contents unknown)	1960	$25
7-34243	Days of Wine and Roses/Blue Velvet/As Usual//I Love You Because/I'm Confessin' (That I Love You)/My Whole World Is Falling Down	1954	$25

— Jukebox issue; small hole, plays at 33 1/3 rpm; Part 2 of two-record set

Number	Title	Yr	NM
ED2702	Dum Dum/Eventually//When I Fall in Love/Build a Big Fence	1961	$25
ED2683	Dynamite/Heading Home//I'm Sorry/That's All You Gotta Do	1960	$25
ED2725 [PS]	Everybody Loves Me But You	1962	$25
ED2745 [PS]	Fly Me to the Moon	1962	$25
ED2712	Fool #1/Anybody But Me//You Can Depend on Me/It's Never Too Late	1961	$25
DL 734528 [PS]	For the First Time	1968	$25

— With Pete Fountain

Number	Title	Yr	NM
ED2725	Here Comes That Feeling/Everybody Loves Me But You//You've Got Me Crying Again/Lazy River	1962	$25
ED2683 [PS]	I'm Sorry	1960	$25
ED2730	It Started All Over Again/Heart in Hand//You Always Hurt the One You Love/Cry	1962	$25
7-4439 [DJ]	I Wanna Be Around/Our Day Will Come/You're the Reason I'm in Love//End of the World/Losing You/Break It to Me Gently	1963	$25

— Jukebox EP, stereo, small hole, plays at 33 1/3 rpm

Number	Title	Yr	NM
ED2695	I Want to Be Wanted/Just a Little//Teach Me Tonite/Walkin' to New Orleans	1961	$25
7-4439 [PS]	Let Me Sing	1963	$25
7-34204 [PS]	Let Me Sing	1963	$30
ED2704	Lover Come Back to Me	1961	$25
ED2704	Lover Come Back to Me/All the Way//Kansas City/On the Sunny Side of the Street	1961	$25
7-34254 [PS]	Merry Christmas	1964	$30

— Sleeve says this is "DL 74583"; price includes title strips

Number	Title	Yr	NM
7-34242	More (From the Film "Mondo Cane")/I Wonder/Danke Schoen//Tammy/Why Don't You Believe Me/The Grass Is Greener	1964	$25

— Jukebox issue; small hole, plays at 33 1/3 rpm; Part 1 of two-record set

Number	Title	Yr	NM
ED2745	My Coloring Book/I Left My Heart in San Francisco//What Kind of Fool Am I/Fly Me to the Moon	1962	$25
7-4216 [PS]	Sincerely	1962	$25
ED2678 [PS]	Sweet Nothin's	1960	$25
ED2801	Thanks a Lot/Think//Is It True/When You Love Me	1965	$25
7-34204	The End of the World/Our Day Will Come/You're the Reason I'm Living//I Wanna Be Around/Night and Day/Out in the Cold Again	1963	$30

— Jukebox issue; small hole, plays at 33 1/3 rpm

Number	Title	Yr	NM
ED2764 [PS]	The Grass Is Greener	1963	$25
ED2764	The Grass Is Greener/I Wonder//My Whole World Is Falling Down/Losing You	1963	$25
7-34254	This Time of the Year/Blue Christmas/Jingle Bell Rock//Rockin' Around the Christmas Tree/Marshmallow World/Winter Wonderland	1964	$30

— Jukebox EP, stereo, small hole, plays at 33 1/3 rpm

Number	Title	Yr	NM
ED2682 [PS]	(title unknown)	1960	$25
ED2695 [PS]	(title unknown)	1961	$25
ED2702 [PS]	(title unknown)	1961	$25
ED2712 [PS]	(title unknown)	1961	$25
ED2730 [PS]	(title unknown)	1962	$25
ED2801 [PS]	(title unknown)	1965	$25
7-34341 [PS]	Too Many Rivers	1965	$25
7-4825 [DJ]	What Now My Love/You Don't Have to Say You Love Me/You've Got Your Troubles//Up Tight/Strangers in the Night/Call Me	1966	$25

— Jukebox EP, stereo, small hole, plays at 33 1/3 rpm

LEE, BRENDA (2)
APOLLO

Number	Title	Yr	NM
490	I Ain't Gonna Give Nobody None/I'll Never Get Rich Again	1956	$40

LEE, CURTIS
DUNES

Number	Title	Yr	NM
801	California GH-903/Then I'll Know	1960	$30
2015	Does He Mean That Much to You/The Wobble	1962	$30
2020	Lonely Weekends/Better Him Than Me	1963	$30
2021	Pickin' Up the Pieces of My Heart/Mr. Mistaker	1963	$30
2003	Pledge of Love/Then I'll Know	1961	$30
2003 [PS]	Pledge of Love/Then I'll Know	1961	$30
2007	Pretty Little Angel Eyes/Gee, How I Wish You Were Here	1961	$30
2001	Special Love/"D" in Love	1960	$30

HOT

Number	Title	Yr	NM
7	I Never Knew What Love Could Do/Gotta Have You	1960	$80

MIRA

Number	Title	Yr	NM
240	Sweet Baby/Is She In Your Town	1967	$30

ROJAC

Number	Title	Yr	NM
114	Get In My Bag/Everybody's Going Wild	1967	$15

SABRA

Number	Title	Yr	NM
517	Let's Take a Ride/I'm Asking Forgiveness	1960	$30

WARRIOR

Number	Title	Yr	NM
1555	With All My Heart/Pure Love	1959	$40

LEE, DICKEY
ATCO

Number	Title	Yr	NM
6580	All My Life/Hang-Ups	1968	$8

DOT

Number	Title	Yr	NM
16087	Life in a Teenage World/Why Don't You Write On	1960	$20

HALLWAY

Number	Title	Yr	NM
1924	Big Brother/She's Walking Away	1964	$12

MERCURY

Number	Title	Yr	NM
57017	Don't Look Back/I'm Trustin' a Feelin'	1980	$4
76129	Everybody Loves a Winner/You Won't Be Here Tonight	1982	$4
57005	He's an Old Rock 'N' Roller/It Hurts to Be in Love	1979	$4
57052	Honky Tonk Hearts/Best I Hit the Road	1981	$4
55068	I'm Just a Heartache Away/Midnight Flyer	1979	$4
57056	I Wonder If I Care As Much/Further Than a Country Mile	1981	$4
57036	Lost in Love/Again	1980	$4

— A-side with Kathy Burdick

Number	Title	Yr	NM
❏ 57027	Workin' My Way to Your Heart/If You Want Me	1980	$4

RCA

Number	Title	Yr	NM
❏ PB-10764	9,999,999 Tears/I Never Will Get Over You	1976	$4
❏ PB-10914	If You Gotta Make a Fool of Somebody/My Love Shows Thru	1977	$4
❏ PB-11389	It's Not Easy/I've Been Honky-Tonkin' Too Long	1978	$4
❏ PB-11191	Love Is a Word/I'll Be Leaving Alone	1978	$4
❏ PB-11294	My Heart Won't Cry Anymore/Danna	1978	$4
❏ PB-11125	Peanut Butter/Breezy Was Her Name	1977	$4

RCA VICTOR

Number	Title	Yr	NM
❏ 47-9862	All Too Soon/Charlie	1970	$6
❏ PB-10543	Angels, Roses and Rain/Danna	1976	$4
❏ 74-0710	Ashes of Love/The Kingdom I Call Home	1972	$5
❏ 74-0798	Baby, Bye Bye/She Thinks I Still Care	1972	$5
❏ 74-0892	Crying Over You/My World Around You	1973	$5
❏ PB-10014	Give Me One Good Reason/Sweet Fever	1974	$5
❏ 47-9941	Home To/Special	1971	$6
❏ 74-0623	I Saw My Lady/What We Used to Hang On To	1971	$5
❏ APBO-0227	I Use the Soap/Strawberry Women	1974	$5
❏ PB-10684	Makin' Love Don't Always Make Love Grow/I Never Will Get Over You	1976	$4
❏ 74-0980	Put Me Down Softly/If She Turns Up in Atlanta	1973	$5
❏ APBO-0082	Sparklin' Brown Eyes/Country Song	1973	$5
❏ PB-10091	The Busiest Memory in Town/Way to Go On	1974	$5
❏ 47-9988	The Mahogany Pulpit/Everybody's Reaching Out for Someone	1971	$6

RENDEZVOUS

Number	Title	Yr	NM
❏ 188	Dream Boy/Stay True Baby	1962	$30

SMASH

Number	Title	Yr	NM
❏ 1808	Don't Wanna Talk About Paula/Just a Friend	1963	$15
❏ 1822	I Go Lonely/Ten Million Faces	1963	$15
❏ 1791	I Saw Linda Yesterday/The Girl I Can't Forget	1962	$15
❏ 1913	Me and My Teardrops/Only Trust in Me	1964	$15
❏ 1758	Patches/More or Less	1962	$20
❏ 1844	She Wants to Be Bobby's Girl/The Day the Sawmill Closed Down	1963	$15
❏ 1871	To the Aisle/Mother Nature	1964	$15

SUN

Number	Title	Yr	NM
❏ 297	Dreamy Nights/Fool, Fool, Fool	1958	$100
❏ 280	Good Lovin'/Memories Never Grow Old	1957	$40

TAMPA

Number	Title	Yr	NM
❏ 131	Dream Boy/Stay True Baby	1957	$40

TCF HALL

Number	Title	Yr	NM
❏ 118	Good Girl Goin' Bad/Pretty White Dress	1965	$10
❏ 128	Good Guy/Annie	1966	$10
❏ 102	Laurie (Strange Things Happen)/Party Doll	1965	$12
❏ 111	The Girl from Peyton Place/The Girl I Used to Know	1965	$10

LEE, ERNIE

MGM

Number	Title	Yr	NM
❏ 11517	Hangin' My Heart Out to Dry/How Come You Never Answer	1953	$30

RCA VICTOR

Number	Title	Yr	NM
❏ 48-0158	My Home Is the Dust of the Road/You're Next to Heaven	1950	$40

—Originals on green vinyl

Number	Title	Yr	NM
❏ 48-0182	Second Hand Heart/Headin' Home	1950	$40

—Originals on green vinyl

Number	Title	Yr	NM
❏ 48-0341	Tormented/I'm a Lonesome Man	1950	$40

—Originals on green vinyl

LEE, HAROLD

CARTWHEEL

Number	Title	Yr	NM
❏ 219	Lila/Outside of Wichita	1972	$6
❏ 198	Mountain Woman/If I Never Hear Goodbye	1971	$6
❏ 204	Outside of Wichita/Way Down I Think I Love You	1971	$6

COLUMBIA

Number	Title	Yr	NM
❏ 4-44649	Mother, Brother and Sweet Darlin' Now/Boys Kept Hanging Around	1968	$8

Number	Title	Yr	NM
❏ 4-44458	The Two Sides of Me/Bringing Daddy Home	1968	$8

GRT

Number	Title	Yr	NM
❏ 088	Trouble Workin' Overtime/(B-side unknown)	1976	$5

LEE, JACKIE, AND THE RAINDROPS

LONDON INT'L.

Number	Title	Yr	NM
❏ 10602	The Last One to Know/There's No One in the Whole Wide World	1962	$15

LEE, JACKIE (1)

ABC

Number	Title	Yr	NM
❏ 11146	One for the Road/Darkest Days	1968	$30

CAPITOL

Number	Title	Yr	NM
❏ 3145	25 Miles to Louisiana/Pershing Square	1971	$6

KEYMEN

Number	Title	Yr	NM
❏ 114	African Boo-Ga-Loo/Bring It Home	1968	$10
❏ 109	Glory of Love/Bring It Home	1968	$10

MIRWOOD

Number	Title	Yr	NM
❏ 5528	Baby I'm Satisfied/Whether It's Right or Wrong	1966	$12

—With Dolores Hall

Number	Title	Yr	NM
❏ 5527	Don't Be Ashamed/Oh, My Darlin'	1966	$12
❏ 5502	The Duck/Let Your Conscience Be Your Guide	1965	$15
❏ 5510	The Shotgun and the Duck/Do the Temptation Walk	1966	$10

UNI

Number	Title	Yr	NM
❏ 55206	The Chicken/I Love You	1970	$8

LEE, JACKIE (2)

ABC-PARAMOUNT

Number	Title	Yr	NM
❏ 9892	The Storm/Bye Bye Blues	1958	$10

CORAL

Number	Title	Yr	NM
❏ 61534	Aloha Oe/More, More, More	1955	$15
❏ 61579	A String of Pearls/Always Love Me	1956	$10
❏ 61827	Baby Buggy Boogie/Sippin' Soda	1957	$12
❏ 61259	Bei Mir Bist Du Schoen/Missouri Waltz	1954	$15
❏ 61461	Cannibal King/The Spoon Song	1955	$15
❏ 61734	Chatterbox/Dardanella	1956	$10
❏ 61400	Chop Sticks/Luigi's Wedding	1955	$15
❏ 61638	Crazy Polka/Elmer's Tune	1956	$12
❏ 61304	I Can't Give You Anything But Love/Blue Boogie	1954	$15
❏ 61214	The Donkey Serenade/Mr. Hot Piano	1954	$15
❏ 1738	Do the New Hully Gully/Patricia	1962	$12
❏ 1767	Hungarian Rhapsody Boogie/Bumpy	1962	$10

SWAN

Number	Title	Yr	NM
❏ 4034	Happy Vacation/The Hucklebuck	1959	$15
❏ 4039	Like Sunset/Rancho	1959	$15

LEE, JACKIE (3)

EPIC

Number	Title	Yr	NM
❏ 9807	I Cry Alone/'Cause I Love Him	1965	$10
❏ 10183	Love Is Gone/The Lonely Clown	1967	$8

LEE, JENNY, AND THE STARLETS

CONGRESS

Number	Title	Yr	NM
❏ 107	What I Gotta Do/Show Me a Man	1962	$80

LEE, JOHNNY

ABC DOT

Number	Title	Yr	NM
❏ 17603	Sometimes/Get Off My Back	1975	$5

ASYLUM

Number	Title	Yr	NM
❏ 47301	Be There for Me Baby/Finally Fallin'	1982	$4
❏ 47215	Bet Your Heart on Me/Highways Run On Forever	1981	$4
❏ 47076	One in a Million/Anni	1980	$4
❏ 47105	Pickin' Up Strangers/Never Lay My Lovin' Down	1981	$4
❏ 47138	Prisomer of Home/Fool for Love	1981	$4

CURB

Number	Title	Yr	NM
❏ 10564	I Can Be a Heartbreaker, Too/Anniversary Song	1989	$3
❏ 10552	I'm Not Over You/Anniversary Song	1989	$3
❏ 10536	Maybe I Won't Love You Anymore/Annie	1989	$3

ELEKTRA

Number	Title	Yr	NM
❏ 47230 [DJ]	Please Come Home for Christmas/Silver Bells	1981	$6

—B-side by Tompall and the Glaser Brothers

FULL MOON

Number	Title	Yr	NM
❏ 29605	Hey Bartender/Blue Monday	1983	$4

FULL MOON/ASYLUM

Number	Title	Yr	NM
❏ 69945	Cherokee Fiddle/You Know Me	1982	$4
❏ 47004	Looking for Love/Lyin' Eyes	1980	$4

—B-side by Eagles

Number	Title	Yr	NM
❏ 47004 [PS]	Looking for Love/Lyin' Eyes	1980	$5
❏ 69848	Sounds Like Love/The Deeper We Fall	1983	$4
❏ 47444	When You Fall in Love/Crossfire	1982	$4

GRT

Number	Title	Yr	NM
❏ 125	Country Party/This Should Go On Forever	1977	$5
❏ 137	Dear Alice/It's Gonna Be Me	1977	$5
❏ 144	This Time/Frisco	1978	$5

WARNER BROS.

Number	Title	Yr	NM
❏ 28747	I Could Get Used to This/It Ain't the Leaving	1986	$3

—A-side with Lane Brody

Number	Title	Yr	NM
❏ 29486	My Baby Don't Slow Dance/You Really Got a Hold on Me	1983	$3
❏ 29270	One More Shot/The Eyes of Love	1984	$3
❏ 29021	Save the Last Chance/It Ain't the Leaving	1985	$3
❏ 28839	The Loneliness in Lucy's Eyes (The Life Sue Ellen Is Living)/If I Knew Then What I Know Now	1985	$3
❏ 28901	They Never Had to Get Over You/Rock 'n' Roll Money	1985	$3

LEE, JULIA

CAPITOL

Number	Title	Yr	NM
❏ F838	Ain't It a Crime/Don't Save It Too Long	1950	$50

—Note: Julia Lee singles before 838 are unknown on 45 rpm

Number	Title	Yr	NM
❏ F1896	Charmaine/Out in the Cold Again	1951	$40
❏ F956	Do You Want It/Decent Woman Blues	1950	$50
❏ F1252	It Won't Be Long/Bleeding Hearted Blues	1950	$50
❏ F2203	Last Call for Alcohol/Goin' to Chicago Blues	1952	$60
❏ F1376	Lotus Blossom/Pipe Dreams	1951	$40
❏ F1589	Mama Don't Allow It/The Breeze	1951	$40
❏ F1111	My Man Stands Out/Don't Come Too Soon	1950	$60
❏ F1149	Pagan Love Song/I'm Forever Blowing Bubbles	1950	$60
❏ F1798	Scream in the Night/If You Hadn't Gone Away	1951	$40
❏ F1009	There Goes My Heart/Nobody Knows You When You're Down and Out	1950	$50

LEE, LAURA

ARIOLA AMERICA

Number	Title	Yr	NM
❏ 7652	Love's Got Me Tired (But I Ain't Tired of Love)/You're Barking Up the Wrong Tree	1976	$5

CHESS

Number	Title	Yr	NM
❏ 2041	As Long As I Got You/A Man with Some Backbone	1968	$10
❏ 2013	Dirty Man/It's Mighty Hard	1967	$12
❏ 2062	Hang It Up/It's How You Make It Good	1968	$12
❏ 2068	Mama's Got a Good Thing/Love More Than Pride	1969	$10
❏ 1989	Stop Giving Your Man Away/You Need Me	1967	$15
❏ 2030	Wanted: Lover, No Experience Necessary/Up Tight, Good Man	1967	$10

COTILLION

Number	Title	Yr	NM
❏ 44073	Together/But You Know I Love You	1970	$8
❏ 44054	What a Man/Separation Line	1970	$8

FANTASY

Number	Title	Yr	NM
❏ 865	Sat-Is-Fac-Tion/Your Song	1979	$5

HOT WAX

Number	Title	Yr	NM
❏ 7111	Love and Liberty/I Don't Want Nothing Old But Money	1971	$8
❏ 7007	Wedlock Is a Padlock/Her Picture Matches Mine	1970	$8
❏ 7105	Women's Love Rights/Her Picture Matches Mine	1971	$8

INVICTUS

Number	Title	Yr	NM
❏ 1273	Don't Leave Me Starving for Your Love/Remember Me	1974	$6
❏ 1264	I Need It Just As Bad As You/If I'm Good Enough to Love	1974	$6

RIC-TIC

Number	Title	Yr	NM
❏ 111	To Win Your Heart/So Will I	1966	$20

Number	Title	Yr	NM
LEE, LONDON			
PHILIPS			
❏ PEP-1 [DJ]	Monologue 1/Monologue 2	1969	$8
UNITED ARTISTS			
❏ 877	Who Is London Lee/Mutiny	1965	$15
LEE, MICHELE			
ABC-PARAMOUNT			
❏ 10411	He's Not Good Enough for You/I See It All Now	1963	$20
❏ 10365	I'm Sorry Missus Murray (But I Cannot Baby-Sit for You Tonight)/Havin' a Party for One	1962	$20
❏ 10365 [PS]	I'm Sorry Missus Murray (But I Cannot Baby-Sit for You Tonight)/Havin' a Party for One	1962	$40
COLUMBIA			
❏ 4-44165	Being Good Isn't Good Enough/I Believe in You	1967	$8
❏ 4-43376	Call Me/You Were There	1965	$8
❏ 4-43476	Feeling Good/Steady, Steady	1965	$8
❏ 4-44554	I Can't Believe I'm Losing You/I Didn't Come to New York to Meet a Guy from My Home Town	1968	$8
❏ 4-43923	If You Go Away/Wednesday's Child	1966	$8
❏ 4-44835	It's a Long Way to Fall/You'll Remember Me	1969	$6
❏ 4-43575	Laugh, Clown, Laugh/I'll Never Go There Anymore	1966	$8
❏ 4-44413	L. David Sloane/Everybody Loves My Baby (But My Baby Don't Love Nobody But Me)	1967	$8
❏ 4-43288	Pretty Lies, Pretty Make Believe/Somewhere in the World	1965	$8
LEE, NANCY			
ACME			
❏ 711	So They Say/Meet Me at the Cross Roads	1957	$200
LEE, PEGGY			
CAPITOL			
❏ EAP 1-864	The Man I Love/Just One Way to Say I Love You//There Is No Greater Love/Something Wonderful	1957	$12
A&M			
❏ 1771	I Remember/Some Cats Know	1975	$4
ATLANTIC			
❏ 3215	Let's Love/Always	1974	$4
CAPITOL			
❏ 4942	Alley Cat Song/O Barquinho (Little Boat)	1963	$10
❏ F4115	Alright, OK, You Win/My Man	1959	$15
❏ 54-547	Bali Ha'i/There Is Nothing Like a Dame	1949	$50
❏ 5404	Bewitched/Sneakin' Up on You	1965	$8
❏ 5557	Big Spender/Trapped	1965	$8
❏ 4576	Boston Beans/Yes Indeed	1961	$10
❏ F1544	Boulevard Café/If You Turn Me Down	1951	$20
❏ 4498	Bucket of Tears/I Love Being Here with You	1961	$10
❏ F1366	Climb Up the Mountain/The Mill on the Floss	1951	$20
❏ 5653	Come Back to Me/You've Got Possibilities	1966	$8
❏ F898	Crazy He Calls Me/Them There Eyes	1950	$30
❏ F961	Cry, Cry, Cry/Once Around the Moon	1950	$30
❏ 5521	Everybody Has the Right to Be Wrong/Free Spirits	1965	$8
❏ F3722	Every Night/Baby, Baby, Wait for Me	1957	$15
❏ F2025	Everytime/Goin' On a Hayride	1952	$20
❏ F3998	Fever/You Don't Know	1958	$15
❏ F4189	Hallelujah I Love Him So/I'm Looking Out the Window	1959	$15
❏ 2817	Have You Seen My Baby/You'll Remember Me	1970	$5
❏ 4349	Heart/C'est Magnifique	1960	$12
❏ F1513	He's Only Wonderful/It Never Happens to Me	1951	$20
❏ 4610	Hey, Look the Over/When He Makes Music	1961	$12
❏ F1667	I Can't Give You Anything But Love/I Don't Know Enough About You	1951	$20
—*Reissue of 78 rpm recordings from the 1940s*			
❏ 5121	I Can't Stop Loving You/A Lot of Livin' to Do	1964	$10
❏ 5988	I Feel It/Lonesome Road	1967	$6
❏ 5488	I Go to Sleep/Stop Living in the Past	1965	$8

Number	Title	Yr	NM
❏ 4474	I Like a Sleighride (Jingle Bells)/Christmas Carousel	1960	$15
❏ 4474 [PS]	I Like a Sleighride (Jingle Bells)/Christmas Carousel	1960	$50
❏ F1749	I Love You But I Don't Like You/Wandering Swallow	1951	$20
❏ 4888	I'm a Woman/Big Bad Bill	1962	$10
❏ 4449	I'm Gonna Go Fishin'/My Gentle Young Johnny	1960	$10
❏ 5241	In the Name of Love/My Sin	1964	$10
❏ 2602	Is That All There Is/Me and My Shadow	1969	$6
❏ F1601	It's a Good Day/Them There Eyes	1951	$20
—*Reissue of 78 rpm recordings from the 1940s*			
❏ F4071	Light of Love/Sweetheart	1958	$15
❏ F3811	Listen to the Rockin' Bird/Uninvited Dream	1957	$15
❏ X4-1475 [S]	Love and Marriage/Ole	1961	$20
—*Small hole, plays at 33 1/3 rpm*			
❏ F1161	Lover Come Back to Me/Helpless	1950	$30
❏ SM-1857 [S]	Mack the Knife/Mama's Gone, Goodbye	1963	$20
—*Small hole, plays at 33 1/3 rpm*			
❏ F1602	Manana (Is Soon Enough for Me)/Why Don't You Do It Right	1951	$20
—*Reissue of 78 rpm recordings from the 1940s*			
❏ 2308	Misty Roses/It'll Never Happen Again	1968	$6
❏ F1586	My Magic Heart/So Far So Good	1951	$20
❏ 2721	My Old Flame/Love Story	1970	$5
❏ F801	My Small Senor/When You Speak with Your Eyes	1950	$30
❏ F1244	Once in a Lifetime/Love Is So Peculiar	1950	$30
❏ 2910	One More Ride on the Merry-Go-Round/Pieces of Dreams	1970	$5
❏ F810	Save Your Sorrow for Tomorrow/Sugar	1950	$30
❏ F1926	Shame on You/Would You Dance	1952	$20
❏ F1105	Show Me the Way to Get Out of This World ('Cause That's Where Everything Is)/Happy Music	1950	$30
❏ 3439	Someone Who Cares/Love Song	1972	$5
❏ 2696	Something/Whistle for Happiness	1969	$6
❏ 5758	So What's New/Walking Happy	1966	$8
❏ 2477	Spinning Wheel/Lean On Me	1969	$6
❏ 5678	Stay with Me/Happy Feet	1966	$8
❏ F849	Sunshine Cake/Goodbye John	1950	$30
❏ 5289	Talk to Me Baby/After You've Gone	1964	$10
❏ 4812	Tell All the World About You/Amazing	1962	$10
❏ 5605	That Man/You Don't Know	1966	$8
❏ F1450	That Ol' Devil/Cannonball Express	1951	$20
❏ F1609	That Old Feeling/Solitude	1951	$20
—*B-side by the Capitol Jazzmen; reissue of 1940s material*			
❏ 5346	That's What It Takes/Pass Me By	1965	$8
❏ 54-90035	The Christmas Spell/Song at Midnight	1949	$50
❏ 5001	The Doodlin' Song/Got That Magic	1963	$10
❏ F791	The Old Master Painter/Bless You	1949	$30
—*With Mel Torme*			
❏ 5469	The Sandpiper Love Theme (The Shadow of Your Smile)/Maybe This Summer	1965	$8
❏ 4750	The Sweetest Sounds/Loads of Love	1962	$10
❏ 4311	The Tree/The Christmas List	1959	$20
❏ 4311 [PS]	The Tree/The Christmas List	1959	$30
❏ X1-1475 [S]	titles unknown	1961	$20
—*Small hole, plays at 33 1/3 rpm*			
❏ X2-1475 [S]	titles unknown	1961	$20
—*Small hole, plays at 33 1/3 rpm*			
❏ X3-1475 [S]	titles unknown	1961	$20
—*Small hole, plays at 33 1/3 rpm*			
❏ F1573	(When I Dance with You) I Get Ideas/Tonight You Belong to Me	1951	$20
❏ F1298	Where Are You/Ay-Ay-Chug-a-Lug	1950	$30
❏ 3113	Where Did They Go/All I Want	1971	$5
❏ F1776	While We're Young/Birmingham Jail	1951	$20
DECCA			
❏ 28889	Apples, Peaches and Cherries/Night Holds No Fear	1953	$20
❏ 28890	Baubles, Bangles and Beads/Love You So	1953	$20
❏ 28142	Be Anything/Forgive Me	1952	$20
❏ 29460	Bella Notte/La La Lu	1955	$15

Number	Title	Yr	NM
❏ 29342	God Rest Ye Merry Gentlemen/White Christmas	1954	$20
—*A-side with Trudi Stevens; B-side by Bing Crosby and Danny Kaye*			
❏ 29003	Go You Where You Go/Where Can I Go Without You	1954	$20
❏ 29427	He's a Tramp/The Siamese Cat Song	1955	$15
❏ 29429	I Belong to You/How Bitter, My Sweet	1955	$15
❏ 30879	It Ain't Necessarily So/Swing Low Sweet Chariot	1959	$10
❏ 29359	It Must Be So/Straight Ahead	1954	$15
—*With the Mills Brothers*			
❏ 28737	I've Got You Under My Skin/My Heart Belongs to Daddy	1953	$20
❏ 29373	Let Me Go Lover/Bouquet of Roses	1954	$15
❏ 29250	Love, You Didn't Do Right by Me/Sisters	1954	$20
❏ 28215	Lover/You Go to My Head	1952	$20
❏ 29681	Me/Pablo Pasablo	1955	$15
❏ 29834	Mr. Wonderful/Crazy in the Heart	1956	$15
❏ 29534	Ooh, That Kiss/Oh! No!	1955	$15
❏ 28395	San Souci/River, River	1952	$20
❏ 29605	Sing a Rainbow/He Needs Me	1955	$15
❏ 29164	Summer Vacation/That's What a Woman Is For	1954	$20
❏ 29994	That's Alright Honey/We Laughed at Love	1956	$15
❏ 29837	The Comeback/You've Got to See Mamma Every Night	1956	$15
❏ 28565	This Is a Very Special Day/I Hear the Music Now	1953	$20
❏ 27238	Watermelon Weather/The Moon Came Up	1950	$20
—*With Bing Crosby*			
❏ 29608	What Can I Say After I Say I'm Sorry/Sugar	1955	$15
❏ 30117	Where Flamingos Fly/Gypsy with Fire in Her Shoes	1956	$15
❏ 28631	Who's Gonna Pay the Check/Sorry, Baby, You Let My Love Get Cold	1953	$20

7-Inch Extended Plays

Number	Title	Yr	NM
CAPITOL			
❏ SXA-1772	Ain't That Love/I Believe in You/Teach Me Tonight//Tell All the World About Us/I've Got the World on a String/Big Bad Bill	1962	$15
—*Jukebox issue; small hole, plays at 33 1/3 rpm*			
❏ SU-2475 [PS]	Big Spender	1966	$12
❏ SU-2475	Come Back to Me/You've Got Possibilities/I Must Know//Alright, Okay, You Win/I'll Only Miss Him When I Think of Him/Big Spender	1966	$10
—*Stereo jukebox issue; small hole, plays at 33 1/3 rpm*			
❏ EAP 3-864	(contents unknown)	1957	$15
❏ SXA-1969 [PS]	In Love Again	1963	$15
❏ SXA-1969	I've Got Your Number/(I'm) In Love Again/That's My Style//Little by Little/I Got Lost in His Arms/Got That Magic	1963	$15
—*Jukebox issue; small hole, plays at 33 1/3 rpm*			
❏ SXA-2320 [PS]	Pass Me By	1965	$12
❏ EAP 2-864	Please Be Kind/If I Should Lose You//He's My Guy/Then I'll Be Tired of You	1957	$15
❏ SXA-2320	Sneakin' Up on You/I Wanna Be Around/You Always Hurt the One That You Love//Quiet Nights/Love/Dear Heart	1965	$10
—*Jukebox issue; small hole, plays at 33 1/3 rpm*			
❏ SXA-2320 [PS]	Sugar 'n' Spice	1962	$15
❏ EAP 1-864 [PS]	The Man I Love, Part 1	1957	$15
❏ EAP 2-864 [PS]	The Man I Love, Part 2	1957	$15
❏ EAP 3-864 [PS]	The Man I Love, Part 3	1957	$15
❏ EAP 1-864	The Man I Love/Just One Way to Say I Love You//There Is No Greater Love/Something Wonderful	1957	$15
❏ SU-2338 [PS]	Then Was Then	1966	$12
❏ SU-2338	Trapped (In the Web of Love)/Losers Weepers/Leave It to Love//They Say/Seventh Son/Then Was Then (And Now Is Now)	1966	$10
—*Jukebox issue; small hole, plays at 33 1/3 rpm*			
LEE, ROBIN			
ATLANTIC AMERICA			
❏ 7-99264	Before You Cheat on Me Once (You Better Think Twice)/Serious Afffection	1988	$4
❏ 7-99264 [PS]	Before You Cheat on Me Once (You Better Think Twice)/Serious Afffection	1988	$4
❏ 7-99307	Shine a Light on a Lie/I'm Gettin' Good at Bein' Bad	1988	$4

Number	Title	Yr	NM
❏ 7-99307 [PS]	Shine a Light on a Lie/I'm Gettin' Good at Bein' Bad	1988	$4
❏ 7-99353	This Old Flame/Maybe I Will, Maybe I Won't	1988	$4
❏ 7-99353 [PS]	This Old Flame/Maybe I Will, Maybe I Won't	1988	$4

EVERGREEN

Number	Title	Yr	NM
❏ 1016	Angel in Your Arms/Turning Back the Covers (Don't Turn Back the Time)	1983	$5
❏ 1023	Cold in July/Breaking the Chains	1984	$5
❏ 1006	Heart for a Heart/Turning Back the Covers (Don't Turn Back the Time)	1983	$5
❏ 1043	If You're Anything Like Your Eyes/Paint the Town Blue	1986	$5
❏ 1026	I Heard It on the Radio/Angel in Your Arms	1984	$5
❏ 1026 [PS]	I Heard It on the Radio/Angel in Your Arms	1984	$6
❏ 1039	I'll Take Your Love Anytime/Between the Lies	1986	$5
❏ 1012	Love Always Leaves Me Lonely/(B-side unknown)	1983	$5
❏ 1033	Paint the Town Blue/Angel in Your Arms	1985	$5

— A-side with Lobo

Number	Title	Yr	NM
❏ 1037	Safe in the Arms of Love/Between the Lies	1985	$5
❏ 1003	Turning Back the Covers (Don't Turn Back the Time)/Angel in Your Arms	1983	$5
❏ 1003 [PS]	Turning Back the Covers (Don't Turn Back the Time)/Angel in Your Arms	1983	$8
❏ 1018	Want Ads/Breaking the Chains	1984	$5

LEFEVRE, RAYMOND

4 CORNERS OF THE WORLD

Number	Title	Yr	NM
❏ 147	Ame Caline (Soul Coaxing)/If I Were a Carpenter	1968	$5
❏ 151	Delilah/If I Only Had Time	1968	$5
❏ 145	Groovin'/A Whiter Shade of Pale	1967	$5
❏ 149	La, La, La (He Gives Me Love)/C'est La Rose	1968	$5
❏ 142	When a Man Loves a Woman/Black Is Black	1967	$5

ATLANTIC

Number	Title	Yr	NM
❏ 2093	Come Softly to Me/Havah Nagilah	1961	$10

BUDDAH

Number	Title	Yr	NM
❏ 269	Mammy Blue/What Have They Done to My Song, Ma	1971	$5
❏ 809	Spanish Eyes/Stars of the Way	1967	$6
❏ 231	The Day the Rains Came/Butterfingers	1958	$12

MERCURY

Number	Title	Yr	NM
❏ 71599	What Good Does It Do Me/(Instrumental)	1960	$10

VERVE

Number	Title	Yr	NM
❏ 10263	Come Une Symphonie/Un Voms Vivo	1962	$8

LEFT BANKE, THE

SMASH

Number	Title	Yr	NM
❏ 2209	Bryant Hotel/Give the Man a Hand	1969	$15
❏ 2165	Dark Is the Bark/My Friend Today	1968	$15
❏ 2119	Desiree/I've Got Something on My Mind	1967	$15
❏ 2119 [PS]	Desiree/I've Got Something on My Mind	1967	$30
❏ 2198	Goodbye Holly/Sing, Little Bird, Sing	1968	$15
❏ 2089	Ivy, Ivy/And Suddenly	1967	$15
❏ 2243	Myrah/Pedestal	1969	$50

— Picture sleeves are bootlegs

Number	Title	Yr	NM
❏ 2074	Pretty Ballerina/Lazy Day	1966	$20
❏ 2097	She May Call You Up Tonight/Barterers and Their Wives	1967	$15
❏ 2041	Walk Away Renee/I Haven't Got the Nerve	1966	$20

LEGARDE TWINS, THE

4 STAR

Number	Title	Yr	NM
❏ 1037	I Can Almost Touch the Feelin'/True Love	1979	$5

— As "The LeGardes"

BEAR

Number	Title	Yr	NM
❏ 194	Crocodile Man (From Walk-About Creek)/(B-side unknown)	1988	$6

DOT

Number	Title	Yr	NM
❏ 17377	Another Glass of Beer/From New South Wales to Nashville	1971	$8
❏ 15608	Freight Train Yodel/Poison Darts	1959	$30

INVITATION

Number	Title	Yr	NM
❏ 101	Daddy's Makin' Records in Nashville/Grady Family Band	1980	$6

RAINDROP

Number	Title	Yr	NM
❏ 012	True Love/25 Years and 15 Days	1978	$8

— As "The LeGardes"

LEGENDARY MASKED SURFERS, THE

UNITED ARTISTS

Number	Title	Yr	NM
❏ XW270	Summer Means Fun/Gonna Hustle You	1973	$30

— Original pressings have a Jan & Dean recording on them by mistake

Number	Title	Yr	NM
❏ XW270	Summer Means Fun/Gonna Hustle You	1973	$120

— With the intended recording, a newly-recorded vocal track

Number	Title	Yr	NM
❏ XW270 [PS]	Summer Means Fun/Gonna Hustle You	1973	$40
❏ 50958	Summertime, Summertime/Gonna Hustle You	1972	$40

LEGENDARY STARDUST COWBOY, THE

MERCURY

Number	Title	Yr	NM
❏ 72891	Down in the Wrecking Yard/I Took a Trip on a Gemini Spaceship	1969	$30
❏ 72912	Everything's Getting Bigger But Our Love/Kiss and Run	1969	$30
❏ 72862	Paralyzed/Who's Knocking on My Door	1968	$30

PSYCHO-SUAVE

Number	Title	Yr	NM
❏ 1033	Paralyzed/Who's Knocking on My Door	1968	$40

LEGENDS, THE

CALDWELL

Number	Title	Yr	NM
❏ 410	Go Away with Me/Jungle Lullaby	1962	$30

CAPITOL

Number	Title	Yr	NM
❏ 5014	Summertime Blues/Run to the Movies	1963	$30

COLUMBIA

Number	Title	Yr	NM
❏ 41949	Theme from "Exodus"/Later	1961	$15

DOC HOLLIDAY

Number	Title	Yr	NM
❏ 107	Surf's Up/Dance with the Drummer Man	1963	$50
❏ 107 [PS]	Surf's Up/Dance with the Drummer Man	1963	$60

ERMINE

Number	Title	Yr	NM
❏ 43	Bop-A-Lena/I Wish I Knew	1962	$60
❏ 41	Lariat/Late Train	1962	$50
❏ 39	My Love for You/Say Mama	1962	$60
❏ 45	Temptation/Marionette	1962	$50

HART-VAN

Number	Title	Yr	NM
❏ 18003	Traction/As Long As I Live	1962	$40

HULL

Number	Title	Yr	NM
❏ 727	The Legend of Love/Now I'm Telling You	1958	$125

— Red label

Number	Title	Yr	NM
❏ 727	The Legend of Love/Now I'm Telling You	1962	$40

— Multicolor label

JAMIE

Number	Title	Yr	NM
❏ 1228	Tell the Truth/You'll Never See the Forest	1962	$30

KEY

Number	Title	Yr	NM
❏ 1002	Lariat/Gail	1961	$50
❏ 1002	Lariat/Late Train	1961	$50

MELBA

Number	Title	Yr	NM
❏ 109	I'll Never Fall in Love Again/Eyes of an Angel	1957	$200

— Label with double horizontal lines

Number	Title	Yr	NM
❏ 109	I'll Never Fall in Love Again/Eyes of an Angel	1961	$50

— Label with no horizontal lines

PARROT

Number	Title	Yr	NM
❏ 45011	Alright/How Can I Find Her	1965	$15

RAILROAD HOUSE

Number	Title	Yr	NM
❏ 12003	High Towers/Fever Games	1969	$30
❏ 12003 [PS]	High Towers/Fever Games	1969	$40

UP

Number	Title	Yr	NM
❏ 2202	Baby, Get Your Head Screwed On/Why	1968	$60

WARNER BROS.

Number	Title	Yr	NM
❏ 5457	Here Comes the Rain/Don't Be Ashamed	1964	$20

LEGRAND, MICHEL

20TH CENTURY

Number	Title	Yr	NM
❏ 2346	The Other Side of Midnight (Noelle's Theme)/Drive to Demeris	1977	$4

BELL

Number	Title	Yr	NM
❏ 45171	Brian's Song/Theme from "The Go-Between	1972	$5
❏ 45118	The Summer Knows/I Will Say Goodbye	1971	$5

COLUMBIA

Number	Title	Yr	NM
❏ 41312	Cheek to Cheek/Only You	1958	$10
❏ 40751	Friendly Persuasion/Lovers and Lollipops	1956	$15
❏ 40732	Love Theme from "La Strada"/Paris Canaille	1956	$15
❏ 40692	Smile/Bon Jour, Paris	1956	$15

DECCA

Number	Title	Yr	NM
❏ 32287	Pretty Polly/The Race Is to the Swift	1968	$6

MCA

Number	Title	Yr	NM
❏ 40523	Gable and Lombard Love Theme/I Can't Give You Anything But Love, Baby	1976	$4
❏ 40160	Walking on the Beach/Breezy's Song	1973	$4

MGM

Number	Title	Yr	NM
❏ 13894	Love Theme from "Elvira Madigan"/Melange	1968	$6
❏ 13816	Tara's Theme (Part 1)/Tara's Theme (Part 2)	1967	$6
❏ 13816	Tara's Theme (Part 1)/Theme from Orfell Negro	1967	$6

PHILIPS

Number	Title	Yr	NM
❏ 40357	I Will Wait for You/Melody from the Stars	1966	$8
❏ 40098	Love Is a Ball/Millie's Theme	1963	$8
❏ 40257	Love Theme from Parapailies de Cherbourg/Garage Scene	1965	$8
❏ 40188	Monkey Business/Come Ray or Come Charles	1964	$8

RCA VICTOR

Number	Title	Yr	NM
❏ PB-10234	Blue, Green, Gray and Gone/Brian's Song	1975	$4

UNITED ARTISTS

Number	Title	Yr	NM
❏ 50662	What Are You Doing the Rest of Your Life (English)/What Are You Doing the Rest of Your Life (French)	1970	$6

WARNER BROS.

Number	Title	Yr	NM
❏ 7486	Theme from "Summer of '42"/Summer Song	1971	$5

LEHR, ZELLA

COLUMBIA

Number	Title	Yr	NM
❏ 18-02677	Blue Eyes Don't Make an Angel/Doin' a Lot	1982	$4
❏ 18-02816	Didn't Mean to Fall in Love Again/He's a Gypsy	1982	$4
❏ 18-02431	Feedin' the Fire/What a Man, My Man Is	1981	$4
❏ 38-03593	Haven't We Loved Somewhere Before/Get Out of My Heart	1983	$4
❏ 18-03164	What a Way to Spend the Night/Ain't It Funny	1982	$4

COMPLEAT

Number	Title	Yr	NM
❏ 129	All Heaven Is About to Break Loose/I'll Get You Back	1984	$5

MEGA

Number	Title	Yr	NM
❏ 1229	I Can't Help Myself/Red Skies Over Georgia	1975	$6

RCA

Number	Title	Yr	NM
❏ PB-11359	Danger, Heartbreak Ahead/I Can't Imagine Laying Down (With Anyone But You)	1978	$4
❏ PB-12073	Love Crazy Love/It Feels Good Enough to Call It Love	1980	$4
❏ PB-11754	Love Has Taken Its Time/If You Only Knew	1979	$4
❏ PB-11648	Once in a Blue Moon/All He Did Was Tell Me Lies (To Try to Woo Me)	1979	$4
❏ PB-11543	Only Diamonds Are Forever/Music Maker	1979	$4
❏ PB-11433	Play Me a Memory/Expert at Everything	1978	$4
❏ PB-11174	Two Doors Down/Two Sides to Every Woman	1977	$4
❏ PB-11265	When the Fire Gets Hot/Can't Help But Wonder	1978	$4

LEHRER, TOM

REPRISE

Number	Title	Yr	NM
❏ 0862	Pollution/Who's Next	1969	$8

7-Inch Extended Plays

LEHRER

Number	Title	Yr	NM
❏ F8-OH-0421/2	Fight Fiercely, Harvard/The Old Dope Peddler/Be Prepared//The Wild West/I Wanna Go Home to Dixie/Lobachevsky	1955	$50

— Side 1 and Side 2 of 2-EP set

Number	Title	Yr	NM
❏ TLEP-1 [PS]	Songs by Tom Lehrer	1955	$60

— Cover for F8-OH-0421/0422 and F8-OH-0423/0424

Number	Title	Yr	NM
❑ F8-OH-0423/4	The Irish Ballad/The Hunting Song/My Home Town//When You Are Old and Grey/I Hold Your Hand in Mine/The Wiener Schnitzel Waltz	1955	$50

—Side 3 and Side 4 of 2-EP set

LEIBERT, DICK

RCA VICTOR

Number	Title	Yr	NM
❑ 47-2968	Deck The Halls / God Rest Ye Merry Gentlemen/We Three Kings / Good King Wenceslaus	1949	$15
❑ 47-2966	Hark The Herald Angels Sing/The First Noel / As With	1949	$15
❑ 47-2965	It Came Upon A Midnight Clear/Joy To The World / Away In A Manger	1949	$15
❑ 47-2967	O Come All Ye Faithful/ Angels From The Realms	1949	$15

LEIGH, BONNIE

R.C.P.

Number	Title	Yr	NM
❑ 020	Moon Walking/(B-side unknown)	1987	$6
❑ 016	That's When (You Can Call Me Your Own)/(B-side unknown)	1987	$6

LEIGH, LINDA

AMERICAN INT'L.

Number	Title	Yr	NM
❑ 543	Beri-Beri/The Plan	1959	$60
❑ 546	Foolish Dreams/The Scent	1960	$30
❑ 540	I Promise You/My Guy	1959	$30

KASH

Number	Title	Yr	NM
❑ 1028	Heart/Here I Go Out of Your Life	1965	$15

RENDEZVOUS

Number	Title	Yr	NM
❑ 103	Move Out/It's Real	1958	$30
❑ 106	Please Please (Let Me Go Steady)/Teardrops	1959	$30

REPRISE

Number	Title	Yr	NM
❑ 20078	Lover's Beach/A Thousand Violins	1962	$15
❑ 20060	Someone Special/Please	1962	$15

LEMMON, DAVE

SCP

Number	Title	Yr	NM
❑ 9781	Too Good to Be Through/ Maggie	1983	$8

LEMMON, JACK

EPIC

Number	Title	Yr	NM
❑ 9318	Daphne/Sleepy Lagoon	1959	$12
❑ 9364	I Cover the Waterfront/I'm Forever Blowing Bubbles	1960	$10
❑ 9399	Theme from The Apartment/ Lemmon Flavored Blues	1960	$10
❑ 9399 [PS]	Theme from The Apartment/ Lemmon Flavored Blues	1960	$30

LEMON PIPERS, THE

BUDDAH

Number	Title	Yr	NM
❑ 23	Green Tambourine/No Help from Me	1967	$15
❑ 136	I Was Not Born to Follow/ Rainbow Tree	1969	$8
❑ 11	Turn Around and Take a Look/Danger	1967	$10
❑ 63	Wine and Violet/Lonely Atmosphere	1968	$10

LEMONGELLO, PETER

PRIVATE STOCK

Number	Title	Yr	NM
❑ 45,119	Do I Love You/(B-side unknown)	1976	$8

—May only exist as a mono/stereo promo

Number	Title	Yr	NM
❑ 45,099	If You Walked Away/All You Get from Love Is a Love Song	1976	$6
❑ 45,131	Miss You Nights/(B-side unknown)	1977	$8

—May only exist as a mono/stereo promo

LEMONHEADS, THE

TAANG!

Number	Title	Yr	NM
❑ 31	Luka//Strange/Mad	1989	$4

—White vinyl

Number	Title	Yr	NM
❑ 31 [PS]	Luka//Strange/Mad	1989	$3

—With "Colored Vinyl Limited Edition" sticker

Number	Title	Yr	NM
❑ 31	Luka//Strange/Mad	1989	$3

—Black vinyl

Number	Title	Yr	NM
❑ 31	Luka//Strange/Mad	1989	$6

—Blue vinyl

Number	Title	Yr	NM
❑ 31	Luka//Strange/Mad	1989	$8

—Blue/yellow vinyl

Number	Title	Yr	NM
❑ 31	Luka//Strange/Mad	1989	$15

—Red vinyl

7-Inch Extended Plays

ARMORY ARMS/HUH-BAG

Number	Title	Yr	NM
❑ 1/2	Glad I Don't Know/I Like To//I Am a Rabbit/So I Fucked Up...	1986	$70

—Original pressing on black vinyl; any copy on colored vinyl (usually blue) is a reproduction

Number	Title	Yr	NM
❑ 1/2 [PS]	Laughing All the Way to the Cleaners	1986	$70

—Also has lyric insert; both record and sleeve have been counterfeited

LENNON, FREDDIE

JERDEN

Number	Title	Yr	NM
❑ 792	That's My Life (My Love and My Home)/Next Time You Feel Important	1966	$100

LENNON, JOHN

Includes records as "Plastic Ono Band," "John Ono Lennon," "John Lennon/Plastic Ono Band" and other records he made with Yoko Ono. Also see THE BEATLES.

APPLE

Number	Title	Yr	NM
❑ P-1878 [DJ]	#9 Dream (edited mono/ stereo)	1974	$60
❑ 1878	#9 Dream/What You Got	1974	$8
❑ P-1883 [DJ]	Ain't That a Shame (mono/ stereo)	1975	$200

—No stock copies issued

Number	Title	Yr	NM
❑ 1813 [PS]	Cold Turkey/Don't Worry Kyoko (Mummy's Only Looking for a Hand in the Snow)	1969	$50

—As "Plastic Ono Band

Number	Title	Yr	NM
❑ 1813	Cold Turkey/Don't Worry Kyoko (Mummy's Only Looking for a Hand in the Snow)	1969	$5

—As "Plastic Ono Band"; most copies skip on A-side on the third chorus because of a pressing defect

Number	Title	Yr	NM
❑ 1813	Cold Turkey/Don't Worry Kyoko (Mummy's Only Looking for a Hand in the Snow)	1969	$10

—As "Plastic Ono Band"; some copies don't skip on A-side. They tend to have wider, bolder print than those that do.

Number	Title	Yr	NM
❑ 1809	Give Peace a Chance/ Remember Love	1969	$5

—As "Plastic Ono Band

Number	Title	Yr	NM
❑ 1809 [PS]	Give Peace a Chance/ Remember Love	1969	$20

—As "Plastic Ono Band

Number	Title	Yr	NM
❑ S45X0 [DJ]	Happy Xmas (War Is Over)/ Listen, the Snow Is Falling	1971	$750

—As "John & Yoko/Plastic Ono Band with the Harlem Community Choir"; white label on styrene

Number	Title	Yr	NM
❑ 1842	Happy Xmas (War Is Over)/ Listen, the Snow Is Falling	1971	$20

—As "John & Yoko/Plastic Ono Band with the Harlem Community Choir"; green vinyl, faces label

Number	Title	Yr	NM
❑ 1842	Happy Xmas (War Is Over)/ Listen, the Snow Is Falling	1971	$12

—As "John & Yoko/Plastic Ono Band with the Harlem Community Choir"; green vinyl, Apple label

Number	Title	Yr	NM
❑ 1842 [PS]	Happy Xmas (War Is Over)/ Listen, the Snow Is Falling	1971	$30

—As "John & Yoko/Plastic Ono Band with the Harlem Community Choir

Number	Title	Yr	NM
❑ S45X-47663/4 [DJ]	Happy Xmas (War Is Over)/ Listen, the Snow Is Falling	1971	$1000

—As "John & Yoko/Plastic Ono Band with the Harlem Community Choir"; white label on styrene

Number	Title	Yr	NM
❑ 1840	Imagine/It's So Hard	1971	$8

—As "John Lennon Plastic Ono Band"; tan label

Number	Title	Yr	NM
❑ 1840	Imagine/It's So Hard	1975	$15

—As "John Lennon Plastic Ono Band"; green label with "All Rights Reserved

Number	Title	Yr	NM
❑ 1818 [DJ]	Instant Karma! (We All Shine On)	1970	$200

—As "John Ono Lennon"; one-sided promo

Number	Title	Yr	NM
❑ 1818 [DJ]	Instant Karma! (We All Shine On)	1970	$200

—As "John Ono Lennon"; one-sided promo

Number	Title	Yr	NM
❑ 1818	Instant Karma! (We All Shine On)/Who Has Seen the Wind?	1970	$10

—As "John Ono Lennon"; B-side by "Yoko Ono Lennon

Number	Title	Yr	NM
❑ 1818 [PS]	Instant Karma! (We All Shine On)/Who Has Seen the Wind?	1970	$25

—As "John Ono Lennon"; B-side by "Yoko Ono Lennon

Number	Title	Yr	NM
❑ 1868	Mind Games/Meat City	1973	$6
❑ 1868 [PS]	Mind Games/Meat City	1973	$20
❑ P-1868 [DJ]	Mind Games (mono/stereo)	1973	$60
❑ P-1868 [DJ]	Mind Games (mono/stereo)	1973	$60
❑ 1827	Mother/Why	1970	$10

—As "John Lennon/Plastic Ono Band"; B-side by "Yoko Ono/ Plastic Ono Band

Number	Title	Yr	NM
❑ 1827 [PS]	Mother/Why	1970	$120

—As "John Lennon/Plastic Ono Band"; B-side by "Yoko Ono/ Plastic Ono Band

Number	Title	Yr	NM
❑ 1827	Mother/Why	1970	$15

—As "John Lennon/Plastic Ono Band"; star on A-side label

Number	Title	Yr	NM
❑ 1827	Mother/Why	1970	$50

—As "John Lennon/Plastic Ono Band"; "MONO" on A-side label

Number	Title	Yr	NM
❑ 1830	Power to the People/ Touch Me	1971	$12

—As "John Lennon/Plastic Ono Band"; B-side by "Yoko Ono/ Plastic Ono Band

Number	Title	Yr	NM
❑ 1830 [PS]	Power to the People/ Touch Me	1971	$50

—As "John Lennon/Plastic Ono Band"; B-side by "Yoko Ono/ Plastic Ono Band

Number	Title	Yr	NM
❑ 1830	Power to the People/ Touch Me	1971	$8

—As "John Lennon/Plastic Ono Band"; with star on A-side label

Number	Title	Yr	NM
❑ P-1883 [DJ]	Slippin' and Slidin' (mono/ stereo)	1975	$200

—No stock copies issued

Number	Title	Yr	NM
❑ P-1883 [DJ]	Slippin' and Slidin' (mono/ stereo)	1975	$200

—No stock copies issued

Number	Title	Yr	NM
❑ P-1881 [DJ]	Stand By Me (mono/stereo)	1975	$60
❑ P-1881 [DJ]	Stand By Me (mono/stereo)	1975	$60
❑ 1881	Stand By Me/Move Over Ms. L.	1975	$8
❑ 1874	Whatever Gets You Thru the Night/Beef Jerky	1974	$6

—As "John Lennon and the Plastic Ono Nuclear Band

Number	Title	Yr	NM
❑ P-1874 [DJ]	Whatever Gets You Thru the Night (mono/stereo)	1974	$60

—As "John Lennon and the Plastic Ono Nuclear Band

Number	Title	Yr	NM
❑ P-1874 [DJ]	Whatever Gets You Thru the Night (mono/stereo)	1974	$60

—As "John Lennon and the Plastic Ono Nuclear Band

Number	Title	Yr	NM
❑ P-1878 [DJ]	What You Got (mono/stereo)	1974	$125
❑ P-1878 [DJ]	What You Got (mono/stereo)	1974	$125
❑ 1848	Woman Is the Nigger of the World/Sisters O Sisters	1972	$10

—As "John Lennon/Plastic Ono Band..."; B-side by "Yoko Ono/Plastic Ono Band...

Number	Title	Yr	NM
❑ 1848 [PS]	Woman Is the Nigger of the World/Sisters O Sisters	1972	$30

—As "John Lennon/Plastic Ono Band..."; B-side by "Yoko Ono/Plastic Ono Band...

APPLE/AMERICOM

Number	Title	Yr	NM
❑ 1809P/M-435	Give Peace a Chance/ Remember Love	1969	$750

—As "Plastic Ono Band"; four-inch flexi-disc sold in vending machines

CAPITOL

Number	Title	Yr	NM
❑ 1878	#9 Dream/What You Got	1976	$50

—Orange label

Number	Title	Yr	NM
❑ 1878	#9 Dream/What You Got	1978	$6

—Purple late-1970s label

Number	Title	Yr	NM
❑ 1878	#9 Dream/What You Got	1983	$12

—Black colorband label

Number	Title	Yr	NM
❑ 1842	Happy Xmas (War Is Over)/ Listen, the Snow Is Falling	1976	$60

—As "John & Yoko/Plastic Ono Band with the Harlem Community Choir"; orange label

Number	Title	Yr	NM
❑ 1842	Happy Xmas (War Is Over)/ Listen, the Snow Is Falling	1978	$6

—As "John & Yoko/Plastic Ono Band with the Harlem Community Choir"; purple late-1970s label

Number	Title	Yr	NM
❑ 1842	Happy Xmas (War Is Over)/ Listen, the Snow Is Falling	1983	$6

—As "John & Yoko/Plastic Ono Band with the Harlem Community Choir"; black colorband label

Number	Title	Yr	NM
❑ 1842	Happy Xmas (War Is Over)/ Listen, the Snow Is Falling	1988	$30

—As "John & Yoko/Plastic Ono Band with the Harlem Community Choir"; purple late-1980s label (wider)

Number	Title	Yr	NM
❑ 1840	Imagine/It's So Hard	1978	$6

—As "John Lennon Plastic Ono Band"; purple late 1970s label

Number	Title	Yr	NM
❑ 1840	Imagine/It's So Hard	1983	$6

—As "John Lennon Plastic Ono Band"; black colorband label

Number	Title	Yr	NM
❑ 1840	Imagine/It's So Hard	1988	$5

—As "John Lennon Plastic Ono Band"; purple late-1980s label (wider)

Number	Title	Yr	NM
❑ 1868	Mind Games/Meat City	1978	$6

—Purple late-1970s label

Number	Title	Yr	NM
❑ 1868	Mind Games/Meat City	1983	$15

—Black colorband label

Number	Title	Yr	NM
❑ 1874	Whatever Gets You Thru the Night/Beef Jerky	1978	$6

—Purple late-1970s label

Number	Title	Yr	NM
❏ 1874	Whatever Gets You Thru the Night/Beef Jerky	1983	$6
— Black colorband label			
❏ 1874	Whatever Gets You Thru the Night/Beef Jerky	1988	$6
— Purple late-1980s label			

GEFFEN

❏ 29855	Happy Xmas (War Is Over)/Beautiful Boy (Darling Boy)	1982	$5
❏ 29855 [PS]	Happy Xmas (War Is Over)/Beautiful Boy (Darling Boy)	1982	$5
❏ 49695	Watching the Wheels/Yes, I'm Your Angel	1981	$4
— B-side by Yoko Ono			
❏ 49695 [PS]	Watching the Wheels/Yes, I'm Your Angel	1981	$4
— B-side by Yoko Ono			
❏ 49644	Woman/Beautiful Boys	1980	$4
— B-side by Yoko Ono			
❏ 49644 [PS]	Woman/Beautiful Boys	1980	$4
— B-side by Yoko Ono			

POLYDOR

❏ 821204-7	Borrowed Time/Your Hands	1984	$8
— B-side by Yoko Ono			
❏ 821204-7 [PS]	Borrowed Time/Your Hands	1984	$5
❏ 881378-7	Every Man Has a Woman Who Loves Him/It's Alright	1984	$8
— B-side by Sean Ono Lennon			
❏ 881378-7 [PS]	Every Man Has a Woman Who Loves Him/It's Alright	1984	$8
❏ 821107-7	I'm Stepping Out/Sleepless Night	1984	$4
— B-side by Yoko Ono			
❏ 821107-7 [PS]	I'm Stepping Out/Sleepless Night	1984	$4

QUAKER GRANOLA DIPPS

❏ 0(no cat #)	A Tribute to John Lennon	1986	$20
— Cardboard record included in specially marked boxes of Quaker Granola Dipps			

LENNON, JULIAN
ATLANTIC

❏ 89567	Say You're Wrong/Big Mama	1985	$4
❏ 89567 [PS]	Say You're Wrong/Big Mama	1985	$4
❏ 89437	Stick Around/Always Think Twice	1986	$4
❏ 89437 [PS]	Stick Around/Always Think Twice	1986	$4
❏ 89385	This Is My Day/Everyday	1986	$4
❏ 89589	Too Late for Goodbyes/Let Me Go	1985	$4
❏ 89589 [PS]	Too Late for Goodbyes/Let Me Go	1985	$4
❏ 89405	Want Your Body/Everyday	1986	$4

CAPITOL

❏ B-5618	Time Will Teach Us All/(Instrumental)	1986	$4

LENNON SISTERS, THE
BRUNSWICK

❏ 55075	Bubble Gum/Have You Ever Been Lonely	1958	$10
— With Larry Dean			
❏ 55058	Dear One/Mr. Clarinet Man	1958	$12
❏ 55063	How Will I Know My Love/Graduation Dance	1958	$10
❏ 55044	Let's Light the Christmas Tree/Merry, Merry Christmas	1957	$15
❏ 55028	Shake Me I Rattle/Pocahontas	1957	$10
❏ 55113	The Children's Marching Song/Slumber Party	1959	$12
❏ 55051	To Know You Is to Love You/Hide Your Troubles Behind a Smile	1958	$10
❏ 55082	Walk with Me/Goodnight God	1958	$10
❏ 55013	White Silver Sands/One Day a Little Girl	1957	$10

DOT

❏ 15965	A Hundred and One in the Sun/Vacation Waltz	1959	$8
❏ 16423	Bei Mir Bist Du Schoen/Lida Rose	1963	$8
❏ 16748	Chim Chim Cheree/A Step in Time	1965	$6
❏ 16215	Darlin' Meggie/On the Double	1961	$8
❏ 16184	Did'Ja Know/What a Sky	1961	$8
❏ 16131	Freckles/I Wakled with the Wind	1960	$8
❏ 17010	He's Got a Lotta Lovin'/I'm Coming Back to You	1967	$6
❏ 17046	I Love/Gypsy, What Can I Do	1967	$6
❏ 16681	Little Stranger/Little Lady Make Believe	1964	$6
❏ 16255	Sad Movies (Make Me Cry)/I Don't Know Why	1961	$8
❏ 16489	The Heartstrings/Speak, Sugar, Speak	1963	$8

Number	Title	Yr	NM
MERCURY			
❏ 72830	As Long As There's an Apple Tree/I'm So Glad That You've Found Me	1968	$6
❏ 72883	The Christmas Waltz/Lullaby for Christmas	1968	$6

LENNOX, ANNIE, AND AL GREEN
A&M

❏ 1255	Put a Little Love in Your Heart/A Great Big Piece of Love	1988	$3
— B-side by Spheres of Celestial Influence			
❏ 1255 [PS]	Put a Little Love in Your Heart/A Great Big Piece of Love	1988	$3
— Scrooged" sleeve with large hole in center			

LENNY AND THE CHIMES
VEE JAY

❏ 605	Only Forever/Two Times Two	1964	$15

LENNY AND THE THUNDERTONES
DOT

❏ 16177	The Street Beat/Happy Little Jug	1961	$30

LENOIR, J.B.
CHECKER

❏ 901	Daddy Talk to Your Son/She Don't Know	1958	$40
❏ 856	Don't Touch My Head/I've Been Down So Long	1957	$50
❏ 844	Let Me Die with the One I Love/If I Give My Love to You	1956	$50
❏ 874	What About Your Daughter/Five Years	1957	$40

J.O.B.

❏ 1102	Play a Little While/Louise	1952	$120
❏ 1012	The Mojo/How Can I Leave	1952	$200

PARROT

❏ 802	Eisenhower Blues/I'm in Korea	1954	$400
❏ 821	Fine Girls/I Lost My Baby	1955	$200
❏ 809	Mama Talk to Your Daughter/Man, Watch Your Woman	1955	$100
❏ 814	Mama Your Daughter Is Going to Miss Me/What Have I Done	1955	$125
❏ 802	Tax Paying Blues/I'm in Korea	1954	$1000
— A-side is similar, though not identical, to "Eisenhower Blues			
❏ 802	Tax Paying Blues/I'm in Korea	1954	$2000
— Red vinyl			

SHAD

❏ 5012	Back Door/Louella	1959	$30

U.S.A.

❏ 744	I Feel So Good/Sing Um the Way I Feel	1963	$30

VEE JAY

❏ 352	Do What I Say/Oh Baby	1960	$15
— As "J.B. Lenore"			

LEON AND THE DREAMERS
PARKWAY

❏ 843	Haircut/If It Hadn't Been for You	1962	$20

LEONARD, BILLY
FAIRMOUNT

❏ 1007	Tell Me Do You Love Me/Tears for Love	1966	$100

LES CHANSONETTES
SHRINE

❏ 114	Don't Let Him Hurt You/Deeper	1966	$800

LES THUGS
SUB POP

❏ 29	Chess and Crimes/Sunday Time	1989	$30
— #4 in Sub Pop Singles Club series			
❏ 29 [PS]	Chess and Crimes/Sunday Time	1989	$30

LESTER, BOBBY, AND THE MOONLIGHTERS
CHECKER

❏ 806	So All Alone/Shoo Doo-Be Do (My Loving Baby)	1954	$125
— Maroon label with checkerboard top			

Number	Title	Yr	NM
❏ 806	So All Alone/Shoo Doo-Be Do (My Loving Baby)	1958	$50
— Maroon label, vertical logo			

LESTER, KETTY
ERA

❏ 3080	But Not for Me/Once Upon a Time	1962	$10
❏ 3103	Fallen Angel/Lullaby for Lovers	1963	$10
❏ 3068	Love Letters/I'm a Fool to Want You	1962	$15
❏ 3094	This Land Is Your Land/Love Is for Everyone	1962	$10

PETE

❏ 706	I Wil Lead You/Now That I Need Him	1968	$6
❏ 710	Measure of a Man/Cracker Box Living	1968	$6
❏ 714	Show Me/Since I Fell for You	1969	$6

RCA VICTOR

❏ 47-8424	I Trust You Baby/Theme from The Luck of Ginger Coffey	1964	$30
❏ 47-8573	(Looking for a) Better World/Pretty Lies, Pretty Make Believes	1965	$30
❏ 47-8371	Please Don't Cry Anymore/Roses Grow With Thorns	1964	$125
❏ 47-8331	The House Is Haunted/Some Things Are Better Left Unsaid	1964	$125

TOWER

❏ 166	I'll Be Looking Back/West Coast	1965	$8
❏ 208	Secret Love/Love Me Just a Little Bit	1966	$8
❏ 236	When a Woman Loves a Man/We'll Be Together Again	1966	$8

LETHAL YELLOW
7-Inch Extended Plays
TPOS/STENCH

❏ 09	Declaration of Retardation	1983	$35
❏ 09 [PS]	Declaration of Retardation	1983	$35
— Yellow sleeve			
❏ 09 [PS]	Declaration of Retardation	1983	$35
— Pink sleeve			

LETTERMEN, THE
ALPHA OMEGA

❏ 078501	It Feels Like Christmas/I Believe	1985	$4
❏ 078501 [PS]	It Feels Like Christmas/I Believe	1985	$4

APPLAUSE

❏ 104	What I Did for Love/Cherish-Precious and Few	1983	$4

CAPITOL

❏ 4851	Again/A Tree in the Meadow	1962	$15
❏ 4851 [PS]	Again/A Tree in the Meadow	1962	$30
❏ 2196	Anyone Who Had a Heart/All the Gray-Haired Men	1968	$6
❏ 3619	A Summer Song/Mac Arthur Park	1973	$4
❏ 5749	Chanson D'Amour/She Don't Want Me Now	1966	$8
❏ 4699	Come Back Silly Girl/A Song for Young Love	1962	$15
❏ 4699 [PS]	Come Back Silly Girl/A Song for Young Love	1962	$30
❏ 3020	Everything Is Good About You/It's Over	1971	$5
❏ 2054	Goin' Out of My Head-Can't Take My Eyes Off You/I Believe	1967	$8
❏ 3810	Goodbye/The You Part of Me	1973	$4
❏ 2774	Hang On Sloopy/For Love	1970	$5
❏ 2938	Hey Girl/Worlds	1970	$5
❏ 4746	How Is Julie?/Turn Around, Look at Me	1962	$15
❏ 4746 [PS]	How Is Julie?/Turn Around, Look at Me	1962	$30
❏ 2482	Hurt So Bad/Catch the Wind	1969	$6
❏ 5544	I Believe/Sweet September	1965	$8
❏ 4161	If You Feel the Way I Do/Love Me Like a Stranger	1975	$4
❏ 2414	I Have Dreamed/The Pendulum Swings Both Ways	1969	$6
❏ 5649	I Only Have Eyes for You/Love Letters	1966	$8
❏ 5649 [PS]	I Only Have Eyes for You/Love Letters	1966	$15
❏ 3098	Love Is a Hurtin' Thing/Feelings	1971	$5
❏ 2218	Love Is Blue-Greensleeves/Where Were You When the Lights Went Out	1968	$6
❏ 3192	Love/Maybe Tomorrow	1971	$5
❏ 3449	Maybe We Should/Spin Away	1972	$4
❏ 3285	Oh My Love/An Old Fashioned Love Song	1972	$4

Number	Title	Yr	NM
3285 [PS]	Oh My Love/An Old Fashioned Love Song	1972	$6
5813	Our Winter Love/Warm	1966	$8
2254	Playing the Piano/Sally Le Roy	1968	$6
5218	Put Away Your Teardrops/Seventh Dawn Theme	1964	$10
2324	Put Your Head on My Shoulder/Mary's Rainbow	1968	$6
3512	Sandman/Love Song	1973	$4
5499	Secretly/The Things We Did Last Summer	1965	$8
5499 [PS]	Secretly/The Things We Did Last Summer	1965	$15
2643	Shangri-La/When Summer Ends	1969	$6
2820	She Cried/For Love	1970	$5
2132	Sherry Don't Go/Never My Love	1968	$6
4810	Silly Boy (She Doesn't Love You)/I Told the Stars	1962	$15
4810 [PS]	Silly Boy (She Doesn't Love You)/I Told the Stars	1962	$30
4005	Song from Some Came Running (To Love and Be Loved)/Eastward	1974	$4
4226	Storms of Troubled Times?/The Way You Look Tonight	1976	$4
5370	The Girl with a Little Tin Heart/It's Over	1965	$8
5437	Theme from "A Summer Place"/Sealed with a Kiss	1965	$8
3912	The Way We Were-Isn't It a Shame/Touch Me in the Morning	1974	$4
4586	The Way You Look Tonight/That's My Desire	1961	$15
4586 [PS]	The Way You Look Tonight/That's My Desire	1961	$30
2697	Traces-Memories Medley/For Once in a Lifetime	1969	$6
4976	Two Brothers/The Allentown Jail	1963	$10
4658	When I Fall in Love/Smile	1961	$15
4658 [PS]	When I Fall in Love/Smile	1961	$30
5273	When Summer Ends/You Don't Know Just How Lucky You Are	1964	$10
5091	Where or When/Be My Girl	1963	$10

WARNER BROS.

Number	Title	Yr	NM
5152	Their Hearts Were Full of Spring/When	1960	$20
5178	Two Hearts/Magic Sound	1960	$20

LETTERMEN, THE (2)
LIBERTY

Number	Title	Yr	NM
55141	Hey, Big Brain/Guiro	1958	$12

LEVEL 42
A&M

Number	Title	Yr	NM
2631	Micro-Kid/Standing in the Light	1984	$5
2667	The Sun Goes Down (Living It Up)/Dance On Heavy Weather	1984	$5

POLYDOR

Number	Title	Yr	NM
885155-7	Hot Water	1986	$3
887277-7	It's Over/MICR Kid	1987	$3
811538-7	Last Chance/Chinese Way	1983	$5
885284-7	Leaving Me Now/Sleep on My Heart	1986	$3
883956-7	Lessons in Love/Hot Water (Live)	1986	$3
883956-7 [PS]	Lessons in Love/Hot Water (Live)	1986	$3
2221	Love Games/Weave Your Spell	1982	$5
883362-7	Something About You/	1985	$3
887136-7	To Be with You Again/Physical Presence (Live)	1987	$3
871438-7	Tracie/Man	1989	$3
2207	Turn It On/Star Child	1982	$5

LEVERETT, CHICO
BETHLEHEM

Number	Title	Yr	NM
3062	Baby (Don't Leave)/Work, Work	1963	$50

TAMLA

Number	Title	Yr	NM
54024	Solid Sender/I'll Never Love Again	1959	$2000

— VG 1000; VG+ 1500

LEVON AND THE HAWKS
ATCO

Number	Title	Yr	NM
6625	He Don't Love You (And He'll Break Your Heart)/Go Go Lisa Jane	1968	$40
6383	He Don't Love You (And He'll Break Your Heart)/Stones I Throw	1965	$40

LEWIS AND CLARKE EXPEDITION, THE
CHARTMAKER

Number	Title	Yr	NM
402	Expedition West/For Your Freedom Tonight	1966	$8

COLGEMS

Number	Title	Yr	NM
66-1022	Chain Around the Flowers/Why Need They Pretend	1968	$8
66-1028	Daddy's Plastic Child/Gypsy Song Man	1968	$8
66-1011	Destination Unknown/Freedom Bird	1967	$8
66-1011 [PS]	Destination Unknown/Freedom Bird	1967	$20
66-1006	I Feel Good (I Feel Bad)/Blue Revelations	1967	$8
66-1006 [PS]	I Feel Good (I Feel Bad)/Blue Revelations	1967	$20

LEWIS, BARBARA
ATLANTIC

Number	Title	Yr	NM
2283	Baby, I'm Yours/I Say Love	1965	$20
2255	Come Home/Pushin' a Good Thing Too Far	1964	$30
2316	Don't Forget About Me/It's Magic	1965	$30
2413	Fool, Fool, Fool/Only All the Time	1967	$30
2184	Hello Stranger/Think a Little Sugar	1963	$20
2550	I'm All You've Got/You're a Dream Maker	1968	$30
2361	I Remember the Feeling/Baby What You Want Me to Do	1966	$60
2400	Love Makes the World Go Round/I'll Make Him Love Me	1967	$30
2346	Make Me Belong to You/Girls Need Loving Care	1966	$30
2300	Make Me Your Baby/Love to Be Loved	1965	$30
2141	My Heart Went Do Dat Da/The Longest Night of the Year	1962	$10
2159	My Mama Told Me/Gonna Love You Till the Day I Die	1962	$50
2514	On Bended Knees/I'll Keep Believing	1968	$30
2214	Puppy Love/Snap Your Fingers	1963	$50
2227	Someday We're Gonna Love Again/Spend a Little Time	1964	$50
2200	Straighten Up Your Heart/If You Love Her	1963	$50
2482	Thankful for What I Got/Sho Nuff	1968	$30

ENTERPRISE

Number	Title	Yr	NM
9029	Anyway/That's the Way I Like It	1970	$10
9027	Ask the Lonely/Why Did It Take You So Long	1970	$40

KAREN

Number	Title	Yr	NM
313	My Heart Went Do Dat Da/The Longest Night of the Year	1961	$50

LEWIS, BOBBY (1)
R&B singer.

ABC-PARAMOUNT

Number	Title	Yr	NM
10565	That's Right/Fannie Lewis	1964	$15

BELTONE

Number	Title	Yr	NM
2018	A Man's Gotta Be a Man/Day by Day I Need Your Love	1962	$20
2023	I'm Tossin' and Turnin' Again/Nothin' But the Blues	1962	$20
2026	Lonely Teardrops/Boom-a-Chick-Chick	1962	$20
1012	One Track Mind/Are You Ready	1961	$30
1002	Tossin' and Turnin'/Oh Yes I Love You	1961	$30
1015	What a Walk/Cry No More	1961	$20

MERCURY

Number	Title	Yr	NM
71245	Mumbles Blues/Oh Baby	1957	$30

PHILIPS

Number	Title	Yr	NM
40519	Soul Seekin'/Give Me Your Yesterdays	1968	$30

ROULETTE

Number	Title	Yr	NM
4382	Solid as a Rock/Oh Mr. Somebody	1961	$20

SPOTLIGHT

Number	Title	Yr	NM
394	Mumbles Blues/Oh Baby	1957	$40
397	Solid as a Rock/You Even Forgot My Name	1957	$40

LEWIS, BOBBY (2)
Country singer.

ACE OF HEARTS

Number	Title	Yr	NM
0463	Already Gone to My Heart/Mr. President	1973	$6
0466	Here with You/Where Happiness Is	1973	$6
0480	I Never Get Through Missing You/Lady Lover	1974	$6
7503	It's So Nice to Be with You/(B-side unknown)	1975	$6
0502	Let Me Take Care of You/Where Happiness Is	1975	$6
0472	Too Many Memories/With Meaning	1973	$6

CAPRICORN

Number	Title	Yr	NM
0331	Love Won't Be Love Without You/This Is a Man and Woman Kind of Thing	1979	$5
0318	She's Been Keeping Me Up Nights/I Keep Falling in Love with You	1979	$5

GRT

Number	Title	Yr	NM
008	I See Love/Your Love	1974	$6
007	Lady Lover/I Never Get Through Missing You	1974	$6

HME

Number	Title	Yr	NM
04853	Love Is An Overload/Treat Her Like a Stranger	1985	$4

RPA

Number	Title	Yr	NM
7603	For Your Love/(B-side unknown)	1976	$6
7613	I'm Getting High Remembering/With Meaning	1976	$6
7622	What a Diff'rence a Day Made/I Can Feel It	1977	$6

UNITED ARTISTS

Number	Title	Yr	NM
50476	Each and Every Part of Me/My (Is Such a Lonely Word)	1969	$8
842	Everybody's Baby/Perfect Example of a Fool	1965	$12
50327	From Heaven to Heartache/Only for Me	1968	$8
50067	How Long Has It Been/Easy to Say, Hard to Do	1966	$8
50208	I Doubt It/Laughing Girl, She's Not Happy	1967	$8
50620	I'm Going Home/I May Never Be Free	1969	$8
50161	Love Me and Make It All Better/My Tears Don't Care (They Fall Anywhere)	1967	$8
50263	Ordinary Miracle/These Are Things I Miss	1968	$8
50573	Things for You and I/Somebody Lied to Me	1969	$8
50528	Til Something Better Comes Along/I'm Only a Man	1969	$8
50133	Two of the Usual/Your B.A.B.Y. Baby Don't Love You	1967	$8
920	Why Me/Six Days a Week, Twice on Sunday	1965	$10

LEWIS, CLARENCE
FURY

Number	Title	Yr	NM
1032	Cupid's Little Helper/Half a Heart	1960	$20

RED ROBIN

Number	Title	Yr	NM
136	Lost Everything/Your Heart Must Be Made of Stone	1955	$100

LEWIS, GARY, AND THE PLAYBOYS
EPIC

Number	Title	Yr	NM
50068	One Good Woman/Ooh Baby	1975	$8

— Gary Lewis solo

LIBERTY

Number	Title	Yr	NM
56075	C.C. Rider/Main Street	1968	$6
55778	Count Me In/Little Miss Go-Go	1965	$12
65-227 [PS]	Doin' the Flake//This Diamond Ring/Little Miss Go-Go	1965	$60

— Kellogg's Corn Flakes giveaway

Number	Title	Yr	NM
65-227	Doin' the Flake//This Diamond Ring/Little Miss Go-Go	1965	$30

— Record available by mail order from Kellogg's Corn Flakes; all copies have black labels with silver print

Number	Title	Yr	NM
55818	Everybody Loves a Clown/Time Stands Still	1965	$12
55818 [PS]	Everybody Loves a Clown/Time Stands Still	1965	$20
56093	Every Day I Have to Cry Some/Mister Memory	1969	$6
55971	Girls in Love/Let's Be More Than Friends	1967	$8
56158	Great Balls of Fire/I'm On the Road Right Now	1970	$6
55880	Green Grass/I Can Read Between the Lines	1966	$10
55880 [PS]	Green Grass/I Can Read Between the Lines	1966	$20
56011	Has She Got the Nicest Eyes/Happiness	1967	$8
56121	Hayride/Gary's Groove	1969	$6
56144	I Saw Elvis Presley Last Night/Something's Wrong	1969	$15
55898	My Heart's Symphony/Tina	1966	$10
55898 [PS]	My Heart's Symphony/Tina	1966	$20
55809	Save Your Heart for Me/Without a Word of Warning	1965	$10
56037	Sealed with a Kiss/Sara Jane	1968	$8
55846	She's Just My Style/I Won't Make That Mistake Again	1965	$10

Number	Title	Yr	NM
❏ 55846 [PS]	She's Just My Style/I Won't Make That Mistake Again	1965	$20
❏ 55865	Sure Gonna Miss Her/I Don't Wanna Say Goodnight	1966	$10
❏ 55865 [PS]	Sure Gonna Miss Her/I Don't Wanna Say Goodnight	1966	$20
❏ 55949	The Loser (With a Broken Heart)/Ice Melts in the Sun	1967	$10
❏ 55949 [PS]	The Loser (With a Broken Heart)/Ice Melts in the Sun	1967	$20
❏ 55756	This Diamond Ring/Hard to Find	1964	$15
❏ 55756	This Diamond Ring/Tijuana Wedding	1964	$10
❏ 0 (no cat #) [DJ]	Way Way Out (same on both sides)	1967	$500
❏ 55933	Where Will the Words Come From/May the Best Man Win	1966	$10

SCEPTER

Number	Title	Yr	NM
❏ 12359	Peace of Mind/Then Again Maybe	1972	$8

— *Gary Lewis solo*

UNITED ARTISTS

Number	Title	Yr	NM
❏ 0065	Count Me In/Save Your Heart for Me	1973	$4
❏ 0066	Everybody Loves a Clown/Sure Gonna Miss Her	1973	$4
❏ 0067	She's Just My Style/Green Grass	1973	$4

— *0064 through 0067 are "Silver Spotlight Series" reissues*

Number	Title	Yr	NM
❏ 0064	This Diamond Ring/My Heart's Symphony	1973	$4

LEWIS, HUEY, AND THE NEWS

CHRYSALIS

Number	Title	Yr	NM
❏ VS443143	Doing It All for My Baby/Naturally	1987	$3
❏ VS443143 [PS]	Doing It All for My Baby/Naturally	1987	$3
❏ 2589	Do You Believe in Love/Is It Me	1981	$5
❏ VS842947	Do You Believe in Love/Working for a Living	1986	$4

— *Silver label reissue*

Number	Title	Yr	NM
❏ VS443335	Give Me the Keys (And I'll Drive You Crazy)/It's All Right (Live)	1989	$4
❏ VS443335 [PS]	Give Me the Keys (And I'll Drive You Crazy)/It's All Right (Live)	1989	$3
❏ VS842948	Heart and Soul/I Want a New Drug	1986	$4

— *Silver label reissue*

Number	Title	Yr	NM
❏ VS442726	Heart and Soul/You Crack Me Up	1983	$3
❏ VS442726 [PS]	Heart and Soul/You Crack Me Up	1983	$3
❏ VS443065	Hip to Be Square/Some of My Lies Are True	1986	$3
❏ VS443065 [PS]	Hip to Be Square/Some of My Lies Are True	1986	$3
❏ 2604	Hope You Love Me Like You Say You Do/Whatever Happened to True Love	1982	$5
❏ 2604 [PS]	Hope You Love Me Like You Say You Do/Whatever Happened to True Love	1982	$5
❏ VS442803	If This Is It/Change of Heart	1984	$3
❏ VS442803 [PS]	If This Is It/Change of Heart	1984	$3
❏ VS443108	I Know What I Like/Forest for the Trees	1987	$3
❏ VS443108 [PS]	I Know What I Like/Forest for the Trees	1987	$3
❏ VS442766	I Want a New Drug/Finally Found a Home	1983	$3
❏ VS442766 [PS]	I Want a New Drug/Finally Found a Home	1983	$5
❏ VS443265	Perfect World/Slammin'	1988	$3
❏ VS443265 [PS]	Perfect World/Slammin'	1988	$3
❏ VS442876	Power of Love/Bad Is Bad	1985	$5

— *Original edition*

Number	Title	Yr	NM
❏ VS443306	Small World/(Instrumental)	1988	$3
❏ VS443306 [PS]	Small World/(Instrumental)	1988	$3
❏ 2446	Some of My Lies Are True/Hearts	1980	$12
❏ 2446 [PS]	Some of My Lies Are True/Hearts	1980	$20

— *Newspaper-like sleeve with "The Bay Area's Free Daily SPECIAL EDITION" on front*

Number	Title	Yr	NM
❏ VS443019	Stuck with You/Don't Ever Tell Me That You Love Me	1986	$3
❏ VS443019 [PS]	Stuck with You/Don't Ever Tell Me That You Love Me	1986	$3
❏ VS842949	The Heart of Rock 'n' Roll/If This Is It	1986	$4

— *Silver label reissue*

Number	Title	Yr	NM
❏ VS442782	The Heart of Rock 'n' Roll/Workin' for a Livin' (Live)	1984	$3
❏ VS442782 [PS]	The Heart of Rock 'n' Roll/Workin' for a Livin' (Live)	1984	$4
❏ VS442876	The Power of Love/Bad Is Bad	1985	$3

— *Later edition, with "The" added to A-side title*

Number	Title	Yr	NM
❏ VS442876 [PS]	The Power of Love/Bad Is Bad	1985	$5

— *All of the picture sleeves have this title on them*

Number	Title	Yr	NM
❏ VS442825	Walking on a Thin Line/The Only One	1984	$3
❏ VS442825 [PS]	Walking on a Thin Line/The Only One	1984	$3
❏ 2630	Workin' for a Livin'/(Live)	1982	$5

LEWIS, JERRY

CAPITOL

Number	Title	Yr	NM
❏ F1482	A-Hunting We Will Go/Never Been Kissed	1951	$20
❏ F2141	Crazy Words/I Can't Carry a Tune	1952	$20
❏ F2576	Give Me a Little Kiss, Will Ya Huh/Yyyup	1953	$20
❏ F2481	If You Love Me Truly/Little Man You've Had a Busy Day	1953	$20

— *With Patti Lewis*

Number	Title	Yr	NM
❏ F1740	I Like It, I Like It/I'll Tell a Policeman on You	1951	$20
❏ F1868	I Love Girls/Lay Something on the Bar	1951	$20
❏ F1045	I'm a Little Busybody/Sunday Driving	1950	$30
❏ F2317	I've Had a Very Merry Christmas/Strictly for the Birds	1952	$30
❏ F1969	The Book Was So Much Better Than the Picture/North Dakota, South Dakota	1952	$20
❏ F2202	They Go Wild, Simply Wild Over Me/I Keep Her Picture Hanging	1952	$20

DECCA

Number	Title	Yr	NM
❏ 30370	By Myself/No One	1957	$10
❏ 30664	Dormi-Dormi-Dormi/Love Is a Lonely Thing	1958	$12
❏ 30263	Let Me Sing and I'm Happy/It All Depends on You	1957	$12
❏ 30607	Long Black Nylons/Back to Kenya	1958	$10
❏ 31019	Makin' Whoopee/Have a Girl, Have a Boy	1959	$10
❏ 31400	My Mammy/Let Me Sing and I'm Happy	1962	$8
❏ 30345	My Mammy/With These Hands	1957	$10
❏ 30503	Sad Sack/The Lord Loves a Laughing Man	1957	$10
❏ 31115	Smile/Everything's Coming Up Roses	1960	$8
❏ 30808	Song from "The Geisha Boy"/The More I See	1959	$12

DOT

Number	Title	Yr	NM
❏ 16772	Green, Green/I'll See Your Light	1965	$6

— *As "The Jerry Lewis Singers"*

Number	Title	Yr	NM
❏ 16164	Somebody/Turn It On	1960	$8

7-Inch Extended Plays

DECCA

Number	Title	Yr	NM
❏ ED2457	Birth of the Blues/Bye Bye Baby//Back in Your Own Backyard/Sometimes I'm Happy	1957	$20
❏ ED2455 [PS]	Come Rain or Come Shine/Shine On Your Shoes//How Long Has This Been Going On/Get Happy	1957	$20
❏ ED2456	(contents unknown)	1957	$20

LEWIS, JERRY LEE, AND LINDA GAIL LEWIS

SMASH

Number	Title	Yr	NM
❏ 2220	Don't Let Me Cross Over/We Live in Two Different Worlds	1969	$12
❏ 2220 [PS]	Don't Let Me Cross Over/We Live in Two Different Worlds	1969	$30

LEWIS, JERRY LEE

ELEKTRA

Number	Title	Yr	NM
❏ 46642	Honky Tonk Stuff/Rockin' Jerry Lee	1980	$4
❏ 69962	I'd Do It All Again/Who Will Buy the Wine	1982	$4
❏ 47026	Over the Rainbow/Folsom Prison Blues	1980	$4
❏ 47095	Thirty-Nine and Holding/Change Places with Me	1980	$4
❏ 46591	When Two Worlds Collide/Good News Travels Fast	1980	$4
❏ 46067	Who Will the Next Fool Be/Rita May	1979	$4

MCA

Number	Title	Yr	NM
❏ 52188	Come As You Were/Circumstantial Evidence	1983	$3
❏ 52369	I Am What I Am/That Was the Way It Was Then	1984	$3
❏ 52151	My Fingers Do the Talkin'/Forever Forgiving	1983	$3
❏ 52233	She Sings Amazing Grace/Why You Been Gone So Long	1983	$3

MERCURY

Number	Title	Yr	NM
❏ 73729	A Damn Good Country Song/When I Take My Vacation in Heaven	1975	$6
❏ 73685	Boogie Woogie Country Man/I'm Still Jealous of You	1975	$6
❏ 73273	Chantilly Lace/Think About It Darlin'	1972	$8
❏ 55021	Come On In/Who's Sorry Now	1977	$6
❏ 73763	Don't Boogie Woogie/That Kind of Fool	1976	$6
❏ 73374	Drinking Wine Spo-Dee O'Dee/Rock and Roll Medley	1973	$8
❏ 73618	He Can't Fill My Shoes/Tomorrow's Taking Baby Away	1974	$6
❏ 73661	I Can Still Hear the Music in the Restroom/Remember Me	1975	$6
❏ 73155	I Can't Have a Merry Christmas, Mary (Without You)/In Loving Memories	1970	$10
❏ 55028	I'll Find It Where I Can/Don't Let the Stars Get In Your Eyes	1977	$6
❏ 73452	I'm Left, You're Right, She's Gone/I've Fallen to the Bottom	1974	$8
❏ 76148	I'm So Lonesome I Could Cry/Pick Me Up on Your Way Down	1982	$5
❏ 73822	Let's Put It Back Together Again/Jerry Lee's Rock and Roll Revival Show	1976	$6
❏ 73296	Lonely Weekends/Turn On Your Love Light	1972	$8
❏ 73462	Meat Man/Just a Little Bit	1974	$8
❏ 55011	Middle Age Crazy/Georgia on My Mind	1977	$6
❏ 73423	Sometimes a Memory Ain't Enough/I Think I Need to Pray	1973	$8
❏ 73491	Tell Tale Signs/Cold, Cold Morning Light	1974	$8
❏ 73872	The Closest Thing to You/You Belong to Me	1976	$6
❏ 73099	There Must Be More to Love Than This/Home Away from Home	1970	$8
❏ 73192	Touching Home/Woman, Woman	1971	$8
❏ 73227	When He Walks on You (Like You Have Walked on Me)/Foolish Kind of Man	1971	$8
❏ 73328	Who's Gonna Play This Old Piano/No Honky Tonks in Heaven	1972	$8
❏ 73248	Would You Take Another Chance on Me/Me and Bobby McGee	1971	$8

PHILLIPS INT'L.

Number	Title	Yr	NM
❏ 3559	In the Mood/I Get the Blues When It Rains	1960	$60

— *As "The Hawk"*

POLYDOR

Number	Title	Yr	NM
❏ 889312-7	Breathless/Great Balls of Fire	1989	$4
❏ 889312-7 [PS]	Breathless/Great Balls of Fire	1989	$4
❏ 889798-7	Crazy Arms/Great Balls of Fire	1989	$4

SCR

Number	Title	Yr	NM
❏ 386	Get Out Your Big Roll, Daddy/Honky Tonkin' Rock 'N' Roll Piano Man	1985	$5

SMASH

Number	Title	Yr	NM
❏ 2146	Another Place, Another Time/Walking the Floor Over You	1968	$10
❏ 1969	Baby Hold Me Close/I Believe in You	1965	$20
❏ 2006	Green, Green Grass of Home/You've Got What It Takes	1965	$20
❏ 1930	High Heel Sneakers/You Went Back on Your Word	1964	$20
❏ 2103	Holding On/It's a Hang-Up, Baby	1967	$15
❏ 2053	If I Had It All to Do Over/Memphis Beat	1966	$15
❏ 1886	I'm on Fire/Bread and Butter Man	1964	$50
❏ 2257	Once More with Feeling/You Went Out of Your Way (To Walk on Me)	1970	$10
❏ 2224	One Has My Name (The Other Has My Heart)/I Can't Stop Loving You	1969	$10
❏ 1857	Pen and Paper/Hit the Road Jack	1963	$20
❏ 2244	She Even Woke Me Up to Say Goodbye/Echoes	1969	$10
❏ 2186	She Still Comes Around (To Love What's Left of Me)/Slipping Around	1968	$10
❏ 1906	She Was My Baby (He Was My Friend)/The Hole He Said He'd Dig for Me	1964	$20
❏ 884934-7	Sixteen Candles/Rock and Roll (Fais-Do-Do)	1986	$4

— *B-side with Roy Orbison, Carl Perkins and Johnny Cash*

Number	Title	Yr	NM
❏ 2027	Sticks and Stones/What a Heck of a Mess	1966	$15
❏ 1992	This Must Be the Place/Rocking Pneumonia and the Boogie Woogie Flu	1965	$20

Number	Title	Yr	NM
❏ 2202	To Make Love Sweeter for You/Let's Talk About Us	1968	$10
❏ 2122	Turn On Your Love Light/Shotgun Man	1967	$15
❏ 888142-7	We Remember the King/Class of '55	1987	$4

— With Johnny Cash, Roy Orbison and Carl Perkins; B-side by Carl Perkins solo

Number	Title	Yr	NM
❏ 2164	What's Made Milwaukee Famous (Has Made a Loser Out of Me)/All the Good Is Gone	1968	$10

SUN

Number	Title	Yr	NM
❏ 1151	Be-Bop-a-Lula/The Breakup	1980	$4

— B-side by Charlie Rich; both sides are duets with Orion

Number	Title	Yr	NM
❏ 288	Breathless/Down the Line	1958	$50
❏ 396	Carry Me Back to Old Virginny/I Know What It Means	1965	$30
❏ 1141	Cold, Cold Heart/Hello Josephine	1979	$4
❏ 364	Cold, Cold Heart/It Won't Happen with Me	1961	$30
❏ 259	Crazy Arms/End of the Road	1957	$125

— As "Jerry Lee Lewis

Number	Title	Yr	NM
❏ 259	Crazy Arms/End of the Road	1957	$60

— As "Jerry Lee Lewis and His Pumping Piano

Number	Title	Yr	NM
❏ 382	Good Golly Miss Molly/I Can't Trust Me	1962	$30
❏ 1130	Good Rockin' Tonight/I Can't Trust Me in Your Arms Anymore	1973	$5
❏ 281	Great Balls of Fire/You Win Again	1957	$50
❏ 281 [PS]	Great Balls of Fire/You Win Again	1957	$100
❏ 344	Hang Up My Rock and Roll Shoes/John Henry	1960	$30
❏ 296	High School Confidential/Fools Like Me	1958	$40
❏ 296 [PS]	High School Confidential/Fools Like Me	1958	$100
❏ 1115	I Can't Seem to Say Goodbye/Goodnight Irene	1970	$5
❏ 303	I'll Make It All Up to You/Break-Up	1958	$40
❏ 312	I'll Sail My Ship Alone/It Hurt Me So	1958	$30
❏ 1101	Invitation to Your Party/I Could Never Be Ashamed of You	1969	$6
❏ 374	I've Been Twistin'/Ramblin' Rose	1962	$30
❏ 324	Let's Talk About Us/Ballad of Billy Joe	1959	$30
❏ 301	Lewis Boogie/The Return of Jerry Lee	1958	$40

— B-side by George and Louis

Number	Title	Yr	NM
❏ 330	Little Queenie/I Could Never Be Ashamed of You	1959	$30
❏ 352	Love Made a Fool of Me/When I Get Paid	1960	$30
❏ 1125	Love on Broadway/Matchbox	1971	$5
❏ 317	Lovin' Up a Storm/Big Blon' Baby	1959	$30
❏ 1138	Matchbox/Am I to Be the One	1978	$4
❏ 371	Money/Bonnie B	1961	$30
❏ 337	Old Black Joe/Baby Baby, Bye Bye	1960	$30
❏ 1107	One Minute Past Eternity/Frankie and Johnny	1969	$6
❏ 1139	Save the Last Dance for Me/Am I to Be the One	1978	$4

— With uncredited "duet" partner, actually Orion (Jimmy Ellis); a shameless attempt to concoct a "lost Elvis Presley duet

Number	Title	Yr	NM
❏ 367	Save the Last Dance for Me/As Long As I Live	1961	$30
❏ 379	Sweet Little Sixteen/How's My Ex Treating You	1962	$30
❏ 384	Teenage Letter/Seasons of My Heart	1963	$30
❏ 1119	Waiting for the Train (All Around the Watertank)/Big Legged Woman	1970	$5
❏ 356	What'd I Say/Livin' Lovin' Wreck	1961	$30
❏ 267	Whole Lot of Shakin' Going On/It'll Be Me	1957	$50
❏ EPA-108	Don't Be Cruel/Goodnight Irene//Put Me Down/It All Depends	1958	$60
❏ EPA-110	High School Confidential/When the Saints Go Marching In//Matchbox/It'll Be Me	1958	$60
❏ EPA-107	Mean Woman Blues/I'm Feelin' Sorry//Whole Lot of Shakin' Goin' On/Turn Around	1958	$100
❏ EPA-107 [PS]	The Great Ball of Fire	1958	$100

LEWIS, JIMMY, AND THE ELFS

HIT

Number	Title	Yr	NM
❏ 306	Come Back When You Grow Up/How Can I Be Sure	1967	$8

— B-side by the Olives

LEWIS, JUNIOR

ATCO

Number	Title	Yr	NM
❏ 6242	Please Send Me Someone to Love/Tumbling Down	1962	$30

COLUMBIA

Number	Title	Yr	NM
❏ 4-42361	Forty Days and Forty Nights/The Only Girl	1962	$50
❏ 4-42129	Hear What I Say/Where the World Begins	1961	$30
❏ 4-42129 [PS]	Hear What I Say/Where the World Begins	1961	$50
❏ 4-42236	Too Bad/Tears on My Face	1961	$30

MGM

Number	Title	Yr	NM
❏ K13728	All About Love/Why Take It Out on Me	1967	$40

SCEPTER

Number	Title	Yr	NM
❏ 1268	Hi Dee You All/(Tell Me) Where Do I Go from Here	1964	$40

LEWIS, LINDA GAIL

MERCURY

Number	Title	Yr	NM
❏ 73463	I Wanna Be a Sensuous Woman/I Should Not Have Fallen in Love with You	1974	$6

SMASH

Number	Title	Yr	NM
❏ 2240	He's Loved Me Much Too Much (Much Too Long)/Southside Soul Society Chapter No. 1	1969	$8
❏ 2261	My Heart Was the Last One to Know)/Gather Round Children	1970	$8
❏ 2211	T-H-E E-N-D/Then We Said Goodbye	1969	$8
❏ 2193	Turn Back the Hands of Time/Good	1968	$10

LEWIS, MARGARET

CAPITOL

Number	Title	Yr	NM
❏ 5385	If You Ever Wonder/Nobody's Darling But Mine	1965	$10

SSS INTERNATIONAL

Number	Title	Yr	NM
❏ 741	Honey (I Miss You Too)/Milk and Honey	1968	$8

LEWIS, PAT

GOLDEN WORLD

Number	Title	Yr	NM
❏ 42	Can't Shake It Loose/Let's Go Together	1966	$40

SOLID HIT

Number	Title	Yr	NM
❏ 101	Look at What I Almost Missed/No, Baby, No	1967	$50
❏ 105	Warning/I'll Wait	1967	$125

LEWIS, RAMSEY

ARGO

Number	Title	Yr	NM
❏ 5303	Black Eyed Peas/Carmen	1958	$15
❏ 5423	Blueberry Hill/Memphis in June	1962	$10
❏ 5387	Blues for the Night Owl/Hello, Cello	1961	$10
❏ 5413	Blue Spring/Spring Fever	1962	$10
❏ 5344	C.C. Rider/Consider the Source	1959	$15
❏ 5467	Dance Mystique/For the Love of a Princess	1964	$8
❏ 5411	I Got Plenty of Nothin'/Thanks for the Memory	1962	$10
❏ 5496	Let It Be Me/It Had Better Be Tonight	1965	$8
❏ 5362	Little Liza Jane/Put Your Little Foot Right Out	1960	$15
❏ 5454	Lonely Avenue/Come On Baby	1963	$8
❏ 5438	Look-a Here/Andaluza	1963	$8
❏ 5431	Maha de Carnaval/Tangleweed 'Round My Heart	1963	$8
❏ 5351	Ol' Devil Moon/Please Send Me Someone to Love	1959	$15
❏ 5377	Santa Claus Is Coming to Town/Winter Wonderland	1960	$15
❏ 108#NAME? [S]	Scarlet Ribbons/Here 'Tis	1960	$30
❏ 110#NAME? [S]	Solo Para Ti/These Foolish Things	1960	$30
❏ 5481	Something You Got/My Babe	1964	$8
❏ 5407	Sound of Christmas/Merry Christmas Baby	1961	$15
❏ 5352	The Chant/Here 'Tis	1959	$15
❏ 5506	The "In" Crowd/Since I Fell for You	1965	$12
❏ 5322	Tracy Blues/Delilah	1958	$15
❏ 5474	Why Don't You Do It Right/Travel On	1964	$8

CADET

Number	Title	Yr	NM
❏ 5525	A Hard Day's Night/All My Love Belongs to You	1966	$8
❏ 5423	Blueberry Hill/Memphis in June	1966	$6
❏ 5681	Candida/Love Me Now	1971	$6
❏ 5573	Dancing in the Street/Girls Talk	1967	$8

Number	Title	Yr	NM
❏ 5678	Do Whatever Sets You Free/Close Your Eyes and Remember	1970	$6
❏ 5668	Everybody's Talkin'/Love I Feel for You	1970	$6
❏ 5562	Function at the Junction/Hey, Mrs. Jones	1967	$8
❏ 5522	Hang On Sloopy/Movin' Easy	1965	$8
❏ 5684	He Ain't Heavy, He's My Brother/Up in Yonder	1971	$6
❏ 5531	Hi Heel Sneakers -- Pt. 1/Hi Heel Sneakers -- Pt. 2	1966	$8
❏ 5645	If You've Got It, Flaunt It/Wanderin' Rose	1969	$6
❏ 5496	Let It Be Me/It Had Better Be Tonight	1966	$6
❏ 5431	Maha de Carnaval/Tangleweed 'Round My Heart	1966	$6
❏ 5629	Mary's Boy Child/Have Yourself a Merry Little Christmas	1968	$6
❏ 5662	Mary's Boy Child/My Cherie Amour	1969	$6
❏ 5556	One, Two, Three/Down by the Riverside	1967	$8
❏ 5377	Santa Claus Is Coming to Town/Winter Wonderland	1966	$6

— Reissue of Argo 5377

Number	Title	Yr	NM
❏ 5565	Saturday Night After the Movies/China Gate	1967	$6
❏ 5609	Since You've Been Gone/Les Fleurs	1968	$6
❏ 5481	Something You Got/My Babe	1966	$6
❏ 5583	Soul Man/Struttin' Lightly	1967	$8
❏ 5695	Summertime/Look-a There	1973	$6
❏ 5506	The "In" Crowd/Since I Fell for You	1966	$6
❏ 5593	The Look of Love/Bear Mash	1968	$6
❏ 5674	Them Changes/Unsilent Minority	1970	$6
❏ 5541	Wade in the Water/Ain't That Peculiar	1966	$8

COLUMBIA

Number	Title	Yr	NM
❏ 07220	7-11/My Love Will Lead You Home	1987	$3
❏ 10827	All the Way Live/Toccata	1978	$5
❏ 10932	Aquarius-Let the Sunshine In/Just Can't Give You Up	1979	$5
❏ 10382	Brazilica/Salongo	1976	$5
❏ 10293	Don't It Feel Good/Fish Bite	1976	$5
❏ 45847	Dreams/Hang On Sloopy	1973	$5
❏ 45973	Hi-Heel Sneakers/Wade in the Water	1973	$5
❏ 10056	Hot Dawgit/R.L. Tambura	1974	$5

— A-side with Earth, Wind and Fire

Number	Title	Yr	NM
❏ 02572	Lakeshore Cowboy/Michelle	1981	$4
❏ 10643	Skippin'/Camino El Bueno	1977	$5
❏ 45634	Slipping Into Darkness/Collage	1972	$5
❏ 02043	So Much More/Romance Me	1981	$4
❏ 10571	Spring High/The Messenger	1977	$5
❏ 46037	Summer Breeze/Everywhere Calypso	1974	$5
❏ 10103	Sun Goddess/Jungle Strut	1975	$5

— A-side with Earth, Wind and Fire

Number	Title	Yr	NM
❏ 10698	Tequila Mockingbird/My Angel's Smile	1978	$5
❏ 04524	The Two of Us/Song Without Words (Remembering)	1984	$4
❏ 05640	This Ain't No Fantasy/The Quest	1985	$3
❏ 11042	Wearin' It Out/Spanoletta	1979	$5
❏ 10235	What's the Name of This Funk (Spider Man)/Juacklyn	1975	$5

7-Inch Extended Plays

ARGO

Number	Title	Yr	NM
❏ EP-1084	Sleigh Ride/Christmas Blues//Sound of Christmas/The Christmas Song	1961	$10
❏ EP-1084 [PS]	Sound of Christmas	1961	$15

LEWIS, RAY

ATCO

Number	Title	Yr	NM
❏ 6846	Cool Love/Sugar Toe	1971	$50

FAIRMOUNT

Number	Title	Yr	NM
❏ 1013	Give My Love a Try/Getting Over You	1966	$300

SMASH

Number	Title	Yr	NM
❏ 2134	I Still Love You/Sorry, You've Got the Wrong Number	1967	$80

LEWIS, ROBERT Q.

MGM

Number	Title	Yr	NM
❏ 12740	Santa Claus Jr./(I Love That) Little Green Girl	1958	$10

LEWIS, RUDY

ATLANTIC

Number	Title	Yr	NM
❏ 2193	I've Loved You So Long/Baby I Dig Love	1963	$50

Number	Title	Yr	NM

RCA VICTOR
❏ 47-7792	Moonbeam/Beer, Beer and More Beer	1960	$30

— With the Sputnicks

LEWIS, SABBY
ABC-PARAMOUNT
❏ 9685	Ding-a-Ling/Kenny's Blues	1956	$50
❏ 9687	Forgive Me, My Love/ Regretting	1956	$50

GONE
❏ 5074	Swana/Sabby	1959	$30

— With the Uniques

LEWIS, SAMMIE
SUN
❏ 218	So Long Baby Goodbye/I Feel So Worried	1955	$100

LEWIS, SHARI, AND LAMB CHOP
MUSICOR
❏ 1140	Some Things For Xmas/ Mr. Santa	1965	$20
❏ 1140 [PS]	Some Things For Xmas/ Mr. Santa	1965	$30

LEWIS, SMILEY
DOT
❏ 16674	I Wonder/Lookin' for My Woman	1964	$10

IMPERIAL
❏ 5478	Bad Luck Blues/School Days Are Back Again	1957	$40
❏ 5241	Caldonia's Party/Oh Baby	1953	$100
❏ 5296	Can't Stop Loving You/That Certain Door	1954	$100
❏ 5268	Down the Road/Blue Monday	1954	$100
❏ 5404	Down Yonder We Go Ballin'/ Someday You'll Want Me	1956	$100
❏ 5450	Go On Fool/Goin' to Jump and Shout	1957	$40
❏ 5208	Gumbo Blues/It's So Peaceful	1952	$125
❏ 5820	Gumbo Blues/Tee Nah Nah	1962	$20
❏ 5224	Gypsy Blues/You're Not the One	1953	$125
❏ 5356	I Hear You Knocking/ Bumpity Bump	1955	$100
❏ 5279	I Love You for Sentimental Reasons/The Rocks	1954	$100
❏ 5676	Last Night/Ain't Goin' There No More	1960	$20
❏ 5531	Lil' Liza Jane/My Love Is Gone	1958	$30
❏ 5252	Little Fernandez/It's Music	1953	$100
❏ 5662	Oh Red!/I Want to Be with Her	1960	$20
❏ 5380	One Night/Ain't Gonna Do It	1956	$100
❏ 5234	Play Girl/Big Mamou	1953	$100
❏ 5234	Play Girl/Big Mamou	1953	$250

— Red vinyl

❏ 5418	Shame, Shame, Shame/ No No	1957	$70
❏ 5389	She's Got Me (Hook, Line and Sinker)/Please Listen to Me	1956	$100
❏ 5719	Stormy Monday Blues/Tell Me Who	1961	$20
❏ 5194	The Bells Are Ringing/ Lillie Mae	1952	$120

— Note: Smiley Lewis records on Imperial before 5194 are unconfirmed on 45 rpm.

❏ 5316	Too Many Drivers/Ooh La La	1954	$100

KNIGHT
❏ 2007	Baby Please/I Shall Not Be Moved	1959	$20
❏ 2011	Lost Weekend/By the Water	1959	$20

LOMA
❏ 2024	Bells Are Ringing/Walkin' the Girl	1965	$12

OKEH
❏ 7146	I'm Coming Down with the Blues/Tune-Up	1962	$15

LEWIS, TEXAS JIM
CORAL
❏ 60856	Sweet Face but a Cold Heart/Banjo Schottische	1952	$30

LEYTON, JOHN
ABC-PARAMOUNT
❏ 10292	Son, This Is She/Six White Horses	1962	$15

ATCO
❏ 6319	Make Love to Me/I'll Cut Your Tail Off	1964	$15

LIVERPOOL SOUND
❏ 901	Beautiful Dreamer/I Guess You Are Always On My Mind	1964	$15

LIBERACE
AVI
❏ 112	My Melody of Love/El Bimbo	1976	$4
❏ 101	The Way We Were/The Entertainer	1976	$4

COLUMBIA
❏ 40395	Alexander's Ragtime Band/ El Cumbanchero	1954	$10
❏ 39778	As Time Goes By/ Liebestraum	1952	$15
❏ 40099	A Story of Three Loves/ Maiden's Wish Samba	1953	$20
❏ 39986	Autumn Nocturne/Concerto #2 in A Major for Piano and Orchestra	1953	$15
❏ 48001	Ave Maria/Christmas Medley (White Christmas/Jingle Bells/O Come All Ye Faithful/ Silent Night)	1954	$20
❏ 48001 [PS]	Ave Maria/Christmas Medley (White Christmas/Jingle Bells/O Come All Ye Faithful/ Silent Night)	1954	$30
❏ 39779	Carioca/Warsaw Concerto	1952	$15
❏ 40397	Cement Mixer/Beer Barrel Polka	1954	$10

— The above four comprise a box set

❏ 39921	Cement Mixer/Slaughter on Tenth Avenue	1953	$15
❏ 39920	Chopsticks/The Old Piano Roll Blues	1953	$15
❏ 40394	Cornish Rhapsody/ Rhapsody by Candlelight	1954	$12
❏ 39922	Cumana/Lover	1953	$15

— The above four comprise a box set

❏ 40147	Dream of Owlen/Laura (Conclusion)	1953	$15
❏ 40337	Etude No. 3 in E Major (Beginning)/Etude in F Minor	1954	$12
❏ 40338	Etude No. 3 in E Major (Conclusion)/Waltz No. 6 in D-Flat Major	1954	$12

— The above four comprise a box set

❏ 40686	Faith Unlocks the Door/ Nocturne No. 2	1956	$15
❏ 40333	Fantasie-Impromptu (Beginning)/Nocturne No. 2 in E Flat Major (Conclusion)	1954	$10
❏ 40334	Fantasie-Impromptu (Conclusion)/Nocturne No. 2 in E Flat Major (Beginning)	1954	$10

— The above four comprise a box set

❏ 40381	Gesu Bambino/Sleigh Ride// Star Bright/Ave Maria	1954	$15
❏ 40067	Grieg's Piano Concerto (Beginning)/Chopin's Fantasia (Conclusion)	1953	$15
❏ 40068	Grieg's Piano Concerto (Conclusion)/Chopin's Fantasia (Beginning)	1953	$15

— The above four comprise a box set

❏ 39985	I Don't Care/Jalousie	1953	$15
❏ 40454	I'll Get By/Finger of Suspicion	1955	$15
❏ 48008	I Love You Truly/Oh Promise Me	1954	$15
❏ 48008 [PS]	I Love You Truly/Oh Promise Me	1954	$20
❏ 39895	I Miss You So/I Don't Care	1952	$20
❏ 39995	I'm Loved/I'd Never Forgive Myself	1953	$20
❏ 40396	My TV Sponsors/Clair de Lune	1954	$10
❏ 39780	Polish National Dance/ Moonlight Sonata	1952	$15

— The above four comprise a box set

❏ 40335	Polonaise in A-Flat Major (Beginning)/Grande Valse	1954	$10
❏ 40336	Polonaise in A-Flat Major (Conclusion)/Prelude No. 4 in E Minor	1954	$10
❏ 40285	Polonaise/Liebestraum (Love's Dream)	1954	$15
❏ 39709	September Song/I Want My Mama	1952	$20
❏ 40570	Sincerely Yours/Under Paris Skies	1955	$15
❏ 40145	Spellbound Concerto (Beginning)/Rachmaninoff Fantasia (Conclusion)	1953	$15
❏ 40146	Spellbound Concerto (Conclusion)/Rachmaninoff Fantasia (Beginning)	1953	$15
❏ 39777	Star Dust/Malaguena	1952	$15
❏ 40148	Stella by Starlight/Laura (Beginning)	1953	$15

— The above four comprise a box set

❏ 39987	Tales from the Vienna Woods/I'll Be Seeing You	1953	$15

— The above four comprise a box set

❏ 39984	Tchakovsky's Piano Concerto #1/September Song	1953	$15
❏ 40380	The Christmas Song/The Toy Piano//The Beauty of Holiness/Santa Claus Medley	1954	$15
❏ 40768	The Magic of Believing/Cuba	1956	$15
❏ 40379	The Spirit of Christmas/O Holy Night	1954	$15

Number	Title	Yr	NM
❏ 40382	Twas the Night Before Christmas/Christmas Medley	1954	$15
❏ 40217	Twelfth Street Rag/Beer Barrel Polka	1954	$15
❏ 40331	Waltz in C-Sharp Minor/ Polonaise in A Major	1954	$10
❏ 40065	Warsaw Concerto (Beginning)/Cornish Rhapsody (Conclusion)	1953	$15
❏ 40066	Warsaw Concerto (Conclusion)/Cornish Rhapsody (Beginning)	1953	$15
❏ 40647	We All Need Love/Dancing Skeletons	1956	$15

CORAL
❏ 62112	Gigi/This Earth Is Mine	1959	$10
❏ 65539	I Believe/Gigi	1961	$8
❏ 65556	I'll Be Seeing You/Laura	1961	$8

DOT
❏ 16594	Alley Cat/Theme from "Outer Space	1964	$6
❏ 17033	Happy Barefoot Boy/Two for the Road	1967	$6

MGM
❏ 14518	The Morning After/Theme from "Above San Francisco	1973	$5

WARNER BROS.
❏ 7465	Ciao/Theme from Love Story	1971	$5
❏ 5-2051	O Holy Night/The Toy Piano//Sleigh Ride/The Christmas Song	1954	$15

— Alternate numbers are "B-454-3" and "B-454-4"

❏ 5-2050	The Spirit of Christmas/ Christmas Medley//Star Bright/The Beauty of Holiness	1954	$15

— Alternate numbers are "B-454-2" and "B-454-5"

❏ B-454 [PS]	(title unknown)	1954	$20

LIFEGUARDS, THE (1)
ABC-PARAMOUNT
❏ 10021	Everybody Out'a the Pool/ Teenage Tango	1959	$50

CASA BLANCA
❏ 5535	Everybody Out'a the Pool/ Teenage Tango	1959	$60

DR
❏ 69	Everybody Out'a the Pool/ Teenage Tango	1965	$20

LIFEGUARDS, THE (2)
CATCH
❏ 104	State Beach/Big Swim	1964	$40

REPRISE
❏ 0277	Swim Party/Swimtime U.S.A.	1964	$30

LIGHT, ENOCH
COMMAND
❏ 4050	A Hard Day's Night/Carribe	1964	$8
❏ 4067	Downtown/Easy Baby, Go Easy Baby	1965	$8
❏ 4068	Forget Domani/Love Me Now	1965	$8
❏ 4072	Love Theme from "The Sandpiper"/Forget Domani	1966	$8
❏ 4010	Mack the Knife Cha Cha/ (B-side unknown)	1960	$10
❏ 4029	Meditation (Meditacao)/Big Ben Bossa	1962	$8
❏ 4028	Perdido/Rio Junction	1962	$8
❏ 4019	Satan Never Sleeps/The Four Horsemen of the Apocalypse	1961	$8
❏ 4069	Theme from "Zorba the Greek"/Von Ryan's Express	1965	$8
❏ 4008	The Private Life of a Private Eye/Gum Shoe Lullaby	1960	$10

GRAND AWARD
❏ 1026	Baby, It's Cold Outside Cha Cha/Chiquita Cha Cha	1958	$15
❏ 1020	I Want to Be Happy Cha Cha/Cara Mia Cha Cha	1958	$15
❏ 1035	Scarlet Ribbons/ Greensleeves	1959	$15
❏ 1032	With My Eyes Wide Open I'm Dreaming/I Cried for You	1959	$15
❏ 1367	Alice's Restaurant/ Raindrops Keep Fallin' on My Head	1970	$5
❏ 1344	A Man Without Love/ Whoever You Are, I Love You	1969	$6
❏ 1354	Blowin' in the Wind/Happy Ever After	1969	$6
❏ 1310	Come On, Come On, Come On, Don't Be Timid/I Love, I Live, I Love	1967	$6
❏ 1369	Day of Anger/Song from "The Wild Bunch	1970	$5
❏ 1348	Funny Girl/Ol' Devil Moon	1969	$6
❏ 1330	Green Tambourine/I Wonder What She's Doing Tonight	1968	$6
❏ 1359	Hair/(B-side unknown)	1969	$6

Number	Title	Yr	NM
❑ 1341	Hang 'Em High/The Windmills of Your Mind	1968	$6
❑ 1346	Interlude/Now	1969	$6
❑ 1322	In the Heat of the Night/Live for Life	1967	$6
❑ 1305	Is Paris Burning/And We Were Lovers	1967	$6
❑ 1339	Lullaby from "Rosemary's Baby"/The Windmills of Your Mind	1968	$6
❑ 1368	My Silent Song/Little Fugue for You and Me	1970	$5

LIGHTFOOT, GORDON
ABC-PARAMOUNT

Number	Title	Yr	NM
❑ 10352	Daisy-Doo/I'm the One (Remember Me)	1962	$30

— As "Gord Lightfoot

❑ 10373	It's Too Late, He Wins/Negotiations	1962	$30

CHATEAU

❑ 142	Daisy-Doo/I'm the One (Remember Me)	1962	$60
❑ 152	I'll Meet You in Michigan/Is My Baby Blue Tonight	1962	$50
❑ 148	It's Too Late, He Wins/Negotiations	1962	$60

REPRISE

❑ 1088	Beautiful/Don Quixote	1972	$5
❑ 1145	Can't Depend on You/It's Worth Believin'	1972	$5
❑ 1309	Carefree Highway/Seven Island Suite	1974	$4
❑ 0744	If You Could Read My Mind/Me and Bobby McGee	1972	$4

— Back to Back Hits" series

❑ 0974	If You Could Read My Mind/Poor Little Allison	1970	$6
❑ 0926	Me and Bobby McGee/Pony Man	1970	$5
❑ 1035	Summer Side of Life/Love and Maple Syrup	1971	$5
❑ 1194	Sundown/Too Late for Prayin'	1974	$4
❑ 1020	Talking in Your Sleep/Nous Vivons Ensemble	1971	$5
❑ 0745	Talking in Your Sleep/Summer Side of Life	1972	$4

— Back to Back Hits" series

❑ 1369	The Wreck of the Edmund Fitzgerald/The House You Live In	1976	$4

UNITED ARTISTS

❑ 50447	Does Your Mother Know/Bitter Green	1968	$8
❑ 50055	For Lovin' Me/Spin, Spin	1966	$8
❑ 50765	If I Could/Softly	1971	$5
❑ 50114	I'll Be Alright/Go Go Round	1967	$8
❑ 50281	Pussywillows, Cat-Tails/Black Day in July	1968	$8
❑ 50152	The Way I Feel/Peaceful Waters	1967	$8

WARNER BROS.

❑ 28655	Anything for Love/Let It Ride	1986	$3
❑ 28655 [PS]	Anything for Love/Let It Ride	1986	$4
❑ 50012	Baby Step Back/Thank You for the Promises	1982	$4
❑ 29963	Blackberry Wine/(B-side unknown)	1982	$4
❑ 8579	Daylight Katy/Hangdog Hotel Room	1978	$4
❑ 8644	Dreamland/Songs the Minstrel Sang	1978	$4
❑ 49230	Dream Street Rose/Make Way for the Lady	1980	$4
❑ 28422	East of Midnight/I'll Tag Along	1987	$3
❑ 28222	Ecstasy Made Easy/Morning Glory	1987	$3
❑ 5621	For Lovin' Me/I'm Not Sayin'	1965	$20
❑ 49516	If You Need Me/Mister Rock of Ages	1980	$4
❑ 29859	Shadows/In My Fashion	1982	$4
❑ 29466	Someone to Believe In/Without You	1983	$4
❑ 28553	Stay Loose/Morning Glory	1986	$3
❑ 8518	The Circle Is Small (I Can See It In Your Eyes)/Sweet Guinevere	1978	$4

— Subtitle added to later pressings

❑ 8518	The Circle Is Small/Sweet Guinevere	1978	$5

— Without A-side subtitle

LIGHTFOOT, PAPA
ALADDIN

❑ 3171	After a While (Blue Lights)/P.L.'s Blues	1953	$200
❑ 3304	Blue Lights/Jumpin' with Jarvis	1955	$200

IMPERIAL

❑ 5289	Wine, Women, Whiskey/Mean Old Train	1954	$200

SAVOY

❑ 1161	Mean Old Train/Wild Fire	1955	$40

LIGHTHOUSE
EVOLUTION

Number	Title	Yr	NM
❑ 1076	Broken Guitar Blues/Merlin	1973	$5
❑ 1041	Hats Off/Sing, Sing, Sing	1971	$5
❑ 1061	I'd Be So Happy/Old Man	1972	$5
❑ 1058	I Just Wanna Be Your Friend/1849	1972	$5
❑ 1048	One Fine Morning/Little Kind Words	1971	$6
❑ 1069	Sunny Days/Lonely Places	1972	$5
❑ 1052	Take It Slow (Out in the Country)/Sweet Lullaby	1971	$5

POLYDOR

❑ 14197	Can You Feel It/Bright Side	1973	$4
❑ 14246	Good Day/Going Downtown	1974	$4
❑ 14220	Magic's in the Dancing/Disagreeable man	1974	$4
❑ 14198	Pretty Lady/Bright Side	1973	$4

RCA VICTOR

❑ 74-0224	Eight Miles High/If There Ever Was a Time	1969	$6
❑ 74-0285	Feel So Good/Places on Faces Four Blue Carpet Traces	1969	$6
❑ 47-9808	The Chant (Nam-Myo-Ho Renge Kyo)/Could You Be Concerned	1969	$6

LIGHTNIN' SLIM
ACE

❑ 505	Bad Feeling Blues/Lightning Slim Boogie	1955	$200

EXCELLO

❑ 2258	Baby Please Come Back/You Move Me Baby	1964	$30
❑ 2267	Bad Luck Blues/Can't Live This Life No More	1965	$30
❑ 2240	Blues at Night/Don't Mistreat Me Baby	1963	$30
❑ 2186	Cool Down Baby/Nothin' But the Devil	1960	$30
❑ 2269	Don't Start Me Talkin'/Darlin' You're the One	1965	$30
❑ 2150	Feelin' Awful Blues/I'm Leavin' You Baby	1959	$40
❑ 2080	Goin' Home/Wonderin' and Goin'	1956	$40
❑ 2252	Greyhound Blues/She's My Crazy Little Baby	1964	$30
❑ 2262	Have Mercy on Me Baby/I've Been a Fool for You Darlin'	1965	$30
❑ 2096	Have Your Way/Bad Luck and Trouble	1956	$40
❑ 2203	Hello Mary Lee/I'm Tired Waitin' Baby	1961	$30
❑ 2131	Hoo-Doo Blues/It's Mighty Crazy	1958	$40
❑ 2066	I Can't Be Successful/Lightnin' Blues	1955	$50
❑ 2228	If You Ever Need Me/I'm Evil	1963	$30
❑ 2272	I Hate to See You Leave/Love Is Just a Gamble	1965	$30
❑ 2116	I'm a Rollin' Stone/Love Me Mama	1957	$40
❑ 2234	Loving Around the Clock/You Know You're So Fine	1963	$30
❑ 2106	Mean Old Lonesome Train/I'm Grown	1957	$40
❑ 2215	Mind Your Own Business/You're Old Enough to Understand	1962	$30
❑ 2320	My Babe/Good Morning Heartaches	1971	$10
❑ 2179	My Little Angel Child/Too Close Blues	1960	$30
❑ 2142	My Starter Won't Work/Long Leanie Mama	1958	$40
❑ 2195	Somebody Knockin'/I Just Don't Know	1961	$30
❑ 2075	Sugar Plum/Just Made Twenty One	1956	$40
❑ 2160	Sweet Little Woman/Lightnin's Troubles	1959	$40
❑ 2224	Winter Time Blues/I'm Warnin' You Baby	1962	$30

FEATURE

❑ 3012	Bugger Bugger Boy/Ethel Mae	1954	$70
❑ 3008	I Can't Live Happy/New Orleans Bound	1954	$70

LIGHTNING
P.I.P.

❑ 8921	Hideaway/Freedom	1970	$30

LI'L WALLY
DRUM BOY

❑ 115	Christmas In Your Heart/Hawaiian Christmas	1965	$8

JAY JAY

❑ 229	Auld Lang Syne/Dance Around The Christmas Tree	1968	$6

— Yellow vinyl

❑ 209	Happy New Year/Jesus Was Born	1967	$8
❑ 230	Merry Christmas Mom & Dad/Oh Lovely Christmas Tree	1968	$6

— Yellow vinyl

❑ 228	Santa Claus Is Coming To Town/How Lovely Is Christmas	1968	$6

Number	Title	Yr	NM
— Yellow vinyl			
❑ 150	Sleigh Bells Waltz/Jingle Bells Polka	1966	$8
❑ 253	White Christmas/Winter Wonderland	1969	$6

LIMAHL
EMI AMERICA

❑ B-8318	Love in Your Eyes/Love Will Tear the Soul	1986	$5
❑ B-8318 [PS]	Love in Your Eyes/Love Will Tear the Soul	1986	$5
❑ B-8277	Only for Love/The Waiting Game	1985	$3
❑ B-8277 [PS]	Only for Love/The Waiting Game	1985	$3

LIME SPIDERS
7-Inch Extended Plays
VIRGIN

❑ 99393 [DJ]	Space Cadet/Just One Solution/Action Women/Stone Free	1987	$13

— Promo-only live versions; green vinyl

❑ 99393 [PS]	Space Cadet/Just One Solution/Action Women/Stone Free	1987	$13

LIMELIGHTERS, THE
JOSIE

❑ 795	Cabin Hideaway/My Sweet Norma Lee	1956	$200

LIMELITERS, THE
RCA VICTOR

❑ 47-7859	A Dollar Down/When Twice the Moon Has Come and Gone	1961	$8
❑ 47-7859 [PS]	A Dollar Down/When Twice the Moon Has Come and Gone	1961	$15
❑ 47-8255	Midnight Special/McClintock's Theme	1963	$8
❑ 47-7942	Milk and Honey/Red Roses and White Wine	1961	$8
❑ 47-7913	Paco Peco/A Hundred Years Ago	1961	$8
❑ 47-8094	Who Will Buy/Funk	1962	$8
❑ 47-8094 [PS]	Who Will Buy/Funk	1962	$15

WARNER BROS.

❑ 7254	Time to Gather Seed/The Importance of the Rose	1968	$6
❑ LPC-132	Hey Li Lee Li Lee/Rumania, Rumania	1961	$20

— Compact Double 33" with small hole; this is an extended play record despite having only one song per side

❑ LPC-132 [PS]	Tonight: In Person	1961	$20

LIMEYS, THE
DOT

❑ 16725	Don't Cry/I Can't Find My Way Through	1965	$20

SCEPTER

❑ 12156	Come Back/Scraped: Green and Blue	1966	$20

LIND, BOB
CAPITOL

❑ 3169	Theme from the Music Box/She Can Get Along	1971	$5

UNITED ARTISTS

❑ 0032	Elusive Butterfly/Truly Julie's Blues	1973	$4

— Silver Spotlight Series" reissue

VERVE FOLKWAYS

❑ 5029	Black Night/White Snow	1966	$8
❑ 5018	Wandering/Hey Nellie Hellie	1966	$8

WORLD PACIFIC

❑ 77808	Elusive Butterfly/Cheryl's Goin' Home	1965	$12
❑ 77879	Goodbye Neon Lies/We May Have Touched	1967	$8
❑ 77865	Good Time Special/Just My Love	1967	$8
❑ 77839	San Francisco Woman/Baby Take Me Home	1966	$8
❑ 77830	We've Never Spoken/I Just Let It Take Me	1966	$8

LINDA AND THE VISTAS
SHRINE

❑ 0100	Bad Apple/She Went Away	1965	$400

LINDE, JOHN
CADET

❑ 5611	Accordingly/I Learned Some Things Today	1968	$8

PARKWAY

❑ 856	Bossa Nova Bill/Round Sound	1962	$15

Number	Title	Yr	NM

LINDEN, KATHY
CAPITOL
❏ 4811	If You Really Love Me/Jimmy	1962	$8
❏ 5018	People Say/There'll Always Be Sadness	1963	$8
❏ 4770	Words/There'll Always Be Sadness	1962	$8

FELSTED
❏ 8510	Billy/If I Could Hold You in My Arms	1958	$20
❏ 8571	Goodbye, Jimmy, Goodbye/Heartaches at Sweet Sixteen	1959	$20
❏ 8533	Oh Johnny Oh/Georgie	1958	$20
❏ 8554	Somebody Loves You/You Walked Into My Life	1959	$20
❏ 8596	Think Love/Mary Lou Wilson and Johnny Brown	1959	$15

MONUMENT
❏ 420	Allentown Jail/That's What Love Is	1960	$10
❏ 423	Midnight/The Willow Weeps	1960	$10
❏ 436	So in Love (With You)/Take Me Home, Jimmy	1961	$12
❏ 428	Take Me Home (To My Lover)/We Had Words	1960	$10

LINDSAY, MARK
COLUMBIA
❏ 45229	And the Grass Won't Pay No Mind/Funny How Little Men Care	1970	$6
❏ 45462	Are You Old Enough/Don't You Know	1971	$5
❏ 45037	Arizona/Man from Houston	1969	$6
❏ 45385	Been Too Long on the Road/All I Really See Is You	1971	$5
❏ 45895	California/Someone's Been Hiding	1973	$5
❏ 44875	First Hymn from Grand Terrace/The Old Man at the Fair	1969	$6
❏ 10081	Mamacita/Song for a Friend	1974	$5
❏ 45125	Miss America/Small Town Woman	1970	$6
❏ 10114	Photograph/Song for a Friend	1975	$5
❏ 45506	Pretty Pretty/Something Big	1971	$5
❏ 45286	Problem Child/Bookends	1970	$6
❏ 45180	Silver Bird/So Hard to Leave You	1970	$6

ELKA
❏ 310	Sing Your Own Song/Sing Your Own Song (Theme)	1976	$10

GREEDY
❏ 106	Sing Your Own Song/Sing Your Own Song (Theme)	1976	$6

WARNER BROS.
❏ 8479	Little Ladies of the Night/Flips-Eyed	1977	$4
❏ 8359	Sing Me High, Sing Me Low/Flips-Eyed	1977	$4

LINDSEY, GEORGE
CAPITOL
❏ 2450	96 Miles to Bakersfield/It's Such a Pretty World Today	1969	$12
❏ 2685	Freaked Out/My Home Town	1969	$10

COLUMBIA
❏ 4-44215	Call Me Country/The World's Biggest Whopper	1967	$15

LINDSEY, LAWANDA, AND KENNY VERNON
CHART
❏ 1063	Eye to Eye/Looking Over Our Shoulders	1968	$8
❏ 5090	Let's Think About Where We're Going/Puzzles of My Mind	1970	$6
❏ 5055	Pickin' Wild Mountain Berries/We Don't Deserve Each Other	1970	$6
❏ 5114	The Crawdad Song/Wrong Number	1971	$6

LINDSEY, THERESA
❏ 5840	Gotta Find a Way/Wonderful One	1963	$50
❏ 5841	Sugar Mountain/Why Oh Why	1963	$50

GOLDEN WORLD
❏ 43	I'll Bet You/Daddy-O	1966	$60

LINE MATERIAL
MCGRAW-EDISON
❏ NO9W-1867	Let's Trim the Christmas Tree/The Sounds of Christmas	1962	$15
❏ LO9H-3092	Santa's Factoree/The Kinds of Christmas	1960	$20
❏ HO8W-0439	Santa's North Pole Band	1957	$30
—Blank B-side			

❏ JO8W-1438	The Sounds of Christmas/Santa's North Pole Band	1958	$20

—Note: All of these are identified by the A-side matrix number. The B-side matrix number is the same as earlier releases of the same title.

LINK-EDDY COMBO
REPRISE
❏ 20002	Big Mr. C./The Man with the Golden Arm	1961	$20

LINKLETTER, BOB
CHATTAHOOCHIE
❏ 702	The Out Crowd/Final Season	1965	$30

LINKS, THE
TEENAGE
❏ 1009	Ba-Bee/She's the One	1958	$1000

LINN, ROBERTA
KEEN
❏ 2013	Merry Christmas Darling/Katie the Kangaroo	1958	$20

LINNEAS, THE
DIAMOND
❏ 241	It's a Good Kind of Hurt/Forever Baby	1968	$15
❏ 248	My Baby Comes Home Today/Born to Be Your Baby	1968	$15

LINTON, SHERWIN
BLACK GOLD
❏ 6913	I'm Not Among the Loving/(B-side unknown)	1969	$8
❏ 7217	Little Peace of Mind/Livin' My Life with a Cheater	1972	$8

BREAKER
❏ 3902	Santa Got a DWI/An Old Christmas Card	1986	$4
❏ 3902 [PS]	Santa Got a DWI/An Old Christmas Card	1986	$6

HICKORY
❏ 1541	Sunshine/Working for the Man	1969	$10
❏ 1553	Then I Miss You/I'm Leaving for Good This Time	1969	$10

SOUNDWAVES
❏ 4696	Football Junkie/Thank You to the NFL	1983	$5
—With Patti Trobec			
❏ 4568	I Fell in Love with Dolly Parton/Put Another Log on the Fire	1978	$6

TWIN TOWN
❏ 716	House of Blue Lights/Gimme Another Bottle of Beer	1965	$30

LIONS, THE
IMPERIAL
❏ 5678	Hickory Dickory/The Yodel	1960	$20

RENDEZVOUS
❏ 116	The Feast of the Beasts/Two-Timing Lovers	1960	$20

LIPHAM, CURLY
DECCA
❏ 9-46372	Blue Fedora/I'm Afraid of Your Kisses	1951	$30
❏ 9-46323	Maybe Someday/Hearts That Could Never Be True	1951	$30

LIPPS, INC.
CASABLANCA
❏ 2348	Designer Music/Background Singer	1981	$4
❏ 2233	Funkytown/All Night Dancing	1980	$5
❏ 2342	Hold Me Down/Always Lookin'	1981	$4
❏ 2303	How Long/There They Are	1980	$4
❏ 2326	The Gossip Song/Jazzy	1981	$4

LIPTON, PEGGY
ODE
❏ 111	Let Me Pass By/Stoney End	1968	$8
❏ 124	Lu/Let Me Pass By	1969	$8
❏ 124 [PS]	Lu/Let Me Pass By	1969	$15
❏ 114	San Francisco Glide/Stoney End	1968	$8
❏ 114 [PS]	San Francisco Glide/Stoney End	1968	$15
❏ 66001	Wear Your Love Like Heaven/Honey Won't Let Me	1970	$6
❏ 66001 [PS]	Wear Your Love Like Heaven/Honey Won't Let Me	1970	$15

LIQUID SMOKE
AVCO EMBASSY
❏ 4546	Hard to Handle/(B-side unknown)	1970	$8
❏ 4522	I Who Have Nothing/Warm Touch	1970	$8
❏ 4532	The Shelter of Your Arms/Let Me Down Easy	1970	$8

ROULETTE
❏ 7166	Dance, Dance, Dance/Where's Our Love	1975	$6

LISA LISA AND CULT JAM
COLUMBIA
❏ 38-05844	All Cried Out/Behind My Eyes	1986	$5
—As "Lisa Lisa and Cult Jam with Full Force featuring Paul Anthony and Bow Legged Lou			
❏ 38-05669	Can You Feel the Beat/Feel the Beat You Can	1985	$4
—As "Lisa Lisa and Cult Jam with Full Force			
❏ 38-05669 [PS]	Can You Feel the Beat/Feel the Beat You Can	1985	$4
❏ 38-07737	Everything Will B-Fine/Everything's Instrumental	1988	$3
❏ 38-07737 [PS]	Everything Will B-Fine/Everything's Instrumental	1988	$3
❏ 38-07982	Go for Yours/I Promise You	1988	$3
—As "Lisa Lisa and Cult Jam with Full Force			
❏ 38-07982 [PS]	Go for Yours/I Promise You	1988	$3
❏ 13-08382	Head to Toe/I Wonder If I Take You Home	1989	$3
—Reissue			
❏ 38-07008	Head to Toe/You'll Never Change	1987	$3
❏ 38-07008 [PS]	Head to Toe/You'll Never Change	1987	$3
❏ 38-04886	I Wonder If I Take You Home/If I Take You Home Tonight (Cult Jam Dub)	1985	$4
—As "Lisa Lisa and Cult Jam with Full Force			
❏ 38-68674	Little Jackie Wants to Be a Star/Star (The Jackie Mix)	1989	$3
❏ 38-68674 [PS]	Little Jackie Wants to Be a Star/Star (The Jackie Mix)	1989	$3
❏ 13-08383	Lost in Emotion/All Cried Out	1989	$3
—Reissue			
❏ 38-07267	Lost in Emotion/Motion Is Lost	1987	$3
❏ 38-07267 [PS]	Lost in Emotion/Motion Is Lost	1987	$3
❏ CS7 02869 [DJ]	Someone to Love Me for Me (Edit)/(LP Version)	1987	$5
❏ 38-07619	Someone to Love Me for Me/Spanish Fly	1987	$3
❏ 38-07619 [PS]	Someone to Love Me for Me/Spanish Fly	1987	$3

LISTENING
VANGUARD
❏ 35077	I Can Teach You/Cuando	1968	$30
❏ 35094	Life Stories/Hello You	1968	$30

LITTER
PROBE
❏ 467	Blue Ice/On Our Minds	1969	$30
❏ 461	Silly People/Feeling	1968	$30

SCOTTY
❏ 6710	Action Woman/A Legal Matter	1967	$125

WARICK
❏ 6712	Action Woman/Whatcha Gonna Do About It	1967	$200
❏ 6711	Somebody Help Me/I'm a Man	1967	$200

LITTLE, "BIG" TINY
CORAL
❏ 62294	Tiny's Christmas Medley/Silver Bells	1961	$10

LITTLE ANGELS, THE
RIVERDALE
❏ 1960	(I'll Be a) Little Angel/The Santa Claus Parade	1960	$30

WARWICK
❏ 672	(I'll Be a) Little Angel/The Santa Claus Parade	1961	$20

LITTLE ANTHONY AND THE IMPERIALS
APOLLO
❏ 521	The Fires Burn No More/Lift Up Your Hands	1957	$70
—As "The Chesters			

AVCO
❏ 4651	Hold On (Just a Little Bit Longer)/I've Got to Let You Go (Part 1)	1975	$5
❏ 4645	I Don't Have to Worry/Loneliest House on the Block	1974	$5

Number	Title	Yr	NM
❏ 4655	I'll Be Loving You Sooner or Later/Young Girl	1975	$5
❏ 4635	I'm Falling in Love with You/What Good Am I Without You	1974	$5

DCP

❏ 1119	Goin' Out of My Head/Make It Easy on Yourself	1964	$10
❏ 1154	Hurt/Never Again	1966	$8
❏ 1128	Hurt So Bad/Reputation	1965	$10
❏ 1128 [PS]	Hurt So Bad/Reputation	1965	$50
❏ 1149	I Miss You So/Get Out of My Life	1965	$8
❏ 1104	I'm On the Outside (Looking In)/Please Go	1964	$10
❏ 1136	Take Me Back/Our Song	1965	$8

END

❏ 1047	A Prayer and a Juke Box/River Path	1959	$30
❏ 1104	Dream/A Lovely Way to Spend an Evening	1961	$20
❏ 1083	Formula of Love/Dream	1961	$20
❏ 1074	I'm Taking a Vacation from Love/Only Sympathy	1960	$20
❏ 1080	Limbo (Part 1)/Limbo (Part 2)	1960	$20
❏ 1067	My Empty Room/Bayou, Bayou, Baby	1960	$20
❏ 1086	Please Say You Want Me/So Near Yet So Far	1961	$20
❏ 1060	Shimmy, Shimmy, Ko-Ko Bop/I'm Still in Love with You	1959	$40
❏ 1036	So Much/Oh Yeah	1958	$30
❏ 1053	So Near and Yet So Far/I'm Alright	1959	$30
❏ 1027	Tears on My Pillow/Two People in the World	1958	$50

— As "The Imperials

| ❏ 1027 | Tears on My Pillow/Two People in the World | 1958 | $30 |

— As "Little Anthony and the Imperials

❏ 1038	The Diary/Cha Cha Henry	1959	$30
❏ 1091	Traveling Stranger/Say Yea	1961	$20
❏ 1039	When You Wish Upon a Star/Wishful Thinking	1959	$30

JANUS

❏ 160	Father, Father/Each One, Teach One	1971	$6
❏ 166	Madeline/Universe	1971	$6
❏ 178	(Where Do I Begin) Love Story/There's an Island	1972	$6

LIBERTY

| ❏ 55119 | The Glory of Love/C'mon Tiger (Gimme a Growl) | 1958 | $40 |

— As "The Imperials

MCA

| ❏ 41258 | Daylight/Your Love | 1980 | $4 |

— Little Anthony solo

PCM

| ❏ 202 | This Time We're Winning/Your Love | 1983 | $4 |

ROULETTE

| ❏ 4477 | Lonesome Romeo/I've Got a Lot to Offer Darling | 1963 | $15 |

— Little Anthony solo

| ❏ 4379 | That Lil' Ole Lovemaker Me/It Just Ain't Fair | 1961 | $15 |

— Little Anthony solo

UNITED ARTISTS

| ❏ 0117 | Goin' Out of My Head/I'm On the Outside (Looking In) | 1973 | $4 |

— Silver Spotlight Series" reissue

| ❏ 50720 | Help Me Find a Way (To Say I Love You)/If I Love You | 1970 | $6 |
| ❏ 0118 | Hurt So Bad/Take Me Back | 1973 | $4 |

— Silver Spotlight Series" reissue

❏ 50625	It'll Never Be the Same Again/Don't Get Close	1970	$6
❏ 50552	Out of Sight, Out of Mind/Summer's Comin'	1969	$6
❏ 50598	The Ten Commandments of Love/Let the Sunshine In	1969	$6
❏ 50677	World of Darkness/The Change	1970	$6

VEEP

❏ 1303	Anthem (Revelation)/Goodbye Good Times	1969	$8
❏ 1275	Beautiful People/If I Remember to Forget	1967	$8
❏ 1228	Better Use Your Head/The Wonder of It All	1966	$8
❏ 1228 [PS]	Better Use Your Head/The Wonder of It All	1966	$50
❏ 1255	Don't Tie Me Down/Where There's a Will There's a Way	1967	$8
❏ 1241	Goin' Out of My Head/Shing-a-Ling	1966	$6
❏ 1262	Hold On to Someone/Lost in Love	1967	$8
❏ 1245	Hurt/Never Again	1966	$6
❏ 1242	Hurt So Bad/Reputation	1966	$6
❏ 1278	I'm Hypnotized/Hungry Heart	1968	$8
❏ 1244	I Miss You So/Get Out of My Life	1966	$6
❏ 1240	I'm On the Outside (Looking In)/Please Go	1966	$6
❏ 1248	It's Not the Same/Down on Love	1966	$8

❏ 1243	Take Me Back/Our Song	1966	$6
❏ 1239	Tears on My Pillow/Who's Sorry Now	1966	$6
❏ 1293	The Flesh Failures (Let the Sunshine In)/Gentle Rain	1969	$8
❏ 1283	What Greater Love/In the Back of My Heart	1968	$8

7-Inch Extended Plays

END

❏ 203	*The Diary/Tears on My Pillow/Traveling Stranger/So Much	1959	$250
❏ 203 [PS]	Little Anthony and the Imperials	1959	$300
❏ 204 [PS]	We Are Little Anthony and the Imperials	1959	$300
❏ 204	When You Wish Upon a Star/Over the Rainbow/Love Is a Many-Splendored Thing/What Did I Do	1959	$250

LITTLE BILL AND THE BLUENOTES
DOLTON

| ❏ 4 | I Love an Angel/Bye Bye Baby | 1959 | $40 |

LITTLE BILLY
ABC-PARAMOUNT

| ❏ 9896 | I Found Me a Girl/Say It Like You Mean It | 1958 | $20 |

LITTLE BOOKER
ACE

| ❏ 547 | Open the Door/Teen-Age Rock | 1958 | $30 |

IMPERIAL

| ❏ 5293 | Thinkin' 'Bout My Baby/Doing the Ham Bone | 1954 | $125 |

LITTLE BOY BLUES
FONTANA

| ❏ 1623 | It's Only You/Is Love? | 1968 | $20 |

IRC

❏ 6939	I Can Only Give You Everything/You Don't Love Me	1966	$40
❏ 6936	I'm Ready/Little Boy Blues' Blues	1966	$40
❏ 6928	Look at the Sun/Love for a Day	1966	$30

LITTLE BUBBER
IMPERIAL

| ❏ 5225 | High Class Woman/Come Back Baby | 1953 | $100 |

LITTLE CAESAR
RCA VICTOR

| ❏ 47-7270 | Who Slammed the Door/I'm Reachin' | 1958 | $30 |

RECORDED IN HOLLYWOOD

❏ 239	Atomic Love/You Can't Bring Me Down	1953	$70
❏ 238	Do Right/Money Ain't Long Enough	1953	$70
❏ 235	Goodbye Baby/If I Could See My Baby	1952	$70
❏ 234	Long Time Baby/(Going Down to) The River	1952	$70
❏ 236	Move Me/Lying Woman	1953	$70

RPM

| ❏ 393 | Chains of Love Have Disappeared/Tried to Reason with You Baby | 1953 | $70 |

LITTLE CAESAR AND THE CONSULS
MALA

| ❏ 523 | Hey Girl/You Laugh Too Much | 1966 | $15 |
| ❏ 512 | (My Girl) Sloopy/Poison Ivy | 1965 | $20 |

LITTLE CAESAR AND THE EMPIRE
PARKWAY

| ❏ 152 | Everybody Dance Now!/(Instrumental) | 1967 | $30 |

LITTLE CAESAR AND THE ROMANS
DEL-FI

❏ 4164	Hully Gully Again/Frankie and Johnny	1961	$30
❏ 4166	Memories of Those Oldies But Goodies/Fever	1961	$70
❏ 4176	Popeye One More Time/Yoyo Yo Yoyo	1962	$30
❏ 4170	Ten Commandments of Love/C.C. Rider	1961	$60
❏ 4158	Those Oldies But Goodies (Remind Me of You)/She Don't Wanna Dance	1961	$40

SCEPTER

| ❏ 12237 | Baby Love/When Will I Get Over You | 1969 | $8 |

— As "Caesar and the Romans"

LITTLE CHARLES AND THE SIDEWINDERS
DECCA

❏ 31980	I'm Available/It's a Heartache	1966	$300
❏ 32321	Sweet Lorene/Twice as Much for My Baby	1968	$40
❏ 32095	Talkin' About You, Babe/A Taste of the Good Life	1967	$300
❏ 32233	The Loner (Part 1)/The Loner (Part 2)	1967	$80

JEWEL

| ❏ 752 | Give Me a Chance/Guess I'll Have to Take What's Left | 1965 | $50 |

LITTLE CHERYL
CAMEO

❏ 292	Come On Home/I Love You Conrad	1964	$15
❏ 270	Heaven Only Knows/Can't We Just Be Friends	1963	$50
❏ 276	Mama Let the Phone Bell Ring/Can't We Just Be Friends	1963	$15

LITTLE EVA
AMY

| ❏ 943 | Stand By Me/That's My Man | 1965 | $8 |

BELL

| ❏ 45264 | The Loco-Motion/Will You Love Me Tomorrow | 1972 | $5 |

DIMENSION

❏ 1019	Let's Start the Party Again/Please Hurt Me	1963	$15
❏ 1006	Let's Turkey Trot/Down Home	1963	$15
❏ 1035	Makin' with the Magilla/Conga	1964	$10
❏ 1035	Makin' with the Magilla/Run to Her	1964	$10
❏ 1035 [PS]	Makin' with the Magilla/Run to Her	1964	$50
❏ 1011	Old Smokey Locomotion/Just a Little Girl	1963	$15
❏ 1021	The Christmas Song/I Wish You a Merry Christmas	1963	$20

— With Big Dee Irwin

| ❏ 1021 [PS] | The Christmas Song/I Wish You a Merry Christmas | 1963 | $50 |

— With Big Dee Irwin

❏ 1000	The Loco-Motion/He Is the Boy	1962	$20
❏ 1013	The Trouble with Boys/What I Gotta Do	1963	$30
❏ 1042	Wake Up John/Takin' Back What I Said	1964	$70

SPRING

| ❏ 101 | Mama Said/Something About You Boy | 1970 | $30 |

VERVE

| ❏ 10459 | Bend It/Just One Word Isn't Enough | 1966 | $40 |
| ❏ 10529 | Everything Is Beautiful About You Boy/Take a Step in My Direction | 1967 | $50 |

LITTLE FEAT
WARNER BROS.

❏ 8219	All That You Dream/One Love Stand	1976	$5
❏ 7689	Dixie Chicken/Lafayette Railroad	1973	$6
❏ 7553	Easy to Slip/Cat Fever	1972	$8
❏ 49801	Front Page News/Easy to Sleep	1981	$5
❏ 27728	Hate to Lose Your Lovin'/Cajun Girl	1988	$3
❏ 27728 [PS]	Hate to Lose Your Lovin'/Cajun Girl	1988	$3
❏ 8174	Long Distance Love/Romance Dance	1975	$5
❏ 8054	Oh Atlanta/Down the Road	1974	$5
❏ 8566	Oh Atlanta/Willin'	1978	$5
❏ 27684	One Clear Moment/Changin' Luck	1988	$3
❏ 27684 [PS]	One Clear Moment/Changin' Luck	1988	$3
❏ 49841	Strawberry Flats/Gringo	1981	$5
❏ 7431	Strawberry Flats/Hamburger Midnight	1970	$8
❏ 8420	Time Loves a Hero/Sailin' Shoes	1977	$5
❏ 49169	Wake Up Dreaming/Front Page News	1980	$5

LITTLE FOLK OF MT. ROSKILL, THE
RCA VICTOR

| ❏ HR383 | Hooray for Santa Claus/Come Go with Me | 1969 | $10 |

— New Zealand import

LITTLE GUY AND THE GIANTS
LAWN

| ❏ 103 | It's You/So Young | 1960 | $200 |

LITTLE IKE
CHAMPION

| ❏ 1011 | She Can Rock/Am I Losin' You | 1959 | $125 |

Number	Title	Yr	NM

LITTLE IVA AND HER BAND
MIRACLE
❏ 2	When I Needed You/Continental Strut	1960	$1500

LITTLE JOE
BRUNSWICK
| ❏ 55369 | Holiday/Fool on the Hill | 1968 | $8 |

LITTLE JOE AND THE THRILLERS
ENJOY
| ❏ 2011 | Peanuts and Popcorn/Chicken Little Boo Boo | 1964 | $10 |

EPIC
| ❏ 9293 | Mine/It's Too Bad We Had to Say Goodbye | 1958 | $20 |

MGM
❏ 14466	Baby I Could Be So Good at Lovin' You/Cherry Pink and Apple Blossom White	1972	$5
❏ 14290	Don't Take the Rain Away/The Children	1971	$5
❏ 14662	Folks Who Live on the Hill/Baby I Could Be So Good at Lovin' You	1973	$5
❏ 14230	People Show/Baby I Could Be So Good at Lovin' You	1971	$5
❏ 14361	Shelly Made Me Smile/Words and Music	1972	$5
❏ 14129	Somehow, Someway/Days 'Til Morning	1970	$5

OKEH
❏ 7116	Cherry (Part 1)/Cherry (Part 2)	1959	$15
❏ 7099	Don't Leave Me Alone/What's Happened to Your Halo	1958	$20
❏ 7134	Ev'ry Now and Then/Goodnight, Little Girl	1960	$15
❏ 7127	Give Me All Your Love/I'll Never Let You Go	1959	$15
❏ 7121	I'm Tryin'/Strange Dreams	1959	$15
❏ 7075	Let's Do the Slop/This I Know	1956	$20
❏ 7094	Lonesome/The Echoes Keep Calling Me	1957	$20
❏ 7107	Mine/It's Too Bad We Had to Say Goodbye	1958	$20
❏ 7088	Peanuts/Lilly Lou	1957	$30
❏ 7136	Stay/Please Don't Go	1960	$40

REPRISE
| ❏ 20142 | Peanuts/No, No, I Can't Stop | 1963 | $10 |

7-Inch Extended Plays

EPIC
| ❏ EG-7198 | (contents unknown) | 1958 | $125 |
| ❏ EG-7198 [PS] | Little Joe and the Thrillers | 1958 | $125 |

LITTLE JOEY
FIDELITY
| ❏ 3014 | Comin' Down The Chimney #2/Comin' Down The Chimney #1 | 1959 | $15 |

—*B-side by Little Tootsie*

LITTLE JOEY AND THE FLIPS
CAMEO
| ❏ 327 | The Beachcomber/Fool, Fool, Fool | 1964 | $50 |

—*As "Joey and the Flips*

JOY
| ❏ 268 | Bongo Gully/It Was Like Heaven | 1962 | $15 |
| ❏ 262 | Bongo Stomp/Lost Love | 1962 | $20 |

LITTLE KIDS, THE
TOWER
| ❏ 298 | Santa Claus Is Stuck in the Chimney/Tambourine Jingle | 1966 | $20 |

LITTLE MILTON
BOBBIN
❏ 120	Dead Love/My Baby Pleases Me	1960	$30
❏ 117	Hold Me Tight/Same Old Blues	1959	$30
❏ 101	I'm a Lonely Man/That Will Never Do	1958	$30
❏ 128	I'm in Love/Cross My Heart	1961	$30
❏ 125	Let It Be Known/Hey Girl	1960	$30
❏ 103	Long Distance Operator/I Found Me a New Love	1959	$30
❏ 112	Strange Dreams/I'm Tryin'	1959	$30

CHECKER
❏ 1203	At the Dark End of the Street/I (Who Have Nothing)	1968	$15
❏ 1186	A Whole Lot of Fun Before the Weekend Is Done/Real True Love	1967	$15
❏ 1227	Baby I Love You/Don't Talk Back	1970	$15

Number	Title	Yr	NM
❏ 1096	Blind Man/Blues in the Night	1964	$20
❏ 1162	Feel So Bad/You Colored My Blues Right	1966	$30
❏ 1212	Grits Ain't Groceries (All Around the World)/I Can't Quit You Baby	1969	$40
❏ 1118	Help Me Love You/Without My Sweet Baby	1965	$20
❏ 1226	If Walls Could Talk/Loving You	1969	$15
❏ 1194	I Know What I Want/You Mean Everything to Me	1968	$15
❏ 1172	I'll Never Turn My Back on You/Don't Leave Her	1967	$15
❏ 1138	I'm Mighty Grateful/When Does Heartache End	1966	$20
❏ 1178	I'm Shorty/Sitting Home Alone	1967	$15
❏ 1239	I Play Dirty/Nothing Beats a Failure	1971	$8
❏ 1020	I Wonder Why/Losing Hand	1962	$20
❏ 1208	Let Me Down Easy/Lonely Drifter	1968	$15
❏ 1225	Let's Get Together/I'll Always Love You	1969	$15
❏ 1149	Man Loves Two/Believe in Me	1966	$20
❏ 1236	Many Rivers to Cross/Mother's Love	1970	$15
❏ 1063	Meddlin'/One of These Old Days	1963	$20
❏ 1189	More and More/Cost of Living	1967	$15
❏ 1128	My Baby's Something Else/Your People	1965	$15
❏ 1221	Poor Man/So Blue	1969	$15
❏ 1078	Sacrifice/What Kind of Love Is This	1964	$20
❏ 1012	Satisfied/Someone to Love	1962	$20
❏ 977	Saving My Love for You/Lonely No More	1961	$20
❏ 1048	She Put a Spell on Me/Never Too Old	1963	$20
❏ 994	So Mean to Me/I Need Somebody	1961	$20
❏ 1231	Somebody's Changin' My Sweet Baby's Mind/I'm Tired	1970	$15

—*As "Little Milton Campbell"*

❏ 1132	Sometimes/We Got the Winning Hand	1965	$20
❏ 1105	We're Gonna Make It/Can't Hold Back the Tears	1965	$20
❏ 1113	Who's Cheating Who?/Ain't No Big Deal on You	1965	$20

GLADES
❏ 1738	Baby It Ain't No Way/Bring It On Back	1976	$5
❏ 1734	Friend of Mine/(Instrumental)	1976	$5
❏ 1743	Loving You (Is the Best Thing to Happen to Me)/9:59 A.M.	1977	$5
❏ 1747	Me for You, You for Me/My Thing Is You	1977	$5
❏ 2127	I Will Survive/4:59 A.M.	1986	$4
❏ 2123	Lonesome Christmas/Come To Me	1985	$4
❏ 2108	Misty Blue/Catch You on the Way Down	1985	$4
❏ 2104	The Blues Is All Right/Come Back Kind of Loving	1985	$4

MCA
| ❏ 52184 | Age Ain't Nothin' But a Number/(Instrumental) | 1983 | $4 |
| ❏ 52254 | Living on the Dark Side of Love/Why Are You So Hard to Please | 1983 | $4 |

METEOR
| ❏ 5045 | Let My Baby Be/Oh My Little Baby | 1957 | $800 |
| ❏ 5040 | Love at First Sight/Let's Boogie Baby | 1957 | $200 |

STAX
❏ 0210	Behind Closed Doors/Bet You I Win	1974	$6
❏ 0252	How Could You Do It to Me/Packed Up and Took My Mind	1975	$6
❏ 0100	If That Ain't a Reason (For Your Woman to Leave You)/Mr. Mailman	1971	$6
❏ 0238	If You Talk in Your Sleep/Sweet Woman of Mine	1975	$6
❏ 0141	I'm Gonna Cry a River/What It Is	1972	$6
❏ 0229	Let Me Back In/Let Your Loss Be Your Lesson	1974	$6
❏ 0148	Lovin' Stick/Rainy Day	1972	$6
❏ 0111	That's What Love Will Make You Do/I'm Livin' Off the Love You Give	1972	$6
❏ 0191	Tin Pan Alley/Sweet Woman of Mine	1974	$6
❏ 0124	Walking the Back Streets and Crying/Before the Honeymoon	1972	$6
❏ 0174	What It Is/Who Can Handle Me Is You	1973	$6

SUN
| ❏ 194 | Beggin' My Baby/Somebody Told Me | 1954 | $300 |
| ❏ 200 | If You Love Me/Alone and Blue | 1954 | $600 |

Number	Title	Yr	NM
❏ 220	Lookin' for My Baby/Homesick for My Baby	1955	$800

LITTLE OTIS
TAMLA
| ❏ 54058 | I Out-Duked the Duke/Baby I Need You | 1962 | $40 |

LITTLE RICHARD
ATLANTIC
| ❏ 2181 | Crying in the Chapel/Hole in the Wall | 1963 | $15 |
| ❏ 2192 | It Is No Secret (What God Can Do)/Travelin' Shoes | 1963 | $15 |

BELL
| ❏ 45385 | Good Golly Miss Molly/Good Golly Miss Molly (Part 2) | 1973 | $5 |

BRUNSWICK
❏ 55362	She's Together/Try Some of Mine	1968	$8
❏ 55386	Soul Train/Can I Count on You	1968	$8
❏ 55377	Stingy Jenny/Baby Don't You Tear My Clothes	1968	$8

CORAL
| ❏ 62366 | Milky White Way/Need Him | 1963 | $10 |

CRITIQUE
| ❏ 99392 | Happy Endings/California Girls | 1987 | $4 |

—*A-side with the Beach Boys; B-side is The Beach Boys without Little Richard*

ELEKTRA
| ❏ 69385 | Tutti Frutti/Kokomo | 1988 | $3 |

—*B-side by the Beach Boys*

| ❏ 69384 | Tutti Frutti/Powerful Stuff | 1988 | $3 |

—*B-side by the Fabulous Thunderbirds*

| ❏ 69370 | Tutti Frutti/Rave On | 1988 | $3 |

—*B-side by John Cougar Mellencamp*

END
| ❏ 1058 | Milky White Way/I've Just Come From the Fountain | 1959 | $20 |
| ❏ 1057 | Troubles of the World/Save Me Lord | 1959 | $20 |

GREEN MOUNTAIN
| ❏ 413 | In the Middle of the Night/Where Will I Find a Place to Sleep This Evening | 1973 | $5 |

KENT
| ❏ 4568 | Don't You Know I/In the Name | 1972 | $5 |

MAINSTREAM
| ❏ 5572 | Try to Help Your Brother/Funk Proof | 1975 | $5 |

MANTICORE
| ❏ 7007 | Call My Name/Steal Miss Liza (Miss Liza Jane) | 1975 | $4 |

MCA
| ❏ 52780 | Great Gosh A-Mighty! (It's a Matter of Time)/The Ride | 1986 | $3 |

—*B-side by Charlie Midnight*

| ❏ 52780 [PS] | Great Gosh A-Mighty! (It's a Matter of Time)/The Ride | 1986 | $3 |

MERCURY
❏ 71911	Do You Care/Ride On King Jesus	1962	$20
❏ 71884	He's Not Just a Soldier/Joy, Joy, Joy	1962	$20
❏ 71965	Why Don't You Change Your Ways/He Got What He Wanted	1962	$20

MODERN
❏ 1043	Baby What You Want Me to Do (Part 1)/Baby What You Want Me to Do (Part 2)	1967	$15
❏ 1022	Directly from My Heart to You/I'm Back	1966	$15
❏ 1019	Do You Feel It (Part 1)/Do You Feel It (Part 2)	1966	$15
❏ 1018	Holy Mackeral/Baby, Don't You Want a Man Like Me	1966	$15
❏ 1018 [PS]	Holy Mackeral/Baby, Don't You Want a Man Like Me	1966	$30
❏ 1030	Slippin' and Slidin'/Bring It Back Home to Me	1967	$15

OKEH
❏ 7278	Don't Deceive Me (Please Don't Go)/Never Gonna Let You Go	1967	$15
❏ 7271	Hurry Sundown/I Don't Want to Discuss It	1967	$15
❏ 7262	I Need Love/Commandments of Love	1966	$15
❏ 7325	Lucille/Whole Lotta Shakin' Goin' On	1969	$10
❏ 7286	Money/Little Bit of Something	1967	$15
❏ 7251	Poor Dog (Who Can't Wag His Own Tail)/Well	1966	$20
❏ 7251 [PS]	Poor Dog (Who Can't Wag His Own Tail)/Well	1966	$30

Number	Title	Yr	NM

PEACOCK

Number	Title	Yr	NM
❏ 1658	Little Richard's Boogie/Directly from My Heart to You	1956	$200
❏ 1673	Maybe I'm Right/I Love My Baby	1957	$100

RCA VICTOR

❏ 47-4582	Get Rich Quick/Thinkin' 'Bout My Mother	1952	$800
❏ 47-5025	Please Have Mercy on Me/I Brought It All on Myself	1952	$600
❏ 47-4392	Taxi Blues/Every Hour	1951	$900
❏ 47-4772	Why Did You Leave Me?/Ain't Nothin' Happenin'	1952	$800

REPRISE

❏ 0907	Freedom Blues/Dew Drop Inn	1970	$10
❏ 1043	Green Power/Dancing in the Street	1971	$8
❏ 0942	Greenwood Mississippi/I Saw Her Standing There	1970	$10
❏ 1130	Mockingbird Sally/Nuki Suki	1972	$8
❏ 1062	Money Is/Money Runner	1972	$8

—B-side by Quincy Jones

| ❏ 1005 | Shake a Hand (If You Can)/Somebody Saw You | 1971 | $8 |

SPECIALTY

❏ 645	Baby Face/I'll Never Let You Go	1958	$30
❏ 692	Bama Lama Bama Loo/Annie Is Back	1964	$20
❏ 660	By the Light of the Silvery Moon/Wonderin'	1959	$30
❏ 734	Chicken Little Baby/Oh Why	1974	$6
❏ 624	Good Golly, Miss Molly/Hey-Hey-Hey-Hey!	1958	$40
❏ 624 [PS]	Good Golly, Miss Molly/Hey-Hey-Hey-Hey!	1958	$60
❏ 584	Heebie-Jeebies/She's Got it	1956	$50
❏ 681	I Got It/Baby	1960	$30
❏ 572	Long Tall Sally/Slippin' and Slidin' (Peepin' and Hidin')	1956	$50
❏ 598	Lucille/Send Me Some Lovin'	1957	$50
❏ 633	Ooh! My Soul/True, Fine Mama	1958	$30
❏ 633 [PS]	Ooh! My Soul/True, Fine Mama	1958	$60
❏ 633/624	Ooh! My Soul/True, Fine Mama	1958	$100

—Some copies have the B-side misnumbered; all other information is correct, including the master number

❏ 699	Poor Boy Paul/Wonderin'	1964	$20
❏ 670	Shake a Hand/All Night Long	1959	$30
❏ 652	She Knows How to Rock/Early One Morning	1958	$30
❏ 591	The Girl Can't Help It/All Around the World	1956	$50
❏ 686	The Most I Can Offer/Directly from My Heart	1964	$20
❏ 561	Tutti-Frutti/I'm Just a Lonely Guy	1955	$60
❏ 680	Whole Lotta Shakin' Goin' On/Maybe I'm Right	1959	$30

VEE JAY

❏ 625	Blueberry Hill/Cherry Red	1964	$10
❏ 698	I Don't Know What You've Got But It's Got Me -- Part I/I Don't Know What You've Got But It's Got Me -- Part II	1965	$10
❏ 652	It Ain't Whatcha Do/Cross Over	1965	$10
❏ 612	Whole Lotta Shakin' Goin' On/Goodnight Irene	1964	$10
❏ 665	Without Love/Dance What You Wanna	1965	$10

WARNER BROS.

| ❏ 28491 | Big House Reunion/Somebody's Comin' | 1987 | $4 |

WTG

| ❏ 08492 | Twins (Long)/Twins (Short) | 1988 | $4 |

—With Philip Bailey

7-Inch Extended Plays

RCA CAMDEN

❏ CAE-416	Ain't Nothin' Happenin'/Why Did You Leave Me//Every Hour/I Brought It All on Myself	1955	$175
❏ CAE-416 [PS]	Little Richard	1955	$175
❏ CAE-446 [PS]	Little Richard Rocks	1956	$125
❏ CAE-446	Taxi Blues/Please Have Mercy on Me//Get Rich Quick/Thinkin' 'Bout My Mother	1956	$125

SPECIALTY

❏ SEP-405	Boo Hoo Hoo Hoo/The Girl Can't Help It//Send Me Some Lovin'/Heeby-Jeebies	1958	$100
❏ SEP-400 [PS]	Here's Little Richard	1957	$125
❏ SEP-401 [PS]	Here's Little Richard	1957	$125
❏ SEP-402 [PS]	Here's Little Richard	1957	$125
❏ SEP-403 [PS]	Little Richard	1958	$100
❏ SEP-404 [PS]	Little Richard	1958	$100
❏ SEP-405 [PS]	Little Richard	1958	$100

Number	Title	Yr	NM
❏ SEP-400	Long Tall Sally/Miss Ann//She's Got It/Can't Believe You Wanna Leave	1957	$125
❏ SEP-404	Ooh! My Soul/All Around the World//Good Golly, Miss Molly/Babyface	1958	$100
❏ SEP-401	Slippin' and Slidin'/Oh Why//Ready Teddy/Baby	1957	$125
❏ SEP-402	Tutti-Frutti/True, Fine Mama//Rip It Up/Jenny, Jenny	1957	$125

LITTLE RIVER BAND

CAPITOL

❏ B-5469	Blind Eyes/Butterfly	1985	$3
❏ 4789	Cool Change/Middle Man	1979	$4
❏ 4862	It's Not a Wonder/Man on the Run	1980	$4
❏ B-5579	It Was the Night/Time for Love	1986	$3
❏ 4748	Lonesome Loser/Shut Down Turn Off	1979	$4
❏ A-5061	Man on Your Mind/Orbit Zero	1982	$4
❏ A-5061 [PS]	Man on Your Mind/Orbit Zero	1982	$4
❏ B-5609	Paper Paradise/Face in a Crowd	1986	$3
❏ B-5411	Playing to Win/Through Her Eyes	1984	$3

—As "LRB

❏ B-5411 [PS]	Playing to Win/Through Her Eyes	1984	$4
❏ A-5057	Take It Easy on Me/Orbit Zero	1981	$4
❏ A-5057 [PS]	Take It Easy on Me/Orbit Zero	1981	$4
❏ B-5185	The Other Guy/No More Tears	1982	$4
❏ B-5185 [PS]	The Other Guy/No More Tears	1982	$4
❏ B-5231	We Two/Falling	1983	$3

HARVEST

❏ 4524	Happy Anniversary/Changed and Different	1978	$4
❏ 4428	Help is On Its Way/Inner Light	1977	$4
❏ 4380	I'll Always Call Your Name/Man in Black	1976	$4
❏ 4318	It's a Long Way There/Meanwhile	1976	$4
❏ 4667	Lady/Take Me Home	1978	$4
❏ 4667 [PS]	Lady/Take Me Home	1978	$12

MCA

❏ 53767	If I Get Lucky/Piece of My Heart	1989	$3
❏ 53424	It's Cold Out Tonight/The Great Unknown	1988	$3
❏ 53677	Listen to Your Heart/High Wire	1989	$3

—B-side by Glenn Medeiros

| ❏ 53201 | Love Is a Bridge/Inside Story | 1988 | $3 |

LITTLE ROGER AND THE GOOSEBUMPS

GOOSEBUMP

| ❏ 0(no cat #) | Hit and Run/Now That I've Lost You | 1974 | $6 |

SPLASH

| ❏ 901 | Stairway to Gilligan's Island/The Wet Look | 1978 | $30 |

LITTLE SAMMY AND THE TONES

JACLYN

| ❏ 1761 | Christine/Over the Rainbow | 1962 | $60 |

LITTLE SIS

PARKWAY

| ❏ 815 | The Twist/The Pony | 1960 | $20 |

LITTLE SISTERS, THE

LIBERTY

| ❏ 55220 | Are My Ears On Straight/A Little Star Came Down | 1959 | $15 |

LITTLE SUSIE

MGM

| ❏ 12396 | Who Put the Gum in Santa's Whiskers/Christmas Season | 1956 | $20 |

LITTLE TOMMY

LAURIE

| ❏ 3077 | (All I Want for Christmas Is) My Two Front Teeth/Cuddly Wuddly | 1960 | $20 |

—As "Little Tommy

| ❏ 3077 | (All I Want For Christmas Is) My Two Front Teeth/Mister Cuddly Wuddly | 1960 | $20 |

—As "Little Tommy Tucker

Number	Title	Yr	NM

LITTLE TOOTSIE

FIDELITY

| ❏ 3014 | Comin' Down The Chimney #1/Comin' Down The Chimney #2 | 1959 | $15 |

—B-side by Little Joey

LITTLE WALTER

CHANCE

| ❏ 1116 | That's All Right/Just Keep Loving Her | 1952 | $3000 |

—As "Little Walter J." VG 1000; VG+ 2000

CHECKER

❏ 945	Ah'w Baby/I Had My Fun	1960	$30
❏ 780	Blues with a Feeling/Quarter to Twelve	1953	$125
❏ 867	Boom, Boom -- Out Goes the Light/Temperature	1957	$50
❏ 938	Break It Up/Me and Piney Brown	1960	$30
❏ 986	Crazy Legs/Crazy for My Baby	1961	$30
❏ 1081	Dead Presidents/I'm a Business Man	1964	$20
❏ 1071	Diggin' My Potatoes/Snake Dancer	1964	$20
❏ 767	Don't Have to Hunt No More/Tonight with a Fool	1953	$100
❏ 859	Everybody Needs Somebody/Nobody But You	1957	$50
❏ 930	Everything's Gonna Be All Right/Back Track	1959	$30
❏ 838	Flying Saucer/One More Chance with You	1956	$50
❏ 968	I Don't Play/As Long As I Have You	1961	$30
❏ 852	It's Too Late Brother/Take Me Back	1957	$50
❏ 805	Last Night/Mellow Down Easy	1954	$70
❏ 786	Lights Out/You're So Fine	1953	$60
❏ 764	Mean Old World/Sad Hours	1952	$120
❏ 1117	Mean Ole Frisco/Blue and Lonesome	1965	$20
❏ 955	My Babe/Blue Midnight	1960	$30
❏ 811	My Babe/Thunder Bird	1955	$30
❏ 919	My Baby's Sweeter/Crazy Mixed-Up World	1959	$30
❏ 770	Off the Wall/Tell Me Mama	1953	$100

—Black vinyl

| ❏ 770 | Off the Wall/Tell Me Mama | 1953 | $3000 |

—Red vinyl

❏ 793	Oh Baby/Rocker	1954	$50
❏ 845	Teenage Beat/What a Feeling	1956	$50
❏ 890	The Toddle/Confessin' the Blues	1958	$40
❏ 825	Too Late/I Hate to See You Go	1955	$50
❏ 833	Who/It Ain't Right	1956	$50

LITTLE WHEELS, THE

DOT

| ❏ 16676 | Four Wheels, Ball Bearing Surfing Board/The Bumper | 1964 | $40 |

LITTLEFIELD, LITTLE WILLIE

FEDERAL

❏ 12174	Goofy Dust Blues/Falling Tears	1954	$100
❏ 12148	Miss K.C.'s Fine/Rock-a-Bye Baby	1953	$125
❏ 12163	Please Don't Go-o-o-o-oh/Don't Take My Heart Little Girl	1954	$100
❏ 12101	Sticking on You Baby/Blood Is Redder Than Wine	1952	$125
❏ 12137	The Midnight Hour Was Shining/My Best Wishes and Regards	1953	$125

RHYTHM

| ❏ 107 | Baby Shame/Mistreated | 1956 | $200 |

LITTLEJOHN, JIMMY

COLUMBIA

| ❏ 4-21320 | Haunted Blues/I'm Mean When I'm Mad | 1954 | $30 |
| ❏ 4-21259 | Tequila Mama/No Parking Here | 1954 | $30 |

LITTLES, HATTIE

GORDY

| ❏ 7004 | Back in My Arms Again/(B-side unknown) | 1962 | $800 |
| ❏ 7007 | Here You Come/Your Love Is Wonderful | 1962 | $100 |

LITTLETON, JOHN, AND THE CAPISTRANOS

DUKE

| ❏ 179 | Po Mary/Now Darling | 1959 | $100 |

LIVELY ONES, THE

DEL-FI

❏ 4184	Guitarget/Crying Guitar	1962	$40
❏ 4210	High Tide/Goofy Foot	1963	$30
❏ 4189	Misirlou/Blue Tears	1962	$40
❏ 4189	Misirlou/Livin'	1962	$40
❏ 4217	Surf City/Telstar Surf	1963	$30
❏ 4205	Surfer Boogie/Ric-a-Tic	1963	$30
❏ 4196	Surf Rider/Surfer's Lament	1963	$40

Number	Title	Yr	NM
MGM			
❏ 13691	Bugalu Movement/Take It While You Can	1967	$20

LIVERBIRDS, THE
PHILIPS

Number	Title	Yr	NM
❏ 40276	Shop Around/It's Got to Be You	1965	$10
❏ 40288	Why Do You Hang Around Me/Diddley Daddy	1965	$10

LIVERPOOL SPINNERS, THE
FONTANA

Number	Title	Yr	NM
❏ 1574	Seth Davey/All For Me Grog	1967	$10

LIVERS, THE
CONSTELLATION

Number	Title	Yr	NM
❏ 118	Beatle Time/This Is the Night	1964	$20

LIVING COLOUR
EPIC

Number	Title	Yr	NM
❏ 68611	Cult of Personality/Funny Vibe	1989	$3
❏ 68548	Glamour Boys/Cult of Personality (Live)	1989	$3
❏ 68934	Open Letter (To a Landlord)/Talkin' About a Revolution	1989	$3

LLOYD, CHARLES
A&M

Number	Title	Yr	NM
❏ 1415	Seagull/TM	1973	$5
ATLANTIC			
❏ 5078	Forest Flower Sunday (Part 1)/Forest Flower Sunday (Part 2)	1967	$8
❏ 2435	Love-In/Sunday Morning	1967	$8
❏ 5071	Sombrero Sam (Part 1)/Sombrero Sam (Part 2)	1966	$8
COLUMBIA			
❏ 43290	She's a Woman/You Know	1965	$10
KAPP			
❏ 2118	Moonman/I Don't Care What You Tell Me	1971	$6

LLOYD, JIMMY
ROULETTE

Number	Title	Yr	NM
❏ 4062	I Got a Rocket in My Pocket/You're Gone Baby	1958	$125
❏ 7001	Where the Rio De Rosa Flows/The Beginning of the End	1957	$70

LOAD OF MISCHIEF
HOLIDAY INN

Number	Title	Yr	NM
❏ 2205	I'm a Lover/Back in My Arms Again	1967	$30
SUN			
❏ 407	I'm a Lover/Back in My Arms Again	1967	$100

— *The last of the Sam Phillips Sun 45s*

LOBO
ATLANTIC

Number	Title	Yr	NM
❏ 3851 [DJ]	Caribbean Carnival (same on both sides)	1981	$5

— *May be promo only*

BIG TREE

Number	Title	Yr	NM
❏ 141	A Simple Man/Don't Expect Me to Be Your Friend	1972	$5
❏ 119	California Kid and Reemo/A Little Different	1971	$5
❏ 158	Don't Expect Me to Be Your Friend/A Big Red Kite	1973	$4
❏ 16033	Don't Tell Me Goodnight/My Mama Had Soul	1975	$4
❏ 16004	How Can I Tell Her/Hope You're Proud of Me Girl	1973	$4
❏ 147	I'd Love You to Want Me/Am I True to Myself	1972	$5
❏ 16001	It Sure Took a Long, Long Time/Running Deer	1973	$4
❏ 112	Me and You and a Dog Named Boo/Walk Away from It All	1971	$6
❏ 116	She Didn't Do Magic/I'm the Only One	1971	$5
❏ 15001	Standing at the End of the Line/Stoney	1974	$4
❏ 134	The Albatross/We'll Make It, I Know We Will	1972	$5
❏ 16012	There Ain't No Way/Love Me for What I Am	1973	$4
❏ 16040	Would I Still Have You/Morning Sun	1975	$4
ELEKTRA			
❏ 47099	I Can't Believe You Anymore/Fight Fire with Fire	1980	$4

Number	Title	Yr	NM
EVERGREEN			
❏ 1028 [DJ]	Am I Going Crazy (Or Just Out of Her Mind) (same on both sides)	1985	$6

— *Promo copies have incorrect title*

Number	Title	Yr	NM
❏ 1028	Am I Going Crazy (Or Just Out of My Mind)/I Don't Want to Want You	1985	$5

— *Stock copies have corrected title*

LAURIE

Number	Title	Yr	NM
❏ 3526	Happy Days in New York City/My Friend Is Here	1969	$20

— *As "Kent LaVoie"*

LOBO

Number	Title	Yr	NM
❏ IV	Come Looking for Me/I Don't Want to Want You	1982	$5
❏ I	I Don't Want to Want You/No One Will Ever Know	1981	$5
❏ X	Living My Life Without You/A Simple Man	1982	$5
MCA			
❏ 41152	Holdin' On for Dear Love/Gus, the Dancing Dog	1979	$4
❏ 41065	Where Were You When I Was Falling in Love/I Don't Wanna Make Love Anymore	1979	$4
WARNER BROS.			
❏ 8493	Afterglow/Our Best Time	1977	$4

LOCKETS, THE
ARGO

Number	Title	Yr	NM
❏ 5455	Little Boy/Don'tcha Know	1963	$15

LOCKLIN, HANK
4 STAR

Number	Title	Yr	NM
❏ 1624	Alone at a Table for Two/Golden Wristwatch	1953	$40
❏ 1605	Could You/Down Texas Way	1952	$40
❏ 1556	I Could Love You Darling/The Song of the Whispering Leaves	1951	$50
❏ 1641	Let Me Be the One/I'm Tired of Runnin' Around	1953	$40
❏ 1574	Send Me the Pillow You Dream On, No. 2/I Always Lose	1951	$50
❏ 1582	Stumpy Joe/I'm Going to Copyright Your Kisses	1951	$50
❏ 1594	Tell Me You Love Me/Tomorrow's Just Another Day to Cry	1952	$50
❏ 1747	The Same Sweet Girl/You Burned a Hole in My Heart	1960	$20
❏ 1608	Who's Knocking at My Heart/The Harvest Is Ripe	1952	$40
❏ 1688	Who Will It Be/Empty Bottle, Empty Heart	1954	$40
❏ 1632	Won't You Change Your Mind/Crazy Over You	1953	$40
DECCA			
❏ 9-29270	Baby You Can Count on Me/Whispering Scandal	1954	$30
❏ 9-28740	I Can't Run Away/Red Rose	1953	$30
❏ 9-28526	I Like to Play with Your Kisses/Picking Sweethearts	1953	$30
❏ 9-28826	Lessons in Love/Shadows	1953	$30
❏ 9-29599	Let Me Confess/I'll Always Be Standing By	1955	$30
KING			
❏ 5283	Send Me the Pillow You Dream On/Let Me Be the One	1959	$20
MGM			
❏ 14802	Irish Eyes/Please Let Me Have You	1975	$5
❏ 14753	Send Me Your Coffee Cup/True Love Is Always Hard to Find	1974	$5
❏ 14777	The Sweetest Mistake/Hang My Picture in Your Heart	1975	$5
PLANTATION			
❏ 142	Daytime Love Affair/You Never Miss the Water	1976	$5
❏ 160	There Never Was a Time/(B-side unknown)	1977	$5
❏ 135	These Arms You Push Away/Baby I Need You	1976	$5
RCA VICTOR			
❏ 47-6778	14 Karat Gold/By the Sweat of My Brow	1956	$30
❏ 74-0941	Before My Time/If Loving You Means Anything	1973	$6
❏ 47-9894	Bless Her Heart...I Love Her/Morning	1970	$8
❏ 74-0772	Eventually/I Forgot to Live Today	1972	$6
❏ 47-9582	Everlasting Love/I'm Slowly Going Out of Your Mind	1968	$12
❏ 47-9849	Flying South/Rosalita	1970	$8
❏ 47-8156	Flyin' South/Behind the Footlights	1963	$15
❏ 47-8318	Followed Closely by My Teardrops/You Never Want to Love Me	1964	$15

Number	Title	Yr	NM
❏ 47-7472	Foreign Car/When the Band Plays the Blues	1959	$20
❏ 47-8560	Forty Nine, Fifty One/Faith and Trust	1965	$10
❏ 47-7871	From Here to There to You/This Song Is Just for You	1961	$15
❏ 47-6967	Geisha Girl/Livin' Alone	1957	$30
❏ 47-6867	Goin' Home All By Myself/The Rich and the Poor	1957	$30
❏ 74-0848	Goodbye Dear Ole Ryman/Just Call Me Darling	1972	$6
❏ 47-7965	Happy Journey/I Need You Now	1961	$15
❏ 47-9092	Hasta Luego (See You Later)/Wishing on a Star	1967	$12
❏ 47-8399	Hello Heartache/I Was Coming Home to You	1964	$15
❏ 47-7561	Hiding in My Heart/The Border of the Blues	1959	$20
❏ 47-6672	How Much/She's Better Than Most	1956	$30
❏ SP-45-177 [DJ]	Hurt Me Again (same on both sides)	1968	$30
❏ 47-7393	I Gotta Talk to Your Heart/The Other Side of the Door	1958	$20
❏ 47-6434	I'm a Fool/A Good Woman's Love	1956	$30
❏ 74-0634	Imagination Running Wild/Love Has a Mind of Its Own	1972	$6
❏ 47-8497	I'm Blue/Give Your Wife a Kiss for Me	1965	$10
❏ 47-8783	Insurance/I Feel a Cry Coming On	1966	$10
❏ 47-7203	It's a Little More Like Heaven/Blue Grass Skirt	1958	$20
❏ 47-9476	Love Song for You/Little Geisha Girl	1968	$10
❏ 47-9646	Lovin' You (The Way I Do)/Hot Pepper Doll	1968	$10
❏ 47-9986	My Heart Needs a Friend/Only a Fool	1971	$8
❏ 47-7813	One Step Ahead of My Past/Toujours Moi	1960	$15
❏ 74-0287	Please Help Me, I'm Falling/Anna	1969	$8
❏ 47-7692	Please Help Me, I'm Falling/My Old Home Town	1960	$20
❏ 47-7127	Send Me the Pillow You Dream On/Why Don't You Haul Off and Love Me	1957	$30
❏ 47-7612	Seven Days (The Humming Song)/Blues in Advance	1959	$20
❏ 47-6571	Seven or Eleven/You Can't Never Tell	1956	$30
❏ 47-9955	She's As Close As I Can Get to Loving You/I Like a Woman	1971	$8
❏ 47-7317	That Inner Glow/The Upper Room	1958	$20
❏ 47-8928	The Best Part of Loving You/The Last Thing on My Mind	1966	$12
❏ 47-9323	The Country Hall of Fame/Evergreen	1967	$12
❏ 48-1014	The Devil Out of Me/Softly	1971	$8
❏ 47-8695	The Girls Get Prettier (Every Day)/To Him	1965	$10
❏ 47-8891	There's More Pretty Girls Than One/A Good Woman's Love	1966	$10
❏ 47-8106	Wabash Cannonball/Once More	1962	$15
❏ 47-8034	We're Gonna Go Fishin'/Welcome Home, Mister Blues	1962	$15
❏ 47-9710	Where the Blue of the Night Meets the Gold of the Day/The Girls Who Wait	1969	$8
❏ 47-6242	Who Am I to Cast the First Stone/These Ruins Belong to You	1955	$20
❏ 47-6347	Why Baby Why/Love or Spite	1955	$30
❏ APBO-0226	Wildwood Flower/Sweet Inspiration	1974	$6
❏ 47-8248	Wooden Soldier/Kiss on the Door	1963	$15
7-Inch Extended Plays			
❏ EPA-4366 [PS]	Please Help Me, I'm Falling	1960	$25
❏ EPA-4366	Please Help Me, I'm Falling/Seven Days (The Humming Song)/Livin' Alone/Hiding in My Heart	1960	$25

LOCOMOTIONS, THE
GONE

Number	Title	Yr	NM
❏ 5142	Little Eva/Adios My Love	1962	$30
SWAN			
❏ 4237	Weekend Workout/Make It Saturday Night	1965	$10

LODI
MOWEST

Number	Title	Yr	NM
❏ 5003	Happiness/I Hope I See It in My Lifetime	1971	$8

LOE AND JOE
HARVEY

Number	Title	Yr	NM
❏ 112	Little Ole Boy, Little Ole Girl/That's How I Am Without You	1962	$40

Number	Title	Yr	NM
LOFGREN, NILS			

Also see GRIN. Also was a member of BRUCE SPRINGSTEEN's E Street Band in the 1980s.

A&M

Number	Title	Yr	NM
❏ 1692	Back It Up/If I Say It, It's So	1975	$5
❏ 1812	Cry Tough/Share a Little	1976	$5
❏ 1927	I Came to Dance/Code of the Road	1977	$4
❏ 1839	It's Not a Crime/Share a Little	1976	$5

COLUMBIA

Number	Title	Yr	NM
❏ 05598	Delivery Night/Flip Ya Flip	1985	$3
❏ 05406	Secrets in the Street/From the Heart	1985	$3

LOGGINS AND MESSINA

Also see KENNY LOGGINS; JIM MESSINA.

COLUMBIA

Number	Title	Yr	NM
❏ 10222	A Lover's Question/Oh, Lonesome Me	1975	$5
❏ 10444	Angry Eyes/Watching the River Run	1976	$5
❏ 10077	Changes/Get a Hold	1974	$5
❏ 10118	Growin'/Keep Me in Mind	1975	$5
❏ 10188	I Like It Like That/Angry Eyes	1975	$5
❏ 45952	My Music/A Love Song	1973	$5
❏ 45664	Peace of Mind/House at Pooh Corner	1972	$6

— As "Kenny Loggins and Jim Messina"

❏ 45550	Same Old Wine/Vahevelia	1972	$6

— As "Kenny Loggins and Jim Messina"

❏ 45815	Thinking of You/Till the Ends Meet	1973	$5

— A-side is a different version than on most LPs

❏ 46010	Watching the River Run/Travelin' Blues	1974	$5
❏ 10311	When I Was a Child/Peacemaker	1976	$5

LOGGINS, KENNY

COLUMBIA

Number	Title	Yr	NM
❏ 11-11417	Celebrate Me Home (Live)/Celebrate Me Home (Studio)	1980	$5
❏ 3-10652	Celebrate Me Home/Why Do People Lie	1977	$5
❏ 38-05893	Danger Zone/I'm Gonna Do It Right	1986	$3
❏ 38-05893 [PS]	Danger Zone/I'm Gonna Do It Right	1986	$3
❏ CNR-03270	Don't Fight It/(B-side blank)	1982	$6

— Kenny Loggins with Steve Perry; one-sided budget release

❏ 18-03192	Don't Fight It/The More We Try	1982	$3

— A-side with Steve Perry

❏ 18-03192 [PS]	Don't Fight It/The More We Try	1982	$4
❏ 3-10866	Easy Driver/Somebody Knows	1978	$5
❏ 38-04310	Footloose/Swear Your Love	1984	$3
❏ 38-04310 [PS]	Footloose/Swear Your Love	1984	$6
❏ 38-04931	Forever/At Last	1985	$3
❏ 38-04931 [PS]	Forever/At Last	1985	$3
❏ CNR-03427	Heart to Heart/(B-side blank)	1982	$8

— One-sided budget release

❏ 38-03377	Heart to Heart/The More We Try	1982	$3
❏ 3-10569	I Believe in Love/Enter My Dream	1977	$5
❏ 38-05625	I'll Be There/No Lookin' Back	1985	$4
❏ 1-11317	I'm Alright (Theme from "Caddyshack")/Lead the Way	1980	$4
❏ AE71216 [DJ]	I'm Alright (Theme from "Caddyshack") (Soundtrack Version 3:25)/(Live Album Version 4:47)	1980	$6
❏ 13-02167	I'm Alright (Theme from "Caddyshack")/This Is It	1981	$3

— Reissue

❏ 38-04452	I'm Free (Heaven Helps the Man)/Welcome to Heartlight (Live)	1984	$3
❏ 38-04452 [PS]	I'm Free (Heaven Helps the Man)/Welcome to Heartlight (Live)	1984	$3
❏ 38-08091	I'm Gonna Miss You/Isabella's Eyes	1988	$3
❏ 38-08091 [PS]	I'm Gonna Miss You/Isabella's Eyes	1988	$3
❏ 1-11290	Love Has Come of Age/Junkanoo Holiday (Fallin', Flyin')	1980	$6
❏ 38-06690	Meet Me Half Way/Semifinal	1987	$3

— B-side by Giorgio Moroder

❏ 38-06690 [PS]	Meet Me Half Way/Semifinal	1987	$3
❏ 38-05902	Playing with the Boys/Love Will Follow	1986	$3
❏ 38-05902 [PS]	Playing with the Boys/Love Will Follow	1986	$3
❏ 38-68531	Tell Her/Hope for the Runaway	1989	$4
❏ CS7-01466 [DJ]	Tell Her (Short Intro 3:11)/(3:35)	1989	$6
❏ 1-11109	This Is It/Will It Last	1979	$5

Number	Title	Yr	NM
❏ 38-03555	Welcome to Heartlight/Only a Miracle	1983	$3
❏ 38-03555 [PS]	Welcome to Heartlight/Only a Miracle	1983	$4
❏ 3-10794	Whenever I Call You "Friend"/Angelique	1978	$5

— With Stevie Nicks on A-side (uncredited)

LOGSDON, JIMMIE

DECCA

Number	Title	Yr	NM
❏ 9-28726	As Long As We're Together/The Love You Gave to Me	1953	$40
❏ 9-29075	Good Deal Lucille/Midnight Boogie	1954	$30
❏ 9-29337	I'm Goin' Back to Tennessee/You Ain't Nothing But the Blues	1954	$30
❏ 9-28913	In the Mission of St. Augustine/Papaya Mama	1953	$40
❏ 9-28502	I Wanna Be Mama'd/That's When I Love You the Best	1952	$40
❏ 9-28584	The Death of Hank Williams/Hank Williams Sings the Blues No More	1953	$60

— Lines on either side of "Decca

❏ 9-28584	The Death of Hank Williams/Hank Williams Sings the Blues No More	1955	$40

— Star under "Decca

❏ 9-29122	These Lonesome Blues/My Sweet French Baby	1954	$30
❏ 9-28864	Where the Old Red River Flows/Let's Have a Happy Time	1953	$40

DOT

Number	Title	Yr	NM
❏ 1274	Cold Cold Rain/Midnight Blues	1956	$40

KING

Number	Title	Yr	NM
❏ 5846	Daddy Don't Go/The Loneliest Guy in Town	1964	$15
❏ 5795	Gear Jammer/Truck Drivin' Daddy	1963	$15
❏ 5748	I Know You're Married/Mother's Flower Garden	1963	$15
❏ 5872	I've Got Over You/I Have to Laugh	1964	$15
❏ 5827	Making Believe/I Guess I've Let You Down	1963	$15
❏ 5752	The Life of Hank Williams (Part 1)/The Life of Hank Williams (Part 2)	1963	$20

LOLITA

KAPP

Number	Title	Yr	NM
❏ 370	Cowboy Jimmy Joe (Die Sterne Der Prarie)/Theme from "A Summer Place	1961	$8
❏ 370 [PS]	Cowboy Jimmy Joe (Die Sterne Der Prarie)/Theme from "A Summer Place	1961	$30
❏ 402	For the First Time (I've Fallen in Love)/Souvenir d'Amour	1961	$8
❏ 349	Sailor (Your Home Is the Sea)/La Luna (Quando La Luna)	1960	$15

— Maroon and silver label

❏ 349	Sailor (Your Home Is the Sea)/La Luna (Quando La Luna)	1960	$8

— Black label

❏ 349 [PS]	Sailor (Your Home Is the Sea)/La Luna (Quando La Luna)	1960	$30

LOLLIPOP SHOPPE, THE

SHAMLEY

Number	Title	Yr	NM
❏ 44005	Someone I Know/Through My Window	1969	$15

LOLLIPOPS, THE (1)

GORDY

Number	Title	Yr	NM
❏ 7089	Cheating Is Telling On You/Need Your Love	1969	$800

IMPACT

Number	Title	Yr	NM
❏ 1021	Lovin' Good Feelin'/Step Aside Baby	1967	$200

V.I.P.

Number	Title	Yr	NM
❏ 25051	Cheating Is Telling On You/Need Your Love	1968	$300

LOLLIPOPS, THE (3)

WARNER BROS.

Number	Title	Yr	NM
❏ 5122	Mister Santa/Little Donkey (Carry Mary Safely on Her Way)	1959	$15

LOLLIPOPS, THE (U)

RCA VICTOR

Number	Title	Yr	NM
❏ 47-8430	Billy, Billy Baby/Big Brother	1964	$30
❏ 47-8494	Busy Signal/I Want You Back Again	1965	$125

Number	Title	Yr	NM
❏ 47-8390	Don't Monkey With Me/Love Is the Only Answer	1964	$80
❏ 47-8344	Peggy Got Engaged/I'll Set My Love to Music	1964	$30

SMASH

Number	Title	Yr	NM
❏ 2057	He's the Boy/Gee Whiz Baby	1966	$125

LOLLYPOPS, THE

HOLLAND

Number	Title	Yr	NM
❏ 7420	My Love Is Real/Believe in Me	1958	$3000

UNIVERSAL INT'L.

Number	Title	Yr	NM
❏ 7420	My Love Is Real/Believe in Me	1958	$4000

LOMBARDO, GUY

CAPITOL

Number	Title	Yr	NM
❏ 4392	Better Than a Dream/Sweet Sue	1960	$8
❏ F3470	Bistro/You Dance with Me	1956	$10
❏ F3540	Cannon Ball/Love Me Sweet and Love Me Long	1956	$10
❏ F3411	Charleston Parisien/Rinka-Tinka Man	1956	$10
❏ F3371	Our Melody/You Can't Help But Be Wonderful	1956	$10
❏ F3954	Over and Over/The Letter Gets Better	1958	$8
❏ 4152	Silver Dollar/La Valse Julie	1959	$8
❏ F4098	St. Louis Blues Cha Cha/Exactly Like You Cha Cha	1958	$8
❏ F3613	Tears in Your Eyes/I Won't Let You Out of My Heart	1957	$8
❏ F3682	Want What Ya Got/Our Little Ranch House	1957	$8

DECCA

Number	Title	Yr	NM
❏ 9-27118	All My Love (Bolero)/The Swiss Bellringer	1950	$20
❏ 9-28535	Annie Laurie/Blue Bells of Scotland	1953	$10
❏ 9-27560	Anniversary Song/Together	1951	$15
❏ 9-27133	Arkansas Traveler Square Dance/Old Dan Tucker Square Dance	1950	$15

— The above three are part of a box set

❏ 9-28271	Auf Wiederseh'n Sweetheart/Half As Much	1952	$20
❏ 9-24260	Auld Lang Syne/Home on the Range	1950	$20
❏ 9-28905	Auld Lang Syne/Hot Time in the Old Town Tonight	1953	$20

— Black label, lines on either side of "Decca

❏ 9-28905	Auld Lang Syne/Hot Time in the Old Town Tonight	1955	$12

— Black label, star under "Decca

❏ 28905	Auld Lang Syne/Hot Time in the Old Town Tonight	1960	$8

— Black label with color bars

❏ 9-28476	Because You're Mine/Why Don't You Believe Me	1952	$20
❏ 9-29074	Bimbo/Slowly	1954	$15
❏ 9-28751	Blue Dancing Shoes/Always Someone You Can't Forget	1953	$15
❏ 9-28031	Blue Tango/At Last, At Last	1952	$20
❏ 9-28693	Blue Willows/I'm in Love	1953	$15
❏ 9-27015	Boo Hoo/A Sailboat in the Moonlight	1950	$15
❏ 9-28537	Camellia/Al Fresco	1953	$10
❏ 9-29510	Cherry Pink (And Apple Blossom White)/Darling, Je Vous Aime Beaucoup	1955	$10
❏ 9-27800	Children's Songs (Part 1)/(Part 2)	1951	$30
❏ 9-27469	Confessin' (That I Love You)/Somebody Loves Me	1951	$15

— The above four comprise a box set

❏ 9-28456	Congratulations to You/Meet Mister Callaghan	1952	$20
❏ 9-27888	Crazy Heart/Whispering Shadows	1951	$20
❏ 9-29283	Curiosity Killed a Cat/Hula Rhumba	1954	$15
❏ 9-27640	Dark Is the Night/Wonder Why	1951	$20
❏ 9-28655	Downhearted/Seven Lonely Days	1953	$15
❏ 9-27607	Down the Trail of Aching Hearts/The Strange Little Girl	1951	$20
❏ 9-29121	Do You/Dream, Dream, Dream	1954	$15
❏ 9-27584	Evertrue, Evermore/Just for Love's Sake	1951	$20
❏ 9-29591	Far Away from Everybody/Simpatico	1955	$10
❏ 9-29587	Freddy/Pass the Plate of Happiness Around	1955	$10
❏ 9-27257	Frosty the Snowman/If I Were Santa Claus	1950	$30
❏ 9-27692	Glockenspiel/The Circus Day Parade	1951	$20
❏ 9-27502	Golden Earrings/Where or When	1951	$15
❏ 9-27280	Green Grass and Peaceful Pastures/Sea of the Moon	1950	$20
❏ 9-29377	Greensleeves/Blue Mirage	1954	$15

Number	Title	Yr	NM
❑ 9-28742	Half a Photograph/Don't You Care	1953	$15
❑ 9-27516	Happiness/Always You	1951	$20
❑ 9-27208	Harbor Lights/The Petite Waltz (La Petite Valse)	1950	$20
❑ 9-27802	He'll Be Coming Down the Chimney/Christmas Chopsticks	1951	$20
❑ 9-27613	Hello Young Lovers/Getting to Know You	1951	$20
❑ 9-29173	Hernando's Hideaway/Vas Villet Du Haben	1954	$15
❑ 9-28385	Hide-Away Harbor/My Heart's in the Ring	1952	$20
❑ 9-27503	How Deep Is the Ocean/If I Had My Way	1951	$15
❑ 9-28523	How Do You Speak to an Angel/I Feel Like I'm Gonna Live Forever	1952	$20
❑ 9-27132	Ida Red Square Dance/Virginia Reel Square Dance	1950	$15
❑ 9-27449	If/Wait for Me	1951	$20
❑ 9-27911	I'll See You in My Dreams/Goodnight Sweetheart	1951	$20
❑ 9-27468	I'll Walk Alone/I Love You	1951	$15
❑ 9-28546	I'm Skipping Home with a Rainbow/John, John, John	1953	$15
❑ 9-28942	I Saw Mommy Kissing Santa Claus/Please Bring My Daddy a Train, Santa	1953	$20
❑ 9-29215	It's Great to Be Alive/Marry the One You Love	1954	$15
❑ 9-27624	I've Got to Fall in Love Again/Mine	1951	$20
❑ 9-28411	I Went to Your Wedding/Somewhere Along the Way	1952	$20
❑ 9-27776	Laura Lee/Blue Fedora	1951	$20
❑ 9-27127	La Vie En Rose/It All Begins and Ends with You	1950	$20
❑ 9-28763	Limelight/Gigi	1953	$15
❑ 9-27017	Little Dutch Mill/When the Organ Played at Twilight	1950	$15

— The above four comprise a box set

Number	Title	Yr	NM
❑ 9-27327	Long Before I Knew You/It's Raining Sundrops	1950	$20
❑ 9-29303	Looking Back to See/More and More	1954	$15
❑ 9-27962	Marshmallow Moon/Stolen Love	1952	$20
❑ 9-29516	Marty/Hey, Mr. Banjo	1955	$10
❑ 9-27719	Mary Rose/Sweetheart of Yesterday	1951	$20
❑ 9-27562	Meet Me in St. Louis, Louis/Dreamy Old New England Moon	1951	$15

— The above three are part of a box set

Number	Title	Yr	NM
❑ 9-27561	Missouri Waltz/That Naughty Waltz	1951	$15
❑ 9-27016	Moonlight Saving Time/Swingin' on a Hammock	1950	$15
❑ 9-28132	More Than Love/Come Back	1952	$20
❑ 9-27467	My Extraordinary Gal/Singin' in the Rain	1951	$15
❑ 9-29486	My Honey's Lovin' Arms/When the Saints Go Marching In	1955	$10
❑ 9-27487	Oh What a Face/A Nickel Ain't Worth a Cent Today	1951	$20
❑ 9-27131	Old Joe Clark Square Dance/Little Brown Jug Square Dance	1950	$15
❑ 9-27466	Once in a While/Soon	1951	$15
❑ 9-27995	One Little Word/Honestly and Truly	1952	$20
❑ 9-29022	Our Heartbreaking Waltz/Till We Two Are One	1954	$15
❑ 9-27092	Our Little Ranch House/Here, Pretty Kitty	1950	$20
❑ 9-28536	Pizzicato/Ever Lovin' Rag	1953	$10
❑ 9-29628	Present Arms/Nevada	1955	$12
❑ 9-28576	Pretend/That's Me Without You	1953	$15
❑ 9-29859	Sand Dance/Doggone Blues	1956	$10
❑ 9-28408	Santa Claus Is Coming To Town/Jingle Bells	1952	$15
❑ 9-27452	Shenanigans/Get Out Those Old Records	1951	$20
❑ 9-27014	St. Louis Blues/You're Driving Me Crazy	1950	$15
❑ 9-28352	Sunshowers/You Like?	1952	$20
❑ 9-27504	Symphony/(All of a Sudden) My Heart Sings	1951	$15

— The above three are part of a box set

Number	Title	Yr	NM
❑ 9-27336	Tennessee Waltz/Get Out Those Old Records	1950	$20
❑ 9-24839	The 3rd Man Theme/The Cafe Mozart Waltz	1950	$30
❑ 9-27523	The Coconut Song/Enjoy Yourself	1951	$20
❑ 9-27202	The Glory of Love/A Rainy Day Refrain	1950	$20

— With the Andrews Sisters

Number	Title	Yr	NM
❑ 9-28047	The Little Engine That Could/Let's Have a Party	1952	$20
❑ 9-29301	The Mama Doll Song/Hold My Hand	1954	$15
❑ 9-27398	The Most Beautiful Girl in the World/I Remember Cornfields	1951	$20
❑ 9-28952	Think/Florida	1953	$15
❑ 9-27005	Tiddley Winkie Woo/Where Are You Gonna Be When the Moon Shines	1950	$30

Number	Title	Yr	NM
❑ 9-27669	Tin Pan Alley Rag/Little Fairy Waltz	1951	$20
❑ 9-29113	Trees/My Desire	1954	$15
❑ 9-28277	Walkin' My Baby Back Home/Once in a While	1952	$20
❑ 9-29434	Wedding Bells/Softly, Softly	1955	$10
❑ 9-28858	When I Plunk on My Guitar/Would It Be Wrong	1953	$15
❑ 9-30014	Where the Shy Little Violets Grow/After I Say I'm Sorry	1956	$10
❑ 9-28409	White Christmas/Merry Christmas Waltz	1952	$15
❑ 9-28308	Wish You Were Here/Honky Tonk Sweetheart	1952	$20
❑ 9-27993	With a Song in My Heart/I Could Write a Book	1952	$20
❑ 9-27645	With These Hands/Lonesome and Sorry	1951	$20
❑ 9-28985	Woman/The Jones Boy	1954	$15
❑ 9-28471	Wonderful Copenhagen/Thumbelina	1952	$20

MCA

Number	Title	Yr	NM
❑ 60147	The 3rd Man Theme/The Cafe Mozart Waltz	1973	$5

— Reissue; black label with rainbow

Number	Title	Yr	NM
❑ ED2220 [PS]	Dance Time with Guy Lombardo	1955	$15

RCA VICTOR

Number	Title	Yr	NM
❑ 947-0154	The Perfect Song/Ti-Pi-Tin//Liebestraum/Yours and Mine	1954	$10

— Record 1 of 2-EP set EPBT 3059

Number	Title	Yr	NM
❑ EPBT3059 [PS]	This Is Guy Lombardo and His Orchestra	1954	$12

— Cover for 2-EP set (947-0154, 947-0155)

Number	Title	Yr	NM
❑ 947-0155	When My Dream Boat Comes Home/I'll See You in My Dreams//The Old Apple Tree/It Looks Like Rain in Cherry Blossom Lane	1954	$10

— Record 2 of 2-EP set EPBT 3059

LONDON, JULIE

BETHLEHEM

Number	Title	Yr	NM
❑ 11015	Don't Worry 'Bout Me/You're Blase	1959	$15
❑ 11003	Sometimes I Feel Like a Motherless Child/A Foggy Day	1958	$30

LIBERTY

Number	Title	Yr	NM
❑ 55009	Baby, Baby, All the Time/Shadow Woman	1955	$12
❑ 33008 [S]	Blue Moon/I Guess I'll Have to Change My Plan	1960	$30
❑ 55157	Blue Moon/Man of the West	1958	$10
❑ 33009 [S]	Bye Bye Blues/Basin Street Blues	1960	$30
❑ 55175	Come On-a My House/My Strange Affair	1959	$10
❑ 55216	Comin' Through the Rye/Makin' Whoopee	1959	$10
❑ 55227	Cry Me a River/It's a Blue World	1959	$12
❑ 55006	Cry Me a River/S'Wonderful	1955	$15
❑ 33010 [S]	Daddy/Bye Bye Blackbird	1960	$30

— The above four are 33 1/3 rpm jukebox singles

Number	Title	Yr	NM
❑ 55512	Desafinado/Where Did the Gentleman Go	1962	$8
❑ 55702	Girl (Boy) from Ipanema/My Lover Is a Stranger	1964	$6
❑ 55830	Girl Talk/Won't Somebody Please Belong to Me	1965	$6
❑ 55666	Guilty Heart/I Want to Find Out for Myself	1964	$6
❑ 55108	I'd Like You for Christmas/Saddle the Wind	1957	$15
❑ 55605	I'm Coming Back to You/When Snowflakes Fall in the Summer	1963	$8
❑ 55269	In the Wee Small Hours of the Morning/Time for Lovers	1960	$10
❑ 55076	It Had to Be You/Dark	1957	$10
❑ 55139	It's Easy/Voice in the Mirror	1958	$10
❑ 33006 [S]	Lonesome Road/Goodbye	1960	$30
❑ 56085	Louie Louie/Hushabye Mountain	1969	$5
❑ 55966	Mickey Mouse March/Baby Won't You Please	1967	$6
❑ 55182	Must Be Catchin'/Something I Dreamed Last Night	1959	$10
❑ 55337	My Darling, My Darling/My Love, My Love	1961	$8
❑ 55309	Sanctuary/Every Chance I Get	1961	$8
❑ 55300	Send for Me/Evenin'	1961	$8
❑ 55025	September in the Rain/Lonely Girl	1956	$10
❑ 55032	Tall Boy/Now, Baby, Now	1956	$10
❑ 55131	Tell Me You're Home/The Freshman	1958	$10
❑ 55052	The Meaning of the Blues/Boy on a Dolphin	1957	$10
❑ 55759	We Proved Them Wrong/You're Free to Go	1964	$6
❑ 33007 [S]	When I Fall in Love/The More I See You	1960	$30

UNITED ARTISTS

Number	Title	Yr	NM
❑ 0013	Cry Me a River/Come On-a My House	1973	$4

Number	Title	Yr	NM
	— Silver Spotlight Series" reissue		

7-Inch Extended Plays

LIBERTY

Number	Title	Yr	NM
❑ LEP-1-9002	*June in January/February Brings the Rain/Melancholy March/I'll Remember April	1956	$15
❑ LEP-1-3012	*Lonely Girl/Fools Rush In/How Deep Is the Ocean/Mean to Me	1956	$15
❑ LEP-2-9002	*People Who Are Born in May/Memphis in June/Sleigh Ride in July/Time for August	1956	$15
❑ LEP-3-9002	*September in the Rain/This October/November Twilight/Warm December	1956	$15
❑ LEP-2-3012	*When Your Lover Has Gone/All Alone/Remember/Moments Like This/I Lost My Sugar in Salt Lake City	1956	$15
❑ LEP-1-9002 [PS]	Calendar Girl, Part One	1956	$15
❑ LEP-3-9002 [PS]	Calendar Girl, Part Three	1956	$15
❑ LEP-2-9002 [PS]	Calendar Girl, Part Two	1956	$15
❑ LEP-2-3006	(contents unknown)	1956	$15
❑ LEP-3-3006	(contents unknown)	1956	$15
❑ LEP-3-3012	Don't Take Your Love from Me/Where or When//It's the Talk of the Town/What'll I Do	1956	$15
❑ LEP-1-3006	Laura/S' Wonderful/I'm in the Mood for Love/Can't Help Lovin' That Man	1956	$15
❑ LEP-1-3012 [PS]	Lonely Girl, Part One	1956	$15
❑ LEP-3-3012 [PS]	Lonely Girl, Part Three	1956	$15
❑ LEP-2-3012 [PS]	Lonely Girl, Part Two	1956	$15
❑ LST-7342	Since I Fell for You/Fools Rush In/You Don't Have to Be a Baby to Cry//I Wish You Love/Charade/Wives and Lovers	1964	$20

— Jukebox issue; small hole, plays at 33 1/3 rpm

LONDON, LAURIE

CAPITOL

Number	Title	Yr	NM
❑ F3891	He's Got the Whole World (In His Hands)/Handed Down	1958	$20
❑ F4133	My Mother/Three O'Clock	1959	$15

ROULETTE

Number	Title	Yr	NM
❑ 4176	Pretty Eyed Baby/Boom Ladda Boom Boom	1959	$10

7-Inch Extended Plays

CAPITOL

Number	Title	Yr	NM
❑ EAP 1-10182	He's Got the Whole World in His Hands/Handed Down/The Gospel Train/Boomerang	1958	$25
❑ EAP 1-10182 [PS]	Laurie London!	1958	$25

LONDON, MARK

CAMEO

Number	Title	Yr	NM
❑ 362	Moanin'/Stranger in the World	1965	$20

LONE JUSTICE

GEFFEN

Number	Title	Yr	NM
❑ 28470	I Found Love/If You Don't Like Pain	1987	$3
❑ 28520	Shelter/Belfry	1986	$3
❑ 28520 [PS]	Shelter/Belfry	1986	$3
❑ 28965	Sweet Sweet Baby (I'm Falling)/Don't Toss Us Away	1985	$3
❑ 28965 [PS]	Sweet Sweet Baby (I'm Falling)/Don't Toss Us Away	1985	$3
❑ 29023	Ways to Be Wicked/Cactus Rose	1985	$3
❑ 29023 [PS]	Ways to Be Wicked/Cactus Rose	1985	$3

LONESOME DRIFTER, THE

K

Number	Title	Yr	NM
❑ 5812	Eager Boy/Teardrop Valley	1958	$2000

LONESOME RHODES

RCA VICTOR

Number	Title	Yr	NM
❑ 47-9305	The Delight of My Day/(B-side unknown)	1967	$30

LONESOME STRANGERS, THE

HIGHTONE

Number	Title	Yr	NM
❑ 508	Goodbye Lonesome, Hello Baby Doll/We Used to Fuss	1989	$6

LONG, HUEY

FIDELITY

Number	Title	Yr	NM
❑ 4055	Elvis Stole My Gal/Ballad of John Glenn	1962	$60
❑ 4054	How to Tell My Heart/Waiting for a Letter	1962	$30

Number	Title	Yr	NM

LONG, SHORTY (1)
R&B singer. (45)

SOUL

Number	Title	Yr	NM
❏ 35064	A Whiter Shade of Pale/When You Are Available	1969	$10
❏ 35031	Chantilly Lace/Your Love Is Amazing	1966	$20
❏ 35001	Devil with the Blue Dress/Wind It Up	1964	$30
❏ 35021	Function at the Junction/Call On Me	1966	$20
❏ 35044	Here Comes the Judge/Sing What You Wanna	1968	$12
❏ 35054	I Had a Dream/Ain't No Justice	1969	$10
❏ 35005	It's a Crying Shame/Out to Get You	1964	$30

TRI-PHI

Number	Title	Yr	NM
❏ 1006	I'll Be There/Bad Willie	1962	$60
❏ 1015	Too Smart/I'll Be There	1962	$75
❏ 1021	What's the Matter/Going Away	1963	$70

LONG, SHORTY (2)
C&W singer.

DOT

Number	Title	Yr	NM
❏ 1154	Pretend/Crying Street Guitar Waltz	1953	$30

KING

Number	Title	Yr	NM
❏ 953	Goodnight Cincinnati/Just Like Two Drops of Water	1951	$50
❏ 5605	Take Me to the Happy Land/Mary, Oh Mary	1962	$30

RCA VICTOR

Number	Title	Yr	NM
❏ 48-0347	A Bottle and a Blonde/Waltz of Colorado	1950	$50

— Originals on green vinyl; second pressing on black vinyl is unconfirmed

Number	Title	Yr	NM
❏ 47-6804	Another Love Has Ended/Little White Horse	1957	$125
❏ 47-6472	Hey, Doll Baby/Luscious	1956	$125
❏ 48-0134	I Wasted a Nickel/This Cold War with You	1950	$50

— Originals on green vinyl; second pressing on black vinyl is unconfirmed

Number	Title	Yr	NM
❏ 48-0057	The Morning After/Please Daddy Forgive	1949	$50

— Originals on green vinyl; second pressing on black vinyl is unconfirmed

Number	Title	Yr	NM
❏ 48-0098	The Warm Red Wine/I Got Mine	1949	$50

— Originals on green vinyl; second pressing on black vinyl is unconfirmed

X

Number	Title	Yr	NM
❏ 024	Standing in the Station/Make with Me De Love	1954	$30

LONGBRANCH PENNYWHISTLE

AMOS

Number	Title	Yr	NM
❏ 121	Don't Talk Now/Jubilee Anne	1969	$20
❏ 129	Lucky Love/Rebecca	1969	$20
❏ 148	Star Spangled Bus/Bring Back Founky Women	1970	$20

LONNIE AND THE CAROLLONS

MOHAWK

Number	Title	Yr	NM
❏ 112	Back Yard Rock/You Say	1958	$60
❏ 108	Chapel of Tears/My Heart	1958	$200

— Green label

Number	Title	Yr	NM
❏ 108	Chapel of Tears/My Heart	1961	$40

— Red label

Number	Title	Yr	NM
❏ 108	Chapel of Tears/My Heart	1965	$30

— White label

Number	Title	Yr	NM
❏ 111	Hold Me Close/Trudy	1958	$60
❏ 113	The Gang All Knows/Ike Hammer	1959	$70

LONNIE AND THE CRISIS

UNIVERSAL

Number	Title	Yr	NM
❏ 103	Bells in the Chapel/Santa Town USA	1961	$200

LONZO AND OSCAR

CAPITOL

Number	Title	Yr	NM
❏ F939	If Texas Told What Arkansaw/Onions, Onions	1950	$40
❏ F40269	My Dreams Turned Into a Nightmare/I'll Go Chasing Women	1950	$40
❏ F1446	Pretty Little Indian Maid/Tickle Tomcats Tail	1951	$30

CHALET

Number	Title	Yr	NM
❏ 1058	Heartaches for Fun and Profit/Wood	1969	$12
❏ 1052	Hertz Rent-a-Chick/Dolly	1969	$12
❏ 1067	My Business Ain't Doin' So Good/Ants A-Go-Go	1970	$10

COLUMBIA

Number	Title	Yr	NM
❏ 4-44400	Did You Have to Bring That Up/Give Me a King-Sized Cola and a Moon Pie	1967	$8

DECCA

Number	Title	Yr	NM
❏ 9-28624	Baby Me Baby/Skunk Skin Britches	1953	$30
❏ 9-28961	Frosty the De-Frosted Snowman/Jangle Bells	1953	$30
❏ 9-30374	Gone #2/A Fallen Star	1957	$30
❏ 9-28363	Goodbye Little Darlin' #2/Honky Tonk Sweetheart	1952	$30
❏ 9-28972	Hey Joe #2/It Can't Be Done	1954	$30
❏ 9-46359	I Courted the Sunshine/Extravagant Baby	1951	$30
❏ 9-46299	I Lithp/Metro Polka	1951	$30
❏ 9-46312	I'm Movin' On Number Two/Give Me an RC Cola	1951	$30
❏ 9-46378	Let's Live a Little Number Two/Strange Little Girl	1951	$30
❏ 9-46393	Mona Lisa Number Two/Charming Betsy	1952	$30
❏ 9-28060	Music Makin' Mama Second Hand/Let Old Mother Nature #2	1952	$30
❏ 9-29425	See Saw Baby/One Love for Me	1955	$30

DOT

Number	Title	Yr	NM
❏ 1216	Crazy 'Bout You Baby/Got It on My Mind	1954	$30
❏ 1196	Let Me Be the One #2/Wild Oats	1954	$30

GRC

Number	Title	Yr	NM
❏ 2013	Any Old Wind That Blows/Railroad Take Your Whistle Home	1974	$8
❏ 2054	Bitter Grapes/When I Stop Dreaming	1975	$8
❏ 2022	Catfish Dinner/Don't Want to Change It Now	1974	$8
❏ 2029	From Your Shoulders to Mine/God Is the Color of Love	1974	$8
❏ 2035	He Came Back/God Is the Color of Love	1975	$8
❏ 1006	Traces of Life/Lubbock	1973	$8
❏ 2063	When the Fields in the Valley Turn Green/He Came Back	1975	$8
❏ 201	Hand Holdin'/Uh, What's Her Name	1962	$20

STARDAY

Number	Title	Yr	NM
❏ 463	Bare Faced Bird Brain/I'm My Own Grandpa	1959	$30
❏ 543	Country Music Time/Can't Pitch Woo (In an Igloo)	1961	$30
❏ 404	Deep Thinking/Have a Little Faith in Me	1958	$30
❏ 436	Gotta Find Julie/Hills of East Tennessee	1959	$30
❏ 563	Honey Babe/The Touch of You	1961	$30
❏ 491	I Lost an Angel/Blue Love	1960	$30
❏ 523	Takin' a Chance with You/Punkin Raiser	1960	$30

LOOKING GLASS

EPIC

Number	Title	Yr	NM
❏ 10874	Brandy (You're a Fine Girl)/One by One	1972	$6
❏ 11061	City Lady/Who's Gonna Sing My Rock 'N' Roll Song	1973	$5
❏ 10834	Don't It Make You Feel Good/Catherine Street	1972	$5
❏ 10953	Sweet Somethin'/Rainbow Man	1973	$5
❏ 11085	Sweet Somethin'/Who's Gonna Sing My Rock 'N' Roll Song	1974	$5

LOOKING GLASS, THE
This group pre-dates the one on Epic, which did not use the word "The" in its name.

VALIANT

Number	Title	Yr	NM
❏ 750	Silver and Sunshine (How Wonderful My Love)/If I Never Love Again	1966	$10

WARNER BROS.

Number	Title	Yr	NM
❏ 7050	Lonely Stranger/Love Is Not Everything	1967	$10

LOOKINLAND, MIKE

CAPITOL

Number	Title	Yr	NM
❏ 3914	Gum Drop/Love Doesn't Care Who's In It	1974	$10
❏ 3914 [PS]	Gum Drop/Love Doesn't Care Who's In It	1974	$20

LOPEZ, TRINI

CAPITOL

Number	Title	Yr	NM
❏ 3402	Mammy Blue/Viva	1972	$5
❏ 3195	Some Kind of a Summer/Poor Old Billy	1971	$5

GRIFFIN

Number	Title	Yr	NM
❏ 508	Bring Back the Sunshine/We Gotta Make It Together	1974	$5
❏ 504	Butterfly/Don't Burn Your Bridges Behind You	1973	$5

KING

Number	Title	Yr	NM
❏ 5304	Chain of Love/Sweet Thing	1960	$30
❏ 5820	Don't Go/It Seems	1963	$15
❏ 5234	Don't Let Your Sweet Love Die/I'm Grateful	1959	$30
❏ 5418	Don't Treat Me That Way/Then You Know	1960	$30
❏ 5344	It Hurts to Be in Love/The Search Goes On	1960	$30
❏ 5198	Love Me Tonight/Here Comes Sally	1959	$30
❏ 5487	One Heart, One Life, One Love/You Broke the Only Heart	1961	$30
❏ 5324	Schemes/Jeannie Marie	1960	$30
❏ 5187	Since I Don't Have You/Rock On	1959	$30
❏ 6021	The Search Goes On/Chain of Love	1966	$8

PRIVATE STOCK

Number	Title	Yr	NM
❏ 45,044	Heavy Makes You Happy (Sha-La-Boom-Boom-Yeah)/Satisfaction	1975	$5
❏ 45,035	Seco Sulto Y Tonton	1975	$5
❏ 45,024	Somethin' 'Bout You Baby I Like/Sweet Life	1975	$5

REPRISE

Number	Title	Yr	NM
❏ 0912	5 O'Clock World/You Make My Day	1970	$5
❏ 20168	A-M-E-R-I-C-A/Let It Be Known	1963	$10
❏ 0376	Are You Sincere/You'll Be Sorry	1965	$8
❏ 0596	Ballad of the Dirty Dozen/The Bramble Bush	1967	$6
❏ 20224	Bye Bye Blackbird/Medley	1963	$20

— Released only in Holland

Number	Title	Yr	NM
❏ 0814	Come a Little Bit Closer/My Baby Loves Sad Songs	1969	$6
❏ 0825	Don't Let the Sun Catch You Crryin'/My Baby Loves Sad Songs	1969	$6
❏ 0801 [DJ]	El Nino Del Tambor/Nocho De Paz (Let There Be Peace)	1968	$8

— Stock copy may not exist

Number	Title	Yr	NM
❏ 0879	Games People Play/Love Story	1969	$6
❏ 0547	Gonna Get Along Without Ya' Now/Love Letters	1967	$6
❏ 0687	Good Old Mountain Dew/Mental Journey	1968	$6
❏ 0508	Hall of Fame/Pancho Lopez	1966	$8
❏ 20218	If I Had a Hammer/La Bamba	1963	$20

— Released only in Italy

Number	Title	Yr	NM
❏ 0700	If I Had a Hammer/Lemon Tree	1968	$5

— Back to Back Hits" series

Number	Title	Yr	NM
❏ 20198	If I Had a Hammer/Unchain My Heart	1963	$15
❏ 0574	In the Land of Plenty/Up To Now	1967	$6
❏ 0648	It's a Great Life/Let's Take a Walk	1967	$6
❏ 0618	I Wanna Be Free/Together	1967	$6
❏ 0239	La Bamba/Granada	1963	$20

— Released only in Latin America

Number	Title	Yr	NM
❏ 0725	La Bamba/Kansas City	1968	$5

— Back to Back Hits" series

Number	Title	Yr	NM
❏ 20190	La Bamba (Part 1)/La Bamba (Part 2)	1963	$10
❏ 0480	La Bamba -- Part 1/Trini's Tune	1966	$8
❏ 0336	Lemon Tree/Pretty Eyes	1965	$12
❏ 0336 [PS]	Lemon Tree/Pretty Eyes	1965	$20
❏ 0975	Let's Think About Living/There Was a Crooked Man	1970	$5
❏ 0435	Made in Paris/Pretty Little Girl	1965	$8
❏ 0435 [PS]	Made in Paris/Pretty Little Girl	1965	$20
❏ 0933	Mexican Medicine Man/Time to Get It Together	1970	$5
❏ 0300	Michael/San Fancisco De Assisi	1964	$8
❏ 0328	Sad Tomorrows/I've Lost My Love for You	1964	$8
❏ 0328 [PS]	Sad Tomorrows/I've Lost My Love for You	1964	$20
❏ 0659	Sally Was a Good Old Girl/It's a Great Life	1968	$6
❏ 0405	Sinner Man/Double Trouble	1965	$8
❏ 0405 [PS]	Sinner Man/Double Trouble	1965	$20
❏ 0770	Something Tells Me/Malaguena Salerosa	1968	$6
❏ 0947	Su-Kal-De-Don/Mexican Medicine Man	1970	$5

Number	Title	Yr	NM
❑ 0455	The 32nd of May/I'm Coming Home, Cindy	1966	$8
❑ 20223	This Land Is Your Land/Cielito Lindo	1963	$20

—*Released only in Holland*

❑ 20234	This Land Is Your Land/La Bamba	1963	$20

—*Released only in West Germany*

ROULETTE
❑ 7214	Beautiful People/Helplessly	1977	$5

7-Inch Extended Plays

FRESCA
❑ ZTEP-124178	A-Mer-I-Ca/Kansas City//If I Had a Hammer/The Blizzard Song	1967	$10
❑ ZTEP-124178 [PS]	Trini Lopez Sings His Greatest Hits	1967	$20

—*Available on specially marked packages of Fresca soda*

REPRISE
❑ SR6215	Spanish Harlem (Aquella Rosa)/Amor/Tengo Nada//Yours (Quiereme Mucho)/My Love, Forgive Me (Amor Perdoname)/You Belong to My Heart (Solamenta Una Vez)	1966	$10

—*Jukebox issue; small hole, plays at 33 1/3 rpm*

❑ SR6255	There's a Kind of Hush/Hold Me Now and Forever/Born Free//Sunny/You Talk Too Much/Guantanamera (Lady of Guantanamo)	1967	$10

—*Jukebox issue; small hole, plays at 33 1/3 rpm*

❑ SR6215 [PS]	The Second Latin Album	1966	$12
❑ SR6255 [PS]	Trini Lopez -- Now!	1967	$12
❑ SR6171	Wee Wee Hours/Double Trouble/Don't Let Go//She's About a Mover/Let the Four Winds Blow/Ooh Poo Pah Doo	1965	$10

—*Jukebox issue; small hole, plays at 33 1/3 rpm*

LORD, BOBBY
COLUMBIA
❑ 41030	Am I a Fool/I Know It Was You	1957	$30
❑ 41824	Before I Lose My Mind/When the Snow Falls	1960	$30
❑ 21539	Everybody's Rockin' But Me/Without Your Love	1956	$100

—*Without Your Love" was the hit, but "Everybody's Rockin' But Me" is the collectible side*

❑ 40666	Fire of Love/Beautiful Baby	1956	$40
❑ 41596	Give Me a Woman/Where Did My Woman Go	1960	$30
❑ 21437	Hawk-Eye/I Can't Make My Dreams Understand	1955	$40
❑ 40927	High Voltage/Just Wonderful	1957	$50
❑ 21459	I Can't Do Without You Anymore/Don't Make Me Laugh	1955	$30
❑ 21367	I'm the Devil Who Made Her That Way/Ain'tcha Ever Gonna	1955	$30
❑ 41352	Party Pooper/What a Thrill	1959	$30
❑ 41155	Sack/Fire of Love	1958	$30
❑ 21498	So Doggone Lonesome/Pie Peachie Pie Pie	1956	$30
❑ 21397	Something's Missing/Sittin' Home Prayin' for Rain	1955	$30
❑ 41505	Too Many Miles/Swamp Fox	1959	$30
❑ 41288	When I've Learned/Walking Alone	1958	$30

DECCA
❑ 32797	Do It to Someone You Love/So in Love with You	1970	$8
❑ 32932	Everybody's Here/Sweet Inspiration	1972	$6
❑ 32797	Goodbye Jukebox/Do It to Someone You Love	1971	$6
❑ 32277	Live Your Life Out Loud/Charlotte, North Carolina	1968	$6
❑ 32115	Look What You're Doing/On and On Goes the Hurt	1967	$8
❑ 32174	Shadows on the Wall/One Day Down	1967	$8
❑ 32373	The True and Lasting Kind/It's My Life	1968	$6
❑ 32841	They've Got Something in the Country/Peace of Mind	1971	$6
❑ 32718	Wake Me Up Early in the Morning/Violets Are Red	1970	$6

HICKORY
❑ 1259	A Man Needs a Woman/Take a Bucket to the Wall	1964	$10
❑ 1361	Cash on the Barrelhead/That's Love	1965	$10
❑ 1210	Cry, Cry Darling/Shopping Center	1963	$12
❑ 1190	Don't Shed Any Tears for Me/Out Behind the Barn	1962	$15
❑ 1158	I'll Go On Alone/My Heart Tells Me So	1961	$15

Number	Title	Yr	NM
❑ 1310	I'm Going Home Next Summer/That Room in the Corner of the House	1965	$10
❑ 1389	It Only Hurts When I'm Laughing/Losers Like Me	1966	$8
❑ 1232	Life Can Have Meaning/Pickin' White Gold	1963	$12
❑ 1169	Precious Jewel/Trail of Tears	1962	$15

RICE
❑ 5062	Hello Wine/(B-side unknown)	1973	$8
❑ 5056	I've Had You/Got Yourself Something	1973	$8
❑ 5063	Looking for a Cold, Lonely Winter/Hello Wine	1973	$8
❑ 5068	The Look of Love/Your Song	1974	$8

LORD, BRIAN, AND THE MIDNIGHTERS
CAPITOL
❑ 4981	Big Surfer/Not Another One	1963	$200

VIGAH
❑ 001	Big Surfer/Not Another One	1963	$300

LORRAINE AND THE SOCIALITES
MERCURY
❑ 72163	Any Old Way/The Conqueror	1963	$15

LORRIE, MYRNA/BUDDY DEVAL
ABBOTT
❑ 172	Are You Mine/You Bet I Kissed Him	1954	$30
❑ 177	I'm Your Man/Underway	1955	$30

LORY, DICK
COLUMBIA
❑ 41276	Crazy Little Daisy/Don't Be a Fool for Love	1958	$50
❑ 41224	Wild Blooded Woman/No One But You Knows When	1958	$60

DOT
❑ 15496	Cool It Baby/Ball Room Baby	1956	$70

LIBERTY
❑ 55600	Crazy Arms/There's Going to Be a Fight	1963	$20
❑ 55319	Hello Walls/City of Love	1961	$20
❑ 55529	I Got Over You/Welcome Home Again	1963	$20
❑ 55707	I Will/I Catch Myself Crying	1964	$15
❑ 55306	The Pain Is Here/You	1961	$20

LOS ADMIRADORES
COMMAND
❑ LPSAM8 [S]	Golden Earrings/Birth of the Blues	1960	$10

—*Small hole, plays at 33 1/3 rpm*

❑ LPSAM6 [S]	How High the Moon/Caravan	1960	$10

—*Small hole, plays at 33 1/3 rpm*

❑ LPSAM10 [S]	Laura/I Can Dream, Can't I	1960	$12

—*Small hole, plays at 33 1/3 rpm*

❑ LPSAM7 [S]	My Funny Valentine/Makin' Whoopie	1960	$10

—*Small hole, plays at 33 1/3 rpm*

❑ LPSAM9 [S]	titles unknown	1960	$10

—*Small hole, plays at 33 1/3 rpm*

LOS BRAVOS
PARROT
❑ 3020	Bring a Little Lovin'/Make It Last	1968	$15
❑ 3023	Dirty Street/Two People in Me	1968	$12

PRESS
❑ 60002	Black Is Black/I Want a Name	1966	$20
❑ 60003	Going Nowhere/Brand New Baby	1966	$10

LOS LOBOS
SLASH
❑ 7-28186	Come On, Let's Go/Ooh My Head	1987	$3
❑ 7-28336DJ [DJ]	La Bamba (2:54)/(Fade 2:13)	1987	$8
❑ 7-28336	La Bamba/Charlena	1987	$4
❑ 7-28336 [PS]	La Bamba/Charlena	1987	$4
❑ 7-28464	One Time One Night/All I Wanted to Do Was Dance	1987	$4
❑ 7-28464 [PS]	One Time One Night/All I Wanted to Do Was Dance	1987	$6
❑ 7-28390	Set Me Free (Rosa Lee)/Tears of Crying	1987	$6
❑ 7-29093	Will the Wolf Survive?/The Breakdown	1985	$5
❑ 7-29093 [PS]	Will the Wolf Survive?/The Breakdown	1985	$6

Number	Title	Yr	NM

LOST & FOUND
INTERNATIONAL ARTISTS
❑ 120	Everybody's Here/Forever Lasting Plastic Words	1968	$30
❑ 125	When Will You Come Through/Professor Black	1968	$30

LOST, THE
CAPITOL
❑ 5519	Back Door Blues/Maybe More Than You Do	1965	$20
❑ 5708	Mean Motorcycle/Violet Gown	1966	$20

JANUS
❑ 109	I Shall Be Released/Shame	1969	$10

LOU, HERB B., AND THE LEGAL EAGLES
ARCH
❑ 1607	The Trial/Kiss Me	1958	$50

LOUDERMILK, JOHN D.
COLONIAL
❑ 435	1000 Concrete Blocks/In My Simple Way	1958	$40

—*As "Johnny Dee*

❑ 430	Sittin' in the Balcony/A-Plus in Love	1957	$40

—*As "Johnny Dee*

❑ 430 [PS]	Sittin' in the Balcony/A-Plus in Love	1957	$400

—*As "Johnny Dee*

❑ 433	Teenage Queen/It's Gotta Be You	1957	$40

—*As "Johnny Dee*

COLUMBIA
❑ 4-41247	Goin' Away to School/This Cold War with You	1958	$20
❑ 4-41209	Lover's Lane/Yo Yo	1958	$20
❑ 4-41507	The Happy Wanderer/Red Headed Stranger	1959	$20
❑ 4-41562	Tobacco Road/Midnight Bus	1960	$30

DOT
❑ 15699	Somebody Sweet/They Were Right	1958	$40

—*As "Johnny Dee*

RCA VICTOR
❑ 47-8154	Bad News/The Guitar Player	1963	$15
❑ 47-8308	Blue Train (Of the Heartbreak Line)/Rhythm and Blues	1962	$15
❑ 74-0121	Brown Girl/The Jones'	1969	$8
❑ 47-8054	Callin' Doctor Casey/Oh How Sad	1962	$15
❑ 47-8973	I Hear It Now/You're the Guilty One	1966	$10
❑ 47-9189	It's My Time/Bahama Mama	1967	$10
❑ 47-7938	Language of Love/Darling Jane	1961	$15
❑ 47-9592	Sidewalks/The Odd Folks of Okracoke	1968	$8
❑ 47-8579	That Ain't All/Then You Can Tell Me Goodbye	1965	$15

—*B-side is the original version of the future hit*

❑ 47-7993	Thou Shalt Not Steal/Mister Jones	1962	$15
❑ 47-8389	Th' Wife/Nothing to Gain	1964	$15

LOUIS, BOBBY
CAPITOL
❑ F4224	Adult Western/Love at First Sight	1959	$40
❑ F4272	I'm a Coward/Cell of Love	1959	$40

LOUVIN BROTHERS, THE
CAPITOL
❑ F4200	Blue from Now On/While You're Cheating on Me	1959	$20
❑ F2510	Born Again/From Mother's Arms to Korea	1952	$30
❑ F2381	Broadminded/I Know What You're Talking About	1953	$30
❑ 4757	Broken Engagement/Time Goes So Slow	1962	$20
❑ F3804	Call Me/I Wish You Knew	1957	$30
❑ F3871	Dog Sled/When I Loved You	1958	$20
❑ F3630	Don't Laugh/New Partner Waltz	1957	$30
❑ 5075	Every Time You Leave/There Is No Easy Way	1963	$15
❑ F2753	God Bless Her/No One to Sing for Me	1954	$30
❑ F3413	Hoping That You're Hoping/Childish Love	1956	$30
❑ 4628	How's the World Treating You/It Hurts Me More	1961	$20
❑ 4559	I Ain't Gonna Work Tomorrow/I Can't Keep You in Love with Me	1961	$20
❑ F3300	I Don't Believe You've Met My Baby/In the Middle of Nowhere	1955	$30

Number	Title	Yr	NM
❏ F2852	If We Forget God/Satan Lied to Me	1954	$30
❏ 4506	I Love You Best of All/Scared of the Blues	1961	$20
❏ 4999	I'm Glad That I'm Not Him/ Message to Your Heart	1963	$15
❏ 4430	Love Is a Lonely Street/ What a Change	1960	$20
❏ F3083	Love Thy Neighbor As Thyself/Make Him a Soldier	1955	$30
❏ 4941	Love Turns to Hate/I Cried After You Left	1963	$15
❏ 4822	Must You Throw Dirt in My Face/The First Time in Life	1962	$20
❏ F3974	My Baby Came Back/She Didn't Even Know I Was Gone	1958	$20
❏ F4055	My Baby's Gone/Lorene	1958	$20
❏ F3715	Plenty of Everything But You/The First One to Love You	1957	$30
❏ F3770	Praying/There's No Excuse	1957	$30
❏ F2612	Preach the Gospel/I Love God's Way of Living	1953	$30
❏ 4473	Santa Claus Parade/It's Christmas Time	1960	$20
❏ 4473 [PS]	Santa Claus Parade/It's Christmas Time	1960	$40
❏ F2965	Satan and the Saint/Swing Low Sweet Chariot	1954	$30
❏ F2296	The Family Who Prays Together/Let Us Travel On	1952	$30
❏ 4686	Weapon of Prayer/Great Atomic Power	1962	$20
❏ F3177	When I Stop Dreaming/ Pitfall	1955	$30
❏ F3467	Where Will You Build/That's All He's Asking of Me	1956	$30

MGM

Number	Title	Yr	NM
❏ K11392	Do You Live What You Preach/I'll Live with God	1953	$40
❏ K11221	Get Acquainted/My Love Song	1952	$40
❏ K11277	Insured Before the Grave/ Great Atomic Power	1952	$40
❏ K10988	Weapon of Prayer/ They've Got the Church Outnumbered	1951	$40

7-Inch Extended Plays

CAPITOL

Number	Title	Yr	NM
❏ EAP 3-825	*I Won't Have to Cross Jordan Alone/This Little Light of Mine/Lord, I'm Coming Home/I Steal Away and Pray	1957	$15
❏ EAP 2-825	*Nearer My God to Thee/ There's No Excuse/Praying/I Can't Say No	1957	$15
❏ EAP 1-825	*Wait a Little Longer, Please Jesus/Last Chance to Pray/ Are You Washed in the Blood/Thankful	1957	$15

MGM

Number	Title	Yr	NM
❏ X1324	(contents unknown)	1956	$20
❏ X1325	(contents unknown)	1956	$20
❏ X1326	(contents unknown)	1956	$20
❏ X1324 [PS]	The Louvin Brothers (Ira and Charles), Vol. 1	1956	$20
❏ X1325 [PS]	The Louvin Brothers (Ira and Charles), Vol. 2	1956	$20
❏ X1326 [PS]	The Louvin Brothers (Ira and Charles), Vol. 3	1956	$20

LOUVIN, CHARLIE, AND ROY ACUFF

HAL KAT

Number	Title	Yr	NM
❏ 63058	The Precious Jewel/Buried Alive	1989	$8

LOUVIN, CHARLIE, AND MELBA MONTGOMERY

CAPITOL

Number	Title	Yr	NM
❏ 3508	A Man Likes Things Like That/That Don't Mean I Don't Love You	1973	$8
❏ 3388	Baby, What's Wrong with Us/Unmatched Wedding Bands	1972	$8
❏ 3111	Baby, You've Got What It Takes/If We Don't Make It	1971	$8
❏ 3029	Did You Ever/Don't Believe Me	1971	$8
❏ 3208	I'm Gonna Leave You/When I Stop Dreaming	1971	$8
❏ 2915	Something to Brag About/ Let's Help Each Other to Forget	1970	$8

LOUVIN, CHARLIE

Also see JIM AND JESSE; THE LOUVIN BROTHERS.

CAPITOL

Number	Title	Yr	NM
❏ 3528	Bottom of the Fifth/The Roses and the Rain	1973	$8
❏ 2824	Come and Get It Mama/Is Home Sweet Home	1970	$8
❏ 3607	Funny Man/Harvest Time	1973	$8
❏ 2703	Here's a Toast to Mama/ Show Me the Way Back to Your Heart	1969	$8
❏ 2231	Hey Daddy/She Will Get Lonesome	1968	$8

Number	Title	Yr	NM
❏ 5173	I Don't Love You Anymore/ My Book of Memories	1964	$10
❏ 5948	I Forgot to Cry/Drive Me Out of My Mind	1967	$10
❏ 3243	I Placed a Call/I'm Going Home	1971	$8
❏ 5296	Less and Less/I Don't Want It	1964	$12
❏ 2448	Let's Put Our World Back Together/Heart of Clay	1969	$8
❏ 2612	Little Reasons/After Awhile	1969	$8
❏ 3048	Love Has to Die All By Itself/I Wish It Had Been a Dream	1971	$8
❏ 5791	Off and On/Still Loving You	1967	$10
❏ 5872	On the Other Hand/ Someone's Heartache	1967	$10
❏ 5369	See the Big Man Cry/I Just Don't Understand	1965	$10
❏ 2972	Sittin' Bull/It Ain't No Big Thing	1970	$8
❏ 5665	Something's Wrong/I Want a Happy Life	1966	$12
❏ 2007	The Only Way Out (Is to Walk Over Me)/Too Little and Too Late	1967	$10
❏ 5729	The Proof Is in the Kissing/ Scared of the Blues	1966	$10
❏ 5475	Think I'll Go Somewhere and Cry Myself to Sleep/Life Begins at Love	1965	$10
❏ 2770	Tiny Wings/I Ain't Gonna Work Tomorrow	1970	$8
❏ 5606	To Tell the Truth (I Told a Lie)/That's What Your Leaving's Done to Me	1966	$10
❏ 2350	What Are Those Things (With Big Black Wings)/ What Then	1968	$8
❏ 2106	Will You Visit Me on Sundays?/Tears, Wine and Flowers	1968	$8

LITTLE DARLIN'

Number	Title	Yr	NM
❏ 7922	Love Don't Care/Who's Gonna Love Me Now	1979	$5

—A-side with Emmylou Harris

UNITED ARTISTS

Number	Title	Yr	NM
❏ XW689	I Just Went Out, That's All/Is I Love You That Easy to Say	1975	$6
❏ XW430	It Almost Felt Like Love/Until I'm Out of Sight	1974	$6
❏ XW919	Sweet Texas/(B-side unknown)	1976	$6
❏ XW540	When Love Is Gone/I Want to See You One More Time	1974	$6
❏ XW616	When You Have to Fly Alone/I Just Want a Happy Life	1975	$6

LOUVIN, IRA

Also see THE LOUVIN BROTHERS.

CAPITOL

Number	Title	Yr	NM
❏ 5190	Make Believe It's Me/Who Threw Dat Rock	1964	$10

LOVE

BLUE THUMB

Number	Title	Yr	NM
❏ 106	Stand Out/I'll Pray for You	1970	$6

ELEKTRA

Number	Title	Yr	NM
❏ 45605	7 and 7 Is/No. Fourteen	1966	$10
❏ 45629	Alone Again Or/A House Is Not a Home	1968	$10
❏ 45700	Alone Again Or/Good Times	1970	$8
❏ 45633	Laughing Stock/You're Mine and We Belong Together	1968	$20
❏ 45603	My Little Red Book/Message to Pretty	1966	$10
❏ 45608	She Comes in Colors/ Orange Sky	1966	$10
❏ 45608	Stephanie Knows Who/ Orange Sky	1966	$40

RSO

Number	Title	Yr	NM
❏ 506	Good Old Fashioned Dream/You Said You Would	1975	$5
❏ 502	Time Is Like a River/With a Little Energy	1974	$5

LOVE AFFAIR, THE

DATE

Number	Title	Yr	NM
❏ 2-1627	A Day Without Love/I'm Happy	1968	$10
❏ 2-1652	Bringing On Back the Good Times/Another Day	1969	$10
❏ 2-1591	Everlasting Love/Gone Are the Songs of Yesterday	1968	$12
❏ 2-1646	Let Me Know/One Road	1969	$12

LOVE AND ROCKETS

BAUHAUS related.

BIG TIME

Number	Title	Yr	NM
❏ 8956-7-R	So Alive/Dreamtime	1989	$3
❏ 8956-7-R [PS]	So Alive/Dreamtime	1989	$3

LOVE, DARLENE

COLUMBIA

Number	Title	Yr	NM
❏ 07984	He's Sure the Man I Love/ Everybody Needs	1988	$5

PASSPORT

Number	Title	Yr	NM
❏ 7926	Christmas (Baby Please Come Home)/Playing for Keeps	1983	$15

PHILLES

Number	Title	Yr	NM
❏ 117	A Fine Fine Boy/Nino & Sonny (Big Trouble)	1963	$30
❏ 119	Christmas (Baby Please Come Home)/Harry and Milt Meet Hal B.	1963	$50
❏ 125X	Christmas (Baby Please Come Home)/Winter Wonderland	1965	$30
❏ 125	Christmas (Baby Please Come Home)/X-Mas Blues	1964	$400
❏ 123 [DJ]	Stumble and Fall/(He's a) Quiet Guy	1964	$200

—White label promo

Number	Title	Yr	NM
❏ 123	Stumble and Fall/(He's a) Quiet Guy	1964	$800

—Yellow and red label stock copy; has been verified to exist

Number	Title	Yr	NM
❏ 123	Stumble and Fall/(He's a) Quiet Guy	1964	$300

—Yellow and red label, "D.J. Copy Not for Sale" on label

Number	Title	Yr	NM
❏ 111	(Today I Met) The Boy I'm Gonna Marry/My Heart Beat a Little Bit Faster	1963	$40
❏ 111	(Today I Met) The Boy I'm Gonna Marry/Playing for Keeps	1963	$30
❏ 114	Wait 'Til My Bobby Gets Home/Take It From Me	1963	$30

REPRISE

Number	Title	Yr	NM
❏ 0534	Too Late to Say You're Sorry/If	1966	$200

WARNER/SPECTOR

Number	Title	Yr	NM
❏ 0401	Christmas (Baby Please Come Home)/Winter Wonderland	1974	$30
❏ 0410	Lord, If You're a Woman/ Stumble and Fall	1975	$10

LOVE EXCHANGE, THE

UPTOWN

Number	Title	Yr	NM
❏ 755	Swallow the Sun/Mellow Memory	1968	$30

LOVE GENERATION, THE

IMPERIAL

Number	Title	Yr	NM
❏ 66243	Groovy Summertime/Playin' on the Strings of the Wind	1967	$8
❏ 66336	Let the Good Time In/ Catching Up on Fun	1968	$8
❏ 66289	Love and Sunshine/Magic Land	1968	$8
❏ 66275	Maman (Mama)/W.C. Fields	1968	$8
❏ 66254	Meet Me at the Love-In/She Touched Me	1967	$8
❏ 66310	Montage from "How Sweet It Is" (I Know That You Know)/ Consciousness Expansion	1968	$8

LOVE, HONEY, AND THE LOVE NOTES

CAMEO

Number	Title	Yr	NM
❏ 409	Baby Baby You/Beg Me	1966	$50

—As "The Lovenotes"

Number	Title	Yr	NM
❏ 380	We Belong Together/Mary Ann	1965	$70

LOVE, HOT SHOT

SUN

Number	Title	Yr	NM
❏ 196	Wolf Call Boogie/Harmonica Jam	1954	$4000

LOVE NOTES, THE (1)

HOLIDAY

Number	Title	Yr	NM
❏ 2607	If I Could Make You Mine/ Don't Go	1957	$50

LOVE NOTES, THE (2)

IMPERIAL

Number	Title	Yr	NM
❏ 5254	Surrender Your Heart/Get On My Train	1953	$1200

RAINBOW

Number	Title	Yr	NM
❏ 266	I'm Sorry/Sweet Lulu	1954	$300

RIVIERA

Number	Title	Yr	NM
❏ 970	I'm Sorry/Sweet Lulu	1954	$800
❏ 975	Since I Fell for You/Don't Be No Fool	1954	$1000

—Authentic copies have a lavender (light purple) label, counterfeits have a pink label

Number	Title	Yr	NM
LOVE NOTES, THE (3)			
WILSHIRE			
❏ 203	Gloria/The Mathematics of Love	1963	$125
LOVE POTION, THE			
KAPP			
❏ 979	This Love/Moby Binks	1969	$8
TCB			
❏ 1601	This Love/Mr. Farouk	1968	$20
LOVE, RONNIE			
DOT			
❏ 16144	Chills and Fever/No Use Pledging My Love	1960	$30
❏ 1027	'Deed I Do/Always Be Good	1964	$40
MERCURY			
❏ 71575	Because You Love Me/While Our Hearts Are Young	1960	$30
—As "Johnny Love"			
❏ 71492	Bless Your Heart/Lead Me	1959	$30
—As "Johnny Love"			
❏ 71667	There Goes My Heart/I Love You, Yes I Do	1960	$30
—As "Johnny Love"			
STARTIME			
❏ 5001	Chills and Fever/No Use Pledging My Love	1960	$60
—As "Johnny Love"			
❏ 5003	Shakin' and a Breakin'/ (B-side unknown)	1961	$40
LOVE SCULPTURE			
DAVE EDMUNDS was in this group.			
PARROT			
❏ 362	In the Land of the Few/ Farandole	1970	$20
❏ 335	Sabre Dance/Think of Love	1969	$20
LOVE UNLIMITED ORCHESTRA			
20TH CENTURY			
❏ 2145	Baby Blues/What a Groove	1974	$5
❏ 2348	Brazilian Love Song/My Sweet Summer Suite	1977	$5
❏ 2367	Don't You Know How Much I Love You/Hey Look at Me, I'm in Love	1978	$5
❏ 2197	Forever in Love/Only You Can Make Me Blue	1975	$5
❏ 2069	Love's Theme/Sweet Moments	1973	$5
❏ 2281	Midnight Groove/It's Only What I Feel	1976	$5
❏ 2301	My Sweet Summer Suite/ Just Living It Up	1976	$5
❏ 2162	Satin Soul/Just Living It Up	1975	$5
❏ 2325	Theme from King Kong (Pt. 1)/Theme from King Kong (Pt. 2)	1977	$5
❏ 2399	Theme from "Superman"/ Theme from "Shaft"	1978	$5
❏ 2107	Theme from "Together Brothers"/Find the Man Brothers	1974	$5
❏ 2364	Whisper Softly/Hey Look at Me, I'm in Love	1978	$5
UNLIMITED GOLD			
❏ 1421	I Wanna Boogie and Woogie with You/I'm in the Mood	1980	$5
❏ 02134	Lift Your Voice and Say (United We Can Live in Peace Today)/My Fantasies	1981	$4
❏ 03881	My Laboratory Is Ready for You/Goodbye Concerto	1983	$4
❏ 02478	Welcome Aboard/Strange	1981	$4
LOVEJOYS, THE			
RED BIRD			
❏ Oct-004	Payin'/It's Mighty Nice	1964	$40
LOVELESS, PATTY			
MCA			
❏ 53097	After All/I Did	1987	$4
❏ 53097 [DJ]	After All (same on both sides)	1987	$10
—Promo only on yellow vinyl			
❏ 53333	A Little Bit in Love/I Can't Get You Off My Mind	1988	$3
❏ 53418	Blue Side of Town/I'll Never Grow Tired of You	1988	$3
❏ 53764	Chains/I'm On Your Side	1989	$4
❏ 53477	Don't Toss Us Away/After All	1989	$3
❏ 52787	I Did/Lonely Days, Lonely Nights	1986	$6
❏ 52787 [DJ]	I Did (same on both sides)	1986	$15
—Promo only on blue vinyl			
❏ 53040 [DJ]	I Did (same on both sides)	1987	$10
—Promo only on blue vinyl			
❏ 53040	I Did/You Are Everything	1987	$4

Number	Title	Yr	NM
❏ 53270	If My Heart Had Windows/ So Good to Be in Love	1988	$3
❏ 52694	Lonely Days, Lonely Nights/ Country I'm Coming Home to You	1985	$4
❏ 52694 [PS]	Lonely Days, Lonely Nights/ Country I'm Coming Home to You	1985	$6
❏ 52694 [DJ]	Lonely Days, Lonely Nights (same on both sides)	1985	$10
—Promo only on yellow vinyl			
❏ 53702	The Lonely Side of Love/I'll Never Grow Tired of You	1989	$3
❏ 53641	Timber, I'm Falling in Love/ Go On	1989	$4
❏ 52969	Wicked Ways/Half Over You	1986	$4
LOVELITES, THE			
BANDERA			
❏ 2515	I Found Me a Lover/You Better Stop It	1967	$20
LOVERBOY			
Includes members of STREETHEART and MOXY.			
COLUMBIA			
❏ 05711	Dangerous/Too Much Too Soon	1985	$3
❏ 05711 [PS]	Dangerous/Too Much Too Soon	1985	$3
❏ 06178	Heaven in Your Eyes/Friday Night	1986	$3
❏ 06178 [PS]	Heaven in Your Eyes/Friday Night	1986	$3
❏ 38-03941	Hot Girls in Love/Meltdown	1983	$3
❏ 38-03941 [PS]	Hot Girls in Love/Meltdown	1983	$3
❏ 05867	Lead a Double Life/Steal the Thunder	1986	$3
❏ 05867 [PS]	Lead a Double Life/Steal the Thunder	1986	$3
❏ 07652	Love Will Rise Again/Read My Lips	1987	$3
❏ 05569	Lovin' Every Minute of It/ Bullet in the Chamber	1985	$3
❏ 05569 [PS]	Lovin' Every Minute of It/ Bullet in the Chamber	1985	$3
❏ 03054	Lucky Ones/Gangs in the Streets	1982	$4
❏ 05765	This Could Be the Night/It's Your Life	1986	$3
❏ 05765 [PS]	This Could Be the Night/It's Your Life	1986	$3
❏ 11421 [DJ]	Turn Me Loose (Long)/Turn Me Loose (Short)	1981	$8
❏ 11421 [DJ]	Turn Me Loose (Long)/Turn Me Loose (Short)	1981	$8
❏ 11421	Turn Me Loose/Prissy Prissy	1981	$5
❏ 03108	Turn Me Loose/The Kid Is Hot Tonite	1982	$3
—Reissue			
❏ 02814	When It's Over/It's Your Life	1982	$4
❏ 02814 [PS]	When It's Over/It's Your Life	1982	$4
❏ 02589	Working for the Weekend/ Emotional	1981	$4
❏ 02589 [PS]	Working for the Weekend/ Emotional	1981	$4
❏ 03866	Working for the Weekend/ When It's Over	1983	$3
—Reissue			
LOVERS, THE (1)			
ALADDIN			
❏ 3419	Tell Me/Love Bug Bit Me	1958	$50
IMPERIAL			
❏ 5845	Darling It's Wonderful/I Want to Be Loved	1962	$30
❏ 66055	Darling It's Wonderful/I Want to Be Loved	1964	$20
❏ 5960	Tell Me/Let's Elope	1963	$30
LAMP			
❏ 2005	Darling It's Wonderful/Gotta Whole Lot of Livin' to Do	1957	$60
❏ 2013	I Wanna Be Loved/Let's Elope	1957	$60
❏ 2018	Tell Me/Love Bug Bit Me	1958	$60
POST			
❏ 10007	Darling It's Wonderful/Gotta Whole Lot of Livin' to Do	1963	$20
LOVERS, THE (2)			
AGON			
❏ 1011	Caravan of Lonely Men/In My Tenement	1965	$30
GATE			
❏ 501	Someone/Do This for Me	1965	$200
PHILIPS			
❏ 40353	Someone/Do This for Me	1966	$40
LOVERS, THE (3)			
CASINO			
❏ 103	Let's/Big Axe	1958	$30

Number	Title	Yr	NM
LOVERS, THE (4)			
MARLIN			
❏ 3313	Discomania (Part 1)/ Discomania (Part 2)	1977	$5
LOVERS, THE (U)			
CHECKER			
❏ 1100	It's Too Late/Security	1965	$50
DECCA			
❏ 29862	Don't Touch Me/Let Me Be the First to Know	1956	$50
KELLER			
❏ 101	Party Line/Strange As It Seems	1961	$50
LOVETONES, THE			
PLUS			
❏ 108	Talk to an Angel/Take It Easy, Baby	1956	$500
LOVETT, LYLE			
MCA			
❏ 52818 [DJ]	Farther Down the Line (same on both sides)	1986	$8
—Green vinyl			
❏ 52818 [DJ]	Farther Down the Line (same on both sides)	1986	$10
—Promo only on green vinyl			
❏ 52818	Farther Down the Line/Why I Don't Know	1986	$3
MCA/CURB			
❏ 52951 [DJ]	Cowboy Man (same on both sides)	1986	$8
—Clear vinyl			
❏ 52951 [DJ]	Cowboy Man (same on both sides)	1986	$20
—Promo only on clear vinyl			
❏ 52951	Cowboy Man/The Waltzing Fool	1986	$3
❏ 53157	Give Back My Heart/Simple Song	1987	$3
❏ 53030	God Will/An Acceptable Level of Ecstasy (The Wedding Song)	1987	$3
❏ 53030 [DJ]	God Will (same on both sides)	1987	$10
—Promo only on blue vinyl			
❏ 53401	If I Had a Boat/Black and Blue	1988	$3
❏ 53703	If I Were the Man You Wanted/Cryin' Shame	1989	$3
❏ 53316	I Loved You Yesterday/L.A. County	1988	$3
❏ 53471	I Married Her Just Because She Looks Like You/If I Had a Boat	1988	$3
❏ 53246	She's No Lady/Pontiac	1988	$3
❏ 53611	Stand By Your Man/ Wallisville Road	1989	$3
❏ 53102	Why I Don't Know/If I Were the Man You Wanted	1987	$3
LOVICH, LENE			
STIFF/EPIC			
❏ 03863	Blue Hotel/Savages	1983	$15
❏ 50767	Home/The Writing on the Wall	1979	$15
❏ 03499	It's You, Only You (Mein Schmerz)/Blue	1983	$10
❏ 50725	Lucky Number/Lucky Number (Slavic Dance Version)	1979	$15
LOVIN' SPOONFUL, THE			
Also see JOE BUTLER; JOHN SEBASTIAN; ZALMAN YANOVSKY.			
KAMA SUTRA			
❏ 220	Darling Be Home Soon/ Darlin' Companion	1967	$12
❏ 220 [PS]	Darling Be Home Soon/ Darlin' Companion	1967	$20
❏ 608 [DJ]	Daydream (mono/stereo)	1976	$6
—Stock copy not known to exist			
❏ 608 [DJ]	Daydream (mono/stereo)	1976	$6
—Stock copy not known to exist			
❏ 208	Daydream/Night Owl Blues	1966	$20
—Mostly red-orange label			
❏ 208	Daydream/Night Owl Blues	1966	$15
—Mostly yellow label with "Kama Sutra" in red			
❏ 208	Daydream/Night Owl Blues	1966	$12
—Mostly yellow label with "Kama Sutra" in black			
❏ 208 [PS]	Daydream/Night Owl Blues	1966	$20
❏ 209	Did You Ever Have to Make Up Your Mind/Didn't Want to Have to Do It	1966	$12
❏ 209 [PS]	Did You Ever Have to Make Up Your Mind/Didn't Want to Have to Do It	1966	$20

Number	Title	Yr	NM
❏ 201	Do You Believe in Magic/On the Road Again	1965	$20

—Mostly red-orange label

Number	Title	Yr	NM
❏ 201	Do You Believe in Magic/On the Road Again	1965	$12

—Mostly yellow label with "Kama Sutra" in red

Number	Title	Yr	NM
❏ 201	Do You Believe in Magic/On the Road Again	1965	$8

—Mostly yellow label with "Kama Sutra" in black

Number	Title	Yr	NM
❏ 231	Lonely (Amy's Theme)/You're a Big Boy Now	1967	$20
❏ 255	Me About You/Amazing Air	1968	$8
❏ 241	Money/Close Your Eyes	1967	$8
❏ 239	She Is Still a Mystery/Only Pretty, What a Pity	1967	$10
❏ 239 [PS]	She Is Still a Mystery/Only Pretty, What a Pity	1967	$20
❏ 225	Six O'Clock/The Finale	1967	$12
❏ 225 [PS]	Six O'Clock/The Finale	1967	$20
❏ 211	Summer in the City/Butchie's Tune	1966	$10
❏ 211 [PS]	Summer in the City/Butchie's Tune	1966	$20
❏ 551	Summer in the City/You and Me and Rain on the Roof	1972	$6
❏ 551 [PS]	Summer in the City/You and Me and Rain on the Roof	1972	$20

— Sleeve evidently is promo only

7-Inch Extended Plays

Number	Title	Yr	NM
❏ EK-1 [DJ]	It's Not Time Now/Nashville Cats//Henry Thomas/Darlin' Companion	1967	$25
❏ EK-1 [PS]	The Lovin' Spoonful	1967	$60

LOWE, JIM
20TH CENTURY FOX
Number	Title	Yr	NM
❏ 426	Hootenanny Granny/These Bones Gonna Rise Again	1963	$8

BUDDAH
Number	Title	Yr	NM
❏ 44	Michael J. Polalrd for President/The Ol' Racetrack	1968	$6

DECCA
Number	Title	Yr	NM
❏ 31153	Someone Else's Arms/Man of the Cloth	1960	$12
❏ 31198	That Do Make It Nice/Two Sides to Every Story	1961	$12

DOT
Number	Title	Yr	NM
❏ 16636	Addis Ababa/Have You Ever Been Lonely	1964	$6
❏ 15525	By You, By You, By You/I Feel the Beat	1957	$10
❏ 15832	Chapel Bells on Chapel Hill/Ja, Ja, Ja	1958	$10
❏ 15381	Close the Door/Nuevo Laredo	1955	$15
❏ 15569	Four Walls/Talkin' to the Blues	1957	$15
❏ 15611	From a Jack to a King/Slow Train	1957	$10
❏ 16046	He'll Have to Go/Dress Rehearsal	1960	$12
❏ 15954	I'm Movin' On/Without You	1959	$10
❏ 15407	Maybellene/Rene La Rue	1955	$15
❏ 15869	Play Number Eleven/Come Away from Her Arms	1958	$10
❏ 15753	Take Us To Your President/Later On Tonight	1958	$10
❏ 15486	The Green Door/(The Story of) The Little Man in Chinatown	1956	$20

— Originals have maroon labels

Number	Title	Yr	NM
❏ 15486	The Green Door/(The Story of) The Little Man in Chinatown	1956	$15

— Second pressings have black labels

Number	Title	Yr	NM
❏ 16074	The Midnight Ride of Paul Revere/A Tomorrow That Never Comes	1960	$10
❏ 15456	The Sixty-Four Thousand Dollar Question/Blue Suede Shoes	1956	$15

MERCURY
Number	Title	Yr	NM
❏ 70163	Gambler's Guitar/The Martins and the Coys	1953	$30
❏ 70319	Goodbye Little Sweetheart/River Boat	1954	$30
❏ 71016	Prince of Peace/Santa Claus Rides a Strawberry Roan	1956	$20
❏ 70265	Santa Claus Rides a Strawberry Roan/Love in Both Directions	1953	$30

UNITED ARTISTS
Number	Title	Yr	NM
❏ 50124	Gambler's Guitar/Blotson Bottom	1967	$6
❏ 874	Mr. Moses/Make Your Back Strong	1965	$6

LOWE, NICK
Also see DAVE EDMUNDS; ROCKPILE.

COLUMBIA
Number	Title	Yr	NM
❏ 3837 [DJ]	Cool Reaction (same on both sides)	1983	$3
❏ 03837 [DJ]	Cool Reaction (same on both sides)	1983	$3

Number	Title	Yr	NM
❏ 11018	Cruel to Be Kind/Endless Grey Ribbon	1979	$5
❏ 04486	Half a Boy and Half a Man/Awesome	1984	$3
❏ 05570	I Knew the Bride (When She Used to Rock and Roll)/Long Walk Back	1985	$3

— Label credit: Nick Lowe And His Cowboy Outfit

Number	Title	Yr	NM
❏ 10844	(I Love the Sound of) Breaking Glass/Endless Sleep	1978	$5
❏ 07734	Lovers Jamboree/Crying in My Sleep	1988	$3
❏ 10734	So It Goes/Heart of the City (Live)	1978	$5
❏ 02813	Stick It Where the Sun Don't Shine/My Heart Hurts	1982	$3
❏ 11131	Switch Board Susan/Basin Street	1979	$5
❏ 03837	Wish You Were Here/How Do You Talk to An Angel	1983	$3

LOWE, VIRGINIA
MELBA
Number	Title	Yr	NM
❏ 107	I'm in Love with Elvis Presley/Empty Feeling	1956	$60

LOWES, THE
API
Number	Title	Yr	NM
❏ 1001	Cry Baby/(B-side unknown)	1986	$6
❏ 1002	I Ain't Never/(B-side unknown)	1986	$6

SOUNDWAVES
Number	Title	Yr	NM
❏ 4775	Good and Lonesome/He's Got a Heartache on His Mind	1986	$5

LUCAS, AL
CHALLENGE
Number	Title	Yr	NM
❏ 59042	She's My Baby/Got the Ring	1959	$70
❏ 59050	Sweet Tooth for My Baby Ruth/Always	1959	$50

LUCK, RANDY
ART
Number	Title	Yr	NM
❏ 170	I Was a Teenage Caveman/Twelve O'Clock	1958	$600

LUKE, ROBIN
BERTRAM INTERNATIONAL
Number	Title	Yr	NM
❏ 212	Five Minutes More/Who's Gonna Hold Your Hand	1959	$40
❏ 208	My Girl/Chicka Chicka Honey	1958	$40
❏ 210	Strollin' Blues/You Can't Stop Me from Dreaming	1959	$40
❏ 206 [PS]	Susie Darlin'/Living's Loving You	1958	$125
❏ 206	Susie Darlin'/Living's Loving You	1958	$70

DOT
Number	Title	Yr	NM
❏ 16040	Bad Boy/School Bus Love Affair	1960	$30
❏ 16096	Everlovin'/Well Oh Well Oh	1960	$30
❏ 16096 [PS]	Everlovin'/Well Oh Well Oh	1960	$70
❏ 15959	Five Minutes More/Who's Gonna Hold Your Hand	1959	$30
❏ 16366	Foggin' Up the Windows/Time	1962	$20

— With Roberta Shore

Number	Title	Yr	NM
❏ 16001	Make Me a Dreamer/Walkin' in the Moonlight	1959	$30
❏ 15839	My Girl/Chicka Chicka Honey	1958	$30
❏ 16229	Part of a Fool/Poor Little Rich Boy	1961	$20
❏ 16170	So Alone/All Because of You	1960	$30
❏ 15899	Strollin' Blues/You Can't Stop Me from Dreaming	1959	$30
❏ 15781	Susie Darlin'/Living's Loving You	1958	$30

INTERNATIONAL
Number	Title	Yr	NM
❏ 206	Susie Darlin'/Living's Loving You	1958	$1000

— Light blue label

7-Inch Extended Plays
DOT
Number	Title	Yr	NM
❏ DEP-1092 [PS]	Susie Darlin'	1958	$400
❏ DEP-1092	Susie Darlin'/Bad Boy//Won't You Please Be Mine/Chicka Chicka Honey	1958	$400

LULU
ALFA
Number	Title	Yr	NM
❏ 7006	I Could Never Miss You (More Than I Do)/Dance to the Feeling	1981	$4
❏ 7006 [PS]	I Could Never Miss You (More Than I Do)/Dance to the Feeling	1981	$5

— With Lulu wearing a spotted headband

Number	Title	Yr	NM
❏ 7006 [PS]	I Could Never Miss You (More Than I Do)/Dance to the Feeling	1981	$6

— With Lulu not wearing a headband (original)

Number	Title	Yr	NM
❏ 7011	If I Were You/You Win, I Lose	1981	$4
❏ 7011 [PS]	If I Were You/You Win, I Lose	1981	$5
❏ 7021	Who's Foolin' Who/You Win, I Lose	1982	$4

ATCO
Number	Title	Yr	NM
❏ 6819	Goodbye My Love, Goodbye/Everybody's Got to Clap	1971	$6
❏ 6761	Good Day Sunshine/After the Feeling Is Gone	1970	$6
❏ 6749	Hum a Song (From Your Heart)/Where's Eddie	1970	$6
❏ 6885	It Takes a Real Man/You Ain't Wrong, You Just Ain't Right	1972	$6
❏ 6774	Melody Fair/To the Other Woman	1970	$6
❏ 6722	Oh Me Oh My (I'm a Fool for You Baby)/Sweep Around Your Own Back Door	1969	$8

CHELSEA
Number	Title	Yr	NM
❏ 3019	Boy Meets Girl/(B-side unknown)	1975	$10
❏ 3038	Heaven and Earth and the Stars/(B-side unknown)	1976	$30
❏ 78-0121	Make Believe World/Help Me Help You	1973	$8
❏ 3011	Take Your Mama for a Ride (Long)/Take Your Mama for a Ride (Short)	1975	$10
❏ 3001	The Man Who Sold the World/Watch That Man	1974	$40

—A David Bowie song on the A-side...and produced by Bowie, too

Number	Title	Yr	NM
❏ 3009	The Man with a Golden Gun/Baby I Don't Care	1974	$30

EPIC
Number	Title	Yr	NM
❏ 10260/65 [DJ]	Best of Both Worlds/Everybody Knows	1968	$30

—B-side by the Dave Clark Five; odd promo

Number	Title	Yr	NM
❏ 10260	Best of Both Worlds/Love Loves to Love Love	1967	$8
❏ 10260 [PS]	Best of Both Worlds/Love Loves to Love Love	1967	$30
❏ 10210	Dreamy Nights and Days/Let's Pretend	1967	$8
❏ 10302	Me, the Peaceful Heart/Look Out	1968	$8
❏ 10302 [PS]	Me, the Peaceful Heart/Look Out	1968	$30
❏ 10367	Morning Dew/You and I	1968	$8
❏ 10346	Sad Memories/Boy	1968	$8
❏ 10187	To Sir with Love/The Boat That I Row	1967	$10
❏ 10403	Without Him/This Time	1968	$8

PARROT
Number	Title	Yr	NM
❏ 9714	Here Comes the Night/I'll Come Running	1964	$30
❏ 9778	Leave a Little Love/He Don't Want Your Love Anymore	1965	$30
❏ 9678	Shout/Forget Me Baby	1964	$30
❏ 40021	Shout/When He Touches Me	1967	$10
❏ 9791	Try to Understand/Not in This Whole World	1965	$30

ROCKET
Number	Title	Yr	NM
❏ YB-11355	Don't Take Love for Granted/Love Is the Sweetest Mistake	1978	$5

7-Inch Extended Plays
EPIC
Number	Title	Yr	NM
❏ 5-26339 [PS]	To Sir with Love	1967	$20
❏ 5-26339 [DJ]	To Sir With Love/Morning Dew/Love Loves to Love Love//Best of Both Worlds/Day Tripper/Take Me in Your Arms (And Love Me)	1967	$20

—Jukebox mini-LP, small hole, plays at 33 1/3 rpm

LULU BELLE AND SCOTTY
MERCURY
Number	Title	Yr	NM
❏ 6389	Ay-Round the Corner/Wishin'	1952	$40
❏ 70824	Have I Told You Lately That I Love You/In My Heart	1956	$30
❏ 6414	Imagination/Honey Bunch	1952	$40
❏ 70155	Lips That Touch Liquor/God Put a Rainbow in the Cloud	1953	$30
❏ 6354	Saturday Night Waltz/All Night Long	1951	$40
❏ 6304	Shenandoah Waltz/My Heart Cries for You	1951	$40
❏ 70092	That's Only Half of It/Walk Me By the River	1953	$30
❏ 6400	Tied Down/I'm No Communist	1952	$40

STARDAY
Number	Title	Yr	NM
❏ 746	Try to Live Some (When You're Here)/I'll Be All Smiles Tonight	1965	$15

LUMAN, BOB

CAPITOL

Number	Title	Yr	NM
❏ F4059	Precious/Svengali	1958	$40
❏ F3972	Try Me/I Know My Baby Cares	1958	$40

EPIC

Number	Title	Yr	NM
❏ 10786	A Chain Don't Take to Me/Don't Let Love Pass You By	1971	$5
❏ 10994	A Good Love Is Like a Good Song/Have I Ever Said "I Love You" to a Lady	1973	$4
❏ 10312	Ain't Got Time to Be Unhappy/I Can't Remember to Forget	1968	$6
❏ 50183	A Satisfied Mind/Cleanin' Up the Streets of Memphis	1975	$4
❏ 10439	Come On Home and Sing the Blues to Daddy/Big, Big World	1969	$6
❏ 10480	Every Day I Have to Cry Some/Livin' in a House Full of Love	1969	$6
❏ 10581	Gettin' Back to Norma/Maybelline	1970	$6
❏ 50323	He's Got a Way with Women/Here We Are Making Love Again	1976	$4
❏ 10631	Honky Tonk Man/I Ain't Built That Way	1970	$6
❏ 50247	How Do You Start Over/Red Cadillac and Black Mustache	1976	$4
❏ 10755	I Got a Woman/One Hundred Songs on the Jukebox	1971	$5
❏ 10381	I Like Trains/A World of Unhappiness	1968	$6
❏ 10416	I'm In This Town for Good/A Woman Without Love	1968	$6
❏ 10699	Is It Any Wonder That I Love You?/Give Us One More Chance	1971	$5
❏ 10869	It Takes You/Let's Think About Livin'	1972	$5
❏ 50297	Labor of Love/Blond Haired Woman	1976	$4
❏ 11138	Let Me Make the Bright Lights Shine for You/The Closest Thing to Heaven That I Love	1974	$4
❏ 10905	Lonely Women Make Good Lovers/Love Ought to Be a Happy Thing	1972	$5
❏ 50065	Proud of You Baby/Tonight Your Baby's Coming Home	1975	$4
❏ 50136	Shame on Me/How Do You Start Over	1975	$4
❏ 11039	Still Loving You/I'm Gonna Write a Song	1973	$4
❏ 10535	The Gun/Cleanin' Up the Streets of Memphis	1969	$6
❏ 50216	The Man from Bowling Green/It's Only Make Believe	1976	$4
❏ 10667	What About the Hurt/The Time to Remember	1970	$6
❏ 10823	When You Say Love/Have a Little Faith	1972	$5

HICKORY

Number	Title	Yr	NM
❏ 1289	Bad, Bad Day/Tears from Out of Nowhere	1965	$12
❏ 1219	Can't Take the Country from the Boy/I'm Gonna Write a Song of Love	1963	$15
❏ 1410	Come On and Sing/It's a Sin	1966	$10
❏ 1277	Fire Engine Red/Old George Dickel	1964	$15
❏ 1355	Five Miles from Home (Soon I'll See Mary)/(I Get So) Sentimental	1965	$10
❏ 1430	Hardly Anymore/Freedom of Living	1967	$8
❏ 1460	If You Don't Love Me (Then Why Don't You Leave Me Alone)/Throwin' Kisses	1967	$8
❏ 1333	I Love You Because/Love Worked a Miracle	1965	$10
❏ 1536	It's All Over (But the Shouting)/Still Loving You	1969	$6
❏ 1266	Lonely Room (Empty Walls)/Run On Home Baby Brother	1964	$15
❏ 1382	Poor Boy Blues/(Can't Get You) Off My Mind	1966	$12
❏ 1564	Still Loving You/Meet Mr. Mud	1970	$6
❏ 1238	The File/Bigger Men Than I (Have Cried)	1964	$15
❏ 1221	Too Hot to Dance/I Like Your Kind of Love	1963	$15

—With Sue Thompson

IMPERIAL

Number	Title	Yr	NM
❏ 8315	Make Up Your Mind, Baby/Your Love	1958	$70

—The same coupling was slated for Imperial 8314 but not released.

POLYDOR

Number	Title	Yr	NM
❏ 14444	A Christmas Tribute/Give Someone You Love (A Little Bit of Love This Year)	1977	$4
❏ 14408	I'm a Honky-Tonk Woman's Man/Lonely Women Make Good Lovers	1977	$4
❏ 14454	Proud Lady/Let Me Love Him Out of You	1978	$4
❏ 14431	The Pay Phone/He'll Be the One	1977	$4

ROLLIN' ROCK

Number	Title	Yr	NM
❏ 028	Stranger Than Fiction/You're the Cause of It All	1978	$4

WARNER BROS.

Number	Title	Yr	NM
❏ 5272	Big River Rose/Belonging to You	1962	$30
❏ 5506	Boston Rocker/Old Friends// Bad Bad Day/Let's Think About Living	1960	$125

—Part of Warner Bros. "+2" series, with two new songs and excerpts of two prior hits

Number	Title	Yr	NM
❏ 5506 [PS]	Boston Rocker/Old Friends// Bad Bad Day/Let's Think About Living	1960	$125
❏ 5105	Dreamy Doll/Buttercup	1959	$30
❏ 5105 [PS]	Dreamy Doll/Buttercup	1959	$70
❏ 5299	Hey Joe/The Fool	1962	$30
❏ 5172	Let's Think About Living/You've Got Everything	1960	$30
❏ 5172 [PS]	Let's Think About Living/You've Got Everything	1960	$50
❏ 5255	Louisiana Man/Rocks of Reno	1962	$30
❏ 5081	My Baby Walks All Over Me/Class of '59	1959	$30
❏ 5233	Private Eyes/You've Turned Down the Lights	1961	$30
❏ 5233 [PS]	Private Eyes/You've Turned Down the Lights	1961	$50
❏ 5204	The Great Snow Man/The Pig Latin Song	1961	$30
❏ 5204 [PS]	The Great Snow Man/The Pig Latin Song	1961	$50
❏ 5184	Why, Why, Bye, Bye/Oh Lonesome Me	1960	$30
❏ 5184 [PS]	Why, Why, Bye, Bye/Oh Lonesome Me	1960	$50

LUMPKIN, HENRY

MOTOWN

Number	Title	Yr	NM
❏ 1005	I've Got a Notion/We Really Love Each Other	1961	$125
❏ 1029	Mo Jo Hanna/Break Down and Sing	1962	$60
❏ 1013	What Is a Man/Don't Leave Me	1961	$70

LUTCHER, NELLIE

CAPITOL

Number	Title	Yr	NM
❏ F1789	Birth of the Blues/I Want to Be Near You	1951	$30
❏ F1604	Fine Brown Frame/Hurry On Down	1951	$30

—Reissue of early tracks making their first appearance on 45

Number	Title	Yr	NM
❏ F847	For You My Love/Can I Come In for a Second	1950	$30

—With Nat King Cole

Number	Title	Yr	NM
❏ F1728	Humoresque/The Song Is Ended	1951	$30
❏ F878	I'll Never Get Tired/That's a Plenty	1950	$40
❏ F798	Little Sally Walker/Only You	1950	$40

—Capitol 45s in the 15000, 40000 and 70000 series are unknown

Number	Title	Yr	NM
❏ F1829	Mean to Me/Let the Worry Bird Worry You	1951	$30
❏ F1420	Pa's Not Home/I Really Couldn't Love You	1951	$30
❏ F2038	That's How It Goes/Keepin' Out of Mischief Now	1952	$30
❏ F1978	The Heart of a Clown/What a Difference a Day Made	1952	$30
❏ F1217	To Be Forgotten/That'll Just About Knock Me Out	1950	$40

DECCA

Number	Title	Yr	NM
❏ 9-29464	Please Come Back/It's Been Said	1955	$20

EPIC

Number	Title	Yr	NM
❏ 5-9005	Whee, Baby/Blues for Bill Bailey	1953	$30

LIBERTY

Number	Title	Yr	NM
❏ F-55027	All of a Sudden/Have You Ever Been Lonely	1956	$20
❏ F-55018	Blue Skies/You Made Me Love You	1956	$20

OKEH

Number	Title	Yr	NM
❏ 5-6935	Muchly, Verily/How Many More	1953	$40

LUTHER, FRANK

DECCA

Number	Title	Yr	NM
❏ 27897	Ting-a-Ling Jingle/Santa Claus Is Coming to Town	1951	$20
❏ 88078 [PS]	Ting-a-Ling Jingle/Santa Claus Is Coming to Town	1951	$30

—Children's Series release

Number	Title	Yr	NM
❏ 88078	Ting-a-Ling Jingle/Santa Claus Is Coming to Town	1951	$15

—Children's Series release

LUVWORTH, RITCHIE

DATE

Number	Title	Yr	NM
❏ 2-1624	Can You Dig It/Let's Dance	1968	$10
❏ 2-1597	Girl of Mine/Hey Baby, Where You Gonna Go	1968	$10

LY-DELLS, THE

MASTER

Number	Title	Yr	NM
❏ 111	Genie of the Lamp/Teenage Tears	1961	$250
❏ 251	Wizard of Love/Let This Night Last	1961	$70

PAM

Number	Title	Yr	NM
❏ 103	There Goes the Boy/Talking to Myself	1959	$200

PARKWAY

Number	Title	Yr	NM
❏ 897	There Goes the Boy/Talking to Myself	1964	$30

SCA

Number	Title	Yr	NM
❏ 18001	Book of Songs/Hear That Train	1962	$50

SOUTHERN SOUND

Number	Title	Yr	NM
❏ 122	Three Little Monkeys/Playing Hide and Seek	1965	$70

LYMAN, ARTHUR

GNP CRESCENDO

Number	Title	Yr	NM
❏ 349	Cast Your Fate to the Wind/Night Train	1965	$6
❏ 315	Shangri-La/Pearly Shells	1964	$6
❏ 497	Skybird/Puka Shells	1975	$4

HIFI

Number	Title	Yr	NM
❏ 533	76 Trombones/House on a Haunted Hill	1959	$10
❏ 5096	Afro Blues/Waltzing Matilda	1965	$8
❏ 5057	America (West Side Story)/Planning Rice	1962	$10
❏ 5055	Anna/(B-side unknown)	1962	$10
❏ 564	Bahia/Jungle Jalopy	1959	$12
❏ 5078	Blowin' in the Wind/I've Been Workin' on the Railroad	1963	$8
❏ 5080	Charade/Arthur's Line	1963	$8
❏ 5071	Cottonfields/Limbo Rock	1963	$8
❏ 5091	Hello, Dolly/Get Me to the Church On Time	1964	$8
❏ 5079	He's Gone Away/Suzy's Waltz	1963	$8
❏ 591	Legend of the Rain/Vera Cruz	1960	$12
❏ 5100	Lemon Tree/The Car	1966	$8
❏ 5066	Love for Sale/Dahil Sayo	1963	$8
❏ 5049	Moanin'/Aloha No Honolulu	1962	$10
❏ 5065	Mutiny on the Bounty/Pagan Love Song	1963	$8
❏ 5082	Petticoat Junction/Gently, Gently	1963	$15
❏ 5076	Sentimental Journey/Jungle Drums	1963	$8
❏ 5088	Swingin' Shephard Blues/(B-side unknown)	1964	$8
❏ 5092	Taboo/Black Orchid	1965	$8
❏ 550	Taboo/Dahil Sayo	1959	$10
❏ 5002	Taboo Tu/Ebb Tide	1960	$10
❏ 5101	The Shadow of Your Smile/Imua Kamehameha	1966	$8
❏ 5040	(The Sloop) John B/Honolulu Nites	1961	$10
❏ 5105	The Windmills of Your Mind/Lonely Winds	1969	$8
❏ 5058	We Three Kings/Little Drummer Boy	1962	$15
❏ 5083	We Three Kings/Little Drummer Boy	1963	$15
❏ 5089	Wheel of Fortune/La Montana	1964	$8
❏ 5081	Winter Wonderland/Rudolph, the Red-Nosed Reindeer	1963	$15

LYMAN, JONI

REPRISE

Number	Title	Yr	NM
❏ 0378	Happy Birthday Blue/I Just Don't Know What to Do with Myself	1965	$50

LYME AND CYBELLE

WHITE WHALE

Number	Title	Yr	NM
❏ 228	Follow Me/Like the Seasons	1966	$30
❏ 232	If You Gotta Go, Go Now/I'll Go On	1966	$30
❏ 245	Song No. 7/Write If You Get Work	1967	$30

LYMON, FRANKIE, AND THE TEENAGERS

GEE

Number	Title	Yr	NM
❏ 1039	Goody Goody/Creation of Love	1957	$50

—Actually a Frankie Lymon solo recording; the first pressing credited the entire group

Number	Title	Yr	NM
❑ 1026	I'm Not a Juvenile Delinquent/Baby Baby	1957	$40
❑ 1018	I Promise to Remember/Who Can Explain	1956	$40
❑ 1012	I Want You to Be My Girl/I'm Not a Know-It-All	1956	$60

— As "The Teenagers featuring Frankie Lymon"

❑ 1012	I Want You to Be My Girl/I'm Not a Know-It-All	1956	$40

— As "Frankie Lymon and the Teenagers

❑ 1036	Miracle of Love/Out in the Cold Again	1957	$40
❑ 1032	Teenage Love/Paper Castles	1957	$40
❑ 1022	The ABC's of Love/Share	1956	$40
❑ 1002	Why Do Fools Fall in Love/My Girl	1958	$30

— White label, "Gee Records" at top; note different B-side

❑ 1002	Why Do Fools Fall in Love/Please Be Mine	1956	$100

— Red and gold label

❑ 1002	Why Do Fools Fall in Love/Please Be Mine	1956	$60

— Red and black label; vocal duet on B-side

❑ 1002	Why Do Fools Fall in Love/Please Be Mine	1956	$40

— Red and black label; vocal solo on B-side. All of the above credit "The Teenagers featuring Frankie Lymon

❑ 1002	Why Do Fools Fall in Love/Please Be Mine	1959	$20

— Gray label, "Gee Records" at bottom; label credit is "The Teenagers featuring Frankie Lymon

7-Inch Extended Plays

Number	Title	Yr	NM
❑ GEP-602	Paper Castles/Share//Am I Fooling Myself Again/I'm Not a Know-It-All	1957	$250
❑ GEP-601	Teenage Love/Why Do Fools Fall in Love//I Want You to Be My Girl/Love Is a Clown	1956	$175
❑ GEP-601 [PS]	The Teenagers Go Rock'n	1956	$250
❑ GEP-602 [PS]	The Teenagers Go Romantic	1957	$250

LYMON, FRANKIE

BIG KAT
Number	Title	Yr	NM
❑ 7008	I Want You to Be My Girl/Portable on My Shoulder	1968	$10
❑ 7008 [PS]	I Want You to Be My Girl/Portable on My Shoulder	1968	$15

COLUMBIA
❑ 43094	Somewhere/Sweet and Lovely	1964	$60

GEE
❑ 1039	Goody Goody/Creation of Love	1957	$30
❑ 1052	I'm Not Too Young to Dream/Goody Good Girl	1959	$30

ROULETTE
❑ 4150	Before I Fall Asleep/What a Little Moonlight Can Do	1959	$30
❑ 4283	Buzz, Buzz, Buzz/Waitin' in School	1960	$30
❑ 4348	Change Partners/So Young	1961	$30
❑ 4044	Footsteps/Thumb Thumb	1958	$30
❑ 4391	I Put the Bomp/So Young	1962	$30
❑ 4035	It's Christmas Once Again/Little Girl	1957	$30
❑ 4257	Little Bitty Pretty One/Creation of Love	1960	$30
❑ 4068	Mama Don't Allow It/Portable on My Shoulder	1958	$30
❑ 4093	Melinda/The Only Way to Love	1958	$30
❑ 4026	So Goes My Love/My Girl	1957	$30

TCF
❑ 11	Teacher Teacher/To Each His Own	1964	$20

7-Inch Extended Plays

ROULETTE
❑ EPR-1-304 [PS]	Frankie Lymon at the London Palladium	1958	$250
❑ EPR-1-304	Let's Fall in Love/My Baby Just Cares for Me//Goody Goody/Somebody Loves Me	1958	$250

LYMON, LEWIS, AND THE TEENCHORDS

END
Number	Title	Yr	NM
❑ 1007	I Found Out Why/Tell Me Love	1958	$100
❑ 1003	Too Young/Your Last Chance	1957	$125
❑ 1113	Too Young/Your Last Chance	1962	$30

FURY
❑ 1003	Honey, Honey (You Don't Know)/Please Tell the Angels	1957	$100
❑ 1006	I'm Not Too Young to Fall in Love/Falling in Love	1957	$100
❑ 1000	I'm So Happy (Tra-La-La-La-La)/Lydia	1957	$200

— Maroon label

Number	Title	Yr	NM
❑ 1000	I'm So Happy (Tra-La-La-La-La)/Lydia	1958	$50

— Yellow label

JUANITA
❑ 101	Dance Girl/Them There Eyes	1958	$60

LYNDEN, TRACY

RCA
Number	Title	Yr	NM
❑ PB-14059	Straight Laced Lady/(B-side unknown)	1985	$4
❑ JK-14059 [DJ]	Straight Laced Lady (same on both sides)	1985	$10

— Promo only on red vinyl

LYNDON, FRANK

LAURIE
❑ 3322	Santa's Jet/Sing Along with Santa's Jet	1965	$30

LYNN, BARBARA

ATLANTIC
Number	Title	Yr	NM
❑ 2880	(Daddy Hotstuff) You're Too Hot to Hold/You Better Quit It	1972	$6
❑ 2553	Love Ain't Never Hurt Nobody/You're Gonna See a Lot More	1968	$8
❑ 2585	People Like Me/He Ain't Gonna Do Right	1968	$8
❑ 2450	This Is the Thanks I Get/Ring, Telephone, Ring	1967	$8
❑ 2513	Why Can't You Love Me/You're Losing Me	1968	$8

JAMIE
❑ 1304	All I Need Is Your Love/You're Gonna Be Sorry	1965	$8
❑ 1301	Can't Buy Me Love/That's What Friends Are For	1965	$8
❑ 1244	Don't Be Cruel/You Can't Be Satisfied	1963	$15
❑ 1295	(Don't Pretend) Just Lay It on the Line/Careless Hands	1965	$8

— With Lee Maye

❑ 1286	Don't Spread It Around/Let Her Knock Herself Out	1964	$15
❑ 1265	Everybody Loves Somebody/Dedicate the Blues to Me	1963	$15
❑ 1260	(I Cried at) Laura's Wedding/You Better Stop	1963	$15
❑ 1292	It's Better to Have It/People Gonna Talk	1964	$15
❑ 1269	Money/Jealous Love	1964	$15
❑ 1277	Oh! Baby (We Got a Good Thing Goin')/Unfair	1964	$15
❑ 1233	Second Fiddle Girl/Letter to Mommy and Daddy	1962	$15
❑ 1251	To Love or Not to Love/Promises	1963	$15

TRIBE
❑ 8324	I Don't Want a Playboy/New Kind of Love	1967	$125
❑ 8322	Watch the One That Brings Bad News/AUB A-Go-Go	1967	$50

LYNN, LORETTA

DECCA
Number	Title	Yr	NM
❑ 31541	Before I'm Over You/Where Were You	1963	$12
❑ 31769	Blue Kentucky Girl/Two Steps Forward	1965	$10
❑ 32749	Coal Miner's Daughter/Man of the House	1970	$10
❑ 32749 [PS]	Coal Miner's Daughter/Man of the House	1970	$15
❑ 31893	Dear Uncle Sam/Hurtin' for Certain	1966	$12
❑ 32045	Don't Come Home a-Drinkin' (With Lovin' on Your Mind)/A Saint to a Sinner	1966	$12
❑ 32264	Fist City/Slowly Killing Me	1968	$8
❑ 31707	Happy Birthday/When Lonely Hits Your Heart	1964	$12
❑ 32900	Here in Topeka/Kinfolks Holler	1971	$30
❑ 32127	If You're Not Gone Too Long/A Man I Hardly Know	1967	$10
❑ 32637	I Know How/The End of My World	1970	$8
❑ 32043	It Won't Seem Like Christmas/To Heck with Santa Claus	1966	$10
❑ 32043 [PS]	It Won't Seem Like Christmas/To Heck with Santa Claus	1966	$20
❑ 31384	Success/Hundred Proof Heartache	1962	$15
❑ 31323	The Girl That I Am Now/I Walked Away from the Wreck	1961	$20
❑ 31836	The Home You're Tearin' Down/The Farther You Go	1965	$10
❑ 31471	The Other Woman/Who'll Help Me Get Over You	1963	$10
❑ 32513	To Make a Man (Feel Like a Man)/One Little Reason	1969	$8

Number	Title	Yr	NM
❑ 32184	What Kind of a Girl (Do You Think I Am?)/Bargain Basement Dress	1967	$10
❑ 31879	When I Hear My Children Play/Everybody Wants to Go to Heaven	1965	$15
❑ 31608	Wine, Women and Song/This Haunted House	1964	$10
❑ 32586	Wings Upon Your Horns/Let's Get Back Down to Earth	1969	$8
❑ 32439	Woman of the World (Leave My World Alone)/Sneakin' In	1969	$8
❑ 31435	World of Forgotten People/Get Set for a Heartache	1962	$20

MCA
❑ 52158	Breakin' It/There's All Kinds of Smoke (In the Barroom)	1983	$4
❑ 51015	Cheatin' On a Cheater/Until I Met You	1980	$4
❑ 53397	Fly Away/Your Used to Be	1988	$3
❑ 52621	Heart Don't Do This to Me/Adam's Rib	1985	$3
❑ 52621 [PS]	Heart Don't Do This to Me/Adam's Rib	1985	$4
❑ 40150	Hey Loretta/Turn Me Any Way But Loose	1973	$5
❑ 40438	Home/You Take Me to Heaven Every Night	1975	$5
❑ 41021	I Can't Feel You Anymore/True Love Needs to Keep in Touch	1979	$4
❑ 52005	I Lie/If I Ain't Got It	1982	$4
❑ 51226	I Lie/If I Ain't Got It	1982	$5
❑ 41129	I've Got a Picture of Us on My Mind/I Don't Feel Like a Movie Tonight	1979	$4
❑ 40058	Love Is the Foundation/What Sundown Does to You	1973	$5
❑ 52219	Lyin', Cheatin', Woman Chasin', Honky Tonkin', Whiskey Drinkin' You/Star Light, Star Bright	1983	$4
❑ 52092	Making Love from Memory/Don't It Feel Good	1982	$4
❑ 40832	Out of My Head and Back in My Bed/Old Rooster	1977	$5
❑ 41185	Pregnant Again/You're a Cross I Can't Bear	1980	$4
❑ 65034	Shadrack, the Black Reindeer/Let's Put Christ Back in Christmas	1974	$4

— Black label with rainbow

❑ 65034	Shadrack, the Black Reindeer/Let's Put Christ Back in Christmas	1980	$3

— Blue label with rainbow

❑ 40679	She's Got You/The Lady That Lived Here Before	1977	$5
❑ 51058	Somebody Led Me Away/Everybody's Lookin' for Somebody New	1981	$4
❑ 40607	Somebody Somewhere (Don't Know What He's Missin' Tonight)/Sundown Tavern	1976	$5
❑ 40910	Spring Fever/God Bless the Children	1978	$4
❑ 40358	The Pill/Will You Be There	1975	$5
❑ 40223	They Don't Make 'Em Like My Daddy/Nothin'	1974	$5
❑ 40283	Trouble in Paradise/We've Already Tasted Love	1974	$5
❑ 52289	Walking with My Memories/It's Gone	1983	$4
❑ 40954	We've Come a Long Way, Baby/I Can't Feel You Anymore	1978	$4
❑ 40954 [PS]	We've Come a Long Way, Baby/I Can't Feel You Anymore	1978	$6
❑ 40484	When the Tingle Becomes a Chill/All I Want from You (Is Away)	1975	$5
❑ 53320	Who Was That Stranger/Elsie Banks	1988	$3
❑ 40747	Why Can't He Be You/I Keep On Putting On	1977	$5
❑ 52706	Wouldn't It Be Great/One Man Band	1985	$3

ZERO
❑ 107	I'm a Honky Tonk Girl/Whispering Sea	1960	$500
❑ 112	The Darkest Day/Gonna Pack My Troubles	1961	$400

7-Inch Extended Plays

DECCA
Number	Title	Yr	NM
❑ 7-34226	Alone with You/The Other Woman/Success//Color of the Blues/A Hundred Proof Heartache/Act Naturally	1963	$35

— Jukebox issue; small hole, plays at 33 1/3 rpm

❑ DL 734731	Big Ole Hurt/I'm Dynamite//When I Reach the Bottom//Wings Upon Your Horns/I'll Still Be Missing You/Let's Get Back to Earth	1970	$15

— Jukebox issue; small hole, plays at 33 1/3 rpm

❑ 7-34333 [PS]	Blue Kentucky Girl	1965	$30

Number	Title	Yr	NM
❑ 7-34333	Blue Kentucky Girl/Night Girl/Farther to Go/The Race Is On/The Beginning of the End/Send Me the Pillow You Dream On	1965	$30

—*Jukebox issue; small hole, plays at 33 1/3 rpm*

Number	Title	Yr	NM
❑ ED2784	(contents unknown)	1965	$25
❑ ED2793	(contents unknown)	1965	$25
❑ ED2800	(contents unknown)	1965	$25
❑ DL 734531 [PS]	Fist City	1968	$20
❑ DL 734531	Fist City/What Kind of Girl (Do You Think I Am)/How Long Will It Take//Somebody's Back in Town/I Don't Wanna Play House/A Satisfied Mind	1968	$20

—*Jukebox issue; small hole, plays at 33 1/3 rpm*

Number	Title	Yr	NM
❑ 7-34318	Happy Birthday/You've Made Me What I Am/It Just Looks That Way//A Boy Like You/I Don't Believe I'll Fall in Love Today/A Wound Time Can't Erase	1965	$30

—*Jukebox issue; small hole, plays at 33 1/3 rpm*

Number	Title	Yr	NM
❑ 34877	He's All I Got/One's on the Way/I Can't See Me Without You/L-O-V-E, Love/Too Wild to Be Tamed/It's Not the Miles You Traveled	1972	$15

—*Stereo jukebox issue; small hole, plays at 33 1/3 rpm*

Number	Title	Yr	NM
❑ 7-34374 [PS]	I Like 'Em Country	1966	$25
❑ 7-34226 [PS]	Loretta Lynn Sings	1963	$35
❑ 34877 [PS]	One's on the Way	1972	$15
❑ 7-34318 [PS]	Songs from My Heart...	1965	$30
❑ ED2800 [PS]	Songs from the Heart	1965	$25
❑ ED2793 [PS]	The End of the World	1965	$25
❑ ED2762 [PS]	The Other Woman	1964	$25
❑ ED2762	The Other Woman/Where Were You?/Success/Before I'm Over You	1964	$25
❑ ED2784 [PS]	Wine, Women and Song	1965	$25
❑ DL 734731 [PS]	Wings Upon Your Horns	1970	$15

LYNN, MICKI

CAPITOL

Number	Title	Yr	NM
❑ 5495	I've Got the Blues/Some of This and Some of That	1965	$60

REVUE

Number	Title	Yr	NM
❑ 11042	In the Meantime/Sure Is Something	1969	$30

LYNN, SANDRA

CONSTELLATION

Number	Title	Yr	NM
❑ 140	Where Would I Be/Sometime	1964	$15

LYNN, TRISHA

OAK

Number	Title	Yr	NM
❑ 1083	I Can't Help Myself/(B-side unknown)	1989	$6
❑ 1053	I Go to Pieces/(B-side unknown)	1988	$6

LYNN, VERA

DJM

Number	Title	Yr	NM
❑ 70009	Fool on the Hill/Goodnight	1969	$8

LONDON

Number	Title	Yr	NM
❑ 1773	Across the Bridge/If I Were You	1958	$10
❑ 1208	A Little Love/Marryin' Time	1952	$20
❑ 1830	Almost in Your Arms/Love Song from "Houseboat"	1959	$10
❑ 1227	Auf Wiederseh'n Sweetheart/From the Time We Say Goodbye (The Parting Song)	1952	$20
❑ 1202	Be Anything (But Be Mine)/Sleeping Beauty	1952	$20
❑ 1845	Be Happy/Window	1959	$12
❑ 1196	Blue Fool/A House Is a Home	1952	$20
❑ 1169	Cry/And Love Was Born	1951	$20
❑ 1729	Don't Cry My Love (The Faithful Hussar)/By the Fountains of Rome	1957	$15
❑ 1596	Doonaree/Tell Me What Have They Told You	1955	$15
❑ 1434	Du Bist Mein Liebchen/Two Easter Sunday Sweethearts	1954	$20
❑ 1688	Ev'ry Day of My Life/Come Back to Me	1956	$15
❑ 1811	Ev'ry Hour, Ev'ry Day of My Life/Say	1958	$10
❑ 1265	Forget Me Not/What a Day We'll Have	1952	$20
❑ 1870	Have I Told You Lately That I Love You/I'm a Fool to Forgive You	1959	$12
❑ 1431	Have You Ever Bought a Smile/Next Time You Feel Important	1954	$20
❑ 1249	Homing Waltz/When Swallows Say Goodbye	1952	$20
❑ 1550	I Do/Addio Amore	1955	$15
❑ 1412	If You Love Me (Really Love Me)/C'est La Vie	1954	$20

Number	Title	Yr	NM
❑ 1298	I'll Always Love You/No More	1953	$20
❑ 1317	I'll Wait for You/My Love, My Life, My Happiness	1953	$20
❑ 1501	My Son, My Son/Our Heaven on Earth	1954	$20
❑ 1233	Padam Padam (How It Echoes the Beat of My Heart)/By the Fireside	1952	$20
❑ 1793	Seventy-Six Trombones/Another Time, Another Place	1958	$10
❑ 1642	Such a Day/Unfaithful You	1956	$15
❑ 1475	The Greatest Love of All/Du Bist Mein Liebschen	1954	$20
❑ 9640	Theme from "Dr. Strangelove"/We'll Meet Again	1964	$10
❑ 1774	Tonight/I Would Love You Too	1958	$10
❑ 1752	Travellin' Home/If I Were You	1957	$15
❑ 1489	Try Again/Now and Forever	1954	$20
❑ 1302	Waiting for You/I Lived When I Met You	1953	$20
❑ 9635	We'll Meet Again/If You Love Me (Really Love Me)	1964	$10
❑ 1348	We'll Meet Again/Windsor Waltz	1953	$20
❑ 1146	Wish Me Luck/We'll Meet Again	1951	$20

MGM

Number	Title	Yr	NM
❑ K12976	Accordion/Again	1961	$10
❑ K13028	Adios, My Love/May Your Heart Stay Young Forever	1961	$10

UNITED ARTISTS

Number	Title	Yr	NM
❑ 50119	It Hurts to Say Goodbye/In the Snow	1967	$10

LYNNE, GLORIA

ABC IMPULSE!

Number	Title	Yr	NM
❑ 31003	Out of This World/Thank You Early Bird	1976	$4

CANYON

Number	Title	Yr	NM
❑ 36	Love's Finally Found Me/If You Don't Get It Yourself	1970	$5

EVEREST

Number	Title	Yr	NM
❑ 19326	Be My Love/My Prayer for You	1960	$12
❑ 19308	But Not for Me/Just in Time	1959	$15
❑ 29344 [S]	Bye Bye Blackbird/April in Paris	1960	$15

—*Jukebox issue, small hole, plays at 33 1/3 rpm*

Number	Title	Yr	NM
❑ 19373	Condemned Without Trial/Dreamy	1960	$10
❑ 2044	Don't Take Your Love from Me/You Don't Know What Love Is	1964	$8
❑ 2055	Fly Me to the Moon/The Night Has a Thousand Eyes	1965	$8
❑ 2061	Folks Who Live on the Hill/That's a Joy	1965	$8
❑ 29345 [S]	For All We Know/'Tis Autumn	1960	$15

—*Jukebox issue, small hole, plays at 33 1/3 rpm*

Number	Title	Yr	NM
❑ 19367	Gypsy Boy/Recommend to Love	1960	$10
❑ 19337	Happiness Is Just a Thing Called Joe/My Reverie	1960	$12
❑ 19409	He Needs the Lamp Is Low	1961	$8
❑ 20008	I Know Love/It Just Happened to Me	1962	$8
❑ 2023	I'll Buy You a Star/Record Company Blues	1963	$8
❑ 19431	I'm Glad There Is You/And This Is My Beloved	1962	$8
❑ 19418	Impossible/This Little Boy of Mine	1961	$8
❑ 2042	I Should Care/Indian Love Call	1964	$8
❑ 2036	I Wish You Love/Through a Long and Sleepless Night	1963	$8
❑ 29346 [S]	Little Girl Blue/Am I Blue	1960	$15

—*Jukebox issue, small hole, plays at 33 1/3 rpm*

Number	Title	Yr	NM
❑ 2059	Lonely Street/Try a Little Tenderness	1965	$8
❑ 2062	My Devotion/I'm Glad There Is You	1965	$8
❑ 2051	On Christmas Day/Wouldn't It Be Loverly	1964	$8
❑ 2058	Out of This World/Squeeze Me	1965	$8
❑ 29343 [S]	Perdido/June Night	1960	$15

—*Jukebox issue, small hole, plays at 33 1/3 rpm*

Number	Title	Yr	NM
❑ 2047	Serenade in Blue/Without a Song	1964	$8
❑ 2030	Stormy Monday Blues/Humming Blues	1963	$8
❑ 29347 [S]	Without a Song/They Didn't Believe Me	1960	$15

—*Jukebox issue, small hole, plays at 33 1/3 rpm*

FONTANA

Number	Title	Yr	NM
❑ 1890	Be Anything (But Be Mine)/Soul Serenade	1964	$8
❑ 1890 [PS]	Be Anything (But Be Mine)/Soul Serenade	1964	$15
❑ 1594	Foolish Dreamer/I Can't Stand It	1967	$6
❑ 1674	Hold It/Untouched by Human Love	1969	$5

Number	Title	Yr	NM
❑ 1560	Honey Machine/I Got What You Want	1966	$6
❑ 1639	I've Got to Be Someone/Problem Child	1969	$5
❑ 1617	I've Never Ever Loved Before/Down Here on the Ground	1968	$5
❑ 1567	Love Is/It's Not the Truth	1967	$6
❑ 1966	Soul Serenade/Do Anything	1965	$6
❑ 1538	Speaking of Happiness/Sometimes It Be's That Way	1966	$6
❑ 1554	Strangers in the Night/Hey, Candy Man	1966	$6
❑ 1627	The Guy Who Lived Up There/Hold Back the Dawn	1968	$5
❑ 1507	The Touch of Your Lips/Intimate Moments	1965	$6
❑ 1523	The Whisperers/I Understand	1965	$6
❑ 1511	Watermelon Man/All Alone	1965	$6

HIFI

Number	Title	Yr	NM
❑ 5103	I Wish You Love/Long Long Story	1966	$6

SEECO

Number	Title	Yr	NM
❑ 6077	Is There Someone for Me/I'm Not Afraid Anymore	1961	$10
❑ 6037	Little Boy Blues/Way Beyond the Hills	1959	$15

LYNNE, JEFF
Also see ELECTRIC LIGHT ORCHESTRA.

JET

Number	Title	Yr	NM
❑ AE71220 [DJ]	Doin' That Crazy Thing/(B-side blank)	1980	$6

—*Small hole, plays at 33 1/3 rpm; later edition than Jet 1060*

Number	Title	Yr	NM
❑ XW1060	Doin' That Crazy Thing/Going Down to Rio	1977	$6

LYNOTT, PHIL
Also see THIN LIZZY.

WARNER BROS.

Number	Title	Yr	NM
❑ 49272	Ode to a Black Man/King's Call	1980	$15

LYNYRD SKYNYRD

MCA

Number	Title	Yr	NM
❑ 40532	Double Trouble/Roll Gypsy Roll	1975	$5
❑ 40957	Down South Jukin'/Wino	1978	$5
❑ 40328	Free Bird/Down South Jukin'	1974	$5
❑ 40665	Free Bird/Searching	1976	$5
❑ 40565	Gimme Back My Bullets/All I Can Do Is Write About It	1976	$5
❑ L45-1966 [DJ]	Gimme Back My Bullets (same on both sides)	1976	$30
❑ 40647	Gimme Three Steps/Travelin' Man	1976	$5
❑ 40416	Saturday Night Special/Made in the Shade	1975	$5
❑ 60191	Sweet Home Alabama/Saturday Night Special	1976	$4

—*Reissue*

Number	Title	Yr	NM
❑ 40258	Sweet Home Alabama/Take Your Time	1974	$5
❑ 40819	What's Your Name/I Know a Little	1977	$5

—*"What's Your Name" is a different mix than that on the Street Survivors LP.*

Number	Title	Yr	NM
❑ 53206	When You Got Good Friends/Truck Drivin' Man	1987	$4

SOUNDS OF THE SOUTH

Number	Title	Yr	NM
❑ 40231	Don't Ask Me No Questions/Take Your Time	1974	$8
❑ 40158	Gimme Three Steps/Mr. Banker	1973	$8
❑ 40258	Sweet Home Alabama/Take Your Time	1974	$8

LYRICS, THE

ABC-PARAMOUNT

Number	Title	Yr	NM
❑ 10560	So Hard to Get Along/Side Wind	1964	$15

CORAL

Number	Title	Yr	NM
❑ 62322	The Girl I Love/Oh, Please Love Me	1962	$30

FERNWOOD

Number	Title	Yr	NM
❑ 129	Let's Bee Sweethearts Again/You and Your Fellow	1960	$800

—*This edition misspelled the A-side*

FLEETWOOD

Number	Title	Yr	NM
❑ 233	Let's Be Sweethearts Again/You and Your Fellow	1961	$400

—*This edition spelled the A-side correctly*

VEE JAY

Number	Title	Yr	NM
❑ 285	Come On Home/Why Don't You Stop	1958	$100

LYZER, TONY

LAURIE

Number	Title	Yr	NM
❑ 3019	Six Little Men/Loco	1958	$200

M

M/A/R/R/S
4TH & B'WAY

Number	Title	Yr	NM
❏ 7452	Pump Up the Volume (From Bright Lights Big City)/Anitina	1987	$3
❏ 7452 [PS]	Pump Up the Volume (From Bright Lights Big City)/Anitina	1987	$3

—Both versions have same picture sleeve

❏ 7452	Pump Up the Volume (Radio Edit)/Anitina	1987	$4

—No mention of "Bright Lights Big City" on label

M.H. ROYALS, THE
ABC

Number	Title	Yr	NM
❏ 10957	Old Town/Now She's Crying	1967	$30
❏ 10907	Tomorrow's Dead/She's Gone Forever	1967	$30

M.P.D. LIMITED
LTD

Number	Title	Yr	NM
❏ 400	Little Boy Sad/Wendy Don't Go	1965	$50

M-3'S, THE
ABC-PARAMOUNT

Number	Title	Yr	NM
❏ 10772	Funny Cafe/So Give Me Love	1966	$30

UNITED ARTISTS

❏ 889	Three Lonely Nights/I See a Rainbow	1965	$15
❏ 737	When the Party's Over/Magic Kiss	1964	$15

MABLEY, MOMS
MERCURY

Number	Title	Yr	NM
❏ 72935	Abraham, Martin and John/Sunny	1969	$6
❏ 72958	His Way/Yes Indeed	1969	$6
❏ 73240	I Surrender Dear/That's Pops	1971	$5
❏ 72974	It's Your Thing/He's Got the Whole World in His Hands	1969	$6

MACGREGOR, MARY
ARIOLA AMERICA

Number	Title	Yr	NM
❏ 7667	For a While/Lady I Am	1977	$5
❏ 7677	I've Never Been to Me/In Your Eyes	1977	$5
❏ 7708	Memories/Seashells on the Windows, Candles and a Magic Stone	1978	$5
❏ 7662	This Girl (Has Turned Into a Woman)/Good Together	1977	$5
❏ 7638	Torn Between Two Lovers/I Just Want to Love You	1976	$5
❏ 7726	Wedding Song (There Is Love)/Benjamin	1978	$5

RSO

❏ 1025	Dancin' Like Lovers/I Can't Hold On	1980	$4
❏ 1044	Dominoes/Somebody Please	1980	$4
❏ 938	Good Friend/Rudy and Tripper	1979	$4

MACK, BILL
HICKORY

Number	Title	Yr	NM
❏ 1628	End of the Road/La Donna	1972	$8
❏ 1601	That's Love/That's Why I Cry	1971	$8
❏ 1660	Today I'm Bringing You Roses/Waitin' for the River to Rise	1973	$8

STARDAY

❏ 313	A Million Miles Away/Cheatin' on Your Mind	1957	$60
❏ 360	Blue/Faded Rose	1958	$50
❏ 252	Cat Just Got in Town/Sweet Dreams Baby	1956	$200
❏ 418	I'll Still Be Here Tomorrow/Long, Long Train	1959	$50
❏ 280	It's Saturday Night/That's Why I Cry	1957	$200

MACK, LONNIE
ELEKTRA

Number	Title	Yr	NM
❏ 45715	Lay It Down/She Even Woke Me Up to Say Goodbye	1971	$8
❏ 45715 [PS]	Lay It Down/She Even Woke Me Up to Say Goodbye	1971	$20
❏ 45638	Memphis/Why	1968	$10
❏ 45652	Save Your Money/In the Band	1969	$10

EPIC

❏ 08117	Hard Life/50's-60's Man	1988	$4

Number	Title	Yr	NM
❏ 07973	Too Rock for Country, Too Country for Rock and Roll/Lucille	1988	$4

FRATERNITY

❏ 918	Baby, What's Wrong/Where There's a Will	1963	$15
❏ 932	Chicken Pickin'/Sa-Ba-Hoola	1964	$15
❏ 957	Crying Over You/Are You Guilty	1966	$15
❏ 942	Crying Over You/Coastin'	1965	$15
❏ 938	Don't Make My Baby Blue/Oh Boy	1964	$15
❏ 951	Honky Tonk '65/Chicken Pickin'	1965	$15
❏ 981	I Left My Heart in San Francisco/Omaha	1967	$10
❏ 925	I've Had It/Nashville	1964	$15
❏ 906	Memphis/Down in the Dumps	1963	$20
❏ 986	Save Your Money/Snow on the Mountain	1967	$10
❏ 920	Say Something Nice to Me/Lonnie on the Move	1964	$15
❏ 1004	Soul Express/Down and Out	1968	$12
❏ 967	Tension (Part 1)/Tension (Part 2)	1966	$15
❏ 959	The Circus/Bucaroo	1966	$15
❏ 946	Tonky Go Go/When I'm Alone	1965	$15
❏ 912	Wham!/Susie-Q	1963	$20
❏ 969	Wildwood Flower/Snow on the Mountain	1966	$15

ROULETTE

❏ 7175	All We Need Is Love, You and Me/Highway 56	1975	$6

MACK, VONNIE
COLUMBIA

Number	Title	Yr	NM
❏ 4-21541	Blue Mountain Waltz/Slowly I'm Losing You	1956	$30
❏ 4-40809	Please Forgive Me/I Live for You	1956	$30

MACK, WARNER
DECCA

Number	Title	Yr	NM
❏ 31436	Afraid to Look Back/I Wake Up Crying	1962	$20
❏ 32394	Don't Wake Me I'm Dreaming/When the Walls Come Tumblin' Down	1968	$8
❏ 32082	Driftin' Apart/When We Are Alone at Night	1967	$12
❏ 32142	How Long Will It Take/As Long As I Keep Wantin' (I'll Keep Wanting You)	1967	$10
❏ 32211	I'd Give the World (To Be Back Loving You)/It's Been a Good Life Loving You	1967	$10
❏ 32547	I'l Still Be Missing You/Sunshine (Bring Back My Sunshine)	1969	$8
❏ 32308	I'm Gonna Move On/Tell Me to Go	1968	$8
❏ 9-30587	Is It Wrong (For Loving You)/Baby, Squeeze Me	1957	$30
❏ 32004	It Takes a Lot of Money/A Million Thoughts from My Mind	1966	$10
❏ 32473	Leave My Dream Alone/You're Always Turnin' Up Again	1969	$8
❏ 32725	Live for the Good Times/Another Mountain to Climb	1970	$8
❏ 9-30645	Lonesome for You Now/Your Fool	1958	$30
❏ 32646	Love Hungry/Love Is Where the Heart Is	1970	$8
❏ 32365	Pray for Your Country/Be Good to Your Neighbor Every Day	1968	$8
❏ 31684	Sittin' in an All Nite Cafe/Blue Mood	1964	$15
❏ 31853	Sittin' on a Rock (Cryin' in a Creek)/The Way It Feels to Die	1965	$15
❏ 31559	Surely/This Little Hurt	1963	$15
❏ 31911	Talkin' to the Wall/One Mile More	1966	$10
❏ 9-30587	That's My Heart's Desire/Falling in Love	1958	$30
❏ 31774	The Bridge Washed Out/The Biggest Part of Me	1965	$12
❏ 9-30714	The First Chance I Get/Going Back to School	1958	$30
❏ 31626	The Least Little Thing Would Make Me Stay/I'll Be Alright in the Morning	1964	$15
❏ 9-30841	Too Bashful/Yes, There's a Reason	1959	$30
❏ 31506	Working Girl/I'll Step Out of the Picture	1963	$15

KAPP

❏ 392	Tears for Two/Forever We'll Walk Hand in Hand	1961	$20
❏ 656	Wild Side of Life/Forever We'll Walk Hand in Hand	1965	$8

MCA

❏ 40064	After the Lights Go Out/Then	1973	$5
❏ 40452	Baby, You've Built a Fire/Who's Makin' the Changes	1975	$5

Number	Title	Yr	NM
❏ 40398	Don't Bring the Rain Down on Me/One Step Away	1975	$5
❏ 40137	Goodbyes Don't Come Easy/Christie, Christie	1973	$5
❏ 40516	I've Got a Friend (Just Over the Mountain)/Nothin' Ain't Right	1976	$5

MOON SHINE

❏ 3035	Go Around Again/(B-side unknown)	1985	$6

PAGEBOY

❏ 30	Brush Arbor in the White House/She's a Sweet Talkin' Woman	1977	$5
❏ 31	These Crazy Thoughts (Run Through My Mind)/I Wanna Go Back	1977	$5

SCARLET

❏ 4002	My Love for You/Someone Somewhere	1960	$30

TOP RANK

❏ 2053	I'll Run Back to You/Prison of Love	1960	$30

7-Inch Extended Plays
DECCA

Number	Title	Yr	NM
❏ DL 734533	How Long Will It Take/Tell Me to Go (Tell Me to Stay)/Then//I'm Gonna Move On/Paper Mansions/You're the Reason	1968	$15

—Jukebox issue; small hole, plays at 33 1/3 rpm

❏ DL 734533 [PS]	The Many Country Moods of Warner Mack	1968	$15

MACKENZIE, GISELE
CAPITOL

Number	Title	Yr	NM
❏ F2156	Adios/Darling You Can't Love Two	1952	$15
❏ F2695	A Letter and a Ring/Le Gros Bill	1954	$15
❏ F2266	Crazy Waltz/Water Can't Quench the Fire of Love	1952	$15

—With Helen O'Connell

❏ F2743	Doggone It Baby, I'm in Love/Ridin' to Tennessee	1954	$15
❏ F2256	Don't Let the Stars Get In Your Eyes/My Favorite Song	1952	$15
❏ F1997	Eggbert the Easter Egg/Benny the Bob-Tailed Bunny	1952	$20
❏ F2827	El Recicario/The One Who Broke My Heart Is Back in Town	1954	$15
❏ F2521	Give Me a Name/When the Hands of the Clock Pray at Midnight	1953	$15

—With Helen O'Connell

❏ F2307	Gone/The New Wears Off Too Fast	1952	$15
❏ F2556	Half Hearted/Till They've All Come Home	1953	$15
❏ F2501	I'd Rather Die Young/I Didn't Want to Love You	1953	$15
❏ F1907	La Fiacre/Thu Pocket Thu Pocket	1951	$20
❏ F2354	Let Me Know/Friend of the Family	1953	$15
❏ F2404	Lipstick and Powder and Paint/Get It While You're Young	1953	$15

—With Helen O'Connell

❏ F1959	My Buick, My Lover and I/Lovers' Waltz	1952	$15

—With Gordon MacRae

❏ F1807	On Rosary Hill/Lovers' Waltz	1951	$20

—With Gordon MacRae

❏ F1878	Please/Love Makes the World Go Round	1951	$20
❏ F1826	Sans Souci/I Never Was Loved by Anyone Else	1951	$20
❏ F1865	Sweetheart/It's All Over But the Memories	1951	$20
❏ F2600	Walkin' Tune/Embrasse	1953	$15
❏ F2059	What'll I Do/I'm So Easy to Satisfy	1952	$15
❏ F1983	Wishin'/Goodbye Sweetheart	1952	$15

EVEREST

❏ 19352	In Milano/You Dream of Me (And I'll Dream of You)	1960	$8

RCA VICTOR

❏ 47-7183	They're Playing Our Song/Come to Me My True Love	1958	$8

VIK

❏ 0249	He Knows/Hello There	1957	$12
❏ 0233	The Star You Wished Upon Last Night/It's Delightful to Be Married	1956	$10
❏ 0274	The Waltz That Broke My Heart/Oh Pain, Oh Agony	1957	$10
❏ 0300	Too Fat for the Chimney/Jingle Bells	1957	$15
❏ 0300 [PS]	Too Fat for the Chimney/Jingle Bells	1957	$30

Number	Title	Yr	NM
X			
❑ 0137	Hard to Get/Boston Fancy	1955	$15
❑ 0137 [PS]	Hard to Get/Boston Fancy	1955	$30
❑ 0202	Mr. Telephone/Dance If You Want to Dance	1956	$10
❑ 0172	Pepper Hot Baby/That's the Chance I've Got to Take	1955	$10
VIK			
❑ EXA-211 [PS]	Autumn and Gisele	1956	$25
❑ EXA-211	Autumn Leaves/The River Seine//Tell Me That You Love Me/Hands Across the Table	1956	$25
❑ EXA-181	Between the Devil and the Deep Blue Sea/Tiptoe Thru the Tulips//Swinging Down the Lane/At Sundown	1956	$25
❑ EXA-209	C'est Si Bon/September in the Rain//Comme Ci, Comme Ca/Cherry Pink and Apple Blossom White (contents unknown)	1956	$25
❑ EXA-269		1957	$25
❑ EXA-271	Dans Cette Etable (In This Stable)/Les Anges Dans Nos Campagnes (The Angels in Our Fields)/La Marche Des Rois (The March of the Kings)/Parade of the Wooden Soldiers//White Christmas/Rudolph the Red-Nosed Reindeer	1957	$25
❑ EXA-180	Do You Ever Think of Me/You Are My Lucky Star//You're My Everything/Don't Worry About Me	1956	$25
❑ EXA-179	Everytime We Say Goodbye/Beyond the Sea//These Foolish Things Remind Me of You/On Top of the World, Alone	1956	$25
❑ EXA-210 [PS]	Gisele in Paris	1956	$25
❑ EXA-179 [PS]	Gisele MacKenzie, Vol. 1	1956	$25
❑ EXA-180 [PS]	Gisele MacKenzie, Vol. 2	1956	$25
❑ EXA-181 [PS]	Gisele MacKenzie, Vol. 3	1956	$25
❑ EXA-210	La Vie En Rose/Under Paris Skies//Dinner for One Please, James/Passing By Mam'selle Gisele	1956	$25
❑ EXA-209 [PS]		1956	$25
❑ EXA-269 [PS]	Season's Greetings	1957	$25

MACLAINE, SHIRLEY

DECCA

Number	Title	Yr	NM
❑ 32446	My Personal Property/Where Am I Going	1969	$8
❑ 32446 [PS]	My Personal Property/Where Am I Going	1969	$15

RCA VICTOR

Number	Title	Yr	NM
❑ 47-9699	The Way That I Live/Mr. Blossom Goes "Bust	1968	$8

— B-side by Riz Ortolani

MACRAE, GORDON

CAPITOL

Number	Title	Yr	NM
❑ F1941	Baby Doll/Green Acres, Purple Mountains	1952	$15
❑ F3122	Bella Notte/Follow Your Heart	1955	$12
❑ F1836	Be My Guest/Laughing at Love	1951	$20
❑ F2196	Blame it on My Youth/There's a Lull in My Life	1952	$15
❑ F1990	Call Her Sweetheart/900 Miles	1952	$15
❑ F2465	C'est Magnifique/Homin' Time	1953	$15
❑ F2784	Coney Island Boat/Open Your Arms	1954	$15

— With June Hutton

Number	Title	Yr	NM
❑ F2352	Congratulations to Someone/How Do You Speak to an Angel	1953	$15
❑ F2927	Count Your Blessings Instead of Sheep/Cara Mia	1954	$15
❑ F1545	Cuban Love Song/Last Night When We Were Young	1951	$20
❑ F1750	Cuddle Up a Little Closer/Down Old Ox Road	1951	$20
❑ 4483	Dolce Par Niente/If Ever I Would Leave You	1960	$8
❑ F2760	Face to Face/Backward Turn Backward	1954	$15
❑ 4613	Face to Face/Sail Away	1961	$8
❑ F3315	Fate/Never Before and Never Again	1956	$10
❑ F4116	Fly Little Bluebird/Little Do You Know	1959	$8
❑ F2010	Gentle Hands/These Things Shall Pass	1952	$15
❑ F3284	(Here's to) A Wonderful Christmas/A Woman in Love	1955	$15
❑ F2988	Here's What I'm Here For/Love Can Change the Stars	1954	$15
❑ F1193	Honestly, I Love You!/Just the Way You Are	1950	$30
❑ F3438	I Asked the Lord/One Misty Morning	1956	$10
❑ F3864	If I Forget You/Now	1957	$10
❑ 4626	Impossible/Ordinary People	1961	$8
❑ F812	I'm Yours/Just One More Chance	1950	$30

Number	Title	Yr	NM
❑ F1471	I'm Yours to Command/I'll Buy You a Star	1951	$20
❑ F2603	I Still Dream of You/I Don't Want to Walk Without You	1953	$15
❑ F3384	I've Grown Accustomed to Your Face/Who Are We	1956	$10
❑ F1168	Love 'Em All/Pigskin Polka	1950	$30
❑ 4773	Lovely/Warmer Than a Whisper	1962	$8
❑ 54-90034	Merry Christmas Waltz/Adeste Fideles	1949	$50
❑ 54-777	Mule Train/Dear Hearts and Gentle People	1949	$30
❑ F1959	My Buick, My Lover and I/Lovers' Waltz	1952	$15

— With Gisele MacKenzie

Number	Title	Yr	NM
❑ F1846	My Love/How Close	1951	$20
❑ F924	Oh, Oh, Ophelia/Two-Faced Heart	1950	$30
❑ F1374	O Kive Neabs Kive (Love Means Love)/Wait for Me	1951	$20
❑ F1705	Ol' Man River/On Sunday at Coney Island	1951	$20
❑ 4357	Our Love Story/You Were There	1960	$8

— With Sheila MacRae

Number	Title	Yr	NM
❑ F2115	Peace in the Valley/Mansion Over the Hilltop	1952	$15
❑ F3214	People Will Say We're in Love/Surrey with the Fringe on Top	1955	$10
❑ F842	Poison Ivy/Half a Heart Is All You Left Me (When You Broke My Heart in Two)	1950	$30
❑ F3816	Sayonara/Never Till Now	1957	$10
❑ F1684	So in Love/Ramona	1951	$15

— Reissue

Number	Title	Yr	NM
❑ F2672	Soothe My Lonely Heart/High on a Windy Hill	1953	$15
❑ F2311	Starlight and Narrow/Brotherly Love	1952	$15
❑ F2652	Stranger in Paradise/Never in a Million Years	1953	$15
❑ F4179	Stranger/Palace of Love	1959	$8
❑ 54-755	The Prairie Is Still/Sunshine of Your Smile	1949	$30
❑ F4033	The Secret/A Man Once Said	1958	$10
❑ 4323	The Sound of Music/When Did I Fall in Love	1959	$8
❑ F1021	The Stars and Stripes Forever/Hongi-Tongi-Goki-Poki	1950	$30
❑ 54-711	The Wedding of Lilli Marlene/Twenty-Four Hours of Sunshine	1949	$30
❑ F3641	Till We Meet Again/Lonely	1957	$10
❑ 54-628	Ting-a-Ling/Lover's Gold	1949	$30
❑ F3724	When You Kiss Me/Endless Love	1957	$10
❑ F3519	Without Love/Obey	1956	$10
MGM			
❑ K10734	They Say It's Wonderful/Prisoner of Love	1950	$40

7-Inch Extended Plays

CAPITOL

Number	Title	Yr	NM
❑ EAP 3-834	*The Last Round-Up/Green Grow the Lilacs/Wagon Wheels/I Went to the City	1957	$10
❑ EAP 2-765	(contents unknown)	1956	$10
❑ EAP 1-765	(contents unknown)	1956	$10
❑ EAP 3-765	(contents unknown)	1956	$10
❑ EAP 3-834 [PS]	Cowboy's Lament, Part 3	1957	$12
❑ EAP 1-765 [PS]	The Best Things in Life Are Free, Part 1	1956	$12
❑ EAP 2-765 [PS]	The Best Things in Life Are Free, Part 2	1956	$12
❑ EAP 3-765 [PS]	The Best Things in Life Are Free, Part 3	1956	$12

MACRAY, MACK

DECCA

Number	Title	Yr	NM
❑ 9-46327	One More Beer/That's a Horse of a Different Color	1951	$30

— in Sub Pop Singles Club series

MAD HATTERS, THE

ASCOT

Number	Title	Yr	NM
❑ 2197	I Need Love/Blowin' in the Wind	1965	$30

FONTANA

Number	Title	Yr	NM
❑ 1582	I'll Come Running/Hello Girl	1967	$30

MAD LADS, THE

CAPITOL

Number	Title	Yr	NM
❑ 5284	Don't Cry at the Party/I'll Survive	1964	$20

STAX

Number	Title	Yr	NM
❑ 160	Surf Jerk/Sidewalk Surf	1964	$20

VOLT

Number	Title	Yr	NM
❑ 4016	By the Time I Get to Phoenix/No Strings Attached	1969	$8
❑ 135	Come Closer to Me/Sugar Sugar	1966	$10

Number	Title	Yr	NM
❑ 127	Don't Have to Shop Around/Tear-Maker	1965	$12
❑ 4068	Gone! The Promises of Yesterday/I'm So Glad I Fell in Love with You	1971	$8
❑ 4098	I Forgot to Be Your Lover/I'm So Glad I Fell in Love with You	1973	$8
❑ 137	I Want a Girl/What Will Love Tend to Make You Do	1966	$10
❑ 131	I Want Someone/Nothing Can Break Through	1965	$10
❑ 4080	Let Me Repair Your Heart/Did My Baby Call	1972	$8
❑ 4009	Love Is Here Today and Gone Tomorrow/Make This Young Lady Mine	1969	$8
❑ 150	My Inspiration/Mr. Fix-It	1967	$10
❑ 139	Patch My Heart/You Mean So Much to Me	1966	$10
❑ 4041	Seeing Is Believing/These Old Memories	1970	$8
❑ 4003	So Nice/Make Room	1968	$8
❑ 143	These Simple Reasons/I Don't Want to Lose Your Love	1967	$10
❑ 162	Whatever Hurts You/No Time Is Better Than Right Now	1968	$10
WAND			
❑ 11221	Let's Have Some Fun (Part 1)/Let's Have Some Fun (Part 2)	1970	$12

MAD MILO

COMBO

Number	Title	Yr	NM
❑ 131	Elvis on Trial/A Date with Elvis	1957	$60

MILLION

Number	Title	Yr	NM
❑ 20018	Elvis for Christmas/New Year	1957	$60

— B-side by Ron Tan and Combo

MAD, THE

DISGUSTING

Number	Title	Yr	NM
❑ 781	Eyeball/I Hate Music	1979	$60
❑ 781 [PS]	Eyeball/I Hate Music	1979	$60
❑ 123	Fried Egg//The Hell/Disgusting	1979	$60
❑ 123 [PS]	Fried Egg//The Hell/Disgusting	1979	$60

MADDOX BROTHERS AND ROSE

Also see ROSE MADDOX.

4 STAR

Number	Title	Yr	NM
❑ 1596	8:30 Blues/Your Love Light Never Shone	1952	$40
❑ 1671	Baby You Should Live So Long/You've Been Talking in Your Sleep	1955	$30
❑ 1604	Detour #2/I'll Still Write Your Name in the Sand	1952	$40
❑ 1626	I Just Steal Away and Pray/I'd Rather Have Jesus	1953	$40
❑ 1639	I'll Fly Away/The Land Where We'll Never Grow Old	1953	$40
❑ 1664	I'll Never Do It Again/I've Stopped My Dreaming	1954	$30
❑ 1586	I Wish I Was a Single Girl Again/I Want to Live and Love	1952	$40
❑ 1657	Momma Says It's Naughty/Old Pal of Yesterday	1954	$30
❑ 1570	Shimmy Shakin' Daddy/No One Is Sweeter Than You	1951	$50
❑ 1618	Texas Guitar Stomp/Country Bugle Boy	1952	$40
❑ 1633	The Meanest Man in Town/Rosalie by the Rio	1953	$40

COLUMBIA

Number	Title	Yr	NM
❑ 4-21513	Away This Side of Heaven/It's a Dark, Dark Place	1956	$30
❑ 4-21146	A-Wooin' We Will Go/On Mexico's Beautiful Shore	1953	$30
❑ 4-21099	Green Grow the Lilacs/Empty Mansion	1953	$30
❑ 4-21127	I'd Rather Die Young/The Nightingale Song	1953	$30
❑ 4-21546	I'll Find Her/Wish You Would	1956	$30
❑ 4-20924	I'll Make Sweet Love to You/Coquita of Laredo	1952	$30
❑ 4-21405	I've Got Four Big Brothers/No More Time	1955	$30
❑ 4-40895	Love Is Strange/My Life with You	1957	$30
❑ 4-21466	Old Black Choo Choo/Let This Be the Last Time	1955	$30
❑ 4-41020	Stop Whistlin' Wolf/Let Me Love You	1957	$30
❑ 4-21217	This Is Spring/Beautiful Bouquet	1954	$30
❑ 4-21297	Waltz of the Pines/The Life That You've Led	1954	$30
❑ 4-20955	Wedding Blues/I'll Make Sweet	1952	$30

DECCA

Number	Title	Yr	NM
❑ 9-28784	I'll Be No Stranger There/The Unclouded Day	1953	$30

Number	Title	Yr	NM
❏ 9-28551	Why Not Confess/Hangover Blues	1953	$30

MADDOX, JOHNNY
DOT

Number	Title	Yr	NM
❏ 15057	12th Street Rag/Little Girl	1953	$20
❏ 15286	After the Ball/Bye Bye Blues	1955	$15
❏ 186	After the Ball/Bye Bye Blues	1967	$5
—Reissue of 15286			
❏ 15077	Ain't She Sweet/Do You Ever Think of Me	1953	$15
❏ 178	Ain't She Sweet/Do You Ever Think of Me	1967	$5
—Reissue of 15077			
❏ 15730	(All That I'm Asking Is) Sympathy/Don't Get Around Much Anymore	1958	$10
❏ 15069	Angry/Shine	1953	$15
❏ 170	Angry/Shine	1967	$5
—Reissue of 15069			
❏ 16185	Asia Minor/Shell Happy	1961	$8
❏ 15026	At the Georgia Camp Meeting/Elite Syncopations	1952	$20
❏ 15075	Avalon/Tip Toe Through the Tulips	1953	$15
❏ 176	Avalon/Tip Toe Through the Tulips	1967	$5
—Reissue of 15075			
❏ 15072	Baby Face/Moonlight and Roses	1953	$15
❏ 173	Baby Face/Moonlight and Roses	1967	$5
—Reissue of 15072			
❏ 16404	Ballin' the Jack/Ragtime Johnny	1962	$8
❏ 15070	Blue Moon/A Shanty in Old Shanty Town	1953	$15
❏ 171	Blue Moon/A Shanty in Old Shanty Town	1967	$5
—Reissue of 15070			
❏ 15452	Boppin'/Farewell to Thee	1956	$15
❏ 15972	Broken Hearted/Summer Serenade	1959	$10
❏ 15076	Bye Bye Blackbird/The Sheik of Araby	1953	$15
❏ 177	Bye Bye Blackbird/The Sheik of Araby	1967	$5
—Reissue of 15076			
❏ 15281	Camptown Races/I'm Looking Over a Four Leaf Clover	1955	$15
❏ 181	Camptown Races/I'm Looking Over a Four Leaf Clover	1967	$5
—Reissue of 15281			
❏ 16023	Coconut Grove/In the Mood	1960	$8
—Reissue			
❏ 1005	Crazy Bone Rag/St. Louis Tickle	1950	$30
❏ 163	Crazy Bone Rag/St. Louis Tickle	1967	$5
—Reissue of 1005			
❏ 15102	Dipsy Doodle/Alexander's Ragtime Band	1953	$20
❏ 15408	Do It Again/When You Were a Tulip	1955	$20
❏ 15090	Eight Beat Boogie/Learning	1953	$20
❏ 16267	Flip, Flop and Bop/Golden Wildwood Flowers	1961	$8
❏ 16320	Glad Rag Doll/Frenchy	1961	$8
❏ 15289	Glow-Worm/Chicken Reel	1955	$15
❏ 189	Glow-Worm/Chicken Reel	1967	$5
—Reissue of 15289			
❏ 15287	Golden Slippers/Washington and Lee Swing	1955	$15
❏ 187	Golden Slippers/Washington and Lee Swing	1967	$5
—Reissue of 15287			
❏ 15488	Heart and Soul/Dixieland Band	1956	$15
❏ 15074	Hindustan/Carolina in the Morning	1953	$15
❏ 175	Hindustan/Carolina in the Morning	1967	$5
—Reissue of 15074			
❏ 15059	Honey Song/Alice Blue Gown	1953	$20
❏ 15467	Honey/Where the Lazy Daisies Grow	1956	$15
❏ 15432	Hop Scotch Boogie/Hands Off	1955	$20
❏ 1012	Hula Blues/I Get the Blues When It Rains	1950	$30
❏ 164	Hula Blues/I Get the Blues When It Rains	1967	$5
—Reissue of 1012			
❏ 15284	Humoresque/The Stars and Stripes Forever	1955	$15
❏ 184	Humoresque/The Stars and Stripes Forever	1967	$5
—Reissue of 15284			
❏ 15892	Hurdy Gurdy Song/Tempest	1959	$10
❏ 15066	Ida/School Days	1953	$15

Number	Title	Yr	NM
❏ 167	Ida/School Days	1967	$5
—Reissue of 15066			
❏ 15427	I Never Knew/Chicken Reel	1955	$20
❏ 15045	In the Mood/By the Light of the Silvery Moon	1953	$20
❏ 15992	In the Mood/Sweet Georgia Brown	1959	$10
❏ 15120	I Saw Mommy Kissing Santa Claus/Rudolph the Red-Nosed Reindeer	1953	$20
❏ 15270	Lady in Red/Blue Night	1954	$20
❏ 179	Lady in Red/Blue Night	1967	$5
—Reissue of 15270			
❏ 15015	Listen to the Mocking Bird/Molly Darling	1952	$20
❏ 15020	Little Grass Shack/Coconut Grove	1952	$20
❏ 15067	Margie/Swanee River	1953	$15
❏ 168	Margie/Swanee River	1967	$5
—Reissue of 15067			
❏ 15068	Me and My Shadow/Peggy O'Neil	1953	$15
❏ 169	Me and My Shadow/Peggy O'Neil	1967	$5
—Reissue of 15068			
❏ 1023	Memphis Blues/Alabama Jubilee	1951	$30
❏ 165	Memphis Blues/Alabama Jubilee	1967	$5
—Reissue of 1023			
❏ 15280	Oh Lady Be Good/Oh You Beautiful Doll	1955	$15
❏ 180	Oh Lady Be Good/Oh You Beautiful Doll	1967	$5
—Reissue of 15280			
❏ 15226	Pattona Rag/Blue Hawaii	1954	$20
❏ 15169	Peg o' My Heart/Teddy Bear Blues	1954	$20
❏ 15027	Porcupine Rag/Sunflower Slow Drag	1952	$20
❏ 15282	Pretty Baby/Shine On Harvest Moon	1955	$15
❏ 182	Pretty Baby/Shine On Harvest Moon	1967	$5
—Reissue of 15282			
❏ 16214	Sabre Dance/Glow-Worm	1961	$8
❏ 152	San Antonio Rose/Beg Your Pardon	1966	$5
—Reissue			
❏ 15001	San Antonio Rose/Bully of the Town	1951	$20
❏ 15841	San Antonio Rose/Long Gone	1958	$10
❏ 15071	Should I/You Were Meant for Me	1953	$15
❏ 172	Should I/You Were Meant for Me	1967	$5
—Reissue of 15071			
❏ 15288	Sidewalks of New York/Chinatown, My Chinatown	1955	$15
❏ 188	Sidewalks of New York/Chinatown, My Chinatown	1967	$5
—Reissue of 15288			
❏ 15021	Sioux City Sue/Johnny Maddox Special	1952	$20
❏ 15028	Sleepy Sidney/African Pass	1952	$20
❏ 15283	Smiles/Over the Waves	1955	$15
❏ 183	Smiles/Over the Waves	1967	$5
—Reissue of 15283			
❏ 15029	Smokey Mokes/Tickled to Death	1952	$20
❏ 15509	Solitude/Nickelodeon Tango	1956	$15
❏ 15006	Star Dust/Piano Polka	1952	$20
❏ 1057	Sweet Georgia Brown/Dill Pickles	1951	$30
❏ 166	Sweet Georgia Brown/Dill Pickles	1967	$5
—Reissue of 1057			
❏ 15058	Sweet Leilani/Goodbye Girls, I'm Through	1953	$20
❏ 16029	The Crazy Otto (Medley)/Eight Beat Boogie	1960	$8
—Reissue			
❏ 15325	The Crazy Otto (Medley)/Humoresque	1955	$20
❏ 16077	The Maddox Medley (Part 1)/(Part 2)	1960	$8
❏ 15128	There's a Star Spangled Banner Waving Somewhere/I Don't Love Nobody	1954	$20
❏ 15062	Twilight Time/Alice Blue Gown	1953	$20
❏ 15285	Whispering/Dixie-Yankee Doodle	1955	$15
❏ 185	Whispering/Dixie-Yankee Doodle	1967	$5
—Reissue of 15285			
❏ 15014	Why Worry/Friday Night Stomp	1952	$20

MADDOX, ROSE
Also see THE MADDOX BROTHERS AND ROSE.
CAPITOL

Number	Title	Yr	NM
❏ 5110	Alone with You/When the Sun Goes Down	1964	$15
❏ 4432	Billy Cline/Shining Silver, Gleaming Gold	1960	$20
❏ 5186	Blue Bird Let Me Tag Along/Stand Up Fool	1964	$15
❏ 4598	Conscience, I'm Guilty/Lonely Street	1961	$20
❏ F4241	Custer's Last Stand/My Little Baby	1959	$30
❏ 4975	Down to the River/I Don't Hear You	1963	$20
❏ 4709	Fool Me Again/Here We Go Again	1962	$20
❏ F4177	Gambler's Love/What Makes Me Hang Around	1959	$30
❏ 5439	I'll Always Be Loving You/Mad at the World	1965	$15
❏ F4296	I'm Happy Every Day I Live/I Lost Today	1959	$30
❏ 4905	Lonely Teardrops/George Carter	1963	$20
❏ 4347	Please Help Me, I'm Falling/Down, Down, Down	1960	$20
❏ 5263	Silver Threads and Golden Needles/Tia Lisa Lynn	1964	$15
❏ 4845	Sing a Little Song of Heartache/Tie a Ribbon on the Apple Tree	1962	$20
❏ 5038	Somebody Told Somebody/Let Me Kiss You for Old Times	1963	$20
❏ 4771	Take Me Back Again/Let's Pretend We're Strangers	1962	$20
❏ 4651	There Ain't No Love/Your Kind of Lovin' Won't Do	1961	$20

COLUMBIA

Number	Title	Yr	NM
❏ 4-21533	Burrito Jo/False Hearted	1956	$30
❏ 4-21306	Forever Yours/You Won't Believe This	1954	$30
❏ 4-21453	Hasty Baby/When the Sun Goes Down	1955	$30
❏ 4-21490	Hey Little Dreamboat/Tall Men	1956	$30
❏ 4-21419	Hummingbird/Words Are So Easy to Say	1955	$30
❏ 4-21345	I Could Never Stop Loving You/Fountain of Youth	1955	$30
❏ 4-41047	I'll Go Steppin' Too!/Let Those Brown Eyes Smile at me	1957	$30
❏ 4-21155	I'm a Little Red Caboose/These Wasted Years	1953	$30
❏ 4-21333	I Wonder If I Can Lose the Blues/There's No Right Way to Do Me	1954	$30
❏ 4-21062	Little Willie Waltz/The Hiccough Song	1953	$30
❏ 4-40814	Looky There, Over There/Your Sweet, Mean Heart	1957	$30
❏ 4-40948	Old Man Blues/Tomorrow Land	1957	$30
❏ 4-21253	Poor Little Heartbroken Rose/Marry Me Again	1954	$30
❏ 4-40873	Take a Gamble on Me/1-2-3 Anyplace Road	1957	$30
❏ 4-21016	Take These Shackles/Cocquita of Laredo	1952	$30
❏ 4-21215	The Birthday Card Song/Waltz of the Pines	1954	$30
❏ 4-21559	The Death of Rock and Roll/Paul Bunyon Love	1956	$40
❏ 4-21394	Wild Wild Young Men/Second Chance	1955	$30

STARDAY

Number	Title	Yr	NM
❏ 895	The Bigger the Pride/Faded Love	1970	$8
❏ 921	Two of Us/Get It Over	1971	$8

UNI

Number	Title	Yr	NM
❏ 55040	Bottom of the Glass/Step Right In	1967	$10

MADHATTANS, THE
ATLANTIC

Number	Title	Yr	NM
❏ 1142	Wowie/A Basketful of Blueberries	1957	$30

MADISONS, THE
LAWN

Number	Title	Yr	NM
❏ 240	Can You Imagine It/The Wind and the Rain	1964	$50

LIMELIGHT

Number	Title	Yr	NM
❏ 3018	Bad Baboon/Because I Got You	1964	$30

MGM

Number	Title	Yr	NM
❏ 13312	Cheryl Anne/Looking for True Love	1965	$50

Number	Title	Yr	NM

MADNESS
GEFFEN

Number	Title	Yr	NM
❏ 29562	It Must Be Love/ Calling Cards	1983	$3
❏ 29562 [PS]	It Must Be Love/ Calling Cards	1983	$3
❏ 29668	Our House/Cardiac Arrest	1983	$3
❏ 29668 [PS]	Our House/Cardiac Arrest	1983	$3
❏ 29350	The Sun and the Rain/ Time for Tea	1984	$3
❏ 29350 [PS]	The Sun and the Rain/ Time for Tea	1984	$3

SIRE

Number	Title	Yr	NM
❏ 49205	Madness/Mistakes	1980	$5
❏ 0204	One Step Beyond/Mistakes	1979	$10

—Canada-only single

MADONNA
GEFFEN

Number	Title	Yr	NM
❏ 29051	Crazy for You/No More Words	1985	$3

—B-side by Berlin

Number	Title	Yr	NM
❏ 29051 [PS]	Crazy for You/No More Words	1985	$3

SIRE

Number	Title	Yr	NM
❏ 29008	Angel/(12" Remix Edit)	1985	$3
❏ 29008 [PS]	Angel/(12" Remix Edit)	1985	$3
❏ 29354	Borderline/Think of Me	1984	$4
❏ 29354 [PS]	Borderline/Think of Me	1984	$100

—Fold-out poster sleeve

Number	Title	Yr	NM
❏ 28224	Causing a Commotion/ Jimmy, Jimmy	1987	$3
❏ 28224 [PS]	Causing a Commotion/ Jimmy, Jimmy	1987	$3
❏ 22883	Cherish/Supernatural	1989	$3
❏ 22883 [PS]	Cherish/Supernatural	1989	$3
❏ 28919	Dress You Up/Shoo-Be-Doo	1985	$3
❏ 28919 [PS]	Dress You Up/Shoo-Be-Doo	1985	$60
❏ 29841	Everybody/(Instrumental)	1982	$30
❏ 22948	Express Yourself/ The Look of Love	1989	$3
❏ 22948 [PS]	Express Yourself/ The Look of Love	1989	$3
❏ 29478	Holiday/I Know It	1983	$4
❏ 29478 [PS]	Holiday/(Instrumental)	1983	$4
❏ 28425	La Isla Bonita/(Instrumental)	1987	$3
❏ 28425 [PS]	La Isla Bonita/(Instrumental)	1987	$3
❏ 27539 [DJ]	Like a Prayer (7" Remix Edit)/(7" Version with Fade)	1989	$12
❏ 27539	Like a Prayer/Act of Contrition	1989	$3
❏ 27539 [PS]	Like a Prayer/Act of Contrition	1989	$3
❏ 29210	Like a Virgin/Stay	1984	$3
❏ 29210 [PS]	Like a Virgin/Stay	1984	$3
❏ 28717	Live to Tell/(Instrumental)	1986	$3
❏ 28717 [PS]	Live to Tell/(Instrumental)	1986	$3
❏ 29177	Lucky Star/I Know It	1984	$4
❏ 29083	Material Girl/Pretender	1985	$3
❏ 29083 [PS]	Material Girl/Pretender	1985	$3
❏ 22723	Oh Father/Pray for Spanish Eyes	1989	$3
❏ 28508	Open Your Heart/White Heat	1986	$3
❏ 28508 [PS]	Open Your Heart/White Heat	1986	$3
❏ 28660	Papa Don't Preach/ Pretender	1986	$3
❏ 28660 [PS]	Papa Don't Preach/ Pretender	1986	$3
❏ PRO-S-2023 [DJ]	Physical Attraction (same on both sides)	1983	$60
❏ 28591	True Blue/Ain't No Big Deal	1986	$5

—Blue vinyl

Number	Title	Yr	NM
❏ 28591 [PS]	True Blue/Ain't No Big Deal	1986	$5

—Limited edition blue vinyl pressing" on sleeve

Number	Title	Yr	NM
❏ 28591	True Blue/Ain't No Big Deal	1986	$3
❏ 28591 [PS]	True Blue/Ain't No Big Deal	1986	$3

—No mention of limited edition on sleeve

Number	Title	Yr	NM
❏ 28341	Who's That Girl?/White Heat	1987	$3
❏ 28341 [PS]	Who's That Girl?/White Heat	1987	$3

MAESTRO, JOHNNY
Also see THE BROOKLYN BRIDGE; THE CRESTS.

APT

Number	Title	Yr	NM
❏ 25075	Phone Booth on the Highway/She's All Mine Alone	1965	$200

BUDDAH

Number	Title	Yr	NM
❏ 289 [DJ]	Snow (mono/stereo)	1971	$12

—May be promo only

CAMEO

Number	Title	Yr	NM
❏ 305	Lean on Me/(It's Harder to) Make Up My Mind	1964	$30
❏ 256	Over the Weekend/I'll Be There	1963	$40

COED

Number	Title	Yr	NM
❏ 562	Besame Baby/ It Must Be Love	1962	$125
❏ 557	I.O.U./The Way You Look Tonight	1961	$40

Number	Title	Yr	NM
❏ 545	Model Girl/We've Got to Tell Them	1961	$30

—As "Johnny Mastro

Number	Title	Yr	NM
❏ 552	Mr. Happiness/Test of Love	1961	$30
❏ 527	Say It Isn't So/The Great Physician	1960	$30

—As "Johnny Masters

Number	Title	Yr	NM
❏ 549	What a Surprise/ Warning Voice	1961	$30

PARKWAY

Number	Title	Yr	NM
❏ 987 [DJ]	Heartburn	1966	$70

—One-sided white label promo

Number	Title	Yr	NM
❏ 987	Heartburn/Try Me	1966	$20
❏ 999	I Care About You/Come See Me (I'm Your Man)	1966	$20
❏ 118	My Times/Is It You	1966	$30

UNITED ARTISTS

Number	Title	Yr	NM
❏ 474	Before I Loved Her/Fifty Million Heartbeats	1962	$50

MAGGOTS, THE
7-Inch Extended Plays
WIGGLETEENS

Number	Title	Yr	NM
❏ 37689	Tammy Wynette/2-2-79/ Rough Dub	1980	$35
❏ 37689 [PS]	Tammy Wynette/2-2-79/ Rough Dub	1980	$35

MAGIC FERN, THE
JERDEN

Number	Title	Yr	NM
❏ 813	Maggie/I Wonder Why	1966	$30

MAGIC LANTERNS
ATLANTIC

Number	Title	Yr	NM
❏ 2600	Give Me Love/ Biding My Time	1969	$8
❏ 2626	Melt All Your Troubles Away/Bossa Nova 1940-Hello You Lovers	1969	$8
❏ 2715	One Night Stand/ Frisco Annie	1970	$8
❏ 2560	Shame, Shame, Baby, I Gotta Go Now	1968	$10

BIG TREE

Number	Title	Yr	NM
❏ 113	Let the Sunshine In/ Old Pa Bradley	1971	$6
❏ 109	One Night Stand/ Frisco Annie	1970	$6

CHARISMA

Number	Title	Yr	NM
❏ 100	Country Woman/Pa Bradley	1972	$5

EPIC

Number	Title	Yr	NM
❏ 10062	Excuse Me Baby/ Greedy Girl	1966	$8
❏ 10062 [PS]	Excuse Me Baby/ Greedy Girl	1966	$30

MAGIC MUSHROOM, THE
WARNER BROS.

Number	Title	Yr	NM
❏ 5846	I'm Gone/Cry Baby	1966	$30

MAGIC MUSHROOMS, THE
A&M

Number	Title	Yr	NM
❏ 815	It's a-Happening/Never More	1966	$20

PHILIPS

Number	Title	Yr	NM
❏ 40483	Look in My Face/ Never Let Go	1968	$20

MAGIC REIGN, THE
JAMIE

Number	Title	Yr	NM
❏ 1364	Pop Goes the Weasel/Mirrors	1968	$40

MAGNETS, THE (1)
GROOVE

Number	Title	Yr	NM
❏ 58-0058	Surprise/You Just Say the Word	1965	$70

MAGNETS, THE (2)
LONDON INT'L.

Number	Title	Yr	NM
❏ 10036	Drag Race/Joker	1963	$30

MAGNETS, THE (3)
RCA VICTOR

Number	Title	Yr	NM
❏ 47-7391	When the School Bells Ring/ Don't Tarry, Little Mary	1958	$30

MAGNIFICENT FOUR, THE
BLAST

Number	Title	Yr	NM
❏ 210	The Closer You Are/ Uncle Sam	1963	$50

WHALE

Number	Title	Yr	NM
❏ 506	The Closer You Are/ Uncle Sam	1961	$100

MAGNIFICENT 7, THE
DIAL

Number	Title	Yr	NM
❏ 4074	Ooh, Baby Baby/Never Will I (Make My Baby Cry)	1968	$60

DIMENSION

Number	Title	Yr	NM
❏ 1050	Show Me/Boogidy	1965	$30

—As "Magnificent VII

EASTERN

Number	Title	Yr	NM
❏ 611	She's Called a Woman/ Since You've Been Gone So Long	1966	$200

MAGNIFICENTS, THE
CHECKER

Number	Title	Yr	NM
❏ 1016	The Dribble Twist/ Do You Mind	1962	$20

KANSOMA

Number	Title	Yr	NM
❏ 03	The Dribble Twist/ Do You Mind	1962	$40

VEE JAY

Number	Title	Yr	NM
❏ 281	Don't Leave Me/Ozeta	1958	$125
❏ 208	Hiccup/Caddy Bo	1956	$125
❏ 235	Off the Mountain/Lost Lovers	1957	$80

MAHAL, TAJ
COLUMBIA

Number	Title	Yr	NM
❏ 45455	Ain't Gwine to Whistle Dixie Anymore (Part 1/Part 2)	1971	$5
❏ 10368	Ain't Nobody's Business/ Easy to Love	1976	$4
❏ 45990	Buck Dancer's Choice/ Little Red Hen	1974	$5
❏ 46031	Built for Comfort/Teacup's Jazzy Blues Tune	1974	$5
❏ 45539	Chevrolet/Oh Susanna	1972	$5
❏ 44767	Corinna/A Lot of Love	1969	$8
❏ 44405	E-Z Rider/Leaving Trunk	1967	$8
❏ 45419	Fishin' Blues/Diving Duck Blues	1971	$5
❏ 44051	Let the Good Times Roll/ Shimmy Like My Sister Kate	1967	$8
❏ 10109	Salve Drive/Cajun Waltz	1975	$4
❏ 44991	Six Days on the Road/ Light Rain Blues	1969	$8
❏ 44476	Statesboro Blues/ Everybody's Got to Change Sometime	1968	$8
❏ 10260	Why, And We Repeat Why, And We Repeat…/ (B-side unknown)	1975	$4
❏ 10055	Why Did You Have to Desert Me/Cajun Waltz	1974	$4

WARNER BROS.

Number	Title	Yr	NM
❏ 8528	Sing a Happy Song/ Southbound with the Hammer Down	1978	$4

MAHARIS, GEORGE
EPIC

Number	Title	Yr	NM
❏ 9555	Baby Has Gone Bye Bye/After One Kiss	1962	$8
❏ 9555 [PS]	Baby Has Gone Bye Bye/After One Kiss	1962	$12
❏ 9569	Don't Fence Me In/ Alright, Okay, You Win	1963	$8
❏ 9569 [PS]	Don't Fence Me In/ Alright, Okay, You Win	1963	$12
❏ 9753	I'm Coming Back for You/Lonely People Do Foolish Things	1965	$6
❏ 9653	It's a Sin to Tell a Lie/ Sara Darling	1964	$6
❏ 9858	Ivy/A World Without Sunshine	1965	$6
❏ 9522	Love Me as I Love You/ They Knew About You	1962	$8
❏ 9522 [PS]	Love Me as I Love You/ They Knew About You	1962	$10
❏ 9772	More I Cannot Do/Where Does Happiness Go	1965	$6
❏ 9504	Teach Me Tonight/After the Lights Go Down Low	1962	$8
❏ 9504 [PS]	Teach Me Tonight/After the Lights Go Down Low	1962	$10
❏ 9613	That's How It Goes/ It Isn't There	1963	$8
❏ 9613 [PS]	That's How It Goes/ It Isn't There	1963	$12
❏ 9696	The Object of My Affection/ Tonight You Belong to Me	1964	$6
❏ 9696 [PS]	The Object of My Affection/ Tonight You Belong to Me	1964	$15
❏ 9600	Where Can You Go (For a Broken Heart)/Kiss Me	1963	$8
❏ 9600 [PS]	Where Can You Go (For a Broken Heart)/Kiss Me	1963	$10

MAHOGANY RUSH
Featuring Frank Marino.

20TH CENTURY

Number	Title	Yr	NM
❏ 2166	Buddy/Satisfy Your Soul	1975	$5

NINE

Number	Title	Yr	NM
❏ 369	Buddy/All in Your Mind	1973	$8

Number	Title	Yr	NM

MAIDS, THE
ANEMIC
❏ 1	Back to Bataan/I Do I Do	1979	$70
❏ 1 [PS]	Back to Bataan/I Do I Do	1979	$70

MAINER, WADE
KING
❏ 1035	Dreaming of a Little Cabin/ That Star Belongs to Me	1952	$40
❏ 975	He's Passing This Way/ God's Radio Phone	1951	$50
❏ 1093	Little Birdie/The Girl I Left in Sunny Tennessee	1952	$40
❏ 5514	My Soldier Boy/I'm a Free Little Bird	1961	$15
❏ 5499	On the Banks of the Ohio/ My Home Is Down in Dixie	1961	$15
❏ 1074	Standing Outside/I'm Not Looking Backward	1952	$40
❏ 955	Those Blue Eyes I Love/Little Book	1951	$50

MAJESTICS, THE (1)
CHESS
❏ 1802	Oasis (Part 1)/Oasis (Part 2)	1961	$30

V.I.P.
❏ 25028 [DJ]	Say You/All for Someone	1965	$600

—*Promo only; stock copies credited "The Monitors*

MAJESTICS, THE (2)
CHEX
❏ 1009	Baby/Teach Me How to Limbo	1963	$30
❏ 1000	Give Me a Cigarette/ Shoppin' and Hoppin'	1962	$125
❏ 1000	Give Me a Cigarette/ So I Can Forget	1962	$50
❏ 1006	Lonely Heart/Gwendolyn	1962	$40

MAJESTICS, THE (3)
20TH FOX
❏ 171	The Lone Stranger/ Sweet One	1959	$30

CONTOUR
❏ 501	Teen Age Gossip/ Hard Times	1960	$100

FARO
❏ 592	TV Cowboys/So You Want to Rock	1959	$30

FOXIE
❏ 7004	The Lone Stranger/ Sweet One	1960	$30

NRC
❏ 502	Please Don't Say No/ Divided Heart	1958	$250

SIOUX
❏ 91459	The Lone Stranger/ Sweet One	1959	$60

MAJESTICS, THE (4)
DUNES
❏ 2014	The Boss Walk (Part 1)/ The Boss Walk (Part 2)	1962	$50

MAJESTICS, THE (5)
JORDAN
❏ 1057	Angel of Love/Searching for a New Love	1961	$300

—*Yellow vinyl*
❏ 1057	Angel of Love/Searching for a New Love	1961	$60

—*Black vinyl*

LINDA
❏ 121	Girl of My Dreams/ It Hurts Me	1963	$600

—*Yellow label*
❏ 121	Girl of My Dreams/ It Hurts Me	1963	$750

—*Violet label*
❏ 111	Strange World/Everything Is Gonna Be All Right	1963	$80

NU-TONE
❏ 123	Angel of Love/Searching for a New Love	1961	$75

PIXIE
❏ 6901	Angel of Love/Searching for a New Love	1961	$40

MAJESTICS, THE (7)
MGM
❏ 13488	Love Has Forgotten Me/ Smile Through My Tears	1966	$15

MAJORETTES, THE
TROY
❏ 1000	White Levi's/Please Come Back	1963	$30
❏ 1000 [PS]	White Levi's/Please Come Back	1963	$50

MAJORS, THE (1)
IMPERIAL
❏ 5855	A Wonderful Dream/ Time Will Tell	1962	$30
❏ 66009	I'll Be There/Ooh Wee Baby	1963	$15
❏ 5968	One Happy Ending/ Get Up Now	1963	$15
❏ 5879	She's a Troublemaker/A Little Bit Now, A Little Bit Later	1962	$40
❏ 5936	Tra La La/What Have You Been Doin'	1963	$15
❏ 5914	What in the World/ Anything You Can Do	1963	$50
❏ 5991	Which Way Did She Go/ Your Life Begins (Sweet 16)	1963	$15

UNITED ARTISTS
❏ 0110	A Wonderful Dream/ Mother-in-Law	1973	$5

—*Silver Spotlight Series" reissue; B-side by Ernie K-Doe*

MAJORS, THE (2)
DERBY
❏ 763	At Last/You Ran Away from My Heart	1951	$800
❏ 779	Laughing on the Outside/ Come On Up to My Room	1951	$600

MAJORS, THE (3)
FELSTED
❏ 8501	Blue Sunset/Rockin' the Boogie	1958	$40
❏ 8576	Come Go with Me/Les Qua	1959	$30
❏ 8707	Come Go with Me/Les Qua	1964	$20

MAJORS, THE (4)
ORIGINAL
❏ 1003	Big Eyes/Go 'Way	1954	$400

MAKEBA, MIRIAM
KAPP
❏ 452	Carnival/Can't Cross Over	1962	$15

LONDON
❏ 1610	Lovely Lies/Kilimanjaro	1956	$20

—*With the Manhattan Brothers*

MERCURY
❏ 72642	Ballad of the Sad Young Men/Mommy, Mommy, What Is Heaven Like	1966	$8

RCA VICTOR
❏ 47-8326	Dubula/Forbidden Games	1964	$12

REPRISE
❏ 0755	Ibabalazie/Emavungivini (Down in the Dumps)	1968	$6
❏ 0804	I Shall Be Released/ Iphi Ndilela	1969	$6
❏ 0921	I Shall Sing/In My Life	1970	$6
❏ 0654	Malaysha/Ring Bell, Ring Bell	1967	$8
❏ 0606	Pata Pata/Ballad of the Sad Young Men	1967	$8
❏ 0732	Pata Pata/Malaysha	1969	$4

—*Back to Back Hits" series*
❏ 0671	What Is Love/Ho Po Zamani	1968	$6

MALLETT, SAUNDRA, AND THE VANDELLAS
TAMLA
❏ 54067	Camel Walk/It's Gonna Be Hard Times	1962	$1000

MALLIE ANN AND SLIM
COLUMBIA
❏ 4-21223	I Can Hear Harbor Bells/ Undo Latch Strings	1954	$30
❏ 4-21396	If You Know Where You're Going/I Want to Know More About Jesus	1955	$30
❏ 4-21342	I'll Bear the Shame/There's No Tomorrow for Me	1955	$30
❏ 4-21456	Light Up the Old Flame/I'll Always Love You	1955	$30
❏ 4-21332	Love of Jesus/ Better Than Gold	1954	$30
❏ 4-21273	Love You/Hillbilly Rhumba	1954	$30

MALTAIS, GENE
DECCA
❏ 30387	Crazy Baby/Deep River Blues	1957	$200

REGAL
❏ 7502	Lovemakin'/The Bug	1958	$200

MAMAS AND THE PAPAS, THE
ABC DUNHILL
❏ 4171	Do You Wanna Dance/My Girl	1968	$8
❏ 4150	For the Love of Ivy/ Strange Young Girls	1968	$8
❏ 4125	Safe in My Garden/Too Late	1968	$8
❏ 4301	Step Out/Shooting Star	1972	$6

DUNHILL
❏ 4020	California Dreamin'/ Somebody Groovy	1966	$10

—*Most of the 1966 Dunhill singles credited "The Mama's and the Papa's*
❏ 4020 [PS]	California Dreamin'/ Somebody Groovy	1966	$300

—*Sleeve is promo only*
❏ 4083	Creeque Alley/Did You Ever Want to Cry	1967	$12
❏ 4083 [PS]	Creeque Alley/Did You Ever Want to Cry	1967	$50

—*Sleeve is promo only*
❏ 4113	Dancing Bear/ John's Music Box	1967	$12
❏ 4113 [PS]	Dancing Bear/ John's Music Box	1967	$15
❏ 4077	Dedicated to the One I Love/Free Advice	1967	$12
❏ 4107	Glad to Be Unhappy/ Hey Girl	1967	$10
❏ 4018 [DJ]	Go Where You Wanna Go/Somebody Groovy	1966	$30

—*Withdrawn before stock copies were released*
❏ 4018 [PS]	Go Where You Wanna Go/Somebody Groovy	1966	$400

—*Yes, a picture sleeve has been confirmed!*
❏ 4031	I Saw Her Again/ Even If I Could	1966	$10
❏ 4050	Look Through My Window/ Once Was a Time I Thought	1966	$10
❏ 4026	Monday, Monday/ Got a Feeling	1966	$10
❏ 4026 [PS]	Monday, Monday/I Call Your Name	1966	$600

—*The sleeve was printed, but after Dunhill changed the flip side of the 45 before release, most of them were destroyed*
❏ 4125	Safe in My Garden/Too Late	1968	$30

—*Without the "ABC" logo at top of label*
❏ 4099	Twelve Thirty (Young Girls Are Coming to the Canyon)/Straight Shooter	1967	$10
❏ 4057	Words of Love/Dancing in the Street	1966	$10

7-Inch Extended Plays
ABC DUNHILL
❏ PRO-50106 [PS]	People Like Us	1972	$35
❏ PRO-50106	People Like Us/I Wanna Be a Star/Pearl//Pacific Coast Highway/Snowqueen of Texas/Step Out	1972	$25

—*Jukebox issue; small hole, plays at 33 1/3 rpm*
❏ LP-DS-50031	Safe in My Garden/For the Love of Ivy//Mansions/ Dream a Little Dream of Me	1968	$20

—*Jukebox issue; small hole, plays at 33 1/3 rpm*
❏ LP-DS-50031 [PS]	The Papas and the Mamas	1968	$20

DUNHILL
❏ LP DS-50006 [PS]	If You Can Believe Your Eyes and Ears	1966	$30
❏ LP DS-50006	Monday, Monday/I Call Your Name/Go Where You Wanna Go/California Dreamin'/You Baby/In Crowd	1966	$30

—*Jukebox issue; small hole, plays at 33 1/3 rpm*
❏ EP-DS-50010 [PS]	The Mamas and the Papas	1966	$25

MANCHA, STEVE
GROOVESVILLE
❏ 1005	Don't Make Me a Storyteller/I Won't Love and Leave You	1967	$70
❏ 1004	Friday Night/Monday Through Thursday	1966	$500
❏ 1002	I Don't Want to Lose You/ Need to Be Needed	1966	$50

WHEELSVILLE
❏ 102	Did My Baby Call/Whirlpool	1965	$1000

MANCHESTER, MELISSA

ARISTA

Number	Title	Yr	NM
❏ 0183	Better Days/Sing, Sing, Sing	1976	$4
❏ 1028	Come In from the Rain/Hey Ricky (You're a Low Down Heel)	1982	$4
❏ 0237	Dirty Work/Be Somebody	1977	$4
❏ 0373	Don't Cry Out Loud/We Had This Time	1978	$4

— Originals have black labels

❏ 0373	Don't Cry Out Loud/We Had This Time	1979	$3

— Second pressings have whitish labels

❏ 0485	Fire in the Morning/Lights of Dawn	1980	$4
❏ 0196	Happy Endings/Rescue Me	1976	$4
❏ 9162	I Don't Care What the People Say/Emergency	1984	$3
❏ 0551	If This Is Love/Talk	1980	$4
❏ 0267	I Wanna Be Where You Are/No One's Ever Seen This Side of Me	1977	$4
❏ 0587	Lovers After All/Happier Than I've Ever Been	1981	$4

— With Peabo Bryson

❏ 0116	Midnight Blue/I Got Eyes	1975	$4
❏ 0218	Monkey See, Monkey Do/So's My Old Man	1976	$4
❏ 1057	My Boyfriend's Back/Looking for the Perfect Aah	1983	$4
❏ 9014	My Boyfriend's Back/Looking for the Perfect Aah	1983	$3
❏ 0456	Pretty Girls/It's All in the Sky Above	1979	$4
❏ 0405	Theme from "Ice Castles"/Such a Night	1979	$4
❏ 0579	Without You/Boys in the Back Room	1980	$4

BELL

❏ 45465	Heaven/Inclined	1974	$5

CASABLANCA

❏ 880308-7	Thief of Hearts/(B-side unknown)	1984	$3

MB

❏ 1005	Beautiful People/A Song for You	1967	$20

MCA

❏ 52616	Energy/So Full of Yourself	1985	$3
❏ 52616 [PS]	Energy/So Full of Yourself	1985	$3
❏ 52575	Mathematics/So Full of Yourself	1985	$3
❏ 52575 [PS]	Mathematics/So Full of Yourself	1985	$3
❏ 52784	Music of Goodbye (Love Theme from Out of Africa)/Have You Got a Story for Me	1986	$3

— With Al Jarreau

❏ 52784 [PS]	Music of Goodbye (Love Theme from Out of Africa)/Have You Got a Story for Me	1986	$3

— With Al Jarreau

RCA VICTOR

❏ 74-0366	Tellin' the World/(B-side unknown)	1970	$15

— With Grover Kimball

MANCHESTERS, THE (2)

VEE JAY

❏ 700	I Don't Come from England/Dragonfly	1965	$30

MANCINI, HENRY

AVCO EMBASSY

❏ 4531	Love Theme from Sunflower/Giovanna	1970	$5

CORAL

❏ 61990	Love Theme from "The Brothers Karamazov"/Tana's Theme	1958	$15
❏ 61974	The Long Hot Summer/Paris Holiday	1958	$15

LIBERTY

❏ 55060	Hot Rod/Big Band Rock and Roll	1957	$15
❏ 55045	(Main Theme from) Four Girls in Town/Cha Cha Cha for Gia	1956	$15
❏ 55184	Pow/Cha Cha Cha for Gia	1959	$12
❏ 1489	Trail of the Pink Panther (Soundtrack)/The Inspector Clouseau Theme (Soundtrack)	1983	$4

RCA

❏ PB-11423	Theme from Battlestar Galactica/NBC Nightly News Theme	1978	$5
❏ PB-10888	Theme from "Charlie's Angels"/Bumper's Theme	1977	$5
❏ PB-11142	The Money Changers/Just You and Me Together, Love	1977	$5
❏ PB-11054	What's Happening Theme/Silver Streak	1977	$5

RCA VICTOR

Number	Title	Yr	NM
❏ 47-9654	A Man, a Horse, and a Gun/Las Cruces	1968	$6
❏ 47-8856	Arabesque/We've Loved Before	1966	$6
❏ 47-8381	A Shot in the Dark/The Shadows of Paris	1964	$8
❏ 47-8381 [PS]	A Shot in the Dark/The Shadows of Paris	1964	$15
❏ 47-8184	Banzai Pipeline/Rhapsody in Blue	1963	$30
❏ 47-8184 [PS]	Banzai Pipeline/Rhapsody in Blue	1963	$30
❏ 47-7785	Big Noise from Winnetka/The Blues	1960	$15
❏ 47-7785 [PS]	Big Noise from Winnetka/The Blues	1960	$20
❏ 47-7682	Bijou/Let's Walk	1960	$15
❏ 47-8256	Charade/Orange Tamoure	1963	$8
❏ 47-8256 [PS]	Charade/Orange Tamoure	1963	$20
❏ 47-8120	Days of Wine and Roses/Seventy Six Trombones	1962	$8
❏ 47-8120 [PS]	Days of Wine and Roses/Seventy Six Trombones	1962	$20
❏ 47-8458	Dear Heart/How Soon	1964	$8
❏ 47-8458 [PS]	Dear Heart/How Soon	1964	$15
❏ 47-8008	Experiment in Terror/Tooty Tooty	1962	$8
❏ 47-8008 [PS]	Experiment in Terror/Tooty Tooty	1962	$20
❏ 47-7442	Fallout/Dreamsville	1959	$15
❏ 47-7902	Fanny/My Cousin from Naples	1961	$10
❏ APBO-0323	Hangin' Out/Send a Little Love My Way	1974	$5
❏ 47-8951	Hawaii/Driftwood and Dreams	1966	$6
❏ 47-8951 [PS]	Hawaii/Driftwood and Dreams	1966	$15
❏ 47-8691	He Shouldn't-A, Hadn't-A, Oughtn't-A Swang on Me/Push the Button, Man	1965	$8
❏ 47-7791	High Time/The Second Time Around	1960	$15
❏ 47-8798	House of the Rising Sun/Turtles	1966	$6
❏ 47-8099	Love Theme from Phaedra/Dreamsville	1962	$8
❏ 47-8099 [PS]	Love Theme from Phaedra/Dreamsville	1962	$20
❏ 74-0131	Love Theme from Romeo and Juliet/The Windmills of Your Mind	1969	$10
❏ 47-9857	Love Theme from Sunflower/Darling Lili	1970	$5
❏ APBO-0117	Ludmila's Theme/Pretty Girls	1973	$5
❏ 74-0297	Midnight Cowboy/There's Enough to Go Around	1969	$6
❏ 47-8718	Moment to Moment/Soldier in the Rain	1965	$8
❏ 74-0212	Moonlight Sonata/Natalie	1969	$6
❏ 47-7916	Moon River/Breakfast at Tiffany's	1961	$8
❏ 47-7916 [PS]	Moon River/Breakfast at Tiffany's	1961	$20
❏ 47-7705	Mr. Lucky/Floating Pad	1960	$15
❏ 74-0575	Mystery Movie Theme/Theme from "Cade's Country"	1971	$5
❏ 74-0974	Oklahoma Crude/Amazing Grace	1973	$5
❏ APBO-0249	Olympic Village/Dolce	1974	$5
❏ PB-10355	Once Is Not Enough/The Greatest Gift	1975	$5
❏ 47-7460	Peter Gunn/The Brothers Go to Mother's	1959	$15
❏ 47-8624	Pie in the Face Polka/Sweetheart Tree	1965	$8
❏ 47-8624 [PS]	Pie in the Face Polka/Sweetheart Tree	1965	$15
❏ PB-10463	Satin Soul/African Symphony	1975	$5
❏ 47-8574	Senor Peter Gunn/La Raspa	1965	$8
❏ PB-10060	Sex Symbol/Theme from "White Dawn	1974	$5
❏ PB-10731	Slow Hot Wind/Symphonic Soul	1976	$5
❏ 47-7512	Spook!/Timothy	1959	$15
❏ PB-10288	The Greatest Gift/The Pink Penther Theme	1975	$5
❏ 47-9585	The Magnificent Seven/Springtime for Hitler	1968	$8
❏ 47-8037	Theme from "Hatari!"/Your Father's Feathers	1962	$8
❏ 47-8037 [PS]	Theme from "Hatari!"/Your Father's Feathers	1962	$20
❏ 47-9927	Theme from Love Story/Phone Call to the Past	1970	$5
❏ 47-7830	Theme from The Great Impostor/Love Music	1961	$10
❏ 47-7830 [PS]	Theme from The Great Impostor/Love Music	1961	$20
❏ 74-0756	Theme from The Mancini Generation/Bluish Bag	1972	$5
❏ 74-0315	Theme from "The Molly Maguires"/Theme from "Z	1970	$5
❏ 74-0454	Theme from "The Night Visitor"/Whistling Away the Dark	1971	$5
❏ 74-0890	Theme from "The Thief Who Came to Dinner"/Charade	1973	$5
❏ 74-0890 [PS]	Theme from "The Thief Who Came to Dinner"/Charade	1973	$8
❏ 47-9483	The Party/Party Poop	1968	$6
❏ 47-9483 [PS]	The Party/Party Poop	1968	$10
❏ 47-8286	The Pink Panther Theme/It Had Better Be Tonight	1963	$8
❏ 47-8286 [PS]	The Pink Panther Theme/It Had Better Be Tonight	1963	$20
❏ 47-8857	The Swing March/In the Arms of Love	1966	$6
❏ 47-8857 [PS]	The Swing March/In the Arms of Love	1966	$15
❏ 47-9200	Two for the Road/Happy Barefoot Boy	1967	$6
❏ 47-9200 [PS]	Two for the Road/Happy Barefoot Boy	1967	$10
❏ 47-9340	Wait Until Dark/Theme for Three	1967	$6
❏ 47-9340 [PS]	Wait Until Dark/Theme for Three	1967	$10

UNITED ARTISTS

❏ XW1237	Pink Panther Theme '78/Touch of Red	1978	$4

WARNER BROS.

❏ 5019	The Star Spangled Banner/The Stars and Stripes Forever	1959	$10
❏ 29697	The Thorn Birds Theme/Luke and Meggie	1983	$4
❏ 29697 [PS]	The Thorn Birds Theme/Luke and Meggie	1983	$6

7-Inch Extended Plays

RCA VICTOR

❏ EPA-4339 [M]	*Walkin' Bass/Spook!/The Little Man Theme/Goofin' at the Coffee House	1959	$15
❏ ESP-4339 [S]	*Walkin' Bass/Spook!/The Little Man Theme/Goofin' at the Coffee House (contents unknown)	1959	$20
❏ LPC-104		1961	$10

— Compact 33 Double"; small hole, plays at 33 1/3 rpm

❏ LPC-104 [PS]	Henry Mancini Showcase	1961	$12
❏ EPA-4339 [PS]	More Music from Peter Gunn	1959	$15
❏ ESP-4339 [PS]	More Music from Peter Gunn	1959	$20
❏ LPC-130 [PS]	Mr. Lucky Goes Latin	1961	$12
❏ LPC-130	Mr. Lucky (Goes Latin)/Lu Jon//No-Cal Sugar Loaf/Siesta	1961	$12

— Compact 33 Double"; small hole, plays at 33 1/3 rpm

❏ EPA-4363	Mr. Lucky/My Friend Andamo/Lightly Latin/Tipsy	1960	$15
❏ EPA-4363 [PS]	Music from Mr. Lucky	1960	$15
❏ EPA-4333 [M]	Peter Gunn/A Profound Gass//Fallout!/Sorta Blue	1959	$15
❏ ESP-4333 [S]	Peter Gunn/A Profound Gass//Fallout!/Sorta Blue	1959	$25
❏ EPA-4333 [PS]	The Music from Peter Gunn	1959	$15
❏ ESP-4333 [PS]	The Music from Peter Gunn	1959	$25

MANDRELL, BARBARA

ABC

❏ 12451	(If Loving You Is Wrong) I Don't Want to Be Right/I Feel the Hurt Coming On	1979	$5
❏ 12403	Sleeping Single in a Double Bed/Just One More of Your Goodbyes	1978	$4
❏ 12362	Tonight/If I Were a River	1978	$4

ABC DOT

❏ 17623	Beginning of the End/That's What Friends Are For	1976	$4
❏ 17716	Hold Me/This Is Not Another Cheatin' Song	1977	$4
❏ 17644	Love Is Thin Ice/Will We Ever Make Love In Love Again	1976	$4
❏ 17688	Married But Not to Each Other/Fools Gold	1977	$4
❏ 17668	Midnight Angel/I Count on You	1976	$4
❏ 17601	Standing Room Only/Can't Help But Wonder	1975	$4
❏ 17736	Woman to Woman/Let the Rain Out	1977	$4

CAPITOL

❏ B-44220	I Wish That I Could Fall in Love Today/I'll Be Your Jukebox Tonight	1988	$3
❏ B-44383	Mirror Mirror/Blanket of Love	1989	$3
❏ B-44276	My Train of Thought/Blanket of Love	1989	$3

COLUMBIA

❏ 45307	Do Right Woman -- Do Right Man/The Letter	1971	$5
❏ 45819	Give a Little, Take a Little/Ain't It Good	1973	$5
❏ 45702	Holdin' On (To the Love I Got)/Smile, Somebody Loves You	1972	$5
❏ 44955	I've Been Loving You Too Long (To Stop Now)/Baby Come Home	1969	$6
❏ 45143	Playin' Around with Love/I Almost Lost My Mind	1970	$5
❏ 45580	Show Me/Satisfied	1972	$5
❏ 45904	The Midnight Oil/In the Name of Love	1973	$5
❏ 46054	This Time I Almost Made It/Son-of-a-Gun	1974	$5

Number	Title	Yr	NM
❑ 45505	Tonight My Baby's Coming Home/He'll Never Take the Place of You	1971	$5
❑ 45391	Treat Him Right/Break My Mind	1971	$5
❑ 10082	Wonder When My Baby's Comin' Home/Kiss the Hurt Away	1974	$5

EMI AMERICA
Number	Title	Yr	NM
❑ 43042	Angels Love Bad Men/Sunshine Street	1988	$3
❑ 43032	Child Support/I'm Glad I Married You	1987	$3
❑ 43032 [PS]	Child Support/I'm Glad I Married You	1987	$4

EMI MANHATTAN
Number	Title	Yr	NM
❑ 50102	Sure Feels Good/Sunshine Street	1987	$3

MCA
Number	Title	Yr	NM
❑ 52645	Angel in Your Arms/Don't Look in My Eyes	1985	$3
❑ 41263	Crackers/Using Him to Get to You	1980	$3
❑ 52465	Crossword Puzzle/If It's Not One Thing It's Another	1984	$3
❑ 52737 [DJ]	Fast Lanes and Country Roads (same on both sides)	1985	$10

— Promo only on yellow vinyl

Number	Title	Yr	NM
❑ 52737	Fast Lanes and Country Roads/You Only You	1985	$3
❑ 52737 [PS]	Fast Lanes and Country Roads/You Only You	1985	$3
❑ 41077	Fooled by a Feeling/Love Takes a Long Time to Die	1979	$3
❑ 52340	Happy Birthday Dear Heartache/A Man's Not a Man ('Til He's Loved by a Woman)	1984	$3
❑ 12451	(If Loving You Is Wrong) I Don't Want to Be Right/I Feel the Hurt Coming On	1979	$4

— Reissue of ABC 12451

Number	Title	Yr	NM
❑ 52206	In Times Like These/Loveless	1983	$3
❑ 51107	I Was Country When Country Wasn't Cool/Woman's Got a Right	1981	$4
❑ 51062	Love Is Fair/Sometime, Somewhere, Somehow	1981	$3
❑ 52258	One of a Kind Pair of Fools/As Well As Can Be Expected	1983	$3
❑ 52397	Only a Lonely Heart Knows/I Wonder What the Rich Folk Are Doin' Tonight	1984	$3
❑ 52111	Operator, Long Distance Please/Black and White	1982	$3
❑ S45-1241 [DJ]	Santa, Bring My Baby Back Home//It Must Have Been the Mistletoe (Our First Christmas)/From Our House to Yours	1984	$10
❑ 51001	The Best of Strangers/Sometime, Somewhere, Somehow	1980	$3
❑ 52537	There's No Love in Tennessee/Sincerely I'm Yours	1985	$3
❑ 52537 [PS]	There's No Love in Tennessee/Sincerely I'm Yours	1985	$3
❑ 52038	'Till You're Gone/You're Not Supposed to Be Here	1982	$3
❑ 52802 [DJ]	When You Get to the Heart (same on both sides)	1986	$10

— Promo only on red vinyl

Number	Title	Yr	NM
❑ 52802	When You Get to the Heart/Survivors	1986	$3

— With the Oak Ridge Boys

Number	Title	Yr	NM
❑ 51171	Wish You Were Here/She's Out There Dancin' Alone	1981	$3

MANDRELL, BARBARA, AND LEE GREENWOOD
MCA
Number	Title	Yr	NM
❑ 52525	It Should Have Been Love By Now/Can't Get Too Much of a Good Thing	1985	$4
❑ 52415	To Me/We Were Meant for Each Other	1984	$3
❑ 52415 [PS]	To Me/We Were Meant for Each Other	1984	$3

MANDRELL, LOUISE, AND R.C. BANNON
EPIC
Number	Title	Yr	NM
❑ 50668	I Thought You'd Never Ask/Yes, I Do	1979	$4
❑ 50951	One False Move (And I'm Yours)/The Pleasure's All Mine	1980	$4
❑ 50789	We Love Each Other/I Want to (Do Everything to You)	1979	$4

RCA
Number	Title	Yr	NM
❑ PB-13358	Christmas Is Just a Song for Us This Year/Christmas in Dixie	1982	$5

— B-side by Alabama

Number	Title	Yr	NM
❑ PB-13095	Our Wedding Band/Just Married	1982	$4

Number	Title	Yr	NM
❑ PB-12359	Where There's Smoke There's Fire/Before You	1981	$4

MANDRELL, LOUISE
EPIC
Number	Title	Yr	NM
❑ 50682	Band of Gold/Everlasting Love	1979	$6
❑ 50896	Beggin' for Mercy/Come Here	1980	$4
❑ 50651	Everlasting Love/You Never Cross My Mind	1978	$5
❑ 50752	I Never Loved Anyone Like I Love You/Surrender to My Heart	1979	$5
❑ 50935	Love Insurance/When It Hurts You Most	1980	$4
❑ 50565	Put It On Me/Yes, I Do	1978	$5
❑ 50856	Wake Me Up/That Song Called Forever	1980	$4

RCA
Number	Title	Yr	NM
❑ 5115-7-R	Do I Have to Say Goodbye/Keep What We Had Going	1987	$3
❑ PB-13752	I'm Not Through Loving You Yet/A New Girl in Town	1984	$3
❑ PB-14364	I Wanna Hear It from Your Lips/Summer Nights	1986	$3
❑ PB-14151	I Wanna Say Yes/There'll Never Be Another for Me	1985	$3
❑ PB-14039	Maybe My Baby/Are You Just Playing with Me	1985	$3
❑ PB-13450	Save Me/Trust	1983	$3
❑ PB-14251	Some Girls Have All the Luck/How Did It Get So Late, So Early	1985	$3
❑ PB-13278	Some of My Best Friends Are Old Songs/689-Double-2-0-3	1982	$4
❑ PB-14320	Talkin' About My Baby/(B-side unknown)	1986	$4
❑ 5208-7-R	Tender Time/Take Me Back	1987	$3
❑ PB-13954	This Bed's Not Big Enough/Paying Through the Heart	1984	$3
❑ PB-13954 [PS]	This Bed's Not Big Enough/Paying Through the Heart	1984	$4
❑ PB-13567	Too Hot to Sleep/We Put On Quite a Show	1983	$3
❑ PB-13567 [PS]	Too Hot to Sleep/We Put On Quite a Show	1983	$4

MANGIONE, CHUCK
A&M
Number	Title	Yr	NM
❑ 1919	Bellavia/Doin' Everything With You	1977	$4
❑ 1773	Bellavia/Listen to the Wind	1975	$4
❑ 2118	Bellavia/Lullaby	1979	$4
❑ 2354	Cannonball Run Theme/Can't We Do This All Night	1981	$3
❑ 1707	Chase the Clouds Away/Soft	1975	$4
❑ 2088	Children of Sanchez/Doin' Everything with You	1978	$4
❑ 2088 [PS]	Children of Sanchez/Doin' Everything with You	1978	$5
❑ 2001	Feels So Good/Maui-Waui	1977	$4
❑ 2001 [PS]	Feels So Good/Maui-Waui	1977	$5
❑ 2236	Fun and Games/Children of Sanchez (Finale)	1980	$4
❑ 2236 [PS]	Fun and Games/Children of Sanchez (Finale)	1980	$4
❑ 2341	Give It All You Got, But Slowly/Neapolitan Tarantella	1981	$3
❑ 2211	Give It All You Got/B'Bye	1980	$4
❑ 2211 [PS]	Give It All You Got/B'Bye	1980	$4
❑ 2167	Land of Make Believe/Children of Sanchez	1979	$4
❑ 1886	Main Squeeze/Come Take a Ride with Me	1976	$4
❑ 1886 [PS]	Main Squeeze/Come Take a Ride with Me	1976	$6
❑ 1827	Soft/Can't We Do This All Night	1976	$4

COLUMBIA
Number	Title	Yr	NM
❑ 04649	Diana "D"/Josephine	1984	$3
❑ 07917	Long Hair Soulful/Do You Ever Think About Me	1988	$3
❑ 05866	Save Tonight for Me/T.J.'s Gingerbread Man	1986	$3
❑ 03008	Steppin' Out/Memories of Scirocco	1982	$3

MERCURY
Number	Title	Yr	NM
❑ 73238	And In the Beginning/Feel a Vision	1972	$6
❑ 73453	As Long As We're Together/Legend of the One-Eyed Sailor	1974	$6
❑ 73262	Freddie's Walkin'/Look to the Children	1972	$6
❑ 73208	Hill Where the Lord Hides/Friends and Lovers	1971	$8
❑ 74016	Hill Where the Lord Hides/Land of Make Believe	1978	$5
❑ 73635	Land of Make Believe/As Long As We're Together	1975	$6
❑ 73920	Land of Make Believe/As Long As We're Together	1977	$5
❑ 73371	Last Tango in Paris/Legend of the One-Eyed Sailor	1973	$6

MANHATTAN TRANSFER
ATLANTIC
Number	Title	Yr	NM
❑ 89720	American Pop/Why Not!	1983	$4

— Featuring Frankie Valli

Number	Title	Yr	NM
❑ 89720 [PS]	American Pop/Why Not!	1983	$4
❑ 89594	Baby Come Back to Me (Morse Code of Love)/That's the Way It Goes	1984	$12
❑ 3636	Birdland/Shaker Song	1979	$5
❑ 3816	Boy from New York City/(The World of) Confirmation	1981	$4
❑ 3374	Chanson d'Amour/Popsicle Toes	1976	$5
❑ 3491	Four Brothers/It's Not the Spotlight	1978	$5
❑ 3349	Helpless/My Cat Fell in the Well	1976	$5
❑ 89695	Mystery/Goodbye Love	1984	$4
❑ 3292	Operator/Tuxedo Junction	1975	$5
❑ 3855	Smile Again/Until I Met You	1981	$4
❑ 89156	Soul Food to Go/Hear the Voices	1988	$4
❑ 89156 [PS]	Soul Food to Go/Hear the Voices	1988	$4
❑ 89094	So You Say/Notes from the Underground	1988	$4
❑ 89094 [PS]	So You Say/Notes from the Underground	1988	$4
❑ 89786	Spice of Life/The Night That Monk Returned to Heaven	1983	$4
❑ 89786 [PS]	Spice of Life/The Night That Monk Returned to Heaven	1983	$5
❑ 3877	Spies in the Night/Kafka	1981	$4
❑ 3277	Sweet Talking Guy/Clap Your Hands	1975	$8
❑ 89467	That's Killer Joe/Airegin II	1985	$5
❑ 89647	This Independence/Code of Ethics	1984	$5
❑ 3772	Trickle, Trickle/Foreign Affair	1980	$10
❑ 3649	Twilight Zone-Twilight Tone/Body and Soul	1980	$5
❑ 3472	Where Did Our Love Go/Inside and Out	1978	$5

CAPITOL
Number	Title	Yr	NM
❑ 2968	Care for Me/Rosianna	1970	$10

— With Gene Pistilli

Number	Title	Yr	NM
❑ 3036	Maybe Mexico/Winterlude	1971	$10

— With Gene Pistilli

(NO LABEL)
Number	Title	Yr	NM
❑ 1984 [DJ]	The Christmas Song (same on both sides)	1984	$50
❑ 1984 [PS]	The Christmas Song (same on both sides)	1984	$50

— Above sleeve and record are a private pressing for friends and associates of the group

MANHATTANS, THE (1)
CARNIVAL
Number	Title	Yr	NM
❑ 526	All I Need Is Your Love/Our Love Will Never Die	1967	$20
❑ 514	Baby I Need You/Teach Me the Philly Dog	1966	$20
❑ 517	Can I/That New Girl	1966	$20
❑ 512	Follow Your Heart/The Boston Money	1965	$20
❑ 522	I Betcha (Couldn't Love Me)/Sweet Little Girl	1966	$20
❑ 533	I Call It Love/Manhattan Stomp	1967	$20
❑ 542	I Don't Wanna Go/Love Is Breaking Out	1968	$20
❑ 524	It's That Time of the Year/Alone on New Year's Eve	1966	$30
❑ 504	I've Got Everything But You/For the Very First Time	1964	$30
❑ 507	I Wanna Be (Your Everything)/What's It Gonna Be	1965	$20
❑ 509	Searchin' for My Baby/I'm the One That Love Forgot	1965	$20
❑ 506	There Goes a Fool/Call Somebody Please	1964	$50
❑ 545	Til You Come Back to Me/Call Somebody Please	1968	$20
❑ 529	When We're Made As One/Baby I'm Sorry	1967	$20

COLUMBIA
Number	Title	Yr	NM
❑ 10674	Am I Losing You/Movin'	1978	$5
❑ 03939	Crazy/Gonna Find You	1983	$4
❑ 04930	Don't Say No/Dreamin'	1985	$4
❑ 10045	Don't Take Your Love/The Day the Robins Sang to Me	1974	$5
❑ 60511	Do You Really Mean Goodbye/Rendezvous	1981	$4
❑ 10766	Everybody Has a Dream/Happiness	1978	$5
❑ 04110	Forever By Your Side/Locked Up in Your Love	1983	$4
❑ 11321	Girl of My Dreams/The Closer You Are	1980	$4
❑ 10921	Here Comes the Hurt Again/Don't Say Goodbye	1979	$5
❑ 10140	Hurt/Nursery Rhymes	1975	$5
❑ 10430	I Kinda Miss You/Gypsy Man	1976	$5
❑ 11398	I'll Never Find Another (Another Just Like You)/Rendezvous	1980	$4

Number	Title	Yr	NM
❏ 10495	It Feels So Good to Be Loved By You/On the Street (Where I Live)	1977	$5
❏ 02548	Let Your Love Come Down/I Gotta Thank You	1981	$4
❏ 02666	Money, Money/I Wanta Thank You	1982	$4
❏ 07010	Mr. D.J./All I Need	1987	$4
❏ 11222	Shining Star/I'll Never Run Away from Love Again	1980	$4
❏ 02164	Shining Star/Summertime in the City	1981	$3

— Reissue

Number	Title	Yr	NM
❏ 46081	Summertime in the City/The Other Side of Me	1974	$6
❏ 45838	There's No Me Without You/I'm Not a Run-Around	1973	$6
❏ 11024	The Way We Were-Memories/New York City	1979	$5
❏ 10586	We Never Danced to a Love Song/Let's Start It All Over Again	1977	$5
❏ 06376	Where Did We Go Wrong/Maybe Tomorrow	1986	$4

— With Regina Belle

Number	Title	Yr	NM
❏ 45971	Wish That You Were Mine/It's So Hard Loving You	1973	$6

DELUXE

Number	Title	Yr	NM
❏ 137	A Million to One/Cry If You Wanna Cry	1971	$10
❏ 144	Back Up/Fever	1972	$12
❏ 136	Do You Ever/I Can't Stand for You to Leave Me	1971	$12
❏ 152	Do You Ever/If My Heart Could Speak	1973	$12
❏ 129	From Atlanta to Goodbye/Fantastic Journey	1970	$10
❏ 122	If My Heart Could Speak/Loneliness	1970	$10
❏ 115	It's Gonna Take a Lot to Bring Me Back/Give Him Up	1970	$10
❏ 132	Let Them Talk/Straight to My Heart	1970	$12
❏ 139	One Life to Live/It's the Only Way	1972	$10
❏ 109	The Picture Became Quite Clear/Oh Lord, How I Wish I Could Sleep	1969	$10

STARFIRE

Number	Title	Yr	NM
❏ 121	Alone on New Year's Eve/It's That Time of the Year	1979	$5

VALLEY VUE

Number	Title	Yr	NM
❏ 75723	Sweet Talk/(B-side unknown)	1989	$6
❏ 75749	Why You Wanna Love Me Like That/(B-side unknown)	1989	$6

MANHATTANS, THE (2)

COLPIX

Number	Title	Yr	NM
❏ 115	Big Wheel Express/Powder Blue	1959	$40

MANHATTANS, THE (U)

AVANTI

Number	Title	Yr	NM
❏ 1401	What Should I Do/Later for You	1963	$80

CAPITOL

Number	Title	Yr	NM
❏ 4730	La La La/Sing All the Day	1962	$30
❏ 4591	Molly Brown Medley/I Ain't Down Yet	1961	$30

ENJOY

Number	Title	Yr	NM
❏ 2008	Come On Back/Long Time No See	1964	$30

— As "Ronnie and the Manhattans

KING

Number	Title	Yr	NM
❏ 5228	Ebb Tide (Part 1)/Ebb Tide (Part 2)	1959	$20
❏ 5259	Sugar Tooth/Like Saying Something	1959	$20

PINEY

Number	Title	Yr	NM
❏ 108	Crazy Love/The Hawk and the Crow	1962	$60
❏ 107	Live It Up/Go Baby Go	1962	$70

WARNER

Number	Title	Yr	NM
❏ 1015	How Do I Say I'm Sorry/Love Is Where You Find It	1958	$120

MANILOW, BARRY

ARISTA

Number	Title	Yr	NM
❏ 0305	Can't Smile Without You/Sunrise	1978	$4
❏ 0339	Copacabana (Short Version)/Copacabana (Long Version)	1978	$4
❏ 0126	Could It Be Magic/I Am Your Child	1975	$4
❏ 0273	Daybreak/Jump Shout Boogie	1977	$4
❏ 0330	Even Now/I Was a Fool (To Let You Go)	1978	$4
❏ 0330 [PS]	Even Now/I Was a Fool (To Let You Go)	1978	$4

Number	Title	Yr	NM
❏ 9666	Hey Mambo/When October Goes	1988	$3

— With Kid Creole and the Coconuts

Number	Title	Yr	NM
❏ 9666 [PS]	Hey Mambo/When October Goes	1988	$3
❏ 0501	I Don't Want to Walk Without You/One Voice	1980	$4
❏ 0566	I Made It Through the Rain/Only in Chicago	1980	$4
❏ 0108	It's a Miracle/One of These Days	1975	$4
❏ SP-11 [DJ]	It's Just Another New Year's Eve (same on both sides)	1977	$8
❏ SP-11 [PS]	It's Just Another New Year's Eve (same on both sides)	1977	$15
❏ 0157	I Write the Songs/A Nice Boy Like Me	1975	$4
❏ 0675	Let's Hang On/No Other Love	1982	$4
❏ 0596	Lonely Together/The Last Duet	1981	$4

— B-side with Lily Tomlin

Number	Title	Yr	NM
❏ 0244	Looks Like We Made It/New York City Rhythm	1977	$4
❏ 1025	Memory/Heart of Steel	1982	$4
❏ 0698	Oh Julie/Break Down the Door	1982	$4
❏ 9811	Please Don't Be Scared/A Little Traveling Music, Please	1989	$3
❏ 0464	Ships/They Gave In to the Blues	1979	$4
❏ 1046	Some Kind of Friend/Heaven	1983	$4
❏ 9003	Some Kind of Friend/Heaven	1983	$3
❏ 0658	Somewhere Down the Road/Let's Take All Night to Say Goodbye	1982	$4
❏ 0382	Somewhere in the Night/Leavin' in the Morning	1978	$4
❏ 0633	The Old Songs/Don't Fall in Love with Me	1981	$4
❏ 0206	This One's for You/Riders to the Stars	1976	$4
❏ 0172	Tryin' to Get the Feeling Again/Beautiful Music	1976	$4
❏ 0212	Weekend in New England/Say the Words	1976	$4
❏ 0481	When I Wanted You/Bobbie Lee (What's the Difference I Gotta Live)	1979	$4
❏ 9873 [DJ]	When the Good Times Come Again (same on both sides)	1989	$10

— Record appears to be promo only

BELL

Number	Title	Yr	NM
❏ 45422	Cloudburst/Could It Be Magic	1973	$6
❏ 45443	Let's Take Some Time to Say Goodbye/Seven More Years	1974	$6
❏ 45613	Mandy/Something's Comin' Up	1974	$5
❏ 45357	Sweetwater Jones/One of These Days	1973	$6

RCA

Number	Title	Yr	NM
❏ PB-14302	He Doesn't Care (But I Do)/It's All Behind Us Now	1986	$3
❏ PB-14302 [PS]	He Doesn't Care (But I Do)/It's All Behind Us Now	1986	$4
❏ PB-14397	I'm Your Man/I'm Your Man (Dub)	1986	$3
❏ PB-14397 [PS]	I'm Your Man/I'm Your Man (Dub)	1986	$3
❏ PB-14223	In Search of Love/At the Dance	1985	$3
❏ PB-14223 [PS]	In Search of Love/At the Dance	1985	$4

MANN, BARRY

ABC-PARAMOUNT

Number	Title	Yr	NM
❏ 10180	Happy Birthday, Broken Heart/Millionaire	1961	$30
❏ 10356	Hey Baby I'm Dancin'/Like I Don't Love You	1962	$30
❏ 10263	Little Miss U.S.A./Find Another Fool	1961	$30
❏ 10380	Teenage Has-Been/Bless You	1962	$30
❏ 10143	War Paint/Counting Teardrops	1960	$30
❏ 10237	Who Put the Bomp (In the Bomp, Bomp, Bomp)/Love, True Love	1961	$30

ARISTA

Number	Title	Yr	NM
❏ 0194	The Princess and the Punk/Jennifer	1976	$4

CAPITOL

Number	Title	Yr	NM
❏ 2217	I Just Can't Help Believin'/Where Do I Go from Here	1968	$10
❏ 5695	Looking at Tomorrow/Angelica	1966	$10
❏ 5894	Where Do I Go from Here/She Is Today	1967	$10

CASABLANCA

Number	Title	Yr	NM
❏ 2287	Brown-Eyed Woman/In My Own Way	1980	$4

COLPIX

Number	Title	Yr	NM
❏ 691	Graduation Time/Johnny Surfboard	1963	$30

JDS

Number	Title	Yr	NM
❏ 5002	I Love to Last a Lifetime/All the Things You Are	1959	$40

NEW DESIGN

Number	Title	Yr	NM
❏ 1000	Carry Me Home/Sundown	1971	$5
❏ 1006	Too Many Mornings/Lay It All Out	1972	$5
❏ 1006	Too Many Mornings/On Broadway	1972	$5
❏ 1005	When You Get Right Down to It/Don't Give Up on Me	1972	$5

RCA VICTOR

Number	Title	Yr	NM
❏ PB-10319	Don't Seem Right/I'm a Survivor	1975	$5

RED BIRD

Number	Title	Yr	NM
❏ Oct-0015	Talk to Me Baby/Amy	1964	$20

SCEPTER

Number	Title	Yr	NM
❏ 12281	Feelings/Let Me Stay with You	1970	$6

UNITED ARTISTS

Number	Title	Yr	NM
❏ XW1021	Best That I Know How/Lettin' Good Times Get Away	1977	$4

WARNER BROS.

Number	Title	Yr	NM
❏ 8752	For No Reason at All/Almost Gone	1979	$4
❏ 8752 [PS]	For No Reason at All/Almost Gone	1979	$5

MANN, GLORIA

ABC-PARAMOUNT

Number	Title	Yr	NM
❏ 9805	My Heart Has a Mind of Its Own/Why Can't I Make You Understand	1957	$15

DECCA

Number	Title	Yr	NM
❏ 9-30140	Faded Photographs/You Can't Be Mine	1956	$20
❏ 9-29886	Friendship Ring/One Heart	1956	$30
❏ 9-30069	It Happened Again/Love, Sweet Love	1956	$20
❏ 9-29961	My Secret Sin/Cashmere Sweater	1956	$20
❏ 9-29832	Why Do Fools Fall in Love?/Partners for Life	1956	$30

DERBY

Number	Title	Yr	NM
❏ 841	All Dressed Up/Made Me a Present of You	1954	$40

JUBILEE

Number	Title	Yr	NM
❏ 5142	Goodnight, Sweetheart, Goodnight/Love-Me-Boy	1954	$30

— With the Carter Rays

SOUND

Number	Title	Yr	NM
❏ 109	Earth Angel Will You Be Mine/I Love You, Yes I Do	1955	$40
❏ 121	I Can Tell/Bon Soir Cherie	1955	$40
❏ 122	I Don't Know — I Don't Care/My Gift from Heaven	1955	$40
❏ 114	I Played the Fool/Pretty Eyes	1955	$40
❏ 126	Teen Age Prayer/Gypsy Lady	1955	$30
❏ 102	The Waltz You Saved for Me/I'm Living My Life for You	1954	$40

MANN, HERBIE

ATLANTIC

Number	Title	Yr	NM
❏ 3037	Anata/Sound of Wood Wind	1974	$5
❏ 5031	Bag's Groove/New York Is a Jungle Festival	1963	$12
❏ 2661	Battle Hymn of the Republic/Hold On, I'm Comin'	1969	$6
❏ 3390	Birdwalk/Aria	1977	$4
❏ 5026	Blues Walk Bossa Nova/It Must Be Love Bossa Nova	1962	$15
❏ 2498	By the Time I Get to Phoenix/Sports Car	1968	$6
❏ 3343	Cajun Moon/So Git It While You Can	1976	$4
❏ 5019	Carnival/La La La	1962	$15
❏ 2451	Cottage for Sale/Live for Life	1967	$6

— With Carmen McRae

Number	Title	Yr	NM
❏ 2392	Day Tripper/A Good Thing (Is Hard to Come By)	1967	$60

— With Tamiko Jones

Number	Title	Yr	NM
❏ 2960	Do It Again/Turtle Baby	1973	$5
❏ 5038	Down By the Riverside/Insensatez	1964	$12
❏ 5037	Harlem Nocturne/Not Now -- Not Later	1964	$12
❏ 3246	Hijack/Orient Express	1975	$4
❏ 2363	Is Paris Burning?/Happy Brass	1966	$8
❏ 2671	It's a Funky Thing -- Right On (Part 1)/It's a Funky Thing -- Right On (Part 2)	1969	$6
❏ 5036	Love in Peace/One Note Samba	1964	$10
❏ 2621	Memphis Underground/New Orleans	1969	$6
❏ 3219	My Girl/Rivers of Babylon	1974	$5
❏ 5065	Our Man Flint/Yesterday	1966	$8

Number	Title	Yr	NM
❏ 5074	Philly Dog/Frere Jacques	1966	$8
❏ 5044	Soul Guajira/Hushi Mushi	1965	$8
❏ 3313	Stars and Stripes Forever (Part 1)/Stars and Stripes Forever (Part 2)	1976	$5
❏ 5020	Sumemrtime/Comin' Home Baby	1962	$15
❏ 3547	Superman/Etagui	1978	$4
❏ 3547 [PS]	Superman/Etagui	1978	$6
❏ 2399	The Beat Goes On/Free for All	1967	$6
❏ 3536	The Closer I Get to You/Watermelon Man	1978	$4
❏ 5032	The Girl from Ipanema/Soft Winds	1964	$10
❏ 2379	The Honeydripper/The Puppet	1967	$6
❏ 2262	Theme from Malamondo/Fiddler on the Roof	1964	$10
❏ 5070	Theme from This Is My Beloved/Scratch	1966	$8
❏ 89880	Theme from "Tootsie"/(B-side unknown)	1983	$4
❏ 5015	This Little Girl of Mine/Why Don't You Do Right	1961	$15
❏ 5064	Today/Arrastao	1966	$8
❏ 2444	To Sir with Love/Hold Back (Just a Little Longer)	1967	$6
❏ 5010	Walkin'/(B-side unknown)	1961	$15
❏ 3282	Waterbed/Body Oil	1975	$4

BETHLEHEM

Number	Title	Yr	NM
❏ 3040	Chicken Little/My Little Suede Shoes	1962	$10
❏ 11038	Cuban Love Song/Scuffles	1959	$15
❏ 11036	Love Is a Simple Thing/Jasmine	1959	$15
❏ 11037	Surrey with the Fringe on Top/Sorimao	1959	$15

PRESTIGE

Number	Title	Yr	NM
❏ 318	Cherry Point/Early Morning Blues	1964	$10
❏ 113	Let's March (Part 1)/Let's March (Part 2)	1957	$30
❏ 416	Tutti Flutee (Part 1)/Tutti Flutee (Part 2)	1966	$8

MANN, JOHNNY, SINGERS

EPIC

Number	Title	Yr	NM
❏ 10895	Stand Up and Cheer/America, There's So Much to Say	1972	$5

LIBERTY

Number	Title	Yr	NM
❏ 55653	African Noel/Children, Board That Train	1963	$8

— By "The Johnny Mann Children's Choir

Number	Title	Yr	NM
❏ 56107	Carolina on My Mind/Little Sister	1969	$6
❏ 55871	Cinnamint Shuffle/Rovin' Gambler	1966	$6
❏ 55525	Cotton Fields/Shenandoah	1962	$8
❏ 56010	Don't Look Back/Instant Happy	1967	$6
❏ 55355	Don't/Love Me	1961	$8
❏ 55327	East of the Sun/(B-side unknown)	1961	$8
❏ 56083	Snow/If I Only Had Time	1968	$8
❏ 55466	Summersong/Mr. and Mrs. Millionaire	1962	$8
❏ 55938	Whither Thou Goest/A Joyful Noise	1966	$6

MANN, MANFRED

ASCOT

Number	Title	Yr	NM
❏ 2170	Come Tomorrow/What Did I Do Wrong	1965	$10
❏ 2170 [PS]	Come Tomorrow/What Did I Do Wrong	1965	$30
❏ 2157	Do Wah Diddy Diddy/What You Gonna Do?	1964	$20
❏ 2151	Hubble Bubble (Toil and Trouble)/I'm Your Kingpin	1964	$200
❏ 2194	If You Gotta Go, Go Now/The One in the Middle	1965	$10
❏ 2241	My Little Red Book/I Can't Believe What You Say	1967	$10
❏ 2184	My Little Red Book/What Am I Doing Wrong	1965	$10
❏ 2165	Sha La La/John Hardy	1964	$10
❏ 2165 [PS]	Sha La La/John Hardy	1964	$30
❏ 2210	She Needs Company/Hi Lili, Hi Lo	1966	$10

MERCURY

Number	Title	Yr	NM
❏ 72879	Fox on the Run/Too Many People	1968	$8
❏ 72675	Ha, Ha, Said the Clown/Feeling So Good	1967	$10
❏ 72822	My Name Is Jack/There Is a Man	1968	$8
❏ 72822 [PS]	My Name Is Jack/There Is a Man	1968	$20
❏ 72629	Semi-Detached Suburban Mr. Jones/Each and Every Day	1966	$10
❏ 72770	The Mighty Quinn (Quinn the Eskimo)/By Request -- Edwin Garvey	1968	$10

— Orange and red swirl label

Number	Title	Yr	NM
❏ 72770	The Mighty Quinn (Quinn the Eskimo)/By Request -- Edwin Garvey	1968	$15

— Red label with "Mercury" in all capital letters

Number	Title	Yr	NM
❏ 72770	The Mighty Quinn (Quinn the Eskimo)/By Request -- Edwin Garvey	1968	$8

— Red label with white "Mercury" in a circle

Number	Title	Yr	NM
❏ 72770	The Mighty Quinn (Quinn the Eskimo)/By Request -- Edwin Garvey	1968	$20

— Black label, silver print, "Mercury Records" in double oval at top; as this label was last used in 1964, this shouldn't exist, but it does

POLYDOR

Number	Title	Yr	NM
❏ 14097	Please Mrs. Henry/Prayers	1971	$5
❏ 14026	Sometimes/Snakeskin Garter	1970	$6

PRESTIGE

Number	Title	Yr	NM
❏ 312	5-4-3-2-1/Without You	1964	$50
❏ 314	Blue Brave/Brother Jack	1964	$125

UNITED ARTISTS

Number	Title	Yr	NM
❏ 0048	Do Wah Diddy Diddy/Sha La La	1973	$5

— Silver Spotlight Series" reissue

Number	Title	Yr	NM
❏ 0049	Pretty Flamingo/Come Tomorrow	1973	$5

— Silver Spotlight Series" reissue

Number	Title	Yr	NM
❏ 50040	Pretty Flamingo/You're Standing By	1966	$10
❏ 50066	When Will I Be Loved/Do You Have to Do That	1966	$10

MANN, MANFRED, EARTH BAND

POLYDOR

Number	Title	Yr	NM
❏ 14225	Father of Night/Solar Fire Two	1974	$5
❏ 14191	Get Your Rocks Off/Wind	1973	$5
❏ 14130	I'm Up and Leaving/Part Time Man	1972	$5
❏ 14130 [PS]	I'm Up and Leaving/Part Time Man	1972	$10
❏ 14160	It's All Over Now, Baby Blue/Ashes	1973	$5
❏ 14113	Living Without You/Tribute	1972	$5
❏ 14173	Mardi Gras Day/Sad Joy	1973	$5

WARNER BROS.

Number	Title	Yr	NM
❏ 49762	Adolescent Dream/Lies (Through the 80's)	1981	$4
❏ 8252	Blinded by the Light/Starbird No. 2	1976	$5
❏ 8252 [PS]	Blinded by the Light/Starbird No. 2	1976	$8
❏ 8574	California/Bouillabaise	1978	$5
❏ 8620	Davy's on the Road Again/Bouillabaise	1978	$5
❏ 49678	For You/Fool I Am	1981	$5
❏ 8152	Spirit in the Night/As Above So Below	1975	$8
❏ 8176	Spirit in the Night/As Above So Below	1976	$6
❏ 8176 [DJ]	Spirit in the Night (Long)/Spirit in the Night (Short)	1976	$6
❏ 8355	Spirit in the Night/Questions	1977	$5

— This has newly-recorded vocal tracks by Chris Thompson

Number	Title	Yr	NM
❏ 8355 [DJ]	Spirit (same on both sides)	1977	$10

— Newly-recorded vocal tracks by Chris Thompson; some early promos use this title in error and include a card that says "The correct title should be 'Spirit in the Night. WBS 8355

MANNERS, ZEKE

CAPITOL

Number	Title	Yr	NM
❏ F1906	Piano Players/Good Humoresque Boogie	1951	$30
❏ F1552	Satins and Lace/There's a Rainbow in the Sky	1951	$30

RCA VICTOR

Number	Title	Yr	NM
❏ 48-0052	There Is Nothin' Like a Dame/When It's Springtime in the Rockies	1949	$50

— Originals on green vinyl

MANNHEIM STEAMROLLER

AMERICAN GRAMAPHONE

Number	Title	Yr	NM
❏ AGS1984	Deck the Halls/Silent Night	1984	$5
❏ AGS1984 [PS]	Deck the Halls/Silent Night	1984	$5

MANNING, LINDA

Number	Title	Yr	NM
❏ 6429	Turning Back the Tables/Hello Little Lover	1963	$15

MERCURY

Number	Title	Yr	NM
❏ 72875	Since They Fired the Band Director (At Murphy High)/Talk of the Town	1968	$8
❏ 72803	Someone Up There Still Loves Me/Hurt Me Now	1968	$8
❏ 72906	The Peaceful Protest of Charlie McDugg/Billy Christian	1969	$8

SOUNDWAVES

Number	Title	Yr	NM
❏ 4792	Out with the Boys/(B-side unknown)	1987	$5

MANNO, TOMMY

ATLANTIC

Number	Title	Yr	NM
❏ 2149	Too Good to Be True/That's for Me to Know	1962	$15

MANZAREK, RAY

Keyboardist for THE DOORS.
Also see THE DOORS; RICK AND THE RAVENS.

MERCURY

Number	Title	Yr	NM
❏ 73601	Downbound Train/Choose Up and Choose Off	1974	$5
❏ 73477	Solar Boat/Moorish Idol	1974	$5
❏ 73644	The Whole Thing Started with Rock and Roll (And Now It's Out of Control)/Art Deco Fandango	1974	$5

MAPHIS, JOE

COLUMBIA

Number	Title	Yr	NM
❏ 4-41579	Del Rio/Jubilo	1959	$20
❏ 4-21547	Floggin' the Banjo/Bully of the Town	1956	$30
❏ 4-21518	Guitar Rock and Roll/Tennessee Two-Step	1956	$40
❏ 4-41353	Moonshot/Short Recess	1959	$20
❏ 4-40882	Town Hall Shuffle/Sweet Fern	1957	$30

REPUBLIC

Number	Title	Yr	NM
❏ 2006	Water Baby Boogie/Black Combrero	1960	$20

STARDAY

Number	Title	Yr	NM
❏ 683	Hot Rod Guitar/Lonesome Jailhouse Blues	1964	$10

7-Inch Extended Plays

COLUMBIA

Number	Title	Yr	NM
❏ B-10051	*Fire on the Strings/Guitar Rock and Roll/Flying Fingers/Twin Banjo Special	1957	$30

MAPHIS, JOE AND ROSE LEE

CAPITOL

Number	Title	Yr	NM
❏ 5077	Maple on the Hill/Whiskey Is the Devil in Liquid Form	1963	$10

CHART

Number	Title	Yr	NM
❏ 5029	Gee, Aren't We Lucky/Guitar Happy	1969	$8

CMH

Number	Title	Yr	NM
❏ 1520	Somewhere Between/Fiddle Pickin'	1979	$6

COLUMBIA

Number	Title	Yr	NM
❏ 4-41004	A Picture, a Ring and a Curl/I Gotta Lotta Lovin'	1957	$30
❏ 4-21389	Honky Tonk Down Town/Parting of the Way	1955	$30
❏ 4-21479	I Love You Deeply/Fire on the Strings	1956	$30
❏ 4-21568	I'm Willin' to Try/Let's Pull Together	1956	$30

Lariat

Number	Title	Yr	NM
❏ 1203	Let's Fly Away/You Can't Take the Heart Out of Me	1952	$50
❏ 290	Tunin' Up for the Blues/Lifetime of Love	1966	$10

STARDAY

Number	Title	Yr	NM
❏ 675	Hoot'n Annie/Remember, I'm Just As Close As the Phone	1964	$10
❏ 710	Hot Time in Nashville/I've Come to Take You Home	1965	$10

MAR-KEYS

SATELLITE

Number	Title	Yr	NM
❏ 107	Last Night/Night Before	1960	$40

STAX

Number	Title	Yr	NM
❏ 114	About Noon/Sack-O-Woe	1961	$15
❏ 156	Beach Bash/Bush Bash	1964	$12
❏ 115	Foxy/One Degree North	1961	$15
❏ 181	Grab This Thing (Part 1)/Grab This Thing (Part 2)	1965	$10
❏ 112	Morning After/Diana	1961	$15
❏ 185	Philly Dog/Honey Pot	1966	$10
❏ 121	Pop-Eye Stroll/Po-Dunk	1962	$15
❏ 129	Sailor Man Waltz/Sack-O-Woe	1963	$15
❏ 133	The Dribble/Bo Time	1963	$15
❏ 166	The Shovel/Banana Juice	1965	$10
❏ 124	What's Happening/You Got It	1962	$15

Number	Title	Yr	NM

MAR-VELS, THE
ANGIE
☐ 1005	Go On and Have Yourself a Ball/How Do I Keep the Girls Away	1963	$30

BUTANE
| ☐ 778 | Go On and Have Yourself a Ball/How Do I Keep the Girls Away | 1963 | $20 |

IN
| ☐ 102 | Surfing at Makeha/Endless Nights | 1964 | $60 |

LOVE
| ☐ 5011/2 | Cherry Lips/Could Be You | 1958 | $40 |

TAMMY
| ☐ 1019 | My Guardian Angel/Marble Stomp | 1961 | $300 |
| ☐ 1016 | Somewhere in Life/Voo Doo Hurt | 1961 | $300 |

MARAINEY, BIG MEMPHIS
SUN
| ☐ 184 | Call Me Anything, But Call Me/Baby No, No | 1953 | $4000 |

— VG 2000; VG+ 3000

MARATHONS, THE (1)
ARGO
| ☐ 5389 | Peanut Butter/Down in New Orleans | 1961 | $20 |

— As "Vibrations Named By Others As MARATHONS

ARVEE
☐ 5048	Chicken Spaceman/You Bug Me Baby	1962	$15
☐ 5027	Peanut Butter/Talkin' Trash	1961	$30
☐ 5038	Tight Sweater/C. Percy Mercy of Scotland	1961	$15

CHESS
| ☐ 1790 | Peanut Butter/Down in New Orleans | 1961 | $20 |

PLAZA
| ☐ 507 | Mashed Potatoes One More Time/Little Pancho | 1962 | $15 |

MARATHONS, THE (2)
SABRINA
| ☐ 334 | Don't Know Why/The Stranger | 1959 | $120 |

MARAUDERS, THE
ALMO
| ☐ 221 | Like You/Slippin' and Slidin' | 1965 | $20 |

HAWK
| ☐ 4002 | Sand Flea/Stomp Watch | 1962 | $60 |

LAURIE
| ☐ 3356 | Out of Sight, Out of Mind/Jug Band Music | 1966 | $30 |

SKYVIEW
| ☐ 01 | Since I Met You/I Don't Know How | 1966 | $30 |
| ☐ 01 [PS] | Since I Met You/I Don't Know How | 1966 | $60 |

MARBLE PHROGG, THE
DERRICK
| ☐ 8568 | Fire/(B-side unknown) | 1968 | $100 |

MARCELS, THE
888
| ☐ 101 | How Deep Is the Ocean/Lonely Boy | 1964 | $20 |

ALL EARS
| ☐ 810085 | Blue Moon/Clap Your Hands (When I Clap My Hands) | 1981 | $6 |

COLPIX
☐ 665	Alright, Okay, You Win/Lollipop Baby	1962	$30
☐ 186	Blue Moon/Goodbye to Love	1961	$40
☐ 186 [PS]	Blue Moon/Goodbye to Love	1961	$70
☐ 640	Flowerpot/Hold On	1962	$40
☐ 629	Footprints in the Sand/Twistin' Fever	1962	$60
☐ 687	Give Me Back Your Love/I Wanna Be the Leader	1963	$40
☐ 612	Heartaches/My Love for You	1961	$30
☐ 612 [PS]	Heartaches/My Love for You	1961	$125
☐ 651	Loved Her the Whole Week Through/Friendly Loans	1962	$30
☐ 617	Merry Twist-Mas/Don't Cry for Me This Christmas	1961	$30
☐ 617 [PS]	Merry Twist-Mas/Don't Cry for Me This Christmas	1961	$120
☐ 624	My Melancholy Baby/Really Need Your Love	1962	$30
☐ 694	One Last Kiss/Teeter-Totter Love	1963	$125
☐ 694	One Last Kiss/You Got to Be Sincere	1963	$200
☐ 196	Summertime/Teeter-Totter Love	1961	$30
☐ 683	That Old Black Magic/Don't Turn Your Back on Me	1963	$30

KYRA
| ☐ 100 | Comes Love/Your Red Wagon | 1964 | $125 |

—Red vinyl
| ☐ 100 | Comes Love/Your Red Wagon | 1964 | $60 |

MONOGRAM
☐ 112	I'll Be Forever Loving You/A Fallen Tear	1974	$15
☐ 113	Sweet Was the Wine/Over the Rainbow	1974	$15
☐ 115	Two People in the World/Most of All	1974	$15

QUEEN BEE
| ☐ 47001 | In the Still of the Night/High on a Hill | 1973 | $20 |

MARCH, LITTLE PEGGY
OLDE WORLD
| ☐ 1105 | Average People/Isn't This the Way We Are | 1975 | $8 |

RCA VICTOR
☐ 74-0136	Boom Bang-a Bang/Lilac Skies	1969	$10
☐ 47-8840	Ein Boy Wie Du (A Boy Like You)/Sechs Tage Lang (Six Long Days)	1966	$30
☐ 47-9033	Fool, Fool, Fool (Look in the Mirror)/Try to See It My Way	1966	$10
☐ 47-9359	Have a Good Time/Let Me Down Hard	1967	$12
☐ 47-8710	He Couldn't Care Less/Heaven for Lovers	1965	$12
☐ 47-8221	Hello Heartache, Goodbye Love/Boy Crazy	1963	$20
☐ 47-8221 [PS]	Hello Heartache, Goodbye Love/Boy Crazy	1963	$40
☐ 47-8903	He's Back Again/Running Scared	1966	$12
☐ 47-9494	If You Would Love Me/Thinking Through My Tears	1968	$10
☐ 47-8302	(I'm Watching) Every Little Move You Make/After You	1963	$15
☐ 47-9627	I've Been Here Before/Aren't You Glad	1968	$10
☐ 47-8139	I Will Follow Him/Wind-Up Doll	1963	$30
☐ 47-8189	I Wish I Were a Princess/My Teenage Castle	1963	$20
☐ 47-8189 [PS]	I Wish I Were a Princess/My Teenage Castle	1963	$40
☐ 47-8605	Let Her Go/Your Girl	1965	$12
☐ 47-8107	Little Me/Pagan Love Song	1962	$20
☐ 47-9223	Mama Dear, Papa Dear/Your Good Girl's Gonna Go Bad	1967	$10
☐ 47-8418	Oh My, What a Guy/Only You Could Do That to My Heart	1964	$10
☐ 47-8877	Play a Simple Melody/Old Fashioned Wedding	1966	$10

— With Gary Marshall
| ☐ 47-9718 | Purple Hat/Try to See It My Way | 1969 | $10 |
| ☐ 47-8357 | Takin' the Long Way Home/Leave Me Alone | 1964 | $10 |

— All records from 1964 on are as "Peggy March"
☐ 47-8267	The Impossible Happened/Waterfall	1963	$15
☐ 47-9283	This Heart Wasn't Made to Kick Around/Foolin' Around	1967	$10
☐ 47-8460	Watch What You Do With My Baby/Can't Stop Thinking About Him	1964	$10
☐ 47-8534	Why Can't He Be You/Losin' My Touch	1965	$10

MARCHAN, BOBBY
ACE
☐ 3016	Baby Get Your Yo-Yo/What Can I Do	1975	$5
☐ 523	Chickee Wah-Wah/Don't Take Your Love from Me	1956	$50
☐ 3008	God Bless Our Love/My Day Is Coming	1975	$5
☐ 532	I'll Never Let You Go/I Can't Stop Loving You	1957	$40
☐ 3004	Push the Button/My Day Is Coming	1974	$5

BOBBY ROBINSON
| ☐ 0(# unknown) | There's Something on Your Mind/(B-side unknown) | 1973 | $6 |

CAMEO
☐ 453	Meet Me in Church/Hooked	1967	$8
☐ 429	Shake Your Tambourine/Just Be Yourself	1966	$10
☐ 405	There's Something About My Baby/Everything a Poor Man Needs	1966	$10

DIAL
☐ 1152	Bump Your Bootie/Ain't Nothing Wrong with Whitey	1975	$5
☐ 4002	Get Down to It/Half a Mind	1964	$10
☐ 4007	Hello Happiness/Funny Style	1965	$12
☐ 4020	I Feel It Coming/Gimme Your Love	1965	$10
☐ 3022	I Gotta Sit Down and Cry/I Got a Thing Going	1964	$10
☐ 4065	I Just Want What Belongs to Me/Sad Sack	1967	$8

FIRE
☐ 1035	All in My Mind/I Miss You So	1961	$20
☐ 1027	Booty Green/It Hurts Me to My Heart	1960	$20
☐ 1014	Snoopin' and Accusin'/This Is the Life	1959	$20
☐ 1022	There's Something On Your Mind (Part 1)/There's Something On Your Mind (Part 2)	1960	$30
☐ 1037	What You Don't Know Don't Hurt You/I Need Someone (I Need You)	1961	$20

GALE
| ☐ 4M-101 | Chickee Wah Wah/Give a Helping Hand | 1957 | $30 |

GAMBLE
| ☐ 216 | (Ain't No Reason) For Girls to Be Lonely Part 1/Part 2 | 1968 | $8 |

MERCURY
| ☐ 73908 | I Wanna Bump with the Big Fat Woman/Disco Rabbit | 1977 | $5 |

VOLT
| ☐ 108 | What Can I Do (Part 1)/What Can I Do (Part 2) | 1963 | $15 |

MARENO, LEE
NEW ART
| ☐ 103 | Goddess of Love/He's Gone | 1961 | $120 |

SCEPTER
| ☐ 1222 | Goddess of Love/He's Gone | 1961 | $40 |
| ☐ 12222 | Goddess of Love/Lonely Summer | 1968 | $15 |

—As "Lee

MARESCA, ERNIE
LAURIE
☐ 3496	Blind Date/People Get Jealous	1969	$8
☐ 3371	My Son/My Shadow and Me	1967	$10
☐ 3345	The Good Life/A Bum Can't Cry	1966	$10
☐ 3519	The Spirit of Woodstock/Web of Love	1969	$8
☐ 3447	What Is a Marine/The Night My Papa Died	1968	$8

RUST
| ☐ 5076 | The Beetle Dance/Theme from Lilly, Lilly | 1964 | $20 |

SEVILLE
☐ 119	Down on the Beach/Mary Jane	1962	$20
☐ 119 [PS]	Down on the Beach/Mary Jane	1962	$30
☐ 138	I Can't Dance/It's Their World	1965	$20
☐ 107	Lonesome Blues/I Don't Know Why	1960	$20
☐ 125	Love Express/Lorelei	1963	$60
☐ 45-117	Shout! Shout! (Knock Yourself Out)/Crying Like a Baby	1962	$30
☐ 122	Something to Shout About/How Many Times	1962	$20

MARGO AND THE MARVETTES
AMERICAN ARTS
| ☐ 8 | Cherry Pie/Say You Will | 1965 | $20 |

MARGULIS, CHARLIE
CARLTON
| ☐ 456 | Heartache for Sale/Gigi | 1958 | $15 |
| ☐ 494 | Malaguena/Theme from El Salon Mexico | 1959 | $15 |

MARIE AND REX
CARLTON
| ☐ 502 | I Can't Sit Down/Miracles | 1959 | $20 |

MARIE AND THE DECCORS
CUB
| ☐ 9115 | I'm the One/Queen of Fools | 1962 | $30 |

MARIE ANN
EPIC
| ☐ 5-9465 | (I Know That) Your Heart's Not Made of Wood/Dear Teddy | 1961 | $15 |

WARWICK
| ☐ 605 | Dream Boy/High Heel Sneakers | 1960 | $15 |

Number	Title	Yr	NM

MARINERS, THE
COLUMBIA
❏ 1-873	Our Lady of Fatima/ The Rosary	1950	$50

— Microgroove 7-inch, 33 1/3 rpm single

❏ 6-873	Our Lady of Fatima/ The Rosary	1950	$40
❏ 4-39042	Our Lady of Fatima/ The Rosary	1951	$30

MARIONETTES, THE
LONDON
❏ 9738	Whirlpool of Love/ Nobody But You	1965	$15

MARIS, TOMMY
CAMEO
❏ 406	Don't Come Cryin' to Me/ Wait for Me My Love	1966	$40

MARK IV, THE
COSMIC
❏ 704	(Make with) The Shake/45 RPM	1957	$70

MERCURY
❏ 71445	Dante's Inferno/ Move Over Rover	1959	$50
❏ 71403	I Got a Wife/Ah-Ooo-Gah	1959	$50
❏ 71481	Mairsy Doats/Ring, Ring, Ring Those Bells	1959	$50

MARKAY, GRACE
CAPITOL
❏ 5999	For Those in Love/It's a Happening World	1967	$30
❏ 2161	Sally Go 'Round the Roses/Sonny Boy	1968	$30

PARAMOUNT
❏ 0137	Merry Xmas/Times Have Changed	1971	$15

MARKETTS, THE
ARVEE
❏ 5063	Beach Bum/Sweet Potatoes	1962	$30

CALLIOPE
❏ 8009	City Nights/Soul Coaxing	1977	$5

— As "The New Marketts

❏ 8003	Mary Hartman, Mary Hartman/(B-side unknown)	1977	$5

— As "The New Marketts

FARR
❏ 021	Looking for Mr. Goodbar (Terry's Theme)/Black	1977	$5

— As "Danny Welton and the New Marketts

❏ 007	Song from M.A.S.H./ Song from M.A.S.H. (Disco Version)	1976	$5

— As "The New Marketts

❏ 019	The Hustle/Song from M.A.S.H.	1977	$5

— As "The New Marketts

LIBERTY
❏ 55443	Balboa Blue/Stompede	1962	$30

— As "The Mar-Kets

❏ 55506	Stomping Room Only/ Canadian Sunset	1962	$30

— As "The Mar-Kets

❏ 55401	Surfer's Stomp/Start	1962	$30

— As "The Mar-Kets

MERCURY
❏ 73433	Mystery Movie Theme/ Sister Candy	1973	$8

SEMINOLE
❏ 501	Song from M.A.S.H./ Song from M.A.S.H. (Disco Version)	1976	$8

— As "The New Marketts

UNION
❏ 504	Balboa Blue/Stompede	1962	$40
❏ 507	Stomping Room Only/ Canadian Sunset	1962	$40
❏ 501	Surfer's Stomp/Start	1961	$40

UNITED ARTISTS
❏ 0043	Surfer's Stomp/Balboa Blue	1973	$5

— Silver Spotlight Series" reissue

WARNER BROS.
❏ 5696	Batman Theme/ Richie's Theme	1966	$15
❏ 5468	Come See, Come Ska/ Look for a Star	1964	$15
❏ 5641	Miami's Blue/ Napoleon's Solo	1965	$10
❏ 5391	Outer Limits/Bella Dalena	1963	$40

— Original title of A-side

❏ 7116	Out of Limits/Batman Theme	1968	$6

—Back to Back Hits" series -- originals have green labels with "W7" logo

❏ 5391	Out of Limits/Bella Dalena	1963	$30
❏ 5847	Tarzan/Stirrin' Up Some Soul	1966	$10
❏ 5814	Theme from "The Avengers"/A Touch of Velvet, a Sting of Brass	1966	$30
❏ 5365	Woody Wagon/Cobra	1963	$20

WORLD PACIFIC
❏ 77899	California Summer (People Moving West)/Groovin' Time	1968	$10
❏ 77874	Sunshine Girl/Sun Power	1967	$10

MARKEYS, THE
20TH CENTURY
❏ 1210	Eternal Love/You've Got Me on a String	1956	$60

GONE
❏ 5028	Special Delivery/ Along Came Love	1958	$40

RCA VICTOR
❏ 47-7256	Hot Rod/Yakkaty Yal	1958	$30
❏ 47-7412	Time to Love/Make a Record Man	1958	$30

MARKIE, BIZ
COLD CHILLIN'
❏ 27784	This Is Something for the Radio/(Dub Dash Apella)	1989	$5

PRISM
❏ 2008	Make the Music with Your Mouth/(B-side unknown)	1986	$10

MARKSMEN, THE (2)
ABC-PARAMOUNT
❏ 9745	Hands/The Story of a Star	1956	$20

CORAL
❏ 9-61453	Hot Rod/Red Sails in the Sunset	1955	$30
❏ 9-61270	The Owata Song/Oh Ma Ma	1954	$30

MARKSMEN, THE (3)
SARA
❏ 65128	Black Pepper/ (B-side unknown)	1965	$30

MARKSMEN, THE (U)
JUBILEE
❏ 5531	Coming In on a Wing and a Prayer/Just One More Mile	1966	$15

STARDAY
❏ 320	Don't Gamble with My Heart/You Hurt Me So	1957	$600

MARLEY, BOB, AND THE WAILERS
BLACK HEART
❏ 8042	African Herbsman/ Stand Alone	1974	$15

CLOCK TOWER
❏ 505	Duppy Conqueror/ Duppy Version	1971	$30

COTILLION
❏ 46029	Chances Are/ (B-side unknown)	1981	$5

ISLAND
❏ 99740	Blackman Redemption/ Is This Love	1984	$4
❏ 99882	Buffalo Soldier/Buffalo Dub	1983	$4
❏ 99882 [PS]	Buffalo Soldier/Buffalo Dub	1983	$6
❏ 1215	Concrete Jungle/ No More Trouble	1973	$8
❏ 1218	Get Up, Stand Up/ Slave Driver	1973	$8
❏ 005	I Shot the Sheriff/Put It On	1974	$6
❏ 099	Is This Love/Crisis	1978	$6
❏ 027	Lively Up Yourself/ So Jah Seh	1975	$6
❏ 99837	Mix Up, Mix Up/French Town	1983	$4
❏ PR670 [DJ]	Stir It Up (same on both sides)	1984	$10
❏ 092	Waiting in Vain/Roots	1977	$6
❏ 072	Who the Cap Fit/ (B-side unknown)	1976	$6

JAD
❏ 211	Bend Down Low/ Mellow Mood	1968	$125

— As "Bob, Rita and Peter

TRANQUILITY
❏ T0024	It Hurts to Be Alone/ (B-side unknown)	1965	$200

— As "The Wailers

UPSETTER
❏ 07	Cross the Nation/All in One (Medley)	1970	$30

❏ 07	Cross the Nation/Version	1970	$30

— B-side by the Upsetters

❏ 0(# unknown)	More Axe/The Axe Man	1971	$30
❏ 9001	Secondhand/ Secondhand Part 2	1971	$30
❏ 09	Small Axe/Version	1970	$30

— B-side by the Upsetters

MARLINS, THE
CAMEO
❏ 333	(Everybody Do) The Swim (Part 1)/(Part 2)	1964	$20

MARLO, MICKI
ABC-PARAMOUNT
❏ 9807	Ain't That Love/The Beginning of Love	1957	$20
❏ 9762	Little By Little/It All Started With Your Kiss	1956	$30
❏ 9841	What You've Done to Me/That's Right	1957	$40

— With "Vocal assist by Paul Anka

❏ 9841	What You've Done to Me/That's Right	1957	$20

— New mix, without "Vocal assist by Paul Anka

CAPITOL
❏ F3016	Don't Go, Don't Go, Don't Go/Can You	1955	$20
❏ F3346	How Come You Love Me Like You Do/Way Down by the Cherry Tree	1956	$20
❏ F2874	I'm Flying/Why Should I Cry	1954	$20
❏ F2801	I'm Going to Sit Right Down and Cry Over You/Forever Is Now	1954	$30
❏ F2736	I'm Gonna Rock, Rock, Rock/Love's Like That	1954	$30
❏ F3148	I've Got Rhythm in My Nursery Rhymes/Dream Boy	1955	$20
❏ F3266	Pet Me, Poppa/Like I Love Nobody Before	1955	$20
❏ F3062	Prize of Gold/Foolish Notion	1955	$20
❏ F2932	Show Me/Every Road Must Have a Turning	1954	$20

MARMALADE, THE
ARIOLA AMERICA
❏ 7619	Falling Apart at the Seams/Fly, Fly, Fly	1976	$4
❏ 7631	My Everything/ Walking a Tightrope	1976	$4

EMI
❏ 3676	Engine Driver/Wishing Well	1973	$4

EPIC
❏ 10162	Can't Stop Now/There Ain't No Use in Hanging On	1967	$10
❏ 10284	Cry/Man in a Shop	1968	$8
❏ 10340	Hey Joe/Lovin' Things	1968	$8
❏ 10428	Ob-La-Di, Ob-La-Da/Chains	1969	$10
❏ 10236	Otherwise It's Been a Perfect Day/I See the Rain	1967	$10
❏ 10493	Time Is On My Side/ Baby Make It Soon	1969	$8
❏ 10404	Wait for Me Mary-Ann/ Mess Around	1968	$8

LONDON
❏ 20068	Lonely Man/Cousin Norman	1971	$5
❏ 20066	My Little One/Is Your Life Your Own	1971	$5

MARQUEES, THE (1)
DAY-SEL
❏ 1001	Ecstasy/Close to Me	1959	$600

MARQUEES, THE (2)
GRAND
❏ 141	The Bells/The Rain	1956	$300

— With no address on label

MARQUEES, THE (3)
JO-ANN
❏ 130	I Need a Helping Hand/ Don't You Do Me Like That	1961	$125
❏ 128	Stay with Me/That's the Way I Feel	1960	$200

MARQUEES, THE (4)
LEN
❏ 100	Say Hey/I'm in Misery	1958	$125

MARQUEES, THE (5)
OKEH
❏ 7096	Hey Little School Girl/Wyatt Earp	1957	$120

Number	Title	Yr	NM

MARQUEES, THE (6)
WARNER BROS.
| ☐ 5127 | Christmas in the Crowd/Sunset to Sunrise | 1959 | $50 |
| ☐ 5072 | Who Will Be the First One/Love Machine | 1959 | $50 |

MARQUIS, THE
ONYX
| ☐ 505 | Bohemian Daddy/(B-side unknown) | 1956 | $2000 |

MARSH, RICHIE
ACAMA
| ☐ 125 | Baby, Baby, Baby/Half Angel | 1960 | $40 |
AVA
| ☐ 122 | Goodbye/Crying Inside My Heart | 1963 | $30 |
ROSCO
| ☐ 412 | There's Only One Girl/What Chance Have I | 1960 | $30 |
SHEPHERD
| ☐ 2203 | They Say Darling/I Swear That It's True | 1962 | $30 |

MARSHALL BROTHERS, THE
SAVOY
| ☐ 825 | Mr. Santa's Boogie/Who'll Be the Fool from Now On | 1951 | $500 |
| ☐ 833 | Why Make a Fool Out of Me/Just a Poor Boy in Love | 1952 | $400 |

MARSHALL, SAMMY
ROXIE
| ☐ 324 | It's Christmas Time Again/Maybe We'll Have Snow for Christmas | 1961 | $20 |
SILVER
| ☐ 108 | Manger of Bethlehem/Holy Day | 1958 | $30 |

MARSHALL TUCKER BAND, THE
CAPRICORN
☐ 0049	Another Cruel Love/Blue Ridge Mountain Sky	1974	$5
☐ 0278	Can't You See/Fly Like an Eagle	1977	$5
☐ 0021	Can't You See/See You Later, I'm Gone	1973	$6
☐ 0300	Dream Lover/A Change Is Gonna Come	1978	$5
☐ 0244	Fire on the Mountain/Bop Away My Blues	1975	$5
☐ 0270	Heard It in a Love Song/Life in a Song	1977	$5
☐ 0307	I'll Be Seeing You/Everybody Needs Somebody	1978	$5
☐ 0258	Long Hard Ride/Windy City Blues	1976	$5
☐ 0251	Searchin' for a Rainbow/Walkin' and Talkin'	1976	$5
☐ 0030	Take the Highway/Jesus Told Me So	1973	$6
☐ 0228	This Ol' Cowboy/Try One More Time	1975	$5
MERCURY
☐ 870505-7	Dancin' Shoes/I'm Glad It's Gone	1988	$3
☐ 888774-7	Hangin' Out in Smokey Places/He Don't Know	1987	$3
☐ 870050-7	Once You Get the Feel of It/Slow Down	1987	$3
☐ 872096-7	Still Holdin' On/Same Old Moon	1989	$3
WARNER BROS.
☐ 29619	A Place I've Never Been/8:05	1983	$4
☐ 49259	Disillusioned/Without You	1980	$4
☐ 29355	I May Be Easy But You Make It Hard/Shot Down Where You Stand	1984	$4
☐ 49215	It Takes Time/Jimi	1980	$5
☐ 8841	Last of the Singing Cowboys/Pass It On	1979	$5
☐ 8841 [PS]	Last of the Singing Cowboys/Pass It On	1979	$6
☐ 29995	Mr. President/The Sea, Dreams and Fairy Tales	1982	$4
☐ 49724	This Time I Believe/Tell the Blues to Take Off the Night	1981	$4
☐ 49764	Time Has Come/Love Some	1981	$4

7-Inch Extended Plays
CAPRICORN
| ☐ SCP 0124 | 24 Hours at a Time/Blue Ridge Mountain Sky//A New Life | 1973 | $10 |

—*Jukebox issue; small hole, plays at 33 1/3 rpm*

MARSHANS, THE
ETIQUETTE
| ☐ 8 | I Remember/It's Almost Tomorrow | 1964 | $30 |
JOHNSON
| ☐ 736 | My Letter To Santa/Main Man | 1966 | $30 |

MARTELLS, THE
BELLA
| ☐ 45 | Forgotten Spring/Va Va Voom | 1961 | $60 |
CESSNA
| ☐ 477 | Forgotten Spring/Va Va Voom | 1961 | $100 |
RELIC
| ☐ 517 | Forgotten Spring/Va Va Voom | 1964 | $10 |

MARTERIE, RALPH
MERCURY
☐ 54280	Across the Wide Missouri/Silver Moon	1950	$30
☐ 57050	Alice Blue Gown/I Only Have Eyes for You	1951	$20
☐ 57120	Alice Blue Gown/Once in a While	1951	$20
☐ 702480	All That Oil in Texas/Love for Three Oranges	1953	$20
☐ 57820	Autumn Leaves/Goodbye Sweetheart	1952	$20
☐ 56790	Beautiful Ohio/A Trumpeter's Lullaby	1951	$20
☐ 705350	Blue Mirage (Don't Go)/Remember Me	1955	$15
☐ 704820	Bongo Guitar/Kiss Crazy Baby	1954	$15
☐ 715470	B'wana/Trumpet Soliliquy	1959	$10
☐ 700970	Caravan/While We Dream	1953	$20
☐ 710070	Carla/Guaglione	1956	$15
☐ 56580	Castle Rock/September Song	1951	$20
☐ 706550	Cha-Cha-Cha/One Fine Day	1955	$15
☐ 57340	Christmas in Killarney/When Your Lover Has Gone	1951	$20
☐ 706140	Ciribiri Mambo/O Mio Balbino Caro	1955	$15
☐ 712790	College Man/Cinderella Tango	1958	$10
☐ 714240	Compulsion/Words of Love	1959	$10
☐ 701530	Crazy, Man, Crazy/Go Away	1953	$30

—*Vocal by Larry Ragon & the Smarty-Aires*
☐ 58820	Dark Eyes/Peanut Vendor	1952	$20
☐ 56580	Didn't Yer Mother Ever Tell Ya Nothin'/You Better Stop	1951	$20
☐ 704930	Dig That Crazy Santa Claus/Rock, Rock	1954	$20
☐ 703580	Dry Marterie/Until Six	1954	$15
☐ 706920	Dry Marterie with an Olive/The Toy Tiger	1955	$15
☐ 58240	Frenesi/What Is This Thing Called Love	1952	$20

—*With the Harmonicats*
☐ 712040	Hesitation Hop/Driftwood	1957	$12
☐ 71594	I Can't Give You Anything But Love/Diga Diga Doo	1960	$10
☐ 58520	I'm Yours/The Music Goes Round and Round	1952	$20
☐ 58600	In a Persian Market/Street Scene	1952	$20
☐ 55070	I Only Have Eyes for You/I'll Never Smile Again	1950	$30
☐ 54570	It Ain't Necessarily So/Sweet and Lovely	1950	$30
☐ 57160	It's All in the Game/Tenderly	1951	$20
☐ 713380	Love Song from "Houseboat"/Lou's Blues	1958	$10
☐ 706820	Maybellene/The Toy Tiger	1955	$20
☐ 54730	My Silent Love/Say It Isn't So	1950	$30
☐ 57870	Perdido/Lulu (Had a Baby)	1952	$20
☐ 700450	Pretend/After Midnight	1953	$20
☐ 713790	Pretend Cha Cha/Flighty	1958	$10
☐ 710920	Shish-Kebab/Bop-a-Doo Bop-a-Doo	1957	$10
☐ 705880	Silver Moon/Chicken Boogie	1955	$15
☐ 704320	Skokiaan/Crazy 'Bout Lollipop	1954	$15
☐ 55700	So Long (It's Been Good to Know Yuh)/Here's to Happiness	1951	$20
☐ 55620	Sonny Boy/Danse Arabe	1950	$30
☐ 58270	Stompin' at the Savoy/Boulevard of Broken Dreams	1952	$20
☐ 59030	Takes Two to Tango/Ol' Man Mose	1952	$20
☐ 704060	Tantalizin' Melody/Bumble Boogie	1954	$15
☐ 57670	Tell Me Why/Perdido	1951	$20
☐ 709760	That Mellow Saxophone/Do You Ever Think of Me	1956	$15
☐ 700080	The Continental/Indian Summer	1952	$20
☐ 702810	The Creep/Love Theme	1953	$20
☐ 701990	The Girl of the Golden West/The Moon Is Blue	1953	$20

☐ 707710	The Grass Is Green/Where the Wind Blows	1956	$15
☐ 708360	Theme from Picnic/Rock and Roll the Barrel	1956	$15
☐ 57590	The Object of My Affection/Lulu Had a Baby	1951	$20
☐ 714880	Thin Man/When My Sugar Walks Down the Street	1959	$10
☐ 710500	Tricky/Travel at Your Own Risk	1957	$10
☐ 703280	Tularosa/Big Noise from Winnetka	1954	$15
☐ 714730	Wampum/Cleopatra's Dream	1959	$10
☐ 702210	Warsaw Concerto/Lazy River	1953	$20
☐ 707600	Wondrous Love/Misirlou	1955	$15
UNITED ARTISTS
☐ 315	Bacardi/The Shuck	1961	$8
☐ 352	Caravan/Tonight	1961	$8
☐ 447	Caravan Twist/Dry Marterie with a Twist	1962	$8
☐ 409	Lili Marlene/Schwalbenwinkel	1962	$8
☐ 554	Little Girl Blue/My Romance	1963	$8
☐ 284	Moonlight Becomes You/Truly	1961	$8
☐ 465	Smoke Rings/Skyliner	1962	$8
☐ 498	Theme from Carnival/Moonlight in Vermont	1962	$8

MARTHA AND THE VANDELLAS
GORDY
☐ 7127	Baby Don't Leave Me/I Won't Be the Fool I've Been Again	1973	$8
☐ 7110	Bless You/Hope I Don't Get My Heart Broke	1971	$8
☐ 7014	Come and Get These Memories/Jealous Love	1963	$40
☐ 7033	Dancing in the Street/There He Is (At My Door)	1964	$20
☐ 7033 [PS]	Dancing in the Street/There He Is (At My Door)	1964	$120
☐ 7022	Heat Wave/A Love Like Yours	1963	$30
☐ 7067	Honey Chile/Show Me the Way	1967	$12

—*Starting here, as "Martha Reeves and the Vandellas"*
☐ 7075	I Can't Dance to That Music You're Playin'/I Tried	1968	$10
☐ 7103	I Gotta Let You Go/You're the Loser Now	1970	$8
☐ 7011	I'll Have to Let Him Go/My Baby Won't Come Back	1962	$30
☐ 7056	I'm Ready for Love/He Doesn't Love Her Anymore	1966	$20

—*Gordy" logo at top*
| ☐ 7056 | I'm Ready for Love/He Doesn't Love Her Anymore | 1966 | $15 |

—*Gordy" logo at left*
☐ 7113	In and Out of My Life/Your Love Makes It All Worthwhile	1972	$8
☐ 7031	In My Lonely Room/A Tear for the Girl	1964	$20
☐ 7070	I Promise to Wait My Love/Forget Me Not	1968	$10
☐ 7098	I Should Be Proud/Love, Guess Who	1970	$8
☐ 7027	Live Wire/Old Love	1964	$20
☐ 7062	Love Bug Leave My Heart Alone/One Way Out	1967	$10
☐ 7048	My Baby Loves Me/Never Leave Your Baby's Side	1965	$15
☐ 7080	Sweet Darlin'/Without You	1968	$10
☐ 7094	Taking My Love (And Leaving Me)/Heartless	1969	$8
☐ 7118	Tear It On Down/I Want You Back	1972	$8
☐ 7085	(We've Got) Honey Love/I'm In Love (And I Know It)	1969	$8
☐ 7053	What Am I Gonna Do Without Your Love/Go Ahead and Laugh	1966	$15
☐ 7036	Wild One/Dancing Slow	1964	$15
TOPPS/MOTOWN
| ☐ 7 | Dancing in the Street | 1967 | $80 |

—*Cardboard record*
| ☐ 14 | Love Is Like a Heat Wave | 1967 | $80 |

—*Cardboard record*

7-Inch Extended Plays
GORDY
| ☐ G-60917 | Come and Get These Memories/Love Is Like a Heat Wave/Dancing in the Street//Love (Makes Me Do Foolish Things)/A Love Like Yours (Don't Come Knocking Everyday)/Nowhere to Run | 1966 | $60 |

—*Jukebox issue; small hole, plays at 33 1/3 rpm*
| ☐ G-60917 [PS] | Greatest Hits | 1966 | $60 |
| ☐ G-60920 | I'm Ready for Love/One Way Out/Jimmy Mack//I'll Follow You/No More Tearstained Makeup/Tell Me I'll Never Be Alone | 1966 | $50 |

—*Jukebox issue; small hole, plays at 33 1/3 rpm*

Number	Title	Yr	NM
❏ G-60920 [PS]	Watchout!	1966	$50

MARTIN, BENNY
DECCA
Number	Title	Yr	NM
❏ 9-30712	Border Baby/My Fortune	1958	$30
❏ 9-31050	Top Gun/Going Down This Road	1960	$30

JAB
| ❏ 9002 | I'm a Father Alone/Salvation Army | 1967 | $8 |

MERCURY
❏ 70560	Ice Cold Love/You Know That I Know	1955	$40
❏ 70794	If I Didn't Have a Conscience/You're Guilty Darlin'	1956	$40
❏ 70883	Lover of the Town/Whippoor-Will	1956	$40
❏ 70508	Me and My Fiddle/The Law of My Heart	1954	$40
❏ 70664	Take My Word/Who Put Those Tears in Your Eyes	1955	$40

RCA VICTOR
❏ 47-7100	Do Me a Favor/(B-side unknown)	1957	$30
❏ 47-7003	I Saw Your Face in the Moon/Torch of Love	1957	$30
❏ 47-6855	That's the Story of My Life/Look What You've Done	1957	$30

STARDAY
❏ 519	A Dime's Worth of Dreams/Pretty Girl	1960	$30
❏ 646	Down in the Shinnery/Two Take Away One Equals Lonesome	1963	$20
❏ 743	Hello City Limits/I'll Never Get Over Loving You	1965	$15
❏ 725	One Way or the Other/Weekend Ellie	1965	$15
❏ 705	Stick Your Finger in a Glass of Water/The Other Me	1964	$20

MARTIN, DEAN, AND JERRY LEWIS
7-Inch Extended Plays
CAPITOL
❏ EAP 1-533	(contents unknown)	1954	$100
❏ EAP 1-733	(contents unknown)	1956	$75
❏ EAP 1-533 [PS]	Living It Up	1954	$100
❏ EAP 1-733 [PS]	Pardners	1956	$75

MARTIN, DEAN
CAPITOL
❏ 4420	Ain't That a Kick in the Head/Humdinger	1960	$8
❏ F1975	All I Have to Give/When You're Smiling	1952	$20
❏ F3988	Angel Baby/I'll Gladly Make the Same Mistake Again	1958	$8
❏ F1921	As You Are/Oh Boy	1952	$20
❏ F3680	Bamboozled/Only Trust Your Heart	1957	$12
❏ 4551	Bella, Bella Bambina/All in a Night's Work	1961	$8
❏ F1458	Beside You/Who's Sorry Now	1951	$20
❏ F2071	Bet-i-Cha/I Passed Your House Tonight	1952	$20
❏ F1052	Bye Bye Blackbird/Happy Feet	1950	$20
❏ F3648	Captured/The Man Who Plays the Mandolino	1957	$10
❏ F3133	Chee Chee Oo-Chee/Ridin' Into Love	1955	$10
❏ F981	Choo'n Gum/I Don't Care If the Sun Don't Shine	1950	$20
❏ F3011	Confused/Belle from Barcelona	1955	$10
❏ F1160	Don't Rock the Boat/I'm in Love with You	1950	$20

— With Margaret Whiting
❏ F1724	Go Go Go Go/Luna Mezzo Mare	1951	$20
❏ F1797	Hanging Around with You/Aw C'mon	1951	$20
❏ F2749	Hey Brother Pour the Wine/I'd Cry Like a Baby	1954	$15
❏ 4472	How Sweet It Is/Sogni D'Oro	1960	$8
❏ F4287	I Ain't Gonna Lead This Life No More/Career	1959	$8
❏ F3718	I Can't Give You Anything But Love/I Never Had a Chance	1957	$10
❏ F2555	If I Could Sing Like Bing/Don't You Remember	1953	$15
❏ F1342	If/I Love the Way	1950	$20
❏ F2240	I Know a Dream When I See One/Second Chance	1952	$20
❏ F3238	I Like Them All/In Napoli	1955	$10
❏ F1028	I'll Always Love You/Baby Obey Me	1950	$20
❏ F3352	Innamorata/Lady with a Big Umbrella	1956	$10
❏ F1703	In the Cool, Cool, Cool of the Evening/Bonne Nuit	1951	$20

Number	Title	Yr	NM
❏ F1002	I Still Get a Thrill/Be Honest with Me	1950	$20
❏ F4124	It Takes So Long/You Were Made for Love	1959	$8
❏ F2378	Little Did We Know/There's My Lover	1953	$15
❏ F2485	Love Me, Love Me/Till I Find You	1953	$15
❏ 4328	Love Me, My Love/Who Was That Lady	1960	$8
❏ F3842	Makin' Love Ukulele Style/Good Morning Life	1957	$10
❏ F1811	Meanderin'/Bella Bimba	1951	$20
❏ F3295	Memories Are Made of This/Change of Heart	1955	$15
❏ F3521	Mississippi Dreamboat/Test of Time	1956	$10
❏ F2818	Money Burns a Hole in My Pocket/Sway	1954	$15
❏ F948	Muskrat Ramble/I'm Gonna Paper All My Walls with Love Letters	1950	$20
❏ F2140	Oh Marie/Come Back to Sorrento	1952	$20
❏ F1682	Oh Marie/I'll Always Love You	1951	$15
❏ F4222	On an Evening in Roma/You Can't Love 'Em All	1959	$8
❏ F4222 [PS]	On an Evening in Roma/You Can't Love 'Em All	1959	$30
❏ F4065	Once Upon a Time/The Magician	1958	$8
❏ F2985	Open Up the Doghouse/Long, Long Ago	1954	$20

— With Nat King Cole
❏ F1139	Peddler's Serenade/Wham, Bam, Thank You, Ma'am	1950	$20
❏ F2001	Pretty as a Picture/Won't You Surrender	1952	$20
❏ F3787	Promise Her Anything/Triche Trache	1957	$10
❏ F3153	Simpatico/Love Is All That Matters	1955	$10
❏ F1817	Solitaire/I Ran All the Way Home	1951	$20
❏ 4518	Sparklin' Eyes/Tu Sei Bella Signorina	1961	$8
❏ F3414	Standing on the Corner/Watching the World Go By	1956	$10
❏ F3468	Street of Love/I'm Gonna Steal You Away	1956	$10
❏ 54-726	That Lucky Old Sun/Vieni Su	1949	$30
❏ B-44153	That's Amore/It Must Be Him	1988	$4

— B-side by Vikki Carr
❏ B-44153 [PS]	That's Amore/It Must Be Him	1988	$5
❏ F2589	That's Amore/You're the Right One	1953	$20
❏ F2870	That's What I Like/Peddler Man	1954	$15
❏ F2640	The Christmas Blues/If I Should Love Again	1953	$15
❏ F3577	The Look/Give Me a Sign	1956	$10
❏ 4570	The Story of Life/Giuggiola	1961	$8
❏ F2911	Try Again/One More Time	1954	$15
❏ F3196	Two Sleepy People/Relax Ay Voo	1955	$10

— With Line Renaud
| ❏ F2319 | What Could Be More Beautiful/The Kiss | 1953 | $15 |
| ❏ F3752 | Write to Me from Naples/Beau James | 1957 | $10 |

MCA
| ❏ 52662 | L.A. Is My Home/Drinking Champagne | 1985 | $4 |

REPRISE
❏ 20150	Ain't Gonna Try Anymore/A Face in the Crowd	1963	$10
❏ 0500	A Million and One/Shades	1966	$6
❏ 1141	Amor Mio/You Made Me Love You	1972	$5
❏ 0761	April Again/That Old Time Feelin'	1968	$5
❏ 20082	Baby-O/Dame Su Amor	1962	$12
❏ 0542	Blue Christmas/A Marshmallow World	1966	$6
❏ 20076	C'est Si Bon/The Poor People of Paris	1962	$30

— Released only in Italy
❏ 0466	Come Running Back/Bouquet of Roses	1966	$6
❏ 20194	Corrine, Corrina/My Sugar's Gone	1963	$12
❏ 0857	Crying Time/One Cup of Happiness	1969	$5
❏ 0955	Detroit City/Turn the World Around	1970	$5
❏ 0893	Down Home/Come On Down	1970	$5
❏ 0281	Everybody Loves Somebody/A Little Voice	1964	$12
❏ 0709	Everybody Loves Somebody/A Million and One	1968	$5
❏ 0765	Five Card Stud/One Lonely Boy	1968	$5
❏ 0973	For the Good Times/Georgia Sunshine	1970	$5
❏ 0915	For the Love of a Woman/The Tracks of My Tears	1970	$5

Number	Title	Yr	NM
❏ 20116	From the Bottom of My Heart (Dammi, Dammi, Dammi)/Who's Got the Action	1962	$10
❏ 20116 [PS]	From the Bottom of My Heart (Dammi, Dammi, Dammi)/Who's Got the Action	1962	$30
❏ 20217	Fugue for Tinhorns/The Oldest Established (Permanent Floating Crap Game in New York)	1963	$20

— By Frank Sinatra/Bing Crosby/Dean Martin
| ❏ 20217 [PS] | Fugue for Tinhorns/The Oldest Established (Permanent Floating Crap Game in New York) | 1963 | $100 |

— By Frank Sinatra/Bing Crosby/Dean Martin
❏ 0812	Gentle on My Mind/That's When I See the Blues	1969	$5
❏ 0393	Houston/Bumming Around	1965	$8
❏ 0714	Houston/I Will	1968	$5
❏ 1085	I Can Give You What You Want Now/Guess Who	1972	$5
❏ 0730	In the Chapel in the Moonlight/Little Ole Wine Drinker, Me	1968	$5
❏ 0601	In the Chapel in the Moonlight/Welcome to My World	1967	$6
❏ 0735	In the Misty Moonlight/Not Enough Indians	1970	$4

— 0703 through 0735 are "Back to Back Hits" reissues
❏ 0640	In the Misty Moonlight/The Glory of Love	1967	$6
❏ 0640	In the Misty Moonlight/Wallpaper Roses	1967	$6
❏ 0841	I Take a Lot of Pride in What I Am/Drowning in My Tears	1969	$5
❏ 0415	I Will/You're the Reason I'm in Love	1965	$8
❏ 0252	La Giostra (Merry-Go-Round)/Grazie, Prego, Scusi	1964	$8
❏ 0703	Lay Some Happiness on Me/(Open Up the Door) Let the Good Times In	1968	$5
❏ 0571	Lay Some Happiness on Me/Think About Me	1967	$6
❏ 0608	Little Ole Wine Drinker, Me/I Can't Help Remembering You	1967	$6
❏ 0934	My Woman, My Woman, My Wife/Here We Go Again	1970	$5
❏ 0538	(Open Up the Door) Let the Good Times In/I'm Not the Marrying Kind	1966	$6
❏ 20128	Sam's Song/Me and My Shadow	1962	$20

— A-side with Sammy Davis, Jr.; B-side: Sammy Davis Jr. and Frank Sinatra
❏ 20128 [PS]	Sam's Song/Me and My Shadow	1962	$50
❏ 0344	Send Me the Pillow You Dream On/I'll Be Seeing You	1965	$8
❏ 0718	Send Me the Pillow You Dream On/The Door Is Still Open to My Heart	1968	$5
❏ 1004	She's a Little Bit Country/Raining in My Heart	1971	$5
❏ 1166	Smile/Get On With Your Livin'	1973	$5
❏ 0711	Somewhere There's a Someone/Come Running Back	1968	$5
❏ 0443	Somewhere There's a Someone/That Old Clock on the Wall	1965	$6
❏ 0307	The Door Is Still Open to My Heart/Every Minute, Every Hour	1964	$8
❏ 1060	What's Yesterday/The Right Kind of Woman	1971	$5
❏ PRO248 [DJ]	White Christmas (same on both sides)	1966	$10
❏ 20140	Who's Got the Action/Send a Fine	1963	$10

WARNER BROS.
❏ 29480	Drinking Champagne/Since I Met You Baby	1983	$4
❏ 29584	My First Country Song/Hangin' Around	1983	$4
❏ EAP 1-702 [PS]	Artists and Models	1956	$20
❏ EAP 1-1285 [PS]	A Winter Romance, Part 1	1959	$15
❏ EAP 2-1285 [PS]	A Winter Romance, Part 2	1959	$15
❏ EAP 3-1285 [PS]	A Winter Romance, Part 3	1959	$15
❏ EAP 1-702	(contents unknown)	1956	$20
❏ EAP 1-849	(contents unknown)	1957	$15
❏ EAP 2-849	(contents unknown)	1957	$15
❏ EAP 3-849	(contents unknown)	1957	$15
❏ EAP 1-806	(contents unknown)	1957	$20
❏ EAP 1-840	(contents unknown)	1957	$20
❏ EAP 1-1285	(contents unknown)	1959	$15
❏ EAP 2-1285	(contents unknown)	1959	$15
❏ EAP 3-1285	(contents unknown)	1959	$15
❏ EAP-1-9123 [PS]	Dean Martin	1955	$20

Number	Title	Yr	NM
☐ MA 1-1580 [PS]	Dean Martin	1961	$20
☐ EAP 1-806 [PS]	Hollywood or Bust	1957	$20
☐ EAP-1-9123	Let Me Go, Lover/The Naughty Lady of Shady Lane//Mambo Italiano/ That's All I Want from You	1955	$20
☐ EAP 1-701 [PS]	Memories Are Made of This	1956	$20
☐ EAP 1-701	Memories Are Made of This/I Like Them All//Change of Heart//Ridin' Into Love	1956	$20
☐ EAP 1-849 [PS]	Pretty Baby, Part 1	1957	$15
☐ EAP 2-849 [PS]	Pretty Baby, Part 2	1957	$15
☐ EAP 3-849 [PS]	Pretty Baby, Part 3	1957	$15
☐ EAP 1-481 [PS]	Sunny Italy	1954	$25
☐ EAP 1-840 [PS]	Ten Thousand Bedrooms	1957	$20
☐ MA 1-1580	That's Amore/Memories Are Made of This// Volare/Return to Me	1961	$20

— Small hole, plays at 33 1/3 rpm

Number	Title	Yr	NM
☐ EAP 1-481	That's Amore/Oh Marie// Come Back to Sorrento/ Luna Mezzo Mare	1954	$25

REPRISE

Number	Title	Yr	NM
☐ SR6301 [PS]	Dean Martin's Greatest Hits! Vol. 1	1968	$12
☐ SR6320 [PS]	Dean Martin's Greatest Hits! Vol. 2	1968	$12
☐ SR2053 [PS]	Dino	1972	$12

— Part of "Little LP" series (#179)

Number	Title	Yr	NM
☐ SR6213	Don't Let the Blues Make You Bad/A Million and One//I'm Living in Two Worlds//Shades/ Today Is Not the Day/I Ain't Gonna Try Anymore	1966	$10

— Jukebox issue; small hole, plays at 33 1/3 rpm

Number	Title	Yr	NM
☐ SR6123 [PS]	Dream with Dean	1964	$12
☐ 6130 [PS]	Everybody Loves Somebody	1964	$12

— Both versions have virtually identical sleeves

Number	Title	Yr	NM
☐ 6130	Everybody Loves Somebody/ Corrine Corrina/Face in the Crowd//Just Close Your Eyes/ Things/My Heart Cries for You	1964	$20

— Jukebox issue; small hole, plays at 33 1/3 rpm; white label with "Promotion" at bottom

Number	Title	Yr	NM
☐ SR6301	Everybody Loves Somebody/ You're Nobody 'Til Somebody Loves You/In the Chapel in the Moonlight//Every Minute, Every Hour/Bumming Around/You'll Always Be the One I Love	1968	$10

— Jukebox issue; small hole, plays at 33 1/3 rpm

Number	Title	Yr	NM
☐ SR6330 [PS]	Gentle on My Mind	1968	$12
☐ SR2053	Guess Who/Just the Other Side of Nowhere/What's Yesterday//Blue Memories/ Party Dolls & Wine/I Can Give You What You Want	1972	$10

— Jukebox issue; small hole, plays at 33 1/3 rpm

Number	Title	Yr	NM
☐ SR6181 [PS]	Houston	1965	$12
☐ SR6181	Houston/Snap Your Fingers/ Little Lovely One//I Will/The First Thing Ev'ry Morning (And the Last Thing Ev'ry Night)/Down Home	1965	$10

— Jukebox issue; small hole, plays at 33 1/3 rpm

Number	Title	Yr	NM
☐ SR6123	I Don't Know Why (I Just Do)/Baby Won't You Please Come Home//I'm Confessin'// "Gimme" A Little Kiss Will "Ya" Huh?/I'll Buy That Dream/Smile	1964	$10

— Jukebox issue; small hole, plays at 33 1/3 rpm

Number	Title	Yr	NM
☐ SR6320	In the Misty Moonlight/ Send Me the Pillow That You Dream On/Little Old Wine Drinker, Me//Lay Some Happiness on Me/ You've Still Got a Place in My Heart/King of the Road	1968	$10

— Jukebox issue; small hole, plays at 33 1/3 rpm

Number	Title	Yr	NM
☐ SR2113	I Wonder Who's Kissing Her Now/At Sundown/ Almost Like Being in Love//It's a Good Day/ Ramblin' Rose/I'm Sittin' on Top of the World	1973	$10

— Jukebox issue; small hole, plays at 33 1/3 rpm

Number	Title	Yr	NM
☐ SR6250	Little Old Wine Drinker, Me/The Green, Green Grass of Home/Wallpaper Roses//In the Chapel in the Moonlight/Welcome to My World/Release Me (And Let Me Love Again)	1967	$10

— Jukebox issue; small hole, plays at 33 1/3 rpm

Number	Title	Yr	NM
☐ SR6201	Second Hand Rose/ Bouquet of Roses/Just a Little Lovin'//Somewhere There's a Someone/I Can't Help It/Anytime	1966	$10

— Jukebox issue; small hole, plays at 33 1/3 rpm

Number	Title	Yr	NM
☐ SR2113 [PS]	Sittin' on Top of the World	1973	$12

— Part of "Little LP" series (#228)

Number	Title	Yr	NM
☐ SR6201 [PS]	Somewhere There's a Someone	1966	$12
☐ SR6330	That Old Time Feelin'/ Welcome to My Heart/ By the Time I Get to Phoenix//Gentle on My Mind/That's When I See the Blues (In Your Pretty Brown Eyes)/April Again	1968	$10

— Jukebox issue; small hole, plays at 33 1/3 rpm

Number	Title	Yr	NM
☐ SR6211	The Glory of Love/Empty Saddles in the Old Corral/ Side by Side//On the Sunny Side of the Street/ The Last Round-up/Red Sails in the Sunset	1966	$10

— Jukebox issue; small hole, plays at 33 1/3 rpm

Number	Title	Yr	NM
☐ SR6213 [PS]	The Hit Sound of Dean Martin	1966	$12
☐ SR6211 [PS]	The Silencers	1966	$12
☐ SR6170	Walk On By/King of the Road//(Remember Me) I'm the One Who Loves You//Here Comes My Baby/My Shoes Keep Walking Back to You/ The Birds and the Bees	1965	$10

— Jukebox issue; small hole, plays at 33 1/3 rpm

Number	Title	Yr	NM
☐ SR6250 [PS]	Welcome to My World	1967	$12

MARTIN, GEORGE

UNITED ARTISTS

Number	Title	Yr	NM
☐ 750	A Hard Day's Night/I Should Have Known Better	1964	$125
☐ 750 [PS]	A Hard Day's Night/I Should Have Known Better	1964	$2000
☐ 831	All Quiet on the Mersey Front/Cast Your Fate to the Wind	1965	$20
☐ 873	I Feel Fine/Downtown	1965	$20
☐ 50148	Love in the Open Air/ Bahama Sound	1967	$40

MARTIN, GRADY

DECCA

Number	Title	Yr	NM
☐ 9-28588	A Fool Such as I/ Side by Side	1953	$30
☐ 9-30022	Allegheny Moon/When My Dreamboat Comes Home	1956	$20
☐ 9-30453	All the Way/Chicago	1957	$20
☐ 9-28472	Anniversary Song/ Happy Birthday	1952	$30
☐ 9-29328	A Pretty Girl Is Like a Melody/What's the Use	1954	$30
☐ 9-28689	Bandera/Poor Butterfly	1953	$30
☐ 9-28987	Bimbo/Mexicali Rose	1954	$30
☐ 9-29691	Don't Take Your Love from Me/Nashville	1955	$20
☐ 31990	Double-o-Dobro/Last Letter	1966	$12
☐ 9-28845	Dragnet/The Velvet Glove	1953	$30
☐ 9-31013	Elmer's Tune/You've Got Me Crying Again	1959	$15
☐ 9-28074	Get Up and Give/ Don't Stay Away	1952	$30
☐ 25642	Heartaches by the Number/ The Velvet Glove	1964	$8
☐ 25668	He'll Have to Go/ Bully of the Town	1965	$8
☐ 9-30940	Hey Chick/Tuxedo Junction	1959	$15
☐ 9-29146	Isle of Capri/Twelfth Street Rag	1954	$30
☐ 9-28388	I Went to Your Wedding/ You Belong to Me	1952	$30
☐ 9-29468	Long John Boogie/Gorgeous	1955	$20
☐ 31885	May the Bird of Paradise Fly Up Your Nose/The Battle of New Orleans	1965	$10
☐ 25629	Melody of Love/ Around the World	1964	$8
☐ 9-46375	San Antonio Rose/ Bully of the Town	1951	$30
☐ 9-28613	Shenanigans (Part 1)/ Shenanigans (Part 2)	1953	$30
☐ 9-29558	Singing the Blues Till My Daddy Comes Home/Hot Lips	1955	$20
☐ 9-28497	Sioux City Sue/ September Song	1952	$30
☐ 9-27838	Stardust/Beer Barrel Polka	1951	$30
☐ 31211	The Fuzz/Tippin' In	1961	$15
☐ 31691	Theme from "Malamondo" (Funny World)/El Paso	1964	$10

Number	Title	Yr	NM
☐ 31381	Twist and Turn/Good, Good, Good	1962	$10

7-Inch Extended Plays

Number	Title	Yr	NM
☐ ED2747	*Colonel Bogey March/ Fraulein/Happy Birthday/ Red River Valley	1963	$10
☐ ED2747 [PS]	Happy Birthday	1963	$12

MARTIN, JANIS

PALETTE

Number	Title	Yr	NM
☐ 5058	Hard Times Ahead/Here Today and Gone Tomorrow	1960	$30
☐ 5071	Teen Street/Cry Guitar	1961	$30

RCA VICTOR

Number	Title	Yr	NM
☐ 47-7104	All Right Baby/Billy Boy, Billy Boy	1957	$40
☐ 47-7184	Cracker Jack/Good Love	1958	$40
☐ 47-6491	Drugstore Rock and Roll/ Will You, Willyum	1956	$50
☐ 47-6744	Let's Elope, Baby/ Barefoot Baby	1956	$40
☐ 47-6983	Love and Kisses/I'll Never Be Free	1957	$40
☐ 47-6832	Love Me to Pieces/ Two Long Years	1957	$40
☐ 47-6652	My Boy Elvis/Little Bit	1956	$75
☐ 47-6560	Ooby-Dooby/One More Year to Go	1956	$50

MARTIN, MARY

BUENA VISTA

Number	Title	Yr	NM
☐ 332	Making Believe It's Christmas Eve/ Motherless Child	1958	$20

MARTIN, RAY

CAPITOL

Number	Title	Yr	NM
☐ F3767	Heladero/Manhattan Tango	1957	$15
☐ F3516	Street Symphony/ Tambourine	1956	$15
☐ F3393	Tickled Pink/If Hearts Could Talk	1956	$15
☐ F3670	Whistling Sergeant/ Tango in the Rain	1957	$15

ESSEX

Number	Title	Yr	NM
☐ 335	Begorrah/Hi-Lilli, Hi-Lo	1953	$20
☐ 346	Tango Waltz/Carnivalito	1954	$20

RCA VICTOR

Number	Title	Yr	NM
☐ 47-7920	The Boulevard of Broken Dreams/The Mime's Theme	1961	$8
☐ 47-7344	Wild Gypsy/Big Dipper	1958	$10

UNITED ARTISTS

Number	Title	Yr	NM
☐ 116	Argentina Ballerina/ Spring in Spain	1958	$10
☐ 103	Song from "The Quiet American"/The Grape Stompers	1958	$12

MARTIN, TONY

CHART

Number	Title	Yr	NM
☐ 5078	Coast of California/ Inseparable	1970	$8
☐ 5059	Hills of Yesterday/Strangers	1970	$6

DOT

Number	Title	Yr	NM
☐ 16402	As Long As She Needs Me/I'll Be Seeing You	1962	$8
☐ 16361	In Other Words (Fly Me to the Moon)/The Rest of My Days	1961	$8

MERCURY

Number	Title	Yr	NM
☐ 5708x45	If I Love Again/Make Believe	1951	$20
☐ 5489x45	That Old Black Magic/ Tea for Two	1950	$30

MOTOWN

Number	Title	Yr	NM
☐ 1088	Ask Any Man/Spanish Rose	1966	$50
☐ 1071	Talkin' to Your Picture/ Our Rhapsody	1964	$70
☐ 1082	The Bigger Your Heart Is (The Harder You'll Fall)/Two of Us	1965	$30

NAN

Number	Title	Yr	NM
☐ 3002	Sellisima/Winter Sun	1964	$10

PARK AVENUE

Number	Title	Yr	NM
☐ 129	Broadway Broken Heart/ Footsteps of a Fool	1963	$10

RCA VICTOR

Number	Title	Yr	NM
☐ 47-5946	All of You/Vera Cruz	1954	$15
☐ 47-2790	All Through the Night/ Blue Is the Night	1949	$20

— The above four comprise a box set

Number	Title	Yr	NM
☐ 47-3254	All Through the Night/ Blues in the Night	1950	$30
☐ 47-2918	Angels Never Leave Heaven/My Heart Beats Faster	1949	$30
☐ 47-3777	An Ordinary Broom/I Theenk	1950	$30

— With Fran Warren

Number	Title	Yr	NM
☐ 47-4019	A Penny a Kiss/In Your Arms	1951	$30

— With Dinah Shore

Number	Title	Yr	NM
❏ 47-5279	April in Portugal (The Whisp'ring Serenade)/ Now Hear This	1953	$20
❏ 47-4477	At Last, At Last/Make with the Magic	1952	$20
❏ 47-7007	At Last/Scusami	1957	$12
❏ 47-4277	Big Chief Hole in the Ground/Let the Worry Bird Worry for You	1951	$15
❏ 47-5757	Boulevard of Nightingales/ Angels in the Sky	1954	$15
❏ 47-5414	Caribbean/Relax	1953	$20
❏ 47-7099	Carioca/Souvenir d'Italie	1957	$10
❏ 47-4216	Casey at the Bat/Take Me Out to the Ball Game	1951	$30
❏ 47-6317	Christmas in America/ Christmas in Rio	1955	$20
❏ 47-2947	Circus/No, No and No	1949	$30
❏ 47-3056	Come, Josephine, in My Flying Machine/There's a Broken Heart for Every Light on Broadway	1949	$20

— The above three comprise a box set

Number	Title	Yr	NM
❏ 47-5008	Dance of Destiny/ Sleepy Time Gal	1952	$20
❏ 47-3243	Darn It Baby, That's Love/ That "We" Is Me and You	1950	$30

— With Fran Warren

Number	Title	Yr	NM
❏ 47-6863	Do I Love You (Because You're Beautiful)/ Ten Minutes Ago	1957	$12
❏ 47-3803	Dolores/Rosalie	1950	$20
❏ 47-6167	Domani/What's the Time in Nicaragua	1955	$12
❏ 47-4343	Domino/It's All Over But the Memories	1951	$20
❏ 47-7494	Do You Remember As I Remember/Lilly Lu	1959	$12
❏ 47-4098	Faithfully Yours/ No One But You	1951	$30
❏ 47-3941	Fascination/Johannesburg	1950	$30
❏ 47-4944	Forgive and Forget/ Don't Tempt Me	1952	$20
❏ 47-7170	Gigi/Noche de Amour	1958	$10
❏ 47-3024	Give Me Your Tired, Your Poor/If We Hadn't Broken Up on Wednesday Night, Thursday Would Have Been a Year	1949	$30
❏ 47-2787	Goodnight, Sweetheart/You and the Night and the Music	1949	$20
❏ 47-5665	Here/Philosophy	1954	$15
❏ 47-6283	Hold Me in Your Heart/ Everywhere	1955	$12
❏ 47-4544	I Could Write a Book/ Jump Through the Ring	1952	$20
❏ 47-4049	I Cried for You/You Are My Lucky Star	1951	$20
❏ 47-4141	I Get Ideas/Tahiti, My Island	1951	$20
❏ 47-3119	I Said My Pajamas (And Put On My Pray'rs)/Have I Told You Lately That I Love You	1949	$30

— With Fran Warren

Number	Title	Yr	NM
❏ 47-6597	It's Better in the Dark/ Your Place in the Sun	1956	$10
❏ 47-4136	I Wish, I Wish/The Kissing Song	1951	$20

— With Dinah Shore

Number	Title	Yr	NM
❏ 47-3819	La Vie En Rose/Tonight	1950	$30
❏ 47-7376	Lolita/She Serves a Nice Cup of Tea	1958	$10
❏ 47-6888	Mail, Mail, There Ain't No Mail/Look at 'Er	1957	$10
❏ 47-4345	Manhattan/If You Catch a Little Cold	1951	$20

— With Dinah Shore

Number	Title	Yr	NM
❏ 47-7633	Marina/I'll Take Romance	1959	$10
❏ 47-5975	Melody of Love/ You're Getting to Be a Habit with Me	1955	$10

— With Dinah Shore

Number	Title	Yr	NM
❏ 47-6682	Moderation/Since You've Been Mine	1956	$10
❏ 47-3883	Music, Maestro, Please!/ The Big Dipper	1950	$30
❏ 47-5907	My Bambino/Restless Heart	1954	$15
❏ 47-6797	My Budapest/The Rainmaker	1957	$10
❏ 47-3228	My Sin/Begin the Beguine	1950	$30
❏ 47-7728	My Sin/Once When the World Was Mine	1960	$10
❏ 47-2788	Oh, How I Miss You Tonight/Deep Night	1949	$20
❏ 47-3054	Oh You Beautiful Doll/I Want You to Want Me (To Want You)	1949	$20
❏ 47-4268	Old Soft Shoe/Be Mine Tonight	1951	$20

— With Dinah Shore

Number	Title	Yr	NM
❏ 47-3972	Once Upon a Rhumba/ Tambarina	1950	$30
❏ 47-4220	Over a Bottle of Wine/ You'll Know	1951	$20
❏ 47-4758	Padam, Padam/Where Did the Night Go	1952	$20
❏ 47-3799	Peace of Mind/I Still Get a Thrill	1950	$30
❏ 47-5208	Please, Please/ Golden Years	1953	$20
❏ 47-7210	Say Darling/Try to Love Me Just As I Am	1958	$10

Number	Title	Yr	NM
❏ 47-4048	Singin' in the Rain/ Pagan Love Song	1951	$20
❏ 47-4836	Some Day/Luna Rossa (Blushing Moon)	1952	$20
❏ 47-5352	Sorta on the Border/Unfair	1953	$20
❏ 47-5538	Stranger in Paradise/I Love Paris	1953	$15
❏ 47-3804	Sweet Sue/Dinah	1950	$20

— The above three comprise a box set

Number	Title	Yr	NM
❏ 47-4169	Tell Me/Do You Really Love Me	1951	$20
❏ 47-3987	Tell Me Tonight/The Sea of the Moon	1950	$30
❏ 47-5596	That's What a Rainy Day Is For/Look Out, I'm Romantic	1954	$15
❏ 47-4488	The Closer You Are/ Prologue from "Pagliacci"	1952	$20
❏ 47-4225	The Musicians/How D'Ya Do and Shake Hands	1951	$30

— With Phil Harris, Dinah Shore and Betty Hutton

Number	Title	Yr	NM
❏ 47-5473	There's Danger in Your Eyes, Cherie/I Just Love You	1953	$20
❏ 47-3078	There's No Tomorrow/A Thousand Violins	1949	$30
❏ 47-4278	There's No Tomorrow/ Prologue from "Pagliacci"	1951	$15

— The above three comprise a box set

Number	Title	Yr	NM
❏ 47-3756	The Thrill Is Gone/Spring Made a Fool of Me	1950	$30
❏ 47-6731	This Much I Know/ Lonely Winter	1956	$10
❏ 47-3874	Till We Meet Again/Take a Letter, Miss Smith	1950	$30
❏ 47-3049	Toot, Toot, Tootsie, Goodbye/You Call It Madness, I Call It Love	1949	$30
❏ 47-6493	Walk Hand in Hand/ Flamenco Love	1956	$10
❏ 47-7298	Walk with Me/Indiscreet	1958	$10
❏ 47-3055	When I Get You Alone Tonight/Peg o' My Heart	1949	$20
❏ 47-4056	Would I Love You (Love You, Love You)/I Apologize	1951	$30

MARTIN, TRADE

BUDDAH

Number	Title	Yr	NM
❏ 266	I Can't Do It for You/ To Know the Girl	1971	$10

COED

Number	Title	Yr	NM
❏ 579	Hot Diggity/Loveability	1963	$20
❏ 573	Hula Hula Dancin' Doll/ Something in the Wind	1962	$30
❏ 575	Lucky Boy, Happy Girl, Lonely Me/Strategy	1963	$20
❏ 590	Send for Me/Spend Your Life with Me	1964	$20
❏ 570	That Stranger Used to Be My Girl/We'll Be Dancing on the Moon	1962	$20

GEE

Number	Title	Yr	NM
❏ 1053	La Mer/Loving You	1959	$30

RCA VICTOR

Number	Title	Yr	NM
❏ 47-9210	Sixteen Tons/She's Got the Wind in Her Hair	1967	$30
❏ 47-9112	Take Me for a Little While/Moanin'	1967	$60
❏ 47-8926	Work Song/So This Is Love	1966	$60

ROULETTE

Number	Title	Yr	NM
❏ 4258	My Song of Love/Pomp and Circumstance	1960	$20

TOOT

Number	Title	Yr	NM
❏ 610	I Couldn't Make You Love Me (The Way That You Loved Him)/ You're the Cause of It	1968	$10
❏ 606	If I Were a Rich Man/ (B-side unknown)	1968	$10

MARTINDALE, WINK

ABC DOT

Number	Title	Yr	NM
❏ 17606	Deck of Cards/Black Land Farmer	1976	$5

DOT

Number	Title	Yr	NM
❏ 16282	A Man Needs a Woman/ Three Steps to the Phone	1961	$10
❏ 16243	Black Land Farmer/ Make Him Happy	1961	$10
❏ 16051	Blue Bobby Sox/Steal Away	1960	$10
❏ 16628	Born Too Late/Hey Girl, Hey Boy	1964	$8
❏ 16491	Deck of Cards/Black Land Farmer	1963	$8
❏ 15968	Deck of Cards/Now You Know How It Feels	1959	$15
❏ 15968 [PS]	Deck of Cards/Now You Know How It Feels	1959	$30
❏ 16138	Glory of Love/I Wanna Play House	1960	$10
❏ 15728	I Don't Suppose/All Love Broke Loose	1958	$15
❏ 16531	I Heard the Bluebirds Sing/Nevertheless	1963	$8
❏ 16020	Life Gets Tee-Jus, Don't It/I Never See Maggie Alone	1959	$12
❏ 16083	Lincoln's Gettysburg Address/Love's Old Sweet Song	1960	$12

Number	Title	Yr	NM
❏ 16316	Melody of Love/The Thing	1961	$10
❏ 16698	My True Love/A String, an Eraser, and a Blotter	1965	$8
❏ 16555	The First Kiss/ Our Love Affair	1963	$8
❏ 16347	The World's Greatest Man/ Sweet Little Loveable You	1961	$10
❏ 16597	Why Don't They Understand/Big Buildin'	1964	$8

RANWOOD

Number	Title	Yr	NM
❏ 1005	America: An Affirmation/ The People	1974	$6

MARTINI, LUIGI, AND THE BAY CITY 5

JAGUAR

Number	Title	Yr	NM
❏ 3001	Basin Street Blues/Please Don't Talk About Me	1954	$300
❏ 3002	Oh Marie/I'm Sorry I Made You Cry	1954	$300

MARTINO, AL

20TH CENTURY FOX

Number	Title	Yr	NM
❏ 530	I Can't Get You Out of My Heart/Come Back to Me	1964	$8
❏ 575	Mama/My Bella Amore	1965	$8
❏ 508	My Side of the Story/It's All Over But the Shouting	1964	$8

20TH FOX

Number	Title	Yr	NM
❏ 232	Come Back to Me/It's All Over But the Shouting	1960	$15
❏ 153	Darling, I Love You/ Memory of You	1959	$15
❏ 184	Dearest (Cara)/ Hello My Love	1960	$15
❏ 213	Heart of Hearts/ Our Concerto	1960	$15
❏ 132	I Can't Get You Out of My Heart/Two Hearts Are Better Than One	1959	$15
❏ 173	I Sold My Heart/ Summertime	1960	$15
❏ 237	Little Boy, Little Girl/ My Side of the Story	1961	$15
❏ 180	Mama/And I Have You My Love	1960	$15

BBS

Number	Title	Yr	NM
❏ 101	Here in My Heart/I Cried Myself to Sleep	1952	$40

— With "BBS Records" at top of label

Number	Title	Yr	NM
❏ 101	Here in My Heart/I Cried Myself to Sleep	1952	$50

— With "BBS Record Co., Phila. 7, Pa." at top of label

Number	Title	Yr	NM
❏ 101	Here in My Heart/I Cried Myself to Sleep	1952	$70

— Red vinyl

CAPITOL

Number	Title	Yr	NM
❏ F2535	All I Want Is a Chance/ You Can't Go On Forever Breaking My Heart	1953	$30
❏ 4897	Almost Gone/Doors	1980	$4
❏ 5239	Always Together/Thank You for Loving Me	1964	$8
❏ F2649	Before/Sweetheart of Mine	1953	$30
❏ 2746	Can't Help Falling in Love/You're All the Woman That I Need	1970	$5
❏ 4071	Charmer/Wake Up	1975	$4
❏ F3307	Close to Me/The Journey's End	1955	$20
❏ 3056	Come Into My Life/ One Pair of Hands	1971	$5
❏ 3918	Daddy Loves You Honey/ More Than Ever Now	1974	$4
❏ 5825	Daddy's Little Girl/Devotion	1967	$6
❏ F2899	Don't Go to Strangers/When	1954	$30
❏ 4362	Dream of Me/There's Nothing Greater Than Our Love	1976	$4
❏ 4710	Exodus/Love, Where Are You Now	1962	$10
❏ 5506	Forgive Me/What Now My Love	1965	$8
❏ F2431	Here in My Arms/ There's Music in You	1953	$30
❏ 4593	Here in My Heart/Granada	1961	$12
❏ 2355	I Can't Help It (If I'm Still in Love with You)/I Can Only See You	1968	$6
❏ 3604	If I Give My Heart to You/Hey Mama	1973	$4
❏ 4930	I Love You Because/ Merry-Go-Round	1963	$8
❏ 5108	I Love You More and More Every Day/I'm Living My Heaven with You	1964	$8
❏ F3605	I'm Sorry/I'm a Funny Guy	1956	$20
❏ 2674	I Started Loving You Again/Let Me Stay Awhile (With You)	1969	$6
❏ 4798	I Think About You/ Only a Dream Away	1979	$4

— With Kathy Keates

Number	Title	Yr	NM
❏ 2158	Lili Marlene/Georgia	1968	$6
❏ 5060	Living a Lie/I Love You Truly	1963	$8
❏ 4957	Look Around (You'll Find Me There)/More Than Ever Now	1980	$4

Number	Title	Yr	NM
❏ 2102	Love Is Blue/I'm Carrying the World on My Shoulders	1968	$6
❏ F3080	Love Is Eternal/Snowy, Snowy Mountains	1955	$20
❏ 4797	Make Me Believe/Because You're Mine	1962	$10
❏ 3771	Mary Go Lightly (Como Un Nino)/Daddy Let's Play	1973	$4
❏ 5904	Mary in the Morning/I Love You and You Love Me	1967	$6
❏ 4322	May I Have the Next Dream with You/Sing My Love Song	1976	$4
❏ F2737	Melancholy Serenade/Way Paesano	1954	$30
❏ 3256	More Than Ever Now/The Summer Knows	1972	$5
❏ 5989	More Than the Eye Can See/Red Is Red	1967	$6
❏ 5434	My Cherie/Romana	1965	$8
❏ 5341	My Heart Would Know/Hush, Hush, Sweet Charlotte	1965	$8
❏ 5341 [PS]	My Heart Would Know/Hush, Hush, Sweet Charlotte	1965	$15
❏ F2826	On and On/Give Me Something to Go with the Wine	1954	$30
❏ 4551	One Last Time/Here I Go Again	1978	$4
❏ F2353	One Lonely Night/Rachel	1953	$30
❏ 5000	Painted, Tainted Rose/That's the Way It's Got to Be	1963	$8
❏ 4643	Pardon/Another Time, Another Place	1961	$12
❏ 2468	Sausalito/Take My Hand for Awhile	1969	$6
❏ F2982	Say It Again/The Story of Tina	1954	$30
❏ F2185	Say You'll Wait for Me/I've Never Seen	1952	$30
❏ 3763	She/Mary Go Lightly (Como Un Nino)	1973	$4
❏ 5311	Silver Bells/You're All I Want for Christmas	1964	$8
❏ 5384	Somebody Else Is Taking My Place/With All My Heart	1965	$8
❏ 5542	Spanish Eyes/Melody of Love	1965	$8
❏ 3313	Speak Softly Love/I Have But One Heart	1972	$4
❏ 3444	Take Me Back/Canta Libre	1972	$4
❏ F2122	Take My Heart/I Never Cared	1952	$30
❏ 5183	Tears and Roses/A Year Ago Tonight	1964	$8
❏ F3501	The Girl I Left in Rome/Love to Call My Own	1956	$20
❏ 4241	The More I See You/My Thrill	1976	$4
❏ 5741	The Wheel of Hurt/Somewhere in This World	1966	$6
❏ 5598	Think I'll Go Somewhere and Cry Myself to Sleep/Hello Memory	1966	$6
❏ F2480	This Night I'll Remember/When You're Mine	1953	$30
❏ 3120	Too Many Mornings/Losing My Mind	1971	$5
❏ F3171	To Please My Lady/The Man from Laramie	1955	$20
❏ 4681	Torero/Now That I Found You	1979	$4
❏ 3987	To the Door of the Sun (Alle Porte Del Sol)/Mary Go Lightly	1974	$4
❏ 2956	True Love Is Greater Than Friendship/The Call	1970	$5
❏ 2285	Wake Up to Me Gentle/If You Must Leave My Life	1968	$6
❏ 2830	Walking in the Sand/One More Mile (And Darlin' I'll Be Home)	1970	$5
❏ 5293	We Could/Sunrise to Sunrise	1964	$8
❏ B-5191	What Your Love Did for Me/Warm Is When You Touch Me	1982	$3
❏ 5652	Wiederseh'n/The Minute You're Gone	1966	$6
❏ 5652 [PS]	Wiederseh'n/The Minute You're Gone	1966	$10

MARTY
NOVELTY

Number	Title	Yr	NM
❏ 101	Marty on Planet Mars (Part 1)/Marty on Planet Mars (Part 2)	1956	$50

MARVELETTES, THE
A&M

Number	Title	Yr	NM
❏ 1201	Danger Heartbreak Dead Ahead/Baby Please Don't Go	1988	$4

—B-side by Them

| ❏ 1201 [PS] | Danger Heartbreak Dead Ahead/Baby Please Don't Go | 1988 | $4 |

—Good Morning Vietnam" sleeve

GORDY

| ❏ 7024 | Too Hurt to Cry, Too Much in Love to Say Goodbye/Come On Home | 1963 | $100 |

—As "The Darnells

TAMLA

Number	Title	Yr	NM
❏ 54213	A Breath Taking Guy/You're the One for Me Baby	1972	$8
❏ 54088	As Long As I Know He's Mine/Little Girl Blue	1963	$15
❏ 54065	Beechwood 4-5789/Someday, Someway	1962	$30
❏ 54120	Danger, Heartbreak Dead Ahead/Your Cheating Ways	1965	$12
❏ 54171	Destination: Anywhere/What's So Easy for Two Is So Hard for One	1968	$12
❏ 54126	Don't Mess with Bill/Anything You Wanna Do	1965	$12
❏ 54077	Forever/Locking Up My Heart	1963	$20
❏ 54166	Here I Am Baby/Keep Off, No Trespassing	1968	$12
❏ 54091	He's a Good Guy (Yes He Is)/Goddess of Love	1964	$15
❏ 54116	I'll Keep Holding On/No Time for Tears	1965	$10
❏ 54177	I'm Gonna Hold On Long As I Can/Don't Make Hurting Me a Habit	1968	$10
❏ 54198	Marionette/After All	1970	$8
❏ 54158	My Baby Must Be a Magician/I Need Someone	1967	$10
❏ 54060	Playboy/All the Love I've Got	1962	$30
❏ 54046	Please Mr. Postman/So Long Baby	1961	$30
❏ 54046 [PS]	Please Mr. Postman/So Long Baby	1961	$120
❏ 54072	Strange I Know/Too Strong to Be Strung Along	1962	$20
❏ 54186	That's How Heartaches Are Made/Rainy Mourning	1969	$12
❏ 54143	The Hunter Gets Captured by the Game/I Think I Can Change You	1967	$10
❏ 54082	Tie a String Around My Finger/My Daddy Knows Best	1963	$30
❏ 54105	Too Many Fish in the Sea/A Need for Love	1964	$10
❏ 54054	Twistin' Postman/I Want a Guy	1962	$30
❏ 54054 [PS]	Twistin' Postman/I Want a Guy	1962	$125
❏ 54105	Two Many Fish in the Sea/A Need for Love	1964	$50

—Some copies feature the above incorrect A-side title

| ❏ 54150 | When You're Young and In Love/The Day You Take One, You Have to Take the Other | 1967 | $10 |

TOPPS/MOTOWN

| ❏ 12 | Please Mr. Postman | 1967 | $80 |

—Cardboard record

7-Inch Extended Plays
TAMLA

Number	Title	Yr	NM
❏ TM-60253	Don't Mess with Bill/Locking Up My Heart/Too Many Fish in the Sea//Please Mr. Postman/Forever/Beechwood 4-5789	1967	$50

—Stereo jukebox issue; small hole, plays at 33 1/3 rpm

| ❏ TM-60253 [PS] | Greatest Hits | 1967 | $50 |

MARVELLOS, THE (1)
CHA CHA

Number	Title	Yr	NM
❏ 756	Come Back My Love/Boyee Yoing	1963	$40

STEPHENY

| ❏ 1818 | Come Back My Love/Boyee Yoing | 1958 | $200 |

MARVELLOS, THE (2)
EXODUS

Number	Title	Yr	NM
❏ 6216	I Ask of You/Hip Enough	1962	$120
❏ 6214	Salty Sam/She Told Me Lies	1962	$200

REPRISE

| ❏ 20088 | Salty Sam/She Told Me Lies | 1962 | $40 |

MARVELLOS, THE (3)
LOMA

Number	Title	Yr	NM
❏ 2045	Something's Burning/We Go Together	1966	$200

MODERN

| ❏ 1054 | Down in the City/In the Sunshine | 1967 | $40 |

WARNER BROS.

| ❏ 7011 | Don't Play with My Heart/Let Me Keep You Satisfied | 1967 | $50 |
| ❏ 7054 | Piece of Silk/Yes I Do | 1967 | $60 |

MARVELOWS, THE
ABC

Number	Title	Yr	NM
❏ 10820	Fade Away/You've Been Going to Sally	1966	$50
❏ 11139	Hey, Hey Girl/Wait, Be Cool	1968	$40

—As "The Mighty Marvelows

| ❏ 11073 | I'm So Confused/I'm Without a Girl | 1968 | $50 |

—As "The Mighty Marvelows

| ❏ 11011 | In the Morning/Talkin' 'Bout Ya, Baby | 1967 | $50 |

—As "The Mighty Marvelows

ABC-PARAMOUNT

❏ 10613	A Friend/Hey, Hey Baby	1965	$10
❏ 10756	Do It/I've Got My Eyes on You	1965	$12
❏ 10629	I Do/My Heart	1965	$20
❏ 10708	Shim Sham/Your Little Sister	1965	$10

MARVELS, THE (1)
ABC-PARAMOUNT

Number	Title	Yr	NM
❏ 9771	I Won't Have You Breaking My Heart/Jump Rock and Roll	1956	$600

MARVELS, THE (2)
LAURIE

| ❏ 3106 | I Shed So Many Tears/So Young, So Sweet | 1958 | $75 |

—Also released as "The Marvells

MARVELS, THE (U)
WINN

| ❏ 1916 | For Sentimental Reasons/Come Back | 1961 | $200 |

MARVIN AND JOHNNY
ALADDIN

Number	Title	Yr	NM
❏ 3439	It's Christmas/The Valley of Love	1958	$40

FELSTED

| ❏ 8681 | Hot Biscuits and Gravy/Tired of Being Alone | 1963 | $15 |

JAMIE

| ❏ 1188 | Once Upon a Time/Tick Tock | 1961 | $15 |

LIBERTY

| ❏ 1394 | It's Christmas/It's Christmas Time | 1980 | $5 |

—B-side by the Five Keys

MODERN

❏ 974	Ain't That Right/Let Me Know	1956	$40
❏ 959	Butler Ball/Sugar Mama	1955	$50
❏ 952	I Love You, Yes I Do/Baby Won't You Marry Me	1955	$50
❏ 946	Little Honey/Honey Girl	1955	$60
❏ 941	Sugar/Kiss Me	1954	$60
❏ 933	Tick Tock/Cherry Pie	1954	$80
❏ 968	Will You Love Me/Sweet Dreams	1956	$40

SPECIALTY

| ❏ 479 | Baby Doll/I'm Not a Fool | 1953 | $70 |
| ❏ 479 | Baby Doll/I'm Not a Fool | 1953 | $125 |

—Red vinyl

❏ 530	Day In -- Day Out/Flip	1954	$70
❏ 554	Ding Dong Baby/Mamo Mamo	1955	$60
❏ 498	School of Love/Boy Loves Girl	1954	$70

SWINGIN'

| ❏ 641 | I'm Tired of Being Alone/Baby You Don't Know | 1962 | $15 |
| ❏ 645 | Pretty One/Second Helping of Cherry Pie | 1963 | $15 |

Number	Title	Yr	NM
MARVIN AND THE CHIRPS			
TIP TOP			
❏ 202	I'll Miss You This Christmas/Sixteen Tons	1958	$200
MARX, RICHARD			
EMI			
❏ B-50218	Angelia/Endless Summer Nights (Live)	1989	$3
❏ B-50189	Satisfied/Shoud've Known Better (Live)	1989	$3
❏ B-50189 [PS]	Satisfied/Shoud've Known Better (Live)	1989	$5
—Fold-open poster sleeve			
EMI MANHATTAN			
❏ B-50113	Endless Summer Nights/Have Mercy	1988	$3
❏ B-50113 [PS]	Endless Summer Nights/Have Mercy	1988	$3
❏ B-50106	Hold On to the Nights/Lonely Heart	1988	$3
❏ B-50106 [PS]	Hold On to the Nights/Lonely Heart	1988	$3
MANHATTAN			
❏ B-50079	Don't Mean Nothing/The Flame of Love	1987	$3
❏ B-50079 [PS]	Don't Mean Nothing/The Flame of Love	1987	$4
❏ B-50083	Should've Known Better/Rhythm of Life	1987	$3
❏ B-50083 [PS]	Should've Known Better/Rhythm of Life	1987	$4
MARY SUE AND THE TRAMS			
HIT			
❏ 145	Dancing in the Street/(I've Got a) Tiger in My Tank	1964	$12
—B-side by the Jalopy Five			
MARYLANDERS, THE			
JUBILEE			
❏ 5114	Fried Chicken/Good Old 99	1953	$400
—Red vinyl			
❏ 5114	Fried Chicken/Good Old 99	1953	$300
❏ 5079	I'm a Sentimental Fool/Sittin' By the River	1952	$400
❏ 5091	Make Me Thrill Again/Please Love Me	1952	$400
MASCOTS, THE (1)			
ABC			
❏ 11152	Baby, You're So Wrong/Moreen	1968	$8
MASCOTS, THE (2)			
BLAST			
❏ 206	Once Upon a Love/Hey Little Angel	1963	$50
—Red label			
❏ 206	Once Upon a Love/Hey Little Angel	1963	$30
—White label			
MERMAID			
❏ 107	Bluebirds Over the Mountain/Timberlands	1962	$100
MASCOTS, THE (3)			
KING			
❏ 5435	Lonely Rain/That's the Way I Feel	1960	$70
❏ 5377	The Story of My Heart/Do the Wiggle	1960	$125
MASCOTS, THE (4)			
MGM			
❏ 12236	Who Put the Devil in Evelyn's Eyes/Java Jive	1956	$30
MASH, THE			
COLUMBIA			
❏ 45130	Song from M*A*S*H/M*A*S*H March	1970	$8
—Alternate A-side title			
❏ 45130	Suicide Is Painless/M*A*S*H March	1970	$15

Number	Title	Yr	NM
MASKED MARAUDERS, THE			

Fictional supergroup from a Rolling Stone magazine album review, which noted the presence of Bob Dylan, Mick Jagger, John Lennon and Paul McCartney. The below, recorded using the bogus review as a guide, was actually THE CLEANLINESS AND GODLINESS SKIFFLE BAND.

Number	Title	Yr	NM
DEITY			
❏ 0870	I Can't Get No Nookie/Cow Pie	1969	$20
MASON, BARBARA			
ARCTIC			
❏ 146	Don't Ever Go Away/I'm No Good for You	1968	$30
❏ 116	Don't Ever Want to Lose Your Love/Is It Me	1965	$50
❏ 102	Girls Have Feelings Too/Come to Me	1964	$50
❏ 142	Half a Love/(I Can Feel Your Love) Slipping Away	1968	$40
❏ 126	Hello Baby/Poor Girl in Trouble	1966	$20
❏ 140	I Don't Want to Lose You/Dedicated to the One I Love	1968	$30
❏ 120	I Need Love/Bobby Is My Baby	1966	$70
❏ 137	Oh, How It Hurts/Ain't Got Nobody	1967	$125
❏ 108	Sad, Sad Girl/Come to Me	1965	$30
❏ 148	Take It Easy/You Never Loved Me	1969	$30
BUDDAH			
❏ 296	Bed and Board/Yes It's You	1972	$15
❏ 395	Caught in the Middle/Give Him Up	1973	$8
❏ 375	Child of Tomorrow/Out of This World	1973	$8
❏ 441	From His Woman to You/When You Wake Up in Georgia	1974	$8
❏ 331	Give Me Your Love/You Can Be with the One You Don't Love	1972	$8
❏ 481	Make It Last/We Got Each Other	1975	$60
—With the Futures			
❏ 481 [PS]	Make It Last/We Got Each Other	1975	$70
❏ 424	Our Day Will Come/Half Sister, Half Brother	1974	$10
❏ 459	Shackin' Up/One Man Between Us	1975	$10
❏ 409	The Devil Is Busy/All in Love Is Fair	1974	$8
❏ 249	The Pow Pow Song (Sorry Sorry Baby)/Your Old Flame	1971	$8
❏ 319	Woman and Man/Who Will You Hurt Next	1972	$6
❏ 405	World War III/I Miss You Gordon	1974	$10
CRUSADER			
❏ 111	Dedicated to You/Trouble Child	1965	$50
NATIONAL GENERAL			
❏ 018	I Can't Help It/Jean (Gene)	1971	$30
❏ 017	When You Look at Me/I Should Be Leaving You	1971	$20
PRELUDE			
❏ 71111	Darling Come Back Home Soon/It Was You Boy	1978	$6
❏ 71103	I Am Your Woman, She Is Your Wife/Take Me Tonight	1978	$6
WEST END			
❏ 1264	Another Man (Vocal)/Another Man (Rap)	1984	$5
WMOT			
❏ 5352	I'll Never Love the Same Way Twice/(B-side unknown)	1980	$5
❏ 70077	On and Off/You're All Inside of Me	1981	$10
❏ WS9 02506	She's Got the Papers (But I've Got the Man)/(Instrumental)	1981	$8
MASON, DAVE			
BLUE THUMB			
❏ 205	A Heartache, a Shadow, a Lifetime/Can't Stop Worrying	1972	$6
❏ 114	Only You Know and I Know/Sad and Deep As You	1970	$6
❏ 276	Only You Know and I Know/Sad and Deep As You	1975	$5
❏ 7117	Satin and Red Velvet Woman/Shouldn't Have Took More Than You Gave	1971	$6
❏ 209	To Be Free/Pearly Queen	1972	$6
❏ 112	World and Changes/Can't Stop Worrying	1970	$6
CHUMLEY			
❏ 45-01	I Love the Music/In Love with You	1987	$8
COLUMBIA			
❏ 10469	All Along the Watchtower/Sad and Deep As You	1976	$5

Number	Title	Yr	NM
❏ 45947	Baby... Please/Side-Tracked	1973	$5
❏ 10074	Bring it On Home to Me/Harmony and Melody	1974	$5
❏ 10104	Every Woman/Relationships	1975	$5
❏ 10662	Let it Go, Let It Flow/Takin' the Time to Find	1978	$5
❏ 10246	Long Lost Friend/Split Coconut	1975	$5
❏ 11289	Save Me/Tryin' to Get Back to You	1980	$4
❏ 10162	Show Me Some Affection/Get a Hold on Love	1975	$5
❏ 10509	So High (Rock Me Baby and Roll Me Away)/You Just Have to Wait Now	1977	$5
❏ 10819	Warm Desire/Don't It Make You Wonder	1978	$5
❏ 10575	We Just Disagree/Mystic Traveler	1977	$5
❏ 10749	Will You Still Love Me Tomorrow/Mystic Traveler	1978	$5
MCA			
❏ 53205	Dreams I Dream/Fighting for Love	1987	$4
—A-side with Phoebe Snow			
❏ 53205 [PS]	Dreams I Dream/Fighting for Love	1987	$4
MASON DIXON			
CAPITOL			
❏ B-44381	A Mountain Ago/When It Hurts You Most	1989	$3
❏ B-44189	Dangerous Road/Where Does Love Go	1988	$3
❏ B-44331	Exception to the Rule/A Woman Like You	1989	$3
❏ B-44249	When Karen Comes Around/Where Does Love Go	1988	$3
PREMIER ONE			
❏ 112	3935 West End Avenue/Baby's Song	1987	$5
❏ 115	Don't Say No Tonight/Natchez Queen	1987	$5
❏ 101	Home Grown/Savin' the Best for Last	1986	$5
TEXAS			
❏ 5502	Every Breath You Take/Armadillo Country	1983	$6
—Black vinyl			
❏ 5502	Every Breath You Take/Armadillo Country	1983	$12
—Yellow vinyl			
❏ 5557	Gettin' Over You/(B-side unknown)	1984	$6
❏ 5510	Got My Heart Set on You/Armadillo Country	1985	$6
❏ 5508	Houston Heartache/Mason Dixon Lines	1985	$6
❏ 5556	I Never Had a Chance with You/Circle	1984	$6
❏ 5555	Mason Dixon Lines/(B-side unknown)	1983	$6
❏ 5558	Only a Dream Away/Buried Treasure	1985	$6
❏ 5511	Silent Night/O Come All Ye Faithful	1985	$6
MASON, JACKIE			
VERVE			
❏ 10289	Don't Blame the Bossa Nova/I Gave My Love	1963	$15
MASON PROFFIT			
AMPEX			
❏ 11048	Hope/Jewel	1971	$6
HAPPY TIGER			
❏ 570	Hard Luck Woman/Good Friend of Mary's	1971	$6
❏ 552	Two Hangmen/Sweet Lady of Love	1970	$6
WARNER BROS.			
❏ 7709	I Saw the Light/Lilly	1973	$5
MASQUERADERS, THE			
ABC/HBS			
❏ 12141	Baby It's You/Listen	1975	$12
❏ 12157	(Call Me) The Traveling Man/Sweet Sweetning	1976	$10
AGP			
❏ 108	I'm Just an Average Guy/I Ain't Gonna Stop	1969	$40
❏ 122	Love, Peace and Understanding/Tell Me You Love Me	1969	$15
❏ 114	Say It/The Grass Was Green	1969	$20
BANG			
❏ ZS94806	Desire/Into Your Soul	1980	$12
BELL			
❏ 932	Brotherhood/Steamroller	1970	$40
❏ 874	How Big Is Big/Please Take Me Back	1970	$200

Number	Title	Yr	NM
❏ 733	I Ain't Got to Love Nobody Else/I Got It	1968	$30

HI

❏ 2251	Let the Love Bells Ring/ Now That I Found You	1973	$30
❏ 2264	Wake Up Fool/Now That I've Found You	1974	$30

LA BEAT

❏ 6605	A Family (Part 1)/(Part 2)	1966	$30
❏ 6701	Be Happy for Me/ (Instrumental)	1967	$200
❏ 6704	I Got the Power/Together That's the Only Way	1967	$300
❏ 6606	I'm Gonna Make It/How	1966	$1200
❏ 6702	One More Chance/Together That's the Only Way	1967	$300

SOULTOWN

❏ 201	That's the Same Thing/ Talk About a Woman	1965	$750

—As "The Masquaders"

STAIRWAY

❏ 71A	Let Me Show the World I Love You/ Masqueraders' Theme	1971	$200
❏ 72A	The Truth Is Here/Let Me Show the World I Love You	1972	$200
❏ 72B	The Truth Is Here/(Part 2)	1972	$40

TOWER

❏ 281	A Family (Part 1)/(Part 2)	1966	$15

WAND

❏ 1172	Do You Love Me Baby/ Sweet Lovin' Woman	1968	$600
❏ 1168	I Don't Want Nobody to Lead Me On/Let's Face Facts	1968	$50

MASTER-TONES, THE

BRUCE

❏ 111	What'll You Do/Tell Me	1954	$500

—Black vinyl, "New York 19, N.Y." address

❏ 111	What'll You Do/Tell Me	1954	$300

—Blue vinyl

❏ 111	What'll You Do/Tell Me	1962	$60

—Black vinyl, "New York, N.Y." address

MASTER FLEET

SUSSEX

❏ 625	Let Love Stand/ Until Tomorrow	1974	$20
❏ 516	Well, Phase I/Well, Phase II	1974	$20

MASTERS FAMILY, THE

COLUMBIA

❏ 4-20940	Cry from the Cross/ Glory Land March	1952	$30
❏ 4-21413	Everlasting Joy/Coming to Carry Me Home	1955	$30
❏ 4-21357	Filled with the Spirit of God/Don't You Wait to Go to Heaven	1955	$30
❏ 4-20888	From 40 to 65/When the Wagon Was New	1952	$30
❏ 4-21272	God Owns It All/When He Heard My Plea	1954	$30
❏ 4-20851	Hand Me Down My Trumpet/ Happiness Comes	1951	$30
❏ 4-21549	Heaven/I Wasn't There	1956	$30
❏ 4-20785	I'll Be Going to Heaven Sometime/Let the Spirit Descend	1951	$30
❏ 4-21136	Singing in the Promised Land/I Have Changed	1953	$30
❏ 4-21044	Southbound Passenger Train/My Heart's Like a Beggar	1952	$30
❏ 4-20996	The Old World Is Rocking in Sin/Stop Kicking God's Children	1952	$30
❏ 4-21094	They've Made a New Bible/ Marching On to Glory	1953	$30

DECCA

❏ 31378	Great Gilded Hall/ Medals for Mother	1962	$15

MASTERS, KEN

DECCA

❏ 31084	Too Late/Parting Hour	1960	$30

MATADORS, THE (1)

CHART MAKER

❏ 404	Let Me Dream/ Wiggle Wobble	1966	$200

FORBES

❏ 230	Let Me Dream/ Wiggle Wobble	1966	$30

MATADORS, THE (2)

COLPIX

❏ 698	Ace of Hearts/Perfidia	1963	$30
❏ 741	C'mon, Let Yourself Go (Part 1)/C'mon, Let Yourself Go (Part 2)	1964	$30
❏ 718	I've Gotta Drive/La Corrida	1963	$60

—A-side is a Jan and Dean track with a new spoken introduction

MATADORS, THE (3)

KEITH

❏ 6502	If You Left Me Today/It Ain't Nothin' But Rock 'N' Roll	1962	$50

MATADORS, THE (4)

SUE

❏ 701	Be Good to Me/ Have Mercy Baby	1957	$100
❏ 700	Pennies from Heaven/ Vengeance	1957	$120

MATADORS, THE (U)

JAMIE

❏ 1226	Listen/So Near	1962	$30

MATCHHEADS, THE

ARTISTE

❏ 0(# unknown)	Cadillac/Pearl Harbor/ Fat Bitch	1981	$60
❏ 0(# unknown) [PS]	Cadillac/Pearl Harbor/ Fat Bitch	1981	$60

MATHERS, JERRY

ATLANTIC

❏ 2156	Don'tcha Cry/Wind-Up Toy	1962	$30
❏ 2156 [PS]	Don'tcha Cry/Wind-Up Toy	1962	$50

MATHIS, BOBBY, AND THE SEVILLES

SIOUX

❏ 51860	Girl in the Drugstore/ Going to the City	1960	$200

MATHIS, COUNTRY JOHNNY

The "original" Johnny Mathis, the "Country" prefix was added to his name after the "other" Johnny Mathis became far more popular.

D

❏ 1130	Caryl Chessman/ Tears and Gold	1960	$20
❏ 1119	Come On In/Chances Are	1960	$20
❏ 1054	From a Kiss to the Blues/Since I Said Goodbye to Love	1959	$20
❏ 1027	Lonely Night/I've Been Known to Cry	1958	$30
❏ 1152	When I Came Through Town/Only Time Will Tell	1960	$20

HILLTOP

❏ 3008	Welcome Home/ Carolina Sunshine Girl	1965	$10

LITTLE DARLIN'

❏ 037	A Heart Needs a Heart/ No Place to Go	1967	$10
❏ 051	Big Old Heart Full of Love/ Take Your Heart and Go	1968	$12
❏ 09	Black Sheep/Something in Your World	1966	$10
❏ 067	Bring Back My Life/ Sweet Rita	1970	$10
❏ 056	Come Here to My Heart/I'll Cry When I Call Your Name	1969	$10
❏ 015	I Could Never Forget Your Love/Sugar Thief	1966	$10

MERCURY

❏ 71273	Harbor of Love/One Life	1958	$30
❏ 71202	Moonlight Magic/ You Don't Care	1957	$30

UNITED ARTISTS

❏ 460	Every Road Must Have a Turn/I'm Still in Love with Kay	1962	$15
❏ 633	If I Could Keep You Off My Mind/Love Gone Wrong	1963	$15
❏ 536	Please Talk to My Heart/ Let's Go Home	1963	$15
❏ 396	Thinking Too Far Behind/ Wouldn't That Be Something	1961	$15
❏ 697	Was It You/Little Girl	1964	$10

MATHIS, JOHNNY

COLUMBIA

❏ 41193	A Certain Smile/Let It Rain	1958	$10
❏ 41193 [PS]	A Certain Smile/Let It Rain	1958	$20
❏ 41152	All the Time/ Teacher, Teacher	1958	$10
❏ 44357	Among the First to Know/ Long Winter Nights	1967	$5
❏ JZSP45265 [DJ]	An Open Fire/I Concentrate on You	1959	$30
❏ 3-10574	Arianne/99 Miles from L.A.	1977	$5
❏ 3-11001	Begin the Beguine/ Gone, Gone, Gone	1979	$4
❏ 41253	Call Me/Stairway to the Sea	1958	$10
❏ 41253 [PS]	Call Me/Stairway to the Sea	1958	$20
❏ 40993	Chances Are/The Twelfth of Never	1957	$10
❏ 40993 [PS]	Chances Are/The Twelfth of Never	1957	$30
❏ 31238 [S]	Christmas Eve/My Kind of Christmas	1961	$30

—Stereo Seven" single, small hole, plays at 33 1/3 rpm

❏ 1-11158	Christmas in the City of the Angels/The Very First Christmas Day	1979	$5
❏ 45281	Christmas Is/Sign of the Dove	1970	$5
❏ 45513	Christmas Is/Sign of the Dove	1971	$5
❏ AE71148 [DJ]	Christmas Is/Sleigh Ride	1977	$8
❏ AE71148 [PS]	Christmas Is/Sleigh Ride	1977	$15

—Above single and sleeve were the 1977 Christmas Seals record

❏ 0(no cat #) [DJ]	Columbia Records Presents Johnny Mathis -- Take 2	1957	$40

—Promo-only gatefold sleeve containing white-label promos of 40784 and 40851

❏ 41082	Come to Me/When I Am With You	1957	$10
❏ S731347 [S]	Crazy in the Heart/ Too Much Too Soon	1962	$15
❏ 45223	Darling Lili/Pieces of Dreams	1970	$5
❏ 38-08524	Daydreamin'/Love Brought Us Here Tonight	1988	$3
❏ 1-11313	Different Kinda Different/ The Lights of Rio	1980	$4

—A-side with Paulette

❏ 3-10404	Do Me Wrong, But Do Me/Send In the Clowns	1976	$5
❏ 42799	Every Step of the Way/No Man Can Stand Alone	1963	$8
❏ 42799 [PS]	Every Step of the Way/No Man Can Stand Alone	1963	$12
❏ 3-42799	Every Step of the Way/No Man Can Stand Alone	1963	$30

—Columbia Single 33"; small hole

❏ 31799 [S]	Every Step of the Way/No Man Can Stand Alone	1963	$20

—Stereo Seven" single, small hole, plays at 33 1/3 rpm

❏ S730828 [S]	Everything's Coming Up Roses/I Wish I Were in Love Again	1960	$15
❏ 45371	Evie/Think About Things	1971	$5
❏ 45104	For All We Know/ Odds and Ends	1970	$5
❏ 42582	Gina/I Love Her That's Why	1962	$8
❏ 42582 [PS]	Gina/I Love Her That's Why	1962	$10
❏ 3-42582	Gina/I Love Her That's Why	1962	$20

—Columbia Single 33"; small hole

❏ 31582 [S]	Gina/I Love Her That's Why	1962	$30

—Stereo Seven" single, small hole, plays at 33 1/3 rpm

❏ 42582 [DJ]	Gina (same on both sides)	1962	$30

—Promo only on red vinyl

❏ 45035	Give Me Your Love for Christmas/Calypso Noel	1969	$6
❏ 45100 [DJ]	Give Me Your Love for Christmas/Calypso Noel	1969	$8
❏ 45100 [PS]	Give Me Your Love for Christmas/Calypso Noel	1969	$10

—The above sleeve and record were the 1969 Christmas Seals promo

❏ 45035 [PS]	Give Me Your Love for Christmas/Calypso Noel	1969	$8
❏ 30598 [S]	Heavenly/Hello, Young Lovers	1959	$20

—Stereo Seven" single, small hole, plays at 33 1/3 rpm

❏ AS93 [PS]	Helena Rubenstein Presents Johnny Mathis for Courant	1974	$20

—Promo sleeve with above single

❏ S731733 [S]	Here I'll Stay/My Darling, My Darling	1963	$15
❏ S731348 [S]	Hey Look Me Over/Love	1962	$15

—The above five are "Stereo Seven" 33 1/3 rpm jukebox singles from set "JS7-47" entitled "Live It Up!

❏ 3-10611	Hold Me, Thrill Me, Kiss Me/ The Most Beautiful Girl	1977	$5
❏ 45470	How Can You Mend a Broken Heart/If We Only Have Love	1971	$5
❏ 41866	How to Handle a Woman/ While You're Young	1960	$8
❏ 41866 [PS]	How to Handle a Woman/ While You're Young	1960	$15
❏ 3-41866	How to Handle a Woman/ While You're Young	1960	$20

—Columbia Single 33"; small hole

Number	Title	Yr	NM
❑ 30866 [S]	How to Handle a Woman/While You're Young	1960	$20
—Stereo Seven" single, small hole, plays at 33 1/3 rpm			
❑ S730832 [S]	I Am in Love/Love Eyes	1960	$15
—The above five are "Stereo Seven" 33 1/3 rpm jukebox singles from set "JS7-9" entitled "The Rhythms and Ballads of Broadway			
❑ S730830 [S]	I Could Have Danced All Night/A Cock-Eyed Optimist	1960	$15
❑ 45559	If We Only Have Love/This Way, Mary	1972	$5
❑ S730831 [S]	I Just Found Out About Love/Let's Do It	1960	$15
❑ 44837	I'll Never Fall in Love Again/Whoever You Are, I Love You	1969	$5
❑ 42916	I'll Search My Heart/All the Sad Young Men	1963	$8
❑ 31916 [S]	I'll Search My Heart/All the Sad Young Men	1963	$20
—Stereo Seven" single, small hole, plays at 33 1/3 rpm			
❑ 42916 [DJ]	I'll Search My Heart (same on both sides)	1963	$30
—Promo only on red vinyl			
❑ 45908	I'm Coming Home/Stop, Look, and Listen to Your Heart	1973	$5
❑ 38-07797	I'm on the Outside Looking In/Just Like You	1988	$3
❑ 10112	I'm Stone in Love with You/Foolish	1975	$5
❑ 46048	I'm Stone in Love with You/Sweet Child	1974	$5
❑ JZSP39330 [DJ]	In Other Words (Complete Version)/In Other Words (Short Version)	1956	$30
—Promo only, possibly his first single. Came with a "Columbia Records Introduces" sleeve, the presence of which doubles the value			
❑ 38-69092	In the Still of the Night/True Love Ways	1989	$4
—A-side with Take 6			
❑ 40851	It's Not for Me to Say/Warm and Tender	1957	$15
❑ 45323	I Was There/Ten Times Forever More	1971	$5
❑ S731346 [S]	I Won't Dance/Johnny One Note	1962	$15
❑ 31048 [S]	Laurie, My Love/Should I Wait	1961	$20
—Stereo Seven" single, small hole, plays at 33 1/3 rpm			
❑ 42048	Laurie My Love/Should I Wait (Or Should I Run to Her)	1961	$8
❑ 42048 [PS]	Laurie My Love/Should I Wait (Or Should I Run to Her)	1961	$15
❑ 3-42048	Laurie My Love/Should I Wait (Or Should I Run to Her)	1961	$20
—Columbia Single 33"; small hole			
❑ 41304	Let's Love/You Are Beautiful	1958	$12
❑ 45975	Life Is a Song Worth Singing/I Just Wanted to Be Me	1973	$5
❑ S731344 [S]	Live It Up/Just Friends	1962	$15
❑ 45415	Long Ago and Far Away/For All We Know	1971	$5
❑ S731735 [S]	Lost in Loveliness/Stella by Starlight	1963	$15
—The above five are "Stereo Seven" 33 1/3 rpm jukebox singles from "JS7-76" entitled "Rapture			
❑ 44915	Love Theme from Romeo and Juliet (A Time for Us)/The World I Threw Away	1969	$5
❑ 3-10496	Loving You, Losing You/World of Laughter	1977	$5
❑ 45635	Make It Easy on Yourself/Sometimes	1972	$5
❑ 41684	Maria/Hey Love	1960	$8
—Reissued in 1961 with the same catalog number			
❑ 30684 [S]	Maria/Hey Love	1960	$20
—Stereo Seven" single, small hole, plays at 33 1/3 rpm			
❑ 42420	Marianna/Unaccustomed As I Am	1962	$8
❑ 42420 [PS]	Marianna/Unaccustomed As I Am	1962	$15
❑ 3-42420	Marianna/Unaccustomed As I Am	1962	$20
—Columbia Single 33"; small hole			
❑ 31420 [S]	Marianna/Unaccustomed As I Am	1962	$30
—Stereo Seven" single, small hole, plays at 33 1/3 rpm			
❑ JZSP55369 [DJ]	Maria/Tonight	1959	$30
❑ 45022	Midnight Cowboy/We	1969	$5
❑ 44266	Misty Roses/Don't Talk to Me	1967	$5
❑ 30599 [S]	Misty/Stranger in Paradise	1959	$20
—Stereo Seven" single, small hole, plays at 33 1/3 rpm			
❑ 41483	Misty/The Story of Our Love	1959	$10
❑ 41483 [PS]	Misty/The Story of Our Love	1959	$20
❑ 30483 [S]	Misty/The Story of Our Love	1959	$30
—Stereo Seven" single, small hole, plays at 33 1/3 rpm			
❑ S731732 [S]	Moments Like This/You've Come Home	1963	$15

Number	Title	Yr	NM
❑ 4-42238	My Kind of Christmas/Christmas Eve	1961	$15
❑ 3-42238	My Kind of Christmas/Christmas Eve	1961	$30
—Columbia Single 33"; small hole			
❑ 4-42238 [PS]	My Kind of Christmas/Christmas Eve	1961	$30
❑ 41764	My Love for You/Oh That Feeling	1960	$8
❑ 3-41764	My Love for You/Oh That Feeling	1960	$20
—Columbia Single 33"; small hole			
❑ 30764 [S]	My Love for You/Oh That Feeling	1960	$20
—Stereo Seven" single, small hole, plays at 33 1/3 rpm			
❑ 3-10291	One Day in Your Life/Midnight Blue	1976	$5
❑ 10080	Sail On White Moon/The Heart of a Woman	1974	$5
❑ 30601 [S]	Secret Love/And This Is My Beloved	1959	$20
—Stereo Seven" single, small hole, plays at 33 1/3 rpm			
❑ 45835	Show and Tell/Happy (Theme from Lady Sings the Blues)	1973	$5
❑ 38-04468	Simple/Lead Me to Your Love	1984	$3
❑ 41410	Small World/You Are Everything to Me	1959	$12
❑ 30410 [S]	Small World/You Are Everything to Me	1959	$30
—Stereo Seven" single, small hole, plays at 33 1/3 rpm			
❑ 41355	Someone/Very Much in Love	1959	$12
❑ 30355 [S]	Someone/Very Much in Love	1959	$30
—Stereo Seven" single, small hole, plays at 33 1/3 rpm			
❑ 42836	Sooner or Later/In Wisconsin	1963	$8
❑ 3-42836	Sooner or Later/In Wisconsin	1963	$30
—Columbia Single 33"; small hole			
❑ 31836 [S]	Sooner or Later/In Wisconsin	1963	$20
—Stereo Seven" single, small hole, plays at 33 1/3 rpm			
❑ 45729	Soul and Inspiration-Just Once in My Life/I	1972	$5
❑ 41583	Starbright/All Is Well	1960	$8
❑ 41583 [PS]	Starbright/All Is Well	1960	$15
❑ 10250	Stardust/What I Did for Love	1975	$5
❑ S731734 [S]	Stars Fell on Alabama/I Was Telling Her About You	1963	$15
❑ 42261	Sweet Thursday/One Look	1962	$8
❑ 3-42261	Sweet Thursday/One Look	1962	$20
—Columbia Single 33"; small hole			
❑ 42261 [PS]	Sweet Thursday/One Look	1962	$15
❑ 31261 [S]	Sweet Thursday/One Look	1962	$30
—Stereo Seven" single, small hole, plays at 33 1/3 rpm			
❑ 42509	That's the Way It Is/I'll Never Be Lonely Again	1962	$8
❑ 42509 [PS]	That's the Way It Is/I'll Never Be Lonely Again	1962	$12
❑ 3-42509	That's the Way It Is/I'll Never Be Lonely Again	1962	$20
—Columbia Single 33"; small hole			
❑ 31509 [S]	That's the Way It Is/I'll Never Be Lonely Again	1962	$30
—Stereo Seven" single, small hole, plays at 33 1/3 rpm			
❑ 41491	The Best of Everything/Cherie	1959	$12
❑ 41491 [PS]	The Best of Everything/Cherie	1959	$20
❑ 30583 [S]	The Best of Everything/Cherie	1959	$30
—Stereo Seven" single, small hole, plays at 33 1/3 rpm			
❑ SS-7 [S]	The Best of Everything/The Theme from "A Summer Place	1960	$20
—B-side by Percy Faith; "Stereo Seven" single, small hole, plays at 33 1/3 rpm			
❑ JZSP44991 [DJ]	The Christmas Song (Merry Christmas to You)/What Child Is This?	1958	$30
❑ 44728	The End of the World/The 59th Street Bridge Song (Feelin' Groovy)	1968	$5
❑ 10175	The Greatest Gift/You're As Right As Rain	1975	$5
❑ AS93 [DJ]	The Heart of a Woman (same on both sides)	1974	$10
—Promo release for the Helena Rubenstein cosmetics firm			
❑ 3-10902	The Last Time I Felt Like This/As Time Goes By	1979	$4
—A-side with Jane Olivor			
❑ 45183	The Last Time I Saw Her/Wherefore and Why	1970	$5
❑ 30600 [S]	Tonight/Maria	1959	$20
—Stereo Seven" single, small hole, plays at 33 1/3 rpm			
❑ 45777	Walking Tall (Theme)/Take Good Care of Her	1973	$5
❑ 42156	Wasn't the Summer Short/There You Are	1961	$8
❑ 42156 [PS]	Wasn't the Summer Short/There You Are	1961	$15

Number	Title	Yr	NM
❑ 3-42156	Wasn't the Summer Short/There You Are	1961	$20
—Columbia Single 33"; small hole			
❑ 42666	What Will Mary Say/Quiet Girl	1963	$10
❑ 42666 [PS]	What Will Mary Say/Quiet Girl	1963	$15
❑ 3-42666	What Will Mary Say/Quiet Girl	1963	$30
—Columbia Single 33"; small hole			
❑ 31666 [S]	What Will Mary Say/Quiet Girl	1963	$30
—Stereo Seven" single, small hole, plays at 33 1/3 rpm			
❑ 42666	What Will My Mary Say/Quiet Girl	1963	$8
—Revised A-side title			
❑ 3-42666	What Will My Mary Say/Quiet Girl	1963	$20
—Columbia Single 33"; small hole; revised A-side title			
❑ 31666 [S]	What Will My Mary Say/Quiet Girl	1963	$30
—Stereo Seven" single, small hole, plays at 33 1/3 rpm; revised A-side title			
❑ 42666 [DJ]	What Will My Mary Say (same on both sides)	1963	$30
—Promo only on red vinyl			
❑ 3-10640	When a Child Is Born/Every Time You Touch Me (I Get High)	1977	$5
❑ 11-11409	When a Child Is Born/The Lord's Prayer	1980	$4
—With Gladys Knight and the Pips			
❑ 3-10447	When a Child Is Born/Turn the Lights Down	1976	$5
❑ 38-03222	When the Lovin' Goes Out of the Lovin'/Warm	1982	$3
❑ 38-06561	Where Can I Find Christmas?/It's Beginning to Look a Lot Like Christmas	1986	$4
❑ S731345 [S]	Why Not/On a Cold and Rainy Day	1962	$15
❑ 40784	Wonderful! Wonderful!/When Sunny Gets Blue	1956	$15

MERCURY

Number	Title	Yr	NM
❑ 72229	Bye Bye Barbara/A Great Night for Cryin'	1964	$6
❑ 72229 [PS]	Bye Bye Barbara/A Great Night for Cryin'	1964	$10
❑ DJ-72 [DJ]	Chim Chim Cheree (same on both sides?)	1964	$20
❑ 72184	Come Back/Your Teenage Dreams	1963	$6
❑ 72184 [PS]	Come Back/Your Teenage Dreams	1963	$10
❑ 72432	Dianacita/Take the Time	1965	$6
❑ 72432 [PS]	Dianacita/Take the Time	1965	$12
❑ 72339	Listen Lonely Girl/All I Wanted	1964	$6
❑ 72339 [PS]	Listen Lonely Girl/All I Wanted	1964	$12
❑ 72464	Mirage/The Sweetheart Tree	1965	$6
❑ 72464 [PS]	Mirage/The Sweetheart Tree	1965	$10
❑ 72539	Moment to Moment/Glass Mountain	1966	$6
❑ 72493	On a Clear Day You Can See Forever/Come Back to Me	1965	$6
❑ 72653	Saturday Sunshine/Two Tickets and a Candy Heart	1967	$6
❑ 72653 [PS]	Saturday Sunshine/Two Tickets and a Candy Heart	1967	$10
❑ 72287	Taste of Tears/White Roses from a Blue Valentine	1964	$6
❑ 72610	The Impossible Dream/So Nice	1966	$6
❑ 72610 [PS]	The Impossible Dream/So Nice	1966	$10
❑ 72217	The Little Drummer Boy/Have Reindeer, Will Travel	1963	$10
❑ 72217 [PS]	The Little Drummer Boy/Have Reindeer, Will Travel	1963	$30
❑ 72568	The Shadow of Your Smile (Love Theme from "The Sandpiper")/The Sweetheart Tree	1966	$6

7-Inch Extended Plays

COLUMBIA

Number	Title	Yr	NM
❑ B-8871	*Autumn in Rome/Love, Your Magic Spell Is Everywhere/Cabin in the Sky/In Other Words	1957	$20
❑ B-11193	*Ave Maria (Bach-Gounod)/The Rosary/May the Good Lord Bless and Keep You/Ave Maria (Schubert)	1958	$10
❑ B-10782	*By Myself/I've Grown Accustomed to Her Face/Baby, Baby, Baby/What'll I Do	1958	$15
❑ B-8872	*Caravan/Star Eyes/It Might As Well Be Spring/Street of Dreams	1957	$20
❑ B-15262	*Corner to Corner/The Folks Who Live on the Hill/I'm in the Mood for Love/Stay Warm	1960	$10
❑ B-8873	*Easy to Love/Prelude to a Kiss/Babalu/Angel Eyes	1957	$20

Number	Title	Yr	NM
❏ B-11192	*Eli Eli/Kol Nidre/Where Can I Go?/One God	1958	$10
❏ B-12702	*Embraceable You/ My Funny Valentine/I'll Be Seeing You/I'm Just a Boy in Love	1959	$10
❏ B-14222	*Faithfully/One Starry Night/Nobody Knows/ You Better Go Now	1959	$10
❏ B-11191	*Good Night, Dear Lord/I Heard a Forest Praying/ Deep River/Swing Low, Sweet Chariot	1958	$10
❏ B-13511	*Heavenly/Misty/ Hello, Young Lovers/I'll Be Easy to Find	1959	$10
❏ B-10783	*I'm Glad There Is You/ The Lovely Things You Do/There Goes My Heart/ Then I'll Be Tired of You	1958	$15
❏ B-15263	*I'm Gonna Laugh You Right Out of My Life/How High the Moon/April in Paris/In Return	1960	$10
❏ B-10282	*It Could Happen to You/ That Old Black Magic/ Too Close for Comfort/ In the Wee Small Hours of the Morning	1957	$15
❏ B-2129	*It's Not for Me to Say/Warm and Tender/Wonderful, Wonderful/Babalu	1957	$20
❏ B-11653	*Love Walked In/Easy to Say/This Heart of Mine/ Like Someone in Love	1958	$15
❏ B-12701	*Open Fire/Please Be Kind/ Bye Bye Blackbird/Tenderly	1959	$10
❏ B-13512	*Something I Dreamed Last Night/Moonlight Becomes You/They Say It's Wonderful/ More Than You Know	1959	$10
❏ B-11652	*Sweet Lorraine/Can't Get Out of This Mood/ You Hit the Spot/Get Me to the Church on Time	1958	$15
❏ B-10283	*Year After Year/Early Autumn/You Stepped Out of a Dream/Day In, Day Out	1957	$15
❏ B-13513	A Lovely Way to Spend an Evening/That's All//A Ride on a Rainbow/ Stranger in Paradise	1959	$10
❏ B-14223	And This Is My Beloved/ Tonight//Follow Me/ Blue Gardenia	1959	$10
❏ B-11193 [PS]	Ave Maria	1958	$12
❏ 7-8634	Chances Are/The Twelfth of Never/Wonderful! Wonderful!//It's Not for Me to Say/Come to Me/ Wild Is the Wind	1963	$10

—Jukebox issue; small hole, plays at 33 1/3 rpm

Number	Title	Yr	NM
❏ 7-30210 [PS]	Close to You	1970	$12
❏ 7-30210	Come Saturday Morning/ Yellow Days/(If You Can Let Me Make Love To You) Why Can't I Touch You?/ Until It's Time for You to Go/ Everything Is Beautiful	1970	$10

—Jukebox issue; small hole, plays at 33 1/3 rpm

Number	Title	Yr	NM
❏ B-2143	Come to Me/Wild Is the Wind//No Love (But Your Love)/When I Am with You	1957	$20
❏ B-10283 [PS]	Day In, Day Out	1957	$15
❏ B-11192 [PS]	Eli Eli	1958	$12
❏ B-14221 [PS]	Faithfully, Vol. 1	1959	$12
❏ B-14222 [PS]	Faithfully, Vol. 2	1959	$12
❏ B-14223 [PS]	Faithfully, Vol. 3	1959	$12
❏ B-11191 [PS]	Good Night, Dear Lord	1958	$12
❏ B-15261	Goodnight My Love/There's No Love//Once/I'm So Lost	1960	$10
❏ B-13511 [PS]	Heavenly, Vol. 1	1959	$12
❏ B-13512 [PS]	Heavenly, Vol. 2	1959	$12
❏ B-13513 [PS]	Heavenly, Vol. 3	1959	$12
❏ B-12703	I Concentrate on You/You'll Never Know//When I Fall in Love/In the Still of the Night	1959	$10
❏ B-11952	I'll Be Home for Christmas/ Oh Holy Night//The Christmas Song/Silver Bells	1958	$15
❏ 7-9637	I Say a Little Prayer/Love Is Blue/Never My Love/Venus/ Moon River/Walk On By	1968	$10

—Jukebox issue; small hole, plays at 33 1/3 rpm

Number	Title	Yr	NM
❏ B-10281 [PS]	Looking at You	1957	$15

—Same contents, different title

Number	Title	Yr	NM
❏ 7-9637 [PS]	Love Is Blue	1968	$12
❏ B-11951 [PS]	Merry Christmas, Vol. 1	1958	$15
❏ B-11952 [PS]	Merry Christmas, Vol. 2	1958	$15
❏ B-11953 [PS]	Merry Christmas, Vol. 3	1958	$15
❏ B-12701 [PS]	Open Fire, Two Guitars, Vol. 1	1959	$12
❏ B-12702 [PS]	Open Fire, Two Guitars, Vol. 2	1959	$12
❏ B-12703 [PS]	Open Fire, Two Guitars, Vol. 3	1959	$12
❏ B-14221	Secret Love/Where Are You//Maria/Where Do You Think You're Going	1959	$10
❏ B-2129 [PS]	Songs from "Lizzie" and Other Favorites	1957	$20
❏ B-11651 [PS]	Swing Softly, Vol. 1	1958	$15
❏ B-11652 [PS]	Swing Softly, Vol. 2	1958	$15

Number	Title	Yr	NM
❏ B-11653 [PS]	Swing Softly, Vol. 3	1958	$15
❏ B-11953	The First Noel/It Came Upon a Midnight Clear// What Child Is This?/ Silent Night, Holy Night	1958	$15
❏ B-2537	The Twelfth of Never/ Chances Are// Wonderful, Wonderful/ It's Not for Me to Say	1959	$15
❏ B-11651	To Be in Love/You'd Be So Nice to Come Home To//It's De-Lovely/I've Got the World on a String	1958	$15
❏ B-10282 [PS]	Too Close for Comfort	1957	$15
❏ B-10781 [PS]	Warm, Vol. 1	1958	$15
❏ B-10782 [PS]	Warm, Vol. 2	1958	$15
❏ B-10783 [PS]	Warm, Vol. 3	1958	$15
❏ B-10781	Warm/A Handful of Stars// My One and Only Love/ While We're Young	1958	$15
❏ B-10281 [PS]	Will I Find My Love Today	1957	$15
❏ B-10281	Will I Find My Love Today/ Looking at You//All Through the Night	1957	$15
❏ B-11951	Winter Wonderland/ Blue Christmas//White Christmas/Sleigh Ride	1958	$15

MERCURY

Number	Title	Yr	NM
❏ SR-665-C [PS]	So Nice	1966	$15
❏ SR-665-C	What Now My Love/ What the World Needs Now Is Love/Man of La Mancha//I Will Wait for You/ Elusive Butterfly/So Nice	1966	$15

—Jukebox issue; small hole, plays at 33 1/3 rpm

MATTEA, KATHY
MERCURY

Number	Title	Yr	NM
❏ 874672-7	Burnin' Old Memories/ Hills of Alabam	1989	$3
❏ 872766-7	Come from the Heart/ True North	1989	$3
❏ 870148-7	Eighteen Wheels and a Dozen Roses/ Like a Hurricane	1988	$4
❏ 870148-7 [PS]	Eighteen Wheels and a Dozen Roses/ Like a Hurricane	1988	$5
❏ 888874-7	Goin' Gone/Every Love	1987	$3
❏ 888874-7 [PS]	Goin' Gone/Every Love	1987	$5
❏ 884177-7	Heart of the Country/ Talkin' to Myself	1985	$4
❏ 880867-7	He Won't Give In/I Believe I Could Fall in Love	1985	$4
❏ 880595-7	It's Your Reputation Talkin'/ Never Look Back	1985	$4
❏ 872082-7	Life As We Knew It/As Long As I Have a Heart	1988	$3
❏ 884573-7	Love at the Five & Dime/Can't Run Away from Your Heart	1986	$3
❏ 818289-7	Someone in Love/ That's Easy for You to Say	1984	$4
❏ 814375-7	Street Talk/Heartbeat	1983	$4
❏ 880192-7	That's Easy for You to Say/ Somewhere Down the Road	1984	$4
❏ 888574-7	Train of Memories/Evenin'	1987	$3
❏ 884978-7	Walk the Way the Wind Blows/Come Home to West Virginia	1986	$3
❏ 876262-7	Where've You Been/I'll Take Care of You	1989	$6

MATTHEWS, FAT MAN
BAYOU

Number	Title	Yr	NM
❏ 016	I'm Thankful/Goin' Down	1952	$200

IMPERIAL

Number	Title	Yr	NM
❏ 5235	Down the Line/You Know It	1953	$125
❏ 5211	When Boy Meets Girl/Later Baby	1952	$2000

—VG 1000; VG+ 1500

MATTY, JAY
LUTE

Number	Title	Yr	NM
❏ 6021	Merry Twist Mas/ Teenage Monster	1961	$30

MAUDS, THE
DUNWICH

Number	Title	Yr	NM
❏ 160	Hold On/C'mon and Move	1967	$15

MERCURY

Number	Title	Yr	NM
❏ 72919	Brother Chickie/ Satisfy My Hunger	1969	$8
❏ 72832	Forever Gone/Soul Drippin'	1968	$8
❏ 72760	He Will Break Your Heart/ You Must Believe Me	1967	$8
❏ 72694	Hold On/C'mon and Move	1967	$8
❏ 72877	Only Love Can Save You/ Sergeant Sunshine	1968	$8
❏ 72720	When Something Is Wrong (With My Baby)/You Make Me Feel So Bad	1967	$8

RCA VICTOR

Number	Title	Yr	NM
❏ 74-0377	Forget It, I've Got It/A Man Without a Dream	1970	$6

MAXEDON, SMILEY
COLUMBIA

Number	Title	Yr	NM
❏ 4-20910	Crazy to Care/In the Window	1952	$30
❏ 4-21188	Give Me a Red Hot Mama/Why Can't You Look Me in the Eye	1953	$30
❏ 4-21244	If I Should Change Your Ways/Too Late to Cry Over You	1954	$30
❏ 4-21337	I Want You/Oh Why Did I Cheat	1955	$30
❏ 4-21301	That's All Right/Blue as Blue Can Be	1954	$40
❏ 4-21095	What Good Is My Love/ We Can't Live Together	1953	$30

MAXIMILLIAN
BIG TOP

Number	Title	Yr	NM
❏ 3095	The Twistin' Ghost/ The Breeze and I-Peter Gunn Theme	1961	$30
❏ 3068	The Wanderer/The Snake	1961	$70

CUB

Number	Title	Yr	NM
❏ 9046	Gee Baby, You're the Utmost/Blowing My Brains Out (Over You)	1959	$30

MAXWELL, HOLLY
CONSTELLATION

Number	Title	Yr	NM
❏ 162	Let Him Go for Himself/ Only When You're Lonely	1965	$30
❏ 152	One Thin Dime/ It's Impossible	1965	$200

MAXWELL, LEN
20TH FOX

Number	Title	Yr	NM
❏ 551	A Merry Monster Christmas/ The Sounds of Christmas	1964	$30

MAXWELL, ROBERT
DECCA

Number	Title	Yr	NM
❏ 31734	April in Portugal/ The Right to Love	1965	$6
❏ 25671	A Summer Song/ Summertime	1965	$6
❏ 31668	One O'Clock Jump/Rosebud	1964	$6
❏ 25637	Peg o' My Heart/Little Dipper	1964	$6
❏ 25622	Shangri-La/That Old Black Magic	1964	$8
❏ 31839	Song of the Nairobi Trio/ Theme from "Morituri	1965	$6

MERCURY

Number	Title	Yr	NM
❏ 5773	Chinatown, My Chinatown/ Shuffle Off to Buffalo	1952	$20

—As "Bobby Maxwell

Number	Title	Yr	NM
❏ 70159	Hindustan/Bobble, Bobble, Bobble	1953	$20
❏ 5844	Limehouse Blues/ Plink, Plank, Plunk	1952	$20
❏ 70033	Shangri-La/Mary Lou	1953	$30

—As "Bobby Maxwell

MGM

Number	Title	Yr	NM
❏ 12293	Hot Tamale/Freckles	1956	$15
❏ 12351	Injury Music for Football Games/Cumana	1956	$15
❏ 12546	I've Told Every Little Star/ Come Follow Me Baby	1957	$15
❏ 12488	Mary Lou/Open Your Mouth and Sing	1957	$15
❏ 12410	Song of the Nairobi Trio/Accidental Slip on an Oriental Rug	1957	$15
❏ 12254	Spaghetti Rag/Can't Keep Running	1956	$15

ROULETTE

Number	Title	Yr	NM
❏ 4338	Bazaar in Barcelona/ Little Dipper	1961	$12

—Roulette titles as "Mickey Mozart

Number	Title	Yr	NM
❏ 4148	Little Dipper/Mexican Hop	1959	$12
❏ 4180	Pink Parfait/Flower of Budapest	1959	$10
❏ 4241	The Man with the Monocle/ Ver Boten Liebe	1960	$10

MAY, BILLY
CAPITOL

Number	Title	Yr	NM
❏ CCF349 [PS]	A Band Is Born!	1952	$10

—Empty box for 15905, 15906 and 15907

Number	Title	Yr	NM
❏ F2297	A Cute Piece of Property/Driftwood	1952	$20
❏ F1793	All of Me/Lean, Baby	1951	$20
❏ F1995	Always/There Is No Greater Love	1952	$20
❏ KCF329 [PS]	Big Band Bash	1952	$12

—Empty box for 15859, 15860 and 15861

Number	Title	Yr	NM
❏ F3123	Cha Cha Cha/Shaner Maidel	1955	$15
❏ 6F15906	Charmaine/Lean, Baby	1952	$10
❏ F1919	Charmaine/When I Take My Sugar to Tea	1952	$20
❏ F3598	Christopher Columbus/ Floater	1956	$15

Number	Title	Yr	NM
❏ F2364	Cocktails for Two/Little Brown Jug	1953	$20
❏ F2653	Cool Water/Dixieland Band	1953	$20
❏ F2113	Easy Street/Mayhem	1952	$20
❏ F1794	Fat Man Boogie/My Silent Love	1951	$20
❏ F2575	Gone with the Wind/Romance	1953	$20
❏ F2474	Good Grief/From the Land of the Sky Blue Water	1953	$20
❏ F2840	Hernando's Hideaway/Anything Can Happen Mambo	1954	$20
❏ F2849	Hi Fi/The Song Is You	1954	$20
❏ F2284	High Noon/Do You Ever Think of Me	1952	$20
❏ F2054	Honest and Truly/When the Swallows Come Back to Capistrano	1952	$20
❏ F3066	How Important Can It Be?/Let It Happen	1955	$15
❏ F15731	If I Had You/All of Me	1951	$15
❏ F2157	Love Is Just Around the Corner/Gin and Tonic	1952	$20
❏ 4752	Love Makes the World Go Round/The Sweetest Sounds	1962	$10
❏ F3372	Main Title -- Theme from "The Man with the Golden Arm"/Our Melody	1956	$15
❏ F3221	Oklahoma!/Por Favor	1955	$15
❏ F2227	Orchids in the Moonlight/Fat Man Mambo	1952	$20
❏ 6F15861	Perfidia/Diane	1952	$10

— Above three comprise box set KCF-329, "Big Band Bash"

Number	Title	Yr	NM
❏ F3846	Seventy-Six Trombones/Young and Dangerous	1957	$15
❏ F3297	Street of Dreams/Suzette	1955	$15
❏ F2721	The Breeze and I/Whistle Stop	1954	$20
❏ 6F15907	The Fat Man Boogie/There Is No Greater Love	1952	$10

— Above three comprise box set CCF-349, "A Band Is Born!

Number	Title	Yr	NM
❏ F3697	Theme from "The Strange One"/Laurel Is Out	1957	$15
❏ F3104	Whatever Lola Wants/Just Between Friends	1955	$15
❏ F1795	When My Sugar Walks Down the Street/I Guess I'll Have to Change My Plans	1951	$20
❏ 6F15905	When My Sugar Walks Down the Street/I Guess I'll Have to Change My Plans	1952	$10
❏ 6F15860	When Your Lover Has Gone/Please Be Kind	1952	$10

MCA
Number	Title	Yr	NM
❏ 40352	Front Page Rag/Reunion	1974	$8

REPRISE
Number	Title	Yr	NM
❏ 20054	Ballad of the Sergeants 3/Sergeant Boswell's Rock	1962	$12
❏ 20062	Sergeants 3 March/Girls from the Antler Bar	1962	$10

TIME
Number	Title	Yr	NM
❏ 1050	Advise and Consent/Bashful Billie	1962	$10
❏ EAP 1-1043	Big Fat Brass, Part 1	1958	$10
❏ EAP 1-1043	(contents unknown)	1958	$10

MAYALL, JOHN

ABC
Number	Title	Yr	NM
❏ 12216	Sunshine/Turn Me Loose	1976	$5

BLUE THUMB
Number	Title	Yr	NM
❏ 264	Step in the Sun/Al Goldstein Blues	1975	$5

IMMEDIATE
Number	Title	Yr	NM
❏ 502	Telephone Blues/I'm Your Witch Doctor	1967	$8

LONDON
Number	Title	Yr	NM
❏ 20024	All Your Love/Hideaway	1966	$10
❏ 20039	Broken Wings/Sonny Boy Blue	1967	$8
❏ 20042	Living Alone/Walking on Sunset	1968	$8
❏ 20035	Oh, Pretty Woman/Suspicions	1967	$8

POLYDOR
Number	Title	Yr	NM
❏ 14004	Don't Waste My Time/Don't Pick a Flower	1969	$6
❏ 14253	Let Me Give/Passing Through	1974	$6
❏ 14151	Moving On/Keep Our Country Green	1972	$6
❏ 14243	The 1974 Gasoline Blues/Brand New Band	1974	$6

MAYE, LEE

ABC
Number	Title	Yr	NM
❏ 11028	If You Leave Me/The Greatest Love I've Ever Known	1967	$40

BUDDAH
Number	Title	Yr	NM
❏ 141	He'll Have to Go/Jus' Lookin'	1969	$6

CASH
Number	Title	Yr	NM
❏ 1065	All I Want Is Someone to Love/Pounding	1958	$120

Number	Title	Yr	NM
❏ 1063	Will You Be Mine/Honey Honey	1958	$200

DIG
Number	Title	Yr	NM
❏ 133	A Fool's Prayer/(B-side unknown)	1957	$200
❏ 124	This Is the Night for Love/(B-side unknown)	1956	$250

FLIP
Number	Title	Yr	NM
❏ 330	Hey Pretty Baby/'Cause You're Mine Alone	1958	$100

— As "Arthur Lee Maye

IMPERIAL
Number	Title	Yr	NM
❏ 5790	Will You Be Mine/Honey Honey	1961	$30

JAMIE
Number	Title	Yr	NM
❏ 1295	(Don't Pretend) Just Lay It on the Line/Careless Hands	1965	$8

— With Barbara Lynn

Number	Title	Yr	NM
❏ 1287	Even a Nobody/Who Made You What You Are	1964	$12
❏ 1276	How's the World Treating You?/Loving Fool	1964	$50

— As "Lee Maye of the Milwaukee Braves

Number	Title	Yr	NM
❏ 1284	Only a Dream/The Breaks of Life	1964	$10
❏ 1272	Who Made You What You Are/Loving Fool	1964	$10

LENOX
Number	Title	Yr	NM
❏ 5566	Half Way (Out of Love with You)/I Can't Please You	1963	$30

MODERN
Number	Title	Yr	NM
❏ 944	Set My Heart Free/I Wanna Love	1954	$600

— As "Arthur Lee Maye and the Crowns

RPM
Number	Title	Yr	NM
❏ 438	Do the Bop/Please Don't Leave Me	1955	$200

— As "Arthur Lee Maye and the Crowns

Number	Title	Yr	NM
❏ 429	Loop De Loop/Love Me Always	1955	$120

— As "Arthur Lee Maye

Number	Title	Yr	NM
❏ 424	Truly/Oochie Pachie	1955	$200

— As "Arthur Lee Maye and the Crowns

SPECIALTY
Number	Title	Yr	NM
❏ 573	Gloria/Oo-Rooba-Lee	1956	$70

— As "Arthur Lee Maye and the Crowns

TOWER
Number	Title	Yr	NM
❏ 243	When My Heart Hurts No More/At the Party	1966	$40

MAYER, NATHANIEL

Number	Title	Yr	NM
❏ 557	Going Back to the Village of Love/My Last Dance with You	1963	$70
❏ 547	Hurting Love/Leave Me Alone	1962	$30
❏ 487	Hurting Love/Leave Me Alone	1962	$40

— Fortune 449 and 487 were part of the United Artists numbering system

Number	Title	Yr	NM
❏ 554	I Had a Dream/I'm Not Gonna Cry	1963	$20
❏ 550	Mr. Santa Claus/(B-side unknown)	1962	$40
❏ 542	My Last Dance with You/My Little Darling	1962	$30
❏ 550	Work It Out/Well, I've Got News	1962	$50

MAYFIELD, CURTIS
Also see THE IMPRESSIONS. (45)

Number	Title	Yr	NM
❏ 9806 [PS]	He's a Flyguy/(Instrumental)	1989	$3

— With Fishbone

BOARDWALK
Number	Title	Yr	NM
❏ NB7-11-169	Dirty Laundry/Nobody But You	1982	$4
❏ NB7-11-155	Hey Baby (Give It All to Me)/Summer Hot	1982	$4
❏ NB7-11-122	She Don't Let Nobody (But Me)/You Get All My Love	1981	$4
❏ NB7-11-132	Toot An'Toot An'Toot/Come Free Your People	1981	$4

COLUMBIA
Number	Title	Yr	NM
❏ 10147	Stash That Butt, Sucker/Zanzibar	1975	$5

CRC
Number	Title	Yr	NM
❏ 001	Baby It's You/Breakin' in the Streets	1985	$6

CURTOM
Number	Title	Yr	NM
❏ 1960	Beautiful Brother of Mine/Give It Up	1971	$6
❏ 1972	Beautiful Brother of Mine/Love to Keep You In My Mind	1972	$6
❏ 1993	Can't Say Nothin'/Future Song	1973	$6

Number	Title	Yr	NM
❏ 0131	Do Do Wap Is Strong in Here/Need Someone to Love	1977	$5
❏ 0141	Do It All Night/Party Party	1978	$5
❏ 1955	(Don't Worry) If There's a Hell Below We're All Going to Go/The Makings of You	1970	$6
❏ 1975	Freddie's Dead (Theme from "Superfly")/Underground	1972	$6
❏ 1987	Future Shock/The Other Side of Town	1973	$6
❏ 1966	Get Down/We're a Winner	1971	$6
❏ 1991	If I Were Only a Child Again/Think	1973	$6
❏ 0142	In Love, In Love, In Love/Keeps Me Loving You	1978	$5
❏ 1963	Mighty Mighty (Spade and Whitey)/(B-side unknown)	1971	$6
❏ 2006	Mother's Son/Love Me	1974	$6
❏ 1974	Move On Up/Underground	1972	$6
❏ 0118	Only You Babe/Love to the People	1976	$5
❏ 0122	Party Night/P.S. I Love You	1976	$5
❏ 0125	Show Me Love/Just Want to Be with You	1977	$5
❏ 0105	So in Love/Hard Times	1975	$5
❏ 1978	Superfly/Underground	1972	$6
❏ 1978 [PS]	Superfly/Underground	1972	$8
❏ 2005	Sweet Exorcist/Suffer	1974	$6
❏ 1968	We Got to Have Peace/We're a Winner	1972	$6
❏ 1968 [PS]	We Got to Have Peace/We're a Winner	1972	$8

RSO/CURTOM
Number	Title	Yr	NM
❏ 1036	Love Me, Love Me Now/It's Alright	1980	$5
❏ 1029	Love's Sweet Sensation/(Instrumental)	1980	$5

— With Linda Clifford

Number	Title	Yr	NM
❏ 919	This Year/(Instrumental)	1979	$5
❏ 1046	Tripping Out/Never Stop Loving	1980	$5

7-Inch Extended Plays

CURTOM
Number	Title	Yr	NM
❏ CRS-8014#NAME?	Pusherman/Think (Instrumental)//Give Me Your Love/Eddie You Should Know Better/Junkie Chase (Instrumental)	1972	$20

— Jukebox issue; small hole, plays at 33 1/3 rpm

Number	Title	Yr	NM
❏ CRS-8014#NAME? [PS]	Super Fly	1972	$20

MAYFIELD, PERCY

ATLANTIC
Number	Title	Yr	NM
❏ 3207	I Don't Want to Be President/Nothin' Stays the Same Forever	1974	$5

BRUNSWICK
Number	Title	Yr	NM
❏ 55390	Walking on a Tightrope/P.M. Blues	1968	$8

CHESS
Number	Title	Yr	NM
❏ 1599	Double Dealing/Are You Out There	1955	$70

IMPERIAL
Number	Title	Yr	NM
❏ 5620	My Heart Is a Prisoner/My Memories	1959	$20
❏ 5577	One Love/My Reward	1959	$20

KING
Number	Title	Yr	NM
❏ 4480	Two Years of Torture/Half Awake	1951	$70

RCA VICTOR
Number	Title	Yr	NM
❏ 74-0348	A Highway Is Like a Woman/You Wear Your Hair Too Long	1970	$6
❏ 74-0379	Daddy Wants You to Come Home/Weakness Is a Thing Called Man	1970	$6
❏ 74-0462	The Flirt/California Blues	1971	$6
❏ 74-0307	To Live the Past/Lying Woman (Not Trustworthy)	1970	$6

SPECIALTY
Number	Title	Yr	NM
❏ 544	Baby You're Rich/The Voice Within	1955	$40
❏ 416	Cry Baby/Hopeless	1952	$50
❏ 607	Diggin' the Moonglow/Please Believe Me	1956	$40
❏ 485	I Need Love So Bad/Loose Lips	1954	$50
❏ 439	Lonesome Highway/My Heart	1952	$50
❏ 390	Lost Love/Life Is Suicide	1951	$70
❏ 460	Lost Mind/Lonely One	1953	$50

— Black vinyl

Number	Title	Yr	NM
❏ 460	Lost Mind/Lonely One	1953	$100

— Colored vinyl

Number	Title	Yr	NM
❏ 723	Lost Mind/River's Invitation	1973	$6
❏ 432	Louisiana/Two Hearts Are Greater Than One	1952	$50
❏ 537	My Heart Is Cryin'/You Were Lyin' to Me	1954	$50
❏ 375	Please Send Me Someone to Love/Strange Things Happening	1950	$100

Number	Title	Yr	NM
❏ 408	Prayin' For Your Return/My Blues	1951	$70
❏ 473	The Bachelor Blues/How Deep Is the Well	1953	$50
—Black vinyl			
❏ 473	The Bachelor Blues/How Deep Is the Well	1953	$100
—Colored vinyl			
❏ 425	The Big Question/The Hurt Is On	1952	$50
❏ 400	What a Fool I Was/Nightless Lover	1951	$70
❏ 690	When Did You Leave Heaven/What Must I Do	1960	$30

TANGERINE

Number	Title	Yr	NM
❏ 977	As Long As You're Mine/Ha Ha in the Daytime	1967	$8
❏ 979	Don't Start Lyin' to Me/Pretty Eyed Baby	1967	$8
❏ 950	Fading Love/Stand By	1965	$8
❏ 957	Give Me Time to Explain/My Jug and I	1965	$8
❏ 966	It's Time to Make a Change/We Both Must Cry	1966	$8
❏ 973	My Love/My Bottle Is My Companion	1966	$8
❏ 941	Stranger in My Own Home Town/Maybe It's Because of Love	1964	$10
❏ 934	The Hunt Is On/Cookin' in Style	1963	$10

MAYO, FRANKIE, AND THE FALCONS
RCA VICTOR

Number	Title	Yr	NM
❏ 47-7076	Stepping Stone/Jigsaw Puzzle	1957	$30

MAYS, WILLIE
DUKE

Number	Title	Yr	NM
❏ 350	My Sad Heart/If You Love Me	1962	$10
❏ 418	My Sad Heart/If You Love Me	1967	$8

EPIC

Number	Title	Yr	NM
❏ 9066	Say Hey (The Willie Mays Song)/Out of the Bushes	1954	$30

—With the Treniers

MC5
AMG

Number	Title	Yr	NM
❏ 1001	I Can Only Give You Everything/I Just Don't Know	1969	$80
—Black label			
❏ 1001	I Can Only Give You Everything/One of the Guys	1969	$80
—Yellow label			
❏ 1000 [DJ]	I Can Only Give You Everything (same on both sides)	1966	$100

A-SQUARE

Number	Title	Yr	NM
❏ 333	Looking at You/Borderline	1967	$300
—500 copies of this record were pressed			
❏ 333 [PS]	Looking at You/Borderline	1967	$80

ATLANTIC

Number	Title	Yr	NM
❏ 2724	The American Ruse/Shakin' Street	1970	$25
❏ 2678	Tonight/Looking at You	1969	$40

MCALLISTER, BILLY JOE
LITTLE DARLIN'

Number	Title	Yr	NM
❏ 044	My Worst Is the Best/These Things I'm Not	1968	$10

MCAULIFFE, LEON
CAPITOL

Number	Title	Yr	NM
❏ 5066	Shape Up or Ship Out/I Don't Love Nobody	1963	$10
❏ 5168	Things to Remember/Bluesville U.S.A.	1964	$10

CIMARRON

Number	Title	Yr	NM
❏ 4046	Bear Creek Hop/Boogie on Strings	1960	$20
❏ 4052	Choo Choo Ch'Boogie/Honky Tonk Song	1961	$20
❏ 4050	Cozy Inn/Ain't Gonna Hurt No More	1961	$20
❏ 4057	Faded Love/My Little Red Wagon	1962	$20
❏ 4043	Lookin' Glass/Wapanuka	1959	$20
❏ 4054	My Ace in the Hole/Night Life	1962	$20
❏ 4049	Orange Blossom Special/Cimarron (Roll On)	1961	$20
❏ 4039	Steel Guitar Rag/Panhandle Rag	1959	$30
❏ 4047	Water Baby Boogie/The Three Bears	1960	$20

COLUMBIA

Number	Title	Yr	NM
❏ 4-20907	Blacksmith Blues/I'm Going Back to Birmingham	1952	$30
❏ 4-20845	Blue Guitar Stomp/I Didn't Know How Much	1951	$40
❏ 2-700(?)	Bonaparte's Retreat/What, Where and When	1950	$50
—Microgroove 33 1/3 rpm small-holed 7-inch single			
❏ 2-520(?)	Chattanoogie Shoe Shine Boy/Rag Mop	1950	$50
—Microgroove 33 1/3 rpm small-holed 7-inch single			
❏ 2-600(?)	Cimarron Rag/Birmingham Bounce	1950	$50
—Microgroove 33 1/3 rpm small-holed 7-inch single			
❏ 4-21115	Eating Right Out of Your Hand/Heart Attacks	1953	$30
❏ 4-21398	Hard Hearted Gal/Dial Love for Me	1955	$30
❏ 4-20872	Makin' Believe You're There/Search My Heart	1952	$30
❏ 4-21319	One Little Dream of You/Mr. Steel Guitar	1954	$30
❏ 2-346	Panhandle Waltz/Sugar and Salt	1949	$50
—Microgroove 33 1/3 rpm small-holed 7-inch single			
❏ 4-21283	Sh-Boom/Smooth Sailing	1954	$30
❏ 4-21020	Stolen Love/Hear Me Now	1952	$30
❏ 4-20782	Take It Away Leon/Tulsa Straight Ahead	1951	$40
❏ 4-20807	There's a Right Way and a Wrong Way/I've Never Lived in Tennessee	1951	$40
❏ 2-420(?)	The Three Bears/Twin Fiddle Rag	1949	$50
—Microgroove 33 1/3 rpm small-holed 7-inch single			
❏ 4-20952	This Side of Town/Who Took My Ring from Your Finger	1952	$30
❏ 4-21227	Wished You Would/Tie Your Apron Strings	1954	$30

DOT

Number	Title	Yr	NM
❏ 15741	My Love/Lone Star Rag	1958	$30
❏ 15845	There's That Smile Again/Johnny Can Read	1958	$30

MCBRIDE, DALE
CON BRIO

Number	Title	Yr	NM
❏ 127	Always Lovin' Her Man/I Know the Feeling	1977	$5
❏ 131	A Sweet Love Song the World Can Sing/I'm Savin' Up Sunshine	1978	$5
❏ 151	Getting Over You Again/She Makes Love Feel Good	1979	$5
❏ 109	Getting Over You Again/You Have Missed Nothing	1976	$5
❏ 158	Get Your Hands on Me Baby/I Knew the Feeling	1979	$5
❏ 135	I Don't Like Cheatin' Songs/My Girl	1978	$5
❏ 117	I'm Savin' Up Sunshine/She's My Heaven	1977	$5
❏ 145	It's Hell to Know She's Heaven/You Have Missed Nothing	1979	$5
❏ 140	Let's Be Lonely Together/She Makes Me Feel Good	1978	$5
❏ 121	Love I Need You/A Love for All Seasons	1977	$5
❏ 124	My Girl/She Makes Love Feel Good	1977	$5
❏ 114	Ordinary Man/Mexicali Rose	1976	$5

FAME

Number	Title	Yr	NM
❏ 507	Prissy Missy/Class Beyond Compare	1959	$100

MCA

Number	Title	Yr	NM
❏ 40853	My World Is Empty Without You/Quiet Moments	1978	$4

POMPEII

Number	Title	Yr	NM
❏ 66681	Country Boy/Born to Love You	1968	$12

REPRISE

Number	Title	Yr	NM
❏ 0331	Barbara/I Can't Ever Free My Mind	1964	$12

TEAR DROP

Number	Title	Yr	NM
❏ 3062	Am I That Easy to Forget/Our Hearts Beat as One	1965	$15
❏ 3041	Barbara/I Can't Ever Free My Mind	1964	$15
❏ 3029	Lovely Little One/Guess Who	1964	$15
❏ 3020	Old Enough to Break a Heart/The Rest of My Life	1964	$15
❏ 3077	Prissy Missy/Two Steps from the Blues	1965	$15
❏ 539	Corpus Christi Wind/Is Anybody Going to San Antone	1971	$8
❏ 528	Life to Me/Guess You've Made Your Mind Up	1970	$8

MCCALL, C.W.
AMERICAN GRAMAPHONE

Number	Title	Yr	NM
❏ 351	Old Home Filler-Up An' Keep On-a-Truckin' Café/Old 30	1974	$20

MGM

Number	Title	Yr	NM
❏ 14825	Black Bear Road/Four Wheel Drive	1975	$4
❏ 14801	Classified/I've Trucked All Over This Land	1975	$4
❏ 14839	Convoy/Long Lonesome Road	1975	$5
❏ 14738	Old Home Filler-Up An' Keep On-a-Truckin' Café/Old 30	1974	$4
❏ 14764	Wolf Creek Pass/Sloan	1974	$4

POLYDOR

Number	Title	Yr	NM
❏ 14377	Audubon/Ratchetjaw	1977	$4
❏ 14331	Crispy Critters/Jackson Hole	1976	$4
❏ 14352	Four Wheel Cowboy/Aurora Borealis	1976	$4
❏ 14550	Milton/The Little Things in Life	1979	$4
❏ 14458	Old Glory/Watch the Wildwood Flowers	1978	$4
❏ 14527	Outlaws and Lone Star Beer/Silver Cloud Breakdown	1978	$4
❏ 14445	Sing Silent Night/Old Glory	1977	$5
❏ 14310	There Won't Be No Country Music (There Won't Be No Rock 'n' Roll)/Green River	1976	$4

MCCANN, LES, AND EDDIE HARRIS
ATLANTIC

Number	Title	Yr	NM
❏ 2694	Compared to What/Cold Duck	1969	$6

MCCANN, LES
ATLANTIC

Number	Title	Yr	NM
❏ 2713	What I Call Soul/Comment	1970	$6
❏ 2918	What's Going On (Part 1)/What's Going On (Part 2)	1972	$5
❏ 3253	When It's Over/Someday We'll Meet Again	1975	$5
❏ 2615	With These Hands/Burnin' Coal	1969	$6

LIMELIGHT

Number	Title	Yr	NM
❏ 3077	All/Bucket O' Grease	1967	$8
❏ 3060	But Not Really/Jack V. Schwartz	1965	$8
❏ 3078	Caper of the Golden Bulls/Loves of July	1967	$8
❏ 3066	Green Green Rocky Road/Great City	1965	$8
❏ 3081	The Shout (Part 1)/The Shout (Part 2)	1967	$8

PACIFIC JAZZ

Number	Title	Yr	NM
❏ 306	C Jam Blues/The Shout	1960	$15
❏ 311	Fish This Week/Vacushna	1961	$15
❏ 318	Gone Up and Get That Church (Part 1)/Gone Up and Get That Church (Part 2)	1961	$15
❏ 317	I Am in Love/Big Jim	1961	$15
❏ 350	Shampoo/Kathleen's Theme	1963	$15
❏ 329	Sweet Georgia Brown/I Cried for You	1961	$15
❏ 820	They Can't Take That Away from Me/Little Girl from Casper	1960	$15
❏ 309	Truth/Little Girl from Casper	1961	$15
❏ 341	Twist Cha Cha/Little 3/4 for God & Co.	1962	$15

WORLD PACIFIC

Number	Title	Yr	NM
❏ 404	Back at the Chicken Shack/Sack o' Woe	1964	$12
❏ 422	Basuto Baby/McCanna	1965	$12
❏ 411	Big City/Route 66	1964	$12
❏ 406	Bluesette/Spanish Castles	1964	$10
❏ 389	Bye and Bye/Get That Soul	1963	$10
❏ 418	It Had Better Be Tonight/Que Rico	1964	$10
❏ 387	The Gospel Truth/Send It On Down to Me	1963	$10
❏ 88133	The Shout/Spanish Onions	1966	$8

MCCANTS, JUNIOR
KING

Number	Title	Yr	NM
❏ 6076	A Boy Needs a Girl/Help My Love	1967	$125
❏ 6106 [B]	Try Me for Your New Love/She Wrote It -- I Read It	1967	$5000

—Promo has sold for 15,000

Number	Title	Yr	NM

MCCARTNEY, PAUL, AND STEVIE WONDER

COLUMBIA

❑ 18-02860 Ebony and Ivory/Rainclouds 1982 $4

—B-side by McCartney solo

❑ 18-02860 [PS] Ebony and Ivory/Rainclouds 1982 $4

MCCARTNEY, PAUL

Includes Thrillington and Wings. Also see THE BEATLES. Includes duets with Linda McCartney plus his work with Wings. Also see THE BEATLES; MICHAEL JACKSON AND PAUL McCARTNEY.

APPLE

❑ 1829 Another Day/Oh Woman, Oh Why 1971 $15

—With star on A-side label

❑ 1829 Another Day/Oh Woman, Oh Why 1971 $8

❑ PRO-6193/4 [DJ] Another Day/Oh Woman, Oh Why 1971 $100

❑ P-1873 [DJ] Band on the Run (Edited Mono)/Band on the Run (Full-length Stereo) 1974 $50

—Paul McCartney and Wings

❑ P-1873 [DJ] Band on the Run (mono/stereo, both edits) 1974 $125

—Paul McCartney and Wings

❑ 1873 Band on the Run/Nineteen Hundred and Eighty-Five 1974 $8

—Paul McCartney and Wings

❑ PRO-6787 [DJ] Country Dreamer (mono/stereo) 1973 $400

—Paul McCartney and Wings

❑ 1847 Give Ireland Back to the Irish/Give Ireland Back to the Irish (Version) 1972 $10

—Wings

❑ 1847 [PS] Give Ireland Back to the Irish/Give Ireland Back to the Irish (Version) 1972 $40

—Wings; title sleeve with large center hole

❑ 1869 Helen Wheels/Country Dreamer 1973 $8

—Paul McCartney and Wings

❑ P-1869 [DJ] Helen Wheels/Country Dreamer 1973 $2000

—Paul McCartney and Wings; a very rare promo, as most promos have the same song on both sides (see 6786 and 6787 below)

❑ PRO-6786 [DJ] Helen Wheels (mono/stereo) 1973 $60

—Paul McCartney and Wings

❑ 1857 Hi Hi Hi/C Moon 1972 $12

—Wings; red label

❑ 1863 Live and Let Die/I Lie Around 1973 $8

—Wings

❑ 1851 Mary Had a Little Lamb/Little Woman Love 1972 $10

—Wings

❑ 1851 [PS] Mary Had a Little Lamb/Little Woman Love 1972 $30

—Wings; without "Little Woman Love" on sleeve

❑ 1851 [PS] Mary Had a Little Lamb/Little Woman Love 1972 $50

—Wings; with "Little Woman Love" on sleeve

❑ 1851 [DJ] Mary Had a Little Lamb/Little Woman Love 1972 $300

—White label promo, lists artist as Paul McCartney

❑ 1861 My Love/The Mess 1973 $8

—Paul McCartney and Wings; custom "Red Rose Speedway" label

❑ 1861 [DJ] My Love/The Mess 1973 $200

—Paul McCartney and Wings; white label

❑ P-1875 [DJ] Sally G (mono/stereo) 1974 $100

—Paul McCartney and Wings

CAPITOL

❑ 1829 Another Day/Oh Woman, Oh Why 1976 $20

—Black label

❑ 1873 Band on the Run/Nineteen Hundred and Eighty-Five 1976 $20

—Credited to "Paul McCartney and Wings"; black label

❑ 7PRO-79889 [DJ] Figure of Eight (same on both sides) 1989 $125

—Test pressings with blank label; most known copies come in a Capitol sleeve; number taken from dead wax

❑ 4504 Girls' School/Mull of Kintyre 1977 $5

—Credited to "Wings"; black label (more common version)

❑ 4504 [PS] Girls' School/Mull of Kintyre 1977 $15

❑ 4504 Girls' School/Mull of Kintyre 1978 $120

—Credited to "Wings"; purple label, label has reeded edge

❑ 1847 Give Ireland Back to the Irish/Give Ireland Back to the Irish 1976 $30

—Credited to "Wings"; black label

❑ 1869 Helen Wheels/Country Dreamer 1976 $20

—Credited to "Paul McCartney and Wings"; black label

❑ 1857 Hi Hi Hi/C Moon 1976 $20

—Credited to "Wings"; black label

❑ 4594 I've Had Enough/Deliver Your Children 1978 $4

—Credited to "Wings

❑ 4293 Let 'Em In/Beware My Love 1976 $6

—Credited to "Wings"; black label (more common version)

❑ 4293 Let 'Em In/Beware My Love 1976 $4

—Credited to "Wings"; "Speed of Sound" label

❑ 4145 Letting Go/You Gave Me the Answer 1975 $5

—Credited to "Wings

❑ 4091 Listen to What the Man Said/Love in Song 1975 $5

—Credited to "Wings

❑ 4091 [PS] Listen to What the Man Said/Love in Song 1975 $15

❑ 1863 Live and Let Die/I Lie Around 1976 $15

—Credited to "Wings"; black label

❑ 4625 London Town/I'm Carrying 1978 $4

—Credited to "Wings

❑ 1851 Mary Had a Little Lamb/Little Woman Love 1976 $15

—Credited to "Wings"; black label

❑ SPRO-8570/1 [DJ] Maybe I'm Amazed (3:43) (stereo/mono) 1977 $40

—As "Wings

❑ 4385 Maybe I'm Amazed/Soily 1976 $4

—Credited to "Wings"; custom label (more common version)

❑ 4385 Maybe I'm Amazed/Soily 1976 $30

—Credited to "Wings"; black label

❑ B-44367 My Brave Face/Flying to My Home 1989 $10

—Version 1: Both title and artist in block print, time of A-side is "3:17

❑ B-44367 My Brave Face/Flying to My Home 1989 $8

—Version 2: Artist in custom print, title in block print, time of A-side is "3:17

❑ B-44367 My Brave Face/Flying to My Home 1989 $5

—Version 3: Same as Version 2, time of A-side is "3:16

❑ B-44367 [PS] My Brave Face/Flying to My Home 1989 $5

❑ 1861 My Love/The Mess 1976 $30

—Credited to "Paul McCartney and Wings"; black label; "The Mess" plays too fast

❑ 1861 My Love/The Mess 1976 $30

—Credited to "Paul McCartney and Wings"; black label; "The Mess" plays normally

❑ B-5672 Only Love Remains/Tough on a Tightrope 1987 $5

❑ B-5672 [PS] Only Love Remains/Tough on a Tightrope 1987 $5

❑ B-5597 Press/It's Not True 1986 $5

❑ B-5597 [PS] Press/It's Not True 1986 $5

❑ 4256 Silly Love Songs/Cook of the House 1976 $8

—Credited to "Wings"; black label

❑ 4256 Silly Love Songs/Cook of the House 1976 $4

—Credited to "Wings"; "Speed of Sound" label (more common version)

❑ 7PRO-9552/3 [DJ] Spies Like Us (4:40)/(3:46) 1985 $30

❑ B-5537 Spies Like Us/My Carnival 1985 $3

❑ B-5537 [PS] Spies Like Us/My Carnival 1985 $6

❑ B-5636 Stranglehold/Angry 1986 $5

❑ B-5636 [PS] Stranglehold/Angry 1986 $5

❑ 7PRO-79700 [DJ] This One (same on both sides) 1989 $400

—Vinyl is promo only

❑ 4559 With a Little Luck/Backwards Traveller-Cuff Link 1978 $4

—Credited to "Wings

COLUMBIA

❑ 1-11070 Arrow Through Me/Old Siam, Sir 1979 $6

—Credited to "Wings

❑ 13-33409 Band on the Run/Helen Wheels 1980 $12

—Credited to "Paul McCartney and Wings"; red label "Hall of Fame" series

❑ 13-33409 Band on the Run/Helen Wheels 1985 $40

—Credited to "Paul McCartney and Wings"; briefly available grayish label reissue

❑ 1-11263 Coming Up//Coming Up (Live at Glasgow)/Lunch Box-Odd Sox 1980 $4

—The first song on side 2 is credited to "Paul McCartney & Wings

❑ 1-11263 [PS] Coming Up//Coming Up (Live at Glasgow)/Lunch Box-Odd Sox 1980 $5

❑ AE71204 [DJ] Coming Up (Live at Glasgow)/(B-side blank) 1980 $8

—Small hole, plays at 33 1/3 rpm; this was the bonus single included with most early pressings of the "McCartney II" LP (Columbia FC 36511) and was not distributed separately

❑ 3-11020 Getting Closer/Spin It On 1979 $6

—Credited to "Wings

❑ 3-11020 [PS] Getting Closer/Spin It On 1979 $40

—Title sleeve with large center hole

❑ 3-10939 Goodnight Tonight/Daytime Nighttime Suffering 1979 $6

—Credited to "Wings

❑ 13-33405 Goodnight Tonight/Getting Closer 1980 $10

—Credited to "Wings"; red label "Hall of Fame" series

❑ 13-33407 My Love/Maybe I'm Amazed 1980 $10

—Credited to "Paul McCartney and Wings"; red label "Hall of Fame" series; B-side is the studio version, making its first appearance on U.S. 45 here

❑ 13-33407 My Love/Maybe I'm Amazed 1985 $40

—Credited to "Paul McCartney and Wings"; briefly available grayish label reissue

❑ 18-02171 Silly Love Songs/Cook of the House 1981 $30

—Credited to "Wings"; despite label information, this has an edited version of A-side

❑ 38-04296 So Bad/Pipes of Peace 1983 $5

❑ 38-04296 [PS] So Bad/Pipes of Peace 1983 $5

❑ 18-03018 Take It Away/I'll Give You a Ring 1982 $3

❑ 18-03018 [PS] Take It Away/I'll Give You a Ring 1982 $3

❑ 38-03235 Tug of War/Get It 1982 $15

❑ 1-11335 Waterfalls/Check My Machine 1980 $6

❑ 1-11335 [PS] Waterfalls/Check My Machine 1980 $30

❑ 1-11162 Wonderful Christmastime/Rudolph the Red-Nosed Reggae 1979 $10

❑ 1-11162 [PS] Wonderful Christmastime/Rudolph the Red-Nosed Reggae 1979 $20

❑ 38-04127 Wonderful Christmastime/Rudolph the Red-Nosed Reggae 1983 $40

—Scarce reissue with B-side in stereo

EMI

❑ 3977 Walking in the Park with Eloise/Bridge on the River Suite 1974 $70

❑ 3977 [PS] Walking in the Park with Eloise/Bridge on the River Suite 1974 $100

—As "The Country Hams

MCCLAIN, CHARLY

EPIC

❑ 34-07244 And Then Some/What Makes Love Go Round N' Round 1987 $3

❑ 34-04423 Band of Gold/His Love Is Out of My Hands 1984 $3

❑ 14-02975 Dancing Your Memory Away/Love This Time 1982 $3

❑ 34-06980 Don't Touch Me There/I Know the Way By Heart 1987 $3

❑ 34-03808 Fly Into Love/The Best That Never Was 1983 $3

❑ 50378 It's Too Late to Love Me Now/You Can Love It Away 1977 $4

❑ 50285 Lay Down/Pride and Sorrow 1976 $4

❑ 50338 Lay Something on My Bed Besides a Blanket/Love Me 'Til the Morning Comes 1977 $4

❑ 50525 Let Me Be Your Baby/Your Eyes 1978 $4

❑ 50873 Let's Put Our Love in Motion/I'm Puttin' My Love Inside You 1980 $4

❑ 50436 Make the World Go Away/Leanin' on the Bottle (And Slowly Fallig Down) 1977 $4

❑ 50825 Men/Come Take Care of Me 1979 $4

❑ 34-04172 Sentimental Ol' You/I'll Get You Back 1983 $3

❑ 14-02421 Sleepin' with the Radio On/That's All a Woman Lives For 1981 $3

❑ 34-04586 Some Hearts Get All the Breaks/Someone Just Like You 1984 $3

❑ 34-06167 So This Is Love/Too Many Tears Too Late 1986 $3

❑ 34-07670 Still I Stay/If You Didn't Need Me 1988 $3

❑ 19-01045 Surround Me with Love/He's Back 1981 $3

❑ 50653 Take Me Back/Bedtime Comes Earlier at Our House 1978 $4

❑ 50598 That's What You Do to Me/1 + 1 = Love 1978 $4

Number	Title	Yr	NM
❏ 50706	When a Love Ain't Right/You Can't Make Love by Yourself	1979	$4
❏ 50948	Who's Cheatin' Who/Love Scenes	1980	$4
❏ 34-03308	With You/Crazy Hearts	1982	$3
❏ 50916	Women Get Lonely/I'd Rather Fall in Love with You	1980	$4
MERCURY			
❏ 872036-7	Down the Road/You Can Be You (And Be Mine Too)	1988	$3
❏ 872506-7	One in Your Heart One on Your Mind/You Got the Job	1989	$3
❏ 870508-7	Sometimes She Feels Like a Man/You Can Be You (And Be Mine Too)	1988	$3

MCCLINTON, DELBERT

Number	Title	Yr	NM
ABC			
❏ 12218	Blue Monday/Special Love Song	1976	$5
❏ 12132	Object of My Affection/Two More Bottles of Wine	1975	$5
BOBILL			
❏ 101	I Know She Knows/Please Help Me, I'm Falling	1967	$10
BROWNFIELD			
❏ 303	I Know She Knows/Please Help Me, I'm Falling	1964	$30
CAPITOL/MSS			
❏ 4948	Giving It Up for Your Love/My Sweet Baby	1980	$4
❏ 5003	Going Back to Louisiana/Jealous Kind	1981	$4
❏ 5069	Sandy Beaches/I Wanna Thank You	1981	$4
❏ 4984	Shotgun Rider/Baby Ruth	1981	$4
CAPRICORN			
❏ 0328	Shot from the Saddle (mono/stereo)	1979	$8
— Only released as a promo			
❏ 0302	Take It Easy/Lovingest Man	1978	$5
JUBILEE			
❏ 9012	I Know She Knows/Please Help Me, I'm Falling	1965	$15
LONDON			
❏ 9544	Angel Eyes/Dunkirk	1962	$30
— As "Del McClinton			
MCA			
❏ 51124	Special Love Song/Let Love Come Between Us	1981	$4
PARAMOUNT			
❏ 016	Fannie Mae/I Know She Knows	1969	$10
SOFT			
❏ 1041	100 Pounds of Honey/Zip-a-Dee-Do-Dah	1970	$12

MCCOO, MARILYN, AND BILLY DAVIS, JR.

Number	Title	Yr	NM
ABC			
❏ 12170	I Hope We Get to Love in Time/There's Got to Be a Happy Ending	1976	$4
❏ 12298	Look What You've Done to My Heart/In My Lifetime	1977	$4
❏ 12324	My Reason to Be Is You/Two of Us	1978	$4
❏ 12316	Wonderful/Hard Road Down	1977	$4
COLUMBIA			
❏ 3-10806	Shine On Silver Moon/I Got the Words, You Got the Music	1978	$4

MCCOO, MARILYN

Number	Title	Yr	NM
RCA			
❏ PB-13677	Heart Stop Beating in Time/Understand Your Man	1983	$4
❏ PB-13761	I Believe in You/Just Like You	1984	$4

MCCORMICK, GAYLE

Number	Title	Yr	NM
ABC DUNHILL			
❏ 4281	Gonna Be Alright Now/Save Me	1971	$5
❏ 4288	It's a Cryin' Shame/If Only You Believe	1971	$5
MCA			
❏ 40007	Sweet Feelings/Take Me Back	1973	$4
SHADY BROOK			
❏ 45017	Coming In Out of the Rain/Simon Said	1977	$10

MCCORMICK, MAUREEN

Number	Title	Yr	NM
PARAMOUNT			
❏ 0292	Love's in the Roses/Harmonize	1974	$20

MCCOY, BUDD

Number	Title	Yr	NM
RCA VICTOR			
❏ 47-7453	The Midnight Ride of Paul Revere/Hiawatha	1959	$30

MCCOY, CHARLIE

Number	Title	Yr	NM
CADENCE			
❏ 1390	Cherry Berry Wine/My Little Woman	1960	$10
❏ 1415	I Just Want to Make Love to You/Rooster Blues	1962	$10
MONUMENT			
❏ 45-224	Amazing Grace/Squeezing	1977	$5
❏ 8633	Blue Christmas/Christmas Cheer	1974	$5
❏ 1938	Blue Christmas/Christmas Cheer	1976	$3
— Golden Series" reissue			
❏ 8660	Blues Stay Away from Me/Pots and Pans	1975	$4
❏ 8611	Boogie Woogie (A/K/A T.D.'s Boogie Woogie)/Keep On Harpin'	1974	$4
— With Barefoot Jerry			
❏ 45-292	Carolina Morning/Appalachian Fever	1979	$5
❏ 45-296	Cold, Cold Heart/Station Break	1980	$5
❏ 998	Cold Cold World/You've Got to Face Life	1967	$8
❏ 8672	Columbus Stockade Blues/(I Heard That) Lonesome Whistle	1975	$4
❏ 45-272	Drifting Lovers/West Virginia Mountain Melody	1978	$5
❏ 8638	Everybody Stand Up and Holler for the Union/New River Gorge	1975	$4
❏ 45-258	Fair and Tender Ladies/18th Century Rosewood Clock	1978	$5
❏ 45-239	Foggy River/Last Letter	1977	$5
❏ 1076	Gimme Some Lovin'/Boy from England	1968	$6
❏ 893	Girl (Those Were the Good Old Days)/It's a Man Down There	1965	$8
❏ 1093	Harper Valley P.T.A./Juke	1968	$6
❏ 870	I'm Ready/Harpoon Man	1965	$8
❏ 8546	I'm So Lonesome I Could Cry/Grade A	1972	$5
❏ 8554	I Really Don't Want to Know/Minor, Minor	1972	$5
❏ 8529	I Started Loving You Again/The Real McCoy	1971	$5
❏ 926	Let Him Go/Screamin', Shoutin', Beggin', Pleadin'	1966	$8
❏ 45-282	Midnight Flyer/Cripple Creek	1979	$5
❏ 842	My Babe/Will You Love Me Tomorrow	1964	$15
❏ 8566	Orange Blossom Special/Hangin' On	1973	$5
❏ 8650	Please Don't Tell Me How the Story Ends/Juke	1975	$4
❏ 8576	Shenandoah/John Henry	1973	$5
❏ 8600	Silver Threads and Golden Needles/I Just Can't Stand to See You Cry	1974	$5
❏ 975	Stubborn Kind of Fellow/My Baby's Back Again	1966	$8
❏ 45-210	Summit Ridge Drive/Play It Again Charlie	1977	$5
❏ 8683	The Star-Spangled Banner/Silver Wings	1976	$4
❏ 03518	The State of Our Union/Just Doin' Nothin' with You (Is Really Somethin')	1983	$4
— With Laney Hicks			
❏ 8625	The Way We Were/I Can't Help It	1974	$4
❏ 8703	Wabash Cannonball/Ode to Billie Joe	1976	$4

7-Inch Extended Plays

Number	Title	Yr	NM
❏ AEZ-00001 [PS]	Free Bonus 7	1973	$12
— Sleeve with large flap at left; may have been included with purchase of certain Charlie McCoy LPs in 1973			

MCCOY, CLYDE

Number	Title	Yr	NM
CAPITOL			
❏ F1986	Always Late/Hells Bells	1952	$20
❏ F2045	I Love to Hear a Choo Choo Train/To Be Loved by You	1952	$20
— Vocal by Liz Tilton			
❏ F1937	Sugar Blues Boogie/I Just Love Affection	1952	$20
❏ F2138	Tear It Down/Where's My Sweetie Hiding	1952	$20
❏ F2321	The Music Goes Round and Round/Mr. Wah Wah	1953	$20

Number	Title	Yr	NM
DECCA			
❏ 9-25014	Sugar Blues/I've Found a New Baby	1950	$30
— Recorded in 1935 for a 78 (Decca 381); this 45 is a reissue of a 78 with the same number that came out in the 1940s			
MERCURY			
❏ 5667x45	A Stranger in Town/How Ya Gonna Keep 'Em Down on the Farm	1951	$20
❏ 71938	Fidgety Feet/St. Louis Blues	1962	$10
❏ 5550x45	Memphis Blues/Wait for Me	1950	$30
❏ 5551x45	Stack-O-Lee/When You're Sailing	1950	$30
❏ 5648x45	St. Louis Blues/Because of Rain	1951	$20
❏ 5118x45	Sugar Blues/Way Down Yonder in New Orleans	1950	$40
— 78 rpm was issued in 1948			
❏ 5559x45	Tear It Down/Stormy Weather	1950	$30
❏ 5621x45	When You're Smiling/Memphis Blues	1951	$20
TODD			
❏ 1067	Lonely Wine/My World	1961	$10
❏ 1023	Swinging Shepherd Blues/Hot Sugar Blues	1959	$10

MCCOY, VAN

Number	Title	Yr	NM
AVCO			
❏ 4648	Boogie Down/Rainy Night in Georgia	1975	$5
❏ 4660	Change with the Times/Goodnight Baby	1975	$4
❏ 4639	Love Is the Answer/Killing Me Softly	1974	$5
❏ 4653	The Hustle/Hey Girl, Come and Get It	1975	$4
COLUMBIA			
❏ 43694	I Will Wait for You/The House That Love Built	1966	$8
❏ 43495	Starlight Starbright/This Is the Way We Fall in Love	1965	$8
H&L			
❏ 4670	Party/The Disco Kid	1976	$4
❏ 4682	Soul Cha Cha/Oriental Boogie	1977	$4
❏ 4677	The Shuffle/That's the Joint	1976	$4
LIBERTY			
❏ 55457	Follow Your Heart/Lonely	1962	$15
MCA			
❏ 40984	Lonely Dancer/Decisions	1979	$4
❏ 40885	My Favorite Fantasy/You're So Right for Me	1978	$4
❏ 40938	Trying to Make the Best of It/Two Points	1978	$4
ROCK'N			
❏ 101	Mr. D.J./Never Trust a Friend	1961	$60

MCCOYS, THE
Also see RICK DERRINGER.

Number	Title	Yr	NM
BANG			
❏ 543	Beat the Clock/Like You Do to Me	1967	$12
❏ 522	Come On Let's Go/Little People	1966	$10
❏ 532	Don't Worry Mother, Your Son's Heart Is Pure/Ko-Ko	1966	$12
❏ 511	Fever/Sorrow	1965	$10
❏ 506	Hang On Sloopy/I Can't Explain It	1965	$20
❏ 538	I Got to Go Back (And Watch That Little Girl Dance)/Dynamite	1966	$10
❏ 549	I Wonder If She Remembers Me/Say Those Magic Words	1967	$10
MERCURY			
❏ 72897	Daybreak/Epilogue	1969	$8
❏ 72967	Don't Fight It/Rosa Rodriguez	1969	$20
PHILCO-FORD			
❏ HP-6	Fever/Hang On Sloopy	1967	$30
— 4-inch plastic "Hip Pocket Record" with color sleeve			
RCA VICTOR			
❏ 47-7204	Daddy's Geisha Girl/Our Love Goes On and On	1958	$30
❏ 47-7354	Full Grown Cat/Throwing Kisses	1958	$30

MCCRACKEN, HUGH

Number	Title	Yr	NM
CONGRESS			
❏ 257	Buzz in My Head/You Blow My Mind	1965	$30

MCCRACKLIN, JIMMY

ART-TONE

Number	Title	Yr	NM
❑ 826	Christmas Time (Part 1)/ Christmas Time (Part 2)	1961	$15
❑ 827	Shame, Shame, Shame/I'm the One	1962	$15
❑ 831	That's No Big Thing/ Susie and Pat	1962	$15

CHECKER

Number	Title	Yr	NM
❑ 893	Everybody Rock/Get Tough	1958	$20
❑ 885	The Walk/I'm to Blame	1958	$30

CHESS

Number	Title	Yr	NM
❑ 1809	I Know/Later On	1961	$10
❑ 1826	One Track Love/Trottin'	1962	$10

HI

Number	Title	Yr	NM
❑ 2023	Things I Meant to Say/Here Today and Gone Tomorrow	1960	$15

HOLLYWOOD

Number	Title	Yr	NM
❑ 1054	It's All Right/Fare You Well	1955	$60

IMPERIAL

Number	Title	Yr	NM
❑ 5911	Advice/No No	1963	$10
❑ 66116	Arkansas (Part 1)/ Arkansas (Part 2)	1965	$8
❑ 66067	Believe in Me/Set Six	1964	$8
❑ 5892	Bitter Pill/Head Over Flip	1962	$10
❑ 66168	Come On Home (Back Where You Belong)/ Something That Belongs to Me	1966	$8
❑ 66094	Every Night, Every Day/ Can't Raise Me	1965	$8
❑ 5977	Every Night/The Slightest Idea	1963	$12
❑ 66010	I Did Wrong/Someone	1964	$8
❑ 5906	I Don't Care/Just Got to Know	1963	$10
❑ 66207	It's Got to Be Love/Sorry	1966	$8
❑ 66147	My Answer/Beulah	1966	$8
❑ 5982	Sooner or Later/ Looking for a Woman	1963	$12
❑ 5955	That's the Way (It Goes)/I'll See It Through	1963	$12
❑ 5926	The Bitter and the Sweet/ Just Pretending	1963	$12
❑ 66129	Think/Steppin' Up in Class	1965	$8

IRMA

Number	Title	Yr	NM
❑ 109	Beer Tavern Girl/ Love for You	1957	$40
❑ 107	I'm the One/Savoy's Jump	1957	$40
❑ 103	Take a Chance/Fare Well	1956	$40

KENT

Number	Title	Yr	NM
❑ 369	I've Got Eyes for You/I'm Gonna Tell Your Mother	1962	$10

LIBERTY

Number	Title	Yr	NM
❑ 56198	Believe Me/I Never Thought	1970	$5

MERCURY

Number	Title	Yr	NM
❑ 71613	Doomed Lover/By Myself	1960	$15
❑ 71516	Let's Do It (The Chicken Scratch)/Georgia Slop	1959	$20
❑ 71412	The Wobble/With Your Love	1959	$20
❑ 71747	What's That (Part 1)/ The Bridge	1961	$15

MINIT

Number	Title	Yr	NM
❑ 32022	Dog (Part 1)/Dog (Part 2)	1967	$6
❑ 32064	Drown in My Own Tears/ What's Going On	1969	$6
❑ 32033	Get Together/How You Like Your Love	1967	$6
❑ 32086	I Had to Get With It/You Ain't Nothin' But a Devil	1969	$6
❑ 32018	Let the Door Hit You/ This Thing	1967	$6
❑ 32052	Love, Love, Love/ Married Life	1968	$6
❑ 32044	Pretty Little Sweet Thing/A & I	1968	$6
❑ 32092	Stick to My Mind/I Just Live by the Rules	1970	$6

MODERN

Number	Title	Yr	NM
❑ 926	Blues Blasters' Boogie/ The Panic's On	1954	$50
❑ 934	Darlin' Share Your Love/ Give My Heart a Break	1954	$50
❑ 967	Gonna Tell Your Mother/ That Ain't Right	1955	$50
❑ 951	Please Forgive Me Baby/ Couldn't Be a Dream	1954	$50

PEACOCK

Number	Title	Yr	NM
❑ 1634	I Cried/The End	1953	$70
❑ 1683	I Need Your Loving/ The Swinging Thing	1958	$30
❑ 1605	My Days Are Limited/ She's Gone	1952	$70
❑ 1615	She Felt Too Good/ Share and Share Alike	1953	$70
❑ 1639	The Cheater/My Story	1954	$70

MCCULLERS, MICKEY

TAMLA

Number	Title	Yr	NM
❑ 54064	Same Old Story/I'll Cry a Million Tears	1962	$50

V.I.P.

Number	Title	Yr	NM
❑ 25009	Same Old Story/Who You Gonna Run To	1964	$60

MCCURN, GEORGE

A&M

Number	Title	Yr	NM
❑ 759	As Tears Go By/ Georgia Town	1965	$20
❑ 731	Guess Who/I've Got to Move	1964	$20
❑ 705	I'm Just a Country Boy/In My Little Corner of the World	1963	$10
❑ 715	Please Send Me Someone to Love/How's the World Treating You	1963	$30
❑ 741	Well/Clap Your Hands	1964	$20
❑ 726	When the Wind Blows (In Chicago)/Georgia Town	1963	$10

MCDANIELS, GENE

ATLANTIC

Number	Title	Yr	NM
❑ 2805	The Lord Is Back/Tell Me Mr. President	1971	$6

—As "Eugene McDaniels"

COLUMBIA

Number	Title	Yr	NM
❑ 43800	Something Blue/Cause I Love You So	1966	$40
❑ 44010	Touch of Your Lips/ Sweet Lover No More	1967	$40

LIBERTY

Number	Title	Yr	NM
❑ 55308	A Hundred Pounds of Clay/ Take a Chance on Love	1961	$20
❑ 55805	A Miracle/Walk with a Winner	1965	$200
❑ 55344	A Tear/She's Come Back	1961	$20
❑ 55405	Chip Chip/Another Tear Falls	1962	$20
❑ 55752	Emily/Forgotten Man	1964	$125
❑ 55444	Funny/Chapel of Tears	1962	$20
❑ 55834	Hang On/Will It Last Forever	1965	$125
❑ 55231	In Times Like These/ Once Before	1959	$20
❑ 55597	It's a Lonely Town/ False Friends	1963	$40
❑ 55723	Make Me a Present of You/ In Times Like These	1964	$15
❑ 55637	Old Country/Anyone Else	1963	$15
❑ 55480	Point of No Return/ Warmer Than a Whisper	1962	$20
❑ 55510	Spanish Lace/ Somebody's Waiting	1962	$20
❑ 55265	The Green Door/ Facts of Life	1960	$20
❑ 55541	The Puzzle/Cry Baby Cry	1963	$15
❑ 55371	Tower of Strength/ The Secret	1961	$20

MGM

Number	Title	Yr	NM
❑ 14613	Ol' Heartbreak Top Ten/River	1973	$5

ODE

Number	Title	Yr	NM
❑ 66107	Lady Fair/Natural Juices	1975	$4

UNITED ARTISTS

Number	Title	Yr	NM
❑ 0053	A Hundred Pounds of Clay/Tower of Strength	1973	$4

—Silver Spotlight Series" reissue

Number	Title	Yr	NM
❑ 0054	Chip Chip/Point of No Return	1973	$4

—Silver Spotlight Series" reissue

MCDEVITT, CHAS., AND HIS SKIFFLE GROUP

CHIC

Number	Title	Yr	NM
❑ 1008	Freight Train/The Cotton Song	1957	$20

EPIC

Number	Title	Yr	NM
❑ 9244	Face in the Rain/ Sporting Life	1957	$20

KAPP

Number	Title	Yr	NM
❑ 216	Sing, Sing, Sing/Johnny-O	1958	$20
❑ 238	Stack-O-Lee/Real Love	1958	$20

MCDONALD, MICHAEL

Also see THE DOOBIE BROTHERS; THE REGENTS (5).

BELL

Number	Title	Yr	NM
❑ 45182	Dear Me/I Think I Love You Again	1972	$20

—As "Mike McDonald"

Number	Title	Yr	NM
❑ 45259 [DJ]	Drivin' Wheel/ (B-side unknown)	1972	$15

—As "Mike McDonald"; stock copy may not exist

Number	Title	Yr	NM
❑ 45219	Good Old Time Love Song/When I'm Home	1972	$20

—As "Mike McDonald"

Number	Title	Yr	NM
❑ 45308 [DJ]	Where Do I Go from Here/ (B-side unknown)	1973	$15

—As "Mike McDonald"; stock copy may not exist

MCA

Number	Title	Yr	NM
❑ S45-17156 [DJ]	Sweet Freedom (Short Version 4:10)/ (Radio Edit 6:48)	1986	$8
❑ 52857	Sweet Freedom/The Freedom Eights	1986	$3
❑ 52857 [PS]	Sweet Freedom/The Freedom Eights	1986	$3

RCA VICTOR

Number	Title	Yr	NM
❑ 74-0405	God Knows/If You Won't, I Will	1970	$30

—As "Mike McDonald

WARNER BROS.

Number	Title	Yr	NM
❑ 7-29862	I Gotta Try/Believe in It	1982	$4
❑ 7-29862 [PS]	I Gotta Try/Believe in It	1982	$4
❑ 7-29933	I Keep Forgettin' (Every Time You're Near)/Losin' End	1982	$4

—Second pressing has subtitle on A-side

Number	Title	Yr	NM
❑ 7-29933 [PS]	I Keep Forgettin' (Every Time You're Near)/Losin' End	1982	$6

—Second pressing has subtitle on A-side

Number	Title	Yr	NM
❑ 7-29933	I Keep Forgettin'/Losin' End	1982	$6

—First pressing has no subtitle on A-side

Number	Title	Yr	NM
❑ 7-29933 [PS]	I Keep Forgettin'/Losin' End	1982	$6

—First pressing has no subtitle on A-side

Number	Title	Yr	NM
❑ 7-28847	Lost in the Parade/By Heart	1985	$4
❑ 7-28847 [PS]	Lost in the Parade/By Heart	1985	$4
❑ 7-28596	Our Love (Theme from "No Mercy")/Don't Let Me Down	1986	$3
❑ 7-28596 [PS]	Our Love (Theme from "No Mercy")/Don't Let Me Down	1986	$3
❑ 7-29743	Playin' by the Rules/ Believe in It	1983	$4

MCDONALD, SKEETS

CAPITOL

Number	Title	Yr	NM
❑ F1890	Baby Brown Eyes/ Fuss and Fight	1951	$30
❑ F2523	Baby I'm Courtin'/ It's Your Life	1953	$30
❑ F3312	Baby I'm Lost Without You/I Got a New Field to Plow	1956	$20
❑ F4147	Baby Wait/What a Lonesome Life It's Been	1959	$20
❑ F1570	Bless Your Little Old Heart/ Today I'm Moving Out	1951	$30
❑ F2885	But I Do/Your Love Is Like a Faucet	1954	$30
❑ F2073	Curtain of Tears/ Please Come Back	1952	$30
❑ F2216	Don't Let the Stars Get In Your Eyes/ Big Family Trouble	1952	$30
❑ F3600	Don't Push Me Too Far/ You Better Not Go	1956	$20
❑ F3378	Fallen Angel/It'll Take Me a Long, Long Time	1956	$20
❑ F3778	Fingertips/Bless Your Little Ol' Heart	1957	$20
❑ F2573	Hi Diddle Dee/Worried Mind	1953	$30

—With Helen O'Connell

Number	Title	Yr	NM
❑ F2434	I Can't Last Long/I've Got to Win Your Love Again	1953	$30
❑ F2774	I Love You Mama Mia/ Remember You're Mine	1954	$30
❑ F3833	I'm Hurtin'/Love Wind	1957	$20
❑ F1771	I'm Hurtin'/Ridin' with the Blues	1951	$30
❑ F2326	Let Me Know/I'm Sorry to Say I'm Sorry	1953	$30
❑ F2607	Looking at the Moon and Wishing/I Need Your Love	1953	$30
❑ F2696	Look Who's Cryin' Now/ Walkin' on Teardrops	1954	$30
❑ F1518	Scoot, Git and Begone/ The Blues Is Bad News	1951	$30
❑ F2976	Smoke Comes Out My Chimney/Each Time a New Love Dies	1954	$30
❑ F3215	Strollin'/You Turned Me Down	1955	$30
❑ F1967	Tell Me Why/Be My Life's Companion	1952	$30
❑ F3741	Welcome Home/Your Sweet Love Is Gone	1957	$20
❑ F4095	What I Know About Her/ What Am I Doing Here	1958	$20

Number	Title	Yr	NM
❏ F1993	Wheel of Fortune/Love That Hurt Me So	1952	$30

COLUMBIA

Number	Title	Yr	NM
❏ 4-43573	A Member of the Blues/Polly Brown	1966	$10
❏ 4-43425	Big Chief Buffalo Nickel (Desert Blues)/Day Sleeper	1965	$12
❏ 4-42807	Call Me Mr. Brown/This Old Broken Heart	1963	$10
❏ 4-41556	Cheek to Cheek with the Blues/Where You Go (I'll Follow)	1960	$15
❏ 4-42960	Chin Up, Chest Out/I'd Hate to See Him	1963	$10
❏ 4-42655	Dear John/I've Gotta Show You	1962	$15
❏ 4-43152	Down in Mexico/Teardrop Inn	1964	$12
❏ 4-41667	Gotta Get Away from That Crowd/The Everglades	1960	$15
❏ 4-43946	Mabel/Too Much of Me (Walked Away with You)	1966	$10
❏ 4-43275	Me and My Heart and My Shoes/Mrs. Right's Divorcing Mr. Wrong	1965	$10
❏ 4-42252	Same Old Town/I Write You Letters	1961	$15
❏ 4-43791	There Sits an Angel/She's Never Gone That Route	1966	$10
❏ 4-41773	This Old Heart/Make Room for the Blues	1960	$15
❏ 4-43065	Too Many Times Away from You/Think of Me	1964	$10

UNI

Number	Title	Yr	NM
❏ 55041	It's Genuine/Old Indians Never Die	1967	$10

7-Inch Extended Plays

CAPITOL

Number	Title	Yr	NM
❏ EAP 1-451	*Don't Let the Stars Get In Your Eyes/Let Me Know/ Bless Your Little Ol' Heart (You're Mine)/I'm Hurtin'	1954	$20
❏ EAP 1-451 [PS]	Country & Hillbilly Songs	1954	$20

MCDOWELL, RONNIE

CURB

Number	Title	Yr	NM
❏ 10508	I'm Still Missing You/ Suspicion	1988	$3
❏ 10501	It's Only Make Believe/ Baby Me Baby	1987	$3
❏ 10525	Sea of Heartbreak/ Ain't Love Wonderful	1989	$3
❏ 10558	She's a Little Past Forty/ Under These Conditions	1989	$3
❏ 10544	Who'll Turn Out the Lights/ Hey Hey Miss Lucy	1989	$3

EPIC

Number	Title	Yr	NM
❏ 50925	Gone/24 Hours of Love	1980	$4
❏ 50895	How Far Do You Want Me to Go/You've Already Gone to My Heart	1980	$4
❏ 34-04367	I Dream of Women Like You/ Your Baby's Not My Baby	1984	$4
❏ 34-04499	I Got a Million of 'Em/ My Baby Don't Wear No Pajamas	1984	$4
❏ 14-02884	I Just Cut Myself/World's Greatest Lover	1982	$4
❏ 34-04816	In a New York Minute/ Something Special	1985	$4
❏ 50753	Love Me Now/Never Seen a Mountain So High	1979	$4
❏ 34-05404	Love Talks/She Lays Me Down	1985	$4
❏ 50857	Lovin' a Livin' Dream/When the Right Time Comes	1980	$4
❏ 19-02129	Older Women/No Body's Perfect	1981	$4
❏ 34-03526	Personally/You Make My Day Pay Off (All Night Long)	1982	$4
❏ 14-03203	Step Back/I Never Felt So Much Love (In One Bed)	1982	$4
❏ 50962	Wandering Eyes/What Would Heaven Say	1980	$4
❏ 14-02614	Watchin' Girls Go By/ Good Time Lovin' Man	1981	$4
❏ 50696	World's Most Perfect Woman/Rockin' You Easy, Lovin' You Slow	1979	$4

MCA

Number	Title	Yr	NM
❏ 53126	Make Me Late for Work Today/Hold Me Tight	1987	$3

MCA CURB

Number	Title	Yr	NM
❏ 52816	All Tied Up/Strings of Silver Satin	1986	$3
❏ 52994	Lovin' That Crazy Feelin'/I Don't Want to Set the World on Fire	1986	$3
❏ 52994 [DJ]	Lovin' That Crazy Feelin' (same on both sides)	1986	$10

—Promo only on red vinyl

Number	Title	Yr	NM
❏ 52907	When You Hurt, I Hurt/Whoopla	1986	$3

SCORPION

Number	Title	Yr	NM
❏ 0533	Only the Lonely/The Bridge Washed Out	1977	$10

MCENTIRE, REBA

MCA

Number	Title	Yr	NM
❏ 53638	Cathy's Clown/Walk On	1989	$4
❏ 52604	Have I Got a Deal for You/Whose Heartache Is This Anyway	1985	$3
❏ 52604 [PS]	Have I Got a Deal for You/Whose Heartache Is This Anyway	1985	$5
❏ 52404	He Broke Your Mem'ry Last Night/If Only	1984	$3
❏ 52468	How Blue/That's What He Said	1984	$3
❏ 53402	I Know How He Feels/ So, So, Long	1988	$3
❏ S45-17725 [DJ]	I'll Be Home for Christmas/ The Christmas Guest	1987	$10
❏ 52990	Let the Music Lift You Up/ Lookin' for a New Love Story	1986	$3
❏ 52990 [DJ]	Let the Music Lift You Up (same on both sides)	1986	$12

—Promo only on yellow vinyl

Number	Title	Yr	NM
❏ 53763	Little Girl/Am I the Only One Who Cares	1989	$4
❏ 52848	Little Rock/If You Only Knew	1986	$3
❏ 53244	Love Will Find Its Way to You/Someone Else	1988	$3
❏ 53092 [DJ]	One Promise Too Late (same on both sides)	1987	$10

—Promo only on yellow vinyl

Number	Title	Yr	NM
❏ 53092	One Promise Too Late/ Why Not Tonight	1987	$4
❏ 52691	Only in My Mind/She's the Only One Loving You Now	1985	$3
❏ 52527	Somebody Should Leave/ Don't You Believe Him	1985	$3
❏ 52527 [PS]	Somebody Should Leave/ Don't You Believe Him	1985	$5
❏ 53315	Sunday Kind of Love/ So, So Long	1988	$3
❏ S45-17446 [DJ]	The Christmas Song (Chestnuts Roasting on an Open Fire)/O Holy Night	1987	$12
❏ 53159	The Last One to Know/I Don't Want to Be Alone	1987	$3
❏ 53694	'Til Love Comes Again/ You Must Really Love Me	1989	$3
❏ 52922	What Am I Gonna Do About You/I Heard Her Crying	1986	$3
❏ 52922 [DJ]	What Am I Gonna Do About You (same on both sides)	1986	$15

—Promo only on blue vinyl

Number	Title	Yr	NM
❏ 52767	Whoever's in New England/Can't Stop Now	1986	$4

MERCURY

Number	Title	Yr	NM
❏ 76180	Can't Even Get the Blues/Sweet Dreams	1982	$6
❏ 73929	Glad I Waited Just for You/ Invitation to the Blues	1977	$10
❏ 73788	I Don't Want to Be a One Night Stand/I'm Not Your Kind of Girl	1976	$10
❏ 76157	I'm Not That Lonely Yet/ Over, Under and Around	1982	$6
❏ 55014	I've Waited All My Life for You/One to One	1977	$15
❏ 55036	Last Night, Ev'ry Night/ Angel in Your Arms	1978	$8
❏ 57062 [PS]	Only You (And You Alone)/Love by Love	1981	$10
❏ 814629-7	There Ain't No Future in This/Reasons	1983	$5
❏ 73879	(There's Nothing Like the Love) Between a Woman and a Man/I Was Glad to Give My Everything to You	1977	$10
❏ 812632-7	Why Do We Want (What We Know We Can't Have)/I Can See Forever in Your Eyes	1983	$5

MCENTIRE, REBA, AND JERRY FULLER

MERCURY

Number	Title	Yr	NM
❏ 888027-7	It's Another Silent Night/Hold On	1986	$5

MCFADDEN, BOB

BRUNSWICK

Number	Title	Yr	NM
❏ 55156	Bingo/Shake, Rattle and Roll	1959	$30
❏ 55120	Frankie and Igor at a Rock and Roll Party/ Children Cross the Bridge	1959	$30
❏ 55140	The Mummy/The Beat Generation	1959	$30

—As "Bob McFadden and Dor"

Number	Title	Yr	NM
❏ 55140 [PS]	The Mummy/The Beat Generation	1959	$50

—As "Bob McFadden and Dor"

CORAL

Number	Title	Yr	NM
❏ 62209	Dracula Cha-Cha/ Transylvania Polka	1959	$40

MCFADDEN, RUTH, AND THE SUPREMES

OLD TOWN

Number	Title	Yr	NM
❏ 1017	Darling Listen to the Words of This Song/Since My Baby's Been Gone	1956	$60

MCFADDEN, RUTH

OLD TOWN

Number	Title	Yr	NM
❏ 1020	Two in Love/(B-side unknown)	1956	$125

MCFARLAND, GARY

IMPULSE!

Number	Title	Yr	NM
❏ 250	Winter Samba/ Summer's Gone Away	1966	$8

SKYE

Number	Title	Yr	NM
❏ 4511	80 Miles an Hour Through Beer-Can Country/ (B-side unknown)	1969	$6
❏ 453	By the Time I Get to Phoenix/Flea Market	1968	$6
❏ 4516	Slaves/(Instrumental)	1970	$6

VERVE

Number	Title	Yr	NM
❏ 10342	And I Love Her/A Hard Day's Night	1964	$10
❏ 10380	Fried Bananas/ Wine and Bread	1966	$10
❏ 10272	How to Succeed in Business Without Really Trying/I Believe in You	1962	$10

MCFERRIN, BOBBY

ELEKTRA/MUSICIAN

Number	Title	Yr	NM
❏ 7-69949	Moondance/Jubilee	1982	$5

EMI MANHATTAN

Number	Title	Yr	NM
❏ B-50146	Don't Worry Be Happy/ Simple Pleasures	1988	$3
❏ B-50163	Good Lovin'/Don't Worry Be Happy	1988	$3
❏ B-50163 [PS]	Good Lovin'/Don't Worry Be Happy	1988	$3

MCGHEE, BROWNIE

DOT

Number	Title	Yr	NM
❏ 1184	Cheatin' and Lyin'/Need Someone to Love	1954	$250

HARLEM

Number	Title	Yr	NM
❏ 2329	My Confession (I Want to Thank You)/ Bluebird, Bluebird	1954	$70
❏ 2323	Worrying Over You/Christina	1954	$70

JAX

Number	Title	Yr	NM
❏ 310	Guitar Strangers Blues/ Dissatisfied Woman	1952	$120
❏ 304	I Feel So Good/Key to the Highway	1952	$120
❏ 312	I'm 10,000 Years Old/ Cherry Red	1952	$120
❏ 307	Meet You in the Morning/ Brownie's Blues	1952	$120
❏ 302	Smiling and Crying Blues/A Letter to Lightnin' Hopkins	1951	$120

RED ROBIN

Number	Title	Yr	NM
❏ 111	Don't Dog Your Woman/Daisy	1953	$250

SAVOY

Number	Title	Yr	NM
❏ 835	Diamond Ring/So Much Trouble	1952	$40
❏ 1177	I'd Love to Love You/ Anna Mae	1955	$30
❏ 1564	Living with the Blues/ Be My Friend	1959	$20
❏ 899	Sweet Baby Blues/4 O'Clock in the Morning	1953	$40
❏ 872	Tell Me Baby/Bad Nerves	1952	$40
❏ 1185	When It's Love Time/My Fault	1956	$30

MCGHEE, STICK

ATLANTIC

Number	Title	Yr	NM
❏ 873	Drinkin' Wine Spo-Dee-O-Dee/Blues Mixture (I'd Rather Drink Muddy Water)	1971	$30

—Yellow label, "fan" logo at lower left; first issue of this number on 45

Number	Title	Yr	NM
❏ 955	Wee Wee Hours (Part 1)/ Wee Wee Hours (Part 2)	1952	$125

—Note: Stick McGhee records on Atlantic before 955 are unconfirmed on 45 rpm

HERALD

Number	Title	Yr	NM
❏ 553	Money Fever/Sleep-In Job	1960	$20

KING

Number	Title	Yr	NM
❏ 4783	Double Crossin' Liquor/Six to Eight	1955	$120
❏ 4800	Get Your Mind Out the Gutter/Sad, Bad, Glad	1955	$125
❏ 4700	I'm Doin' All This Time/ Wiggle Waggin' Woo	1954	$125
❏ 4610	Little Things We Used to Do/Head Happy with Wine	1953	$125
❏ 4628	Whiskey, Women and Loaded Dice/Blues in My Heart and Tears in My Eyes	1953	$125

SAVOY

Number	Title	Yr	NM
❏ 1148	Things Have Changed/ Help Me Baby	1955	$40

Number	Title	Yr	NM

MCGILL, JERRY
SUN
| ❏ 326 | Love Struck/I Wanna Make Sweet Love | 1959 | $40 |

MCGOVERN, MAUREEN
20TH CENTURY
❏ 2213	Even Better Than I Know Myself/All I Want (All I Need)	1975	$4
❏ 2107	Give Me a Reason to Be Gone/Love Knots	1974	$4
❏ 2051	I Won't Last a Day Without You/Darlene	1973	$4
❏ 2234	Love Songs Are Getting Harder to Sing/Stop Me	1975	$4
❏ 2234 [PS]	Love Songs Are Getting Harder to Sing/Stop Me	1975	$8

— No titles on sleeve, but catalog number is on it plus the words "The new Maureen McGovern in more ways than one!

| ❏ 2010 | The Morning After (Song from The Poseidon Adventure)/Midnight Storm | 1973 | $4 |
| ❏ 2158 | We May Never Love Like This Again/Wherever Love Takes Me | 1974 | $4 |

CBS
| ❏ 39-07689 | The Same Moon/Why Can't I Forget | 1988 | $4 |
| ❏ 39-07689 [PS] | The Same Moon/Why Can't I Forget | 1988 | $4 |

MAIDEN VOYAGE
| ❏ 120 | Halfway Home/You Love Me Too Late | 1981 | $4 |

WARNER BROS.
❏ 49525	Bottom Line/Don't Stop Now	1980	$4
❏ 49129	Can't Take My Eyes Off You/A Very Special Love	1979	$4
❏ 8750	Can You Read My Mind/You Love Me Too Late	1979	$4
❏ 8835	Different Worlds/Carolina Moon	1979	$4
❏ 49177	We Could Have It All/Don't Stop Now	1980	$4

MCGRATH, BAT, AND DON POTTER
EPIC
| ❏ 5-10582 | Me and Bobby McGee/Jefferson Queen | 1970 | $10 |
| ❏ 5-10562 | Mr. Cadillac/Walking Bird | 1969 | $8 |

MCGRIFF, JIMMY
BLUE NOTE
| ❏ 1968 | Black Pearl/Groove Alley | 1971 | $5 |
CAPITOL
| ❏ 2875 | Sugar Sugar/Fat Cakes | 1970 | $5 |
| ❏ 3019 | The Bird/Plain Brown Bag | 1971 | $5 |
GROOVE MERCHANT
❏ 1014	Everyday I Have the Blues/It's You I Adore	1973	$5
❏ 1003	Groove Grease/Mr. Lucky	1972	$5
❏ 1025	If You're Ready (Come Go with Me)/(B-side unknown)	1974	$5
❏ 1029	Main Squeeze/The Sermon	1975	$5
❏ 1033	Stump Juice/The Worm Turns	1976	$5
❏ 1006	Theme from Shaft/Let's Stay Together	1972	$5
JELL
| ❏ 503 | Soul Song Of Christmas (Silent Nite)/Chip! Chip! | 1965 | $8 |
MILESTONE
| ❏ 313 | I'm Walkin'/(B-side unknown) | 1984 | $4 |
SOLID STATE
❏ 2534	Back on the Street/Chris Cross	1970	$6
❏ 2531	Charlotte/Trying to Come By	1969	$6
❏ 2502	Cherry/The Comeback	1966	$8
❏ 2516	Days of Wine and Roses/You Are My Sunshine	1967	$8
❏ 2522	Honey/Since You've Been Gone	1968	$6
❏ 2510	I Can't Give You Anything But Love, Baby/(I Can't Get No) Satisfaction	1967	$8
❏ 2501	I Cover the Waterfront/Slow But Sure	1966	$8
❏ 2520	I've Got a Woman/Kiko	1968	$6
❏ 2528	Step One/South Wes	1969	$6
❏ 2515	Tennessee Waltz/Swingin' Shepherd Blues	1967	$8
❏ 2524	The Worm/Keep Loose	1968	$6
SUE
❏ 777	All About My Girl/M.G. Blues	1963	$8
❏ 110	All Day Long/When You're Smiling	1964	$8
❏ 804	Christmas with McGriff Part 1/Part 2	1963	$15
❏ 123	Discotheque U.S.A./People	1965	$8
❏ 105	Hello Betty/Close Your Eyes	1964	$8
❏ 770	I've Got a Woman (Part 1)/I've Got a Woman (Part 2)	1962	$10
❏ 802	Lonely Avenue (Part 1)/Lonely Avenue (Part 2)	1963	$8

❏ 791	One of Mine/Broadway	1963	$8
❏ 120	Sho 'Nuff/Bilbo	1965	$8
❏ 786	The Last Minute (Part 1)/The Last Minute (Part 2)	1963	$8
❏ 112	Topkapi/Theme from "The Man with the Golden Arm	1964	$8
❏ 128	Turn Blue/Bump De Bump	1965	$8
❏ 804	Winter with McGriff Pt. 1/Winter with McGriff Pt. 2	1963	$10
UNITED ARTISTS
| ❏ 50826 | Pretty Baby/I Need Love So Bad | 1971 | $5 |

— With Junior Parker

MCGUINN, ROGER
Also see THE BYRDS; McGUINN AND HILLMAN; McGUINN, CLARK AND HILLMAN.

COLUMBIA
❏ 10543	American Girl/I'm Not Lonely Anymore	1977	$6
❏ 45931	Draggin'/Time Cube	1973	$6
❏ 10019	Gate of Horn/Same Old Sound	1974	$6
❏ 10201	Lover of the Bayou/Easy Does It	1975	$6
❏ 10181	Somebody Loves You/Easy Does It	1975	$6
❏ 10385	Take Me Away/Friend	1976	$6

MCGUIRE, BARRY, AND BARRY KANE
HORIZON
| ❏ 354 | Another Man/Bull 'Gine Run | 1962 | $15 |

MCGUIRE, BARRY
Also see THE NEW CHRISTY MINSTRELS.

DUNHILL
❏ 4014	Child of Our Times/Upon a Painted Ocean	1965	$10
❏ 4014 [PS]	Child of Our Times/Upon a Painted Ocean	1965	$20
❏ 4028	Cloudy Summer Afternoon (Raindrops)/I'd Have to Be Outta My Mind	1966	$10
❏ 4009	Eve of Destruction/What Exactly's the Matter with Me	1965	$15
❏ 4124	Grasshopper Song/Top o' the Hill	1968	$10
❏ 4124 [PS]	Grasshopper Song/Top o' the Hill	1968	$20
❏ 4116	Lollipop Train/Inner-Manipulations	1968	$8
❏ 4098	Masters of War/Stop Now and Dig It While You Can	1967	$8
❏ 4048	There's Nothing Else on My Mind/Why Not Stop and Dig It	1966	$10
❏ 4019	This Precious Time/Don't You Wonder Where It's At	1966	$15

— A-side backing group: The Mamas and The Papas

HORIZON
| ❏ 8 | Oh, Miss Mary/So Long, Stay Well | 1963 | $15 |
| ❏ 4 | One by One/Town and Country | 1963 | $15 |
MIRA
| ❏ 205 | Greenback Dollar/Oh, Miss Mary | 1965 | $10 |
MOSAIC
| ❏ 1004 | I've Got a Secret/Cindy and Johnny | 1962 | $15 |
| ❏ 1001 | The Three/Theme from The Tree | 1961 | $15 |
MYRRH
| ❏ 119 | Love Is/David and Goliath | 1973 | $5 |
ODE
| ❏ 66010 | Old Farm/South of the Border | 1970 | $6 |

7-Inch Extended Plays
DUNHILL
| ❏ LP-DS-50005 [PS] | This Precious Time | 1966 | $15 |
| ❏ LP-DS-50005 | This Precious Time/California Dreamin'/Hide Your Love Away//Let Me Be/Do You Believe in Magic/Don't You Wonder Where It's At | 1966 | $15 |

— Jukebox issue, small hole, plays at 33 1/3 rpm

MCGUIRE SISTERS, THE
ABC-PARAMOUNT
| ❏ 10776 | Grazia/Truer Than You Are | 1966 | $6 |
CORAL
❏ 61073	Are You Looking for a Sweetheart/You'll Never Know Till Monday	1953	$15
❏ 61856	Around the World in 80 Days/Interlude	1957	$10
❏ 61303	Christmas Alphabet/Give Me Your Heart for Christmas	1954	$15

| ❏ 61126 | Cling to Me/Pine Tree, Pine Over Me | 1954 | $15 |

— With Johnny Desmond and Eileen Barton

❏ 61991	Ding Dong/Since You Went Away to School	1958	$12
❏ 61815	Drownin' in Memories/Please Don't Do That to Me	1957	$12
❏ 61703	Every Day of My Life/Endless	1956	$12
❏ 61888	Forgive Me/Kiss Them for Me	1957	$10
❏ 61494	Give Me Love/Sweet Song of India	1955	$15
❏ 61187	Goodnight, Sweetheart, Goodnight/Heavenly Feeling	1954	$15
❏ 61748	Goodnight My Love, Pleasant Dreams/Mommy	1956	$10
❏ 61335	Hearts of Stone/The Naughty Lady of Shady Lane	1955	$15
❏ 61501	He/If You Believe	1955	$15
❏ 61798	He's Got Time/Blue Skies	1957	$12
❏ 61002	Hey, Mister Cotton Picker/Where Good Times Are	1954	$15
❏ 62296	I Can Dream, Can't I/I'm Just Taking My Time	1961	$8
❏ 62333	I Really Don't Want to Know/Mama's Gone, Goodbye	1962	$8
❏ 61369	It May Sound Silly/Doesn't Anybody Love Me?	1955	$15
❏ 62162	Livin' Dangerously/Lover's Lullaby	1960	$8
❏ 62162 [PS]	Livin' Dangerously/Lover's Lullaby	1960	$10
❏ 62059	May You Always/Achoo Cha Cha	1958	$10
❏ 61587	Missing/Tell Me Now	1956	$10
❏ 60969	Miss You/Tootle-Ooh Siana	1953	$15
❏ 61278	Muskrat Ramble/Lonesome Polecat	1954	$15
❏ 61258	Muskrat Ramble/Not as a Stranger	1954	$15
❏ 61532	My Baby's Got Such Lovin' Ways/(Baby, Baby) Be Good to Me	1955	$15
❏ 61334	Open Up Your Heart (And Let the Sun Shine In)/Melody of Love	1955	$15
❏ 60917	Picking Sweethearts/One, Two, Three, Four	1953	$15
❏ 61627	Picnic/Delilah Jones	1956	$10
❏ 61911	Santa Claus Is Comin' to Town/Honorable Congratulations	1957	$10
❏ 61323	Sincerely/No More	1954	$15
❏ 62155	Some of These Days/Have a Nice Weekend	1959	$12
❏ 61423	Something's Gotta Give/Rhythm 'N' Blues (Mama's Got the Rhythm -- Papa's Got the Blues)	1955	$15
❏ 61924	Sugartime/Banana Split	1958	$15
❏ 62305	Sugartime Twist/More Hearts Are Broken That Way	1962	$8
❏ 62106	Summer Dreams/Peace	1959	$10
❏ 62047	Sweetie Pie/I'll Think of You	1958	$10
❏ 62276	Tears on My Pillow/Will There Be Room in the Space Ship	1961	$8
❏ 62276 [PS]	Tears on My Pillow/Will There Be Room in the Space Ship	1961	$10
❏ 62216	The Last Dance/Nine O'Clock	1960	$8
❏ 61531	The Littlest Angel/I'd Like to Trim a Tree with You	1955	$15
❏ 62235	To Be Loved/I Don't Know Why	1960	$8

REPRISE
❏ 0330	Dear Heart/Candy Heart	1964	$6
❏ 0338	I'll Walk Alone/Ticket to Anywhere	1965	$6
❏ 20197	Summertime (Is the Time for Love)/Cordially Invited	1963	$6

7-Inch Extended Plays
CORAL
❏ EC81098 [PS]	By Request	1955	$20
❏ EC81165	(contents unknown)	1958	$15
❏ EC81184 [M]	(contents unknown)	1959	$15
❏ EC 7-81184 [S]	(contents unknown)	1959	$25
❏ EC81174 [PS]	Four by Three	1958	$15
❏ EC81184 [PS]	I'll Think of You	1959	$15
❏ EC 7-81184 [PS]	I'll Think of You	1959	$25
❏ EC81098	Melody of Love/Hearts of Stone//Open Up Your Heart/The Naughty Lady of Shady Lane	1955	$20
❏ EC81507	Something's Gotta Give/Sincerely//Goodnight, Sweetheart, Goodnight/Muskrat Ramble	1959	$15
❏ EC81145	Sugartime/Banana Split//I Tried/Lullaby of Birdland	1958	$15
❏ EC81174	Summer Dreams/Ding Dong//Since You Went Away to School/Think of Me Kindly	1958	$15
❏ EC81145 [PS]	The McGuire Sisters	1958	$15
❏ EC81507 [PS]	The McGuire Sisters	1959	$15
❏ EC81165 [PS]	While the Lights Are Low	1958	$15

Number	Title	Yr	NM
MCHUGH, JIMMY			
HUNCH			
❏ 346	Do the Kangaroo/I Don't Want Everything	1965	$30
SUCCESS			
❏ 106	Do the Kangaroo/I Don't Want Everything	1963	$20
MCKAY, SCOTTY			
ACE			
❏ 608	Brown Eyed Handsome Man/Cry Me a River	1960	$70
❏ 8003	Half a Heartache/ Little Miss Blue	1962	$40
❏ 636	I've Got My Eyes on You/ Shattered Dreams	1961	$50
❏ 603	Let the Good Times Roll/Little Liza Jane	1960	$60
❏ 623	Ole King Cole/Pull Down the Sky	1961	$60
❏ 652	Olive Learned to Pop-Eye/Shame	1962	$50
CLARIDGE			
❏ 309	Batman/All Around the World	1966	$30
HANNA-BARBERA			
❏ 495	I'm Gonna Love Ya/ Waikiki Beach	1966	$30
LAWN			
❏ 102	I've Been Thinkin'/ It's a Fun Thing	1960	$30
PHILIPS			
❏ 40109	Mess Around/Sittin' Down and Cryin'	1963	$30
SWAN			
❏ 4049	Little Lump of Sugar/ Midnight Cryin' Time	1960	$70
UNI			
❏ 55205	High on Life/If You Really Want Me To, I'll Go	1970	$15
MCKENZIE, BOB AND DOUG			
MERCURY			
❏ 76134	Take Off/Elron McKenzie	1981	$6
❏ 76134 [PS]	Take Off/Elron McKenzie	1981	$15
❏ 810323-7	Take Off/Twelve Days Of Christmas	1983	$5
—Reissue			
❏ 76133 [DJ]	Twelve Days of Christmas (same on both sides)	1981	$10
—May be promo only			
MCKENZIE, SCOTT			
CAPITOL			
❏ 5348	All I Want Is You/ Look in Your Eyes	1965	$10
❏ 5961	All I Want Is You/ Look in Your Eyes	1967	$6
❏ 5500	There Stands the Glass/Wipe the Tears (From Your Face)	1965	$10
ODE			
❏ 66012	Going Home Again/ Take a Moment	1970	$5
❏ 107	Holy Man/What's the Difference, Chapter III	1968	$6
❏ 105	Like and Old Time Movie/What's the Difference, Chapter II	1967	$6
❏ 103	San Francisco (Be Sure to Wear Flowers in Your Hair)/ What's the Difference	1967	$8
—Revised title and revised mix			
❏ 103	San Francisco "Wear Some Flowers in Your Hair"/ What's the Difference	1967	$20
—Original title; also has a different mix (echoey bass drum in bridge) than the later, more common version			
MCKUEN, ROD			
A&M			
❏ 712	Hi Lonesome/Ballad of Hollywood	1963	$12
BUDDAH			
❏ 372	Cycles/I Have Loved You	1973	$4
❏ 401	Seasons in the Sun/ (B-side unknown)	1974	$4
BUENA VISTA			
❏ 482	Pastures Green/ Scandalous John	1971	$5
❏ 482 [PS]	Pastures Green/ Scandalous John	1971	$20
DECCA			
❏ 30840	Lonesome Boy/Time's A-Gettin' Hard	1959	$20
❏ 30902	Sure/Take It Like a Man	1959	$20
❏ 30660	Two Brothers/Jump Up	1958	$20

Number	Title	Yr	NM
HORIZON			
❏ 3	Advice to Folk Singers/ There's a Hoot Tonight	1963	$10
JUBILEE			
❏ 5420	Oliver Twist Meets the Duke of Oil/Steel Men	1962	$15
KAPP			
❏ 366	In a Lonely Place/ Marie, Marie	1961	$15
LIBERTY			
❏ 55034	Happy Is a Boy Named Me/Repeat After Me	1956	$15
RCA VICTOR			
❏ 47-9376	Listen to the Warm/A Cat Named Sloopy	1967	$8
❏ 47-8772	So Long, San Francisco/ Some Trust in Chariots	1965	$8
❏ 47-8613	Summer in My Eye/ So Many Others	1965	$8
❏ 47-9139	The Ever Constant Sea/ Baby Be My Love	1967	$8
❏ 47-9478	The Importance of the Rose/The Single Man	1968	$8
SPIRAL			
❏ 1407	Oliver Twist/Celebrity Twist	1962	$20
STANYAN			
❏ 34	Simple Christmas/A Hand To Hold At Christmas	1974	$5
—B-side by Glenn Yarbrough			
WARNER BROS.			
❏ 7274	Boat Ride/I'll Catch the Sun	1969	$6
❏ 7346	Bring Her a Rose/Mister Kelly-Kelly and Me	1969	$6
❏ 7454	Champion Charlie Brown/ Something for Snoopy	1971	$6
❏ 7699	Good for Nothin' Bill/The World I Used to Know	1973	$4
❏ 7533	Hit 'Em in the Head with Love/Soldiers Want to Be Heroes	1971	$5
❏ 7389	I Think It's Going to Rain Today/Lonely	1970	$5
❏ 7259	Ivy That Clings to the Wall/Kaleidoscope	1969	$6
❏ 7288	Look Away/Trashy	1969	$6
❏ 7420	My Mother's Eyes/Soldiers Want to Be Heroes	1970	$5
❏ 7243	Seasons in the Sun/ To Watch the Trains	1968	$6
❏ 7542 [PS]	The Carols of Christmas/So My Sheep May Safely Graze	1971	$6
❏ 7542	The Carols of Christmas/So My Sheep May Safely Graze	1971	$5
❏ 7332	The Things Men Do/The Time It Takes to Love You	1969	$6
❏ 7620	Time to Sing My Song/ Minute-Thirty-Second Waltz	1972	$5
7-Inch Extended Plays			
❏ PRO298 [DJ]	A Personal Message from Rod McKuen//The Language of Hello/Concerto for 4 Hands/Boat Ride	1968	$20
—Promo-only item; small hole, plays at 33 1/3 rpm			
❏ PRO298 [PS]	Lonesome Cities	1968	$25
MCLAIN, DENNY			
CAPITOL			
❏ 2282	Extra Innings/Lonely Is the Name	1968	$15
MCLAIN, TOMMY			
JIN			
❏ 229	Barefootin'/Together Again	1968	$40
❏ 228	Before I Grow Too Old/Domino '68	1968	$12
❏ 197	Sweet Dreams/I Need You So	1966	$30
❏ 230	Tender Years/My Heart Remembers	1968	$10
❏ 197	Sweet Dreams/I Need You So	1966	$15
STARFLITE			
❏ 4901	(I Don't Love You) Since You Walked Out on Me/ That's Good Enough for Me	1979	$6
MCLAWLER, SARAH			
KING			
❏ 4549	Please Try to Love Me/ Ready, Willing, and Able	1952	$125
VEE JAY			
❏ 199	Babe in the Woods/Flamingo	1956	$40
❏ 239	Snowfall/Relax Miss Frisky	1957	$40
—With Richard Otto			

Number	Title	Yr	NM
MCLEAN, DON			
ARISTA			
❏ 0379	It Doesn't Matter Anymore/If We Try	1978	$4
❏ 0284	Prime Time/The Statue	1977	$4
CAPITOL			
❏ B-44258	Eventually/It's Not Your Fault	1988	$3
❏ B-44186	Love in the Heart/ Every Day's a Miracle	1988	$3
❏ B-44098	Perfect Love/Can't Blame the Train	1987	$3
EMI AMERICA			
❏ 8375	He's Got You/To Have and To Hold	1987	$3
❏ 43025	Superman's Ghost/ (B-side unknown)	1987	$3
MEDIARTS			
❏ 108	And I Love You So/ Castles in the Air	1970	$10
MILLENNIUM			
❏ YB-11819	Castles in the Air/Crazy Eyes	1981	$4
❏ YB-11799	Crying/Genesis (In the Beginning)	1980	$4
❏ GB-13477	Crying/Since I Don't Have You	1983	$3
—Gold Standard Series			
❏ YB-11809	It's Just the Sun/ Words and Music	1981	$4
❏ YB-11804	Since I Don't Have You/ Your Cheating Heart	1981	$4
UNITED ARTISTS			
❏ 50856 [PS]	American Pie	1971	$10
—Comes with both promos and stock copies			
❏ 50856 [DJ]	American Pie (mono/stereo)	1971	$8
—With a different edit than the Part 1/Part 2 stock copy			
❏ XW520	American Pie (Part 1)/ American Pie (Part 2)	1974	$4
—Reissue			
❏ 50856	American Pie -- Part 1/ American Pie -- Part 2	1971	$5
❏ 50796	And I Love You So/ Castles in the Air	1971	$6
❏ 51100	Dreidel/Bronco Bill's Lament	1973	$4
❏ XW363	Fool's Paradise/Happy Trails	1973	$4
❏ XW579	Homeless Brothers/ La La Love You	1974	$4
❏ XW206	If We Try/The More You Pay	1973	$4
❏ XW541	Sitting on Top of the World/ Mule Skinner Blues	1974	$4
❏ XW614	Wonderful Baby/ Birthday Song	1975	$4
MCLEAN, PHIL			
VERSATILE			
❏ 108	Big Mouth Bill/Come with Us	1962	$12
❏ 107	Small Sad Sam/Chicken	1961	$12
MCLOLLIE, OSCAR			
CLASS			
❏ 243	Convicted/My Heart Speaks	1959	$20
❏ 206	Here I Am/Say	1957	$20
❏ 228	Hey Girl -- Hey Boy/Let Me Know Let Me Know	1958	$20
—With Jeanette Baker			
❏ 238	Let's Get Together/ Rock-a-Cha	1958	$20
—With Jeanette Baker			
❏ 265	The Honey Jump/ Call It Love	1960	$20
MERCURY			
❏ 70964	Blue Velvet/The Penalty	1956	$30
MODERN			
❏ 915	Be Cool My Heart/ All the Oil in Texas	1952	$60
❏ 920	Falling in Love with You/Lolly Pop	1953	$60
❏ 976	God Gave Us Christmas/ (B-side unknown)	1955	$40
❏ 943	God Gave Us Christmas/ Dig That Crazy Santa Claus	1954	$50
❏ 938	Hot Banana/Wiggle Toe	1954	$50
❏ 955	Pagliacci (With a Broken Heart)/Eternal Love	1955	$50
❏ 950	Pretty Girl/Hey Lolly Lolly	1955	$50
❏ 902	The Honey Jump (Part 1)/ The Honey Jump (Part 2)	1952	$70
WING			
❏ 90083	God's Green Earth/Got Your Love in My Heart	1956	$30
MCMAHON, ED			
CAMEO			
❏ 474	Beautiful Girl/The Loving Heart	1967	$15

Number	Title	Yr	NM

MCMANUS, ROSS
IMPERIAL
| ❏ 66042 | Patsy Girl/I'm the Greatest | 1964 | $15 |

MCNABB, CECIL
KING
| ❏ 5116 | Clock Tickin' Rhythm/ Nothing Like This | 1958 | $250 |

MCNAIR, BARBARA
AUDIO FIDELITY
| ❏ 162 | After St. Francis/I Can Tell | 1969 | $10 |
| ❏ 153 | Love Has a Way/ (B-side unknown) | 1969 | $10 |

CORAL
❏ 62071	Goin' Steady with the Moon/I Feel a Feeling	1959	$30
❏ 61972	He's Got the Whole World in His Hands/Flipped Over You	1958	$40
❏ 61996	Indiscreet/Waltz Me Around	1958	$30
❏ 62116	Lover's Prayer/ Old Devil Moon	1959	$30
❏ 61923	Till There Was You/Bobby	1958	$30
❏ 62020	Too Late This Spring/ See If I Care	1958	$30

KC
| ❏ 112 | A Little Bird Told Me/ Nobody Rings My Bell | 1963 | $50 |
| ❏ 109 | Cross Over the Bridge/Gloryland | 1962 | $60 |

MOTOWN
❏ 1106	Here I Am Baby/My World Is Empty Without You	1966	$30
❏ 1112	Steal Away Tonight/ For Once in My Life	1967	$500
❏ 1087	Touch of Time/You're Gonna Love My Baby	1965	$300
❏ 1099	What a Day/Everything Is Good About You	1966	$30
❏ 1123	Where Would I Be Without You/For Once in My Life	1968	$30

SIGNATURE
| ❏ 12033 | All About Love/You Done Me Wrong | 1960 | $30 |
| ❏ 12024 | He's a King/Murray, What's Your Hurry | 1960 | $125 |

WARNER BROS.
| ❏ 5633 | Wanted Me/It Was Never Like This | 1965 | $200 |

MCNEELY, BIG JAY
BAYOU
| ❏ 018 | Catastrophe/Calamity | 1953 | $100 |
| ❏ 014 | Hometown Jamboree/ Teenage Hop | 1953 | $100 |

FEDERAL
❏ 12151	3-D/Texas Turkey	1953	$50
❏ 12191	Beachcomber/Strip Tease Swing	1954	$50
❏ 12179	Hot Cinders/Whipped Cream	1954	$50
❏ 12186	Let's Work/Hard Tack	1954	$50
❏ 12168	Mule Walk/Ice Water	1954	$50
❏ 12102	The Goof/Big Jay Shuffle	1952	$50

IMPERIAL
| ❏ 5219 | Deacon's Express/Jet Fury | 1953 | $60 |

—Note: Earlier Big Jay McNeely releases on Imperial are unknown on 45 rpm

SAVOY
| ❏ 1143 | Deacon Hop/The Hucklebuck | 1955 | $40 |

—With Paul Williams
| ❏ 798 | The Deacon's Hop/ Thirty Five Thirty | 1951 | $70 |

SWINGIN'
❏ 629	After Midnight/ Before Midnight	1961	$20
❏ 618	I Got the Message/ Psycho Serenade	1959	$20
❏ 627	I Love You, Oh Darling/ Oh, What a Fool	1960	$20
❏ 622	Minnie/My Darling Dear	1960	$20
❏ 614	There Is Something on Your Mind/Back...Shack...Track	1959	$30
❏ 637	Without a Love/The Squat	1962	$20

VEE JAY
| ❏ 142 | Big Jay's Hop/ Three Blind Mice | 1955 | $50 |

7-Inch Extended Plays
FEDERAL
❏ EP-301	*Mule Milk/Hot Cinders/Ice Water/Whipped Cream	1954	$250
❏ EP-246	Big Jake Shuffle/3-D// Nervous Man Nervous/ The Goof	1953	$300
❏ EP-301 [PS]	Big Jay McNeely, Volume 2	1954	$250
❏ EP-332	(contents unknown)	1954	$250
❏ EP-373	(contents unknown)	1955	$125
❏ EP-246 [PS]	Go! Go! Go! With Big Jay McNeely	1953	$300
❏ EP-332 [PS]	Wild Man of the Saxophone	1954	$250

Number	Title	Yr	NM

MCPHATTER, CLYDE
Also see THE DRIFTERS.

AMY
❏ 968	A Shot of Rhythm and Blues/ I'm Not Going to Work Today	1966	$15
❏ 941	Everybody's Somebody's Fool/I Belong to You	1965	$20
❏ 993	I Dreamt I Died/Lonely People Can't Afford to Cry	1967	$300
❏ 950	Little Bit of Sunshine/ Everybody Loves a Good Time	1966	$15
❏ 975	Sweet and Innocent/ Lavender Lace	1967	$15

ATLANTIC
❏ 1199	A Lover's Question/I Can't Stand Up Long	1958	$30
❏ 1185	Come What May/ Let Me Know	1958	$30
❏ 2060	Deep Sea Ball/Let the Boogie-Woogie Roll	1960	$30

—B-side actually the "old" Drifters (uncredited)
| ❏ 1070 | Everybody's Laughing/ Hot Ziggity | 1955 | $40 |
| ❏ 2082 | If I Didn't Love You Like I Do/Go! Yes Go! | 1960 | $30 |

—B-side actually the "old" Drifters (uncredited)
| ❏ 1149 | Long Lonely Nights/ Heartaches | 1957 | $30 |
| ❏ 1077 | Love Has Joined Us Together/I Gotta Have You | 1955 | $40 |

—With Ruth Brown
❏ 2018	Lovey Dovey/My Island of Dreams	1959	$30
❏ 1081	Seven Days/I'm Not Worthy	1956	$40
❏ 2028	Since You've Been Gone/Try, Try Baby	1959	$30

—B-side actually the "old" Drifters (uncredited)
❏ 1170	That's Enough for Me/ No Love Like Her Love	1958	$30
❏ 1106	Thirty Days/I'm Lonely Tonight	1956	$40
❏ 1092	Treasure of Love/ When You're Sincere	1956	$50
❏ 1117	Without Love (There Is Nothing)/I Make Believe	1956	$40

DECCA
| ❏ 32719 | Book of Memories/I'll Belong to You | 1970 | $8 |
| ❏ 32753 | Why Can't We Get Together/Mixed-Up Cup | 1970 | $8 |

DERAM
| ❏ 85039 | Baby You've Got It/ Baby I Could Be So Good at Loving You | 1969 | $12 |
| ❏ 85032 | Thank You Love/Only a Fool | 1968 | $10 |

MERCURY
❏ 71809	A Whole Heap o'Love/ You're Movin' Me	1961	$20
❏ 71809 [PS]	A Whole Heap o'Love/ You're Movin' Me	1961	$40
❏ 72407	Crying Won't Help You Now/I Found My Love	1965	$20
❏ 72407 [PS]	Crying Won't Help You Now/I Found My Love	1965	$40
❏ 72220	Deep in the Heart of Harlem/ Happy Good Times	1963	$20
❏ 72220 [PS]	Deep in the Heart of Harlem/ Happy Good Times	1963	$40
❏ 71692	I Just Want to Love You/You're for Me	1960	$20
❏ 71692 [PS]	I Just Want to Love You/You're for Me	1960	$40
❏ 71841	I Never Knew/Happiness	1961	$20
❏ 71841 [PS]	I Never Knew/Happiness	1961	$30
❏ 71987	Little Bitty Pretty One/ Next to Me	1962	$20
❏ 71987 [PS]	Little Bitty Pretty One/ Next to Me	1962	$50
❏ 71941	Lover Please/Let's Forget About the Past	1962	$30
❏ 71941 [PS]	Lover Please/Let's Forget About the Past	1962	$50
❏ 72317	Lucille/Baby, Baby	1964	$20
❏ 72025	Maybe/I Do Believe	1962	$20
❏ 72025 [PS]	Maybe/I Do Believe	1962	$40
❏ 71740	One More Chance/Before I Fall in Love Again	1960	$20
❏ 71740 [PS]	One More Chance/Before I Fall in Love Again	1960	$40
❏ 71868	Same Time, Same Place/ Your Second Choice	1961	$20
❏ 71868 [PS]	Same Time, Same Place/ Your Second Choice	1961	$40
❏ 72253	Second Window, Second Floor/In My Tenement	1964	$20
❏ 72166	So Close to Being in Love/From One to One	1963	$20
❏ 72166 [PS]	So Close to Being in Love/From One to One	1963	$40
❏ 71660	Ta Ta/I Ain't Givin' Up Nothin'	1960	$20
❏ 72051	The Best Man Cried/Stop	1962	$20
❏ 72051 [PS]	The Best Man Cried/Stop	1962	$40
❏ 71783	Tomorrow Is a-Comin'/I'll Love You Till the Cows Come Home	1961	$20
❏ 71783 [PS]	Tomorrow Is a-Comin'/I'll Love You Till the Cows Come Home	1961	$40

Number	Title	Yr	NM

MGM
❏ 12780	I Told Myself a Lie/The Masquerade Is Over	1959	$30
❏ 12843 [M]	Let's Try Again/Bless You	1959	$30
❏ SK-50134 [S]	Let's Try Again/Bless You	1959	$50
❏ 12949	One Right After Another/ This Is Not Goodbye	1960	$30
❏ 12988	The Glory of Love/ Take a Step	1961	$30
❏ 12877	Think Me a Kiss/When the Right Time Comes Along	1960	$30
❏ 12816	Twice As Nice/Where Did I Make My Mistake	1959	$30

7-Inch Extended Plays
ATLANTIC
❏ EP605	*Honey Love/What'cha Gonna Do/Seven Days/ Long Lonely Nights	1958	$250
❏ EP584	*Without Love (There Is Nothing)/Thirty Days/I Make Believe/Treasure of Love	1958	$250
❏ EP618	A Lover's Question/I Can't Stand Up Alone/Lovey Dovey/My Island of Dreams	1959	$250
❏ EP584 [PS]	Clyde McPhatter	1958	$250
❏ EP618 [PS]	Clyde McPhatter	1959	$250

MCRAE, CARMEN
ATLANTIC
❏ 2776	Carry That Weight/ Goodbye Joe	1971	$5
❏ 2485	Elusive Butterfly/I'm Always Drunk in San Francisco	1968	$6
❏ 2421	For Once in My Life/Got to Get You Into My Life	1967	$6
❏ 2581	Gloomy Sunday/My Heart Reminds Me	1968	$6
❏ 2691	I Love You More Than You'll Ever Know/ Just a Dream Ago	1969	$5
❏ 2736	I Want You/Just a Little Lovin'	1970	$5
❏ 2807	Silent Spring/I Love the Life I Lead	1971	$5

BETHLEHEM
| ❏ 11009 | If I'm Lucky/Tip Toe Gently | 1958 | $15 |

COLUMBIA
❏ 42642	Am I Going Out of Your Mind/Baby, Baby	1962	$10
❏ 42376	How Does the Wine Taste/Nightlife	1962	$10
❏ 42292	Take Five/Easy As You Go	1962	$10

DECCA
❏ 29793	Come Down to Earth, Mr. Smith/I Guess I'll Dress for the Blues	1956	$15
❏ 29555	Get Set/You Don't Have to Tell Me	1955	$15
❏ 30274	How Many Stars Have to Shine/It's Like Gettin' a Donkey	1957	$15
❏ 29620	I Go for You/A Fine Romance	1955	$15

—With Sammy Davis, Jr.
❏ 30727	I Love the Ground You Walk On/I'll Love You	1958	$15
❏ 30075	I'm Putting All My Eggs in One Basket/Namely You	1956	$15
❏ 30618	Invitation/Lo and Behold	1958	$15
❏ 29675	Love Is Here to Stay/This Will Make You Laugh	1955	$15
❏ 29324	Ooh (What'cha Doin' to Me/If I'm Lucky	1954	$20
❏ 30540	Passing Fancy/ As I Love You	1958	$15
❏ 30004	Skyliner/If You Should Leave Me	1956	$15
❏ 30667	So Nice to Be Wrong/ Moon Ray	1958	$15
❏ 29890	Star Eyes/Tonight He's Out to Break Another Heart	1956	$15
❏ 30112	The Party's Over/I'm a Dreamer, Aren't We All	1956	$15
❏ 29472	Whatever Lola Wants/ Am I the One to Blame	1955	$15

GROOVE MERCHANT
| ❏ 1018 | It Takes a Whole Lot of Human Feeling/Straighten Up and Fly Right | 1973 | $5 |
| ❏ 1022 | The Good Life/How Could I Settle for Less | 1973 | $5 |

KAPP
❏ 327	Big Town/What Has She Got	1960	$10
❏ 290	Talk to Me/Show Me the Way	1959	$10
❏ 302	The More I See You/ Don't Cry Joe	1959	$10
❏ 259	Which Way Is Love/ Play for Keeps	1959	$10

MAINSTREAM
❏ 650	Alfie/Modesty	1966	$8
❏ 630	Go and Buy Yourself a Dream/(B-side unknown)	1965	$8
❏ 613	Haven't We Met?/Life Is Just a Bowl of Cherries	1965	$8

Number	Title	Yr	NM

7-Inch Extended Plays

ATLANTIC
❏ EP-8165 [DJ]	Elusive Butterfly/I'm Always Drunk in San Francisco// Ask Any Woman/My Very Own Person	1968	$20

— White label, large hole

❏ EP-8165 [PS]	Portrait of Carmen	1968	$20

DECCA
❏ ED2342	But Beautiful/If You'd Stay the Way I Dream About You// I'm a Dreamer Aren't We All/ Good Morning Heartache	1956	$15
❏ ED2341	(contents unknown)	1956	$15
❏ ED2343	(contents unknown)	1956	$15
❏ ED2341 [PS]	Torchy! Part 1	1956	$15
❏ ED2342 [PS]	Torchy! Part 2	1956	$15
❏ ED2343 [PS]	Torchy! Part 3	1956	$15

MCVIE, CHRISTINE
Also see CHICKEN SHACK; FLEETWOOD MAC.

EPIC
❏ 10536	I'd Rather Go Blind/Get Like You Used to Be	1969	$15

— As "Christine Perfect

SIRE
❏ 732	I'd Rather Go Blind/ Close to Me	1976	$8

WARNER BROS.
❏ GWB 0488	Got a Hold on Me/Love Will Show Us How	1986	$3

— Back to Back Hits" series

❏ 29372	Got a Hold on Me/Who's Dreaming This Dream	1984	$3
❏ 29372 [PS]	Got a Hold on Me/Who's Dreaming This Dream	1984	$3
❏ 29160	I'm the One/The Challenge	1984	$3
❏ 29313	Love Will Show Us How/The Challenge	1984	$3
❏ 29313 [PS]	Love Will Show Us How/The Challenge	1984	$3

MCWILLIAMS, DAVID

COLUMBIA
❏ 4-43793	Blue Eyes/God and My Country	1966	$15

KAPP
❏ 896	Days of Pearly Spencer/ There's No Lock Upon My Door	1968	$12
❏ 952	This Side of Heaven/Can I Get There by Candlelight?	1968	$8

ME & YOU

PARKWAY
❏ 121	Let the World In/I've Got My Time Baby	1966	$30

ME AND THEM

U.S. SONGS
❏ 601	Everything I Do Is Wrong/ Show You Mean It Too	1964	$20

MEADER, VAUGHN

MGM
❏ K13169	Elephant Song/ No Hiding Place	1963	$12

VERVE
❏ 10309	St. Nick Visits the White House/'Twas the Night Before Christmas	1963	$30

7-Inch Extended Plays

CADENCE
❏ CSBLL-1	The Experiment/After Dinner Conversations/Relatively Speaking/Motorcade//But Vote!/Economy Lunch/ Press Conference	1962	$10

— Jukebox issue; small hole, plays at 33 1/3 rpm

❏ CSBLL-1 [PS]	The First Family	1962	$12

MEAT LOAF
Also see STONEY AND MEATLOAF. MEAT LOAF also contributed vocals to TED NUGENT'S Free For All album. Also see THE POPCORN BLIZZARD; STONEY AND MEATLOAF.

ATLANTIC
❏ 89340	Getting Away with Murder/ Rock 'N' Roll Hero	1986	$3

CLEVELAND INT'L.
❏ 02490	I'm Gonna Love Her for Both of Us/Peel Out	1981	$4

EPIC
❏ 50588	Paradise by the Dashboard Light/"Bat" Overture	1978	$5
❏ 50513	Two Out of Three Ain't Bad (3:50)/For Crying Out Loud	1978	$5
❏ 50513	Two Out of Three Ain't Bad (5:12)/For Crying Out Loud	1978	$6

RCA
❏ PB-14101	(Give Me the Future with a) Modern Girl/Sailor to a Siren	1985	$3
❏ PB-14101 [PS]	(Give Me the Future with a) Modern Girl/Sailor to a Siren	1985	$3
❏ PB-14149	Surf's Up/Jumpin' the Sun	1985	$3

RSO
❏ 407	More Than You Deserve/ Presence of the Lord	1974	$15

MEAT PUPPETS

SST
❏ E39 [DJ]	Swimming Ground/ Up on the Sun	1985	$6
❏ E39 [PS]	Swimming Ground/ Up on the Sun	1985	$6

— Stamped sleeve promoting upcoming LP

WORLD IMITATION
❏ PRC-1 [PS]	In a Car	1981	$25
❏ PRC-1	In a Car/Big House/ Dolfin Field/Out in the Gardiner/Foreign Lawns	1981	$25

MEATMEN, THE
7-Inch Extended Plays

TOUCH N GO
❏ 0(no cat #)	Blood Sausage	1982	$38
❏ 0(no cat #) [PS]	Blood Sausage	1982	$38
❏ 8	Crippled Children Suck	1982	$38
❏ 8 [PS]	Crippled Children Suck	1982	$38

— With insert

MECO

ARISTA
❏ 0686	Big Band Medley (Part 1)/ Big Band Medley (Part 2)	1982	$4
❏ 9045	Ewok Celebration/Lapti Nek	1983	$4
❏ 9218	Musicmakers/Anything Goes	1984	$3
❏ 0660	Pop Goes the Movies (Part 1)/Pop Goes the Movies (Part 2)	1982	$4

CASABLANCA
❏ 2339	Blue Moon/You Gotta Hurt Me	1981	$4
❏ 998	Devil Delight/Grazing in the Grass	1979	$6
❏ 2239	Theme from Star Trek/ (B-side unknown)	1980	$4
❏ 964	Theme from Superman/ Can You Read My Mind	1979	$4

MILLENNIUM
❏ 604	Star Wars Theme- Cantina Band/Funk	1977	$5
❏ 608 [DJ]	Theme from Close Encounters (4:33)/(2:59)	1978	$5
❏ 608	Theme from Close Encounters/Roman Nights	1978	$4
❏ 620	Theme from the Wizard of Oz/Fantasy	1978	$4
❏ 613	Topsy/Lady Marion	1978	$4

RSO
❏ 1038	Empire Strikes Back (Medley)/The Force Theme	1980	$4
❏ 1052	Main Theme from "Shogun"/ Love Theme from "Shogun" (Mariko's Theme)	1980	$4
❏ 815718-7	Sleigh Ride/Christmas in the Stars	1983	$8

— With R2D2 and C3PO

❏ 815718-7 [PS]	Sleigh Ride/Christmas in the Stars	1983	$12
❏ 1058	What Can You Get a Wookiee for Christmas (When He Already Owns a Comb)/R2D2 We Wish You a Merry Christmas	1980	$4

— A-side as "The Star Wars Intergalactic Droid Choir and Chorale"; B-side as "The Original Star Wars Cast: R2D2/ Anthony Daniels as C-3PO"; silver label

❏ 1058	What Can You Get a Wookiee for Christmas (When He Already Owns a Comb)/R2D2 We Wish You a Merry Christmas	1980	$8

— A-side as "The Star Wars Intergalactic Droid Choir and Chorale"; B-side as "The Original Star Wars Cast: R2D2/ Anthony Daniels as C-3PO"; tan label

❏ 1058 [PS]	What Can You Get a Wookiee for Christmas (When He Already Owns a Comb)/We Wish You a Merry Christmas	1980	$10

MEDALLIONS, THE (1)

DOOTO
❏ 425	A Lover's Prayer/Unseen	1957	$40

—As "Vernon Green and the Medallions

❏ 454	Behind the Door/ Rocket Ship	1959	$30

—As "Vernon Green and the Medallions

❏ 419	For Better or For Worse/I Wonder, Wonder, Wonder	1957	$40

—As "Vernon Green and the Medallions

❏ 446	Magic Mountain/59 Volvo	1959	$30

—As "Vernon Green and the Medallions

DOOTONE
❏ 479	Can You Talk/You Don't Know	1964	$20
❏ 379	Dear Darling/Don't Shoot Baby	1955	$75
❏ 364	Edna/Speeding	1955	$70
❏ 393	I Want a Love/ Dance and Swing	1956	$60
❏ 407	My Mary Lou/Did You Have Fun	1956	$70

—As "Vernon Green and the Medallions

❏ 373	My Pretty Baby/I'll Never Love Again	1955	$70

—As "Johnny Twovoice and the Medallions

❏ 400	Shedding Tears for You/ Push Button Automobile	1956	$70

—As "Vernon Green and the Medallions

❏ 347	The Letter/Buick 59	1955	$200

— Red label

❏ 347	The Letter/Buick 59	1955	$70

— Black label

❏ 357	The Telegram/Coupe de Ville Baby	1955	$70

— Maroon label

❏ 357	The Telegram/Coupe de Ville Baby	1955	$200

— Blue label

MINIT
❏ 32034	Look at Me, Look at Me/Am I Ever Gonna See My Baby	1968	$30

—As "Vernon Green and the Medallions

PAN WORLD
❏ 71	Dear Ann/Shimmy Shimmy Shake	1962	$60

— As "Vernon Green and the Medallions

7-Inch Extended Plays

DOOTONE
❏ 202	(contents unknown)	1958	$125

MEDALLIONS, THE (2)

ESSEX
❏ 901	I Know/Laki-Lani	1955	$400

MEDALLIONS, THE (4)

SINGULAR
❏ 1002	A Broken Heart/Lolo Baby	1957	$60

SULTAN
❏ 4004	Love That Girl/Carachi	1959	$100

MEDALLIONS, THE (U)

SARG
❏ 191	I Love You True/ My Baby's Gone	1961	$50
❏ 194	Lovin' Time/Home Town	1961	$50

MEDLEY, BILL

A&M
❏ 1371	A Simple Man/Missing You Too Long	1972	$4
❏ 1285	A Song for You/We've Only Just Begun	1971	$5
❏ 1311	A Song for You/We've Only Just Begun	1971	$4
❏ 1350	Freedom for the Stallion/ Damn Good Friend	1972	$4
❏ 1336	Help Me Make It Through the Night/Hung on You	1972	$4
❏ 1434	Put a Little Love Away/ It's Not Easy	1973	$4

CURB
❏ 10542	Most of All You/I'm Gonna Be Strong	1989	$3

LIBERTY
❏ 1402	Don't Know Much/Woman	1981	$4
❏ 1412	Stay the Night/Grandma and Grandpa	1981	$4

MCA
❏ 53443	Brown Eyed Woman/You've Lost That Lovin' Feelin'	1988	$3

Number	Title	Yr	NM
MGM			
❏ 13959	Brown Eyed Woman/Let the Good Times Roll	1968	$8
❏ 14099	Evie/Let Me Love Again	1969	$8
❏ 14179	Gone/What Have You Got to Lose	1970	$6
❏ 14119	Hold On, I'm Comin'/Makin' My Way	1970	$6
❏ 13931	I Can't Make It Alone/One Day Girl	1968	$8
❏ 14000	Peace Brother Peace/Winter Won't Come This Year	1968	$8
❏ 14025	Something's So Wrong/This Is a Love Song	1969	$8
❏ 14202	Wasn't It Easy/Gone	1970	$6
PARAMOUNT			
❏ 0089	Swing Low, Sweet Chariot/(B-side unknown)	1971	$6
PLANET			
❏ YB-13474	For You/I Need You in My Life	1983	$3
❏ YB-13425	I'm No Angel/I Need You in My Life	1983	$3
RCA			
❏ PB-14021	Is There Anything I Can Do/Old Friend	1985	$3
❏ PB-13753	I Still Do/I've Got Dreams to Remember	1984	$3
❏ PB-13692	I've Got Dreams to Remember/Till Your Memory's Gone	1983	$3
❏ 5224-7-RX	(I've Had) The Time of My Life/Love Is Strange	1987	$3

—A-side: With Jennifer Warnes; B-side by Mickey and Sylvia

Number	Title	Yr	NM
❏ 5224-7-RX [PS]	(I've Had) The Time of My Life/Love Is Strange	1987	$4

—A-side: With Jennifer Warnes; B-side by Mickey and Sylvia

Number	Title	Yr	NM
❏ PB-13851	Turn It Loose/I've Always Got the Heart to Sing the Blues	1984	$3
❏ PB-14081	Women in Love/Stand Up	1985	$3
REPRISE			
❏ 0413	I Surrender to Your Touch/Leavin' Town	1965	$20
SCOTTI BROTHERS			
❏ ZS4-07938	He Ain't Heavy, He's My Brother/The Bridge	1988	$3

—B-side by Georgio Moroder

Number	Title	Yr	NM
❏ ZS4-07938 [PS]	He Ain't Heavy, He's My Brother/The Bridge	1988	$3
UNITED ARTISTS			
❏ 1349	Hello Rock & Roll/Still a Fool	1980	$4
❏ XW1256	Lay a Little Lovin' On Me/Wasn't That You Last Night	1978	$4
❏ XW1270	Statue of a Fool/Wasn't That You Last Night	1978	$4
VERVE			
❏ 10569	That Lucky Old Sun/My Darling Clementine	1967	$12

MEEHAN, DON
DATE

Number	Title	Yr	NM
❏ 2-1654	Sir, My Men Refuse to Go/That's the Reason Why	1969	$10

MEGATRONS, THE
AUDICON

Number	Title	Yr	NM
❏ 107	Dance of the Silhouettes/Ranchero	1960	$12
❏ 104	Whispering Winds/Tootie Flutie	1960	$10
LAURIE			
❏ 3310	A Love That Will Last Forever/The Detroit Sound	1965	$8

MEISNER, RANDY
Also see EAGLES.
ASYLUM

Number	Title	Yr	NM
❏ 45502	I Really Want You Here Tonight/Heart Song	1978	$5
EPIC			
❏ 9-50939	Deep Inside My Heart/I Need You Bad	1980	$4
❏ 02059	Gotta Get Away/Trouble Ahead	1981	$4
❏ 50964	Hearts on Fire/Anyway Bye Bye	1981	$4
❏ 03352	Strangers Still/Runnin'	1982	$4

MEL AND TIM
BAMBOO

Number	Title	Yr	NM
❏ 107	Backfield in Motion/Do It Right Baby	1969	$8

—White label, not a promo

Number	Title	Yr	NM
❏ 107	Backfield in Motion/Do It Right Baby	1969	$6

—Multicolor label

Number	Title	Yr	NM
❏ 112	Feeling Bad/I've Got Puredee	1970	$6
❏ 109	Good Guys Only Win in the Movies/I Found That I Was Wrong	1970	$6
❏ 118	I'm the One/Put An Extra Plus to Your Love	1971	$6
❏ 106	I've Got Puredee/(Instrumental)	1969	$6
❏ 114	Mail Call Time/Forget It, I've Got It	1970	$6
❏ 116	We've Got a Groove to Move On/Never on Time	1970	$6
STAX			
❏ 0224	Forever and a Day/That's the Way I Want to Live My Life	1974	$5
❏ 0160	Heaven Knows/Don't Mess with My Money, My Honey, Oh My Woman	1973	$5
❏ 0154	I May Not Be What You Want/Too Much Wheelin' and Dealin'	1973	$5
❏ 0127	Starting All Over Again/It Hurts to Want It So Bad	1972	$5
❏ 0202	Those Little Things That Count/The Same Folks	1974	$5

MEL-O-DOTS, THE
APOLLO

Number	Title	Yr	NM
❏ 1192	One More Time/Just How Long	1952	$3000

MELA, DENNY
PARKWAY

Number	Title	Yr	NM
❏ 802	Forget My Past/Blondie	1959	$20

MELACHRINO, GEORGE
7-Inch Extended Plays
RCA VICTOR

Number	Title	Yr	NM
❏ EPC-1045 [PS]	Christmas in High Fidelity	1954	$12

—Cover for 3-EP set (547-0440, 547-0441, 547-0442)

Number	Title	Yr	NM
❏ 547-0440	Once More It's Christmas/Rudolph the Red Nosed Reindeer/Little Brown Jug//White Christmas/Sleigh Ride	1954	$10

—Side 1" and "Side 6" of EPC-1045

Number	Title	Yr	NM
❏ 547-0441	Silent Night/Adeste Fideles/Fairy on the Christmas Tree//Jingle Bells/The First Noel/Mrs. Santa Claus	1954	$10

—Side 2" and "Side 5" of EPC-1045

Number	Title	Yr	NM
❏ 547-0442	The Skaters Waltz/I Saw Mommy Kissing Santa Claus//Winter Wonderland/Hark! The Herald Angels Sing/Good King Wenceslas	1954	$10

—Side 3" and "Side 4" of EPC-1045

MELANIE
AMHERST

Number	Title	Yr	NM
❏ 300	Who's Been Sleeping in My Bed (Edited)/Who's Been Sleeping in My Bed	1985	$4
ATLANTIC			
❏ 3380	If I Needed You/Cyclone	1977	$5
BLANCHE			
❏ 1	Imaginary Heroes/Detroit or Buffalo	1982	$4
❏ 110	When You're Dead and Gone/Detroit or Buffalo	1982	$4
BUDDAH			
❏ 135	Beautiful People/Any Guy	1969	$6
❏ 113	Bo Bo's Party/I'm Back in Town	1969	$6
❏ 304	I'm Back in Town/Johnny Boy	1972	$5
❏ 167	Lay Down (Candles in the Rain)/Candles in the Rain	1970	$6
❏ 167 [PS]	Lay Down (Candles in the Rain)/Candles in the Rain	1970	$8
❏ 186	Peace Will Come (According to Plan)/Close to It All	1970	$5
❏ 186	Peace Will Come (According to Plan)/Stop (I Don't Want to Hear It Anymore)	1970	$5
❏ 186 [PS]	Peace Will Come (According to Plan)/Stop (I Don't Want to Hear It Anymore)	1970	$6
❏ 161 [DJ]	Take Me Home (mono/stereo)	1970	$6

—May be promo only

Number	Title	Yr	NM
❏ 224	We Don't Know Where We're Going/The Good Book	1971	$5
COLUMBIA			
❏ 44524	Garden in the City/Why Didn't My Mother Tell Me	1968	$10
❏ 44524 [PS]	Garden in the City/Why Didn't My Mother Tell Me	1968	$30
❏ 44349	My Beautiful People/God's Only Daughter	1967	$10
❏ 44349 [PS]	My Beautiful People/God's Only Daughter	1967	$30

MIDSONG INT'L.

Number	Title	Yr	NM
❏ 40858	I'd Rather Leave While I'm in Love/Record People	1978	$5
NEIGHBORHOOD			
❏ 4210	Bitter Bad/Do You Believe	1973	$4
❏ 4201	Brand New Key/Some Say (I Got Devil)	1971	$6

—White label (not a promo)

Number	Title	Yr	NM
❏ 4201	Brand New Key/Some Say (I Got Devil)	1971	$5

—Multicolor label

Number	Title	Yr	NM
❏ 4215	Lover's Cross/Holding Out	1974	$4
❏ 4214	Love to Love Again/Fine and Feather	1974	$4
❏ 4214 [PS]	Love to Love Again/Fine and Feather	1974	$6
❏ 4212	Seeds/Some Say (I Got Devil)	1973	$4
❏ 4204	Steppin'/Someday I'll Be a Farmer	1972	$4
❏ 4204 [PS]	Steppin'/Someday I'll Be a Farmer	1972	$8
❏ 4209	Stoneground Woman/Do You Believe	1972	$4
❏ 10001	Sweet Misery/Record Machine	1975	$4
❏ 4207	Together Alone/Center of the Circle	1972	$4
❏ 4207 [PS]	Together Alone/Center of the Circle	1972	$5
❏ 4213	Will You Love Me Tomorrow/Here I Am	1973	$4
❏ 4213 [PS]	Will You Love Me Tomorrow/Here I Am	1973	$5
PORTRAIT			
❏ 51001	One More Try/Apathy	1981	$4
STORK			
❏ 0(no cat #)	Timothy Scott Bogart	1970	$15

—One-sided promo of "Christopher Robin" to celebrate the birth of Neil Bogart's son

Number	Title	Yr	NM
WORLD UNITED			
❏ 1947	Oh Boy/Brand New Key	1978	$5

7-Inch Extended Plays
BUDDAH

Number	Title	Yr	NM
❏ SP2 [PS]	I'm Back in Town	1971	$12
❏ SP2 [DJ]	Merry Christmas/Christopher Robin//I'm Back In Town/I Really Loved Harold	1971	$12

MELCHER, TERRY
COLUMBIA

Number	Title	Yr	NM
❏ 42678	Be a Soldier/I Love You Betty	1963	$30

—As "Terry Day

Number	Title	Yr	NM
❏ 42678 [PS]	Be a Soldier/I Love You Betty	1963	$50
❏ 42427	I Waited Too Long/That's All I Want	1962	$30

—As "Terry Day

Number	Title	Yr	NM
❏ 42427 [PS]	I Waited Too Long/That's All I Want	1962	$50

—As "Terry Day

Number	Title	Yr	NM
RCA VICTOR			
❏ PB-10587	Fire in a Rainstorm/So Right Tonight	1976	$10

MELIS, JOSE
COLUMBIA

Number	Title	Yr	NM
❏ 4-39181	Moon Over Miami/Isle of Capri	1951	$15
❏ 4-39182	On a Little Street in Singapore/Cherokee	1951	$15
❏ 4-39184	Playera/Orientale	1951	$15

—The above four comprise a box set

Number	Title	Yr	NM
❏ 4-39183	The Love Nest/Moon Over Miami	1951	$15
❏ 71821	Hello My Heart/Summertime in Venice	1961	$8
❏ 5757x45	In a Little Spanish Town/Tamanaco	1952	$20
❏ 72006	Meadowland/On Top of Old Smokey	1962	$8
MGM			
❏ K12464	Mandolina/Argentina Ballerina	1957	$15
SEECO			
❏ 6019	Anniversary Song/Linger Awhile	1959	$10
❏ 6003	Chop Stick Rock/Rockin' the Keys	1958	$10
❏ 6001	Sweet and Lovely/Bright Lights of Brussels	1958	$10
❏ 6015	The Story Of Christmas/Sleigh Ride	1958	$15

Number	Title	Yr	NM

MELLENCAMP, JOHN
Includes records as "Johnny Cougar," "John Cougar," and "John Cougar Mellencamp."

MCA
❏ 40634	American Dream/ Oh, Pretty Woman	1976	$10

—As "Johnny Cougar

MERCURY
❏ 870126-7	Check It Out/We Are the People	1988	$3

—Mercury releases starting with "870" and "888" are by "John Cougar Mellecamp

❏ 870126-7 [PS]	Check It Out/We Are the People	1988	$3
❏ 888934-7	Cherry Bomb/Shama Lama Ding Dong	1987	$3
❏ 888934-7 [PS]	Cherry Bomb/Shama Lama Ding Dong	1987	$3
❏ 874932-7	Let It All Hang Out/ Country Gentleman	1989	$4
❏ 874932-7 [PS]	Let It All Hang Out/ Country Gentleman	1989	$4
❏ 888763-7	Paper in Fire/Never Too Old	1987	$3
❏ 888763-7 [PS]	Paper in Fire/Never Too Old	1987	$3
❏ 874012-7	Pop Singer/J.M.'s Question	1989	$3
❏ 874012-7 [PS]	Pop Singer/J.M.'s Question	1989	$3

RIVA
❏ 207	Ain't Even Done with the Night/Make Me Feel	1981	$4
❏ 204	A Little Night Dancin'/ Pray for Me	1980	$5
❏ 216	Authority Song/Pink Houses (Acoustic Version)	1984	$4
❏ 216 [PS]	Authority Song/Pink Houses (Acoustic Version)	1984	$5
❏ 214	Crumblin' Down/ Golden Gates	1983	$4

—Riva 214 on as "John Cougar Mellencamp

❏ 214 [PS]	Crumblin' Down/ Golden Gates	1983	$5
❏ 211	Hand to Hold On To/ Small Paradise	1982	$4
❏ 211 [PD]	Hand to Hold On To/ Small Paradise	1982	$30

—Promo-only 7-inch picture disc with small hole

❏ 209	Hurts So Good/ Close Enough	1982	$4
❏ 209 [PS]	Hurts So Good/ Close Enough	1982	$10
❏ 202 [DJ]	I Need a Lover (Short Version 3:40)/(Long Version 5:35)	1979	$8
❏ 202	I Need a Lover/Welcome to Chinatown	1979	$4

—Riva 202-211 as "John Cougar

❏ 202 [PS]	I Need a Lover/Welcome to Chinatown	1979	$10
❏ 880984-7	Lonely Ol' Night/The Kind of Fella I Am	1985	$3
❏ 880984-7 [PS]	Lonely Ol' Night/The Kind of Fella I Am	1985	$4
❏ 215 [DJ]	Pink Houses (Long Version 4:43)/(Short Version 3:59)	1983	$30

—Promo only on pink vinyl

❏ 215 [DJ]	Pink Houses (Long Version 4:43)/(Short Version 3:59)	1983	$30
❏ 215 [PS]	Pink Houses/ Serious Business	1983	$6
❏ 203	Small Paradise/Sugar Marie	1980	$4
❏ 884202-7	Small Town/(Acoustic Version)	1985	$3
❏ 884202-7 [PS]	Small Town/(Acoustic Version)	1985	$4
❏ 205	This Time/Don't Misunderstand Me	1980	$4

MELLO-HARPS, THE
CASINO
❏ 104	Gumma Gumma/No Good	1959	$70

DO-RE-MI
❏ 203	Love Is a Vow/Valerie	1956	$8000

—VG 4000; VG+ 6000

TIN PAN ALLEY
❏ 159	I Couldn't Believe/ My Bleeding Heart	1956	$600
❏ 145/6	I Love Only You/Ain't Got the Money	1955	$400
❏ 157/8	What Good Are My Dreams/Gone	1956	$600

MELLO-KINGS, THE
HERALD
❏ 511	Baby Tell Me Why Why Why/The Only Girl I'll Ever Know	1958	$40
❏ 507	Chapel on the Hill/Sassafras	1957	$40
❏ 536	Chip Chip/Running to You	1959	$40

—Both sides play as labeled

❏ 536	Chip Chip/Running to You	1959	$200

—Mispressing; plays "Rockin' at the Bandstand"/"Down in Cuba" by the Royal Holidays

❏ 567	Love at First Sight/ She's Real Cool	1961	$30

❏ 548	Our Love Is Beautiful/ Dear Mr. Jock	1960	$30
❏ 561	Penny/Till There Were None	1961	$30
❏ 502	Tonite Tonite/Do Baby Do	1957	$500

—First pressing credits "The Mellotones

❏ 502	Tonite Tonite/Do Baby Do	1957	$60

—Label corrected to "The Mello-Kings"; script print inside flag

❏ 502	Tonite Tonite/Do Baby Do	1961	$30

—Reissue; block print inside flag

LESCAY
❏ 3009	Walk Softly/But You Lied	1962	$40

7-Inch Extended Plays
HERALD
❏ HEP-451 [PS]	The Fabulous Mello-Kings	1957	$400
❏ HEP-451	Tonite, Tonite/She's Real Cool//The Only Girl/Do Baby Do	1957	$300

MELLO-MOODS, THE
GAMBLE
❏ 2512	Stop Taking My Love for Granted/ Inspirational Pleasure	1972	$10

HAMILTON
❏ 143	I'm Lost/I Woke Up This Morning	1953	$125

PRESTIGE
❏ 799	Call on Me/I Tried and Tried and Tried	1953	$700
❏ 856	I'm Lost/I Woke Up This Morning	1953	$700

RED ROBIN
❏ 104	I Couldn't Sleep a Wink Last Night/And You Just Can't Go Through Life Alone	1952	$1000

—Despite the lower number, this came out after Robin/Red Robin 105

❏ 105	Where Are You (Now That I Need You)/How Could You	1952	$1000

—Reissue of Robin 105

ROBIN
❏ 105	Where Are You (Now That I Need You)/How Could You	1951	$5000

—Despite the higher number, this record pre-dates both of the Red Robin releases

MELLO-TONES, THE
COLUMBIA
❏ 39215	Looking for a City/ Flysing Saucers	1951	$300
❏ 6-904	When the Rain Gates Unfold/What Are They Doing in Heaven	1950	$400

—Originally released on Columbia's short-lived special numbering system for 7-inch records

❏ 39051	When the Rain Gates Unfold/What Are They Doing in Heaven	1950	$300
❏ 1-904	When the Rain Gates Unfold/What Are They Doing in Heaven	1950	$400

—Microgroove 33 1/3 rpm 7-inch record, small hole

DECCA
❏ 48319	I'm Just Another One in Love with You/I'm Gonna Get	1954	$400
❏ 48318	Winos on Parade/ Man Loves Woman	1954	$400

GEE
❏ 1040	Ca-Sandra/Rattle Shake Roll	1957	$50

MELLOW DROPS, THE
IMPERIAL
❏ 5324	When I Grow Too Old to Dream/The Crazy Song	1955	$200

MELLOWLARKS, THE
ARGO
❏ 5285	Sing a Silly Sing Song/ Farewell to You, My Nancy	1958	$30

MELLOWS, THE
CANDLELIGHT
❏ 1012	Farewell Farewell/ No More Loneliness	1956	$200
❏ 1011	Moon of Silver/You're Gone	1956	$200

CELESTE
❏ 3004	I'm Yours/Sweet Lorraine	1956	$600
❏ 3002	Lucky Guy/My Darling	1956	$120

JAY DEE
❏ 793	How Sentimental Can I Be/Nothin' to Do	1954	$200
❏ 801	I Was a Fool to Let You Go/I Still Care	1955	$200
❏ 797	Smoke from Your Cigarette/Pretty Baby	1954	$250

MELO GENTS, THE
WARNER BROS.
❏ 5056	Baby Be Mine/Get Off My Back	1959	$60

MELODEARS, THE
GONE
❏ 5040	It's Love Because/ They Don't Say	1958	$20
❏ 5033	Summer Romance/Charock	1958	$20

MELODY MAKERS, THE
HOLLIS
❏ 1001	Carolina Moon/Let's Make Love Worthwhile	1957	$125

MELTON, JAMES
RCA VICTOR
❏ 49-0485	Silent Night/Oh Come, All Ye Faithful	1949	$20

—Red vinyl

MELVIN, HAROLD, AND THE BLUE NOTES
ABC
❏ 12268	After You Love Me, Why Do You Leave Me/ Big Singing Star	1977	$5

—With Sharon Paige

❏ 12327	Baby, You Got My Nose Open/Try to Live a Day	1978	$5
❏ 12368	Power of Love/ Now Is the Time	1978	$5

ARCTIC
❏ 135	Go Away/What Can a Man Do	1967	$80

LANDA
❏ 703	Get Out (And Let Me Cry)/ You May Not Love Me	1964	$200

—As "The Blue Notes"

MCA
❏ 51190	Hang On In There/If You Love Me, Really Love Me	1982	$4
❏ 41291	Tonight's the Night/ If You're Looking for Someone to Love	1980	$4

—With Sharon Paige

PHILADELPHIA INT'L.
❏ 3562	Bad Luck (Part 1)/ Bad Luck (Part 2)	1975	$5
❏ 3569	Hope That We Can Be Together Soon/Be for Real	1975	$5

—With Sharon Paige

❏ 3520	If You Don't Know Me By Now/Let Me Into Your World	1972	$5
❏ 3516	I Miss You (Part I)/I Miss You (Part II)	1972	$5
❏ 3543	Satisfaction Guaranteed (Or Take Your Love Back)/I'm Weak for You	1974	$5
❏ 3588	Tell the World How I Feel About 'Cha Baby/ You Know How to Make Me Feel So Good	1976	$5
❏ 3533	The Love I Lost (Part 1)/ The Love I Lost (Part 2)	1973	$20
❏ 3579	Wake Up Everybody (Part 1)/Wake Up Everybody (Part 2)	1975	$5
❏ 3552	Where Are All My Friends/Let It Be You	1974	$20

PHILLY WORLD
❏ 99761	Don't Give Me Up/ (Instrumental)	1984	$4
❏ 99709	I Really Love You/I Can't Let Go	1984	$4
❏ 99735	Today's Your Lucky Day (Long)/Today's Your Lucky Day (Short)	1984	$4

SOURCE
❏ 41231	I Should Be Your Lover (Part 1)/I Should Be Your Lover (Part 2)	1980	$4
❏ 41156	Prayin'/(Instrumental)	1979	$40
❏ 41157	Tonight's the Night/ Your Love Is Taking Me on a Journey	1979	$4

—As "Sharon Paige with Harold Melvin and the Blue Notes

STARFLITE
❏ 4903	Lose the Blues/It's Not Fun Anymore	1979	$6

7-Inch Extended Plays
PHILADELPHIA INT'L.
❏ ZS731648	Be for Real/Ebony Woman/Let It Be You	1971	$25

—Stereo jukebox issue; small hole, plays at 33 1/3 rpm

❏ ZS731648 [PS]	Harold Melvin and the Blue Notes	1971	$25

Number	Title	Yr	NM

MELVINS, THE
BONER
| ❏ BR21 | Sweet Young Thing Ain't Sweet No More/I Dreamed I Dream | 1989 | $30 |

— *B-side by Steel Pole Bathtub; orange vinyl*

| ❏ BR21 [PS] | Sweet Young Thing Ain't Sweet No More/I Dreamed I Dream | 1989 | $30 |

LEOPARD GECKO
| ❏ LG 004 | Oven/Revulsion/We Reach | 1989 | $30 |

— *Originals on pink vinyl*

| ❏ LG 004 [PS] | Oven/Revulsion/We Reach | 1989 | $30 |

— *With insert of cut-out clothes*

MAKE 'EM BLEED AND SUFFER
| ❏ 0(no cat #) | Symptom of the Universe/ Hate the Police (Live) | 1988 | $30 |

— *B-side by Mudhoney*

| ❏ 0(no cat #) [PS] | Symptom of the Universe/ Hate the Police (Live) | 1988 | $30 |

— *Actually a large envelope that contained this single, which was enclosed in a Japanese porno magazine*

7-Inch Extended Plays
C/Z
| ❏ 1705 | Easy As It Was | 1986 | $30 |
| ❏ 1705 [PS] | Easy As It Was | 1986 | $30 |

MEMORIES, THE
WAY-LIN
| ❏ 101 | Love Bells/I Promise | 1959 | $400 |

MEMPHIS MINNIE
CHECKER
| ❏ 771 | Broken Heart/Me and My Chauffeur | 1953 | $3000 |

— *VG 1000; VG+ 2000*

MEMPHIS SLIM
JOSIE
| ❏ 973 | Come Again/Little Lonely Girl | 1967 | $10 |

KING
| ❏ 6301 | Messin' Around with the Blues/Mistake in Life | 1970 | $8 |

MERCURY
| ❏ 70063x45 | The Train Is Coming/ Drivin' Me Mad | 1953 | $50 |
| ❏ 8251x45 | Train Time/Blue Evening | 1951 | $60 |

MONEY
| ❏ 212 | My Country Gal/Treat Me Like I Treat You | 1955 | $50 |

PEACOCK
| ❏ 1602 | Sitting and Thinking/ Living Like a King | 1952 | $60 |

STRAND
| ❏ 25041 | Four Walls/Lonesome | 1961 | $30 |

UNITED
| ❏ 138 | Back Alley/Living the Life I Love | 1952 | $70 |
| ❏ 166 | Call Before You Go Home/ This Is My Lucky Day | 1953 | $70 |

— *Black vinyl*

| ❏ 166 | Call Before You Go Home/ This Is My Lucky Day | 1953 | $200 |

— *Red vinyl*

❏ 201	Go to Find My Baby/ Blue and Lonesome	1956	$50
❏ 182	I Love My Baby/Four Years of Torment	1954	$60
❏ 186	Memphis Slim U.S.A./ Blues All Around My Head	1954	$60
❏ 189	She's Alright/Two of a Kind	1955	$60
❏ 156	The Come Back/ Five O'Clock Blues	1953	$70

— *Black vinyl*

| ❏ 156 | The Come Back/ Five O'Clock Blues | 1953 | $200 |

— *Red vinyl*

| ❏ 176 | Wish Me Well/Sassy Mae | 1954 | $70 |

— *Black vinyl*

| ❏ 176 | Wish Me Well/Sassy Mae | 1954 | $200 |

— *Red vinyl*

VEE JAY
❏ 330	Steppin' Out/My Gal Keeps Me Crying	1959	$30
❏ 271	Stroll On Little Girl/ Guitar Cha Cha Cha	1958	$30
❏ 343	The Come Back/ Slim's Blues	1960	$20
❏ 294	This Time I'm Through/ What's the Matter	1958	$30

WARNER BROS.
| ❏ 7500 | Chicago Seven/Boogie Woogie 1-9-7-0 | 1971 | $8 |

MEN AT WORK
COLUMBIA
| ❏ CNR-03373 | Down Under/(B-side blank) | 1982 | $5 |

— *One-sided budget release*

| ❏ 38-03303 | Down Under/Crazy | 1982 | $4 |
| ❏ 38-04111 [PS] | Dr. Heckyll & Mr. Jive | 1983 | $5 |

— *Demonstration -- Not for Sale" on rear*

❏ 38-04111	Dr. Heckyll & Mr. Jive/I Like To (Live)	1983	$3
❏ 38-04111 [PS]	Dr. Heckyll & Mr. Jive/I Like To (Live)	1983	$3
❏ 38-04929 [PS]	Everything I Need	1985	$5

— *Demonstration -- Not for Sale" on rear*

❏ 38-04929	Everything I Need/ Sail to You	1985	$3
❏ 38-04929 [PS]	Everything I Need/ Sail to You	1985	$3
❏ 38-05649	Hard Luck Story/ Snakes and Ladders	1985	$3
❏ 38-03959	It's a Mistake/Shintano	1983	$3
❏ 38-03959 [PS]	It's a Mistake/Shintano	1983	$3
❏ 38-05454	Maria/Snakes and Ladders	1985	$3
❏ 38-05454 [PS]	Maria/Snakes and Ladders	1985	$3
❏ AE71633 [DJ]	Overkill (same on both sides)	1983	$5
❏ AE71633 [PS]	Overkill (same on both sides)	1983	$5

— *Special color sleeve, different from stock version*

❏ 38-03795	Overkill/Till the Money Runs Out	1983	$3
❏ 38-03795 [PS]	Overkill/Till the Money Runs Out	1983	$3
❏ 18-02888	Who Can It Be Now?/ Anyone for Tennis	1982	$4

MEN WITHOUT HATS
BACKSTREET
| ❏ 52232 | The Safety Dance/ Living in China | 1983 | $3 |
| ❏ 52232 [PS] | The Safety Dance/ Living in China | 1983 | $5 |

MCA
❏ 52293	I Like/Things in My Life	1983	$3
❏ 52293 [PS]	I Like/Things in My Life	1983	$3
❏ 52332	I've Got the Message/ Great Ones Remember	1983	$3
❏ 52460	Where Do the Boys Go?/Unsatisfaction	1984	$3

MERCURY
❏ 870153-7	Moonbeam/Jenny Wore Black	1988	$3
❏ 870153-7 [PS]	Moonbeam/Jenny Wore Black	1988	$3
❏ 888859-7	Pop Goes the World/ End of the World	1987	$3
❏ 888859-7 [PS]	Pop Goes the World/ End of the World	1987	$3
❏ 870432-7	Walk on Water/Lose My Way	1988	$3

MENTAL AS ANYTHING
A&M
❏ 2592	Brian Brain/Not Enough	1983	$3
❏ 2514	If You Leave Me, Can I Come Too?/Let's Cook	1982	$3
❏ 2503	Too Many Times/Let's Cook	1982	$3

COLUMBIA
❏ 07763	Don't Tell Me Now/ The Mad King	1988	$3
❏ 05798	Live It Up/Good Friday	1986	$3
❏ 05798 [PS]	Live It Up/Good Friday	1986	$3

MENTALLY ILL, THE
AUTISTIC
| ❏ MI1 | Gacy's Place/Padded Cell/Tumor Boy | 1979 | $40 |
| ❏ MI1 [PS] | Gacy's Place/Padded Cell/Tumor Boy | 1979 | $40 |

MEPHISTOPHELES
REPRISE
| ❏ 0832 | Cricket Song/Take a Jet | 1969 | $15 |

MERCED BLUE NOTES, THE
GALAXY
| ❏ 744 | Mama Rufus/Bad Bad Whiskey | 1965 | $40 |

SOUL
| ❏ 35007 | Do the Pig/Thumping | 1965 | $350 |

TRI-PHI
| ❏ 1011 | Midnight Sessions (Part 1)/ Midnight Sessions (Part 2) | 1962 | $60 |
| ❏ 1023 | Whole Lotta Nothin'/Fragile | 1963 | $50 |

MERCER, BARBARA
CAPITOL
| ❏ 2059 | Call on Me/So Real | 1967 | $50 |

GOLDEN WORLD
| ❏ 21 | Hey/Can't Stop Loving You Baby | 1965 | $40 |

| ❏ 27 | Hungry for Love/The Things We Do Together | 1965 | $200 |

SIDRA
| ❏ 9012 | Call on Me/So Real | 1967 | $100 |

MERCER, JOHNNY
CAPITOL
| ❏ 54-582 | Baby It's Cold Outside/I Never Heard You Say | 1949 | $40 |

— *With Margaret Whiting*

❏ F15512	Candy/Ac-Cent-Tchu-Ate the Positive	1950	$20
❏ F15513	G.I. Jive/I Lost My Sugar in Salt Lake City	1950	$20
❏ F1618	One for My Baby/ St. Louis Blues	1951	$20

— *Reissue of material first issued on 78*

| ❏ F15514 | On the Atchison, Topeka and the Santa Fe/Strip Polka | 1950 | $20 |

— *The above three comprise CCF-214; all are reissues of hits that charted from 1942-45*

| ❏ F982 | She's Shimmyun on the Beach Again/At the Jazzland Ball | 1950 | $30 |
| ❏ F1641 | Sugar Blues/Goofus | 1951 | $20 |

— *Reissue of material first issued on 78*

| ❏ F2248 | The Glow-Worm/ New Ashmolean | 1952 | $20 |
| ❏ F1285 | Winter Wonderland/Goofus | 1950 | $20 |

MERCER, WILL
CONSTELLATION
| ❏ 109 | Penny Candy/Willowy Billowy Land | 1963 | $20 |

MERCURY, ERIC
AVCO EMBASSY
| ❏ 4523 | Everybody Has the Right to Know/You Bring Me to My Knees | 1969 | $30 |
| ❏ 4516 | Hurdy Gurdy Man/ Enter My Love | 1969 | $30 |

ENTERPRISE
❏ 9041	I Can Smell That Funky Music/Listen with Your Eyes	1971	$20
❏ 9080	Love Is Taking Over/Take a Walk Down My Street	1973	$15
❏ 9089	Sweet Sara/Don't Lose Faith in Me Lord	1973	$15
❏ 9047	The Truth Will Set You Free/ What's Usual Seems Natural	1972	$20

MERCURY, FREDDIE
Also see QUEEN.
ANTHEM
| ❏ 104 | I Can Hear Music/ Going Back | 1973 | $125 |

— *As "Larry Lurex"; A-side matrix number on label is "A-0009-REMIX*

| ❏ 104 | I Can Hear Music/ Going Back | 1973 | $200 |

— *As "Larry Lurex"; A-side matrix number on label is "A-0009*

CAPITOL
| ❏ B-5696 | The Great Pretender/ Exercises in Free Love | 1987 | $3 |
| ❏ B-5696 [PS] | The Great Pretender/ Exercises in Free Love | 1987 | $4 |

COLUMBIA
❏ 04869	I Was Born to Love You/. Stop All the Fighting	1985	$4
❏ 04869 [PS]	I Was Born to Love You/. Stop All the Fighting	1985	$4
❏ 05455	Living on My Own/She Blows Hot and Cold	1985	$4
❏ 04606	Love Kills/Rotwang's Party (Robot Dance)	1984	$4
❏ 04606 [PS]	Love Kills/Rotwang's Party (Robot Dance)	1984	$4

MERCY
SUNDI
| ❏ 6811 | Love (Can Make You Happy)/Fire Ball | 1969 | $8 |

WARNER BROS.
❏ 7297	Forever/The Morning's Come	1969	$6
❏ 7331	Hello Baby/Heard You Went Away	1969	$6
❏ 7291	Love Can Make You Happy/ Happy As Can Be, La La La	1969	$20

— *Pressed in U.S. for export only; A-side is a re-recording of the hit on Sundi*

Number	Title	Yr	NM

MERLIN, JACK

CAMEO
❑ 311	My Debbie/Drip Drop Sha-La-La Blues	1964	$20

DOT
❑ 16332	Girl of My Dreams/I Beat the Blues	1962	$60

HICKORY
❑ 1322	Are You/Love Life of Crime	1965	$30
❑ 1296	One Song/Mechanical Man	1965	$60

MERRI-MEN, THE

APT
❑ 25051	Big Daddy/St, Louis Blues	1960	$30

MERRIAM, CHUCK

CAMEO
❑ 301	Broken Glass/ Chuck's Monster	1964	$15

MERRY-GO-ROUND, THE

A&M
❑ 857	Gonna Fight the World/ We're in Love	1967	$10
❑ 886	Had to Run Around/ She Laughed Loud	1967	$10
❑ 957	Highway/'Til the Day After	1968	$12
❑ 834	Live/Time Will Show the Wiser	1967	$10
❑ 920	Missing You/Listen, Listen	1968	$10

MERSEYBEATS, THE

FONTANA
❑ 1905	Don't Turn Around/ Really Mystified	1964	$20
❑ 1532	I Love You, Yes I Do/ See Me Back	1965	$20
❑ 1513	It Would Take a Long Time/ Don't Let It Happen to Us	1965	$20
❑ 1882	Mr. Moonlight/I Think of You	1964	$20
❑ 1950	See Me Back/Last Night	1964	$20

MERSEYS, THE

MERCURY
❑ 72582	Sorrow/Some Other Day	1966	$30

MERTENS, TEDDY

4 CORNERS OF THE WORLD
❑ 143	Puppet on a String/Il Doit Faire Beaux La Bas	1967	$10
❑ 135	Trumpet in the Night/ Farewell Waltz	1966	$10

CAMEO
❑ 328	This Is My Prayer/My River of Memories	1964	$30

PALETTE
❑ 5107	Lonesome Heart/ Sunset Prayer	1963	$20

MESHEL, BILLY

OLD TOWN
❑ 1181	My Little Angel/Tiger and the 71st Street Sharks	1965	$15

PROBE
❑ 459	I Say Hello When I'm Leaving/(It Ain't Easy Being) Shirley Newman's Boyfriend	1969	$10
❑ 462	Today Has Been Cancelled/ That's What Sends Him to the Bowery	1969	$10

MESSENGERS, THE (1)

RARE EARTH
❑ 5032	That's the Way a Woman Is/In the Jungle	1971	$5

SOUL
❑ 35037	Window Shopping/ California Soul	1967	$40

U.S.A.
❑ 866	Midnight Hour/ Hard Hard Year	1967	$20

—As "The Messengers"

❑ 866	Midnight Hour/Up 'Til Now	1967	$15

—As "Michael and the Messengers"

MESSENGERS, THE (2)

ERA
❑ 3143	Let Me Be Your Man/ You've Got Me Cryin'	1964	$15

MESSENGERS, THE (3)

MGM
❑ 13293	I'm Stealin' Back/This Little Light of Mine	1964	$15
❑ 13346	When Did You Leave Heaven/More Pretty Girls Than One	1965	$15

MESSENGERS, THE (4)

U.S.A.
❑ 897	Gotta Take It Easy/I Need Her Here	1968	$8

—As "Michael and the Messengers"

MESSINA, JIM
Also see BUFFALO SPRINGFIELD; LOGGINS AND MESSINA; POCO. (45)

AUDIO FIDELITY
❑ 098	The Breeze and I/ Straight Man	1964	$40

COLUMBIA
❑ 11182	Do You Want to Dance/ Seeing You (For the First Time)	1980	$4

FEATURE
❑ 101	Panther Pounce/Tiger Tail	1964	$40

ULTIMA
❑ 705	Drag Bike Boogie/A-Rab	1964	$40

VIV
❑ 1000	Side Track/Sherrie	1965	$30

WARNER BROS.
❑ 29278	Big Tease/The Island	1984	$4
❑ 29457	Forever My Love/ One More Mile	1983	$4
❑ 49839	It's All Right Here/ Move Into Your Heart	1981	$4
❑ 49784	Move Into Your Heart/ Stay the Night	1981	$4

—With Pauline Wilson

METALLICA

ELEKTRA
❑ 69357	Eye of the Beholder/ Breadfan	1988	$10
❑ 69357 [PS]	Eye of the Beholder/ Breadfan	1988	$15
❑ 69329 [PS]	One/The Prince	1988	$15

METERS, THE

JOSIE
❑ 1024	A Message from the Meters/Zony Mash	1970	$10
❑ 1018	Chicken Strut/Hey! Last Minute	1970	$10
❑ 1005	Cissy Strut/Here Comes the Meter Man	1969	$10
❑ 1013	Dry Spell/Look-Ka Py Py	1969	$12
❑ 1008	Ease Back/Ann	1969	$12
❑ 1031	Good Old Funky Music/Sassy Lady	1971	$10
❑ 1021	Hand Clapping Song/Joog	1970	$12
❑ 1015	Look-Ka Py Py/This Is My Last Affair	1970	$10
❑ 1001	Sophisticated Cissy/ Sehorn's Farm	1968	$12
❑ 1026	Stretch Your Rubber Band/Groovy Lady	1971	$10
❑ 1029	(The World Is a Bit Under the Weather) Doodle-Oop/I Need More Time	1971	$10

REPRISE
❑ 1106	Cabbage Alley/The Flower Song	1972	$8
❑ 1135	Chug Chug Chug-A-Lug (Part 1)/Chug Chug Chug-A-Lug (Part 2)	1972	$8
❑ 1357	Disco Is the Thing Today/Mister Moon	1976	$6
❑ 1086	Do the Dirt/Smiling	1972	$8
❑ 1307	Hey Pocky A-Way/Africa	1974	$6
❑ 1314	People Say/Loving You Is On My Mind	1974	$6
❑ 1372	Trick Bag/Find Yourself	1976	$6

WARNER BROS.
❑ 8434	Be My Lady/No More Okey Doke	1977	$5

METRONOMES, THE (1)

CADENCE
❑ 1339	How Much I Love You/Dear Don	1957	$120
❑ 1310	I Love My Girl/I'm Gonna Get Me a Girl Somehow	1957	$125

METRONOMES, THE (2)

CHALLENGE
❑ 9157	Hot Time/Tears, Tears, Tears	1962	$20

MAUREEN
❑ 1000	My Dearest Darling/ The Chickie-Goo	1962	$60

METROS, THE (1)

1-2-3
❑ 1720	If You Can Feel/The Dampness from Your Kiss	1969	$10

RCA VICTOR
❑ 47-9331	Let's Groove/The Replacer	1967	$70
❑ 47-9159	Since I Found My Baby/No Baby	1967	$300
❑ 47-8994	Sweetest One/Time Changes Things	1966	$40

METROS, THE (2)

JUST
❑ 1502	All of My Life/Lookin'	1959	$400

METROS, THE (3)

MTM
❑ B-72070	After the Passion's Gone/Don't Let Our Love Go (Baby)	1986	$4

METROTONES, THE

COLUMBIA
❑ 40420	A-Ting-a-Ling/Tonight	1955	$30
❑ 40486	Write Me Baby/Even Though	1955	$30

RESERVE
❑ 116	Please Come Back/ Skitter Skatter	1957	$250

7-Inch Extended Plays

COLUMBIA
❑ B-2026	(contents unknown)	1955	$25
❑ B-2026 [PS]	Tops in Rock and Roll, Vol. 1	1955	$25
❑ B-2027 [PS]	Tops in Rock and Roll, Vol. 2	1955	$25
❑ B-2027	Tweedlee Dee/Pledging My Love/Rock Love/ Hearts of Stone	1955	$25

MIAMI SOUND MACHINE

AUDIOFON
❑ AU-282	Live Again/(Instrumental)	1977	$60

CBS INTERNATIONAL
❑ DBS10051	A Todo Maquine/Olivadate	1984	$30
❑ DBS10019	Baila Conmingo/Atiendeme	1981	$30
❑ DBS10056	Comunicacion/Entregate	1985	$30
❑ DBS10049	Dr. Beat/Eyes of Innocence	1984	$30
❑ DBS10070	Hablas De Mi/Conga	1985	$30
❑ DBS10044	Luchare/Dr. Beat	1984	$30
❑ DBS10080	Primitive Love/Words Get in the Way Spanish Version (No Me Vuelvo a Enamorar)	1986	$30
❑ DBS10029	Sola/Quedemos Como Amigos	1981	$30
❑ DBS10120	Words Get in the Way/ Spanish Version (No Me Vuelvo a Enamorar)	1986	$30

ELECTRIC CAT
❑ 1704	I Want You to Love Me/ Different Kind of Love	1978	$125

EPIC
❑ 34-05805	Bad Boy/Surrender Paradise	1986	$3
❑ 34-05805 [PS]	Bad Boy/Surrender Paradise	1986	$4
❑ 15-69121	Conga/Bad Boy	1989	$3
—Reissue
❑ 34-05457	Conga/Mucho Money	1985	$3
❑ 34-05457 [PS]	Conga/Mucho Money	1985	$4
❑ 34-04574	Dr. Beat/When Someone Comes Into Your Life	1984	$12
❑ 34-06352	Falling in Love (Uh-Oh)/Primitive Love	1986	$3
❑ 34-06352 [PS]	Falling in Love (Uh-Oh)/Primitive Love	1986	$4
❑ 34-04674	I Need a Man/ Orange Express	1984	$10
❑ 15-69122	Words Get in the Way/ Betcha Say That	1989	$3

—Reissue; B-side as "Gloria Estefan and Miami Sound Machine

❑ 34-06120	Words Get In the Way/Movies	1986	$3

—A picture sleeve is rumored to exist, but we've never seen one

MICHAEL, GEORGE, AS GENE EARLHART

WFIL
❑ DM84514	Between the Periods -- The Fantastic Philadelphia Flyers (same on both sides)	1974	$30

MICHAEL, GEORGE

COLUMBIA
❑ 38-05888	A Different Corner/ (Instrumental)	1986	$3
❑ 38-05888 [PS]	A Different Corner/ (Instrumental)	1986	$3
❑ 38-68704	A Different Corner/ (Instrumental)	1989	$3
—Reissue
❑ 38-07623	Faith/Hand to Mouth	1987	$3

Number	Title	Yr	NM
38-07623 [PS]	Faith/Hand to Mouth	1987	$3
38-07682	Father Figure/(Instrumental)	1988	$3
38-07682 [PS]	Father Figure/(Instrumental)	1988	$3
38-07164	I Want Your Sex (Rhythm 1 Lust)/(Rhythm 2 Brass in Love)	1987	$3
38-07164 [PS]	I Want Your Sex (Rhythm 1 Lust)/(Rhythm 2 Brass in Love)	1987	$3
38-07941	Monkey/(Instrumental)	1988	$3
38-07941 [PS]	Monkey/(Instrumental)	1988	$3
38-07773	One More Try/Look At Your Hands	1988	$3
38-07773 [PS]	One More Try/Look At Your Hands	1988	$3

MICHAELS, DICK
EXPLOSIVE
Number	Title	Yr	NM
101/102	Coffee Date/Teen Age Blues	1961	$70

MICHAELS, JERRI
CAMEO
Number	Title	Yr	NM
414	Give It All to Me/Like a Madness	1966	$70

MICHAELS, MARILYN
RCA VICTOR
Number	Title	Yr	NM
47-7831	Past the Age of Innocence/Danny	1961	$20
47-7771	Tell Tommy I Miss Him/Everyone Was There But You	1960	$30

MICHAELS, TONY
GOLDEN WORLD
Number	Title	Yr	NM
41	I Love the Life I Live/Picture Me and You	1966	$300

MICKEY AND KITTY
ATLANTIC
Number	Title	Yr	NM
2036	First Love/St. Louis Blues	1959	$20
2046	My Reverie/Buttercup	1959	$20
2024	Ooh-Sha-Lala/The Kid Brother	1959	$20

MICKEY AND SYLVIA
Also see MICKEY BAKER; SYLVIA (1).

ALL PLATINUM
Number	Title	Yr	NM
2310	Anytime/Souling with Mickey and Sylvia	1969	$6
2307	Lovedrops/Because You Do It to Me	1969	$6

CAT
Number	Title	Yr	NM
102	Fine Love/Speedy Life	1954	$50

—As "Little" Sylvia Vanderpool and Mickey Baker

GROOVE
Number	Title	Yr	NM
0175	Love Is Strange/I'm Going Home	1956	$40

KING
Number	Title	Yr	NM
5737	Baby, Let's Dance/Oh Yea, Ah Ah	1963	$15
6006	Love Is Strange/Darling	1965	$10

RAINBOW
Number	Title	Yr	NM
318	Forever and a Day/Ride, Sally, Ride	1955	$40
316	I'm So Glad/Se De Boom Run Dun	1955	$40

RCA
Number	Title	Yr	NM
5224-7-RX	Love Is Strange/(I've Had) The Time of My Life	1987	$3

—B-side by Bill Medley and Jennifer Warnes

RCA VICTOR
Number	Title	Yr	NM
47-8582	Fallin' in Love/From the Beginning of Time	1965	$15
47-8517	Let's Shake Some More/Gypsy	1965	$15
APAO-0080	Love Is Strange/Dearest	1973	$6
47-7877	Love Is the Only Thing/Love Lesson	1961	$20
37-7877	Love Is the Only Thing/Love Lesson	1961	$60

—Compact Single 33" (small hole, plays at LP speed)
Number	Title	Yr	NM
47-7774 [M]	Sweeter As the Days Go By/Mommy Out De Light	1960	$20
61-7774 [S]	Sweeter As the Days Go By/Mommy Out De Light	1960	$50

—Living Stereo" (large hole, plays at 45 rpm)
Number	Title	Yr	NM
47-7403	To the Valley/Oh Yeah! Uh-Huh	1958	$30
47-7811 [M]	What Would I Do/This Is My Story	1960	$30
61-7811 [S]	What Would I Do/This Is My Story	1960	$50

—Living Stereo" (large hole, plays at 45 rpm)

STANG
Number	Title	Yr	NM
5047	Baby You're So Fine/Anytime You Want To	1973	$6

VIK
Number	Title	Yr	NM
0334	It's You I Love/True, True Love	1958	$30
0290	Love Is a Treasure/Let's Have a Picnic	1957	$30
0252	Love Is Strange/I'm Going Home	1957	$40
0297	There'll Be No Backin' Out/Where Is My Honey	1957	$30
0267	There Oughta Be a Law/Dearest	1957	$30
0280	Two Shadows on Your Window/Love Will Make You Fail in School	1957	$30

WILLOW
Number	Title	Yr	NM
23000	Baby, You're So Fine/Lovedrops	1961	$20
23002	Darling (I Miss You So)/I'm Guilty	1961	$20
23006	Love Is Strange/Walking in the Rain	1962	$20
23004	Since I Fell for You/He Gave Me Everything	1962	$20

7-Inch Extended Plays
GROOVE
Number	Title	Yr	NM
EGA-18 [PS]	Love Is Strange	1957	$175
EGA-18	Love Is Strange/I'm Going Home//Walkin' in the Rain/No Good Lover	1957	$175

VIK
Number	Title	Yr	NM
262	*There Oughta Be a Law/I'm So Glad/Dearest/Se De Boom Run Dun	1957	$100
262 [PS]	Love Is Strange	1957	$100

MIDDLETON, TONY
A&M
Number	Title	Yr	NM
1084	Angela/Keep On Dancing	1969	$40
1124	Harlem Lady/Sound of Goodbye	1969	$20

ALFA
Number	Title	Yr	NM
113	My Home Town/Please Take Me	1962	$40

EL DORADO
Number	Title	Yr	NM
508	First Taste of Love/Only My Heart	1957	$40

GONE
Number	Title	Yr	NM
5015	Let's Fall in Love/Say Yeah	1957	$70

MALA
Number	Title	Yr	NM
544	Out of This World/My Baby Likes to Boogaloo	1966	$500

MGM
Number	Title	Yr	NM
13493	Don't Ever Leave Me/To the Ends of the Earth	1966	$400

MR. G
Number	Title	Yr	NM
815	Good Morning World/(B-side unknown)	1968	$15
811	Let Me Down Easy (Part 1)/Let Me Down Easy (Part 2)	1968	$15

PHILIPS
Number	Title	Yr	NM
40151	I Need You Tonight/Send Me Away	1963	$40
40184	Too Hot to Handle/I Just Couldn't Help Myself	1964	$15

ROULETTE
Number	Title	Yr	NM
4345	Is It This or Is It That/I'm Gonna Try Love One More Time	1961	$30

ROYAL FLUSH
Number	Title	Yr	NM
102	Lady Fingers/A Garden in the Ghetto	1976	$6

SAXONY
Number	Title	Yr	NM
104	I'm On My Way/(B-side unknown)	1958	$60

SCEPTER
Number	Title	Yr	NM
12290	Border Song (Holy Moses)/Silliest People	1970	$10

TRIUMPH
Number	Title	Yr	NM
600	Count Your Blessings (See What Love Has Done)/I Just Want Somebody	1959	$30

UNITED ARTISTS
Number	Title	Yr	NM
410	Drifting/Memories Are Made of This	1962	$50

MIDLER, BETTE
ATLANTIC
Number	Title	Yr	NM
7-89789 [DJ]	All I Need to Know (2:59)/(4:08)	1983	$8
7-89789	All I Need to Know/My Eye on You	1983	$5
7-89789 [PS]	All I Need to Know/My Eye on You	1983	$6
7-89712	Beast of Burden/Come Back Jimmy Dean	1984	$5
3628	Big Noise from Winnetka/Rain	1979	$6
2964	Boogie Woogie Bugle Boy/Delta Dawn	1973	$5
2980 [DJ]	Chapel of Love (stereo/mono)	1973	$10

Number	Title	Yr	NM
2928	Do You Want to Dance/Superstar	1972	$5
7-89761	Favorite Waste of Time/My Eye on You	1983	$5
2980	Friends/Chapel of Love	1973	$6
3616	Hang On In There Baby/Cradle Days	1979	$6
3004	In the Mood/Drinking Again	1974	$6
3582	Married Men/Bang, You're Dead	1979	$5
3771	My Mother's Eyes/Chapel of Love	1980	$6
3325	Old Cape Cod/Tragedy	1976	$6
3475	Paradise/Red	1978	$6
3431	Storybook Children (Daybreak)/Empty Bed Blues	1977	$5
3319	Stranger in the Night/Samedi Et Vendredi	1976	$6
3643	When a Man Loves a Woman/Love Me with a Feeling	1980	$4
7-88972	Wind Beneath My Wings/Oh Industry	1989	$3
7-88972 [PS]	Wind Beneath My Wings/Oh Industry	1989	$6

7-Inch Extended Plays
ATLANTIC
Number	Title	Yr	NM
SD 7-7270 [PS]	Bette Midler	1973	$20
SD 7-7270	(contents unknown)	1973	$20

—Jukebox issue; small hole, plays at 33 1/3 rpm

MIDNIGHT ANGELS, THE
APEX
Number	Title	Yr	NM
77073	I'm Sufferin'/In the Moonlight	1967	$40
77073 [PS]	I'm Sufferin'/In the Moonlight	1967	$50

MIDNIGHT OIL
COLUMBIA
Number	Title	Yr	NM
07433	Beds Are Burning/Bullroarer	1987	$4

—With copyright notice "1987 Midnight Oil
Number	Title	Yr	NM
07433	Beds Are Burning/Bullroarer	1987	$3

—With copyright notice "1987 CBS Records Pty. Ltd.
Number	Title	Yr	NM
08093	Dreamworld/Progress	1988	$3
08093 [PS]	Dreamworld/Progress	1988	$3
07964	The Dead Heart/Kosciusko	1988	$3
07964 [PS]	The Dead Heart/Kosciusko	1988	$3
04349 [PS]	The Power and the Passion	1984	$5

—Demonstration -- Not for Sale" on rear
Number	Title	Yr	NM
04349	The Power and the Passion/Tin Legs and Tin Mines	1984	$3
04349 [PS]	The Power and the Passion/Tin Legs and Tin Mines	1984	$3

MIDNIGHT STAR
SOLAR
Number	Title	Yr	NM
74002	90 Days (Same as Cash)/(Instrumental)	1989	$3
69638	Body Snatchers/Curious	1985	$3
48003	Can't Give You Up/Hold Out	1982	$4
70027	Don't Rock the Boat/(B-side unknown)	1988	$3
69501	Engine No. 9/Searching for Love	1986	$3
70011	Freak-A-Zoid/Curious	1988	$3
69828	Freak-A-Zoid/Move Me	1983	$4
69547	Headlines/Headlines (Dub)	1986	$3
69547 [PS]	Headlines/Headlines (Dub)	1986	$4
47947	Hold Out/I Won't Let You Be Lonely	1981	$4
48012	Hot Spot/I Won't Let You Be Lonely	1982	$4
YB-12221	I've Been Watching You/Searching for Love	1981	$5
47933	I've Been Watching You/Searching for Love	1981	$4
68961	Love Song/(Instrumental)	1989	$3
YB-11903	Make It Last/Follow the Path	1980	$4
69525	Midas Touch/Searching for Love	1986	$3
69684	Operator/Playmates	1984	$3
69659	Scientific Love/Make Time (To Fall in Love)	1985	$3
B-44284	Snake in the Grass/Snake in the Grass (TV Mix)	1988	$3
69472	Stay Here by My Side/Searching for Love	1987	$3
47948	Tuff/I Got What You Need	1981	$4
YB-12035	Two in Love/You're the Star	1980	$4
69790	Wet My Whistle/You Can't Stop Me	1983	$4

MIDNIGHTERS, THE
FEDERAL
Number	Title	Yr	NM
12195	Annie Had a Baby/She's the One	1954	$70
12200	Annie's Aunt Fanny/Crazy Loving	1954	$70
12210	Ashamed of Myself/Ring-a-Ling-Ling	1955	$70
12339	Baby Please/Ow-Wow-Oo-Wee	1958	$50
12243	Don't Change Your Pretty Ways/We'll Never Meet Again	1955	$70

Number	Title	Yr	NM
❏ 12293	E Basta Cosi/In the Doorway Crying	1957	$60
❏ 12177	Give It Up/That Woman	1954	$100

—As "The Midnighters Formerly the Royals

Number	Title	Yr	NM
❏ 12230	Give It Up/That Woman	1955	$70
❏ 12224	Henry's Got Flat Feet (Can't Dance No More)/ Whatsoever You Do	1955	$70
❏ 12285	I'll Be Home Some Day/ Come On and Get It	1957	$60
❏ 12227	It's Love Baby (24 Hours a Day)/Looka Here	1955	$70
❏ 12305	Let 'Em Roll/What Made You Change Your Mind	1957	$50
❏ 12288	Let Me Hold Your Hand/ Oh Bah Baby	1957	$60
❏ 12299	Oh, So Happy/Is Your Love for Real	1957	$50
❏ 12251	Partners for Life/Sweet Mama, Do Right	1956	$70
❏ 12185	Sexy Ways/Don't Say Your Last Goodbye	1954	$100

—As "The Midnighters Formerly the Royals

Number	Title	Yr	NM
❏ 12205	She's the One/Moonrise	1955	$70
❏ 12317	Stay By My Side/ Daddy's Little Baby	1958	$50
❏ 12202	Tell Them/Stingy Little Thing	1954	$70
❏ 12270	Tore Up Over You/ Early One Morning	1956	$60
❏ 12220	Why Are We Apart/ Switchie, Witchie, Titchie	1955	$70
❏ 12169	Work With Me Annie/ Until I Die	1954	$125

—Silver top label; as " The Midnighters (Formerly Known As the Royals)

Number	Title	Yr	NM
❏ 12169	Work With Me Annie/ Until I Die	1954	$50

—All-green label; as "The Midnighters (Formerly Known As the Royals)

7-Inch Extended Plays

Number	Title	Yr	NM
❏ 333 [PS]	The Midnighters Sing Their Greatest Hits	1955	$250

—Pink cover

Number	Title	Yr	NM
❏ 333 [PS]	The Midnighters Sing Their Greatest Hits	1955	$250

—Purple cover

Number	Title	Yr	NM
❏ 333	Work with Me Annie/ Moonrise//Sexy Ways/Get It	1955	$300

—Green label, silver top

Number	Title	Yr	NM
❏ 333	Work with Me Annie/ Moonrise//Sexy Ways/Get It	1955	$175

—All-green label

MIGHTY JOE YOUNG
POWERHAUS

Number	Title	Yr	NM
❏ MJ 004	(There'll Be Other Girls) Hoss/Chump	1989	$20

— 1,000 copies were pressed

Number	Title	Yr	NM
❏ MJ 004 [PS]	(There'll Be Other Girls) Hoss/Chump	1989	$250

— Only 25 came with picture sleeves; value is conjecture

MIGHTY LEMON DROPS, THE
SIRE

Number	Title	Yr	NM
❏ 27906	Inside Out/Head on the Block	1988	$3

MIGIL FIVE, THE
CAMEO

Number	Title	Yr	NM
❏ 316	Mockin' Bird Hill/Long Ago (And Far Away)	1964	$10

HICKORY

Number	Title	Yr	NM
❏ 1334	I'm in Love Again/ One Hundred Years	1965	$10

MIKE AND BILL
ARISTA

Number	Title	Yr	NM
❏ 0130	Somebody's Gotta Go (Sho Ain't Me)/(Instrumental)	1975	$20
❏ 0180	Things Won't Be This Bad Always/(Instrumental)	1976	$10

MOVING UP

Number	Title	Yr	NM
❏ 124	Somebody's Gotta Go (Sho Ain't Me)/(Instrumental)	1975	$30

MIKE AND LULU
TOP RANK

Number	Title	Yr	NM
❏ 2036	Baby's Lullaby/Baby Talk	1959	$15

MIKE AND THE CENSATIONS HIGHLAND

Number	Title	Yr	NM
❏ 1189	Baby What You Gonna Do/Don't Sell Your Soul	1968	$70
❏ 1186	Be Mine Forever/I Need Your Lovin'	1968	$50
❏ 1181	Don't Mess with Me/There Is Nothing I Can Do About It	1967	$60
❏ 1203	I Need Your Lovin'/Baby What You Gonna Do	1968	$50

REVUE

Number	Title	Yr	NM
❏ 11068	Gonna Try to Get You Back/A Man Ain't Nothin' But a Man	1970	$75
❏ 11056	Shopping for Love/ The Straw (That Broke the Camel's Back)	1969	$40
❏ 11041	Split Personality/ You're Living a Lie	1969	$40

MIKE AND THE JAYS
DOYL

Number	Title	Yr	NM
❏ 1001	My Only Girl/Dingle Dangle Doll	1960	$100

MIKE + THE MECHANICS
ATLANTIC

Number	Title	Yr	NM
❏ 7-89450	All I Need Is a Miracle/ You Are the One	1986	$3
❏ 7-89450 [PS]	All I Need Is a Miracle/ You Are the One	1986	$4
❏ 7-88921	Seeing Is Believing/Don't	1989	$3
❏ 7-88921 [PS]	Seeing Is Believing/Don't	1989	$3
❏ 7-89488	Silent Running (On Dangerous Ground)/ Par Avion	1985	$3
❏ 7-89488 [PS]	Silent Running (On Dangerous Ground)/ Par Avion	1985	$4
❏ 7-89404	Taken In/A Call to Arms	1986	$3
❏ 7-89404 [PS]	Taken In/A Call to Arms	1986	$4
❏ 7-88964 [DJ]	The Living Years (Edit)/ (LP Version)	1989	$5
❏ 7-88964	The Living Years/ Too Many Friends	1989	$3
❏ 7-88964 [PS]	The Living Years/ Too Many Friends	1989	$8

MIKE AND THE MODIFIERS
GORDY

Number	Title	Yr	NM
❏ 7006	I Found Myself a Brand New Baby/It's Too Bad	1962	$70

MIKE AND THE UTOPIANS
CEE JAY

Number	Title	Yr	NM
❏ 574	Erlene/I Found a Penny	1958	$200
❏ 574	Erlene/I Wish	1958	$300

MIKE, JOHN AND BILL
OMNIBUS

Number	Title	Yr	NM
❏ 239	How Can You Kiss Me/ Just a Little Love	1963	$300

MILAN
MIGON

Number	Title	Yr	NM
❏ 1962	Santa's Doing The Twist/ (B-side unknown)	1962	$20

MILANO, BOBBY
CHALLENGE

Number	Title	Yr	NM
❏ 59005	Life Begins at 4 O'Clock/ Double Talking Baby	1958	$125

WARNER BROS.

Number	Title	Yr	NM
❏ 5027	Water Under the Bridge/ My Yiddishe Momma	1959	$15

MILBURN, AMOS
ALADDIN

Number	Title	Yr	NM
❏ 3093	Ain't Nothin' Shaking/ Just One More Drink	1951	$100
❏ 3293	All Is Well/My Happiness Depends on You	1955	$50
❏ 3068	Bad, Bad Whiskey/I'm Going to Tell My Mama	1950	$500

— Note: Amos Milburn singles on Aladdin before 3068 are unconfirmed on 45 rpm except those listed

Number	Title	Yr	NM
❏ 3018	Bewildered/A and M Blues	1950	$120

—78 originally released in 1948

Number	Title	Yr	NM
❏ 3146	Button Your Lip/Everything I Do Is Wrong	1952	$100
❏ 3014	Chicken Shack Boogie/It Took a Long, Long Time	1950	$200

—78 originally released in 1948

Number	Title	Yr	NM
❏ 3332	Chicken Shack Boogie/ Juice, Juice, Juice	1956	$50
❏ 3090	Everybody Clap Hands/That Was Your Last Mistake	1951	$100
❏ 3125	Flying Home/Put Something in My Hand	1952	$100
❏ 3320	French Fried Potatoes and Ketchup/I Need Someone	1956	$50

Number	Title	Yr	NM
❏ 3340	Girl of My Dreams/ Everyday of the Week	1956	$50
❏ 3248	Glory of Love/Baby, Baby All the Time	1954	$70
❏ 3218	Good, Good Whiskey/ Let's Have a Party	1954	$100
❏ 3370	Greyhound/Dear Angel	1957	$40
❏ 3306	House Party/I Guess I'll Go	1955	$50
❏ 3226	How Could You Hurt Me So/Rocky Mountain	1954	$70
❏ 3133	I Won't Be Your Fool Anymore/Roll Mr. Jelly	1952	$100
❏ 3164	Let Me Go Home, Whiskey/ Three Times a Fool	1953	$70
❏ 3080	Let's Rock a While/ Tears, Tears, Tears	1951	$100
❏ 3168	Long, Long Day/ Please Mr. Johnson	1953	$70
❏ 3240	Milk and Water/I'm Still a Fool for You	1954	$70
❏ 3197	One Scotch, One Bourbon, One Beer/What Can I Do	1953	$125
❏ 3105	She's Gone Again/ Boogie Woogie	1951	$100
❏ 3269	That's It/One, Two, Three Everybody	1954	$70
❏ 3124	Thinking and Drinking/ Trouble in Mind	1952	$100
❏ 3383	Thinking of You Baby/ If I Could Be with You	1957	$40
❏ 3281	Why Don't You Do Right/I Love You Anyway	1955	$50

IMPERIAL

Number	Title	Yr	NM
❏ 5831	I'm Still a Fool for You/ Rocky Mountain	1962	$15

KING

Number	Title	Yr	NM
❏ 5405	Christmas (Comes But Once a Year)/Please Come Home for Christmas	1960	$15

—B-side by Charles Brown

Number	Title	Yr	NM
❏ 5464	I Wanna Go Back Home/My Little Baby	1961	$15

— With Charles Brown

Number	Title	Yr	NM
❏ 5529	Movin' Time/The Hammer	1961	$15
❏ 5483	My Sweet Baby's Love/ Heartaches That Make You Cry	1961	$15
❏ 6095	Whiz O Shoo Pepi/ Same Old Thing	1967	$10

MOTOWN

Number	Title	Yr	NM
❏ 1038	I'll Make It Up to You Somehow/My Baby Gave Me Another Chance	1963	$40
❏ 1046	My Daily Prayer/ (B-side unknown)	1963	$40

UNITED ARTISTS

Number	Title	Yr	NM
❏ 0149	Chicken Shack Boogie/ Revitalized	1973	$4

— Silver Spotlight Series" reissue

MILDRED AND C. P.
MAC GREGOR

Number	Title	Yr	NM
❏ 0(no cat #)	Season's Greetings From (Side 1)/Season's Greetings From (Side 2)	1958	$15

— Yellow vinyl

MILES, BUDDY
ATLANTIC

Number	Title	Yr	NM
❏ 3852 [DJ]	Can You Hold Me (same on both sides)	1981	$4

— May be promo only

Number	Title	Yr	NM
❏ 4006 [DJ]	Sunshine of Your Love (same on both sides)	1982	$4

— May be promo only

COLUMBIA

Number	Title	Yr	NM
❏ 45969	Crazy Love/Thinking of You	1973	$5
❏ 45876	Elvira/Hear No Evil	1973	$5
❏ 45826	Love Affair/Life Is What You Make It	1973	$5
❏ 10030	Pain/We Get Love	1974	$20
❏ 10089	Pull Yourself Together/I'm Just a Kiss Away	1975	$200

MERCURY

Number	Title	Yr	NM
❏ 73086	Down By the River/ Hearts Delight	1970	$6
❏ 73119	Dreams/Your Feeling Is Mine	1970	$6
❏ 73261	Give Away None of My Love/Take It Off Him and Put It On Me	1972	$5
❏ 73277	Life Is What You Make It (Part 1)/Life Is What You Make It (Part 2)	1972	$5
❏ 72945	Memphis Train/My Chant	1969	$6
❏ 73008	Them Changes/ Spot on the Wall	1970	$6
❏ 73238	Them Changes/The Way I Feel Tonight	1971	$5
❏ 72860	The Train (Part 1)/ The Train (Part 2)	1968	$8
❏ 72903	This Lady/'69 Freedom Special	1969	$8
❏ 73159	We Got to Live Together (Part 1)/We Got to Live Together (Part 2)	1970	$6

Number	Title	Yr	NM
❏ 73205	Wholesale Love/That's the Way Life Is	1971	$5

MILLER, BOBBY
CONSTELLATION
Number	Title	Yr	NM
❏ 134	I'm For the Girls/Love Take the Case	1964	$40
❏ 103	The Big Question/I Don't Believe You	1963	$30
❏ 111	The Big Question/Uncle Willie Time	1963	$30
❏ 127	This Is My Dance/Simon Says	1964	$30
❏ 116	Whoa (She's All Mine)/Take It in Stride	1964	$30

MILLER, CHUCK
CAPITOL
Number	Title	Yr	NM
❏ F2613	Am I to Blame/Count Your Blessings	1953	$30
❏ F2841	Hopahula Boogie/I'll Know My Love	1954	$30
❏ F2766	Idaho Red/The Joker (In the Card Game of Life)	1954	$30

— With Dave Cavanaugh
| ❏ F2700 | The Pucker-Nut Free/After All | 1954 | $30 |

MERCURY
❏ 70767	Boogie Along/Lookout Mountain	1955	$20
❏ 70842	Bright Red Convertible/Baltimore Jones	1956	$20
❏ 71308	Down the Road Apiece/Mad About Her Blues	1958	$15
❏ 70697	Hawk Eye/Something to Live For	1955	$20
❏ 71056	Me Head in De Barrel/Good Mornin' Darlin'	1957	$15
❏ 71173	Plaything/After Yesterday	1957	$15
❏ 71001	The Auctioneer/Baby Doll	1956	$20
❏ 70627	The House of Blue Lights/Can't Help Wonderin'	1955	$30

MILLER, CLINT
ABC-PARAMOUNT
❏ 9979	A Lover's Prayer/No, Never, My Love	1958	$30
❏ 9878	Bertha Lou/Doggone It Baby, I'm in Love	1957	$60
❏ 9938	Polka Dotted Poliwampus/Teenage Dance	1958	$40
❏ 9938 [PS]	Polka Dotted Poliwampus/Teenage Dance	1958	$70

BIG TOP
| ❏ 3013 | Lonely Traveler/You Must Have Read My Mind | 1959 | $30 |

HEADLINE
❏ 1013	I Still Write Your Name in the Sand/The Girl with a Ribbon in Her Hand	1961	$40
❏ 1011	London Town/Till the End of the World Rolls Around	1961	$40
❏ 1010	Silly Billy Boy/Do You Remember	1960	$60

LENOX
| ❏ 5574 | Bridge Across the River/Crabs Walk Sideways | 1963 | $15 |
| ❏ 5557 | Forget Me Nots/Drummer Boy of Shiloh | 1962 | $15 |

MILLER, DREW, AND THE BEL-AIRES
MGM
| ❏ 11627 | When Christmas Angels Sing/Mystery Trail | 1953 | $30 |

MILLER, FRANKIE
COLUMBIA
❏ 4-21510	Day by Day/I Don't Know Why I Love You	1956	$30
❏ 4-21314	It's No Big Thing to Me/Hey, Where Ya Goin'	1954	$30
❏ 4-21420	Paid in Full/My Wedding Song for You	1955	$30
❏ 4-21472	Pain, Powder and Perfume/What You Do from Now On	1955	$30

MERCURY
| ❏ 884450-7 | Game of Love/I'd Lie to You for Your Love | 1986 | $4 |

STARDAY
❏ 655	A Little South of Memphis/Too Hot to Handle	1963	$15
❏ 496	Baby Rocked Her Dolly/Rain Rain	1960	$20
❏ 424	Black Land Farmer/True Blue	1959	$20
❏ 777	Charlie's Got a Good Thing Goin'/Tough Road to Hoe	1966	$15
❏ 739	Country Music Who's Who/Bringing Mary Home	1965	$15
❏ 457	Family Man/Poppin' Johnny	1959	$20
❏ 793	Fickle Hand of Fate/She's My Antibiotic	1967	$15

Number	Title	Yr	NM
❏ 577	Gotta Win My Baby Back Again/The Picture at St. Helene	1962	$20
❏ 709	I Can Almost Forget/Big Talk of the Town	1965	$15
❏ 537	I'll Write to You/Richest Poor Boy	1961	$20
❏ 691	It Took a Lot of Love/Mean Old Greyhound	1964	$15
❏ 550	Lookin' Around Downtown/A Little Bit Later	1961	$20
❏ 525	Out of Bounds/Two Lips Away	1960	$20

— With Dottie Sills
❏ 673	Out of This World/Fifteen Acres of Peanut Land	1964	$15
❏ 513	Strictly Nothin'/Young Widow Brown	1960	$20
❏ 566	The Cat and the Mouse/It's Not Easy	1961	$20
❏ 481	The Money Side of Life/Reunion (With Dinner on the Ground)	1960	$20

MILLER, GLENN, ORCHESTRA (BUDDY DEFRANCO, DIRECTOR)
7-Inch Extended Plays
EPIC
| ❏ 5-26206 [S] | A Taste of Honey/What Now My Love/Whipped Cream/Tijuana Taxi/The Lonely Bull/Spanish Flea | 1966 | $10 |
| ❏ 5-26206 [PS] | Something New | 1966 | $12 |

MILLER, GLENN
20TH FOX
| ❏ 122 | Boom Shot/You Say the Sweetest Things | 1959 | $10 |
| ❏ 47-2852 | American Patrol/Song of the Volga Boatmen | 1949 | $30 |

—Aqua label
| ❏ 47-2852 | American Patrol/Song of the Volga Boatmen | 1951 | $20 |

— Black label, outline of dog at right
❏ 47-2858	A String of Pearls/Chattanooga Choo Choo	1949	$30
❏ 47-2877	Bugle Call Rag/Runnin' Wild	1949	$30
❏ 27-0026	Chattanooga Choo Choo/(I've Got a Gal in) Kalamazoo	1951	$20

— Silver label, red print
| ❏ 47-4086 | In the Mood/A String of Pearls | 1951 | $20 |
| ❏ 47-2853 | In the Mood/Little Brown Jug | 1949 | $30 |

—Aqua label
| ❏ 47-2853 | In the Mood/Little Brown Jug | 1951 | $20 |

— Black label, outline of dog at right
| ❏ 447-0029 | Poinciana/It Must Be Jelly | 1956 | $20 |
| ❏ 47-2854 | Star Dust/Pennsylvania Six-Five Thousand | 1949 | $30 |

—Aqua label
| ❏ 47-2854 | Star Dust/Pennsylvania Six-Five Thousand | 1951 | $20 |

— Black label, outline of dog at right
| ❏ 27-0028 | Sunrise Serenade/Moonlight Serenade | 1951 | $20 |

— Silver label, red print

UNITED STATES ARMY
| ❏ HO7H-1760/1 [DJ] | In the Mood/American Patrol | 1958 | $50 |

— Promo-only "Recruiting Service" record; white label with red and blue print

RCA VICTOR
❏ EPA 1-1494	*Star Dust/A Lovely Way to Spend an Evening/Long Ago and Far Away/My Ideal	1957	$15
❏ EPAT426 [PS]	Ah! Spring	1954	$25
❏ 947-0178	Along the Santa Fe Trail/Swingin' at the Seance/I'll Never Smile Again/V for Victory Hop	1954	$10

— Side 1 and 30 of 15-EP set EPOT 6701
| ❏ 947-0124 | American Patrol/Ida//Flagwaver/One O'Clock Jump | 1953 | $10 |

— Side 9 and 20 of EPNT 6700
| ❏ 947-0182 | A Million Dreams Ago/Daisy Mae//Let's Have Another Cup of Coffee/The Rhumba Jumps | 1954 | $10 |

— Side 5 and 26 of 15-EP set EPOT 6701
| ❏ EPAT426 | April Played the Fiddle/Blue Rain//Vagabond Dreams/The Story of a Starry Night | 1954 | $25 |

— Silver label, red print
| ❏ EPAT429 | At Last/Blue Evening//Delilah/Elmer's Tune | 1954 | $25 |

— Silver label, red print
| ❏ 947-0184 | At Sundown/My Last Goodbye//So Little Time/Down South Camp Meetin' | 1954 | $10 |

Number	Title	Yr	NM
— Side 7 and 24 of 15-EP set EPOT 6701			
❏ 947-0128	Baby Me/There'll Be Some Changes Made//Wishing Will Make It So/Rug Cutter's Swing	1953	$10
— Side 13 and 16 of EPNT 6700			
❏ EPA727	Beautiful Ohio/Adios//Serenade in Blue/Bugle Call Rag	1956	$20
❏ 947-0192	Bluebirds in the Moonlight/I Want to Be Happy//My Heart Belongs to Daddy/Deep Purple	1954	$10
— Side 15 and 16 of 15-EP set EPOT 6701			
❏ 947-0191	Blue Skies/Heaven Can Wait//After All/St. Louis Blues	1954	$10
— Side 14 and 17 of 15-EP set EPOT 6701			
❏ 947-0118	Boulder Bluff/Caribbean Clipper//Sliphorn Jive/Here We Go Again	1953	$10
— Side 3 and 26 of EPNT 6700			
❏ EPA5081 [PS]	Chattanooga Choo Choo	1958	$15
❏ 599-9110	Chattanooga Choo Choo/American Patrol/Oh So Good//Rhapsody in Blue/Rug Cutter's Swing/King Porter Stomp	1956	$15
— Side 8 and 13 of 10-EP set SPD 18; pink label			
❏ 599-9110	Chattanooga Choo Choo/American Patrol/Oh So Good//Rhapsody in Blue/Rug Cutter's Swing/King Porter Stomp	1956	$15
— Side 8 and 13 of 10-EP set SPD 18; gray label			
❏ EPA5081	Chattanooga Choo Choo/American Patrol//Tuxedo Junction/(I've Got a Gal in) Kalamazoo	1958	$15
❏ 947-0123	Devil may Care/Chip Off the Old Block//Don't Sit Under the Apple Tree/Lady Be Good	1953	$10
— Side 8 and 21 of EPNT 6700			
❏ 599-9111	Devil May Care/Sleepy Town Train/One O'Clock Jump//Sun Valley Jump/String of Pearls/Flagwaver	1956	$15
— Side 9 and 12 of 10-EP set SPD 18; pink label			
❏ 599-9111	Devil May Care/Sleepy Town Train/One O'Clock Jump//Sun Valley Jump/String of Pearls/Flagwaver	1956	$15
— Side 9 and 12 of 10-EP set SPD 18; gray label			
❏ EPAT429 [PS]	Elmer's Tune	1954	$25
❏ 947-0183	Falling Leaves/Crosstown//Anchors Aweigh/Body and Soul	1954	$10
— Side 6 and 25 of 15-EP set EPOT 6701			
❏ EPNT6700	Glenn Miller and His Orchestra -- Limited Edition	1953	$250
— With 14 records (947-0116 through 947-0129), white loose-leaf folder and numbered booklet			
❏ EPOT6701	Glenn Miller and His Orchestra -- Limited Edition, Volume Two	1954	$250
— With 15 records (947-0178 through 947-0192), gold loose-leaf folder and numbered booklet			
❏ EPA729 [PS]	Glenn Miller Concert	1956	$20
❏ EPA5035 [PS]	Glenn Miller (Gold Standard Series)	1958	$15
❏ EPA5032 [PS]	Glenn Miller (Gold Standard Series)	1958	$15
❏ EPA-733 [PS]	Glenn Miller Plays Selections from The Glenn Miller Story	1956	$20
❏ LPC-101 [PS]	Glenn Miller Serenade	1961	$15
— Cover for "Compact Double 33			
❏ EPA729	Going Home/April in Paris//Everybody Loves My Baby/Georgia on My Mind	1956	$20
❏ 947-0125	Guess I'll Have to Change My Plan/Glen Island Special//Sleepy Town Train/My Devotion/Fresh as a Daisy	1953	$10
— Side 10 and 19 of EPNT 6700			
❏ 947-0185	Hallelujah/I'm Sorry for Myself//A Stone's Throw from Heaven/Humoresque	1954	$10
— Side 8 and 23 of 15-EP set EPOT 6701			
❏ E3CW-3349/50 [DJ]	Highlights from the Great Glenn Miller Limited Edition 1953	1953	$60
— Promo-only sampler from the limited box sets			
❏ 599-9107	I Guess I'll Have to Change My Plan/Twenty-Four Robbers/Lady Be Good//Wishing Will Make it So/Say Si Si/Mister Meadowlark	1956	$15
— Side 5 and 16 of 10-EP set SPD 18; pink label			

Number	Title	Yr	NM
❑ 599-9107	I Guess I'll Have to Change My Plan/Twenty-Four Robbers/Lady Be Good//Wishing Will Make it So/Say Si Si/Mister Meadowlark	1956	$15

— Side 5 and 16 of 10-EP set SPD 18; gray label

❑ 947-0122	Imagination/It Must Be Jelly//Fools Rush In/Twenty-Four Robbers	1953	$10

— Side 7 and 22 of EPNT 6700

❑ 947-0179	In a Sentimental Mood/Frenesi//Dancing in a Dream/Sophisticated Lady	1954	$10

— Side 2 and 29 of 15-EP set EPOT 6701

❑ EPA5032	In the Mood/A String of Pearls//Moonlight Serenade/Sunrise Serenade	1958	$15
❑ 547-1102	In the Mood/Sunrise Serenade//Bugle Call Rag/Moonlight Serenade	1957	$20

— "Side 3" and "Side 4" of EPC 1506

❑ 947-0180	Isn't That Just Like Love/I Dreamt I Dwelt in Harlem//On the Alamo/April in Paris	1954	$10

— Side 3 and 28 of 15-EP set EPOT 6701

❑ EPA5035	Make Believe Ballroom Time/I Guess I'll Have to Dream the Rest//Juke Box Saturday Night/It Happened in Sun Valley	1958	$15
❑ 947-0119	Make Believe/Say Si Si/Introduction to a Waltz//Sweet Eloise/Rhapsody in Blue	1953	$10

— Side 4 and 25 of EPNT 6700

❑ EPA 1-1494 [PS]	Marvelous Miller Moods, Vol. 1	1957	$15
❑ EPAT430 [PS]	Moonlight Cocktail	1954	$25
❑ EPAT430	Moonlight Cocktail/Perfidia//Serenade in Blue/It Happened in Hawaii	1954	$25

— Silver label, red print

❑ 947-0136	Moonlight Serenade/American Patrol//Pennsylvania Six-Five Thousand/In the Mood	1954	$25

— Silver label, red print; part of 2-EP set EPBT 3057

❑ EPA-733	Moonlight Serenade/In the Mood//Tuxedo Junction/String of Pearls	1956	$20
❑ 599-9103	Moonlight Serenade/Perfidia//Love with a Capital "You"/Down for the Count	1956	$15

— Side 1 and 20 of 10-EP set SPD 18; pink label

❑ 599-9103	Moonlight Serenade/Perfidia//Love with a Capital "You"/Down for the Count	1956	$15

— Side 1 and 20 of 10-EP set SPD 18; gray label

❑ 947-0116	Moonlight Serenade-Perfidia/Wonderful One//The Lamplighter's Serenade/Farewell Blues	1953	$10

— Sides 1 and 28 of EPNT 6700

❑ 547-1100	Moonlight Serenade/Running Wild/Londonderry Air (Danny Boy)//One O'Clock Jump	1957	$20

— Side 1" and "Side 6" of EPC 1506

❑ 599-9108	Moon Over Miami-A Million Dreams Ago-Aloha-Baby Me-Rainbow Rhapsody//Boulder Buff/Sweet Eloise/Caribbean Clipper	1956	$15

— Side 6 and 15 of 10-EP set SPD 18; pink label

❑ 599-9108	Moon Over Miami-A Million Dreams Ago-Aloha-Baby Me-Rainbow Rhapsody//Boulder Buff/Sweet Eloise/Caribbean Clipper	1956	$15

— Side 6 and 15 of 10-EP set SPD 18; gray label

❑ 947-0129	Moon Over Miami-A Million Dreams Ago-Aloha/Sun Valley Jump//String of Pearls/Love with a Capital "You	1953	$10

— Side 14 and 15 of EPNT 6700

❑ 947-0126	My Darling-Blueberry Hill-Can't Get Started/Bugle Call Rag//Chattanooga Choo Choo/My Melancholy Baby-Moon Love-Stompin' at the Savoy-Blue Moon	1953	$10

— Side 11 and 18 of EPNT 6700

❑ 599-9109	My Darling-Blueberry Hill-I Can't Get Started-Don't Sit Under the Apple Tree-There'll Be Some Changes Made//Here We Go Again/Imagination/Angel Child	1956	$15

— Side 7 and 14 of 10-EP set SPD 18; pink label

Number	Title	Yr	NM
❑ 599-9109	My Darling-Blueberry Hill-I Can't Get Started-Don't Sit Under the Apple Tree-There'll Be Some Changes Made//Here We Go Again/Imagination/Angel Child	1956	$15

— Side 7 and 14 of 10-EP set SPD 18; gray label

❑ 599-9106	On a Little Street in Singapore/Fools Rush In/The Hop//Ida/Fresh As a Daisy/Careless	1956	$15

— Side 4 and 17 of 10-EP set SPD 18; pink label

❑ 599-9106	On a Little Street in Singapore/Fools Rush In/The Hop//Ida/Fresh As a Daisy/Careless	1956	$15

— Side 4 and 17 of 10-EP set SPD 18; gray label

❑ 947-0127	On a Little Street in Singapore/Oh So Good//Angel Child/King Porter Stomp	1953	$10

— Side 12 and 17 of EPNT 6700

❑ EPBT3057 [PS]	Selections from the Film "The Glenn Miller Story	1954	$25

— Cover for 2-EP set (947-0136, 947-0137)

❑ EPA5049 [PS]	Serenade in Blue	1958	$15
❑ LPC-101	Serenade in Blue//In the Mood//Moonlight Serenade/Sunrise Serenade	1961	$15

— Compact Double 33"; small hole, plays at 33 1/3 rpm

❑ EPA5049	Serenade in Blue/Little Brown Jug//Don't Sit Under the Apple Tree (With Anyone Else But Me)/Pennsylvania Six-Five Thousand	1958	$15
❑ 599-9112	Sliphorn Jive/Little Brown Jug//Farewell Blues/It Must Be Jelly/Chip Off the Old Block/Glen Island Special	1956	$15

— Side 10 and 11 of 10-EP set SPD 18; pink label

❑ 599-9112	Sliphorn Jive/Little Brown Jug//Farewell Blues/It Must Be Jelly/Chip Off the Old Block/Glen Island Special	1956	$15

— Side 10 and 11 of 10-EP set SPD 18; gray label

❑ 547-1101	Stairway to the Stars/To You/Little Brown Jug//Jim Jam Jump/For Jones/Hold Tight	1957	$20

— Side 2" and "Side 5" of EPC 1506

❑ 947-0188	Sunrise Serenade/Blue Orchids/I Don't Want to Walk Without You/Limehouse Blues	1954	$10

— Side 11 and 20 of 15-EP set EPOT 6701

❑ VLP-3377(e) [PS]	The Best of Glenn Miller	1966	$12
❑ EPC-1506 [PS]	The Glenn Miller Carnegie Hall Concert	1957	$20

— Cover for 3-EP set (547-1100, 547-1101, 547-1102)

❑ 947-0186	The Hour of Parting/The Jumpin' Jive//This Can't Be Love	1954	$10

— Side 9 and 22 of 15-EP set EPOT 6701

❑ EPAT428 [PS]	The Spirit Is Willing	1954	$25
❑ EPAT428	The Spirit Is Willing/Long Tall Mama//Rainbow Rhapsody/Take the "A" Train	1954	$25

— Silver label, red print

❑ EPA727 [PS]	This Is Glenn Miller	1956	$20
❑ SPD18 [PS]	(title unknown)	1956	$175

— Includes 10 records (599-9105 through 599-9114) plus box and booklet insert

❑ 947-0137	Tuxedo Junction/St. Louis Blues//String of Pearls/Little Brown Jug	1954	$25

— Silver label, red print; part of 2-EP set EPBT 3057

❑ 947-0187	Twilight Interlude/And the Angels Sing//Daddy/Deep in the Heart of Texas	1954	$10

— Side 10 and 21 of 15-EP set EPOT 6701

❑ 947-0189	We Can Live on Love/Pagan Love Song//Georgia on My Mind/Be Happy	1954	$10

— Side 12 and 19 of 15-EP set EPOT 6701

❑ 947-0117	Weekend of a Private Secretary/Always in My Heart//Mister Meadowlark/Just a Little Bit South of North Carolina/Under a Blanket of Blue	1953	$10

— Side 2 and 27 of EPNT 6700

❑ 947-0190	We've Come a Long Way Together/Get Out of Town//Indian Summer/Tiger Rag	1954	$10

— Side 13 and 18 of 15-EP set EPOT 6701

Number	Title	Yr	NM

MILLER, HAL, AND THE RAYS

AMY
❑ 920	A Blessing in Disguise/Cry Like the Rain	1965	$100
❑ 909	I Still Care/On My Own Two Feet	1964	$200

TOPIX
❑ 6003	An Angel Cried/Faith, Hope, Dreams	1961	$70

MILLER, LESLEY

MGM
❑ K13748	Teach Me to Love You/Think of Rain	1967	$20

RCA VICTOR
❑ 47-8455	Heartache Is Over/Walk with Me	1964	$20
❑ 47-8753	He Doesn't Need Your Pity/I'm Going Back to My First Love	1965	$40
❑ 47-8786	He Wore the Green Beret/(You Got a Way of) Bringing Out My Tears	1966	$40
❑ 47-8815	Mountain of Our Love/Everybody Knows But Me	1966	$40

MILLER, LISA

CANTERBURY
❑ 519	The Loneliest Christmas Tree/Love	1967	$30

MILLER, MITCH

COLUMBIA
❑ 42399	Ain't We Got Fun/You're An Old Smoothie	1962	$6
❑ 42215	Aura Lee/The Fog and the Grog	1961	$8
❑ 39835	Au Revoir Again/Song of Delilah	1952	$12

— The above four comprise box set B-315

❑ 50033	Autumn Leaves/(B-side unknown)	1955	$12

— Early "Hall of Fame Series" reissue, this charted with this number in 1955

❑ 6-790(?)	Autumn Leaves/Song of Delilah	1950	$30
❑ 1-790(?)	Autumn Leaves/Song of Delilah	1950	$30

— Microgroove 33 1/3 rpm 7-inch single

❑ 42401	Black Bottom/Bidin' My Time	1962	$6
❑ 41235	Bluebell/It Seems Like Only Yesterday	1958	$8
❑ S731079 [S]	Cecelia/When the Red, Red Robin Comes Bob, Bob, Bobbin' Along	1961	$10
❑ 39300	Cider Night/By the Moonlight	1951	$20
❑ 39742	Cuban Nightingale/Bunk House Boogie	1952	$15
❑ 41499	Do-Re-Mi/Alouette March	1959	$8
❑ 41499 [PS]	Do-Re-Mi/Alouette March	1959	$15
❑ 40409	Follow Me/The Singing Lesson	1955	$10
❑ 40244	Frou! Frou!/Sail! Sail! Sail!	1954	$15
❑ 41128	Ginny, My Joy/Bonnie Eloise	1958	$8
❑ 42214	God Rest Ye Merry Gentlemen/O Come, All Ye Faithful	1961	$8
❑ S730441 [S]	Goodnight Irene/On Top of Old Smoky	1960	$10

— Stereo Seven" 33 1/3 single, small hole

❑ 39617	Greensleeves/Love Makes the World Go Round	1951	$20
❑ 42305	Happy Whistlin' Blues/(Instrumental)	1962	$6
❑ 41375	Holiday for Lovers/This Here Goat	1959	$8
❑ 1-789	In My Arms/Au Revoir Again	1950	$30

— Microgroove 33 1/3 rpm 7-inch single

❑ 6-789	In My Arms/Au Revoir Again	1950	$30
❑ 42400	I Wanna Be Happy/Tea for Two	1962	$6
❑ 40635	Lisbon Antigua (In Old Lisbon)/Willy Can	1956	$12
❑ 41301	Lover's Gold/Moonlight and Roses	1958	$8
❑ 40655	Madeira/Bolero Gaucho	1956	$10
❑ 41066	March from the River Kwai and Coloney Bogey/Hey Little Baby	1957	$10
❑ 39851	Meet Mister Callaghan/How Strange	1952	$15
❑ B-315 [PS]	Mmmmitch!	1952	$10

— Box for 4-record set

❑ 4-42240	Must Be Santa/Be a Santa	1961	$8
❑ 3-42240	Must Be Santa/Be a Santa	1961	$15

— Columbia Single 33" with small hole; orange label

❑ 41814	Must Be Santa/Christmas Spirit	1960	$10
❑ 39982	Oriental Polka/Tira Lira Madeira	1953	$15
❑ 42914	Pine Cones and Holly Berries/Whispering Hope	1963	$8
❑ 42914 [PS]	Pine Cones and Holly Berries/Whispering Hope	1963	$10

Number	Title	Yr	NM
41992	Poor Butterfly/I'm Looking Over a Four-Leaf Clover	1961	$8
40302	Sabrina/Wooden Shoes and Happy Hearts	1954	$15
39727	Serenade for Horns/Horn Belt Boogie	1952	$15
41989	Shine On Harvest Moon/For Me and My Gal/My Wild Irish Rose/When Irish Eyes Are Smiling	1961	$8
42213	Silent Night, Holy Night/Deck The Halls With Boughs Of Holly	1961	$8
41716	Silly Little Tune/Walkin' Down to Washington	1960	$8
41616	Sing Along/Pink Polemoniums	1960	$8
42210	Sleigh Ride/The Christmas Song	1961	$8
40772	Song of the Sparrow/(Instrumental)	1956	$12
40683	That Girl/St. Lawrence River	1956	$12
40575	The Bonnie Blue Gal/Bel Sante	1955	$12
41317	The Children's Marching Song/Carolina in the Morning	1959	$8
41317 [PS]	The Children's Marching Song/Carolina in the Morning	1959	$15
42813	The Great Escape March/Shenandoah	1963	$6
42016	The Guns of Navarone/Bye Bye Blackbird	1961	$8
42797	The House Is Haunted/It's a Darn Good Thing	1963	$6
42585	The Longest Day/(Instrumental)	1962	$6
40493	Theme from "I Am a Camera"/On Honolulu Bay	1955	$10
40730	Theme Song from "Song for a Summer Night" (Vocal)/(Instrumental)	1956	$10
40715	The President on the Dollar/Trapeze	1956	$10
41991	The Prisoner's Song/Where Do You Work/Yes! We Have No Bananas	1961	$8
41990	There Is a Tavern in the Town/Show Me the Way to Go Home/That Old Gang of Mine	1961	$8
39833	The Sea of the Moon/Greensleeves	1952	$10
39053	The Sea of the Moon/Smile, Smile, Smile	1950	$20
41988	The Whiffenpoof Song/Sweet Adeline/Let Me Call You Sweetheart	1961	$8
31020 [S]	titles unknown	1961	$10
31021 [S]	titles unknown	1961	$10
31022 [S]	titles unknown	1961	$10
31023 [S]	titles unknown	1961	$10
31024 [S]	titles unknown	1961	$10
31080 [S]	titles unknown	1961	$10
31081 [S]	titles unknown	1961	$10
31082 [S]	titles unknown	1961	$10
31083 [S]	titles unknown	1961	$10
31364 [S]	titles unknown	1962	$10
31365 [S]	titles unknown	1962	$10
31366 [S]	titles unknown	1962	$10
31367 [S]	titles unknown	1962	$10
31368 [S]	titles unknown	1962	$10
31565 [S]	titles unknown	1962	$10
31566 [S]	titles unknown	1962	$10
31567 [S]	titles unknown	1962	$10
31568 [S]	titles unknown	1962	$10
31569 [S]	titles unknown	1962	$10

— *The above all are Columbia "Stereo 7" singles*

Number	Title	Yr	NM
43247	To Be with You/Major Dundee March	1965	$6
41941	Tunes of Glory/Shlub-a-Dubba-Due	1961	$8
41941 [PS]	Tunes of Glory/Shlub-a-Dubba-Due	1961	$10
39834	Tzena, Tzena, Tzena/Autumn Leaves	1952	$10
1-706	Tzena, Tzena, Tzena/The Sleigh	1950	$30

— *Microgroove 33 1/3 rpm 7-inch single*

Number	Title	Yr	NM
6-706	Tzena, Tzena, Tzena/The Sleigh	1950	$30
42398	We're In the Money/Chinatown, My Chinatown	1962	$6
43053	Whip Out Your Ukulele/Song for a Summer Night	1964	$6
40999	Whistle Stop/The Bowery Grenadiers	1957	$10
39901	Without My Love/Just Dreaming	1952	$15

DECCA

Number	Title	Yr	NM
31883	Ballad from Vietnam/That's All for Now	1965	$6
31934	Into Each Life Some Rain Must Fall/He Who Hesitates Is Lost	1966	$6

DIAMOND

Number	Title	Yr	NM
251	Dear World/One Person	1968	$5

UNITED ARTISTS

Number	Title	Yr	NM
50260	Soft Is the Sparrow/Waking Up Son	1968	$5

7-Inch Extended Plays

COLUMBIA

Number	Title	Yr	NM
B-13311	*I Love You Truly/Meet Me Tonight in Dreamland/The Sweetest Story Ever Told/I Wonder Who's Kissing Her Now	1960	$8
B-12831	*In a Shanty in Old Shanty Town/Smiles/Beer Barrel Polka/Hinky Dinky Parlez-Vous - She'll Be Coming 'Round the Mountain	1959	$8
B-12051	*Joy to the World/We Three Kings of Orient Are/Hark! The Herald Angels Sing/It Came Upon a Midnight Clear	1958	$8
B-13891	*Polly Wolly Doodle-Wait for the Wagon-The Old Gray Mare/Juanita-Sweet Genevieve/Drink to Me Only with Thine Eyes-Vive L'Amour/Drunk Last Night	1960	$8
B-11601	*That Old Gang of Mine/Down by the Old Mill Stream/You Are My Sunshine/By the Light of the Silvery Moon	1958	$8
B-12051 [PS]	Christmas Sing Along with Mitch, Vol. 1	1958	$8
B-12052 [PS]	Christmas Sing Along with Mitch, Vol. 2	1958	$8
B-12053 [PS]	Christmas Sing Along with Mitch, Vol. 3	1958	$8
B-11602	(contents unknown)	1958	$8
B-11603	(contents unknown)	1958	$8
B-12432	(contents unknown)	1958	$8
B-12433	(contents unknown)	1958	$8
B-12053	(contents unknown)	1958	$8
B-13892	(contents unknown)	1960	$8
B-13893	(contents unknown)	1960	$8
B-13312	(contents unknown)	1960	$8
B-13313	(contents unknown)	1960	$8
B-13162	(contents unknown)	1960	$8
B-13163	(contents unknown)	1960	$8
B-13891 [PS]	Fireside Sing Along with Mitch, Vol. 1	1960	$8
B-13892 [PS]	Fireside Sing Along with Mitch, Vol. 2	1960	$8
B-13893 [PS]	Fireside Sing Along with Mitch, Vol. 3	1960	$8
B-13161 [PS]	Folk Songs Sing Along with Mitch, Vol. I	1960	$8
B-13162 [PS]	Folk Songs Sing Along with Mitch, Vol. II	1960	$8
B-13163 [PS]	Folk Songs Sing Along with Mitch, Vol. III	1960	$8
B-12431 [PS]	More Sing Along with Mitch, Vol. 1	1958	$8
B-12432 [PS]	More Sing Along with Mitch, Vol. 2	1958	$8
B-12433 [PS]	More Sing Along with Mitch, Vol. 3	1958	$8
B-13161	On Top of Old Smokey/Medley: Camptown Races-Oh, Susanna//Down in the Valley/Blue Tail Fly	1960	$8
B-13311 [PS]	Party Sing Along with Mitch, Volume 1	1960	$8
B-13312 [PS]	Party Sing Along with Mitch, Volume 2	1960	$8
B-13313 [PS]	Party Sing Along with Mitch, Volume 3	1960	$8
B-12431	Pretty Baby-Be My Little Baby Bumble Bee/Moonlight and Roses//Sweet Adeline-Let Me Call You Sweetheart/The Whiffenpoof Song	1958	$8
B-11601 [PS]	Sing Along with Mitch, Vol. 1	1958	$8
B-11602 [PS]	Sing Along with Mitch, Vol. 2	1958	$8
B-11603 [PS]	Sing Along with Mitch, Vol. 3	1958	$8
C7791 [PS]	Singin' Up a Blizzard	1966	$8

— *Free with a 6-pack of Fresca (sleeve is designed to slip over the neck of a bottle)*

Number	Title	Yr	NM
B-12831 [PS]	Still More! Sing Along with Mitch	1959	$8
C7791	The Blizzard Song/Frosty The Snow Man//Let It Snow/Sleigh Ride	1966	$6
B-12052	What Child Is This?/Silent Night, Holy Night//Deck the Halls with Boughs of Holly/THe First Noel	1958	$8

MILLER, MRS.

AMARET

Number	Title	Yr	NM
114	I've Gotta Be Me/Renaissance of Smut	1970	$8

CAPITOL

Number	Title	Yr	NM
5640	Downtown/A Lover's Concerto	1966	$12

MILLER, NED

CAPITOL

Number	Title	Yr	NM
4652	Dark Moon/Go On Back, You Fool	1961	$15
2074	Endless/Only a Fool	1968	$6
5502	Fall of the King/Down the Street	1965	$8
5742	Lorraine/Teardrop Lane	1966	$8

Number	Title	Yr	NM
5568	Lovin' Pains/If the World Turned Into Ashes	1965	$8
4607	My Heart Waits at the Door/Cold Gray Bars	1961	$15
5868	The Hobo/Echo of the Pines	1967	$8
5431	Whistle Walkin'/Two Voices, Two Shadows, Two Faces	1965	$8

DOT

Number	Title	Yr	NM
15601	From a Jack to a King/Parade of Broken Hearts	1957	$50
15651	Turn Back/Lights in the Street	1957	$20

FABOR

Number	Title	Yr	NM
121	Another Fool Like Me/Magic Moon	1963	$10
125	Big Love/Sunday Morning Tears	1964	$12
137	Do What You Do Well/Dusty Guitar	1964	$8
114	From a Jack to a King/Parade of Broken Hearts	1962	$15
128	Invisible Tears/Old Restless Ocean	1964	$10
116	One Among the Many/Man Behind the Gun	1963	$10
139	What I Know/Lights in the Street	1965	$8

JACKPOT

Number	Title	Yr	NM
48020	Girl from the Second World/Ring the Bell for Johnny	1960	$15

— *With Jan Howard*

RADIO

Number	Title	Yr	NM
105	Gypsy/With Enough Love	1958	$30

REPUBLIC

Number	Title	Yr	NM
1404	Autumn Winds/My Last Go-Round	1969	$5
1416	Back to Oklahoma/I Hang My Head and Cry	1970	$5
1410	Breakin'/Just Walkin' in the Rain	1970	$5
1411	The Lover's Song/Cold Gray Bars	1970	$5

MILLER, ROGER

20TH CENTURY

Number	Title	Yr	NM
2421	The Hat/Pleasing the Crowd	1979	$4

BUENA VISTA

Number	Title	Yr	NM
493	Whistle Stop/Not in Nottingham	1973	$5
493 [PS]	Whistle Stop/Not in Nottingham	1973	$5

COLUMBIA

Number	Title	Yr	NM
45948	I Believe in the Sunrise/Shannon's Song	1973	$5
10107	I Love a Rodeo/Lovin' You Is Always on My Mind	1975	$5
02681	Old Friends/When a House Is Not a Home	1982	$4

— *Roger Miller/Willie Nelson/Ray Price*

Number	Title	Yr	NM
45873	Open Up Your Heart/Qua La Linta	1973	$5
10052	Our Love/Yester Waltz	1974	$5
46000	Whistle Stop/The 4th of July	1974	$5

DECCA

Number	Title	Yr	NM
30953	Sweet Ramona/Jason Fleming	1959	$20
30838	Wrong Kind of Girl/A Man Like Me	1959	$20

ELEKTRA

Number	Title	Yr	NM
47192	Everyone Gets Crazy Now and Then/Aladam Bama	1981	$4

MCA

Number	Title	Yr	NM
52855	Some Hearts Get All the Breaks/Arkansas	1986	$3

MERCURY

Number	Title	Yr	NM
73354	Hoppy's Gone/I Jumped from Uncle Harvey's Plane	1972	$5
73230	Loving Her Was Easier (Than Anything I'll Ever Do Again)/Que La Linta	1971	$5
71212	Poor Little John/My Fellow	1957	$30
73102	South/Don't We All Have the Right	1970	$5
73190	Tomorrow Night in Baltimore/A Million Years or So	1971	$5
73268	We Found It in Each Other's Arms/Sunny Side of My Life	1972	$5

MUSICOR

Number	Title	Yr	NM
1102	Can't Stop Loving You/You're Forgetting Me	1965	$10

RCA VICTOR

Number	Title	Yr	NM
47-7958	Burma Shave/Fair Swiss Maiden	1961	$20
47-7776	Footprints in the Snow/You Don't Want My Love	1960	$20
47-8651	If You Want Me To/Hey Little Star	1965	$10
47-8175	Lock, Stock and Teardrops/I Know Who It Is	1963	$15
47-8028	Sorry, Willie/Hitch-Hiker	1962	$15
47-8091	Trouble on the Turnpike/Hey Little Star	1962	$15

Number	Title	Yr	NM
❏ 47-7878	When Two Worlds Collide/Every Which-A-Way	1961	$20

SMASH

Number	Title	Yr	NM
❏ 1926	Chug-a-Lug/Reincarnation	1964	$10
❏ 1881	Dang Me/Got Two Again	1964	$12
❏ 1881 [PS]	Dang Me/Got Two Again	1964	$20

— Red sleeve

❏ 1881 [PS]	Dang Me/Got Two Again	1964	$30

— Yellow sleeve

❏ 1947	Do-Wacka-Do/Love Is Not for Me	1964	$12
❏ 1947 [PS]	Do-Wacka-Do/Love Is Not for Me	1964	$20
❏ 1983	Engine, Engine #9/The Last Word in Lonesome Is Me	1965	$8
❏ 2010	England Swings/Good Old Days	1965	$8
❏ 2066	Heartbreak Hotel/Less and Less	1966	$8
❏ 2024	Husbands and Wives/I've Been a Long Time Leavin'	1966	$8
❏ 2148	Little Green Apples/Our Little Love	1968	$8
❏ 2148 [PS]	Little Green Apples/Our Little Love	1968	$15
❏ 2230	Me and Bobby McGee/I'm Gonna Teach My Heart to Bend (Instead of Break)	1969	$6
❏ 2055	My Uncle Used to Love Me But She Died/You're My Kingdom	1966	$8
❏ 2130	Old Toy Trains/Silent Night	1967	$10
❏ 2130 [PS]	Old Toy Trains/Silent Night	1967	$15
❏ 1994	One Dyin' and a-Buryin'/It Happened Just That Way	1965	$8
❏ 1994 [PS]	One Dyin' and a-Buryin'/It Happened Just That Way	1965	$20
❏ 2121	The Ballad of Waterhole #3 (Code of the West)/Rainbow Valley	1967	$8
❏ 2121 [PS]	The Ballad of Waterhole #3 (Code of the West)/Rainbow Valley	1967	$20
❏ 2258	The Tom Green County Fair/I Know Who It Is	1970	$6
❏ 2081	Walkin' in the Sunshine/Home	1967	$8
❏ 2183	What I'd Give (To Be the Wind)/Toliver	1968	$8
❏ 2246	Where Have All the Average People Gone/Boeing Boeing 707	1969	$6

STARDAY

❏ 356	Can't Stop Loving You/You're Forgetting Me	1958	$30
❏ 718	Playboy/Poor Little John	1965	$10

WINDSONG

❏ CB-11072	Baby Me Baby/Dark Side of the Moon	1977	$4
❏ CB-11166	Oklahoma Woman/There's Nobody Like You	1977	$4

7-Inch Extended Plays

SMASH

❏ SRS-702-C [PS]	Dang Me	1964	$15

— This is the title on the cover

❏ SRS-702-C	Dang Me/I Ain't Comin' Home Tonight/If You Want Me To//Chug-a-Lug/The Moon Is High/Squares Make the World Go Round	1964	$15

— Jukebox issue; small hole, plays at 33 1/3 rpm; label has title "Roger and Out (Dang Me)

❏ SRS-706-C [PS]	Golden Hits	1965	$15
❏ SRS-705-C	Love Is Not for Me/You Can't Roller Skate in a Buffalo Herd/Do-Wacka-Do//There I Go Dreamin'/Ain't That Fine/King of the Road	1965	$15

— Jukebox issue; small hole, plays at 33 1/3 rpm

❏ SRS-705-C [PS]	The Return of Roger Miller	1965	$15

MILLER SISTERS, THE

ACME

Number	Title	Yr	NM
❏ 111	Let's Start Anew/The Flip Skip	1957	$60
❏ 721	Let's Start Anew/The Flip Skip	1958	$50

EMBER

❏ 1004	Guess Who/How Am I to Know	1956	$40

FLIP

❏ 504	Someday You Will Pay/I Knew You Would	1955	$200

GLODIS

❏ 1003	Pop Your Finger/You Got to Reap What You Sow	1961	$20

GMC

❏ 10006	I'm Telling It Like It Is/Until You Come Home I'll Walk Alone	1967	$10

HERALD

❏ 455	Hippity Ha/Until You're Mine	1955	$60
❏ 527	Hippity Ha/Until You're Mine	1958	$30

HULL

Number	Title	Yr	NM
❏ 752	I Cried All Night/Hully Gully Reel	1962	$30
❏ 718	Please Don't Leave/Do You Wanna Go	1956	$50

MILLER

❏ 1140	Oh Lover/Remember That	1960	$30
❏ 1143	Please Mr. D.J./(B-side unknown)	1960	$30
❏ 1141	Pony Dance/Give Me Some Old Fashioned Love	1960	$30

ONYX

❏ 507	Sugar Candy/My Own	1957	$60

RAYNA

❏ 5001	I Miss You So/Dance Little Sister	1962	$20
❏ 5004	Oh Why/Walk On	1962	$20

RIVERSIDE

❏ 4535	Dance Close/Tell Him	1962	$30

ROULETTE

❏ 4491	Baby Your Baby/Silly Girl	1963	$15

STARDUST

❏ 3001	Feel Good/Cooncha	1964	$10

SUN

❏ 255	Finders Keepers/Ten Cats Down	1956	$60
❏ 504	Someday You Will Pay/I Knew You Would	1955	$200
❏ 230	There's No Right Way to Do Me Wrong/You Can Tell Me	1956	$60

YORKTOWN

❏ 75	Looking Over My Life/Si Senor	1965	$10

MILLER, STEVE, BAND

CAPITOL

Number	Title	Yr	NM
❏ B-5126 [PS]	Abracadabra	1982	$4

— Same sleeve has been found with record of either B-side

❏ B-5126	Abracadabra/Baby Wanna Dance	1982	$3
❏ B-5126	Abracadabra/Give It Up	1982	$4
❏ B-5442	Bongo Bongo/Get On Home	1985	$3
❏ B-5442 [PS]	Bongo Bongo/Get On Home	1985	$3
❏ B-5223	Buffalo's Serenade/Living in the U.S.A.	1983	$3
❏ A-5086	Circle of Love/(Instrumental)	1982	$3
❏ B-5162	Cool Magic/Young Girl's Heart	1982	$3
❏ B-5162 [PS]	Cool Magic/Young Girl's Heart	1982	$4
❏ 2638	Don't Let Nobody Turn You Around/Little Girl	1969	$8
❏ 3344	Fandango/Love's Riddle	1972	$6
❏ 4372	Fly Like an Eagle/Lovin' Cup	1976	$4
❏ B-5194	Give It Up/Heart Like a Wheel	1982	$3
❏ 2945	Going to Mexico/Steve Miller's Midnight Tango	1970	$6
❏ 2878	Going to the Country/Never Kill Another Man	1970	$6
❏ A-5068	Heart Like a Wheel/True Fine Love	1981	$3
❏ A-5068 [PS]	Heart Like a Wheel/True Fine Love	1981	$3
❏ B-5476	Italian X-Rays/Who Do You Love	1985	$3
❏ B-5704	I Wanna Be Loved/I Wanna Be Loved	1987	$3
❏ B-5704 [PS]	I Wanna Be Loved/I Wanna Be Loved	1987	$3
❏ B-5646	I Want to Make the World Turn Around/Slinky	1986	$3
❏ B-5646 [PS]	I Want to Make the World Turn Around/Slinky	1986	$3
❏ 3884	Living in the U.S.A./Kow Kow Calqulator	1974	$5
❏ 2287	Living in the U.S.A./Quicksilver Girl	1968	$15
❏ 2520	My Dark Hour/Song for Our Ancestors	1969	$8
❏ B-5407	Shangri-La/Circle of Love	1984	$3
❏ B-5407 [PS]	Shangri-La/Circle of Love	1984	$3
❏ 4496	Swingtown/Winter Time	1977	$4
❏ 4260	Take the Money and Run/Sweet Maree	1976	$4

MILLER, STEVE

HIT

Number	Title	Yr	NM
❏ 313	Everlasting Love/In and Out of Love	1967	$8

— B-side by Jenny and the Jewels

❏ 330	This Guy's in Love with You/The Good, the Bad, and the Ugly	1968	$8

— B-side by the New Society Group

MILLETT, LOU

COLUMBIA

Number	Title	Yr	NM
❏ 4-21086	Bayou Pigeon/Get a Grip on Your Heart	1953	$30
❏ 4-21143	God Only Knows/Memories from Your Cedar Chest	1953	$30

Number	Title	Yr	NM
❏ 4-21225	That's How I Need You/Since the Devil Moved In	1954	$125
❏ 4-21029	Worried, Lonesome and Blue/Your Own Heart You Must Mend	1952	$30

MILLINDER, LUCKY

KING

Number	Title	Yr	NM
❏ 4571	Backslider's Ball/Please Be Careful	1952	$125
❏ 4449	Chew Tobacco Rag/Georgia Rose	1951	$70
❏ 4803	Goody Good Love/I'm Here, Love	1955	$40
❏ 5240	Heavy Sugar/Honeydripper	1959	$15
❏ 4453	I'm Waiting Just for You/Bongo Boogie	1951	$70
❏ 4792	It's a Sad, Sad Feeling/Ow	1955	$100

— With the Admirals

❏ 4557	Lord Knows I Tried/Heavy Sugar	1952	$125
❏ 4476	The Grape Vine/No One Else Could Be	1951	$70
❏ 4545	When I Have You My Love/Please Be Careful	1952	$125

RCA VICTOR

❏ 47-3005	Awful Natural/In the Middle of the Night	1949	$60
❏ 50-0054	D Natural Blues/Little Girl, Don't Cry	1949	$70

— Gray label, orange vinyl

❏ 47-3128	I'll Never Be Free/Journey's End	1949	$60
❏ 50-0088	Let It Be/Sweet Slumber	1950	$60
❏ 47-2961	Tomorrow/I Ain't Got Nothin' to Lose	1949	$60

WARWICK

❏ 582	Big Fat Mama/Slide My Trombone	1960	$15

MILLS BROTHERS, THE

DECCA

Number	Title	Yr	NM
❏ 9-29115	A Carnival in Venice/Go In and Out the Window	1954	$15
❏ 25516	Across the Alley from the Alamo/Don't Be a Baby, Baby	1961	$8
❏ 9-29781	All the Way 'Round the World/I've Changed My Mind a Thousand Times	1956	$10
❏ 9-27400	Around the World/You Don't Have to Drop a Heart to Break It	1951	$20
❏ 9-27184	A Star for Everyone/I'm Afraid to Love You	1950	$30
❏ 9-27889	Be My Life's Companion/Love Lies	1951	$20
❏ 9-27236	Daddy's Little Boy/I Still Love You	1950	$30
❏ 9-29564	Daddy's Little Girl/Daddy's Little Boy	1955	$15
❏ 9-24872	Daddy's Little Girl/If I Live to Be a Hundred	1950	$30
❏ 9-30024	Don't Get Caught (Short on Love)/That's Right	1956	$12
❏ 9-29853	Dream of You/In a Mellow Tone	1956	$12
❏ 9-33 [PS]	Famous Barber Shop Ballads, Volume One	1950	$20

— Box for 24761, 24762 and 24763

❏ 9-27267	Funny Feelin'/I Don't Mind Being Alone	1950	$30
❏ 9-28021	High and Dry/You're Not Worth My Tears	1952	$20
❏ 9-29185	How Blue/Why Do I Keep Lovin' You	1954	$15
❏ 9-29754	I Believe in Santa Claus/You Don't Have to Be a Santa Claus	1955	$15
❏ 9-24756	If I Had My Way/Sweet Genevieve	1950	$30
❏ 9-29019	I Had to Call You Up to Say I'm Sorry/You Didn't Want Me When You Had Me	1954	$15
❏ 9-29977	I'm the Guy/Ninety-Eight Cents	1956	$10
❏ 9-30224	In De Banana Tree/Knocked-Out Nightingale	1957	$10
❏ 9-27762	I Ran All the Way Home/Get Her Off My Hands	1951	$20
❏ 9-25046	Lazy River/Cielito Lindo	1950	$30
❏ 9-28458	Lazy River/Wish Me Good Luck, Amigo	1952	$20
❏ 9-27683	Lord Ups an' Downs/A Cottage with a Prayer	1951	$30
❏ 9-27615	Love Me/Who Knows Love	1951	$20
❏ 9-24763	Meet Me Tonight in Dreamland/Can't You Hear Me Callin', Caroline	1950	$20

— The above three comprise "Album 9-33

❏ 9-27579	Mister and Mississippi/Wonderful, Wasn't It	1951	$20
❏ 9-24762	My Gal Sal/Just a Dream of You, Dear	1950	$20
❏ 9-29496	Opus One/There You Are	1955	$15
❏ 9-27157	Paper Doll/I'll Be Around	1950	$30

— Reissue of 78 from 1943; black label with lines on either side of "Decca

Number	Title	Yr	NM
❏ 9-27157	Paper Doll/I'll Be Around	1955	$15

— Black label with star under "Decca

❏ 27157	Paper Doll/I'll Be Around	1960	$8

— Black label with color bar

❏ 9-29382	Paper Valentine/The Urge	1954	$15
❏ 9-27447	Please Don't Talk About Me When I'm Gone/You Know You Belong to Someone Else	1951	$20

— With Tommy Dorsey

❏ 9-28180	Pretty As a Picture/When You Come Back to Me	1952	$20
❏ 9-28736	Pretty Butterfly/Don't Let Me Dream	1953	$15
❏ 9-28670	Say Si Si/I'm With You	1953	$15
❏ 9-29511	Smack Dab in the Middle/Kiss Me and Kill Me with Love	1955	$15
❏ 9-24694	Someday/On a Chinese Honeymoon	1950	$30
❏ 9-28459	Someone Loved Someone/A Shoulder to Weep On	1952	$20
❏ 9-29897	Standing on the Corner/King Porter Stomp	1956	$10
❏ 9-29686	Suddenly There's a Valley/Gum Drop	1955	$15
❏ 9-29621	That's All I Ask of You/My Muchacha (Little Girl)	1955	$15
❏ 9-30136	That's All I Need/Tell Me More	1956	$12
❏ 30546	The Barbershop Quartet/You Only Told Me Half	1958	$12
❏ 9-28384	The Glow-Worm/After All	1952	$20
❏ 9-28586	Twice As Much/I Want Someone to Care For	1953	$15
❏ 30430	Two Minute Tango/Change for a Penny	1957	$10
❏ 9-28818	Who Put the Devil in Evelyn's Eyes/Beware	1953	$15

DOT

❏ 17235	A Guy on the Go/What Have I Done for Her Lately	1969	$6
❏ 17041	Cab Driver/Fortuosity	1967	$6
❏ 17198	Dream/Jimtown Road	1969	$6
❏ 15695	Get a Job!/I Found a Million Dollar Baby	1958	$20
❏ 16091	Highways Are Happy Ways/I Got You	1960	$8
❏ 16360	I Found the Only Girl for Me/Queen of the Senior Prom	1961	$8
❏ 17285	I'll Never Forgive Myself/Up to Maggie Jones	1969	$6
❏ 16258	I'll Take Care of Your Cares/Ballerina	1961	$8
❏ 16049	I Miss You So/Oh Ma Ma	1960	$8
❏ 17321	It Ain't No Big Thing/Help Yourself to Some Tomorrow	1969	$6
❏ 15950	Lullaby in Ragtime/Te Quiero	1959	$10
❏ 15827	Me and My Shadow/Music, Maestro, Please	1958	$10
❏ 17096	My Shy Violet/Flower Road	1968	$6
❏ 16037	Paper Doll/Smack Dab in the Middle	1960	$8
❏ 16972	Smack Dab in the Middle/Honeysuckle Rose Blues Bossa Nova	1967	$6
❏ 17162	The Ol' Race Track/But for Love	1968	$6

PARAMOUNT

❏ 0147	Come Summer/Sally Sunshine	1972	$5
❏ 0095	Happy Songs of Love/I'm Sorry I Answered the Phone	1971	$5
❏ 0117	L-O-V-E/Strollin'	1971	$5
❏ 0046	Smile Away Every Rainy Day/Between Winston-Salem and Nashville, Tennessee	1970	$5
❏ 0181	There's No Life on the Moon/A Donut and a Dream	1972	$5
❏ 1003	Tiger Rag/On a Chinese Honeymoon	1974	$4
❏ 961	Truck Stop/He Gives Me Love	1973	$4
❏ ED2118	Basin Street Blues/This One Today-That One Tomorrow//A Carnival In Venice/I Cried Like a Baby	1954	$20
❏ ED2118 [PS]	Four Boys and a Guitar, Vol. 1	1954	$20
❏ DL 734820 [PS]	Golden Favorites, Volume II	1970	$12

— Part of "Little LP" series (#129)

❏ DL 734820	How Blue?/One Dozen Roses/You're Nobody 'Til Somebody Loves You//The Jones Boys/Someday (You'll Want Me to Love You)/She Was Five and He Was Ten	1970	$10

— Jukebox issue; small hole, plays at 33 1/3 rpm

MILLS, GARRY

IMPERIAL

❏ 5674	Look for a Star -- Part 1/Look for a Star -- Part 2	1960	$20

LONDON

❏ 9504	I'll Step Down/Treasure Island	1962	$20

TOP RANK

❏ 2071	Top Teen Baby/Don't Forget	1960	$20

UNITED ARTISTS

❏ 0099	Look for a Star/Look for a Star	1973	$5

— Silver Spotlight Series" reissue; B-side by Gary Miles

MILLS, HAYLEY

BUENA VISTA

❏ 408	Castaway/Sweet River	1962	$10
❏ 408 [PS]	Castaway/Sweet River	1962	$30
❏ 420	Flitterin'/Beautiful Beulah	1963	$10

— With Eddie Hodges

❏ 420 [PS]	Flitterin'/Beautiful Beulah	1963	$30
❏ 409	Let's Climb/Enjoy It	1962	$12

— With Maurice Chevalier

❏ 409 [PS]	Let's Climb/Enjoy It	1962	$30
❏ 385	Let's Get Together/Cobbler, Cobbler	1961	$15
❏ 385 [PS]	Let's Get Together/Cobbler, Cobbler	1961	$30
❏ 401	Side by Side/Ching Ching and a Ring Ding Ding	1962	$10
❏ 401 [PS]	Side by Side/Ching Ching and a Ring Ding Ding	1962	$30

MAINSTREAM

❏ 656	Gypsy Girl/Younger Than Seventeen	1966	$8

MILSAP, RONNIE

BOBLO

❏ 524	Make Love Sweet/(B-side unknown)	1977	$5

CHIPS

❏ 2889	Loving You Is a Natural Thing/So Hung Up on Sylvia	1970	$8

FESTIVAL

❏ 5002	Wishing You Were Here/Your Tears Leave Me Cold	1977	$5

PACEMAKER

❏ 245	Wishing You Were Here/A Loving Background	1967	$8

RCA

❏ PB-12194	Am I Losing You/He'll Have to Go	1981	$4
❏ PB-13216	Any Day Now/It's Just a Room	1982	$4
❏ GB-13785	Any Day Now/Stranger in My House	1984	$3

— Gold Standard Series

❏ 9027-7-R	A Woman in Love/Starting Today	1989	$3
❏ GB-11994	Back on My Mind Again/Nobody Likes Sad Songs	1980	$4

— Gold Standard Series

❏ PB-11421	Back on My Mind Again/Santa Barbara	1978	$4
❏ 8389-7-R	Button Off My Shirt/One Night	1988	$3
❏ 5351-7-R	Christmas Medley: Carol of the Bells/O Come, O Come Emmanuel/Silent Night/Joy to the World//I'll Be Home for Christmas	1987	$3
❏ PB-12006	Cowboys and Clowns/Misery Loves Company	1980	$4
❏ PB-12006 [PS]	Cowboys and Clowns/Misery Loves Company	1980	$5
❏ 8746-7-R	Don't You Ever Get Tired (Of Hurtin' Me)/I Never Expected to See You	1988	$3
❏ PB-13564	Don't You Know How Much I Love You/Feelings Change	1983	$4
❏ GB-13784	Don't You Know How Much I Love You/Show Her	1984	$3

— Gold Standard Series

❏ PB-14286	Happy Happy Birthday Baby/I'll Take Care of You	1986	$3
❏ PB-13286	He Got You/I Love New Orleans Music	1982	$4
❏ 8868-7-R	Houston Solution/If You Don't Want Me To	1989	$3
❏ 5033-7-R	How Do I Turn You On/Don't Take It Tonight	1986	$3
❏ 9071-7-R	I'll Be Home for Christmas/We're Here to Love	1989	$3
❏ GB-10931	(I'm a) Stand By My Woman Man/What Goes On When the Sun Goes Down	1977	$4

— Gold Standard Series

❏ PB-14365	In Love/Old Fashioned Girl Like You	1986	$3
❏ PB-11695	In No Time at All/Get It Up	1979	$4
❏ PB-13362	Inside/Carolina Dreams	1982	$4
❏ PB-13665	It's Christmas/We're Here to Love	1983	$4
❏ PB-10976	It Was Almost Like a Song/It Don't Hurt to Dream	1977	$4
❏ GB-11496	It Was Almost Like a Song/Only One Love in My Life	1979	$4

— Gold Standard Series

❏ PB-12342	I Wouldn't Have Missed It For the World/It Happens Every Time (I Think of You)	1981	$4
❏ PB-10843	Let My Love Be Your Pillow/Busy Makin' Plans	1976	$4

Number	Title	Yr	NM
❏ PB-11333	Let My Love Be Your Pillow/Busy Makin' Plans	1978	$4
❏ PB-11369	Let's Take the Long Way Around the World/Not Trying to Forget	1978	$4
❏ JH-11369 [DJ]	Let's Take the Long Way Around the World (same on both sides)	1978	$15

— Promo only on yellow vinyl

❏ PB-14135	Lost in the Fifties Tonight (In the Still of the Night)/I Might Have Said	1985	$4
❏ PB-14135 [PS]	Lost in the Fifties Tonight (In the Still of the Night)/I Might Have Said	1985	$4
❏ GB-14349	Lost in the Fifties Tonight (In the Still of the Night)/She Keeps the Home Fires Burning	1986	$3

— Gold Standard Series

❏ 5209-7-R	Make No Mistake, She's Mine/You're My Love	1987	$3

— With Kenny Rogers

❏ 5209-7-R [PS]	Make No Mistake, She's Mine/You're My Love	1987	$4
❏ PB-11952	My Heart/Silent Night (After the Fight)	1980	$4
❏ GB-12315	My Heart/Silent Night (After the Fight)	1981	$3

— Gold Standard Series

❏ 6896-7-R	Old Folks/Earthquake	1988	$3

— A-side with Mike Reid

❏ 6896-7-R [PS]	Old Folks/Earthquake	1988	$5

— A-side with Mike Reid

❏ PB-11270	Only One Live in My Life/Back on My Mind Again	1978	$4
❏ 5049-7-R	Only One Night of the Year/It's Just Not Christmas (If I Can't Spend It With You)	1986	$3
❏ PB-14034	She Keeps the Home Fires Burning/Is It Over	1985	$3
❏ JK-14034 [DJ]	She Keeps the Home Fires Burning (same on both sides)	1985	$10

— Promo only on green vinyl

❏ JD-13869 [DJ]	She Loves My Car/(Instrumental)	1984	$8
❏ PB-13847	She Loves My Car/Prisoner of the Highway	1984	$4
❏ PB-13658	Show Her/Watch Out for the Other Guy	1983	$4
❏ PB-12084	Smoky Mountain Rain/Crystal Fallin' Rain	1980	$4
❏ 5169-7-R	Snap Your Fingers/This Time Last Year	1987	$3
❏ PB-13805	Still Losing You/I'll Take Care of You	1984	$4
❏ PB-13470	Stranger in My House/Is It Over	1983	$4
❏ 9120-7-R	Stranger Things Have Happened/Southern Roots	1989	$3
❏ PB-12264	(There's) No Gettin' Over Me/I Live My Whole Life at Night	1981	$4
❏ GB-13491	(There's) No Gettin' Over Me/I Wouldn't Have Missed It for the World	1983	$3

— Gold Standard Series

❏ GB-11987	What a Difference You've Made in My Life/Let's Take the Long Way Around the World	1980	$4

— Gold Standard Series

❏ PB-11146	What a Difference You've Made in My Life/Selfish	1977	$4
❏ 5259-7-R	Where Do the Nights Go/If You Don't Want Me To	1987	$3
❏ PB-11909	Why Don't You Spend the Night/Heads I Go, Hearts I Stay	1980	$4
❏ GB-12314	Why Don't You Spend the Night/Smoky Mountain Rain	1981	$3

— Gold Standard Series

RCA VICTOR

❏ GB-10672	Daydreams About Night Things/Just in Case	1976	$4

— Gold Standard Series

❏ PB-10335	Daydreams About Night Things/Play Born to Lose	1975	$5
❏ PB-10112	(I'd Be) A Legend in My Time/The Biggest Lie	1974	$5
❏ PB-10112 [PS]	(I'd Be) A Legend in My Time/The Biggest Lie	1974	$8
❏ GB-10502	(I'd Be) A Legend in My Time/The Biggest Lie	1975	$4

— Gold Standard Series

❏ 74-0969	I Hate You/(All Together Now) Let's Fall Apart	1973	$6
❏ PB-10724	(I'm a) Stand By My Woman Man/Lovers, Friends and Strangers	1976	$5
❏ APBO-0313	Please Don't Tell Me How the Story Ends/Streets of Gold	1974	$6
❏ GB-10500	Please Don't Tell Me How the Story Ends/Streets of Gold	1975	$4

— Gold Standard Series

Number	Title	Yr	NM
❏ APBO-0237	Pure Love/Love the Second Time Around	1974	$6
❏ GB-10503	Pure Love/Love the Second Time Around	1975	$4
— Gold Standard Series			
❏ GB-10167	That Girl Who Waits on Tables/I Hate You	1975	$4
— Gold Standard Series			
❏ APBO-0097	That Girl Who Waits on Tables/You're Drivin' Me Out of My Mind	1973	$6
❏ PB-10228	Too Late to Worry, Too Blue to Cry/Country Cookin'	1975	$5
❏ GB-10501	Too Late to Worry, Too Blue to Cry/Country Cookin'	1975	$4
— Gold Standard Series			
❏ PB-10593	What Goes On When the Sun Goes Down/Love Takes a Long Time to Die	1976	$5
SCEPTER			
❏ 12127	A Thousand Miles from Nowhere/When It Comes to My Baby	1966	$15
❏ 12228	Do What You Gotta Do/Mr. Mailman	1968	$8
❏ 12206	House of the Rising Sun/I Can't Tell a Lie	1967	$10
❏ 12109	Let's Go Get Stoned/Never Had It So Good	1965	$15
❏ 12145	The End of the World/I Saw Pity in the Face of a Friend	1966	$15
❏ 12272	What's Your Game/Love Will Never Pass Us By	1970	$8
❏ 12161	When the Boys Talk About the Girls/Ain't No Sole in These Old Shoes	1966	$15
❏ 12161	When the Boys Talk About the Girls/Another Branch from the Old Branch	1966	$15
WARNER BROS.			
❏ 8218	Crying/Why	1976	$4
❏ 7629	Magic Me Again/Me and You, You and Me	1972	$6
❏ 8127	She Even Woke Me Up to Say Goodbye/Loving You's a Natural Thing	1975	$4
❏ 7540	Sunday Rain/Why	1971	$6
❏ 5405	Total Disaster/It Went to Your Head	1963	$20

MILTON, ROY

CENCO

Number	Title	Yr	NM
❏ 114	I Can't Go On/Thelma Lou	1960	$20
DOOTONE			
❏ 398	Baby I'm Gone/Cry Some Baby	1956	$60
❏ 363	I Can't Go On/Fools Are Getting Scarcer	1955	$60
❏ 377	I Want to Go Home/I Never Would Have Made It	1955	$60
KING			
❏ 5035	Succotash/I'm Grateful	1957	$30
SPECIALTY			
❏ 480	Baby, You Don't Know	1953	$60
— Original pressings have a white line through the black bars on either side of the center hole			
❏ 480	Baby, You Don't Know	1961	$30
— Reissues have solid black bars on either side of the center hole			
❏ 446	Believe Me Baby/Blue Turning Gray All Over	1952	$125
❏ 414	Best Wishes/Short, Sweet and Snappy	1951	$70
❏ 464	Early in the Morning/Let Me Give You All My Love	1953	$60
— Black vinyl			
❏ 464	Early in the Morning/Let Me Give You All My Love	1953	$200
— Red vinyl			
❏ 436	Flying Saucer/As Time Goes By	1952	$100
❏ 538	How Can I Live Without You?/Tell It Like It Is	1954	$50
❏ 403	It's Later Than You Think/Numbers Blues	1951	$70
❏ 526	It's Too Late/Gonna Leave You Baby	1954	$50
❏ 489	Make Me Know It/A Bird in Hand	1954	$50
❏ 455	Some Day/Don't You Remember Baby	1953	$60
❏ 429	So Tired/Thelma Lou	1952	$100
❏ 407	T-Town Twist/I Have News for You	1951	$70
❏ 545	What Can I Do?/Baby, Don't Do That to Me	1955	$40
WARWICK			
❏ 549	Early in the Morning/Bless Your Heart	1960	$30

MIMMS, GARNET, AND THE ENCHANTERS

ARISTA

Number	Title	Yr	NM
❏ 0239	What It Is (Part 1)/What It Is (Part 2)	1977	$4

GSF

Number	Title	Yr	NM
❏ 6874	Another Place/Stop and Check Yourself	1972	$6
❏ 6887	I'll Keep On Loving/Somebody, Someplace	1972	$6
UNITED ARTISTS			
❏ 796	A Little Bit of Soap/I'll Make It Up to You	1964	$30
❏ 658	Baby Don't You Weep/For Your Precious Love	1963	$30
❏ 658 [PS]	Baby Don't You Weep/For Your Precious Love	1963	$40
❏ 629	Cry Baby/Don't Change Your Heart	1963	$20
❏ 0109	Cry Baby/For Your Precious Love	1973	$4
— Silver Spotlight Series" reissue			
❏ 887	Everytime/That Goes to Show You	1965	$20
❏ 951	Looking for You/More Than a Miracle	1965	$200
❏ 715	One Girl/A Quiet Place	1964	$30
❏ 773	One Woman Man/Look Away	1964	$40
❏ 995	Prove It to Me/I'll Take Good Care of You	1966	$50
❏ 848	So Close/It Was Easier to Hurt Her	1965	$40
❏ 694	Tell Me Baby/Anytime You Want Me	1964	$20
❏ 868	Welcome Home/The Adventures of Moll Flanders	1965	$10
VEEP			
❏ 1252	All About Love/The Truth Hurts	1967	$40
❏ 1234	My Baby/Keep On Smilin'	1966	$50
❏ 1232	Thinkin'/It's Been Such a Long Time Comin'	1966	$30
VERVE			
❏ 10624	Can You Top This/We Can Find That Love	1968	$40
❏ 10650	Sad Song/Get It While You Can	1970	$40
❏ 10596	Stop and Think It Over/I Can Hear My Baby Crying	1968	$40
❏ 10642	Take Me/Happy Landing	1969	$20

MINEO, SAL

DECCA

Number	Title	Yr	NM
❏ 31692	Why Don't You Love Me/A Girl Across the Way	1964	$15
EPIC			
❏ 9287	Baby Face/Souvenirs of Summertime	1958	$30
❏ 9345	I'll Never Be Myself Again/The Words That I Whisper	1959	$30
❏ 9227	Lasting Love/You Shouldn't Do That	1957	$30
❏ 9227 [PS]	Lasting Love/You Shouldn't Do That	1957	$40
❏ 9260	Little Pigeon/Cuttin' In	1958	$30
❏ 9246	Party Time/The Words That I Whisper	1957	$30
❏ 9246 [PS]	Party Time/The Words That I Whisper	1957	$40
❏ 9271	Seven Steps to Love/A Couple of Crazy Kids	1958	$30
❏ 9216	Start Movin' (In My Direction)/Love Affair	1957	$30
❏ 9216 [PS]	Start Movin' (In My Direction)/Love Affair	1957	$50
FONTANA			
❏ 1504	Save the Last Dance for Me/Take Me Back	1965	$15

7-Inch Extended Plays

EPIC

Number	Title	Yr	NM
❏ EG-7194	Baby Face/Too Young// The Words That I Whisper/Blue-Eyed Baby	1958	$50
❏ EG-7187	(contents unknown)	1958	$60
❏ EG-7195	(contents unknown)	1958	$50
❏ EG-7194 [PS]	Sal	1958	$50
❏ EG-7195 [PS]	Sal	1958	$50
❏ EG-7187 [PS]	Sal Mineo	1958	$60
❏ EG-7204 [PS]	Souvenirs of Summertime	1959	$60
❏ EG-7204	Souvenirs of Summertime/Seven Steps to Love//A Couple of Crazy Kids/Secret Doorway	1959	$60

MINIATURE MEN, THE

DOLTON

Number	Title	Yr	NM
❏ 57	Baby Elephant Walk/Bool-Ya-Base	1962	$15
❏ 52	Miniature Blues/Soupy's Theme	1962	$15

MINISTRY

ARISTA

Number	Title	Yr	NM
❏ 9068	I Wanted to Tell Her/A Walk in the Park	1983	$6

MINK DEVILLE

ATLANTIC

Number	Title	Yr	NM
❏ 89750	Each Word's a Beat of My Heart/River of Tears	1983	$3
❏ 89470	I Must Be Dreaming/In the Heart of the City	1985	$3
❏ 89443	Italian Shoes	1986	$3
❏ 3880	Maybe Tomorrow	1981	$4
❏ 89682	Pick Up the Pieces/Demasiado Corazon	1983	$3
CAPITOL			
❏ 4607	Guardian Angel/Easy Slider	1978	$4
❏ 4938	Lipstick Traces/Just to Walk That Little Girl Home	1980	$4
❏ 4510	Little Girl/Cadillac Walk	1977	$4
❏ 4461	Mixed-Up, Shook-Up Girl/Spanish Stroll	1977	$4

MINNELLI, LIZA

A&M

Number	Title	Yr	NM
❏ 1173	Come Saturday Morning/Wherefore and Why	1970	$6
❏ 1244	(I Wonder Where My) Easy Rider's Gone/The Man I Love	1971	$6
❏ 915	Married/You Better Sit Down Kids//Waiting for My Friends	1968	$6
CADENCE			
❏ 1436	What Do You Think I Am/You Are For Living	1963	$15
CAPITOL			
❏ 5103	Day Dreaming/His Woman	1964	$12
❏ 5473	Did I Hurt Your Feelings/Imprevu	1965	$8
❏ 5761	I Who Have Nothing/Middle of the Street	1966	$8
❏ 4994	One Summer Love/How Much Do I Love You	1963	$10
COLUMBIA			
❏ 10178	All That Jazz/My Own Best Friend	1975	$4
❏ 45846	Don't Let Me Be Lonely Tonight/Mr. Emery Won't Be Home	1973	$5
❏ 45995	Harbour/More Than I Like You	1974	$5
❏ 45746	The Singer/Mr. Emery Won't Be Home	1972	$5
EPIC			
❏ 73011	Losing My Mind/Tonight Is Forever	1989	$5
UNITED ARTISTS			
❏ XW1014	Theme from "New York, New York"/Hazy	1977	$5

MINNIE PEARL

KING

Number	Title	Yr	NM
❏ 978	On Top of Old Smoky/In the Shadow of the Pine	1951	$50
RCA VICTOR			
❏ 47-5699	How to Catch a Man/And That's Good Enough for Me	1954	$30
❏ 47-5812	I Wonder Where That Man of Mine Has Went/Never Been Kissed	1954	$30
❏ 47-5605	Man (Uh-Huh)/I Wish They Would	1954	$30
❏ 47-5982	Me/Hurtin' Season	1955	$30
STARDAY			
❏ 754	Giddyup Go -- Answer/Road Runner	1966	$10
❏ 764	What Is an American/Live Some While You're Here	1966	$10

MINOR THREAT

DISCHORD

Number	Title	Yr	NM
❏ 15	Salad Days/Stumped/Good Guys	1985	$5
❏ 15 [PS]	Salad Days/Stumped/Good Guys	1985	$5

7-Inch Extended Plays

Number	Title	Yr	NM
❏ 3	Filler/I Don't Wanna Hear It/Seeing Red/Straight Edge//Small Man, Big Mouth/Screaming at a Wall/Bottled Violence/Minor Threat	1981	$40
— First pressing of 1000: Yellow label			
❏ 3	Filler/I Don't Wanna Hear It/Seeing Red/Straight Edge//Small Man, Big Mouth/Screaming at a Wall/Bottled Violence/Minor Threat	1981	$40
— Second pressing of 1000: Blue label			
❏ 3	Filler/I Don't Wanna Hear It/Seeing Red/Straight Edge//Small Man, Big Mouth/Screaming at a Wall/Bottled Violence/Minor Threat	1981	$35
Third and fourth pressings: Silver label			
❏ 5	In My Eyes/Out of Step//Guilty of Being White/Steppin' Stone	1981	$40
— First pressing of 1000: Red vinyl			

Number	Title	Yr	NM
❏ 5 [PS]	In My Eyes/Out of Step// Guilty of Being White/ Steppin' Stone	1981	$50

—First 125 issued with photocopied cover

| ❏ 5 | In My Eyes/Out of Step// Guilty of Being White/ Steppin' Stone | 1981 | $40 |

—Black vinyl, yellow label

| ❏ 5 [PS] | In My Eyes/Out of Step// Guilty of Being White/ Steppin' Stone | 1981 | $40 |

—Printed, as opposed to photocopied, sleeve

| ❏ 5 | In My Eyes/Out of Step// Guilty of Being White/ Steppin' Stone | 1981 | $35 |

—Black vinyl, blue label

| ❏ 5 [PS] | In My Eyes/Out of Step// Guilty of Being White/ Steppin' Stone | 1981 | $35 |

—Heavy cover stock, as opposed to thinner paper stock

| ❏ 3 [PS] | Minor Threat | 1981 | $50 |

—First pressing of 1000: Red cover

| ❏ 3 [PS] | Minor Threat | 1981 | $50 |

—Second pressing of 1000: Yellow cover

| ❏ 3 [PS] | Minor Threat | 1981 | $50 |

—Third pressing of 1000: Green cover

| ❏ 3 [PS] | Minor Threat | 1981 | $35 |

—Fourth pressing of 2000: Blue cover

MINT JULEPS, THE

HERALD

| ❏ 481 | Bells of Love/Vip-a-Dip | 1956 | $125 |

—With script logo inside flag

| ❏ 481 | Bells of Love/Vip-a-Dip | 1956 | $30 |

—With block logo inside flag

MINUTE MEN, THE

ARGO

| ❏ 5469 | Please Keep the Beatles in England/My Love Is Gone | 1964 | $20 |

MINUTEMEN

Also see FIREHOSE. Featuring Mike Watt.

SST

| ❏ PSST E-58 | Courage/What Is It?/Stories | 1985 | $8 |
| ❏ PSST E-58 [PS] | Courage/What Is It?/Stories | 1985 | $15 |

—Rubberstamped sleeve

7-Inch Extended Plays

REFLEX

| ❏ 0L | Tour-Spiel | 1984 | $13 |
| ❏ 0L [PS] | Tour-Spiel | 1984 | $13 |

SST

| ❏ 002 | Paranoid Time | 1980 | $6 |
| ❏ 002 [PS] | Paranoid Time | 1980 | $6 |

THERMIDOR

| ❏ 8 | Bean-Spill | 1981 | $8 |

—Came in generic Thermidor sleeve (add 25%)

MIRACLES, THE

CHESS

| ❏ 1734 | Bad Girl/I Love Your Baby | 1959 | $70 |

—Blue label with vertical Chess logo (original)

| ❏ 1734 | Bad Girl/I Love Your Baby | 1963 | $30 |

—Black label

| ❏ 1734 | Bad Girl/I Love Your Baby | 1966 | $30 |

—Blue label with "Chess" at top

| ❏ 1768 | I Need a Change/ All I Want (Is You) | 1960 | $50 |

COLUMBIA

❏ 3-10706	Mean Machine/The Magic of Your Eyes (Laura's Eyes)	1978	$5
❏ 3-10464	Spy for Brotherhood/ The Bird Must Fly Away	1976	$5
❏ 3-10517	Women (Make the World Go 'Round)/I Can Touch the Sky	1977	$5

END

| ❏ 1016 | Got a Job/My Mama Done Told Me | 1958 | $70 |
| ❏ 1029 | Money/I Cry | 1958 | $60 |

—Mostly gray-white label, no mention of Roulette Records

| ❏ 1029 | Money/I Cry | 1958 | $50 |

—Multicolor label with "A Division of Roulette Records Inc." on label

| ❏ 1084 | Money/I Cry | 1961 | $30 |

MOTOWN

| ❏ G1/G 2 | Bad Girl/I Love Your Baby | 1959 | $2500 |

—VG 1250; VG+ 1875

| ❏ TLX-2207 | Bad Girl/I Love Your Baby | 1959 | $2500 |

—VG 1250; VG+ 1875

Number	Title	Yr	NM
STANDARD GROOVE			
❏ 13090 [DJ]	I Care About Detroit	1968	$200

—With Tamla globe logo on label

| ❏ 13090 [DJ] | I Care About Detroit | 1968 | $200 |

—With no Tamla logo on label

TAMLA

❏ 54184	Abraham, Martin, and John/Much Better Off	1969	$8
❏ 54036	Ain't It Baby/The Only One I Love	1961	$200
❏ 54078	A Love She Can Count On/I Can Take a Hint	1963	$30
❏ 54178	Baby, Baby Don't Cry/Your Mother's Only Daughter	1968	$8
❏ 54109	Come On Do the Jerk/ Baby Don't You Go	1964	$20
❏ 54140	Come 'Round Here -- I'm the One You Need/Save Me	1966	$10
❏ 54140 [PS]	Come 'Round Here -- I'm the One You Need/Save Me	1966	$125
❏ 54206	Crazy About the La La La/ Oh Baby Baby I Love You	1971	$6
❏ 54248	Do It Baby/I Wanna Be with You	1974	$5
❏ 54256	Don't Cha Love It/Up Again	1974	$5
❏ 54237	Don't Let It End (Til You Let It Begin)/Wigs and Lashes	1973	$5

—Starting here, name reverts to The Miracles

❏ 54048	Everybody's Gotta Pay Some Dues/I Can't Believe	1961	$60
❏ 54048 [PS]	Everybody's Gotta Pay Some Dues/I Can't Believe	1961	$200
❏ 54240	Give Me Just Another Day/I Wanna Be with You	1973	$5
❏ 54127	Going to A-Go-Go/ Choosey Beggar	1965	$20
❏ 54127 [PS]	Going to A-Go-Go/ Choosey Beggar	1965	$125
❏ 54183	Here I Go Again/ Doggone Right	1969	$8
❏ 54225	I Can't Stand to See You Cry/With Your Love Came	1972	$6
❏ 54205	I Don't Blame You at All/That Girl	1971	$6
❏ 54162	If You Can Want/When the Words from Your Heart Get Caught Up in Your Throat	1968	$8

—Tamla" in box on label

| ❏ 54162 | If You Can Want/When the Words from Your Heart Get Caught Up in Your Throat | 1968 | $20 |

—Tamla" in globe on label

❏ 54089	I Gotta Dance to Keep from Crying/Such Is Love, Such Is Life	1963	$20
❏ 54098	I Like It Like That/You're So Fine and Sweet	1964	$20
❏ 54098 [PS]	I Like It Like That/You're So Fine and Sweet	1964	$120
❏ 54059	I'll Try Something New/You Never Miss a Good Thing	1962	$30
❏ 54059 [PS]	I'll Try Something New/You Never Miss a Good Thing	1962	$120
❏ 54159	I Second That Emotion/ You Must Be Love	1967	$8
❏ 54262	Love Machine (Part 1)/ Love Machine (Part 2)	1975	$5
❏ 54083	Mickey's Monkey/Whatever Makes You Happy	1963	$30
❏ 54044	Mighty Good Lovin'/ Broken Hearted	1961	$60
❏ 54044 [PS]	Mighty Good Lovin'/ Broken Hearted	1961	$200
❏ 54152	More Love/Swept for You Baby	1967	$8
❏ 54123	My Girl Has Gone/Since You Won My Heart	1965	$20
❏ 54113	Ooo Baby Baby/ All That's Good	1965	$20
❏ 54189	Point It Out/Darling Dear	1969	$8
❏ 54211	Satisfaction/Flower Girl	1971	$6
❏ 54034	Shop Around/ Who's Lovin' You	1960	$180

—Original take, withdrawn shortly after release; "H55518A" in trail-off wax

| ❏ 54034 | Shop Around/ Who's Lovin' You | 1960 | $40 |

—Hit take; "L-1" in trail-off wax; horizontal lines label

| ❏ 54034 | Shop Around/ Who's Lovin' You | 1960 | $50 |

—Hit take; "ZTSC-67018" on label and in trail-off wax of Side 1 and "ZTSC-67019" on label and in trail-off wax of Side 2; horizontal lines label

❏ 54172	Special Occasion/ Give Her Up	1968	$8
❏ 54102	That's What Love Is Made Of/Would I Love You	1964	$20
❏ EX-009 [DJ]	The Christmas Song/ Christmas Everyday	1963	$200
❏ 54028	The Feeling Is So Fine/ You Can Depend On Me	1960	$500

—With alternate take of B-side; matrix number followed by "A" in trail-off wax

| ❏ 54028 | The Feeling Is So Fine/ You Can Depend On Me | 1960 | $400 |

Number	Title	Yr	NM
❏ 54145	The Love I Saw in You Was Just a Mirage/ Come Spy with Me	1967	$8

—Starting here, through Tamla 54225, as "Smokey Robinson and the Miracles

❏ 54199	The Tears of a Clown/ Promise Me	1970	$6
❏ 54118	The Tracks of My Tears/A Fork in the Road	1965	$20
❏ 54028	Way Over There/ Depend On Me	1960	$70

—With overdubbed strings on A-side

| ❏ 54028 | Way Over There/ Depend On Me | 1960 | $200 |

—No strings on A-side recording

❏ 54069	Way Over There/If Your Mother Only Knew	1962	$30
❏ 54220	We've Come Too Far to End It Now/When Sundown Comes	1972	$6
❏ 54053	What's So Good About Good-By/I've Been Good to You	1962	$40
❏ 54053 [PS]	What's So Good About Good-By/I've Been Good to You	1962	$120
❏ 54134	Whole Lot of Shakin' in My Heart (Since I Met You)/Oh Be My Lover	1966	$10
❏ 54194	Who's Gonna Take the Blame/I Gotta Thing For You	1970	$8

TOPPS/MOTOWN

| ❏ 11 | Shop Around | 1967 | $80 |

—Cardboard record

7-Inch Extended Plays

TAMLA

| ❏ TM-60267 [PS] | Going to a Go-Go | 1966 | $60 |
| ❏ TM-60267 | The Tracks of My Tears/ Going To a Go-Go/Ooo Baby Baby//My Girl Has Gone/Choosey Beggar/ In Case You Need Love | 1966 | $60 |

—Jukebox issue; small hole, plays at 33 1/3 rpm

MIRACLES, THE (2)

BATON

| ❏ 210 | A Lover's Chant/Come Home with Me | 1955 | $200 |

MISFITS, THE

The famous punk band. Also see GLENN DANZIG; SAMHAIN.

BLANK

| ❏ A101 | Cough Cool/She | 1977 | $200 |

—500 copies were pressed

| ❏ A101 [PS] | Cough Cool/She | 1977 | $200 |

PLAN 9

| ❏ PL1013 [PS] | 3 Hits from Hell: London Dungeon/Horror Hotel/ Ghouls Night Out | 1981 | $60 |
| ❏ PL1001 | Bullet/We Are 138/Attitude/ Hollywood Babylon | 1978 | $125 |

—Black vinyl

| ❏ PL1001 | Bullet/We Are 138/Attitude/ Hollywood Babylon | 1978 | $125 |

—Red vinyl

| ❏ PL1001 [PS] | Bullet/We Are 138/Attitude/ Hollywood Babylon | 1978 | $125 |

—First edition with gatefold and lyric sheet

| ❏ PL1001 [PS] | Bullet/We Are 138/Attitude/ Hollywood Babylon | 1978 | $125 |

—Second edition with new back cover "Better Dead on Red

| ❏ PL1017 | Halloween I/Halloween II | 1981 | $60 |
| ❏ PL1017 [PS] | Halloween I/Halloween II | 1981 | $70 |

—Orange sleeve with lyric sheet

| ❏ PL1017 [PS] | Halloween I/Halloween II | 1981 | $400 |

—Black and white test sleeve; approximately 10 were made

| ❏ PL1009 | Horror Business/Teenagers from Mars/Children in Heat | 1979 | $70 |

—Yellow vinyl

| ❏ PL1009 [B] | Horror Business/Teenagers from Mars/Children in Heat | 1979 | $15000 |

—25 (!!) on black vinyl, no picture sleeve

| ❏ PL1009 [PS] | Horror Business/Teenagers from Mars/Children in Heat | 1979 | $125 |

—With insert (deduct 40 percent if missing)

| ❏ PL1009 [PS] | Horror Business/Teenagers from Mars/Children in Heat | 1979 | $300 |

—Withdrawn sleeve; these have a back cover with a group photo and were never used, but some have hit the collector's market

| ❏ PL1013 | London Dungeon/Horror Hotel/Ghouls Night Out | 1981 | $60 |

—3,000 with gray label

| ❏ PL1013 | London Dungeon/Horror Hotel/Ghouls Night Out | 1981 | $60 |

—7,000 with orange label

Number	Title	Yr	NM
❏ PL1013	London Dungeon/Horror Hotel/Ghouls Night Out	1981	$60
— Second pressing: 400 on black vinyl, smal center hole			
❏ PL1013	London Dungeon/Horror Hotel/Ghouls Night Out	1981	$60
— Second pressing: 400 on white vinyl			

7-Inch Extended Plays

Number	Title	Yr	NM
❏ PL1019	20 Eyes/Night Of The Living Dead/Astro Zombies/Horror Business//London Dungeon/All Hell Breaks Loose/We Are 138	1982	$60
— Yellow label			
❏ PL1019	20 Eyes/Night Of The Living Dead/Astro Zombies/Horror Business//London Dungeon/All Hell Breaks Loose/We Are 138	1982	$60
— Orange label			
❏ PL1019 [PS]	Evilive	1982	$80
— Numbered sleeve with insert			
❏ PL1019 [PS]	Evilive	1982	$50
— Unnumbered sleeve			
❏ PL1019 [PS]	Evilive	1982	$800
— 33 sets of 3 each with individual sleeves by the three band members, available through the Fiend Club (fan club)			

MISFITS, THE (2)
BLACK & WHITE

Number	Title	Yr	NM
❏ (no #)	Pretty Boy/Laughing Lover/Mommi I'm a Misfit/When I Was Young	1982	$60
❏ (no #) [PS]	Pretty Boy/Laughing Lover/Mommi I'm a Misfit/When I Was Young	1982	$60
— Most picture sleeves have a sticker with the band's new name, The Tragics			

MISFITS, THE (U)
ARIES

Number	Title	Yr	NM
❏ 3	Midnight Star/I Don't Know	1961	$200

HUSH

| ❏ 105 | Give Me Your Heart/My Mother-in-Law | 1960 | $400 |

IMPERIAL

| ❏ 66054 | This Little Piggy (I'm a Hog for You)/Lost Love | 1964 | $30 |

SOUND STAGE 7

| ❏ 2538 | It's Up to You/Skiing Time | 1965 | $30 |

MR. CLEAN
ORIGINAL SOUND

| ❏ 40 | Mr. Clean/Jessie Lee | 1964 | $200 |
| — Written, produced and performed on by Frank Zappa | | | |

MR. EPP AND THE CALCULATIONS
7-Inch Extended Plays
PRAVDA

❏ 711	Of Course I'm Happy	1982	$35
— With Mark Arm, pre-Green River and Mudhoney			
❏ 711 [PS]	Of Course I'm Happy	1982	$35

MR. LUCKY AND THE GAMBLERS
DOT

| ❏ 16930 | Take a Look at Me/I Told You (Once Before) | 1966 | $30 |

PANORAMA

| ❏ 52 | Alice Designs/You Don't Need Me | 1967 | $20 |
| ❏ 37 | Take a Look at Me/I Told You (Once Before) | 1966 | $30 |

MR. WIGGLES
PARKWAY

| ❏ 104 | Fat Back Part 1/Part 2 | 1966 | $60 |

MITCHELL, BILLY
ATLANTIC

❏ 974	Ghost Train/Bald Headed Woman	1952	$200
— With Joe Morris			
❏ 950	If I Had Known/Verna Lee	1951	$200
❏ 954	Let's Have a Ball Tonight/Someday You'll Be Sorry	1952	$200
❏ 933	My Love, My Desire/Pack Up All Your Bags	1951	$300

CALLA

| ❏ 165 | Oh Happy Day/The Chokin' Kind | 1969 | $8 |
| ❏ 167 | Too Busy Thinking 'Bout My Baby/Crystal Blue Persuasion | 1969 | $8 |

Number	Title	Yr	NM
IMPERIAL			
❏ 5520	Satellite Be-Bop/Pickin' on the Wrong Chicken	1958	$30
JUBILEE			
❏ 5400	Short Skirts/You Know I Do	1961	$20
UNITED ARTISTS			
❏ 235	Call to Me (I'll Be Here)/Where	1960	$20
WARWICK			
❏ 501	It Doesn't Matter to Me/Stop a Little While	1959	$20

MITCHELL, BOBBY
IMPERIAL

Number	Title	Yr	NM
❏ 5282	Angel Child/School Boy Blues	1954	$120
❏ 5270	Baby's Gone/Sister Lucy	1954	$120
❏ 5392	Goin' Round in Circles/I Try So Hard	1956	$60
❏ 5558	Hearts of Fire/You're Going to Be Sorry	1959	$50
❏ 5346	I Cried/I'm in Love	1955	$70
❏ 5923	I Don't Want to Be a Wheel No More/I Got to Call That Number	1963	$15
❏ 5511	I Love to Hold You/64 Hours	1958	$50
❏ 5309	I'm a Young Man/She Couldn't Be Found	1954	$120
❏ 5236	I'm Cryin'/Rack 'Em Back	1953	$200
❏ 5475	I'm Gonna Be a Wheel Someday/You Better Go Home	1957	$60
❏ 5326	I Wish I Knew/Nothing Sweet As You	1955	$100
❏ 5882	My Southern Bell/When First We Met	1962	$15
❏ 5250	One Friday Morning/Four-Eleven-Forty-Four	1953	$200
❏ 5295	The Wedding Bells Are Ringing/Meant for Me	1954	$120
❏ 5378	Try Rock and Roll/No, No, No	1956	$60
RON			
❏ 342	Mama Don't Allow/There's Only One of You	1961	$15
❏ 337	Sand Me Your Picture/You're Doing Me Wrong	1961	$15

MITCHELL, CHAD, TRIO
COLPIX

Number	Title	Yr	NM
❏ 157	Devil Road/Paddy West	1960	$15
❏ 144	I Do Adore Her/The Gallows Tree	1960	$15
❏ 133	Sally Ann/Vaya Con Dios	1959	$15
❏ 610	Six Men/I'm Going Home	1961	$12
— B-side by Eugene Lamarr			
❏ 154	The Ballad of Herbie Spear/Pretty Saro	1960	$15
KAPP			
❏ 481	Alberta/Come Along Home	1962	$10
❏ 510	Blowing in the Wind/Adios, Mi Corazon	1963	$10
❏ 518	Green Grow the Lilacs/Leave Me If You Want To	1963	$10
❏ 439	Lizzie Borden/Super Skier	1961	$15
❏ 439 [PS]	Lizzie Borden/Super Skier	1961	$30
MAY			
❏ 116	The Ballad of Herbie Spear/Sally Ann	1962	$12
MERCURY			
❏ 72197	The Marvelous Toy/Bonny Streets of Fyve-10	1963	$10
❏ 72197 [PS]	The Marvelous Toy/Bonny Streets of Fyve-10	1963	$20
❏ 72234	The Tarriers Song/Tell Old Bill	1964	$8
❏ 72234 [PS]	The Tarriers Song/Tell Old Bill	1964	$20
❏ 72257	What Did You Learn in School Today/Barry's Boys	1964	$8

MITCHELL, GUY
CHALICE

Number	Title	Yr	NM
❏ 711	My Angel/Bit of Love	1963	$40
❏ 711	My Angel/Mr. Hobo	1963	$40
❏ 712	Take Your Time/(B-side unknown)	1963	$40
COLUMBIA			
❏ 40987	A Cure for the Blues/Call Rosie on the Phone	1957	$10
❏ 41359	Alias Jesse James/Pride o' Dixie	1959	$8
❏ 6-760(?)	Angels Cry/You're Not in My Arms Tonight	1950	$30
❏ 1-760(?)	Angels Cry/You're Not in My Arms Tonight	1950	$40
— Microgroove 33 1/3 rpm 7-inch single			
❏ 39512	Belle, Belle, My Liberty Belle/Sweetheart of Yesterday	1951	$20
❏ 39879	('Cause I Love You) That's-a Why/Train of Love	1952	$20
— With Mindy Carson			

Number	Title	Yr	NM
❏ 40035	Cloud Lucky Seven/Chicka-Boom	1953	$15
❏ 41033	C'mon Let's Go/The Unbeliever	1957	$10
❏ 42143	Divorce/I'll Just Pretend	1961	$8
❏ 39886	Don't Rob Another Man's Castle/Why Should I Go Home	1952	$20
❏ 39822	Feet Up (Pat Him on the Po-Po)/Jenny Kissed Me	1952	$20
❏ 40724	Finders Keepers/I'd Like to Say a Few Words About Texas	1956	$10
❏ 41970	Follow Me/Your Goodnight Kiss	1961	$8
❏ 1-640(?)	Giddy Up/Where in the World	1950	$40
— Microgroove 33 1/3 rpm 7-inch single			
❏ 40700	Give Me a Carriage with Eight White Horses/I Used to Hate Ya	1956	$10
❏ 40128	Got a Hole in My Sweater/The Cuff of My Shirt	1953	$15
❏ 41311	Guilty Heart/Half As Much	1958	$8
❏ 41177	Hangin' Around/Honey Brown Eyes	1958	$8
❏ 40008	Hannah Lee/Look at That Girl	1953	$15
❏ 41476	Heartaches By the Number/Two	1959	$12
❏ 41476 [PS]	Heartaches By the Number/Two	1959	$20
❏ 41146	Hey, Madame/Till We're Engaged	1958	$8
❏ 40389	I Met the Cutest Little Eyeful (At the Eiffel Tower)/Gee But You Gotta Come Home	1954	$15
❏ 39950	I Want You for a Sunbeam/So Am I	1953	$15
❏ 41215	Let It Shine, Let It Shine/Butterfly Doll	1958	$8
❏ 40531	Let Us Be Sweethearts Again/Too Late	1955	$12
❏ 41397	Loosen Up, Lucy/I'm Gonna Leave You Now	1959	$8
❏ 1-680(?)	Me and My Imagination/To Me You're a Song	1950	$40
— Microgroove 33 1/3 rpm 7-inch single			
❏ 6-918	My Heart Cries for You/The Roving Kind	1950	$30
❏ 1-918	My Heart Cries for You/The Roving Kind	1950	$40
— Microgroove 33 1/3 rpm 7-inch single			
❏ 39067	My Heart Cries for You/The Roving Kind	1950	$20
❏ 41274	My Heart Cries for You/Under the Rainbow	1958	$8
❏ 41725	My Shoes Keep Walking Back to You/Silver Moon Upon the Golden Sands	1960	$8
❏ 39415	My Truly, Truly Fair/Who Knows Love	1951	$20
❏ 41075	One Way Street/The Lord Made a Peanut	1957	$10
❏ 40507	Otto's Gotta Go (Otto Drives Me Crazy)/Man Overboard	1955	$15
❏ 39663	Pittsburgh, Pennsylvania/Doll with a Sawdust Heart	1952	$20
❏ 39909	She Wears Red Feathers/Pretty Little Blackeyed Susie	1952	$20
❏ 40769	Singing the Blues/Crazy with Love	1956	$10
❏ 40769 [PS]	Singing the Blues/Crazy with Love	1956	$30
❏ 40077	Sippin' Soda/Strollin' Blues	1953	$15
❏ 42231	Soft Rain/Big Big Chance	1961	$8
❏ 42231 [PS]	Soft Rain/Big Big Chance	1961	$15
❏ 40672	Solo/Green Grows the Grass	1956	$12
❏ 39190	Sparrow in the Tree Top/Christopher Columbus	1951	$20
❏ 3-39190	Sparrow in the Tree Top/Christopher Columbus	1951	$40
— Microgroove 33 1/3 rpm 7-inch single			
❏ 41853	Sunshine Guitar/Ridin' Around in the Rain	1960	$8
❏ 41853 [PS]	Sunshine Guitar/Ridin' Around in the Rain	1960	$15
❏ 40940	Sweet Stuff/In the Middle of a Dark, Dark Night	1957	$10
❏ 41653	Symphony of Spring/Cry Hurtin' Heart	1960	$8
❏ 40175	Tear Down the Mountains/A Dime and a Dollar	1954	$15
❏ 39753	The Day of Jubilo/You'll Never Be Mine	1952	$30
❏ 40240	There Once Was a Man/My Heaven on Earth	1954	$15
❏ 39595	There's Always Room at Our House/I Can't Help It (If I'm Still in Love with You)	1951	$20
❏ 39992	There's Nothing As Sweet As My Baby/Tell Us Where the Good Times Are	1953	$15
— With Mindy Carson			
❏ 41576	The Same Old Me/Build Up My Gallows High	1960	$8
❏ 40278	What Am I Doin' in Kansas City/You've Ruined Me	1954	$15
❏ 40560	When Binky Blows/Belonging	1955	$10
❏ 39639	Wimmin/We Don't Live in a Castle	1952	$30

Number	Title	Yr	NM
❏ 39962	Wise Man or Fool/Walkin' and Wanderin'	1953	$15

JOY

Number	Title	Yr	NM
❏ 270	Go Tiger Go/If You Ever Go Away	1962	$8
❏ 273	Have I Told You Lately That I Love You/Blue Violet	1963	$8

REPRISE

Number	Title	Yr	NM
❏ 0477	Best Thing That Ever Happened to Me/If I Had My Life to Live Over	1966	$6

STARDAY

Number	Title	Yr	NM
❏ 828	Alabam/Irene Good-By	1968	$6
❏ 846	Frisco Line/Singing the Blues	1968	$6
❏ 866	Get It Over/Just Wish You'd Change Your Mind	1969	$6
❏ 878	Smokey Blue Eyes/Heartaches by the Number	1969	$6
❏ 819	Traveling Shoes/Every Night Is a Lifetime	1967	$6

7-Inch Extended Plays

COLUMBIA

Number	Title	Yr	NM
❏ B-2502	*My Heart Cries for You/The Roving Kind/My Truly, Truly Fair/Pittsburgh, Pennsylvania	1957	$15
❏ B-2133	*Rock-A-Billy/Finders Keepers/Hoot Owl/A House Without Love	1957	$15
❏ B-2502 [PS]	Guy Mitchell (Hall of Fame Series)	1957	$15

MITCHELL, JONI

ASYLUM

Number	Title	Yr	NM
❏ 45221	Big Yellow Taxi/Rainy Night House	1974	$4
❏ 45377	Coyote/Blue Motel Room	1976	$4
❏ 45467	Dreamland/Jericho	1978	$4
❏ 11041	Free Man in Paris/People's Parties	1974	$5
❏ 11034	Help Me/Just Like This Train	1974	$5
❏ 45298	In France They Kiss on Main Street/Boho Dance	1976	$4
❏ 46506	The Dry Cleaner from Des Moines/God Must Be a Boogie Man	1979	$4
❏ 47038	Why Do Fools Fall in Love/Black Crow	1980	$4

GEFFEN

Number	Title	Yr	NM
❏ 28840	Good Friends/Smokin' Empty (Try Another)	1985	$4
❏ 28840 [PS]	Good Friends/Smokin' Empty (Try Another)	1985	$5
❏ 27887	My Secret Place/Lakota	1988	$4
❏ 28675	Shiny Toys/Three Great Stimulants	1986	$4

REPRISE

Number	Title	Yr	NM
❏ 1155	Big Yellow Taxi/Carey	1972	$5

—Back to Back Hits" series

Number	Title	Yr	NM
❏ 0906	Big Yellow Taxi/Woodstock	1970	$8
❏ 1154	Both Sides Now/Chelsea Morning	1972	$5

—Back to Back Hits" series

Number	Title	Yr	NM
❏ 1029	Carey/This Flight Tonight	1971	$8
❏ 1049	Case of You/California	1971	$6
❏ 0694	I Had a King/Night in the City	1968	$8

MITCHELL, LEE

PHILLIPS INT'L.

Number	Title	Yr	NM
❏ 3530	The Frog/A Little Bird Told Me	1958	$20

MITCHELL, MARLON

VENA

Number	Title	Yr	NM
❏ 100	Ice Cold Baby/Bermuda Shorts	1957	$120

MITCHELL, PRISCILLA

MERCURY

Number	Title	Yr	NM
❏ 72635	Acres of Heartaches/Look at the Laughter	1966	$10
❏ 72565	Almost Everything a Lonely Girl Needs/Sweet Talk	1966	$10
❏ 72681	He's Not for Real/Take Me Home to Your Mama	1967	$8
❏ 72499	It Comes and Goes/The Teen Years	1965	$10

MITCHELL, ROSE

IMPERIAL

Number	Title	Yr	NM
❏ 5260	Live My Life/Baby Please Don't Go	1954	$70
❏ 5243	Slipping In/I'm Searching	1953	$70

MITCHELL, STAN

GONE

Number	Title	Yr	NM
❏ 5106	Devil in Disguise/Lovin' Man	1961	$40

MITCHELL TRIO, THE

MERCURY

Number	Title	Yr	NM
❏ 72591	Dark Shadows and Empty Hallways/Stay with Me	1966	$8
❏ 72340	I Can't Help But Wonder/Stewball and Griselda	1964	$8
❏ 72340 [PS]	I Can't Help But Wonder/Stewball and Griselda	1964	$20
❏ 72518	That's the Way It's Gonna Be/Violets of Dawn	1966	$8

REPRISE

Number	Title	Yr	NM
❏ 0588	Leaving on a Jet Plane/Baby, That's Where It Is	1967	$6
❏ 0630	She Loves You/Like to Deal with the Ladies	1967	$6

MITCHELL, WILLIE

HI

Number	Title	Yr	NM
❏ 2075	20-75/Secret Home	1964	$8
❏ 2154	30-60-90/Take Five	1969	$6
❏ 2125	Au Shucks/Slippin' and Slidin'	1967	$6
❏ 2103	Bad Eye/Sugar T	1966	$6
❏ 2196	Breaking Point/Roadhouse	1971	$5
❏ 2091	Buster Browne/Woodchopper's Ball	1965	$8
❏ 2053	Drippin'/Buddy Bear	1962	$12
❏ 2058	Easy Now/Sunrise Serenade	1962	$12
❏ 2237	Last Tango in Paris/Six to Go	1973	$4
❏ 2132	Lucky/Ooh Baby, You Turn Me On	1967	$6
❏ 2112	Mercy/Sticks and Stones	1966	$6
❏ 2119	Misty/Barefootin'	1967	$6
❏ 2167	My Babe/Teenie's Dream	1969	$6
❏ 2083	Percolatin'/Check Me	1964	$8
❏ 2066	Percolatin'/Empty Rooms	1963	$10
❏ 2147	Prayer Meetin'/Run Daddy	1968	$6
❏ 2175	Six to Go/Robin's Nest	1970	$5
❏ 2140	Soul Serenade/Mercy, Mercy, Mercy	1968	$6
❏ 2097	That Driving Beat/Everything Is Gonna Be Alright	1965	$8
❏ 2044	The Crawl (Part 1)/The Crawl (Part 2)	1962	$12
❏ 2190	Too Sweet/Restless	1971	$5
❏ 2181	Wade in the Water/Tails Out	1970	$5

HOME OF THE BLUES

Number	Title	Yr	NM
❏ 123	I Like It/Willie's House Party	1961	$15
❏ 119	One Mint Julep/I've Got a Right	1961	$15
❏ 111	Thirty-Five Thirty/Yvonne	1960	$15

7-Inch Extended Plays

HI

Number	Title	Yr	NM
❏ SBG-56	20-75/My Girl/Mustang Sally//Tequila/Honky Tonk/Pin Head	1968	$10

—Jukebox issue; small hole, plays at 33 1/3 rpm

Number	Title	Yr	NM
❏ SBG-47	Bad Eye/Shadow of Your Smile/Secret Agent Man//Taste of Honey/Hot Cha/What Now My Love	1966	$10

—Jukebox issue; small hole, plays at 33 1/3 rpm

Number	Title	Yr	NM
❏ SBG-44	Everything Is Gonna Be Alright/Nick-O-Demus/The Champion Pt. 1//That Driving Beat/Fat Cat/Smiley	1966	$10

—Jukebox issue; small hole, plays at 33 1/3 rpm

Number	Title	Yr	NM
❏ SBG-65	Grazing in the Grass/Sunrise Serenade/Up-Hard//Monkey Jump/Strawberry Solo/Hideaway	1968	$10

—Jukebox issue; small hole, plays at 33 1/3 rpm

Number	Title	Yr	NM
❏ SBG-28 [PS]	Hold It!! Here's Willie Mitchell	1964	$15
❏ SBG-28	Hold It/You Can't Sit Down/The Dog//20-75/Mashed Potatoes/Last Date	1964	$15

—Jukebox issue; small hole, plays at 33 1/3 rpm

Number	Title	Yr	NM
❏ SBG-32	In the Mood/Woodchopper's Ball/Apple Jack//Ram-Bunk-Shush/Since I Met You Baby/When My Dreamboat Comes Home	1965	$10

—Jukebox issue; small hole, plays at 33 1/3 rpm

Number	Title	Yr	NM
❏ SBG-32 [PS]	It's Dance Time	1965	$12
❏ SBG-47 [PS]	It's What Happening	1966	$12
❏ SBG-72 [PS]	On Top	1969	$12
❏ SBG-65 [PS]	Solid Soul	1968	$12
❏ SBG-59 [PS]	Soul Serenade	1968	$12
❏ SBG-59	Soul Serenade/Ooh Baby, You Turn Me On/Soul Finger//Papa's Got a Brand New Bag/Sunny/Respect	1968	$10

—Jukebox issue; small hole, plays at 33 1/3 rpm

Number	Title	Yr	NM
❏ SBG-72	Take Five/Poppin'/Canadian Sunset//Louie, Louie/I Say a Little Prayer/Sunshine of Your Love	1969	$10

—Jukebox issue; small hole, plays at 33 1/3 rpm

Number	Title	Yr	NM
❏ SBG-44 [PS]	The Driving Beat	1966	$12
❏ SBG-56 [PS]	Willie Mitchell Live	1968	$12

MITCHUM, ROBERT

CAPITOL

Number	Title	Yr	NM
❏ 3741	The Ballad of Thunder Road/My Baby's Lovin' Arms	1973	$6
❏ F3986	The Ballad of Thunder Road/My Honey's Lovin' Arms	1958	$20

—Purple label with "F" prefix

Number	Title	Yr	NM
❏ F3986 [PS]	The Ballad of Thunder Road/My Honey's Lovin' Arms	1958	$30
❏ 3986	The Ballad of Thunder Road/My Honey's Lovin' Arms	1960	$12

—Purple label, Capitol logo at left, no "F" prefix

Number	Title	Yr	NM
❏ 3986	The Ballad of Thunder Road/My Honey's Lovin' Arms	1962	$8

—Orange and yellow swirl label, no "F" prefix

Number	Title	Yr	NM
❏ 3986	The Ballad of Thunder Road/My Honey's Lovin' Arms	1969	$6

—Red and orange "target" label

Number	Title	Yr	NM
❏ 3986	The Ballad of Thunder Road/My Honey's Lovin' Arms	1973	$4

—Orange label, "Capitol" at bottom

Number	Title	Yr	NM
❏ F3672	What Is This Generation Coming To/Mama Looka Boo Boo	1957	$20

COLUMBIA

Number	Title	Yr	NM
❏ 03483	The Ballad of Thunder Road/That Little Ole Wine Drinker Me	1983	$5

MIXTURES, THE (1)

LINDA

Number	Title	Yr	NM
❏ 113	Chinese Checkers/Dig These Blues	1963	$10
❏ 108	Olive Oyl/Canadian Sunset	1963	$10
❏ 115	Sen-Say-Shun/The Last Minute	1964	$10
❏ 109	Tiki/Poochum	1963	$10

MIXTURES, THE (2)

SIRE

Number	Title	Yr	NM
❏ 350	The Pushbike Song/Who Loves Ya	1971	$6

MIZZY, VIC

RCA VICTOR

Number	Title	Yr	NM
❏ 47-8477	Main Theme: The Addams Family/Main Theme: Kentucky Jones	1964	$30

MOB, THE

CAMEO

Number	Title	Yr	NM
❏ 421	Wait (Please Don't Walk Away)/Mystery Man	1966	$20

COLOSSUS

Number	Title	Yr	NM
❏ 134	Give It to Me/I'd Like to See More of You	1971	$6
❏ 134 [PS]	Give It to Me/I'd Like to See More of You	1971	$8
❏ 130	I Dig Everything About You/Love Had a Hold on Me	1970	$6
❏ 145	Money/Once a Man, Twice a Child	1971	$6

MERCURY

Number	Title	Yr	NM
❏ 72791	Disappear/I Wish You'd Leave Me Alone	1968	$8

MGM

Number	Title	Yr	NM
❏ 14406	Feel Like Dancin'/You Give Me the Strength	1972	$6

PRIVATE STOCK

Number	Title	Yr	NM
❏ 45,053	All the Dudes Are Dancing/(B-side unknown)	1975	$5
❏ 45,084	Don't Let It Get You Down/(B-side unknown)	1976	$5
❏ 45,031	Hot Music/I Can't Stop This Love Song	1975	$5
❏ 45,159	Love Connection/(B-side unknown)	1977	$5

MOBY GRAPE

Also see ALEXANDER "SKIP" SPENCE.

COLUMBIA

Number	Title	Yr	NM
❏ 44172	8:05/Mister Blues	1967	$8
❏ 44172 [PS]	8:05/Mister Blues	1967	$30
❏ 44567	Can't Be So Bad/Bitter Wind	1968	$6
❏ 44170	Changes/Fall on You	1967	$8
❏ 44170 [PS]	Changes/Fall on You	1967	$30
❏ 44174	Hey Grandma/Come in the Morning	1967	$8
❏ 44174 [PS]	Hey Grandma/Come in the Morning	1967	$30
❏ 44789	If You Can't Learn From My Mistakes/Trucking Man	1969	$6
❏ JZSP118972 [DJ]	Omaha/8:05	1967	$15

—Yellow label promo; "Rush Reserive

Number	Title	Yr	NM
❏ 44173	Omaha/Someday	1967	$8
❏ 44173 [PS]	Omaha/Someday	1967	$30
❏ 44885	Ooh Mama Ooh/It's a Beautiful Day Today	1969	$6
❏ 44171	Sitting by the Window/Indifference	1967	$8

Number	Title	Yr	NM
❏ 44171 [PS]	Sitting by the Window/Indifference	1967	$30

REPRISE

Number	Title	Yr	NM
❏ 1055	Goin' Down to Texas/About Time	1971	$5
❏ 1096	Gone Fishin'/Gypsy Wedding	1972	$5
❏ 1040	Gypsy Wedding/Apocalypse	1971	$5

MOCKINGBIRDS, THE

ABC-PARAMOUNT

Number	Title	Yr	NM
❏ 10653	That's How/I Never Should Have Kissed You	1965	$20

MODELS, THE

GEFFEN

Number	Title	Yr	NM
❏ 7-28644	Cold Fever//Preacher from the Black Lagoon/Out of Mind, Out of Sight (Live)	1986	$4
❏ 7-28644 [PS]	Cold Fever//Preacher from the Black Lagoon/Out of Mind, Out of Sight (Live)	1986	$4
❏ 7-28762	Out of Mind Out of Sight/Down in the Garden	1986	$3
❏ 7-28762 [PS]	Out of Mind Out of Sight/Down in the Garden	1986	$3

MGM

Number	Title	Yr	NM
❏ 13775	Bend Me, Shape Me/In a World of Pretty Faces	1967	$30

MODERN ENGLISH

SIRE

Number	Title	Yr	NM
❏ 7-29339	Hands Across the Sea/Reflection	1984	$5
❏ 7-29775	I Melt with You/After the Snow	1983	$6
❏ 7-28741	Ink and Paper/Love Forever	1986	$4
❏ 7-29598	Someone's Calling/Carry Me Down	1983	$5

MODERN JAZZ QUARTET, THE

ATLANTIC

Number	Title	Yr	NM
❏ 2085	England's Carol (Part 1)/England's Carol (Part 2)	1960	$30

MODERNAIRES, THE

CAPITOL

Number	Title	Yr	NM
❏ 2633	Theme from "The Mod Squad" (Alone Too Long)/I'll See Your Light	1969	$8

COLUMBIA

Number	Title	Yr	NM
❏ 1-612	Down the Lane/Rubber Knuckle Sam (Leader of the Washboard Band)	1950	$50

—*Microgroove 33 1/3 rpm 7-inch single, small hole*

Number	Title	Yr	NM
❏ 1-468(?)	Home Town Band/Olly Olly Oxen Free	1950	$50

—*Microgroove 33 1/3 rpm, 7-inch single, small hole*

Number	Title	Yr	NM
❏ 1-245(?)	Senora/Beautiful Blond from Bashful Bend	1949	$50

—*Microgroove 33 1/3 rpm 7-inch single, small hole*

Number	Title	Yr	NM
❏ 1-472(?)	The Big Movie Show in the Sky/The Yodel Blues	1950	$50

—*Microgroove 33 1/3 rpm 7-inch single, small hole*

CORAL

Number	Title	Yr	NM
❏ 9-61949	Act Your Age/As Long As I Have You	1958	$10
❏ 9-61873	A Foggy Day/Makin' Whoopee	1957	$10
❏ 9-61513	Alright, Okay, You Win/At My Front Door	1955	$15
❏ 9-61599	April in Paris/Hi Diddlee I Di	1956	$15
❏ 9-61110	A Salute to Glenn Miller (Part 1)/(Part 2)	1953	$15
❏ 9-61837	Cinderella Baby/Calypso Melody	1957	$10
❏ 9-60726	Goody Goody/Bugle Call Rag	1952	$20
❏ 9-61555	Go On with the Wedding/Ain't She Sweet	1956	$15
❏ 9-60881	Gotta Be This or That/Wild Flower	1952	$20
❏ 9-60658	I'll Always Be Following You/The Dipsy Doodle	1952	$20
❏ 9-60439	I'm Late/Alice in Wonderland	1951	$30
❏ 9-61764	I'm Ready to Love Again/Noah	1956	$15
❏ 9-61568	Let's Dance Medley (Part 1)/(Part 2)	1956	$15
❏ 9-61348	Mine, Mine, Mine/Birds and Puppies and Tropical Fish	1955	$15
❏ 9-60609	October 32nd, 1992/Stompin' at the Savoy	1952	$20
❏ 9-61037	Put Some Money in the Juke Box/Rock-a-Bye Boogie	1953	$20
❏ 9-61779	Salute to Tommy Dorsey (Part 1)/(Part 2)	1957	$10
❏ 9-61547	Santa's Little Sleigh Bells/Sleepy Little Space Cadet	1955	$20
❏ 9-60982	Say You're Mine Again/He Who Has Love	1953	$20
❏ 9-61199	That's You, That's Me, That's Love/I Know Why	1954	$15

Number	Title	Yr	NM
❏ 9-61378	Tops 'n Pops (Part 1)/(Part 2)	1955	$15
❏ 9-61490	Wake Up the Place/Milkman's Matinee	1955	$15

—*With Les Brown and His Band of Renown*

Number	Title	Yr	NM
❏ 9-60824	When My Love Comes Back to Me/Four or Five Times	1952	$20
❏ 9-61412	Wine, Women and Gold/Slue Foot	1955	$15

—*With Bob Crosby and His Bob Cats*

Number	Title	Yr	NM
❏ 9-60408	Wishing You Were Here Tonight/Lovely Is the Evening	1951	$30

MERCURY

Number	Title	Yr	NM
❏ 71529	Like Young/Don't Dream	1959	$12

UNITED ARTISTS

Number	Title	Yr	NM
❏ 422	Mr. Lucky/Bill Bailey (Won't You Please Come Home)	1962	$8

MODUGNO, DOMENICO

DECCA

Number	Title	Yr	NM
❏ 31401	Addio...Addio/Lupi E Percorelle	1962	$8
❏ 31171	Ciao Ciao Bambino/Si, Si, Si	1960	$8
❏ 30777	Coma Prima/Strada 'Nfosa	1958	$10
❏ 31359	La Novia/Se Dio Vorra	1962	$8
❏ 31071	Olympia/O Solo Mio	1960	$8
❏ 30845	Piove (Ciao, Ciao Bambino)/Farfalle	1959	$10
❏ 30747	Stay Here with Me/Io	1958	$10
❏ 30950	The Bandit/Lunga Notte	1959	$12
❏ 31718	Tu Si' 'Na Casa Grande/Tu Si O' Mare	1964	$6

JUBILEE

Number	Title	Yr	NM
❏ 5339	La Petit Reveil/Cavudduzzu	1958	$12

MGM

Number	Title	Yr	NM
❏ 13487	Dio, Come Ti Amo (English Version)/Dio, Come Ti Amo (Italian Version)	1966	$6

RCA VICTOR

Number	Title	Yr	NM
❏ 48-1022	Love Is Like the Wind/How Did You	1972	$4
❏ 47-9502	Meraviglioso (Part 1)/Meraviglioso (Part 2)	1968	$5
❏ 47-7321	Musetto/Io Mammeta E Tu	1958	$10

7-Inch Extended Plays

DECCA

Number	Title	Yr	NM
❏ ED2633	*Nel Blu Dipinto Di Blu (Volare)/Mariti in Citta/A Pizza C' 'A Pummarola/Ventu D'Estati	1958	$20

MODULATIONS, THE

BUDDAH

Number	Title	Yr	NM
❏ 418	I Can't Fight Your Love/I'm Hopelessly in Love	1974	$30
❏ 418	I Can't Fight Your Love/Your Love Has Me Locked Up	1974	$70
❏ 398	I'm Hopelessly in Love/What Good Am I	1974	$70
❏ 497	Worth Your Weight in Gold/I'll Always Love You	1975	$30

MOE, ADRIAN, AND THE SCULPTORS

COLUMBIA

Number	Title	Yr	NM
❏ 4-43445	Love Train/Shotgun	1965	$10
❏ 4-43445 [PS]	Love Train/Shotgun	1965	$20

MOGEN DAVID AND THE GRAPES OF WRATH

CHA CHA

Number	Title	Yr	NM
❏ 757	Little Girl Gone/Go Away Girl	1967	$4000

—*VG 2000; VG+ 3000*

MOJO MEN, THE

AUTUMN

Number	Title	Yr	NM
❏ 19	Dance with Me/The Loneliest Boy in Town	1965	$20
❏ 11	Mama's Little Baby/Off the Hook	1965	$20
❏ 27	She's My Baby/Fire in My Heart	1966	$20

GRT

Number	Title	Yr	NM
❏ 8	Candle to Burn/Make You at Home	1969	$10
❏ 16	Everyday Love/There Goes My Mind	1969	$12
❏ 5	Flower of Love/I Can't Let Go	1969	$10

REPRISE

Number	Title	Yr	NM
❏ 0759	Don't Be Cruel/Let It Be Him	1968	$12
❏ 0580	Me About You/When You're in Love	1967	$10
❏ 0486	She's My Baby/Do the Hanky Panky	1966	$30
❏ 0689	Should I Cry/You to Me	1968	$10
❏ 0539	Sit Down, I Think I Love You/Don't Leave Me Crying Like Before	1966	$10

Number	Title	Yr	NM
❏ 0707	Sit Down, I Think I Love You/Me About You	1968	$6

—*Back to Back Hits" series*

Number	Title	Yr	NM
❏ 0617	Whatever Happened to Happy/Make You at Home	1967	$10

TIDE

Number	Title	Yr	NM
❏ 2000	Surfin' Fat Man/Paula	1964	$50

MOJOS, THE

PARROT

Number	Title	Yr	NM
❏ 45001	Everything's Alright/Give Your Loving to Me	1964	$15
❏ 9707	Seven Daffodils/Nothin' at All	1964	$10
❏ 45002	Why Not Tonight/Don't Do It Anymore	1964	$15

MOLES, GENE

CHALLENGE

Number	Title	Yr	NM
❏ 59249	Burning Rubber/Twin Pipes	1964	$30

MOLLY HATCHET

EPIC

Number	Title	Yr	NM
❏ 50943	Beatin' the Odds/Few and Far Between	1980	$4
❏ 50822	Flirtin' with Disaster/Gunsmoke	1980	$5
❏ 50773	Gunsmoke/Jukin' City	1979	$4
❏ 50809	It's All Over Now/Good Rockin'	1979	$4
❏ 50669	The Creeper/Dreams I'll Never See	1979	$4

MONARCHS, THE (1)

MONUMENT

Number	Title	Yr	NM
❏ 03484	Look Homeward, Angel/This Old Heart	1983	$5

SOUND STAGE 7

Number	Title	Yr	NM
❏ 2530	Climb Every Mountain/Take Me Home	1964	$15
❏ 2516	Look Homeward, Angel/What Made You Change Your Mind	1964	$15
❏ 2502	This Old Heart/'Til I Hear It From You	1963	$15

MONARCHS, THE (2)

DOT

Number	Title	Yr	NM
❏ 15228	Gravy/Caravan Mambo	1954	$50

MONARCHS, THE (3)

MELBA

Number	Title	Yr	NM
❏ 101	Pretty Little Girl/In My Younger Days	1956	$100

NEIL

Number	Title	Yr	NM
❏ 103	Always Be Faithful/How Are You	1956	$120
❏ 101	Pretty Little Girl/In My Younger Days	1956	$200

MONARCHS, THE (U)

LIBAN

Number	Title	Yr	NM
❏ 1002	Love You That's Why/Coming Home	1959	$2000

WING

Number	Title	Yr	NM
❏ 90040	Angels in the Sky/Wanna Go Home	1955	$100

YUCCA

Number	Title	Yr	NM
❏ 172	Forever Lost/Cuckoo	1964	$60

ZONE

Number	Title	Yr	NM
❏ 1067	Friday Night/El Bandito	1963	$20

MONDAY BLUES

VAULT

Number	Title	Yr	NM
❏ 963	Be My Baby/Do I Love You	1970	$8

MONDAY MORNING QUARTERBACK, THE

WARNER BROS.

Number	Title	Yr	NM
❏ 7664	The Twelve Days of Christmas (The Game Plan to Beat Miami)//Santa Claus Medley: Santa Claus Is Comin' to Town/Here Comes Santa Claus	1972	$10
❏ 7664 [PS]	The Twelve Days of Christmas (The Game Plan to Beat Miami)//Santa Claus Medley: Santa Claus Is Comin' to Town/Here Comes Santa Claus	1972	$20

—*Picture sleeve is a slick pasted onto a plain white sleeve*

Number	Title	Yr	NM

MONDELLOS, THE
RHYTHM
Number	Title	Yr	NM
❏ 102	Come Back Home/100 Years from Today	1956	$200

—As "Alice Jean and the Mondellos

| ❏ 109 | Hard to Please/ Happiness Street | 1957 | $200 |
| ❏ 114 | My Heart/That's What I Call Love | 1957 | $200 |

—As "Rudy Lambert and the Mondellos

| ❏ 105 | Over the Rainbow/ Never Leave Me Alone | 1956 | $200 |

—As "Yul McClay and the Mondellos

| ❏ 128 | That Old Feeling/ Sunday Kind of Love | 1957 | $200 |

—As "Rudy Lambert and the Mondellos

| ❏ 106 | That's What I Call Love/ Daylight Saving Time | 1956 | $200 |

MONEY, EDDIE
COLUMBIA
Number	Title	Yr	NM
❏ 10663	Baby Hold On/Save a Little Room in Your Heart for Me	1978	$5
❏ 10981	Can't Keep a Good Man Down/Nightmare	1979	$5
❏ 04376	Club Michelle/Back on the Road Again	1984	$3
❏ 04376 [PS]	Club Michelle/Back on the Road Again	1984	$3
❏ 07035	Endless Nights/ Bring On the Rain	1987	$3
❏ 07035 [PS]	Endless Nights/ Bring On the Rain	1987	$3
❏ 11064	Get a Move On/Don't You Ever Say No	1979	$5
❏ 06569	I Wanna Go Back/ Broken Down Chevy	1987	$3
❏ 06569 [PS]	I Wanna Go Back/ Broken Down Chevy	1987	$3
❏ 68739	Let Me In/Forget About Love	1989	$3
❏ 11377	Let's Be Lovers Again/ Million Dollar Girl	1980	$4

—With Valerie Carter

❏ 11030	Maureen/Love the Way You Love Me	1979	$5
❏ 10900	Maybe I'm a Fool/ Life for the Taking	1979	$5
❏ 03252	Shakin'/My Friends, My Friends	1982	$3
❏ 06231	Take Me Home Tonight/ Calm Before the Storm	1986	$4

—With Ronnie Spector

| ❏ 06231 [PS] | Take Me Home Tonight/ Calm Before the Storm | 1986 | $30 |

—Sleeve is promo only (no stock sleeves are known)

| ❏ 08428 | Take Me Home Tonight/ Calm Before the Storm | 1988 | $3 |

—Reissue

❏ 04199	The Big Crash/Backtrack	1983	$3
❏ 68532	The Love in Your Eyes/ (B-side unknown)	1989	$3
❏ 02964	Think I'm in Love/ Drivin' Me Crazy	1982	$4
❏ 02964 [PS]	Think I'm in Love/ Drivin' Me Crazy	1982	$4
❏ 03867	Think I'm in Love/Shakin'	1983	$3

—Reissue

❏ 11414	Trinidad/Million Dollar Girl	1980	$4
❏ 10765	Two Tickets to Paradise/ Don't Worry	1978	$5
❏ 08060	Walk on Water/Dancing with Mr. Jitters	1988	$3
❏ 08060 [PS]	Walk on Water/Dancing with Mr. Jitters	1988	$3
❏ 07359	We Should Be Sleeping/I Can't Hold Back	1987	$3
❏ 07359 [PS]	We Should Be Sleeping/I Can't Hold Back	1987	$3

MONEY, ZOOT
EPIC
Number	Title	Yr	NM
❏ 5-10077	Big Time Operator/ Zoot's Sermon	1966	$12

MONIQUES, THE
CENTAUR
Number	Title	Yr	NM
❏ 105	I'm With You All the Way/ Rock Pretty Baby	1963	$30

MONITORS, THE (1)
SOUL
Number	Title	Yr	NM
❏ 35049	Step by Step (Hand in Hand)/Time Is Passing By	1968	$20

V.I.P.
❏ 25046	Bring Back the Love/ The Further You Look, The Less You See	1967	$30
❏ 25032	Greetings (This Is Uncle Sam)/Number One in Your Heart	1965	$50
❏ 25028	Say You/All for Someone	1965	$40

Number	Title	Yr	NM
❏ 25039	Since I Lost You Girl/ Don't Put Off Till Tomorrow What You Can Do Today	1966	$40
❏ 25049	Step by Step (Hand in Hand)/Time Is Passing By	1968	$60

MONITORS, THE (2)
ALADDIN
Number	Title	Yr	NM
❏ 3309	Tonight's the Night/ Candy Coated Kisses	1955	$125

MONITORS, THE (U)
BUDDAH
Number	Title	Yr	NM
❏ 278	Fence Around Your Heart/ Have You Seen Her	1972	$125

CIRCUS
| ❏ 219 | A Boyfriend's Prayer/Nita | 1957 | $200 |

SPECIALTY
❏ 622	Closer to Heaven/ Rock 'N' Roll Forever	1957	$200
❏ 636	Mamma Linda/Hop Scotch	1958	$70
❏ 595	Our Schooldays/I've Got a Dream	1957	$100

MONK, THELONIOUS
COLUMBIA
Number	Title	Yr	NM
❏ 42825	Bye-Ya/Hackensack	1963	$10

MONKEES, THE
Also see DOLENZ, JONES & TORK; DOLENZ, JONES, BOYCE & HART; MICKEY DOLENZ; DAVY JONES; MICHAEL NESMITH.
ARISTA
Number	Title	Yr	NM
❏ 0201	Daydream Believer/ Monkee's Theme	1976	$12
❏ 9532	Daydream Believer/ Randy Scouse Git	1986	$4
❏ 9532 [PS]	Daydream Believer/ Randy Scouse Git	1986	$4
❏ 9505	That Was Then, This Is Now/ (Theme from) The Monkees	1986	$20

—First pressings list both sides' artist as "The Monkees

| ❏ 9505 | That Was Then, This Is Now/ (Theme from) The Monkees | 1986 | $15 |

—Without "By Mickey Dolenz and Peter Tork (of the Monkees)" on sleeve

| ❏ 9505 | That Was Then, This Is Now/ (Theme from) The Monkees | 1986 | $3 |

—With A-side artist listed as " Mickey Dolenz and Peter Tork (of the Monkees)

| ❏ 9505 [PS] | That Was Then, This Is Now/ (Theme from) The Monkees | 1986 | $3 |

—With "By Mickey Dolenz and Peter Tork (of the Monkees)" on sleeve

| ❏ 66-1003 [PS] | A Little Bit Me, A Little Bit You/She Hangs Out | 1967 | $1200 |

—Though the record does not exist, this picture sleeve does. It uses the same photo that appears on the "Pleasant Valley Sunday" sleeve.

❏ 66-1004	A Little Bit Me, A Little Bit You/The Girl I Knew Somewhere	1967	$20
❏ 66-1012	Daydream Believer/ Goin' Down	1967	$25
❏ 66-1012 [PS]	Daydream Believer/ Goin' Down	1967	$50
❏ 66-1023	D.W. Washburn/It's Nice to Be with You	1968	$20
❏ 66-1023 [PS]	D.W. Washburn/It's Nice to Be with You	1968	$50
❏ 66-5005	Good Clean Fun/ Mommy and Daddy	1969	$25
❏ 66-5005 [PS]	Good Clean Fun/ Mommy and Daddy	1969	$40
❏ 66-1002	I'm a Believer/(I'm Not Your) Steppin' Stone	1966	$20
❏ 66-1002 [PS]	I'm a Believer/(I'm Not Your) Steppin' Stone	1966	$40
❏ 66-1001	Last Train to Clarksville/ Take a Giant Step	1966	$20
❏ 66-1001 [PS]	Last Train to Clarksville/ Take a Giant Step	1966	$40

—Version 1: Black & white photo, no red strip at bottom

| ❏ 66-1001 [PS] | Last Train to Clarksville/ Take a Giant Step | 1966 | $30 |

—Version 2: Black & white photo, red strip at bottom with "Ask For The Monkees LP Album" in white

| ❏ 66-1001 [PS] | Last Train to Clarksville/ Take a Giant Step | 1966 | $30 |

—Version 3: Color photo, white strip at bottom of each side. Side 1 type reads "Ask For The Monkees LP Album"; Side 2 has "Write To Monkees." Note: At least one source claims that there are seven (7) different variations of the "Last Train to Clarksville" picture sleeve, but these are the ones we know about

| ❏ 66-5004 | Listen to the Band/ Someday Man | 1969 | $12 |
| ❏ 66-5004 [PS] | Listen to the Band/ Someday Man | 1969 | $30 |

—Listen to the Band" listed first

| ❏ 66-5011 | Oh My My/I Love You Better | 1970 | $25 |

Number	Title	Yr	NM
❏ 66-5011 [PS]	Oh My My/I Love You Better	1970	$50
❏ 66-1007	Pleasant Valley Sunday/Words	1967	$25
❏ 66-1007 [PS]	Pleasant Valley Sunday/Words	1967	$40
❏ 66-1031	Porpoise Song/ As We Go Along	1968	$20
❏ 66-1031 [PS]	Porpoise Song/ As We Go Along	1968	$50
❏ 66-5004	Someday Man/ Listen to the Band	1969	$30

—Someday Man" listed first

| ❏ 66-5000 | Tear Drop City/A Man Without a Dream | 1969 | $20 |
| ❏ 66-5000 [PS] | Tear Drop City/A Man Without a Dream | 1969 | $35 |

RHINO
❏ 74410	Every Step of the Way/ (I'll) Love You Forever	1987	$3
❏ 74410 [PS]	Every Step of the Way/ (I'll) Love You Forever	1987	$4
❏ RNSI74411	Every Step of the Way/ (I'll) Love You Forever	1987	$12

—Picture disc in plastic sleeve with small hole

| ❏ 74408 | Heart and Soul/M.G.B.G.T. | 1987 | $3 |

—Black vinyl

| ❏ 74408 [PS] | Heart and Soul/M.G.B.G.T. | 1987 | $4 |
| ❏ 74408 | Heart and Soul/M.G.B.G.T. | 1987 | $12 |

—Pink vinyl

7-Inch Extended Plays
COLGEMS
Number	Title	Yr	NM
❏ CGLP-102	I'm a Believer/Mary, Mary/When Love Comes Knockin' (At Your Door)// (I'm Not Your) Steppin' Stone/The Kind of Girl I Could Love/She	1966	$200

—Jukebox issue; small hole, plays at 33 1/3 rpm

| ❏ CGLP-102 [PS] | More of the Monkees | 1966 | $300 |
| ❏ CGLP-101 | Theme from The Monkees/I Wanna Be Free/Take a Giant Step//Last Train to Clarksville/Saturday's Child/Tomorrow's Gonna Be Another Day | 1966 | $250 |

—Jukebox mini-LP, small hole, plays at 33 1/3 rpm

| ❏ CGLP-101 [PS] | The Monkees | 1966 | $175 |

MONO MEN
ESTRUS
Number	Title	Yr	NM
❏ ES71	Burning Bush/Rat Fink	1989	$28

—Gold vinyl

| ❏ ES71 | Burning Bush/Rat Fink | 1989 | $8 |
| ❏ ES71 [PS] | Burning Bush/Rat Fink | 1989 | $8 |

MONORAYS, THE
RED ROCKET
Number	Title	Yr	NM
❏ 476	Guardian Angel/Five Minutes to Love You	1959	$50

TAMMY
| ❏ 1005 | Guardian Angel/Five Minutes to Love You | 1959 | $200 |

MONOTONES, THE (1)
ARGO
Number	Title	Yr	NM
❏ 5290	Book of Love/You Never Loved Me	1958	$40
❏ 5339	Tell It to the Judge/ Fools Will Be Fools	1959	$60
❏ 5321	The Legend of Sleepy Hollow/Soft Shadows	1958	$40
❏ 5301	Tom Foolery/Zombi	1958	$40

HULL
| ❏ 743 | Daddy's Home, But Momma's Gone/Tattle Tale | 1961 | $60 |

MASCOT
| ❏ 124 | Book of Love/You Never Loved Me | 1957 | $800 |

MONOTONES, THE (2)
HICKORY
Number	Title	Yr	NM
❏ 1250	Is It Right/What Would You Do	1964	$30
❏ 1306	When Will I Be Loved/ If You Can't Give Me All	1965	$30

MONOTONES, THE (U)
ABC-PARAMOUNT
Number	Title	Yr	NM
❏ 10796	Crystal Ball/A Thousand Faces	1966	$30

MONROE, BILL
COLUMBIA
Number	Title	Yr	NM
❏ 2-275	Along About Daybreak/ Heavy Traffic Ahead	1949	$50

—Microgroove 7-inch, small hole, 33 1/3 rpm single

| ❏ 2-423 | Blue Grass Stomp/Girl in the Blue Velvet Band | 1950 | $50 |

Number	Title	Yr	NM
—Microgroove 7-inch, small hole, 33 1/3 rpm single			
❏ 2-323	I'm Going Back to Old Kentucky/Molly and Tenbooks	1949	$50
—Microgroove 7-inch, small hole, 33 1/3 rpm single			
❏ 2-207	The Old Cross Road/Remember the Cross	1949	$50
—Microgroove 7-inch, small hole, 33 1/3 rpm single			
❏ 2-540(?)	Travelling This Lonesome Road/Can't You Hear Me Calling	1950	$50
—Microgroove 7-inch, small hole, 33 1/3 rpm single; With Mac Wiseman			

DECCA

Number	Title	Yr	NM
❏ 31487	Big Sandy River/There Was Nothing We Could Do	1963	$15
❏ 31346	Blue Grass/Flowers of Love	1962	$15
❏ 9-29289	Blue Moon of Kentucky/Close By	1954	$30
❏ 31456	Blue Ridge Mountain Blues/How Will I Explain About You	1963	$15
❏ 9-46254	Boat of Love/I'm Blue, I'm Lonesome	1950	$50
❏ 9-46380	Brake Man's Blues/Travelin' Blues	1951	$40
❏ 9-28749	Cabin of Love/Country Waltz	1953	$30
❏ 9-29021	Chainging Partners/Y'All Come	1954	$30
❏ 9-29406	Cheyenne/Roanoke	1955	$30
❏ 9-46386	Christmas Time's A-Comin'/The First Whip-Poor-Wills	1951	$40
❏ 31802	Cindy/Jimmy Brown the Newsboy	1965	$10
❏ 9-31031	Come Go with Me/Lonesome Wind Blues	1959	$20
❏ 32502	Crossing the Cumberlands/I Haven't Seen Mary in Years	1969	$8
❏ 31409	Danny Boy/Toy Heart	1962	$15
❏ 9-30944	Dark as the Night, Blue as the Day/Tomorrow I'll Be Gone	1959	$20
❏ 31596	Darling Corey/Salt Creek	1964	$12
❏ 9-28416	Footprints in the Snow/In the Pines	1952	$30
❏ 9-30327	Four Walls/A Fallen Star	1957	$30
❏ 9-46351	Get Down on Your Knees/I'll Meet You in Church	1951	$40
❏ 9-29141	Get Up John/White House Blues	1954	$30
❏ 31943	Going Home/The Master Builder	1966	$10
❏ 32827	Goin' Up Caney/Tallahassee	1971	$8
❏ 32404	Gold Rush/Virginia Darlin'	1968	$8
❏ 9-30809	Gotta Travel On/No One But My Darling	1959	$20
❏ 9-29196	Happy on My Way/We Will Set Your Fields Afire	1954	$30
❏ 9-46369	Highway of Sorrow/Sugar Coated Love	1951	$40
❏ 31878	I Live in the Past/Old, Old House	1965	$10
❏ 9-30486	I'm Sitting on Top of the World/Molly and Tenbrooks	1957	$30
❏ 9-29348	I'm Working on a Building/A Voice from On High	1954	$30
❏ 9-46392	Letter from My Darlin'/Rawhide	1952	$40
❏ 9-29436	Let the Light Shine Down on Me/Wait a Little Longer Jesus	1955	$30
❏ 31218	Linda Lou/Put Your Rubber Doll Away	1961	$15
❏ 32966	Lonesome Moonlight Waltz/My Old Kentucky	1972	$8
❏ 9-46344	Lonesome Truck Driver's Blues/Rotation Blues	1951	$40
❏ 9-46305	Lord, Protect My Soul/River of Death	1951	$40
❏ 31658	Mary at the Home Place/Shenandoah Breakdown	1964	$10
❏ 32654	McKinley's March/Walk Softly on My Heart	1970	$8
❏ 9-46266	Memories of You/Blue Grass Ramble	1950	$50
❏ 9-29886	On and On/I Believe in You Darling	1956	$30
❏ 9-46298	On the Old Kentucky Shore/Poison Love	1951	$40
❏ 9-28356	Pike County Breakdown/A Mighty Pretty Waltz	1952	$30
❏ 9-28183	Sailor's Plea/When the Cactus Is in Bloom	1952	$30
❏ 9-30647	Sally-Jo/Brand New Shoes	1958	$20
❏ 9-30739	Scotland/Panhandle Country	1958	$20
❏ 9-46325	Swing Low, Sweet Chariot/Angels Rock Me to Sleep	1951	$40
❏ 9-28878	The Little Girl and the Dreadful Snake/Memories of Mother and Dad	1953	$30
❏ 9-46236	The Old Fiddler/Alabama Waltz	1950	$50
❏ 32245	Train 45/Is the Blue Moon Still Shining	1968	$8
❏ 9-29645	Wheel Hoss/Put My Little Shoes Away	1955	$30
❏ 32075	When My Blue Moon Turns to Gold Again/Pretty Fair Maiden in the Garden	1967	$10
❏ 9-29009	Wishing Waltz/I Hope You Have Learned	1954	$30
❏ 32574	With Body and Soul/Fireball Mail	1969	$8

MCA

Number	Title	Yr	NM
❏ 40220	Down Yonder/Swing Low Sweet Chariot	1974	$5
❏ 51129	My Last Days on Earth/Go Hither to Go Yonder	1981	$4
❏ 40675	My Sweet Blue-Eyed Darlin'/Monroe Blues	1976	$5

MONROE, CHARLIE

DECCA

Number	Title	Yr	NM
❏ 9-28281	Find 'Em, Fool 'Em and Leave 'Em Alone/These Triflin' Women	1952	$30
❏ 9-46406	I'm Old Kentucky Bound/An Angel in Disguise	1952	$30
❏ 9-30307	Weep and Cry/I'm Weary of Heartaches	1957	$30
❏ 9-30048	Why Did You Say Goodbye/That's What I Like About You	1956	$30

RCA VICTOR

Number	Title	Yr	NM
❏ 48-0222	Bringin' In the Georgia Mail/Down in the Willow Garden	1950	$40
—Originals on green vinyl			
❏ 20-3249	Campin' in Canaan's Land/Don't Forget to Pray	1949	$15
❏ 48-0195	Campin' in Canaan's Land/Don't Forget to Pray	1950	$40
—Originals on green vinyl			
❏ 48-0456	Gold Star Mother/I'm Gonna Sing, Sing, Sing	1951	$30
❏ 48-0417	Good Morning to You/'Neath a Cold Gray Tomb of Stone	1951	$30
❏ 48-0327	I Know He's Been Dealing with Me/You'd Better Be Somewhere	1950	$40
—Originals on green vinyl			
❏ 48-0194	Mother's Not Dead, She's Only Sleeping/There's No Depression in Heaven	1950	$40
—Originals on green vinyl			
❏ 48-0326	My Saviour's Train/Springtime in Glory	1950	$40
—Originals on green vinyl			
❏ 48-0103	Our Mansion Is Ready/A Valley of Peace	1949	$50
—Originals on green vinyl			
❏ 48-0361	So Blue/Without Me Are You Blue	1950	$40
—Originals on green vinyl			
❏ 48-0391	Sugar Cane Mama/Down in Carolina	1950	$40
—Originals on green vinyl			
❏ 48-0193	When the Angels Carry Me Home/If We Never Meet Again	1950	$40
—Originals on green vinyl			

MONROE, MARILYN

RCA VICTOR

Number	Title	Yr	NM
❏ 47-6033	Heat Wave/After You Get What You Want	1955	$40
❏ 47-6033 [PS]	Heat Wave/After You Get What You Want	1955	$120

UNITED ARTISTS

Number	Title	Yr	NM
❏ 161	I Wanna Be Loved By You/I'm Through with Love	1959	$30

MONROE, MELISSA

COLUMBIA

Number	Title	Yr	NM
❏ 2-844	Guilty Tears/Oh How I Miss You	1950	$60
—Microgroove 33 1/3 rpm 7-inch record, small hole			
❏ 4-20752	Guilty Tears/Oh How I Miss You	1950	$50
❏ 4-20868	I'm Waiting Just for You/There's No Room in My Heart	1952	$40
❏ 4-20856	Oceans of Tears/Peppermint Sticks and Lemon Drops	1951	$40
❏ 4-20783	Stop, Look and Listen/You Rule My Heart	1951	$40

MONROE, VAUGHN

DOT

Number	Title	Yr	NM
❏ 16536	Desert Flower/Ballad of Shadow Mountain	1963	$6
❏ 16308	Mr. Moto/If You Gotta Make a Fool of Somebody	1961	$8
❏ 16482	Pee Wee Valley/Valley Forge	1963	$6
❏ 16434	There! I've Said It Again!/I Really Love You	1963	$6

JUBILEE

Number	Title	Yr	NM
❏ 5412	Bye Bye Blackbird/One Hour Before the Posse	1961	$8

MGM

Number	Title	Yr	NM
❏ 12968	Learn to Ski by Mail/Song of the Skier	1960	$8

RCA VICTOR

Number	Title	Yr	NM
❏ 47-5608	Always, Always in My Dreams/Talkin' to a Sparrow	1954	$10

Number	Title	Yr	NM
❏ 47-4942	A Man's Best Friend Is His Horse/You'll Never Get Away	1952	$15
❏ 47-3942	A Marshmallow World/Snowy White Snow and Jingle Bells	1950	$20
❏ 47-2883	Anniversary Song/Something Special	1949	$20
❏ 47-3257	Ballerina/The Stars Will Remember	1949	$30
❏ 47-3143	Bamboo/A Little Golden Cross	1949	$30
❏ 47-2884	Because/Oh, Promise Me	1949	$20
❏ 47-6260	Black Denim Trousers and Motorcycle Boots/All By Myself	1955	$10
❏ 47-5943	Butterscotch World/Goodnight Mrs. Jones	1954	$10
❏ 47-4375	Charmaine/Once	1951	$20
❏ 47-5236	Co-Ed/Don't Build Your Dreams Too High	1953	$15
❏ 47-4180	Dark Is the Night/Wonder Why	1951	$20
❏ 47-4173	Don't Fence Me In/What Is This Thing Called Love	1951	$15
❏ 47-6358	Don't Go to Strangers/Steel Guitar	1955	$12
❏ 47-5329	Don't You Care/My Good Girl	1953	$15
❏ 47-4760	Do You Care/Faith	1952	$15
❏ 47-3929	Dream a Little Dream of Me/Dream Awhile	1950	$20
❏ 47-2835	Dream/My Dreams Are Getting Better All the Time	1949	$20
— The above three comprise a box set			
❏ 47-2833	Drifting and Dreaming/I'll See You in My Dreams	1949	$20
❏ 47-2794	Easy to Remember/Roses for Remembrance	1949	$20
❏ 47-4059	Faithful/They're Playing Our Song	1951	$20
❏ 47-3915	Frosty the Snowman/Could Be	1950	$20
❏ 47-4299	Frosty the Snowman/The Jolly Old Man in the Bright Red Suit	1951	$20
❏ 47-7345	Ghost Train/Ten Chaperones	1958	$10
❏ 47-3164	Gypsy Love Song/I'm Falling in Love with Someone	1949	$20
❏ 47-4941	Hound Dog/A Man Don't Life Who Can Die Alone	1952	$20
❏ 47-4172	I Get a Kick Out of You/Easy to Love	1951	$15
❏ 47-5490	I Know for Sure/Fiesta	1953	$15
❏ 47-6619	In the Middle of the House/Rollin' Heart	1956	$10
❏ 47-2830	It's Only a Paper Moon/Moonlight and Roses	1949	$20
❏ 47-2804	I've Got a Pocketful of Dreams/Did You Ever See a Dream Walking	1949	$30
❏ 47-4611	Lady Love/Idaho State Fair	1952	$15
❏ 47-4218	Laura Lee/Got Her Off My Hands	1951	$20
❏ 47-4850	Learn to Lose/Dancing Girl	1952	$15
❏ 47-7284	Left Right Out of Your Heart/Double Dutch	1958	$12
❏ 47-2944	Look for the Silver Lining/Kiss in the Night	1949	$20
❏ 47-4838	Man on the Misty Mountain/When My Love Comes Back to Me	1952	$15
❏ 47-4638	Marionette/California Rose	1952	$15
❏ 47-4888	Marionette/California Rose	1952	$15
❏ 47-4271	Meanderin'/They Call the Wind Maria	1951	$20
❏ 47-2834	Meet Me Tonight in Dreamland/My Isle of Golden Dreams	1949	$20
❏ 47-2791	Memory Lane/Memories	1949	$20
❏ 47-2831	Moon of Manakoora/Moonglow	1949	$20
❏ 47-4479	Mountain Laurel/Ooh What You Did	1952	$15
❏ 47-3106	Mule Train/Singing My Way Back Home	1949	$30
❏ 47-3031	My Hot Tamale Want Chilly On Me/Gee, It's Tough to Be a Skunk	1949	$30
❏ 47-4146	Old Soldiers Never Die/Love and Devotion	1951	$20
❏ 47-4726	On Top of Old Smoky/Ballerina	1952	$10
❏ 47-4114	On Top of Old Smoky/Shall We Dance	1951	$20
❏ 47-3806	Our Very Own/Violins from Nowhere	1950	$20
❏ 47-3711	Over and Over/It's Easter Time	1950	$20
❏ 47-2945	Shine On Harvest Moon/Who	1949	$20
❏ 47-5145	Small World/Lonely Eyes	1953	$15
❏ 47-4171	So in Love/I Concentrate on You	1951	$15
❏ 47-2986	Someday (You'll Want Me to Want You)/And It Still Goes	1949	$30
❏ 47-3068	Sonny Boy/I Only Have Eyes for You	1949	$30
❏ 47-3112	So This Is Love/There's No One Here But Me	1949	$30
❏ 47-4113	Sound Off (The Duckworth Chant)/Oh Marry, Marry Me	1951	$20
❏ 47-2934	Telephone to My Heart/It Looked So Good in De Window	1949	$30
❏ 47-4403	Tenderly/I Like It, I Like It	1951	$20

Number	Title	Yr	NM
❏ 47-3773	Thanks, Mr. Florist/Tell Her You Love Her	1950	$20
❏ 47-2793	Thanks for the Memory/ Remember	1949	$20
❏ 47-3018	That Lucky Old Sun (Just Rolls Around Heaven All Day)/Make Believe	1949	$30
❏ 47-7495	The Battle of New Orleans/Hercules	1959	$8
❏ 47-3880	The Beer That I Left on the Bar/Why Fight the Feeling	1950	$20
❏ 47-7093	The Best Dream of All/Stargazer	1957	$12
❏ 47-7443	The Clown/There! I've Said It Again	1959	$8
❏ 47-5970	The Holy Bible/The Ten Commandments	1954	$15
❏ 47-6216	The Moon Was Yellow/You Could Hear a Pin Drop	1955	$10
❏ 47-3810	The Phantom Stagecoach/ Gonna Ride 'n' Ride	1950	$15
❏ 47-3818	The Phantom Stagecoach/ Mexicali Trail	1950	$20
❏ 47-3812	The Pony Express/ Rounded Up in Glory	1950	$15

— The above three comprise a box set

Number	Title	Yr	NM
❏ 47-7193	There's No Piano in This House/Somebody This Is Taking My Place	1958	$10
❏ 47-2885	The Whiffenpoof Song/ Without a Song	1949	$20

— The above three comprise a box set

Number	Title	Yr	NM
❏ 47-5767	They Were Doin' the Mambo/Mister Sandman	1954	$10
❏ 47-3907	This Is My Country/The Great American Dream	1950	$20
❏ 47-2946	Time on My Hands/Avalon	1949	$20
❏ 47-7019	Tomorrow, Tomorrow/ Miss You	1957	$10
❏ 47-3162	Toyland/Ah! Sweet Mystery of Life	1949	$20
❏ 47-6703	Wait for Love/Not for a Long, Long Time	1956	$10
❏ WBY-56	Westward Ho, the Wagons/ Wringle Wrangle	1957	$30

— From the "Bluebird Children's Records" series

Number	Title	Yr	NM
❏ 47-6002	What a Diff'rence a Day Made/The Main Event	1955	$10
❏ 47-4138	Where or When/The Most Beautiful Girl in the World	1951	$20
❏ 47-3811	While I'm Smokin' My Last Cigarette/No Range to Ride Anymore	1950	$15

UNITED ARTISTS

Number	Title	Yr	NM
❏ 214	Love Me Forever/Ballerina	1960	$8

MONSTER MAGNET
CIRCUIT

Number	Title	Yr	NM
❏ CIRCA7001	Lizard Johnny/ Freak Shop USA	1989	$70

— Red vinyl

Number	Title	Yr	NM
❏ CIRCA7001	Lizard Johnny/ Freak Shop USA	1989	$30
❏ CIRCA7001 [PS]	Lizard Johnny/ Freak Shop USA	1989	$30

MONTAGUE
CLASS

Number	Title	Yr	NM
❏ 218	Thanks for Christmas (Narration)/Thanks for Christmas	1957	$30

— B-side by Judy Lynn Phelps

MONTANA SLIM
DECCA

Number	Title	Yr	NM
❏ 9-29585	A Strawberry Roan/ Dynamite Trail	1955	$30
❏ 9-30340	Away Out on the Mountain/ Padlock on Your Heart	1957	$30
❏ 9-31034	Blind Boy's Prayer/There's a Bluebird on Your Windowsill	1959	$20
❏ 9-29942	I'm Ragged But I'm Right/Yodeling Song	1956	$30
❏ 9-30907	My French Canadian Girl/My Prairie Rose	1959	$20
❏ 9-30079	My Little Lady/ Silver Bell Yodel	1956	$30
❏ 9-29384	My Mountain High Yodel Song/Shoo Shoo Shoo Sh'La La	1954	$30
❏ 9-29671	The Alpine Milkman/There's a Tree on Every Road	1955	$30
❏ 9-29535	The Sunshine Bird/ Maple Leaf Rag	1955	$30

RCA VICTOR

Number	Title	Yr	NM
❏ 47-8205	32 Wonderful Years/A Cashbox for a Heartache	1963	$15
❏ 47-4846	Alabama Saturday Night/Manhunt	1952	$30
❏ 48-0054	Bluebird on Your Windowsill/All I Need Is Some More Lovin'	1949	$50

— Originals on green vinyl

Number	Title	Yr	NM
❏ 47-4523	Goodbye Maria/ Driftwood on the River	1952	$30
❏ 47-5045	Huggin' Squeezin' Kissin' Teasin'/Sweet Little Love	1952	$30

Number	Title	Yr	NM
❏ 48-0457	Let's Go Back to the Bible/She'll Be There	1951	$40
❏ 48-0419	My Heart's Closed for Repairs/Just a Woman's Smile	1951	$40
❏ 47-4446	My Oklahoma Rose/I Wish There Were Three Days in the Year	1952	$30
❏ 48-0477	My Wife Is On a Diet/ Sick, Sober and Sorry	1951	$40
❏ 47-5276	Sleep, Little One, Sleep/ Mockingbird Love	1953	$30
❏ 48-0090	Streamlined Yodel Song/My Swiss Moonlight Lullaby	1949	$50

— Originals on green vinyl

Number	Title	Yr	NM
❏ 48-0352	Take It Easy Blues/Apple, Cherry, Mince, Chocolate	1950	$40

— Originals on green vinyl

Number	Title	Yr	NM
❏ 47-4252	Wha' Hoppen/Tears Don't Always	1951	$30
❏ 48-0139	When the Ice Warms Next Again/Shackles and Chains	1950	$50

— Originals on green vinyl

STARDAY

Number	Title	Yr	NM
❏ 686	Grandad's Yodeling Song/The Little Shirt My Mother Made for Me	1964	$15

MONTCLAIRS, THE (1)
PAULA

Number	Title	Yr	NM
❏ 409	Baby, You Know I'm Gonna Miss You (Part 1)/Baby, You Know I'm Gonna Miss You (Part 2)	1974	$5
❏ 375	Beggin' Is Hard to Do/ Unwanted Love	1973	$5
❏ 363	Dreaming Out of Season/I Just Can't Get Away	1972	$5
❏ 390	I'm Calling You/Hung Up on Your Love	1973	$5
❏ 382	I Need You More Than Ever/ Prelude to a Heartbreak	1973	$5
❏ 345	Is This for Real/All I Really Care About Is You	1971	$5
❏ 381	Make Up for Lost Time/ How Can One Man Live	1973	$5

MONTCLAIRS, THE (2)
ABC-PARAMOUNT

Number	Title	Yr	NM
❏ 10463	I Believe (In Your Love)/No Baby	1963	$20

MONTCLAIRS, THE (3)
AUDICON

Number	Title	Yr	NM
❏ 111	Goodnight, Well, It's Time to Go/A Broken Promise	1961	$40

MONTCLAIRS, THE (4)
HI-Q

Number	Title	Yr	NM
❏ 5001	Golden Angel/Don Juan	1957	$300

PREMIUM

Number	Title	Yr	NM
❏ 404	Give Me a Chance/ My Every Dream	1956	$400

SONIC

Number	Title	Yr	NM
❏ 104	All I Want Is Love/I've Heard About You	1956	$800

MONTCLAIRS, THE (U)
SUNBURST

Number	Title	Yr	NM
❏ 115	Poopsie/Sore Feet	1965	$15
❏ 106	Wait for Me/Happy Feet Time	1965	$15

UNITED INT'L.

Number	Title	Yr	NM
❏ 1007	Lisa/Tap Tap Daisy	1963	$30

MONTE, LOU
AFE

Number	Title	Yr	NM
❏ 102	Darktown Strutters Ball/ The Sheik of Araby	1981	$4

GWP

Number	Title	Yr	NM
❏ 530	I Really Don't Want to Know/I Have an Angel in Heaven	1972	$5

LAURIE

Number	Title	Yr	NM
❏ 3652	Crabs Walk Sideways/ Nicolena	1977	$4
❏ 3643	Paul Revere's Ride/ Jerusalem, Jerusalem	1976	$4

RCA VICTOR

Number	Title	Yr	NM
❏ 47-5496	Baby Cried/One Moment More	1953	$15
❏ 47-6133	Bella Notte/With You Beside Me	1955	$12
❏ 47-6848	Calypso Italiano/Someone Else Is Taking You Home	1957	$10
❏ 47-5963	Cat's Whiskers/Roulette	1954	$15
❏ 47-8831	Cheech the Cat/ Makin' Whoopee	1966	$6
❏ 47-5611	Darktown Strutters Ball/I Know How You Feel	1954	$20

Number	Title	Yr	NM
❏ 47-9328	Digga Digga Baby/A Girl, A Girl	1967	$6
❏ 47-7265	Eh, Marie, Eh, Marie/ The Shiek of Araby	1958	$8
❏ 47-6704	Elvis Presley for President/ If I Were a Millionaire	1956	$40
❏ 47-7061	Ha! Ha! Ha!/Round and Round in My Heart	1957	$10
❏ 47-5993	How Important Can It Be/Truly Yours	1955	$10
❏ 47-9405	I Don't Play with Matches Anymore/All for the Kids	1967	$6
❏ 47-6522	If I Knew You Were Comin' I'd've Baked a Cake/Ask Your Heart	1956	$6
❏ 47-5832	Italian Hucklebuck/ Just Like Before	1954	$15
❏ 47-7160	Lazy Mary/Angelique	1958	$12
❏ 47-8716	Mama Get the Hammer (There's a Fly on Papa's Head)/Six O'Clock Supper	1965	$6
❏ 47-7346	Marianne/Strada 'Nfosa	1958	$8
❏ 47-9021	Oh How I Miss You Tonight/Seventeen	1966	$6
❏ 47-8754	Paul Revere's Horse (Ba-Cha-Ca-Loop)/ Oh Lonesome Me	1965	$6
❏ 47-7554	Pistol Packin' Mama/ Have Another	1959	$8
❏ 47-7641	Santa Nicola/All Because It's Christmas	1959	$15
❏ 47-6320	Santo Natale/Italian Jingle Bells	1955	$15
❏ 47-5691	Somewhere There Is Someone/Won't You Forgive Me	1954	$15
❏ 47-7523	The Angel in the Fountain/ Sole Per Te (Only for You)	1959	$8
❏ 47-7467	The Italian Cowboy Song/ Pizza Boy U.S.A.	1959	$8
❏ 47-6072	The Italian Wallflower/ Dreamboat	1955	$10
❏ 47-6951	The Wife/Musica Bella	1957	$10
❏ 47-6287	Tombolee-Tombola/Rosina	1955	$10
❏ 47-5883	When I Hold You in My Arms/In My Dreams	1954	$15
❏ 47-9216	When You Get What You Want/There'll Be Some Changes Made	1967	$6
❏ 47-7423	Where Do You Work, Marie/Skinny Lena	1958	$8

REGALIA

Number	Title	Yr	NM
❏ 6600	Goombar Custer's Last Stand/Tattooed Susie	1969	$6

REPRISE

Number	Title	Yr	NM
❏ 0267	A Baby Cried/The Rooster and the Hen	1964	$6
❏ 20015	A Good Man Is Hard to Find/Sixteen Tons	1961	$10
❏ 0384	Don't Wish Your Heartbreak on Me/No, No, Don't Cry, My Love	1965	$6
❏ 0241	Down Little Doggie/La Luna Si Vuola Sposane	1963	$6
❏ 0284	Hello Dolly/Jungle Louie	1964	$6
❏ 20219	Hootenanny Italian Style/ Who Stole My Provolone	1963	$8
❏ 0326	I Want to Hold Your Hand/ My Parson's Across the Way	1964	$8
❏ 20171	Limbo Italiano/Bossa Nova Italiano	1963	$8
❏ 20037	Oh Mein Papa (Oh Mio Papa)/Tici Ti Tici To Tici Ti	1961	$10
❏ 20146	Pepino's Friend Pasqual (The Italian Pussy-Cat)/I Like You, You Like Me, Eh, Paisan?	1963	$8
❏ 20146 [PS]	Pepino's Friend Pasqual (The Italian Pussy-Cat)/I Like You, You Like Me, Eh, Paisan?	1963	$15
❏ 20106	Pepino the Italian Mouse/ What Did Washington Say (When He Crossed the Delaware)	1962	$8
❏ 20106 [PS]	Pepino the Italian Mouse/ What Did Washington Say (When He Crossed the Delaware)	1962	$15
❏ 0724	Pepino the Italian Mouse/ What Did Washington Say (When He Crossed the Delaware)	1968	$4

— Back to Back Hits" series

Number	Title	Yr	NM
❏ 20085	Please Mr. Columbus (Turn the Ship Around)/ Addio, Addio (Good-Bye)	1962	$10
❏ 0352	The Mixed-Up Bull from Palermo/I Know How You Feel	1965	$6
❏ 20044	Twist Italiano/Oh Tessie	1962	$10

ROULETTE

Number	Title	Yr	NM
❏ 4266	Bim Bam Bu/Oh, Oh, Rosie	1960	$8
❏ 4308	Christmas at Our House/ Dominick the Donkey	1960	$15
❏ 4253	The Darktown Strutter's Ball/Half a Love	1960	$8
❏ 4294	The Huckle-Buck/ Always You	1960	$8
❏ 4366	The Sheriff of Sicily/ Katareena	1961	$8

MONTEREYS, THE

ARWIN

Number	Title	Yr	NM
❏ 130	Goodbye My Love/ It Hurts Me So	1961	$50

BLAST

Number	Title	Yr	NM
❏ 219	Face in the Crowd/ Step Right Up	1965	$400

DOMINION

| ❏ 1019 | First Kiss/Just One
More Kiss | 1964 | $50 |

EASTWEST

| ❏ 121 | I'll Love You Again/
The American Teens | 1958 | $30 |

GNP CRESCENDO

| ❏ 314 | For Sentimental Reasons/I
Still Love You | 1964 | $30 |

IMPALA

| ❏ 213 | Without a Girl/So Deep | 1959 | $120 |

MAJOR

| ❏ 1009 | A Crowded Room/You
Said That You Loved Me | 1959 | $75 |

SATURN

| ❏ 1002 | My Girl/With You | 1956 | $50 |

TRANS AMERICAN

| ❏ 1000/1 | Darlin' Send Me a
Letter/Late Darlin' | 1960 | $600 |

MONTEZ, CHRIS

A&M

Number	Title	Yr	NM
❏ 839	Because of You/Elena	1967	$8
❏ 780	Call Me/Go Head On	1965	$8
❏ 855	Foolin' Around/ Dindi (Jin-Jee)	1967	$6
❏ 958	Love Is Here to Stay/ Nothing to Hide	1968	$6
❏ 906	Once in a While/ The Face I Love	1968	$6
❏ 796	The More I See You/ You, I Love You	1966	$10
❏ 810	There Will Never Be Another You/You Can Hurt the One You Love	1966	$8
❏ 985	Where Are You Now/ Watch What Happens	1968	$6

JAMIE

| ❏ 1410 | Let's Dance/Somebody
Loves You | 1973 | $5 |

MONOGRAM

❏ 500	All You Had to Do (Was Tell Me)/Love Me	1962	$15
❏ 513	In An English Towne/My Baby Loves to Dance	1963	$15
❏ 522	(It's Not) Puppy Love/He's Been Leading You On	1964	$15
❏ 520	It Takes Two/To Shoot the Curl	1964	$15

—With Kathy Young

| ❏ 505 | Let's Dance/You're the One | 1962 | $30 |
| ❏ 507 | Some Kinda Fun/Tell Me | 1962 | $15 |

PARAMOUNT

| ❏ 0109 | We Can Make the World
a Whole Lot Brighter/
The End of the Line | 1971 | $5 |

MONTGOMERY, BOB

BRUNSWICK

| ❏ 55157 | Because I Love You/
Taste of the Blues | 1959 | $50 |

MONTGOMERY, CHRISTOPHER

DOLTON

| ❏ 84 | My Paradise/Giants
of Bombora | 1963 | $40 |

MONTGOMERY, JACK

REVUE

| ❏ 11009 | Baby, Baby, Take a Chance
on Me/(Instrumental) | 1968 | $200 |

SCEPTER

| ❏ 12152 | Dearly Beloved/
Do You Believe It | 1966 | $300 |

—Correct title of A-side

| ❏ 12152 | My Dear Beloved/
Do You Believe It | 1966 | $400 |

—Misprinted A-side title

MONTGOMERY, MELBA

Also see GEORGE JONES AND MELBA MONTGOMERY.

CAPITOL

❏ 2513	As Far As My Forgetting's Got/You Let Me Win	1969	$8
❏ 4290	He Called Me Baby/ Country Child	1976	$4
❏ 3091	He's My Man/We Don't Live Here Anymore	1971	$8

Number	Title	Yr	NM
❏ 3297	Hope I Never Love That Way Again/Say You'll Never Leave Me	1972	$8
❏ 2758	The Closer She Gets/Where Do We Go from Here	1970	$8
❏ 2825	Together Again/ Eloy Crossing	1970	$8

COMPASS

| ❏ 45-7 | Straight Talkin'/
(B-side unknown) | 1986 | $6 |

ELEKTRA

❏ 45229	Don't Let the Good Times Fool You/It Sure Gets Lonely	1975	$5
❏ 45875	He'll Come Home/ Country Written Up and Down Your Face	1973	$6
❏ 45272	If I Ever Needed Someone/ He Loved You Right Out of My Mind	1975	$5
❏ 45211	If You Want the Rainbow/ Love, I Need You	1974	$5
❏ 45296	Love Was the Wind/I Never Dreamed That Love Could Be This Good	1975	$5
❏ 45247	Searchin' (For Someone Like You)/Hiding in the Darkness of My Mind	1975	$5
❏ 45866	Wrap Your Love Around Me/ Let Me Show You How I Can	1973	$6

KARI

| ❏ 111 | The Star/Carolina
in My Mind | 1980 | $6 |

MUSICOR

❏ 1175	Crossing Over Jordan/The Dead Shall Live Again	1966	$12
❏ 1157	Don't Keep Me Lonely Too Long/I'm Looking for the Man	1966	$12
❏ 1324	Hallelujah Road/Life Beyond Death	1968	$10
❏ 1182	He's Out There With Her Somewhere/My Tiny Music Box	1966	$12
❏ 1209	He Stayed Away (Long As He Could)/Won't Take Long	1966	$12
❏ 1291	He Wrote Forgive Me/ You Put Me Here	1968	$12
❏ 1311	Our Little Man/Tell Me Your Troubles	1968	$10
❏ 1278	The Day Your Memory Came to Town/Twilight Years	1967	$12
❏ 1241	What Can I Tell the Folks Back Home/The Right Time to Lose My Mind	1967	$10
❏ 1344	What's to Become of What's Left of Me/Every Day's a Happy Day for Fools	1969	$10

UNITED ARTISTS

❏ XW1115	Angel of the Morning/ Pinkerton's Flowers	1977	$5
❏ 768	Big City Heartaches/ Why Does the Lady Cry	1964	$15
❏ 964	Big Joke/Constantly	1965	$15
❏ 576	Hall of Shame/What's Bad for You Is Good for Me	1963	$15
❏ 803	I Can't Change Overnight/I Can't Get Used to Being Lonely	1965	$15
❏ XW1175	Leavin' Me in Your Mind/We've Been Lyin' Here Too Long	1978	$5
❏ 705	The Face/I Will Always Keep Loving You	1964	$15
❏ 652	The Greatest One of All/Lies Can't Hide What's On My Mind	1963	$15
❏ 850	White Lightning/I Saw It	1965	$15

MONTGOMERY, RITA

LIBERTY

| ❏ 55049 | I Believe in Santa
Claus/Many, Many
Christmases Ago | 1956 | $20 |

MONTGOMERY, TAMMY

CHECKER

| ❏ 1072 | If I Would Marry You/
This Time Tomorrow | 1964 | $50 |

—Maroon label

| ❏ 1072 | If I Would Marry You/
This Time Tomorrow | 1964 | $30 |

—Mostly blue label with red and black checkers

SCEPTER

| ❏ 1224 | If You See Bill/It's Mine | 1961 | $70 |

TRY ME

| ❏ 28001 | I Cried/If You Don't Think | 1962 | $40 |

—As "Tana Montgomery"

MONTGOMERY, WES

A&M

| ❏ 865 | A Day in the Life (Part 1)/A
Day in the Life (Part 2) | 1967 | $8 |
| ❏ 940 | Georgia on My Mind/I
Say a Little Prayer | 1968 | $8 |

Number	Title	Yr	NM
❏ 916	Goin' On to Detroit/ Wind Song	1968	$8
❏ 1008	Where Have All the Flowers Gone/Fly Me to the Moon	1968	$8
❏ 883	Windy/Watch What Happens	1967	$8

PACIFIC JAZZ

| ❏ 301 | Summertime/Fingerpickin' | 1960 | $15 |

VERVE

❏ 10442 [DJ]	Bumpin' on Sunset (Part 1)/ Bumpin' on Sunset (Part 2)	1966	$10
❏ 10441 [DJ]	Bumpin' (Part 1)/ Bumpin' (Part 2)	1966	$10
❏ 10489	California Dreaming/ Mr. Walker	1967	$8
❏ CS?-5	Celebrity Scene: Wes Montgomery	1966	$70

—Box set of five singles (10440-10444). Price includes box, all 5 singles, jukebox title strips, bio. Records are sometimes found by themselves, so they are also listed separately.

❏ 10384	Goin' Out of My Head/Boss City	1966	$8
❏ 10440 [DJ]	Goin' Out of My Head/Tequila	1966	$10
❏ 10373	Love Theme from "The Sandpiper"/Bumpin'	1965	$8
❏ 10444 [DJ]	Love Theme from "The Sandpiper" (The Shadow of Your Smile)/A Quiet Thing	1966	$10

—CS2-5 Record Number 5

| ❏ 10443 [DJ] | Phoenix Love
Theme/Caravan | 1966 | $10 |
| ❏ 10432 | Tequila/Bumpin' On Sunset | 1966 | $8 |

MONTGOMERYS, THE

AMY

Number	Title	Yr	NM
❏ 883	Promise of Love/Gotta Make a Hit Record	1963	$250

MONTY PYTHON

ARISTA

| ❏ 0130 | The Single/(B-side unknown) | 1975 | $8 |
| ❏ 0578 | They Won't Play This
Song on the Radio/Sit
on My Face-Farewell
to John Denver | 1980 | $8 |

WARNER BROS.

| ❏ 49112 | Always Look on the
Bright Side of Life/Brian | 1979 | $10 |

MOODS, THE (1)

BANG

| ❏ 555 | Gotta Figure Out/
Genuine Jade | 1968 | $8 |

MOODS, THE (2)

KOOL

❏ 1024	High School Days/ The Broken Hip	1964	$12
❏ 1032	Only the Young/ (B-side unknown)	1965	$10
❏ 1028	Oop-Sy-Do/Stay with Me	1965	$10

MOODS, THE (3)

SARG

❏ 176	Easy Going/Duck Walk	1959	$50
❏ 179	Let Me Have Your Love/Broke Up	1959	$60
❏ 162	Little Alice/Lady of the Sea	1959	$100
❏ 185	On the Move/ Teenager's Past	1960	$50

MOODY BLUES, THE

Also see GRAEME EDGE; JUSTIN HAYWARD; DENNY LAINE; JOHN LODGE; RAY THOMAS. (45)

| ❏ 85028 | Tuesday Afternoon (Forever
Afternoon)/Another Morning | 1968 | $8 |

LONDON

❏ 273	Driftwood/I'm Your Man	1978	$5
❏ 9799	Ev'ry Day/You Don't	1965	$20
❏ 20030	Fly Me High/I Really Haven't Got the Time	1967	$15
❏ 9764	From the Bottom of My Heart (I Love You)/ And My Baby's Gone	1965	$20
❏ 9726V [DJ]	Go Now!/It's Easy Child	1965	$30

—Orange and brown swirl label; may be promo only

| ❏ 5N-9726 | Go Now!/It's Easy Child | 1978 | $6 |

—Reissue on "sunrise" label

| ❏ 9726 | Go Now!/Lose Your Money | 1965 | $30 |

—White, purple and blue label

| ❏ 9726 | Go Now!/Lose Your Money | 1965 | $15 |

—Blue swirl label, "London" in white

| ❏ 9726 | Go Now!/Lose Your Money | 1965 | $8 |

—Blue swirl label, "London" in black

| ❏ 5N-9726 | Go Now!/Lose Your Money | 1975 | $6 |

—Blue swirl label; new prefix

| ❏ 270 | Steppin' in a Slide Zone/I'll
Be Level with You | 1978 | $4 |

Number	Title	Yr	NM
❏ 9810	Stop!/Bye Bye Bird	1966	$20
❏ 1005	This Is My House (But Nobody Calls)/Boulevard de la Madelaine	1967	$15

POLYDOR

Number	Title	Yr	NM
❏ 871270-7	Al Fin Voy a Encontrarte (I Know You're Out There Somewhere -- Spanish Version)/I Know You're Out There Somewhere	1989	$5
❏ 887815-7	Here Comes the Weekend/ River of Endless Love	1988	$3
❏ 887600-7	I Know You're Out There Somewhere/Miracle	1988	$3
❏ 887600-7 [PS]	I Know You're Out There Somewhere/Miracle	1988	$3
❏ 885201-7	The Other Side of Life/The Spirit	1986	$5

— Blue vinyl

Number	Title	Yr	NM
❏ 885201-7 [PS]	The Other Side of Life/The Spirit	1986	$5

— Special sleeve for blue vinyl version

Number	Title	Yr	NM
❏ 885212-7	The Other Side of Life/The Spirit	1986	$3
❏ 885212-7 [PS]	The Other Side of Life/The Spirit	1986	$3

THRESHOLD

Number	Title	Yr	NM
❏ 605	Blue World/Sorry	1983	$4
❏ 601	Gemini Dream/ Painted Smile	1981	$4
❏ 67012	I'm Just a Singer (In a Rock and Roll Band)/For My Lady	1973	$5
❏ 67009	Isn't Life Strange/ After You Came	1972	$5
❏ 604	Sitting at the Wheel/ Going Nowhere	1983	$4
❏ 604 [PS]	Sitting at the Wheel/ Going Nowhere	1983	$6
❏ 603	Talking Out of Turn/ Veteran Cosmic Rocker	1981	$4
❏ 67006	The Story in Your Eyes/ Melancholy Man	1971	$6
❏ 67006 [PS]	The Story in Your Eyes/ Melancholy Man	1971	$15

MOODY, CLYDE

DECCA

Number	Title	Yr	NM
❏ 9-28662	Mexican Joe/The Kind of Love I Can't Forget	1953	$30
❏ 9-28785	What a Life/Canadian Waltz	1953	$30

KING

Number	Title	Yr	NM
❏ 1147	Forgive Me/Hard Hearted	1952	$40
❏ 1031	If You Only Knew/You Are the Rainbow in My Dreams	1952	$70

— Red vinyl

Number	Title	Yr	NM
❏ 1031	If You Only Knew/You Are the Rainbow in My Dreams	1952	$40

— Black vinyl

Number	Title	Yr	NM
❏ 1125	Landslide of Love/I Love You Dear Forever	1952	$40
❏ 987	She Cooked My Goose/I'm Sorry If That's the Way You Feel	1951	$50
❏ 977	Too Young/Tend to Your Business	1951	$50
❏ 968	West Virginia Waltz/You're a Real Sweetheart to Me	1951	$50
❏ 1072	When You Have No One to Love You/Why Don't You Come Back to Me	1952	$40

LITTLE DARLIN'

Number	Title	Yr	NM
❏ 069	California Dream/While My Heart Is Breaking	1970	$10

STARDAY

Number	Title	Yr	NM
❏ 702	Dark Midnight/What It Means to Be Lonely	1964	$15
❏ 671	Where There's Smoke (There's Bound to Be Fire)/Whispering Pines	1964	$15

MOON BEAMS, THE

GRATE

Number	Title	Yr	NM
❏ 100	A Lover's Plea/ Don't Go Away	1959	$200

MOON, KEITH
Also see THE WHO.

TRACK

Number	Title	Yr	NM
❏ 40435	In My Life/Crazy Like a Fox	1975	$20
❏ 40387	Solid Gold/Move Over Ms. L.	1975	$20
❏ 40316	Teenage Idol/Don't Worry Baby	1974	$20

MOON, THE

IMPERIAL

Number	Title	Yr	NM
❏ 66330	Faces/John Automaton	1968	$30
❏ 66285	Mothers and Fathers/ Someday Girl	1968	$40

MOONEY, ART

MGM

Number	Title	Yr	NM
❏ K12461	A Face in the Crowd/ Mama Guitar	1957	$10
❏ K12000	Alabama Jubilee/Paddlin' Madeline Home	1955	$15
❏ K12847	A Merry Merry Christmas to You/Sunset to Sunrise	1959	$10
❏ K12847 [PS]	A Merry Merry Christmas to You/Sunset to Sunrise	1959	$15
❏ K12703	Autumn Sunset/Saw My Baby on TV	1958	$12
❏ K11456	Baby Don't Do It/ All Night Long	1953	$15
❏ K12908	Banjo Boy/Captain Buffalo	1960	$8
❏ K11725	Barefoot Days/ Wanderlust Blues	1954	$15
❏ K11871	Bip Bam/Big Boy Blue	1954	$15
❏ K11171	Blacksmith Blues/You're Not Worth Tears	1952	$20
❏ K10851	Christmas Choo Choo/ Candyland Parade	1950	$30
❏ K11072	Daddy/The Tinkle Song	1951	$20
❏ K12277	Daydreams/Somebody Stole My Muchacha (Cha-Cha-Cha)	1956	$12
❏ K12869	Diddy Boppers/Goodtime Special, Part 2	1960	$8
❏ K10906	Faithful/Just for Tonight	1951	$20
❏ K11486	Gee Whiz/Miss You	1953	$15
❏ K12320	Giant/Rock and Roll Tumbleweed	1956	$10
❏ K10969	Goodnight Cincinnati/Sarah Kelly from Plumbnelly	1951	$20
❏ K11306	Hesitation/You're the One I Care For	1952	$20
❏ K11900	Honey-Babe/No Regrets	1955	$15
❏ K13246	I Ain't Down Yet/ Dolce Far Niente	1964	$8

— B-side by Leroy Holmes

Number	Title	Yr	NM
❏ K12957	I Ain't Down Yet/'Till Tomorrow	1960	$8
❏ K11434	I Just Can't Take It Baby/I Played the Fool	1953	$15
❏ K10839	I'll Never Be Free/To Think You've Chosen Me	1950	$30
❏ K12009	I'm Looking Over a Four Leaf Clover/Baby Face	1955	$15
❏ 8014	I'm Looking Over a Four Leaf Clover/The Big Brass Band from Brazil	1949	$40

— Originally issued on 78 in 1948 with the number 10119

Number	Title	Yr	NM
❏ K12545	In Italy/Let the Rest of the World Go By	1957	$10
❏ K11258	I Painted It/I May Hate Myself in the Morning	1952	$20
❏ K11347	Lazy River/Honestly	1952	$20
❏ K12649	Louella/Something's Always Happening on the River	1958	$10
❏ K11570	Love Birds/Night Must Fall	1953	$15
❏ K12989	Malibu/Yancey Special	1961	$8
❏ K12133	Memories of You/The Lord Is a Busy Man	1955	$15
❏ K11610	Mogambo/Off Shore	1953	$15
❏ K11772	Mothballs/Corn Belt Symphony	1954	$15
❏ K11196	Move It Over/Honky Tonk Blues	1952	$20
❏ K12832	My Dreams Are Getting Better All the Time/Till the End of the World	1959	$10
❏ K10984	My Truly Fair/Love I'd Give My Life	1951	$20
❏ K11542	O (Oh!)/Cloverleaf Special	1953	$15
❏ K11330	Over the Hill/Window Shopping	1952	$20
❏ K10822	Serenade in Blue/I'm a Dreamer	1950	$30
❏ K11669	Silhouette/Promises	1954	$15
❏ K12403	Sinner's Train/Wheeling, West Virginia	1957	$10
❏ K11115	Slow Poke/Keep On the Sunny Side	1951	$20
❏ K12802	Smile/Sunset to Sunrise	1959	$12
❏ K10924	Sparrow in the Tree Top/ Beautiful Brown Eyes	1951	$20
❏ K11033	Stay Awhile/Oh How I Love You	1951	$20
❏ K12219	Tally Ho/You Are the One	1956	$10
❏ K11651	The Creep/Plantation Waltz	1954	$15
❏ K12435	The Donkey Got Drunk/I Never Had a Worry in the World	1957	$10
❏ K12073	The Girl I Left Behind Me/Give Me a Band and My Baby	1955	$15
❏ K12312	Theme from "Rebel Without a Cause"/Theme from "East of Eden"	1956	$20
❏ K12312 [PS]	Theme from "Rebel Without a Cause"/Theme from "East of Eden"	1956	$60
❏ K12503	The Parade Is Passing Me By/Honest Love	1957	$10

Number	Title	Yr	NM
❏ K12190	The Phonograph Song/ Is There a Teen-Ager in the House	1956	$15
❏ K12590	The River Kwai March and Colonel Bogey/Bullfight	1958	$10
❏ K11015	The Song Is Ended/ Maybe It's Because	1951	$20
❏ K12165	Tutti-Frutti/You Can Take My Heart	1956	$15
❏ K12039	Twenty Tiny Fingers/A Happy Song	1955	$15
❏ K11690	Way, Paesano/Si Petite	1954	$15
❏ K10765	Wham Bam Thank You Ma'am/There'll Never Be Another You	1950	$30
❏ K11386	Winter/Heartbreaker	1952	$20

RIVERSIDE

Number	Title	Yr	NM
❏ 4543	St. Louis Blues Bossa Nova/Sugar Loaf	1963	$20

MOONGLOWS, THE

BIG P

Number	Title	Yr	NM
❏ 101	Sincerely '72/You've Chosen Me	1972	$10

CHAMPAGNE

Number	Title	Yr	NM
❏ 7500	I Just Can't Tell No Lie/I've Been Your Dog (Ever Since I've Been Your Man)	1952	$1500

CHANCE

Number	Title	Yr	NM
❏ 1147	Baby Please!/ Whistle My Love	1953	$1000

— Black vinyl

Number	Title	Yr	NM
❏ 1147	Baby Please!/ Whistle My Love	1953	$3000

— Red vinyl. VG 1500; VG+ 2250

Number	Title	Yr	NM
❏ 1156	I Was Wrong/Ooh Rockin' Daddy	1954	$600

— Yellow and black label

Number	Title	Yr	NM
❏ 1156	I Was Wrong/Ooh Rockin' Daddy	1954	$600

— Black and white label

Number	Title	Yr	NM
❏ 1161	My Gal/219 Train	1954	$5000

— VG 2500; VG+ 3750

Number	Title	Yr	NM
❏ 1152	Secret Love/Real Gone Mama	1954	$1500

— Silver and blue label

Number	Title	Yr	NM
❏ 1152	Secret Love/Real Gone Mama	1954	$1000

— Yellow and black label

CHESS

Number	Title	Yr	NM
❏ 1770	Beatnick/Junior	1960	$30
❏ 1811	Blue Velvet/Penny Arcade	1962	$30

— As "Bobby Lester and the Moonglows"

Number	Title	Yr	NM
❏ 1598	Foolish Me/Slow Down	1955	$70

— Blue label, silver top

Number	Title	Yr	NM
❏ 1651	I'm Afraid the Masquerade Is Over/Don't Say Goodbye	1957	$60

— Blue label, silver top

Number	Title	Yr	NM
❏ 1611	In My Diary/Lover, Love Me	1955	$70

— Blue label, silver top

Number	Title	Yr	NM
❏ 1689	In the Middle of the Night/Soda Pop	1958	$40
❏ 1717	Love Is a River/I'll Never Stop Wanting You	1959	$30
❏ 1738	Mama Loocie/ Unemployment	1959	$30

— As "Harvey and the Moonglows"

Number	Title	Yr	NM
❏ 1589	Most of All/She's Gone	1955	$70

— Blue label, silver top

Number	Title	Yr	NM
❏ 1646	Over and Over Again/I Knew from the Start	1957	$70

— With slower version of A-side; "8119A" in in the run-off area

Number	Title	Yr	NM
❏ 1646	Over and Over Again/I Knew from the Start	1957	$60

— With normal version of A-side; blue label, silver top

Number	Title	Yr	NM
❏ 1661	Please Send Me Someone to Love/Mr. Engineer (Bring Her Back to Me)	1957	$60

— Blue label, silver top

Number	Title	Yr	NM
❏ 1629	See Saw/When I'm With You	1956	$60

— Blue label, silver top

Number	Title	Yr	NM
❏ 1581	Sincerely/Tempting	1954	$70

— Blue label, silver top

Number	Title	Yr	NM
❏ 1605	Starlite/In Love	1955	$70

— Blue label, silver top

Number	Title	Yr	NM
❏ 1705	Ten Commandments of Love/Mean Old Blues	1958	$40

— As "Harvey and the Moonglows"

Number	Title	Yr	NM
❏ 1669 [PS]	The Beating of My Heart/ Confess It to Your Heart	1957	$60

— In general, for the above singles, the blue label with vertical "Chess" versions are 60% of the above values; yellow early-1960s label versions and black mid-1960s versions are 40% of above; and blue late-1960s versions, with "Chess" on top, are about 20%

Number	Title	Yr	NM
❏ 1701	This Love/Sweeter Than Words	1958	$40

Number	Title	Yr	NM
❏ 1681	Too Late/Here I Am	1958	$40
❏ 1619	We Go Together/ Chickie Um Bah	1956	$60

—Blue label, silver top

CRIMSON

Number	Title	Yr	NM
❏ 1003	My Imagination/Gee	1964	$30

RCA VICTOR

Number	Title	Yr	NM
❏ 74-0759	Sincerely/I Was Wrong	1972	$5
❏ 74-0839	When I'm With You/ You've Chosen Me	1972	$5

VEE JAY

Number	Title	Yr	NM
❏ 423	Secret Love/Real Gone Mama	1962	$30

7-Inch Extended Plays

CHESS

Number	Title	Yr	NM
❏ 5122	(contents unknown)	1959	$250
❏ 5122 [PS]	Look! It's the Moonglows	1959	$250
❏ 5123 [PS]	Look! It's the Moonglows, Vol. 2	1959	$250
❏ 5123	True Love/Penny Arcade//I'll Stop Waiting/ Sweeter Than Words	1959	$250

MOORE, BOBBY, AND THE RHYTHM ACES

CHECKER

Number	Title	Yr	NM
❏ 1129	Searching for My Love/Hey Mr. D.J.	1966	$20

—Maroon label, vertical "Checker

Number	Title	Yr	NM
❏ 1129	Searching for My Love/Hey Mr. D.J.	1966	$10

—Blue label

Number	Title	Yr	NM
❏ 1156	Try My Love Again/Go Ahead and Burn Baby	1966	$10

MOORE, DOROTHY

AVCO

Number	Title	Yr	NM
❏ 4599	Same Old Feeling/ (B-side unknown)	1972	$15
❏ 4590	See How They've Done My Love/(B-side unknown)	1972	$15

CHIMNEYVILLE

Number	Title	Yr	NM
❏ 10204	Don't Let Go/Two of a Kind	1975	$6
❏ 10207	We Can Love/Making Love	1975	$6

—With King Floyd

GSF

Number	Title	Yr	NM
❏ 6908	Cry Like a Baby/Just the One I've Been Looking For	1973	$20

—B-side is sought by Northern Soul aficionados

HANDSHAKE

Number	Title	Yr	NM
❏ WS9-02879	What's Forever For/ Someone's Lover Before (But Never Someone's Girl)	1982	$5

MALACO

Number	Title	Yr	NM
❏ 2064	Angel of the Morning/ Make It Soon	1980	$5
❏ 1037	For Old Time Sake/ Daddy's Eyes	1976	$6
❏ 1033	Funny How Time Slips Away/Ain't That a Mother's Luck	1976	$6
❏ 1042	I Believe You/Love Me	1977	$6
❏ 1048	Let the Music Play/1-2-3 (You and Me)	1978	$5
❏ 1029	Misty Blue/Here It Is	1976	$6
❏ 1059	Once or Twice/Love Me	1979	$5
❏ 1052	Special Occasion/ Girl Overboard	1978	$20

—B-side is sought by Northern Soul aficionados

Number	Title	Yr	NM
❏ 2062	Talk to Me-Every Beat of My Heart/Lonely	1980	$5
❏ 1054	(We Need More) Loving Time/Write a Little Prayer	1978	$5
❏ 1040	We Should Really Be in Love/I'll Never Be Loved	1977	$5

—With Eddie Floyd

Number	Title	Yr	NM
❏ 1047	With Pen in Hand/ Too Blind to See	1977	$5

VOLT

Number	Title	Yr	NM
❏ 990	Can't Get Over You (Once Again I'm Misty Blue)/ Don't Hold Your Breath	1988	$5
❏ 301	Endless Summer Nights/ Walk Through This Pain	1988	$5

MOORE, GATEMOUTH

KING

Number	Title	Yr	NM
❏ 4492	Christmas Blues/Happy New Year, Darling	1951	$60

—B-side by Lonnie Johnson

MOORE, HARV

AMERICAN ARTS

Number	Title	Yr	NM
❏ 20	Interview of the Fab Four/I Feel So Fine	1964	$300

MOORE, JACKIE

ATLANTIC

Number	Title	Yr	NM
❏ 2989	Both Ends Against the Middle/Clean Up Your Own Yard	1973	$5
❏ 2861	Darling Baby/ Something in a Love	1972	$5
❏ 2902	It Ain't Who You Know/They Tell Me of an Uncloudy Day	1972	$5
❏ 2681	Precious Precious/ Will Power	1969	$5
❏ 2798	Sometimes It's Got to Rain (In Your Love Life)/ Wonderful Marvelous	1971	$5
❏ 2956	Sweet Charlie Babe/If	1973	$5
❏ 2830	Time/Cover Me	1971	$5

CATAWBA

Number	Title	Yr	NM
❏ 1010	Holding Back/ (B-side unknown)	1983	$4

COLUMBIA

Number	Title	Yr	NM
❏ 11288	Helpless/With Your Love	1980	$4
❏ 11140	How's Your Love Life Baby/ Do Ya Got What It Takes	1979	$4
❏ 11363	Love Won't Let Me Wait/ With Your Love	1980	$4
❏ 10779	Personally/Ain't No Trouble Like Love Trouble	1978	$4
❏ 10993	This Time Baby/Let's Go Somewhere and Make Love	1979	$4
❏ 04599	This Time Baby/Let's Go Somewhere and Make Love	1984	$3

KAYVETTE

Number	Title	Yr	NM
❏ 5127	Disco Body (Shake It to the East, Shake It to the West)/Tired of Hiding	1976	$5
❏ 5139	Heart Be Still/Singin' Funky Music Turns Me On	1981	$4
❏ 5125	It's Harder to Leave/ (B-side unknown)	1976	$5
❏ 5122	Make Me Feel Like a Woman/Singin' Funky Music Turns Me On	1975	$5
❏ 5129	Make Me Yours/ Somebody Loves You	1977	$5
❏ 5124	Puttin' It Down to You/ Never Is Forever	1975	$5
❏ 5140	Who's Next/Singin' Funky Music Turns Me On	1981	$4

SHOUT

Number	Title	Yr	NM
❏ 232	Dear John/Here I Am	1968	$8
❏ 239	Why Don't You Call on Me/(B-side unknown)	1968	$8

MOORE, JIM, AND SIDEWINDER

WILLOW WIND

Number	Title	Yr	NM
❏ 0511	Ain't She Shinin' Tonight/ (B-side unknown)	1988	$6

MOORE, JOHNNY'S, BLAZERS

HOLLYWOOD

Number	Title	Yr	NM
❏ 1045	Christmas Everyday/ Christmas Eve, Baby	1955	$50

—With Frankie Ervin; also see "Ervin, Frankie

MOORE, LATTIE

KING

Number	Title	Yr	NM
❏ 4955	100,000 Women Can't Be Wrong/Lonesome Man Blues	1956	$60
❏ 5370	Cajun Doll/Mine Again	1960	$50
❏ 5413	Drunk Again/Driving Nails	1960	$30
❏ 1194	Foolish Castles/I'm Gonna Tell You Something	1953	$60
❏ 5762	Honky Tonk Heaven/ Lonesome Man Blues	1963	$20
❏ 1250	I Gotta Go Home/A Brand New Case of Love	1953	$60
❏ 5685	I Told You So/Heaven All Around Me	1962	$20
❏ 5723	Out of Control/Just About Then	1963	$20
❏ 1350	Pull Down the Blinds/What Am I Supposed to Do	1954	$60
❏ 5526	Sundown and Sorrow/If the Good Lord's Willing	1961	$30
❏ 1327	They're Not Worth the Paper They're Printed On/ Under a Mexico Moon	1954	$60

STARDAY

Number	Title	Yr	NM
❏ 441	Too Hot to Handle/ Just a-Waitin'	1959	$40

WPL

Number	Title	Yr	NM
❏ 1001	Old Ex-Husbands/Beat Years of Your Life	1970	$125

MOORE, MELBA

BUDDAH

Number	Title	Yr	NM
❏ 452	I Am His Lady/If I Lose You	1975	$5
❏ 596	I Don't Know No One Else to Turn To/Just Another Link	1978	$5
❏ 535	Lean On Me/One Less Morning	1976	$5
❏ 572	My Sensitive, Passionate Man/The Greatest Feeling	1977	$5

Number	Title	Yr	NM
❏ 589	Standing Right Here/ Living Free	1977	$5
❏ 496	Starting to Fall/ Must Be Dues	1975	$5

—With Jo Ellen Cohn

Number	Title	Yr	NM
❏ 568	The Long and Winding Road/Ain't No Love Lost	1977	$5
❏ 562	The Way You Make Me Feel/So Many Mountains	1977	$5
❏ 519	This Is It/Stay Awhile	1976	$5
❏ 519 [PS]	This Is It/Stay Awhile	1976	$8

CAPITOL

Number	Title	Yr	NM
❏ B-5632	A Little Bit More/ When We Touch	1986	$3

—A-side with Freddie Jackson

Number	Title	Yr	NM
❏ B-5415	(Can't Take Half) All of You/Let Me Be Yours	1984	$3

—With Lillo Thomas

Number	Title	Yr	NM
❏ B-5415 [PS]	(Can't Take Half) All of You/Let Me Be Yours	1984	$4
❏ B-5651	Falling/(B-side unknown)	1986	$3
❏ B-5520	I Can't Believe It (It's Over)/King of No Heart	1985	$3
❏ B-44148	I Can't Complain/There I Go Falling in Love Again	1988	$3

—A-side with Freddie Jackson

Number	Title	Yr	NM
❏ B-44148 [PS]	I Can't Complain/There I Go Falling in Love Again	1988	$3
❏ B-44195	I'm in Love/Stay	1988	$3

—With Kashif

Number	Title	Yr	NM
❏ B-44195 [PS]	I'm in Love/Stay	1988	$3
❏ B-44012	I'm Not Gonna Let You Go/Dreams	1987	$3
❏ B-44012 [PS]	I'm Not Gonna Let You Go/Dreams	1987	$3
❏ B-5681	It's Been So Long/ Don't Go Away	1987	$3
❏ B-5681 [PS]	It's Been So Long/ Don't Go Away	1987	$3
❏ B-5308	Livin' for Your Love/Got to Have Your Love	1984	$3
❏ B-5308 [PS]	Livin' for Your Love/Got to Have Your Love	1984	$4
❏ B-44265	Love and Kisses/I'm in Love	1988	$3
❏ B-5343	Love Me Right/ Never Say Never	1984	$3
❏ B-5343 [PS]	Love Me Right/ Never Say Never	1984	$4
❏ B-5577	Love the One I'm With (A Lot of Love)/Don't Go Away	1986	$3

—With Kashif

Number	Title	Yr	NM
❏ B-5577 [PS]	Love the One I'm With (A Lot of Love)/Don't Go Away	1986	$3
❏ B-5180	Mind Up Tonight/ (Instrumental)	1982	$3
❏ B-5484	When You Love Me Like This/Winner	1985	$3
❏ B-5484 [PS]	When You Love Me Like This/Winner	1985	$4

EMI AMERICA

Number	Title	Yr	NM
❏ 8104	Let's Stand Together/ What a Woman Needs	1981	$4
❏ 8126	Love's Comin' At Ya/ (Instrumental)	1982	$4
❏ 8114	Piece of the Rock/ (Instrumental)	1982	$4
❏ 8092	Take My Love/Just You, Just Me	1981	$4

EPIC

Number	Title	Yr	NM
❏ 50909	Everything So Good About You/Next to You	1980	$4
❏ 50805	Hot and Tasty/Night People	1979	$4
❏ 50762	Miss Thing/Need Love	1979	$4
❏ 50663	Pick Me Up, I'll Dance/ Where Did You Ever Go	1979	$4

MERCURY

Number	Title	Yr	NM
❏ 73217	He Ain't Heavy, He's My Brother/Take Up a Course in Happiness	1971	$8
❏ 73183	If I Had a Million/Loving You Comes So Easy	1971	$8
❏ 73072	I Got Love/I Love Making Love to You	1970	$8
❏ 72942	I Messed Up a Good Thing/I'll Do It All Over Again	1969	$8
❏ 73134	Look What You're Doing to the Man/ Patience Is Rewarded	1970	$8
❏ 73289	Love Letters/I Ain't Got to Love Nobody Else	1972	$8
❏ 73040	Time and Love/ (B-side unknown)	1970	$8
❏ 72989	We're Living to Give (Each Other)/(B-side unknown)	1969	$8

MUSICOR

Number	Title	Yr	NM
❏ 1189	Does Love Believe in Me/Don't Cry, Sing Along with the Music	1966	$12

MOORE, MELVIN

KING

Number	Title	Yr	NM
❏ 4539	Possessed/Hold Me, Kiss Me, Squeeze Me	1952	$125

Number	Title	Yr	NM
MOORE, PHIL			
RCA VICTOR			
❏ 47-5538	Blink Before Christmas/ Chincy Old Scrooge	1953	$30
MOORE, RUDY			
FEDERAL			
❏ 12280	Bobbie Dobbie/I'll Be Home to See You Tomorrow Night	1956	$60
❏ 12253	My Little Angel/I'm Mad with You	1956	$60
❏ 12276	Step It Up and Go/ Let Me Come Home	1956	$125
❏ 12259	The Buggy Ride/ Ring-a-Ling-Dong	1956	$60
MOORE, SCOTTY			
FERNWOOD			
❏ 107	Have Guitar Will Travel/Rest	1958	$40
MOORE, TIM			
ABC DUNHILL			
❏ 4337	Fool Like You/ Thinking About You	1973	$5
A SMALL RECORD COMPANY			
❏ 0601	Second Avenue/ (B-side unknown)	1974	$10
ASYLUM			
❏ 45214	Charmer/I'll Be Your Time	1974	$4
❏ 45214 [PS]	Charmer/I'll Be Your Time	1974	$6
❏ 46047	Fallen Angel/Crisis in the Finyard	1979	$4
❏ 45265	If Somebody Needs It/ Sweet Navel Lightning	1975	$4
❏ 45394	In the Middle/ Strengthen My Love	1977	$4
❏ 45287	Lay Down the Line to Me/ Sweet Navel Lightning	1975	$4
❏ 45208	Second Avenue/ Aviation Man	1974	$4
❏ 45427	Second Avenue/ Strengthen My Love	1977	$4
MORALES, NORO & HIS ORCHESTRA			
RCA VICTOR			
❏ 47-5674	Santa/Me And My Shadow	1954	$15
MORANDI, CHRISTIAN			
DECCA			
❏ 31343	Dear Gesu Bambino/ Caro Gesu Bambino	1961	$15
— B-side by Bruno Pallesi			
MORGAN, AL			
COLUMBIA			
❏ 4-41022	Bouquet of Roses/The Wanderer Came Home	1957	$20
❏ 4-40943	Easy Goin' Heart/Don't Rob Another Man's Castle	1957	$20
❏ 4-40755	I'm Paying for Yesterday's Mistakes/ Let's Dance Ragtime	1956	$20
DECCA			
❏ 9-27908	Good Night, Sweet Jesus/Mother At Your Feet Is Kneeling	1951	$30
❏ 9-28585	If I Had a Penny/Things I Might Have Been	1953	$30
❏ 9-27902	I'll Never Let You Cry/ The Bluest Word I Know Is "Lonesome	1951	$30
❏ 9-28229	Is It True What They Say About Dixie/ Someday Sweetheart	1952	$30
❏ 9-28040	Mistakes/My Castle in Spain	1952	$30
❏ 9-27794	Sin/Jealous Eyes	1951	$30
❏ 9-27887	Too Good to Be True/ Blue Smoke	1951	$30
LONDON			
❏ 885	If I Had My Way/You Tell Me Your Dream	1950	$40
❏ 887	Smile, Darn Ya, Smile/ Gee But It's Great	1950	$40
❏ 30006	Tears on My Pillow/ (B-side unknown)	1950	$40
RENDEZVOUS			
❏ 113	I'll Take Care of Your Cares/Me and the Moon	1959	$30
X			
❏ 04	Sweet Kentucky Sue/ You Told Me to Go	1954	$30
❏ 052	Tell Me Now/Bells of Memory	1954	$30
❏ 015	That Silver-Haired Daddy of Mine/My Mom	1954	$30
MORGAN, BILL			
COLUMBIA			
❏ 4-21450	Adios, So Long, Goodbye/ I'm a Fool to Think You Care	1955	$30

Number	Title	Yr	NM
❏ 4-21373	Mucher We Do It/Mighty, Mighty Lonesome	1955	$30
MORGAN, BILLIE			
STARDAY			
❏ 464	Country Girl at Heart/ Treatin' Me	1959	$20
❏ 420	Life to Live/Thinking All Night	1959	$20
MORGAN, FREDDY			
CHALLENGE			
❏ 59044	64 Rue Blondell/Side Saddle	1959	$12
MORGAN, GEORGE			
4 STAR			
❏ 1009	From This Moment On/ One Wife Five Kids Later	1975	$5
❏ 1034	I Just Want You to Know/I Will Take Care of You	1978	$5
❏ 1040	I'm Completely Satisfied with You/From This Moment On	1979	$5
— With Lorrie Morgan			
❏ 1001	In the Misty Moonlight/ Welcome Back to My World	1975	$5
COLUMBIA			
❏ 4-21344	A Cheap Affair/So Lonesome	1955	$30
❏ 4-20944	Almost/There's No Reason	1952	$30
—B-side by Neal Burris; one record of a 4-record various-artists box			
❏ 4-20906	Almost/You're a Little Girl	1952	$30
❏ 2-550(?)	Angel Mother/Lucky Seven	1950	$50
— Microgroove 33 1/3 rpm small hole 7-inch single			
❏ 4-41063	A Perfect Romance/ Sweet, Sweet Lips	1957	$30
❏ 4-43393	A Picture That's New/Roses	1965	$15
❏ 4-21321	A Shot in the Dark/ Oceans of Tears	1954	$30
❏ 4-21390	Best Mistake/I'd Like to Know	1955	$30
❏ 4-20945	Be Sure You Know/ Whistle My Love	1952	$30
❏ 4-42757	Beyond My Heart/ Where Is My Love	1963	$20
❏ 4-42650	Blue Snowfall/Mach Nichts (It Makes No Difference)	1962	$20
❏ 4-20870	Broken Candy Heart/I Wish I May, I Wish I Might	1952	$30
❏ 4-41246	Candy Kisses/ Rockabilly Bungalow	1958	$40
❏ 2-355(?)	Cry-Baby Heart/I Love Everything About You	1949	$50
— Microgroove 33 1/3 rpm small hole 7-inch single			
❏ 4-42060	Every Day of My Life/Our Love	1961	$20
❏ 4-21170	Every Prayer Is a Flower/ How Many Times	1953	$30
❏ 4-21465	Every So Often/ Lonesome Record	1955	$30
❏ 2-700(?)	Greedy Fingers/Warm Hands, Cold Heart	1950	$50
— Microgroove 33 1/3 rpm small hole 7-inch single			
❏ 4-21108	Half Hearted/I Passed By Your Window	1953	$30
❏ 4-43216	Happy Endings/Dear John	1965	$15
❏ 4-43653	Home Is Where the Heart Is/No Man Could Hurt As Much As I	1966	$15
❏ 4-42505	I Can Hear My Heart Break/ Across the Wide Missouri	1962	$20
❏ 4-21070	(I Just Had a Date) A Lover's Quarrel/Most of All	1953	$30
❏ 4-20747	I Know You'll Never Change/ Don't Be Afraid to Love Me	1950	$40
❏ 4-20774	I Love No One But You/ Somebody Robbed Me	1951	$40
❏ 4-41318	I'm in Love Again/It Was All in Your Mind	1959	$20
❏ 4-41188	I'm Not Afraid/Loveable You	1958	$20
❏ 4-21237	It's Been Nice/I Think I'm Going to Cry	1954	$30
❏ 4-20811	I Wish I May/Broken Candy Heart	1951	$40
❏ 4-41420	Little Dutch Girl/The Last Thing I Want to Know	1959	$20
❏ 4-21430	Little Pioneer/Ain't Love Grand	1955	$30
❏ 4-42277	Lonely Room/Let Me Live and Love Today	1962	$20
❏ 4-21151	Lonesome Waltz/I'll Furnish the Shoulder You Cry On	1953	$30
❏ 4-21178	Look What Followed Me Home/No One Knows It Better Than Me	1953	$30
❏ 4-21204	Love, Love, Love/The First Time I Told You a Lie	1954	$30
❏ 4-20850	My Baby Lied to Me/ Waltzing by the Ohio	1951	$40
❏ 4-40967	My House Is Divided/ Late Date	1957	$30
❏ 4-42882	One Dozen Roses (And Our Love)/All Right (I'll Sign the Papers)	1963	$20
❏ 4-41794	One Empty Chair/ It's Best You Know	1960	$20
❏ 4-21006	One Woman Man/ Everything Rolled Into One	1952	$30
❏ 4-41957	Only One Minute More/ The Little Green Men	1961	$20

Number	Title	Yr	NM
❏ 4-40978	Our Summer Vacation/It Always Ends Too Soon	1957	$30
❏ 4-21052	Please Believe/A Stranger in the Night	1952	$30
❏ 4-21548	Stay Away from Me Baby/Now You Know	1956	$30
❏ 4-21517	Take a Look at Yourself/ Send for My Baby	1956	$30
❏ 4-43098	Tears and Roses/ You're Not Home Yet	1964	$15
❏ 4-20822	Tennessee Hillbilly Ghost/ My Heart Keeps Telling Me	1951	$40
❏ 4-20884	The Cry of the Lamb/ Mansion Over the Hilltop	1952	$30
❏ 4-40792	There Goes My Love/ Can I Be Dreaming	1956	$30
❏ 4-43899	There Goes My World/ Speak Well of Me	1966	$15
❏ 4-40859	The Tears Behind the Smile/ Don't Cry, For You I Love	1957	$30
❏ 4-21276	Walking Shoes/Sweetheart	1954	$30
❏ 4-21318	Whither Thou Goest/ Oh Gentle Shepherd	1954	$30
❏ 4-41701	Who Knows You the Best/Where There's a Will There's a Way	1960	$20
❏ 4-21071	Withered Roses/You Love Me Just Enough to Hurt Me	1953	$30
DECCA			
❏ 32886	Gentle Rains of Home/ Walking Shadow, Talking Mem'ry	1971	$6
❏ 33037	Makin' Heartaches/Sing My Blues and Birthday Song	1972	$6
MCA			
❏ 40298	A Candy Mountain Melody/You're That Much Woman to Me	1974	$5
❏ 40069	Mr. Ting-a-Ling (Steel Guitar Man)/Our Wedding Song	1973	$5
❏ 40227	Somewhere Around Midnight/I Never Knew Love	1974	$5
STARDAY			
❏ 825	Barbara/Sad Bird	1967	$12
❏ 804	I Couldn't See/Look at the Lonely	1967	$10
❏ 860	I'll Sail My Ship Alone/Live and Let Live and Be Happy	1969	$10
❏ 834	Living/Rosebuds and You	1968	$10
❏ 814	Shiny Red Automobile/ Have Some of Mine	1967	$10
❏ 850	Sounds of Goodbye/Ballad of the Grand Ole Opry	1968	$12
STOP			
❏ 357	I Walk on the Outside/ The Enemy	1970	$8
❏ 252	Like a Bird/Left Over Feelings	1969	$8
❏ 365	Lilacs and Fire/ Hardest Easy Thing	1970	$8
❏ 384	One and the Same/I Wouldn't Have You Any Other Way	1971	$8
❏ 297	We've Done All the Lovin' We Can Do/Color of a Bird	1969	$8
MORGAN, JANE			
ABC			
❏ 11002	Him's a Dope/I Promise You	1967	$6
❏ 11092	Look What You've Done to Me/There's Nothing Else in My Mind	1968	$5
❏ 11034	Masquerade/Smile	1968	$5
❏ 11054	My Funny Valentine/A Child	1968	$5
❏ 10969	Somebody Someplace/This Is My World Without You	1967	$6
❏ 11024	The Marvelous Toy/Smile	1967	$6
COLPIX			
❏ 761	After the Fall/Oh, How I Lie	1965	$8
❏ 734	C'est Si Bon/Once Upon a Summertime	1964	$8
❏ 713	Does Goodnight Mean Goodbye/Bless 'Em All	1963	$8
❏ 713 [PS]	Does Goodnight Mean Goodbye/Bless 'Em All	1963	$15
❏ 754	Dominique/Funny World	1964	$8
❏ 727	Frum Russia with Love/The Song from Moulin Rouge (Where Is Your Heart)	1964	$8
❏ 755	The Poor People of Paris/Funny World	1964	$8
EPIC			
❏ 10058	Elusive Butterfly/Good Lovin'	1966	$6
❏ 10012	I Will Wait for You/ Love Me True	1966	$6
❏ 9881	Little Hands/Everyone Come to My Party	1965	$8
❏ 9819	Maybe/Walking the Streets in the Rain	1965	$8
❏ 9847	Side by Side/Till I Waltz Again with You	1965	$8
❏ 10159	The Three Bells/I Want to Be with You	1967	$6
KAPP			
❏ 478	Ask Me to Dance/Waiting for Charlie to Come Home	1962	$8
❏ 104	Baseball, Baseball/ Fairweather Friends	1954	$20

Number	Title	Yr	NM
❏ AS-928X [DJ]	Black Coffee/Guess I'll Hang My Tears Out to Dry	1962	$30
— Special Disc Jockey Record" and "Album Sample			
❏ 172	Come Home, Come Home, Come Home/From the First Hello to Our Last Goodbye	1957	$10
❏ 221	Enchanted Island/Once More, My Love, Once More	1958	$12
❏ 191	Fascination/(Instrumental)	1957	$10
❏ 191 [PS]	Fascination/(Instrumental)	1957	$30
— With color picture of Jane Morgan only			
❏ 191 [PS]	Fascination/(Instrumental)	1957	$40
— With photos of Gary Cooper, Audrey Hepburn and Jane Morgan on sleeve			
❏ 115	Flyin' High/Give Me Your World	1955	$15
❏ 305	Happy Anniversary/C'est La Vie, C'est L'Amour	1959	$12
❏ 305 [PS]	Happy Anniversary/C'est La Vie, C'est L'Amour	1959	$20
❏ 332	I Am a Heart/Romantica	1960	$10
❏ 304	I'm in Love/Was It Day, Was It Night	1959	$10
❏ 121	In Paree/Take Me Away	1955	$15
❏ 111	I Try to Forget You/Why Don't They Leave Us Alone	1955	$15
❏ 200	It's Been a Long, Long Time/I'm New at the Game of Romance	1957	$10
❏ 185	It's Not for Me to Say/Around the World	1957	$10
❏ 418	It Takes Love/Homesick for New England	1961	$8
❏ 148	La Ronde/Midnight Blues	1956	$15
❏ 140	Let's Go Steady/Take Care	1956	$15
❏ 351	Lord and Master/Where's the Boy (I Never Met)	1960	$10
❏ 390	Love Makes the World Go 'Round/He Makes Me Feel I'm Lonely	1961	$8
❏ 431	Moon River/Blue Hawaii	1961	$8
❏ 214	Only One Love/I've Got Bells on My Heart	1958	$10
❏ 358	The Angry Sea/Somebody	1960	$12
❏ 317	The Bells of St. Mary's/Ballad of Lady Jane	1960	$12
❏ 235	The Day the Rains Came/The Day the Rains Came (French Version)	1958	$12
❏ AS-924X [DJ]	The Second Time Around (same on both sides)	1961	$30
❏ 264	To Each His Own/Love Is Like Champagne	1959	$10
❏ 253	To Love and Be Loved/If Only I Could Live My Life Again	1958	$10
❏ 161	Two Different Worlds/Nights in Verona	1956	$10
— With Roger Williams			
❏ 450	What Now My Love/Forever My Love	1962	$8
❏ AS904X [DJ]	When the World Was Young/J'Attendrai	1956	$30
— Album Sample" promo-only single			
❏ 284	With Open Arms/I Can't Begin to Tell You	1959	$10
❏ 284 [PS]	With Open Arms/I Can't Begin to Tell You	1959	$20

RCA VICTOR

Number	Title	Yr	NM
❏ 47-9839	A Girl Named Johnny Cash/Charley	1970	$5
❏ 47-9727	Congratulations, I Guess/All of My Laughter	1969	$5
❏ 74-0316	He Gives Me Love/He's Never Too Busy	1970	$5
❏ 74-0153	Marry Me, Marry Me/Three Rest Stops	1969	$5
❏ 47-9901	The First Day/I'm Only a Woman	1970	$5
❏ 74-0194	Traces/Where Do I Go	1969	$5

7-Inch Extended Plays

EPIC

Number	Title	Yr	NM
❏ 5-26166 [S]	I'm Sorry/You Belong to Me/Downtown//Fascination/Why Don't You Believe Me/We'll Sing in the Sunshine	1965	$10
— 33 1/3 rpm, small hole, "For Jukebox Use Only			
❏ 5-26166 [PS]	In My Style	1965	$12

KAPP

Number	Title	Yr	NM
❏ KE-752 [PS]	All the Way	1958	$20
❏ KE-752	All the Way/Till//Melodie d'Amour (Song of Love)/Tammy	1958	$20
❏ KE-756	Arrivederci Roma/Who's Sorry Now?//Catch a Falling Star/Be My Little Bumble Bee	1958	$20
❏ KE-747 [PS]	Fascination	1957	$20
❏ KE-747	Fascination/It's Not for Me to Say//My Heart Reminds Me/An Affair to Remember	1957	$20
❏ SE-415	Fascination/My Heart Reminds Me//It's Not for Me to Say/Around the World	1959	$30
— Stereo, large hole			
❏ KE-731 [PS]	From the First Hello to the Last Goodbye	1957	$20

Number	Title	Yr	NM
❏ KE-731	From the First Hello to the Last Goodbye/Come Home, Come Home, Come Home//I'll Be Seeing You/Thanks for the Memory	1957	$20
❏ SE-405	The Day the Rains Came/Everybody Loves a Lover//It's All in the Game/Wrap Your Troubles in Dreams	1959	$30
— Stereo, large hole			
❏ KE-758	The Day the Rains Came/Volare//It's All in the Game/Everybody Loves a Lover	1958	$20
❏ SE-405 [PS]	(title unknown)	1959	$30
❏ SE-406 [PS]	(title unknown)	1959	$30

MORGAN, JAYE P.

BEVERLY HILLS

Number	Title	Yr	NM
❏ 9367	A Song fo You/Do You Really Have a Heart	1971	$6
❏ 9337	Billy Sunshine/Love of a Gentle Man	1969	$6
❏ 9349	He's Too Good to Me/I've Got an Awful Lot of Losing You to Do	1970	$6
❏ 9386	That Man Is My Weakness/Love of a Gentle Man	1972	$6
❏ 9344	What Are You Doing the Rest of Your Life/Applause	1970	$6

DECCA

Number	Title	Yr	NM
❏ 9-29501	Life Was Made for Living/Have You Ever Been Lonely	1955	$15

DERBY

Number	Title	Yr	NM
❏ 855	I Ain't Got the Man/Baby Don't Do It	1954	$30
❏ 837	Life Is Just a Bowl of Cherries/Operator 299	1953	$30
❏ 852	Life Was Meant for Living/Nobody Met the Train	1954	$30

MGM

Number	Title	Yr	NM
❏ K12752	Are You Lonesome Tonight/Miss You	1959	$10
❏ K13049	Brotherhood of Man/Nobody's Sweetheart	1961	$8
❏ K12984	Catch Me a Kiss/Close Your Eyes	1961	$8
❏ K12879	Half As Much/I Don't Want to Walk Without You	1960	$10
❏ K13076	He Thinks I Still Care/Heartache Named Johnny	1962	$8
❏ K12904	I Understand/I Wish I Didn't Love You So	1960	$10
❏ K12924	I Walk the Line/Wondering Where You Are	1960	$10
❏ K12838	Left My Gal in the Mountains/That Funny Feeling	1959	$12
❏ K13021	Let Me Know/No One to Cry To	1961	$8
❏ K13114	Ma, He's Making Eyes at Me/Slowly	1962	$8
❏ K12861	My Darling, My Darling/Thoughts of Love	1959	$10
❏ K12786	My Reputation/(It Took) One Kiss	1959	$10
❏ K12815	Somebody Loses, Somebody Wins/Somebody Else Is Taking My Place	1959	$12
❏ K13142	The Longest Walk/Will He Love Me	1963	$8
❏ K12956	When You Get What You Want/World I Can't Live In	1960	$10

RCA VICTOR

Number	Title	Yr	NM
❏ 47-7364	All I Have to Do Is Dream/Just You, Just Me	1958	$10
❏ 47-6137	Chee Chee O-Chee (Sang the Little Bird)/Two Lost Souls	1955	$10
— With Perry Como			
❏ 47-6016	Danger! Heartbreak Ahead/Softly, Softly	1955	$20
❏ 47-7326	Easy Does It/Star Dust	1958	$12
❏ 47-6441	Get Up! Get Up! (You Sleepyhead)/Sweet Lips	1956	$15
❏ 47-6938	Graduation Ring/You, You Romeo	1957	$15
❏ 47-6282	If You Don't Want My Love/Pepper-Hot Baby	1955	$20
❏ 47-7263	I Love You So Much It Hurts/I Know, I Know, I Know	1958	$10
❏ 47-6798	I Thought It Was Over/I Pledge Allegiance to Your Heart	1957	$15
❏ 47-6505	Lost in the Shuffle/Play for Keeps	1956	$15
❏ 47-6708	Mutual Admiration Society/If'n	1956	$20
— With Eddy Arnold			
❏ 47-7178	My Blind Date/Tell Me More	1958	$10
❏ 47-6842	One/Do You Love Me	1957	$15
— With Eddy Arnold			
❏ 47-5896	That's All I Want from You/Dawn	1954	$20
❏ 47-6182	The Longest Walk/Swanee	1955	$20
❏ 47-7064	There's a Dream in My Heart/Take a Chance	1957	$15

MORGAN, LEE

BLUE NOTE

Number	Title	Yr	NM
❏ 1930	Cornbread, Part 1/Cornbread, Part 2	1967	$8
❏ 1947	Hey Chico/Sweet Honey Bee	1968	$8
❏ 1951	Midnight Cowboy/Popi	1969	$8
❏ 1911	The Sidewinder, Part 1/The Sidewinder, Part 2	1964	$8

VEE JAY

Number	Title	Yr	NM
❏ 401	Expoobedient/Just in Time	1961	$15
❏ 360	I'm a Fool to Want You/Terrible "T	1960	$15

MORGAN, LORRIE

ABC HICKORY

Number	Title	Yr	NM
❏ 54041	Two People in Love/I Don't Care	1979	$6

MCA

Number	Title	Yr	NM
❏ 52331	Don't Go Changing/Everything You Say	1983	$4
❏ 52439	Easy Love/If You Came Back Tonight	1984	$4
❏ 52280	Someday We'll Be Together/Everything You Say	1983	$4
❏ 41052	Tell Me I'm Only Dreaming/In for Rain	1979	$5

RCA

Number	Title	Yr	NM
❏ 8866-7-R	Dear Me/Eight Days a Week	1989	$3
❏ 9016-7-R	Out of Your Shoes/One More Last Time	1989	$4
❏ 8638-7-R	Trainwreck of Emotion/One More Last Time	1988	$4

MORGAN, LOUMELL

ATLANTIC

Number	Title	Yr	NM
❏ 953	Charmaine/Jock-O-Mo	1952	$200

MORGAN, RUSS

DECCA

Number	Title	Yr	NM
❏ 24766	Blue Christmas/The Mistletoe Kiss	1950	$20
❏ 30147	The Santa Claus March/I Will Always Believe in Santa Claus	1956	$15

MORGAN TWINS, THE

RCA VICTOR

Number	Title	Yr	NM
❏ 47-7373	Let's Get Goin'/While It Lasted	1958	$30
❏ 47-7300	TV Hop/This Feeling's Bound to Be Love	1958	$30

MORGEN

PROBE

Number	Title	Yr	NM
❏ 474	Of Dreams/She's the Nighttime	1969	$30

MORISSETTE, ALANIS

LAMOR

Number	Title	Yr	NM
❏ LMR-10-12 [PS]	Fate Stay With Me/Find the Right Man	1987	$400
— As "Alanis"; Canadian release only, this was her first record			
❏ LMR-10-12	Fate Stay With Me/Find the Right Man	1987	$400

MORLEY, COZY

ABC-PARAMOUNT

Number	Title	Yr	NM
❏ 9811	I Love My Girl/Why Don't You Fall in Love	1957	$30

MORRIS, BOB

CAPITOL

Number	Title	Yr	NM
❏ 2444	All I Had Going for Me/What's Wrong with Staying Home (With Julie)	1969	$8
❏ 2293	Going Home to Mama/Wicked Wind	1968	$8

CHALLENGE

Number	Title	Yr	NM
❏ 59313	Fool Enough/Something to Think About	1965	$40
❏ 59324	I Bumped Into It/Ordinarily	1966	$20
❏ 59247	See the Monkey Walk Through the Door/I Tried to Make You Over	1964	$30
❏ 59215	Silly Willy/Pur Your Arms Around Him	1963	$30
❏ 59284	Walkin' Talkin' Livin' Doll/Don't Underestimate Me	1965	$40

TOWER

Number	Title	Yr	NM
❏ 307	Fishin' on the Mississippi/Little Bit of You	1966	$10
❏ 375	That Old Letter from Home/All That's Missing Here Tonight Is You	1967	$12
❏ 338	The First Thing I Think Of/Queen Bee	1967	$10

MORRIS, GARY
WARNER BROS.

Number	Title	Yr	NM
❑ 28823	100% Chance of Rain/Back in Her Arms Again	1986	$3
❑ 28713	Anything Goes/Draggin' the Lake for the Moon	1986	$3
❑ 29131	Baby Bye Bye/West Texas Highway and Me	1984	$3
❑ 29321	Between Two Fires/All She Said Was Yes	1984	$3
❑ 50017	Don't Look Back/She Gave Me Till Friday	1982	$4
❑ 29967	Dreams Die Hard/(B-side unknown)	1982	$3
❑ 27706 [PS]	Every Christmas/Silver Bells	1988	$4
❑ 27706	Every Christmas/Silver Bells	1988	$4
❑ 28218	Finishing Touches/Mama You Can't Give Me No Whippin'	1987	$3
❑ 49668	Fire in Your Eyes/Heartaches by the Number	1981	$4
❑ 49829	Headed for a Heartache/I'm So Tired of Losing	1981	$4
❑ 28654	Honeycomb/Whoever's Watchin'	1986	$3
❑ 28947	I'll Never Stop Loving You/Heaven's Hell Without You	1985	$3
❑ 29028	Lasso the Moon/When I Close My Eyes	1985	$3
❑ 28542	Leave Me Lonely/Eleventh Hour	1986	$3
❑ 49564	May I Borrow Some Sugar for You/Sweet Red Wine	1980	$5
❑ 28468	Plain Brown Wrapper/Moonshine	1987	$3
❑ 29230	Second Hand Heart/Whoever's Watchin'	1984	$3
❑ 28388	Simply Meant to Be/Simply Meant to Be	1987	$3

— A-side with Jennifer Warnes; B-side by Henry Mancini

Number	Title	Yr	NM
❑ 29683	The Love She Found in Me/That's the Way It Is	1983	$3
❑ 29532	The Wind Beneath My Wings/The Way I Love You Tonight	1983	$6
❑ 29450	Why Lady Why/The Way I Love You Tonight	1983	$3

MORRIS, HOWARD
ROULETTE

Number	Title	Yr	NM
❑ 4309	Department Store Santa Claus (Before Christmas)/Department Store Santa Claus (After Christmas)	1960	$20

MORRIS, JOE
ATLANTIC

Number	Title	Yr	NM
❑ 914	Any Time, Any Place, Any Where/Come Back Daddy Daddy	1950	$500

— With Laura Tate; Atlantic's earliest number on 45; Morris' 78s on Atlantic before 914 were not issued on 45

Number	Title	Yr	NM
❑ 1160	Going, Going, Gone/Sinner Woman	1957	$30
❑ 985	I'm Goin' to Leave You/That's What Makes My Baby Fat	1953	$125

HERALD

Number	Title	Yr	NM
❑ 446	Be Careful/Way Down Yonder	1955	$40
❑ 420	Travelin' Man/No, It Can't Be Done	1954	$50

— Black vinyl

Number	Title	Yr	NM
❑ 420	Travelin' Man/No, It Can't Be Done	1954	$100

— Red vinyl

MORRISON, VAN
BANG

Number	Title	Yr	NM
❑ 545	Brown Eyed Girl/Goodbye, Baby	1967	$15
❑ 552	Chick-a-Boom/Ro Ro Rosey	1967	$10
❑ 585	Spanish Rose/Midnight Special	1971	$8

MERCURY

Number	Title	Yr	NM
❑ 880669-7	Haunts of Ancient Peace/Tore Down A La Rimbaud	1985	$4
❑ 884841-7	Ivory Tower/New Kind of Man	1986	$4
❑ 884841-7 [PS]	Ivory Tower/New Kind of Man	1986	$4

PHILCO-FORD

Number	Title	Yr	NM
❑ HP-16	Brown Eyed Girl/Midnight Special	1968	$30

— 4-inch plastic "Hip Pocket Record" with color sleeve

WARNER BROS.

Number	Title	Yr	NM
❑ 7797	Ain't Nothin' You Can Do/Wild Children	1974	$5
❑ 7462	Blue Money/Sweet Thing	1971	$6
❑ 8029	Bulbs/Cul-De-Sac	1974	$5
❑ 7488	Call Me Up in Dreamland/Street Choir	1971	$6
❑ 8805	Checkin' It Out/Kingdom Hall	1979	$4
❑ 7383	Come Running/Crazy Love	1970	$6
❑ 7434	Domino/Sweet Janine	1970	$6

Number	Title	Yr	NM
❑ 49162	Full Force Gale/You Make Me Feel So Free	1980	$4
❑ 7786	Gloria/(B-side unknown)	1973	$5
❑ 7744	Green/Wild Children	1973	$5
❑ 7665	Gypsy/Saint Dominic's Preview	1972	$5
❑ 8743	Lifetimes/Natalia	1979	$4
❑ 8450	Moondance/Cold Wind in August	1977	$5
❑ 50031	Scandinavia/Cleaning Windows	1982	$4
❑ 7573	Straight to My Heart Like a Cannonball/Old Old Woodstock	1972	$5
❑ 7543	Tupelo Honey/Starting a New Life	1971	$6
❑ 7706	Warm Love/I Will Be There	1973	$5
❑ 8661	Wavelength/Checkin' It Out	1978	$5
❑ 7518	Wild Night/When That Evening Sun Goes Down	1971	$6

MORRISSEY
Also see THE SMITHS. (45)

SIRE

Number	Title	Yr	NM
❑ 27837	Everyday Is Like Sunday/Disappointed	1988	$6
❑ 27907	Suedehead/I Know Very Well How I Got My Name	1988	$6

MORROW, BUDDY
EPIC

Number	Title	Yr	NM
❑ 5-9765	The Bostella (Part 1)/(Part 2)	1965	$8
❑ 5-9765 [PS]	The Bostella (Part 1)/(Part 2)	1965	$15
❑ LPC-119	(contents unknown)	1961	$10

— Compact 33 Double"; small hole, plays at 33 1/3 rpm

MORSE, ELLA MAE
7-Inch Extended Plays
CAPITOL

Number	Title	Yr	NM
❑ EAP 1-513 [PS]	Barrelhouse, Boogie, and the Blues	1955	$20

MORTIMER
PHILIPS

Number	Title	Yr	NM
❑ 40524	Dedicated Music Man/To Understand Someone	1968	$8
❑ 40524 [PS]	Dedicated Music Man/To Understand Someone	1968	$15
❑ 40567	Ingenue's Theme/Slicker Beauty Hints	1968	$8

MORTIMER, AZIE
BIG TOP

Number	Title	Yr	NM
❑ 3041	Lips/Wrapped Up in a Dream	1960	$400

EPIC

Number	Title	Yr	NM
❑ 5-9584	Cry Me a River/Little Boy (I Keep On Changing My Mind)	1963	$30

OKEH

Number	Title	Yr	NM
❑ 4-7337	I Don't Care/Prove It	1970	$15

PALETTE

Number	Title	Yr	NM
❑ 5097	Mama, What Should I Do/When You're Talking Love	1962	$30

— As "A.Z. Mortimer

RCA VICTOR

Number	Title	Yr	NM
❑ 47-8985	Little Miss Everything/Best Years	1966	$20

REGATTA

Number	Title	Yr	NM
❑ 2002	Brother Love/Treat Me Like You Love Me	1961	$30

SWAN

Number	Title	Yr	NM
❑ 4158	Put Yourself in My Place/Bring Back Your Love	1963	$20

UNITED ARTISTS

Number	Title	Yr	NM
❑ 847	The Other Half of Me/(I Get the Feeling) You're Ashamed of Me	1965	$50

MORTON, ANN J.
CHART

Number	Title	Yr	NM
❑ 5183	Housewife's Union/Welcome Home	1973	$8
❑ 5227	Somebody Bigger Than Me/(B-side unknown)	1974	$8

PRAIRIE DUST

Number	Title	Yr	NM
❑ 7621	Black and Blue Heart/Me and My Horse Named Daddy	1977	$5
❑ 7619	Blueberry Hill/Onions and Love Affairs	1977	$5
❑ 7612	Don't Call Me No Lady/Onions and Love Affairs	1977	$5
❑ 7631	Don't Stay on Your Side of the Bed Tonight/It's Written All Over Your Face	1979	$5

Number	Title	Yr	NM
❑ 7617	Don't Want to Take a Chance (On Loving You)/Tainted Rose	1977	$5
❑ 7634	Hey Vern/I'll Do It 'Cause I Love You	1980	$5
❑ 7629	I'm Not in the Mood (For Love)/Willie I Will	1978	$5
❑ 7632	My Empty Arms/Don't Stay on Your Side of the Bed Tonight	1979	$5
❑ 7606	Poor Wilted Rose/Molly Jones (Is a Happy Hooker)	1976	$5
❑ 7636	Share Your Love Tonight/(B-side unknown)	1980	$5
❑ 7627	Share Your Love Tonight/Willie I Will	1978	$5
❑ 7633	(We Used to Kiss Each Other on the Lips But It's) All Over Now/I Like Being Lonely	1979	$5
❑ 7603	Willie I Will/Onions and Love Affairs	1976	$5

MORTON, TEX
OKEH

Number	Title	Yr	NM
❑ 18014	I Was Born in Old Wyoming/I've Known the Truth	1954	$50

MOSBY, JOHNNY AND JONIE
CAPITOL

Number	Title	Yr	NM
❑ 2978	A Little of Me, A Little of You/Someone to Take My Place	1970	$6
❑ 2258	Come In the Back Door (Go 'Round, Go 'Round)/You Be the Mama, I'll Be the Papa	1968	$6
❑ 2505	Hold Me, Thrill Me, Kiss Me/Comparing Him with You	1969	$6
❑ 2608	I'll Never Be Free/Pattern of Our Lives	1969	$6
❑ 2796	I'm Leavin' It Up to You/If It's Left Up to Me	1970	$6
❑ 3141	Let's Get This Show on the Road/Souvenirs of Love	1971	$6
❑ 3613	Let's Try Love Again/It's All Because of You	1973	$6
❑ 5980	Make a Left and Then a Right/Take Back the World	1967	$6
❑ 2087	Mr. and Mrs. John Smith/Hello There Stranger	1968	$6
❑ 3277	Music to My Ears/I'll Say It Again	1972	$6
❑ 3332	My Ecstasy/Ain't You Ever	1972	$6
❑ 2865	My Happiness/Let Your Sun Shine on Me	1970	$6
❑ 2865 [PS]	My Happiness/Let Your Sun Shine on Me	1970	$10
❑ 3039	Oh, Love of Mine/Closing Time Till Dawn	1971	$6
❑ 2179	Our Golden Wedding Day/Two Dollar Honeymoon Room	1968	$6
❑ 2730	Third World/You Go Back to Your World (I'll Go Back to Mine)	1970	$6

CHALLENGE

Number	Title	Yr	NM
❑ 59088	He Wouldn't Take Me Home to Meet His Mother/Hard Luck and Misery	1960	$20

COLUMBIA

Number	Title	Yr	NM
❑ 42668	Don't Call Me from a Honky Tonk/Wrong Side of Town	1963	$12
❑ 43631	Heartbreak U.S.A./Identity	1966	$8
❑ 43100	How the Other Half Lives/Stolen Paradise	1964	$10
❑ 42449	I'd Fight the World/Answer to Charlie's Shoes	1962	$15
❑ 43218	Strawberry Wine/Wrong Company	1965	$8
❑ 43344	The High Cost of Loving/The Home She's Tearing Down	1965	$8
❑ 42841	Trouble in My Arms/Who's Been Cheatin' Who	1963	$10

TOPPA

Number	Title	Yr	NM
❑ 1047	Dear Okie/You Can't Hurt Me Anymore	1962	$20
❑ 1039	Making Believe/Ain't You Ever	1961	$20

MOSES, LEE
FRONT PAGE

Number	Title	Yr	NM
❑ 2301	Time and Place/I Can't Take No Chances	1970	$30

GATES

Number	Title	Yr	NM
❑ 1502	Bad Girl/Dark End of the Street	1967	$100

MUSICOR

Number	Title	Yr	NM
❑ 1242	Bad Girl (Part 1)/(Part 2)	1967	$40

Number	Title	Yr	NM
MOSS, ROY			
FASCINATION			
❏ 1002	Wiggle Walkin' Baby/ (B-side unknown)	1957	$200
MERCURY			
❏ 70858	Corinne, Corinna/You Don't Know My Mind	1956	$200
MOST, MICKIE			
LAWN			
❏ 236	Sea Cruise/It's a Little Bit Hot	1964	$30
MOTELS, THE			
Also see MARTHA DAVIS.			
CAPITOL			
❏ 4896	Danger/Cry Baby	1980	$5
❏ 4937	Envy/Whose Problem	1980	$5
❏ 5182	Forever Mine/So L.A.	1982	$3
❏ 5182 [PS]	Forever Mine/So L.A.	1982	$3
❏ 5114	Only the Lonely/ Change My Mind	1982	$3
❏ 5114 [PS]	Only the Lonely/ Change My Mind	1982	$4
—A moderately tough sleeve to find			
❏ 5497	Shame/Save the Last Dance for Love	1985	$3
❏ 5497 [PS]	Shame/Save the Last Dance for Love	1985	$3
❏ 5529	Shock/In the Jungle (Concrete Jungle)	1985	$3
❏ 5529 [PS]	Shock/In the Jungle (Concrete Jungle)	1985	$3
❏ 5271	Suddenly Last Summer/ Some Things Never Change	1983	$3
❏ 5271 [PS]	Suddenly Last Summer/ Some Things Never Change	1983	$3
❏ 5149	Take the L/Mission of Mercy	1982	$3
❏ 5149 [PS]	Take the L/Mission of Mercy	1982	$3
❏ 4796	Total Control/Love Don't Help	1979	$5
❏ 4796 [PS]	Total Control/Love Don't Help	1979	$5
MOTHER EARTH			
MERCURY			
❏ 72878	Down So Long/Goodbye Nelda Greeby	1968	$8
❏ 72909	Mother Earth/I Did My Part	1969	$8
❏ 72943	Painted Girls and Wine/ Your Time's Comin'	1969	$8
REPRISE			
❏ 1041	I'll Be Long Gone/ Bring Me Home	1971	$6
❏ 1019	Soul of Sadness/Temptation Took Control of Me and I Fell	1971	$6
MOTIONS, THE (1)			
ABC-PARAMOUNT			
❏ 10529	Big Chief/Where Is Your Heart	1964	$15
CONGRESS			
❏ 237	It's Gone/I've Got Money	1965	$15
MERCURY			
❏ 72297	Beatle Drums/Long Hair	1964	$30
❏ 72413	Bumble Bee '65/Motions	1965	$30
❏ 72368	I Can Dance/Land Beyond the Moon	1964	$30
MOTIONS, THE (2)			
LAURIE			
❏ 3112	Make Me a Love/Mr. Night	1961	$120
MOTIONS, THE (3)			
PHILIPS			
❏ 40624	Freedom/What's Your Name	1969	$8
MOTLEY CRUE			
ELEKTRA			
❏ 7-69429	All I Need/All in the Name	1987	$4
❏ 7-69271	Dr. Feelgood/Sticky Sweet	1989	$3
❏ 7-69271 [PS]	Dr. Feelgood/Sticky Sweet	1989	$3
❏ 7-69465	Girls, Girls, Girls/ Sumthin' for Nuthin'	1987	$3
❏ 7-69465 [PS]	Girls, Girls, Girls/ Sumthin' for Nuthin'	1987	$3
❏ 7-69591	Home Sweet Home/Red Hot	1985	$5
❏ 7-69756	Looks That Kill/Piece of Your Action	1984	$5
❏ 7-69756 [PS]	Looks That Kill/Piece of Your Action	1984	$5
❏ 7-69625	Smokin' in the Boys' Room/Use It or Lose It	1985	$4
❏ 7-69625 [PS]	Smokin' in the Boys' Room/Use It or Lose It	1985	$4
❏ 7-69732	Too Young to Fall in Love/ Take Me to the Top	1984	$5
❏ 7-69732 [PS]	Too Young to Fall in Love/ Take Me to the Top	1984	$5
❏ 7-69449	Wild Side/Five Years Dead	1987	$3
❏ 7-69449 [PS]	Wild Side/Five Years Dead	1987	$3

Number	Title	Yr	NM
LEATHUR			
❏ 01	Stick to Your Guns/ Toast of the Town	1981	$100
❏ 001 [PS]	Stick to Your Guns/ Toast of the Town	1981	$120
MOTORS, THE			
DUCKS DELUXE and BRAM TCHAIKOVSKY related. (45)			
VIRGIN			
❏ ZS89519	Airport/Mamma Rock 'N' Roller	1978	$4
❏ ZS89517	Cold Love/Phoney Heaven	1977	$4
❏ ZS89515	Dancing the Night Away/ Whiskey and Wine	1977	$4
❏ ZS89520	Forget About You/Breathless	1978	$4
❏ 67007	Love and Loneliness/ Time for Makeup	1980	$3
❏ 67007 [PS]	Love and Loneliness/ Time for Makeup	1980	$3
❏ ZS89521	Today/The Hustler	1978	$4
MOTT THE HOOPLE			
COLUMBIA			
❏ 45920	All the Way from Memphis/I Wish I Was Your Mother	1973	$10
❏ 4-45673	All the Young Dudes/ One of the Boys	1972	$6
—A-side is the British single version with "unlocked cars" lyric; matrix number in dead wax ends in "1" plus a letter			
❏ 4-45673 [PS]	All the Young Dudes/ One of the Boys	1972	$30
❏ 4-45673	All the Young Dudes/ One of the Boys	1972	$8
—A-side is the LP version with "Marks and Sparks" lyric; matrix number in dead wax ends in the number "2" plus a letter			
❏ 3-10091	All the Young Dudes/Rose	1975	$5
❏ 45882	Honaloochie Boogie/Rose	1973	$10
❏ 45754	One of the Boys/Sucker	1973	$15
❏ 45784	Sweet Jane/Jerkin' Crocus	1973	$15
❏ 46035	The Golden Age of Rock 'N' Roll/Rest in Peace	1974	$15
MOULD, BOB			
Also see HUSKER DU; SUGAR.			
VIRGIN			
❏ 99190	See a Little Light/All Those People Know	1989	$4
❏ 99190 [PS]	See a Little Light/All Those People Know	1989	$6
MOULE, BOB'S, DIXIELAND EXPRESS			
MSK			
❏ 709	Santa Claus Is Comin' to Town/Let It Snow	1975	$4
MOULTRY, MARY			
KING			
❏ 6038	Last Year's Senior Prom/They're Trying to Tear Us Apart	1966	$40
MOUNTAIN			
WINDFALL			
❏ 533	For Yasgur's Farm/ To My Friend	1970	$8
❏ 532	Mississippi Queen/The Laird	1970	$8
❏ 535	Silver Paper/Travelin' in the Dark	1971	$10
❏ 534	The Animal Trainer and the Toad/Tired Angels	1971	$15
❏ 537	Waiting to Take You Away/ (B-side unknown)	1972	$10
MOURNING REIGN, THE			
CONTOUR			
❏ 601	Evil Hearted You/Get Out of My Life, Woman	1967	$30
LINK			
❏ 2	Evil Hearted You/Get Out of My Life, Woman	1966	$40
❏ 1	Satisfaction Guaranteed/ Our Fate	1966	$40
❏ 1 [PS]	Satisfaction Guaranteed/ Our Fate	1966	$600
MOUSE AND THE TRAPS			
CAPITOL			
❏ 2460	Streets of a Dusty Town/Mouse	1969	$10
FRATERNITY			
❏ 956	A Public Execution/ All for You	1966	$30
❏ 1000	Beg, Borrow, and Steal/L.O.V.E. Love	1967	$20
❏ 1011	I Satisfy/Good Times	1968	$20
❏ 1015	Look at the Sun/ Requiem for Sarah	1968	$20

Number	Title	Yr	NM
❏ 966	Mad of Sugar/I Am the One	1966	$20
❏ 973	Promises, Promises/ Do the Best You Can	1966	$20
❏ 1005	Sometimes You Just Can't Win/Cryin' Inside	1968	$20
❏ 1005 [PS]	Sometimes You Just Can't Win/Cryin' Inside	1968	$100
❏ 971	Would You Believe/ Like I Know You Do	1966	$20
SMUDGE			
❏ 0703	Bottom Line/Gypsy Girl	1981	$15
MOUTH AND MACNEIL			
PHILIPS			
❏ 40715	How Do You Do?/Land of Milk and Honey	1972	$5
—Light blue label			
❏ 40715	How Do You Do?/Land of Milk and Honey	1972	$4
—Dark blue label			
❏ 40721	Sing Along/Hello	1973	$4
❏ 40721 [PS]	Sing Along/Hello	1973	$15
❏ 40717	Why Did You, Why?/ Hey, You Love	1972	$4
TARA			
❏ 110	I See a Star/My Friends	1974	$4
MOVE, THE			
Also see ELECTRIC LIGHT ORCHESTRA; ROY WOOD.			
A&M			
❏ 1020	Blackberry Way/Something	1969	$15
❏ 1197	Brontosaurus/Lightning Never Strikes Twice	1970	$15
❏ 884	Flowers in the Rain/ (Here We Go Round the) Lemon Tree	1967	$15
❏ 1119	This Time Tomorrow/Curly	1969	$15
❏ 914	Walk Upon the Water/ Fire Brigade	1968	$20
❏ 1239	When Alice Comes Back to the Farm/What?	1971	$15
CAPITOL			
❏ 3126	Tonight/Don't Mess Me Up	1971	$30
DERAM			
❏ 7506	I Can Hear the Grass Grow/Wave the Flag and Stop the Train	1967	$20
❏ 7504	The Disturbance/ Night of Fear	1967	$20
MGM			
❏ 14332 [DJ]	Chinatown/Down by the Bay	1971	$30
—Evidently not released as stock copy			
UNITED ARTISTS			
❏ 50876	Chinatown/Down on the Bay	1972	$8
❏ 50928	Do Ya/California Man	1972	$8
❏ XW202	Tonight/My Marge	1973	$6
MOVING SIDEWALKS, THE			
TANTARA			
❏ 3101	99th Floor/What Are You Going to Do	1967	$50
❏ 3113	Flashback/(B-side unknown)	1969	$40
❏ 3103	I Want to Hold Your Hand/Joe Blues	1968	$50
WAND			
❏ 1156	99th Floor/What Are You Going to Do	1967	$30
MUD			
RAK			
❏ 187 [PS]	Lonely This Christmas/I Can't Stand It	1973	$20
❏ 187	Lonely This Christmas/I Can't Stand It	1973	$15
MUDCRUTCH			
SHELTER			
❏ 40357	Depot Street/Wild Eyes	1975	$40
MUDHONEY			
MAKE 'EM BLEED AND SUFFER			
❏ 0(no cat #)	Hate the Police (Live)/ Symptom of the Universe	1988	$30
—B-side by the Melvins			
❏ 0(no cat #) [PS]	Hate the Police (Live)/ Symptom of the Universe	1988	$30
—Actually a large envelope that contained this single, which was enclosed in a Japanese porno magazine			
SUB POP			
❏ 26	Halloween/Touch Me I'm Sick	1988	$60
—B-side by Sonic Youth; first 500 on clear vinyl			
❏ 26	Halloween/Touch Me I'm Sick	1988	$20
—B-side by Sonic Youth; last 2,500 on black vinyl			

Number	Title	Yr	NM
❏ 26 [PS]	Halloween/Touch Me I'm Sick	1988	$30
—#2 in Sub Pop Singles Club series			
❏ 44a	This Gift/Baby Help Me Forget	1989	$5
❏ 44a [PS]	This Gift/Baby Help Me Forget	1989	$5
❏ 44a	This Gift/Baby Help Me Forget	1989	$40
—Purple vinyl			
❏ 18	Touch Me I'm Sick/ Sweet Young Thing	1988	$100
—First 800 were pressed on brown vinyl			
❏ 18	Touch Me I'm Sick/ Sweet Young Thing	1988	$125
—Standard black vinyl pressing, toilet label			
❏ 18	Touch Me I'm Sick/ Sweet Young Thing	1988	$200
—Any of accidental purple, red, yellow or blueish vinyl pressings			
❏ 18	Touch Me I'm Sick/ Sweet Young Thing	1988	$8
—Regular Sub Pop label, black vinyl			
❏ 18 [PS]	Touch Me I'm Sick/ Sweet Young Thing	1988	$8
—Only accompanied regular Sub Pop label pressings			

MUDLARKS, THE
ROULETTE
❏ 4143	Love Game/My Grandfather's Clock	1959	$15

MUDSLINGER, ROGER
RED BIRD
❏ Oct-0013	The Election Year 1964 (Part 1)/The Election Year 1964 (Part 2)	1964	$30

MUGWUMPS, THE
SIDEWALK
❏ 900	Bald Headed Woman/ Jug Band Music	1966	$30
❏ 909	Season of the Witch/My Gal	1967	$30

WARNER BROS.
❏ 5471	I'll Remember Tonight/I Don't Wanna Know	1964	$20
❏ 7018	Searchin'/Here It Is, Another Day	1967	$10

MULDAUR, GEOFF & MARIA
REPRISE
❏ 0807	Open Up Your Soul/Sittin' Alone in the Moonlight	1969	$8

MULDAUR, MARIA
REPRISE
❏ 1319	I'm a Woman/Cool River	1974	$4
❏ 1183	Midnight at the Oasis/ Any Old Time	1973	$5
❏ 1331	Oh Papa/Gringo de Mexico	1975	$4
❏ 1352	Sad Eyes/Wild Bird	1976	$4
❏ 1362	Sweet Harmony/ Jon the Generator	1976	$4

WARNER BROS.
❏ 49058	Dancin' in the Street/ Birds Fly South (When Winter Comes)	1979	$4
❏ 49131	Fall in Love Again/ Love Is Everything	1979	$4
❏ 8580	Make Love to the Music/I'll Keep My Light in My Window	1978	$4

MULL, MARTIN
ABC
❏ 12251	Boogie Man/Bombed Away	1977	$5
❏ 12304	Humming Song/Get Up, Get Down	1977	$5

CAPRICORN
❏ 0241	Do the Dog/ Thousands of Girls	1975	$8
❏ 0019	Dueling Tubas/2001 Polkas	1973	$8
❏ 0024	In the Eyes of My Dog (Part 1)/In the Eyes of My Dog (Part 2)	1973	$8
❏ 037	Santafly/Santa Doesn't Cop Out On Dope	1973	$15
❏ 0282	Santafly/Santa Doesn't Cop Out On Dope	1977	$10

ELEKTRA
❏ 46057	Bernie Don't Disco/Bun and Run Part 1 and 3	1979	$5
❏ 46056	The Fruit Song/ Pig in a Blanket	1979	$5

MULLICAN, MOON
CORAL
❏ 9-62042	Sweet Rockin' Music/ Moon's Rock	1958	$30

DECCA
❏ 9-30962	Writin' on the Wall/ Cush Cush Ky-Yay	1960	$30

HALLWAY
❏ 1923	Colinda/I'll Pour the Wine	1964	$20
❏ 1914	Fools Like Me/Make Friends	1963	$20
❏ 1208	Mr. Tears/Big, Big City	1965	$15
❏ 1907	The Coffee Song/I'll Pour the Wine	1962	$20

KAPP
❏ 2055	Big Big City/Fools Like Me	1969	$8
❏ 2027	I'll Pour the Wine/ Make Friends	1969	$8

KING
❏ 1152	1001 Sleepless Nights/A Crushed Red Rose	1952	$40
❏ 1343	All I Need Is You/Don't Let Temptation Turn You Round	1954	$40
❏ 984	Another Night Is Coming/ Heartless Lover	1951	$50
❏ 965#NAME?	Cherokee Boogie (Eh-Oh-Aleena)/Love Is the Light That Leads Me Home	1951	$50
❏ 1007	Country Boogie/ Moonshine Blues	1951	$50
❏ 1427	Crippled for Life/There Goes the Bride	1955	$30
❏ 1408	Downstream/You Got the Best of Me	1954	$40
❏ 1355	End of the Rainbow/Where the Beautiful Flowers Are	1954	$40
❏ 1337	Good Deal, Lucille/Wanted	1954	$40
❏ 5223	Goodnight Irene/Mona Lisa	1959	$20
❏ 1221	Hey Mr. Corn Picker/Leaving You with a Worried Mind	1953	$40
❏ 4937	Hey Shah/Maybe It's All for the Best	1956	$30
❏ 4894	Honolulu Rock-a Roll-a/ Seven Nights to Rock	1956	$50
❏ 1244	I Done It/Grandpa Stole My Baby	1953	$40
❏ 5473	I Don't Know What to Do/I'll Take Your Hat Right Off My Rack	1961	$20
❏ 5828	I'll Sail My Ship Alone/ New Jole Blon	1963	$15
❏ 5172	I'll Sail My Ship Alone/ Seven Nights to Rock	1959	$30
❏ 1366	I'm Hanging Up All My Work Clothes/No Stranger	1954	$40
❏ 5354	I Was Sorta Wondering/ Sweeter Than the Flowers	1960	$20
❏ 1006	Memphis Blues/ Piano Breakdown	1951	$50
❏ 1481	Mexicali Rose/ Panhandle Rag	1955	$30
❏ 1060	My Tears Will Fall/ Triflin' Woman Blues	1952	$40
❏ 1164	Ooglie Ooglie Ooglie/ So Long	1953	$40
❏ 1461	San Antonio Rose/ Cedarwood Blues	1955	$30
❏ 1078	Save a Little Dream for Me/Trouble, Trouble	1952	$40
❏ 1043	Shoot the Moon/A Million Regrets	1952	$40
❏ 1137	Sugar Beet/Pipeliner's Blues	1952	$40
❏ 1447	When Love Dies/What's the Matter with the Mill	1955	$30

MUSICOR
❏ 1126	Love That Might Have Been/Custer's Last Stand	1965	$10

STARDAY
❏ 596	Ain't Nothin' Like Lovin'/Good Times Gonna Roll Again	1962	$20
❏ 594	Ballad of Frank Clement/Good Times Gonna Roll Again	1962	$20
❏ 562	I'll Sail My Ship Alone/ Mona Lisa	1961	$30

MULLIGAN, GERRY
PACIFIC JAZZ
❏ 614	Winter Wonderland/I Fall in Love Too Easily	1953	$30

MULLINS, DEE
MEL-O-DY
❏ 117	Love Makes the World Go, But Money Greases the Wheel/Come On Back	1964	$30

PLANTATION
❏ 31	Guilt Box/California, the Promised Land	1969	$6
❏ 54	Irma Jackson/ In a Small Time	1970	$6
❏ 17	The Big Man/Run Willie Run	1969	$6

SSS INTERNATIONAL
❏ 707	War Baby/Parking for Cheaters	1967	$8

TRIUNE
❏ 7205	Circle Me/Friday's Wine	1973	$6

MUMMIES, THE
HIT
❏ 193	Tell Her No/For Me	1965	$15
—B-side by Wayne Harris			

REKKIDS
❏ 01	Skinny Minnie/You Can't Sit Down	1989	$30
❏ 01 [PS]	Skinny Minnie/You Can't Sit Down	1989	$30

7-Inch Extended Plays
❏ 05	Greg Lowery	1989	$30
❏ 05 [PS]	Greg Lowery	1989	$30

MUNGO JERRY
BELL
❏ 45383	Alright, Alright, Alright/ Little Miss Hipshake	1973	$4
❏ 45123	Lady Rose/Little Louis	1971	$4
❏ 45451	Long Legged Woman Dressed in Black/ Gonna Bop Till I Drop	1974	$4
❏ 45427	Wild Love/Glad I'm a Rocker	1973	$4

JANUS
❏ 148	Baby Jump/The Man Beside the Piano	1971	$5
❏ 125	In the Summertime/ Mighty Man	1970	$6

PYE
❏ 65009	Going Back Home/Open Up	1972	$4
❏ 71032	In the Summertime/ (B-side unknown)	1975	$4

MUNSTERS, THE
DECCA
❏ 31670	Munster Creep/ Make It Go Away	1964	$30

MURE, BILLY
DANCO
❏ 506	Mon Coeur Brise (My Broken Heart)/ Rose of Cherry Bay	1965	$8

FORD
❏ 2552	See the Fait from the Air/See Lanny Ross	1963	$10

MGM
❏ K13190	Fascination/Mona Lisa	1963	$8
❏ K13565	Five Foot Two, Eyes of Blue/ Yes Sir, That's My Baby	1966	$8
❏ K13252	Ma, What Time Is It/ Sticky Fingers	1964	$8
—With Benny Mure			
❏ K13161	Maria Elena/In the Cool of the Day	1963	$8

PARIS
❏ 545	Theme for the Lonely/Ambush	1960	$10

RCA VICTOR
❏ 47-7394	Haggis Baggis/Tara Lara	1958	$20

RIVERSIDE
❏ 4547	Diamonds/String of Guitars	1963	$12

SPLASH
❏ 800	A String of Trumpets/ Tea and Trumpets	1959	$15
—As "Billy Mure and the Trumpeteers"			
❏ 800	A String of Trumpets/ Tea and Trumpets	1959	$15
—As "The Trumpeteers"			

SRG
❏ 102	Theme for the Lonely/ Little Reuben	1960	$20

STRAND
❏ 25037	Hawaiian Drums/ Pink Hawaii	1961	$8

7-Inch Extended Plays
RCA VICTOR
❏ EPA-4271	(contents unknown)	1958	$15
❏ EPA-4271 [PS]	The Big Guitar	1958	$15

MURMAIDS, THE
CHATTAHOOCHIE
❏ 636	Heartbreak Ahead/ He's Good to Me	1964	$12
❏ 711	Little Boys/Go Away	1966	$12
❏ 628	Popsicles and Icicles/ Blue Dress	1963	$30
❏ 628	Popsicles and Icicles/ Bunny Stomp	1963	$20
❏ 628	Popsicles and Icicles/ Comedy and Tragedy	1963	$20

Number	Title	Yr	NM
❏ 628	Popsicles and Icicles/ Huntington Flats	1963	$20
❏ 668	Stuffed Animals/ Little White Lies	1965	$10
❏ 641	Wild and Wonderful/Bull Talk	1964	$10
LIBERTY			
❏ 56078	Paper Sun/Song Through Perception	1968	$10

MURPHEY, MICHAEL

A&M

Number	Title	Yr	NM
❏ 1459	Calico Silver/Blessing in Disguise	1973	$5
❏ 1447	Cosmic Cowboy/ Temperature Train	1973	$5
❏ 1712	Geronimo's Cadillac/ Blessing in Disguise	1975	$4
❏ 1368	Geronimo's Cadillac/ Boy from the Country	1972	$5
❏ 1368 [PS]	Geronimo's Cadillac/ Boy from the Country	1972	$6
EMI AMERICA			
❏ 8265	Carolina in the Pines/ Cherokee Fiddle	1985	$3
❏ 8243	What She Wants/Still Taking Chances	1984	$3
❏ 8243 [PS]	What She Wants/Still Taking Chances	1984	$3
EPIC			
❏ 50131	Carolina in the Pines/ Without My Lady There	1975	$4
❏ 50369	Changing Woman/A North Wind and a New Moon	1977	$4
❏ 50319	Cherokee Fiddler/ Running Wide Open	1976	$4
❏ 11130	Holy Roller/Rye By-The-Sea	1974	$4
❏ 11130 [PS]	Holy Roller/Rye By-The-Sea	1974	$6
❏ 50686	Lightning/Chain Gang	1979	$4
❏ 50184	Mansion on the Hill/ Renegade	1976	$4
❏ 50572	Paradise Tonight/Song Dog	1978	$4
❏ 50739	South Coast/ Backsliders Wine	1979	$4
❏ 02075	Take It As It Comes/ Hard Country	1981	$4

—A-side with Katy Moffatt

Number	Title	Yr	NM
❏ 50084	Wildfire/Night Thunder	1975	$5
LIBERTY			
❏ 1494	Crystal/Love Affairs	1983	$3
❏ 1517	Disenchanted/Sacred Heart	1984	$3

— Starting here, as "Michael Martin Murphey

Number	Title	Yr	NM
❏ 1455	Lost River/The Two-Step Is Easy	1982	$3
❏ 1486	Still Taking Chances/ Lost River	1982	$3
❏ 1505	The Heart Never Lies/Don't Count the Rainy Days	1983	$3
❏ 1505 [PS]	The Heart Never Lies/Don't Count the Rainy Days	1983	$4
❏ 1466	What's Forever For/Crystal	1982	$3
❏ 1514	Will It Be Love by Morning/ Goodbye Money Mountain	1983	$3
❏ 1514 [PS]	Will It Be Love by Morning/ Goodbye Money Mountain	1983	$4
WARNER BROS.			
❏ 28471	A Face in the Crowd/ You're History	1987	$3

— With Holly Dunn

Number	Title	Yr	NM
❏ 28370	A Long Line of Love/ Worlds Apart	1987	$3
❏ PRO-S-2869 [DJ]	Colorado Christmas/The Cowboy's Christmas Ball	1987	$6

— B-side by Nitty Gritty Dirt Band

Number	Title	Yr	NM
❏ 22765	Family Tree/Wood Smoke in the Wind	1989	$3
❏ 28598	Fiddlin' Man/Ghost Town (Messages from the Ghost Ranch)	1986	$3
❏ 27668	From the Word Go/ Vanishing Breed	1989	$3
❏ 28168	I'm Gonna Miss You, Girl/Running Blood	1987	$3
❏ 27810	Pilgrims on the Way (Matthew's Song)/ Still Got the Fire	1988	$3
❏ 27947	Talkin' to the Wrong Man/What Am I Doin' Hangin' 'Round	1988	$3
❏ 27947 [PS]	Talkin' to the Wrong Man/What Am I Doin' Hangin' 'Round	1988	$3
❏ 28797	Tonight We Ride/ Santa Fe Cantina	1986	$3

MURPHY, CHUCK

COLUMBIA

Number	Title	Yr	NM
❏ 4-21376	Gonne Run, Not Walk/ Friday Night Free-for-All	1955	$30
❏ 4-21258	Hocus Pocus/Hard Headed	1954	$30
❏ 4-21322	Santa Plays the Trombone (In the North Pole Band)/ Let's Have an Old-Fashioned Christmas	1954	$30
CORAL			
❏ 9-61014	A 2-D Gal in a 3-D Town/One Beer	1953	$40

Number	Title	Yr	NM
❏ 9-60800	Who Drank My Beer While I Was in the Rear?/Oceana Roll	1952	$40

MURPHY, EDDIE

COLUMBIA

Number	Title	Yr	NM
❏ 38-05772	How Could It Be/C-O-N Confused	1986	$3
❏ 38-05772 [PS]	How Could It Be/C-O-N Confused	1986	$3
❏ 38-05609	Party All the Time/ (Instrumental)	1985	$3
❏ 38-05609 [PS]	Party All the Time/ (Instrumental)	1985	$12
❏ 13-08423	Party All the Time/ (Instrumental)	1988	$3

—Reissue

Number	Title	Yr	NM
❏ 38-68897	Put Your Mouth on Me/ With All I Know	1989	$3
❏ AE71768 [DJ]	Singers/The Barbecue	1983	$6
❏ 38-73018	Till the Money's Gone/ Let's Get With It	1989	$4
THE ENTERTAINMENT COMPANY			
❏ 18-03209	Boogie in Your Butt/ Enough Is Enough	1982	$5
❏ 18-03047	Enough Is Enough// Buckwheat/Talking Cars	1982	$5
❏ 18-03047 [PS]	Enough Is Enough// Buckwheat/Talking Cars	1982	$5

MURPHY, JIMMY

ARK

Number	Title	Yr	NM
❏ 259	I Love to Hear Hank Sing the Blues/Swing Steel Blues	1963	$20

—B-side by Paul Smith

Number	Title	Yr	NM
❏ 260	My Feet's on Solid Ground/ Wake Me Up Sweet Jesus	1963	$15
COLUMBIA			
❏ 4-21569	Baboon Boogie/ Grandpaw's Cat	1956	$200
❏ 4-21486	Here Kitty Kitty/I'm Looking for a Mustard Patch	1956	$200
❏ 4-21534	Sixteen Tons Rock and Roll/My Gal Dottie	1956	$200
ENCORE			
❏ 10033	Two Sides/What Would the World Be Without Music?	1986	$5
RCA VICTOR			
❏ 48-0474	Big Mama Blues/We Live a Long Time	1951	$60
❏ 48-0447	Electricity/Mother, Where Is Your Daughter	1951	$60
❏ 47-4609	That First Guitar of Mine/ Love That Satisfies	1952	$50
REV			
❏ 3508	I'm Gone Mama/Plum Crazy	1957	$60

MURPHY, KEITH, AND THE DAZE

KING

Number	Title	Yr	NM
❏ 6171	Dirty Ol' Sam/Slightly Reminiscent of Her	1968	$125

MURRAY, ANNE, AND GLEN CAMPBELL

CAPITOL

Number	Title	Yr	NM
❏ 3200	I Say a Little Prayer-By the Time I Get to Phoenix/ All Through the Night	1971	$5

MURRAY, ANNE

CAPITOL

Number	Title	Yr	NM
❏ B-5264	A Little Good News/I'm Not Afraid Anymore	1983	$3
❏ B-5264 [PS]	A Little Good News/I'm Not Afraid Anymore	1983	$5
❏ A-5083	Another Sleepless Night/ It Should Have Been Easy	1982	$4
❏ B-44053	Anyone Can Do the Heartbreak/Without You	1987	$3
❏ B-44005	Are You Still in Love with Me/Give Me Your Love	1987	$3
❏ 4072	A Stranger in My Place/ Dream Lover	1975	$4
❏ 3059	A Stranger in My Place/ Sycamore Slick	1971	$5
❏ 4987	Blessed Are the Believers/Only Love	1981	$4
❏ 4987 [PS]	Blessed Are the Believers/Only Love	1981	$5
❏ 3352	Bobbie's Song for Jesus/You Can't Have a Hand on Me	1972	$5
❏ 4773	Broken Hearted Me/Why Don't You Stick Around	1979	$4
❏ 4402	Canterbury Song/Shilo Song	1977	$4

— With Gene MacLellan

Number	Title	Yr	NM
❏ SPRO-9723 [DJ]	Christmas Medley: Silver Bells/I'll Be Home for Christmas/ Winter Wonderland (same on both sides)	1981	$8
❏ 3260	Cotton Jenny/Destiny	1972	$5
❏ 4920	Could I Have This Dance/ Somebody's Waiting	1980	$4
❏ 4920 [PS]	Could I Have This Dance/ Somebody's Waiting	1980	$5

Number	Title	Yr	NM
❏ 3481	Danny's Song/Drown Me	1972	$4
❏ 4813	Daydream Believer/ Do You Think of Me	1979	$4
❏ 4000	Day Tripper/Lullaby	1974	$4
❏ B-44219	Flying On Your Own/ Slow All Night	1988	$3
❏ B-44219 [PS]	Flying On Your Own/ Slow All Night	1988	$3
❏ 4265	Golden Oldie/Together	1976	$4
❏ B-5536	Go Tell It On the Mountain/O Holy Night	1985	$4
❏ B-5536 [PS]	Go Tell It On the Mountain/O Holy Night	1985	$5
❏ B-5145	Hey! Baby!/Song for the Mira	1982	$3
❏ B-5145 [PS]	Hey! Baby!/Song for the Mira	1982	$3
❏ B-44495	I'd Fall in Love Tonight/Now and Forever (You and Me)	1989	$3
❏ B-5472	I Don't Think I'm Ready for You/Take Good Care of My Baby	1985	$3
❏ B-5472 [PS]	I Don't Think I'm Ready for You/Take Good Care of My Baby	1985	$4
❏ B-44432	If I Ever Fall in Love Again/ Just Another Woman in Love	1989	$3

—A-side: With Kenny Rogers

Number	Title	Yr	NM
❏ 4675	I Just Fall in Love Again/Just to Feel This Love from You	1979	$4
❏ 4675 [PS]	I Just Fall in Love Again/Just to Feel This Love from You	1979	$5
❏ 4878	I'm Happy Just to Dance with You/What's Forever For	1980	$4
❏ A-5023	It's All I Can Do/If a Heart Must Be Broken	1981	$4
❏ B-5384	Let Your Heart Do the Talking/I Don't Think I'm Ready for You	1984	$3
❏ 3776	Love Song/You Can't Go Back	1973	$4
❏ 4848	Lucky Me/Somebody's Waiting	1980	$4
❏ B-5610	My Life's a Dance/ Call Us Fools	1986	$3
❏ B-5655	On and On/Gotcha	1986	$3
❏ B-44134	Perfect Strangers/It Happens All the Time	1988	$3

— With Doug Mallory

Number	Title	Yr	NM
❏ 3082	Put Your Hand in the Hand/It Takes Time	1971	$5
❏ 3648	Send a Little Love My Way/ Head Above the Water	1973	$4
❏ 4716	Shadows in the Moonlight/ Yucatan Cafe	1979	$4
❏ 2988	Sing High -- Sing Low/ Days of the Looking Glass	1970	$5
❏ B-44272	Slow Passin' Time/ Flying on Your Own	1989	$3
❏ 2738	Snowbird/Just Bidin' My Time	1970	$6
❏ B-5183	Somebody's Always Saying Goodbye/That'll Keep Me Dreamin'	1982	$4
❏ B-5183 [PS]	Somebody's Always Saying Goodbye/That'll Keep Me Dreamin'	1982	$3
❏ 4375	Sunday School to Broadway/Dancin' All Night Long	1976	$4
❏ 4142	Sunday Sunrise/Out on the Road Again	1975	$4
❏ 3159	Talk It Over in the Morning/ Head Above the Water	1971	$5
❏ B-5305	That's Not the Way (It's S'posed to Be)/ The More We Try	1983	$3
❏ 4207	The Call/Lady Bug	1976	$4
❏ 4329	Things/Caress Me Pretty Music	1976	$4
❏ B-5436	Time Don't Run Out on Me/Let Your Heart Do the Talking	1985	$3
❏ B-5436 [PS]	Time Don't Run Out on Me/Let Your Heart Do the Talking	1985	$3
❏ 4527	Walk Right Back/a Million More	1978	$4
❏ A-5013	We Don't Have to Hold Out/ Call Me with the News	1981	$4
❏ A-5013 [PS]	We Don't Have to Hold Out/ Call Me with the News	1981	$4
❏ 3600	What About Me/Let Sunshine Have Its Day	1973	$4
❏ B-44341	Who But You/You Make Me Curious	1989	$3
❏ B-5576	Who's Leaving Who/ Reach for Me	1986	$3
❏ B-5576 [PS]	Who's Leaving Who/ Reach for Me	1986	$3

MURRAY, JACK

LAURIE

Number	Title	Yr	NM
❏ 3199	Surfin' with Me/What Do You Think of Me Baby	1963	$20

MURRAY, RAY, AND THE DYNAMICS

ARBO

Number	Title	Yr	NM
❏ 222	With All My Love/Baby, What You Want Me to Do	1960	$125

Number	Title	Yr	NM

MURRAY THE "K

BRS
☐ 1/2	Murray the "K" and The Beatles As It Happened	1964	$50
☐ 1/2 [PS]	Murray the "K" and The Beatles As It Happened	1964	$120

IBC
☐ F4KM-0082/3	Murray the "K" and The Beatles As It Happened	1976	$10
☐ F4KM-0082/3 [PS]	Murray the "K" and The Beatles As It Happened	1976	$10

RED BIRD
☐ Oct-0045	It's What's Happening, Baby/Sins of a Family	1966	$20

MUSIC MACHINE, THE

BELL
☐ 764	Mother Nature--Father Earth/Advise and Consent	1969	$8

ORIGINAL SOUND
☐ 71	Double Yellow Line/Absolutely Positive	1967	$12
☐ 82	Hey Joe/Wrong	1968	$12
☐ 75	I've Loved You/The Eagle Never Hunts the Fly	1967	$10
☐ 61	Talk Talk/Come On In	1966	$15
☐ 0 (no cat #) [PS]	The Music Machine	1967	$10

—*Custom sleeve, large center hole, not assigned to any one record, with pictures of band members on front and ads for "Oldies But Goodies" LPs on back*

☐ 67	The People in Me/Masculine Institution	1967	$10

WARNER BROS.
☐ 7093	Bottom of the Soul/Astrologically Incompatible	1968	$8
☐ 7093 [PS]	Bottom of the Soul/Astrologically Incompatible	1968	$20
☐ 7199	To the Light/You'll Love Me Again	1968	$8

MYLES, ALANNAH

ATLANTIC
☐ 7-88742	Black Velvet/If You Want To	1989	$6

—*Original pressings on red and black label*

☐ 7-88918	Love Is/Rock This Joint	1989	$4

MYLES, BILLY

EMBER
☐ 1046	I'm Gonna Walk/Price of Your Love	1958	$30
☐ 1040	Price of Your Love/I'm Too Sentimental	1958	$30

KING
☐ 5395	Dance Little Girlie/Two Empty Arms	1960	$20

MYSTERY TOUR, THE

MGM
☐ 14097	The Ballad of Paul/The Ballad of Paul (Follow the Bouncing Ball)	1969	$30

MYSTICS, THE

BLACK CAT
☐ 101	Snoopy/Ooh Poo Pah Doo	1966	$50

CONSTELLATION
☐ 138	She's Got Everything/Just a Loser	1964	$15

KING
☐ 5678	Mashed Potatoes With Me/The Hoppy Hop	1962	$20

LAURIE
☐ 3047	All Through the Night/To Think of You Again	1960	$30
☐ 3038	Don't Take the Stars/So Tenderly	1959	$30
☐ 3028 [M]	Hushabye/Adam and Eve	1959	$40
☐ S-3028 [S]	Hushabye/Adam and Eve	1959	$120
☐ 3086	Star Crossed Lovers/Goodbye Mr. Blue	1961	$30
☐ 3104	Sunday Kind of Love/Darling I Know How	1961	$40
☐ 3058	White Cliffs of Dover/Blue Star	1960	$30

NOLTA
☐ 353	The Fox/Dan	1963	$20

N

N.W.A.

RUTHLESS
☐ 7206	Express Yourself/Straight Outta Compton	1989	$10
☐ 7206 [PS]	Express Yourself/Straight Outta Compton	1989	$10

NABAY

IMPACT
☐ 1032	Believe It or Not/(Instrumental)	1967	$3000

NABORS, JIM

COLUMBIA
☐ 45636	(At) The End (Of a Rainbow)/It Won't Hurt to Try It	1972	$5
☐ AE1028 [DJ]	Ave Maria/How Great Thou Art	1971	$6
☐ 45321	God Bless America/The Star-Spangled Banner	1971	$5
☐ 45271	I'll Begin Again/Louisiana Lady	1970	$5
☐ 44965	It's My Life/Young Hearts	1969	$6
☐ 43553	Love Me with All Your Heart/Rock-a-Bye	1966	$8
☐ 45932	Oh Babe, What Would You Say/Cardboards, Crayons and Clay	1973	$5
☐ 45053	O Holy Night/I Was a King at Jesus' Birth	1969	$6
☐ 43395	Shazam!/Old Blue	1965	$15
☐ 10035	That's What Friends Are For/Lena the Queen of the Honky-Tonk Angels	1974	$4
☐ 44462	The Impossible Dream/Time After Time	1968	$6
☐ 44537	To Give (The Reason I Live)/I Must Have Been Out of My Mind	1968	$6
☐ 45126	Tomorrow Never Comes/It's My Life	1970	$5
☐ 45126 [PS]	Tomorrow Never Comes/It's My Life	1970	$8
☐ 44359	White Christmas/In A Humble Place	1967	$6

RANWOOD
☐ 1081	Always Leave 'Em Laughing/Sing Me a Love Song	1977	$4

ROULETTE
☐ 4105	There's No Tomorrow/I'm Working	1958	$30

—*As "Jimmy Nabors*

NAKED EYES

EMI AMERICA
☐ SPRO-9923 [DJ]	Always Something There to Remind Me (Remix 5:41)/Voices in My Head (3:47)	1983	$15
☐ B-8155	Always Something There to Remind Me/The Time Is Now	1983	$4
☐ B-8170	Promises, Promises/A Very Hard Act to Follow	1983	$4
☐ B-8170 [PS]	Promises, Promises/A Very Hard Act to Follow	1983	$4
☐ B-8219	(What) In the Name of Love/Two Heads Together	1984	$4
☐ B-8219 [PS]	(What) In the Name of Love/Two Heads Together	1984	$4
☐ B-8183	When the Lights Go Out/Low Life	1983	$4

NAKED RAYGUN
7-Inch Extended Plays

RUTHLESS
☐ 0 (# unknown)	Flammable Solid	1983	$60
☐ 0 (# unknown) [PS]	Flammable Solid	1983	$60

—*With stickered cover and parchment lyric sheet*

NAKED SKINNIES

NAKED HOUSE
☐ 0 (# unknown)	All My Life/This Is the Beautiful Night	1981	$50
☐ 0 (# unknown) [PS]	All My Life/This Is the Beautiful Night	1981	$50

NAPOLEON XIV

WARNER BROS.
☐ 5853	I'm in Love with My Little Red Tricycle/Doin' the Napoleon	1966	$10
☐ 7726	They're Coming to Take Me Away, Ha-Haaa!/!Aaah-Ah, Yawa Em Ekat ot Gnimoc Er'yeht	1973	$8
☐ 5831	They're Coming to Take Me Away, Ha-Haaa!/Yawa Em Ekat ot Gnimoc Er'yeht, !Aaah-Ah	1966	$15

NASH, GRAHAM, AND DAVID CROSBY

ABC
☐ 12165	Bittersweet/Take the Money and Run	1976	$4
☐ 12140	Carry Me/Mama Lion	1975	$4
☐ 12217	Foolish Man/Spotlight	1976	$4
☐ 12185	Love Workout/Bittersweet	1976	$4
☐ 12199	Out of the Darkness/Broken Bird	1976	$4

ATLANTIC
☐ 2873	Immigration Man/Whole Cloth	1972	$5
☐ 2892	Southbound Train/The Wall Song	1972	$5

NASH, GRAHAM
Also see CROSBY, STILLS AND NASH; CROSBY, STILLS, NASH & YOUNG; THE HOLLIES.

ATLANTIC
☐ 2804	Chicago/Simple Man	1971	$6
☐ 89373	Chippin' Away/Newday	1986	$3
☐ 89434	Innocent Eyes/I Got a Rock	1986	$3
☐ 89434 [PS]	Innocent Eyes/I Got a Rock	1986	$4
☐ 2827	Military Madness/Sleep Song	1971	$5
☐ 2990	Prison Song/Hey You (Looking at the Moon)	1973	$5
☐ 89396	Sad Eyes/Newday	1986	$3

CAPITOL
☐ 4879	Earth and Sky/Magical Child	1980	$4
☐ 4849	Helicopter Song/Out on the Island	1980	$4
☐ 4812	In the 80's/T.V. Guide	1979	$4

NASH, JOHNNY

ABC-PARAMOUNT
☐ 9960	Almost in Your Arms/Midnight Moonlight	1958	$30
☐ 10026	And the Angels Sing/Baby, Baby, Baby	1959	$30
☐ 10076	A Place in the Sun/Goodbye	1960	$20
☐ 9996	As Time Goes By/The Voice of Love	1959	$30
☐ 9996 [PS]	As Time Goes By/The Voice of Love	1959	$50
☐ 10212	A Thousand Miles Away/I Need Someone to Stand By Me	1961	$15
☐ 10230	I'm Counting on You/I Lost My Baby	1961	$15
☐ 10205	I Need Someone to Stand By/A House on the Hill	1961	$15
☐ 10112	Let the Rest of the World Go By/Music of Love	1960	$20
☐ 10137	(Looks Like) The End of the World/We Kissed	1960	$20
☐ 9894	My Pledge to You/It's So Easy to Say	1958	$30
☐ 9743	Out of Town/A Teenager Sings the Blues	1956	$30
☐ 9927	Please Don't Go/I Lost My Love Last Night	1958	$30
☐ 10046	Take a Giant Step/But Not for Me	1959	$30
☐ 9844	The Ladder of Love/I'll Walk Alone	1957	$30
☐ 10060	The Wish/Too Proud	1959	$30
☐ 10251	Too Much Love/Love's Young Dream	1961	$50
☐ 9942	Truly Love/You're Looking at Me	1958	$30
☐ 10181	World of Tears/Some of Your Lovin'	1961	$125

ARGO
☐ 5492	Spring Is Here/Strange Feeling	1965	$50
☐ 5471	Talk to Me/Love Ain't Nothin'	1964	$80
☐ 5501	Teardrops in the Rain/I Know What I Want	1965	$8
☐ 5479	Then You Can Tell Me Goodbye/Always	1964	$8

ATLANTIC
☐ 2344	Big City/Somewhere	1966	$30

CADET
☐ 5528	Teardrops in the Rain/Get Myself Together	1966	$20

EPIC
☐ 50386	Back in Time/That Woman	1977	$4
☐ 50051	Beautiful Baby/Celebrate Life	1974	$5
☐ 50737	Closer/Mr. Sea	1979	$4
☐ 50091	Good Vibrations/The Very First Time	1975	$5
☐ 10902	I Can See Clearly Now/How Good It Is	1972	$6
☐ 11070	Loving You/Gonna Open Up My Heart Again	1973	$5
☐ 11003	My Merry-Go-Round/We're Trying to Get Back to You	1973	$5
☐ 11034	Ooh What a Feeling/Yellow House	1973	$5

Number	Title	Yr	NM
❑ 10949	Stir It Up/Ooh Baby You've Been Good to Me	1973	$6
❑ 50138	Tears on My Pillow (I Can't Take It)/Beautiful Baby	1975	$5
❑ 50219	(What a) Wonderful World/Rock It Baby (We've Got a Date)	1976	$5

GROOVE

Number	Title	Yr	NM
❑ 58-0021	Deep in the Heart of Harlem/What Kind of Love Is This	1963	$50
❑ 58-0021 [PS]	Deep in the Heart of Harlem/What Kind of Love Is This	1963	$60
❑ 58-0018 [PS]	Helpless/I've Got a Lot to Offer, Darling	1963	$40
❑ 58-0018	Helpless/I've Got a Lot to Offer, Darling	1963	$12
❑ 58-0030	I'm Leaving/Oh Mary Don't You Weep	1964	$10
❑ 58-0026	It's No Good for Me/Town of Lonely Hearts	1963	$10

JAD

Number	Title	Yr	NM
❑ 220	Cupid/Hold Me Tight	1969	$6
❑ 207	Hold Me Tight/Cupid	1968	$8
—Mostly light green label with purple trim			
❑ 218	Love and Peace/People in Love	1969	$6
❑ 214	Lovey Dovey/You Got Soul	1969	$6
❑ 215	Sweet Charity/People in Love	1969	$6
❑ 223	What a Groovy Feeling/You Got Soul (Part 1)	1970	$6

JANUS

Number	Title	Yr	NM
❑ 136	Falling In and Out of Love/You've Got to Change Your Ways	1970	$6

JODA

Number	Title	Yr	NM
❑ 102	Let's Move and Groove (Together)/Understanding	1965	$12
❑ 105	One More Time/Got to Find Her	1965	$10
❑ 106	Somewhere/Big City	1966	$12

MGM

Number	Title	Yr	NM
❑ 13637	Amen/Perfumed Flower	1966	$8
❑ 13683	Good Goodness/You Never Know	1967	$8
❑ 13805	Stormy/(I'm So) Glad You're My Baby	1967	$8

WARNER BROS.

Number	Title	Yr	NM
❑ 5336	Cigarettes, Whiskey and Wild, Wild Women/I'm Movin' On	1963	$15
❑ 5270	Don't Take Your Love Away/Moment of Weakness	1962	$15
❑ 5301	Ol' Man River/My Dear Little Sweetheart	1962	$15

NASHVILLE FIVE, THE
HIT

Number	Title	Yr	NM
❑ 231	A Taste of Honey/England Swings	1965	$8
—B-side by Bobby Brooks			
❑ 243	Batman Theme/Husbands and Wives	1966	$8
❑ 119	Cotton Candy/Love Me with All Your Heart	1964	$8
—B-side by the Music City Singers			
❑ 135	Walk Don't Run '64/Because	1964	$10
—B-side by the Roamers			

NATIONAL LAMPOON
BANANA

Number	Title	Yr	NM
❑ 218	Deteriorata/Thise Fabulous Sixties	1972	$8
❑ 233	Pizza Man/Lemmings Lament	1974	$8
❑ 240	The Watergate Tapes/The Silent Majority	1973	$8

NATIVE BOYS, THE
COMBO

Number	Title	Yr	NM
❑ 119	Laughing Love/Valley of Lovers	1956	$75
❑ 120	Oh Let Me Dream/I've Got a Feeling	1956	$70
❑ 113	Strange Love/Cherrlyn	1956	$70
❑ 115	Tears/When I Met You	1956	$75

NATURAL FOUR, THE
ABC

Number	Title	Yr	NM
❑ 11253	Hurt/I Thought You Were Mine	1969	$30
❑ 11257	Message from a Black Man/Stepping On Up	1970	$500
❑ 11236	Same Thing in Mind/The Situation Needs No Explanation	1969	$15
❑ 11205	Why Should We Stop Now/You Did This for Me	1969	$8

CURTOM

Number	Title	Yr	NM
❑ 1990	Can This Be Real/Try Love Again	1973	$5

Number	Title	Yr	NM
❑ 0119	Free/Nothing Beats a Failure (But a Try)	1976	$5
❑ 0101	Heaven Right Here on Earth/While We're Away	1975	$5
❑ 0114	It's the Music/It's the Music (Disco Version)	1976	$5
❑ 0104	Love's So Wonderful/What's Happening Here	1975	$5
❑ 1995	Love That Really Counts/Love's Society	1974	$5
❑ 1981	Things Will Be Better Tomorrow/Eddie, You Should Know Better	1973	$5
❑ 1984	Try Love Again/Eddie, You Should Know Better	1973	$5

NATURALS, THE (1)
CALLA

Number	Title	Yr	NM
❑ 181	I Can't Share You/Young Generation	1972	$6

MOTOWN

Number	Title	Yr	NM
❑ 1208	Good Things/Where Was I When Love Came By	1972	$6

NATURALS, THE (4)
ERA

Number	Title	Yr	NM
❑ 1089	The Mummy/Don't Send Me Away	1959	$20

NATURALS, THE (5)
HUNT

Number	Title	Yr	NM
❑ 325	Blue Moon/How Strange	1959	$20

RED TOP

Number	Title	Yr	NM
❑ 113	Blue Moon/How Strange	1959	$40

NATURALS, THE (6)
LIBERTY

Number	Title	Yr	NM
❑ 55741	I Should Have Known Better/Didn't I	1964	$15
❑ 55758	It Was You/Look at Me Now	1964	$15

NATURALS, THE (7)
MGM

Number	Title	Yr	NM
❑ K11970	Marty/The Jitterbug Waltz	1955	$20
❑ K11970 [PS]	Marty/The Jitterbug Waltz	1955	$100
—With photos of Ernest Borgnine and Betsy Blair, plus a synopsis of the play			
❑ K12576	Patti Ann/Missing	1957	$15
❑ K12576 [PS]	Patti Ann/Missing	1957	$30

NATURALS, THE (8)
SMASH

Number	Title	Yr	NM
❑ 1925	Different Girls/Hey Fellas	1964	$15

NATURALS, THE (U)
20TH CENTURY FOX

Number	Title	Yr	NM
❑ 545	Caravan/Whole Lotta Rockin'	1964	$15

CUB

Number	Title	Yr	NM
❑ 9026	The Flower Song/Three Young Men	1959	$20
—B-side by Lee Davis			

NATURE BOY & FRIENDS
BERTRAM INT'L.

Number	Title	Yr	NM
❑ 255	Surfer John/John John	1964	$50

NAVARRO, TOMMY, AND THE SUNDIALERS
URANIA

Number	Title	Yr	NM
❑ 1401	I'll Be Satisfied/Summertime	1961	$125

NAYLOR, JERRY
COLUMBIA

Number	Title	Yr	NM
❑ 4-44874	Gotta Travel On/Posters on the Wall	1969	$8
❑ 4-44809	The Chokin' Kind/Helga	1969	$8

HITSVILLE

Number	Title	Yr	NM
❑ 6041	The Bad Part of Me/I Hate to Drink Alone	1976	$5
❑ 6046	The Last Time You Love Me/Born to Fool Around	1976	$5

MC

Number	Title	Yr	NM
❑ 5004	If You Don't Want to Love Her/Love Away Her Memory Tonight	1978	$5

MELODYLAND

Number	Title	Yr	NM
❑ 6012	He'll Have to Go/Once Again	1975	$5
❑ 6003	Is This All There Is to a Honky Tonk?/You're the One	1974	$5
❑ 6020	What's a Nice Girl Like You Doing in a Honky Tonk/Prayin' for My Mind	1975	$5

MGM

Number	Title	Yr	NM
❑ 14497	Bitter Memories/Love You Most of All	1973	$6
❑ 14439	Continental Highway/In This World	1972	$6
❑ 14637	Honky Tonk Women/You Are a Song	1973	$6
❑ 14546	If You Don't Know Me by Now/Bitter Memories	1973	$6
❑ 14393	That'll Be the Day/Hands	1972	$6
❑ 14312	With This Ring/Goodtime Charlie	1971	$6

OAK

Number	Title	Yr	NM
❑ 1014	Cheating Eyes/America, I'm Coming Home to You	1980	$6

SMASH

Number	Title	Yr	NM
❑ 1971	I'll Take You Home/I Found You	1965	$20

TOWER

Number	Title	Yr	NM
❑ 264	Almost Persuaded/I'll Get My Life the Way I Want It	1966	$15
❑ 162	City Lights/Life	1965	$20
❑ 280	Drinkin' and Thinkin'/Johnny Brown	1966	$15
❑ 365	High on Happiness/Today and Tomorrow	1967	$15
❑ 139	It's Only Make Believe/Leave Him and Come to My Loving Arms	1965	$20
❑ 214	My Special Angel/Would You Believe	1966	$15
❑ 327	Sweet Violets/Temptation Leads Me	1967	$15

WARNER BROS.

Number	Title	Yr	NM
❑ 8767	But for Love/Part Time Lover, Full Time Fool	1979	$5
❑ 8881	She Wears It Well/Part Time Lover, Full Time Fool	1979	$5

WEST

Number	Title	Yr	NM
❑ 723	For Old Time Sake/I Want to Be Loved	1986	$6
❑ 726	Lean on Me/I Wanna Be Loved	1987	$6

NAZARETH
A&M

Number	Title	Yr	NM
❑ 1469	Bad Bad Boy/Razamanaz	1973	$5
❑ 1453	Broken Down Angel/Hard Living	1973	$5
❑ 2444	Dream On/Take the Rap	1982	$4
❑ 2324	Dressed to Kill/Pop the Silo	1981	$4
❑ 2116	Expect No Mercy/May the Sunshine	1979	$4
❑ 1511	Go Down Fighting/This Flight Tonight	1974	$5
❑ 2029	Gone Dead Train/Kentucky Fried Blues	1978	$4
❑ 2389	Hair of the Dog/Holiday	1982	$4
❑ 2237	Hearts Grown Cold/Ship of Dreams	1980	$4
❑ 2219	Holiday/Ship of Dreams	1980	$4
❑ 1895	I Want To (Do Everything for You)/I Don't Want to Go On Without You	1976	$4
❑ 1854	Loretta/Lift the Lid	1976	$4
❑ 1671	Love Hurts/Hair of the Dog	1975	$4
❑ 1671 [PS]	Love Hurts/Hair of the Dog	1975	$6
❑ 2421	Love Leads to Madness/Take the Rap	1982	$4
❑ 1936	Somebody to Roll/This Flight Tonight	1976	$4
❑ 2158	Star/Expect No Mercy	1979	$4
❑ 1548	Sunshine/This Flight Tonight	1974	$5
❑ 2130	Whatever You Want Babe/Expect No Mercy	1979	$4

WARNER BROS.

Number	Title	Yr	NM
❑ 7599	Morning Dew (Take Me for a Walk)/Dear John	1972	$8

NAZZ (1)
Also see TODD RUNDGREN.

SGC

Number	Title	Yr	NM
❑ 01	Hello It's Me/Open My Eyes	1969	$30
—First pressing: Light yellow label, no horizontal lines on label			
❑ 01	Hello It's Me/Open My Eyes	1969	$15
—Second pressing: Darker yellow label with horizontal lines			
❑ 001	Hello It's Me/Open My Eyes	1969	$8
—Third printing: Mostly green label with some yellow. Red vinyl copies on any label are bootlegs.			
❑ 01 [PS]	Hello It's Me/Open My Eyes	1969	$30
—Legitimate sleeves are paper, not cardboard			
❑ 09	Magic Me/Kicks	1970	$30
❑ 09	Magic Me/Some People	1970	$15

NAZZ (2)
VERY

Number	Title	Yr	NM
❑ 001	Lay Down and Die, Goodbye/Wonder Who's Loving Her Now	1967	$2000
—Warning! Reproductions of this record were made in the 1990s with white promo labels and picture sleeves. They are NOT the real thing. VG 1000; VG+ 1500			

Number	Title	Yr	NM
NEAL, JERRY			
DOT			
❏ 15810	I Hates Rabbits/Scratchin'	1958	$100
—With Eddie Cochran on guitar on B-side			
NECROS			
GASATANKA			
❏ JC9019	Tangled Up/The Nile Song	1985	$10
❏ JC9019 [PS]	Tangled Up/The Nile Song	1985	$10
7-Inch Extended Plays			
TOUCH N GO			
❏ 14422	Conquest for Death	1983	$35
❏ 14422 [PS]	Conquest for Death	1983	$35
❏ 001	Sex Drive/Police Brutality// Better Never Than Late/Caste System	1981	$250
❏ 001 [PS]	Sex Drive/Police Brutality// Better Never Than Late/Caste System	1981	$250
—Beware! Both record and sleeve have been heavily bootlegged.			
TOUCH N GO/DISCHORD			
❏ 13118	I.Q. 32	1981	$50
❏ 13118 [PS]	I.Q. 32	1981	$50
NED AND GARY			
LIBERTY			
❏ 55160	Lovin'/I Bust My Seams	1958	$70
NED AND NELDA			
VIGAH			
❏ 02	Hey Nelda/Surf Along	1963	$200
NEIGHB'RHOOD CHILDREN			
ACTA			
❏ 828	Behold the Lilies/I Want Action	1968	$30
❏ 823	Happy Child/Please Leave Me Alone	1968	$20
❏ 813	Maintain/Just No Way	1967	$30
—As "Neighborhood			
DOT			
❏ 17238	On Our Way/Woman Thing	1969	$20
NEIL AND JACK			
DUEL			
❏ 517	I'm Afraid/Till You've Tried Love	1962	$400
❏ 508	What Will I Do/You Are My Love at Last	1962	$400
NEIL, FRED			
BRUNSWICK			
❏ 55117	Listen Kitten/Take Me Back Again	1959	$40
—As "Freddie Neil			
CAPITOL			
❏ 2604	Everybody's Talkin'/Badi-Da	1969	$30
❏ 2256	Everybody's Talkin'/ That's the Bag I'm In	1968	$40
❏ 2091	Felicity/Please Send Me Someone to Love	1968	$40
❏ 2047	The Dolphins/I've Got a Secret	1967	$40
EPIC			
❏ 5-9435	Four Chaplains/The Rainbow and the Rose	1961	$30
❏ 5-9334	Love's Funny/Secret, Secret	1959	$30
❏ 5-9403	Slippin' Around/You Don't Have to Be a Baby to Cry	1960	$30
NEKTAR			
PASSPORT			
❏ 7904	Astral Man/Nelly the Elephant	1975	$25
NELMS, JOHNNY			
DECCA			
❏ 9-46318	I Told My Heart/Crossroads	1951	$30
❏ 9-46346	Should I Come Back/I've Been Lonesome Before	1951	$30
NELSON, KATHY			
LIBERTY			
❏ 55115	Santa Dear/Gimmie a Little Kiss, Will Ya Huh?	1957	$30
NELSON, RICKY			
CAPITOL			
❏ 4962	Almost Saturday Night/ The Loser Babe Is You	1981	$5
❏ 4988	Believe What You Say/ The Loser Babe Is You	1981	$5

Number	Title	Yr	NM
❏ 4974	Call It What You Want/ It Hasn't Happened Yet	1981	$5
DECCA			
❏ 31703	A Happy Guy/Don't Breathe a Word	1964	$15
❏ 31703 [PS]	A Happy Guy/Don't Breathe a Word	1964	$40
❏ 32026	Alone/Things You Gave Me	1966	$15
❏ 32026 [PS]	Alone/Things You Gave Me	1966	$100
❏ 32298	Barefoot Boy/Don't Make Promises	1968	$12
❏ 32284	Don't Blame It on Your Wife/ Promenade in Green	1968	$12
❏ 32222	Dream Weaver/Baby Close Your Eyes	1967	$12
❏ 32635	Easy to Be Free/ Come On In	1970	$8
❏ 32635 [PS]	Easy to Be Free/ Come On In	1970	$20
❏ 34193/7 [PS]	Envelope, bonus photo and intact jukebox title strips for these 5 singles	1963	$125
❏ 31533	Fools Rush In/Down Home	1963	$20
❏ 31533 [PS]	Fools Rush In/Down Home	1963	$40
❏ 31574	For You/That's All She Wrote	1963	$20
❏ 31574 [PS]	For You/That's All She Wrote	1963	$40
❏ 32980	Garden Party/So Long Mama	1972	$10
❏ 34193 [S]	Gypsy Woman/For Your Sweet Love	1963	$125
❏ 32739	How Long/Down Along the Bayou Country	1970	$8
❏ 32676	I Shall Be Released/If You Gotta Go, Go Now	1970	$8
❏ 34197 [S]	I Will Follow You/ What Comes Next	1963	$125
—34193-34197 are 33 1/3 rpm, small hole jukebox singles. The set came with a package, priced separately.			
❏ 34196 [S]	Let's Talk the Whole Thing Over/I Got a Woman	1963	$125
❏ 32779	Life/California	1971	$8
❏ 32711	Look at Mary/We Got Such a Long Way to Go	1970	$8
❏ 31956	Louisiana Man/You Just Can't Quit	1966	$15
❏ 31956 [PS]	Louisiana Man/You Just Can't Quit	1966	$70
❏ 31845	Love and Kisses/ Say You Love Me	1965	$15
❏ 31845 [PS]	Love and Kisses/ Say You Love Me	1965	$50
❏ 32906	Love Minus Zero-No Limit/Gypsy Pilot	1971	$8
❏ 31756	Mean Old World/When the Chips Are Down	1965	$15
❏ 31756 [PS]	Mean Old World/When the Chips Are Down	1965	$40
❏ 32176	Moonshine/Suzanne on a Sunday Morning	1967	$10
❏ 34195 [S]	One Boy Too Late/Everytime I Think About You	1963	$125
❏ 34194 [S]	Pick Up the Pieces/Every Time I See You Smilin'	1963	$125
❏ 32550	She Belongs to Me/ Promises	1969	$8
❏ 31495	String Along/Gypsy Woman	1963	$20
❏ 31495 [PS]	String Along/Gypsy Woman	1963	$40
❏ 32120	Take a City Bride/I'm Called Lonely	1967	$10
❏ 32120 [PS]	Take a City Bride/I'm Called Lonely	1967	$70
❏ 32860	Thank You Lord/ Sing Me a Song	1971	$8
❏ 31656	There's Nothing I Can Say/Lonely Corner	1964	$15
❏ 31656 [PS]	There's Nothing I Can Say/Lonely Corner	1964	$40
❏ 32055	They Don't Give Medals (To Yesterday's Heroes)/ Take a Broken Heart	1966	$15
EPIC			
❏ 34-06066	Dream Lover/Rave On	1986	$4
❏ 34-06066 [PS]	Dream Lover/Rave On	1986	$4
❏ 50674	Dream Lover/That Ain't the Way Love's Supposed to Be	1979	$5
❏ 50501	Gimme A Little Sign/ Something You Can't Buy	1978	$5
❏ 50458	It's Another Day/ You Can't Dance	1977	$5
IMPERIAL			
❏ 5958	A Long Vacation/ Mad Mad World	1963	$30
❏ 5958	A Long Vacation/ Mad Mad World	1963	$300
—Red vinyl			
❏ 5770	A Wonder Like You/ Everlovin'	1961	$30
—Starting here, Imperial singles by "Rick Nelson"			
❏ 5770 [PS]	A Wonder Like You/ Everlovin'	1961	$50
❏ 5463	Be-Bop Baby/Have I Told You Lately That I Love You	1957	$60
—Red label			
❏ 5463	Be-Bop Baby/Have I Told You Lately That I Love You	1957	$30
—Black label			
❏ 5463 [PS]	Be-Bop Baby/Have I Told You Lately That I Love You	1957	$100

Number	Title	Yr	NM
❏ 5503	Believe What You Say/My Bucket's Got a Hole in It	1958	$40
—Black label			
❏ 5503 [PS]	Believe What You Say/My Bucket's Got a Hole in It	1958	$75
❏ 5503	Believe What You Say/My Bucket's Got a Hole in It	1958	$60
—Red label			
❏ 66017	Congratulations/One Minute to One	1964	$20
❏ 66039	Everybody But Me/ Lucky Star	1964	$20
❏ 5685	I'm Not Afraid/Yes Sir, That's My Baby	1960	$30
❏ 5685 [PS]	I'm Not Afraid/Yes Sir, That's My Baby	1960	$75
❏ 5901	It's Up to You/I Need You	1962	$30
❏ 5901 [PS]	It's Up to You/I Need You	1962	$50
❏ 5614	I Wanna Be Loved/ Mighty Good	1959	$30
❏ 5614 [PS]	I Wanna Be Loved/ Mighty Good	1959	$75
❏ 5545	Lonesome Town/I Got a Feeling	1958	$40
❏ 5545	Lonesome Town/I Got a Feeling	1958	$600
—Red vinyl			
❏ 5545 [PS]	Lonesome Town/I Got a Feeling	1958	$75
❏ 5935	Old Enough to Love/ If You Can't Rock Me	1963	$30
❏ 5935 [PS]	Old Enough to Love/ If You Can't Rock Me	1963	$50
❏ 5935	Old Enough to Love/ If You Can't Rock Me	1963	$500
—Red vinyl			
❏ 5528	Poor Little Fool/Don't Leave Me This Way	1958	$40
❏ 5483	Stood Up/Waitin' in School	1957	$50
—Red label			
❏ 5483	Stood Up/Waitin' in School	1957	$30
—Black label			
❏ 5483 [PS]	Stood Up/Waitin' in School	1957	$75
❏ 5864	Teen Age Idol/I've Got My Eyes on You	1962	$30
❏ 5864 [PS]	Teen Age Idol/I've Got My Eyes on You	1962	$50
❏ 5910	That's All/I'm in Love Again	1963	$30
❏ 5985	Time After Time/ There's Not a Minute	1963	$30
❏ 66004	Today's Teardrops/ Thank You Darlin'	1963	$20
❏ 66004 [PS]	Today's Teardrops/ Thank You Darlin'	1963	$50
❏ 5741	Travelin' Man/ Hello Mary Lou	1961	$30
—Black vinyl			
❏ 5741	Travelin' Man/ Hello Mary Lou	1961	$800
—Red vinyl			
❏ 5741 [PS]	Travelin' Man/ Hello Mary Lou	1961	$75
MCA			
❏ 40130	Evil Woman Child/Lifestream	1973	$6
❏ 40392	Louisiana Belle/Try (Try to Fall in Love)	1975	$6
❏ 40214	One Night Stand/Lifestream	1974	$6
❏ 40001	Palace Guard/A Flower Opens Gently By	1973	$6
❏ 40187	Windfall/Legacy	1974	$6
UNITED ARTISTS			
❏ 0080	A Wonder Like You/ Everlovin'	1973	$5
—0071 through 0080 are "Silver Spotlight Series" reissues			
❏ 0071	Be-Bop Baby/Stood Up	1973	$5
❏ 0079	Hello Mary Lou/ Sweeter Than You	1973	$5
❏ 0072	Lonesome Town/ It's Up to You	1973	$5
❏ 0073	Poor Little Fool/My Bucket's Got a Hole in It	1973	$5
❏ 0075	Teen Age Idol/ Young Emotions	1973	$5
❏ 0074	Travelin' Man/Believe What You Say	1973	$5
UNIVERSAL PICTURES			
❏ CPM 7-112/3 [DJ]	Love and Kisses Radio Spots	1965	$300
—Red vinyl; three segments on one side, three on the other; double the value if a six-page transcription is with the record			
VERVE			
❏ 10047	I'm Walkin'/A Teenager's Romance	1957	$60
—Orange and yellow label			
❏ 10047	I'm Walkin'/A Teenager's Romance	1957	$50
—Black and white label			
7-Inch Extended Plays			
DECCA			
❏ 7-34319 [PS]	Best Always	1965	$35
—With title strips			

Number	Title	Yr	NM
❑ 7-34319 [S]	I'm Not Ready for You Yet/ Lonely Corner/Mean Old World//I Know a Place/It's Beginning to Hurt/When the Chips Are Down	1965	$35

— 33 1/3 rpm, small hole jukebox edition

Number	Title	Yr	NM
❑ ED2760	I Will Follow You/Pick Up the Pieces//One Boy Too Late/Let's Talk the Whole Thing Over	1963	$175
❑ ED2760 [PS]	One Boy Too Late	1963	$175

IMPERIAL

Number	Title	Yr	NM
❑ IMP153	Be-Bop Baby/Have I Told You Lately That I Love You//Honeycomb/ Boppin' the Blues	1957	$60
❑ IMP159	Be True to Me/One of These Mornings// Lonesome Town/It's Late	1959	$60
❑ IMP164	Don't Leave Me/That's All//A Long Vacation/ Sweeter Than You	1959	$70

— Revised track order; "RE" before master number at 3 o'clock on label

Number	Title	Yr	NM
❑ IMP164	Don't Leave Me/That's All//Sweeter Than You/A Long Vacation	1959	$60

— Original track order

Number	Title	Yr	NM
❑ IMP157	Down the Line/Don't Leave Me This Way//I'm in Love Again/My Babe	1958	$60
❑ IMP165	Glory Train/I Bowed My Head in Shame//March with the Band of the Lord/If You Believe It	1959	$125
❑ LP 4-2232 [PS]	Million Sellers	1964	$100
❑ IMP161	Old Enough to Love/ Tryin' to Get to You// Never Be Anyone Else But You/I Can't Help It	1959	$60
❑ IMP163	One Minute To One/Blood from a Stone//Half Breed/ Just a Little Too Much	1959	$60
❑ IMP156	Shirley Lee/There's Good Rockin' Tonight// Someday/I'm Feelin' Sorry	1958	$60
❑ IMP164 [PS]	Songs by Ricky (Don't Leave Me)	1959	$60
❑ IMP163 [PS]	Songs by Ricky (One Minute to One)	1959	$60
❑ IMP162 [PS]	Songs by Ricky (You'll Never Know What You're Missin')	1959	$60
❑ IMP154	Teenage Doll/If You Can't Rock Me//Whole Lotta Shakin' Goin' On/ Baby I'm Sorry	1957	$60
❑ LP 4-2232	Travelin' Man/Never Be Anyone Else But You/It's Late//Young Emotions/ Hello Mary Lou/Yes Sir, That's My Baby	1964	$100

— 33 1/3 rpm, small hole, jukebox edition

VERVE

Number	Title	Yr	NM
❑ 5048	I'm Walkin'/A Teenager's Romance//You're My One and Only Love/Honey Rock	1957	$175

NELSON, SANDY

IMPERIAL

Number	Title	Yr	NM
❑ 66284	Alligator Boogaloo/ Midnight Magic	1968	$10
❑ 5860	All Night Long/Rompin' and Stompin'	1962	$15
❑ 66146	A Lover's Concerto/ Treat Her Right	1965	$10
❑ 5870	And Then There Were Drums/Live It Up	1962	$15
❑ 5904	Be-Bop Baby/Let the Four Winds Blow	1962	$15
❑ 5745	Big Noise from the Jungle/Get With It	1961	$15
❑ 5672	Bouncy/Lost Dreams	1960	$15
❑ 5988	Caravan/Sandy	1963	$15
❑ 66034	Castle Rock/You Don't Say	1964	$10
❑ 66093	Chop Chop/Reach for a Star	1965	$10
❑ 5708	Cool Operator/Jive Talk	1960	$15
❑ 5829	Drummin' Up a Storm/ Drum Stomp	1962	$15
❑ 5630	Drum Party/Big Noise from Winnetka	1959	$15
❑ 66127	Drums A-Go-Go/Caesar	1965	$12
❑ 5809	Drums Are My Beat/ The Birth of the Beat	1962	$15
❑ 66019	Drum Shack/Kitty's Theme	1964	$12
❑ 5965	Here We Go Again/Just Bill	1963	$15
❑ 66107	Land of 1000 Dances/ Let There Be Drums	1965	$12
❑ 66209	Let's Go Trippin'/Pipeline	1966	$15
❑ 66402	Let There Be Drums and Brass/Leap Frog	1969	$12
❑ 5775	Let There Be Drums/ Quite a Beat	1961	$20
❑ 66375	Manhattan Spiritual/ The Stripper	1969	$10
❑ 5932	Ooh Poo Pah Doo/ Feel So Good	1963	$15
❑ 5648	Party Time/The Wiggle	1960	$15
❑ 66253	Peter Gunn/You Got Me Hummin'	1967	$10

Number	Title	Yr	NM
❑ 5884	Teenage House Party/Day Train	1962	$15
❑ 66060	Teen Beat '65/Kitty's Theme	1964	$15
❑ 66246	The Drums Go On/ Lawdy Miss Clawdy	1967	$10

ORIGINAL SOUND

Number	Title	Yr	NM
❑ 5	Teen Beat/Big Jump	1959	$30

UNITED ARTISTS

Number	Title	Yr	NM
❑ 0082	Teen Beat/Let There Be Drums	1973	$5

— Silver Spotlight Series" reissue

NELSON, WILLIE, AND KRIS KRISTOFFERSON

COLUMBIA

Number	Title	Yr	NM
❑ 38-04652	How Do You Feel About Foolin' Around/ Eye of the Storm	1984	$3

NELSON, WILLIE, AND ROGER MILLER

COLUMBIA

Number	Title	Yr	NM
❑ 02681	Old Friends/When a House Is Not a Home	1982	$4

— With Ray Price

NELSON, WILLIE, AND WEBB PIERCE

COLUMBIA

Number	Title	Yr	NM
❑ 03231	In the Jailhouse Now/ Back Street Affair	1982	$4

NELSON, WILLIE, AND RAY PRICE

COLUMBIA

Number	Title	Yr	NM
❑ 11405	Don't You Ever Get Tired (Of Loving Me)/Funny How Time Slips Away	1980	$4
❑ 11329	Faded Love/This Cold World with You	1980	$4

NELSON, WILLIE, AND LEON RUSSELL

COLUMBIA

Number	Title	Yr	NM
❑ 11023	Heartbreak Hotel/ Sioux City Sue	1979	$4
❑ 11119	Trouble in Mind/One for My Baby (And One More for the Road)	1979	$4

NELSON, WILLIE

ATLANTIC

Number	Title	Yr	NM
❑ 2979	Devil in a Sleepin' Bag/ Stay All Night	1973	$5
❑ 3008	Heaven and Hell/I Still Can't Believe You're Gone	1974	$5
❑ 3334	Heaven and Hell/I Still Can't Believe You're Gone	1976	$5
❑ 3020	Phases and Stages/ Bloody Mary Morning	1974	$5
❑ 2968	Shotgun Willie/Sad Songs and Waltzes	1973	$5
❑ 3228	Sister's Coming Home/ Pick Up the Tempo	1974	$5

BETTY

Number	Title	Yr	NM
❑ 5703	Man with the Blues/The Storm Has Just Begun	1964	$30
❑ 5702	What a Way to Love/ Misery Mansion	1964	$30

CHALLENGE

Number	Title	Yr	NM
❑ 59280	I'm Talking About Love/I'm in Love with a Dancing Girl Working at Metropole	1965	$20

COLUMBIA

Number	Title	Yr	NM
❑ 10834	All of Me/Unchained Melody	1978	$5
❑ 02741	Always on My Mind/ The Party's Over	1982	$4
❑ 11418	Angel Flying Too Close to the Ground/I Guess I've Come to Live Here in Your Eyes	1981	$4
❑ 03123	Angel Flying Too Close to the Ground/Mona Lisa	1982	$3

— Reissue

Number	Title	Yr	NM
❑ 05566	Are There Any More Real Cowboys/I'm a Memory	1985	$3

— A-side with Neil Young

Number	Title	Yr	NM
❑ 04495	As Time Goes By/ You'll Never Know	1984	$30

— Willie Nelson and Julio Iglesias; withdrawn immediately upon release

Number	Title	Yr	NM
❑ 04495 [PS]	As Time Goes By/ You'll Never Know	1984	$30

— Willie Nelson and Julio Iglesias; withdrawn immediately upon release

Number	Title	Yr	NM
❑ 03674	Beer Barrel Polka/Little Old Fashioned Karma	1983	$4
❑ 10176	Blue Eyes Cryin' in the Rain/Bandera	1975	$5
❑ 10784	Blue Skies/Moonlight in Vermont	1978	$5
❑ 04568	City of New Orleans/Why Are You Pickin' On Me	1984	$3
❑ 04568 [PS]	City of New Orleans/Why Are You Pickin' On Me	1984	$4

Number	Title	Yr	NM
❑ 05594	Desperadoes Waiting for a Train/The Twentieth Century Is Almost Over	1985	$3

— A-side: Willie Nelson/Waylon Jennings/Johnny Cash/Kris Kristofferson; B-side: Nelson, Cash

Number	Title	Yr	NM
❑ 04847	Forgiving You Was Easy/ You Wouldn't Cross the Street (To Say Goodbye)	1985	$3
❑ 10704	Georgia on My Mind/On the Sunny Side of the Street	1978	$5
❑ 03124	Heartache of a Fool/ Midnight Rider	1982	$3

— Reissue

Number	Title	Yr	NM
❑ 02558	Heartaches of a Fool/ Uncloudy Day	1981	$4
❑ 07007	Heart of Gold/So Much Like My Dad	1987	$3
❑ 11126	Help Me Make It Through the Night/The Pilgrim: Chapter 33	1979	$4
❑ 08406	Highwayman/Desperadoes Waiting for a Train	1988	$3

— Waylon Jennings/Willie Nelson/Johnny Cash/Kris Kristofferson; reissue

Number	Title	Yr	NM
❑ 04881	Highwayman/The Human Condition	1985	$3

— A-side: Willie Nelson/Waylon Jennings/Johnny Cash/Kris Kristofferson; B-side: Nelson, Cash

Number	Title	Yr	NM
❑ 04881 [PS]	Highwayman/The Human Condition	1985	$4

— A-side: Willie Nelson/Waylon Jennings/Johnny Cash/Kris Kristofferson; B-side: Nelson, Cash

Number	Title	Yr	NM
❑ 10327	I'd Have to Be Crazy/ Amazing Grace	1976	$5
❑ 10383	If You've Got the Money, I've Got the Time/The Sound in Your Mind	1976	$5
❑ 10588	I Love You a Thousand Ways/Mom and Dad's Waltz	1977	$5
❑ 02187	I'm Gonna Sit Right Down and Write Myself a Letter/ Over the Rainbow	1981	$4
❑ 06246	I'm Not Trying to Forget You/ I've Got the Craziest Feeling	1986	$3
❑ 07202	Island in the Sun/There Is No Easy Way (But There Is a Way)	1987	$3
❑ 05749	I Told a Lie to My Heart/ Slow Movin' Outlaw	1986	$3

— A-side with Hank Williams, Jr.; B-side: with Lacy J. Dalton

Number	Title	Yr	NM
❑ 03385	Last Thing I Needed First Thing This Morning/Old Fords and a Natural Stone	1982	$4
❑ 03073	Let It Be Me/ Permanently Lonely	1982	$4
❑ 05834	Living in the Promiseland/ Bach Minuet in G	1986	$3
❑ 08395	Living in the Promiseland/ Forgiving You Was Easy	1988	$3

— Reissue

Number	Title	Yr	NM
❑ 05597	Me and Paul/I Let My Mind Wander	1985	$3
❑ 11257	Midnight Rider/Do You Think You're a Cowboy	1980	$4
❑ 02000	Mona Lisa/Twinkle, Twinkle Little Star	1981	$4
❑ 11186	My Heroes Have Always Been Cowboys/Rising Star (Love Theme)	1980	$4
❑ 11351	On the Road Again/ Jumpin' Cotton-Eyed Joe	1980	$4

— B-side by Johnny Gimble

Number	Title	Yr	NM
❑ 02166	On the Road Again/ September Song	1981	$3

— Reissue

Number	Title	Yr	NM
❑ 06530	Partners After All/Home Away from Home	1986	$3
❑ AE71183 [DJ]	Pretty Paper/Rudolph the Red-Nosed Reindeer	1979	$30

— Red vinyl

Number	Title	Yr	NM
❑ 03476	Pretty Paper/White Christmas	1982	$5
❑ AE71775 [DJ]	Pretty Paper/White Christmas	1982	$6
❑ 10929	September Song/Don't Get Around Much Anymore	1979	$4
❑ 04715	Seven Spanish Angels/ Who Cares	1984	$3

— A-side: Ray Charles and Willie Nelson; B-side: Ray Charles and Janie Frickie

Number	Title	Yr	NM
❑ 05677	Slow Movin' Outlaw/They All Went to Mexico	1985	$3

— A-side with Lacy J. Dalton; B-side with Carlos Santana

Number	Title	Yr	NM
❑ 10644	Something to Brag About/Anybody's Darlin' (Anybody But Mine)	1977	$5

— With Mary Kay Place

Number	Title	Yr	NM
❑ 08044	Spanish Eyes/Ole Buttermilk Sky	1988	$3

— With Julio Iglesias

Number	Title	Yr	NM
❑ 73015	There You Are/Spirit	1989	$3
❑ 04217	To All the Girls I've Loved Before/I Don't Want to Wake You	1984	$3

— Julio Iglesias & Willie Nelson; B-side by Julio Iglesias solo

Number	Title	Yr	NM
❏ 04217 [PS]	To All the Girls I've Loved Before/I Don't Want to Wake You	1984	$5

—Julio Iglesias & Willie Nelson; first sleeve has artists' names in both capital and small letters

Number	Title	Yr	NM
❏ 04217 [PS]	To All the Girls I've Loved Before/I Don't Want to Wake You	1984	$4

—Julio Iglesias & Willie Nelson; second sleeve has artists' names in all capital letters

Number	Title	Yr	NM
❏ 08541	Twilight Time/Ac-Cent-Tchu-Ate the Positive	1989	$3
❏ 10877	Whiskey River/Under the Double Eagle	1978	$5
❏ AE71182 [DJ]	White Christmas/Blue Christmas	1979	$30

—Green vinyl

Number	Title	Yr	NM
❏ 03965	Why Do I Have to Choose/Would You Lay with Me (In a Field of Stone)	1983	$4
❏ 04263	Without a Song/I Can't Begin to Tell You	1983	$3

D

Number	Title	Yr	NM
❏ 1084	Man with the Blues/The Storm Has Just Begun	1959	$40
❏ 1131	What a Way to Love/Misery Mansion	1960	$40

LIBERTY

Number	Title	Yr	NM
❏ 55661	Am I Blue/There'll Be No Teardrops Tonight	1964	$10
❏ 55532	Half a Man/The Last Letter	1963	$15
❏ 55638	How Long Is Forever/You Took My Happy Away	1963	$15
❏ 55386	Mr. Record Man/The Part Where I Cry	1961	$30
❏ 55591	Take My Word/Feed It a Memory	1963	$15
❏ 55439	Touch Me/Where My House Lives	1962	$20
❏ 55494	Wake Me When It's Over/There's Gonna Be Love in My House	1962	$20
❏ 55403	Willingly/Chain of Love	1962	$20

—A-side with Shirley Collie

LONE STAR

Number	Title	Yr	NM
❏ 703	The End of Understanding/Will You Remember Mine	1978	$5

MONUMENT

Number	Title	Yr	NM
❏ 03408	Everything Is Beautiful (In Its Own Way)/Put It Off Until Tomorrow	1982	$4

—A-side: Willie Nelson and Dolly Parton; B-side: Dolly Parton and Kris Kristofferson

Number	Title	Yr	NM
❏ 855	I Never Cared for You/You Left Me	1964	$20

PARADISE

Number	Title	Yr	NM
❏ 629	Wabash Cannonball/Tennessee Waltz	1984	$4

—A-side with Hank Wilson (a.k.a. Leon Russell); B-side by Wilson solo

RCA

Number	Title	Yr	NM
❏ PB-11673	Crazy Arms/Hurricane Shirley	1979	$5

—B-side by Bobby Bare

Number	Title	Yr	NM
❏ PB-12254	Good Times/Where Do You Stand	1981	$4
❏ PB-12254 [PS]	Good Times/Where Do You Stand	1981	$5
❏ PB-11235	If You Can Touch Her at All/Rainy Day Blues	1978	$5
❏ PB-10969	I'm a Memory/It Should Be Easier Now	1977	$5

—With Darrell McCall

Number	Title	Yr	NM
❏ PB-12328	Mountain Dew/Laying My Burdens Down	1981	$4
❏ GB-11995	Sweet Memories/If You Can Touch Her At All	1980	$3

—Gold Standard Series

Number	Title	Yr	NM
❏ PB-11465	Sweet Memories/Little Things	1979	$5

RCA VICTOR

Number	Title	Yr	NM
❏ 74-0635	A Moment Isn't Very Long/Words Don't Fit the Picture	1972	$6
❏ 47-9202	Blackjack County Chain/Some Other World	1967	$10
❏ 47-9684	Bring Me Sunshine/Don't Say Love or Nothing	1968	$10
❏ 47-8801	Columbus Stockade Blues/He Sits at My Table	1966	$15
❏ 47-9536	Good Times/Don't You Ever Get Tired	1968	$10
❏ 47-8594	Healing Hands of Time/One Day at a Time	1965	$15
❏ 47-8682	I Just Can't Let You Say Goodbye/And So Will You, My Love	1965	$15
❏ PB-10429	I'm a Memory/Fire and Rain	1975	$5
❏ 47-9951	I'm a Memory/I'm So Lonesome I Could Cry	1971	$6
❏ 47-8852	I'm Still Not Over You/I Love You Because	1966	$15
❏ 47-9903	Laying My Burdens Down/Truth Number One	1970	$8
❏ 47-9427	Little Things/I'll Stay Around	1968	$10

Number	Title	Yr	NM
❏ 74-0816	Mountain Dew/Phases, Stages, Circles, Cycles, and Scenes	1972	$6
❏ 47-8933	One in a Row/San Antonio Rose	1966	$15
❏ 47-8484	Pretty Paper/What a Merry Christmas This Could Be	1964	$20
❏ 47-9029	Pretty Paper/What a Merry Christmas This Could Be	1966	$15
❏ 47-9931	Pretty Paper/What a Merry Christmas This Could Be	1970	$8
❏ PB-10461	Pretty Paper/What a Merry Christmas This Could Be	1975	$8
❏ 47-9324	San Antonio/To Make a Long Story Short	1967	$10
❏ 47-8519	She's Not for You/Permanently Lonely	1965	$15
❏ PB-10591	Summer of Roses/I Gotta Get Drunk	1976	$5
❏ 47-9100	The Party's Over/Make Way for a Better Man	1967	$10
❏ 47-9798	Who Do I Know in Dallas/Once More with Feeling	1969	$8

SONGBIRD

Number	Title	Yr	NM
❏ 41313	Family Bible/In God's Eyes	1980	$4

UNITED ARTISTS

Number	Title	Yr	NM
❏ XW1165	Hello Walls/The Last Letter	1978	$5
❏ XW771	The Last Letter/There Goes a Man	1976	$5
❏ XW1254	There'll Be Teardrops Tonight/Blue Must Be the Color of the Blues	1978	$5

NELSON, WILLY
LIBERTY

Number	Title	Yr	NM
❏ 55155	Susie/No Dough	1958	$40

—As "Willie Nelson"

Number	Title	Yr	NM
❏ 55155	Susie/No Dough	1958	$30

—As "Willy Nelson"

NENA
EPIC

Number	Title	Yr	NM
❏ 04108	99 Luftballons/99 Red Balloons	1983	$5

—B-side label had "Balloons" misspelled

Number	Title	Yr	NM
❏ 04108	99 Luftballons/99 Red Balloons	1983	$3

—B-side label corrects spelling error

Number	Title	Yr	NM
❏ 08472	99 Luftballons/99 Red Balloons	1988	$3

—Reissue

NEON BOYS
7-Inch Extended Plays
SHAKE

Number	Title	Yr	NM
❏ SHK101 [PS]	That's All I Know (Right Now)/Love Comes in Spurts//Don't Die/Time	1980	$13
❏ SHK101	That's All I Know (Right Now)/Love Comes in Spurts//Don't Die/Time	1980	$13

—Neon Boys later became Television; B-side tracks by Richard Hell and the Voidoids

NEONS, THE (1)
CHALLENGE

Number	Title	Yr	NM
❏ 9147	Magic Moment/Fat Girls	1962	$125
❏ 59147	Magic Moment/Fat Girls	1962	$60

NEONS, THE (2)
GONE

Number	Title	Yr	NM
❏ 5090	Angel Face/Golden Dreams	1960	$50

TETRA

Number	Title	Yr	NM
❏ 4444	Angel Face/Kiss Me Quickly	1956	$100

VINTAGE

Number	Title	Yr	NM
❏ 1016	Honey Bun/Golden Dreams	1974	$5

NEONS, THE (3)
WALDON

Number	Title	Yr	NM
❏ 1001	My Lover/Tucson	1961	$700

NEPTUNES, THE
CHECKER

Number	Title	Yr	NM
❏ 967	She'll Understand/So Little Time	1960	$15

GLORY

Number	Title	Yr	NM
❏ 269	Fraidy Cat/As Long As	1959	$30

INSTANT

Number	Title	Yr	NM
❏ 3255	Make a Memory/House of Heartaches	1963	$60

PAYSON

Number	Title	Yr	NM
❏ 101/2	If You Care/She Went That-a-Way	1958	$30

RCA VICTOR

Number	Title	Yr	NM
❏ 47-7931	Curiosity Killed the Cat/This Is Love	1961	$15

VICTORIA

Number	Title	Yr	NM
❏ 102	I'm Coming Home/I Don't Cry Anymore	1964	$300

WARNER BROS.

Number	Title	Yr	NM
❏ 5453	Shame Girl/I've Got Plans	1964	$15

NERO, PETER
ARIOLA AMERICA

Number	Title	Yr	NM
❏ 7650	Tara's Theme/Always Lovely Times	1976	$4
❏ 7635	There'll Be Time/Always Lovely Times	1976	$4

ARISTA

Number	Title	Yr	NM
❏ 0112	Emmanuelle/Soul Ballet	1975	$4
❏ 0125	Theme from "The Young and the Restless"/Superstition	1975	$4

COLUMBIA

Number	Title	Yr	NM
❏ 44934	Be-In/Theme from Picasso Summer	1969	$5
❏ 45731	Ben (Theme from "Ben")/His World	1972	$4
❏ 45544	Brian's Song/Just for Her	1972	$4
❏ 45077	Come Saturday Morning/Maybe Tomorrow	1970	$4
❏ 45167	Company/Raindrops Keep Fallin' on My Head	1970	$4
❏ 45756	Lady Sings the Blues/Love Is Waiting	1973	$4
❏ 45756 [PS]	Lady Sings the Blues/Love Is Waiting	1973	$5
❏ 45651	Love Theme from "The Godfather"/A Love That Never Ends	1972	$4
❏ 44846	Soulful Strut/For Once in My Life	1969	$5
❏ 45198	The Great Hits of Summer Medley/Something	1970	$4
❏ 45825	Theme from "Baxter"/Love Is Waiting	1973	$4
❏ 45279	Theme from "Love Story"/El Condor Pasa	1970	$4
❏ 45399	Theme from "Summer of '42"/Theme from "Jesus Christ Superstar	1971	$4
❏ 45959	The Morning After/Daydream	1973	$4

RCA VICTOR

Number	Title	Yr	NM
❏ 47-8892	Born Free/Who's Afraid	1966	$6
❏ 47-9556	Elvira/A Heart Without Love	1968	$6
❏ 47-9247	Guantanamera/Xochimilco	1967	$6
❏ 47-7932	Maria/On the Street Where You Live	1961	$8
❏ 47-8620	Ship of Fools/Why Did I Choose You	1965	$6
❏ 47-8161	Space Flight/It's a Darn Good Thing	1963	$8
❏ 47-8322	Sunday in New York/More in Love	1964	$6
❏ 47-8503	Theme from "36 Hours"/If You've Got a Heart	1965	$6
❏ 47-7956	Theme from "Summer and Smoke"/Maria	1961	$8
❏ 47-7956 [PS]	Theme from "Summer and Smoke"/Maria	1961	$15
❏ 47-9429	Theme from The Fox/Who Will Answer	1968	$6
❏ 47-9125	Theme from The Quiller Memorandum/Amy's Theme	1967	$6
❏ 47-8715	Thunderball/Theme from "The Spy Who Came In from the Cold	1965	$6

NERVES, THE
7-Inch Extended Plays
NERVES

Number	Title	Yr	NM
❏ 4501	Hanging on the Telephone	1976	$25
❏ 4501 [PS]	Hanging on the Telephone	1976	$25

NERVOUS EATERS
ELEKTRA

Number	Title	Yr	NM
❏ 47072	Loretta/Get Stuffed	1980	$30
❏ 47072 [DJ]	Loretta (mono/stereo)	1980	$20

RAT

Number	Title	Yr	NM
❏ 5282	Loretta/Rock with Me	1979	$10
❏ 5282 [PS]	Loretta/Rock with Me	1979	$10
❏ 5282 [PS]	Loretta/Rock with Me	1979	$50

—First pressing has cardboard sleeve

NERVOUS NORVUS
BIG BEN

Number	Title	Yr	NM
❏ 101	Pure Gold/Let's Worship God Each Sunday	1960	$30

DOT

Number	Title	Yr	NM
❏ 15485	Ape Call/Wild Dog of Kentucky	1956	$40

—Originals have maroon labels

Number	Title	Yr	NM
❏ 15485	Ape Call/Wild Dog of Kentucky	1956	$30

—Second pressings have black labels

Number	Title	Yr	NM
❏ 15500	The Fang/The Bullfrog	1956	$40

—*Originals have maroon labels*

❏ 15500	The Fang/The Bullfrog	1956	$30

—*Second pressings have black labels*

❏ 16765	Transfusion/Ape Call	1965	$15
❏ 15470	Transfusion/Dig	1956	$60

—*Originals have maroon labels*

❏ 15470	Transfusion/Dig	1956	$40

—*Second pressings have black labels*

EMBEE

❏ 117	I Like Girls/Stone Age Woo	1959	$30

NESBITT, JIM

ACE

❏ 621	Please Mr. Kennedy/The Horse Race	1961	$30

CAPRICORN

❏ 0236	Shaving Cream/Suckin' Up Suds	1975	$6

CHART

❏ 1165	A Tiger in My Tank/I Can't Stand This Living Alone	1965	$8
❏ 5193	Bars Put Me Behind These Bars/Mr. Jones	1973	$8
❏ 1043	Clean the Slate in '68/The Husband Is the Last to Know	1968	$8
❏ 5150	Going Home to Die/I Am a Married Man	1972	$8
❏ 5131	Having Fun in '71/Here Today and Here Tomorrow	1971	$8
❏ 1350	Heck of a Fix in '66/I'm from the Country	1966	$8
❏ 1445	Husbands-in-Law/I Want to Have My Operation on TV	1967	$8
❏ 5112	I Love Them Old Nasty Cigarettes/Nice Guys Always Finish Last	1971	$8
❏ 5004	I'm Yeller/If You See My Brother	1969	$8
❏ 5023	It's Great to Stay in the U.S.A./Intoxicated, Frustrated Me	1969	$8
❏ 1055	Living the Life of Riley/Six Broken Hearts	1968	$8
❏ 1065	Looking for More in '64/Cry Me a River	1964	$8
❏ 1100	Mother-in-Law/If You Don't Love Me	1964	$8
❏ 5070	My Old Drinking Friends/When They Sent My Old Lady to the Moon	1970	$8
❏ 5096	Pollution/Spiro	1970	$8
❏ 1320	She Didn't Come Home/Working All My Life	1966	$8
❏ 1200	Still Alive in '65/I Laughed When You Said You Were Leaving	1965	$8
❏ 1410	Stranded/These Modern Things	1966	$8
❏ 1240	The Friendly Undertaker/Crying and Waiting for You	1965	$8
❏ 1018	Truck Drivin' Cat with Nine Wives/Social Security	1968	$8
❏ 5202	Whiskey Sampler/From the Moment You're Born	1973	$8

DOT

❏ 16424	Livin' Offa Credit/I'm a Married Man	1963	$15
❏ 16197	Please Mr. Kennedy/The Horse Race	1961	$15

SCORPION

❏ 0500	Phone Call from the Devil/Drop in the Bucket	1975	$6
❏ 0505	The Short Sheriff/Overseas by Mail	1976	$5
❏ 0513	Twenty Years and Holding/Run for a Life	1976	$5

—*With Tammy Haney*

NESMITH, MICHAEL

Also see MIKE, JOHN AND BILL; THE MONKEES.

HIGHNESS

❏ HN-13	Wanderin'/Well Well Well	1963	$400

—*As "Mike Nesmith*

PACIFIC ARTS

❏ 108	Cruisin'/Horserace	1979	$6
❏ 6373	Life, the Unsuspecting Captive/Rio	1976	$12
❏ 084	Life, the Unsuspecting Captive/Rio	1977	$8
❏ 106	Magic (This Night Is Magic)/Dance	1979	$6

RCA VICTOR

❏ 74-0629	Lazy Lady/Mama Rocker	1971	$8
❏ 74-0540	Only Bound/Propinquity	1971	$8
❏ 74-0399	Silver Moon/Lady of the Valley	1970	$10
❏ 74-0491	Tumbling Tumbleweeds/Texas Morning	1971	$8

NESSER, JACK

BRIAR

❏ 125	The Christmas Day Song/Still In Love	1961	$12

NETTLES, BILL

MERCURY

❏ 6350	Smiles Won't Hide an Achin' Heart/Long Road to Travel	1951	$40

STARDAY

❏ 174	Wine-O Boogie/Gumbo Mumbo	1955	$125

NEUMAN, ALFRED E., AND THE FURSHLUGGINER FIVE

ABC-PARAMOUNT

❏ 10013	What -- Me Worry?/Potrzebie	1959	$50
❏ 10013 [PS]	What -- Me Worry?/Potrzebie	1959	$70

NEVIL, ROBBIE

EMI

❏ B-50176	Somebody Like You/Can I Count on You	1989	$3

EMI MANHATTAN

❏ B-50152	Back on Holiday/Too Soon	1988	$3
❏ B-50152 [PS]	Back on Holiday/Too Soon	1988	$3

MANHATTAN

❏ B-50047	C'est La Vie/Time Waits for No One	1986	$3
❏ B-50047 [PS]	C'est La Vie/Time Waits for No One	1986	$4
❏ B-50053	Dominoes/Neighbors	1987	$3
❏ B-50053 [PS]	Dominoes/Neighbors	1987	$3
❏ B-50075	Wot's It To Ya/(To Ya Remix)	1987	$3
❏ B-50075 [PS]	Wot's It To Ya/(To Ya Remix)	1987	$10
❏ 7PRO-79064 [DJ]	Wot's It To Ya/(To Ya Remix)	1987	$10

NEVILLE, AARON

BELL

❏ 834	All These Things/She's On My Mind	1969	$8
❏ 781	Speak to Me/You Don't Love Me Anymore	1969	$8

MERCURY

❏ 73310	Baby I'm-a Want You/Mojo Hannah	1972	$6
❏ 73387	Hercules/Going Home	1973	$200

MINIT

❏ 624	Don't Cry/Reality	1961	$15
❏ 639	How Many Times/I'm Waitin' at the Station	1962	$15
❏ 650	Humdinger/Sweet Little Mama	1962	$15
❏ 631	Let's Live/I Found Another Love	1961	$15
❏ 612	Over You/Every Day	1960	$20

—*As "Arron Neville*

❏ 618	Show Me the Way/Get Out of My Life	1960	$15
❏ 657	Wrong Number/How Could I Help But Love You	1963	$15

PAR-LO

❏ 103	She Took You for a Ride/Space Man	1967	$8
❏ 101	Tell It Like It Is/Why Worry	1966	$30

—*Black and white label*

❏ 101	Tell It Like It Is/Why Worry	1966	$30

—*Turquoise label, silver print*

❏ 101	Tell It Like It Is/Why Worry	1966	$30

—*Yellow label, red and black print*

POLYDOR

❏ 14426	Greatest Love/Performance	1977	$4

SAFARI

❏ 201	Forever More/Ape Man	1967	$10

WHO DAT?

❏ VPAG-4476/7	Who Dat? (The History of the Saints)/(Extended Version)	1987	$8

NEW BRICK WINDOW, THE

VENDETTA

❏ 126	Little Girl/Baby Come Running	1968	$60

NEW CHRISTY MINSTRELS, THE

At one time or another, KIM CARNES, Gene Clark of THE BYRDS, BARRY McGUIRE, KENNY ROGERS and RANDY SPARKS were members, as were most of the original FIRST EDITION.

COLUMBIA

❏ 43822	A Corner in the Sun/Beautiful, Beautiful World	1966	$6
❏ 44577	Alice's Restaurant/Summertime Love	1968	$5
❏ 44528	Ballad for Americans/Gallant Men	1968	$5
❏ 43470	Born to Be Free/Everybody Loves Saturday Night	1965	$8
❏ 43215	Chim Chim Cheree/They Gotta Quit Kickin' My Dog Around	1965	$8
❏ 4-44631	Chitty Chitty Bang Bang/Me Old Bam-Boo	1968	$6
❏ 43533	Dance My Troubles Away (Zorba's Dance)/There But for Fortune	1966	$6
❏ 42673	Denver/Liza Jane	1963	$12
❏ 43178	Down the Road I Go/Gotta Get a-Goin'	1964	$8
❏ 42805	Green, Green/The Banjo	1963	$10
❏ 43644	If I Could Start My Life Again/The Music of the World a-Turnin'	1966	$6
❏ 44176	I'll Coat Your Mind with Honey/Night and Day	1967	$6
❏ 43961	It Should Have Been You/Sleep Comes Easy	1967	$6
❏ 43137	Same Ol' Huckleberry Finn/The Ol' Riverboat	1964	$8
❏ 42887	Saturday Night/The Wheeler-Dealers	1963	$10
❏ 43092	Silly Ol' Summertime/The Far Side of the Hill	1964	$8
❏ 44355	The Clown/No Matter What People	1967	$6
❏ 42592	This Land Is Your Land/Don't Cry, Suzanne	1962	$10
❏ 42592 [PS]	This Land Is Your Land/Don't Cry, Suzanne	1962	$20
❏ 43000	Today/Miss Katy Cruel	1964	$8
❏ 43940	We Need a Little Christmas/Oh Holy Night	1966	$10
❏ JZSP116417/8 [DJ]	We Need a Little Christmas/Sleigh Ride	1966	$15

—*Yellow label*

❏ JZSP116417/8 [DJ]	We Need a Little Christmas/Sleigh Ride	1966	$15

—*White label*

GREGAR

❏ 71-0106	Brother/I Still Do	1970	$4
❏ 71-0114	The Age of Not Believing/Love It Along	1972	$4

NEW COLONY SIX, THE

CENTAUR

❏ 1201	I Confess/Dawn Is Breaking	1966	$20
❏ 1202	I Like Awake/At the River's Edge	1966	$20

MCA

❏ 40288	I Really Don't Want to Go/Run	1974	$40

MERCURY

❏ 73004	Barbara, I Love You/Prairie Grey	1970	$8
❏ 72817	Can't You See Me Cry/Summertime's Another Name for Love	1968	$8
❏ 72817 [PS]	Can't You See Me Cry/Summertime's Another Name for Love	1968	$20
❏ 73093	Close Your Eyes Little Girl/Love, That's the Best I Can Do	1970	$30

—*Promo copies go for less*

❏ 72920	I Could Never Lie to You/Just Feel Worse	1969	$8
❏ 72961	I Want You to Know/Free	1969	$8
❏ 72775	I Will Always Think About You/Hold Me with Your Eyes	1968	$10

—*Orange and red swirl label*

❏ 72775	I Will Always Think About You/Hold Me with Your Eyes	1968	$15

—*Red label with "Mercury" logo in all capital letters*

❏ 73063	People and Me/Ride the Wicked Wind	1970	$20
❏ 72858	Things I'd Like to Say/Come and Give Your Love to Me	1968	$10

—*Red label with "Mercury" logo in an oval*

❏ 72858	Things I'd Like to Say/Come and Give Your Love to Me	1968	$15

—*Orange and red swirl label*

❏ 72737	Treat Her Groovy/Rap-a-Tap	1967	$10

—*Orange and red swirl label*

❏ 72737 [PS]	Treat Her Groovy/Rap-a-Tap	1967	$20
❏ 72737	Treat Her Groovy/Rap-a-Tap	1967	$15

—*Red label with "Mercury" logo in all capital letters*

SENTAR

❏ 1204	(Ballad of the) Wingbat Marmaduke/Power of Love	1966	$20
❏ 1203	Cadillac/Sunshine	1966	$20
❏ 1207	I'm Just Waiting Anticipating for Her to Show Up/Hello Lonely	1967	$20
❏ 1205	Love You So Much/Let Me Love You	1967	$20

SENTAUR

❏ 1202	I Like Awake/At the River's Edge	1966	$30

—*Reissue of Centaur 1202, but harder to find*

Number	Title	Yr	NM
SUNLIGHT			
❏ 1004	Long Time to Be Alone/Never Be Lonely	1971	$6
❏ 1005	Someone, Sometime/Come On Down	1972	$8
NEW DAWN, THE			
GARLAND			
❏ 2020	Why Did You Go/Tears	1970	$30
IMPERIAL			
❏ 66397	Melody Fair/Sometimes in the Morning	1969	$8
MAINSTREAM			
❏ 652	If I Can't Have Your Love/Loser	1966	$30
❏ 664	Slave of Desire/Funny Feeling	1966	$30
RCA VICTOR			
❏ 47-9569	Listen to the Music/Someday	1968	$8
NEW EDITION			
MCA			
❏ 52768	A Little Bit of Love (Is All It Takes)/Sneakin' Around	1986	$3
❏ 52768 [PS]	A Little Bit of Love (Is All It Takes)/Sneakin' Around	1986	$3
❏ 53464	Can You Stand the Rain/(Instrumental)	1988	$3
❏ 53464 [PS]	Can You Stand the Rain/(Instrumental)	1988	$3
❏ 52455	Cool It Now/(Instrumental)	1984	$4
❏ 52455 [PS]	Cool It Now/(Instrumental)	1984	$4
❏ 52703	Count Me Out/Good Boys	1985	$3
❏ 52703 [PS]	Count Me Out/Good Boys	1985	$3
❏ 53500	Crucial (Dance Remix)/Crucial (Uptown Mix Instrumental)	1989	$3
❏ 53500 [PS]	Crucial (Dance Remix)/Crucial (Uptown Mix Instrumental)	1989	$3
❏ 53079	Duke of Earl/What's Your Name	1987	$3
❏ 52905	Earth Angel/With You All the Way	1986	$3
❏ 53164	Helplessly in Love/(Instrumental)	1987	$3
❏ 53264	If It Isn't Love/(Instrumental)	1988	$3
❏ 53264 [PS]	If It Isn't Love/(Instrumental)	1988	$3
❏ 52745	It's Christmas (All Over the World)/All I Want for Christmas Is My Girl	1985	$4
—Red vinyl stock copy			
❏ 52745 [PS]	It's Christmas (All Over the World)/All I Want for Christmas Is My Girl	1985	$4
❏ 52745 [DJ]	It's Christmas (All Over the World) (same on both sides)	1985	$6
—Promo on red vinyl			
❏ 52553	Lost in Love/Gold Mine	1985	$4
❏ 52553 [PS]	Lost in Love/Gold Mine	1985	$4
❏ 52484	Mr. Telephone Man/(Instrumental)	1984	$4
❏ 52484 [PS]	Mr. Telephone Man/(Instrumental)	1984	$4
❏ 52627	My Secret (Didja Gitit Yet?)/I'm Leaving You Again	1985	$4
❏ 52627 [PS]	My Secret (Didja Gitit Yet?)/I'm Leaving You Again	1985	$4
❏ 52959	Once in a Lifetime Groove/Once in a Lifetime Groove (Acapella)	1986	$3
❏ 52959 [PS]	Once in a Lifetime Groove/Once in a Lifetime Groove (Acapella)	1986	$3
❏ 53019	Tears on My Pillow/Bring Back the Memories	1987	$5
—Little Anthony appears on this record			
❏ 53019 [PS]	Tears on My Pillow/Bring Back the Memories	1987	$5
❏ 52829	With You All the Way/All for Love	1986	$3
❏ 52829 [PS]	With You All the Way/All for Love	1986	$3
STREETWISE			
❏ 1108	Candy Girl/(Instrumental)	1983	$8
❏ 1111	Is This the End/(Instrumental)	1983	$8
❏ 1116	Popcorn Love/Jealous Girl	1983	$8
NEW FACES, THE			
DOT			
❏ 16747	Blue Mist/So Small	1965	$30
PARROT			
❏ 40030	If You Love Me/The Road and the Miles to Dundee	1968	$20
❏ 40026	We Can Get There by Candlelight/The Yellow Road	1968	$20

Number	Title	Yr	NM
NEW GRASS REVIVAL			
CAPITOL			
❏ B-44357	Callin' Baton Rouge/Let Me Be Your Man	1989	$5
❏ B-44128	Can't Stop Now/I Can Talk to You	1988	$3
EMI AMERICA			
❏ B-8347	Ain't That Peculiar/Seven by Seven	1986	$4
❏ B-8329	What You Do to Me/Sweet Release	1986	$4
STARDAY			
❏ 965	Great Balls of Fire/I Wish I Said	1972	$10
❏ 974	Prince of Peace/(B-side unknown)	1973	$10
NEW KIDS ON THE BLOCK			
COLUMBIA			
❏ 38-05883	Be My Girl/(Instrumental)	1986	$8
❏ 38-69088	Cover Girl/Merry, Merry Christmas	1989	$3
❏ 38-06619	Didn't I (Blow Your Mind)/New Kids on the Block	1987	$6
❏ 38-68960	Hangin' Tough/Didn't I (Blow Your Mind)	1989	$3
❏ 38-68671	I'll Be Loving You (Forever)/(Instrumental)	1989	$3
❏ 38-07700	Please Don't Go Girl/Whatcha Gonna Do About It	1988	$3
❏ 38-07700 [PS]	Please Don't Go Girl/Whatcha Gonna Do About It	1988	$3
❏ 38-06293	Stop It Girl/New Kids on the Block	1986	$6
❏ 38-73064	This One's for the Children/Funky, Funky Christmas	1989	$3
NEW ORDER			
Also see JOY DIVISION.			
FACTORY			
❏ FAC53	Procession/Everything's Gone Green	1982	$5
—All copies pressed in England; U.S. records are indistinguishable from records meant for U.K. distribution			
❏ FAC53 [PS]	Procession/Everything's Gone Green	1982	$30
—American edition; yellow print with gray background (all other colors are UK-only editions) and a "Rough Trade" sticker on cover			
QWEST			
❏ 7-28421	Bizarre Love Triangle/Every Little Bit Counts	1987	$20
❏ 7-28421 [DJ]	Bizarre Love Triangle (same on both sides)	1987	$8
❏ 7-27979	Blue Monday 1988/Touched by the Hand of God	1988	$8
❏ 7-27979 [PS]	Blue Monday 1988/Touched by the Hand of God	1988	$10
❏ PRO-S-3450 [DJ]	Fine Time (7" Edit) (same on both sides)	1988	$30
—May only exist as a test pressing			
❏ 7-28968	The Perfect Kiss/(Instrumental)	1985	$6
❏ 7-28968 [PS]	The Perfect Kiss/(Instrumental)	1985	$10
❏ 7-28271	True Faith/1963	1987	$4
❏ 7-28271 [PS]	True Faith/1963	1987	$4
❏ 7-28271DJ [DJ]	True Faith (Album Edit)/(Remix)	1987	$5
NEW ORDER, THE			
WARNER BROS.			
❏ 5870	Sailing Ship/Had I Loved Her Less	1966	$15
❏ 5836	Why Can't I?/Pucci Girl	1966	$30
NEW ORLEANS BAND, THE			
HIT			
❏ 275	Winchester Cathedral/Born Free	1966	$8
—B-side by Floyd Tiller			
NEW RIDERS OF THE PURPLE SAGE			
JERRY GARCIA was briefly in this group.			
A&M			
❏ 2327	Fly Right/Night for Making Love	1981	$4
❏ 2352	Full Moon at Midnite/No Other Love	1981	$4
COLUMBIA			
❏ 45526	Garden of Eden/I Don't Know You	1972	$5
❏ 45763	Groupie/She's No Angel	1973	$5
❏ 45607	I Don't Need No Doctor/Runnin' Back to You	1972	$5
❏ 45469	Louisiana Lady/The Last Lonely Eagle	1971	$6
❏ 45976	Panama Red/Cement, Clay, and Glass	1973	$6

Number	Title	Yr	NM
MCA			
❏ 40591	Dead Flowers/She's Looking Better Every Beer	1976	$4
❏ 40564	Don't Put Her Down/Fifteen Days Under the Hood	1976	$4
NEW SEEKERS, THE			
COCA-COLA			
❏ 0(no cat #) [DJ]	Buy the World a Coke//Bring a Little Sunshine/It's the Real Thing	1971	$15
—All three songs are Coca-Coca jingles. The A-side became "I'd Like to Teach the World to Sing			
ELEKTRA			
❏ 45710	Beautiful People/When There's No Love Left	1970	$5
❏ 45780	Beg, Steal or Borrow/Mystic Queen	1972	$5
❏ 45787	Circles/I Can Say You're Beautiful	1972	$5
❏ 45805	Dance, Dance, Dance/I Can Say You're Beautiful	1972	$5
❏ 45762	I'd Like to Teach the World to Sing/Boom Town	1971	$6
❏ 45699	Look What They've Done to My Song, Ma/It's a Beautiful Day	1970	$6
❏ 45747	Tonight/Sweet Louise	1971	$5
MGM			
❏ 14691	Song for You and Me/You Won't Find Another Fool Like Me	1974	$5
❏ 14586	The Greatest Song I've Ever Heard/Woman Grows	1973	$5
MGM VERVE			
❏ 10698	Come Softly to Me/Unwithered Rose	1972	$5
❏ 10698 [PS]	Come Softly to Me/Unwithered Rose	1972	$5
❏ 10709	Pinball Wizard-See Me, Feel Me/Come Softly to Me	1973	$5
❏ 10709	Pinball Wizard-See Me, Feel Me/Time Limit	1973	$6
NEW SOCIETY GROUP, THE			
HIT			
❏ 319	Love Is Blue/I Can Take or Leave Your Loving	1968	$8
—B-side by the Chords (2)			
❏ 280	Mercy, Mercy, Mercy/Green, Green Grass of Home	1967	$8
—B-side by Ed Hardin			
❏ 355	Soulful Strut/You Showed Me	1969	$8
—B-side by the Fantastics			
❏ 330	The Good, the Bad, and the Ugly/This Guy's in Love with You	1968	$8
—B-side by Steve Miller			
NEW SOCIETY, THE			
RCA VICTOR			
❏ 47-8807	Buttermilk/Do Not Ask for Love	1966	$10
❏ 47-9149	I've Been Thinking About You Baby/Love Thee Till I Die	1967	$10
❏ 47-8958	We Have So Little Time!/Dawn of Sorrow	1966	$10
NEW SURVIVORS, THE			
SCEPTER			
❏ 12227	The Pickle Protest/But I Know	1968	$20
NEW THINGS, THE			
ACCENT			
❏ 1228	Dumbo/I Want You Back	1967	$50
NEW TWEEDY BROTHERS, THE			
DOT			
❏ 16910 [B]	Good Time Car/Terms of You Love Me	1966	$150
NEW WAVE, THE			
CANTERBURY			
❏ 512	Little Dreams/Autre Fois	1967	$12
❏ 503	Where Do We Go from Here/Not from You	1967	$10
NEW WORLD			
RAK			
❏ ZS74514	Living Next Door to Alice/Something to Say	1973	$8

Number	Title	Yr	NM

NEW YORK CITY
CHELSEA
Number	Title	Yr	NM
❏ 3031	Can't Survive Without My Sweets/Take My Hand	1975	$5
❏ 3010	Got to Get You Back In My Life/Reach Out	1975	$5
❏ 3000	Happiness Is/Darling Take Me Back	1974	$5
❏ 78-0113	I'm Doin' Fine Now/Ain't It So	1973	$5
❏ 3008	Love Is What You Make It/Do You Remember Yesterday	1974	$5
❏ BCBO-0025	Make Me Twice the Man/Uncle James	1973	$5

NEW YORK DOLLS
MERCURY
Number	Title	Yr	NM
❏ DJ-387 [DJ]	Personality Crisis (mono/stereo)	1973	$20
❏ 73615	Puss 'N' Boots/Showmen	1974	$30
❏ 73478	Stranded in the Jungle/Who Are the Mystery Girls	1974	$20
❏ DJ-378 [DJ]	Trash (mono/stereo)	1973	$20
❏ DJ-378 [PS]	Trash (mono/stereo)	1973	$80

— Promo-only numbered sleeve

Number	Title	Yr	NM
❏ 73414	Trash/Personality Crisis	1973	$70
❏ 73414 [PS]	Trash/Personality Crisis	1973	$20

NEW YORK SOUNDS, THE
RED BIRD
Number	Title	Yr	NM
❏ Oct-0060	Drag Street/Good Lovin'	1966	$30

NEW YORKERS FIVE, THE
DANICE
Number	Title	Yr	NM
❏ 801	Gloria My Darling/Cha Cha Baby	1955	$400

NEW YORKERS, THE (1)
WALL
Number	Title	Yr	NM
❏ 547	Miss Fine/Dream a Little Dream	1961	$40
❏ 548	Tears in My Eyes/A Little Bit	1961	$40

NEW YORKERS, THE (2)
DECCA
Number	Title	Yr	NM
❏ 32569	I Guess the Lord Must Be in New York City/Do Wah Diddy	1969	$10

JERDEN
Number	Title	Yr	NM
❏ 906	Adrienne/Ice Cream World	1968	$15
❏ 908	Land of Ur/Michael Glover	1969	$15

SCEPTER
Number	Title	Yr	NM
❏ 12207	Again/Show Me the Way to Love	1968	$15
❏ 12199	Mr. Kirby/Seeds of Spring	1967	$20

WARNER BROS.
Number	Title	Yr	NM
❏ 7318	Lonely/There'll Come a Time	1969	$10

NEWBAG, JOHNNY
ATLANTIC
Number	Title	Yr	NM
❏ 2355	The Poorer the Man (The Higher His Love)/Got to Get You Back	1966	$125

PORT
Number	Title	Yr	NM
❏ 3008	Sweet Thing/Little Samson	1965	$125

NEWBEATS, THE
BUDDAH
Number	Title	Yr	NM
❏ 390	The Way You Do the Things You Do/Does Your Body Need Lovin'	1973	$8

HICKORY
Number	Title	Yr	NM
❏ 1522	Ain't That Lovin' You/The Girls and the Boys	1968	$8
❏ 1600	Am I Not My Brother's Keeper/Run, Baby, Run (Back Into My Arms)	1971	$10
❏ 1496	Bad Dreams/Swinger	1968	$8
❏ 1408	Bird Dog/Evil Eva	1966	$8
❏ 1269	Bread and Butter/Tough Little Buggy	1964	$20
❏ 326	Bread and Butter/Tough Little Buggy	1974	$6
❏ 1290	Break Away (From That Boy)/Hey-O Daddy-O	1965	$10
❏ 1485	Don't Turn Me Loose/You and Me and Happiness	1967	$8
❏ 1282	Everything's All Right/Pink Dally Rue	1964	$15
❏ 1539	Great Balls of Fire/Thou Shalt Not Steal	1969	$8
❏ 1552	Groovin' (Out on Life)/Bread and Butter	1969	$10
❏ 1467	Hide the Moon/It's Really Goodbye	1967	$8
❏ 1569	I'm a Teardrop/She Won't Hang Her Love (Out on the Line)	1970	$6

Number	Title	Yr	NM
❏ 1510	I've Been a Long Time Loving You/Michelle de Ann	1968	$8
❏ 1562	Laura (What's He Got That I Ain't Got)/Break Away (From That Boy)	1970	$6
❏ 1320	Little Child/I Can't Hear You No More	1965	$12
❏ 1637	Love Gets Sweeter/Everything's All Right	1972	$10
❏ 1422	My Yesterday Love/Patent on Love	1966	$8
❏ 1624	Oh, Pretty Woman/Remember Love	1972	$10
❏ 1366	Shake Hands (And Come Out Crying)/Too Sweet to Be Forgotten	1966	$10
❏ 1387	Short on Love/Crying My Heart Out	1966	$8
❏ 1436	So Fine/Top Secret	1967	$8
❏ 1305	(The Bees Are For the Birds) The Birds Are For the Bees/Better Watch Your Step	1965	$12

PLAYBOY
Number	Title	Yr	NM
❏ 6013	I Believe I'm in Love with You/I Know (You Don't Want Me No More)	1974	$6

7-Inch Extended Plays
HICKORY
Number	Title	Yr	NM
❏ HSP120005	A Patent on Love/So Fine/Thou Shalt Not Steal//There Outa Be a Law/I'm Blue (The Gong Gong Song)/Ain't That Lovin' You Baby	1965	$30

— Jukebox issue; small hole, plays at 33 1/3 rpm

Number	Title	Yr	NM
❏ HSP120005 [PS]	Bread & Butter	1965	$50

— Sleeve calls this "Special Promotion Six-Pac" and calls the first song on side 2 "There Oughta Be a Law"

NEWCOMERS, THE
MERCURY
Number	Title	Yr	NM
❏ 74011	Do Yourself a Favor/That's When You Know Your Woman Wants to Be Free	1978	$40

STAX
Number	Title	Yr	NM
❏ 0099	Pin the Tail on the Donkey/Mannish Boy	1971	$8

TRUTH
Number	Title	Yr	NM
❏ 3213	(Too Much in Common to Be Lovers) Too Much Going to Say Good-Bye/The Whole World's a Picture Show	1974	$40

VOLT
Number	Title	Yr	NM
❏ 4022	Open Up Your Heart/Girl, This Boy Loves You	1969	$40

NEWLEY, ANTHONY
ACAPELLA
Number	Title	Yr	NM
❏ 778	Tribute/Lament for a Hero	1964	$15

KAPP
Number	Title	Yr	NM
❏ 984	I'm All I Need/When You Gotta Go	1969	$6

LONDON
Number	Title	Yr	NM
❏ 1972	And the Heavens Cried/Lonely Boy and Pretty Girl	1961	$10
❏ 9531	Deep River/Letters to My Love	1962	$12
❏ 1918	Do You Mind/Girls Were Made to Love and Kiss	1960	$12
❏ 5205	Father of Girls/Young Only Yesterday	1963	$10
❏ 9501	Gone with the Wind/Pop Goes the Weasel	1961	$10
❏ 1929	If She Should Come to You/A Lifetime of Happiness	1960	$10
❏ 5202	I Saw Her Standing There/I Love Everything About Her	1963	$30

— One of the first cover versions of a Beatles song to be released in the U.S.

Number	Title	Yr	NM
❏ 1871	I've Waited So Long/Sat'day Night Rock-a-Boogie	1959	$15
❏ 1882	My Blue Angel/Idle Rock	1959	$10
❏ 5201	There's No Such Thing/She's Just Another Girl	1963	$10
❏ 9546	What Kind of Fool Am I/Gonna Build a Mountain	1962	$15
❏ 9518	What Now My Love/Why	1961	$10
❏ 9512	When Your Lover Has Gone/Yes, We Have No Bananas	1961	$10

MGM
Number	Title	Yr	NM
❏ 14479	A Fool Who Dared to Dream/Ain't It Funny	1973	$4
❏ 14307	Cheer Up Charlie/Pop Goes the Weasel	1971	$5
❏ 14627	Good Old Bad Old Days/Ain't It Funny	1973	$4
❏ 14724	If I Were Free/Long Live Hope	1974	$4
❏ 14220	Pure Imagination/Love Story (Where Do I Begin)	1971	$5
❏ 14252	The Candy Man/Pure Imagination	1971	$5

Number	Title	Yr	NM

RCA VICTOR
Number	Title	Yr	NM
❏ 47-8785	Is There a Way Back to Your Arms/Why Can't You Try to Didgeridoo	1966	$8
❏ 47-9310	I Think I Love You/Something in Your Smile	1967	$8
❏ 47-8485	Who Can I Turn To/The Joker	1964	$8

UNITED ARTISTS
Number	Title	Yr	NM
❏ XW825	Shelby/Teach the Children	1976	$4
❏ XW1012	The Hollywood Seven/Lunch with a Friend	1977	$4

WARNER BROS.
Number	Title	Yr	NM
❏ 7174	Sweet November/Sara's Theme	1968	$6

—B-side by Michel Legrand

NEWLYWEDS, THE
HOMOGENIZED SOUL
Number	Title	Yr	NM
❏ 601	Love Walked Out/The Quarrel	1961	$3000

— VG 1500; VG+ 2250

NEWMAN, BOB
KING
Number	Title	Yr	NM
❏ 45-1057	Around the Corner/Lonesome Sailor's Dream	1952	$60
❏ 45-1082	Chic-a-Choo Freight/Sand Boogie	1952	$60
❏ 45-1008	Hangover Boogie/I'm Gonna Give You a Dose of Your Own Medicine	1951	$60
❏ 45-1044	Haulin' Freight/Baby, Take Me Home with You	1952	$60
❏ 45-973	It Hurts Me/Rover, Rover	1951	$60
❏ 45-1186	It's Momma, She's the One/Sweet Music	1953	$60
❏ 45-5216	Lonesome Truck Driver's Blues/Haulin' Freight	1959	$30
❏ 45-5789	Lonesome Truck Driver's Blues/Haulin' Freight	1963	$20
❏ 45-959	Lonesome Truck Driver's Blues/Turtle Boogie	1951	$70
❏ 45-1131	Phfft! You Were Gone/Doodle Bug	1952	$60
❏ 45-1155	Sweet Orchard Vine/Strange Love	1953	$60
❏ 45-1108	Tonight's the Night/Greetings	1952	$60

NEWMAN, JACK
D
Number	Title	Yr	NM
❏ 1251	Daddy's Baby/Ship for Lonely Men	1964	$20
❏ 1201	One Little Room/Blue Me	1961	$30
❏ 1230	The Sun Turned Blue/Make Me a Member	1962	$20

RENNER
Number	Title	Yr	NM
❏ 230	Everybody/These Arms	1963	$30
❏ 218	I'm Beginning Again/Walking Through the Years	1962	$30

—Black vinyl

Number	Title	Yr	NM
❏ 218	I'm Beginning Again/Walking Through the Years	1962	$50

—Red vinyl

TNT
Number	Title	Yr	NM
❏ 160	After Night Falls/Sirens in the Distance	1959	$30
❏ 179	Candy Town/Bronco Buster	1959	$30
❏ 170	House of Blue Lovers/I Didn't Think This Could Happen to Me	1959	$40
❏ 178	I Just Can't Stand These Blues/I Could Be the One	1959	$30
❏ 183	Make Room for One More/Out in the World Alone	1960	$30

NEWMAN, JIMMY
DECCA
Number	Title	Yr	NM
❏ 31416	After Dark Affair/You Must Be True	1962	$10
❏ 31324	Alligator Man/Give Me Heaven	1961	$10
❏ 31503	Already I'm Falling/Everything	1963	$10
❏ 31609	Angel on Leave/Summer Skies and Golden Sands	1964	$8
❏ 31841	Artificial Rose/My Love for You	1965	$8
❏ 31745	Back in Circulation/City of the Angels	1965	$8
❏ 31916	Back Pocket Money/For Better or For Worse	1966	$8
❏ 31440	Bayou Talk/I May Fall Again	1962	$12
❏ 32668	Be Proud of Your Man/Washington, D.C.	1970	$6
❏ 31281	Big Mamou/Finally	1961	$12
❏ 32202	Blue Lonely Winter/The Devil Was Laughing at Me	1967	$6
❏ 32484	Boo Dan/Surrounded by Your Love	1969	$6
❏ 32366	Born to Love You/Carmelita	1968	$6
❏ 31994	Bring Your Heart Home/Unwanted Feeling	1966	$8
❏ 31374	Crazy Old Heart/Of All the Things (You Left)	1962	$12

Number	Title	Yr	NM
❑ 31553	D.J. for a Day/The Mover	1963	$12
❑ 32067	Dropping Out of Sight/ We Lose a Little Ground	1966	$8
❑ 31217	Everybody's Dying for Love/Just One More Night (With You)	1961	$12
❑ 32609	Foolishly/Louisana Dirty Rice	1970	$6
❑ 32440	Future Farmers of America/ My Prayer for Today	1969	$6
❑ 32740	I'm Holding Your Memory (But He's Holding You)/ It'll Take a Lot of Love	1970	$6
❑ 32805	Is It Really Over/As Long As There's a Honky Tonk	1971	$6
❑ 32130	Louisana Saturday Night/ Gentleman Loafer	1967	$6
❑ 32285	Sunshine and Bluebirds/I'm Sorry Letters	1968	$6
❑ 32549	Three/There'll Always Be a Song	1969	$6

DOT

❑ 1289	A Fallen Star/I Can't Go On This Way	1957	$30
❑ 15574	A Fallen Star/I Can't Go On This Way	1957	$20
❑ 15627	A Sweet Kind of Love/Need Me	1957	$20
❑ 1260	Blue Darlin'/Let Me Stay in Your Arms	1955	$30
❑ 15766	Carry On/Bop-a-Hula	1958	$50
❑ 1283	Come Back to Me/I Wanta Tell All the World	1956	$30
❑ 1195	Cry, Cry Darling/You Didn't Have to Go	1954	$30
❑ 15659	Cry, Cry Darling/You're the Idol of My Dreams	1957	$20
❑ 1237	Daydreamin'/Crying for a Pastime	1955	$30
❑ 1270	God Was So Good/I Thought I'd Fall in Love Again	1955	$30
❑ 1286	Honky Tonk Tears/Let the Whole World Talk	1956	$30
❑ 1278	Seasons of My Heart/ Let's Stay Together	1956	$30
❑ 1288	The Way That You're Living/ I've Got You on My Mind	1957	$30
❑ 15704	With Tears in My Eyes/ Step Aside Shallow Water	1958	$20

FEATURE

❑ 1060	I Made a Big Mistake/I Don't Know What to Do	1953	$60

KHOURY'S

❑ 530	Cry, Cry Darling/You Didn't Have to Go	1954	$40

MGM

❑ 12894	A Lovely Work of Art/ What About Me	1960	$15
❑ 12812	Grin and Bear It/The Ballad of Baby Doe	1959	$15
❑ 12864	I Miss You Already/ The End of the Line	1960	$15
❑ 12790	Lonely Girl/I'd Be Fool Enough	1959	$15
❑ 12749	So Soon/What'cha Gonna Do	1959	$15
❑ 12830	Walkin' Down the Road/Angels Cryin'	1959	$15
❑ 12945	Wanting You with Me Tonight/Now That You're Gone	1960	$15

MONUMENT

❑ 8545	Big Bayou/Not as a Sweetheart	1972	$5
❑ 8535	Happy Cajun Man/You Have a Secret Lover	1972	$5

PLANTATION

❑ 188	A Cajun Man Can/ Sweet Suzanna	1980	$5
❑ 153	Alligator Man/Lache Las La Patate	1977	$5
❑ 143	Big Mamou/Diggy Liggy Lo	1976	$5
❑ 162	Billy's Brother/ (B-side unknown)	1977	$6
❑ 155	Hello, Dolly/(B-side unknown)	1977	$6
❑ 140	Lafayette/Shrimp Boats	1976	$5
❑ 166	Louisana Cajun Rock Band/Everywhere I Go	1978	$5
❑ 186	Sugar Bee/Big Texan	1980	$5
❑ 182	The Happy Cajun/The More Happy Cajun	1979	$5

— Green vinyl

❑ 175	Thibodeaux and the Cajun Band/Lousiana Saturday Night	1979	$5

PLAYBACK

❑ 1314	Louisana Love/There Ain't No Ugly Girls	1988	$6

SHANNON

❑ 807	Good Time Charlie's Got the Blues/Wild Rose	1973	$6

SOUNDWAVES

❑ 4788	Laissez Les Bon Temps Rouler/(B-side unknown)	1987	$5

Number	Title	Yr	NM

NEWMAN, RANDY

DOT

❑ 16411	Golden Gridiron Boy/ Country Boy	1962	$60

—May be promo only

REPRISE

❑ 27856	Falling in Love/Bad News from Home	1989	$3
❑ 0945	Gone Dead Train/ Harry Flowers	1970	$20
❑ 1324	Guilty/Naked Man	1975	$5
❑ 0917	Have You Seen My Baby/Hold On	1970	$20
❑ 22798	I'd Love to See You Smile/End Title (I'd Love to See You Smile)	1989	$3
❑ 0692	I Think It's Going to Rain Today/The Beehive State	1968	$20
❑ 27709	It's Money That Matters/ Roll with the Punches	1988	$3
❑ 27709 [PS]	It's Money That Matters/ Roll with the Punches	1988	$3
❑ 0771	Last Night I Had a Dream/I Think He's Hiding	1968	$30

—May be promo only

❑ 1387	Louisiana 1927/Marie	1977	$5
❑ 1102	Sail Away/Political Science	1972	$6

WARNER BROS.

❑ 8550	Baltimore/You Can't Fool the Fat Man	1978	$4
❑ 49149	Half a Man/The Story of a Rock and Roll Band	1979	$4
❑ 29687	I Love L.A./Song for the Dead	1983	$4
❑ 49088	It's Money That I Love/Ghosts	1979	$4
❑ 8492	Short People/Old Man on the Farm	1977	$5
❑ 49223	Spies/Political Science (Let's Drop the Big One)	1980	$4
❑ 29803	The Blues/The Same Girl	1983	$4

—A-side: With Paul Simon

❑ 29803 [PS]	The Blues/The Same Girl	1983	$4

NEWMAN, TED

RCA VICTOR

❑ 47-7251	Hey Little Freshman/Brigette	1958	$20
❑ 47-7197	It's Hot in Here/Why Did You Break My Heart	1958	$20

REV

❑ 3511	I Double Dare You/ None of Your Tears	1957	$20
❑ 3505	Plaything/Unlucky Me	1957	$30

NEWPORTS, THE (1)

GUYDEN

❑ 2067	If I Could Tonight/A Fellow Needs a Girl	1962	$40
❑ 2116	Tears/Disillusioned Love	1964	$40

NEWPORTS, THE (2)

KENT

❑ 380	The Wonder of Love/ Dixie Women	1962	$300

NEWPORTS, THE (3)

LAURIE

❑ 3327	The Trouble Is You/I Want You	1966	$30

NEWPORTS, THE (U)

PARROT

❑ 45008	Party Night/Listen to Your Big Brother	1966	$20

NEWTON-JOHN, OLIVIA

ATLANTIC

❑ 89420	The Best of Me/Sage	1986	$3

—With David Foster

❑ 89420 [PS]	The Best of Me/Sage	1986	$3

MCA

❑ 40975	A Little More Love/ Borrowed Time	1978	$4
❑ 40975 [PS]	A Little More Love/ Borrowed Time	1978	$5
❑ 53438	Can't We Talk It Over in Bed/Get Out	1988	$3
❑ 53438 [PS]	Can't We Talk It Over in Bed/Get Out	1988	$4
❑ 40525	Come On Over/Small Talk and Pride	1976	$4
❑ 41009	Deeper Than the Night/Please Don't Keep Me Waiting	1979	$4
❑ 40600	Don't Stop Believin'/ Greensleeves	1976	$4
❑ 40600 [PS]	Don't Stop Believin'/ Greensleeves	1976	$5
❑ 40642	Every Face Tells a Story/ Love You Hold the Key	1976	$4

Number	Title	Yr	NM
❑ 40349	Have You Never Been Mellow/Water Under the Bridge	1974	$5
❑ 52100	Heart Attack/ Strangers Touch	1982	$3
❑ 52100 [PS]	Heart Attack/ Strangers Touch	1982	$3
❑ 40209	If You Love Me (Let Me Know)/Brotherly Love	1974	$5
❑ 40811	I Honestly Love You/Don't Cry for Me Argentina	1977	$5
❑ 40811 [PS]	I Honestly Love You/Don't Cry for Me Argentina	1977	$10
❑ 40280	I Honestly Love You/Home Ain't Home Anymore	1974	$5
❑ 52069	Landslide/Recovery	1982	$3
❑ 52069 [PS]	Landslide/Recovery	1982	$4
❑ 40495	Let It Shine/He Ain't Heavy, He's My Brother	1975	$5
❑ 40101	Let Me Be There/Maybe Then I'll Think of You	1973	$5
❑ 52341	Livin' in Desperate Times/Landslide	1984	$3
❑ 52341 [PS]	Livin' in Desperate Times/Landslide	1984	$3
❑ 41247	Magic/Fool Country	1980	$5

—Custom pink "Xanadu" label

❑ 41247 [PS]	Magic/Fool Country	1980	$5
❑ 41247	Magic/Fool Country	1980	$4

—Standard blue rainbow label

❑ 52000	Make a Move on Me/Falling	1982	$3
❑ 52000 [PS]	Make a Move on Me/Falling	1982	$5
❑ 40737	Making a Good Thing Better/I Think I'll Say Goodbye	1977	$4
❑ 51182	Physical/The Promise (The Dolphin Song)	1981	$3
❑ 51182 [PS]	Physical/The Promise (The Dolphin Song)	1981	$4
❑ 40418	Please Mr. Please/ And In the Morning	1975	$5
❑ 40418 [PS]	Please Mr. Please/ And In the Morning	1975	$10
❑ 40670	Sam/I'll Bet You a Kangaroo	1976	$4
❑ 40459	Something Better to Do/He's My Rock	1975	$5
❑ 40459 [PS]	Something Better to Do/He's My Rock	1975	$6
❑ 52686	Soul Kiss/Electric	1985	$3
❑ 52686 [PS]	Soul Kiss/Electric	1985	$3
❑ 41286	Suddenly/You Made Me Love You	1980	$5

—A-side with Cliff Richard

❑ 51007 [PS]	Suddenly/You Made Me Love You	1980	$5
❑ 51007	Suddenly/You Made Me Love You	1980	$4

—A-side with Cliff Richard

❑ 40043 [DJ]	Take Me Home, Country Roads (mono/stereo)	1973	$30
❑ 40043	Take Me Home, Country Roads/Sail Into Tomorrow	1973	$40

—This has (finally) been proven to exist

❑ 52155	Tied Up/Silvery Rain	1983	$3
❑ 52155 [PS]	Tied Up/Silvery Rain	1983	$3
❑ 41074	Totally Hot/Dancing Round and Round	1979	$4
❑ 41074 [PS]	Totally Hot/Dancing Round and Round	1979	$5
❑ 52757	Toughen Up/Driving Music	1986	$3
❑ 52757 [PS]	Toughen Up/Driving Music	1986	$3
❑ 52284	Twist of Fate/Take a Chance	1983	$3
❑ 52284 [PS]	Twist of Fate/Take a Chance	1983	$3

RSO

❑ 903	Hopelessly Devoted to You/Love Is a Many-Splendored Thing	1978	$4

UNI

❑ 55304	Banks of the Ohio/It's So Hard to Say Goodbye	1971	$8
❑ 55281	If Not for You/The Biggest Clown	1971	$10
❑ 55317	What Is Life/I'm a Small and Lonely Light	1972	$8

NEWTON, BOBBY

ATLANTIC

❑ 2932	There's an Island/A Little Bit of Soap	1973	$30
❑ 2992	When the World's at Peace/ If You Can't Be My Woman	1973	$40

FOXIE

❑ 7003	Dance Craze/These Empty Arms	1960	$50

LORRAINE

❑ 1401	Don't Fight the Feeling/ Alone and Lonely Nights	1966	$30

MERCURY

❑ 72894	Do the Whip/(Instrumental)	1969	$40

Number	Title	Yr	NM

NEWTON, JUICE

CAPITOL

Number	Title	Yr	NM
4976	Angel of the Morning/Headin' for a Heartache	1981	$3
4976 [PS]	Angel of the Morning/Headin' for a Heartache	1981	$4
4768	Any Way That You Want Me/A Dream Never Dies	1979	$5
B-5148	Break It to Me Gently/Adios Mi Corazon	1982	$3
B-5148 [PS]	Break It to Me Gently/Adios Mi Corazon	1982	$4
4499	Come to Me/Save a Heart	1977	$6
B-5289	Dirty Looks/20 Years Ago	1983	$3
B-5289 [PS]	Dirty Looks/20 Years Ago	1983	$4
B-5192	Heart of the Night/Love Sail Away	1982	$3
B-5192 [PS]	Heart of the Night/Love Sail Away	1982	$4
4611	Hey Baby/It's Not Impossible	1978	$6
4552	It's a Heartache/Wouldn't Mind the Rain	1978	$6
4714	Lay Back in the Arms of Someone/It's Not Impossible	1979	$5
4679	Let's Keep It That Way/Tell My Baby Goodbye	1979	$5
B-5120	Love's Been a Little Bit Hard on Me/Ever True	1982	$3
B-5120 [PS]	Love's Been a Little Bit Hard on Me/Ever True	1982	$4
4818	Sunshine/Go Easy on Me	1980	$4
B-5265	Tell Her No/Stranger at My Door	1983	$3
B-5265 [PS]	Tell Her No/Stranger at My Door	1983	$4
A-5046	The Sweetest Thing (I've Ever Known)/Ride 'Em Cowboy	1981	$3
A-5046 [PS]	The Sweetest Thing (I've Ever Known)/Ride 'Em Cowboy	1981	$4

RCA

Number	Title	Yr	NM
PB-13823	A Little Love/Waiting for the Sun	1984	$3
PB-13823 [PS]	A Little Love/Waiting for the Sun	1984	$4
PB-14377	Both to Each Other (Friends and Lovers)/A World Without Love	1986	$3

— With Eddie Rabbitt

Number	Title	Yr	NM
PB-14377 [PS]	Both to Each Other (Friends and Lovers)/A World Without Love	1986	$5
PB-13863	Can't Wait All Night/Restless Heart	1984	$3
PB-13863 [PS]	Can't Wait All Night/Restless Heart	1984	$4
PB-14417	Cheap Love/Old Flame	1986	$3
5170-7-R	First Time Caller/Til You Cry	1987	$3
PB-14199	Hurt/Eye of a Hurricane	1985	$3
GB-14355	Hurt/You Make Me Want to Make You Mine	1986	$3
PB-10828	If I Ever/Bye, Bye Baby	1976	$8
PB-14295	Old Flame/One Touch	1986	$3
5283-7-R	Tell Me True/If I Didn't Love You	1987	$3
5068-7-R	What Can I Do with My Heart/Let Your Woman Take Care of You	1986	$3
8815-7-R	When Love Comes Around the Bend/(B-side unknown)	1989	$3

RCA VICTOR

Number	Title	Yr	NM
PB-10354	Catwillow River/It's High Time	1975	$8

— With Silver Spur

Number	Title	Yr	NM
PB-10538	Love Is a Word/The Sweetest Thing (I've Ever Known)	1976	$8

— With Silver Spur

Number	Title	Yr	NM
PB-10412	The Sweetest Thing (I've Ever Known)/The Shelter of Your Love	1975	$8

— With Silver Spur

NEWTON, WAYNE

20TH CENTURY

Number	Title	Yr	NM
2393	Hold Me Like You Never Had Me/Housewife	1978	$4

ARIES II

Number	Title	Yr	NM
107	I Apologize/It's Nice to Be with You	1979	$4

CAPITOL

Number	Title	Yr	NM
5553	A Little Bit of Heaven/Some Sunday Morning	1965	$8
3044	Apartment 21/Me and Bobby McGee	1971	$5
5171	Bill Bailey/When the Saints Go Marching In	1964	$10
5338	Comin' On Too Strong/Lookin' Through a Tear	1965	$30

— Bruce Johnston and Terry Melcher help out on this record

Number	Title	Yr	NM
4989	Danke Schoen/Better Now Than Later	1963	$15
5124	Dream Baby (How Long Must I Dream)/I'm Looking Over a Four-Leaf Clover	1964	$12
5954	Dream Street Rose/Summer Colors	1967	$6
5692	Excuse Me/How Loud a Sound	1966	$8
2980	For the Good Times/Little Dreamer	1970	$5
5793	Happy Is Gone/How D'Ya Talk to a Girl	1966	$8
4920	Heart! (I Hear You Beating)/So Long Lucy	1963	$12
4920	Heart/So Long Lucy	1963	$15

— Original pressing has no subtitle on A-side

Number	Title	Yr	NM
3189	I Ain't That Easy to Love/Leavin' Ya Going My Way	1971	$5
5842	If I Only Had a Song to Sing/Sunny Day Girl	1967	$6
5419	I'll Be With You in Apple Blossom Time/Laura Lee	1965	$8
2016	Love of the Common People/It's Still Loving You	1967	$6
5203	Only You/Too Late to Meet	1964	$10
5058	Shirl Girl/Someone's Ahead of You	1963	$10
5643	Somebody to Love/Stagecoach to Cheyenne	1966	$8
5643 [PS]	Somebody to Love/Stagecoach to Cheyenne	1966	$20
5470	Summer Wind/I'll Be Standing By	1965	$8
5754	The Games That Lovers Play/Half a World Away	1966	$8
5993	Through the Eyes of Love/Just a Memory	1967	$6

CHALLENGE

Number	Title	Yr	NM
59228	I Want to Mean Everything to You/I Still Love You	1964	$10
59238	The Little White Cloud That Cried/Born When You Kissed Me	1964	$10
59238	The Little White Cloud That Cried/Calorie Date	1964	$10

CHELSEA

Number	Title	Yr	NM
3018	All Alone Am I/You Don't Have to Ask	1975	$4
78-0109	Anthem/Fool	1972	$4
78-0105	Can't You Hear the Song?/You Don't Have to Ask	1972	$4
78-0100	Daddy Don't You Walk So Fast/Echo Valley 2-6809	1972	$6

— White label (not a promo)

Number	Title	Yr	NM
78-0100	Daddy Don't You Walk So Fast/Echo Valley 2-6809	1972	$5

— Mostly pink label

Number	Title	Yr	NM
AMBO-0126	Daddy Don't You Walk So Fast/Fool	1973	$4

— Gold Standard Series reissue

Number	Title	Yr	NM
78-0124	Help Me Help You/We Didn't Know the Time of Day	1973	$4
3058	It Could Have Been a Wonderful Christmas/Jingle Bell Hustle	1976	$5
3003	Lay Lady Lay/Walking in the Sand	1974	$4
BCBO-0091	May the Road Rise to Meet You/Pour Me a Little More Wine	1973	$4
3041	The Hungry Years/In Dreams	1976	$4

CURB

Number	Title	Yr	NM
10520	Cowboy's Christmas/(B-side unknown)	1988	$3
10559	While the Feeling's Good/Our Wedding Band	1989	$3

— A-side with Tammy Wynette

ELEKTRA

Number	Title	Yr	NM
45528	Last Exit for Love/Too Good to Be True	1978	$4

GEORGE

Number	Title	Yr	NM
7777	The Little White Cloud That Cried/(B-side unknown)	1962	$30

MGM

Number	Title	Yr	NM
13891	All the Time/Like Everything Else	1968	$5
14019	Christmas Prayer/Santa Claus Is Comin' to Town	1968	$5
13955	Dreams of the Everyday Housewife/The Tip of My Fingers	1968	$5
14046	Everything's Gone Today/The Silence Says	1969	$5
14014	I Just Can't Help Believin'/Husbands and Wives	1968	$5
14098	It's Such a Lonely Time of the Year/The Country	1969	$5
13993	Silence Says/Town and Country	1968	$5
14430	With Pen in Hand/Town and Country	1972	$4

WARNER BROS.

Number	Title	Yr	NM
8415	I Want You with Me/Midnight Sun	1977	$4

7-Inch Extended Plays

ARIES II

Number	Title	Yr	NM
102	White Christmas/It's the Season/I'll Be Home for Christmas/Blue Snow at Christmas	1979	$4

NEXT, THE
7-Inch Extended Plays

SHARP

Number	Title	Yr	NM
0(# unknown) [B]	Make It Quick	1979	$80
0(# unknown) [PS]	Make It Quick	1979	$80

— Actualy a 15x22 poster with the white side facing out, wrapped around the record

Number	Title	Yr	NM
0(# unknown) [PS]	Make It Quick	1979	$100

— A few copies of the poster had "The Next -- Make It Quick" stamped on the white side

NIC NACS, THE

RPM

Number	Title	Yr	NM
342	Gonna Have a Merry Christmas/Found Me a Sugar Daddy	1951	$200

NICE, THE
Keith Emerson, later of EMERSON, LAKE AND PALMER, was in this group.

IMMEDIATE

Number	Title	Yr	NM
5008	America/Diamnd Hard Apples of the Moon	1968	$15
5004	Azrial (Angel of Death)/Thoughts of Emerlist Davjack	1968	$15

MERCURY

Number	Title	Yr	NM
73272	Country Pie-Brandenburg Concerto No. 6 (Part 1)/Finale-5th Bridge	1972	$6
73114	Country Pie/(B-side unknown)	1970	$8

NICHOLS, SAM

MGM

Number	Title	Yr	NM
K11417	Blue Bonnet Waltz/Texas Lady	1953	$40

NICK AND THE JAGUARS

TAMLA

Number	Title	Yr	NM
5501F	Ich-I-Bon #1/Cool and Crazy	1960	$300

NICKIE AND THE NITELITES

BRUNSWICK

Number	Title	Yr	NM
55155	I'm Lonely/Tell Me You Care	1959	$125

NICKS, STEVIE
Also see FLEETWOOD MAC; TOM PETTY AND THE HEARTBREAKERS.

ATLANTIC OLDIES SERIES

Number	Title	Yr	NM
OS13258	Edge of Seventeen/Stand Back	1985	$3
84998	If Anyone Falls/Nightbird	1986	$3
OS13236	Stop Draggin' My Heart Around/Leather and Lace	1983	$3
84964	Talk to Me/I Can't Wait	1987	$3

MODERN

Number	Title	Yr	NM
7405 [PS]	After the Glitter Fades/Think About It	1982	$8
7405	After the Glitter Fades/Think About It	1982	$6
7401	Edge of Seventeen (Just Like the White Winged Dove)/Edge of Seventeen (Live)	1982	$4
7401 [PS]	Edge of Seventeen (Just Like the White Winged Dove)/Edge of Seventeen (Live)	1982	$6
99532	Has Anyone Ever Written Anything for You/Imperial Hotel	1986	$3
99532 [PS]	Has Anyone Ever Written Anything for You/Imperial Hotel	1986	$8
99565 [DJ]	I Can't Wait (Remix)/I Can't Wait (Soft Intro)	1986	$8
99565 [PS]	I Can't Wait (Remix)/I Can't Wait (Soft Intro)	1986	$15
99565	I Can't Wait/The Nightmare	1986	$3
99565 [PS]	I Can't Wait/The Nightmare	1986	$3
99832	If Anyone Falls/Wild Heart	1983	$4
99832 [PS]	If Anyone Falls/Wild Heart	1983	$5
7341	Leather and Lace/Bella Donna	1981	$5

— With Don Henley; first pressing states "Written for Waylon Jennings and Jessi Colter"

Number	Title	Yr	NM
7341	Leather and Lace/Bella Donna	1981	$4

— With Don Henley; with no reference to Waylon Jennings and Jessi Colter on label

Number	Title	Yr	NM
7341 [PS]	Leather and Lace/Bella Donna	1981	$12
99863	Stand Back/Garbo	1983	$3
99863 [PS]	Stand Back/Garbo	1983	$4

Number	Title	Yr	NM
❑ 7336	Stop Draggin' My Heart Around/Kind of Woman	1981	$4

— *With Tom Petty and the Heartbreakers*

Number	Title	Yr	NM
❑ 7336 [PS]	Stop Draggin' My Heart Around/Kind of Woman	1981	$6
❑ 99582	Talk to Me/One More Big Time Rock and Roll Star	1985	$3
❑ 99582 [PS]	Talk to Me/One More Big Time Rock and Roll Star	1985	$3
❑ 99179	Two Kinds of Love/Real Tears	1989	$3
❑ 99179 [PS]	Two Kinds of Love/Real Tears	1989	$5
❑ 99150	Whole Lotta Trouble/Ghosts	1989	$3

NICKY AND THE NOBLES
END
| ❑ 1098 | School Bells/School Day Crush | 1961 | $30 |
| ❑ 1021 | Schoolhouse Rock/A Way to Tell Her | 1958 | $60 |

GONE
| ❑ 5039 | School Bells/School Day Crush | 1958 | $70 |

— *Black label*

| ❑ 5039 | School Bells/School Day Crush | 1958 | $30 |

— *Multicolor label*

| ❑ 5039 | School Bells/School Days | 1958 | $125 |

— *With B-side title variation*

NICOL, JIMMY
PARROT
| ❑ 9752 | Sweet Clementine/Roaring Blue | 1965 | $30 |

NIGHT RANGER
DAMN YANKEES related. Guitarist Brad Gillis was briefly in OZZY OSBOURNE's band.
BOARDWALK
| ❑ NB7-11-171 | Don't Tell Me You Love Me/Night Ranger | 1983 | $5 |
| ❑ NB7-11-175 | Sing Me Away/Play Rough | 1983 | $5 |
MCA
❑ 53495	Don't Start Thinkin' (I'm Alone Tonight)/Kiss Me Where It Hurts	1989	$3
❑ 52350	Sister Christian/Chippin' Away	1984	$4
❑ 52420	When You Close Your Eyes/Why Does Love Have to Change	1984	$3
❑ 52420 [PS]	When You Close Your Eyes/Why Does Love Have to Change	1984	$4
MCA CAMEL
❑ 52661	Four in the Morning (I Can't Take Any More)/The Boy Needs to Rock	1985	$3
❑ 52661 [PS]	Four in the Morning (I Can't Take Any More)/The Boy Needs to Rock	1985	$3
❑ 52729	Goodbye/Seven Wishes	1985	$3
❑ 52729 [PS]	Goodbye/Seven Wishes	1985	$15
❑ 53131	Hearts Away/Better Let it Go	1987	$3
❑ 53364	I Did It for Love/Woman in Love	1988	$3
❑ 53364 [PS]	I Did It for Love/Woman in Love	1988	$3
❑ 52591	Sentimental Street/Night Machine	1985	$3
❑ 52591 [PS]	Sentimental Street/Night Machine	1985	$3
❑ 53013	The Secret of My Success/Carry On	1987	$3
❑ 53013 [PS]	The Secret of My Success/Carry On	1987	$3

NIGHT WATCH, THE
ABC
| ❑ 10862 | Closed Time/Lips to Your Heart | 1966 | $30 |

NIGHTCRAWLERS, THE
KAPP
❑ 746	A Basket of Flowers/Washboard	1966	$20
❑ 826	My Butterfly/Today I'm Happy	1967	$40
❑ 709	The Little Black Egg/You're Running Wild	1965	$20
❑ KE-110	The Little Black Egg/You're Running Wild	1966	$10
LEE
| ❑ 101 | Cry/Marie | 1964 | $70 |
| ❑ 1012 | The Little Black Egg/You're Running Wild | 1965 | $60 |
MARLIN
| ❑ 1904 | A Basket of Flowers/Washboard | 1966 | $30 |

NIGHTHAWK, ROBERT
STATES
| ❑ 131 | The Moon Is Rising/Maggie Campbell | 1954 | $300 |

NIGHTINGALE, MAXINE
UNITED ARTISTS
❑ XW1015	How Much Love/Will You Be My Lover	1977	$4
❑ XW944	If I Ever Lose This Heaven/Love Hit Me	1977	$4
❑ XW865	Life Has Just Begun/(I Think I Wanna) Possess You	1976	$4
❑ XW983	Love Hit Me (Part 1)/Love Hit Me (Part 2)	1977	$4
❑ XW820	One Last Ride/Gotta Be the One	1976	$4
WINDSONG
❑ CB-12117	All Night with Me/Tight Spot	1980	$4
❑ CB-11729	(Bringing Out) The Girl in Me/Hideaway	1979	$4
❑ CB-11729 [PS]	(Bringing Out) The Girl in Me/Hideaway	1979	$4
❑ CB-11530	Lead Me On/Love Me Like You Mean It	1979	$4
❑ CB-12020	Take Your Heart/Why Did You Turn Me On	1980	$4

NILES, JOHNNY
MERCURY
| ❑ 72132 | Donna, I Understand/Wig Job | 1963 | $12 |

NILSSON
CRUSADER
| ❑ 103 | Baa Baa Black Sheep/Baa Baa Black Sheep (Part 2) | 1964 | $40 |

— *As "Bo Pete*

MUSICOR
| ❑ 6308 | Please Mr. Music Man/Foolish Clock | 1977 | $4 |
POLYDOR
| ❑ 881177-7 | Silver Horse/Loneliness | 1984 | $4 |
RCA
❑ PB-11193	Ain't It Kinda Wonderful/I'm Bringing a Red, Red Rose	1978	$4
❑ PB-11144	All I Think About Is You/I Never Thought I'd Get This Lonely	1977	$4
❑ PB-11059 [PS]	Perfect Day/Who Done It	1977	$5
❑ PB-11059	Perfect Day/Who Done It	1977	$4
❑ PB-11318	Spaceman/Me and My Arrow	1978	$4
RCA VICTOR
❑ APBO-0039	As Time Goes By/Lullabye in Ragtime	1973	$6
❑ 74-0336	Caroline/Yellow Man	1970	$6
❑ 74-0718	Coconut/Down	1972	$5
❑ APBO-0246	Daybreak/Down	1974	$4
❑ APBO-0246 [PS]	Daybreak/Down	1974	$6
❑ 74-0362	Down to the Valley/Buy My Album	1970	$6
❑ 47-9544	Everybody's Talkin'/Don't Leave Me	1968	$15
❑ 74-0161	Everybody's Talkin'/Rainmaker	1969	$12
❑ 74-0261	I Guess the Lord Must Be in New York City/Maybe	1969	$8
❑ 74-0310	I'll Be Home/Waiting	1970	$6
❑ PB-10139	Loop De Loop/Don't Forget Me	1974	$4
❑ PB-10001	Many Rivers to Cross/Don't Forget Me	1974	$8
❑ 74-0207	Maybe/Marchin' Down Broadway	1969	$8
❑ 74-0443	Me and My Arrow/Are You Sleeping	1971	$6
❑ 47-9442	One/Sister Marie	1968	$8
❑ PB-10634	Sail Away/Moonshine Bandit	1976	$4
❑ 74-0788	Spaceman/Turn On Your Radio	1972	$5
❑ PB-10078	Subterranean Homesick Blues/Mucho Mungo	1974	$8
❑ 47-9206	Without Her/Freckles	1967	$8
❑ 74-0524	Without Her/Good Old Desk	1971	$6
❑ 74-0604	Without You/Gotta Get Up	1971	$5
TOWER
❑ 518	Good Time/Growin' Up	1969	$20
❑ 244	She's Yours/Growing Up	1966	$20
❑ 103	Sixteen Tons/I'm Gonna Lose My Mind	1964	$20
TRY
| ❑ 501 | Do You Wanna/Groovy Little Suzie | 1964 | $50 |

— *As "Bo Pete*

7-Inch Extended Plays
RCA
| ❑ DTF0-2005 [PS] | A Little Touch of Schmilsson in the Night | 1973 | $25 |
| ❑ DTF0-2005 | Makin' Whoopee/Nevertheless (I'm in Love with You)/You Made Me Love You (I Didn't Want to Do It)/I Wonder Who's Kissing Her Now/For Me and My Gal/It Had to Be You | 1973 | $25 |

— *Stereo jukebox issue; small hole, plays at 33 1/3 rpm*

NIMBLE, JACK B. AND THE QUICKS
DEL RIO
| ❑ 2303/4 | Like Keyed/Babes in Toyland | 1962 | $30 |

NIMOY, LEONARD
DOT
❑ 17175	Consilium/Here We Go 'Round Again	1968	$20
❑ 17125	I'd Love Making Love to You/Please Don't Try to Change My Mind	1968	$20
❑ 17028	The Ballad of Bilbo Baggins/Cotton Candy	1967	$20
❑ 17038	Theme from "Star Trek"/Visit to a Sad Planet	1967	$30
❑ 17330	The Sun Will Rise/Time to Get It Together	1969	$20

NINCHUKS, THE
BRYAN
| ❑ BP-1 [DJ] | Bruce Lee's "Return of the Dragon" (mono/stereo) | 1974 | $10 |

— *Stock copies may not exist*

999
POLYDOR
| ❑ 2076 | Boiler/Hollywood | 1980 | $20 |
| ❑ 2172 | Obsessed/Fortune Teller | 1981 | $20 |

1910 FRUITGUM COMPANY
ATTACK
| ❑ 10293 | Lawdy, Lawdy/The Clock | 1970 | $15 |
BUDDAH
❑ 54	1,2,3, Red Light/Sticky, Sticky	1968	$10
❑ 71	Goody Goody Gumdrops/Candy Kisses	1968	$8
❑ 91	Indian Giver/Pow Wow	1969	$10
❑ 39	May I Take a Giant Step (Into Your Heart)/(Poor Old) Mr. Jensen	1968	$8
❑ 24	Simon Says/Reflections from the Looking Glass	1968	$10
❑ 114	Special Delivery/No Good Annie	1969	$8
❑ 130	The Train/Eternal Light	1969	$8
❑ 146	When We Get Married/Baby Sweet	1969	$8
SUPER K
| ❑ 115 | Go Away/The Track | 1970 | $15 |

NINO AND THE EBB TIDES
ACME
| ❑ 720 | Franny Franny/Darling I'll Love Only You | 1958 | $300 |
MADISON
| ❑ 162 | Those Oldies But Goodies (Remind Me of You)/Don't Run Away | 1961 | $50 |
MALA
| ❑ 480 | Automatic Reaction/Linda Lou Garrett Like 24 Karat | 1964 | $30 |
MARCO
| ❑ 105 | Little Miss Blue/Someday | 1961 | $60 |
MR. PEACOCK
| ❑ 117 | Lovin' Time/Stamps, Baby, Stamps | 1962 | $30 |
| ❑ 102 | Wished I Was Home/Happy Guy | 1961 | $30 |
MR. PEEKE
| ❑ 123 | Tonight I'll Be Lonely/Nursery Rhymes | 1963 | $30 |
RECORTE
❑ 413	Don't Look Around/I Love Girls	1959	$125
❑ 409	I'm Confessin'/Tell the World I Do	1959	$60
❑ 405	Puppy Love/You Make Me Rock 'N' Roll	1958	$60

Number	Title	Yr	NM

NIRVANA
The 1990s grunge group fronted by Kurt Cobain. Dave Grohl now leads FOO FIGHTERS

SUB POP
❏ 23	Love Buzz/Big Cheese	1988	$500

—#1 in Sub Pop Singles Club series

❏ 23 [PS]	Love Buzz/Big Cheese	1988	$500

— Hand-numbered edition of 1,000

NIRVANA (1)
The 1960s psychedelic group.

BELL
❏ 739	Trapeze/The Touchables	1968	$10
❏ 715	We Can Help You/Pentecost Hotel	1968	$10

NITE RIDERS, THE

MGM
❏ 12487	Sippin' Coffee/Tank Town	1957	$40

TEEN
❏ 118	Got Me a Six-Button Benny/Don't Hang Up the Phone	1955	$50
❏ 116	Starlight and You/I Know You're In There	1955	$50
❏ 120	When a Man Cries/Waiting in the Schoolroom	1955	$50

NITTY GRITTY DIRT BAND

LIBERTY
❏ 1449	Badlands/Jealousy	1982	$4

— As "The Dirt Band"

❏ 55948	Buy for Me the Rain/Candy Man	1967	$10
❏ 1513	Colorado Christmas/Mr. Bojangles	1983	$6
❏ 1429	Fire in the Sky/EZ Slow	1981	$4

— As "The Dirt Band"

❏ 1389	High School Yearbook/Too Good to Be True	1980	$4

— As "The Dirt Band"

❏ 1499	Let's Go/Shot Full of Love	1983	$4
❏ 1507	Mary Anne/Dance Little Jean	1983	$4
❏ 56197	Mr. Bojangles/Mr. Bojangles (Prelude: Uncle Charlie and His Dog Teddy)	1970	$6
❏ 56197	Mr. Bojangles (Prelude: Uncle Charlie and His Dog Teddy)/Spanish Fandango	1970	$6
❏ 56134	Some of Shelley's Blues/Yukon Railroad	1969	$6
❏ 56054	These Days/Collegiana	1968	$8
❏ 1467	Too Close for Comfort/Circular Man	1982	$4

— As "The Dirt Band"

UNITED ARTISTS
❏ XW655	(All I Have to Do Is) Dream/Raleigh-Durham Reel	1975	$5
❏ 1330	An American Dream/Take Me Back	1979	$5

— As "The Dirt Band"

❏ 1378	Badlands/Too Good to Be True	1980	$4

— As "The Dirt Band"

❏ 50921	Baltimore/Fish Song	1972	$6
❏ XW936	Buy for Me the Rain/Mother Earth (Provides for Me)	1976	$4

— As "The Dirt Band"

❏ XW263	Cosmic Cowboy (Part 1)/Cosmic Cowboy (Part 2)	1973	$5
❏ XW830	Cosmic Cowboy/Stars and Stripes Forever	1976	$4

— As "The Dirt Band"

❏ XW1268	For a Little While/On the Loose	1978	$4

— As "The Dirt Band"

❏ XW247	Grand Ole Opry Song/Orange Blossom Special	1973	$5
❏ 50965	Honky Tonkin'/Jamaica	1972	$6
❏ 50769	House at Pooh Corner/Travelin' Mood	1971	$6
❏ 50769 [PS]	House at Pooh Corner/Travelin' Mood	1971	$8
❏ 1312	In Her Eyes/Jas' Moon	1979	$4

— As "The Dirt Band"

❏ 50861	I Saw the Light/Sixteen Tracks	1971	$6
❏ 1356	Make a Little Magic/Jas' Moon	1980	$4

— As "The Dirt Band"

❏ XW741	Mother of Love/The Moon Just Turned Blue	1975	$5
❏ 0061	Mr. Bojangles/Buy for Me the Rain	1973	$4

— Silver Spotlight Series" reissue

❏ XW1164	Orange Blossom Special/Will the Circle Be Unbroken	1978	$4

❏ 50849	Precious Jewel/I Saw the Light	1971	$6

— With Roy Acuff

❏ XW321	Tennessee Stud/Way Down Town	1973	$5

— With Doc Watson

❏ XW544	The Battle of New Orleans/Mountain Whipporwill	1974	$5
❏ XW544 [PS]	The Battle of New Orleans/Mountain Whipporwill	1974	$6
❏ 50817	The Cure/Some of Shelly's Blues	1971	$6
❏ XW1228	Wild Nights/In for the Night	1978	$4

— As "The Dirt Band"

❏ XW177	Will the Circle Be Unbroken/Honky Tonkin'	1973	$5
❏ XW177 [PS]	Will the Circle Be Unbroken/Honky Tonkin'	1973	$8

UNIVERSAL
❏ UVL-66009	Turn of the Century/Blueberry Hill	1989	$3
❏ UVL-66023	When It's Gone/I'm Sittin' on Top of the World	1989	$4

WARNER BROS.
❏ 28443	Baby's Got a Hold on Me/Oleanna	1987	$3
❏ 28547	Cadillac Ranch/Fire in the Sky	1986	$3
❏ 27679	Down That Road Tonight/A Lot Like Me	1989	$3
❏ 28311	Fishin' in the Dark/Keepin' the Road Hot	1987	$3
❏ 29099	High Horse/Must Be Love	1985	$4
❏ 28897	Home Again in My Heart/Telluride	1985	$4
❏ 29203	I Love Only You/Face on the Cutting Room Floor	1984	$4
❏ 27750	I've Been Lookin'/Must Be Love	1988	$3
❏ 29282	Long Hard Road (The Sharecropper's Dream)/Video Tape	1984	$4
❏ 29027	Modern Day Romance/Queen of the Road	1985	$4
❏ 28173	Oh What a Love/America, My Sweetheart	1987	$3
❏ 28173 [PS]	Oh What a Love/America, My Sweetheart	1987	$4
❏ 28780	Partners, Brothers and Friends/Redneck Riviera	1986	$3
❏ 28690	Stand a Little Rain/Miner's Night Out	1986	$3
❏ 27940	Workin' Man/Brass Sky	1988	$3

WARNER BROS
❏ PRO-S-2869 [DJ]	Colorado Christmas/The Cowboy's Christmas Ball	1987	$6

— B-side by Michael Martin Murphey

NITZSCHE, JACK

FANTASY
❏ 760	One Flew Over the Cuckoo's Next/The Last Dance	1976	$6
❏ 760 [PS]	One Flew Over the Cuckoo's Next/The Last Dance	1976	$10

— Jack Nicholson is pictured on the sleeve

MCA
❏ 40897	Coke Machine/Hard Workin' Man	1978	$4

REPRISE
❏ 0364	Senorita from Detroit/Puerto Vallarta	1965	$30
❏ 0337	The Green Grass of Texas/Night Walker	1965	$30
❏ 0262	The Last Race/Man with the Golden Arm	1964	$30
❏ 20202	The Lonely Surfer/Song for a Summer Night	1963	$40
❏ 20202 [PS]	The Lonely Surfer/Song for a Summer Night	1963	$125
❏ 0285	Theme from The Long Ships/Zapata	1964	$30

NIX, WILLIE

SABRE
❏ 104	All By Myself/Just Can't Stay	1953	$2000

NO NAMES, THE

GUYDEN
❏ 2114	Love/Jam	1964	$60

NOACK, EDDIE

D
❏ 1060	A Thinking Man's Woman/Don't Look Behind	1959	$30
❏ 1148	Firewater Luke/Too Weak to Go	1960	$30
❏ 1019	Have Blues -- Will Travel/The Price of Love	1958	$40
❏ 1220	It's Hard to Tell an Old Love Goodbye/Love's Other Face	1961	$30
❏ 1124	Shake Hands with the Blues/Sunflower Song	1960	$30
❏ 1037	Walk 'Em Off/I Don't Live There Anymore	1959	$70

STARDAY
❏ 334	Dust on the River/What's the Matter, Joe?	1957	$40
❏ 213	Fair Today, Cold Tomorrow/Don't Worry 'Bout Me Baby	1955	$40
❏ 201	If It Ain't on the Menu/Wind Me Up	1955	$40
❏ 225	It Ain't Much But It's Home/When the Bright Lights Grow Dim	1956	$40
❏ 169	Left Over Lovin'/I'll Be So Good to You	1955	$40
❏ 316	Scarecrow/Think of Her Now	1957	$40
❏ 159	Take It Away Lucky/Don't Trade	1954	$40
❏ 276	The Worm Has Turned/She Can't Stand the Light of Day	1956	$40

TNT
❏ 110	Too Hot to Handle/How Does It Feel to Be the Winner	1954	$40

NOBELLS, THE

MAR
❏ 101	Searchin' for My Love/Crying Over You	1962	$125

NOBLE, NICK

20TH CENTURY FOX
❏ 6612	The Girl with the Long Red Hair/Simple, Simple	1965	$8

CAPITOL
❏ 3677	It's All Up to You/Let Me Be a Man	1973	$5

CHESS
❏ 1909	Don't Forget/Not Like I Used to Be	1964	$8
❏ 1876	Sleep Walk/Flying Over Rainbows	1963	$12
❏ 1879	Stay with Me/Flying Over Rainbows	1963	$8

CHURCHILL
❏ 7755	Big Man's Cafe/My Country Kind of Girl	1980	$6
❏ 7701	May God Be With You/(B-side unknown)	1978	$6
❏ 7713	Stay with Me/My Country Kind of Girl	1978	$6

COLUMBIA
❏ 4-44887	I'm Gonna Make You Love Me/I'm So Busy Being Broken Hearted	1969	$6

CORAL
❏ 62233	Excuse Me (I Think I've Got a Heartache)/Island Farewell	1960	$10
❏ 62280	For Just a Little While Tonight/The Beat of My Soul	1961	$10
❏ 9-62075	How Much Can a Heart Take/My Darling's Earrings	1959	$10
❏ 62262	(I'm Gonna) Cry Some Tears/They Call Me the Fool	1961	$10
❏ 9-62124	I Need Someone/Thank Heaven for Little Girls	1959	$10
❏ 62246	Someplace to Cry/Over Someone's Shoulder	1961	$12
❏ 9-62144	Somethin' Cha Cha/I Surrender Dear	1959	$12
❏ 62495	The Tip of My Fingers/Someplace to Cry	1966	$8
❏ 62213	The Tip of My Fingers/Sweet Love	1960	$15

EPIC
❏ 50327	Forgetting Someone/If We Could Live Our Life Away	1977	$4

FRATERNITY
❏ 817	Fountains Cry/There's a Church in Your Heart	1958	$10
❏ 825	One Track Mind/Lonely Star	1958	$10

LIBERTY
❏ 55534	A Legend in My Time/Closer to Heaven	1963	$8
❏ 55576	Gee Little Girl/A Rose and a Star	1963	$8
❏ 55488	Hello Out There/We Could	1962	$8
❏ 55442	The Twelfth Dark Hour/My Heart Came Running Back to You	1962	$8

MERCURY
❏ 71124	A Fallen Star/Let Me Hold You in My Arms	1957	$10
❏ 71117	A Fallen Star/They're Playing Our Song	1957	$15
❏ 70959	Autumn Concerto/Mom, Oh Mom	1956	$15
❏ 71233	Halo of Love/Sweet Treat	1957	$10
❏ 71169	Moonlight Swim/Lucy Lou	1957	$10
❏ 70496	Tara's Theme/Please Don't Break My Heart	1954	$20
❏ 70821	To You, My Love/You Are My Only Love	1956	$15

TMS
❏ 612	I Wanna Go Back/I Keep On Breathin' You	1979	$6
❏ 601	The Girl on the Other Side/Why Don't You Believe Me	1979	$6

Number	Title	Yr	NM

WING

❏ 90042	Lovely Lies/Bella Bella Perzicella	1955	$15
❏ 90028	The Best Is Yet to Come/ If It Happened to You	1955	$15
❏ 90003	The Bible Tells Me So/ Army of the Lord	1955	$15
❏ 90045	To You My Love/You Are My Only Love	1955	$20

NOBLES, CLIFF

ATLANTIC

❏ 2352	My Love Is Getting Stronger/Too Fond of You	1966	$300

JAMIE

❏ 1406	The Horse/If You Don't	1972	$20

MOON SHOT

❏ 6710	Pony the Horse/ Little Claudie	1969	$30

PHIL-L.A. OF SOUL

❏ 318	Horse Fever/Judge Baby, I'm Back	1968	$8
❏ 324	Switch It On/Burning Desire	1969	$8
❏ 329	The Camel/Goin' Away	1969	$8
❏ 313	The Horse/Love Is All Right	1968	$10
❏ 310	The More I Do for You Baby/This Love Will Last	1968	$8

ROULETTE

❏ 7142	This Feeling of Loneliness/ We Got Our Thing Together	1973	$20

NOBLES, THE (1)

ABC-PARAMOUNT

❏ 9984	Till the End of Time/ Standing Loose	1958	$30

NOBLES, THE (2)

KLIK

❏ 305	Poor Rock and Roll/ Ting-a-Ling	1958	$200

TIMES SQUARE

❏ 12	Crime Doesn't Pay/Darkness	1963	$30
— All copies on blue vinyl

❏ 1	Poor Rock and Roll/ Ting-a-Ling	1963	$40
— Blue vinyl

❏ 1	Poor Rock and Roll/ Ting-a-Ling	1963	$30
— Green vinyl

❏ 33	Why Be a Fool/The Search	1964	$30

NOBLES, THE (3)

SELBON

❏ 1005	Black Widow/Jaguar	1963	$50

NOBLES, THE (4)

STACY

❏ 926	Serenade/You Ain't Right	1962	$50

NOBLES, THE (5)

U.S.A.

❏ 788	Marlene/That Special One	1965	$30

NOBLES, THE (U)

TEE GEE

❏ 101	Oops Oh Lawdy/Stop Crying	1958	$60

NOCTURNES, THE

CARLSON INT'L

❏ 4105	My Christmas Star/ (B-side unknown)	1964	$70

MGM

❏ K11525	As You Desire Me/ Giuseppe's Serenade	1953	$20
❏ K12057	Ballads, Boogie and Blues/ Por Favor (Please)	1955	$15
❏ K11906	Hey Punchinello/These Are the Things We'll Share	1955	$15
❏ K11700	I Saw a Stranger/ Sing It Paisan	1954	$15
❏ K10835	Malaguena/After My Laughter Came Tears	1950	$30
❏ K11158	Misirlou/I'll Never Let You Cry	1952	$20
❏ K10768	Oh! Marie/Lucky, Lucky, Lucky Me	1950	$30
❏ K11644	Poppa Piccolino/For the First Time in a Long Time	1953	$15
❏ K11863	Somebody Ought to Write a Song/Remember Mama	1954	$15
❏ K12084	Toodle-Oo Igaloo/ Birmin'ham	1955	$15
❏ K11783	Who Dat (Buck Dance)/ The Knicka-Knacka Song (My Old Gal)	1954	$15

Number	Title	Yr	NM

NOEL, SID

ALADDIN

❏ 3331	The Flying Saucer (Part 1)/ The Flying Saucer (Part 2)	1956	$50
— Cover version of the Buchanan and Goodman break-in record

NOGUEZ, JACKY

JAMIE

❏ 1148	Amapola/Mahzel	1959	$15
❏ 1148 [PS]	Amapola/Mahzel	1959	$20
❏ 1127	Ciao, Ciao Bambina (Chiow, Chiow, Bambeena)/ De Serait Dommage	1959	$15
❏ 1137	Marina/Adonis	1959	$15

NOLAN, BOB

RCA VICTOR

❏ 47-5241	I Can't Lie to Myself/The House of Broken Dreams	1953	$30
❏ 47-5127	The Mystery of His Way/ An Angel in the Choir	1953	$30
❏ 47-5403	Tumbling Tumbleweeds/ Manhunt	1953	$30

NOLAN, FRANKIE

ABC-PARAMOUNT

❏ 10231	I Still Care/(I Wish It Were) Summer All Year Round	1961	$50
— Frankie Valli also appears on this record

NOLAND, TERRY

APT

❏ 25065	There Goes a Girl/ Long Gone Baby	1962	$20

BRUNSWICK

❏ 55069	Crazy Dream/ Everyone But One	1958	$40
❏ 55122	Guess I'm Gonna Fall/ Teenage Teardrops	1959	$40
❏ 55010	Hypnotized/Ten Little Women	1957	$40
❏ 55036	Patty Baby/Don't Do Me This Way	1957	$40
❏ 55054	Puppy Love/Oh Baby, Look at Me	1958	$40
❏ 55092	There Was a Fungus Among Us/Sugar Drop	1958	$50

CORAL

❏ 62274	There Was a Fungus Among Us/Sugar Drop	1961	$30

NOLTE, NANCY

LE CAM

❏ 704	Christmas Night/Christmas Tree in Heaven	1960	$15

NON-CONFORMISTS, THE

SCEPTER

❏ 12184	Two-Legged Big Eyed Yellow Haired Crying Canary/Bird Walk	1967	$40

NOONE, PETER

BELL

❏ 45131	Oh You Pretty Thing/ Because You're There	1971	$60
— Allegedly features David Bowie on A-side piano

❏ 45266	Should I/(B-side unknown)	1972	$8

CASABLANCA

❏ 0017	Meet Me at the Corner Down at Joe's Cafe/(Blame It)On the Pony Express	1974	$5
❏ 0106	Meet Me at the Corner Down at Joe's Cafe/(Blame It)On the Pony Express	1974	$4
❏ 802	Meet Me at the Corner Down at Joe's Cafe/(Blame It)On the Pony Express	1974	$4
❏ 823	Something Old, Something New/(B-side unknown)	1975	$4

JOHNSTON

❏ 02838	(I Don't Wanna Love You But) You Got Me Anyway/I'm One of the Glory Boys	1982	$4

PHILIPS

❏ 40730	All SIng Together/ Getting Over You	1974	$5

Number	Title	Yr	NM

NORMA JEAN

COLUMBIA

❏ 4-41400	Chapel Bells/ Honolulu Queen	1959	$30
❏ 4-41795	I Didn't Mean It/ Some Place to Cry	1960	$20
❏ 4-41636	What Does a Poor Girl Do/Just Like I Knew	1960	$20

MCA

❏ 52475	Shot in the Dark/ (Instrumental)	1984	$3

RCA VICTOR

❏ 47-9983	Back to His-Hers/That Song Writin' Man	1971	$8
❏ 48-1016	Chicken Every Sunday/Heavenly	1971	$8
❏ 47-9147	Conscience Keep an Eye on Me/Still	1967	$10
❏ 47-8989	Don't Let That Doorknob Hit You/Company's Comin'	1966	$15
❏ 74-0115	Dusty Road/Love's a Woman's Job	1969	$8
❏ 47-8433	Go Cat Go/Lonesome Number One	1964	$15
❏ 47-9362	Heaven Help the Working Girl/Your Alibi Called Today	1967	$12
❏ 74-0214	Home-Made Love/ These Flowers	1969	$8
❏ 47-8518	I Cried All the Way to the Bank/You Have to Be Out of Your Mind	1965	$15
❏ 47-8623	I Wouldn't Buy a Used Car from Him/I'm No Longer in Your Heart	1965	$15
❏ 47-8261	Let's Go All the Way/ Private Little World	1963	$15
❏ 47-9645	One Man Band/I Can't Leave Him	1968	$10
❏ 47-8887	Pursuing Happiness/It Wasn't God Who Made Honky Tonk Angels	1966	$15
❏ 47-8328	Put Your Arms Around Her/ I'm a Walkin' Advertisement (For the Blues)	1964	$15
❏ 47-8790	The Shirt/Please Don't Hurt Me	1966	$15
❏ 47-9466	Truck Driving Woman/ Supper Time	1968	$10
❏ 47-9809	Two Good Reasons/ Somebody's Gonna Plow Your Field	1969	$8
❏ 47-9854	What More Can I Do/ Another Man Loved Me Last Night	1970	$8
❏ 47-9900	Whiskey-Six Years Old/I'm Givin' Up	1970	$8

NORMA JEAN (2)

BEARSVILLE

❏ 49119	High Society/Hold Me Lonely Boy	1979	$5

NORMAN, GENE, AND THE ROCKIN' ROCKETS

SNAG

❏ 101	Snaggle Tooth Ann/ Long Gone Night Train	1958	$1000

NORMAN, JIMMY

BUDDAH

❏ 439	Funk Don't Mean a Scent/In the Palm of Another's Hand	1974	$20
❏ 504	I Wanna Make Love to You/Fallin' in Love	1975	$15

DOT

❏ 16016	Green Stamps/Just to Get to You	1959	$40

JOSIE

❏ 994	Gangster of Love/ Gangster of Love Pt. 2	1968	$30

LITTLE STAR

❏ 113	I Don't Love You No More (I Don't Care About You)/Tell Her for Me	1962	$30
❏ 126	Love Is Wonderful/What's the Word, Do the Bird	1963	$40

MERCURY

❏ 72658	Family Tree/It's Beautiful When You're Falling in Love	1967	$30
❏ 72727	If You Love Her (Show It)/I'm Leaving (This Old Town)	1967	$50

POLO

❏ 211	Dotted Line/You Crack Me Up	1964	$70

RAY STAR

❏ 781	I'll Never Be Free/ Lovesick Feeling	1961	$50
❏ 783	One of These Days/ Someone to Care For	1962	$50

SAMAR

❏ 116	Can You Blame Me/ This I Beg of You	1966	$30

Number	Title	Yr	NM

NORMAN, LARRY
A founding father of Christian rock. Also see PEOPLE.

CAPITOL
❏ 2766	Sweet Sweet Song of Salvation/Walking Backwards Down the Stairs	1970	$30

MGM
| ❏ 14676 | Christmas Time/The Same Old Story | 1973 | $20 |

SOLID ROCK
| ❏ 202 | Christmas Time/The Christmas Song | 1976 | $8 |

VERVE
| ❏ 10718 | I've Got to Learn to Live Without You/Readers Digest | 1973 | $30 |
| ❏ 10720 | I've Got to Learn to Live Without You/The Outlaw | 1973 | $30 |

NORMANAIRES, THE
MGM
| ❏ 11622 | My Greatest Sin/Wrap It Up | 1953 | $100 |

NORRIS, CHARLES
ATLANTIC
| ❏ 994 | Messin' Up/Let Me Know | 1953 | $70 |

NORTH, FREDDIE
ABET
❏ 9418	Don't Make Me Look So Bad/Hold Back	1967	$15
❏ 9440	Follow the Lamb/From the Blind Side	1969	$10
❏ 9430	I Have a Dream/(Instrumental)	1968	$10
❏ 9439	Love to Hate/Thank That Woman	1969	$10
❏ 9436	Oh Lord, What Are You Doing to Me/Long Hard Road	1968	$10

MANKIND
❏ 12022	Cuss the Wind/Love to Hate	1975	$12
❏ 12019	Lovin' on Back Streets/Love to Hate	1973	$8
❏ 12004	She's All I Got/Ain't Nothin' in the News (But the Blues)	1971	$8
❏ 12016	Song #29 (I'm Your Man)/Laid Back and Easy	1972	$8
❏ 12011	Sweeter Than Sweetness/I Did the Woman Wrong	1972	$8
❏ 12020	Taking Her Love Ain't Gonna Be Easy/Raining on a Sunny Day	1973	$8

PHILLIPS INT'L.
| ❏ 3574 | Don't Make Me Cry/Sometime She'll Come Along | 1962 | $30 |

RIC
| ❏ 119 | The Hurt/It's No Good for Me | 1964 | $200 |

UNIVERSITY
| ❏ 605 | How to Cry/OK, So What? | 1960 | $40 |

NORTH, JAY
KEM
| ❏ 2756 | The Cat And The Christmas Tree/Christmas For Tommy | 1960 | $20 |

NORTHERN LIGHTS, THE
UNITED ARTISTS
| ❏ 991 | Time to Move Along/No Time | 1966 | $30 |

NORWOOD, DOROTHY
GRC
| ❏ 2009 | Mama Loves Her Children All The Time (Part 1)/(Part 2) | 1974 | $8 |
| ❏ 1011 | There's Got to Be Rain in Your Life (To Appreciate the Sunshine)/Get Aboard the Soul Train | 1973 | $8 |

JEWEL
| ❏ 262 | He's a Friend/There Is Someone Who Cares for You | 1978 | $6 |

SAVOY
❏ 4261	A Boy and His Kite/(B-side unknown)	1966	$15
❏ 4223	I'm Thine, Oh Lord/The Old Lady's House	1964	$20
❏ 4301	In That Little Town/Prescription	1969	$10
❏ 4338	Precious Lord/(B-side unknown)	1970	$12
❏ 4282	The Singing Slave/(B-side unknown)	1967	$15

NOTES, THE
CAPITOL
| ❏ F3332 | Don't Leave Me Now/Cha Jezebel | 1956 | $300 |

MGM
| ❏ 12338 | Trust in Me/Round and Round | 1956 | $200 |

SARG
| ❏ 177 | Little Girl/G.I. Blues | 1959 | $60 |

NOVA LOCAL, THE
DECCA
| ❏ 32138 | Games/If You Only Had the Time | 1967 | $30 |
| ❏ 32194 | Other Girls/John Knight's Body (I Wanna Get Out) | 1967 | $30 |

NOVAS, THE
PARROT
| ❏ 45005 | The Crusher/Take 7 | 1964 | $100 |

NRBQ
BUTTON
| ❏ 037 | Froggy Went a-Courtin'/Bless Your Beautiful Hide | 1975 | $60 |

COLUMBIA
❏ 44937	C'mon Everybody/Rocket No. 9	1969	$6
❏ 44865	Stomp/I Didn't Know Myself	1969	$6
❏ 45019	Sure to Fall (In Love With You)/Down in My Heart	1969	$6

KAMA SUTRA
❏ 575	C'mon If You're Comin'/RC Cola and a Moon Pie	1973	$6
❏ 586	Get That Gasoline Blues/Mona	1974	$6
❏ 544	Howard Johnson's Got His Hojo Workin'/Do You Feel It	1972	$6
❏ 549	Only You/Magnet	1972	$6

MERCURY
| ❏ 73991 | Green Lights/I Love Her, She Loves Me | 1978 | $5 |

RED ROOSTER
❏ 1006	Christmas Wish/Jolly Old St. Nicholas	1978	$10
❏ 1006 [PS]	Christmas Wish/Jolly Old St. Nicholas	1978	$10
❏ 1002	I Got a Rocket in My Pocket/Tapdancin' Bats	1977	$6
❏ 1002 [PS]	I Got a Rocket in My Pocket/Tapdancin' Bats	1977	$10

ROUNDER
❏ 1010	Captain Lou!/Boardin' House Pie	1982	$4
❏ 1010 [PS]	Captain Lou!/Boardin' House Pie	1982	$4
❏ 4525	Christmas Wish/Jolly Old St. Nicholas	1979	$5
❏ 4525 [PS]	Christmas Wish/Jolly Old St. Nicholas	1979	$6
❏ 4522	Get That Gasoline Blues/Wacky Tobacky	1979	$5
❏ 4521	Hot Biscuits and Sweet Marie/She Don't Look Good	1979	$5
❏ 4531	Me and the Boys/People	1980	$5
❏ 4531 [PS]	Me and the Boys/People	1980	$10
❏ 4556	Things to Do/I Can't Stop Loving You Now	1985	$4
—With Skeeter Davis

SCEPTER
| ❏ 12322 | Sho' Need Love/Don't Talk About My Music1 | 1971 | $60 |
—As "The Dickens"

SELECT-O-HIT
| ❏ 022 | Sourpuss/Rumors | 1974 | $60 |

VIRGIN
| ❏ 99130 | If I Don't Have You/Boozoo, That's Who | 1989 | $4 |
| ❏ 99161 [DJ] | Wild Weekend/This Love Is True | 1989 | $4 |

7-Inch Extended Plays
RED ROOSTER
| ❏ EP-1 | Christmas Wish/Here Comes Santa Claus//God Rest Ye Merry Gentlemen/Message from the North Pole | 1979 | $20 |
—Called "Merry Christmas from NRBQ"; not issued with cover

NU SHOOZ
ATLANTIC
❏ 89033	Are You Lookin' for Somebody New/The Truth	1988	$3
❏ 89345	Don't Let Me Be the One/Secret Message	1986	$3
❏ 88978	Driftin'/Doin' Alright	1989	$3
❏ 89446	I Can't Wait/Make Up Your Mind	1986	$3
❏ 89446 [PS]	I Can't Wait/Make Up Your Mind	1986	$6
❏ 89392	Point of No Return/Goin' Thru the Motions	1986	$3
❏ 89392 [PS]	Point of No Return/Goin' Thru the Motions	1986	$6

| ❏ 89108 | Should I Say Yes?/Monte Carlo Nite | 1988 | $3 |
| ❏ 89108 [PS] | Should I Say Yes?/Monte Carlo Nite | 1988 | $4 |

POOLSIDE
| ❏ 1001 | I Can't Wait/Don't Turn Back | 1985 | $10 |
| ❏ 1001 [PS] | I Can't Wait/Don't Turn Back | 1985 | $20 |
—Fold-open poster sleeve

NU-TONES, THE
COMBO
| ❏ 127 | At Midnight/Beans 'N' Greens | 1957 | $200 |

HOLLYWOOD STAR
| ❏ 798 | Annie Kicked the Bucket/Believe | 1955 | $8000 |

NU TORNADOS, THE
CARLTON
| ❏ 492 | Philadelphia, U.S.A./Magic Record | 1959 | $30 |
| ❏ 497 | The "Ole Mummers" Strut/Let's Have a Party | 1959 | $30 |

FELSTED
| ❏ 8577 | Cry Baby Cry/Keep a Flower Growing in Your Heart | 1959 | $30 |

NUGENT, TED
Also see THE AMBOY DUKES; ST. PARADISE. One-time vocalist Charlie Huhn is now in FOGHAT.

ATLANTIC
❏ 89998	Bound and Gagged/Habitual Offender	1982	$3
❏ 89998 [PS]	Bound and Gagged/Habitual Offender	1982	$5
❏ 89442	High Heels in Motion/Angry Young Man	1986	$3
❏ 89442 [PS]	High Heels in Motion/Angry Young Man	1986	$4
❏ 89661	Lean Mean R&R Machine/(Where Do You) Draw the Line	1984	$3
❏ 89436	Little Miss Dangerous/Angry Young Man	1986	$3
❏ 89705	Tied Up in Love/Lean Mean R&R Machine	1984	$5
—Promo copies, with "Tied Up in Love" on both sides, go for less
| ❏ 89705 [PS] | Tied Up in Love/Lean Mean R&R Machine | 1984 | $5 |

EPIC
❏ 50425	Cat Scratch Fever/Wang Dang Sweet Poontang	1977	$5
❏ 50493	Death by Misadventure/Home Bound	1977	$4
❏ 50301	Dog Eat Dog/Light My Way	1976	$5
❏ 50363	Free-for-All/Street Rags	1977	$4
❏ 50197	Hey Baby/Stormtroopin'	1976	$5
❏ 50713	I Want to Tell You/Bite Down Hard	1979	$4
❏ 01046	Land of a Thousand Dances/The TNT Overture	1981	$4
❏ 50172	Motor City Madness/Where Have You Been All My Life	1975	$5
❏ 50907	Wango Tango/Scream Dream	1980	$4

NUGGETS, THE (1)
CAPITOL
| ❏ F-3052 | Anxious Heart/Shtiggy Boom | 1955 | $20 |
| ❏ F-2989 | So Help Me I Love You/Quirl Up in My Arms | 1954 | $30 |

NUGGETS, THE (2)
RCA VICTOR
| ❏ 47-7930 | Before We Say Goodnight/Angel on the Dance Floor | 1961 | $40 |

NUMAN, GARY
ATCO
❏ 7206	Are Friends Electric?/You Are In My Vision	1979	$4
❏ 7211	Cars/Metal	1980	$4
❏ 7308	I Die; You Die/Sleep by Windows	1980	$4

NUMBERS, THE
BONNEVILLE
| ❏ 101 | Big Red/My Pillow | 1962 | $200 |

DORE
| ❏ 641 | Big Red/My Pillow | 1962 | $60 |

NUNLEY, BILL
CANNERY
| ❏ 0402 | I'll Know the Good Times/That's How Long I'll Wait for You | 1988 | $6 |
| ❏ 0525 | The Way You Got Over Me/(B-side unknown) | 1988 | $6 |

Number	Title	Yr	NM
NUNS, THE			
415 RECORDS			
❏ S-0001	Savage/Decadent Jew/Suicide Child	1978	$30
❏ S-0001 [PS]	Savage/Decadent Jew/Suicide Child	1978	$30
ROSCO			
❏ 0(no cat #)	The Beat/Media Control	1979	$20
❏ 0(no cat #) [PS]	The Beat/Media Control	1979	$20
❏ 4166	World War III/Cock in My Pocket	1980	$20
❏ 4166 [PS]	World War III/Cock in My Pocket	1980	$20
— Insert and rubberstamped sleeve			
NUTMEGS, THE			
BABY GRAND			
❏ 800	Story Untold '72/Tell Me	1972	$8
HERALD			
❏ 492	Love So True/Comin' Home	1956	$50
❏ 538	My Sweet Dream/My Story	1959	$50
❏ 459	Ship of Love/Rock Me	1955	$50
❏ 452	Story Untold/Make Me Lose My Mind	1955	$75
❏ 466	Whispering Sorrows/Betty Lou	1955	$60
NIGHTRAIN			
❏ 905	Shifting Sands/Take Me and Make Me	1973	$8
TEL			
❏ 1014	A Dream of Love/Someone, Somewhere (Help Me)	1960	$125
TIMES SQUARE			
❏ 27	Down in Mexico/My Sweet Dreams	1964	$30
❏ 19	Down to Earth/Coo Coo Cuddle Coo	1963	$30
— B-side by the Admirations			
❏ 6	Let Me Tell You/Hello	1963	$30
— Blue vinyl			
❏ 14	The Way Love Should Be/Wide Hoop Skirts	1963	$30
❏ 22	Why Must We Go to School/Ink Dries Quicker Than Tears	1963	$30
— B-side by the Volumes			
7-Inch Extended Plays			
HERALD			
❏ 452	*Story Untold/Betty Lou/Comin' Home/ Whispering Sorrows	1960	$125
❏ 452 [PS]	Story Untold	1960	$120
NUTTY SQUIRRELS, THE			
COLUMBIA			
❏ 41818	Please Don't Take Our Tree for Christmas/Nutty Noel	1960	$30
❏ 41818 [PS]	Please Don't Take Our Tree for Christmas/Nutty Noel	1960	$50
HANOVER			
❏ 4551	Eager Beaver/Zowee	1960	$30
RCA VICTOR			
❏ 47-8287	Hello Again/Bluesette	1963	$20
7-Inch Extended Plays			
HANOVER			
❏ 301 [PS]	(title unknown)	1960	$75
— Paper sleeve (not cardboard)			
NYRO, LAURA			
COLUMBIA			
❏ 44786	Once It Was Alright (Farmer Joe)/Lu	1969	$6
❏ 45089	Save the Country/New York Tendaberry	1970	$6
❏ 44531	Sweet Blindness/Eli's Comin'	1968	$8
❏ JZSP139152/3 [DJ]	Sweet Blindness/ Stoned Soul Picnic	1968	$20
❏ 45041	Time and Love/A Man Who Sends Me Home	1969	$6
❏ 45298	When I Was a Freeport and You Were the Main Drag/Been On a Train	1971	$6
VERVE FOLKWAYS			
❏ 5051	And When I Die/ Flim Flam Man	1967	$10
❏ 5038	Billie's Blues/Goodbye Joe	1967	$10
❏ 5024	Wedding Bell Blues/ Stoney End	1966	$10
VERVE FORECAST			
❏ 5104	And When I Die/I Never Meant to Hurt You	1969	$8
❏ 5112	Goodbye Joe/I Never Meant to Hurt You	1969	$8
❏ 5095	Stoney End/Flim Flam Man	1968	$8

O

Number	Title	Yr	NM
OAK RIDGE BOYS, THE			
ABC			
❏ 12434	Come On In/ Morning Glory Do	1978	$4
❏ 12397	Cryin' Again/I Can Love You	1978	$4
❏ 12350	I'll Be True to You/Old Time Family Bluegrass Band	1978	$4
❏ 12463	Sail Away/Only One	1979	$4
CADENCE			
❏ 1362	The Mocking Bird/The House of the Lord	1959	$30
— As "The Oak Ridge Quartet"			
CAPITOL			
❏ F2181	A Mother's Prayer/My Lord's Gonna Move This Wicked Race	1952	$40
❏ F2182	Give Me That Old Time Religion/No Tears in Heaven	1952	$40
❏ F2183	Her Mansion Is Higher Than Mine/I've Found a Hidin' Place	1952	$40
— The above three as "The Oak Ridge Quartet			
COLUMBIA			
❏ 10419	All Our Favorite Songs/ Whoever Finds This, I Love You	1976	$5
❏ 10349	Family Reunion/ Don't Be Late	1976	$5
❏ 10226	Heaven Bound/ Look Away Mama	1975	$5
❏ 46001	He's Gonna Shine on Me/ Put Your Arms Around Me, Blessed Jesus	1974	$5
❏ 46044	Loves Me Like a Rock/He	1974	$5
❏ 10320	Where the Soul Never Dies/No Earthly Good	1976	$5
MCA			
❏ 52179	American Made/The Cure for My Broken Heart	1983	$4
❏ 53705	An American Family/ Too Many Heartaches	1989	$3
❏ 52095	Back in Your Arms Again/I Wish I Could Have Turned My Head	1982	$4
❏ 53625	Beyond Those Years/ Too Many Heartaches	1989	$3
❏ 51231	Bobbie Sue/Live In Love	1982	$4
❏ 52006	Bobbie Sue/Live In Love	1982	$4
❏ 53460	Bridges and Walls/ Never Together (But Close Sometimes)	1988	$3
❏ 52722	Come On In (You Did the Best You Could Do)/ Roll Tennessee River	1985	$3
❏ 52722 [PS]	Come On In (You Did the Best You Could Do)/ Roll Tennessee River	1985	$4
❏ 52722 [DJ]	Come On In (You Did the Best You Could Do) (same on both sides)	1985	$10
— Promo only on blue vinyl			
❏ 41078	Dream On/Sometimes the Rain Won't Let Me Sleep	1979	$4
❏ 51084	Elvira/A Woman Like You	1981	$4
❏ 52419	Everyday/Ain't No Cure for the Rock 'N' Roll	1984	$3
❏ 51169	Fancy Free/How Long Has It Been	1981	$4
❏ 53381	Gonna Take a Lot of River/Private Lives	1988	$3
❏ 52342	I Guess It Never Hurts to Hurt Sometimes/ Through My Eyes	1984	$3
❏ 53010	It Takes a Little Rain (To Make Love Grow)/ Looking for Love	1987	$3
❏ 41154	Leaving Louisiana in the Broad Daylight/I Gotta Get Over This	1979	$4
❏ 52556	Little Things/Secret of Love	1985	$3
❏ 52224	Love Song/Heart on the Line	1983	$4
❏ 41280	Love Takes Two/ Heart of Mine	1980	$4
❏ 52488	Make My Life with You/ Break My Mind	1984	$3
❏ 52288	Ozark Mountain Jubilee/ Down Deep Inside	1983	$4
❏ 12463	Sail Away/Only One	1979	$3
❏ S45-1154 [DJ]	Santa's Song/Happy Christmas Eve	1982	$15
❏ 52065	So Fine/I Wish You Were Here	1982	$4
❏ S45-1705 [DJ]	Star Spangled Banner (stereo/mono)	1980	$10
❏ 52145	Thank God for Kids/ Christmas Is Paintin' the Town	1982	$4
❏ S45-1250 [DJ]	Thank God for Kids/ Jesus Is Born Today	1982	$15
❏ S45-1741 [DJ]	The Boy Scout Way/Check Out the Boy Scouts	1981	$20
— Label calls this a "Public Service Recording (Not for Sale)			
❏ S45-17450 [DJ]	There's A New Kid In Town/From a Distance	1986	$10
— B-side by Nanci Griffith			
❏ 53023 [DJ]	This Crazy Love (same on both sides)	1987	$10
— Promo only on blue vinyl			
❏ 53023	This Crazy Love/Where the Fast Lane Ends	1987	$3
❏ 53175	Time In/A Little More Coal on the Fire	1987	$3
❏ 52646	Touch a Hand, Make a Friend/Only One I Love	1985	$3
❏ 53272	True Heart/Love Without Mercy	1988	$3
❏ 41217	Trying to Love Two Women/ Hold On 'Til Sunday	1980	$4
❏ S45-17233 [DJ]	When You Give It Away/The Voices Of Rejoicing Love	1986	$20
— Promo only on green vinyl			
WARNER BROS.			
❏ 5359	This Ole House/Early in the Morning	1963	$30
O'BRIAN, HUGH			
7-Inch Extended Plays			
ABC-PARAMOUNT			
❏ A-203	(contents unknown)	1957	$25
❏ B-203	(contents unknown)	1957	$25
❏ C-203	Don't Move/Timothy//I'm Walkin' Away/Down in the Meadow	1957	$25
❏ A-203 [PS]	Hugh O'Brian (TV's Wyatt Earp) Sings, Vol. I	1957	$25
❏ B-203 [PS]	Hugh O'Brian (TV's Wyatt Earp) Sings, Vol. II	1957	$25
❏ C-203 [PS]	Hugh O'Brian (TV's Wyatt Earp) Sings, Vol. III	1957	$25
O'BRIEN, RHYS			
MGM			
❏ 13862	The Word Called Love/ Christmas Morning	1967	$8
O'BRYAN			
CAPITOL			
❏ B-5376	Breakin' Together/(Dub)	1984	$4
❏ B-5376 [PS]	Breakin' Together/(Dub)	1984	$4
❏ B-5673	Driving Force/Surrender	1987	$4
❏ B-5673 [PS]	Driving Force/Surrender	1987	$4
❏ B-5414	Go On and Cry/ You Gotta Use It	1984	$4
❏ B-5203	I'm Freaky/(Instrumental)	1983	$4
❏ B-5329	Lovelite/(Instrumental)	1984	$4
❏ B-5329 [PS]	Lovelite/(Instrumental)	1984	$4
❏ B-5291	Soul Train's a-Comin'/ Soft Touch	1983	$6
❏ B-5117	Still Water (Love)/ Right from the Start	1982	$4
❏ B-5117 [PS]	Still Water (Love)/ Right from the Start	1982	$5
❏ B-5617	Tenderoni/(Instrumental)	1986	$4
❏ A-5067	The Gigolo/Can't Live Without Your Love	1981	$4
OBSESSIONS, THE			
ACCENT			
❏ 1182	Love Always/A Fool	1964	$200
OCASEK, RIC			
GEFFEN			
❏ 28617	Emotion in Motion/P.F.J.	1986	$3
❏ 28617 [PS]	Emotion in Motion/P.F.J.	1986	$3
❏ 29784	Something to Grab For/ Connect Up to Me	1983	$4
❏ 29784 [PS]	Something to Grab For/ Connect Up to Me	1983	$4
❏ 28504	True to You/Hello Darkness	1986	$3
❏ 28504 [PS]	True to You/Hello Darkness	1986	$3
OCEAN			
KAMA SUTRA			
❏ 525	Deep Enough for Me/ No Other Woman	1971	$4
❏ 556	One More Chance/Will the Circle Be Unbroken	1972	$4
❏ 519	Put Your Hand in the Hand/ Tear Down the Fences	1971	$5
❏ 529	We Got a Dream/Will the Circle Be Unbroken	1971	$4
OCEAN, BILLY			
ARIOLA AMERICA			
❏ 7630	L.O.D. (Love On Delivery)/ Mr. Business Man	1976	$6
❏ 7621	Love Really Hurts Without You/You're Running Out of Fools	1976	$6
EPIC			
❏ 8-50810	American Hearts/My Love	1979	$5
❏ 14-02485	Another Day Won't Matter/ Whatever Turns You On	1981	$4
❏ 14-02464	Are You Ready/ Taking Chances	1981	$4
❏ 14-02942	Calypso Funkin'/City Limits	1982	$4

Number	Title	Yr	NM
❏ 14-03174	Inner Feelings/Tryin' to Get Through to You	1982	$4
JIVE			
❏ 1283-7-J	Licence to Chill/Pleasure	1989	$3
❏ 1283-7-J [PS]	Licence to Chill/Pleasure	1989	$3
JIVE/ARISTA			
❏ 9199	Caribbean Queen (No More Love on the Run)/ (Instrumental)	1984	$3
❏ 9678	Get Outta My Dreams, Get Into My Car/Showdown	1988	$3
❏ 9678 [PS]	Get Outta My Dreams, Get Into My Car/Showdown	1988	$3
❏ 9540	Love Is Forever/Dance Floor	1986	$3
❏ 9540 [PS]	Love Is Forever/Dance Floor	1986	$3
❏ 9284	Loverboy/(Dub)	1984	$3
❏ 9284 [PS]	Loverboy/(Dub)	1984	$3
❏ 9510	Love Zone/(Instrumental)	1986	$3
❏ 9510 [PS]	Love Zone/(Instrumental)	1986	$3
❏ 9374	Mystery Lady/African Queen (No More Love on the Run)	1985	$3
❏ 9374 [PS]	Mystery Lady/African Queen (No More Love on the Run)	1985	$3
❏ 9323	Suddenly/Lucky Man	1985	$3
❏ 9323 [PS]	Suddenly/Lucky Man	1985	$3
❏ 9740	Tear Down These Walls/Without You	1988	$3
❏ 9740 [PS]	Tear Down These Walls/Without You	1988	$3
❏ 9707	The Colour of Love/It's Never Too Late to Try	1988	$3
❏ 9707 [PS]	The Colour of Love/It's Never Too Late to Try	1988	$3
❏ 9465	There'll Be Sad Songs (To Make You Cry)/ If I Should Lose You	1986	$3
❏ 9465 [PS]	There'll Be Sad Songs (To Make You Cry)/ If I Should Lose You	1986	$3
❏ 9432	When the Going Gets Tough, the Tough Get Going/(Instrumental)	1985	$3
❏ 9432 [PS]	When the Going Gets Tough, the Tough Get Going/(Instrumental)	1985	$3

OCHS, PHIL
A&M

Number	Title	Yr	NM
❏ 881	Flower Lady/Cross My Heart	1967	$10
❏ 1509	Here's to the State of Richard Nixon/ Power and Glory	1974	$8
❏ 1180	My Kingdom for a Car/ One Way Ticket Home	1970	$8
❏ 1070	My Life/The World Began in Eden and Ended in Los Angeles	1969	$8
❏ 891	Outside of a Small Circle of Friends/Miranda	1967	$10
❏ 932	The War Is Over/The Harder They Fall	1968	$8

O'CONNOR, CARROLL, AND JEAN STAPLETON
ATLANTIC

Number	Title	Yr	NM
❏ 2847	Those Were the Days/ Those Were the Days	1971	$5
❏ 2847 [PS]	Those Were the Days/ Those Were the Days	1971	$8

O'CONNOR, SINEAD
CHRYSALIS

Number	Title	Yr	NM
❏ VS4-43232	I Want Your (Hands on Me)/Just Call Me Joe	1988	$5
❏ VS4-43232 [PS]	I Want Your (Hands on Me)/Just Call Me Joe	1988	$5
❏ VS4-43207	Mandinka/Drink Before the War	1988	$4
❏ VS4-43207 [PS]	Mandinka/Drink Before the War	1988	$4

OCTOBER COUNTRY
EPIC

Number	Title	Yr	NM
❏ 5-10320	My Girlfriend Is a Witch/I Just Don't Know	1968	$10
❏ 5-10252	October Country/ Baby What I Mean	1967	$10

O'DAY, ALAN
PACIFIC

Number	Title	Yr	NM
❏ 100	Oh Johnny!/(B-side unknown)	1979	$6
❏ 004	Satisfied/Catch My Breath	1978	$5
❏ 101	Skinny Girls/(B-side unknown)	1979	$6
❏ 003	Soldier of Fortune/ (B-side unknown)	1978	$5
❏ 002	Started Out Dancing, Ended Up Making Love/Angie Baby	1977	$5
VIVA			
❏ 7679	Somewhere She Is Sleeping/A Song	1974	$6

O'DAY, TOMMY
NU TRAYL

Number	Title	Yr	NM
❏ 929	Accentuate the Positive/Blue River	1979	$6
❏ 912	Candy Bars, Lollipops/ Wrote This Song for You	1977	$6
❏ 933	Daddy Went Out Walking/ Don't Stepping Out Mean	1979	$6
❏ 924	From a Jack to a King/ The Wayward Wind	1978	$6
❏ 926	I Heard a Song Today/ Today's Woman	1978	$6
❏ 922	I Wrote This Song for You/Sweeter Than Mountain Water	1978	$6
❏ 1001	Look at All the Angels/ (B-side unknown)	1980	$6
❏ 919	Memories Are Made of This/ Up and Over Your Love	1977	$6
❏ 916	Mr. Sandman/Winter Winds of Love	1977	$6
❏ 931	Secretly/I'm Gonna Kiss Your Past Goodbye	1979	$6
❏ 909	The Man in Her Sleep/ Up and Over Your Love	1977	$6
❏ 923	When a Woman Cries/ Round and Round	1978	$6

ODDIS, RAY
V.I.P.

Number	Title	Yr	NM
❏ 25012	Happy Ghoul Tide/Ray the Newspaper Boy	1964	$30

ODDS AND ENDS
RED BIRD

Number	Title	Yr	NM
❏ Oct-0083	Before You Go (Hey Little Girl)/Never Learn	1967	$15

O'DELL, DOYE
ERA

Number	Title	Yr	NM
❏ 1024	According to the Evidence/ Bow Your Head and Pray	1956	$30
LIBERTY			
❏ 55347	Dreamboat, Still Afloat/ Lights in the Streets	1961	$20
RADIO			
❏ 115	Strange Nights/Bring a Hammer and a Needle	1958	$30

ODETTA
ABC DUNHILL

Number	Title	Yr	NM
❏ 4213	Ballad of Easy Rider/ Visa Versa	1969	$6
POLYDOR			
❏ 14045	Take Me to the Pilot/ Hit or Miss	1970	$5
RCA VICTOR			
❏ 47-8262	Got My Mind on Freedom/ It's a Mighty World	1963	$10
RIVERSIDE			
❏ 4524	Make Me a Pallet on Your Floor/Oh, My Babe	1962	$10
VANGUARD			
❏ 35007	Motherless Children/ The Ox-Driver Song	1959	$30
VERVE FORECAST			
❏ 5087	Peace and Harmony/Until It's Time for You to Go	1968	$6

OERTLING, JIM
HAMMOND

Number	Title	Yr	NM
❏ 267	Old Moss Back/A Wilde Rose	1959	$400

OFF KEYS, THE
ROWE

Number	Title	Yr	NM
❏ 03	Our Wedding Day/ Singing Bells	1962	$125
TECHNICHORD			
❏ 1001	Our Wedding Day/ Singing Bells	1962	$60

— Glossy red label

Number	Title	Yr	NM
❏ 1001	Our Wedding Day/ Singing Bells	1962	$30

— Flat maroon label

OGNIR AND THE NIGHT PEOPLE
SAMRON

Number	Title	Yr	NM
❏ 102	I Found a New Love/ All My Heart	1965	$50
WARNER BROS.			
❏ 5687	I Found a New Love/ All My Heart	1965	$30

O'GWYNN, JAMES
D

Number	Title	Yr	NM
❏ 1022	Blue Memories/You Don't Want to Hold Me	1958	$40
❏ 1006	Talk to Me Lonesome Heart/Changeable	1958	$40
MERCURY			
❏ 72008	Does He Mean That Much to You/What Do You Want from Me	1962	$20
❏ 72053	Don't We All Have the Right/That's How It Is	1962	$20
❏ 71807	Down on the Corner of Love/ I'm Getting Nowhere Fast	1961	$20
❏ 71513	Easy Money/Tears of Tomorrow	1959	$20
❏ 71731	House of Blue Lovers/ Another Falling Tear	1960	$20
❏ 71419	How Can I Think of Tomorrow/Were You Ever a Stranger	1959	$20
❏ 71127	I Cry/Do You Miss Me	1957	$30
❏ 71066	Mule Skinner Blues/ Who'll Be the Next One	1957	$30
❏ 71935	My Name Is Mud/You're Getting All Over Me	1962	$20
❏ 71584	Someone Sweet to Love/ That's All I Got from You	1960	$20
❏ 71864	Too Much of You/Your Heart	1961	$20
❏ 71452	Trying to Forget You/ Take the Last Look	1959	$20
❏ 71234	Two Little Hearts/ You've Always Won	1957	$20
PLANTATION			
❏ 83	House of Blue Lovers/ Tomorrow Ends Like Today	1972	$8
❏ 130	Talk to Me, Lonely Heart/Tender Years	1975	$6
STARDAY			
❏ 266	If I Never Get to Heaven/ Losing Game	1956	$40

O'HENRY, LENNY
ABC-PARAMOUNT

Number	Title	Yr	NM
❏ 10222	Billy the Continental Kid/Cheated Heart	1961	$20
❏ 10272	Goin' to a Party/Touch of You	1961	$20
ATCO			
❏ 6291	Across the Street/ Saturday Angel	1964	$15
❏ 6525	Across the Street/ Saturday Angel	1967	$8
❏ 6312	Sweet Young Love/ Savin' All My Love	1964	$15
SMASH			
❏ 1800	Burning Memories/ Mr. Moonlight	1963	$15

OHIO EXPRESS, THE
BUDDAH

Number	Title	Yr	NM
❏ 70	Chewy Chewy/Firebird	1968	$10
❏ 147	Cowboy Convention/The Race (That Took Place)	1970	$8
❏ 56	Down at Lulu's/She's Not Coming Home	1968	$8
❏ 160	Love Equals Love/Peanuts	1970	$8
❏ 102	Mercy/Roll It Up	1969	$8
❏ 117	Pinch Me (Baby, Convince Me)/Peanuts	1969	$8
❏ 129	Sausalito (Is the Place to Go)/Make Love Not War	1969	$8

— With Graham Gouldman, later of 10CC, on lead vocal

Number	Title	Yr	NM
❏ 92	Sweeter Than Sugar/ Bitter Than Lemon	1969	$8
❏ 386	Wham Bam/Slow and Steady	1973	$20

— As "Ohio Ltd.

Number	Title	Yr	NM
CAMEO			
❏ 483	Beg, Borrow and Steal/Maybe	1967	$15
❏ 2001	Try It/Soul Struttin'	1967	$15
SUPER K			
❏ 114	Hot Dog/Ooh La La	1970	$10

OHIO PLAYERS, THE
AIR CITY

Number	Title	Yr	NM
❏ 1007	Follow Me/(B-side unknown)	1984	$5
❏ 402	Sight for Sore Eyes/ (Instrumental)	1984	$4
❏ 402 [PS]	Sight for Sore Eyes/ (Instrumental)	1984	$4
ARISTA			
❏ 0440	Don't Say Goodbye/Say It	1979	$4
❏ 0408	Everybody Up/Take De Funk Off, Fly	1979	$4
BOARDWALK			
❏ WS8-02063	Skinny/Call Me	1981	$4
❏ NB7-11-133	Star of the Party/I Better Take a Coffee Break	1981	$30
❏ 5708	Try a Little Tenderness/ Try to Be a Man	1981	$4

Number	Title	Yr	NM
CAPITOL			
❏ 2385	Bad Bargain/Here Today and Gone Tomorrow	1969	$12
❏ 2523	Find Someone to Love/Over the Rainbow	1969	$10
COMPASS			
❏ 7018	It's a Crying Shame/I've Got to Hold On	1968	$30
❏ 7015	Tresspassin'/You Don't Mean It	1967	$60
MERCURY			
❏ 73913	Body Vibes/Don't Fight My Love	1977	$5
❏ 73860	Far East Mississippi/Only a Child Can Love	1976	$5
❏ 73881	Feel the Beat (Everybody Disco)/Contradiction	1976	$5
❏ 73643	Fire/Together	1974	$5
❏ 73775	Fopp/Let's Love	1976	$5
❏ 74014	Funk-O-Nots/Sleepwalkin'	1978	$5
❏ 73974	Good Luck Charm (Part 1)/Good Luck Charm (Part 2)	1977	$5
❏ 73753	Happy Holidays (Part 1)/Happy Holidays (Part 2)	1975	$6
❏ 73675	I Want to Be Free/Smoke	1975	$5
❏ 73734	Love Rollercoaster/It's All Over	1975	$5
❏ 73983	Magic Trick/Mr. Mean	1978	$5
❏ 73956	Merry Go Round/Angel	1977	$5
❏ 73932	O-H-I-O/Can You Still Love Me	1977	$5
❏ 73609	Skin Tight/Heaven Must Be Like This	1974	$5
❏ 73713	Sweet Sticky Thing/Alone	1975	$5
❏ 74031	Time Slips Away/Nott Enuff	1978	$5
❏ 73814	Who'd She Coo?/Bi-Centennial	1976	$5
TRACK			
❏ 58812	Let's Play (From Now On)/Show Off	1988	$3
❏ 58815	Sweat/Rock the House	1988	$3
WESTBOUND			
❏ 216	Ecstasy/Not So Sad and Lonely	1973	$6
❏ 214	Funky Worm/Paint Me	1973	$6
❏ 188	Pain (Part 1)/Pain (Part 2)	1971	$6
❏ 204	Pleasure/I Wanna Hear from You	1972	$6
❏ 228	Sleep Talk/Food Stamps Y'All	1974	$6
❏ 208	Walt's First Trip/Varce Is Love	1972	$6

OHIO UNTOUCHABLES, THE

Number	Title	Yr	NM
LUPINE			
❏ 116/7	I'm Tired/Uptown	1962	$50
❏ 1011	I'm Tired/Uptown	1964	$20
❏ 110	Love Is Amazing/Forgive Me Darling	1962	$60
❏ 1010	Love Is Amazing/Forgive Me Darling	1964	$30
❏ 109	She's My Heart's Desire/What to Do	1962	$60
❏ 1009	She's My Heart's Desire/What to Do	1964	$30

OINGO BOINGO

Number	Title	Yr	NM
A&M			
❏ 2439	Private Life/Islands	1982	$5
❏ 2610	Wake Up (It's 1984)/No Spill Blood	1983	$5
❏ 2504 [DJ]	Whole Day Off (stereo/mono)	1982	$10

—*Apparently, no stock copy exists*

Number	Title	Yr	NM
MCA			
❏ 42013	BOI-NGO	1987	$60

—*Boxed set of five 45s, comprising the album of the same name*

Number	Title	Yr	NM
❏ 52789	Stay/Heard Somebody Cry	1986	$4
❏ 52789 [PS]	Stay/Heard Somebody Cry	1986	$4
❏ 53105	We Close Our Eyes/Where Do All My Friends Go	1987	$4
❏ 53105 [PS]	We Close Our Eyes/Where Do All My Friends Go	1987	$4
❏ 52633	Weird Science/Weird Mama	1985	$4

—*B-side by Ira & the Geeks*

Number	Title	Yr	NM
❏ 52633 [PS]	Weird Science/Weird Mama	1985	$4

O'JAYS, THE

Number	Title	Yr	NM
APOLLO			
❏ 759	Miracles/Can't Take It	1961	$40
ASTROSCOPE			
❏ 110	Peace/Don't You Know a True Love (When You See Her)	1974	$8
❏ 106	Wisdom of a Child/Peace	1974	$8
BELL			
❏ 770	Don't You Know a True Love/That's All Right	1969	$8
❏ 691	I'll Be Sweeter Tomorrow (Than I Was Today)/I Dig Your Act	1967	$10

Number	Title	Yr	NM
❏ 749	I Miss You/Now That I Found You	1968	$10
❏ 45378	Look Over Your Shoulder/Four for the Price of One	1973	$5
❏ 704	Look Over Your Shoulder/I'm So Glad I Found You	1968	$10
❏ 737	The Choice/Going, Going, Gone	1968	$12
EMI			
❏ B-50180	Have You Had Your Love Today/Pot Can't Call the Kettle Black	1989	$3
❏ B-50212	Out of My Mind (Radio Mix)/(Soul 2 Mix)	1989	$3
❏ B-50230	Serious Hold on Me/(Instrumental)	1989	$4
IMPERIAL			
❏ 66197	Friday Night/Stand In for Love	1966	$10
❏ 66076	Girl Machine/Oh How You Hurt Me	1964	$10
❏ 5942	How Does It Feel/Crack Up Laughing	1963	$20
❏ 66162	I'll Never Forget You/Pretty Words	1966	$300
❏ 66145	I'll Never Let You Go/It Won't Hurt	1965	$10
❏ 66025	I'll Never Stop Loving You/My Dearest Beloved	1964	$10
❏ 66102	Lipstick Traces/Think It Over, Baby	1965	$12
❏ 5976	Lonely Drifter/That's Enough	1963	$10
❏ 66200	Lonely Drifter/That's Enough	1966	$10
❏ 66007	Stand Tall/The Storm Is Over	1963	$10
❏ 66121	Whip It On Me Baby/I've Cried My Last Tear	1965	$10
LITTLE STAR			
❏ 125	Dream Girl/Joey St. Vincent	1963	$30
❏ 124	How Does It Feel/Crack Up Laughing	1963	$30
MINIT			
❏ 32015	Hold On/Working on Your Case	1967	$12
NEPTUNE			
❏ 18	Branded Bad/You're the Best Thing Since Candy	1969	$8
❏ 33	Christmas Ain't Christmas New Year's Ain't New Year's Without the One You Love/Just Can't Get Enough	1970	$8
❏ 20	Christmas Ain't Christmas New Year's Ain't New Year's Without the One You Love/There's Someone Waiting	1969	$10
❏ 22	Deeper (In Love with You)/I've Got the Groove	1970	$8
❏ 31	Looky Looky (Look at Me Girl)/Let Me in Your World	1970	$8
❏ 12	One Night Affair/There's Someone (Waiting Back Home)	1969	$8
PHILADELPHIA INT'L.			
❏ 3522	992 Arguments/Listen to the Clock on the Wall	1972	$5
❏ 3517	Back Stabbers/Sunshine	1972	$5
❏ 3652	Brandy/Take Me to the Stars	1978	$5
❏ 3537	Christmas Ain't Christmas New Year's Ain't New Year's Without the One You Love/Just Can't Get Enough	1973	$6
❏ 3581	Christmas Ain't Christmas New Year's Ain't New Year's Without the One You Love/Just Can't Get Enough	1975	$5
❏ 3666	Cry Together/Strokety Stroke	1978	$5
❏ 3610	Darlin' Darlin' Baby (Sweet, Tender, Love)/A Prayer	1976	$5
❏ B-50067	Don't Take Your Love Away/I Just Want Somebody to Love Me	1987	$3
❏ ZS4-04437	Extraordinary Girl/I Really Need You Now	1984	$4
❏ 3596	Family Reunion/Unity	1976	$5
❏ 3727	Forever Mine/Get On Out and Party	1979	$5
❏ ZS8-02096	Forever Mine/Girl, Don't Let It Get You Down	1981	$3

—*Reissue*

Number	Title	Yr	NM
❏ 3544	For the Love of Money/People Keep Tellin' Me	1974	$5
❏ 3565	Give the People What They Want/What Am I Waiting For	1975	$5
❏ 3101	Hurry Up and Come Back/Identify	1979	$5
❏ ZS4-03892	I Can't Stand the Pain/A Letter to My Friends	1983	$4
❏ B-50122	I Just Want Someone to Love Me/Lovin' You	1988	$3
❏ ZS5-02834	I Just Want to Satisfy/Don't Walk Away Mad	1982	$4
❏ 3577	I Love Music (Part 1)/I Love Music (Part 2)	1975	$5
❏ 3726	I Want You Here with Me/Get On Out and Party	1979	$5
❏ 3573	Let Me Make Love to You/Survival	1975	$5
❏ ZS4-04535	Let Me Show You (How Much I Really Love You)/Love You Direct	1984	$4
❏ B-50104	Let Me Touch You/Undercover Lover	1987	$3

Number	Title	Yr	NM
❏ 3587	Livin' for the Weekend/Stairway to Heaven	1976	$5
❏ 3524	Love Train/Who Am I	1973	$5
❏ B-50084	Lovin' You/Don't Let the Dream Get Away	1987	$3
❏ 3601	Message in Our Music/She's Only a Woman	1976	$5
❏ ZS4-02982	My Favorite Person/One by One	1982	$4
❏ ZS4-04069	Put Our Heads Together/Nice and Easy	1983	$4
❏ 3535	Put Your Hands Together/You Got Your Hooks in Me	1973	$5
❏ 3707	Sing a Happy Song/One in a Million (Girl)	1979	$5
❏ 3558	Sunshine (Part 1)/Sunshine (Part 2)	1974	$5
❏ 3531	Time to Get Down/Shiftless, Shady, Jealous Kind of People	1973	$5
❏ B-50021	What a Woman!/Love America	1985	$3
❏ 3631	Work On Me/Let's Spend Some Time Together	1977	$5
SARU			
❏ 1220	Shattered Man/La De Da (Means I'm Out to Get You)	1971	$6
TSOP			
❏ 3771	Christmas Ain't Christmas New Year's Ain't New Year's Without the One You Love/Just Can't Get Enough	1980	$5
❏ 4790	Girl, Don't Let It Get You Down/You're the Girl of My Dreams	1980	$4
❏ 4791	Once Is Not Enough/To Prove I Love You	1980	$4

O'KAYSIONS, THE

Number	Title	Yr	NM
ABC			
❏ 11094	Girl Watcher/Deal Me In	1968	$8
❏ 11153	Love Machine/Dedicated to the One I Love	1968	$6
❏ 11207	Twenty-Four Hours from Tulsa/Colors	1969	$6
COTILLION			
❏ 44089	Happiness/Watch Out Girl	1970	$5
❏ 44134	Life and Things/Travelin' Life	1971	$5
NORTH STATE			
❏ 1001	Girl Watcher/Deal Me In	1968	$125
❏ 1001 [PS]	Girl Watcher/Deal Me In	1968	$300

O'KEEFE, DANNY

Number	Title	Yr	NM
ATLANTIC			
❏ 2978	Angel, Spread Your Wings/Mad Ruth the Babe	1973	$5
❏ 3267	The Delta Queen/Quits	1975	$5
JERDEN			
❏ 806	Don't Wake Me in the Morning/That Old Sweet Song	1966	$12
PICCADILLY			
❏ 228	Don't Wake Me in the Morning/That Old Sweet Song	1967	$8
❏ 237	Today One Day Later/Baby	1967	$8
SIGNPOST			
❏ 70006	Good Time Charlie's Got the Blues/The Valentine Pieces	1972	$6

O'KEEFE, JOHNNY

Number	Title	Yr	NM
LIBERTY			
❏ 55262	Come On and Take My Hand/Don't You Know Little Baby	1960	$50
❏ 55228	She's My Baby/It's Too Late	1959	$40
❏ 55228 [PS]	She's My Baby/It's Too Late	1959	$60
❏ 55223	She's My Baby/Own True Self	1959	$50
MR. PEACOCK			
❏ 111	I'm Counting on You/The Steady Game	1962	$50
SIMS			
❏ 337	So Why/Cryin' Is the One Thing I Do Very Well	1968	$8

O'KEEFE, PAUL

Number	Title	Yr	NM
EVEREST			
❏ 19322	(Santa Claus) What Would You Like for Christmas?/A Baby in a Basket	1959	$15
❏ 19322 [PS]	(Santa Claus) What Would You Like for Christmas?/A Baby in a Basket	1959	$20

OL' 55 AND THE O.K. CHORALE

Number	Title	Yr	NM
MUSHROOM			
❏ 6587	(I Want A) Rockin' Christmas/Little Saint Nick	1976	$15

—*U.K. import*

OLA AND THE JANGLERS

GNP CRESCENDO

Number	Title	Yr	NM
❏ 432	California Sun/Baby, Baby, Baby	1970	$8
❏ 423	Let's Dance/Strolling Along	1969	$8
❏ 427	What a Way to Die/That's Why I Cry	1969	$8

LONDON

Number	Title	Yr	NM
❏ 20034	Eeny Meeny Miney Moe/I Can Wait	1967	$12

OLDFIELD, MIKE

VIRGIN

Number	Title	Yr	NM
❏ PR223 [DJ]	Hergest Ridge (two different edits?)	1974	$40
❏ 99402	Magic Touch/Wind Chimes Part 1	1987	$4
❏ 99402 [PS]	Magic Touch/Wind Chimes Part 1	1987	$4
❏ 9510	Portsmouth/Argiers	1975	$6
❏ 9505	Theme: From Ommadawn/On Horseback	1975	$6
❏ 55100	Tubular Bells (Now the Original Theme from the Movie "The Exorcist")/Tubular Bells	1973	$8
❏ PR199 [DJ]	Tubular Bells (same on both sides?)	1974	$30

VIRGIN/EPIC

Number	Title	Yr	NM
❏ 14-02877	Family Man/Mount Teidi	1982	$6

7-Inch Extended Plays

VIRGIN

Number	Title	Yr	NM
❏ PR196 [DJ]	Tubular Bells Excerpts	1974	$30

—Six different edits; promo only

OLDHAM, ANDREW

PARROT

Number	Title	Yr	NM
❏ 9745	I Get Around/Save It For Me	1965	$40
❏ 9684	Theme from The Dick Van Dyke Show/I'd Like to See Me on the "B" Side	1964	$40

OLENN, JOHNNY

ANTLER

Number	Title	Yr	NM
❏ 1105	Born Reckless/You, Loveable You	1959	$50
❏ 1101	My Sweetie Pie/For the First Time	1959	$50
❏ 4009	My Sweetie Pie/Smile	1957	$50
❏ 4018	The Magic Touch/Football Freddy	1957	$50

LIBERTY

Number	Title	Yr	NM
❏ 55053	Candy Kisses/My Idea of Love	1957	$30

PERSONALITY

Number	Title	Yr	NM
❏ 1002	Teenie/Devil Darling	1959	$60

TNT

Number	Title	Yr	NM
❏ 1016	Candy Kisses/Sally Let Your Bangs Hang Down	1955	$60
❏ 1018	I Ain't Gonna Cry No More/Blues Stay Away from Me	1955	$60

OLIVER

CREWE

Number	Title	Yr	NM
❏ 341	Angelica/Anna	1970	$6
❏ 346	I Can Remember/Where There's a Heartache	1970	$6
❏ 337	Sunday Mornin'/Let Me Kiss You with a Dream	1969	$6

JUBILEE

Number	Title	Yr	NM
❏ 5659	Good Morning Starshine/Can't You See	1969	$8

MCA

Number	Title	Yr	NM
❏ 52063	Don't Take Your Love Away/Everybody Wants to Be the Boss	1982	$3
❏ 52113	I Want Your Love, I Need Your Love/Make Up Your Mind	1982	$3

PARAMOUNT

Number	Title	Yr	NM
❏ 0198	Everybody I Love You/I Am Reaching	1973	$4

UNITED ARTISTS

Number	Title	Yr	NM
❏ 50762	Early Morning Rain/Catch Me If You Can	1971	$5
❏ 0130	Good Morning Starshine/Jean	1973	$4

—"Silver Spotlight Series" reissue

Number	Title	Yr	NM
❏ 50735	Sweet Kindness/Light the Way	1970	$5
❏ 50814	Walkin' Down the Line/Firelight	1971	$5
❏ 50862	Why You Been Gone So Long/Please	1971	$5

OLIVER AND THE TWISTERS

COLPIX

Number	Title	Yr	NM
❏ 615	Mother Goose Twist/Locomotion Twist	1961	$15
❏ 615 [PS]	Mother Goose Twist/Locomotion Twist	1961	$30

OLIVER, BIG DANNY

TREND

Number	Title	Yr	NM
❏ 016	Blues for the 49/In the Bottom of My Heart	1958	$50
❏ 012	Sapphire/I Wanna Go Steady with You	1958	$70

OLIVERS, THE

PHALANX

Number	Title	Yr	NM
❏ 1022	Bleecker Street/I Saw What You Did	1967	$70

RCA VICTOR

Number	Title	Yr	NM
❏ 47-9113	Bleecker Street/I Saw What You Did	1967	$30

OLIVES, THE

HIT

Number	Title	Yr	NM
❏ 306	How Can I Be Sure/Come Back When You Grow Up	1967	$8

—B-side by Jimmy Lewis and the Elfs

OLSEN, DOROTHY

RCA VICTOR

Number	Title	Yr	NM
❏ 47-7654	The Christmas Spirit/Little Donkey	1959	$20

OLYMPICS, THE

ARVEE

Number	Title	Yr	NM
❏ 562	(Baby) Hully Gully/Private Eye	1959	$30
❏ 5056	Baby It's Hot/The Scotch	1962	$20
❏ 6501	Big Boy Pete '65/Stay Where You Are	1965	$15
❏ 595	Big Boy Pete/The Slop	1960	$30
❏ 5020	Dance by the Light of the Moon/Dodge City	1960	$30
❏ 5051	Everybody Likes to Cha Cha Cha/The Twist	1962	$20
❏ 5023	Little Pedro/The Bullfight	1961	$30
❏ 5044	Mash Them 'Taters/The Stomp	1961	$30
❏ 5006	Shimmy Like Kate/Workin' Hard	1960	$30
❏ 5031	Stay Where You Are/Dooley	1961	$50
❏ 5073	What'd I Say (Part 1)/What'd I Say (Part 2)	1963	$20

DEMON

Number	Title	Yr	NM
❏ 1512	Dance with the Teacher/Everybody Needs Love	1958	$30
❏ 1508	Western Movies/Well!	1958	$40

DUO DISC

Number	Title	Yr	NM
❏ 104	The Boogler (Part 1)/The Boogler (Part 2)	1964	$15

JUBILEE

Number	Title	Yr	NM
❏ 5674	The Cartoon Song/Things That Make Me Laugh	1969	$8

LOMA

Number	Title	Yr	NM
❏ 2017	Baby I'm Yours/No More Will I Cry	1965	$12
❏ 2013	Good Lovin'/Olympic Shuffle	1965	$10
❏ 2010	I'm Comin' Home/Rainin' in My Heart	1965	$10

MGM

Number	Title	Yr	NM
❏ 14505	Worm in Your Wheatgerm/The Apartment	1973	$5

MIRWOOD

Number	Title	Yr	NM
❏ 5523	Baby Do the Philly Dog/Western Movies	1966	$8
❏ 5533	Big Boy Pete/(Baby) Hully Gully	1967	$8
❏ 5513	Mine Exclusively/Secret Agents	1966	$8
❏ 5525	The Bounce/The Duck	1966	$8
❏ 5529	The Same Old Thing/I'll Do a Little Bit More	1967	$8
❏ 5504	We Go Together (Pretty Baby)/Secret Agents	1966	$8

PARKWAY

Number	Title	Yr	NM
❏ 6003	Lookin' for a Love/Good Things	1968	$8

TITAN

Number	Title	Yr	NM
❏ 1718	The Chicken/Cool Short	1961	$30

TRI DISC

Number	Title	Yr	NM
❏ 110	Bounce Again/A New Dancin' Partner	1963	$20
❏ 107	Dancin' Holiday/Do the Slauson Shuffle	1963	$20
❏ 106	The Bounce/Fireworks	1963	$20
❏ 112	The Broken Hip/So Goodbye	1963	$20

WARNER BROS.

Number	Title	Yr	NM
❏ 7369	Girl, You're My Kind of People/Please, Please, Please	1970	$6

7-Inch Extended Plays

ARVEE

Number	Title	Yr	NM
❏ 423	(contents unknown)	1960	$250
❏ 423 [PS]	Doin' the Hully Gully	1960	$250

OMAR AND THE HOWLERS

COLUMBIA

Number	Title	Yr	NM
❏ 38-07380	Dancing in the Canebrake/You Ain't Foolin' Nobody	1987	$4

OMEGAS, THE (1)

DECCA

Number	Title	Yr	NM
❏ 31138	Falling in Love/No One Will Ever Know	1960	$30
❏ 31094	So How Come (No One Loves Me)/Study Hall	1960	$30
❏ 31008	When You Touch Me/Froze	1959	$30

GROOVE

Number	Title	Yr	NM
❏ 4	I Wanna Go Home/Midnight Run	1961	$20

OMEGAS, THE (2)

UNITED ARTISTS

Number	Title	Yr	NM
❏ 50247	I Can't Believe/Mr. Yates	1968	$40

100 PROOF AGED IN SOUL

HOT WAX

Number	Title	Yr	NM
❏ 7108	90 Day Freeze (On Her Love)/Not Enough Love to Satisfy	1971	$6
❏ 7206	Don't Scratch/If I Could See the Light in the Window	1972	$6
❏ 7104	Driveway/Love Is Sweeter	1971	$6
❏ 7202	Everything Good Is Bad/I'd Rather Fight Than Switch	1972	$6
❏ 7009	One Man's Leftovers (Is Another Man's Feast)/If I Could See the Light in the Window	1970	$6
❏ 7004	Somebody's Been Sleeping/I've Come to Save You	1970	$6
❏ 6904	Too Many Cooks (Spoil the Soup)/Not Enough Love to Satisfy	1969	$15

—First pressings as "Aged in Soul

Number	Title	Yr	NM
❏ 6904	Too Many Cooks (Spoil the Soup)/Not Enough Love to Satisfy	1969	$6

—Later pressings as "100 Proof Aged in Soul

O'NEAL, COLEMAN

CHANCELLOR

Number	Title	Yr	NM
❏ 108	Mr. Heartache, Move On/Make Him Know	1962	$15

O'NEAL, POLLY

COLUMBIA

Number	Title	Yr	NM
❏ 4-21331	I've Been Cryin'/That New Girl Down the Street	1954	$30

ONO, YOKO

Also see JOHN LENNON.

APPLE

Number	Title	Yr	NM
❏ 1859	Death of Samantha/Yang Yang	1973	$20
❏ GM/OYB-1 [DJ]	Greenfield Morning/Open Your Box	1971	$2000

—Exactly six copies made for the personal use of Yoko Ono.

Number	Title	Yr	NM
❏ 1839	Mrs. Lennon/Midsummer New York	1971	$12

—As "Yoko Ono/Plastic Ono Band

Number	Title	Yr	NM
❏ 1867	Woman Power/Men, Men, Men	1973	$20

GEFFEN

Number	Title	Yr	NM
❏ 49849	Goodbye Sadness/I Don't Know Why	1981	$5
❏ PRO-S-935 [DJ]	Walking on Thin Ice (3:23) (5:58)	1981	$15
❏ 49683	Walking on Thin Ice/It Happened	1981	$5
❏ 49683 [PS]	Walking on Thin Ice/It Happened	1981	$5

—Includes picture sleeve and lyric insert

POLYDOR

Number	Title	Yr	NM
❏ 883455-7	Hell in Paradise/(Instrumental)	1985	$4
❏ 883455-7 [PS]	Hell in Paradise/(Instrumental)	1985	$4
❏ 2224	My Man/Let the Tears Dry	1982	$4
❏ 2224 [PS]	My Man/Let the Tears Dry	1982	$4

OPALS, THE (1)
APOLLO
Number	Title	Yr	NM
462	My Heart's Desire/Oh But She Did	1954	$200

— Original with flat (non-glossy) label

Number	Title	Yr	NM
462	My Heart's Desire/Oh But She Did	1958	$50

— Reissue with glossy label

OPALS, THE (2)
BELTONE
Number	Title	Yr	NM
2025	Love/Two-Sided Love	1962	$30

OPALS, THE (3)
OKEH
Number	Title	Yr	NM
7188	Does It Matter/Tender Lover	1964	$30
7224	I'm So Afraid/Restless Lover	1965	$30

ORANGE COLORED SKY
UNI
Number	Title	Yr	NM
55115	Happiness Is/Another Sky	1969	$15
55088	Orange Colored Sky/The Shadow of Summer	1968	$15
55156	The Sun and I/Sweet Potato	1969	$15

ORBISON, ROY
ASYLUM
Number	Title	Yr	NM
46541	Poor Baby/Lay It Down	1979	$5
46048	Tears/Easy Way Out	1979	$5

JE-WEL
Number	Title	Yr	NM
101	Ooby Dooby/Tryin' to Get to You	1956	$4000

— As "The Teen Kings"; with "Vocal: Roy Orbison" credit (spelled correctly). VG 1500; VG+ 2750

Number	Title	Yr	NM
101	Ooby Dooby/Tryin' to Get to You	1956	$4000

— As "The Teen Kings"; with "Vocal: Roy Oribson" credit (spelled incorrectly). VG 1500 ; VG+ 2750

MERCURY
Number	Title	Yr	NM
73652	Hung Up on You/Spanish Nights	1975	$6
73705	It's Lonely/Still	1975	$6
73610	Sweet Mama Blue/Heartache	1974	$8

MGM
Number	Title	Yr	NM
13757	Breakin' Up Is Breakin' My Heart/Too Soon to Know	1967	$20

— Part of Celebrity Scene CS9-5

Number	Title	Yr	NM
13446	Breakin' Up Is Breakin' My Heart/Wait	1966	$10
13446 [PS]	Breakin' Up Is Breakin' My Heart/Wait	1966	$30
CS9-5	Celebrity Scene: Roy Orbison	1967	$125

— Box set of five singles (13756-13760). Price includes box, all 5 singles, jukebox title strips, bio. Records are sometimes found by themselves, so they are also listed separately.

Number	Title	Yr	NM
14358	Changes/God Loves You	1972	$10
14293	Close Again/Last Night	1971	$10
13634	Communication Breakdown/Going Back to Gloria	1966	$10
13410	Crawling Back/If You Can't Say Something Nice	1965	$12
13410 [PS]	Crawling Back/If You Can't Say Something Nice	1965	$30
13764	Cry Softly Lonely One/Pistolero	1967	$12
13764 [PS]	Cry Softly Lonely One/Pistolero	1967	$30
13950	Flowers/Walk On	1968	$10
13991	Heartache/Sugar Man	1968	$12
14105	How Do You Start Over/She Cheats on Me	1970	$10
14441	I Can Read Between the Lines/Memphis, Tennessee	1972	$10
14626	I Wanna Live/You Lay So Easy on My Mind	1973	$10
14079	Penny Arcade/Tennessee Own My Soul	1969	$10
13817	She/Here Comes the Rain Baby	1967	$10
13889	Shy Away/Born to Be Loved by You	1968	$10
13685	So Good/Memories	1967	$12
14039	Southbound Jericho Parkway/My Friend	1969	$10
14121	So Young/If I Had a Woman Like You	1970	$12
13759	Sweet Dreams/Going Back to Gloria	1967	$20

— Part of Celebrity Scene CS9-5

Number	Title	Yr	NM
13549	Too Soon to Know/You'll Never Be Sixteen Again	1966	$10
13549 [PS]	Too Soon to Know/You'll Never Be Sixteen Again	1966	$125
13498	Twinkle Toes/Where Is Tomorrow	1966	$10
13498 [PS]	Twinkle Toes/Where Is Tomorrow	1966	$30
13758	Twinkle Toes/Where Is Tomorrow?	1967	$20

— Part of Celebrity Scene CS9-5

MONUMENT
Number	Title	Yr	NM
8690	Belinda/All These Chains	1976	$5
425	Blue Angel/Today's Teardrops	1960	$30
447	Crying/Candy Man	1961	$30
447 [PS]	Crying/Candy Man	1961	$50
456	Dream Baby (How Long Must I Dream)/The Actress	1962	$30
456 [PS]	Dream Baby (How Long Must I Dream)/The Actress	1962	$50
45-215	Drifting Away/Under Suspicion	1977	$5
815	Falling/Distant Drums	1963	$30
815 [PS]	Falling/Distant Drums	1963	$60
873	Goodnight/Only with You	1965	$20
45-200	(I'm a) Southern Man/Born to Love Me	1976	$5
433	I'm Hurtin'/I Can't Stop Loving You	1960	$30
433 [PS]	I'm Hurtin'/I Can't Stop Loving You	1960	$120
806	In Dreams/Shahdaroba	1963	$30
806 [PS]	In Dreams/Shahdaroba	1963	$50
837	It's Over/Indian Wedding	1964	$30
837 [PS]	It's Over/Indian Wedding	1964	$50
939	Lana/Our Summer Song	1966	$20
467	Leah/Workin' for the Man	1962	$30
467 [PS]	Leah/Workin' for the Man	1962	$50
906	Let the Good Times Roll/Distant Drums	1965	$20
824	Mean Woman Blues/Blue Bayou	1963	$30
851	Oh Pretty Woman/Yo Te Amo Maria	1964	$30

— Revised title

Number	Title	Yr	NM
421	Only the Lonely (Know the Way I Feel)/Here Comes That Song Again	1960	$30
409	Paper Boy/With the Bug	1959	$100

— White label with vertical lines

Number	Title	Yr	NM
830	Pretty Paper/Beautiful Dreamer	1963	$30
1936	Pretty Paper/Beautiful Dreamer	1976	$4

— Golden Series" reissue

Number	Title	Yr	NM
851	Pretty Woman/Yo Te Amo Maria	1964	$40

— Original title

Number	Title	Yr	NM
891	(Say) You're My Girl/Sleepy Hollow	1965	$20
461	The Crowd/Mama	1962	$30
461 [PS]	The Crowd/Mama	1962	$50

RCA VICTOR
Number	Title	Yr	NM
47-7447	Almost Eighteen/Julie	1959	$50
47-7381	Sweet and Innocent/Seems to Me	1958	$50

SUN
Number	Title	Yr	NM
284	Chicken Hearted/I Like Love	1958	$60
265	Devil Doll/Sweet and Easy to Love	1957	$100
353	Devil Doll/Sweet and Easy to Love	1960	$250
242	Ooby Dooby/Go! Go! Go!	1956	$125

VIRGIN
Number	Title	Yr	NM
99202	California Blue/In Dreams	1989	$3
99202 [PS]	California Blue/In Dreams	1989	$3
99388	Crying/Falling	1988	$3

— A-side with k.d. lang

Number	Title	Yr	NM
99388 [PS]	Crying/Falling	1988	$3
99434	In Dreams/Leah	1987	$3
99434 [PS]	In Dreams/Leah	1987	$4
99159	Oh Pretty Woman/Claudette	1989	$3
99159 [PS]	Oh Pretty Woman/Claudette	1989	$3
99227	She's a Mystery to Me/Dream Baby	1989	$3
99227 [PS]	She's a Mystery to Me/Dream Baby	1989	$3

WARNER BROS.
Number	Title	Yr	NM
49262	That Lovin' You Feeling Again/Lola	1980	$5

— A-side with Emmylou Harris; B-side by Craig Hundley

7-Inch Extended Plays
MONUMENT
Number	Title	Yr	NM
MSP-2	Crying/Our Summer Song/Let's Make a Memory//Lana/Loneliness/Night Life	1962	$125

— Probably a jukebox single; small hole, plays at 33 1/3 rpm; picture sleeve is unconfirmed

Number	Title	Yr	NM
MSP-003	In Dreams/Lonely Wine/Shadharoba//Dream/Blue Bayou/Gigolette (They Call You)	1963	$60

— Stereo jukebox issue; small hole, plays at 33 1/3 rpm

Number	Title	Yr	NM
SSP-512	Oh, Pretty Woman/Dance//Let the Good Times Roll//(I Get So) Sentimental/Wedding Day/I'd Be a Legend in My Time	1965	$50

— Jukebox issue; small hole, plays at 33 1/3 rpm

Number	Title	Yr	NM
SSP-512 [PS]	Orbisongs, Volume One	1965	$50

ORBITS, THE
ARGO
Number	Title	Yr	NM
5286	Who Are You/Mr. Bad Luck	1958	$50

FLAIR-X
Number	Title	Yr	NM
5000	Message of Love/I Really Do	1956	$40

ORCHESTRAL MANOEUVRES IN THE DARK
A&M
Number	Title	Yr	NM
3002	Dreaming/Satellite	1988	$3
3002 [PS]	Dreaming/Satellite	1988	$3
2872	(Forever) Live and Die/This Town	1986	$5

— White label stock copy

Number	Title	Yr	NM
2872	(Forever) Live and Die/This Town	1986	$3

— Black label

Number	Title	Yr	NM
2872 [PS]	(Forever) Live and Die/This Town	1986	$3

— The same sleeve was used with both stock pressings

Number	Title	Yr	NM
2811 [PS]	If You Leave/La Femme Accident	1986	$5
2811	If You Leave/La Femme Accident (2:42)	1986	$5
2811	If You Leave/La Femme Accident (6:15)	1986	$3
2671	Locomotion/Her Body in My Soul	1984	$4
2671 [PS]	Locomotion/Her Body in My Soul	1984	$4
2794	Secret/Firegun	1985	$3
2794 [PS]	Secret/Firegun	1985	$3
1209	Secret/Telegraph (Live)	1988	$3
1209 [PS]	Secret/Telegraph (Live)	1988	$3
2746	So in Love/Concrete Hands	1985	$3
2746 [PS]	So in Love/Concrete Hands	1985	$3
2897	We Love You/(Dub)	1986	$5
2897 [PS]	We Love You/(Dub)	1986	$20

VIRGIN/EPIC
Number	Title	Yr	NM
14-02766	Souvenir/New Stone Age	1982	$5
34-03891	Telegraph/This Is Helena	1983	$6

ORCHIDS, THE (1)
COLUMBIA
Number	Title	Yr	NM
43175	Christmas Is the Time to Be With Your Baby/It Doesn't Matter	1964	$30
43066	Tell Me a Story/From Bad to Worse	1964	$30
42913	That Boy Is Messin' Up My Mind/Harlem Tango	1963	$30

ORCHIDS, THE (2)
HARLOW
Number	Title	Yr	NM
101	I Don't Think You Missed Me/We're in Love	1962	$30

ORCHIDS, THE (3)
KING
Number	Title	Yr	NM
4663	I've Been a Fool from the Start/Beginning to Miss You	1953	$400
4661	Oh Why/All Night Baby	1953	$400

PARROT
Number	Title	Yr	NM
819	I Can't Refuse/You Said You Loved Me	1955	$250

ORCHIDS, THE (U)
ROULETTE
Number	Title	Yr	NM
4633	Good Good Time/Love Is What You Make It	1965	$15
4412	Pony Walk/Good Time Stomp	1962	$30

WALL
Number	Title	Yr	NM
549	Soft Shadows/Good Gully	1961	$30

ORGAN GRINDERS, THE
SMASH
Number	Title	Yr	NM
2242	Babylon/Precious Time	1969	$12

ORIGINAL CASTE, THE
DOT
Number	Title	Yr	NM
17138	Snakes and Ladders/I'm So Much in Love	1968	$20

T-A
Number	Title	Yr	NM
192	Mr. Monday/Highway	1970	$10
186	One Tin Soldier/Live for Tomorrow	1969	$15
186 [PS]	One Tin Soldier/Live for Tomorrow	1969	$15
211	Sault Ste. Marie/When Love Is Near	1971	$10
204	Sweet Chicago/Ain't That Tellin' You People	1970	$10

ORIGINAL CASUALS, THE
BACK BEAT
Number	Title	Yr	NM
503	So Tough/I Love My Darling	1958	$50

— Original pressings by "The Casuals

Number	Title	Yr	NM
503	So Tough/I Love My Darling	1958	$30
514	Three Kisses Past Midnight/It's Been a Long Time	1958	$30

ORIGINALS, THE (1)

FANTASY

Number	Title	Yr	NM
❑ 847	Blue Moon/Ladies (We Need You)	1979	$5
❑ 820	Take This Love/Ladies (We Need You)	1978	$5

MOTOWN

Number	Title	Yr	NM
❑ 1370	50 Years/Financial Affair	1975	$6
❑ 1379	Everybody's Got to Do Something/(Instrumental)	1975	$6
❑ 1355	Good Lovin' Is Just a Dime Away/Nothing Can Take the Place (Of Your Love)	1975	$6

PHASE II

Number	Title	Yr	NM
❑ WS8-02061	Baby I'm for Real/Share Your Love with Me	1981	$4
❑ ZS5-02724	Baby I'm for Real/ The Magic Is You	1982	$4

—As "Hank Dixon and the Originals

Number	Title	Yr	NM
❑ WS8-02147	The Magic Is You/ Let Me Dance	1981	$4
❑ 5653	Waitin' on a Letter/Mr. Postman//(B-side unknown)	1981	$5

SOUL

Number	Title	Yr	NM
❑ 35066	Baby I'm for Real/The Moment of Truth	1969	$8
❑ 35102	Be My Love/Endlessly Love	1973	$6
❑ 35121 [DJ]	Call On Your Six Million Dollar Man (mono/stereo)	1977	$6
❑ 35119	Down to Love Town/Just to Be Closer to You	1976	$6
❑ 35109	First Lady (Sweet Mother's Love)/There's a Chance When You Love, You Love	1973	$6
❑ 35113	Game Called Love/Ooh You Put a Spell on Me	1974	$6
❑ 35079	God Bless Whoever Sent You/Desperate Young Man	1970	$8
❑ 35029	Goodnight Irene/Need Your Loving (Want It Back)	1967	$15
❑ 35061	Green Grow the Lilacs/ You're the One	1969	$15
❑ 35093	I'm Someone Who Cares/ Once I Have You	1972	$6
❑ 35112	Supernatural Voodoo Woman (Part 1)/ Supernatural Voodoo Woman (Part 2)	1974	$6
❑ 35069	The Bells/I'll Wait for You	1970	$8
❑ 35117	Touch/Ooh You Put a Spell on Me	1975	$6
❑ 35074	We Can Make It Baby/I Like Your Style	1970	$8
❑ 35074	We Can Make It/I Like Your Style	1970	$15
❑ 35056	We've Got a Way Out Love/You're the One	1969	$15

ORIGINALS, THE (2)

DIAMOND

Number	Title	Yr	NM
❑ 102	At Times Like These/Gimme a Little Kiss, Will Ya, Huh?	1961	$50
❑ 116	Summer Schoo/You and I	1962	$50

ORIGINALS, THE (3)

JACKPOT

Number	Title	Yr	NM
❑ 48012	Anna/Sleepless Nights	1959	$40
❑ 48007	The Whip/The Blue Kat	1959	$40

ORIGINALS, THE (4)

ORIGINAL SOUND

Number	Title	Yr	NM
❑ 13	Little Lonely Girl/I Still Love You	1960	$30

—As "Tony Allan and the Originals

Number	Title	Yr	NM
❑ 10	Wishing Star/Let Me Hear You Say Yeah	1960	$40

ORIGINALS, THE (U)

7-Inch Extended Plays

SOMERSET

Number	Title	Yr	NM
❑ EX-6000	Lazy Mary/Billy// (B-side unknown)	1958	$25

ORIOLES, THE

ABNER

Number	Title	Yr	NM
❑ 1016	Sugar Girl/Didn't I Say	1958	$70

CHARLIE PARKER

Number	Title	Yr	NM
❑ 213	Back to the Chapel Again/(It's Gonna Be a) Lonely Christmas	1962	$30
❑ 219	I Miss You So/Hey! Little Woman	1963	$20
❑ 212	In the Chapel in the Moonlight/Hey! Little Woman	1962	$30
❑ 215	It's Too Soon to Know/I Miss You So	1963	$20
❑ 211	Secret Love/The Wobble	1962	$30
❑ 214	What Are You Doing New Year's Eve/Don't Mess Around with My Love	1962	$30
❑ 216	Write and Tell Me Why/ Don't Tell Her What Happens to Me	1963	$20

JUBILEE

Number	Title	Yr	NM
❑ 5231	Angel/Don't Go to Strangers	1956	$70
❑ 5025	At Night/Every Dog-Gone Time	1951	$1000
❑ 5065	Baby, Please Don't Go/ Don't Tell Her What's Happened to Me	1951	$2000

—Red vinyl. VG 1,000; VG+ 1,500

Number	Title	Yr	NM
❑ 5065	Baby, Please Don't Go/ Don't Tell Her What's Happened to Me	1951	$600

—Black vinyl

Number	Title	Yr	NM
❑ 5115	Bad Little Girl/Dem Days	1953	$400
❑ 5084	Barfly/Getting Tired, Tired, Tired	1952	$400
❑ 5384	Come On Home/The First of Summer	1960	$20

—As "Sonny Til and the Orioles

Number	Title	Yr	NM
❑ 5122	Crying in the Chapel/Don't You Think I Ought to Know	1953	$100
❑ 6001	Crying in the Chapel/ Forgive and Forget	1959	$20

—As "Sonny Til and the Orioles

Number	Title	Yr	NM
❑ 5092	Don't Cry Baby/ See See Rider	1952	$1500

—Red vinyl

Number	Title	Yr	NM
❑ 5092	Don't Cry Baby/ See See Rider	1952	$400
❑ 5120	I Cover the Waterfront/ One More Time	1953	$1200

—Red vinyl

Number	Title	Yr	NM
❑ 5120	I Cover the Waterfront/ One More Time	1953	$400
❑ 5040	I Cross My Fingers/Can't Seem to Laugh Anymore	1951	$2000
❑ 5161	If You Believe/Longing	1954	$60
❑ 5177	I Love You Mostly/ Fair Exchange	1955	$50
❑ 5107	I Miss You So/Till Then	1952	$1500

—Red vinyl

Number	Title	Yr	NM
❑ 5107	I Miss You So/Till Then	1952	$400
❑ 5107	I Miss You So/Till Then	1963	$30

—Reissue, credited to "Sonny Til and the Orioles

Number	Title	Yr	NM
❑ 5051	I Miss You So/You Are My First Love	1951	$2000

—Red vinyl. VG 1000; VG+ 1500

Number	Title	Yr	NM
❑ 5051	I Miss You So/You Are My First Love	1951	$800
❑ 5061	I'm Just a Fool in Love/ Hold Me, Squeeze Me	1951	$800
❑ 5189	I Need You Baby/The Good Lord Will Smile	1955	$50
❑ 5154	In the Chapel in the Moonlight/Thank the Lord, Thank the Lord	1954	$60
❑ 5127	In the Mission of St. Augustine/Write and Tell Me Why	1953	$60
❑ 5082	It's All Over Because We're Through/Waiting	1952	$500
❑ 5000	It's Too Soon to Know/ Barbara Lee	1951	$4000
❑ 5143	Maybe You'll Be There/ Drowining Every Hope I Ever Had	1954	$100
❑ 5045	Oh Holy Night/The Lord's Prayer	1951	$600

—Original on blue label

Number	Title	Yr	NM
❑ 5045 [PS]	Oh Holy Night/The Lord's Prayer	1954	$600
❑ 5055	Pal of Mine/Happy Go Lucky Local Blues	1951	$800
❑ 5221	Please Sing My Blues Tonight/Moody Over You	1955	$50
❑ 5076	Proud of You/You Never Cared for Me	1952	$500
❑ 5137	Secret Love/Don't Go to Strangers	1954	$60
❑ 5016	So Much/Forgive and Forget	1951	$2000
❑ 5108	Teardrops on My Pillow/ Hold Me, Thrill Me, Kiss Me	1953	$1500

—Red vinyl

Number	Title	Yr	NM
❑ 5108	Teardrops on My Pillow/ Hold Me, Thrill Me, Kiss Me	1953	$400
❑ 5363	Tell Me So/At Night	1959	$20

—As "Sonny Til and the Orioles

Number	Title	Yr	NM
❑ 5005	Tell Me So/Deacon Jones	1951	$2000
❑ 5134	There's No One But You/Robe of Calvary	1954	$60
❑ 5074	Trust in Me/Shrimp Boats	1952	$500
❑ 5017	What Are You Doing New Year's Eve/Lonely Christmas	1951	$800
❑ 5017 [PS]	What Are You Doing New Year's Eve/Lonely Christmas	1954	$1000
❑ 5071	When You're Not Around/ How Blind Can You Be	1952	$600

VEE JAY

Number	Title	Yr	NM
❑ 228	For All We Know/Never Leave Me Baby	1956	$40
❑ 196	I Just Got Lucky/ Happy 'Til the Letter	1956	$40
❑ 244	Sugar Girl/Didn't I Say	1957	$50

VIRGO

Number	Title	Yr	NM
❑ 6017	What Are You Doing New Year's Eve/ Crying in the Chapel	1972	$4

7-Inch Extended Plays

JUBILEE

Number	Title	Yr	NM
❑ 5000 [PS]	The Orioles Sing	1954	$1000
❑ 5000	Too Soon to Know/Forgive and Forget//Tell Me So/At Night	1954	$1000

ORION

KRISTAL

Number	Title	Yr	NM
❑ 2338	100 Pounds of Clay/ Because He Lived	1986	$4
❑ 2292/2308	I'm Saving Up My Pennies/I'm Starting Over	1985	$4

SUN

Number	Title	Yr	NM
❑ 1156	Am I That Easy to Forget/Crazy Arms	1980	$4
❑ 1156 [DJ]	Am I That Easy to Forget (same on both sides)	1980	$10

—Yellow vinyl promo

Number	Title	Yr	NM
❑ 1172	Baby Please Say Yes/Feelings	1982	$4
❑ 1151	Be-Bop-a-Lula/The Breakup	1980	$4

—A-side with Jerry Lee Lewis; B-side with Charlie Rich

Number	Title	Yr	NM
❑ 1147	Before the Next Teardrop Falls/Washing Machine	1979	$4
❑ 1165	Born/If I Can't Have You	1981	$4
❑ 1165 [DJ]	Born (same on both sides)	1981	$10

—Yellow vinyl promo

Number	Title	Yr	NM
❑ 1162	Crazy Little Thing Called Love/Matchbox	1981	$4
❑ 1142	Honey/Ebony Eyes	1979	$4
❑ 1175	Honky Tonk Heaven/ Morning, Noon and Night	1982	$4
❑ 1175 [DJ]	Honky Tonk Heaven (same on both sides)	1982	$12

—Yellow vinyl promo

Number	Title	Yr	NM
❑ 1152 [DJ]	It Ain't No Mystery (same on both sides)	1980	$10

—Yellow vinyl promo

Number	Title	Yr	NM
❑ 1152	It Ain't No Mystery/ Stranger in My Place	1980	$4
❑ 1170	Some You Win, Some You Lose/Ain't No Good	1981	$4
❑ 1170 [DJ]	Some You Win, Some You Lose (same on both sides)	1981	$12

—Yellow vinyl promo

Number	Title	Yr	NM
❑ 1153	Texas Tea/Faded Love	1980	$4
❑ 1153 [DJ]	Texas Tea (same on both sides)	1980	$10

—Yellow vinyl promo

7-Inch Extended Plays

Number	Title	Yr	NM
❑ 1152 [DJ]	Stranger in My Place Greetings: Wedding Anniversary/Good Music/Great Station//Favorite Station/Best Music/Birthday	1981	$50

—Came with insert but no cover

ORION THE HUNTER

With Barry Goudreau, formerly of BOSTON.

PORTRAIT

Number	Title	Yr	NM
❑ 37-04483	So You Ran/Fast Talk	1984	$5

ORLANDO, TONY

ATCO

Number	Title	Yr	NM
❑ 6376	Think Before You Act/She Loves Me (For What I Am)	1965	$10

CAMEO

Number	Title	Yr	NM
❑ 471	Sweet Sweet/Manuelito (Little Manuel	1967	$10

CASABLANCA

Number	Title	Yr	NM
❑ 2249	Pullin' Together/She Always Knew	1980	$4
❑ 2229	San Pedros Children/ High Steppin'	1979	$4
❑ 991	Sweets for My Sweet/ High Steppin'	1979	$4
❑ 967	They're Playing Our Song (Medley)/Moonlight	1979	$4

EPIC

Number	Title	Yr	NM
❑ 9519	At the Edge of Tears/Chills	1962	$15
❑ 9519 [PS]	At the Edge of Tears/Chills	1962	$30
❑ 9562	Beautiful Dreamer/ The Loneliest	1962	$12
❑ 9452	Bless You/Am I the Guy	1961	$20
❑ 9452 [PS]	Bless You/Am I the Guy	1961	$30
❑ 9441	Halfway to Paradise/ Lonely Tomorrows	1961	$20
❑ 9441 [PS]	Halfway to Paradise/ Lonely Tomorrows	1961	$30
❑ 9476	Hapy Times (Are Here to Stay)/Lonely Am I	1961	$15
❑ 9476 [PS]	Hapy Times (Are Here to Stay)/Lonely Am I	1961	$30
❑ 9502	I'd Never Find Another You/Love on Your Lips	1962	$15
❑ 9622	I'll Be There/What Am I Gonna Do	1963	$10
❑ 9491	My Baby's a Starnger/ Talkin' About You	1962	$15
❑ 9491 [PS]	My Baby's a Starnger/ Talkin' About You	1962	$30
❑ 9668	She Doesn't Know It/ Tell Me What I Can Do	1964	$10

ORLANDO, TONY (2)

MILO

Number	Title	Yr	NM
❏ 101	Ding Dong/You and Only You	1959	$125

ORLEANS

ABC

Number	Title	Yr	NM
❏ 11420	If/Stoned	1974	$5
❏ 11408	Please Be There/Mountains	1973	$5

ASYLUM

Number	Title	Yr	NM
❏ 45447	Business As Usual/Time Passes On	1977	$4
❏ 45261	Dance with Me/Ending of a Song	1975	$5
❏ 45243	Let There Be Music/Give One Heart	1975	$4
❏ 45336	Still the One/Siam Sam	1976	$5

— Clouds label

Number	Title	Yr	NM
❏ 45336	Still the One/Siam Sam	1976	$6

— Dark blue label with white stylized "a" at top

Number	Title	Yr	NM
❏ 45391	The Bum/Spring Fever	1977	$4

ATLANTIC AMERICA

Number	Title	Yr	NM
❏ 99981	One of a Kind/Beatin' Around the Bush	1982	$4

INFINITY

Number	Title	Yr	NM
❏ 50017	Don't Throw Our Love Away/The Flame and the Moth	1979	$4
❏ 50036	Forever/Keep On Rollin'	1979	$4
❏ 50006	Love Takes Time/Isn't It Easy	1979	$4

MCA

Number	Title	Yr	NM
❏ 41228	Change Your Mind/When Are You Coming Home	1980	$4
❏ 52909	Grown-Up Children/On Hold	1986	$3
❏ 52862	Lady Liberty/On Hold	1986	$3

ORLONS, THE

ABC

Number	Title	Yr	NM
❏ 10894	Everything/Keep Your Hands Off My Baby	1967	$10

CALLA

Number	Title	Yr	NM
❏ 113	Spinnin' Top/Anyone Who Had a Heart	1966	$10

CAMEO

Number	Title	Yr	NM
❏ 105 [DJ]	Big Girls Don't Cry/Pop Pop Pop-Pie	1962	$50

— Yellow label, black print, promo only

Number	Title	Yr	NM
❏ 287	Bon-Doo-Wah/Don't Throw Your Love Away	1963	$20
❏ 287 [PS]	Bon-Doo-Wah/Don't Throw Your Love Away	1963	$40
❏ 352	Come On Down Baby/I Ain't Coming Back	1965	$15
❏ 273	Cross Fire!/It's No Big Thing	1963	$30
❏ 273 [PS]	Cross Fire!/It's No Big Thing	1963	$40
❏ 231	Don't Hang Up/The Conservative	1962	$30
❏ 231 [PS]	Don't Hang Up/The Conservative	1962	$50
❏ 372	Don't You Want My Lovin'/I Can't Take It	1965	$15
❏ 346	I Ain't Coming Back/Envy (In My Eyes)	1965	$15
❏ 198	I'll Be True/Heart Darling Angel	1961	$60
❏ 211	Mr. 21/Please Let It Be Me	1961	$60
❏ 295	Shimmy Shimmy/Everything Nice	1964	$20
❏ 295 [PS]	Shimmy Shimmy/Everything Nice	1964	$30
❏ 243	South Street/Them Terrible Boots	1963	$30
❏ 243 [PS]	South Street/Them Terrible Boots	1963	$50
❏ 218	The Wah-Watusi/Holiday Hill	1962	$30

ORPHEUS

BELL

Number	Title	Yr	NM
❏ 45128	Big Green Pearl/Sweet Life	1971	$5

MGM

Number	Title	Yr	NM
❏ 14022	Brown Arms in Houston/I Can Make the Sun Rise	1969	$6
❏ 14022 [PS]	Brown Arms in Houston/I Can Make the Sun Rise	1969	$10
❏ 13882	Can't Find the Time/Lesley's Girl	1967	$10

— Originals have black labels

Number	Title	Yr	NM
❏ 13882	Can't Find the Time/Lesley's Girl	1969	$6

— Reissues (same number) have blue and gold labels

Number	Title	Yr	NM
❏ 13947	I've Never Seen Love Like This/Congress Alley	1968	$6

RED BIRD

Number	Title	Yr	NM
❏ Oct-0041	My Life/Music Minus Orpheus	1965	$20

ORR, CHERYL

SUMMIT

Number	Title	Yr	NM
❏ 107	What I Saw on Christmas Night/Why Does My Daddy Come Here	1958	$60

ORR, J.D.

SUMMIT

Number	Title	Yr	NM
❏ 105	Hula-Hoop Boogie/Lonesome Hearted Blues	1958	$400

ORRELL, DAVID

FELSTED

Number	Title	Yr	NM
❏ 8515	Be My Baby/You're the One	1958	$100

ORSI, PHIL, AND THE LITTLE KINGS

LUCKY

Number	Title	Yr	NM
❏ 1009	Come On Everybody/Oh My Darling	1963	$80
❏ 1015	Don't You Just Know It/(B-side unknown)	1964	$30

U.S.A.

Number	Title	Yr	NM
❏ 841	Sorry (I Ran All the Way Home)/Whoever He May Be	1965	$30
❏ 837	Stay/Whoever He May Be	1965	$30

OSBORNE, ARTHUR

BRUNSWICK

Number	Title	Yr	NM
❏ 55068	Hey Ruby/Don't Give Me Heartaches	1958	$70

OSBORNE BROTHERS, THE

CMH

Number	Title	Yr	NM
❏ 1524	I Can Hear Kentucky Calling Me/Shawnee	1980	$4
❏ 1522	Shackles and Chains/Midnight Flyer	1979	$4

— With Mac Wiseman

DECCA

Number	Title	Yr	NM
❏ 31595	Bluegrass Express/Cuckoo Bird	1964	$8
❏ 31655	Charlie Cotton/This Heart of Mine	1964	$8
❏ 32325	Cut the Cornbread, Mama/If I Could Count on You	1968	$8
❏ 32794	Georgia Pineywoods/Searching for Yesterday	1971	$8
❏ 31977	Hard Times/A World of Unwanted	1966	$8
❏ 31751	Hey, Hey, Bartender/Me and My Old Banjo	1965	$8
❏ 32680	Listen to the Rain/Midnight Angel	1970	$8
❏ 31823	Lonesome Day/I'll Be Alright Tomorrow	1965	$8
❏ 33028	Midnight Flyer/Tears Will Kiss the Morning Dew	1972	$8
❏ 32979	Miss You Mississippi/Today I Started Loving You Again	1972	$8
❏ 32864	Muddy Bottom/Beneath Still Waters	1971	$8
❏ 32746	My Old Kentucky Home (Turpentine and Dandelion Wine)/No Good Son of a Gun	1970	$8
❏ 32382	Son of a Sawmill Man/That Was Yesterday	1968	$8
❏ 32908	Take Me Home, Country Roads/Tears Are No Stranger	1971	$8
❏ 31546	Take This Hammer/Don't Even Look at Me	1963	$8
❏ 32516	Tennessee Hound Dog/Thanks for All the Yesterdays	1969	$8
❏ 32942	Windy City/Shelly's Winter Love	1972	$8
❏ 32451	Working Man/World of Forgotten	1969	$8

MCA

Number	Title	Yr	NM
❏ 40226	Bluegrass Melodies/The Seventh of December	1974	$4
❏ 40113	Blue Heartache/You're Heavy on My Mind	1973	$4
❏ 40509	Don't Let Smokey Mountain Smoke Get In Your Eyes/Born a Ramblin' Man	1976	$4
❏ 40346	El Rancho/A Heartache Looking for a Home	1974	$4
❏ 40028	Lizzie Lou/Tears	1973	$4
❏ 40169	Sled Ridin'/Fastest Grass Alive	1973	$4

MGM

Number	Title	Yr	NM
❏ 12970	At the First Fall of Snow/Fair and Tender Ladies	1960	$12
❏ 13098	Banjo Boys/Poor Old Cora	1962	$12
❏ 13045	Black Sheep Returned to the Fold/Each Season Changes You	1961	$10
❏ 12930	Blame Me/Lonely, Lonely Me	1960	$10
❏ 12527	Della Mae/Wild Mountain Honey	1957	$15

— With Red Allen

Number	Title	Yr	NM
❏ 13073	Five Days of Heaven/It Ain't Gonna Rain No Mo'	1962	$10
❏ 12420	Ho Honey Ho/Down in the Willow Garden	1957	$15

— With Red Allen

Number	Title	Yr	NM
❏ 12762	I Love You Only/Give This Message to Your Heart	1959	$15
❏ 12805	Lost Highway/You'll Never Know	1959	$15
❏ 12689	Love Pains/It Hurts to Know	1958	$15

— With Red Allen

Number	Title	Yr	NM
❏ 13126	Mule Skinner Blues/Lovey Told Me Goodbye	1963	$10
❏ 12308	My Aching Heart/Ruby Are You Mad	1956	$20

— With Red Allen

Number	Title	Yr	NM
❏ 12633	My Destiny/If You Don't Somebody Else Will	1958	$15

— With Red Allen

Number	Title	Yr	NM
❏ 12583	Once More/She's No Angel	1957	$15

— With Red Allen

Number	Title	Yr	NM
❏ 12839	Sweethearts Again/There's a Woman Behind Every Man	1959	$15
❏ 12383	Whu Dun It!/Teardrops in My Eyes	1956	$20

— With Red Allen

OSBORNE, JEFFREY

A&M

Number	Title	Yr	NM
❏ 1266	All Because of You/La Cuenta, Por Favor	1989	$3
❏ 1250	Can't Go Back on a Promise/La Cuenta, Por Favor	1988	$3
❏ 2687	Don't Stop/Forever Mine	1984	$4
❏ 2687 [PS]	Don't Stop/Forever Mine	1984	$4
❏ 2561	Don't You Get So Mad/So Much Love	1983	$4
❏ 2530	Eenie Meenie/New Love	1983	$4
❏ 2894	In Your Eyes/Come Midnight	1986	$3
❏ 2410	I Really Don't Need No Light/One Million Kisses	1982	$4
❏ 2724	Let Me Know/Live for Today	1985	$4
❏ 2434	On the Wings of Love/I'm Beggin'	1982	$4
❏ 2434 [PS]	On the Wings of Love/I'm Beggin'	1982	$5
❏ 1227	She's on the Left/A Second Chance	1988	$3
❏ 1227 [PS]	She's on the Left/A Second Chance	1988	$3
❏ 2863	Soweto/Love's Not Ready	1986	$3
❏ 2863 [PS]	Soweto/Love's Not Ready	1986	$3
❏ 2591	Stay with Me Tonight/Baby	1983	$4
❏ 2695	The Borderlines/I'll Make Believe	1984	$4
❏ 2618	We're Going All the Way/Two Wrongs Don't Make a Right	1984	$4
❏ 2618 [PS]	We're Going All the Way/Two Wrongs Don't Make a Right	1984	$4

OSBORNE, JIMMIE

KING

Number	Title	Yr	NM
❏ 1048	A Million People Have Died/God Has Taken My Flower	1952	$40
❏ 1268	A Tribute to Robert A. Taft/Korean Story	1953	$30
❏ 1363	Blue Days and Lonely Nights/Invest Your Little Heart	1954	$30
❏ 1144	Don't Slam the Door!/This Evil Life Don't Pay	1952	$40
❏ 1231	Hills of Roan County/My Main Trial Is Yet to Come	1953	$30
❏ 1354	I Did and I Does and I Do/A Tennessee Ocean	1954	$30
❏ 958	I Hate to Be Jealous/Tell Me Daddy	1951	$50
❏ 1012	It's Me Who Has to Suffer/Love Me or Leave Me	1951	$40
❏ 1117	Mama Won't Agree/Automobile Baby	1952	$40
❏ 1412	Married on Paper/When You Told Me You Love Me	1954	$30
❏ 1038	Missing in Action/Give Me Back My Ring and Picture	1952	$40
❏ 1314	My Tissue Paper Heart/It Just Tears Me All to Pieces	1954	$30
❏ 971	The Arm of God/He'll Come Like a Thief in the Night	1951	$50
❏ 1393	The First One to Know/An Empty Old Cottage	1954	$30
❏ 1484	Too Many Friends/You Can't Sometimes	1955	$30
❏ 1066	We Can't Take It With Us/How Many Hearts Can You Break	1952	$40

OSBORNE, KELL, AND THE CHICKS

CLASS

Number	Title	Yr	NM
❏ 302	Little Chick-A-Dee/Do You Mind	1962	$20

LOMA

Number	Title	Yr	NM
❏ 2023	That's What's Happening/You Can't Outsmart a Woman	1965	$200

TREY

Number	Title	Yr	NM
❏ 3006	The Bells of St. Mary's/That's Alright, Baby	1960	$30

Number	Title	Yr	NM

OSBOURNE, OZZY

Also see BLACK SABBATH; QUIET RIOT; URIAH HEEP; RAINBOW; BADLANDS; NIGHT RANGER.

CBS ASSOCIATED

Number	Title	Yr	NM
❏ ZS4-04318	Bark at the Moon/Spiders	1984	$5
❏ ZS4-68534	Crazy Babies/ Demon Alcohol	1989	$5
❏ ZS4-07168	Crazy Train (Live)/ Crazy Train (Original)	1987	$5
❏ ZS4-08516	Miracle Man/Man You Said It All	1988	$5
❏ ZS8-08463	Shot in the Dark/Crazy Train	1988	$4
—Reissue			
❏ ZS4-05810	Shot in the Dark/ You Said It All	1986	$4
❏ ZS4-05810 [PS]	Shot in the Dark/ You Said It All	1986	$6
❏ ZS4-04383	So Tired/"B" Side	1984	$5

JET

Number	Title	Yr	NM
❏ ZS6-02079	Crazy Train/Steal Away (The Night)	1981	$6
❏ ZS5-02582	Flying High Again/I Don't Know	1981	$5
❏ ZS4-03392	Paranoid/Iron Man	1982	$5
❏ ZS5-02707	Tonight/Little Dolls	1982	$5

O'SHEA, SHAD

FRATERNITY

Number	Title	Yr	NM
❏ 3385	Big John D/Ginger Cookies	1976	$6
❏ 3494	Centerfolds Bare She Is/(B-side unknown)	1984	$6
❏ 3381	Colorado Call/Bub-Bub-Bub-Boo	1975	$8
❏ 3386	What Is America?/ One Small Voice	1976	$6
❏ 3491	Where's the Beef?/ (B-side unknown)	1984	$6

GRT

Number	Title	Yr	NM
❏ 068	What Is America?/ One Small Voice	1976	$5

NORMAN

Number	Title	Yr	NM
❏ 521	Hit Record Pt. 2/Shad's Tune	1963	$15
❏ 529	The Club/The Golden Miracle	1963	$15

PLANTATION

Number	Title	Yr	NM
❏ 101	Goodbye Sam/The Applegate Free Food Band	1973	$6
❏ 210	McLove Story (same on both sides)	1982	$8

PRIVATE STOCK

Number	Title	Yr	NM
❏ 45,071	Colorado Call/Bub-Bub-Bub-Boo	1976	$5

SOUND STAGE 7

Number	Title	Yr	NM
❏ 2527	Hal-a-Loo-Yah, I'm a Bum/Snipe Hunt	1964	$10
❏ 2539	Little General/I Got the Miz-Er-Ees	1965	$12

OSHINS, MILT

PELVIS

Number	Title	Yr	NM
❏ 169	All About Elvis/All About Elvis (Part 2)	1956	$80

OSLIN, K.T.

ELEKTRA

Number	Title	Yr	NM
❏ 47132	Clean Your Own Tables/ Nelda Jean Prudy	1981	$5
—As "Kay T. Oslin"			

RCA

Number	Title	Yr	NM
❏ 5154-7-R	80's Ladies/Old Pictures	1987	$3
❏ 5154-7-R [PS]	80's Ladies/Old Pictures	1987	$4
❏ 9029-7-R	Didn't Expect It to Go Down This Way/Round the Clock Lovin'	1989	$3
❏ 8380-7-R	Do Ya'/80's Ladies	1988	$3
—Gold Standard Series" reissue			
❏ 5239-7-R	Do Ya'/Lonely But Only for You	1987	$3
❏ 8865-7-R	Hey Bobby/Where Is a Woman to Go	1989	$3
❏ 8725-7-R	Hold Me/She Don't Talk Like Us No More	1988	$3
❏ 5330-7-R	I'll Always Come Back/ Old Pictures	1987	$3
❏ 8388-7-R	Money/Dr., Dr.	1988	$3
❏ 8943-7-R	This Woman/Younger Men	1989	$3
❏ 5066-7-R	Wall of Tears/Two Hearts Are Better Than One	1986	$3
❏ 5066-7-R [PS]	Wall of Tears/Two Hearts Are Better Than One	1986	$4

OSMOND BOYS, THE

ARO

Number	Title	Yr	NM
❏ 1987	Santa Claus Is Coming to Town/Kay Thompson's Jingle Bells	1987	$5

OSMOND, DONNY

CAPITOL

Number	Title	Yr	NM
❏ 7PRO-79683	Hold On (same on both sides)	1989	$6
—7-inch vinyl is promo only			
❏ B-44379	Sacred Emotion/Groove	1989	$3
❏ 7PRO-79608 [PS]	Sacred Emotion (same on both sides)	1989	$5
—Picture sleeve appears to have been released only with promo copies			
❏ 7PRO-79608	Sacred Emotion (same on both sides)	1989	$5
—7-inch vinyl originally was promo only			
❏ B-44369	Soldier of Love/My Secret Touch	1989	$3
❏ B-44369 [PS]	Soldier of Love/My Secret Touch	1989	$5
❏ 7PRO-79585	Soldier of Love (same on both sides)	1989	$8
—Promo-only pressing			

MGM

Number	Title	Yr	NM
❏ 14583	A Million to One/Young Love	1973	$5
❏ 14677	Are You Lonesome Tonight/ When I Fall in Love	1973	$5
❏ 14285	Go Away Little Girl/The Wild Rover (Time to Ride)	1971	$5
—Altered B-side title			
❏ 14285	Go Away Little Girl/Time to Ride	1971	$6
❏ 14322	Hey Girl/I Knew You When	1971	$6
❏ 14781	I Have a Dream/I'm Dyin'	1975	$4
❏ 14424	Lonely Boy/Why	1972	$6
❏ 14367	Puppy Love/Let My People Go	1972	$6
❏ 14227	Sweet and Innocent/Flirtin'	1971	$6
❏ 14227 [PS]	Sweet and Innocent/Flirtin'	1971	$8
❏ 14503	The Twelfth of Never/Life Is Just What You Make It	1973	$5
❏ 14503 [PS]	The Twelfth of Never/Life Is Just What You Make It	1973	$8
❏ 14407	Too Young/Love Me	1972	$6

POLYDOR

Number	Title	Yr	NM
❏ 14320	C'mon Marianne/Ol' Man Auctioneer	1976	$4

OSMOND, DONNY AND MARIE

MGM

Number	Title	Yr	NM
❏ 14840	Deep Purple/Take Me Back Again	1975	$4
❏ 14735	I'm Leaving It (All) Up to You/The Umbrella Song	1974	$5
❏ 14807	Make the World Go Away/ Living on My Suspicion	1975	$4
❏ 14765	Morning Side of the Mountain/ One of These Days	1974	$4

POLYDOR

Number	Title	Yr	NM
❏ 14363	Ain't Nothin' Like the Real Thing/Sing	1976	$4
❏ 14456	Baby, I'm Sold on You/ Sure Would Be Nice	1978	$4
❏ 14474	May Tomorrow Be a Perfect Day/I Want to Give You My Everything	1978	$4
❏ 14510	On the Shelf/Certified Honey	1978	$4

OSMOND, MARIE

CAPITOL

Number	Title	Yr	NM
❏ B-44044	Cry Just a Little/More Than Dancing	1987	$3
❏ B-5703	Everybody's Crazy 'Bout My Baby/Making Music	1987	$3
❏ B-44269	I'm in Love and He's in Dallas/ My Home Town Boy	1989	$3
❏ B-5663	I Only Wanted You/We're Gonna Need a Love Song	1986	$3
❏ B-5478	Meet Me in Montana/What Do Lonely People Do	1985	$3
—With Dan Seals			
❏ B-5478 [PS]	Meet Me in Montana/What Do Lonely People Do	1985	$4
❏ 7PRO-79808	Slowly But Surely (same on both sides)	1989	$5
—Vinyl originally was promo only			
❏ B-44468	Slowly But Surely/What Would You Do About You	1989	$4
❏ B-44412	Steppin' Stone/What Would You Do About Me If You Were Me	1989	$3
❏ B-44215	Sweet Life/My Home Town Boy	1988	$3
—A-side: With Paul Davis			
❏ B-5521	There's No Stopping Your Heart/Blue Sky Shinin'	1985	$3
❏ B-5521 [PS]	There's No Stopping Your Heart/Blue Sky Shinin'	1985	$5
❏ B-44176	Without a Trace/ Baby's Blue Eyes	1988	$3

ELEKTRA

Number	Title	Yr	NM
❏ 69995	Back to Believing Again/Look Who's Getting Over Who	1982	$4
❏ 69882	I'm Learning/Look Who's Getting Over Who	1982	$4

MGM

Number	Title	Yr	NM
❏ 14694	My Little Corner of the World/ It's Just the Other Way Around	1974	$4
❏ 14609	Paper Roses/Least of All You	1973	$5
❏ 14609 [PS]	Paper Roses/Least of All You	1973	$8
❏ 14786	Who's Sorry Now/ This I Promise You	1975	$4

POLYDOR

Number	Title	Yr	NM
❏ 14333 [B]	A" My Name Is Alice/ Weeping Willow	1976	$4
❏ 14405	Cry, Baby, Cry/Please Tell Him I Said Hello	1977	$4
❏ 14385	This Is the Way That I Feel/ Play the Music Loud	1977	$4
❏ 14385 [PS]	This Is the Way That I Feel/ Play the Music Loud	1977	$5

RCA

Number	Title	Yr	NM
❏ PB-13680	Who's Counting/'Til the Best Comes Along	1983	$4

OSMONDS, THE

Includes records as "The Osmond Brothers." (Most of these were pre-1970, before Donny was a member of the group.) Also see DONNY OSMOND.

BARNABY

Number	Title	Yr	NM
❏ 2004	I've Got Loving on My Mind/Mollie-"A	1968	$10
❏ 2002	Mary Elizabeth/ Speak Like a Child	1968	$10
❏ 2005	Taking a Chance on Love/ Groove With What You Got	1969	$10

ELEKTRA

Number	Title	Yr	NM
❏ 47438	I Think About Your Lovin'/ Working Man's Blues	1982	$4
❏ 69969	It's Like Falling in Love/ Your Leaving Was the Last Thing on My Mind	1982	$4

EMI AMERICA

Number	Title	Yr	NM
❏ 8313	Baby Wants/Lovin' Proof	1986	$3
❏ 8298	Baby When Your Heart Breaks Down/Love Burning Down	1985	$3
❏ 8360	Looking for Suzanne/ Back in Your Arms	1986	$3
❏ 43033	Slow Ride/Heartbreak Radio	1987	$3

MERCURY

Number	Title	Yr	NM
❏ 74079	Emily/Rainin'	1979	$4
❏ 74056	Love on the Line/You're Mine	1979	$4

MGM

Number	Title	Yr	NM
❏ 13162	Be My Little Baby Bumble Bee/I Wouldn't Trade the Silver in My Mother's Hair	1963	$20
❏ 14450	Crazy Horses/That's My Girl	1972	$5
❏ 14259	Double Lovin'/Chilly Winds	1971	$6
❏ 14324	Down by the Lazy River/ He's the Light of the World	1971	$6
❏ 14562	Goin' Home/Are You Up There	1973	$5
❏ 14405	Hold Her Tight/Love Is	1972	$5
❏ 14617	Let Me In/One Way Ticket to Anywhere	1973	$5
❏ 14617 [PS]	Let Me In/One Way Ticket to Anywhere	1973	$8
❏ 14746	Love Me for a Reason/Fever	1974	$5
❏ 14159	Movin' Along/Open Up Your Heart	1970	$8
❏ 13281	Mr. Sandman/My Mom	1964	$30
❏ 13281 [PS]	Mr. Sandman/My Mom	1964	$60
❏ 14193	One Bad Apple/He Ain't Heavy, He's My Brother	1970	$6
❏ 14193 [PS]	One Bad Apple/He Ain't Heavy, He's My Brother	1970	$60
—Sleeve calls the group "The Osmond Brothers," rather than "The Osmonds" as the 45 does, which may explain its rarity			
❏ 14831	Thank You/I'm Still Gonna Need You	1975	$5
❏ 14831 [PS]	Thank You/I'm Still Gonna Need You	1975	$6
❏ 13174 [PS]	Theme from "The Travels of Jamie McPheeters"/Aura Lee	1963	$40
❏ 13174	Theme from "The Travels of Jamie McPheeters"/Aura Lee	1963	$20
❏ 14791	The Proud One/The Last Day Is Coming	1975	$5

POLYDOR

Number	Title	Yr	NM
❏ 14348	Check It Out/I Can't Live a Dream	1976	$4

UNI

Number	Title	Yr	NM
❏ 55015	I Can't Stop/Flower Music	1967	$10
❏ 55276	I Can't Stop/Flower Music	1971	$6

WARNER BROS.

Number	Title	Yr	NM
❏ 28982	Any Time/Desperately	1985	$3
❏ 29312	If Every Man Had a Woman Like You/Come Back to Me	1984	$4
❏ 29594	She's Ready for Someone to Love Her/You Make the Long Road Shorter with Your Love	1983	$4
❏ 29387	Where Does An Angel Go When She Cries/ One More for Lovers	1984	$4

O'SULLIVAN, GILBERT

EPIC

Number	Title	Yr	NM
❏ 50967	What's in a Kiss/ Down, Down, Down	1981	$4

MAM

Number	Title	Yr	NM
❏ 3619	Alone Again (Naturally)/Save It	1972	$6
❏ 3641	A Woman's Place/Too Bad	1974	$4
❏ 3645	Christmas Song/ Just As You Are	1975	$5

Number	Title	Yr	NM
❏ 3626	Clair/Ooh Wakka Doo Wakka Day	1972	$5
❏ 3626 [PS]	Clair/Ooh Wakka Doo Wakka Day	1972	$6
❏ 3629	Get Down/A Very Extraordinary Sort of Girl	1973	$5
❏ 3636	Happiness Is Me and You/Breakfast, Dinner and Tea	1974	$4
❏ 3644	I Don't Love You But I Think I Like You/That's a Fact	1975	$4
❏ 3643	Marriage Machine/Tell Me Why	1975	$4
❏ 3633	Ooh Baby/Good Company	1973	$4
❏ 3628	Out of the Question/Everybody Knows	1973	$5
❏ 3613	We Will/I Didn't Know What to Do	1971	$6

OTHER HALF, THE (1)
ACTA
❏ 801	Flight of the Dragon Lady/Wonderful Day	1967	$30
❏ 806	I Need You/No Doubt About It	1967	$30
❏ 825	Morning Fire/Ozlee Eaves Drop	1968	$20
❏ 819	What Can I Do for You/Bad Day	1968	$20
GNP CRESCENDO
| ❏ 378 | I've Come So Far/Mr. Pharmacist | 1966 | $30 |

OTHER ONES, THE
ABC-PARAMOUNT
| ❏ 10793 | Stop/Dreaming Out Loud | 1966 | $15 |
VIRGIN
❏ 99428	Holiday/Dark Ages	1987	$3
❏ 99428 [PS]	Holiday/Dark Ages	1987	$3
❏ 99473	We Are What We Are/Islands	1987	$3
❏ 99473 [PS]	We Are What We Are/Islands	1987	$3

OTHERS, THE (1)
FONTANA
| ❏ 1944 | Oh Yeah!/I'm Taking Her Home | 1964 | $40 |

OTHERS, THE (U)
RCA VICTOR
| ❏ 47-8669 | I Can't Stand This Love, Goodbye/Until I Heard It From You | 1965 | $40 |
| ❏ 47-8776 | Lonely Street/(I Remember) The First Time I Saw You | 1965 | $20 |

OTIS AND CARLA
Also see OTIS REDDING; CARLA THOMAS.
ATCO
| ❏ 6665 | When Something Is Wrong with My Baby/Ooh Carla, Ooh Otis | 1968 | $10 |
STAX
| ❏ 244 | Lovey Dovey/New Year's Resolution | 1968 | $10 |
| ❏ 216 | Tramp/Tell It Like It Is | 1967 | $10 |

OTIS, JOHNNY
CAPITOL
❏ F3852	Bye Bye Baby/Good Golly	1957	$30
❏ F3799	Can't You Hear Me Callin'/My Ding-a-Ling	1957	$60
❏ F4168 [M]	Castin' My Spell/Telephone Baby	1959	$30
❏ F4168 [S]	Castin' My Spell/Telephone Baby	1959	$60
❏ F3802	It's Too Soon to Know/Star of Love	1957	$60
❏ F4260	Let the Sun Shine in My Life/Baby, Just You	1959	$30
❏ F3800	Ma, He's Makin' Eyes at Me/In the Dark	1957	$60
❏ 4326	Mumblin' Mosie/Hey Baby, Don't You Know	1960	$20
❏ F4156	My Dear/You	1959	$30
❏ F3801	Stay with Me/Tell Me So	1957	$60
❏ F4226	Three Girls Named Molly (Doin' the Hully Gully)/I'll Do the Same for You	1959	$30
❏ F3889	Well, Well, Well/You Just Kissed Me Goodbye	1958	$30
❏ F3966	Willie and the Hand Jive/Ring-a-Ling	1958	$40
❏ F4060	Willie Did the Cha Cha/Crazy Country Hop	1958	$30
DIG
❏ 119	Hey! Hey! Hey! Hey!/Let the Sunshine in My Heart	1956	$40
❏ 132	My Eyes Are Full of Tears/Turtle Dove	1957	$40
❏ 139	Stop, Look and Love Me/The Night Is Young	1957	$40
❏ 122	The Midnite Creeper (Part 1)/The Midnite Creeper (Part 2)	1956	$40
❏ 134	Wa Wa (Part 1)/Wa Wa (Part 2)	1957	$40
ELDO
| ❏ 153 | Long Distance/Banana Peels | 1968 | $8 |

EPIC
| ❏ 5-10757 | Willie and the Hand Jive/Goin' Back to L.A. | 1971 | $6 |

—B-side with Delmar Evans

KENT
| ❏ 506 | Country Girl/Bye Bye Baby | 1969 | $8 |
| ❏ 4521 | Shuggie's Blues/Cool Ade | 1969 | $8 |
KING
❏ 5790	Bye, Bye Baby/The Hash	1963	$15
❏ 5581	Hand Jive One More Time/Baby I Got News for You	1961	$20
❏ 5606	She's All Right/It Must Be Love	1962	$20
❏ 5707	Somebody Call the Station/Yes	1963	$15
❏ 5690	The Hey Hey Hey Song/Early in the Morning Blues	1962	$20
MERCURY
❏ 8289	Call Operator 210/Baby Baby Blues	1952	$60
❏ 8295	Gypsy Blues/The Candle's Burning Low	1952	$60
❏ 70050	Love Bug Boogie/Brown Skin Butterball	1953	$60
❏ 8273	One-Nighter Blues/Goomp Blues	1952	$60
❏ 8263	Oopy Doo/Stardust	1952	$60
❏ 70038	Why Don't You Believe Me/Wishing Well	1953	$60
OKEH
| ❏ 7332 | Watts Breakaway/You Can Depend On Me | 1969 | $6 |
PEACOCK
❏ 1675	Butter Ball/Dandy's Boogie	1957	$60
❏ 1636	Shake It/I Won't Be Your Fool No More	1954	$60
❏ 1648	Sittin' Here Drinkin'/You Got Me Crying	1955	$60
SAVOY
❏ 788	All Nite Long/New Love	1951	$60
❏ 750	Cupid Boogie/Just Can't Get Free	1950	$70
❏ 780	Doggin' Blues/Living and Loving You	1951	$60
❏ 731	Double Crossing Blues/Ain't Nothin' Shakin'	1950	$120
❏ 731	Double Crossing Blues/Back Alley Blues	1950	$125

—B-side by the Beale Street Gang

❏ 777	Gee Baby/Mambo Boogie	1951	$60
❏ 824	Get Together Blues/Chittlin' Switch	1951	$60
❏ 815	Harlem Nocturne/Midnight in the Barrelhouse	1951	$60
❏ 787	I Dream/Hangover Blues	1951	$60
❏ 855	It Ain't the Beauty/Gonna Take a Train	1952	$60
❏ 812	Warning Blues/I'll Ask My Heart	1951	$60
❏ 764	Wedding Blues/Far Away Blues (Xmas Blues)	1950	$70

7-Inch Extended Plays
CAPITOL
| ❏ EAP 1-940 | Hum Ding a Ling/It's Too Soon to Know/Stay with Me/Ma (He's Makin' Eyes at Me) | 1958 | $175 |

O'TOOLE, KNUCKLES
7-Inch Extended Plays
GRAND AWARD
| ❏ EP2001 | If You Knew Susie/Paper Doll/Peg o' My Heart/Shine On Harvest Moon-Bicycle Built for Two/The Bowery-The Sidewalks of New York | 1958 | $8 |

OTT, PAUL
ELEKTRA
| ❏ 46066 | A Salute to the Duke/Listen to the Eagle | 1979 | $5 |
MONUMENT
❏ 8655	I'm the South/Keep Me Comin' 'Round	1975	$5
❏ 8691	Listen to the Eagle/Ole Blue	1976	$5
❏ 8605	Ole Blue/Plant a Tree	1974	$5
❏ 45-293	Our First Night/Turn to Me	1980	$5
SHOW BIZ
| ❏ 502 | Soldier's Prayer/Danny Boy | 1972 | $6 |
| ❏ 503 | The Twenty-Second Day/Danny Boy | 1972 | $6 |
THUNDER INT'L.
| ❏ 1024 | Times Have Changed/White Rose | 1960 | $125 |

OTTO'S CHEMICAL LOUNGE
7-Inch Extended Plays
REFLEX
| ❏ 0H [PS] | Fire | 1983 | $60 |
| ❏ 0H | Fire/Trip with Me/Noodle Man/I'm Otto Your Mind | 1983 | $60 |

OUR GANG
BR'ER BIRD
| ❏ 001 | Summertime Summertime/Theme from Leon's Garage | 1966 | $200 |

OUTCASTS, THE (1)
ASKEL
| ❏ 104 | I'll Set You Free/Everyday | 1966 | $40 |
| ❏ 102 | I'm in Pittsburgh (And It's Raining)/Price of Victory | 1966 | $100 |
GALLANT
| ❏ 101 | 1523 Blair/Smokestack Lightning | 1967 | $60 |

OUTCASTS, THE (2)
CAMEO
| ❏ 477 | Today's the Day/I Didn't Have to Love Her Anymore | 1967 | $30 |
DECCA
| ❏ 32036 | Set Me Free/You'd Be Surprised | 1966 | $20 |

OUTCASTS, THE (U)
DOT
| ❏ 16828 | I Gotta Find Cupid/Mexican Maiden | 1966 | $15 |
| ❏ 16897 | I'll Keep Coming Back/Hava Nagila | 1966 | $15 |

OUTFIELD, THE
COLUMBIA
❏ 38-05894	All the Love in the World/Taking My Chances	1986	$3
❏ 38-05894 [PS]	All the Love in the World/Taking My Chances	1986	$3
❏ 38-06295	Everytime You Cry/Tiny Lights	1986	$3
❏ 38-06295 [PS]	Everytime You Cry/Tiny Lights	1986	$3
❏ 38-68943	My Paradise/Somewhere in America '89	1989	$3
❏ 38-05447	Say It Isn't So/Mystery Man	1985	$8
❏ 38-05447 [PS]	Say It Isn't So/Mystery Man	1985	$8
❏ 38-08426	Say It Isn't So/Mystery Man	1988	$3

—Reissue

| ❏ 38-07170 | Since You've Been Gone/Better Than Nothing | 1987 | $3 |
| ❏ 38-07170 [PS] | Since You've Been Gone/Better Than Nothing | 1987 | $3 |

OUTLAWS
"Southern rock" band; few, if any, of their releases used the word "The" before their name. Also see LYNYRD SKYNYRD.
ARISTA
❏ 0188	Breaker-Breaker/South Carolina	1976	$4
❏ 0582	(Ghost) Riders in the Sky/Devil's Road	1981	$4
❏ 0338	Green Grass and High Tides/Holiday	1978	$4
❏ 0213	Green Grass and High Tides/Prisoner	1976	$5
❏ 0282	Hearin' My Heart Talkin'/Holiday	1977	$4
❏ 0258	Hurry Sundown/So Afraid	1977	$4
❏ 0378	Take It Anyway You Want It/Cry Some More	1978	$4
❏ 0150	There Goes Another Love Song/Keep Prayin'	1975	$4
❏ 0597	Wishing Well/I Can't Stop Loving You	1981	$4
PASHA
| ❏ ZS4-06550 | One Last Ride/Saved by the Bell | 1987 | $3 |

OUTLAWS, THE (2)
CRUSADE
| ❏ 92765 | Chains/(B-side unknown) | 1965 | $40 |

OUTLAWS, THE (3)
DOT
| ❏ 16512 | Hold-Up/Somethin' Else | 1963 | $50 |

OUTLAWS, THE (U)
SMASH
| ❏ 2025 | Don't Cry/Only for You | 1966 | $15 |

OUTSIDERS, THE
BELL
| ❏ 904 | Changes/Lost in My World | 1970 | $6 |
CAPITOL
❏ 5646	Girl in Love/What Makes You So Bad	1966	$10
❏ 5646 [PS]	Girl in Love/What Makes You So Bad	1966	$30
❏ 5759	Help Me Girl/You Gotta Look	1966	$12
❏ 5759 [PS]	Help Me Girl/You Gotta Look	1966	$30
❏ 5892	I Just Can't See You Anymore/Gotta Leave Us Alone	1967	$8

Number	Title	Yr	NM
❑ 5843	I'll Give You Time/I'm Not Trying to Hurt You	1967	$8
❑ 5843 [PS]	I'll Give You Time/I'm Not Trying to Hurt You	1967	$30
❑ 5955	I'll See You in the Summertime/And Now You Want My Sympathy	1967	$8
❑ 5955 [PS]	I'll See You in the Summertime/And Now You Want My Sympathy	1967	$30
❑ 2055	Little Bit of Lovin'/I Will Love You	1967	$8
❑ 2216	Oh How It Hurts/We Ain't Gonna Make It	1968	$8
❑ 5573	Time Won't Let Me/Was It Really Real	1966	$15

KAPP

Number	Title	Yr	NM
❑ 2104	Tinker, Tailor/Oh You're Not So Pretty	1970	$6

OUTSIDERS, THE (U)
KARATE

Number	Title	Yr	NM
❑ 505	The Guy with the Long Liverpool Hair/Outsider	1964	$30

OVATIONS, THE (1)
GOLDWAX

Number	Title	Yr	NM
❑ 300	Don't Cry/I Need a Lot of Loving	1966	$20
❑ 341	Happiness/Rockin' Chair	1969	$20
❑ 306	I Believe I'll Go Back Home/Qualifications	1966	$20
❑ 117	I'm Living Good/Recipe for Love	1965	$20
❑ 113	It's Wonderful to Be in Love/Dance Party	1965	$20
❑ 322	I've Gotta Go/Kiss My Troubles and Blues Away	1967	$20
❑ 314	Me and My Imagination/They Say	1967	$20
❑ 110	Pretty Little Angel/Won't You Call	1964	$20

MGM

Number	Title	Yr	NM
❑ 14623	Having a Party" Medley/Just Too Good to Be True	1973	$8
❑ 14705	I'm in Love/Don't Say You Love Me	1974	$8

—As "Louis Williams and the Ovations"

SOUNDS OF MEMPHIS

Number	Title	Yr	NM
❑ 712	Hooked on a Feeling/Take It From One Who Knows	1972	$8
❑ 717	One in a Million/So Nice to Be Loved by You	1973	$8
❑ 708	Touching Me/Don't Break Your Promise	1972	$8

OVATIONS, THE (2)
ANDIE

Number	Title	Yr	NM
❑ 5017	My Lullaby/Whole Wide World	1960	$50

BARRY

Number	Title	Yr	NM
❑ 101	My Lullaby/The Day We Fell in Love	1961	$50

EPIC

Number	Title	Yr	NM
❑ 9470	Oh, What a Day/Real True Love	1961	$50

OVATIONS, THE (3)
CAPITOL

Number	Title	Yr	NM
❑ 5082	I Don't Wanna Cry/Loneliness Never Entered My Mind	1963	$40

OVATIONS, THE (U)
HAWK

Number	Title	Yr	NM
❑ 153	I Still Love You/Runaround	1963	$200

JOSIE

Number	Title	Yr	NM
❑ 916	Who Needs Love/Remembering	1964	$30

OVERLANDERS, THE
HICKORY

Number	Title	Yr	NM
❑ 1362	Michelle/Cradle of Love	1965	$15
❑ 1275	Movin'/Don't It Make You Feel Good	1964	$15
❑ 1384	My Life/Girl from Indiana	1966	$15
❑ 1427	Shanghai Rooster/Leaves Are Falling	1966	$15

MERCURY

Number	Title	Yr	NM
❑ 72165	Call of the Wild/Summer Skies and Golden Sands	1963	$20

OVERMAN, RUNE
PARKWAY

Number	Title	Yr	NM
❑ 859	Madison Piano/Big Bass Boogie	1962	$20

STACY

Number	Title	Yr	NM
❑ 970	Beatnik Walk/Smorgasbord	1964	$12

OVERSTREET, PAUL
MTM

Number	Title	Yr	NM
❑ B-72113	Love Helps Those/What God Has Joined Together	1988	$4

RCA

Number	Title	Yr	NM
❑ 9015-7-R	All the Fun/Homemaker	1989	$4
❑ PB-13042	Beautiful Baby/Feels Good	1982	$4
❑ 9116-7-R	Seein' My Father in Me/Love Never Sleeps	1989	$4
❑ 8919-7-R	Sowin' Love/Love Helps Those	1989	$3

SCR

Number	Title	Yr	NM
❑ 146	While I'm Warm/(B-side unknown)	1977	$15

OVERSTREET, TOMMY
ABC

Number	Title	Yr	NM
❑ 12367	Better Me/Tell My Woman I Miss Her	1978	$5
❑ 12456	Cheater's Kit/Stolen Wine	1979	$5
❑ 12408	Fadin' In, Fadin' Out/If This Is Freedom (Then I Want Out)	1978	$5

ABC DOT

Number	Title	Yr	NM
❑ 17697	Don't Go City Girl on Me/I'll Give Up (When You Give Up on Me)	1977	$5
❑ 17580	From Woman to Woman/Grass Don't Grow in Heaven	1975	$5
❑ 17630	Here Comes That Girl Again/I'll Give Up (When You Give Up on Me)	1976	$5
❑ 17672	If Love Was a Bottle of Wine/I Never Really Missed You	1976	$5
❑ 17533	I'm a Believer/This Land Is a Big Land	1974	$5
❑ 17552	That's When My Woman Begins/A Small Quiet Table (In the Corner)	1975	$5
❑ 17721	This Time I'm In It for the Love/(Don't Make Me) A Memory Before My Time	1977	$5

AMI

Number	Title	Yr	NM
❑ 1314	Dream Maker/More Than You Can Stand	1983	$5
❑ 1317	Heart of Dixie/(B-side unknown)	1983	$5

DOT

Number	Title	Yr	NM
❑ 17402	Ann (Don't Go Runnin')/Within This World of Mine	1971	$6
❑ 17418	A Seed Before the Rose/How'd We Ever Get This Way	1972	$6
❑ 17350	Good Day Sunshine/Playing with Fire	1970	$6

—With Peggy Little

Number	Title	Yr	NM
❑ 17375	Gwen (Congratulations)/One Love, Two Hearts, Three Lives	1971	$6
❑ 17428	Heaven Is My Woman's Love/Baby's Gone	1972	$6
❑ 17428 [PS]	Heaven Is My Woman's Love/Baby's Gone	1972	$12
❑ 17387	I Don't Know You (Anymore)/I Still Love You Enough (To Love You All Over Again)	1971	$6
❑ 17515	If I Miss You Again Tonight/I'm Not Ready Yet	1974	$6
❑ 17357	If You're Looking for a Fool/The Smartest Fool	1970	$6
❑ 17474	I'll Never Break These Chains/Woman, Your Name Is My Song	1973	$6
❑ 17331	Painted by the Wine/You Can't Walk in the Sunshine	1969	$6
❑ 17455	Send Me No Roses/Your Love Controls My Life	1973	$6

DUNHILL

Number	Title	Yr	NM
❑ 4011	Lonely Again/Little Bit of Devil	1965	$15

ELEKTRA

Number	Title	Yr	NM
❑ 46600	Down in the Quarter/Forever in Blue Jeans	1980	$4
❑ 46564	Fadin' Renegade/Smokey Mountain Lullaby	1979	$4
❑ 46023	I'll Never Let You Down/You Needed Me	1979	$4
❑ 47041	Me and the Boys in the Band/You	1980	$4
❑ 46658	Sue/Her Heart Still Belongs to Me	1980	$4
❑ 46516	What Would Could a Man Need/Only a Fool	1979	$4

GERVASI

Number	Title	Yr	NM
❑ 665	I Still Love Your Body/(B-side unknown)	1984	$5

TINA

Number	Title	Yr	NM
❑ 523	Tears (There's Nowhere Else to Hide)/Lord, If I Make It to Heaven	1978	$6

OVERTON, C.B.
SHOCK

Number	Title	Yr	NM
❑ 9	If I Can't Stop You/(Instrumental)	1978	$20
❑ 13	Superstar Lady/(B-side unknown)	1978	$20

OWEN BROTHERS, THE
AUDIOGRAPH

Number	Title	Yr	NM
❑ 470	Southern Women/(B-side unknown)	1983	$6

OWEN, MACK
SUN

Number	Title	Yr	NM
❑ 336	Walkin' and Talkin'/Somebody Like You	1960	$30

OWEN, REG
PALETTE

Number	Title	Yr	NM
❑ PZ-5005	Manhattan Spiritual/Ritual Blues	1958	$10

OWENS, A.L. "DOODLE
RAINDROP

Number	Title	Yr	NM
❑ 010 [PS]	Honky Tonk Toys/California Rose	1977	$10

OWENS, BONNIE
CAPITOL

Number	Title	Yr	NM
❑ 5755	Consider the Children/I Know He Loves Me	1966	$10
❑ 2029	Don't Tell Me/Somewhere Between	1967	$8
❑ 5529	Excuse Me for Living/Souvenirs	1965	$10
❑ 2210	How Can Our Cheatin' Be Wrong/Yes I Love You Only	1968	$8
❑ 5977	I'd Be More of a Woman/Everything That's Fastened Down Is Coming Loose	1967	$10
❑ 2586	It Don't Take Much to Make Me Cry/My Hi-Fi to Cry By	1969	$8
❑ 2340	Lead Me On/I'll Always Be Glad to Take You Back	1968	$8
❑ 5618	Merry-Go-Round/Livin' on Your Love	1966	$10
❑ 2716	Philadelphia Lawyer/That Little Boy of Mine	1970	$8
❑ 5847	Someone Else You've Known/The Best Part of Me	1967	$12

MAR-VEL

Number	Title	Yr	NM
❑ 102	A Dear John Letter/Wonderful World	1953	$60

—With Fuzzy Owens

TALLY

Number	Title	Yr	NM
❑ 156	Don't Take Advantage of Me/Stop the World	1964	$30
❑ 184	Lie a Little/I'll Try Again Tomorrow	1964	$30
❑ 149	Why Don't Daddy Live Here Anymore/Waggin' Tongues	1963	$30

X

Number	Title	Yr	NM
❑ 028	I Traded My Heart for His Gold/Take Me	1954	$50

OWENS, BUCK, AND ROSE MADDOX
CAPITOL

Number	Title	Yr	NM
❑ 4550	Mental Cruelty/Loose Talk	1961	$20
❑ 4992	We're the Talk of the Town/Sweethearts in Heaven	1963	$20

OWENS, BUCK, AND SUSAN RAYE
CAPITOL

Number	Title	Yr	NM
❑ 3368	Looking Back to See/Cryin' Time	1972	$6
❑ 3368 [PS]	Looking Back to See/Cryin' Time	1972	$10
❑ 4100	Love Is Strange/Sweethearts in Heaven	1975	$6
❑ 3225	Santa's Gonna Come in a Stagecoach/One of Everything You Got	1971	$8
❑ 3601	The Good Old Days (Are Here Again)/When You Get to Heaven (I'll Be There)	1973	$6
❑ 2871	The Great White Horse/Your Tender Loving Care	1970	$8
❑ 2871 [PS]	The Great White Horse/Your Tender Loving Care	1970	$10
❑ 2791	Togetherness/Fallin' for You	1970	$8
❑ 2791 [PS]	Togetherness/Fallin' for You	1970	$10
❑ 2731	We're Gonna Get Together/Everybody Needs Somebody	1970	$8
❑ 2731 [PS]	We're Gonna Get Together/Everybody Needs Somebody	1970	$10

OWENS, BUCK
CAPITOL

Number	Title	Yr	NM
❑ 4043	41st Street Lonely Hearts Club/Weekend Daddy	1975	$6
❑ B-44295	A-11/Sweethearts in Heaven	1989	$4
❑ 4337	Above and Beyond/Till These Dreams Come True	1960	$20
❑ 3011	Act Naturally/My Heart Skips a Beat	1971	$15

—As "Buck Owens' Bakersfield Brass"

Number	Title	Yr	NM
❑ 4937	Act Naturally/Over and Over Again	1963	$20
❑ B-44409	Act Naturally/The Key's in the Mailbox	1989	$20

—A-side with Ringo Starr

Number	Title	Yr	NM
❑ 3563	Ain't It Amazing, Gracie/The Good Old Days	1973	$6
❑ 3688	Arms Full of Empty/Songwriter's Lament	1973	$6
❑ 5410	Before You Go/No One But You	1965	$12
❑ 5410 [PS]	Before You Go/No One But You	1965	$20

Number	Title	Yr	NM
❏ 3769	Big Game Hunter/ That Loving Feeling	1973	$6
❏ 2646	Big in Vegas/White Satin Bed	1969	$8
❏ 2646 [PS]	Big in Vegas/White Satin Bed	1969	$15
❏ 3023	Bridge Over Troubled Water/(I'm Goin') Home	1971	$6
❏ 3023 [PS]	Bridge Over Troubled Water/(I'm Goin') Home	1971	$10
❏ 5517	Buckaroo/If You Want a Love	1965	$10
❏ 2962	Buckaroo/Okie from Muskogee	1970	$15

— As "Buck Owens' Bakersfield Brass"

Number	Title	Yr	NM
❏ 3066	Cajun Brass/Waitin' in Your Welfare Line	1971	$10

— As "Buck Owens' Bakersfield Brass"

Number	Title	Yr	NM
❏ 2328	Christmas Shopping/One of Everything You Got	1968	$8
❏ F3824	Come Back/I Know What It Means	1957	$30
❏ 4412	Excuse Me (I Think I've Got a Heartache)/I've Got a Right to Know	1960	$20
❏ 4496	Foolin' Around/High As the Mountains	1961	$20
❏ 7PRO-79805 [DJ]	Gonna Have Love (same on both sides)	1989	$10

— Vinyl is promo only

Number	Title	Yr	NM
❏ 3976	Great Expectations/ Let the Fun Begin	1974	$6
❏ B-44248	Hot Dog/Second Fiddle	1988	$4
❏ B-44248 [PS]	Hot Dog/Second Fiddle	1988	$5
❏ 2080	How Long Will My Baby Be Gone/Everybody Needs Somebody	1968	$8
❏ 2080 [PS]	How Long Will My Baby Be Gone/Everybody Needs Somebody	1968	$15
❏ 5240	I Don't Care (Just As Long As You Love Me)/ Don't Let Her Know	1964	$15
❏ 3262	I'll Still Be Waiting for You/ Full Time Daddy	1972	$6
❏ F4090	I'll Take a Chance on Loving You/Walk the Floor	1958	$30
❏ 3504	In the Palm of Your Hand/Get Out of Town Before Sundown	1972	$6
❏ 3907	(It's a) Monsters' Holiday/ Great Expectations	1974	$6
❏ 2001	It Takes People Like You (To Make People Like Me)/You Left Her Lonely Too Long	1967	$8
❏ 2001 [PS]	It Takes People Like You (To Make People Like Me)/You Left Her Lonely Too Long	1967	$15
❏ 5336	I've Got a Tiger by the Tail/Cryin' Time	1965	$10
❏ 5336 [PS]	I've Got a Tiger by the Tail/Cryin' Time	1965	$20
❏ 2300	I've Got You on My Mind Again/That's All Right with Me (If It's All Right with You)	1968	$8
❏ 2300 [PS]	I've Got You on My Mind Again/That's All Right with Me (If It's All Right with You)	1968	$15
❏ 2947	I Wouldn't Live in New York City (If They Gave Me the Whole Dang Town)/No Milk and Honey in Baltimore	1970	$8
❏ 2947 [PS]	I Wouldn't Live in New York City (If They Gave Me the Whole Dang Town)/No Milk and Honey in Baltimore	1970	$10
❏ 2237	Let the World Keep On a-Turnin'/I'll Love You Forever and Ever	1968	$8

— With Buddy Alan

Number	Title	Yr	NM
❏ 2237 [PS]	Let the World Keep On a-Turnin'/I'll Love You Forever and Ever	1968	$15

— As "Buck Owens and Buddy Alan and the Buckaroos"

Number	Title	Yr	NM
❏ 5025	Love's Gonna Live Here/ Getting Used to Losing You	1963	$15
❏ 3314	Made in Japan/Black Texas Dirt	1972	$6
❏ 4181	Meanwhile Back at the Ranch/ Country Singer's Prayer	1976	$6
❏ 5136	My Heart Skips a Beat/ Together Again	1964	$15
❏ 5465	Only You (Can Break My Heart)/Gonna Have Love	1965	$10
❏ 5465 [PS]	Only You (Can Break My Heart)/Gonna Have Love	1965	$20
❏ 3841	On the Cover of the Music City News/Stony Mountain, West Virginia	1974	$6
❏ 5705	Open Up Your Heart/ No More Me and You	1966	$10
❏ 5705 [PS]	Open Up Your Heart/ No More Me and You	1966	$20
❏ B-44356	Put a Quarter in the Jukebox/ Don't Let Her Know	1989	$4
❏ 5865	Sam's Place/Don't Ever Tell Me Goodbye	1967	$8
❏ 5865 [PS]	Sam's Place/Don't Ever Tell Me Goodbye	1967	$15
❏ 5537	Santa Looked a Lot Like Daddy/All I Want for Christmas Dear Is You	1965	$10
❏ 5537 [PS]	Santa Looked a Lot Like Daddy/All I Want for Christmas Dear Is You	1965	$20
❏ 5537	Santa Looked a Lot Like Daddy/All I Want for Christmas Dear Is You	1973	$4

— Orange label, "Capitol" at bottom

Number	Title	Yr	NM
❏ 4765	Save the Last Dance for Me/King of Fools	1962	$20
❏ F4172	Second Fiddle/Everlasting Love	1959	$30
❏ 2142	Sweet Rosie Jones/Happy Times Are Here Again	1968	$8
❏ 2142 [PS]	Sweet Rosie Jones/Happy Times Are Here Again	1968	$15
❏ F3957	Sweet Thing/I Only Know That I Love You So	1957	$30
❏ 2570	Tall Dark Stranger/Sing That Kind of Song	1969	$8
❏ 2570 [PS]	Tall Dark Stranger/Sing That Kind of Song	1969	$15
❏ 4138	The Battle of New Orleans/Run Him to the Roundhouse Nellie	1975	$6
❏ 5647	Think of Me/Heart of Glass	1966	$10
❏ 5647 [PS]	Think of Me/Heart of Glass	1966	$20
❏ 3215	Too Old to Cut the Mustard/Wham Bam	1971	$6

— As "Buck and Buddy" (Buck Owens and BUDDY ALAN)

Number	Title	Yr	NM
❏ 3215 [PS]	Too Old to Cut the Mustard/Wham Bam	1971	$10
❏ 2330	Turkish Holiday/Things I Saw Happening at the Fountain	1968	$8
❏ 5566	Waitin' in Your Welfare Line/ In the Palm of Your Hand	1965	$10
❏ 5811	Where Does the Good Times Go/The Way That I Love You	1967	$8
❏ 5811 [PS]	Where Does the Good Times Go/The Way That I Love You	1967	$15
❏ 2377	Who's Gonna Mow Your Grass/There's Gotta Be Some Chances Made	1969	$8
❏ 2377 [PS]	Who's Gonna Mow Your Grass/There's Gotta Be Some Chances Made	1969	$15

DIXIE

Number	Title	Yr	NM
❏ 505	Hot Dog/Rhythm and Booze	1956	$400

— As "Corky Jones

PEP

Number	Title	Yr	NM
❏ 107	Hot Dog/Rhythm and Booze	1956	$250

— As "Corky Jones

Number	Title	Yr	NM
❏ 105	It Don't Show on Me/Down on the Corner of Love	1956	$60
❏ 106	The House Down the Block/ Right After the Dance	1956	$60
❏ 109	There Goes My Love/ Sweethearts in Heaven	1957	$60

REPRISE

Number	Title	Yr	NM
❏ 27964 [PS]	Streets of Bakersfield/ One More Name	1988	$4
❏ 27964	Streets of Bakersfield/ One More Name	1988	$3

— With Dwight Yoakam

STARDAY

Number	Title	Yr	NM
❏ 588	Down on the Corner of Love/ Right After the Dance	1962	$20
❏ 571	There Goes My Love/ It Don't Show on Me	1961	$20

WARNER BROS.

Number	Title	Yr	NM
❏ 8255	California Okie/Child Support	1976	$5
❏ 8701	Do You Wanna Make Love/ Seasons of My Heart	1978	$4
❏ 49046	Hangin' In and Hangin' On/ Sweet Molly Brown's	1979	$4
❏ 8223	Hollywood Waltz/Rain on Your Parade	1976	$5
❏ 8395	It's Been a Long, Long Time/ Rain on Your Parade	1977	$5
❏ 49118	Let Jesse Rob the Train/Victim of Life's Circumstances	1979	$4
❏ 8486	Let the Good Times Roll/ Texas Tornado	1977	$5
❏ 49200	Love Is a Warm Cowboy/I Don't Want to Live in San Francisco	1980	$4
❏ 49278	Moonlight and Magnolia/ Nickels and Dimes	1980	$4
❏ 8433	Our Old Mansion/How Come My God Don't Bark	1977	$5
❏ 8830	Play Together Again Again/He Don't Deserve You Anymore	1979	$4

— A-side with Emmylou Harris

Number	Title	Yr	NM
❏ 49651	Without You/Love Don't Make the Bars	1981	$4
❏ 8316	World Famous Holiday Inn/He Don't Deserve You Anymore	1977	$10
❏ 8316	World Famous Paradise Inn/He Don't Deserve You Anymore	1977	$5

7-Inch Extended Plays

CAPITOL

Number	Title	Yr	NM
❏ R-5446 [PS]	4-By Buck Owens	1965	$30
❏ SXA-2283 [PS]	I've Got a Tiger by the Tail	1965	$25
❏ SXA-2283	I've Got a Tiger by the Tail/ Trouble and Me/Wham Bam// Fallin' for You/We're Gonna Let the Good Times Roll/Memphis	1965	$25

— Jukebox issue; small hole, plays at 33 1/3 rpm

Number	Title	Yr	NM
❏ R-5446	Memphis/Let the Bad Times Roll On//Fallin' for You/ If You Fall Out of Love	1965	$20

OWENS, DUSTY

COLUMBIA

Number	Title	Yr	NM
❏ 4-21362	Give Me a Little Chance/ Wouldn't You	1955	$30
❏ 4-21202	Hello Operator/The Life You Want to Live	1954	$30
❏ 4-21310	They Didn't Know the Difference/A Love That Once Was Mine	1954	$30
❏ 4-21440	Who Do You Think They Would Blame/Forget My Broken Heart	1955	$30

OWENS, MARIE

4 STAR

Number	Title	Yr	NM
❏ 1019	Someone Loves You Honey/The Devil's Song	1975	$6
❏ 1007	Will the Circle Be Unbroken/ You Gave Me a Mountain	1975	$6

LOBO

Number	Title	Yr	NM
❏ VII	Long Loving Night/ (B-side unknown)	1982	$6

MCA

Number	Title	Yr	NM
❏ 40308	I Want to Lay Down Beside You/Broken Wings	1974	$6

OXFORD CIRCUS, THE

ZIG ZAG

Number	Title	Yr	NM
❏ 101	Tracy/4th Street Carnival	1967	$50

OXFORD, VERNON

RCA

Number	Title	Yr	NM
❏ PB-10872	A Good Old Fashioned Saturday Night Honky Tonk Barrom Brawl/One More Night to Spare	1977	$4
❏ PB-10787	Clean Your Own Tables/ Baby Sister	1976	$4
❏ PB-10952	Only the Shadows Know/ We Sure Danced Us Some Goodin's	1977	$4

RCA VICTOR

Number	Title	Yr	NM
❏ 47-9117	A Field of Flowers/ Stone by Stone	1967	$10
❏ 47-8943	Baby Sitter/Goin' Home	1966	$12
❏ PB-10348	Giving the Pill/Country Singer	1975	$6
❏ PB-10098	How High Does the Cotton Grow Mama/I've Got to Get Peter Off Your Mind	1974	$6
❏ PB-10185	I Wish You Would Leave Me Alone/Soft and Warm	1975	$6
❏ 47-8843	Let's Take a Cold Shower/Hide	1966	$12
❏ 47-9306	Little Sister Throw Your Red Shoes Away/Old Folks' Home	1967	$10
❏ PB-10442	Shadows of My Mind/ She's Always There	1975	$5
❏ 47-9467	This Woman Is Mine/The Touch of God's Hand	1968	$10
❏ 47-8759	Woman, Let Me Sing You a Song/Watermelon Time in Georgia	1966	$10

OZARK MOUNTAIN DAREDEVILS

A&M

Number	Title	Yr	NM
❏ 1842	Chicken Train Stomp/Journey to the Center of Your Heart	1976	$4
❏ 1709	Colorado Song/Thin Ice	1975	$4
❏ 1477	Country Girl/Within Without	1973	$5
❏ 1989	Crazy Lovin'/Stinghead	1977	$4
❏ 2016	Following (The Way That I Feel)/Snowbound	1978	$4
❏ 1772	If I Only Knew/Dreams	1975	$4
❏ 1515	If You Wanna Get to Heaven/ Spaceship Orion	1974	$5
❏ 1623	Look Away/It Probably Always Will	1974	$4

COLUMBIA

Number	Title	Yr	NM
❏ 1-11357	Oh Darlin'/Sailin' Around the World	1980	$4
❏ 1-11247	Take You Tonight/Runnin' Out	1980	$4

Number	Title	Yr	NM

P

P.F.M.
MANTICORE
❏ 2002	Celebration/(B-side unknown)	1973	$6
❏ 7003	Mr. Nine Til Five/Celebration	1974	$5

P. FUNK ALL STARS
CBS ASSOCIATED
❏ 04032	Generator Pop/Hydraulic Pump	1983	$4

HUMP
❏ 1	Hydraulic Pump (Part 1)/Hydraulic Pump (Part 2)	1981	$5
❏ 3	One of Those Summers/It's Too Funky in Here	1982	$5

UNCLE JAM
❏ 04408	Pumpin' It Up/Pumpin' It Up (Special Mix)	1984	$4

P.J.
TAMLA
❏ 54215	T.L.C./It Takes a Man to Teach a Woman How to Love	1972	$30

V.I.P.
❏ 25062	It Takes a Man to Teach a Woman How to Love/The Best Years of My Life	1970	$50

PABLO CRUISE
A&M
❏ 2570	Another World/Will You, Won't You	1983	$3
❏ 1910	A Place in the Sun/El Verano	1977	$4
❏ 1976	A Place in the Sun/El Verano	1977	$4
❏ 1999	Atlanta June/Never Had a Love	1977	$4
❏ 2349	Cool Love/Jenny	1981	$3
❏ 1876	Crystal/Look to the Sky	1976	$4
❏ 1834	Don't Believe It/Look to the Sky	1976	$4
❏ 2076	Don't Want to Live Without It/Raging Fire	1978	$4
❏ 2112	I Go to Rio/Raging Fire	1979	$4
❏ 1695	Island Woman/Denny	1975	$4
❏ 1815	(I Think) It's Finally Over/Look to the Sky	1976	$4
❏ 2195	I Want You Tonight/Family Man	1979	$4
❏ 2048	Love Will Find a Way/Always Be Together	1978	$4
❏ 2048 [PS]	Love Will Find a Way/Always Be Together	1978	$5
❏ 2217 [DJ]	Part of the Game (mono/stereo)	1980	$5
—No stock copies known			
❏ 2373	Slip Away/That's When	1981	$3
❏ 2373 [PS]	Slip Away/That's When	1981	$3
❏ 1920	Whatcha Gonna Do?/Atlanta June	1977	$4
❏ 1920 [PS]	Whatcha Gonna Do?/Atlanta June	1977	$6
❏ 1742	What Does It Take/In My Own Quiet Way	1975	$4

PACERS, THE
CALICO
❏ 101/2	I Found a Dream/I Wanna Dance with You	1958	$40

CORAL
❏ 62398	Sassy Sue/You Got Me Bugged	1964	$10

GUYDEN
❏ 2064	How Sweet/No Wonder	1962	$1500

RAZORBACK
❏ 125	Batman/Gotham City	1966	$30
❏ 108	Confound It/Skeeter Dape	1960	$30
❏ 112	Don't Get Around Much/Sad Sad	1962	$30
❏ 103	Fright Street/Sooie	1958	$30
❏ 137	Short Squashed Texan/Sock It To 'Em Soobey	1967	$30
❏ 118	Tennessee Stud/Beautiful Debbie	1964	$30
❏ 123	The Pit/Pace Setter	1965	$30
❏ 115	West Memphis/Dollar, Two Ninety-Eight	1963	$30

PACIFIC DRIFT
DERAM
❏ 85063	Tomorrow Morning Brings/Yes You Do	1970	$8

PACIFIC GAS & ELECTRIC
COLUMBIA
❏ 45158	Are You Ready?/Staggolee	1970	$6
—Available with at least three different label variations, all equal in value			
❏ 45221	Elvira/Father Come On Home	1970	$5
❏ 45621	Heat Wave/We Did What We Could	1972	$5
❏ 45444	One More River to Cross/Rocky Roller's Lament	1971	$5
❏ 45519	Thank God for You Baby/See the Monkey Run	1971	$5
❏ 45304	The Time Has Come/Death Row No. 172	1971	$5

KENT
❏ 4538	The Hunter/Long Handled Shovel	1971	$15

POWER
❏ 1701	Wade in the Water/Live Love	1969	$10

PACIFIC STEEL CO.
PACIFIC ARTS
❏ 111	Fat 'n Sassy/Rio	1980	$6

PACK, RAY
HAPPY MAN
❏ 818	Where Was I/(B-side unknown)	1989	$6

PACKARDS, THE
PARADISE
❏ 105	Dream of Love/Ding Dong	1956	$400

PLA-BAC
❏ 106	Ladise/My Doctor of Love	1956	$2000

PAGANS, THE
BONA FIDE
❏ 7004	Don't Leave Me Alone/Real World	1987	$30
—Red vinyl (all copies)			
❏ 7004 [PS]	Don't Leave Me Alone/Real World	1987	$30
—Poster sleeve, numbered edition of 200			

DROME
❏ DR-7	Dead End America/Little Black Egg	1979	$50
❏ DR-7 [PS]	Dead End America/Little Black Egg	1979	$12
❏ DR-7	Dead End America/Little Black Egg	1987	$12
—New record manufactured by Treehouse, accompanied by original picture sleeve			
❏ DR-1	Street Where Nobody Lives/What's This Shit Called Love?	1978	$13
❏ DR-1 [PS]	Street Where Nobody Lives/What's This Shit Called Love?	1978	$63
❏ DR-1 [PS]	Street Where Nobody Lives/What's This Shit Called Love?	1987	$13
—New picture sleeve with original records (500 made)			

NECK
❏ 1143	Six & Change/Six & Change	1977	$200
—Not issued with picture sleeve; 200 copies were pressed			
❏ 002 [PS]	Six & Change/Six & Change	1977	$175
—250 copies were made			

TREEHOUSE
❏ 003	Dead End America 87/Secret Agent Man	1987	$13
❏ 003 [PS]	Dead End America 87/Secret Agent Man	1987	$13

PAGE BOYS, THE
ABC-PARAMOUNT
❏ 10323	Lonely Sea/Road of Life	1962	$10

DECCA
❏ 31505	If Tears Could Speak/Ole Buttermilk Skies	1963	$15

HAMILTON
❏ 50025	Barracuda/Peter Gunn	1960	$15

PREP
❏ 117	Waiting/This I Give to You	1957	$30

PAGE, HOT LIPS
KING
❏ 1404	Cadillac Song/Ain't Nothing Wrong	1954	$125
❏ 4594	I Bongo You/Ruby	1953	$200
❏ 4584	Last Call for Alcohol/Old Parie	1952	$300

RCA VICTOR
❏ 50-0120	Let Me In/That's the One for Me	1951	$125
❏ 50-0129	Strike While the Iron's Hot/I Wanna Ride Like the Cowboys Do	1951	$125

PAGE, JIMMY
Also see THE HONEYDRIPPERS; LED ZEPPELIN; THE YARDBIRDS.
GEFFEN
❏ 27821	Wasting My Time/Fires of Winter	1988	$5

PAGE, PATTI, AND TOM T. HALL
MERCURY
❏ 73347	Hello We're Lonely/We're Not Getting Older	1972	$5

PAGE, PATTI
AVCO
❏ 603	I May Not Be Lovin' You/Whoever Finds This, I Love You	1974	$4
❏ 613	Less Than the Song/Did He Ask About Me	1975	$4
❏ 607	Pour Your Lovin' on Me/Big Wind from Dallas	1975	$4

COLUMBIA
❏ 4-44257	All the Time/Pretty Bluebird	1967	$5
❏ 4-43794	Almost Persuaded/It's the World Outside	1966	$6
❏ 4-44778	A Mighty Fortress Is Our Love/The Love Song	1969	$5
❏ 4-44989	Boy from the Country/You Don't Need a Heart	1969	$70
❏ 4-43647	Can I Trust You?/In This Day and Age	1966	$6
❏ 4-43183	Don't You Pass Me By/Days of the Waltz	1964	$6
❏ 4-43078	Drina (Little Soldier Boy)/Promises	1964	$6
❏ 4-43019	Drive-In Movie/I'd Rather Be Sorry	1964	$6
❏ 4-44353	Gentle on My Mind/Excuse Me	1967	$5
❏ 4-43447 [PS]	Happy Birthday, Jesus (A Child's Prayer)/Christmas Bells	1965	$12
❏ JZSP111907/8 [DJ]	Happy Birthday, Jesus (A Child's Prayer)/Christmas Bells	1965	$12
—Green vinyl			
❏ JZSP111907/8 [DJ]	Happy Birthday, Jesus (A Child's Prayer)/Christmas Bells	1965	$8
—Black vinyl			
❏ 4-43447	Happy Birthday, Jesus (A Child's Prayer)/Christmas Bells	1965	$8
❏ 4-43251	Hush, Hush, Sweet Charlotte/Longing to Hold You Again	1965	$8
❏ 4-42963	I Adore You/I Wonder, I Wonder, I Wonder	1964	$6
❏ 4-43761	It's the World Outside/Detour	1966	$6
❏ 4-45159	I Wish I Had a Mommy Like You/He'll Never Take the Place of You	1970	$5
❏ 4-44556	Little Green Apples/This House	1968	$5
❏ 4-42902	Love Letters/If and When	1963	$8
❏ 4-45059	Pickin' Up the Pieces/Tied Down	1969	$5
❏ 4-42671	Pretty Boy Lonely/Just a Simple Melody	1963	$8
❏ 4-42791	Say Wonderful Things/I Knew I Would See Him Again	1963	$8
❏ 4-44666	Stand By Your Man/Red Summer Roses	1968	$5
❏ 4-43909	The Wishing Doll/Music and Memories	1966	$6
❏ 4-43517	Till You Come Back to Me/Custody	1966	$6
❏ 4-44115	Walkin' -- Just Walkin'/Same Old You	1967	$5
❏ 4-44242	What's She Got That I Ain't Got (Darlin')/Pretty Bluebird	1967	$5
❏ 4-43990	Wish Me a Rainbow/This Is the Sunday	1967	$5

EPIC
❏ 11032	Love Lives Again/I Can't Sit Still	1973	$4
❏ 11109	Someone Came to See Me/One Final Stand	1974	$4

MERCURY
❏ 71792	A City Girl Stole My Country Boy/Dondi	1961	$8
❏ 71792 [PS]	A City Girl Stole My Country Boy/Dondi	1961	$20
❏ 70878	Allegheny Moon/The Strangest Romance	1956	$15
❏ 5512	All My Love (Bolero)/Back in Your Own Backyard	1950	$30
❏ 5455	All My Love (Bolero)/Roses Remind Me of You	1950	$30
❏ 5706	And So to Sleep Again/One Sweet Letter	1951	$20

Number	Title	Yr	NM
❑ 71294	Another Time, Another Place/These Worldly Wonders	1958	$10
❑ 71059	A Poor Man's Roses (Or a Rich Man's Gold)/The Wall	1957	$10
❑ 70190	Arfie, the Doggie in the Window/Arfie Goes to School	1953	$30
❑ 5463	Back in Your Own Backyard/Right Kind of Love	1950	$30
❑ 71247	Belonging to Someone/Bring Up Together	1957	$12
❑ 5729	Boogie Woogie Santa Claus/Christmas Bells	1951	$20
❑ 71870	Broken Heart and a Pillow Filled with Tears/Dark Moon	1961	$8
❑ 71870 [PS]	Broken Heart and a Pillow Filled with Tears/Dark Moon	1961	$20
❑ 70183	Butterflies/This Is My Song	1953	$20
❑ 70295	Changing Partners/Don't Get Around Much Anymore	1954	$20
❑ 70260	Changing Partners/Where Did My Snowman Go	1953	$20
❑ 73306	Come What May/Love Is a Friend of Mine	1972	$5
❑ 5772	Come What May/Retreat (Cries My Heart)	1952	$20
❑ 505	Confess/Money, Marbles and Chalk	1950	$40
—Reissue of her first hit from 1948			
❑ 5511	Confess/That Old Feeling	1950	$30
❑ 70713	Croce di Oro (Cross of Gold)/Search My Heart	1955	$15
❑ 70302	Cross Over the Bridge/My Restless Lover	1954	$20
❑ 5682	Detour/Who's Gonna Shoe My Pretty Little Feet	1951	$20
❑ 71745	Don't Read the Letter/That's All I Need to Know	1960	$8
❑ 71745 [PS]	Don't Read the Letter/That's All I Need to Know	1960	$20
❑ 5751	Down in the Valley/I Want to Be a Cowboy's Sweetheart	1951	$20
❑ 5579	Down the Trail of Achin' Hearts/Ever True Ever More	1951	$20
❑ 70528	Everlovin'/You Too Can Be a Dreamer	1955	$15
❑ 72044	Everytime I Hear Your Name/Let's Cry Together	1962	$8
❑ 70222	Father, Father/The Lord's Prayer	1953	$30
❑ 71355	Fibbin'/You Will Find Your Love (In Paris)	1958	$10
❑ 71355 [PS]	Fibbin'/You Will Find Your Love (In Paris)	1958	$30
❑ 73162	Give Him Love/Wish I Could Take That Little Boy Home	1970	$5
❑ 71510	Goodbye Charlie/Because Him Is a Baby	1959	$10
❑ 71906	Go On Home/Too Late to Cry	1961	$8
❑ 71906 [PS]	Go On Home/Too Late to Cry	1961	$20
❑ 70766	Go On with the Wedding/The Voice Inside	1955	$15
❑ 72078	High on the Hill of Hope/By a Long Shot	1963	$8
❑ 5396	I Don't Care If the Sun Don't Shine/I'm Gonna Paper All My Walls with Your Love Letters	1950	$30
❑ 73222	I'd Rather Be Sorry/Words	1971	$5
❑ 70532	I Got It Bad/Don't Get Around Much Anymore	1955	$15
❑ 71189	I'll Remember Today/My How the Time Goes By	1957	$10
❑ 72123	I'm Walkin'/Invitation to the Blues	1963	$8
❑ 5899	I Went to Your Wedding/You Belong to Me	1952	$20
❑ 71695	I Wish I'd Never Been Born/I Need You	1960	$8
❑ 71695 [PS]	I Wish I'd Never Been Born/I Need You	1960	$20
❑ 71331	Left Right Out of Your Heart (Hi Lee Hi Lo Hi Lup Up Up)/Longing to Hold You Again	1958	$12
❑ 70511	Let Me Go, Lover!/Hocus Pocus	1954	$20
❑ 70579	Little Crazy Quilt/Keep Me in Mind	1955	$15
❑ 73199	Make Me Your Kind of Woman/I Wish I Was a Little Boy Again	1971	$5
❑ 70971	Mama from the Train/Every Time (I Feel His Spirit)	1956	$15
❑ 5645	Mister and Mississippi/These Things I Offer You	1951	$20
—Black vinyl			
❑ 5645	Mister and Mississippi/These Things I Offer You	1951	$50
—Red vinyl			
❑ 5595	Mockin' Bird Hill/I Love You Because	1951	$20
❑ 71950	Most People Get Married/You Don't Know Me	1962	$8
❑ 71950 [PS]	Most People Get Married/You Don't Know Me	1962	$15
❑ 70230	My World Is You/Milwaukee Polka	1953	$20
❑ 71101	Old Cape Cod/Wondering	1957	$10
❑ 5867	Once in Awhile/I'm Glad You're Happy with Someone Else	1952	$20

Number	Title	Yr	NM
❑ 71639	One of Us (Will Weep Tonight)/What Will My Future Be	1960	$8
❑ 71639 [PS]	One of Us (Will Weep Tonight)/What Will My Future Be	1960	$20
❑ 70127	Oo What You Do to Me/Now That I'm in Love	1953	$20
❑ 70657	Piddily Patter Patter/Every Day	1955	$15
❑ 70506	Pretty Snowflakes/I Wanna Go Dancing with Willie	1954	$20
❑ 5731	Santa Claus Is Coming to Town/Silent Night	1951	$20
❑ 5521	So in Love/Why Can't You Behave	1950	$30
❑ 70380	Steam Heat/Lonely Days	1954	$20
❑ 5592	Tag-a-Long/Soft and Tenderly	1951	$30
—With Rex Allen			
❑ 70137	Tell Me Why/Big Mamou	1953	$20
—With Rusty Draper			
❑ 5715	That's All I Ask of You/I'm Glad You're Happy with Someone Else	1951	$20
❑ 72013	The Boys' Night Out/Three Fools	1962	$8
❑ 72013 [PS]	The Boys' Night Out/Three Fools	1962	$15
❑ 70070	The Doggie in the Window/My Jealous Eyes	1953	$20
❑ 70458	The Mama Doll Song/I Can't Tell a Waltz from a Tango	1954	$20
❑ 71555	The Sound of Music/Little Donkey	1959	$10
❑ 5534	The Tennessee Waltz/Boogie Woogie Santa Claus	1950	$30
❑ 5534	The Tennessee Waltz/Long, Long Ago	1951	$20
❑ 71428	The Walls Have Ears/My Promise	1959	$10
❑ 73249	Think Again/A Woman Left Lonely	1971	$5
❑ 70820	Too Young to Go Steady/My First Formal Gown	1956	$15
❑ 71400	Trust in Me/Under the Sun Valley Moon	1958	$10
❑ 71597	Two Thousand, Two Hundred, Twenty-Three Miles/Promise Her, Thomas	1960	$8
❑ 70416	What a Dream/I Cried	1954	$20
❑ 5707	Whispering/Cabaret	1951	$20
❑ 5816	Whispering Winds/Love Where You Are	1952	$20
❑ 5732	White Christmas/The Christmas Song	1951	$20
—The above four comprise a box set			
❑ 70025	Why Don't You Believe Me/Conquest	1952	$20
❑ 71469	With My Eyes Wide Open I'm Dreaming/My Mother's Eyes	1959	$10
❑ 5571	Would I Love You (Love You, Love You)/Sentimental Music	1951	$20
PLANTATION			
❑ 212	Barbara's Daughter/(B-side unknown)	1982	$4
❑ 208	My Man Friday/Tennessee Waltz	1982	$4
❑ 201	On the Inside/A Poor Man's Roses	1981	$4
❑ 199	Wasn't It Good/Detour	1981	$4
❑ EP-1-3038 [PS]	Christmas with Patti Page	1956	$15
❑ EP-1-3038	The Christmas Song/The First Noel//Christmas Choir/Christmas Bells	1956	$15

PAGENTS, THE
BAMBOO

Number	Title	Yr	NM
❑ 525	Pa-Cha/Sad and Lonely	1963	$60

ERA

Number	Title	Yr	NM
❑ 3119	Enchanted/The Big Daddy	1963	$40
❑ 3124	Glenda/Shake	1964	$40
❑ 3134	Pa-Cha/Sad and Lonely	1964	$30

IKE

Number	Title	Yr	NM
❑ 631	Enchanted Surf/The Big Daddy	1963	$125

PAIGE, HAL
ATLANTIC

Number	Title	Yr	NM
❑ 1032	Big Foot May/Please Say You Do	1954	$200
❑ 996	Drive It Home/Break of Day Blues	1953	$200

CHECKER

Number	Title	Yr	NM
❑ 873	Don't Have to Cry No More/Pour the Corn	1957	$30

FURY

Number	Title	Yr	NM
❑ 1024	After Hours Blues/Going Back to My Home Town	1959	$30
❑ 1002	Don't Have to Cry No More/Pour the Corn	1957	$100

J&S

Number	Title	Yr	NM
❑ 1601	Thunderbird/Sugar Bare	1957	$40

PAIN, JOE
LITTLE DARLIN'

Number	Title	Yr	NM
❑ 039	Deaf, Dumb and Blind/True Love Dies	1968	$12
❑ 025	Down at Kelly's/A Thousand Times Paid	1967	$12

PAIR, THE
LIBERTY

Number	Title	Yr	NM
❑ 55748	Patience Baby/Fight for Your Girl	1965	$8
—As "The Pair Extraordinaire"			

PALACE GUARD, THE
ORANGE EMPIRE

Number	Title	Yr	NM
❑ 332	A Girl You Can Depend On/If You Need Me	1965	$20
❑ 331	All Night Long/Playgirl	1965	$20
❑ 400	Falling Sugar/Oh Blue	1965	$20

PARKWAY

Number	Title	Yr	NM
❑ 124	Calliope/Creed	1966	$15
❑ 111	Saturday's Child/Party Lights	1966	$15

VERVE

Number	Title	Yr	NM
❑ 10410	Falling Sugar/Oh Blue	1966	$10

PALISADES, THE
CALICO

Number	Title	Yr	NM
❑ 113	Close Your Eyes/I Can't Quit	1960	$30

CHAIRMAN

Number	Title	Yr	NM
❑ 4401	Heaven Is Being with You/Make the Night a Little Longer	1963	$30
—With Carole King			

DEBRA

Number	Title	Yr	NM
❑ 1003	Chapel Bells/She Can't Stop Dancing	1963	$200
—Also released credited to "The Magics			

DORE

Number	Title	Yr	NM
❑ 609	Hometown Girl/Oh My Love	1961	$20

LEADER

Number	Title	Yr	NM
❑ 806	Dear Joan/The Shrine	1960	$30

MEDIEVAL

Number	Title	Yr	NM
❑ 205	This Is the Night/Relic Rock	1962	$30

PALLESI, BRUNO
DECCA

Number	Title	Yr	NM
❑ 31343	Caro Gesu Bambino/Dear Gesu Bambino	1961	$15
—B-side by Christian Morandi			

PALM BEACH BAND BOYS, THE
RCA VICTOR

Number	Title	Yr	NM
❑ 47-9003	Bend It/Gypsy Caravan	1966	$6
❑ 47-9026	I'm Gonna Sit Right Down and Write Myself a Letter/I Don't Want to Set the World on Fire	1966	$6
❑ 47-9207	More and More/Fernanda's Theme	1967	$6
❑ 47-9141	The Object of My Affection/Strangers in the Night	1967	$6

PALMER, ROBERT
EMI

Number	Title	Yr	NM
❑ 50183	She Makes My Day/Casting a Spell	1989	$3
❑ 50183 [PS]	She Makes My Day/Casting a Spell	1989	$3
❑ 7PRO-04311 [DJ]	Tell Me I'm Not Dreaming/Tell Me I'm Not Dreaming (12" Edit)	1989	$5
—Vinyl is promo only			

EMI MANHATTAN

Number	Title	Yr	NM
❑ 50157	Early in the Morning/Disturbing Behavior	1988	$3
❑ 50157 [PS]	Early in the Morning/Disturbing Behavior	1988	$3
❑ 50133	Simply Irresistible/Nova	1988	$3
❑ 50133 [PS]	Simply Irresistible/Nova	1988	$3

ISLAND

Number	Title	Yr	NM
❑ 99570	Addicted to Love/Let's Fall in Love Tonight	1986	$3
❑ 99570 [PS]	Addicted to Love/Let's Fall in Love Tonight	1986	$4
—First version: Close-up photo of Robert Palmer			
❑ 99570 [PS]	Addicted to Love/Let's Fall in Love Tonight	1986	$4
—Second version: Photo of "models" band from video			
❑ 49016	Bad Case of Loving You (Doctor, Doctor)/Love Can Run Faster	1979	$4
❑ 99139	Bad Case of Loving You/Sweet Lies	1989	$3
❑ 99139 [PS]	Bad Case of Loving You/Sweet Lies	1989	$4

Number	Title	Yr	NM
❏ 49137	Can We Still Be Friends/Remember to Remember	1979	$4
❏ 99597	Discipline of Love (Why Did You Do It)/Dance for Me	1985	$3
❏ 99597 [PS]	Discipline of Love (Why Did You Do It)/Dance for Me	1985	$3
❏ 100	Every Kinda People/How Much Fun	1978	$4
❏ 015	Get Ta Steppin'/Get Right On Down	1975	$5
❏ 99545	Hyperactive/Woke Up Laughing	1986	$3
❏ 99537	I Didn't Mean to Turn You On/Get It Through Your Heart	1986	$3
❏ 99537 [PS]	I Didn't Mean to Turn You On/Get It Through Your Heart	1986	$3
❏ 49094	In Walks Love Again/Jealous	1979	$4
❏ 49620	Looking for Clues/Woke Up Laughing	1980	$4
❏ 075	Man Smart, Woman Smarter/Keep in Touch	1976	$5
❏ 081	One Last Look/Some People Can Do What They Want	1977	$5
❏ 049	Pressure Drop/Give Me an Inch Girl	1976	$5
❏ 99835	Pride/(B-side unknown)	1983	$3
❏ 99835 [PS]	Pride/(B-side unknown)	1983	$4
❏ 006	Sneakin' Sally Through the Alley/Epidemic	1974	$5
❏ 50042	Some Guys Have All the Luck/Too Good to Be True	1982	$4
❏ 49554	Style Kills/Johnny and Mary	1980	$4
❏ 99377	Sweet Lies/Want You More	1988	$3
❏ 99377 [PS]	Sweet Lies/Want You More	1988	$3
❏ 8697	Where Can It Go/You're Gonna Get What's Coming	1978	$4
❏ 042	Which One of Us Is the Fool/Get Outside	1975	$5

MCA

Number	Title	Yr	NM
❏ 52643	All Around the World/It's Not Difficult	1985	$3

PALS, THE

GUYDEN

Number	Title	Yr	NM
❏ 2019	My Baby Likes to Rock/Summer Is Here	1959	$30

TURF

Number	Title	Yr	NM
❏ 1000	My Baby Likes to Rock/Summer Is Here	1958	$50

PANICS, THE

ABC-PARAMOUNT

Number	Title	Yr	NM
❏ 10072	Heartaches/You're Driving Me Crazy	1959	$20

CHANCELLOR

Number	Title	Yr	NM
❏ 1109	Panicsville/Bony Moronie	1962	$20
❏ 1127	Skinnie Minnie Olive Oil/Voodoo Walk	1962	$20

SWAN

Number	Title	Yr	NM
❏ 4247	Beans/Show Her You Care	1966	$15

PAPA DOO RUN RUN

EQUINOX

Number	Title	Yr	NM
❏ PB-10404	Disney Girls/Be True to Your School	1975	$12

PAPER DOLLS, THE

MGM

Number	Title	Yr	NM
❏ 13766	'Cause I Love You/You're the Boy I Want to Marry	1967	$15

UNI

Number	Title	Yr	NM
❏ 55104	Someday/Any Old Time You're Lonely and Sad	1969	$12

WARNER BROS.

Number	Title	Yr	NM
❏ 7191	All the Time in the World/Something Here in My Heart (Keeps a-Tellin' Me No)	1968	$10

PAPER LACE

BANG

Number	Title	Yr	NM
❏ 700	Martha/You Can't Touch Me	1972	$5

MERCURY

Number	Title	Yr	NM
❏ 73479	Billy, Don't Be a Hero/Celia	1974	$6
❏ 73694	So What If I Am/Himalayan Lullaby	1975	$4
❏ 73620	The Black-Eyed Boys/Jean	1974	$4

PAPPALARDI, FELIX

COLUMBIA

Number	Title	Yr	NM
❏ 43773	Love Someday/You Lie to Me	1966	$30

PARADE, THE

A&M

Number	Title	Yr	NM
❏ 950	A.C.-D.C./She Sleeps Alone	1968	$6
❏ 887	Frog Prince/Hallelujah Rocket	1967	$6

Number	Title	Yr	NM
❏ 904	I Can See Love/Radio Song	1968	$6
❏ 970	Laughing Lady/Hallelujah Rocket	1968	$6
❏ 867	She's Got the Magic/Welcome, You're in Love	1967	$6
❏ 841	Sunshine Girl/This Old Melody	1967	$10

PARADONS, THE

MILESTONE

Number	Title	Yr	NM
❏ 2005	Bells Ring/Please Tell Me	1960	$40
❏ 2003	Diamonds and Pearls/I Want Love	1960	$60

—Maroon label

Number	Title	Yr	NM
❏ 2003	Diamonds and Pearls/I Want Love	1960	$40

—Red label

Number	Title	Yr	NM
❏ 2003	Diamonds and Pearls/I Want Love	1960	$30

—Green label

Number	Title	Yr	NM
❏ 2015	I Had a Dream/Never, Never	1962	$50

WARNER BROS.

Number	Title	Yr	NM
❏ 5186	Take All of Me/So Fine, So Fine, So Fine	1960	$30

PARAGONS, THE

BUDDAH

Number	Title	Yr	NM
❏ 478	Oh Lovin' You/Con Me	1975	$6

MUSIC CLEF

Number	Title	Yr	NM
❏ 3001/2	Time After Time/Baby, Take My Hand	1963	$30

MUSICRAFT

Number	Title	Yr	NM
❏ 1102	Wedding Bells/Blue Velvet	1960	$30

TAP

Number	Title	Yr	NM
❏ 500	If/Hey Baby	1961	$60
❏ 503	In the Midst of the Night/Begin the Beguine	1961	$50
❏ 504	These Are the Things I Love/If You Love Me	1961	$50

TIMES SQUARE

Number	Title	Yr	NM
❏ 9	So You Will Know/Don't Cry Baby	1963	$30

WINLEY

Number	Title	Yr	NM
❏ 236	Darling, I Love You/Doll Baby	1959	$50
❏ 228	Don't Cry Baby/So You Will Know	1958	$50
❏ 215	Hey Little School Girl/Florence	1957	$60
❏ 220	Let's Start All Over Again/Stick With Me Baby	1957	$60
❏ 240	So You Will Know/Doll Baby	1959	$40
❏ 227	The Wows of Love/Twilight	1958	$1000

—With misspelled A-side title

Number	Title	Yr	NM
❏ 223	Two Hearts Are Better Than One/Give Me Love	1958	$50

PARAKEETS, THE (1)

BIG TOP

Number	Title	Yr	NM
❏ 3130	I Love You Like I Do/I Want You Right Now	1962	$30

JUBILEE

Number	Title	Yr	NM
❏ 5407	Come Back/Shangri-La	1961	$30

PARAKEETS, THE (2)

GEM

Number	Title	Yr	NM
❏ 218	Give Me Time/I'm Losing My Mind Over You	1954	$400

PARAMOR, NORRIE

CAPITOL

Number	Title	Yr	NM
❏ F3629	Every Street's a Boulevard/Magic Banjo	1957	$12
❏ F3714	Taurus Tango/Gemini Waltz	1957	$10
❏ F4266	Waltzing Matilda/Barcelona	1959	$10

ESSEX

Number	Title	Yr	NM
❏ 337	Callahan's Monkey/Melodia	1953	$20
❏ 356	Wedding Day/Luxembourg Polka	1954	$15

PARAMOUNTS, THE (1)

CARLTON

Number	Title	Yr	NM
❏ 524	Girl Friend/Trying	1960	$50

PARAMOUNTS, THE (2)

CENTAUR

Number	Title	Yr	NM
❏ 103	When I Dream/Where's Carolyn Tonight	1963	$70

PARAMOUNTS, THE (3)

DOT

Number	Title	Yr	NM
❏ 16201	When You Dance/Year 17	1961	$30
❏ 16175	Why Do You Have to Go/Congratulations	1961	$30

PARAMOUNTS, THE (4)

LIVERPOOL SOUND

Number	Title	Yr	NM
❏ 903	Poison Ivy/I Feel Good All Over	1964	$80

PARAMOUNTS, THE (U)

COMBO

Number	Title	Yr	NM
❏ 156	Take My Heart/Thunderbird Baby	1960	$120

FLEETWOOD

Number	Title	Yr	NM
❏ 1014	I Know You'll Be My Love/Christopher Columbus	1960	$125

MAGNUM

Number	Title	Yr	NM
❏ 722	Time Will Bring a Change/Under Your Spell	1964	$40

MERCURY

Number	Title	Yr	NM
❏ 72429	Girl with the Big Black Boots/I Won't Share Your Love	1965	$15

PARAMOURS, THE

MOONGLOW

Number	Title	Yr	NM
❏ 214	That's All I Want Tonight/There She Goes	1962	$30
❏ 214	That's All I Want Tonight/There She Goes	1962	$50

—Red vinyl

SMASH

Number	Title	Yr	NM
❏ 1718	Cutie Cutie/Miss Social Climber	1961	$30
❏ 1701	That's the Way We Love/Prison Break	1961	$30

PARIS, BOBBY

CAPITOL

Number	Title	Yr	NM
❏ 3592	Baby, Spread Your Love on Me/You're a Friend	1973	$12
❏ 5929	I Walked Away/Kansas City	1967	$500

—Counterfeits exist with B-sides by other artists

Number	Title	Yr	NM
❏ 3727	Love Looks So Good on You/Day Dreamer	1973	$10

CHATTAHOOCHEE

Number	Title	Yr	NM
❏ 631	Little Miss Dreamer/Who Needs You	1963	$15
❏ 672	Love Passed Me By/The Fight	1965	$20

JAIRICK

Number	Title	Yr	NM
❏ 204	Are You the One/Torch Is Out	1963	$20

JOLAR

Number	Title	Yr	NM
❏ 1001	Is It You/Wishing Well	1962	$20

MAGENTA

Number	Title	Yr	NM
❏ 03	Dark Continent (Part 1)/(Part 2)	1961	$30

TETRAGRAMMATON

Number	Title	Yr	NM
❏ 1509	Let Me Show You the Way/Bye, Bye, Blackbird	1968	$30
❏ 1517	Let the Sunshine In (The Flesh Failures)/You	1969	$12
❏ 1504	Per-So-Nal-Ly/Tragedy	1968	$100

—Authentic copies are on styrene; counterfeits are on vinyl

PARIS BROTHERS, THE

BRUNSWICK

Number	Title	Yr	NM
❏ 55132	This Is It/Our Love Is Here to Stay	1959	$40

CORAL

Number	Title	Yr	NM
❏ 62220	Funny Feeling/(B-side unknown)	1959	$30

PARIS, FREDDIE

RCA VICTOR

Number	Title	Yr	NM
❏ 47-9358	Little Things Can Make a Woman Cry/Face It, Boy, It's Over	1967	$10
❏ 47-9232	Take Me As I Am/It's Okay to Cry Now	1967	$10
❏ 47-9571	There She Goes/Young Hearts, Young Hands	1968	$30

PARIS SISTERS, THE
Also see PRISCILLA PARIS.

CAPITOL

Number	Title	Yr	NM
❏ 2081	Golden Days/Greener Days	1968	$8

DECCA

Number	Title	Yr	NM
❏ 29488	Baby, Honey, Baby/Huckleberry Pie	1955	$30
❏ 29970	Daughter! Daughter!/So Much -- So Very Much	1956	$30
❏ 30554	Don't Tell Anybody/Mind Reader	1958	$30
❏ 29527	His and Hers/Truly Do	1955	$30

—With Gary Crosby

Number	Title	Yr	NM
❏ 29891	I Love You Dear/Mistaken	1956	$30
❏ 29744	Lover Boy/Oh Yes You Do	1955	$30

Number	Title	Yr	NM
❏ 29372	Ooh La La/Whose Arms Are You Missing	1954	$30

GNP CRESCENDO

Number	Title	Yr	NM
❏ 410	Stand Naked Clown/Ugliest Girl in Town	1968	$8

GREGMARK

Number	Title	Yr	NM
❏ 2	Be My Boy/I'll Be Crying Tomorrow	1961	$30
❏ 10	He Knows I Love Him Too Much/Lonely Girl's Prayer	1962	$30
❏ 6	I Love How You Love Me/All Through the Night	1961	$30
❏ 12	Let Me Be the One/What Am I to Do	1962	$30

IMPERIAL

Number	Title	Yr	NM
❏ 5465	Old Enough to Cry/Tell Me More	1957	$30
❏ 5487	Some Day/My Original Love	1958	$30

MERCURY

Number	Title	Yr	NM
❏ 72468	Always Waitin'/Why Do I Take It from You	1965	$10
❏ 72468 [PS]	Always Waitin'/Why Do I Take It from You	1965	$30
❏ 72320	Once Upon a Time/When I Fall in Love	1964	$10
❏ 72320 [PS]	Once Upon a Time/When I Fall in Love	1964	$30

MGM

Number	Title	Yr	NM
❏ 13236	Dream Lover/Lonely Girl	1964	$20
❏ 13236 [PS]	Dream Lover/Lonely Girl	1964	$30

REPRISE

Number	Title	Yr	NM
❏ 0472	I'm Me/You	1966	$10
❏ 0511	It's My Party/My Good Friend	1966	$10
❏ 0440	Sincerely/Too Good to Be True	1965	$10
❏ 0548	Some of Your Lovin'/Long After Tonight Is All Over	1967	$12

PARKER, BILLY (1)

CANYON CREEK

Number	Title	Yr	NM
❏ 0315	It's Time for Your Dreams to Come True/You Are My Angel	1989	$5
❏ 0801	She's Sittin' Pretty/(B-side unknown)	1988	$5

DECCA

Number	Title	Yr	NM
❏ 32652	I Get a Happy Feeling/If These Tears Could Talk	1970	$8
❏ 32913	Ladder of Success/Looking for a Woman	1972	$8
❏ 32462	The Pillow/I'll Drink to That	1969	$8

OAK

Number	Title	Yr	NM
❏ 47565	Better Side of Thirty/Lord If I Make It	1981	$6

SCR

Number	Title	Yr	NM
❏ 120	Average Man/(B-side unknown)	1975	$6
❏ 157	If There's One Angel Missing (She's Here in My Arms Tonight)/Tough Act to Follow	1978	$5
❏ 157 [PS]	If There's One Angel Missing (She's Here in My Arms Tonight)/Tough Act to Follow	1978	$8
❏ 148	If You Got to Have It Your Way (I'll Go Mine)/The Line Between Love and Hate	1977	$6
❏ 129	I'll Hold You in My Heart/These Hard Times	1976	$6
❏ 133	It's Bad When You're Caught (With the Goods)/I Guess I Owe That Much to You	1976	$6
❏ 185	Lord, If I Make It to Heaven Can I Bring My Own Angel Along/(B-side unknown)	1980	$5
❏ 136	Lord, If I Make It to Heaven Can I Bring My Own Angel Along/Jerri Again	1976	$6
❏ 127	More Than One Kind of Love/(B-side unknown)	1976	$6
❏ 162	Pleasin' My Woman/Thanks E.T. Thanks a Lot	1978	$5
❏ 177	Thanks a Lot/Until the Next Time	1979	$5
❏ 181	Tough Act to Follow/(B-side unknown)	1979	$5
❏ 118	Travelin' Truckin' Man/The Man from Galilee	1975	$6
❏ 144	What Did I Promise Her Last Night/Let a Fool Take a Bow	1977	$6

SIMS

Number	Title	Yr	NM
❏ 184	Sounds Like a Winner/Tattooed Lover	1964	$15
❏ 146	The Line Between Love and Hate/I Hurt Me (Instead of You)	1963	$20

SOUNDWAVES

Number	Title	Yr	NM
❏ 4773	Her Lovin' Already Told Me She Was Gone/I Found a Miracle in You	1986	$5
❏ 4678	If I Ever Need a Lady/Can I Have What's Left	1982	$5

—A-side as "Billy Parker and Friend"

Number	Title	Yr	NM
❏ 4643	I'll Drink to That/One More Last Time	1981	$5
❏ 4659	I See an Angel Every Day/Hello Out There	1981	$5
❏ 4708	Love Don't Know a Lady (From a Honky Tonk Girl)/It's Not Me	1983	$5

—A-side as "Billy Parker and Friends"

Number	Title	Yr	NM
❏ 4719	Memory #1/Why Do I Keep Calling You Honey	1983	$5

—A-side with Webb Pierce

Number	Title	Yr	NM
❏ 4686	Too Many Irons in the Fire/Honky Tonk Girl	1982	$5

—A-side with Cal Smith

Number	Title	Yr	NM
❏ 4729	When I Need Love Bad/Tomorrow Never Comes	1984	$5

—With Ernest Tubb

Number	Title	Yr	NM
❏ 4699	Who Said Love Was Fair/Take Me Back to Tulsa	1983	$5

—A-side as "Billy Parker and Friends"

Number	Title	Yr	NM
❏ 4670	(Who's Gonna Sing) The Last Country Song/What's a Nice Girl Like You	1982	$5

—A-side as "Billy Parker and Friend"

Number	Title	Yr	NM
❏ 4746	Why Do I Keep Calling You Honey, Honey/I Believe I'm Entitled to You	1984	$5

PARKER, BOBBY

V-TONE

Number	Title	Yr	NM
❏ 223	Watch Your Step/Steal Your Heart Away	1961	$30

—45-V Tone 223-A" in hit side trail-off area

Number	Title	Yr	NM
❏ 223	Watch Your Step/Steal Your Heart Away	1961	$20

—223-AAX" in hit side trail-off area

PARKER, CHARLIE

CLEF

Number	Title	Yr	NM
❏ 89129	Cosmic Rays/Kim	1955	$30
❏ 89144	I Hear Music/Laird Baird	1955	$30
❏ 89138	I Remember You/Chi Chi	1955	$30

PARKER, FESS, AND BUDDY EBSEN

COLUMBIA

Number	Title	Yr	NM
❏ 4-40510	Be Sure You're Right (Then Go Ahead)/Old Betsy (Davy Crockett's Rifle)	1955	$30
❏ B-2031	Davy Crockett, Indian Fighter	1955	$50

—Cover for 40476 and 40477

Number	Title	Yr	NM
❏ 4-40476	Davy Crockett, Indian Fighter (Part 1)/Davy Crockett, Indian Fighter (Part 4)	1955	$30
❏ 4-40477	Davy Crockett, Indian Fighter (Part 2)/Davy Crockett, Indian Fighter (Part 3)	1955	$30
❏ B-2033	Davy Crockett at the Alamo	1955	$50

—Cover for 40480 and 40481

Number	Title	Yr	NM
❏ 4-40480	Davy Crockett at the Alamo (Part 1)/Davy Crockett at the Alamo (Part 4)	1955	$30
❏ 4-40481	Davy Crockett at the Alamo (Part 2)/Davy Crockett at the Alamo (Part 3)	1955	$30
❏ B-2032	Davy Crockett Goes to Congress	1955	$50

—Cover for 40478 and 40479

Number	Title	Yr	NM
❏ 4-40478	Davy Crockett Goes to Congress (Part 1)/Davy Crockett Goes to Congress (Part 4)	1955	$30
❏ 4-40479	Davy Crockett Goes to Congress (Part 2)/Davy Crockett Goes to Congress (Part 3)	1955	$30

PARKER, FESS

BUENA VISTA

Number	Title	Yr	NM
❏ F-426	Ballad of Davy Crockett/Farewell	1963	$15
❏ F-426 [PS]	Ballad of Davy Crockett/Farewell	1963	$20

CASCADE

Number	Title	Yr	NM
❏ 5910	Eyes of an Angel/Strong Man	1959	$20
❏ 5913	Lonely/Jayhawkers	1959	$20

COLUMBIA

Number	Title	Yr	NM
❏ 4-40449	Ballad of Davy Crockett/I Gave My Love (Riddle Song)	1955	$20
❏ J4-242	Ballad of Davy Crockett/I Gave My Love (Riddle Song)	1955	$30

—Yellow label "Children's Series" release

Number	Title	Yr	NM
❏ J4-242 [PS]	Ballad of Davy Crockett/I Gave My Love (Riddle Song)	1955	$50

—Yellow label "Children's Series" release

Number	Title	Yr	NM
❏ 4-40450	Farewell/I'm Lonely My Darlin'	1955	$20

DISNEYLAND

Number	Title	Yr	NM
❏ F-049	A Hole in the Sky/Wedding Bell Calypso	1957	$15
❏ F-049 [PS]	A Hole in the Sky/Wedding Bell Calypso	1957	$30
❏ F-053	Gonna Find Me a Bluebird/Catch Me Fish	1957	$30
❏ F-045	Pioneer's Prayer/The Ballad of John Coulter	1957	$15
❏ F-045 [PS]	Pioneer's Prayer/The Ballad of John Coulter	1957	$30
❏ F-039	Wringle Wrangle/(Instrumental)	1957	$40

—B-side by Camarata

Number	Title	Yr	NM
❏ F-043	Wringle Wrangle/The Ballad of John Coulter	1957	$15
❏ F-043 [PS]	Wringle Wrangle/The Ballad of John Coulter	1957	$30

GUSTO

Number	Title	Yr	NM
❏ 900	Ballad of Davy Crockett/Lonely	1963	$12

RCA VICTOR

Number	Title	Yr	NM
❏ 74-0249	Comin' After Jimmy/Sittin' Here Drinkin'	1969	$10
❏ 47-8429	Daniel Boone/The Ballad of Davy Crockett	1964	$15
❏ 47-8429 [PS]	Daniel Boone/The Ballad of Davy Crockett	1964	$30

PARKER, GRAHAM
Includes records with THE RUMOUR.

ARISTA

Number	Title	Yr	NM
❏ 0549	Endless Nights/No Holding Back	1980	$4

—A-side: Guest vocals by Bruce Springsteen

Number	Title	Yr	NM
❏ 9065	Life Gets Better/Beyond a Joke	1983	$3
❏ 0420	Local Girls/I Want You Back	1979	$4
❏ 0420 [PS]	Local Girls/I Want You Back	1979	$4
❏ 0439	Mercury Poisoning/I Want You Back (Alive)	1979	$4
❏ 0523	Stupefaction/Women in Charge	1980	$4
❏ 0523 [PS]	Stupefaction/Women in Charge	1980	$4
❏ 0652	Temporary Beauty/No More Excuses	1981	$4

ELEKTRA

Number	Title	Yr	NM
❏ 69654	Wake Up (Next to You)/Bricks and Mortar	1985	$4
❏ 69654 [PS]	Wake Up (Next to You)/Bricks and Mortar	1985	$5

MERCURY

Number	Title	Yr	NM
❏ 73876	Heat Treatment/Back Door Love	1976	$8
❏ 74000	Hold Back the Night/(Let Me Get) Sweet on You//White Honey/Soul Shoes	1977	$5

—Pink vinyl

Number	Title	Yr	NM
❏ DJ-491 [DJ]	Hold Back the Night (same on both sides)	1977	$15
❏ DJ-491 [DJ]	Hold Back the Night (same on both sides)	1977	$15
❏ 73834	Soul Shoes/You've Got to Be Kidding	1976	$8
❏ DJ-531 [DJ]	Stick to Me (same on both sides)	1977	$15
❏ DJ-531 [DJ]	Stick to Me (same on both sides)	1977	$15
❏ 73970	Stick to Me/The Heat in Harlem	1977	$8
❏ 74000 [PS]	The Pink Parker": Hold Back the Night/(Let Me Get) Sweet on You//White Honey/Soul Shoes, The	1977	$5

RCA

Number	Title	Yr	NM
❏ 8639-7-R	(Get Started) Start a Fire/Ordinary Girl	1988	$3
❏ 8639-7-R [PS]	(Get Started) Start a Fire/Ordinary Girl	1988	$3

PARKER, JUNIOR

BLUE ROCK

Number	Title	Yr	NM
❏ 4080	Ain't Gon' Be No Cuttin' Loose/I'm So Satisfied	1969	$8
❏ 4088	Easy Lovin'/You Can't Keep a Good Woman Down	1969	$8
❏ 4064	I Got Money/Lover to Friend	1968	$8

CAPITOL

Number	Title	Yr	NM
❏ 2997	Drownin' on Dry Land/River's Invitation	1970	$6
❏ 2951	Lady Madonna/Tomorrow Never Knows	1970	$12
❏ 2857	The Outside Man/Darling, Depend on Me	1970	$6

DUKE

Number	Title	Yr	NM
❏ 345	Annie Get Your Yo-Yo/Mary Jo	1961	$15
❏ 137	Backtracking/I Wanna Ramble	1954	$75
❏ 193	Barefoot Rock/What Did I Do	1958	$30

Number	Title	Yr	NM
❏ 389	Crying for My Baby/Guess You Don't Know (The Golden Rule)	1965	$15
❏ 315	Dangerous Woman/Belinda Marie	1960	$20
❏ 120	Dirty Friend Blues/Can't Understand	1954	$70
❏ 147	Driving Me/There Better Not Be No Feel	1956	$60
❏ 335	Driving Wheel/Seven Days	1961	$30
❏ 306	Five Long Years/I'm Holding On	1959	$30
❏ 357	Foxy Devil/Someone Somewhere	1962	$15
❏ 406	Get Away Blues/Why Do You Make Me Cry	1966	$15
❏ 351	I Feel Alright Again/Sweeter As the Days Go By	1962	$15
❏ 364	If You Don't Love Me/I Can't Forget About You	1963	$15
❏ 326	I'll Learn to Love Again/That's Just Alright	1960	$20
❏ 384	I'm in Love/Jivin' Woman	1964	$15
❏ 341	In the Dark/How Long Can This Go On	1961	$15
❏ 362	It's a Pity/Last Night	1963	$15
❏ 413	Man or Mouse/Wait for Another Day	1966	$15
❏ 157	Mother-in-Law Blues/That's My Baby	1956	$60
❏ 177	Peaches/Pretty Little Doll	1957	$40
❏ 127	Please Baby Please/Sittin', Drinkin' and Thinkin'	1954	$70
❏ 330	Stand By Me/I'll Forget About You	1960	$20
❏ 309	Stranded/Blue Letter	1959	$30
❏ 371	Strange Things Happening/I'm Gonna Stop	1964	$15
❏ 301	Sweet Home Chicago/Sometimes	1959	$30
❏ 168	That's Alright/Pretty Baby	1957	$40
❏ 394	These Kind of Blues (Part 1)/These Kind of Blues (Part 2)	1966	$15
❏ 367	The Tables Have Turned/Yonders Wall	1963	$15
❏ 376	Things I Used to Do/That's Why I'm Always Crying	1964	$15
❏ 398	Walking the Floor Over You/Goodbye Little Girl	1966	$15
❏ 184	Wondering/Sitting and Thinking	1958	$30

GROOVE MERCHANT

❏ 1004	I Like Your Style/I Need Love So Bad	1972	$10
❏ 1010	Love Ain't Nothin' But a Business Goin' On/Losing Battle	1972	$10
❏ 1002	Way Back Home/(B-side unknown)	1971	$15

MERCURY

❏ 72620	Baby Please/Just Like a Fish	1966	$12
❏ 72672	Country Girl/Sometimes I Wonder	1967	$12
❏ 72733	Hurtin' Inside/What a Fool I Was	1967	$10
❏ 72699	I Can't Put My Finger On It/If I Had Your Love	1967	$10
❏ 72793	It Must Be Love/Your Love's All Over	1968	$8

MINIT

| ❏ 32080 | Worried Life Blues/Let the Good Times Roll | 1969 | $6 |

SUN

| ❏ 187 | Feelin' Good/Fussin' and Fightin' Blues | 1953 | $400 |

—As "Little Junior's Blue Flames

| ❏ 192 | Mystery Train/Love My Baby | 1954 | $300 |

—As "Little Junior's Blue Flames

UNITED ARTISTS

| ❏ 50855 | Funny How Time Slips Away/No One Knows | 1971 | $10 |

PARKER, RAY, JR.

ARISTA

| ❏ 0592 | A Woman Needs Love (Just Like You Do)/So Into You | 1981 | $4 |

—As "Ray Parker Jr. and Raydio

| ❏ 1030 | Bad Boy/Let's Get Off | 1982 | $4 |
| ❏ 0554 | Can't Keep from Cryin'/It's Time to Party Now | 1980 | $4 |

—As "Ray Parker Jr. and Raydio

❏ 1035	Christmas Time Is Here/(Instrumental)	1982	$5
❏ 1035 [PS]	Christmas Time Is Here/(Instrumental)	1982	$6
❏ 0522	For Those Who Like to Groove/Can't Keep from Cryin'	1980	$4

—As "Ray Parker Jr. and Raydio

❏ 9212	Ghostbusters/(Instrumental)	1984	$3
❏ 9352	Girls Are More Fun/I'm in Love	1985	$3
❏ 9352 [PS]	Girls Are More Fun/I'm in Love	1985	$3

Number	Title	Yr	NM
❏ 0353	Honey I'm Rich/Betcha You Can't Love Me Just Once	1978	$5

—As "Raydio

| ❏ 9198 | In the Heat of the Night/N2 U2 | 1984 | $4 |
| ❏ 0328 | Is This a Love Thing/Let's Go All the Way | 1978 | $5 |

—As "Raydio

❏ 9116	I Still Can't Get Over Losing You/She Still Feels the Need	1983	$4
❏ 1014	It's Our Own Affair/Just Havin' Fun	1982	$4
❏ 0641	It's Your Night/Old Pro	1981	$4

—As "Ray Parker Jr. and Raydio

| ❏ 0695 | Let Me Go/Stop, Look Before You Fall | 1982 | $4 |
| ❏ 0575 | Little Bit of You/It's Time to Party Now | 1980 | $4 |

—As "Ray Parker Jr. and Raydio

| ❏ 0441 | More Than One Way to Love a Woman/Hot Stuff | 1979 | $5 |

—As "Raydio

| ❏ 9451 | One Sided Love Affair/Men Have Feelings Too | 1985 | $4 |
| ❏ 0616 | That Old Song/Old Pro | 1981 | $4 |

—As "Ray Parker Jr. and Raydio

| ❏ 0616 [PS] | That Old Song/Old Pro | 1981 | $4 |

—As "Ray Parker Jr. and Raydio

❏ 0669	The Other Woman/Stay the Night	1982	$4
❏ 1051	The People Next Door/Streetlove	1983	$4
❏ 0494	Two Places at the Same Time/Everybody Makes Mistakes	1980	$4

—As "Ray Parker Jr. and Raydio

| ❏ 9048 | Woman Out of Control/She Still Feels the Need | 1983 | $4 |

ATLANTIC

| ❏ 89456 | One Sunny Day-Dueling Bikes from Quicksilver/How Long | 1986 | $3 |

—A-side with Helen Terry; B-side by the Motor Band

| ❏ 89456 [PS] | One Sunny Day-Dueling Bikes from Quicksilver/How Long | 1986 | $3 |

FLASHBACK

| ❏ 9288 | Christmas Time Is Here/(Instrumental) | 1984 | $3 |

—Reissue

GEFFEN

❏ 28417	I Don't Think That Man Should Sleep Alone/After Midnight	1987	$3
❏ 28417 [PS]	I Don't Think That Man Should Sleep Alone/After Midnight	1987	$3
❏ 28152	Over You/After Midnite	1987	$3
❏ 28152 [PS]	Over You/After Midnite	1987	$3

—With Natalie Cole

PARKER, ROBERT

IMPERIAL

| ❏ 5842 | Mash Potatoes All Night Long/Twistin' Out of Space | 1962 | $15 |
| ❏ 5916 | Please Forgive Me/You Got It | 1963 | $15 |

ISLAND

| ❏ 074 | A Little Bit Something/Better Luck in the Summer | 1976 | $4 |
| ❏ 044 | Give Me the Country Side of Life/It's Hard But It's Fair | 1975 | $4 |

NOLA

❏ 730	A Letter To Santa/C.C. Rider	1966	$15
❏ 721	Barefootin'/Let's Go Baby (Where the Action Is)	1966	$30
❏ 735	Everybody's Hip-Hugging/Foxy Mama	1967	$15
❏ 726	Happy Feet/The Scratch	1966	$15
❏ 738	I Caught You in a Lie/Holdin' Out	1967	$15
❏ 729	Tip Toe/Soul Kind of Loving	1966	$15

RON

| ❏ 327 | All Nite Long (Part 1)/All Nite Long (Part 2) | 1959 | $20 |
| ❏ 331 | Walkin'/Across the Track | 1960 | $20 |

PARKS, GINO

FORTUNE

| ❏ 528 | Last Night I Cried/Just Go | 1957 | $100 |

GOLDEN WORLD

| ❏ 32 | My Sophisticated Lady/Talkin' About My Baby | 1966 | $30 |

MIRACLE

| ❏ 3 | Don't Say Bye Bye/Blibber Blabber | 1960 | $800 |

TAMLA

| ❏ 54066 | For This I Thank You/Fire | 1962 | $100 |
| ❏ 54042 | That's No Lie/Same Thing | 1961 | $125 |

Number	Title	Yr	NM

PARKS, MICHAEL

MGM

❏ 14104	Long Lonesome Highway/Mountain High	1970	$6
❏ 14154	Sally/Save a Little, Spend a Little	1970	$5
❏ 14092	Tie Me to Your Apron Strings Again/Won't You Ride in My Little Red Wagon	1969	$5
❏ 14363	Won't You Ride in My Little Red Wagon/Big "T" Water	1972	$5

VERVE

| ❏ 10653 | Drownin' on Dry Land/River's Invitation | 1971 | $5 |

PARKS, VAN DYKE

MGM

| ❏ 13570 | Come to the Sunshine/Farther Along | 1966 | $15 |
| ❏ 13441 | Do What You Wanta/Number Nine | 1966 | $15 |

WARNER BROS.

| ❏ 7026 | Donovan's Colors Part 1/Part 2 | 1967 | $15 |

—As "George Washington Brown

| ❏ 7609 | Occapella/Ode to Tobago | 1972 | $6 |
| ❏ 7409 | On the Rolling Sea When Jesus Speaks to Me/The Eagle and Me | 1970 | $10 |

PARLETTES, THE

JUBILEE

| ❏ 5467 | Tonight I Met An Angel/Because We're Very Young | 1964 | $15 |

PARLIAMENT

Also see GEORGE CLINTON; FUNKADELIC; PARLET; THE PARLIAMENTS.

CASABLANCA

❏ 2317	Agony of DeFeet/The Freeze	1980	$5
❏ 950	Aqua Boogie (A Psychoalphadisco betabioaquadoloop)/(You're a Fish and I'm a) Water Sign	1978	$5
❏ 950 [PS]	Aqua Boogie (A Psychoalphadisco betabioaquadoloop)/(You're a Fish and I'm a) Water Sign	1978	$10
❏ 900	Bop Gun (Endangered Species)/I've Been Watchin' You	1977	$5
❏ 831	Chocolate City/Chocolate City (Part 2)	1975	$5
❏ 2330	Crush It/Body Language	1981	$5
❏ 871	Do That Stuff/Handcuffs	1976	$5
❏ 875	Dr. Funkenstein/Children of Production	1977	$5
❏ 892	Fantasy Is Reality/The Landing (Of the Mothership)	1977	$5
❏ 909	Flash Light/Swing Down, Sweet Chariot	1978	$5
❏ 921	Funkentelechy/Funkentelechy (Part 2)	1978	$5
❏ 2222	Party People/Party People (Part 2)	1979	$5
❏ 852	P. Funk (Wants to Get Funked Up)/Night of the Tempasaurus Peoples	1976	$5
❏ 864	Star Child (Mothership Connection)/Supergroovealistic	1976	$5
❏ 856	Tear the Roof Off the Sucker (Give Up the Funk)/P-Funk	1976	$5

—Blue label

| ❏ 856 | Tear the Roof Off the Sucker (Give Up the Funk)/P-Funk | 1976 | $4 |

—Tan label

❏ 811	Testify/I Can Move You	1974	$5
❏ 2250	The Big Bang Theory/The Big Bang Theory (Part 2)	1980	$5
❏ 0003	The Goose (Part 1)/The Goose (Part 2)	1974	$6
❏ 2235	Theme from The Black Hole/(You're a Fish and I'm a) Water Sign	1980	$5

INVICTUS

❏ 9095	Breakdown/Little Ole Country Boy	1971	$10
❏ 9123	Come In Out of the Rain/Little Ole Country Boy	1972	$8
❏ 9077	I Call My Baby Pussy Cat/Little Ole Country Boy	1970	$10

PARLIAMENTS, THE

APT

| ❏ 25036 | Poor Willie/Party Boys | 1959 | $50 |

FLIPP

| ❏ 100/1 | Lonely Island/You Make Me Wanna Cry | 1960 | $50 |

—Red label

| ❏ 100/1 | Lonely Island/You Make Me Wanna Cry | 1960 | $40 |

—Yellow label

Number	Title	Yr	NM
GOLDEN WORLD			
❑ 46	Heart Trouble/That Was My Girl	1966	$200
LEN			
❑ 101	Don't Need You Anymore/ Honey, Take Me Home with You	1958	$100
REVILOT			
❑ 211	All Your Goodies Are Gone (The Loser's Seat)/Don't Be Sore at Me	1967	$20
❑ 223	Good Old Music/Time	1968	$20
❑ 207	(I Wanna) Testify/I Can Feel the Ice Melting	1967	$20
❑ 214	Little Man/The Goose (That Laid the Golden Egg)	1968	$20
❑ 217	Look at What I Almost Missed/What You Been Growing	1968	$20
U.S.A.			
❑ 719	My Only Love/To Be Alone	1961	$30

PARRAMOR, NORRIE
7-Inch Extended Plays

Number	Title	Yr	NM
CAPITOL			
❑ EAP 1-10073	An Aries Aria/Taurus Tango// Mood Aquarius/Ode to Pisces	1957	$10
❑ EAP 2-10073	The Gemini Waltz/Cancerian Concerto//The Sagacious Sagittarius/Capricious Capricorn	1957	$10

PARRIS, FRED

Number	Title	Yr	NM
ATCO			
❑ 6439	Land of the Broken Hearts/ Bring It Home to Daddy	1966	$12
GREEN SEA			
❑ 106	Blushing Bride/Giving My Love to You	1966	$10
❑ 107	I'll Be Hangin' On/I Can Really Satisfy	1966	$10
MAMA SADIE			
❑ 1001	In the Still of the Nite "67"/ Heck No	1967	$10

PARROTS, THE (1)

Number	Title	Yr	NM
CHECKER			
❑ 772	Don't Leave Me/Weep, Weep, Weep	1953	$500

PARROTS, THE (2)

Number	Title	Yr	NM
MALA			
❑ 558	They All Got Carried Away/ Hey, Put the Clock Back on the Wall	1967	$15

PARSONS, ALAN, PROJECT

Number	Title	Yr	NM
20TH CENTURY			
❑ 2297	(The System of) Doctor Tarr and Professor Fether/Dream Within a Dream	1976	$5
❑ 2333	To One in Paradise/The Cask of Amontillado	1977	$6
ARISTA			
❑ 0454	Damned If I Do/If I Could Change Your Mind	1979	$4
❑ 0310	Day After Day/Breakdown	1978	$4
❑ 9349	Days Are Numbers (The Traveller)/Somebody Out There	1985	$3
❑ 9160	Don't Answer Me/Don't Let It Show	1984	$3
❑ 9160 [PS]	Don't Answer Me/Don't Let It Show	1984	$3
❑ 0696	Eye in the Sky/Gemini	1982	$4
❑ 0573	Games People Play/Ace of Swords	1980	$4
❑ 0288	I Robot/Don't Let It Show	1977	$4
❑ 0260	I Wouldn't Want to Be Like You/Nucleus	1977	$4
❑ 9282	Let's Talk About Me/ Hawkeye	1984	$3
❑ 9282 [PS]	Let's Talk About Me/ Hawkeye	1984	$3
❑ 1048	Old and Wise/You're Gonna Get Your Fingers Burned	1983	$4
❑ 9208	Prime Time/Gold Bug	1984	$3
❑ 1029	Psychobabble/Children of the Moon	1982	$4
❑ 0635	Snake Eyes/I Don't Wanna Go Home	1981	$4
❑ 9576	Standing on Higher Ground/ Inside Looking Out	1987	$3
❑ 9576 [PS]	Standing on Higher Ground/ Inside Looking Out	1987	$3
❑ 9443	Stereotomy/Urbania	1985	$3
❑ 0598	Time/The Gold Bug	1981	$4
❑ 0352	What Goes Up/In the Lap of the Gods	1978	$4

Number	Title	Yr	NM
PARSONS, BILL			
FRATERNITY			
❑ 838	Educated Rock and Roll/ Carefree Wanderer	1959	$40
❑ 835	The All American Boy/ Rubber Dolly	1959	$50
— *This record is actually by Bobby Bare miscredited*			
STARDAY			
❑ 526	Hod Rod Volkswagen/Guitar Blues	1960	$40
❑ 544	The Price We Pay for Livin'/A-Waitin'	1960	$30

PARSONS, GRAM
Also see THE BYRDS; THE FLYING BURRITO BROTHERS; THE INTERNATIONAL SUBMARINE BAND.

Number	Title	Yr	NM
REPRISE			
❑ 1192	Love Hurts/In My Hour of Darkness	1974	$6
❑ 1139	That's All It Took/She	1972	$6
SIERRA			
❑ 105	Love Hurts/The New Soft Shoe	1982	$5
❑ 104	Medley (Bony Moronie/40 Days/Almost Grown)// Conversations/Hot Burrito #1	1982	$5
— *Second song on side 2 by Gene Parsons*			

PARTON, DOLLY

Number	Title	Yr	NM
COLUMBIA			
❑ 07727	I Know You by Heart/Could I Have Your Autograph	1988	$3
— *With Smokey Robinson*			
❑ 07727 [PS]	I Know You by Heart/Could I Have Your Autograph	1988	$3
❑ 07995	Make Love Make Two Lovers	1988	$3
❑ 68760	Why'd You Come In Here Lookin' Like That/Wait Til I Get You Home	1989	$3
GOLDBAND			
❑ 1086	Puppy Love/Girl Left Alone	1959	$600
— *Originals have a red label*			
MERCURY			
❑ 71982	It's Sure Gonna Hurt/The Love You Gave	1962	$300
MONUMENT			
❑ 913	Busy Signal/I Took Him for Granted	1965	$20
❑ 922	Control Yourself/Don't Drop Out	1966	$20
❑ 982	Dumb Blonde/The Giving and the Taking	1967	$12
❑ 03408	Everything Is Beautiful (In Its Own Way)/Put It Off Until Tomorrow	1982	$4
— *A-side with Willie Nelson; B-side with Kris Kristofferson*			
❑ 1047	I'm Not Worth the Tears/ Ping Pong	1968	$8
❑ 869	I Wasted My Tears/What Do You Think About Lovin'	1965	$20
❑ 948	Little Things/I'll Put It Off Until Tomorrow	1966	$20
❑ 897	Old Enough to Know Better (Too Young to Resist)/ Happy, Happy Birthday Baby	1965	$20
❑ 1007	Something Fishy/I've Lived My Life	1967	$12
❑ 03781	What Do You Think About Lovin'/You're Gonna Love Yourself (In the Morning)	1983	$4
— *A-side: Dolly Parton and Brenda Lee; B-side: Willie Nelson and Brenda Lee*			
❑ 1032	Why, Why, Why/I Couldn't Wait Forever	1967	$10
RCA			
❑ GB-12316	9 to 5/Old Flames Can't Hold a Candle to You	1981	$3
— *Gold Standard Series*			
❑ JH-12133 [DJ]	9 to 5 (same on both sides)	1980	$20
— *Promo only on blue vinyl*			
❑ PB-12133	9 to 5/Sing for the Common Man	1980	$4
❑ PB-12133 [PS]	9 to 5/Sing for the Common Man	1980	$5
❑ PB-11420	Baby I'm Burning/I Really Got the Feeling	1978	$4
❑ JB-11420 [DJ]	Baby I'm Burning (same on both sides)	1978	$12
— *Promo only on red vinyl*			
❑ GB-11993	Baby I'm Burnin'/ Heartbreaker	1980	$3
— *Gold Standard Series*			
❑ PB-12200	But You Know I Love You/ Poor Folks' Town	1981	$4
❑ 5001-7-R	Do I Ever Cross Your Mind/ We Had It All	1986	$3
❑ GB-14346	Don't Call It Love/Real Love	1986	$3
— *Gold Standard Series*			
❑ PB-13987	Don't Call It Love/We Got Too Much	1985	$3

Number	Title	Yr	NM
❑ JB-11705 [DJ]	Great Balls of Fire (same on both sides)	1979	$10
— *Promo only on red vinyl*			
❑ PB-13361	Hard Candy Christmas/Me and Little Andy	1982	$4
❑ JK-13361 [DJ]	Hard Candy Christmas (same on both sides)	1982	$15
— *Promo only on red vinyl*			
❑ JB-11296 [DJ]	Heartbreaker (same on both sides)	1978	$12
— *Promo only on red vinyl*			
❑ PB-11296	Heartbreaker/Sure Thing	1978	$4
❑ PB-13234	Heartbreak Express/Act Like a Fool	1982	$4
❑ PB-11123	Here You Come Again/Me and Little Andy	1977	$4
❑ GB-11505	Here You Come Again/Two Doors Down	1979	$3
— *Gold Standard Series*			
❑ PB-13260	I Will Always Love You/Do I Ever Cross Your Mind	1982	$4
— *A-side is the same song, but a different recording than that on APBO-0234*			
❑ PB-13260 [PS]	I Will Always Love You/Do I Ever Cross Your Mind	1982	$5
❑ PB-10935	Light of a Clear Blue Morning/There	1977	$4
❑ JK-13944 [DJ]	Medley: Winter Wonderland/ Sleigh Ride (same on both sides)	1984	$4
❑ PB-13944	Medley: Winter Wonderland- Sleigh Ride/The Christmas Song	1984	$3
— *B-side by Kenny Rogers*			
❑ PB-12040	Old Flames Can't Hold a Candle to You/I Knew You When	1980	$4
❑ PB-13514	Potential New Boyfriend/ One of Those Days	1983	$3
❑ JK-13514 [DJ]	Potential New Boyfriend (same on both sides)	1983	$15
— *Promo only on blue vinyl*			
❑ JK-13514 [DJ]	Potential New Boyfriend (Short) (same on both sides)	1983	$15
— *Promo only on yellow vinyl*			
❑ PB-13703	Save the Last Dance for Me/ Elusive Butterfly	1983	$3
❑ JK-13703 [DJ]	Save the Last Dance for Me (same on both sides)	1983	$10
— *Promo only on green vinyl*			
❑ PB-13057	Single Women/Barbara on Your Mind	1982	$4
❑ JK-13057 [DJ]	Single Women (same on both sides)	1982	$15
— *Promo only on red vinyl*			
❑ JH-11926 [DJ]	Starting Over Again (same on both sides)	1980	$15
— *Promo only on green vinyl*			
❑ PB-11926	Starting Over Again/Sweet Agony	1980	$4
❑ PB-13883	Sweet Lovin' Friends/God Won't Get You	1984	$3
— *With Sylvester Stallone*			
❑ PB-11705	Sweet Summer Lovin'/Great Balls of Fire	1979	$4
❑ PB-13619	Tennessee Homesick Blues/ Butterflies	1984	$3
❑ GB-14070	Tennessee Homesick Blues/ Hard Candy Christmas	1985	$3
— *Gold Standard Series*			
❑ PB-13756	The Great Pretender/ Downtown	1984	$3
❑ PB-13756 [PS]	The Great Pretender/ Downtown	1984	$3
❑ PB-12282	The House of the Rising Sun/Working Girl	1981	$4
❑ PB-14218	Think About Love/Come Back to Me	1985	$3
❑ PB-14297	Tie Our Love (In a Double Knot)/I Hope You're Never Happy	1986	$3
❑ PB-11240	Two Doors Down/It's All Wrong, But It's All Right	1978	$4
RCA VICTOR			
❑ PB-10730	All I Can Do/Falling Out of Love with Me	1976	$4
❑ 74-0538	Coat of Many Colors/Here I Am	1971	$6
❑ 74-0538 [PS]	Coat of Many Colors/Here I Am	1971	$10
❑ 47-9971	Comin' For to Carry Me Home/Golden Streets of Glory	1971	$10
❑ 47-9784	Daddy Come and Get Me/ Chas	1969	$6
❑ 74-0132	Daddy/He's a Go-Getter	1969	$6
❑ PB-10564	Hey, Lucky Lady/Most of All, Why	1976	$4
❑ 74-0192	In the Ghetto/Bridge	1969	$6
❑ 47-9657	In the Good Old Days (When Times Were Bad)/Try Being Lonely	1968	$8
❑ APBO-0234	I Will Always Love You/ Lonely Comin' Down	1974	$5
❑ GB-10505	I Will Always Love You/ Lovely Comin' Down	1975	$3
— *Gold Standard Series*			

Number	Title	Yr	NM
❏ 74-0797	Lord, Hold My Hand/When I Sing for Him	1972	$5
❏ PB-10031	Love Is Like a Butterfly/Sacred Memories	1974	$4
❏ GB-10504	Love Is Like a Butterfly/Sacred Memories	1975	$3
— Gold Standard Series			
❏ JK-13944 [DJ]	Medley: Winter Wonderland/Sleigh Ride (same on both sides)	1984	$4
❏ 47-9863	Mule Skinner Blues/More Than Their Share	1970	$6
❏ 74-0243	My Blue Ridge Mountain Boy/'Til Death Do Us Part	1969	$6
❏ 47-9999	My Blue Tears/The Mystery of the Mystery	1971	$6
❏ 74-0868	My Tennessee Mountain Home/Better Part of Life	1973	$5
❏ PB-10164	The Bargain Store/I'll Never Forget	1975	$4
❏ GB-10676	The Bargain Store/The Seeker	1976	$3
— Gold Standard Series			
❏ PB-10310	The Seeker/Love with Feeling	1975	$8
❏ 74-0662	Touch Your Woman/Mission Chapel Memories	1972	$5
❏ 74-0950	Traveling Man/I Remember	1973	$5
❏ 74-0757	Washday Blues/Just As Good As Gone	1972	$10
❏ PB-10396	We Used To/My Heart Started Breaking	1975	$4

PARTON, DOLLY/LINDA RONSTADT/EMMYLOU HARRIS
WARNER BROS.

Number	Title	Yr	NM
❏ 28371	Telling Me Lies/Rosewood Casket	1987	$3
❏ 28248	Those Memories of You/My Dear Companion	1987	$3
❏ 28248 [PS]	Those Memories of You/My Dear Companion	1987	$4
❏ 28492	To Know Him Is to Love Him/Farther Along	1987	$3
❏ 28492 [PS]	To Know Him Is to Love Him/Farther Along	1987	$4
❏ 27970	Wildflowers/Hobo's Meditation	1988	$3

PARTON, RANDY
RCA

Number	Title	Yr	NM
❏ PB-13608	A Stranger in Her Bed/Waltz Across Texas	1983	$4
❏ PB-12351	Don't Cry Baby/Again and Again	1981	$4
❏ PB-10877	Down/Just As Good As Gone	1977	$5
❏ PB-12137	Hold Me Like You Never Had Me/My Blue Tears	1981	$4
❏ JK-13087 [PS]	Oh, No	1982	$10
— Sleeve is promo only			
❏ PB-13087	Oh, No/Hold Me Like You Never Had Me	1982	$4
❏ JK-13087 [DJ]	Oh, No (same on both sides)	1982	$10
— Promo only on yellow vinyl			
❏ PB-12271	Shot Full of Love/Please Don't Lie	1981	$4
❏ JK-12271 [DJ]	Shot Full of Love (same on both sides)	1981	$10
— Promo only on red vinyl			

RCA VICTOR

Number	Title	Yr	NM
❏ PB-10261	If You Were Mine/Tennessee Born	1975	$5
❏ PB-10432	In Love/Losing Everything	1975	$5

PARTRIDGE FAMILY, THE
BELL

Number	Title	Yr	NM
❏ 45200	Am I Losing You/If You Ever Go	1972	$10
❏ 45235	Breaking Up Is Hard to Do/I'm Here, You're Here	1972	$10
❏ 963	Doesn't Somebody Want to Be Wanted/You Are Always on My Mind	1971	$10
❏ 963 [PS]	Doesn't Somebody Want to Be Wanted/You Are Always on My Mind	1971	$12
❏ 45336	Friend and a Lover/Something's Wrong	1973	$10
❏ 996	I'll Meet You Halfway/Morning Rider on the Road	1971	$10
❏ 910	I Think I Love You/Somebody Wants to Love You	1970	$10
❏ 910 [PS]	I Think I Love You/Somebody Wants to Love You	1970	$12
❏ 910	I Think I Love You/Somebody Wants to Love You	1970	$50
— Artist erroneously listed on both sides as "The PATRIDGE Family			
❏ 45160	It's One of Those Nights (Yes Love)/One Night Stand	1971	$10
❏ 45130	I Woke Up in Love This Morning/Twenty-Four Hours a Day	1971	$10

Number	Title	Yr	NM
❏ 45414	Lookin' for a Good Time/Money Money	1973	$100
— Extremely rare as a stock copy			
❏ 45414 [PS]	Lookin' for a Good Time/Money Money	1973	$100
❏ 45301	Looking Through the Eyes of Love/Storybook Love	1972	$10

PARTY BROTHERS, THE
CANUSA

Number	Title	Yr	NM
❏ 505	A&T's Party/Let Me Be the One	1967	$50

REVUE

Number	Title	Yr	NM
❏ 11046	Do the Ground Hog/Nassau Daddy	1969	$50

PASSIONS, THE (1)
ABC-PARAMOUNT

Number	Title	Yr	NM
❏ 10436	The Bully/The Empty Seat	1963	$30

AUDICON

Number	Title	Yr	NM
❏ 108	Beautiful Dreamer/One Look Is All It Took	1960	$40
❏ 106	Gloria/Jungle Drums	1960	$40
❏ 105	I Only Want You/This Is My Love	1960	$40
— Red label			
❏ 105	I Only Want You/This Is My Love	1960	$30
— Red, black and white label			
❏ 112	Made for Lovers/You Don't Have Me Anymore	1961	$50

DIAMOND

Number	Title	Yr	NM
❏ 146	Sixteen Candles/The Third Floor	1963	$50

JUBILEE

Number	Title	Yr	NM
❏ 5406	Lonely Road/One Look Is All It Took	1961	$30

OCTAVIA

Number	Title	Yr	NM
❏ 8005	Aphrodite/I've Gotta Know	1962	$800

PASSIONS, THE (2)
BACK BEAT

Number	Title	Yr	NM
❏ 573	Baby I Do/Man About Town	1966	$12

TOWER

Number	Title	Yr	NM
❏ 485	Hijacked/Hijacked	1969	$8
❏ 443	I Can See My Way Through/Just Another Reason	1968	$8
❏ 443	I Can See My Way Through/Without a Warning	1968	$8
❏ 424	Without a Warning/Just Like a Rolling Seal	1968	$8

PASSIONS, THE (U)
GSF

Number	Title	Yr	NM
❏ 6880	One Night Affair/A Toast (May There Be No Last Time)	1972	$40

PASSPORT
ATLANTIC

Number	Title	Yr	NM
❏ 3659	Departure/(B-side unknown)	1979	$5
❏ 3487	Loco-Motive/Mandrake	1978	$5
❏ 89697	Man in the Mirror/(B-side unknown)	1983	$5

PASTEL SIX, THE
CHATTAHOOCHIE

Number	Title	Yr	NM
❏ 696	I Can't Dance/Red River Quetzal	1966	$10

DOWNEY

Number	Title	Yr	NM
❏ 102	Braum's Nightmare/Open House at the Cinder	1962	$30
❏ 101	Twitchin'/Open House at the Cinder	1962	$40
❏ 101	Twitchin'/Wino Stomp	1962	$40

ZEN

Number	Title	Yr	NM
❏ 111	Miss Sue/Baby Please Don't Go	1963	$30
❏ 105	Sing Along Song/The Strange Ghost	1963	$30
❏ 102	The Cinnamon Cinder (It's a Very Nice Dance)/Bandido	1962	$30
❏ 108	The Milkshake/Parchman Farm	1963	$30

PASTELS, THE
ARGO

Number	Title	Yr	NM
❏ 5287	Been So Long/My One and Only Dream	1958	$30
❏ 5314	So Far Away/Don't Knock	1958	$30

JUBILEE

Number	Title	Yr	NM
❏ 5495	First Star/Tokyo Melody	1965	$15

MASCOT

Number	Title	Yr	NM
❏ 123	Been So Long/My One and Only Dream	1957	$300

UNITED

Number	Title	Yr	NM
❏ 196	Put Your Arms Around Me/Boom De De Boom	1957	$100

PATIENCE AND PRUDENCE
CHATATHOOCHIE

Number	Title	Yr	NM
❏ 665	Tonight You Belong to Me (New Version)/How Can I Tell Him	1965	$10

LIBERTY

Number	Title	Yr	NM
❏ 55154	All I Do Is Dream of You/Your Careless Love	1958	$30
❏ 55058	Dreamer's Bay/We Can't Sing Rhythm and Blues	1957	$30
❏ 55169	Golly Oh Gee/Tom Thumb's Tune	1958	$30
❏ 55040	Gonna Get Along Without Ya Now/The Money Tree	1956	$30
— Blue-green label, silver print			
❏ 55040	Gonna Get Along Without Ya Now/The Money Tree	1956	$50
— Maroon label, gold print			
❏ 55125	Heavenly Angel/Little Wheel	1958	$30
❏ 55207	Should I/Whisper Whisper	1959	$20
— With Mike Clifford			
❏ 55022	Tonight You Belong to Me/A Smile and a Ribbon	1956	$40
❏ 55107	Witchcraft/Over Here	1957	$30

UNITED ARTISTS

Number	Title	Yr	NM
❏ 0012	Tonight You Belong to Me/Gonna Get Along Without You Now	1973	$5
— Silver Spotlight Series" reissue			

PATRICK, MILT
DEMON

Number	Title	Yr	NM
❏ 1518	A Fountain of Love/You Are My Inspiration	1959	$15

EVEREST

Number	Title	Yr	NM
❏ 2014	I Don't Think I Wanna Do It/No Fool Like an Old Fool	1963	$8

TERRI-ANN

Number	Title	Yr	NM
❏ 101	Merry Twistmas/Just A Doggone Dream	1962	$10

PATTERSON, MIKE, AND THE FUGITIVES
IMPERIAL

Number	Title	Yr	NM
❏ 66083	Cookin' Beans/Jerky	1965	$15
❏ 66118	Don't You Just Know It/Righteous Theme	1965	$15

PATTON, JIMMY
SAGE AND SAND

Number	Title	Yr	NM
❏ 261	Call Me/Forty-Nine Women	1958	$120
❏ 282	Ocean Full of Tears/Twinklin' Teardrops	1959	$50

SIMS

Number	Title	Yr	NM
❏ 227	Blue Darling/Preacher and a Girl in the Night	1965	$15
❏ 256	Can't Shake the Blues/(B-side unknown)	1965	$15
❏ 103	Careful/Guilty	1955	$60
— With Ann Jones			
❏ 105	Ocean of Tears/I Don't Want It	1955	$60
❏ 117	Okie's in the Pokie/Lonely Nights	1960	$200
❏ 104	Teenage Haert/Jalopy	1955	$60

PATTY AND THE EMBLEMS
CONGRESS

Number	Title	Yr	NM
❏ 263	Easy Come, Easy Go/It's the Little Things	1966	$30

HERALD

Number	Title	Yr	NM
❏ 595	And We Danced/You Can't Get Away from Me	1964	$20
❏ 590	Mixed-Up, Shook-Up, Girl/Ordinary Guy	1964	$30
❏ 593	The Sound of Music Makes Me Want to Dance/You Took Advantage of a Good Thing	1964	$20

KAPP

Number	Title	Yr	NM
❏ 870	I'll Cry Later/One Man Woman	1967	$30
❏ 897	I'm Gonna Love You a Long, Long Time/My Heart's So Full of You	1968	$20
❏ 791	Let Him Go Little Heart/Try It, You Won't Forget It	1966	$30
❏ 850	Please Don't Ever Leave Me/All My Tomorrows Are Gone	1967	$30

PATTY FLABBIE'S COUGHED ENGINE
DIAMOND

Number	Title	Yr	NM
❏ 252	Billy Got a Goat/Tin Can Eater	1968	$20

Number	Title	Yr	NM
PAUL AND PAULA			
❏ 315	Hey Paula ('77 Disco)/ (Instrumental)	1977	$4
❏ 979	Hey Paula/Bobbie Is the One	1962	$60

—As "Jill and Ray"

Number	Title	Yr	NM
❏ 321	Hey Paula/Paula (My Love)	1978	$4

— Reissued in 1982 with the same catalog number

Number	Title	Yr	NM
❏ 99	The Beginning of Love/All I Want Is You	1963	$30
PHILIPS			
❏ 40352	All I Want Is You/The Beginning of Love	1966	$10
❏ 40296	Dear Paula/All the Love	1965	$8
❏ 40142	First Day Back at School/A Perfect Pair	1963	$15
❏ 40114	First Quarrel/School Is Thru	1963	$15
❏ 40114 [PS]	First Quarrel/School Is Thru	1963	$30
❏ 40084	Hey Paula/Bobby Is the One	1962	$20
❏ 40158	Holiday for Teens/Holiday Hootenanny	1963	$15
❏ 40130	Something Old, Something New/Flipped Over You	1963	$15
❏ 40268	True Love/Any Way You Want Me	1965	$8
❏ 40168	We'll Never Break Up for Good/Crazy Little Things	1964	$10
UNI			
❏ 55052	All These Things/Wedding	1968	$8
UNITED ARTISTS			
❏ 50712	Moments Like These/Mrs. Bean	1970	$6
PAUL, BILLY			
GAMBLE			
❏ 232	Somewhere/Bluesette	1968	$15
JUBILEE			
❏ 5081	That's Why I Dream/Why Am I	1952	$40
NEPTUNE			
❏ 30	Mrs. Robinson/Let's Fall in Love All Over	1970	$10
PHILADELPHIA INT'L.			
❏ 3526	Am I Black Enough for You/I'm Gonna Make It This Time	1973	$5
❏ 3551	Be Truthful to Me/I Wish It Was Yesterday	1974	$5
❏ 3563	Billy's Back Home/I've Got So Much to Live For	1975	$5
❏ 3676	Bring the Family Back/It's Critical	1979	$5
❏ 3639	Everybody's Breakin' Up/Sooner or Later	1978	$5
❏ 3699	False Faces/I Gotta Put This Life Down	1979	$5
❏ 3613	How Good Is Your Game/I Think I'll Stay Home Today	1977	$5
❏ 3630	I Trust You/Love Won't Come Easy	1977	$5
❏ 3621	Let 'Em In/We All Got a Mission	1977	$5
❏ 3584	Let's Make a Baby/My Head's On Straight	1976	$5
❏ 3509	Love Buddies/Magic Carpet Ride	1971	$6
❏ 3521	Me and Mrs. Jones/Your Song	1972	$5
❏ 3645	One Man's Junk/Don't Give Up on Love	1978	$5
❏ 3635	Only the Strong Survive/Where I Belong	1977	$5
❏ 3593	People Power/I Want Cha Baby	1976	$5
❏ 3538	Thanks for Saving My Life/I Was Married	1974	$5
❏ 3515	This Is Your Life/I Wish It Were Yesterday	1972	$6
❏ 3572	When It's Your Turn to Go/July, July, July, July	1975	$5
TOTAL EXPERIENCE			
❏ 2419	Lately/(Instrumental)	1985	$5
❏ 2434	Sexual Therapy/Hot Date	1986	$5

7-Inch Extended Plays

Number	Title	Yr	NM
PHILADELPHIA INT'L.			
❏ ZS731793 [PS]	360 Degrees of Billy Paul	1972	$15
❏ ZS731793	I'm Just a Prisoner//Am I Black Enough for You/I'm Gonna Make It This Time	1972	$15

—Jukebox issue; small hole, plays at 33 1/3 rpm

Number	Title	Yr	NM
PAUL, BUDDY			
MURCO			
❏ 1022	They Stuck to Their Guns/Trust Me	1960	$30
❏ 1018	This Old Town/Foolish Me	1960	$30
PAUL, BUNNY			
BRUNSWICK			
❏ 55022	Breedle-Lump-Bump/The One You Love	1957	$20
❏ 55003	Poor Joe/Buzz Me	1957	$20

Number	Title	Yr	NM
CAPITOL			
❏ F3288	Open the Door/Who Am I Foolin'	1955	$20
❏ F3074	Please Have Mercy/These Are the Things We'll Share	1955	$20
❏ F3178	Song of the Dreamer/For the Very First Time	1955	$20
❏ F3224	Take a Chance/Tell the Man	1955	$20
❏ F3109	Two Castanets/Leave My Heart Alone	1955	$20
DOT			
❏ 15107	Magic Guitar/Never Let Me Go	1953	$30
ESSEX			
❏ 385	Brown Jug/Pam-Poo-Dey	1955	$70
❏ 364	Honey Love/I'll Never Tell	1954	$125
❏ 359	Lovey Dovey/Answer the Call	1954	$70
❏ 352	Such a Night/I'm Gonna Have Some Fun	1954	$70
GORDY			
❏ 7017	We're Only Young Once/I'm Hooked	1963	$30
POINT			
❏ 5	Sweet Talk/History	1956	$50
ROULETTE			
❏ 4186	Such a Night/A Million Miles from Nowhere	1959	$20

Number	Title	Yr	NM
PAUL, JOYCE			
CHANCELLOR			
❏ 105	Big Girls Don't Cry/The One Who Carries the Torch	1962	$20
DOT			
❏ 15703	Baby, You've Had It/Bad News	1958	$50
❏ 16246	Cold, Cold Heart/Captured	1961	$15
IMPERIAL			
❏ 66008	I'll Give You Me (If You'll Give Me You)/Don't Send Flowers	1964	$10
❏ 66024	Lasting Love/Painted Smile	1964	$12
REPUBLIC			
❏ 7053	I've Forgotten More Than You'll Ever Know/Caribbean	1953	$30
UNITED ARTISTS			
❏ 50149	Calico Doll/Been Rained On	1967	$10
❏ 50454	Do Right Woman, Do Right Man/You Didn't Come Home Last Night	1968	$8
❏ 50226	I Loved Him Much Longer Than You/Mama's Gonna Fix the Baby's Wagon	1967	$10
❏ 902	I'm the Girl on the Billboard/Changing World	1965	$10
❏ 50315	Phone Call to Mama/Don't Keep Me Hanging On	1968	$8

PAUL, LES, AND MARY FORD

Included are the Capitol listings for LES PAUL solo works. Some of these appear on B-sides of duet hits.

Number	Title	Yr	NM
CAPITOL			
❏ F3248	Amukiriki (The Lord Willing)/Magic Melody	1955	$15
❏ F3825	A Pair of Fools/Fire	1957	$10
❏ F3570	Blow the Smoke Away/Running Wild	1956	$10
❏ F1600	Brazil/Lover	1951	$15

—As "Les Paul"

Number	Title	Yr	NM
❏ F2316	Bye Bye Blues/Mammy's Boogie	1953	$20
❏ F3444	Cimarron/San Antonio Rose	1956	$10
❏ F3612	Cinco Robles (Five Oaks)/Ro-Ro-Robinson	1957	$10
❏ F2614	Don'cha Hear Them Bells/The Kangaroo	1953	$20
❏ F1088	Dry My Tears/Cryin'	1950	$30
❏ F3858	Goodnight My Someone/The Night of the Fourth	1957	$10
❏ F1192	Goofus/Sugar Sweet	1950	$30
❏ F1451	How High the Moon/Walkin' Whistlin' Blues	1951	$30
❏ F3165	Hummingbird/Goodbye My Love	1955	$15
❏ F3776	I Don't Want You No More/Strollin' Blues	1957	$10
❏ F2839	I'm a Fool to Care/Auctioneer	1954	$15
❏ F2080	I'm Confessin' (That I Love You)/Carioca	1952	$20
❏ F15750	I'm Forever Blowing Bubbles/The Lonesome Road	1951	$20

— Part 3" and "Part 4" of CCF-286

Number	Title	Yr	NM
❏ F2400	I'm Sitting on Top of the World/Sleep	1953	$20
❏ F15748	In the Good Old Summertime/La Rosita	1951	$20

— Part 1" and "Part 6" of CCF-286

Number	Title	Yr	NM
❏ F2735	I Really Don't Want to Know/South	1954	$15
❏ PRO233/4 [DJ]	Magic Melody/Magic Melody -- Part II	1955	$40

—Promo-only release; B-side's running time listed as "One Second"!

Number	Title	Yr	NM
❏ F2193	Meet Mister Callaghan/Take Me in Your Arms and Hold Me	1952	$20
❏ F1373	Mockin' Bird Hill/Chicken Reel	1951	$30
❏ F3934	More and More Each Day/A Small Island	1958	$10
❏ F3329	Moritat (Theme from Threepenny Opera)/Nuevo Laredo	1956	$10
❏ F2265	My Baby's Coming Home/Lady of Spain	1952	$20
❏ F3389	Say the Words I Love to Hear/Send Me Some Money	1956	$10
❏ F2123	Smoke Rings/In the Good Old Summertime	1952	$20
❏ F3015	Someday Sweetheart/Song in Blue	1955	$15
❏ F1316	Tennessee Waltz/Little Rock Getaway	1950	$30
❏ F3301	Texas Lady/Alabamy Bound	1955	$15
❏ F1748	The World Is Waiting for the Sunrise/Whispering	1951	$20
❏ F15749	Three Little Words/Moon Over Manakoora	1951	$20

—Part 2" and "Part 5" of CCF-286

Number	Title	Yr	NM
❏ F1920	Tiger Rag/It's a Lonesome Old Town	1951	$20
❏ F3725	Tuxedos and Flowers/Hummin' and Waltzin'	1957	$10
❏ F2928	Whither Thou Goest/Mandolino	1954	$15
COLUMBIA			
❏ S731386 [S]	A Cottage for Sale/Chasing Shadows	1962	$15
❏ 41350	All I Need Is You/At the Save-a-Penny Super Store	1959	$10
❏ S731388 [S]	Am I Blue/You Brought a New Kind of Love to Me	1962	$15
❏ S731385 [S]	'Deed I Do/Makin' Whoopee!	1962	$15
❏ 42754	Gentle Is Your Love/Move Along Baby (Don't Waste My Time)	1963	$8
❏ 42754 [PS]	Gentle Is Your Love/Move Along Baby (Don't Waste My Time)	1963	$15
❏ 42241	Goodnight Irene/Lonely Guitar	1961	$8
❏ 42241 [PS]	Goodnight Irene/Lonely Guitar	1961	$15
❏ S731387 [S]	It's Been a Long, Long Time/After You've Gone	1962	$15
❏ 42179	It's Too Late/Mountain Railroad	1961	$8
❏ 42602	Playing Make Believe/I Just Don't Understand	1962	$8
❏ 42602 [PS]	Playing Make Believe/I Just Don't Understand	1962	$15
❏ 41222	Put a Ring on My Finger/Fantasy	1958	$10
❏ 41222 [PS]	Put a Ring on My Finger/Fantasy	1958	$20
❏ 41592	The Poor People of Paris/All Night Long	1960	$8
❏ S731389 [S]	(titles unknown)	1962	$15

— The above five are "Stereo Seven" 33 1/3 rpm jukebox singles from "JS7-52

Number	Title	Yr	NM
❏ 41660	Wonderful Rain/Take a Warning	1960	$8
❏ EAP 4-577	Baby Won't You Please Come Home/Dangerous Curves//I'm Movin' On/Farewell for Just Awhile	1955	$20
❏ EAP 1-802	(contents unknown)	1956	$20
❏ EAP 2-802	(contents unknown)	1956	$20
❏ EAP 3-802	(contents unknown)	1956	$20
❏ EAP 1-577	Falling with Love//On the Sunny Side of the Street//Just One of Those Things//Twelfth Street Rag	1955	$20
❏ EAP 1-554 [PS]	I'm a Fool to Care	1956	$20
❏ EAP 1-554	I'm a Fool to Care/I Really Don't Want to Know//Auctioneer/It's a Lonesome Old Town	1956	$20
❏ EAP 1-577 [PS]	Les and Mary, Part 1	1955	$20
❏ EAP 2-577 [PS]	Les and Mary, Part 2	1955	$20
❏ EAP 3-577 [PS]	Les and Mary, Part 3	1955	$20
❏ EBF 1-577 [PS]	Les and Mary, Parts 1 and 2	1955	$25
❏ EBF 2-577 [PS]	Les and Mary, Parts 3 and 4	1955	$25

—Gatefold cover for some editions of 3-577 and 4-577

Number	Title	Yr	NM
❏ EAP 1-9121 [PS]	Les Paul and Mary Ford	1955	$20
❏ EAP 2-577	Lies/Turista//Swing Low Sweet Chariot/Nuevo Laredo	1955	$20
❏ EAP 1-9121	Mister Sandman/That's What I Like//I Need You Now/The Things I Didn't Do	1955	$20
❏ EAP 3-577	The Best Things in Life Are Free/Theme from "Laughing Eyes"//Some of These Days/Tico Tico	1955	$20
❏ EAP 1-802 [PS]	Time to Dream, Volume 1	1956	$20
❏ EAP 2-802 [PS]	Time to Dream, Volume 2	1956	$20
❏ EAP 3-802 [PS]	Time to Dream, Volume 3	1956	$20
❏ EAP 1-559 [PS]	Whither Thou Goest	1955	$25
❏ EAP 1-559	Whither Thou Goest/Nola//Take Me in Your Arms and Hold Me/Mandolino	1955	$25

Number	Title	Yr	NM
PAUL, LES			
DECCA			
❏ 27903	Blue Skies/Dark Eyes	1951	$20
❏ 29013	Steel Guitar Rag/Guitar Boogie	1954	$20
LONDON			
❏ 120	Los Angeles/The System	1969	$6
PAUL, LOUIS			
COTILLION			
❏ 44064	Annie Mae/Railroad Man	1970	$10
ENTERPRISE			
❏ 9056	Gotta Get Away/With a Little Bit of Love	1972	$6
❏ 9094	I Like Rock and Roll/My Dream	1974	$6
❏ 9060	It's Christmas Time/Santa Claus Is on His Way Again	1972	$6
❏ 9077	Merry-Go-Round/Mister Crystal	1973	$6
PAULA, MARLENA			
REGENT			
❏ 7506	I Wanna Spend Christmas with Elvis/Once More It's Christmas	1956	$60
PAUPERS, THE			
VERVE FOLKWAYS			
❏ 5033	Copper Penny/If I Call You by Some Other Name	1966	$12
❏ 5043	Let Me Be/Simple Deed	1967	$12
VERVE FORECAST			
❏ 5094	Another Man's Hair on My Razor/Cairo Hotel	1968	$10
❏ 5062	Magic People/Black Thank You Package	1967	$10
❏ 5056	One Rainy Day/Tudor Impressions	1967	$10
❏ 5074	Think I Care/White Song	1967	$10
PAVAROTTI, LUCIANO			
LONDON			
❏ 20102	Ave Maria (Schubert)/Ave Maria (Bach-Gounod)	1978	$5
PAVEMENT			
TREBLE KICKER			
❏ TK 001	Slay Tracks: You're Killing Me/Box Elder	1989	$60
❏ TK 001 [PS]	Slay Tracks: You're Killing Me/Box Elder	1989	$60
—Numbered edition of 1,000; already has been counterfeited			
PAVLOV'S DOG			
ABC			
❏ 12086	Episode/Julia	1975	$12
PAVONE, RITA			
POLYDOR			
❏ 15011	'Til Tomorrow/Try It and See	1970	$6
RCA VICTOR			
❏ 47-8212	Cuore/Ballo del Mattone	1963	$8
❏ 47-8538	I Don't Wanna Be Hurt/Eyes of Mine	1965	$8
❏ 47-8612	Oh My Mama/Right Now	1965	$8
❏ 47-9485	Okay, Okay/Wenn Ich Ein Junge War	1968	$10
❏ 47-8420	Wait for Me/It's Not Easy	1964	$8
❏ 47-8420 [PS]	Wait for Me/It's Not Easy	1964	$10
PAXTON, GARY			
CAPITOL			
❏ 5707	Goin' Through the Motions/You Got to Do the Best You Can	1966	$20
❏ 5975	Mother-in-Law/Miles and Cities	1967	$20
❏ 5467	My Heart Won't Let My Lips Say Goodbye/It's My Way (Of Lovin' You)	1965	$20
FELSTED			
❏ 8691	Sweet Senorita from Santa Fe/Kansas City	1964	$30
GARPAX			
❏ 44172	It Had to Be You/We're Going Back Together	1963	$30
❏ 44177	The Scavenger/How to Be a Fool (In Six Easy Lessons)	1963	$30
❏ 44180	Two Duel Bump Camel Named Robert E. Lee/Your Past Is Back Again	1964	$30
LIBERTY			
❏ 55584	Spooky Movies (Part 1)/Spooky Movies (Part 2)	1963	$30
❏ 55485	Stop Twistin' Baby/Alley Oop Was a Two Dab Man	1962	$30

Number	Title	Yr	NM
❏ 55407	Teen Age Crush/It's So Funny I Could Cry	1962	$30
LONDON			
❏ 5208	Super Torque/Cute Little Coly	1964	$30
MGM			
❏ 14306	Carin' for Karen/Out on a Limb	1971	$6
NEW PAX			
❏ 6	Different World/(B-side unknown)	1976	$8
PRIVATE STOCK			
❏ 45,007	The Clone Affair/(B-side unknown)	1975	$5
RCA VICTOR			
❏ APBO-0081	It's Hard to Be a Rock and Roll Star When You're Old and Fat/White Tornado Alias Gary S. Paxton	1973	$5
❏ 74-0916	Shadow of Your Memory/This Little Light of Mine	1973	$5
❏ PB-10449	Too Far Gone (To Care What You Do to Me)/Freedom Lives in a Country Song	1975	$5
PAXTON, TOM			
ELEKTRA			
❏ 45667	Crazy John/Things I Notice Now	1969	$6
❏ 45703	Whose Garden Was This?/Annie's Going to Sing Her Song	1970	$6
REPRISE			
❏ 1110	Peace Will Come (According to Plan)/Jesus Christ S.R.O.	1972	$5
VANGUARD			
❏ 35206	The Death of Stephen Biko/Anita O.J.	1977	$5
PAYCHECK, JOHNNY, AND MERLE HAGGARD			
EPIC			
❏ 19-51012	I Can't Hold Myself in Line/Carolyn	1981	$4
PAYCHECK, JOHNNY			
AMI			
❏ 1327	Everything Is Changing/Palimony	1985	$5
❏ 1322	I Never Got Over You/Ole Pay Ain't Checked Out Yet	1984	$5
CERTRON			
❏ 10003	Forever Ended Yesterday/It's For Sure I Can't Go On	1970	$8
DAMASCUS			
❏ 2001	Scars/(B-side unknown)	1989	$6
DECCA			
❏ 31283	Go Ring the Bells/I Guess I Had It Coming	1961	$30
❏ 9-30763	On This Mountaintop/It's Been a Long, Long Time for Me	1958	$40
—A-side as "Donny Young and Roger Miller"; B-side as "Donny Young"			
❏ 31077	Shakin' the Blues/Miracle of Love	1960	$50
—As "Donny Young"			
❏ 9-30881	The Old Man and the River/Pictures Can't Talk Back	1959	$30
—As "Donny Young"			
DESPERADO			
❏ 1001	Out of Beer/Oklahoma Lady	1988	$6
EPIC			
❏ 8-50249	11 Months and 29 Days/Live with Me (Till I Can Learn to Live Again)	1976	$6
❏ 8-50146	All-American Man/The Fool Strikes Again	1975	$6
❏ 14-03052	D.O.A. (Drunk On Arrival)/Gonna Get Right (And Do Something Wrong)	1982	$4
❏ 9-50818	Drinkin' and Drivin'/Just Makin' Love Don't Make It Love	1979	$5
❏ 9-50863	Fifteen Beers/Who Was That Man Who Beat Me So	1980	$5
❏ 8-50040	For a Minute There/She's All I Live For	1974	$6
❏ 8-50621	Friend, Lover, Wife/Leave It to Me	1978	$6
❏ 8-50539	Georgia in a Jug/Me and the I.R.S.	1978	$6
❏ 8-50215	Gone at Last/Live with Me	1976	$6
❏ 8-50291	I Can See Me Lovin' You Again/I Sleep with Her Memory Every Night	1976	$6
❏ 8-50111	I Didn't Love Her Anymore/Loving Her Is All I Thought It Would Be	1975	$6

Number	Title	Yr	NM
❏ 8-50391	I'm the Only Hell (Mama Ever Raised)/She's Still Lookin' Good	1977	$6
❏ 9-50923	In Memory of a Memory/New York Town	1980	$5
❏ 8-50073	Loving You Beats All I've Ever Seen/Touch of the Master's Hand	1975	$6
❏ 5-10999	Mr. Lovemaker/Once You've Had the Best	1973	$6
❏ 5-11090	My Part of Forever/If Love Gets Any Better	1974	$6
❏ 8-50334	Slide Off of Your Satin Sheets/That's What the Outlaws in Texas Want to Hear	1977	$6
❏ 5-10947	Something About You I Love/Your Love Is the Key to It All	1973	$6
❏ 5-11046	Song and Dance Man/Love Is a Strange and Wonderful Thing	1973	$6
❏ 9-50777	(Stay Away From) The Cocaine Train/Billy Bardo	1979	$5
❏ 8-50469	Take This Job and Shove It/Colorado Kool-Aid	1977	$8
❏ 8-50193	The Feminine Touch/Rhythm Guitar	1976	$6
❏ 14-02684	The Highlight of '81/Sharon Rae	1982	$4
❏ 8-50655	The Outlaw's Prayer/Armed and Crazy	1979	$6
HILLTOP			
❏ 3007	A-11/Where (In the World)	1965	$20
❏ 3002	Don't Start Countin' on Me/I'd Rather Be Your Fool	1964	$30
❏ 3006	For Those Who Think Young/The Girl They Talk About	1965	$20
❏ 3009	Heartbreak Tennessee/Help Me Hank, I'm Fallin'	1966	$20
❏ 3015	I'm Barely Hangin' On to Me/The Real Mr. Heartache	1966	$20
LITTLE DARLIN'			
❏ 7918	California Dreams/The Loser	1979	$6
❏ 035	Don't Monkey with Another Monkey's Monkey/You'll Recover in Time	1967	$12
❏ 7808	Down on the Corner at a Bar Named Kelly's/Something He'll Have to Learn	1978	$6
❏ 7923	Gentle on My Mind/Everything You Touch Turns to Hurt	1979	$6
❏ 052	If I'm Gonna Sink/The Loser	1968	$10
❏ 7810	I'll Place My Order Early/The Old Year Is Gone	1978	$6
❏ 042	(It Won't Be Long) And I'll Be Hating You/Fools Hall of Fame	1968	$10
❏ 7804	It Won't Be Long/If I'm Gonna Sink (Might As Well Go to the Bottom)	1978	$6
❏ 016	Motel Time Again/If You Should Come Back Today	1966	$10
❏ 046	My Heart Keeps Running to You/Yesterday, Today and Tomorrow	1968	$10
❏ 057	My World of Memories/(B-side unknown)	1969	$10
❏ 011	The Ballad of the Green Berets/A Dying Hero	1966	$12
❏ 032	The Cave/Then Love Dies	1967	$12
❏ 08	The Lovin' Machine/Pride Covered Ears	1966	$10
❏ 043	The Old Year Is Gone/According to the Bible	1968	$10
❏ 060	Wherever You Are/I Can't Promise You Won't Get Lonely	1969	$10
❏ 072	Wildfire/Basin Street Mama	1969	$10
MERCURY			
❏ 888341-7	Come to Me/Ragtime Redneck	1987	$4
❏ 888088-7	Don't Bury Me 'Til I'm Ready/Ex-Wives and Lovers	1986	$4
❏ 888651-7	I Grow Old Too Fast (And Smart Too Slow)/Caught Between a Rock and a Soft Place	1987	$4
❏ 888925-7	Modern Times/She Don't Love Me All the Time	1987	$4
❏ 884720-7	Old Violin/Comin' Home to Baby	1986	$4
❏ 71900	On Second Thought/One Day a Week	1962	$30
—As "Donny Young"			
TODD			
❏ 1098	Don't You Get Lonesome Without Me/I'm Glad to Have Her Back Again	1964	$30
—As "Donny Young"			

PAYNE, FREDA

ABC

Number	Title	Yr	NM
❏ 12139	Lost in Love/You	1975	$5
❏ 12079	Shadows on the Wall/I Get Carried Away	1975	$5

ABC DUNHILL

Number	Title	Yr	NM
❏ 15018	It's Yours to Have/Run for Life	1974	$5

ABC-PARAMOUNT

Number	Title	Yr	NM
❏ 10366	Desafinado/He Who Laughs Last	1962	$30
❏ 10437	Pretty Baby/Grin and Bear It	1963	$30

CAPITOL

Number	Title	Yr	NM
❏ 4431	Baby, You've Got What It Takes/Bring Back the Joy	1977	$5
❏ 4805	Can't Wait/Longest Night	1979	$5
❏ 4537	Feed Me Your Love/Stares and Whispers	1978	$5
❏ 4631	Happy Days Are Here Again/Happy Music (Dance the Night Away)/Falling in Love	1978	$5
❏ 4383	I Can't Live on a Memory/I Get High (On Your Memory)	1976	$5
❏ 4695	I'll Do Anything for You (Part 1)/I'll Do Anything for You (Part 2)	1979	$5
❏ 4494	Love Magnet/Loving You Means So Much to Me	1977	$5

IMPULSE!

Number	Title	Yr	NM
❏ 221	It's Time/Sweet September	1963	$30

INVICTUS

Number	Title	Yr	NM
❏ 9075	Band of Gold/Easiest Way to Fall	1970	$6
❏ 9092	Bring the Boys Home/I Shall Not Be Moved	1971	$6
❏ 9085	Cherish What Is Dear to You (While It Is Near to You)/They Don't Owe Me a Thing	1971	$6
❏ 9085 [PS]	Cherish What Is Dear to You (While It Is Near to You)/They Don't Owe Me a Thing	1971	$10
❏ 9080	Deeper and Deeper/The Unhooked Genration	1970	$6
❏ 1257	For No Reason/Mother Misery's Favorite Child	1973	$6
❏ 9109	I'm Not Getting Any Better/The Road We Didn't Take	1972	$6
❏ 9128	She's in My Life/Through the Memory of My Mind	1972	$6
❏ 1255	Two Wrongs Don't Make a Right/We've Gotta Find a Way Back to Love	1973	$6

SUTRA

Number	Title	Yr	NM
❏ 117	In Motion/(Instrumental)	1982	$5

PAYNE, JIMMY

CINNAMON

Number	Title	Yr	NM
❏ 780	If It Pleases You/You and Me and Love on the Open Road	1974	$6
❏ 796	Sweet Fantasy/(B-side unknown)	1974	$6

EPIC

Number	Title	Yr	NM
❏ 5-10301	Baby Don't Cry/Boston	1968	$8
❏ 5-10261	He Will Break Your Heart/Where Has All the Love Gone	1967	$8
❏ 5-10027	My Most Requested Song/What Does It Take	1966	$8
❏ 5-10222	What Does It Take (To Keep a Woman Like You Satisfied/Woman, Woman	1967	$8
❏ 5-10173	Woman, Woman/Money Cannot Make the Man	1967	$8

KIK

Number	Title	Yr	NM
❏ 907	Turnin' My Love On/She's Free But She's Not Easy	1981	$6

VEE JAY

Number	Title	Yr	NM
❏ 517	Why Can't We Love Each Other/Sweet Little Pretty Girl	1963	$20

PAYNE, LEON

CAPITOL

Number	Title	Yr	NM
❏ F1580	A Million Years Ago/Lonely and Blue Over Someone	1951	$30
❏ F1321	Because You Love Me/My Daddy	1950	$40
❏ F1164	Did I Forget to Call/I Miss That Girl	1950	$40
❏ F1463	Empty Dreams/Farewell Waltz	1951	$30
❏ F1872	Gentle Hands/He Is the Light of the World	1951	$30
❏ F1093	I Couldn't Do a Thing Without You/You Still Got a Place	1950	$40
❏ F1405	I Don't Know Why/If I Could Live My Life Over	1951	$30
❏ F40270	I Hate to Leave You/Find Them, Fool Them, and Leave Them	1950	$40
❏ F920	I'm a Lone Wolf/I Just Said Goodnight to My Dreams	1950	$40
❏ F2454	I Need Your Love/Wouldn't It Be Wonderful	1953	$30
❏ F1782	It's Many a Mile Back Home/Teach Me to Forget	1951	$30

Number	Title	Yr	NM
❏ F1910	I Want You to Love Me/How Can I Help It	1951	$30
❏ F2295	Mailman/Lying to My Heart	1952	$30
❏ F2055	Polk Salad Green/Weeping Willow	1952	$30
❏ F2561	Sister Sue Polka/If I Took the Time	1953	$30
❏ F1338	The Great American Eagle/Fatal Letter	1950	$40

D

Number	Title	Yr	NM
❏ 1108	Brothers of a Bottle/Mitzie McGraw	1960	$20
❏ 1138	There's No Justice/With Half a Heart	1960	$20
❏ 1150	Things Have Gone to Pieces/Blue Side of Lonesome	1960	$20

DECCA

Number	Title	Yr	NM
❏ 9-29333	A Lifetime to Regret/The Moon, Your God and You	1954	$30
❏ 9-28851	Don't Be Afraid/Pedro the Hot Tamale Man	1953	$30
❏ 9-29046	The Face in the Crowd/You Haven't Got a Heart	1954	$30

LONGHORN

Number	Title	Yr	NM
❏ 555	Truth Is In My Pocket/Everybody's Buddy	1965	$15

MERCURY

Number	Title	Yr	NM
❏ 71063	Lumberjack/A Million to One	1957	$30

STARDAY

Number	Title	Yr	NM
❏ 250	All the Time/One More Chance	1956	$30
❏ 215	Christmas Everyday/Christmas Love Song	1955	$30
❏ 637	Close to You/The Log Train	1963	$15
❏ 220	Doorstep to Heaven/You Are the One	1956	$30
❏ 666	September Memory/Six Foot Six	1964	$15
❏ 267	Sweet Sweet Love/A Prisoner's Diary	1956	$30
❏ 245	That Ain't It/Little Rock Rock	1956	$300
— As "Rock Rogers"			
❏ 232	Two by Four/You Can't Lean on Me	1956	$30
❏ 208	We're on the Main Line/I Die 10,000 Times a Day	1955	$30

TNT

Number	Title	Yr	NM
❏ 168	My Ship of Dreams/I'll Still Be Around	1959	$30

PEACHEROOS, THE

EXCELLO

Number	Title	Yr	NM
❏ 2044	Be-Bop Baby/Everyday My Love Is True	1954	$400

PEACHES AND HERB

COLUMBIA

Number	Title	Yr	NM
❏ 45554	God Save This World/I Can't Forget the One I Love	1972	$5
❏ 04081	In My World/Keep On Smiling	1983	$4
❏ 45386	The Sound of Silence/The Two of Us	1971	$5

DATE

Number	Title	Yr	NM
❏ 1549	Close Your Eyes/I Will Watch Over You	1967	$10
❏ 1549 [PS]	Close Your Eyes/I Will Watch Over You	1967	$20
❏ 1655	Cupid/Darling, How Long	1969	$8
❏ 1555	Cupid-Venus/Darling, How Long	1967	$20
❏ 1563	For Your Love/I Need Your Love So Desperately	1967	$10
❏ 1563 [PS]	For Your Love/I Need Your Love So Desperately	1967	$20
❏ 1669	It's Just a Game, Love/Satisfy My Hunger	1970	$8
❏ 1649	Let Me Be the One/I Need Your Love So Desperately	1969	$8
❏ 1523	Let's Fall in Love/We're In This Thing Together	1966	$12
❏ 1623	Let's Make a Promise/Me and You	1968	$8
❏ 1623 [PS]	Let's Make a Promise/Me and You	1968	$20
❏ 1574	Love Is Strange/It's True I Love You	1967	$10
❏ 1574 [PS]	Love Is Strange/It's True I Love You	1967	$20
❏ 1676	Soothe Me with Your Love/We're So Much in Love	1970	$8
❏ 1592	The Ten Commandments of Love/What a Lovely Way (To Say Goodnight)	1968	$8
❏ 1586	Two Little Kids/We've Got to Love One Another	1967	$8
❏ 1633	We've Got to Love One Another/So True	1968	$10
❏ 1637	When He Touches Me (Nothing Else Matters)/Thank You	1969	$8

MCA

Number	Title	Yr	NM
❏ 40782	It Will Never Be the Same Again/I'm Counting on You	1977	$5
❏ 40701	We're Still Together/Love Is Here Beside Us	1977	$5

MERCURY

Number	Title	Yr	NM
❏ 73388	Can't It Wait/Thank Heaven for You	1973	$5

POLYDOR

Number	Title	Yr	NM
❏ 2187	Bluer Than Blue/Go with the Flow	1981	$4
❏ 2178	Freeway/Pickin' Up the Pieces	1981	$4
❏ 2115	Funtime (Part 1)/Funtime (Part 2)	1980	$4
❏ 2053	I Pledge My Love/(I Want Us) Back Together	1980	$4
❏ 2140	One Child of Love/Hearsay	1980	$4
❏ 14514	Shake Your Groove Thing/All Your Love (Get It Here)	1978	$4
❏ 2157	Surrender/Love Stealers	1981	$4
❏ 14577	We've Got Love/Four's a Traffic Jam	1979	$4

PEANUT BUTTER CONSPIRACY, THE

CHALLENGE

Number	Title	Yr	NM
❏ 500	Back in L.A./Have a Little Faith	1969	$8
❏ 500 [PS]	Back in L.A./Have a Little Faith	1969	$50

COLUMBIA

Number	Title	Yr	NM
❏ 44667	I'm a Fool/It's So Hard	1968	$8
❏ 43985	It's a Happening Thing/Twice Is Life	1967	$10
❏ 43985 [PS]	It's a Happening Thing/Twice Is Life	1967	$60
❏ 44063	Then Came Love/Dark on You Now	1967	$8
❏ 44356	Turn On a Friend (To the Good Life)/Captain Sandwich	1967	$8

VAULT

Number	Title	Yr	NM
❏ 933	Time Is After You/Floating Dream	1966	$20

PEARL HARBOUR AND THE EXPLOSIONS

415 RECORDS

Number	Title	Yr	NM
❏ S-0003	Drivin'/Release It	1979	$4
❏ S-0003 [PS]	Drivin'/Release It	1979	$4

WARNER BROS.

Number	Title	Yr	NM
❏ 49207	Drivin'/The Big One	1980	$4

PEARLS BEFORE SWINE

ESP-DISK'

Number	Title	Yr	NM
❏ 4575	Images of April/There Was a Man	1968	$50
❏ 4554	Morning Song/Drop Out	1967	$40

REPRISE

Number	Title	Yr	NM
❏ 0916	God Save the Child/Rocket Man	1970	$15
❏ 0873	If You Don't Want To/These Things Too	1969	$15

PEARLS, THE (1)

AMBER

Number	Title	Yr	NM
❏ 2003	I Cried/It Must Be Love	1961	$500

— Originals have matrix muber stamped into trail-off wax

PEARLS, THE (2)

ATCO

Number	Title	Yr	NM
❏ 6066	Bells of Love/Come On Home	1956	$50
❏ 6057	Shadows of Love/Yum Yummy	1956	$40

ON THE SQUARE

Number	Title	Yr	NM
❏ 320	Band of Angels/Ugly Face	1959	$30

ONYX

Number	Title	Yr	NM
❏ 511	Ice Cream Baby/Yuz-a-Ma-Tuz	1957	$70
❏ 503	Let's You and I Go Steady/Zippidy Zippidy Zoom	1956	$70
❏ 506	My Oh My/Tree in the Meadow	1956	$200
❏ 516	The Wheel of Love/It's Love, Love, Love	1957	$120

PEARLS, THE (3)

PRIVATE STOCK

Number	Title	Yr	NM
❏ 45-060	Pearly/I'll See You in My Dreams	1975	$5

PEARLS, THE (4)

WARNER BROS.

Number	Title	Yr	NM
❏ 5300	Happy Over You/If I Had a Choice	1962	$30

PEARSON, DUKE

BLUE NOTE

Number	Title	Yr	NM
❏ 1754	Black Coffee/Gate City	1960	$10
❏ 1755	Taboo/Like Somebody in Love	1960	$10

Number	Title	Yr	NM

PEBBLES AND BAMM BAMM
HANNA-BARBERA
❏ 449	Open Up Your Heart/The Lord Is Counting on You	1965	$30
❏ 449 [PS]	Open Up Your Heart/The Lord Is Counting on You	1965	$60
❏ 484	The World Is Full of Toys/Daddy	1966	$30

7-Inch Extended Plays
❏ CS7044	Little Drummer Boy/We Three Kings//Silent Night/It Came Upon a Midnight Clear	1965	$60
❏ CS7044 [PS]	We Wish You a Merry Christmas	1965	$125

PECK, GREGORY
DECCA
❏ 9-69 [PS]	Lullaby of Christmas	1950	$10

— Box for 3-record set (9-24731, 9-24732 and 9-24733)

❏ 9-24731	Lullaby of Christmas (Part 1)/(Part 6)	1950	$10

— Side 1 and Side 6 of "Album No. 9-69

❏ 9-24732	Lullaby of Christmas (Part 2)/(Part 5)	1950	$10

— Side 2 and Side 5 of "Album No. 9-69

❏ 9-24733	Lullaby of Christmas (Part 3)/(Part 4)	1950	$10

— Side 3 and Side 4 of "Album No. 9-69

PEDICIN, MIKE
ABC-PARAMOUNT
❏ 10303	Gotta Twist/When the Cats Come Twistin' In	1962	$15

APOLLO
❏ 534	Hey Pop, Give Me the Keys/St. James Infirmary	1959	$50

CAMEO
❏ 125	Shake a Hand/The Dickie Doo	1957	$30

FEDERAL
❏ 12417	Burnt Toast/You Gotta Go, You Gotta Go	1961	$20

MALVERN
❏ 101	The Dickie Doo/(B-side unknown)	1957	$40

RCA VICTOR
❏ 47-6150	Fe-Fi-Fo-Fum/The Hot Barcarolle	1955	$30
❏ 47-6043	I'm Hip/I Wanna Hug You, Kiss You, Squeeze You	1955	$30
❏ 47-6051	Mambo Rock/D-E-V-I-L	1955	$30
❏ 47-6676	Teenage Fairy Tales/Close All the Doors	1956	$30
❏ 47-6546	The Beat/Save Us, Preacher Davis	1956	$30
❏ 47-6847	The Hucklebuck/Calypso Rock	1957	$30
❏ 47-6369	The Large, Large House/Hotter Than a Pistol	1955	$30

PEE WEE CHILDREN'S CHORUS, THE
CCP
❏ 1002	Pee Wee The Pink Pine Tree/Santa Claus Junior	1976	$4

—B-side by Reta, Alita & Marilyn

PEEBLES, ANN
HI
❏ 2284	Beware/You Got to Feed the Fire	1975	$6
❏ 2205	Breaking Up Somebody's Home/Troubles, Heartaches and Sadness	1972	$6
❏ 2294	Come to Mama/I'm Leaving You	1975	$6
❏ 2271	Do I Need You/Love Vibration	1974	$6
❏ 2302	Dr. Love Power/I Still Love You	1976	$6
❏ 2320	Fill This World with Love/It Was Jealousy	1976	$6
❏ 2173	Generation Gap Between Us/I'll Get Along	1970	$6
❏ 2165	Give Me Some Credit/Solid Foundation	1969	$6
❏ 2248	I Can't Stand the Rain/I've Been There Before	1973	$6
❏ 78518	I Didn't Take Your Man/Being Here with You	1978	$5
❏ 2309	I Don't Lend My Man/I Need Somebody	1976	$6
❏ 80533	I'd Rather Leave While I'm in Love/Heartaches	1980	$5
❏ 77502	If This Is Heaven/Sailing	1977	$5
❏ 79528	If You've Got the Time (I've Got the Love)/Let Your Lovelight Shine	1979	$5
❏ 2232	I'm Gonna Tear Your Playhouse Down/One Way Street	1973	$6

❏ 2186	I Pity the Fool/Heartaches, Heartaches	1971	$6
❏ 81534	Mon Belle-Amour/(B-side unknown)	1981	$5
❏ 78509	Old Man with Young Ideas/A Good Day for Lovin'	1978	$5
❏ 2178	Part Time Love/I Still Love You	1970	$6
❏ 2198	Slipped, Tripped and Fell in Love/99 Lbs.	1971	$6
❏ 2219	Somebody's On Your Case/I've Been There Before	1972	$6
❏ 2157	Walk Away/I Can't Let You Go	1969	$6

PEEK, EVERETT
COMMERCIAL
❏ 00016	Sea Cruise/(B-side unknown)	1977	$8

PEEL, DAVE
CHART
❏ 5143	Cracklin' Rosie/I Thought of You Today	1971	$6
❏ 5037	I'm Walkin'/My Baby	1969	$8
❏ 5159	Ordinary Day/Wax Museum	1972	$6
❏ 5086	Sad Man's Song/You're Walking Through the Rooms	1970	$6
❏ 5123	The Day/My Baby	1971	$6
❏ 5054	Wax Museum/If You've Been Better Than I've Been	1970	$6

PEEL, DAVID
APPLE
❏ PRO-6498/9 [DJ]	F Is Not a Dirty Word/The Ballad of New York City	1972	$120
❏ PRO-6545/6 [DJ]	Hippie from New York City/The Ballad of New York City	1972	$120

ORANGE
❏ 1001	Bring Back the Beatles/Imagine	1977	$10

PEELS, THE
KARATE
❏ 527	Scrooey Mooey/Time Marches On	1966	$8

PEERCE, JAN
RCA VICTOR
❏ 47-7109	A Child's First Christmas/Faith	1957	$15

7-Inch Extended Plays
❏ ERA132 [PS]	Five Christmas Songs	1953	$20

— Ornament-shaped sleeve

❏ ERA132	Gesu Bambino/Oh, Holy Night (Cantique de Noel)//Maria on the Mountain/Behold a Branch Is Growing/O Sanctissima	1953	$15

PEEVEY, GAYLA
COLUMBIA
❏ 40602	77 Santas/Rubberlegs (The Knock-Kneed Monkey)	1955	$20
❏ 4-224	Got A Cold In The Node For Christmas/The Angel In The Christmas Play	1954	$20

— Yellow-label "Children's Series" record

❏ 40364	Got A Cold In The Node For Christmas/The Angel In The Christmas Play	1954	$20
❏ 40106	I Want a Hippopotamus for Christmas/Are My Ears On Straight?	1953	$30
❏ 4-186	I Want a Hippopotamus for Christmas/Are My Ears On Straight?	1953	$20

— Yellow-label "Children's Series" record

PEGGY SUE
DECCA
❏ 32640	After the Preacher's Gone/You Can't Pull the Wool Over My Eyes	1970	$6
❏ 32698	All American Husband/I'm Leaving the Bottle and You	1970	$6
❏ 32754	Apron Strings/You're Leaving Me for Her Again	1970	$6
❏ 32984	Coffee and Tears/Bread Upon the Waters	1972	$6
❏ 32812	I Say "Yes Sir"/Do it Girl Before It's Too Late	1971	$6
❏ 32917	L-O-V-E, Love/You're Leavin' Me for Her Again	1972	$6

DOOR KNOB
❏ 069	All Night Long/Good Evening Henry	1978	$5
❏ 021	Every Beat of My Heart/This Time It's Love	1976	$5
❏ 121	For as Long as You Want Me/Only One Thing Left to Do	1980	$5

❏ 036	Good Evening Henry/Fire in Texas	1977	$5
❏ 079	How I Love You in the Morning/Where Your Memories Play	1978	$5
❏ 029	I Just Came In Here (To Let a Little Hurt Out)/Jody Come Home	1977	$5
❏ 094	I Want to See Me in Your Eyes/Let Me Down Easy	1979	$5
❏ 052	Let Me Down Easy/Come and Lay Down with Me	1978	$5
❏ 043	Mama's Country Christmas/Donkey Without a Name	1977	$5
❏ 137	Slow Motion/The Love Song and the Dream Belong to Me	1980	$5
❏ 102	The Love Song and the Dream Belong to Me/Rainy Day Lovin'	1979	$5
❏ 045	To Be Loved/I've Been Close to Love (Too Many Times)	1978	$5
❏ 160	Too Late to Go Dancing/The Love Song and the Dream Belong to Me	1981	$5
❏ 131	Why Don't You Go to Dallas/Only One Thing Left to Do	1980	$5

MCA
❏ 40323	Lookin' in a Devil's Eye/Never Say Never	1974	$5
❏ 40125	Love What 'Cha Got at Home/Kick It Again	1973	$5
❏ 40189	My Heart Keeps Getting in My Way/Poverty Hill	1974	$5

PEGGY SUE AND SONNY WRIGHT (2)
❏ 180	Two Ring Circus/(B-side unknown)	1983	$5

DOOR KNOB
❏ 113	Gently Hold Me/If This Is What Love's All About	1979	$5
❏ 038	If This Is What Love Is All About/Someone I Can't Say No To	1977	$5

PEJOE, MORRIS
CHECKER
❏ 781	Can't Get Along/It'll Plumb Get It	1953	$400

— Black vinyl

❏ 781	Can't Get Along/It'll Plumb Get It	1953	$1000

— Red vinyl

❏ 766	Tired of Crying Over You/Gonna Buy Me a Telephone	1953	$500

— Black vinyl

❏ 766	Tired of Crying Over You/Gonna Buy Me a Telephone	1953	$3000

— Red vinyl. VG 1500; VG+ 2250

PELICANS, THE
IMPERIAL
❏ 5307	Chimes/Ain't Gonna Do It	1954	$1000

PARROT
❏ 793	White Cliffs of Dover/Aurelia	1954	$3000

— Black vinyl

❏ 793	White Cliffs of Dover/Aurelia	1954	$6000

— Red vinyl. VG 3000; VG+ 4500

PELL, DAVE
7-Inch Extended Plays
RCA VICTOR
❏ EPA 2-1394	Arkansas/South of the Border//Wagon Wheels/Across the Alley from the Alamo	1956	$10
❏ EPA 2-1394 [PS]	Swingin' in the Ol' Corral, Vol. 2	1956	$15

PENDARVIS, TRACY
SUN
❏ 335	A Thousand Guitars/Is It Too Late	1960	$30
❏ 359	Eternally/Belle of the Swanee	1961	$30
❏ 345	Is It Me/South Bound Line	1960	$30

PENDERGRASS, TEDDY
Also see HAROLD MELVIN AND THE BLUE NOTES. (45)

ASYLUM
❏ 69422	2 A.M./(Instrumental)	1988	$4
❏ 69720	Hold Me/Love	1984	$4

— With Whitney Houston

❏ 69720 [PS]	Hold Me/Love	1984	$4
❏ 69669	In My Time/Stay with Me	1985	$4
❏ 69538	Lert Me Be Closer/Love Emergency	1986	$4
❏ 69568	Love 4/2//One of Us Feels in Love	1986	$4

Number	Title	Yr	NM
❑ 69628	Somewhere I Belong/Hot Love	1985	$4
❑ 69628 [PS]	Somewhere I Belong/Hot Love	1985	$4

ELEKTRA

Number	Title	Yr	NM
❑ 69422	2 A.M./(Instrumental)	1988	$3
❑ 69358	Love Is the Power/I'm Ready	1988	$3
❑ 69358 [PS]	Love Is the Power/I'm Ready	1988	$3
❑ 69312	The Last Time/(B-side unknown)	1989	$3

PHILADELPHIA INT'L.

Number	Title	Yr	NM
❑ 3107	Can't We Try/Plenty Good Lovin'	1980	$5
❑ 02095	Can't You Try/Love T.K.O.	1981	$4
❑ 3648	Close the Door/Get Up, Get Down, Get Funky, Get Loose	1978	$5
❑ 3717	Come Go with Me/Do Me	1979	$5
❑ 02462	I Can't Live Without Your Love/You Must Live On	1981	$4
❑ 03325	I Can't Win for Losing	1982	$6
—One-sided budget release			
❑ 03284	I Can't Win for Losing/Don't Lead Me Out Along the Road	1982	$4
❑ 3622	I Don't Love You Anymore/Somebody Told Me	1977	$5
❑ 70062	Is It Still Good to You/Girl You Know	1981	$4
❑ 3742	It's You I Love/Where Did All the Lovin' Go	1980	$5
❑ 3669	Life Is a Song Worth Singing/Cold, Cold World	1978	$5
❑ 04302	Life Is for the Living/I Want My Baby Back	1984	$4
❑ 3116	Love T.K.O./I Just Called to Say	1980	$5
❑ 03116	Love T.K.O./I Just Called to Say	1982	$3
—Reissue			
❑ 3657	Only You/It Don't Hurt Now	1978	$5
❑ 3733	Shout and Scream/Close the Door	1979	$5
❑ 3633	The Whole Town's Laughing at Me/The More I Get, The More I Want	1977	$5
❑ 3696	Turn Off the Lights/If You Know Like I Know	1979	$5

PENDLETONS, THE

DOT

Number	Title	Yr	NM
❑ 16511	Board Party/Barefoot Adventure	1963	$125

RENDEZVOUS

Number	Title	Yr	NM
❑ 194	The Waddle/Itchy Bon Mash	1962	$50

PENDULUM, THE

KAMA SUTRA

Number	Title	Yr	NM
❑ 257	Dead Dog/Now I'll Cry	1968	$8
❑ 268	High on a Hill/She Can Blow Your Mind	1969	$12
❑ 253	Silly Sally Sunday/I Do You	1968	$8

PENGUINS, THE

ATLANTIC

Number	Title	Yr	NM
❑ 1132	Pledge of Love/I Knew I'd Fall in Love	1957	$40

DOOTO

Number	Title	Yr	NM
❑ 435	Do Not Pretend/If You're Mine	1958	$40
❑ 348	Earth Angel/Hey Senorita	1959	$30
—Reissue on altered label name and yellow label			
❑ 432	Sweet Love/Let Me Make Up Your Mind	1958	$40
❑ 428	That's How Much I Need You/Be My Lovin' Baby	1957	$50

DOOTONE

Number	Title	Yr	NM
❑ 362	Baby, Let's Make Some Love/Kiss a Fool Goodbye	1955	$60
❑ 348	Earth Angel/Hey Senorita	1954	$200
—First pressings on glossy red labels			
❑ 348	Earth Angel/Hey Senorita	1955	$60
—Maroon label			
❑ 348	Earth Angel/Hey Senorita	1955	$50
—Blue label			
❑ 348	Earth Angel/Hey Senorita	1955	$40
—Black label			
❑ 353	Love Will Make Your Mind Go Wild/Ookey Ook	1954	$75
—First pressings on glossy red label			
❑ 353	Love Will Make Your Mind Go Wild/Ookey Ook	1955	$60
—Maroon label			
❑ 353	Love Will Make Your Mind Go Wild/Ookey Ook	1955	$50
—Blue label			
❑ 353	Love Will Make Your Mind Go Wild/Ookey Ook	1955	$40
—Black label			

MERCURY

Number	Title	Yr	NM
❑ 70762	A Christmas Prayer/Jingle Jangle	1955	$100
❑ 71033	Cool Baby Cool/Will You Be Mine	1957	$50
❑ 70610	Don't Do It/Be Mine or Be a Fool	1955	$60
—Black vinyl			
❑ 70610	Don't Do It/Be Mine or Be a Fool	1955	$200
—Red vinyl			
❑ 70943	Earth Angel/Ice	1956	$50
—Not the same recording as the hit on Dootone			
❑ 70799	My Troubles Are Not At an End/She's Gone, Gone	1956	$60
—Maroon label			
❑ 70799	My Troubles Are Not At an End/She's Gone, Gone	1956	$30
—Black label			
❑ 70703	Promises, Promises, Promises/The Devil That I See	1955	$60
❑ 70654	Walkin' Down Broadway/It Only Happens with You	1955	$60

ORIGINAL SOUND

Number	Title	Yr	NM
❑ 54	Heavenly Angel/Big Bobo's Party Train	1965	$30
❑ 27	Memories of El Monte/Be Mine	1963	$125
—Black and red label			
❑ 27	Memories of El Monte/Be Mine	1963	$60
—Black and silver label; A-side written by Frank Zappa			

SUN STATE

Number	Title	Yr	NM
❑ 01	Believe Me/The Pony Rock	1962	$30

WING

Number	Title	Yr	NM
❑ 90076	Dealer of Dreams/Peace of Mind	1956	$40

7-Inch Extended Plays

DOOTO

Number	Title	Yr	NM
❑ 241	Butterball/Heart of a Fool//Money Talks/Lover or Fool	1959	$120
❑ 243	(contents unknown)	1959	$120
❑ 244	(contents unknown)	1959	$120
❑ 243 [PS]	The Cool, Cool Penguins, Vol. 2	1959	$120
❑ 244 [PS]	The Cool, Cool Penguins, Vol. 3	1959	$120
❑ 241 [PS]	The Cool, Cool Penguins Vol. 1	1959	$120

DOOTONE

Number	Title	Yr	NM
❑ 101	Earth Angel/I Ain't Gonna Cry No More//Love Will Make Your Mind Go Wild/Baby Let's Make Some Love	1955	$250
❑ 101 [PS]	The Penguins	1955	$250
—Issued in "Dootone" jacket rather than custom jacket			

PENN, LITTLE "LAMBSIE"

ATCO

Number	Title	Yr	NM
❑ 6082	I Wanna Spend Christmas With Elvis/Painted Lips and Pigtails	1956	$60

PENN, WILLIAM, AND THE QUAKERS

MELRON

Number	Title	Yr	NM
❑ 5013	California Sun/No More Love	1966	$60
❑ 5024	Santa Needs Ear Muffs on His Nose/Philly	1966	$70
❑ 5024	Santa Needs Ear Muffs on His Nose/Sweet Caroline	1966	$70

THUNDERBIRD

Number	Title	Yr	NM
❑ 502	Blow My Mind/Swami	1966	$50
—As the "William Penn Fyve			

TWILIGHT

Number	Title	Yr	NM
❑ 410	Ghost of the Monks/Goodbye My Love	1967	$40

UPTOWN

Number	Title	Yr	NM
❑ 745	Chrome Dome Wheeler Dealer/Scrapped	1967	$50

PENNANTS, THE

WORLD

Number	Title	Yr	NM
❑ 102	Don't Go/Workin' Man	1961	$125

PENNELL, ZAG

COLUMBIA

Number	Title	Yr	NM
❑ 4-21302	Day and Night Patrol/Some Kinna	1954	$30
❑ 4-21408	How Could It Be Wrong/Everything Needs Something	1955	$30
❑ 4-21365	Tender Lovin' Care/I'm Doing All Right	1955	$30

PENNER, DICK

SUN

Number	Title	Yr	NM
❑ 282	Cindy Lou/Your Honey Love	1958	$60

PENNINGTON, RAY

CAPITOL

Number	Title	Yr	NM
❑ 2118	Hush, Hush, Sweet Charlotte/Someday You'll Fall Back to Home	1968	$8
❑ 5751	Who's Been Mowing the Lawn (While I Was Gone)/I Don't Feel at Home	1966	$8
❑ 2006	Who's Gonna Walk the Dog (And Put Out the Cat)/You Turned the Lights On	1967	$8

DIMENSION

Number	Title	Yr	NM
❑ 1039	For Christmas/Don't Let Me Lie Again	1982	$5
❑ 1043	While I Was Slippin' In (She Was Steppin' Out)/I Can Forget About You	1983	$5

EMH

Number	Title	Yr	NM
❑ 0029	Drowning My Troubles (Till They've Learned How to Swim)/Till the Fear Slips Away	1984	$5
❑ 0027	For Christmas/Dark Haired Woman	1983	$5
❑ 0022	The Memories That Last/Nothing to Go On	1983	$5

KING

Number	Title	Yr	NM
❑ 5783	The First Step Down Is the Longest/Your Diary	1963	$15

LEE

Number	Title	Yr	NM
❑ 502	Boogie Woogie Country Girl/ (B-side unknown)	1958	$250
❑ 504	My Steady Baby/(B-side unknown)	1958	$200

MONUMENT

Number	Title	Yr	NM
❑ 8553	Let Them Talk/Happy Times	1972	$6
❑ 8537	My Church/This Song Don't Care Who Sings It	1971	$6
❑ 8527	The Best Worst Thing/My Daddy Was a Travelin' Man	1971	$6
❑ 8540	Woman Go On Home/Dark Haired Woman	1972	$6

MRC

Number	Title	Yr	NM
❑ 1022	She Wanted a Little Bit More/(B-side unknown)	1978	$5

RUBY

Number	Title	Yr	NM
❑ 290	Fancy Free/You'll Want Me Back But I Won't Care	1957	$70

STEP ONE

Number	Title	Yr	NM
❑ 403	Blue of a Kind/Fat Boy Rag	1989	$5
❑ 362	Good Ole Country Mood/In the Mood	1986	$5

ZODIAC

Number	Title	Yr	NM
❑ 1003	I Can't Get Up Myself/ (B-side unknown)	1976	$6
❑ 1010	Steppin' Aside Just Ain't My Style/The Good Old Days Are Right Now	1976	$6

PENNY AND JEAN

RCA VICTOR

Number	Title	Yr	NM
❑ 47-7844	I Forgot More Than You'll Ever Know/How Come I'm Crying Now?	1961	$15

PENNY AND THE OVERTONES

RIM

Number	Title	Yr	NM
❑ 2021	What Made You Forget/ (B-side unknown)	1958	$125

PENNY, ED

DECCA

Number	Title	Yr	NM
❑ 29727	What Is Christmas?/Lonely Old Shepherd	1955	$15

ESSEX

Number	Title	Yr	NM
❑ 376	What Is Christmas/Lonely Old Shepherd	1954	$20
—As "Edward Penny and Larry Forbes			

PENNY, HANK

DECCA

Number	Title	Yr	NM
❑ 9-29597	A Letter from Home/Bloodshot Eyes	1955	$30
❑ 9-29560	I Can't Get You Out of My Mind/When They Ask About You	1955	$30
❑ 9-30313	The Cricket Song/Big Footed Sam	1957	$30
❑ 9-30179	Wham! Bam! Thank You Ma'am/Texas Never Woulda	1957	$30

KING

Number	Title	Yr	NM
❑ 1020	Alabama Jubilee/Back Up a Little Bit	1951	$50
❑ 1090	Back Up a Little Bit/Don't You Know It's Wrong	1952	$40

Number	Title	Yr	NM
❏ 1500	Bloodshot Eyes/Wham, Bam, Thank You Ma'am	1955	$30
❏ 1021	Steel Guitar Polka/Won't You Ride in My Little Red Wagon	1951	$50
❏ 1122	Two Timin' Mama/Low Down Woman Blues	1952	$40

RCA VICTOR

❏ 48-0501	Catch 'Em Young, Treat 'Em Rough/I Like Molasses	1951	$40
❏ 47-5283	Fan It/You Can't Pull the Wool	1953	$30

— With Jaye P. Morgan

❏ 47-4862	Hadicillin Boogie/If I Can't Wear the Pants	1952	$30
❏ 47-4363	I Want My Rib/White Shotgun	1951	$30
❏ 47-5023	Makin' Love Tennessee Style/Sweet Mama Put Him in Low	1952	$30
❏ 48-0406	Tater Pie/Just for Old Time's Sake	1950	$40
❏ 47-4633	Taxes, Taxes/You're Bound to Look Like a Monkey	1952	$30
❏ 47-4414	That Mink on Her Back/My Little Red Wagon	1951	$30
❏ 47-5150	That's My Weakness Now/I Want to Live a Little	1953	$30
❏ 48-0466	What She's Got Is Mine/Hold the Phone	1951	$40

PENNY, JOE
FEDERAL

❏ 12322	Mercy, Mercy Percy/Bip a Little, Bop a Little	1958	$200

SIMS

❏ 173	Frosty Window Pane/Hatty Fatty	1964	$30

PENTAGONS, THE
DONNA

❏ 1344	I Like the Way You Look (At Me)/For a Love That Is Mine	1961	$40
❏ 1337	To Be Loved (Forever)/Down at the Beach	1961	$40

FLEET INT'L.

❏ 100	Down at the Beach/To Be Loved (Forever)	1960	$200

— Original record has "Down at the Beach" labeled as "100-1" and "To Be Loved (Forever)" as "100-2"

JAMIE

❏ 1201	I Wonder/She's Mine	1961	$20

PENTANGLE, THE
REPRISE

❏ 0843	I Saw an Angel/Once I Had a Sweetheart	1969	$8
❏ 0784	Let No Man Steal Your Throne/Way Behind the Sun	1968	$8
❏ PRO391 [DJ]	Light Flight/Sally Go 'Round the Roses	1969	$12

PEOPLE
CAPITOL

❏ 2251	Apple Cider/Ashes of Me	1968	$10
❏ 2078	I Love You/Somebody Tell Me My Name	1968	$15
❏ 5920	Organ Grinder/Riding High	1967	$10
❏ 2499	Turnin' Me In/Ulla	1969	$10

PARAMOUNT

❏ 0019	For What It's Worth/Maple Street	1970	$6
❏ 0005	Love Will Take Us Higher and Higher/Livin' It Up	1969	$6
❏ 0028	One Chain Don't Make No Prison/Keep It Alive	1970	$6
❏ 0011	Sunshine Lady/Crosstown Bus	1969	$6

POLYDOR

❏ 14087	Chant for Peace/I Don't Carry No Guns	1971	$6

ZEBRA

❏ 102	Come Back Beatles (same on both sides)	1978	$10

PEOPLE'S CHOICE
CASABLANCA

❏ 2322	My Feet Won't Move, But My Shoes Did the Boogie/You Ought to Be Dancin'	1980	$4

PALMER

❏ 5020	Easy to Be True/Savin' My Love for You	1967	$250

PHILADELPHIA INT'L.

❏ 3649	Turn Me Loose/Soft and Tender	1978	$4

PHIL-L.A. OF SOUL

❏ 349	I Likes to Do It/Big Ladies Man	1971	$6
❏ 358	Let Me Do My Thing/On a Cloudy Day	1972	$6

Number	Title	Yr	NM
❏ 356	Magic/Oh How I Love It	1972	$6
❏ 352	Wootie-T-Woo/'Cause That's the Way I Know	1971	$6

TSOP

❏ 4784	Cold Blooded & Down-Right Funky/Jam, Jam, Jam (All Night Long)	1976	$5
❏ 4769	Do It Any Way You Wanna/The Big Hurt	1975	$5
❏ 4781	Here We Go Again/Mickey D's	1976	$5
❏ 4786	If You Gonna Do It (Put Your Mind To It) (Part I)/If You Gonna Do It (Put Your Mind To It) (Part II)	1977	$5
❏ 4751	Love Shot/The Big Hurt	1973	$5
❏ 4782	Movin' In All Directions/Mellow Hood	1976	$5
❏ 4759	Party Is a Groovy Thing/Asking for Trouble	1974	$5

PEPPERMINT RAINBOW, THE
DECCA

❏ 32498	Don't Wake Me Up in the Morning, Michael/Rosemary	1969	$8
❏ 32498 [PS]	Don't Wake Me Up in the Morning, Michael/Rosemary	1969	$15
❏ 32601	Good Morning Means Goodbye/Don't Love Me Unless It's Forever	1969	$8
❏ 32316	Pink Lemonade/Walking in Different Circles	1968	$8
❏ 32410	Will You Be Staying After Sunday/And I'll Be There	1968	$10

PEPPERMINT TROLLEY COMPANY, THE
ACTA

❏ 815	Baby You Come Rollin' Across My Mind/9 O'Clock Business Man	1968	$12
❏ 809	It's a Lazy Summer Day/Blue Eyes	1967	$8
❏ 807	She's the Kind of Girl/Little Miss Sunshine	1967	$8
❏ 835	Spinnin' 'n' Whirlin' Around/New York City	1969	$8
❏ 834	The Last Thing on My Mind/Memphis City Letter	1969	$20
❏ 829	Trust/I Remember Long Along	1968	$8

VALIANT

❏ 752	Lollipop Train/Bored to Tears	1966	$30

PEPPERS, THE
BIG TREE

❏ 16041	Doctor's Music/Velvet Moon	1975	$8

EVENT

❏ 221	Do It, Do It/Just a Rock	1974	$8
❏ 215	Hot Caramel/Blue Ballad	1974	$8
❏ 213	Pepper Box/Pinch of Salt	1974	$10

PERE UBU
Pioneering Cleveland industrialists, featuring Dave Thomas.

HEARTHAN

❏ HR-101	30 Seconds Over Tokyo/Heart of Darkness	1975	$60

—First issue: Black label

❏ HR-101 [PS]	30 Seconds Over Tokyo/Heart of Darkness	1975	$125

—First 1,000 issued with picture sleeve

❏ HR-101	30 Seconds Over Tokyo/Heart of Darkness	1975	$50

— Second issue: Brown on white label

❏ HR-102	Final Solution/Cloud 149	1976	$30
❏ HR-102 [PS]	Final Solution/Cloud 149	1976	$200

—First 600 issued with picture sleeve

❏ HR-103	Street Waves/My Dark Ages	1976	$30
❏ HR-103 [PS]	Street Waves/My Dark Ages	1976	$60

—Most issued with picture sleeve

❏ HR-104	The Modern Dance/Heaven	1977	$30
❏ HR-104 [PS]	The Modern Dance/Heaven	1977	$60

—First 1,000 issued with picture sleeve

PERENNIALS, THE
BALL

❏ 1016	My Big Mistake/I'm Yours 'Til the End	1963	$400

PERFIDIANS, THE
HUSKY

❏ 1	La Paz/Whiplash	1962	$100

— Red vinyl

❏ 1	La Paz/Whiplash	1962	$50

— Black vinyl

PERKINS, CARL
COLUMBIA

❏ 45107	All Mama's Children/Step Aside	1970	$8

— With NRBQ

❏ 42061	Anyway the Wind Blows/The Unhappy Girls	1961	$30
❏ 44993	C.C. Rider/Soul Beat	1969	$8
❏ 45466	Cotton Top/About All I Can Give You Is My Love	1971	$5
❏ 44883	For Your Love/Four Letter Word	1969	$8
❏ 45582	High on Love/Take Me Back to Memphis	1972	$5
❏ 42405 [PS]	Hollywood City/The Fool I Used to Be	1962	$120
❏ 42405	Hollywood City/The Fool I Used to Be	1962	$30
❏ 41825	Honey, 'Cause I Love You/Just for You	1960	$30
❏ 42753	I Just Got Back from There!/Forget Me Next Time Around	1963	$30
❏ 41207	Levi Jacket/Pop, Let Me Have the Car	1958	$30
❏ 41651	L-O-V-E-V-I-L-L-E/Too Much for a Man to Understand	1960	$30
❏ 45347	Me Without You/Red Headed Woman	1971	$5
❏ 41449	One Ticket to Loneliness/I Don't See Me in Your Eyes Anymore	1959	$30
❏ 41131	Pink Pedal Pushers/Jive After Five	1958	$40
❏ 41131 [PS]	Pink Pedal Pushers/Jive After Five	1958	$120
❏ 41379	Pointed Toe Shoes/Highway of Love	1959	$30
❏ 42514	Sister Twister/Hambone	1962	$30
❏ 42514 [PS]	Sister Twister/Hambone	1962	$400
❏ 45694	Someday/The Trip	1972	$5
❏ 45132	State of Confusion/My Son, My Son	1970	$6
❏ 45253	What Every Little Boy Ought to Know/Just As Long	1970	$5

DECCA

❏ 31591	After Sundown/I Wouldn't Have Told You	1964	$20
❏ 31548	Help Me Find My Baby/For a Little While	1963	$20
❏ 31786	One of These Days/Mama of My Song	1965	$20
❏ 31709	The Monkeyshine/Let My Baby Be	1964	$20

DOLLIE

❏ 505	Country Boy's Dream/If I Could Come Back	1966	$15
❏ 516	It's You/Lake County Cotton Country	1968	$15
❏ 514	My Old Home Town/Back to Tennessee	1967	$15
❏ 508	Shine, Shine, Shine/Almost Love	1967	$15
❏ 512	Without You/You Can Take the Boy Out of the Country	1967	$15

FLIP

❏ 501	Movie Magg/Turn Around	1955	$1000

JET

❏ 5054	Blue Suede Shoes/Rock Around the World	1979	$4

MERCURY

❏ 73993	Help Me Dream/You Tore My Heaven All to Hell	1973	$6
❏ 73425	(Let's Get) Dixiefried/One More Loser Goin' Home	1973	$6
❏ 73690	The E.P. Express/Big Bad Blues	1975	$5
❏ 55009	The E.P. Express/Big Bad Blues	1977	$4

MMI

❏ 1016	Don't Get Off Gettin' It On/Georgia Court Room	1977	$4
❏ 1019	Standing in the Need of Love/Georgia Court Room	1977	$4

MUSIC MILL

❏ 1007	Born to Boogie/Take Me Back	1976	$4

SMASH

❏ 884760-7	Birth of Rock and Roll/Rock and Roll (Fais-Do-Do)	1986	$4

—B-side with Jerry Lee Lewis, Roy Orbison and Johnny Cash

❏ 884760-7 [PS]	Birth of Rock and Roll/Rock and Roll (Fais-Do-Do)	1986	$4

—B-side with Jerry Lee Lewis, Roy Orbison and Johnny Cash

❏ 888142-7	Class of '55/We Remember the King	1987	$4

—B-side with Jerry Lee Lewis, Roy Orbison and Johnny Cash

❏ 884934-7	Sixteen Candles/Rock & Roll (Fais-Do-Do)	1986	$4

—B-side with Jerry Lee Lewis, Roy Orbison and Johnny Cash; A-side by Jerry Lee Lewis

SUEDE

❏ 101	I Don't Want to Fall in Love Again/We Did It in '54	1978	$4
❏ 6777	Little Teardrops/Green Grass of Home	1977	$4

Number	Title	Yr	NM
SUN			
❏ 234	Blue Suede Shoes/Honey Don't	1956	$70
❏ 243	Boppin' the Blues/All Mama's Children	1956	$50
❏ 249	Dixie Fried/I'm Sorry, I'm Not Sorry	1956	$40
❏ 287	Glad All Over/Lend Me Your Comb	1958	$40
❏ 224	Gone, Gone, Gone/Let the Jukebox Keep On Playing	1955	$125
❏ 261	Matchbox/Your True Love	1957	$40
❏ 274	That's Right/Forever Yours	1957	$40
UNIVERSAL			
❏ UVL-66002	Charlene/Love Makes Dreams Come True	1989	$4
❏ UVL-66019	Hambone/Love Makes Dreams Come True	1989	$4

7-Inch Extended Plays

Number	Title	Yr	NM
COLUMBIA			
❏ B-12341 [PS]	Whole Lotta Shakin'	1958	$250
❏ B-12341	Whole Lotta Shakin' Goin' On/That's All Right/Tutti Frutti/I Got a Woman	1958	$250
SUN			
❏ EPA-115	Blue Suede Shoes/Movie Magg//Sure to Fall/Gone, Gone, Gone	1958	$400
❏ EPA-115 [PS]	Carl Perkins	1958	$400

PERKINS, DAL

Number	Title	Yr	NM
CHALLENGE			
❏ 59288	If You Were Mine/Money Greases the Wheel	1965	$20
❏ 59262	Last of the Lovers/It's So Nice to See You	1964	$20
❏ 59318	Second Choice/Standing in Your Shadow	1965	$20
COLUMBIA			
❏ 4-44343	Helpless/Woman in the Darkness	1967	$12
❏ 4-44204	Here's to the Girls/One Day a Week	1967	$12

PERKINS, LAURA LEE

Number	Title	Yr	NM
IMPERIAL			
❏ 5507	Don't Wait Up/Oh La Baby	1958	$50

PERKINS, ROY

Number	Title	Yr	NM
MELADEE			
❏ 111	Bye Bye Baby/You're on My Mind	1958	$125
MERCURY			
❏ 71278	Drop Top/That's What the Mailman Had to Say	1958	$50

PERKINS, TONY

Number	Title	Yr	NM
EPIC			
❏ 9201	A Fool in Love/Melody for Lovers	1957	$30
—As "Anthony Perkins			
❏ 9181	Friendly Persuasion/If You Were the Only Girl	1956	$30
—As "Anthony Perkins			
❏ 9165	If You'll Be Mine/A Little Love Can Go a Long Way	1956	$30
—As "Anthony Perkins			
RCA VICTOR			
❏ 47-7155	Indian Giver/Just Being of Age	1958	$15
❏ 47-7155 [PS]	Indian Giver/Just Being of Age	1958	$30
❏ 47-7020	Moon-Light Swim/First Romance	1957	$15
❏ 47-7295	Moonlight Swim/She Used to Be My Girl	1958	$15
❏ 47-7244	The Prettiest Girl in School/ No, No, No	1958	$15
❏ 47-7415	Treasure Island/Gonna Get Some Lovin'	1958	$15
❏ 47-7078	When School Starts Again/ Rocket to the Moon	1957	$15

PERRIN, SUE

Number	Title	Yr	NM
GOLDEN WORLD			
❏ 2	Candy Store Man/Recipe of Love	1963	$40

PERRY, FRANK

Number	Title	Yr	NM
BELLE			
❏ 251	Santa's Caught On The Freeway/Young & Innocent	1959	$15

PERRY, JOE, PROJECT

Number	Title	Yr	NM
COLUMBIA			
❏ 02497	Buzz Buzz/East Coast, West Coast	1981	$5
❏ 11250	Let the Music Do the Talking/ Bone to Bone	1980	$5

PERRY, STEVE

Number	Title	Yr	NM
COLUMBIA			
❏ 04693	Foolish Heart/It's Only Love	1984	$3
❏ 04391	Oh Sherrie/Don't Tell Me Why You're Leaving	1984	$3
❏ 04391 [PS]	Oh Sherrie/Don't Tell Me Why You're Leaving	1984	$3
❏ 04496	She's Mine/You Should Be Happy	1984	$3
❏ 04496 [PS]	She's Mine/You Should Be Happy	1984	$3
❏ 04598	Strung Out/Captured by the Moment	1984	$3

PERSIANS, THE (1)

Number	Title	Yr	NM
ABC			
❏ 11145	I Only Have Eyes for You/ The Sun's Gotta Shine in Your Heart	1968	$8
❏ 11087	Too Much Pride/That's If You Want Me To	1968	$8
CAPITOL			
❏ 3414	Give Me a Little Tune/I Won't Cry for You Anymore	1972	$6
❏ 3333	I Want to Go Home/Baby Come Back Home	1972	$6

PERSIANS, THE (2)

Number	Title	Yr	NM
GOLD EAGLE			
❏ 1813	Love Me Tonight/Gee What a Girl	1962	$30
GOLDISC			
❏ 17	Let's Monkey Again/When You Said Let's Get Married	1963	$40
❏ 1	Teardrops Are Falling/Vault of Memories	1963	$70
MUSIC WORLD			
❏ 102	Let's Monkey Again/When You Said Let's Get Married	1963	$15
PAGEANT			
❏ 601	Get a Hold of Yourself/The Steady Kind	1963	$20
RSVP			
❏ 114	Tears of Love/Dance Now	1962	$40
RTO			
❏ 100	Sunday Kind of Love/When We Get Married	1963	$20

PERSONALITIES, THE

Number	Title	Yr	NM
SAFARI			
❏ 1002	Woe Woe Baby/Yours to Command	1957	$200
—With giraffe on label			
❏ 1002	Woe Woe Baby/Yours to Command	1957	$60
—No giraffe on label			

PERSUADERS, THE

Number	Title	Yr	NM
ATCO			
❏ 6943	Some Guys Have All the Luck/Love Attack	1973	$8
❏ 6822	Thin Line Between Love and Hate/Thigh Spy	1971	$10
CALLA			
❏ 3006	I Need Love/Sure Shot	1977	$6
❏ 3007	Trying to Love Two Women/ Quickest Way Out	1977	$6
CARLTON			
❏ 568	Arabella/Viva El Matador	1962	$20
WINLEY			
❏ 235	Tears/What Could It Be	1959	$200
WIN OR LOSE			
❏ 222	If This Is What You Call Love (I Don't Want No Part of It)/ Thanks for Loving Me	1972	$8
❏ 220	Love Gonna Pack Up (And Walk Out)/You Musta Put Something In Your Love	1971	$8
❏ 225	Peace in the Valley of Love/ What Is the Definition of Love	1972	$8

PERSUADERS, THE (2)

Surf group.

Number	Title	Yr	NM
SATURN			
❏ 405	Caught in the Soup/ Gremmie Bread	1963	$40
❏ 404	Surfing Strip/Hanging Ten	1963	$40

PERSUASIONS, THE

Number	Title	Yr	NM
A&M			
❏ 1658	I Just Want to Sing with My Friends/Somewhere to Lay My Head	1975	$6
❏ 1531	I Really Got It Bad for You/ We're All Goin' Home	1974	$6

Number	Title	Yr	NM
❏ 1698	One Thing on My Mind/ Darlin'	1975	$6
❏ 1631	With This Ring/Somewhere to Lay My Head	1974	$6
CAPITOL			
❏ 3242	Don't Know Why I Love You/ Tempts Jam	1971	$8
❏ 3162	Let It Be/It's You That I Need	1971	$8
❏ 3317	People Get Ready/Buffalo Soldier	1972	$8
❏ 3425	The Ten Commandments of Love/Good Times	1972	$8
❏ 3492	Three Angels (Part 1)/Three Angels (Part 2)	1972	$8
ELEKTRA			
❏ 45396	Papa-Oom-Mow-Mow/ Women and Drinkin'	1977	$5
MCA			
❏ 40118	Chapel of Love/Love You Most of All	1973	$6
❏ 40080	Good Old Accapella/You Must Believe in Me	1973	$6
REPRISE			
❏ 0977	Since I Fell for You/Without a Song	1970	$8
TOWER			
❏ 197	Big Brother/Deep Down Love	1966	$12
❏ 146	Try Me/I'll Go Crazy	1965	$10

PET SHOP BOYS

Number	Title	Yr	NM
EMI AMERICA			
❏ B-43027	It's a Sin/You Know Where You Went Wrong	1987	$4
❏ B-43027 [PS]	It's a Sin/You Know Where You Went Wrong	1987	$6
—With forthcoming album identified as "Jealousy" on back cover			
❏ B-43027 [PS]	It's a Sin/You Know Where You Went Wrong	1987	$4
—With forthcoming album correctly identified as "Actually" on back cover, or not identified at all			
❏ B-8338	Love Comes Quickly/That's My Impression	1986	$4
❏ B-8338 [PS]	Love Comes Quickly/That's My Impression	1986	$4
❏ B-8321	Opportunities (Let's Make Lots of Money)/In the Night	1986	$15
—Withdrawn shortly after release; has different mix than 8330			
❏ B-8321 [PS]	Opportunities (Let's Make Lots of Money)/In the Night	1986	$15
❏ B-8330	Opportunities (Let's Make Lots of Money)/Was That What It Was?	1986	$4
❏ B-8330 [PS]	Opportunities (Let's Make Lots of Money)/Was That What It Was?	1986	$4
❏ B-8355	Suburbia/Jack the Lad	1986	$4
❏ B-8355 [PS]	Suburbia/Jack the Lad	1986	$4
❏ B-8307	West End Girls/A Man Could Get Arrested	1986	$4
❏ B-8307 [PS]	West End Girls/A Man Could Get Arrested	1986	$4
❏ B-50107	What Have I Done to Deserve This?/A New Life	1987	$4
—A-side with Dusty Springfield; original label is gray			
EMI MANHATTAN			
❏ B-50123	Always on My Mind/Do I Have To?	1988	$4
❏ B-50161	Domino Dancing/Don Juan	1988	$4
❏ B-50161 [PS]	Domino Dancing/Don Juan	1988	$4
—Cover has orange sticker on front			
❏ B-50171	Left to My Own Devices/The Sound of the Atom Splitting	1988	$4
❏ B-50171 [PS]	Left to My Own Devices/The Sound of the Atom Splitting	1988	$12
—Sleeve may only have been issued with promo copies			
❏ B-50107 [PS]	What Have I Done to Deserve This?/A New Life	1987	$4
—Record sleeve says "EMI Manhattan" but the record was at least first issued as "EMI America"; we're not sure if the record exists with a white, black and yellow "EMI Manhattan" label			

PETER AND GORDON

Number	Title	Yr	NM
CAPITOL			
❏ 5175	A World Without Love/If I Were You	1964	$15
❏ 5532	Don't Pity Me/Crying in the Rain	1965	$12
❏ 2071	Greener Days/Never Ever	1968	$10
❏ 2544	I Can Remember (Not Too Long Ago)/Hard Time, Rainy Day	1969	$10
❏ 5272	I Don't Want to See You Again/I Would Buy You Presents	1964	$15
❏ 5272 [PS]	I Don't Want to See You Again/I Would Buy You Presents	1964	$20
❏ 5335	I Go to Pieces/Love Me, Baby	1965	$15
❏ 5335 [PS]	I Go to Pieces/Love Me, Baby	1965	$20

Number	Title	Yr	NM
❑ 5740	Lady Godiva/Morning's Calling	1966	$12
❑ 5740	Lady Godiva/The House I Live In	1966	$20
❑ 5864	Sunday for Tea/Hurtin' Is Lovin'	1967	$10
❑ 5864 [PS]	Sunday for Tea/Hurtin' Is Lovin'	1967	$20
❑ 5650	There's No Living Without Your Loving/A Stranger with a Black Dove	1966	$10
❑ 5650 [PS]	There's No Living Without Your Loving/A Stranger with a Black Dove	1966	$20
❑ 5461	To Know You Is to Love You/I Told You So	1965	$10
❑ 5461 [PS]	To Know You Is to Love You/I Told You So	1965	$20
❑ 5684	To Show I Love You/Start Trying Someone Else	1966	$10
❑ 5684 [PS]	To Show I Love You/Start Trying Someone Else	1966	$20
❑ 5406	True Love Ways/If You Wish	1965	$15
❑ 5406 [PS]	True Love Ways/If You Wish	1965	$20
❑ 5579	Woman/Wrong from the Start	1966	$15

— *A-side composer listed as "Bernard Webb*

Number	Title	Yr	NM
❑ 5579	Woman/Wrong from the Start	1966	$10

— *A-side composer listed as "A. Smith*

CAPITOL CREATIVE PRODUCTS

Number	Title	Yr	NM
❑ 51 [DJ]	Wrong from the Start/You've Lost That Lovin' Feelin'	1966	$15

— *B-side by the Lettermen*

Number	Title	Yr	NM
❑ 51 [DJ]	Wrong from the Start/You've Lost That Lovin' Feelin'	1966	$15

— *B-side by the Lettermen*

CAPITOL STARLINE

Number	Title	Yr	NM
❑ 6076	A World Without Love/Nobody I Know	1965	$8

— *Green swirl label original*

Number	Title	Yr	NM
❑ 6103	I Go to Pieces/Love Me Baby	1966	$8

— *Green swirl label original*

Number	Title	Yr	NM
❑ 6104	There's No Living Without Your Loving/Stranger with a Black Dove	1966	$8

— *Green swirl label original*

PETER, PAUL AND MARY

(NO LABEL)

Number	Title	Yr	NM
❑ 0(no cat #) [DJ]	Eugene McCarthy for President	1968	$30

PETER, PAUL AND MARY

(NO LABEL)

Number	Title	Yr	NM
❑ 0(no cat #) [DJ]	El Salvador/Light One Candle	1983	$20
❑ 0(no cat #) [DJ]	Eugene McCarthy for President	1968	$30

WARNER BROS.

Number	Title	Yr	NM
❑ 5402	A-Soalin'/High-A-Bye	1963	$15
❑ 5402 [PS]	A-Soalin'/High-A-Bye	1963	$30
❑ 5325	Big Boat/Tiny Sparrow	1962	$12
❑ 5325 [PS]	Big Boat/Tiny Sparrow	1962	$30
❑ 5368	Blowin' in the Wind/Flora	1963	$10
❑ 7359	Christmas Dinner/The Marvelous Toy	1969	$10
❑ 7279	Day Is Done/Make Believe Town	1969	$8
❑ 5385	Don't Think Twice, It's All Right/Autumn to May	1963	$12
❑ 5659	Early Morning Rain/The Rising of the Moon	1965	$8
❑ 5883	For Baby (For Bobbie)/Hurry Sundown	1967	$8
❑ 8728	Forever Young/Best of Friends	1978	$4
❑ 5496	For Lovin' Me/Monday Morning	1965	$8
❑ 7067	I Dig Rock and Roll Music/The Great Mandella (The Wheel of Life)	1967	$10
❑ 5296	If I Had a Hammer/Gone the Rainbow	1962	$10
❑ 7340	Leaving on a Jet Plane/The House Song	1969	$12
❑ 5274	Lemon Tree/Early in the Morning	1962	$12
❑ 8684	Like the First Time/Best of Friends	1978	$4
❑ PRO149 [DJ]	Morning Train/Gone the Rainbow	1963	$20

— *Stereo 33 1/3 rpm, 7-inch single with small hole; "Promotion" at 10 o'clock on label*

Number	Title	Yr	NM
❑ 5442	Oh, Rock My Soul (Part 1)/Oh, Rock My Soul (Part 2)	1964	$10
❑ 5348	Puff/Pretty Mary	1963	$15

— *First pressings have no subtitle on A-side*

Number	Title	Yr	NM
❑ 5348	Puff (The Magic Dragon)/Pretty Mary	1963	$10

— *Later pressings add subtitle*

Number	Title	Yr	NM
❑ 5334	Settle Down (Goin' Down That Highway)/500 Miles	1963	$10

Number	Title	Yr	NM
❑ 5399	Stewball/The Cruel War	1963	$10
❑ 5418	Tell It on the Mountain/Old Coat	1964	$10
❑ 5809	The Cruel War/Mon Vrai Destin	1966	$8
❑ 5849	The Other Side of This Life/Sometime Lover	1966	$8
❑ 7092	Too Much of Nothing/The House Song	1967	$8
❑ 5625	When the Ship Comes In/The Times They Are a-Changin'	1965	$8
❑ S1751 [PS]	Late Again	1968	$12
❑ S1751	Moments of Soft Persuasion/Too Much of Nothing/Reason to Believe//She Dreams/Hymn/I Shall Be Released	1968	$10

— *Jukebox issue; small hole, plays at 33 1/3 rpm*

PETERIK, JIM

EPIC

Number	Title	Yr	NM
❑ 50272	Don't Fight the Feeling/Hard Day at the World	1976	$5
❑ 50311	Last Tango/Lay Back	1976	$5
❑ 50406	The Closest Thing to My Mind/Don't Fight the Feeling	1977	$5

PETERS AND LEE

PHILIPS

Number	Title	Yr	NM
❑ 40732	Don't Stay Away Too Long/The Old-Fashioned Way	1974	$6
❑ 40729	Welcome Home/Can't Keep My Mind on the Game	1974	$6

PETERS, BEN

CAPITOL

Number	Title	Yr	NM
❑ 3687	Would You Still Love Me/This Has Got to Last	1973	$6

LIBERTY

Number	Title	Yr	NM
❑ 56174	Can't Get Over You/Downtown U.S.A.	1970	$8
❑ 56139	For My Woman's Love/It's Time for Me to Go	1969	$8
❑ 56114	San Francisco Is a Lonely Town/You're the Happy Song I Sing	1969	$8

PETERS, DEBBIE

FREE FLIGHT

Number	Title	Yr	NM
❑ JH-11486 [DJ]	Boogie with Me Baby (same on both sides)	1979	$15

— *Promo only on yellow vinyl*

Number	Title	Yr	NM
❑ PB-11486	Boogie with Me Baby/Turnin' You Off	1979	$6

OAK

Number	Title	Yr	NM
❑ 1012	It Can't Wait/I Can't Get Enough of You	1980	$6

RCA

Number	Title	Yr	NM
❑ PB-11159	I'd Rather Give It Away/Feel Like a Little Love	1977	$5

PETERS, JIMMIE

MCA

Number	Title	Yr	NM
❑ 40361	Danger Zone/Put My Love in Your Pocket	1975	$6
❑ 40270	Everyday with You/What's Left of Her	1974	$6
❑ 40203	I Overlooked a Good Thing Way Too Long/What About the Good Times	1974	$6
❑ 40336	This Kind of Fool Again/The Farther We Go	1974	$6

MERCURY

Number	Title	Yr	NM
❑ 55016	634-5789/Just Because It Feels Good	1978	$5
❑ 55025	I Will Always Love You/Just Because It Feels Good	1978	$5
❑ 55005	Lipstick Traces/Even If It's Wrong	1977	$5
❑ 73911	Somebody Took Her Love (And Never Gave It Back)/I'm What I Am (Because You're Mine)	1977	$5

SUNBIRD

Number	Title	Yr	NM
❑ 105	Hearts/Let's Write a Love Song	1980	$5
❑ 105 [PS]	Hearts/Let's Write a Love Song	1980	$6

PETERSEN, PAUL

COLPIX

Number	Title	Yr	NM
❑ 676	Amy/Goody Goody	1963	$15
❑ 676	Amy/I Only Have Eyes for You	1963	$15
❑ 697	Girls in the Summertime/Mama, Your Little Boy Fell	1963	$15
❑ 763	Happy/Little Dreamer	1965	$15
❑ 649	Lollipops and Roses/Please Mr. Sun	1962	$15
❑ 663	My Dad/Little Boy Sad	1962	$20
❑ 663 [PS]	My Dad/Little Boy Sad	1962	$40

Number	Title	Yr	NM
❑ 620	She Can't Find Her Keys/Very Likely	1962	$20
❑ 620 [PS]	She Can't Find Her Keys/Very Likely	1962	$40

— *Sleeve spells his last name "Peterson" in error*

Number	Title	Yr	NM
❑ 720	She Rides with Me/Poorest Boy in Town	1964	$100

— *A-side produced by Brian Wilson*

Number	Title	Yr	NM
❑ 707	The Cheer Leader/Polka Dots and Moonbeams	1963	$15
❑ 631	What Did They Do Before Rock and Roll/Very Unlikely	1962	$30

— *With Shelly Fabares*

Number	Title	Yr	NM
❑ 631 [PS]	What Did They Do Before Rock and Roll/Very Unlikely	1962	$400
❑ 730	Where Is She/Hey There Beautiful	1964	$15

MOTOWN

Number	Title	Yr	NM
❑ 1129	A Little Bit for Sandy/Your Love's Got Me Runnin'	1968	$30
❑ 1108	Chained/Don't Let It Happen	1967	$30

PETERSON, EARL

COLUMBIA

Number	Title	Yr	NM
❑ 21406	Be Careful of the Heart You're Going to Break/I'm Not Buying Baby	1955	$60
❑ 21364	Boogie Blues/Believe Me	1955	$60
❑ 21467	I Ain't Gonna Fall in Love/I'll Live My Life Alone	1955	$60

SUN

Number	Title	Yr	NM
❑ 197	Boogie Blues/In the Dark	1954	$500

PETERSON, OSCAR

CLEF

Number	Title	Yr	NM
❑ 89093	Autumn in New York/I Hear Music	1954	$20
❑ 89077	Begin the Beguine/Let's Do It	1953	$20
❑ 89078	Cheek to Cheek/I've Got My Love to Keep Me Warm	1953	$20
❑ 89113	It's Easy to Remember/Pooper	1954	$20
❑ 89076	I Was Doing All Right/Oh, Lady Be Good	1953	$20
❑ 89106	One for My Baby/Polka Dots and Moonbeams	1954	$20
❑ 89139	Pettiford's Tune/(B-side unknown)	1955	$15
❑ 89148	Soft Winds/Sweet Lorraine	1955	$15
❑ 89079	Sophisticated Lady/Cottontail	1953	$20

LIMELIGHT

Number	Title	Yr	NM
❑ 3062	Lover's Promenade/The Smudge	1965	$8
❑ 3056	March Past/Place St. Henri	1965	$8
❑ 3072	Straighten Up and Fly Right/When My Sugar Walks Down the Street	1966	$8

MERCURY

Number	Title	Yr	NM
❑ 8923	All the Things You Are/Three O'Clock in the Morning	1950	$30
❑ 89009	Blue Moon/They Can't Take That Away from Me	1952	$20
❑ 89039	Blue Skies/Isn't This a Lovely Day	1953	$20
❑ 8917	Debut/Tenderly	1950	$30
❑ 89008	East of the Moon (West of the Sun)/These Foolish Things	1952	$20
❑ 8930	Exactly Like You/Robin's Nest	1951	$30
❑ 8933	Get Happy/Jumping with Symphony Sid	1951	$30
❑ 8943	How High the Moon/Nameless	1951	$30
❑ 89007	I Can't Get Started/Small Hotel	1952	$20
❑ 89062	I Can't Give You Anything But Love, Baby/Spring Is Here	1953	$20
❑ 72342	Incoherent Blues/Mumbles	1964	$8
❑ 89040	In the Still of the Night/What Is This Thing Called Love	1953	$20
❑ 8926	Little White Lies/Lover	1951	$30
❑ 8959	Love for Sale/Until the Real Thing Comes Along	1952	$30
❑ 8921	Lover Come Back to Me/They Didn't Believe Me	1950	$30
❑ 89041	Prelude to a Kiss/John Hardy's Wife	1953	$20
❑ 8940	Squatty Roo/Salute to Garne	1951	$30
❑ 89038	The Man I Love/It Ain't Necessarily So	1953	$20
❑ 8952	What's New/I Get a Kick Out of You	1951	$30
❑ 8922	Where or When/Oscar's Blues	1950	$30

PRESTIGE

Number	Title	Yr	NM
❑ 727	Girl Talk/On a Clear Day	1969	$6
❑ 711	Sandy's Blues (Part 1)/Sandy's Blues (Part 2)	1969	$6

VERVE

Number	Title	Yr	NM
❑ 10268	Billy Boy/Yours Is My Heart Alone	1962	$10
❑ 10145	Bye Bye Blackbird/Golden Striker	1958	$15

Number	Title	Yr	NM
❑ 10207	Gentleman Jimmy/'Til Tomorrow	1960	$10
❑ 10302	Hallelujah Time/Hymn to Freedom	1963	$10
❑ 10192	On the Street Where You Live/I Could Have Danced All Night	1959	$15
❑ 10354	People/Quiet Nights of Quiet Stars	1965	$8
❑ 10056	Soft Sands/Echoes	1957	$15
❑ 10320	Someday My Prince Will Come/Come Sunday	1964	$8
❑ 10084	Song to the Stars/Chanel	1957	$15
❑ 10292	This Could Be the Start of Something Big/Gravy Waltz	1963	$10
❑ 10073	Why, Oh Why/I've Never Left Your Arms	1957	$15

PETERSON, RAY
DECCA
Number	Title	Yr	NM
❑ 32861	Stamp Out Loneliness/There's a Better Way	1971	$5

DUNES
Number	Title	Yr	NM
❑ 2022	A Love to Remember/I'm Not Jimmy	1963	$20
❑ 2002	Corrina, Corinna/Be My Girl	1960	$30

— Produced by Phil Spector
Number	Title	Yr	NM
❑ 2002 [PS]	Corrina, Corinna/Be My Girl	1960	$70
❑ 2025	Give Us Your Blessing/Without Love (There Is Nothing)	1963	$20
❑ 2009	I Could Have Loved You So Well/Why Don't You Write Me	1961	$30

— Produced by Phil Spector
Number	Title	Yr	NM
❑ 2018	If Only Tomorrow/You Didn't Care	1962	$20
❑ 2027	I Forgot What It Was Like/Be My Girl	1963	$20
❑ 2019	Is It Wrong/Slowly	1963	$20
❑ 2006	Missing You/You Thrill Me	1961	$20
❑ 2030	Promises/Sweet Little Kathy	1963	$20
❑ 2004	Sweet Little Kathy/You Didn't Care	1961	$20
❑ 2024	Where Are You/Deep Are the Roots	1963	$20

MGM
Number	Title	Yr	NM
❑ 13299	Across the Street (Is a Million Miles Away)/When I Stop Dreaming	1964	$10
❑ 13336	A House Without WIndows/Wish I Could Say No to You	1965	$8
❑ 13508	Amanda/I'm Gonna Change Everything	1966	$8
❑ 13269	If You Were Here/Oh No	1964	$10
❑ 13269 [PS]	If You Were Here/Oh No	1964	$20
❑ 13388	I'm Only Human/One Lonesome Rose	1965	$8
❑ 13436	Love Hurts/Everybody	1966	$8

RCA
Number	Title	Yr	NM
❑ GB-11758	Tell Laura I Love Her/The Wonder of You	1979	$3

— Gold Standard Series

RCA VICTOR
Number	Title	Yr	NM
❑ 47-7703	Answer Me, My Love/What Do You Want to Make Those Eyes At Me For	1960	$30
❑ 47-7336	Dream Way/I'll Always Want You Near	1958	$30
❑ 47-7087	Fever/We're Old Enough to Cry	1957	$30
❑ 47-7635	Goodnight My Love (Pleasant Dreams)/Till Then	1959	$30
❑ 47-7635 [PS]	Goodnight My Love (Pleasant Dreams)/Till Then	1959	$40
❑ 47-7165	Let's Try Romance/Shirley Purley	1958	$30
❑ 47-7578	My Blue Angel/Come and Get It	1959	$30
❑ 61-7578 [S]	My Blue Angel/Come and Get It	1959	$100

— Living Stereo" (large hole, plays at 45 rpm)
Number	Title	Yr	NM
❑ 47-7845	My Blue Angel/I'm Tired	1961	$30
❑ 37-7845	My Blue Angel/I'm Tired	1961	$60

— Compact Single 33" (small hole, plays at LP speed)
Number	Title	Yr	NM
❑ 47-7303	Patricia/The Blue-Eyed Baby	1958	$30
❑ 47-7255	Suddenly/Tall Light	1958	$30
❑ 47-7779	Teenage Heartache/I'll Always Want You Near	1960	$30
❑ 47-7745	Tell Laura I Love Her/Wedding Days	1960	$30
❑ 61-7745 [S]	Tell Laura I Love Her/Wedding Days	1960	$125

— Living Stereo" (large hole, plays at 45 rpm)
Number	Title	Yr	NM
❑ 47-8333	The Wonder of You/Goodnight My Love	1964	$10
❑ 47-7513	The Wonder of You/I'm Gone	1959	$30

REPRISE
Number	Title	Yr	NM
❑ 0811	Love Rules the World/Together	1969	$8

UNI
Number	Title	Yr	NM
❑ 55275	Fever/Changes	1971	$6
❑ 55249	Love the Understanding Way/Oklahoma City Rimes	1970	$8

Number	Title	Yr	NM
❑ 55268	Tell Laura I Love Her/To Wait for Love	1971	$6

7-Inch Extended Plays
RCA VICTOR
Number	Title	Yr	NM
❑ EPA-4367 [PS]	Tell Laura I Love Her	1960	$120
❑ EPA-4367	Tell Laura I Love Her/Suddenly//Fever/The Wonder of You	1960	$120

PETRIFIED FOREST, THE
FONTANA
Number	Title	Yr	NM
❑ 1596	So Mystifying/She's the Only Thing That's Kept Me Going	1967	$20

PETS, THE
ARWIN
Number	Title	Yr	NM
❑ 109	Cha-Hua-Hua/Cha-Kow-Ski	1958	$20
❑ 116	Guitarro/Whatever Will Be, Will Be	1958	$20
❑ 112	Wow-Ee!!!/Beyond the Sea	1958	$20

PETTICOATS, THE (1)
CHALLENGE
Number	Title	Yr	NM
❑ 9211	Surfin' Sally/Why Does Billy Play in Your Yard	1963	$30

PETTICOATS, THE (2)
DOT
Number	Title	Yr	NM
❑ 16052	By the Light of the Silvery Moon/Troubadour	1960	$30
❑ 16155	For Sentimental Reasons/Cincinnati	1960	$30

PETTICOATS, THE (3)
PREP
Number	Title	Yr	NM
❑ 125	I Ain't Gonna Do It No More/Manhattan Mountains	1957	$30

UNIQUE
Number	Title	Yr	NM
❑ 363	High Heels/I'll Go Along with You	1956	$30
❑ 387	In My Loving Heart/Michigan Bankroll	1957	$30
❑ 344	The Motorboat Song/The First One	1956	$30

PETTIS, RAY
DREXEL
Number	Title	Yr	NM
❑ 911	Does It Have To Be Christmas/Christmas Here, Christmas There	1956	$60

PETTY, FRANK, TRIO
MGM
Number	Title	Yr	NM
❑ 11629	Italian Christmas Bells/Let It Snow, Let It Snow, Let It Snow	1953	$20

PETTY, NORMAN, TRIO
ABC-PARAMOUNT
Number	Title	Yr	NM
❑ 9787	Almost Paradise/It's Been a Long, Long Time	1957	$15

COLUMBIA
Number	Title	Yr	NM
❑ 41039	Moondreams/Toy Boy	1957	$125

— With Buddy Holly on guitar
Number	Title	Yr	NM
❑ 40929	The First Kiss/(Instrumental)	1957	$15

FELSTED
Number	Title	Yr	NM
❑ 8647	Mood Indigo/On the Alamo	1962	$10

JARO
Number	Title	Yr	NM
❑ 77027	Ditty Dum/Bring Your Heart	1960	$15

X
Number	Title	Yr	NM
❑ 0104	I Wonder Why/Three Little Kisses	1955	$15
❑ 040	Mood Indigo/Petty's Little Polka	1954	$15
❑ 0130	Oh! You Pretty Woman/Hey! Good Lookin'	1955	$15
❑ 071	On the Alamo/Echo Polka	1954	$15
❑ 0167	Solitude/When It's Darkness on the Delta	1955	$15

7-Inch Extended Plays
COLUMBIA
Number	Title	Yr	NM
❑ B-10921	(contents unknown)	1958	$125
❑ B-10921 [PS]	Moondreams	1958	$125

X
Number	Title	Yr	NM
❑ EXA-82	(contents unknown)	1955	$25

PETTY, TOM, AND THE HEARTBREAKERS
Includes Tom Petty solo. Also see STEVIE NICKS; TRAVELING WILBURYS. (45)

BACKSTREET
Number	Title	Yr	NM
❑ 51136	A Woman in Love (It's Not Me)/Gator on the Lawn	1981	$4
❑ 51136 [PS]	A Woman in Love (It's Not Me)/Gator on the Lawn	1981	$4

Number	Title	Yr	NM
❑ 52181	Change of Heart/Heartbreakers Beach Party	1983	$8

— Red vinyl in clear plastic sleeve with sticker
Number	Title	Yr	NM
❑ 52181	Change of Heart/Heartbreakers Beach Party	1983	$3
❑ 52181 [PS]	Change of Heart/Heartbreakers Beach Party	1983	$4

— Only issued with black-vinyl versions
Number	Title	Yr	NM
❑ 41138	Don't Do Me Like That/Casa Dega	1979	$4
❑ 41138 [PS]	Don't Do Me Like That/Casa Dega	1979	$5
❑ 41227	Here Comes My Girl/Louisiana Rain	1980	$4
❑ 41227 [PS]	Here Comes My Girl/Louisiana Rain	1980	$5
❑ 51100	The Waiting/Nightwatchman	1981	$4
❑ 51100 [PS]	The Waiting/Nightwatchman	1981	$4

MCA
Number	Title	Yr	NM
❑ 53153	All Mixed Up/Let Me Up (I've Had Enough)	1987	$3
❑ 53153 [PS]	All Mixed Up/Let Me Up (I've Had Enough)	1987	$3
❑ 52496	Don't Come Around Here No More/Trailer	1985	$4

— Original copies have a 4:19 version of the A-side
Number	Title	Yr	NM
❑ 52496	Don't Come Around Here No More/Trailer	1985	$4

— Second pressings feature a 5-plus-minute version of the A-side
Number	Title	Yr	NM
❑ 52496 [PS]	Don't Come Around Here No More/Trailer	1985	$4
❑ 53748	Free Fallin'/Down the Line	1989	$5
❑ 53369	I Won't Back Down/The Apartment Song	1989	$4
❑ 53369	I Won't Back Down/The Apartment Song	1989	$30

— Special vinyl promo cover
Number	Title	Yr	NM
❑ 52605	Make It Better (Forget About Me)/Crackin' Up	1985	$3
❑ 52605 [PS]	Make It Better (Forget About Me)/Crackin' Up	1985	$3

SHELTER
Number	Title	Yr	NM
❑ 62007	American Girl/Luna	1977	$6
❑ 62008	Breakdown/Fooled Again (I Can't Take It)	1977	$6
❑ 62006 [DJ]	Breakdown (Mono)/Breakdown (Stereo)	1976	$10
❑ 62006 [DJ]	Breakdown (Mono)/Breakdown (Stereo)	1976	$10
❑ 62010	I Need to Know/No Second Thoughts	1978	$5
❑ 62011	Listen to Her Heart/I Don't Know What to Say to You	1978	$5
❑ 62011 [PS]	Listen to Her Heart/I Don't Know What to Say to You	1978	$5

PHAETONS, THE
HI-Q
Number	Title	Yr	NM
❑ 5012	Fling/Homemade	1959	$30

SAHARA
Number	Title	Yr	NM
❑ 102	I'm So Lonely/Road of Blues	1963	$30
❑ 103	The Beatle Walk/Frantic	1964	$60

— B-side by the Premiers

VIN
Number	Title	Yr	NM
❑ 1015	I Love My Baby/As You Know	1959	$70

WARNER BROS.
Number	Title	Yr	NM
❑ 7205	Leave It to Me/You'd Better Come Home	1968	$12
❑ 7082	She Came Like the Rain/Three Weeks, Four Days and Fifteen Hours	1967	$10

PHAFNER
DRAGON
Number	Title	Yr	NM
❑ 1001	Overdrive/Plea from the Soul	1971	$200

PHANTOM, THE (1)
CAPITOL
Number	Title	Yr	NM
❑ F3427	Whispering/Five Foot Two, Eyes of Blue	1956	$30

PHANTOM, THE (2)
DOT
Number	Title	Yr	NM
❑ 16056	Love Me/Whisper Your Love	1960	$200
❑ 16056 [PS]	Love Me/Whisper Your Love	1960	$300

PHANTOM'S DIVINE COMEDY
HIDEOUT
Number	Title	Yr	NM
❑ 1080	Calm Before the Storm/Black Magic, White Magic	1974	$30

Number	Title	Yr	NM

PHELPS, JAMES
ARGO
❑ 5509	La De Da, I'm a Fool in Love/Wasting Time	1965	$8
❑ 5499	Love Is a Five-Letter Word/I'll Do the Best I Can	1965	$8

CADET
❑ 5534	Oh, What a Feeling/Action	1966	$8

FONTANA
❑ 1581	Don't Be a Cry Baby/Walking the Floor Over You	1967	$6
❑ 1600	Fabulous One/The Wrong Number	1967	$6

PARAMOUNT
❑ 0136	My Lover's Prayer/Check Yourself	1971	$5

PHELPS, JUDY LYNN
CLASS
❑ 218	Thanks for Christmas/Thanks for Christmas (Narration)	1957	$30

— *B-side by Montague*

PHIL AND DEL
LINDA
❑ 105	My Girl/Don't Play with Love	1962	$15

PHILADELPHIA MINSTRELS, THE
CAMEO
❑ 284	The Girl That I'll Adore/Grandma's House	1963	$10

— *B-side by the Squirrels*

PHILADELPHIA ORCHESTRA, THE
COLUMBIA
❑ 42621	Adeste Fideles/O Come, Little Children	1962	$10
❑ 43155	We Wish You a Merry Christmas/Little Drummer Boy	1964	$10

— *With the Temple University Choir (side A) and the De Sales Boys Choir (side B)*

PHILADELPHIA STRUMMERS, THE
PARKWAY
❑ 816	I Ain't Down Yet/Every Moment You Live	1961	$10

PHILIP AND STEPHAN
INTERPHON
❑ 7711	Meet Me Tonight Little Girl/When You're Near, You're So Far Away	1964	$20

PHILIPS, TERRY
CORAL
❑ 62247	Fear/Find a Horseshoe	1961	$20

UNITED ARTISTS
❑ 351	My Foolish Ways/Hands of a Fool	1961	$100

PHILLIPS, BILL
AVCO
❑ 608	Four Roses/Typical Day	1975	$6
❑ 602	I've Loved You All Over the World/We Gave Birth to Passion	1974	$6

COLUMBIA
❑ 4-41646	Empty Hours/All Night Long	1960	$20
❑ 4-41323	Foolish Me/The Tears That Fall	1959	$20
❑ 4-41827	How Could You/I Found a True Love	1960	$20
❑ 4-42158	Love Never Dies/The Outsider	1961	$20
❑ 4-41218	Lying Lips/There's a Change in Me	1958	$30
❑ 4-41954	Walk with Me Baby/The Blues Are Settin' In	1961	$20

DECCA
❑ 32782	Big Rock Candy Mountain/I Didn't Forget	1971	$8
❑ 31848	Friends Tell Friends/It Happens Every Time	1965	$10
❑ 31584	I Can Stand It (As Long As She Can)/Wheeling Dealing Daddy	1964	$10
❑ 31781	I'd Be Better Off Without You/Wanted	1965	$10
❑ 31733	I Guess You Made a Fool Out of Me/A Kiss Must Last Forever	1965	$10
❑ 32141	I Learn Something New Everyday/I Didn't Forget	1967	$8
❑ 32432	I Only Regret/She's an Angel	1969	$8

Number	Title	Yr	NM
❑ 32295	I Talked About You Too/Everything Turns Out for the Best	1968	$8
❑ 32375	I've Got a Wonderful Future Behind Me/I'm Thankful	1968	$8
❑ 31480	Let's Walk Away Strangers/Lying to Be Together	1963	$15
❑ 32565	Little Boy Sad/I'm Living in Two Worlds	1969	$8
❑ 32207	Love's Dead End/Oh, What It Did to Me	1967	$8
❑ 31901	Put It Off Until Tomorrow/Lonely Lonely Boy	1966	$20
❑ 32707	Same Old Story, Same Old Lie/You Can't Love Me When I'm Gone	1970	$8
❑ 32638	She's Hungry Again/You've Still Got a Place in My Heart	1970	$8
❑ 31648	Stop Me/Stepping Out	1964	$10
❑ 31996	The Company You Keep/The Lies Just Can't Be True	1966	$12
❑ 32074	The Words I'm Gonna Have to Eat/Falling Back to You	1967	$8

SOUNDWAVES
❑ 4587	At the Moonlite/I'm Turning You Loose	1979	$5
❑ 4570	Divorce Suit (You Were Named Co-Respondent)/I've Been Loving You Too Long	1978	$5
❑ 4575	I Love My Neighbor/I'm Turning You Loose	1978	$5
❑ 4598	Memory Bound/When Can We Do This Again	1979	$5

UNITED ARTISTS
❑ 50879	I Am, I Said/Son	1972	$6
❑ XW266	It's Only Over Now and Then/I've Got Yesterday	1973	$6
❑ XW332	Teach Your Children/New World Tomorrow	1973	$6
❑ 50937	We'll Make It/My Intentions	1972	$6

PHILLIPS, CHARLIE
COLUMBIA
❑ 42526	Cancel the Call/You're Moving Away	1962	$10
❑ 42289	I Guess I'll Never Learn/Now That It's Over	1962	$10
❑ 42851	Later Tonight/This Is the House	1963	$12
❑ 43014	Street of Loneliness/Please Help Me Believe	1964	$10

CORAL
❑ 61970	Be My Bride/Too Many Tears	1958	$30
❑ 61908	Sugartime/One Faded Rose	1958	$30

REPRISE
❑ 0581	Be Careful, Go Easy, Go Slow/Souvenirs of Sorrow	1967	$8

PHILLIPS, ESTHER
ATLANTIC
❑ 2281	And I Love Him/Shangri-La	1965	$15
❑ 2745	Brand New Day/Set Me Free	1970	$6
❑ 2783	Catch Me I'm Falling/Woman Will Do Wrong	1971	$6
❑ 2775	Crazy Love/All God Has Is Us	1970	$6
❑ 2800	Cry Me a River Blues/I'm Getting 'Long Alright	1971	$6
❑ 2370	Fever/Try Me	1966	$15
❑ 2265	Half a Heart/Some Things You Never Get Used To	1964	$20
❑ 2223	Hello Walls/Double Crossing Blues	1964	$20

— *With Jimmy Ricks*

❑ 2417	I'm Sorry/Cheater Man	1967	$10
❑ 2251	It's Too Soon to Know/You're the Reason I'm Living	1964	$20
❑ 2304	Let Me Know When It's Over/I Saw Me	1965	$15
❑ 2294	Moonglow & Theme from Picnic/Makin' Whoopee	1965	$15
❑ 2360	Somebody Else Is Taking My Place/When Love Comes to the Human Race	1966	$15
❑ 2335	When a Woman Loves a Man/Ups and Downs	1966	$15

DECCA
❑ 28804	If You Want Me/Talkin' All Out of My Head	1953	$50
❑ 48305	Please Don't Send Me/Stop Crying	1953	$50
❑ 48314	Sit Back Down/He's a No Good Man	1954	$70

FEDERAL
❑ 12078	Aged and Mellow/Bring My Lovin' Back to Me	1952	$75
❑ 12065	Better Beware/I'll Be There	1952	$75
❑ 12142	Cherry Wine/Love Oh Love	1953	$75
❑ 12042	Cryin' and Singin' the Blues/Tell Him That I Need Him	1951	$100
❑ 12036	Heart to Heart/Looking for a Man to Satisfy My Soul	1951	$500

— *With the Dominoes*

❑ 12115	Hollerin' and Screamin'/Turn the Lamp Down Low	1953	$75

— *With Little Willie Littlefield*

Number	Title	Yr	NM
❑ 12126	Hound Dog/Sweet Lips	1953	$75
❑ 12023	I'm a Bad, Bad Girl/Don't Make a Fool Out of Me	1951	$100
❑ 12108	Last Laugh Blues/Flesh, Blood and Bones	1952	$75

— *With Little Willie Littlefield*

❑ 12100	Saturday Night Daddy/Mainliner	1952	$300

— *With Bobby Nunn*

❑ 12090	Somebody New/Ramblin' Blues	1952	$75
❑ 12063	Summertime/The Storm	1952	$75

KUDU
❑ 906	Baby I'm for Real/That's All Right with Me	1972	$5
❑ 936	Boy I Really Tied One On/Magic's in the Air	1976	$5
❑ 922	Disposable Society/(B-side unknown)	1974	$5
❑ 929	For All We Know/Fever	1976	$5
❑ 938	Higher and Higher/All the Way Down	1976	$5
❑ 904	Home Is Where the Hatred Is/Til My Back Ain't Got No Bone	1972	$5
❑ 910	I've Never Found a Man (To Love Me Like You Do)/Cherry Red	1972	$5
❑ 921	Such a Night/Can't Trust Your Neighbor	1974	$5
❑ 925	What a Difference a Day Makes/Turn Around, Look at Me	1975	$5

LENOX
❑ 5577	A Lover's Hymn/God Bless the Child Who's Got His Own	1963	$30
❑ 5560	Am I That Easy to Forget/I Really Don't Want to Know	1963	$30
❑ 5575	Don't Let Me Go/Why Was I Born	1963	$30
❑ 5570	Why Should We Try Anymore/While It Lasted	1963	$30

MERCURY
❑ 73967	Love Addict/I've Never Been a Woman Before	1977	$4
❑ 74060	Oo-Oop-Oo-Oop/I'll Close My Eyes	1979	$4
❑ 74077	Our Day Will Come/Mr. Melody	1979	$4
❑ 74030	There You Go Again (There She Goes Again)/Stormy Weather	1978	$4

SAVOY
❑ 1563	It's So Good/Do You Ever Think of Me	1959	$20
❑ 1516	Longing in My Heart/If It's News to Me	1957	$30

WARWICK
❑ 610	Gee Baby/Wild Child	1961	$20

WINNING
❑ 1001	Turn Me Out/(B-side unknown)	1983	$5

PHILLIPS, PHIL
KHOURY'S
❑ 711	Sea of Love/Juella	1959	$1500

MERCURY
❑ 71657	Come Back/My Darling/Nobody Knows-Nobody Cares	1960	$30
❑ 71550	Providing/Don't Leave Me	1960	$30
❑ 71465	Sea of Love/Juella	1959	$30
❑ 71649	Stormy Weather/Don't Cry Baby	1960	$30
❑ 71817	Sweet Affection/Betray	1961	$30
❑ 71531 [M]	Take This Heart/Verdie Mae	1959	$30
❑ 10021 [S]	Take This Heart/Verdie Mae	1959	$60
❑ 71611	What Will I Tell My Heart/Your True Love Once More	1960	$30

PHILLIPS, SHAWN
A&M
❑ 1238	A Christmas Song/Lovely Lady	1970	$10
❑ 1238 [PS]	A Christmas Song/Lovely Lady	1970	$10
❑ 1507	All the Kings and Castles/Salty Tears	1974	$5
❑ 1435	Anella/Hey Miss Lonely	1973	$5
❑ 1750	Do You Wonder/Summer Vignette	1975	$5
❑ 1482	Dream Queen/Bright White	1973	$5
❑ 1405	Lost Horizon/Landscape	1973	$5
❑ 1402	We/"L" Ballade	1972	$5

PHILLIPS, STU
CAPITOL
❑ 5466	Feels Like Lovin'/Kathy Keep Playing	1965	$10

COLUMBIA
❑ 4-42978	Heart/Here She Comes Again	1964	$15

Number	Title	Yr	NM
❏ 4-42393	One Day Early/This Heart of Mine	1962	$15
MCA			
❏ 40970	Theme from "Battlestar Galactica"/(B-side unknown)	1978	$6
RCA VICTOR			
❏ 47-8771	Bracero/Angel of Love	1966	$8
❏ 47-9673	Bring Love Back Into Our World/Speak Softly, My Love	1968	$8
❏ 74-0134	Let the Guitars Play/Rings of Grass	1969	$8
❏ 74-0227	Little Tin God/Secret of the Summer Wind	1969	$8
❏ 47-8868	The Great El Tigre (The Tiger)/Another Day Has Gone	1966	$8
❏ 47-9557	The Top of the World/That Completely Destroys My Plans	1968	$8
❏ 47-9066	Walk Me to the Station/Guess Things Happen That Way	1967	$8

PHLUPH
VERVE

Number	Title	Yr	NM
❏ 10564	Another Day/Doctor Mind	1967	$20
❏ 10575	Patterns/In Her Way	1967	$30

PIANO RED
CHECKER

Number	Title	Yr	NM
❏ 911	Get Up Mare/So Worried	1958	$40
GROOVE			
❏ 023	Decatur Street Blues/Big Rock Joe from Kokomo	1954	$40
❏ 0145	I'm Nobody's Fool/That's My Desire	1956	$40
❏ 0101	Pay It No Mind/Jump, Man, Jump	1955	$40
❏ 0118	Six O'Clock Bounce/Goodbye	1955	$40
❏ 0169	Woo-Ee/You Were Mine for Awhile	1956	$40
JAX			
❏ 1006	Guitar Walk/I've Been Walkin'	1959	$20
❏ 1000	This Old World/I Feel Good	1959	$20
KING			
❏ 6330	I Want a Bowlegged Woman/Underground Atlanta	1970	$5
RCA VICTOR			
❏ 47-4524	Bouncin' with Red/Count the Days I'm Gone	1952	$70
❏ 47-7217	Comin' On/One Glimpse of Heaven	1958	$30
❏ 47-5337	Decatur Street Boogie/Your Mouth's Got a Hole in It	1953	$50
❏ 47-4265	Diggin' the Boogie/Let's Have a Good Time Tonight	1951	$70
❏ 47-4380	Hey Good Lookin'/It Makes No Difference Now	1951	$70
❏ 47-5101	I'm Gonna Rock Some More/Everybody's Boogie	1952	$60
❏ 50-0130	Layin' the Boogie/Baby What's Wrong	1951	$70
❏ 47-6953	Peachtree Parade/Please Don't Talk About Me	1957	$30
❏ 47-5224	She's Dynamite/I'm Gonna Tell Everybody	1953	$50
❏ 47-4766	She Walks Right In/Sales Tax Boogie	1952	$70
❏ 47-7065	South/Coo Cha	1957	$30
❏ 50-0106	The Wrong Yo-Yo/My Gal Jo	1951	$70
❏ 47-6856	Wild Fire/Rock Baby	1957	$30

7-Inch Extended Plays
GROOVE

Number	Title	Yr	NM
❏ EGA-3	(contents unknown)	1956	$125
❏ EGA-26	(contents unknown)	1956	$75
❏ EGA-27	(contents unknown)	1956	$75
❏ EGA-28	(contents unknown)	1956	$75
❏ EGA-26 [PS]	Piano Red In Concert, Vol. 1	1956	$75
❏ EGA-27 [PS]	Piano Red In Concert, Vol. 2	1956	$75
❏ EGA-28 [PS]	Piano Red In Concert, Vol. 3	1956	$75
RCA VICTOR			
❏ EPA-5091	(contents unknown)	1959	$125
—Maroon label			
❏ EPA-5091	(contents unknown)	1959	$60
—Black label			

PICKARD, SORRELLS
BOONE

Number	Title	Yr	NM
❏ 1061	There Ain't Enough of You to Go Around/See Ruby Fall	1967	$8
DECCA			
❏ 33023	Is That All San Francisco Did for You/Lovely Lady	1972	$6
❏ 32963	Marianne/Who Really Cares	1972	$6

PICKETT, BOBBY "BORIS"
ANTHEM

Number	Title	Yr	NM
❏ 205	Monster Concert/Am I	1973	$6
CAPITOL			
❏ 5063	Simon the Sensible Surfer/Simon Says So What	1963	$30
GARPAX			
❏ 44185	Blood Bank Blues/Me and My Mummy	1965	$30
❏ 44175	Graduation Day/The Humpty Dumpty	1963	$30
❏ 44175 [PS]	Graduation Day/The Humpty Dumpty	1963	$50
❏ 724	I'm Down to My Last Heartbreak/I Can't Stop	1962	$30
❏ 44167	Monster Mash/Monster's Mash Party	1962	$30
❏ 44167 [PS]	Monster Mash/Monster's Mash Party	1962	$70
❏ P-1	Monster Mash/Monster's Mash Party	1962	$40
—Orange label, first release of 44167?			
❏ 44171	Monster's Holiday/Monster's Motion	1962	$30
❏ 44171 [PS]	Monster's Holiday/Monster's Motion	1962	$50
METROMEDIA			
❏ BMBO-0089	Me and My Mummy/It's Not the Same Without You	1973	$10
—B-side by Pickett and Payne			
PARROT			
❏ 348	Monster Mash/Monster's Mash Party	1970	$10
—Reissued in 1973 with the same number and label design			
❏ 366	Monster's Holiday/Monster Minuet	1971	$10
PIZZERIA			
❏ 1	Star Drek/Mangy Old Sidewinder	1977	$10
—With Peter Ferrara; originals are autographed on the label by both			
RCA VICTOR			
❏ 47-8312	Smoke! Smoke! Smoke! (That Cigarette)/Gotta Leave This Town	1964	$20
❏ 47-8459	The Werewolf Watusi/Monster Swim	1964	$20
WHITE WHALE			
❏ 365	Monster Concert/(B-side unknown)	1970	$30
❏ 363	Monster Man Jam/Am I	1970	$30
—B-side by Bobby and Joan Pickett			

PICKETT, CHARLIE, AND THE EGGS
OPEN

Number	Title	Yr	NM
❏ 1	Feelin'/White Light White Heat	1981	$20
❏ 1 [PS]	Feelin'/White Light White Heat	1981	$20
❏ 2 [PS]	If This Is Love Can I Get My Money Back (Remixed Version)/Slow Death	1981	$20
❏ 2	If This Is Love Can I Get My Money Back (Remixed Version)/Slow Death	1982	$30
❏ 2	If This Is Love Can I Get My Money Back/Slow Death	1981	$20

PICKETT, WILSON
ATLANTIC

Number	Title	Yr	NM
❏ 2320	634-5789 (Soulsville, U.S.A.)/That's a Man's Way	1966	$20
❏ 2575	A Man and a Half/People Make the World (What It Is)	1968	$10
❏ 2631	Born to Be Wild/Toe Hold	1969	$8
❏ 2824	Call My Name, I'll Be There'/Woman Let Me Down Home	1971	$6
❏ 2271	Come Home Baby/Take a Little Love	1965	$20
❏ 2961	Come Right Here/International Playboy	1973	$6
❏ 2306	Don't Fight It/It's All Over	1965	$20
❏ 2797	Don't Knock My Love (Part 1)/Don't Knock My Love (Part 2)	1971	$6
❏ 2781	Don't Let the Green Grass Fool You/Ain't No Doubt About It	1971	$6
❏ 2765	Engine Number Nine/International Playboy	1970	$6
❏ 2381	Eveybody Needs Somebody to Love/Nothing You Can Do	1967	$15
❏ 2852	Fire and Water/Pledging My Love	1971	$6
❏ 2878	Funk Factory/One Step Away	1972	$6
❏ 2430	Funky Broadway/I'm Sorry About That	1967	$15
❏ 2648	Hey Joe/Night Owl	1969	$8
❏ 2591	Hey Jude/Search Your Heart	1968	$12
❏ 2394	I Found a Love – Part I/I Found a Love – Part II	1967	$15
❏ 2558	I Found a True Love/For Better or Worse	1968	$10

Number	Title	Yr	NM
❏ 2528	I'm a Midnight Mover/Deborah	1968	$10
❏ 2233	I'm Gonna Cry/For Better or Worse	1964	$20
❏ 2289	In the Midnight Hour/I'm Not Tired	1965	$20
❏ 2348	Land of 1000 Dances/You're So Fine	1966	$20
❏ 2909	Mama Told Me Not to Come/Covering the Same Old Ground	1972	$6
❏ 2611	Mini-Skirt Minnie/Back in Your Arms	1969	$8
❏ 2365	Mustang Sally/Three Time Loser	1966	$20
❏ 2753	She Said Yes/It's Still Good	1970	$6
❏ 2504	She's Lookin' Good/We've Got to Have Love	1968	$10
❏ 2412	Soul Dance Number Three/You Can't Stand Alone	1967	$15
❏ 2448	Stag-O-Lee/I'm In Love	1967	$15
❏ 2722	Sugar, Sugar/Cole, Cooke, and Redding	1970	$8
BIG TREE			
❏ 16129	Groovin'/Time to Let the Sun Shine In	1978	$5
❏ 16121	Who Turned You On/Dance You Down	1978	$5
CORREC-TONE			
❏ 501	Let Me Be Your Boy/My Heart Belongs to You	1962	$70
CUB			
❏ 9113	Let Me Be Your Boy/My Heart Belongs to You	1962	$40
DOUBLE L			
❏ 713	If You Need Me/Baby Call on Me	1963	$30
❏ 724	I'm Down to My Last Heartbreak/I Can't Stop	1963	$20
❏ 717	It's Too Late/I'm Gonna Love You	1963	$30
EMI AMERICA			
❏ 8070	Ain't Gonna Give You No More/Don't Underestimate the Power of Love	1981	$5
❏ 8082	Back on the Right Track/It's You	1981	$5
❏ 8027	I Want You/Love of My Life	1979	$5
❏ 8034	Live with Me/Granny	1980	$5
ERVA			
❏ 318	Love Dagger/Time to Let the Sun Shine on Me	1977	$5
MOTOWN			
❏ 1898	Don't Turn Away/Can't Stop Now	1987	$4
❏ 1916	In the Midnight Hour/Just Let Her Know	1987	$4
❏ 53407	Love Never Let Me Down/Just Let Her Know	1988	$4
❏ 1938	Love Never Let Me Down/Just Let Her Know	1988	$4
PHILCO-FORD			
❏ HP-11	Land of a 1000 Dances/Midnight Hour	1967	$20
—4-inch plastic "Hip Pocket Record" with color sleeve			
RCA VICTOR			
❏ PB-10067	I Was Too Nice/Isn't That So	1974	$6
❏ 74-0908	Mr. Magic Man/I Sho' Love You	1973	$6
❏ APBO-0174	Soft Soul Boogie Woogie/Take That Pollution Out of Your Throat	1973	$6
❏ APBO-0049	Take a Closer Look at the Woman You're With/Two Woman and a Wife	1973	$6
❏ APBO-0309	Take Your Pleasure Where You Find It/What Good Is a Lie	1974	$6
VERVE			
❏ 10378	Let Me Be Your Boy/My Heart Belongs to You	1966	$30
WICKED			
❏ 8102	Love Will Keep Us Together/It's Gonna Be Good	1976	$6
❏ 8101	The Best Part of a Man/How Will I Ever Know	1975	$6

7-Inch Extended Plays
ATLANTIC

Number	Title	Yr	NM
❏ SD 7-8250	Groovy Little Woman/Funky Way/It's Still Good//This Old Town/You Keep Me Hangin' On	1970	$15
—Jukebox issue; small hole, plays at 33 1/3 rpm			
❏ SD8129	Something You Got/Barefootin'/Land of 1000 Dances//In the Midnight Hour/Ninety-Nine and a Half (Won't Do)/I'm Drifting	1966	$20
—Jukebox issue; small hole, plays at 33 1/3 rpm			
❏ SD8129 [PS]	The Exciting Wilson Pickett	1966	$20

PICKS, THE

COLUMBIA

Number	Title	Yr	NM
41096	Moondreams/Look to the Future	1958	$60

PICKWICKS, THE

PARROT

Number	Title	Yr	NM
9679	Apple Blossom Time/I Don't Want to Tell You Again	1964	$20

WARNER BROS.

Number	Title	Yr	NM
5492	Little by Little/I Took My Baby Home	1965	$20

PIERCE, WEBB, AND NANCY DEE

DECCA

Number	Title	Yr	NM
32884	Above Suspicion/I Owe It to My Heart	1971	$8

PIERCE, WEBB

4 STAR

Number	Title	Yr	NM
1616	Georgia Rag/Lucky Lee	1952	$40
1610	Hawaiian Echoes/I Saw Your Face in the Moon	1952	$40
1601	Heebie Jeebie Blues/High Geared Daddy	1952	$40

DECCA

Number	Title	Yr	NM
31347	Alla My Love/You Are My Life	1962	$15
9-29974	Any Old Time/We'll Find a Way	1956	$30
7-34137 [S]	Are You Sincere?/(B-side unknown)	1963	$20
—33 1/3 rpm jukebox single, small hole			
9-30858	A Thousand Miles Ago/What Goes On in Your Heart	1959	$20
9-28369	Back Street Affair/I'll Always Take Care of You	1952	$30
9-28431	Bow Thy Head/The Country Church	1952	$40
9-30321	Bye Bye, Love/Missing You	1957	$40
9-46332	California Blues/You Scared the Love Right Out of Me	1951	$40
31867	Christmas at Home/Sweet Memories	1965	$15
7-34015 [S]	Cow Town/(B-side unknown)	1962	$20
—33 1/3 rpm jukebox single, small hole			
31421	Cow Town/Sooner or Later	1962	$15
9-30623	Cryin' Over You/You'll Come Back	1958	$20
31118	Drifting Texas Sand/All I Need Is You	1960	$15
9-29107	Even Tho/Sparkling Brown Eyes	1954	$30
31165	Fallen Angel/Truck Driver's Blues	1960	$15
7-34016 [S]	First to Have a Second Chance/(B-side unknown)	1962	$20
—33 1/3 rpm jukebox single, small hole			
32167	Fool Fool Fool/Bottles and Babies	1967	$8
32098	Goodbye City, Goodbye Girl/That Same Old Street	1967	$8
32924	Hey Good Lookin'/Wonderful, Wonderful, Wonderful	1972	$8
7-34014 [S]	Hideaway Heart/(B-side unknown)	1962	$20
—33 1/3 rpm jukebox single, small hole			
9-30419	Holiday for Love/Don't Do It Darlin'	1957	$20
9-30255	Honky Tonk Song/Someday	1957	$30
9-30923	I Ain't Never/Shanghaied	1959	$20
7-34138 [S]	I Can't Stop Loving You/(B-side unknown)	1963	$20
—33 1/3 rpm jukebox single, small hole			
9-29480	I Don't Care/Your Good for Nothing Heart	1955	$30
9-46322	If Crying Would Make You Care/Drifting Texas Sand	1951	$40
32438	If I Had Last Night to Live Over/No Tears Tonight	1969	$8
7-34139 [S]	If I Lost Your Love/(B-side unknown)	1963	$20
—33 1/3 rpm jukebox single, small hole			
9-28534	I'll Go On Alone/That's Me Without You	1953	$30
32973	I'm Gonna Be a Swinger/Someday	1972	$8
9-46385	I'm Gonna See My Baby/You Know I'm Still in Love	1952	$30
9-30789	I'm Letting You Go/Sittin' Alone	1958	$20
9-30155	I'm Tired/It's My Way	1956	$30
7-34018 [S]	I'm Walking Behind You/(B-side unknown)	1962	$20
—33 1/3 rpm jukebox single, small hole			
9-29391	In the Jailhouse Now/I'm Gonna Fall Out of Love with You	1955	$30
7-38099 [S]	In the Jailhouse Now/Poison Love	1959	$30
—Small hole, plays at 33 1/3 rpm			
31058	Is It Wrong (For Loving You)/(Doin' the) Lovers Leap	1960	$15
9-28725	It's Been So Long/Don't Throw Your Life Away	1953	$30
7-34135 [S]	I've Got a New Heartache/(B-side unknown)	1963	$20
—33 1/3 rpm jukebox single, small hole			
31197	Let Forgiveness In/There's More Pretty Girls Than One	1961	$15
33044	Let the Children Pick the Flowers/You're Letting Me Go	1973	$8
9-29662	Love, Love, Love/If You Were Me	1955	$30
32577	Love Ain't Never Gonna Be No Better/The Other Side of You	1969	$8
31982	Love's Something (I Can't Understand)/A Loner	1966	$10
31737	Loving You Then Losing You/Let Me Live a Little	1965	$10
32246	Luzianna/Somebody Please Kiss My Sweet Thing	1967	$8
31617	Memory No. 1/French Riviera	1964	$10
32641	Merry-Go-Round World/Fools Night Out	1970	$8
9-29252	More and More/You're Not Mine Anymore	1954	$30
9-29155	Mother Calling My Name in Prayer/Bugle Call from Heaven	1954	$40
31488	Sands of Gold/Nobody's Darlin' But Mine	1963	$10
32388	Saturday Night/I Tried Everything to Please	1968	$8
31451	Sawmill/If I Could Come Back	1963	$10
32762	Showing His Dollar/The Way We Were Back Then	1970	$8
9-28991	Slowly/You Just Can't Be True	1954	$30
32855	Someone Stepped In (And Stole Me Blind)/I Miss the Little Things	1971	$8
32339	Stranger in a Strange, Strange City/In Another World	1968	$8
31249	Sweet Lips/Last Night	1961	$15
31380	Take Time/Crazy Wild Desire	1962	$15
9-30045	Teenage Boogie/I'm Really Glad You Hurt Me	1956	$50
32787	Tell Him That You Love Him/Heartaches Are for Lovers, Not for Friends	1971	$8
7-34017 [S]	Tennessee Waltz/(B-side unknown)	1962	$20
—33 1/3 rpm jukebox single, small hole			
9-28091	That Heart Belongs to Me/So Used to Loving You	1952	$30
31704	That's Where My Money Goes/Broken Engagement	1964	$12
9-28594	The Last Waltz/I Haven't Got the Heart	1953	$30
32694	The Man You Want Me to Be/Too Long	1970	$8
9-28834	There Stands the Glass/I'm Walking the Dog	1953	$30
33015	There Stands the Glass/Valentino of the Hobos	1972	$8
32508	This Thing/Does My Memory Ever Cross Your Mind	1969	$8
31544	Those Wonderful Years/If the Back Door Could Talk	1963	$10
9-30711	Tupelo County Jail/Falling Back to You	1958	$20
31582	Waiting a Lifetime/Love Come to Me	1964	$10
31298	Walking the Streets/How Do You Talk to a Baby	1961	$15
7-34076 [S]	Waterloo/Cry, Cry Darling	1962	$20
—33 1/3 rpm jukebox single, small hole			
7-34136 [S]	What Good Will It Do/One More Time	1963	$20
—33 1/3 rpm jukebox single, small hole			
32033	Where'd Ya Stay Last Night/She's Twenty-One	1966	$10
31816	Who Do I Think I Am/Hobo and the Rose	1965	$10
9-46364	Wondering/New Silver Bells	1951	$30

MCA

Number	Title	Yr	NM
40255	Honey (Open That Door)/Take the Time It Takes	1974	$6
40181	I'd Be Number One/You Better Treat Her Right	1974	$6
40310	I Know, I Know, I Know/I'm Ashamed to Be Here	1974	$6
40128	Lo-Lenna/When You're Living in Hell	1973	$6

PLANTATION

Number	Title	Yr	NM
145	Christmas Time's a Coming/The Family Christmas Tree	1976	$6
149	Got You on My Mind/Love Brought Us Together	1977	$5
—With Carol Channing			
136	I've Got Leaving on My Mind/Shame, Shame, Shame	1976	$6
141	That's Me Without You/Appleton	1976	$6
131	The Good Lord Giveth (And Uncle Sam Taketh Away)/Send My Love to Me	1975	$6

7-Inch Extended Plays

DECCA

Number	Title	Yr	NM
ED2653 [M]	*After the Boy Gets the Girl/I Owe It to Myself/My Shoes Keep Walking Back to You/Life to Go	1959	$25
ED 7-2653 [S]	*After the Boy Gets the Girl/I Owe It to Myself/My Shoes Keep Walking Back to You/Life to Go	1959	$35
ED2761	*Cow Town/If I Could Come Back/Sooner or Later/Sawmill	1964	$35
ED2734	*Crazy Wild Desire/Take Time/I'm Falling in Love with You/There's More Pretty Girls Than One	1962	$30
ED2709	*Hideaway Heart/Tender Years/Pictures on the Wall/First to Have a Second Chance	1962	$30
ED2668 [M]	*I Ain't Never/Shanghaied/A Thousand Miles Ago/What Goes On in Your Heart	1959	$25
ED 7-2668 [S]	*I Ain't Never/Shanghaied/A Thousand Miles Ago/What Goes On in Your Heart	1959	$35
ED2694	*Is It Wrong/Lover's Leap/No Love Have I/Whirlpool of Love	1961	$30
ED2581	*New Love Affair/I Care No More/Just Imagination/I Love	1958	$25
ED2685	*Walking the Streets/All I Need Is You/Drifting Texas Sand/Drinking My Blues Away	1960	$30
ED2715 [PS]	Alla My Love	1962	$30
ED2715	Alla My Love/You Are My Life//Sweet Lips/How Do You Talk to a Baby	1962	$30
ED2355	(contents unknown)	1956	$25
ED2364	(contents unknown)	1956	$25
ED2719	(contents unknown)	1962	$30
ED2748	(contents unknown)	1963	$35
ED2785	(contents unknown)	1965	$50
ED2799	(contents unknown)	1966	$50
ED2761 [PS]	Cow Town	1964	$35
ED2734 [PS]	Crazy Wild Desire	1962	$30
ED2748 [PS]	Fallen Angel	1963	$35
ED2709 [PS]	Hideaway Heart	1962	$30
ED2668 [PS]	I Ain't Never	1959	$25
ED 7-2668 [PS]	I Ain't Never	1959	$35
ED2694 [PS]	Is It Wrong	1961	$30
ED2799 [PS]	Loving You Then Losing You	1966	$50
ED2786 [PS]	Softly and Tenderly	1965	$50
ED2786	Softly and Tenderly/If Jesus Came to Your House//What Would You Give in Exchange for Your Soul/Bow Thy Head	1965	$50
ED2355 [PS]	The Country Church	1956	$25
ED2364 [PS]	The Wondering Boy, Vol. 3	1956	$25
ED2685 [PS]	Walking the Streets	1960	$30
ED2653 [PS]	Webb	1959	$25
ED 7-2653 [PS]	Webb	1959	$35
ED2719 [PS]	Webb Pierce	1962	$30

PIKE, PETE

CORAL

Number	Title	Yr	NM
61522	Old Fashioned Christmas/Happy Birthday, Dear Jesus	1955	$15

PILGRIM TRAVELERS, THE

SPECIALTY

Number	Title	Yr	NM
837	I'll Be Home for Christmas/Move Up to Heaven	1952	$60
856	Silent Night/I'll Be Home for Christmas	1953	$50

PILLOW, RAY

ABC DOT

Number	Title	Yr	NM
17560	Dog Tired of Cattin' Around/Rita Faye	1975	$5
17543	I Slipped But Didn't Fall/The Simple Things in Life	1975	$5
17526	Livin' in the Sunshine of Your Love/The Party	1974	$5
17628	Love Is Comin' Over Me/She Never Likes Nothing for Long	1976	$5

CAPITOL

Number	Title	Yr	NM
5597	Common Colds and Broken Hearts/You've Got a Good Thing Going	1966	$8
2030	Gone with the Wine/No Milk Today	1967	$8
5953	I Just Want to Be Alone/I Like a Whole Lot	1967	$8
5405	I'm Here to Make a Deal/Long Way Home	1965	$8
5180	Left Out/What's the World Coming To	1964	$12
5323	Take Your Hands Off My Heart/Even the Bad Times Are Good	1964	$8
5518	Thank You Ma'am/"If" Is a Mighty Big Word	1965	$8
5851	The First Chance I Get/Two Minus One Leaves Blue	1967	$8

Number	Title	Yr	NM

FIRST GENERATION

Number	Title	Yr	NM
☐ 011	One Too Many Memories/ Friday Night Blues	1981	$6

HILLTOP

| ☐ 130 | Who's Gonna Tie My Shoes/ Can I Have What's Left | 1978 | $6 |

MCA

| ☐ 40994 | Heaven Help the Tempted Man/Hungry Man's Dream | 1979 | $5 |
| ☐ 41047 | Super Lady/Nighttime Masquerade | 1979 | $5 |

MEGA

☐ 0040	Book It/Haven't You Heard	1971	$6
☐ 1202	Countryfied/I'm Doing What I Love, Loving You	1973	$6
☐ 0088	Excuse Me/I'm Doing What I Love, Loving You	1972	$6
☐ 0025	She Knows What Love Can Do/The Waitress	1971	$6
☐ 0072	She's Doing It to Me Again/ Everytime	1972	$6
☐ 0055	Since Then/While I'm Gone	1972	$6
☐ 0095	Slipping Around/Too Much One Too Many Times	1972	$6

PLANTATION

| ☐ 36 | It Takes All Kinds of People/ They Left Me Holding the Bottle | 1969 | $6 |
| ☐ 49 | Slice of Life/House of Glass | 1970 | $6 |

PILTDOWN MEN, THE

CAPITOL

☐ 4703	Big Lizard/A Pretty Girl Is Like a Melody	1962	$20
☐ 4414	Brontosaurus Stomp/ McDonald's Cave	1960	$30
☐ 4581	Fossil Rock/Gargantua	1961	$20
☐ 4501	Goodnight Mrs. Flintstone/ The Great Impostor	1961	$20
☐ 4460	Piltdown Rides Again!/ Bubbles in the Tar	1960	$20
☐ 4875	Tequila Bossa Nova/Night Surfin'	1962	$20

PIN-UPS, THE

STORK

| ☐ STK-1 | Lookin' for Boys/Kenny | 1964 | $20 |

PINERA, MIKE

CAPRICORN

| ☐ 0288 | Alone with You/Lady Divine | 1978 | $6 |

SPECTOR

| ☐ 00002 | Can't You Believe/I Am the Bubble | 1979 | $6 |
| ☐ 03 | Goodnight My Love/Looking for the Light | 1979 | $15 |

PINETOPPERS, THE

CORAL

| ☐ 9-61151 | American Patrol/National Emblem March | 1954 | $20 |
| ☐ 9-61074 | As Long As I'm Dreaming/It's Written in the Stars | 1953 | $20 |

— *With the Marlin Sisters*

| ☐ 9-61245 | Blossoms in the Springtime (Melody Version)/Blossoms in the Springtime (Harmony Version) | 1954 | $20 |

— *With the Marlin Sisters*

| ☐ 9-61032 | Blue Canary/Mama What'll I Do | 1953 | $20 |

— *With the Marlin Sisters*

☐ 9-64095	Cherry Beer Polka/All Alone 'Neath the Blue Grass	1951	$30
☐ 9-64074	Metro Polka/Waltz of the Roses	1951	$30
☐ 9-64061	Mockin' Bird Hill/Big Parade Polka	1950	$30

— *Note: Earlier Coral 45s in the 64000 series by the Pinetoppers may exist*

| ☐ 9-60830 | My Little Girl/Tennessee Warbler | 1952 | $20 |
| ☐ 9-61192 | Pretty Rainbow/Boom Boom Polka | 1954 | $20 |

— *With the Marlin Sisters*

☐ 9-60949	Small World/Seven Lonely Days	1953	$20
☐ 9-60783	The Irish Polka/Twin Mazurka	1952	$20
☐ 9-60922	The Stars and Stripes Forever/Washington Post March	1953	$20
☐ 9-64114	The Woodpecker Polka/Jolly Cop Polka	1952	$30
☐ 9-60811	Till the End of the World/Bell Bottom Polka	1952	$20

DECCA

☐ 9-29639	A Big Stack o' Barley/A Sailor Is Always True	1955	$15
☐ 9-29824	Bye Bye My Baby/Forgetful	1956	$15
☐ 9-29458	Home in the Hills/Roly Polka	1955	$15

— *As "Vaughn Horton's Pinetoppers*

PING PONGS, THE

CUB

| ☐ 9062 | Big Ben/In the Chapel in the Moonlight | 1960 | $30 |

PINK CLOUD, THE

TOWER

| ☐ 376 | Midnight Sun (Vocal)/ Midnight Sun (Instrumental) | 1967 | $30 |

PINK FLOYD

Also see SYD BARRETT; ROGER WATERS; RICHARD WRIGHT.

COLUMBIA

| ☐ 03118 | Another Brick in the Wall, Part 2/One of My Turns | 1982 | $3 |

— *Reissue*

| ☐ 11187 | Another Brick in the Wall (Part 2)/One of My Turns | 1980 | $5 |

— *Custom "wall" label*

| ☐ 11187 | Another Brick in the Wall (Part 2)/One of My Turns | 1980 | $4 |

— *Regular Columbia orange label*

☐ 11187 [PS]	Another Brick in the Wall (Part 2)/One of My Turns	1980	$8
☐ 11311	Comfortably Numb/Hey You	1980	$4
☐ 10248	Have a Cigar/Welcome to the Machine	1975	$15
☐ 07363	Learning to Fly/Terminal Frost	1987	$4
☐ 07363 [PS]	Learning to Fly/Terminal Frost	1987	$4
☐ 07660	On the Turning Away/Run Like Hell	1987	$4
☐ 07660 [PS]	On the Turning Away/Run Like Hell	1987	$8
☐ 03142	When the Tigers Broke Free/ Bring the Boys Back Home	1982	$4
☐ X18-03176	When the Tigers Broke Free/ Bring the Boys Back Home	1982	$10
☐ X18-03176 [PS]	When the Tigers Broke Free/ Bring the Boys Back Home	1982	$10

— *Fold-open cardboard sleeve*

| ☐ 03142 [PS] | When the Tigers Broke Free/ Bring the Boys Back Home | 1982 | $8 |

— *Fold-open cardboard sleeve*

HARVEST

☐ 3240	Fearless/One of These Days	1971	$30
☐ 3609	Money/Any Colour You Like	1973	$20
☐ SPRO-6669 [DJ]	Money (Censored Edited Mono)/Money (Censored Edited Stereo)	1973	$20

— *This promo was sent to radio stations with a frantic note telling them to disregard the first promo*

☐ P-3609 [DJ]	Money (Edited Mono)/ Money (Edited Stereo)	1973	$30
☐ 3391	Stay/Free Four	1972	$30
☐ 3832	Time/Us and Them	1974	$30

TOWER

| ☐ 333 | Arnold Layne/Candy and a Currant Bun | 1967 | $200 |
| ☐ 333 [PS] | Arnold Layne/Candy and a Currant Bun | 1967 | $700 |

— *Only issued with promotional copies*

☐ 426	It Would Be So Nice/Julia Dream	1968	$250
☐ 440	Let There Be More Light/ Remember a Day	1968	$300
☐ 356	See Emily Play/Scarecrow	1967	$200
☐ 356 [PS]	See Emily Play/Scarecrow	1967	$700

— *Title sleeve; only issued with some promotional copies*

| ☐ 356 [PS] | See Emily Play/Scarecrow | 1967 | $800 |

— *Photo sleeve; only issued with some promotional copies*

| ☐ 378 | The Gnome/Flaming | 1967 | $200 |

PINKERTON'S ASSORTED COLOURS

LONDON

| ☐ 9820 | Mirror, Mirror/She Don't Care | 1966 | $30 |

PARROT

| ☐ 40001 | Don't Stop Loving Me Baby/ Will You | 1966 | $30 |

PINKNEY, BILL

FONTANA

| ☐ 1956 | Don't Call Me/I Do the Jerk | 1964 | $15 |

PHILLIPS INT'L.

| ☐ 3524 | After the Hop/Sally's Got a Sister | 1958 | $30 |

— *As "Bill Pinky*

VEEP

| ☐ 1264 | I Found Some Lovin'/The Masquerade Is Over | 1967 | $10 |

PINKY & PERKY
7-Inch Extended Plays

COLUMBIA

| ☐ SEG8122 [PS] | Christmas with Pinky and Perky | 1963 | $12 |

—*U.K. import*

| ☐ SEG8122 | (contents unconfirmed) | 1963 | $10 |

PIPER, WARDELL

MIDSONG INT'L.

☐ MI1001	Captain Boogie/(Long Version)	1978	$6
☐ 72000	Gimme Something Real/The Power of Love	1980	$10
☐ MI1005	Super Sweet/Don't Turn Away from Me Baby	1979	$10

PIPES, THE (1)

CARLTON

| ☐ 575 | Teamwork/Soon I Will Be Done | 1962 | $30 |

PIPES, THE (2)

DOOTO

| ☐ 388 | Be Fair/Let Me Give You Money | 1958 | $30 |

DOOTONE

| ☐ 388 | Be Fair/Let Me Give You Money | 1956 | $300 |

PIPSQUEEKS, THE

WARNER BROS.

| ☐ 5878 | Santa's Little Helpers/ Santa's Magic Flute | 1966 | $10 |

PIRATES, THE

MEL-O-DY

| ☐ 105 | Mind Over Matter (I'm Gonna Make You Mine)/I'll Love You Till I Die | 1962 | $125 |

PITNEY, GENE, AND GEORGE JONES

MUSICOR

☐ 1097	I'm a Fool to Care/Louisiana Man	1965	$15
☐ 1097 [PS]	I'm a Fool to Care/Louisiana Man	1965	$20
☐ 1066	I've Got Five Dollars and It's Saturday Night/Wreck on the Highway	1965	$15

PITNEY, GENE, AND MELBA MONTGOMERY

MUSICOR

| ☐ 1135 | Baby, Ain't That Fine/ Everybody Knows But You and Me | 1965 | $15 |

PITNEY, GENE

BLAZE

| ☐ 351 | Going Back to My Love/ Cradle of My Arms | 1958 | $40 |

— *As "Billy Bryan*

EPIC

| ☐ 50332 | Dedication AKA This Song I Want to Dedicate to You/ Sandman | 1977 | $5 |
| ☐ 50461 | It's Over, It's Over/Walkin' in the Sun | 1977 | $5 |

FESTIVAL

| ☐ 25002 | Please Come Back/I'll Find You | 1960 | $40 |

MUSICOR

☐ 1394	All the Young Women/I Remember	1970	$6
☐ 1405	A Street Called Hope/Think of Us	1970	$6
☐ 1442	A Thousand Arms (Five Hundred Hearts)/Gene, Are You There?	1971	$6
☐ 1348	Baby, You're My Kind of Woman/Hate	1969	$8
☐ 1171	Backstage/Blue Color	1966	$12
☐ 1171 [PS]	Backstage/Blue Color	1966	$20
☐ 1331	Billy, You're My Friend/ Lonely Drifter	1968	$8
☐ 1331 [PS]	Billy, You're My Friend/ Lonely Drifter	1968	$15
☐ 1331	Billy, You're My Friend/She Believes in Me	1968	$8
☐ 1235	Don't Mean to Be a Preacher/Animal Crackers (In Cellophane Boxes)	1967	$12
☐ 1011	Every Breath I Take/Mr. Moon, Mr. Cupid and I	1961	$40

—*Produced by Phil Spector; mostly gunmetal gray label with color inserts*

| ☐ 1011 [PS] | Every Breath I Take/Mr. Moon, Mr. Cupid and I | 1961 | $30 |

Number	Title	Yr	NM
❏ 1011	Every Breath I Take/Mr. Moon, Mr. Cupid and I	1961	$30

— *Produced by Phil Spector; mostly brown label*

Number	Title	Yr	NM
❏ 1233	For Me, This Is Happy/I'm Gonna Listen to Me	1967	$10
❏ 1026	Half Heaven-Half Heartache/Tower Tall	1962	$30

— *Mostly brown label*

Number	Title	Yr	NM
❏ 1026	Half Heaven-Half Heartache/Tower Tall	1962	$20

— *Mostly black label*

Number	Title	Yr	NM
❏ 1439	Higher and Higher/Beautiful Sounds	1971	$6
❏ 1453	I Just Can't Help Myself/Beautiful Sounds	1972	$6
❏ 1045	I'm Gonna Be Strong/Aladdin's Lamp	1964	$30
❏ 1045	I'm Gonna Be Strong/E Se Domani	1964	$20
❏ 1045 [PS]	I'm Gonna Be Strong/E Se Domani	1964	$30
❏ 1070	I Must Be Seeing Things/Marianne	1965	$15
❏ 1070 [PS]	I Must Be Seeing Things/Marianne	1965	$20
❏ 1200	(In the) Cold Light of Day/The Boss' Daughter	1966	$10
❏ 1200 [PS]	(In the) Cold Light of Day/The Boss' Daughter	1966	$20
❏ 1040	It Hurts to Be in Love/Hawaii	1964	$20
❏ 1040 [PS]	It Hurts to Be in Love/Hawaii	1964	$30
❏ 1002	(I Wanna) Love My Life Away/I Laughed So Hard I Cried	1960	$20
❏ 1002 [PS]	(I Wanna) Love My Life Away/I Laughed So Hard I Cried	1960	$50
❏ 1093	Last Chance to Turn Around/Save Your Love	1965	$15
❏ 1155	Lei Mi Aspetta/Nessuno Mi Puo' Guidcare	1966	$20
❏ 1103	Looking Through the Eyes of Love/There's No Living Without Your Loving	1965	$15
❏ 1006	Louisiana Mama/Take Me Tonight	1961	$20
❏ 1006 [PS]	Louisiana Mama/Take Me Tonight	1961	$40
❏ 1358	Maria Elena/The French Horn	1969	$8
❏ 1028	Mecca/Teardrop by Teardrop	1963	$20
❏ 1028 [PS]	Mecca/Teardrop by Teardrop	1963	$30
❏ 1022	Only Love Can Break a Heart/If I Didn't Have a Dime	1962	$20

— *Mostly brown label*

Number	Title	Yr	NM
❏ 1361	Playing Games of Love/California	1969	$8
❏ 1130	Princess in Rags/Amore Mio	1965	$15
❏ 1419	Shady Lady/Billy, You're My Friend	1970	$6
❏ 1474	Shady Lady/Run, Run Roadrunner	1973	$6
❏ 1384	She Lets Her Hair Down (Early in the Morning)/I Remember	1969	$8
❏ 1306	She's a Heartbreaker/Conquistador	1968	$10
❏ 1252	Somethin' Gotten Hold of My Heart/Building Up My Dream World	1967	$12
❏ 1308	Somewhere in the Country/Lonely Drifter	1968	$8
❏ 1461	Summertime Dreaming/A Thousand Arms (Five Hundred Hearts)	1972	$6
❏ 1036	That Girl Belongs to Yesterday/Who Needs It	1964	$30

— *A-side written by Mick Jagger and Keith Richards and produced by Andrew Oldham*

Number	Title	Yr	NM
❏ 1036 [PS]	That Girl Belongs to Yesterday/Who Needs It	1964	$30
❏ 1020	(The Man Who Shot) Liberty Valance/Take It Like a Man	1962	$20

— *Mostly brown label*

Number	Title	Yr	NM
❏ 1299	The More I Saw of Her/Won't Take Long	1968	$8
❏ 1009	Town Without Pity/Air Mail Special Delivery	1961	$20
❏ 1245	Tremblin'/Where Did the Magic Go	1967	$10
❏ 1032	True Love Never Runs Smooth/Donna Means Heartbreak	1963	$20
❏ 1034	Twenty-Four Hours from Tulsa/Lonely Night Dream	1963	$20
❏ 1034 [PS]	Twenty-Four Hours from Tulsa/Lonely Night Dream	1963	$30

PITTMAN, BARBARA
PHILLIPS INT'L.

Number	Title	Yr	NM
❏ 3527	Cold, Cold Heart/Everlasting Love	1958	$50
❏ 3553	Handsome Man/The Eleventh Commandment	1960	$30
❏ 3518	Two Young Fools in Love/I'm Getting Better All the Time	1957	$50

SUN

Number	Title	Yr	NM
❏ 253	I Need a Man/No Matter Who's to Blame	1956	$200

PITTS, GLORIA JEAN
IMPERIAL

Number	Title	Yr	NM
❏ 5406	I Don't Stand No Quittin'/Things You Should Know	1956	$60

PITTSBURGH POPS ORCHESTRA
UNITED ARTISTS

Number	Title	Yr	NM
❏ 785	Holiday for Trumpet/Hello Dolly	1964	$12

PIXIES
Features Frank Black, now a prolific solo artist.
ELEKTRA

Number	Title	Yr	NM
❏ 69287	Here Comes Your Man/Into the White	1989	$8

PIXIES, THE
BALBOA

Number	Title	Yr	NM
❏ 07	Santa's Too Fat for the Hula Hoop/Kitty Kats on Parade	1958	$30

PIXIES THREE, THE
MERCURY

Number	Title	Yr	NM
❏ 72130	Birthday Party/Our Love	1963	$20
❏ 72130 [PS]	Birthday Party/Our Love	1963	$30
❏ 72208	Cold, Cold Winter/442 Glenwood Avenue	1963	$20
❏ 72208 [PS]	Cold, Cold Winter/442 Glenwood Avenue	1963	$30
❏ 72250	Gee/After the Party	1964	$20
❏ 72250 [PS]	Gee/After the Party	1964	$40
❏ 72288	It's Summertime U.S.A./The Hootch	1964	$20
❏ 72288 [PS]	It's Summertime U.S.A./The Hootch	1964	$30
❏ 72357	Love Me, Love Me/Your Way	1964	$20
❏ 72331	Love Walked In/Orphan Boy	1964	$20

PLACE, MARY KAY
COLUMBIA

Number	Title	Yr	NM
❏ 3-10422	Baby Boy/Streets of This Town (Ode to Fernwood)	1976	$5

— *Credited to "Mary Kay Place as Loretta Haggers*

Number	Title	Yr	NM
❏ 3-10707	Don't Make Love (To a Country Music Singer)/Marlboro Man	1978	$5
❏ 3-10644	Something to Brag About/Anybody's Darling (Anything But Mine)	1977	$5

— *A-side with Willie Nelson*

PLAIDS, THE
DARL

Number	Title	Yr	NM
❏ 1003	Halfway to Heaven/Al-Lee-O, Al-Lee-Ay	1956	$30

ERA

Number	Title	Yr	NM
❏ 3002	Around the Corner/He Stole Flo	1959	$30

LIBERTY

Number	Title	Yr	NM
❏ 55167	Hungry for Your Love/Chit-Chat	1958	$400

NASCO

Number	Title	Yr	NM
❏ 6011	Till the End of the Dance/My Pretty Baby	1958	$30

PLANET P
Features Tony Carey of RAINBOW and solo fame.
GEFFEN

Number	Title	Yr	NM
❏ 29705	Why Me?/Only You and Me	1983	$3
❏ 29705 [PS]	Why Me?/Only You and Me	1983	$3

MCA

Number	Title	Yr	NM
❏ 52515	What I See/Beyond the Barrier	1984	$3

— *As "Planet P Project*

Number	Title	Yr	NM
❏ 52515 [DJ]	What I See (same on both sides)	1984	$8

— *Pink vinyl; as "Planet P Project*

PLANETS, THE (1)
ALJON

Number	Title	Yr	NM
❏ 1244	Be Sure/Once Upon a Lifetime	1962	$300

PLANETS, THE (2)
ERA

Number	Title	Yr	NM
❏ 1049	Be Sure/Wild Leaves	1957	$60

NU-CLEAR

Number	Title	Yr	NM
❏ 7422	I Need You So/Sharin' Lockers	1959	$70

PLANETS, THE (4)
MOTOWN

Number	Title	Yr	NM
❏ 1485	Break It To Me Gently/Secret	1980	$4

PLANT & SEE
WHITE WHALE

Number	Title	Yr	NM
❏ 309	Henrietta/Put Out the Fire	1969	$15

PLANT LIFE
DATE

Number	Title	Yr	NM
❏ 1572	Flower Girl/Say It Over Again	1967	$10

PLANT, ROBERT
Also see THE HONEYDRIPPERS; LED ZEPPELIN; LISTEN.
ES PARANZA

Number	Title	Yr	NM
❏ 99844	Big Log/Far Post	1983	$3
❏ 99844 [PS]	Big Log/Far Post	1983	$5
❏ 99373	Heaven Knows/Walking Towards Paradise	1988	$3
❏ 99373 [PS]	Heaven Knows/Walking Towards Paradise	1988	$3
❏ 99820	In the Mood/Horizontal Departure	1983	$3
❏ 99820 [PS]	In the Mood/Horizontal Departure	1983	$5
❏ 99644	Little by Little/Trouble Your Money	1985	$3
❏ 99644 [PS]	Little by Little/Trouble Your Money	1985	$4
❏ 99333	Ship of Fools/Billy's Revenge	1988	$3
❏ 99333 [PS]	Ship of Fools/Billy's Revenge	1988	$3
❏ 99348	Tall Cool One/White, Clean and Neat	1988	$3
❏ 99348 [PS]	Tall Cool One/White, Clean and Neat	1988	$10
❏ 99622	Too Loud/Kallalou Kallalou	1985	$3
❏ 99622 [PS]	Too Loud/Kallalou Kallalou	1985	$4

SWAN SONG

Number	Title	Yr	NM
❏ 99979	Burning Down One Side/Moonlight in Samosa	1982	$4
❏ 99979 [PS]	Burning Down One Side/Moonlight in Samosa	1982	$6
❏ 99952	Pledge Pin/Fat Lip	1982	$4
❏ 99952 [PS]	Pledge Pin/Fat Lip	1982	$40

PLANTS, THE
J&S

Number	Title	Yr	NM
❏ 1602	Dear, I Swear/It's You	1957	$400

— *Address under label name*

Number	Title	Yr	NM
❏ 1602	Dear, I Swear/It's You	1957	$50

— *No address under label name*

Number	Title	Yr	NM
❏ 248/9	I Searched the Seven Seas/I Took a Trip Way Over the Sea	1956	$400

PLASMATICS
VICE SQUAD

Number	Title	Yr	NM
❏ VS101/102	Butcher Baby/Fast Food Service/Concrete Shoes	1978	$30

— *All copies on red vinyl*

Number	Title	Yr	NM
❏ VS101/102 [PS]	Butcher Baby/Fast Food Service/Concrete Shoes	1978	$30
❏ VS103/104	Dream Lover/Corruption/Want You Baby	1978	$30

— *All copies on purple vinyl*

Number	Title	Yr	NM
❏ VS103/104 [PS]	Dream Lover/Corruption/Want You Baby	1978	$30

PLASTIC BERTRAND
SIRE

Number	Title	Yr	NM
❏ 1020	Ca Plane Pour Moi/Pogo Pogo	1978	$8
❏ 1020 [PS]	Ca Plane Pour Moi/Pogo Pogo	1978	$10

PLASTIC COW, THE
DOT

Number	Title	Yr	NM
❏ 17300	Lady Jane/One Many, One Vault	1969	$12
❏ 17284	The Plastic Cow/Medicine Man	1969	$10

PLASTIC IDOLS
VISION

Number	Title	Yr	NM
❏ 25	Einstein Experience/Uncircumsised Twin/Siamese Lust	1980	$30
❏ 25 [PS]	Einstein Experience/Uncircumsised Twin/Siamese Lust	1980	$30
❏ 23	I.U.D./Sophistication	1979	$15
❏ 23 [PS]	I.U.D./Sophistication	1979	$15

PLATINUM BLONDE
EPIC

Number	Title	Yr	NM
❏ 07606	Contact/Tough Enough	1987	$3
❏ 05593	Crying Over You/It Ain't Love Anyway	1985	$3
❏ 05593 [PS]	Crying Over You/It Ain't Love Anyway	1985	$3

Number	Title	Yr	NM
❏ 05593	Crying Over You/It Ain't Love Anyway	1985	$3
❏ 05804	Somebody Somewhere/Red Light	1985	$3

PLATO
PARKWAY
❏ 914	Copy Cat/Claude's Theme	1964	$12

PLATTERS, THE
More than one group has used this name over the years, but all are related. Also see TONY WILLIAMS.

ANTLER
❏ 3000/1	I Do It All the Time/Shake What Your Mama Gave You	1982	$6

AVALANCHE
❏ XW224	Sunday with You/If the World Loved	1973	$8

—As "The Buck Ram Platters

ENTREE
❏ 107	Won't You Be My Friend/Run While It's Dark	1965	$8

—As "The Platters 1965

FEDERAL
❏ 12153	Give Thanks/Hey Now	1953	$400

—As "Tony Williams and the Platters

❏ 12271	Give Thanks/I Need You All the Time	1956	$100
❏ 12164	I'll Cry When You're Gone/I Need You All the Time	1954	$1000
❏ 12204	Maggie Doesn't Work Here Anymore/Take Me Back, Take Me Back	1955	$200
❏ 12244	Only You (And You Alone)/You Made Me Cry	1955	$300
❏ 12250	Tell the World/I Need You All the Time	1956	$120
❏ 12188	Tell the World/Love All Night	1954	$200

MERCURY
❏ 71624	Ebb Tide/(I'll Be With You) In Apple Blossom Time	1960	$30
❏ 71427	Enchanted/The Sound and the Fury	1959	$30
❏ 71563	Harbor Lights/Sleepy Lagoon	1960	$30
❏ 71563 [PS]	Harbor Lights/Sleepy Lagoon	1960	$50
❏ 71246	Helpless/Indifferent	1957	$30
❏ 71749	If I Didn't Care/True Lover	1961	$20
❏ 71749 [PS]	If I Didn't Care/True Lover	1961	$40
❏ 71847	I'll Never Smile Again/You Don't Say	1961	$20
❏ 71847 [PS]	I'll Never Smile Again/You Don't Say	1961	$40
❏ 71032	I'm Sorry/He's Mine	1957	$40

—Maroon label

❏ 71032	I'm Sorry/He's Mine	1957	$30

—Black label

❏ 71921	It's Magic/Reaching for a Star	1962	$20
❏ 71921 [PS]	It's Magic/Reaching for a Star	1962	$40
❏ 71353	I Wish/It's Raining Outside	1958	$30

—Black label

❏ 71353	I Wish/It's Raining Outside	1958	$40

—Blue label

❏ 72359	Love Me Tender/Little Things Mean a Lot	1964	$10
❏ 72060	Memories/Heartbreak	1962	$15
❏ 71986	More Than You Know/Every Little Moment	1962	$15
❏ 71093	My Dream/I Wanna	1957	$40

—Maroon label

❏ 71093	My Dream/I Wanna	1957	$30

—Black label

❏ 70893	My Prayer/Heaven on Earth	1956	$50

—Maroon label

❏ 70893	My Prayer/Heaven on Earth	1956	$30

—Black label

❏ 71538	My Secret/What Does It Matter	1959	$30
❏ 72107	Once in a While/I'll See You in My Dreams	1963	$10
❏ 71011	One in a Million/On My Word of Honor	1956	$40
❏ 71184	Only Because/The Mystery of You	1957	$30
❏ 70633	Only You (And You Alone)/Bark, Battle and Ball	1955	$60

—Earliest pressings have pink labels

❏ 70633	Only You (And You Alone)/Bark, Battle and Ball	1955	$50

—Black label

❏ 76160	Platterama Medley/Red Sails in the Sunset	1982	$6
❏ 72305	Sincerely/P.S. I Love You	1964	$10
❏ 71383	Smoke Gets In Your Eyes/No Matter What You Are	1958	$30

—Black label

❏ 71383	Smoke Gets In Your Eyes/No Matter What You Are	1958	$40

—Blue label

❏ 10001 [S]	Smoke Gets In Your Eyes/No Matter What You Are	1959	$60
❏ 71904	Song for the Lonely/You'll Never Know	1961	$20
❏ 71904 [PS]	Song for the Lonely/You'll Never Know	1961	$40
❏ 72129	Strangers/Here Comes Heaven Again	1963	$10
❏ 70753	The Great Pretender/I'm Just a Dancing Partner	1955	$50

—Maroon label

❏ 70753	The Great Pretender/I'm Just a Dancing Partner	1955	$30

—Black label

❏ 71697	To Each His Own/Down the River of Golden Dreams	1960	$30
❏ 71697 [PS]	To Each His Own/Down the River of Golden Dreams	1960	$40
❏ 71791	Trees/Immortal Love	1961	$20
❏ 71791 [PS]	Trees/Immortal Love	1961	$40
❏ 71289	Twilight Time/Out of My Mind	1958	$30
❏ 71502	Where/Wish It Were Me	1959	$30

MUSICOR
❏ 1195	Alone in the Light (Without You)/Devri	1966	$8
❏ 1443	Be My Love/Sweet Sweet Lovin'	1971	$8
❏ 1341	Fear of Loving You/Sonata	1968	$8
❏ 1322	Hard to Get a Thing Called Love/Why	1968	$8
❏ 1211	I'll Be Home/(You've Got) The Magic Touch	1966	$8
❏ 1166	I Love You 1000 Times/Don't Hear, Speak, See No Evil	1966	$8
❏ 1288	Love Must Go On/How Beautiful Our Love Is	1968	$8
❏ 1262	On Top of My Mind/Shing-a-Ling-a-Loo	1967	$8
❏ 1302	So Many Tears/Think Before You Walk Away	1968	$8
❏ 1275	Sweet, Sweet Lovin'/Sonata	1967	$8
❏ 1251	Washed Ashore (On a Lonely Island in the Sea)/One in a Million	1967	$8
❏ 1251	Washed Ashore (On a Lonely Island in the Sea)/What Name Shall I Give You, My Love	1967	$8
❏ 1229	With This Ring/If I Had a Love	1967	$10

OWL
❏ 320	Sixteen Tons/Are You Sincere	1973	$8

RAM
❏ 1004/5	My Ship Is Coming In/Guilty	1977	$8
❏ 1002	Only You/Here Comes the Boogie Man	1977	$8
❏ 4852	Personality/Who's Sorry Now	1978	$8

7-Inch Extended Plays
FEDERAL
❏ EP-378	*Only You (And You Alone)/I Need You All the Time/Tell the World/Give Thanks	1956	$400
❏ EP-378 [PS]	The Platters Sing for Only You	1956	$400

KING
❏ 378	(contents unknown)	1956	$175
❏ 651 [B]	(contents unknown)	1956	$175

—Federal" 651 is a counterfeit; all originals are on King

❏ 378 [PS]	The Platters	1956	$175

—Reissue of Federal EP

❏ 651 [PS]	The Platters	1956	$175
❏ EP 1-3343	Heart of Stone/I'd Climb the Highest Mountain//September in the Rain/You've Changed	1957	$50
❏ EP 1-3344	I'll Get By/I'll Give You My Word//In the Still of the Night/Wagon Wheels	1957	$50
❏ EP 1-3355	Mean to Me/Oh Promise Me//Time and Tide/Don't Forget	1958	$50
❏ EP 1-3336	My Prayer/Have Mercy//On My Word of Honor/I'm Sorry	1957	$50
❏ EP 1-3354	Only Because/Love, You Funny Thing//I'm Gonna Sit Right Down and Write Myself a Letter/In the Middle of Nowhere	1958	$50
❏ EP 1-3345	Take Me in Your Arms/You Can Depend on Me//Temptation/I Don't Know Why	1957	$50
❏ EP 1-3355 [PS]	The Flying Platters	1958	$50
❏ EP 1-3353 [PS]	The Flying Platters (Part 1)	1958	$50
❏ EP 1-3354 [PS]	The Flying Platters (Part 2)	1958	$50
❏ EP 1-3336 [PS]	The Platters	1957	$50
❏ EP 1-3343 [PS]	The Platters (Part 1)	1957	$50
❏ EP 1-3344 [PS]	The Platters (Part 2)	1957	$50
❏ EP 1-3345 [PS]	The Platters (Part 3)	1957	$50
❏ EP 1-3393 [PS]	Twilight Time	1958	$50
❏ EP 1-3393	Twilight Time/For the First Time//Don't Blame Me/But Not Like You	1958	$50

PLAYBOYS, THE (1)
CAMEO
❏ 142	Over the Weekend/Double Talk	1958	$30

MARTINIQUE
❏ 101	Over the Weekend/Double Talk	1958	$60
❏ 400	Please Forgive Me/Sing Along	1959	$50

PLAYBOYS, THE (3)
ACE
❏ 670	Gotta Feelin'/How Could You Forget	1963	$15

PLAYBOYS, THE (4)
CAT
❏ 115	Good Golly Miss Molly/Honey Run	1955	$60
❏ 108	Tell Me/Rock, Moan and Cry	1954	$60

PLAYBOYS, THE (5)
CATALINA
❏ 1069	Shortnin' Bread/Cheater Stomp	1964	$40

PLAYBOYS, THE (6)
TETRA
❏ 4447	One Question/So Good	1956	$200

PLAYBOYS, THE (U)
CHANCELLOR
❏ 1074	Boston Hop/What'd I Say	1961	$20

—B-side by the Cousins

❏ 1106	Duck Walk/If I Had My Way	1962	$20

COTTON
❏ 1008	Careful with My Heart/Girl of My Dreams	1962	$30

DOLTON
❏ 8	Party Ice/Icy Fingers	1959	$30

HEARTBEAT
❏ 60	Harlem Nocturne/Blue Moon	1963	$30

IMPERIAL
❏ 5586	Sweet Talk/Crazy Daisy	1959	$30

LEGATO
❏ 101	Mope De Mope/The Night Before Christmas	1963	$40

MERCURY
❏ 71228	Why Do I Love You, Why Do I Care/Don't Do Me Wrong	1957	$30

SOUVENIR
❏ 1001	Believe It or Not/Hawaiian War Chant	1959	$20

TITAN
❏ 1732	The Scramble/Cat Walk	1963	$30

ZIPP
❏ 101	Sweet Talk/Crazy Daisy	1959	$50

PLAYER
CASABLANCA
❏ 2295	Givin' It All/Tip of the Iceberg	1980	$4
❏ 2265	It's for You/Tip of the Iceberg	1980	$4

RCA
❏ PB-13006	If Looks Could Kill/Born to Be with You	1981	$4
❏ PB-13089	My Mind's Made Up/Thank You for the Use of Your Love	1982	$4

RSO
❏ 879	Baby Come Back/Love Is Where You Find It	1977	$5
❏ 920	I Just Wanna Be with You/Let Me Down Easy	1979	$4
❏ 908	Prisoner of Your Love/Join In the Dance	1978	$4
❏ 914	Silver Lining/Forever	1978	$4
❏ 890	This Time I'm In It for Love/Every Which Way	1978	$4

PLAYMATES, THE
ABC-PARAMOUNT
❏ 10422 [B]	A" My Name Is Alice/Just a Little Bit	1963	$10
❏ 10522	Guy Behind the Wheel/One Guy Left on the Corner	1964	$10
❏ 10492	I Cross My Fingers/I'll Never Get Over You	1963	$10
❏ 10468	She Never Looked Better/But Not Through Tears	1963	$10

BELL
❏ 45149	Foundation of Love/Davenu	1971	$6

Number	Title	Yr	NM

COLPIX

Number	Title	Yr	NM
□ 760	Fiddler on the Roof/Piece of the Sky	1964	$8
□ 769	One by One the Roses Died/Spanish Perfume	1965	$8

CONGRESS

| □ 245 | Ballad of Stanley the Lifeguard/Should I Ask Someone Else to Tell Her | 1965 | $8 |

ROULETTE

□ 4003	Barefoot Girl/Pretty Woman	1957	$20
□ 4115	Beep Beep/Your Love	1958	$30
□ 4022	Darling It's Wonderful/Island Girl	1957	$20
□ 4022	Darling It's Wonderful/Magic Shoes	1957	$20
□ 4072	Don't Go Home/Can't You Get It Through Your Head	1958	$20
□ 4200	First Love/A-Ciu-E	1959	$15
□ 4056	Let's Be Lovers/Give Me Another Chance	1958	$20
□ 4322	Little Mis Stuck-Up/Real Life	1961	$15
□ 4211	On the Beach/The Song Everybody's Singing	1959	$15
□ 4252	Parade of Pretty Girls/Our Wedding Day	1960	$15
□ 4227	Second Chance/These Things I Offer You	1960	$15
□ 4136	Star Love/The Thing-A-Ma-Jig	1959	$15
□ 4370	Tell Me What She Said/Cowboys Never Cry	1961	$15
□ 4100	The Day I Died/While the Record Goes Around	1958	$20
□ 4276	Wait for Me/Eyes of Angel	1960	$15
□ 4464	What a Funny Way to Show It/Petticoats Fly	1962	$10
□ 4160	What Is Love/I Am	1959	$15
□ 4393	Wimoweh/One Little Kiss	1961	$15

PLEASE, BOBBY

ERA

| □ 1044 | Heartache Street/Your Driver's License Please | 1957 | $20 |

IMPERIAL

| □ 5508 | I'm Girl Crazy/My Tummy Flip | 1958 | $20 |

JAMIE

| □ 1118 | The Monster/The Switch | 1959 | $20 |

PLEASURE FAIR, THE
With Robb Royer, later of BREAD.

UNI

| □ 55016 | Morning Glory Days/Fade In, Fade Out | 1967 | $8 |
| □ 55078 | Today/I'm Gonna Hafta Let You Go | 1968 | $8 |

PLEASURE SEEKERS

CAPITOL

| □ 2050 | (Theme from) Valley of the Dolls/If You Climb on the Tiger's Back | 1967 | $30 |

MERCURY

| □ 72800 | Good Kind of Hurt/Light of Love | 1968 | $30 |

PLEBS, THE

MGM

| □ 13320 | Bad Blood/Babe I'm Gonna Leave You | 1965 | $15 |

PLEDGES, THE

REV

| □ 3517 | Betty Jean/Her Bermuda Shorts | 1958 | $30 |

PLIMSOULS, THE

GEFFEN

□ 29600	A Million Miles Away/Play the Breaks	1983	$4
□ 29600 [PS]	A Million Miles Away/Play the Breaks	1983	$15
□ 29496	Oldest Story in the World/Hobo	1983	$10

SHAKY CITY

| □ 134 | A Million Miles Away/I'll Get Lucky | 1982 | $4 |
| □ 134 [PS] | A Million Miles Away/I'll Get Lucky | 1982 | $4 |

PLUGZ

FATIMA

| □ 79 | La Bamba/Achin' | 1981 | $20 |
| □ 79 [PS] | La Bamba/Achin' | 1981 | $20 |

SLASH

| □ 102 | Move/Let Go/Mindless Contentment | 1978 | $30 |

| □ 102 [PS] | Move/Let Go/Mindless Contentment | 1978 | $125 |

—Black on yellow sleeve with band photo and lyrics

| □ 102 [PS] | Move/Let Go/Mindless Contentment | 1978 | $30 |

—Gray folder with necktie and "Singi" button artwork

PLUMB, EVE

RCA VICTOR

| □ 74-0409 | How Will It Be/Fortune Cookie Song | 1970 | $20 |
| □ 74-0409 [PS] | How Will It Be/Fortune Cookie Song | 1970 | $30 |

PO' BOYS, THE

DECCA

□ 31915	Dear Heart/Orange Blossom Special	1966	$8
□ 32170	Faded Love/Sunny-Gem	1967	$8
□ 32821	Louisiana Man/Sidewalkin'	1971	$8
□ 32944	Sunnyside Up/Guitar Boy	1972	$8
□ 32281	White Rabbit/Up & Atom	1968	$8

MCA

| □ 40117 | Pass Me By/Fire Ball Mail | 1973 | $6 |

POCO

ABC

□ 12439	Crazy Love/Barbados	1978	$5
□ 12295	Indian Summer/Me and You	1977	$5
□ 12159	Makin' Love/Flyin' Solo	1976	$5

ATLANTIC

□ 89851	Break of Hearts/Love's So Cruel	1983	$5
□ 89674	Days Gone By/Daylight	1984	$3
□ 89970	Ghostown/High Sierra	1982	$3
□ 89970 [PS]	Ghostown/High Sierra	1982	$4
□ 89629	Save a Corner of Your Heart/The Storm	1984	$5
□ 89919	Shoot for the Moon/The Midnight Rodeo	1982	$3
□ 89650	This Old Flame/The Storm	1984	$3

EPIC

□ 50076	Bitter Blue/High and Dry	1975	$6
□ 10714	C'Mon/I Guess You Made It	1971	$8
□ 10890	Good Feeling to Know/Early Times	1972	$6
□ 11055	Here We Go Again/Fools Gold	1973	$6
□ 10958	I Can See Everything/Go and Say Goodbye	1973	$6
□ 11092	Magnolia/Blue Water	1974	$6
□ 10543	My Kind of Love/Hard Luck	1969	$10
□ 10501	Pickin' Up the Pieces/First Love	1969	$10

MCA

□ 51172	Down on the River Again/Widowmaker	1981	$4
□ 51034	Everlasting Kind/Friends in the Distance	1980	$4
□ 41023	Heart of the Night/Last Goodbye	1979	$4
□ 41103	Legend/Indian Summer	1979	$4
□ 41326	Midnight Rain/Fool's Paradise	1980	$4
□ 52001	Seas of Heartbreaks/Feudin'	1982	$4

RCA

| □ 9038-7-R | Call It Love/Lovin' You Every Minute | 1989 | $3 |
| □ 9038-7-R [PS] | Call It Love/Lovin' You Every Minute | 1989 | $3 |

POETS, THE (1)

SYMBOL

□ 219	I'm Particular/I've Only Two Hearts	1966	$15
□ 214	She Blew a Good Thing/Out to Lunch	1966	$20
□ 216	So Young (And So Innocent)/A Sure Thing	1966	$15

VEEP

| □ 1286 | The Hustler/Soul Brothers Holiday | 1968 | $30 |

POETS, THE (4)

IMPERIAL

| □ 5664 | Honey Chile/I'm in Love | 1960 | $20 |

POETS, THE (U)

CHAIRMAN

| □ 4408 | Coffee House/Number One (More Time) | 1963 | $15 |

RED BIRD

| □ Oct-0046 | Merry Christmas Baby/I'm Stuck on You | 1965 | $15 |

POGO THE CLOWN

AMPHETAMINE REPTILE

| □ SCALE15 | Lederhosen/Sesame Street | 1988 | $30 |
| □ SCALE15 [PS] | Lederhosen/Sesame Street | 1988 | $30 |

POINDEXTER, BUSTER

RCA

□ 9007-7-R	All Night Party (Hot Mix)/All Night Party (Power Mix)	1989	$3
□ 9007-7-R [PS]	All Night Party (Hot Mix)/All Night Party (Power Mix)	1989	$3
□ 8914-7-R	Hit the Road Jack/Heart of Gold	1989	$3
□ 8914-7-R [PS]	Hit the Road Jack/Heart of Gold	1989	$3
□ 5357-7-R	Hot Hot Hot/Cannibal	1987	$3
□ 5357-7-R [PS]	Hot Hot Hot/Cannibal	1987	$3
□ 7638-7-R	Oh Me Oh My (I'm a Fool for You Baby)/Cannibal	1988	$3
□ 7638-7-R [PS]	Oh Me Oh My (I'm a Fool for You Baby)/Cannibal	1988	$3

POINTER, BONNIE

MOTOWN

| □ 1484 | Deep Inside My Soul/I Love to Sing to You | 1980 | $4 |
| □ 1451 | Free Me from My Freedom-Tie Me to a Tree (Handcuff Me)/(Instrumental) | 1978 | $4 |

—Black vinyl

| □ 1451 [PS] | Free Me from My Freedom-Tie Me to a Tree (Handcuff Me)/(Instrumental) | 1978 | $6 |
| □ 1451 | Free Me from My Freedom-Tie Me to a Tree (Handcuff Me)/(Instrumental) | 1978 | $8 |

—Stock copy on red vinyl

| □ 1459 | Heaven Must Have Sent You/Heaven Must Have Sent You (LP Version) | 1979 | $4 |
| □ 1478 | I Can't Help Myself (Sugar Pie, Honey Bunch)/I Wanna Make It (In Your World) | 1979 | $4 |

PRIVATE I

□ ZS4-04658	Premonition/Tight Blue Jeans	1984	$3
□ ZS4-04819	The Beast in Me/There's Nobody Quite Like You	1985	$3
□ ZS4-04819 [PS]	The Beast in Me/There's Nobody Quite Like You	1985	$3

POINTER, JUNE

COLUMBIA

| □ 38-68748 | Tight on Time (I'll Fit U In)/Fool for Love | 1989 | $3 |

PLANET

| □ YB-13592 | Don't Mess With Bill/I Understand | 1983 | $4 |

POINTER, RUTH

EPIC

| □ 34-08115 | Enemies Like You and Me/I Need You | 1988 | $3 |

—With Billy Vera

POINTER SISTERS, THE

ATLANTIC

| □ 2893 | Destination No More Heartaches/Send Him Back | 1972 | $50 |
| □ 2845 | Don't Try to Take the Fifth/Tulsa County | 1971 | $30 |

BLUE THUMB

| □ 254 | Fairytale/Love In Them Thar Hills | 1974 | $10 |

—First pressing has a gray to white label and no reference to ABC

| □ 254 | Fairytale/Love In Them Thar Hills | 1974 | $5 |

—Second pressing has a multicolor label with ABC logo

□ 268	Going Down Slowly/Sleeping Alone	1975	$5
□ 275	Having a Party/Lonely Gal	1977	$5
□ 265	How Long (Betcha' Got a Chick on the Side)/Easy Days	1975	$5
□ 277	I Need a Man/I'll Get By Without You	1978	$5
□ 262	Live Your Life Before You Die/Shaky Flat Blues	1975	$5
□ 248	Steam Heat/Shaky Flat Blues	1974	$6
□ 243	Wang Dang Doodle/Cloudburst	1973	$6

COLUMBIA

| □ 08015 | Power of Persuasion/(Instrumental) | 1988 | $3 |
| □ 08015 [PS] | Power of Persuasion/(Instrumental) | 1988 | $3 |

MCA

| □ 53120 | Be There/(Instrumental) | 1987 | $3 |
| □ 53120 [PS] | Be There/(Instrumental) | 1987 | $3 |

PLANET

Number	Title	Yr	NM
GB-13485	American Music/I'm So Excited	1983	$3
—Gold Standard Series			
YB-13254	American Music/I Want to Do It with You	1982	$4
YB-13730	Automatic/Nightline	1984	$4
YB-14041	Baby Come and Get It/Operator	1985	$4
YB-14041 [PS]	Baby Come and Get It/Operator	1985	$4
45906	Blind Faith/The Shape I'm In	1979	$4
47920	Could I Be Dreaming/Evil	1980	$4
47918	Es Tan Timido/Cosas Especiales	1980	$6
GB-14076	Fire/He's So Shy	1985	$3
—Gold Standard Series			
45901	Fire/Love Is Like a Rolling Stone	1978	$4
45901 [PS]	Fire/Love Is Like a Rolling Stone	1978	$6
45902	Happiness/Too Late	1979	$4
47916	He's So Shy/Movin' On	1980	$4
YB-13430	If You Wanna Get Back Your Lady/I'm So Excited	1983	$4
YB-13857	I'm So Excited/Dance Electric	1984	$4
YB-13327	I'm So Excited/Nothing But a Heartache (Live)	1982	$4
YB-13639	I Need You/If You Wanna Get Back Your Lady	1983	$4
GB-13795	I Need You/If You Wanna Get Back Your Lady	1984	$3
—Gold Standard Series			
47960	Should I Do It/We're Gonna Make It	1982	$4
47929	Slow Hand/Holdin' Out for Love	1981	$4
GB-14077	Slow Hand/Should I Do It	1985	$3
—Gold Standard Series			
47945	Sweet Lover Man/Got to Find Love	1981	$4
47937	What a Surprise/Fall in Love Again	1981	$4
47925	Where Did the Time Go/Special Things	1981	$4

RCA

Number	Title	Yr	NM
5112-7-R	All I Know Is the Way I Feel/Translation	1987	$3
PB-14126	Dare Me/I'll Be There	1985	$3
PB-14126 [PS]	Dare Me/I'll Be There	1985	$3
PB-14224	Freedom/Telegraph Your Love	1985	$3
PB-14224 [PS]	Freedom/Telegraph Your Love	1985	$3
5062-7-R	Goldmine/Sexual Power	1986	$3
5062-7-R [PS]	Goldmine/Sexual Power	1986	$3
6865-7-R	He Turned Me Out/Translation	1988	$3
6865-7-R [PS]	He Turned Me Out/Translation	1988	$3
8378-7-R	I'm in Love/Uh-Oh	1988	$3
5230-7-R	Mercury Rising/Say the Word	1987	$3
PB-14197	Twist My Arm/Easy Persuasion	1986	$3
PB-14197 [PS]	Twist My Arm/Easy Persuasion	1986	$3

POISON
First name in "hair metal."

CAPITOL

Number	Title	Yr	NM
B-5686	Talk Dirty to Me/Want Some, Need Some	1987	$3
—Originals have Capitol logo at top with colorband			
B-5686 [PS]	Talk Dirty to Me/Want Some, Need Some	1987	$4

ENIGMA

Number	Title	Yr	NM
B-44203	Every Rose Has Its Thorn/Livin' for the Minute	1988	$3
B-44203 [PS]	Every Rose Has Its Thorn/Livin' for the Minute	1988	$3
B-44191	Fallen Angel/Bad to Be Good	1988	$3
B-44191 [PS]	Fallen Angel/Bad to Be Good	1988	$3
B-44004	I Want Action/Play Dirty	1987	$3
B-44004 [PS]	I Want Action/Play Dirty	1987	$4
—Fold-out poster sleeve			
B-44038	I Won't Forget You/Blame It on You	1987	$3
B-44038 [PS]	I Won't Forget You/Blame It on You	1987	$3

POISON IDEA
7-Inch Extended Plays

AMERICAN LEATHER

Number	Title	Yr	NM
01	Darby Crash Rides Again	1988	$20
—Blue vinyl			
01 [PS]	Darby Crash Rides Again	1988	$20
—Black and white sleeve			

FATAL ERECTION

Number	Title	Yr	NM
TR-001	Pick Your King	1983	$38
—First pressing on clear vinyl			
TR-001	Pick Your King	1983	$25
—Second pressing on black vinyl			
TR-001	Pick Your King	1983	$13
—Third pressing on blue vinyl			
TR-001 [PS]	Pick Your King	1983	$38
—First sleeve: white with two inserts			
TR-001 [PS]	Pick Your King	1983	$25
—Second sleeve: Blue, no inserts			
TR-001 [PS]	Pick Your King	1983	$13
—Third sleeve: Cream or white, no inserts			

SHITFOOL

Number	Title	Yr	NM
0 (# unknown)	Filth Kick	1988	$15
0 (# unknown) [PS]	Filth Kick	1988	$15
—2,000 pressed			

POLICE, THE
Also see KLARK KENT; STING; ANDY SUMMERS.

A&M

Number	Title	Yr	NM
2218	Bring On the Night/Visions of the Night	1980	$5
2147	Can't Stand Losing You/No Time This Time	1979	$5
2147 [PS]	Can't Stand Losing You/No Time This Time	1979	$10
2275	De Do Do Do, De Da Da Da/Friends	1980	$4
—Standard A&M late-1970s label			
2275	De Do Do Do, De Da Da Da/Friends	1980	$3
—Yellowish custom label with blueish triangle (most common version)			
2275	De Do Do Do, De Da Da Da/Friends	1980	$4
—Red custom label with silver triangle			
2275 [PS]	De Do Do Do, De Da Da Da/Friends	1980	$6
—Actually a title sleeve with large center hole			
25000	De Do Do Do, De Da Da Da (Japanese)/De Do Do Do, De Da Da Da (Spanish)	1981	$5
—Small center hole			
25000 [PS]	De Do Do Do, De Da Da Da (Japanese)/De Do Do Do, De Da Da Da (Spanish)	1981	$5
2879	Don't Stand So Close to Me '86/Don't Stand So Close to Me (Live)	1986	$3
2879 [PS]	Don't Stand So Close to Me '86/Don't Stand So Close to Me (Live)	1986	$3
2301	Don't Stand So Close to Me/A Sermon	1981	$3
2301 [PS]	Don't Stand So Close to Me/A Sermon	1981	$3
PR-4401 [PD]	Don't Stand So Close to Me/De Do Do Do, De Da Da Da	1981	$12
—Star-shaped badge picture disc in folder; promo only			
2542	Every Breath You Take/Murder by Numbers	1983	$3
2542 [PS]	Every Breath You Take/Murder by Numbers	1983	$3
2371	Every Little Thing She Does Is Magic/Shambelle	1981	$3
2371 [PS]	Every Little Thing She Does Is Magic/Shambelle	1981	$3
2190	Message in a Bottle/Landlord	1979	$5
2190 [PS]	Message in a Bottle/Landlord	1979	$10
—Fold-out poster sleeve			
2190 [PS]	Message in a Bottle/Landlord	1979	$15
—Regular sleeve			
PR-4400 [PD]	Message in a Bottle/Message in a Bottle (Live)	1980	$10
—Star-shaped badge picture disc in folder; promo only			
2408	Secret Journey/Darkness	1982	$3
2408 [PS]	Secret Journey/Darkness	1982	$3
2390	Spirits in the Material World/Flexible Strategies	1982	$3
2390 [PS]	Spirits in the Material World/Flexible Strategies	1982	$3
2571	Synchronicity II/Once Upon a Daydream	1983	$3
2571 [PS]	Synchronicity II/Once Upon a Daydream	1983	$3
0 (no cat #) [DJ]	The Police File	1985	$60
—Boxed set of five "A&M Memories" singles released to radio. Price is mostly for the box.			
2908	Walking on the Moon/Message in a Bottle	1986	$5
2908 [PS]	Walking on the Moon/Message in a Bottle	1986	$5
2614	Wrapped Around Your Finger/Tea in the Sahara (Live)	1984	$3
2614 [PS]	Wrapped Around Your Finger/Tea in the Sahara (Live)	1984	$3

POLLARD, RAY

DECCA

Number	Title	Yr	NM
32111	Lie, Lips, Lie/This Is My Song	1967	$50
32189	This Is No Laughing Matter/Wanderlust	1967	$120

OMNIPOTENT

Number	Title	Yr	NM
1001	Soulmate?/(B-side unknown)	1973	$800

UNITED ARTISTS

Number	Title	Yr	NM
50012	All the Things You Are/It's a Sad Thing	1966	$125
856	Darling Take Me Back/My Girl and I	1965	$100
916	The Drifter/Let Him Go (And Let Me Love You)	1965	$100

POLLUTION

CAPITOL

Number	Title	Yr	NM
2458	Getting Together/Angela Jerome	1969	$10

PROPHECY

Number	Title	Yr	NM
55001	Do You Really Have a Heart/(B-side unknown)	1971	$8

POLNAREFF, MICHEL

4 CORNERS OF THE WORLD

Number	Title	Yr	NM
141	Time Will Tell/Under What Star Was I Born	1967	$20

ATLANTIC

Number	Title	Yr	NM
3330	Lipstick (Part 1)/Lipstick (Part 2)	1976	$5
3314	Since I Saw You/If You Only Believe	1976	$5

KAPP

Number	Title	Yr	NM
786	Love Me, Please Love Me/No, No, No, No, No	1966	$8

PONI-TAILS, THE

ABC-PARAMOUNT

Number	Title	Yr	NM
10077	Before We Say Goodnight/Come Be My Love	1960	$30
9934	Born Too Late/Come On Joey Dance With Me	1958	$30
9934 [DJ]	Born Too Late/Come On Joey Dance With Me	1958	$60
—White label promo with artist's name spelled "Pony-Tails			
9969	Close Friends/Seven Minutes in Heaven	1958	$30
9995	Early to Bed/Father Time	1959	$30
10047	I'll Be Seeing You/I'll Keep Tryin'	1959	$30
10027	Moody/Ooh-Pah Polka	1959	$30
10114	Who, When and Why/Oh My, You	1960	$30
9846	Wild Eyes and Tender Lips/It's Just My Luck to Be Fifteen	1957	$30

MARC

Number	Title	Yr	NM
1001	Can I Be Sure/Still in Your Teens	1957	$30

PONTRELLI, PETE

SKYWAY

Number	Title	Yr	NM
103	Season's Greetings (A Cheerful Hello)/Season's Greetings (A Cheerful Hello)	1960	$8
—B-side by Gaylord Carter			
101	Season's Greetings/There's Room In My Heart	1960	$10

PONTY, JEAN-LUC

ATLANTIC

Number	Title	Yr	NM
4009	As/Rhythms of Hope	1982	$4
3639	Beach Girl/Sunset Drive	1979	$8
3523	Cosmic Messenger/The Art of Happiness	1978	$5
3778	Demagomania/(B-side unknown)	1980	$4
89787	Far from Beaten Paths/(B-side unknown)	1983	$4

POOBAH

A.E.I.

Number	Title	Yr	NM
04/005	Through These Eyes/Watch Me!	1976	$60

POOH AND THE HEFFALUMPS

LAURIE

Number	Title	Yr	NM
3281	Lady Godiva/Rooty Toot	1965	$15

Number	Title	Yr	NM

POOLE, BRIAN, AND THE TREMELOES
AUDIO FIDELITY
Number	Title	Yr	NM
❏ 121	Good Lovin'/Could It Be You	1966	$10
❏ 112	I Go Crazy/Love Me Baby	1965	$10

LONDON
| ❏ 9625 | Do You Love Me/Why Can't You Love Me | 1964 | $20 |

MONUMENT
❏ 882	After a While/Don't Cry	1965	$15
❏ 840	Candy Man/I Can Dream	1964	$15
❏ 846	Someone, Someone/(Meet Me) Where We Used to Meet	1964	$15

POOLE, BRIAN
DATE
| ❏ 1539 | Everything I Touch Turns to Tears/I Need Her Tonight | 1966 | $12 |

POOLE, CHERYL
PAULA
❏ 251	Every Chance You Get/Throwing In the Crying Towel	1966	$8
❏ 263	Heart Trouble/His Wife	1967	$8
❏ 1205	How About Your Love for Christmas/It's Christmas Every Day of the Year	1968	$8
❏ 277	Second Hand Girl/There's Got to Be a Woman Too	1967	$8
❏ 297	Swingin' Blue/Ruby's Stool	1968	$8
❏ 309	Three Playing Love/I'm Not Your Woman (You're Not My Man)	1968	$8

POPCORN AND THE MOHAWKS
MOTOWN
| ❏ 1002 | Custer's Last Man/Shimmy Gully | 1960 | $70 |

POPCORN BLIZZARD, THE (1)
DE-LITE
| ❏ 522 | Good Good Day/I Just Saw a Face | 1969 | $30 |
| ❏ 516 | Good Thing Going/My Suzanne | 1969 | $30 |

POPCORN BLIZZARD, THE (2)
MAGENDA
| ❏ 7411 | Once Upon a Time/Hello! | 1967 | $125 |
| *— The first recorded performance by MEAT LOAF* | | | |

POPCORN REBELLION, THE
DATE
| ❏ 1632 | The Christmas Game/Dance to the Music of the Christmas Game | 1968 | $12 |

POPE, RAYMOND, AND THE LOVETONES
SQUALOR
| ❏ 1313 | I Love Nadine/Star | 1962 | $200 |

POPPIES, THE
EPIC
❏ 10059	Do It with Soul/He Means So Much to Me	1966	$15
❏ 10019	He's Ready/He's Got Real Love	1966	$12
❏ 10019 [PS]	He's Ready/He's Got Real Love	1966	$30
❏ 9893	I Wonder Why/Lullaby of Love	1966	$10
❏ 10086	There's a Pain in My Heart/My Love and I	1966	$30

POPPY FAMILY, THE
LONDON
❏ 128	Another Year, Another Day/You Don't Know What Love Is	1970	$10
—Deleted quickly; a more common Margaret Whiting single was also issued as London 128			
❏ 172	Good Friends/Tryin'	1972	$5
❏ 148	I Was Wondering/Where Evil Grows	1971	$5
❏ 139	That's When I Went Wrong/Shadows on My Wall	1970	$5
❏ 129	Which Way You Goin' Billy/Endless Sleep	1970	$6

POPSICLES, THE (1)
GNP CRESCENDO
| ❏ 336 | I Don't Want to Be Your Baby Anymore/Baby I Miss You | 1965 | $10 |

POPSICLES, THE (2)
KNIGHT
| ❏ 2002 | Thumb Print/This is the End | 1958 | $50 |

POPULAIRES, THE
MARVELLO
| ❏ 5001 | Island of Paradise/I Lost My Heart | 1957 | $200 |

PORTER, BOB
LITTLE DARLIN'
| ❏ 0070 | There's No Easy Way to Die/I Think I'll Wait Awhile | 1970 | $8 |

PORTER, DAVID
ENTERPRISE
❏ 9049	Ain't That Loving You (For More Reasons Than One)/Baby I'm-a Want You	1972	$5
— With Isaac Hayes			
❏ 9071	As Long As You're the One Somebody in the World/When You Have to Sneak	1973	$5
❏ 9014	Can't See You When I Want To/One Part, Two Parts	1970	$6
❏ 9090	Falling Out, Falling In/I Got You and I'm Glad	1973	$5
❏ 9050	I'm Afraid the Masquerade Is Over/Sloopy	1972	$5
❏ 9055	Wanna Be Your Somebody/When the Chips Are Down	1972	$5

STAX
| ❏ 163 | Can't See You When I Want To/Win You Over | 1965 | $30 |

PORTER, JIM
HIT
| ❏ 05 | Dr. Feelgood/Shout | 1962 | $8 |
| *—B-side by Bill Austin* | | | |

PORTER, NOLAN
ABC
❏ 11343	If I Could Only Be Sure/Work It Out in the Morning	1972	$125
❏ 11367 [DJ]	Singer Man (mono/stereo)	1973	$6
❏ 11367	Singer Man/Oh Baby	1973	$70

LIZARD
❏ 21003	Crazy Love/What Would You Do (If I Did That to You)	1971	$15
— As "Nolan			
❏ 1008	I Like What You Give/Somebody's Cryin'	1971	$20
— As "Nolan			

PORTER, ROCKY
COLUMBIA
❏ 4-21325	I Knew It All Along/Don't Forget to Remember	1954	$30
❏ 4-20903	I've Fallen in Love with an Angel/Keep On Keeping On	1952	$30
❏ 4-21028	Please Say a Prayer/All Seeing Eye	1952	$30
❏ 4-20980	Suppose/I'm in Love with No One	1952	$30
❏ 4-21264	The World Is a Monster/I Talked to the Man in the Moon	1954	$30

PORTER, ROYCE
D
| ❏ 1026 | Lookin'/I Still Belong to You | 1958 | $125 |

MERCURY
| ❏ 71314 | Good Time/Beach of Love | 1958 | $125 |

PORTRAITS, THE (1)
CAPITOL
| ❏ F-4181 | Close to You/Easy Cash | 1959 | $40 |

PORTRAITS, THE (2)
SIDEWALK
| ❏ 928 | A Million to One/Let's Tell the World | 1967 | $20 |
| ❏ 935 | Over the Rainbow/Runaround Girl | 1968 | $30 |

PORTRAITS, THE (3)
TRI-DISC
| ❏ 109 | We're Gonna Party/Three Blind Mice | 1963 | $20 |

POSEY, SANDY
AUDIOGRAPH
| ❏ 449 | Can't Get Used to Sleeping Without You/(B-side unknown) | 1983 | $4 |

COLUMBIA
❏ 45458	Bring Him Safely Home To Me/A Man in Need of Love	1971	$5
❏ 45828	Don't/Thank the Lord for New York City	1973	$5
❏ 45828	Don't/Thank the Lord for New York City	1973	$5
❏ 45703	Happy Happy Birthday Baby/Thank the Lord for New York City	1972	$5
❏ 45360	Losing Out on You/You Say Beautiful Things to Me	1971	$5
❏ 45596	Why Don't We Go Somewhere and Love/Together	1972	$5

MGM
❏ 14006	All Hung Up in Your Green Eyes/Your Conception of Love	1968	$6
❏ 13824	Are You Never Coming Home/I Can Show You How to Live	1967	$8
❏ 13501	Born a Woman/Caution to the Wind	1967	$8
❏ 13744	I Take It Back/The Boy I Love	1967	$8
❏ 13744 [PS]	I Take It Back/The Boy I Love	1967	$15
❏ 13892	Silly Girl, Silly Boy/Something I'll Remember	1968	$6
❏ 13612	Single Girl/Blue Is My Best Color	1966	$8
❏ 13612 [PS]	Single Girl/Blue Is My Best Color	1966	$15
❏ 13967	Ways of the World/Wonderful World of Summer	1968	$6
❏ 13702	What a Woman in Love Won't Do/Shattered	1967	$8

MONUMENT
| ❏ 8698 | Trying to Live Without You Kind of Days/Why Do We Carry On | 1976 | $5 |

WARNER BROS.
❏ 49104	Black Is the Night/Best Things in My Life	1979	$4
❏ 8540	Born to Be with You/It's Not Too Late	1978	$4
❏ 8289	It's Midnight (Do You Know Where Your Baby Is)/Long Distance Kissing	1976	$4
❏ 8610	Love, Love, Love-Chapel of Love/I Believe in Love	1978	$4
❏ 8731	Love Is Sometimes Easy/I Believe in Love	1979	$4
❏ 8852	Try Home/Love Is Sometimes Easy	1979	$4

POSITIVELY 13 O'CLOCK
HANNA-BARBERA
| ❏ 500 | Psychotic Reaction/13 O'Clock Theme for Psychotics | 1966 | $50 |

POSSUM
HIGHLAND
| ❏ 10 | The Cockroach That Ate Cincinnati/Chula Vista | 1966 | $20 |

POSSUM, POLLY
COLUMBIA
❏ 4-21196	Bimbo/I'm a Stranger in My Home	1954	$30
❏ 4-21140	Castanets/Between You and the Birds	1953	$30
❏ 4-20947	Lord Oh Lord/Hurry	1952	$30
❏ 4-20908	Sad Singin', Slow Ridin'/Don't Cry	1952	$30
❏ 4-21090	Sin Is Satin/Don't Talk to Me About Man	1953	$30
❏ 4-21238	Takes All Kinds of People/Something Happened to You	1954	$30

POST, MIKE
ELEKTRA
❏ 47477	School's Out/Aaron's Tune	1982	$4
❏ 47400	Theme from Magnum, P.I./Gumbus Bed	1982	$4
❏ 47400 [PS]	Theme from Magnum, P.I./Gumbus Bed	1982	$4
❏ 47186	The Theme from Hill Street Blues/Aaron's Tune	1981	$4
❏ 47186 [PS]	The Theme from Hill Street Blues/Aaron's Tune	1981	$4

EPIC
| ❏ 50325 | Theme from "Baa Baa Black Sheep"/Southbound | 1976 | $4 |

MGM
| ❏ 14829 | Manhattan Spiritual/Lay Back Lafayette | 1975 | $4 |

MUSIC FACTORY
| ❏ 419 | Harper Valley P.T.A./Walking to San Francisco | 1968 | $8 |

POLYDOR
| ❏ 887145-7 | Theme from "L.A. Law"/Jenny's Ayre | 1987 | $4 |

Number	Title	Yr	NM
❏ 887145-7 [PS]	Theme from "L.A. Law"/ Jenny's Ayre	1987	$4

RCA

PB-13859	The A Team//6/24	1984	$5

REPRISE

❏ 0406	For My Home/Long Time Alone	1965	$10
❏ 0468	Hard Times/Louisiana Man	1966	$12

WARNER BROS.

❏ 7357	Bubble Gum Breakthrough/ Not a Blade of Grass	1969	$8

POSTA, ADRIENNE
LONDON

❏ 9782	When a Girl Really Loves You/Winds That Bloe	1966	$10

POTTER, CURTIS
DOT

❏ 17153	Drowning Man/Dumb Dumb	1968	$12
❏ 17302	Handful/Heartaches Can Be Fun	1969	$8
❏ 17348	It's My Day/My First Stop Is Omaha	1970	$8

FOX

❏ 409	I'm a Real Glad Daddy/ (B-side unknown)	1958	$250

HILLSIDE

❏ 7903	Fraulein (The Texas National Anthem)/The Story Behind the Photograph	1979	$6
❏ 8003	It's the Cheatin' She Loves/ Undo the Right	1980	$6
❏ 7905	Part-Time Lover, Full-Time Heartache/Soft Rain	1979	$6
❏ 8001	San Antonio Medley/Thank God for Country Music	1980	$6

— With Darrell McCall

❏ 8104	She Wears Faded Jeans/ You Left a Long, Long Time Ago	1981	$6
❏ 8101	Texas Proud/When My Baby Double Talks to Me	1981	$6

RCA VICTOR

❏ APBO-0247	All I Need Is Time/You Can Always Come to Me	1974	$6
❏ PB-10195	Close Every Door Behind You/I Can't Keep My Mind Off of You	1975	$6
❏ PB-10016	If She Keeps Loving Me/The Farther I Go with You	1974	$6
❏ PB-10087	Too Much Woman/Am I What's the Matter with You	1974	$6

STEP ONE

❏ 376	All I Need Is Time/Am I Blue	1987	$5
❏ 367	Chicago Dancin' Girls/Then I Can Face Your Memory	1986	$5
❏ 372	Close Your Eyes/All I Need Is Time	1987	$5
❏ 348	I Wish It Was That Easy/If This Was Texas	1985	$5

WINSTON

❏ 1042	Can I Be Sure/Who Do You Miss	1959	$30

ZODIAC

❏ 1009	Far Away Feeling/Let Me Love in Peace	1976	$6

POWELL, AUSTIN
ATLANTIC

❏ 968	Wrong Again/What More Can I Ask	1952	$200

DECCA

❏ 48206	All This Can't Be True/Some Other Spring	1951	$100

POWELL, CHRIS, AND THE FIVE BLUE FLAMES
COLUMBIA

❏ 39272	Country Girl Blues/Man with a Horn	1951	$200
❏ 39407	My Love Has Gone/In the Cool of the Evening	1951	$500

GRAND

❏ 124	Anniversary Waltz/Sweet Georgia Brown	1955	$50
❏ 116	Dinah/Song of the Vagabond	1954	$60
❏ 127	Mandolin Mambo/The Whiffenpoof Song	1955	$50
❏ 120	Mr. Sandman/Mambo Gunch	1954	$60
❏ 112	Secret Love Mambo/I Love Paris Mambo	1954	$60
❏ 108	Sweet Sue Mambo/Uh Uh Baby	1953	$60

GROOVE

❏ 0105	Break It Up/Love Ya Like Crazy	1955	$30
❏ 0128	Goodbye Little Girl/ Chinatown	1955	$30
❏ 0144	Moritat/The Poor People of Paris	1956	$30

OKEH

Number	Title	Yr	NM
❏ 6900	Blue Boy/I Come from Jamaica	1952	$125
❏ 6875	Ida Red/Darn That Dream	1952	$125
❏ 6850	October Twilight/That's Right	1952	$125
❏ 6818	The Masquerade Is Over/ Talkin'	1951	$300

POWELL, JEROME
PARKWAY

❏ 927	Home to Stay/Live and Let Live	1964	$15

POWELL, JIMMY (1)
DECCA

❏ 32685	Stranger on a Train/Sugar Man	1970	$6

LONDON

❏ 9545	I Love You/Dance Her By Me (One More Time)	1962	$10

POWELL, JIMMY (2)
JUBILEE

❏ 5533	The Shadow of Your Smile/ On a Clear Day You Can See Forever	1966	$8

POWELL, PATTI
HICKORY

❏ 1659	High on Jesus/Satisfied	1973	$8
❏ 1602	Long Haul Widow/To See the Kids Again	1971	$8
❏ 1616	The Best Way to Hold a Man/Your Boots Are By the Door	1971	$8

POWELL, SANDY
HERALD

❏ 557	Bon Bon/Pistol-Packin' Mama	1961	$125

IMPALA

❏ 211	Bon Bon/Pistol-Packin' Mama	1961	$300

SINGULAR

❏ 714	My Jimmie/Next Thing to Paradise	1958	$30

POWER, DUFFY
EPIC

❏ 10650	Hellhound/Hummingbird	1970	$6

VEEP

❏ 1204	Where Am I/I Don't Care	1964	$30

POWER STATION, THE
CAPITOL

❏ B-5511	Communication/Murderess	1985	$3
❏ B-5511 [PS]	Communication/Murderess	1985	$3
❏ B-5479	Get It On/Go To Zero	1985	$3
❏ B-5479 [PS]	Get It On/Go To Zero	1985	$3
❏ B-5444	Some Like It Hot/The Heat Is On	1985	$3

— Custom label claims this is "Extended Version" but it is the 45 rpm edit

❏ B-5444 [PS]	Some Like It Hot/The Heat Is On	1985	$3

POWERS, JOEY
AMY

❏ 898	Billy Old Buddy/In the Morning Gloria	1964	$10
❏ 986	Gimmie Gimmie/Baila Maria	1967	$8
❏ 903	Love Is a Season/You Comb Her Hair	1964	$10
❏ 892	Midnight Mary/Where Do You Want the World Delivered	1963	$15
❏ 914	Tears Keep Falling/Where Did the Summer Go	1964	$10

MGM

❏ 13421	I Love You/Leave Me Alone	1965	$8

RCA VICTOR

❏ 47-8119	Don't Envy Me/Me, Myself and I	1962	$12
❏ 47-9790	Hard to Be Without You/ You're in a Bad Way	1969	$5

— As "Joey Powers' Flower"

❏ 74-0326	Land of the Midnight Sun/ So Sing the Children on the Avenue	1970	$5

— As "Joey Powers' Flower

❏ 47-8039	Two Tickets and a Candy Heart/Jenny, Won't You Walk Up?	1962	$10

POWERS, JOHNNY
FORTUNE

Number	Title	Yr	NM
❏ 199	Honey Let's Go (To a Rock and Roll Show)/Your Love	1955	$200

SUN

❏ 327	With Your Love, With Your Kiss/Be Mine, All Mine	1959	$60

TRIODEX

❏ 103	A Teenage Prayer/A Young Boy's Heart	1960	$30

POWERS OF BLUE, THE
MTA

❏ 118	Cool Jerk/You Blow My Mind	1967	$8
❏ 113	Good Lovin'/(I Can't Get No) Satisfaction	1966	$10

POWERS, TINA
PARKWAY

❏ 847	Making Up Is Fun to Do/ Back to School	1962	$30

POWERSOURCE
POWERVISION

❏ 8603	Dear Mr. Jesus/Love, Sharon	1987	$30

POZO-SECO SINGERS, THE
DON WILLIAMS was in this group.

CERTRON

❏ 10006	Apartment #9/Comin' Apart	1970	$5
❏ 10033	Bringing It Down to Me/He's a Friend of Mine	1971	$5
❏ 10020	Strawberry Fields & Something/There's Never Been a Time	1970	$5

COLUMBIA

❏ 44690	Good Morning Today/ Remember Suzie	1968	$6
❏ 44598	Gotta Come Up with Something/The Renegade	1968	$6
❏ 45065	High on Life/Till You Hear Your Mama Call	1970	$6
❏ 44041	I Believed It All/Excuse Me Dear Martha	1967	$8
❏ 43784	I Can Make It With You/ Come a Little Bit Closer	1966	$8
❏ 43646	I'll Be Gone/It Ain't Worth the Lonely Road Back	1966	$8
❏ 44168	It's All Right/Morning Dew	1967	$8
❏ 44841	Leavin'/Creole Woman	1969	$6
❏ 43927	Look What You've Done/ Almost Persuaded	1966	$8
❏ 44263	Louisiana Man/Tomorrow Proper	1967	$8
❏ 44980	Morning Mama Memories/ The Proper Mrs. Brown	1969	$10

— As "Don Williams and Pozo Seco"; his first "solo" credit

❏ 43437	Time/Down the Road I Go	1965	$8
❏ 44979	Woman in Love/God Save the Children	1969	$6

— As "Susan Taylor and Pozo Seco

EDMARK

❏ 10017	Time/Down the Road I Go	1965	$30

PRADO, PEREZ
RCA VICTOR

❏ 47-5281	A La Billy May/Beautiful	1953	$15
❏ 47-7120	A Lo Loco/Kilindini Dance	1957	$10
❏ 47-5367	Anna/Silvana Mangano	1953	$15
❏ 47-7963	Arrividerci Roma/Moliendo Café	1961	$8
❏ 47-6990	Beautiful Margaret/Leyende Mexicana (Legend of Mexico)	1957	$12
❏ 47-6752	Bongo Bash/Donna	1956	$10
❏ 47-6960	Calypso Man/Cucara Cha Cha Cha	1957	$10
❏ 47-8356	Caravan/Papa Mi	1964	$8
❏ 47-4319	C'est Si Bon Mambo/In a Little Spanish Town Mambo	1951	$20
❏ 47-3873	Chattanoogie Shoe Shine Boy/More Mambo Jambo	1950	$20
❏ 47-5965	Cherry Pink and Apple Blossom White/Rhythm Sticks	1954	$15
❏ 47-7630	Clap Hands/Divina	1959	$8
❏ 47-6214	Crazy, Crazy/Monitor Mambo	1955	$12
❏ 47-3988	Cuban Mambo/Mambo del Papelero	1950	$20
❏ 47-6538	Cuban Rock/Hawaiian War Chant	1956	$15
❏ 47-3782	El Mambo/Mambo #5	1950	$30
❏ 47-7337	Guaglione/Paris	1958	$8
❏ 47-6776	Hawaiian Cha Cha Cha/ Mambo Japanese	1956	$12
❏ 47-8077	La Raggaza (The Girl)/Via Veneto	1962	$8
❏ 47-3917	Mambo #8/Babarabatiri	1950	$20
❏ 47-5892	Marilyn Monroe Mambo/ Steam Heat Mambo	1954	$30

Number	Title	Yr	NM
❏ 47-6085	Mood Indigo/Back Bay Shuffle (Mambo)	1955	$10
❏ 47-7768	Oh, Oh, Rosie/Rockambo Baby	1960	$8
❏ 47-3918	Pachito E-Che/Mambo #5	1950	$20
❏ 47-8006	Patricia Twist/Ti-Pi-Tin Twist	1962	$8
❏ 47-7245	Patricia/Why Wait	1958	$10
❏ 47-6684	Petticoats of Portugal/Bandido	1956	$10
❏ 47-6277	Pretty Doll/La Macarena	1955	$10
❏ 47-5839	Skokiaan/The High and the Mighty	1954	$15
❏ 47-5820	St. Louis Blues Mambo/Tomcat Mambo	1954	$15
❏ 47-5393	Suby/Jazz Me Blues	1953	$15
❏ 47-5738	Such a Night/Ballin' the Jack	1954	$15
❏ 47-4196	Syncopated Clock Mambo/Broadway Mambo	1951	$20
❏ 47-7873	Teresita La Chunga/Ritmo De Chunga	1961	$8
❏ 47-7456	The Millionaire/Catalania	1959	$8
❏ 47-6477	The Story of Love/Tomorrow I Will Live	1956	$10
❏ 47-7540	Tic Toc Polly Woc/My Roberta	1959	$8
❏ 47-6122	Whatever Lola Wants/Dilo (Mambo)	1955	$10

UNITED ARTISTS

Number	Title	Yr	NM
❏ 765	The Girl with the Green Eyes/Woman of Straw	1964	$8

7-Inch Extended Plays

RCA VICTOR

Number	Title	Yr	NM
❏ LPC-114 [PS]	Big Hits by Prado	1961	$15
❏ LPC-114	Cherry Pink and Apple Blossom White/Mambo No. 5//In a Little Spanish Town/Patricia	1961	$15

—Compact 33 Double"; small hole, plays at 33 1/3 rpm

Number	Title	Yr	NM
❏ EPA-5022	Cherry Pink and Apple Blossom White/St. Louis Blues Mambo//Mambo Jambo/Mambo No. 5	1958	$15
❏ EPA-732	Mambo Jambo/Mambo No. 5//Perdido/Mambo No. 8	1956	$15
❏ EPA-4322 [PS]	Patricia	1958	$15
❏ EPA-4322	Patricia/Mood Indigo//Pretty Doll/Whistling Rock	1958	$15
❏ EPA-5022 [PS]	Perez Prado (Gold Standard Series)	1958	$15
❏ EPA-732 [PS]	(title unknown)	1956	$15

PRAIRIE RAMBLERS, THE

COLUMBIA

Number	Title	Yr	NM
❏ 4-20800	I'll Be Back in a Year (Little Darlin')/Answer to I'll Be Back in a Year (Little Darlin')	1951	$50

MERCURY

Number	Title	Yr	NM
❏ 6283	Open Up That Door Hiram/Wrangler Boogie	1950	$50

—B-side by the Willis Brothers as "The Oklahoma Wranglers

PREACHERS, THE

MOONGLOW

Number	Title	Yr	NM
❏ 5006	Pain and Sorrow/Stay Out of My World	1965	$30
❏ 240	Who Do You Love/Chicken Poppa	1965	$30

PRECISIONS, THE (1)

ATCO

Number	Title	Yr	NM
❏ 6643	Don't Double (With Trouble)/Into My Life	1969	$15

DREW

Number	Title	Yr	NM
❏ 1003	If This Is Love (I'd Rather Be Lonely)/You'll Soon Be Gone	1967	$30
❏ 1004	Instant Heartbreak (Just Add Tears)/Dream Girl	1968	$20
❏ 1001	Such Misery/A Lover's Plea	1967	$30
❏ 1002	Why Girl/Sugar Ain't Sweet	1967	$2500

—VG 1000; VG+ 1750

Number	Title	Yr	NM
❏ 1002	Why Girl/What I Want	1967	$20

D-TOWN

Number	Title	Yr	NM
❏ 1055	Mexican Love Song/You're Sweet	1965	$30
❏ 1033	My Lover Come Back/I Wanna Tell My Baby	1965	$200

PRECISIONS, THE (2)

HIGHLAND

Number	Title	Yr	NM
❏ 300	Eight Reasons Why I Love You/(B-side unknown)	1962	$400

PREFAB SPROUT

EPIC

Number	Title	Yr	NM
❏ 05769	Appetite/When the Angels	1986	$3
❏ 07922	Cars and Girls/Vendetta	1988	$3
❏ 07922 [PS]	Cars and Girls/Vendetta	1988	$3
❏ 05464	When Love Breaks Down/The Yearning Loins	1985	$3
❏ 05464 [PS]	When Love Breaks Down/The Yearning Loins	1985	$3

PRELUDE

ISLAND

Number	Title	Yr	NM
❏ 002	After the Goldrush/Johnson Boy	1974	$6
❏ IXPI1 [DJ]	Christmas Message (same on both sides)	1974	$10
❏ 018	Fly/Lady from a Small Town	1975	$5

PYE

Number	Title	Yr	NM
❏ 71045	For a Dancer/Best of a Bad Time	1975	$5

PRELUDES FIVE, THE

PIK

Number	Title	Yr	NM
❏ 231	Starlight/Don't You Know Love?	1961	$30

PRELUDES, THE (1)

ARLISS

Number	Title	Yr	NM
❏ 1004	Lorraine/Oh Please, Genie	1961	$100

OCTAVIA

Number	Title	Yr	NM
❏ 8008	A Place for You (In My Heart)/That Would Be So Good	1962	$50

PRELUDES, THE (3)

EMPIRE

Number	Title	Yr	NM
❏ 103	Don't Fall in Love Too Soon/I Want Your Arms Around Me (All the Time)	1956	$125

PREMEERS, THE

HERALD

Number	Title	Yr	NM
❏ 577	Diary of Our Love/Gee Oh Gee	1963	$40

PREMICE, JOSEPHINE

GNP CRESCENDO

Number	Title	Yr	NM
❏ 117	Mommy, Give Me What You Give To Santa/The Little Christmas Tree	1956	$15

PREMIERS, THE (1)

FARO

Number	Title	Yr	NM
❏ 624	Come On and Dance/Get On the Plane	1966	$15
❏ 615	Farmer John/Duffy's Blues	1964	$40
❏ 621	Get Your Baby/Little Ways	1965	$15

WARNER BROS.

Number	Title	Yr	NM
❏ 5464	Annie Oakley/Blues for Arlene	1964	$15
❏ 5443	Farmer John/Duffy's Blues	1964	$20

PREMIERS, THE (2)

FURY

Number	Title	Yr	NM
❏ 1029	I Pray/Pigtails, Eyes Are Blue	1960	$50

RUST

Number	Title	Yr	NM
❏ 5032	Falling Star/She Gives Me Fever	1961	$125

PREMIERS, THE (3)

CINDY

Number	Title	Yr	NM
❏ 3008	China Doll/Life Is Grand	1958	$100

DIG

Number	Title	Yr	NM
❏ 113	My Darling/Have a Heart	1956	$250

FORTUNE

Number	Title	Yr	NM
❏ 527	When You Are in Love/The Trap of Love	1956	$100

GONE

Number	Title	Yr	NM
❏ 5009	Is It a Dream/Valerie	1957	$500

—With correct track on side 1

Number	Title	Yr	NM
❏ 5009	Is It a Dream/Valerie	1957	$200

—With "Let Me Share Your Dream" by The Deltas (Gone 5010) on Side 1 by mistake

PREMIERS, THE (4)

KING

Number	Title	Yr	NM
❏ 6061	She's Always There/I'm Better Off Now	1966	$30

STAX

Number	Title	Yr	NM
❏ 177	Make It Me/You Make a Strong Girl Weak	1965	$40

PREMIERS, THE (5)

MINK

Number	Title	Yr	NM
❏ 21	Tonight/I Think I Love You	1959	$125

PARKWAY

Number	Title	Yr	NM
❏ 807	Tonight/I Think I Love You	1959	$30

PREMIERS, THE (6)

NU-PHI

Number	Title	Yr	NM
❏ 367/8	Cruisin'/(B-side unknown)	1959	$40
❏ 701	Firewater/Younger Than You	1960	$40

PREMIERS, THE (U)

BOND

Number	Title	Yr	NM
❏ 5803/4	Hop and Skip/Uh-Huh	1958	$30

PRESENT, THE

PHILIPS

Number	Title	Yr	NM
❏ 40466	I Know/Many's the Slip Twixt the Cup and the Lip	1966	$40

PRESIDENTS, THE (1)

SUSSEX

Number	Title	Yr	NM
❏ 207	5-10-15-20 (25-30 Years of Love)/I'm Still Dancing	1970	$8

PRESIDENTS, THE (2)

DELUXE

Number	Title	Yr	NM
❏ 113	Gold Walk/I Want My Baby	1969	$8
❏ 134	Lover's Psalm/Our Meeting	1971	$6

—As "The President's Band"

Number	Title	Yr	NM
❏ 120	Snoopy/Stinky	1969	$8
❏ 127	Which Way/Peter Rabbit	1970	$8

PRESIDENTS, THE (3)

MERCURY

Number	Title	Yr	NM
❏ 72016	Pots 'n' Pans/The Toasts	1962	$30

PRESIDENTS, THE (U)

HOLLYWOOD

Number	Title	Yr	NM
❏ 1137	Shoeshine (Part 1)/Shoeshine (Part 2)	1968	$10

WARNER BROS.

Number	Title	Yr	NM
❏ 5240	Hot Toddy March/I Do Love You (Do I Love You)	1961	$20

PRESLEY, ELVIS

The King of Rock 'n' Roll, Elvis created the most coveted 45s known to collectors -- his first five singles originally released by Sun Records in Memphis. RCA later re-released the 45s under its label.

SUN RECORDS

Number	Title	Yr	NM
❏ 217	Baby Let's Play House/I'm Left, You're Right, She's Gone	1955	$3000
❏ 210	Good Rockin' Tonight/I Don't Care If the Sun Don't Shine	1954	$3500
❏ 223	I Forgot to Remember to Forget/Mystery Train	1955	$2500
❏ 215	Milkcow Blues Boogie/You're a Heartbreaker	1955	$5000
❏ 209	That's All Right/Blue Moon of Kentucky	1954	$10000

COLLECTABLES

Number	Title	Yr	NM
❏ COL-4508	A Big Hunk o'Love/My Wish Came True	1986	$3

—Black vinyl

Number	Title	Yr	NM
❏ COL-4502	Baby Let's Play House/I'm Left, You're Right, She's Gone	1986	$3

—Black vinyl

Number	Title	Yr	NM
❏ COL-4521	Big Boss Man/Paralyzed	1986	$3

—Black vinyl

Number	Title	Yr	NM
❏ COL-4513	Bossa Nova Baby/Such a Night	1986	$3

—Black vinyl

Number	Title	Yr	NM
❏ COL-4515	Follow That Dream/When My Blue Moon Turns to Gold Again	1986	$3

—Black vinyl

Number	Title	Yr	NM
❏ COL-4522	Fools Fall in Love/Blue Suede Shoes	1986	$3

—Black vinyl

Number	Title	Yr	NM
❏ COL-4516	Frankie and Johnny/Love Letters	1986	$3

—Black vinyl

Number	Title	Yr	NM
❏ COL-4500	Good Rockin' Tonight/I Don't Care If the Sun Don't Shine	1986	$3

—Black vinyl

Number	Title	Yr	NM
❏ COL-4520	How Great Thou Art/His Hand in Mine	1986	$3

—Black vinyl

Number	Title	Yr	NM
❏ COL-4510	I Feel So Bad/Wild in the Country	1986	$3

—Black vinyl

Number	Title	Yr	NM
❏ COL-4503	I Got a Woman/I'm Counting on You	1986	$3

—Black vinyl

Number	Title	Yr	NM
❏ COL-4504	I'll Never Let You Go (Little Darlin')/I'm Gonna Sit Right Down and Cry (Over You)	1986	$3

—Black vinyl

Number	Title	Yr	NM
COL-4514	Love Me/Flaming Star	1986	$3
—Black vinyl			
COL-4506	Money Honey/One-Sided Love Affair	1986	$3
—Black vinyl			
COL-4518	Old Shep/You'll Never Walk Alone	1986	$3
—Black vinyl			
COL-4512	One Broken Heart for Sale/Devil in Disguise	1986	$3
—Black vinyl			
COL-4519	Poor Boy/An American Trilogy	1986	$3
—Black vinyl			
COL-4511	She's Not You/Jailhouse Rock	1986	$3
—Black vinyl			
COL-4509	Stuck on You/Fame and Fortune	1986	$3
—Black vinyl			
COL-4564	The Elvis Medley/Always on My Mind	1986	$3
COL-4507	Too Much/Playing for Keeps	1986	$3
—Black vinyl			
COL-4505	Tryin' to Get to You/I Love You Because	1986	$3
—Black vinyl			

RCA

Number	Title	Yr	NM
PP-11301	15 Golden Records, 30 Golden Hits	1977	$70
—Includes 15 records (11099-11113) and outer box			
PP-11340	20 Golden Hits in Full Color Sleeves	1977	$100
—Includes 10 records (11099, 11100, 11102, 11104-11109, 11111) and outer box			
447-0626	A Big Hunk o'Love/My Wish Came True	1977	$4
447-0649	Ain't That Loving You Baby/Ask Me	1977	$4
447-0667	A Little Less Conversation/Almost in Love	1977	$4
PB-13888	All Shook Up/(Let Me Be Your) Teddy Bear	1984	$4
—From box "Elvis' Greatest Hits, Golden Singles, Volume 1"; gold vinyl			
PB-13888 [PS]	All Shook Up/(Let Me Be Your) Teddy Bear	1984	$4
PB-11106	All Shook Up/That's When Your Heartaches Begin	1977	$4
PB-11106 [PS]	All Shook Up/That's When Your Heartaches Begin	1977	$4
—From boxes "15 Golden Records, 30 Golden Hits" and "20 Golden Hits in Full Color Sleeves"			
447-0618	All Shook Up/That's When Your Heartaches Begin	1977	$4
PB-14090	Always on My Mind/My Boy	1985	$10
—Purple vinyl			
PB-14090 [PS]	Always on My Mind/My Boy	1985	$10
JK-14090 [DJ]	Always on My Mind (same on both sides)	1985	$30
—Purple vinyl; "Not for Sale" on label			
447-0685	An American Trilogy/Until It's Time for You to Go	1977	$4
PB-13895	Are You Lonesome Tonight/Can't Help Falling in Love	1984	$4
—From box "Elvis' Greatest Hits, Golden Singles, Volume 2"; gold vinyl			
PB-13895 [PS]	Are You Lonesome Tonight/Can't Help Falling in Love	1984	$4
PB-11104	Are You Lonesome To-Night?/I Gotta Know	1977	$4
PB-11104 [PS]	Are You Lonesome To-Night?/I Gotta Know	1977	$4
—From boxes "15 Golden Records, 30 Golden Hits" and "20 Golden Hits in Full Color Sleeves"			
447-0629	Are You Lonesome To-Night?/I Gotta Know	1977	$4
JB-11533 [DJ]	Are You Sincere/Solitaire	1979	$10
—Yellow label, dog near top, "Not for Sale" on label			
PB-11533	Are You Sincere/Solitaire	1979	$5
PB-11533 [PS]	Are You Sincere/Solitaire	1979	$10
PB-13875	Baby Let's Play House/Hound Dog	1984	$50
—Gold vinyl, custom label			
PB-13875 [PS]	Baby Let's Play House/Hound Dog	1984	$50
JB-13875 [DJ]	Baby Let's Play House/Hound Dog	1984	$200
—Gold vinyl, custom label			
447-0604	Baby Let's Play House/I'm Left, You're Right, She's Gone	1977	$4
447-0662	Big Boss Man/You Don't Know Me	1977	$4
447-0647	Blue Christmas/Santa Claus Is Back in Town	1977	$4
447-0647 [PS]	Blue Christmas/Santa Claus Is Back in Town	1977	$10
—Does not mention "Gold Standard Series" on sleeve			
447-0613	Blue Moon/Just Because	1977	$4

Number	Title	Yr	NM
PB-13929	Blue Suede Shoes/Promised Land	1984	$20
—Blue vinyl; incorrect label -- "Blue Suede Shoes" side says "Stereo" and "Promised Land" side says "Mono"			
PB-13929	Blue Suede Shoes/Promised Land	1984	$15
—Blue vinyl; correct label -- "Blue Suede Shoes" side says "Mono" and "Promised Land" side says "Stereo"			
PB-13929 [PS]	Blue Suede Shoes/Promised Land	1984	$10
JK-13929 [DJ]	Blue Suede Shoes (same on both sides)	1984	$30
—Blue vinyl promo, "Not for Sale" on label			
PB-11107	Blue Suede Shoes/Tutti Frutti	1977	$4
PB-11107 [PS]	Blue Suede Shoes/Tutti Frutti	1977	$4
—From boxes "15 Golden Records, 30 Golden Hits" and "20 Golden Hits in Full Color Sleeves"			
447-0609	Blue Suede Shoes/Tutti Frutti	1977	$4
PB-13885	Blue Suede Shoes/Tutti Frutti	1984	$4
—From box "Elvis' Greatest Hits, Golden Singles, Volume 1"; gold vinyl			
PB-13885 [PS]	Blue Suede Shoes/Tutti Frutti	1984	$4
447-0642	Bossa Nova Baby/Witchcraft	1977	$4
PB-11102	Can't Help Falling in Love/Rock-a-Hula Baby	1977	$4
PB-11102 [PS]	Can't Help Falling in Love/Rock-a-Hula Baby	1977	$4
—From boxes "15 Golden Records, 30 Golden Hits" and "20 Golden Hits in Full Color Sleeves"			
447-0635	Can't Help Falling in Love/Rock-a-Hula Baby	1977	$4
447-0672	Clean Up Your Own Back Yard/The Fair Is Moving On	1977	$4
PB-11113	Crying in the Chapel/I Believe in the Man in the Sky	1977	$4
PB-11113 [PS]	Crying in the Chapel/I Believe in the Man in the Sky	1977	$4
—From box "15 Golden Records, 30 Golden Hits"			
447-0643	Crying in the Chapel/I Believe in the Man in the Sky	1977	$4
PB-13886	Don't Be Cruel/Hound Dog	1984	$4
—From box "Elvis' Greatest Hits, Golden Singles, Volume 1"; gold vinyl			
PB-13886 [PS]	Don't Be Cruel/Hound Dog	1984	$4
447-0674	Don't Cry Daddy/Rubberneckin'	1977	$4
447-0621	Don't/I Beg of You	1977	$4
447-0648	Do the Clam/You'll Be Gone	1977	$4
PB-13897	Elvis' Greatest Hits, Golden Singles, Volume 1	1984	$20
—Box set of six 45s with sleeves (13885-13890) with box			
PB-13898	Elvis' Greatest Hits, Golden Singles, Volume 2	1984	$20
—Box set of six 45s with sleeves (13891-13896) with box			
447-0656	Frankie and Johnny/Please Don't Stop Loving Me	1977	$4
447-0636	Good Luck Charm/Anything That's Part of You	1977	$4
447-0602	Good Rockin' Tonight/I Don't Care If the Sun Don't Shine	1977	$4
PB-12158	Guitar Man/Faded Love	1981	$5
PB-12158 [PS]	Guitar Man/Faded Love	1981	$10
447-0663	Guitar Man/High Heel Sneakers	1977	$4
JH-12158 [DJ]	Guitar Man (mono/stereo)	1981	$300
—Promo only on red vinyl			
JH-12158 [DJ]	Guitar Man (mono/stereo)	1981	$20
—Promo only on black vinyl			
447-0623	Hard Headed Woman/Don't Ask Me Why	1977	$4
8760-7 [DJ]	Heartbreak Hotel/Heartbreak Hotel	1988	$30
—B-side by "David Keith & Charlie Schlatter with Zulu Time"; white label promo, "Not for Sale" on label			
8760-7-R	Heartbreak Hotel/Heartbreak Hotel	1988	$5
—B-side by "David Keith & Charlie Schlatter with Zulu Time			
8760-7-R [PS]	Heartbreak Hotel/Heartbreak Hotel	1988	$6
—Stock version with pink Cadillac pictured			
8760-7 [PS]	Heartbreak Hotel/Heartbreak Hotel	1988	$100
—Promo-only sleeve with "The Infamous Butch Waugh as Elvis Presley"			
PB-11105	Heartbreak Hotel/I Was the One	1977	$4
PB-11105 [PS]	Heartbreak Hotel/I Was the One	1977	$4
—From boxes "15 Golden Records, 30 Golden Hits" and "20 Golden Hits in Full Color Sleeves"			
447-0605	Heartbreak Hotel/I Was the One	1977	$4

Number	Title	Yr	NM
PB-13892	Heartbreak Hotel/Jailhouse Rock	1984	$4
—From box "Elvis' Greatest Hits, Golden Singles, Volume 2"; gold vinyl			
PB-13892 [PS]	Heartbreak Hotel/Jailhouse Rock	1984	$4
PB-11099	Hound Dog/Don't Be Cruel	1977	$4
PB-11099 [PS]	Hound Dog/Don't Be Cruel	1977	$4
—From boxes "15 Golden Records, 30 Golden Hits" and "20 Golden Hits in Full Color Sleeves"			
447-0608	Hound Dog/Don't Be Cruel	1977	$4
447-0670	How Great Thou Art/His Hand in Mine	1977	$4
PB-10601	Hurt/For the Heart	1976	$125
—Second pressings (very rare) on the 1976-88 "dog near top" black label			
447-0631	I Feel So Bad/Wild in the Country	1977	$4
447-0681	If Every Day Was Like Christmas/How Would You Like to Be	1977	$4
447-0668	If I Can Dream/Edge of Reality	1977	$4
447-0600	I Forgot to Remember to Forget/Mystery Train	1977	$4
—Note: All RCA releases with a "447" prefix are from the Gold Standard Series and are black label, dog near top			
447-0683	I'm Leavin'/Heart of Rome	1977	$4
447-0654	I'm Yours/(It's a) Long, Lonely Highway	1977	$4
447-0659	Indescribably Blue/Fools Fall in Love	1977	$4
PB-11100	In the Ghetto/Any Day Now	1977	$4
PB-11100 [PS]	In the Ghetto/Any Day Now	1977	$4
—From boxes "15 Golden Records, 30 Golden Hits" and "20 Golden Hits in Full Color Sleeves"			
447-0671	In the Ghetto/Any Day Now	1977	$4
PB-13890	In the Ghetto/If I Can Dream	1984	$4
—From box "Elvis' Greatest Hits, Golden Singles, Volume 1"; gold vinyl			
PB-13890 [PS]	In the Ghetto/If I Can Dream	1984	$4
447-0679	I Really Don't Want to Know/There Goes My Everything	1977	$4
PB-11110	It's Now or Never/A Mess of Blues	1977	$4
PB-11110 [PS]	It's Now or Never/A Mess of Blues	1977	$4
—From box "15 Golden Records, 30 Golden Hits"			
447-0628	It's Now or Never/A Mess of Blues	1977	$4
PB-13889	It's Now or Never/Surrender	1984	$4
—From box "Elvis' Greatest Hits, Golden Singles, Volume 1"; gold vinyl			
PB-13889 [PS]	It's Now or Never/Surrender	1984	$4
447-0684	It's Only Love/The Sound of Your Cry	1977	$4
447-0677	I've Lost You/The Next Step Is Love	1977	$4
PB-13887	I Want You, I Need You, I Love You/Love Me	1984	$4
—From box "Elvis' Greatest Hits, Golden Singles, Volume 1"; gold vinyl			
PB-13887 [PS]	I Want You, I Need You, I Love You/Love Me	1984	$4
447-0607	I Want You, I Need You, I Love You/My Baby Left Me	1977	$4
PB-13500	I Was the One/Wear My Ring Around Your Neck	1983	$5
PB-13500 [PS]	I Was the One/Wear My Ring Around Your Neck	1983	$10
JB-13500 [DJ]	I Was the One/Wear My Ring Around Your Neck	1983	$300
—Promo only on gold vinyl			
JB-13500 [DJ]	I Was the One/Wear My Ring Around Your Neck	1983	$20
—Promo only on black vinyl, "Not for Sale" on label			
447-0615	Lawdy Miss Clawdy/Shake, Rattle, and Roll	1977	$4
JH-10951 [DJ]	Let Me Be There (mono/stereo)	1977	$200
—Promo only			
PB-11109	(Let Me Be Your) Teddy Bear/Loving You	1977	$4
PB-11109 [PS]	(Let Me Be Your) Teddy Bear/Loving You	1977	$4
—From boxes "15 Golden Records, 30 Golden Hits" and "20 Golden Hits in Full Color Sleeves"			
447-0620	(Let Me Be Your) Teddy Bear/Loving You	1977	$4
JH-11320 [DJ]	(Let Me Be Your) Teddy Bear/Puppet on a String	1978	$20
—Light yellow label promo, "Not for Sale" on label			
PB-11320	(Let Me Be Your) Teddy Bear/Puppet on a String	1978	$5
PB-11320 [PS]	(Let Me Be Your) Teddy Bear/Puppet on a String	1978	$12
447-0666	Let Yourself Go/Your Time Hasn't Come Yet, Baby	1977	$4
447-0682	Life/Only Believe	1977	$4
PB-13547	Little Sister/Paralyzed	1983	$5
PB-13547 [PS]	Little Sister/Paralyzed	1983	$10
JB-13547 [DJ]	Little Sister/Paralyzed	1983	$300
—Promo only on blue vinyl			
JB-13547 [DJ]	Little Sister/Paralyzed	1983	$20

Number	Title	Yr	NM
—Promo only, black vinyl, "Not for Sale" on label			
❏ 447-0657	Love Letters/Come What May	1977	$4
❏ PB-11108	Love Me Tender/Any Way You Want Me (That's How I Will Be)	1977	$4
❏ PB-11108 [PS]	Love Me Tender/Any Way You Want Me (That's How I Will Be)	1977	$4
—From boxes "15 Golden Records, 30 Golden Hits" and "20 Golden Hits in Full Color Sleeves			
❏ 447-0616	Love Me Tender/Anyway You Want Me (That's How I Will Be)	1977	$4
❏ PB-13893	Love Me Tender/Loving You	1984	$4
—From box "Elvis' Greatest Hits, Golden Singles, Volume 2"; gold vinyl			
❏ PB-13893 [PS]	Love Me Tender/Loving You	1984	$4
❏ PB-12205	Lovin' Arms/You Asked Me To	1981	$6
—Not issued with picture sleeve (bootlegs exist)			
❏ JB-12205 [DJ]	Lovin' Arms/You Asked Me To	1981	$300
—Yellow label promo, "Not for Sale" on label, green vinyl			
❏ JB-12205 [DJ]	Lovin' Arms/You Asked Me To	1981	$20
—Yellow label promo, "Not for Sale" on label, black vinyl			
❏ 447-0634	(Marie's the Name) His Latest Flame/Little Sister	1977	$4
❏ PB-13894	(Marie's the Name) His Latest Flame/Little Sister	1984	$4
—From box "Elvis' Greatest Hits, Golden Singles, Volume 2"; gold vinyl			
❏ PB-13894 [PS]	(Marie's the Name) His Latest Flame/Little Sister	1984	$4
❏ 447-0669	Memories/Charro	1977	$4
❏ PB-14237	Merry Christmas Baby/Santa Claus Is Back in Town	1985	$20
—Elvis 50th Anniversary" label			
❏ PB-14237	Merry Christmas Baby/Santa Claus Is Back in Town	1985	$5
—Normal black RCA label			
❏ PB-14237 [PS]	Merry Christmas Baby/Santa Claus Is Back in Town	1985	$15
❏ PB-14237	Merry Christmas Baby/Santa Claus Is Back in Town	1985	$20
—Green vinyl			
❏ 447-0603	Milkcow Blues Boogie/You're a Heartbreaker	1977	$4
❏ 447-0614	Money Honey/One-Sided Love Affair	1977	$4
❏ GB-11326	Moody Blue/For the Heart	1978	$4
—Gold Standard Series			
❏ JB-10857 [DJ]	Moody Blue/She Thinks I Still Care	1976	$20
—Light yellow label promo, "Not for Sale" on label			
❏ PB-10857	Moody Blue/She Thinks I Still Care	1976	$5
❏ PB-10857 [PS]	Moody Blue/She Thinks I Still Care	1976	$10
❏ JB-10857 [DJ]	Moody Blue/She Thinks I Still Care	1976	$1000
—Colored vinyl pressings exist in five different colors -- red, white, gold, blue, green. Value is for any of them.			
❏ GB-10489	My Boy/Thinking About You	1977	$4
—Gold Standard Series; black label			
❏ JH-11165 [DJ]	My Way/America	1977	$30
—Light yellow label promo, "Not for Sale" on label			
❏ PB-11165	My Way/America	1977	$5
❏ PB-11165 [PS]	My Way/America	1977	$10
❏ PB-11165	My Way/America the Beautiful	1977	$30
❏ PB-11165 [PS]	My Way/America the Beautiful	1977	$30
❏ 447-0640	One Broken Heart for Sale/They Remind Me Too Much of You	1977	$4
❏ PB-11112	One Night/I Got Stung	1977	$4
❏ PB-11112 [PS]	One Night/I Got Stung	1977	$4
—From box "15 Golden Records, 30 Golden Hits			
❏ 447-0624	One Night/I Got Stung	1977	$4
❏ GB-10488	Promised Land/It's Midnight	1977	$4
—Gold Standard Series; black label			
❏ 447-0650	Puppet on a String/Wooden Heart	1977	$4
❏ GB-10486	Separate Ways/Always on My Mind	1977	$4
—Gold Standard Series; black label			
❏ 447-0637	She's Not You/Just Tell Her Jim Said Hello	1977	$4
❏ 447-0658	Spinout/All That I Am	1977	$4
❏ 447-0627	Stuck on You/Fame and Fortune	1977	$4
❏ 447-0653	(Such An) Easy Question/It Feels So Right	1977	$4
❏ 447-0645	Such a Night/Never Ending	1977	$4
❏ 447-0630	Surrender/Lonely Man	1977	$4
❏ PB-13896	Suspicious Minds/Burning Love	1984	$4
—From box "Elvis' Greatest Hits, Golden Singles, Volume 2"; gold vinyl			
❏ PB-13896 [PS]	Suspicious Minds/Burning Love	1984	$4

Number	Title	Yr	NM
❏ PB-11103	Suspicious Minds/You'll Think of Me	1977	$4
❏ PB-11103 [PS]	Suspicious Minds/You'll Think of Me	1977	$4
—From box "15 Golden Records, 30 Golden Hits			
❏ 447-0673	Suspicious Minds/You'll Think of Me	1977	$4
❏ GB-13275	Suspicious Minds/You'll Think of Me	1982	$4
—Gold Standard Series			
❏ GB-10485	Take Good Care of Her/I've Got a Thing About You, Baby	1977	$4
—Gold Standard Series; black label			
❏ 447-0655	Tell Me Why/Blue River	1977	$4
❏ 447-0601	That's All Right/Blue Moon of Kentucky	1977	$4
❏ PB-13891	That's All Right/Blue Moon of Kentucky	1984	$4
—From box "Elvis' Greatest Hits, Golden Singles, Volume 2"; gold vinyl			
❏ PB-13891 [PS]	That's All Right/Blue Moon of Kentucky	1984	$4
❏ PB-13351	The Elvis Medley/Always on My Mind	1982	$5
❏ PB-13351 [PS]	The Elvis Medley/Always on My Mind	1982	$10
❏ JB-13351 [DJ]	The Elvis Medley (Long Version)/The Elvis Medley (Short Version)	1982	$300
—Promo only on gold vinyl			
❏ JB-13351 [DJ]	The Elvis Medley (Long Version)/The Elvis Medley (Short Version)	1982	$20
—Promo only on black vinyl			
❏ JH-13302	The Impossible Dream (The Quest)/An American Trilogy	1982	$125
❏ JH-13302 [PS]	The Impossible Dream (The Quest)/An American Trilogy	1982	$125
—Promo only, distributed to visitors to Elvis' birthplace in Tupelo, Mississippi, in 1982.			
❏ JB-13058 [DJ]	There Goes My Everything/You'll Never Walk Alone	1982	$20
—Light yellow label promo, "Not for Sale" on label			
❏ PB-13058	There Goes My Everything/You'll Never Walk Alone	1982	$5
❏ PB-13058 [PS]	There Goes My Everything/You'll Never Walk Alone	1982	$10
❏ JB-11679 [DJ]	There's a Honky Tonk Angel (Who Will Take Me Back In)/I Got a Feelin' in My Body	1979	$15
—Light yellow label promo, "Not for Sale" on label			
❏ PB-11679 [PS]	There's a Honky Tonk Angel (Who Will Take Me Back In)/I Got a Feelin' in My Body	1979	$10
❏ PB-11679	There's a Honky Tonk Angel (Who Will Take Me Back In)/I Got a Feelin' in My Body	1979	$20
—Has full production credits (background vocals, strings) listed in error on both sides			
❏ PB-11679	There's a Honky Tonk Angel (Who Will Take Me Back In)/I Got a Feelin' in My Body	1979	$5
—Has production credits removed; only producers are listed			
❏ 447-0661	There's Always Me/Judy	1977	$4
❏ 447-0676	The Wonder of You/Mama Liked the Roses	1977	$4
❏ 447-0617	Too Much/Playing for Keeps	1977	$4
❏ GB-10487	T-R-O-U-B-L-E/Mr. Songman	1977	$4
—Gold Standard Series; black label			
❏ GB-11504	Way Down/My Way	1979	$4
—Gold Standard Series			
❏ JB-10998 [DJ]	Way Down/Pledging My Love	1977	$30
—Light yellow label promo, "Not for Sale" on label			
❏ JB-10998 [DJ]	Way Down/Pledging My Love	1977	$120
—White label promo, "Elvis Presley" is twice as large as the song titles			
❏ PB-10998	Way Down/Pledging My Love	1977	$5
❏ PB-10998 [PS]	Way Down/Pledging My Love	1977	$10
❏ 447-0622	Wear My Ring Around Your Neck/Don'tcha Think It's Time	1977	$4
❏ 447-0680	Where Did They Go, Lord/Rags to Riches	1977	$4
RCA VICTOR			
❏ 47-7600	A Big Hunk o'Love/My Wish Came True	1959	$30
❏ 47-7600 [PS]	A Big Hunk o'Love/My Wish Came True	1959	$75
❏ 447-0626	A Big Hunk o'Love/My Wish Came True	1962	$20
—Black label, dog on top			
❏ 447-0626	A Big Hunk o'Love/My Wish Came True	1965	$10
—Black label, dog on left			
❏ 447-0626	A Big Hunk o'Love/My Wish Came True	1969	$30
—Orange label			

Number	Title	Yr	NM
❏ 447-0626	A Big Hunk o'Love/My Wish Came True	1970	$8
—Red label			
❏ 47-8440 [DJ]	Ain't That Loving You Baby/Ask Me	1964	$70
—White label promo			
❏ 47-8440	Ain't That Loving You Baby/Ask Me	1964	$10
❏ 47-8440 [PS]	Ain't That Loving You Baby/Ask Me	1964	$30
—Coming Soon" on sleeve			
❏ 47-8440 [PS]	Ain't That Loving You Baby/Ask Me	1964	$30
—Ask For" on sleeve			
❏ 447-0649	Ain't That Loving You Baby/Ask Me	1965	$10
—Black label, dog on left			
❏ 447-0649	Ain't That Loving You Baby/Ask Me	1970	$8
—Red label			
❏ 47-9610 [DJ]	A Little Less Conversation/Almost in Love	1968	$50
—Yellow label promo, "Not for Sale" on label			
❏ 47-9610	A Little Less Conversation/Almost in Love	1968	$10
❏ 47-9610 [PS]	A Little Less Conversation/Almost in Love	1968	$30
❏ 447-0667	A Little Less Conversation/Almost in Love	1970	$8
❏ 47-6870	All Shook Up/That's When Your Heartaches Begin	1957	$40
—No horizontal line on label			
❏ 47-6870	All Shook Up/That's When Your Heartaches Begin	1957	$40
—With horizontal line on label			
❏ 47-6870 [PS]	All Shook Up/That's When Your Heartaches Begin	1957	$100
❏ 447-0618	All Shook Up/That's When Your Heartaches Begin	1959	$20
—Black label, dog on top			
❏ 447-0618 [DJ]	All Shook Up/That's When Your Heartaches Begin	1964	$125
❏ 447-0618 [PS]	All Shook Up/That's When Your Heartaches Begin	1964	$200
❏ 447-0618	All Shook Up/That's When Your Heartaches Begin	1965	$10
—Black label, dog on left			
❏ 447-0618	All Shook Up/That's When Your Heartaches Begin	1969	$30
—Orange label			
❏ 447-0618	All Shook Up/That's When Your Heartaches Begin	1970	$8
—Red label			
❏ 74-0672 [DJ]	An American Trilogy/The First Time Ever I Saw Your Face	1972	$30
—Yellow label promo, "Not for Sale" on label			
❏ 74-0672	An American Trilogy/The First Time Ever I Saw Your Face	1972	$30
❏ 74-0672 [PS]	An American Trilogy/The First Time Ever I Saw Your Face	1972	$50
❏ 447-0685	An American Trilogy/Until It's Time for You to Go	1973	$8
❏ 61-7810 [S]	Are You Lonesome To-Night?/I Gotta Know	1960	$600
—Living Stereo" (large hole, plays at 45 rpm)			
❏ 47-7810	Are You Lonesome To-Night?/I Gotta Know	1960	$30
❏ 47-7810 [PS]	Are You Lonesome To-Night?/I Gotta Know	1960	$70
❏ 447-0629	Are You Lonesome To-Night?/I Gotta Know	1962	$20
—Black label, dog on top			
❏ 447-0629	Are You Lonesome To-Night?/I Gotta Know	1965	$10
—Black label, dog on left			
❏ 447-0629	Are You Lonesome To-Night?/I Gotta Know	1969	$30
—Orange label			
❏ 447-0629	Are You Lonesome To-Night?/I Gotta Know	1970	$8
—Red label			
❏ 47-6383	Baby Let's Play House/I'm Left, You're Right, She's Gone	1955	$70
—With horizontal line on label			
❏ 47-6383	Baby Let's Play House/I'm Left, You're Right, She's Gone	1955	$70
—No horizontal line on label			
❏ 447-0604	Baby Let's Play House/I'm Left, You're Right, She's Gone	1959	$20
—Black label, dog on top			
❏ 447-0604	Baby Let's Play House/I'm Left, You're Right, She's Gone	1965	$12
—Black label, dog on left			

Number	Title	Yr	NM
❑ 447-0604	Baby Let's Play House/I'm Left, You're Right, She's Gone	1970	$8
—Red label			
❑ 47-9341 [DJ]	Big Boss Man/You Don't Know Me	1967	$50
—White label promo, "Not for Sale" on label			
❑ 47-9341	Big Boss Man/You Don't Know Me	1967	$12
❑ 47-9341 [PS]	Big Boss Man/You Don't Know Me	1967	$30
❑ 447-0662	Big Boss Man/You Don't Know Me	1970	$12
❑ HO7W-0808 [DJ]	Blue Christmas (same on both sides)	1957	$1500
❑ 447-0647 [DJ]	Blue Christmas/Santa Claus Is Back in Town	1965	$50
—White label promo, "Not for Sale" on label			
❑ 447-0647	Blue Christmas/Santa Claus Is Back in Town	1965	$15
—Black label, dog on side			
❑ 447-0647 [PS]	Blue Christmas/Santa Claus Is Back in Town	1965	$40
—Has "Gold Standard Series" on sleeve			
❑ 447-0647	Blue Christmas/Santa Claus Is Back in Town	1969	$30
—Orange label			
❑ 447-0647	Blue Christmas/Santa Claus Is Back in Town	1970	$8
—Red label			
❑ 447-0720 [DJ]	Blue Christmas/Wooden Heart	1964	$50
—White label promo, "Not for Sale" on label			
❑ 447-0720	Blue Christmas/Wooden Heart	1964	$20
❑ 447-0720 [PS]	Blue Christmas/Wooden Heart	1964	$70
❑ 47-6640	Blue Moon/Just Because	1956	$70
—No horizontal line on label			
❑ 47-6640	Blue Moon/Just Because	1956	$70
—With horizontal line on label			
❑ 447-0613	Blue Moon/Just Because	1959	$20
—Black label, dog on top			
❑ 447-0613	Blue Moon/Just Because	1965	$10
—Black label, dog on left			
❑ 447-0613	Blue Moon/Just Because	1969	$30
—Orange label			
❑ 447-0613	Blue Moon/Just Because	1970	$8
—Red label			
❑ 47-6636	Blue Suede Shoes/Tutti Frutti	1956	$100
—No horizontal line on label			
❑ 47-6636	Blue Suede Shoes/Tutti Frutti	1956	$100
—With horizontal line on label			
❑ 447-0609	Blue Suede Shoes/Tutti Frutti	1959	$20
—Black label, dog on top			
❑ 447-0609	Blue Suede Shoes/Tutti Frutti	1965	$10
—Black label, dog on left			
❑ 447-0609	Blue Suede Shoes/Tutti Frutti	1969	$30
—Orange label			
❑ 447-0609	Blue Suede Shoes/Tutti Frutti	1970	$8
—Red label			
❑ 47-8243	Bossa Nova Baby/Witchcraft	1963	$15
❑ 47-8243 [PS]	Bossa Nova Baby/Witchcraft	1963	$40
—Coming Soon" on sleeve			
❑ 47-8243 [PS]	Bossa Nova Baby/Witchcraft	1963	$40
—Ask For" on sleeve			
❑ 47-8243 [PS]	Bossa Nova Baby/Witchcraft	1963	$40
—No reference to another album on sleeve			
❑ 447-0642	Bossa Nova Baby/Witchcraft	1964	$30
—Black label, dog on top			
❑ 447-0642	Bossa Nova Baby/Witchcraft	1965	$10
—Black label, dog on left			
❑ 447-0642	Bossa Nova Baby/Witchcraft	1969	$30
—Orange label			
❑ 447-0642	Bossa Nova Baby/Witchcraft	1970	$8
—Red label			
❑ JA-10401 [DJ]	Bringing It Back/Pieces of My Life	1975	$30
—Yellow label promo; both sides are mono			
❑ PB-10401	Bringing It Back/Pieces of My Life	1975	$200
—Orange label			
❑ PB-10401	Bringing It Back/Pieces of My Life	1975	$5
—Tan label			
❑ PB-10401 [PS]	Bringing It Back/Pieces of My Life	1975	$10
❑ 74-0769 [DJ]	Burning Love/It's a Matter of Time	1972	$30
—Yellow label promo, "Not for Sale" on label			
❑ 74-0769	Burning Love/It's a Matter of Time	1972	$6
—Originals have orange labels			
❑ 74-0769 [PS]	Burning Love/It's a Matter of Time	1972	$20
❑ 74-0769	Burning Love/It's a Matter of Time	1974	$200
—Very rare reissues have gray labels			
❑ GB-10156	Burning Love/Steamroller Blues	1975	$8
—Gold Standard Series; red label			
❑ GB-10156	Burning Love/Steamroller Blues	1977	$4
—Gold Standard Series; black label			
❑ 47-7968	Can't Help Falling in Love/ Rock-a-Hula Baby	1961	$30
❑ 47-7968 [PS]	Can't Help Falling in Love/ Rock-a-Hula Baby	1961	$50
❑ 37-7968	Can't Help Falling in Love/ Rock-a-Hula Baby	1961	$2000
—Compact Single 33" (small hole, plays at LP speed). VG 1000; VG+ 1500			
❑ 37-7968 [PS]	Can't Help Falling in Love/ Rock-a-Hula Baby	1961	$4000
—Special picture sleeve for above record. VG 2000; VG+ 3000			
❑ 447-0635	Can't Help Falling in Love/ Rock-a-Hula Baby	1962	$15
—Black label, dog on top			
❑ 447-0635	Can't Help Falling in Love/ Rock-a-Hula Baby	1965	$10
—Black label, dog on left			
❑ 447-0635	Can't Help Falling in Love/ Rock-a-Hula Baby	1969	$30
—Orange label			
❑ 447-0635	Can't Help Falling in Love/ Rock-a-Hula Baby	1970	$8
—Red label			
❑ 47-9747 [DJ]	Clean Up Your Own Back Yard/The Fair Is Moving On	1969	$40
—Yellow label promo, "Not for Sale" on label			
❑ 47-9747	Clean Up Your Own Back Yard/The Fair Is Moving On	1969	$8
❑ 47-9747 [PS]	Clean Up Your Own Back Yard/The Fair Is Moving On	1969	$30
❑ 447-0672	Clean Up Your Own Back Yard/The Fair Is Moving On	1970	$8
❑ 447-0643 [DJ]	Crying in the Chapel/I Believe in the Man in the Sky	1965	$40
—White label promo, "Not for Sale" on label			
❑ 447-0643	Crying in the Chapel/I Believe in the Man in the Sky	1965	$12
—Black label, dog on left			
❑ 447-0643 [PS]	Crying in the Chapel/I Believe in the Man in the Sky	1965	$40
❑ 447-0643	Crying in the Chapel/I Believe in the Man in the Sky	1970	$8
—Red label			
❑ 47-6604	Don't Be Cruel/Hound Dog	1956	$40
—No horizontal line on label			
❑ 47-6604	Don't Be Cruel/Hound Dog	1956	$40
—With horizontal line on label			
❑ 47-6604 [PS]	Don't Be Cruel/Hound Dog	1956	$200
—Don't Be Cruel" listed on top of "Hound Dog!			
❑ 47-6604 [PS]	Don't Be Cruel/Hound Dog	1956	$120
—Hound Dog!" listed on top of "Don't Be Cruel			
❑ 47-9768 [DJ]	Don't Cry Daddy/ Rubberneckin'	1969	$40
—Yellow label promo, "Not for Sale" on label			
❑ 47-9768	Don't Cry Daddy/ Rubberneckin'	1969	$8
❑ 47-9768 [PS]	Don't Cry Daddy/ Rubberneckin'	1969	$20
❑ 447-0674	Don't Cry Daddy/ Rubberneckin'	1970	$8
❑ 47-7150	Don't/I Beg of You	1958	$30
—No horizontal line on label			
❑ 47-7150	Don't/I Beg of You	1958	$30
—With horizontal line on label			
❑ 47-7150 [PS]	Don't/I Beg of You	1958	$100
❑ 447-0621	Don't/I Beg of You	1961	$15
—Black label, dog on top			
❑ 447-0621	Don't/I Beg of You	1965	$12
—Black label, dog on left			
❑ 447-0621	Don't/I Beg of You	1969	$30
—Orange label			
❑ 447-0621	Don't/I Beg of You	1970	$8
—Red label			
❑ SP-45-76 [DJ]	Don't/Wear My Ring Around Your Neck	1960	$800
❑ SP-45-76 [PS]	Don't/Wear My Ring Around Your Neck	1960	$2000
—VG 1000; VG+ 1500			
❑ 47-8500 [DJ]	Do the Clam/You'll Be Gone	1965	$60
—White label promo, "Not for Sale" on label			
❑ 47-8500	Do the Clam/You'll Be Gone	1965	$12
❑ 47-8500 [PS]	Do the Clam/You'll Be Gone	1965	$30
❑ 447-0648	Do the Clam/You'll Be Gone	1965	$12
—Black label, dog on left			
❑ 447-0648	Do the Clam/You'll Be Gone	1970	$12
—Red label			
❑ 47-8780 [DJ]	Frankie and Johnny/Please Don't Stop Loving Me	1966	$60
—White label promo, "Not for Sale" on label			
❑ 47-8780	Frankie and Johnny/Please Don't Stop Loving Me	1966	$10
❑ 47-8780 [PS]	Frankie and Johnny/Please Don't Stop Loving Me	1966	$30
❑ 447-0656	Frankie and Johnny/Please Don't Stop Loving Me	1968	$10
—Black label, dog on left			
❑ 447-0656	Frankie and Johnny/Please Don't Stop Loving Me	1969	$30
—Orange label			
❑ 447-0656	Frankie and Johnny/Please Don't Stop Loving Me	1970	$8
—Red label			
❑ 47-7992	Good Luck Charm/Anything That's Part of You	1962	$30
❑ 47-7992 [PS]	Good Luck Charm/Anything That's Part of You	1962	$50
—Titles in blue and pink letters			
❑ 47-7992 [PS]	Good Luck Charm/Anything That's Part of You	1962	$50
—Titles in rust and lavender letters			
❑ 37-7992	Good Luck Charm/Anything That's Part of You	1962	$2500
—Compact Single 33" (small hole, plays at LP speed). VG 1250; VG+ 1875			
❑ 37-7992 [PS]	Good Luck Charm/Anything That's Part of You	1962	$5000
—Special picture sleeve for above record. VG 2500; VG+ 3750			
❑ 447-0636	Good Luck Charm/Anything That's Part of You	1962	$15
—Black label, dog on top			
❑ 447-0636	Good Luck Charm/Anything That's Part of You	1965	$10
—Black label, dog on left			
❑ 447-0636	Good Luck Charm/Anything That's Part of You	1969	$30
—Orange label			
❑ 447-0636	Good Luck Charm/Anything That's Part of You	1970	$8
—Red label			
❑ 47-6381	Good Rockin' Tonight/I Don't Care If the Sun Don't Shine	1955	$70
—With horizontal line on label			
❑ 47-6381	Good Rockin' Tonight/I Don't Care If the Sun Don't Shine	1955	$70
—No horizontal line on label			
❑ 447-0602	Good Rockin' Tonight/I Don't Care If the Sun Don't Shine	1959	$20
—Black label, dog on top			
❑ 447-0602	Good Rockin' Tonight/I Don't Care If the Sun Don't Shine	1959	$6000
—One-of-a-kind red vinyl pressing. VG 2000; VG+ 4000			
❑ 447-0602 [PS]	Good Rockin' Tonight/I Don't Care If the Sun Don't Shine	1964	$200
❑ 447-0602 [DJ]	Good Rockin' Tonight/I Don't Care If the Sun Don't Shine	1964	$125
❑ 447-0602	Good Rockin' Tonight/I Don't Care If the Sun Don't Shine	1965	$10
—Black label, dog on left			
❑ 447-0602	Good Rockin' Tonight/I Don't Care If the Sun Don't Shine	1970	$8
—Red label			
❑ 47-9425 [DJ]	Guitar Man/High Heel Sneakers	1968	$40
—White label promo, "Not for Sale" on label			
❑ 47-9425	Guitar Man/High Heel Sneakers	1968	$10
❑ 47-9425 [PS]	Guitar Man/High Heel Sneakers	1968	$30
—Coming Soon" on sleeve			
❑ 47-9425 [PS]	Guitar Man/High Heel Sneakers	1968	$30
—Ask For" on sleeve			
❑ 447-0663	Guitar Man/High Heel Sneakers	1970	$8
❑ 47-7280	Hard Headed Woman/Don't Ask Me Why	1958	$30
❑ 47-7280 [PS]	Hard Headed Woman/Don't Ask Me Why	1958	$75
❑ 447-0623	Hard Headed Woman/Don't Ask Me Why	1961	$20
—Black label, dog on top			
❑ 447-0623	Hard Headed Woman/Don't Ask Me Why	1965	$12
—Black label, dog on left			
❑ 447-0623	Hard Headed Woman/Don't Ask Me Why	1969	$30
—Orange label			

Number	Title	Yr	NM
❏ 447-0623	Hard Headed Woman/Don't Ask Me Why	1970	$8

— Red label

❏ 47-6420	Heartbreak Hotel/I Was the One	1956	$50

— No horizontal line on label

❏ 47-6420	Heartbreak Hotel/I Was the One	1956	$50

— With horizontal line on label

❏ 447-0605	Heartbreak Hotel/I Was the One	1959	$20

— Black label, dog on top

❏ 447-0605 [PS]	Heartbreak Hotel/I Was the One	1964	$200
❏ 447-0605 [DJ]	Heartbreak Hotel/I Was the One	1964	$125
❏ 447-0605	Heartbreak Hotel/I Was the One	1965	$12

— Black label, dog on left

❏ 447-0605	Heartbreak Hotel/I Was the One	1969	$30

— Orange label

❏ 447-0605	Heartbreak Hotel/I Was the One	1970	$8

— Red label

❏ 74-0651 [DJ]	He Touched Me/The Bosom of Abraham	1972	$120

— Yellow label promo, "Not for Sale" on label

❏ 74-0651	He Touched Me/The Bosom of Abraham	1972	$200

— He Touched Me" actually plays at about 35 rpm in error. A-side has "AWKS-1277" stamped in trail-off wax.

❏ 74-0651	He Touched Me/The Bosom of Abraham	1972	$8

— He Touched Me" plays correctly. A-side has "APKS-1277" stamped in trail-off wax.

❏ 74-0651 [PS]	He Touched Me/The Bosom of Abraham	1972	$120
❏ 447-0608	Hound Dog/Don't Be Cruel	1959	$20

— Black label, dog on top

❏ 447-0608 [PS]	Hound Dog/Don't Be Cruel	1964	$200
❏ 447-0608 [DJ]	Hound Dog/Don't Be Cruel	1964	$125
❏ 447-0608	Hound Dog/Don't Be Cruel	1965	$10

— Black label, dog on left

❏ 447-0608	Hound Dog/Don't Be Cruel	1969	$30

— Orange label

❏ 447-0608	Hound Dog/Don't Be Cruel	1970	$8

— Red label

❏ 74-0130 [DJ]	How Great Thou Art/His Hand in Mine	1969	$120

— Yellow label promo, "Not for Sale" on label

❏ 74-0130	How Great Thou Art/His Hand in Mine	1969	$30
❏ 74-0130 [PS]	How Great Thou Art/His Hand in Mine	1969	$200
❏ 447-0670	How Great Thou Art/His Hand in Mine	1970	$10
❏ SP-45-162 [DJ]	How Great Thou Art/So High	1967	$200
❏ SP-45-162 [PS]	How Great Thou Art/So High	1967	$200
❏ JB-10601 [DJ]	Hurt/For the Heart	1976	$30

— Yellow label promo, "Not for Sale" on label

❏ PB-10601	Hurt/For the Heart	1976	$5

— Originals on tan labels

❏ PB-10601 [PS]	Hurt/For the Heart	1976	$10
❏ 47-7880	I Feel So Bad/Wild in the Country	1961	$30
❏ 47-7880 [PS]	I Feel So Bad/Wild in the Country	1961	$60
❏ 37-7880	I Feel So Bad/Wild in the Country	1961	$1000

— Compact Single 33" (small hole, plays at LP speed)

❏ 37-7880 [PS]	I Feel So Bad/Wild in the Country	1961	$1200

— Special picture sleeve for above record

❏ 447-0631	I Feel So Bad/Wild in the Country	1962	$15

— Black label, dog on top

❏ 447-0631	I Feel So Bad/Wild in the Country	1965	$10

— Black label, dog on left

❏ 447-0631	I Feel So Bad/Wild in the Country	1970	$8

— Red label

❏ 47-8950 [DJ]	If Every Day Was Like Christmas/How Would You Like to Be	1966	$60

— White label promo, "Not for Sale" on label

❏ 47-8950	If Every Day Was Like Christmas/How Would You Like to Be	1966	$30
❏ 47-8950 [PS]	If Every Day Was Like Christmas/How Would You Like to Be	1966	$50
❏ 447-0681	If Every Day Was Like Christmas/How Would You Like to Be	1972	$8
❏ 47-9670 [DJ]	If I Can Dream/Edge of Reality	1968	$40

— Yellow label promo, "Not for Sale" on label

Number	Title	Yr	NM
❏ 47-9670	If I Can Dream/Edge of Reality	1968	$8

— First Elvis single on orange label

❏ 47-9670 [PS]	If I Can Dream/Edge of Reality	1968	$30

— Mentions his NBC-TV special on sleeve

❏ 47-9670 [PS]	If I Can Dream/Edge of Reality	1968	$30

— Does not mention his NBC-TV special on sleeve

❏ 447-0668	If I Can Dream/Edge of Reality	1970	$8
❏ 47-6357	I Forgot to Remember to Forget/Mystery Train	1955	$70

— No horizontal line on label

❏ 47-6357	I Forgot to Remember to Forget/Mystery Train	1955	$70

— With horizontal line on label

❏ 447-0600	I Forgot to Remember to Forget/Mystery Train	1959	$20

— Note: All RCA Victor releases with a "447" prefix are from the Gold Standard Series. Black label, dog on top

❏ 447-0600	I Forgot to Remember to Forget/Mystery Train	1965	$10

— Black label, dog on left

❏ 447-0600	I Forgot to Remember to Forget/Mystery Train	1969	$30

— Orange label

❏ 447-0600	I Forgot to Remember to Forget/Mystery Train	1970	$8

— Red label

❏ DJAO-0280 [DJ]	If You Talk in Your Sleep/Help Me	1974	$30

— Light yellow label promo, "Not for Sale" on label; both sides are mono

❏ APBO-0280	If You Talk in Your Sleep/Help Me	1974	$15

— On label, the title "If You Talk in Your Sleep" is all on one line

❏ APBO-0280	If You Talk in Your Sleep/Help Me	1974	$6

— On label, the title "If You Talk" is on one line and "In Your Sleep" is on another line

❏ APBO-0280 [PS]	If You Talk in Your Sleep/Help Me	1974	$20
❏ 47-6637	I Got a Woman/I'm Countin' On You	1956	$100

— With horizontal line on label

❏ 47-6637	I Got a Woman/I'm Countin' On You	1956	$100

— No horizontal line on label

❏ 447-0610	I Got a Woman/I'm Countin' On You	1959	$20

— Black label, dog on top

❏ 4-834-115 [DJ]	I'll Be Back	1966	$8000

— One-sided promo with designation "For Special Academy Consideration Only". VG 4000; VG+ 6000

❏ 47-6638	I'm Gonna Sit Right Down and Cry (Over You)/I'll Never Let You Go (Little Darlin')	1956	$75

— No horizontal line on label

❏ 47-6638	I'm Gonna Sit Right Down and Cry (Over You)/I'll Never Let You Go (Little Darlin')	1956	$75

— With horizontal line on label

❏ 447-0611	I'm Gonna Sit Right Down and Cry (Over You)/I'll Never Let You Go (Little Darlin')	1959	$20

— Black label, dog on top

❏ 47-9998 [DJ]	I'm Leavin'/Heart of Rome	1971	$30

— Yellow label promo, "Not for Sale" on label

❏ 47-9998	I'm Leavin'/Heart of Rome	1971	$6
❏ 47-9998 [PS]	I'm Leavin'/Heart of Rome	1971	$30
❏ 447-0683	I'm Leavin'/Heart of Rome	1972	$8
❏ 47-8657 [DJ]	I'm Yours/(It's a) Long, Lonely Highway	1965	$50

— White label promo, "Not for Sale" on label

❏ 47-8657	I'm Yours/(It's a) Long, Lonely Highway	1965	$10
❏ 47-8657 [PS]	I'm Yours/(It's a) Long, Lonely Highway	1965	$30
❏ 447-0654	I'm Yours/(It's a) Long, Lonely Highway	1966	$10

— Black label, dog on left

❏ 447-0654	I'm Yours/(It's a) Long, Lonely Highway	1970	$8

— Red label

❏ 47-9056 [DJ]	Indescribably Blue/Fools Fall in Love	1966	$50

— White label promo, "Not for Sale" on label

❏ 47-9056	Indescribably Blue/Fools Fall in Love	1966	$10
❏ 47-9056 [PS]	Indescribably Blue/Fools Fall in Love	1966	$30
❏ 447-0659	Indescribably Blue/Fools Fall in Love	1969	$30

— Orange label

❏ 447-0659	Indescribably Blue/Fools Fall in Love	1970	$8

— Red label

Number	Title	Yr	NM
❏ 47-9741 [DJ]	In the Ghetto/Any Day Now	1969	$40

— Yellow label promo, "Not for Sale" on label

❏ 47-9741	In the Ghetto/Any Day Now	1969	$8
❏ 47-9741 [PS]	In the Ghetto/Any Day Now	1969	$30

— Coming Soon" on sleeve

❏ 47-9741 [PS]	In the Ghetto/Any Day Now	1969	$30

— Ask For" on sleeve

❏ 447-0671	In the Ghetto/Any Day Now	1970	$8
❏ 47-9960 [DJ]	I Really Don't Want to Know/There Goes My Everything	1971	$30

— Yellow label promo, "Not for Sale" on label

❏ 47-9960	I Really Don't Want to Know/There Goes My Everything	1971	$6
❏ 47-9960 [PS]	I Really Don't Want to Know/There Goes My Everything	1971	$20

— Coming Soon" on sleeve

❏ 47-9960 [PS]	I Really Don't Want to Know/There Goes My Everything	1971	$20

— Ask For" on sleeve

❏ 447-0679	I Really Don't Want to Know/There Goes My Everything	1972	$8
❏ 47-7777	It's Now or Never/A Mess of Blues	1960	$1000

— An early mispress is missing the piano part on the A-side. Has the number "L2WW-0100-3S" or "L2WW-0100-4S" in trail-off wax.

❏ 47-7777	It's Now or Never/A Mess of Blues	1960	$30

— All other pressings with overdubbed piano

❏ 47-7777 [PS]	It's Now or Never/A Mess of Blues	1960	$70
❏ 61-7777 [S]	It's Now or Never/A Mess of Blues	1960	$400

— Living Stereo" (large hole, plays at 45 rpm)

❏ 447-0628	It's Now or Never/A Mess of Blues	1962	$15

— Black label, dog on top

❏ 447-0628	It's Now or Never/A Mess of Blues	1965	$10

— Black label, dog on left

❏ 447-0628	It's Now or Never/A Mess of Blues	1969	$30

— Orange label

❏ 447-0628	It's Now or Never/A Mess of Blues	1970	$8

— Red label

❏ 48-1017 [DJ]	It's Only Love/The Sound of Your Cry	1971	$40

— Yellow label promo, "Not for Sale" on label

❏ 48-1017	It's Only Love/The Sound of Your Cry	1971	$6
❏ 48-1017 [PS]	It's Only Love/The Sound of Your Cry	1971	$20
❏ 447-0684	It's Only Love/The Sound of Your Cry	1972	$8
❏ 47-9873 [DJ]	I've Lost You/The Next Step Is Love	1970	$30

— Yellow label promo, "Not for Sale" on label

❏ 47-9873	I've Lost You/The Next Step Is Love	1970	$6
❏ 47-9873 [PS]	I've Lost You/The Next Step Is Love	1970	$20
❏ 447-0677	I've Lost You/The Next Step Is Love	1971	$8
❏ 47-6540	I Want You, I Need You, I Love You/My Baby Left Me	1956	$50

— No horizontal line on label

❏ 47-6540	I Want You, I Need You, I Love You/My Baby Left Me	1956	$50

— With horizontal line on label

❏ 447-0607	I Want You, I Need You, I Love You/My Baby Left Me	1959	$20

— Black label, dog on top

❏ 447-0607	I Want You, I Need You, I Love You/My Baby Left Me	1965	$10

— Black label, dog on left

❏ 447-0607	I Want You, I Need You, I Love You/My Baby Left Me	1969	$30

— Orange label

❏ 447-0607	I Want You, I Need You, I Love You/My Baby Left Me	1970	$8

— Red label

❏ 47-6642	Lawdy Miss Clawdy/Shake, Rattle, and Roll	1956	$50

— No horizontal line on label

❏ 47-6642	Lawdy Miss Clawdy/Shake, Rattle, and Roll	1956	$200

— With horizontal line on label, but with no dog

❏ 47-6642	Lawdy Miss Clawdy/Shake, Rattle, and Roll	1956	$50

— With horizontal line on label, dog on label as usual

❏ 447-0615	Lawdy Miss Clawdy/Shake, Rattle, and Roll	1959	$20

— Black label, dog on top

❏ 447-0615	Lawdy Miss Clawdy/Shake, Rattle, and Roll	1965	$12

— Black label, dog on left

❏ 447-0615	Lawdy Miss Clawdy/Shake, Rattle, and Roll	1969	$30

Number	Title	Yr	NM
—Orange label			
447-0615	Lawdy Miss Clawdy/Shake, Rattle, and Roll	1970	$8
—Red label			
47-7000	(Let Me Be Your) Teddy Bear/Loving You	1957	$50
—Label says "Let Me Be Your TEDDY BEAR" (no parentheses)			
47-7000	(Let Me Be Your) Teddy Bear/Loving You	1957	$40
—Parentheses around "Let Me Be Your", no horizontal line on label			
47-7000	(Let Me Be Your) Teddy Bear/Loving You	1957	$40
—Parentheses around "Let Me Be Your", with horizontal line on label			
47-7000 [PS]	(Let Me Be Your) Teddy Bear/Loving You	1957	$120
447-0620	(Let Me Be Your) Teddy Bear/Loving You	1959	$20
—Black label, dog on top			
447-0620	(Let Me Be Your) Teddy Bear/Loving You	1965	$12
—Black label, dog on left			
447-0620	(Let Me Be Your) Teddy Bear/Loving You	1969	$30
—Orange label			
447-0620	(Let Me Be Your) Teddy Bear/Loving You	1970	$8
—Red label			
47-9547 [DJ]	Let Yourself Go/Your Time Hasn't Come Yet, Baby	1968	$70
—Yellow label promo, "Not for Sale" on label			
47-9547	Let Yourself Go/Your Time Hasn't Come Yet, Baby	1968	$12
47-9547 [PS]	Let Yourself Go/Your Time Hasn't Come Yet, Baby	1968	$30
—Coming Soon" on sleeve			
47-9547 [PS]	Let Yourself Go/Your Time Hasn't Come Yet, Baby	1968	$30
—Ask For" on sleeve			
447-0666	Let Yourself Go/Your Time Hasn't Come Yet, Baby	1970	$8
47-9985 [DJ]	Life/Only Believe	1971	$40
—Yellow label promo, "Not for Sale" on label			
47-9985	Life/Only Believe	1971	$6
47-9985 [PS]	Life/Only Believe	1971	$40
447-0682	Life/Only Believe	1972	$8
47-9115 [DJ]	Long Legged Girl (With the Short Dress On)/That's Someone You Never Forget	1967	$50
—White label promo, "Not for Sale" on label			
47-9115	Long Legged Girl (With the Short Dress On)/That's Someone You Never Forget	1967	$10
47-9115 [PS]	Long Legged Girl (With the Short Dress On)/That's Someone You Never Forget	1967	$30
—Coming Soon" on sleeve			
47-9115 [PS]	Long Legged Girl (With the Short Dress On)/That's Someone You Never Forget	1967	$30
—Ask For" on sleeve			
447-0660	Long Legged Girl (With the Short Dress On)/That's Someone You Never Forget	1970	$50
47-8870 [DJ]	Love Letters/Come What May	1966	$60
—White label promo, "Not for Sale" on label			
47-8870	Love Letters/Come What May	1966	$10
47-8870 [PS]	Love Letters/Come What May	1966	$30
—Coming Soon" on sleeve			
47-8870 [PS]	Love Letters/Come What May	1966	$30
—Ask For" on sleeve			
447-0657	Love Letters/Come What May	1968	$10
—Black label, dog on left			
447-0657	Love Letters/Come What May	1970	$8
—Red label			
47-6643	Love Me Tender/Anyway You Want Me (That's How I Will Be)	1956	$40
—No horizontal line on label			
47-6643	Love Me Tender/Anyway You Want Me (That's How I Will Be)	1956	$40
—With horizontal line on label			
47-6643	Love Me Tender/Anyway You Want Me (That's How I Will Be)	1956	$50
—No reference to the movie "Love Me Tender" on label			
47-6643 [PS]	Love Me Tender/Anyway You Want Me (That's How I Will Be)	1956	$180
—Black and white sleeve			
47-6643 [PS]	Love Me Tender/Anyway You Want Me (That's How I Will Be)	1956	$80
—Black and green sleeve			
47-6643 [PS]	Love Me Tender/Anyway You Want Me (That's How I Will Be)	1956	$50
—Black and dark pink sleeve			
47-6643 [PS]	Love Me Tender/Anyway You Want Me (That's How I Will Be)	1956	$40
—Black and light pink sleeve			
447-0616	Love Me Tender/Anyway You Want Me (That's How I Will Be)	1959	$20
—Black label, dog on top			
447-0616	Love Me Tender/Anyway You Want Me (That's How I Will Be)	1965	$10
—Black label, dog on left			
447-0616	Love Me Tender/Anyway You Want Me (That's How I Will Be)	1969	$30
—Orange label			
447-0616	Love Me Tender/Anyway You Want Me (That's How I Will Be)	1970	$8
—Red label			
47-7908	(Marie's the Name) His Latest Flame/Little Sister	1961	$30
—All copies of this record actually read "Marie's the Name HIS LATEST FLAME" (no parentheses)			
47-7908 [PS]	(Marie's the Name) His Latest Flame/Little Sister	1961	$60
37-7908	(Marie's the Name) His Latest Flame/Little Sister	1961	$1500
—Compact Single 33" (small hole, plays at LP speed)			
37-7908 [PS]	(Marie's the Name) His Latest Flame/Little Sister	1961	$2000
—Special picture sleeve for above record. VG 1000 ; VG+ 1500			
37-7908 [PS]	(Marie's the Name) His Latest Flame/Little Sister	1961	$2250
—Special picture sleeve for above record; says "Stereo-Orthophonic" on sleeve in error. VG 2250; VG+ 1687.50			
447-0634	(Marie's the Name) His Latest Flame/Little Sister	1962	$15
—Black label, dog on top			
447-0634	(Marie's the Name) His Latest Flame/Little Sister	1965	$10
—Black label, dog on left			
447-0634	(Marie's the Name) His Latest Flame/Little Sister	1969	$30
—Orange label			
447-0634	(Marie's the Name) His Latest Flame/Little Sister	1970	$8
—Red label			
47-9731 [DJ]	Memories/Charro	1969	$40
—Yellow label promo, "Not for Sale" on label			
47-9731	Memories/Charro	1969	$8
47-9731 [PS]	Memories/Charro	1969	$30
447-0669	Memories/Charro	1970	$8
74-0572 [DJ]	Merry Christmas Baby/O Come All Ye Faithful	1971	$40
—Yellow label promo, "Not for Sale" on label			
74-0572	Merry Christmas Baby/O Come All Ye Faithful	1971	$20
74-0572 [PS]	Merry Christmas Baby/O Come All Ye Faithful	1971	$50
47-6382	Milkcow Blues Boogie/You're a Heartbreaker	1955	$70
—No horizontal line on label			
47-6382	Milkcow Blues Boogie/You're a Heartbreaker	1955	$70
—With horizontal line on label			
447-0603	Milkcow Blues Boogie/You're a Heartbreaker	1959	$20
—Black label, dog on top			
447-0603	Milkcow Blues Boogie/You're a Heartbreaker	1965	$10
—Black label, dog on left			
447-0603	Milkcow Blues Boogie/You're a Heartbreaker	1969	$30
—Orange label			
447-0603	Milkcow Blues Boogie/You're a Heartbreaker	1970	$8
—Red label			
447-0652 [DJ]	Milky White Way/Swing Down Sweet Chariot	1966	$120
—White label promo, "Not for Sale" on label			
447-0652	Milky White Way/Swing Down Sweet Chariot	1966	$20
—Black label, dog on left			
447-0652 [PS]	Milky White Way/Swing Down Sweet Chariot	1966	$200
447-0652	Milky White Way/Swing Down Sweet Chariot	1970	$8
—Red label			
47-6641	Money Honey/One-Sided Love Affair	1956	$60
—With horizontal line on label			
47-6641	Money Honey/One-Sided Love Affair	1956	$60
—No horizontal line on label			
447-0614	Money Honey/One-Sided Love Affair	1959	$20
—Black label, dog on top			
447-0614	Money Honey/One-Sided Love Affair	1965	$10
—Black label, dog on left			
447-0614	Money Honey/One-Sided Love Affair	1969	$30
—Orange label			
447-0614	Money Honey/One-Sided Love Affair	1970	$8
—Red label			
RCA-2458EX	My Boy/Loving Arms	1975	$500
—Gray label; pressed in the U.S. for export			
RCA-2458EX [PS]	My Boy/Loving Arms	1975	$200
—Not a sleeve, but a paper insert with no number on it; white with green and black print			
JH-10191 [DJ]	My Boy (mono/stereo)	1975	$40
—Light yellow label promo, "Not for Sale" on label			
PB-10191	My Boy/Thinking About You	1975	$5
—Orange label			
PB-10191	My Boy/Thinking About You	1975	$5
—Tan label			
PB-10191 [PS]	My Boy/Thinking About You	1975	$10
GB-10489	My Boy/Thinking About You	1975	$8
—Gold Standard Series; red label			
CR-15 [DJ]	Old Shep	1956	$1000
—One-sided promo			
47-8134	One Broken Heart for Sale/They Remind Me Too Much of You	1963	$15
47-8134 [PS]	One Broken Heart for Sale/They Remind Me Too Much of You	1963	$40
447-0640	One Broken Heart for Sale/They Remind Me Too Much of You	1964	$30
—Black label, dog on top			
447-0640	One Broken Heart for Sale/They Remind Me Too Much of You	1965	$15
—Black label, dog on left			
447-0640	One Broken Heart for Sale/They Remind Me Too Much of You	1969	$30
—Orange label			
447-0640	One Broken Heart for Sale/They Remind Me Too Much of You	1970	$8
—Red label			
47-7410 [DJ]	One Night/I Got Stung	1958	$30
47-7410 [PS]	One Night/I Got Stung	1958	$75
447-0624	One Night/I Got Stung	1961	$15
—Black label, dog on top			
447-0624	One Night/I Got Stung	1965	$10
—Black label, dog on left			
447-0624	One Night/I Got Stung	1969	$30
—Orange label			
447-0624	One Night/I Got Stung	1970	$8
—Red label			
JA-10074 [DJ]	Promised Land/It's Midnight	1974	$30
—Light yellow label promo, "Not for Sale" on label; both sides are mono			
PB-10074	Promised Land/It's Midnight	1974	$5
—Orange label (available at the same time as gray label)			
PB-10074	Promised Land/It's Midnight	1974	$5
—Gray label (available at the same time as orange label)			
PB-10074	Promised Land/It's Midnight	1975	$30
—Tan label (reissue)			
PB-10074 [PS]	Promised Land/It's Midnight	1975	$10
GB-10488	Promised Land/It's Midnight	1975	$8
—Gold Standard Series; red label			
447-0650 [DJ]	Puppet on a String/Wooden Heart	1965	$40
—White label promo, "Not for Sale" on label			
447-0650	Puppet on a String/Wooden Heart	1965	$10
—Black label, dog on left			
447-0650 [PS]	Puppet on a String/Wooden Heart	1965	$40
447-0650	Puppet on a String/Wooden Heart	1970	$8
—Red label			
74-0815 [DJ]	Separate Ways/Always on My Mind	1972	$30
—Yellow label promo, "Not for Sale" on label			
74-0815	Separate Ways/Always on My Mind	1972	$6

Number	Title	Yr	NM
❑ 74-0815 [PS]	Separate Ways/Always on My Mind	1972	$20
❑ GB-10486	Separate Ways/Always on My Mind	1975	$8
—Gold Standard Series; red label			
❑ 47-8041	She's Not You/Just Tell Her Jim Said Hello	1962	$30
❑ 47-8041 [PS]	She's Not You/Just Tell Her Jim Said Hello	1962	$50
❑ 447-0637	She's Not You/Just Tell Her Jim Said Hello	1963	$15
—Black label, dog on top			
❑ 447-0637	She's Not You/Just Tell Her Jim Said Hello	1965	$10
—Black label, dog on left			
❑ 447-0637	She's Not You/Just Tell Her Jim Said Hello	1969	$30
—Orange label			
❑ 447-0637	She's Not You/Just Tell Her Jim Said Hello	1970	$8
—Red label			
❑ 47-8941 [DJ]	Spinout/All That I Am	1966	$60
—White label promo, "Not for Sale" on label			
❑ 47-8941	Spinout/All That I Am	1966	$10
❑ 47-8941 [PS]	Spinout/All That I Am	1966	$30
—Watch For" on sleeve			
❑ 47-8941 [PS]	Spinout/All That I Am	1966	$30
—Ask For" on sleeve			
❑ 447-0658	Spinout/All That I Am	1968	$10
—Black label, dog on left			
❑ 447-0658	Spinout/All That I Am	1970	$8
—Red label			
❑ 74-0910 [DJ]	Steamroller Blues/Fool	1973	$20
—Light yellow label promo, "Nof for Sale" on label			
❑ 74-0910	Steamroller Blues/Fool	1973	$6
❑ 74-0910 [PS]	Steamroller Blues/Fool	1973	$20
❑ 47-7740	Stuck on You/Fame and Fortune	1960	$30
❑ 47-7740 [PS]	Stuck on You/Fame and Fortune	1960	$70
❑ 61-7740 [S]	Stuck on You/Fame and Fortune	1960	$400
—Living Stereo" (large hole, plays at 45 rpm)			
❑ 447-0627	Stuck on You/Fame and Fortune	1962	$15
—Black label, dog on top			
❑ 447-0627	Stuck on You/Fame and Fortune	1965	$10
—Black label, dog on left			
❑ 447-0627	Stuck on You/Fame and Fortune	1969	$30
—Orange label			
❑ 447-0627	Stuck on You/Fame and Fortune	1970	$8
—Red label			
❑ 47-8585 [DJ]	(Such An) Easy Question/It Feels So Right	1965	$60
—White label promo, "Not for Sale" on label			
❑ 47-8585	(Such An) Easy Question/It Feels So Right	1965	$10
❑ 47-8585 [PS]	(Such An) Easy Question/It Feels So Right	1965	$30
—Coming Soon" on sleeve			
❑ 47-8585 [PS]	(Such An) Easy Question/It Feels So Right	1965	$30
—Ask For" on sleeve			
❑ 447-0653	(Such An) Easy Question/It Feels So Right	1966	$10
—Black label, dog on left			
❑ 447-0653	(Such An) Easy Question/It Feels So Right	1970	$8
—Red label			
❑ 47-8400	Such a Night/Never Ending	1964	$15
❑ 47-8400 [PS]	Such a Night/Never Ending	1964	$30
❑ 47-8400 [DJ]	Such a Night/Never Ending	1964	$5000
—White label promo, "Not for Sale" on label. VG 2500; VG+ 3750			
❑ 447-0645	Such a Night/Never Ending	1965	$50
—Black label, dog on top			
❑ 447-0645	Such a Night/Never Ending	1965	$10
—Black label, dog on left			
❑ 447-0645	Such a Night/Never Ending	1969	$30
—Orange label			
❑ 447-0645	Such a Night/Never Ending	1970	$8
—Red label			
❑ 47-7850	Surrender/Lonely Man	1961	$30
❑ 47-7850 [PS]	Surrender/Lonely Man	1961	$70
❑ 37-7850	Surrender/Lonely Man	1961	$600
—Compact Single 33" (small hole, plays at LP speed)			
❑ 37-7850 [PS]	Surrender/Lonely Man	1961	$1000
—Special picture sleeve for above record			
❑ 68-7850 [S]	Surrender/Lonely Man	1961	$2000
—Compact Stereo 33" in "Living Stereo". VG 1000; VG+ 1500			
❑ 61-7850 [S]	Surrender/Lonely Man	1961	$800
—Living Stereo" (large hole, plays at 45 rpm)			

Number	Title	Yr	NM
❑ 447-0630	Surrender/Lonely Man	1962	$30
—Black label, dog on top			
❑ 447-0630	Surrender/Lonely Man	1965	$10
—Black label, dog on left			
❑ 447-0630	Surrender/Lonely Man	1969	$30
—Orange label			
❑ 447-0630	Surrender/Lonely Man	1970	$8
—Red label			
❑ 47-9764 [DJ]	Suspicious Minds/You'll Think of Me	1969	$40
—Yellow label promo, "Not for Sale" on label			
❑ 47-9764	Suspicious Minds/You'll Think of Me	1969	$8
❑ 47-9764 [PS]	Suspicious Minds/You'll Think of Me	1969	$30
❑ 447-0673	Suspicious Minds/You'll Think of Me	1970	$8
❑ DJBO-0196 [DJ]	Take Good Care of Her/I've Got a Thing About You, Baby	1973	$30
—Light yellow label promo, "Not for Sale" on label			
❑ APBO-0196	Take Good Care of Her/I've Got a Thing About You, Baby	1973	$6
❑ APBO-0196 [PS]	Take Good Care of Her/I've Got a Thing About You, Baby	1973	$20
❑ GB-10485	Take Good Care of Her/I've Got a Thing About You, Baby	1975	$8
—Gold Standard Series; red label			
❑ 47-8740 [DJ]	Tell Me Why/Blue River	1965	$60
—White label promo, "Not for Sale" on label			
❑ 47-8740	Tell Me Why/Blue River	1965	$10
❑ 47-8740 [PS]	Tell Me Why/Blue River	1965	$30
❑ 447-0655	Tell Me Why/Blue River	1968	$10
—Black label, dog on left			
❑ 447-0655	Tell Me Why/Blue River	1970	$8
—Red label			
❑ 47-6380	That's All Right/Blue Moon of Kentucky	1955	$70
—No horizontal line on label			
❑ 47-6380	That's All Right/Blue Moon of Kentucky	1955	$70
—With horizontal line on label			
❑ 447-0601	That's All Right/Blue Moon of Kentucky	1959	$20
—Black label, dog on top			
❑ 447-0601 [PS]	That's All Right/Blue Moon of Kentucky	1964	$200
❑ 447-0601 [DJ]	That's All Right/Blue Moon of Kentucky	1964	$125
❑ 447-0601	That's All Right/Blue Moon of Kentucky	1965	$12
—Black label, dog on left			
❑ 447-0601	That's All Right/Blue Moon of Kentucky	1969	$8
—Red label; B-side artist credit is misspelled "Elvis Presely"			
❑ 47-9287 [DJ]	There's Always Me/Judy	1967	$50
—White label promo, "Not for Sale" on label			
❑ 47-9287	There's Always Me/Judy	1967	$10
❑ 47-9287 [PS]	There's Always Me/Judy	1967	$30
❑ 447-0661	There's Always Me/Judy	1970	$20
❑ 47-9835 [DJ]	The Wonder of You/Mama Liked the Roses	1970	$40
—Yellow label promo, "Not for Sale" on label			
❑ 47-9835	The Wonder of You/Mama Liked the Roses	1970	$8
❑ 47-9835 [PS]	The Wonder of You/Mama Liked the Roses	1970	$20
❑ 447-0676	The Wonder of You/Mama Liked the Roses	1971	$8
❑ 47-6357 [PS]	This Is His Life: Elvis Presley	1955	$1500
—Promo-only sleeve issued with above single; no stock picture sleeve was issued. This was formerly listed under "I Want You, I Need You, I Love You," as the sleeve does not have a number. Consensus opinion now places it with "Mystery Train."			
❑ 47-6800	Too Much/Playing for Keeps	1957	$40
—No horizontal line on label			
❑ 47-6800	Too Much/Playing for Keeps	1957	$200
—With horizontal line on label, but with no dog			
❑ 47-6800	Too Much/Playing for Keeps	1957	$40
—With horizontal line on label, dog on label as normal			
❑ 47-6800 [PS]	Too Much/Playing for Keeps	1957	$100
❑ 447-0617	Too Much/Playing for Keeps	1959	$20
—Black label, dog on top			
❑ 447-0617	Too Much/Playing for Keeps	1965	$10
—Black label, dog on left			
❑ 447-0617	Too Much/Playing for Keeps	1969	$30
—Orange label			
❑ 447-0617	Too Much/Playing for Keeps	1970	$8
—Red label			
❑ JH-10278 [DJ]	T-R-O-U-B-L-E (mono/ stereo)	1975	$40
—Light yellow label promo, "Not for Sale" on label			

Number	Title	Yr	NM
❑ PB-10278	T-R-O-U-B-L-E/Mr. Songman	1975	$5
—Orange label			
❑ PB-10278	T-R-O-U-B-L-E/Mr. Songman	1975	$125
—Gray label			
❑ PB-10278	T-R-O-U-B-L-E/Mr. Songman	1975	$10
—Tan label			
❑ PB-10278 [PS]	T-R-O-U-B-L-E/Mr. Songman	1975	$10
❑ GB-10487	T-R-O-U-B-L-E/Mr. Songman	1975	$8
—Gold Standard Series; red label			
❑ 47-6639	Tryin' to Get to You/I Love You Because	1956	$75
—With horizontal line on label			
❑ 47-6639	Tryin' to Get to You/I Love You Because	1956	$75
—No horizontal line on label			
❑ 447-0612	Tryin' to Get to You/I Love You Because	1959	$20
—Black label, dog on top			
❑ 47-7240	Wear My Ring Around Your Neck/Don'tcha Think It's Time	1958	$30
❑ 47-7240 [PS]	Wear My Ring Around Your Neck/Don'tcha Think It's Time	1958	$100
❑ 447-0622	Wear My Ring Around Your Neck/Don'tcha Think It's Time	1961	$15
—Black label, dog on top			
❑ 447-0622	Wear My Ring Around Your Neck/Don'tcha Think It's Time	1965	$10
—Black label, dog on left			
❑ 447-0622	Wear My Ring Around Your Neck/Don'tcha Think It's Time	1969	$30
—Orange label			
❑ 447-0622	Wear My Ring Around Your Neck/Don'tcha Think It's Time	1970	$8
—Red label			
❑ 47-9980 [DJ]	Where Did They Go, Lord/ Rags to Riches	1971	$40
—Yellow label promo, "Not for Sale" on label			
❑ 47-9980	Where Did They Go, Lord/ Rags to Riches	1971	$6
❑ 47-9980 [PS]	Where Did They Go, Lord/ Rags to Riches	1971	$30
❑ 447-0680	Where Did They Go, Lord/ Rags to Riches	1972	$8

SUN

Number	Title	Yr	NM
❑ 217	Baby Let's Play House/I'm Left, You're Right, She's Gone	1955	$3000
—VG 1,000; VG+ 2,000			
❑ 210	Good Rockin' Tonight/I Don't Care If the Sun Don't Shine	1954	$3500
—VG 1500; VG+ 2500			
❑ 223	I Forgot to Remember to Forget/Mystery Train	1955	$2500
❑ 215	Milkcow Blues Boogie/You're a Heartbreaker	1955	$5000
—VG 2000 ; VG+ 3500			
❑ 209 [B]	That's All Right/Blue Moon of Kentucky	1954	$10000
—A mint copy of this has sold for over $17,000, but so far that is an aberration. VG 2000 ; VG+ 4000			

7-Inch Extended Plays

RCA

Number	Title	Yr	NM
❑ DTF0-2006 [PS]	Aloha from Hawaii Via Satellite	1973	$125
❑ DTF0-2006 [S]	Something/You Gave Me a Mountain/I Can't Stop Loving You//My Way/What Now My Love/I'm So Lonesome I Could Cry	1973	$100
—Jukebox issue; small hole, plays at 33 1/3 rpm			

RCA VICTOR

Number	Title	Yr	NM
❑ EPA-5141	All Shook Up/Don't Ask Me Why//Too Much/Blue Moon of Kentucky	1959	$80
—Black label, dog on top			
❑ EPA-5141	All Shook Up/Don't Ask Me Why//Too Much/Blue Moon of Kentucky	1959	$400
—Maroon label			
❑ EPA-5141	All Shook Up/Don't Ask Me Why//Too Much/Blue Moon of Kentucky	1959	$40
—Black label, dog on top			
❑ EPA-5141	All Shook Up/Don't Ask Me Why//Too Much/Blue Moon of Kentucky	1959	$100
—Orange label			
❑ EPA-965 [PS]	Anyway You Want Me	1956	$60

Number	Title	Yr	NM

— With song titles and catalog number on front

| ☐ EPA-965 | Anyway You Want Me (That's How I Will Be)/I'm Left, You're Right, She's Gone//I Don't Care If the Sun Don't Shine/Mystery Train | 1956 | $50 |

— Without horizontal line on label

| ☐ EPA-965 | Anyway You Want Me (That's How I Will Be)/I'm Left, You're Right, She's Gone//I Don't Care If the Sun Don't Shine/Mystery Train | 1956 | $50 |

— With horizontal line on label

| ☐ EPA-965 | Anyway You Want Me (That's How I Will Be)/I'm Left, You're Right, She's Gone//I Don't Care If the Sun Don't Shine/Mystery Train | 1956 | $250 |

— With horizontal line on label, but with no dog

| ☐ EPA-965 | Anyway You Want Me (That's How I Will Be)/I'm Left, You're Right, She's Gone//I Don't Care If the Sun Don't Shine/Mystery Train | 1965 | $35 |

— Black label, dog on left

| ☐ EPA-965 | Anyway You Want Me (That's How I Will Be)/I'm Left, You're Right, She's Gone//I Don't Care If the Sun Don't Shine/Mystery Train | 1969 | $100 |

— Orange label

☐ EPA-5088 [PS]	A Touch of Gold	1959	$75
☐ EPA-5141 [PS]	A Touch of Gold, Volume 3	1959	$80
☐ EPA-5101 [PS]	A Touch of Gold, Volume II	1959	$75
☐ 599-9141	Blue Moon of Kentucky/Love Me Tender//Mystery Train/Milkcow Boogie Blues	1957	$400

— This is "Side 6" and "Side 15" of various artists box set SPD-26, "Great Country/Western Hits"; notice the error in title on the second side

| ☐ EPA-747 | Blue Suede Shoes/Tutti Frutti//I Got a Woman/Just Because | 1956 | $60 |

— Without horizontal line on label

| ☐ EPA-747 | Blue Suede Shoes/Tutti Frutti//I Got a Woman/Just Because | 1956 | $60 |

— With horizontal line on label

| ☐ EPA-747 | Blue Suede Shoes/Tutti Frutti//I Got a Woman/Just Because | 1956 | $250 |

— With horizontal line on label, but with no dog

| ☐ EPA-747 | Blue Suede Shoes/Tutti Frutti//I Got a Woman/Just Because | 1956 | $250 |

— With incorrect label on Side 1 that lists, as song 3, "I'm Gonna Sit Right Down and Cry (Over You)," which does not appear on this record. Known copies of this version do not have horizontal line on label.

| ☐ EPA-747 | Blue Suede Shoes/Tutti Frutti//I Got a Woman/Just Because | 1965 | $35 |

— Black label, dog on left

| ☐ EPA-747 | Blue Suede Shoes/Tutti Frutti//I Got a Woman/Just Because | 1969 | $100 |

— Orange label

| ☐ EPA-4340 [PS] | Christmas with Elvis | 1958 | $100 |

— With copyright notice and "Printed in U.S.A." at lower right

| ☐ EPA-4340 [PS] | Christmas with Elvis | 1965 | $50 |

— Without copyright notice and "Printed in U.S.A." at lower right

| ☐ EPA-940 | Don't Be Cruel/I Want You, I Need You, I Love You//Hound Dog/My Baby Left Me | 1956 | $60 |

— Without horizontal line on label

| ☐ EPA-940 | Don't Be Cruel/I Want You, I Need You, I Love You//Hound Dog/My Baby Left Me | 1956 | $60 |

— With horizontal line on label

| ☐ EPA-940 | Don't Be Cruel/I Want You, I Need You, I Love You//Hound Dog/My Baby Left Me | 1956 | $250 |

— With horizontal line on label, but with no dog

| ☐ EPA-5120 | Don't Be Cruel/I Want You, I Need You, I Love You//Hound Dog/My Baby Left Me | 1959 | $80 |

— Black label, dog on top

| ☐ EPA-5120 | Don't Be Cruel/I Want You, I Need You, I Love You//Hound Dog/My Baby Left Me | 1959 | $600 |

— Maroon label

Number	Title	Yr	NM
☐ EPA-5120	Don't Be Cruel/I Want You, I Need You, I Love You//Hound Dog/My Baby Left Me	1965	$30

— Black label, dog on left

| ☐ EPA-5120 | Don't Be Cruel/I Want You, I Need You, I Love You//Hound Dog/My Baby Left Me | 1969 | $100 |

— Orange label

| ☐ EPA-4387 [PS] | Easy Come, Easy Go | 1967 | $35 |
| ☐ EPA-4387 | Easy Come, Easy Go/The Love Machine/Yoga Is As Yoga Does/You Gotta Shop/Sing You Children/I'll Take Love | 1967 | $35 |

— All copies appear to be black label, dog on left

| ☐ LPC-128 [PS] | Elvis By Request | 1961 | $50 |
| ☐ EPA-747 [PS] | Elvis Presley | 1956 | $1000 |

— Temporary envelope sleeve with dark blue print, "Blue Suede Shoes by Elvis Presley" in big letters

| ☐ EPA-747 [PS] | Elvis Presley | 1956 | $600 |

— Temporary envelope sleeve with black print, "Blue Suede Shoes by Elvis Presley" in big letters

| ☐ EPA-747 [PS] | Elvis Presley | 1956 | $60 |

— Five different back covers exist, all with titles on front cover; any are of equal value

| ☐ EPB-1254 | Elvis Presley | 1956 | $250 |

— Without horizontal line on label; eight songs on two discs; value is for both discs together

| ☐ EPB-1254 | Elvis Presley | 1956 | $250 |

— With horizontal line on label; eight songs on two discs; value is for both discs together

| ☐ EPB-1254 [PS] | Elvis Presley | 1956 | $250 |

— Three different back covers exist hyping other non-Elvis RCA Victor releases; any are of equal value

| ☐ EPB-1254 [PS] | Elvis Presley | 1956 | $175 |

— With no hype of other non-Elvis releases on back

| ☐ SPD-22 | Elvis Presley | 1956 | $400 |

— Value is for both discs together

| ☐ SPD-22 [PS] | Elvis Presley | 1956 | $400 |

— Bonus given to buyers of a Victrola

| ☐ SPD-23 | Elvis Presley | 1956 | $3000 |

— Value is for all three discs together. VG 1000; VG+ 2000

| ☐ SPD-23 [PS] | Elvis Presley | 1956 | $3000 |

— Bonus given to buyers of a more expensive Victrola. VG 1000; VG+ 2000

| ☐ EPA-830 [PS] | Elvis Presley | 1956 | $60 |
| ☐ EPB-1254 | Elvis Presley | 1956 | $1500 |

— Two records have three songs on each side (12 total), as opposed to the two of the standard release

| ☐ EPA-747 [PS] | Elvis Presley | 1965 | $35 |

— No titles at top of front cover

| ☐ EPA-4325 [PS] | Elvis Sails | 1958 | $100 |

— With 1959 calendar and a hole to make it suitable for hanging

☐ EPA-5157 [PS]	Elvis Sails	1965	$35
☐ EPA-4108 [PS]	Elvis Sings Christmas Songs	1957	$50
☐ EPA-992 [PS]	Elvis (Volume 1)	1956	$60
☐ EPA-993 [PS]	Elvis (Volume 2)	1956	$60

— Titles at top of front cover

| ☐ EPA-993 [PS] | Elvis (Volume 2) | 1965 | $35 |

— No titles at top of front cover

| ☐ EPA-4368 [PS] | Follow That Dream | 1962 | $175 |

— Paper sleeve with "Coin Operator -- DJ Prevue" at top; print is in red

| ☐ EPA-4368 [PS] | Follow That Dream | 1962 | $50 |

— Incorrect playing times on back cover; "Follow That Dream" is listed as 1:35 but is actually 1:38, and two others are wrong also

| ☐ EPA-4368 [PS] | Follow That Dream | 1965 | $30 |

— Correct playing times on back cover

| ☐ EPA-4368 | Follow That Dream/Angel//What a Wonderful Life/I'm Not the Marrying Kind | 1962 | $35 |

— Black label, dog on top, no playing times on label

| ☐ EPA-4368 | Follow That Dream/Angel//What a Wonderful Life/I'm Not the Marrying Kind | 1962 | $50 |

— Black label, dog on top, with playing times on label

| ☐ EPA-4368 | Follow That Dream/Angel//What a Wonderful Life/I'm Not the Marrying Kind | 1965 | $30 |

— Black label, dog on left

| ☐ EPA-4368 | Follow That Dream/Angel//What a Wonderful Life/I'm Not the Marrying Kind | 1969 | $100 |

— Orange label

| ☐ EPA-5088 | Hard Headed Woman/Good Rockin' Tonight//Don't/I Beg of You | 1959 | $70 |

— Black label, dog on top

| ☐ EPA-5088 | Hard Headed Woman/Good Rockin' Tonight//Don't/I Beg of You | 1959 | $400 |

Number	Title	Yr	NM

— Maroon label

| ☐ EPA-5088 | Hard Headed Woman/Good Rockin' Tonight//Don't/I Beg of You | 1965 | $35 |

— Black label, dog on left

| ☐ EPA-5088 | Hard Headed Woman/Good Rockin' Tonight//Don't/I Beg of You | 1969 | $100 |

— Orange label

| ☐ EPA-821 [PS] | Heartbreak Hotel | 1956 | $60 |
| ☐ EPA-821 | Heartbreak Hotel/I Was the One//Money Honey/I Forgot to Remember to Forget | 1956 | $60 |

— Without horizontal line on label

| ☐ EPA-821 | Heartbreak Hotel/I Was the One//Money Honey/I Forgot to Remember to Forget | 1956 | $60 |

— With horizontal line on label

| ☐ EPA-821 | Heartbreak Hotel/I Was the One//Money Honey/I Forgot to Remember to Forget | 1956 | $250 |

— With horizontal line on label, but with no dog

| ☐ EPA-821 | Heartbreak Hotel/I Was the One//Money Honey/I Forgot to Remember to Forget | 1965 | $35 |

— Black label, dog on left

| ☐ EPA-821 | Heartbreak Hotel/I Was the One//Money Honey/I Forgot to Remember to Forget | 1969 | $100 |

— Orange label

| ☐ EPA-4383 | I Feel That I've Known You Forever/Slowly But Surely//Night Rider/Dirty Feeling | 1965 | $35 |

— Black label, dog on left

| ☐ EPA-4383 | I Feel That I've Known You Forever/Slowly But Surely//Night Rider/Dirty Feeling | 1969 | $100 |

— Orange label

| ☐ EPA-4382 | If You Think I Don't Need You//I Need Somebody to Lean On//C'mon Everybody/Today, Tomorrow and Forever | 1964 | $50 |

— Black label, dog on top

| ☐ EPA-4382 | If You Think I Don't Need You//I Need Somebody to Lean On//C'mon Everybody/Today, Tomorrow and Forever | 1965 | $35 |

— Black label, dog on left

| ☐ EPA-4382 | If You Think I Don't Need You//I Need Somebody to Lean On//C'mon Everybody/Today, Tomorrow and Forever | 1969 | $100 |

— Orange label

| ☐ EPA-4041 | I Need You So/Have I Told You Lately//Blueberry Hill/Is It So Strange | 1957 | $250 |

— With horizontal line on label, but with no dog

| ☐ EPA-4041 | I Need You So/Have I Told You Lately//Blueberry Hill/Is It So Strange | 1957 | $60 |

— Without horizontal line on label

| ☐ EPA-4041 | I Need You So/Have I Told You Lately//Blueberry Hill/Is It So Strange | 1957 | $60 |

— With horizontal line on label

| ☐ EPA-4041 | I Need You So/Have I Told You Lately//Blueberry Hill/Is It So Strange | 1965 | $35 |

— Black label, dog on left

| ☐ EPA-4041 | I Need You So/Have I Told You Lately//Blueberry Hill/Is It So Strange | 1969 | $100 |

— Orange label

| ☐ EPA-2-1515 | Lonesome Cowboy/Hot Dog//Mean Woman Blues/Got a Lot of Livin' to Do | 1957 | $50 |

— Without horizontal line on label

| ☐ EPA-2-1515 | Lonesome Cowboy/Hot Dog//Mean Woman Blues/Got a Lot of Livin' to Do | 1957 | $50 |

— With horizontal line on label

| ☐ EPA-2-1515 | Lonesome Cowboy/Hot Dog//Mean Woman Blues/Got a Lot of Livin' to Do | 1965 | $35 |

— Black label, dog on left

| ☐ EPA-2-1515 | Lonesome Cowboy/Hot Dog//Mean Woman Blues/Got a Lot of Livin' to Do | 1969 | $100 |

— Orange label

| ☐ EPA-994 | Long Tall Sally/First in Line//How Do You Think I Feel/How's the World Treating You | 1956 | $60 |

— Without horizontal line on label

| ☐ EPA-994 | Long Tall Sally/First in Line//How Do You Think I Feel/How's the World Treating You | 1956 | $60 |

Number	Title	Yr	NM
—With horizontal line on label			
❑ EPA-994	Long Tall Sally/First in Line//How Do You Think I Feel/How's the World Treating You	1956	$250
—With horizontal line on label, but with no dog			
❑ EPA-994	Long Tall Sally/First in Line//How Do You Think I Feel/How's the World Treating You	1965	$35
—Black label, dog on left			
❑ EPA-994	Long Tall Sally/First in Line//How Do You Think I Feel/How's the World Treating You	1969	$100
—Orange label			
❑ EPA-4006 [PS]	Love Me Tender	1956	$60
—With song titles on top of front cover			
❑ EPA-4006 [PS]	Love Me Tender	1965	$35
—No song titles on top of front cover			
❑ DJ-7 [DJ]	Love Me Tender/Anyway You Want Me (That's How I Will Be)//Welcome to the Club/I Won't Be Rockin' Tonight	1956	$250
—B-side tracks by Jean Chapel; white label; each side is labeled with the corresponding nuimber for the regular 45 rpm issue			
❑ EPA-4006	Love Me Tender/Let Me//Poor Boy/We're Gonna Move	1956	$60
—Without horizontal line on label			
❑ EPA-4006	Love Me Tender/Let Me//Poor Boy/We're Gonna Move	1956	$60
—With horizontal line on label			
❑ EPA-4006	Love Me Tender/Let Me//Poor Boy/We're Gonna Move	1956	$250
—With horizontal line on label, but with no dog			
❑ EPA-4006	Love Me Tender/Let Me//Poor Boy/We're Gonna Move	1965	$35
—Black label, dog on left			
❑ EPA-4006	Love Me Tender/Let Me//Poor Boy/We're Gonna Move	1969	$100
—Orange label			
❑ EPA-1-1515 [PS]	Loving You, Vol. I	1957	$50
❑ EPA-2-1515 [PS]	Loving You, Vol. II	1957	$50
—With song titles on top of front cover			
❑ EPA-2-1515 [PS]	Loving You, Vol. II	1965	$35
—No song titles on top of front cover			
❑ EPA-1-1515	Loving You/Party//(Let Me Be Your) Teddy Bear/True Love	1957	$50
—Without horizontal line on label			
❑ EPA-1-1515	Loving You/Party//(Let Me Be Your) Teddy Bear/True Love	1957	$50
—With horizontal line on label			
❑ EPA-1-1515	Loving You/Party//(Let Me Be Your) Teddy Bear/True Love	1965	$35
—Black label, dog on left			
❑ EPA-1-1515	Loving You/Party//(Let Me Be Your) Teddy Bear/True Love	1969	$100
—Orange label			
❑ EPA-4054 [PS]	Peace in the Valley	1957	$50
❑ EPA-5121 [PS]	Peace in the Valley	1959	$50
—Three slightly different cover variations with no difference in value			
❑ SPA-7-37 [DJ]	Perfect for Parties	1956	$75
—Without horizontal line on label			
❑ SPA-7-37 [DJ]	Perfect for Parties	1956	$75
—With horizontal line on label			
❑ SPA-7-37 [PS]	Perfect for Parties	1956	$75
❑ EPA-4325	Press Interview with Elvis Presley/Elvis Presley's Newsreel Interview/Pat Hernon Interviews Elvis...	1958	$100
❑ EPA-5157	Press Interview with Elvis Presley/Elvis Presley's Newsreel Interview/Pat Hernon Interviews Elvis...	1965	$35
—Black label, dog on top			
❑ EPA-5157	Press Interview with Elvis Presley/Elvis Presley's Newsreel Interview/Pat Hernon Interviews Elvis...	1969	$100
—Orange label			
❑ EPA-4108	Santa Bring My Baby Back (To Me)/Blue Christmas//Santa Claus Is Back in Town/I'll Be Home for Christmas	1957	$50
—Black label, dog on top			
❑ EPA-4108	Santa Bring My Baby Back (To Me)/Blue Christmas//Santa Claus Is Back in Town/I'll Be Home for Christmas	1965	$35
—Black label, dog on left			
❑ EPA-4108	Santa Bring My Baby Back (To Me)/Blue Christmas//Santa Claus Is Back in Town/I'll Be Home for Christmas	1969	$100
—Orange label			
❑ EPA-830	Shake, Rattle and Roll/I Love You Because//Blue Moon/Lawdy, Miss Clawdy	1956	$60
—Without horizontal line on label			
❑ EPA-830	Shake, Rattle and Roll/I Love You Because//Blue Moon/Lawdy, Miss Clawdy	1956	$60
—With horizontal line on label			
❑ EPA-830	Shake, Rattle and Roll/I Love You Because//Blue Moon/Lawdy, Miss Clawdy	1956	$250
—With horizontal line on label, but with no dog			
❑ EPA-830	Shake, Rattle and Roll/I Love You Because//Blue Moon/Lawdy, Miss Clawdy	1965	$35
—Black label, dog on left			
❑ EPA-830	Shake, Rattle and Roll/I Love You Because//Blue Moon/Lawdy, Miss Clawdy	1969	$100
—Orange label			
❑ EPA-993	So Glad You're Mine/Old Shep//Ready Teddy/Anyplace Is Paradise	1956	$50
—Without horizontal line on label			
❑ EPA-993	So Glad You're Mine/Old Shep//Ready Teddy/Anyplace Is Paradise	1956	$50
—With horizontal line on label			
❑ EPA-993	So Glad You're Mine/Old Shep//Ready Teddy/Anyplace Is Paradise	1956	$250
—With horizontal line on label, but with no dog			
❑ EPA-993	So Glad You're Mine/Old Shep//Ready Teddy/Anyplace Is Paradise	1965	$35
—Black label, dog on left			
❑ EPA-993	So Glad You're Mine/Old Shep//Ready Teddy/Anyplace Is Paradise	1969	$100
—Orange label			
❑ EPA-994 [PS]	Strictly Elvis (Elvis, Vol. 3)	1956	$60
—With titles listed on front cover			
❑ EPA-994 [PS]	Strictly Elvis (Elvis, Vol. 3)	1965	$35
—No titles listed on front cover			
❑ EPA-4054	(There'll Be) Peace in the Valley (For Me)/It Is No Secret (What God Can Do)/I Believe/Take My Hand, Precious Lord	1957	$50
—Without horizontal line on label			
❑ EPA-4054	(There'll Be) Peace in the Valley (For Me)/It Is No Secret (What God Can Do)/I Believe/Take My Hand, Precious Lord	1957	$50
—With horizontal line on label			
❑ EPA-5121	(There'll Be) Peace in the Valley (For Me)/It Is No Secret (What God Can Do)/I Believe/Take My Hand, Precious Lord	1959	$35
—Black label, dog on top			
❑ EPA-5121	(There'll Be) Peace in the Valley (For Me)/It Is No Secret (What God Can Do)/I Believe/Take My Hand, Precious Lord	1959	$400
—Maroon label			
❑ EPA-5121	(There'll Be) Peace in the Valley (For Me)/It Is No Secret (What God Can Do)/I Believe/Take My Hand, Precious Lord	1965	$30
—Black label, dog on left			
❑ EPA-5121	(There'll Be) Peace in the Valley (For Me)/It Is No Secret (What God Can Do)/I Believe/Take My Hand, Precious Lord	1969	$100
—Orange label			
❑ EPA-4383 [PS]	Tickle Me	1965	$35
—Coming Soon" on front cover			
❑ EPA-4383 [PS]	Tickle Me	1965	$35
—Ask For" on front cover			
❑ EPA-4383 [PS]	Tickle Me	1969	$40
—No blurb for new album on front cover			
❑ DJ-56 [DJ]	Too Much/Playing for Keeps//Chantez-Chantez/Honkytonk Heart	1956	$250
—B-side tracks by Dinah Shore; white label; each side is labeled with the corresponding nuimber for the regular 45 rpm issue			
❑ EPA-4321	Trouble/Young Dreams//Crawfish/Dixieland Rock	1958	$50
—Black label, dog on top			
❑ EPA-4321	Trouble/Young Dreams//Crawfish/Dixieland Rock	1965	$35
—Black label, dog on left			
❑ EPA-4321	Trouble/Young Dreams//Crawfish/Dixieland Rock	1969	$100
—Orange label			
❑ G8-MW-8705 [DJ]	TV Guide Presents Elvis Presley	1956	$1200
—Blue label, locked grooves (needle has to be lifted to play each of the four excerpts)			
❑ EPA-5101	Wear My Ring Around Your Neck/Treat Me Nice//One Night/That's All Right	1959	$75
—Black label, dog on top			
❑ EPA-5101	Wear My Ring Around Your Neck/Treat Me Nice//One Night/That's All Right	1959	$400
—Maroon label			
❑ EPA-5101	Wear My Ring Around Your Neck/Treat Me Nice//One Night/That's All Right	1965	$35
—Black label, dog on left			
❑ EPA-5101	Wear My Ring Around Your Neck/Treat Me Nice//One Night/That's All Right	1969	$100
—Orange label			
❑ EPA-4340	White Christmas/Here Comes Santa Claus//Oh Little Town of Bethlehem/Silent Night	1958	$80
—Black label, dog on top			
❑ EPA-4340	White Christmas/Here Comes Santa Claus//Oh Little Town of Bethlehem/Silent Night	1965	$50
—Black label, dog on left			
❑ EPA-4340	White Christmas/Here Comes Santa Claus//Oh Little Town of Bethlehem/Silent Night	1969	$100
—Orange label			

PRESTON, BILLY, AND SYREETA

MOTOWN

Number	Title	Yr	NM
❑ 1520	Searchin'/Hey You	1981	$4
❑ 1477	With You I'm Born Again/All I Wanted Was You	1979	$4
❑ 1460	With You I'm Born Again/Go For It	1979	$5

TAMLA

Number	Title	Yr	NM
❑ 54312	Dance For Me Children/One More Time for Love	1980	$4
❑ 54319	Please Stay/Signed, Sealed, Delivered (I'm Yours)	1980	$4

PRESTON, BILLY

A&M

Number	Title	Yr	NM
❑ 1980	A Whole New Thing/Wide Stride	1977	$4
❑ 1536	Creature Feature/My Soul Is a Witness	1974	$4
❑ 1768	Do It While You Can/Song of Joy	1975	$4
❑ 1892	Do What You Want/I've Got the Spirit	1976	$4
❑ 1735	Fancy Lady/Song of Joy	1975	$4
❑ 1735 [PS]	Fancy Lady/Song of Joy	1975	$6
❑ 2071	Get Back/Space Race	1978	$4
❑ 1925	Girl/Ecstasy	1977	$4
❑ 2012	I Really Miss You/Attitudes	1978	$4
❑ 1320	Outa-Space/I Wrote a Simple Song	1972	$5
❑ 1340	Should Have Known Better/The Bus	1972	$5
❑ 1380	Slaughter/God Loves You	1972	$5
❑ 1380 [PS]	Slaughter/God Loves You	1972	$6
❑ 1463	Space Race/We're Gonna Make It	1973	$4
❑ 1463 [PS]	Space Race/We're Gonna Make It	1973	$6
❑ 1644	Struttin'/You Are So Beautiful	1974	$4
❑ 1954	Wide Stride/When You Are Mine	1977	$4
❑ 1411	Will It Go Round in Circles/Blackbird	1973	$4

APPLE

Number	Title	Yr	NM
❑ 1817	All That I've Got (I'm Gonna Give It to You)/As I Get Older	1970	$8
❑ 1817 [PS]	All That I've Got (I'm Gonna Give It to You)/As I Get Older	1970	$20
❑ 1814	Everything's All Right/I Want to Thank You	1969	$8
❑ 1826	My Sweet Lord/Little Girl	1970	$8
❑ 1826	My Sweet Lord/Little Girl	1970	$15
—With star on A-side label			

Number	Title	Yr	NM
☐ P-1808/PRO 6555 [DJ]	That's the Way God Planned It (Parts 1 & 2) (mono/stereo)	1969	$70
☐ 1808	That's the Way God Planned It/What About You	1969	$8
☐ 1808 [PS]	That's the Way God Planned It/What About You	1969	$12
☐ 1808	That's the Way God Planned It/What About You	1972	$8

— With "Mono" on both sides of record and reference to LP

APPLE/AMERICOM

☐ 1808P/M-433	That's the Way God Planned It (Edit)/What About You	1969	$400

— Four-inch flexi-disc sold from vending machines

CAPITOL

☐ 2309	Hey Brother (Part 1)/Hey Brother (Part 2)	1968	$8
☐ 5660	In the Midnight Hour/Advice	1966	$8
☐ 5797	Phony Friends/Can't She Tell	1966	$8
☐ 5730	Sunny/Let the Music Play	1966	$8
☐ 5611	The Girl's Got "It"/The Night	1966	$8

DERBY

☐ 1002	Greazee (Part 1)/(Part 2)	1963	$30

MGM

☐ 14001	The Split/It's Just a Love Game	1968	$8

MOTOWN

☐ 1511	A Change Is Gonna Come/You	1981	$4
☐ 1625	I'm Never Gonna Say Goodbye/Love You So	1982	$4
☐ 1470	It Will Come In Time/All I Wanted Was You	1979	$4
☐ 1505	Sock-It Rocket/Hope	1981	$4

MYRRH

☐ 216	One with the Lord/Universal Love	1979	$8

VEE JAY

☐ 653	Don't Let the Sun Catch You Cryin'/Billy's Bag	1965	$12
☐ 692	Log Cabin/Drown in My Own Tears	1965	$10

PRESTON, JOHN

HIT

☐ 69	Blue on Blue/Those Lazy-Hazy-Crazy Days of Summer	1963	$8

— B-side by Frank Clark

☐ 207	Long Lonely Nights/Once You've Been in Love	1965	$8
☐ 177	Speaking of Broken Hearts/You're Nobody Till Somebody Loves You	1965	$8

— B-side by Marty Wood

☐ 92	Walking Proud/500 Miles Away from Home	1963	$8

— B-side by Mitch Wood

PRESTON, JOHNNY

ABC

☐ 11085	I'm Only Human/There's No One Like You	1968	$10

HALLWAY

☐ 1201	All Around the World/Just Plain Hurt	1964	$20
☐ 1204	Willie and the Hand Jive/I've Got My Eyes on You	1964	$20

IMPERIAL

☐ 5947	I've Got My Eyes on You/I Couldn't Take It Again	1963	$10
☐ 5924	This Little Bitty Tear/The Day the World Stood Still	1963	$10

MERCURY

☐ 71691	Charming Billy/Up in the Air	1960	$30
☐ 71598 [M]	Cradle of Love/City of Tears	1960	$30
☐ 71598 [PS]	Cradle of Love/City of Tears	1960	$40
☐ 10027 [S]	Cradle of Love/City of Tears	1960	$60
☐ 71651 [M]	Feel So Fine/I'm Starting to Go Steady	1960	$30
☐ 10036 [S]	Feel So Fine/I'm Starting to Go Steady	1960	$70
☐ 71651 [PS]	Feel So Fine/I'm Starting to Go Steady	1960	$40
☐ 71908	Free Me/Kissin' Tree	1961	$30
☐ 71908 [PS]	Free Me/Kissin' Tree	1961	$40
☐ 71803	I Feel Good/Willy Walk	1961	$30
☐ 71803 [PS]	I Feel Good/Willy Walk	1961	$50
☐ 71761	Leave My Kitten Alone/Token of Love	1961	$30
☐ 71761 [PS]	Leave My Kitten Alone/Token of Love	1961	$40
☐ 71951	Let's Leave It That Way/Broken Hearts Anonymous	1962	$20
☐ 72049	Let the Big Boss Man (Pull You Through)/The Day After Forever	1962	$20
☐ 71865	Let Them Talk/She Once Belonged to Me	1961	$30

TCF HALL

Number	Title	Yr	NM
☐ 120	I'm Askin' Forgiveness/Good Good Lovin'	1965	$10
☐ 110	Sounds Like Trouble/You Can Make It If You Try	1965	$20

PRESTON, MIKE

LONDON

☐ 1834	A House, a Car and a Wedding Ring/My Lucky Love	1958	$15
☐ 9601	Careless Love/Little Grain of Sand	1963	$10
☐ 1865	Girl Without a Heart/In Surabaya	1959	$10
☐ 1981	Girl Without a Heart/Marry Me	1960	$10
☐ 1903	'Till Tomorrow/An Ordinary Couple	1960	$10

PRESTON, ROBERT

CAPITOL CUSTOM

☐ CF-1000	Chicken Fat (School Version)/Chicken Fat (Disc Jockey Version)	1962	$20

— White label, small hole, plays at 33 1/3 rpm

PRETENDERS

POLYDOR

☐ 887816-7	Window of the World/1969	1988	$3
☐ 887816-7 [PS]	Window of the World/1969	1988	$3

SIRE

☐ 29840	Back on the Chain Gang/My City Was Gone	1982	$3
☐ 29840 [PS]	Back on the Chain Gang/My City Was Gone	1982	$3
☐ 49181	Brass in Pocket (I'm Special)/Space Invader	1980	$4
☐ 28630	Don't Get Me Wrong/Dance!	1986	$3
☐ 28630 [PS]	Don't Get Me Wrong/Dance!	1986	$3
☐ 28354	Hymn to Her (She Will Always Carry On)/Tradition of Love	1987	$3
☐ 28354 [PS]	Hymn to Her (She Will Always Carry On)/Tradition of Love	1987	$3
☐ 49861	I Go to Sleep/Waste Not Want Not	1981	$4
☐ 49819	Louie Louie/In the Sticks	1981	$4
☐ 49819 [PS]	Louie Louie/In the Sticks	1981	$4
☐ PRO-S-942 [DJ]	Message of Love/Talk of the Town	1981	$10
☐ 29444	Middle of the Road/2000 Miles	1983	$3
☐ 29444 [PS]	Middle of the Road/2000 Miles	1983	$3
☐ 28496	My Baby/Room Full of Mirrors	1987	$3
☐ 28496 [PS]	My Baby/Room Full of Mirrors	1987	$3
☐ 29317	Show Me/Fast or Slow (The Law Is The Law)	1984	$3
☐ 29317 [PS]	Show Me/Fast or Slow (The Law Is The Law)	1984	$3
☐ 49506	Stop Your Sobbing/Phone Call	1980	$4
☐ 49506 [PS]	Stop Your Sobbing/Phone Call	1980	$8
☐ 29249	Thin Line Between Love and Hate/Time the Avenger	1984	$3
☐ 29249 [PS]	Thin Line Between Love and Hate/Time the Avenger	1984	$3

WARNER BROS.

☐ 28259	If There Was a Man/Into Vienna	1987	$3

— B-side by John Barry

☐ 28259 [PS]	If There Was a Man/Into Vienna	1987	$3

— B-side by John Barry

WEA/REAL

☐ ARE20	2000 Miles/Fast Or Slow (The Law's The Law)	1983	$5
☐ ARE20 [PS]	2000 Miles/Fast Or Slow (The Law's The Law)	1983	$5

— Above record and sleeve are U.K. imports

PRETENDERS, THE (2)

APT

Number	Title	Yr	NM
☐ 25026	Blue and Lonely/Daddy Needs Baby	1959	$500

CENTRAL

☐ 2605	Blue and Lonely/Daddy Needs Baby	1958	$1500

PRETENDERS, THE (3)

BETHLEHEM

☐ 3050	The Day You Are Mine/Ding Dong Bells	1962	$200

PRETENDERS, THE (4)

CHATTAHOOCHIE

☐ 685	Pepita's Theme/Tijuana Taxi	1965	$30

PRETENDERS, THE (U)

POWER-MARTIN

☐ 1001	Smile/I'm So Happy	1961	$125

RAMA

☐ 198	Possessive Love/I've Got to Have You Baby	1956	$120

WHIRLIN' DISC

☐ 106	Close Your Eyes/Part-Time Sweetheart	1957	$250

PRETTY POISON

POISON POPS

☐ 0(no cat #)	Gimme Gimme (Your Autograph)/Kill You	1981	$30

— Small center hole; original paper sleeve has handwritten phone number

☐ 0(no cat #) [PS]	Gimme Gimme (Your Autograph)/Kill You	1981	$30

SVENGALI

☐ 2913	Expiration/The Realm of Existence	1981	$20

— Plays at 33 1/3 rpm

☐ 2913 [PS]	Expiration/The Realm of Existence	1981	$20

— Fold-over sleeve

VIRGIN

☐ 99416	Catch Me (I'm Falling)/(Spanish Mix)	1987	$3
☐ 99416 [PS]	Catch Me (I'm Falling)/(Spanish Mix)	1987	$5

— Hiding Out" sleeve

☐ 99310	When I Look Into Your Eyes/(Hip Hop Mix)	1988	$3

PRETTY THINGS, THE

FONTANA

☐ 1916	Big Boss Man/Rosalyn	1964	$30
☐ 1550	Come See Me/Judgment Day	1966	$30
☐ 1550	Come See Me/Progress	1966	$40
☐ 1518	Cry to Me/I Can Never Say	1965	$40
☐ 1518	Cry to Me/Judgment Day	1965	$20
☐ 1941	Don't Bring Me Down/We'll Be Together	1964	$30
☐ 1508	I Can Never Say/Honey, I Need	1965	$30
☐ 1540	Midnight to Six Man/Can't Stand Pain	1966	$30

LAURIE

☐ 3458	Talkin' About the Good Times/Walking Through My Dreams	1968	$60

RARE EARTH

☐ 5005	Private Sorrow/Balloon Burning	1969	$30

SWAN SONG

☐ 70104	Come Home Momma/Joey	1975	$5
☐ 70107	It Isn't Rock & Roll/Remember That Boy	1975	$5

PREVIN, ANDRE

COLUMBIA

☐ JZSP55071/0 [DJ]	God Rest Ye Merry, Gentlemen/Let No Walls Divide	1961	$15

— B-side by Doris Day

☐ 43136	Goodbye, Charlie/Kiss Me, Stupid	1964	$8
☐ 41683	Love Me or Leave Me/Like Love	1960	$8
☐ 42596	Song from "Two for the Seesaw"/Song from "Long Day's Journey Into Night"	1962	$8
☐ 30833 [S]	(titles unknown)	1960	$10
☐ 30834 [S]	(titles unknown)	1960	$10
☐ 30835 [S]	(titles unknown)	1960	$10
☐ 30836 [S]	(titles unknown)	1960	$10
☐ 30837 [S]	(titles unknown)	1960	$10
☐ 31074 [S]	(titles unknown)	1961	$10
☐ 31075 [S]	(titles unknown)	1961	$10

Number	Title	Yr	NM
❏ 31076 [S]	(titles unknown)	1961	$10
❏ 31077 [S]	(titles unknown)	1961	$10
❏ 31078 [S]	(titles unknown)	1961	$10
❏ 31540 [S]	(titles unknown)	1962	$10
❏ 31541 [S]	(titles unknown)	1962	$10
❏ 31542 [S]	(titles unknown)	1962	$10
❏ 31543 [S]	(titles unknown)	1962	$10
❏ 31544 [S]	(titles unknown)	1962	$10

— *Anyone who can fill in these gaps -- the above 15 all are Columbia "Stereo 7" singles -- please let us know.*

DECCA

❏ 25529	Moonlight Becomes You/ Let's Fall in Love	1961	$8

MGM

❏ 12792	Like Young/Young Man's Lament	1959	$12

— *With David Rose*

RCA VICTOR

❏ WP214 [PS]	Andre Previn Plays the Piano	1949	$20

— *Empty box for 47-2764, 47-2765 and 47-2766*

❏ 47-3123	Anything Goes/Bewitched, Bothered and Bewildered	1949	$20
❏ 47-2764	But Not for Me/Hallelujah	1949	$20
❏ 47-3080	Dardanella/The Gypsy in My Soul	1949	$20
❏ 47-4163	Dearly Beloved/Love Is Just Around the Corner	1951	$20
❏ 47-2767	I Didn't Know What Time It Was/Should I	1949	$20
❏ 47-3263	I Didn't Know What Time It Was/Should I	1949	$20
❏ 47-4354	I'll String Along/Jeepers Creepers	1951	$15

— *The above four comprise a box set*

❏ 47-4351	Lullaby of Broadway/I Only Have Eyes for You	1951	$15
❏ 47-2766	Mad About the Boy/Just One of Those Things	1949	$20

— *The above three comprise box set WP-214, "Andre Previn Plays the Piano*

❏ 47-2765	My Shining Hour/This Can't Be Love	1949	$20
❏ 47-4161	Skylark/You Took Advantage of Me	1951	$20
❏ 47-9122	Theme from Hotel/The Bad Guys	1967	$6
❏ 47-4780	The Story of a Piano (Part 1)/Romance, Op. 28, No. 2	1952	$15
❏ 47-4781	The Story of a Piano (Part 2)/Valse Brilliance in A Minor	1952	$15
❏ 47-4782	The Story of a Piano (Part 3)/Traumere Op. 15	1952	$15
❏ 47-4783	The Story of a Piano (Part 4)/Adagio Cantabile	1952	$15

— *The above four comprise a box set*

❏ 47-4352	This Head of Mine/ September in the Rain	1951	$15
❏ 47-4353	This Heart of Mine/I Know Why and So Do You	1951	$15
❏ 47-3836	Three Little Words/Thinking of You	1950	$20
❏ 47-3125	Who Cares/Who	1949	$20

— *The above three comprise a box set*

❏ 47-3837	Who's Sorry Now/All Alone	1950	$20

UNITED ARTISTS

❏ 50080	Bad Guys/Waltz of the Fortune Cookie	1966	$6

PRICE, ALAN
Also see THE ANIMALS.

COTILLION

❏ 44044	Falling in Love Again/Sly Sadie	1969	$6

— *Might be promo only*

EPIC

❏ 04319	I Don't Feel No Pain No More (Time and Tide)/Rowf and Snitter Run to Sea	1984	$4

— *Might be promo only*

JET

❏ XW1119	I Wanna Dance/Just for You	1978	$4
❏ 5056	This Is Your Lucky Day/ Mama Don't Go Home	1979	$4

PARROT

❏ 3007	Hi-Lili, Hi-Lo/Take Me Home	1966	$12
❏ 3001	I Put a Spell on You/ Iechyd-Da	1966	$10
❏ 3014	Shame/Don't Do That Again	1967	$8
❏ 3009	Tickle Me/Simon Smith and His Amazing Dancing Bears	1966	$10
❏ 3013	Who Cares/The House That Jack Built	1967	$8

WARNER BROS.

❏ 7717	Poor People/O Lucky Man	1973	$5

PRICE, CHUCK

PLAYBOY

❏ 6067	Cadillac Johnson/Trouble in Mind	1976	$5

Number	Title	Yr	NM
❏ 6030	Cheatin' Again/What Is It	1975	$5
❏ 5811	Cowboy Lemonade/What Is It	1977	$5
❏ 6072	I Don't Want It/Trouble in Mind	1976	$5
❏ 6099	Is Anybody Goin' to San Antone/My Memories	1977	$5
❏ 6052	Last of the Outlaws/Angels Have Days They Can't Fly	1975	$5
❏ 6010	Slow Down/West Virginia Woman	1974	$5

PRICE, DAVID

EPIC

❏ 5-9494	Please Dim the Lights/Save a Little Room	1962	$15

GAYLORD

❏ 6430	Good Morning Self/You Make It Easy	1963	$20
❏ 5075	Love Him Tender, Sweet Jesus/I Need a Friend	1977	$8
❏ 1001	The World Lost a Man/I Need a Friend	1964	$20

ROULETTE

❏ 4639	If It's the Last Thing I Do/You Gotta Go Where It Is	1965	$10

PRICE, DENISE

DIMENSION

❏ 1037	Two Hearts Can't Be Wrong/ Somebody Everybody's Had	1982	$5
❏ 1037 [PS]	Two Hearts Can't Be Wrong/ Somebody Everybody's Had	1982	$6

PRICE, KENNY

BOONE

❏ 1070	Going Home for the Last Time/Blame It on Me	1968	$8
❏ 1035	Goin' Out of Style/Hunky Dory	1966	$10
❏ 1063	Grass Won't Grow on a Busy Street/Somebody Told Mary	1967	$10
❏ 1051	Happy Tracks/The Clock	1966	$12
❏ 1081	It Don't Mean a Thing to Me/ Big Operator	1968	$8
❏ 1067	My Goal for Today/Say Something Nice to Me	1967	$10
❏ 1056	Pretty Girl, Pretty Clothes, Pretty Sad/You Made Me Lie to You	1967	$10
❏ 1075	Southern Bound/After All	1968	$8
❏ 1042	Walking on New Grass/ Wasting My Time	1966	$10
❏ 1085	Who Do I Know in Dallas/I'm a Long Way from Home	1969	$8

DIMENSION

❏ 1010	She's Leavin' (And I'm Almost Gone)/In Vain	1980	$5
❏ 1003	Well Rounded Traveling Man/Everybody Needs Something	1980	$5

MRC

❏ 1007	Afraid You'd Come Back/ Walkin' in That California Sunshine	1977	$5
❏ 1025	Hey There/Pickin' Up the Pieces	1979	$5
❏ 1001	I'd Buy You Chattanooga/ Mortar Mixing Mama	1977	$5
❏ 1004	Leavin'/Boone County Weight Watchers of America	1977	$5
❏ 1012	Sunshine Man/Sidewalk Satin Salesman	1978	$5

RCA VICTOR

❏ 74-0936	30 California Women/Love's Not Hard to Take	1973	$6
❏ PB-10260	Birds and Children Fly Away/ Born in Country Music (Raised on Dixieland)	1975	$5
❏ AMAO-0127	Charlotte Fever/The Sheriff of Boone County	1973	$5

— *Gold Standard Series" reissue*

❏ 74-0872	Don't Tell Me Your Troubles/ Front of the Bus, Back of the Church	1973	$6
❏ PB-10141	Easy Look/Country Blues	1974	$5
❏ PB-10376	I've Changed Since I've Been Unchained/She Even Loves Me	1975	$5
❏ PB-10039	Let's Truck Together/Super Hillbilly	1974	$5
❏ 74-0781	Sea of Heartbreak/Smiley	1972	$6
❏ 74-0617	Super Sideman/From Here to There	1971	$6
❏ PB-10460	Too Big a Price to Pay/Don't Boogie Woogie When You Say Your Prayers Tonight	1975	$5
❏ APBO-0198	Turn On Your Light (And Let It Shine)/The First Song That Wasn't the Blues	1973	$6

PRICE, LLOYD

ABC

❏ 11016	Personality/Just Because	1967	$8

Number	Title	Yr	NM
❏ 1237	Stagger Lee/Personality	1969	$6

— *Golden Treasure Chest" reissue; contains the "samitized" version of "Stagger Lee" with Mr. Lee and Billy arguing over a woman*

ABC-PARAMOUNT

❏ 10288	Be a Leader/'Nother Fairy Tale	1962	$20
❏ 10177	Boo Hoo/I Made You Cry	1961	$20
❏ 10062	Come Into My Heart/Won't Cha Come Home	1959	$20
❏ S-10062 [S]	Come Into My Heart/Won't Cha Come Home	1959	$60
❏ 10342	Counterfeit Friends/Your Picture	1962	$20
❏ 10032 [M]	I'm Gonna Get Married/ Three Little Pigs	1959	$30
❏ S-10032 [S]	I'm Gonna Get Married/ Three Little Pigs	1959	$60
❏ 10075	Lady Luck/Never Let Me Go	1960	$20
❏ 10221	Mary and Man-O/I Ain't Givin' Up Nothin'	1961	$20
❏ 10197	One Hundred Percent/Say I'm the One	1961	$20
❏ 10018 [M]	Personality/Have You Ever Had the Blues	1959	$30
❏ S-10018 [S]	Personality/Have You Ever Had the Blues	1959	$60
❏ 9972 [M]	Stagger Lee/You Need Love	1958	$30

— *Most, if not all, copies contain the "raunchy" version of "Stagger Lee" with Mr. Lee and Billy playing cards*

❏ S-9972 [S]	Stagger Lee/You Need Love	1958	$50
❏ 10206	String of Pearls/Chantilly Lace	1961	$20
❏ 10229	Talk to Me/I Cover the Waterfront	1961	$20
❏ 10299	Twistin' the Blues/Pop Eye's Irresistable You	1962	$20
❏ 9997 [M]	Where Were You (On Our Wedding Day)?/Is It Really Love	1959	$30
❏ S-9997 [S]	Where Were You (On Our Wedding Day)?/Is It Really Love	1959	$50
❏ 10412	Who's Sorry Now/Hello Bill	1963	$20

DOUBLE-L

❏ 729	Billie Baby/Try a Little Bit of Tenderness	1964	$10
❏ 729 [PS]	Billie Baby/Try a Little Bit of Tenderness	1964	$30
❏ 739	Every Night/Peeping and Hiding	1966	$12
❏ 736	Go On Little Girl/You're Reading Me	1965	$10
❏ 730	I'll Be a Fool for You/You're Nobody Till Somebody Loves You	1964	$10
❏ 728	Merry Christmas Mama/Auld Lang Syne	1963	$15
❏ 722	Misty/Cry On	1963	$10
❏ 714	Pistol Packin' Mama/ Tennessee Waltz	1963	$10
❏ 740	Send Me Some Loving/ Somewhere Along the Way	1966	$10

GSF

❏ 6894	Love Music/Just for Baby	1973	$6
❏ 6882	Sing a Song/(B-side unknown)	1972	$6
❏ 6904	Trying to Slip (Away)/They Get Down	1973	$6

HURD

❏ 82	Misty '66/Saturday Night	1966	$8

JAD

❏ 212	Don't Stop Now/The Truth	1968	$8
❏ 208	Luv, Luv, Luv/Take All	1968	$8
❏ 303	Hello Little Girl/Georgianna	1957	$30
❏ 305	How Many Times/To Love and Be Loved	1957	$30
❏ 301	Lonely Chair/The Chicken and the Bop	1957	$60

LPG

❏ 111	What Did You Do with My Love/Love Music	1976	$6

MONUMENT

❏ 865	Amen/I'd Fight the World	1964	$10
❏ 856	Don't Cry/I Love You, I Just Love You	1964	$12
❏ 887	If I Had My Life to Live Over/ Two for Love	1965	$10
❏ 877	Oh, Lady Luck/Woman	1965	$10

PARAMOUNT

❏ 0168	In the Eyes of God/The Legend of Nigger Charley	1972	$6

REPRISE

❏ 0499	I Won't Cry Anymore/The Man Who Took the Valise Off the Floor at Grand Central Station at Noon	1966	$8

SCEPTER

❏ 12310	Hooked on a Feeling/If You Really Love Him	1971	$6
❏ 12327	Mr. and Mrs. Untrue/Natural Slnner	1971	$6

SPECIALTY

❏ 452	Ain't It a Shame?/Tell Me Pretty Baby	1953	$125

Number	Title	Yr	NM
❏ 452	Ain't It a Shame?/Tell Me Pretty Baby	1953	$200
— Red vinyl			
❏ 602	Baby Please Come Home/Breaking My Heart (All Over Again)	1957	$40
❏ 578	Country Boy Rock/Rock 'N' Dance	1956	$60
❏ 582	Forgive Me, Clawdy/I'm Glad	1956	$40
❏ 471	I Wish Your Picture Was You/Frog Legs	1953	$125
❏ 428	Lawdy Miss Clawdy/Mailman Blues	1952	$250
❏ 428	Lawdy Miss Clawdy/Mailman Blues	1952	$1500
— Red vinyl			
❏ 661	Lawdy Miss Clawdy/Mailman Blues	1959	$30
❏ 483	Let Me Come Home, Baby/Too Late for Tears	1954	$100
❏ 483	Let Me Come Home, Baby/Too Late for Tears	1954	$200
— Red vinyl			
❏ 535	Oo-Ee Baby/Chee-Koo Baby	1954	$50
❏ 440	Oooh-Oooh-Oooh/Restless Heart	1952	$125
❏ 540	Trying to Find Someone to Love/Lord, Lord, Amen!	1955	$50
❏ 494	Walkin' the Track/Jimmie Lee	1954	$100
❏ 457	What's the Matter Now/So Long	1953	$125
❏ 457	What's the Matter Now/So Long	1953	$200
— Red vinyl			
❏ 463	Where You At?/Baby Don't Turn Your Back on Me	1953	$125
❏ 463	Where You At?/Baby Don't Turn Your Back on Me	1953	$200
— Red vinyl			
❏ 571	Woe Ho Ho/I Yi Yi Gomen-a-Sai (I'm Sorry)	1956	$50

TURNTABLE

Number	Title	Yr	NM
❏ 506	Bad Conditions/The Truth	1969	$8
❏ 502	I Heard It Through the Grapevine/It's Your Thing	1969	$8
❏ 501	I Understand/The Grass Will Sing (For You)	1969	$8
❏ 509	Lawdy Miss Clawdy/Little Volcano	1969	$8

7-Inch Extended Plays

ABC-PARAMOUNT

Number	Title	Yr	NM
❏ A-315	Ain't Nobody's Business/Just to Hold Your Hand//Talk to Me/I Cover the Waterfront	1960	$125
❏ A-324	Lady Luck/Personality//Stagger Lee/I'm Gonna Get Married	1960	$125
❏ A-277 [PS]	Lawdy Miss Clawdy/Just Because//You Need Love/Why	1959	$125
❏ A-324 [PS]	Mr. Personality's Big Hits	1960	$125
❏ A-315 [PS]	Mr. Personality Sings the Blues	1960	$125
❏ A-277 [PS]	The Exciting Lloyd Price	1959	$125

PRICE, RAY

ABC

Number	Title	Yr	NM
❏ 12095	Farthest Thing from My Mind/All That Keeps Me Going	1975	$4

ABC DOT

Number	Title	Yr	NM
❏ 17666	A Mansion on the Hill/Hey, Good Lookin'	1976	$4
❏ 17718	Born to Love Me/The Only Way to Say Good Morning	1977	$4
❏ 17690	Different Kind of Flower/Don't Let the Stars Get in Your Eyes	1977	$4
❏ 17588	Say I Do/I'll Still Love You	1975	$4
❏ 17616	That's All She Wrote/I Didn't Feel Nothing	1976	$4
❏ 17637	To Make a Long Story Short/We're Getting There	1976	$4

COLUMBIA

Number	Title	Yr	NM
❏ 21404	A Man Called Peter/Call the Lord and He'll Be There	1955	$30
❏ 45005	April's Fool/Make It Rain	1969	$6
❏ 43162	A Thing Called Sadness/Here Comes My Baby Back Again	1964	$10
❏ 43560	A Way to Survive/I'm Not Crazy Yet	1966	$8
❏ 10631	Born to Love Me/I'm Sorry for the Hateful Thing I Did	1977	$4
❏ 42971	Burning Memories/That's All That Matters	1964	$10
❏ 41191	City Lights/Invitation to the Blues	1958	$15
❏ 21117	Cold Shoulder/You Weren't Ashamed to Kiss Me	1953	$30
❏ 21510	Crazy Arms/You Done Me Wrong	1956	$20
❏ 41105	Curtain in the Window/It's All Your Fault	1958	$15
❏ 44042	Danny Boy/I'll Let My Mind Wander	1967	$8

Number	Title	Yr	NM
❏ 44042 [PS]	Danny Boy/I'll Let My Mind Wander	1967	$15
❏ 21025	Don't Let the Stars Get In Your Eyes/I Lost the Only Love I Know	1952	$30
❏ 43427	Don't You Ever Get Tired of Hurting Me/Unloved, Unwanted	1965	$8
❏ 45178	For the Good Times/Grazin' in Greener Pastures	1970	$6
❏ 41374	Heartaches By the Number/Wall of Tears	1959	$15
❏ 20863	Heart Aching Blues/Till Death Do Us Part	1951	$40
❏ 41947	Heart Over Mind/The Twenty-Fourth Hour	1961	$12
❏ 10503	Help Me/Nobody Wins	1977	$4
❏ 20943	Hot Diggity Dog/I've Got to Hurry, Hurry, Hurry	1952	$30
— With Jimmy Dickens			
❏ 21015	I Can't Escape from You/Won't You Please Be Mine	1952	$30
❏ 21442	I Can't Go On Like This/I Don't Want It on My Conscience	1955	$20
❏ 21299	I Could Love You More/What If He Don't Love You	1954	$30
❏ 45425	I'd Rather Be Sorry/When I Loved Her	1971	$5
❏ 21315	If You Don't, Somebody Else Will/Oh Yes Darling	1954	$30
❏ 10150	If You Ever Change Your Mind/Just Enough to Make Me Stay	1975	$4
❏ 21214	I'll Be There (If You Ever Want Me)/Release Me	1954	$30
❏ 40889	I'll Be There (When You Get Lonely)/Please Don't Leave Me	1957	$20
❏ 20883	I Made a Mistake and I'm Sorry/Weary Blues	1952	$30
❏ 44195	I'm Still Not Over You/Crazy	1967	$8
❏ 20833	I Saw My Castles Fall Today/Hey Lala	1951	$40
❏ 44505	I've Been There Before/Night Life	1968	$8
❏ 21562	I've Got a New Heartache/Wasted Words	1956	$20
❏ 42310	I've Just Destroyed the World (I'm Living In)/Big Shoes	1962	$10
❏ 41767	I Wish I Could Fall in Love Today/I Can't Run Away from Myself	1960	$15
❏ 45329	I Won't Mention It Again/Kiss the World Goodbye	1971	$5
❏ 21173	Leave Her Alone/You Always Get By	1953	$30
❏ 10006	Like a First Time Thing/You Are the Song	1974	$5
❏ 42827	Make the World Go Away/Night Life	1963	$10
❏ 21249	Much Too Young to Die/I Love You So Much	1954	$30
❏ 40951	My Shoes Keep Walking Back to You/Don't Do This to Me	1957	$20
❏ 21354	One Broken Heart/I'm Alone Because I Love You	1955	$20
❏ 41590	One More Time/Who'll Be the First	1960	$15
❏ 43086	Please Talk to My Heart/I Don't Know Why	1964	$10
❏ 21089	Price for Loving You/That's What I Got for Loving You	1953	$30
❏ 42518	Pride/I'm Walking Slow	1962	$10
❏ 44747	Set Me Free/Trouble	1969	$6
❏ 45724	She's Got to Be a Saint/Oh Lonesome Me	1972	$5
❏ 44628	She Wears My Ring/Goin' Away	1968	$8
❏ 42132	Soft Rain/Here We Are Again	1961	$12
❏ 46015	Storms of Troubled Times/Some Things Never Change	1974	$5
❏ 44761	Sweetheart of the Year/How Can I Write on Paper (What I Feel in My Heart)	1969	$6
❏ 21402	Sweet Little Miss Blue Eyes/Let Me Talk to You	1955	$20
❏ 44374	Take Me As I Am (Or Let Me Go)/In the Summer of My Life	1967	$8
❏ 20913	Talk to Your Heart/I've Got to Hurry, Hurry, Hurry	1952	$30
❏ 41309	That's What It's Like to Be Lonesome/Kissing Your Picture	1958	$15
❏ 45583	The Lonesomest Lonesome/That's What Leaving's About	1972	$5
❏ 43264	The Other Woman/Tearful Earful	1965	$8
❏ 41477	The Same Old Me/Under Your Spell Again	1959	$15
❏ 31428 [S]	(titles unknown)	1962	$20
❏ 31429 [S]	(titles unknown)	1962	$20
❏ 31430 [S]	(titles unknown)	1962	$20
❏ 31431 [S]	(titles unknown)	1962	$20
❏ 31432 [S]	(titles unknown)	1962	$20

—Anyone who can fill in these gaps -- the above 5 all are Columbia "Stereo 7" singles -- please let us know.

Number	Title	Yr	NM
❏ 43795	Touch My Heart/It Should Be Easier Now	1966	$8

Number	Title	Yr	NM
❏ 42658	Walk Me to the Door/You Took Her Off My Hands (Now Please Take Her Off My Mind)	1963	$10
❏ 21149	Wrong Side of Town/Who Stole That Train	1953	$30

DIMENSION

Number	Title	Yr	NM
❏ 1024	Diamonds in the Stars/Grazing in Greener Pastures	1981	$4
❏ 1031	Forty and Fadin'/Something to Forget You By	1982	$4
❏ 1018	Getting Over You Again/Circle Driveway	1981	$4
❏ 1021	It Don't Hurt Me Half As Bad/She's the Right Kind of Woman (Loving the Wrong Kind of Man)	1981	$4
❏ 1038	Somewhere in Texas/Getting Down and Getting High	1982	$4
❏ 1035	Will Till Those Bridges Are Gone/Angel in My Heart (Devil in My Mind)	1982	$4

MONUMENT

Number	Title	Yr	NM
❏ 45-267	Feet/Let's Make a Nice Memory (Today)	1978	$4
❏ 45-290	Misty Morning Rain/We Can't Build a Fire in the Rain	1979	$4
❏ 45-283	That's the Only Way to Say Good Morning/All the Good Things Are Gone	1979	$4
❏ 45-277	There's Always Me/If It All the Same to You (I'll Be Leaving in the Morning)	1979	$4

MYRRH

Number	Title	Yr	NM
❏ 146	Like Old Times Again/My First Day Without Her	1974	$5

STEP ONE

Number	Title	Yr	NM
❏ 355	All the Way/Bummin' Around	1986	$4
❏ 383	Big Ole Teardrops/The Season for Missing You	1988	$4
❏ 388	Don't the Morning Always Come Too Soon/All You Have to Do Is Come Back	1988	$4
❏ 350	Five Fingers/Lonely Like a Rose	1985	$4
❏ 381	For Christmas/With Christmas Near	1987	$4
❏ 393	I'd Do It All Over Again/Wind Beneath My Wings	1988	$4
❏ 344	I'm Not Leaving (I'm Just Getting Out of Your Way)/Why Don't Love Just Go Away	1985	$4
❏ 410	Love Me Down to Size/(B-side unknown)	1989	$4
❏ 361	Please Don't Talk About Me When I'm Gone/For the Good Times	1986	$4
❏ 370	Sentimental Journey/Better Class of Loser	1987	$4
❏ 341	(She Got a Hold of Me Where It Hurts) She Won't Let Go/Memories to Burn	1985	$4
❏ 366	When You Gave Your Love to Me/Forty and Fadin'	1986	$4

VIVA

Number	Title	Yr	NM
❏ 29217	Better Class of Loser/Everytime I Sing a Love Song	1984	$3
❏ 29458	Coors in Colorado/Living Her Life in a Song	1983	$4
❏ 29543	Scotch and Soda/I Love You Eyes	1983	$3
❏ 29147	What Am I Gonna Do Without You/You've Been Leaving Me for Years	1984	$3

WARNER BROS.

Number	Title	Yr	NM
❏ 29830	One Fiddle, Two Fiddle/San Antonio Rose	1982	$4
❏ 29691	Willie, Write Me a Song/I Love You Eyes	1983	$3
❏ B-10153	I'll Sail My Ship Alone/I Can't Help It//A Mansion on the Hill/Pins and Needles in My Heart	1957	$20
❏ B-10151	I Love You Because/Let Me Talk to You//Blues, Stay Away from Me/Many Tears Ago	1957	$20
❏ B-10152	Letters Have No Arms/Faded Love//Remember Me (I'm the One Who Loves You)/I Saw My Castles Fall Today	1957	$20

PRIDE, CHARLEY

16TH AVENUE

Number	Title	Yr	NM
❏ 70435	Amy's Eyes/I Made Love to You in My Mind	1989	$4
❏ 70400	Have I Got Some Blues for You/Ever Knowin'	1987	$4
❏ 70402	If You Still Want a Fool Around/You Took Me There	1987	$4
❏ 70414	I'm Gonna Love Her on the Radio/Shouldn't It Be Easier Than This	1988	$4
❏ 70408	Shouldn't It Be Easier Than This/Look in Your Mirror	1987	$4
❏ 70429	The More I Do/Heaven Help Us All	1989	$4

Number	Title	Yr	NM
❏ 70420	Where Was I/A Whole Lotta Lovin' (Goes a Long, Long Way)	1988	$4
❏ 70425	White Houses/Shouldn't It Be Easier Than This	1989	$4

RCA

Number	Title	Yr	NM
❏ PB-10757	A Whole Lotta Things to Sing About/The Hardest Part of Livin's Lovin' Me	1976	$4
❏ PB-11391	Burgers and Fries/Nothing's Prettier Than Rose Is	1978	$4
❏ GB-11992	Burgers and Fries/Where Do I Put Her Memory	1980	$3

—*Gold Standard Series" reissue*

| ❏ PB-11736 | Dallas Cowboys/When I Stop Leaving | 1979 | $15 |

—*Special blue and silver label edition*

| ❏ PB-11736 | Dallas Cowboys/When I Stop Leaving | 1979 | $6 |

—*Regular black-label edition*

❏ PB-14045	Down on the Farm/Now and Then	1985	$3
❏ PB-13648	Ev'ry Heart Should Have One/Lovin' It Up (Livin' It Down)	1983	$3
❏ PB-11912	Honky Tonk Blues/I'm So Lonesome I Could Cry	1980	$3
❏ GB-12371	Honky Tonk Blues/You Win Again	1981	$3

—*Gold Standard Series" reissue*

❏ PB-13096	I Don't Think She's in Love Anymore/Oh What a Beautiful Love Song	1982	$3
❏ PB-10975	I'll Be Leaving Alone/We Need Lovin'	1977	$4
❏ PB-14134	Let a Little Love Come In/Night Games	1985	$3
❏ PB-13667	Let It Snow, Let It Snow, Let It Snow/O Holy Night	1983	$4
❏ PB-13359	Let It Snow, Let It Snow, Let It Snow/Peace on Earth	1982	$5

—*B-side by Razzy Bailey*

❏ PB-14296	Love on a Blue Rainy Day/I Used It All on You	1986	$3
❏ PB-13936	Missin' Mississippi/Falling in Love Again	1984	$3
❏ PB-11751	Missin' You/Heartbreak Mountain	1979	$4
❏ PB-13451	More and More/Radio Heroes	1983	$3
❏ PB-11086	More to Me/Heaven Watches Over Fools Like Me	1977	$4
❏ PB-13014	Mountain of Love/Love Is a Shadow	1981	$3
❏ GB-11331	My Eyes Can Only See As Far As You/A Whole Lotta Things to Sing About	1978	$3

—*Gold Standard Series" reissue*

❏ PB-10875	She's Just An Old Love Turned Memory/Country Music	1977	$4
❏ PB-11201	Someone Loves You Honey/Days of Our Lives	1978	$4
❏ GB-11498	Someone Loves You Honey/When I Stop Leaving (I'll Be Gone)	1979	$3

—*Gold Standard Series" reissue*

| ❏ JK-13754 | Stagger Lee (same on both sides) | 1984 | $10 |

—*Promo on red vinyl*

❏ PB-14265	The Best There Is/The Tumbleweed and the Rose	1986	$3
❏ PB-13732	The Late Show/Love on a Blue Rainy Day	1984	$4
❏ PB-13821	The Power of Love/Ellie	1984	$3
❏ PB-11287	When I Stop Leaving (I'll Be Gone)/I Can See the Lovin' in Your Eyes	1978	$4
❏ PB-11477	Where Do I Put Her Memory/The Best in the World	1979	$4
❏ PB-13397	Why Baby Why/It's So Good to Be Together	1982	$3

RCA VICTOR

Number	Title	Yr	NM
❏ 74-0624	All His Children/You'll Still Be the One	1972	$5
❏ 74-0167	All I Have to Offer You (Is Me)/Brand New Bed of Roses	1969	$8
❏ GB-10509	Amazing Love/Blue Ridge Mountains Turning Green	1975	$3

—*Gold Standard Series" reissue*

| ❏ APBO-0073 | Amazing Love/Blue Ridge Mountains Turnin' Green | 1973 | $5 |
| ❏ AMBO-0128 | A Shoulder to Cry On/Don't Fight the Feelings of Love | 1973 | $4 |

—*Gold Standard Series" reissue*

❏ 74-0884	A Shoulder to Cry On/I'm Learning to Love Her	1973	$5
❏ 47-8738	Atlantic Coastal Line/Snakes Crawl at Night	1966	$20
❏ 47-9933	Christmas in My Home Town/Santa and the Kids	1970	$8
❏ 447-0935	Christmas in My Home Town/Santa and the Kids	1972	$4

—*Gold Standard Series*

Number	Title	Yr	NM
❏ 47-9281	Does My Ring Hurt Your Finger/The Spell of the Freight Train	1967	$15

—*Above three labeled as "Country Charley Pride*

❏ 74-0942	Don't Fight the Feelings of Love/Tennessee Girl	1973	$5
❏ PB-10344	Hope You're Feelin' Me (Like I'm Feelin' You)/Searching for the Morning Sun	1975	$4
❏ PB-10236	I Ain't All Bad/Hard Times Will Be the Best Times	1975	$4
❏ GB-10674	I Ain't All Bad/Hope You're Feelin' Me (Like I'm Feelin' You)	1976	$4

—*Gold Standard Series" reissue*

❏ 47-9902	I Can't Believe That You've Stopped Loving Me/Time	1970	$6
❏ 47-9952	I'd Rather Love You/You Don't Belong	1971	$6
❏ 47-9162	I Know One/The Best Banjo Picker	1967	$15
❏ 47-9996	I'm Just Me/A Place for the Lonesome	1971	$6
❏ 447-0920	I'm Just Me/Jeanie Norman	1972	$6

—*Gold Standard Series on red label; B-side makes its first 45 rpm appearance here*

❏ 74-0265	(I'm So) Afraid of Losing You Again/Good Chance of Tear-Fall Tonight	1969	$8
❏ PB-10643	In Jesus' Name I Pray/I Don't Deserve a Mansion	1976	$6
❏ 47-9806	Is Anybody Goin' to San Antone/Things Are Looking Up	1970	$6
❏ 74-0707	It's Gonna Take a Little Bit Longer/You're Wanting Me to Stop Loving You	1972	$5
❏ 74-0707 [PS]	It's Gonna Take a Little Bit Longer/You're Wanting Me to Stop Loving You	1972	$8
❏ 47-9974	Let Me Live/Did You Think to Pray	1971	$8
❏ 47-9622	Let the Chips Fall/She Made Me Go	1968	$8
❏ 47-8862	Miller's Cave/Before I Met You	1966	$20
❏ PB-10030	Mississippi Cotton Picking Delta Town/Mary Go Round	1974	$4
❏ GB-10508	Mississippi Cotton Picking Delta Town/Mary Go Round	1975	$3

—*Gold Standard Series" reissue*

❏ PB-10592	My Eyes Can Only See As Far As You/Oklahoma Morning	1976	$4
❏ 74-0802	She's Too Good to Be True/She's That Kind	1972	$5
❏ 47-9403	The Day the World Stood Still/Gone, On the Other Hand	1967	$8
❏ 47-9514	The Easy Part's Over/Right to Do Wrong	1968	$8
❏ PB-10455	The Happiness of Having You/Right Back Missing You Again	1975	$4
❏ PB-10126	Then Who Am I/Completely Helpless	1974	$4
❏ GB-10507	Then Who Am I/Completely Helpless	1975	$3

—*Gold Standard Series" reissue*

❏ APBO-0257	We Could/Love Put a Song in My Heart	1974	$5
❏ 47-9777	Wings of a Dove/They Stood in Silent Prayer	1969	$15
❏ 47-9855	Wonder Could I Live There Anymore/Piroque Joe	1970	$6

PRIESMAN, MAGEL

SUN

Number	Title	Yr	NM
❏ 294	Memories of You/I Feel So Blue	1958	$30

PRIMA, LOUIS, AND KEELY SMITH

CAPITOL

Number	Title	Yr	NM
❏ F4140	I've Got You Under My Skin/Don't Take Your Love from Me	1959	$10
❏ F4063	That Old Black Magic/You Are My Love	1958	$15

DOT

❏ 16249	Because of You/Absent Minded Lover	1961	$12
❏ 16192	Begin the Beguine/Surprise Package	1961	$12
❏ 15956	Bei Mir Bist Du Schoen/I Don't Know Why	1959	$12
❏ 16221	Mustapha/The Shepard Man	1961	$10

PRIMA, LOUIS

ABC

Number	Title	Yr	NM
❏ 11093	Almost Persuaded/Waitin' in Your Welfare Line	1968	$6
❏ 11166	Flooby Dooby Doo/I Never Opened My Eyes	1969	$6
❏ 12047	Time Heals Everything/When Hazel Comes in the Room	1974	$4

BRUNSWICK

Number	Title	Yr	NM
❏ 55485	I Left My Heart in San Francisco/I Never Promised You a Rose Garden	1972	$6

BUENA VISTA

| ❏ F-461 | I Wanna Be Like You/The Bare Necessities | 1967 | $20 |

—*B-side by Phil Harris*

| ❏ 454 | Santa, How Come Your Eyes Are Green When Last Year They Were Blue/Senor Santa Claus | 1966 | $15 |

CAPITOL

| ❏ F3566 | A Banana Spilt for My Baby/ Five Months, Two Weeks, Two Days | 1956 | $15 |

—*With Sam Butera*

| ❏ F3856 | Beep Beep/Buona Sera | 1957 | $15 |
| ❏ 4805 | Big Daddy/Ooh, Look What You've Done to Me | 1962 | $12 |

—*With Gia Maione*

| ❏ F3667 | Midnight Melody/The Wild Ones | 1957 | $15 |

—*With Sam Butera*

| ❏ 4732 | Twist All Night/Everybody Knows | 1962 | $10 |
| ❏ F3615 | Whistle Stop/Be Mine | 1957 | $15 |

—*With Sam Butera*

COLUMBIA

❏ 40064	Barncale Bill the Sailor/ Shepherd Boy	1953	$30
❏ 39692	Basta/Ooh Dah Dilly Dah	1952	$30
❏ 39823	Chili Sauce/One Mint Julep	1952	$30
❏ 39969	Oh Marie/Luigi	1953	$30
❏ 40015	Paul Revere/It's As Good As New	1953	$30
❏ 39614	Shake Hands with Santa/ Eleanor	1951	$30
❏ 39735	The Bigger the Figure/Boney Bones	1952	$30

DECCA

| ❏ 29128 | Happy Wanderer/Until Sunrise | 1954 | $20 |
| ❏ 29162 | Paper Doll/The Dummy Song | 1954 | $20 |

DOT

❏ 15978	Confessin'/Night and Day	1959	$10
❏ 16301	Continental Twist/Oh Ma Ma Twist	1962	$10
❏ 16108	Don't You Know/Brooklyn Bridge	1960	$12
❏ 16193	Enchantment/Chapel by the Sea	1961	$12
❏ 16009	Hey Ba-Ba-Re-Bop/My Cucuzza	1959	$12
❏ 16273	Mod Indigo/Come Back to Sorrento	1961	$10
❏ 16211	My Prayer/You Can Depend on Me	1961	$10
❏ 16060	When My Baby Smiles at Me/Paradise	1960	$10
❏ 16151	Wonderland by Night/Ol' Man Moses	1960	$10

HANNA-BARBERA

| ❏ 467 | I'm Gonna Sit Right Down and Write Myself a Letter/ Civilization (Bongo, Bongo, Bongo) | 1966 | $10 |

MERCURY

❏ 5406	Francis, the Talking Mule/A Good Time Was Had By All	1950	$40
❏ 5451	Here, Pretty Kitty/Buona Sera	1950	$40
❏ 5386	Over the Rainbow/Tears on My Tie	1950	$40

—*Note: Earlier Louis Prima 45s on Mercury may exist.*

RCA VICTOR

| ❏ 47-2960 | Five Foot Two, Eyes of Blue/ For Mari-Yooten | 1949 | $30 |

ROBIN HOOD

| ❏ 102 | Goodbye Joe/My Conchetta | 1950 | $40 |
| ❏ 101 | Oh Babe!/Piccolina Lena | 1950 | $40 |

UNITED ARTISTS

❏ 50175	Illya Darling/I Believe in You	1967	$6
❏ 50200	My Cup Runneth Over/ Cabaret	1967	$6
❏ 50223	The Impossible Dream/Poor Old Marat	1967	$6

7-Inch Extended Plays

CAPITOL

❏ EAP 1-908	*On the Sunny Side of the Street/Exactly Like You/ Robin Hood/Oh Babe	1957	$20
❏ EAP 2-908	Foggy Day/How High the Moon//Come Back to Sorrento/I Gotta Right to Sing the Blues	1957	$20
❏ EAP 1-755	Medley: Just a Gigolo-I Ain't Got Nobody-Nobody Cares for Me//Night Train/(I'll Be Glad When You're Dead) You Rascal You	1956	$20

Number	Title	Yr	NM
❏ EAP 1-836	Medley: When You're Smiling (The Whole World Smiles with You)-The Shiek of Araby/Blow, Red, Blow//When the Saints Go Marching In	1957	$20
❏ EAP 1-836 [PS]	The Call of the Wildest, Part 1	1957	$20
❏ EAP 1-755 [PS]	The Wildest! Part 1	1956	$20
❏ EAP 1-908 [PS]	The Wildest Show at Tahoe, Part 1	1957	$20
❏ EAP 2-908 [PS]	The Wildest Show at Tahoe, Part 2	1957	$20

COLUMBIA

Number	Title	Yr	NM
❏ B-12061	*Chop Suey Chow Mein/ Basta/Barnacle Bill the Sailor/Shepherd Boy	1959	$20
❏ B-12061 [PS]	Breakin' It Up!	1959	$20

PRIMETTES, THE

LUPINE

Number	Title	Yr	NM
❏ 120	Tears of Sorrow/Pretty	1962	$300

PRIMITIVES, THE (1)

PARKWAY

Number	Title	Yr	NM
❏ 940	Help Me/Let Them Fall	1965	$30

PRIMITIVES, THE (2)

PICKWICK

Number	Title	Yr	NM
❏ 1001	The Ostrich/Sneaky Pete	1964	$300

PRINCE

Includes records as "Prince and the Revolution," "Prince and the N.P.G." (or New Power Generation); plus later releases as an unpronounceable glyph. Also see 94 EAST.

PAISLEY PARK

Number	Title	Yr	NM
❏ 27900	Alphabet St./Alphabet St. (Cont.)	1988	$3
❏ 27900 [PS]	Alphabet St./Alphabet St. (Cont.)	1988	$3
—Heavy PVC sleeve with title sticker			
❏ 27900 [DJ]	Alphabet St./Alphabet St. (Cont.)	1988	$8
❏ 28999	America/Girl	1985	$4
❏ 28999 [PS]	America/Girl	1985	$4
❏ 28999 [DJ]	America (same on both sides)	1985	$8
❏ 28620	Anotherloverholenyohead/ Girls and Boys	1986	$3
❏ 28620 [PS]	Anotherloverholenyohead/ Girls and Boys	1986	$3
❏ 28620 [DJ]	Anotherloverholenyohead (same on both sides)	1986	$8
❏ 28620 [DJ]	Girls and Boys (same on both sides)	1986	$15
❏ 27806	Glam Slam/Escape	1988	$3
❏ 27806 [PS]	Glam Slam/Escape	1988	$3
—Heavy plastic sleeve with title sticker			
❏ 27806 [DJ]	Glam Slam (same on both sides)	1988	$8
❏ PRO-S-3211 [DJ]	Glam Slam (Shep Pettibone Remix 4:22)/(Edit 3:28)	1988	$20
❏ PRO-S-2939 [DJ]	Hot Thing (same on both sides)	1987	$15
❏ 28288	I Could Never Take the Place of Your Man/Hot Thing	1987	$3
❏ 28288 [PS]	I Could Never Take the Place of Your Man/Hot Thing	1987	$3
❏ 28288 [DJ]	I Could Never Take the Place of Your Man (same on both sides)	1987	$8
❏ 28334 [DJ]	If I Was Your Girlfriend (same on both sides)	1987	$8
❏ 28334	If I Was Your Girlfriend/ Shockadelica	1987	$3
❏ 28334 [PS]	If I Was Your Girlfriend/ Shockadelica	1987	$3
❏ PRO-S-3371 [DJ]	I Wish U Heaven (Radio Edit of Remix 4:25)/(Single Edit of Remix 5:45)	1988	$20
❏ 27745 [DJ]	I Wish U Heaven (same on both sides)	1988	$8
❏ 27745	I Wish U Heaven/Scarlet Pussy	1988	$3
❏ 27745 [PS]	I Wish U Heaven/Scarlet Pussy	1988	$5
❏ 28711	Mountains/Alexa de Paris	1986	$3
❏ 28711 [PS]	Mountains/Alexa de Paris	1986	$3
❏ 28711 [DJ]	Mountains (same on both sides)	1986	$8
❏ 29052 [PS]	Paisley Park/She's Always In My Hair	1985	$500
—Evidently, some U.S. picture sleeves exist (not to be confused with European sleeves for this record)			
❏ GWB 0529	Pop Life/America	1986	$3
—Back to Back Hits" reissue			
❏ 28998	Pop Life/Hello	1985	$3
❏ 28998 [PS]	Pop Life/Hello	1985	$3
❏ 28998 [DJ]	Pop Life (same on both sides)	1985	$8
❏ GWB 0528	Purple Rain/Raspberry Beret	1986	$3
—Back to Back Hits" reissue			
❏ 28399	Sign "O" the Times/La, La, La, Hee, Hee, Hee	1987	$3
❏ 28399 [PS]	Sign "O" the Times/La, La, La, Hee, Hee, Hee	1987	$3

Number	Title	Yr	NM
❏ 28399 [DJ]	Sign "O" the Times (same on both sides)	1987	$8

WARNER BROS.

Number	Title	Yr	NM
❏ 29896	1999/How Come U Don't Call Me Anymore?	1982	$5
❏ 29896 [PS]	1999/How Come U Don't Call Me Anymore?	1982	$12
❏ GWB 0468	1999/Little Red Corvette	1984	$3
—Back to Back Hits" reissue			
❏ 29896 [DJ]	1999 (stereo/mono)	1982	$8
❏ 21980	Anotherloverholenyohead/ Mountains	1987	$3
—Back to Back Hits" series			
❏ 22924	Batdance/200 Balloons	1989	$3
❏ 22924 [PS]	Batdance/200 Balloons	1989	$3
❏ 21859	Batdance/Partyman	1989	$3
—Back to Back Hits" series			
❏ 22924 [DJ]	Batdance (same on both sides)	1989	$12
❏ 49808 [DJ]	Controversy (stereo/mono)	1981	$8
❏ 49808	Controversy/When You Were Mine	1981	$20
❏ 29503	Delirious/Horny Toad	1983	$6
—Label erroneously lists A-side time at 3:56			
❏ 29503 [PS]	Delirious/Horny Toad	1983	$60
—Fold-out poster sleeve			
❏ 29503	Delirious/Horny Toad	1983	$5
—Label lists correct A-side time of 2:36			
❏ GWB 0476	Delirious/Let's Pretend We're Married	1984	$3
—Back to Back Hits" reissue			
❏ 29503 [DJ]	Delirious (stereo/mono)	1983	$12
—Label on both sides lists incorrect A-side time of 3:56			
❏ 49638 [DJ]	Dirty Mind (stereo/mono)	1980	$8
❏ 49638	Dirty Mind/When We're Dancing Close and Slow	1980	$20
❏ 29942	Do Me, Baby/Private Joy	1982	$20
❏ 29942 [DJ]	Do Me, Baby (stereo/mono)	1982	$8
❏ 21858	I Could Never Take the Place of Your Man/Alphabet St.	1989	$3
—Back to Back Hits" series			
❏ 49050	I Wanna Be Your Lover/My Love Is Forever	1979	$10
❏ 49050 [DJ]	I Wanna Be Your Lover (stereo/mono)	1979	$20
❏ GWB 0392	I Wanna Be Your Lover/ Why You Wanna Treat Me So Bad?	1982	$4
—Back to Back Hits" reissue			
❏ 29121	I Would Die 4 U/Another Lonely Christmas	1984	$4
❏ 29121 [PS]	I Would Die 4 U/Another Lonely Christmas	1984	$4
❏ 29121 [DJ]	I Would Die 4 U (same on both sides)	1984	$8
❏ GWB 0517	I Would Die 4 U/Take Me With U	1985	$3
—Back to Back Hits" reissue			
❏ 29216	Let's Go Crazy/Erotic City	1984	$4
❏ 29216 [PS]	Let's Go Crazy/Erotic City	1984	$8
❏ 29216 [DJ]	Let's Go Crazy (same on both sides)	1984	$8
❏ 29548	Let's Pretend We're Married/ Irresistible Bitch	1983	$5
❏ 29548 [PS]	Let's Pretend We're Married/ Irresistible Bitch	1983	$12
❏ 29548 [DJ]	Let's Pretend We're Married (stereo/mono)	1983	$8
❏ 50002	Let's Work/Ronnie Talk to Russia	1982	$20
❏ 50002 [DJ]	Let's Work (stereo/mono)	1982	$8
❏ 20129 [PD]	Little Red Corvette/1999	1983	$50
—7-inch picture disc with custom sticker; numbered as if a 12-inch single			
❏ 29746	Little Red Corvette/All the Critics Love U in New York	1983	$5
❏ 29746 [DJ]	Little Red Corvette (Edit 3:08)/(Dance Remix 4:32)	1983	$15
❏ 49050 [PS]	My Love Is Forever	1979	$100
—Promo-only sleeve; withdrawn when "I Wanna Be Your Lover" was pushed as the A-side			
❏ 49050 [DJ]	My Love Is Forever (stereo/ mono)	1979	$30
❏ 22814	Partyman/Feel U Up	1989	$3
❏ 22814 [PS]	Partyman/Feel U Up	1989	$3
❏ 22814 [DJ]	Partyman (same on both sides)	1989	$15
❏ 29174	Purple Rain/God	1984	$4
—Purple vinyl			
❏ 29174 [PS]	Purple Rain/God	1984	$8
—Plastic semi-transparent sleeve			
❏ 29174 [DJ]	Purple Rain (same on both sides)	1984	$8
—Purple vinyl			
❏ 22824 [DJ]	Scandalous (same on both sides)	1989	$30

—The last Prince promo 45 -- though "Partyman" has a lower number, it was released earlier, as opposed to the usual backwards numbering of Warner Bros. from 1982 on

Number	Title	Yr	NM
❏ 22824	Scandalous/When 2 R In Love	1989	$3
❏ 22824 [PS]	Scandalous/When 2 R In Love	1989	$3
❏ 21938	Sign "O" the Times/U Got the Look	1988	$3
—Back to Back Hits" series			
❏ 8619	Soft and Wet/So Blue	1978	$40
—Two slightly different variations exist; one has the time of each side under the catalog number, the other has the time of each side after the titles			
❏ 8619 [DJ]	Soft and Wet (stereo/mono)	1978	$20
❏ 49226	Still Waiting/Bambi	1980	$20
❏ 49226 [DJ]	Still Waiting (stereo/mono)	1980	$8
❏ 29079	Take Me With U/Baby I'm a Star	1985	$4
❏ 29079 [PS]	Take Me With U/Baby I'm a Star	1985	$4
❏ 29079 [DJ]	Take Me With U (same on both sides)	1985	$8
❏ 22757	The Arms of Orion/I Love U in Me	1989	$3
❏ 22757 [PS]	The Arms of Orion/I Love U in Me	1989	$3
—With Sheena Easton			
❏ 29286 [DJ]	When Doves Cry (3:49)/ (5:52)	1984	$10
—Purple vinyl promo			
❏ 29286 [DJ]	When Doves Cry (3:49)/ (5:52)	1984	$8
—Black vinyl			
❏ 29286	When Doves Cry/17 Days	1984	$30
—Purple vinyl			
❏ 29286	When Doves Cry/17 Days	1984	$3
—Black vinyl			
❏ 29286 [PS]	When Doves Cry/17 Days	1984	$3
❏ GWB 0516	When Doves Cry/Let's Go Crazy	1985	$3
—Back to Back Hits" reissue			
❏ 49178	Why You Wanna Treat Me So Bad?/Baby	1980	$40
❏ 49178 [PS]	Why You Wanna Treat Me So Bad?/Baby	1980	$70
❏ 49178 [DJ]	Why You Wanna Treat Me So Bad? (stereo/mono)	1980	$20

PRINCE, BOBBY

CHANCE

Number	Title	Yr	NM
❏ 1158	Better Think It Over/If You Only Knew	1954	$400
❏ 1128	Tell Me Why, Why, Why/I Want to Hold You	1953	$500

EXCELLO

Number	Title	Yr	NM
❏ 2039	Too Many Keys/Please Give Me Your Love	1954	$100

PRINCE BUSTER

AMY

Number	Title	Yr	NM
❏ 906	Everybody Ska/30 Pieces of Silver	1964	$20

PHILIPS

Number	Title	Yr	NM
❏ 40427	Ten Commandments/Don't Make Me Cry	1967	$15

RCA VICTOR

Number	Title	Yr	NM
❏ 47-9114	Ten Commandments from Woman to Man/Ain't That Saying a Lot	1967	$15

PRINE, JOHN

ASYLUM

Number	Title	Yr	NM
❏ 45509	Fish and Whistle/Sabu Visits the Twin Cities Alone	1978	$4
❏ 45550	There She Goes/That's the Way That the World Goes 'Round	1978	$4

ATLANTIC

Number	Title	Yr	NM
❏ 2925	Clocks and Spoons/ Everybody	1972	$5
❏ 3297	Common Sense/Come Back to Us Barbara Lewis, Harre Krishna, Beauregard	1975	$4
❏ 3013	Grandpa Was a Carpenter/ Onomatopoeia	1974	$4
❏ 3276	Middle Man/Saddle in the Rain	1975	$4
❏ 2815	Sam Stone/Blue Umbrella	1971	$5

PRISCO, TOMMY

EPIC

Number	Title	Yr	NM
❏ 5-9267	Chewin' Gum/O Bella Mia	1958	$30
❏ 5-9239	I Don't Want to Love You/ Hasty Words	1957	$30
❏ 5-9219	Maybe Someday/Teardrops in My Heart	1957	$30
❏ 5-9315	Stingaree/Only Once	1959	$40
❏ 5-9302	Till There Was You/For Me and My Girl	1959	$30

Number	Title	Yr	NM

PRISONAIRES, THE
SUN
❏ 191	A Prisoner's Prayer/I Know	1953	$500
❏ 189	Softly and Tenderly/My God Is Real	1953	$700
❏ 207	There Is Love in You/What'll You Do Next	1954	$12000

— VG 5000; VG+ 8500

PRIX
ORK
| ❏ 81979 [B] | Girl, Everytime I Close My Eyes/Zero | 1977 | $35 |

PRIZES, THE
PARKWAY
| ❏ 917 | Summer's Here at Last/I Found Someone New | 1964 | $10 |

PROBY, P.J.
BETA
| ❏ 1008 | Loud Perfume/(B-side unknown) | 1958 | $200 |

— As "Jett Powers"

DESIGN
| ❏ 811 | Go Girl Go/Teen-Age Quarrel | 1957 | $300 |

— As "Jett Powers"

LIBERTY
❏ 55989	Butterfly High/Just Holding On	1967	$10
❏ 55850	Good Things Are Coming My Way/Maria	1965	$15
❏ 55915	I Can't Make It Alone/If I Ruled the World	1966	$15
❏ 55915 [PS]	I Can't Make It Alone/If I Ruled the World	1966	$20
❏ 56031	It's Your Day Today/I Apologize	1968	$8
❏ 55875	My Prayer/Wicked Woman	1966	$15
❏ 55588	So Do I/I Can't Take It Like You Can	1963	$20
❏ 55757	Somewhere/Just Like Him	1964	$15
❏ 55791	Stagger Lee/Mission Bell	1965	$15
❏ 55806	That Means a Lot/Let the Water Run Down	1965	$30

— The A-side is a Lennon-McCartney song; the Beatles' own version was not released until 1996

❏ 55505	The Other Side of Town/Watch Me Walk Away	1962	$20
❏ 55367	There Stands the One/Try to Forget Her	1961	$20
❏ 56051	What's Wrong with My World/Turn Her Away	1968	$8
❏ 55974	Work with Me Annie/You Can't Come Home Again (If You Leave Me Now)	1967	$10
❏ 55974 [PS]	Work with Me Annie/You Can't Come Home Again (If You Leave Me Now)	1967	$20

LONDON
❏ 9648	Hold Me/The Tip of My Fingers	1964	$20
❏ 9688	Hold Me/The Tip of My Fingers	1964	$20
❏ 9705	Sweet and Tender Romance/Together	1964	$20

PROCESSION
SMASH
| ❏ 2225 | Adelaide, Adelaide/One Day in Every Week | 1969 | $8 |
| ❏ 2239 | Every American Citizen/You-Me | 1969 | $8 |

PROCLAIMERS, THE
CHRYSALIS
| ❏ VS443283 | I'm Gonna Be (500 Miles)/Better Days | 1988 | $5 |
| ❏ VS443283 [PS] | I'm Gonna Be (500 Miles)/Better Days | 1988 | $5 |

PROCOL HARUM
Also see THE PARAMOUNTS (4); ROBIN TROWER.

A&M
❏ 1069	A Salty Dog/Long Gone Geek	1969	$8
❏ 1389	A Whiter Shade of Pale/Lime Street Blues	1972	$5
❏ 1389 [PS]	A Whiter Shade of Pale/Lime Street Blues	1972	$5
❏ 1347	Conquistador/A Salty Dog	1972	$5
❏ 1347 [PS]	Conquistador/A Salty Dog	1972	$8
❏ 885	Homburg/Good Captain Clack	1967	$15
❏ 927	In the Wee Small Hours of Sixpence/Quite Rightly So	1968	$15
❏ 1264	Power Failure/Broken Barricades	1971	$6
❏ 1287	Song for a Dreamer/Simple Sister	1971	$6

| ❏ 1111 | The Devil Came from Kansas/Boredom | 1969 | $8 |
| ❏ 1218 | Whiskey Train/About to Die | 1970 | $6 |

CHRYSALIS
| ❏ 2011 [DJ] | Bringing Home the Bacon (mono/stereo) | 1973 | $8 |

— May be promo only

❏ 2013	Grand Hotel/Fires	1973	$5
❏ 2013 [PS]	Grand Hotel/Fires	1973	$10
❏ 2109	Pandora's Box/Piper's Tune	1975	$5

DERAM
| ❏ 7507 | A Whiter Shade of Pale/Lime Street Blues | 1967 | $20 |

WARNER BROS.
| ❏ CRS2115 | Wizard Man/Something Magic | 1977 | $6 |

— Warner Bros. label with Chrysalis number; possible factory mispress?

PROCTOR, BILLY
EPIC
| ❏ 50160 | (I'm Gonna) Chop Down That Oak Tree/Keeping Up with the Joneses | 1975 | $5 |

SOUL
| ❏ 35099 | What Is Black/I Can Take It All | 1972 | $30 |

PROCTOR, PAUL
19TH AVENUE
| ❏ 1009 | Ain't We Got Love/(B-side unknown) | 1987 | $6 |
| ❏ 1012 | Tied to the Wheel of a Runaway Heart/Feelin' My Way Through the Dark | 1988 | $6 |

AURORA
| ❏ 1005 | He's Not Good Enough/(B-side unknown) | 1987 | $6 |

PRODUCERS, THE
PORTRAIT
❏ 03255	Chinatown/She Sheila	1982	$3
❏ 02092	What She Does to Me (The Diana Song)/Here's to You	1981	$4
❏ 02445	What's He Got/Boys Say When -- Girls Say Why	1981	$4

PROFESSOR MORRISON'S LOLLIPOP
WHITE WHALE
❏ 288	Angela/Duba Duba Doo	1968	$10
❏ 275	Gypsy Lady/You Got the Love	1968	$10
❏ 293	Oo Poo Pah Susie/You Can Take It	1969	$10

PROFILES, THE (1)
BAMBOO
❏ 115	A Little Misunderstanding/Got to Be Love	1970	$8
❏ 108	Be Careful/I Still Love You	1969	$8
❏ 104	Got to Be Love (Something Stupid)/You Don't Care About Me	1969	$8

DUO
| ❏ 7449 | If I Didn't Love You/(B-side unknown) | 1968 | $10 |

PROGRESSIVES, THE
DOT
| ❏ 16514 | Hot Cinders/Man of Mystery | 1963 | $30 |

PROPHET, ORVAL
DECCA
❏ 9-46404	Don't Trade Your Love for Gold/I'm Going Back to Birmingham	1952	$30
❏ 9-28338	Molly Darling/Tears on My Bridal Bouquet	1952	$30
❏ 9-29302	Tired Little Mother/My Heart's on the Borderline	1954	$30
❏ 9-28870	With God's Hand in Mine/Beautiful Bells	1953	$30

STARDAY
| ❏ 771 | Big River Joe/Traveling Snowman | 1966 | $12 |

PROPHETS, THE
DELPHI
| ❏ 009 | Don't You Think It's Time/I Don't Love You No More | 1967 | $120 |
| ❏ 07 | Talk Don't Bother Me/Don't Look Back | 1967 | $200 |

JUBILEE
| ❏ 5596 | Don't You Think It's Time/I Don't Love You No More | 1967 | $40 |
| ❏ 5565 | Talk Don't Bother Me/Don't Look Back | 1967 | $30 |

SHRINE
| ❏ 116 | If I Had One Gold Piece/Huh Baby | 1966 | $3000 |

— VG 1500; VG+ 2250

SMASH
| ❏ 2161 | I Got the Fever/Soul Control | 1967 | $10 |

PROVINE, DOROTHY
WARNER BROS.
| ❏ 5202 | Bye Bye Blackbird/Crazy Words-Crazy Tune | 1961 | $15 |
| ❏ 5249 | The Whisper Song/Don't Bring Lulu | 1961 | $15 |

PROVISOR, DENNY
20TH CENTURY-FOX
| ❏ 506 | Mickey Mouse/Walk On with Him | 1964 | $15 |

VALIANT
| ❏ 717 | Little Girl Lost/Dead Letter | 1965 | $15 |
| ❏ 728 | She's Not Mine Anymore/It Really Tears Me Up | 1965 | $15 |

PROW, JIMMY LEE
KING
| ❏ 4929 | Shopping List/You Tell Her, I Stutter | 1956 | $40 |

PRUETT, JEANNE
AUDIOGRAPH
| ❏ 467 | Lady of the Eighties/Ain't No Way to Make a Bad Love Grow | 1983 | $4 |
| ❏ 454 | Love Me/Safely in the Arms of Jesus | 1983 | $5 |

— A-side with Marty Robbins

| ❏ 441 | Star-Studded Nights/Wild Side of Life | 1984 | $4 |
| ❏ 477 | We Came So Close/(B-side unknown) | 1983 | $4 |

DECCA
❏ 32977	Call On Me/Stay on His Mind	1972	$6
❏ 32857	Hold On to My Unchanging Love/He's Calling Me Baby Again	1971	$6
❏ 33013	I Forgot More Than You'll Ever Know (About Him)/Don't Hold Your Breath	1972	$6
❏ 32614	It Ain't Fair That It Ain't Right/At the Sight of You	1970	$6
❏ 32929	Love Me/I'm Out Looking for You	1972	$6
❏ 32435	Make Me Feel Like a Woman Again/Don't Hold Your Breath	1969	$8
❏ 32383	One Woman Man/One Day Ahead of My Tears	1968	$8

IBC
❏ 0005	Back to Back/Wild Side of Life	1979	$5
❏ 00010	It's Too Late/I Can't Feel at Home	1980	$5
❏ 0002	Please Sing Satin Sheets for Me/Love All the Leavin' Out of You	1979	$5
❏ 0008	Temporarily Yours/Ain't We Sad Today	1980	$5

MCA
❏ 40440	A Poor Man's Woman/Momma Let Me Find Shelter (In Your Sweet Woman's Arms)	1975	$4
❏ 40527	Driftin' Too Far Away/Sweet Sorrow	1976	$4
❏ 40395	Honey on His Hands/One of These Days	1975	$4
❏ 40678	I'm Living a Lie/My First Pay Day	1977	$4
❏ 40116	I'm Your Woman/Your Memory's Comin' On	1973	$4
❏ 40569	It Doesn't Hurt to Ask/If I'm Not Girl Enough to Hold You	1976	$4
❏ 40605	I've Taken/Sweet and Warm and Right	1976	$4
❏ 40490	My Baby's Gone/But Not Today	1975	$4
❏ 40015	Satin Sheets/Sweet Sweetheart	1973	$6
❏ 40723	She's Still All Over You/Fancy Place to Cry	1977	$4
❏ 40284	Welcome to the Sunshine (Sweet Baby Jane)/What My Thoughts Do All the Time	1974	$4

MERCURY
| ❏ 55034 | I Guess I'm Not That Good at Being Bad/Where Do You Draw the Line | 1978 | $4 |
| ❏ 55017 | I'm a Woman/Midnight Exchange | 1978 | $4 |

PAID
| ❏ 136 | I Ought to Feel Guilty/Who'll Turn Out the Lights (In Your World) | 1981 | $4 |

Number	Title	Yr	NM
❏ 118	Sad Ole Shade of Gray/When I Stop Dreaming	1981	$4

RCA VICTOR

Number	Title	Yr	NM
❏ 47-8157	Another Heart to Break/Just a Little After Heartaches	1963	$20
❏ 47-8297	As a Matter of Fact/Sing Me a Song I Can Cry By	1963	$20
❏ 47-8232	Little Black Book/The Things I Don't Know	1963	$20

PRUETT, LEWIS

DECCA

Number	Title	Yr	NM
❏ 31201	Crazy Bullfrog/The Hand That Held the Hand	1961	$70
❏ 31095	Softly and Tenderly (I'll Hold You in My Arms)/Riches and Gold	1960	$20
❏ 31295	This Little Girl (Has a Magic Touch)/I'll Never Forget You	1961	$20
❏ 31038	Timbrook/(You'll Make) A Fool of Me	1959	$20

— National reissue of Peach 725

GREAT

Number	Title	Yr	NM
❏ 1135	Big Wheel from Boston/I'll Never Take Another Drink Again	1968	$10

MUSIC TOWN

Number	Title	Yr	NM
❏ 020	If You've Been Better Than I've Been (You're Bored)/We're Going Down Together	1969	$8

PEACH

Number	Title	Yr	NM
❏ 703	Pretty Baby/I'm in a Daze	1959	$200
❏ 710	This Little Girl/I'll Never Forget	1959	$200
❏ 725	Timbrook/(You'll Make) A Fool of Me	1959	$30

VEE JAY

Number	Title	Yr	NM
❏ 502	Point of No Return/Thanks a Lot	1963	$15
❏ 601	The Worst Is Yet to Come/I'd Rather Say Goodbye	1964	$15

PRYOR, CACTUS

4 STAR

Number	Title	Yr	NM
❏ 1689	16 Hours/Merrimac (Radio Service of NBZ)	1956	$30
❏ 1631	Don't Let the Stars Get In Your Eyes #2/I'll Ride Alone	1953	$30
❏ 1558	My Heart Bawls for You/Hog Calling Champ of Arkansas	1951	$50
❏ 1580	On Top of Old Baldy/Too Young #75	1951	$40
❏ 1661	Point of Order with the Senator and the Private (Parts 1 and 2)	1954	$30
❏ 1676	Tweedlee Dee/What's the Score, Podner	1955	$40

PRYOR, SNOOKY

J.O.B.

Number	Title	Yr	NM
❏ 1014	Cryin' Shame/Eight, Nine, Ten	1953	$400

PARROT

Number	Title	Yr	NM
❏ 807	Crosstown Blues/I Want You for Myself	1954	$1500

— Black vinyl

Number	Title	Yr	NM
❏ 807	Crosstown Blues/I Want You for Myself	1954	$2500

— Red vinyl

PRYSOCK, ARTHUR

BETHLEHEM

Number	Title	Yr	NM
❏ 3100	The Girls I Never Kissed/Funny World	1972	$6

DECCA

Number	Title	Yr	NM
❏ 27871	A Man Ain't Supposed to Cry/I Didn't Sleep a Wink Last Night	1951	$20
❏ 31775	Baby, Don't You Cry/I Didn't Sleep a Wink Last Night	1965	$8
❏ 29118	Baby Don't You Cry/My Last Goodbye	1954	$20
❏ 27722	Blue Velvet/Morning Side Of the Mountain	1951	$20
❏ 28700	I'd Give Anything/This Is the Time	1953	$20
❏ 27978	I Hear a Rhapsody/Am I to Blame	1952	$20
❏ 28867	My Mood/Temptation	1953	$20
❏ 28270	School of Love/Sentimental Fool	1952	$20
❏ 27769	Sin/The Love of a Gypsy	1951	$20
❏ 31710	Wheel of Fortune/I Cover the Waterfront	1964	$8
❏ 27967	Wheel of Fortune/'Til the Stars Fall in the Ocean	1952	$20
❏ 25684	When Day Is Done/What Will I Tell My Heart	1965	$8

GUSTO

Number	Title	Yr	NM
❏ 9023	Today I Started Loving You Again/It Ain't No Big Thing	1979	$6

KING

Number	Title	Yr	NM
❏ 6353	Cry/Unforgettable	1971	$6
❏ 6279	Go Ahead and Fly/How Do I Tell Her	1969	$6
❏ 6307	Have a Good Time/Frisco Line	1970	$6
❏ 6354	It Ain't No Big Thing/Big Blue Diamonds	1971	$6
❏ 6315	Lord, Is That Me/My Home Is Not a Home Without You	1970	$6
❏ 6364	Precious Memories/Just a Closer Walk with Thee	1971	$6
❏ 6276	Save Your Love for Me/If I Were Young Again	1969	$6
❏ 6243	Soul Soliloquy/(I Wanna Go) Where the Soul Trees Grow	1969	$6
❏ 6271	The 23rd Psalm/I Believe	1969	$6

MCA

Number	Title	Yr	NM
❏ 40943	Here's to Good Friends/All I Can Do Is Cry	1978	$8

— The song that became the "Tonight, let it be Lowenbrau" commercial

MERCURY

Number	Title	Yr	NM
❏ 70599	I Have Lied/Morning, Noon and Night	1955	$20
❏ 70502	Show Me How to Mambo/I'm in Heaven Tonight	1954	$20
❏ 70352	Take Care of Yourself/I'll Never Let You Cry	1954	$20
❏ 70414	This I Know/If You Don't, Somebody Will	1954	$20

OLD TOWN

Number	Title	Yr	NM
❏ 1188	Again/I Got the Blues So Bad	1965	$8
❏ 1115	April in Paris/When I Fall in Love	1962	$10
❏ 1196	Because/Let It Be Me	1966	$8
❏ 1163	Close Your Eyes/My Everlasting Love	1964	$8
❏ 103	Color My World/Good Morning News	1974	$5
❏ 1155	Ebb Tide/Are You Ready for a Laugh	1964	$8
❏ 1170	Fly Me to the Moon/Without the One You Love	1964	$8
❏ 1174	Full Moon and Empty Arms/You Always Hurt the One You Love	1964	$8
❏ 1092	Good Rockin' Tonight/My Everything	1960	$10
❏ 106	Hurt So Bad/Love Makes It Right	1974	$5
❏ 1060	I Just Want to Make Love to You/Keep a Light in the Window	1958	$15
❏ 1055	I Love You So/The Greatest Gift	1958	$15
❏ 100	In the Rain/Thank Heaven for You	1973	$5
❏ 1183	It's Too Late, Baby Too Late/Who Can I Turn To	1965	$8
❏ 108	I Wantcha Baby/One Broken Heart	1975	$5
❏ 1001	I Wantcha Baby/One Broken Heart	1977	$5
❏ 1073	I Worry About You/My Faith	1959	$15
❏ 1191	My Funny Valentine/House by the Side of the Road	1966	$8
❏ 1138	My Special Prayer/You Can't Come In	1963	$10
❏ 1106	One More Time/Speak to Me	1961	$10
❏ 1185	Open Up Your Heart/Only a Fool Breaks His Own Heart	1965	$8
❏ 1132	Our Love Will Last/Come and See This Old Fool	1963	$10
❏ 1003	Since I Fell for You/Between Hello and Goodbye	1978	$5
❏ 1146	Stella by Starlight/My Wish	1963	$10
❏ 1177	Teardrops in the Rain/I'm Crossing Over	1965	$8
❏ 1144	There Will Never Be Another You/Crawdad	1963	$10
❏ 1087	This Is My Love/Do You Believe	1960	$10
❏ 1101	This Time/I Wonder Where Our Love Has Gone	1961	$10
❏ 1000	When Love Is New/All I Need Is You	1976	$5
❏ 1125	Where Can I Go/Pianissimo	1962	$10

VERVE

Number	Title	Yr	NM
❏ 10574	A Working Man's Prayer/No More in Life	1967	$6
❏ 10544	Before You Break My Heart/Goodbye, So Long	1967	$6
❏ 10620	I Must Be Doing Something Right/Young Runaways	1968	$6
❏ 10515	Love Me/She's a Woman	1967	$6
❏ 10592	Madam/No Sun Today	1968	$6
❏ 10633	My Special Prayer/Pretty Girl	1969	$6

PRYSOCK, RED

CHESS

Number	Title	Yr	NM
❏ 2042	I Heard It Through the Grapevine/Groovy Sax	1968	$8

KING

Number	Title	Yr	NM
❏ 5595	Hand Clapping One More Time/Smokestack	1962	$12
❏ 5669	Harem Girl/Ride Away	1962	$12
❏ 5704	Here We Go Again/Can't Sit Down	1963	$12

MERCURY

Number	Title	Yr	NM
❏ 71358	Billie's Blues/Willow Weep for Me	1958	$15
❏ 71786	Charleston Twist/Bony Maronie	1961	$15
❏ 71573	Deep Purple/Offshore	1960	$15
❏ 70733	Finger Tips/Short Circuit	1955	$30
❏ 70674	Hand Clappin'/Shoe String	1955	$30
❏ 70419	Happy Feet/Blow Your Horn	1954	$30
❏ 71054	Head Snappin'/Pog Wog	1957	$20
❏ 70460	Hey There/Fats' Place	1954	$30
❏ 71411	Margie/Chop Suey	1959	$15
❏ 71735	More Handclappin'/Twistin' 'n' Bendin'	1960	$15
❏ 70985	Teen-Age Rock/Paquino Walk	1956	$20
❏ 71214	What's the Word, Thunderbird/Satellite	1957	$20

RED ROBIN

Number	Title	Yr	NM
❏ 117	Hard Rock/Jump for George	1953	$125
❏ 107	Wiggles/Crying My Heart Out	1952	$120

PSEUDO ECHO

EMI AMERICA

Number	Title	Yr	NM
❏ 8256	Beat for You/Walk Away	1984	$4
❏ 8232	Listening/In Their Time	1984	$4

RCA

Number	Title	Yr	NM
❏ 5323-7-R	A Beat for You/Try	1987	$3
❏ 5217-7-R	Funky Town/Lies or Nothing	1987	$4

— First pressing had A-side title as two words

Number	Title	Yr	NM
❏ 5217-7-R	Funkytown/Lies or Nothing	1987	$3

— Second pressing correctly had A-side title as one word

Number	Title	Yr	NM
❏ 5272-7-R	Listening/Lonely Without You	1987	$3
❏ 5125-7-R	Living in a Dream/Don't Go	1987	$3

PSYCHEDELIC FURS

A&M

Number	Title	Yr	NM
❏ 2826	Pretty in Pink (Long)/Pretty in Pink (Short)	1986	$3
❏ 2826 [PS]	Pretty in Pink (Long)/Pretty in Pink (Short)	1986	$30

COLUMBIA

Number	Title	Yr	NM
❏ 07974	All That Money Wants/Birdland	1988	$3
❏ 07974 [PS]	All That Money Wants/Birdland	1988	$3
❏ 07440	Angels Don't Cry/Mack the Knife	1987	$3
❏ 06420	Heartbreak Beat/New Dream	1986	$3
❏ 06420 [PS]	Heartbreak Beat/New Dream	1986	$3
❏ 04627	Heaven/Alice's House	1984	$3
❏ 08499	Heaven/India	1988	$3
❏ 04577	Here Come Cowboys/Another Edge	1984	$3
❏ 03340	Love My Way/I Don't Want to Be Your Shadow	1982	$4
❏ 07224	Shock/President Gas (Live)	1987	$3
❏ 04416	The Ghost in You/Heartbeat (Remix)	1984	$3
❏ 04416 [PS]	The Ghost in You/Heartbeat (Remix)	1984	$3

PSYCHOTIC PINEAPPLE, THE

PYNOTIC

Number	Title	Yr	NM
❏ 0(no cat #)	I Want Her So Bad/Say That You Will	1978	$30
❏ 0(no cat #) [PS]	I Want Her So Bad/Say That You Will	1978	$30

RICHMOND

Number	Title	Yr	NM
❏ 1	I Wanna Wanna Wanna Wanna Wanna Wanna Wanna Get Rid of You/Ahead of My Time	1979	$8
❏ 1 [PS]	I Wanna Wanna Wanna Wanna Wanna Wanna Wanna Get Rid of You/Ahead of My Time	1979	$8

PUBLIC ENEMY

DEF JAM

Number	Title	Yr	NM
❏ 38-68613	Black Steel in the Hour of Chaos/Caught, Can We Get a Witness	1989	$5
❏ WS4-07934	Don't Believe the Hype/Prophets of Rage	1988	$4
❏ 38-06670	Public Enemy #1/(B-side unknown)	1987	$6

MOTOWN

Number	Title	Yr	NM
❏ 1972	Fight the Power/(Flavor Flav Meets Spike Lee Version)	1989	$5

Number	Title	Yr	NM

PUCKETT, GARY, AND THE UNION GAP
COLUMBIA
Number	Title	Yr	NM
❏ 45678	Bless the Child/Leavin' in the Morning	1972	$5
❏ 44788	Don't Give In to Him/Could I	1969	$6
❏ 45438	Hello Morning/Gentle Woman	1971	$5
❏ 45509	Hello Morning/I Can't Hold On	1971	$5
❏ 45249	I Just Don't Know What to Do With Myself/All That Matters	1970	$5
❏ 44547	Lady Willpower/Daylight Strangers	1968	$8
❏ 44547 [PS]	Lady Willpower/Daylight Strangers	1968	$15

— As "The Union Gap"

❏ 45097	Let's Give Adam and Eve Another Chance/The Beggar	1970	$6
❏ 45097 [PS]	Let's Give Adam and Eve Another Chance/The Beggar	1970	$8
❏ 45358	Life Has Its Little Ups and Downs/Shimmering Eyes	1971	$5
❏ 44644	Over You/If the Day Would Come	1968	$6
❏ 44644 [PS]	Over You/If the Day Would Come	1968	$15
❏ 44967	This Girl Is a Woman Now/His Other Woman	1969	$6
❏ 44297	Woman, Woman/Don't Make Promises	1967	$8
❏ 44297 [PS]	Woman, Woman/Don't Make Promises	1967	$15

— As "The Union Gap

PUFNSTUF
DECCA
| ❏ 32702 | Pufnstuf/Nonsense | 1970 | $20 |

PULLEN, WHITEY
CARLTON
| ❏ 455 | Sunglasses After Dark/Teenage Bug | 1958 | $300 |

— As "Dwight Pullen

ROLLIN' ROCK
❏ 010	Drinkin' Wine/Everybody's Rockin'	1978	$5
❏ 005	Let's All Go Wild/Moonshine Liquor	1978	$5
❏ 017	Tuscaloosa Lucy/Tight Slacks	1979	$5

SAGE
| ❏ 279 | By You, By the Bayou/It's Over With | 1959 | $200 |

— As "Dwight Pullen

| ❏ 372 | Crazy in Love/I Won the Day I Lost You | 1962 | $50 |
| ❏ 283 | I Live a Lifetime Last Night/You'll Get Yours Some Day | 1959 | $200 |

— As "Dwight Pullen

❏ 303	I'm Beggin' Your Pardon/Let Your Left Hand Know	1960	$125
❏ 294	Let's All Go Wild Tonight/Gently	1959	$200
❏ 313	Tuscaloosa Lucy/Waltz of the Steel Guitar	1960	$120
❏ 274	Walk My Way Back Home/Don't Make Me Cry	1958	$250

PUMPKIN
BRUNSWICK
| ❏ 55004 | Half Past Seventeen/Boom Boom | 1957 | $50 |

PUNSTERS, THE
7-Inch Extended Plays
ROSEBUD
| ❏ 001 [PS] | Boardwalk Santa/In Her Disarray/We're Drunk Again/Oh! Sarah | 1980 | $8 |
| ❏ 001 | Boardwalk Santa/In Her Disarray/We're Drunk Again/Oh! Sarah | 1980 | $8 |

PURCELL, BOOTS, COMBO
HIT
| ❏ 39 | Desafinado/Release Me | 1962 | $8 |

— B-side by Lucille Johns.

PURE ENERGY
PRISM
| ❏ PFF-311 | Party On/(Instrumental) | 1980 | $20 |
| ❏ PFF-317 | When You're Dancin'/What Are You In the Mood For? | 1980 | $20 |

PURE LOVE AND PLEASURE
ABC DUNHILL
| ❏ 4232 | All in My Mind/What Cha Gonna Do | 1970 | $8 |

PURE PRAIRIE LEAGUE
CASABLANCA
Number	Title	Yr	NM
❏ 2319	I Can't Stop the Feelin'/A Lifetime of Nightime	1980	$4
❏ 2294	I'm Almost Ready/You're My True Love	1980	$4
❏ 2266	Let Me Love You Tonight/Janny Lou	1980	$4
❏ 2332	Still Right Here in My Heart/Don't Keep Me Hangin'	1981	$4

RCA
❏ PB-10880	All the Way/Fade Away	1977	$4
❏ PB-11678	Can't Hold Back/Restless Woman	1979	$4
❏ PB-10829	Dance/Help Yourself	1976	$4
❏ PB-11282	Love Will Grow/Slim Pickin's	1978	$4
❏ PB-11148	The Sun Shone Lightly/Lucille Crawfield	1977	$4
❏ PB-11260	Working in the Coal Mine/Bad Cream	1978	$4

RCA VICTOR
| ❏ PB-10184 | Amie/Memories | 1975 | $5 |
| ❏ GB-10490 | Amie/Memories | 1975 | $3 |

— Gold Standard Series

❏ 74-0794	Early Morning Riser/Angel #9	1972	$6
❏ PB-10580	Long Cold Winter/The Sun Shone Brightly	1976	$4
❏ 48-1028	Tears/You're Between Me	1972	$6
❏ PB-10679	That'll Be the Day/I Can Only Dream of You	1976	$4
❏ PB-10302	Two-Lane Highway/Sister's Keeper	1975	$4
❏ 74-0742	Woman/She Darked the Sun	1972	$6

PURIFY, JAMES AND BOBBY
BELL
❏ 700	Do Unto Me/Everybody Needs Somebody	1967	$8
❏ 735	Help Yourself (To All of My Lovin')/Last Piece of Love	1968	$8
❏ 721	I Can Remember/I Was Born to Lose Out	1968	$8
❏ 774	I Don't Know What It Is You Got/Section C	1969	$8
❏ 648	I'm Your Puppet/So Many Reasons	1966	$20
❏ 680	I Take What I Want/Sixteen Tons	1967	$8
❏ 685	Let Love Come Between Us/I Don't Want to Have to Wait	1967	$8
❏ 669	Shake a Tail Feather/Goodness Gracious	1967	$15
❏ 660	Wish You Didn't Have to Go/You Can't Keep a Good Man Down	1967	$8

CASABLANCA
❏ 830	All the Love I Got/(B-side unknown)	1975	$5
❏ 812	Do Your Thing/Why Love	1974	$5
❏ 827	Man Can't Be a Man Without a Woman/You and Me Together Forever	1975	$5

MERCURY
❏ 73893	Get Closer/What's Better Than Love	1977	$5
❏ 73884	I Ain't Got to Love Nobody Else/What's Better Than Love	1977	$5
❏ 73767	I'm Your Puppet/Lay Me Down Easy	1976	$5
❏ 73806	Morning Glory/Turning Back the Pages	1976	$5

PHILCO-FORD
| ❏ HP-28 | I'm Your Puppet/Goodnight Gracious | 1968 | $20 |

— 4-inch plastic "Hip Pocket Record" with color sleeve

PURSELL, BILL
COLUMBIA
❏ 43090	Crying/I'll Never Be Free	1964	$6
❏ 42876	Dark Alley/Autumn Magic	1963	$6
❏ 42780	Loved/Stranger	1963	$6
❏ 43593	Love Theme from Superman/Soul Shall It Be	1966	$10
❏ 43255	Madrilena/Remembered Love	1965	$6
❏ 42619	Our Winter Love/A Wound Can't Erase	1962	$8
❏ 42832	Pride/Farewell to Adra	1963	$6
❏ 42970	The Theme from Captain Newman/Remember Me (I'm the One Who Loves You)	1964	$6

DOT
| ❏ 17217 | Geary Street/Winter Waves | 1969 | $5 |

PUSSY GALORE
SUB POP
| ❏ 37 | Damaged 2/Damaged 1 | 1989 | $20 |

— B-side by Tad.

| ❏ 37 [PS] | Damaged 2/Damaged 1 | 1989 | $20 |

— B-side by Tad; #8 in Sub Pop Singles Club series

Number	Title	Yr	NM

7-Inch Extended Plays
ADULT CONTEMPORARY
| ❏ 04 | Feel Good About Your Body | 1985 | $60 |
| ❏ 04 [PS] | Feel Good About Your Body | 1985 | $60 |

PUTMAN, CURLY
ABC
| ❏ 10934 | My Elusive Dreams/Hurtin' Like a Heartache | 1967 | $8 |
| ❏ 10984 | Set Me Free/Hummin' a Heartache | 1967 | $8 |

CHEROKEE
| ❏ 504 | The Prison Song/Forsaken | 1960 | $40 |

EVEREST
| ❏ 19334 | The Prison Song/Forsaken | 1960 | $30 |

RCA VICTOR
❏ 47-9850	Army of Heartaches/Waiting for the Next Rainbow	1970	$6
❏ 47-9910	Country Dreams/Woke Up with a Stranger	1970	$6
❏ 47-9959	Danny the D.J./Goin' Home Blues	1971	$6
❏ 48-1004	Divorce Sale/One Time	1971	$6
❏ 74-0577	Old Ramblin' Alabama Me/You Love Me Into Staying	1971	$6

PUZZLE
ABC
| ❏ 11181 | Hey Medusa/Make the Children Happy | 1969 | $8 |

PYLE, PETE
FORTUNE
| ❏ 172 | Making a Fool of Me/Wildcat Boogie | 1952 | $40 |

PYRAMIDS, THE (1)
BEST
| ❏ 102 | Penetration/Here Comes Marsha | 1963 | $50 |
| ❏ 13002 | Penetration/Here Comes Marsha | 1964 | $30 |

— No mention of London Records on label

| ❏ 13002 | Penetration/Here Comes Marsha | 1964 | $20 |

— With "Dist. by London" or similar wording on label

| ❏ 13002 [PS] | Penetration/Here Comes Marsha | 1964 | $50 |

— Red sleeve

| ❏ 13002 [PS] | Penetration/Here Comes Marsha | 1964 | $50 |

— Black sleeve

| ❏ 1 | Pyramid's Stomp/Paul | 1963 | $40 |
| ❏ 13001 | Pyramid's Stomp/Paul | 1963 | $30 |

CEDWICKE
| ❏ 13006 | Contact/Pressure | 1964 | $50 |
| ❏ 13005 | Midnight Run/Custom Caravan | 1964 | $50 |

PYRAMIDS, THE (2)
CUB
| ❏ 9112 | I'm the Playboy/Cryin' | 1962 | $30 |

SONBERT
| ❏ 82861 | I'm the Playboy/Cryin' | 1962 | $50 |

VEE JAY
| ❏ 489 | What Is Love/Shakin' Fit | 1963 | $30 |

PYRAMIDS, THE (U)
DAVIS
| ❏ 453 | At Any Cost/Okay, Baby! | 1956 | $60 |
| ❏ 457 | Why Did You Go/Before It's Too Late | 1957 | $60 |

FEDERAL
| ❏ 12233 | Deep in My Heart for You/And I Need You | 1955 | $400 |

HOLLYWOOD
| ❏ 1047 | Someday/Bow Wow | 1955 | $500 |

RCA VICTOR
| ❏ 47-7556 | Long Long Time/Oh No You Won't (Oh Yes You Will) | 1959 | $20 |

SHELL
| ❏ 711 | Ankle Bracelet/Hot Dog Dooly Wah | 1958 | $60 |
| ❏ 304 | Ankle Bracelet/Hot Dog Dooly Wah | 1961 | $30 |

— As "The Original Pyramids

PYTHON LEE JACKSON
GNP CRESCENDO
❏ 462	Cloud Nine/Rod's Blues	1973	$6
❏ 449	In a Broken Dream/Doin' Fine	1972	$6
❏ 449	In a Broken Dream/Turn the Music Down	1972	$6

Number	Title	Yr	NM

Q

Q
EPIC
Number	Title	Yr	NM
❏ 8-50335	Dancin' Man/Love Pollution	1977	$5
❏ 8-50440	Feel It in Your Backbone, Got It in Your Feet/Jump for Joy	1977	$5
❏ 8-50404	Sweet Summertime/If It Ain't One Thing It's Another	1977	$5
❏ 8-50404 [PS]	Sweet Summertime/If It Ain't One Thing It's Another	1977	$10

QUADRANGLE, THE
PHILIPS
Number	Title	Yr	NM
❏ 40408	She's Too Familiar Now/No More Time	1966	$40

QUADRANT SIX
ATLANTIC
Number	Title	Yr	NM
❏ 89892	Body Mechanic/ (Instrumental)	1982	$5
❏ 89800	The Lone Wolf/(B-side unknown)	1983	$5

QUADRELLS, THE
WHIRLIN' DISC
Number	Title	Yr	NM
❏ 103	What Can the Matter Be/ Come to Me	1957	$75

QUADS, THE
VAULT
Number	Title	Yr	NM
❏ 907	Surfin' Hearse/Little Queenie	1963	$50

QUAILS, THE (2)
HARVEY
Number	Title	Yr	NM
❏ 120	I Thought/Over the Hump	1963	$60
❏ 116	My Love/Never Felt Like This Before	1961	$60

QUAITE, CHRISTINE
WORLD ARTISTS
Number	Title	Yr	NM
❏ 1028	Mr. Stuck Up/Will You Be the Same Tomorrow	1964	$15
❏ 1022	Tell Me Mamma/In the Middle of the Floor	1964	$15

QUAKER CITY BOYS, THE
SWAN
Number	Title	Yr	NM
❏ 4026	Everywhere You Go/Love Me Tonight	1959	$10
❏ 4045	Goodbye 50's, Hello 60's/ You Call Everybody Darlin'	1959	$10
❏ 4023	Teasin'/Won't Ya Come Out Mary Ann	1958	$15

QUARTER NOTES, THE (1)
BISON
Number	Title	Yr	NM
❏ 757	Frantic Flip/Canadian Sunset	1960	$40
IMPERIAL
Number	Title	Yr	NM
❏ 5647	Frantic Flip/Canadian Sunset	1960	$20

QUARTER NOTES, THE (2)
BOOM
Number	Title	Yr	NM
❏ 60018	Hey Little Girl/I've Been Loved	1966	$20

QUARTER NOTES, THE (3)
DELUXE
Number	Title	Yr	NM
❏ 6116	Loneliness/Come De Nite	1957	$30
❏ 6129	My Fantasy/Ten Minutes to Midnight	1957	$30

QUARTER NOTES, THE (U)
DOT
Number	Title	Yr	NM
❏ 15685	Please Come Home/Like You Bug Me	1958	$30
GUYDEN
Number	Title	Yr	NM
❏ 2083	Pretty Pretty Eyes/I Don't Wanna Go Home	1963	$30
RCA VICTOR
Number	Title	Yr	NM
❏ 47-7327	The Interview/Punkanilla	1958	$20

QUARTERFLASH
GEFFEN
Number	Title	Yr	NM
❏ 29882	Critical Times/Try to Make It True	1982	$4
❏ 50006	Find Another Fool/Cruisin' with the Deuce	1982	$4
❏ 50006 [PS]	Find Another Fool/Cruisin' with the Deuce	1982	$4

Number	Title	Yr	NM
❏ PRO-S-1012 [DJ]	Find Another Fool (Remix Edit)/(LP Version)	1982	$8
❏ 49824	Harden My Heart/Don't Be Lonely	1981	$4
❏ GGEF 0426	Harden My Heart/Find Another Fool	1983	$3

—"Back to Back Hits" reissue series
Number	Title	Yr	NM
❏ 29523	Take Another Picture/One More Round to Go	1983	$4
❏ 29523 [PS]	Take Another Picture/One More Round to Go	1983	$4
❏ 29603	Take Me to Heart/Nowhere Left to Hide	1983	$4
❏ 29603 [PS]	Take Me to Heart/Nowhere Left to Hide	1983	$4
❏ 28908	Talk to Me/Grace Under Fire	1985	$3
❏ 28908 [PS]	Talk to Me/Grace Under Fire	1985	$3
❏ 28894	Walking on Ice/Come to Me	1985	$3
❏ 28894 [PS]	Walking on Ice/Come to Me	1985	$3

QUATEMAN, BILL
COLUMBIA
Number	Title	Yr	NM
❏ 4-45858	Get It Right On Out There/ Your Love Can Make It Real	1973	$5
❏ 4-45792	Only Love/Keep Dreaming	1973	$5
❏ 4-45792 [PS]	Only Love/Keep Dreaming	1973	$8
RCA
Number	Title	Yr	NM
❏ PB-11254	Shot in the Dark/All Over Now	1978	$4
❏ PB-11180	Wait Until Tomorrow/ Josephine	1977	$4

QUATRO, MICHAEL
EVOLUTION
Number	Title	Yr	NM
❏ 1062	Circus/Time Spent in Dreams	1972	$15

—As "Mike Quatro Jam Band
Number	Title	Yr	NM
❏ 1083	Tomorrows/(B-side unknown)	1973	$15
PRODIGAL
Number	Title	Yr	NM
❏ 0631	Pure Chopin/One by One	1976	$6
SPECTOR
Number	Title	Yr	NM
❏ 00014	Bottom Line/Melody	1981	$5
❏ 00012	Let It Ride/Melody	1981	$5
UNITED ARTISTS
Number	Title	Yr	NM
❏ XW672#NAME?	In Collaboration with the Gods/Neptune's Nicromea	1975	$15

QUATRO, SUZI
BELL
Number	Title	Yr	NM
❏ 45401	48 Crash/Little Bitch Blue	1973	$6
❏ 45477	All Shook Up/Glycerine Queen	1974	$6
❏ 45609	Devil Gate Drive/In the Morning	1974	$6
BIG TREE
Number	Title	Yr	NM
❏ 16053	Can the Can/Don't Mess Around	1975	$6
DREAMLAND
Number	Title	Yr	NM
❏ 107	Lipstick/Woman Cry	1980	$4
RAK
Number	Title	Yr	NM
❏ 4512	Brain Confusion (For All the Lonely People)/Rolling Stone	1972	$15
RSO
Number	Title	Yr	NM
❏ 929	If You Can't Give Me Love/ Non-Citizen	1979	$4
❏ 1001	I've Never Been in Love/ Space Cadets	1979	$4
❏ 1014	She's in Love with You/ Starlight Lady	1979	$4
❏ 917	Stumblin' In/A Stranger to Paradise	1979	$4

—With Chris Norman (lead singer of Smokie)

QUATTLEBAUM, DOUG
GOTHAM
Number	Title	Yr	NM
❏ 519	Don't Be Funny Baby/ Lizzie Lou	1953	$125

QUAZAR
ARISTA
Number	Title	Yr	NM
❏ 0349	Funk 'n' Roll (Dancin' in the Funkshine)/Savin' My Love for a Rainy Day	1978	$6
❏ 0349 [PS]	Funk 'n' Roll (Dancin' in the Funkshine)/Savin' My Love for a Rainy Day	1978	$6
❏ 0386	Funk with a Big Foot/ Starlight Circus	1979	$5

QUEEN
Also see FREDDIE MERCURY. (45)

CAPITOL
Number	Title	Yr	NM
❏ 7PRO-79685	Breakthru (same on both sides)	1989	$15

—Vinyl is promo only
Number	Title	Yr	NM
❏ B-5424	Hammer to Fall/Tear It Up	1984	$5

Number	Title	Yr	NM
❏ B-5424 [PS]	Hammer to Fall/Tear It Up	1984	$5
❏ B-5372	It's a Hard Life/Is This the World We Created?	1984	$5
❏ B-5372 [PS]	It's a Hard Life/Is This the World We Created?	1984	$6
❏ B-44372	I Want It All/Hang On In There	1989	$5
❏ B-44372 [PS]	I Want It All/Hang On In There	1989	$5
❏ B-5350	I Want to Break Free/ Machines (Or Back to Humans)	1984	$4
❏ B-5350 [PS]	I Want to Break Free/ Machines (Or Back to Humans)	1984	$5

— With Freddie Mercury in center
Number	Title	Yr	NM
❏ B-5350 [PS]	I Want to Break Free/ Machines (Or Back to Humans)	1984	$5

— With Brian May in center
Number	Title	Yr	NM
❏ B-5350 [PS]	I Want to Break Free/ Machines (Or Back to Humans)	1984	$5

— With Roger Taylor in center
Number	Title	Yr	NM
❏ B-5350 [PS]	I Want to Break Free/ Machines (Or Back to Humans)	1984	$5

— With John Deacon in center
Number	Title	Yr	NM
❏ 7PRO-9114 [DJ]	I Want to Break Free (same on both sides)	1984	$15

— White label, no song title or name of group on label
Number	Title	Yr	NM
❏ 7PRO-9546/7 [DJ]	One Vision (4:00)/(3:46)	1985	$15
❏ B-5530	One Vision/Blurred Vision	1985	$4
❏ B-5530 [PS]	One Vision/Blurred Vision	1985	$5
❏ B-5633	Pain Is So Close to Pleasure/Don't Lose Your Head	1986	$4
❏ B-5633 [PS]	Pain Is So Close to Pleasure/Don't Lose Your Head	1986	$5
❏ B-5568	Princes of the Universe/A Dozen Red Roses for My Darling	1985	$4
❏ B-5568 [PS]	Princes of the Universe/A Dozen Red Roses for My Darling	1985	$5
❏ 7PRO-79779	Scandal (same on both sides)	1989	$15

— Vinyl is promo only

ELEKTRA
Number	Title	Yr	NM
❏ 47031	Another One Bites the Dust/ Don't Try Suicide	1980	$4
❏ 45106	Another One Bites the Dust/ Keep Yourself Alive	1981	$4

—Spun Gold" reissue
Number	Title	Yr	NM
❏ 69941	Back Chat/Staying Power	1982	$4
❏ 69941 [PS]	Back Chat/Staying Power	1982	$5
❏ 45541	Bicycle Race/Fat Bottomed Girls	1978	$6
❏ 45541 [PS]	Bicycle Race/Fat Bottomed Girls	1978	$15
❏ 47452	Body Language/Life Is Real (Song for Lennon)	1982	$4

— Most copies of this did not come with picture sleeves
Number	Title	Yr	NM
❏ 47452 [PS]	Body Language/Life Is Real (Song for Lennon)	1982	$20

— Nude bodies sleeve
Number	Title	Yr	NM
❏ 47452 [PS]	Body Language/Life Is Real (Song for Lennon)	1982	$10

— All-white sleeve
Number	Title	Yr	NM
❏ 45297	Bohemian Rhapsody/I'm in Love with My Car	1975	$8

— Butterfly label
Number	Title	Yr	NM
❏ 45297	Bohemian Rhapsody/I'm in Love with My Car	1976	$10

— Red label, much scarcer than butterfly label
Number	Title	Yr	NM
❏ 45083	Bohemian Rhapsody/You're My Best Friend	1977	$4

— Spun Gold" reissue
Number	Title	Yr	NM
❏ 69981	Calling All Girls/Put Out the Fire	1982	$4
❏ 69981 [PS]	Calling All Girls/Put Out the Fire	1982	$6
❏ 45103	Crazy Little Thing Called Love/Bicycle Race	1981	$4

— Spun Gold" reissue
Number	Title	Yr	NM
❏ 46579	Crazy Little Thing Called Love/Spread Your Wings	1979	$4
❏ 46008	Don't Stop Me Now/More of That Jazz	1979	$6
❏ 47092	Flash's Theme AKA Flash/ Football Fight	1980	$4
❏ 47092 [PS]	Flash's Theme AKA Flash/ Football Fight	1980	$5
❏ 45478	It's Late/Sheer Heart Attack	1978	$6
❏ 45478 [PS]	It's Late/Sheer Heart Attack	1978	$10
❏ 45884	Liar/Doing All Right	1974	$30
❏ 45412	Long Away/You and I	1977	$8
❏ 46652	Play the Game/A Human Body	1980	$4
❏ 46652 [PS]	Play the Game/A Human Body	1980	$5
❏ 45891	Seven Seas of Rhye/See What a Fool I've Been	1974	$30

Number	Title	Yr	NM
❏ 45362	Somebody to Love/White Man	1976	$6
—Butterfly label			
❏ 45362	Somebody to Love/White Man	1976	$12
—Red label, much scarcer than butterfly label			
❏ 45385	Tie Your Mother Down/Drowse	1977	$6
❏ 45441	We Are the Champions/We Will Rock You	1977	$6
❏ 45441 [PS]	We Are the Champions/We Will Rock You	1977	$10
❏ 45090	We Are the Champions/We Will Rock You	1979	$4
—Spun Gold" reissue			
❏ 46532	We Will Rock You (Live)/Let Me Entertain You	1979	$8
EMI			
❏ QUEEN5	Thank God It's Christmas//Man on the Prowl/Keep Passing the Open Windows	1984	$10
❏ QUEEN5 [PS]	Thank God It's Christmas//Man on the Prowl/Keep Passing the Open Windows	1984	$10
—Above record and sleeve are U.K. imports			

QUEEN, THE
MERCURY

Number	Title	Yr	NM
❏ 71389	Honky Tonky/Somewhere Along the Line	1958	$30

QUEEN'S NECTORINE MACHINE, THE
ABC

Number	Title	Yr	NM
❏ 11172	I Got Trouble/Gypsy Lady	1969	$20

QUEENSRYCHE
EMI

Number	Title	Yr	NM
❏ 7PRO-04281	Eyes of a Stranger (same on both sides)	1989	$10
—Promo only number			
❏ B-50201	Eyes of a Stranger/The Mission	1989	$8
❏ 7PRO-04345	I Don't Believe in Love (same on both sides)	1989	$10
—Vinyl is promo only			

QUEERS, THE
7-Inch Extended Plays

DOHENY

Number	Title	Yr	NM
❏ E210X85	We'd Have a Riot Doing Heroin/Terminal Rut/Fagtown/I Want Cunt/Trash This Place/Love Me	1982	$175
—Not issued with picture sleeve			

QUESTELL, CONNIE
DECCA

Number	Title	Yr	NM
❏ 31783	Don't Let It Break Your Heart/Straighten Up	1965	$125
❏ 31986	Girl Can't Take It/Tell Me What to Do	1966	$125
❏ 31855	Give Up Girl/World of Trouble	1965	$200

? (QUESTION MARK) AND THE MYSTERIANS
ABKCO

Number	Title	Yr	NM
❏ 4020	96 Tears/Can't Get Enough of You, Baby	1973	$15
—Reissue; contains full-length version of A-side (most Cameo singles are edited)			
❏ 4033	I Need Somebody/Girl (You Captivate Me)	1973	$15
—Reissue			

CAMEO

Number	Title	Yr	NM
❏ 428	96 Tears/Midnight Hour	1966	$30
—Contains an early fade of the A-side and the LP version of the B-side; trail-off wax markings are "C 428 A R" and "C 428 B R"; composer of both songs listed as "Rudy Martinez"			
❏ 428	96 Tears/Midnight Hour	1966	$40
—Contains the LP version of the A-side and an alternate version (different vocal and words) of the B-side; trail-off wax markings are "C 428 A-1A" and "C 428 B-1B			
❏ 428	96 Tears/Midnight Hour	1966	$20
—Contains an early fade of the A-side and the LP version of the B-side; trail-off wax markings are "C 428 A R" and "C 428 B R"; composer of both songs listed as "The Mysterians"			
❏ 428	96 Tears/Midnight Hour	1966	$20
—Label credit is "? and the Mysterians"; contains an early fade of the A-side (even though the time is listed as "2:53") and the LP version of the B-side; trail-off wax markings are "C 428 A" and "62831" on Side 1 and "C 428 B" and "62831-X" on Side 2; composer of both songs listed as "The Mysterians"			
❏ 467	Can't Get Enough of You, Baby/Smokes	1967	$20

Number	Title	Yr	NM
❏ 496	Do Something to Me/Love Me, Baby	1967	$20
❏ 479	Girl (You Captivate Me)/Got To	1967	$20
❏ 441	I Need Somebody/"8" Teen	1966	$20
CAPITOL			
❏ 2162	Make You Mine/I Love You, Baby (Like Nobody's Business)	1968	$60
CHICORY			
❏ 410	Talk Is Cheap/She Goes to Church on Sunday	1968	$60
LUV			
❏ 159	Funky Lady/Hot N' Groovin'	1975	$30
PA-GO-GO			
❏ 102	96 Tears/Midnight Hour	1965	$300
SUPER K			
❏ 102	Hang In/Sha La La	1969	$20
TANGERINE			
❏ 989	Ain't It a Shame/Turn Around Baby (Don't Ever Look Back)	1970	$50

QUICK, THE
A&M

Number	Title	Yr	NM
❏ 2870	Down the Wire/Lonely Girl	1986	$4
EPIC			
❏ 10516	Ain't Nothing Gonna Stop Me/Southern Comfort	1969	$30
❏ 14-03046	One Light in a Blackout/Small Blond Box	1982	$5

QUICKLY, TOMMY
LIBERTY

Number	Title	Yr	NM
❏ 55732	It's As Simple As That/You Might As Well Forget Him	1964	$10
❏ 55753	Wild Side of Life/Forget the Other Guy	1964	$10

QUICKSILVER MESSENGER SERVICE
CAPITOL

Number	Title	Yr	NM
❏ 3349	Doin' Time in the U.S.A./Changes	1972	$8
❏ 2920	Fresh Air/Freeway Flyer	1970	$10
❏ 3417	Fresh Air/Freeway Flyer	1972	$8
❏ 3046	Good Old Rock and Roll/What About Me	1971	$8
❏ 4206	Gypsy Lights/Witches' Moon	1976	$6
❏ 3233	Hope/I Found Love	1971	$8
❏ 2194	Pride of Man/Dino's Song	1968	$20
❏ 2800	Shady Grove/Three or Four Feet from Home	1970	$20
❏ 2320	Stand By Me/Bears	1968	$20
❏ 2320 [PS]	Stand By Me/Bears	1968	$750
❏ 2557	Who Do You Love/Which Do You Love	1969	$20
❏ 2670	Words Can't Say/Holy Holy	1969	$20

QUIET RIOT
OZZY OSBOURNE guitarist Randy Rhoads was on this band's first two albums, issued only in Japan.

PASHA

Number	Title	Yr	NM
❏ ZS4-04267	Bang Your Head (Metal Health)/(Live)	1983	$4
❏ ZS4-04267 [PS]	Bang Your Head (Metal Health)/(Live)	1983	$4
❏ ZS4-04005	Cum On Feel the Noize/Run for Cover	1983	$4
❏ ZS4-04505	Mama Weer All Crazee Now/Bad Boy	1984	$4
❏ ZS4-04505 [PS]	Mama Weer All Crazee Now/Bad Boy	1984	$4
❏ ZS4-08096	Stay With Me Tonight/Callin' the Shots	1988	$5
❏ ZS4-06174	The Wild and the Young/Rise or Fall	1986	$4
❏ ZS4-06174 [PS]	The Wild and the Young/Rise or Fall	1986	$4

QUIN-TONES, THE
HUNT

Number	Title	Yr	NM
❏ 321	Down the Aisle of Love/Please Dear	1958	$60
❏ 322	There'll Be No Sorrow/What Am I to Do	1958	$70
RED TOP			
❏ 108	Down the Aisle of Love/Please Dear	1958	$120
—Red label			
❏ 108	Down the Aisle of Love/Please Dear	1958	$50
❏ 116	Heavenly Father/I Watch the Stars	1959	$125

QUINN, CARMEL
COLUMBIA

Number	Title	Yr	NM
❏ 40611	The Story of the Magi/Santa's Coming	1955	$15

QUINN, CAROLE
MGM

Number	Title	Yr	NM
❏ K-13326	Do Those Little Things/I'll Do It for You	1965	$12
❏ K-13265	Good Boy Gone Bad/What's So Sweet About Sweet Sixteen	1964	$10

QUINNS, THE
CYCLONE

Number	Title	Yr	NM
❏ 111	Oh Starlight/Hong Kong	1957	$200
—No address on label			
❏ 111	Oh Starlight/Hong Kong	1958	$100
—Address on label under company name			

QUINTEROS, EDDIE
BRENT

Number	Title	Yr	NM
❏ 7009	Come Dance with Me/Vivian	1960	$40
❏ 7012	Please Don't Go/Lookin' for My Baby	1960	$40
❏ 7014	Slow Down Sandy/Lindy Lou	1960	$60

QUINTO SISTERS, THE
COLUMBIA

Number	Title	Yr	NM
❏ 43166	A Holly Jolly Christmas/Confidence	1964	$10

QUINTONES, THE (1)
CHESS

Number	Title	Yr	NM
❏ 1685	I Try So Hard/Ding Dong	1957	$50

QUINTONES, THE (2)
GEE

Number	Title	Yr	NM
❏ 1009	I'm Willing/Strange As It Seems	1956	$1000

QUINTONES, THE (3)
PHILLIPS INT'L.

Number	Title	Yr	NM
❏ 3586	Times Sho' Gettin' Ruff/Softie	1963	$30

QUINTONES, THE (U)
PARK

Number	Title	Yr	NM
❏ 111/2	South Sea Island/More Than a Notion	1957	$400

QUIST, JACK
GRUDGE

Number	Title	Yr	NM
❏ 4756	Where Does Love Go (When It Dies)/South for the Winter	1989	$6
❏ 4756 [PS]	Where Does Love Go (When It Dies)/South for the Winter	1989	$8
MEMORY MACHINE			
❏ 1015	Memory Machine/I'm Comin' Home	1982	$6

QUOTATIONS, THE
ADMIRAL

Number	Title	Yr	NM
❏ 753	In the Night/Oh No, I Still Love Her	1964	$30
DEVENUS			
❏ 107	It Can Happen to You/You Don't Have to Worry	1968	$15
IMPERIAL			
❏ 66338	Havin' a Good Time/Can I Have Someone	1968	$12
❏ 66368	Havin' a Good Time (With My Baby)/Can I Have Someone (For Once)	1969	$12
LIBERTY			
❏ 55527	Listen, My Children, And You Shall Hear/Speak Softly and Carry a Big Horn	1962	$30
VERVE			
❏ 10245	Imagination/Ala-Men-Say	1961	$40
❏ 10261	See You in September/Sumemrtime Goodbye	1962	$60
❏ 10252	This Love of Mine/We'll Reach Heaven Together	1962	$40

Number	Title	Yr	NM

R

R.E.M.

EVATONE

Number	Title	Yr	NM
❑ 105900-15	Dark Globe (one-sided)	1989	$6

—5-inch black flexi-disc included in issue of Sassy magazine (double value if record is still attached to magazine)

FAN CLUB

❑ 122589 [DJ]	Good King Wenceslas/ Academy Fight Song	1989	$60
❑ 122589 [PS]	Good King Wenceslas/ Academy Fight Song	1989	$60

—Fold-out poster sleeve

❑ U-23518M [DJ]	Parade of the Wooden Soldiers/See No Evil	1988	$70

—Green vinyl

❑ U-23518M [PS]	Parade of the Wooden Soldiers/See No Evil	1988	$70

I.R.S.

❑ 52642	Can't Get There from Here/ Bandwagon	1985	$6
❑ 52642 [PS]	Can't Get There from Here/ Bandwagon	1985	$6
❑ 9931	(Don't Go Back to) Rockville/ Catapult (Live)	1984	$12
❑ 9931 [PS]	(Don't Go Back to) Rockville/ Catapult (Live)	1984	$20
❑ 52678	Driver 8/Crazy	1985	$6
❑ 52678 [PS]	Driver 8/Crazy	1985	$6
❑ 52883	Fall on Me/Rotary Ten	1986	$5
❑ 52883 [PS]	Fall on Me/Rotary Ten	1986	$5
❑ 53220	It's the End of the World As We Know It (And I Feel Fine)/Last Date	1987	$3
❑ 53220 [PS]	It's the End of the World As We Know It (And I Feel Fine)/Last Date	1987	$4
❑ 9927	So. Central Rain (I'm Sorry)/ King of the Road	1984	$6
❑ 9927 [PS]	So. Central Rain (I'm Sorry)/ King of the Road	1984	$20
❑ 52971	Superman/White Tornado	1986	$5
❑ 52971 [PS]	Superman/White Tornado	1986	$5
❑ 53171	The One I Love/Maps and Legends	1987	$3
❑ 53171 [PS]	The One I Love/Maps and Legends	1987	$3

THE BOB

❑ 20	Femme Fatale (one-sided)	1986	$20

—Flexi-disc included with The Bob magazine; black

❑ 20	Femme Fatale (one-sided)	1986	$20

—Flexi-disc included with The Bob magazine; red

❑ 20 [PS]	Femme Fatale (one-sided)	1986	$50

—Picture sleeve sent to The Bob subscribers only

WARNER BROS.

❑ 22791	Get Up/Funtime	1989	$3
❑ 22791 [PS]	Get Up/Funtime	1989	$3
❑ 27640	Pop Song 89/Pop Song 89 (Acoustic Version)	1989	$3
❑ 22780	Singleactiongreen	1989	$30

—Box set of 4 7-inch 45s, each with picture sleeve, plus poster. All have WB 27688, 27640 and 22791; all also are supposed to have W2960, but some contain 927 652 in error. No difference in value.

❑ 27688	Stand/Memphis Train Blues	1988	$3
❑ 27688 [PS]	Stand/Memphis Train Blues	1988	$3
❑ 21864	Stand/Pop Song 89	1989	$3

—Back to Back Hits" series

RABBITT, EDDIE

20TH FOX

❑ 474	Six Nights and Seven Days/ Next to the Note	1964	$30

DATE

❑ 2-1599	The Bed/Holding On	1968	$15
❑ 2-1599 [PS]	The Bed/Holding On	1968	$30

ELEKTRA

❑ 45381	Could You Love a Poor Boy, Dolly/There's Someone She Lies To (To Lie Here with Me)	1977	$6
❑ 45301	Drinkin' My Baby (Off My Mind)/When I Was Young	1976	$5
❑ 46656	Drivin' My Life Away/Pretty Lady	1980	$4
❑ 45554	Every Which Way But Loose/Under the Double Eagle	1978	$4
❑ 45237	Forgive and Forget/Pure Love	1975	$5
❑ 46613	Gone Too Far/Loveline	1980	$4
❑ 45461	Hearts on Fire/Girl on My Mind	1978	$4
❑ 45390	I Can't Help Myself/She Loves Me Like She Means It	1977	$4
❑ 47435	I Don't Know Where to Start/ Skip-A-Beat	1982	$4
❑ 45531	I Just Want to Love You/ Crossin' the Mississippi	1978	$4

Number	Title	Yr	NM
❑ 47066	I Love a Rainy Night/Short Road to Love	1980	$4
❑ 45269	I Should Have Married You/ Sweet Janine	1975	$5
❑ 46558	Pour Me Another Tequila/I Will Never Let You Go	1979	$4
❑ 47239	Someone Could Lose a Heart Tonight/Nobody Loves Me Like My Baby	1981	$4
❑ 378 [DJ]	Song of Ireland (same on both sides)	1978	$20

—Promo only on green vinyl; small center hole

❑ 47174	Step By Step/My Only Wish	1981	$4
❑ 47174 [PS]	Step By Step/My Only Wish	1981	$6
❑ 46053	Suspicions/I Don't Want to Make Love (With Anyone But You)	1979	$4
❑ 45357	Two Dollars in the Jukebox/ Don't Wanna Make Love	1976	$5

—Butterfly label

❑ 45357	Two Dollars in the Jukebox/ Don't Wanna Make Love	1976	$6

—Red label

❑ 45418	We Can't Go On Living Like This/We Made Love Beautiful	1977	$4

RCA

❑ PB-14192	A World Without Love/1-2-3, You Really Got a Hold on Me (The Wrestling Song)	1985	$3
❑ PB-14377	Both to Each Other (Friends and Lovers)/A World Without Love	1986	$3

—With Juice Newton

❑ PB-14377 [PS]	Both to Each Other (Friends and Lovers)/A World Without Love	1986	$5
❑ 5012-7-R	Gotta Have You/Singing in the Subway	1986	$3
❑ 8819-7-R	That's Why I Fell in Love with You/She's An Old Cadillac	1988	$3
❑ 8306-7-R	The Wanderer/Workin' Out	1988	$3
❑ 5238-7-R	Wanna Dance with You/ Gotta Have You	1987	$3
❑ 8716-7-R	We Must Be Doing Something Right/He's a Cheater	1988	$3
❑ 5093-7-R	When We Make Love/ (B-side unknown)	1987	$3

UNIVERSAL

❑ UVL-66025	On Second Thought/Only One Love in My Life	1989	$4

WARNER BROS.

❑ 29279	B-B-B-Burnin' Up with Love/747	1984	$4
❑ 29512	Our Love Will Survive/You Put the Beat in My Heart	1983	$4
❑ 28976	She's Comin' Back to Say Goodbye/Dial That Telephone	1985	$4
❑ 29186	The Best Year of My Life/ Over There	1984	$4
❑ 29089	Warning Sign/Go to Sleep, Big Bertha	1985	$4

RABIN, MIKE, AND THE DEMONS

TOWER

❑ 109	Head Over Heels/I'm Leaving You	1964	$20

RACKET SQUAD, THE

JUBILEE

❑ 5591	Hung Up/Higher Than High	1967	$40
❑ 5657	I'll Never Forget Your Love/ (B-side unknown)	1969	$30
❑ 5682	In Your Arms/(B-side unknown)	1969	$40
❑ 5623	Let's Dance to the Beat of My Heart/Higher Than High	1968	$30
❑ 5601	Little Red Wagon/(Just Like) Romeo and Juliet	1967	$30
❑ 5638	Suburban Life/The Loser	1968	$30
❑ 5628	That's How Much I Love My Baby/Movin' In	1968	$30
❑ 5613	The Loser/No Fair at All	1968	$30

RACONTEURS, THE (2)

TOWER

❑ 194	Like a Dribbling Fram/ Someday	1965	$40

RADER, JOHN

CLONE

❑ CL-009 [B]	One Step At a Time/Get You Back	1979	$25

RADHA KRISHNA TEMPLE

APPLE

❑ SPRO-5067/8 [DJ]	Govinda (Edit)/Govinda	1970	$50
❑ 1821	Govinda/Govinda Jai Jai	1970	$8
❑ 1821	Govinda/Govinda Jai Jai	1970	$10

—With Capitol logo on B-side label bottom

Number	Title	Yr	NM
❑ PRO-5013/4 [DJ]	Govinda/Govinda Jai Jai	1970	$30

—With an edit of the A-side

❑ 1821 [PS]	Govinda/Govinda Jai Jai	1970	$10
❑ 1810	Hare Krishna Mantra/Prayer to the Spiritual Masters	1969	$8
❑ 1810 [PS]	Hare Krishna Mantra/Prayer to the Spiritual Masters	1969	$400

—Only one copy is known to exist. The price is highly speculative.

RADIANTS, THE

ABC

❑ 12394	I Need a Vacation/Just Like You	1978	$5

CHESS

❑ 2078	Book of Love/Another Mule Is Kicking In Your Stall	1969	$10
❑ 2066	Choo Choo/Ida Mae Foster	1969	$10
❑ 1986	(Don't It Make You) Feel Kind of Bad/Anything You Do Is Alright	1967	$15
❑ 2021	Don't Take Your Love/The Clown Is Clever	1967	$15
❑ 1832	Father Knows Best/One Day I'll SHow You	1962	$20
❑ 2037	Hold On/I'm Glad I'm the Loser	1968	$15
❑ 1872	I'm in Love/Shy Guy	1963	$20
❑ 2083	I'm So Glad I'm the Loser/ Shadow of a Doubt	1970	$10
❑ 1925	It Ain't No Big Thing/I Got a Girl	1965	$15
❑ 1954	I Want to Thank You, Baby/ Baby You've Got It	1966	$15

—As "Maurice and the Radiants"

❑ 1849	Please Don't Leave Me/ Heartbreak Society	1963	$20
❑ 2057	Tears of a Clown/I'm Just a Man	1968	$15
❑ 1939	Whole Lot of Love/Tomorrow	1965	$15

TWINIGHT

❑ 153	My Sunshine Girl/Don't Wanna Face the Truth	1971	$8

RADICE, MARK

DECCA

❑ 32411	Three Cheers/Ten Thousand Year Old Blues	1968	$50

—Supposedly includes Steve Tallerico (a.k.a. Steve Tyler), later of Aerosmith

PARAMOUNT

❑ 0170	Hey, My Love/Your Love Is Like Fire	1972	$12

RCA VICTOR

❑ 47-9420	Save Your Money/Wooden Girl	1967	$20
❑ 47-9420 [PS]	Save Your Money/Wooden Girl	1967	$40

UNITED ARTISTS

❑ UA-XW840-Y	If You Can't Beat 'Em, Join' Em/The Whole Wide World Ain't Nothin' But a Party	1976	$8
❑ UA-XW897-Y	The Answer Is You/Monkey See, Monkey Do	1976	$8

RAFFERTY, GERRY

BLUE THUMB

❑ 231	Can I Have My Money Back/ Sign on the Dotted Line	1973	$8

LIBERTY

❑ 1482	Good Intentions/Standing at the Gates	1982	$4

SIGNPOST

❑ 70001	Make You, Break You/Mary Skeffington	1972	$10

UNITED ARTISTS

❑ XW1192	Baker Street/Big Change in the Weather	1978	$8

—Mispress with the full-length album version of "Baker Street" on A-side There is no "E" in the trail-off wax.

❑ XW1192	Baker Street/Big Change in the Weather	1978	$4

—Regular press with the edited, slightly sped-up version of "Baker Street" on A-side

❑ XW1298	Days Gone Down (Still Got That Light in Your Eyes)/ Why Won't You Talk to Me	1979	$4
❑ 1316	Get It Right Next Time/It's Gonna Be a Long Night	1979	$4
❑ XW1266	Home and Dry/Mattie's Rag	1978	$4
❑ XW1098	Mattie's Rag/City to City	1977	$5

Number	Title	Yr	NM

RAG DOLLS, THE
MALA
❑ 499	Baby's Gone/We Almost Made It	1965	$12
❑ 493	Dusty/Hey Hoagy	1964	$12
❑ 506	Little Girl Tears/Put a Ring on My Finger	1965	$12

PARKWAY
❑ 921	Society Girl/Ragen (Society Girl Bossa Nova)	1964	$15

RAGING STORMS, THE
FLAME
❑ 1019	High Octane/Madison Blues	1959	$50

TRANS ATLAS
❑ 691	So Hard to Take/Down at the Corner	1962	$12
❑ 677	The Dribble (Twist)/Hound Dog	1962	$10

WARWICK
❑ 677	The Dribble (Twist)/Hound Dog	1962	$10

RAGLAND, LOU
AMY
❑ 988	Travel Alone/Big Wheel	1967	$200

RAGSDALE, JOHNNY
ARIOLA AMERICA
❑ 7641	Head On Collision/Wake Up Darlin'	1976	$5

COLUMBIA
❑ 4-21422	Stand-In Sweetheart/Someone Parted Our Love	1955	$30
❑ 4-21232	Ten Thousand Cows/Blue Memory	1954	$30
❑ 4-21123	The Engineer's Song/Calamity Jane	1953	$30
❑ 4-21346	Words I Didn't Say/I'm Taking My Marbles Home	1955	$30
❑ 4-21163	Wrong Side of the Fence/Come Right In and Set	1953	$30

MONUMENT
❑ 45-257	Somewhere There's a Love Song/You're My Jamaica	1978	$4

RAIDERS, THE (2)
BRUNSWICK
❑ 55090	Walking Through the Jungle/My Steady Girl	1958	$50

RAIDERS, THE (3)
LIBERTY
❑ 55393	Dardanella/What Time Is It	1961	$40

RAIDERS, THE (5)
VAN
❑ 0663	On a Straight Away/It's Motivation	1963	$30
❑ 0262	Stick Shift/Skipping Around	1962	$60
❑ 0763	Supercharger/Cruisin' Low	1963	$30

VEE JAY
❑ 504	Stick Shift/Skipping Around	1963	$30

RAIN
A.P.I.
❑ 336	Outta My Life/E.S.P.	1967	$60
❑ 337	Substitute/Hear You Cry	1967	$60

BELL
❑ 45206	Caught in the Middle of It/Stop Me from Believing in You	1972	$5

LONDON
❑ 107	Outta My Life/E.S.P.	1967	$50
❑ 111	Substitute/Hear You Cry	1967	$50

MGM
❑ 13622	Take It Away/City Lovin'	1966	$30

PARAMOUNT
❑ 087	Show Me the Road Home/Funky Junky Blues	1971	$30

RAINBOW
Also see DEEP PURPLE; ELF; DIO; RONNIE DIO; FANDANGO; YNGWIE MALMSTEEN; MSG.

MERCURY
❑ 76146	Stone Cold/Rock Fever	1982	$4
❑ 76146 [PS]	Stone Cold/Rock Fever	1982	$5
❑ 815660-7	Street of Dreams/Anybody There	1983	$4
❑ 815660-7 [PS]	Street of Dreams/Anybody There	1983	$4

POLYDOR
❑ 2163	I Surrender/Vielleicht Das Nachster Leit	1981	$4

❑ 14481	Long Live Rock 'n Roll/Sensitive to Light	1978	$4
❑ 2014	Since You Been Gone/Bad Girls	1979	$4
❑ 14290	Snake Charmer/Man on the Silver Mountain	1975	$6

—As "Blackmore's Rainbow"

RAINBOW PRESS, THE
MR. G
❑ 821	Great White Whale/The Last Platoon	1969	$20
❑ 817	There's a War On/Better Way	1968	$20

RAINBOWS, THE (1)
ARGYLE
❑ 1012	Shirley/Stay	1962	$30

FIRE
❑ 1012	Mary Lee/Evening	1960	$30

PILGRIM
❑ 703	Mary Lee/Evening	1956	$60
❑ 711	Shirley/Stay	1956	$200

RAMA
❑ 209	Minnie/They Say	1956	$600

RED ROBIN
❑ 134	Mary Lee/Evening	1955	$600

—Note: Red Robin 141 is a bootleg

RAINBOWS, THE (2)
DAVE
❑ 908	I Know/Only a Picture	1963	$40
❑ 909	It Wouldn't Be Right/Family Monkey	1963	$40

RAINBOWS, THE (3)
DOT
❑ 16920	Color of Love/Down the Block	1966	$10
❑ 16612	My Ringo/He's Hooked on J's	1964	$20

RAINBOWS, THE (4)
EPIC
❑ 9900	Balla Balla/Ju Ju Hand	1966	$12

JAMIE
❑ 1339	Balla Balla/Ju Ju Hand	1967	$8

RAINBOWS, THE (U)
MERCURY
❑ 72068	Gonna Go Down/Dreamwalk	1962	$20

MGM
❑ 13058	Old Man's Twist/Straight Ahead	1962	$30

RAINDROPS, THE (1)
JUBILEE
❑ 5469	Book of Love/I Won't Cry	1964	$30
❑ 5497	Don't Let Go/My Mama Don't Like Him	1965	$30
❑ 5531	Hanky Panky/Hanky Panky	1965	$60

—Very rare promo release

❑ 5475	Let;s Go Together/You Got What I Like	1964	$30
❑ 5487	One More Tear/Another Boy Like Mine	1964	$30
❑ 5466	That Boy John/Hanky Panky	1963	$30
❑ 5444	What a Guy/It's So Wonderful	1963	$30

RAINDROPS, THE (3)
CORSAIR
❑ 104	Maybe/Love Is Like a Mountain	1960	$100

DORE
❑ 561	Maybe/Love Is Like a Mountain	1960	$30

RAINDROPS, THE (4)
IMPERIAL
❑ 5785	I Remember in the Still of the Night/Sweet Song	1961	$40

RAINDROPS, THE (5)
SPIN-IT
❑ 104	(I Found) Heaven in Love/I Prayed for Gold	1956	$200
❑ 106	Little One/Rockin' on the Farm	1956	$200

RAINDROPS, THE (U)
HAMILTON
❑ 50021	Oh Why/Without Love, Love, Love	1960	$30

RAINES, RITA
CADENCE
❑ 1331	I Told a Stranger/Sleepy Sunday Afternoon	1957	$10

DEED
❑ 1006	Don't Touch Me/Until Death Do Us Part	1955	$15
❑ 1006	Don't Touch Me/Wedding Song	1955	$15
❑ 1003	If I Were You/Boy Meets Girl	1955	$15
❑ 1015	I'm Crying/Little Mary	1956	$10
❑ 1010	Such a Day (So Ein Tag)/Ol' Devil Moon	1956	$10
❑ 1020	There's a Time/I Volunteer	1956	$10

JAMIE
❑ 1041	I Told a Stranger/Sleepy Sunday Afternoon	1957	$20
❑ 1036	Someone Else/Silence Is Golden	1957	$20

RAINWATER, MARVIN
❑ 1001	Part Time Lover/That Aching Heart	1963	$12

—With Bill Guess

CORAL
❑ 9-61342	I Gotta Go Get My Baby/Daddy's Glad You Came Home	1955	$30

MGM
❑ 12370	Get Off the Stool/(Sometimes) I Feel Like Leaving Town	1956	$40
❑ 12412	Gonna Find Me a Bluebird/So You Think You've Got Troubles	1957	$30
❑ 12803	Half-Breed/A Song of Love	1959	$30
❑ 12891	Hard Luck Blues/She's Gone	1960	$20
❑ 12240	Hot and Cold/Mr. Blues	1956	$50
❑ 12665	I Dig You Baby/Moanin' the Blues	1958	$30
❑ 12739	Lonely Island/Born to Be Lonesome	1958	$30
❑ 12773	Love Me Baby (Like There's No Tomorrow)/That's When I'll Stop Loving You	1959	$30
❑ 12586	Lucky Star/Look for Me	1957	$30
❑ 12653	Moanin' the Blues/Gamblin' Man	1958	$30
❑ 12511	My Brand of Blues/My Love Is Real	1957	$30
❑ 12865	Pale Faced Indian/Wayward Angel	1960	$20
❑ 12071	Sticks and Stones/Albino Stallion	1955	$30
❑ 12090	Tennessee Houn' Dog Yodel/Tea Bag Romeo	1955	$30
❑ 12152	Where Do We Go from Here/Dem Low Down Blues	1955	$30
❑ 12609	Whole Lotta Woman/Baby Don't Go	1958	$30
❑ 12313	Why Did You Have to Go and Leave Me/What Am I Supposed to Do	1956	$30

NU TRAYL
❑ 902	Haircut/Looking Good	1976	$6

UNITED ARTISTS
❑ 917	Black Sheet/Indian Burial Ground	1965	$10
❑ 837	It Wasn't Enough/My Old Home Town	1965	$10
❑ 50023	Sorrow Brings a Good Man Down/The Troubles My Little Boy Had	1966	$12

WARWICK
❑ 666	Boo Hoo/I Can't Forget	1961	$50
❑ 674	Tough Top Cat/(There's a) Honky Tonk in Your Heart	1962	$30

7-Inch Extended Plays
MGM
❑ X1466	(contents unknown)	1957	$30
❑ X1464	Gonna Find Me a Bluebird/Where Do We Go from Here//Dem Lowdown Blues/Cause I'm a Dreamer	1957	$30
❑ X1464 [PS]	Songs by Marvin Rainwater, Vol. 1	1957	$30
❑ X1466 [PS]	Songs by Marvin Rainwater, Vol. 3	1957	$30
❑ X1465 [PS]	Songs by Marvin Rainwater Vol. 2	1957	$30
❑ X1465	Tennessee Houn' Dog Yodel/What Am I Supposed to Do//Why Did You Have to Go and Leave Me/Mr. Blues	1957	$30

Number	Title	Yr	NM

RAINY DAYS, THE
JUBILEE
| ❏ 5517 | He Was a Friend of Mine/Don't Want No Fool | 1965 | $15 |

PANIK
| ❏ 7566 | I Can Only Give You Anything/(B-side unknown) | 1966 | $30 |
| ❏ 7542 | Turn on Your Lovelight/Go On and Cry | 1966 | $30 |

RAINY DAZE, THE
CHICORY
| ❏ 404 | That Acapulco Gold/In My Mind Lives a Forest | 1967 | $20 |

UNI
❏ 55011	Discount City/Good Morning, Mr. Smith	1967	$12
❏ 55026	Fe Fi Fo Fum/Fe Fi Fo Fum	1967	$30
—Original title of song (first pressing)			
❏ 55026	Stop Sign/Blood of Oblivion	1967	$10
❏ 55002	That Acapulco Gold/In My Mind Lives a Forest	1967	$10

WHITE WHALE
| ❏ 279 | My Door Is Always Open/Make Me Laugh | 1968 | $10 |

RAITT, BONNIE
A&M
❏ 1249	Baby Mine/Mickey Mouse March	1988	$4
—A-side with Was (Not Was); B-side by Aaron Neville			
❏ 1249 [PS]	Baby Mine/Mickey Mouse March	1988	$4

CAPITOL
| ❏ B-44365 | Thing Called Love/The Road's My Middle Name | 1989 | $4 |
| ❏ B-44365 [PS] | Thing Called Love/The Road's My Middle Name | 1989 | $4 |

FULL MOON
| ❏ 49612 | Once in a Lifetime/You're Only Lonely | 1980 | $4 |
| —B-side by J.D. Souther | | | |

FULL MOON/ASYLUM
❏ 47033	Don't Make You Wanna Dance/Orange Blossom Special	1980	$5
—B-side by Gilley's Urban Cowboy Band			
❏ 47033 [PS]	Don't It Make You Wanna Dance/Orange Blossom Special	1980	$6

REPRISE
| ❏ 1370 | When You Touch Me This Way/Since I've Been With You Babe | 1976 | $5 |
| —By Geoff Muldaur and Bonnie Raitt | | | |

WARNER BROS.
❏ 7554	Bluebird/Women Be Wise	1972	$8
❏ 50022	Can't Get Enough/Keep This Heart in Mind	1982	$4
❏ 28450	Crimes of Passion/Stand Up to the Night	1987	$4
❏ 7758	Everybody's Cryin' Mercy/You've Been in Love Too Long	1973	$6
❏ 8485	Gamblin' Man/About to Make Me Leave Home	1977	$5
❏ 8166	Good Enough/My First Night Alone Without You	1975	$6
❏ 8044	I Got Plenty/You Got to Be Ready for Love	1974	$6
❏ 7645	Too Long at the Fair/Under the Falling Sky	1972	$8
❏ 7645 [DJ]	Too Long at the Fair/Under the Falling Sky	1972	$20
—Cardboard picture sleeve and booklet			
❏ 8430	Two Lives/Three Time Loser	1977	$5
❏ 49185	Wild for You Baby/(I Could Have Been Your) Best Old Friend	1980	$4

RAJAHS, THE
KLIK
| ❏ 7805 | I Fell in Love/Shifting Sands | 1957 | $300 |

RALLY PACKS, THE
IMPERIAL
| ❏ 66036 | Move Out Little Mustang/Bucket Seats | 1964 | $70 |

RAM
POLYDOR
| ❏ 14099 | The Want in You/Mother's Day Song | 1971 | $8 |

RAM JAM
EPIC
| ❏ 50357 | Black Betty/I Should Have Known | 1977 | $5 |
| ❏ 50587 | Pretty Poison/Runaway Runaway | 1978 | $6 |

RAMAL, BILL
20TH CENTURY FOX
| ❏ 432 | Exodus/Theme from "Dr. No | 1963 | $10 |
MGM
| ❏ 13123 | Hard Times/Sax Fifth Ave. | 1963 | $12 |

RAMBEAU, EDDIE
20TH CENTURY FOX
| ❏ 491 | Come Closer/She's Smilin' at Me | 1964 | $10 |

BELL
| ❏ 873 | Don't Leave Me/Solitary Man | 1970 | $6 |
| ❏ 847 | Who Will Buy-Where Is Love/Solitary Man | 1969 | $6 |

DYNO VOICE
❏ 204	Concrete and Clay/Don't Believe Him	1965	$10
❏ 217	I Just Need Your Love/I'm the Sky	1966	$8
❏ 207	I Just Need Your Love/My Name Is Mud	1965	$8
❏ 221	I Miss You/Thinkin' About You Baby	1966	$8
❏ 225	The Clock/If I Were You	1966	$8
❏ 211	The Train/Yesterday's Newspapers	1966	$8

SWAN
❏ 4145	Lover's Medley/The Car Hop and the Hard Top	1963	$10
❏ 4105	My Four Leaf Clover/Anyone Want More Flowers	1962	$10
❏ 4077	Skin Divin'/Toni	1961	$12
❏ 4112	Summertime Guy/Last Night Was My Last Night with You	1962	$10

RAMBLERS, THE (2)
ALMONT
❏ 311	Father Sebastian/Barbara (I Loved You)	1964	$30
❏ 313	School Girl/Birdland Baby	1964	$30
❏ 315	Surfin' Santa/Silly Little Boy	1964	$30

RAMBLERS, THE (3)
FEDERAL
| ❏ 12286 | Don't You Know?/The Heaven and Earth | 1957 | $200 |

RAMBLERS, THE (4)
JAX
| ❏ 319 | Search My Heart/50-50 Love | 1953 | $500 |
| —Red vinyl | | | |

RAMBLERS, THE (5)
MGM
| ❏ 55006 | Bad Girl/Rickey-Do, Rickey-Do | 1955 | $200 |

RAMBLERS, THE (6)
TRUMPET
| ❏ 102 | So Sad/Come On Back | 1963 | $1000 |

RAMBLERS, THE (U)
RCA VICTOR
| ❏ 47-5240 | Mama He Treats Your Daughter Mean/And the Bull Walked Around Olay | 1953 | $400 |
SIDEWINDER
| ❏ 101 | Ticonderoga/Mozart Stomp | 1964 | $50 |

RAMONES, THE
Marky Ramone was in DUST; also see DEE DEE RAMONE.
BEGGARS BANQUET
❏ BEG-201	Merry Christmas (I Don't Want to Fight Tonight)/I Wanna Live	1987	$8
❏ BEG-201 [PS]	Merry Christmas (I Don't Want to Fight Tonight)/I Wanna Live	1987	$8
—Above record and sleeve are U.K. imports			

RSO
| ❏ 1055 | I Wanna Be Sedated/The Return of Jackie and Judy | 1980 | $8 |

SIRE
❏ 49182	Baby I Love You/High Risk Insurance	1980	$10
❏ 725	Blitzkrieg Bop/Havana Affair	1976	$80
—Promo copies worth slightly less			
❏ 1025	Don't Come Close/I Don't Want You	1978	$12
❏ 49261	Do You Remember Rock & Roll Radio/Let's Go	1980	$12
❏ 1017	Do You Wanna Dance?/Baby Sitter	1978	$12
❏ 1017 [PS]	Do You Wanna Dance?/Baby Sitter	1978	$50
❏ 29107	Howling at the Moon (Sha La La)/Wart Hog	1985	$8
❏ 27663	I Wanna Be Sedated/I Wanna Be Sedated (Ramones On 45 Mega-Mix)	1988	$8
❏ 27663 [PS]	I Wanna Be Sedated/I Wanna Be Sedated (Ramones On 45 Mega-Mix)	1988	$8
❏ 734	I Wanna Be Your Boyfriend// California Sun/I Don't Wanna Walk Around with You	1976	$10
❏ 734 [PS]	I Wanna Be Your Boyfriend// California Sun/I Don't Wanna Walk Around with You	1976	$25
❏ 22911	Pet Sematary/Sheena is a Punk Rocker	1989	$8
❏ 22911 [PS]	Pet Sematary/Sheena is a Punk Rocker	1989	$8
❏ 746	Sheena Is a Punk Rocker/I Don't Care	1977	$10
❏ 746 [PS]	Sheena Is a Punk Rocker/I Don't Care	1977	$15
❏ 1006	Sheena Is a Punk Rocker/I Don't Care	1977	$8
❏ 1006 [PS]	Sheena Is a Punk Rocker/I Don't Care	1977	$10
❏ 28599	Something to Believe In/Animal Boy	1986	$8
❏ 738	Swallow My Pride/Pinhead	1977	$20
❏ 738 [PS]	Swallow My Pride/Pinhead	1977	$25
❏ 29606	The Time Has Come Today/Psycho Therapy	1983	$8
❏ 49812	We Want the Airwaves/All's Quiet on the Western Front	1981	$8

RAMRODS
AMY
❏ 813	(Ghost) Riders in the Sky/Zig Zag	1961	$30
❏ 817	Loch Lomond Rock/Take Me Back to My Boots and Saddle	1961	$30
❏ 846	War Cry/Boing!	1962	$30
QUEEN
❏ 240145	Slee-Zee/Slouchee	1962	$30
R&H
❏ 1001	Moonlight Surf/Night Ride	1963	$60

RAMS, THE
FLAIR
| ❏ 1066 | Sweet Thing/Rock Bottom | 1955 | $200 |

RAN-DELLS, THE
CHAIRMAN
❏ 4403	Martian Hop/Forgive Me, Darling (I Have Lied)	1963	$30
❏ 4403 [PS]	Martian Hop/Forgive Me, Darling (I Have Lied)	1963	$60
❏ 4407	Sound of the Sun/Come On and Love Me	1964	$20

R.S.V.P.
| ❏ 1104 | Beyond the Stars/Wintertime | 1964 | $20 |

RANCHEROS, THE
DOT
| ❏ 16572 | Linda's Tune/Little Linda | 1964 | $30 |
LONNIE
| ❏ 5005 | Linda's Tune/Little Linda | 1963 | $60 |

RANDAZZO, TEDDY
ABC-PARAMOUNT
❏ 10228	Broken Bell/Let the Sunshine In	1961	$10
❏ 10127	But You Broke My Heart/Misery	1960	$15
❏ 10350	Dance to the Locomotion/Cotton Fields	1962	$12
❏ 10247	Don't Go Away/One More Chance	1961	$12
❏ 10377	Echoes/It Wasn't a Dream	1962	$12
❏ 10193	Happy Ending/But You Broke My Heart	1961	$12
❏ 10068	How I Need You/You Don't Care Anymore	1959	$15
❏ 10014	Laughing on the Outside/Awkward Age	1959	$15
❏ 10043	Lies/I'm On a Merry-Go Round	1959	$15
❏ 10287	Mother Goose Twist/It's a Pity to Say Goodbye	1961	$10
❏ 9998	Papito/You Are Always in My Heart	1959	$15
❏ 10312	Teenage Senorita/Blue Hawaii Moon	1962	$10
❏ 10088	The Way of a Clown/Cherie	1960	$15
❏ 10103	Triste Pagliaccio (The Way of a Clown)/Cherie	1960	$20

Number	Title	Yr	NM
COLPIX			
❏ 662	Big Wide World/Be Sure My Love	1962	$15
❏ 684	Dear Heart/Just Hold My Hand	1963	$12
DCP			
❏ 1108	Less Than Tomorrow/Lost Without You	1964	$8
❏ 1003	Pretty Blue Eyes/Doo Dah	1964	$8
MGM			
❏ 13682	A Fistful of Dollars/Take Me Back	1967	$8
❏ 13648	I'm Losing You/Trick or Treat	1966	$8
❏ 13448	Lara's Theme/The Old and the New	1966	$8
❏ 13449	Theme from "A Patch of Blue"/The Old and New	1966	$8
❏ 13511	Watch What Happens/Per Un Pugno Di Dollari	1966	$8
VERVE FOLKWAYS			
❏ 5050	A World Without Love/Just One More Time	1967	$8
VIK			
❏ 0319	Dutch Treat/To Belong	1958	$15
❏ 0310	I'll Never Smile Again/Red Ruby Lips	1957	$15
❏ 0330	Little Serenade/Be My Kitten, Little Chicken	1958	$20

RANDELL, BUDDY
UNI			
❏ 55209	Be My Baby/Randi Randi	1970	$6

RANDELL, LYNNE
ABC			
❏ 11112	Open Letter/Right to Cry	1968	$30
EPIC			
❏ 10197	I Need You Boy/That's a Hoe-Down	1967	$40
❏ 10147	Stranger in My Arms/Ciao Baby	1967	$40

RANDI, DON
CAPITOL			
❏ 2475	Love Theme from Romeo and Juliet/The Windmills of Your Mind	1969	$6
WORLD PACIFIC			
❏ 812	Our Last Dance/Oh Yeah	1960	$15

RANDOLPH, BARBARA
SOUL			
❏ 35050	Can I Get a Witness/You Got Me Hurtin' All Over	1968	$30
❏ 35038	I Got a Feeling/You Got Me Hurtin' All Over	1967	$30

RANDOLPH, BOOTS
MONUMENT			
❏ 8616	Behind Closed Doors/Old Joe Clarke	1974	$4
❏ 460	Bluebird of Happiness/Keep a Light in Your Window Tonight	1962	$10
❏ 443	Fancy Dan/Hey, Daddy Daddy	1961	$10
❏ 1125	Games People Play/By the Time I Get to Phoenix	1969	$6
❏ 1081	Gentle on My Mind/Jackson	1968	$6
❏ 835	Hey, Mr. Sax Man/Baby, Go to Sleep	1964	$8
❏ 1165	Hey Jude/Down Yonder	1969	$6
❏ 45-209	Honky Tonk/Memphis	1977	$4
❏ 45-294	I Write the Songs/Motherland-Oluwa	1980	$4
❏ 821	Lonely Street/Windy and Warm	1963	$8
❏ 8541	Lonesome Ladies/Mountain Minuet	1972	$4
❏ 8534	Lookin'/Alligator Annie	1972	$4
❏ 1038	Love Letters/Big Daddy	1967	$6
❏ 8552	Love Theme from "The Godfather"/Rocky Top	1972	$4
❏ 8588	Marie/Sentimental Journey	1973	$4
❏ 852	Mickey's Tune/I'll Take You Home Again, Kathleen	1964	$8
❏ 8500	My Sweet Lord/(B-side unknown)	1971	$5
❏ 1226	Proud Mary/Without Love (There Is Nothing)	1970	$5
❏ 8634	Sanford & Son Theme/Ebb Tide	1974	$5
❏ 1176	Sleigh Ride/White Christmas	1969	$8
❏ 8632	Sleigh Ride/White Christmas	1974	$5
❏ 1937	Sleigh Ride/White Christmas	1976	$4
— *Golden Series*			
❏ 1199	Spanish Harlem/Anna	1970	$5
❏ 1219	Sunday Morning Coming Down/Those Were the Days	1970	$5
❏ 1233	Take a Letter Maria/See See Rider	1970	$5
❏ 1009	Temptation/You've Lost That Lovin' Feelin'	1967	$6

Number	Title	Yr	NM
❏ 928	These Boots Are Made for Walking/Honey in Your Heart	1966	$8
❏ 976	The Shadow of Your Smile/I'll Just Walk Away	1966	$8
❏ 1056	Wonderland by Night/Fred	1968	$6
RCA VICTOR			
❏ 47-7515	Blue Guitar/Greenback Dollar	1959	$15
— *As "Randy Randolph*			
❏ 47-7835	Bog Daddy/Bongo Band	1961	$15
❏ 47-7278	Difficult/I'm Getting Your Message Baby	1958	$20
— *As "Randy Randolph*			
❏ 47-7611	Temptation/Sweet Talk	1959	$15

7-Inch Extended Plays

Number	Title	Yr	NM
MONUMENT			
❏ SMN-361 [DJ]	Sleigh Ride/Rudolph The Red-Nosed Reindeer/White Christmas/I'll Be Home For Christmas	1969	$25

RANDOLPH, WILLIAM
HIT			
❏ 214	Come Back to Me/I'll Never Find Another You	1965	$8
— *B-side by the Broadway Singers*			
❏ 201	I'm in a Very Romantic Mood/I Know a Place	1965	$8
— *B-side by Betty Coleson*			
❏ 196	Madrid/Red Roses for a Blue Lady	1965	$8
❏ 173	Song of Love/The Wedding	1965	$8
— *B-side by Betty Coleson*			
❏ 188	Swinging Spiritual/No Arms Can Ever Hold You	1965	$8
— *B-side by Danny Woods*			
❏ 205	Theme from "Peyton Place"/Tower Suite	1965	$8

RANDOMS, THE
DANGERHOUSE			
❏ PT1	ABCD/Let's Get Rid of New York	1977	$20
❏ PT1 [PS]	ABCD/Let's Get Rid of New York	1977	$20

RANDY AND THE RADIANTS
SUN			
❏ 398	My Way of Thinking/Truth from My Eyes	1966	$30
❏ 395	The Mountain's High/Peek-a-Boo	1965	$30

RANDY AND THE RAINBOWS
AMBIENT SOUND			
❏ 02872	Debbie/Try the Impossible	1982	$5
B.T. PUPPY			
❏ 535	I'll Be Seeing You/Oh to Get Away	1967	$10
MIKE			
❏ 4008	Bonnie's Part of Town/Can It Be	1966	$15
❏ 4001	Lovely Lies/I'll Forget Her Tomorrow	1966	$15
RUST			
❏ 5059	Denise/Come Back	1963	$40
— *Blue label*			
❏ 5059	Denise/Come Back	1963	$30
— *Mostly white label*			
❏ 5080	Happy Teenager/Dry Your Eyes	1964	$20
❏ 5091	Little Star/Sharin'	1964	$20
❏ 5073	She's My Angel/Why Do Kids Grow Up	1964	$20

RANDY AND THE ROCKETS
VIKING			
❏ 1000	If You Really Care/Genevieve	1959	$30
❏ 1003	Is It True/Crazy Notion	1959	$30
❏ 1004	That's Life/Sweet Love	1959	$30

RANEY, SUE
CAPITOL			
❏ 4360	Biology/Too Soon	1960	$15
❏ F3745	Careless Years/What's the Good Word, Mr. Bluebird?	1957	$15
❏ F3806	Don't Take My Happiness/Please Hurry Home	1957	$15
❏ F4110	Ever/Restless Sea	1959	$12
❏ 4429	One Finger Symphony/Word Got Around	1960	$10
❏ F4038	Periwinkle Blue/My, How the Time Goes By	1958	$15
IMPERIAL			
❏ 66265	A Banda/Wait Until Dark	1967	$8

Number	Title	Yr	NM
❏ 66151	Before the Rain/Now Is the Hour	1965	$12
❏ 66340	Early Morning Blues and Greens/Knowing When to Leave	1968	$8
❏ 66184	Little Things Mean a Lot/Who's Afraid	1966	$8
❏ 66211	Smile/Any Old Time of Day	1966	$8
❏ 66222	There Goes My Everything/Try to See It My Way	1986	$8

RANEY, WAYNE
DECCA			
❏ 31004	Four Aces and a Queen/I Ain't Got Time	1959	$20
❏ 30212	Shake Baby Shake/Fortieth and Plum	1957	$70
KING			
❏ 1259	Adam/Roosters Are Crowing	1953	$40
❏ 1187	Betrayed Waltz/Falling	1953	$40
❏ 989	Blues at My Door/You Better Treat Your Man Right	1951	$50
❏ 1058	Catfish Baby/Heads or Tails I Win	1952	$40
❏ 1149	Child's Side of Life/If You Never Slip Around	1952	$40
❏ 5327	Gathering in the Sky/Book of Revelations	1960	$20
❏ 1480	Gone with the Wind This Morning/Tear Down the Mountains	1955	$30
❏ 1229	Gonna Row My Boat/Burning Your Love Letters	1953	$40
❏ 1036	I'd Feel Just Like a Millionaire/Real Good Feelin'	1952	$40
❏ 1087	I'm Really Needin' You/Beatin' Round the Bush	1952	$40
❏ 939	I've Gone and Sold My Soul/I Love My Little Yo-Yo	1951	$60
❏ 974	I Want a Home in Dixie/I Had My Fingers Crossed	1951	$50
❏ 1469	I Was There/We Love to Live	1955	$30
❏ 956	Lost John Boogie/I'm On My Way	1951	$50
❏ 1331	Trying to Live Without You/Mama	1954	$40
❏ 1116	When They Let the Hammer Down/Undertakin' Daddy	1952	$40
STARDAY			
❏ 663	Mail Order Heart/Don't Try to Be What You Ain't	1964	$15
❏ 677	Strictly Nothing/Love Thief	1964	$15

RANGERS QUARTET, THE
DECCA			
❏ 9-46331	He Bore It All/I Shall Go Home in the Morning	1951	$30

RANGERS, THE
CHALLENGE			
❏ 59229	Snow Skiing/Mogul Monster	1964	$30
FTP			
❏ 404	Four on the Floor/Riders in the Sky	1961	$40

RANK AND FILE
SLASH			
❏ 29591	Amanda Ruth/Lucky Day	1983	$4
❏ 29297	Sound of the Rain/Long Gone Road	1984	$4

RANK, KEN
FENTON			
❏ 2194	Twin City Saucer/Ken's Thing	1968	$40

RANKIN, KENNY
ABC-PARAMOUNT			
❏ 10268	Funny That's Love/Go Home Little Girl	1961	$15
— *As "Ken Rankin*			
COLUMBIA			
❏ 43885	Haven't We Met/In the Name of Love	1966	$12
❏ 42881	Soft Guitar/Baby Goodbye	1963	$12
❏ 43036	Where Did My Little Girl Go/U.S. Mail	1964	$10
DECCA			
❏ 31124	Casey Jones/It Started in Naples	1960	$15
❏ 30852	Cindy Loo/Catch Love	1959	$20
❏ 30954	I Cry By Night/Have Pity Miss Kitty	1959	$20
❏ 30691	My Popular Baby/You Be the Judge	1958	$20
❏ 30485	Saturday After the Game/I'll Be Waiting	1957	$30
❏ 31162	Sure As You're Born/Teasin' Heart	1960	$15
❏ 31054	What Do You Want to Make Those Eyes at Me For?/Tonight I'm Speaking Love	1960	$15

LITTLE DAVID

Number	Title	Yr	NM
❏ 729	Catfish/Silver Morning	1975	$5
❏ 8093	Catfish/Silver Morning	1975	$5
❏ 733	Creepin'/Lost Up in Loving You	1976	$5
❏ 735	On and On/Through the Eyes of the Eagle	1977	$5
❏ 726	Peaceful/Sometimes	1973	$5
❏ 728	Penny Lane/Killed a Cat	1974	$5
❏ 8072	Penny Lane/Killed a Cat	1975	$5
❏ 725	String Man/Comin' Down	1972	$5
❏ 732	Sunday Kind of Love/Inside	1975	$5
❏ 737	When Sunny Gets Blue/I Love You	1977	$5
❏ 727	Why Do Fools Fall in Love/ (B-side unknown)	1973	$5

MERCURY

Number	Title	Yr	NM
❏ 72956	Minuet/Peaceful	1969	$8
❏ 72768	Peaceful/The Dolphin	1968	$8
❏ 72768 [PS]	Peaceful/The Dolphin	1968	$15

RAPEMAN

RUTHLESS

Number	Title	Yr	NM
❏ 0(# unknown)	Marmoset/Hated Chinee	1989	$38
❏ 0(# unknown) [PS]	Marmoset/Hated Chinee	1989	$38

SUB POP

Number	Title	Yr	NM
❏ 40	Inki's Butt Crack/Song Number One	1989	$33

—First 1,000 on clear vinyl

| ❏ 40 | Inki's Butt Crack/Song Number One | 1989 | $18 |

—Black vinyl

| ❏ 40 [PS] | Inki's Butt Crack/Song Number One | 1989 | $18 |

—#10 in Sub Pop Singles Club series

RARE BREED, THE

ATTACK

Number	Title	Yr	NM
❏ 1401	Beg, Borrow and Steal/Jeri's Theme	1966	$40
❏ 1403	Come and Take a Ride in My Boat/Take Me to This World of Yours	1966	$30

RARE EARTH

PRODIGAL

Number	Title	Yr	NM
❏ 0637	Crazy Love/Is Your Teacher Cool	1977	$5
❏ 0643	I Can Feel My Love Risin'/S.O.S. (Stop Her On Sight)	1978	$5
❏ 0640	Warm Ride/Would You Like to Come Along	1978	$5

RARE EARTH

Number	Title	Yr	NM
❏ 5056	Big John Is My Name/Ma	1974	$6
❏ 5021	Born to Wander/Here Comes the Night	1970	$6
❏ 5057	Chained/Fresh from the Can	1974	$6
❏ 5010	Generation (Light of the Sky)/Magic Key	1969	$15
❏ 5012	Get Ready/Magic Key	1970	$6
❏ 5048	Good Time Sally/Love Shines Down	1972	$6
❏ 5038	Hey Big Brother/Under God's Light	1971	$6
❏ 5054	Hum Along and Dance/ Come with Me	1973	$6
❏ 5031	I Just Want to Celebrate/ The Seed	1971	$6
❏ 5031 [PS]	I Just Want to Celebrate/ The Seed	1971	$10
❏ 5017	(I Know) I'm Losing You/ When Joanie Smiles	1970	$6
❏ 5058	It Makes You Happy (But It Ain't Gonna Last Too Long)/ Boogie with Me Children	1975	$6
❏ 5059	Let Me Be Your Sunshine/ Keep Me Out of the Storm	1976	$6
❏ 5053	Ma/(Instrumental)	1973	$6
❏ 5060	Midnight Lady/Walking Shtick	1976	$6
❏ 5052	We're Gonna Have a Good Time/Would You Like to Come Along	1973	$6
❏ 5043	What'd I Say/Nice to Be with You	1972	$6
❏ 960/961 [DJ]	What'd I Say (stereo/mono)	1972	$30

—Blue vinyl, promo only, white label

VERVE

Number	Title	Yr	NM
❏ 10622	Stop-Where Did Our Love Go/Mother's Oats	1968	$15

RASCALS, THE

ATLANTIC

Number	Title	Yr	NM
❏ 2493	A Beautiful Morning/Rainy Day	1968	$6

—First record as "The Rascals"

❏ 2493 [PS]	A Beautiful Morning/Rainy Day	1968	$30
❏ 2424	A Girl Like You/It's Love	1967	$8
❏ 2424 [PS]	A Girl Like You/It's Love	1967	$30
❏ 2664	Carry Me Back/Real Thing	1969	$6
❏ 2664 [PS]	Carry Me Back/Real Thing	1969	$15
❏ 2353	Come On Up/What Is the Reason	1966	$10
❏ 2743	Glory Glory/You Don't Know	1970	$6
❏ 2743 [PS]	Glory Glory/You Don't Know	1970	$15
❏ 2321	Good Lovin'/Mustang Sally	1966	$20
❏ 2428	Groovin' (Spanish)/Groovin' (Italian)	1967	$30
❏ 2401	Groovin'/Sueno	1967	$8
❏ 2401 [PS]	Groovin'/Sueno	1967	$30
❏ 2599	Heaven/Baby I'm Blue	1969	$6
❏ 2695	Hold On/I Believe	1969	$6
❏ 2695 [PS]	Hold On/I Believe	1969	$15
❏ 2438	How Can I Be Sure/I'm So Happy Now	1967	$8
❏ 2312	I Ain't Gonna Eat Out My Heart Anymore/Slow Down	1965	$20

—From here through Atlantic 2463, as "The Young Rascals"

❏ 2463	It's Wonderful/Of Course	1967	$8
❏ 2377	I've Been Lonely Too Long/If You Knew	1967	$10
❏ 2377 [PS]	I've Been Lonely Too Long/If You Knew	1967	$30
❏ 2537	People Got to Be Free/My World	1968	$6
❏ 2537 [PS]	People Got to Be Free/My World	1968	$15
❏ 2634	See/Away Away	1969	$6
❏ 2634 [PS]	See/Away Away	1969	$15

COLUMBIA

Number	Title	Yr	NM
❏ 45568	Brother Tree/Saga of New York	1972	$6
❏ 45600	Echoes/Hummin' Song	1972	$6
❏ 45400	Love Me/Happy Song	1971	$6
❏ 45491	Lucky Day/Love Letter	1971	$6

PHILCO-FORD

Number	Title	Yr	NM
❏ HP-18	A Girl Like You/I've Been Lonely Too Long	1967	$20

—4-inch plastic "Hip Pocket Record" with color sleeve

7-Inch Extended Plays

ATLANTIC

Number	Title	Yr	NM
❏ SD 7-8169 [PS]	Once Upon a Dream	1968	$25
❏ SD 7-8169	Please Love Me/It's Wonderful/I'm Gonna Love You/Easy Rollin'/Rainy Day	1968	$25

—Jukebox issue; small hole, plays at 33 1/3 rpm

RASPBERRIES

Also see ERIC CARMEN; THE CHOIR.

CAPITOL

Number	Title	Yr	NM
❏ PRO-6426 [DJ]	Don't Want to Say Goodbye (3:48 Mono)/(5:00 Stereo)	1972	$30
❏ 3826	Don't Want to Say Goodbye/ Ecstasy	1974	$6
❏ 3280	Don't Want to Say Goodbye/ Rock and Roll Mama	1972	$8
❏ 3280 [PS]	Don't Want to Say Goodbye/ Rock and Roll Mama	1972	$30
❏ 3885	Drivin' Around/Might As Well	1974	$6
❏ 3348	Go All the Way/With You in My Life	1972	$6
❏ 3765	I'm a Rocker/Money Down	1973	$6
❏ 3473	I Wanna Be with You/Goin' Nowhere Tonight	1972	$6
❏ 3546	Let's Pretend/Every Way I Can	1973	$6
❏ 3546 [PS]	Let's Pretend/Every Way I Can	1973	$15
❏ 3946	Overnight Sensation (Hit Record)/Hands on You	1974	$6
❏ 4001	The Party's Over/Cruisin' Music	1974	$6
❏ 3610	Tonight/Had to Get Over a Heartbreak	1973	$6

RATIONALS, THE

A-SQUARE

Number	Title	Yr	NM
❏ 103	Feelin' Lost/Little Girls Cry	1966	$30
❏ 103	Feelin' Lost/Respect	1966	$30
❏ 402	I Need You/Get the Picture	1967	$30

—B-side by SRC (Scott Richard Case)

❏ 107	I Need You/Out in the Streets	1968	$30
❏ 104/3	Leavin' Here/Feelin' Lost	1966	$30
❏ 104	Leavin' Here/Respect	1966	$40

—This is the original issue of this single

| ❏ 101 | Look What You Doin'/I Gave My Love | 1966 | $30 |

CAMEO

Number	Title	Yr	NM
❏ 455	Hold On Baby/Sing	1967	$20
❏ 481	Leavin' Here/Not Like It Is	1967	$20

CAPITOL

Number	Title	Yr	NM
❏ 2124	I Need You/Out in the Streets	1968	$20

CREWE

Number	Title	Yr	NM
❏ 340	Handbags and Gladrags/ Guitar Army	1969	$20

DANBY'S

Number	Title	Yr	NM
❏ 0(no cat #)	Turn On/Irrational	1966	$60

—Made for Danby's clothiers

GENESIS

Number	Title	Yr	NM
❏ 1	Guitar Army/Sunset	1969	$20

RATS, THE

LAURIE

Number	Title	Yr	NM
❏ 3276	Spoonful/I've Got My Eyes on You Baby	1964	$15

RUST

Number	Title	Yr	NM
❏ TR-2	Spoonful/I've Got My Eyes on You Baby	1965	$20

RATTLES, THE

LONDON

Number	Title	Yr	NM
❏ 1037	Devil's on the Loose/I Know You Don't Know	1972	$5
❏ 1047	Devil's Sun/Why Do I Care	1973	$5

MERCURY

Number	Title	Yr	NM
❏ 72554	Sha La La La Lee/Dance	1966	$15
❏ 72403	Shame, Shame, Shame/ Someone Who Is Just Like You	1965	$15

PROBE

Number	Title	Yr	NM
❏ 480	The Witch/Geraldine	1970	$8

RAUSCH, LEON

Number	Title	Yr	NM
❏ 106	Ginny/My Friend, My Friend	1976	$6
❏ 119	I'm Satisfied with You/ (B-side unknown)	1978	$5
❏ 122	Let's Have a Heart to Heart Talk/Did We Have to Come This Far to Say Goodbye	1978	$5
❏ 128	Palimony/Love, Love, Love	1979	$5
❏ 107	She's the Trip That I've Been On/I'll Say Your Goodbyes	1976	$5
❏ 105	Through the Bottom of the Glass/Louisiana, My Home	1975	$6
❏ 583	Dim Lights, Thick Smoke/ You Bring Out the Worst in Me	1967	$8
❏ 580	Painted Angels/I'm So Glad Momo Can't See Me Now	1967	$8

SIMS

Number	Title	Yr	NM
❏ 232	Dance Toward the Door/Are You Really Worth It	1965	$15
❏ 213	Glass of Pride/Heart of a Clown	1964	$15

RAVEN, EDDY

ABC

Number	Title	Yr	NM
❏ 12037	Ain't She Somethin' Else/If Is a Bird on a Chain	1974	$5
❏ 11370	Arkansas Sun/Killer of the Class of '53	1973	$6
❏ 11449	Carolina Country Morning/ Killer of the Class of '53	1974	$5
❏ 12083	Good News, Bad News/Sam	1975	$5
❏ 11392	Sam/Southern Queen	1973	$6
❏ 11421	The Last of the Sunshine Cowboys/Sugah Kane	1974	$5

ABC DOT

Number	Title	Yr	NM
❏ 17595	Free to Be/Country Green	1975	$5
❏ 17663	I'm Losing It All/Touch This Morning	1976	$5
❏ 17618	I Wanna Live/I Don't Want to Talk It Over	1976	$5
❏ 17646	The Curse of a Woman/ Thank God for Kids	1976	$6

COSMOS

Number	Title	Yr	NM
❏ (# unknown)	Once a Fool/(B-side unknown)	1962	$40

DIMENSION

Number	Title	Yr	NM
❏ 1011	Another Texas Song/Day After Day	1980	$5
❏ 1005	Dealin' with the Devil/She Don't Cry	1980	$5
❏ 1017	Peace of Mind/Just Leave Me Alone	1980	$5
❏ 1001	Sweet Mother Texas/I Should've Called	1979	$5

ELEKTRA

Number	Title	Yr	NM
❏ 47413	A Little Bit Crazy/Loving Arms and Lying Eyes	1982	$4
❏ 47233 [DJ]	Blue Christmas/White Christmas	1981	$6

—B-side by Mel Tillis

❏ 47136	I Should've Called/Young Girl	1981	$4
❏ 69929	San Antonio Nights/Free to Be	1982	$4
❏ 47469	She's Playing Hard to Forget/Desperate Dreams	1982	$4
❏ 47216	Who Do You Know in California/Thinking It Over	1981	$4

MONUMENT

Number	Title	Yr	NM
❏ 45-245	Colinda (Dancer Petite)/ Touch and Go	1978	$5

RCA

Number	Title	Yr	NM
❏ PB-13839	I Could Use Another You/ Folks Out on the Road	1984	$3
❏ PB-13746	I Got Mexico/Love Burning Down	1984	$3
❏ 6831-7-R	I'm Gonna Get You/Other Than Montreal	1988	$3

Number	Title	Yr	NM
❑ PB-14164	I Wanna Hear It from You/Room to Run	1985	$3
❑ PB-14044	Operator, Operator/Just for the Sake of the Thrill	1985	$3
❑ JK-14044 [DJ]	Operator, Operator (same on both sides)	1985	$10

— Promo only on red vinyl

Number	Title	Yr	NM
❑ PB-13939	She's Gonna Win Your Heart/Looking for Ways	1984	$3
❑ 5221-7-R	Shine, Shine, Shine/Stay with Me	1987	$3
❑ PB-14319	Sometimes a Lady/Just for the Sake of a Thrill	1986	$3
❑ 8798-7-R	'Til You Cry/Just for the Sake of the Thrill	1988	$3

UNIVERSAL

Number	Title	Yr	NM
❑ UVL-66016	Bayou Boys/Angel Fire	1989	$3
❑ UVL-66003	In a Letter to You/Risky Business	1989	$3
❑ UVL-66029	Sooner or Later/Little Sheba	1989	$5

RAVEN, PAUL

DECCA

Number	Title	Yr	NM
❑ 32714	Goodbye Seattle/Wait for Me	1970	$20

RAVENS, THE

ARGO

Number	Title	Yr	NM
❑ 5261	A Simple Prayer/Water Boy	1956	$100
❑ 5284	Here Is My Heart/Lazy Mule	1957	$40
❑ 5276	That'll Be the Day/Dear One	1957	$40

CHECKER

Number	Title	Yr	NM
❑ 871	That'll Be the Day/Dear One	1957	$30

COLUMBIA

Number	Title	Yr	NM
❑ 6-903	Don't Look Now/Time Takes Care of Everything	1950	$700
❑ 1-903	Don't Look Now/Time Takes Care of Everything	1950	$1500

— Microgroove 33 1/3 single

Number	Title	Yr	NM
❑ 1-925	My Baby's Gone/I'm So Crazy for Love	1950	$1500

— Microgroove 33 1/3 single

Number	Title	Yr	NM
❑ 6-925	My Baby's Gone/I'm So Crazy for Love	1950	$600

JUBILEE

Number	Title	Yr	NM
❑ 45-5184	Bye Bye Baby Blues/Happy Go Lucky Baby	1955	$40
❑ 45-5203	Green Eyes/The Bells of San Rafael	1955	$40

— As "Jimmy Ricks and the Ravens

Number	Title	Yr	NM
❑ 45-5237	I'll Always Be in Love with You/(Take Me Back To My) Boots and Saddles	1956	$40

— As "Jimmy Ricks and the Ravens

Number	Title	Yr	NM
❑ 45-5217	On Chapel Hill/We'll Raise a Ruckus Tonight	1955	$40

MERCURY

Number	Title	Yr	NM
❑ 5800x45	Begin the Beguine/Looking for My Baby	1952	$250
❑ 70119x45	Come a Little Bit Closer/She's Got to Go	1953	$200
❑ 70330x45	Going Home/Lonesome Road	1954	$200
❑ 70060x45	I'll Be Back/Don't Mention My Name	1953	$200
❑ 70413x45	I've Got You Under My Skin/Love Is No Dream	1954	$250

— Pink label

Number	Title	Yr	NM
❑ 70413x45	I've Got You Under My Skin/Love Is No Dream	1954	$125

— Black label

Number	Title	Yr	NM
❑ 70554x45	Ol' Man River/Write Me a Letter	1955	$200

— Pink label

Number	Title	Yr	NM
❑ 70554x45	Ol' Man River/Write Me a Letter	1955	$125

— Black label

Number	Title	Yr	NM
❑ 70307x45	September Song/Escortin' Or Courtin'	1954	$200
❑ 5764x45	There's No Use Pretending/Wagon Wheels	1951	$300
❑ 8259x45	There's No Use Pretending/Wagon Wheels	1951	$400
❑ 70505x45	White Christmas/Silent Night	1954	$200

— Pink label

Number	Title	Yr	NM
❑ 70505x45	White Christmas/Silent Night	1954	$125

— Black label

Number	Title	Yr	NM
❑ 70213x45	Who'll Be the Fool/Rough Ridin'	1953	$200
❑ 5853x45	Why Did You Leave Me/Chloe	1952	$250
❑ 70240x45	Without a Song/Walkin' My Blues Away	1953	$200

NATIONAL

Number	Title	Yr	NM
❑ 9111-X45	Count Every Star/I'm Gonna Paper All My Walls with Your Love	1950	$3000

— The only known Ravens single on a National 45. VG 1500; VG+ 2250

OKEH

Number	Title	Yr	NM
❑ 6888	Mam'selle/Calypso Song	1952	$400

Number	Title	Yr	NM
❑ 6843	That Old Gang of Mine/Everything But You	1951	$500
❑ 6825	The Whiffenpoof Song/I Get All My Lovin' on a Saturday Night	1951	$500

SAVOY

Number	Title	Yr	NM
❑ 1540	White Christmas/Silent Night	1958	$30

TOP RANK

Number	Title	Yr	NM
❑ 2003	Into the Shadows/The Rising Sun	1959	$30
❑ 2016	Solitude/Hole in the Middle of the Moon	1959	$30

7-Inch Extended Plays

KING

Number	Title	Yr	NM
❑ 310	*Honey/Bye Bye Baby Blues/Out of a Dream/My Sugar Is So Refined	1954	$500

RAVERS, THE

ZOMBIE/ARIOLA

Number	Title	Yr	NM
❑ 7683	(It's Gonna Be a) Punk Rock Christmas/Silent Night	1977	$8
❑ 7683 [PS]	(It's Gonna Be a) Punk Rock Christmas/Silent Night	1977	$10

RAW SPITT

UNITED ARTISTS

Number	Title	Yr	NM
❑ 50813	That Ain't My Wife/Song to Sing	1971	$15

RAWLS, LOU

ARISTA

Number	Title	Yr	NM
❑ 0103	Baby You Don't Know How Good You Are/Hour Glass	1975	$6

BELL

Number	Title	Yr	NM
❑ 45608	She's Gone/Hour Glass	1974	$6
❑ 45616	Who Can Tell Us Why?/Now You're Coming Back Michelle	1974	$6

CANDIX

Number	Title	Yr	NM
❑ 305	In My Little Black Book/Just Thought You'd Like to Know	1960	$30
❑ 312	When We Get Old/Eighty Ways	1961	$30

CAPITOL

Number	Title	Yr	NM
❑ 2856	Bring It On Home/Can You Dig It-Take Me for What I Am	1970	$8
❑ 5869	Dead End Street/Yes It Hurts, Doesn't It	1967	$12
❑ 2252	Down Here on the Ground/I'm Satisfied (The Duffy Theme)	1968	$8
❑ 2084	Evil Woman/My Ancestors	1968	$8
❑ 2668	I Can't Make It Alone/Make the World Go Away	1969	$8
❑ 2408	It's You/Sweet Charity	1969	$8
❑ 2026	Little Drummer Boy/A Child with a Toy	1967	$8
❑ 5709	Love Is a Hurtin' Thing/Memory Lane	1966	$10
❑ 5227	Love Is Blind/I Fell in Love	1964	$15
❑ 4761	Save Your Love for Me/Trust Me	1962	$15
❑ 5941	Show Business/When Love Goes Wrong	1967	$10
❑ 2172	Soul Serenade/You're Good for Me	1968	$8
❑ 4803	Stormy Monday/Sweet Lover	1962	$15

— With Les McCann

Number	Title	Yr	NM
❑ 4622	That Lucky Old Sun/In My Heart	1961	$20
❑ 5160	The House Next Door/Come On In, Mr. Blues	1964	$15
❑ 5655	The Shadow of Your Smile/Southside Blues	1966	$10
❑ 2348	The Split/Why Can't I Speak	1968	$8
❑ 4695	The Wedding (The Bride)/The Biggest Lover in Town	1962	$15
❑ 5424	Three O'Clock in the Morning/Nothing Really Feels the Same	1965	$15
❑ 5049	Tobacco Road/Blues for Four-String Guitar	1963	$15
❑ 5824	Trouble Down Here Below/The Life That I Lead	1967	$10
❑ 5824 [PS]	Trouble Down Here Below/The Life That I Lead	1967	$10
❑ 4743	Trust Me/Please Let Me Be the First to Know	1962	$15
❑ 5505	What'll I Do/Can I Please	1965	$15
❑ 2942	Win Your Love for Me/Coppin' a Plea	1970	$8

EPIC

Number	Title	Yr	NM
❑ 04550	All-Time Lover/When We Were Young	1984	$4
❑ 05831	Are You With Me/(Instrumental)	1986	$4
❑ 05831 [PS]	Are You With Me/(Instrumental)	1986	$4
❑ 04773	Close Company/Forever I Do	1985	$4
❑ 04677	Close Company/The Lady in My Life	1984	$4

Number	Title	Yr	NM
❑ 03944	Couple More Years/Upside Down	1983	$4
❑ 05714	Learn to Love Again/Ready or Not	1985	$4
❑ 03357	Let Me Show You How/Watch Your Back	1982	$4
❑ 06145	Stop Me from Starting This Feeling/Never Entered My Mind	1986	$4
❑ 04079	The One I Sing My Love Songs To/You Can't Take It With You	1983	$4
❑ 03299	Together Again/Here Comes Garfield	1982	$4

— Lou Rawls and Desiree Goyette

Number	Title	Yr	NM
❑ 03758	Wind Beneath My Wings/Midnight Sun	1983	$4

GAMBLE & HUFF

Number	Title	Yr	NM
❑ 310	I Wish You Belonged to Me/It's a Tough Job	1987	$5
❑ 316	Two Happy Hearts/Jealous Lover	1988	$5

MGM

Number	Title	Yr	NM
❑ 14652	Dead End Street/Love Is a Hurtin' Thing	1973	$6
❑ 14349	His Song Shall Be Sung/I'm Waiting	1972	$6
❑ 14489	Man of Value/Learning Cup	1973	$6
❑ 14428	Politician/Walk On In	1972	$6
❑ 14574	Send for Me/Morning Comes Around	1973	$6
❑ 14527	Star Spangled Banner/Just a Closer Walk with Thee	1973	$6

PHILADELPHIA INT'L.

Number	Title	Yr	NM
❑ ZS93102	Ain't That Loving You (For More Reasons Than One)/(B-side unknown)	1980	$5
❑ ZS83604	Groovy People/This Song Will Last Forever	1976	$5
❑ 70051	Hoochie Coochie Man/You've Lost That Lovin' Feelin'	1981	$5
❑ ZS93114	I Go Crazy/Be Anything (But Be Mine)	1980	$5
❑ ZS83634	Lady Love/Not the Staying Kind	1977	$5
❑ ZS83684	Let Me Be Good to You/Lover's Holiday	1979	$5
❑ ZS83643	One Life to Live/If I Coulda, Woulda, Shoulda	1978	$5
❑ ZS83623	See You When I Git There/Spring Again	1977	$5
❑ ZS83672	Send In the Clowns/This Song Will Last Forever	1978	$5
❑ ZS93738	Sit Down and Talk to Me/When You Get Home	1979	$5
❑ ZS83653	There Will Be Love/Unforgettable	1978	$5
❑ ZS93715	What's the Matter with the World/Tomorrow	1979	$5
❑ SU-2632 [PS]	Carryin' On	1967	$20
❑ SU-2459 [PS]	Lou Rawls Live	1966	$20
❑ SU-2566	Love Is a Hurtin' Thing/Autumn Leaves/A Whole Lotta Woman//It Was a Very Good Year/Breaking My Back (Instead of Using My Mind)/So Hard to Laugh, So Easy to Cry	1966	$20

— Stereo jukebox issue; small hole, plays at 33 1/3 rpm

Number	Title	Yr	NM
❑ SU-2632	Mean Black Snake/Walking Proud/Find Out What's Happening//The Life I Lead/Trouble Down Here Below/A Woman Who's a Woman	1967	$20

— Stereo jukebox issue; small hole, plays at 33 1/3 rpm

Number	Title	Yr	NM
❑ SU-2566 [PS]	Soulin'	1966	$20
❑ SU-2459	The Shadow of Your Smile/Southside Blues/World of Trouble//Stormy Monday/I'd Rather Drink Muddy Water/Goin' to Chicago Blues	1966	$20

— Stereo jukebox issue; small hole, plays at 33 1/3 rpm

CAPITOL CREATIVE PRODUCTS

Number	Title	Yr	NM
❑ SU-479	Another Saturday Night/Chain Gang/Cool Train//Take Me for What I Am/Win Your Love/What Makes the Ending So Sad	1970	$15

— Stereo jukebox issue; small hole, plays at 33 1/3 rpm

Number	Title	Yr	NM
❑ SU-479 [PS]	Bring It on Home	1970	$15

RAY, ALDER

LIBERTY

Number	Title	Yr	NM
❑ 55715	'Cause I Love Him/A Little Love (Will Go a Long Way)	1964	$20

MINIT

Number	Title	Yr	NM
❑ 32005	I Need You Baby/My Heart Is in Danger	1966	$10

REVUE

Number	Title	Yr	NM
❑ 11014	Love Will Let You Down/Run, Baby, Run	1968	$8

RAY AND ELLEN

CAMEO

Number	Title	Yr	NM
❑ 383	All Right/Two Little People	1965	$20

RAY AND THE DARCHAES

ALJON

Number	Title	Yr	NM
❑ 1249	Carol/Little Girl So Fine	1962	$120

BUZZY

Number	Title	Yr	NM
❑ 202	Darling Forever/There Will Always Be	1962	$125

RAY, DANNY

VIN

Number	Title	Yr	NM
❑ 1025	Love Me/Gone	1960	$125

RAY, DIANE

MERCURY

Number	Title	Yr	NM
❑ 72276	Happy Happy Birthday Baby/That Boy's Gonna Be Mine	1964	$20
❑ 72195	My Summer Love/Where Is the Boy	1963	$20
❑ 72195 [PS]	My Summer Love/Where Is the Boy	1963	$70
❑ 72117	Please Don't Talk to the Lifeguard/That's All I Want from You	1963	$20
❑ 72117 [PS]	Please Don't Talk to the Lifeguard/That's All I Want from You	1963	$125
❑ 72223	Snow Man/Just So Bobby Can See	1963	$20
❑ 72223 [PS]	Snow Man/Just So Bobby Can See	1963	$70

RAY, JAMES

CAPRICE

Number	Title	Yr	NM
❑ 110	If You Gotta Make a Fool of Somebody/It's Been a Drag	1961	$40
❑ 114	Itty Bitty Pieces/You Remember the Face	1962	$30
❑ 117	Things Are Gonna Be Different/A Miracle	1962	$30

CONGRESS

Number	Title	Yr	NM
❑ 201	Do the Monkey/Put Me in Your Diary	1963	$30
❑ 109	Marie/The Old Man and the Mule	1963	$30
❑ 203	The Masquerade Is Over/One by One	1963	$30
❑ 218	We Got a Thing Goin' On/On That Day	1964	$30

DYNAMIC SOUND

Number	Title	Yr	NM
❑ 503	I've Got My Mind Set on You/Always	1963	$50

— The A-side was remade by George Harrison in 1987 as "Got My Mind Set on You"

7-Inch Extended Plays

CAPRICE

Number	Title	Yr	NM
❑ 1002	The Old Man & the Mule/Lazy Bones//Come Rain or Come Shine/St. James Infirmary	1962	$60

RAY-JAY BAND

RAY-JAY

Number	Title	Yr	NM
❑ 101	Touchdown Cleveland Browns/Dance Big C	1980	$20

RAY, JOHNNIE

CADENCE

Number	Title	Yr	NM
❑ 1387	In the Heart of a Fool/Let's Forget It Now	1960	$15

COLUMBIA

Number	Title	Yr	NM
❑ 40649	Ain't Misbehavin'/Walk Along with Kings	1956	$15
❑ 40391	Alexander's Ragtime Band/If You Believe	1954	$15
❑ 40046	All I Do Is Dream of You/Tell the Lady I Said Goodbye	1953	$15
❑ 39788	All of Me/A Sinner Am I	1952	$20
❑ 39703	All of Me/Give Me Time	1952	$15

— The above four comprise a box set

Number	Title	Yr	NM
❑ 40392	As Time Goes By/Nobody's Sweetheart	1954	$15
❑ 39908	A Touch of God's Hand/I'm Gonna Walk and Talk with the Lord	1952	$20
❑ 40695	Because I Love You/Goodbye, Au Revoir, Adios	1956	$15
❑ 40942	Build Your Love (On a Strong Foundation)/Street of Memories	1957	$10
❑ 41372	Call Me Yours/Here and Now	1959	$10
❑ 39700	Coffee and Cigarettes/Don't Blame Me	1952	$15
❑ 39659	Cry/Because of You	1952	$15

— B-side by Tony Bennett; early reissue

Number	Title	Yr	NM
❑ 41705	Don't Leave Me Now/Tell Me	1960	$12

Number	Title	Yr	NM
❑ 39702	Don't Take Your Love from Me/The Lady Drinks Champagne	1952	$15
❑ 41162	Endlessly/Lonely for a Letter	1958	$12
❑ 40471	Flip, Flop and Fly/Thine Eyes Are As the Eyes of a Dove	1955	$15
❑ 39814	Gee But I'm Lonesome/Don't Say Love Has Ended	1952	$20
❑ 40252	Going-Going-Gone/To Ev'ry Girl-To Ev'ry Boy	1954	$15
❑ 40224	Hernando's Hideaway/Hey There	1954	$15
❑ 41626	I'll Make You Mine/Before You	1959	$10
❑ 41438	I'll Never Fall in Love Again/You're All That I Live For	1959	$10
❑ 39837	Love Me (Baby Can't You Love Me)/Faith Can Move Mountains	1952	$20
❑ 41069	Miss Me Just a Little/Soliloquy of a Fool	1957	$10
❑ 39939	Mr. Midnight/Oh, What a Sad, Sad Day	1953	$15
❑ 41327	One Man's Love Song Is Another Man's Blues/When's Your Birthday, Baby	1959	$10
❑ 40324	Papa Loves Mambo/The Only Girl I'll Ever Love	1954	$15
❑ 40435	Parade of Broken Hearts/Paths of Paradise	1955	$15
❑ 41002	Pink Sweater Angel/Texas Tambourine	1957	$10
❑ 41124	Plant a Little Seed/Strollin' Girl	1958	$10
❑ 40090	Please Don't Talk About Me When I'm Gone/An Orchid for the Lady	1953	$15
❑ 39636	Please Mr. Sun/Here Am I – Broken Hearted	1952	$20
❑ 40006	Satisfied/With These Hands	1953	$15
❑ 39961	Somebody Stole My Gal/Glad Rag Doll	1953	$15
❑ 40528	Song of the Dreamer/I've Got So Many Million Miles	1955	$15
❑ 40200	Such a Night/Destiny	1954	$20
❑ 39897	The Thing I Might Have Been/The Commandments of Love	1952	$20
❑ 39701	Walking My Baby Back Home/Out in the Cold Again	1952	$15
❑ 39750	Walkin' My Baby Back Home/Give Me Time	1952	$20
❑ 41280	What More Can I Say/You're the One Who Knows	1958	$10
❑ 39729	What's the Use?/A Guy Is a Guy	1952	$10

— B-side by Doris Day

Number	Title	Yr	NM
❑ 39698	What's the Use?/Mountains in Moonlight	1952	$20
❑ 41528	When It's Springtime in the Rockies/An Ordinary Couple	1959	$10
❑ 40613	Who's Sorry Now/A Heart Comes In Handy	1955	$15
❑ 40154	Why Should I Be Sorry?/You'd Be Surprised	1954	$15

DECCA

Number	Title	Yr	NM
❑ 31459	After My Laughter Came Tears/Lookout Chattanooga	1963	$8
❑ 31601	Can't I/Break My Heartbreak	1964	$8
❑ 31507	Lonely Wine/I Can't Stop Crying for You	1963	$8

GROOVE

Number	Title	Yr	NM
❑ 58-0044	One Life/Sometime Love	1964	$8

LIBERTY

Number	Title	Yr	NM
❑ 55404	A Lover's Question/Nothing Goes Up Without Coming Down	1962	$8
❑ 55431	Cry/Scotch and Soda	1962	$8
❑ 55400	I Believe/A Mother's Love	1961	$10

— With Timi Yuro

OKEH

Number	Title	Yr	NM
❑ 6840	Cry/The Little White Cloud That Cried	1951	$40

— Label listed as "Okeh Rhythm and Blues" at top

Number	Title	Yr	NM
❑ 6840	Cry/The Little White Cloud That Cried	1951	$30

— Label listed as "Okeh" at top

Number	Title	Yr	NM
❑ 6809	Whiskey and Gin/Tell the Lady I Said Goodbye	1951	$30

UNITED ARTISTS

Number	Title	Yr	NM
❑ 341	How Many Nights, How Many Days/I'll Bring Along My Banjo	1961	$10
❑ B-9612	I'm Gonna Move to the Outskirts of Town/How Long, How Long Blues//I Miss You So/Trouble in Mind	1957	$25
❑ B-9611	Pretty-Eyed Baby/Lotus Blossom//Shake a Hand/I'll Never Be Free	1957	$25
❑ B-9611 [PS]	The Big Beat, Part 1	1957	$25
❑ B-9612 [PS]	The Big Beat, Part 2	1957	$25

EPIC

Number	Title	Yr	NM
❑ EG-7021	Cry/The Little White Cloud That Cried//Whiskey and Gin/Tell the Lady I Said Goodbye	1957	$30

RAY-O-VACS, THE

ATCO

Number	Title	Yr	NM
❑ 6085	Party Time/Crying All Alone	1957	$30

DECCA

Number	Title	Yr	NM
❑ 48162	Besame Mucho/You Gotta Love My Baby Too	1950	$30
❑ 48260	Charmaine/Hands Across the Table	1951	$30
❑ 48197	Goodnight My Love/Take Me Back to My Boots and Saddle	1951	$30
❑ 48221	My Baby's Gone/Let's	1951	$30
❑ 48234	What's Mine Is Mine/I Still Love You Baby	1951	$30
❑ 48274	When the Swallows Come Back to Capistrano/She's a Real Lovin' Baby	1952	$30

JOSIE

Number	Title	Yr	NM
❑ 763	Darling/Ridin' High	1954	$40
❑ 781	I Still Love You/Daddy	1955	$40

JUBILEE

Number	Title	Yr	NM
❑ 5124	Outside of Paradise/You Know	1953	$40
❑ 5098	What Can I Say/Start Lovin' Me	1952	$40

KAISER

Number	Title	Yr	NM
❑ 384	Crying All Alone/Party Time	1956	$40
❑ 389	Wine-O/Hong Kong	1956	$40

SHARP

Number	Title	Yr	NM
❑ 103	I'll Always Be in Love with You/Little Boy	1960	$30

RAY, WADE

CAPITOL

Number	Title	Yr	NM
❑ 54-40232	Cuddle Bug/I Want My Dime Back	1949	$60
❑ 54-40204	Flop-Eared Mule/Hell Amongst the Yearlin's	1949	$60
❑ 54-40205	Forty Years Ago/Hilo Schottische	1949	$60

DOT

Number	Title	Yr	NM
❑ 15600	Two Red Red Lips/Burning Desire	1957	$20

RCA VICTOR

Number	Title	Yr	NM
❑ 47-6219	Albino Stallion/I'll Keep On Being a Fool	1955	$30
❑ 47-5302	Burned Fingers/Don't Wait to Baby Your Baby	1953	$30
❑ 47-5199	Call Me Up/If They Should Ask	1953	$30
❑ 47-6110	Dipsey Doodle/A Sentimental Journey	1955	$30
❑ 47-6061	Excuse Me/I Couldn't Be So Happy	1955	$30
❑ 47-6457	Going Home All Alone/Any Old Time	1956	$30
❑ 47-4429	Heart of a Clown/Just Like Taking Candy from a Baby	1951	$40
❑ 47-5624	Idaho Red/A Penny for Your Thoughts	1954	$30
❑ 47-5091	It's All Your Fault/The Things I Might Have Been	1952	$30
❑ 47-4580	I Was Just Walkin' Out the Door/Fiddlin' Rag	1952	$30
❑ 47-5440	Let Me Go, Devil/Too Late Too	1953	$40
❑ 47-5518	Saturday Night/First, Last and Always	1953	$30
❑ 47-5377	That Love Makin' Melody/Did I Do Wrong	1953	$30
❑ 47-5696	The Best Man Must Smile/Easy Pickins	1954	$30
❑ 47-4930	The Echo of Your Voice/Bill Bailey Won't You Please Come Home	1952	$30
❑ 47-5957	There's No Fool Like a Young Fool/No Mama, No Papa	1954	$30
❑ 47-6818	When I Lost You/All or Nothin' Man	1957	$30
❑ 47-6931	Wild Heart/Little Green Valley	1957	$30

RAYBURN, MARGIE

CAPITOL

Number	Title	Yr	NM
❑ F3180	Alley Oop/I Laughed and Laughed	1955	$20
❑ F3338	Basin Street Blues/Can I Tell Them That You're Mine	1956	$20
❑ 5396	Maker of Raindrops and Roses/Are You Sure	1965	$10

CHALLENGE

Number	Title	Yr	NM
❑ 9110	Cast a Little Spell on Me/Here I Am	1961	$15
❑ 59100	Try Me/I've Tried So Hard Not to Love You	1960	$15

DOME

Number	Title	Yr	NM
❑ 506	Hi-De-Ho/I'm Only Human	1967	$20
❑ 501	Wish Me a Rainbow/So Nice (Summer Samba)	1966	$20

DOT

Number	Title	Yr	NM
❑ 16363	Bobby Is My Hobby/Somebody Else Is Taking My Place	1961	$10

Number	Title	Yr	NM
❏ 16327	Hello, Mr. Heartbreak/ Mud Pies	1961	$12
❏ 16840	Play #10 on the Juke Box/ Happy Jose	1966	$10

LIBERTY

Number	Title	Yr	NM
❏ 55072	Dreamy Eyes/Freight Train	1957	$20
❏ 55102	I'm Available/If You Were	1957	$20
❏ 55273	I Miss You Already/Maid of Honor	1960	$15
❏ 55134	I Would/Alright, But It Won't Be Easy	1958	$15
❏ 55195	Laddie-O/Unexpectedly	1959	$15
❏ 55088	Mississippi Moon/The Get Acquainted Waltz	1957	$20
❏ 55120	Ooh What a Doll/Smoochin'	1958	$15
❏ 55238	Sentimental Journey/Magic Words	1959	$15
❏ 55043	Take a Gamble on Love/ Every Minute of the Day	1956	$20
❏ 55183	Tell Him No/A Boy and a Girl	1959	$15
❏ 55159	To Each His Own/And He Told Me a Lie	1958	$15
❏ 55174	Wait/Make Me Queen Again	1959	$15
❏ 55059	Walking Around in a Dream/ Teenage Heart Throb	1957	$20

RAYE, SUSAN
CAPITOL

Number	Title	Yr	NM
❏ 3289	A Song to Sing/Adios, Farewell, Goodbye, Good Luck, So Long	1972	$5
❏ 3569	Cheating Game/I'll Love You Forever and Ever	1973	$5
❏ 4063	Ghost Story/Beginner's Luck	1975	$4
❏ 4140	He Gives Me Something (To Forgive Him For)/You're the Piece That's Always Gone	1975	$4
❏ 4197	Honey Toast and Sunshine/ Only a Good Love Lasts Forever	1975	$4
❏ 2620	I Ain't Gonna Be Treated That-a-Way/Maybe If I Close My Eyes (It'll Go Away)	1969	$6
❏ 3209	(I've Got a) Happy Heart/ How Long Will My Baby Be Gone	1971	$6
❏ 3035	L.A. International Airport/ Merry-Go-Round of Love	1971	$6
❏ 3499	Love Sure Feels Good in My Heart/I've Got You on My Mind Again	1972	$5
❏ 3327	My Heart Has a Mind of Its Own/You'll Never Miss the Water	1972	$5
❏ 2833	One Night Stand/She Don't Deserve You Anymore	1970	$6
❏ 3129	Pitty, Pitty, Patter/I'll Be Gone	1971	$6
❏ 3699	Plastic Trains, Paper Planes/I Won't Be Needing You	1973	$5
❏ 2701	Put a Little Love in Your Heart/I've Carried This Torch Much Too Long	1969	$6
❏ 3850	Stop the World (And Let Me Off)/Love's Ups and Downs	1974	$4
❏ 3980	Whatcha Gonna Do with a Dog Like That/That Loving Feeling	1974	$4
❏ 3438	Wheel of Fortune/My Heart Skips a Beat	1972	$5
❏ 3782	When You Get Back from Nashville/Nobody's Fool But Yours	1973	$5
❏ 2950	Willy Jones/I'll Love You Forever (If You're Sure You'll Want Me Then)	1970	$6

UNITED ARTISTS

Number	Title	Yr	NM
❏ XW1026	It Didn't Have to Be a Diamond/My Hiding Place	1977	$4
❏ XW934	Mr. Heartache/Turn Away	1977	$4
❏ XW870	Ozark Mountain Lullaby/ Johnny Sunshine	1976	$4
❏ XW976	Saturday Night to Sunday Quiet/My Hiding Place	1977	$4

WESTEXAS AMERICA

Number	Title	Yr	NM
❏ 1	Put Another Notch in Your Belt/I Just Can't Take the Leaving Anymore	1984	$4

RAYS, THE
AMY

Number	Title	Yr	NM
❏ 900	Love Another Girl/Sad Saturday	1964	$8

CAMEO

Number	Title	Yr	NM
❏ 117	Silhouettes/Daddy Cool	1957	$30

CHESS

Number	Title	Yr	NM
❏ 1678	How Long Must I Wait/ Second Fiddle	1957	$30
❏ 1613	Tippity Top/Moo-Goo-Gai-Pan	1956	$30

UNART

Number	Title	Yr	NM
❏ 2001	Souvenirs of Summertime/ Elevator Operator	1958	$50

XYZ

Number	Title	Yr	NM
❏ 605	It's a Cryin' Shame/ Mediterranean Moon	1959	$50

Number	Title	Yr	NM
❏ 607	Magic Moon/Louie Hoo Hoo	1960	$50
—Blue label			
❏ 607	Magic Moon/Louie Hoo Hoo	1960	$30
—Red label			
❏ 100	My Steady Girl/No One Loves You Like I Do	1957	$70
❏ 608	Old Devil Moon/Silver Starlight	1960	$30
❏ 102	Silhouettes/Daddy Cool	1957	$200
—Gray label			
❏ 102	Silhouettes/Daddy Cool	1957	$70
—Blue label			
❏ 106	Souvenirs of Summertime/ Elevator Operator	1958	$60
❏ 600	Why Do You Love the Other Way/Zimbo Lula	1959	$60

7-Inch Extended Plays
CHESS

Number	Title	Yr	NM
❏ 5120	(contents unknown)	1958	$400

RAYS, THE (2)
PERRI

Number	Title	Yr	NM
❏ 1004	Are You Happy Now/Bright Brown Eyes	1962	$40
—Frankie Valli performed on this record			

RE-VELS, THE
ATLAS

Number	Title	Yr	NM
❏ 1035	My Lost Love/Love Me, Baby	1954	$400
—As "The Re-Vels Quartette"			

CHESS

Number	Title	Yr	NM
❏ 1708	False Alarm/When You Come Back to Me	1958	$200

SOUND

Number	Title	Yr	NM
❏ 135	Dream, My Darlin', Dream/ Cha Cha Toni	1956	$200

TEEN

Number	Title	Yr	NM
❏ 122	So in Love/It Happened to Me	1955	$600

REACTORS, THE
CAMEO

Number	Title	Yr	NM
❏ 446	Do That Thing/1-A	1966	$30

READY FOR THE WORLD
MCA

Number	Title	Yr	NM
❏ 52735	Ceramic Girl/(Instrumental)	1986	$10
❏ 53635	Cowboy/(Instrumental)	1989	$4
❏ 52561	Deep Inside Your Love/I'm the One Who Loves You	1985	$4
❏ 52561 [PS]	Deep Inside Your Love/I'm the One Who Loves You	1985	$4
❏ 52734	Digital Display/I'm the One Who Loves You	1985	$4
❏ 52734 [PS]	Digital Display/I'm the One Who Loves You	1985	$4
❏ 53469	Gently/(Instrumental)	1988	$4
❏ 53174	Here I Am/(Percusapella)	1987	$4
❏ 53174 [PS]	Here I Am/(Percusapella)	1987	$4
❏ 53099	Long Time Coming/ (Instrumental)	1987	$4
❏ 53099 [PS]	Long Time Coming/ (Instrumental)	1987	$4
❏ 52947	Love You Down/Human Toy	1986	$4
❏ 52947 [PS]	Love You Down/Human Toy	1986	$4
❏ 53004	Mary Goes 'Round/It's All a Game	1987	$4
❏ 53004 [PS]	Mary Goes 'Round/It's All a Game	1987	$4
❏ 53337	My Girly/(Instrumental)	1988	$4
❏ 53337 [PS]	My Girly/(Instrumental)	1988	$4
❏ 52636	Oh Sheila/I'm the One Who Loves You	1985	$4
❏ 52636 [PS]	Oh Sheila/I'm the One Who Loves You	1985	$4
❏ 52713	Slide Over/I'm the One Who Loves You	1986	$4
❏ 52713 [PS]	Slide Over/I'm the One Who Loves You	1986	$4
❏ 52507	Tonight (same on both sides)	1984	$5

REAL ORIGINAL BEATLES, THE
DOT

Number	Title	Yr	NM
❏ 16655	The Beatle Story (Part 1)/ The Beatle Story (Part 2)	1964	$30

REALLY RED
C.I.A.

Number	Title	Yr	NM
❏ 01	Crowd Control/Corporate Settings	1979	$12
❏ 01 [PS]	Crowd Control/Corporate Settings	1979	$12
❏ 02	Modern Needs/White Lies	1980	$10
❏ 02 [PS]	Modern Needs/White Lies	1980	$10

7-Inch Extended Plays

Number	Title	Yr	NM
❏ 03	Despise Moral Majority	1981	$10
—Recorded live in Texas in 1980			
❏ 03 [PS]	Despise Moral Majority	1981	$12

REBB, JOHNNY, AND HIS REBELS
BULLSEYE

Number	Title	Yr	NM
❏ 1027	Pathway to Paradise/ Rock On	1959	$600

REBELS, THE (2)
KING'S X

Number	Title	Yr	NM
❏ 3362	In the Park/In My Heart	1959	$1000

REBELS, THE (3)
PEACOCK

Number	Title	Yr	NM
❏ 1909	The Donkey Step/Just Give Me Your Heart	1962	$30

REBOUNDS, THE
TOWER

Number	Title	Yr	NM
❏ 288	Since I Fell for You/I'm Not Your Steppin' Stone	1966	$20

RED HOT CHILI PEPPERS
WTG

Number	Title	Yr	NM
❏ 68678	Taste the Rain/All for Love	1989	$4
—B-side by Nancy Wilson (of Heart)			

RED, WHITE AND BLUE (GRASS)
GRC

Number	Title	Yr	NM
❏ 2015	Linda Ann/(B-side unknown)	1974	$8

REDBONE
EPIC

Number	Title	Yr	NM
❏ 10910	Already Here/Fais-Do	1972	$5
❏ 11035	Come and Get Your Love/ Day to Day Life	1973	$5
❏ 11035	Come and Get Your Love/ Your Miserable Face	1973	$5
❏ 10597	Crazy Cajun Cade Walk Band/Night Come Down	1970	$6
❏ 10670	Maggie/New Blue Sermonette	1970	$6
❏ 10866	One Monkey (Don't Stop No Show)/Message from a Drum	1972	$5
❏ 50043	One More Time/Blood, Sweat and Tears	1974	$4
❏ 50074	Only You and Rock and Roll/ Interstate Highway 101	1975	$4
❏ 50107	Physical Attraction/I've Got to Find the Right Woman	1975	$4
❏ 10946	Poison Ivy/Condition Your Condition	1973	$5
❏ 50015	Suzie Girl/Interstate Highway 101	1974	$4
❏ 10749	The Witch Queen of New Orleans/Chant: 13th Hour	1971	$6
❏ 10979	We Were All Wounded at Wounded Knee/Speakeasy	1973	$5
❏ 10839	When You Got Trouble/ (B-side unknown)	1972	$5
❏ 10712	Who Can Say/Light as a Feather	1971	$6
❏ 11131	Wovoka/Clouds in My Sunshine	1974	$4

RCA

Number	Title	Yr	NM
❏ PB-11182	Checkin' It Out/Funky Silk	1977	$4
❏ PB-11096	Give Our Love Another Try/ Funny Silk	1977	$4

REDCOATS, THE
KITE

Number	Title	Yr	NM
❏ 2003	Perkin/Hi Ho	1957	$60
❏ 2003	Perkins/Hi Ho	1957	$60
—Note slight variation in A-side title			

REDD, BARBARA
S.P.Q.R.

Number	Title	Yr	NM
❏ 3311	I'll Be All Alone/Dancing Teardrops	1963	$600

REDD, GENE
FEDERAL

Number	Title	Yr	NM
❏ 12119	I Dreamed the Blues/In the Redd	1953	$40

KING

Number	Title	Yr	NM
❏ 5262	Teen Beat/Old Virginny Rock	1959	$15

REDDING, OTIS
ATCO

Number	Title	Yr	NM
❏ 6654	A Lover's Question/You Made a Man Out of Me	1969	$10
❏ 6742	Demonstration/Johnny's Heartbreak	1970	$8
❏ 6700	Free Me/Higher and Higher	1969	$10
❏ 6766	Giving Away None of My Love/Snatch a Little Piece	1970	$8
❏ 6592	Hard to Handle/Amen	1968	$12

Number	Title	Yr	NM
❏ 6612	I've Got Dreams to Remember/Nobody's Fault But Mine	1968	$10
❏ 6723	Look at the Girl/That's a Good Idea	1969	$10
❏ 6677	Love Man/I Can't Turn You Loose	1969	$10
❏ 6907	My Girl/Good to Me	1972	$5
❏ 6636	Papa's Got a Brand New Bag/Direct Me	1968	$10
❏ 6802	Try a Little Tenderness/I've Been Loving You Too Long (To Stop Now)	1971	$6
❏ 6631	White Christmas/Merry Christmas, Baby	1968	$10
❏ 7069	White Christmas/Merry Christmas, Baby	1976	$5
❏ 7321	White Christmas/Merry Christmas, Baby	1980	$4
❏ 99955	White Christmas/Merry Christmas, Baby	1982	$4

BETHLEHEM
❏ 3083	Shout Bamalama/Fat Girl	1964	$30

CONFEDERATE
❏ 135	Shout Bamalama/Fat Girl	1962	$60

FINER ARTS
❏ 2016	She's Alright/Tough Enuff	1961	$60

— *Originally released on Trans World by "The Shooters*

KING
❏ 6149	Shout Bamalama/Fat Girl	1968	$10

ORBIT
❏ 135	Shout Bamalama/Fat Girl	1961	$300

PHILCO-FORD
❏ HP-13	Shake/Fa-Fa-Fa-Fa-Fa	1967	$30

— *4-inch plastic "Hip Pocket Record" with color sleeve*

VOLT
❏ 121	Chained and Bound/Your One and Only Man	1964	$20
❏ 116	Come to Me/Don't Leave Me This Way	1964	$20
❏ 138	Fa-Fa-Fa-Fa-Fa (Sad Song)/Good to Me	1966	$20
❏ 152	Glory of Love/I'm Coming Home	1967	$15
❏ 130	I Can't Turn You Loose/Just One More Day	1965	$20
❏ 146	I Love You More Than Words Can Say/Let Me Come On Home	1967	$15
❏ 126	I've Been Loving You Too Long (To Stop Now)/I'm Depending on You	1965	$20
❏ 124	Mr. Pitiful/That's How Strong My Love Is	1965	$20
❏ 136	My Lover's Prayer/Don't Mess with Cupid	1966	$20
❏ 112	Pain in My Heart/Something Is Worrying Me	1963	$30
❏ 132	Satisfaction/Any Ole Way	1966	$20
❏ 117	Security/I Want to Thank You	1964	$20
❏ 149	Shake/You Don't Miss Your Water	1967	$15
❏ 157	(Sittin' On) The Dock of the Bay/Sweet Lorene	1968	$15

— *Black and red label*
❏ 157	(Sittin' On) The Dock of the Bay/Sweet Lorene	1968	$12

— *Multicolor (mostly brown) label*
❏ 109	That's What My Heart Needs/Mary's Little Lamb	1963	$30
❏ 163	The Happy Song (Dum-Dum)/Open That Door	1968	$10
❏ 103	These Arms of Mine/Hey, Hey Baby	1962	$30
❏ 141	Try a Little Tenderness/I'm Sick Y'All	1966	$20

7-Inch Extended Plays

ATCO
❏ SD 37-265	I Can't Turn You Loose/Pain in My Heart/Mr. Pitiful/Any Ole Way/Respect	1968	$30

— *Stereo jukebox issue; small hole, plays at 33 1/3 rpm*
❏ SD 37-265 [PS]	Otis Redding In Person at the Whiskey A-Go-Go	1968	$30

ATLANTIC
❏ SD70419	(Sittin' on) The Dock of the Bay/Let Me Come On Home/Open the Door//The Glory of Love/Tramp/Ole Man Trouble	1968	$30

— *Stereo jukebox issue; small hole, plays at 33 1/3 rpm*
❏ SD70419 [PS]	The Dock of the Bay	1968	$30

— *Cover says "Volt" but the label of the record is Atlantic*

REDDY, HELEN
CAPITOL
Number	Title	Yr	NM
❏ 4128	Ain't No Way to Treat a Lady/Long Time Looking	1975	$4
❏ 3972	Angie Baby/I Think I'll Write a Song	1974	$4
❏ 4108	Bluebird/You Don't Need a Reason	1975	$4
❏ 4521	Candle on the Water/Brazzle Dazzle Day	1977	$4
❏ 4521 [PS]	Candle on the Water/Brazzle Dazzle Day	1977	$6
❏ 3138	Crazy Love/Best Friend	1971	$5
❏ 3645	Delta Dawn/If We Could Still Be Friends	1973	$4
❏ 4021	Emotion/I've Been Waiting for You So Long	1974	$4
❏ 3350	I Am Woman/More Than You Could Take	1972	$5

— *Red and orange "target" label*
❏ 3350	I Am Woman/More Than You Could Take	1972	$4

— *Orange label, "Capitol" at bottom*
❏ 4312	I Can't Hear You No More/Music Is My Life	1976	$4
❏ 3027	I Don't Know How to Love Him/I Believe in Music	1971	$5
❏ 4628	Lady of the Night/Poor Little Fool	1978	$4
❏ 3768	Leave Me Alone (Ruby Red Dress)/The Old Fashioned Way	1973	$4
❏ 4867	Love's Not the Question/Take What You Find	1980	$4
❏ 4712	Make Love to Me/More Than You Could Take	1979	$4
❏ 4654	Mama/West Wind Circus	1978	$4
❏ 3527	Peaceful/What Would They Say	1973	$4
❏ 4192	Somewhere in the Night/Ten to Eight	1975	$4
❏ 4487	The Happy Girls/Laissez Les Bontemps Rouler	1977	$4
❏ 4786	Trying to Get to You/Let Me Be Your Woman	1979	$4
❏ 4918	Way with the Ladies/Killer Barracuda	1980	$4
❏ 4555	We'll Sing in the Sunshine/I'd Rather Be Alone	1978	$4

FONTANA
❏ 1611	One Way Ticket/Go	1968	$20

MCA
❏ 52170	Don't Tell Me Tonight/Yesterday Can't Hurt Me	1983	$4
❏ 51106	I Can't Say Goodbye to You/Let's Just Stay Home Tonight	1981	$4
❏ 52221	Imagination/The Way I Feel	1983	$4
❏ 51143	Stars Fell on California/When I Dream	1981	$4
❏ 51186	Theme from "Continental Divide"/When I Dream	1981	$4

REDELL, TEDDY
HI
❏ 2024	Pipeliner/I Want to Hold You	1960	$30

VADEN
❏ 115	Goldust/Corrine, Corrina	1960	$120
❏ 305	I'll Sail My Ship Alone/Don't Grow Old Alone	1961	$100
❏ 117	Pipeliner/I Want to Hold You	1960	$120
❏ 301	Pipeliner/I Want to Hold You	1961	$100

REDJACKS, THE
APT
❏ 25006	Big Brown Eyes/To Make You Mine	1958	$30

OKLAHOMA
❏ 5005	Big Brown Eyes/To Make You Mine	1958	$60

REDWOODS, THE
EPIC
❏ 9505	Please, Mr. Scientist/Where You Need to Be	1962	$50
❏ 9447	Shake, Shake Sherry/The Memory Lingers On	1961	$50

— *As "The Flairs*
❏ 9447	Shake, Shake Sherry/The Memory Lingers On	1961	$40

— *As "The Redwoods*

REED, A.C.
AGE
❏ 29103	Come On Home/I Wanna Be Free	1961	$40
❏ 29123	I Stay Mad/Whole Lotta Lovin'	1964	$40
❏ 29112	Mean Cop/That Ain't Right	1962	$40
❏ 29101	This Little Voice/Apache War Dance	1961	$40

— *B-side by Earl Hooker*

COOL
Number	Title	Yr	NM
❏ 5001	My Baby's Been Cheating (I Know)/My Baby Is Fine	1966	$200

ICE CUBE
❏ 5928	Fast Food Annie/This Little Voice	1982	$8
❏ 5927	I Am Fed Up with This Music (DJ Version)/Got the Blues	1982	$10
❏ 5926	I Am Fed Up with This Music (X-Rated)/Got the Blues	1982	$6

NIKE
❏ 2002	Boogaloo - Tramp/Talkin' 'Bout My Friends	1966	$50

U.S.A.
❏ 813	I'd Rather Fight Than Switch/I've Got Money to Burn	1963	$30

REED, DEAN
CAPITOL
❏ F4198	A Pair of Scissors/I Kissed a Queen	1959	$20
❏ 4384	Don't Let Her Go/No Wonder	1960	$20
❏ F4273	Our Summer Romance/I Ain't Got You	1959	$20
❏ 4438	Pistolero/Hummingbird	1960	$20
❏ F4121	The Search/Annabelle	1959	$20

IMPERIAL
❏ 5733	I Forgot More Than You'll Ever Know/Once Again	1961	$15

REED, JAMES
BIG TOWN
❏ 117	Things Ain't What They Used to Be/You Better Hold Me	1954	$200

FLAIR
❏ 1042	Dr. Brown/You Better Hold Me	1954	$200
❏ 1034	My Mama Told Me/This Is the End	1954	$200

MONEY
❏ 201	Oh People/My Love Is Real	1954	$200

RHYTHM
❏ 1775	Tin Pan Alley/Biggest Place in Town	1954	$500

REED, JERRY
CAPITOL
❏ B-5531	Big Time Fool/What Comes Around	1985	$3
❏ B-5556	Country's Alive and Doing Well/Let It Go	1986	$3
❏ F3992	How Can I Go On This Way/Your Money Makes You Purty	1958	$20
❏ F3294	If the Good Lord's Willing and the Creeks Don't Rise/Here I Am	1955	$30
❏ F3381	I'm a Lover, Not a Fighter/Honey Chile	1956	$30
❏ F3823	In My Own Back Yard/Ba-Bee	1957	$20
❏ F3657	It's High Time/Forever	1957	$20
❏ B-5612	This Missin' You's a Whole Lotta Fun/There Was You	1986	$3
❏ F3592	Too Busy Cryin' the Blues/You're Braggin', Boy	1956	$30
❏ F3882	Too Young to Be Blue/Bessie Baby	1958	$20
❏ F3429	When I Found You/Mister Whiz	1956	$30

COLUMBIA
❏ 42183	Hit and Run/Sure Is Blue Out Tonight	1961	$12
❏ 42417	I'm Movin' On/Goodnight Irene	1962	$10
❏ 42704	I Want to Be Loved/I'll See You in My Dreams	1963	$10
❏ 42047	Love and War (Ain't Much Difference in the Two)/Love Is the Cause of It All	1961	$10
❏ 42311	Pity the Fool/I've Got Everybody Fooled But Me	1962	$10
❏ 42863	The Mountain Man/Love Don't Grow on Trees	1963	$10
❏ 42808	The Shock/Let's Get Ready for the Summer	1963	$10
❏ 42639	Too Old to Cut the Mustard/Overlooked and Underloved	1962	$10
❏ 42533	Twist-a-Roo/Hully Gully Guitar	1962	$10
❏ 42533 [PS]	Twist-a-Roo/Hully Gully Guitar	1962	$40

NRC
❏ 014	Have Blues Will Travel/This Can't Be Happening to Me	1958	$20
❏ 5008	Little Lovin' Liza/Soldier's Joy	1959	$15

RCA
❏ PB-11944	Age/Workin' at the Car Wash Blues	1980	$4

Number	Title	Yr	NM
❏ PB-12157	Caffein, Nicotine, Benzedrine (And Wish Me Luck)/If Love's Not Around the House	1981	$4
❏ JK-13666 [DJ]	Christmas Time's a-Coming (same on both sides)	1983	$5
❏ PB-13666	Christmas Time's a-Coming/ The Best I Ever Had	1983	$5
❏ PB-13422	Down on the Corner/Good Times	1983	$4
❏ JK-13422 [DJ]	Down on the Corner (same on both sides)	1983	$12

— Promo only on green vinyl

Number	Title	Yr	NM
❏ PB-11056	East Bound and Down/(I'm Just A) Redneck in a Rock and Roll Bar	1977	$4
❏ GB-11986	East Bound and Down/(I'm Just A) Redneck in a Rock and Roll Bar	1980	$3

— Gold Standard Series

Number	Title	Yr	NM
❏ PB-11407	Gimme Back My Blues/ Honkin'	1978	$4
❏ PB-12253	Good Friends Make Good Lovers/The Devil Went Down to Georgia	1981	$4
❏ JK-13527 [DJ]	Good Ole Boys (same on both sides)	1983	$10

— Promo only on green vinyl

Number	Title	Yr	NM
❏ JB-13527 [DJ]	Good Ole Boys/She's Ready for Someone to Love Her	1983	$15

— Promo only on blue vinyl

Number	Title	Yr	NM
❏ PB-13527	Good Ole Boys/She's Ready for Someone to Love Her	1983	$4
❏ PB-11698	Hot Stuff/Nervous Breakdown	1979	$4
❏ PB-11281	(I Love You) What Can I Say/High Rollin'	1978	$4
❏ PB-11281	(I Love You) What Can I Say/I Feel for You	1978	$4
❏ PB-13663	I'm a Slave/Nobody Ever Loved Me	1983	$4
❏ JK-12318 [DJ]	Patches (same on both sides)	1981	$10

— Promo only on blue vinyl

Number	Title	Yr	NM
❏ PB-12318	Patches/Stray Dogs and Stray Women	1981	$4
❏ PB-11472	Second-Hand Satin Lady (And a Bargain Basement Boy)/Jiffy Jam	1979	$4
❏ PB-10893	Semolita/Phantom of the Opry	1977	$4
❏ PB-13268	She Got the Goldmine (I Got the Shaft)/44	1982	$5
❏ GB-14069	She Got the Goldmine (I Got the Shaft)/The Bird	1985	$3

— Gold Standard Series

Number	Title	Yr	NM
❏ PB-11370	Stars and Stripes Forever/ Reedology	1978	$4
❏ PB-11764	Sugar Foot Rag/I Wanna Go Back Home to Georgia	1979	$4
❏ PB-11232	Sweet Love Feelings/You're Gonna Need Someone	1978	$4
❏ PB-12083	Texas Bound and Flyin'/ Concrete Sailor	1980	$4
❏ PB-13355	The Bird/The Hobo	1982	$5

— As "Jerry Reed and Friends

Number	Title	Yr	NM
❏ PB-12034	The Friendly Family Inn/ Bandit	1980	$4
❏ PB-13081	The Man with the Golden Thumb/East Bound and Down	1982	$4
❏ PB-12210	The Testimony of Soddy Hoe/Dreaming Fairy Tales	1981	$4
❏ PB-11638	(Who Was the Man Who Put) The Line in Gasoline/ Piece of Cake	1979	$4
❏ PB-11008	With His Pants in His Hand/ We Called It Everything Else	1977	$4

RCA VICTOR

Number	Title	Yr	NM
❏ APBO-0273	A Good Woman's Love/ Everybody Needs Someone	1974	$5
❏ 47-8667	Ain't That Just Like a Fool/ Love's Battleground	1965	$8
❏ 74-0738	Alabama Wildman/Take It Easy	1972	$5
❏ 74-0738 [PS]	Alabama Wildman/Take It Easy	1972	$10
❏ 47-9623	Alabama Wild Man/Twelve Bar Midnight	1968	$8
❏ 47-9904	Amos Moses/The Preacher and the Bear	1970	$6
❏ 74-0613	Another Puff/Love Man	1971	$5
❏ 74-0211	Are You From Dixie/A Worried Man	1969	$6
❏ 74-0124	Blues Land/There's Better Things in Life	1969	$6
❏ PB-10063	Boogie Woogie Rock and Roll/In Between	1974	$5
❏ 47-8730	Fighting for the U.S.A./Navy Blues	1965	$8
❏ PB-10717	Gator/Good for Him	1976	$5
❏ 47-9870	Georgia Sunshine/Swinging '69	1970	$6
❏ 47-9152	Guitar Man/It Don't Work That Way	1967	$10
❏ 47-8565	If I Don't Live Up to It/I Feel a Sin Coming On	1965	$8
❏ PB-10132	Let's Sing Our Song/Grab Bag	1974	$5
❏ 74-0960	Lord, Mr. Ford/2-Timin'	1973	$5

Number	Title	Yr	NM
❏ GB-10510	Lord, Mr. Ford/Two-Timin'	1975	$3

— Gold Standard Series

Number	Title	Yr	NM
❏ PB-10247	Mind Your Love/Struttin'	1975	$5
❏ 47-9701	Oh, What a Woman/Losing Your Love	1968	$8
❏ 74-0667	Smell the Flowers/If It Comes to That	1972	$5
❏ 47-9804	Talk About the Good Times/ Alabama Jubilee	1969	$6
❏ 47-9890	Tennessee Stud/Cannonball Rag	1970	$6

— With Chet Atkins

Number	Title	Yr	NM
❏ APBO-0224	The Crude Oil Blues/Pickie, Pickie, Pickie	1974	$5
❏ PB-10325	The Telephone/City of New Orleans	1975	$5
❏ 47-9334	Tupelo Mississippi Flash/ Wabash Cannonball	1967	$8
❏ 47-9976	When You're Hot, You're Hot/You've Been Crying Again	1971	$6
❏ 47-8957	Woman Shy/I Feel for You	1966	$8

REED, JIMMY

ABC

Number	Title	Yr	NM
❏ 10887	Got Nowhere to Go/Two Ways to Skin (A Cat)	1966	$8

BLUESWAY

Number	Title	Yr	NM
❏ 61013	Buy Me a Hound Dog/Crazy About Oklahoma	1968	$8
❏ 61025	Don't Light My Fire/The Judge Should Know	1969	$8
❏ 61006	Don't Press Your Luck Woman/Feel Like I Want to Ramble	1967	$8
❏ 61003	I Wanna Know/Two Heads Are Better Than One	1967	$8
❏ 61020	Peepin' and Hidin'/My Baby Told Me	1968	$8

CHANCE

Number	Title	Yr	NM
❏ 1142	High and Lonesome/Roll and Rhumba	1953	$2100

— VG 700; VG+ 1400

EXODUS

Number	Title	Yr	NM
❏ 2008	Cousin Peaches/Crazy 'Bout Oklahoma	1966	$12

VEE JAY

Number	Title	Yr	NM
❏ 168	Ain't That Lovin' You Baby/ Baby, Don't Say That No More	1956	$50
❏ 425	Aw, Shucks, Hush Your Mouth/Baby, What's Wrong	1962	$30
❏ 333	Baby What You Want Me to Do/Caress Me, Baby	1959	$40
❏ 380	Big Boss Man/I'm a Love You	1961	$30
❏ 398	Bright Lights, Big City/I'm Mr. Luck	1961	$30
❏ 186	Can't Stand to See You Go/ Rockin' with Reed	1956	$50
❏ 709	Don't Think I'm Through/ When Girls Do It	1966	$20
❏ 347	Found Love/Where Can You Be	1960	$30
❏ 593	Help Yourself/Heading for a Fall	1964	$20
❏ 100	High and Lonesome/Roll and Rumba	1953	$1200

— Red vinyl

Number	Title	Yr	NM
❏ 100	High and Lonesome/Roll and Rumba	1953	$600
❏ 253	Honest I Do/Signals of Love	1957	$40
❏ 237	Honey, Where You Going/ Little Rain	1957	$40
❏ 357	Hush Hush/Going to the River, Part 2	1960	$30
❏ 153	I Don't Go for That/She Don't Want Me No More	1955	$60
❏ 105	I Found My Baby/Jimmy's Boogie	1953	$400

— Red vinyl

Number	Title	Yr	NM
❏ 105	I Found My Baby/Jimmy's Boogie	1953	$200
❏ 287	I Know It's a Sin/Down in Virginia	1958	$40
❏ 459	I'll Change My Style/Too Much	1962	$30
❏ 203	I Love You Baby/My First Plea	1956	$40
❏ 622	I'm Going Upside Your Head/The Devil's Shoestring	1964	$20
❏ 298	I'm Gonna Get My Baby/ Odds and Ends	1958	$40
❏ 702	I'm the Man Down There/ Left Handed Woman	1965	$20
❏ 304	I Told You Baby/Ends and Odds (Instrumental)	1958	$40
❏ 642	I Wanna Be Loved/A New Leaf	1965	$20
❏ 326	I Wanna Be Loved/Going to New York	1959	$40
❏ 373	Laughing at the Blues/Close Together	1961	$30
❏ 473	Let's Get Together/Oh, John	1962	$30
❏ 552	Mary Mary/I'm Gonna Help You	1963	$20
❏ 616	Oh John/Down in Mississippi	1964	$20
❏ 570	Outskirts of Town/St. Louis Blues	1963	$20

Number	Title	Yr	NM
❏ 132	Pretty Thing/I'm Gonna Ruin You	1955	$125
❏ 584	See See Rider/Wee Wee Baby Blues	1964	$20
❏ 314	Take Out Some Insurance/ You Know I Love You	1959	$40
❏ 449	Tell Me You Love Me/Good Lover	1962	$30
❏ 509	There'll Be a Day/Shame, Shame, Shame	1963	$20
❏ 248	The Sun Is Shining/Baby, What's On Your Mind	1957	$40

REED, LOU
Also see THE PRIMITIVES; THE VELVET UNDERGROUND.

A&M

Number	Title	Yr	NM
❏ 2781	September Song/Oh Heavenly Salvation	1985	$4

— B-side by Mark Bingham/Johnny Adams/Aaron Neville

Number	Title	Yr	NM
❏ 2883	Soul Man/Sweet Sarah	1986	$3

— With Sam Moore

ARISTA

Number	Title	Yr	NM
❏ 0431	City Lights/I Want to Boogie with You	1979	$4
❏ 0535	Growing Up in Public/The Power of Positive Drinking	1980	$4
❏ 0215	I Believe in Love/ Senselessly Cruel	1976	$4

ATLANTIC

Number	Title	Yr	NM
❏ 89468	My Love Is Chemical/People Have Got to Move	1985	$3

— B-side by Jenny Burton

Number	Title	Yr	NM
❏ 89468 [PS]	My Love Is Chemical/People Have Got to Move	1985	$5

RCA

Number	Title	Yr	NM
❏ PB-13841	I Love You Suzanne/My Friend George	1984	$3
❏ JB-13558	Martial Law/Don't Talk to Me About Work	1983	$3

RCA VICTOR

Number	Title	Yr	NM
❏ PB-10573	Charley's Girl/Nowhere At All	1976	$4
❏ PB-10648	Crazy Feeling/Nowhere At All	1976	$4
❏ 74-0727	I Can't Stand It/Going Down	1972	$6
❏ APBO-0172	Lady Day/How Do You Think It Feels	1973	$5
❏ PB-10081	Sally Can't Dance/Ennui	1974	$4
❏ PB-10053	Sally Can't Dance/Vicious	1974	$4
❏ 74-0964	Satellite of Love/Walk and Talk It	1973	$6
❏ APBO-0238	Sweet Jane/Lady Day	1974	$40

— Part of U.S. numbering system, but pressed for export.

Number	Title	Yr	NM
❏ 74-0784	Walk and Talk It/Wild Child	1972	$6
❏ 74-0887	Walk on the Wild Side/ Perfect Day	1973	$6
❏ GB-10162	Walk on the Wild Side/ Vicious	1975	$3

— Gold Standard Series reissue

REED, LULA

KING

Number	Title	Yr	NM
❏ 4649	Don't Make Me Love You/ Goin' Back to Mexico	1953	$60
❏ 4996	Every Second/Waste No More Tears	1956	$30
❏ 4590	Heavenly Road/My Mother's Prayer	1953	$60
❏ 4714	If the Sun Isn't Shining in Your Window/Just Whisper	1954	$50
❏ 4811	I'm Giving All My Love/Why Don't You Come Home	1955	$30
❏ 4630	I'm Losing You/My Poor Heart	1953	$60
❏ 4578	Let Me Be Your Love/My Story	1952	$100
❏ 4899	Let's Call It a Day/I'll Drown in My Own Tears	1956	$30
❏ 4969	Sample Man/Three Men	1956	$30
❏ 4748	Sick and Tired/Jealous Love	1954	$50
❏ 4703	Troubles on Your Mind/ Bump on a Log	1954	$50
❏ 4737	What Could I Do But Believe in Jesus/A Quiet Time with Jesus	1954	$60
❏ 4796	Without Love/Caught Me When My Love Was Down	1955	$30
❏ 4726	Wonderful Love/I'll Upset You Baby	1954	$50

REED, TAWNEY

CONGRESS

Number	Title	Yr	NM
❏ 270	My Heart Cried/Can't Take It Away	1966	$15

REED, VIVIAN

ATCO

Number	Title	Yr	NM
❏ 6938	Save Your Love for Me/I Didn't Mean to Love You	1973	$600

EPIC

Number	Title	Yr	NM
❏ 5-10290	Baby, Baby/I	1968	$20
❏ 5-10752	I Feel the Earth Move/Don't Close the Door on Me	1971	$40
❏ 5-10683	Lean on Me/Missing You	1970	$20

Number	Title	Yr	NM
❏ 5-10382	Mama Open the Door/Medley: Soul and Inspiration-You've Lost That Lovin' Feelin'	1968	$20
❏ 5-10422	Somewhere/Shape of Things to Come	1968	$20
❏ 5-10533	Then I'll Be Over You/Unbelievable	1969	$30
❏ 5-10453	Walk on My Side/Look the Other Way	1969	$30

H&L

Number	Title	Yr	NM
❏ 4666	Bubbling Brown Sugar/(B-side unknown)	1976	$8
❏ 4672	God Bless the Child/Sweet Georgia Brown	1976	$8

UNITED ARTISTS

Number	Title	Yr	NM
❏ X-1239#NAME?	It's Alright (This Feeling I'm Feeling)/When You Touch Me	1978	$20
❏ X-1260#NAME?	Start Dancin'/Sweet Harmony	1979	$15

REEDER, BILL

HI

Number	Title	Yr	NM
❏ 2041	Secret Love/Judy	1961	$30
❏ 2037	Till I Waltz Again with You/There Was a Time	1961	$100

VOLL

Number	Title	Yr	NM
❏ 100	Till I Waltz Again with You/There Was a Time	1961	$200

REEKERS, THE

RY-JAC

Number	Title	Yr	NM
❏ 13	Grindin'/Don't Call Me Flyface	1964	$60

REESE, DELLA

ABC

Number	Title	Yr	NM
❏ 11051	I Gotta Be Me/Never My Love	1968	$6
❏ 10962	I Heard You Cried Last Night/On the South Side of Chicago	1967	$6
❏ 10841	It Was a Very Good Year/Solitary Woman	1966	$8
❏ 11017	Let's Make the Most of a Beautiful Thing/Sorry Baby	1967	$6
❏ 10931	Soon/Every Other Day	1967	$6
❏ 10815	Stranger on Earth/If It's the Last Thing I Do	1966	$8
❏ 10876	Sunny/That's Life	1966	$8

ABC-PARAMOUNT

Number	Title	Yr	NM
❏ 10691	After Loving You/How Do You Keep from Crying	1965	$8
❏ 10721	And That Reminds Me/I Only Want a Buddy, Not a Sweetheart	1965	$8
❏ 10759	'T'Ain't Nobody's Bizness If I Do/I Ain't Ready for That	1965	$8

AVCO

Number	Title	Yr	NM
❏ 4586	If It Feels Good Do It/Good Lovin' Makes It Right	1972	$5

AVCO EMBASSY

Number	Title	Yr	NM
❏ 4545	Billy My Love/(B-side unknown)	1970	$6
❏ 4515	Games People Play/Compared to What	1969	$6
❏ 4566	The Troublemaker/The Love I've Been Looking For	1971	$6

CHI-SOUND

Number	Title	Yr	NM
❏ XW978	I'll Be Your Sunshine/Nothing But a True Love	1977	$4

JUBILEE

Number	Title	Yr	NM
❏ 5292	And That Reminds Me/I Cried for You	1957	$15
❏ 5247	Headin' Home/Daybreak Serenade	1956	$20
❏ 5278	How About You/How Can You Not Believe	1957	$20
❏ 5317	How Can You Lose (What You Never Had)/If Not for You	1958	$15
❏ 5375	I Don't Want to Walk Without You/I'm Nobody's Baby	1959	$15
❏ 5263	In the Meantime/The More I See You	1956	$20
❏ 5198	In the Still of the Night/Kiss My Love Goodbye	1955	$20
❏ 5307	I Only Want to Love You/By Love Possessed	1957	$15
❏ 5323	I've Got a Feelin' You're Foolin'/C'mon, C'mon	1958	$15
❏ 5233	I've Got My Love to Keep Me Warm/Years from Now	1956	$20
❏ 5332	I Wish/You Gotta Love Everybody	1958	$15
❏ 5251	My Melancholy Baby/One for My Baby	1956	$20
❏ 5345	Sermonette/Dreams End at Dawn	1958	$15
❏ 5453	Sermonette/You Gotta Love Somebody	1963	$10
❏ 5214	Time After Time/Fine Sugar	1955	$20
❏ 5369	Time Was/Once Upon a Dream	1959	$15

Number	Title	Yr	NM
❏ 5346	When I Grow Too Old to Dream/You're Just in Love	1958	$15

— *Della Reese and Kirk Stuart*

RCA VICTOR

Number	Title	Yr	NM
❏ 47-7784	And Now/There's Nothin' Like a Boy	1960	$10
❏ 47-7784 [PS]	And Now/There's Nothin' Like a Boy	1960	$30
❏ 47-8260	Angel D'Amore/Forbidden Games	1963	$10
❏ 47-8093	As Long As He Needs Me/It Makes No Difference Now	1962	$10
❏ 47-8093 [PS]	As Long As He Needs Me/It Makes No Difference Now	1962	$20
❏ 47-8145	Be My Love/I Behold You	1963	$12
❏ 47-8145 [PS]	Be My Love/I Behold You	1963	$20
❏ 47-7591	Don't You Know/Soldier Won't You Marry Me	1959	$12
❏ 47-7750	Everyday/There's No Two Ways About It	1960	$12
❏ 47-7750 [PS]	Everyday/There's No Two Ways About It	1960	$30
❏ 47-8394	If I Didn't Care/Wind in the Willows	1964	$8
❏ 47-8070	I Love You So Much It Hurts/Blow Out the Sun	1962	$10
❏ 47-7884	I Possess/A Far, Far Better Thing	1961	$10
❏ 47-8187	More/Serenade	1963	$10
❏ 47-7961	One/What Do You Think, Joe	1961	$10
❏ 47-7683	Someday/The Lady Is a Tramp	1960	$12
❏ 47-7706	Someday You'll Want Me to Want You/Faraway Boy	1960	$12
❏ 47-8337	The Bottom of Old Smokey/A Clock That's Got No Hands	1964	$8
❏ 47-7833	The Most Beautiful Words/You Mean All the World to Me	1961	$10
❏ 47-7867	The Touch of Your Lips/Won'cha Come Home, Bill Bailey	1961	$10
❏ 37-7867	The Touch of Your Lips/Won'cha Come Home, Bill Bailey	1961	$30

— *Compact Single 33" (small hole, plays at 33 1/3 rpm)*

7-Inch Extended Plays

Number	Title	Yr	NM
❏ EPA-4349 [PS]	Don't You Know	1959	$20
❏ EPA-4349	Don't You Know/Soldier, Won't You Marry Me//Not One Minute More/You're My Love	1959	$20

REESE, JAXON

PARKWAY

Number	Title	Yr	NM
❏ 129	Hurry Sundown/How Do You Speak to an Angel	1967	$50
❏ 142	Pretty Girl/Cry Me a River	1967	$50

REESE, LLOYD, AND THE SOLID ROCK CHORUS

VERVE

Number	Title	Yr	NM
❏ 10461	Sweet Little Lord Jesus/Nino Chiquito	1966	$10

REEVES, DEL

CAPITOL

Number	Title	Yr	NM
❏ F3819	Love, Love, Love/You're Not the Changing Kind	1957	$40

— *With Chester Smith*

Number	Title	Yr	NM
❏ F3979	The Trot/Cool Drool	1958	$40
❏ F4045	Two Teen Hearts/Baby I Love You	1958	$40

CHART

Number	Title	Yr	NM
❏ 5082	Stand In/Bad, Bad Tuesday	1970	$8

COLUMBIA

Number	Title	Yr	NM
❏ 4-43044	Talking to the Night Lights/Not Since Adam	1964	$10

DECCA

Number	Title	Yr	NM
❏ 31307	Be Quiet Mind/As Far As I Can See	1961	$15
❏ 31417	He Stands Real Tall/Empty House	1962	$15

KOALA

Number	Title	Yr	NM
❏ 339	Ain't Nobody Gonna Get My Body But You/Let's Think About Livin'	1981	$5
❏ 324	Good Ole Girls/Doin' Soft Time	1980	$5
❏ 336	Slow Hand/Take Off Time	1981	$5
❏ 333	Swinging Doors/Who Left the Door to Heaven Open	1981	$5
❏ 584	Take Me to Your Heart/What the Love of a Lady Can Do	1980	$5
❏ 347	That's What I Like About the South/(B-side unknown)	1982	$5
❏ 594	What Am I Gonna Do?/Night Out	1980	$5
❏ 329	White Christmas/White Christmas (Second Version)	1980	$5

PEACH

Number	Title	Yr	NM
❏ 746	Time After Time/I Don't Wonder	1961	$30

PLAYBACK

Number	Title	Yr	NM
❏ 1301	Dear Dr. Ruth/Anywhere U.S.A.	1988	$6
❏ 1303	I Used My Doodle-De-Doos/I Wish I Had Loved	1988	$6
❏ 1302	Louisiana Legs/(B-side unknown)	1988	$6
❏ 1103	The Second Time Around/(B-side unknown)	1986	$5

REPRISE

Number	Title	Yr	NM
❏ 20228	I Closed My Eyes and Saw the Light/Once a Fool	1963	$10
❏ 20158	The Only Girl I Can't Forget/The Love She Offered Me	1963	$10

UNITED ARTISTS

Number	Title	Yr	NM
❏ 50210	A Dime at a Time/So Much Got Lost	1967	$8
❏ 50840	A Dozen Pairs of Boots/A Rose Is Hard to Beat	1971	$6
❏ XW1047	Am I in Heaven/Rita Ballow	1977	$5
❏ 50743	Bar Room Talk/I'm Not Through Loving You	1971	$6
❏ 50964	Before Goodbye/Buck Jones Guitar	1972	$6
❏ 50128	Blame It On My Do Wrong/I Don't Have Sense Enough	1967	$8
❏ XW593	But I Do/One More Round of Gin	1975	$5
❏ 50115	Christmas Is Lonely/Sajo	1966	$10
❏ XW1230	Dig Down Deep/Darlin' I Love You	1978	$5
❏ 50035	Gettin' Any Feed for Your Chickens/Plain as the Tears on My Face	1966	$8
❏ 0141	Girl on the Billboard/Bar Room Talk	1973	$4

— *Silver Spotlight Series" reissue*

Number	Title	Yr	NM
❏ 824	Girl on the Billboard/Eyes Don't Come Crying to Me	1965	$8
❏ XW760	I Ain't Got Nobody/I Would Like to See You Again	1976	$5
❏ XW989	Ladies Night/Cryin' in Arkansas Tonight	1977	$5
❏ XW308	Lay a Little Lovin' on Me/Lay Me to Sleep	1973	$5
❏ XW249	Mm-Mm Good/Bridge That Wouldn't Burn	1973	$5
❏ XW885	My Better Half/Dig a Little Deeper in the Well	1976	$5
❏ 50001	One Bum Town/Dead and Gone	1966	$8
❏ XW564	Pour It All on Me/Belles of Broadway	1974	$5
❏ XW427	Prayer from a Mobile Home/Three Years Late	1974	$5
❏ XW639	Puttin' In Overtime at Home/Homemade Love	1975	$5
❏ XW532	She Likes Country Bands/A Rose Is Hard to Beat	1974	$5
❏ 890	The Belles of Southern Bell/Nothing to Write Home About	1965	$8
❏ 50877	The Best Is Yet to Come/Truth Can Hurt a Woman	1972	$6
❏ 50802	The Philadelphia Fillies/Belles of Broadway	1971	$6
❏ 50157	The Private/Things Her Memory Makes	1967	$8
❏ 50157 [PS]	The Private/Things Her Memory Makes	1967	$30
❏ 50081	This Must Be the Bottom/Laughter Keeps Running Down My Cheeks	1966	$8
❏ 51106	Trucker's Paradise/Gathering of My Memories	1973	$6
❏ XW378	What a Way to Go/Sometimes Woman	1974	$5
❏ XW1191	When My Angel Turns Into a Devil/How Can Anything That Feels So Good (Hurt So Bad)	1978	$5
❏ 940	Women Do Funny Things to Me/My Half of Our Part	1965	$8
❏ 50763	Working Like the Devil (For the Lord)/Sidewalks of Chicago	1971	$6

REEVES, JIM, AND PATSY CLINE

MCA

Number	Title	Yr	NM
❏ 52052	So Wrong/I Fall to Pieces	1982	$4

RCA

Number	Title	Yr	NM
❏ PB-12346	Have You Ever Been Lonely (Have You Ever Been Blue)/Welcome to My World	1981	$4

REEVES, JIM

ABBOTT

Number	Title	Yr	NM
❏ 184	Are You the One/How Many	1955	$30

— *With Alvadean Coker*

Number	Title	Yr	NM
❏ 148	Bimbo/Gypsy Heart	1953	$30

— *Black vinyl*

Number	Title	Yr	NM
❏ 148	Bimbo/Gypsy Heart	1953	$70

— *Red vinyl*

Number	Title	Yr	NM
❏ 178	Drinking Tequila/Red Eyed and Rowdy	1955	$30
❏ 160	Echo Bonita/Then I'll Stop Loving You	1954	$30
❏ 143	El Rancho Del Rio/It's Hard to Love Just One	1953	$30

Number	Title	Yr	NM
❑ 143	El Rancho Del Rio/It's Hard to Love Just One	1953	$70
— Red vinyl			
❑ 180	Give Me One More Kiss/Tahiti	1955	$30
❑ 137	Let Me Love You Just a Little/Butterfly Love	1953	$30
❑ 137	Let Me Love You Just a Little/Butterfly Love	1953	$70
— Red vinyl			
❑ 186	Let Me Remember/Hillbilly Waltz	1956	$30
❑ 116	Mexican Joe/I Could Cry	1953	$70
— Red vinyl			
❑ 116	Mexican Joe/I Could Cry	1953	$30
❑ 168	Padre of Old San Antone/Mother Went A-Walkin'	1954	$30
❑ 170	Penny Candy/I'll Follow You	1954	$30
❑ 115	Wagon Load of Love/What Were You Doing Last Nite	1953	$30
❑ 115	Wagon Load of Love/What Were You Doing Last Nite	1953	$70
— Red vinyl			
❑ 174	Where Does a Broken Heart Go/The Wilder Your Heart Beats, The Sweeter You Love	1954	$30
RCA			
❑ PB-11564	Don't Let Me Cross Over/I've Enjoyed As Much of This As I Can Stand	1979	$4
❑ PB-10956	It's Nothin' to Me/I Won't Forget You	1977	$4
❑ PB-11060	Little Ole Dime/A Letter to My Heart	1977	$4
❑ PB-11737	Oh, How I Miss You Tonight/The Talking Walls	1979	$4
❑ PB-11946	Take Me in Your Arms and Hold Me/Missing Angel	1980	$4
— A-side with Deborah Allen (overdubbed)			
❑ PB-13693	The Image of Me/Won't Come In While He's There	1983	$4
❑ PB-12118	There's Always Me/Somewhere Along the Line	1980	$4
RCA VICTOR			
❑ 47-6620	According to My Heart/The Mother of a Honky Tonk Girl	1956	$30
— With Carol Johnson			
❑ 47-8019	Adios Amigo/A Letter to My Heart	1962	$10
❑ 47-7800	Am I Losing You/I Missed Me	1960	$15
❑ 47-7800 [PS]	Am I Losing You/I Missed Me	1960	$30
❑ 47-6749	Am I Losing You/Waitin' for a Train	1956	$30
❑ 74-0963	Am I That Easy to Forget/Rosa Rio	1973	$4
❑ 47-9880	Angels Don't Lie/You Kept Me Awake Last Night	1970	$6
❑ 47-7070	Anna Marie/Everywhere You Go	1957	$20
❑ 47-8252	An Old Christmas Card/Senor Santa Claus	1963	$20
❑ 47-8252 [PS]	An Old Christmas Card/Senor Santa Claus	1963	$50
❑ 447-0884	An Old Christmas Card/Senor Santa Claus	1972	$4
— Gold Standard Series			
❑ 47-7380	Billy Bayou/I'd Like to Be	1958	$20
❑ 47-6625	Bimbo/Penny Candy	1956	$30
❑ 47-7266	Blue Boy/Theme of Love (I Love to Say I Love You)	1958	$20
❑ 74-0859	Blue Christmas/Snowflake	1972	$5
❑ 47-8902	Blue Side of Lonesome/It Hurts So Much (To See You Go)	1966	$8
❑ 47-8789	Distant Drums/Old Tige	1966	$8
❑ 47-6874	Four Walls/I Know and You Know	1957	$20
❑ 47-8193	Guilty/Little Ole You	1963	$10
❑ 47-8193 [PS]	Guilty/Little Ole You	1963	$20
❑ 47-9969	Gypsy Feet/He Will	1971	$6
❑ 47-7643	He'll Have to Go/In a Mansion Stands My Love	1959	$15
❑ EP-10133	He Will/We Thank Thee	1974	$4
❑ 47-7479	Home/If Heartache Is the Fashion	1959	$20
❑ APBO-0255	I'd Fight the World/What's In It for Me	1974	$4
❑ 47-6401	If You Were Mine/That's a Sad Affair	1956	$30
❑ 47-8383	I Guess I'm Crazy/Not Until the Next Time	1964	$10
❑ 47-9343	I Heard a Heart Break Last Night/Golden Memories and Silver Tears	1967	$8
❑ 47-7171	I Love You More/Overnight	1958	$20
❑ 47-7756	I'm Gettin' Better/I Know One	1960	$15
❑ 47-7756 [PS]	I'm Gettin' Better/I Know One	1960	$30
❑ 47-8080	I'm Gonna Change Everything/Pride Goes Before a Fall	1962	$10
❑ 47-8625	Is It Really Over?/Rosa Rio	1965	$8
❑ 47-8625 [PS]	Is It Really Over?/Rosa Rio	1965	$15
❑ 47-8127	Is This Me?/Missing Angel	1963	$10
❑ 47-8127 [PS]	Is This Me?/Missing Angel	1963	$30

Number	Title	Yr	NM
❑ 47-6274	I've Lived a Lot in My Time/Jimbo Jenkins	1955	$30
❑ 47-9057	I Won't Come In While He's There/Maureen	1966	$8
❑ 47-8461	I Won't Forget You/Highway to Nowhere	1964	$10
❑ 47-7950	Losing Your Love/(How Can I Write on Paper) What I Feel in My Heart	1961	$15
❑ 47-8324	Love Is No Excuse/Look Who's Talking	1964	$10
— With Dottie West			
❑ 47-6626	Mexican Joe/How Many	1956	$30
❑ GB-10511	Missing You/I'd Fight the World	1975	$4
— Gold Standard Series			
❑ 74-0744	Missing You/The Tie That Binds	1972	$5
❑ 47-6517	My Lips Are Sealed/Pickin' a Chicken	1956	$30
❑ 47-7557	Partners/I'm Beginning to Forget You	1959	$20
❑ 47-8719	Snowflake/Take My Hand, Precious Lord	1965	$8
❑ 447-0885	Snowflake/Take My Hand, Precious Lord	1972	$4
— Gold Standard Series			
❑ 47-9455	That's When I See the Blues (In Your Pretty Brown Eyes)/I've Lived a Lot in My Time	1968	$8
❑ 47-7855	The Blizzard/Danny Boy	1961	$15
❑ 47-6627	Then I'll Stop Loving You/Drinking Tequila	1956	$30
❑ 47-9238	The Storm/Trying to Forget	1967	$8
❑ 74-0626	The Writing on the Wall/You're Free to Go	1971	$6
❑ 47-8508	This Is It/There's That Smile Again	1965	$8
❑ 47-8289	Welcome to My World/Good Morning Self	1963	$10
❑ 47-7905	What Would You Do?/Stand At Your Window	1961	$15
❑ 74-0135	When Two Worlds Collide/Could I Be Falling in Love	1969	$6
❑ 47-9614	When You Are Gone/How Can I Write on Paper	1968	$8
❑ 74-0286	Why Do I Love You (Melody of Love)/Nobody's Fool	1969	$6
7-Inch Extended Plays			
❑ EPA-5145 [PS]	Am I Losing You (Gold Standard Series)	1958	$20
❑ EPA-5145	Am I Losing You/Home//Billy Bayou/Partners	1958	$20
❑ VLP-3793 [PS]	Blue Side of Lonesome	1967	$20
❑ VLP-3793	Blue Side of Lonesome/Trying to Forget/I Know One//I Won't Come In While He's There/Teardrops on the Rocks/Deep Dark Water	1967	$20
— Stereo jukebox issue; small hole, plays at 33 1/3 rpm			
❑ EPA-4062 [PS]	Four Walls	1957	$25
❑ EPA-5124	Four Walls/Blue Boy//Bimbo/Mexican Joe	1958	$20
❑ EPA-4062	Four Walls/I Know (And You Know)//The Gods Were Angry with Me/Look Behind You	1957	$25
❑ EPA-4357 [PS]	He'll Have to Go	1960	$25
❑ EPA-4357	He'll Have to Go/Wishful Thinking//Please Come Home/After Awhile	1960	$25
❑ EPA-757 [PS]	(title unknown)	1956	$25
REEVES, MARTHA			
ARISTA			
❑ 0124	Love Blind/This Time I'll Be Sweeter	1975	$5
— Also see "Martha and the Vandellas"			
FANTASY			
❑ 868	Dancin' in the Streets (Skatin' in the Streets)/When You Came	1979	$4
❑ 825	Love Don't Come No Stronger/You're Like Sunshine	1978	$4
MCA			
❑ 40329	My Man/Facsimile	1974	$5
❑ 40194	Power of Love/Stand By Me	1974	$5
❑ 40274	Stand By Me/Wild Night	1974	$5
REFLECTIONS, THE (1)			
ABC			
❑ 10794	Like Adam and Eve/Vito's House	1966	$125
GOLDEN WORLD			
❑ 29	Girl in the Candy Store/Your Kind of Love	1965	$20
❑ 16	Henpecked Guy/Don't Do That to Me	1964	$20
❑ 12	Like Columbus Did/Lonely Girl	1964	$20
❑ 15	Oowee Now/Talkin' 'Bout My Girl	1964	$20
❑ 20	Poor Man's Son/Comin' At You	1965	$20
❑ 22	Wheelin' and Dealin'/Deborah Ann	1965	$20

Number	Title	Yr	NM
REFLECTIONS, THE (2)			
CAPITOL			
❑ 4222	Are You Ready (Here I Am)/Day After Day (Night After Night)	1976	$5
❑ 4358	Gift Wrap My Love/She's My Summer Breeze	1976	$30
❑ 4137	Love on Delivery/One Into One	1975	$5
❑ 4078	Three Steps from True Love/How Could We Let the Love Get Away	1975	$6
RCA			
❑ PB-11408	Boogie City/I'm Gonna Let You Go This Time	1978	$5
REFLECTIONS, THE (3)			
CROSSROADS			
❑ 401	I Really Must Know/Maybe Tomorrow	1961	$70
REFLECTIONS, THE (U)			
KAY-KO			
❑ 1003	Helpless/You Said Goodbye	1963	$200
TIGRE			
❑ 602	In the Still of the Night/Tic Toc	1962	$50
REGALS, THE (1)			
ATLANTIC			
❑ 1062	I'm So Lonely/Got the Water Boiling	1955	$70
MGM			
❑ 11869	There'll Always Be a Christmas/When You're Home with the Ones You Love	1954	$50
REGALS, THE (2)			
LAST CHANCE			
❑ 109	See You in the Morning/Yes My Love	1961	$10
LAVENDER			
❑ 1452	See You in the Morning/Yes My Love	1960	$40
UNITED ARTISTS			
❑ 380	Icy Fingers/Tiger Tears	1961	$40
REGAN, DENISE			
DEE GEE			
❑ 3005 [PS]	A Date with Santa Claus/Hole in the Stocking	1965	$30
❑ 3005	A Date with Santa Claus/Hole in the Stocking	1965	$10
REGAN, EDDIE			
ABC			
❑ 10795	Playin' Hide and Seek/Talk About Heartaches	1966	$40
REGAN, PHIL			
RCA VICTOR			
❑ 47-3936	Christmas Story/Leprechaun Lullaby	1950	$20
REGAN, RUSS			
CAPITOL			
❑ F4280	Adults Only/Just the Two of Us	1959	$15
REGAN, TOMMY			
COLPIX			
❑ 725	I'll Never Stop Loving You/This Time I'm Losing You	1964	$125
TELL STAR			
❑ 5001	Santa Twist/(B-side unknown)	1962	$15
WORLD ARTISTS			
❑ 1049	I Adore You/9 to 5	1965	$20
REGENTS, THE (1)			
COUSINS			
❑ 1002	Barbara-Ann/I'm So Lonely	1961	$1200
GEE			
❑ 1065	Barbara-Ann/I'm So Lonely	1961	$40
❑ 1073	Don't Be a Fool/Liar	1961	$30
❑ 1075	Lonesome Boy/Oh Baby	1961	$30

Number	Title	Yr	NM
REGENTS, THE (2)			
ARGO			
5268	Isle of Trinidad/Bamboo Tree	1957	$30
REGENTS, THE (3)			
BLUE CAT			
110	Playmates/Me and You	1965	$10
PENTHOUSE			
502	Words/Worryin' Kind	1966	$10
REGENTS, THE (4)			
KAYO			
101	(That's What I Call) A Real Good Time/No Hard Feelings	1960	$30
REGENTS, THE (5)			
REPRISE			
0430	She's Got Her Own Way of Lovin'/When I Die, Don't You Cry	1965	$40
REGOS, EUGENIA			
FLAIR			
1024	I'm Gonna Write a Letter to Santa Claus/I Wanna Be a Hollywood Cowboy	1953	$30
REID, BILL & MARY			
COLUMBIA			
4-21497	Blue Ridge Waltz/In My Heart I Love You Yet	1956	$30
4-21529	I'll Never Be Lonesome/Get Down on Your Knees and Pray	1956	$30
REID, CLARENCE			
ALSTON			
3717	Baptize Me in Your Love/Whatever It Takes	1975	$5
4584	Chicken Hawk/That's How It Is	1970	$6
3720	Come On With It/Mr. Smith's Wife	1976	$5
4592	Direct Me/You Knock Me Out	1971	$6
4572	Fools Are Not Born (They Are Made)/Part-Time Lover	1969	$8
4621	Funky Party/Winter Man	1974	$6
4603	Good Old Days/Ten Tons of Dynamite	1972	$6
4598	I Get My Kicks/Gotta Take It Home to Mother	1971	$6
4578	I'm a Man of My Word/I'm Gonna Tear You a New Heart	1969	$8
4608	I'm Gonna Do Something Good to You/Real Woman	1972	$6
4582	I've Been Trying/Don't Look Too Hard	1970	$6
4602	Love Every Woman You Can/Ten Tons of Dynamite	1971	$6
4588	Masterpiece/Down the Road of Love	1970	$6
3723	Shake Your Butt/Caution! Love Ahead	1976	$5
4616	Till I Get My Share/With Friends Like These	1973	$6
ATCO			
7025	See Through/I Bet You Believe Me Now	1975	$8
DIAL			
4040	Gimmie a Try/Part of Your Love	1966	$15
3018	I Got My Shake/There'll Come a Day	1964	$20
4019	I Refuse to Give Up/Somebody Will	1965	$15
PHIL-L.A. OF SOUL			
301	Cadillac Annie/Tired Blood	1967	$10
WAND			
1121	I'm Your Yes Man/Your Love Is All the Help I Need	1966	$200
1106	Somebody Will/I Refuse to Give Up	1966	$30
REID, MATTHEW			
ABC-PARAMOUNT			
10305	Tarzan Twist (Bwana Ungava)/Through My Tears	1962	$30
DECCA			
31662	One More Minute/Hurt Me	1964	$15
PHILIPS			
40634	Outward Bound/Hey There Sweet Sue	1969	$10
SCEPTER			
1238	Faded Roses/Tomorrow	1962	$30
TOPIX			
6006	Cry Myself to Sleep/Lollipops Went Out of Style	1961	$50
REINHART, DICK			
COLUMBIA			
2-115	Cross My Heart/A Broken Heart for a Souvenir	1949	$60
— Microgroove 33 1/3 rpm 7-inch single, small hole			
RELATIVES, THE			
MUSICOR			
1063	Eternally/Hadn't Been for Baby	1965	$12
RELF, KEITH			
EPIC			
10044	Mr. Zero/Knowing	1966	$60
10044 [DJ]	Mr. Zero/Knowing	1966	$200
— Promo on red vinyl... Reportedly, two promos were released for this single; the second, a different mix, was accompanied by a note telling the radio people not to play the first one, but to use the second one instead. This has not been confirmed.			
10110	Shapes in My Mind/Blue Sands	1966	$60
10110 [PS]	Shapes in My Mind/Blue Sands	1966	$125
10110 [DJ]	Shapes in My Mind (same on both sides)	1966	$200
— Promo on red vinyl			
MCCM			
002	Together Now/All the Falling Angels	1989	$5
— Purple marbled vinyl			
002 [PS]	Together Now/All the Falling Angels	1989	$6
RELLA, CINDY			
CARLTON			
583	He Don't Love Me Anymore/I Want Him to Come Back Home	1962	$15
601	Phil Will/To Tommy with Love	1964	$15
DRUM BOY			
112	Bring Me A Beatle for Christmas/Cla-wence	1964	$15
REMAINS, THE			
EPIC			
9872	But I Ain't Got You/I Can't Get Away from You	1965	$100
10001	Diddy Wah Diddy/Once Before	1966	$100
10001 [DJ]	Diddy Wah Diddy/Once Before	1966	$200
— Promo on red vinyl			
10060	Don't Look Back/Me Right Now	1966	$100
9783	My Babe/Why Do I Cry	1965	$100
10001 [PS]	To Be Seen and Heard: Diddy Wah Diddy	1966	$125
— Promo-only sleeve			
SPOONFED			
SR-4505 [PS]	Why Do I Cry/Mercy, Mercy	1978	$20
SR-4505	Why Do I Cry/Mercy, Mercy	1978	$10
REMARKABLES, THE			
CHASE			
1600	Write Me/Whirl-A-Round	1964	$250
REMINGTON, HERB			
D			
1129	Coo Coo Creek Hop/Chime Out for Love	1960	$30
— As "Herby Remington			
1186	Soft Shoe Slide/Fiddle Steel	1961	$20
— As "Herby Remington			
STARDAY			
332	Slush Pump/Station Break	1957	$30
— As "Herby Remington			
UNITED ARTISTS			
482	Swinging Cow Bells/Pedal Softly	1962	$20
— As "Herby Remington			
REMINISCENTS, THE			
MARCEL			
1000	Cards of Love/Flames	1962	$120
RENAY, DIANE			
20TH CENTURY FOX			
514	Growin' Up Too Fast/Waitin' for Joey	1964	$10
533	It's In Your Tears/Present from Eddie	1964	$10
ATCO			
6262	Dime a Dozen/Tender	1963	$15
6240	Falling Star/Little White Lies	1962	$15
FONTANA			
1679	Hold Me, Thrill Me, Kiss Me/Yesterday	1969	$12
MGM			
13296	Billy Blue Eyes/Watch Out Sally	1964	$10
13335	I Had a Dream/Troublemaker	1965	$30
NEW VOICE			
803	Cross My Heart, Hope to Die/Happy Birthday, Broken Heart	1965	$12
800	Words/The Company You Keep	1965	$10
UNITED ARTISTS			
50048	Dynamite/Please Gypsy	1966	$20
RENDEZVOUS			
REPRISE			
20089	Congratulations Baby/Faithfully	1962	$40
RUST			
5041	It Breaks My Heart/Take a Break	1961	$50
RENDEZVOUS STOMPERS, THE			
DORE			
626	Gremmies Unite/Rock Me Gently	1962	$50
RENE AND RENE			
ABC			
10699	Chantilly Lace/I'm Not the Only One (No Soy El Unico)	1965	$8
ARV INTERNATIONAL			
A-5011	Lo Mucho Que Te Quiero/Mornin'	1968	$20
— Silver label			
A-5011	Lo Mucho Que Te Quiero/Mornin'	1968	$15
— Blue label			
CERTRON			
10011	My Amigo Jose/Good Old Days	1970	$5
COLUMBIA			
43045	Angelito/Write Me Soon	1964	$8
43045 [PS]	Angelito/Write Me Soon	1964	$15
43163	Please Don't Bother/Undecided	1964	$8
EPIC			
10443	Muchachita/Our Day Will Come	1969	$5
JOX			
017	Angelito/Write Me Soon	1964	$15
032	Chantilly Lace/I'm Not the Only One	1965	$10
041	Little Peanuts/Little Vagabond	1965	$10
050	Loving You Could Hurt Me So/Little Diamonds	1966	$10
025	Pretty Flowers/Fade Away	1965	$10
WHITE WHALE			
303	Enchilada Jose/Lloraras	1969	$5
298	Las Cosas/You Will Cry	1969	$5
281	Lo Mucho Que Te Quiero/Lloraras	1968	$6
287	Lo Mucho Que Te Quiero/Mornin'	1968	$5
327	Love Is for the Two of Us/Sally Tosis	1969	$5

Number	Title	Yr	NM

RENE, GOOGIE
CLASS
Number	Title	Yr	NM
❏ 214	At the Break of Dawn/Twilight Walk	1957	$30
❏ 212	Beautiful Weekend/Rock-a-Boogie	1957	$30
❏ 239	Big Foot/Rebecca	1958	$20
❏ 262	Caesar's Pad/Serenade in the Night	1959	$20
❏ 1518	Chica-Boo/Mercy Mercy	1966	$30
❏ 270	Cool It at the Coliseum/Cafe Roman Candle	1960	$20
❏ 706	Cool Swimming Pool/(B-side unknown)	1965	$30
❏ 1519	Downtown/Beautiful Weekend	1966	$20
❏ 264	Ez-Zee/Forever	1960	$20
❏ 305	Flapjacks (Part I)/(Part II)	1962	$20
❏ 205	Midnight/Big Time	1957	$30
❏ 208	Side-Track/Break It Up	1957	$30
❏ 1517	Smokey Joe's La La/Needing You	1966	$30
❏ 702	Soul Zone '65/Wild Bird	1965	$30
❏ 310	Soul Zone/Walk Right In	1963	$30
❏ 233	Sunrise/Moonglow	1958	$20
❏ 227	Swingin' Summer Love/Shine On Harvest Moon	1958	$20
❏ 309	Tamba Shake/Bossa Baby	1963	$20
❏ 312	The Chiller/Young Folk	1964	$30
❏ 1515	There I Was/Vikki's Lament	1965	$200
❏ 201	Wham Bam/Sad Fool	1957	$50
— B-side by the Rollettes			
❏ 221	Wiggle Tail (Part 1)/(Part 2)	1958	$20

RENDEZVOUS
Number	Title	Yr	NM
❏ 144	April Is Her Name/Little Cupid Blues	1961	$20
❏ 157	Caesar's Pad/Ez-Zee	1961	$20
❏ 134	The Slide (Part 1)/(Part 2)	1960	$30
❏ 134 [PS]	The Slide (Part 1)/(Part 2)	1960	$40

RENEGADES, THE (1)
AMERICAN INT'L.
Number	Title	Yr	NM
❏ 537	Charge/Geronimo	1959	$60

RENEGADES, THE (2)
CONGRESS
Number	Title	Yr	NM
❏ 241	Cadillac/Matelot (Sailor Boy)	1965	$40

RENEGADES, THE (3)
DORSET
Number	Title	Yr	NM
❏ 5007	Stolen Angel/Keep Laughin'	1961	$60

RENEGADES, THE (U)
KARATE
Number	Title	Yr	NM
❏ 519	Take a Heart/If It Gets Lonesome	1966	$20

RENO, AL
KAPP
Number	Title	Yr	NM
❏ 432	Cheryl/Congratulations	1961	$50

RENO AND SMILEY
DOT
Number	Title	Yr	NM
❏ 15760	One More Hill/Banjo Medley	1958	$30
❏ 15835	One Teardrop and One Step Away/Unforgiveable You	1958	$30
❏ 15588	Sawing on the Strings/Sweethearts in Heaven	1957	$30
❏ 15649	Where Did Our Young Years Go/Cotton-Eyed Joe	1957	$30

KING
Number	Title	Yr	NM
❏ 5184	A Brighter Mansion Over There/Keep Me Humble	1959	$30
❏ 5936	A Lonely Road When You're All Alone/I Know Your Burdens	1964	$10
❏ 1199	A Pretty Wreath for Mother's Grave/A Rose on God's Shore	1953	$40
❏ 1490	Barefoot Nellie/Reno Ride	1955	$30
❏ 5905	Black and White Rag/Dill Pickles	1964	$10
❏ 5432	Bringin' In the Georgia Trail/Please Remember That I Love You	1960	$20
❏ 1458	Charlotte Breakdown/It's Grand to Have Someone	1955	$30
❏ 5937	Chinese Breakdown/Just a Country Banjo	1964	$10
❏ 1235	Choking the Strings/I'm the Talk of the Town	1953	$40
❏ 5814	Christmas Reunion/The True Meaning of Christmas	1963	$15
❏ 5169	Country Latin Special/Wall Around Your Heart	1959	$30
❏ 1104	Crazy Finger Blues/Maybe You Will Change Your Mind	1952	$40
❏ 1510	Cumberland Gap/Country Boy Rock and Roll	1955	$40
❏ 5002	Cumberland Rock/Country Boy Rock and Roll	1956	$30
❏ 5369	Dark as a Dungeon/East Bound Freight Train	1960	$20

Number	Title	Yr	NM
❏ 1390	Dixie Breakdown/Your Tears Are Just Interest on the Loan	1954	$30
❏ 5469	Don't Let Your Sweet Love Die/Born to Lose	1961	$20
❏ 1509	Double Banjo Blues/Trail of Sorrow	1955	$30
❏ 1360	Emotions/Tally Ho	1954	$30
❏ 5935	Forever/Tragic Romance	1964	$10
❏ 5024	Forgotten Men/Kneel Down	1957	$30
❏ 5320	Freight Train Boogie/Money, Marbles and Chalk	1960	$20
❏ 4944	Get Behind Me Satan/Jesus Answers My Prayers	1956	$30
❏ 1474	Green Mountain Hop/Home Sweet Home	1955	$30
❏ 1045	Hear Jerusalem Mount/I'm Using My Bible for a Roadmap	1952	$50
❏ 4962	Hen Scratchin' Stomp/Cruel Love	1956	$40
❏ 1263	He's Coming Back to Earth Again/My Mother's Bible	1953	$40
❏ 1303	I Can Hear the Angels Sing/The Mountain Church	1954	$30
❏ 5046	I Know You're Married/Beer Barrel Polka	1957	$30
❏ 5697	I'll See It Happen to You/Don't Let Temptation Turn You 'Round	1962	$15
❏ 5401	I'm Blue and I'm Lonesome/The Lord's Last Supper	1960	$20
❏ 1409	I'm Building a Mansion in Heaven/Springtime in Heaven	1954	$30
❏ 5808	I'm Jealous of You/Only in a Dream World	1963	$15
❏ 4875	I'm So Happy/Family Altar	1956	$30
❏ 5065	I Never Get to Hold You in My Arms/When You and I...	1957	$30
❏ 5728	It's a Sin/Grandfather's Clock	1963	$15
❏ 6060	I Want to Know/He's Not Ashamed of You	1966	$10
❏ 1079	I Want to Live Like Christ/Let In the Guiding Light	1952	$40
❏ 5200	I Wouldn't Change You/Little Rock Getaway	1959	$30
❏ 5296	Lonesome Wind Blues/She Has Forgotten	1959	$30
❏ 5520	Love Oh Love, Please Come Home/Double Eagle	1961	$20
❏ 1433	Mack's Hoedown/I'm the Biggest Liar in Town	1955	$30
❏ 5921	Mansion in the Sky/Amazing Grace	1964	$10
❏ 5346	Mountain Rosa Lee/Eight More Miles to Louisville	1960	$20
❏ 1377	My Shepherd Is God/Since I've Used My Bible for a Roadmap	1954	$30
❏ 4921	Old Home Place/Banjo Riff	1956	$30
❏ 6010	Open Road/Little Mountain Road	1965	$10
❏ 1332	Please Don't Feel Sorry for Me/Love Call Waltz	1954	$30
❏ 5260	Pretending/Sockeye	1959	$30
❏ 1162	Some Beautiful Day/Jesus Is Standing at My Right	1953	$40
❏ 5126	Springtime in Dixie/Always Be Kind to Your Mother	1958	$30
❏ 6082	Sundown and Sorrow/The Last Mile	1967	$8
❏ 1283	Tennessee Breakdown/I Could Cry	1953	$40
❏ 1150	Tennessee Cutup Breakdown/I'm Gone Long Gone	1952	$40
❏ 5554	That Moon Is No Stopping Place/Holiday Religion	1961	$20
❏ 5673	The Everglades/Ten Faces	1962	$15
❏ 1128	The Lord's Last Supper/There's a Highway to Heaven	1952	$40
❏ 5915	There Ain't Nobody Gonna Kiss Me/I Don't Blame You	1964	$10
❏ 1063	There's Another Baby Waitin'/Drifting with the Tide	1952	$40
❏ 5875	Things Are Gonna Be Different/Too Many Teardrops	1964	$10
❏ 1352	Tree of Life/Someone Will Love Me in Heaven	1954	$30
❏ 5650	When It's Time for the Whip-Poor-Will to Sing/Washington and Lee Swing	1962	$15

RENO, DON, AND BENNY MARTIN
MONUMENT
Number	Title	Yr	NM
❏ 912	Soldier's Prayer in Viet Nam/Five by Eight	1965	$15
❏ 931	Too Bad That You're No Good for Me/You Can't Make a Heel Toe the Line	1966	$15

RENO, DON
DOT
Number	Title	Yr	NM
❏ 16693	Military Five String/Now I'm Willing to Give You My Heart	1965	$10

EMH
Number	Title	Yr	NM
❏ 0020	Dueling Banjos/Tennessee Pride	1983	$6

MONUMENT
Number	Title	Yr	NM
❏ 966	I'm Worried About Me/My Daddy's Uncle Sam (My Mommy's Miss America)	1966	$15

RENO, MIKE, AND ANN WILSON
COLUMBIA
Number	Title	Yr	NM
❏ 04418	Almost Paradise...Love Theme from Footloose/Strike Zone	1984	$3
❏ 04418 [PS]	Almost Paradise...Love Theme from Footloose/Strike Zone	1984	$4

REO SPEEDWAGON
EPIC
Number	Title	Yr	NM
❏ 5-10847	157 Riverside Avenue/Five Men Were Killed Today	1972	$20
❏ 5-10847 [DJ]	157 Riverside Avenue (stereo/mono)	1972	$8
❏ 34-04713	Can't Fight This Feeling/Break His Spell	1984	$3
❏ 34-04713 [PS]	Can't Fight This Feeling/Break His Spell	1984	$6
❏ 19-02127	Don't Let Him Go/I Wish You Were There	1981	$4
❏ 19-02127 [PS]	Don't Let Him Go/I Wish You Were There	1981	$5
❏ 9-50764	Easy Money/I Need You Tonight	1979	$6
❏ 34-07901 [DJ]	Here with Me (4:29)/(4:53)	1988	$4
❏ 34-07901	Here with Me/Wherever You're Goin' (It's Alright)	1988	$3
❏ 34-07901 [PS]	Here with Me/Wherever You're Goin' (It's Alright)	1988	$3
❏ 34-08030	I Don't Want to Lose You/On the Road Again	1988	$3
❏ 34-04659	I Do'Wanna Know/Rock 'N Roll Star	1984	$3
❏ 34-04659 [PS]	I Do'Wanna Know/Rock 'N Roll Star	1984	$4
❏ 34-07255	In My Dreams/Over the Edge	1987	$3
❏ 34-07255 [PS]	In My Dreams/Over the Edge	1987	$3
❏ 15-03847	In Your Letter/Don't Let Him Go	1983	$3
— Reissue			
❏ 14-02457	In Your Letter/Shakin' It Loose	1981	$4
❏ 5-10892	Lay Me Down/Gypsy Woman's Passion	1972	$20
❏ 5-10892 [DJ]	Lay Me Down (stereo/mono)	1972	$8
❏ 5-10975	Little Queenie/Golden Country	1973	$20
❏ 5-10975 [DJ]	Little Queenie (stereo/mono)	1973	$8
❏ 34-05412	Live Every Moment/Gotta Feel More	1985	$3
❏ 34-04848	One Lonely Night/Wheels Are Turnin'	1985	$3
❏ 34-04848 [PS]	One Lonely Night/Wheels Are Turnin'	1985	$4
❏ 9-50790	Only the Strong Survive/Drop It (An Old Disguise)	1979	$6
❏ 5-11132	Open Up/Start a New Life	1974	$15
❏ 5-11132 [DJ]	Open Up (stereo/mono)	1974	$6
❏ 8-50120	Out of Control/Running Blind	1975	$8
❏ 5-10827	Sophisticated Lady/Prison Women	1972	$20
❏ 5-10827 [DJ]	Sophisticated Lady (stereo/mono)	1972	$6
❏ ENR-03264	Sweet Time/(B-side blank)	1982	$5
— One-sided budget release			
❏ 14-03175	Sweet Time/Stillness of the Night	1982	$4
❏ 14-03175 [PS]	Sweet Time/Stillness of the Night	1982	$5
❏ 19-01054	Take It on the Run/Someone Tonight	1981	$4
❏ 34-06656	That Ain't Love/Accidents Can Happen	1987	$3
❏ 34-06656 [PS]	That Ain't Love/Accidents Can Happen	1987	$3
❏ 8-50059	Throw the Chains Away/Sky Blues	1975	$8
❏ 9-50858	Time for Me to Fly/Lightning	1980	$5
❏ 8-50582	Time for Me to Fly/Runnin' Blind	1978	$6

REPARATA AND THE DELRONS
KAPP
Number	Title	Yr	NM
❏ 2010	San Juan/We're Gonna Hold the Night	1969	$6
❏ 989	(That's What Sends Men to) The Bowery/I've Got an Awful Lot of Losing to Do	1969	$6
❏ 2050	Waking in the Rain/Got Fear of Losing You	1969	$6

LAURIE
Number	Title	Yr	NM
❏ 3589	Octopus' Garden/Your Life Is Gone	1972	$5
— As "Reparata			

MALA
Number	Title	Yr	NM
❏ 589	Captain of Your Ship/Toom Toom Is a Little Boy	1968	$15
❏ 12026	Heaven Only Knows/Summer Laughter	1968	$6

Number	Title	Yr	NM
❑ 573	I Believe/It's Waiting There for You	1967	$6
❑ 12000	Saturday Night Didn't Happen/Panic	1968	$6

NAMI

❑ N-2024	Whenever a Teenager Cries/ Whenever a Teenager Cries	1974	$6

—Remake

POLYDOR

❑ 14271	Shoes/Song for All	1975	$4

—As "Reparata

RCA VICTOR

❑ 47-9123	Boys and Girls/That Kind of Trouble That I Love	1967	$10
❑ 47-9185	I Can Hear the Rain/Always Waitin'	1967	$10
❑ 47-8721	I Can Tell/Take a Look Around You	1965	$10
❑ 47-8820	I'm Nobody's Baby Now/The Loneliest Girl in Town	1966	$20
❑ 47-8921	Mama's Little Girl/He Don't Want You	1966	$10

WORLD ARTISTS

❑ 1057	He's the Greatest/A Summer Thought	1965	$15
❑ 1062	The Boy I Love/I Found My Place	1965	$15
❑ 1051	Tommy/Mama Don't Allow	1965	$15
❑ 1036	Whenever a Teenager Cries/ He's My Guy	1964	$15

REPLACEMENTS, THE
Featuring PAUL WESTERBERG.

SIRE

❑ 7-28151	Can't Hardly Wait/Cool Water	1987	$5
❑ 7-28151 [PS]	Can't Hardly Wait/Cool Water	1987	$12
❑ 7-22992	I'll Be You/Date to Church	1989	$4

TWIN/TONE

❑ TTR8120	I'm in Trouble/If Only You Were Lonely	1981	$50
❑ TTR8120 [PS]	I'm in Trouble/If Only You Were Lonely	1981	$50

RESIDENTS, THE

CRYPTIC

❑ RZ-SP-1SP 1	Earth Vs. the Flying Saucers	1986	$30

—Green vinyl, one-sided, bonus with collector's edition of book "The Cryptic Guide to the Residents

EVA-TONE

❑ 10371900-1	Diskomo (Live)	1988	$5

—Flexi-disc included with April 1988 issue of Reflex

RALPH

❑ RR 0577	Beyond the Valley of A Day in the Life/Flying	1977	$200
❑ RR 0577 [PS]	Beyond the Valley of A Day in the Life/Flying	1977	$200

—Also known as "The Residents Meet the Beatles and The Beatles Meet the Residents

❑ RR1272	Fire/Aircraft Damage	1972	$200

—Part of "Santa Dog" two-7" single set

❑ RR8721 [PD]	Hit the Road Jack/For Elsie (Excerpt)	1987	$20

—Picture disc

❑ RR8722	Hit the Road Jack/For Elsie (Excerpt)	1987	$3
❑ RR8722 [PS]	Hit the Road Jack/For Elsie (Excerpt)	1987	$3
❑ RZ8422	It's a Man's Man's Man's World/Safety Is a Cootie Wootie	1984	$20

—White vinyl; blue "iris" label and plastic sleeve with red lines; corrected labels

❑ RZ8422	It's a Man's Man's Man's World/Safety Is a Cootie Wootie	1984	$5

—Black vinyl

❑ RZ8422 [PS]	It's a Man's Man's Man's World/Safety Is a Cootie Wootie	1984	$5

—Sleeve with black vinyl edition

❑ RZ8422	It's a Man's Man's Man's World/Safety Is a Cootie Wootie	1984	$30

—White vinyl; blue "iris" label and plastic sleeve with red lines; labels reversed

❑ RR1272	Lightning/Explosion	1972	$200

—Part of "Santa Dog" two-7" single set

❑ RR1272 [PS]	Santa Dog: Fire/Aircraft Damage; Lightning/ Explosion	1972	$600

—Signed, intentionally misnumbered sleeve for above two records

❑ RR7812	Santa Dog '78/Fire	1978	$30
❑ RR7812 [PS]	Santa Dog '78/Fire	1978	$30
❑ RR 0776	Satisfaction/Loser Is Congruent to Weed	1976	$200

Number	Title	Yr	NM
❑ RR 0776 [PS]	Satisfaction/Loser Is Congruent to Weed	1976	$200
❑ RR7803	Satisfaction/Loser Is Congruent to Weed	1978	$4
❑ RR7803 [PS]	Satisfaction/Loser Is Congruent to Weed	1978	$4

7-Inch Extended Plays

❑ RR1177	*Laughing Song/Blue Rosebuds/Constantinople/ The Booker Tease/Sinister Exaggerator/Bach Is Dead/ Elvis and His Boss	1978	$8

—Red label

❑ RR 0377	*Monstrous Intro/Death in Barstow/Melon Collie Lassie/Flight of the Bumble Roach/Walter Westinghouse	1979	$125

—Also known as "Babyfingers"; first edition not issued with picture sleeve

❑ RR 0377	*Monstrous Intro/Death in Barstow/Melon Collie Lassie/Flight of the Bumble Roach/Walter Westinghouse	1979	$275

—Label hand-decorated with felt-tip pens

❑ RR 0377 [PS]	Babyfingers	1979	$250

—Actually a modified "Santa Dog '78" sleeve; this was sent with the felt-tip decorated copies to 10 people who had been waiting two years for a limited-edition copy of "The Third Reich 'n' Roll" LP

❑ WEIRD1	Babyfingers	1981	$25

—Pink vinyl on labels left over from fan club issue

❑ WEIRD1 [PS]	Babyfingers	1981	$25
❑ RR1177 [PS]	Duck Stab	1978	$5

—Matte cover

❑ RR1177 [PS]	Duck Stab	1978	$60

—Shiny cover

W.E.I.R.D.

❑ WEIRD1	Babyfingers	1981	$25

—Fan club reissue

❑ WEIRD1 [PS]	Babyfingers	1981	$25

RESTIVO, JOHNNY

20TH FOX

❑ 279	Doctor Love/The Magic Age Is Seventeen	1961	$20
❑ 279 [PS]	Doctor Love/The Magic Age Is Seventeen	1961	$40
❑ 260	Sweet Lovin'/Looka Here Now	1961	$20

CAMEO

❑ 416	I'm Just a Boy (Looking for a Girl)/Suzanne	1966	$30

EPIC

❑ 9537	My Reputation/You Can't Turn Back the Clock	1962	$20

RCA VICTOR

❑ 47-7601	Dear Someone/I Like Girls	1959	$20
❑ 47-7601 [PS]	Dear Someone/I Like Girls	1959	$40
❑ 47-7697	High School Play/But I Love You	1960	$20
❑ 47-7636	Our Wedding Day/Come Closer	1959	$30
❑ 47-7758	That's Good That's Bad/I Can't Take It	1960	$20
❑ 47-7559 [M]	The Shape I'm In/Ya Ya	1959	$30
❑ 61-7559 [S]	The Shape I'm In/Ya Ya	1959	$60

—Living Stereo" issue with large hole

❑ 47-7559 [PS]	The Shape I'm In/Ya Ya	1959	$60
❑ 47-7818	Two Crazy Kids/Give Me a Little Whistle (And I'll Be There)	1960	$20

RESTLESS HEART

RCA

❑ 8714-7-R	A Tender Lie/This Time	1988	$3
❑ PB-14190	(Back to the) Heartbreak Kid/She Danced Her Way (Into My Heart)	1985	$3
❑ PB-14190 [PS]	(Back to the) Heartbreak Kid/She Danced Her Way (Into My Heart)	1985	$4
❑ 8816-7-R	Big Dreams in a Small Town/ The Ride of Your Life	1989	$3
❑ 8386-7-R	Bluest Eyes in Texas/ Eldorado	1988	$3
❑ 9115-7-R	Fast Movin' Train/The Truth Hurts	1989	$3
❑ 5065-7-R	I'll Still Be Loving You/Victim of the Game	1986	$4
❑ PB-14086	I Want Everyone to Cry/ She's Coming Home	1985	$3
❑ PB-14086 [PS]	I Want Everyone to Cry/ She's Coming Home	1985	$4
❑ PB-13969	Let the Heartache Ride/Few and Far Between	1984	$3
❑ JK-13969 [DJ]	Let the Heartache Ride (same on both sides)	1984	$12

—Promo only on yellow vinyl

❑ 9034-7-R	Say What's in Your Heart/ Jenny Come Back	1989	$3
❑ PB-14376	That Rock That Won't Roll/You Can't Outrun the Night	1986	$3

Number	Title	Yr	NM
❑ PB-14292	Til I Loved You/Shakin' the Night Away	1986	$3
❑ 5280-7-R	Wheels/New York (Hold Her Tight)	1987	$3
❑ 5280-7-R [PS]	Wheels/New York (Hold Her Tight)	1987	$4
❑ 8382-7-R	Wheels/Why Does It Have to Be (Wrong or Right)	1988	$3

—Gold Standard Series

❑ 5132-7-R	Why Does It Have to Be (Wrong or Right)/ Hummingbird	1987	$3

REV-LONS, THE

GARPAX

❑ 44168	Boy Trouble/Give Me One More Chance	1962	$20

REPRISE

❑ 0251	After Last Night/It's Gonna Happen Someday	1964	$15
❑ 20200	I Can't Forget About You/ Love Can't Be a One-Way Deal	1963	$15

REVALONS, THE

PET

❑ 802	Dreams Are for Fools/This Is the Moment	1958	$120

RE'VELLS, THE

ROMAN PRESS

❑ 201	Let It Please Be You/Love Walked In	1962	$125

REVELONS, THE

ORK

❑ NYC3 [B]	The Way You Touch My Hand/96 Tears	1978	$20

REVELS, THE (1)

NORGOLDE

❑ 103	Dead Man's Stroll/Talking to My Heart	1959	$120
❑ 103	Midnight Stroll/Talking to My Heart	1959	$30

—Same A-side as above, but with revised title

❑ 104	Tweedlee Dee/Foo Man Choo	1959	$30

REVELS, THE (2)

CT

❑ 1	Church Key/Vesuvius	1960	$125

DOWNEY

❑ 123	Intoxica/Comanche	1964	$30

IMPACT

❑ 1	Church Key/Vesuvius	1960	$30

—Black vinyl

❑ 1	Church Key/Vesuvius	1960	$60

—Red vinyl

❑ 7	Comanche/Rampage	1961	$30

—Black vinyl

❑ 7	Comanche/Rampage	1961	$60

—Yellow vinyl

❑ 22	Conga Twist/Revellion	1962	$30

—Black vinyl

❑ 22	Conga Twist/Revellion	1962	$60

—Yellow vinyl; Both A-sides of Impact 22 are the same song

❑ 3	Intoxica/Tequila	1961	$30
❑ 13	Party Time/Soft Top	1961	$30
❑ 22	The Monkey Bird/Revellion	1962	$30

—Black vinyl

❑ 22	The Monkey Bird/Revellion	1962	$60

—Yellow vinyl

LYNN

❑ 1302	Six Pak/Good Grief	1960	$70

SWINGIN'

❑ 620	Six Pak/Good Grief	1960	$50

WESTCO

❑ 3/4	Party Time/Soft Top	1963	$60

—Red and yellow vinyl

REVELS, THE (3)

DIAMOND

❑ 143	Lots of Luck/Gonna Have Some Fun	1963	$20

REVELS, THE (4)

JAMIE

❑ 1318	True Love/Everybody Can Do the New Dog But Me	1966	$10

Number	Title	Yr	NM

REVELS, THE (U)
ANDIE
| ❏ 5077 | Please/Two Little Monkeys (In a Banana Tree) | 1960 | $30 |

KAPP
| ❏ 621 | Downtown/Dollar Sign | 1964 | $40 |

PALETTE
| ❏ 5074 | O How I Love You/I Met My Lost Love | 1961 | $30 |

REVENGERS, THE
MGM
| ❏ 13465 | Batman Theme/Back Side Blues | 1966 | $15 |

REVERE, PAUL, AND THE RAIDERS
20TH CENTURY
| ❏ 2283 | The British Are Coming/ Surrender at Appomattox | 1976 | $6 |

—B-side by Susie Allanson

COLUMBIA
| ❏ 45898 | All Over You/Seaboard Line Boogie | 1973 | $8 |

—As "Raiders

| ❏ 45453 | Birds of a Feather/The Turkey | 1971 | $6 |

—As "Raiders

| ❏ 44655 | Cinderella Sunshine/It's Happening | 1968 | $8 |
| ❏ 45535 | Country Wine/It's So Hard Getting Up Today | 1972 | $6 |

—As "The Raiders"; orange label with "COLUMBIA" background

| ❏ 45535 | Country Wine/It's So Hard Getting Up Today | 1972 | $5 |

—As "The Raiders"; gray label

❏ 44553	Don't Take It Too Hard/ Observation from Flight 285 (In 3/4 Time)	1968	$6
❏ 44553 [PS]	Don't Take It Too Hard/ Observation from Flight 285 (In 3/4 Time)	1968	$12
❏ 45150	Gone Movin' On/Interlude (To Be Forgotten)	1970	$6

—As "Raiders

❏ 10126	Gonna Have a Good Time/ Your Love (Is the Only Love)	1975	$10
❏ 43907	Good Thing/Undecided Man	1966	$10
❏ 43907 [PS]	Good Thing/Undecided Man	1966	$30
❏ 44094	Him or Me -- What's It Gonna Be?/Legend of Paul Revere	1967	$12
❏ 44094 [PS]	Him or Me -- What's It Gonna Be?/Legend of Paul Revere	1967	$20
❏ 43678 [DJ]	Hungry (same on both sides)	1966	$60

—Red vinyl promo

❏ 43678	Hungry/There She Goes	1966	$10
❏ 43678 [PS]	Hungry/There She Goes	1966	$30
❏ 44227	I Had a Dream/Upon Your Leaving	1967	$8
❏ 44227 [PS]	I Had a Dream/Upon Your Leaving	1967	$10
❏ 45332	Indian Reservation (The Lament of the Cherokee Reservation Indian)/Terry's Tune	1971	$8

—As "Raiders"; red label, black print

| ❏ 45332 | Indian Reservation (The Lament of the Cherokee Reservation Indian)/Terry's Tune | 1971 | $6 |

—As "Raiders"; orange label with "Columbia" background print

❏ 44854	Let Me/I Don't Know	1969	$6
❏ 43008	Louie Go Home/Have Love Will Travel	1964	$20
❏ 42814	Louie Louie/Night Train	1963	$50
❏ 45759	Love Music/Goodbye, No. 9	1973	$8

—As "Raiders

❏ 44744	Mr. Sun, Mr. Moon/Without You	1969	$6
❏ 44744 [PS]	Mr. Sun, Mr. Moon/Without You	1969	$10
❏ 43273	Ooh Poo Pah Doo/ Sometimes	1965	$20
❏ 43114	Over You/Swim	1964	$20
❏ 44335	Peace of Mind/Do Unto Others	1967	$8
❏ 44335 [PS]	Peace of Mind/Do Unto Others	1967	$10
❏ 45601	Powder Blue Mercedes Queen/Golden Girls Sometimes	1972	$8

—As "Raiders

| ❏ 45688 | Song Seller/A Simple Song | 1972 | $8 |

—As "Raiders

| ❏ CSM-466 [PS] | SS 396/Camaro | 1967 | $60 |

—B-side by The Cyrkle

| ❏ CSM-466 | SS 396/Camaro | 1967 | $30 |

—B-side by The Cyrkle

❏ CSP-262	SS 396/Corvair Baby	1965	$30
❏ 43375	Steppin' Out/Blue Fox	1965	$10
❏ 43375 [DJ]	Steppin' Out (same on both sides)	1965	$60

—Red vinyl promo

❏ 43810	The Great Airplane Strike/In My Community	1966	$10
❏ 43810 [PS]	The Great Airplane Strike/In My Community	1966	$20
❏ 43810 [DJ]	The Great Airplane Strike (same on both sides)	1966	$60

—Red vinyl promo

❏ 44444	Too Much Talk/Happening '68	1968	$8
❏ 44444 [PS]	Too Much Talk/Happening '68	1968	$10
❏ 44970	We Gotta All Get Together/ Frankfort Side Street	1969	$6

DRIVE
| ❏ 6248 | Ain't Nothing Wrong/You're Really Saying Something | 1976 | $5 |

GARDENA
❏ 124	All Night Long/Groovey	1962	$50
❏ 106	Beatnick Sticks/Orbit (The Spy)	1960	$40
❏ 127	Like, Bluegrass/Leatherneck	1962	$50
❏ 118	Like, Charleston/Midnite Ride	1961	$30
❏ 116	Like, Long Hair/Sharon	1961	$40
❏ 115	Paul Revere's Ride/ Unfinished Fifth	1960	$50
❏ 131	Shake It Up (Part 1)/Shake It Up (Part 2)	1962	$50
❏ 137	Tall Cool One/Road Runner	1963	$60

JERDEN
| ❏ 807 | So Fine/Blues Stay Away | 1966 | $30 |

SANDE
| ❏ 101 | Louie Louie/Night Train | 1963 | $250 |

7-Inch Extended Plays
COLUMBIA
| ❏ 7-9665 [PS] | Happening '68 | 1968 | $30 |
| ❏ 7-9665 | Happening '68// Communication Part 1/ Communication Part 2// Happens Every Day/Love Makes the World Go Round (Don't You Let It Stop Now)/ Free | 1968 | $30 |

—Jukebox issue, small hole, plays at 33 1/3 rpm

JERDEN
| ❏ LP JRLS-7004 [PS] | In the Beginning | 1966 | $60 |
| ❏ LP JRLS-7004 | Shake Rattle & Roll/Work with Me Annie/So Fine//Mojo Workout/Blues Stay Away/ Irresistible You | 1966 | $60 |

—Jukebox issue; small hole, plays at 33 1/3 rpm

REVERES, THE (1)
GLORY
| ❏ 272 | Leonore/Honeystroller | 1958 | $30 |

—B-side by the Honeystrollers

REVERES, THE (2)
JUBILEE
| ❏ 5463 | Beyond the Sea/The Show Must Go On | 1963 | $30 |

REVERES, THE (3)
VALIANT
| ❏ 6041 | Big "T"/Me and My Spider | 1964 | $60 |

REVLONS, THE
CAPITOL
| ❏ 4739 | Dry Your Eyes/She'll Come to Me | 1962 | $40 |

RAE COX
| ❏ 105 | This Restless Heart/I Promise Love | 1961 | $40 |

TOY
| ❏ 101 | What a Love This Is/Did I Make a Mistake | 1962 | $30 |

REX
Hard rock band with two records; later solo albums are as REX SMITH.
COLUMBIA
| ❏ AE71116 [DJ] | Trouble/Call Her Easy | 1976 | $6 |

—Small hole, white label

| ❏ AE71116 [PS] | Trouble/Call Her Easy | 1976 | $10 |

REYNOLDS, ALLEN
JMI
| ❏ 13 | Back to the Country/If She Just Helps Me (Get Over You) | 1973 | $6 |
| ❏ 44 | Mississippi Memory/Gone Girl | 1974 | $6 |

RCA VICTOR
| ❏ 47-8190 | Here Comes Raggedy Ann/ She Really Lied | 1963 | $12 |
| ❏ 47-7885 | Through the Eyes of Love/ What a Pretty Little Girl | 1961 | $15 |

TRIPLE I
| ❏ 496 | Wrong Road Again/Ready for the Times to Get Better | 1978 | $8 |

REYNOLDS, BURT
MCA
| ❏ 51004 | Let's Do Something Cheap and Superficial/Rockin' Lone Star Style | 1980 | $5 |

—B-side by the Bandit Band

| ❏ 51004 [PS] | Let's Do Something Cheap and Superficial/Rockin' Lone Star Style | 1980 | $6 |

MERCURY
| ❏ 73454 | I Like Having You Around/ She's Taken a Gentle Lover | 1974 | $6 |
| ❏ 73441 | Till I Get It Right/Room for a Boy Never Used | 1973 | $6 |

REYNOLDS, DEBBIE
ABC-PARAMOUNT
| ❏ 10709 | The Sweetheart Tree/From Where I Sit | 1965 | $8 |

BEVERLY HILLS
| ❏ 9375 | The Age of Not Believing/ (B-side unknown) | 1972 | $6 |

CORAL
❏ 9-62030	Hungry Eyes/Faces There Are Fairer	1958	$15
❏ 9-61851	Tammy/French Heels	1957	$20
❏ 9-61986	This Happy Feeling/Hillside in Scotland	1958	$15

DOT
❏ 15884	Aba Daba Honeymoon/Love Is a Thing	1958	$15
❏ 15985	Am I That Easy to Forget/ Ask Me to Go Steady	1959	$10
❏ 15985 [PS]	Am I That Easy to Forget/ Ask Me to Go Steady	1959	$20
❏ 16071	City Lights/Just for a Touch of Your Love	1960	$10
❏ 16071 [PS]	City Lights/Just for a Touch of Your Love	1960	$20
❏ 16465	Home in the Meadow/My Six Loves	1963	$8
❏ 16473	Is Goodbye That Easy to Say/The Apple, the Wind and the Storm	1963	$8
❏ 16156	It Looks Like Rain in Cherry Blossom Lane/Satisfied, Part 2	1960	$10
❏ 16199	Lonely People/Just a Little Girl	1961	$10
❏ 15937	Love Is a Simple Thing/I Can't Love You Anymore	1959	$10
❏ 16337	People Will Say We're in Love/(Answer to) You Better Move On	1961	$10
❏ 16119	Please/I'll Pretend	1960	$10
❏ 16446	Tammy/Am I That Easy to Forget	1963	$8

JANUS
| ❏ 111 | With a Little Love/ Conversations | 1970 | $6 |

MGM
| ❏ K30282 | Aba Daba Honeymoon/Row, Row, Row | 1951 | $30 |

—Credited to "Debbie Reynolds and Carleton Carpenter

❏ K12560	All Grown Up/Wall Flower	1957	$20
❏ K12086	Canoodlin' Rag/The Tender Trap	1955	$20
❏ K11939	Carolina in the Morning/ Never Mind the Noise in the Market	1955	$20
❏ K13492	Dominique/Brother John	1966	$8
❏ K13140	Home in the Meadow/Raise a Ruckus Tonight	1963	$8
❏ K12819	Love Is a Gamble/It Started with a Kiss	1959	$10
❏ K30493	Ooops!/Oogie Oogie Wa Wa	1951	$30
❏ K12761	The Mating Game/Right Away	1959	$10

PARAMOUNT
| ❏ 0220 | Mother Earth and Father Time/Charlotte's Web | 1973 | $10 |

REYNOLDS, JODY

DEMON

Number	Title	Yr	NM
1511	Closin' In/Elope with Me	1958	$30
1507	Endless Sleep/Tight Capris	1958	$40
1509	Fire of Love/Daisy Mae	1958	$30
1515	Golden Idol/Beulah Lee	1959	$30
1524	Stone Cold/(The Girl with) The Raven Hair	1960	$30
1519	The Storm/Please Remember	1959	$30
1523	Whipping Post/I Wanna Be with You Tonight	1960	$30

INDIGO

Number	Title	Yr	NM
127	Tarantula/Thunder	1961	$60

PULSAR

Number	Title	Yr	NM
2419	Endless Sleep/My Baby's Eyes	1969	$6

SMASH

Number	Title	Yr	NM
1810	Don't Jmp/Stormy	1963	$15

TITAN

Number	Title	Yr	NM
1734	Devil Girl/A Tear for Hesse	1963	$20

RHEIMS, ROBERT

RHEIMS

Number	Title	Yr	NM
101 [PS]	Silent Night/O Come All Ye Faithful	1959	$20

— Sleeve calls the B-side "Adeste Fidelis"

| 101 | Silent Night/O Come All Ye Faithful | 1959 | $10 |

RHINO 39

DANGERHOUSE

Number	Title	Yr	NM
RH39	Prolixin Stomp/Xerox/No Compromise	1979	$30
RH39 [PS]	Prolixin Stomp/Xerox/No Compromise	1979	$30

RHINOCEROS

ELEKTRA

Number	Title	Yr	NM
45647	Apricot Brandy/When You Say You're Sorry	1969	$8
45677	Back Door/In a Little Room	1970	$6
45694	Better Times/It's a Groovy World	1970	$6
45659	I Need Love/Velvuekus	1969	$6
45691	Let's Party/Old Age	1970	$6

RHODES, EMITT

A&M

Number	Title	Yr	NM
1254	Till the Day After/You're a Very Lovely Woman	1971	$6

— As "Emitt Rhodes with the Merry-Go-Round"

ABC DUNHILL

Number	Title	Yr	NM
4280	A Lullaby/With My Face on the Floor	1971	$5
4267	Fresh as a Daisy/You Take the Dark Out of the Night	1970	$6
4274	Live Till You Die/Promises I've Made	1971	$5
4303	Take You Far Away/Golden Child of God	1972	$5
4315	Tame the Lion/Golden Child of God	1972	$5
4315	Tame the Lion/Golden Child of God	1972	$20

— With insert

RHODES, SLIM

SUN

Number	Title	Yr	NM
225	Are You Ashamed of Me/The House of Sin	1955	$300
238	Bad Girl/Gonna Romp and Stomp	1956	$125
216	Don't Believe/Uncertain Blues	1955	$125
256	Do What I Do/Take and Give	1956	$60

RHODES, TODD

KING

Number	Title	Yr	NM
4755	Chicken Strut/Echoes	1954	$40
4469	Gin, Gin, Gin/I Shouldn't Cry But I Do	1951	$125
4486	Good Man/Evening Breeze	1951	$70
4583	Hog Maw and Cabbage Slaw/Must I Cry Again	1952	$60

— B-side by La Vern Baker

4666	Let Down Blues/Beet Patch	1953	$50
4566	Pig Latin Blues/Blue Autumn	1952	$60
4736	Silver Sunset/Specks	1954	$40
4556	Snuff Dipper/Trying	1952	$60

— B-side by La Vern Baker

| 4601 | Thunderbolt Boogie/Lost Child | 1953 | $60 |

— B-side by La Vern Baker

RHYTHM ACES, THE (1)

VEE JAY

Number	Title	Yr	NM
124	I Wonder Why/Get Lost	1954	$2000

—Red vinyl

| 124 | I Wonder Why/Get Lost | 1954 | $200 |

—Black vinyl

| 160 | That's My Sugar/Flippety Flop | 1955 | $120 |
| 138 | Whisper to Me/Olly, Olly, Oxsen Free | 1955 | $2000 |

—Red vinyl

| 138 | Whisper to Me/Olly, Olly, Oxsen Free | 1955 | $200 |

—Black vinyl

RHYTHM ACES, THE (2)

MARK-X

Number	Title	Yr	NM
8004	Boppin' Sloppin' Baby/Crazy Jealousy	1960	$40

RHYTHM ACES, THE (3)

ROULETTE

Number	Title	Yr	NM
4268	Mohawk Rock/It'll Do	1960	$20

SIOUX

Number	Title	Yr	NM
82260	Allan's Rock/Go Get It	1960	$40

UNIVERSAL ARTISTS

Number	Title	Yr	NM
3160	Mohawk Rock/It'll Do	1960	$50

RHYTHM CADETS, THE

VESTA

Number	Title	Yr	NM
501/2	Dearest Doryce/Rocking Jimmy	1957	$800

RHYTHM HERITAGE

ABC

Number	Title	Yr	NM
12177	Baretta's Theme (Keep Your Eye on the Sparrow)/My Cherie Amour	1976	$4
12205	Disco-Fied/(It's Time to) Boogie Down	1976	$4
12243	Gonna Fly Now (Theme from "Rocky")/Last Night on Earth	1976	$4
12334 [DJ]	Holdin' Out for You Love (mono/stereo)	1978	$4

— May be promo only

12378	Language of Love/Sail Away with Me	1978	$4
12273	Theme from "Starsky and Hutch"/Disco Queen	1977	$4
12135	Theme from S.W.A.T./I Wouldn't Treat a Dog (The Way You Treated Me)	1975	$5

— Version 1: With short version of A-side

| 12135 | Theme from S.W.A.T./I Wouldn't Treat a Dog (The Way You Treated Me) | 1975 | $4 |

— Version 2: With long version of A-side; "RE-1" on label next to matrix number

| 12063 | Theme from "Young Frankenstein"/I Wouldn't Treat a Dog (The Way You Treated Me) | 1975 | $5 |

RHYTHM, JOHNNY

MGM

Number	Title	Yr	NM
13043	This Is It/Wouldn't It Be Nice	1961	$50

RHYTHM MASTERS, THE (1)

ACE

Number	Title	Yr	NM
610	The Devil and His Old Suitcase/Holding My Savior's Hand	1961	$30

RHYTHM MASTERS, THE (2)

FLIP

Number	Title	Yr	NM
314	Baby We Two/Patricia	1956	$300

RHYTHM ROCKERS (2)

SATIN

Number	Title	Yr	NM
921	Oh Boy/We Belong Together	1960	$70
921 [PS]	Oh Boy/We Belong Together	1960	$125

RHYTHM ROCKERS (3)

SUN

Number	Title	Yr	NM
248	Fiddle Bop/Juke Box, Help Me Find My Baby	1956	$125

RHYTHM ROCKERS (U)

FENTON

Number	Title	Yr	NM
944	Surf Around/Three Strikes	1962	$60

WIPE OUT

Number	Title	Yr	NM
1001	Foot Cruising/Get It On	1962	$50

RHYTHMMETTES, THE

BRUNSWICK

Number	Title	Yr	NM
55083	Elaine/Bow Legged Woman	1958	$15
55097	I'll Be With You in Apple Blossom Time/Page from the Future	1958	$15
55012	Mind Reader/Mister Love	1957	$20
55050	That's a-Plenty/Till My Baby Comes Home	1958	$15

CORAL

Number	Title	Yr	NM
62186	High School Lovers/Snow Queen	1960	$12

RCA VICTOR

Number	Title	Yr	NM
47-6539	Homin' Pigeon/Boom-Boom	1956	$20
47-6089	Only You/Him	1955	$30
47-6244	Show Me the Way/The Bridge of Love	1955	$20
47-6349	Take My Hand, Show Me the Way/I've Got to Know	1955	$20
47-6742	Winter Snow/Take a Look in the Mirror	1956	$20

RHYZE

20TH CENTURY

Number	Title	Yr	NM
2603	Tonight's Gonna Be My Night/What Can I Do About This Feelin'	1982	$10

SAM

Number	Title	Yr	NM
80-5016	Free/Singing and Dancing	1980	$8

RIA AND THE REASONS

AMY

Number	Title	Yr	NM
888	Memories Linger On/Sorry I Lied	1963	$30
888	Memories Linger On/Sorry I Lied	1963	$100

—Blue vinyl

RSVP

Number	Title	Yr	NM
1110	He's Not There/She Fell in Love	1965	$30

— As "Ria and the Revellons"

RIALTOS, THE

CB

Number	Title	Yr	NM
5009	Let Me In/It Hurts	1962	$300

RIBBONS, THE

MARSH

Number	Title	Yr	NM
203	After Last Night/This Is Our Melody	1963	$15
202	Ain't Gonna Kiss Ya/My Baby Said	1963	$20

PARKWAY

Number	Title	Yr	NM
912	Meoldie D'Amour/They Played a Sad Song	1964	$15

RIC-A-SHAYS, THE

LOLA

Number	Title	Yr	NM
02	Groovy/Turn On	1964	$30

RICARDOS, THE

STAR-X

Number	Title	Yr	NM
512	Mary's Little Lamb/I Mean Really	1958	$160

RICE, JIMMY

RED BIRD

Number	Title	Yr	NM
Oct-0022	The Grass Is Always Greener/Spanish Perfume	1965	$30

RICE, TONY

ACTION

Number	Title	Yr	NM
100	My Darling Y-O-U/I Thank You Baby	1961	$40

PRINCETON

Number	Title	Yr	NM
101	Summer's Love/Please Don't	1960	$70

RAE COX

Number	Title	Yr	NM
106	Little School Girl/Blue Bird of Happiness	1961	$30

Number	Title	Yr	NM

RICH, BUDDY

ARGO
❏ 5384	Makin' Whoopee/Lulu's Back in Town	1961	$8

CLEF
❏ 89094	Let's Fall in Love/Me and My Jaguar	1954	$15
❏ 89066	Sleepyhead/Bugle Call Rag	1953	$15

MCA
❏ 51116	Fantasy/Listen Here Goes Funky	1981	$4

PACIFIC JAZZ
❏ 88145	Mercy, Mercy, Mercy/Big Mama Cass	1968	$6
❏ 88140	The Beat Goes On/Mexicali Rose	1967	$5

RCA VICTOR
❏ PB-10712	Speak No Evil/Sophisticated Lady (She's a Different Lady)	1976	$4

RICH, CHARLIE

ELEKTRA
❏ 47047	A Man Just Doesn't Know What a Woman Goes Through/Marie	1980	$4
❏ 47104	Are We Dreamin' the Same Dream/Angelina	1981	$4
❏ 45553	I'll Wake You Up When I Get Home/Salty Dog Blues	1978	$4

EPIC
❏ 50142	All Over Me/You & I	1975	$4
❏ 50222	America the Beautiful (1976)/Down By the Riverside	1976	$4
❏ 10809	A Part of Your Life/A Sunday Kind of Woman	1971	$5
❏ 10745	A Woman Left Lonely/Have a Heart	1971	$5
❏ 50562	Beautiful Woman/Everybody Wrote That Song for Me	1978	$4
❏ 10950	Behind Closed Doors/A Sunday Kind of Woman	1973	$5
— Originals have yellow labels			
❏ 10950	Behind Closed Doors/A Sunday Kind of Woman	1973	$4
— Repressings have orange labels			
❏ 50328	Easy Look/My Lady	1976	$4
❏ 50869	Even a Fool Would Let Go/Pretty People	1980	$4
❏ 50103	Every Time You Touch Me (I Get High)/Pass On By	1975	$4
❏ 20006	I Love My Friend/Why Oh Why	1974	$4
❏ 10867	I Take It On Home/Peace on You	1972	$5
❏ 10492	Life's Little Ups and Downs/It Takes Time	1969	$6
❏ 50064	My Elusive Dreams/Whatever Happened	1975	$4
❏ 50616	On My Knees/Mellow Melody	1978	$4
❏ 10287	Set Me Free/I'll Just Go Away	1968	$6
❏ 50182	Since I Fell for You/She	1975	$4
❏ 50701	Spanish Eyes/I Do My Swingin' at Home	1979	$4
❏ 11040	The Most Beautiful Girl/I Feel Like Going Home	1973	$4
❏ 03165	Try a Little Tenderness/As Time Goes By	1982	$4

GROOVE
❏ 58-0025	Big Boss Man/Let Me Go My Merry Way	1963	$20
❏ 58-0032	Lady Love/Why, Oh Why	1964	$20
❏ 58-0020	The Grass Is Always Greener/She Loved Everybody But Me	1963	$20
❏ 58-0020 [PS]	The Grass Is Always Greener/She Loved Everybody But Me	1963	$40
❏ 58-0035	The Ways of a Woman in Love/My Mountain Dew	1964	$20

HI
❏ 2134	Hurry Up Freight Train/Only Me	1967	$10
❏ 2116	Love Is After Me/Pass On By	1966	$10
❏ 2123	My Heart Would Know/Nobody's Lonesome for Me	1967	$10

MERCURY
❏ 73498	A Field of Yellow Daisies/Party Girl	1974	$5
❏ 73466	I Washed My Hands in Muddy Water/No Home	1974	$5
❏ 73646	Something Just Came Over Me/Best Years	1974	$5

PHILLIPS INT'L.
❏ 3576	Easy Money/Midnight Blues	1962	$30
❏ 3552	Lonely Weekends/Everything I Do Is Wrong	1960	$30
❏ 3562	On My Knees/Stay	1960	$30
❏ 3560	School Days/Gonna Be Waiting	1960	$30
❏ 3582	Sittin' and Thinkin'/Finally Found Out	1962	$30

❏ 3584	There's Another Place I Can't Go/I Need Your Love	1963	$30
❏ 3532	Whirlwind/Philadelphia Baby	1959	$30
❏ 3566	Who Will the Next Fool Be/Caught in the Middle	1961	$30

RCA
❏ PB-10859	My Mountain Dew/Nice 'N Easy	1976	$4

RCA VICTOR
❏ APBO-0260	I Don't See Me in Your Eyes Anymore/No Room to Dance	1974	$4
❏ PB-10256	It's All Over Now/Big Jack	1975	$4
❏ 47-8468	It's All Over Now/Too Many Teardrops	1964	$20
❏ PB-10062	She Called Me Baby/$10 and a Clean White Shirt	1974	$4
❏ GB-10512	She Called Me Baby/$10 and a Clean White Shirt	1975	$3
— Gold Standard Series			
❏ 47-8536	There Won't Be Anymore/Gentleman Jim	1965	$30
❏ APBO-0195	There Won't Be Anymore/It's All Over Now	1973	$5
❏ GB-10159	There Won't Be Anymore/Tomorrow Night	1975	$3
— Gold Standard Series			
❏ 74-0983	Tomorrow Night/The Ways of a Woman in Love	1973	$4

SMASH
❏ 2012	Dance of Love/I Can't Go On	1965	$20
❏ 2022	Hawg Jaw/Something Just Came Over Me	1966	$20
❏ 1993	Mohair Sam/I Washed My Hands in Muddy Water	1965	$30
❏ 2060	That's the Way/When My Baby Comes Home	1966	$20

SUN
❏ 1151	The Breakup/Be-Bop-a-Lula	1980	$4
—B-side by Jerry Lee Lewis; both sides are duets with Orion			
❏ 1110	Who Will the Next Fool Be/Stay	1970	$5

UNITED ARTISTS
❏ 1340	I'd Build a Bridge/All You Ever Have to Do Is Touch Me	1980	$4
❏ XW1280	I Lost My Head/She Knows Just How to Touch Me	1979	$4
❏ XW1223	I Still Believe in Love/Wishful Thinking	1978	$4
❏ XW1307	Life Goes On/Standing Tall	1979	$4
❏ XW1193	Puttin' In Overtime at Home/Ghost of Another Man	1978	$4
❏ XW1269	The Fool Strikes Again/I Loved You All the Way	1978	$4

7-Inch Extended Plays

EPIC
❏ AE71065 [DJ]	Big Boss Man/Nice 'n' Easy// Life Has Its Little Ups and Downs/I Take It on Home	1972	$6
— Small hole, plays at 33 1/3 rpm; came as a bonus with some copies of KE 31933, "The Best of Charlie Rich			
❏ AE71065 [PS]	The Best of Charlie Rich Bonus Record	1972	$6
— Special sleeve for above disc; came as a bonus with some copies of KE 31933, "The Best of Charlie Rich			

RICH, DAVE

DECCA
❏ 31573	It's Not for Me to Understand/When They Ring Those Golden Bells	1963	$15
❏ 31513	The Great Speckled Bird/I Want to Know You Lord	1963	$15

RCA VICTOR
❏ 47-7045	Chicken House/I've Learned	1957	$40
❏ 47-7247	City Lights/Burn On Love Fire	1958	$40
❏ 47-6327	I Forgot/I Think I'm Gonna Die	1955	$40
❏ 47-6435	I'm Glad/Darling, I'm Lonesome	1956	$40
❏ 47-6687	I'm Sorry, Goodbye/I Love 'Em All	1956	$40
❏ 47-6753	Lonely Street/Didn't Work Out, Did It	1956	$40
❏ 47-7141	School Blues/I've Thought It Over	1958	$40
❏ 47-6824	Tuggin' on My Heart Strings/Our Last Night Together	1957	$40
❏ 47-7656	Where Else Would I Want to Be/Brand New Feeling	1959	$30

REPUBLIC
❏ 390	Because You're Gone/Cheatin', Stealin', Steel Guitar Man	1977	$5
❏ 116	The Sea of Galilee/King Jesus	1978	$6

RICH KIDS, THE

STEED
❏ 702	Plastic Flowers/Got to Find a Woman	1967	$10

RICHARD AND THE YOUNG LIONS

PHILIPS
❏ 40381	Open Up Your Door/Once Upon Your Smile	1966	$30
❏ 40381 [PS]	Open Up Your Door/Once Upon Your Smile	1966	$30
❏ 40438	To Have and to Hold/You Can Make It	1967	$50

RICHARD, CLIFF

ABC-PARAMOUNT
❏ 10175	Catch Me, I'm Falling/"D" in Love	1961	$30
❏ 10109	Fall in Love with You/Choppin' 'N' Changin'	1960	$30
❏ 10042	Living Doll/Apron Strings	1959	$30
❏ 10136	Please Don't Tease/Where Is My Heart	1960	$30
❏ 10195	Theme for a Dream/Mumblin' Mosie	1961	$50
❏ 10066	Travellin' Light/Dynamite	1959	$30

CAPITOL
❏ F4154	Livin' Lovin' Doll/Steady with You	1959	$50
❏ F4096	Move It/High Class Baby	1958	$50

COLUMBIA
❏ DB8293	All My Love/Sweet Little Jesus Boy	1967	$10
—U.K. import			

DOT
❏ 16399	Wonderful to Be Young/Got a Funny Feeling	1962	$30

EMI
❏ EMP78 [PS]	Mistletoe and Wine/Marmaduke	1988	$5
—Record and sleeve are U.K. imports; with poster/calendar sleeve			
❏ EMP78	Mistletoe and Wine/Marmaduke	1988	$5
❏ EMS78 [PS]	Mistletoe and Wine/Marmaduke/True Love Ways	1988	$4
—Record and sleeve are U.K. imports			
❏ EMS78	Mistletoe and Wine/Marmaduke/True Love Ways	1988	$4

EMI AMERICA
❏ 8068	A Little in Love/Everyman	1980	$4
❏ 8035	Carrie/Language of Love	1980	$4
❏ 8103	Daddy's Home/Summer Rain	1982	$4
❏ 8193	Donna/Ocean Deep	1984	$4
❏ 8057	Dreaming/Dynamite	1980	$5
— Green label			
❏ 8057	Dreaming/Dynamite	1980	$4
— Gray label			
❏ 8076	Give a Little Bit More/Keep Lookin'	1981	$4
❏ 8076 [PS]	Give a Little Bit More/Keep Lookin'	1981	$5
❏ 8149	Little Town/Be in My Heart	1982	$4
❏ 8135	The Only Way Out/Be in My Heart	1982	$4
❏ 8025	We Don't Talk Anymore/Count Me Out	1979	$4
❏ 8095	Wired for Sound/Hold On	1981	$4

EPIC
❏ 9757	Again/The Minute You're Gone	1965	$20
❏ 9691	Bachelor Boy/True, True Lovin'	1964	$30
❏ 10018	Blue Turns to Grey/I'll Walk Alone	1966	$20
❏ 9810	I Could Easily Fall (In Love with You)/On My Word	1965	$20
❏ 9737	I Don't Wanna Love You/Look in My Eyes Maria	1964	$20
❏ 9670	I'm the Lonely One/I Only Have Eyes for You	1964	$30
❏ 9670 [PS]	I'm the Lonely One/I Only Have Eyes for You	1964	$30
❏ 9633	It's All in the Game/I'm Looking Out the Window	1963	$30
❏ 10178	It's All Over/Heartbeat	1967	$20
❏ 9597	Lucky Lips/Next Time	1963	$30
❏ 9597 [PS]	Lucky Lips/Next Time	1963	$30
❏ 9839	The Twelfth of Never/Paradise Lost	1965	$20
❏ 10101	Time Drags By/The La La La Song	1966	$20
❏ 9866	Wind Me Up (and Let Me Go)/Eye of a Needle	1965	$20

MONUMENT
❏ 1211	Goodbye Sam, Hello Samantha/You Never Can Tell	1970	$6
❏ 1229	I Ain't Got Time Anymore/Morning Comes Too Soon	1970	$6

Number	Title	Yr	NM

POLYDOR
❏ 885336-7	All I Ask of You/Phantom of the Opera Overture, Act 2	1987	$3

— With Sarah Brightman

| ❏ 885336-7 [PS] | All I Ask of You/Phantom of the Opera Overture, Act 2 | 1987 | $3 |

ROCKET
❏ 40574	Devil Woman/Love On (Shine On)	1976	$5
❏ 40724	Don't Turn the Light Out/Nothing Left for Me to Say	1977	$4
❏ YB-11463	Green Light/Needing a Friend	1979	$4
❏ 40531	Miss You Nights/Love Enough	1976	$4

SIRE
| ❏ 703 | Living in Harmony/Jesus | 1973 | $5 |
| ❏ 707 | Power to All Our Friends/Come Back Billie Joe | 1973 | $5 |

STRIPED HORSE
❏ 7008	My Pretty One/Love Ya	1988	$3
❏ 7008 [PS]	My Pretty One/Love Ya	1988	$3
❏ 7011	Some People/Love Ya	1988	$3
❏ 7011 [PS]	Some People/Love Ya	1988	$3

UNI
❏ 55061	All My Love/Our Story Book	1968	$10
❏ 55069	Congratulations/High 'N' Dry	1968	$10
❏ 55145	The Day I Met Marie/Sweet Little Jesus Boy	1969	$15

WARNER BROS.
| ❏ 7344 | Throw Down a Line/Reflections | 1969 | $8 |

—A-side by Cliff and Hank (Marvin)

RICHARDS, BARRY
EPIC
| ❏ 9564 | Baby Sittin' Santa/Kissin' Doll | 1962 | $40 |

RICHARDS, DICK
COLUMBIA
❏ 4-40957	Blue Jean Baby/We've Got a Right to Love	1957	$50
❏ 4-41035	I Love You So Much It Hurts/Not Until I Pray for You	1957	$30
❏ 4-40786	Time Alone/Fourteen Karat Gold	1957	$50

RICHARDS, KATY
HIT
| ❏ 34 | All Alone Am I/He Thinks I Still Care | 1962 | $8 |

—B-side by Connie Landers

| ❏ 66 | Losing You/Still | 1963 | $10 |

—B-side by Bobby Russell

RICHARDS, KEITH
VIRGIN
| ❏ 99240 | Make No Mistake/It Means a Lot | 1988 | $4 |
| ❏ 99297 | Take It So Hard/I Could Have Stood You Up | 1988 | $4 |

RICHARDS, SYLVIA
HIT
| ❏ 53 | Blame It on the Bossa Nova/Let's Limbo Some More | 1963 | $8 |

—B-side by Leroy Jones

RICHARDS, TOM
RAMA
| ❏ 26 | Christmas Dreaming/When Santa Comes This Year | 1953 | $50 |

RICHARDSON, RUDI
SUN
| ❏ 271 | Fools Hall of Fame/Why Should I Cry | 1957 | $40 |

RICHIE AND THE ROYALS
GOLDEN CREST
| ❏ 573 | Be My Girl/We're Strollin' | 1962 | $60 |

RELLO
| ❏ 1 | And When I'm Near You/Goody Goody | 1961 | $100 |
| ❏ 3 | Be My Girl/We're Strollin' | 1962 | $200 |

RICHIE, LIONEL
MOTOWN
| ❏ 1698 | All Night Long (All Night)/Wandering Stranger | 1983 | $4 |
| ❏ 1873 | Ballerina Girl/Deep River Woman | 1986 | $3 |

—B-side with Alabama

❏ 1873 [PS]	Ballerina Girl/Deep River Woman	1986	$4
❏ 1843	Dancing on the Ceiling/Love Will Find a Way	1986	$3
❏ 1843 [PS]	Dancing on the Ceiling/Love Will Find a Way	1986	$3
❏ 1519	Endless Love/(Instrumental)	1981	$4

— With Diana Ross

❏ 1722	Hello/You Mean More to Me	1984	$4
❏ 1866	Love Will Conquer All/The Only One	1986	$3
❏ 1866 [PS]	Love Will Conquer All/The Only One	1986	$3
❏ 1677	My Love/Round and Round	1983	$4
❏ 1677 [PS]	My Love/Round and Round	1983	$5
❏ 1762	Penny Lover/Tell Me	1984	$4
❏ 1762 [PS]	Penny Lover/Tell Me	1984	$5
❏ 1819	Say You, Say Me/Can't Slow Down	1985	$3
❏ 1819 [PS]	Say You, Say Me/Can't Slow Down	1985	$4

— Two different sleeves were released, each of equal value

❏ 1883	Se La/Serves You Right	1987	$3
❏ 1883 [PS]	Se La/Serves You Right	1987	$3
❏ 1746	Stuck on You/Round and Round	1984	$4
❏ 1746 [PS]	Stuck on You/Round and Round	1984	$4
❏ 1644	Truly/Just Put Some Love in Your Heart	1982	$4

MOTOWN YESTERYEAR
| ❏ Y-678F | All Night Long (All Night)/Running with the Night | 1984 | $3 |

—Reissue

| ❏ Y-691F | Dancing on the Ceiling/Love Will Conquer All | 1985 | $3 |

—Reissue

| ❏ Y-677F | Hello/Stuck on You | 1984 | $3 |

—Reissue

| ❏ Y-679F | My Love/You Mean More to Me | 1984 | $3 |

—Reissue

| ❏ Y-686F | Penny Lover/Love Will Find a Way | 1985 | $3 |

—Reissue

| ❏ Y-694F | Say You, Say Me/Ballerina Girl | 1987 | $3 |

—Reissue

| ❏ Y-674F | Truly/You Are | 1984 | $3 |

—Reissue

RICHMOND, RUSTY
SARG
| ❏ 125 | Santa's Here To Stay/You Ought To Know | 1956 | $20 |

RICHY, PAUL
SUN
| ❏ 338 | The Legend of the Big Steeple/Broken Hearted Willie | 1960 | $30 |

RICK AND DONNA
A&M
| ❏ 710 | I'm a Losing Guy/Wedding Bells Will Ring | 1963 | $15 |

TOWER
| ❏ 112 | A.B.C./What Good Is Love | 1965 | $12 |

RICK AND THE KEENS
AUSTIN
| ❏ 303 | Peanuts/I'll Be Home | 1961 | $60 |

LE CAM
| ❏ 133 | Darla/Someone New | 1964 | $40 |
| ❏ 721 | Peanuts/I'll Be Home | 1961 | $60 |

SMASH
| ❏ 1722 | Maybe/Popcorn | 1961 | $30 |
| ❏ 1705 | Peanuts/I'll Be Home | 1961 | $30 |

TOLLIE
| ❏ 9016 | Darla/Someone New | 1964 | $30 |

RICK AND THE MASTERS
CAMEO
| ❏ 226 | Flame of Love/Here Come Nancy | 1962 | $60 |
| ❏ 247 | Let It Please Be You/I Don't Want Your Love | 1963 | $60 |

HARAL
| ❏ 776 | Bewitched, Bothered and Bewildered/A Kissin' Friend | 1962 | $70 |

TABA
| ❏ 101 | Flame of Love/Here Come Nancy | 1962 | $200 |

RICK AND THE RANDELLS
ABC-PARAMOUNT
| ❏ 10055 | Let It Be You/Honey Doll | 1959 | $50 |

RICK AND THE RAVENS
AURA
| ❏ 4506 | Henrietta/Just for Me | 1965 | $70 |
| ❏ 4511 | Soul Train/Geraldine | 1965 | $60 |

RICK, ROBIN & HIM
V.I.P.
| ❏ 25035 | Three Choruses of Despair/Cause You Know Me | 1965 | $30 |

RICKIE AND THE HALLMARKS
AMY
| ❏ 877 | Wherever You Are/Joanie Don't You Cry | 1963 | $50 |

RICKS, JIMMY
Also see THE RAVENS. (45)
ARNOLD
| ❏ 1011 | Canadian Sunset/Change of Heart | 1961 | $20 |

ATCO
| ❏ 6220 | Daddy Rolling Stone/Homesick | 1962 | $30 |

ATLANTIC
| ❏ 2246 | Trouble in Mind/Romance in the Dark | 1964 | $20 |

BATON
| ❏ 236 | I'm a Fool to Want You/Bad Man of Missouri | 1957 | $50 |

DECCA
| ❏ 30443 | What Have I Done/Lazy Mule | 1957 | $30 |

FELSTED
| ❏ 8582 | Leaning On Your Love/Here Come the Tears Again | 1959 | $30 |
| ❏ 8560 | Secret Love/If It Didn't Hurt So Much | 1959 | $30 |

FURY
| ❏ 1070 | I Wonder/Let Me Down Easy | 1962 | $30 |

JOSIE
| ❏ 796 | She's Fine, She's Mine/The Unbeliever | 1956 | $50 |

JUBILEE
❏ 5579	Don't Go to Strangers/Lonely Man	1967	$15
❏ 5608	It's All in the Game/Baby Don't Leave Me	1967	$15
❏ 5559	Lonely Man/If You Ever Loved Someone	1967	$15
❏ 5619	Snap Your Fingers/Wigglin' and Gigglin'	1968	$15
❏ 5561	Wigglin' and Gigglin'/Long, Long Arm of Love	1967	$15

MAINSTREAM
| ❏ 625 | Girl of My Dreams/Glow Worm | 1965 | $20 |

MERCURY
| ❏ 8296 | Love Is the Thing/Too Soon | 1952 | $100 |

PARIS
| ❏ 504 | Do You Promise/The Sugar Man Song | 1957 | $40 |

SIGNATURE
❏ 12013	At Sunrise/Goodnight My Love	1959	$30
❏ 12040	I Needed Your Love/Timber	1960	$30
❏ 12051	The Christmas Song/Love Is the Thing	1960	$30

RICKY AND THE VACELS
EXPRESS
| ❏ 711 | Lorraine/Bubble Gum | 1962 | $40 |

FARGO
| ❏ 1050 | His Girl/Don't Want Your Love No More | 1963 | $40 |
| ❏ 1050 | His Girl/Don't Want Your Love No More | 1963 | $100 |

— Blue vinyl

Number	Title	Yr	NM

RICO AND THE RAVENS

AUTUMN

❏ 6	Don't You Know/In My Heart	1965	$20

RALLY

❏ 1601	Don't You Know/In My Heart	1965	$50

RIDDLE, ALLAN

PLAID

❏ 1001	The Moon Is Crying/(B-side unknown)	1960	$30

RIDDLE, NELSON

20TH CENTURY FOX

❏ 6626	Batman Theme/Nelson's Riddler	1966	$20

CAPITOL

❏ F3631	Accordion Willy/Holiday in Naples	1957	$15
❏ F3225	All Er Nothin'/Pore Jud Is Daid	1955	$20
❏ F4075	Birds of Paradise/Uma Casa Portugese	1958	$15
❏ F3794	Blame It on Paree/In a Small Forgotten Town	1957	$15
❏ F2744	Brother John/Deep Blue Sea	1954	$20
❏ F4175	De Guello/Blue Safari	1959	$15
❏ F3877	I'm Getting Sentimental Over You/The Girl Most Likely	1958	$15
❏ F2846	In the Chapel in the Moonlight/Shadow Waltz	1954	$20
❏ F3287	Lisbon Antigua/Robin Hood	1955	$20
❏ 4521	Little Old New York/My Gentle Young Johnny	1961	$10
❏ F3980	Love Theme from St. Louis Blues/The Seventh Voyage of Sinbad	1958	$15
❏ F4244	Markham Theme/Ting-a-Lay-O	1959	$15
❏ F2609	Martin Kane Theme/Make Believe That You're in Love	1953	$20
❏ 4691	O Mein Liebchen/Come a-Wandering with Me	1962	$10
❏ F3374	Port-au-Prince/Midnight Blues	1956	$15
❏ F4005	Song from "Kings Go Forth"/Siesta in Sevilla	1958	$15
❏ F2893	Song from "The Caine Mutiny" (I Can't Believe That You're in Love)/Vilia	1954	$20
❏ F3758	Tangi Tahiti/Rue Madeleine	1957	$15
❏ 4896	The Ballad of Jed Clampett/Stoney Burke Theme	1962	$12
❏ F3559	The Farmer's Tango/Could You	1956	$15
❏ 4448	The Green Leaves of Summer/De Guelle	1960	$10
❏ F3717	Theme from "The New Girl in Town"/Matinee Theatre	1957	$15
❏ F3472	Theme from "The Proud Ones"/The Love of Genevieve	1956	$15
❏ 4378	Theme -- The Untouchables/The Untouchables Strike Back	1960	$20
❏ 4378 [PS]	Theme -- The Untouchables/The Untouchables Strike Back	1960	$30
❏ F3206	Three Little Stars/Take It or Leave It	1955	$20

EPIC

❏ 5-10175 [PS]	El Dorado (Vocal)/(Instrumental)	1967	$12

REPRISE

❏ 20169	Come Blow Your Horn/Connie's Theme	1963	$8
❏ 0476	Don't Drink the Water/Freddie's New Slacks	1966	$8
❏ 0319	Fiddler on the Roof/Gabriel	1965	$8
❏ 0270	Hello, Dolly!/My True Carrie Love	1964	$8
❏ 20230	It's a Mad, Mad, Mad, Mad World/My Special Dream	1963	$8
❏ 0412	Marriage on the Rocks/Theme from "Skyscraper"	1965	$8
❏ 0386	Me and My Shadow/Melancholie	1965	$8
❏ 0467	Time for Singing/Freddie's New Slacks	1966	$8

VERVE

❏ 10194	March of the Swiss Soldiers/Walking the Dog	1960	$15

7-Inch Extended Plays

CAPITOL

❏ EAP 1-814	(contents unknown)	1957	$15
❏ EAP 2-814	(contents unknown)	1957	$15
❏ EAP 3-814	(contents unknown)	1957	$15
❏ EAP 1-814 [PS]	Hey, Let Yourself Go, Part 1	1957	$15
❏ EAP 2-814 [PS]	Hey, Let Yourself Go, Part 2	1957	$15
❏ EAP 3-814 [PS]	Hey, Let Yourself Go, Part 3	1957	$15

RIDERS IN THE SKY

ROUNDER

❏ 4537	Blue Bonnet Lady/Blue Montana Skies	1980	$8
❏ 4530	Cowboy Song/Here Comes the Santa Fe	1980	$8
❏ 4551	Prairie Serenade/Old El Paso	1982	$8
❏ 4543	Soon As the Roundup's Through/Back in the Saddle Again	1981	$8

RIDGLEY, TOMMY

ATLANTIC

❏ 1009	Ooh Lawdy My Baby/I'm Gonna Cross That River	1953	$70

DECCA

❏ 48226	Anything But Love/Once in a Lifetime	1951	$100

HERALD

❏ 508	Baby Do Liddle/Just a Memory	1957	$30
❏ 513	Come back Baby/Woncha Gone	1958	$30
❏ 537	I'll Be True/Girl Across the Street	1959	$30
❏ 526	Mairzy Doats and Dozy Doats/I've Heard That Story Before	1958	$30
❏ 540	Tina/How I Feel	1959	$30
❏ 501	When I Meet My Girl/Whatcha Gonna Do	1957	$30

IMPERIAL

❏ 5223	Good Times/A Day Is Coming	1953	$200
❏ 5198	I Live My Life/Lavinia	1952	$200
❏ 5203	Looped/Junie Mae	1952	$200
❏ 5214	Monkey Man/Nobody Cares	1953	$200

RIC

❏ 978	Double Eye Whammy/Should I Ever Love Again	1961	$20
❏ 973	Do You Remember/Please Hurry Home	1960	$20
❏ 993	Heavenly/I Love You Yes I Do	1963	$15
❏ 994	Honest I Do/I've Heard That Story Before	1963	$15
❏ 968	Is It True/Let's Try and Talk It Over	1959	$20
❏ 990	My Ordinary Girl/She's Got What It Takes	1962	$15
❏ 984	The Girl from Kooka Monga/In the Same Old Way	1961	$20
❏ 982	Three Times/The Only Girl for Me	1961	$20

RONN

❏ 36	It's the Same Old Way/I'm Not the Same Person	1969	$10

WHITE CLIFFS

❏ 260	Hey Little Chick/Did You Tell Him	1967	$12

RIFFS, THE

JAMIE

❏ 1296	Tell Her/I Been Thinkin'	1965	$15

OLD TOWN

❏ 1179	Tell Tale Friends/Why Are the Nights So Cold	1965	$60

SUNNY

❏ 22	Little Girl/Why Are the Nights So Cold	1964	$200

RIG

CAPITOL

❏ 2952	Last Time Around/Have a Cigar	1970	$15

RIGHTEOUS BROTHERS, THE

HAVEN

❏ 7006	Dream On/Dr. Rock and Roll	1974	$4
❏ 7004	Give It to the People/Love Is Not a Dirty Word	1974	$4
❏ 7011	High Blood Pressure/Never Say I Love You	1975	$4
❏ 800	Hold On to What You Got/Let Me Make the Music	1976	$4

MOONGLOW

❏ 238	Bring Your Love to Me/Fannie Mae	1965	$20
❏ 234	Bring Your Love to Me/If You're Lying, You'll Be Crying	1964	$30
❏ 243	For Your Love/Gotta Tell You How I Feel	1965	$20
❏ 244	Georgia on My Mind/My Tears Will Go Away	1966	$20
❏ 221	Gotta Tell You How I Feel/If You're Lying, You'll Be Crying	1963	$30
❏ 245	I Need a Girl/Bring Your Love to Me	1966	$20
❏ 215	Little Latin Lupe Lu/I'm So Lonely	1963	$30
❏ 215 [DJ]	Little Latin Lupe Lu/I'm So Lonely	1963	$60

—Red vinyl promo

❏ 223	My Babe/Fee-Fi-Fidily-I-Oh	1963	$30
❏ 235	This Little Girl of Mine/If You're Lying, You'll Be Crying	1964	$20
❏ 231	Try to Find Another Man/I Still Love You	1964	$30

PHILLES

❏ 130	Ebb Tide/(I Love You) For Sentimental Reasons	1965	$20
❏ 130 [PS]	Ebb Tide/(I Love You) For Sentimental Reasons	1965	$40
❏ 132	The White Cliffs of Dover/She's Mine, All Mine	1966	$30
❏ 132 [PS]	The White Cliffs of Dover/She's Mine, All Mine	1966	$50

VERVE

❏ 10479	Along Came Jones/Jimmy's Blues	1967	$8
❏ 10648	And the Party Goes On/Woman, Man Needs Ya	1968	$8
❏ CS8-5	Celebrity Scene: The Righteous Brothers	1967	$70

—Box set of five singles (10520-10524). Price includes box, all 5 singles, jukebox title strips, bio. Records are sometimes found by themselves, so they are also listed separately.

❏ 10430	Go Ahead and Cry/Things Didn't Go Your Way	1966	$10
❏ 10649	Good N' Nuff/Po' Folks	1968	$8
❏ 10406	He/He Will Break Your Heart	1966	$12
❏ 10406 [PS]	He/He Will Break Your Heart	1966	$30
❏ 10577	Here I Am/So Many Lonely Nights Ahead	1968	$8
❏ 10521	Hold On, I'm Coming/He Will Break Your Heart	1967	$12
❏ 10523	I (Who Have Nothing)/Island in the Sun	1967	$10
❏ 10637	Let the Good Times Roll/You've Lost That Lovin' Feelin'	1968	$8
❏ 10507	Melancholy Music Man/Don't Give Up on Me	1967	$8
❏ 10522	Melancholy Music Man/I Believe	1967	$10
❏ 10524	My Girl/Something You Got	1967	$10
❏ 10449	On This Side of Goodbye/A Man Without a Dream	1966	$10
❏ 10551	Stranded in the Middle of No Place/Been So Nice	1967	$8
❏ 10551 [PS]	Stranded in the Middle of No Place/Been So Nice	1967	$20

7-Inch Extended Plays

MOONGLOW

❏ SD71004	Little Latin Lupe Lu/Georgia on My Mind/Bye Bye Love/Fannie Mae/My Prayer/This Little Girl of Mine	1965	$35

—Jukebox issue; small hole, plays at 33 1/3 rpm

❏ SD71004 [PS]	The Best of the Righteous Brothers	1965	$35

RILEY, BILLY LEE

ATLANTIC

❏ 2525	Sittin' and a Waitin'/Happy Man	1968	$8

ENTRANCE

❏ 7508	I Got a Thing About You Baby/You Don't Love Me	1972	$5

GNP CRESCENDO

❏ 371	Gonna Find a Cave/That's the Bag I'm In	1966	$10
❏ 377	The Way I Feel/St. James Infirmary	1966	$10

HIP

❏ 8006	Family Portrait/Going Back to Memphis	1968	$8
❏ 8011	Show Me Your Soul/Midnight Hour	1968	$8

HOME OF THE BLUES

❏ 233	Flip, Flop, and Fly/Teenage Letter	1961	$40

MERCURY

❏ 72314	Bo Diddley/Memphis	1964	$20
❏ 72385	Mojo Workout/Charlene	1965	$15

MOJO

❏ 1933	Southern Soul/Midnight Hour	1967	$10

SUN

❏ 289	Baby Please Don't Go/Wouldn't You Know	1958	$60
❏ 313	Down by the Riverside/No Name Girl	1959	$30
❏ 260	Flying Saucers Rock and Roll/I Want You Baby	1957	$125
❏ 322	One More Time/Got the Water Boilin'	1959	$60
❏ 1105	Pilot Town L.A./Workin' on the River	1969	$6
❏ 1116	Tallahassee/Old Home Place	1970	$5
❏ 245	Trouble Bound/Rock with Me, Baby	1956	$120

Number	Title	Yr	NM

RILEY, BOB
CORAL
| ❏ 62125 | I Think It's a Shame/Blue Guitar Waltz | 1959 | $30 |

DOT
| ❏ 15625 | Baby Sittin'/Without Your Love | 1957 | $30 |

MGM
| ❏ 12612 | Wanda Jean/The Midnight Line | 1958 | $200 |

RILEY, JEANNIE C.
CAPITOL
| ❏ 2449 | I Don't Know What I'm Doing Here/You've Got Me Singing Nursery Rhymes | 1969 | $5 |
| ❏ 2378 | The Price I Pay to Stay/How Can Anything So Right Be So Wrong | 1969 | $5 |

LITTLE DARLIN'
| ❏ 0048 | I Don't Know What I'm Doing Here/I'll Be a Woman of the World | 1968 | $6 |
| ❏ 031 | What About Them/You Write the Music | 1967 | $20 |
— As "Jean Riley

MCA
| ❏ 52018 | From Harper Valley to the Mountain/I Don't Have to Die to Get Into Heaven | 1982 | $3 |

MERCURY
| ❏ 73616 | Plain Vanilla/Country Girl | 1974 | $4 |
MGM
❏ 14666	Another Football Year/Mother America	1973	$4
❏ 14341	Give Myself a Party/Why You Been Gone So Long	1972	$4
❏ 14382	Good Morning Country Rain/This Is for You	1972	$4
❏ 14310	Houston Blues/How Hard I'm Trying	1971	$4
❏ 14554	Hush/Not Looking Back	1973	$4
❏ 14696	Missouri/Sing Jeannie Sing	1974	$4
❏ 14427	One Night/Without You	1972	$4
❏ 14495	When Love Has Gone Away/Thou Shalt Not Kill	1973	$4

PLANTATION
❏ 44	Country Girl/We Were Raised on Love	1970	$5
❏ 59	Duty Not Desire/Holdin' On	1970	$5
❏ 75	Good Enough to Be Your Wife/Light Your Light	1971	$5
❏ 173	Harper Valley P.T.A. (Soundtrack Version)/I've Done a Lot of Living Since Then	1979	$6
❏ 3	Harper Valley P.T.A./Yesterday All Day Long Today	1968	$8
— Yellow label
| ❏ 3 | Harper Valley P.T.A./Yesterday All Day Long Today | 1968 | $8 |
— Blue label
| ❏ 3 | Harper Valley P.T.A./Yesterday All Day Long Today | 1968 | $6 |
— Green and white label
❏ 93	If You Could Read My Mind/Will the Real Jesus Please Stand Up	1972	$5
❏ 65	My Man/The Generation Gap	1970	$5
❏ 72	Oh, Singer/I'll Take What's Left of You	1971	$5
❏ 29	The Back Side of Dallas/Things Go Better with Love	1969	$5
❏ 7	The Girl Most Likely/My Scrapbook	1968	$5
❏ 85	The Lion's Club/Tell the Truth and Shame the Devil	1972	$5
❏ 16	There Never Was a Time/Back to School	1969	$5

PLAYBACK
| ❏ 1350 | Here's to the Cowboys/Free | 1989 | $6 |

WARNER BROS.
| ❏ 8290 | Pure Gold/Take Time | 1976 | $4 |
| ❏ 8226 | The Best I've Ever Had/Thank You for Forgiving | 1976 | $4 |

7-Inch Extended Plays
PLANTATION
| ❏ PEP-1 [PS] | Harper Valley P.T.A. | 1968 | $12 |
| ❏ PEP-1 | Harper Valley P.T.A./Shed Me No Tears/Widow Jones// No Brass Band/The Cotton Patch/The Little Town Square | 1968 | $10 |
— Jukebox issue; small hole, plays at 33 1/3 rpm

RINGO, JIMMY
DOT
| ❏ 15787 | I Like This Kind of Music/No One Else | 1958 | $40 |
| ❏ 15997 | I Like This Kind of Music/No One Else | 1959 | $30 |

RIO, BOBBY
ABC-PARAMOUNT
| ❏ 10656 | Boy Meets Girl/Don't Break My Heart and Run Away | 1965 | $20 |
LENOX
| ❏ 5569 | Don Diddley/I Got You | 1963 | $20 |

RIO, CHUCK
CHALLENGE
| ❏ 59019 | Bad Boy/Denise | 1958 | $30 |
JACKPOT
| ❏ 48016 | Margarita/C'est La Vie | 1960 | $40 |
KENT
| ❏ 308 | Bye Bye Baby/No Matter What You Do | 1958 | $30 |
TEQUILA
| ❏ 100 | Caravan/El Bracero | 1961 | $30 |
| ❏ 103 | La Cha Cha Twist/If You Were the Only Girl in the World | 1961 | $30 |

RIOS, AUGIE
METRO
| ❏ 20010 | Donde Esta Santa Claus?/Ol' Fatso | 1958 | $50 |
| ❏ 20027 | Trip to the Island/Teacher Walked Out of the Room | 1959 | $40 |
MGM
| ❏ 13292 | Donde Esta Santa Claus?/Ol' Fatso | 1964 | $15 |
| ❏ 12966 | Feliz Navidades/Gypsy Boy | 1960 | $30 |
SHELLEY
❏ 181	I've Got a Girl/There's a Girl Down the Way	1963	$50
❏ 192	Teach Me Tonight/Linda Lou	1964	$30
❏ 186	When You Dance/No One	1963	$40

RIOS, MIGUEL
A&M
❏ 1193	A Song of Joy (Himno A La Alegria)/El Rio	1970	$5
❏ 1193 [PS]	A Song of Joy (Himno A La Alegria)/El Rio	1970	$8
❏ 1203	Himno A La Alegria/El Rio	1970	$6

RIOT SQUAD, THE
HANNA-BARBERA
| ❏ 485 | I Take It That We're Through/Working Man | 1966 | $20 |
REPRISE
| ❏ 0457 | Cry, Cry, Cry/How Is It Done? | 1966 | $20 |
ROULETTE
| ❏ 4621 | Gonna Make You Mine/I Wanna Talk About My Baby | 1965 | $20 |
| ❏ 4621 [PS] | Gonna Make You Mine/I Wanna Talk About My Baby | 1965 | $60 |
— Promotional copy

RIP CHORDS, THE
COLUMBIA
| ❏ 43221 | Don't Be Scared/Bunny Hill | 1965 | $20 |
| ❏ 42812 [DJ] | Gone (same on both sides) | 1963 | $60 |
— Blue vinyl promo
| ❏ 42812 [PS] | Gone (same on both sides) | 1963 | $60 |
— Sleeve is promo only
| ❏ 42812 | Gone/She Thinks I Still Care | 1963 | $20 |
| ❏ 42687 [PS] | Here I Stand | 1963 | $60 |
— Sleeve is promo only
| ❏ 42687 | Here I Stand/Karen | 1963 | $20 |
| ❏ 42687 [DJ] | Here I Stand (same on both sides) | 1963 | $60 |
— Green vinyl promo
| ❏ 42687 [DJ] | Here I Stand (same on both sides) | 1963 | $30 |
— Black vinyl promo
| ❏ 42921 [DJ] | Hey, Little Cobra (same on both sides) | 1963 | $60 |
— Yellow vinyl promo
❏ 42921	Hey, Little Cobra/The Queen	1963	$30
❏ 43093	One Piece Topless Bathing Suit/Wah-Wahini	1964	$20
❏ 43035	Three Window Coupe/Hot Rod U.S.A.	1964	$20
❏ 43035 [DJ]	Three Window Coupe (same on both sides)	1964	$60
— Red vinyl promo

RIP-CHORDS, THE
ABCO
| ❏ 105 | I Love You the Most/Let's Do the Razzle Dazzle | 1956 | $600 |
— Black vinyl
| ❏ 105 | I Love You the Most/Let's Do the Razzle Dazzle | 1956 | $1500 |
— Red vinyl

RIPPLES AND WAVES PLUS MICHAEL, THE
STEELTOWN
| ❏ 689 | Let Me Carry Your School Books/I Never Had a Girl | 1969 | $100 |

RIPPY, RODNEY ALLEN
BELL
| ❏ 45403 | Take Life a Little Easier/World of Love | 1973 | $8 |

RISING SUNS, THE
COLUMBIA
| ❏ 43534 | Candy Man/The Devil's Got My Woman | 1966 | $50 |

RITA AND THE TIARAS
DORE
| ❏ 783 [B] | Gone with the Wind Is My Love/Wild Times | 1967 | $3500 |

RITES OF SPRING, THE
PARKWAY
| ❏ 109 | Why/Comin' On to Me | 1966 | $40 |

RITES, THE
DECCA
| ❏ 32218 | Things/Hour Glass | 1967 | $30 |

RITTER, TEX
Also see STAN KENTON AND TEX RITTER.
CAPITOL
❏ 2388	A Funny Thing Happened (On the Way to Miami)/The Governor and the Kid	1969	$8
❏ F1977	As Long As the River Flows On/When My Blue Moon Turns to Gold	1952	$30
❏ F3003	A Whale of a Tale/High on a Mountain Top	1954	$30
❏ 5966	A Working Man's Prayer/William Barrett Travis: A Message from the Alamo	1967	$8
❏ F1058	Bad Brahma Bull/Blood on the Saddle	1950	$40
❏ 54-40181	Blood on the Saddle/Rounded Up in Glory	1949	$40
❏ F2174	Boll Weevil Song/Have I Told You Lately That I Love You	1952	$30
❏ F928	Boogie Woogie Cowboy/He's a Cowboy Auctioneer	1950	$50
❏ F2756	Brave Man/Turn Around Boy	1954	$30
❏ 5474	Bummin' Around/Take Him Fishin'	1965	$10
❏ 2097	Bump Tiddle Dee Bum Bum/I Just Can't Get Away	1968	$8
❏ F3640	Children and Fools/I Leaned on a Man	1957	$30
❏ F1188	Coal Smoke, Valve Oil and Steam/Nobody's Fool	1950	$40
❏ F4217	Conversation with a Gun/Rye Whiskey	1959	$20
❏ 4849	Coo Se Coo/The Cookson Hills	1962	$15
❏ F1267	Daddy's Last Letter/Onward Christian Soldiers	1950	$40
❏ F4285	Deck of Cards/Conversation with a Gun	1959	$20
❏ F885	Deck of Cards/Rye Whiskey	1950	$40
❏ 5224	Fool's Paradise/Gimme Some	1964	$10
❏ 4239	God Bless America Again/Lucy Let Your Lovelight Shine	1976	$5
❏ F3589	Green Grow the Lilacs/He Is There	1956	$30
❏ 2541	Growin' Up/A Letter to My Sons	1969	$8
❏ F3230	Gunsmoke/Remember the Alamo	1955	$30
❏ F3903	Here Was a Man/It Came Upon the Midnight Clear	1959	$20
❏ F2120	High Noon (Do Not Forsake Me)/Go On! Get Out!	1952	$40
❏ 4567	I Dreamed of a Hill-Billy Heaven/The Wind and the Tree	1961	$15
❏ F1453	If I Could Steal You/There's No One to Cry Over Me	1951	$30
❏ F3363	If Jesus Came to Your House/Touch of the Master's Hand	1956	$30
❏ F2957	Is There a Santa Claus/Ole Tex Kringle	1954	$30
❏ F1071	I've Got $5 and It's Saturday Night/Boiled Crawfish	1950	$40

Number	Title	Yr	NM
❑ F2594	Let Me Go, Devil!/Long Black Rifle	1953	$30
❑ 4644	Lonely Soldier Boy/Strange Little Melody	1961	$15
❑ F2836	Lovely Veil of White/The Best Time of All	1954	$30
❑ F1264	Merry Christmas Polka/Christmas Carols by the Old Corral	1950	$40
❑ 5697	Mommy, Daddy, Tell Us/Remember Us	1966	$8
❑ F2368	My Woman Ain't Pretty/Buffalo Dream	1953	$30
❑ 3570	One Night for Willie/Sweet Bird of Youth	1973	$6
❑ F2916	Prairie Home (Theme from The Vanishing Prairie)/The Bandit	1954	$30
❑ 5347	She Loved This House/I Dreamed of a Hill-Billy Heaven	1965	$10
❑ F1334	Stay Away from My Heart/Big Blue Diamonds	1950	$40
❑ F1783	Tennessee Blues/Rock All Babies	1951	$30
❑ 2232	Texas/Stranger on Boot Hill	1968	$8
❑ 5159	That Son of a Saginaw Fisherman/Gallows Pole	1964	$12
❑ 3814	The Americans (A Canadian's Opinion)/He Who Is Without Sin	1974	$6
❑ 54-40179	The Chisholm Trail/San Antonio Rose	1949	$40
❑ 5004	The Gods Were Angry with Me/Will	1963	$10
❑ F4043	The History Song/I Look for a Love	1958	$20
❑ F3538	The Last Wagon/Paul Bunyan Love	1956	$30
❑ F2034	The Letter Edged in Black/There Shall Be Showers	1952	$30
❑ F2475	The Marshall's Daughter/The San Antone Story	1953	$30
❑ 5574	The Men in My Little Girl's Life/Custody	1966	$8
❑ F1141	The Pledge of Allegiance/Fiery Bear	1950	$40
❑ 4753	The Pledge of Allegiance/Ol' Shorty	1962	$15
❑ F3324	These Hands/The Last Frontier	1956	$30
❑ F3430	The Wayward Wind/The Searchers (Ride Away)	1956	$30
❑ F1098	Thief on the Cross/Beautiful Life	1950	$40
❑ F3754	Trooper Hook (Chapter 1)/Trooper Hook (Chapter 2)	1957	$30
❑ 54-40180	Try Me One More Time/Boll Weevil Song	1949	$40
❑ 2677	Wand'rin' Star/Chuckwagon Son of a Gun	1969	$8
❑ F1581	Wearin' Out Your Walkin' Shoes/Coffee Pot	1951	$30
❑ F3179	Wichita/September Song	1955	$30
❑ 3705	Willie, the Wandering Gypsy, and Me/Wind of Oklahoma	1973	$6

RITUALS, THE
ARWIN

Number	Title	Yr	NM
❑ 120	Girl in Zanzibar/Guitarro	1963	$40
❑ 128	Surfers Rule/Gone	1964	$50
❑ 127	This Is Paradise/Gone	1964	$40

RIVERA, LUCY
END

Number	Title	Yr	NM
❑ 1041	Make Me Queen/Ific	1959	$30

RIVERS, BOB, COMEDY CORP
CRITIQUE

Number	Title	Yr	NM
❑ PR2135 [DJ]	I'm Dressing Up Like Santa (When I Get Out on Parole) (same on both sides)	1987	$5
❑ 99263	The Twelve Pains of Christmas/A Message from the King	1988	$5
❑ 99263 [PS]	The Twelve Pains of Christmas/A Message from the King	1988	$5
❑ PR2119 [DJ]	Wreck The Malls/The Twelve Pains Of Christmas	1987	$5

RIVERS, JACK
CORAL

Number	Title	Yr	NM
❑ 9-64072	Haunted House Boogie/Bugle Call Baby	1951	$40
❑ 9-64084	Shame, Shame on Jolie/Summer or Winter	1951	$40

LISTEN

Number	Title	Yr	NM
❑ 1445	titles unknown	1952	$40

RIVERS, JOHNNY
ATLANTIC

Number	Title	Yr	NM
❑ 3011	Sitting in Limbo/Artists and Poets	1974	$5
❑ 3028	Six Days on the Road/Artists and Poets	1974	$5

BIG TREE

Number	Title	Yr	NM
❑ 16106	Curious Mind (Um, Um, Um, Um, Um, Um)/Ashes and Sand	1977	$4
❑ 16094	Swayin' to the Music (Slow Dancin')/Outside Help	1977	$4

CAPITOL

Number	Title	Yr	NM
❑ 4913	If You Want It, I've Got It/My Heart Is In Your Hands	1963	$20
❑ 5232	Long Black Veil/Don't Look Now	1964	$20
❑ 4850	Long Black Veil/This Could Be the One	1962	$20

CHANCELLOR

Number	Title	Yr	NM
❑ 1070	I Get So Doggone Lonesome/Knock Three Times	1961	$30
❑ 1108	To Be Loved/Too Good to Last	1962	$30

CORAL

Number	Title	Yr	NM
❑ 62425	That's My Baby/Your First and Last Love	1964	$20

CUB

Number	Title	Yr	NM
❑ 9058	Answer Me My Love/The Customary Thing	1960	$30
❑ 9047	Everyday/Darling Talk to Me	1959	$30

DEE DEE

Number	Title	Yr	NM
❑ 239	The White Cliffs of Dover/Your First and Last Love	1959	$30

EPIC

Number	Title	Yr	NM
❑ 50150	Can I Change My Mind/John Lee Hooker	1975	$4
❑ 50121	Help Me Rhonda/New Lovers and Old Friends	1975	$5

—A-side features Brian Wilson on backing vocals

Number	Title	Yr	NM
❑ 50248	Linda Lue/Outside Help	1976	$4
❑ 50208	Welcome Home/Outside Help	1976	$4

ERA

Number	Title	Yr	NM
❑ 3037	Call Me/Andersonville	1961	$30

GONE

Number	Title	Yr	NM
❑ 5026	Baby Come Back/Long Long Walk	1958	$50

IMPERIAL

Number	Title	Yr	NM
❑ 66227	Baby I Need Your Lovin'/Gettin' Ready for Tomorrow	1967	$12
❑ 66227 [PS]	Baby I Need Your Lovin'/Gettin' Ready for Tomorrow	1967	$20
❑ 66453	Fire and Rain/Apple Tree	1970	$8
❑ 66448	Into the Mystic/Jesus Is a Soul Man	1970	$8
❑ 66175	(I Washed My Hands In) Muddy Water/Roogalator	1966	$10
❑ 66286	Look to Your Soul/Something's Strange	1968	$8
❑ 66286 [PS]	Look to Your Soul/Something's Strange	1968	$15
❑ 66056	Maybelline/Walk Myself On Home	1964	$10
❑ 66056 [PS]	Maybelline/Walk Myself On Home	1964	$20
❑ 66032	Memphis/It Wouldn't Happen with Me	1964	$15
❑ 66087	Midnight Special/Cupid	1965	$10
❑ 66075	Mountain of Love/Moody River	1964	$10
❑ 66386	Muddy River/Resurrection	1969	$8
❑ 66386 [PS]	Muddy River/Resurrection	1969	$15
❑ 66418	One Woman/Ode to John Lee	1969	$8
❑ 66205	Poor Side of Town/A Man Can Cry	1966	$15
❑ 66205 [PS]	Poor Side of Town/A Man Can Cry	1966	$20
❑ 66159	Secret Agent Man/You Dig	1966	$15
❑ 66159 [PS]	Secret Agent Man/You Dig	1966	$20
❑ 66112	Seventh Son/Unsquare Dance	1965	$10
❑ 66112 [PS]	Seventh Son/Unsquare Dance	1965	$20
❑ 66267	Summer Rain/Memory of the Coming Good	1967	$10
❑ 66360	These Are Not My People/Going Back to Big Sur	1969	$8
❑ 66244	The Tracks of My Tears/Rewind Medley	1967	$10
❑ 66244 [PS]	The Tracks of My Tears/Rewind Medley	1967	$20
❑ 66133	Where Have All the Flowers Gone/Love Me While You Can	1965	$10

MCA

Number	Title	Yr	NM
❑ 52502	Heartbreak Love/Why Can't We Communicate	1984	$4

MGM

Number	Title	Yr	NM
❑ 13266	Answer Me, My Love/Customary Thing	1964	$20

RIVERAIRE

Number	Title	Yr	NM
❑ 1001	Don't Bug Me Baby/Haunting Black Eyes	1959	$40

ROULETTE

Number	Title	Yr	NM
❑ 4565	Baby Come Back/Long Long Walk	1964	$30

RSO

Number	Title	Yr	NM
❑ 1045	China/The Price	1980	$4

SOUL CITY

Number	Title	Yr	NM
❑ 007	Ashes and Sand/Outside Help	1977	$5
❑ 010	Little White Lie/Be My Baby	1980	$5
❑ 008	Swayin' to the Music (Slow Dancin')/Outside Help	1977	$8

SUEDE

Number	Title	Yr	NM
❑ 1401	Little Girl/Two by Two	1957	$125

—As "Johnny Ramistella"

UNITED ARTISTS

Number	Title	Yr	NM
❑ XW198	Blue Suede Shoes/Stories to a Child	1973	$5
❑ 769	Dream Doll/To Be Loved	1964	$15
❑ XW310	I'll Feel a Whole Lot Better/Over the Line	1973	$5
❑ 0101	Memphis/Secret Agent Man	1973	$4
❑ 0102	Mountain of Love/Maybellene	1973	$4
❑ 741	Oh What a Kiss/Knock Three Times	1964	$15
❑ 50948	On the Borderline/Come Home America	1972	$5
❑ 0104	Poor Side of Town/Baby I Need Your Lovin'	1973	$4
❑ 50778	Sea Cruise/Our Lady of the Well	1971	$6
❑ XW226	Searchin'-So Fine/New York City Dues	1973	$5
❑ 0103	Seventh Son/Midnight Special	1973	$4
❑ 0105	Summer Rain/The Tracks of My Tears	1973	$4

—0101 through 0105 are "Silver Spotlight Series" reissues

Number	Title	Yr	NM
❑ 50822	Think His Name/Permanent Change	1971	$6
❑ XW523	Where Have All the Flowers Gone/(I Washed My Hands in) Muddy Water	1974	$4

—Reissue

RIVERS, TONY, AND THE CASTAWAYS
CONSTELLATION

Number	Title	Yr	NM
❑ 128	I Love the Way You Walk/I Love You	1964	$20

RIVIERAS, THE (1)
COED

Number	Title	Yr	NM
❑ 529	Blessing of Love/Moonlight Cocktails	1960	$30
❑ 503	Count Every Star/True Love Is Hard to Find	1958	$60
❑ 542	Easy to Remember/Stay in My Heart	1960	$30
❑ 551	El Doreado/Refrigerator	1961	$30
❑ 592	Moonlight Cocktails/Midnight Flyer	1964	$20
❑ 508	Moonlight Serenade/Neither Rain Nor Snow	1959	$50
❑ 538	My Friend/Great Big Eyes	1960	$30
❑ 513	Our Love/Midnight Flyer	1959	$40
❑ 513	Our Love/True Love Is Hard to Find	1959	$40
❑ 522	Since I Made You Cry/11th Hour Melody	1959	$40

RIVIERAS, THE (2)
RIVIERA

Number	Title	Yr	NM
❑ 1409	Bug Juice/Never Feel the Pain	1965	$30
❑ 1401	California Sun/H.B. Goose Step	1964	$30
❑ 1401	California Sun/Played On	1964	$50

—Possibly as few as 1,000 were pressed with this B-side

Number	Title	Yr	NM
❑ 1406	Let's Go to Hawaii/Lakeview Lane	1965	$20
❑ 1402	Little Donna/Let's Have a Party	1964	$20
❑ 1407	Somebody Asked Me/Somebody New	1965	$20

—Credited to the Rivieras, but actually by Bobby Whiteside

Number	Title	Yr	NM
❑ 1405	Whole Lotta Shakin'/Lakeview Lane	1965	$30
❑ 1405	Whole Lotta Shakin'/Rip It Up	1965	$20

RIVIERAS, THE (3)
ALGONQUIN

Number	Title	Yr	NM
❑ 718	Together Forever/A Night to Remember	1958	$200

—Reissued as "The Ravenairs"

RIVILEERS, THE
BATON

Number	Title	Yr	NM
❑ 200	A Thousand Stars/Hey Chiquita	1953	$200
❑ 241	A Thousand Stars/Who Is the Girl	1957	$50
❑ 205	Carolyn/Eternal Love	1954	$120
❑ 201	Forever/Darling Farewell	1954	$120
❑ 207	(I Love You) For Sentimental Reasons/I Want to See My Baby	1955	$70
❑ 209	Little Girl/Don't Ever Leave Me	1955	$70

Number	Title	Yr	NM

RIVINGTONS, THE

AGC

Number	Title	Yr	NM
❏ 5	I Lost the Love/Mind Your Man	1968	$8

A.R.E. AMERICAN

| ❏ 100 | All That Glitters/You Move Me Baby | 1964 | $20 |

BATON MASTER

| ❏ 202 | Teach Me Tonight/Reach Our Goal | 1967 | $8 |

J.D.

| ❏ 122 | Don't Hate Your Father (Part 1)/Don't Hate Your Father (Part 2) | 1976 | $5 |

LIBERTY

❏ 55671	Fairy Tales/Wee Jee Walk	1964	$20
❏ 55610	Little Sally Walker/Cherry	1963	$40
❏ 55528	Mama-Oom-Mow-Mow/Waiting	1962	$20
❏ 55427	Papa-Oom-Mow-Mow/Deep Water	1962	$30
❏ 1484 [DJ]	Papa-Oom-Mow-Mow (same on both sides)	1982	$6

— *Reissue; promo only*

| ❏ 55553 | The Bird's the Word/I'm Losing My Grip | 1963 | $30 |
| ❏ 55585 | The Shaky Bird (Part 1)/The Shaky Bird (Part 2) | 1963 | $20 |

QUAN

| ❏ 1379 | I Don't Want a New Baby/You're Gonna Pay | 1967 | $10 |

RCA VICTOR

| ❏ 74-0301 | Pop Your Corn (Part 1)/Pop Your Corn (Part 2) | 1969 | $8 |

REPRISE

| ❏ 0293 | I Tried/One Monkey Don't Stop No Show | 1964 | $15 |

UNITED ARTISTS

| ❏ 0096 | Papa-Oom-Mow-Mow/The Bird's the Word | 1973 | $4 |

— *Silver Spotlight Series" reissue*

VEE JAY

❏ 634	All That Glitters/You Move Me Baby	1964	$15
❏ 649	I Love You Always/Years of Tears	1965	$15
❏ 677	The Willy/Just Got to Be Mine	1965	$15

WAND

| ❏ 11253 | Papa-Oom-Mow-Mow/I Don't Want a New Baby | 1973 | $5 |

ROAD RUNNERS, THE

CHALLENGE

| ❏ 9197 | Dead Man/Pretty Girls | 1963 | $30 |

MIRAMAR

| ❏ 116 | Take Me/I'll Make It Up to You | 1965 | $20 |

MOROCCO

| ❏ 01 | Goodbye/Tell Her You Love Her | 1966 | $30 |

REPRISE

| ❏ 0418 | Take Me/I'll Make It Up to You | 1965 | $20 |

ROAD, THE

BLUE ONION

| ❏ 106 | It's So Hard to Find/You Rub Me the Wrong Way | 1969 | $40 |

KAMA SUTRA

❏ 531	Alone/If You Ever Needed a Woman	1971	$6
❏ 267	Mr. Soul/I Can Only Give You Everything	1969	$8
❏ 504	Mr. Soul/The Grass Looks Greener on the Other Side	1970	$6
❏ 256	She's Not There/A Bummer	1968	$8
❏ 266	The Grass Looks Greener on the Other Side/In Love	1969	$8

ROAMERS, THE

HIT

| ❏ 135 | Because/Walk Don't Run '64 | 1964 | $12 |

— *B-side by the Nashville Five*

| ❏ 94 | Be True to Your School/Wonderful Summer | 1963 | $8 |

— *B-side by Joanne Kay*

| ❏ 250 | Be True to Your School/Wonderful Summer | 1966 | $8 |

— *B-side by Joanne Kay*

| ❏ 118 | Bits and Pieces/(Just Like) Romeo and Juliet | 1964 | $10 |
| ❏ 115 | Dead Man's Curve/Ronnie | 1964 | $8 |

— *B-side by the Chellows*

| ❏ 221 | Eve of Destruction/I Got You Babe | 1965 | $15 |

— *B-side by Wayne and Dee*

Number	Title	Yr	NM
❏ 158	Everything's Alright/Dance, Dance, Dance	1964	$15

— *B-side by the Spartas*

| ❏ 140 | G.T.O./In the Misty Moonlight | 1964 | $8 |

— *B-side by Marty Wood*

| ❏ 222 | Hang On Sloopy/The "In" Crowd | 1965 | $15 |

— *B-side by Just Three*

| ❏ 102 | Hey Little Cobra/Daisy Petal Pickin' | 1964 | $8 |

— *B-side by Ricky Dickens*

| ❏ 126 | I Get Around/Yesterday's Gone | 1964 | $8 |
| ❏ 217 | I Want Candy/(I Can't Get No) Satisfaction | 1965 | $15 |

— *B-side by the Jalopy Five*

| ❏ 218 | I Want Candy/I Like It Like That | 1965 | $15 |

— *B-side by the Jalopy Five*

| ❏ 172 | Love Potion Number Nine/Never Forget Me | 1965 | $15 |
| ❏ 141 | Save It for Me/Selfish One | 1964 | $8 |

— *B-side by Betty Wrigley*

| ❏ 132 | The Little Old Lady from Pasadena/Can't You See That She's Mine | 1964 | $10 |

— *B-side by the Jalopy Five*

| ❏ 151 | Tobacco Road/I Know Johnny Loves Me | 1964 | $10 |

— *B-side by Amy and the Jarretts*

| ❏ 227 | Treat Her Right/You're the One | 1965 | $8 |

— *As "Cal York and the Roamers"; B-side by the Crests (2)*

| ❏ 160 | We Build a 409/Big Man in Town | 1964 | $15 |

— *B-side by the Chellows*

| ❏ 147 | When I Grow Up (To Be a Man)/Matchbox | 1964 | $10 |

— *B-side by the Jalopy Five*

ROBB, DEE

ARGO

| ❏ 5439 | Bye Bye Baby/The Prom | 1963 | $15 |

SCORE

| ❏ 1006 | He's Got the Whole World in His Hands/Say That Thing | 1964 | $20 |

ROBBINS, HARGUS "PIG"

CHART

❏ 5022	Penguin Walk (Cool Theme)/Unknown Love	1969	$8
❏ 5039	Tequila Float/Funk Chunkin'	1969	$8
❏ 1060	The Bridge Washed Out/Love's Apparition	1968	$8

ELEKTRA

❏ 45469	Canadian Sunset/Roamin' 'Round	1978	$5
❏ 46037	Chunky People/Whatever Happened to the Girls I Knew	1979	$5
❏ 45440	Diggin' In/Near You	1977	$5
❏ 45514	Little Bitty Pretty One/Forever	1978	$5

TIME

| ❏ 1070 | Forever/Happy Boy | 1963 | $15 |

ROBBINS, DENNIS

MCA

| ❏ 52809 | Hard Lovin' Man/Baby It's You | 1986 | $4 |
| ❏ 52809 [DJ] | Hard Lovin' Man (same on both sides) | 1986 | $12 |

— *Promo only on blue vinyl*

| ❏ 52584 | I've Got Your Number/Work for Love | 1985 | $4 |

— *As "Rockie Robbins"*

❏ 52987	Long Gone Lonesome Blues/The Mountain Man and Me	1986	$3
❏ 52913	The First of Me/Sweet Sweet Lovin'	1986	$4
❏ 53143	Two of a Kind (Workin' on a Full House)/The Church on Cumberland Road	1987	$5
❏ 52516	We Belong Together/Work for Love	1984	$4

— *As "Rockie Robbins"*

NSD

| ❏ 169 | If I Could Get Over You/A Fire in Me | 1983 | $6 |

ROBBINS, EDDIE

DOT

| ❏ 15702 | A Girl Like You/Dear Parents | 1958 | $50 |

POWER

| ❏ 214 | A Girl Like You/Dear Parents | 1958 | $120 |

Number	Title	Yr	NM

ROBBINS, MARTY

COLUMBIA

❏ 21111	A Castle in the Sky/A Half-Way Chance with You	1953	$40
❏ 10472	Adios Amigo/Helen	1977	$5
❏ 41282	Ain't I the Lucky One/The Last Time I Saw My Heart	1958	$30
❏ 11016	All Around Cowboy/The Dreamer	1979	$5
❏ 10396	Among My Souvenirs/She's Just a Drifter	1976	$5
❏ 11372	An Occasional Rose/Holding On to You	1980	$4
❏ S731125 [S]	Answer Me My Love/Clara	1961	$30
❏ S731192 [S]	Answer Me My Love/Half As Much	1961	$30
❏ S731127 [S]	Are You Sincere?/Guess I'll Be Going	1961	$30
❏ 40864	A White Sport Coat (And a Pink Carnation)/Grown Up Tears	1957	$30
❏ 40864 [PS]	A White Sport Coat (And a Pink Carnation)/Grown Up Tears	1957	$50
❏ 03927	Baby That's Love/What If I Said I Love You	1983	$4
❏ 41809 [M]	Ballad of the Alamo/A Time and a Place for Everything	1960	$20
❏ 41809 [PS]	Ballad of the Alamo/A Time and a Place for Everything	1960	$40
❏ S730809 [S]	Ballad of the Alamo/A Time and a Place for Everything	1960	$40

— *Stereo Seven" single (small hole, plays at 33 1/3 rpm)*

❏ 42890	Begging to You/Over High Mountain	1963	$15
❏ 41589 [M]	Big Iron/Saddle Tramp	1960	$20
❏ S730589 [S]	Big Iron/Saddle Tramp	1960	$40

— *Stereo Seven" single (small hole, plays at 33 1/3 rpm)*

❏ 21172	Blesserd Jesus Should I Fall Don't Let Me Lay/Kneel and Let the Lord Take Your Load	1953	$40
❏ 11102	Buenos Dias Argentina/Ballad of a Small Man	1979	$5
❏ 21291	Call Me Up (And I'll Come Calling on You)/I'm Too Big to Cry	1954	$40
❏ 45024	Camelia/Virginia	1969	$5
❏ 41408	Cap and Gown/Last Night About This Time	1959	$30
❏ 03789	Change of Heart/Devil in a Cowboy Hat	1983	$4
❏ 3-39020 [S]	Change That Dial/You Won't Have Her Long	1964	$40

— *Jukebox single, small hole, plays at 33 1/3 rpm; rather than the usual rainbow "target" label of Columbia "Stereo Seven" singles, this one has green labels*

❏ 42701	Cigarettes and Coffee Blues/Teenager's Dad	1963	$15
❏ 42701 [PS]	Cigarettes and Coffee Blues/Teenager's Dad	1963	$30
❏ 11425	Completely Out of Love/Another Cup of Coffee	1981	$4
❏ 43500	Count Me Out/Private Wilson White	1965	$8
❏ 20965	Crying 'Cause I Love You/I Wish Somebody Loved Me	1952	$40
❏ 21388	Daddy Loves You/Pray for Me, Mother of Mine	1955	$30
❏ 42486	Devil Woman/April Fool's Day	1962	$20
❏ 42486 [PS]	Devil Woman/April Fool's Day	1962	$30

— *Sleeve has a photo of Marty with a green background*

| ❏ 42486 [PS] | Devil Woman/April Fool's Day | 1962 | $30 |

— *Sleeve has a photo of Marty with a brown background*

| ❏ S731747 [S] | Devil Woman/Time Can't Make Me Forget | 1963 | $30 |

— *Stereo Seven" single, small hole, plays at 33 1/3 rpm*

❏ 10629	Don't Let Me Touch You/Tomorrow, Tomorrow, Tomorrow	1977	$5
❏ 21176	Don't Make Me Ashamed/It's a Long, Long Ride	1953	$40
❏ 41922	Don't Worry/Like All the Other Times	1961	$20
❏ 41922 [PS]	Don't Worry/Like All the Other Times	1961	$30
❏ 45442	Early Morning Sunshine/Another Day Has Gone By	1971	$5
❏ JZSP49158/ 48863 [DJ]	El Paso (2:58)/El Paso (4:37)	1959	$50
❏ 10305	El Paso City/When I'm Gone	1976	$5
❏ 41511 [M]	El Paso/Running Gun	1959	$30
❏ 41511 [PS]	El Paso/Running Gun	1959	$40
❏ S730511 [S]	El Paso/Running Gun	1959	$40

— *Stereo Seven" (small hole, plays at 33 1/3 rpm)*

| ❏ 41771 [M] | Five Brothers/Ride, Cowboy, Ride | 1960 | $20 |
| ❏ S730771 [S] | Five Brothers/Ride, Cowboy, Ride | 1960 | $40 |

— *Stereo Seven" single (small hole, plays at 33 1/3 rpm)*

❏ 44271	Gardenias in Her Hair/In the Valley of the Rio Grande	1967	$6
❏ 42968	Girl from Spanish Town/Kingston Girl	1964	$10
❏ 44968	Girl from Spanish Town/Kingston Girl	1969	$8

Number	Title	Yr	NM
❏ 21352	God Understands/Have Thine Own Way, Lord	1955	$30
❏ S731126 [S]	Half As Much/Unchained Melody	1961	$30
❏ 42672	Hawaii's Calling Me/Ka-Lu-A	1963	$15
❏ 44895	I Can't Say Goodbye/Hello Daily News	1969	$5
❏ 21075	I Couldn't Keep from Crying/After You Leave	1953	$40
❏ 40868	I Cried Like a Baby/Where D'Ja Go	1957	$30

— With Lee Emerson

Number	Title	Yr	NM
❏ 10536	I Don't Know Why (I Just Do)/Inspiration for a Song	1977	$5
❏ 43196	I Eish-Tay-Mah-Su (I Love You)/A Whole Lot Easier	1964	$10
❏ 21022	I'll Go On Alone/You're Breaking My Heart	1952	$40
❏ 21525	I'll Know Tomorrow You're Gone/How Long Will It Be	1956	$30

— With Lee Emerson

Number	Title	Yr	NM
❏ S731748 [S]	In the Ashes of an Old Love Affair/The Hands You're Holding Now	1963	$30

— Stereo Seven" single, small hole, plays at 33 1/3 rpm

Number	Title	Yr	NM
❏ 41686	Is There Any Chance/I Told My Heart	1960	$20
❏ 44641	It Finally Happened/Big Mouthin' Around	1968	$6

— By "Marty Robbins Jr. and Sr.

Number	Title	Yr	NM
❏ 21414	It Looks Like I'm Just in the Way/I'll Love You Till the Day I Die	1955	$30
❏ 42246	I Told the Brook/Sometimes I'm Tempted	1961	$20
❏ 42246 [PS]	I Told the Brook/Sometimes I'm Tempted	1961	$30
❏ 44739	It's a Sin/I Feel Another Heartache Coming On	1969	$5
❏ 42065	It's Your World/You Told Me So	1961	$20
❏ 42065 [PS]	It's Your World/You Told Me So	1961	$30
❏ 45668	I've Got a Woman's Love/A Little Spot in Heaven	1972	$5
❏ 44633	I Walk Alone/Lily of the Valley	1968	$6
❏ 45775	Laura (What's He Got That I Ain't Got)/It Kind of Reminds Me of You	1973	$5
❏ 45346	Little Spot in Heaven/Wait a Little Longer Please, Jesus	1971	$6
❏ 40679	Long Tall Sally/Mr. Teardrop	1956	$60
❏ 42375	Love Can't Wait/Too Far Gone	1962	$20
❏ 42375 [PS]	Love Can't Wait/Too Far Gone	1962	$30
❏ 44509	Love Is in the Air/I've Been Leaving Everyday	1968	$6
❏ 02854	Lover, Lover/Some Memories Just Won't Die	1982	$4
❏ 21446	Maybellene/This Broken Heart of Mine	1955	$60
❏ 43870	Mr. Shorty/Tall Handsome Strangers	1966	$8
❏ 21213	My Isle of Golden Dreams/Aloha Oe	1954	$40
❏ 45091	My Woman, My Woman, My Wife/Martha Ellen Jenkins	1970	$5
❏ 43377	Old Red/Matilda	1965	$8
❏ 11291	One Man's Trash (Is Another Man's Treasure)/I Can't Wait Until Tomorrow	1980	$4
❏ 43134	One of These Days/Up in the Air	1964	$10
❏ 45273	Padre/At Times	1970	$6
❏ 40969	Please Don't Blame Me/Teen-Age Dream	1957	$30
❏ 10821	Please Don't Play a Love Song/Jenny	1978	$5
❏ 21461	Pretty Mama/Don't Let Me Hang Around	1955	$60
❏ 21246	Pretty Words/Your Heart's Turn to Break	1954	$40
❏ S731750 [S]	Progressive Love/Love Is a Hurting Thing	1963	$30

— Stereo Seven" single, small hole, plays at 33 1/3 rpm

Number	Title	Yr	NM
❏ 11240	She's Made of Faith/Misery in My Soul	1980	$4
❏ 41208	She Was Only Seventeen (He Was One Year More)/Sittin' in a Tree House	1958	$30
❏ 41208 [PS]	She Was Only Seventeen (He Was One Year More)/Sittin' in a Tree House	1958	$50
❏ 21508	Singing the Blues/I Can't Quit (I've Gone Too Far)	1956	$50
❏ 21545	Singing the Blues/I Can't Quit (I've Gone Too Far)	1956	$40
❏ 21145	Sing Me Something Sentimental/At the End of Long, Lonely Days	1953	$40
❏ 02575	Teardrops on My Heart/Honeycomb	1981	$4
❏ 21477	Tennessee Toddy/Mean Mama Blues	1955	$60
❏ 21351	That's All Right/Gossip	1955	$60
❏ 45520	The Best Part of Living/Gone with the Wind	1971	$5
❏ 45377	The Chair/Seventeen Years	1971	$5
❏ 43049	The Cowboy in the Continental Suit/Man Walks Among Us	1964	$12

Number	Title	Yr	NM
❏ 41325	The Hanging Tree/The Blues, Country Style	1959	$30
❏ 41325 [PS]	The Hanging Tree/The Blues, Country Style	1959	$50
❏ 43680	The Shoe Goes On the Other Foot Tonight/It Kind of Reminds Me of You	1966	$8
❏ 41013	The Story of My Life/Once-a-Week Date	1957	$30
❏ 41013 [PS]	The Story of My Life/Once-a-Week Date	1957	$50
❏ 03236	Tie Your Dream to Mine/That's All She Wrote	1982	$4
❏ 21324	Time Goes By/It's a Pity What Money Can Do	1954	$40
❏ S731124 [S]	To Each His Own/I Can't Help It	1961	$30
❏ S731191 [S]	To Each His Own/I Can't Help It	1961	$30
❏ 20925	Tomorrow You'll Be Gone/Love Me or Leave Me Alone	1952	$40
❏ 44128	Tonight Carmen/Waiting in Reno	1967	$6
❏ S731128 [S]	To Think You've Chosen Me/Too Young	1961	$30

— The above five are "Stereo Seven" 33 1/3 rpm jukebox singles from set "JS7-32" entitled "Just a Little Sentimental

Number	Title	Yr	NM
❏ S731194 [S]	To Think You've Chosen Me/Too Young	1961	$30

— The above five are "Stereo Seven" 33 1/3 rpm jukebox singles from set "JS7-37," an alternate compilation of "Just a Little Sentimental

Number	Title	Yr	NM
❏ 10905	Touch Me with Magic/Confused and Lonely	1979	$5
❏ 43428	While You're Dancing/Lonely Too Long	1965	$8
❏ S731749 [S]	Worried/Little Rich Girl	1963	$30

— Stereo Seven" single, small hole, plays at 33 1/3 rpm

MCA

Number	Title	Yr	NM
❏ 40067	A Man and a Train/Las Vegas, Nevada	1973	$5
❏ 40236	Don't You Think/I Couldn't Believe It Was True	1974	$5
❏ 40012	Franklin, Tennessee/Walking Piece of Heaven	1973	$5
❏ 40172	I'm Wanting To/Twentieth Century Drifter	1973	$5
❏ 40342	Life/It Takes Faith	1974	$5
❏ 40134	Love Me/Crawling on My Knees	1973	$5
❏ 40425	These Are My Souvenirs/Shotgun Rider	1975	$5
❏ 52197	Two Gun Daddy/Life	1983	$5
❏ 40296	Two-Gun Daddy/Queen of the Big Rodeo	1974	$5

WARNER BROS.

Number	Title	Yr	NM
❏ 29847	Honkytonk Man/Shotgun Rag	1982	$4

— B-side by Johnny Gimble and the Texas Swing Band

Number	Title	Yr	NM
❏ B-14812	*Five Brothers/Little Joe the Wrangler/Song of the Bandit/I've Got No Use for the Woman	1960	$15
❏ B-14811	*San Angelo/Prairie Fire/Streets of Laredo	1960	$15
❏ B-14813	*She Was Young and She Was Pretty/My Love/Ride Cowboy Ride/This Peaceful Sod	1960	$15
❏ B-2116	*Singing the Blues/I Can't Quit/Long Gone Lonesome Blues/Lorelei	1956	$60
❏ B-10871	*Song of the Islands/Now Is the Hour/Sweet Leilani/Aloha Oe	1957	$20
❏ B-2134 [PS]	A White Sport Coat	1957	$50
❏ B-2134	A White Sport Coat/Mean Mama Blues//Grown-Up Tears/Long Tall Sally	1957	$50
❏ B-2814	A White Sport Coat/Singing the Blues//The Story of My Life/I'm So Lonesome I Could Cry	1958	$15
❏ B-13492	Big Iron/In the Valley//Running Gun/Utah Carol	1959	$15
❏ B-13493	Cool Water/The Master's Call//Billy the Kid/The Little Green Valley	1959	$20
❏ B-13491	El Paso/A Hundred and Sixty Acres//They're Hanging Me Tonight/The Strawberry Roan	1959	$15
❏ B-13491 [PS]	Gunfighter Ballads and Trail Songs, Vol. I	1959	$15
❏ B-13492 [PS]	Gunfighter Ballads and Trail Songs, Vol. II	1959	$15
❏ B-13493 [PS]	Gunfighter Ballads and Trail Songs, Vol. III	1959	$20
❏ B-2808	I Couldn't Keep from Crying/Sing Me Something Sentimental//Tennessee Toddy/You Don't Owe Me a Thing	1957	$60
❏ H-1785	I'll Go On Alone/Crying 'Cause I Love You//I Couldn't Keep from Crying/A Half-Way Chance with You	1953	$70
❏ B-9763	I'll Step Aside/All the World Is Lonely Now//Bouquet of Roses/Have I Told You Lately That I Love You?	1957	$20

Number	Title	Yr	NM
❏ B-9762	I Never Let You Cross My Mind/I Hang My Head and Cry/You Only Want Me When You're Lonely/Moanin' the Blues	1957	$20
❏ B-9761	Lovesick Blues/I'm So Lonesome I Could Cry//It's Too Late Now/Rose of Ol' Pawnee	1957	$20
❏ H-1785 [PS]	Marty Robbins	1953	$70
❏ B-2153 [PS]	Marty Robbins	1957	$35
❏ B-2814 [PS]	Marty Robbins	1958	$15
❏ B-11891 [PS]	Marty Robbins	1958	$20
❏ B-2808 [PS]	Marty Robbins (Hall of Fame Series)	1957	$60
❏ B-14811 [PS]	More Gunfighter Ballads and Trail Songs, Vol. I	1960	$15
❏ B-14812 [PS]	More Gunfighter Ballads and Trail Songs, Vol. II	1960	$15
❏ B-14813 [PS]	More Gunfighter Ballads and Trail Songs, Vol. III	1960	$15
❏ B-2116 [PS]	Singing the Blues	1956	$60
❏ B-10871 [PS]	Song of the Islands	1957	$20
❏ B-2153	The Letter Edged in Black/The Little Rosewood Casket//The Dream of the Miner's Child/The Convict and the Rose	1957	$35
❏ B-9763 [PS]	The Song of Robbins, Vol. III	1957	$20
❏ B-9761 [PS]	The Song of Robbins Vol. I	1957	$20
❏ B-9762 [PS]	The Song of Robbins Vol. II	1957	$20

ROBBINS, MEL

ARGO

Number	Title	Yr	NM
❏ 5340	Save It/To Know You	1959	$125

ROBBS, THE

ABC

Number	Title	Yr	NM
❏ 11270	I'll Never Get Enough/It All Comes Back	1970	$6

ABC DUNHILL

Number	Title	Yr	NM
❏ 4208	Write to You/Movin'	1969	$10
❏ 4233	Written in the Dust/Last of the Wine	1970	$8

ATLANTIC

Number	Title	Yr	NM
❏ 2578	A Good Time Song/Changin' Winds	1968	$10
❏ 2511	Castles in the Air/I Don't Want to Discuss It	1968	$10

MERCURY

Number	Title	Yr	NM
❏ 72641	Bittersweet/End of the Week	1966	$10
❏ 72641 [PS]	Bittersweet/End of the Week	1966	$20
❏ 72730	Girls, Girls/Violets of Dawn	1967	$10
❏ 72616	I Don't Feel Alone/Next Time You Call Me	1966	$10

ROBBY AND THE ROBBINS

TODD

Number	Title	Yr	NM
❏ 1089	Surfer's Life/She Cried	1963	$50

ROBERT AND JOHNNY

OLD TOWN

Number	Title	Yr	NM
❏ 1043	Broken Hearted Man/Indian Marriage	1957	$50
❏ 1038	Don't Do It/Baby Come Home	1957	$50
❏ 1068	Dream Girl/Oh My Love	1959	$40
❏ 1058	Eternity with You/I'm Truly, Truly Yours	1958	$40
❏ 1065	Give Me the Key to Your Heart/Truly in Love	1959	$40
❏ 1078	Hear My Heartbeat/Try Me Pretty Baby	1960	$30
❏ 1052	I Believe in You/Marry Me	1958	$50
❏ 1021	I Believe You/Train to Paradise	1956	$60
❏ 1052	I Know/Marry Me	1958	$50
❏ 1108	Togetherness/I Got You	1961	$30
❏ 1072	Wear This Ring/Bad Dan	1959	$40
❏ 1117	Wear This Ring/Broken Hearted Man	1962	$30
❏ 1047	We Belong Together/In the Rain	1958	$60
❏ 1086	We Belong Together/In the Rain	1960	$30

SUE

Number	Title	Yr	NM
❏ 792	A Perfect Wife/Brown, Pretty Brown Eyes	1963	$30

Number	Title	Yr	NM
ROBERTS, ART			
IMPERIAL			
❑ 5504	Give Her the Ax, Max/Terrible Ivan	1958	$30
ROBERTS, BILL, AND THE WAYNE SINGERS			
ACCENT			
❑ 1266	Christmas Is For Everyone/Have A Heart	1967	$8
ROBERTS, BOBBY, AND THE RAVONS			
CAMEO			
❑ 339	How Can I Make Her Mine/I'm in Love Again	1965	$40
GMA			
❑ 10	How Can I Make Her Mine/I'm in Love Again	1964	$120
ROBERTS, BOBBY			
HUT			
❑ 881	Cravin'/Hop Skip and Jump	1958	$250
KING			
❑ 4868	Her and My Best Friend/I'm Pullin' Stakes and Leavin' You	1956	$125
❑ 4837	I'm Gonna Comb You Outta My Hair/My Undecided Heart	1955	$60
SKY			
❑ 56-101	Big Sandy/She's My Woman	1956	$2000
— VG 1000; VG+ 1500			
ROBERTS, DEREK			
ROULETTE			
❑ 4656	There Won't Be Any Snow (Christmas In The Jungle)/A World Without Sunshine	1965	$10
ROBERTS, HOUSTON			
LITTLE DARLIN'			
❑ 024	If the Price Is Right/The Tie That Binds	1967	$10
❑ 012	The All American Boy/Sorry, Wrong Number	1966	$12
ROBERTS, JOEY, JR.			
CAMEO			
❑ 418	Once in a Lifetime/That Man's Got No Luck	1966	$20
ROBERTS, KENNY, AND TOMMY SOSEBEE			
CORAL			
❑ 9-64112	It's Great to Be a Christian/Let Jesus Come Into Your Heart	1951	$30
❑ 9-64108	The Sissy Song/She Said	1951	$30
ROBERTS, KENNY			
BETHLEHEM			
❑ 3052	Cheer Up/Sing Me a Hurtin' Song	1962	$15
CORAL			
❑ 9-61035	A Dear John Letter/She Taught Me How to Yodel	1953	$30
❑ 9-60540	Beautiful Ohio/I Miss My Swiss	1951	$30
❑ 9-64151	Call of the Wild/Love Makes a New Fool Every Day	1952	$30
❑ 9-64070	Cry Baby Blues/One Way Ticket	1950	$40
❑ 9-60696	Ding Dong Bells (Are Ringing Again)/I'd Like to Kiss Susie Again	1952	$30
❑ 9-64115	F.O.B. Tennessee/Good Old Mountain Dew	1952	$30
❑ 9-64105	He'll Be Coming Down the Chimney/Grandfather Kringle	1951	$30
❑ 9-64142	Hillbilly Style/The Yodel Polka	1952	$30
❑ 9-60818	Honky Tonk Sweetheart/Mighty Pretty Waltz	1952	$30
❑ 9-64089	I Believe I'm Entitled to You/Just a Yodel for Me	1951	$30
❑ 9-64059	I Finally Got Maggie Alone/Choo Choo Ch' Boogie	1950	$40
❑ 9-64064	If You've Got the Money, I've Got the Time/Molasses, Molasses	1950	$40
❑ 9-64073	May the Good Lord Bless and Keep You/Wide Is the Gate	1951	$30
❑ 9-64079	Mickey the Chickey/Casper, the Candy Cowboy	1951	$30
❑ 9-60884	Sleighbell Polka/Elfie the Elf	1952	$30
❑ 9-60932	Sweet Little Cherokee/Hush Puppies	1953	$30
❑ 9-61133	Wicked Little Cricket/Buzzy the Bumble Bee	1954	$30
DECCA			
❑ 9-30472	Arizona Yodeler/Dream Little Cowboy	1957	$30
❑ 9-30073	Broken Teen-Age Heart/I'm Looking for the Bully of the Town	1956	$20

Number	Title	Yr	NM
DOT			
❑ 15140	Smoke Gets in Your Eyes/Wagon Wheels	1954	$30
KING			
❑ 5773	Choc'late Ice Cream Cone/24 Hours with the Blues	1963	$15
❑ 5543	Goodbye for Him (Hello for Me)/Two Steps Forward (Three Steps Back)	1961	$20
❑ 5911	I Never See Maggie Alone/I'm Crying on the Inside	1964	$15
STARDAY			
❑ 769	Anytime/Tying the Leaves	1966	$10
❑ 869	Artificial Flowers/Gonna Whistle Me a Tune	1969	$8
❑ 788	Blue/Sioux City Sue	1966	$15
❑ 851	Country Music Singing Sensation/Fugitive of Love	1968	$8
❑ 736	Fly Away Mockingbird/If I'm a Man	1965	$10
❑ 716	Tavern Town/Guitar Ringing	1965	$10
ROBERTS, LANCE			
SUN			
❑ 348	The Good Guy Always Wins/The Time Is Right	1960	$30
ROBERTS, LOU			
MGM			
❑ 13387	Don't Count on Me/Ten to One	1965	$30
❑ 13347	Gettin' Ready/You Fooled Me	1965	$40
ROBERTS, PADDY			
LONDON			
❑ 9573	...And A Happy New Year/Got 'n' Idea	1962	$15
ROBERTS, ROCKY, AND THE AIREDALES			
BRUNSWICK			
❑ 55357	Buzz Buzz Buzz/Too Much	1967	$10
❑ 55368	Tell Me/Gotta Thing Going	1968	$10
ROBERTS, WAYNE			
20TH CENTURY FOX			
❑ 644	Little Girl/One Piece Bathing Suit	1966	$30
ROBERTSON, DON			
CAPITOL			
❑ F4282	Mery Men/A Fine Day	1959	$15
❑ F3391	The Happy Whistler/You're Free to Go	1956	$20
MONUMENT			
❑ ZS88674	Must Be a Better Way to Say Goodbye/Marguerita	1975	$5
❑ ZS88694	She Comes Home to Me/When I Was With You	1976	$5
RCA VICTOR			
❑ 47-7862	Bobby-O/Buttons and Bows	1961	$10
❑ 47-8269	Dictionary Song/What a Day	1963	$12
❑ 47-9289	Don't Keep Me Lonely Too Long/Jamaica Rum	1967	$8
❑ 47-7909	Feather in the Wind/Tennessee Waltz	1961	$10
❑ 47-8177	It's Hard for a King to Step Down/Life Goes On	1963	$10
ROBERTSON, ROBBIE			
GEFFEN			
❑ 28175	Showdown at Big Sky/Hell's Half Acre	1987	$4
❑ 28175 [PS]	Showdown at Big Sky/Hell's Half Acre	1987	$4
❑ 28111	Somewhere Down the Crazy River/Hell's Half Acre	1988	$4
ROBERTSON, TEXAS JIM			
MGM			
❑ 11787	Hide-a-Way Love/Automatic Woman	1954	$30
❑ 11860	Pride of My Heart/Walkin' and Talkin' with the Lord	1954	$30
RCA VICTOR			
❑ 47-4906	Blue Eyed Ellen/Life Passed Me By	1952	$30
❑ 48-0492	Deadly Weapon/Bite Your Tongue and Say You're Sorry	1951	$30
❑ 48-0427	Don't You Angel Me/You Can't Do Nothin' with a Woman	1951	$30
❑ 48-0398	I Don't Want No More of the Army Life/If You've Got the Money, I've Got the Time	1950	$40
— Originals on green vinyl			
❑ 48-0097	I Heard the Angels Weep/I'm So Low	1949	$40
— Originals on green vinyl			
❑ 48-0133	I'll Never Slip Around Again/Revenge	1949	$40
— Originals on green vinyl			

Number	Title	Yr	NM
❑ 48-0178	I'll Walk This Weary Road Alone/I'm Back to Where I Started	1950	$40
— Originals on green vinyl			
❑ 47-4326	Lonesome Whistle/Gotta Git a Glitter	1951	$30
❑ 48-0334	One Kind Word/Yesterday's Kisses	1950	$40
— Originals on green vinyl			
❑ 47-4710	Put Your Arms Around Me/Low in the Lehigh Valley	1952	$30
❑ 48-0071	Slipping Around/Wedding Bells	1949	$50
— Originals on green vinyl			
❑ 48-0071	Slipping Around/Wedding Bells	1950	$30
— Reissues on black vinyl			
❑ 47-4548	Taffy/I'm Gonna Be Long Gone	1952	$30
❑ 48-0463	Wildcat Baby/Why Don't You Marry the Girl	1951	$30
ROBIN AND THE MERRY MEN			
MOHAWK			
❑ 130	Mr. Santa, Bring Me a Doll/Ellen	1960	$20
ROBIN HOOD BRIANS			
UNI			
❑ 55226	Crazy 'Bout Your Sunshine/Miami	1970	$8
❑ 55166	Web of Love/Goodbye, So Long, Honolulu	1969	$8
ROBIN, RICHIE			
GOLDISC			
❑ 3002	Sugar Love/Bonnie Come Home	1960	$20
❑ 3008	This Little Girl of Mine/A Little Bit Is Better Than Nothing	1960	$20
GONE			
❑ 5083	Branded/Strange Dreams	1959	$30
❑ 5077	Mama, I Wanna Dance/Jiving with the Saints	1959	$30
ROBIN SISTERS, THE			
POLARIS			
❑ 100	Chimney Top Twist/Santa's Little Workshop	1962	$20
ROBIN, TINA			
CORAL			
❑ 62015	A Little Bird Told Me/We've All Gotta Live in This House	1958	$15
❑ 61862	All of Me/Little Gray Cat	1957	$15
❑ 61935	Everyday/Believe Me	1958	$15
❑ 61848	Lady Fair/Over Somebody Else's Shoulder	1957	$15
❑ 61822	My Mammy/I Have a Heart	1957	$15
❑ 62076	Sunshine/The Power of Prayer	1959	$15
❑ 62055	Winter Wonderland Cha Cha/I've Got My Love To Keep Me Warm	1958	$15
MERCURY			
❑ 71852	Dear Mr. D.J. Play It Again/Nothing's Impossible	1961	$12
❑ 72074	Get Out of My Life/Why Did You Go	1963	$10
ROBINS, THE (1)			
ATCO			
❑ 6059	Smokey Joe's Cafe/Just Like a Fool	1956	$60
CROWN			
❑ 106	I Made a Vow/Double Crossing Baby	1954	$400
KNIGHT			
❑ 2008	It's Never Too Late/A Little Bird Told Me	1958	$100
RCA VICTOR			
❑ 47-5564	Get It Off Your Mind/Don't Stop Now	1953	$200
❑ 47-5434	How Would You Know/Let's Go to the Dance	1953	$400
❑ 47-5486	My Baby Done Told Me/I'll Do It	1953	$300
❑ 47-5271	Oh Why/All Night Baby	1953	$400
❑ 20-5271	Oh Why/All Night Baby	1953	$100
❑ 47-5489	Ten Days in Jail/Empty Bottles	1953	$200
SPARK			
❑ 110	If Teardrops Were Kisses/Whadaya Want	1955	$300
— Red label			
❑ 110	If Teardrops Were Kisses/Whadaya Want	1955	$125
— Blue label			
❑ 116	I Must Be Dreamin'/The Hatchet Man	1955	$200
— Red label			
❑ 116	I Must Be Dreamin'/The Hatchet Man	1955	$60
— Yellow label			

Number	Title	Yr	NM
❑ 107	Loop De Loop Mambo/Framed	1954	$300
— Silver top label			
❑ 107	Loop De Loop Mambo/Framed	1954	$125
— Red label			
❑ 113	One Kiss/I Love Paris	1955	$300
❑ 122	Smokey Joe's Cafe/Just Like a Fool	1955	$350
WHIPPET			
❑ 206	A Fool in Love/All of a Sudden My Heart Sings	1957	$75
❑ 200	Cherry Lips/Out of the Picture	1956	$100
❑ 208	Every Night/Where's the Fire	1957	$75
❑ 201	Hurt Me/Merry-Go-Rock	1956	$75
❑ 211	In My Dreams/Keep Your Mind on Me	1957	$75
❑ 212	Snowball/You Wanted Fun	1958	$75
❑ 203	That Old Black Magic/Since I First Met You	1956	$75

ROBINS, THE (2)
ARDENT

Number	Title	Yr	NM
❑ 106	Batman/Batarang	1966	$40

ROBINS, THE (3)
LAVENDER

Number	Title	Yr	NM
❑ 02	Magic of a Dream/Mary Lou Loves to Hootchy Kootchy Koo	1961	$50
❑ 01	The White Cliffs of Dover/How Many More Times	1961	$50

ROBINS, THE (U)
ARVEE

Number	Title	Yr	NM
❑ 5013	Live Wire Suzie/Oh No	1960	$30
DOT			
❑ 16519	Blue Grass Blues/Top 40 Blues	1963	$15
GONE			
❑ 5101	Baby Love/We Loved	1961	$40
MUSICOR			
❑ 1050	Cry Over You/Lucy Watusi	1964	$20

ROBINSON, BILL, AND THE QUAILS
DATE

Number	Title	Yr	NM
❑ 1620	Do I Love You/Lay My Head on Your Shoulder	1969	$12
DELUXE			
❑ 6057	A Little Bit of Love/Somewhere Somebody Cares	1954	$200
❑ 6047	I Know She's Gone/Baby Don't Want Me No More	1954	$300
❑ 6030	Lonely Star/Quit Pushin'	1954	$200
❑ 6074	Love of My Life/Oh Sugar	1955	$200
❑ 6085	The Things She Used to Do/Pretty Huggin' Baby	1955	$75
— As "The Quails"			
❑ 6059	Why Do I Wait/Heaven Is the Place	1954	$200

ROBINSON, FLOYD
DOT

Number	Title	Yr	NM
❑ 16352	I Need You/Show Boat	1961	$15
❑ 16290	The Art of Making Love/Don't Let Me Fall	1961	$15
GROOVE			
❑ 58-0040	My Little Martian/Surprise	1964	$100
JAMIE			
❑ 1186	Mother Nature/Is There Something I Ought to Know?	1961	$20
RCA VICTOR			
❑ 47-7789	A Girl Like You/Why Can't It Go On	1960	$20
❑ 47-7736	Boys and Girls/Sonja	1960	$20
❑ 47-7685	Little Sir Echo/Alphabet Song	1960	$20
❑ 47-7529	Makin' Love/My Girl	1959	$30
❑ 47-7827	Out of Gas/Magic Lamp	1960	$40
❑ 47-7693	Tattletale/I Believe in Love	1960	$30
❑ 47-7637	Tonight You Belong to Me/Let It Be Me	1959	$20
UNITED ARTISTS			
❑ 534	Heartaches/I've Got a Sweetheart	1963	$15
❑ 986	Sidewalk Surfer/Motorcycle Man	1966	$20

7-Inch Extended Plays
RCA VICTOR

Number	Title	Yr	NM
❑ EPA-4350	(contents unknown)	1959	$60
❑ EPA-4350 [PS]	Makin' Love	1959	$60

ROBINSON, FREDDY
CHECKER

Number	Title	Yr	NM
❑ 1143	The Creeper/Go Go Girl	1966	$12
LIBERTY			
❑ 56214	Carmalita/Stone Stallion	1970	$6
MERCURY			
❑ 71270	Be Mine/You and Me	1958	$15

PACIFIC JAZZ

Number	Title	Yr	NM
❑ 88152	Before Six/The Coming Atlantis	1969	$6
❑ 88155	Black Fox/The Oogue Boogum Song	1970	$6

ROBINSON, JOHNNY
EPIC

Number	Title	Yr	NM
❑ 10578	God Is Love/Kansas City	1970	$10
❑ 10607	Person to Person/Lady Doctor	1970	$10
MERCURY			
❑ 72434	I Gotta Kick the Habit (Part 1)/I Gotta Kick the Habit (Part 2)	1965	$30
OKEH			
❑ 7307	Gone But Not Forgotten/I Need Your Love So Bad	1968	$125
❑ 7328	Green Green Grass of Home/You've Been With Him	1969	$30
❑ 7317	Poor Man/When a Man Cries	1968	$30

ROBINSON, MARK
JAMIE

Number	Title	Yr	NM
❑ 1103	Pretty Jane/Want Me	1958	$30
TEE GEE			
❑ 104	Pretty Jane/Want Me	1958	$50

ROBINSON, REVEREND CLEOPHUS
PEACOCK

Number	Title	Yr	NM
❑ 3044	Go Tell It On The Mountain/Just Ask Him	1964	$10
❑ 3071	Silent Night/Amen	1965	$10
❑ 1789	Silent Night/I'm Not Tired Yet	1958	$20

ROBINSON, SMOKEY, AND THE MIRACLES
See THE MIRACLES.

ROBINSON, SMOKEY
COLUMBIA

Number	Title	Yr	NM
❑ 07727	I Know You by Heart/Could I Have Your Autograph	1988	$3
— With Dolly Parton			
MOTOWN			
❑ 1925	Love Don't Give No Reason/Hanging On by a Thread	1988	$3
❑ 1925 [PS]	Love Don't Give No Reason/Hanging On by a Thread	1988	$5
❑ 1897	One Heartbeat/Love Will Set You Free (Theme from Solarbabies)	1987	$3
❑ 1897 [PS]	One Heartbeat/Love Will Set You Free (Theme from Solarbabies)	1987	$6
❑ 1911	What's Too Much/I've Made Love to You a Thousand Times	1987	$3
❑ 1911 [PS]	What's Too Much/I've Made Love to You a Thousand Times	1987	$5
TAMLA			
❑ 1735	And I Don't Love You/Dynamite	1984	$4
❑ 54276	An Old Fashioned Man/Just Passing Through	1976	$5
❑ 54325	Aquicontigo/Being with You (Aquicontigo)	1981	$4
❑ 1630	Are You Still Here/Yes It's You Lady	1982	$4
❑ 54239	Baby Come Close/A Silent Partner in a Three-Way Love Affair	1973	$5
❑ 54258	Baby That's Backatcha/Just Passing Through	1975	$5
❑ 54321	Being with You/What's In Your Life for Me	1981	$4
❑ 1684	Blame It on Love/Even Tho'	1983	$4
— With Barbara Mitchell			
❑ 54306	Cruisin'/Ever Had a Dream	1979	$4
❑ 54293	Daylight and Darkness/Why You Wanna See My Bad Side	1978	$5
❑ 1700	Don't Play Another Love Song/Wouldn't You Like to Know	1983	$4
❑ 1786	First Time on a Ferris Wheel/Train of Thought	1985	$4
❑ 54301	Get Ready/Ever Had a Dream	1979	$4
❑ 1855	Girl I'm Standing There/Because of You (It's the Best It's Ever Been)	1986	$4
❑ 54313	Heavy on Pride/I Love the Nearness of You	1980	$4
❑ 1828	Hold On to Your Love/Train of Thought	1985	$4
❑ 1828 [PS]	Hold On to Your Love/Train of Thought	1985	$6
❑ 54251	I Am, I Am/The Family Song	1974	$5
❑ 1756	I Can't Find/Gimme What You Want	1984	$4
❑ 54296	I'm Loving You Softly/Shoe Soul	1978	$5
❑ 54246	It's Her Turn to Live/Just My Soul Responding	1974	$5
❑ 1655	I've Made Love to You a Thousand Times/Into Each Rain Some Life Must Fall	1983	$4
❑ 54318	I Want to Be Your Love/Wine, Women and Song	1980	$4
❑ 54311	Let Me Be the Clock/Travelin' Through	1980	$4

Number	Title	Yr	NM
❑ 1868	Love Will Set You Free (Theme from Solarbabies) (Parts 1 & 2)	1986	$4
❑ 1615	Old Fashioned Love/Destiny	1982	$4
❑ 54267	Open/Coincidentally	1976	$5
❑ 1839	Sleepless Nights/Close Encounters of the First Kind	1986	$4
❑ 1839 [PS]	Sleepless Nights/Close Encounters of the First Kind	1986	$5
❑ 54233	Sweet Harmony/Want to Know My Mind	1973	$5
❑ 1601	Tell Me Tomorrow (Part 1)/Tell Me Tomorrow (Part 2)	1982	$4
❑ 54261	The Agony and the Ecstasy/Wedding Song	1975	$5
❑ 54288	Theme from Big Time (Part 1)/Theme from Big Time (Part 2)	1977	$5
❑ 54279	There Will Come a Day (I'm Gonna Happen to You)/Humming Song	1977	$5
❑ 1678	Touch the Sky/All My Life's a Lie	1983	$4
❑ 54269	When You Came/Coincidentally	1976	$15
— Released only in Canada			
❑ 54332	Who's Sad/Food for Thought	1981	$4

ROBINSON, SUGAR CHILE
CAPITOL

Number	Title	Yr	NM
❑ F1526	Baby Blues/The Donkey Song	1951	$30
❑ F1386	Broken Down Piano/I'll Get My Spinach	1951	$30
❑ F1259	Christmas Boogie/Rudolph the Red-Nosed Reindeer	1950	$30
❑ F1719	The Hunkie Man/The Green Grass Grows All Around	1951	$30

ROBISON, CARSON
MGM

Number	Title	Yr	NM
❑ K10949	6 P.M./Our Silver Anniversary	1951	$25
❑ K10053	Bob's Favorite/Maverick	1949	$30
— Reissue of 78 from 1947			
❑ K11688	Denver, Dragon (Part 1)/Denver, Dragon (Part 2)	1954	$30
❑ K10051	Head Couples Separate/Hook and Whirl	1949	$30
— Reissue of 78 from 1947			
❑ K11432	Ike's Letter to Harry/Harry's Reply	1953	$40
❑ K12355	I'm Going Back to Where I Come From/Will Someone Please Tell Me Who	1956	$20
❑ K11293	I'm No Communist/Will Someone Please Tell Me	1952	$40
❑ K10052	Lady Round the Lady/Devil's Britches	1949	$30
— Reissue of 78 from 1947			
❑ K11091	Old Tom the Turkey/Barnyard Square Dance	1951	$30
❑ K11044	Plumb Aggrevatin' Ain't It/Sunday Drivers	1951	$30
❑ K10054	Pokeberry Promenade/When Work's All Done This Fall	1949	$30
— Reissue of 78 from 1947; the above four comprise 45 rpm box set K-5, "Square Dances"			
❑ K11475	Spring! Spring! (Part 1)/Spring! Spring! (Part 2)	1953	$30
❑ K11159	Square Dance Polka/Promenade Indian	1952	$30
❑ K10837	Texas Dan/The Devil Calls a Meeting	1950	$40
❑ K10732	Trail Drive/That Horse Named Pete	1950	$40
RCA VICTOR			
❑ 47-2871	Golden Slippers/Turkey in the Straw	1949	$30
— The above four comprise box set WP 155			
❑ 47-2868	Irish Washerwoman/Spanish Caballero	1949	$30
❑ 47-2869	Solomon Levi/Comin' Round the Mountain	1949	$30

ROCCO, LENNY
DELSEY

Number	Title	Yr	NM
❑ 301	Sugar Girl/Rochelle	1961	$300

ROCHELL AND THE CANDLES
CHALLENGE

Number	Title	Yr	NM
❑ 9191	Annie's Not an Orphan Anymore/Let's Run Away and Get Married	1963	$30
❑ 9158	Turn Her Down/Each Night	1962	$50
SWINGIN'			
❑ 652	Big Boy Pete/A Long Time Ago	1963	$30
❑ 623	Once Upon a Time/When My Baby Is Gone	1960	$30
❑ 640	Peg of My Heart/Squat with Me, Baby	1962	$30
❑ 634	So Far Away/Hey, Pretty Baby	1961	$30

ROCHES, THE
WARNER BROS.

Number	Title	Yr	NM
❑ 29815	The Hallelujah Chorus/Second Family	1982	$30

Number	Title	Yr	NM
ROCK-A-FELLAS, THE			
ABC-PARAMOUNT			
❑ 9923	Don't Torment Me/Red Lips	1958	$30
DEVERE			
❑ 313	Don't Torment Me/Red Lips	1958	$60
ROCK-A-TEENS, THE			
DORAN			
❑ 3515	Woo Hoo/Untrue	1959	$200
ROULETTE			
❑ 4217	Twangy/Doggone It, Baby	1959	$30
❑ 4192	Woo Hoo/Untrue	1959	$40
ROCK BROTHERS, THE			
KING			
❑ 4851	Dungaree Doll/Livin' It Up	1955	$40
❑ 4882	Oh, Didn't I Ramble/I Gotta Get Back	1956	$30
ROCK GARDEN, THE			
B.T. PUPPY			
❑ 536	Sweet Pajamas/Perhaps the Joy of Giving	1967	$10
ROCK ISLAND			
PROJECT 3			
❑ 1382	Babe I'm Gonna Leave You/ Hard and Never Easy	1970	$12
ROCKA, BILLY			
BRUNSWICK			
❑ 55049	Listen Pretty Baby/I'm Gonna Sit Right Down and Cry	1958	$70
ROCKAWAYS, THE			
RED BIRD			
❑ Oct-005	Top Down Time/Don't Cry	1964	$30
ROCKERS, THE			
CARTER			
❑ 3029	Tell Me Why/Count Every Star	1955	$800
FEDERAL			
❑ 12273	Down in the Bottom/Why Don't You Believe Me	1956	$125
❑ 12267	What Am I to Do/I'll Die in Love with You	1956	$200
ROCKETEERS, THE (1)			
GLAD HAMP			
❑ 2017	Drag Strip/Summertime	1963	$50
ROCKETEERS, THE (2)			
HERALD			
❑ 415	Foolish One/Gonna Feed My Baby Poison	1953	$700
—Black vinyl			
❑ 415	Foolish One/Gonna Feed My Baby Poison	1953	$2000
—Red vinyl			
ROCKETEERS, THE (3)			
MODERN			
❑ 999	Talk It Over Baby/Hey Rube	1956	$60
ROCKETEERS, THE (4)			
M.J.C.			
❑ 501	My Reckless Heart/They Turned the Party Out Down at Bessie's House	1958	$2000
ROCKETONES, THE			
MELBA			
❑ 113	Mexico/Dee I	1957	$60
❑ 113	Mexico/I Do	1957	$70
ROCKETS			
Founded by guitarist Jimmy McCarty and drummer Johnny "Bee" Badanjek, both former members of Mitch Ryder & The Detroit Wheels.			
CAPITOL			
❑ 5262	Turn Up the Radio/Can't Sleep	1983	$3
❑ 5262 [PS]	Turn Up the Radio/Can't Sleep	1983	$4
ELEKTRA			
❑ 47212	Lift You Up/Tired of Wearing Black	1981	$3
RSO			
❑ 926	Can't Sleep/Something Ain't Right	1979	$3
❑ 1022	Desire/Troublemaker	1980	$3
❑ 935	Oh Well/Love Me Once More	1979	$3

Number	Title	Yr	NM
❑ 1028	Sad Song/Takin' It Back	1980	$3
TORTOISE INT'L.			
❑ TB-11207	She's a Pretty One/I've Got to Move	1978	$4
ROCKETS, THE (2)			
ATLANTIC			
❑ 988	Open the Door/Big Leg Mama	1953	$125
ROCKETS, THE (3)			
COLUMBIA			
❑ 41512	Gibraltar Rock/Walkin' Home	1959	$30
ROCKETS, THE (5)			
WHITE WHALE			
❑ 270	Hole in My Pocket/Let Me Go	1968	$20
ROCKETTES, THE			
PARROT			
❑ 789	I Can't Forget/Love Nobody	1954	$3000
—VG 1000; VG+ 2000			
ROCKIN' BERRIES, THE			
REPRISE			
❑ 0442	Doesn't Time Fly/The Water Is Over My Head	1965	$12
❑ 0329	He's in Town/Flashback	1964	$15
❑ 0377	Poor Man's Son/Follow Me	1965	$12
❑ 0355	What in the World's Come Over You/You Don't Know What to Do	1965	$10
ROCKIN' CHAIRS, THE			
RECORTE			
❑ 412	Memories of Love/Girl of Mine	1959	$60
❑ 404	Please Mary/Come On Baby	1958	$60
ROCKIN' DUKES, THE			
O.J.			
❑ 1007	Angel and a Rose/My Baby Left Me	1957	$300
ROCKIN' KIDS, THE			
DOT			
❑ 15749	Black Stockings/Yea Yea (I'm in the Mood)	1958	$40
ROCKIN' RAMRODS, THE			
BON-BON			
❑ 1315	She Lies/The Girl Can't Help It	1964	$200
CLARIDGE			
❑ 301	Don't Fool with Fu Manchu/Tears	1965	$50
❑ 317	Play It/Got My Mojo Workin'	1966	$40
PLYMOUTH			
❑ 2965	Flowers in My Mind/Mary, Mary	1967	$40
—As "The Ramrods"			
❑ 2961	I Wanna Be Your Man/I'll Be On My Way	1964	$60
❑ 2961 [PS]	I Wanna Be Your Man/I'll Be On My Way	1964	$125
❑ 2963	Mister Wind/Bright Lit Blue Skies	1966	$30
—As "The Ramrods"			
SOUTHERN SOUND			
❑ SS305	Wild About You/Cry in My Room	1965	$60
❑ SS305	Wild About You/Cry in My Room	1965	$60
—Promo only			
ROCKIN' REBELS, THE			
ITZY			
❑ 8	Wild Weekend/Wild Weekend Cha Cha	1963	$30
MAR-LEE			
❑ 095	Buffalo Blues/Donkey Walk	1961	$40
—As "The Buffalo Rebels"			
❑ 096	Theme from Rebel/Any Way You Want Me	1961	$40
—As "The Buffalo Rebels"			
❑ 094	Wild Weekend/Wild Weekend Cha Cha	1960	$125
—As "The Rebels"			
STORK			
❑ STK-3	Bongo Blue Beat/Burn Baby Burn	1964	$30
SWAN			
❑ 4150	Another Wild Weekend/Happy Popcorn	1963	$30
❑ 4161	Monday Morning/Flibbity Jibbit	1963	$30
❑ 4248	Wild Weekend/Donkey Twine	1966	$30

Number	Title	Yr	NM
❑ 4125	Wild Weekend/Wild Weekend Cha Cha	1962	$50
—First pressings credit "The Rebels"			
❑ 4125	Wild Weekend/Wild Weekend Cha Cha	1962	$40
—Second pressings credit "Rockin' Rebels" and do not have "Don't Drop Out" on the label			
❑ 4125	Wild Weekend/Wild Weekend Cha Cha	1963	$30
—Later pressings credit "Rockin' Rebels" and have "Don't Drop Out" on the label			
ROCKIN' R'S, THE			
STEPHENY			
❑ 1842	Walkin' You to School/ Bewitched (Bothered and Bewildered)	1960	$30
TEMPUS			
❑ 7541	Crazy Baby/The Beat	1959	$50
❑ 1515	Mustang/I'm Still in Love with You	1959	$40
VEE JAY			
❑ 346	Hum Bug/The Mix	1960	$30
❑ 334	Mustang/I'm Still in Love with You	1959	$30
ROCKIN' SAINTS, THE			
DECCA			
❑ 31144	Cheat on Me, Baby/Half and Half	1960	$100
❑ 30990	Saints Rock/Alright Baby	1959	$40
ROCKIN' SIDNEY			
EPIC			
❑ 34-05430	My Toot Toot/Jalapeno Lena	1985	$4
❑ 1183	Soul Christmas (Part 1)/Soul Christmas (Part 2)	1966	$15
❑ 1186	The Grandpa/Feel Delicious	1967	$10
❑ 110	My Little Girl/Don't Say Goodbye	1959	$60
❑ 141	Walking Out on You/Rocky	1960	$40
❑ 1024	My Toot Toot/Zydeco Shoes	1984	$8
❑ 1025	Party This Christmas/Christmas Without You	1984	$6
ROCKIN' VICKERS			
COLUMBIA			
❑ 43818	Dandy/I Don't Need Your Love	1966	$20
ROCKING BROTHERS, THE			
IMPERIAL			
❑ 5341	Blow Torch/Evening Shadows	1955	$40
SAVOY			
❑ 1144	Play Boy Hop/The Grinder	1955	$60
ROCKPILE			
Also see DAVE EDMUNDS; NICK LOWE.			
COLUMBIA			
❑ 60503	Heart/Take a Message to Mary	1981	$4
—B-side by Dave Edmunds and Nick Lowe			
❑ 11388	Teacher Teacher/Fool Too Long	1980	$4
ROCKWELL			
MOTOWN			
❑ 1845	Carme (Part 1)/(Part 2)	1986	$4
❑ 1863	Grow Up/(Instrumental)	1986	$4
❑ 1772	He's a Cobra/Change Your Ways	1984	$4
❑ 1772 [PS]	He's a Cobra/Change Your Ways	1984	$6
❑ 1731	Obscene Phone Caller/ (Instrumental)	1984	$4
❑ 1731 [PS]	Obscene Phone Caller/ (Instrumental)	1984	$4
❑ 1782	Peeping Tom/Tokyo	1985	$4
❑ 1702	Somebody's Watching Me/ (Instrumental)	1984	$4
ROCKY FELLERS, THE			
DONNA			
❑ 1383	Don't Sit Down/The Beachcomber Song	1963	$15
PARKWAY			
❑ 836	Long Tall Sally/South Pacific Twist	1962	$15
SCEPTER			
❑ 1263	Bye Bye Baby/She Makes Me Wanna Dance	1963	$15
❑ 1258	Ching-a-Ling Baby/Hey Little Donkey	1963	$15
❑ 1254	Like the Big Guys Do/Great Big World	1963	$15
❑ 1254 [PS]	Like the Big Guys Do/Great Big World	1963	$30
❑ 1271	My Prayer/Two Guys from Trinidad	1964	$15

Number	Title	Yr	NM
❑ 1245	Santa Santa/Great Big World	1962	$30

—A-side is a very early Neil Diamond composition

Number	Title	Yr	NM
❑ 1245 [DJ]	Santa Santa/Santa's Grove	1963	$15

—Promo reissue with new B-side. All-white label (no black oval)

VALMOR

Number	Title	Yr	NM
❑ 2004	Opus/Orange Peel	1962	$20

WARNER BROS.

Number	Title	Yr	NM
❑ 5459	Better Let Her Go/Nina	1964	$12
❑ 5440	(Everybody Wants to Be a) Tiger/Jeannie Memsoh	1964	$12
❑ 5497	Man with the Blue Guitar/Don't Throw My Toys Away	1965	$10

ROD AND CAROLYN

PARKWAY

Number	Title	Yr	NM
❑ 934	Love Is Where You Are/I've Got You on My Mind	1964	$10

RODCAY, HARRY

IMPERIAL

Number	Title	Yr	NM
❑ 8232	My Heart Keeps On Beatin'/ Love You Dearly	1954	$30
❑ 8244	What She Did to Me/Don't Tell a Soul	1954	$30

RODGERS, JIMMIE (1)

RCA VICTOR

Number	Title	Yr	NM
❑ 27-0105	Blue Yodel No. 2/Tuck Away My Lonesome Blues	1950	$30
❑ 27-0103	Blue Yodel No. 3/I'm Sorry We Met	1950	$30

—The above three comprise box set WPT 22

Number	Title	Yr	NM
❑ 27-0101	Blue Yodel No. 4/Waiting for a Train	1950	$30
❑ 27-0106	Blue Yodel No. 6/Dear Old Sunny South by the Sea	1950	$30

—The above three comprise box set WPT 23

Number	Title	Yr	NM
❑ 27-0098	Blue Yodel (T for Texas)/Away Out on the Mountain	1950	$30
❑ 27-0100	Frankie and Johnny/The Brakeman's Blues	1950	$30

—The above three comprise box set WPT 21

Number	Title	Yr	NM
❑ 47-6092	In the Jailhouse Now No. 2/ Peach Pickin' Time Down in Georgia	1955	$30
❑ 47-6205	Mule Skinner Blues/Mother, the Queen of My Heart	1955	$30
❑ AMAO-0130	Mule Skinner Blues/Waiting for a Train	1973	$8

—Gold Standard Series reissue

Number	Title	Yr	NM
❑ 27-0102	My Old Pal/Desert Blues	1950	$30
❑ 27-0104	Sleep, Baby, Sleep/My Carolina Sunshine Girl	1950	$30

7-Inch Extended Plays

Number	Title	Yr	NM
❑ EPAT23	*My Carolina Sunshine Girl/ Sleep, Baby, Sleep/Blue Yodel No. 2/Tuck Away My Lonesome Blues	1952	$25
❑ 547-0902	Blue Yodel No. 4/Waiting for a Train//Prairie Lullaby/Blue Yodel No. 6	1955	$25

—Side 2" and "Side 3" of EPB-1232

RODGERS, JIMMIE (2)

A&M

Number	Title	Yr	NM
❑ 871	Child of Clay/Turnaround	1967	$6
❑ 1152	Cycles/Tomorrow My Friends	1969	$6
❑ 1120	Father Paul/Me About You	1969	$6
❑ 930	How Do You Say Goodbye/I Wanna Be Free	1968	$6
❑ 902	I Believe It All/You Pass Me By	1968	$6
❑ 898	If I Were the Man/What a Strange Town	1967	$6
❑ 842	I'll Say Goodbye/Shadows	1967	$6
❑ 1055	The Windmills of Your Mind/L.A. Break Down (And Take Me Back In)	1969	$6
❑ 976	Today/The Lovers	1968	$6
❑ 1213	Troubled Times/The Dum Dum Song	1970	$5

DOT

Number	Title	Yr	NM
❑ 16826	A Falen Star/Brother, Where Are You	1966	$8
❑ 16694	(All My Friends Are Gonna Be) Strangers/Bon Soir Mademoiselle	1965	$8
❑ 16749	Are You Going My Way (Little Beachcomber)/Little Schoolgirl	1965	$8
❑ 16781	Bye Bye Love/Hollow Words	1965	$8
❑ 16720	Careless Love/When I'm Right You Don't Remember	1965	$8
❑ 16467	(I Don't Know Why) I Just Do/ Load 'Em Up (And Keep a Steppin')	1963	$10
❑ 16428	I'll Never Stand in Your Way/ Afraid	1963	$10
❑ 16861	It's Over/Anita, You're Dreaming	1966	$10
❑ 16450	Lonely Tears/A Face in the Crowd	1963	$10
❑ 16973	Love Me, Please Love Me/ Wonderful You	1966	$8
❑ 16916	Morning Means Tomorrow/ New Ideas	1966	$8
❑ 16490	Poor Little Raggedy Ann/I'm Gonna Be the Winner	1963	$12
❑ 16795	The Chipmunk Song (Christmas Don't Be Late)/In the Snow	1965	$8
❑ 16595	The World I Used to Know/I Forgot More Than You'll Ever Know	1964	$10
❑ 17040	Time/Yours and Mine	1967	$8
❑ 16561	Together/Mama Was a Cotton Picker	1963	$10
❑ 16527	Two-Ten Six-Eighteen (Doesn't Anybody Know My Name)/The Banana Boat Song	1963	$10
❑ 16673	Two Tickets/I Forgot More Than You'll Ever Know	1964	$10
❑ 16653	Water Boy/Someplace Green	1964	$10

EPIC

Number	Title	Yr	NM
❑ 10828	Froggy's Fable/Daylight Lights the Dawning	1972	$5

MGM

Number	Title	Yr	NM
❑ 11732	Mama, Don't Cry at My Wedding/You Don't Live Here No More	1954	$30

ROULETTE

Number	Title	Yr	NM
❑ 4384	A Little Dog Cried/Englidh Country Garden	1961	$15
❑ 4090	Are You Really Mine/The Wizard	1958	$20
❑ 4090 [PS]	Are You Really Mine/The Wizard	1958	$50
❑ 4116	Bimbombey/You Understand Me	1958	$20
❑ SSR-8001 [S]	Bo Diddley/Soldier Won't You Marry Me	1959	$40
❑ 4349	Everytime My Heart Sings/I'm On My Way	1961	$15
❑ SSR-8007 [S]	Froggy Went a-Courtin'/Lisa	1959	$40
❑ 4015	Honeycomb/Their Hearts Were Full of Spring	1957	$30
❑ 4129	I'm Never Gonna Tell/Because You're Young	1959	$20
❑ 4205	It's Christmas Once Again/ Wistful Willie	1959	$30
❑ 4045	Oh-Oh, I'm Falling in Love Again/The Long Hot Summer	1958	$30

—Red label

Number	Title	Yr	NM
❑ 4045	Oh-Oh, I'm Falling in Love Again/The Long Hot Summer	1958	$20

—White label with colored spokes

Number	Title	Yr	NM
❑ 4070	Secretly/Make Me a Miracle	1958	$30
❑ 4070 [PS]	Secretly/Make Me a Miracle	1958	$50
❑ SSR-8010 [S]	St. James Infirmary/Just a Wearyin' for You	1959	$40
❑ 4260	The Wreck of the John B/Four Little Girls in Boston	1960	$15
❑ 4218 [M]	T.L.C. Tender Love and Care/ Waltzing Matilda	1960	$15
❑ SSR-4218 [S]	T.L.C. Tender Love and Care/ Waltzing Matilda	1960	$40
❑ 4191	Tucumcari/That Night You Became Seventeen	1959	$20
❑ 4318	When Love Is Young/The Little Shepherd of Kingdom Come	1960	$15
❑ 4293	Woman from Liberia/Come Along Julie	1960	$15
❑ 4293 [PS]	Woman from Liberia/Come Along Julie	1960	$30

SCRIMSHAW

Number	Title	Yr	NM
❑ 1313	A Good Woman Likes to Drink with the Boys/Dancing on the Moon	1977	$4
❑ 1319/20	Easy to Love/Easy	1979	$4

—With Michele

Number	Title	Yr	NM
❑ 1314	Everytime I Sing a Love Song/ Just a Little Time	1978	$4
❑ 1318	Secretly/Shovelin' Coal	1978	$4
❑ 1316	When Our Love Began (Cowboys and Indians)/(B-side unknown)	1978	$4
❑ EPR-1-315	Bo Diddley/Riddle Song//The Fox and the Goose/Black Is the Color	1960	$60
❑ EPR-1-317	Soldier, Won't You Marry Me?/ Lassie O'Mine//Liza/Froggy Went a-Courtin'	1960	$60
❑ EPR-1-303	Woman from Liberia/The Mating Call//Hey Little Baby/ Water Boy	1957	$60

RODNEY AND THE BRUNETTES

BOMP!

Number	Title	Yr	NM
❑ 127	Little G.T.O./Holocaust on Sunset Blvd.	1980	$4

—Regular pressing features Rodney Bingenheimer of KROQ with Blondie as backup band

Number	Title	Yr	NM
❑ 127 [PS]	Little G.T.O./Holocaust on Sunset Blvd.	1980	$4
❑ 127	Little G.T.O./Holocaust on Sunset Blvd.	1980	$125

—First pressing, issued by mistake in Europe, is a demo with Deborah Harry of Blondie on vocals

RODRIGUEZ, JOHNNY

CAPITOL

Number	Title	Yr	NM
❑ B-44403	Back to Stay/Someday I'm Gonna Finish Leaving You	1989	$4
❑ B-44071	I Didn't (Every Chance I Had)/I'm Not That Good at Goodbye	1987	$4
❑ B-44204	I Wanta Wake Up with You/ Someday I'm Gonna Finish Leaving You	1988	$4

COLUMBIA

Number	Title	Yr	NM
❑ 02987	The Most Beautiful Girl/Too Far Gone	1982	$4

—With Ray Conniff; B-side by Zella Lehr with Ray Conniff

EPIC

Number	Title	Yr	NM
❑ 04206	Back on Her Mind Again/Eleven Roses	1983	$3
❑ 50671	Down on the Rio Grande/ Mexico Holiday	1979	$4
❑ 04562	First Time Burned/Hand Me Another of Those	1984	$3
❑ 03598	Foolin'/Because of You	1983	$3
❑ 50735	Fools for Each Other/Street Walker	1979	$4
❑ 04838	Here I Am Again/Full Circle	1985	$3
❑ 03275	He's Not Entitled to Your Love/ Starting All Over Again	1982	$3
❑ 03972	How Could I Love Her So Much/Somethin' About a Jukebox	1983	$3
❑ 50791	I Hate the Way I Love It/Almost Persuaded	1979	$4

—With Charly McClain

Number	Title	Yr	NM
❑ 02638	It's Not the Same Old You/Born with the Blues	1981	$3
❑ 01033	I Want You Tonight/Your Love Isn't Mine Anymore	1981	$3
❑ 04460	Let's Leave the Lights On Tonight/What a Movie You'd Make	1984	$3
❑ 50859	Love, Look At Us Now/Where Did It Go	1980	$4
❑ 05863	Maxine/Full Circle	1986	$3
❑ 05732	She Don't Cry Like She Used To/Back on Her Mind Again	1985	$3
❑ 04336	Too Late to Go Home/No Memories Hangin' 'Round	1984	$3
❑ 02411	Trying Not to Love You/Mexico Rain	1981	$3
❑ 50808	What'll I Tell Virginia/Whatever Gets Me Through the Night	1979	$4

MERCURY

Number	Title	Yr	NM
❑ 55050	Alibis/Rest Your Love on Me	1978	$4
❑ 73493	Dance with Me (Just One More Time)/Faded Love	1974	$5

—Red label

Number	Title	Yr	NM
❑ 73493	Dance with Me (Just One More Time)/Faded Love	1974	$4

—Chicago skyline label

Number	Title	Yr	NM
❑ 73878	Desperado/There'll Always Be Honky-Tonks in Texas	1976	$4
❑ 55004	Eres Tu/You Put a Hold on Me	1977	$4
❑ 73855	Hillbilly Heart/Commonly Known As the Blues	1976	$4
❑ 73769	I Couldn't Be Me Without You/ Sometimes I Wish I Were You	1976	$4
❑ 73914	If Practice Makes Perfect/Hard Times	1977	$4
❑ 73659	I Just Can't Get Her Out of My Mind/Have I Told You Lately	1975	$4
❑ 73815	I Wonder If I Ever Said Goodbye/Louisiana	1976	$4
❑ 55029	Love Me with All Your Heart (Cuando Caliente El Sol)	1978	$4
❑ 73715	Love Put a Song in My Heart/ Steppin' Out on You	1975	$4
❑ 73334	Pass Me By (If You're Only Passing Through)/Jealous Heart	1972	$5
❑ 55012	Savin' This Love Song for You/ Que Te Quiero	1977	$4
❑ 73471	Something/Born to Lose	1974	$5
❑ 73446	That's the Way Love Goes/I Really Don't Want to Know	1973	$5
❑ 55020	We Believe in Happy Endings/ The Immigrant	1978	$4
❑ 73621	We're Over/Oh I Miss You	1974	$4

ROE, TOMMY

ABC

Number	Title	Yr	NM
❑ 11076	An Oldie But a Goodie/Sugar Cane	1968	$8
❑ 11164	Dizzy/The You I Need	1969	$12
❑ 11039	Dottie I Like It/Soft Words	1968	$8
❑ 11211	Heather Honey/Money Is My Pay	1969	$6
❑ 10852	Hooray for Hazel/Need Your Love	1966	$10
❑ 11140	It's Gonna Hurt Me/Gotta Keep Rolling Along	1968	$8
❑ 10888	It's Now Winters Day/Kick Me Charlie	1966	$8
❑ 10888 [PS]	It's Now Winters Day/Kick Me Charlie	1966	$20
❑ 11287	Little Miss Goodie Two Shoes/ Traffic Jam	1971	$6
❑ 10945	Little Miss Sunshine/You I Need	1967	$8
❑ 10989	Melancholy Mood/Paisley Dreams	1967	$8

Number	Title	Yr	NM
❏ 10933	Moon Talk/Sweet Sounds	1967	$8
❏ 11266	Pearl/A Dollar's Worth of Pennies	1970	$6
❏ 10908	Sing Along with Me/Night Time	1967	$8
❏ 11307	Stagger Lee/Back Streets and Alleys	1971	$6
❏ 11258	Stir It Up and Serve It/Fire Fly	1970	$6
❏ 10762	Sweet Pea/Much More Love	1966	$10

—Reissue; this was the common version when this song was a hit; earliest copies have "ABC Records" standing alone (not in a circle)

❏ 11273	We Can Make Music/Gotta Keep Rolling Along	1970	$6
❏ 11273 [PS]	We Can Make Music/Gotta Keep Rolling Along	1970	$6

ABC-PARAMOUNT

❏ 10543	Carol/Be a Good Little Girl	1964	$10
❏ 10515	Come On/There Will Be Better Years	1964	$10
❏ 10555	Dance with Henry/Wild Water Skiing Weekend	1964	$30
❏ 10738	Doesn't Anybody Know My Name/Everytime a Bluebird Cries	1965	$12
❏ 10389	Don't Cry Donna/Gonna Take a Chance	1962	$15
❏ 10478	Everybody/Sorry I'm Late, Lisa	1963	$20
❏ 10665	Fourteen Pair of Shoes/Combo Music	1965	$10
❏ 10706	I Keep Remembering (Things I Forgot)/Wish You Didn't Have to Go	1965	$10
❏ 10623	Love Me, Love Me/Diane from Manchester Square	1965	$15
❏ 10579	Oh So Right/I Think I Love You	1964	$15
❏ 10604	Party Girl/Oh How I Could Love You	1964	$12
❏ 10329	Sheila/Save Your Kisses	1962	$20
❏ 10362	Susie Darlin'/Piddle De Pat	1962	$15
❏ 10362 [PS]	Susie Darlin'/Piddle De Pat	1962	$30
❏ 10762	Sweet Pea/Much More Love	1966	$30
❏ 10423	The Folk Singer/Count on Me	1963	$10
❏ 10696	The Gunfighter/I'm a Rambler, I'm a Gambler	1965	$30
❏ 10379	Town Crier/Rainbow	1962	$15
❏ 10379 [PS]	Town Crier/Rainbow	1962	$40

AWESOME

❏ 104	First Things First/(B-side unknown)	1984	$6
❏ 108	Sittin' on a Mood/(B-side unknown)	1984	$6

BGO

❏ 1003	She Do Run Run/(B-side unknown)	1982	$10

JUDD

❏ 1018	Caveman/I Gotta Girl	1960	$60
❏ 1022	Sheila/Pretty Girl	1960	$200

MARK IV

❏ 01	Caveman/I Gotta Girl	1960	$125

MCA CURB

❏ 52711	Some Such Foolishness/Barbara Lou	1985	$4

MERCURY

❏ 888497-7	Back When It Really Mattered/Radio Romance	1987	$3
❏ 888206-7	Let's Be Fools Like That Again/Barbara Lou	1986	$3

MGM SOUTH

❏ 7001	Mean Little Woman, Rosalie/Skyline	1972	$5
❏ 7008	Sarah My Love/Chewing on Sugar Cane	1972	$5
❏ 7025	Silver Eyes/Memphis Me	1973	$6
❏ 7013	Working Class Hero/Sun in My Eyes	1973	$5

MONUMENT

❏ 45-205	Early in the Morning/Bad News	1976	$5
❏ 8705	Everybody/Energy	1976	$5
❏ 8644	Glitter and Gleam/Bad News	1975	$5
❏ 8684	Slow Dancing/Burn On Love Light	1976	$5
❏ 8662	Snowing Me Under/Rita and Her Band	1975	$5

TRUMPET

❏ 1401	Caveman/I Gotta Girl	1960	$200

WARNER BROS.

❏ 49235	Charlie, I Love Your Wife/There Is No Sun on Sunset Boulevard	1980	$4
❏ 8660	Dreamin' Again/Love the Way You Love Me Up	1978	$4
❏ 8800	Massachusetts/Just Look at Me	1979	$5

ROECKER, SHERRILL

SWAN

❏ 4173	Don't Say Nothin' (If You Can't Say Anything Nice)/It's All Over	1964	$12

ROEMANS, THE

ABC

❏ 10871	All the Good Things/Pleasing You Pleases Me	1966	$20
❏ 10814	When the Sun Shines in the Mornin'/Love (That's All I Want)	1966	$20

Number	Title	Yr	NM

ABC-PARAMOUNT

❏ 10583	Give Me a Chance/Your Friend	1964	$30
❏ 10757	Listen to Me/You Make Me Feel Good	1965	$30
❏ 10671	Miserlou/Don't	1965	$30

ROGERS, CHARLIE

HIT

❏ 155	The Spirit of This Land/Ringo	1964	$8

—B-side by John Preston

ROGERS, CHUCK

DECCA

❏ 9-46394	Five Little Girls/Ragtime Annie	1952	$30

ROGERS, DAVID

ATLANTIC

❏ 4022	Hey There Girl/Someone That I Can Forget	1974	$6
❏ 4204	I Just Can't Help Believin'/Now That You're a Woman	1974	$6
❏ 4005	It'll Be Her/Singin' Star	1973	$6
❏ 4012	Loving You Has Changed My Life/You Be You and I'll Be Gone	1973	$6

COLUMBIA

❏ 4-45351	Bottle Do Your Thing/A Stranger in My Place	1971	$8
❏ 4-44561 [PS]	I'm in Love with My Wife/Tessie's Bar Mystery	1968	$15

HAL KAT

❏ 2083	I'm a Country Song/(B-side unknown)	1984	$6

KARI

❏ 120	Houston Blue/Here's to You Darling	1981	$6
❏ 108	The Only Way to Go/(B-side unknown)	1980	$6

MR. MUSIC

❏ 018	The Devil Is a Woman/Time for Lovin'	1983	$6

MUSIC MASTER

❏ 012	Crown Prince of the Barroom/Me and Ms. Chablis	1982	$6
❏ 1004	Hold Me/Chuck Berry Music	1983	$6

REPUBLIC

❏ 038	Darlin'/How Long Has It Been	1979	$5
❏ 006	Do You Hear My Heart Beat/They Went Together	1977	$5
❏ 015	I'll Be There (When You Get Lonely)/Just for the Love of It	1978	$5
❏ 001	I Love What My Woman Does to Me/(B-side unknown)	1977	$5
❏ 343	I'm Gonna Love You Right Out of This World/Burning Bridges	1976	$5
❏ 020	Let's Try to Remember/That Woman Keeps This Cowboy Comin' Home	1978	$5
❏ 311	Mahogany Bridge/It's a Crying Shame (That People Change)	1976	$6
❏ 382	The Lady and the Baby/That Woman Keeps This Cowboy Coming Home	1977	$6
❏ 029	When a Woman Cries/The Power of Positive Drinking	1978	$5
❏ 256	Whispers and Grins/Use Me Up	1976	$6

UNITED ARTISTS

❏ XW720	Got You on My Mind Again/The Part of Me You Left Behind	1975	$5
❏ XW617	It Takes a Whole Lotta Livin' in a House/Since Never	1975	$5

ROGERS, JESSE

ARCADE

❏ 162	Say It Again/Nightwind	1961	$30

MGM

❏ K11369	An Old-Fashioned Christmas/Red, White and Blue	1952	$30
❏ K11742	Foldin' Money/I'm Sorry for Yourself	1954	$30
❏ K11422	Howlin' and a Prowlin'/The Devil's Pitchfork	1953	$30
❏ K11884	I Gotta Love Just Like I Like/I Never Knew I Needed You	1954	$30
❏ K11983	The Waltz You Saved for Me/Impatient Heart	1955	$30

RCA VICTOR

❏ 48-0350	A Great Big Needle/I've Got Five Dollars	1950	$40

—Originals on green vinyl

❏ 48-0454	Beautiful Brown Eyes/Tellin' My Baby Bye	1951	$30
❏ 48-0100	Blue Christmas/Here Comes Santa Claus	1949	$60

—Originals on green vinyl

❏ 48-0389	I Can Fool the World/Plain Old Lovin'	1950	$40

—Originals on green vinyl

❏ 48-0359	Slippin' Around with Jole Blon/Finder's Keepers	1950	$40

—Originals on green vinyl

Number	Title	Yr	NM

ROGERS, JIMMY

CHESS

❏ 1574	Chicago Bound/Sloppy Drunk	1954	$300
❏ 1506	I Used to Love a Woman/Back Door Friend	1952	$200

—Earlier Jimmy Rogers 45s on Chess are not known to exist

❏ 1543	Left Me with a Broken Heart/Act Like You Love Me	1953	$200
❏ 1659	One Kiss/I Can't Believe	1957	$60
❏ 1519	The Last Time/Out on the Road	1952	$200
❏ 1643	Walking By Myself/If It Ain't Me	1956	$60
❏ 1687	What Have I Done/Trace of You	1958	$50

ROGERS, JULIE

MEGA

❏ 0075	Almost Close to You/Where Do You Go	1972	$5

MERCURY

❏ 72535	Another Year, Another Love, Another Heartache/Don't Waste Your Young Years on Him	1966	$8
❏ 72646	Climb Ev'ry Mountain/While the Angelus Was Ringing	1966	$8
❏ 72426	Hawaiian Wedding Song/Turn Around, Look at Me	1965	$8
❏ 72380	Like a Child/The Love of a Boy	1965	$8
❏ 72380 [PS]	Like a Child/The Love of a Boy	1965	$15
❏ 72332	The Wedding/Without Your Love	1964	$10

—Black label

❏ 72332	The Wedding/Without Your Love	1964	$8

—Red label

ROGERS, KENNY, AND DOLLY PARTON

RCA

❏ PB-14261	Christmas Without You/A Christmas to Remember	1985	$3
❏ PB-14261 [PS]	Christmas Without You/A Christmas to Remember	1985	$4
❏ 5352-7-R	Christmas Without You/I Believe in Santa Claus	1987	$3

—B-side by Dolly Parton

❏ 9070-7-R	Christmas Without You/Medley: Winter Wonderland-Sleigh Ride	1989	$3

—B-side by Dolly Parton

❏ GB-14073	Islands in the Stream/Eyes That See in the Dark	1985	$3

— Gold Standard Series; B-side by Kenny Rogers

❏ PB-13615	Islands in the Stream/I Will Always Love You	1983	$3
❏ PB-13615 [PS]	Islands in the Stream/I Will Always Love You	1983	$5

— Version 1: With "(Duet with Dolly Parton)" in small letters

❏ PB-13615 [PS]	Islands in the Stream/I Will Always Love You	1983	$4

— Version 2: With Dolly Parton's name the same size as Kenny Rogers'

❏ PB-13945	The Greatest Gift of All/White Christmas	1984	$4

ROGERS, KENNY, AND THE FIRST EDITION
See THE FIRST EDITION.

ROGERS, KENNY, AND DOTTIE WEST

LIBERTY

❏ 1516	Baby I'm-a Want You/Together Again	1984	$3

UNITED ARTISTS

❏ XW1276	All I Ever Need Is You/Another Somebody Done Somebody Wrong Song	1979	$4
❏ XW1234	Anyone Who Isn't Me Tonight/You and Me	1978	$4
❏ XW1137	Every Time Two Fools Collide/We Love Each Other	1978	$4
❏ XW1299	Till I Can Make It on My Own/Midnight Flyer	1979	$4

ROGERS, KENNY

CARLTON

❏ 468	For You Alone/I've Got a Lot to Learn	1958	$70
❏ 454	That Crazy Feeling/We'll Always Have Each Other	1958	$125

—As "Kenneth Rogers

❏ 454	That Crazy Feeling/We'll Always Have Each Other	1958	$125

—As "Kenny Rogers

LIBERTY

❏ 1526	Abraham, Martin and John/Goodbye Marie	1985	$3
❏ 1495	All My Life/The Farther I Go	1983	$3
❏ 1495 [PS]	All My Life/The Farther I Go	1983	$4
❏ 1485	A Love Song/Fool in Me	1982	$3
❏ 1524	A Stranger in My Place/Love Is What We Make It	1985	$3
❏ 1441	Blaze of Glory/The Good Life	1981	$3
❏ 1415	I Don't Need You/Without You in My Life	1981	$3

Number	Title	Yr	NM
❑ 1415 [PS]	I Don't Need You/Without You in My Life	1981	$4
❑ 1380	Lady/Sweet Music Man	1980	$4
❑ 1380 [PS]	Lady/Sweet Music Man	1980	$5
❑ 1391	Long Arm of the Law/You Were a Good Friend	1980	$4
❑ 1471	Love Will Turn You Around/I Want a Son	1982	$3
❑ 1471 [PS]	Love Will Turn You Around/I Want a Son	1982	$5
❑ 1503	Scarlet Fever/What I Learned from Loving You	1983	$3
❑ 1430	Share Your Love with Me/ Greybeard	1981	$3
❑ 1430 [PS]	Share Your Love with Me/ Greybeard	1981	$4
❑ 1444	Through the Years/So In Love with You	1981	$3
❑ 1525	Twentieth Century Fool/It Turns Me Inside Out	1985	$3
❑ 1492	We've Got Tonight/You Are So Beautiful	1983	$4

—A-side with Sheena Easton

Number	Title	Yr	NM
❑ 1492 [PS]	We've Got Tonight/You Are So Beautiful	1983	$5

MERCURY

Number	Title	Yr	NM
❑ 72545	Here's That Rainy Day/Take Life in Stride	1966	$30

RCA

Number	Title	Yr	NM
❑ JK-13713 [DJ]	Buried Treasure (same on both sides)	1984	$5
❑ GB-14353	Crazy/Morning Desire	1986	$3

—Gold Standard Series

Number	Title	Yr	NM
❑ PB-13975	Crazy/The Stranger	1984	$3
❑ PB-13975 [PS]	Crazy/The Stranger	1984	$4
❑ PB-13832	Evening Star/Midsummer Nights	1984	$3
❑ PB-13774	Eyes That See in the Dark/ Hold Me	1984	$3
❑ 8390-7-R	I Don't Call Him Daddy/We're Doin' Alright	1988	$3
❑ 8381-7-R	I Prefer the Moonlight/Make No Mistake, She's Mine	1988	$3

—Gold Standard Series; B-side with Ronnie Milsap

Number	Title	Yr	NM
❑ 5258-7-R	I Prefer the Moonlight/We're Doin' Alright	1987	$3
❑ 5209-7-R	Make No Mistake, She's Mine/ You're My Love	1987	$3

—With Ronnie Milsap

Number	Title	Yr	NM
❑ PB-14194	Morning Desire/People in Love	1985	$3
❑ PB-14194 [PS]	Morning Desire/People in Love	1985	$4

—Fold-out poster sleeve

Number	Title	Yr	NM
❑ PB-13944	The Christmas Song/Medley: Winter Wonderland-Sleigh Ride	1984	$4

—B-side by Dolly Parton

Number	Title	Yr	NM
❑ 6832-7-R	The Factory/One More Day	1987	$3
❑ PB-14384	The Pride Is Back/Didn't We?	1986	$4

—A-side: With Nickie Ryder

Number	Title	Yr	NM
❑ PB-14384 [PS]	The Pride Is Back/Didn't We?	1986	$4
❑ 5016-7-R	They Don't Make Them Like They Used To/Just the Thought of Losing You	1986	$3
❑ 5016-7-R [PS]	They Don't Make Them Like They Used To/Just the Thought of Losing You	1986	$3
❑ PB-13710	This Woman/Buried Treasure	1984	$3
❑ PB-13710 [PS]	This Woman/Buried Treasure	1984	$4
❑ GB-14074	This Woman/What About Me	1985	$3

—Gold Standard Series; B-side by Kenny Rogers, Kim Carnes and James Ingram

Number	Title	Yr	NM
❑ PB-14298	Tomb of the Unknown Love/Our Perfect Song	1986	$3
❑ PB-14298 [PS]	Tomb of the Unknown Love/Our Perfect Song	1986	$4
❑ 5078-7-R	Twenty Years Ago/The Heart of the Matter	1986	$3
❑ PB-13899	What About Me/The Rest of Last Night	1984	$3

—With Kim Carnes and James Ingram

Number	Title	Yr	NM
❑ PB-13899 [PS]	What About Me/The Rest of Last Night	1984	$4

REPRISE

Number	Title	Yr	NM
❑ 22750	Christmas in America/Joy to the World	1989	$3
❑ 22750 [PS]	Christmas in America/Joy to the World	1989	$3
❑ 27690	Planet Texas/When You Put Your Heart in It	1988	$3
❑ 27690 [PS]	Planet Texas/When You Put Your Heart in It	1988	$3
❑ 22853	(Something Inside) So Strong/ When You Put Your Heart In It	1989	$3
❑ 27812	When You Put Your Heart In It/ (Instrumental)	1988	$3
❑ 27812 [PS]	When You Put Your Heart In It/ (Instrumental)	1988	$3

UNITED ARTISTS

Number	Title	Yr	NM
❑ 1327	Coward of the County/I Wanna Make You Smile	1979	$4
❑ XW1153	Daytime Friends/But You Know I Love You	1978	$4
❑ XW1027	Daytime Friends/We Don't Make Love Anymore	1977	$4
❑ 1345	Don't Fall in Love with a Dreamer/Intro: Goin' Home to the Rock-Gideon Tanner	1980	$4

—A-side: With Kim Carnes

Number	Title	Yr	NM
❑ 1345 [PS]	Don't Fall in Love with a Dreamer/Intro: Goin' Home to the Rock-Gideon Tanner	1980	$5
❑ XW812	I Would Like to See You Again/ While the Feeling's Good	1976	$4
❑ XW868	Laura (What's He Got That I Ain't Got)/I Wasn't Mad Enough	1976	$4
❑ XW746	Love Lifted Me/Home-Made Love	1975	$4
❑ XW1151	Love Lifted Me/Reuben James	1978	$4
❑ XW1210	Love Or Something Like It/ Starting Again	1978	$4
❑ 1359	Love the World Away/Sayin' Goodbye-Requiem	1980	$4
❑ XW1154	Lucille/Something's Burning	1978	$4
❑ XW929	Lucille/Till I Get It Right	1976	$4
❑ XW1273	She Believes in Me/Morgana Jones	1979	$4
❑ XW1273 [PS]	She Believes in Me/Morgana Jones	1979	$5
❑ XW1095	Sweet Music Man/Lying Again	1977	$4
❑ XW1155	Sweet Music Man/Ruby, Don't Take Your Love to Town	1978	$4

—B-sides of the above five singles are re-recordings of First Edition hits paired with early United Artists country hits

Number	Title	Yr	NM
❑ XW1250	The Gambler/Momma's Waiting	1978	$4
❑ XW798	There's an Old Man in Our Town/Home-Made Love	1976	$4
❑ XW1152	Today I Started Loving You Again/Just Dropped In (To See What Condition My Condition Was In)	1978	$4

ROGERS, MORRIS, AND THE CONTINENTALS

DELTA

Number	Title	Yr	NM
❑ 601/2	The Leg/Wonders of Love	1963	$200

ROGERS, ROY, AND SPADE COOLEY

RCA VICTOR

Number	Title	Yr	NM
❑ 48-0132	Oh Dem Golden Slippers/Lucky Leather Breeches	1949	$50

—Originals on green vinyl

Number	Title	Yr	NM
❑ 48-0131	Old Joe Clark/Sycamore Reel	1949	$50

—Originals on green vinyl

Number	Title	Yr	NM
❑ 48-0130	Skip to My Lou/Rickett's Reel	1949	$50

—Originals on green vinyl

ROGERS, ROY, AND DALE EVANS

CAPITOL

Number	Title	Yr	NM
❑ 2022	Merry Christmas My Darling/ Sleigh Ride-Jingle Bells	1967	$10

RCA VICTOR

Number	Title	Yr	NM
❑ 48-0128	Christmas on the Plains/ Wonderful Christmas Night	1949	$60

—Originals on green vinyl

Number	Title	Yr	NM
❑ 48-0337	He Is So Precious to Me/ When Jesus Came Into My Heart	1950	$50

—Originals on green vinyl

Number	Title	Yr	NM
❑ 47-0373	May the Good Lord Bless and Keep You/Smiles Are Made Out of Sunshine	1950	$50

—Originals on green vinyl

Number	Title	Yr	NM
❑ 48-0490	Snow on the Mountain/ Strawberry Tears	1951	$40
❑ 48-0344	The Old Rugged Cross/In the Garden	1950	$50

—Originals on green vinyl

Number	Title	Yr	NM
❑ 48-0336	What a Friend We Have in Jesus/I Love to Tell the Story	1950	$50

—Originals on green vinyl

Number	Title	Yr	NM
❑ 48-0338	Where He Leads Me/Love Lifted Me	1950	$50

—Originals on green vinyl

ROGERS, ROY

20TH CENTURY

Number	Title	Yr	NM
❑ 2209	Cowboy Heaven/Don't Ever Wear It for Him	1975	$6
❑ 2173	Happy Trails/Don't Cry, Baby	1975	$6
❑ 2154	Hoppy, Gene & Me/Good News, Bad News	1974	$6

CAPITOL

Number	Title	Yr	NM
❑ 3117	Happy Anniversary/If I Ever Get That Close Again	1971	$8
❑ 3338	Homemade Love/Love Rides a Big White Horse	1972	$8
❑ 3016	Lovenworth/Vision at the Peace Table	1971	$8
❑ 2895	Money Can't Buy Love/You and Me Against the World	1970	$8
❑ 3490	Talkin' About Love/In Another Lifetime	1972	$8
❑ 3263	These Are the Good Old Days/Pass It On	1972	$8

RCA VICTOR

Number	Title	Yr	NM
❑ 48-0035	Blue Shadows on the Trail/ (There'll Never Be Another) Pecos Bill	1949	$60

—Originals on green vinyl

Number	Title	Yr	NM
❑ 48-0479	Buckeye Cowboy/I Wish I Wuz	1951	$40
❑ 48-0331	Buffalo Billy/Me and My Teddy Bear	1950	$50

—Originals on green vinyl

Number	Title	Yr	NM
❑ 47-4301	Daddy's Cowboy/The Three Little Dwarfs	1951	$40
❑ 48-0008	Don't Fence Me In/Roll On Texas Moon	1949	$50

—Originals on green vinyl

Number	Title	Yr	NM
❑ 47-2806	Don't Fence Me In/Roll On Texas Moon	1949	$50
❑ 48-0423	Easter Parade/Peter Cottontail	1951	$40
❑ 47-0306	Egbert the Easter Egg/Peter Cottontail	1951	$50

—Blue label, yellow vinyl

Number	Title	Yr	NM
❑ 47-0306 [PS]	Egbert the Easter Egg/Peter Cottontail	1951	$100

—Blue label, yellow vinyl

Number	Title	Yr	NM
❑ 47-4526	Egbert the Easter Egg/Peter Cottontail	1952	$40
❑ 47-4634	Four Legged Friend/There's a Cloud in My Valley of Sunshine	1952	$40
❑ 47-0255	Frosty the Snowman/Gabby the Gobbler	1950	$50

—Blue label, yellow vinyl

Number	Title	Yr	NM
❑ 48-0374	Frosty the Snowman/Gabby the Gobbler	1950	$50

—Originals on green vinyl

Number	Title	Yr	NM
❑ 47-4709	Happy Trails/California Rose	1952	$50
❑ 47-4950	Hazy Mountains/You've Got a Rope Around My Heart	1952	$40
❑ 48-0011	Home in Oklahoma/A Gay Ranchero	1949	$50

—Originals on green vinyl

Number	Title	Yr	NM
❑ 47-2809	Home in Oklahoma/A Gay Ranchero	1949	$50
❑ 48-0074	Home on the Range/That Palomino Pal of Mine	1949	$60

—Originals on green vinyl

Number	Title	Yr	NM
❑ 47-4424	Horseshoe Moon/Home Sweet Oklahoma	1951	$40
❑ 48-0152	Little Hula Honey/Mommy Can I Take My Doll to Heaven	1950	$50

—Originals on green vinyl

Number	Title	Yr	NM
❑ 48-0115	My Chickashay Gal/A Little White Cross on the Hill	1949	$50

—Originals on green vinyl

Number	Title	Yr	NM
❑ 48-0117	My Heart Went That-a-Way/ Dusty	1949	$50

—Originals on green vinyl

Number	Title	Yr	NM
❑ 48-0028	My Heart Went That-a-Way/ No Children Allowed	1949	$60

—Originals on green vinyl

Number	Title	Yr	NM
❑ 47-4732	Peace in the Valley/Precious Memories	1952	$40
❑ 47-0200	Pecos Bill -- Part 1/Pecos Bill -- Part 4	1949	$50

—Blue label, yellow vinyl

Number	Title	Yr	NM
❑ 47-0201	Pecos Bill -- Part 2/Pecos Bill -- Part 3	1949	$50

—Blue label, yellow vinyl; the above two records comprise set "WY 389

Number	Title	Yr	NM
❑ 48-0458	Pliney Jane/Cowboy's Heaven	1951	$40
❑ 47-4237	Punky Punkin/The Kiwi Bird	1951	$40
❑ 48-0010	San Fernando Valley/Along the Navajo Trail	1949	$50

—Originals on green vinyl

Number	Title	Yr	NM
❑ 47-2808	San Fernando Valley/Along the Navajo Trail	1949	$50
❑ 48-0161	Stampede/Church Music	1950	$50

—Originals on green vinyl

Number	Title	Yr	NM
❑ 48-0496	The Lamp of Faith/Good Luck, Good Health	1951	$40
❑ 47-4664	The Little White Duck/The Kiwi Bird	1952	$40
❑ 48-0414	The Story of Bucky 'n' Dan/ Ride, Son, Ride	1951	$40

ROGERS, SMOKEY

CAPITOL

Number	Title	Yr	NM
❑ F40284	(Without Your) Wedding Ring/Dimples or Dumplin's	1950	$50

ROGERS, TIMMIE

CADET

Number	Title	Yr	NM
❑ 5685	Super Soul Brothers/It Rolls Through Everything	1971	$5

CAMEO

Number	Title	Yr	NM
❑ 116	Back to School Again/I've Got a Dog Who Loves Me	1957	$40

Number	Title	Yr	NM
❑ 131	Take Me to Your Leader/ Fla-Ga-La-Pa	1958	$30

CAPITOL

Number	Title	Yr	NM
❑ F2509	Oh Yeah/Nothin' Wrong with Nothin'	1953	$30
❑ F2406	Saturday Night/If I Were You, Baby	1953	$30

EPIC

Number	Title	Yr	NM
❑ 9899	Everybody Wants to Go to Heaven, But Nobody Wants to Die/Too Young to Go Steady	1966	$8
❑ 9813	If You Can't Smile and Say Yes (Please Don't Cry and Say No)/Chum Goy Tum Toy Fricasee (Soy Soy Soo)	1965	$8

MERCURY

Number	Title	Yr	NM
❑ 70451	If I Give My Heart to You/ Teedle-Dee Teedle-Dum	1954	$50

PARKWAY

Number	Title	Yr	NM
❑ 814	I Love Ya, I Love Ya, I Love Ya/Tee-Hee	1960	$20

PAR-TEE

Number	Title	Yr	NM
❑ 1303	Watergate/Snake Hips	1973	$5

PHILIPS

Number	Title	Yr	NM
❑ 40074	Oh Yeah/Fla-Ga-La-Pa	1962	$10

SIGNATURE

Number	Title	Yr	NM
❑ 12037	First Proposal/Underwater Cha Cha Cha	1960	$20

ROGERS, WELDON

IMPERIAL

Number	Title	Yr	NM
❑ 5451	So Long, Good Luck and Goodbye/Trying to Get to You	1957	$200

—B-side is actually The Teen Kings' version rather than Rogers'; by mistake, the wrong recording left Norman Petty's studio for Imperial.

JE-WEL

Number	Title	Yr	NM
❑ 103	Everybody Wants You/This Song's Just for You	1956	$1000

ROKES, THE

RCA VICTOR

Number	Title	Yr	NM
❑ 47-9199	Let's Live for Today/Change of Papers	1967	$15
❑ 47-9546	When the Wind Arises/The Works of Bartholomew	1968	$15

ROLAND, ADRIAN

ALLSTAR

Number	Title	Yr	NM
❑ 7207	Imitation of Love/It Takes More Than a While	1960	$30
❑ 7189	Mr. Bass Fiddle/Now I Know	1959	$30

ROLLERS, THE

LIBERTY

Number	Title	Yr	NM
❑ 55303	Bonneville/Got My Eye on You	1961	$30
❑ 55357	The Bounce/Teenager's Waltz	1961	$30
❑ 55320	The Continental Walk/I Want You So	1961	$30

ROLLETTES, THE

CLASS

Number	Title	Yr	NM
❑ 201	Sad Fool/Wham Bam	1957	$50

—B-side by Googie Rene

ROLLING STONES, THE

Also see MICK JAGGER; KEITH RICHARDS; MICK TAYLOR; RONNIE WOOD; BILL WYMAN.

ABKCO

Number	Title	Yr	NM
❑ 4701 [DJ]	I Don't Know Why (same on both sides)	1975	$30
❑ 4701	I Don't Know Why/Try a Little Harder	1975	$5

—With A-side writing credits of "Wonder, Riser, Hunter, Hardaway

Number	Title	Yr	NM
❑ 4701	I Don't Know Why/Try a Little Harder	1975	$10

—With A-side writing credits of "Jagger, Richards, Taylor

Number	Title	Yr	NM
❑ 4702	Out of Time/Jiving Sister Fanny	1975	$6
❑ 4702 [DJ]	Out of Time/Jiving Sister Fanny	1975	$30

LONDON

Number	Title	Yr	NM
❑ 9823	19th Nervous Breakdown/ Sad Day	1966	$20
❑ 9823 [PS]	19th Nervous Breakdown/ Sad Day	1966	$75
❑ 9823 [DJ]	19th Nervous Breakdown/ Sad Day	1966	$100

—Orange swirl label

Number	Title	Yr	NM
❑ 9808	As Tears Go By/Gotta Get Away	1965	$20
❑ 9808 [PS]	As Tears Go By/Gotta Get Away	1965	$70
❑ 9808 [DJ]	As Tears Go By/Gotta Get Away	1965	$80

—Orange swirl label

Number	Title	Yr	NM
❑ 905	Dandelion/We Love You	1967	$30
❑ 9792	Get Off of My Cloud/I'm Free	1965	$30
❑ 9792 [PS]	Get Off of My Cloud/I'm Free	1965	$70
❑ 9792 [DJ]	Get Off of My Cloud/I'm Free	1965	$80

—Orange swirl label

Number	Title	Yr	NM
❑ 903	Have You Seen Your Mother, Baby, Standing in the Shadow?/Who's Driving My Plane	1966	$20
❑ 903 [PS]	Have You Seen Your Mother, Baby, Standing in the Shadow?/Who's Driving My Plane	1966	$70
❑ 9725 [PS]	Heart of Stone/What a Shame	1964	$800
❑ 9725 [DJ]	Heart of Stone/What a Shame	1964	$80

—Orange swirl label

Number	Title	Yr	NM
❑ 910	Honky Tonk Women/You Can't Always Get What You Want	1969	$20
❑ 910 [PS]	Honky Tonk Women/You Can't Always Get What You Want	1969	$40
❑ 9766	(I Can't Get No) Satisfaction/ The Under Assistant West Coast Promotion Man	1965	$30
❑ 9766 [PS]	(I Can't Get No) Satisfaction/ The Under Assistant West Coast Promotion Man	1965	$500
❑ 9766 [DJ]	(I Can't Get No) Satisfaction/ The Under Assistant West Coast Promotion Man	1965	$80

—Orange swirl label

Number	Title	Yr	NM
❑ 907	In Another Land/The Lantern	1967	$30

—A-side credited to Bill Wyman, though taken from "Their Satanic Majesties Request

Number	Title	Yr	NM
❑ 907 [PS]	In Another Land/The Lantern	1967	$80
❑ 907 [DJ]	In Another Land/The Lantern	1967	$80

—A-side credited to Bill Wyman; orange swirl label

Number	Title	Yr	NM
❑ 9687	It's All Over Now/Good Times, Bad Times	1964	$50

—White, purple and blue label

Number	Title	Yr	NM
❑ 9687 [PS]	It's All Over Now/Good Times, Bad Times	1964	$125
❑ 9687 [DJ]	It's All Over Now/Good Times, Bad Times	1964	$80

—Orange swirl label

Number	Title	Yr	NM
❑ 9687	It's All Over Now/Good Times Bad Times	1964	$10

—Blue swirl label

Number	Title	Yr	NM
❑ 9641	I Wanna Be Your Man/ Stoned	1964	$9000

—VG 3000; VG+ 6000

Number	Title	Yr	NM
❑ 9641 [DJ]	I Wanna Be Your Man/ Stoned	1964	$1000

—With similar label to stock copy, except in white, black and gray

Number	Title	Yr	NM
❑ 9641 [DJ]	I Wanna Be Your Man/ Stoned	1964	$1500

—White label, black print, script "London" at top

Number	Title	Yr	NM
❑ 904 [PS]	Let's Spend the Night Together/Ruby Tuesday	1967	$70
❑ 902	Mothers Little Helper/Lady Jane	1966	$20
❑ 902 [PS]	Mothers Little Helper/Lady Jane	1966	$70
❑ 902 [DJ]	Mothers Little Helper/Lady Jane	1966	$80

—Orange swirl label

Number	Title	Yr	NM
❑ 901	Paint It, Black/Stupid Girl	1966	$20
❑ 901 [DJ]	Paint It, Black/Stupid Girl	1966	$80

—Orange swirl label

Number	Title	Yr	NM
❑ 901 [PS]	Paint It, Black/Stupid Girl	1966	$70
❑ 906	She's a Rainbow/2000 Light Years from Home	1967	$30
❑ 906 [PS]	She's a Rainbow/2000 Light Years from Home	1967	$60
❑ 906 [DJ]	She's a Rainbow/2000 Light Years from Home	1967	$80

—Orange swirl label

Number	Title	Yr	NM
❑ 909	Street Fighting Man/No Expectations	1968	$30
❑ 909 [PS]	Street Fighting Man/No Expectations	1968	$15000

—VG 4000; VG+ 8000

Number	Title	Yr	NM
❑ 909 [DJ]	Street Fighting Man/No Expectations	1968	$80

—Orange swirl label

Number	Title	Yr	NM
❑ 9682	Tell Me (You're Coming Back)/I Just Want to Make Love to You	1964	$50

—White, purple and blue label

Number	Title	Yr	NM
❑ 9682 [PS]	Tell Me (You're Coming Back)/I Just Want to Make Love to You	1964	$175
❑ 9682	Tell Me (You're Coming Back)/I Just Want to Make Love to You	1964	$10

—Blue swirl label

Number	Title	Yr	NM
❑ 9682 [DJ]	Tell Me (You're Coming Back)/I Just Want to Make Love to You	1964	$80

—Orange swirl label

Number	Title	Yr	NM
❑ 5N9682	Tell Me (You're Coming Back)/I Just Want to Make Love to You	1977	$15

—Sunrise label; this version plays the LP version rather than the single edit, even though the label says "Time: 2:35"; number in trail-off wax is "5N-9682-A

Number	Title	Yr	NM
❑ 9741	The Last Time/Play with Fire	1965	$10

—Blue swirl label, "London" in black letters

Number	Title	Yr	NM
❑ 9741 [PS]	The Last Time/Play with Fire	1965	$200
❑ 9741 [DJ]	The Last Time/Play with Fire	1965	$80

—Orange swirl label

Number	Title	Yr	NM
❑ 9741	The Last Time/Play with Fire	1965	$20

—Blue swirl label, "London" in white letters

Number	Title	Yr	NM
❑ 9741	The Last Time/Play with Fire	1965	$30

—White, purple and blue label

Number	Title	Yr	NM
❑ 9708	Time Is On My Side/ Congratulations	1964	$40

—White, purple and blue label

Number	Title	Yr	NM
❑ 9708 [PS]	Time Is On My Side/ Congratulations	1964	$125
❑ 9708	Time Is On My Side/ Congratulations	1964	$10

—Blue swirl label

Number	Title	Yr	NM
❑ 9708 [DJ]	Time Is On My Side/ Congratulations	1964	$80

—Orange swirl label

Number	Title	Yr	NM
❑ 905 [PS]	We Love You/Dandelion	1967	$600

ROLLING STONES

Number	Title	Yr	NM
❑ 19302	Ain't Too Proud to Beg/ Dance Little Sister	1974	$5
❑ 19302 [DJ]	Ain't Too Proud to Beg (mono/stereo)	1974	$40
❑ 38-73093	Almost Hear You Sigh/Break the Spell	1989	$3
❑ 19105 [DJ]	Angie (mono/stereo)	1973	$40
❑ 19105	Angie/Silver Train	1973	$5

—With "Angie" listed as "Side One" and "Silver Train" listed as "Side Two", or with no reference at all to "Side One" and "Side Two

Number	Title	Yr	NM
❑ 19309 [DJ]	Beast of Burden (long/short versions)	1978	$40
❑ 19309	Beast of Burden/When the Whip Comes Down	1978	$4
❑ 19309 [PS]	Beast of Burden/When the Whip Comes Down	1978	$2000

—Beware of counterfeits! Original copies have a 1/2-inch inner fold on the inside of the picture sleeve (counterfeits have a much smaller fold). Also, the originals are a light lavender, almost pink, color (counterfeits are a grape or purple color).. VG 1000 ; VG+ 1500

Number	Title	Yr	NM
❑ PR316 [DJ]	Before They Make Me Run (mono/stereo)	1978	$30
❑ PR316 [PS]	Before They Make Me Run (mono/stereo)	1978	$60
❑ 19100	Brown Sugar/Bitch	1971	$5
❑ 19100 [DJ]	Brown Sugar (mono/stereo)	1971	$40
❑ 19109	Doo Doo Doo Doo Doo (Heartbreaker)/Dancing with Mr. D.	1973	$5
❑ 19109 [DJ]	Doo Doo Doo Doo Doo (Heartbreaker) (mono/ stereo)	1973	$40
❑ 20001	Emotional Rescue/Down in the Hole	1980	$4
❑ 20001 [PS]	Emotional Rescue/Down in the Hole	1980	$4
❑ 20001 [DJ]	Emotional Rescue (edit/LP versions)	1980	$30
❑ 19307 [DJ]	Far Away Eyes (same on both sides)	1978	$250
❑ 19304	Fool to Cry/Hot Stuff	1976	$4
❑ 19304 [DJ]	Fool to Cry/Hot Stuff	1976	$200
❑ 19304 [DJ]	Fool to Cry (long/short versions)	1976	$40
❑ 19304 [DJ]	Fool to Cry (same on both sides)	1976	$40
❑ 21301	Going to A-Go-Go/Beast of Burden	1982	$4
❑ 21301 [PS]	Going to A-Go-Go/Beast of Burden	1982	$4
❑ 21301 [DJ]	Going to A-Go-Go/Beast of Burden	1982	$30
❑ 21300	Hang Fire/Neighbours	1982	$4
❑ 21300 [DJ]	Hang Fire (same on both sides)	1982	$30
❑ 19104	Happy/All Down the Line	1972	$5
❑ 19104 [DJ]	Happy/All Down the Line	1972	$40
❑ 38-05802 [PS]	Harlem Shuffle	1986	$30

—Demonstration Not for Sale" on sleeve, and no B-side listed

Number	Title	Yr	NM
❑ 38-05802	Harlem Shuffle/Had It with You	1986	$3
❑ 38-05802 [PS]	Harlem Shuffle/Had It with You	1986	$3
❑ 38-05802 [DJ]	Harlem Shuffle (same on both sides)	1986	$30
❑ 19304 [DJ]	Hot Stuff (long/short versions)	1976	$40

Number	Title	Yr	NM
❏ 19304 [DJ]	Hot Stuff (same on both sides)	1976	$40
❏ 19301 [DJ]	It's Only Rock 'N' Roll (But I Like It) (Edit/Long Version)	1974	$40
❏ 19301	It's Only Rock 'N' Roll (But I Like It)/Through the Lonely Nights	1974	$5
❏ 19307	Miss You/Far Away Eyes	1978	$4
❏ 19307 [PS]	Miss You/Far Away Eyes	1978	$4
❏ 19307 [DJ]	Miss You (same on both sides)	1978	$40
❏ 99724 [DJ]	Miss You	1984	$40
❏ 38-69008	Mixed Emotions/Fancy Man Blues	1989	$3
❏ 38-69008 [DJ]	Mixed Emotions (same on both sides)	1989	$50
❏ 38-05906 [PS]	One Hit (To the Body)	1986	$30
—Demonstration Not for Sale" on sleeve, and no B-side listed			
❏ 38-05906	One Hit (To the Body)/Fight	1986	$3
❏ 38-05906 [PS]	One Hit (To the Body)/Fight	1986	$3
❏ 38-05906 [DJ]	One Hit (To the Body) (same on both sides)	1986	$30
❏ 19310	Shattered/Everything Is Turning to Gold	1978	$4
❏ 19310 [PS]	Shattered/Everything Is Turning to Gold	1978	$6
❏ 19310 [DJ]	Shattered (same on both sides)	1978	$30
❏ 21001 [DJ]	She's So Cold (edit/LP versions)	1980	$30
❏ 21001	She's So Cold/Send It to Me	1980	$4
❏ 21001 [PS]	She's So Cold/Send It to Me	1980	$6
❏ 99788 [DJ]	She Was Hot (long/short versions)	1984	$40
❏ 99788	She Was Hot/Think I'm Going Mad	1984	$3
❏ 99788 [PS]	She Was Hot/Think I'm Going Mad	1984	$3
❏ 19105	Silver Train/Angie	1973	$15
— With "Silver Train" listed as "Side One" and "Angie" listed as "Side Two"			
❏ 21003	Start Me Up/No Use in Crying	1981	$4
❏ 21003 [PS]	Start Me Up/No Use in Crying	1981	$4
❏ 21003 [DJ]	Start Me Up (same on both sides)	1981	$30
❏ 99978 [DJ]	Time Is On My Side (Live) (same on both sides)	1982	$30
❏ 99978	Time Is On My Side (Live)/ Twenty Flight Rock	1982	$5
❏ 99978 [PS]	Time Is On My Side (Live)/ Twenty Flight Rock	1982	$5
❏ PR228 [DJ]	Time Waits for No One (mono/stereo)	1974	$80
❏ PR228 [PS]	Time Waits for No One (mono/stereo)	1974	$175
❏ 0 (no cat #)	Tongue Sleeve	1972	$8
— Sleeve used on some copies of "Tumbling Dice" and "Hang Fire," and possibly some other Rolling Stones Records 45s			
❏ 99724	Too Tough/Miss You	1984	$50
❏ 19103 [DJ]	Tumbling Dice (mono/stereo)	1972	$40
❏ 19103	Tumbling Dice/Sweet Black Angel	1972	$5
❏ 21004	Waiting on a Friend/Little T & A	1981	$4
❏ 21004 [PS]	Waiting on a Friend/Little T & A	1981	$4
❏ 21004 [DJ]	Waiting on a Friend (same on both sides)	1981	$30
❏ 19101 [DJ]	Wild Horses (long version/ short version)	1971	$60
❏ 19101 [DJ]	Wild Horses (mono/stereo, both full length)	1971	$40
❏ 19101	Wild Horses/Sway	1971	$5

7-Inch Extended Plays

LONDON

Number	Title	Yr	NM
❏ SBG23 [PS]	12x5	1964	$250
❏ SBG23	Around and Around/2120 South Michigan Avenue/ Confessin' the Blues//Time Is On My Side/Grown Up Wrong/It's All Over Now	1964	$275
— Jukebox issue; small hole, plays at 33 1/3 rpm			
❏ SBG43 [PS]	December's Children (and Everybody's)	1965	$275
❏ SBG34	Down the Road Apiece/ Off the Hook/Oh Baby (We Got a Good Thing Goin')//Everybody Needs Somebody to Love/Heart of Stone/Surprise, Surprise	1965	$250
— Jukebox issue; small hole, plays at 33 1/3 rpm			
❏ SBG37 [PS]	Out of Our Heads	1965	$250
❏ SBG43	Talkin' 'Bout You/Look What You've Done/Get Off of My Cloud//I'm Free/Gotta Get Away/As Tears Go By	1965	$250
— Jukebox issue; small hole, plays at 33 1/3 rpm			
❏ SBG54 [PS]	Their Satanic Majesties Request	1967	$250
❏ SBG37	The Spider and the Fly/ One More Try//Hitch Hike// The Last Time/Good Times/ Mercy Mercy	1965	$250
— Jukebox issue; small hole, plays at 33 1/3 rpm			

Number	Title	Yr	NM
ROLLING STONES			
❏ COC 7-22900 [PS]	Exile on Main St.	1972	$100
—Part of "Little LP" series (LLP #199)			
❏ CO7-59101 [PS]	Goats Head Soup	1973	$100
❏ PR287 [DJ]	If You Can't Rock Me/Get Off of My Cloud/Brown Sugar// Jumpin' Jack Flash/Hot Stuff	1977	$35
—Large hole; promo-only sampler from "Love You Live			
❏ PR287 [PS]	Love You Live	1977	$60
❏ CO7-59101	Star Star/Hide Your Love// Can You Hear the Music/100 Years Ago	1973	$100
—Jukebox issue; small hole, plays at 33 1/3 rpm			

Number	Title	Yr	NM
ROLLINS, SONNY			
BLUE NOTE			
❏ 1669	Decision (Part 1)/Decision (Part 2)	1957	$15
❏ 1670	Plain Jane (Part 1)/Plain Jane (Part 2)	1957	$15
❏ 1698	Sonny Moon for Two (Part 1)/ Sonny Moon for Two (Part 2)	1958	$15
IMPULSE!			
❏ 247	Alfie's Theme (Part 1)/Alfie's Theme (Part 2)	1966	$8
❏ 305	Isn't She Lovely/Arroz Con Pollo	1977	$5
RCA VICTOR			
❏ 47-8111	If Ever I Would Leave You/ Brown Skin Girl	1962	$8

Number	Title	Yr	NM
ROMAN NUMERALS, THE			
COLUMBIA			
❏ 44314	The Come-On/Matchstick in a Whirlpool	1967	$30
❏ 44314 [PS]	The Come-On/Matchstick in a Whirlpool	1967	$40

Number	Title	Yr	NM
ROMANTICS, THE			
BOMP!			
❏ 120	Tell It to Carrie/First in Line	1978	$5
❏ 120 [PS]	Tell It to Carrie/First in Line	1978	$5
NEMPEROR			
❏ 7537	Forever Yours/New Cover Story	1981	$4
❏ 05684	Mystified/Make It Last	1985	$3
❏ 05684 [PS]	Mystified/Make It Last	1985	$4
❏ ZS4-04373	One in a Million/Do Me Anyway You Wanna	1984	$3
❏ ZS4-04373 [PS]	One in a Million/Do Me Anyway You Wanna	1984	$3
❏ 04135	Talking in Your Sleep/I'm Hip	1983	$3
❏ 7531	Tell It to Carrie/Hung on You	1980	$3
❏ 05587 [PS]	Test of Time	1985	$5
—Demonstration -- Not for Sale" on back			
❏ 05587	Test of Time/Better Make a Move	1985	$3
❏ 05587 [PS]	Test of Time/Better Make a Move	1985	$3
❏ 7527	What I Like About You/First in Line	1979	$5
❏ 7527 [PS]	What I Like About You/First in Line	1979	$10
❏ 7530	When I Look in Your Eyes/Little White Lies	1980	$3
SPIDER			
❏ SPDR-101	Little White Lies/I Can't Tell You Anything	1977	$10
❏ SPDR-101 [PS]	Little White Lies/I Can't Tell You Anything	1977	$10

Number	Title	Yr	NM
ROME, RICHARD			
PARKWAY			
❏ 978	Happiness Is/Back in Sixty Seconds	1966	$12
SWAN			
❏ 4021	Bluebird of Happiness/Leaf in the Wind	1959	$15

Number	Title	Yr	NM
ROMEO VOID			
415 RECORDS			
❏ 0012	White Sweater/Apache	1982	$3
❏ 0012 [PS]	White Sweater/Apache	1982	$3
COLUMBIA			
❏ 04534	A Girl in Trouble (Is a Temporary Thing)/Going to Be Neon	1984	$3
❏ 04704 [PS]	Say No	1984	$5
—Demonstration -- Not for Sale" on back			
❏ 04704	Say No/Six Days and One	1984	$3
❏ 04704 [PS]	Say No/Six Days and One	1984	$3

Number	Title	Yr	NM
ROMEOS, THE (1)			
MARK II			
❏ 103	A Tear and a Smile/Seaching	1967	$20
❏ 101	Precious Memories/Juicy Lucy	1967	$20

Number	Title	Yr	NM
ROMEOS, THE (2)			
AMY			
❏ 840	The Tiger's Wide Awake (The Lion Sleeps Tonight)/Hitch-Hikin'	1962	$20
ROMEOS, THE (3)			
APOLLO			
❏ 461	Love Me/I Beg You Please	1954	$600
ROMEOS, THE (4)			
ATCO			
❏ 6107	Moments to Remember You By/Fine, Fine Baby	1958	$70
FOX			
❏ 749	Gone, Gone, Get Away/Let's Be Partners	1957	$300
—Cream label			
❏ 749	Gone, Gone, Get Away/Let's Be Partners	1957	$120
—Yellow label			
❏ 846	Moments to Remember You By/Fine, Fine Baby	1957	$500
—Cream label			
❏ 846	Moments to Remember You By/Fine, Fine Baby	1957	$120
—Yellow label			
ROMEOS, THE (5)			
COLUMBIA			
❏ 43074	Baby Stay in Line/Two of the Chosen Few	1964	$12
ROMEOS, THE (U)			
FELSTED			
❏ 8528	Two Innocent Loves/Love-Mobile	1958	$40
LOMA			
❏ 2041	Calypso Chili/Mon Petite Chow	1966	$15
❏ 2028	Mucho Soul/Are You Ready for That	1966	$15
ROMERO, CHAN			
CHALLENGE			
❏ 59285	The Funniest Things/It's Not Fine	1965	$20
DEL-FI			
❏ 4126	I Don't Care Now/My Little Rudy	1959	$70
❏ 4119	The Hippy Hippy Shake/If I Had My Way	1959	$125
PHILIPS			
❏ 40391	Humpy Bumpy/Man Can't Dog a Woman	1966	$10
RON AND BILL			
ARGO			
❏ 5350	It/Don't Say Bye Bye	1959	$60
TAMLA			
❏ 54025	It/Don't Say Bye Bye	1960	$120
RON-DELLS, THE			
ARLEN			
❏ 723	I'll Be Gone/Slow Down	1963	$20
RON-DELS, THE			
BROWNFIELD			
❏ 18	If You Really Want Me To, I'll Go/Walk About	1965	$30
DOT			
❏ 16593	Far Horizons/On the Run	1964	$30
❏ 17323	Matilda/Tina	1970	$10
SHALIMAR			
❏ 104	Matilda/Tina	1963	$20
SMASH			
❏ 2014	A Picture of You/Lose Your Money	1965	$8
❏ 1986	If You Really Want Me To, I'll Go/Walk About	1965	$10
❏ 2002	She's My Girl/Over	1965	$8
RONDELLS, THE			
ABC-PARAMOUNT			
❏ 10690	Don't Say That You Love Me/ Parking in the Ko Ko Mo	1965	$20
CARLTON			
❏ 467	Good Good/Dreamy	1958	$30

Number	Title	Yr	NM

RONDELS, THE
AMY
❏ 825	Back Beat #1/Shades of Green	1961	$30
❏ 839	Caldonia/110 Lbs. of Drums	1962	$30
❏ 857	Meet Us at the Peppermint Lounge/Cover Charge	1962	$30
❏ 830	My Prayer/Satan's Theme	1961	$30

RONDO, DON
ATLANTIC
❏ 2194	Malibu/So Did I	1963	$8
CARLTON
| ❏ 531 | Friends/Hoot an' a Holler | 1960 | $8 |
| ❏ 536 | Wanderlust/The King of Holiday Island | 1960 | $8 |
DECCA
❏ 29738	Evening Star/Beyond the Mighty River	1955	$15
❏ 30248	I Offer You My Heart/Evening Star	1957	$15
❏ 32561	Statue of a Fool/I'll Be True	1969	$5
JUBILEE
❏ 5381	Because of You/Alone in the World	1960	$8
❏ 5334	City Lights/As Long As I Have You	1958	$10
❏ 5270	Don't/The Love I Never Had	1957	$15
❏ 5325	Dormi, Dormi, Dormi/Her Hair Was Yellow	1958	$12
❏ 5297	Forsaking All Others/There's Only You	1957	$15
❏ 5341	I Could Be a Mountain/Great Adventure	1958	$10
❏ 5522	Love Me Back/Play the Other Side	1966	$6
❏ 5313	Made for Each Other/What a Shame	1958	$10
❏ 5364	My Foolish Heart/Leave Your Trouble on My Lips	1959	$10
❏ 5320	School Dance/I've Got Bells in My Heart	1958	$10
❏ 5354	Song from "Geisha Boy"/Gretna Green	1958	$12
❏ 5319	There Goes My Heart Again/Blonde Bombshell	1958	$10
❏ 5282	To Belong/On Forgotten Street	1957	$15
❏ 5421	Two Different Worlds/Blonde Bombshell	1962	$8
❏ 5256	Two Different Worlds/He Made You Mine	1956	$15
❏ 5305	Wanderin' Heart/In Chi-Chi-Chihuahua	1957	$10
❏ 5288	White Silver Sands/Stars Fell on Alabama	1957	$15
ROULETTE
❏ 4202	Batch of Love/Quiet Girl	1959	$12
❏ 4236	That's My Girl/Even the Heavens Cried	1960	$12
❏ 4216	Wall to Wall Tears/The Golden Rule	1959	$10
TUBA
| ❏ 1301 | My Way/A Warmer World | 1965 | $8 |
UNITED ARTISTS
| ❏ 50191 | Let's Live for Today/Oh Why My Love | 1967 | $6 |
| ❏ 50111 | Till the World Knows You're Mine/Is There Room in Your Tomorrow | 1967 | $6 |

RONETTES, THE
BUDDAH
❏ 384	Go Out and Get It/Lover, Lover	1973	$30
—As "Ronnie Spector and the Ronettes
| ❏ 408 | I Wish I Never Saw the Sunshine/I Wonder What He's Doing | 1974 | $30 |
COLPIX
| ❏ 646 | I'm Gonna Quit While I'm Ahead/I'm On the Wagon | 1962 | $70 |
| ❏ 601 | I Want a Boy/Sweet Sixteen | 1961 | $125 |
—As "Ronnie and the Relatives
DIMENSION
| ❏ 1046 | He Did It/Recipe for Love | 1965 | $60 |
MAY
| ❏ 138 | Memory/Good Girls | 1963 | $60 |
| ❏ 111 | My Darling Angel/I'm Gonna Quit While I'm Ahead | 1961 | $200 |
—As "Ronnie and the Relatives
| ❏ 114 | Silhouettes/You Bet I Would | 1962 | $60 |
PAVILLION
| ❏ 03333 | I Saw Mommy Kissing Santa Claus/Rudolph the Red-Nosed Reindeer | 1982 | $5 |
—B-side by The Crystals
PHILLES
| ❏ 118 | Baby I Love You/Miss Joan and Mr. Sam | 1963 | $40 |
| ❏ 116 | Be My Baby/Tedesco and Pittman | 1963 | $40 |

❏ 126	Born to Be Together/Blues for Baby	1965	$30
❏ 126 [PS]	Born to Be Together/Blues for Baby	1965	$200
❏ 121	Do I Love You?/Bebe and Susu	1964	$40
❏ 133	I Can Hear Music/When I Saw You	1966	$40
❏ 128	Is This What I Get for Loving You?/Oh, I Love You	1965	$30
❏ 128 [PS]	Is This What I Get for Loving You?/Oh, I Love You	1965	$200
❏ 120	(The Best Part of) Breakin' Up/Big Red	1964	$40
❏ 123	Walkin' in the Rain/How Does It Feel	1964	$50
❏ 123 [PS]	Walkin' in the Rain/How Does It Feel	1964	$200

RONNIE AND THE HI-LITES
ABC-PARAMOUNT
| ❏ 10685 | High School Romance/Too Young | 1965 | $30 |
JOY
| ❏ 265 | Be Kind/Send My Love (Special Delivery) | 1962 | $30 |
| ❏ 260 | I Wish That We Were Married/Twistin' and Kissin' | 1962 | $30 |
WIN
❏ 250	A Slow Dance/What the Next Day May Bring	1963	$30
❏ 252	High School Romance/Uptown-Downtown	1963	$30
❏ 251	The Fact of the Matter/You Keep Me Guessin'	1963	$30

RONNIE AND THE POMONA CASUALS
DONNA
| ❏ 1402 | I Wanna Do the Jerk/Sloopy | 1965 | $15 |
| ❏ 1400 | Swimming at the Rainbow/Casual Blues | 1964 | $15 |

RONNIE AND THE RED CAPS
REB
| ❏ 45-105 | Conquest/Lover | 1958 | $250 |

RONNY AND THE DAYTONAS
MALA
❏ 531	Antique '32 Studebaker Dictator Coupe/Then the Rains Came	1966	$30
❏ 503	Beach Boy/No Wheels	1965	$30
❏ 492	Bucket "T"/Little Rail Job	1964	$30
❏ 490	California Bound/Hey Little Girl	1964	$30
❏ 525	Goodbye Baby/Somebody to Love Me	1966	$30
❏ 481	G.T.O./Hot Rod Baby	1964	$30
❏ 542	I'll Think of Summer/Little Scrambler	1966	$20
❏ 497	Little Scrambler/Teenage Years	1965	$30
❏ 513	Sandy/(Instrumental)	1965	$30
RCA VICTOR
❏ 47-8896	All American Girl/Dianne, Dianne	1966	$15
❏ 47-8896 [PS]	All American Girl/Dianne, Dianne	1966	$30
❏ 47-9253	Brave New World/Hold Onto Your Heart	1968	$15
❏ 47-9435	The Girls and the Boys/Alfie	1968	$15
❏ 47-9107	Walk with the Sun/The Last Letter	1967	$15
❏ 47-9022	Winter Weather/Young	1966	$15
SHOW BIZ
| ❏ 21207 [DJ] | 4-Cast She'll Love Me Again | 1968 | $30 |
—One-sided promo
| ❏ 21207 [DJ] | 4-Cast She'll Love Me Again | 1968 | $30 |
—One-sided promo

RONSON, MICK
Also see DAVID BOWIE; MOTT THE HOOPLE.
RCA VICTOR
❏ PB-10237 [B]	Billy Porter/Seven Days	1975	$30
❏ APBO-0212	Love Me Tender/Only After Dark	1974	$6
❏ APBO-0291	Slaughter on Tenth Avenue/Leave My Heart Alone	1974	$6
7-Inch Extended Plays
| ❏ DJEO-259 [DJ] | Slaughter on 10th Avenue/Growing Up and I'm Fine//All Cut Up on You/Andy Warhol | 1974 | $15 |
—Promo-only EP with B-side by Dana Gillespie
| ❏ DJEO-0259 [DJ] | Slaughter on 10th Avenue/Growing Up and I'm Fine//All Cut Up on You/Andy Warhol | 1974 | $15 |
—Promo-only EP with B-side by Dana Gillespie

RONSTADT, LINDA
Also see CHRISTMAS SPIRIT; STONE PONEYS.
ASYLUM
❏ 46034	Alison/Mohammed's Radio	1979	$4
❏ 45519	Back in the U.S.A./White Rhythm and Blues	1978	$4
❏ 45519 [PS]	Back in the U.S.A./White Rhythm and Blues	1978	$6
❏ 45431	Blue Bayou/Old Paint	1977	$4
❏ 11039	Desperado/Colorado	1974	$5
❏ 69838	Easy for You to Say/Mr. Radio	1983	$4
❏ 69948	Get Closer/Sometimes You Just Can't Win	1982	$4
❏ 69948 [PS]	Get Closer/Sometimes You Just Can't Win	1982	$5
❏ 45282	Heat Wave/Love Is a Rose	1975	$4
❏ 46602	How Do I Make You/Rambler Gambler	1980	$4
❏ 46602 [PS]	How Do I Make You/Rambler Gambler	1980	$5
❏ 46624	Hurt So Bad/Justine	1980	$4
❏ 46654	I Can't Let Go/Look Out for My Love	1980	$4
❏ 69853	I Knew You When/Talk to Me of Mendocino	1982	$4
❏ 69853 [PS]	I Knew You When/Talk to Me of Mendocino	1982	$5
❏ 69476	(I Love You) For Sentimental Reasons/Straighten Up and Fly Right	1987	$4
❏ 45438	It's So Easy/Lo Siento Mi Vida	1977	$4
❏ 69752	I've Got a Crush on You/Lover Man	1984	$4
❏ 45464	Lago Azul/Lo Siento Mi Vida	1978	$15
❏ 45402	Lose Again/Lo Siento Mi Vida	1977	$8
❏ 11026	Love Has No Pride/I Can Almost See It	1973	$5
❏ 45271	Love Is a Rose/Silver Blue	1975	$6
❏ 69671	Lush Life/Skylark	1985	$4
❏ 45546	Ooh Baby Baby/Blowing Away	1978	$4
❏ 45462	Poor Poor Pitiful Me/Simple Man, Simple Dream	1978	$4
❏ 11032	Silver Threads and Golden Needles/Don't Cry Now	1974	$5
❏ 45361	Someone to Lay Down Beside Me/Crazy	1976	$4
❏ 69725	Someone to Watch Over Me/What'll I Do	1984	$4
❏ 45340	That'll Be the Day/Try Me Again	1976	$4
—Clouds label
| ❏ 45340 | That'll Be the Day/Try Me Again | 1976 | $5 |
—All-blue label
| ❏ 45295 | Tracks of My Tears/The Sweetest Gift | 1975 | $4 |
—B-side with Emmylou Harris
❏ 45479	Tumbling Dice/I Never Will Marry	1978	$4
❏ 69780	What's New/Crazy He Calls Me	1983	$4
❏ 69653	When I Fall in Love/It Never Entered My Mind	1985	$4
❏ 69507	When You Wish Upon a Star/Little Girl Blue	1986	$4
❏ 69507 [PS]	When You Wish Upon a Star/Little Girl Blue	1986	$4
CAPITOL
❏ 2438	Dolphins/The Long Way Around	1969	$15
❏ 3210	I Fall to Pieces/Can It Be True	1971	$6
❏ 2846	Long Long Time/Nobody's	1970	$8
❏ 2767	Lovesick Blues/Will You Love Me Tomorrow	1970	$8
❏ 3021	The Long Way Around/(She's a) Very Lovely Woman	1971	$6
❏ 4050	When Will I Be Loved/It Doesn't Matter Anymore	1975	$4
ELEKTRA
| ❏ 69261 | Don't Know Much/Cry Like a Rainstorm | 1989 | $3 |
—With Aaron Neville
ELEKTRA SPUN GOLD
| ❏ 45102 | Back in the U.S.A./Ooh, Baby, Baby | 1980 | $3 |
—Reissue
| ❏ 45089 | Blue Bayou/It's So Easy | 1979 | $3 |
—Reissue
| ❏ 45081 | Heat Wave/Tracks of My Tears | 1977 | $3 |
—Reissue
| ❏ 45116 | Hurt So Bad/How Do I Make You | 1981 | $3 |
—Reissue
| ❏ 65989 | I Knew You When/Get Closer | 1985 | $3 |
—Reissue
| ❏ 45073 | Love Has No Pride/Silver Threads and Golden Needles | 1975 | $4 |

Number	Title	Yr	NM
— Reissue			
❏ 45092	Poor, Poor, Pitiful Me/ Tumbling Dice	1979	$3
— Reissue			
❏ 65988	What's New/I've Got a Crush on You	1985	$3
— Reissue			
❏ 65965	When You Wish Upon a Star/(I Love You) For Sentimental Reasons	1988	$3
— Reissue			
MCA			
❏ 52973	Somewhere Out There/ (Instrumental)	1986	$3
— With James Ingram			
❏ 52973 [PS]	Somewhere Out There/ (Instrumental)	1986	$4

ROOFTOP SINGERS, THE
ATCO

Number	Title	Yr	NM
❏ 6526	My Life Is My Own/Kites	1967	$6
PHILCO-FORD			
❏ HP-37	Walk Right In/Tom Cat	1969	$20
— 4-inch plastic "Hip Pocket Record" with color sleeve			
VANGUARD			
❏ 35034	Ham and Eggs/Somebody Came Home	1965	$8
❏ 35020	Mama Don't Allow/It Don't Mean a Thing	1963	$8
❏ 35020 [PS]	Mama Don't Allow/It Don't Mean a Thing	1963	$15
❏ 35024	Sail Away Ladies/Twelve String	1964	$8
❏ 35019	Tom Cat/Shoes	1963	$8
❏ 35019 [PS]	Tom Cat/Shoes	1963	$15
❏ 35017	Walk Right In/Cool Water	1962	$10
❏ 35017 [PS]	Walk Right In/Cool Water	1962	$30

ROOMATES, THE
BAN

Number	Title	Yr	NM
❏ 691	A Place Called Love/ Knowing You	1985	$5
CAMEO			
❏ 233	Sunday Kind of Love/A Lovely Way to Spend An Evening	1962	$40
CANADIAN AMERICAN			
❏ 166	My Heart/Just for Tonight	1964	$50
PHILIPS			
❏ 40105	Gee/Answer Me, My Love	1963	$30
VALMOR			
❏ 010	Band of Gold/O Baby Love	1961	$30
❏ 08	Glory of Love/Never Know	1961	$30
❏ 013	My Foolish Heart/My Kisses for Your Thoughts	1962	$30

ROONEY, TEDDY
IMPERIAL

Number	Title	Yr	NM
❏ 5644	Bite Your Tongue/After the Dance	1960	$50

ROOSTERS, THE
A&M

Number	Title	Yr	NM
❏ 746	Shake a Tail Feather/ Rooster Walk	1964	$15
EPIC			
❏ 9487	Let's Try Again/Pretty Girl	1962	$20
FELSTED			
❏ 8642	Chicken Hop/Fun House	1962	$20
PHILIPS			
❏ 40559	Good Good Lovin'/Home Down Right	1968	$8
❏ 40504	Love Machine/I'm Suspectin'	1968	$10
SHAR-DEE			
❏ 704	Chicken Hop/Fun House	1959	$30

ROSE, BIFF
BUDDAH

Number	Title	Yr	NM
❏ 218	The Captain/I Forgot to Tell You	1971	$5
TETRAGRAMMATON			
❏ 1510	Buzz the Fuzz/Gentle People	1969	$6
❏ 1543	Take Care of My Brother/ Myrtle's Files	1970	$6
❏ 1506	What's Gnawing at Me/Molly	1969	$6

ROSE, DAVID
CAPITOL

Number	Title	Yr	NM
❏ 2094 [PS]	Theme from The High Chaparral/Merci, Cherie	1968	$10
❏ K12492	Ama Casa Portuguesa/ Arianne	1957	$15

Number	Title	Yr	NM
❏ K30120	Bewitched (Bothered and Bewildered)/Moon of Manakoora	1950	$30
❏ 8009	Bewitched (Bothered and Bewildered)/Moon of Manakoora	1950	$30
— Original 45 rpm issue			
❏ K13211	Bird Brain/The Grasshopper	1964	$8
❏ K13377	Brazilian Summer/Mae	1965	$8
❏ K12554	Ca, C'est L'Amour/Autumn Holiday	1957	$15
❏ K12430	Calypso Melody/Theme from "Wings of Eagles	1957	$15
❏ K12652	Chapo/Punch and Judy	1958	$15
❏ SK-50114 [S]	Chief Rocky Boy/Sorry for Myself	1959	$30
❏ K12750	Circus Elephants/Our Waltz	1959	$10
❏ K13030	Concerto/The Truth	1961	$10
❏ K12270	Cool Tango/Catered Affair (Theme)	1956	$15
❏ K13289	Emily/A World of Our Own	1964	$8
❏ K30019	Estrellita/4:20 A.M.	1950	$30
❏ K13314	Fiddler on the Roof/Theme from "Quick, Before It Melts	1965	$8
❏ K12243	Forbidden Planet/Theme from "The Swan	1956	$15
❏ K12336	Friendly Persuasion (Thee I Love)/There's Never Been Anyone Else	1956	$15
❏ K30125	Gaucho Serenade/Serenade in Blue	1950	$30
❏ K30017	Holiday for Strings/Deserted City	1950	$30
❏ K12376	Holiday for Trombones/ Midnight on the Cliffs	1956	$15
❏ K12714	How High the Moon/Stroll Along	1958	$15
❏ K13131	How the West Was Won/ Whistle Bait	1963	$8
❏ K30839	I Live for You/Migraine Melody	1955	$15
❏ K30020	Intermezzo/Manhattan Square Dance	1950	$30
❏ K30850	I've Got the World on a String/It's Only a Paper Moon	1955	$15
❏ K12792	Like Young/Young Man's Lament	1959	$12
— With Andre Previn			
❏ SK-50124 [S]	Like Young/Young Man's Lament	1959	$30
— With Andre Previn			
❏ K30883	Love Is a Many-Splendored Thing/You and You Alone (Gelsomina)	1955	$15
❏ K13250	Love Theme from "The Carpetbaggers/Lefty Louie	1964	$8
❏ K30865	Love Walked In/Fascinating Rhythm	1955	$15
❏ K13245	March from the River Kwai/ Our Waltz	1964	$8
❏ K30887	Pam Pam/Serenade	1955	$15
❏ K30824	Parade of the Clowns/Our Waltz	1954	$15
❏ K30858	Satan and the Polar Bear/ Sleepy Lagoon	1955	$15
❏ K12585	Savanna/Little Bisquit	1957	$15
❏ K30123	Serenade/Penny Serenade	1950	$30
❏ K30126	Serenade to a Lemonade/ Puppet Serenade	1950	$30
❏ K12997	Silent Thunder/Theme from "Carnival	1961	$10
❏ K12974	Spellbound/Cimarron	1960	$10
❏ K30124	Sunrise Serenade/ Penthouse Serenade	1950	$30
❏ K30018	Sweet Sue -- Just You/Laura	1950	$30
❏ K12608	Swinging Shepherd Blues/ Rock Fiddle	1958	$15
❏ K30875	Take My Love/Love Is Eternal	1955	$15
❏ K30886	That Old Black Magic/ Happiness Is a Thing Called Joe	1955	$15
❏ K12965	Theme from "Bonanza"/ Choria's Theme (From "Butterfield-8")	1960	$10
❏ K13086	Theme from "The Wonderful World of the Brothers Grimm"/Black and Tan Fantasy	1962	$10
❏ K12631	The Night They Invented Champagne/Waltz at Maxim's	1958	$15
❏ K13064	The Stripper/Ebb Tide	1962	$10
❏ K30885	Time for Parting/Barcelona	1955	$15
❏ K13006	Too Young to Go Steady/It's a Most Unusual Day	1961	$10
RCA VICTOR			
❏ 47-2753	Begin the Beguine/Love for Sale	1949	$30
❏ WP158 [PS]	Cole Porter Review	1949	$30
— Box for 47-2752, 2753, 2754 and 2755			
❏ 47-2755	I Get a Kick Out of You/In the Still of the Night	1949	$30
❏ 47-2752	What Is This Thing Called Love/I've Got You Under My Skin	1949	$30
❏ X1001	(contents unknown)	1952	$10
❏ X1016	(contents unknown)	1952	$10
❏ X1179	(contents unknown)	1955	$10
❏ X1178 [PS]	Lover's Serenade, Vol. 2	1955	$12
❏ X1179 [PS]	Lover's Serenade, Vol. 3	1955	$12

Number	Title	Yr	NM
❏ X1016 [PS]	Motion Picture Themes	1952	$12
❏ X1001 [PS]	Portrait of a Flirt	1952	$12
❏ X1178	Serenade in Blue/Sunrise Serenade//Puppet Serenade/The Gaucho Serenade	1955	$10

ROSE, FRED
MGM

Number	Title	Yr	NM
❏ K11909	Old Man of the Sea/New Flame	1955	$30

ROSE GARDEN, THE
ATCO

Number	Title	Yr	NM
❏ 6564	Here's Today/If My World Falls Through	1968	$12

ROSE, JUANITA
CHART

Number	Title	Yr	NM
❏ 1400	Pillow Filled with Tears/Drop the World in My Arms	1966	$10
HICKORY			
❏ 1667	Go On Back to the Honky Tonk/Tonight I'm Wantin' You Again	1973	$8

ROSE ROYCE
ATLANTIC

Number	Title	Yr	NM
❏ 88942	Perfect Lover/When You Get Right Down To It	1989	$4
C&R			
❏ 7687	Holding On to Love/(B-side unknown)	1984	$12
❏ 7684	Magic Touch/You're So Fine	1984	$8
EPIC			
❏ 14-02818	Best Love/Dance with Me	1982	$8
❏ 14-02996	Fire in the Funk/Still in Love	1982	$8
❏ 34-03319	Somehow We Made It Through the Rain/You Blew It	1982	$8
MCA			
❏ 40615	Car Wash/Water	1976	$5
— With Rose Royce's name prominent on label			
❏ 40615	Car Wash/Water	1976	$8
— With "Music Composed and Produced by Norman Whitfield" and no mention of Rose Royce on either side			
❏ 40721	I'm Going Down/Yo Yo	1977	$5
❏ 40662	I Wanna Get Next to You/ Sunrise	1976	$5
❏ 40814	Put Your Money Where Your Mouth Is/You're On My Mind	1977	$5
OMNI			
❏ 99488	Doesn't Have to Be That Way/You're My Peace of Mind	1986	$4
❏ 99476	Lonely Road/I Found Someone	1987	$4
WHITFIELD			
❏ 8440	Do Your Dance -- Part 1/Do Your Dance -- Part 2	1977	$5
❏ 8789	First Come, First Serve/Let Me Be the First to Know	1979	$5
❏ 49681	Golden Touch/Love Is in the Air	1981	$6
❏ 8629	I'm in Love (And I Love the Feeling)/Get Up Off Your Fat	1978	$5
❏ 49049	Is It Love You're After/You Can't Run from Yourself	1979	$5
❏ 49735	I Wanna Make It with You/ Love Is in the Air	1981	$8
❏ 8712	Love Don't Live Here Anymore/That's What's Wrong with Me	1978	$5
❏ 8491	Ooh Boy/You Can't Please Everybody	1977	$5
❏ 49274	Pop Your Fingers/I Wonder Where You Are Tonight	1980	$5
❏ 49127	What You Waitin' For/Shine Your Light	1979	$5
❏ 8531	Wishing on a Star/Love, More Love	1978	$5

ROSE, TIM
CAPITOL

Number	Title	Yr	NM
❏ 3001	I've Gotta Get a Message to You/Janie Sue	1970	$6
COLUMBIA			
❏ 44792	Angela/Whatcha Gonna Do	1969	$6
❏ 44849	Babe Do You Turn Me On/ Roanoke	1969	$6
❏ 43648	Hey Joe/The Lonely Blue King	1966	$8
❏ 43563	I'm Bringing It Home/Mother, Father, Where Are You	1966	$8
❏ 43958	I'm Gonna Be Strong/I Got a Loneliness	1967	$8
❏ 44603	Long-Haired Boy/Looking at a Baby	1968	$6
❏ 44387	Long Time Man/Come Away Melinda	1967	$8
❏ 44031	Morning Dew/You're Slipping Away from Me	1967	$8

Number	Title	Yr	NM
❏ 43722	Where Was I/I Gotta Do Things My Way	1966	$8
PLAYBOY			
❏ 50012	Goin' Down in Hollywood/ (B-side unknown)	1972	$5
❏ 50005	It Takes a Little Longer/Ride Your Love Away	1972	$5

ROSEBUDS, THE (1)
GEE

Number	Title	Yr	NM
❏ 1033	Dearest Darling/ Unconditional Surrender	1957	$60

ROSEBUDS, THE (2)
TOWER

Number	Title	Yr	NM
❏ 104	Say You'll Be Mine/Mama Said	1964	$15

ROSELLA, CARMELA
NANCY

Number	Title	Yr	NM
❏ 1004	Oh, It Was Elvis/Where?	1961	$50

ROSELLI, JIMMY
LENOX

Number	Title	Yr	NM
❏ 5571	Mala Femmina/Her Eyes Shone Like Diamonds	1963	$8
❏ 5576	Passione/Satte Vincino A Me	1963	$8
M&R			
❏ 2010	When Your Old Wedding Ring Was New/Little Pal	1982	$8
RIC			
❏ 148	Don't Cry Little Girl, Don't Cry/Just Say I Love Her	1965	$8
UNITED ARTISTS			
❏ 50273	Bella/O Surdato 'Enammurato	1968	$6
❏ 50490	Buona Sera, Mrs. Campbell/ I'll Take Care of You	1969	$5
❏ 50496	Buona Sera, Mrs. Campbell (Italian)/Te Purtavo Na Rosa	1969	$8
❏ 1659	Buon Natale (Means Merry Christmas To You)/ Christmas	1966	$6

— Silver Spotlight Series

Number	Title	Yr	NM
❏ 50546	E Rose Parlano/Senza Mamma E Inamurata	1969	$5
❏ 50287	Get Out of My Heart/Oh What It Seemed to Be	1968	$6
❏ 928	Have You Ever Been Lonely/ Rage to Live	1965	$6
❏ 50234	I Don't Want to Walk Without You/Please Believe Me	1967	$6
❏ 996	I'll Never Let You Cry/I'm Gonna Change Everything	1966	$6
❏ 50624	I'm Coming Home, Los Angeles/Angelina	1970	$5
❏ 866	Laugh It Off/Why Don't We Do This More Often	1965	$6
❏ 50059	Love Me Love/Lusingame	1966	$6
❏ 50480	My Heart Cries for You/Why Did You Leave Me	1969	$5
❏ 50179	There Must Be a Way/I'm Yours to Command	1967	$6
❏ 50064	This Planet Earth/Who Can Say (Africa Addio)	1966	$6
❏ 50217	Walkin' My Baby Back Home/All the Time	1967	$6

ROSES, THE
DOT

Number	Title	Yr	NM
❏ 15816	Almost Paradise/I Kissed An Angel	1958	$30

ROSIE AND RETTA
COLUMBIA

Number	Title	Yr	NM
❏ 4-21385	Hoot Owl Melody/I'm Gonna Be Loved Tonight	1955	$30
❏ 4-21447	Was There a Teardrop/ Wild Wind	1955	$30

ROSIE AND THE ORIGINALS
BRUNSWICK

Number	Title	Yr	NM
❏ 55205	Lonely Blue Nights/We'll Have a Chance	1961	$30

— By "Rosie, formerly with the Originals

Number	Title	Yr	NM
❏ 55212	My Darling Forever/The Time Is Near	1961	$30

— By "Rosie, formerly with the Originals

HIGHLAND

Number	Title	Yr	NM
❏ 1011	Angel Baby/Give Me Love	1960	$30

ROSS, CHARLIE
BIG TREE

Number	Title	Yr	NM
❏ 16025	Can't Live With You, Can't Live Without You/Thanks for the Smiles	1974	$6
❏ 16068	Give Her What She Wants/ (B-side unknown)	1976	$6
❏ 16014	She's My Lady/(B-side unknown)	1974	$6

Number	Title	Yr	NM
❏ 16056	Without Your Love (Mr. Jordan)/Sneaking Round Corners	1976	$6
TOWN HOUSE			
❏ 1061	Are We in Love (Or Am I)/ Shoot First, Ask Questions Later	1982	$5
❏ 1060	Let's Start Over/(B-side unknown)	1982	$6
❏ 1057	The High Cost of Loving/ She Sure Got Away with My Heart	1982	$5
ZODIAC			
❏ 1022	Lady Loretta/Without Your Love, Mr. Jordan, Part 2	1977	$6

ROSS, DIANA; MARVIN GAYE; SMOKEY ROBINSON; AND STEVIE WONDER
MOTOWN

Number	Title	Yr	NM
❏ 1455	Pops, We Love You/ (Instrumental)	1979	$8

— Original version is 3:59 and has a monologue by Diana Ross

Number	Title	Yr	NM
❏ 1455	Pops, We Love You/ (Instrumental)	1979	$4

— Later version is 3:30 and has no monologue

Number	Title	Yr	NM
❏ M9-1455	Pops, We Love You/ (Instrumental)	1979	$20

— Heart-shaped red vinyl record in plastic sleeve

Number	Title	Yr	NM
❏ 1455 [DJ]	Pops, We Love You (same on both sides)	1979	$12

— Original version is 3:59 and has a monologue by Diana Ross

ROSS, DIANA, AND MARVIN GAYE
MOTOWN

Number	Title	Yr	NM
❏ 1296	Don't Knock My Love/Just Say Just Say	1974	$5
❏ 1269	My Mistake (Was to Love You)/Include Me in Your Life	1973	$5

ROSS, DIANA, AND THE SUPREMES
See THE SUPREMES.

ROSS, DIANA
MCA

Number	Title	Yr	NM
❏ 40947	Ease On Down the Road/ Poppy Girls	1978	$5

— With Michael Jackson; B-side by Quincy Jones

Number	Title	Yr	NM
❏ 40947 [PS]	Ease On Down the Road/ Poppy Girls	1978	$5

— With Michael Jackson

Number	Title	Yr	NM
❏ 53448	If We Hold On Together/ (Instrumental)	1988	$3
❏ 53448 [PS]	If We Hold On Together/ (Instrumental)	1988	$3
MOTOWN			
❏ 1169	Ain't No Mountain High Enough/Can't It Wait Until Tomorrow	1970	$4
❏ 1169 [PS]	Ain't No Mountain High Enough/Can't It Wait Until Tomorrow	1970	$15
❏ 2003	Bottom Line/(Instrumental)	1989	$3
❏ 0(no cat #) [PS]	Diana Ross TV Special 4/8/71	1971	$8

— Special sleeve issued with some Motown (usually Diana Ross) 45s in March and April 1971

Number	Title	Yr	NM
❏ 1377	Do You Know Where You're Going To/No One's Gonna Be a Fool Forever	1975	$15

— Possibly Canadian release only, with different A-side title

Number	Title	Yr	NM
❏ 1519	Endless Love/(Instrumental)	1981	$4

— With Lionel Richie

Number	Title	Yr	NM
❏ 1427	Gettin' Ready for Love/ Confide in Me	1977	$5
❏ 1211	Good Morning Heartache/ God Bless the Child	1972	$5
❏ 1211 [PS]	Good Morning Heartache/ God Bless the Child	1972	$10
❏ 1491	I'm Coming Out/Give Up	1980	$4
❏ 1192	I'm Still Waiting/A Simple Thing Like Cry	1971	$5
❏ 1387	I Thought It Took a Little Time (But Today I Fell in Love)/After You	1976	$5
❏ 1387 [PS]	I Thought It Took a Little Time (But Today I Fell in Love)/After You	1976	$10
❏ 1471	It's My House/Sparkle	1979	$4
❏ 1496	It's My Turn/Together	1980	$4
❏ 1496 [PS]	It's My Turn/Together	1980	$15
❏ 1278	Last Time I Saw Him/Save the Children	1973	$5
❏ 1392	Love Hangover/Kiss Me Now	1976	$5
❏ 1531	My Old Piano/Now That You're Gone	1981	$4
❏ 1398	One Love in My Lifetime/ Smile	1976	$5
❏ 1508	One More Chance/After You	1981	$4
❏ 1295	Sleepin'/You	1974	$5

Number	Title	Yr	NM
❏ 1335	Sorry Doesn't Always Make It Right/Together	1975	$5
❏ 1335 [PS]	Sorry Doesn't Always Make It Right/Together	1975	$15
❏ 1188	Surrender/I'm a Winner	1971	$5
❏ 1462	The Boss/I'm in the World	1979	$4
❏ 1377	Theme from Mahogany (Do You Know Where You're Going To)/No One's Gonna Be a Fool Forever	1975	$5
❏ 1377 [PS]	Theme from Mahogany (Do You Know Where You're Going To)/No One's Gonna Be a Fool Forever	1975	$30
❏ 1998	This House/Paradise	1989	$3
❏ 1513	To Love Again/Crying My Heart Out for You	1981	$4
❏ 1449 [DJ]	Top of the World (same on both sides)	1978	$60

— Promo only; withdrawn before stock copies were pressed

Number	Title	Yr	NM
❏ 1239	Touch Me in the Morning/I Won't Last a Day Without You	1973	$5
❏ 1626	We Can Never Light That Old Flame Again/Old Funky Rolls	1982	$4
❏ 1456	What You Gave Me/ Together	1979	$4
❏ S45-17886 [DJ]	Workin' Overtime (4:18) (same on both sides)	1989	$10
❏ 1964	Workin' Overtime/ (Instrumental)	1989	$3
❏ 1964 [PS]	Workin' Overtime/ (Instrumental)	1989	$3
RCA			
❏ PB-14244	Chain Reaction/More and More	1985	$4
❏ PB-14244 [PS]	Chain Reaction/More and More	1985	$3
❏ PB-14244	Chain Reaction (Special New Mix)/More and More	1986	$3
❏ 5172-7-R	Dirty Looks/So Close	1987	$3
❏ 5172-7-R [PS]	Dirty Looks/So Close	1987	$3
❏ PB-14181	Eaten Alive/(Instrumental)	1985	$3
❏ PB-14181 [PS]	Eaten Alive/(Instrumental)	1985	$3
❏ JB-13013 [DJ]	Endless Love (Long)/ Endless Love (Short)	1981	$12

— Promo only

Number	Title	Yr	NM
❏ JB-13013 [DJ]	Endless Love (Long)/(Short)	1981	$15

— Promo only

Number	Title	Yr	NM
❏ PB-13671	Let's Go Up/Girls	1983	$4
❏ PB-13021	Mirror, Mirror/Sweet Nothings	1981	$4
❏ GB-14342	Missing You/Swept Away	1986	$3

— Gold Standard Series

Number	Title	Yr	NM
❏ PB-13966	Missing You/We Are the Children of the World	1984	$3
❏ PB-13966 [PS]	Missing You/We Are the Children of the World	1984	$3
❏ PB-13348	Muscles/I Am Me	1982	$4
❏ PB-13348 [PS]	Muscles/I Am Me	1982	$4
❏ GB-13798	Muscles/Pieces of Ice	1984	$3

— Gold Standard Series

Number	Title	Yr	NM
❏ PB-13549	Pieces of Ice/Still in Love	1983	$4
❏ PB-13549 [PS]	Pieces of Ice/Still in Love	1983	$4
❏ PB-13424	So Close/Fool for Your Love	1983	$4
❏ PB-13864	Swept Away/Fight for It	1984	$3
❏ PB-13864 [PS]	Swept Away/Fight for It	1984	$3
❏ PB-14032	Telephone/Fool for Your Love	1985	$3
❏ PB-14032 [PS]	Telephone/Fool for Your Love	1985	$3
❏ 5297-7-R	Tell Me Again/I Am Me	1987	$3
❏ 5297-7-R [PS]	Tell Me Again/I Am Me	1987	$3
❏ GB-13479	Why Do Fools Fall in Love/ Mirror, Mirror	1983	$3

— Gold Standard Series

Number	Title	Yr	NM
❏ PB-12349	Why Do Fools Fall in Love/ Think I'm in Love	1981	$4
❏ PB-13201	Work That Body/You Can Make It	1982	$4

7-Inch Extended Plays
MOTOWN

Number	Title	Yr	NM
❏ M60724 [PS]	Everything Is Everything	1970	$15

— Part of "Little LP" series (LLP #133)

Number	Title	Yr	NM
❏ M60724	My Place/Baby It's Love/ The Long and Winding Road//How About You/I'm Still Waiting/Everything Is Everything	1970	$15

— Jukebox issue; small hole, plays at 33 1/3 rpm

ROSS, JACKIE
BRUNSWICK

Number	Title	Yr	NM
❏ 55361	Mr. Sunshine/Walk on My Side	1968	$8
CAPITOL			
❏ 4308	I Can't Stand to See You Go/ Ain't No Fun to Me	1976	$4
CHESS			
❏ 1915	Haste Makes Waste/ Wasting Time	1964	$8
❏ 1913	I've Got the Skill/Change Your Ways	1964	$8

Number	Title	Yr	NM
❏ 1903	Selfish One/Everything But Love	1964	$8
❏ 1938	Take Me for a Little While/Honey Dear	1965	$8
❏ 1940	We Can Do It/Honey Dear	1965	$8

GSF
❏ 6895	A One Woman Man/Take the Weight Off Me	1973	$5
❏ 6886	Woman Get Nothing from Love/Do I	1972	$5

MERCURY
❏ 73041	Angel of the Morning/Showcase	1970	$6
❏ 73185	Glory Be/I Must Give You Time	1971	$6

SAR
❏ 129	Hard Times/Hold Me	1962	$20

—As "Jacki Ross

SCEPTER
❏ 12345	The World's in a Hell of a Shape/What Would You Give	1972	$5

ROSS, JERIS
ABC
❏ 12038	Chapel of Love/Funny How the Bad Times Fade Away	1974	$5
❏ 12004	Come to Me/I Can Feel Love	1974	$5
❏ 11436	I Know the Feeling/Everything You Always Wanted to Know	1974	$6
❏ 11397	Moontan/People Just Like You	1973	$6
❏ 12064	Pictures on Paper/Won't You Meet Me at the Church	1975	$5

ABC DOT
❏ 17615	All the Cryin' in the World/Just Like Your Daddy	1976	$5
❏ 17573	I'd Rather Be Picked Up Here (Than Be Put Down at Home)/Sing a Love Song to Your Baby	1975	$5

DOOR KNOB
❏ 108	Little Bit More/Ease Me to the Ground	1979	$5

GAZELLE
❏ 431	I Think I'll Say Goodbye/Rock Me	1977	$5

ROSSI, STEVE
ROULETTE
❏ 4773	Christmas Story/The Night Before Christmas	1967	$8

ROSSINGTON-COLLINS BAND
MCA
❏ 41284	Don't Misunderstand Me/Winners and Losers	1980	$4
❏ 51218	Don't Stop Me Now/Gotta Get It Straight	1981	$4
❏ 51023	Getaway/Sometimes You Can Put It Out	1980	$4

ROSSINI, TONI
SUN
❏ 349	I Gotta Know/Is It Too Late	1960	$30
❏ 378	Meet Me After School/Just Around the Corner	1962	$30
❏ 366	Well I Ask Ya/Darlena	1961	$30

ROTARY CONNECTION
CADET CONCEPT
❏ 7008	Aladdin/Magical World	1968	$10
❏ 7028	Hey Love/If I Sing My Song	1971	$12

—As "New Rotary Connection
❏ DJ-1 [DJ]	Lady Jane/Amen	1968	$20
❏ 7000	Like a Rollin' Stone/Turn Me On	1967	$12
❏ 7021	Love Me Now/May Our Amens Be True	1970	$10
❏ 7007	Paper Castle/Teach Me How to Fly	1968	$10
❏ 7009	Silent Night Chant/Peace At Least	1968	$15
❏ 7027	Stormy Monday Blues/Teach Me How to Fly	1970	$10
❏ 7014	The Weight/Respect	1969	$10
❏ 7018	Want You to Know/Memory Band	1969	$10

JANUS
❏ 249	Living Alone/Magical World	1975	$5

—As "Minnie Riperton and Rotary Connection

ROTATIONS, THE (1)
FRANTIC
❏ 202	Changed Man/Heartaches	1967	$125
❏ 200	Put a Nickel on D-9 (Pt. 1)/Put a Nickel on D-9 (Pt. 2)	1965	$200

MALA
❏ 576	Misty Roses/Trying to Make You My Own	1967	$40

Number	Title	Yr	NM

ROTATIONS, THE (2)
ORIGINAL SOUND
❏ 41	The Crusher/Heavies	1964	$125

—Produced by FRANK ZAPPA

ROTH, CHERYL
ECHO MOUNTAIN
❏ 111185	GB The Cosmic Snowball (same on both sides)	1985	$3

ROTH, DAVID LEE
Also see VAN HALEN.
WARNER BROS.
❏ 29102	California Girls/California Girls (Remix)	1985	$3
❏ 29102 [PS]	California Girls/California Girls (Remix)	1985	$3
❏ 27825	Damn Good/Skyscraper	1988	$3
❏ 27825 [PS]	Damn Good/Skyscraper	1988	$3
❏ 28584	Goin' Crazy!/Loco Del Calor!	1986	$3
❏ 28584 [PS]	Goin' Crazy!/Loco Del Calor!	1986	$3
❏ 28108	Stand Up/Knucklebones	1988	$3
❏ 28108 [PS]	Stand Up/Knucklebones	1988	$3
❏ 28511	That's Life/Bump and Grind	1986	$3
❏ 28511 [PS]	That's Life/Bump and Grind	1986	$3

ROTTERS, THE
ROTTEN
❏ TR 003	Sink the Whales Buy Japanese Goods/Disco Queen	1979	$125
❏ TR 003 [PS]	Sink the Whales Buy Japanese Goods/Disco Queen	1979	$125
❏ TR 002	Sit on My Face Stevie Nicks/Amputee	1978	$20
❏ TR 002 [PS]	Sit on My Face Stevie Nicks/Amputee	1978	$30

ROULETTES, THE
ANGLE
❏ 1001	Surfer's Charge/Archibald II (Duke of Nothing)	1963	$60

CHAMP
❏ 102	I See a Star/Come On, Baby	1958	$100

EBB
❏ 124	The Way You Carry On/You Don't Care Anymore	1957	$40

SCEPTER
❏ 1204	Hasten Jason/Wouldn't It Be Goin' Steady	1959	$600

UNITED ARTISTS
❏ 718	Can You Go/Soon You'll Be Leaving Me	1964	$30
❏ 990	Long Cigarette/Junk	1966	$10

ROUND, JONATHAN
WESTBOUND
❏ 186	Don't It Make You Want to Go Home/Train a-Comin'	1971	$8
❏ 199	Sympathy for the Devil/Travelin' Mama Blues	1972	$10

ROUND ROBIN
CAPITOL
❏ 5962	Ton of Joy/Vulture	1967	$15

DOMAIN
❏ 1407	Don't Let Go/Up and Down	1964	$20
❏ 1400	Do the Slauson/Slauson Shuffle Time	1963	$20
❏ 1019	Do the Slauson/Slauson Shuffle Time	1963	$20
❏ 1406	I Know/Giddyap Kick	1964	$20
❏ 1424	I'm the Wolfman/Sit and Dance	1965	$15
❏ 1420	Land of 1000 Dances/Yea Yea	1965	$15
❏ 1422	Sit and Dance/Little People	1965	$15
❏ 1402	Slauson Town/Malloy, The Engineer	1963	$20

ROUSSEAU, JACK
GONE
❏ 5045	Christmas in the Snow/Piney	1958	$20

ROUTERS, THE
MERCURY
❏ 73418	Superbird/Sack of Woe	1973	$6

WARNER BROS.
❏ 5379	A-Ooga/Big Band	1963	$15
❏ 5444	Crack Up/Let's Dance	1964	$15
❏ 5332	Half Time/Make It Snappy	1963	$15
❏ 5283	Let's Go (pony)/Mashy	1962	$20
❏ 7117	Let's Go (pony)/Mashy	1967	$12
❏ 5403	Snap, Crackle and Pop/Amoeba	1963	$15
❏ 5467	Stamp and Shake/Ah-Ya	1964	$15
❏ 5349	Sting Ray/Snap Happy	1963	$15

Number	Title	Yr	NM

ROUZAN SISTERS, THE
FRISCO
❏ 113	Men of War/Dance Every Dance	1965	$10

ROVER BOYS, THE
ABC-PARAMOUNT
❏ 9659	Come to Me/Love Me Again	1955	$20
❏ 9732	From a School Ring to a Wedding Ring/Young Love	1956	$20
❏ 9700	Graduation Day/I Hear Music	1956	$20
❏ 9779	Little Did I Know/Again and Again	1957	$20
❏ 9678	My Queen/Sixteen Teens	1956	$20
❏ 9760	The Piano Tuner/Whoop Doodly Baby	1956	$20

CORAL
❏ 61271	Show Me/You've Got It	1954	$30

DECCA
❏ 31485	Shalom/I Hear Havana	1963	$8

RCA VICTOR
❏ 47-7432	Magic Lamp/Little Darlin'	1959	$15
❏ 47-7482	Sweet Violets/Julia	1959	$15

UNITED ARTISTS
❏ 331	For Every Boy or Girl/If You Plant a Little Kiss	1961	$10
❏ 288	Is It Me/Marry Young	1961	$10

VIK
❏ 0317	Blind Date/Make Room for Me	1958	$30
❏ 0313	Blue Willow/You're My Everything	1958	$30
❏ 0338	S'Agapo/Ask Me Who Loves You	1958	$30
❏ 0283	Soft Sands/My Baby's Steppin' Out	1957	$30
❏ 0302	What Can I Do for a Heartache/I Got to You	1957	$30

ROVERS, THE
CLEVELAND INT'L.
❏ 02148	Mexican Girl/Pheasant Pluckers Son	1981	$4
❏ 02728	Pain in My Past/Daddies (Bobby's Song)	1982	$4
❏ 02911	People Who Read People Magazine/Roly Poly Ladies	1982	$4
❏ 51007	Wasn't That a Party/Matchstalk Men and Matchstalk Cats & Dogs	1981	$5

EPIC
❏ 03089	Wasn't That a Party/Pain in My Past	1982	$3

—Reissue

ROVERS, THE (1)
CAPITOL
❏ F3078	Why Oh-h/Ichi-Bon Tami Dachi	1955	$60

MUSIC CITY
❏ 780	Salute to Johnny Ace/Jadda	1955	$100

—Black vinyl
❏ 780	Salute to Johnny Ace/Jadda	1955	$250

—Red vinyl
❏ 750	Why Oh-h/Ichi-Bon Tami Dachi	1954	$100

—Black vinyl
❏ 750	Why Oh-h/Ichi-Bon Tami Dachi	1954	$250

—Red vinyl

ROVERS, THE (2)
CHATTAHOOCHIE
❏ 653	The Web/Can't Be the First	1964	$10

ROVERS, THE (3)
KAPP
❏ 278	Delia's Gone/I Know Where I'm Goin'	1959	$15

ROVERS, THE (4)
ATTIC
❏ 275	Grandma Got Run Over by a Reindeer/Merry Bloody Christmas	1982	$6

Number	Title	Yr	NM

ROVIN' KIND, THE
DUNWICH
❑ 146	My Generation/Girl	1967	$30
❑ 154	She/Didn't Want to Have to Do It	1967	$30

ROWE, JACK
DECCA
❑ 9-46388	Bomb Bosh Boogie/Texas Stomp	1952	$40
❑ 9-46320	Hill Top Rag/Steelin' the Theme	1951	$30

ROWE, STACEY
SABRE
❑ 4510	I Couldn't Live Without Your Love/(B-side unknown)	1979	$8

ROWELL, ERNIE
GRASS
❑ 05	I'm Leavin' You Alone/He's the One	1979	$6
❑ 07	Music in the Mountains/He's the One	1981	$6

PRIZE
❑ 02	Fire and Rain/Facing You	1971	$8
❑ 19	Four Roses/Those Two X's	1972	$8
❑ 08	Going Back to Louisiana/This Bottle Hides the Weakness in Me	1971	$8

ROWLAND, DAVE, AND SUGAR
ELEKTRA
❑ 47234 [DJ]	Winter Wonderland/Rudolph the Red-Nosed Reindeer	1981	$8

— *B-side by Mel and Nancy (Tillis and Sinatra)*

ROXETTE
CAPITOL
❑ B-5380	Teaser Japanese/Can You Touch Me	1984	$60
❑ PB-5380 [DJ]	Teaser Japanese (same on both sides)	1984	$30

EMI
❑ B-50204	Dressed for Success/The Look	1989	$4
❑ 7PRO-4409 [DJ]	Listen to Your Heart (same on both sides)	1989	$8

— *Vinyl originally was promo only*

❑ 7PRO-04409/22 [DJ]	Listen to Your Heart (U.S. Remix)/(Remix Short Version)	1989	$15

— *Vinyl originally was promo only*

❑ B-50190	The Look/Silver Blue	1989	$4

ROXY MUSIC
Also see BRYAN FERRY.
ATCO
❑ 7204	Angel Eyes/My Little Girl	1979	$4
❑ 7100	Dance Away/Trash 2	1979	$4
❑ 7315	In the Midnight Hour/(B-side unknown)	1980	$4
❑ 7042	Love Is the Drug/Both Ends Burning	1975	$4
❑ 7310	Oh Yeah (On the Radio)/Rain, Rain, Rain	1980	$4
❑ 7301	Over You/My Only Love	1980	$4
❑ 7018	The Thrill of It All/The Application Failed	1975	$4

WARNER BROS.
❑ 7719	Do the Strand/Editions of You	1973	$12
❑ 29912	More Than This/Always Unknowing	1982	$3
❑ 29978	Take a Chance with Me/India	1982	$3
❑ 29978 [PS]	Take a Chance with Me/India	1982	$4

ROY, BOBBIE
CAPITOL
❑ 3587	Baby, I've Waited/Love Makes a Woman Feel Good	1973	$6
❑ 3513	I Am Woman/Till I Get It Right	1973	$6
❑ 3477	I Like Everything About Loving You/I Wanted So to Say It	1972	$6
❑ 3428	Leavin' on Your Mind/Candle in the Wind	1972	$6
❑ 3301	One Woman's Trash (Another Woman's Treasure)/Due to a Heartache	1972	$6
❑ 3711	Things Are Looking Good/The World's Not Ready Yet	1973	$6

DIAL
❑ 1151	Till the Feeling Goes Away/What You Got at Home	1975	$6

ROY C
ALAGA
❑ 1005	A Merry Black Christmas/I Don't Want To Worry	1970	$10
❑ 1003	Falling in Love/I Found a Man in My Bed	1970	$10
❑ 1006	Got to Get Enough (Of Your Sweet Love Stuff)/An Open Letter to the President	1971	$10
❑ 1013	I Caught You in the Act/Back Into My Arms	1973	$10
❑ 1008	I'll Never Leave You Lonely/I'm Gonna Love (Somebody Else's Woman)	1972	$10
❑ 1000	In Divorce Court/I Don't Want to Worry	1970	$10
❑ 1007	I Wasn't There/Those Days Are Gone	1971	$10
❑ 1014	Since God Made a Woman/We're On the Road to Hell	1973	$10
❑ 1009	Since I Met You Baby/Lonely I Was	1972	$10

— *With Linda Caver*

BLACK HAWK
❑ 12101	Shotgun Wedding/I'm Gonna Make It	1965	$15

MERCURY
❑ 73391	Don't Blame the Man/I'm Bustin' My Rocks	1973	$6
❑ 73780	Every Woman Has a Right/Don't Stop Short of Satisfaction	1976	$5
❑ 73981	From the Outside Looking In (He Used to Be My Friend)/After Loving You	1977	$5
❑ 73605	Loneliness Has Got a Hold on Me/If I Could Love You Forever	1974	$5
❑ 73672	Love Me Till Tomorrow Comes/Virgin Girl	1975	$5
❑ 73735	My Girl (Reggae)/The Second Time Around	1975	$5
❑ 73445	She Kept On Walkin'/Back Into My Arms	1973	$6

SHOUT
❑ 206	Gone Gone/Stop What You're Doing	1966	$10

UPTOWN
❑ 731	Shotgun Wedding/High School Dropout	1966	$10

ROYAL, BILLY JOE
ALL WOOD
❑ 401	Wait for Me Baby/If It Wasn't for a Woman	1962	$30

ATLANTIC AMERICA
❑ 99555	Boardwalk Angel/Out of Sight and On My Mind	1986	$3
❑ 99599	Burned Like a Rocket/Lonely Loving You	1985	$3
❑ 99404	I'll Pin a Note on Your Pillow/A Place for a Heartache	1987	$3
❑ 99404 [PS]	I'll Pin a Note on Your Pillow/A Place for a Heartache	1987	$3
❑ 99519	I Miss You Already/Another Endless Night	1986	$3
❑ 99295	It Keeps Right On Hurtin'/Let It Rain	1988	$3
❑ 99295 [PS]	It Keeps Right On Hurtin'/Let It Rain	1988	$3
❑ 99217	Love Has No Right/Cross My Heart and Hope to Try	1989	$3
❑ 99217 [PS]	Love Has No Right/Cross My Heart and Hope to Try	1989	$4
❑ 99485	Old Bridges Burn Slow/We've Both Got a Lot to Learn	1987	$3
❑ 99485 [PS]	Old Bridges Burn Slow/We've Both Got a Lot to Learn	1987	$3
❑ 99364	Out of Sight and On My Mind/She Don't Cry Like She Used To	1988	$3
❑ 99364 [PS]	Out of Sight and On My Mind/She Don't Cry Like She Used To	1988	$3
❑ 99242	Tell It Like It Is/Losing You	1989	$3
❑ 99242 [PS]	Tell It Like It Is/Losing You	1989	$4

COLUMBIA
❑ 44743	Bed of Roses/The Greatest Love	1969	$6
❑ 45220	Burning a Hole/Every Night	1970	$5
❑ 43740	Campfire Girls/Should I Come Back	1966	$8
❑ 44902	Cherry Hill Park/Helping Hand	1969	$8
❑ 45620	Child of Mine/Natchez Trace	1972	$6
❑ 45495	Colorado Rain/We Go Back	1971	$5
❑ 44468	Don't You Be Ashamed (To Call My Name)/Don't You Think It's Time	1968	$8
❑ 43305	Down in the Boondocks/Oh, What a Night	1965	$12
❑ 43305 [DJ]	Down in the Boondocks (same on both sides)	1965	$50

— *Red vinyl promo*

❑ 43305 [DJ]	Down in the Boondocks (same on both sides)	1965	$50

— *Red vinyl promo*

❑ 43622	Heart's Desire/Keep Inside Me	1966	$8
❑ 44277	Hush/Watching from the Bandstand	1967	$8

❑ 43390 [DJ]	I Knew You When (same on both sides)	1965	$50

— *Red vinyl promo*

❑ 43390	I Knew You When/Steal Away	1965	$10
❑ 43538	It's a Good Time/Don't Wait Up for Me Mama	1966	$8
❑ 43465 [DJ]	I've Got to Be Somebody (same on both sides)	1965	$40

— *Red vinyl promo*

❑ 43465	I've Got to Be Somebody/You Make Me Feel Like a Man	1965	$8
❑ 45557	Later/The Family	1972	$6
❑ 45085	Mama's Song/Me Without You	1970	$5
❑ 44677	Movies in My Mind/Gabriel	1968	$6
❑ 45406	Poor Little Pearl/Lady Lives to Love	1971	$5
❑ 44574	Storybook Children/Just Between You and Me	1968	$8
❑ 44103	These Are Not My People/The Greatest Love	1967	$8
❑ 45289	Tulsa/Pick Up the Pieces	1970	$5
❑ 44003	Wisdom of a Fool/Everything Turned Blue	1967	$8

FAIRLANE
❑ 21013	Dark Glasses/Perhaps	1962	$40

KAT FAMILY
❑ 02297	Wasted Time/Outrun the Sun	1981	$4
❑ 01044	(Who is Like You) Sweet America/No Love Like a First Love	1981	$4

MERCURY
❑ 76069	Mr. Kool/Let's Talk It Over	1980	$4

MGM SOUTH
❑ 7022	If This Is the Last Time/Perfect Harmony	1973	$5
❑ 7032	Star Again/Sugar Blue	1974	$5
❑ 7018	Summertime Skies/Look What I Found	1973	$5
❑ 7011	This Magic Moment/Mountain Woman	1973	$5

PLAYER'S
❑ 1	I'm Specialized/Really You	1965	$30

PRIVATE STOCK
❑ 45212 [DJ]	Anchors Aweigh (mono/stereo)	1979	$5
❑ 45,212 [DJ]	Anchors Aweigh (mono/stereo)	1979	$5

SCEPTER
❑ 12419	All Night Rain/Time Don't Pass By Here	1976	$4

TOLLIE
❑ 9011	Mama Didn't Raise No Fools/Get Behind Me, Devil	1964	$20

ROYAL DEBS, THE
TIFCO
❑ 826	I Do/Jerry	1962	$30

ROYAL DRIFTERS, THE
TEEN
❑ 506	S'Why Hard/Little Linda	1959	$125
❑ 508	To Each His Own/Da Kind	1959	$200

ROYAL GUARDSMEN, THE
LAURIE
❑ 3391	Airplane Song (My Airplane)/Om	1967	$8
❑ 3461	Baby Let's Wait/Biplane "Evermore"	1968	$8
❑ 3359	Baby Let's Wait/Leaving Me	1966	$80
❑ 3461	Baby Let's Wait/So Right (To Be in Love)	1968	$8
❑ 3428	I Say Love/I'm Not Gonna Stay	1968	$8
❑ 3494	Magic Window/Mother, Where's Your Daughter	1969	$30
❑ 3451	Snoopy for President/Down Behind the Lines	1968	$8
❑ 3590	Snoopy for President/Down Behind the Lines	1972	$6
❑ 3646	Snoopy for President/Sweetmeats Slide	1976	$5
❑ 3416	Snoopy's Christmas/It Kinda Looks Like Christmas	1967	$12
❑ 3416 [PS]	Snoopy's Christmas/It Kinda Looks Like Christmas	1967	$30
❑ 3366	Snoopy vs. the Red Baron/I Needed You	1966	$15

— *Regular red, black and white label*

❑ 3366	Snoopy vs. the Red Baron/I Needed You	1966	$20

— *Light blue label*

❑ 3397	Wednesday/So Right (To Be in Love)	1967	$8

Number	Title	Yr	NM

ROYAL HALOS, THE
ALADDIN
| ❏ 3460 | My Love Is True/Nobody But Me and My Girl | 1959 | $50 |

ROYAL HOLIDAYS, THE
CARLTON
| ❏ 472 | Margaret/I'm Sorry | 1958 | $30 |
PENTHOUSE
| ❏ 9357 | Margaret/I'm Sorry | 1958 | $200 |

ROYAL ROBINS, THE
ABC-PARAMOUNT
| ❏ 10542 | How High the Moon/Something You've Got, Baby | 1964 | $40 |
| ❏ 10504 | Turn Me Loose/Country Fool | 1963 | $40 |

ROYAL TEENS, THE
ABC-PARAMOUNT
❏ 9918	Big Name Button/Sham Rock	1958	$30
❏ 9945	Harvey's Got a Girl Friend/Hangin' Around	1958	$30
❏ 9955	Open the Door/My Kind of Dream	1958	$30
❏ 9882	Short Shorts/Planet Rock	1958	$40
ALLNEW
| ❏ 1415 | Short Short Twist/Royal Twist | 1962 | $30 |
CAPITOL
❏ F4261	Believe Me/Little Cricket	1959	$40
❏ 4335	The Moon's Not Meant for Lovers/Was It a Dream	1960	$40
❏ 4402	With You/It's the Talk of the Town	1960	$40
JUBILEE
| ❏ 5418 | Short Short Twist/Royal Twist | 1962 | $20 |
MIGHTY
❏ 112	Cave Man/Wounded Heart	1959	$40
❏ 111	Leotards/Royal Blues	1959	$30
❏ 200	My Memories of You/Little Trixie	1961	$50
MUSICOR
| ❏ 1398 | Smile a Little Smile for Me/Hey Jude | 1969 | $12 |
POWER
| ❏ 113 | Mad Gass/Sittin' with My Baby | 1959 | $50 |
| ❏ 215 | Short Shorts/Planet Rock | 1957 | $200 |
SWAN
| ❏ 4200 | I'll Love You ('Til the End of Time)/(Instrumental) | 1965 | $125 |
TCF HALL
| ❏ 117 | Bad Girl/Do the Montoona | 1965 | $20 |

ROYAL TONES, THE
TITANIC
| ❏ 5014 | Black Lightnin'/Surfer's Junction | 1964 | $70 |

ROYALETTES, THE
CHANCELLOR
| ❏ 1140 | Willie the Wolf/Blue Summer | 1963 | $20 |
MGM
❏ 13283	He's Gone/Don't You Cry	1964	$15
❏ 13544	I Don't Want to Be the One/An Affair to Remember	1966	$15
❏ 13507	It's a Big Mistake/It's Better Not to Know	1966	$15
❏ 13366	It's Gonna Take a Miracle/Out of Sight, Out of Mind	1965	$20
❏ 13405	I Want to Meet Him/Never Again	1965	$15
❏ 13588	Love Without An End/When Summer's Gone	1966	$15
❏ 13627	My Man/Take My Love	1966	$15
❏ 13327	Poor Boy/Watch What Happens	1965	$15
WARNER BROS.
| ❏ 5439 | There He Goes/Come to Me | 1964 | $20 |

ROYALS, THE
FEDERAL
| ❏ 12177 [DJ] | Give It Up/That Woman | 1954 | $125 |

—*Evidently, some promos exist crediting The Royals. For stock copies, see "Midnighters, The*

ROYALS, THE (1)
FEDERAL
| ❏ 12098 | A Love in My Heart/I'll Never Let You Go | 1952 | $1000 |
| ❏ 12113 | Are You Forgetting?/What Did I Do | 1952 | $600 |

| ❏ 12064AA | Every Beat of My Heart/All Night Long | 1952 | $3000 |

—*Blue vinyl. VG 1,000; VG+ 2,000*

❏ 12064	Every Beat of My Heart/All Night Long	1952	$1500
❏ 12133	Get It/No It Ain't	1953	$200
❏ 12177 [DJ]	Give It Up/That Woman	1954	$300

—*Evidently, some promos exist crediting The Royals*

❏ 12150	Hello Miss Fine/I Feel That-A-Way	1953	$200
❏ 12077	I Know I Love You So/Starting From Tonight	1952	$2500
❏ 12088	Moonrise/Fifth Street Blues	1952	$2000
❏ 12088	Moonrise/Fifth Street Blues	1952	$3000

—*Blue vinyl. VG 1000; VG+ 2000*

❏ 12160	That's It/Someone Like You	1953	$250
❏ 12121	The Shrine of St. Cecelia/I Feel So Blue	1953	$800
❏ 12169	Work With Me Annie/Until I Die	1954	$250

—*Original pressing; for reissues, see "Midnighters, The*

ROYALS, THE (2)
OKEH
| ❏ 6832 | If You Love Me/Dreams of You | 1951 | $1000 |

ROYALS, THE (3)
PENGUIN
| ❏ 1008 | Thunder Wagon/Teen Beat | 1959 | $40 |

ROYALS, THE (4)
VAGABOND
| ❏ 444 | Christmas Party/White Christmas | 1963 | $60 |

—*Black vinyl*

| ❏ 444 | Christmas Party/White Christmas | 1963 | $125 |

—*Red vinyl*

| ❏ 134 | Surfin' Lagoon/Wild Safari | 1962 | $60 |

ROYALS, THE (5)
VENUS
| ❏ 103 | Someday We'll Meet Again/I Want You to Be My Mambo Baby | 1954 | $400 |

ROYALTONES, THE
GOLDISC
❏ 3016	Butterscotch/Dixie Cup	1961	$8
❏ 3028	Do the Early Bird/Scotch and Soda	1962	$8
❏ 3011	Flamingo Express/Secret Love	1960	$10
❏ 3011	Flamingo Express/Tacos	1960	$10
❏ 3026	Peppermint Twist/Scotch and Soda	1962	$8
❏ 3004	Short Line/Big Wheel	1960	$10
JUBILEE
| ❏ 5338 | Poor Boy/Wail! | 1958 | $30 |

—*Dark blue label, silver print*

| ❏ 5338 | Poor Boy/Wail! | 1958 | $20 |

—*Black label with rainbow*

| ❏ 5362 | Seesaw/Little Bo | 1959 | $15 |
MALA
| ❏ 482 | El Toro/Lonely World | 1964 | $8 |
| ❏ 473 | Holy Smokes/Our Faded Love | 1964 | $8 |
OLD TOWN
| ❏ 1018 | Crazy Love/Never Let Me Go | 1956 | $125 |
PORT
| ❏ 70037 | Poor Boy/See Saw | 1963 | $15 |

ROZA, LITA
LONDON
| ❏ 1398 | The Little Boy That Santa Forgot/Saint Nicholas Waltz | 1953 | $15 |

ROZZI, LITTLE SAMMY
PELHAM
| ❏ 722 | Christine/Over the Rainbow | 1961 | $200 |

RUBBER BAND, THE (1)
ABC
| ❏ 10849 | Plastic Soul/Let's Sail Away | 1966 | $10 |
COLUMBIA
| ❏ 44013 | In and Out of My Life/Bring Your Love | 1967 | $10 |
REPRISE
| ❏ 0637 | I'm Gonna Make It/Messin' Up the Mind of a Young Girl | 1967 | $10 |

RUBBER BAND, THE (2)
GRT
| ❏ 1 | Sunshine of Your Love/Deserted Cities of the Heart | 1969 | $6 |

RUBBISH, JONNY
UNITED ARTISTS
| ❏ 36479 [DJ] | Santa's Alive/Policeman (I Got Pulled Over By A) | 1978 | $10 |

—*U.K. import*

RUBEN AND THE JETS
MERCURY
| ❏ 73411 | Charlena/Mah Man Flash | 1973 | $6 |
| ❏ 73381 | If I Could Be Your Love Again/Wedding Bells | 1973 | $6 |

RUBIN, DAN, ORCHESTRA
HIT
| ❏ 42 | The Lonely Bull/Telstar | 1962 | $10 |

—*B-side by the Tides*

RUBINOOS, THE
BESERKLEY
❏ 5738	Gorilla/Cats and Dogs	1976	$5
❏ 5750	Hold Me/Lightning Love Affair	1977	$4
❏ 5741	I Think We're Alone Now/As Long As I'm with You	1977	$4
❏ 5741 [PS]	I Think We're Alone Now/As Long As I'm with You	1977	$4
❏ 46518	I Wanna Be Your Boyfriend/Lightning Love Affair	1979	$4

RUBY AND THE ROMANTICS
A&M
| ❏ 1042 | Hurting Each Other/Baby, I Could Be So Good at Loving You | 1969 | $8 |
ABC
❏ 11065	On a Clear Day You Can See Forever/More Than Yesterday, Less Than Tomorrow	1968	$10
❏ 10941	Only Heaven Knows/This Is No Laughing Matter	1967	$10
❏ 10911	Twilight Time/Una Bella Brazilian Melody	1967	$10
KAPP
❏ 601	Baby Come Home/Every Day's a Holiday	1964	$15
❏ 646	Does He Really Care for Me/Nevertheless (I'm in Love with You)	1965	$15
❏ 544	Hey There Lonely Boy/Not a Moment Too Soon	1963	$15
❏ 544 [PS]	Hey There Lonely Boy/Not a Moment Too Soon	1963	$20
❏ 773	Hey There Lonely Boy/Think	1966	$12
❏ 839	I Know/We'll Love Again	1967	$10
❏ 525	My Summer Love/Sweet Love and Sweet Forgiveness	1963	$15
❏ 501	Our Day Will Come/Moonlight and Music	1963	$20
❏ 578	Our Everlasting Love/Much Better Off Than I've Ever Been	1964	$15
❏ 759	We Can Make It/Remember Me	1966	$10
❏ 665	We'll Meet Again/Your Baby Doesn't Love You Anymore	1965	$15
❏ 615	When You're Young and In Love/I Cry Alone	1964	$15

RUFFIN, DAVID, AND EDDIE KENDRICK
RCA
| ❏ 5313-7-R | I Couldn't Believe It/Don't Know Why You're Dreamin' | 1987 | $3 |
| ❏ 6925-7-R | One More for the Lonely Hearts Club/Don't Know Why You're Dreaming | 1988 | $3 |

RUFFIN, DAVID
Also see DARYL HALL AND JOHN OATES; JIMMY AND DAVID RUFFIN; THE TEMPTATIONS; THE VOICE MASTERS.

ANNA
| ❏ 1127 | I'm in Love/One of These Days | 1961 | $70 |
CHECK MATE
| ❏ 1010 | Mr. Bus Driver -- Hurry!/Knock You Out (With Love) | 1962 | $70 |
MOTOWN
❏ 1204	A Day in the Life of a Working Man/A Little More Trust	1972	$6
❏ 1223	Blood Donors Needed/Go On with Your Bad Self	1973	$6
❏ 1259	Common Man/I'm Just a Mortal Man	1973	$6

Number	Title	Yr	NM
❏ 1178	Each Day Is a Lifetime/Don't Stop Loving Me	1971	$6
❏ 1393	Everything's Coming Up Love/No Matter Where	1976	$5
❏ 1388	Heavy Love/Love Can Be Hazardous To Your Health	1976	$5
❏ 1158	I'm So Glad I Fell for You/I Pray Every Day You Won't Regret Loving Me	1969	$6
❏ 1149	I've Lost Everything I've Ever Loved/We'll Have a Good Thing Going On	1969	$6
❏ 1327	Me and Rock and Roll (Are Here to Stay)/Smiling Faces Sometimes	1974	$6
❏ 1140	My Whole World Ended (The Moment You Left Me)/I've Got to Find Myself a Brand New Baby	1968	$6
❏ 1405	On and Off/Statue of a Fool	1976	$5
❏ 1336	Superstar/No Matter Where	1975	$5
❏ 1376	Walk Away from Love/Love Can Be Hazardous to Your Health	1975	$5

WARNER BROS.

Number	Title	Yr	NM
❏ 49123	I Get Excited/Chain on the Brain	1979	$4
❏ 49030	Sexy Dancer/Break My Heart	1979	$4
❏ 49277	Slow Dance/Don't You Go Home	1980	$4
❏ 49577	Still in Love with You/I Wanna Be with You	1980	$4

RUFFIN, JIMMY

ATCO

Number	Title	Yr	NM
❏ 6926	Tears of Joy/Goin' Home	1973	$8

CHESS

Number	Title	Yr	NM
❏ 2160	Tell Me What You Want/Do You Know Me	1974	$5
❏ 2168	What You See (Ain't Always What You Get)/Boy from Mississippi	1975	$5

EPIC

Number	Title	Yr	NM
❏ 50339	Fallin' in Love with You/Fallin' in Love with You	1977	$5
❏ 50384	Fallin' in Love with You/Fallin' in Love with You	1977	$5

MIRACLE

Number	Title	Yr	NM
❏ 1	Don't Feel Sorry for Me/Heart	1961	$200

RSO

Number	Title	Yr	NM
❏ 1021	Hold On to My Love/(Instrumental)	1980	$5

SOUL

Number	Title	Yr	NM
❏ 35016	As Long As There Is L-O-V-E/How Can I Say I'm Sorry	1965	$10
❏ 35046	Don't Let Him Take Your Love from Me/Lonely, Lonely Man Am I	1968	$8
❏ 35035	Don't You Miss Me A Little Bit Baby/I Want Her Love	1967	$8
❏ 35060	Farewell Is a Lonely Sound/If You Will Let Me, I Know I Can	1969	$8
❏ 35032	Gonna Give Her All the Love I've Got/World So Wide (Nowhere to Hide from Your Heart)	1967	$8
❏ 35043	I'll Say Forever My Love/Everybody Needs Love	1968	$8
❏ 35027	I've Passed This Way Before/Tomorrow's Tears	1966	$10
❏ 35077	Maria (You Were the Only One)/Living in a World I Created For Myself	1970	$8
❏ 35092	Our Favorite Melody/You Gave Me Love	1972	$6
❏ 35053	Sad and Lonesome Feeling/Gonna Keep On Trying Till I Win Your Love	1968	$8
❏ 35002	Since I've Lost You/I Want Her Love	1964	$50
❏ 35022	What Becomes of the Brokenhearted/Baby I've Got It	1966	$20

RUFFIN, JIMMY AND DAVID

SOUL

Number	Title	Yr	NM
❏ 35086	Lo and Behold/The Things We Have to Do	1971	$5
❏ 35076	Stand By Me/Your Love Was Worth Waiting For	1970	$5
❏ 35082	When My Love Hand Comes Do Down/Steppin' On a Dream	1971	$5

RUFUS

ABC

Number	Title	Yr	NM
❏ 12239	At Midnight (My Love Will Lift You Up)/Better Days	1976	$5
❏ 12390	Blue Love/Turn	1978	$5
❏ 12179	Dance Wit' Me/Everybody's Got an Aura	1976	$5
❏ 12296	Everlasting Love/Close the Door	1977	$5
❏ 11394	Feel Good/Keep It Coming	1973	$6
❏ 12269	Holywood/Earth Song	1977	$5
❏ 12066	Once You Get Started/Rufusized	1975	$5
❏ 12099	Please Pardon Me (You Remind Me of a Friend)/Somebody's Watching You	1975	$5
❏ 11356	Slip 'N Slide/I Finally Found You	1973	$8
❏ 12349	Stay/My Ship Will Sail	1978	$5
❏ 12149	Sweet Thing/Circles	1975	$5
❏ 11427	Tell Me Something Good/Smokin' Room	1974	$6
❏ 12010	Tell Me Something Good/Smokin' Room	1974	$5
❏ 11376	Whoever's Thrilling You (Is Killing Me)/I Finally Found You	1973	$6

EPIC

Number	Title	Yr	NM
❏ 10726	Follow the Lamb/Fire One, Fire Two, Fire Three	1971	$15

MCA

Number	Title	Yr	NM
❏ 41025	Ain't Nobody Like You/You're to Blame	1979	$4
❏ 41131	Do You Love What You Feel/Dancin' Mood	1979	$4
❏ 41230	I'm Dancing for Your Love/Walk the Rockway	1980	$4
❏ 51125	Party 'Til You're Broke/Hold On to a Friend	1981	$4
❏ 51203	Sharing the Love/We Got the Way	1981	$4
❏ 51070	Tonight We Love/Afterwards	1981	$4
❏ 52002	True Love/Better Together	1982	$4
❏ 41191	What Am I Missing/Any Love	1980	$4

WARNER BROS.

Number	Title	Yr	NM
❏ 29555	Ain't Nobody/Sweet Thing	1983	$4
❏ 29675	Blinded by the Boogie/You're Really Out of Line	1983	$4
❏ 29406	One Million Kisses/Stay	1983	$4
❏ 29790	Take It to the Hop/Distant Lover	1983	$4

RUFUS AND CARLA

ATCO

Number	Title	Yr	NM
❏ 6177	Cause I Love You/Deep Down Inside	1960	$30

—As "Carla and Rufus"

Number	Title	Yr	NM
❏ 6199	I Didn't Believe/Yeah, Yea-Ah	1961	$30

—As "Rufus and Friend"

SATELLITE

Number	Title	Yr	NM
❏ 102	Cause I Love You/Deep Down Inside	1960	$50

STAX

Number	Title	Yr	NM
❏ 184	Birds and Bees/Never Let You Go	1966	$15
❏ 151	That's Really Some Good/Night Time Is the Right Time	1964	$15
❏ 176	When You Move You Lose/We're Tight	1965	$15

RUGBYS, THE

AMAZON

Number	Title	Yr	NM
❏ 4	The Light/Wendeghal Warlock	1970	$8

RUMBLERS, THE

DOT

Number	Title	Yr	NM
❏ 16480	Angry Sea (Walmea)/Bugged	1963	$20
❏ 16421	Boss/I Don't Need You No More	1963	$20
❏ 16455	Boss Strikes Back/Sorry	1963	$20
❏ 16521	It's a Gas/Tootananny	1963	$20

DOWNEY

Number	Title	Yr	NM
❏ 107	Angry Sea (Walmea)/Bugged	1963	$40
❏ 103	Boss/I Don't Need You No More	1962	$40
❏ 133	Boss Soul/Till Always	1965	$30
❏ 106	Boss Strikes Back/Sorry	1963	$40
❏ 114	High Octane/Night Scene	1964	$30
❏ 111	It's a Gas/Tootananny	1963	$40
❏ 127	Soulful Jerk/Hey-Did-a-Da-Do	1964	$30
❏ 119	The Hustler/Riot in Cell Block #9	1964	$30

HIGHLAND

Number	Title	Yr	NM
❏ 1026	Intersection/Stomping Theme	1962	$60

RUMBLES LTD., THE

DAD'S

Number	Title	Yr	NM
❏ 103 [PS]	The Wildest Christmas/Santa Claus Is Coming To Town	1968	$15
❏ 103	The Wildest Christmas/Santa Claus Is Coming To Town	1968	$20

RUMOUR, THE

GRAHAM PARKER's band.

ARISTA

Number	Title	Yr	NM
❏ 0451	Emotional Traffic/Hard Enough to Show	1979	$4

MERCURY

Number	Title	Yr	NM
❏ 73949	I'm So Glad/This Town	1977	$4

RUN-D.M.C.

MCA

Number	Title	Yr	NM
❏ 53680	Ghost Busters/(Ghost Power Instrumental)	1989	$8

PROFILE

Number	Title	Yr	NM
❏ 5051	30 Days/30 Days (instrumental)	1984	$5
❏ 5088	Can You Rock Like This?/Together Forever	1986	$5
❏ 5235	Christmas in Hollis/Let the Jingle Bells Rock	1988	$4

—B-side by Sweet Tee; red vinyl

Number	Title	Yr	NM
❏ 5036	Hard Times-Jam Master Jay/Hard Times-Jam Master Jay (instrumental)	1983	$5
❏ 5058	Hollis Crew/Hollis Crew (instrumental)	1984	$5
❏ 5224	I'm Not Going Out Like That/How'd Ya Do It Dee	1988	$4
❏ 5224 [PS]	I'm Not Going Out Like That/How'd Ya Do It Dee	1988	$4
❏ 5019	It's Like That/It's Like That (instrumental)	1983	$5
❏ 5131	It's Tricky/Proud to Be Black	1987	$4
❏ 5131 [PS]	It's Tricky/Proud to Be Black	1987	$4
❏ 5211	Mary, Mary/Rock Box	1988	$4
❏ 5211 [PS]	Mary, Mary/Rock Box	1988	$4
❏ 5102	My Adidas/Peter Piper	1986	$4
❏ 5102 [PS]	My Adidas/Peter Piper	1986	$4
❏ 5112	Walk This Way/King of Rock	1986	$4

—A-side with Steven Tyler and Joe Perry of Aerosmith

Number	Title	Yr	NM
❏ 5112 [PS]	Walk This Way/King of Rock	1986	$4

RUNAROUNDS, THE

CAPITOL

Number	Title	Yr	NM
❏ 5644	Perfect Woman/You're a Drag	1966	$30

COUSINS

Number	Title	Yr	NM
❏ 1004	Mashed Potato Mary/I'm All Alone	1964	$30

FELSTED

Number	Title	Yr	NM
❏ 8704	Send Her Back/Carrie, You're An Angel	1964	$40

MGM

Number	Title	Yr	NM
❏ 13763	My Little Girl/You Lied	1967	$20

TARHEEL

Number	Title	Yr	NM
❏ 065	Are You Looking for a Sweetheart/Let Them Talk	1963	$30

RUNAWAYS, THE

Also see JOAN JETT AND THE BLACKHEARTS.

MERCURY

Number	Title	Yr	NM
❏ 73819	Cherry Bomb/Blackmail	1976	$20
❏ 73890 [B]	Heartbeat/Neon Angels on the Road to Ruin	1977	$15

RUNDGREN, TODD

Also see NAZZ (1); UTOPIA.

AMPEX

Number	Title	Yr	NM
❏ 31001	We Gotta Get You a Woman/Medley	1970	$10

—As "Runt"

BEARSVILLE

Number	Title	Yr	NM
❏ 0020	A Dream Goes On Forever/Heavy Metal Kids	1974	$6
❏ 31004	A Long Time, A Long Way to Go/Parole	1971	$8

—As "Runt-Todd Rundgren"

Number	Title	Yr	NM
❏ 29686	Bang the Drum All Day/Chant	1983	$6
❏ 31002	Be Nice to Me/Broke Down and Busted	1971	$8

—As "Runt-Todd Rundgren"

Number	Title	Yr	NM
❏ 0301	Breathless/Wolfman Jack	1974	$6
❏ 0324	Can We Still Be Friends/Determination	1978	$5
❏ 0324	Can We Still Be Friends/Out of Control	1978	$5
❏ 49771	Compassion/Pulse	1981	$5
❏ 0007	Couldn't I Just Tell You/Wolfman Jack	1972	$6

Number	Title	Yr	NM
❑ 29759	Emperor of the Highway/Hideaway	1983	$4
❑ 0309	Good Vibrations/When I Pray	1976	$5
❑ 0009	Hello It's Me/Cold Morning Light	1973	$6
❑ 03	I Saw the Light/Marlene	1972	$15
—Blue vinyl			
❑ 03	I Saw the Light/Marlene	1972	$15
❑ 0335	It Wouldn't Have Made Any Difference/Did You Ever Learn	1979	$5
❑ 0310	Love of the Common Man/Black and White	1976	$5
❑ 49696	Time Heals/Tiny Demons	1981	$4
❑ 0030	We Gotta Get You a Woman/I Saw the Light	1973	$4
—Back to Back Hits" series			
COLUMBIA			
❑ 06151	Loving You's a Dirty Job (But Somebody's Gotta Do It)/Before This Night Is Through	1986	$4
—With Bonnie Tyler			
RHINO			
❑ 74426	Bang the Drum All Day/Can We Still Be Friends	1987	$4
WARNER BROS.			
❑ 22868 [PS]	I Love My Life/Parallel Lines	1989	$3
❑ 28821	Something to Fall Back On/Lockjaw	1986	$4

7-Inch Extended Plays

Number	Title	Yr	NM
BEARSVILLE			
❑ SB2066	I Saw the Light/You Left Me Sore/Hello It's Me//Piss Aaron/It Takes Two to Tango/Sweeter Memories	1972	$15
—Jukebox issue; small hole, plays at 33 1/3 rpm			
❑ SB2066 [PS]	Something/Anything?	1972	$15
—Part of "Little LP" series (LLP #236)			
❑ BHS3522-EP	Time Heals/Tiny Demons	1981	$5
—33 1/3 rpm, small hole; bonus record included with the LP "Healing"			

RUSH

Number	Title	Yr	NM
MERCURY			
❑ 76124	Closer to the Heart/Freewill	1981	$8
❑ 73958	Closer to the Heart/Madrigal	1977	$10
❑ 76060	Entre Nous/Different Strings	1980	$12
❑ DJ-407-73623 [DJ]	Finding My Way (mono/stereo)	1974	$70
❑ 73623	Finding My Way/Need Some Love	1974	$100
❑ 73681	Fly by Night/Anthem	1975	$100
❑ DJ-553-73681 [DJ]	Fly by Night/Anthem	1975	$70
❑ 73990	Fly by Night/Anthem	1978	$10
❑ 73873	Fly by Night-In the Mood/Something for Nothing	1976	$10
❑ DJ-417-73647 [DJ]	In the Mood (mono/stereo)	1974	$70
❑ 73647	In the Mood/What You're Doing	1974	$100
❑ 73737 [DJ]	Lakeside Park (3:16) (mono/stereo)	1975	$70
❑ 73737	Lakeside Park/Bastille Day	1975	$100
❑ 76095	Limelight/XYZ	1981	$12
❑ 73912	Making Memories/The Temples of Syrinx	1977	$10
❑ 76196	Subdivisions/Countdown	1982	$10
❑ PRO383-7 [DJ]	The Big Money (5:35)/(4:32)	1985	$30
❑ 884191-7	The Big Money/Red Sector A	1985	$5
❑ 880050-7	The Body Electric/Between the Wheels	1984	$12
❑ 76044	The Spirit of Radio/Circumstances	1980	$10
❑ 74051	The Trees/Circumstances	1979	$10
❑ 73803	The Twilight Zone/Lessons	1976	$100
❑ 73803 [DJ]	The Twilight Zone (mono/stereo)	1976	$70
❑ 888891-7	Time Stand Still/High Water	1987	$5
❑ 76109	Tom Sawyer/Witch Hunt	1981	$10
❑ 76109 [PS]	Tom Sawyer/Witch Hunt	1981	$30

RUSH, RAY

Number	Title	Yr	NM
PARKWAY			
❑ 846	So What/Can This Be Love	1962	$20

RUSH, TOM

Number	Title	Yr	NM
COLUMBIA			
❑ 4S-45149	Drop Down Mama/Child's Song	1970	$6
❑ 10021	Ladies Love Outlaws/Maggie	1974	$4
❑ 45185	Old Man's Song/Lost My Drivin' Wheel	1970	$5
❑ 45584	Wind on the Water/Mother Earth	1972	$5
❑ 45364	Wrong End of the Rainbow/Merrimac County	1971	$5

Number	Title	Yr	NM
ELEKTRA			
❑ 45718	Something in the Way She Moves/Who Do You Love	1971	$6
❑ 45607	Sugar Babe/Urge for Going	1967	$8
❑ 45604	Who Do You Love/On the Road Again	1966	$8
PRESTIGE			
❑ 289	Diamond Joe/Every Day in the Week	1964	$15

RUSHEN, PATRICE

Number	Title	Yr	NM
ARISTA			
❑ 9604	Anything Can Happen/All My Love	1987	$3
❑ 9604 [PS]	Anything Can Happen/All My Love	1987	$3
❑ 9644	Come Back to Me/Somewhere	1987	$3
❑ 9644 [PS]	Come Back to Me/Somewhere	1987	$3
❑ 9562	Watch Out/Over the Phone	1987	$3
❑ 9562 [PS]	Watch Out/Over the Phone	1987	$3
ELEKTRA			
❑ 69992	Breakout!/Haven't You Heard	1982	$4
❑ 46044	Changes (In Your Life)/Music of the Heart	1979	$5
❑ 47143	Don't Blame Me/Time Will Tell	1981	$4
❑ 69742	Feels So Real (Won't Let Go)/(Instrumental)	1984	$4
❑ 47427	Forget Me Nots/(She Will) Take You Down to Love	1982	$5
❑ 47427 [PS]	Forget Me Nots/(She Will) Take You Down to Love	1982	$5
❑ 69702	Get Off (You Fascinate Me)/(Instrumental)	1984	$4
❑ 46647	Givin' It Up Is Givin' Up/Settle for My Love	1980	$4
—A-side with D.J. Rogers			
❑ 45549	Hang It Up/It's Just a Natural Thing	1978	$5
❑ 46551	Haven't You Heard/Keepin' Faith in Love	1979	$4
❑ 69678	Heartache Heartbreak/Gotta Find It	1984	$4
❑ 69930	I Was Tired of Being Alone (Glad I Got Cha)/Where There Is Love	1982	$4
❑ 46604	Let the Music Take Me/Message in the Music	1980	$4
❑ 47067	Look Up/The Dream	1980	$4
❑ 46024	When I Found You/Play!	1979	$5
PRESTIGE			
❑ 766	Let Your Heart Be Free/Sojourn	1977	$12

RUSHING, JIM

Number	Title	Yr	NM
OVATION			
❑ 1153	Dixie Dirt/Two Hearts Don't Always Make a Pair	1980	$5
❑ 1161	I've Loved Enough to Know/Two Hearts Don't Always Make a Pair	1980	$5

RUSS, LONNIE

Number	Title	Yr	NM
4J			
❑ 504	Flip Flop/Tell Me Now	1963	$30
❑ 510	Lil' Evett/Them Greens	1963	$30
❑ 501	My Wife Can't Cook/Something Old, Something New	1962	$20
❑ 507	We Belong Together (same on both sides)	1963	$30

RUSSELL, AL

Number	Title	Yr	NM
OKEH			
❑ 6845	I Don't Want to Be Alone for Christmas/I Love Each Move You Make	1951	$120

RUSSELL, BOBBY

Number	Title	Yr	NM
BUENA VISTA			
❑ 474	The Ballad of Smith & Gabriel Billyboy/Summer Sweet	1969	$12
❑ 473	The Ballad of Smith & Gabriel Jimmy Boy/Summer Sweet	1969	$12
COLUMBIA			
❑ 45901	Mid American Manufacturing Tycoon/Ships in the Night	1973	$4
ELF			
❑ 90020	1432 Franklin Pike Circle Hero/Let's Talk About It	1968	$6
❑ 90031	Better Homes and Gardens/Summer Sweet	1969	$6
❑ 90023	Carlie/Ain't Society Great	1969	$6
❑ 90014	Dusty/I Made You This Way	1968	$6
❑ 90027	Then She's a Lover/He Wrote a Song	1969	$6

Number	Title	Yr	NM
F&L			
❑ 518	Camp Getcha 'Losa Ya/Arm Chair Quarterback	1982	$6
HIT			
❑ 66	Still/Losing You	1963	$10
—B-side by Katy Richards			
IMAGE			
❑ 1014	Goin' Steady Dream/To the Ones with Broken Hearts	1961	$15
MONUMENT			
❑ 929	Friends and Memories/Wish I'd Say That	1966	$8
❑ 899	Once a Day/You Were Mine	1965	$8
NATIONAL GENERAL			
❑ 006	As Far As I'm Concerned/Traveling with a Star	1970	$8
PRIVATE STOCK			
❑ 45,046	Little Boxes/(B-side unknown)	1975	$5
RISING SONS			
❑ 700	Bluebird/Tears Tell	1967	$8
UNITED ARTISTS			
❑ 50888	Easy Made for Lovin'/The Bell	1972	$5
❑ 50853	Goodbye/It Hurts	1971	$5
❑ 50788	Saturday Morning Confusion/Little Ole Song About Love	1971	$5
❑ 50959	Welcome to the U.S. Army/This Is the Life	1972	$5

RUSSELL, CLIFFORD

Number	Title	Yr	NM
SUGARTREE			
❑ 0509	She Feels Like a New Man Tonight/Sometimes When We Touch	1983	$8
❑ 0509 [PS]	She Feels Like a New Man Tonight/Sometimes When We Touch	1983	$10

RUSSELL, JOHNNY

Number	Title	Yr	NM
MERCURY			
❑ 57008	Ain't No Way to Make a Bad Love Grow/Keep the Change	1979	$4
❑ 57050	Here's to the Horses/Take Me to Heart	1981	$4
❑ 55045	How Deep in Love Am I?/Shall We Gather at the Ridge	1978	$4
❑ 55060	I Might Be Awhile in New Orleans/Make Up My Mind	1979	$4
❑ 57038	Song of the South/I'm Gettin' Holes in My Boots (From Climbing the Walls)	1980	$4
❑ 57026	We're Back in Love Again/Love Makes a Fool of Us All	1980	$4
❑ 57016	While the Choir Sang the Hymn (I Thought of Her)/Falsely Accused	1980	$4
RCA			
❑ PB-11160	Leona/Your Fool	1977	$5
❑ PB-10984	Obscene Phone Call/If I Want to Get It Right	1977	$5
❑ PB-10853	The Son of Hickory Holler's Tramp/I Wonder How She's Doing Now	1976	$5
RCA VICTOR			
❑ 74-0810	Catfish John/Promise of Your Love	1972	$6
❑ 74-0908	Chained/Drinkin' a Beer and Singin' a Country Song	1973	$6
❑ PB-10258	Hello I Love You/You Ain't Got No Class	1975	$5
❑ PB-10563	I'm a Trucker/Your Fool	1976	$5
❑ 48-1000	Mr. and Mrs. Untrue/I'm Stayin'	1971	$6
❑ 74-0665	Mr. Fiddle Man/Crying Takes More Practice Everyday	1972	$6
❑ PB-10403	Our Marriage Was a Failure/Catfish John	1975	$5
❑ PB-10038	She Burn't the Little Roadside Tavern Down/It Sure Seemed Right	1974	$5
❑ APBO-0248	She's in Love with a Rodeo Man/Someday I'll Sober Up	1974	$5
❑ PB-10135	That's How My Baby Builds a Fire/Act Naturally	1974	$5
❑ APBO-0165	The Baptism of Jesse Taylor/Making Plans	1973	$6
❑ PB-10667	This Man and Woman Thing/Over Georgia	1976	$5
❑ 74-0570	What a Price/Listening to the Rain	1971	$6

RUSSELL, KURT

Number	Title	Yr	NM
CAPITOL			
❑ 2823	I Believe in Love/It Ain't Gonna Rain Anymore	1970	$10

Number	Title	Yr	NM

RUSSELL, LEON, AND MARC BENNO
See ASYLUM CHOIR.

RUSSELL, LEON
A&M
❏ 734	Cindy/Misty	1964	$30

DOT
| ❏ 16771 | Everybody's Talkin' 'Bout the Young/It's Alright with Me | 1965 | $50 |

PARADISE
| ❏ 8438 | Easy Love/Hold On to This Feeling | 1977 | $4 |

—As "Leon and Mary Russell"

❏ 8667	Elvis and Marilyn/Anita Bryant	1978	$5
❏ 8667 [PS]	Elvis and Marilyn/Anita Bryant	1978	$5
❏ 628	Good Time Charlie's Got the Blues/Ain't No Love in the City	1984	$4
❏ 8369	Love Crazy/Say You Will	1977	$4

—As "Leon and Mary Russell"

❏ 8719	Midnight Lover/From Maine to Mexico	1978	$5
❏ 49662	Over the Rainbow/I've Just Seen a Face	1981	$4
❏ 8274	Satisfy You/Windsong	1976	$4

—As "Leon and Mary Russell"

| ❏ 629 | Wabash Cannonball/Tennessee Waltz | 1984 | $4 |

—As "Hank Wilson"; A-side with Willie Nelson

RCA VICTOR
| ❏ 47-6884 | (I Tasted) Tears on Your Lips/A Catchy Tune | 1957 | $40 |

—As "Lee Russell"

ROULETTE
| ❏ 4049 | Honky Tonk Woman/Rainbow at Midnight | 1958 | $30 |

—As "Lee Russell"

SHELTER
| ❏ 7305 | A Hard Rain's A-Gonna Fall/Me and Baby Jane | 1971 | $6 |
| ❏ 7338 | A Six Pack to Go/Uncle Pen | 1973 | $5 |

—As "Hank Wilson"

❏ 7316	A Song for You/A Hard Rain's A-Gonna Fall	1971	$6
❏ 40483	Back to the Island/Little Hideaway	1975	$4
❏ 62004	Bluebird/Back to the Island	1976	$4
❏ 40210	If I Were a Carpenter/Wild Horses	1974	$4
❏ 40210 [PS]	If I Were a Carpenter/Wild Horses	1974	$8
❏ 7302	It Takes a Lot to Laugh, It Takes a Train to Cry/Home Sweet Oklahoma	1970	$6
❏ 40378	Lady Blue/Laying Right Here in Heaven	1975	$4
❏ 7328	Slipping Into Christmas/Christmas in Chicago	1972	$5
❏ 7328 [PS]	Slipping Into Christmas/Christmas in Chicago	1972	$30
❏ 65033	Slipping Into Christmas/Christmas in Chicago	1975	$5

—Reissue of 7328

| ❏ 7325 | Tight Rope/This Masquerade | 1972 | $5 |
| ❏ 40277 | Time for Love/Leaving Whipporwhill | 1974 | $4 |

RUTLES, THE
WARNER BROS.
| ❏ 8560 | I Must Be in Love/Doubleback Alley | 1978 | $15 |

RYAN, BUCK
GILT EDGE
| ❏ 5088 | West Virginia Express/Lee Highway Swing | 1954 | $40 |

MERCURY
| ❏ 70670 | Cincinnati Rag/Red Apple Rag | 1955 | $30 |
| ❏ 70931 | Follow the Fiddle/Nightingale Waltz | 1956 | $30 |

RYAN, CATHY
KING
❏ 4848	Come Home/The Cricket, the Dove, and the Goldfish	1955	$40
❏ 4916	Lazy River/Love You with All My Might	1956	$40
❏ 4890	Only a Dream/High Falutin' Heart	1956	$40

RYAN, CHARLIE
4 STAR
❏ 1749	Hot Rod Hades/Hot Rod Guitar	1961	$30
❏ 1733	Hot Rod Lincoln/Thru the Mill	1959	$30
❏ 1761	Hot Rod Race/Hot Rod Lincoln	1963	$30
❏ 1745	Side Car Cycle/Steel Rock	1960	$30

SOUVENIR
| ❏ 101 | Hot Rod Lincoln//(B-side unknown) | 1955 | $70 |

RYAN, PAUL AND BARRY
MGM
❏ 13442	Don't Bring Me Your Heartaches/To Remind You of Our Love	1966	$12
❏ 13472	Have Pity on the Boy/There You Go	1966	$12
❏ 13609	Have You Ever Loved Somebody/I'll Tell You Later	1966	$12
❏ 13911	Madrigal/Pictures of Today	1968	$8
❏ 13546	Silent Street/'Twas on a Night Like This	1966	$10

RYDELL, BOBBY
CAMEO
❏ 164	All I Want Is You/For You, For You	1959	$30
❏ 320	A World Without Love/Our Faded Love	1964	$20
❏ 320 [PS]	A World Without Love/Our Faded Love	1964	$30
❏ 242	Butterfly Baby/Love Is Blind	1963	$20
❏ 242 [PS]	Butterfly Baby/Love Is Blind	1963	$30
❏ 361	Ciao, Ciao Bambino/Voce de la Notte	1965	$20
❏ 1070	Forget Him/A Message from Bobby	1963	$30

—Bonus single with Cameo LP C-1070, "Top Hits of 1963"

❏ 280	Forget Him/Love, Love Go Away	1963	$15
❏ 280 [PS]	Forget Him/Love, Love Go Away	1963	$30
❏ 186	Good Time Baby/Cherie	1961	$20
❏ 186 [PS]	Good Time Baby/Cherie	1961	$30
❏ 217	I'll Never Dance Again/Gee It's Wonderful	1962	$15
❏ 217 [PS]	I'll Never Dance Again/Gee It's Wonderful	1962	$30
❏ 209	I've Got Bonnie/Lose Her	1962	$15
❏ 209 [PS]	I've Got Bonnie/Lose Her	1962	$30
❏ 201	I Wanna Thank You/The Door to Paradise	1961	$20
❏ 201 [PS]	I Wanna Thank You/The Door to Paradise	1961	$30
❏ 272	Let's Make Love Tonight/Childhood Sweetheart	1963	$15
❏ 272 [PS]	Let's Make Love Tonight/Childhood Sweetheart	1963	$30
❏ 265	Little Queenie/The Woodpecker Song	1963	$20
❏ 265 [PS]	Little Queenie/The Woodpecker Song	1963	$30
❏ 309	Make Me Forget/Little Girl, You've Had a Busy Day	1964	$15
❏ 309 [PS]	Make Me Forget/Little Girl, You've Had a Busy Day	1964	$30
❏ 160	Please Don't Be Mad/Makin' Time	1959	$60
❏ 0(no cat #) [DJ]	Steel Pier	1963	$30

—One-sided "Steel Pier Promotion"

❏ 182	Sway/Groovy Tonight	1961	$20
❏ 182 [PS]	Sway/Groovy Tonight	1961	$30
❏ 175	Swingin' School/Ding-a-Ling	1960	$20
❏ 175 [PS]	Swingin' School/Ding-a-Ling	1960	$30
❏ 190	That Old Black Magic/Don't Be Afraid (To Fall in Love)	1961	$20
❏ 190 [PS]	That Old Black Magic/Don't Be Afraid (To Fall in Love)	1961	$30
❏ 228	The Cha-Cha-Cha/The Best Man Cried	1962	$20
❏ 228 [PS]	The Cha-Cha-Cha/The Best Man Cried	1962	$30
❏ 192	The Fish/The Third House	1961	$20
❏ 192 [PS]	The Fish/The Third House	1961	$30
❏ 169	We Got Love/I Dig Girls	1959	$20
❏ 169 [PS]	We Got Love/I Dig Girls	1959	$30
❏ 171	Wild One/Little Bitty Girl	1960	$20
❏ 171 [PS]	Wild One/Little Bitty Girl	1960	$30
❏ 252	Wildwood Days/Will You Be My Baby	1963	$15
❏ 252 [PS]	Wildwood Days/Will You Be My Baby	1963	$30

CAPITOL
❏ 5352	Diana/Stranger in the World	1965	$12
❏ 5305	I Just Can't Say Goodbye/Two Is the Loneliest Number	1964	$10
❏ 5305 [PS]	I Just Can't Say Goodbye/Two Is the Loneliest Number	1964	$20
❏ 5780	Open for Business As Usual/You Gotta Enjoy Joy	1966	$10
❏ 5696	She Was the Girl/Not You	1966	$10
❏ 5513	When I See That Girl of Mine/It Takes Two	1965	$10

PERCEPTION
| ❏ 519 | California Sunshine/Honey Buns | 1973 | $5 |
| ❏ 552 | Everything Seemed Better (When I Was Younger)/Sunday Son | 1974 | $5 |

P.I.P.
| ❏ 6531 | It's Getting Better/The Singles Scene | 1976 | $4 |
| ❏ 6515 | Sway/Feels Good | 1976 | $5 |

RCA VICTOR
| ❏ 47-9892 | Chapel on the Hill/It Must Be Love | 1970 | $6 |

REPRISE
| ❏ 0751 | Every Little Bit Hurts/Time and Changes | 1968 | $8 |
| ❏ 0656 | The Lovin' Things/That's What I Call Lovin' | 1968 | $8 |

VEKO
| ❏ 730/1 | Dream Age/Fatty Fatty | 1958 | $120 |

VENISE
| ❏ 201 | Fatty, Fatty/Happy Happy | 1961 | $40 |

7-Inch Extended Plays
CAPITOL
| ❏ SXA-2281 [PS] | Somebody Loves You | 1965 | $12 |

RYDELL, BOBBY/CHUBBY CHECKER
Also see each artist's individual listings.

CAMEO
| ❏ 12E [DJ] | Chubby Sings Bobby-Bobby Sings Chubby | 1962 | $50 |

—B-side blank, promo only

❏ 214	Teach Me to Twist/Swingin' Together	1962	$20
❏ 214 [PS]	Teach Me to Twist/Swingin' Together	1962	$30
❏ 13E [DJ]	What Are You Doing New Year's Eve?	1962	$50

—B-side blank, promo only

RYDER, MITCH, AND THE DETROIT WHEELS
NEW VOICE
❏ 811	Break Out/I Need Help	1966	$10
❏ 817	Devil with a Blue Dress On & Good Golly Miss Molly/I Had It Made	1966	$15
❏ 801	I Need Help/I Hope	1965	$10
❏ 808	Little Latin Lupe Lu/I Hope	1966	$12
❏ 820	Sock It To Me -- Baby!/I Never Had It Better	1967	$30

—Version 1: With lyric "Feels like a punch," mumbled to the point that it sounds obscene. The copy of this we've seen has a multicolor, concentric circle label, but we can't yet say that ALL copies with this label are this version.

| ❏ 820 | Sock It To Me -- Baby!/I Never Had It Better | 1967 | $12 |

—Version 2: With lyric "Hits me like a PUNCH!" with no doubt about the last word. The copies of this we've seen have a blue label, both "painted on" and not "painted on," but we can't say yet that ALL copies with that label have this version.

| ❏ 820 [PS] | Sock It To Me -- Baby!/I Never Had It Better | 1967 | $30 |

—Black strip at the top with white and red print

| ❏ 820 [PS] | Sock It To Me -- Baby!/I Never Had It Better | 1967 | $40 |

—White strip at the top with black print

❏ 814	Takin' All I Can Get/You Get Your Kicks	1966	$10
❏ 822	Too Many Fish in the Sea & Three Little Fishes/One Grain of Sand	1967	$10
❏ 822 [PS]	Too Many Fish in the Sea & Three Little Fishes/One Grain of Sand	1967	$30

RYDER, MITCH
DOT
| ❏ 17290 | I Believe (There Must Be Someone)/Sugar Bee (We Three) | 1970 | $6 |
| ❏ 17325 | It's Been a Long, Long, Long Time/Direct Me | 1970 | $6 |

DYNOVOICE
❏ 934	Baby I Need Your Loving/Ring Your Bell	1969	$8
❏ 916	Lights of the Night/I Need Loving You	1968	$8
❏ 905	Personality-Chantilly Lace/I Make a Fool of Myself	1968	$8
❏ 901	What Now My Love/Blessing in Disguise	1967	$8

NEW VOICE
| ❏ 828 | Come See About Me/A Face in the Crowd | 1968 | $8 |

RIVA
| ❏ 213 | When You Were Mine/Stand | 1983 | $5 |

Number	Title	Yr	NM

S

SA-SHAYS, THE
ALFI
Number	Title	Yr	NM
❏ 1	Boo Hoo Hoo/You Got Love	1961	$30

ZEN
| ❏ 110 | Boo Hoo Hoo/You Got Love | 1961 | $15 |

SABERS, THE
CAL-WEST
| ❏ 847 | Cool, Cool Christmas/ Always and Forever | 1955 | $400 |

SABRE, JOHNNY, AND THE PASSIONS
ADONIS
| ❏ 103 | Wish It Could Be Me/ Dolly in a Toy Shop | 1959 | $200 |

SABU, PAUL
OCEAN/ARIOLA AMERICA
| ❏ 7510 | Loose Lucy Is on the Loose/ You're Mine Forever | 1979 | $20 |

— As "Sabu

SAD SACKS, THE
IMPERIAL
| ❏ 5517 | Sack Dresses/ Guard Your Heart | 1958 | $20 |

SADE
EPIC
❏ 68595	Love Is Stronger Than Pride/Make Some Room	1989	$3
❏ 07904	Paradise/Super Bien Total	1988	$3
❏ 07904 [PS]	Paradise/Super Bien Total	1988	$3
❏ 08465	Smooth Operator/Hang On to Your Love	1988	$3

— Reissue

| ❏ 08467 | The Sweetest Taboo/Never As Good As the First Time | 1988 | $3 |

— Reissue

| ❏ 08503 | Turn My Back on You/ Keep Looking | 1988 | $3 |

PORTRAIT
| ❏ 04664 [PS] | Hang On to Your Love | 1984 | $5 |

— Demonstration -- Not for Sale" on rear

❏ 04664	Hang On to Your Love/Cherry Pie	1984	$3
❏ 04664 [PS]	Hang On to Your Love/Cherry Pie	1984	$3
❏ 06121	Is It a Crime/Punch Drunk	1986	$3
❏ 06121 [PS]	Is It a Crime/Punch Drunk	1986	$3
❏ 04807 [PS]	Smooth Operator	1985	$5

— Demonstration -- Not for Sale" on rear

❏ 04807	Smooth Operator/Spirit	1985	$3
❏ 04807 [PS]	Smooth Operator/Spirit	1985	$3
❏ 05713	The Sweetest Taboo/ You're Not the Man	1985	$3
❏ 05713 [PS]	The Sweetest Taboo/ You're Not the Man	1985	$3

SADLER, SSGT. BARRY
RCA VICTOR
❏ 47-9008	I Won't Be Home This Christmas/A Woman Is a Weepin' Willow Tree	1966	$8
❏ 47-8804	The "A" Team/An Empty Glass	1966	$6
❏ 47-8804 [PS]	The "A" Team/An Empty Glass	1966	$8
❏ 47-8739	The Ballad of the Green Berets/Letter from Vietnam	1966	$6
❏ 47-8739 [PS]	The Ballad of the Green Berets/Letter from Vietnam	1966	$8

7-Inch Extended Plays
| ❏ VLP3547 [PS] | Ballads of the Green Berets | 1966 | $12 |
| ❏ VLP3547 | The Ballad of the Green Berets/I'm a Lucky One/ Letter from Vietnam//I'm Watching the Raindrops Fall/Saigon/Garet Trooper | 1966 | $10 |

— Jukebox issue; small hole, plays at 33 1/3 rpm

SAFARIS, THE
DEE JAY
| ❏ 203 | My Image of a Girl (Is You)/C'mon Everybody | 1989 | $4 |

— Red vinyl

| ❏ 203 [PS] | My Image of a Girl (Is You)/C'mon Everybody | 1989 | $4 |

ELDO
| ❏ 113 | Garden of Love/ Soldier of Fortune | 1961 | $40 |
| ❏ 101 | Image of a Girl/Four Steps to Love | 1960 | $30 |

Number	Title	Yr	NM
❏ 110	In the Still of the Night/Shadows	1960	$40
❏ 105	The Girl with the Story in Her Eyes/Summer Nights	1960	$30

SAGA
ATLANTIC
| ❏ 89195 | Only Time Will Tell/The Way of the World | 1987 | $3 |

PORTRAIT
| ❏ RNR-03532 | On the Loose/(B-side blank) | 1983 | $6 |

— One-sided budget release

❏ 03359	On the Loose/Framed	1982	$4
❏ 04361	Scratching the Surface/ The Sound of Strangers	1984	$3
❏ 04178	The Flyer/The Sounds of Strangers	1983	$4
❏ 04178 [PS]	The Flyer/The Sounds of Strangers	1983	$4
❏ 05463	What Do I Know/ Easy Way Out	1985	$3
❏ 03791	Wind Him Up/Amnesia	1983	$4

SAGES, THE
RCA VICTOR
| ❏ 47-8760 | In the Beginning/I'm Not Going to Cry | 1965 | $30 |

SAGITTARIUS
COLUMBIA
❏ 44398	Another Time/Pisces	1967	$10
❏ 44289	Hotel Indiscreeet/Virgo	1967	$10
❏ 44163	My World Fell Down/Libra	1967	$10
❏ 44503	The Truth Is Not Real/You Know I've Found a Way	1968	$10

TOGETHER
| ❏ 122 | I Can Still See Your Face/I Guess the Lord Must Be in New York City | 1969 | $10 |
| ❏ 105 | In My Room/Navajo Girl | 1969 | $10 |

SAHL, MORT
REPRISE
| ❏ 20038 | About Women (Part 1)/ About Women (Part 2) | 1961 | $10 |

SAHM, DOUG
Also see SIR DOUGLAS QUINTET.
ABC DOT
| ❏ 17656 | Cowboy Peyton Place/I Love the Way You Love (The Way I Love You) | 1976 | $6 |
| ❏ 17674 | Crying Inside Sometimes/ I'm Missing You | 1976 | $6 |

ATLANTIC
| ❏ 2946 | Is Anybody Going to San Antone/Don't Turn Around | 1973 | $8 |

CRAZY CAJUN
| ❏ 2004 | If You Really Want/ Not Tomato Man | 1974 | $5 |

HARLEM
| ❏ 108 | Baby Tell Me/Sapphire | 1960 | $60 |
| ❏ 108 [DJ] | Baby Tell Me/Sapphire | 1960 | $125 |

— Gold vinyl promo

| ❏ 113 | More and More/Slow Down | 1960 | $60 |

MERCURY
| ❏ 73098 | Be Real/I Don't Want to Go Home | 1970 | $30 |

— As "Wayne Douglas

PERSONALITY
| ❏ 260 | Baby, What's On Your Mind/ Crazy, Crazy Feeling | 1962 | $60 |

RENNER
| ❏ 215 | Baby, What's On Your Mind/ Crazy, Crazy Feeling | 1961 | $50 |
| ❏ 215 [DJ] | Baby, What's On Your Mind/ Crazy, Crazy Feeling | 1961 | $125 |

— Red vinyl promo

| ❏ 212 | Big Hat/Makes No Difference | 1961 | $50 |
| ❏ 212 [DJ] | Big Hat/Makes No Difference | 1961 | $125 |

— Red vinyl promo

❏ 232	Little Angel/Cry	1963	$50
❏ 240	Lucky Me/A Year Ago Tonight	1963	$50
❏ 247	Mr. Kool/Bill Beatty	1964	$60
❏ 226	Two Hearts in Love/ Just Because	1962	$50

SATIN
| ❏ 100 | Crazy Daisy/I Can't Believe You Wanna Leave | 1959 | $60 |

SOFT
| ❏ 1031 | Cry/Down the Pike | 1965 | $40 |

SWINGIN'
| ❏ 625 | Why, Why, Why/If You Ever Need Me | 1960 | $30 |

Number	Title	Yr	NM
TEARDROP			
❏ 3481	I'm Not a Fool Anymore/ Don't Fight It	1982	$4

— With Augie Myers

| ❏ 3479 | Who Were You Thinking Of/Velma | 1982 | $4 |

— With Augie Myers

TEAR DROP
| ❏ 3074 | It's a Man Down There/4 A.M. | 1966 | $30 |

— As "Him

WARNER BROS.
| ❏ 7819 | Girls Today/Groover's Paradise | 1974 | $5 |

WARRIOR
| ❏ 507 | Crazy Daisy/If I Ever Need You | 1958 | $100 |

SAINT, CATHY
DAISY
| ❏ 501 | Big Bad World/ Mr. Heartbreak | 1963 | $60 |

ST. CLOUD, ENDLE
INTERNATIONAL ARTISTS
| ❏ 139 | She Wears It Like a Badge/Laughter | 1970 | $30 |
| ❏ 129 | Tell Me One More Time/ (B-side unknown) | 1969 | $30 |

ST. JAMES, HOLLY
ABC
| ❏ 10996 | That's Not Love/Two Good Reasons | 1967 | $70 |
| ❏ 11042 | Waiting for My Friend/ Magic Moments | 1968 | $30 |

ST. JOHN, DICK
DOT
| ❏ 17080 | Childhood/Lady of the Burning Green-Jade | 1968 | $8 |

— Of Dick and Deedee

| ❏ 17140 | Leaving on a Jet Plane/ Brand New Season | 1968 | $8 |

LIBERTY
| ❏ 55380 | Gonna Stick By You/Sha-Ta | 1961 | $15 |

PHILIPS
| ❏ 40256 | Love's a Funny Little Game/Believe Me Baby | 1965 | $10 |
| ❏ 40325 | Swanee River/You Know What I Mean | 1965 | $10 |

POM POM
| ❏ 4156 | Gonna Stick By You/Sha-Ta | 1961 | $30 |

ROMA
| ❏ 1001 | Hey, Little Gal/Boogie Man (I Ain't Afraid of You) | 1961 | $20 |

ST. JOHN, TAMMY
CONGRESS
| ❏ 258 | Dark Shadows and Empty Hallways/I Mustn't Cry | 1965 | $12 |
| ❏ 236 | He's the One for Me/I'm Tired Just Lookin' at You | 1965 | $12 |

ST. JOHN, TOMMY
RCA
| ❏ JK-13561 [DJ] | Stars on the Water (same on both sides) | 1983 | $10 |

— Promo only on blue vinyl

| ❏ PB-13561 | Stars on the Water/ Wallflower | 1983 | $4 |
| ❏ JB-13405 [DJ] | The Light of My Life (Has Gone Out Tonight)/Waitin' In Your Welfare Line | 1982 | $10 |

— Promo only on red vinyl

| ❏ PB-13405 | The Light of My Life (Has Gone Out Tonight)/Waitin' In Your Welfare Line | 1982 | $4 |
| ❏ PB-13475 | Where'd Ya Stay Last Night/She Can't Make Me What I Ain't | 1983 | $4 |

ST. LOUIS JIMMY
DUKE
| ❏ 110 | Drinkin' Woman/Why Work | 1953 | $120 |

HERALD
| ❏ 407 | Hard Luck Boogie/ Good Book Blues | 1953 | $200 |

PARROT
| ❏ 823 | Going Down Slow/Murder in the First Degree | 1955 | $200 |

Number	Title	Yr	NM

ST. LOUIS UNION
PARROT
❑ 9812	Girl/Respect	1966	$8

ST. MARIE, SUSAN
CINNAMON
❑ 768	All or Nothing with Me/Lonely After You	1973	$8
❑ 784	Something's Wrong/Fever	1974	$8

PINNACLE
❑ 101	It's the Love in You/That's the Way Love Should Be	1977	$6

ST. PATRICK'S CATHEDRAL CHOIR
ROULETTE
❑ 4204	Carol of the Bells/Carol of the Drum	1959	$15

ST. PETERS, CRISPIAN
JAMIE
❑ 1334	Almost Persuaded/You Are Gone	1967	$10
❑ 1309	At This Moment/No No No	1966	$12
❑ 1302	At This Moment/You'll Forget Me, Goodbye	1965	$20
❑ 1324	Changes/My Little Brown Eyes	1966	$10
❑ 1344	Free Spirit/I'm Always Crying	1967	$10
❑ 1359	Please Take Me Back/Look Into My Teardrops	1968	$8
❑ 1320	The Pied Piper/Sweet Dawn My True Love	1966	$15

ST. ROMAIN, KIRBY
IMCO
❑ 2103	Baby Doll/Summertime Fun	1964	$12

INETTE
❑ 104	Butterflies/Walk On Mr. Blue	1963	$15
❑ 106	Love Is Magic/I Don't Wanna Fall in Love	1964	$15
❑ 103	Summer's Comin'/Miss You So	1963	$15

TEARDROP
❑ 3036	Oh Baby Doll/Summertime Fun	1964	$10

ST. SHAW, MIKE
REPRISE
❑ 0325	From the Bottom of My Heart/Send Me Some Lovin'	1964	$15
❑ 0282	Mike's Mid-Nite Special/Summer Skies and Golden Sands	1964	$10
❑ 0273	Take This Hammer/What's That I Hear	1964	$10

SAINT STEVEN
PROBE
❑ 463	Louisiana Home/Aye Aye Poe Day	1969	$30

SAINTE-MARIE, BUFFY
ABC
❑ 12203	Look at the Facts/(B-side unknown)	1976	$5
❑ 12183	Starwalker/Free the Lady	1976	$5

MCA
❑ 40193	Can't Believe the Feeling When You're Gone/Waves	1974	$5
❑ 40286	I Can't Take It No More/Native North American Child: An Odyssey	1974	$5
❑ 40368	Love's Got to Breathe and Fly/Nobody Will Ever Know It's Real But You	1975	$5
❑ 40347	Sweet, Fast Hooker Blues/Generation	1975	$5
❑ 40216	Sweet Little Vera/Waves	1974	$5

VANGUARD
❑ 35072	Better to Find Out for Yourself/Sometimes When I Get to Thinkin'	1968	$8
❑ 35053	Circle Game/Until It's Time for You to Go	1967	$8
❑ 35075	From the Bottom of My Heart/I'm Gonna Be a Country Girl Again	1969	$8
❑ 35135	Helpless/Now You've Been Gone a Long Time	1971	$6
❑ 35091	He's a Keeper of the Fire/Better to Find Out for Yourself	1970	$6
❑ 35156	He's an Indian Cowboy in the Rodeo/Not the Lovin' Kind	1972	$5
❑ 35143	I'm Gonna Be a Country Girl Again/Piney Wood Hills	1971	$5
❑ 35172	I Wanna Hold Your Hand Forever/Jeremiah	1972	$5
❑ 35151	Mister Can't You See/Moonshot	1972	$5
❑ 35127	She Used to Wanna Be a Ballerina/Moratorium	1971	$6
❑ 35180	Soldier Blue/(B-side unknown)	1973	$5
❑ 35116	Soldier Blue/Until It's Time for You to Go	1970	$6
❑ 35064	Soulful Shade of Blue/Piney Wood Hills	1968	$8
❑ 35108	The Circle Game/Better to Find Out for Yourself	1970	$6

SAINTS, THE
SIRE
❑ 1005	(I'm) Stranded/No Time	1977	$20

—Promo copy worth 50% less

SAKAMOTO, KYU
CAPITOL
❑ 5016	China Nights (Shina No Yoru)/Benkyo No Cha Cha Cha	1963	$8
❑ 5262	Sayonara Tokyo/I Like You	1964	$8
❑ 4945	Sukiyaka/Anoko No Namaewa Nantenkana	1963	$20

—First pressing: Misspelled A-side

❑ 4945	Sukiyaka/Anoko No Namaewa Nantenkana	1963	$10

—Second pressing: A-side spelled correctly, subtittled "Music of 'Ue O Muite Aruko'

❑ 4945	Sukiyaka/Anoko No Namaewa Nantenkana	1963	$8

—Third pressing: A-side spelled correctly with no subtitle

❑ 5080	The Olympics Song/Tankobushi	1963	$8

EMI
❑ 4150	Why/Elimo	1975	$5

SALAS BROTHERS, THE
FARO
❑ 625	Donde Este Santa Claus/One Like Mine	1966	$8
❑ 614	Leaving You/Darling, Please Bring Your Love	1964	$12

SALEMS, THE
EPIC
❑ 9480	Ol' Man River/Maria	1961	$20

MERCURY
❑ 71754	My Precious Love/I'll Still Go On Loving You	1961	$20

SALES, SOUPY
ABC-PARAMOUNT
❑ 10747	I'm a Bird Watching Man/Where the Blue Folks Go	1965	$10
❑ 10681	Speedy Gonzales/Hey, Pearl	1965	$10
❑ 10646	The Mouse/Pachalafaka	1965	$15

BRUNSWICK
❑ 55472	Break Your Back/Tom Jones (Push and Pull)	1972	$10

CAPITOL
❑ 5766	Backwards Alphabet/Use Your Noggin	1966	$12
❑ 5752	Spanish Flea/That Wasn't No Girl	1966	$10
❑ 5752 [PS]	Spanish Flea/That Wasn't No Girl	1966	$40

MOTOWN
❑ 1141	Muck-Arty Park/Green Grow the Lilacs	1968	$50

REPRISE
❑ 20189	And That's a Shame/Hilly Billy Ding Dong Choo Choo	1963	$20
❑ 20064	Because of Black Tooth/Soupy's Theme	1962	$20
❑ 20041	Hippy's Cha Cha Hips/White Fang	1961	$20
❑ 20108	My Baby's Got a Crush on Frankenstein/Doggone Doggie	1962	$20
❑ 0368	Pie in the Face/Soupy Sez	1965	$20
❑ 244	Santa Claus Is Surfin' to Town/Santa Claus Is Comin' to Town	1963	$40

WIZDOM
❑ W1978	It's My Ego/It's My Ego	1978	$10

—Promo only

SALLEE, VICKIE
DOT
❑ 16710	Little Wishing Star/Oh My Love	1965	$10

REPRISE
❑ 20118	There Goes the Lucky One/Your Favorite Lie	1962	$20

SALT-N-PEPA
NEXT PLATEAU
❑ KF329	Expression (Half-step)/(Brixton Radio Remix)	1989	$6
❑ KF315	Push It (Remix) (same on both sides)	1987	$5
❑ KF319	Shake Your Thang/Spinderella's Not a Fella (But a Girl D.J.)	1988	$3
❑ KF319 [PS]	Shake Your Thang/Spinderella's Not a Fella (But a Girl D.J.)	1988	$3
❑ KF315	Tramp/Push It	1987	$10
❑ KF321	Twist and Shout/Get Up Everybody (Get Up)	1988	$3
❑ KF321 [PS]	Twist and Shout/Get Up Everybody (Get Up)	1988	$3

SALT WATER TAFFY
BUDDAH
❑ 37	Finders Keepers/He'll Pay	1968	$8
❑ 57	Sticks and Stones/Suddenly I See	1968	$8

METROMEDIA
❑ 220	Summertime Girl/Spend the Sunshine	1971	$8

UNITED ARTISTS
❑ 50691	Summertime Girl/One Hand Washes the Other	1970	$10

SALVATORE, BOBBY
IPG
❑ 1012	Stick 'Em Up Santa/Big Al	1963	$20

SAM AND DAVE
ATLANTIC
❑ 2608	Born Again/Get It	1969	$6
❑ 2540	Can't You Find Another Way (Of Doing It)/Still Is the Night	1968	$6
❑ 2839	Don't Pull Your Love/Jody Ryder Got Killed	1971	$6
❑ 2568	Everybody Got to Believe in Somebody/If I Didn't Have a Girl Like You	1968	$6
❑ 2668	Holdin' On/Ooh Ooh Ooh	1969	$6
❑ 2714	I'm Not an Indian Giver/Baby-Baby Don't Stop Now	1970	$6
❑ 2728	One Part Love, Two Parts Pain/When You Steal from Me	1970	$6
❑ 2590	Soul Sister, Brown Sugar/Come On In	1968	$6
❑ 2733	When You Steal from Me (You're Only Hurting Yourself)/You Easily Excite Me	1970	$6

CONTEMPO
❑ 7004	We Can Work It Out/Why Did You Do It	1977	$5

MARLIN
❑ 6100	I Need Love/Keep a-Walkin'	1961	$50

ROULETTE
❑ 4533	I Found Out/I Got a Thing Going On	1963	$15
❑ 4508	If She'll Still Have Me/Listening for My Name	1963	$15
❑ 4419	I Need Love/Keep a-Walkin'	1962	$15
❑ 4671	It Feels So Nice/It Was So Nice While It Lasted	1966	$8
❑ 4480	It Was So Nice While It Lasted/You Ain't No Big Thing, Baby	1963	$15
❑ 4461	She's Alright/It Feels So Nice	1962	$15

STAX
❑ 168	Goodnight Baby/A Place Nobody Can Find	1965	$20
❑ 189	Hold On! I'm A-Comin'/I Got Everything I Need	1966	$20
❑ 175	I Take What I Want/Sweet Home	1965	$15
❑ 242	I Thank You/Wrap It Up	1968	$15
❑ 198	Said I Wasn't Gonna Tell Nobody/If You Got the Loving	1966	$10
❑ 218	Soothe Me/I Can't Stand Up for Falling Down	1967	$12
❑ 231	Soul Man/May I Baby	1967	$15
❑ 210	When Something Is Wrong with My Baby/Small Portion of Your Love	1967	$10

UNITED ARTISTS
❑ XW438	A Little Bit of Good (Cures a Whole Lot of Bad)/Blinded by Love	1974	$6

SAM I AM
OBLONG
❑ 12-25	Santa Claus Is Dead/(Take That) Fascist Groove Thang	1989	$8

SAM THE SHAM AND THE PHARAOHS

ATLANTIC

Number	Title	Yr	NM
❏ 2767	Me and Bobby McGee/ Key to the Highway	1970	$5

— As "Sam Samudio

DINGO

Number	Title	Yr	NM
❏ 001	Haunted House/How Does a Cheating Woman Feel	1964	$200

FRETONE

Number	Title	Yr	NM
❏ 049	Ain't No Lie/Baby You Got It	1977	$10

— As "Sam the Sham

Number	Title	Yr	NM
❏ 048	Wookie (Part 1)/ Wookie (Part 2)	1977	$10

— As "Sam the Sham

MGM

Number	Title	Yr	NM
❏ 13803	Banned in Boston/ Money's My Problem	1967	$12

— As "The Sam the Sham Revue

Number	Title	Yr	NM
❏ 13747	Black Sheep/My Day's Gonna Come	1967	$10
❏ 14642	Fate/Oh Lo	1973	$10
❏ 13649	How Do You Catch a Girl/ Love You Left Behind	1966	$15
❏ 13649 [PS]	How Do You Catch a Girl/ Love You Left Behind	1966	$30
❏ 13972	I Couldn't Spell !!@!/ Down Home Strut	1968	$20
❏ 13506	Lil' Red Riding Hood/ Love Me Like Before	1966	$20
❏ 13713	Oh That's Good, No That's Bad/Take What You Can Get	1967	$10
❏ 13920	Old Mac Donald Has a Boogaloo Farm/I Never Was No One	1968	$10
❏ 13581	The Hair on My Chinny Chin Chin/(I'm In with the) Out Crowd	1966	$15
❏ 13581 [PS]	The Hair on My Chinny Chin Chin/(I'm In with the) Out Crowd	1966	$30
❏ 14021	Wolly Bully/Ain't Gonna Move	1968	$10
❏ 13322	Wooly Bully/Ain't Gonna Move	1965	$20

TUPELO

Number	Title	Yr	NM
❏ 2982	Betty and Dupree/Manchild	1963	$70

XL

Number	Title	Yr	NM
❏ 905	The Signifyin' Monkey/ Juimonos	1964	$60
❏ 906	Wooly Bully/Ain't Gonna Move	1965	$300

SAMMY AND THE DEL-LARKS

EA-JAY

Number	Title	Yr	NM
❏ 100	Baby Come On/I Never Will Forget	1961	$200

SAMMY AND THEODORE

HIT

Number	Title	Yr	NM
❏ 246	Homeward Bound/Woman	1966	$8

— B-side by Bobby and Buddy

Number	Title	Yr	NM
❏ 259	I Am a Rock/Did You Ever Have to Make Up Your Mind	1966	$8

— B-side by the Jalopy Five

Number	Title	Yr	NM
❏ 323	Scarborough Fair (/ Canticle)/(Theme from) Valley of the Dolls	1968	$8

— B-side by Kathy Shannon

Number	Title	Yr	NM
❏ 235	Sounds of Silence/ Flowers on the Wall	1966	$8

— B-side by the Sheridan Brothers

SAMPLES, JUNIOR

CHART

Number	Title	Yr	NM
❏ 1009	Bird Mule/The Disorderly House	1967	$8
❏ 5008	Birds, Bees, Girls and Stuff Like That/(B-side unknown)	1969	$8
❏ 5102	Dippin', Chewin' Acid and Pot/Sports Common Taters	1970	$8
❏ 5026	That's a Hee Haw/ The Rabbit Song	1969	$12
❏ 1460	World's Biggest Whopper/ It Happened to Junior	1967	$10
❏ 1002	World's Biggest Whopper/ It Happened to Junior	1967	$8

— Reissue of 1460

SAMPLES, WILLIE

DOLLIE

Number	Title	Yr	NM
❏ 504	I Sure Was Happy Gettin' Sad/I'm Leaving My Heartaches to You	1966	$10
❏ 507	Lock the Door Between Us/The Other You	1966	$10

LITTLE DARLIN'

Number	Title	Yr	NM
❏ 059	I'll Take You Home Kathleen/Your Little Boy	1969	$10

SAMPSON, JANA, AND RANDALL PARR

ROCK-IT

Number	Title	Yr	NM
❏ 501	(Merry Christmas) From Lisa Marie/(We've Got) Christmas On Our Mind	1979	$15

— Colored vinyl, round

Number	Title	Yr	NM
❏ 2001	(Merry Christmas) From Lisa Marie/(We've Got) Christmas On Our Mind	1979	$30

— Colored vinyl, Santa-shaped

Number	Title	Yr	NM
❏ 2001	(Merry Christmas) From Lisa Marie/(We've Got) Christmas On Our Mind	1979	$30

— Colored vinyl, bell-shaped

Number	Title	Yr	NM
❏ 501	(Merry Christmas) From Lisa Marie/(We've Got) Christmas On Our Mind	1979	$6

— Black vinyl

SAN REMO GOLDEN STRINGS

GORDY

Number	Title	Yr	NM
❏ 7060	Festival Time/Joy Road	1967	$30

RIC-TIC

Number	Title	Yr	NM
❏ 112	Festival Time/Joy Road	1966	$15
❏ 104	Hungry for Love/ All Turned On	1965	$15
❏ 108	I'm Satisfied/Blueberry Hill	1965	$15
❏ 116	International Love Theme/ Quanto Si Bella	1966	$15

SANDALS, THE

AURA

Number	Title	Yr	NM
❏ 4501	School's Out/Wild As the Sea	1964	$30

— As "The Sandells

WORLD PACIFIC

Number	Title	Yr	NM
❏ 421	All Over Again/Always	1965	$20
❏ 77867	Cloudy/House of Painted Glass	1967	$20
❏ 415	Endless Summer/6-Pak	1964	$30
❏ 405	Scrambler/Out Front	1964	$30

— As "The Sandells

Number	Title	Yr	NM
❏ 77852	Tell Us Dylan/Why Should I Cry	1966	$20
❏ 77840	Theme from Endless Summer/6-Pak	1966	$20

SANDERS, BOBBY

KAYBO

Number	Title	Yr	NM
❏ 618	It Was You/I'm On My Way	1961	$125

KENT

Number	Title	Yr	NM
❏ 382	Maybe I'm Wrong/ You've Forgotten Me	1962	$300

SANDERS, NELSON

LA BEAT

Number	Title	Yr	NM
❏ 6608	This Love Is Here to Stay/ Tired of Being Your Fool	1966	$125

SANDERS, RAY

CONCEPT

Number	Title	Yr	NM
❏ 897	Dynamite/(B-side unknown)	1957	$125

— As "Curly Sanders

Number	Title	Yr	NM
❏ 898	This Time/(B-side unknown)	1957	$70

— As "Curly Sanders

GNP CRESCENDO

Number	Title	Yr	NM
❏ 409	I Always Do the Best with What I've Got/ Come Back to Me	1968	$8
❏ 397	Soldier's Last Letter/ Two People	1967	$8

HILLSIDE

Number	Title	Yr	NM
❏ 8103	Don't You Believe Her/Walk On By	1981	$6
❏ 7901	It Was Always Our Song/ Mountain of Love	1979	$6
❏ 7904	Loose Talk/Silver Wings	1979	$6
❏ 8105	There's a Little Bit of Everything in Texas/Another Place, Another Time	1981	$6

JAMBOREE

Number	Title	Yr	NM
❏ 590	Brand New Rock and Roll/(B-side unknown)	1956	$125

— As "Curly Sanders

LIBERTY

Number	Title	Yr	NM
❏ 55267	A World So Full of Love/A Little Bitty Tear	1960	$10
❏ 55373	Don't Tell Nell/When Love Forgets to Die	1961	$12
❏ 55486	If I Can Slip Away/See One Broken Heart	1962	$10
❏ 55304	Lonelyville/I Haven't Gone Far Enough Yet	1961	$10
❏ 55406	Punish Me Tomorrow/ You're Welcome Anytime	1962	$10
❏ 55348	Walk Slow/Two Hearts Are Broken	1961	$10

REPUBLIC

Number	Title	Yr	NM
❏ 016	Here Comes That Feelin'/ (B-side unknown)	1978	$5
❏ 003	I Don't Want to Be Alone Tonight/The Power of Positive Drinkin'	1977	$5
❏ 008	She Was Alone/ (B-side unknown)	1977	$5
❏ 013	Tennessee/You Keep Right On Walking	1978	$5

STADIUM

Number	Title	Yr	NM
❏ 1115	Christmas Letter/Missing Christmas Card	1964	$10

TOWER

Number	Title	Yr	NM
❏ 330	City of Sin/I'll Try to Work You In	1967	$8
❏ 232	My World Is Upside Down/ Graveyard Dance	1966	$8
❏ 270	The Only Way to Fly/Don't Let Our Love Grow Cold	1966	$8

UNITED ARTISTS

Number	Title	Yr	NM
❏ 50827	All I Ever Need Is You/ Before I Met You	1971	$6
❏ XW201	Another Way to Say Goodbye/(B-side unknown)	1973	$6
❏ 50689	Blame It on Rosey/ Waikiki Sand	1970	$6
❏ 50933	Lucius Grinder/You Let My Love Live	1972	$6
❏ 50774	Walk All Over Georgia/ Tonight She'll Make You Happy	1971	$6

SANDFORD, CHRIS

FONTANA

Number	Title	Yr	NM
❏ 1534	(I Wish They Wouldn't Always Say) I Sound Like the Guy from USA Blues/ Little Man-Nobody Cares	1965	$15

SANDMEN, THE (1)

BLUE JAY

Number	Title	Yr	NM
❏ 5002	If You Want Me/Searching for a New Love	1965	$30

SANDMEN, THE (2)

OKEH

Number	Title	Yr	NM
❏ 7052	When I Grow Too Old to Dream/Somebody to Love	1955	$60

SANDPEBBLES, THE

CALLA

Number	Title	Yr	NM
❏ 134	Forget It/Psychedelic Technicolor Dream	1967	$10
❏ 148	If You Didn't Hear Me the First Time (I'll Say It Again)/Flower Power	1968	$30
❏ 153	Let It Be Me/Soul Keeps Rolling Along	1968	$30
❏ 141	Love Power/ Because of Love	1967	$20

SANDPIPERS, THE

A&M

Number	Title	Yr	NM
❏ 1314	A Gift of Song/ Never My Love	1971	$5
❏ 1208	Beyond the Valley of the Dolls/Santo Domingo	1970	$5
❏ 1280	Chotta Matte Kudasel/ Free to Carry On	1971	$5
❏ 1134	Come Saturday Morning/ Pretty Flamingo	1969	$6
❏ 1185	Come Saturday Morning/ To Put Up with You	1970	$5
❏ 1249	Drifter/Sound of Love	1971	$5
❏ 1227	Free to Carry On/The Whole World in His Hands	1970	$5
❏ 806	Guantanamera/What Makes You Dream, Pretty Girl	1966	$6
❏ 851	It's Over/Glass	1967	$6
❏ 835	La Bamba/For Baby	1967	$6
❏ 819	Louie Louie/Things We Said Today	1966	$8
❏ 1372	Old Fashioned Love Song/ Never Can Say Goodbye	1972	$5
❏ 880	Softly, As I Leave You/ Cuando Sali De Cuba	1967	$6
❏ 968	Softly/Cancion de Amor	1968	$6
❏ 997	Suzanne/Let Go!	1968	$6
❏ 1085	Temptations/Wave	1969	$6
❏ 1044	The Wonder of You/ That Night	1969	$6
❏ 1388	The World Is a Circle/ (Baby I Could Be) So Good at Lovin' You	1972	$5
❏ 861	Woman/Bon Soir Dame	1967	$6
❏ 939	Wooden Heart/Quando M'annamoro	1968	$6

SANDS, EVIE

A&M

Number	Title	Yr	NM
❏ 1090	Any Way That You Want Me/I'll Never Be Alone Again	1969	$10
❏ 1175	But You Know I Love You/Maybe Tomorrow	1970	$10

Number	Title	Yr	NM
❏ 1157	Crazy Annie/Maybe Tomorrow	1969	$12
❏ 1026	One Fine Summer Morning/I'll Hold Out My Hand	1969	$10
❏ 980	Shadow of the Evening/Until It's Time for You to Go	1968	$15
❏ 1192	Take Me for a Little While/It's This I Am, I Find	1970	$15

BLUE CAT

Number	Title	Yr	NM
❏ 118	Take Me for a Little While/Run Home to Your Mama	1965	$40

CAMEO

Number	Title	Yr	NM
❏ 475	Angel of the Morning/Dear John	1967	$30
❏ 2002	Billy Sunshine/It Makes Me Laugh	1968	$40
❏ 413	Picture Me Gone/It Makes Me Laugh	1966	$70
❏ 436	The Love of a Boy/We Know Better	1966	$20

GOLD

Number	Title	Yr	NM
❏ 215	Danny Boy, I Love You So/I Was Moved	1964	$20

HAVEN

Number	Title	Yr	NM
❏ 7013	I Love Makin' Love to You/One Thing on My Mind	1975	$6
❏ 806	The Way You Do the Things You Do/Love in the Afternoon	1976	$10

SANDS, JODIE

ABC-PARAMOUNT

Number	Title	Yr	NM
❏ 10376	Hello, Heartache/This Little Fool	1962	$15
❏ 10451	Time to Love/Charming Little Barefoot	1963	$15
❏ 10337	We Had Words/Uno Momento	1962	$15

BERNLO

Number	Title	Yr	NM
❏ 1003	Love Me Always/Everybody Needs Somebody	1957	$30

CHANCELLOR

Number	Title	Yr	NM
❏ 1005	If You're Not Completely Satisfied/Sayonara	1957	$30
❏ 1015	Love Me Again/All I Ask of You	1958	$30
❏ 1023	Someday/Someday in My Heart	1958	$30
❏ 1009	The Way I Love You/Tantalizin' Love	1957	$30
❏ 1003	With All My Heart/More Than Only Friends	1957	$30

PARIS

Number	Title	Yr	NM
❏ 543	I'd Cry No Tears/Kiss By Kiss	1960	$20
❏ 551	Love Me Forever/Give Me a Break	1960	$20

SIGNATURE

Number	Title	Yr	NM
❏ 12015	Turnabout Heart/Solo A Te Mio Amor	1959	$20

TEEN

Number	Title	Yr	NM
❏ 109	Love Me Always/Everybody Needs Somebody	1955	$50

THOR

Number	Title	Yr	NM
❏ 101	Hold Me/What Does It Mean	1959	$30

SANDS, TOMMY

ABC-PARAMOUNT

Number	Title	Yr	NM
❏ 10480	Cinderella/Only 'Cause I'm Lonely	1963	$10
❏ 10466	Connie/Young Man's Fancy	1963	$10
❏ 10591	Something More/Kisses (Love Theme)	1964	$12
❏ 10539	Won't You Be My Girl/Ten Dollars and a Clean White Shirt	1964	$10

CAPITOL

Number	Title	Yr	NM
❏ F3810	A Swingin' Romance/Man, Like Wow!	1957	$30
❏ F3985	Big Date/After the Senior Prom	1958	$30
❏ F3985 [PS]	Big Date/After the Senior Prom	1958	$40
❏ F4082	Bigger Than Texas/The Worryin' Kind	1958	$30
❏ F4036	Blue Ribbon Baby/I Love You Because	1958	$30
❏ 4470	Doctor Heartache/On and On	1960	$20
❏ F3723	Goin' Steady/Ring My Phone	1957	$30
❏ F4259	I'll Be Seeing You/That's the Way I Am	1959	$20
❏ F4259 [PS]	I'll Be Seeing You/That's the Way I Am	1959	$40
❏ F4160	Is It Ever Gonna Happen/I Ain't Gittin' Rid of You	1959	$20
❏ F3743	Let Me Be Loved/Fantastically Foolish	1957	$30
❏ 4580	Love in a Goldfish Bowl/I Love My Baby	1961	$15
❏ F3867	Sing, Boy, Sing/Crazy 'Cause I Love You	1957	$30
❏ F4231	Sinner Man/Bring Me Your Love	1959	$20

Number	Title	Yr	NM
❏ F3639	Teen-Age Crush/Hep Dee Hootie	1957	$30
❏ F3953	Teenage Doll/Hawaiian Rock	1958	$30
❏ 4366	That's Love/Crossroads	1960	$20
❏ 4405	The Old Oaken Bucket/These Are the Things You Are	1960	$20
❏ 4660	Wrong Side of Love/Jimmy's Song	1961	$15

IMPERIAL

Number	Title	Yr	NM
❏ 66174	As Long As I'm Travelin'/It's the Only One I've Got	1966	$8
❏ 66229	Second Star to the Left/Candy Store Prophet	1967	$8

LIBERTY

Number	Title	Yr	NM
❏ 55807	Love's Funny/One Rose Today, One Rose Tomorrow	1965	$8
❏ 55842	The Statue/Little Rosita	1965	$8

(NO LABEL)

Number	Title	Yr	NM
❏ T929 [DJ]	People in Love/That's All I Want from You	1957	$60

—Promotion Record" with no label name; used to promote the movie "Sing Boy Sing"; T 929 is catalog number of LP and the most prominent number on label

RCA VICTOR

Number	Title	Yr	NM
❏ 47-5628	A Dime and a Dollar/Life Is So Lonesome	1954	$40
❏ 47-5800	Don't Drop It/A Place for Girls Like You	1954	$40
❏ 47-6868	Don't Drop It/Love Pains	1957	$30
❏ 47-5435	Love Pains/Transfer	1953	$40

SUPERSCOPE

Number	Title	Yr	NM
❏ 007	Seasons in the Sun/Ain't No Big Thing	1969	$6

7-Inch Extended Plays

CAPITOL

Number	Title	Yr	NM
❏ EAP 2-929	*A Bundle of Dreams/Just a Little Bit More/Soda-Pop Pop/Would I Love You	1958	$35
❏ EAP 1-848	*Goin' Steady/Teach Me Tonight/Gonna Get a Girl Somewhere Along the Way	1957	$35
❏ EAP 1-929	*I'm Gonna Walk and Talk with My Lord/Who Baby/Rock of Ages/Sing Boy Sing	1958	$35
❏ EAP 1-851	*Teen-Age Crush/My Love Song/Hep Dee Hootie (Cutie Wootie)/Ring-a-Ding-a-Ding	1957	$35
❏ PRO351 [DJ]	Goin' Steady/I Don't Know Why (I Just Do)//Graduation Day/A-You're Adorable (The Alphabet Song)	1957	$50

—Promotional sampler from "Steady Date" album

Number	Title	Yr	NM
❏ EAP 3-929	People in Love/Crazy Cause I Love You/Your Daddy Wants to Do Right/That's All I Want from You	1958	$35
❏ EAP 1-929 [PS]	Sing Boy Sing, Part 1	1958	$35
❏ EAP 2-929 [PS]	Sing Boy Sing, Part 2	1958	$35
❏ EAP 3-929 [PS]	Sing Boy Sing, Part 3	1958	$35
❏ EAP 1-848 [PS]	Steady Date with Tommy Sands, Part 1	1957	$35
❏ EAP 2-848 [PS]	Steady Date with Tommy Sands, Part 2	1957	$35
❏ EAP 3-848 [PS]	Steady Date with Tommy Sands, Part 3	1957	$35
❏ EAP 1-851 [PS]	Teen-Age Crush	1957	$35
❏ EAP 2-848	Walkin' My Baby Back Home/Too Young to Go Steady//A-You're Adorable (The Alphabet Song)/Graduation Day	1957	$35

SANDY, FRANK

MARK

Number	Title	Yr	NM
❏ 138	Shamrock/Here She Comes	1959	$50

MGM

Number	Title	Yr	NM
❏ 12678	Let's Go Rock 'N' Roll/Midnight Stomp	1958	$125
❏ 12626	Somebody Loves Me/Tarantella Rock	1958	$60

SANETTES, THE

OHN-J

Number	Title	Yr	NM
❏ 1001	Merry Christmas/Blessings From Above	1964	$10

SANS, PEGGY

TOLLIE

Number	Title	Yr	NM
❏ 9018	Give Your Love/Snow Man	1964	$10

SANTA CLAUS

CAPITOL

Number	Title	Yr	NM
❏ F1260	Do You Believe in Santa Claus/Gabby the Gobbler	1950	$30

—B-side by Ken Carson

Number	Title	Yr	NM
❏ 2335	What Santa Wants for Christmas/Jingle Bells	1968	$8

SANTA CLAUS AND HIS HELPERS

COLUMBIA

Number	Title	Yr	NM
❏ 40577	Santa's Laughing Song/Santa, The Happy Wanderer	1955	$20
❏ 40577 [PS]	Santa's Laughing Song/Santa, The Happy Wanderer	1955	$30

SANTANA

Also see JOURNEY; CARLOS SANTANA; GREGG ROLIE.

COLUMBIA

Number	Title	Yr	NM
❏ 11218	All I Ever Wanted/Lightning in the Sky	1980	$4
❏ AE71064 [DJ]	All the Love of the Universe/Just in Time to See the Sun	1972	$10
❏ 45270	Black Magic Woman/Hope You're Feeling Better	1970	$6
❏ 45270 [PS]	Black Magic Woman/Hope You're Feeling Better	1970	$15
❏ 10677	Black Magic Woman/I'll Be Waiting	1978	$5
❏ 10353	Dance Sister Dance (Baila Mi Hermana)/Let Me	1976	$5
❏ 45472	Everybody's Everything/Guajira	1971	$5
❏ 45069	Evil Ways/Waiting	1970	$6
❏ 10088	Give and Take/Love Is Anew	1975	$5
❏ 10524	Give Me Love/Revelations	1977	$5
❏ 04034	Havana Moon/Lightnin'	1983	$4
❏ 03268	Hold On	1982	$6

—One-sided budget release

Number	Title	Yr	NM
❏ 03160	Hold On/Oxun	1982	$4
❏ 04912	I'm the One Who Loves You/Right Now	1985	$3
❏ 46067	Incident at Neshabur/Samba Pa Ti	1974	$5
❏ 10336	Let It Shine/Tell Me Are You Tired	1976	$5
❏ 10481	Let the Children Play/Carnival	1977	$5
❏ 45753	Look Up/All the Love of the Universe	1973	$5
❏ 10073	Mirage/Flor de Canela	1974	$5
❏ 10938	One Chain (Don't Make a Prison)/Life Is a Lady-Holiday	1979	$4
❏ 45330	Oye Como Va/Samba Pa Ti	1971	$5
❏ 45330 [PS]	Oye Como Va/Samba Pa Ti	1971	$8
❏ 07140	Praise/It Is You	1987	$3
❏ 04758	Say It Again/Touchdown Raiders	1985	$3
❏ 04758 [PS]	Say It Again/Touchdown Raiders	1985	$4
❏ 02519	Searchin'/Tales of Kilimanjaro	1981	$4
❏ 10616	She's Not There/Zulu	1977	$5
❏ 10873	Stormy/Move On	1978	$5
❏ 10421	Take Me with You/Europa (Earth's Cry Heaven's Smile)	1976	$5
❏ 02178	The Sensitive Kind/American Gypsy	1981	$4
❏ 02178 [PS]	The Sensitive Kind/American Gypsy	1981	$5
❏ 05677	They All Went to Mexico/Slow Movin' Outlaw	1985	$3

—A-side: Willie Nelson and Carlos Santana; B-side: Willie and Lacy J. Dalton

Number	Title	Yr	NM
❏ 10839	Well, All Right/Jericho	1978	$5
❏ 45999	When I Look Into Your Eyes/Samba De Sausalito	1974	$5
❏ 01050	Winning/The Brightest Star	1981	$4

7-Inch Extended Plays

Number	Title	Yr	NM
❏ 7-32445	Love, Devotion & Surrender/Light of Life/Yours Is the Light/Samba de Sausalito	1973	$15

—Jukebox issue; small hole, plays at 33 1/3 rpm

Number	Title	Yr	NM
❏ 7-30595	Taboo/Everything's Coming Our Way//Jungle Strut/Batuka	1971	$10

—Jukebox issue; small hole, plays at 33 1/3 rpm

Number	Title	Yr	NM
❏ 7-32445 [PS]	Welcome	1973	$15

SANTANA, CARLOS, AND BUDDY MILES

COLUMBIA

Number	Title	Yr	NM
❏ 45666	Them Changes/Evil Ways	1972	$5

SANTANA, CARLOS

COLUMBIA

Number	Title	Yr	NM
❏ 03925	Tales of Kilimanjaro/Watch Your Step	1983	$4

SANTO AND JOHNNY

CANADIAN AMERICAN

Number	Title	Yr	NM
❏ 177	A Hard Day's Night/And I Love Her	1964	$20
❏ 167	A Thousand Miles Away/Road Block	1964	$15
❏ 167 [PS]	A Thousand Miles Away/Road Block	1964	$30
❏ 189	Brazilian Summer/Off Tempo	1965	$15
❏ 111	Caravan/Summertime	1960	$20
❏ 204	Come with Me/The Young World	1967	$10
❏ 182	Goldfinger/Sleep Walk	1964	$15
❏ 182 [PS]	Goldfinger/Sleep Walk	1964	$30
❏ 124	Hop Scotch/Sea Shells	1961	$20

Number	Title	Yr	NM
❑ 164	I'll Remember (In the Still of the Night)/ Song for Rosemary	1964	$15
❑ 164 [PS]	I'll Remember (In the Still of the Night)/ Song for Rosemary	1964	$30
❑ 161	Love Letters in the Sand/Lido Beach	1963	$15
❑ 118	Love Lost/Annie	1960	$20
❑ 118 [PS]	Love Lost/Annie	1960	$60
❑ 144	Misirlou/Tokyo Twilight	1962	$15
❑ 151	On Your Mark/Manhattan	1963	$15
❑ 103	Sleep Walk/All Night Diner	1959	$30
❑ 137	Spanish Harlem/ Stage to Cimarron	1962	$15
❑ 174	Sugar Stroll/Rattler	1964	$15
❑ 107	Tear Drop/The Long Walk Home	1959	$20
❑ 115	The Breeze and I/Lazy Day	1960	$20
❑ 128	Theme from Come September/The Long Walk Home	1961	$20
❑ 131	The Mouse/Birmingham	1961	$20
❑ 155	The Wandering Sea/ Manhattan Spiritual	1963	$15
❑ 141	Three Caballeros/Step Aside	1962	$15
❑ 120	Twistin' Bells/Bullseye!	1960	$20
❑ 120 [PS]	Twistin' Bells/Bullseye!	1960	$50
❑ 132	Twistin' Bells/Christmas Day	1961	$30
— B-side by Linda Scott			
❑ 148	Twistin' Bells/Manhattan	1962	$15
❑ 194	Watermelon Man/ Return to Naples	1965	$15

IMPERIAL

❑ 66269	Live for Life/See You in September	1968	$10
❑ 66292	Sleep Walk '68/ It Must Be Him	1968	$12

PAUSA

❑ 703	Come Back Soldier/ Flamingo	1976	$5

UNITED ARTISTS

❑ 970	Thunderball/Mister Kiss Kiss Bang Bang	1966	$10

7-Inch Extended Plays

CANADIAN AMERICAN

❑ 1001	(contents unknown)	1959	$100
❑ 1001 [PS]	Santo and Johnny	1959	$100

SANTOS, LARRY
ATLANTIC

❑ 2250	Someday (When I'm Gone)/True	1964	$30
— With the Four Seasons on backup			

BIG TREE

❑ 136	Life Is Beautiful/Touchin' You	1972	$5

CASABLANCA

❑ 844	Can't Get You Off My Mind/ We Can't Hide It Anymore	1975	$6
— With "Can't Get You Off My Mind" listed as "Side A			
❑ 881	Magic Mountain/Don't Let the Music Stop	1977	$4
❑ 844	We Can't Hide It Anymore/ Can't Get You Off My Mind	1976	$4
— With "We Can't Hide It Anymore" listed as "Side A			

EVOLUTION

❑ 1018	Great Divide/Paper Chase	1970	$6
❑ 1043	I Love You More Than Everything/Let It End	1971	$6
❑ 1039	Let It End/Little Bit of You	1971	$6
❑ 1024	Mornin' Sun/Wandering Man	1970	$6
❑ 1010	Subway Man/Woman-Child	1969	$6
❑ 1007	Tomorrow Without Love/You Got Me Where You Want Me	1969	$6

SAPIANS, THE
MERCURY

❑ 72502	Ask Yourself Why Babe/ Love Ain't Makin' It No More	1965	$200

SAPPHIRES, THE (1)
ABC-PARAMOUNT

❑ 10693	Evil One/How Could I Say Goodbye	1965	$20
❑ 10639	Gee I'm Sorry, Baby/ Gotta Have Your Love	1965	$20
❑ 10559	Hearts Are Made to Be Broken/Let's Break Up for Awhile	1964	$20
❑ 10778	Our Love Is Everywhere/ Slow Fizz	1966	$20
❑ 10590	Thank You for Loving Me/ Our Love Is Everywhere	1964	$20

ITZY

❑ 8	Who Do You Love/ Oh So Soon	1963	$50

SWAN

❑ 4184	Gotta Be More Than Friends/Moulin Rouge	1964	$20

Number	Title	Yr	NM
❑ 4177	I Found Out Too Late/I've Got Mine, You Better Get Yours	1964	$20
❑ 4162	Who Do You Love/ Oh So Soon	1963	$20

SAPPHIRES, THE (2)
RCA VICTOR

❑ 47-7357	Everyone Knows/So Glad	1958	$30

SAQQARA DOGS, THE
BLACK

❑ AFTP001	Splatterdance/Merry Xmas Blues	1986	$30
— B-side by the Celibate Rifles			

SARATOGAS, THE
IMPERIAL

❑ 5738	I'll Be Loving You/ Get It in a Minute	1961	$40

SARDO, FRANKIE
20TH FOX

❑ 221	Dream Lover/ Bonnie, Bonnie	1960	$30
❑ 208	I Know Why and So Do You/ When the Bells Stop Ringing	1960	$30

ABC-PARAMOUNT

❑ 9963	Class Room/Fake Out	1958	$30

MGM

❑ 12621	May I/My Story of Love	1958	$30

NEWTOWN

❑ 5005	I Got You Where I Want You/Mr. Make Believe	1962	$30

SARDO, JOHNNY
CHOCK FULL-O-HITS

❑ 104	(Hip Hop) Take a Ride with Me/Hollywood Sign	1958	$125

WARNER BROS.

❑ 5014	I Wanna Rock/Used Heart	1958	$30
❑ 5044	Late, Late, Late to School/ New Kid in Town	1959	$30

SARDUCCI, FATHER GUIDO
WARNER BROS.

❑ 49627	I Won't Be Twisting This Christmas/Parco Mac Arthur	1980	$8
❑ 49627 [PS]	I Won't Be Twisting This Christmas/Parco Mac Arthur	1980	$10

SARNE, MIKE
ASCOT

❑ 2213	An Englishman Sings "America Swings"/ Can't Wait for Spring	1966	$10

CAMEO

❑ 220	Come On Outside/ Fountain of Love	1962	$15

STELLAR

❑ 1506	Come Outside/ Fountain of Love	1962	$15

SATAN AND THE DISCIPLES
GOLDBAND

❑ 1188	Mummies Curse/Cat's Meow	1969	$30

SATAN'S FOUR
B.T. PUPPY

❑ 515	I Can't Find the Girl on My Mind/Oh Cathy	1966	$20

SATELLITES, THE
ABC-PARAMOUNT

❑ 10038	Linda Jean/Rockateen	1959	$50

CLASS

❑ 234	Heavenly Angel/You Ain't Sayin' Nothin'	1958	$40

CUPID

❑ 0 (no cat #)	Linda Jean/Rockateen	1959	$100

D-M-G

❑ 4001	Each Night/Darktown Strutters Ball	1960	$40

MALYNN

❑ 231	Heavenly Angel/You Ain't Sayin' Nothin'	1958	$30

PALACE

❑ 102	Buzz Buzz/We Like Birdland	1960	$30

PARROT

❑ 313	Bodacious/El San Juan	1966	$30

Number	Title	Yr	NM
UNITED ARTISTS			
❑ 141	I Found a Girl/My Piggie's Gotta Dance	1958	$50

SATINTONES, THE
MOTOWN

❑ 1006	Angel/A Love That Can Never Be	1961	$1500
❑ 1010	I Know How It Feels/ My Kind of Love	1961	$200
❑ 1000	Sugar Daddy/My Beloved	1960	$400
— Without strings. Matrix number of A-side is "MNT 12345			
❑ 1000	Sugar Daddy/My Beloved	1960	$400
— With strings. Matrix number of A-side is "1000 G-3			
❑ 1006	Tomorrow and Always/A Love That Can Never Be	1961	$250
— Without strings			
❑ 1006	Tomorrow and Always/A Love That Can Never Be	1961	$250
— With strings			

TAMLA

❑ 54026	Motor City/Going to the Hop	1960	$800

SATISFACTIONS, THE (1)
LIONEL

❑ 3214	God I'm Losing My Baby/O-o-o La La	1971	$20
❑ 3205	One Light Two Lights/ Turn Back the Tears	1970	$15
❑ 3201	This Bitter Earth/ Ol' Man River	1970	$15

SATISFACTIONS, THE (2)
CHESAPEKE

❑ 610	We Will Walk Together/Oh Why	1962	$40

SATISFACTIONS, THE (3)
IMPERIAL

❑ 66170	Bring It All Down/Daddy, You Just Gotta Let Him In	1966	$30

SMASH

❑ 2059	Give Me Your Love/ Stop Following Me	1966	$20
❑ 2098	Take It or Leave It/ You Got to Share	1967	$40

SATISFACTIONS, THE (U)
1-2-3

❑ 1716	Gonna Get Right Tonight/ Living on a Prayer, a Hope and a Hand-Me-Down	1969	$15

TWIN TOWN

❑ 714	Bad Times/Don't Tell Me	1966	$30

SATISFIERS, THE
CORAL

❑ 61727	Come Away, Love/Where'll I Be Tomorrow Night	1956	$20
❑ 61788	Over the Rainbow/Solitude	1957	$20
❑ 61945	Will o' the Wisp/Remember That Crazy Rock and Roll	1958	$20

JUBILEE

❑ 5205	All or Nothing at All/ Lies, Nothing But Lies	1955	$30

VEGAS

❑ 626	Ghost of a Chance/ Fair Exchange	1960	$15

SATURDAY KNIGHTS, THE
NOCTURNE

❑ 1030	Sea Mist/Queen of the Nile	1963	$60

SWAN

❑ 4081	Hawaiian Tears/ Texas Tommy	1961	$30
❑ 4075	Ticonderoga/Tiger Lily	1961	$40
— As "The Saturday Nights			
❑ 4075	Ticonderoga/Tiger Lily	1961	$30
— As "The Saturday Knights			

SATURDAY, PATTY
SWAN

❑ 4022	Ladies Choice/Love Is a Beautiful Thing	1959	$30

SATURDAY'S CHILDREN
DUNWICH

❑ 139	Born on Saturday/You Don't Know Better	1966	$20
❑ 156	Leave That Baby Alone/I Hardly Know Her	1967	$20
❑ 144	The Christmas Song/ Deck Five	1967	$20

Number	Title	Yr	NM

SAUNDERS, LITTLE BUTCHIE
HERALD
| ❏ 491 | Great Big Heart/I Wanna Holler | 1956 | $60 |
| ❏ 485 | Lindy Lou/Rock 'N' Roll Indian Dance | 1956 | $60 |

SAUNDERS, MERL
FANTASY
❏ 620	Five More/Julia	1969	$8
❏ 600	High Heel Sneakers/ (B-side unknown)	1964	$12
❏ 678	My Problems Got Problems/ Welcome to the Basement	1972	$6
❏ 668	Save Mother Earth (Part 1)/ Save Mother Earth (Part 2)	1971	$6
GALAXY
❏ 747	I Pity the Fool/Tighten Up	1966	$8
❏ 776	Iron Horse/A Little Bit of Righteousness	1970	$8
❏ 755	Soul Grooving/Up-Up and Away	1967	$8

SAVAGE GRACE
REPRISE
❏ 1022	Friends/Yonder	1971	$6
❏ 0924	Hymn to Freedom/ Come On Down	1970	$6
❏ 0988	Ivy/Save It for Me	1971	$6
❏ 0952	Watchtower (All Alone)/ Come On Down	1970	$6

SAVAGE RESURRECTION
MERCURY
| ❏ 72778 | Thing in "E"/The Fox Is Sick | 1968 | $30 |
| ❏ 72778 [PS] | Thing in "E"/The Fox Is Sick | 1968 | $50 |

SAVALAS, TELLY
MCA

SAVITT, BUDDY
PARKWAY
| ❏ 857 | Smoke Gets in Your Eyes/ Come Blow Your Horn | 1962 | $15 |

SAVOY BROWN
Also see FOGHAT.

LONDON
| ❏ 206 | Everybody Loves a Drinkin' Man/Ride On Babe | 1974 | $5 |
| ❏ 234 | Walkin' 'n' Talkin'/ Stranger Blues | 1976 | $5 |
PARROT
❏ 40075	Coming Down Your Way/Can't Find You	1973	$6
❏ 40037	Grits Ain't Groceries/She's Got a Ring in His Nose and a Ring on Her Hand	1969	$8
❏ 40046	Hard Way to Go/The Incredible Gnome Meets Jaxman	1970	$6
❏ 40042	I'm Tired/Stay with Me Baby	1969	$8
❏ 40057	Poor Girl/Mr. Hare	1970	$6
❏ 40034	Shake 'Em On Down/ (B-side unknown)	1968	$20
❏ 40060	Sitting and Thinking/ (B-side unknown)	1971	$6
❏ 40066	Tell Mama/Rock and Roll on the Radio	1971	$6
❏ 40039	Train to Nowhere/ Made Up My Mind	1969	$8
TOWN HOUSE
| ❏ 1054 | Lay Back in the Arms of Someone/Don't Tell Me I Told You | 1981 | $4 |
| ❏ 1054 [PS] | Lay Back in the Arms of Someone/Don't Tell Me I Told You | 1981 | $4 |

SAVOY, RONNIE
EPIC
| ❏ 9619 | I Hear Violins/The Marriage | 1963 | $8 |
| ❏ 9708 | Little Rascals/Sally Blue | 1964 | $8 |
GONE
| ❏ 5079 | Ooh, What a Girl/Love Me As I Love You | 1959 | $15 |
MGM
| ❏ 12950 | And the Heavens Cried/Big Chain | 1960 | $30 |
| ❏ 13001 | Bewitched/It's Gotta Be Love | 1961 | $20 |
PHILIPS
| ❏ 40032 | A Fool, A Loser, A Clown/ Big Hand, Little Hand | 1962 | $8 |
| ❏ 40071 | Moonlight to Sunlight/21,000 Happiness Street | 1962 | $8 |
WINGATE
| ❏ 01 | Memories Linger/Loving You | 1965 | $30 |

SAWYER BROWN
CAPITOL
❏ B-5517	Betty's Bein' Bad/ Lonely Girls	1985	$3
❏ B-5517 [PS]	Betty's Bein' Bad/ Lonely Girls	1985	$4
❏ B-44483	Did It for Love/The Heartland	1989	$4
❏ B-5677	Gypsies on Parade/Not Ready to Let You Go	1987	$3
❏ B-5548	Heart Don't Fall Now/ That's a No No	1986	$3
❏ B-5548 [PS]	Heart Don't Fall Now/ That's a No No	1986	$4
❏ B-44282	It Wasn't His Child/Falling Apart at the Heart	1988	$3
❏ B-44282 [PS]	It Wasn't His Child/Falling Apart at the Heart	1988	$5
❏ B-5403	Leona/Staying Afloat	1984	$3
❏ B-44218	My Baby's Gone/ Blue Denim Soul	1988	$3
❏ B-44332	Old Pair of Shoes/What Am I Going to Tell My Heart	1989	$4
❏ B-44143	Old Photographs/ In This Town	1988	$3
❏ B-5629	Out Goin' Cattin'/The House Won't Rock	1986	$3
—A-side with "Cat" Joe Bonsall			
❏ B-5629 [PS]	Out Goin' Cattin'/The House Won't Rock	1986	$4
❏ B-44007	Savin' the Honey for the Honeymoon/Lady of the Evening	1987	$3
❏ B-5585	Shakin'/Billy Does Your Bulldog Bite	1986	$3
❏ B-44054	Somewhere in the Night/ My Baby Drives a Buick	1987	$3
❏ B-44054 [PS]	Somewhere in the Night/ My Baby Drives a Buick	1987	$4
❏ B-5446	Step That Step/Feel Like Me	1985	$3
❏ B-5446 [PS]	Step That Step/Feel Like Me	1985	$4
❏ B-44108	This Missin' You Heart of Mine/A Mighty Big Broom	1987	$3
❏ B-44108 [PS]	This Missin' You Heart of Mine/A Mighty Big Broom	1987	$4

SAWYER, RAY
CAPITOL
❏ 4592	Dancing Fool/Rhythm Guitar	1978	$4
❏ 4820	Drinking Wine Alone/I Don't Feel Like Smilin'	1980	$4
❏ 4344	(One More Year of) Daddy's Little Girl/I Need That High (But I Can't Stand the Taste)	1976	$4
❏ 4416	Walls and Doors/I Need That High (But I Can't Stand the Taste)	1977	$4
❏ 4747	What I'm Holding/I Want Johnny's Job	1979	$4
SANDY
| ❏ 1037 | I'm Gonna Leave/You Gave Me the Right | 1961 | $30 |

SAXON, EDDIE, AND THE PARAMOUNTS
EMPRESS
❏ 106 [DJ]	Blues No More	1962	$200
—Single-sided promo			
❏ 106	Blues No More/ If It's Meant to Be	1962	$200

SAXON, SKY
Later recorded with THE SEEDS. Also see RITCHIE MARSH.
CONQUEST
| ❏ 777 | They Say/Go Ahead and Cry | 1964 | $40 |

SAYER, LEO
WARNER BROS.
❏ 8738	Don't Look Away/ No Looking Back	1979	$5
❏ 8502	Easy to Love/Haunting Me	1977	$5
❏ 50060	Have You Ever Been in Love/I Don't Need Dreaming Anymore	1982	$5
❏ 7-29960	Heart (Stop Beating in Time)/The End of the Game	1982	$6
❏ 8319	How Much I Care/I Hear the Laughter	1977	$5
❏ 49657	Living in a Fantasy/ Only Foolin'	1981	$4
❏ 8043	Long Tall Glasses (I Can Dance)/In My Life	1975	$5
—Later pressings add subtitle to A-side			
❏ 8043	Long Tall Glasses/In My Life	1974	$6
—First pressings have no A-side subtitle			
❏ 8153	Moonlighting/Streets of Your Town	1975	$6
❏ 49565	More Than I Can Say/Millionaire	1980	$4
❏ 49134	Oh Girl/Englishman in the U.S.A.	1979	$5
❏ 8097	One Man Band/Telepath	1975	$5
❏ 7-29904	Paris Dies in the Morning/We've Got Ourselves in Love	1982	$5
❏ PRO579 [DJ]	The Show Must Go On/Drop Back	1974	$10
❏ 7768	The Show Must Go On/ Innocent Bystander	1974	$8
❏ 7768 [DJ]	The Show Must Go On (Long Stereo)/(Edit Mono)	1974	$6
❏ 8465	Thunder in My Heart/ Get the Girl	1977	$5
❏ 8332	When I Need You/I Think We Fell in Love Too Fast	1977	$5
❏ 49714	Where Did We Go Wrong/ She's Not Coming Back	1981	$5

SCAFFOLD, THE
BELL
❏ 821	Charity Bubbles/Goose	1969	$20
❏ 724	Do You Remember/ Carry On Krow	1968	$20
❏ 747	Lily the Pink/Buttons of Your Mind	1968	$20
❏ 701	Thank U Very Much/ Ide B the First	1968	$20
WARNER BROS.
| ❏ 8001 | Liverpool Lou/Ten Years After on Strawberry Jam | 1974 | $6 |

SCAGGS, BOZ
ATLANTIC
| ❏ 2692 | I'm Easy/I'll Be Long Gone | 1969 | $10 |
COLUMBIA
❏ 11241	Breakdown Dead Ahead/Isn't It Time	1980	$4
❏ 02424	Breakdown Dead Ahead/Look What You've Done to Me	1981	$3
—Reissue			
❏ 07981	Cool Running/You'll Never Know	1988	$3
❏ 45670	Dinah Flo/He's a Fool for You	1972	$6
❏ 10606	Hard Times/We're Waiting	1977	$5
❏ 10606 [PS]	Hard Times/We're Waiting	1977	$12
❏ 07780	Heart of Mine/You'll Never Know	1988	$3
❏ 07780 [PS]	Heart of Mine/You'll Never Know	1988	$4
❏ 45540	Here to Stay/Runnin' Blue	1972	$6
❏ 10679	Hollywood/A Clue	1978	$5
❏ 10319	It's Over/Harbor Lights	1976	$5
❏ 10491	Lido Shuffle/We're All Alone	1977	$5
❏ 11349	Look What You've Done to Me/Simone	1980	$4
❏ 10367	Lowdown/Harbor Lights	1976	$5
❏ 11406	Miss Sun/Dinah Flo	1980	$4
❏ 10027	Slow Dancer/Pain of Love	1974	$6
❏ 45353	We Were Always Sweethearts/Painted Bells	1971	$6
❏ 10440	What Can I Say/ We're All Alone	1976	$5
❏ 08068	What's Number 1/Claudia	1988	$3

SCANDAL
COLUMBIA
❏ 04750	Beat of a Heart/Tonight	1985	$4
❏ 03234	Goodbye to You/All My Life	1982	$4
❏ 04650	Hands Tied/Maybe We Went Too Far	1984	$4
❏ 03615	Love's Got a Line on You/ Another Bad Love	1983	$4
❏ 38-04424	The Warrior/Less Than Half	1984	$4
❏ 03987	Win Some, Lose Some/ Another Bad Love	1983	$4

SCARBURY, JOEY
ABC-DUNHILL
| ❏ 4209 | House of the Rising Sun/Midnight Mail | 1969 | $10 |
BELL
❏ 45113	Albuquerque/Foresee the Future	1971	$6
❏ 45146	I'm Home Again/ Foresee the Future	1971	$6
❏ 45314	Memphis Nights/ (B-side unknown)	1973	$6
BIG TREE
| ❏ 16008 | I'm Gonna Sit Right Down and Write Myself a Letter/ Pretending to Make Love | 1973 | $6 |
COLUMBIA
❏ 3-10785	Again and Again/Chances	1978	$5
❏ 3-10538	There's No One Home at My House/Long Time Love	1977	$5
❏ 3-10990	Turn the Light On/ Sunset Boulevard	1979	$5
ELEKTRA
❏ 47147	Theme from "Greatest American Hero" (Believe It or Not)/Little Bit of Us	1981	$5
—Original 45 has no "The" in the title			
❏ 47147	The Theme from "The Greatest American Hero" (Believe It or Not)/Little Bit of Us	1981	$3
—Revised A-side title, with the added word "The			

Number	Title	Yr	NM
❏ 47147 [PS]	The Theme from "The Greatest American Hero" (Believe It or Not)/Little Bit of Us	1981	$5

—*Most picture sleeves have records with the original title*

Number	Title	Yr	NM
❏ 47201	When She Dances/ Everything But Love	1981	$4

LIONEL

Number	Title	Yr	NM
❏ 3208	Mixed-Up Guy/Loved You Darlin' from the Very Start	1971	$6

PLAYBOY

Number	Title	Yr	NM
❏ 6002	California Free/ (B-side unknown)	1974	$6

RCA

Number	Title	Yr	NM
❏ PB-13913	The River's Song/ Billy's Home	1984	$4

REENA

Number	Title	Yr	NM
❏ 1004	I Love You As You Are/I'll Never Set You Free	1968	$10

SCARLETS, THE (1)
DOT

Number	Title	Yr	NM
❏ 16004	Stampede/Park Avenue	1959	$30

PRINCE

Number	Title	Yr	NM
❏ 1207	Stampede/Park Avenue	1959	$60

SCARLETS, THE (2)
EVENT

Number	Title	Yr	NM
❏ 4287	Dear One/I've Lost	1958	$50

RED ROBIN

Number	Title	Yr	NM
❏ 133	Darling, I'm Yours/Love Doll	1954	$500
❏ 128	Dear One/I've Lost	1954	$500
❏ 135	True Love/Cry Baby	1955	$500

SCARLETS, THE (3)
TOWER

Number	Title	Yr	NM
❏ 144	I've Had It/You Don't Love Me	1965	$10

SCARLETS, THE (U)
FURY

Number	Title	Yr	NM
❏ 1036	Truly Yours/East of the Sun	1960	$40

SCAVENGERS, THE
FENTON

Number	Title	Yr	NM
❏ 987	Curfew/Oasis	1964	$60

MOBILE FIDELITY

Number	Title	Yr	NM
❏ 1212	Devil's Reef/Little Annie	1963	$50
❏ 1005	The Angels Listened In/ My Love Waits for Me	1963	$60

STARS OF HOLLYWOOD

Number	Title	Yr	NM
❏ 1212	Devil's Reef/Little Annie	1963	$60
❏ 1210	Shot Gun/Cream Puff	1963	$60
❏ 1211	Shot Gun/Zip Code	1963	$60

—*Cream Puff" and "Zip Code" are different titles for the same recording*

SUEMI

Number	Title	Yr	NM
❏ 4552	Bogus/Ghost Riders '65	1965	$30

SCENE, THE
B.T. PUPPY

Number	Title	Yr	NM
❏ 533	Scenes (From Another World)/You're in a Bad Way	1967	$10

SCHAFF, MURRAY, AND THE ARISTOCRATS
KING

Number	Title	Yr	NM
❏ 4977	How Many Miles/ Tombstone Number 9	1956	$40

SCHIAVONE SISTERS, THE
DE-LITE

Number	Title	Yr	NM
❏ 510	Granny Claus/Christmas Child (O' Bambino)	1968	$8
❏ 510 [PS]	Granny Claus/Christmas Child (O' Bambino)	1968	$15

SCHIFRIN, LALO
20TH CENTURY

Number	Title	Yr	NM
❏ 2150	Ape Shuffle/Escape from Tomorrow	1974	$5
❏ 2205	Bolero/Dona Donna	1975	$5

A&M

Number	Title	Yr	NM
❏ 1756	Theme from "The Master Gunfighter"/Theme from "The Trial of Billy Jack"	1975	$5

CTI

Number	Title	Yr	NM
❏ 29	Turning Point/Flamingo	1976	$4

DOT

Number	Title	Yr	NM
❏ 17059	Mission Impossible/ Jim on the Move	1967	$10

MCA

Number	Title	Yr	NM
❏ 52175	Heliotrope Bouquet/ The Entertainer	1983	$4

—*B-side by Marvin Hamlisch*

Number	Title	Yr	NM
❏ 40748	Magic Carousel/ Merry-Go-Round	1977	$4

MGM

Number	Title	Yr	NM
❏ 13139	Broken Date/Good Life	1963	$10
❏ 14153	Burning Bridges/ Kelly's Heroes	1970	$6
❏ 13163	Haunting/Theme from "Dime with a Halo"	1963	$12
❏ 13151	Hud/Jive Orbit	1963	$10
❏ 13224	Seven Faces of Dr. Lao/The Wave	1964	$10
❏ 13425	The Cincinnati Kid/ So Many Times	1965	$8
❏ 14180	Theme from "Medical Center"/(B-side unknown)	1970	$6
❏ 13251	Theme from "Rhino"/ Rhino Bomp	1964	$8

PARAMOUNT

Number	Title	Yr	NM
❏ 0002	Mannix/End Game	1969	$8
❏ 0001	Self Destruct/The Getaway	1969	$8

TABU

Number	Title	Yr	NM
❏ 5509	Moonlight Gypsies/ Prophecy of Love	1978	$4

TETRAGRAMMATON

Number	Title	Yr	NM
❏ 1533	Theme from "Che"/ Embo Scada	1969	$8

UNITED ARTISTS

Number	Title	Yr	NM
❏ 50649	What's New Pussycat/ Pussycat, Pussycat, I Love You	1970	$5

VERVE

Number	Title	Yr	NM
❏ 10663	Agnus Dei/Sanctus Benedictus	1971	$6
❏ 10290	Broken Date/Good Life	1963	$8
❏ 10365	Man from Thrush/ Blues-A-Go-Go	1965	$10
❏ 10663	Theme from "Medical Center"/All for the Love of Sunshine	1971	$8
❏ 10434	The Wig/Beneath a Weeping Willow Shade	1966	$8

WARNER BROS.

Number	Title	Yr	NM
❏ 7263	Bullitt/That Night	1969	$6
❏ 7173	Foxtail/That Night	1968	$6

SCHOLARS, THE
CUE

Number	Title	Yr	NM
❏ 7927/8	The Poor Little Doggie/ What Did I Do Wrong	1956	$50

DOT

Number	Title	Yr	NM
❏ 15519	If You Listen with Your Heart/Poor Little Doggie	1956	$30

IMPERIAL

Number	Title	Yr	NM
❏ 5459	Eternally Yours/Kan-Gu-Wa	1957	$30
❏ 5449	I Didn't Want to Do It/Beloved	1957	$30

SCHOOL, DANNY
FORD

Number	Title	Yr	NM
❏ 135	Christmas Rings A Bell/ Happy New Year	1964	$10

SCHOOLBOYS, THE
JUANITA

Number	Title	Yr	NM
❏ 103	Angel of Love/The Slide	1958	$200

OKEH

Number	Title	Yr	NM
❏ 7085	I Am Old Enough/Mary	1957	$30
❏ 7090	Pearl/Carol	1957	$30
❏ 7076	Shirley/Please Say You Want Me	1957	$40

—*Shirley" was the hit, but "Please Say You Want Me" is the side that has lived on*

SCHROEDER, JOHN
CAMEO

Number	Title	Yr	NM
❏ 389	Agent 00-Soul/Nightrider	1965	$30
❏ 366	The Fugitive Theme/Don't Break the Heart of Kimble	1965	$30

SCHUMACHER, CHRISTINE, SINGS WITH THE SUPREMES
MOTOWN

Number	Title	Yr	NM
❏ L-294-MO5 [DJ]	Mother You, Smother You (same on both sides)	1968	$300

—*Schumacher won a "Record a Record with the Supremes" contest on WKNR of Detroit. This is the rare result.*

SCHUMANN, WALTER
CAPITOL

Number	Title	Yr	NM
❏ CDF-9016	Christmas In The Air	1951	$60

—*Contains four records (F95017, F95018, F95019, F95020) and box*

Number	Title	Yr	NM
❏ F95017	Christmas in the Air!/ Adeste Fideles	1951	$10

—*Part 1" and "Part 8" of album CDF-9016*

Number	Title	Yr	NM
❏ F95020	Patapan//Wonderful Counselor/Wolcum Yole	1951	$10

—*Part 4" and "Part 5" of album CDF-9016*

Number	Title	Yr	NM
❏ F95018	Silent Night/Carol of the Bells//Winter Wonderland	1951	$10

—*Part 2" and "Part 7" of album CDF-9016*

Number	Title	Yr	NM
❏ F95019	White Christmas/Mary, Mary	1951	$10

—*Part 3" and "Part 6" of album CDF-9016*

Number	Title	Yr	NM
❏ F1841	White Christmas/ Winter Wonderland	1951	$20

RCA VICTOR

Number	Title	Yr	NM
❏ 47-5922	Calypso Christmas/ Christmas Tree	1954	$20
❏ LPM-1141/ LPT-6702 [DJ]	Christmas Chopsticks/ Pearls On Velvet	1955	$15

—*B-side by Glenn Miller (non-Christmas song); promo-only record using the numbers of the LPs from which the songs were taken*

Number	Title	Yr	NM
❏ 47-6318	The First Snowfall/ Christmas Gift	1955	$15
❏ 47-5542	The Sound of Christmas/ Magic Is the Earth	1953	$30

7-Inch Extended Plays

Number	Title	Yr	NM
❏ 547-0702	Sleigh Ride/God Rest Ye Merry, Gentlemen/The Christmas Song//C-H-R-I-S-T-M-A-S/Go Tell It On The Mountain/ Christmas Chopsticks	1955	$8
❏ 547-0704	The First Snowfall/Fum, Fum, Fum/Christmas Tree//Christmas In Killarney/ The First Noell/Frosty The Snowman/Hark! The Herald Angels Sing	1955	$8

SCHUTT, DAWN
MASTER

Number	Title	Yr	NM
❏ 10	Take Time/(B-side unknown)	1989	$6

SCHUYLER, KNOBLOCH & OVERSTREET
MTM

Number	Title	Yr	NM
❏ B-72086	American Me/Country Heart	1987	$4
❏ B-72081	Baby's Got a New Baby/ Bitter Pill to Swallow	1986	$4

—*As "S-K-O*

SCHUYLER, THOM
CAPITOL

Number	Title	Yr	NM
❏ B-5239	A Little at a Time/ The Softer I Try	1983	$4
❏ B-5281	Brave Heart/Two Way Street	1983	$4

SCORPIONS
Rudolph Schenker's brother Michael was briefly a member - twice.

MERCURY

Number	Title	Yr	NM
❏ 870559-7	Believe in Love/ Love on the Run	1988	$3
❏ 76008	Coast to Coast/Loving You Sunday Morning	1979	$4
❏ 880319-7	I'm Leaving You/Same Thrill	1984	$3
❏ 76084	Lady Starlight/ (B-side unknown)	1980	$4
❏ 76070	Make It Real/(B-side unknown)	1980	$4
❏ 872372-7	Passion Rules the Game/Media Overkill	1988	$3
❏ 880082-7	Still Loving You/Bad Boys Running Wild	1984	$3

RCA VICTOR

Number	Title	Yr	NM
❏ PB-10691	In Trance/Night Lights	1976	$6
❏ PB-10574	Speedy's Gone/They Need a Million	1976	$6

SCOTT, BILLY
CAMEO

Number	Title	Yr	NM
❏ 143	A Million Boys/The Town of Never Worry	1958	$30

EVEREST

Number	Title	Yr	NM
❏ 19315	Carole/Stairway to the Stars	1959	$20

LAMON

Number	Title	Yr	NM
❏ 10114	Merry Christmas/A Night to Remember	1983	$4

SCOTT BROTHERS, THE
COMET

Number	Title	Yr	NM
❏ 2161	Love Me Tenderly/It's Gonna Happen Soon	1963	$20
❏ 2153	Welcome Me/Letter from My Baby	1963	$20

FTP

Number	Title	Yr	NM
❏ 409	Mama's Little Baby/ Cindy, Oh Cindy	1960	$20
❏ 418	On Again, Off Again/ Sometimes I Wonder	1961	$20

N.Y. SKYLINE

Number	Title	Yr	NM
❑ 501	Do You Want My Love?/ (B-side unknown)	1960	$50

PARKWAY

Number	Title	Yr	NM
❑ 841	Beggin' for Your Love/Memories	1962	$30

RIBBON

Number	Title	Yr	NM
❑ 6911	Lost Love/Only Then	1960	$30

SMASH

Number	Title	Yr	NM
❑ 2139	Got to Get a Groove/ My Day Has Come	1967	$20

TODDLIN' TOWN

Number	Title	Yr	NM
❑ 125	A Hunk o' Funk/They All Came Back	1969	$20
❑ 131	I Don't Wanna Lose You/ (B-side unknown)	1969	$20
❑ 134	Top of the Mountain/ (B-side unknown)	1969	$20

SCOTT, BUDDY

HIT

Number	Title	Yr	NM
❑ 230	May the Bird of Paradise Fly Up Your Nose/ Turn! Turn! Turn!	1965	$10

—B-side by Jackie and the Giants

SCOTT, CALVIN

ATCO

Number	Title	Yr	NM
❑ 6729	Cry Like a Baby/More Than You'll Ever Know	1970	$15
❑ 6696	I'm Taking You Home to Mama/Sonny Boy (Be a Man)	1969	$15

STAX

Number	Title	Yr	NM
❑ 0110	Goin' Back to Eden/The Sadness for Things	1971	$10
❑ 094	Shame on the Family Name/ I've Made a Reservation	1971	$10

SCOTT, EARL

KAPP

Number	Title	Yr	NM
❑ KCW-854	Then a Tear Fell/Save a Minute (Lose a Wife)	1962	$10

MERCURY

Number	Title	Yr	NM
❑ 72110	Loose Lips/Guess I'll Never Learn	1963	$8

SCOTT, FREDDIE, AND THE CHIMES

ARROW

Number	Title	Yr	NM
❑ 726	Lovin' Baby/A Faded Memory	1958	$50
❑ 724	Please Call/A Letter Came This Morning	1958	$50

SCOTT, FREDDIE

COLPIX

Number	Title	Yr	NM
❑ 692	Hey Girl/The Slide	1963	$15
❑ 709	I Got a Woman/ Brand New World	1963	$10
❑ 752	On Broadway/If I Had a Hammer	1964	$10
❑ 724	Where Does Love Go/ Where Have All the Flowers Gone	1964	$10

COLUMBIA

Number	Title	Yr	NM
❑ 43316	Don't Let It End/ Come Up Singing	1965	$12
❑ 43199	Lonely Man/I'll Try Again	1964	$10
❑ 43112	Mr. Heartache/ Heartache Too Many	1964	$10
❑ 43623	One Iddy Biddy Needle/ Forget Me If You Can	1966	$10

JOY

Number	Title	Yr	NM
❑ 250	Baby, You're a Long Time Dead/Lost the Right	1961	$15
❑ 255	I Gotta Stand Tall/When the Wind Changes	1961	$15
❑ 280	I Gotta Stand Tall/When the Wind Changes	1963	$10

P.I.P.

Number	Title	Yr	NM
❑ 8932	Deep Is the Night/ The Great If	1972	$5

PROBE

Number	Title	Yr	NM
❑ 481	I Shall Be Released/ Girl I Love You	1970	$6

SHOUT

Number	Title	Yr	NM
❑ 212	Am I Grooving You/ Never You Mind	1967	$8
❑ 207	Are You Lonely for Me/ Where Were You	1966	$8
❑ 211	Cry to Me/No One Could Ever Love You	1967	$8
❑ 245	Forever My Darling/ (You) Got What I Need	1969	$10
❑ 220	He Ain't Give You None/Run Joy	1967	$8
❑ 216	He Will Break Your Heart/I'll Be Gone	1967	$8
❑ 238	Loving You Is Killing Me/Eileen	1968	$8

VANGUARD

Number	Title	Yr	NM
❑ 35137	I Guess God Wants It This Way/Please Listen	1971	$5

SCOTT, JACK

ABC

Number	Title	Yr	NM
❑ 10843	Before the Bird Flies/Insane	1966	$30

ABC-PARAMOUNT

Number	Title	Yr	NM
❑ 9818	Baby She's Gone/You Can Bet Your Bottom Dollar	1957	$200
❑ 9860	Two Timin' Woman/I Need Your Love	1957	$200

CAPITOL

Number	Title	Yr	NM
❑ 4554	A Little Feeling (Called Love)/Now That I	1961	$30
❑ 4554 [PS]	A Little Feeling (Called Love)/Now That I	1961	$60
❑ 4955	All I See Is Blue/Meo Myo	1963	$30
❑ 4689	Cry, Cry, Cry/Grizzly Bear	1962	$30
❑ 4689 [PS]	Cry, Cry, Cry/Grizzly Bear	1962	$60
❑ 4855	If Only/Green, Green Valley	1962	$30
❑ 4597	My Dream Came True/ Strange Desire	1961	$30
❑ 4597 [PS]	My Dream Came True/ Strange Desire	1961	$60
❑ 4796	Sad Story/I Can't Hold Your Letters	1962	$30
❑ 4637	Steps 1 and 2/One of These Days	1961	$30
❑ 4637 [PS]	Steps 1 and 2/One of These Days	1961	$60
❑ 4903	Strangers/Laugh and the World Laughs With You	1963	$30
❑ 4738	The Part Where I Cry/ You Only See What You Wanna See	1962	$30

CARLTON

Number	Title	Yr	NM
❑ 493	Goodbye Baby/ Save My Soul	1959	$40
❑ 493 [PS]	Goodbye Baby/ Save My Soul	1959	$70
❑ 504	I Never Felt Like This/Bella	1959	$40
❑ 462	My True Love/Leroy	1958	$40
❑ 519 [M]	There Comes a Time/ Baby Marie	1959	$30
❑ ST-519 [S]	There Comes a Time/ Baby Marie	1959	$50
❑ 514	The Way I Walk/Midgie	1959	$40
❑ 483	With Your Love/Geraldine	1958	$40
❑ 483 [PS]	With Your Love/Geraldine	1958	$70

DOT

Number	Title	Yr	NM
❑ 17475	May You Never Be Alone/ Face to the Wall	1973	$5

GROOVE

Number	Title	Yr	NM
❑ 58-0031	Blue Skies (Moving In on Me)/I Knew You First	1964	$20
❑ 58-0049	Flakey John/Tall Tales	1964	$30
❑ 58-0027	There's Trouble Brewin'/ Jingle Bell Slide	1963	$30
❑ 58-0042	Thou Shalt Not Steal/I Prayed for an Angel	1964	$20
❑ 58-0037	Wiggle On Out/What a Wonderful Night Out	1964	$30

GRT

Number	Title	Yr	NM
❑ 35	Billy Jack/Mary, Marry Me	1971	$5

GUARANTEED

Number	Title	Yr	NM
❑ 209	What Am I Living For/ Indiana Waltz	1960	$40

JUBILEE

Number	Title	Yr	NM
❑ 5606	My Special Angel/I Keep Changin' My Mind	1967	$30
❑ 4104-30	Spirit of '76/(Instrumental)	1976	$4

RCA VICTOR

Number	Title	Yr	NM
❑ 47-8724	Don't Hush the Laughter/ Let's Learn to Live and Love Again	1965	$20
❑ 47-8685	Looking for Linda/I Hope I Think I Wish	1965	$20
❑ 47-8505	Separation's Now Granted/I Don't Believe in Tea Leaves	1965	$20

TOP RANK

Number	Title	Yr	NM
❑ 2041 [M]	Burning Bridges/ Oh Little One	1960	$30
❑ 2041 [PS]	Burning Bridges/ Oh Little One	1960	$70
❑ 2041 [S]	Burning Bridges/ Oh Little One	1960	$70
❑ 2093	Is There Something on Your Mind/Found a Woman	1960	$30
❑ 2093 [PS]	Is There Something on Your Mind/Found a Woman	1960	$70
❑ 2055	It Only Happened Yesterday/Cool Water	1960	$30
❑ 2075	Patsy/Old Time Religion	1960	$30
❑ 2028 [M]	What in the World's Come Over You/Baby Baby	1959	$40
❑ 2028 [S]	What in the World's Come Over You/Baby Baby	1959	$50

7-Inch Extended Plays

CARLTON

Number	Title	Yr	NM
❑ EP 7/1071	Indiana Waltz,/Midgie// My True Love/Leroy	1959	$250
❑ EP 7/1070 [PS]	Presenting Jack Scott (Volume 1)	1959	$250
❑ EP 7/1071 [PS]	Presenting Jack Scott (Volume 2)	1959	$250
❑ EP 7/1070	Save My Soul/I Can't Help It//Geraldine/With Your Love	1959	$250

TOP RANK

Number	Title	Yr	NM
❑ 1001 [PS]	What in the World's Come Over You	1960	$250
❑ 1001	What in the World's Come Over You/My King//Burning Bridges/Oh, Little One	1960	$250

SCOTT, JOEL

PHILLES

Number	Title	Yr	NM
❑ 101	Here I Stand/You're My Only Love	1962	$30

SCOTT, LINDA

CANADIAN AMERICAN

Number	Title	Yr	NM
❑ 134	Bermuda/Lonely for You	1962	$20
❑ 132	Christmas Day/Twistin' Bells	1961	$30

—B-side by Santo and Johnny

Number	Title	Yr	NM
❑ 133	Count Every Star/ Land of Stars	1962	$20
❑ 127	Don't Bet Money Honey/ Starlight, Starbright	1961	$30
❑ 129	I Don't Know Why/ It's All Because	1961	$30
❑ 123	I've Told Every Little Star/Three Guesses	1961	$30

CONGRESS

Number	Title	Yr	NM
❑ 209	I Envy You/Everybody Stopped Laughing at Jane	1964	$20
❑ 106	I Left My Heart in the Balcony/Lopsided Love Affair	1962	$20
❑ 110	I'm Gonna Sit Right Down and Write Myself a Letter/Ain't That Fun	1963	$20
❑ 108	I'm So Afraid of Losing You/ The Loneliest Girl in Town	1962	$20
❑ 200	Let's Fall in Love/I Know It, You Know It	1963	$20
❑ 206	Let's Fall in Love/I Know It, You Know It	1964	$20
❑ 204	Who's Been Sleeping in My Bed/My Baby	1963	$20

KAPP

Number	Title	Yr	NM
❑ 677	Don't Lose Your Head/I'll See You in My Dreams	1965	$12
❑ 641	If I Love Again/Patch It Up	1965	$10
❑ 610	That Old Feeling/ This Is My Prayer	1964	$12
❑ 762	Toys/Take a Walk Bobby	1966	$10

RCA VICTOR

Number	Title	Yr	NM
❑ 47-9424	They Don't Know You/ Three Miles High	1967	$10

SCOTT, MABEL

HOLLYWOOD

Number	Title	Yr	NM
❑ 1023	Boogie Woogie Santa Claus/How I Hate To See Christmas	1954	$40

SCOTT, MARK, TEENS

CHALLENGE

Number	Title	Yr	NM
❑ 9177	Christmas/Christmas Eve	1962	$15

SCOTT, NEIL

CAMEO

Number	Title	Yr	NM
❑ 476	(I Don't Stand) A Ghost of a Chance with You/ Let Me Think It Over	1967	$30

COMET

Number	Title	Yr	NM
❑ 2151	Tomboy/Run to Me	1962	$40

HERALD

Number	Title	Yr	NM
❑ 581	(Chantilly, Silly Sort of Daffy as a Dilly Little Fussy Little Frilly Little) One Piece Bathing Suit/Little Girl	1963	$30

PORTRAIT

Number	Title	Yr	NM
❑ 102	Bobby/I Haven't Found It with Another	1961	$30
❑ 106	It Happened All Over Again/My Confession	1961	$30

SCOTT, RICKY

CUB

Number	Title	Yr	NM
❑ 9079	I Didn't Mean It/Darlin' Darlin'	1960	$30

X-CLUSIVE

Number	Title	Yr	NM
❑ 1001	I Didn't Mean It/Darlin' Darlin'	1960	$100

SCOTT, RODNEY

CANON

Number	Title	Yr	NM
❑ 225	Granny Went Rockin'/ Bitter Tears	1961	$200

MR. PEEKE

Number	Title	Yr	NM
❑ 126	That's the Way It Goes/Bitter Tears	1963	$40

Number	Title	Yr	NM
SCOTT, SHERREE			
ROBBINS			
❏ 1036	Fascinating Baby/You and I	1957	$200
❏ 105	Twinkle Toes (The Littlest Reindeer)/Our Christmas Day	1959	$50
ROCKET			
❏ 101	Whole Lotta Shakin' Goin' On/Unhappy Birthday	1958	$200
❏ 101 [PS]	Whole Lotta Shakin' Goin' On/Unhappy Birthday	1958	$200
SCOTT, SIMON			
IMPERIAL			
❏ 66066	Move It Baby/What Kind of a Woman	1964	$20
❏ 66089	My Baby's Got Soul/Midnight	1965	$30
SCOTT, TERRY			
VALIANT			
❏ 6016	Little Angel/Love Only Me	1962	$15
SCOTT, TOM			
A&M			
❏ 1345	Boss Walk/Looking Out for Number 7	1972	$5
ABC IMPULSE!			
❏ 265	The Honeysuckle Breeze/Baby I Love You	1967	$8
ATLANTIC			
❏ 89763	Lollipoppin'/Come Back to Me	1983	$4
COLUMBIA			
❏ 10914	Beautiful Music/Lost Inside the Love of You	1979	$4
❏ 02496	So White and So Funky/We Belong Together	1981	$4
ODE			
❏ 50433	Gotcha (Theme from Starsky & Hutch)/Smoothin' On Down	1977	$4
❏ 66043	Strut Your Stuff/Sneaking in the Back	1974	$4
❏ 66121	Time and Love/Dirty Old Man	1976	$4
❏ 66105	Tom Cat/Keep On Doin' It	1975	$4
SCOTT, TOMMY			
LONDON			
❏ 9694	Wrap Your Troubles in Dreams/Blueberry Hill	1964	$15
SCOTT, WALTER			
MUSICLAND U.S.A.			
❏ 20014	It's Been a Long Time/Proud	1966	$20
❏ 20009	Watch Out/My Shadow Is Gone	1966	$20
PZAZZ			
❏ 026	Soul Stew Recipe/Feeling Something New Inside	1969	$12
SCRAMBLERS, THE			
ARVEE			
❏ 6502	Super Surfer U.S.A./Go Getera Go	1963	$30
DEL-FI			
❏ 4237	The Beatle Walk/The Beatle Blues	1964	$30
SCREAMING BLUE MESSIAHS			
ELEKTRA			
❏ 69433	I Wanna Be a Flintstone/(B-side unknown)	1987	$5
❏ 69433 [PS]	I Wanna Be a Flintstone/(B-side unknown)	1987	$5
SCREAMING TREES			
7-Inch Extended Plays			
SUB POP			
❏ 48	Change Has Come	1989	$20
—Two 7-inch 45s, one black vinyl, one white			
❏ 48	Change Has Come	1989	$75
—Second pressing of above: red vinyl			
❏ 48 [PS]	Change Has Come	1989	$20
—Poster sleeve			
SCRITTI POLITTI			
WARNER BROS.			
❏ 7-27976	Boom! There She Was/A World Come Back to Life	1988	$3
—A-side with Roger			
❏ 7-27976 [PS]	Boom! There She Was/A World Come Back to Life	1988	$3

Number	Title	Yr	NM
❏ 7-27710	Oh Patti (Don't Feel Sorry for Loverboy)/Best Thing Ever	1988	$3
—With Miles Davis			
❏ 7-27710 [PS]	Oh Patti (Don't Feel Sorry for Loverboy)/Best Thing Ever	1988	$3
❏ 7-28949	Perfect Way/(Way Perfect Version Edit)	1985	$3
❏ 7-28949 [PS]	Perfect Way/(Way Perfect Version Edit)	1985	$3
❏ 7-28949 [PS]	Perfect Way/(Way Perfect Version Edit)	1985	$10
—Promo-only letterpress cardboard sleeve done by Independent roject Records with sheet of stamps enclosed			
❏ 7-29152	Wood Beez (pray like aretha franklin)/(Version)	1984	$6
❏ 7-28811	Wood Beez (pray like aretha franklin)/(Version)	1986	$3
❏ 7-28811 [PS]	Wood Beez (pray like aretha franklin)/(Version)	1986	$3
SCRUGGS, EARL			
COLUMBIA			
❏ 11176	Blue Moon of Kentucky/Give Me a Sign	1980	$5
❏ 38-03777	Could You Love Me One More/Roller Coaster	1983	$4
—A-side vocals by Burrito Brothers			
❏ 4-45326	East Virginia Blues/Lonesome Ruben	1971	$8
❏ 10992	I Could Sure Use the Feeling/Drive to the Country	1979	$5
❏ 11306	It'll Be Alright/Country Comfort	1980	$5
❏ 38-04717	Pedal to the Metal/Leaving Louisiana in the Broad Daylight	1984	$4
❏ 11106	Play Me No Sad Songs/Morning After Kind of Man	1979	$5
❏ 38-03430	Sittin' on Top of the World/Lindsey	1983	$4
—A-side vocals by Rodney Dillard			
❏ 3-10433	Tall Texas Woman/Daydream	1976	$6
❏ 3-10691	The Cabin/Our Love Is Home Grown	1978	$5
SEA, JOHNNY			
CAPITOL			
❏ 4646	Livin' Is Lovin'/The Wayward Wind	1961	$10
❏ 4585	The Torch and the Flame/No Tears Tonight	1961	$10
COLUMBIA			
❏ 4-44805	Cryin' Gray Tombstone/Everybody's Friend	1969	$5
❏ 4-44423	Going Out to Tulsa/There's a Shadow Bar	1968	$5
❏ 4-44268	If/Behind My Baby's Bedroom Door	1967	$6
❏ 4-44717	I've Learned a Lot Today/A Poor Boy Just Trying to Get Along	1968	$5
❏ 4-44542	Mama When I'm Gone Don't Cry for Me/Song Number 9 1/2 on the Album	1968	$5
❏ 4-44634	Three Six-Packs, Two Arms and a Juke Box/I Loved Her Fine for a Time	1968	$5
—As "Johnny Seay"			
NRC			
❏ 019	Frankie's Man, Johnny/Loneliness	1959	$15
❏ 060	Ghost Riders in the Sky/Mr. and Mrs. Sippi	1960	$15
—As "Johnny Seay"			
❏ 06	It Won't Be Easy to Forget/I Love You	1958	$15
❏ 026	Stranger/Judy and Johnny	1959	$15
PHILIPS			
❏ 40214	All Mixed Up/Standing Room Only	1964	$8
❏ 40307	If It Wasn't for Hard Luck/Hitchin' and Hikin'	1965	$8
❏ 40164	My Baby Walks All Over Me/There's Another Man	1964	$8
❏ 40267	My Old Faded Rose/It's a Shame	1965	$8
SOUND FACTORY			
❏ 411	Bobby's Got a Thing About Trains/(B-side unknown)	1980	$6
VIKING			
❏ 1017	Annie's Going to Sing Her Song/Stormy Weather Girl	1971	$6
❏ 1011	Fort Worth Girl/Willie's Drunk and Willie's Dying	1970	$5
WARNER BROS.			
❏ PRO233 [DJ]	Day for Decision/Listen to the Message	1966	$15
—Promo-only edition with different B-side			
❏ 5820	Day for Decision/Mary Rocks Him to Sleep	1966	$6
❏ 5861	Things You Gave Me/Wheels on the Highway	1966	$6

Number	Title	Yr	NM
SEA LEVEL			
ARISTA			
❏ 1008 [DJ]	Make You Feel Love Again (stereo/mono)	1982	$125
—May not exist as a stock copy; not issued on an LP			
❏ 0559	Schoolteacher/Don't Want to Be Wrong	1980	$5
CAPRICORN			
❏ 0292	It Hurts to Want It So Bad/Had to Fall	1978	$5
❏ 0312	Living in a Dream/Sneakers	1979	$6
❏ 0272	Shake a Leg/Just a Good Feeling	1977	$5
❏ 0287	That's Your Secret/Storm Warning	1977	$6
SEA SHELLS, THE			
GOLIATH			
❏ 1357	Love Those Beach Boys/Close to Jimmy	1964	$50
JUBILEE			
❏ 5587	Hit the Surf/Barefoot in the Sand	1967	$30
SEAFOOD MAMA			
WHITEFIRE			
❏ 0(no cat #)	Harden My Heart/City of Roses	1980	$50
❏ 0(no cat #) [PS]	Harden My Heart/City of Roses	1980	$50
SEALS AND CROFTS			
T-A			
❏ 210	Gabriel Go On Home/Robin	1971	$8
❏ 188	In Tune/Seldom's Sister	1969	$8
❏ 191	See My Life/(B-side unknown)	1969	$8
❏ 206	See My Life/In Tune//Hollow Reed/Leave	1970	$10
WARNER BROS.			
❏ 8277	Baby, I'll Give It to You/Advance Guards	1976	$4
❏ 8130	Castles in the Sand/Golden Rainbow	1975	$4
❏ 7708	Diamond Girl/Wisdom	1973	$5
❏ 49522	First Love/Kite Dreams	1980	$4
❏ 8190	Get Closer/Don't Fail	1976	$4
❏ 8190 [PS]	Get Closer/Don't Fail	1976	$30
❏ 7671	Hummingbird/Say	1972	$5
❏ 8075	I'll Play for You/Truth Is But a Woman	1975	$4
❏ 8639	Magnolia Moon/Takin' It Easy	1978	$4
❏ 8405	My Fair Share/East of Ginger Trees	1977	$4
❏ 8405 [PS]	My Fair Share/East of Ginger Trees	1977	$6
❏ 7565	Sudan Village/High on a Mountain	1972	$6
❏ 7606	Summer Breeze/East of Ginger Trees	1972	$5
❏ 7740	We May Never Pass This Way (Again)/Jessica	1973	$5
❏ 7536	When I Meet Them/Irish Linen	1971	$6
SEALS, JIMMY			
CARLTON			
❏ 470	Sneaky Pete/Benguela	1958	$40
CHALLENGE			
❏ 59270	Everybody's Doing the Jerk/Wa-Hoo	1965	$30
❏ 9200	Lady Heartbreak/Grounded	1963	$40
❏ 59299	She's Not a Bad Girl/The Yesterday of Our Love	1965	$30
❏ 9153	Wish for You, Want for You, Wait for You/Runaway Heart	1962	$40
WINSTON			
❏ 1027	Biscayne Bay/Juarez	1958	$60
❏ 1021	Sneaky Pete/Benguela	1958	$60
SEALS, TROY			
ATLANTIC			
❏ 4020	Honky Tonkin'/Let Me Make the Bright Lights Shine	1974	$6
❏ 4004	I Got a Thing About You Baby/Coal Town Blues	1973	$6
❏ 4013	Star of the Bar/You Can't Judge a Book by the Cover	1973	$6
CALLA			
❏ 139	The Wedding of Society's Child/Sweet Love	1967	$10
COLUMBIA			
❏ 3-10173	Easy/I'll Take You Down to San Antonio	1975	$5
❏ 3-10511	Grand Ole Blues/One More Thrill	1977	$5
❏ 3-10227	Honky Tonk Dreams/San Antone-Ee-O	1975	$5
❏ 3-10435	Let's Go for a Ride/Me and Mama Used to Rock and Roll	1976	$5

Number	Title	Yr	NM
❑ 3-10303	Sweet Dreams/ In Our Rooms	1976	$5
❑ 3-10354	Tall Texas Woman/ We're Much Too Close (To Be So Far Apart)	1976	$5

ELEKTRA

Number	Title	Yr	NM
❑ 46573	One Night Honeymoon/ Wanderin' Friends of Mine	1980	$4

POLYDOR

Number	Title	Yr	NM
❑ 14053	Don't Blame Me/20 Miles from Home	1970	$8
❑ 14028	Where Did My Baby Go/ Circles 'Round the Sun	1970	$8

RCA

Number	Title	Yr	NM
❑ JK-13652 [DJ]	Good (Real Good) (same on both sides)	1983	$10

—Promo only on yellow vinyl

Number	Title	Yr	NM
❑ PB-13652	Good (Real Good)/ We Had It All	1983	$4

RISING SONS

Number	Title	Yr	NM
❑ 715	Mama, Hold My Hand/ Ebony and Ivory	1969	$40

SEAN AND THE BRANDYWINES

DECCA

Number	Title	Yr	NM
❑ 31910	She Ain't No Good/Cod'ine	1966	$30

—Produced by Gary Usher

SEARCHERS, THE

KAPP

Number	Title	Yr	NM
❑ 584	Ain't That Just Like Me/ Ain't Gonna Kiss You	1964	$10
❑ 584 [PS]	Ain't That Just Like Me (special promo sleeve)	1964	$60
❑ KJB-49	Bumble Bee/A Tear Fell	1965	$10

—Orange label "Winners Circle Series"; no black label counterpart

Number	Title	Yr	NM
❑ KJB-29	Bumble Bee/ Everything You Do	1964	$10

—Orange label "Winners Circle Series"; no black label counterpart

Number	Title	Yr	NM
❑ KJB-49	Bumble Bee/ Everything You Do	1964	$15

—Orange label "Winners Circle Series"; no black label counterpart

Number	Title	Yr	NM
❑ 593	Don't Throw Your Love Away/I Pretend I'm with You	1964	$12
❑ 706	Don't You Know Why/ You Can't Lie to a Liar	1965	$12
❑ 658	Goodbye My Lover Goodbye/'Til I Met You	1965	$10
❑ 783	Have You Ever Loved Somebody/It's Just the Way	1966	$12
❑ 686	He's Got No Love/ So Far Away	1965	$12
❑ KJB-27	Love Potion Number Nine/Hi-Heel Sneakers	1964	$10

—Orange label "Winners Circle Series"; no black label counterpart

Number	Title	Yr	NM
❑ 811	Lovers/Popcorn Double Feature	1966	$10
❑ 609	Someday We're Gonna Love Again/No One Else Could Love Me	1964	$12
❑ 609 [PS]	Someday We're Gonna Love Again/No One Else Could Love Me	1964	$40
❑ 729	Take Me for What I'm Worth/Too Many Miles	1966	$10
❑ 644	What Have They Done to the Rain/This Feeling Inside	1965	$10
❑ 618	When You Walk in the Room/I'll Be Missing You	1964	$10

LIBERTY

Number	Title	Yr	NM
❑ 55646	Sugar and Spice/ Saints and Sinners	1963	$30
❑ 55689	Sugar and Spice/ Saints and Sinners	1964	$20

MERCURY

Number	Title	Yr	NM
❑ 72390	(Ain't That) Just Like Me/I Can Tell	1964	$20
❑ 72172	Sweets for My Sweet/ It's All Been a Dream	1963	$30

RCA VICTOR

Number	Title	Yr	NM
❑ 74-0484	Desdemona/The World Is Waiting for Tomorrow	1971	$20
❑ 74-0652	Love Is Everywhere/ And the Button	1972	$20

SIRE

Number	Title	Yr	NM
❑ 49175	It's Too Late/Don't Hang On	1980	$4
❑ 49665	Love's Melody/Little Bit of Heaven	1981	$4

SEATRAIN

A&M

Number	Title	Yr	NM
❑ 994	As I Lay Losing/Let the Duchess Know	1968	$8

—As "Sea Train

Number	Title	Yr	NM
❑ 994 [PS]	As I Lay Losing/Let the Duchess Know	1968	$20

—As "Sea Train

CAPITOL

Number	Title	Yr	NM
❑ 3067	13 Questions/Oh My Love-Sally Goodin	1971	$6
❑ 3275	Gramercy/How Sweet Thy Song	1972	$6
❑ 3201	Marblehead Messenger/ Despair Tire	1971	$6
❑ 3140	Song of Job/ Waiting for Elijah	1971	$6

WARNER BROS.

Number	Title	Yr	NM
❑ 7696	Flute Thing/Freedom Is the Reason	1973	$5

SEAWEED

7-Inch Extended Plays

LEOPARD GECKO

Number	Title	Yr	NM
❑ LG 007	Inside	1989	$43

—Blue/green vinyl

Number	Title	Yr	NM
❑ LG 007	Inside	1989	$18
❑ LG 007 [PS]	Inside	1989	$18

SEBASTIAN, JOHN

Also see THE LOVIN' SPOONFUL.

KAMA SUTRA

Number	Title	Yr	NM
❑ 254	She's a Lady/The Room Nobody Lives In	1968	$10
❑ 254 [PS]	She's a Lady/The Room Nobody Lives In	1968	$20

REPRISE

Number	Title	Yr	NM
❑ 0902	Fa-Fana-Fa/Magical Connection	1970	$6
❑ 1074	Give Us a Break/ Music for People Who Don't Speak English	1972	$6
❑ 1355	Hideaway/One Step Forward, Two Steps Back	1976	$4
❑ 1026	I Don't Want Nobody Else/Sweet Muse	1971	$6
❑ 1349	Welcome Back Kotter/ Warm Baby	1976	$8

—Original A-side title

Number	Title	Yr	NM
❑ 1349	Welcome Back/Warm Baby	1976	$4

—Revised A-side title

Number	Title	Yr	NM
❑ 1050	We'll See/Well, Well, Well	1971	$6
❑ 0918	What She Thinks About/ Red-Eye Express	1970	$6

SECOND TIME, THE

TOWER

Number	Title	Yr	NM
❑ 432	Listen to the Music/ Psychedelic Senate	1968	$12

SECRETS, THE (1)

OMEN

Number	Title	Yr	NM
❑ 15	Here I Am/I Feel a Thrill Coming On	1966	$15

PHILIPS

Number	Title	Yr	NM
❑ 40196	Here He Comes Now!/Oh Donnie	1964	$15
❑ 40222	He's the Boy/He Doesn't Want You	1964	$15
❑ 40173	Hey Big Boy/The Other Side of Town	1964	$15
❑ 40173 [PS]	Hey Big Boy/The Other Side of Town	1964	$30
❑ 40146	The Boy Next Door/ Learnin' to Forget	1963	$20

SECRETS, THE (2)

SWAN

Number	Title	Yr	NM
❑ 4097	Hot Toddy/Twin Exhaust	1962	$30
❑ 4097 [PS]	Hot Toddy/Twin Exhaust	1962	$60

SECRETS, THE (3)

HARMONY

Number	Title	Yr	NM
❑ 6958	Hot Night in the City/ Don't Say Goodbye	1982	$4
❑ 6958 [PS]	Hot Night in the City/ Don't Say Goodbye	1982	$5

SECRETS, THE (U)

RED BIRD

Number	Title	Yr	NM
❑ Oct-0076	Every Day/A Smile Upside Down	1966	$12

SEDAKA, NEIL

DECCA

Number	Title	Yr	NM
❑ 30520	Laura Lee/Snowtime	1957	$70

ELEKTRA

Number	Title	Yr	NM
❑ 45421	Alone at Last/Sleazy Love	1977	$4
❑ 45406	Amarillo/The Leaving Game	1977	$4
❑ 45525	Candy Kisses/All You Need Is the Music	1978	$4
❑ 47017	Letting Go/It's Good to Be Alive Again	1980	$6
❑ 47184	My World Keeps Slipping Away/Love Is Spreading Over the World	1981	$4
❑ 46017	Sad, Sad Story/ Tillie the Twirler	1979	$4
❑ 46615	Should've Never Let You Go/You're So Good for Me	1980	$4

—With Dara Sedaka

KIRSHNER

Number	Title	Yr	NM
❑ 63-5024	Beautiful You/Anywhere You're Gonna Be (Leba's Song)	1972	$6
❑ SP-45-370 [DJ]	Beautiful You (Long)/ Beautiful You (Short)	1972	$8

—Promo only number

Number	Title	Yr	NM
❑ 63-5017	I'm a Song (Sing Me)/ Silent Movies	1971	$5

—As "Sedaka

Number	Title	Yr	NM
❑ SP-45-291 [DJ]	I'm a Song (Sing Me)/ Silent Movies	1971	$8

—Promo only number (mono versions)

Number	Title	Yr	NM
❑ 63-5020	Superbird/Rosemary Blue	1972	$5

MGM

Number	Title	Yr	NM
❑ 14661	Alone in New York in the Rain/Suspicions	1973	$5
❑ 14564	Standing on the Inside/ Let Daddy Know	1973	$5

PYRAMID

Number	Title	Yr	NM
❑ 623	Oh Delilah/Neil's Twist	1962	$40

—B-side is an instrumental version of the A-side credited to The Marvels

RCA VICTOR

Number	Title	Yr	NM
❑ 47-8137	Alice in Wonderland/ Circulate	1963	$15
❑ 47-8137 [PS]	Alice in Wonderland/ Circulate	1963	$30
❑ 47-8254	Bad Girl/Wait 'Til You See My Baby	1963	$15
❑ 47-8046	Breaking Up Is Hard to Do/As Long As I Live	1962	$20
❑ 47-8046 [PS]	Breaking Up Is Hard to Do/As Long As I Live	1962	$30
❑ 47-7829	Calendar Girl/The Same Old Fool	1960	$20
❑ 47-7829 [PS]	Calendar Girl/The Same Old Fool	1960	$30
❑ 61-7829 [S]	Calendar Girl/The Same Old Fool	1960	$60

—Living Stereo" (large hole, plays at 45 rpm)

Number	Title	Yr	NM
❑ 37-7829	Calendar Girl/The Same Old Fool	1960	$60

—Compact Single 33" (small hole, plays at LP speed)

Number	Title	Yr	NM
❑ 47-7957	Happy Birthday Sweet Sixteen/Don't Lead Me On	1961	$20
❑ 37-7957	Happy Birthday Sweet Sixteen/Don't Lead Me On	1961	$60

—Compact Single 33" (small hole, plays at LP speed)

Number	Title	Yr	NM
❑ 47-7473	I Go Ape/Moon of Gold	1959	$30
❑ 47-8453	I Hope He Breaks Your Heart/Too Late	1964	$10
❑ 47-8169	Let's Go Steady Again/ Waiting for Never	1963	$15
❑ 47-8169 [PS]	Let's Go Steady Again/ Waiting for Never	1963	$30
❑ 47-8511	Let the People Talk/In the Chapel with You	1965	$12
❑ 47-8511 [PS]	Let the People Talk/In the Chapel with You	1965	$30
❑ 47-7874	Little Devil/I Must Be Dreaming	1961	$20
❑ 47-7874 [PS]	Little Devil/I Must Be Dreaming	1961	$30
❑ 37-7874	Little Devil/I Must Be Dreaming	1961	$60

—Compact Single 33" (small hole, plays at LP speed)

Number	Title	Yr	NM
❑ 47-7595	Oh! Carol/One Way Ticket (To the Blues)	1959	$30
❑ 61-7595 [S]	Oh! Carol/One Way Ticket (To the Blues)	1959	$60

—Living Stereo" (large hole, plays at 45 rpm)

Number	Title	Yr	NM
❑ 47-7709	Stairway to Heaven/ Forty Winks Away	1960	$20
❑ 61-7709 [S]	Stairway to Heaven/ Forty Winks Away	1960	$60

—Living Stereo" (large hole, plays at 45 rpm)

Number	Title	Yr	NM
❑ 47-8382	Sunny/She'll Never Be You	1964	$10
❑ 47-7922	Sweet Little You/I Found My World in You	1961	$20
❑ 47-7922 [PS]	Sweet Little You/I Found My World in You	1961	$30
❑ 37-7922	Sweet Little You/I Found My World in You	1961	$60

—Compact Single 33" (small hole, plays at LP speed)

Number	Title	Yr	NM
❑ 47-8844	The Answer Lies Within/ Grown-Up Games	1966	$12
❑ 47-8737	The Answer to My Prayer/Blue Boy	1965	$12
❑ 47-8341	The Closest Thing to Heaven/Without a Song	1964	$12
❑ 47-8341 [PS]	The Closest Thing to Heaven/Without a Song	1964	$30
❑ 47-7408	The Diary/No Vacancy	1958	$30
❑ 47-7408 [DJ]	The Diary/No Vacancy	1958	$50

—White label promo with Sedaka's photo on label

Number	Title	Yr	NM
❑ 47-8209	The Dreamer/Look Inside Your Heart	1963	$15
❑ 47-8209 [PS]	The Dreamer/Look Inside Your Heart	1963	$30

Number	Title	Yr	NM
❏ 47-8637	The World Through a Tear/ High On a Mountain	1965	$10
❏ 47-8637 [PS]	The World Through a Tear/ High On a Mountain	1965	$30
❏ 47-9004	We Can Make It If We Try/Too Late	1966	$10

ROCKET

Number	Title	Yr	NM
❏ 40460	Bad Blood/Your Favorite Entertainer	1975	$4
❏ 40500	Breaking Up Is Hard to Do/Nana's Song	1975	$4
❏ 40313	Laughter in the Rain/ Endlessly	1974	$4
❏ 40543	Love in the Shadows/Baby Don't Let It Mess Your Mind	1976	$4
❏ 40582	Steppin' Out/I Let You Walk Away	1976	$4
❏ 40426	That's When the Music Takes Me/Standing on the Inside	1975	$4
❏ 40370	The Immigrant/Hey Mister Sunshine	1975	$4

— No mention of John Lennon on label

Number	Title	Yr	NM
❏ 40370	The Immigrant/Hey Mister Sunshine	1975	$10

— With "Dedicated to John Lennon" under title in bold

SGC

Number	Title	Yr	NM
❏ 005	Star-Crossed Lovers/We Had a Good Thing Going	1969	$6

7-Inch Extended Plays

RCA VICTOR

Number	Title	Yr	NM
❏ EPA-4334 [PS]	I Go Ape	1959	$70
❏ EPA-4334	I Go Ape/All I Need Is You// Stop! You're Knocking Me Out/I Belong to You	1959	$70
❏ LPC-135 [PS]	Little Devil	1961	$60
❏ LPC-135	Little Devil/Circulate// Calendar Girl/We Kiss in a Shadow	1961	$60

— Compact Double 33" with small hole

Number	Title	Yr	NM
❏ EPA-4353 [PS]	Oh! Carol	1959	$75
❏ EPA-4353	Oh! Carol/Going Home to Mary Lou//The Girl for Me/I Ain't Hurtin' No More	1959	$75
❏ LPC-105	Oh! Carol/Stairway to Heaven//The Diary/ Run Samson Run	1961	$60

— Compact Double 33" with small hole

SEEDS, THE
Also see SKY SAXON.

GNP CRESCENDO

Number	Title	Yr	NM
❏ 394	A Thousand Shadows/ March of the Flower Children	1967	$8
❏ 394 [PS]	A Thousand Shadows/ March of the Flower Children	1967	$30
❏ 354	Can't Seem to Make You Mine/Daisy Mae	1965	$20
❏ 354	Can't Seem to Make You Mine/I Tell Myself	1967	$10
❏ 354 [PS]	Can't Seem to Make You Mine/I Tell Myself	1967	$60
❏ 422	Fallin' Off the Edge of My Mind/Wild Blood	1969	$10
❏ 383	Mr. Farmer/No Escape	1967	$8
❏ 383	Mr. Farmer/Up in Her Room	1967	$8
❏ 383 [PS]	Mr. Farmer/Up in Her Room	1967	$60
❏ 372	Pushin' Too Hard/ Try to Understand	1966	$20

— With "GNP Crescendo" standing alone at top of label (no box)

Number	Title	Yr	NM
❏ 372	Pushin' Too Hard/ Try to Understand	1966	$15

— With "GNP Crescendo" in box at top of label

Number	Title	Yr	NM
❏ 408	Satisfy You/900 Million People Daily	1968	$8
❏ 370	The Other Place/ Try to Understand	1966	$20
❏ 398	The Wind Blows Your Hair/Six Dreams	1967	$8

MGM

Number	Title	Yr	NM
❏ 14190	Did He Die/Love in a Summer Blanket	1970	$30
❏ 14163	Wish Me Up/Bad Part of Town	1970	$30

PHILCO-FORD

Number	Title	Yr	NM
❏ HP-26	Pushin' Too Hard/Can't Seem to Make You Mine	1968	$30

— 4-inch plastic "Hip Pocket Record" with color sleeve

SEEGER, PETE

COLUMBIA

Number	Title	Yr	NM
❏ 43699	Draft Dodger Rag/ Guantanamera	1966	$8
❏ 43349	Healing River/ Johnny Give Me	1965	$8
❏ 42940	Little Boxes/Mail Myself to You	1963	$8
❏ 44273	Waist Deep in the Big Muddy/Down by the Riverside	1967	$8

FOLKWAYS

Number	Title	Yr	NM
❏ 45-201	The Battle of New Orleans/ My Home's Across the Smokey Mountains	1959	$15

SEEKERS, THE

ATMOS

Number	Title	Yr	NM
❏ 711	Myra (Shake Up the Party)/Wild Rover	1965	$30

CAPITOL

Number	Title	Yr	NM
❏ 5430	A World of Our Own/ Sinner Man	1965	$15
❏ 5430 [PS]	A World of Our Own/ Sinner Man	1965	$30
❏ 5756	Georgy Girl/When the Stars Begin to Fall	1966	$15
❏ 5383	I'll Never Find Another You/Open Up Them Pearly Gates	1965	$15
❏ 5974	I Wish You Could Be Here/ On the Other Side	1967	$10
❏ 2122	Love Is Kind, Love Is Wine/ All I Can Remember	1968	$10
❏ 5787	Morningtown Ride/ Walk with Me	1967	$10
❏ 5622	Some Day, One Day/ Nobody Knows the Trouble I've Seen	1966	$12
❏ 5531	The Carnival Is Over/We Shall Not Be Moved	1965	$12
❏ 2013	When the Good Apples Fall/ Myra (Shake Up the Party)	1967	$10

CAPITOL CREATIVE PRODUCTS

Number	Title	Yr	NM
❏ 50 [DJ]	Island of Dreams/Breaking My Back -- Instead of Using My Mind	1966	$20

— B-side by Lou Rawls

Number	Title	Yr	NM
❏ 50 [PS]	Island of Dreams/Breaking My Back -- Instead of Using My Mind	1966	$30

— Custom sleeve; no titles or artist, but "#50" is at right and "Capitol has specially produced this record for Frito-Lay" is under the center hole

MARVEL

Number	Title	Yr	NM
❏ 1060	Chilly Winds/The Light from the Lighthouse	1965	$20

SEELY, JEANNIE

CHALLENGE

Number	Title	Yr	NM
❏ 59298	Bring It On Back/ World Without You	1965	$10
❏ 59274	If I Can't Have You/Old Memories Never Die	1965	$10
❏ 59308	Today Is Not the Day/ Please Release Me	1965	$10

COLUMBIA

Number	Title	Yr	NM
❏ 3-10664	Take Me to Bed/ Until You Have To	1978	$5
❏ 3-10550	We're Still Hangin' In There Ain't We Jessi/I Don't Need Love Anymore	1977	$5

DECCA

Number	Title	Yr	NM
❏ 33042	Farm in Pennsyltucky/ Between the King and I	1973	$6

MCA

Number	Title	Yr	NM
❏ 40074	Can I Sleep in Your Arms/ He'll Love the One He's With	1973	$5
❏ 40287	He Can Be Mine/So Was He	1974	$5
❏ 40428	How Big a Fire/ Take My Hand	1975	$5
❏ 40372	If I Had the Chance/ First Time	1975	$5
❏ 40225	I Miss You/I'd Do As Much for You	1974	$5
❏ 40162	Lucky Ladies/Hold Me	1973	$5
❏ 40528	Since I Met You Boy/ Home to Him	1976	$5

MONUMENT

Number	Title	Yr	NM
❏ 987	A Wanderin' Man/Darling Are You Ever Coming Home	1966	$8
❏ 933	Don't Touch Me/You Tied Tin Cans to My Heart	1966	$8
❏ 1075	How Is He?/A Little Unfair	1968	$8
❏ 1029	I'll Love You More (Than You Need)/Enough to Lie	1967	$8
❏ 965	It's Only Love/Then Go Home to Her	1966	$8
❏ 1100	Little Things/My Love Dies Hard	1968	$8
❏ 1011	These Memories/Funny Way of Laughin'	1967	$8
❏ 1054	Welcome Home to Nothing/ Maybe I Should Leave	1968	$8
❏ 999	When It's Over/I'd Be Just As Lonely There	1967	$8

SEEVERS, LES

DECCA

Number	Title	Yr	NM
❏ 32363	My Conscience/Lily	1968	$8
❏ 32434	What Kind of Magic/ Stop, Look, Surrender	1969	$8

EVENT

Number	Title	Yr	NM
❏ 4291	Wooden Angel/Something Old, Something New	1959	$30

SEGER, BOB

ABKCO

Number	Title	Yr	NM
❏ 4016	Chain Smokin'/ Persecution Smith	1973	$6
❏ 4015	East Side Story/ East Side Sound	1973	$6
❏ 4017	Heavy Music - Pt. I/ Heavy Music - Pt. II	1973	$6
❏ 4031	Heavy Music - Pt. I/ Heavy Music - Pt. II	1973	$5

CAMEO

Number	Title	Yr	NM
❏ 465	Chain Smokin'/ Persecution Smith	1967	$30
❏ 438	East Side Story/ East Side Sound	1966	$30
❏ 494	Heavy Music/Heavy Music (Part 2)	1967	$30
❏ 444	Sock It To Me, Santa/ Florida Time	1966	$40

CAPITOL

Number	Title	Yr	NM
❏ 2143	2 + 2 = ?/Death Row	1968	$20
❏ 4863	Against the Wind/ No Man's Land	1980	$4
❏ 4863 [PS]	Against the Wind/ No Man's Land	1980	$6
❏ B-5532	American Storm/ Fortunate Son	1986	$3
❏ B-5532 [PS]	American Storm/ Fortunate Son	1986	$3
❏ 4062	Beautiful Loser/Fine Memory	1975	$5
❏ 4300	Beautiful Loser/Travelin' Man	1976	$5
❏ B-5213	Even Now/Little Victories	1983	$3
❏ B-5213 [PS]	Even Now/Little Victories	1983	$4
❏ A-5077	Feel Like a Number/ Hollywood Nights	1981	$4
❏ A-5077 [PS]	Feel Like a Number/ Hollywood Nights	1981	$5
❏ 4836	Fire Lake/Long Twin Silver Line	1980	$4
❏ 4836 [PS]	Fire Lake/Long Twin Silver Line	1980	$6
❏ 4618	Hollywood Nights/ Brave Strangers	1978	$4
❏ B-5623	It's You/The Aftermath (12" Remix)	1986	$3
❏ B-5623 [PS]	It's You/The Aftermath (12" Remix)	1986	$3
❏ 2480	Ivory/The Lost Song (Love Needs to Be Loved)	1969	$8
❏ B-5592	Like a Rock/Livin' Inside My Heart	1986	$3
❏ B-5592 [PS]	Like a Rock/Livin' Inside My Heart	1986	$3
❏ 2640	Lonely Man/ Innervenus Eyes	1970	$8
❏ 3187	Lookin' Back/Highway Child	1971	$8
❏ 2748	Lucifer/Big River	1970	$8
❏ 4422	Mainstreet/Jody Girl	1977	$4
❏ B-5658	Miami/Somewhere Tonight	1986	$3
❏ B-5658 [PS]	Miami/Somewhere Tonight	1986	$30

— May only have been released in the New York metro area, as it quotes reviewers from four different New York newspapers

Number	Title	Yr	NM
❏ 4702	Old Time Rock and Roll/Sunspot Baby	1979	$4
❏ 4702 [PS]	Old Time Rock and Roll/Sunspot Baby	1979	$6
❏ B-5276	Old Time Rock and Roll/Till It Shines	1983	$3
❏ B-5276 [PS]	Old Time Rock and Roll/Till It Shines	1983	$5
❏ B-5187	Shame on the Moon/ House Behind a House	1982	$3
❏ B-5187 [PS]	Shame on the Moon/ House Behind a House	1982	$4
❏ 4581	Still the Same/Feel Like a Number	1978	$4
❏ 4951	The Horizontal Bop/Her Strut	1980	$5
❏ 4951 [PS]	The Horizontal Bop/Her Strut	1980	$125
❏ SPRO8433 [DJ]	Travelin' Man/Beautiful Loser	1976	$10
❏ SPRO8433 [DJ]	Travelin' Man/Beautiful Loser	1976	$10
❏ A-5042	Tryin' to Live My Life Without You/Brave Strangers	1981	$3
❏ A-5042 [PS]	Tryin' to Live My Life Without You/Brave Strangers	1981	$4
❏ 4653	We've Got Tonite/ Ain't Got No Money	1978	$4
❏ 4653 [PS]	We've Got Tonite/ Ain't Got No Money	1978	$6
❏ 4653 [DJ]	We've Got Tonite (mono/stereo)	1978	$10

— Silver vinyl

HIDEOUT

Number	Title	Yr	NM
❏ 1014	Chain Smokin'/ Persecution Smith	1966	$60
❏ 1013	East Side Story/ East Side Sound	1966	$60

MCA

Number	Title	Yr	NM
❏ 53094	Shakedown/The Aftermath	1987	$3
❏ 53094 [PS]	Shakedown/The Aftermath	1987	$4

— Picture of Bob Seger on front cover

Number	Title	Yr	NM
❏ 53094 [PS]	Shakedown/The Aftermath	1987	$20

— Picture of Eddie Murphy as Axel Foley on front cover

PALLADIUM

Number	Title	Yr	NM
❏ 1205	Get Out of Denver/ Long Song Comin'	1974	$10
❏ 1079	If I Were a Carpenter/ Jesse James	1972	$10

Number	Title	Yr	NM
❏ 1316	This Ole House/U.M.C.	1974	$20
❏ 1117	Turn On Your Love Light/ Who Do You Love?	1972	$10

REPRISE

Number	Title	Yr	NM
❏ PRO571 [DJ]	Midnight Rider (same on both sides)	1972	$20
❏ PRO571 [DJ]	Midnight Rider (same on both sides)	1972	$20

SEGO BROTHERS AND NAOMI, THE
SONGS OF FAITH

Number	Title	Yr	NM
❏ 8032	Sorry I Never Knew You/ Since I Got This Feeling	1963	$20

SEIZURE
REGRESSIVE

Number	Title	Yr	NM
❏ 53667	Cutie's Wrong Now/Frontline	1978	$30

—*Not issued with picture sleeve*

SELECTIONS, THE
ANTONE

Number	Title	Yr	NM
❏ 101	Guardian Angel/ Soft and Sweet	1958	$250

MONA LEE

Number	Title	Yr	NM
❏ 129	Guardian Angel/ Soft and Sweet	1959	$70

SELF, JIMMY DEAN
NOR-VA-JAK

Number	Title	Yr	NM
❏ 1333	An Old Christmas Card/ Blue Christmas	1960	$20

SELF, MACK
PHILLIPS INT'L.

Number	Title	Yr	NM
❏ 3548	Mad at You/Willie Brown	1959	$30

SUN

Number	Title	Yr	NM
❏ 273	Easy to Love/Every Day	1957	$40

SELF, RONNIE
ABC-PARAMOUNT

Number	Title	Yr	NM
❏ 9768	Alone/Sweet Love	1956	$125
❏ 9714	Pretty Bad Blues/ Three Hearts Later	1956	$125

AMY

Number	Title	Yr	NM
❏ 11009	High on Life/The Road Keeps Winding	1968	$12

COLUMBIA

Number	Title	Yr	NM
❏ 40989	Ain't I'm a Dog/ Rocky Road Blues	1957	$50
❏ 41166	Big Blon' Baby/Date Bait	1958	$40
❏ 40875	Big Fool/Flame of Love	1957	$50
❏ 41101	Bop-A-Lena/I Ain't Going Nowhere	1958	$40
❏ 41241	Petrified/You're So Right for Me	1958	$100

DECCA

Number	Title	Yr	NM
❏ 30958	Big Town/This Must Be the Place	1959	$30
❏ 31351	Instant Man/Some Things You Can't Change	1962	$30
❏ 31131	I've Been There/So High	1960	$30
❏ 31431	Oh Me, Oh My/Past, Present and Future	1962	$30

KAPP

Number	Title	Yr	NM
❏ 546	Houdini/Bless My Broken Heart	1963	$30

7-Inch Extended Plays

COLUMBIA

Number	Title	Yr	NM
❏ B-2149 [PS]	Ain't I'm a Dog	1957	$250
❏ B-2149	(contents unknown)	1957	$250

SELF, TED
PLAID

Number	Title	Yr	NM
❏ 1000	Little Angel (Come Rock Me to Sleep)/Walk Her Down the Aisle	1960	$30

—*Number also listed as "115"; we're not sure which is correct, or if perhaps both are correct!*

SELLERS, PETER, AND SOPHIA LOREN
CAPITOL

Number	Title	Yr	NM
❏ 4505	Bangers and Mash/ Goodness Gracious Me	1961	$15

SELLERS, PETER
CAPITOL

Number	Title	Yr	NM
❏ 5580	A Hard Day's Night/Help	1966	$20
❏ F4159	I'm So Ashamed/A Drop of the Hard Stuff	1959	$15

UNITED ARTISTS

Number	Title	Yr	NM
❏ X1221	Thank Heaven for Little Girls/Singin' in the Rain	1978	$10

—*As "Inspector Clouseau*

SEMI-COLONS, THE
CAMEO

Number	Title	Yr	NM
❏ 468	Beachcomber/Set Aside	1967	$30

SENATOR BOBBY
PARKWAY

Number	Title	Yr	NM
❏ 137	Mellow Yellow/ White Christmas	1967	$10

—*A-side by "Senator Bobby & Senator McKinley"; B-side by "Bobby the Poet" (Dylan impersonation)*

Number	Title	Yr	NM
❏ 150	The Congressional Record/ The Hardly Worthit Melody	1967	$12

— *By The Hardly Worthit Players*

Number	Title	Yr	NM
❏ 127	Wild Thing/Wild Thing	1966	$15

—*B-side by "Senator McKinley*

RCA VICTOR

Number	Title	Yr	NM
❏ 47-9522	Sock It To Me, Bobby/ Sock It To Me, Baby	1968	$12

— *B-side by the Bobby Sockers*

SENATORS, THE (1)
ABC-PARAMOUNT

Number	Title	Yr	NM
❏ 10178	There's a New Man in the White House/A Sing-Along Song	1961	$20

SENATORS, THE (2)
GOLDEN CREST

Number	Title	Yr	NM
❏ 514	Loretta/Poor Little Puppet	1958	$200

SENATORS, THE (3)
BRISTOL

Number	Title	Yr	NM
❏ 1916	Scheming/Tafu	1959	$400

WINN

Number	Title	Yr	NM
❏ 1917	Wedding Bells/I Shouldn't Care	1962	$250

SENIORS, THE (2)
DECCA

Number	Title	Yr	NM
❏ 31112	I've Lived Before/ Hello Mr. Robin	1960	$30
❏ 31244	When I Fall in Love/ Baby, Say the Word	1961	$30

SENIORS, THE (3)
EXCELLO

Number	Title	Yr	NM
❏ 2130	Why Did You Leave Me/Sloo Foot Soo	1958	$50

TETRA

Number	Title	Yr	NM
❏ 4446	Evening Shadows Falling (I Think of You)/I've Got Plenty of Love	1956	$200

SENIORS, THE (U)
ESV

Number	Title	Yr	NM
❏ 1016	Ah Sweet Mystery of Love/Rock and Rolly	1960	$30

KENT

Number	Title	Yr	NM
❏ 342	Hully Gully Fever/ Pitter Patter Heart	1960	$30

TAMPA

Number	Title	Yr	NM
❏ 163	Who's Gonna Know/ It's Been a Long Time	1959	$50

SENORS, THE
SUE

Number	Title	Yr	NM
❏ 756	May I Have This Dance/ Searching for Olive Oil	1962	$60

SENSATIONAL EPICS, THE
CAMEO

Number	Title	Yr	NM
❏ 450	I've Been Hurt/It's a Gas	1967	$30

CAPITOL

Number	Title	Yr	NM
❏ 2381	All My Hard Times/ Play It by Ear	1969	$20

WARNER BROS.

Number	Title	Yr	NM
❏ 7168	Be Young, Be Foolish, Be Happy/You Warp My Mind Girl	1968	$20

SENSATIONS OF LONDON, THE
YORK

Number	Title	Yr	NM
❏ 406	Look at My Baby/What a Wonderful Feeling	1966	$20

SENSATIONS, THE
ARGO

Number	Title	Yr	NM
❏ 5405	Let Me In/Oh Yes I'll Be True	1961	$15

— *Brown label*

Number	Title	Yr	NM
❏ 5405	Let Me In/Oh Yes I'll Be True	1961	$30

— *Black label*

Number	Title	Yr	NM
❏ 5391	Music, Music, Music/A Part of Me	1961	$10
❏ 5420	Party Across the Hall/ No Changes	1962	$12

— *By "Yvonne Baker and the Sensations*

Number	Title	Yr	NM
❏ 5412	That's My Desire/Eyes	1962	$12

— *By "Yvonne Baker and the Sensations*

Number	Title	Yr	NM
❏ 5446	When My Lover Comes Home/Father Dear	1963	$10

— *By "Yvonne Baker and the Sensations*

ATCO

Number	Title	Yr	NM
❏ 6075	Cry Baby Cry/My Heart Cries for You	1956	$50
❏ 6083	Little Wallflower/Such a Love	1957	$50
❏ 6090	My Debut to Love/You Made Me Love You	1957	$50
❏ 6067	Please Mr. Disc Jockey/ Ain't He Sweet	1956	$50

JUNIOR

Number	Title	Yr	NM
❏ 1010	I Can't Change/Mend the Torn Pieces	1964	$15
❏ 1002	We Were Meant to Be/ It's Good Enough for Me	1963	$15
❏ 1021	We Were Meant to Be/ It's Good Enough for Me	1964	$15

SENTIMENTALS, THE
CHECKER

Number	Title	Yr	NM
❏ 875	I Want to Love You/ Teenie Teenager	1957	$50

CORAL

Number	Title	Yr	NM
❏ 62172	Deep Down in My Heart/ Two Different Worlds	1960	$30
❏ 62100	We Three/ Understanding Love	1959	$30
❏ 803	I'm Your Fool, Always/ Rock Me, Mama	1958	$50
❏ 801	I Want to Love You/ Tommie Teenager	1957	$60
❏ 802	Sunday Kind of Love/ Wedding Bells	1957	$50

VANITY

Number	Title	Yr	NM
❏ 589	Love Is a Gamble/ If It Isn't for You	1959	$30

SENTINALS, THE
DEL-FI

Number	Title	Yr	NM
❏ 4197	Big Surf/Sunset Beach	1963	$40

ERA

Number	Title	Yr	NM
❏ 3097	Christmas Eve/Latin Soul	1962	$40
❏ 3117	Infinity/Encinada	1963	$40

— *As "The Sentinal Six*

Number	Title	Yr	NM
❏ 3082	Torchula/Latin'ia	1962	$40

POINT

Number	Title	Yr	NM
❏ 5101	Blue Booze/Bony Moronie	1962	$60
❏ 5100	The Bee/Over You	1963	$60

WCEB

Number	Title	Yr	NM
❏ 23	Torchula/Latin'ia	1962	$60

WESTCO

Number	Title	Yr	NM
❏ 12	I've Been Blue/Hit the Road	1964	$40
❏ 14	Tell Me/Hit the Road	1964	$40

SEQUINS, THE
A&M

Number	Title	Yr	NM
❏ 761	I'll Be Satisfied/Who Says You Can't Jerk to the Old Time Music	1965	$15

CAMEO

Number	Title	Yr	NM
❏ 161	To Be Young/The Mountains	1959	$30

GOLD STAR

Number	Title	Yr	NM
❏ 101	Hey Romeo/I've Got to Overcome	1970	$6

RED ROBIN

Number	Title	Yr	NM
❏ 140	Why Can't You Treat Me Right/Don't Fall in Love	1956	$400

TERRACE

Number	Title	Yr	NM
❏ 7515	Hideaway/I Ain't Gonna Cry (No More)	1963	$20
❏ 7511	Love Me Forever/ You're Dancing Now	1962	$20

SERENADERS, THE (1)
CHOCK FULL O' HITS

Number	Title	Yr	NM
❏ 102	Dance Darling, Dance/ Give Me a Girl	1957	$200
❏ 101	I Wrote a Letter/ Never Let Me Go	1957	$300

MGM

Number	Title	Yr	NM
❏ 12666	Dance Darling, Dance/ Give Me a Girl	1958	$120
❏ 12623	I Wrote a Letter/ Never Let Me Go	1958	$125

MOTOWN

Number	Title	Yr	NM
❏ 1046	If Your Heart Says Yes/I'll Cry Tomorrow	1963	$2000

— *VG 1000; VG+ 1500*

Number	Title	Yr	NM
RAE COX			
❏ 101	Gotta Go to School/My Girl Flip-Flop	1959	$70
RIVERSIDE			
❏ 4549	Adios, My Love/Two Lovers Make One Fool	1963	$125
V.I.P.			
❏ 25002	If Your Heart Says Yes/I'll Cry Tomorrow	1964	$125
SERENADERS, THE (2)			
CORAL			
❏ 60720	It's Funny/Confession Is Good for the Soul	1952	$300
❏ 65093	Misery/But I Forgive You	1952	$300
DELUXE			
❏ 6022	Please, Please Forgive Me/Baby	1953	$500
JVB			
❏ 2001	Tomorrow Night/Why Don't You Do Right	1952	$400
RED ROBIN			
❏ 115	Will She Know?/I Want to Love You Baby	1953	$1500
SWING TIME			
❏ 347	M-A-Y-B-E-L-L/Ain't Gonna Cry No More	1954	$1200
SERENADERS, THE (3)			
HANOVER			
❏ 4514	Alaska/Where Did You Go	1959	$20
❏ 4507	Honolulu/Summer Job	1959	$20
SERENADERS, THE (U)			
TEEN LIFE			
❏ 9	Love Me Now/Gates of Gold	1958	$700
SERENADETTS, THE			
ENRICA			
❏ 1008	Boyfriend/The Big Night	1961	$15
SERIOUS BROTHERS, THE			
TUNE TOWN			
❏ 101	It's Another Joyful Elvis Presley Christmas/(B-side unknown)	1988	$15
SERRATT, HOWARD			
SUN			
❏ 198	I Must Be Saved/Troublesome Waters	1954	$2000
SESSIONS, RONNIE			
COMPLEAT			
❏ 161	I Bought the Shoes That Just Walked Out on Me/You're a Real Live Wire	1986	$5
❏ 167	If I Owned a Honky Tonk/You Can't Keep a Good Love Down	1987	$5
MCA			
❏ 40758	Ambush/Victim of Life's Circumstances	1977	$5
❏ 40875	Cash on the Barrelhead/Lucy, Ain't Your Loser Lookin' Good	1978	$5
❏ 40326	Cry/Poor Little Rich Girl	1974	$5
❏ 41038	Do You Want to Fly/Hold On to Your Hiney	1979	$5
❏ 41142	Honky Tonkin'/Come By Here	1979	$5
❏ 40831	I Like to Be with You/Sweet Annette	1977	$5
❏ 40917	I Never Go Around Mirrors/Whole Lotta Hound	1978	$5
❏ 40411	Lonesome Almost Always Feels the Same/Love Hangover	1975	$5
❏ 40462	Makin' Love/Messin' Around	1975	$5
❏ 40705	Me and Millie (Stompin' Grapes and Gettin' Silly)/The Losing End	1977	$5
❏ 40581	Support Your Local Honky Tonks/Showdown	1976	$5
❏ 40624	Wiggle Wiggle/Baby Please Don't Stone Me Anymore	1976	$5
MGM			
❏ 14619	If That Back Door Could Talk/My Love Is Deep, My Love Is Wide	1973	$6
❏ 14712	My Rockin' Days/You Say the Sweetest Things	1974	$6
—With Patti Tierney			
❏ 14528	She Feels So Good I Hate to Put Her Down/We May Never Get This Close Again	1973	$6
❏ 14445	Tossin' and Turnin'/Knock and Ring and Tap	1972	$6

Number	Title	Yr	NM
❏ 14482	Wrap Your Tender Love All Around Me/Christine Loves a Loser	1973	$6
PIKE			
❏ 5904	Bunny Rabbit (Without Any Tail)/Mommy's Japanese	1961	$30
—As "Little Ronnie Sessions			
REPUBLIC			
❏ 1412	More Than Satisfied/Sad But It's True	1970	$8
❏ 1401	My Daddy Was a Guitar Man/Walkin' Down the Road	1969	$8
SETTLERS, THE			
HICKORY			
❏ 1451	Early Morning Rain/Do You Wanna Know the Reason	1967	$8
SETZER, BRIAN			
Guitarist formerly with rockabilly revival band Stray Cats, Setzer helped spur the late-1990s "swing" revival.			
EMI AMERICA			
❏ B-8320	Boulevard of Broken Dreams/Keep Your Lovin' Strong	1986	$4
❏ B-8320 [PS]	Boulevard of Broken Dreams/Keep Your Lovin' Strong	1986	$4
❏ B-8336	Chains Around Your Heart/Three Guys	1986	$8
SEVEN OF US			
RED BIRD			
❏ Oct-0069	The Way to Your Heart/How Could You	1966	$40
SEVEN SOULS, THE			
OKEH			
❏ 4-7289	I Still Love You/I'm No Stranger	1967	$500
VENTURE			
❏ 614	Groovin' In/Got to Find a Way	1968	$50
SEVILLE, DAVID			
LIBERTY			
❏ 55041	Armen's Theme/Carousel in Rome	1956	$30
❏ 55113	Bagdad Express/Starlight, Starbright	1957	$30
❏ 55124	Bonjour Tristesse/Dance from Bonjour Tristesse	1958	$30
❏ 55079	Camel Rock/Gotta Get to Your House	1957	$30
❏ 55079 [PS]	Camel Rock/Gotta Get to Your House	1957	$60
❏ 55153	Little Brass Band/Take Five	1958	$30
❏ 55314	Oh Judge, Your Honor, Dear Sir, Sweetheart/Freddy, Freddy	1961	$30
❏ 55105	Pretty Dark Eyes/Cecelia	1957	$30
❏ 55140	The Bird on My Head/Hey There Moon	1958	$30
❏ 55055	The Donkey and the Schoolboy/The Gift	1957	$30
❏ 55163	The Mountain/Mr. Grape	1958	$30
❏ 55132	Witch Doctor/Don't Whistle at Me Baby	1958	$40
❏ 55272	Witch Doctor/Swanee River	1960	$30
UNITED ARTISTS			
❏ 0063	Witch Doctor/The Bird on My Head	1973	$4
—Silver Spotlight Series" reissue			
7-Inch Extended Plays			
LIBERTY			
❏ LSX-1003	(contents unknown)	1958	$50
❏ LSX-1003 [PS]	Witch Doctor	1958	$50
SEVILLES, THE			
CAL-GOLD			
❏ 172	Don't You Know I Care/(B-side unknown)	1962	$30
GALAXY			
❏ 721	Charlena/Loving You	1963	$20
❏ 727	Creation/Baby	1964	$20
❏ 717	Treat You Right/Hey, Hey, Hey	1963	$20
JC			
❏ 116	Charlena/Loving You (Is My Desire)	1960	$40
❏ 120	Fat Sally/Working Hard	1961	$30
❏ 118	Louella/Salt Mine	1961	$30
SEX PISTOLS			
Johnny Rotten would later join Public Image Ltd.			
WARNER BROS.			
❏ 8516 [DJ]	Pretty Vacant (mono/stereo)	1978	$20
❏ 8516	Pretty Vacant/Sub-Mission	1978	$30

Number	Title	Yr	NM
❏ 8516 [PS]	Pretty Vacant/Sub-Mission	1978	$20
SEX PISTOLS, THE			
WARNER BROS.			
❏ 8516 [DJ]	Pretty Vacant (mono/stereo)	1978	$20
SHA NA NA			
KAMA SUTRA			
❏ 555	Bounce in Your Buggy/Bless My Soul	1972	$6
❏ 555 [PS]	Bounce in Your Buggy/Bless My Soul	1972	$10
❏ 578 [DJ]	In the Still of the Night (mono/stereo)	1973	$20
—As "Eddie and the Evergreens"; may be promo only			
❏ 560	In the Still of the Night/Sea Cruise	1972	$5
❏ 503	Lovers Never Say Goodbye/Remember Then	1970	$6
❏ 592	Maybe I'm Old Fashioned/Stroll All Night	1974	$5
❏ 592 [PS]	Maybe I'm Old Fashioned/Stroll All Night	1974	$10
❏ 522	Only One Song/Yakety Yak	1971	$6
❏ 507	Pay Day/Rock and Roll Is Here to Stay	1970	$6
❏ 604	Shanghied/Chills in My Spine	1975	$5
❏ 596	Too Chubby to Boogie/(B-side unknown)	1974	$5
❏ 528	Top Forty of the Lord/I Wonder Why	1971	$6
❏ 528 [PS]	Top Forty of the Lord/I Wonder Why	1971	$10
RSO			
❏ 930	Blue Moon/Sandy	1979	$4
—B-side by John Travolta			
SHADES OF BLUE			
IMPACT			
❏ 1026	All I Want Is Love/How Do You Save a Dying Love	1967	$30
❏ 1015	Happiness/The Night	1966	$30
❏ 1014	Lonely Summer/With This Ring	1966	$30
❏ 1007	Oh, How Happy/Little Orphan Boy	1966	$30
❏ 1028	Penny Arcade/Funny Kind of Love	1967	$30
SHADES OF JOY			
FONTANA			
❏ 1659	Soul Truth/I Do Like Rock	1969	$12
SHADES, THE			
ALADDIN			
❏ 3453	Dear Lori/One Touch of Heaven	1959	$300
AOK			
❏ 1028	Ginger Bread Man/The Hip	1967	$40
BIG TOP			
❏ 3003	Sun Glasses/Undivided Attention	1958	$125
—B-side by The Knott Sisters			
SHADOWS OF KNIGHT, THE			
ATCO			
❏ 6634	Gloria '69/A Spaniard at My Door	1968	$20
❏ 6776	I Am the Hunter/Warwick County Affair	1970	$20
DUNWICH			
❏ 128	Bad Little Woman/Gospel Zone	1966	$20
❏ 128 [PS]	Bad Little Woman/Gospel Zone	1966	$200
❏ 116	Gloria/Dark Side	1966	$30
—Gold label, no mention of Atco Records			
❏ 116	Gloria/Dark Side	1966	$30
—Yellow label, "Distributed by Atco Record Sales Co.			
❏ 116	Gloria/Dark Side	1966	$20
—Dark pink and yellow label; other label variations may exist			
❏ 141	I'm Gonna Make You Mine/I'll Make You Sorry	1966	$30
❏ 122	Oh Yeah/Light Bulb Blues	1966	$30
❏ 122 [PS]	Oh Yeah/Light Bulb Blues	1966	$40
❏ 167	Someone Like Me/There for Love	1967	$30
❏ 151	The Behemoth/Willie Jean	1967	$30
PHONOGRAPH			
❏ 1002/2001	Sweetness in Motion/Nikki-Hoki (No One Else Will Ever Do)	1986	$8
SUPER K			
❏ 108	Taurus/My Fire Department Needs a Fireman	1969	$10

Number	Title	Yr	NM
TEAM			
❏ 520	Shake/From Way Out to Way In	1968	$20
SHADOWS, THE (1)			
ABC-PARAMOUNT			
❏ 10138	Apache/Quartermaster's Stores	1960	$40
❏ 10073	Saturday Dance/Lonesome Fella	1960	$40
ATLANTIC			
❏ 2177	Dance On/The Rumble	1963	$30
❏ 2111	FBI/The Frightened City	1961	$30
❏ 2166	Guitar Tango/What a Lovely Thing	1962	$30
❏ 2235	Theme for Young Lovers/The Rise and Fall of Flingel Bunt	1964	$30
❏ 2146	Wonderful Land/Stars Fell on Stockton	1962	$30
CAPITOL			
❏ F-4270	Driftin'/Jet Black	1959	$50
— As "The Four Jets			
❏ F-4220	Feelin' Fine/Don't Be a Fool	1959	$50
— As "The Drifters			
EPIC			
❏ 9848	Don't Make My Baby Blue/My Grandfather's Clock	1965	$30
❏ 10020	I Met a Girl/Last Night Set	1966	$30
❏ 9793	Mary Anne/Chu Chi	1965	$30
❏ 9826	Stingray/Alice in Sunderland	1965	$30
SHADOWS, THE (2)			
DECCA			
❏ 48322	Big Mouth Mama/Better Than Gold	1954	$300
❏ 48307	Tell Her/Don't Be Bashful	1954	$300
SHADOWS, THE (4)			
DOTTIE			
❏ 1006	I Wonder Why/Tell This Lonely Heart Goodbye	1961	$30
SHADOWS, THE (U)			
DELTA			
❏ 1509	Bop-A-Lena/There Stands the Glass	1958	$200
SHAFTO, BOBBY			
RUST			
❏ 5096	Baby Then/How Could You Do a Thing Like That to Me	1965	$12
❏ 5092	I'll Never Get Over You/Who Wouldn't Love a Girl Like That	1964	$10
❏ 5108	Lonely Is As Lonely Does/The Same Old Room	1966	$15
❏ 5110	See Me Cry/A Little Like You	1966	$10
❏ 5082	She's My Girl/Wonderful You	1964	$10
SHAG, THE			
CAPITOL			
❏ 5995	Stop and Listen/Melissa	1967	$50
SHAGGS, THE (1)			
CAPITOL			
❏ 2511	Mean Woman Blues/She Makes Me Happy	1969	$10
SHAGGY BOYS, THE			
RED BIRD			
❏ Oct-0074	Stop the Clock/In the Morning	1966	$20
UNITED ARTISTS			
❏ 50135	That's the Only Way/Behind These Stained Glass Windows	1967	$20
SHAGS, THE			
CAMEO			
❏ 470	Tell Me/As Long As I Have You	1967	$30
GOLDEN VOICE			
❏ 3114 [PS]	Talk to a Sidewalk/Did I Say (That I Love You)	1967	$80
❏ 3114	Talk to a Sidewalk/Did I Say (That I Love You)	1967	$30
❏ 3112 [PS]	What Am I to Do/It Ain't Easy	1967	$80
❏ 3112	What Am I to Do/It Ain't Easy	1967	$30
KAYDEN			
❏ 408	Breathe in My Ear/Easy Street	1966	$30
❏ 407	Tell Me/As Long As I Have You	1966	$50
LAURIE			
❏ 3353	I Call Your Name/Hide Away	1966	$30

Number	Title	Yr	NM
TAURUS			
❏ 1881	Don't Press Your Luck/Hey Little Girl	1967	$200
SHAKERS, THE			
ABC			
❏ 10960	Love, Love, Love/One Wonderful Moment	1967	$8
AUDIO FIDELITY			
❏ 119	Break It All/Ticket to Ride	1966	$10
SHAKEY JAKE			
BLUESVILLE			
❏ 807	My Foolish Heart/Jake's Blues	1960	$30
SHAM-ETTES, THE			
MGM			
❏ 13618	Big Bad Wolf (Hey There)/I'd Rather Have You	1966	$20
❏ 13798	He'll Come Back/You're Welcome Back	1967	$15
SHANE, BOB			
DECCA			
❏ 32275	Honey/I Don't Think of You Anymore	1968	$12
❏ 32239	Simple Gifts/Weeping Annaleah	1967	$10
SHANGRI-LAS, THE			
MERCURY			
❏ 72670	Footsteps on the Roof/Take the Time	1967	$30
❏ 72645	I'll Never Learn/Sweet Sounds of Summer	1966	$30
RED BIRD			
❏ Oct-0018	Give Him a Great Big Kiss/Twist and Shout	1964	$30
❏ Oct-0030	Give Us Your Blessings/Heaven Only Knows	1965	$30
❏ Oct-0053	He Cried/Dressed in Black	1966	$30
❏ Oct-0043	I Can Never Go Home Anymore/Bull Dog	1965	$30
❏ Oct-0043	I Can Never Go Home Anymore/Sophisticated Boom Boom	1965	$40
❏ Oct-0014	Leader of the Pack/What Is Love	1964	$30
❏ Oct-0048	Long Live Our Love/Bull Dog	1966	$30
❏ Oct-0048	Long Live Our Love/Sophisticated Boom Boom	1966	$30
❏ Oct-0019	Maybe/Shout	1964	$30
❏ Oct-0025	Out in the Streets/The Boy	1965	$30
❏ Oct-0068	Past, Present and Future/Love You More Than Yesterday	1966	$30
❏ Oct-0068	Past, Present and Future/Paradise	1966	$30
SCEPTER			
❏ 1291	Wishing Well/Hate to Say I Told You So	1964	$30
SMASH			
❏ 1866	Simon Says/Simon Speaks	1963	$50
SPOKANE			
❏ 4006	Wishing Well/Hate to Say I Told You So	1964	$40
SHANK AND MAYDIEA			
FLIP			
❏ 361	Why Don't You Tell Me/Bye Bye Baby (My Pride)	1962	$10
SHANK, BUD			
PACIFIC JAZZ			
❏ 88156	Let It Be/Something	1970	$5
❏ 88131	Sidewinder/Time for Love	1966	$8
❏ 320	The Awakening/New Groove	1961	$12
WORLD PACIFIC			
❏ 370	Brassamba/Little Boat	1963	$8
❏ 77824	California Dreamin'/Woman	1966	$6
❏ 410	Don't Think Twice/Freight Train	1964	$8
❏ 77885	I Am the Walrus/Sounds of Silence	1968	$6
❏ 77814	Michelle/I Will Wait for You	1966	$6
❏ 364	Misty/Joao	1963	$8
❏ 77842	Summer Samba (So Nice)/Monday, Monday	1966	$6
❏ 77893	There's Got to Be a Better Way (Theme from Bandolero)/Tour D'Amour	1968	$6
SHANKAR, RAVI			
DARK HORSE			
❏ 10001	I Am Missing You/Lost	1974	$5

Number	Title	Yr	NM
SPARK			
❏ SP-07	Transmigration/(B-side unknown)	1973	$6
— As "R. Shankar			
WORLD PACIFIC			
❏ 77898	Charly Theme/Love Montage	1968	$8
❏ 77871	Pather Panchali/Gat Kirawani	1967	$8
SHANNON, DEL			
ABC DUNHILL			
❏ 4224	Sister Isabelle/Colorado Rain	1970	$20
❏ 4193	Sweet Mary Lou/Comin' Back to me	1969	$20
AMY			
❏ 911	Do You Want to Dance/This Is All I Have to Give	1964	$20
❏ 905	Handy Man/Give Her Lots of Lovin'	1964	$20
❏ 947	I Can't Believe My Ears/I Wish I Wasn't Me Tonight	1966	$50
— Withdrawn shortly after release; promos worth about half these values			
❏ 897	Mary Jane/Stains on My Letter	1964	$30
❏ 937	Move It On Over/She Still Remembers Tony	1965	$20
❏ 919	Stranger in Town/Over You	1965	$20
❏ 925	Why Don't You Tell Him/Break Up	1965	$20
BERLEE			
❏ 501	Sue's Gotta Be Mine/Now She's Gone	1963	$20
❏ 502	That's the Way Love Is/Time of the Day	1964	$20
BIG TOP			
❏ 3112	Cry Myself to Sleep/I'm Gonna Move On	1962	$30
❏ 3152	From Me to You/Two Silhouettes	1963	$70
— A-side is the first American version of a Beatles song			
❏ 3098	Ginny in the Mirror/I Won't Be There	1962	$30
❏ 3075	Hats Off to Larry/Don't Gild the Lily, Lily	1961	$30
❏ 3091	Hey! Little Girl/I Don't Care Anymore	1961	$30
❏ 3131	Little Town Flirt/The Wamboo	1962	$30
❏ 3083	So Long Baby/The Answer to Everything	1961	$30
❏ 3117	The Swiss Maid/You Never Talked About Me	1962	$30
❏ 3143	Two Kinds of Teardrops/Kelly	1963	$30
ISLAND			
❏ 038	Cry Baby Cry/In My Arms Again	1975	$20
❏ 021	Tell Her No/Restless	1975	$20
LIBERTY			
❏ 55889	Hey Little Star/For a Little While	1966	$15
❏ 55961	Led Along/I Can't Be True	1967	$15
❏ 56036	Magical Musical Box/Gemini	1968	$10
❏ 55939	She/What Makes You Run	1967	$15
❏ 55894	Show Me/Never Thought I Could	1966	$15
❏ 55866	The Big Hurt/I Got It Bad	1966	$15
NETWORK			
❏ 47951	Sea of Love/Midnight Train	1981	$5
❏ 48006	To Love Someone/Liar	1982	$5
WARNER BROS.			
❏ 29098	In My Arms Again/You Can't Forgive Me	1985	$5
❏ 28853	Stranger on the Run/What You Gonna Do with That	1985	$5
SHANNON, KATHY			
HIT			
❏ 334	Angel of the Morning/Jumpin' Jack Flash	1968	$8
— B-side by the Jalopy Five			
❏ 296	Don't Sleep in the Subway/Jackson	1967	$8
— B-side by Jack and Sherry Young			
❏ 327	Do You Know the Way to San Jose/Cry Like a Baby	1968	$8
— B-side by the Jalopy Five			
❏ 343	Harper Valley P.T.A./Hey Jude	1968	$8
— B-side by the Jalopy Five			
❏ 298	I Take It Back/Little Bit o' Soul	1967	$8
— B-side by the Chellows			
❏ 310	It Must Be Him/The Rain, the Park, and Other Things	1967	$8
— B-side by the Flowers			
❏ 290	Love Eyes/This Is My Song	1967	$8

Number	Title	Yr	NM
❏ 303	Ode to Billie Joe/White Rabbit	1967	$8
—B-side by the Chords (2)			
❏ 353	Son-of-a-Preacher-Man/Worst That Could Happen	1969	$8
—B-side by the Chords (2)			
❏ 340	The House That Jack Built/1-2-3, Red Light	1968	$8
—B-side by the Fantastics			
❏ 323	(Theme from) Valley of the Dolls/Scarborough Fair (/Canticle)	1968	$8
—B-side by Sammy and Theodore			
❏ 346	Those Were the Days/Girl Watcher	1968	$8
—B-side by the Chords (2)			
❏ 311	To Sir with Love/Even the Bad Times Are Good	1967	$8
—B-side by the Jalopy Five			

SHANNON, PAT

AMOS
❏ 152	I Ain't Got Time Anymore/(B-side unknown)	1970	$5
❏ 163	Liar/Something's Coming My Way	1971	$5

CAPITOL
❏ 3802	Eleanor Jones/102 Times a Day	1973	$4

DECCA
❏ 31072	Everything But You/So Happy Now	1960	$15
❏ 30545	Maybelle/Knock, Knock, Who's There	1958	$15
❏ 30751	Summer's Over/We Found Love	1958	$15
❏ 30905	Summertime's Comin'/The Snake and the Bookworm	1959	$15

UNI
❏ 55191	Back to Dreamin' Again/Moody	1969	$5
❏ 55229	It's So Easy/102 Times a Day	1970	$5
❏ 55229	It's So Easy/The Story of Your Life	1970	$5

WARNER BROS.
❏ 7210	Candy Apple, Cotton Candy/She Sleeps Alone	1968	$6
❏ 7237	Here They Come Again/Run to Home	1968	$6

SHANTONS, THE

JAY-MAR
❏ 1292	The Christmas Song/Santa Claus Is Coming to Town	1960	$200
❏ 241	To Be in Love with You/Lucille	1959	$800
❏ 0(# unknown)	Triangle Love/Lover's March	1959	$400

SHAPIRO, HELEN

CAPITOL
❏ 4561	Don't Treat Me Like a Child/When I'm With You	1961	$15
❏ 4735	Tell Me What He Said/I Apologize	1962	$15
❏ 4662	Walkin' Back to Happiness/Kiss 'N' Run	1961	$15

EPIC
❏ 9549	Little Miss Lonely/Keep Away from Other Girls	1962	$15
❏ 9599	Woe Is Me/No Trespassing	1963	$15

JANUS
❏ 120	A Glass of Wine/Waiting on the Shores of Nowhere	1970	$6

MUSICOR
❏ 1075	It Might As Well Rain Until September/Shop Around	1965	$10

TOWER
❏ 346	Make Me Belong to You/The Way of the World	1967	$8

SHARMEERS, THE

RED TOP
❏ 109	A School Girl in Love/You're My Love	1958	$200

SHARMETTES, THE

KING
❏ 5648	Answer Me/My Dream	1962	$20
❏ 5686	I Want to Be Loved/Tell Me	1962	$20

SHARON MARIE

CAPITOL
❏ 5195	The Story of My Life/Thinkin' 'Bout You Baby	1964	$200
—Both these records were produced by Brian Wilson			

SHARP, DEE DEE, AND CHUBBY CHECKER

CAMEO
❏ 103 [DJ]	Do You Love Me?/One More Time	1962	$50
—Yellow label, black print, promo only			

SHARP, DEE DEE

ATCO
❏ 6502	Baby I Love You/What Am I Gonna Do	1967	$8
❏ 6445	Bye Bye Baby/My Best Friend's Man	1966	$10
❏ 6587	This Love Won't Run Out/Help Me Find My Glove	1968	$8
❏ 6557	We Got a Thing Goin' On/What 'Cha Gonna Do About It	1968	$8
—With Ben E. King			
❏ 6576	Woman Will Do Wrong/You're Just a Fool in Love	1968	$8

CAMEO
❏ 335	Deep Dark Secret/Good	1964	$500
❏ 244	Do the Bird/Lover Boy	1963	$20
❏ 244 [PS]	Do the Bird/Lover Boy	1963	$30
❏ 219	Gravy (For My Mashed Potatoes)/Baby Cakes	1962	$20
❏ 219 [PS]	Gravy (For My Mashed Potatoes)/Baby Cakes	1962	$30
❏ 375	I Really Love You/Standing in the Need of Love	1965	$10
❏ 375 [PS]	I Really Love You/Standing in the Need of Love	1965	$20
❏ 382	It's a Funny Situation/There Ain't Nothin' I Wouldn't Do for You	1965	$10
❏ 357	Let's Twine/That's What My Mama Said	1965	$12
❏ 212	Mashed Potato Time/Set My Heart at Ease	1962	$30
❏ 347	To Know Him Is to Love Him/There Ain't Nothin' I Wouldn't Do for You	1965	$10
❏ 296	Where Did I Go Wrong/Willyam, Willyam	1964	$15
❏ 296 [PS]	Where Did I Go Wrong/Willyam, Willyam	1964	$30
❏ 274	Wild!/Why Doncha Ask Me	1963	$20
❏ 274 [PS]	Wild!/Why Doncha Ask Me	1963	$30

FAIRMOUNT
❏ 1004	(It's Wonderful) The Love I Feel for You/Willyam, Wilyam	1966	$10

GAMBLE
❏ 4005	The Bottle or Me/You're Gonna Miss Me (When I'm Gone)	1969	$20
❏ 219	What Kind of Lady/You're Gonna Miss Me (When I'm Gone)	1968	$30

PHILADELPHIA INT'L.
❏ 02041	Breaking and Entering/I Love You Anyway	1981	$4
❏ 3512	Conquer the World Together/We Gotta Good Thing Goin'	1971	$6
—With Bunny Sigler			
❏ 3625	Flashback/Nobody Can Take Your Place	1977	$5
❏ 3638	I Believe in Love/Just As Long As I Know You're Mine	1978	$5
❏ 3636	I'd Really Love to See You Tonight/What Color Is Love	1977	$5
❏ 70058	I Love You Anyway/Easy Money	1981	$4
—Philadelphia International records as "Dee Dee Sharp Gamble			
❏ 3644	Tryin' to Get the Feeling Again/I Wanna Be Your Woman	1978	$5

TSOP
❏ 4776	Happy 'Bout the Whole Thing/Touch My Life	1976	$5
❏ 4778	I'm Not in Love/Make It Till Tomorrow	1976	$5

SHARPE, RAY

A&M
❏ 1297	Dream On, Donna/Another Piece of the Puzzle	1971	$5

ATCO
❏ 6402	Help Me (Get the Feeling) Part 1/Help Me (Get the Feeling) Part 2	1966	$12
❏ 6437	I Can't Take It/Mary Jane	1966	$10

DOT
❏ 15788	Oh, My Baby's Gone/That's the Way I Feel	1958	$20
❏ 15974	Oh, My Baby's Gone/That's the Way I Feel	1959	$15

GREGMARK
❏ 14	(The New) Linda Lu/The Bus Song	1963	$15

HAMILTON
❏ 50002	Oh, My Baby's Gone/That's the Way I Feel	1959	$10

JAMIE
❏ 1149	Bermuda/Gonna Let It Go This Time	1960	$20
❏ 1155	For You My Love/Red Sails in the Sunset	1960	$20
❏ 1164	Give-in Up/Kewpie Doll	1960	$20
❏ 1128	Linda Lu/Monkey's Uncle	1959	$30
❏ 1128	Linda Lu/Red Sails in the Sunset	1959	$20
❏ 1138	Long John/T.A. Blues	1959	$20

LHI
❏ 1215	Linda Lu/Monkey's Uncle	1967	$8

MONUMENT
❏ 874	Let's Go, Let's Go, Let's Go/It's Too Cold	1965	$12

SHARPS, THE

ALADDIN
❏ 3401	What Will I Gain/Shufflin'	1957	$60
❏ 3401	What Will I Gain/Shufflin'	1957	$400
—Purple vinyl			

CHESS
❏ 1690	6 Months, 3 Weeks, 2 Days/Cha-Cho Bop	1958	$40
—B-side by Jack McVea			

COMBO
❏ 146	All My Love/Look What You've Done to Me	1958	$60

DOT
❏ 15806	All My Love/Look What You've Done to Me	1958	$20

JAMIE
❏ 1108	Have Love, Will Travel/Look at Me	1958	$60
❏ 1114	Here's My Heart/Gig-A-Lene	1958	$40
❏ 1040	Sweet Sweetheart/Come On	1957	$50

LAMP
❏ 2007	Our Love Is Here to Stay/Lock My Heart	1957	$40

STAR-HI
❏ 10406	Double Clutch/If Love Is What You Want	1960	$40

TAG
❏ 2200	6 Months, 3 Weeks, 2 Days/Cha-Cho Bop	1957	$125
—B-side by Jack McVea			

VIK
❏ 0264	Sweet Sweetheart/Come On	1957	$30

WIN
❏ 702	Teenage Girl/We Three	1958	$60

SHARPTONES, THE

POST
❏ 2009	Since I Fell for You/Made to Love	1955	$400

SHATNER, WILLIAM

DECCA
❏ 32399	How Insensitive/Transformed Man	1969	$30

SHAW, ARTIE

DECCA
❏ 27243	White Christmas/Jingle Bells	1951	$20
❏ LPC-100	(contents unknown)	1961	$10
—Compact 33 Double"; small hole, plays at 33 1/3 rpm			

SHAW, JIMMY

IMPERIAL
❏ 5603	Take a Chance on Me/Big Chief Hug-Um An' Kiss-Um	1959	$30

SHAW, JOAN

JAGUAR
❏ 3010	I Want A Man For Christmas/Most Of All	1954	$15

Number	Title	Yr	NM

SHAW, JOHN, AND THE DELL-OS
U-C
❏ 5002	Why Did You Leave Me/Why Does It Have to Be Her	1957	$4000

— VG 2,000; VG+ 3,000

SHAW, MARLENA
BLUE NOTE
❏ XW366	Easy Evil/Just Don't Want to Be Lonely	1973	$5
❏ XW691	Feel Like Makin' Love/You Taught Me How to Speak in Love	1975	$5
❏ XW790	It's Better Than Walkin' Out/Be for Real	1976	$5
❏ XW209	Last Tango in Paris/(B-side unknown)	1973	$5
❏ XW844	Love Has Gone Away/This Time I'll Be Sweeter	1976	$5
❏ 1981	Somewhere/You Must Believe	1972	$6
❏ XW550	The Feeling's Good/But For Now	1974	$5

CADET
❏ 5571	Brother Where Are You/Waiting for Charlie to Come Home	1967	$8
❏ 5638	California Soul/The House That Jack Built	1969	$6
❏ 5549	Let's Wade in the Water/Show Time	1966	$8
❏ 5618	Looking Through the Eyes of Love/Anyone Can Move a Mountain	1968	$6
❏ 5656	Looking Through the Eyes of Love/California Soul	1969	$6
❏ 5592	Matchmaker, Matchmaker/A Couple of Losers	1968	$6
❏ 5557	Mercy, Mercy, Mercy/Go Away Little Boy	1967	$8
❏ 5650	Woman of the Ghetto/I'm Satisfied	1969	$6

COLUMBIA
❏ 10661	Don't Ask to Stay Until Tomorrow/No Deposit, No Return	1978	$5
❏ 10746	Dreamin'/Places	1978	$5
❏ 11034	Love Dancin'/No One Yet	1979	$15

POLYDOR
❏ 887776-7	I Want to Know/Love Is In Flight	1988	$4

SHAW, ROBERT, CHORALE
RCA VICTOR RED SEAL
❏ WDM1711 [PS]	Christmas Hymns and Carols Volume II	1952	$8

— Box for 4-record set (49-3947, 49-3948, 49-3949, 49-3950); add 50 percent if "Program Notes" are in box

❏ 49-3948	Fum, Fum, Fum-Hacia Belen Va Un Borrilo-Ya Vien La Vieja-La Virgen Lava Panales/Carol of the Birds-O Magnum Mysterium	1952	$8

— Red vinyl; "Side 2" and "Side 7" of WDM 1711

❏ 49-3947	I Saw Three Ships-O Tannenbaum-Allon, Gay Gay Bergeres-The Holly and the Ivy/What Child Is This-Masters in This Hall-Break Forth, O Beauteous Heavenly Light	1952	$8

— Red vinyl; "Side 1" and "Side 8" of "WDM 1711

❏ 49-3950	So Blest a Sight-A Virgin Unspotted-The Twelve Days of Christmas/Good King Wenceslas-The Boar's Head Carol-Christ Was Born on Christmas Day-Har Far Is It to Bethlehem	1952	$8

— Red vinyl; "Side 4" and "Side 5" of "WDM 1711

❏ 49-3949	The Cherry Tree Carol-Mary Had a Baby-How Unto Bethlehem/March of the Kings-Here, Mid the Ass and Oxen Mild-Touro-Louro-Louro	1952	$8

— Red vinyl; "Side 3" and "Side 6" of WDM 1711

❏ ERB-43 [PS]	Christmas Hymns and Carols, Volume 1 (Excerpts)	1954	$8

— Cover for 2-EP set (549-5113 and 549-5114)

❏ 549-5114	Coventry Carol-Carol of the Bells/Lo, How a Rose E'er Blooming-Go Tell It on the Mountain//O Little Town of Bethlehem-Silent Night/We Three Kings-The First Noel-Hark! The Herald Angels Sing	1954	$8

— Side 2" and "Side 3" of ERB-43

❏ 549-5113	O Come, All Ye Faithful-Luther's Cradle Hymn-God Rest You Merry, Gentlemen/Joy to the World-It Came Upon a Midnight Clear-Angels We Have Heard on High//O Come, O Come, Emanuel-I Wonder As I Wander-Echo Hymn/Wassail Song-Deck the Halls	1954	$8

— Side 1" and "Side 4" of ERB-43

SHAW, SANDIE
RCA VICTOR
❏ 74-0370	Love Is For the Two of Us/Wight Is Wight	1970	$8
❏ 47-9594	Together/One More Lie	1968	$8

REPRISE
❏ 0342	Girl Don't Come/I'd Be Far Better Off Without You	1965	$10
❏ 0427	If Ever You Need Me/How Can You Tell	1965	$10
❏ 0365	I'll Stop at Nothing/You Can't Blame Him	1965	$10
❏ 0375	Long Live Love/I've Heard About Him	1965	$10
❏ 20191	Me/Now	1963	$15

— B-side by Bob Candee

❏ 0575	Puppet on a String/I Had a Dream Last Night	1967	$10
❏ 0394	Stop Feeling Sorry for Yourself/I'll Stop at Nothing	1965	$10
❏ 0320	(There's) Always Something There to Remind Me/Don't You Know	1964	$15
❏ 0546	Think Sometime About Me/Hide All Emotion	1967	$10
❏ 0449	Tomorrow/Hurting You	1966	$10

SHAY, DOROTHY
COLUMBIA
❏ 1-450(?)	Diamonds Are a Girl's Best Friend/Little Girl from Little Rock	1949	$50

— Microgroove 33 1/3 rpm 7-inch single, small hole

❏ 1-750	Oh Them Dudes/Mr. Berlitz	1950	$50

— Microgroove 33 1/3 rpm 7-inch single, small hole

❏ 1-252(?)	Pappy's Predicament/Another Notch on Father's Shotgun	1949	$50

— Microgroove 33 1/3 rpm 7-inch single, small hole

IMPERIAL
❏ X5462	Always/Hunky Dory	1957	$15
❏ X5472	Feudin' and Fightin'/Stouthearted Men	1957	$15

SHEA, GEORGE BEVERLY
RCA VICTOR
❏ 47-6315	Christmas, Christmas/Sleep Precious Babe	1955	$20
❏ 47-8123	Greenwillow Christmas/He Is No Stranger	1962	$15
❏ 47-5411	I Wonder As I Wander/There's a Song in the Air	1953	$20
❏ 47-5408	O Holy Night/Go Tell It on the Mountain	1953	$20
❏ 47-5409	O Little Town of Bethlehem/Thou Didst Leave Thy Throne	1953	$20
❏ 47-5904	Put Christ Back Into Christmas/Happy Birthday, Savior	1954	$20
❏ 47-5410	Silent Night/Away in a Manger	1953	$20

7-Inch Extended Plays
❏ EPB-3149 [PS]	Christmas Hymns	1953	$15

— Fold-open cover for 2-EP set (547-0318, 547-0319)

❏ 547-0318	O Holy Night/Go Tell It on the Mountain (Christmas Song of the Plantation)//O Little Town of Bethlehem/Thou Did'st Leave Thy Throne	1953	$15
❏ 547-0319	Silent Night/Away in a Manger//I Wonder As I Wander/There's a Song in the Air	1953	$15

— Above two comprise EPB-3149

SHEAN AND JENKYNS
GNP CRESCENDO
❏ 198	Goofy-Footer Ho-Dad/Do the Commercial	1963	$30

SHEARING, GEORGE
CAPITOL
❏ 4418	Blue Malibu/Honeysuckle Rose	1960	$8
❏ 5850	On a Clear Day You Can See Forever/Call Me	1967	$6
❏ 4922	The Stripper/Fairy Tales	1963	$8

MGM
❏ 11876	Adieu/Undecided	1954	$15
❏ 11677	A Sinner Kissed an Angel/Mood for Milt	1954	$15
❏ 11493	Body and Soul/I Hear a Rhapsody	1953	$20
❏ 11046	Don't Blame Me/Brain Waves	1951	$20
❏ 11600	Easy to Love/Wrap Your Troubles in Dreams	1953	$20
❏ 10907	For You/Little White Lies	1951	$20
❏ 12079	Get Off My Back/Love Is Just Around the Corner	1955	$15
❏ 12182	Hallelujah/Basso Profundo	1956	$15
❏ 10720	I Didn't Know What Time It Was/How's Trix	1950	$30
❏ 10956	I'll Be Around/Quintessence	1951	$20
❏ 10687	I'll Remember April/Jumping with Symphony Sid	1950	$30
❏ 12038	Ill Wind/Drune Negrita	1955	$15

❏ 10647	In a Chinese Garden/(B-side unknown)	1950	$30

—Note: Earlier George Shearing 45s on MGM may exist

❏ 11545	Indian Summer/Appreciation	1953	$20
❏ 11754	I've Never Been in Love Before/Mambo Inn	1954	$15
❏ 11833	Lullaby of Birdland/Love Is Here to Stay	1954	$15
❏ 11354	Lullaby of Birdland/When Lights Are Low	1952	$20
❏ 12349	My Silent Love/As Long As There's Music	1956	$15
❏ 12309	Over the Rainbow/Lonely Moments	1956	$15
❏ 11282	Simplicity/5 O'Clock Whistle	1952	$20
❏ 12227	Spring Is Here/Minor Trouble	1956	$15
❏ 12132	Stranger in Paradise/Point and Counterpoint	1955	$15
❏ 10986	The Breeze and I/I Remember You	1951	$20
❏ 11943	The Lady Is a Tramp/Cool Mambo	1955	$15
❏ 11425	There's a Lull in My Life/Midnight Belongs to You	1953	$20
❏ 11153	Thine Alone/Geneva's Move	1952	$20
❏ 11639	Tiempo de Concerro (Part 1)/Tiempo de Concerro (Part 2)	1953	$20
❏ 11199	To a Wild Rose/Swedish Pastry	1952	$20
❏ 10763	When Your Lover Has Gone/Carnegie Horizons	1950	$30

MGM
❏ X1017	(contents unknown)	1953	$20
❏ X1006 [PS]	For You	1953	$20
❏ X1006	For You/I Remember You//Thine Alone/I'll Be Around	1953	$20
❏ X1017 [PS]	In a Chinese Garden	1953	$20

SHEARS, BILLY, AND THE ALL AMERICANS
SILVER FOX
❏ 121	Brother Paul/Message to Seymour	1969	$15

SHEEP, THE
BOOM
❏ 60007	Dynamite/I Feel Good	1966	$30
❏ 60000	Hide and Seek/Twelve Months Later	1966	$30

SHEFFIELDS, THE
DESTINATION
❏ 621	Do You Still Love Me/Nothing I Can Do	1966	$30
❏ 613	My Loving Days Are Through/Please Come Back	1966	$20

DOT
❏ 16722	Plenty of Love/Bags Groove	1965	$20

FENTON
❏ 2118	Fool Minus a Heart/Blowin' in the Wind	1966	$30

SHEIKS, THE
AMY
❏ 807	Come On Back/Please Don't Take Away the Girl I Love	1960	$200

CAT
❏ 116	Walk That Walk/The Kissing Song (Sweetie Lover)	1955	$50

EF-N-DE
❏ 1000	Give Me Another Chance/Baby Don't You Cry	1955	$600

FEDERAL
❏ 12237	So Fine/Sentimental Heart	1955	$200

JAMIE
❏ 1147	Candlelight Cafe/The Song of Old Paree	1959	$30

LEGRAND
❏ 1016	Cocoanut Woman/Twist That Twist	1962	$30
❏ 1013	What I'd Do for Your Love/Why Should I Dance	1961	$125

MGM
❏ 12876	Baghdad Rock (Part 1)/Baghdad Rock (Part 2)	1960	$30

SHELDON, DOUG
CONGRESS
❏ 266	How Can I Tell Her/It's Because of You	1966	$10

MGM
❏ 13261	Lonely Boy/Hello There Lonely Baby	1964	$15

SHELLS, THE
END
❏ 1022	Pretty Little Girl/Sippin' Soda	1958	$200
❏ 1050	Whispering Wings/Shooma Dom Dom	1959	$60

Number	Title	Yr	NM
GONE			
5103	Pretty Little Girl/Sippin' Soda	1961	$30
JOHNSON			
104	Baby Oh Baby/Angel Eyes	1957	$50
104	Baby Oh Baby/What's in An Angel's Eyes	1960	$20
—Note lengthened B-side title			
109	Better Forget Him/Can't Take It	1961	$30
119	Deep in My Heart/(It's a) Happy Holiday	1962	$40
106	Don't Say Goodbye/Pleading	1958	$125
107	Explain It to Me/An Island Unknown	1961	$30
332	Explain It to Me/An Island Unknown	1961	$20
110	In the Dim Light of the Dark/O-Mi Yum-Mi Yum-Mi	1961	$30
099	My Cherie/Explain It to Me	1972	$6
127	On My Honor/My Royal Love	1963	$60
112	Sweetest One/Baby Walk On In	1961	$40
120	The Drive/A Toast to Your Birthday	1962	$40
JOSIE			
912	Deep in My Heart/Our Wedding Day	1963	$30
ROULETTE			
4156	The Thief/She Wasn't Meant for Me	1959	$40

SHELTON, ANNE

Number	Title	Yr	NM
BUENA VISTA			
476	It Won't Be Long 'Til Christmas/The Christmas Star	1969	$8
476 [PS]	It Won't Be Long 'Til Christmas/The Christmas Star	1969	$10

SHELTON BROTHERS, THE

Number	Title	Yr	NM
DELUXE			
2013	MacDonald's Streamlined Farm/With Another's Arms Around You	1953	$40
2011	The Old Grey Goose/Cheatin' on Your Baby	1953	$40

SHELTON, GARY

Number	Title	Yr	NM
ALPINE			
56	Honey Bee/Till the End of the Line	1960	$40
MARK			
145	Goodbye Little Darlin' Goodbye/Stop the World	1960	$200

SHELTON, RICKY VAN

Number	Title	Yr	NM
COLUMBIA			
38-07025	Crime of Passion/Don't We All Have the Right	1987	$3
38-07798	Don't We All Have the Right/Baby, I'm Ready	1988	$3
38-08529	From a Jack to a King/The Picture	1988	$3
38-68694	Hole in My Pocket/Let Me Live with Love (And Die with You)	1989	$3
38-08022	I'll Leave This World Loving You/Sometimes I Cry in My Sleep	1988	$4
38-07672	Life Turned Her That Way/I Don't Care	1987	$3
38-68994	Living Proof/Somebody's Back in Town	1989	$3
38-07311	Somebody Lied/Working Man's Blues	1987	$3
38-73077	Statue of a Fool/He's Got You	1989	$3
13-08391	Wild-Eyed Dream/Crime of Passion	1988	$3
—Hall of Fame" series; gray label			
38-06542	Wild-Eyed Dream/Think It Over	1986	$4

SHENANDOAH

Number	Title	Yr	NM
COLUMBIA			
38-08042	Mama Knows/The Show Must Go On	1988	$3
38-07779	She Doesn't Cry Anymore/What She Wants	1988	$3
38-07654	Stop the Rain/What She Wants	1987	$4
38-68892	Sunday in the South/Changes	1989	$3
38-68550	The Church on Cumberland Road/She Doesn't Cry Anymore	1989	$4
38-69061	Two Dozen Roses/Hard Country	1989	$3
38-07128	We Don't Make Love Like We Used To/Lily of the Alley	1987	$4
38-07128 [PS]	We Don't Make Love Like We Used To/Lily of the Alley	1987	$4

SHEP AND THE LIMELITES

Number	Title	Yr	NM
HULL			
740	Daddy's Home/This I Know	1961	$50
—Pink label			
740	Daddy's Home/This I Know	1961	$30
—Red label			
740	Daddy's Home/This I Know	1961	$30
—Tan label. Note: Any colored vinyl version is a counterfeit.			
761	Easy to Remember (When You Want to Forget)/Why, Why Won't You Believe Me	1964	$30
753	Gee Baby, What About You/Everything Is Going to Be Alright	1962	$30
767	I'm All Alone/Why Did You Fall for Me	1964	$30
772	In Case I Forget/I'm a-Hurting Inside	1965	$30
748	Our Anniversary/Who Told the Sandman	1962	$30
770	Party for Two/You Better Believe	1965	$40
759	Steal Away (With Your Baby)/For All My Love	1963	$30
757	Stick By Me (And I'll Stick By You)/It's All Over Now	1963	$30
747	Three Steps from the Altar/Oh What a Feeling	1961	$30
751	What Did Daddy Do/Teach Me, Teach Me How to Twist	1962	$30

SHEPARD, JEAN, AND RAY PILLOW

Number	Title	Yr	NM
CAPITOL			
5633	I'll Take the Dog/I'd Fight the World	1966	$8
5769	Mr. Do-It-Yourself/Strangers Nine to Five	1966	$8

SHEPARD, JEAN

Number	Title	Yr	NM
CAPITOL			
F3796	Act Like a Married Man/It Scares Me Half to Death	1957	$30
F2502	A Dear John Letter/I'd Rather Die Young	1953	$30
—A-side with "Ferlin Huskey"			
5508	Ain't You Ashamed/It's a Man	1965	$10
2073	An Old Bridge/My New Darlin'	1968	$8
F3118	A Satisfied Mind/Take Possession	1955	$30
5304	A Tear Dropped By/He Plays the Bongos (I Play the Banjo)	1964	$10
F3222	Beautiful Lies/I Thought of You	1955	$30
4365	Did I Turn Down a Better Deal/How Do I Tell It to the Child	1960	$20
F3051	Did You Tell Her About Me/You Sent Her an Orchid	1955	$30
F2905	Don't Fall in Love with Married Men/You'll Come Crawlin'	1954	$30
F2994	Don't Rush Me/Please Don't Divorce Me	1954	$30
2273	Everyday's a Happy Day for Fools/My World Is New	1968	$8
F2586	Forgive Me, John/My Wedding Ring	1953	$30
—A-side with "Ferlin Huskey"			
F4129	Have Heart, Will Love/I'll Take the Blame	1959	$30
5822	Heart, We Did All That We Could/My Momma Didn't Raise No Fools	1967	$8
F4279	Heartaches, Teardrops and Sorrow/Sweetheart Don't Come Back	1959	$30
4584	How Long Does It Hurt/If You Were Losing Him to Me	1961	$20
5983	I Don't See How I Can Make It/Enough Heart to Hurt	1967	$8
5681	If Teardrops Were Silver/Outstanding in Your Field	1966	$8
F3618	If You Can Walk Away/Tomorrow I'll Be Gone	1957	$30
F3340	I Learned It All from You/This Has Been Your Life	1956	$30
4915	I've Learned to Live with You/It's Torture	1963	$15
F4068	I Want to Go Where No One Knows Me/Just Another Girl	1958	$30
4423	Lonely Little World/For the Children's Sake	1960	$20
5585	Many Happy Hangovers to You/Our Past Is In My Way	1966	$10
4858	One Less Heartache/It's Never Too Late	1962	$15
3238	Safe in These Lovin' Arms of Mine/The Closest Thing to Perfect	1971	$6
5169	Second Fiddle (To an Old Guitar)/Two Little Boys	1964	$10
5392	Someone's Gotta Cry/Don't Take Advantage of Me	1965	$12
5062	That's What Lonesome Is/When Your House Is Not a Home	1963	$15
4640	The Biggest Cry/I've Got to Talk to Mary	1961	$20
F2706	The Glass That Stands Beside You/Let's Kiss and Try Again	1954	$30
—With Ferlin Husky			
4321	The One You Slip Around With/Mysteries of Life	1959	$20
F3727	The Other Woman/Under Suspicion	1957	$30
F4013	The Secret of Life/He's My Baby	1958	$30
F2358	Twice the Lovin'/Crying Steel Guitar Waltz	1953	$40
4719	Two Voices, Two Shadows, Two Faces/Your Conscience or Your Heart	1962	$15
F2791	Two Whoops and a Holler/Why Did You Wait	1954	$40
3033	With His Hand in Mine/Just Plain Lonely	1971	$6
SCORPION			
0557	Saturday Night Sin/(B-side unknown)	1978	$6
UNITED ARTISTS			
XW818	Ain't Love Good/I Can Imagine	1976	$5
XW745	Another Neon Night/(Hey, Won't You Play) Another Somebody Done Somebody Wrong Song	1975	$5
XW384	At the Time/Love Came Pouring Down	1974	$5
XW317	Come On Phone/Are You Sincere?	1973	$5
XW956	Hardly a Day Goes By/Lovin' You Comes So Easy	1977	$5
XW442	I'll Do Anything It Takes (To Stay with You)/Safe in the Love of My Man	1974	$5
XW701	I'm a Believer (In a Whole Lot of Lovin')/I Think I'll Wait Until Tomorrow	1975	$5
XW899	I'm Giving You Denver/He Loves Everything He Gets His Hands On	1976	$5
XW776	Mercy/Wife of a Hard Working Man	1976	$5
XW552	Poor Sweet Baby/I'm Not That Good at Goodbye	1974	$5
XW248	Slippin' Away/Think I'll Go Somewhere and Cry Myself to Sleep	1973	$5
XW591	The Tip of My Fingers/Bright Lights and Country Music	1975	$5

SHEPARDS, THE

Number	Title	Yr	NM
ABC-PARAMOUNT			
10758	Little Girl Lost/Let Yourself Go	1965	$30

SHEPHERD, CYBILL

Number	Title	Yr	NM
PARAMOUNT			
0299	My Heart Belongs to Daddy/Anything Goes	1974	$10

SHEPHERD SISTERS

Number	Title	Yr	NM
20TH CENTURY FOX			
468	I've Got a Secret/Finders Keepers	1964	$10
ATLANTIC			
2195	Talk Is Cheap/The Greatest Lover	1963	$10
2176	What Makes Little Girls Cry/Don't Mention My Name	1963	$10
BIG TOP			
3066	Hapsburg Serenade/Schoen-A, Schoen-A	1961	$20
LANCE			
125	Alone (Why Must I Be Alone)/Congratulations to Someone	1957	$30
MELBA			
100	Gone with the Wind/Rock and Roll, Cha Cha	1956	$30
MERCURY			
71350	Dancing Baby/Is It a Crime	1958	$30
71306	Eatin' Pizza/A Boy and a Girl	1958	$30
71244	Gettin' Ready for Freddie/The Best Thing There Is	1957	$30
MGM			
12766	Heart and Soul/(It's No) Sin	1959	$30
PRIVATE STOCK			
45,063	Our Town/(B-side unknown)	1975	$6
UNITED ARTISTS			
350	Deeply/I'm Still Dancin'	1961	$15
456	Lolita Ya Ya/Marvin	1962	$15
WARWICK			
530	Alone/Rocky	1960	$20
511	Here Comes Heaven Again/I Think It's Time	1959	$20

Number	Title	Yr	NM
YORK			
❏ 50002	Alone (New Version)/ Alone (Original Version)	1965	$10
SHEPPARD, BUDDY, AND THE HOLIDAYS			
SABINA			
❏ 506	My Love Is Real/Brahms' Lullaby (Time to Dream)	1962	$60
SHEPPARD, SHANE			
APT			
❏ 25046	One Week from Today/I'm So Lonely (What Can I Do)	1960	$50
❏ 25039	Too Young to Wed/ Two Loving Hearts	1960	$60
SHEPPARD, T.G.			
COLUMBIA			
❏ 38-05591	Doncha?/Hunger for You	1985	$3
❏ 13-08405	Doncha?/In Over My Heart	1988	$3
— Gray label reissue			
❏ 38-08029	Don't Say It with Diamonds (Say It with Love)/ There's a Lot of Heart	1988	$3
❏ 38-04890	Fooled Around and Fell in Love/Livin' on the Edge	1985	$3
❏ 38-04890 [PS]	Fooled Around and Fell in Love/Livin' on the Edge	1985	$5
❏ 38-06347	Half Past Forever (Till I'm Blue in the Heart)/The Bad Thing About Good Love	1986	$3
❏ 38-05747	In Over My Heart/A Great Work of Art	1985	$3
❏ 38-07312	One for the Money/ Come to Me	1987	$3
❏ 13-08392	One for the Money/ You're My First Lady	1988	$3
— Gray label reissue			
❏ 38-68685	She Didn't Break My Heart/ Don't Say It with Diamonds (Say It with Love)	1989	$3
❏ 13-08404	Strong Heart/Half Past Forever (Till I'm Blue in the Heart)	1988	$3
— Gray label reissue			
❏ 38-05905	Strong Heart/What You Gonna Do About Her	1986	$3
HITSVILLE			
❏ 6053	Lovin' On/I'll Always Remember That Song	1977	$5
❏ 6048	May I Spend Every New Years with You/I'll Always Remember That Song	1976	$5
❏ 6040	Show Me a Man/We Just Live Here (We Don't Love Here Anymore)	1976	$5
❏ 6032	Solitary Man/Shame	1976	$5
— Originally on Melodyland label			
MELODYLAND			
❏ 6016	Another Woman/I Can't Help Myself	1975	$5
❏ 6002	Devil in the Bottle/ Rollin' with the Flow	1974	$5
❏ 6028	Motels and Memories/ Pigskin Charade	1975	$5
❏ 6032	Solitary Man/Shame	1976	$12
— Quickly reissued on Hitsville label			
❏ 6006	Tryin' to Beat the Morning Home/I'll Be Satisfied	1975	$5
WARNER BROS.			
❏ 8678	Daylight/Never Ending Crowded Circle	1978	$4
❏ 8525	Don't Ever Say Good-Bye/ She Pretended We Were Married (While I Pretended She Was You)	1978	$4
❏ 49515	Do You Wanna Go to Heaven/How Far Our Love Goes	1980	$4
❏ 50041	Finally/All My Cloudy Days Are Gone	1982	$4
❏ 8721	Happy Together/That's All She Wrote	1978	$4
❏ 49615	I Feel Like Loving You Again/Let the Little Bird Fly	1980	$4
❏ 49110	I'll Be Coming Back for More/Faster Than I Could Dream	1979	$4
❏ 49690	I Loved 'Em Every One/I Could Never Dream the Way You Feel	1981	$4
❏ 49024	Last Cheater's Waltz/You Do It to Me Every Time	1979	$4
❏ 29343	Make My Day/Lucky We Are	1984	$5
— A-side with Clint Eastwood			
❏ 8490	Mister D.J./Easy to Love	1977	$4
❏ 29167	One Owner Heart/I Could Get Used to This	1984	$4
❏ 49858	Only One You/We Belong in Love Tonight	1981	$4
❏ 49761	Party Time/You Waltzed Yourself Right Into My Life	1981	$4
❏ 29469	Slow Burn/First Things First	1983	$4
❏ 49214	Smooth Sailin'/I Came Home to Make Love to You	1980	$4

Number	Title	Yr	NM
❏ 29369	Somewhere Down the Line/It's a Bad Night for Good Girls	1984	$4
❏ 29934	War Is Hell (On the Homefront Too)/In Another Minute	1982	$4
❏ 8593	When Can We Do This Again/Jenny, Don't Worry 'Bout the Kid	1978	$4
❏ 29695	Without You/Where Did We Go Right?	1983	$4
SHEPPARDS, THE			
ABNER			
❏ 7006	Elevator Operator/ Loving You	1961	$15
APEX			
❏ 7760	Come Home, Come Home/Just Like You	1960	$30
❏ 7755	It's Crazy/Meant to Be	1960	$30
❏ 7750	Loving You/Island of Love	1959	$50
❏ 7762	Tragic/Feel Like Lovin'	1961	$30
BUNKY			
❏ 7766	I'm Not Wanted/Your Love (Has a Hole in It)	1969	$6
❏ 7764	Island of Love/Steal Away	1969	$6
CONSTELLATION			
❏ 123	Island of Love/Give a Hug to Me	1964	$10
❏ 176	Island of Love/Give a Hug to Me	1966	$8
IMPACT			
❏ 1018	Poor Man's Thing/ When Johnny Comes Marching Home	1967	$40
OKEH			
❏ 7173	Walkin'/Pretend You're Still Mine	1963	$10
SHARP			
❏ 6039	What's the Name of the Game/Glitter in Your Eyes	1961	$15
UNITED			
❏ 198	Sherry/Mozelle	1957	$250
VEE JAY			
❏ 406	Every Now and Then/ Glitter in Your Eyes	1961	$15
❏ 441	Tragic/Come to Me	1962	$30
SHERIDAN BROTHERS, THE			
HIT			
❏ 235	Flowers on the Wall/ Sounds of Silence	1966	$8
— B-side by Sammy and Theodore			
SHERIDAN, MIKE, AND THE NIGHTRIDERS			
LIVERPOOL SOUND			
❏ 902	Please Mr. Postman/In Love	1964	$120
SHERIFF AND THE RAVELS			
VEE JAY			
❏ 306	Shombalor/Lonely One	1959	$50
SHERLOCKS, THE			
DOT			
❏ 16953	Shades of Blue/Too Good to Be True	1966	$15
❏ 16890	Skin of My Teeth/ Turn Her Down	1966	$30
SHERMAN, ALLAN			
RCA VICTOR			
❏ 47-9693	Fig Leaves Are Falling/Juggling	1968	$6
❏ 47-8412	The End of a Symphony (Part 1)/The End of a Symphony (Part 2)	1964	$10
❏ 47-8412 [PS]	The End of a Symphony (Part 1)/The End of a Symphony (Part 2)	1964	$40
WARNER BROS.			
❏ 5614	Crazy Downtown/The Drop-Outs March	1965	$12
❏ 5378	Hello Mudduh! Hello Fadduh! (A Letter from Camp)/Here's to the Crabgrass	1963	$20
❏ 5378	Hello Mudduh! Hello Fadduh! (A Letter from Camp)/Rat Fink	1963	$15
❏ 5378 [PS]	Hello Mudduh! Hello Fadduh! (A Letter from Camp)/Rat Fink	1963	$30
❏ 7112	Hello Mudduh! Hello Fadduh! (A Letter from Camp)/Sarah Jackman	1968	$6
— Back to Back Hits" series -- originals have green "W7" labels			

Number	Title	Yr	NM
❏ 5449	Hello Mudduh! Hello Fadduh! New 1964 Version/ Hello Mudduh! Hello Fadduh! Original Version	1964	$15
❏ 5449 [PS]	Hello Mudduh! Hello Fadduh! New 1964 Version/ Hello Mudduh! Hello Fadduh! Original Version	1964	$30
❏ 5806	His Own Little Island/ Odd Ball	1966	$12
❏ 5419	My Son the Vampire/I Can't Dance	1964	$15
❏ 5490	Pop Hates the Beatles/ Grow Mrs. Goldfarb	1964	$20
❏ 5435	Skin (Heart)/The Drop-Outs March	1964	$12
❏ 5672	The Drinking Man's Diet/The Laarge Daark Aardvark Song	1965	$10
❏ 5406	The Twelve Gifts of Christmas/You Went the Wrong Way, Old King Louie	1963	$30
❏ 5896	Westchester Hadassah/ Strange Things in My Soup	1967	$10
SHERMAN, BOBBY			
CAMEO			
❏ 403 [DJ]	Happiness Is	1966	$30
— One-sided promo			
❏ 403	Happiness Is/Can't Get Used to Loving You	1966	$12
CONDOR			
❏ 1002	I'll Never Tell You/Telegram	1969	$10
DECCA			
❏ 31779	Hey Little Girl/Well All Right	1965	$20
❏ 31741	It Hurts Me/Give Me Your Word	1965	$20
❏ 31741 [PS]	It Hurts Me/Give Me Your Word	1965	$60
❏ 31672	Man Overboard/You Make Me Happy	1964	$20
DOT			
❏ 16566	I Want to Hear It From Her/ Nobody's Sweetheart	1963	$20
EPIC			
❏ 10181	Cold Girl/Think of Rain	1967	$10
❏ 10181 [PS]	Cold Girl/Think of Rain	1967	$30
JANUS			
❏ 254	Our Last Song Together/ Sunshine Rose	1975	$4
METROMEDIA			
❏ 206	Cried Like a Baby/ Is Anybody There	1971	$5
❏ 206 [PS]	Cried Like a Baby/ Is Anybody There	1971	$5
❏ 68-0100	Early in the Morning/ Unborn Lullaby	1973	$5
❏ 177	Easy Come, Easy Go/ July Seventeen	1970	$5
❏ 177 [PS]	Easy Come, Easy Go/ July Seventeen	1970	$5
❏ 177	Easy Come, Easy Go/ Sounds Along the Way	1970	$5
❏ 204	Goin' Home (Sing a Song of Christmas Cheer)/ Love's What You're Gettin' for Christmas	1970	$6
❏ 204 [PS]	Goin' Home (Sing a Song of Christmas Cheer)/ Love's What You're Gettin' for Christmas	1970	$8
❏ 188	Hey, Mister Sun/ Two Blind Mice	1970	$5
❏ 188 [PS]	Hey, Mister Sun/ Two Blind Mice	1970	$5
❏ 249	I Don't Believe in Magic/ Just a Little While Longer	1972	$5
❏ 150	La La La (If I Had You)/Time	1969	$5
❏ 150 [PS]	La La La (If I Had You)/Time	1969	$5
❏ 121	Little Woman/One Too Many Mornings	1969	$5
❏ 121 [PS]	Little Woman/One Too Many Mornings	1969	$5
❏ 217	The Drum/Free Now to Roam	1971	$5
❏ 217 [PS]	The Drum/Free Now to Roam	1971	$5
❏ 240	Together Again/ Picture a Little Girl	1972	$5
❏ 240 [PS]	Together Again/ Picture a Little Girl	1972	$5
❏ 222	Waiting at the Bus Stop/Run Away	1971	$5
❏ 222 [PS]	Waiting at the Bus Stop/Run Away	1971	$5
PARKWAY			
❏ 967	Goody Galumshus/Anything Your Little Heart Desires	1966	$10
SHERMAN, JOE			
WORLD ARTISTS			
❏ 1015	I Saw A Star/The Stolen Hours	1963	$8
❏ 1015 [PS]	I Saw A Star/The Stolen Hours	1963	$10

Number	Title	Yr	NM
SHERRYS, THE			
GUYDEN			
❏ 2094	Monk, Monk, Monkey/That Boy of Mine	1963	$20
❏ 2068	Pop-Pop-Pop-Eye/Your Hand in Mine	1962	$20
❏ 2084	Saturday Night/I've Got No One	1963	$20
❏ 2077	Slop Time/Let's Stomp Again	1963	$20
ROBERTS			
❏ 701	Slow Jerk/Confusion	1965	$15
SHEVELLES, THE			
WORLD ARTISTS			
❏ 1025	How Would You Like Me to Love You/I Could Conquer the World	1964	$15
❏ 1023	Oo Poo Pa Doo/Like I Love You	1964	$15
SHEVETON, TONY			
PARROT			
❏ 10616	Dance with Me/A Million Drums	1964	$20
SHIBLEY, ARKIE			
4 STAR			
❏ 1737	Pick Pick Pickin' (My Guitar)/I'm a Poor Oakie	1959	$40
GILT EDGE			
❏ 5036	Arkie Meets the Judge (Hot Rod Race No. 3)/Uncle Sam Has Called My Number	1951	$125
❏ 5065	Arkie's Letter from Home/Five String Banjo March	1952	$70
❏ 5078	Arkie's Talking Blues/Blue Guitar Ramble	1953	$60
❏ 5089	Hard Times in Arkansas/Dusty Blossom Boogie	1954	$60
❏ 5021	Hot Rod Race/I'm Living Alone with an Old Love	1950	$125
❏ 5030	Hot Rod Race No. 2/I Wish I Was Somebody's Rose	1951	$125
❏ 5047	Hot Rod Race No. 4 (The Guy in the Mercury)/This Feeling You Brought Over Me	1951	$125
❏ 5054	Hot Rod Race No. 5 (The Kid in the Model-A)/My Beautiful Washington Rose	1951	$125
❏ 5059	Shore Leave/Guitar Hoedown	1952	$70
❏ 5072	Three Day Pass/Hot Woodpecker Rag	1953	$60
SHIELDS, BILLY			
HARBOUR			
❏ 304	I Was a Boy/Moments from Now	1969	$30
SHIELDS, BOBBY			
MELBA			
❏ 105	Land of Rock and Roll/I Wouldn't Change You for the World	1956	$70
SHIELDS, THE			
ATCO			
❏ 7071	The Way I Feel Tonight/All Right by Me	1977	$5
DOT			
❏ 15940	Fare Thee Well/Play the Game Fair	1959	$30
❏ 15856	I'm Sorry Now/Nature Boy	1958	$40
TENDER			
❏ 521	Fare Thee Well/Play the Game Fair	1959	$70
❏ 518	I'm Sorry Now/Nature Boy	1958	$70
TRANSCONTINENTAL			
❏ 1013	The Girl Around the Corner/Fare Thee Well, My Love	1960	$125
SHILOH			
AMOS			
❏ 162	Down on the Farm/Simple Little Down Home Rock & Roll Love Song for Rosie	1971	$15
SHINDIGS, THE			
MUSTANG			
❏ 3003	Thunder Reef/Wolfman	1965	$50
SHINER, MERVIN			
CORAL			
❏ 9-64178	Hide-Away/Bells of Memory	1954	$30
— With Rusty Keefer			

Number	Title	Yr	NM
❏ 9-61080	I Dreamt That I Was Santa Claus/Don't Wait Until the Night Before Christmas	1953	$30
❏ 9-64163	I'm Just Here to Get My Baby Out of Jail/Castaway	1953	$30
❏ 9-64170	Our Heart Breaking Waltz/River of Silver	1954	$30
DECCA			
❏ 9-28121	Almost/Let's Take a Trip to the Moon	1952	$30
— With Grady Martin			
❏ 9-46345	Ball and Chain Boogie/Memories of Mockingbird Hill	1951	$40
❏ 9-28808	Candy Man/Candy Round-Up	1953	$30
❏ 9-27977	Egbert the Easter Egg/The Rabbit with the Two Big Feet	1952	$30
❏ 9-46231	Francis the Talking Mule/Me and My Teddy Bear	1950	$40
❏ 9-46337	If Teardrops Were Pennies/Let's Live a Little	1951	$30
❏ 9-46274	I Overlooked an Orchid/If You've Got the Money (I've Got the Time)	1950	$40
❏ 9-28504	I Saw Mommy Kissing Santa Claus/Snowy White Snow-Jingle Bells	1952	$30
❏ 9-46260	I Think I'm Gonna Cry Again/Ace in the Hole	1950	$30
❏ 9-28466	Landslide of Love/Me Without You	1952	$30
❏ 9-46244	Little Liza Lou/Gra Mamou	1950	$40
❏ 9-29363	Lord I'm Coming Home/Pass Me Not	1954	$30
❏ 9-28424	Our Love Isn't Legal/Settin' the Woods on Fire	1952	$30
— With Grady Martin			
❏ 9-46221	Peter Cottontail/Floppy	1950	$40
❏ 9-46280	Santa, Santa Don't Be Mad At Me/Fee Fi Fiddle	1950	$30
❏ 9-46253	Slippin' Around with Jole Blon/Steppin' Out	1950	$40
❏ 9-27482	Sonny the Bunny/Bunny Round-Up Time	1951	$30
❏ 9-46272	The Lightning Express/Sweet Mama Blues	1950	$30
❏ 9-46273	Walking with the Blues/Beloved, Be Faithful	1950	$30
— With Eddie Crosby			
LITTLE DARLIN'			
❏ 0068	Ain't That Sad/You Can Tell the World	1970	$8
❏ 0065	In the Ghetto/El Bandito	1970	$8
MGM			
❏ 13704	Big Brother/Big Shot, the Pool Shark	1967	$8
❏ 13900	I'd Rather Be a Fool/How Are You, Brown Eyes	1968	$8
RCA VICTOR			
❏ 47-6171	I Ain't Much of a Hand at Lovin'/Don't Believe	1955	$30
❏ 47-5983	Love with No Tomorrow/It's Nothin'	1955	$30
❏ 47-5938	Mister Sandman/Penny Candy	1954	$30
❏ 47-6328	We're Off on a Race/You're Free to Go	1955	$30
SHINES, JOHNNY			
J.O.B.			
❏ 1010	Evening Sun/Brutal Hearted Woman	1953	$2000
SHIRELLES, THE			
BELL			
❏ 760	A Most Unusual Boy/Look What You've Done to My Heart	1969	$10
❏ 787	Looking Glass/Playthings	1969	$10
BLUE ROCK			
❏ 4066	Call Me/There's a Storm Goin' Home in My Heart	1968	$10
❏ 4051	Don't Mess with Cupid/Sweet Sweet Lovin'	1968	$12
DECCA			
❏ 30588	I Met Him on a Sunday/I Want You to Be My Boyfriend	1958	$30
❏ 30669	My Love Is a Charm/Slop Time	1958	$50
❏ 30761	Stop Me/I Got the Message	1958	$50
PHILCO-FORD			
❏ HP-30	Soldier Boy/My Heart Belongs to You	1968	$30
— 4-inch plastic "Hip Pocket Record" with color sleeve			
RCA VICTOR			
❏ 48-1032	Brother, Brother/Sunday Dreaming	1972	$10
❏ 47-0902	Let's Give Each Other Love/Deep in the Night	1973	$8
❏ APBO-0192	Touch the Wind (Eres Tu)/Do What You've a Mind To	1973	$8

Number	Title	Yr	NM
SCEPTER			
❏ 1292	Are You Still My Baby/I Saw a Tear	1964	$15
❏ 1205	A Teardrop and a Lollipop/Doin' the Ronde	1959	$40
— White label			
❏ 1205	A Teardrop and a Lollipop/Doin' the Ronde	1959	$30
— Red label			
❏ 1220	A Thing of the Past/What a Sweet Thing That Was	1961	$30
❏ 1227	Baby It's You/Things I Want to Hear (Pretty Words)	1961	$30
❏ 1223	Big John/Twenty-One	1961	$30
❏ 1203	Dedicated to the One I Love/Look A Here Baby	1958	$50
— White label			
❏ 1203	Dedicated to the One I Love/Look A Here Baby	1958	$30
— Red label			
❏ 12185	Don't Go Home (My Little Baby)/Nobody Baby After You	1967	$12
❏ 1255	Don't Say Goodnight and Mean Goodbye/I Didn't Mean to Hurt You	1963	$15
❏ 1255 [PS]	Don't Say Goodnight and Mean Goodbye/I Didn't Mean to Hurt You	1963	$50
❏ 1243	Everybody Loves a Lover/I Don't Think So	1962	$20
❏ 1248	Foolish Little Girl/Not for All the Money in the World	1963	$20
❏ 1248 [PS]	Foolish Little Girl/Not for All the Money in the World	1963	$50
❏ 12217	Hippie Walk (Part 1)/Hippie Walk (Part 2)	1968	$12
❏ 12132	I Met Him on a Sunday -- '66/Love That Man	1966	$10
❏ 1260	It's a Mad, Mad, Mad, Mad World/31 Flavors	1963	$15
❏ 12198	Last Minute Miracle/No Doubt About It	1967	$12
❏ 12123	(Mama) My Soldier Boy Is Coming Home/Soldier Boy	1965	$10
❏ 1217	Mama Said/Blue Holiday	1961	$30
❏ 12101	March (You'll Be Sorry)/Everybody's Goin' Mad	1965	$10
❏ 1284	Maybe Tonight/Lost Love	1964	$15
❏ 12114	My Heart Belongs to You/Love That Man	1965	$10
❏ 1207	Please Be My Boyfriend/I Saw a Tear	1960	$40
— White label			
❏ 1207	Please Be My Boyfriend/I Saw a Tear	1960	$30
— Red label			
❏ 12162	Shades of Blue/After Midnight	1966	$10
❏ 12162	Shades of Blue/Looking Around	1966	$10
❏ 1267	Sha-La-La/His Lips Get In the Way	1964	$15
❏ 1296	Shh, I'm Watching the Movies/A Plus B	1965	$15
❏ 1228	Soldier Boy/Love Is a Swingin' Thing	1962	$20
❏ 1237	Stop the Music/It's Love That Really Counts	1962	$20
❏ 12178	Teasin' Me/Look Away	1966	$10
❏ 1278	Thank You Baby/Doomsday	1964	$15
❏ 12150	Till My Baby Comes Home/Que Sera, Sera	1966	$10
❏ 1211	Tomorrow/Boys	1960	$50
— Original A-side title			
❏ 1208	Tonight's the Night/The Dance Is Over	1960	$40
— White label			
❏ 1208	Tonight's the Night/The Dance Is Over	1960	$30
— Red label			
❏ 1208	Tonight's the Night/The Dance Is Over	1960	$30
— Pink label			
❏ 1264	Tonight You're Gonna Fall in Love with Me/20th Century Rock and Roll	1963	$15
❏ 12192	Too Much of a Good Thing/Bright Shiny Colors	1967	$10
❏ 1234	Welcome Home Baby/Mama, Here Comes the Bride	1962	$20
❏ 1259	What Does a Girl Do?/Don't Let It Happen to You	1963	$15
❏ 12209	Wild and Sweet/Wait Till I Give the Signal	1968	$10
❏ 1211	Will You Love Me Tomorrow/Boys	1960	$40
— Revised A-side title			
TIARA			
❏ 6112	I Met Him on a Sunday/I Want to Be My Boyfriend	1958	$800
— Note: Copies with any catalog number except 6112 are reproductions with little collector value			

UNITED ARTISTS

Number	Title	Yr	NM
❑ 50693	It's Gonna Take a Miracle/Lost	1970	$8
❑ 50740	Take Me for a Little While/Dedicated to the One I Love	1971	$8
❑ 50648	There Goes My Baby-Be My Baby/Strange, I Still Love You	1970	$8

SHIRKERS, THE
LIMP

Number	Title	Yr	NM
❑ 03	Drunk and Disorderly/Suicide	1978	$20
❑ 03 [PS]	Drunk and Disorderly/Suicide	1978	$20

—Broken bottle" sleeve

Number	Title	Yr	NM
❑ 03 [PS]	Drunk and Disorderly/Suicide	1978	$15

—Gray live photo sleeve

SHIRLEY (AND COMPANY)
VIBRATION

Number	Title	Yr	NM
❑ 535	Cry, Cry, Cry/(Instrumental)	1975	$5
❑ 539	Disco Shirley/Keep On Rolling On	1975	$5
❑ 542	I Like to Dance/Jim Doc C'ain	1976	$5
❑ 532	Shame, Shame, Shame/(Instrumental)	1974	$5

SHIRLEY AND LEE
ALADDIN

Number	Title	Yr	NM
❑ 3173	Baby/Shirley Come Back to Me	1953	$120
❑ 3432	Come On and Have Your Fun/All I Want to Do Is Cry	1958	$30
❑ 3258	Comin' Over/Takes Money	1954	$60
❑ 3244	Confessin'/Keep On	1954	$60
❑ 3418	Everybody's Rocking/Don't Leave Me Here to Cry	1958	$30
❑ 3289	Feel So Good/You'd Be Thinking of Me	1955	$50
❑ 3338	I Feel Good/Now That It's Over	1956	$30
❑ 3153	I'm Gone/Sweethearts	1952	$125
❑ 3369	I Want to Dance/Marry Me	1957	$30
❑ 3302	Let's Dream/I'll Do It	1955	$50
❑ 3325	Let the Good Times Roll/Do You Mean to Hurt Me So	1956	$70
❑ 3405	Love No One But You (I Love You So)/I'll Thrill You	1958	$30
❑ 3192	Shirley's Back/So In Love	1953	$70
❑ 3455	True Love/When Day Is Done	1959	$30
❑ 3205	Two Happy People/The Proposal	1953	$60
❑ 3362	When I Saw You/That's What I Want to Do	1957	$30
❑ 3222	Why Did I/Lee Goofed	1954	$60

IMPERIAL

Number	Title	Yr	NM
❑ 5970	Dancing World/I'm Gone	1963	$12
❑ 5868	Don't Stop Now/A Little Thing	1962	$12
❑ 5854	My Last Letter/I'm Early Enough	1962	$10
❑ 5979	Paper Doll/The Brink of Disaster	1963	$10
❑ 66000	Somebody Put a Jukebox in the Study Hall/Never Let Me Go	1963	$12
❑ 5922	The Golden Rule/Hey Little Boy	1963	$10
❑ 5818	Together We Stand (Divided We Fall)/The Joker	1962	$10

UNITED ARTISTS

Number	Title	Yr	NM
❑ 0087	Let the Good Times Roll/Feel So Good	1973	$4

—Silver Spotlight Series" reissue

Number	Title	Yr	NM
❑ XW274	Let the Good Times Roll/That's What I Wanna Do	1973	$5

WARWICK

Number	Title	Yr	NM
❑ 679	Let's Live It Up/Girl, You're Married Now	1962	$15
❑ 581	Let the Good Times Roll/Keep Loving Me	1960	$15
❑ 609	Two Peas in a Pod/Your Love Makes the Difference	1961	$15
❑ 664	Well-a, Well-a/Our Kids	1961	$15

SHIT DOGS
7-Inch Extended Plays
PANGOLIN PRODUCTIONS

Number	Title	Yr	NM
❑ 0(# unknown)	Present the History of Cheese	1980	$125
❑ 0(# unknown) [PS]	Present the History of Cheese	1980	$125

SHOCK
DOWNTOWN

Number	Title	Yr	NM
❑ DT-502	We're That Noise/Gone for Good	1978	$30

—Small center hole; blue vinyl

Number	Title	Yr	NM
❑ DT-502 [PS]	We Were That Noise/Gone for Good	1978	$30

—Notice the different title on the sleeve (this is actually the correct title)

7-Inch Extended Plays
IMPACT

Number	Title	Yr	NM
❑ IM501 [PS]	This Generation's On Vacation/I Wanna Be Spoiled//Overseas	1978	$60

—Notice the slightly different second song title on the sleeve compared to the record label

Number	Title	Yr	NM
❑ IM501	This Generation's On Vacation/Spoiled//Overseas	1978	$60

— Small center hole; red vinyl; counterfeits exist, but originals have the "Impact" logo in white and the rest of the label print in silver, whereas counterfeits have all print, including the "Impact" logo, in silver

SHOCKED, MICHELLE
MERCURY

Number	Title	Yr	NM
❑ 870611-7	Anchorage/Anchorage (Live Video Version)	1988	$3
❑ 870611-7 [PS]	Anchorage/Anchorage (Live Video Version)	1988	$3
❑ 872590-7	When I Grow Up/Fogtown	1989	$3
❑ 872590-7 [PS]	When I Grow Up/Fogtown	1989	$3

SHOCKING BLUE, THE
BUDDAH

Number	Title	Yr	NM
❑ 258	Sleepless at Midnight/Serenade	1971	$6

COLOSSUS

Number	Title	Yr	NM
❑ 141	Boll Weevil/Long and Lonesome Road	1971	$6
❑ 116	Long and Lonesome Road/Ackaragh	1970	$8
❑ 111	Mighty Joe/I'm a Woman	1970	$8
❑ 111 [PS]	Mighty Joe/I'm a Woman	1970	$15

MGM

Number	Title	Yr	NM
❑ 14543	Oh Love/Inkpot	1973	$6
❑ 14481	When I Was a Girl/Eve and the Apple	1973	$6

SHONDELL, TROY
BRITE STAR

Number	Title	Yr	NM
❑ 4691	Deeper and Deeper in Love/Love Stuff	1974	$8
❑ 2459	Still Loving You/Rip It Up	1973	$8
❑ 2453	This Time/You're Nobody's Child	1973	$8

EVEREST

Number	Title	Yr	NM
❑ 2015	Gone/Some People Never Learn	1963	$10
❑ 2018	I've Got a Woman/No Fool Like an Old Fool	1963	$10
❑ 2041	Trouble/Little Miss Tease	1964	$10

GAYE

Number	Title	Yr	NM
❑ 2010	This Time/I Catch Myself Crying	1961	$100

GOLDCREST

Number	Title	Yr	NM
❑ 161#NAME?	This Time/Girl After Girl	1961	$40

—With no "Distributed by Liberty" on label

Number	Title	Yr	NM
❑ 161#NAME?	This Time/Girl After Girl	1961	$30

—With "Distributed by Liberty Record Sales" on label

LIBERTY

Number	Title	Yr	NM
❑ 55398	Tears from an Angel/Island in the Sky	1961	$20
❑ 55353	This Time/Girl After Girl	1961	$30

RIC

Number	Title	Yr	NM
❑ 184	Big Windy City/I Thought That You Were Mine	1966	$10

STAR-FOX

Number	Title	Yr	NM
❑ 77	Still Loving You/Doctor Love	1979	$8

TELESONIC

Number	Title	Yr	NM
❑ 804	(Sittin' Here) Lovin' You/(Here I Am) Single Again	1980	$8

TRX

Number	Title	Yr	NM
❑ 5003	Head Man/She's Got Everything She Needs	1967	$8
❑ 5015	Let's Go All the Way/Let Me Love You	1968	$8
❑ 5019	Something's Wrong in Indiana/A Rose and a Baby Ruth	1969	$8

SHONDELLES, THE
KING

Number	Title	Yr	NM
❑ 5597	Don't Cry My Soldier Boy/My Love	1962	$30
❑ 5705	Muscle Bound/Special Delivery	1963	$30
❑ 5755	Watusi, One More/Ooo, Sometimes	1963	$30
❑ 5656	Wonderful One/I Gotta Tell It	1962	$30

SHOOK, JACK, AND DOTTIE DILLARD
CORAL

Number	Title	Yr	NM
❑ 64066	There's No Place Like Home At Christmas/Blue Christmas	1950	$20

SHOOTERS, THE
EPIC

Number	Title	Yr	NM
❑ 34-08082	Borderline/She's Steppin' Out	1988	$3
❑ 34-68587	If I Ever Go Crazy/Leave and Learn	1989	$3
❑ 34-07684	I Taught Her Everything She Knows About Love/I'll Cry Instead	1988	$3
❑ 34-07367	Tell It to Your Teddy Bear/Dancing Alone	1987	$3
❑ 34-06623	They Only Come Out at Night/Remote Control	1987	$3
❑ 34-07131	'Til the Old Wears Off/Some Fools Were Made to Be Broken	1987	$3

TRANS WORLD

Number	Title	Yr	NM
❑ 6908	Tuff Enuff/She's All Right	1960	$125

SHORE, DINAH
CAPITOL

Number	Title	Yr	NM
❑ 4476	I Ain't Down Yet/I Gotta Love You	1960	$8
❑ 4618	Mississippi Mud/This Is a Changing World	1961	$8
❑ 4344	So Many Things to Do Today/When the Sparrows Learn to Fly	1960	$8
❑ 4774	That'll Show Him/Just a Brief Encounter	1962	$8

COLUMBIA

Number	Title	Yr	NM
❑ 1-630(?)	A Simple Melody/I Still Get a Thrill	1950	$40

—Microgroove 33 1/3 rpm 7-inch single

Number	Title	Yr	NM
❑ 1-197	A Wonderful Guy/Younger Than Springtime	1949	$40

—Microgroove 33 1/3 rpm 7-inch single

Number	Title	Yr	NM
❑ 1-200	Baby, It's Cold Outside/My One and Only Highland Fling	1949	$40

—With Buddy Clark; Microgroove 33 1/3 rpm 7-inch single

Number	Title	Yr	NM
❑ 1-437	Bibbidi-Bobbidi-Boo (The Magic Song)/Happy Time	1950	$40

—Microgroove 33 1/3 rpm 7-inch single

Number	Title	Yr	NM
❑ 1-759	Can Anyone Explain? (No! No! No!)/Dream a Little Dream of Me	1950	$40

—Microgroove 33 1/3 rpm 7-inch single

Number	Title	Yr	NM
❑ 6-759	Can Anyone Explain? (No! No! No!)/Dream a Little Dream of Me	1950	$30
❑ 1-690(?)	Cotton Candy and a Toy Balloon/1812	1950	$40

—Microgroove 33 1/3 rpm 7-inch single

Number	Title	Yr	NM
❑ 1-368	Dear Hearts and Gentle People/Speak a Word of Love	1949	$40

—Microgroove 33 1/3 rpm 7-inch single

Number	Title	Yr	NM
❑ 1-134	Forever and Ever/I've Been Hit	1949	$40

—Microgroove 33 1/3 rpm 7-inch single

Number	Title	Yr	NM
❑ 1-155	Having Wonderful Time/The Story of My Life	1949	$40

—Microgroove 33 1/3 rpm 7-inch single

Number	Title	Yr	NM
❑ 1-260(?)	Homework/You Can Have Him	1949	$40

—With Doris Day; Microgroove 33 1/3 rpm 7-inch single

Number	Title	Yr	NM
❑ 1-660(?)	I Didn't Know What Time It Was/I'll Always Love You	1950	$40

—Microgroove 33 1/3 rpm 7-inch single

Number	Title	Yr	NM
❑ 1-220(?)	I'm Gonna Wash That Man Right Out of My Hair/Kiss Me, Sweet	1949	$40

—Microgroove 33 1/3 rpm 7-inch single

Number	Title	Yr	NM
❑ 1-770(?)	It's Easy to Remember/Don't Rock the Boat, Dear	1950	$40

—Microgroove 33 1/3 rpm 7-inch single

Number	Title	Yr	NM
❑ 6-770(?)	It's Easy to Remember/Don't Rock the Boat, Dear	1950	$30
❑ 1-469	It's So Nice to Have a Man Around the House/More Than Anything Else	1950	$40

—Microgroove 33 1/3 rpm 7-inch single

Number	Title	Yr	NM
❑ 1-445(?)	Lucky Us/Nobody Home at My House	1950	$40

—Microgroove 33 1/3 rpm 7-inch single

Number	Title	Yr	NM
❑ 1-450(?)	Scarlet Ribbons (For Her Hair)/Sitting by the Window	1950	$40

—Microgroove 33 1/3 rpm 7-inch single

Number	Title	Yr	NM
❑ 1-599	Scottish Samba/Never Had a Worry	1950	$40

—Microgroove 33 1/3 rpm 7-inch single

Number	Title	Yr	NM
❑ 1-111	So in Love/Always True to You in My Fashion	1949	$40

—Microgroove 33 1/3 rpm 7-inch single

Number	Title	Yr	NM
❑ 1-369	Star of Bethlehem/Merry Christmas	1949	$50

—Microgroove 33 1/3 rpm 7-inch single

Number	Title	Yr	NM
❑ 1-440(?)	The Shoe Is on the Other Foot Now/Wedding Dolls	1950	$40

—With George Morgan; Microgroove 33 1/3 rpm 7-inch single

Number	Title	Yr	NM
❑ 1-330(?)	The Story of Annie Laurie/A Thousand Violins	1949	$40

Number	Title	Yr	NM
—Microgroove 33 1/3 rpm 7-inch single			
❏ 1-290(?)	Through a Long and Sleepless Night/I'm Yours	1949	$40
—Microgroove 33 1/3 rpm 7-inch single			
❏ 1-250(?)	Till My Ship Comes In/Lovers Gold	1949	$40
—Microgroove 33 1/3 rpm 7-inch single			
❏ 1-719	Tunnel of Love/With the Wind and the Rain in Your Hair	1950	$40
—Microgroove 33 1/3 rpm 7-inch single			
DECCA			
❏ 32468	Crying Time/Rocky Top	1969	$5
MERCURY			
❏ 73465	Me and Ole Crazy Bill/ Wait a Little Longer	1974	$4
PROJECT 3			
❏ 1313	All at Once It's Love/ Loneliness Is My Lover	1967	$6
❏ 1328	Trains and Boats and Planes/Faces and Voices	1968	$6
RCA VICTOR			
❏ 47-4019	A Penny a Kiss/In Your Arms	1951	$30
— With Tony Martin			
❏ 47-5390	Blue Canary/Eternally	1953	$15
❏ 47-4926	Blues in Advance/ Bella Musica	1952	$15
❏ 47-4107	Cause I Love You/ Three Cornered Tune	1951	$30
❏ 47-5515	Changing Partners/Think	1953	$15
❏ 47-6792	Chantez-Chantez (Shan-Tay, "Sing")/Honkytonk Heart	1957	$10
❏ 47-4436	Cheres/Pure Night	1951	$15
—B-side by Alan Young			
❏ 47-5438	Choo Choo Train/ Reflections on the Water	1953	$15
❏ 47-5725	Come Back to My Arms/ This Must Be the Place	1954	$15
❏ 47-4719	Delicado/The World Has a Promise	1952	$15
❏ 47-4561	Double Shuffle/Senator from Tennessee	1952	$30
— With Tex Williams			
❏ 47-6980	Fascination/Till	1957	$10
❏ 47-4286	Getting to Know You/ End of a Love Affair	1951	$20
❏ 47-6683	High Heels/The Whistling Tree	1956	$12
❏ 47-4666	I Am a Heart/To Be Loved by You	1952	$15
❏ 47-6469	I Could Have Danced All Night/What a Heavenly Lover	1956	$10
❏ 47-5838	If I Give My Heart to You/Tempting	1954	$15
❏ 47-5863	I Have to Tell You/ Never Underestimate	1954	$15
❏ 47-5622	I'll Hate Myself in the Morning/Pass the Jam, Sam	1954	$15
❏ 47-7056	I'll Never Say "Never Again" Again/The Kiss That Rocked the Cradle	1957	$10
❏ 47-7349	I'm Sitting on Top of the World/Scene of the Crime	1958	$10
❏ 47-4045	I'm Through with Love/ Makin' Whoopee	1951	$20
❏ 47-5335	I'm Your Girl/Marriage-Type Love	1953	$15
❏ 47-7138	I Never Left Your Arms/ Thirteen Men	1958	$10
❏ 47-4233	It's All in the Game/ Stay Awhile	1951	$20
❏ 47-4136	I Wish, I Wish/The Kissing Song	1951	$20
— With Tony Martin			
❏ 47-5176	Let Me Know/Salomay	1953	$15
❏ 47-4421	Life Is a Beautiful Thing/Why Should I Believe in Love	1951	$20
❏ 47-4060	Lonesome Gal/ Too Late Now	1951	$30
❏ 47-6266	Love and Marriage/Compare	1955	$10
❏ 47-4345	Manhattan/If You Catch a Little Cold	1951	$20
— With Tony Martin			
❏ 47-4493	Marshmallow Moon/ Warm Hearted Woman	1952	$15
❏ 47-4437	Marshmallow Moon/Why Should I Believe in Love	1951	$15
—The above three are 75% of a box set			
❏ 47-5975	Melody of Love/ You're Getting to Be a Habit with Me	1955	$10
— With Tony Martin			
❏ 47-3978	My Heart Cries for You/ Nobody's Chasing Me	1950	$30
❏ 47-4047	My Isle of Golden Dreams/Wonder Where My Baby Is Tonight	1951	$20
—The above three comprise a box set			
❏ 47-4268	Old Soft Shoe/Be Mine Tonight	1951	$20
— With Tony Martin			
❏ 47-4046	Orchids in the Moonlight/ Around the Corner	1951	$20

Number	Title	Yr	NM
❏ 47-4434	Saturday Night in Punkin' Crick/Life Is a Beautiful Thing	1951	$15
❏ 47-6360	Stolen Love/That's All There Is to That	1955	$10
❏ 47-5247	Sweet Thing/Why Come Crying to Me	1953	$15
❏ 47-4174	Sweet Violets/If You Turn Me Down	1951	$30
❏ 47-5825	Tempting/Anyplace I Hang My Hat Is Home	1954	$15
❏ 47-4175	Ten Thousand Miles/ How Many Times	1951	$20
❏ 47-6897	The Cattle Call/ Promises, Promises	1957	$12
❏ 47-4317	The Lie-De-Lie Song/Oh How I Needed You Joe	1951	$20
❏ 47-4225	The Musicians/When D'Ya Do and Shake Hands	1951	$30
— With Betty Hutton, Tony Martin and Phil Harris			
❏ 47-6010	Then I'll Be Happy/ The Stow-Away	1955	$10
❏ 47-7211	The Secret of Happiness/ It's the Second Time You Meet That Matters	1958	$10
❏ 47-5755	Three Coins in the Fountain/Pakistan	1954	$15
❏ 47-4015	Wait for Me/Down in Nashville, Tennessee	1951	$30
❏ 47-4768	West of the Mountains/From the Time You Say Goodbye	1952	$15
❏ 47-6077	Whatever Lola Wants (Lola Gets)/Church Twice on Sundays	1955	$10
❏ 47-6077 [PS]	Whatever Lola Wants (Lola Gets)/Church Twice on Sundays	1955	$30
— Special "This Is Her Life" promotional sleeve			

7-Inch Extended Plays

Number	Title	Yr	NM
CHEVROLET			
❏ 2886/7 [PS]	Season's Best	1960	$12
RCA VICTOR			
❏ EPA-405	Blues in the Night/ Wabash Blues//I Got It Bad and That Ain't Good/ The Birth of the Blues	1952	$20
❏ DJ-56 [DJ]	Chantez-Chantez/ Honkytonk Heart//Too Much/Playing for Keeps	1956	$250
—B-side tracks by Elvis Presley; white label; each side is labeled with the corresponding nuimber for the regular 45 rpm issue			
❏ EPA-405 [PS]	Dinah Shore Sings the Blues, Vol. 1	1952	$20
❏ EPA-4119	Opening/You Meet the Nicest People/Have Yourself a Merry Little Christmas//Christmas Party/Happy Christmas Little Friend/Closing	1957	$15

SHORT, BOBBY

Number	Title	Yr	NM
ATLANTIC			
❏ 1157	Down in Mexico/ Sand in My Shoes	1957	$15

SHORTER, WAYNE

Number	Title	Yr	NM
VEE JAY			
❏ 363	Black Diamond/ Harry's Last Stand	1960	$15

SHOTGUN EXPRESS

Number	Title	Yr	NM
UPTOWN			
❏ 747	I Could Feel the Whole World Turn/Curtains	1967	$40

SHOWMEN, THE

Number	Title	Yr	NM
AMY			
❏ 11036	Action/What Would It Take	1968	$8
IMPERIAL			
❏ 66071	Country Fool/ Somebody Help Me	1964	$15
❏ 66033	It Will Stand/Country Fool	1964	$15
LIBERTY			
❏ 56166	It Will Stand/Country Fool	1970	$6
MINIT			
❏ 662	39-21-46/Swish Fish	1963	$30
❏ 32007	39-21-46/Swish Fish	1966	$12
❏ 647	Com'n Home/I Love You, Can't You See	1962	$30
❏ 632	It Will Stand/Country Fool	1961	$40
— Orange label			
❏ 632	It Will Stand/Country Fool	1961	$30
— Black label			
❏ 643	The Wrong Girl/Fate Planned It This Way	1962	$60
❏ 654	True Fine Mama/ The Owl Sees You	1962	$30
SWAN			
❏ 4213	In Paradise/Take It Baby	1965	$10

Number	Title	Yr	NM
❏ 4219	Our Love Will Grow/ You're Everything	1965	$10
❏ 4241	Please Try and Understand/ Honey House	1966	$10
UNITED ARTISTS			
❏ 0100	It Will Stand/I'm a Happy Man	1973	$5
— Silver Spotlight Series" reissue; B-side by the Jive Five			

SHUFFLES, THE

Number	Title	Yr	NM
RAYCO			
❏ 508	Do You Remember My Darling/Dancin' Little Girl	1963	$200

SHURFINE SINGERS, THE

Number	Title	Yr	NM
JOSIE			
❏ 969	Go Tell It on the Mountain/ Silent Night & The 11 O'Clock News	1966	$10

SHUT DOWNS, THE

Number	Title	Yr	NM
DIMENSION			
❏ 1016	Four on the Floor/ Beach Buggy	1963	$30
KARSONG			
❏ 501	Four on the Floor/ Straightaway	1963	$60

SICKNICKS, THE

Number	Title	Yr	NM
AMY			
❏ 824	The Presidential Press Conference (Part 1)/ The Presidential Press Conference (Part 2)	1961	$20
❏ 824 [PS]	The Presidential Press Conference (Part 1)/ The Presidential Press Conference (Part 2)	1961	$30
❏ 831	Wadja Say Mr. K (Part 1)/ Wadja Say Mr. K (Part 2)	1961	$20

SIDE OF THE ROAD GANG, THE

Number	Title	Yr	NM
CAPITOL			
❏ 4298	Suitcase Life/Sittin' by the Side of the Road	1976	$5
❏ 4338	What Am I Doin' Hangin' 'Round/People in Dallas Got Hair	1976	$5

SIDEBOTTOM, FRANK
7-Inch Extended Plays

Number	Title	Yr	NM
IN TAPE			
❏ IT 041	Christmas Is Really Fantastic/Oh Come All Ye Faithful//Mull Of Timperley/ Christmas Medley	1987	$5
❏ IT 041 [PS]	(title unknown)	1987	$5
— Both record and sleeve are U.K. imports			

SIDEKICKS, THE

Number	Title	Yr	NM
RCA VICTOR			
❏ 47-8969	Fifi the Flea/Not Now	1966	$10
❏ 47-9079	He's My Friend/ Miss Charlotte	1967	$12
❏ 47-9174	Sight and Sound/You Gave Me Somebody to Love	1967	$10
❏ 47-8864	Suspicions/Up on the Roof	1966	$10

SIDEWALK SURFERS, THE

Number	Title	Yr	NM
JUBILEE			
❏ 5496	Skate Board/Fun Last Summer	1965	$60

SIERRAS, THE

Number	Title	Yr	NM
DOT			
❏ 16569	Plan for Love/Then I'll Still Love You	1963	$15
GOLDISC			
❏ G-4	I Should Have Loved You/I'll Believe It When I See It	1963	$40
KNOX			
❏ 102	So Many Sleepless Nights/Nearer My Heart	1962	$125
MAIL CALL			
❏ 2333/4	Stormy Weather/Chance	1963	$200

SIGLER, BUNNY

Number	Title	Yr	NM
CRAIG			
❏ 501	I Won't Cry/Come On Home	1961	$40
— As Bunny "Mr. Emotions" Sigler			
DECCA			
❏ 31880	Everything's Gonna Be All Right/For Cryin' Out Loud	1965	$30
❏ 31947	Will You Love Me Tomorrow/ Comparatively Speaking	1966	$15

Number	Title	Yr	NM
❏ 32183	Will You Love Me Tomorrow/ Let Them Talk	1967	$10

GOLD MIND

Number	Title	Yr	NM
❏ 4018	By the Way You Dance (I Knew It Was You)/ Glad to Be Your Lover	1979	$5
❏ 4014	Don't Even Try (Give It Up)/I'm a Fool	1978	$5
❏ 4010	I Got What You Need/ It's Time to Twist	1978	$5
❏ 4020	I'm Funking You Tonight with My Music/Glad to Be Your Lover	1979	$5
❏ 4008	Let Me Party with You (Part 1) (Party, Party, Party)/ Let Me Party with You (Part 2) (Party, Party, Party)	1977	$5
❏ 4012	Only You/Good Good Feeling	1978	$6

—A-side with Loleatta Holloway; B-side is Holloway solo

NEPTUNE

Number	Title	Yr	NM
❏ 24	Conquer the World Together/ We're Only Human	1970	$8

—With Cindy Scott

Number	Title	Yr	NM
❏ 25	Don't Stop Doing What You're Doing/Where Do the Lonely Go	1970	$8
❏ 15	We're Only Human/ Sure Didn't Take Long	1969	$8

—With Cindy Scott

Number	Title	Yr	NM
❏ 14	Where Do the Lonely Go/Great Big Liar	1969	$8

PARKWAY

Number	Title	Yr	NM
❏ 6001	Follow Your Heart/ Can You Dig It	1967	$10
❏ 123	Girl Don't Make Me Wait/ Always in the Wrong Place (At the Wrong Time)	1966	$10
❏ 153	Let the Good Times Roll & Feel So Good/There's No Love Left (In This Old Heart of Mine)	1967	$15
❏ 6000	Lovey Dovey & You're So Fine/Sunny Sunday	1967	$10

PHILADELPHIA INT'L.

Number	Title	Yr	NM
❏ 3512	Conquer the World Together/ We Gotta Good Thing Goin'	1971	$6

—With Dee Dee Sharp

Number	Title	Yr	NM
❏ 3505	Everybody Needs Good Lovin' (Part 1)/Everybody Needs Good Lovin' (Part 2)	1971	$6
❏ 3519	Heaven Knows I've Changed/Regina	1972	$6
❏ 3545	Love Train (Part 1)/ Love Train (Part 2)	1974	$6
❏ 3597	My Music/Can't Believe That You Love Me	1976	$6
❏ 3560	Shake Your Booty/ Your Love Is Good	1975	$6
❏ 3575	Somebody Free/That's How Long I'll Be Loving You	1975	$6
❏ 3608	Somebody Loves You/ Woman, Woman	1976	$6
❏ 3536	That's How Long I'll Be Loving You/Heaven Knows I've Changed	1973	$6
❏ 3532	Theme from "Five Fingers of Death"/Regina	1973	$6
❏ 3523	Tossin' and Turnin'/Picture Us	1972	$6

SALSOUL

Number	Title	Yr	NM
❏ 2114	How Can I Tell Her (It's Over)/ Since the Day I First Saw You	1980	$4
❏ 2125	Super Duper Duper Superman/Kool Aid	1980	$4

SILBERMAN, BENEDICT, ORCHESTRA AND CHORUS

PALETTE

Number	Title	Yr	NM
❏ 5037	The Chipmunk Song/ Lovers of Paris	1959	$12

SILHOUETTES, THE

ACE

Number	Title	Yr	NM
❏ 562	Evelyn/Never Will Part	1959	$30

—As "Bill Horton and the Silhouettes"

Number	Title	Yr	NM
❏ 552	I Sold My Heart to the Junkman/ What Would You Do	1958	$30

EMBER

Number	Title	Yr	NM
❏ 1037	Bing Bong/Voodoo Eyes	1958	$30
❏ 1029	Get a Job/I Am Lonely	1958	$40

—Red label

Number	Title	Yr	NM
❏ 1029	Get a Job/I Am Lonely	1958	$50

—Orange label

Number	Title	Yr	NM
❏ 1029	Get a Job/I Am Lonely	1960	$30

—Black label

Number	Title	Yr	NM
❏ 1032	Headin' for the Poorhouse/ Miss Thing	1958	$30

GRAND

Number	Title	Yr	NM
❏ 142	Wish I Could Be There/ Move On Over	1956	$200

IMPERIAL

Number	Title	Yr	NM
❏ 5899	The Push/Which Way Did She Go	1962	$15

JUNIOR

Number	Title	Yr	NM
❏ 400	Evelyn/Never Will Part	1959	$200

Number	Title	Yr	NM
❏ 391	Get a Job/I Am Lonely	1957	$800

—Brown label (first press)

Number	Title	Yr	NM
❏ 391	Get a Job/I Am Lonely	1957	$600

—Blue label (second press)

Number	Title	Yr	NM
❏ 396	I Sold My Heart to the Junkman/What Would You Do	1958	$125

SILK

DECCA

Number	Title	Yr	NM
❏ 32829	Come Over Here/Falling in Love Isn't Easy	1971	$8

SILKIE, THE

FONTANA

Number	Title	Yr	NM
❏ 1551	Born to Be With You/I'm So Sorry	1966	$10

SILVA TONES, THE

ARGO

Number	Title	Yr	NM
❏ 5281	Chi-Wa-Wa (That's All I Want from You)/ Roses Are Blooming	1957	$30
❏ 5281	That's All I Want from You/ Roses Are Blooming	1957	$40

MONARCH

Number	Title	Yr	NM
❏ 615	That's All I Want from You/ Roses Are Blooming	1957	$40

—Black label

Number	Title	Yr	NM
❏ 615	That's All I Want from You/ Weepin' and a-Wailin'	1957	$60

—Yellow label

SILVER

ARISTA

Number	Title	Yr	NM
❏ 0210	Memory/So Much for the Past	1976	$4
❏ 0227	Musician (It's Not An Easy Life)/Goodbye, So Long	1977	$4
❏ 0189	Wham Bam/Right on Time	1976	$4

—Third pressings: Same label as second pressings with altered title

Number	Title	Yr	NM
❏ 0189	Wham Bam Shang-a-Lang/Right on Time	1976	$5

—Originals on white labels with pale blue logo

Number	Title	Yr	NM
❏ 0189	Wham Bam Shang-a-Lang/Right on Time	1976	$6

—Second pressings on pale blue labels with white logo

SILVER APPLES

KAPP

Number	Title	Yr	NM
❏ 923	Whirly Bird/Oscillations	1968	$8

SILVER CHALICE

FINAL GEAR

Number	Title	Yr	NM
❏ 00	Wasted/Hot Tears	1979	$30
❏ 00 [PS]	Wasted/Hot Tears	1979	$40

SILVER CITY BAND

COLUMBIA

Number	Title	Yr	NM
❏ 3-10601	If You Really Want Me To I'll Go/Georgia Girl	1977	$5
❏ 3-10759	I'm Still Missing You/ Valentine Partner	1978	$5

SILVER CONVENTION

MIDLAND INT'L.

Number	Title	Yr	NM
❏ MB-10339	Fly, Robin, Fly/ Chains of Love	1975	$6

—First pressing: "Fly, Robin, Fly" is 3:45, matrix number is 10339-A

Number	Title	Yr	NM
❏ MB-10339	Fly, Robin, Fly/ Chains of Love	1975	$4

—Second pressing: "Fly, Robin, Fly" is 3:05, matrix number is 10339-Z

Number	Title	Yr	NM
❏ MB-10571	Get Up and Boogie (That's Right)/Son of a Gun	1976	$6

—First pressing: "Get Up and Boogie" is 4:05, matrix number is 10571-A

Number	Title	Yr	NM
❏ MB-10571	Get Up and Boogie (That's Right)/Son of a Gun	1976	$4

—Second pressing: "Get Up and Boogie" is under three minutes long

Number	Title	Yr	NM
❏ MB-10571 [PS]	Get Up and Boogie (That's Right)/Son of a Gun	1976	$6
❏ MB-10212	Save Me/Save Me Again	1975	$4
❏ MB-10849	Thank You Mr. D.J./ Dancing in the Aisles (Take Me Higher)	1976	$4

MIDSONG INT'L.

Number	Title	Yr	NM
❏ 40896	Breakfast in Bed/Spend the Night with Me	1978	$4
❏ GB-10939	Fly, Robin, Fly/Get Up and Boogie (That's Right)	1977	$3

—Gold Standard Series

Number	Title	Yr	NM
❏ MB-11062	Save Me '77/Hotshot	1977	$4
❏ MB-10972	Telegram/(B-side unknown)	1977	$4

SILVER FLEET

UNI

Number	Title	Yr	NM
❏ 55271	Look Out World/ C'mon Plane	1971	$30

SILVER, HORACE

Number	Title	Yr	NM
❏ 1751	Blowin' the Blues Away/ The Baghdad Blues	1959	$10
❏ 1750	Break City/Sister Sadie	1959	$10
❏ 1741	Cookin' at the Continental/ Juicy Lucy	1959	$10
❏ 1818	Doin' the Thing (Part 1)/ Doin' the Thing (Part 2)	1961	$12
❏ 1946	Down and Out/ Take a Little Love	1969	$8
❏ 1903	Dragon Lady/Sweet Sweetie Dee	1963	$12
❏ 1817	Filthy McNasty (Part 1)/ Filthy McNasty (Part 2)	1961	$10
❏ 1740	Finger Poppin'/ Come On Home	1959	$10
❏ 1902	Let's Get to the Nitty Gritty/Silver's Serenade	1963	$12
❏ XW325	Liberated Brother/Nothin' Can Stop Me Now	1973	$5
❏ 1742	Mellow D/Swingin' the Samba	1959	$10
❏ 1872	Sayonara Blues (Part 1)/ Sayonara Blues (Part 2)	1962	$10
❏ 1939	Serenade to a Soul Sister/ Psychedelic Sally	1968	$8
❏ XW905	Slow Down (Tranquilizer Suite)/Time and Effort	1976	$5
❏ 1912	Song for My Father (Part 1)/ Song for My Father (Part 2)	1964	$8
❏ 1784	Strollin'/Nica's Dream	1960	$10
❏ 1924	The African Queen (Part 1)/ The African Queen (Part 2)	1965	$8
❏ 1923	The Cape Verdean Blues/Pretty Eyes	1965	$8
❏ XW1032	Togetherness/Out of the Night (Came You)	1977	$5
❏ 1871	Tokyo Blues (Part 1)/ Tokyo Blues (Part 2)	1962	$10
❏ 1873	Too Much Sake (Part 1)/ Too Much Sake (Part 2)	1962	$10
❏ 1785	Where Are You?/ Me and My Baby	1960	$10

SILVERSTEIN, SHEL

COLUMBIA

Number	Title	Yr	NM
❏ 45450	A Front Row Seat to Hear Ole Johnny Sing/26 Second Song	1971	$6
❏ 45885	All About You/ Peace Proposal	1973	$6
❏ 10053	Everybody's Makin' It Big But Me/The Man Who Got No Sign	1974	$5
❏ 45772	Sahra Cynthia Sylvia Stout Would Not Take the Garbage Out/Stacey Brown Got Two	1973	$6
❏ 10153	Sahra Cynthia Sylvia Stout Would Not Take the Garbage Out/The Man Who Got No Sign	1975	$5

RCA VICTOR

Number	Title	Yr	NM
❏ 74-0158	A Boy Named Sue/ Somebody Stole My Rig	1969	$8
❏ 47-9844	Policeman, Woman, Taxicab/Three Legged Man	1970	$8

SIMEONE, HARRY, CHORALE

20TH CENTURY

Number	Title	Yr	NM
❏ 2434	The Little Drummer Boy/Oh Holy Night	1979	$4

20TH FOX

Number	Title	Yr	NM
❏ 121	The Little Drummer Boy/Die Lorelei	1958	$30

—Original pressings have light blue labels with no "Original Version" on label

Number	Title	Yr	NM
❏ 121 [PS]	The Little Drummer Boy/Die Lorelei	1958	$30
❏ 121	The Little Drummer Boy/Die Lorelei	1959	$20

—Second pressings have light blue labels with "Original Version" in a box and a brief outline of the song on label

Number	Title	Yr	NM
❏ 121 [PS]	The Little Drummer Boy/Die Lorelei	1959	$20

—Second version with "Original Version" on front and lyrics on back

Number	Title	Yr	NM
❏ 429	The Little Drummer Boy/O Holy Night	1963	$8
❏ 6429 [PS]	The Little Drummer Boy/O Holy Night	1964	$8
❏ 6429	The Little Drummer Boy/O Holy Night	1964	$6

KAPP

Number	Title	Yr	NM
❏ 628	O Bambino (One Cold and Blessed Winter)/Sing of a Merry Christmas	1964	$8

Number	Title	Yr	NM
❑ 628 [PS]	O Bambino (One Cold and Blessed Winter)/Sing of a Merry Christmas	1964	$15
❑ 711	The Little Drummer Boy/Hallelujah	1965	$8

—Re-recording of 1958 hit

MCA

❑ 65030	The Little Drummer Boy/O Bambino	1973	$4

—Black label with rainbow; this contains the 1965 Kapp re-recording of the A-side

❑ 65030	The Little Drummer Boy/O Bambino	1980	$3

—Blue label with rainbow; this contains the 1965 Kapp re-recording of the A-side

MERCURY

❑ 72065	Do You Hear What I Hear?/March of the Angels	1962	$8

—Maroon label

❑ 72065	Do You Hear What I Hear?/March of the Angels	1962	$8

—Black label

SIMMONS, "JUMPIN'" GENE

AGP

❑ 119	Back Home Again/Don't Worry About Me	1969	$8

CHECKER

❑ 948	Bad Boy Willie/Goin' Back to Memphis	1960	$15

DELTUNE

❑ 1201	Why Didn't I Think of That/Tennessee Party Time	1977	$8

—As "Gene Simmons"

EPIC

❑ 10601	She's There When I Come Home/Magnolia Street	1970	$6

HI

❑ 2050	Caldonia/Be Her Number One	1962	$10
❑ 2113	Go On Shoes/Keep That Meat in the Pan	1966	$10
❑ 2076	Haunted House/Hey, Hey Little Girl	1964	$20

—As "Gene Simmons"

❑ 2076	Haunted House/Hey, Hey Little Girl	1964	$20

—As "Jumpin' Gene Simmons"

❑ 2092	Mattie Rae/Folsom Prison Blues	1965	$10
❑ 2086	Skinnie Minnie/I'm a Ramblin' Man	1965	$12
❑ 2102	The Batman/Bossy Boss	1966	$20
❑ 2080	The Dodo/The Jump	1964	$12

MALA

❑ 12012	I'm Just a Loser/Lila	1968	$10

SANDY

❑ 1027	The Waiting Game/Shenandoah Waltz	1959	$30

—As "Morris Gene Simmons"

SUN

❑ 299	Drinkin' Wine/I Done Told You	1958	$200

—As "Gene Simmons"

SIMMS, LU ANN

COLUMBIA

❑ 40089	I Dreamt That I Was Santa Claus/I Just Can't Wait 'Til Christmas	1953	$20
❑ 170	I Dreamt That I Was Santa Claus/I Just Can't Wait 'Til Christmas	1953	$15
❑ 170 [PS]	I Dreamt That I Was Santa Claus/I Just Can't Wait 'Til Christmas	1953	$20

SIMON AND GARFUNKEL
Also see ART GARFUNKEL; PAUL SIMON; TOM AND JERRY.

ABC-PARAMOUNT

❑ 10788	That's My Story/Tia-Juana Blues	1966	$30

—Outtakes from Tom and Jerry days

COLUMBIA

❑ JZSP116469 [DJ]	7 O'Clock News-Silent Night (same on both sides)	1966	$30

—Promo-only Christmas release for radio stations

❑ JZSP116469 [DJ]	7 O'Clock News-Silent Night (same on both sides)	1966	$30

—Promo-only Christmas release for radio stations

❑ 43873	A Hazy Shade of Winter/For Emily, Wherever I May Find Her	1966	$10
❑ 45663	America/For Emily, Whenever I May Find Her	1972	$6
❑ AS43 [DJ]	America/Keep the Customer Satisfied	1972	$15
❑ 44046	At the Zoo/The 59th Street Bridge Song (Feelin' Groovy)	1967	$12

Number	Title	Yr	NM
❑ 44046 [PS]	At the Zoo/The 59th Street Bridge Song (Feelin' Groovy)	1967	$50
❑ 44785 [DJ]	Baby Driver (mono/stereo)	1969	$20

—Promo 45s exist promoting this song as the "hit"!

❑ 45079	Bridge Over Troubled Water/Keep the Customer Satisfied	1970	$6
❑ 45079 [PS]	Bridge Over Troubled Water/Keep the Customer Satisfied	1970	$8
❑ 45133	Cecilia/The Only Living Boy in New York	1970	$6

—Red label, "Columbia" in black at top

❑ 45133 [PS]	Cecilia/The Only Living Boy in New York	1970	$8
❑ 45133	Cecilia/The Only Living Boy in New York	1970	$10

—Red label, continuous "Columbia Records" in white along outer edge

❑ 45237	El Condor Pasa/Why Don't You Write Me	1970	$6
❑ 44232	Fakin' It/You Don't Know Where Your Interest Lies	1967	$10

—As far as we can tell, all copies have the A-side listed with a time of "2:74"

❑ 43511	Homeward Bound/Leaves That Are Green	1966	$12
❑ 43511 [DJ]	Homeward Bound (same on both sides)	1966	$60

—Red vinyl promo

❑ 43511 [DJ]	Homeward Bound (same on both sides)	1966	$60

—Red vinyl promo

❑ 43617	I Am a Rock/Flowers Never Bend with the Rainfall	1966	$10
❑ 43617 [DJ]	I Am a Rock (same on both sides)	1966	$60

—Red vinyl promo

❑ 43617 [DJ]	I Am a Rock (same on both sides)	1966	$60

—Red vinyl promo

❑ 44511	Mrs. Robinson/Old Friends-Bookends	1968	$10

—Label says "From the Motion Picture 'The Graduate'"

❑ 44511	Mrs. Robinson/Old Friends-Bookends	1968	$8

—Label says "From the Columbia Lp BOOKENDS," etc. with no reference to "The Graduate"

❑ 10230	My Little Town//Art Garfunkel: Rag Doll/Paul Simon: You're Kind	1975	$5
❑ 10230 [PS]	My Little Town//Art Garfunkel: Rag Doll/Paul Simon: You're Kind	1975	$5
❑ 44465	Scarborough Fair (/Canticle)/April Come She Will	1968	$10
❑ 44785	The Boxer/Baby Driver	1969	$6

—B-side mix (mono) is different than stereo LP version, especially near the end of the song

❑ 44785 [PS]	The Boxer/Baby Driver	1969	$8
❑ 43728 [DJ]	The Dangling Conversation (same on both sides)	1966	$60

—Red vinyl promo

❑ 43728 [DJ]	The Dangling Conversation (same on both sides)	1966	$60

—Red vinyl promo

❑ 43728	The Dangling Conversation/The Big Bright Green Pleasure Machine	1966	$12
❑ 43728 [PS]	The Dangling Conversation/The Big Bright Green Pleasure Machine	1966	$30
❑ 43396 [DJ]	The Sounds of Silence (Acoustic)/(Electric)	1965	$60

—Red vinyl promo containing, possibly in error, the acoustic version on one side and the electric version on the other; the acoustic version has ZSP-111384-1D in the trail-off wax and the electric version has ZSP-111384-1C in the trail-off

❑ 43396 [DJ]	The Sounds of Silence (same on both sides)	1965	$60

—Red vinyl promo

❑ 43396	The Sounds of Silence/We've Got a Groovey Thing Goin'	1965	$10

—With the "folk-rock" hit version of the A-side

❑ 43396	The Sounds of Silence/We've Got a Groovey Thing Goin'	1965	$60

—With the original acoustic version of the A-side; a known stock copy is pressed on vinyl rather than styrene and has the number "ZSP 111384-1G" in the dead wax

WARNER BROS.

❑ 50053	Wake Up Little Susie/Me and Julio Down by the Schoolyard	1982	$4

7-Inch Extended Plays

COLUMBIA

❑ 7-9529	A Hazy Shade of Winter/Mrs. Robinson/Bookends Theme//At the Zoo/Old Friends/Fakin' It	1968	$20

—Jukebox issue; small hole, plays at 33 1/3 rpm

❑ 7-9529 [PS]	Bookends	1968	$20
❑ 7-9914 [PS]	Bridge Over Troubled Water	1970	$20

Number	Title	Yr	NM
❑ 7-9914	Song for the Asking/So Long, Frank Lloyd Wright/El Condor Pasa//Keep the Customer Satisfied/Why Don't You Write Me/Bye Bye Love	1970	$20

—Jukebox issue; small hole, plays at 33 1/3 rpm

SIMON, CARLY
Also see THE SIMON SISTERS.

ARISTA

❑ 9653	All I Want Is You/On a Hot Summer Night	1987	$3
❑ 9653 [PS]	All I Want Is You/On a Hot Summer Night	1987	$3
❑ 9525	Coming Around Again/Itsy Bitsy Spider	1986	$3
❑ 9525 [PS]	Coming Around Again/Itsy Bitsy Spider	1986	$8

—With "Heartburn" movie scenes

❑ 9525 [PS]	Coming Around Again/Itsy Bitsy Spider	1986	$4

—Black and white photo of Carly Simon

❑ 9525 [PS]	Coming Around Again/Itsy Bitsy Spider	1986	$4

—Color photo of Carly Simon

❑ 9732 [DJ]	Do the Walls Come Down (same on both sides)	1988	$5

—Not released as stock copy on this number

❑ 9732 [PS]	Do the Walls Come Down (same on both sides)	1988	$5

—Promo-only picture sleeve

❑ 9587	Give Me All Night/Sleight of Hand	1987	$3
❑ 9587 [PS]	Give Me All Night/Sleight of Hand	1987	$3
❑ 9793	Let the River Run/The Turn of the Tide	1988	$3
❑ 9793 [PS]	Let the River Run/The Turn of the Tide	1988	$3
❑ 9619	The Stuff That Dreams Are Made Of/As Time Goes By	1987	$3
❑ 9619 [PS]	The Stuff That Dreams Are Made Of/As Time Goes By	1987	$3

ELEKTRA

❑ 45759	Anticipation/The Garden	1971	$6
❑ 45246	Attitude Dancing/Are You Ticklish	1975	$5
❑ 45506	Devoted to You/Boys in the Trees	1978	$4

—A-side with James Taylor

❑ 45341	Half a Chance/Libby	1976	$4

—Butterfly label

❑ 45341	Half a Chance/Libby	1976	$5

—Red label

❑ 45857	Haven't Got Time for the Pain/Mind on My Man	1974	$5
❑ 69953	Hidin' Away/Fight for It	1982	$5

—With Jesse Colin Young

❑ 69953 [PS]	Hidin' Away/Fight for It	1982	$6

—With Jesse Colin Young

❑ 45325	It Keeps You Runnin'/Look Me in the Eyes	1976	$4
❑ 45774	Legend in Your Own Time/Julie Through the Glass	1972	$6
❑ 45880	Mockingbird/Grownup	1974	$5

—A-side with James Taylor

❑ 45278	More and More/Love Out in the Street	1975	$4
❑ 46514	Spy/Pure Sin	1979	$4
❑ 45724	That's the Way I've Always Heard It Should Be/Alone	1971	$6
❑ 45796	The Girl You Think You Are/Share the Land	1972	$6
❑ 45544	Tranquillo (Melt My Heart)/Back Down to Earth	1978	$4
❑ 45263	Waterfall/After the Storm	1975	$5

EPIC

❑ 05596	My New Boyfriend/The Wives Are in Connecticut	1985	$3
❑ 05419	Tired of Being Blonde/Black Honeymoon	1985	$3
❑ 05419 [PS]	Tired of Being Blonde/Black Honeymoon	1985	$4

MIRAGE

❑ 99963	Why/(Instrumental)	1982	$4
❑ 4051	Why/Why	1982	$4

—B-side by Chic

❑ 4051 [PS]	Why/Why	1982	$6

PLANET

❑ YB-13779	Someone Waits for You/(B-side unknown)	1984	$4

WARNER BROS.

❑ 50027	Body and Soul/Get Along Without You Very Well	1982	$4
❑ 49689	Come Upstairs/Them	1981	$4
❑ 49880	From the Heart/Hurt	1981	$4
❑ 29428	Hello Big Man/Dawn You Get to Me	1983	$4
❑ 49630	Take Me As I Am/James	1980	$4

SIMON, JOE

COMPLEAT

Number	Title	Yr	NM
❑ 140	It Turns Me Inside Out/ Morning, Noon and Night	1985	$4
❑ 146	Mr. Right or Mr. Right Now/Let Me Have My Way with You	1985	$4

HUSH

Number	Title	Yr	NM
❑ 104	Call My Name/Everybody Needs Somebody	1961	$15
❑ 107	I See Your Face/Troubles	1961	$15
❑ 103	It's a Miracle/Land of Love	1960	$15
❑ 108	Land of Love/I Keep Remembering	1962	$15
❑ 106	Pledge of Love/It's All Over	1961	$15

POSSE

Number	Title	Yr	NM
❑ 5010	Are We Breaking Up/ We're Together	1981	$5
❑ 5001	Baby, When Love Is In Your Heart (It's In Your Eyes)/ Are We Breaking Up	1980	$5
❑ 5014	Fallin' in Love with You/Magnolia	1981	$5
❑ 5021	Get Down, Get Down "82"/ It Be's That Way Sometime	1982	$5
❑ 5005	Glad You Came My Way/I Don't Wanna Make Love	1980	$5
❑ 5019	Go Sam/(Instrumental)	1982	$5

SOUND STAGE 7

Number	Title	Yr	NM
❑ 2634	Baby, Don't Be Looking in My Mind/Don't Let Me Lose the Feeling	1969	$6
❑ 2656	Farther On Down the Road/Wounded Man	1970	$6
❑ 1521	Funny How Time Slips Away/ Message from Maria	1976	$5
❑ 2641	It's Hard to Get Along/San Francisco Is a Lonely Town	1969	$6
❑ 2622	Looking Back/Standing in the Safety Zone	1968	$8
❑ 2617	Message from Maria/I Worry About You	1968	$8
❑ 1508	Misty Blue/That's the Way I Want Our Love	1972	$5
❑ 2651	Moon Walk Part 1/ Moon Walk Part 2	1969	$6
❑ 2577	My Special Prayer/Travelin' Man	1966	$8
❑ 2637	Oon-Guela (Part 1)/ Oon-Guela (Part 2)	1969	$8
❑ 2583	Put Your Trust in Me (Depend on Me)/Just a Dream	1967	$8
❑ 1514	Someone to Lean On/I Got a Whole Lotta Lovin'	1974	$5
❑ 2564	Teenager's Prayer/ Long Hot Summer	1966	$8
❑ 2667	That's the Way I Want Our Love/When	1970	$6
❑ 2628	The Chokin' Kind/ Come On and Get It	1969	$6
❑ 2569	Too Many Teardrops/What Makes a Man Feel Good	1966	$8
❑ 1512	Who's Julie/The Girl's Alright with Me	1973	$5

SPRING

Number	Title	Yr	NM
❑ 145	Carry Me/Do You Know What It's Like to Be Lonesome	1974	$5
❑ 166	Come Get to This/Let the Good Times Roll	1976	$5
❑ 120	Drowning in the Sea of Love/Let Me Be the One	1971	$5
❑ 169	Easy to Love/Can't Stand the Pain	1976	$5
❑ 178	For Your Love, Love, Love/I've Got a Jones on You Baby	1977	$5
❑ 118	Georgia Blues/All My Hard Times	1971	$5
❑ 156	Get Down, Get Down (Get On the Floor)/In My Baby's Arms	1975	$5
❑ 194	Going Through These Changes/I Can't Stand a Liar	1979	$5
❑ 113	Help Me Make It Through the Night/To Lay Down Beside You	1971	$5
❑ 113 [PS]	Help Me Make It Through the Night/To Lay Down Beside You	1971	$6
❑ 3006	Hooked on Disco Music/I Still Love You	1980	$5
❑ 163	I Need You, You Need Me/I'll Take Care (Of You)	1975	$5
❑ 184	I.O.U./It Must Be Love	1978	$5
❑ 3003	I Wanna Taste Your Love/ Make Every Moment Count	1979	$5
❑ 190	Love Vibration/(Instrumental)	1978	$5
❑ 159	Music in My Bones/Fire Burning	1975	$5
❑ 176	One Step at a Time/ Track of Your Love	1977	$5
❑ 124	Pool of Bad Luck/Glad to Be Your Lover	1972	$5
❑ 128	Power of Love/The Mirror Don't Lie	1972	$5
❑ 133	Step by Step/Talk Don't Bother Me	1973	$5
❑ 149	The Best Time of My Life/ What We Gonna Do Now	1974	$5
❑ 138	Theme from Cleopatra Jones/Who Is That Lady	1973	$5
❑ 138 [PS]	Theme from Cleopatra Jones/Who Is That Lady	1973	$6
❑ 130	Trouble in My Home/I Found My Dad	1972	$5

VEE JAY

Number	Title	Yr	NM
❑ 694	Let's Do It Over/The Whoo Pee	1965	$8
❑ 609	My Adorable One/Say (That My Love Is True)	1964	$8

Number	Title	Yr	NM
❑ 663	When You're Near/ When I'm Gone	1965	$8

SIMON, PAUL

Includes records under various pseudonyms, such as "Paul Kane," "Jerry Landis" and "True Taylor." Also see SIMON AND GARFUNKEL; TICO AND THE TRIUMPHS; TOM AND JERRY

AMY

Number	Title	Yr	NM
❑ 875	The Lone Teen Ranger/Lisa	1962	$70

—As "Jerry Landis

BIG

Number	Title	Yr	NM
❑ 614	True or False/Teenage Fool	1958	$125

—As "True Taylor

CANADIAN AMERICAN

Number	Title	Yr	NM
❑ 130	I'm Lonely/I Wish I Weren't in Love	1961	$125

—As "Jerry Landis"; the rarest of his pre-Columbia solo singles

COLUMBIA

Number	Title	Yr	NM
❑ 10270	50 Ways to Leave Your Lover/ Some Folks Lives Roll Easy	1975	$5
❑ 45900	American Tune/One Man's Ceiling Is Another Man's Floor	1973	$5
❑ 45900 [PS]	American Tune/One Man's Ceiling Is Another Man's Floor	1973	$10
❑ 45638	Duncan/Run That Body Down	1972	$5
❑ 10197	Gone at Last/Take Me to the Mardi Gras	1975	$5

—A-side with Phoebe Snow and the Jesse Dixon Singers

Number	Title	Yr	NM
❑ 45907	Loves Me Like a Rock/ Learn How to Fall	1973	$5

—With the Dixie Hummingbirds

Number	Title	Yr	NM
❑ 45585	Me and Julio Down by the Schoolyard/Congratulations	1972	$5

—Orange label

Number	Title	Yr	NM
❑ 45585	Me and Julio Down by the Schoolyard/Congratulations	1972	$4

—Gray label

Number	Title	Yr	NM
❑ 45547	Mother and Child Reunion/ Paranoia Blues	1972	$5

—Orange label

Number	Title	Yr	NM
❑ 45547	Mother and Child Reunion/ Paranoia Blues	1972	$4

—Gray label

Number	Title	Yr	NM
❑ 10630	Slip Slidin' Away/ Something So Right	1977	$6

—First pressings claim the A-side came from the LP "Blatant Greatest Hits." The Oak Ridge Boys are not mentioned.

Number	Title	Yr	NM
❑ 10630	Slip Slidin' Away/ Something So Right	1977	$5

—Later pressings correct the LP title to "Greatest Hits, Etc." The Oak Ridge Boys are credited in the fine print.

Number	Title	Yr	NM
❑ 10332	Still Crazy After All These Years/I Do It for Your Love (Live)	1976	$5
❑ 10711	Stranded in a Limousine/ Have a Good Time	1978	$6
❑ 46038	The Sound of Silence/ Mother and Child Reunion	1974	$8

MGM

Number	Title	Yr	NM
❑ 12822	Anna Belle/Loneliness	1959	$60

—As "Jerry Landis

TRIBUTE

Number	Title	Yr	NM
❑ 128	Carlos Dominguez/ He Was My Brother	1963	$70

—As "Paul Kane"; authentic copies make no mention of Paul Simon on the label

WARNER BROS.

Number	Title	Yr	NM
❑ 29453	Allergies/Think Too Much (ii)	1983	$4
❑ 29453 [PS]	Allergies/Think Too Much (ii)	1983	$4
❑ 28389	Diamonds on the Soles of Her Shoes/All Around the World Or the Myth of Fingerprints	1987	$3
❑ 28389 [PS]	Diamonds on the Soles of Her Shoes/All Around the World Or the Myth of Fingerprints	1987	$3
❑ 28522	Graceland/Hearts and Bones	1986	$3
❑ 28522 [PS]	Graceland/Hearts and Bones	1986	$3
❑ 27903	Graceland/Hearts and Bones	1988	$5
❑ 49511	Late in the Evening/How the Heart Approaches What It Yearns	1980	$4
❑ 49511 [PS]	Late in the Evening/How the Heart Approaches What It Yearns	1980	$5
❑ 49675	Oh, Marion/God Bless the Absentee	1981	$4
❑ 49601	One-Trick Pony/Long, Long Day	1980	$4
❑ 28460 [PS]	The Boy in the Bubble/ Crazy Love, Part 2	1987	$3
❑ 28460	The Boy in the Bubble/ Crazy Love, Part 2	1987	$3
❑ 29333	Think Too Much/Song About the Moon	1984	$4

WARWICK

Number	Title	Yr	NM
❑ 588	I'd Like to Be/Just a Boy	1960	$60

—As "Jerry Landis

Number	Title	Yr	NM
❑ 619	Play Me a Sad Song/ It Means a Lot to Them	1961	$60

—As "Jerry Landis

Number	Title	Yr	NM
❑ 552	Shy/Just a Boy	1960	$60

—As "Jerry Landis

Number	Title	Yr	NM
❑ 522	Swanee/Toot, Toot, Tootsie Goodbye	1960	$60

—As "Jerry Landis

SIMON SISTERS, THE

CARLY SIMON and her sister Lucy.

CHILDREN'S RECORDS OF AMERICA

Number	Title	Yr	NM
❑ 100	My Love Is Like a Red, Red Rose/The Lamb	1968	$30

COLUMBIA

Number	Title	Yr	NM
❑ 02675	Maryanne/(B-side unknown)	1982	$4

—As "Carly and Lucy Simon

KAPP

Number	Title	Yr	NM
❑ 624	Cuddlebug/No One to Talk My Troubles To	1964	$20
❑ 586	Winkin', Blinkin' and Nod/ So Glad I'm Here	1964	$20

SIMONE, NINA

BETHLEHEM

Number	Title	Yr	NM
❑ 11055	Don't Smoke in Bed/ African Mailman	1960	$12
❑ 11087	For All We Know/Good Bait	1960	$10
❑ 11089	He's Got the Whole World in His Hands/Central Park Blues	1960	$12
❑ 11021	I Loves You, Porgy/ Love Me or Leave Me	1959	$15
❑ 3099	I Loves You Porgy/My Baby Just Cares for Me	1970	$5
❑ 11052	Little Girl Blue/He Needs Me	1960	$12
❑ 11057	Mood Indigo/Central Park Blues	1960	$10
❑ 3031	My Baby Just Cares for Me/He Needs Me	1962	$8

COLPIX

Number	Title	Yr	NM
❑ 703	Blackbird/Little Liza Jane	1963	$8
❑ 124	Children Go Where I Send Thee/Willow Weep for Me	1959	$10
❑ 614	Come On Back, Jack/You've Been Gone Too Long	1961	$10
❑ 156	If Only for Tonight/ (B-side unknown)	1960	$10
❑ 647	I Got It Bad/I Want a Little Sugar in My Bowl	1962	$8
❑ 635	In the Evening by the Moonlight/ Chilly Winds Don't Blow	1962	$8
❑ 135	It Might As Well Be Spring/ The Other Woman	1959	$10
❑ 151	Since My Love Has Gone/ Tomorrow (We Shall Meet Once More)	1960	$10
❑ 116	Solitaire/Chilly Winds	1959	$12
❑ 143	Summertime/Fine and Mellow	1960	$10
❑ 197	The Work Song/ Memphis in June	1961	$10
❑ 175	Trouble in Mind/ Cotton-Eyed Joe	1960	$10

CTI

Number	Title	Yr	NM
❑ 44	Baltimore/The Family	1978	$5
❑ 46	Forget/Baltimore	1978	$5
❑ 49	The Family/That's All I Want from You	1978	$5

PHILIPS

Number	Title	Yr	NM
❑ 40232	Don't Let Me Be Misunderstood/A Monster	1964	$8
❑ 40418	Don't Pay Them No Mind/ (B-side unknown)	1966	$6
❑ 40337	Either Way I Lose/Break Down and Let It All Out	1965	$8
❑ 40254	I Am Blessed/How Can I	1965	$8
❑ 40194	I Loves You Porgy/Old Jim Crow	1964	$8
❑ 40286	I Put a Spell on You/ Gimme Some	1965	$8
❑ 40216	Mississippi Goddam/ Sea Lion Woman	1964	$8
❑ 40376	See-Line Woman/I Love Your Lovin' Ways	1966	$6
❑ 40404	What More Can I Say/ Four Women	1966	$6
❑ 40359	Why Keep On Breaking My Heart/I Love Your Lovin' Ways	1966	$6

RCA VICTOR

Number	Title	Yr	NM
❑ 47-9686	Ain't Got No; I Got Life/Real, Real	1968	$6
❑ 47-9375	Cherish/I Wish I Knew How It Would Feel to Be Free	1967	$6
❑ 47-9120	Do I Move You/Day and Night	1967	$6
❑ 47-9602	Do What You Gotta Do/ Peace of Mind	1968	$6
❑ 74-0514	Here Comes the Sun/ Angel of the Morning	1971	$6
❑ 47-9286	It Be's That Way Sometime/ You'll Go to Hell	1967	$6
❑ 74-0871	My Sweet Lord-Today Is a Killer/Poppies	1973	$6
❑ 47-9749	Suzanne/Turn, Turn, Turn (To Everything There Is a Season)	1969	$6
❑ 74-0269	To Be Young, Gifted and Black/Save Me	1969	$6
❑ 47-9447	To Love Somebody/I Can't See Nobody	1968	$6
❑ 74-0311	Who Knows Where the Time Goes/The Assignment Song	1970	$6
❑ 47-9532	Why (Part 1)/Why (Part 2)	1968	$6

SIMPLE MINDS

A&M

Number	Title	Yr	NM
❑ 2783	Alive & Kicking/Up on the Catwalk (Live)	1985	$3
❑ 2783 [PS]	Alive & Kicking/Up on the Catwalk (Live)	1985	$3
❑ 2828	All the Things She Said/Don't You (Forget About Me) (Live)	1986	$3
❑ 2828 [PS]	All the Things She Said/Don't You (Forget About Me) (Live)	1986	$8
❑ 2703	Don't You (Forget About Me)/A Brass Bed in Africa	1984	$3
❑ 2703 [PS]	Don't You (Forget About Me)/A Brass Bed in Africa	1984	$3

—No LP cover pictured on front

Number	Title	Yr	NM
❑ 2703 [PS]	Don't You (Forget About Me)/A Brass Bed in Africa	1984	$4

—With "The Breakfast Club" LP cover pictured in full color on front

Number	Title	Yr	NM
❑ 2954	Promised You a Miracle/Book of Brilliant Things	1987	$3
❑ 2954 [PS]	Promised You a Miracle/Book of Brilliant Things	1987	$3
❑ 2523	Promised You a Miracle/The American	1983	$5
❑ 2523 [PS]	Promised You a Miracle/The American	1983	$6
❑ 2556 [DJ]	Someone, Somewhere in Summertime (same on both sides)	1983	$4

—No stock copy was issued

Number	Title	Yr	NM
❑ 2556 [DJ]	Someone, Somewhere in Summertime (same on both sides)	1983	$12

—No stock copy was issued

Number	Title	Yr	NM
❑ 2629	Speed Your Love to Me/Bass Line	1984	$10
❑ 1413	This Is Your Land/Saturday Girl	1989	$6

SIMPSON, RED

CAPITOL

Number	Title	Yr	NM
❑ 5783	Diesel Smoke, Dangerous Curves/I'm Gonna Write Momma for Money	1966	$12
❑ 2035	He Reminds Me a Whole Lot of Me/Honky Tonk Women	1967	$8
❑ 3872	Honky Tonk Lady's Lovin' Man/Yip Yip	1974	$6
❑ 5956	Party Girl/Mini-Skirt Minnie	1967	$8
❑ 5717	Sidewalk Patrol/I'm Turning In My Star	1966	$8
❑ 5637	The Highway Patrol/Big Mack	1966	$10
❑ 3778	Truckin' Trees for Christmas/Blue Blue Christmas	1973	$8

K.E.Y.

Number	Title	Yr	NM
❑ 108	The Flying Saucer and the Truck Driver/I Miss You a Little	1979	$10

WARNER BROS.

Number	Title	Yr	NM
❑ 8259	Truck Driver's Heaven/It Ain't Even Halloween	1976	$6

SIMS, BOBBY

HIT

Number	Title	Yr	NM
❑ 312	An Open Letter to My Teenage Son/Keep the Ball Rollin'	1967	$8

—B-side by Jimmy Lewis and the Elfs

Number	Title	Yr	NM
❑ 339	Dreams of the Everyday Housewife/Hello, I Love You	1968	$8

—B-side by the Chords (2)

Number	Title	Yr	NM
❑ 320	Honey/The Ballad of Bonnie and Clyde	1968	$8

—B-side by Ed Hardin

Number	Title	Yr	NM
❑ 287	I Think We're Alone Now/Penny Lane	1967	$10

—B-side by the Jalopy Five

Number	Title	Yr	NM
❑ 309	Please Love Me Forever/People Are Strange	1967	$8

—B-side by the Fantastics

Number	Title	Yr	NM
❑ 269	Poor Side of Town/If I Were a Carpenter	1966	$8

—B-side by Bobby Brooks

Number	Title	Yr	NM
❑ 297	San Francisco (Be Sure to Wear Flowers in Your Hair)/A Whiter Shade of Pale	1967	$8

—B-side by the Fantastics

Number	Title	Yr	NM
❑ 272	That's Life/Snoopy vs. the Red Baron	1966	$8

—B-side by the Chords (2)

Number	Title	Yr	NM
❑ 348	Who's Making Love/White Room	1968	$8

—B-side by the Fantastics

Number	Title	Yr	NM
❑ 276	Wild Thing/Music to Watch Girls By	1967	$8

—B-side by the Jalopy Five

SIMS, FRANKIE LEE

ACE

Number	Title	Yr	NM
❑ 527	Hey Little Girl/Walking with Frankie	1957	$50
❑ 539	I Warned You Baby/My Talk Didn't Do No Good	1957	$50
❑ 524	What Will Lucy Do/Misery Blues	1957	$50

SPECIALTY

Number	Title	Yr	NM
❑ 487	I'll Get Along Somehow/Rhumba My Boogie	1954	$50
❑ 478	I'm Long, Long Gone/Yeh Baby	1953	$50
❑ 459	Lucky Man Blues/Don't Take It Out on Me	1953	$60

VIN

Number	Title	Yr	NM
❑ 1006	She Likes to Boogie Low/Well Goodbye Baby	1958	$40

SIMS, MARVIN L.

KAREN

Number	Title	Yr	NM
❑ 1547	Sweet Thang/Your Love Is So Wonderful	1969	$20

—As "Marvin Sims

MELLOW

Number	Title	Yr	NM
❑ 1005	Hurting Inside/Disillusioned	1967	$60
❑ 1002	What Can I Do?/Now I'm in Love with You	1966	$125

MERCURY

Number	Title	Yr	NM
❑ 73288	Dream a Dream/I Can't Turn You Loose	1972	$30

—As "Marvin Sims

Number	Title	Yr	NM
❑ 73364	It's Too Late/(B-side unknown)	1973	$30
❑ 73340	Love Is No Sin/You Gotta Go	1972	$30

REVUE

Number	Title	Yr	NM
❑ 11038	Danger/Get Off My Back	1969	$60
❑ 11024	Talkin' 'Bout Soul/Old Man Time	1968	$40

RIVERTOWN

Number	Title	Yr	NM
❑ 498	Love Is on the Way/Blow Away Breeze	1980	$100

UNI

Number	Title	Yr	NM
❑ 55217	I Can't Understand It/It's Your Love	1970	$15

SIMS TWINS, THE

KENT

Number	Title	Yr	NM
❑ 4556	Bring It On Home Where You Belong/Under the Double Eagle	1971	$6

PARKWAY

Number	Title	Yr	NM
❑ 6002	Together/Baby It's Real	1968	$10

SAR

Number	Title	Yr	NM
❑ 130	Double Portion of Love/You're Pickin' in the Right Cotton Patch	1962	$15
❑ 136	I Gopher You/Good Good Lovin'	1963	$15
❑ 117	Soothe Me/I'll Never Come Running Back to You	1961	$20
❑ 138	That's Where It's At/Movin' and a Groovin'	1963	$15
❑ 125	The Smile/Right to Love	1962	$15

SINATRA, FRANK

CAPITOL

Number	Title	Yr	NM
❑ F3793	All the Way/Chicago	1957	$15
❑ 4615	American Beauty Rose/Sentimental Journey	1961	$15
❑ F2560	Anytime, Anywhere/From Here to Eternity	1953	$30
❑ F3608	Can I Steal a Little Love/Your Love for Me	1956	$20
❑ F3703	Crazy Love/So Long, My Love	1957	$15
❑ F2787	Don't Worry 'Bout Me/I Could Have Told You	1954	$30
❑ X2-1594 [S]	Five Minutes More/Almost Like Being in Love	1961	$30

—Stereo jukebox single, 33 1/3 rpm, small hole

Number	Title	Yr	NM
❑ 4729	Five Minutes More/I'll Remember April	1962	$15
❑ F3350	Flowers Mean Forgiveness/You'll Get Yours	1956	$20
❑ X2-1417 [S]	Fools Rush In/I've Got a Crush on You	1960	$30

—Stereo jukebox single, 33 1/3 rpm, small hole

Number	Title	Yr	NM
❑ F4155	French Foreign Legion/Time After Time	1959	$15
❑ F3552	Hey! Jealous Lover/You Forgot All the Words	1956	$20
❑ F4214	High Hopes/All My Tomorrows	1959	$20
❑ F4214 [PS]	High Hopes/All My Tomorrows	1959	$200
❑ F3952	How Are Ya' Fixed for Love?/Nothin' in Common	1958	$15

—By Frank Sinatra and Keely Smith

Number	Title	Yr	NM
❑ F3423	(How Little It Maters) How Little We Know/Five Hundred Guys	1956	$20
❑ X4-1491 [S]	I Concentrate on You/Should I	1961	$30

—Stereo jukebox single, 33 1/3 rpm, small hole

Number	Title	Yr	NM
❑ 4815	I Love Paris/Hidden Persuasion	1962	$15
❑ F2638	I Love You/South of the Border	1953	$30
❑ F2450	I'm Walking Behind You/Lean Baby	1953	$30

—Add 50% for intact center

Number	Title	Yr	NM
❑ X3-1491 [S]	It's Only a Paper Moon/My Blue Heaven	1961	$30

—Stereo jukebox single, 33 1/3 rpm, small hole

Number	Title	Yr	NM
❑ F2922	It Worries Me/When I Stop Loving You	1954	$30
❑ F3102	Learnin' the Blues/If I Had Three Wishes	1955	$20
❑ F3260	Love and Marriage/The Impatient Years	1955	$30
❑ F3290	(Love Is) The Tender Trap/Weep They Will	1955	$20
❑ F3018	Melody of Love/I'm Gonna Live Till I Die	1954	$30
❑ F3900	Mistletoe and Holly/The Christmas Waltz	1957	$20

—The Christmas Waltz" here is a different version than that on Capitol 2954.

Number	Title	Yr	NM
❑ PRO0 [DJ]	Mistletoe and Holly (with spoken intro)/Mistletoe and Holly	1960	$125

—Christmas Seals record for 1960, with Sinatra introducing the song

Number	Title	Yr	NM
❑ PRO1707/8 [DJ]	Mistletoe and Holly (with spoken intro)/Mistletoe and Holly	1960	$125

—Christmas Seals record for 1960, with Sinatra introducing the song

Number	Title	Yr	NM
❑ F4070	Mr. Success/Sleep Warm	1958	$15
❑ 4546	My Blue Heaven/Sentimental Baby	1960	$15
❑ F2505	My One and Only Love/I've Got the World on a String	1953	$30

—Add 50% for intact center

Number	Title	Yr	NM
❑ 4466	Ol' MacDonald/You'll Always Be the One I Love	1960	$15
❑ F3218	Same Old Saturday Night/Fairy Tale	1955	$20
❑ F4003	Same Old Song and Dance/Monique (Song from Kings Go Forth)	1958	$15
❑ X5-1491 [S]	September in the Rain/You Do Something to Me	1961	$30

—Stereo jukebox single, 33 1/3 rpm, small hole

Number	Title	Yr	NM
❑ XE 1-1676 [S]	September Song/When the World Was Young	1962	$30

—Stereo jukebox single; 33 1/3 rpm, small hole

Number	Title	Yr	NM
❑ F4103	Song from "Some Came Running"/No One Ever Tells You	1958	$15
❑ X2-1491 [S]	S'posin'/Blue Moon	1961	$30

—Stereo jukebox single, 33 1/3 rpm, small hole

Number	Title	Yr	NM
❑ F4284	Talk to Me/They Came to Cordura	1959	$15
❑ X1-1417 [S]	That Old Feeling/How Deep Is the Ocean	1960	$30

—Stereo jukebox single, 33 1/3 rpm, small hole

Number	Title	Yr	NM
❑ F2864	The Girl That Got Away/Half as Lovely	1954	$30
❑ 4677	The Moon Was Yellow/I've Heard That Song Before	1962	$15
❑ XE 3-1676 [S]	There Will Never Be Another You/Somewhere Along the Way	1962	$30

—Stereo jukebox single; 33 1/3 rpm, small hole

Number	Title	Yr	NM
❑ XE 4-1676 [S]	These Foolish Things (Remind Me of You)/It's a Blue World	1962	$30

—Stereo jukebox single; 33 1/3 rpm, small hole

Number	Title	Yr	NM
❑ XE-1729 [S]	They Came to Cordura/I Gotta Right to Sing the Blues	1962	$30

—Stereo jukebox single, 33 1/3 rpm, small hole

Number	Title	Yr	NM
❑ F2816	Three Coins in the Fountain/Rain	1954	$30
❑ X1-1594 [S]	titles unknown	1961	$30

—Stereo jukebox single, 33 1/3 rpm, small hole

Number	Title	Yr	NM
❑ XE 2-1676 [S]	titles unknown	1962	$30

—Stereo jukebox single, 33 1/3 rpm, small hole

Number	Title	Yr	NM
❑ F4103	To Love and Be Loved/No One Ever Tells You	1958	$15
❑ F4103 [PS]	To Love and Be Loved/No One Ever Tells You	1958	$125

—Promo-only sleeve

Number	Title	Yr	NM
❑ F3084	Two Hearts, Two Kisses/From the Bottom to the Top	1955	$20
❑ F3507	Well, Did You Evah?/True Love	1956	$20

—A-side by Bing Crosby and Frank Sinatra; B-side by Bing Crosby and Grace Kelly

Number	Title	Yr	NM
❑ X1-1491 [S]	When You're Smiling/It All Depends on You	1961	$30

—Stereo jukebox single, 33 1/3 rpm, small hole

Number	Title	Yr	NM
❑ F2954	White Christmas/The Christmas Waltz	1954	$30
❑ 2954	White Christmas/The Christmas Waltz	1962	$10

—Reissue without the "F" prefix on orange and yellow swirl label

Number	Title	Yr	NM
❑ F3508	Who Wants to Be a Millionaire/Mind If I Make Love to You?	1956	$20
❑ F3050	Why Should I Cry Over You?/Don't Change Your Mind About Me	1954	$30
❑ 6078	Witchcraft/Chicago	1966	$6

—Starline reissue label

Number	Title	Yr	NM
❑ F3859	Witchcraft/Tell Her You Love Her	1957	$15

COLUMBIA

Number	Title	Yr	NM
❑ 38163	All of Me/I Went Down to Virginia	1950	$30
❑ 38686	Always/Why Was I Born?	1950	$30

—The above four comprise the box set Dedicated to You, B-197

Number	Title	Yr	NM
❑ 1-624	American Beauty Rose/Just an Old Stone House	1950	$70
❑ 37161	Among My Souvenirs/September Song	1950	$30

Number	Title	Yr	NM
1-511	Among My Souvenirs/September Song	1950	$70
50003	Among My Souvenirs/September Song	1954	$10
	—Hall of Fame series		
33319	Among My Souvenirs/September Song	1977	$6
	—Hall of Fame series		
39592	April in Paris/London by Night	1951	$20
39819	Azure-Te/Bim Bam Baby	1952	$20
1-174	Bali Ha'i/Some Enchanted Evening	1949	$70
38446	Bali Ha'i/Some Enchanted Evening	1950	$30
39527	Castle Rock/Deep Night	1951	$30
1-496	Chattanoogie Shoe Shine Boy/God's Country	1950	$70
B-167	Christmas Songs by Sinatra	1950	$200
	—Includes records 38256, 38257, 38258 and 38259 plus box		
1-130	Comme Ci, Comme Ca/While the Angelus Was Ringing	1948	$70
1-372	Could'ja/That Lucky Old Sun	1949	$70
B-197	Dedicated to You	1950	$200
	—Includes records 38683, 38684, 38685 and 38686 plus box		
1-315	Don't Cry Joe/The Wedding of Lili Marlene	1949	$70
40522	Dream/American Beauty Rose	1955	$20
39213	Faithful/You're the One	1951	$30
3-39213	Faithful/You're the One	1951	$200
	—Microgroove 33 1/3 rpm, 7-inch single		
39687	Feet of Clay/Don't Ever Be Afraid to Go Home	1952	$30
6-718	Goodnight Irene/My Blue Heaven	1950	$40
38892	Goodnight Irene/My Blue Heaven	1950	$20
	—Reissue of Columbia 6-718		
1-718	Goodnight Irene/My Blue Heaven	1950	$70
38259	Have Yourself a Merry Little Christmas/Santa Claus Is Comin' to Town	1950	$30
	—The above four comprise the box set Christmas Songs by Sinatra, B-167		
39294	Hello, Young Lovers/We Kissed in a Shadow	1951	$20
6-936	I Am Loved/You Don't Remind Me	1950	$40
39079	I Am Loved/You Don't Remind Me	1950	$30
	—Reissue of Columbia 6-936		
1-936	I Am Loved/You Don't Remind Me	1950	$70
39493	I Fall in Love with You Everyday/It's a Long Way from Your House	1951	$30
1-326	If I Ever Love Again/Every Man Should Marry	1949	$70
36814	If You Are But a Dream/Put Your Dreams Away	1950	$30
	—Most Columbia 45s from 36000-39000 are reissues of titles that first appeared on 78s		
39652	I Hear a Rhapsody/I Could Write a Book	1952	$20
41133	I'm a Fool to Want You/If I Forget You	1958	$20
40229	I'm Glad There Is You/You Can Take My Word For It Baby	1954	$30
1-307	I Only Have Eyes for You/It All Depends on You	1949	$70
38999	It All Depends on You/You Do Something to Me	1950	$30
	—The above four comprise the box set Sing and Dance with Frank Sinatra, B-218		
1-222	It Happens Every Spring/The Hucklebuck	1949	$70
39498	It Never Entered My Mind/Try a Little Tenderness	1951	$20
38151	I've Got a Crush on You/Ever Homeward	1950	$30
50028	I've Got a Crush on You/The Birth of the Blues	1954	$10
	—Hall of Fame series		
33306	I've Got a Crush on You/The Birth of the Blues	1977	$6
	—Hall of Fame series		
39346	I Whistle a Happy Tune/Love Me	1951	$20
1-260	Let's Take an Old-Fashioned Walk/Just One Way to Say I Love You	1949	$70
	—With Doris Day		
1-780	Life Is So Peculiar/Dear Little Boy of Mine	1950	$70
39141	Love Means Love/Cherry Pies Ought to Be You	1951	$30
3-39141	Love Means Love/Cherry Pies Ought to Be You	1951	$600
	—Microgroove 33 1/3 rpm, 7-inch single		
38996	Lover/When You're Smiling	1950	$30
39787	Luna Rosa/Tennessee Newsboy	1952	$30
39425	Mama Will Bark/I'm a Fool to Want You	1951	$50
	—Frank Sinatra & Dagmar; the record Ol' Blue Eyes called his worst		
39726	My Girl/Walkin' in the Sunshine	1952	$30
38258	O Little Town Of Bethlehem/It Came Upon A Midnight Clear	1950	$30
1-845	One Finger Melody/Accidents Will Happen	1950	$70
1-380	On the Island of Stromboli/Mad About You	1949	$70
36921	Paradise/Someone to Watch Over Me	1950	$30
	—The above four comprise the box set The Voice of Frank Sinatra, B-112		
1-669	Peachtree Street/This Is the Night	1950	$70
38829	Poinciana/There's No Business Like Show Business	1950	$30
1-650	Poinciana/There's No Business Like Show Business	1950	$70
50069	Saturday Night/Five Minutes More	1955	$10
	—Hall of Fame series		
40565	Sheila/Day by Day	1955	$40
37259	She's Funny That Way/Embraceable You	1950	$30
38998	Should I?/My Blue Heaven	1950	$30
38256	Silent Night/Adeste Fideles	1950	$30
50079	Silent Night/Adeste Fideles	1955	$10
	—Hall of Fame series		
B-218	Sing and Dance with Frank Sinatra	1950	$200
	—Includes records 38996, 38997, 38998 and 38999 plus box		
1-440	Sorry/Why Remind Me	1949	$70
38684	Strange Music/I Love You	1950	$30
1-106	Sunflower/Once in Love with Amy	1948	$70
	—All records with a "1-" prefix are Microgroove 33 1/3 rpm 7-inch singles		
1-491	Sunshine Cake/We've Got a Sure Thing	1949	$70
39118	Take My Love/Come Back to Sorrento	1950	$20
3-39118	Take My Love/Come Back to Sorrento	1950	$200
	—Microgroove 33 1/3 rpm, 7-inch single		
37257	That Old Black Magic/How Deep Is the Ocean?	1950	$30
39882	The Birth of the Blues/Why Try to Change Me Now?	1952	$20
38997	The Continental/It's Only a Paper Moon	1950	$30
38683	The Moon Was Yellow/The Music Stopped	1950	$30
1-427	The Old Master Painter/Lost in the Stars	1949	$70
36919	These Foolish Things/A Ghost of a Chance	1950	$30
1-144	When Is Sometime/If You Stub Your Toe on the Moon	1949	$70
1-154	Where Is the One/Bop Goes My Heart	1949	$70
38685	Where or When/None But the Lonely Heart	1950	$30
JZSP0 [DJ]	White Christmas/Have Yourself A Merry Little Christmas	1966	$60
JZSP116427/8 [DJ]	White Christmas/Have Yourself A Merry Little Christmas	1966	$60
1-112	Why Can't You Behave/No Orchids for My Lady	1948	$70
36920	Why Shouldn't I?/Try a Little Tenderness	1950	$30

(NO LABEL)

Number	Title	Yr	NM
KB-2077/8	High Hopes with Jack Kennedy/Jack Kennedy All the Way	1960	$300
	—No artist or label shown, but Sinatra does sing the A-side		

QWEST

Number	Title	Yr	NM
29223	L.A. Is My Lady/Until the Real Thing Comes Along	1984	$5
29223 [PS]	L.A. Is My Lady/Until the Real Thing Comes Along	1984	$20
29139	Mack the Knife/It's All Right with Me	1984	$5
28844	The Best of Everything/Teach Me Tonight	1985	$4

RCA VICTOR

Number	Title	Yr	NM
27-0151	Daybreak/There Are Such Things	1948	$20
27-0077	I'll Never Smile Again/(B-side unknown)	1949	$20
	—From WDT 15		
447-0116	I'll Never Smile Again/I'll Be Seeing You	1950	$15
27-0095	Somewhere A Voice Is Calling/(B-side unknown)	1949	$20
	—From WDT 20		
27-0076	Stardust/(B-side unknown)	1949	$20
	—From WDT 15		
447-0123	Stardust/There Are Such Things	1950	$15
447-0445	Street of Dreams/East of the Sun	1952	$15
DTAO-3001	Street of Dreams/Whispering	1973	$15
DTBO-3012	The One I Love/This Love of Mine	1973	$15
447-0929	The Song Is You/The Lamplighter's Serenade	1972	$6

REPRISE

Number	Title	Yr	NM
1342	A Baby Just Like You/Christmas Mem'ries	1975	$10
1342 [PS]	A Baby Just Like You/Christmas Mem'ries	1975	$50
	—Blue printing, released with promo copies only		
1342 [PS]	A Baby Just Like You/Christmas Mem'ries	1975	$30
	—Red and black printing, released with stock copies		
S172 [S]	All the Way/The Continental	1964	$30
	—The above five are 33 1/3 rpm, small hole jukebox singles		
0350	Anytime at All/Available	1964	$8
1327	Anytime (I'll Be There)/The Hurt Doesn't Go Away	1975	$8
1196	Bad, Bad Leroy Brown/I'm Gonna Make It All the Way	1974	$8
GRE 0113	Bad, Bad Leroy Brown/Let Me Try Again	1975	$30
	—Back to Back Hits" series		
20157 [DJ]	California/America the Beautiful	1963	$250
	—No stock copies isssued		
20157 [DJ]	California/America the Beautiful	1963	$250
	—No stock copies isssued		
20157 [PS]	California/America the Beautiful	1963	$750
	—No stock copies isssued		
20178 [DJ]	California/America the Beautiful	1978	$200
	—Private pressing of 1,000 for Sinatra's personal use		
20157 [DJ]	California/America the Beautiful	1978	$200
	—Private pressing of 1,000 for Sinatra's personal use		
20151 [DJ]	Call Me Irresponsible/Come Blow Your Horn	1963	$125
20151 [DJ]	Call Me Irresponsible/Come Blow Your Horn	1963	$125
20151 [PS]	Call Me Irresponsible/Come Blow Your Horn	1963	$200
	—Sleeve accompanies promo copies only		
20151	Call Me Irresponsible/Come Blow Your Horn	1963	$500
	—One stock copy is known to exist!		
20151	Call Me Irresponsible/Tina	1963	$10
	—B-side changed for commercial release		
0764	Cycles/My Way of Life	1968	$6
	—From here from 0865, orange/tan label with "W7/:r" logo		
1377	Dry Your Eyes/Like a Sad Song	1976	$8
1343	Empty Tables/The Saddest Thing of All	1976	$8
0410	Everybody Has the Right to Be Wrong/I'll Only Miss Her When I Think of Her	1965	$8
20063	Everybody's Twistin'/Nothin' But the Best	1962	$20
20063 [PS]	Everybody's Twistin'/Nothin' But the Best	1962	$40
0980	Feelin' Kinda Sunday/Kids	1970	$8
	—A-side by Nancy Sinatra and Frank Sinatra; B-side by Nancy Sinatra		
0380	Forget Domani/I Can't Believe I'm Losing You	1965	$8
0493	Frank Sinatra Reads from Gunga Din	1966	$500
	—300 pressed and given away to friends; no stock copies		
20217	Fugue for Tinhorns/The Oldest Established (Permanent Floating Crap Game in New York)	1963	$20
	—By Frank Sinatra/Bing Crosby/Dean Martin		
20217 [PS]	Fugue for Tinhorns/The Oldest Established (Permanent Floating Crap Game in New York)	1963	$80
	—By Frank Sinatra/Bing Crosby/Dean Martin		
0865	Goin' Out of My Head/Forget to Remember	1969	$8
20092	Goody, Goody/Love Is Just Around the Corner	1962	$15
20010	Granada/The Curse of an Aching Heart	1961	$20
	—From here through 0317, originals on peach label		
20010 [PS]	Granada/The Curse of an Aching Heart	1961	$30
243	Have Yourself a Merry Little Christmas/How Shall I Send Thee?	1963	$30
	—B-side by Les Baxter		
29677	Here's to the Band/It's Sunday	1983	$8
1335 [PS]	I Believe I'm Gonna Love You	1975	$50
	—Issued with promo copies only		
1335	I Believe I'm Gonna Love You/The Only Couple on the Floor	1975	$8
0677	I Can't Believe I'm Losing You/How Old Am I?	1967	$8
20184	I Have Dreamed/Come Blow Your Horn	1963	$10
0314	I Heard the Bells on Christmas Day/The Little Drummer Boy	1964	$30
0314 [PS]	I Heard the Bells on Christmas Day/The Little Drummer Boy	1964	$60
20023	I'll Be Seeing You/The One I Love	1961	$20
0053	I'll Be Seeing You/Without a Song	1962	$200
	—Released in Great Britain as 20,053; pressed in the United States later		
1382	I Love My Wife/Send In the Clowns	1976	$10
20024	Imagination/It's Always You	1961	$20

Number	Title	Yr	NM
❑ 20025	I'm Getting Sentimental Over You/East of the Sun (And West of the Moon)	1961	$20
❑ 40040	I'm Gonna Sit Right Down and Write Myself a Letter/I Won't Dance	1963	$30

—Jukebox 33 1/3 rpm, small hole single

Number	Title	Yr	NM
❑ 1347	I Sing the Songs (I Write the Songs)/Empty Tables	1976	$10
❑ S171 [S]	It Might As Well Be Spring/Swinging on a Star	1964	$30
❑ 0429	It Was a Very Good Year/Moment to Moment	1965	$8
❑ 0429 [PS]	It Was a Very Good Year/Moment to Moment	1965	$30
❑ 0713	It Was a Very Good Year/Stay with Me	1968	$5

—Back to Back Hits" series

Number	Title	Yr	NM
❑ 0895	I Would Be in Love (Anyway)/Watertown	1970	$8

—From here through 29903, orange (or tan) label with ":r" logo in square

Number	Title	Yr	NM
❑ 0970	Lady Day/Song of the Sabia	1969	$8
❑ 1181	Let Me Try Again/Send In the Clowns	1973	$8
❑ 1011	Life's a Trippy Thing/I'm Not Afraid	1971	$8

—A-side by Nancy Sinatra and Frank Sinatra

Number	Title	Yr	NM
❑ 20209	Love Isn't Just for the Young/You Brought a New Kind of Love to Me	1963	$15
❑ 20209 [PS]	Love Isn't Just for the Young/You Brought a New Kind of Love to Me	1963	$60
❑ 0852	Love's Been Good to Me/A Man Alone	1969	$8
❑ 20128	Me and My Shadow/Sam's Song	1962	$20

—A-side by Frank Sinatra and Sammy Davis, Jr.; B-side by Sammy Davis Jr. and Dean Martin

Number	Title	Yr	NM
❑ 20128 [PS]	Me and My Shadow/Sam's Song	1962	$60

—A-side by Frank Sinatra and Sammy Davis, Jr.; B-side by Sammy Davis Jr. and Dean Martin

Number	Title	Yr	NM
❑ S168 [S]	Moon River/Days of Wine and Roses	1964	$30
❑ 40038	My Kind of Girl/I Only Have Eyes for You	1963	$30

—Jukebox 33 1/3 rpm, small hole single

Number	Title	Yr	NM
❑ 0279	My Kind of Town/I Like to Lead When I Dance	1964	$10
❑ 0279 [PS]	My Kind of Town/I Like to Lead When I Dance	1964	$200

—Sleeve issued with promo copies only

Number	Title	Yr	NM
❑ 0702	My Kind of Town/That's Life	1968	$5

—Back to Back Hits" series

Number	Title	Yr	NM
❑ 0817	My Way/Blue Lace	1969	$10
❑ 0734	My Way/Cycles	1970	$5

—Back to Back Hits" series

Number	Title	Yr	NM
❑ 40036	Pennies from Heaven/Please Be Kind	1963	$30

—Jukebox 33 1/3 rpm, small hole single

Number	Title	Yr	NM
❑ 40050	Please Be Kind/My Kind of Girl	1963	$30

—Jukebox 33 1/3 rpm, small hole single

Number	Title	Yr	NM
❑ 20040	Pocketful of Miracles/Name It and It's Yours	1961	$20
❑ 20040 [PS]	Pocketful of Miracles/Name It and It's Yours	1961	$70
❑ 49827	Say Hello/Good Thing Going	1981	$8

—B-side listed on label as "RE-1

Number	Title	Yr	NM
❑ 49827	Say Hello/Good Thing Going	1981	$8

—B-side listed on label as "RE-2

Number	Title	Yr	NM
❑ S170 [S]	Secret Love/In the Cool, Cool, Cool of the Evening	1964	$30
❑ 0706	September of My Years/Softly, As I Leave You	1968	$5

—Back to Back Hits" series

Number	Title	Yr	NM
❑ 0301	Softly, As I Leave You/Then Suddenly Love	1964	$12
❑ 0981	Something/Bein' Green	1970	$8
❑ 0561	Somethin' Stupid/Give Her Love	1967	$12

—A-side: Nancy Sinatra and Frank Sinatra

Number	Title	Yr	NM
❑ 0561	Somethin' Stupid/I Will Wait for You	1967	$8

—A-side: Nancy Sinatra and Frank Sinatra

Number	Title	Yr	NM
❑ 0727	Somethin' Stupid/The World We Knew (Over and Over)	1968	$5

—Back to Back Hits" series; A-side with Nancy Sinatra

Number	Title	Yr	NM
❑ 0332	Somewhere in Your Heart/Emily	1964	$8

—From here through 0677, originals on dark brown & orange label

Number	Title	Yr	NM
❑ 20059	Stardust/Come Rain or Come Shine	1962	$20
❑ 1364	Stargazer/The Best I Ever Had	1976	$8
❑ 1364 [PS]	Stargazer/The Best I Ever Had	1976	$20

—Special sleeve: "New Sinatra Single

Number	Title	Yr	NM
❑ 0249	Stay with Me/Talk to Me Baby	1963	$10
❑ 0470	Strangers in the Night/Oh, You Crazy Moon	1966	$10
❑ 0710	Strangers in the Night/Summer Wind	1968	$5

—Back to Back Hits" series

Number	Title	Yr	NM
❑ 0509	Summer Wind/You Make Me Feel So Young	1966	$10
❑ 20028	Take Me/Daybreak	1961	$20
❑ 0373	Tell Her (You Love Her Each Day)/Here's to the Losers	1965	$8
❑ 0531	That's Life/The September of My Years	1966	$12
❑ 0531 [PS]	That's Life/The September of My Years	1966	$30
❑ 20107	The Look of Love/I Left My Heart in San Francisco	1962	$60
❑ 20107	The Look of Love/Indiscreet	1962	$60
❑ 49233	Theme from New York, New York/That's What God Looks Like to Me	1980	$10
❑ 49233 [PS]	Theme from New York, New York/That's What God Looks Like to Me	1980	$20
❑ GRE 0122	Theme from New York, New York/You and Me (We Wanted It All)	1981	$4

—Back to Back Hits" series

Number	Title	Yr	NM
❑ 20026	There Are Such Things/Polkadots and Moonbeams	1961	$20
❑ 20001	The Second Time Around/Tina	1961	$30

—Originals on light blue label

Number	Title	Yr	NM
❑ 40037	The Tender Trap/Looking at the World Thru Rose Colored Glasses	1963	$30

—Jukebox 33 1/3 rpm, small hole single

Number	Title	Yr	NM
❑ 0920	The Train/What's Now Is Now	1969	$8
❑ 0610	The World We Knew (Over and Over)/You Are There	1967	$8
❑ 0631	This Town/This Is My Love	1967	$8
❑ S169 [S]	Three Coins in the Fountain/The Way You Look Tonight	1964	$30
❑ PRO-S-1007	To Love a Child (mono/stereo)	1982	$300

—Special pressing of 500 with small hole, given to Nancy Reagan for distributuion at a White House function.

Number	Title	Yr	NM
❑ 29903	To Love a Child/That's What God Looks Like to Me	1982	$8
❑ 29903 [PS]	To Love a Child/That's What God Looks Like to Me	1982	$20
❑ 0317	We Wish You the Merriest/Go Tell It on the Mountain	1964	$50

—By Frank Sinatra/Bing Crosby/Fred Waring

Number	Title	Yr	NM
❑ 0317 [PS]	We Wish You the Merriest/Go Tell It on the Mountain	1964	$70

—By Frank Sinatra/Bing Crosby/Fred Waring

Number	Title	Yr	NM
❑ 0790	Whatever Happened to Christmas?/I Wouldn't Trade Christmas	1968	$15

—B-side by The Sinatra Family

Number	Title	Yr	NM
❑ 0398	When Somebody Loves You/When I'm Not Near the Girl I Love	1965	$8
❑ 1010	Witchcraft/Young at Heart	1971	$8
❑ 20027	Without a Song/It Started All Over Again	1961	$20

7-Inch Extended Plays

CAPITOL

Number	Title	Yr	NM
❑ EAP 1-1417	*Nice 'n' Easy/That Old Feeling/She's Funny That Way/Dream	1960	$25
❑ EAP 3-1221	*Stormy Weather/Where Do You Go/Why Try to Change Me Now/Just Friends	1959	$20
❑ EAP 1-542 [PS]	3 Coins in the Fountain	1954	$30
❑ EAP 2-488	A Foggy Day/Like Someone I Love//I Get a Kick Out of You/Little Girl Blue	1954	$25
❑ EAP 2-1491	Always/I Can't Believe You're in Love with Me//It's Only a Paper Moon/My Blue Heaven	1961	$30
❑ EAP 1-1159	Angel Eyes/Willow Weep for Me	1958	$35
❑ EAP 1-803 [PS]	A Swingin' Affair, Part 1	1957	$25
❑ EAP 2-803 [PS]	A Swingin' Affair, Part 2	1957	$25
❑ EAP 3-803 [PS]	A Swingin' Affair, Part 3	1957	$25
❑ EAP 4-803 [PS]	A Swingin' Affair, Part 4	1957	$25
❑ EBF 1-803 [PS]	A Swingin' Affair, Parts 1 and 2	1957	$60

—Gatefold sleeve for some editions of EAP 1-803 and 2-803

Number	Title	Yr	NM
❑ EBF 2-803 [PS]	A Swingin' Affair, Parts 3 and 4	1957	$60

—Gatefold sleeve for some editions of EAP 3-803 and 4-803

Number	Title	Yr	NM
❑ EAP 2-920	Autumn in New York//April in Paris/Around the World	1958	$20
❑ EAP 4-581	Can't We Be Friends/When Your Lover Has Gone//What Is This Thing Called Love/Last Night When We Were Young	1955	$25
❑ EAP 1-789 [PS]	Close to You, Part 1	1956	$25
❑ EAP 2-789 [PS]	Close to You, Part 2	1956	$25
❑ EAP 3-789 [PS]	Close to You, Part 3	1956	$25
❑ EAP 4-789 [PS]	Close to You, Part 4	1956	$25
❑ EBF 1-789 [PS]	Close to You, Parts 1 and 2	1956	$60

—Gatefold sleeve for some editions of EAP 1-789 and 2-789

Number	Title	Yr	NM
❑ EBF 2-789 [PS]	Close to You, Parts 3 and 4	1956	$60

—Gatefold sleeve for some editions of EAP 3-789 and 4-789

Number	Title	Yr	NM
❑ EAP 1-789	Close to You/Love Locked Out//The End of a Love Affair	1956	$25
❑ EAP 1-1069 [PS]	Come Dance with Me, Part 1	1958	$20
❑ EAP 2-1069 [PS]	Come Dance with Me, Part 2	1958	$20
❑ EAP 3-1069 [PS]	Come Dance with Me, Part 3	1958	$20
❑ EAP 1-1069	Come Dance with Me/Something's Gotta Give//The Song Is You/The Last Dance	1958	$20
❑ EAP 1-920 [PS]	Come Fly with Me, Part 1	1958	$20
❑ EAP 2-920 [PS]	Come Fly with Me, Part 2	1958	$20
❑ EAP 3-920 [PS]	Come Fly with Me, Part 3	1958	$20
❑ EAP 4-920 [PS]	Come Fly with Me, Part 4	1958	$20
❑ EAP 1-920	Come Fly with Me/Isle of Capri//It's Nice to Go Trav'ling	1958	$20
❑ EAP 1-1594 [PS]	Come Swing with Me, Part 1	1961	$30
❑ EAP 2-1594 [PS]	Come Swing with Me, Part 2	1961	$30
❑ EAP 3-1594 [PS]	Come Swing with Me, Part 3	1961	$30
❑ EAP 1-1594	(contents unknown)	1961	$30
❑ EAP 2-1594	(contents unknown)	1961	$30
❑ EAP 3-1594	(contents unknown)	1961	$30
❑ EAP 3-581	Deep in a Dream/Mood Indigo//Glad to Be Unhappy/Ill Wind	1955	$25
❑ EAP 4-789	Don't Like Goodbyes//It's Easy to Remember/Blame It on My Youth	1956	$25
❑ EAP 3-789	Everything Happens to Me/It Could Happen to You//I've Had My Moments	1956	$25
❑ MA1-1583 [PS]	Frank Sinatra	1961	$30
❑ EAP 1-1013 [PS]	Frank Sinatra!	1958	$35
❑ EAP 1-1159 [PS]	Frank Sinatra Sings Angel Eyes	1958	$35
❑ EAP 1-1053 [PS]	Frank Sinatra Sings for Only the Lonely	1958	$25
❑ EAP 1-571 [PS]	Frank Sinatra Sings Songs from His Warner Bros. Picture "Young at Heart	1954	$30
❑ SEP 1-1233 [PS]	French Foreign Legion	1959	$60
❑ SEP 1-1233 [S]	French Foreign Legion/Mr. Success//Come Dance with Me/The Last Dance	1959	$60
❑ EAP 1-800 [PS]	Hey! Jealous Lover	1956	$35
❑ EAP 1-982	Hey! Jealous Lover/Everybody Loves Somebody//I Believe/Put Your Dreams Away	1958	$25
❑ EAP 1-1224 [PS]	High Hopes	1959	$35
❑ EAP 1-1224	High Hopes/All My Tomorrows//French Foreign Legion/Mr. Success	1959	$35
❑ EAP 2-1417	How Deep Is the Ocean/Mam'selle//Try a Little Tenderness/Embraceable You	1960	$25
❑ EAP 1-800	How Little We Know/Flowers Mean Forgiveness//You Forgot All the Words/Hey! Jealous Lover	1956	$35
❑ EAP 2-1221	I Don't Stand a Ghost of a Chance with You/Here's That Rainy Day//I Can't Get Started	1959	$20
❑ EAP 2-581	I'll Be Around/I Get Along Without You Very Well//It Never Entered My Mind/Dancing on the Ceiling	1955	$25
❑ EAP 2-855	I'm a Fool to Want You//I Cover the Waterfront/Laura	1957	$25
❑ EAP 1-590	I'm Gonna Live Till I Die/Day In -- Day Out//Melody of Love/Ever Since You Went Away	1955	$30

—Second song on B-side by The Skyliners with Ray Anthony (no Sinatra involvement)

Number	Title	Yr	NM
❑ EAP 1-581 [PS]	In the Wee Small Hours, Part 1	1955	$25
❑ EAP 2-581 [PS]	In the Wee Small Hours, Part 2	1955	$25
❑ EAP 3-581 [PS]	In the Wee Small Hours, Part 3	1955	$25
❑ EAP 4-581 [PS]	In the Wee Small Hours, Part 4	1955	$25
❑ EBF 1-581 [PS]	In the Wee Small Hours, Parts 1 and 2	1955	$60

—Gatefold sleeve for some editions of EAP 1-581 and 2-581

Number	Title	Yr	NM
❑ EBF 2-581 [PS]	In the Wee Small Hours, Parts 3 and 4	1955	$60

—Gatefold sleeve for some editions of EAP 3-581 and 4-581

Number	Title	Yr	NM
❑ EAP 1-581	In the Wee Small Hours of the Morning/I See Your Face Before Me//I'll Never Be the Same/This Love of Mine	1954	$25
❑ EAP 2-803	I Won't Dance/At Long Last Love//I Got It Bad and That Ain't Good/I Guess I'll Have to Change My Plan	1957	$25
❑ EAP 3-855	Lonely Town//The Night We Called It a Day/Autumn Leaves	1957	$25
❑ EAP 1-590 [PS]	Melody of Love	1955	$30
❑ EAP 3-920	Moonlight in Vermont//London by Night/Let's Get Away from It All	1958	$20
❑ EAP 1-488	My Funny Valentine/The Girl Next Door//They Can't Take That Away from Me/Violets for Your Furs	1954	$25
❑ EAP 4-803	Oh! Look at Me Now/Stars Fell on Alabama//Night and Day	1957	$25
❑ EAP 2-894	O Little Town of Bethlehem/Adeste Fideles//It Came Upon a Midnight Clear/Silent Night	1957	$15

Number	Title	Yr	NM
❑ EAP 1-1053	Only the Lonely/Blues in the Night	1958	$25
❑ EAP 4-920	On the Road to Mandalay//Blue Hawaii/Brazil	1958	$20
❑ EAP 1-673 [PS]	Our Town	1956	$60
❑ EAP 1-673	Our Town/The Impatient Years//Love and Marriage/Look to Your Heart	1956	$60
❑ EAP 4-653	Pennies from Heaven/Love Is Here to Stay//I've Got You Under My Skin/I Thought About You	1956	$25
❑ EAP 2-789	P.S. I Love You//With Every Breath I Take/I Couldn't Sleep a Wink Last Night	1956	$25
❑ EAP 3-1069	Saturday Night/Day In -- Day Out//Too Close for Comfort/I Could Have Danced All Night	1958	$20
❑ EAP 1-629 [PS]	Session with Sinatra	1955	$30
❑ EAP 3-1491	Should I/September in the Rain//I Concentrate on You/You Do Something to Me	1961	$30
❑ EAP 1-1491 [PS]	Sinatra's Swingin' Session, Part 1	1961	$30
❑ EAP 2-1491 [PS]	Sinatra's Swingin' Session, Part 2	1961	$30
❑ EAP 3-1491 [PS]	Sinatra's Swingin' Session, Part 3	1961	$30
❑ EAP 2-982	Something Wonderful Happens in Summer/Half As Lovely//So Long My Love/It's the Same Old Dreams	1958	$25
❑ EAP 1-653 [PS]	Songs for Swingin' Lovers, Part 1	1956	$30
— With Sinatra facing away from the embracing couple			
❑ EAP 1-653 [PS]	Songs for Swingin' Lovers, Part 1	1957	$25
— With Sinatra facing toward the embracing couple			
❑ EAP 2-653 [PS]	Songs for Swingin' Lovers, Part 2	1956	$30
— With Sinatra facing away from the embracing couple			
❑ EAP 2-653 [PS]	Songs for Swingin' Lovers, Part 2	1957	$25
— With Sinatra facing toward the embracing couple			
❑ EAP 3-653 [PS]	Songs for Swingin' Lovers, Part 3	1956	$30
— With Sinatra facing away from the embracing couple			
❑ EAP 3-653 [PS]	Songs for Swingin' Lovers, Part 3	1957	$25
— With Sinatra facing toward the embracing couple			
❑ EAP 4-653 [PS]	Songs for Swingin' Lovers, Part 4	1956	$30
— With Sinatra facing away from the embracing couple			
❑ EAP 4-653 [PS]	Songs for Swingin' Lovers, Part 4	1957	$25
— With Sinatra facing toward the embracing couple			
❑ EBF 1-653 [PS]	Songs for Swingin' Lovers, Parts 1 and 2	1956	$75
— Gatefold sleeve for some editions of EAP 1-653 and 2-653; with Sinatra facing away from the embracing couple			
❑ EBF 1-653 [PS]	Songs for Swingin' Lovers, Parts 1 and 2	1957	$60
— Gatefold sleeve for some editions of EAP 1-653 and 2-653; with Sinatra facing toward the embracing couple			
❑ EBF 2-653 [PS]	Songs for Swingin' Lovers, Parts 3 and 4	1956	$75
— Gatefold sleeve for some editions of EAP 3-653 and 4-653; with Sinatra facing away from the embracing couple			
❑ EBF 2-653 [PS]	Songs for Swingin' Lovers, Parts 3 and 4	1957	$60
— Gatefold sleeve for some editions of EAP 3-653 and 4-653; with Sinatra facing toward the embracing couple			
❑ EBF488 [PS]	Songs for Young Lovers	1954	$60
— Both of above EPs in gatefold sleeve			
❑ EAP 1-488 [PS]	Songs for Young Lovers, Vol. 1	1954	$25
❑ EAP 2-488 [PS]	Songs for Young Lovers, Vol. 2	1954	$25
❑ EBF528 [PS]	Swing Easy	1954	$60
— Both 1-528 and 2-528 EPs in gatefold sleeve			
❑ EAP 1-528 [PS]	Swing Easy, Part I	1954	$25
❑ EAP 2-528 [PS]	Swing Easy, Part II	1954	$25
❑ EAP 2-528	Taking a Chance on Love/Jeepers Creepers//Get Happy/All of Me	1954	$25
❑ EAP 1-1348 [PS]	Talk to Me	1959	$35
❑ EAP 1-1348	Talk to Me/They Came to Cordura//When No One Cares/Where Do You Go?	1959	$35
❑ EAP 3-894	The Christmas Waltz/Have Yourself a Merry Little Christmas//The First Noel/Hark the Herald Angels Sing	1957	$15
❑ EAP 1-1013	The Lady Is a Tramp/Witchcraft//Come Fly with Me/Tell Her You Love Her	1958	$35
❑ EAP 1-803	The Lonesome Road/You'd Be So Nice to Come Home To//From This Moment On/Nice Work If You Can Get It	1957	$25
❑ EAP 4-855	There's No You//I Think of You/Maybe You'll Be There	1957	$25
❑ EAP 4-982 [PS]	This Is Sinatra, Volume 2, Part 4	1958	$25

Number	Title	Yr	NM
❑ EAP 1-982 [PS]	This Is Sinatra, Volume Two, Part 1	1958	$25
❑ EAP 2-982 [PS]	This Is Sinatra, Volume Two, Part 2	1958	$25
❑ EAP 3-982 [PS]	This Is Sinatra, Volume Two, Part 3	1958	$25
❑ MA1-1583	Three Coins in the Fountain/Learnin' the Blues//Young-at-Heart/Love and Marriage	1961	$30
— Capitol 33 Compact"; small hole, plays at 33 1/3 rpm			
❑ EAP 1-542	Three Coins in the Fountain/My One and Only Love//Don't Worry 'Bout Me/I Love You	1954	$30
❑ EAP 3-653	Too Marvelous for Words/Old Devil Moon//We'll Be Together Again	1956	$25
❑ EAP 1-629	Two Hearts, Two Kisses (Make One Love)/Don't Change Your Mind About Me//Learnin' the Blues/Why Should I Cry Over You?	1955	$30
❑ EAP 1-1221	When No One Cares/I'll Never Smile Again//A Cottage for Sale/None But the Lonely Heart	1959	$20
❑ EAP 1-1491	When You're Smiling (The Whole World Smiles With You)/Blue Moon//S'Posin'/It All Depends on You	1961	$30
❑ EAP 1-855 [PS]	Where Are You? Part 1	1957	$25
❑ EAP 2-855 [PS]	Where Are You? Part 2	1957	$25
❑ EAP 3-855 [PS]	Where Are You? Part 3	1957	$25
❑ EAP 4-855 [PS]	Where Are You? Part 4	1957	$25
❑ EBF 1-855 [PS]	Where Are You? Parts 1 and 2	1957	$60
— Gatefold sleeve for some editions of EAP 1-855 and 2-855			
❑ EBF 2-855 [PS]	Where Are You? Parts 3 and 4	1957	$60
— Gatefold sleeve for some editions of EAP 3-855 and 4-855			
❑ EAP 1-855	Where Are You?/Where Is the One//Baby Won't You Please Come Home	1957	$25

COLUMBIA

Number	Title	Yr	NM
❑ B-9531 [PS]	Adventures of the Heart, Vol. I	1957	$30
❑ B-9532 [PS]	Adventures of the Heart, Vol. II	1957	$30
❑ B-9533 [PS]	Adventures of the Heart, Vol. III	1957	$30
❑ B-9023 [PS]	A Fellow Needs a Girl	1956	$30
❑ B-9023	A Fellow Needs a Girl/Poinciana (Song of the Tree)//For Every Man There's a Woman/Mean to Me	1956	$30
❑ B-2641	All or Nothing at All/You Go to My Head//Why Try to Change Me Now/I Concentrate on You	1958	$30
❑ 5-1193	Always/Blue Skies//How Deep Is the Ocean/They Say It's Wonderful	1952	$30
— Record that goes with cover B-1524			
❑ B-1620 [PS]	Carousel Sung by Frank Sinatra	1952	$35
❑ B-2542	Castle Rock/Farewell, Farewell to Love//A Little Learnin' Is a Dangerous Thing	1957	$60
❑ B-10321 [PS]	Christmas Dreaming, Vol. 1	1957	$50
❑ B-10322 [PS]	Christmas Dreaming, Vol. 2	1957	$50
❑ B-167 [PS]	Christmas Songs by Sinatra	1952	$60
— Gatefold cover for 2-EP set (1322 and 1323)			
❑ B-2626	Close to You/Embraceable You//The Charm of You/I Dream of You	1958	$30
❑ 5-1559	(contents unknown)	1953	$30
— Side 1 and Side 4 of B-337			
❑ B-1872	(contents unknown)	1954	$30
❑ B-7432	(contents unknown)	1955	$30
❑ ZTEP0 [DJ]	(contents unknown)	1958	$60
❑ 5-1560	Deep Purple/Body and Soul//Begin the Beguine/Laura	1953	$30
— Side 2 and Side 3 of B-337			
❑ 5-1555	Embraceable You/I've Got a Crush on You//Someone to Watch Over Me/Where Is My Bess?	1953	$30
— Record that goes with cover B-1673			
❑ B-1984 [PS]	Frankie, Vol. 1	1955	$30
❑ B-1985 [PS]	Frankie, Vol. 2	1955	$30
❑ B-1986 [PS]	Frankie, Vol. 3	1955	$30
❑ B-2515 [PS]	Frank Sinatra (Hall of Fame Series)	1957	$30
❑ B-2516 [PS]	Frank Sinatra (Hall of Fame Series)	1957	$30
❑ B-2517 [PS]	Frank Sinatra (Hall of Fame Series)	1957	$30
❑ B-2559 [PS]	Frank Sinatra (Hall of Fame Series)	1958	$30
❑ B-2564 [PS]	Frank Sinatra (Hall of Fame Series)	1958	$30
❑ B-2589 [PS]	Frank Sinatra (Hall of Fame Series)	1958	$30
❑ B-2614 [PS]	Frank Sinatra (Hall of Fame Series)	1958	$30
❑ B-2626 [PS]	Frank Sinatra (Hall of Fame Series)	1958	$30
❑ B-2638 [PS]	Frank Sinatra (Hall of Fame Series)	1958	$30
❑ B-2641 [PS]	Frank Sinatra (Hall of Fame Series)	1958	$30
❑ B-1815 [PS]	Frank Sinatra Sings Cole Porter	1954	$30

Number	Title	Yr	NM
❑ B-1673 [PS]	Frank Sinatra Sings George Gershwin	1953	$30
❑ B-1608 [PS]	Frank Sinatra Sings Hits from South Pacific and Oklahoma	1952	$35
❑ B-1524 [PS]	Frank Sinatra Sings Irving Berlin	1952	$30
❑ B-1702 [PS]	Frank Sinatra Sings Jerome Kern	1953	$30
❑ B-1872 [PS]	Frank Sinatra Sings Rodgers and Hart	1954	$30
❑ B-2542 [PS]	Frank Sinatra with Harry James and Pearl Bailey	1957	$60
❑ B-1984	Hello Young Lovers/I Only Have Eyes for You//Falling in Love with Love/You'll Never Know	1955	$30
❑ B-1986	How Cute Can You Be/Almost Like Being in Love//Nancy/Oh! What It Seemed to Be	1955	$30
❑ B-1815	I Concentrate on You/Why Can't You Behave//Why Shouldn't I/You Do Something to Me	1954	$30
❑ B-2515	I Couldn't Sleep a Wink Last Night/A Lovely Way to Spend an Evening//People Will Say We're in Love/Oh, What a Beautiful Mornin'	1957	$30
❑ B-2559	I Could Write a Book/If You Are But a Dream//I'm a Fool to Want You/I Should Care	1958	$30
❑ B-7431	I Don't Know Why (I Just Do)/Try a Little Tenderness//(I Don't Stand) A Ghost of a Chance/Paradise	1955	$30
❑ B-9531	I Guess I'll Have to Dream the Rest/If Only She'd Look My Way//Love Me/Nevertheless	1957	$30
❑ 5-1908	I Only Have Eyes for You/The Girl That I Marry//I Hear a Rhapsody/April in Paris	1952	$30
— One record of 2-EP set B-419			
❑ B-1985	It All Depends on You/S'posin'//All of Me/Time After Time	1955	$30
❑ B-419 [PS]	I've Got a Crush on You	1952	$60
— Gatefold cover for 2-EP set (1907 and 1908)			
❑ 5-1907	I've Got a Crush on You/They Say It's Wonderful//If I Loved You/You Do Something to Me	1952	$30
— One record of 2-EP set B-419			
❑ 5-1129	Lover/It's Only a Paper Moon//The Continental/When You're Smiling	1952	$30
— One record of 2-EP version of B-218			
❑ B-9533	Mad About You/Sorry//On the Island of Stromboli/It's Only a Paper Moon	1957	$30
❑ 5-1130	My Blue Heaven/It All Depends on You//You Do Something to Me/Should I	1952	$30
— One record of 2-EP version of B-218			
❑ B-1702	Ol' Man River/All the Things You Are//Why Was I Born/The Song Is You	1953	$30
❑ B-2564	Ol' Man River/You'll Never Walk Alone//Soliloquy	1958	$30
❑ B-2614	One for My Baby/If I Loved You//Put Your Dreams Away/You'll Never Know	1958	$30
❑ B-7433	Over the Rainbow/That Old Black Magic//Spring Is Here/Lover	1955	$30
❑ B-2589	September Song/Among My Souvenirs//The Things We Did Last Summer/Oh! What It Seemed to Be	1958	$30
❑ 5-1323	Silent Night, Holy Night/Adeste Fideles//O Little Town of Bethlehem/It Came Upon a Midnight Clear	1952	$30
— One record of 2-EP version of B-167			
❑ B-10322	Silent Night, Holy Night/Adeste Fideles//O Little Town of Bethlehem/It Came Upon the Midnight Clear	1957	$35
❑ B-218 [PS]	Sing and Dance with Frank Sinatra	1950	$60
— Gatefold sleeve for 2-EP set (1129 and 1130)			
❑ 5-1389	Soliloquy//If I Loved You/You'll Never Walk Alone	1952	$35
— Record that goes with cover B-1673			
❑ 5-1355	Some Enchanted Evening/Bali Ha'i//People Will Say We're in Love/Oh, What a Beautiful Morning	1952	$35
— Record that goes with cover B-1608			
❑ B-2638	Stormy Weather/Why Was I Born//The House I Live In/How Deep Is the Ocean	1958	$30
❑ B-9021 [PS]	That Old Feeling	1956	$30
❑ B-9021	That Old Feeling/Blue Skies//Autumn in New York/Don't Cry Joe	1956	$30
❑ B-2517	The Birth of the Blues/I've Got a Crush on You//Five Minutes More/Someone to Watch Over Me	1957	$30
❑ 5-1116	These Foolish Things/Why Shouldn't I//I Don't Know Why/Try a Little Tenderness	1952	$30
— One record of 2-EP version of B-112			

Number	Title	Yr	NM
❑ B-9532	We Kiss in a Shadow/I Am Loved//Take My Love/I Could Write a Book	1957	$30
❑ 5-1322	White Christmas/Jingle Bells//Have Yourself a Merry Little Christmas/Have Yourself a Merry Little Christmas	1952	$30

—One record of 2-EP version of B-167

Number	Title	Yr	NM
❑ B-10321	White Christmas/Jingle Bells//Have Yourself a Merry Little Christmas/Santa Claus Is Coming to Town	1957	$35

RCA VICTOR

Number	Title	Yr	NM
❑ 947-0177	Everything Happens to Me/I'll Be Seeing You//This Is the Beginning of the End/Street of Dreams	1954	$35

—Part 2 of EPBT 3063

Number	Title	Yr	NM
❑ EPBT-3063 [PS]	Fabulous Frankie	1954	$50

—Cover for 947-0176 and 947-0177

Number	Title	Yr	NM
❑ EPA-5014 [PS]	Frankie and Tommy	1958	$25
❑ EPA-5147 [PS]	Frank Sinatra	1960	$30
❑ EPA-5014	Oh! Look at Me Now/This Love of Mine//I Guess I'll Have to Dream the Rest/How Do You Do Without Me	1958	$25
❑ EPA-5147	The Lamplighter's Serenade/The Night We Called It a Day//The Song Is You/Night and Day	1960	$30

REPRISE

Number	Title	Yr	NM
❑ SR1019	Come Fly with Me/Street of Dreams/You Make Me Feel So Young//Fly Me to the Moon/Where or When/My Kind of Town (reprise)	1966	$25

—Stereo jukebox issue; small hole, plays at 33 1/3 rpm

Number	Title	Yr	NM
❑ SR1011 [PS]	Days of Wine and Roses, Moon River and Other Academy Award Winners	1964	$25
❑ SR1011	Days of Wine and Roses/Moon River/In the Cool, Cool, Cool of the Evening//Swingin' on a Star/All the Way/The Way You Look Tonight	1964	$25

—Stereo jukebox issue; small hole, plays at 33 1/3 rpm

Number	Title	Yr	NM
❑ SR1013	Dear Heart/Pass Me By/I Can't Believe I'm Losing You//Come Blow Your Horn/Softly As I Leave You/Then Suddenly Love	1965	$25

—Jukebox issue; small hole, plays at 33 1/3 rpm

Number	Title	Yr	NM
❑ SR1033	Drinking Water (Aqua de Beber)/Someone to Light Up My Life/Triste//Leaving on a Jet Plane/Bein' Green/One Note Samba	1971	$20

—Stereo jukebox issue; small hole, plays at 33 1/3 rpm

Number	Title	Yr	NM
❑ SR1012	Fly Me to the Moon/I Wanna Be Around/More//I Can't Stop Loving You/The Good Life/I Wish You Love	1965	$25

—33 1/3 rpm, small hole, "Promotion

Number	Title	Yr	NM
❑ SR1024	Follow Me/Sunny//Yellow Days/Indian Summer	1968	$25

—As "Francis A. Sinatra & Edward K. Ellington"; jukebox issue; 33 1/3 rpm, small hole

Number	Title	Yr	NM
❑ SR1024 [PS]	Francis A. and Edward K.	1968	$25
❑ SR1034 [PS]	Frank Sinatra's Greatest Hits, Vol. II	1972	$20

—Part of "Little LP" series (#191)

Number	Title	Yr	NM
❑ SR1022 [PS]	Frank Sinatra (The World We Knew)	1967	$25
❑ R-40026	I Hadn't Anyone Till You/Misty/Stardust//Come Rain or Come Shine/All or Nothing at All	1962	$30

—Jukebox issue; small hole, plays at 33 1/3 rpm

Number	Title	Yr	NM
❑ SR1012 [PS]	It Might As Well Be Swing	1965	$25
❑ SR2155	Let Me Try Again/You Will Be My Music//Winners/You're So Right (For What's Wrong in My Life)	1973	$25

—Jukebox issue; small hole, plays at 33 1/3 rpm

Number	Title	Yr	NM
❑ R-40043	(Love Is) The Tender Trap/Please Be Kind/Nice Work If You Can Get It//My Kind of Girl/Learnin' the Blues	1963	$30

—Stereo jukebox issue; small hole, plays at 33 1/3 rpm

Number	Title	Yr	NM
❑ SR1018 [PS]	Moonlight Sinatra	1966	$25
❑ SR1018	Moon Love/Moonlight Serenade//Moonlight Becomes You/The Moon Got in My Eyes/I Wished on the Moon	1966	$25

—Jukebox issue; 33 1/3 rpm, small hole

Number	Title	Yr	NM
❑ SR1034	My Way/Love's Been Good to Me//Goin' Out of My Head/Star/The September of My Years	1972	$20

—Jukebox issue; small hole, plays at 33 1/3 rpm

Number	Title	Yr	NM
❑ SR2155 [PS]	Ol' Blue Eyes Is Back	1973	$25

—Part of Little LP series (# LLP 233)

Number	Title	Yr	NM
❑ SR1033 [PS]	Sinatra and Company	1971	$20

—Part of "Little LP" series (#178)

Number	Title	Yr	NM
❑ R-40026 [PS]	Sinatra and Strings	1962	$30
❑ SR1019 [PS]	Sinatra at the Sands	1966	$25
❑ R-40043 [PS]	Sinatra-Basie	1963	$30
❑ SR1013 [PS]	Softly As I Leave You	1965	$25
❑ SR2195 [PS]	Some Nice Things I've Missed	1974	$20

—Part of "Little LP" series (#267)

Number	Title	Yr	NM
❑ PRO-S-2115 [PS]	Stereo Review Salutes Frank Sinatra	1984	$25

—Special promo available from "Stereo Review" magazine

Number	Title	Yr	NM
❑ SR1022	The World We Knew (Over and Over)/Don't Sleep in the Subway/You Are There//Somethin' Stupid (Duet with Nancy Sinatra)/This Town/Drinking Again	1967	$25

—Stereo jukebox issue; small hole, plays at 33 1/3 rpm

Number	Title	Yr	NM
❑ SR2195	What Are You Doing the Rest of Your Life?/Bad, Bad Leroy Brown//You Are the Sunshine of My Life/The Summer Knows/Tie a Yellow Ribbon	1974	$20

—Stereo jukebox issue; small hole, plays at 33 1/3 rpm

SINATRA, NANCY

ELEKTRA

Number	Title	Yr	NM
❑ 46659	Let's Keep It That Way/One Jump Ahead of the Storm	1979	$5

PRIVATE STOCK

Number	Title	Yr	NM
❑ 45,022	Annabel of Mobile/(B-side unknown)	1975	$5
❑ 45,108	Indian Summer/Holly and Hawkeye	1976	$5

—With Lee Hazelwood

Number	Title	Yr	NM
❑ 45,158	It's For My Dad/A Gentle Man Like You	1977	$5

RCA VICTOR

Number	Title	Yr	NM
❑ APBO-0029	Ain't No Sunshine/Sugar Me	1973	$5
❑ 47-0864	It's the Love/Kind of a Woman	1973	$8
❑ 74-0614	Paris Summer/Down from Dover	1971	$8

—With Lee Hazlewood

REPRISE

Number	Title	Yr	NM
❑ 0670	100 Years/See the Little Children	1968	$8
❑ 1021	Did You Ever/Back on the Road	1971	$8

—As "Nancy and Lee" (Hazlewood)

Number	Title	Yr	NM
❑ 0851	Drummer Man/Home	1969	$8
❑ 0980	Feelin' Kinda Sunday/Kids	1970	$8

—A-side by Nancy Sinatra and Frank Sinatra

Number	Title	Yr	NM
❑ 0491	Friday's Child/Hutchinson Jail	1966	$10
❑ 1034	Glory Road/Is Anybody Goin' to San Antone	1971	$8
❑ 0813	God Knows I Love You/Just Plain Old Me	1969	$8
❑ 0789	Good Time Girl/Old Devil Moon	1968	$8
❑ 0756	Happy/Nice 'N' Easy	1968	$8
❑ 0932	Hello L.A., Bye Bye Birmingham/White Tattoo	1970	$8
❑ 0821	Here We Go Again/Memories	1969	$8
❑ 0869	Highway Song/(B-side unknown)	1969	$30

—Released only in England

Number	Title	Yr	NM
❑ 0461	How Does That Grab You, Darlin'?/The Last of the Secret Agents	1966	$10
❑ 0890	I Love Them All/Home	1970	$8
❑ 0968	I'm Not a Girl Anymore/How Are Things in California	1970	$8
❑ 0514	In Our Time/Leave My Dog Alone	1966	$10
❑ 0991	Is Anybody Goin' to San Antone/Hook and Ladder	1971	$8
❑ 0991 [PS]	Is Anybody Goin' to San Antone/Hook and Ladder	1971	$20
❑ 0880	It's Such a Lonely Time of the Year/Kids	1969	$10
❑ 0629	Lady Bird/Sand	1967	$8

—With Lee Hazlewood

Number	Title	Yr	NM
❑ 1011	Life's a Trippy Thing/I'm Not Afraid	1971	$8

—A-side by Nancy Sinatra and Frank Sinatra; B-side by Frank Sinatra solo

Number	Title	Yr	NM
❑ 0729	Lightning's Girl/One Velvet Morning	1968	$5

—B-side with Lee Hazlewood; "Back to Back Hits" series

Number	Title	Yr	NM
❑ 0620	Lightning's Girl/Until It's Time for You to Go	1967	$12
❑ 0620 [PS]	Lightning's Girl/Until It's Time for You to Go	1967	$30
❑ 0559	Love Eyes/Coastin'	1967	$10
❑ 20144	Put Your Head on My Shoulder/I See the Moon	1963	$30
❑ 0407	So Long Babe/If He'd Love Me	1965	$20
❑ 0561	Somethin' Stupid/Give Her Love	1967	$12

—A-side: Nancy Sinatra and Frank Sinatra; B-side: Frank Sinatra

Number	Title	Yr	NM
❑ 0561	Somethin' Stupid/I Will Wait for You	1967	$8

—A-side: Nancy Sinatra and Frank Sinatra; B-side: Frank Sinatra

Number	Title	Yr	NM
❑ 0651	Some Velvet Morning/Oh Lonesome Me	1967	$8

—With Lee Hazlewood

Number	Title	Yr	NM
❑ 0527	Sugar Town/Summer Wine	1966	$15
❑ 0721	Sugar Town/Summer Wine	1968	$5

—Back to Back Hits" series

Number	Title	Yr	NM
❑ 0238	Tammy/Thanks to You	1963	$30
❑ 0335	The Answer to Everything/True Love	1965	$20
❑ 20188	The Cruel War/One Way	1963	$30
❑ 0701	These Boots Are Made for Walkin'/Love Eyes	1968	$5

—Back to Back Hits" series

Number	Title	Yr	NM
❑ 0432	These Boots Are Made for Walkin'/The City Never Sleeps at Night	1965	$15
❑ 0292	This Love of Mine/There Goes the Bride	1964	$30
❑ 20045	To Know Him Is to Love Him/Like I Do	1962	$30
❑ 20127	Tonight You Belong to Me/You Can Have Any Boy	1962	$30
❑ 0636	Tony Rome/This Town	1967	$8
❑ 0263	Where Do the Lonely Go/Just Think About the Good Times	1964	$30

7-Inch Extended Plays

Number	Title	Yr	NM
❑ SR6251 [PS]	Country My Way	1967	$20
❑ SR6277	I Gotta Get Out of This Town/Younger Than Springtime/Things//See the Little Children/Up, Up and Away/This Town	1967	$20

—Jukebox issue; small hole, plays at 33 1/3 rpm

Number	Title	Yr	NM
❑ SR6251	It's Such a Pretty World/Jackson/When It's Over//Oh Lonesome Me/End of the World/Lay Some Happiness on Me	1967	$20

—Jukebox issue; small hole, plays at 33 1/3 rpm

Number	Title	Yr	NM
❑ SR6277 [PS]	Movin' with Nancy	1967	$20

SINCERELY, SAN JOSE

KARMA

Number	Title	Yr	NM
❑ 301	What the World Needs Now/You Don't Get Young Anymore	1968	$1500

SINCERES, THE (1)

COLUMBIA

Number	Title	Yr	NM
❑ 43110	Sincerely/Snap Your Fingers	1964	$20

TAURUS

Number	Title	Yr	NM
❑ 377	The Magic of Love/Tell Her	1966	$40

SINCERES, THE (2)

RICHIE

Number	Title	Yr	NM
❑ 545	Please Don't Cheat on Me/If You Should Leave Me	1961	$700

—No mention of Roulette Records on label

Number	Title	Yr	NM
❑ 545	Please Don't Cheat on Me/If You Should Leave Me	1961	$125

—With Roulette Records distribution mentioned on label

SIGMA

Number	Title	Yr	NM
❑ 1003/4	Darling/Do You Remember	1960	$400

SINCEROS, THE

COLUMBIA

Number	Title	Yr	NM
❑ 02121	Disappearing/Torture Myself	1981	$4
❑ 11115	Take Me to Your Leader/Good Luck (To You)	1979	$4
❑ 11178	Worlds Apart/Hanging On Too Long	1980	$4

SINGER, HAL

SAVOY

Number	Title	Yr	NM
❑ 1179	Hot Rod/Rock 'n Roll	1955	$30
❑ 1194	Hound's Tooth/Crossroads	1956	$20
❑ 861	Indian Love Call/The Frog Hop	1952	$30

SINGER, JOHNNY

HIT

Number	Title	Yr	NM
❑ 233	Make the World Go Away/Fever	1965	$8

—B-side by the Chords (2)

Number	Title	Yr	NM
❑ 178	Ode to the Little Brown Shack Out Back/Do-Wacka-Do	1965	$8

—B-side by Charlie Bare

SINGERS, THE

DATE

Number	Title	Yr	NM
❑ 1540	That's What Christmas Is/Johnny's Noel	1966	$8

SINGING DOGS, THE, DON CHARLES PRESENTS

RCA VICTOR

Number	Title	Yr	NM
❑ 47-6432	Hot Dog Rock and Roll/Hot Dog Boogie	1956	$15
❑ 48-1021	Hot Dog Rock and Roll/Hot Dog Boogie	1971	$5
❑ 47-6344	Oh! Susannah//Pat-a-Cake/Three Blind Mice/Jingle Bells	1955	$20

—Jingle Bells" is part of a medley and lasts 1:15

Number	Title	Yr	NM
❑ 47-6344 [PS]	Oh! Susannah//Pat-a-Cake/Three Blind Mice/Jingle Bells	1955	$30

Number	Title	Yr	NM
❏ F2NW [DJ]	Pearl's Jingle Bells/Caesar's Pat-A-Cake/King's Three Blind Mice//Dolly's Oh! Susanna (Fast)/ Dolly'	1955	$50
—Banded version for radio use ("Jingle Bells" is 1:15)			
❏ F2NW-7846/7 [DJ]	Pearl's Jingle Bells/Caesar's Pat-A-Cake/King's Three Blind Mice//Dolly's Oh! Susanna (Fast)/ Dolly's Oh! Susanna (Slow)	1955	$50
—Banded version for radio use ("Jingle Bells" is 1:15)			

SINGING MCENTIRES, THE (PAKE, REBA AND SUSIE)
BOSS

Number	Title	Yr	NM
❏ SPS-194	The Ballad of John McEntire/ Interview by the Grandchildren	1969	$500
— Supposedly only 25 copies were pressed			

SINGING NUN, THE
PHILIPS

Number	Title	Yr	NM
❏ 40152	Dominique/Entres Les Etoiles (Among the Stars)	1963	$6
❏ 40152 [PS]	Dominique/Entres Les Etoiles (Among the Stars)	1963	$15
❏ 40163	Dominique/Les Pieds de Missionnaires	1963	$6
❏ 40163 [PS]	Dominique/Les Pieds de Missionnaires	1963	$20
—Almost identical to the 40152 sleeve			
❏ 40165	Tous Les Chemins/Frere "Tout Le" Monde	1964	$5
❏ 40165 [PS]	Tous Les Chemins/Frere "Tout Le" Monde	1964	$15

SINGLE BULLET THEORY
ARTIFACTS

Number	Title	Yr	NM
❏ 0(# unknown)	Peggy Got Her Eyes Full/ There Is the Boy	1981	$5
❏ 0(# unknown) [PS]	Peggy Got Her Eyes Full/ There Is the Boy	1981	$5
NEMPEROR			
❏ 03890	Too Hot to Handle/Hang On to Your Heart	1983	$3

SINGLETON, MARGIE, AND FARON YOUNG
MERCURY

Number	Title	Yr	NM
❏ 72312	Another Woman's Man -- Another Man's Woman/ Honky Tonk Happy	1964	$15

SINGLETON, MARGIE

Number	Title	Yr	NM
❏ 2090	Chill Winds/Little Darlin'	1968	$10
❏ 5000	Harper Valley P.T.A./ (B-side unknown)	1968	$12
❏ 2011	Ode to Billie Joe/Big Boys Don't Need Mamas	1967	$10
❏ 2000	Sooner or Later/Angel Hands	1967	$12
❏ 2050	Wandering Mind/Your Conscience Sends Me Flowers	1968	$10
D			
❏ 1007	I Want to Be Where You're Gonna Be/Shattered Kingdom	1958	$40
MERCURY			
❏ 72002	Chained to a Promise/ Living in the Danger Zone	1962	$15
❏ 71672	Destination Love/Toss a Pebble	1960	$20
❏ 72363	Don't Be Good to Me/ It's Too Much	1964	$15
❏ 72268	Forget Me Not/I Don't Want You This Way	1964	$15
❏ 72124	I Don't Have to Look Pretty/ Walkin' Back to Happiness	1963	$15
❏ 71928	I'll Just Walk On By/Her Image Keeps Getting in the Way	1962	$15
❏ 72079	Magic Star (Telstar)/Only Your Shadow Knows	1963	$15
❏ 72213	Old Records/How Do You Say Goodbye	1963	$15
❏ 71359	Oo-Wee, You're the One for Me/Teddy	1958	$30
❏ 71733	She Will Break Your Heart/Voices of Love	1960	$20
STARDAY			
❏ 323	Beautiful Dawn/Take Time Out for Love	1957	$30
❏ 502	For the Love of Jim/ My Special Dream	1960	$30
❏ 309	My Picture of You/ Love Is a Treasure	1957	$30
❏ 287	One Step Nearer to You/ Not What He's Got	1957	$30
❏ 472	The Eyes of Love/Angel Hands	1959	$30
UNITED ARTISTS			
❏ 939	I'm Guilty This Time/You Took the Easy Way Out	1965	$10
❏ 896	What Could I Do/You Shake My Hand and Kiss Me on the Cheek	1965	$10

SINNAMON
BECKET

Number	Title	Yr	NM
❏ 45-11	Thanks to You/(Instr.)	1982	$8
JIVE			
❏ 9028	I Need You Now/ (B-side unknown)	1983	$10

SIOUXSIE AND THE BANSHEES
GEFFEN

Number	Title	Yr	NM
❏ 28813	Cities in Dust/An Execution	1986	$3
❏ 28813 [PS]	Cities in Dust/An Execution	1986	$5
❏ 29358	Dear Prudence/Tattoo	1984	$3
❏ 29358 [PS]	Dear Prudence/Tattoo	1984	$5
❏ 27760	Peek-A-Boo/False Face	1988	$3
❏ 27760 [PS]	Peek-A-Boo/False Face	1988	$5
POLYDOR			
❏ 14561	Hong Kong Garden/Overground	1979	$50
PVC			
❏ 1001	Israel/Red Over White	1980	$6
❏ 1001 [PS]	Israel/Red Over White	1980	$8

SIR DOUGLAS QUINTET
Also see THE DEVONS; DOUG SAHM.
ATLANTIC

Number	Title	Yr	NM
❏ 2985	Texas Tornado/Blue Horizon	1973	$8
—As "Sir Douglas Band			
MERCURY			
❏ 73257	Michoacan/Westside Blues Again	1971	$6
PACEMAKER			
❏ 280	Sugar Bee/Blue Norther	1964	$30
PHILIPS			
❏ 40687	Pretty Flower/Catch the Man on the Fly	1970	$8
❏ 40708	Wasted Days, Wasted Nights/ Me and My Destiny	1971	$8
❏ 40676	What About Tomorrow/A Nice Song	1970	$8
❏ 40676 [PS]	What About Tomorrow/A Nice Song	1970	$20
SMASH			
❏ 2169	Are Inlaws Really Outlaws/Sell a Song	1968	$8
❏ 2253	At the Crossroads/Texas Me	1969	$8
❏ 2233	Dynamite Woman/Too Many Dociled Minds	1969	$8
❏ 2222	Lawd, I'm Just a Country Boy in This Great Big Freaky City/ It Didn't Even Bring Me Down	1969	$8
❏ 2191	Mendocino/I Wanna Be Your Mama Again	1968	$8
TRIBE			
❏ 8318	Beginning of the End/ Love Don't Treat Me Fair	1966	$12
❏ 8323	Hang Loose/I'm Sorry	1967	$12
❏ 8312	In Time/The Story of John Hardy	1965	$10
❏ 8321	She Digs My Love/ When I Sing the Blues	1966	$10
❏ 8308	She's About a Mover/We'll Take Our Last Walk Tonight	1965	$20
— White label (not marked as promo)			
❏ 8308	She's About a Mover/We'll Take Our Last Walk Tonight	1965	$15
— Gray label with Indian head			
❏ 8317	She's Gotta Be Boss/ Quarter to Three	1966	$10
❏ 8310	The Tracker/Blue Brother	1965	$15
— White label (not marked as promo)			
❏ 8310	The Tracker/Blue Brother	1965	$10
— Gray label with Indian head			

SIR LORD BALTIMORE
MERCURY

Number	Title	Yr	NM
❏ 73181	I Got a Woman/ Master Headache	1970	$8

SIR WALTER RALEIGH AND THE COUPONS
A&M

Number	Title	Yr	NM
❏ 764	While I Wait/Somethin'	1965	$10
❏ 757	White Cliffs of Dover/ Something or Other	1965	$10
JERDEN			
❏ 760	Tomorrow's Gonna Be Another Day/Whitcomb St.	1965	$15
—As "Sir Raleigh and the Coupons"			
TOWER			
❏ 220	I Don't Want to Cry/Always	1966	$10
❏ 156	Tell Her Tonight/If You Need Me	1965	$10

SISK, SHIRLEY
SUN

Number	Title	Yr	NM
❏ 365	I Forgot to Remember to Forget/The Other Side	1961	$30

SISTER RAY

Number	Title	Yr	NM
❏ 0(# unknown)	Survivors/Your Every Word/Black (Live)	1987	$30
❏ 0(# unknown) [PS]	Survivors/Your Every Word/Black (Live)	1987	$30
7-Inch Extended Plays			
❏ 0(# unknown)	Coming to Terms	1985	$75
❏ 0(# unknown) [PS]	Coming to Terms	1985	$75

SISTER SLEDGE
ATCO

Number	Title	Yr	NM
❏ 7020	Circle of Love (Caught in the Middle)/Cross My Heart	1975	$15
❏ 7008	Love Don't You Go Through No Changes on Me/ Don't You Miss Him	1974	$15
❏ 7035	Love Has Found Me/ Love Ain't Easy	1975	$15
❏ 6940	Mama Never Told Me/Neither One of Us (Wants to Be the First to Say Goodbye)	1973	$70
❏ 6924	The Weatherman/Have You Met My Friend	1973	$50
ATLANTIC			
❏ 7-89520	Dancing on the Jagged Edge/You Need Me	1985	$4
❏ 7-89547	Frankie/Peer Pressure	1985	$4
❏ 7-89547 [PS]	Frankie/Peer Pressure	1985	$5
❏ 7-89357	Here to Stay/Make a Wish	1986	$4
—B-side by Joe Cruz			
COTILLION			
❏ 46007	All American Girls/ Happy Feeling	1981	$5
❏ 47007	All the Man That I Need/ Light Footin'	1982	$5
❏ 44226	Baby, It's the Rain/Hold Onto This Feeling	1977	$6
❏ 44220	Blockbuster Boy/Moondancer	1977	$6
❏ 7-99885	B.Y.O.B. (Bring Your Own Baby)/(B-side unknown)	1983	$5
❏ 44208	Cream of the Crop/ Love Ain't Easy	1976	$8
❏ 7-99834	Gotta Get Back to Love/ Lifetime Lover	1983	$5
❏ 45007	Got to Love Somebody/ Good Girl Now	1979	$5
❏ 46017	He's Just a Runaway (A Tribute to Bob Marley)/(Long Version)	1981	$5
❏ 44245	He's the Greatest Dancer/ Somebody Loves Me	1978	$5
❏ 44234	I've Seen Better Days/ Do It to the Max	1978	$6
❏ 45020	Let's Go on Vacation/ Easy Street	1980	$5
❏ 45001	Lost in Music/Thinking of You	1979	$5
❏ 44202	Thank You for Today/ Have Love Will Travel	1976	$5
❏ 44251	We Are Family/Easier to Love	1979	$5

SISTERS, THE
DEL-FI

Number	Title	Yr	NM
❏ 4302	Happy New Year, Baby/ Ooh Poo Pah Doo	1964	$12

SIX PENTZ, THE
BRENT

Number	Title	Yr	NM
❏ 7064	Don't Say You're Sorry/ Tinkle Talk	1967	$30
❏ 7062	Imitation Situation/ Please Come Home	1967	$30

SIX TEENS, THE
FLIP

Number	Title	Yr	NM
❏ 315	A Casual Look/ Teenage Promise	1956	$30
❏ 351	A Little Prayer/Suddenly in Love	1960	$20
❏ 322	Arrow of Love/Was It a Dream of Mine	1957	$20
❏ 338	Baby-O/Oh, It's Crazy	1958	$30
❏ 326	Baby You're Dynamite/ My Surprise	1957	$20
❏ 333	Danny/Love's Funny That Way	1958	$20
❏ 329	My Secret/Stop Playing Ping Pong	1958	$20
❏ 320	My Special Guy/Only Jim	1956	$20
❏ 317	Send Me Flowers/ Afar Into the Night	1956	$20
❏ 350	So Happy/That Wonderful Secret of Love	1960	$20
❏ 346	Why Do I Go to School/ Heaven Knows I Love You	1959	$30

SIXPENCE, THE
ALL AMERICAN

Number	Title	Yr	NM
❏ 313	Fortune Teller/My Flash on You	1966	$50
❏ 353	Fortune Teller/My Flash on You	1967	$40
❏ 333	Hey Joe/(B-side unknown)	1967	$40
DOT			
❏ 16959	Fortune Teller/My Flash on You	1966	$30
IMPACT			
❏ 1025	What to Do/You're the Love	1967	$30

Number	Title	Yr	NM

SKA KINGS, THE
ATLANTIC
❏ 2236	Last Night Ska/ Watermelon Man Ska	1964	$12

SKAGGS, RICKY
EPIC
❏ 34-07721	(Angel on My Mind) That's Why I'm Walkin'/Lord, She Sure Is Good at Lovin' Me	1988	$4
❏ 15-08454	Cajun Moon/Love's Gonna Get You Someday	1988	$3

— Gray label reissue
❏ 34-05748	Cajun Moon/Rockin' the Boat	1985	$4
❏ 34-04831	Country Boy/Wheel Hoss	1985	$4
❏ 15-08464	Country Boy/You Make Me Feel Like a Man	1988	$3
❏ 14-02692	Crying My Heart Out Over You/Lost to a Stranger	1982	$4
❏ 19-02034	Don't Get Above Your Raising/Low and Lonely	1981	$4
❏ 15-03096	Don't Get Above Your Raising/ You May See Me Walkin'	1982	$3

— Gray label reissue
❏ 34-73078	Heartbreak Hurricane/Casting My Shadows in the Road	1989	$4
❏ 34-03212	Heartbroke/Don't Think I'll Cry	1982	$4
❏ 34-03812	Highway 40 Blues/Don't Let Your Sweet Love Die	1983	$4
❏ 14-02931	I Don't Care/If That's the Way You Feel	1982	$4
❏ 34-07416	I'm Tired/San Antonio Rose	1987	$4
❏ 15-08459	I've Got a New Heartache/Love Can't Ever Get Better Than This	1988	$3

— Gray label reissue
❏ 34-05898	I've Got a New Heartache/ She Didn't Say Why	1986	$4
❏ 34-06650	I Wonder If I Care As Much/ Raisin' the Dickens	1987	$4
❏ 34-03482	I Wouldn't Change You If I Could/One Way Rider	1982	$4
❏ 34-68995	Let It Be You/The Fields of Home	1989	$4
❏ 34-07060	Love Can't Ever Get Better Than This/Daddy Was a Hardworking, Honest Man	1987	$4

— With Sharon White
❏ 34-06327	Love's Gonna Get You Someday/Walkin' in Jerusalem	1986	$4
❏ 34-68693	Lovin' Only Me/Home Is Wherever You Are	1989	$4

— B-side with Sharon White
❏ 34-08063	Old Kind of Love/Woman You Won't Break Mine	1988	$4
❏ 34-04668	Something in My Heart/ Baby, I'm in Love with You	1984	$4
❏ 34-07924	Thanks Again/If You Don't Believe the Bible	1988	$4

SUGAR HILL
❏ 3706	I'll Take the Blame/Could You Love Me One More Time	1980	$10

SUGAR HILL/EPIC
❏ 34-04245	Don't Cheat in Our Hometown/Children Go	1983	$4
❏ 34-04394	Honey (Open That Door)/ She's More to Be Pitied	1984	$4

SKARLETTONES, THE
EMBER
❏ 1053	Do You Remember/ Will You Dream	1959	$120

SKEE BROTHERS, THE
EPIC
❏ 9275	Big Deal/While I'm Away	1958	$125

OKEH
❏ 7108	That's All She Wrote/Four Aces	1959	$60

SKELLERN, PETER
PRIVATE STOCK
❏ 45,054	Hard Times/And Then You'll Fall	1975	$4
❏ 45,028	Hold On to Love/ (B-side unknown)	1975	$4

SKELTON, EDDIE
STARDAY
❏ 294	My Heart Gets Lonely/Let Me Be With You Forever	1957	$200

SKID ROW (2)
New Jersey hard rockers featuring SEBASTIAN BACH.
ATLANTIC
❏ 88883	18 and Life//Midnight/Tornado	1989	$3
❏ 88883 [PS]	18 and Life//Midnight/Tornado	1989	$3
❏ 88886	I Remember You/Makin' a Mess	1989	$3
❏ 88886 [PS]	I Remember You/Makin' a Mess	1989	$3

SKINNER, JIMMIE
CAPITOL
❏ F2108	Dreaming My Weary Life Away/Till Then	1952	$30
❏ F1476	Falling Rain Blues/ It's All the Same	1951	$30
❏ F2351	Help Me Find My Broken Heart/ Your Flyin' Days Are Through	1953	$30
❏ F1935	Holy Life Insurance/ When the Book	1952	$30
❏ F2231	I Ain't Got Time/I Saw Your Face in the Crowd	1952	$30
❏ F1563	It's Bargain Day/I Can't Tell My Heart That	1951	$30
❏ F1339	It's My World/There's Nothing	1950	$40
❏ F2007	It's Our Goodbye/ Women Beware	1952	$30
❏ F2513	I've Got a Lot of Love Baby/By Degrees	1953	$30
❏ F1889	Penny Post Card/'Tis Sweet	1951	$30
❏ F1209	There Won't Be Much More Time/Will You Be Satisfied	1950	$40

DECCA
❏ 9-30665	Beautiful/Jesus Loves Us All	1958	$30
❏ 9-29179	Don't Get Around Much Anymore/John Henry and the Water Boy	1954	$30
❏ 9-29006	Don't Give Your Heart to a Rambler/What a Pleasure	1954	$30
❏ 9-29454	I Don't Need a Doctor/ Blame the Right One	1955	$30
❏ 9-28910	I'm Allergic to Your Kisses/Baby I Could Change My Ways	1953	$30
❏ 9-29053	Too Hot to Handle/My Broken Heart Is Startin' to Show	1954	$30

MERCURY
❏ 70956	Another Saturday Night/ Just Ramblin' On	1956	$30
❏ 71090	Born to Be Wild/ No Fault of Mine	1957	$30
❏ 71704	Careless Love/I'll Weaken and Call	1960	$20
❏ 71387	Dark Hollow/Walkin' My Blues Away	1958	$20
❏ 70854	Dime a Dozen/My Heart's on a Budget	1956	$30
❏ 71785	Don't Let Love Get You Down/ Please Don't Send Cecil Away	1961	$15
❏ 71873	Four Walls, a Floor and a Ceiling/Big City	1961	$15
❏ 71163	Hafta Do Something/No Maybe in My Baby's Eyes	1957	$30
❏ 71952	Hundred Proof Heartaches/I Know You're Married (But I Love You Still)	1962	$15
❏ 71192	I Found My Girl in the USA/ Carroll County Blues	1957	$30
❏ 71606	Lonesome Road Blues/ Two Squares Away	1960	$20
❏ 70894	Muddy Water Blues/Will You Be Satisfied That Way	1956	$30
❏ 72020	One Dead Man Ago/ Wooden Angels	1962	$15
❏ 70792	Steppin' Out on You/I Want You for My Baby	1956	$30
❏ 71719	The Hem of His Garment/ God's Mansion in the Sky	1960	$20
❏ 71256	What Makes a Man Wander/ We've Got Things in Common	1958	$20
❏ 71341	Where My Sweet Baby Goes/ Where Do We Go from Here	1958	$20

STARDAY
❏ 711	Hard Working Man/ How It's Been (Since the Last Heartbreak)	1965	$12
❏ 821	I'd Rather Take the Blame/The Kind of Love She Gave to Me	1967	$10
❏ 669	The Cork and the Bottle/ Let's Say Goodbye Like We Said Hello	1964	$15
❏ 836	The Story of Bonnie and Clyde/ Bonnie and Clyde's Getaway	1968	$10

— B-side by the Stanley Brothers
❏ 687	This Old Road/Things That Might Have Been	1964	$15
❏ 627	Trouble Walked In/Old Bill Dollar	1963	$15
❏ 647	Try to Be Good/ Yesterday's Wrong	1963	$15
❏ 738	Twenty Beers/To Tell the World	1966	$10

SKIP AND FLIP
BRENT
❏ 7010	Cherry Pie/I'll Quit Cryin' Over You	1960	$30
❏ 7005	Fancy Nancy/It Could Be	1959	$30
❏ 7002	It Was I/Lunch Hour	1959	$30
❏ 7028	Over the Mountain/One More Drink for Julie	1962	$30
❏ 7013	Teenage Honeymoon/ Hully Gully Cha Cha Cha	1960	$30
❏ 7017	The Green Door/Willow Tree	1960	$30

CALIFORNIA
❏ 2325	Tossin' and Turnin'/ Everyday I Have to Cry	1963	$20

REV
❏ 3523	Why Not Confess/Johnny Risk	1959	$30

— As "Gary and Clyde

TIME
❏ 1031	Betty Jean/Doubt	1961	$30

SKUNKS, THE
ARVEE
❏ 585	Smitty's Christmas Toy Piano/Smitty's Toy Piano	1959	$20

SKY
RCA VICTOR
❏ 74-0419	Goodie Two Shoes/ Make It in Time	1971	$6
❏ 74-0611	Let It Lie Low/Taking the Long Way Home	1971	$6

SKYLARKS, THE (1)
ADMIRAL
❏ 500	I'll Surf Around the World/ How Many Times	1963	$40

SKYLARKS, THE (2)
DECCA
❏ 48241	The Glory of Love/You and I	1951	$500

SKYLARKS, THE (3)
EVERLAST
❏ 5022	Everybody's Got Somebody/Jeannie	1963	$40

SKYLARKS, THE (4)
RCA VICTOR
❏ 47-5257	Home in Pasadena/I Had the Craziest Dream	1953	$30

SKYLARKS, THE (5)
VERVE
❏ 10082	Ol' Man River/There's a Boat Dat's Leavin' for New York	1957	$30

SKYLINERS, THE
ATCO
❏ 6270	Since I Fell for You/I'd Die	1963	$50

CALICO
❏ 120	Believe Me/Happy Time	1960	$30
❏ 114	How Much/Lorraine from Spain	1960	$30
❏ 109	It Happened Today/Lonely Way	1959	$40
❏ 117	Pennies from Heaven/I'll Be Seeing You	1960	$30
❏ 103/4	Since I Don't Have You/ One Night, One Night	1959	$60
❏ 106	This I Swear/Tomorrow	1959	$40

CAMEO
❏ 215	Three Coins in the Fountain/ Everyone But You	1962	$50

CAPITOL
❏ 3979	Where Have They Gone/I Could Have Loved You So Well	1974	$30

— As "Jimmy Beaumont and the Skyliners"
❏ 613	Close Your Eyes/ Our Love Will Last	1961	$50
❏ 188	I'll Close My Eyes/The Door Is Still Open	1961	$50

DRIVE
❏ 6250	Our Day Is Here/The Day the Clown Cried	1976	$8

JUBILEE
❏ 5520	I Run to You/Don't Hurt Me Baby	1965	$20
❏ 5506	The Loser/Everything Is Fine	1965	$20
❏ 5512	Who Do You Love/ Get Yourself a Baby	1965	$20

MOTOWN
❏ 1046 [DJ]	Since I Fell for You/I'd Die	1963	$2000

— Record never got beyond the test pressing stage (2 known copies)
❏ 1046 [DJ]	Since I Fell for You/I'd Die	1963	$2000

— Record never got beyond the test pressing stage (2 known copies). VG 1000 ; VG+ 1500

ORIGINAL SOUND
❏ 36	Pennies from Heaven/I'll Be Seeing You	1963	$20
❏ 35	Since I Don't Have You/ One Night, One Night	1963	$20
❏ 37	This I Swear/It Happened Today	1963	$20

TORTOISE INT'L.
❏ PB-11243	Oh How Happy/We've Got Love on Our Side	1978	$8
❏ PB-11312	Smile On Me/Love Bug (Done Bit Me Again)	1978	$8

VISCOUNT
❏ 104	Comes Love/Tell Me	1962	$30

SLADE
CBS ASSOCIATED
❏ 04865	Little Sheila/Lock Up Your Daughters	1985	$4
❏ 04528	My Oh My/High and Dry	1984	$4

Number	Title	Yr	NM

COTILLION

Number	Title	Yr	NM
❏ 44139	Cos I Love You/Gotta Keep a-Rockin'	1971	$30
❏ 44128	Get Down and Get With It/The Gospel According to Rasputin	1971	$30
❏ 44150	Look Wot You Dun/Candidate	1972	$30

POLYDOR

❏ 15069	Cum On Feel the Noize/I'm Mee, I'm Now, An' That's Orl	1973	$20
❏ 15044	Cuz I Love You/My Life Is Natural	1972	$12
❏ 15060	Gudbuy T' Jane/I Won't Let It 'Appen Again	1973	$10
❏ 15080	Let the Good Times Roll/Feel So Fine-I Don' Mind	1973	$12
❏ 15041	Look Wot You Dun/Candidate	1972	$10
❏ 15053	Mama Weer All Crazee Now/Man Who Speeks Evil	1972	$10
❏ 2058422	Merry Xmas Everybody/Don't Blame Me	1973	$5

— U.K. import; original issue with regular Polydor label

| ❏ 2058422 [PS] | Merry Xmas Everybody/Don't Blame Me | 1980 | $4 |

— Photo of group on sleeve; both record and sleeve are U.K. imports

| ❏ 2058422 | Merry Xmas Everybody/Don't Blame Me | 1980 | $4 |

— Reissue with green background and "holly leaf" label

| ❏ POSP780 | Merry Xmas Everybody/Don't Blame Me | 1985 | $4 |

— Yet another reissue

| ❏ POSP780 [PS] | Merry Xmas Everybody/Don't Blame Me | 1985 | $4 |

— Both record and sleeve are U.K. imports

| ❏ 15046 | Take Me Back 'Ome/Wondering Why | 1972 | $10 |

RCA

| ❏ 291 [PS] | (And Now the Waltz) C'est La Vie/Merry Xmas Everybody | 1982 | $4 |

— Both record and sleeve are U.K. imports

❏ 291	(And Now the Waltz) C'est La Vie/Merry Xmas Everybody	1982	$4
❏ 373	My Oh My/Merry Xmas Everybody (live)/Keep Your Hands Off My Power Supply	1983	$4
❏ 373 [PS]	My Oh My/Merry Xmas Everybody (live)/Keep Your Hands Off My Power Supply	1983	$4

— Both record and sleeve are U.K. imports

| ❏ PB40549 | Santa Claus Is Coming to Town/Auld Lang Syne/You'll Never Walk Alone | 1985 | $6 |

— Second 45 (no picture sleeve) in a U.K. two-pack (the other is RCA PB 40449)

RECEIVER

| ❏ BOYZ4 [PS] | Merry Xmas Everybody/Don't Blame Me | 1989 | $4 |

— Both record and sleeve are U.K. imports

| ❏ BOYZ4 | Merry Xmas Everybody/Don't Blame Me | 1989 | $4 |

REPRISE

| ❏ 1182 | Skweeze Me Pleeze Me/My Town | 1973 | $8 |

WARNER BROS.

❏ 7777	Good Time Gals/We're Really Gonna Raise the Roof	1974	$8
❏ 7808	How Can It Be/When the Lights Are Out	1974	$8
❏ 8134	How Does It Feel/OK, Yesterday Was Yesterday	1975	$8
❏ 7759	Merry Christmas Everybody/Don't Blame Me	1973	$10

SLADES, THE

DOMINO

| ❏ 906 | It's Your Turn/Take My Heart | 1961 | $50 |
| ❏ 1000 | Summertime/You Must Try | 1961 | $40 |

LIBERTY

| ❏ 55118 | Baby/You Mean Everything to Me | 1957 | $60 |

— As "The Spades," in error

| ❏ 55118 | Baby/You Mean Everything to Me | 1957 | $30 |

SLATKIN, FELIX

LIBERTY

❏ 55487	A Theme Searching for a Picture/Theme from "My Geisha	1962	$8
❏ 55299	My Own True Love/It's Not Forever	1961	$10
❏ 55523	Orange Blossom Special/Maiden's Prayer	1962	$8
❏ 55326	Streets of Laredo/(B-side unknown)	1961	$10
❏ 55329	Theme from The Pleasure of Your Company/Street Scene	1961	$10
❏ 55282	Theme from The Sundowners/Gaythers Gone	1960	$10

SLAVIN, SLICK

IMPERIAL

| ❏ 5540 | Speed Crazy/She Says She's Mine | 1958 | $40 |

SLED, BOB, AND THE TOBOGGANS

CAMEO

| ❏ 400 | Here We Go (Surfer Boys Are Going Skiing)/Sea and Ski | 1966 | $60 |

SLEDGE, PERCY

ATLANTIC

❏ 2616	Any Day Now/The Angels Listened In	1969	$30
❏ 2383	Baby, Help Me/You Got That Something Wonderful	1967	$30
❏ 2453	Cover Me/Behind Every Great Man There Is a Woman	1967	$15
❏ 2679	Faithful and True/True Love Travels on a Gravel Road	1969	$20
❏ 2754	Help Me Make It Through the Night/Thief in the Night	1970	$8
❏ 2358	It Tears Me Up/Heart of a Child	1966	$10
❏ 2414	Love Me Tender/What Am I Living For	1967	$15
❏ 2594	My Special Prayer/Bless Your Little Sweet Soul	1969	$15
❏ 2396	Out of Left Field/It Can't Be Stopped	1967	$15
❏ 2826	Stop the World Tonight/That's the Way I Want to Live My Life	1971	$8
❏ 2539	Sudden Stop/Between These Arms	1968	$20
❏ 2886	Sunday Brother/Everything You'll Ever Need	1972	$8
❏ 2963	Sunshine/Unchanging Love	1973	$10
❏ 2490	Take Time to Know Her/It's All Wrong But It's Alright	1968	$15
❏ 2719	Too Many Rivers to Cross/Push Mr. Pride Aside	1970	$15
❏ 2342	Warm and Tender Love/Sugar Puddin'	1966	$15
❏ 7-89262	When a Man Loves a Woman/Cover Me	1987	$3
❏ 7-89262 [PS]	When a Man Loves a Woman/Cover Me	1987	$4
❏ 2326	When a Man Loves a Woman/Love Me Like You Mean It	1966	$20
❏ 7-88802	When a Man Loves a Woman/Twentieth Century Fox	1989	$10

— B-side by the Escape Club

| ❏ 2646 | Woman of the Night/Kind Woman | 1969 | $15 |

CAPRICORN

❏ 0220	If This Is the Last Time/Behind Closed Doors	1975	$10
❏ 0209	I'll Be Your Everything/Blue Water	1974	$8
❏ 0273	When She's Touching Me/When a Boy Becomes a Man	1977	$8

MONUMENT

| ❏ WS4 03878 | She's Too Pretty to Cry/Home Type Thing | 1983 | $10 |

PHILCO-FORD

| ❏ HP-12 | When a Man Loves a Woman/Baby Help Me | 1967 | $30 |

— 4-inch plastic "Hip Pocket Record" with color sleeve

7-Inch Extended Plays

ATLANTIC

| ❏ SD78180 [PS] | Take Time to Know Her | 1968 | $25 |
| ❏ SD78180 | Take Time to Know Her/Feed the Flame/Out of Left Field//Cover Me/Baby Help Me/I Love Everything About You | 1968 | $25 |

— Jukebox issue; small hole, plays at 33 1/3 rpm

SLEEPERS

ADOLESCENT

| ❏ 0(no cat #) | Mirror/Theory | 1980 | $4 |
| ❏ 0(no cat #) [PS] | Mirror/Theory | 1980 | $4 |

SEARCH & DESTROY

| ❏ 0(# unknown) | Mirror/Theory | 1980 | $5 |
| ❏ 0(# unknown) [PS] | Mirror/Theory | 1980 | $20 |

— White bordered paper sleeve

| ❏ 0(# unknown) [PS] | Mirror/Theory | 1980 | $5 |

— Cardboard borderless black sleeve

7-Inch Extended Plays

WIN

| ❏ 7777777 | Sleepers | 1978 | $35 |
| ❏ 7777777 [PS] | Sleepers | 1978 | $75 |

— Numbered outer sleeve

| ❏ 7777777 [PS] | Sleepers | 1978 | $35 |

— Un-numbered sleeve

| ❏ 7777777 [PS] | Sleepers | 1978 | $35 |

— Numbered inner sleeve

SLICK, GRACE

Also see THE GREAT SOCIETY; JEFFERSON AIRPLANE; JEFFERSON STARSHIP; PAUL KANTNER AND GRACE SLICK; STARSHIP.

GRUNT

| ❏ BFBO-0183 | Theme from "Manhole"/Come Again, Toucan | 1973 | $6 |

RCA

❏ PB-12041	Dreams/Do It the Hard Way	1980	$4
❏ PB-12171	Sea of Love/Full Moon Man	1981	$4
❏ PB-11939	Seasons/Angel of Night	1980	$4
❏ PB-11939 [PS]	Seasons/Angel of Night	1980	$5
❏ PB-13764	Through the Window/Habits	1984	$4

SLICKEE BOYS

DACOIT

❏ 005	Here to Stay/Porcelain Butter Kitchen	1981	$6
❏ 005 [PS]	Here to Stay/Porcelain Butter Kitchen	1981	$6
❏ 004	The Brain That Refused to Die/Love In	1980	$6
❏ 004 [PS]	The Brain That Refused to Die/Love In	1980	$6
❏ 011	When I Go to the Beach/Invisible People	1983	$6

— 3,000 copies were pressed

| ❏ 011 [PS] | When I Go to the Beach/Invisible People | 1983 | $8 |

TWIN/TONE

| ❏ TTR8336 | When I Go to the Beach/Invisible People | 1984 | $3 |

— 3,000 copies were pressed

| ❏ TTR8336 [PS] | When I Go to the Beach/Invisible People | 1984 | $3 |

7-Inch Extended Plays

DACOIT

| ❏ 001 | Hot and Cool | 1976 | $8 |

DSI

| ❏ 8 | 10th Anniversary EP | 1988 | $5 |

— First pressing of 500 on black vinyl

| ❏ 8 | 10th Anniversary EP | 1988 | $5 |

— Second pressing of 500 on white vinyl

| ❏ 8 [PS] | 10th Anniversary EP | 1988 | $5 |

— First pressing of sleeve is beige

| ❏ 8 [PS] | 10th Anniversary EP | 1988 | $5 |

— Second pressing of sleeve is green

LIMP

| ❏ 05 | 3rd EP | 1979 | $10 |
| ❏ 05 [PS] | 3rd EP | 1979 | $12 |

— Includes decal, lyrics and fan club insert

| ❏ 01 | Mersey Mersey Me | 1978 | $15 |

— Yellow labels

| ❏ 01 [PS] | Mersey Mersey Me | 1978 | $15 |

— Blue sleeve

| ❏ 001 | Mersey Mersey Me | 1978 | $8 |

— Blue labels

| ❏ 001 [PS] | Mersey Mersey Me | 1978 | $8 |

— Pink sleeve

SLITS, THE

ANTILLES

| ❏ ANS-102 | Typical Girls/I Heard It Through the Grapevine | 1980 | $10 |

— Presumably an American release

| ❏ ANS-102 [PS] | Typical Girls/I Heard It Through the Grapevine | 1980 | $20 |

— Fold-out poster sleeve

SLOAN, BONNIE

COLUMBIA

❏ 4-21311	Don't Call Me a Tramp/Alone I Cry	1954	$30
❏ 4-21425	Poor Paper Kite/After the Wedding	1955	$30
❏ 4-21463	Silly Boy/Idle Hours	1956	$30

SLOAN, P.F.

ALADDIN

| ❏ 3461 | All I Want Is Lovin'/Little Girl in the Cabin | 1959 | $30 |

— As "Flip Sloan

ATCO

| ❏ 6663 | Star Gazin'/New Design | 1969 | $30 |

DUNHILL

❏ 4037	City Women/Top of a Fence	1966	$20
❏ 4024	From a Distance/Patterns	1966	$30
❏ 4016	Halloween Mary/I'd Have to Be Out of My Mind	1965	$20
❏ 4016 [PS]	Halloween Mary/I'd Have to Be Out of My Mind	1965	$30

— Sleeve is promo only

Number	Title	Yr	NM
❏ 4054	I Found a Girl/A Melody for You	1966	$20
❏ 4007	Sins of the Family/This Mornin'	1965	$20
❏ 4064	Sunflower, Sunflower/The Man Behind the Red Balloon	1967	$30
❏ 4064 [PS]	Sunflower, Sunflower/The Man Behind the Red Balloon	1967	$40

MART

❏ 802	She's My Girl/If You Believe in Me	1960	$100

MUMS

❏ 6010	Let Me Be/Springtime	1972	$30

SLY AND THE FAMILY STONE

EPIC

❏ 10256	Dance to the Music/Let Me Hear It from You	1967	$12
❏ 10407	Everyday People/Sing a Simple Song	1968	$12
❏ 10407 [PS]	Everyday People/Sing a Simple Song	1968	$15
❏ 10805	Family Affair/Luv N' Haight	1971	$6
❏ 50331	Family Again/Nothing Less Than Happiness	1977	$5
❏ 11060	Frisky/If It Were Left Up to Me	1973	$6
❏ 50201	Greed/Crossword Puzzle	1976	$5
❏ 10229	Higher/Underdog	1967	$12
❏ 10497	Hot Fun in the Summertime/Fun	1969	$10
❏ 50119	Hot Fun in the Summertime/Fun	1975	$8
❏ 11017	If You Want Me to Stay/Babies Makin' Babies	1973	$6
❏ 11017	If You Want Me to Stay/Thankful N' Thoughtful	1973	$6
❏ 50135	I Get High on You/That's Lovin' You	1975	$5
❏ 10353	Life/M'Lady	1968	$8
❏ 50175	Li Lo Li/Who Do You Love	1975	$5
❏ 8-50033	Loose Booty/Can't Strain My Brain	1974	$6
❏ 10850	Smilin'/Luv N' Haight	1972	$6
❏ 10450	Stand!/I Want to Take You Higher	1969	$10
❏ 10450 [PS]	Stand!/I Want to Take You Higher	1969	$15
❏ 10555	Thank You Falettinme Be Mice Elf Agin/Everybody Is a Star	1969	$6
❏ 10555 [PS]	Thank You Falettinme Be Mice Elf Agin/Everybody Is a Star	1969	$10
❏ 11140	Time for Livin'/Small Talk	1974	$6

LOADSTONE

❏ 3951	I Ain't Got Nobody/I Can't Turn You Loose	1967	$30

WARNER BROS.

❏ 29682	High Y'All/Ha Ha He He	1983	$4
❏ 49062	Sheer Energy/Remember Who You Are	1979	$4
❏ 49132	Who's to Say/Same Thing	1979	$4

7-Inch Extended Plays

EPIC

❏ 7-30986 [PS]	There's a Riot Goin' On	1971	$20

SMALL, DANNY

UNITED ARTISTS

❏ 542	On Christmas Day/Theme from Taras Bulba (The Wishing Star)	1962	$15

SMALL FACES
Also see FACES.

IMMEDIATE

❏ 5014	Afterglow of Your Love/Wham, Bam, Thank You Ma'am	1969	$20
❏ 1902	Here Come the Nice/Talk to You	1967	$12
❏ 501	Itchykoo Park/I'm Only Dreaming	1967	$15
❏ 5007	Lazy Sunday/Rollin' Over	1968	$12
❏ 5012	Mad John/The Journey	1969	$20
❏ 5003	Tin Soldier/I Feel Much Better	1968	$10
❏ 5003 [PS]	Tin Soldier/I Feel Much Better	1968	$30

PRESS

❏ 5007	Almost Grown/Hey Girl	1969	$30
❏ 9826	Sha-La-La-La-Lee/Grow Your Own	1966	$20
❏ 9794	What 'Cha Gonna Do About It/What's a Matter	1965	$30

RCA VICTOR

❏ 47-9055	My Mind's Eye/I Can't Dance with You	1966	$30

SMALL, MILLIE

ATCO

❏ 6384	Tongue Tied/Blood Shot Eyes	1965	$10

ATLANTIC

Number	Title	Yr	NM
❏ 2266	Bring It On Home to Me/I've Fallen in Love with a Snowman	1965	$10

BRIT

❏ 7002	My Street/Mixed-Up, Lonely, Self-Centered, Spoiled Kind of Boy	1965	$15

SMASH

❏ 1946	Don't You Know/Tom Hark	1964	$15
❏ 1940	I Love the Way You Love/Bring It On Home to Me	1964	$15
❏ 1893	My Boy Lollipop/Something's Gotta Be Done	1964	$20
❏ 1920	Sweet William/What Am I Living For	1964	$15

SMALLEY, LEROY

GOLDEN WORLD

❏ 7	Girls Are Sentimental/Ain't It a Shame	1964	$100

SMART, JIMMY

ALLSTAR

❏ 7211	Broken Dream/It's Too Late for Me	1960	$30

PLAID

❏ 1004	Shorty/In My Dreams	1961	$30

SMART TONES, THE

HERALD

❏ 529	Bob-O-Link/Ginny	1958	$125

SMEGMA

PIGFACE

❏ 02	Can't Look Straight/Flashcards	1979	$40
❏ 02 [PS]	Can't Look Straight/Flashcards	1979	$40

SMILE (1)

MERCURY

❏ 72977	Earth/Step on Me	1968	$200

SMILE (2)

UNI

❏ 55336	Tonight/One Night Stand	1972	$6

SMITH, ARTHUR "GUITAR BOOGIE

CHOICE

❏ 6102	I'm Afraid of Wimmin/Fishin' Fever	1961	$20
❏ 6101	Shhh (With Dialogue)/Shhh (Without Dialogue)	1960	$20

DOT

❏ 16695	The Billy Malone Story/I Look Up	1965	$12
❏ 17013	Today/Whitepoint	1967	$10

MGM

❏ K12791	Banjo Boogie/Hard Boiled Boogie	1959	$30
❏ K10914	Beautiful Brown Eyes (Vocal)/(Instrumental)	1951	$40
❏ K10551	Be-Bop Rag/I Never See Maggie Alone	1949	$50
❏ K11503	Because You Love Me/Rainbow Waltz	1953	$30
❏ K12330	Blue Rock/More Foolish Questions	1956	$30
❏ K10945	Chew Tobacco Rag/Big Mountain Shuffle	1951	$40
❏ K11040	Fence Jumper/Tears Don't Always Mean a Broken Heart	1951	$40
❏ K12006	Feudin' Banjos/Bye 'Bye Back Smoke Choo Choo	1955	$40

—With Don Reno

❏ K11361	Five String Banjo Boogie/Guitar Jamboree	1952	$30
❏ K12436	Freeze It Boogie/I Thought It Couldn't Happen to Me	1957	$30
❏ K10608	Guitar and Piano Boogie/I'm Only Tellin' You	1950	$40
❏ K11558	He Went That-a-Way!/Three "D" Boogie	1953	$30
❏ K11879	Hi-Lo Boogie/Truck Stop Grill	1954	$30
❏ K10881	Hot Rod Race/Rhumba Boogie	1951	$50
❏ K11704	I Get So Lonely/Outboard	1954	$30
❏ K10714	I.H. Boogie/I'm Afraid of Women	1950	$40
❏ K11413	Indian Boogie/Cherokee Strut	1953	$30
❏ K11433	In Memory of Hank Williams/I'm Richer Than You	1953	$50
❏ K11096	Listen to the Mockingbird/BLue Moon Waltz	1951	$40
❏ K11817	Lonesome/Half-Moon	1954	$30
❏ K11324	Make Me Know It/Five Foot Two, Eyes of Blue	1952	$30

Number	Title	Yr	NM
❏ K10791	Mandolin Boogie/Conversation with a Mule	1950	$40
❏ K10807	Memphis Blues/Beer Barrel Polka	1950	$40
❏ K10847	Merry Christmas, Everyone/Guitar Jingle Bells	1950	$40
❏ K11945	Midnight Rag/You're Hooked	1955	$30
❏ K10516	Mountain Be-Bop/Don't Look for Trouble	1949	$50
❏ K10829	Mr. Stalin, You're Eatin' Too High/Banjo Buster	1950	$40
❏ K10577	Mule Train/Banjo Rag	1949	$50
❏ K11605	Oklahoma Polka/You're Off Limits	1953	$30
❏ K11317	Somebody's Knocking/I Know There's a Crown for Me	1952	$30
❏ K12544	Teen-Age Rebel/Easy Rock	1957	$30
❏ K12224	The Gal with the Yaller Shoes/Buzz Saw	1956	$30
❏ K11657	The Honeymoon Is Over/Cotton Patch Rag	1954	$30
❏ K11379	The South/Lady of Spain	1952	$30
❏ K12458	Two Theme Calypso/Stamps	1957	$30
❏ K10991	Who Shot Willie/Express Train Boogie	1951	$40

MONUMENT

❏ 8604	Guitar Boogie/Right On	1974	$6
❏ 8676	Theme from "Death Driver"/Moods from "Death Driver"	1975	$6

STARDAY

❏ 824	British Backbeat/Lynn's Gone	1968	$8
❏ 576	Guitar Boogie Twist/Napoleon's Retreat	1962	$20
❏ 868	Guitar Unlimited/Summer Theme	1969	$8
❏ 590	Heartaches/Foolish Questions -- Silly Answers	1962	$20
❏ 701	I Like Lasses/Flat Top Hari Kari	1964	$20
❏ 634	Master of the Game/Travelin' Blues	1963	$20
❏ 615	Philadelphia Guitar/Hospitality Blues	1962	$20
❏ 656	The Stuttering Song/Back to His Hole He Went	1963	$20
❏ 642	Tie My Hunting Dogs Down. Jed/Guitar Hop	1963	$20
❏ 861	What Is an American?/Psychoanalysis	1969	$8

7-Inch Extended Plays

ABC-PARAMOUNT

❏ ABCS441 [PS]	Arthur "Guitar" Smith and Voices	1963	$25
❏ ABCS441	Guitar Boogie/I Love You So Much/Sioux City Sue/In a Shanty in Old Shanty Town/Dream/Tumbling Tumbleweeds	1963	$25

—Jukebox issue; small hole, plays at 33 1/3 rpm

❏ X4095	Conversation with a Mule/Who Shot Willie/Just Lookin'/He Went That-a-Way	1954	$25

—Part of 2-EP set "X236

❏ X236 [PS]	Foolish Questions	1954	$35

—Cover for 2-EP set (X4094 and X4095)

❏ X4094	Foolish Questions/Don't Look for Trouble//I'm Only Telling You (What They Told Me)/I'm Afraid of Wimmin'	1954	$25

—Part of 2-EP set "X236

SMITH, HUEY "PIANO

ACE

❏ 584	Beatnik Blues/For Cryin' Out Loud	1960	$20
❏ 545	Don't You Just Know It/High Blood Pressure	1958	$30
❏ 553	Don't You Know Yockomo/Well, I'll Be John Brown	1958	$30
❏ 521	Everybody's Wailin'/Little Liza Jane	1956	$30
❏ 672	Every Once in a While/Somebody Told It	1962	$15
❏ 538	Free, Single and Disengaged/Just a Lonely Clown	1957	$30
❏ 548	Havin' a Good Time/We Like Birdland	1958	$30
❏ 8008	Let's Bring 'Em Back Again/Quiet as It's Kept	1963	$20
❏ 649	Pop-Eye/Scald Dog	1962	$20
❏ 638	She Got Low Down/Mean, Mean, Mean	1961	$20
❏ 639	She Got Low Down/Mean, Mean, Mean/Little Liza Jane/Rockin' Pnuemonia	1961	$30
❏ 8002	Talk to Me Baby/If It Ain't One Thing, It's Another	1962	$15
❏ 571	Tu-Ber-Cu-Lucas and the Sinus Blues/Dearest Darling	1959	$30
❏ 562	Would You Believe It (I Have a Cold)/Genevieve	1959	$30

CONSTELLATION

❏ 102	He's Back Again/Quiet As It's Kept	1963	$12

Number	Title	Yr	NM
IMPERIAL			
❏ 5747	Behind the Wheel -- Part 1/ Behind the Wheel -- Part 2	1961	$15
❏ 5789	Don't Knock It/Shag-a-Tooth	1961	$15
❏ 5772	More Girls/Sassy Sara	1961	$15
❏ 5721	The Little Moron/ Someone to Love	1961	$15
INSTANT			
❏ 3305	Ballad of a Black Man/ The Whatcha Call 'Em	1970	$8
❏ 3301	Epitaph of Uncle Tom/ Eight Bars of Amen	1969	$8
❏ 3287	I'll Never Forget/ Bury Me Dead	1967	$8
❏ 3297	Two Way Pockaway (Part 1)/ Two Way Pockaway (Part 2)	1969	$8
VIN			
❏ 1024	I Didn't Do It/They Kept On	1960	$20

SMITH

Number	Title	Yr	NM
ABC DUNHILL			
❏ 4206	Baby It's You/I Don't Believe (I Believe)	1969	$8
❏ 4206 [PS]	Baby It's You/I Don't Believe (I Believe)	1969	$15
❏ 4246	Comin' Back to Me (Ooh Baby)/Minus-Plus	1970	$6
❏ 4228	Take a Look Around/ Mojalesky Ridge	1970	$6
❏ 4238	What Am I Gonna Do/ Born in Boston	1970	$6
❏ 4238 [PS]	What Am I Gonna Do/ Born in Boston	1970	$10

SMITH, ARLENE

Number	Title	Yr	NM
BIG TOP			
❏ 3073	Love, Love, Love/He Knows I Love Him Too Much	1961	$40

SMITH, BETTY, GROUP

Number	Title	Yr	NM
LONDON			
❏ 1787	Bewitched/Hand Jive	1958	$15
❏ 1819	My Foolsih Heart/ Betty's Blues	1958	$15

SMITH, CAL

Number	Title	Yr	NM
DECCA			
❏ 33003	For My Baby/ Handful of Stars	1972	$6
❏ 32815	Free Streets/Goin' Home to Do My Time	1971	$6
❏ 32959	I've Found Someone of My Own/Lights of the Living	1972	$6
❏ 32768	That's What It's Like to Be Lonesome/The Only Girl in the Game	1971	$6
❏ 33040	The Lord Knows I'm Drinking/Sweet Things I Remember About You	1972	$6
❏ 32878	Woman on the Inside/ To Save, My Wife	1971	$6
KAPP			
❏ 884	Destination Atlanta G.A./ Did She Ask About Me	1968	$8
❏ 938	Drinking Champagne/ Honky Tonk Blues	1968	$8
❏ 960	Empty Arms/So Much to Do	1969	$8
❏ 2059	Heaven Is Just a Touch Away/I Overlooked an Orchid	1969	$6
❏ 748	I'll Just Go On Home/ Silver Dew on the Blue Grass Tonight	1966	$10
❏ 834	I'll Never Be Lonesome with You/If I Had My Life to Live Over	1967	$8
❏ 851	I'll Sail My Ship Alone/ You're Not Drowning Your Heartache	1967	$8
❏ 994	It Takes All Night Long/ Daddy's Arms	1969	$8
❏ 2076	The Difference Between Going and Really Gone/ My Happiness Goes Off	1970	$6
❏ 788	The Only Thing I Want/ Stranger in the House	1966	$8
MCA			
❏ 40265	Between Lust and Watching TV/Some Kind of a Woman	1974	$5
❏ 40911	Bits and Pieces of Life/Leona	1978	$4
❏ 40136	Bleep You/An Hour and a Six-Pack	1973	$5
❏ 40714	Come See About Me/ The In Crowd	1977	$4
❏ 40191	Country Bumpkin/It's Not the Miles You Traveled	1974	$5
❏ 60187	Country Bumpkin/ Thunderstorms	1977	$4
— Reissue; black label with rainbow			
❏ 60053	Drinking Champagne/ It Takes All Night Long	1973	$4
— Reissue; black label with rainbow			
❏ 40789	Helen/I'm Forty Now	1977	$4

Number	Title	Yr	NM
❏ 40061	I Can Feel the Leavin' Comin' On/I've Loved You All Over the World	1973	$5
❏ 40671	I Just Came Home to Count the Memories/Feelin' the Weight of My Chains	1976	$4
❏ 40864	I'm Just a Farmer/The Ghost of Jim Bob Wilson	1978	$4
❏ 40335	It's Time to Pay the Fiddler/ Love Is the Foundation	1974	$5
❏ 40563	MacArthur's Hand/Sunday Morning Christian	1976	$4
❏ 41001	One Little Skinny Rib/I Fed Her Love	1979	$4
❏ 40394	She Talked a Lot About Texas/Baby's Gone	1975	$5
❏ 60171	The Lord Knows I'm Drinking/I've Found Someone of My Own	1974	$4
— Reissue; black label with rainbow			
❏ 40839	Throwin' Memories on the Fire/Tabernacle Tom	1977	$4
❏ 40517	Thunderstorms/19 Years and 1800 Miles	1976	$4
❏ 40618	Woman Don't Try to Sing My Song/I Play a Man	1976	$4
PLAID			
❏ 1003	Eleven Long Years/ Tear Stained Pillow	1961	$30
STEP ONE			
❏ 353	Bein' Gone/I Know It's Not Over	1986	$4

SMITH, CARL

Number	Title	Yr	NM
ABC HICKORY			
❏ 54004	A Way with Words/Till I Stop Meeting You	1976	$5
❏ 54037	I Can't Get the Last Memory Down/Silver Tongued Cowboy	1978	$5
❏ 54009	Show Me a Brick Wall/ It's Teardrop Time	1977	$5
❏ 54016	This Kinda Love Ain't Meant for Sunday School/ There Stands the Glass	1977	$5
❏ 54022	This Lady Loving Me/Loose Talk	1978	$5
COLUMBIA			
❏ 4-42222	Air Mail to Heaven/Things That Mean the Most	1961	$15
❏ 4-21507	Answers/My Dream of the Old Rugged Cross	1956	$30
❏ 4-41610	A Pain a Pill Can't Locate/If I Had You (I'd Live for You Only)	1962	$15
❏ 4-42610	A Pain a Pill Can't Locate/If I Had You (I'd Live for You Only)	1962	$15
❏ 4-20922	Are You Teasing Me/It's a Lovely, Lovely World	1952	$30
❏ 4-41948	Are You True to Me/More Habit Than Desire	1961	$15
❏ 4-21411	Baby I'm Ready/I Just Don't Care Anymore	1955	$30
❏ 4-21226	Back Up Buddy/If You Tried As Hard to Love Me	1954	$30
❏ 4-21552	Before I Met You/ Wicked Lies	1956	$30
❏ 4-43266	Be Good to Her/ Keep Me Fooled	1965	$12
❏ 4-45262	Big Murph/My Mother's Eyes	1970	$8
❏ 4-41642	Cut Across Shorty/Why Did You Come My Way	1960	$15
❏ 4-44233	Deep Water/I Really Don't Want to Know	1967	$8
❏ 4-21197	Dog-Gone It, Baby, I'm in Love/What Am I Going to Do	1954	$30
❏ 4-45497	Don't Say You're Mine/ Country Soul Man	1971	$8
❏ 4-21429	Don't Tease Me/I Just Dropped In to Say Goodbye	1955	$30
❏ 4-45293	Don't Worry 'Bout the Mule (Just Load the Wagon)/Darling Days	1970	$8
❏ 4-44702	Faded Love and Winter Roses/Until I Looked at You	1968	$8
❏ 4-44396	Foggy River/With the Rainbow Follow the Rain	1967	$8
❏ 4-42490	Gettin' Even/I Volunteer	1962	$15
❏ 4-21266	Go, Boy, Go/If You Saw Her Through My Eyes	1954	$30
❏ 4-44816	Good Deal, Lucille/Never Gonna Cry No More	1969	$8
❏ 4-41170	Guess I've Been Around Too Long/Goodnight Mr. Sun	1958	$20
❏ 4-20712	Guilty Conscience/Washing My Dreams in Tears	1950	$40
❏ 4-45031	Heartbreak Avenue/It's Nice to See You Once Again	1969	$8
❏ 4-21129	Hey Joe!/Darling Am I the One	1953	$30
❏ 4-21192	How About You/I'll Be Listening	1953	$30
❏ 4-45225	How I Love Them Old Songs/Little Crop of Cotton Tops	1970	$8
❏ 4-41729	If the World Don't End Tomorrow/Lonely Old Room	1960	$15
❏ 4-45648	If This Is Goodbye/ If You Saw Her	1972	$8
❏ 4-44939	I Love You Because/Mister, Come and Get Your Wife	1969	$8

Number	Title	Yr	NM
❏ 4-45923	I Need Help/ Yesterday Is Gone	1973	$8
❏ 4-42768	In the Back Room Tonight/ Take My Love with You, Too	1963	$15
❏ 4-20741	I Overlooked an Orchid/I Betcha My Heart I Love You	1950	$40
❏ 4-44034	I Should Get Away for Awhile (From You)/Mighty Day	1967	$8
❏ 4-41344	It's All My Heartache/I'll Kiss the Past Goodbye	1959	$15
❏ 4-20942	It's a Lovely, Lovely World/ (When You Feel Like You're in Love) Don't Just Stand There	1952	$30
❏ 4-21493	I've Changed/If You Do Dear	1956	$30
❏ 4-20862	Let Old Mother Nature Have Her Way/Me and My Broken Heart	1951	$30
❏ 4-20796	Let's Live a Little/ There's Nothing As Sweet As My Baby	1951	$30
❏ 4-43361	Let's Walk Away Strangers/ Ain't Love a Hurting Thing	1965	$12
❏ 4-42686	Live for Tomorrow/Let's Talk This Thing Over	1963	$15
❏ 4-43124	Lonely Girl/When It's Over	1964	$15
❏ 4-21317	Loose Talk/More Than Anything Else in the World	1954	$30
❏ 4-45382	Lost It on the Road/I'm Wound Up Tight	1971	$8
❏ 4-41557	Make the Waterwheel Roll/Past	1960	$15
❏ 4-45558	Mama Bear/Before My Time	1972	$8
❏ 4-43753	Man with a Plan/You Mean Ol' Moon	1966	$10
❏ 4-40918	Mr. Lost/Try to Take It Like a Man	1957	$20
❏ 4-20825	Mr. Moon/If Teardrops Were Pennies	1951	$30
❏ 4-21087	Orchids Mean Goodbye/Just Wait 'Til I Get You Alone	1953	$30
❏ 4-21008	Our Honeymoon/Sing Her a Love Song	1952	$30
❏ 4-45177	Pick Me Up on Your Way Down/Bonaparte's Retreat	1970	$8
❏ 4-45086	Pull My String and Wind Me Up/It's All Right	1970	$8
❏ 4-21166	Satisfaction Guaranteed/ Who'll Buy My Heartaches	1953	$30
❏ 4-43200	She Called Me Baby/ My Friends Are Gonna Be Strangers	1965	$10
❏ 4-43599	Sweet Temptation/(Is My) Ring on Your Finger	1966	$10
❏ 4-43033	Take My Ring Off Your Finger/The Ballad of Hershel Lawson	1964	$15
❏ 4-41417	Ten Thousand Drums/ The Tall, Tall Gentleman	1959	$15
❏ 4-41417 [PS]	Ten Thousand Drums/ The Tall, Tall Gentleman	1959	$30
❏ 4-21051	That's the Kind of Love I'm Looking For/My Lonely Heart's Runnin' Wild	1952	$30
❏ 4-42349	The Best Dressed Beggar (In Town)/I Used to Be	1962	$15
❏ 4-41290	The Best Years of Your Life/Mr. Moon	1958	$20
❏ 4-21040	The Blood That Stained the Old Rugged Cross/ Gethsemane	1951	$40
— With the Carters			
❏ 4-42949	The Pillow That Whispers/ Sweet Little Country Girl	1964	$15
❏ 4-21382	There She Goes/Old Lonesome Times	1955	$30
❏ 4-44620	There's No More Love/ Remember Me (I'm the One Who Loves You)	1968	$8
❏ 4-20765	This Side of Heaven/I Won't Be at Home	1950	$40
❏ 30848 [S]	(titles unknown)	1960	$20
❏ 30849 [S]	(titles unknown)	1960	$20
❏ 30850 [S]	(titles unknown)	1960	$20
❏ 30851 [S]	(titles unknown)	1960	$20
❏ 30852 [S]	(titles unknown)	1960	$20
❏ 31473 [S]	(titles unknown)	1962	$20
❏ 31474 [S]	(titles unknown)	1962	$20
❏ 31475 [S]	(titles unknown)	1962	$20
❏ 31476 [S]	(titles unknown)	1962	$20
❏ 31477 [S]	(titles unknown)	1962	$20
— The above 10 are "Stereo Seven" 7-inch 33 1/3 rpm singles with small holes			
❏ 4-41489	Tomorrow Night/I'll Walk with You	1959	$15
❏ 4-21119	Trademark/Do I Like It?	1953	$30
❏ 4-42858	Triangle/I Almost Forgot Her Today	1963	$15
❏ 4-21368	Wait a Little Longer Please, Jesus/Works of the Lord	1955	$30
❏ 4-41243	Walking the Slow Walk/A Love Was Born	1958	$20
❏ 4-45832	What a Difference Your Love Would Make/When You're Gone (There Will Be Nothing Left)	1973	$8
❏ 4-20893	(When You Feel Like You're in Love) Don't Just Stand There/The Little Girl in My Home Town	1952	$30
❏ 4-40984	Why, Why/Emotions	1957	$20
❏ 4-43485	Why Do I Keep Doing This to Us/Why Can't You Feel Sorry for Me	1966	$10

Number	Title	Yr	NM
HICKORY/MGM			
☐ 329	Dreaming Again/I Ain't Getting Nowhere with You	1974	$6
☐ 347	Everything I Touch Turns to Sugar/Lost Highway	1975	$5
☐ 371	If You Don't, Somebody Else Will/It's Gonna Be One of Those Days	1976	$5
☐ 363	She Is/I Can't Go On Like This	1976	$5
☐ 352	The Girl I Love/Me and My Broken Heart	1975	$5
☐ 337	The Way I Lose My Mind/Happy Birthday My Darlin'	1975	$5

7-Inch Extended Plays

Number	Title	Yr	NM
COLUMBIA			
☐ B-2801	*Let Old Mother Nature Have Her Way/Me and My Broken Heart/If Teardrops Were Pennies/I Overlooked an Orchid	1959	$25
☐ B-2131	*You Are the One/You Can't Hurt Me Anymore/That's the Way I Like You Best/Before I Met You	1957	$30
☐ B-2801 [PS]	Carl Smith (Hall of Fame Series)	1959	$25
☐ B-2131 [PS]	Four Hits by Carl Smith	1957	$30
☐ B-10222	If I Could Hold Back the Dawn/That's What You Think//Live and Let Live/If You Want It, I've Got It	1957	$25
☐ B-10223	Please Come Back Home/Look What Thoughts Done to Me/The House That Love Built/Come Back to Me	1957	$25
☐ B-10221	San Antonio Rose/Time Changes Everything//Lovin' Is Livin'/Oh, No!	1957	$25
☐ B-10221 [PS]	Smith's the Name, Vol. I	1957	$25
☐ B-10222 [PS]	Smith's the Name, Vol. II	1957	$25
☐ B-10223 [PS]	Smith's the Name, Vol. III	1957	$25

SMITH, CONNIE, AND NAT STUCKEY

Number	Title	Yr	NM
RCA VICTOR			
☐ 47-9805	If God Is Dead (Who's That Living in My Soul)/His Love Takes Care of Me	1970	$8

SMITH, CONNIE

Number	Title	Yr	NM
COLUMBIA			
☐ 45954	Ain't Love a Good Thing/I Still Feel the Same About You	1973	$5
☐ 46008	Dallas/That's the Way Love Goes	1974	$5
☐ 10393	I Don't Wanna Talk It Over Anymore/You Crossed My Mind a Thousand Times	1976	$4
☐ 10086	I Got a Lot of Hurtin' Done Today/Back in the Country	1975	$4
☐ 46058	I Never Knew (What That Song Meant Before)/Did We Have to Come This Far	1974	$5
☐ 10051	I've Got My Baby on My Mind/Why Don't You Love Me	1974	$4
☐ 10345	So Sad (To Watch Good Love Go Bad)/Constantly	1976	$4
☐ 10501	The Latest Shade of Blue/I'm All Wrapped Up in You	1977	$4
☐ 10210	The Song We Fell in Love To/One Little Reason	1975	$4
☐ 10277	('Til) I Kissed You/Ridin' on a Rainbow	1975	$4
☐ 10135	Why Don't You Love Me/Loving You (Has Changed My Whole Life)	1975	$4
EPIC			
☐ 05414	A Far Cry from You/Don't Touch (The Pain's Not Dry)	1986	$3
☐ 06250	Hold Me Back/Walk Me to the Door	1986	$3
MONUMENT			
☐ 45-219	Coming Around/You and Love and I	1977	$4
☐ 45-284	Don't Say Love/I Don't Want to Be Free	1979	$4
☐ 45-231	I Just Want to Be Your Everything/Scrapbook	1977	$4
☐ 45-281	Lovin' You, Lovin' Me/Ten Thousand and One	1979	$4
☐ 45-241	Lovin' You Baby/All of a Sudden	1978	$4
☐ 45-266	Smooth Sailin'/Loving You Has Sure Been Good to Me	1978	$4
☐ 45-252	There'll Never Be Another for Me/The Wayward Wind	1978	$4
RCA VICTOR			
☐ 47-8842	Ain't Had No Lovin'/Five Fingers to Spare	1966	$8
☐ 47-9413	Baby's Back Again/It Only Hurts for a Little While	1967	$8
☐ 47-9335	Burning a Hole in My Mind/Only for Me	1967	$8
☐ 47-9214	Cincinnati, Ohio/Don't Feel Sorry for Me	1967	$8
☐ 47-9624	Cry, Cry, Cry/The Hurt Goes On	1968	$8
☐ 74-0971	Dream Painter/Once a Day	1973	$6

Number	Title	Yr	NM
☐ APBO-0156	Everybody Loves Somebody/I Don't Want Your Memories	1973	$5
☐ 47-8551	I Can't Remember/Senses	1965	$8
☐ 74-0752	If It Ain't Love (Let's Leave It Alone)/Living Without You	1972	$6
☐ 47-8663	If I Talk to Him/I Don't Have Anyplace to Go	1965	$8
☐ 47-9108	I'll Come Runnin'/It's Now or Never	1967	$8
☐ 74-0535	I'm Sorry If My Love Got In Your Way/Plenty of Time	1971	$6
☐ 47-9832	I Never Once Stopped Loving You/The Sun Shines Down on Me	1970	$6
☐ 47-9887	Louisiana Man/Alone with You	1970	$6
☐ 74-0860	Love Is the Look You're Looking For/My Ecstasy	1972	$6
☐ 47-8416	Once a Day/The Threshold	1964	$10
☐ PB-10051	Someone to Give My Love To/I'm Sorry If My Love Got In Your Way	1974	$5
☐ 47-8964	The Hurtin's All Over/Invisible Tears	1966	$8
☐ 47-8489	Then and Only Then/Tiny Blue Transistor Radio	1964	$8
☐ 47-9938	Where Is My Castle/Clinging to a Saving Hand	1970	$6

SMITH, DALE

Number	Title	Yr	NM
BOLO			
☐ 726	When Christmas Bells Are Ringing/Christmas Story	1961	$10

SMITH, DENNIS

Number	Title	Yr	NM
ADONDA			
☐ 79021	California Calling/Get It Together	1979	$8

SMITH, EDDIE

Number	Title	Yr	NM
KING			
☐ 1171	Back in Your Own Back Yard/Exhibition Special	1953	$30
☐ 1041	Beer Barrel Polka/Mourning Dove	1952	$30
☐ 986	Down Yonder/A Sweet Bunch of Daisies	1951	$40
☐ 1002	San Antonio Rose/Bow Wow Boogie	1951	$40
☐ 1095	The Preacher and the Bear/The Snow Deer	1952	$30
☐ 1204	When You and I Were Young Maggie/Hot Shot Rag	1953	$30

SMITH, ETHEL

Number	Title	Yr	NM
DECCA			
☐ 9-92	Christmas Songs	1950	$60

—Contains 4 records (24142, 24734, 24735, 24736) plus box

Number	Title	Yr	NM
☐ 24735	Hark, The Herald Angels Sing/O, Little Town Of Bethlehem	1950	$15

—Side 3 and 4 of "Album No. 9-92"

Number	Title	Yr	NM
☐ 24736	It Came Upon A Midnight Clear/O, Holy Night	1950	$15

—Side 5 and 6 of "Album No. 9-92"

Number	Title	Yr	NM
☐ 24734	Silent Night/Adeste Fideles	1950	$15

—Side 1 and 2 of "Album No. 9-92"

Number	Title	Yr	NM
☐ 24142	White Christmas/Jingle Bells	1950	$15

—Side 7 and 8 of "Album No. 9-92"

SMITH, JERRY

Number	Title	Yr	NM
CHART			
☐ 1440	Annette/Lil' Ol' Me	1967	$8
DECCA			
☐ 32814	By Special Request/Open All Night	1971	$6
☐ 32938	Cream and Sugar/Down in the Dumps	1972	$6
☐ 32679	Drivin' Home/Louisiana Blues	1970	$6
☐ 32869	Gear Jammer/Touch of Love	1971	$6
☐ 32769	Papa Joe's Polka/The Toy Piano	1971	$6
☐ 32730	Steppin' Out/Closing Time	1970	$6
☐ 945	Faded Love/Moonlight and Roses	1973	$5
☐ 1060	Heart and Soul/Louisiana Blues	1976	$5
☐ 1024	Last Night/One Mile North of Town	1975	$5

—As "Papa Joe's Music Box"

Number	Title	Yr	NM
☐ 1002	Laura's Living Room/Give the World a Smile	1974	$5
☐ 1067	Starlite Waltz/Truck Stop	1976	$5
☐ 1065	The Inn Crowd/Sail Along Silvery Moon	1976	$5
☐ 975	White Silver Sands/Lover's Waltz	1974	$5

—As "Papa Joe's Music Box"

Number	Title	Yr	NM
RICE			
☐ 5029	Shaky's Theme/Closing Time	1968	$8

Number	Title	Yr	NM
SOUND STAGE 7			
☐ 2542	Lil' Ol' Me/Wishy Washy	1965	$12

SMITH, JIMMY

Number	Title	Yr	NM
☐ 1851	Ain't She Sweet/Everybody Loves My Baby	1962	$10
☐ 1877	Back at the Chicken Shack (Part 1)/Back at the Chicken Shack (Part 2)	1963	$12
☐ 1927	Bucket!/Sassy Mae	1966	$8
☐ 1852	Honeysuckle Rose/Lulu's Back in Town	1962	$12
☐ 1925	I Cover the Waterfront/I Can't Give You Anything But Love	1966	$8
☐ 1905	Matilda, Matilda/Can Heat	1964	$10
☐ 1819	Midnight Special (Part 1)/Midnight Special (Part 2)	1962	$10
☐ 1878	Minor Chant (Part 1)/Minor Chant (Part 2)	1963	$10
☐ 1906	Pork Chop (Part 1)/Pork Chop (Part 2)	1964	$12
☐ 1909	Prayer Meetin' (Part 1)/Prayer Meetin' (Part 2)	1964	$12
☐ 1879	Sermon (Part 1)/Sermon (Part 2)	1963	$10
☐ 1904	When My Dreamboat Comes Home (Part 1)/When My Dreamboat Comes Home (Part 2)	1964	$10
MERCURY			
☐ 73895	Can't Hide Love/No Place in Space	1977	$4
☐ 73972	I've Got Love on My Mind/Side Mouthin'	1977	$4
PRIDE			
☐ 7602	Groovin'/Why Can't We Live Together	1974	$5
VERVE			
☐ 10724	And I Love You So/Ritual (Funky 5/4)	1973	$6
☐ 10298	Blueberry Hill/Walk Right In	1963	$8
☐ 10467	Cat in a Tree (Part 1)/Cat in a Tree (Part 2)	1966	$8
☐ 10506 [DJ]	Cat in a Tree (Part 1)/Cat in a Tree (Part 2)	1967	$10
☐ 10506 [DJ]	Cat in a Tree (Part 1)/Cat in a Tree (Part 2)	1967	$10
☐ CS6-5	Celebrity Scene: Jimmy Smith	1967	$70

—Box set of five singles (10502-10506). Price includes box, all 5 singles, jukebox title strips, bio. Records are sometimes found by themselves, so they are also listed separately.

Number	Title	Yr	NM
☐ 10583	Chain of Fools (Part 1)/Chain of Fools (Part 2)	1968	$8
☐ 10672	For Everyone Under the Sun/Sag' Shootin' His Arrow	1972	$6
☐ 10346	Goldfinger (Part 1)/Goldfinger (Part 2)	1965	$8
☐ 10393	Got My Mojo Working (Part 1)/Got My Mojo Working (Part 2)	1966	$8
☐ 10504 [DJ]	Got My Mojo Working (Part 1)/Got My Mojo Working (Part 2)	1967	$10
☐ 10504 [DJ]	Got My Mojo Working (Part 1)/Got My Mojo Working (Part 2)	1967	$10
☐ 10652	Groove Drops/By the Time I Get to Phoenix	1970	$6
☐ 10283	Hobo Flats (Part 1)/Hobo Flats (Part 2)	1963	$8
☐ 10505 [DJ]	I'm Your Hoochie Coochie Man (Part 1)/I'm Your Hoochie Coochie Man (Part 2)	1967	$10
☐ 10695	Lolita/Straight Ahead	1972	$6
☐ 10623	Mission: Impossible/Gentle Rain	1968	$8
☐ 10262	Ol' Man River/Bashin'	1962	$8
☐ 10660	One Bad Apple/Theme from "The Night Visitor"	1971	$6
☐ 10278	Step Right Up (Part 1)/Step Right Up (Part 2)	1963	$8
☐ 10330	The Cat/Basin Street Blues	1964	$8
☐ 10503 [DJ]	The Cat/Basin Street Blues	1967	$12
☐ 10299	Theme from "Any Number Can Win"/What'd I Say	1963	$8
☐ 10382	Theme from "Where the Spies Are"/Slow Theme from "Where the Spies Are	1966	$6
☐ 10363	The Organ Grinder's Swing/I'll Close My Eyes	1965	$8

—With Kenny Burrell and Grady Tate

Number	Title	Yr	NM
☐ 10255	Walk on the Wild Side (Part 1)/Walk on the Wild Side (Part 2)	1962	$8
☐ 10502 [DJ]	Walk on the Wild Side (Part 1)/Walk on the Wild Side (Part 2)	1967	$10
☐ 10424	Who Do You Love (Part 1)/Who Do You Love (Part 2)	1966	$8
☐ 10314	Who's Afraid of Virginia Woolf?/Who's Afraid of Virginia Woolf? (Part 2)	1964	$8

SMITH, JOE
HIT
Number	Title	Yr	NM
□ 349	Abraham, Martin and John/Hold Me Tight	1968	$8

—B-side by Ed Hardin

SMITH, KATE
RCA VICTOR
Number	Title	Yr	NM
□ 47-9007	Christmas Eve in My Home Town/Happy Birthday, Dear Christ Child	1966	$10

SMITH, KEELY
ATLANTIC
Number	Title	Yr	NM
□ 2429	One Less Bell to Answer/Begin the Beguine	1967	$6
□ 2457	Open Your Heart/All Fall Down	1967	$6

CAPITOL
Number	Title	Yr	NM
□ F3820	Autumn Leaves/I Keep Forgetting	1957	$15
□ F3545	High School Affair/Hurt Me	1956	$15
□ F3952	How Are Ya' Fixed for Love?/Nothin' in Common	1958	$15

—By Frank Sinatra and Keely Smith

Number	Title	Yr	NM
□ F3445	I Wish You Love/Shy	1956	$20
□ F3663	Sentimental Journey/Baby, Won't You Please Come Home	1957	$15
□ F3975	The Whippoorwill/Sometimes	1958	$15

DOT
Number	Title	Yr	NM
□ 16298	Can't Help Falling in Love/You'll Never Walk Alone	1961	$10
□ 16147	Christmas Island/Silent Night	1960	$20
□ 16089	Close/Tea Leaves	1960	$15
□ 16089 [PS]	Close/Tea Leaves	1960	$30
□ 16338	Confidential/How Deep Is the Ocean	1962	$10
□ 15989	Don't Let the Stars Get In Your Eyes/I'd Climb the Highest Mountain	1959	$15
□ 16146	Here in My Heart/Clearance Sale	1960	$15
□ 16228	I Keep Coming Back for More/Little Lover Boy	1961	$10
□ 16182	La-Bou-Lay-A/Young in Years	1961	$10
□ 16257	Prisoner of Love/The Loveliest Night of the Year	1961	$10
□ 16386	What Kind of Fool Am I/If I Should Lose You	1962	$10

REPRISE
Number	Title	Yr	NM
□ 20149	Going Through the Motions/When You Cry	1963	$8
□ 0452	Good-Bye My Love/Where Are You	1966	$6
□ 0374	Have You Ever Been Lonely/Something Wonderful Happened	1965	$6
□ 0303	I'll Always Love You/I Can't Get You Out of My Heart	1964	$8
□ 0428	It's All in the Way You Look at Life/I'll Bring You Water	1965	$6
□ 0294	Let Me Call You Sweetheart/Sunday Mornin'	1964	$8
□ 20211	Love Again/No One Ever Tells You	1963	$8
□ 0396	Someday (You'll Want Me to Love You)/Standing in the Ruins	1965	$6
□ 0402	That Old Black Magic/Standing in the Ruins	1965	$6
□ 0482	The Wonder of You/Who's Afraid	1966	$6
□ 0313	Turn Around, Look at Me/The Wedding	1964	$8

SMITH, LENDON, AND THE JESTERS
METEOR
Number	Title	Yr	NM
□ 5030	Women/Lost Love	1956	$200

SMITH, LEON
EPIC
Number	Title	Yr	NM
□ 9326	Little 40 Ford/Cry All the Time	1959	$50

WILLIAMETTE
Number	Title	Yr	NM
□ 109	Flip, Flop and Fly/Sweet Love	1960	$40
□ 105	Honey Honey/That's the Way	1959	$40
□ 101	Little 40 Ford/Once I Had a Heart	1959	$120

SMITH, LOGAN
BRAND X
Number	Title	Yr	NM
□ 6	Little Man/Down on the Farm	1973	$8

SMITH, LONNIE
BLUE NOTE
Number	Title	Yr	NM
□ 1955	Soul Talk (Part 1)/Soul Talk (Part 2)	1969	$6
□ 1945	Think/Son of Ice Bag	1969	$6

GROOVE MERCHANT
Number	Title	Yr	NM
□ 1034	Afro-Desia (Part 1)/Afro-Desia (Part 2)	1975	$4

SMITH, LONNIE LISTON
COLUMBIA
Number	Title	Yr	NM
□ 11057	A Song for the Children/A Gift of Love	1979	$4
□ 10810	Bright Moments/We Can Dream	1978	$4
□ 11217	Give Peace a Chance (Make Love Not War)/Free and Easy	1980	$4
□ 11269	Love Is the Answer/Bridge Through Time	1980	$4
□ 10903	Space Princess/Quiet Moments	1979	$4

DOCTOR JAZZ
Number	Title	Yr	NM
□ 04623	If You Take Care of Me/Silhouettes	1984	$3
□ 03996	Mystic Woman/A Lonely Way to Be	1983	$3

FLYING DUTCHMAN
Number	Title	Yr	NM
□ DB-10392	A Chance for Peace/Sunset	1975	$5
□ DB-10214	Expansions -- Part 1/Expansions -- Part 2	1975	$5
□ DB-10616	Goddess of Love/Get Down Everybody (It's Time for World Peace)	1976	$5
□ DB-10702	Peace and Love/Quiet Down	1976	$5

SMITH, LOU
KRCO
Number	Title	Yr	NM
□ 105	Cruel Love/Close to My Heart	1960	$30
□ 103	If the World Was Mine/You're Always a Winner	1960	$30

SALVO
Number	Title	Yr	NM
□ 2862	I'm Wondering/Aching Breaking Heart	1961	$30

TOP RANK
Number	Title	Yr	NM
□ 2069	Cruel Love/Close to My Heart	1960	$20

SMITH, MARTHA
CAMEO
Number	Title	Yr	NM
□ 359	As I Watch You Walk Away/It Always Seems Like Summer	1965	$50

SMITH, O.C.
CADENCE
Number	Title	Yr	NM
□ 1312	If You Don't Love Me/Bad Man of Missouri	1957	$20

—As "Ocie Smith"

Number	Title	Yr	NM
□ 1329	Lighthouse/Too Many	1957	$20

—As "Ocie Smith"

Number	Title	Yr	NM
□ 1304	Slow Walk/Forbidden Fruit	1956	$20

—As "Ocie Smith"

CARIBOU
Number	Title	Yr	NM
□ 9021	Simple Life/Come with Me	1977	$5
□ 9017	Together/Just Couldn't Help Myself	1976	$30

CITATION
Number	Title	Yr	NM
□ 1034	Try a Little Tenderness/How Times Have Changed	1958	$30

—As "Ocie Smith"

COLUMBIA
Number	Title	Yr	NM
□ 4-45206	Baby I Need Your Loving/San Francisco Is a Lonely Town	1970	$30
□ 4-45343	Clean Up Your Own Back Yard/I've Been There	1971	$6
□ 4-44948	Daddy's Little Man/If I Leave You Now	1969	$6
□ 4-44948 [PS]	Daddy's Little Man/If I Leave You Now	1969	$8
□ 4-45655	Don't Misunderstand/If You Touch Me	1972	$6
□ 4-44151	Double Life/The Season	1967	$40
□ 4-45301	Downtown U.S.A./That's What Life Is All About	1971	$12
□ 4-44859	Friend, Lover, Woman, Wife/I Taught Her Everything She Knows	1969	$6
□ 4-45435	Help Me Make It Through the Night/Diamond in the Rough	1971	$6
□ 4-44751	Honey (I Miss You)/Keep On Keepin' On	1969	$6
□ 4-44705	Isn't It Lonely Together/I Ain't the Worryin' Kind	1968	$6
□ 4-45098	Isn't Life Beautiful/Moody	1970	$6
□ 4-45863	La La Peace Song/When Morning Comes	1973	$8
□ 3-10031	La La Peace Song/When Morning Comes	1974	$6
□ 4-44616	Little Green Apples/Long Black Limousine	1968	$8
□ 4-44555	Main Street Mission/Gas Food Lodging	1968	$8
□ 4-45038	Me and You/Can't Take My Eyes Off You	1969	$6
□ 4-43809	On Easy Street/Beyond the Next Hill	1966	$200
□ 4-45160	Primrose Lane/Melodee	1970	$6
□ 4-43525	That's Life/I'm Your Man	1966	$50
□ 4-44425	The Son of Hickory Holler's Tramp/The Best Man	1968	$8

FAMILY
Number	Title	Yr	NM
□ 5000	Dreams Come True/(B-side unknown)	1980	$6

MGM
Number	Title	Yr	NM
□ K12233	Lost Horizon and Shangri-La/Going, Going, Gone	1956	$20

—As "Ocie Smith"

MOTOWN
Number	Title	Yr	NM
□ 1636	I Betcha/That's One for Love	1982	$40
□ 1623	Love Changes/Got to Know	1982	$30

RENDEZVOUS
Number	Title	Yr	NM
□ 103	Brenda/(Instrumental)	1986	$6
□ 101	What'cha Gonna Do/Nothing But the Best	1986	$5

SHADY BROOK
Number	Title	Yr	NM
□ 1049	Living Without Your Love/Can't Be the One to Say It's Over	1978	$6
□ 1045	Love to Burn/Give Me Time	1978	$15

SOUTH BAY
Number	Title	Yr	NM
□ 1003	Love Changes/Got to Know	1982	$40

7-Inch Extended Plays
COLUMBIA
Number	Title	Yr	NM
□ 7-9680 [PS]	Hickory Holler Revisited	1968	$15
□ 7-9680	The Son of Hickory Holler's Tramp/Little Green Apples//By the Time I Get to Phoenix/Sitting on the Dock of the Bay	1968	$15

—Jukebox issue; small hole, plays at 33 1/3 rpm

SMITH, PATTI, GROUP
ARISTA
Number	Title	Yr	NM
□ SP-4 [DJ]	Ask the Angels (mono/stereo)	1977	$30

—With lyric insert (deduct 20% if missing)

Number	Title	Yr	NM
□ 0318	Because the Night/God Speed	1978	$4

—A-side co-written by Bruce Springsteen

Number	Title	Yr	NM
□ 0318 [PS]	Because the Night/God Speed	1978	$12
□ 0427	Frederick/Frederick (Live)	1979	$5
□ 0427 [PS]	Frederick/Frederick (Live)	1979	$10
□ 0171	Gloria/My Generation	1976	$10
□ 0171 [PS]	Gloria/My Generation	1976	$10
□ 9762	I Was (Looking for You)/Up There Down There	1988	$3
□ 9689	People Have the Power/Wild Leaves	1988	$3
□ 9689 [PS]	People Have the Power/Wild Leaves	1988	$4
□ SP-2 [DJ]	Pissing in the River (mono/stereo)	1976	$30
□ 0453	So You Want to Be a Rock and Roll Star/5-4-3-2-1/A Fire of Unknown Origin	1979	$4
□ 0453 [PS]	So You Want to Be a Rock and Roll Star/5-4-3-2-1/A Fire of Unknown Origin	1979	$30

MER
Number	Title	Yr	NM
□ 601	Hey Joe/Piss Factory	1974	$100

SIRE
Number	Title	Yr	NM
□ 1009	Hey Joe/Piss Factory	1977	$12
□ 1009 [PS]	Hey Joe/Piss Factory	1977	$20

SMITH, RAY
CELEBRITY CIRCLE
Number	Title	Yr	NM
□ 6901	I Walk the Line/Fool #1	1964	$20

CINNAMON
Number	Title	Yr	NM
□ 760	It Wasn't Easy/It's Just Not the Same	1973	$5
□ 795	Ten Steps Out in Front/Because of Losing You	1974	$5
□ 773	The First Lonely Weekend/A Handful of Friends	1973	$5
□ 755	Tilted Cup of Love/I'd Traded Better for Worse	1973	$5

COLUMBIA
Number	Title	Yr	NM
□ 2-300(?)	An Old Christmas Card/Jolly Old St. Nicholas	1949	$50

—Microgroove 33 1/3 rpm single, small hole

Number	Title	Yr	NM
□ 2-534(?)	I'm Saving Mother's Wedding Ring for You/Mommy Can I Take My Doll	1950	$50

—Microgroove 33 1/3 rpm single, small hole

Number	Title	Yr	NM
□ 2-310(?)	Pretty Little Eyes of Blue/Tennessee Polka	1949	$50

—Microgroove 33 1/3 rpm single, small hole

Number	Title	Yr	NM
□ 2-290(?)	Snowdeer/Roll Along Kentucky Moon	1949	$50

—Microgroove 33 1/3 rpm single, small hole

Number	Title	Yr	NM
❏ 2-305(?)	Wedding Bells/I'm Throwing Rice (At the Girl I Love)	1949	$50

— Microgroove 33 1/3 rpm single, small hole

DIAMOND

Number	Title	Yr	NM
❏ 193	Everybody's Goin' Somewhere/Au-Go-Go-Go	1965	$20

INFINITY

Number	Title	Yr	NM
❏ 03	After This Night Is Through/Turn On the Moonlight	1961	$20
❏ 07	Let Yourself Go/Johnny the Hummer	1961	$20

JUDD

Number	Title	Yr	NM
❏ 1021	Blonde Hair, Blue Eyes/You Don't Want Me	1960	$40
❏ 1017	Maria Elena/Put Your Arms Around Me Honey	1960	$40
❏ 1019	One Wonderful Love/Makes Me Feel Good	1960	$40

NU-TONE

Number	Title	Yr	NM
❏ 1182	Deep in My Heart/She's Mine	1964	$20

SUN

Number	Title	Yr	NM
❏ 375	Hey Boss Man/Candy Doll	1962	$40
❏ 298	So Right/Right Behind You Baby	1958	$40
❏ 372	Travelin' Salesman/I Won't Miss You ('Til You're Gone)	1961	$40
❏ 308	Why, Why, Why/You Made a Hit	1958	$40

TOLLIE

Number	Title	Yr	NM
❏ 9029	Here Comes My Baby Back Again/Did We Have a Party	1964	$30

TOPPA

Number	Title	Yr	NM
❏ 1071	Almost Alone/A Place Within My Heart	1962	$30

WARNER BROS.

Number	Title	Yr	NM
❏ 5371	I'm Snowed/Turn Over a New Leaf	1963	$20

ZIRKON

Number	Title	Yr	NM
❏ 1055	After This Night Is Through/Turn On the Moonlight	1961	$30

SMITH, ROBERT CURTIS

ARHOOLIE

Number	Title	Yr	NM
❏ 502	Love Each Other/Please Don't Drive Me Away	1961	$30

SMITH, RONNIE

BRUNSWICK

Number	Title	Yr	NM
❏ 55137	Lookie, Lookie, Lookie/Tiny Kisses	1959	$50

HAMILTON

Number	Title	Yr	NM
❏ 50003	My Babe/I've Got a Love	1959	$30

IMPERIAL

Number	Title	Yr	NM
❏ 5679	I Hear You Knocking/I Started Out Walkin'	1960	$40
❏ 5667	It Hurts Me So/Long Time No Love	1960	$40

SMITH, SAMMI

COLUMBIA

Number	Title	Yr	NM
❏ 44905	Brownsville Lumberyard/Shadows of Your Mind	1969	$8
❏ 44212	He Went a Little Bit Farther/Foxy Dan	1967	$12
❏ 4-44663	Sand Covered Angels/It's Not Time Now	1968	$8
❏ 44370	So Long, Charlie Brown, Don't Look for Me Around/Turn Around	1967	$8
❏ 44523	Why Do You Do Me Like You Do/22 Road Markers to a Mile	1968	$8

CYCLONE

Number	Title	Yr	NM
❏ 104	The Letter/It's a Day for Sad Songs	1979	$4
❏ 100	What a Lie/It's Not My Way	1979	$4

ELEKTRA

Number	Title	Yr	NM
❏ 45300	As Long As There's a Sunday/Children	1976	$4
❏ 45429	Days That End in "Y"/Hallelujah for Beer	1977	$4
❏ 45292	Huckleberry Pie/I Won't Sing No Love Songs Anymore	1975	$5

— With Even Stevens

Number	Title	Yr	NM
❏ 45398	I Can't Stop Loving You/De Grazia's Song	1977	$4
❏ 45476	It Just Won't Feel Like Cheating (With You)/I Ain't Got Time to Rock No Babies	1978	$4
❏ 45374	Loving Arms/I Just Wanted to Sing	1977	$4
❏ 45334	Sunday School to Broadway/Goodmornin', Sunshine, Goodbye	1976	$4

MEGA

Number	Title	Yr	NM
❏ 0118	City of New Orleans/Don't Blow No Smoke on Me	1973	$5
❏ 1222	Cover Me/He Makes It Hard to Say Goodbye	1975	$5

Number	Title	Yr	NM
❏ 0039	For the Kids/Saunder's Ferry Lane	1971	$5
❏ 0068	Girl in New Orleans/Isn't It Sad	1972	$5
❏ 0015	Help Me Make It Through the Night/When Michael Calls	1970	$6
❏ 212	Help Me Make It Through the Night/When Michael Calls	1974	$4

— Reissue of 0015

Number	Title	Yr	NM
❏ 0001	He's Everywhere/This Room for Rent	1970	$5
❏ 0109	I Miss You Most When You're Here/Billy Jacks	1973	$5
❏ 0079	I've Got to Have You/Jimmy's in Georgia	1972	$5
❏ 1214	Long Black Veil/Paste Me On Some Feathers`	1974	$5
❏ 1246	My Window Faces the South/Before the Next Teardrop Falls	1976	$5
❏ 1233	She's in Love with a Rodeo Man/Fool for Something Years	1975	$5
❏ 0026	Then You Walk In/Willie	1971	$5
❏ 0097	The Toast of '45/Tony	1972	$5
❏ 1236	Today I Started Loving You Again/Fine As Wine	1975	$5

PLAYBACK

Number	Title	Yr	NM
❏ 1354	Cloudy Days/(B-side unknown)	1989	$5
❏ 1340	Gonna Lay Me Down Beside My Memories/I'd Do It All Over Again	1989	$5

SOUND FACTORY

Number	Title	Yr	NM
❏ 427	Cheatin's a Two-Way Street/The Legend of Wooley Swamp	1981	$4
❏ 433	Gypsy and Joe/(B-side unknown)	1982	$4
❏ 425	I Just Want to Be with You/I've Never Loved You More Than I Do Now	1980	$4
❏ 446	Sometimes I Cry When I'm Alone/Once or Twice	1981	$4
❏ 432	Waltz Across Texas/I Need Thatr Shoulder After All	1981	$6

— With Ernest Tubb

STEP ONE

Number	Title	Yr	NM
❏ 347	An Offer I Couldn't Refuse/One Away from One Too Many	1985	$4
❏ 351	Love Me All Over/Don't Let It Happen Again	1986	$4

ZODIAC

Number	Title	Yr	NM
❏ 1000	Help Me Make It Through the Night/Saunder's Ferry Drive	1976	$4

SMITH, SHUGGY RAY

PZAZZ

Number	Title	Yr	NM
❏ 019	Papa And Santa Claus/The Hitch Hiking Hippie	1968	$8

SMITH, SOMETHIN', AND THE REDHEADS

EPIC

Number	Title	Yr	NM
❏ 5-9389	Ballin' the Jack/It's a Sin to Tell a Lie	1960	$8
❏ 5-9247	Ev'ry Night at 9 O'Clock/I'm Gonna Wrap Up All My Heartaches	1957	$10
❏ 5-9025	Gee/Just in Case You Change Your Mind	1954	$15

— As "Somethin' Smith and the Skylarks

Number	Title	Yr	NM
❏ 5-9179	Heartaches/Cecelia	1956	$12
❏ 5-9280	I Don't Want to Set the World on Fire/You Made Me Love You	1958	$10
❏ 5-9048	If I Could Be with You/Oh Jane	1954	$10
❏ 5-9168	In a Shanty in Old Shanty Town/Coal Dust on the Fiddle	1956	$10
❏ 5-9093	It's a Sin to Tell a Lie/My Baby Just Cares for Me	1955	$10
❏ 5-9208	Ma (She's Makin' Eyes at Me)/Mambo, Tango, Samba, Chalypso Rhumba Blues	1957	$10
❏ 5-9313	Mr. D.J. (Please Play a Song for Me)/That's Togetherness	1959	$10
❏ 5-9269	My Secret Inspiration/The Brush Off	1958	$10
❏ 5-9340	Poor Butterfly/Ten Chaperones	1959	$12
❏ 5-9264	School Bus Rock/I Thank You, Mr. Moon	1958	$15
❏ 5-9197	Sweet Stuff/I Hope You Know What You're Doin'	1957	$10
❏ 5-9106	The Ace in the Hole/Charley, My Boy	1955	$12
❏ 5-9119	When All the Streets Are Dark/Pretty Baby	1955	$10
❏ 5-9188	When I Grow Too Old to Dream/We'll Build a Bungalow	1956	$10

MGM

Number	Title	Yr	NM
❏ 13023	Ain't We Got Fun/We'll Meet Again	1961	$8

SMITH, WARREN

LIBERTY

Number	Title	Yr	NM
❏ 55409	Bad News Gets Around/Five Minutes of the Latest Blues	1962	$30
❏ 55615	Big City Ways/That's Why I Sing in a Honky Tonk	1963	$20
❏ 55699	Blue Smoke/Judge and Jury	1964	$20
❏ 55475	Book of Broken Hearts/160 Pounds of Hurt	1962	$30
❏ 55336	Call of the Wild/Old Lonesome Feeling	1961	$30
❏ 55248	I Don't Believe I'll Fall in Love Today/Cave-In	1960	$30
❏ 55302	Odds and Ends (Bits and Pieces)/A Whole Lot of Nothin'	1961	$30
❏ 55361	Why Baby Why/Why I'm Walking	1961	$30

— With Shirley Collie

MERCURY

Number	Title	Yr	NM
❏ 72825	Lie to Me/When the Heartaches Get to Me	1968	$12

SUN

Number	Title	Yr	NM
❏ 314	Goodbye Mr. Love/Sweet Sweet Girl	1959	$50
❏ 286	I Fell in Love/I've Got Love If You Want It	1958	$40
❏ 268	Miss Froggie/So Long, I'm Gone	1957	$50

WARNER BROS.

Number	Title	Yr	NM
❏ 5125	Dear Santa/The Meaning of Christmas	1959	$30

SMITH, WHISTLING JACK

DERAM

Number	Title	Yr	NM
❏ 85005	I Was Kaiser Bill's Batman/The British Grin 'N' Bear	1967	$8
❏ 85041	Only When I Laff/Early One Morning	1969	$6

SMITHEREENS, THE

CAPITOL

Number	Title	Yr	NM
❏ 7PRO-79842 [DJ]	A Girl Like You (same on both sides)	1989	$20
❏ 7PRO-79842 [DJ]	A Girl Like You (same on both sides)	1989	$20

CAPITOL/ENIGMA

Number	Title	Yr	NM
❏ 44238	Drown in My Own Tears/House We Used to Live In	1988	$6
❏ 44174	House We Used to Live In/Only a Memory	1988	$30

— Approximately 25 copies of this record exist

Number	Title	Yr	NM
❏ 44174 [PS]	House We Used to Live In/Only a Memory	1988	$30

— Approximately 25 copies of this sleeve exist

Number	Title	Yr	NM
❏ 44174 [DJ]	House We Used to Live In (same on both sides)	1988	$10
❏ 44174 [DJ]	House We Used to Live In (same on both sides)	1988	$10
❏ 44150	Only a Memory/The Seeker	1988	$5

— Add 100% to values for promo copy

Number	Title	Yr	NM
❏ 44150 [PS]	Only a Memory/The Seeker	1988	$5

ENIGMA

Number	Title	Yr	NM
❏ 75002	Behind the Wall of Sleep/Blood and Roses	1986	$5
❏ 75002 [PS]	Behind the Wall of Sleep/Blood and Roses	1986	$12
❏ 75003	In a Lonely Place/Blood and Roses (Live)	1986	$5
❏ 75003 [PS]	In a Lonely Place/Blood and Roses (Live)	1986	$10

7-Inch Extended Plays

D-TONE

Number	Title	Yr	NM
❏ DT150 [PS]	Girls About Town	1980	$60
❏ DT150	Girls About Town/Girl Don't Tell Me//Got Me a Girl/Girls Are Like That	1980	$60

SMITHS, THE

Also see MORRISSEY.

SIRE

Number	Title	Yr	NM
❏ 29007	How Soon Is Now?/Shakespear's Sister/Headmaster Ritual	1985	$20
❏ 29007 [PS]	How Soon Is Now?/Shakespear's Sister/Headmaster Ritual	1985	$30
❏ 28136	Stop Me If You Think You've Heard This One Before/Keep Mine Hidden	1987	$5
❏ 28136 [PS]	Stop Me If You Think You've Heard This One Before/Keep Mine Hidden	1987	$10
❏ 29239	What Difference Does It Make/Back to the Old Home	1984	$10
❏ 29239 [PS]	What Difference Does It Make/Back to the Old Home	1984	$30

Number	Title	Yr	NM

SMOKE RINGS, THE

DOT

Number	Title	Yr	NM
❏ 16975	Love's the Thing/She Gives Me Love	1966	$30

PROSPECT

Number	Title	Yr	NM
❏ 101	Love's the Thing/She Gives Me Love	1966	$50

SMOKE RISE, THE

PARAMOUNT

Number	Title	Yr	NM
❏ 0113	I'm Here (Love Me)/Survival	1971	$8

SMOKE, THE (2)
Houston-based group.

ORBIT

Number	Title	Yr	NM
❏ 1126	Mainstream/Church House Blues	1968	$60

UNI

Number	Title	Yr	NM
❏ 55154	Choose It (Part 1)/Choose It (Part 2)	1969	$10

SMOKESTACK LIGHTNIN'

BELL

Number	Title	Yr	NM
❏ 836	Baby Don't Get Crazy/The Blue Albino Shuffle	1969	$6
❏ 861	Hello L.A., Bye-Bye Birmingham/Well Tuesday	1970	$6
❏ 777	I Idolize You/Something's Got a Hold on You	1969	$6
❏ 755	Light in My Window/Long Stemmed Eyes	1968	$6

WHITE WHALE

Number	Title	Yr	NM
❏ 256	Look What You've Done/Got a Good Love	1967	$8

SMOKEY JOE

FLIP

Number	Title	Yr	NM
❏ 228	The Signifying Monkey/Listen to Me Baby	1955	$500

SUN

Number	Title	Yr	NM
❏ 228	The Signifying Monkey/Listen to Me Baby	1956	$300
❏ 393	The Signifying Monkey/Listen to Me Baby	1964	$200

SMOOTHIES, THE

DECCA

Number	Title	Yr	NM
❏ 31105	Softly/Joanie	1960	$30

SMOTHERS BROTHERS, THE

MERCURY

Number	Title	Yr	NM
❏ 72323	Coo Coo/Slithery Dee	1964	$10
❏ 72027	Fly Ezekiel/They Call the Wind Maria	1962	$10
❏ 72483	The Three Song/The World I Used to Know	1965	$8
❏ 72483 [PS]	The Three Song/The World I Used to Know	1965	$20
❏ 72519	The Toy Song/Little Sacha Sugar	1966	$8
❏ 72519 [PS]	The Toy Song/Little Sacha Sugar	1966	$20
❏ 72573	Writer of Songs/Lark Day	1966	$8

SMOTHERS INC.

Number	Title	Yr	NM
❏ 79151 [PS]	The Christmas Bunny Part 1/The Christmas Bunny Part 2	1969	$60
❏ 79151	The Christmas Bunny Part 1/The Christmas Bunny Part 2	1969	$30

SMOTHERS, DICK

MERCURY

Number	Title	Yr	NM
❏ 72717	Saturday Night at the World/They Are Gone	1967	$30
❏ 72717 [PS]	Saturday Night at the World/They Are Gone	1967	$30

SNIFF 'N' THE TEARS

ATLANTIC

Number	Title	Yr	NM
❏ 3604	Driver's Seat/Slide Away	1979	$4

SNOBS, THE

LONDON

Number	Title	Yr	NM
❏ 9671	Buckle Shoe Stomp/Stand and Deliver	1964	$10

SNODGRASS, ELMER

DECCA

Number	Title	Yr	NM
❏ 31145	What a Terrible Feeling/Heartaches Over You	1960	$20

SNOW, EDDIE

SUN

Number	Title	Yr	NM
❏ 226	Ain't That Right/Bring Your Love Back Home	1955	$200

SNOW, HANK

RCA

Number	Title	Yr	NM
❏ PB-11622	A Good Gal Is Hard to Find/I Wish My Heart Could Talk	1979	$5
❏ PB-11153	Breakfast with the Blues/I've Done At Least One Thing	1977	$5
❏ PB-11080	I'm Still Movin' On/I'm Gonna Bid My Blues Goodbye	1977	$5
❏ PB-11734	It Takes Too Long/6 String Tennessee Flattop	1979	$5
❏ PB-11192	That Heart Belongs to Me/Love Is So Elusive	1978	$5
❏ PB-11487	The Mysterious Lady from St. Martinique/Get On My Love Train	1979	$5
❏ PB-11021	Trouble in Mind/Trying to Get My Baby Off My Mind	1977	$5

RCA VICTOR

Number	Title	Yr	NM
❏ 47-7325	A Woman Captured Me/My Lucky Friend	1958	$20
❏ 47-7869	Beggar to a King/Poor Little Jimmie	1961	$15
❏ 37-7869	Beggar to a King/Poor Little Jimmie	1961	$30

— Compact Single 33" with small hole

Number	Title	Yr	NM
❏ 47-4096	Ben Dewberry's Final Run/Engineer's Child	1951	$30
❏ 47-7233	Big Wheels/I'm Hurting All Over	1958	$20
❏ 48-0214	Blue Ranger/Only a Rose from My Mother's Grave	1950	$40

— Originals on green vinyl

Number	Title	Yr	NM
❏ 47-6269	Born to Be Happy/Mainliner (The Hawk with Silver Wings)	1955	$20
❏ 48-0224	Brand on My Heart/I'll Not Forget My Mother's Prayers	1950	$40

— Originals on green vinyl

Number	Title	Yr	NM
❏ 47-8334	Breakfast with the Blues/I Stepped Over the Line	1964	$15
❏ 47-5006	Broken Hearted/I Wonder Where You Are Tonight	1952	$30
❏ 47-6831	Calypso Sweethearts/Marriage and Divorce	1957	$20
❏ 47-7524	Chasin' a Rainbow/I Heard My Heart Break Last Night	1959	$20
❏ 47-9030	Christmas Cannonball/God Is My Santa Claus	1966	$15
❏ 47-5340	Christmas Roses/Reindeer Boogie	1953	$30
❏ PB-10439	Colorado Country Morning/I Keep Dreaming of You All the Time	1975	$6
❏ 47-9907	Come the Morning/Francesca	1970	$8
❏ 47-4976	Confused with the Blues/On That Old Hawaiian Shore	1952	$30

— The above four comprise a box set

Number	Title	Yr	NM
❏ 47-6578	Conscience I'm Guilty/Hula Rock	1956	$30
❏ 47-6154	Cryin', Prayin', Waitin', Hopin'/I'm Glad I Got to See You Once Again	1955	$20
❏ 47-7448	Doggone That Train/Father Time and Mother Love	1959	$20
❏ 47-9188	Down at the Pawn Shop/Listen	1967	$12
❏ 47-9964	Duquesne, Pennsylvania/So Goes My Heart	1971	$8
❏ PB-10108	Easy to Love/Just a Faded Petal from a Beautiful Bouquet	1974	$6
❏ 47-5380	For Now and Always/A Message from the Tradewinds	1953	$30
❏ 47-5249	Glory Land March/In Daddy's Footsteps	1953	$30
❏ GB-10513	Hello Love/Until the End of Time	1976	$4

— Gold Standard Series" reissue

Number	Title	Yr	NM
❏ PB-10338	Hijack/The Last Ride	1975	$6
❏ 47-4095	Hobo Bill's Last Ride/Wreck of the Old 97	1951	$30
❏ 47-5155	Honeymoon on a Rocket Ship/There Wasn't an Organ at Our Wedding	1953	$30
❏ 47-9012	Hula Love/Letter from Vietnam	1966	$10
❏ 47-5698	I Don't Hurt Anymore/My Arabian Baby	1954	$30
❏ 47-5548	I'm Lost I'm On the Inside/Invisible Hands	1953	$30
❏ 47-4593	I'm Movin' On/Marriage Vow	1952	$30
❏ 48-0328	I'm Movin' On/With This Ring I Thee Wed	1950	$50

— Originals on green vinyl

Number	Title	Yr	NM
❏ 48-0328	I'm Movin' On/With This Ring I Thee Wed	1950	$30

— Reissues on black vinyl

Number	Title	Yr	NM
❏ 47-6326	In an Eighteenth Century Drawing Room/La Cucaracha	1955	$20
❏ 47-8072	I've Been Everywhere/Ancient History	1962	$15
❏ 47-8713	I've Cried a Mile/Crazy Little Train (Of Love)	1965	$10
❏ 47-4909	I Went to Your Wedding/Boogie Woogie Flying Cloud	1952	$30
❏ 47-4733	Lady's Man/Married by the Bible, Divorced by the Law	1952	$30

Number	Title	Yr	NM
❏ 47-9300	Learnin' a New Way of Life/Wild Flower	1967	$12
❏ 47-5960	Let Me Go, Lover!/I've Forgotten You	1954	$30
❏ 47-5026	Love Entered the Iron Door/I Cried But My Tears Were Too Late	1952	$30
❏ 48-0056	Marriage Vow/The Star Spangled Waltz	1949	$50

— Originals on green vinyl

Number	Title	Yr	NM
❏ PB-10225	Merry-Go-Round of Love/My Filipino Love	1975	$6
❏ 47-7748	Miller's Cave/The Change of the Tide	1960	$20
❏ 47-4974	Moanin'/I Knew That We'd Meet Again	1952	$30
❏ 47-4594	Music Makin' Mama from Memphis/Down the Trail of Aching Hearts	1952	$30
❏ 47-4346	Music Makin' Mama from Memphis/The Highest Bidder	1951	$30
❏ 48-0104	My Filipino Rose/The Law of Love	1949	$50

— Originals on green vinyl

Number	Title	Yr	NM
❏ 47-4975	My Little Golden Horseshoe/The Yodeling Cowboy	1952	$30
❏ 47-8437	My Memories of You/Ninety Days	1964	$15
❏ 47-4632	My Mother/I Just Telephone Upstairs	1952	$30
❏ 47-5648	My Religion's Not Old Fashioned/Old Rattler	1954	$30

— With Grandpa Jones

Number	Title	Yr	NM
❏ 47-6772	Oh, Wonderful World/Carnival of Venice	1957	$20
❏ 47-5592	Panamama/Act 1, Act 2, Act 3	1954	$30
❏ 47-4398	Pray/These Things Shall Pass	1951	$30
❏ 48-0364	Somewhere Along Life's Highway/Within This Broken Heart of Mine	1950	$30

— Originals on green vinyl

Number	Title	Yr	NM
❏ 47-5222	Southern Cannonball/Anniversary Blue Yodel	1953	$20
❏ 47-5296	Spanish Fire Ball/Between Fire and Water	1953	$30
❏ 47-6715	Stolen Moments/Two Won't Care	1956	$20
❏ 47-6955	Tangled Mind/My Arms Are a House	1957	$20
❏ 47-5912	That Crazy Mambo Thing/The Next Voice You Hear	1954	$30
❏ 74-0251	That's When the Hurtin' Sets In/I'm Movin'	1969	$8
❏ 47-5794	The Alphabet/My Religion's Not Old Fashioned	1954	$30
❏ 48-0088	The Blind Boy's Dog/Anniversary of My Broken Heart	1949	$50

— Originals on green vinyl

Number	Title	Yr	NM
❏ 47-7121	The Blue Danube Waltz/Under the Double Eagle	1957	$20
❏ 47-8808	The Count Down/Isle of Sicily	1966	$12
❏ 48-0303	The Drunkard's Son/I Wonder Where You Are Tonight	1950	$40

— Originals on green vinyl

Number	Title	Yr	NM
❏ 47-4596	The Golden Rocket/Bluebird Island	1952	$30

— The above four comprise a box set

Number	Title	Yr	NM
❏ 48-0400	The Golden Rocket/Paving the Highway with Tears	1950	$40

— Originals on green vinyl

Number	Title	Yr	NM
❏ 47-4522	The Gold Rush Is Over/Why Do You Promise Me	1952	$30
❏ 47-7586	The Last Ride/The Party of the Second Part	1959	$20
❏ 47-9523	The Late and Great Love (Of My Life)/Born for You	1968	$10
❏ 47-7803	The Man Behind the Gun/I'm Asking for a Friend	1960	$20
❏ 47-8151	The Man Who Robbed the Bank at Santa Fe/You're Losing Your Baby	1963	$15
❏ 47-8151 [PS]	The Man Who Robbed the Bank at Santa Fe/You're Losing Your Baby	1963	$30
❏ 47-4097	The Mystery of Number Five/One More Ride	1951	$30

— The above three comprise a box set

Number	Title	Yr	NM
❏ 47-6379	These Hands/I'm Moving In	1956	$20
❏ 47-8488	The Wishing Well (Down in the Well)/Human	1964	$15
❏ 47-8548	Trouble in Mind/In the Misty Moonlight	1965	$10
❏ 48-0363	Wasted Love/My Two Timin' Woman	1950	$30

— Originals on green vinyl

Number	Title	Yr	NM
❏ 47-5221	When Jimmie Rodgers Said Goodbye/Treasure Untold	1953	$20
❏ 47-5490	When Mexican Joe Met Jole Blon/No Longer a Prisoner	1953	$30
❏ 47-7154	Whispering Rain/I Wish I Was the Moon	1958	$20

Number	Title	Yr	NM
❏ PB-10681	Who's Been Here Since I've Been Gone/That's When He Dropped the World in My Hands	1976	$6
❏ 47-9433	Who Will Answer? (Aleluya No. 1)/I Just Wanted to Know (How the Wind Was Blowing)	1968	$10
❏ 47-5223	Why Did You Give Me Your Love/Mississippi River Blues	1953	$20

— The above four comprise a box set

Number	Title	Yr	NM
❏ EPA472 [PS]	A Country Christmas with Hank Snow	1953	$25
❏ 547-0607	Can't Have You Blues/A Scale to Measure Love// Cuba Rhumba/Blossoms in the Springtime	1955	$25

— One record of 2-EP set EPB-1113

Number	Title	Yr	NM
❏ EPA794	Country Classics	1956	$25
❏ EPA472	Frosty the Snowman/Silent Night//Christmas Roses/The Reindeer Boogie	1953	$25
❏ EPA-5062 [PS]	Hank Snow (Gold Standard Series)	1958	$20
❏ EPA-582 [PS]	Hank Snow's Country Guitar	1954	$25
❏ EPA-5062	I'm Moving On/Marriage Vow//The Rhumba Boogie/With This Ring I Thee Wed	1958	$20
❏ EPA794	I'm Movin' On/THe Rhumba Boogie//The Golden Rocket/Music Making Mama from Memphis	1956	$25
❏ EPA582	Twelfth Street Rag/Rainbow Boogie//Vaya Con Dios (May God Be with You)/ Madison Madness	1954	$25

SNOW, HANK, AND ANITA CARTER

RCA VICTOR

Number	Title	Yr	NM
❏ 48-0441	Down the Trail of Achin' Hearts/Bluebird Island	1951	$30

SNOW, HANK, AND KELLY FOXTON

RCA

Number	Title	Yr	NM
❏ PB-11891	Hasn't It Been Good Together/It Was Love	1980	$5
❏ PB-12102	Pain Didn't Shout/Check	1980	$5
❏ PB-11967	There's Something About You/All I Want to Do Is Touch You	1980	$5
❏ PB-12235	Things/Forbidden Lovers	1981	$5

SNOW, JIMMIE RODGERS

RCA VICTOR

Number	Title	Yr	NM
❏ 47-6303	Bee Line/The Meanest Thing in the World Is the Blues	1955	$30
❏ 47-6189	Go Back You Fool/I Care No More	1955	$30
❏ 47-5900	How Do You Think I Feel/Why Don't You Let Me Go	1954	$30
❏ 47-6623	La Strada (The Road)/The One Note Polka	1956	$20
❏ 47-5986	Love Me/I Can't Spell	1955	$30
❏ 47-5693	My Fallen Star/Well Whaddaya Know	1954	$30
❏ 47-6130	The Flame of Love/Someone Else's Heartaches	1955	$30
❏ 47-6430	The Milk Cow Blues/It Won't Do No Good	1956	$30

SNOW MEN, THE

CHALLENGE

Number	Title	Yr	NM
❏ 59227	Ski Storm (Part 1)/Ski Storm (Part 2)	1964	$40

SNOW, PHOEBE

COLUMBIA

Number	Title	Yr	NM
❏ 10351	All Over/No Regrets	1976	$5
❏ 10856	Every Night/Random Time	1978	$5
❏ 10654	Love Makes a Woman/Electra	1977	$5
❏ 10463	Shakey Ground/Don't Sleep with Your Eyes Closed	1976	$5
❏ 10504	Teach Me Tonight/Autobiography (Shine, Shine, Shine)	1977	$5
❏ 10315	Two Fisted Love/Inspired Insanity	1976	$5

ELEKTRA

Number	Title	Yr	NM
❏ 69305	If I Can Just Get Through the Night/Soothin'	1989	$3
❏ 69290	Something Real/Best of My Love	1989	$3

MIRAGE

Number	Title	Yr	NM
❏ 3800	Games/Down in the Basement	1981	$4
❏ 3818	Mercy, Mercy, Mercy/Something Good	1981	$4

SHELTER

Number	Title	Yr	NM
❏ 40400	Easy Street/Harpo's Blues	1975	$5
❏ 40278	Harpo's Blues/Let the Good Times Roll	1974	$5
❏ 40353	Poetry Man/Either or Both	1974	$6

SNOW, WHITNEY

TOWER

Number	Title	Yr	NM
❏ 380	The Christmas Angels Sing/Whitey, the Snow White Lamb	1967	$12

—B-side by Justin Wilson

SNOWMEN, THE

SLACK

Number	Title	Yr	NM
❏ ODB-1	Hokey Cokey/Don't Go Short	1981	$5
❏ ODB-1 [PS]	Hokey Cokey/Don't Go Short	1981	$5

—Both record and sleeve are U.K. imports

SNYDER, JIMMY

WAYSIDE

Number	Title	Yr	NM
❏ 1029	Candy All Over My Face/Here Comes My Sunshine	1969	$8

SNYDER, RICK

CAPITOL

Number	Title	Yr	NM
❏ B-44185	Losing Somebody You Love/I Know the Feeling	1988	$3

SOCIAL DISTORTION

POSH BOY

Number	Title	Yr	NM
❏ PBS11	Mainliner/Playpen	1981	$13
❏ PBS11 [PS]	Mainliner/Playpen	1981	$13

SOCIAL DISTORTION

Number	Title	Yr	NM
❏ 0(# unknown)	1945/Under My Thumb/Playpen	1982	$40
❏ 0(# unknown) [PS]	1945/Under My Thumb/Playpen	1982	$40

—Sleeve notes distribution by Faulty Products

Number	Title	Yr	NM
❏ 4502	Mommy's Little Monster/Another State of Mind	1983	$20
❏ 4502 [PS]	Mommy's Little Monster/Another State of Mind	1983	$20

TRIPLE X

Number	Title	Yr	NM
❏ 51023-7	Another State of Mind/Mommy's Little Monster	1989	$5

—Clear vinyl

Number	Title	Yr	NM
❏ 51023-7 [PS]	Another State of Mind/Mommy's Little Monster	1989	$5

SOCIAL UNREST

INFA RED

Number	Title	Yr	NM
❏ 01	Making Room for Youth/Rush Hour	1981	$30
❏ 01 [PS]	Making Room for Youth/Rush Hour	1981	$30

SOCIETY'S CHILDREN

ATCO

Number	Title	Yr	NM
❏ 6618	A Tribute to the Four Seasons/Golden Child	1968	$30
❏ 6553	Count the Ways/Golden Child	1968	$12
❏ 6597	Live for Today/I'll Let You Know	1968	$10
❏ 6538	White Christmas/I'll Let You Know	1967	$15

SOFT CELL

SIRE

Number	Title	Yr	NM
❏ 29641	Heat/It's a Mugs Game	1983	$4
❏ 29812	Loving You Hating Me/It's a Mugs Game	1983	$10
❏ 29812 [PS]	Loving You Hating Me/It's a Mugs Game	1983	$3
❏ 29812 [DJ]	Loving You Hating Me (mono/stereo)	1983	$3
❏ 29812 [DJ]	Loving You Hating Me (mono/stereo)	1983	$3
❏ 49855	Tainted Love/Memorabilia	1981	$3
❏ 49855 [PS]	Tainted Love/Memorabilia	1981	$6
❏ PRO01028 [DJ]	Tainted Love/Where Did Our Love Go (Long)//Tainted Love/Where Did Our Love Go (Short)	1982	$10
❏ PRO-S-1028 [DJ]	Tainted Love/Where Did Our Love Go (Long)//Tainted Love/Where Did Our Love Go (Short)	1982	$10
❏ GSRE 0435	Tainted Love/Where Did Our Love Go/What	1983	$4

—Back to Back Hits series; First release of medley on U.S. stock 45

Number	Title	Yr	NM
❏ 29976	What!/A Man Could Get Lost	1982	$4

SOLDIER BOYS, THE

SCEPTER

Number	Title	Yr	NM
❏ 1230	I'm Your Soldier Boy/You Picked Me	1962	$70

SOLID GOLD BAND

Number	Title	Yr	NM
❏ 153	Another Night of Pickin' Country Music/Blackjack and Water	1983	$5

Number	Title	Yr	NM
❏ 92	Blackjack and Water/Lonesome Wind	1981	$5
❏ 110	Cherokee Country/It's Just Your Memory	1981	$5
❏ 138	Country Fiddles/The Sun Shines Bright in Oklahoma	1982	$5
❏ 127	Good Friends Are Hard to Find/Me, My Ol' Guitar and Merle	1982	$5
❏ 121	I Never Had the One That I Wanted/Bandera, Texas	1982	$5

SOLITAIRES, THE

ARGO

Number	Title	Yr	NM
❏ 5316	Walking Along/Please Kiss This Letter	1958	$40

MGM

Number	Title	Yr	NM
❏ 13221	Fool That I Am/Fair Weather Lover	1964	$40

OLD TOWN

Number	Title	Yr	NM
❏ 1000	Blue Valentine/Wonder Boy	1954	$400

—Black vinyl

Number	Title	Yr	NM
❏ 1000	Blue Valentine/Wonder Boy	1954	$1500

—Red vinyl

Number	Title	Yr	NM
❏ 1008	Chances I've Taken/Lonely	1954	$700
❏ 1066	Embraceable You/Round Goes My Heart	1959	$50
❏ 1032	Give Me One More Chance/Nothing Like a Little Love	1956	$200
❏ 1010	I Don't Stand a Ghost of a Chance/Girl of Mine	1955	$500
❏ 1044	I Really Love You So/Thrill of Love	1957	$400
❏ 1071	Light a Candle in the Chapel/Helpless	1959	$50
❏ 1096	Lonesome Lover/Pretty Thing	1961	$50
❏ 1015	Magic Rose/Later for You Baby	1955	$125
❏ 1012	My Dear/What Did She Say	1955	$400

—Logo in Old English style

Number	Title	Yr	NM
❏ 1012	My Dear/What Did She Say	1956	$80

—Logo in block letters

Number	Title	Yr	NM
❏ 1059	Please Remember My Heart/Big Mary's House	1958	$50
❏ 1006/8	Please Remember My Heart/Chances I've Taken	1954	$200
❏ 1006/7	Please Remember My Heart/South of the Border	1954	$700

—Black vinyl

Number	Title	Yr	NM
❏ 1006/7	Please Remember My Heart/South of the Border	1954	$3000

—Red vinyl

Number	Title	Yr	NM
❏ 1019	The Honeymoon/Fine Little Girl	1956	$125
❏ 1139	The Time Is Here/Honey Babe	1963	$40
❏ 1014	The Wedding/Don't Fall in Love	1955	$125
❏ 1049	Walkin' and Talkin'/No More Sorrows	1958	$125
❏ 1034	Walking Along/Please Kiss This Letter	1957	$80

— Yellow label

SOLO, PETER, SINGERS

DATE

Number	Title	Yr	NM
❏ 2-1640	Santa Domingo/Natalie	1969	$8

SOME OF CHET'S FRIENDS

RCA VICTOR

Number	Title	Yr	NM
❏ 47-9229	Chet's Tune/Country Gentleman	1967	$10
❏ 47-9229 [PS]	Chet's Tune/Country Gentleman	1967	$20
❏ 74-0799	Chet's Tune (Part 1)/Chet's Tune (Part 2)	1972	$6

SOMETHING WILD

PSYCHEDELIC

Number	Title	Yr	NM
❏ 1691	Trippin' Out/She's Kinda Weird	1966	$300

SOMETHING YOUNG

FONTANA

Number	Title	Yr	NM
❏ 1556	Oh, Don't Come Crying/The Words I'm Seeking	1966	$30

SOMMERS, JOANIE

ABC

Number	Title	Yr	NM
❏ 12323	Peppermint Choo Choo/Peppermint Engineer	1978	$5

CAPITOL

Number	Title	Yr	NM
❏ 5936	Trains and Boats and Planes/Yesterday's Morning	1967	$8

COLUMBIA

Number	Title	Yr	NM
❏ 43731	Alfie/You Take What Comes Along	1966	$8
❏ 43950	It Doesn't Matter Anymore/Take a Broken Heart	1966	$8

Number	Title	Yr	NM
HAPPY TIGER			
❏ 522	Step Inside Love/Little Girl from Greenwood, Ga.	1970	$6
❏ 537	Sunshine After the Rain/Tell Him	1970	$6
WARNER BROS.			
❏ 5177	Be My Love/Why Don't You Do Right	1960	$20
❏ 5629	Don't Pity Me/My Block	1965	$200
❏ 5324	Goodbye Joey/Bobby's Hobbies	1962	$15
❏ 5390	Goodbye Summer/Big Man	1963	$15
❏ 7251	Great Divide/Talk Until Midnight	1968	$8
❏ 5437	I'd Be So Good for You/I'm Gonna Know He's Mine	1964	$10
❏ 5201	I Don't Want to Walk Without You/Seems Like Long, Long Ago	1961	$20
❏ 5201 [DJ]	I Don't Want to Walk Without You/Seems Like Long, Long Ago	1961	$60
—Promo only on gold vinyl			
❏ 5201 [PS]	I Don't Want to Walk Without You/Seems Like Long, Long Ago	1961	$60
—Sleeve is promo only			
❏ 5454	If You Love Him/I Think I'm Gonna Cry Now	1964	$10
❏ 5350	Little Bit of Everything/Henny Penny	1963	$15
❏ 5374	Little Girl Bad/Wishing Well	1963	$15
❏ 5241	Makin' Whoopee/What's Wrong with Me	1961	$20
❏ 5507	Makin' Whoopee/What's Wrong with Me + 2	1961	$30
—Part of Warner Bros. "+2" series, with two new songs and excerpts of two prior hits			
❏ 5507 [PS]	Makin' Whoopee/What's Wrong with Me + 2	1961	$40
❏ 5339	Memories, Memories/Since Randy Moved Away	1963	$15
❏ 5157	One Boy/I'll Never Be Free	1960	$20
❏ 5157 [DJ]	One Boy/I'll Never Be Free	1960	$60
—Promo only on gold vinyl			
❏ 5361	One Boy/June Is Bustin' Out All Over	1963	$15
❏ 5226	Piano Boy/Serenade of the Bells	1961	$20
❏ 5308	When the Boys Get Together/Passing Strangers	1962	$15

SONIC YOUTH

Number	Title	Yr	NM
FORCED EXPOSURE			
❏ 01	Making the Nature Scene/I Killed Christgau with My Big Fuckin' Dick	1984	$60
❏ 01 [PS]	Making the Nature Scene/I Killed Christgau with My Big Fuckin' Dick	1984	$60
—Black and white sleeve			
❏ 01 [PS]	Making the Nature Scene/I Killed Christgau with My Big Fuckin' Dick	1984	$200
—Special multi-color sleeve with live band shot on rear; only released with test pressings (25 made)			
❏ 01	Making the Nature Scene/I Killed Christgau with My Big Fuckin' Dick	1984	$200
—Test pressing (25 made with special sleeve)			
❏ 012	Silver Rocket/You Pose You Lose/Non-Metal Dude Wearing Metal Tee	1988	$30
❏ 012 [PS]	Silver Rocket/You Pose You Lose/Non-Metal Dude Wearing Metal Tee	1988	$30
IRIDESCENCE			
❏ 12	Death Valley 69/Brave Men Run	1984	$13
—With Lydia Lunch			
❏ 12 [PS]	Death Valley 69/Brave Men Run	1984	$13
NEW ALLIANCE			
❏ 030	Burnin' Up/Tuff Titty Rap/Into the Groovey	1986	$10
—As "Ciccone Youth"			
❏ 030 [PS]	Burnin' Up/Tuff Titty Rap/Into the Groovey	1986	$10
SUB POP			
❏ 26	Touch Me I'm Sick/Halloween	1988	$40
—B-side by Mudhoney; clear vinyl			
❏ 26	Touch Me I'm Sick/Halloween	1988	$20
—B-side by Mudhoney; black vinyl			
❏ 26 [PS]	Touch Me I'm Sick/Halloween	1988	$30
—#2 in Sub Pop Singles Club series			

SONICS, THE (1)

Number	Title	Yr	NM
AMCO			
❏ 001	It's You/Preacher Man	1962	$200

Number	Title	Yr	NM
CHECKER			
❏ 922	This Broken Heart/You Made Me Cry	1959	$30
HARVARD			
❏ 801	This Broken Heart/You Made Me Cry	1959	$400
❏ 922	This Broken Heart/You Made Me Cry	1959	$60
JAMIE			
❏ 1235	Sugaree/Beautiful Brown Eyes	1962	$30
X-TRA			
❏ 107	Once in a Lifetime/It Ain't True	1958	$2000

SONICS, THE (2)

Number	Title	Yr	NM
BURDETTE			
❏ 106	Dirty Old Man/Bama Lama Bama Loo	1975	$8
ETIQUETTE			
❏ 18	Don't Be Afraid of the Dark/Shot Down	1965	$40
❏ 22	Don't Believe in Christmas/Christmas Spirit	1965	$40
—B-side by the Wailers			
❏ 23	Louie Louie/Cinderella	1966	$40
❏ 16	The Hustler/Boss Hoss	1965	$40
GREAT NORTHWEST			
❏ 702	The Witch/Bama Lama Bama Loo	1979	$5
JERDEN			
❏ 809	Love Lights/You Got Your Head On Backwards	1966	$20
❏ 811	Psycho/Maintaining My Cool	1966	$20
❏ 810	The Witch/Like No Other	1966	$20
PICCADILLY			
❏ 244	Anyway the Wind Blows/Lost Love	1967	$30
—A-side written by Frank Zappa			
UNI			
❏ 55039	Anyway the Wind Blows/Lost Love	1967	$20
—A-side written by Frank Zappa			

SONICS, THE (U)

Number	Title	Yr	NM
ARMONIA			
❏ 102	Funny/I Get That Feeling	1962	$200
GAITY			
❏ 114	Marlene/(B-side unknown)	1959	$2000
—VG 1000; VG+ 1500			
GROOVE			
❏ 0112	Bumble Bee/As I Live On	1955	$200
NOCTURNE			
❏ 110	Triangle Love/Evil Eye	1959	$100
RKO UNIQUE			
❏ 411	Triangle Love/Evil Eye	1957	$70

SONNETS, THE

Number	Title	Yr	NM
GUYDEN			
❏ 2112	I Can't Get Sentimental/Forever for You	1964	$20
HERALD			
❏ 477	Please Won't You Call Me/Why Should We Break Up	1956	$70

SONNIER, JO-EL

Number	Title	Yr	NM
❏ 1189	Hurricane Audrey/Jump Little Frog	1969	$10
❏ 1195	I Won't Be Lonesome/Secret of Love	1970	$8
❏ 1193	My Girl of the Village/The Monkey Played Fiddle	1969	$10
❏ 1192	Take Me in Your Arms/Top Rocking Joe	1969	$10
❏ 1202	Where Can I Go/His Own Troubles	1970	$8
MERCURY			
❏ 73784	Always Late (With Your Kisses)/Knock, Knock, Knock	1976	$5
❏ 55002	Cajun Born/It Don't Hurt Me Half As Bad	1977	$5
❏ 73655	Cajun Woman/Blue Is Not a Word	1975	$5
❏ 73796	He's Still All Over You/Am I Just Your Friend	1976	$5
❏ 73702	I've Been Around Enough to Know/Brighter Shade of Blue	1975	$5
❏ 73824	Showboat Gambler/Cheatin' Turns Her On	1976	$5
RCA			
❏ 8918-7-R	(Blue, Blue, Blue) Blue, Blue/I've Got Dreams to Remember	1989	$3
❏ 5282-7-R	Come On Joe/Say You Love Me	1987	$3

Number	Title	Yr	NM
❏ 9014-7-R	If You Heart Should Ever Roll This Way Again/You Done Me Wrong	1989	$3
❏ 8304-7-R	Tear-Stained Letter/Say You Love Me	1988	$3

SONNY

Number	Title	Yr	NM
ATCO			
❏ 6369	Laugh at Me/Tony	1965	$15
—B-side credited to "Sonny's Group"			
❏ 6505	Misty Roses/I Told My Girl to Go Away	1967	$10
❏ 6531	Pammie's on a Bummer/My Best Friend's Girl Is Out of Sight	1967	$10
FIDELITY			
❏ 3020	Wearing Black/Don't Have to Tell Me	1960	$30
—As "Don Christy			
GO			
❏ 1001	As Long As You Love Me/I'll Always Be Grateful	1960	$30
—As "Don Christy			
HIGHLAND			
❏ 1160	I'll Change/Try It Out on Me	1963	$40
—As "Sonny Bono			
MCA			
❏ 40271	Our Last Show/Classified 1A	1974	$4
—As "Sonny Bono			
NAME			
❏ 3	As Long As You Love Me/I'll Always Be Grateful	1960	$30
—As "Don Christy			
SPECIALTY			
❏ 733	One Little Answer/Comin' Down the Chimney	1974	$6
—As "Sonny Bono and Little Tootsie			
❏ 672	Wearing Black/One Little Answer	1959	$30
—As "Don Christy			
SWAMI			
❏ 1001	Don't Shake My Tree/(Mama) Come Get Your Baby Boy	1961	$30
—As "Ronny Sommers			
VEE JAY			
❏ 710	Midnight Surf/Ride the Wild Quetzal	1966	$30
—As "Sonny Bono			

SONNY AND CHER

Number	Title	Yr	NM
ATCO			
❏ 6480	A Beautiful Story/Podunk	1967	$10
❏ 6381	But You're Mine/Hello	1965	$15
❏ 6555	Circus/I Would Marry You Today	1968	$10
❏ 6758	Get It Together/Hold Me Tighter	1970	$8
❏ 6541	Good Combination/You and Me	1968	$10
❏ 6420	Have I Stayed Too Long/Leave Me Be	1966	$12
❏ 6359	I Got You Babe/It's Gonna Rain	1965	$15
❏ 6507	It's the Little Things/Don't Talk to Strangers	1967	$10
❏ 6440	Little Man/Monday	1966	$12
❏ 6449	Living for You/Love Don't Come	1966	$10
❏ 6486	Plastic Man/It's the Little Things	1967	$10
❏ 6461	The Beat Goes On/Love Don't Come	1967	$15
❏ 6395	What Now My Love/I Look for You	1965	$15
KAPP			
❏ 2163	A Cowboy's Work Is Never Done/Somebody	1972	$5
❏ 2151	All I Ever Need Is You/I Got You Babe	1971	$5
❏ 2176	When You Say Love/Crystal Clear and Muddy Waters	1972	$4
MCA			
❏ 40026	Mama Was a Rock and Roll Singer, Papa Used to Write All Her Songs (Parts 1 & 2)	1973	$4
❏ 40083	The Greatest Show on Earth/You Know Darn Well	1973	$4
PHILCO-FORD			
❏ HP-8	I Got You Babe/The Beat Goes On	1967	$30
—4-inch plastic "Hip Pocket Record" with color sleeve			
REPRISE			
❏ 0723	Baby Don't Go/Love Is Strange	1968	$5
—Back to Back Hits" series -- originals have both "r:" and "W7" logos			

Number	Title	Yr	NM
0309	Baby Don't Go/Walkin' the Quetzal	1964	$30
0392	Baby Don't Go/Walkin' the Quetzal	1965	$20
0308	Love Is Strange/Do You Want to Dance	1964	$30
— As "Caesar and Cleo			
0419	Love Is Strange/Let the Good Times Roll	1965	$30
— As "Caesar and Cleo			
0419 [PS]	Love Is Strange/Let the Good Times Roll	1965	$50
— As "Caesar and Cleo			

VAULT

Number	Title	Yr	NM
909	The Letter/Spring Fever	1964	$40
— As "Caesar and Cleo			
916	The Letter/Spring Fever	1965	$15
916 [PS]	The Letter/Spring Fever	1965	$60

7-Inch Extended Plays

ATCO

Number	Title	Yr	NM
LSD 33-177	It's Gonna Rain/You've Really Got a Hold on Me//I Got You Babe/The Letter/Why Don't They Let Us Fall in Love	1965	$30
— Jukebox issue; small hole, plays at 33 1/3 rpm			
LSD 33-177 [PS]	Look At Us	1965	$30

KAPP

Number	Title	Yr	NM
34875 [PS]	All I Ever Need Is You	1972	$12
— Part of "Little LP" series (LLP #184)			
34875	More Today Than Yesterday/I Love What You Did With The Love I Gave You/Here Comes That Rainy Day Feeling//Crystal Clear-Muddy Waters/United We Stand/All I Ever Need Is You	1972	$10
— Jukebox issue; small hole, plays at 33 1/3 rpm			

SONS OF CHAMPLIN, THE

ARIOLA AMERICA

Number	Title	Yr	NM
7653	Follow Your Heart/Here Is Where Your Love Belongs	1976	$4
7627	Hold On/Still in Love with You	1976	$4
7606	Look Out/Queen of the Rain	1975	$4
7664	Saved by the Grace of Your Love/West End	1977	$4

CAPITOL

Number	Title	Yr	NM
2437	1982-A/Black and Blue Rainbow	1969	$8
2534	Freedom/Hello Sunlight	1969	$8
2663	It's Time/Why Do People Run	1969	$8

COLUMBIA

Number	Title	Yr	NM
45872	Welcome to the Dance/Swim	1973	$5

GOLDMINE

Number	Title	Yr	NM
101	Look Out/Queen of the Rain	1975	$5

VERVE

Number	Title	Yr	NM
10500	Sing Me a Lullaby/Fat City	1967	$30

SONS OF ROBIN STONE

ATCO

Number	Title	Yr	NM
6929	Got to Get You Back/Love Is Just Around the Corner	1974	$100

EPIC

Number	Title	Yr	NM
8-50257	Let's Do It Now/It Only Happens in the Movies	1976	$75

SONS OF THE PIONEERS

CORAL

Number	Title	Yr	NM
9-61316	Montana/Lonely Little Room	1954	$30
9-64172	Sierra Nevada/If You Would Only Be Mine	1954	$30

DECCA

Number	Title	Yr	NM
9-29814	Cool Water/Tumbling Tumbleweeds	1956	$20

GRANITE

Number	Title	Yr	NM
550	Cool Water/Pretty Painted Ladies	1976	$6
551	Indian Woman/(B-side unknown)	1977	$6

RCA VICTOR

Number	Title	Yr	NM
47-7392	A Fiddle, a Rifle, an Ax and a Bible/My Last Goodbye	1958	$15
47-3983	America Forever/Little White Cross	1950	$30
WBY-27	A Whale of a Tale/Old Betsy	1955	$30
47-7024	Ballad of the Cowboy Sailor/The Piney Woods	1957	$20
47-6184	Be What You Want to Be/Epidemic	1955	$20
48-0007	Blue Prairie/Cowboy Camp Meetin'	1949	$40
— Green vinyl original			
48-0007	Blue Prairie/Cowboy Camp Meetin'	1949	$30
— Black vinyl reissue			
48-0183	Cigareets, Whusky and Wild, Wild Women/My Best to You	1950	$40
— Green vinyl; reissue of hit 78 rpm from 1947			
48-0004	Cool Water/Chant of the Wanderer	1949	$40
— Green vinyl original			
47-2836	Cool Water/Chant of the Wanderer	1949	$40
48-0004	Cool Water/Chant of the Wanderer	1951	$30
— Black vinyl reissue			
47-8310	Crazy Arms/Cattle Call Rondolet	1963	$12
47-4131	Daddy's Little Cowboy/Baby I Ain't Gonna Cry No More	1951	$30
47-8575	Destiny/Green Ice and Mountain Men	1965	$12
47-4639	Diesel Smoke/Almost	1952	$30
47-6655	For the Love of You/Timmy's Tune	1956	$20
47-9509	Gringo's Guitar/Margretta	1968	$8
47-4264	Heart Break Hill/The Wind	1951	$30
47-7079	High Ridin' Woman/God Has His Arms Around Me	1957	$20
WBY-46	Home on the Range/Cheyenne	1957	$30
WBY-46 [PS]	Home on the Range/Cheyenne	1957	$40
47-6376	How Great Thou Art/The Last Frontier	1956	$20
47-4459	I Told Them All About You/Ho-Le-O	1952	$30
47-6109	I Wonder When We'll Ever Know/The King's Highway	1955	$20
48-0366	Land Beyond the Sun/I Told Them All About You	1950	$30
— Green vinyl original			
47-4571	Land Beyond the Sun/Waltz of the Roses	1952	$30
48-0095	Lead Me Gently Home Father/Power in the Blood	1949	$40
— Green vinyl original			
48-0184	Let's Go West Again/Let Me Share Your Name	1950	$40
— Green vinyl original			
47-4937	Let's Pretend/The Everlasting Hills of Oklahoma	1952	$30
48-0101	Lie Low Little Doggies/Bar None Ranch	1949	$40
— Green vinyl original			
48-0486	Lonesome/The Wondrous Word	1951	$30
47-4072	Moonlight and Roses/Bring Your Roses to Her Now	1951	$30
48-0368	Old Man Atom/What This Country Needs	1950	$30
— Green vinyl original			
47-6890	One More Time/Hasta La Vista	1957	$20
47-4431	Outlaws/I Still Do	1951	$30
47-4073	San Antonio Rose/Room Full of Roses	1951	$30
— The above three comprise a box set			
48-0345	Song of the Wagonmaster/Chuckawalla Swing	1950	$30
— Green vinyl original			
74-0199	Talli Wind/Hawaiian Lullaby	1969	$8
48-0220	Teardrops in My Heart/You Don't Know What Lonesome Is	1950	$40
— Green vinyl; reissue of hit 78 from 1947			
47-6055	The Ballad of Davy Crockett/Graveyard Filler of the West	1955	$30
WBY-25	The Ballad of Davy Crockett/The Graveyard Filler of the West	1955	$40
WBY-25 [PS]	The Ballad of Davy Crockett/The Graveyard Filler of the West	1955	$60
47-4347	The Lord's Prayer/Resurectus	1951	$30
48-0096	The Old Rugged Cross/Read the Bible Every Day	1949	$40
— Green vinyl original			
47-6507	The Searchers/Song of the Prodigal Son	1956	$20
48-0221	The Sea Walker/The Touch of God's Hand	1950	$40
— Green vinyl original			
47-6123	The Tennessee Rock 'n' Roll/The Three of Us	1955	$30
48-0006	Trees/The Timber Trail	1949	$40
— Green vinyl original			
48-0006	Trees/The Timber Trail	1949	$30
— Black vinyl reissue			
47-2838	Trees/The Timber Trail	1949	$40
— The above three comprise a box set; quickly reissued as 48-0004, 0005 and 0006			
48-0005	Tumbling Tumbleweeds/Everlasting Hills of Oklahoma	1949	$40
— Green vinyl original			
48-0005	Tumbling Tumbleweeds/Everlasting Hills of Oklahoma	1949	$30
— Black vinyl reissue			
47-2837	Tumbling Tumbleweeds/The Everlasting Hills of Oklahoma	1949	$40
48-0171	Wedding Bells/Love at the County Fair	1950	$40
— With Dale Evans; green vinyl original			
48-0388	Where Are You/What This Country Needs	1950	$30
— Green vinyl original			
EPA651	Cowboy Lament/Pajarillo Barrenquero/So Long to the Red River Valley/Come and Get It/Cool Water/Curly Joe from Idaho/Cowboy's Dream/Along the Santa Fe Trail	1955	$25
EPA422	Empty Saddles/There's a Gold Mine in the Sky//Home on the Range/Old Pioneer	1952	$30
EPA651 [PS]	Favorite Cowboy Songs Vol. 2	1955	$25
EPA650 [PS]	Favorite Cowboy Songs Vol. I	1955	$25
EPA422 [PS]	Sons of the Pioneers Sing Western Favorites	1952	$30
EPA650	Tumbling Tumbleweeds/Press Along to the Big Corral/Wind/Bunkhouse Bugle Boy//Home on the Range/La Borachita/Timber Trail/Happy Cowboy	1955	$25

SOOTZ, MANNY

PIRATE

Number	Title	Yr	NM
841	Cape Canaveral (Part 1)/Cape Canaveral (Part 2)	1957	$30

SOPHISTICATES, THE

VIVA

Number	Title	Yr	NM
61	When Elvis Comes Marching Home/Woody's Place	1960	$60

SOPHOMORES, THE (1)

CHORD

Number	Title	Yr	NM
1302	Charades/What Can I Do	1957	$50

DAWN

Number	Title	Yr	NM
237	Checkers/Each Time I Hold You	1958	$30
216	Cool, Cool Baby/Every Night About This Time	1956	$30
228	I Just Can't Keep the Tears from Tumblin' Down/If I Should Lose Your Love	1957	$30
225	Is There Someone for Me/Everybody Loves Me	1957	$30
218	Linda/I Get a Thrill	1956	$30
223	Ocean Blue/I Left My Sugar	1956	$30

EPIC

Number	Title	Yr	NM
9259	Charades/What Can I Do	1957	$30

SOPHOMORES, THE (2)

SOUND STAGE 7

Number	Title	Yr	NM
2533	Summer of '64/I Know I Should (Every Night)	1964	$10

SOPWITH "CAMEL," THE

KAMA SUTRA

Number	Title	Yr	NM
236	Great Morpheum/Saga of the Lowdown Letdown	1967	$15
236 [PS]	Great Morpheum/Saga of the Lowdown Letdown	1967	$15
217	Hello Hello/Treadin'	1966	$15
224	Postcard from Jamaica/Little Orphan Annie	1967	$15
224 [PS]	Postcard from Jamaica/Little Orphan Annie	1967	$30

REPRISE

Number	Title	Yr	NM
1179	Sleazy Love/Fazon	1973	$8

SORROWS, THE

WARNER BROS.

Number	Title	Yr	NM
5662	Take a Heart/We Should Get Along Fine	1965	$30

SOSEBEE, TOMMY

CORAL

Number	Title	Yr	NM
9-64110	Don't Trade Your Love for Gold/If You Don't Believe I'm Leaving	1951	$30
9-64158	Honky Tonk Waltz/Love Me	1953	$30
9-64120	How Can You Smile/Don't Waste Your Tears	1952	$30
9-64183	If I Give My Heart to You/Don't Count Me Out	1954	$30

Number	Title	Yr	NM
❏ 9-64071	I'm So Lonesome/You Can't Erase My Memory	1951	$30
❏ 9-64154	Love Is Deeper Than Pride/Nervous Feeling	1953	$30
❏ 9-64087	Mail Order Kisses/You're Always Brand New	1951	$30
❏ 9-64134	Many Miles/Pretty Little Girl	1952	$30
❏ 9-64144	Saviour of the Rugged Cross/The Lord Lives at Your House	1952	$30
❏ 9-64080	She's My Easter Lily/Easter Parade	1951	$30
❏ 9-64164	The Barber Shop Boogie/Anywhere, Anyplace, Anytime	1953	$30
❏ 9-64094	The Singing Hills/You're Fixin' to Break My Heart	1951	$30
❏ 9-60916	Till I Waltz Again with You/All Night Boogie	1953	$30
❏ 9-61406	Time/That's What I Call Love	1955	$30
❏ 9-64097	Wedding Blossoms/Honesick, Lonesome and Sorry	1951	$30
❏ 9-64107	Winter Wonderland/New Year Bells	1951	$40

SOUL AGENTS, THE
CAMEO
❏ 350	Let's Make It Pretty Baby/The Seventh Son	1965	$40

INTERPHON
❏ 7702	I Just Want to Make Love to You/Mean Woman Blues	1964	$30

SOUL ASYLUM
TWIN/TONE
❏ TTR8560	Tied to the Tracks/Long Way Home	1985	$15
❏ TTR8560 [PS]	Tied to the Tracks/Long Way Home	1985	$15

SOUL BROTHERS SIX
ATLANTIC
❏ 2592	Somebody Else Is Loving My Baby/Thank You Baby for Loving Me	1969	$15
❏ 2406	Some Kind of Wonderful/I'll Be Loving You	1967	$20
❏ 2645	What You Got (Is So Good for Me)/Drive	1969	$15

PHIL-L.A. OF SOUL
❏ 355	Funky Funky Way of Making Love/Let Me Be the One	1972	$6
❏ 365	Let Me Do What We Ain't Doin'/Lost the Will to Live	1974	$6

SOUL CLAN, THE
ATLANTIC
❏ 2530	Soul Meeting/That's How It Feels	1968	$12
❏ 2530 [PS]	Soul Meeting/That's How It Feels	1968	$20

SOUL COMFORTERS, THE
HOLLYWOOD
❏ 1042	White Christmas/Silent Night	1955	$40

SOUL, DAVID
MGM
❏ 13510	The Covered Man/I Will Warm Your Heart	1966	$12
❏ 13589	Was I Ever So Wrong/Before	1966	$10

PRIVATE STOCK
❏ 45,129	Don't Give Up on Us/Black Bean Soup	1976	$4
❏ 45,150	Going In with My Eyes Open/Topanga	1977	$4
❏ 45,163	Silver Lady/The Rider	1977	$4

SOUL GENERATION, THE
EBONY SOUNDS
❏ 181	I Wonder What She's Doin'/Key to Your Heart	1973	$15
❏ 176	Million Dollars/Super Fine	1973	$10
❏ 181	Praying for a Miracle/In Your Way	1974	$20
❏ 175	That's the Way It's Got to Be (Body and Soul)/Mandingo Woman	1972	$12

SOUL, JIMMY
SPQR
❏ 3314	Change Partners/I Hate You Baby	1963	$15
❏ 3312	Go 'Way Christina/Everybody's Gone Ape	1963	$15
❏ 3304	Guess Things Happen That Way/My Baby Loves to Bowl	1963	$15
❏ 3305	If You Wanna Be Happy/Don't Release Me	1963	$20
❏ 3305 [PS]	If You Wanna Be Happy/Don't Release Me	1963	$40

Number	Title	Yr	NM
❏ 3315	My Girl-She Sure Can Cook/A Woman Is Smarter in Every Kinda Way	1964	$10
❏ 3221	My Little Room/Ella Is Yella	1964	$10
❏ 3310	Treat 'Em Tough/Church Street in the Summertime	1963	$15
❏ 3300	Twistin' Matilda/I Can't Hold Out Any Longer	1962	$15
❏ 3319	Twistin' Matilda/Treat 'Em Tough	1964	$10
❏ 3302	When Matilda Comes Back/Some Kinda Nut	1962	$15

SOUL, JOHNNY
FEDERAL
❏ 12557	I Want Some/Darling, Darling, I Love You	1970	$30

SSS INTERNATIONAL
❏ 763	I Almost Called Your Name/Take Me Where the Sun Never Shines	1969	$50
❏ 785	Lonely Man/Come and Get It	1970	$40

SOUL SISTERS, THE
GUYDEN
❏ 2066	The Warm-Up/Because I Love You	1962	$30

KAYO
❏ 5101	I Can't Let Him Go/(B-side unknown)	1963	$30

SUE
❏ 140	Flashback/Give Me Some Satisfaction	1966	$20
❏ Oct-005	Good Time Tonight/Foolish Dreamer	1964	$20
❏ 799	I Can't Stand It/Blueberry Hill	1964	$20
❏ 107	Loop de Loop/Long Gone	1964	$20
❏ 130	Think About the Good Times/The Right Time	1965	$20

VEEP
❏ 1291	A Thousand Mountains/You Got 'Em Beat	1968	$15

SOUL SOCIETY, THE
DOT
❏ 17136	Sidewinder/Afro-Desia	1968	$10

SOUL SURFERS, THE
CHALLENGE
❏ 9209	Cannonball/Home from Camp	1963	$50
❏ 59249	Cannonball/In the Misty Moonlight	1964	$20

— B-side by Jerry Wallace

SOUL SURVIVORS
ATCO
❏ 6735	Still Got My Head/Tempting 'Bout to Get Me	1970	$8
❏ 6650	Tell Daddy/Mama Soul	1969	$8
❏ 6627	Turn Out the Fire/Go Out Walking	1968	$8

CRIMSON
❏ 1012	Explosion (In My Soul)/Dathon's Theme	1967	$10
❏ 1010	Expressway to Your Heart/Hey Gyp	1967	$15
❏ 1016	Poor Man's Dream/Impossible Mission	1968	$12

DECCA
❏ 32080	Devil with a Blue Dress On/Shakin' with Linda	1967	$20

DOT
❏ 16830	Hung Up on Losin'/Snow Man	1966	$15
❏ 16793	Look at Me/Can't Stand to Be in Love with You	1965	$30

PHILADELPHIA INT'L.
❏ 3595	Happy Birthday America (Part 1)/Happy Birthday America (Part 2)	1976	$5
❏ 3595 [PS]	Happy Birthday America (Part 1)/Happy Birthday America (Part 2)	1976	$8

TSOP
❏ 4756	City of Brotherly Love/The Best Time Was the Last Time	1974	$6
❏ 4760	What It Takes/Virgin Girl	1974	$20

SOULFUL STRINGS, THE
CADET
❏ 5654	A Love Song/Zabezi	1969	$6
❏ 5576	Burning Spear/Within You Without You	1968	$6
❏ 5633	I Wish It Would Rain/Listen Here	1969	$6
❏ 5559	Paint It Black/Love Is a Hurtin' Thing	1967	$6

Number	Title	Yr	NM
❏ 5607	(Sittin' On) The Dock of the Bay/The Stripper	1968	$6
❏ 5617	The Who Who Song/Jericho	1968	$6

SOUND SYMPOSIUM, THE
DOT
❏ 17296	The Mighty Quinn/I'll Be Your Baby Tonight	1969	$10

SOUNDGARDEN
SUB POP
❏ 12a [PS]	Hunted Down/Nothing to Say	1987	$60

— Special blue sleeve (not a PS) with above

SOUNDS, INC.
LIBERTY
❏ 55789	In the Hall of the Mountain King/Time for You	1965	$8
❏ 55844	On the Brink/I Am Comin' Thru	1965	$8
❏ 55709	The Spartans/Detroit	1964	$8

SOUNDS LIKE US
FONTANA
❏ 1570	Outside Chance/Clock on the Wall	1967	$50

JILL ANN
❏ 101	Outside Chance/Clock on the Wall	1966	$70

SOMA
❏ 8108	It Was a Very Good Year/The Other Side of the Record	1967	$60

SOUNDS OF OUR TIMES, THE
CAPITOL
❏ 2291	Hey Jude/Harper Valley P.T.A.	1968	$20

— Collectible for its inexplicable error in composer's credit on "Hey Jude," claiming the song was written by "Paul Lennon" and "John McCartney"!
❏ 2109	The Look of Love/A Whiter Shade of Pale	1968	$8

SOUNDS ORCHESTRAL
JANUS
❏ 124	Love in the Shadows/Louie, Louie	1970	$6

PARKWAY
❏ 968	A Boy and a Girl/Go Home Girl	1966	$8
❏ 155	A Man and a Woman/West of Carnaby	1967	$8
❏ 958	Canadian Sunset/Have Faith in Your Love	1965	$8
❏ 942	Cast Your Fate to the Wind/To Wendy With Love	1965	$10
❏ 120	Pretty Flamingo/Sounds Like Jacques	1966	$8
❏ 973	Thunderball/Mr. Kiss Kiss Bang Bang	1966	$8

SOUNDS UNLIMITED
DUNWICH
❏ 157	A Girl As Sweet As You/Little Brother	1967	$30

SOUTH 40
METROBEAT
❏ 4457	I Want Sunshine/Goin' Someplace Else	1968	$15
❏ 4450	The Penny Song/Good Lovin'	1967	$15

SOUTH, JOE
APT
❏ 25084	Deep Inside Me/I Want to Be Somebody	1965	$12

CAPITOL
❏ 2060	Birds of a Feather/It Got Away	1967	$8
❏ 2532	Birds of a Feather/These Are Not My People	1969	$6
❏ 2755	Children/The Clock Up On the Wall	1970	$5
❏ 2592	Don't It Make You Want to Go Home/Heart's Desire	1969	$6
❏ 3204	Fool Me/Devil May Care	1971	$5
❏ 2248	Games People Play/Mirror of Your Mind	1968	$8
❏ 2169	How Can I Unlove You/She's Almost You	1968	$8
❏ 3487	I'm a Star/Misunderstanding	1972	$5
❏ 2491	Leanin' On You/Don't You Be Ashamed	1969	$6
❏ 3450	One Man Band/Coming Down All Alone	1972	$5

Number	Title	Yr	NM
❑ 2704	Walk a Mile in My Shoes/Sheltered	1969	$6
❑ 2916	Why Does a Man Do What He Has to Do/Be a Believer	1970	$5

COLUMBIA

Number	Title	Yr	NM
❑ 44218	A Fool in Love/Great Day	1967	$15
❑ 43983	Backfield in Motion/I'll Come Back to You	1967	$15

FAIRLANE

Number	Title	Yr	NM
❑ 21010	Masquerade/I'm Sorry for You	1961	$20
❑ 21015	Slippin' Around/Just to Be with You Again	1962	$20

ISLAND

Number	Title	Yr	NM
❑ 034	To Have, to Hold and Let Go/Midnight Rainbows	1975	$4

MGM

Number	Title	Yr	NM
❑ 13196	Concrete Jungle/The Last One to Know	1963	$10
❑ 13145	Same Old Song/Standing Invitation	1963	$10

NRC

Number	Title	Yr	NM
❑ 022	Chills/What a Night	1959	$20
❑ 02	I'm Snowed/It's Only You	1958	$50
❑ 065	Let's Talk It Over/Formality	1961	$20
❑ 041	Little Bluebird/Play It Cool	1959	$20
❑ 5001	One Fool to Another/Texas Ain't the Biggest Anymore	1958	$20
❑ 053	Tell the Truth/If You Only Knew Her	1960	$20
❑ 5000	The Purple People Eater Meets the Witch Doctor/My Fondest Memories	1958	$20

SOUTH STREET MISSION BAND
CAMEO

Number	Title	Yr	NM
❑ 415	Theme from The Young Ones/Hooka Tooka	1966	$10

SOUTHERN REIGN
REGAL

Number	Title	Yr	NM
❑ 2	15 to 33/Sugary Sam	1986	$5
❑ 3	Summer on the Mississippi/(B-side unknown)	1987	$5
❑ 1	The Auction/(B-side unknown)	1986	$5

STEP ONE

Number	Title	Yr	NM
❑ 377	Cheap Motels (And One Night Stands)/Summer on the Mississippi	1987	$4
❑ 385	Please Don't Leave Me Now/I Don't Think I Want to Love You Anymore	1988	$4
❑ 391	There's a Telephone Ringing (In an Empty House)/Excuse Me for Loving You	1988	$4

SOUTHSIDE JOHNNY AND THE ASBURY JUKES
ATLANTIC

Number	Title	Yr	NM
❑ 89356	Tell Me/I Can't Wait	1986	$3
❑ 89394	Walk Away Renee/I Can't Wait	1986	$3

EPIC

Number	Title	Yr	NM
❑ 50393	First Night/Without Love	1977	$5
❑ 50466	Love on the Wrong Side of Town/Some Things You Don't Change	1977	$5
❑ 50238	The Fever/I Don't Want to Go Home	1976	$5
❑ 50646	Trapped Again/This Time Baby's Gone for Good	1979	$4

MERCURY

Number	Title	Yr	NM
❑ 76007	I'm So Anxious/Your Reply	1979	$4
❑ 76074	On the Beach/Goodbye Love	1980	$4
❑ 76023	Wait in Vain/Living in the Real World	1979	$4

MIRAGE

Number	Title	Yr	NM
❑ 99698	Actions Speak Louder Than Words/Love Is the Drug	1984	$4
❑ 99802	Get Your Body on the Job/Slow Burn	1983	$4
❑ 99839	Ms. Park Ave./Trash It Up	1983	$4

SOUTHWEST F.O.B.
GPC

Number	Title	Yr	NM
❑ 1945	Smell of Incense/Green Skies	1968	$30

HIP

Number	Title	Yr	NM
❑ 8022	Feelin' Groovy/Beggar Man	1969	$10
❑ 8015	Independent Me/As I Look at You	1969	$10
❑ 8002	Smell of Incense/Green Skies	1968	$12

SOUTHWEST HIGH SCHOOL CHOIR
COLUMBIA

Number	Title	Yr	NM
❑ 41295	God's Christmas Tree/Great Somebody	1958	$15

SOUVENIRS, THE
DOOTO

Number	Title	Yr	NM
❑ 412	So Long Daddy/Arlene, Sweet Little Texas Queen	1957	$60

INFERNO

Number	Title	Yr	NM
❑ 2001	I Could Have Danced All Night/It's Too Bad	1967	$60

REPRISE

Number	Title	Yr	NM
❑ 20065	The Worm/The Bump	1962	$20

SOVINE, RED, AND GOLDIE HILL
DECCA

Number	Title	Yr	NM
❑ 9-29411	Are You Mine/Ko Ko Mo	1955	$20

SOVINE, RED
CHART

Number	Title	Yr	NM
❑ 5230	Can I Keep Him Daddy/Red's So Fine	1974	$5
❑ 7507	Daddy's Girl/(B-side unknown)	1975	$5
❑ 5161	Down Through the Years/Petunia	1972	$5
❑ 5216	From Champagne to Beer/Mama's Birthday	1974	$5
❑ 5220	It'll Come Back/Down Through the Years	1974	$5
❑ 5207	Midnight Rider/Why the Grass Is Green	1974	$5
❑ 5142	Old Pine Tree/Two Hearts on a Post Card	1971	$5
❑ 5231	Santa Claus Is a Texas Cowboy/The Legend of the Christmas Rose	1974	$5
❑ 5152	Six Broken Hearts/The Greatest Grand Ol' Opry	1972	$5
❑ 5176	The Guilty One/The Day the Preacher Came	1973	$5

DECCA

Number	Title	Yr	NM
❑ 31028	A Lot Like You/Ooooh How I Love You	1959	$10
❑ 30162	A Poor Man's Riches/Down on the Corner of Love	1956	$15
❑ 30920	Cold Hands of Fate/One Sided Love Affair	1959	$10
❑ 30715	Courtin' Time in Tennessee/Where Will Mommie Go	1958	$15
❑ 29211	Don't Drop It/Don't Be the One	1954	$20
❑ 29825	If Jesus Came to Your House/I Got Religion	1956	$20
❑ 29529	I Hope You Don't Care/I'm Glad You Found a Place for Me	1955	$20
❑ 29876	Little Rosa/Hold Everything (Till I Get Home)	1956	$20

—A-side with Webb Pierce

Number	Title	Yr	NM
❑ 29068	My New Love Affair/How Do You Think I Feel	1954	$20
❑ 30595	Once More/For Arms	1958	$15
❑ 29335	Outlaw/Which One Should I Choose	1954	$20
❑ 30018	The Best Years of Your Life/My Little Rat	1956	$15
❑ 29755	Why Baby Why/Missing You	1955	$20

—A-side with Webb Pierce

Number	Title	Yr	NM
❑ 29739	Why Baby Why/Sixteen Tons	1955	$30

—A-side with Webb Pierce

Number	Title	Yr	NM
❑ 30458	Wrong/Who Knows Better Than You and I	1957	$15

GUSTO

Number	Title	Yr	NM
❑ 9005	A Place for Mama's Roses/Does Steppin' Out Mean Daddy Took a Walk	1978	$4
❑ 9015	Christmas Is For Kids/What Does Christmas Look Like	1978	$4
❑ 9030	It'll Come Back/Love Is	1980	$4
❑ 175	Lay Down Sally/The Farmers and the Miners	1978	$4
❑ 180	Lay Down Sally/The King's Last Concert	1978	$6
❑ 9017	Mr. F.C.C./Flesh and Blood	1979	$4
❑ 188	The Days of Me and You/I'd Love to Make Love	1978	$4
❑ 9026	The First Time I Saw Her/18 Wheels a-Hummin' Home Sweet Home	1980	$4
❑ 9021	The Hero/Flesh and Blood	1979	$4
❑ 9028	The Little Family Soldier/She Was Loving Me Goodbye	1980	$4
❑ 9019	The Prettiest Dress/Flesh and Blood	1979	$4
❑ 9016	The Waylon and Willie Machine/Colorado Cool-Aid	1979	$5
❑ 169	Woman Behind the Man Behind the Wheel/Jealous Heart	1977	$4

MGM

Number	Title	Yr	NM
❑ 10887	Billy Goat Boogie/Big Dipper	1951	$30
❑ 10782	Christmas Day/Dear Mister Santa Claus	1950	$30
❑ 11090	Don't Worry/Sundown Sue	1951	$30
❑ 10981	Four Flusher/Farewell, So Long	1951	$30
❑ 11214	It'd Surprise You/Loveless Marriage	1952	$30
❑ 11323	Okey Dokey/Till Today	1952	$30

Number	Title	Yr	NM
❑ 10717	When I Get Rich/You're Barking Up the Wrong Tree	1950	$30

RCA VICTOR

Number	Title	Yr	NM
❑ 47-7981	The Cajun Queen/Big Dreams	1962	$15

RIC

Number	Title	Yr	NM
❑ 131	Big Ol' Ugly Fool/Hiding Out	1964	$8
❑ 168	I Wish I Had Seen Sunshine/Salt on My Eggs	1965	$8
❑ 154	Losing My Grip/Star of the Show	1965	$8

STARDAY

Number	Title	Yr	NM
❑ 774	Alabam/Nobody's Business	1966	$8

— With Minnie Pearl

Number	Title	Yr	NM
❑ 857	Between Closing Time and Dawn/The Father of Judy Ann	1968	$8
❑ 864	Blues Stay Away from Me/Whiskey Flavored Kisses	1969	$6
❑ 510	Burn the School/One Is a Lonely Number	1960	$10
❑ 885	Castle of Shame/Why Don't You Haul Off and Love Me	1969	$6

— With Lois Williams

Number	Title	Yr	NM
❑ 779	Class of '49/I Hope My Wife Don't Find Out	1966	$8
❑ 567	Color of the Blues/Hold Everything	1961	$10
❑ 158	Daddy's Girl/Love Is All She Ever Wants from Me	1977	$4
❑ 650	Dream House for Sale/King of the Open Road	1963	$12
❑ 579	East of West Berlin/Thanks for Nothing	1962	$12
❑ 915	Enough to Take the Me Out of Men/I'm Waiting Just for You	1970	$6
❑ 896	Freightliner Fever/Mr. Sunday Sun	1970	$6
❑ 926	Get in Touch/Violets Blue	1971	$6
❑ 737	Giddyup Go/A Kiss and the Keys	1965	$8
❑ 137	Giddyup Go/Tonight My Lady Learns to Love	1976	$4
❑ 960	Go Hide John/Tear Stained Guitar	1973	$5
❑ 933	Happy Birthday, My Darlin'/I'll Sail My Ship Alone	1971	$6
❑ 553	Heart of a Man/Brand New Low	1961	$12
❑ 934	I Am a Pilgrim/Beautiful Life	1971	$6
❑ 794	I Didn't Jump the Fence/Don't Let My Glass Run Dry	1967	$8
❑ 889	I Know You're Married But I Love You Still/Money, Marbles and Chalk	1970	$6
❑ 152	I'm Only Seventeen/No One's Too Big to Cry	1977	$4
❑ 766	I'm the Man/I Think I Can Sleep Tonight	1966	$8
❑ 147	Last Goodbye/Lonely Arms of Mine	1976	$4
❑ 144	Little Joe/Cold Love to Go	1976	$4
❑ 757	Long Night/Too Much	1966	$8
❑ 842	Loser Making Good/Good Enough for Nothing	1968	$8
❑ 672	Old Pipeliner/Peace of Mind	1964	$10
❑ 101	Phantom 309/(B-side unknown)	1975	$4
❑ 811	Phantom 309/In Your Heart	1967	$10
❑ 616	Sittin' and Thinkin'/A Million to One	1962	$10
❑ 977	Take Time to Remember/(B-side unknown)	1973	$5
❑ 823	Tell Maude I Slipped/Not Like It Was with You	1967	$8
❑ 882	Truck Drivers Prayer/Chairman of the Board	1969	$8
❑ 831	Twenty-One/Sparkling Wine	1968	$8
❑ 632	Waltzing with Sin/I Forgot to Keep Her with Me	1963	$10
❑ 872	Who Am I/Three Hearts in a Tangle	1969	$6
❑ 540	Why Baby Why/Little Rosa	1961	$10

SPACEK, SISSY
ATLANTIC AMERICA

Number	Title	Yr	NM
❑ 99801	If I Can Just Get Through the Night/Honky Tonkin'	1984	$4
❑ 99773	If You Could Only See Me Now/Have I Told You Lately That I Love You	1984	$4
❑ 99847	Lonely But Only for You/Old Home Town	1983	$4
❑ 99847 [PS]	Lonely But Only for You/Old Home Town	1983	$5

MCA

Number	Title	Yr	NM
❑ 41221	Coal Miner's Daughter/I'm a Honky Tonk Girl	1980	$8
❑ 41221 [PS]	Coal Miner's Daughter/I'm a Honky Tonk Girl	1980	$8
❑ 41311	There He Goes/Back in Baby's Arms	1980	$4

SPACEMEN 3
FORCED EXPOSURE

Number	Title	Yr	NM
❑ 017	Transparent Radiation/Honey	1989	$30

Number	Title	Yr	NM
❏ 017 [PS]	Transparent Radiation/Honey	1989	$30
❏ 017	Transparent Radiation/Honey	1989	$80
— Test pressing (25 made)			
❏ 017 [PS]	Transparent Radiation/Honey	1989	$80
—Full-color pasted-on art; accompanied test pressing (25 made)			

SPACEMEN, THE
ALTON

Number	Title	Yr	NM
❏ 254	The Clouds/The Lonely Jet Pilot	1959	$30

SPADES, THE (3)
MAJOR

Number	Title	Yr	NM
❏ 1007	Close to You/I'm on Fire	1959	$70

SPADES, THE (4)
ZERO

Number	Title	Yr	NM
❏ 10001	I Need a Girl/Do You Want to Dance	1965	$70

SPANDAU BALLET
CHRYSALIS

Number	Title	Yr	NM
❏ 2528	Chant No. 1/Feel the Chant	1981	$6
❏ VS842950	Chant No. 1/Lifeline	1985	$3
— Silver label reissue			
❏ VS442770	Communication/ Code of Love	1984	$4
❏ VS842952	Communication/Only When You Leave	1985	$3
— Silver label reissue			
❏ VS442743	Gold/(Live)	1983	$3
❏ VS442743 [PS]	Gold/(Live)	1983	$3
❏ VS442686	Lifeline/Live and Let Live	1983	$6
❏ VS442792	Only When You Leave/ Paint Me Down (Live)	1984	$3
❏ VS442792 [PS]	Only When You Leave/ Paint Me Down (Live)	1984	$3
❏ 2473	To Cut a Long Story Short/(Dub Version)	1981	$6
❏ VS442720	True/Gently	1983	$3
❏ VS442720 [PS]	True/Gently	1983	$3
❏ VS842951	True/Gold	1985	$3
— Silver label reissue			

EPIC

Number	Title	Yr	NM
❏ 34-06664	How Many Lies/ Snakes and Lovers	1987	$3
❏ 34-06664 [PS]	How Many Lies/ Snakes and Lovers	1987	$10
❏ 34-07190	Through the Barricades/ Snakes and Lovers	1987	$6

SPANIELS, THE
BUDDAH

Number	Title	Yr	NM
❏ 153	Goodnight Sweetheart/ Maybe	1969	$8

CALLA

Number	Title	Yr	NM
❏ 172	Fairy Tales/Jealous Heart	1970	$6

CANTERBURY

Number	Title	Yr	NM
❏ 101	Peace of Mind/She Sang to Me/Danny Boy	1974	$5

CHANCE

Number	Title	Yr	NM
❏ 1141	Baby It's You/Bounce	1953	$500
❏ 1141	Baby It's You/Bounce	1953	$2000
— Red vinyl			

NEPTUNE

Number	Title	Yr	NM
❏ 124	I Love You For Sentimental Reasons/Meek Man	1961	$30
— As "Pookie Hudson and the Spaniels			

NORTH AMERICAN

Number	Title	Yr	NM
❏ 1114	Come Back to These Arms/Money Blues	1970	$5
❏ 001	Fairy Tales/Jealous Heart	1970	$5
❏ 002	Stand in Line/Lonely Man	1970	$5

OWL

Number	Title	Yr	NM
❏ 328	Little Goe/The Posse	1973	$5

VEE JAY

Number	Title	Yr	NM
❏ 101	Baby It's You/Bounce	1953	$4500
—Red vinyl			
❏ 101	Baby It's You/Bounce	1953	$800
— Black vinyl, maroon label			
❏ 101	Baby It's You/Bounce	1961	$50
— Black vinyl, black label			
❏ 301	Baby It's You/Heart and Soul	1958	$70
❏ 189	Dear Heart/Why Won't You Dance	1956	$200
❏ 131	Do-Wah/Don'cha Go	1955	$500
— Red vinyl			
❏ 131	Do-Wah/Don'cha Go	1955	$100
❏ 246	Everyone's Laughing/I.O.U.	1957	$70
❏ 178	False Love/Do You Really	1956	$200

Number	Title	Yr	NM
❏ 107	Goodnite, Sweetheart, Goodnite/You Don't Move Me	1953	$800
—Red vinyl; no "Trade Mark Reg" on label			
❏ 107	Goodnite, Sweetheart, Goodnite/You Don't Move Me	1953	$300
— Black vinyl; as "Spanials			
❏ 107	Goodnite, Sweetheart, Goodnite/You Don't Move Me	1953	$200
— Black vinyl, correct spelling			
❏ 350	I Know/Bus Fare Home	1960	$50
❏ 264	I Love You/Crazee Babee	1958	$70
❏ 342	People Will Say We're in Love/The Bells Ring Out	1960	$125
❏ 116	Play It Cool/Let's Make Up	1954	$500
— Red vinyl			
❏ 116	Play It Cool/Let's Make Up	1954	$125
❏ 229	Please Don't Tease/You Gave Me Peace of Mind	1956	$70
❏ 202	Since I Fell for You/Baby Come Along with Me	1956	$200
❏ 290	Stormy Weather/Here Is Why I Love You	1958	$70
❏ 103	The Bells Ring Out/ House Cleaning	1953	$600
— Red vinyl			
❏ 103	The Bells Ring Out/ House Cleaning	1953	$300
❏ 328	These Three Words/100 Years from Today	1959	$70
❏ 278	Tina/Great Googly Moo	1958	$70
❏ 310	Trees/I Like It Like That	1959	$70

SPANKY AND OUR GANG
EPIC

Number	Title	Yr	NM
❏ 50206	L.A. Freeway/Standing Room Only	1976	$5
❏ 50170	When I Wanna/I Won't Brand You	1975	$5

MERCURY

Number	Title	Yr	NM
❏ 72926	And She's Mine/Leopard Skinned Phones	1969	$8
❏ 72598	And Your Bird Can Sing/ Sealed with a Kiss	1966	$30
❏ 72890	Anything You Choose/ Mecca Flat Blues	1969	$8
❏ 72982	Everybody's Talkin'/ (B-side unknown)	1969	$8
❏ DJ-101 [DJ]	Give a Damn (mono/stereo)	1968	$15
— Special promo for the New York Urban Coalition			
❏ DJ-101 [PS]	Give a Damn (mono/stereo)	1968	$30
— Fold-open sleeve with insert letter			
❏ 72831	Give a Damn/Swinging Gate	1968	$8
❏ 72732	Lazy Day/(It Ain't Necessarily) Byrd Avenue	1967	$8
❏ 72732 [PS]	Lazy Day/(It Ain't Necessarily) Byrd Avenue	1967	$12
❏ 72795	Like to Get to Know You/ Three Ways from Tomorrow	1968	$8
— Orange and tan swirl label			
❏ 72795 [PS]	Like to Get to Know You/ Three Ways from Tomorrow	1968	$12
❏ 72795	Like to Get to Know You/ Three Ways from Tomorrow	1968	$12
— Red label with white "Mercury" in all caps across top of label			
❏ 72714	Making Every Minute Count/ If You Could Only Be Me	1967	$8
❏ 72714 [PS]	Making Every Minute Count/ If You Could Only Be Me	1967	$10
❏ 72765	Sunday Morning/Echoes	1968	$8
❏ 72765 [PS]	Sunday Morning/Echoes	1968	$10
❏ 72679	Sunday Will Never Be the Same/Distance	1967	$8

PHILCO-FORD

Number	Title	Yr	NM
❏ HP-19	Making Every Minute Count/Byrd Avenue	1968	$20
—4-inch plastic "Hip Pocket Record" with color sleeve			

SPANN, OTIS
CHECKER

Number	Title	Yr	NM
❏ 807	It Must Have Been the Devil/Five Spot	1954	$1200

SPARKS
ATLANTIC

Number	Title	Yr	NM
❏ 89797	All You Ever Think About Is Sex/I Wish I Looked a Little Better	1983	$3
❏ 89866	Cool Places/Sports	1983	$3
—A-side: Sparks and Jane Wiedlin			
❏ 89866 [PS]	Cool Places/Sports	1983	$4
❏ 4065	Eaten by the Monster of Love/Mickey Mouse	1982	$3
❏ 4030	I Predict/Moustache	1982	$3
❏ 4030 [PS]	I Predict/Moustache	1982	$4
❏ 89616	Pretending to Be Drunk/ Kiss Me Quick	1984	$3

BEARSVILLE

Number	Title	Yr	NM
❏ 06	Wonder Girl/(No More) Mr. Nice Guys	1972	$10

COLUMBIA

Number	Title	Yr	NM
❏ 10579	Forever Young/ Over the Summer	1977	$20

ELEKTRA

Number	Title	Yr	NM
❏ 46045	Tryouts for the Human Race/No. 1 in Heaven	1979	$5

ISLAND

Number	Title	Yr	NM
❏ 043	Looks, Looks, Looks/ The Wedding of Jackie	1975	$20
❏ 023	Something for the Girl with Everything/Achoo	1975	$5
❏ 009	Talent Is an Asset/ Lost and Found	1974	$5
❏ 001	This Town Ain't Big Enough for Both of Us/Barbecutie	1974	$5

MCA CURB

Number	Title	Yr	NM
❏ 52879	Shopping Mall of Love/Music That You Can Dance To	1986	$3

PRIVATE I

Number	Title	Yr	NM
❏ 05627	Armies of the Night/ Give It Up	1985	$3
— B-side by Evelyn "Champagne" King			

SPARKS OF RHYTHM, THE
APOLLO

Number	Title	Yr	NM
❏ 541	Handy Man/Everybody Rock and Roll	1959	$60
❏ 481	Hurry Home/Stars Are in the Sky	1955	$300
❏ 479	Women, Women, Women/ Don't Love You Anymore	1955	$300

SPARKS, THE
ARWIN

Number	Title	Yr	NM
❏ 114	Something's Happened/ Robin Redbreast	1958	$30

CARLTON

Number	Title	Yr	NM
❏ 522	The Genie/Gee, That's Bad	1959	$30

CUB

Number	Title	Yr	NM
❏ 9151	Woe, Woe/Cool It	1967	$10

DECCA

Number	Title	Yr	NM
❏ 30378	Ol' Man River/ Merry, Merry Lou	1957	$15
❏ 30974	Why Did You Leave/ La Macerena	1959	$10

HULL

Number	Title	Yr	NM
❏ 724	Adreann/Finger	1957	$200
❏ 723	Danny Boy/Run Run Run	1957	$400

SPARKY
CAPITOL

Number	Title	Yr	NM
❏ F1204	I Don't Want a Lot for Christmas/Frosty the Snowman	1950	$20

SPARROW ARTISTS
SPARROW

Number	Title	Yr	NM
❏ SGL0 [DJ]	The Christmas Story/ Christmas ID's	1987	$4

—Artists on this disc: Michael Card, Scott Wesley Brown, Margaret Becker, Steve Camp, Richard Souther, Steven Curtis Chapman, Geoff Moore, Rick Florian (White Heart), Deniece Williams, Steve Green and Billy Smiley (White Heart).

Number	Title	Yr	NM
❏ 0SGL CMAS [DJ]	The Christmas Story/ Christmas ID's	1987	$4

—Artists on this disc: Michael Card, Scott Wesley Brown, Margaret Becker, Steve Camp, Richard Souther, Steven Curtis Chapman, Geoff Moore, Rick Florian (White Heart), Deniece Williams, Steve Green and Billy Smiley (White Heart).

SPARROW, THE
COLUMBIA

Number	Title	Yr	NM
❏ 10234	Eli's Coming/Oh Doctor	1975	$12
❏ 43960	Green Bottle Lover/Down Goes Your Love Life	1967	$30
—As "The Sparrows			
❏ 43755	Tomorrow's Ship/ Isn't It Strange	1966	$30
—As "The Sparrows			
❏ 43755 [PS]	Tomorrow's Ship/ Isn't It Strange	1966	$125
—As "The Sparrows			

SPARROWS, THE
DAVIS

Number	Title	Yr	NM
❏ 456	Love Me Tender/ Come Back to Me	1957	$300

JAY DEE

Number	Title	Yr	NM
❏ 790	I'll Be Loving You/Hey!	1954	$500
❏ 783	Tell Me Baby/Why Did You Leave Me	1953	$500

Number	Title	Yr	NM

SPARTAS, THE
HIT
❏ 158	Dance, Dance, Dance/ Everything's Alright	1964	$15

—B-side by the Roamers

❏ 251	Good Lovin'/Soul and Inspiration	1966	$15

—B-side by John Brooks

❏ 137	House of the Rising Sun/ Bread and Butter	1964	$20

—B-side by Danny and Deanie

❏ 154	I'm Crying/Have I the Right	1964	$20
❏ 181	Sha La La/Midnight Special	1965	$15

—B-side by Harvey Frolic

SPATS, THE
ABC-PARAMOUNT
❏ 10640	Billy, the Blue Grasshoper/ Gotta Tell Ya All About It, Baby	1965	$50
❏ 10585	Gator Tails and Monkey Ribs/The Roach	1964	$10
❏ 10711	Go Go Yamaha/Have You Ever Seen Me Crying	1965	$40
❏ 10790	Scoobee Doo/She Done Moved	1966	$60
❏ 10600	She Kissed Me Last Night/There's a Party in the Pad Down Below	1964	$20

ENITH
❏ 1268	Gator Tails and Monkey Ribs/The Roach	1964	$50

SPEARS, BILLIE JO
CAPITOL
❏ 4272	Faded Love/Heart Over Mind	1976	$5
❏ 2279	Harper Valley P.T.A./ Home-Loving Man	1968	$8
❏ 2964	I Stayed Long Enough/ Come On Home	1970	$6
❏ 3055	It Could 'A Been Me/ Break Away	1971	$6
❏ 2844	Marty Gray/True Love	1970	$6
❏ 3258	Souvenirs and California Mem'rys/What a Love I Have in You	1972	$6

LIBERTY
❏ 1409	What the World Needs Now Is Love/Snowbird	1981	$4

PARLIAMENT
❏ 1801	Midnight Blue/Midnight Love	1983	$5

UNITED ARTISTS
❏ XW1229	'57 Chevrolet/The Lovin' Kind	1978	$4
❏ XW584	Blanket on the Ground/ Come On Home	1975	$5
❏ 50022	Conscience Keep an Eye on Me/If That's What It Takes	1966	$10
❏ 50184	Easy to Be Evil/Much Too Busy to Cry	1967	$8
❏ XW985	If You Want Me/Don't Ever Let Go of Me	1977	$5
❏ XW935	I'm Not Easy/Too Far Gone	1977	$5
❏ XW1190	I've Got to Go/There's More to a Tear (Than Meets the Eye)	1978	$4
❏ XW1292	I Will Survive/Rainy Days and Stormy Nights	1979	$4
❏ X1309	Livin' Our Love Together/You	1979	$4
❏ XW1127	Lonely Hearts Club/His Little Something on the Side	1977	$5
❏ XW1251	Love Ain't Gonna Wait for Us/Say It Again	1978	$4
❏ XW813	Misty Blue/Let's Try to Wake It Up Again	1976	$5
❏ XW549	See the Funny Little Clown/All I Want Is You	1974	$5
❏ XW712	Silver Wings and Golden Rings/Then Give Him Back to Me	1975	$5
❏ X1336	Standing Tall/Freedom Song	1980	$4
❏ XW653	Stay Away from the Apple Tree/Before Your Time	1975	$5
❏ XW1041	Too Much Is Not Enough/ The End of Me	1977	$5
❏ XW764	What I've Got in Mind/ Everytime Two Fools Collide	1976	$5

SPECIALS, THE
CHRYSALIS
❏ 42794	Free Nelson Mandela/ Break Down the Door	1984	$10

—As "The Special AKA

CHRYSALIS/2 TONE
❏ 2374	Gangsters/The Selecter	1979	$4

—B-side by The Selecter

❏ 2374 [PS]	Gangsters/The Selecter	1979	$8

—Sleeve says "The Specials," theoretically for use with any Specials single

SPECTOR, PHIL
CHRYSALIS
❏ 3202	Sleigh Ride/Winter Wonderland//White Christmas/Christmas (Baby Please Come Home)	1987	$20

—Also known as "The Phil Spector Christmas Mix

❏ 3202 [PS]	The Phil Spector Christmas Mix	1987	$20

—Sleeve and record are U.K. imports; songs meld into one another on each side

PAVILLION
❏ AE71354 [DJ]	Phil Spector's Christmas Medley (same on both sides)	1981	$20

—Promo-only sampler from the Pavillion reissue of Phil Spector's Christmas Album

❏ AE71354 [DJ]	Phil Spector's Christmas Medley (same on both sides)	1981	$20

—Promo-only sampler from the Pavillion reissue of Phil Spector's Christmas Album

PHILLES
❏ 0(no cat #) [DJ]	Thanks for Giving Me the Right Time! (same on both sides)	1965	$1000

—Has Phil's picture on label; actually plays "Ebb Tide" by the Righteous Brothers

❏ 0(no cat #) [DJ]	Thanks for Giving Me the Right Time! (same on both sides)	1965	$1000

—Has Phil's picture on label; actually plays "Ebb Tide" by the Righteous Brothers

SPECTOR, RONNIE
ALSTON
❏ 3738	It's a Heartache/I Wanna Come Over	1978	$8

APPLE
❏ 1832	Try Some, Buy Some/ Tandoori Chicken	1971	$8

—With star on A-side label

❏ 1832 [PS]	Try Some, Buy Some/ Tandoori Chicken	1971	$10

COLUMBIA
❏ 07300	Love on a Rooftop/Good Love Is Hard to Find	1987	$4
❏ 07082	Who Can Sleep/ When We Danced	1987	$4
❏ 07082 [PS]	Who Can Sleep/ When We Danced	1987	$4

EPIC
❏ 50374	Say Goodbye to Hollywood/ Baby Please Don't Go	1977	$10
❏ 50374 [PS]	Say Goodbye to Hollywood/ Baby Please Don't Go	1977	$30

POLISH
❏ 202	Darlin'/Tonight	1980	$5

WARNER/SPECTOR
❏ 0409	Paradise/When I Saw You	1976	$10

SPECTORS THREE, THE
TREY
❏ 3001	I Really Do/I Know Why	1959	$30
❏ 3005	My Heart Stood Still/Mr. Robin	1960	$30

SPECTRUM
BLACKBURY
❏ 5002	Funky Christmas (Boogie All The Way)/Beautiful Woman	1978	$8

SPEEKS, RONNIE
DIMENSION
❏ 1014	Baby Loved Me/You Almost Slipped My Mind	1980	$5

FRATERNITY
❏ 968	Oh Lonesome Me/I Who Have Nothing	1966	$15

KING
❏ 5548	Please Wait for Me/What Is Your Technique	1961	$125

PALETTE
❏ 5094	Mister Glenn/My Darling (I Love You So)	1962	$10

SPELLING ON THE STONE
CURB
❏ 10522	Spelling on the Stone (same on both sides)	1988	$5

LS
❏ 53	Spelling on the Stone (same on both sides)	1988	$10

SPELLMAN, BENNY
ACE
❏ 630	That's All I Ask of You/ Roll On Big Wheel	1961	$30

ALON
❏ 9027	It Must Be Love/ Spirit of Loneliness	1965	$10
❏ 9031	It's for You/This Is My Love	1966	$10
❏ 9018	Taint the Truth/ No Don't Stop	1965	$10
❏ 9024	The Word Game/I Feel Good	1965	$30

ATLANTIC
❏ 2291	The Word Game/I Feel Good	1965	$10

MINIT
❏ 664	Ammerette/Talk About Love	1963	$15
❏ 613	Darling No Matter Where/I Didn't Know	1960	$20
❏ 652	Every Now and Then/I'm in Love	1962	$15
❏ 606	Life Is Too Short/Ammerette	1960	$20
❏ 644	Lipstick Traces (On a Cigarette)/Fortune Teller	1962	$15
❏ 659	Stickin' Whicha' Baby/ You Got to Get It	1963	$15

SANSU
❏ 462	But If You Love Her/ Sinner Girl	1967	$8

WATCH
❏ 6336	Slow Down Baby (You Drive Too Fast)/Someday They'll Understand	1964	$12

SPELLMAN, JIMMY
DOT
❏ 15607	Doggonit/I'll Never Smile Again	1957	$40
❏ 15564	Here I Am/Make Up Your Mind	1957	$40

SPENCER AND SPENCER
GONE
❏ 5053	Stagger Lawrence/ Strogonoff Cha Cha	1959	$30

SPICES, THE
CARLTON
❏ 480	Tell Me Little Girl/Money, Fortune and Fame	1958	$300

SPIDELLS, THE
CORAL
❏ 62531	Don't You Forget That You're My Baby/If It Ain't One Thing (It's Another)	1967	$30
❏ 62508	Pushed Out of the Picture/ With You in Mind	1966	$60

SPIDERS, THE (1)
IMPERIAL
❏ 5393	A-1 in My Heart/Dear Mary	1956	$40

—As "The Spiders with Chuck Carbo

❏ 5344	Am I the One/Sukey, Sukey, Sukey	1955	$80
❏ 5354	Bells in My Heart/For a Thrill	1955	$125

—Red label

❏ 5354	Bells in My Heart/For a Thrill	1957	$40

—Black label

❏ 5376	Don't Pity Me/How I Feel	1956	$50

—Featuring Chuck Carbo

❏ 5265	I Didn't Want to Do It/ You're the One	1954	$125
❏ 5618	I Didn't Want to Do It/ You're the One	1959	$40
❏ 5291	I'm Searching/I'm Slippin' In	1954	$250
❏ 5366	Is It True/Witchcraft	1955	$125

—Blue label

❏ 5366	Is It True/Witchcraft	1955	$50

—Red label

❏ 5318	She Keeps Me Wondering/ (3 x 7) = "21	1954	$125
❏ 5280	Tears Begin to Flow/I'll Stop Cryin'	1954	$125
❏ 5331	That's Enough/Lost and Bewildered	1955	$80
❏ 5739	Witchcraft/(True) You Don't Love Me	1961	$40

SPIDERS, THE (2)
MASCOT
❏ 112	Why Don't You Love Me/Hitch Hike	1965	$1500

SANTA CRUZ
❏ 003	Don't Blow Your Mind/ No Price Tag	1966	$1000

Number	Title	Yr	NM

SPIKE DRIVERS, THE
OM 1000
| ❑ 1676 | High Time/Baby Won't You Let Me Tell You How I Lost My Mind | 1966 | $40 |

REPRISE
| ❑ 0535 | High Time/Baby Won't You Let Me Tell You How I Lost My Mind | 1966 | $30 |
| ❑ 0558 | Strange Mysterious Sounds/ Break Out the Wine | 1967 | $30 |

SPINAL TAP
ENIGMA
| ❑ 1143 | Christmas With The Devil/ Christmas With The Devil (Scratch Mix) | 1984 | $6 |
| ❑ 1143 [PS] | Christmas With The Devil/ Christmas With The Devil (Scratch Mix) | 1984 | $10 |

SPINDLES, THE
ABC
| ❑ 10802 | To Make You Mine/And the Band Played On | 1966 | $30 |

SPINDRIFTS, THE
ABC-PARAMOUNT
| ❑ 9904 | Belinda/Cha Cha Doo | 1958 | $30 |

SPINNERS
ATLANTIC
❑ 3546	Are You Ready for Love/ Once You Fall in Love	1978	$5
❑ 3619	Body Language/ With My Eyes	1979	$5
❑ 89862	City Full of Memories/ No Other Love	1983	$4
❑ 2927	Could It Be I'm Falling in Love/Just You and Me Baby	1972	$5
❑ 3664	Cupid-I've Loved You for a Long Time/Pipedreams	1980	$4
❑ 3590	Don't Let the Man Get You/I Love the Music	1979	$5
❑ 3462	Easy Come, Easy Go/ Love Is One Step Away	1978	$5
❑ 89922	Funny How Time Slips Away/I'm Calling You Now	1982	$4
❑ 3284	Games People Play/I Don't Want to Lose You	1975	$10
❑ 2973	Ghetto Child/We Belong Together	1973	$5
❑ 3425	Heaven on Earth (So Fine)/I'm Tired of Giving	1977	$5
❑ 3483	If You Wanna Do a Dance/ One in a Life Proposal	1978	$5
❑ 3765	I Just Want to Fall in Love/ Heavy on the Sunshine	1980	$4
❑ 2904	I'll Be Around/How Could I Let You Get Away	1972	$5
❑ 3027	I'm Coming Home/He'll Never Love You Like I Do	1974	$5
❑ 3252	Living a Little, Loving a Little/ Smile, We Have Each Other	1975	$5
❑ 3814	Long Live Soul Music/Give Your Lady What She Wants	1981	$4
❑ 3882 [DJ]	Love Connection (same on both sides)	1981	$5

— May be promo only

| ❑ 3882 [DJ] | Love Connection (same on both sides) | 1981 | $5 |

— May be promo only

❑ 3206	Love Don't Love Nobody (Part 1)/Love Don't Love Nobody (Part 2)	1974	$5
❑ 3309	Love Or Leave/You Made a Promise to Me	1975	$5
❑ 3757	Love Trippin'/Now That You're Mine Again	1980	$4
❑ 89962	Magic in the Moonlight/ So Far Away	1982	$4
❑ 3400	Me and My Music/I'm Riding Your Shadow	1977	$5
❑ 3006	Mighty Love -- Pt. 1/ Mighty Love -- Pt. 2	1974	$5
❑ 2962	One of a Kind (Love Affair)/Don't Let the Green Grass Fool You	1973	$5
❑ 3268	Sadie/Lazy Susan	1975	$5
❑ 89226	Spaceballs/Spaceballs (Dub Version)	1987	$3
❑ 3029	Then Came You/Just As Long As We Have Love	1974	$6

— With Dionne Warwicke

| ❑ 3202 | Then Came You/Just As Long As We Have Love | 1974 | $5 |

— With Dionne Warwicke

| ❑ 3284 | They Just Can't Stop it the (Games People Play)/I Don't Want to Lose You | 1975 | $5 |

— Same A-side, altered title

| ❑ 3341 | Wake Up Susan/If You Can't Be in Love | 1976 | $5 |
| ❑ 89648 | (We Have Come Into) Our Time for All/All Your Love | 1984 | $4 |

Number	Title	Yr	NM
❑ 3848	What You Feel Is Real/Street Talk	1981	$4

— With Gino Soccio

| ❑ 3827 | Winter of Our Love/ The Deacon | 1981 | $4 |
| ❑ 3637 | Working My Way Back to You/Disco Ride | 1979 | $8 |

— Original pressings mention only one song on the A-side

| ❑ 3637 | Working My Way Back to You-Forgive Me, Girl/Disco Ride | 1979 | $4 |

MIRAGE
| ❑ 99604 | Put Us Together Again/ Show Us Your Magic | 1985 | $3 |
| ❑ 99580 | She Does/(B-side unknown) | 1986 | $3 |

MOTOWN
❑ 1109	For All We Know/ Cross My Heart	1967	$20
❑ 1136	I Just Can't Help But Feel the Pain/Bad, Bad Weather	1968	$20
❑ 1078	I'll Always Love You/ Tomorrow May Never Come	1965	$20
❑ 1155	In My Diary/(She's Gonna Love Me) At Sundown	1969	$1500
❑ 1067	Sweet Thing/How Can I	1964	$20
❑ 1235	Together We Can Make Such Sweet Music/ Bad, Bad Weather	1973	$8
❑ 1093	Truly Yours/Where Is That Girl	1966	$20

TRI-PHI
❑ 1013	I've Been Hurt/I Got Your Water Boiling Baby (I'm Gonna Cook Your Goose)	1962	$30
❑ 1004	Love (I'm So Glad I Found You)/Sudbuster	1961	$30
❑ 1018	She Don't Love Me/Too Young, Too Much, Too Soon	1962	$40
❑ 1010	She Loves Me So/ Whistling About You	1962	$30
❑ 1001	That's What Girls Are Made For/Heebie-Jeebies	1961	$30
❑ 1007	What Did She Use/ Itching for My Baby, I Know Where to Scratch	1962	$30

V.I.P.
❑ 25050	In My Diary/(She's Gonna Love Me) At Sundown	1969	$30
❑ 25057	It's a Shame/Together We Can Make Such Sweet Music	1970	$15
❑ 25054	Message from a Black Man/(She's Gonna Love Me) At Sundown	1970	$15
❑ 25060	We'll Have It Made/My Whole World Ended (The Moment You Left Me)	1971	$15

7-Inch Extended Plays
ATLANTIC
| ❑ SD 7-7296 [PS] | Mighty Love | 1974 | $12 |
| ❑ SD 7-7256 | One Of A Kind (Love Affair)/ Just You and Me Baby/ I'll Be Around//Just Can't Get You Out of My Mind/Could It Be I'm Falling in Love | 1973 | $15 |

— Jukebox issue; small hole, plays at 33 1/3 rpm

| ❑ SD 7-7296 | Since I Been Gone/Love Has Gone Away//Ain't No Price on Happiness/I'm Glad You Walked Into My Life | 1974 | $10 |

— Jukebox issue; small hole, plays at 33 1/3 rpm

| ❑ SD 7-7256 | Spinners | 1973 | $15 |

— Part of "Little LP" series (LLP #216)

SPINNERS, THE
CAPITOL
| ❑ F3955 | Love's Prayer/Goofin' | 1958 | $50 |

CRYSTALETTE
| ❑ 736 | Boomerang/Slave Chain | 1960 | $60 |

— Reissued under different titles and on different labels credited to the Crestriders and Duke Mitchell

END
| ❑ 1045 | Bird Watcher/Richard Pry, Private Eye | 1959 | $125 |

— Gray label

| ❑ 1045 | Bird Watcher/Richard Pry, Private Eye | 1959 | $50 |

— Multicolor label

LAWSON
| ❑ 324 | Surfing Monkey/ Beatle Mania | 1964 | $40 |

LIBERTY
| ❑ 55339 | Till the End of Time/Dream | 1961 | $10 |

RCA VICTOR
| ❑ 47-8427 | All I Want/It Must Be Love | 1964 | $10 |

RHYTHM
| ❑ 125 | Marvella/My Love and Your Love | 1958 | $400 |

Number	Title	Yr	NM

SMASH
| ❑ 1845 | Happy Hootenanny/Nothin' | 1963 | $12 |

WARNER BROS.
| ❑ 5084 | Little Otis/Rag Mop | 1959 | $15 |

SPIRAL STARECASE
COLUMBIA
❑ 44566	Inside, Outside, Upside Down/I'll Run	1968	$6
❑ 44442	Makin' My Mind Up/ Baby What I Mean	1968	$6
❑ 44741	More Today Than Yesterday/ Broken Hearted Man	1969	$8
❑ 45048	She's Ready/Judas to the Love We Know	1969	$5
❑ 44924	Sweet Little Thing/No One for Me to Turn To	1969	$5

SPIRALS, THE
SMASH
| ❑ 1719 | Please Be My Love/ Forever and a Day | 1961 | $125 |

SPIRES, BIG BOY
CHANCE
| ❑ 1137 | About to Lose My Mind/ Which One Do I Love | 1953 | $2500 |

SPIRIT
EPIC
❑ 10648	Animal Zoo/Red Light Roll On	1970	$6
❑ 10849	Darkness/Cadillac Cowboys	1972	$5
❑ 10849 [PS]	Darkness/Cadillac Cowboys	1972	$20
❑ 10701	Mr. Skin/Nature's Way	1971	$5
❑ 11020	Mr. Skin/Nature's Way	1973	$4
❑ 10685	Soldier/Mr. Skin	1970	$6

MERCURY
❑ 73697	America the Beautiful-The Times They Are a-Changin'/ Lady of the Lakes	1975	$5
❑ 73837	Atomic Boogie/Farther Along	1976	$4
❑ 73722	Holy Man/Looking Into Darkness	1975	$5

ODE
❑ 128	1984/Sweet Stella Baby	1969	$8
❑ 122	Dark Eyed Woman/ New Dope in Town	1969	$8
❑ 115	I Got a Line on You/ She Smiles	1968	$10
❑ 108	Mechanical World/ Uncle Jack	1967	$10

RHINO
| ❑ 008 | Turn to the Right/Potato Land Theme Song | 1980 | $5 |

SPIRITS AND WORM
A&M
| ❑ 1104 | Fanny Firecracker/ You and I Together | 1969 | $50 |

SPITALNY, PHIL
RCA VICTOR
❑ 47-3877	Adeste Fideles/Hark the Herald Angels Sing	1950	$20
❑ 47-3875	God Rest Ye Merry, Gentlemen/Carol of the Bells	1950	$20
❑ 47-3876	The First Noel/'Twas the Night Before Christmas	1950	$20

SPITTING IMAGE
VIRGIN
| ❑ 921 | Santa Claus Is On The Dole/1st Atheist Tabernacle Choir | 1986 | $8 |
| ❑ 921 [PS] | Santa Claus Is On The Dole/1st Atheist Tabernacle Choir | 1986 | $8 |

— Both record and sleeve are U.K. imports

SPLINTER
DARK HORSE
❑ 10010	After Five Years/ Halfway There	1976	$5
❑ 10003	China Light/Haven't Got Time	1975	$6
❑ 10002	Costafine Town/Elly-Mae	1974	$6
❑ 10002 [PS]	Costafine Town/Elly-Mae	1974	$8
❑ 8523	I Need Your Love/ Motions of Love	1978	$4
❑ 10007	Which Way Will I Get Home/What Is It (If You Never Tried It Yourself)	1975	$6

SPLIT ENZ
Featuring the Finn brothers.
A&M
| ❑ 2430 [DJ] | Dirty Creature (same on both sides) | 1982 | $5 |

Number	Title	Yr	NM
❏ 2430 [DJ]	Dirty Creature (same on both sides)	1982	$8
❏ 2958	I Got You/(B-side unknown)	1987	$10
❏ 2252	I Got You/Double Happy	1980	$5
❏ 2252 [PS]	I Got You/Double Happy	1980	$8
❏ 2285	I Hope I Never/Choral Sea	1980	$8
❏ 2285 [PS]	I Hope I Never/Choral Sea	1980	$8
❏ 2351	Iris/Clumsy	1981	$8
❏ 2652	Message to My Girl/Kia Kaha	1984	$6
❏ 2339	One Step Ahead/In the Wars	1981	$5

—First pressing: Laser-etched design on record

| ❏ 2339 [PS] | One Step Ahead/In the Wars | 1981 | $5 |

—Special picture sleeve for laser-etched single

| ❏ 2339 | One Step Ahead/In the Wars | 1981 | $4 |

—Regular release with no laser etching

| ❏ 2339 [PS] | One Step Ahead/In the Wars | 1981 | $4 |

—No reference to laser-etched single on sleeve

❏ 2411	Six Months in a Leaky Boat/Make Sense of It	1982	$3
❏ 2411 [PS]	Six Months in a Leaky Boat/Make Sense of It	1982	$3
❏ 2293	What's the Matter with You/Nobody Takes Me Seriously	1980	$5

FAN CLUB

| ❏ 0(no cat #) [DJ] | Merry Christmas from Split Enz | 1982 | $10 |

—Green vinyl for members of fan club

| ❏ 0(no cat #) [DJ] | Merry Christmas from Split Enz | 1982 | $30 |

—Green vinyl for members of fan club

SPOKESMEN, THE
DECCA

❏ 32049	I Love How You Love Me/Beautiful Girl	1966	$10
❏ 31874	It Ain't Fair/Have Courage, Be Careful	1965	$10
❏ 31895	Michelle/Better Days Are Yet to Come	1966	$10
❏ 31844	The Dawn of Correction/For You Babe	1965	$15
❏ 31949	Today's the Day/Enchante	1966	$10

WINCHESTER

| ❏ 1001 | Mary Jane/Flashback | 1967 | $15 |

SPOOKY TOOTH
Also see GARY WRIGHT.
A&M

| ❏ 1144 | That Was Only Yesterday/Waitin' for the Wind | 1969 | $8 |

ISLAND

| ❏ 1219 | All Sewn Up/Things Change | 1973 | $6 |
| ❏ 004 | The Mirror/Hell or High Water | 1974 | $5 |

MALA

| ❏ 12013 | Love Really Changed Me/Spooky Blow | 1968 | $10 |
| ❏ 12022 | The Weight/Do Right People | 1968 | $10 |

SPORTONES, THE
MUNICH

| ❏ 101 | In My Dreams/So Sincere | 1959 | $500 |

SPORTSMEN QUARTET, THE
CAPITOL

| ❏ CCF9005 | Carols At Christmas | 1949 | $40 |

—Contains 3 records (F90017, F90018, F90019) plus box

❏ F90019	Good King Wenceslas/Away In A Manger	1949	$10
❏ F90017	Silent Night/Wassail, Wassail	1949	$10
❏ F90018	We Three Kings Of Orient Are/O Little Town Of Bethlehem	1949	$10

SPORTSMEN, THE
RONROY

| ❏ 1004 | Santa's Toy Express/On This Silent Night | 1962 | $8 |

SPOTLIGHTERS, THE
ALADDIN

| ❏ 3436 | Please Be My Girlfriend/Whisper | 1958 | $125 |
| ❏ 3441 | This Is My Story/Preaching | 1959 | $125 |

IMPERIAL

| ❏ 5342 | It's Cold/Bam Jingle Jingle | 1955 | $125 |
| ❏ 5342 | It's Cold/Bam Jingle Jingle | 1955 | $250 |

—Red vinyl

SPOTNICKS, THE
ATCO

| ❏ 6261 | Orange Blossom Special/Hava Nagila | 1963 | $15 |

FELSTED

| ❏ 8649 | Spotnick/Old Spinning Wheel | 1962 | $15 |

LAURIE

❏ 3333	Drum Didley/Orange Blossom Special	1966	$12
❏ 3241	I'm Goin' Home/Orange Blossom Special	1964	$10
❏ 3260	Summer in Sweden/Endless Sleep	1964	$10

SPOTSWOOD, KENDRA
TUFF

| ❏ 407 | Stickin' with My Baby/Jive Guy | 1965 | $10 |

SPRING
UNITED ARTISTS

| ❏ 50907 | Good Times/Sweet Mountain | 1972 | $100 |

SPRINGFIELD, DUSTY
20TH CENTURY

| ❏ 2457 | It Goes Like It Goes/I Wish That Love Would Last | 1980 | $5 |

ABC DUNHILL

❏ 4357	Mama's Little Girl/Learn to Say Goodbye	1973	$8
❏ 4344	Mama's Little Girl/Learn to Say Goodbye	1973	$6
❏ 4341	Who Gets Your Love/Of All the Things	1973	$6

ATLANTIC

❏ 2685	A Brand New Me/Bad Case of the Blues	1969	$6
❏ 2606	Breakfast in Bed/Don't Forget About Me	1969	$8
❏ 2841	I Believe in You/Someone Who Cared	1971	$6
❏ 2673	In the Land of Make Believe/So Much Love	1969	$6
❏ 2729	I Wanna Be a Free Girl/Let Me In Your Way	1970	$6
❏ 2705	Silly, Silly, Fool/Joe	1970	$6
❏ 2580	Son-of-a-Preacher-Man/Just a Little Lovin'	1968	$12
❏ 2580 [PS]	Son-of-a-Preacher-Man/Just a Little Lovin'	1968	$20
❏ 2623	The Windmills of Your Mind/I Don't Want to Hear It Anymore	1969	$8
❏ 2771	What Good Is I Love You/What Do You Do When Love Dies	1970	$6
❏ 2647	Willie & Laura May Jones/That Old Sweet Roll	1969	$6

CASABLANCA

| ❏ 2356 | I Am Curious/Donnez-Moi | 1981 | $4 |

PHILIPS

❏ 40229	All Cried Out/I Wish I'd Never Loved You	1964	$10
❏ 40229 [PS]	All Cried Out/I Wish I'd Never Loved You	1964	$30
❏ 40396	All I See Is You/I'm Gonna Leave You	1966	$10
❏ 40396 [PS]	All I See Is You/I'm Gonna Leave You	1966	$30
❏ 40245	Guess Who/Live It Up	1964	$10
❏ 40245 [PS]	Guess Who/Live It Up	1964	$30
❏ 40319	I Just Don't Know What to Do with Myself/Some of Your Lovin'	1965	$10
❏ 40319 [PS]	I Just Don't Know What to Do with Myself/Some of Your Lovin'	1965	$30
❏ 40439	I'll Try Anything/The Corrupt Ones	1967	$10
❏ 40439 [PS]	I'll Try Anything/The Corrupt Ones	1967	$30
❏ 40303	In the Middle of Nowhere/Baby, Don't You Know	1965	$10
❏ 40303 [PS]	In the Middle of Nowhere/Baby, Don't You Know	1965	$30
❏ 40162	I Only Want to Be with You/Once Upon a Time	1963	$15
❏ 40553	La Bamba/I Close My Eyes and Count to Ten	1968	$10
❏ 40270	Losing You/Here She Comes	1965	$10
❏ 40270 [PS]	Losing You/Here She Comes	1965	$30
❏ 40180	Stay Awhile/Something Special	1964	$10
❏ 40180 [PS]	Stay Awhile/Something Special	1964	$30
❏ 40547	Sweet Ride/No Stranger Am I	1968	$10
❏ 40465	The Look of Love/Give Me Time	1967	$10
❏ 40498	What's It Gonna Be/Small Town Girl	1967	$10
❏ 40498 [PS]	What's It Gonna Be/Small Town Girl	1967	$20
❏ 40207	Wishin' and Hopin'/Do Re Mi (Forget About the One and Think About Me)	1964	$15

UNITED ARTISTS

❏ XW1205	Checkmate/Sandra	1978	$5
❏ XW1225	Give Me the Night/Checkmate	1978	$5
❏ XW1006	Let Me Love You Once Before You Go/I'm Your Child	1977	$5
❏ XW1255	Living Without Your Love/Get Yourself to Love	1978	$5

SPRINGFIELD, RICK
CAPITOL

❏ 3713	Believe in Me/The Liar	1973	$15
❏ 3637	I'm Your Superman/Why Are You Waiting	1973	$8
❏ 3340	Speak to the Sky/Why	1972	$8
❏ 3340 [PS]	Speak to the Sky/Why	1972	$20
❏ 3466	What Would the Children Think/Come On Everybody	1972	$8
❏ 3466 [PS]	What Would the Children Think/Come On Everybody	1972	$20

CHELSEA

| ❏ 3055 | Million Dollar Face/(B-side unknown) | 1976 | $5 |
| ❏ 3051 | Take a Hand/Archangel | 1976 | $5 |

COLUMBIA

❏ 46057	American Girls/Weep No More	1974	$5
❏ 45935	Believe in Me/The Liar	1973	$6
❏ 46032	Streakin' Across the U.S.A./Music to Streak By	1974	$6

MERCURY

| ❏ 880405-7 | Bruce/Guenevere | 1984 | $4 |
| ❏ 880405-7 [PS] | Bruce/Guenevere | 1984 | $5 |

RCA

| ❏ GB-13794 | Affair of the Heart/Human Touch | 1984 | $3 |

—Gold Standard Series

❏ PB-13497	Affair of the Heart/Like Father, Like Son	1983	$3
❏ PB-13497 [PS]	Affair of the Heart/Like Father, Like Son	1983	$4
❏ PB-13861	Bop 'Til You Drop/Taxi Dancing	1984	$3

—B-side: With Randy Crawford

❏ PB-13861 [PS]	Bop 'Til You Drop/Taxi Dancing	1984	$3
❏ PB-14047	Celebrate Youth/Stranger in the House	1985	$3
❏ PB-14047 [PS]	Celebrate Youth/Stranger in the House	1985	$3
❏ PB-13070	Don't Talk to Strangers/Tonight	1982	$4
❏ PB-13070 [PS]	Don't Talk to Strangers/Tonight	1982	$4
❏ GB-13483	Don't Talk to Strangers/What Kind of Fool Am I	1983	$3

—Gold Standard Series

❏ PB-13813	Don't Walk Away/S.F.O.	1984	$3
❏ PB-13813 [PS]	Don't Walk Away/S.F.O.	1984	$3
❏ 8391-7-R	Honeymoon in Beirut/My Father's Chair	1988	$3
❏ 8391-7-R [PS]	Honeymoon in Beirut/My Father's Chair	1988	$3
❏ PB-13576	Human Touch/Alyson	1983	$3
❏ PB-13303	I Get Excited/Kristina	1982	$4
❏ PB-13303 [PS]	I Get Excited/Kristina	1982	$4
❏ PB-12166	I've Done Everything for You/Red Hot and Blue Love	1981	$4
❏ PB-12166 [PS]	I've Done Everything for You/Red Hot and Blue Love	1981	$4
❏ PB-13008	Love Is Alright Tonite/Everybody's Girl	1981	$4
❏ PB-13008 [PS]	Love Is Alright Tonite/Everybody's Girl	1981	$4
❏ PB-13738	Love Somebody/The Great Lost Art of Conversation	1984	$3
❏ PB-13738 [PS]	Love Somebody/The Great Lost Art of Conversation	1984	$3

—Without sticker on sleeve

| ❏ PB-13738 [PS] | Love Somebody/The Great Lost Art of Conversation | 1984 | $6 |

—With "Special Dollar Refund Offer" sticker on sleeve and $1 off coupon for the purchase of the LP "Hard to Hold" inside

❏ PB-13650	Souls/Souls (Live)	1983	$3
❏ PB-13650 [PS]	Souls/Souls (Live)	1983	$4
❏ PB-14120	State of the Heart/The Power of Love (The Tao of Love)	1985	$3
❏ PB-14120 [PS]	State of the Heart/The Power of Love (The Tao of Love)	1985	$3
❏ PB-13245	What Kind of Fool Am I/How Do You Talk to Girls	1982	$4

SPRINGFIELD RIFLE, THE
ABC

| ❏ 10878 | The Bears/There Is Life on Mars | 1966 | $12 |

JERDEN

| ❏ 815 | All She Said/It Ain't Happened | 1967 | $15 |
| ❏ 812 | Stop and Take a Look Around/100 or Two | 1967 | $15 |

TOWER

| ❏ 455 | I Love Her/That's All I Really Need | 1968 | $10 |

SPRINGFIELDS, THE
PHILIPS

❏ 40072	Dear Hearts and Gentle People/Gotta Travel On	1962	$15
❏ 40099	Foggy Mountain Top/Island of Dreams	1963	$15
❏ 40092	Little By Little/Waf-Woof	1963	$15
❏ 40121	Say I Won't Be There/Little Boat	1963	$15

Number	Title	Yr	NM
❏ 40038	Silver Threads and Golden Needles/Aunt Rhody	1962	$20

SPRINGSTEEN, BRUCE
COLUMBIA

Number	Title	Yr	NM
❏ 10801	Badlands/Streets of Fire	1978	$15
❏ 45805 [DJ]	Blinded by the Light (mono/stereo)	1972	$70
❏ 45805 [DJ]	Blinded by the Light (mono/stereo)	1972	$60
❏ 45805	Blinded by the Light/The Angel	1972	$500
❏ 45805 [PS]	Blinded by the Light/The Angel	1972	$400
❏ 04680	Born in the U.S.A./Shut Out the Light	1984	$4
❏ 04680 [PS]	Born in the U.S.A./Shut Out the Light	1984	$5
❏ 08410	Born in the U.S.A./Shut Out the Light	1984	$3

— Gray label reissue

❏ 10209	Born to Run/Meeting Across the River	1975	$30
❏ 33323	Born to Run/Spirit in the Night	1976	$4

— Columbia Hall of Fame" series; red label

❏ 07595	Brilliant Disguise/Lucky Man	1987	$4
❏ 07595 [PS]	Brilliant Disguise/Lucky Man	1987	$4
❏ 04561	Cover Me/Jersey Girl	1984	$12

— First pressings have a spoken intro to "Jersey Girl." Dead wax has matrix number followed by "-1" and a letter.

❏ 04561 [PS]	Cover Me/Jersey Girl	1984	$5
❏ 04561	Cover Me/Jersey Girl	1984	$4

— Spoken intro to "Jersey Girl" is deleted. Dead wax has matrix number followed by "-2" and a letter.

❏ 08409	Cover Me/Jersey Girl	1984	$3

— Gray label reissue

❏ 04463	Dancing in the Dark/Pink Cadillac	1984	$4
❏ 04463 [PS]	Dancing in the Dark/Pink Cadillac	1984	$5
❏ 08408	Dancing in the Dark/Pink Cadillac	1984	$3

— Gray label reissue

❏ 11431	Fade Away/Be True	1981	$4

— Corrected second pressing

❏ 11431 [PS]	Fade Away/Be True	1981	$6
❏ 11431	Fade Away/To Be True	1981	$30

— Erroneous first pressing

❏ 06657	Fire/Incident on 57th Street	1987	$5
❏ 06657 [PS]	Fire/Incident on 57th Street	1987	$5
❏ 04924	Glory Days/Stand On It	1985	$4
❏ 04924 [PS]	Glory Days/Stand On It	1985	$5
❏ 08412	Glory Days/Stand On It	1985	$3

— Gray label reissue

❏ 03243	Hungry Heart/Fade Away	1983	$4

— Columbia Hall of Fame" series; red label

❏ 11391	Hungry Heart/Held Up Without a Gun	1980	$4
❏ 11391 [PS]	Hungry Heart/Held Up Without a Gun	1980	$6
❏ 05603	I'm Goin' Down/Janey, Don't You Lose Heart	1985	$4
❏ 05603 [PS]	I'm Goin' Down/Janey, Don't You Lose Heart	1985	$5
❏ 08413	I'm Goin' Down/Janey, Don't You Lose Heart	1985	$3

— Gray label reissue

❏ 04772	I'm on Fire/Johnny Bye Bye	1985	$4
❏ 04772 [PS]	I'm on Fire/Johnny Bye Bye	1985	$5
❏ 08411	I'm on Fire/Johnny Bye Bye	1985	$3

— Gray label reissue

❏ 05728	My Hometown/Santa Claus Is Coming to Town	1985	$4
❏ 05728 [PS]	My Hometown/Santa Claus Is Coming to Town	1985	$4
❏ 08414	My Hometown/Santa Claus Is Coming to Town	1985	$3

— Gray label reissue; many copies of this were issued with Columbia 05728 picture sleeves

❏ 07726	One Step Up/Roulette	1988	$4
❏ 07726 [PS]	One Step Up/Roulette	1988	$4
❏ 10763	Prove It All Night/Factory	1978	$15
❏ AE71332 [DJ]	Santa Claus Is Coming to Town (same on both sides)	1981	$30
❏ AE71332 [PS]	Santa Claus Is Coming to Town (same on both sides)	1981	$30
❏ 45864	Spirit in the Night/For You	1973	$1500
❏ 45864 [DJ]	Spirit in the Night (mono/stereo)	1973	$60
❏ 45864 [DJ]	Spirit in the Night (mono/stereo)	1973	$60
❏ 10274	Tenth Avenue Freeze-Out/She's the One	1976	$20
❏ 07663	Tunnel of Love/Two for the Road	1987	$4
❏ 07663 [PS]	Tunnel of Love/Two for the Road	1987	$4
❏ 06432	War/Merry Christmas Baby	1986	$4
❏ 06432 [PS]	War/Merry Christmas Baby	1986	$4

SPRINGSTONE, BRUCE
CLEAN CUTS

Number	Title	Yr	NM
❏ CC-902	Bedrock Rap/(Meet the) Flintstones//Take Me Out to the Ballgame	1982	$5
❏ CC-902 [PS]	Bedrock Rap/(Meet the) Flintstones//Take Me Out to the Ballgame	1982	$5

COLD CUTS

❏ CC-902	Bedrock Rap/(Meet the) Flintstones//Take Me Out to the Ballgame	1982	$8
❏ CC-902 [PS]	Bedrock Rap/(Meet the) Flintstones//Take Me Out to the Ballgame	1982	$8

SPURZZ
EPIC

❏ 50911	Cowboy Stomp!/Night Club	1980	$4

SPUTNIKS, THE
CLASS

❏ 217	My Love Is Gone/Hey Maryann	1958	$60
❏ 222	Wait a Little While/Johnny's Little Lamb	1958	$50

PAM MAR

❏ 601	My Love Is Gone/Hey Maryann	1957	$250

SQUEEZE
A&M

❏ 2994	853-5937/Take Me I'm Yours (Live)	1987	$3
❏ 2994 [PS]	853-5937/Take Me I'm Yours (Live)	1987	$8

— A tough sleeve to find

❏ 2518	Annie Get Your Gun/Spanish Guitar	1983	$3
❏ 2263	Another Nail in My Heart//Going Crazy/What the Butler Saw	1980	$4
❏ 2263 [PS]	Another Nail in My Heart//Going Crazy/What the Butler Saw	1980	$8
❏ 2534	Another Nail in My Heart//Going Crazy/What the Butler Saw	1983	$3
❏ 2424	Black Coffee in Bed/The Hunt	1982	$3
❏ 2424 [PS]	Black Coffee in Bed/The Hunt	1982	$10
❏ AMS7495	Christmas Day/Going Crazy	1979	$8

— Black vinyl

❏ AMS7495 [PS]	Christmas Day/Going Crazy	1979	$8

— Both record and sleeve are U.K. imports

❏ AMS7495	Christmas Day/Going Crazy	1979	$15

— White vinyl

❏ 2146	Cool for Cats/Model	1979	$4
❏ 2146 [PS]	Cool for Cats/Model	1979	$4
❏ 3021	Footprints/Black Coffee in Bed (Live)	1988	$3
❏ 2168	Goodbye Girl/Slightly Drunk	1979	$4
❏ 2168 [PS]	Goodbye Girl/Slightly Drunk	1979	$4
❏ 2776	Hits of the Year/Fortnight Saga	1985	$3
❏ 2776 [PS]	Hits of the Year/Fortnight Saga	1985	$3
❏ 2967	Hourglass/Wedding Bells	1987	$3
❏ 2967 [PS]	Hourglass/Wedding Bells	1987	$3
❏ 1616	If I Didn't Love You/Another Nail in My Heart	1980	$10

— 5-inch single with small hole, plays at 33 1/3 RPM

❏ 1616 [PS]	If I Didn't Love You/Another Nail in My Heart	1980	$10

— Special "Tiny Collector's Edition" sleeve with above single

❏ 2229	If I Didn't Love You/Pretty One	1980	$4
❏ 2229 [PS]	If I Didn't Love You/Pretty One	1980	$6
❏ 2413	I've Returned/When the Hangover Strikes	1982	$3
❏ 2377	Messed Around/Yap, Yap, Yap	1981	$3
❏ 2247	Pulling Mussels (From the Shell)/Pretty One	1980	$4
❏ 2247 [PS]	Pulling Mussels (From the Shell)/Pretty One	1980	$4
❏ 2033 [DJ]	Take Me, I'm Yours (mono)/Take Me, I'm Yours (stereo)	1978	$4

— Label credit: U.K. Squeeze

❏ 2033 [DJ]	Take Me, I'm Yours (mono)/Take Me, I'm Yours (stereo)	1978	$4

— Label credit: U.K. Squeeze

❏ 2345	Tempted/Trust	1981	$3
❏ 2345 [PS]	Tempted/Trust	1981	$6

SQUIER, BILLY
CAPITOL

❏ B-5422	All Night Long/Calley Oh	1984	$3
❏ B-5422 [PS]	All Night Long/Calley Oh	1984	$4

Number	Title	Yr	NM
❏ B-5303	Christmas Is the Time to Say "I Love You"/White Christmas	1983	$5
❏ B-5303 [PS]	Christmas Is the Time to Say "I Love You"/White Christmas	1983	$6
❏ SPRO9870 [DJ]	Christmas Is The Time To Say I Love You/White Christmas	1983	$8

— Has the same picture sleeve as B-5303

❏ SPRO9870 [DJ]	Christmas Is The Time To Say I Love You/White Christmas	1983	$8

— Has the same picture sleeve as B-5303

❏ 7PRO-79694 [DJ]	Don't Say You Love Me (same on both sides)	1989	$12

— Vinyl is promo only

❏ 7PRO-79694 [DJ]	Don't Say You Love Me (same on both sides)	1989	$12

— Vinyl is promo only

❏ B-5135	Emotions in Motion/It Keeps You Rockin'	1982	$4
❏ B-5135 [PS]	Emotions in Motion/It Keeps You Rockin'	1982	$5
❏ B-5163	Everybody Wants You/Keep Me Satisfied	1982	$4
❏ B-5163 [PS]	Everybody Wants You/Keep Me Satisfied	1982	$5
❏ B-5416	Eye on You/Calley Oh	1984	$3
❏ B-5416 [PS]	Eye on You/Calley Oh	1984	$4
❏ A-5040	In the Dark/Whadda You Want from Me	1981	$4
❏ A-5040 [PS]	In the Dark/Whadda You Want from Me	1981	$5
❏ B-5619	Love Is the Hero/Learn How to Live (Live)	1986	$3
❏ B-5619 [PS]	Love Is the Hero/Learn How to Live (Live)	1986	$3
❏ A-5037	My Kinda Lover/Christmas Is the Time to Say "I Love You"	1981	$4
❏ A-5037 [PS]	My Kinda Lover/Christmas Is the Time to Say "I Love You"	1981	$5
❏ B-5202	She's a Runner/In Your Eyes	1983	$4
❏ B-5202 [PS]	She's a Runner/In Your Eyes	1983	$5
❏ B-5657	Shot O' Love/One Good Woman	1986	$3
❏ B-5657 [PS]	Shot O' Love/One Good Woman	1986	$3
❏ 4901	The Music's All Right/Big Beat	1980	$5
❏ A-5005	The Stroke/Too Daze Gone	1981	$4
❏ A-5005 [PS]	The Stroke/Too Daze Gone	1981	$5

SQUIRES, THE (1)
ALADDIN

❏ 3360	Dreamy Eyes/Danglin' with My Heart	1957	$125

KICKS

❏ 1	Dream Come True/Lucy Lou	1954	$800

MAMBO

❏ 105	Sindy/Do-Be-Do-Be-Wop-Wop	1955	$200

VITA

❏ 116	Heavenly Angel/Sweet Girl	1955	$125
❏ 105	Sindy/Do-Be-Do-Be-Wop-Wop	1960	$125
❏ 113	Sweet Girl/Me and My Deal	1955	$125

SQUIRES, THE (2)
ATCO

❏ 6442	Go Ahead/Going All the Way	1966	$200

SQUIRES, THE (3)
CHAN

❏ 105	Mean Misery/Chattanooga Choo Choo	1962	$40
❏ 102	Movin' Out/Our Theme	1961	$40

MGM

❏ 13044	Movin' Out/Our Theme	1961	$20

SQUIRES, THE (4)
COMBO

❏ 35	Let's Give Love a Try/Whop	1952	$500
❏ 42	Oh Darling/My Little Girl	1953	$600

SQUIRES, THE (U)
FLAIR

❏ 1030	Sayonara/Mia Bella Donna	1954	$40

GEE

❏ 1082	Don't Accuse Me/So Many Tears Ago	1962	$60

HERALD

❏ 580	Why Should I Suffer/Walkin'	1963	$40

STARLITE

❏ 1/2	Movin'/Night Road	1964	$60

V

❏ 109	The Sultan/Aurora	1961	$3000

— Canadian release only; with a very early Neil Young. VG 1000; VG+ 2000

Number	Title	Yr	NM

SQUIRRELS, THE
CAMEO
| ❏ 284 | Grandma's House/The Girl That I'll Adore | 1963 | $10 |

—B-side by the Philadelphia Minstrels

SRC
As in Scott Richard Case.
A-SQUARE
| ❏ 402 | Get the Picture/I Need You | 1967 | $30 |

—B-side by the Rationals

| ❏ 301 | I'm So Glad/Who Is That Girl | 1967 | $30 |

— As "Scott Richard Case"

CAPITOL
| ❏ 2327 | Black Sheep/Morning Hood | 1968 | $10 |
| ❏ 2457 | Turn Into Love/Up All Night | 1969 | $10 |

STACKRIDGE
DECCA
| ❏ 32923 | Dora the Female Explorer/ (B-side unknown) | 1972 | $12 |

SIRE
| ❏ 717 | The Last Plimsoul/Spin Around the Room | 1974 | $5 |

STAFF, BOBBI
RCA VICTOR
❏ 47-9504	Back Away/A Ring Beats a Promise	1968	$12
❏ 47-9363	Bobby Blows a Blue Note/ He Chickened Out on Me	1967	$10
❏ 47-8833	Chicken Feed/I Didn't Cry Today	1966	$10
❏ 47-9251	I Can't Find My Walking Shoes/Sun Tan and Wind Blown Time	1967	$10
❏ 47-8689	I'm Available (Just for You)/ Where Did the Summer Go	1965	$10

STAFFORD, JIM
COLUMBIA
| ❏ 04339 | Little Bits and Pieces/ Banjo Billy | 1984 | $3 |

ELEKTRA
| ❏ 47013 | Don't Fool Around (When There's a Fool Around)/I Took Your Love Lightly | 1980 | $4 |
| ❏ 47226 | Isabel and Samantha/ Yeller Dog Blues | 1981 | $4 |

MGM
❏ 14819	I Got Stoned and I Missed It/I Ain't Workin'	1975	$4
❏ 14718	My Girl Bill/L.A. Mama	1974	$4
❏ 14648	Spiders and Snakes/ Undecided	1973	$4
❏ 14496	Swamp Witch/Nifty Fifties Blues	1973	$4
❏ 14737	Wildwood Weed/ The Last Chant	1974	$4

TOWN HOUSE
| ❏ 1062 | What Mama Don't Know/ That's What Little Kids Do | 1982 | $4 |

WARNER BROS.
| ❏ 49611 | Cow Patti/Texas Guitar Song | 1980 | $4 |
| ❏ 8299 | Turn Loose of My Leg/The Fight | 1976 | $4 |

STAFFORD, JO, AND VIC DAMONE
COLUMBIA
| ❏ 40968 | Silence Is Golden/Good Nite | 1957 | $10 |

STAFFORD, JO, AND GORDON MACRAE
CAPITOL
❏ 54-782	Bibbidi-Bobbidi-Boo (The Magic Song)/Echoes	1949	$30
❏ F858	Dearie/Monday, Tuesday, Wednesday	1950	$30
❏ F969	Down the Lane/ You Are My Love	1950	$30
❏ F1307	To Think You've Chosen Me/Hold Me, Hold Me	1950	$30
❏ F1523	When It's Springtime...You Tell Me/Nights of Splendor	1951	$30
❏ F1642	Whispering Hope/I'll String Along with You	1951	$20

—Reissue of 1949 hit

| ❏ 54-690 | Whispering Hope/ Thought in the Heart | 1949 | $30 |
| ❏ F1659 | Wunderbar/Beyond the Sunset | 1951 | $20 |

—Reissue

STAFFORD, JO
CAPITOL
| ❏ F946 | Ask Me No Questions/ On the Outgoing Tide | 1950 | $30 |
| ❏ F1248 | Autumn Leaves/ Autumn in New York | 1950 | $30 |

Number	Title	Yr	NM
❏ F998	Ave Maria/Shinin' Through	1950	$20
❏ F997	Baby Won't You Please Come Home/I'll Be With You in Apple Blossom Time	1950	$20
❏ F994	Barbara Allen/He's Gone Away	1950	$20
❏ F989	Begin the Beguine/In the Still of the Night	1950	$20
❏ PRO2756 [DJ]	Christmas Is The Season/ Merry Christmas	1964	$10
❏ F914	Day by Day/When April Comes Again	1950	$30
❏ F824	Diamonds Are a Girl's Best Friend/Open Door, Open Arms	1950	$30
❏ F808	Fools Rush In/Just One of Those Things	1950	$30
❏ F1142	Goodnight Irene/ Our Very Own	1950	$30
❏ F992	Here I'll Stay/Almost Like Being in Love	1950	$20
❏ F1195	In the Middle of a Riddle/Tea for Two	1950	$30
❏ F1153	La Vie En Rose/ La Vie En Rose	1950	$30

—B-side by Paul Weston

❏ F1312	Love Is a Masquerade/ It Was So Beautiful	1950	$30
❏ F996	On the Alamo/ Roses of Picardy	1950	$20
❏ F1039	Play a Simple Melody/ Pagan Love Song	1950	$30
❏ 54-785	Scarlet Ribbons (For Her Hair)/Happy Times	1949	$30
❏ F990	September Song/Yesterdays	1950	$20
❏ 54-90042	Silent Night/White Christmas	1949	$20
❏ F1685	Sometime/No Other Love	1951	$20

—Reissue

❏ F993	Sometimes I'm Happy/ Why Can't You Believe Me	1950	$20
❏ F991	The Best Things in Life Are Free/The Gentleman Is a Dope	1950	$20
❏ F1651	Tumbling Tumbleweeds/On the Sunny Side of the Street	1951	$20

—Reissue

❏ F927	Tumbling Tumbleweeds/ Someone to Love	1950	$30
❏ F995	Walkin' My Baby Back Home/Over the Rainbow	1950	$20
❏ F999	Where Are You Gonna Be/Driftin' Down the Dreamy Old Ohio	1950	$20

— Whether the above 11 (F989-F999) were released individually, as a box set, or as several box sets, we don't know.

| ❏ F1262 | White Christmas/Silent Night | 1950 | $20 |

COLPIX
| ❏ 623 | Misty/Adios My Love | 1962 | $10 |
| ❏ 633 | My Heart Had a Window/Symphony | 1962 | $10 |

COLUMBIA
❏ 40538	Ain'tcha Comin' Out T-Tonight/St. Louis Blues	1955	$15
❏ 40640	All Night Long/As I Love You	1956	$10
❏ 41413	All Yours/Pine Top's Boogie	1959	$10
❏ 40170	April and You/Indiscretion	1954	$15

— With Liberace

❏ 39653	Ay-Round the Corner (Bee-Hind the Bush)/ Heaven Drops the Curtain	1952	$20
❏ 40495	Be Sure, Beloved/ Young and Foolish	1955	$15
❏ 39723	Blue Moon/I'm In the Mood for Love	1952	$15

— The above four comprise a box set

| ❏ 41690 | Candy/Indoor Sport | 1960 | $10 |
| ❏ 39893 | Christmas Roses/ Chow, Willy | 1952 | $20 |

— With Frankie Laine

❏ 40406	Don't Get Around Much Anymore/Darling! Darling! Darling!	1955	$10
❏ 39720	Don't Worry 'Bout Me/ As You Desire Me	1952	$15
❏ 41007	Echoes in the Night/ Beyond the Stars	1957	$12
❏ 41640	Happy Is the Word/ What a Feeling	1960	$12
❏ 41321	How Can We Say Goodbye/ My Heart Is From Missouri	1959	$10
❏ 39082	If/It Is No Secret (What God Can Do)	1950	$30
❏ 3-39082	If/It Is No Secret (What God Can Do)	1950	$40

—Microgroove 33 1/3 rpm 7-inch single

| ❏ 40193 | I Found a Friend/Beautiful Isle of Somewhere | 1954 | $10 |

— The above four comprise a box set

❏ 39130	If You've Got the Money, I've Got the Time/ Handsome Stranger	1950	$30
❏ 40926	I'll Be There (When We Get Lonely)/Underneath the Overpass	1957	$10
❏ 41160	I May Never Pass This Way Again/It Won't Be Easy	1958	$10

Number	Title	Yr	NM
❏ 40190	It Is No Secret (What God Can Do)/Beautiful Garden of Prayer	1954	$10
❏ 40595	It's Almost Tomorrow/ If You Want to Love Me, You Have to Cry	1955	$15
❏ 41517	It's Been So Long/Just Tell 'Em You Love Me	1959	$10
❏ 41281	Lazy Moon/Hibiscus	1958	$12
❏ 40059	Living for Only You/ Cups of Joy	1953	$20
❏ 40745	Love Me Good/A Perfect Love	1956	$10
❏ 40143	Make Love to Me!/ Adi-Adios, Amigo	1953	$15
❏ 39301	Make Man Love Me/ Along the Colorado Trail	1951	$30
❏ 40000	My Dearest, My Darling/ Just Another Polka	1953	$20
❏ 40782	On London Bridge/ Bells Are Ringing	1956	$10
❏ 40451	Please Don't Go So Soon/I Got a Sweetie	1955	$15
❏ 39206	San Antonio Rose/ Lovely Is the Evening	1951	$30
❏ 39722	September in the Rain/ Easy Come, Easy Go	1952	$15
❏ 39581	Shrimp Boats/Love Mystery	1951	$30
❏ 39951	Smoking My Sad Cigarette/ Without My Lover	1953	$20
❏ 39389	Somebody/Allentown Jail	1951	$30
❏ 40021	Someone's Been Readin' My Mail/I'm Your Girl	1953	$20
❏ 39721	Something to Remember You By/Spring Is Here	1952	$15
❏ 1-905(?)	Stardust/You Don't Remind Me	1950	$40

—Microgroove 33 1/3 rpm 7-inch single

| ❏ 6-905(?) | Stardust/You Don't Remind Me | 1950 | $30 |

— First edition of 45

| ❏ 39056 | Stardust/You Don't Remind Me | 1950 | $30 |

— Second edition of this 45

❏ 39448	Star of Hope/He Bought My Soul	1951	$30
❏ 40191	Star of Hope/Peace in the Valley (For Me)	1954	$10
❏ 41006	Star of Love/What's Botherin' You Baby	1957	$10
❏ 40559	Suddenly There's a Valley/ The Night Watch	1955	$15
❏ 41078	Sweet Little Darlin'/I'll Buy It	1957	$10
❏ 41129	Sweet Little Darlin'/It's Never Quite the Same	1958	$10
❏ 40351	Teach Me Tonight/Suddenly	1954	$15
❏ 39129	Tennessee Waltz/ Goodnight Pillow	1950	$30
❏ 1-910(?)	Tennessee Waltz/If You've Got the Money, I've Got the Time	1950	$40

—Microgroove 33 1/3 rpm 7-inch single

| ❏ 6-910(?) | Tennessee Waltz/If You've Got the Money, I've Got the Time | 1950 | $30 |

— First edition of 45

| ❏ 39065 | Tennessee Waltz/If You've Got the Money, I've Got the Time | 1950 | $30 |

— Second edition of this 45

❏ 40250	Thank You for Calling/ Where Are You	1954	$15
❏ 40103	The Christmas Blues/What Good Am I Without You	1953	$20
❏ 40034	Till We Meet Again/ With These Hands	1953	$20

— With Nelson Eddy

| ❏ 40697 | Warm All Over/Big D | 1956 | $10 |
| ❏ 1-900(?) | Where or When/Use Your Imagination | 1950 | $40 |

—Microgroove 33 1/3 rpm 7-inch single

| ❏ 6-900(?) | Where or When/Use Your Imagination | 1950 | $30 |

— First edition of 45

| ❏ 39049 | Where or When/Use Your Imagination | 1950 | $30 |

— Second edition of this 45

| ❏ 40832 | Wind in the Willow/ King of Paris | 1957 | $10 |
| ❏ 40718 | With a Little Bit of Luck/ One Little Kiss | 1956 | $10 |

DECCA
| ❏ 25740 | Make Love to Me/I'll Be Seeing You | 1968 | $6 |

DOT
| ❏ 16791 | Do I Hear a Waltz/ Down in the Valley | 1965 | $8 |
| ❏ 16904 | Falling in Love Again/ Cry, Cry Darling | 1966 | $8 |

REPRISE
| ❏ 20205 | Country Bumpkin/ Writing on the Wall | 1963 | $8 |

Number	Title	Yr	NM

7-Inch Extended Plays

COLUMBIA
Number	Title	Yr	NM
❏ B-2527	*Make Love to Me!/Early Autumn/Stardust/Teach Me Tonight	1957	$20
❏ B-9102	*Winter Song/It Happened in Sun Valley/I've Got My Love to Keep Me Warm/The Nearness of You	1956	$15
❏ B-9101	Baby It's Cold Outside/Moonlight in Vermont//Let It Snow! Let It Snow! Let It Snow!/By the Fireside	1956	$15
❏ B-9101 [PS]	Ski Trails, Vol. 1	1956	$15
❏ B-9102 [PS]	Ski Trails, Vol. 2	1956	$15
❏ B-9103 [PS]	Ski Trails, Vol. 3	1956	$15
❏ B-9103	Winter Wonderland/June in January//The Whiffenpoof Song/Sleigh Ride	1956	$15

STAFFORD, TERRY

A&M
| ❏ 707 | Heartaches on the Way/You Left Me Here to Cry | 1963 | $15 |

ATLANTIC
❏ CY-4006	Amarillo by Morning/Say, Has Anybody Seen My Sweet Gypsy Rose	1973	$8
❏ 4015	Captured/It Sure Is Bad to Love Her	1974	$6
❏ 4026	Stop If You Love Me/We've Grown Close	1974	$6

CASINO
| ❏ 113 | It Sure Is Bad to Love Her/(B-side unknown) | 1977 | $6 |

CRUSADER
❏ 110	A Little Bit Better/Hoping	1964	$15
❏ 109	Follow the Rainbow/Are You a Fool Like Me	1964	$15
❏ 105	I'll Touch a Star/Playing with Fire	1964	$15
❏ 101	Suspicion/Judy	1964	$20

MELODYLAND
| ❏ 6009 | Darling, Think It Over/I Can't Find It | 1975 | $5 |

MERCURY
| ❏ 72538 | Out of the Picture/Forbidden | 1966 | $10 |

MGM
| ❏ 14271 | California Dancer/The Walk | 1971 | $6 |
| ❏ 14232 | Mean Woman Blues-Candy Man/Chilly Chicago | 1971 | $6 |

PLAYER
| ❏ 134 | Lonestar Lonesome/(B-side unknown) | 1989 | $6 |

SIDEWALK
| ❏ 914 | A Step or Two Behind You/The Joke's on Me | 1967 | $10 |
| ❏ 902 | Soldier Boy/When Sin Stops, Love Begins | 1966 | $12 |

WARNER BROS.
| ❏ 7286 | Big in Dallas/Will a Man Ever Learn | 1969 | $6 |

STAINS, THE
7-Inch Extended Plays

GUTTERWORST
| ❏ 01 | Feel Guilty/Give Ireland Back to the Snakes/Sick of Being Sick/Submission | 1980 | $25 |
| ❏ 01 [PS] | Feel Guilty/Give Ireland Back to the Snakes/Sick of Being Sick/Submission | 1980 | $25 |

STALK-FORREST GROUP, THE
ELEKTRA
| ❏ 45693 | What Is Quicksand/Arthur Comics | 1970 | $60 |

STAMEY, CHRIS
CAR
| ❏ 7 | I Thought You Wanted to Know/If and When | 1978 | $15 |
| ❏ 7 [PS] | I Thought You Wanted to Know/If and When | 1978 | $15 |

CAR/ORK
| ❏ 2/81982 | The Summer Sun/Where the Fun Is | 1977 | $25 |
| ❏ 2/81982 [PS] | The Summer Sun/Where the Fun Is | 1977 | $40 |

— *Orange and black sleeve*

| ❏ 2/81982 [PS] | The Summer Sun/Where the Fun Is | 1977 | $25 |

— *Black and white sleeve*

COYOTE
| ❏ 8699 | Christmas Time/Occasional Shivers | 1986 | $10 |

— *Green vinyl*

| ❏ 8699 [PS] | Christmas Time/Occasional Shivers | 1986 | $10 |

— *Actually a plain white sleeve with gold sticker*

STAMPEDERS
BELL
❏ 45154	Devil You/Giant in the Streets	1971	$5
❏ 45188	Monday Morning Choo-Choo/Then Came the White Man	1972	$6
❏ 45331	Oh My Lady/No Destination	1973	$6
❏ 45120	Sweet City Woman/Gator Road	1971	$6
❏ 45226	Wild Eyes/Carryin' On	1972	$6

CAPITOL
| ❏ 3868 | Goodbye Goodbye/Me and My Stone | 1974 | $4 |

MGM
| ❏ 13970 | Be a Woman/I Don't Believe | 1968 | $15 |

POLYDOR
| ❏ 14060 | Carry Me/I Didn't Need You Anyhow | 1970 | $10 |

QUALITY
| ❏ 501 | Hard Lovin' Woman/Hit the Road Jack | 1976 | $4 |
| ❏ 505 | Sweet Love Bandit/Let It Begin | 1976 | $4 |

STAMPLEY, JOE
ABC DOT
❏ 17624	All These Things/My Louisiana Woman	1976	$5
❏ 17575	Cry Like a Baby/Try a Little Tenderness	1975	$5
❏ 17654	Everything I Own/Dallas Alice	1976	$5
❏ 17537	Penny/Backtrackin'	1974	$5

CHESS
| ❏ 1798 | Creation of Love/Teenage Picnic | 1961 | $30 |

DOT
❏ 17452	Bring It On Home (To Your Woman)/You Make Life Easy	1973	$6
❏ 17400	Hello Operator/Hello Charlie	1971	$6
❏ 17502	How Lucky Can One Man Be/Can You Imagine How I Feel	1974	$6
❏ 17421	If You Touch Me (You've Got to Love Me)/All the Praises	1972	$6
❏ 17485	I'm Still Loving You/The Weatherman	1973	$6
❏ 17442	Soul Song/Not Too Long Ago	1972	$6
❏ 17442 [PS]	Soul Song/Not Too Long Ago	1972	$20

— *Sleeve is promo only*

❏ 17522	Take Me Home to Somewhere/Hall of Famous Losers	1974	$6
❏ 17363	Take Time to Know Her/I Live to Love You	1970	$6
❏ 17469	Too Far Gone/Night Time and My Baby	1973	$6
❏ 17383	Two Weeks and a Day/Can You Imagine How I Feel	1971	$6

EPIC
❏ 50854	After Hours/I'm Afraid to Know You That Well	1980	$4
❏ 14-02533	All These Things/Let's Get Together and Cry	1981	$4
❏ 8-50410	Baby, I Love You So/Pour the Wine	1977	$5
❏ 34-03290	Backslidin'/I'm Willing to Try	1982	$4
❏ 8-50147	Billy, Get Me a Woman/She Has Love	1975	$5
❏ 34-04366	Brown Eyed Girl/A Winner Never Quits	1984	$4
❏ 8-50114	Dear Woman/Get On My Love Train	1975	$5
❏ 34-04173	Double Shot (Of My Baby's Love)/Penny	1983	$4
❏ 8-50626	Do You Ever Fool Around/Please Don't Throw Our Love Away	1978	$5
❏ 8-50453	Everyday I Have to Cry Some/What Would I Have	1977	$5
❏ 34-03558	Finding You/I'm Just Crazy Enough	1983	$4
❏ 50893	Haven't I Loved You Somewhere Before/Whiskey Fever	1980	$4
❏ 14-03016	I Didn't Know You Could Break a Broken Heart/I Just Can't Get Over You	1982	$4
❏ 8-50694	I Don't Lie/Draggin' Main	1979	$4
❏ 8-50575	If You've Got Ten Minutes (Let's Fall in Love)/If This Is Freedom	1978	$5
❏ 34-05592	I'll Still Be Loving You/Heart Troubles	1985	$4
❏ 14-02791	I'm Goin' Hurtin'/The Fool	1982	$4
❏ 50972	I'm Gonna Love You Back to Loving Me Again/Back on the Road Again	1981	$4
❏ 15-03095	I'm Gonna Love You Back to Loving Me Again/Whiskey Chasin'	1982	$3

— *Gray label reissue*

Number	Title	Yr	NM
❏ 34-04446	Memory Lane/Could It Wait Until Forever	1984	$4

— *With Jessica Boucher*

❏ 34-03966	Poor Side of Town/It's Over	1983	$4
❏ 50754	Put Your Clothes Back On/I Could Be Persuaded	1979	$4
❏ 8-50199	Sheik of Chicago/Whiskey Talkin'	1976	$5
❏ 8-50179	She's Helping Me Get Over Loving You/Ray of Sunshine	1975	$5
❏ 8-50361	She's Long Legged/Better Part of Me	1977	$5
❏ 50934	There's Another Woman/No Love at All	1980	$5
❏ 8-50316	There She Goes Again/You Lift Me Up	1976	$5
❏ 8-50224	Was It Worth It/Live It Up	1976	$5
❏ 34-05405	When Something Is Wrong with My Baby/Say It Like You Mean It	1985	$4
❏ 34-05758	When You Were Blue and I Was Green/There's No You Left in Us Anymore	1986	$4
❏ 19-02097	Whiskey Chasin'/The Jukebox Never Plays Home Sweet Home	1981	$4
❏ 8-50259	Whiskey Talkin'/Darlin' Raise the Shade	1976	$5

EVERGREEN
| ❏ 1075 | Cry Baby/(B-side unknown) | 1988 | $5 |
| ❏ 1100 | If You Don't Know Me by Now/(B-side unknown) | 1989 | $5 |

IMPERIAL
| ❏ 5617 | Glenda/We're Through | 1959 | $30 |
| ❏ 5637 | Heaven Dreams/Come a-Runnin' | 1960 | $30 |

PARAMOUNT
| ❏ 0025 | All the Good Is GOne/Quonette McGraw | 1970 | $8 |

PAULA
| ❏ 403 | Sometimes/Groovin' Out | 1974 | $6 |

STAMPS QUARTET, THE
COLUMBIA
❏ 4-21263	At the End of the Trail/Heaven Will Surely Be Worth It All	1954	$30
❏ 4-40806	Father, Watch Over Thy Child/I Will Not Be a Stranger	1956	$20
❏ 4-20751	Hallelujah Day/That Lonely Mile	1950	$40
❏ 4-21416	Heaven's Avenue/Sentimental Valley	1955	$30
❏ 4-20993	He's the Lily of the Valley/He Made a Way for Me	1952	$30
❏ 4-21553	Hide Me Rock of Ages/Oh When I Meet You	1956	$30
❏ 4-21201	Hide Me Rock of Ages/This I Know	1954	$30
❏ 4-21492	I Cannot Bring Them Back/Meet Me Up in Heaven	1956	$30
❏ 4-20889	I Heard the Saviour Call My Name/A Little Old Church	1952	$30
❏ 4-20921	I Know My Saviour Is There/I've Put My All in His Care	1952	$30
❏ 4-20875	I'll Tell the World/Somewhere, Someday	1952	$30
❏ 2-700(?)	I'm a Little Bit Closer/What a Saviour	1950	$50

— *Microgroove 33 1/3 rpm 7-inch single, small hole*

❏ 4-21476	It Won't Be Very Long Now/The Road That Leads to Tomorrow	1955	$30
❏ 4-20836	I Want to Know More About My Lord/Peace in the Valley	1951	$30
❏ 4-20711	Lead My Children/Whispering Hope	1950	$40
❏ 4-21349	My Lord Is Caring for Me/God Is Right	1955	$30
❏ 4-21363	My Thanks to Him/Way Up in Glory Land	1955	$30
❏ 4-20773	Paradise Island/The Lord Is Coming By and By	1951	$30
❏ 4-21245	Paradise Is Waiting/Oh When I Meet You	1954	$30
❏ 4-21067	Please Mention My Name/Sing	1953	$30
❏ 4-21005	Save Thy People, Lord/I've Found a City	1952	$30
❏ 4-21055	Sing, Brother, Sing/One of His Own	1952	$30
❏ 4-21100	Somewhere/Headed for the Gloryland	1953	$30
❏ 4-21377	There's a Ranch House in Heaven/I'll Have a Mansion of My Own	1955	$30
❏ 4-21323	This Ole House/Promise You'll Meet Me	1954	$30
❏ 4-20824	What Could I Do/The Love of God	1951	$30
❏ 4-40891	Who?/When God's Chariot Comes	1957	$20
❏ 4-21520	Will the Lord Be With Me/His Name Is Jesus	1956	$30

Number	Title	Yr	NM

STANDARDS, THE

AMOS
Number	Title	Yr	NM
❏ 134	When You Wish Upon a Star/(Instrumental)	1969	$10

CHESS
| ❏ 1869 | My Heart Belongs to You/Hello Love | 1963 | $50 |

DEBRO
| ❏ 3178 | Tears Bring Heartaches/No, No, No | 1963 | $200 |

GLENDEN
| ❏ 1315 | It Isn't Fair/Everybody Knows | 1964 | $30 |

MAGNA
| ❏ 1315 | It Isn't Fair/Everybody Knows | 1963 | $60 |
| ❏ 1314 | My Heart Belongs to You/Hello Love | 1963 | $100 |

ROULETTE
| ❏ 4487 | Tears Bring Heartaches/No, No, No | 1963 | $40 |

STANDELLS, THE

LIBERTY
Number	Title	Yr	NM
❏ 55722	Help Yourself/I'll Go Crazy	1964	$30
❏ 55743	So Fine/Linda Lou	1964	$30
❏ 55680	The Peppermint Beatle/The Shake	1964	$30

MGM
| ❏ 13350 | Someday You'll Cry/Zebra in the Kitchen | 1965 | $40 |

SUNSET
| ❏ 61000 | Ooh Poo Pah Doo/Help Yourself | 1966 | $30 |

TOWER
❏ 398	Animal Girl/Soul Drippin'	1968	$20
❏ 348	Can't Help But Love You/Ninety-Nine and One Half	1967	$20
❏ 185	Dirty Water/Rari	1966	$30
❏ 312	Don't Tell Me What to Do/When I Was a Cowboy	1967	$100

— By "The Sllednats" (Standells backwards)

❏ 257	Sometimes Good Guys Don't Wear White/Why Did You Hurt Me	1966	$20
❏ 310	Try It/Poor Shell of a Man	1967	$20
❏ 310 [PS]	Try It/Poor Shell of a Man	1967	$60
❏ 282	Why Pick on Me/Mr. Nobody	1966	$20

VEE JAY
❏ 679	Big Boss Man/Don't Say Goodbye	1965	$30
❏ 643	The Boy Next Door/B.J. Quetzal	1965	$30
❏ 643 [PS]	The Boy Next Door/B.J. Quetzal	1965	$200

STANDLEY, JOHNNY

CAPITOL
❏ F3544	Get Out and Vote! (Part 1)/(Part 2)	1956	$30
❏ F2249	It's In the Book (Part 1)/(Part 2)	1952	$30
❏ F2569	Proud New Father/Clap Your Hands	1953	$30

STANLEY BROTHERS, THE

COLUMBIA
| ❏ 2-340(?) | Angels Are Singing/It's Never Too Late | 1949 | $50 |

— Microgroove 33 1/3 rpm single, small hole

| ❏ 4-20735 | Drunkards Hell/We'll Be Sweethearts in Heaven | 1950 | $40 |
| ❏ 2-420(?) | Have You Someone/Visions of Mother | 1949 | $50 |

— Microgroove 33 1/3 rpm single, small hole

| ❏ 4-20770 | Hey, Hey, Hey/Pretty Polly | 1950 | $40 |
| ❏ 2-600(?) | I Love No One But You/Too Late to Cry | 1950 | $50 |

— Microgroove 33 1/3 rpm single, small hole

| ❏ 4-20816 | I'm a Man of Constant Sorrow/Lonesome River | 1951 | $30 |
| ❏ 2-250(?) | Let Me Be Your Friend/Little Glass of Wine | 1949 | $50 |

— Microgroove 33 1/3 rpm single, small hole

| ❏ 4-20953 | Sweetest Love/Wandering Boy | 1952 | $30 |
| ❏ 2-490(?) | The Fields Have Turned Brown/The Old Home | 1950 | $50 |

— Microgroove 33 1/3 rpm single, small hole

KING
❏ 5902	A Crown He Wore/John 3:16	1964	$10
❏ 5415	An Old Love Letter/Little Benny	1960	$20
❏ 6053	A Soldier's Grave/Take Me Home	1966	$10
❏ 5384	Daybreak in Dixie/Finger Poppin' Time	1960	$20
❏ 5869	Don't Cheat in Our Home Town/I See Through You	1964	$12

Number	Title	Yr	NM
❏ 5934	Five String Drag/Shout Little Lucie	1964	$10
❏ 6059	God's Highway/I Feel Like Going Home	1966	$10
❏ 5932	He's Passing This Way/Shoutin' on the Hills of Glory	1964	$12
❏ 5920	How Bad I Do Feel/Bully of the Town	1964	$10
❏ 5197	How Can We Thank Him/That Home Far Away	1959	$20
❏ 5306	How Far to Little Rock/Heaven Seems So Near	1960	$20
❏ 5688	I Just Came from Your Wedding/Mama Don't Allow	1962	$15
❏ 5518	I'll Take the Blame/I'd Worship You	1961	$20
❏ 5637	I'm Only Human/Keep Them Cold Icy Fingers Off of Me	1962	$15
❏ 5763	Lips That Lie/He Went to Sleep -- The Hogs Ate Him	1963	$15
❏ 5494	Little Bessie/The Village Church Yard	1961	$20
❏ 5754	Memories of Mother/Paul and Silas	1963	$15
❏ 5367	Mother Left Me Her Bible/Over in Glory Land	1960	$20
❏ 5347	Mountain Dew/Old Rattler	1960	$20
❏ 5269	Mountain Girls Can Love/A Man of Constant Sorrow	1959	$20
❏ 5674	My Deceitful Heart/The Drunkard's Dream	1962	$15
❏ 5732	Old and In the Way/Six Months Ain't Long	1963	$15
❏ 5313	Pass Me Not/When Jesus Beckons Me Home	1960	$20
❏ 5155	She's More to Be Pitied/The Train	1958	$30
❏ 5629	Still Trying to Get to Little Rock/String, Eraser and Blotter	1962	$15
❏ 5809	Stone Walls and Steel Bars/Lonesome Night	1963	$15
❏ 5291	Sunny Side of the Mountain/Shenandoah Waltz	1959	$20
❏ 5355	Sweeter Than the Flowers/Next Sunday, Darling, Is My Birthday	1960	$20
❏ 5441	The Angel of Death/Jordan	1961	$20
❏ 6023	The End of the Road/Pray for the Boys	1966	$10
❏ 6089	The Hills of Roan County/I Don't Want Your Rambling Letters	1967	$10
❏ 5557	There Is a Trap/Fast Express	1961	$20
❏ 5460	The Window Up Above/The Wild Side of Life	1961	$20
❏ 5916	Train 45/I Just Stood There	1964	$10
❏ 6079	Whiskey/A Little Birdie	1967	$10
❏ 5233	White Dove/Mother's Footsteps Guide Me	1959	$20
❏ 5708	Who Will Sing for Me/Drinking from the Fountain	1963	$15

MERCURY
❏ 70886	Baby Girl/Say You'll Take Me Back	1956	$30
❏ 70453	Blue Moon of Kentucky/I Just Got Wise	1954	$30
❏ 70483	Harbor of Love/Calling from Heaven	1954	$30
❏ 70546	Hard Times/I Worship You	1955	$30
❏ 71258	If That's the Way You Feel/I'd Rather Be Forgotten	1957	$30
❏ 70718	I Hear My Savior Calling/Just a Little Talk with Jesus	1955	$30
❏ 70217	I'm Lonesome/That Weary Heart You Stole	1953	$30
❏ 71302	It's a Long Story/No Foolish Fling	1958	$30
❏ 70663	Lonesome and Blue/Orange Blossom Special	1955	$30
❏ 71207	Loving You Too Well/Fling Ding	1957	$30
❏ 70400	Memories of Mother/Could You Love Me	1954	$30
❏ 70270	Our Last Goodbye/Won't You Be Mine	1953	$30
❏ 70612	So Blue/You'd Better Get Right	1955	$30
❏ 71135	The Cry from the Cross/Let Me Walk, Lord, By Your Side	1957	$30
❏ 71064	The Flood/I'm Lost, I'll Never Find the Way	1957	$30

STARDAY
| ❏ 836 | Bonnie and Clyde's Getaway/The Story of Bonnie and Clyde | 1968 | $10 |

— B-side by Jimmie Skinner

❏ 565	Carolina Mountain Home/A Few More Sessions	1961	$20
❏ 413	Christmas Is Near/Holiday Pickin'	1958	$30
❏ 587	Come All Ye Tenderhearted/Choo Choo Comin'	1962	$15
❏ 546	Don't Go Out Tonight/If I Lose	1961	$20
❏ 406	Gonna Paint the Town/That Happy Night	1958	$30
❏ 466	Highway of Regret/Another Night	1959	$30
❏ 522	Little Maggie/God Gave You to Me	1960	$20
❏ 438	Trust Each Other/Beneath the Maple	1959	$30

Number	Title	Yr	NM

STANLEY, MICHAEL, BAND

ARISTA
❏ 0368	Baby If You Wanna Dance/Fool's Parade	1978	$4
❏ 0436	Last Night/Down to the Wire	1979	$4
❏ 0348	Why Should Love Be This Way/Late Show	1978	$4

EMI AMERICA
❏ 8090	Falling in Love Again/Does It Hurt	1981	$3
❏ 8063	He Can't Love You/Carolyn	1980	$3
❏ 8064	Lover/Save a Little Piece for Me	1981	$3
❏ 8178	My Town/Just How Good	1983	$3
❏ 8189	Someone Like You/Highlife	1983	$3
❏ 8146	Take the Time/Just a Little Bit Longer	1982	$3
❏ 8130	When I'm Holding You Tight/In Between the Lines	1982	$3

EPIC
❏ 50151	Face the Music/Song for My Children	1975	$4
❏ 50116	I'm Gonna Love You/Step the Way	1975	$4
❏ 50242	Ladies' Choice/Sweet Refrain	1976	$4
❏ 50416	Love Hasn't Been Here/Nothing's Gonna Change My Mind	1977	$4

STANLEY, PAUL
Also see KISS.

CASABLANCA
| ❏ 940 | Hold Me, Touch Me/Goodbye | 1978 | $6 |

— Casablanca Record and FilmWorks" label

| ❏ 940 | Hold Me, Touch Me/Goodbye | 1978 | $15 |

— Tan label with camel

STANSHALL, VIVIAN

LIBERTY
| ❏ 56171 | Labio-Dental Fricative/Paper-Round | 1970 | $30 |

STANTE, TONI

PARKWAY
| ❏ 970 | Donde Este Santa Claus/It's My Life | 1965 | $12 |

STAPLE SINGERS, THE

20TH CENTURY
| ❏ 2508 | Hold On to Your Dreams/Cold and Windy Night | 1981 | $4 |

CURTOM
| ❏ 0109 | Let's Do It Again/After Sex | 1975 | $4 |

EPIC
❏ 9748	Be Careful of Stones That You Throw/More Than a Hammer and Nail	1964	$12
❏ 10339	Crying in the Chapel/Nothing Lasts Forever	1968	$8
❏ 10264	Deliver Me/He	1967	$8
❏ 9776	Do Something for Yourself/Samson and Delilah	1965	$12
❏ 10220	For What It's Worth/Are You Sure	1967	$8
❏ 10742	For What It's Worth/Why	1971	$6
❏ 9825	Freedom Highway/The Funeral	1965	$10
❏ 10294	Let's Get Together/Power of Love	1968	$8
❏ 10104	Pray On/It's Been a Change	1966	$12
❏ 10158	Why (Am I Treated So Bad)/What Are They Doing (In Heaven Today)	1967	$8
❏ 9880	Why/What Are They Doing	1965	$10

PRIVATE I
❏ 05565	Are You Ready/Love Wonks in Strange Ways	1985	$4
❏ 05565 [PS]	Are You Ready/Love Wonks in Strange Ways	1985	$6
❏ 04384	H-A-T-E (Don't Live Here Anymore)/Can You Hang	1984	$4
❏ 04583	Slippery People/On My Own Again	1984	$4
❏ 04711	This Is Our Night/Turning Point	1984	$4

RIVERSIDE
❏ 4568	Blowing in the Wind/Wish I Had Answered	1963	$15
❏ 4563	Cotton Fields/This Land	1963	$15
❏ 4531	Gambling Man/Use What You Got	1962	$15
❏ 4518	Gloryland/Hammer and Nails	1962	$15
❏ 4553	I Can't Help from Cryin'/Let That Liar Again	1963	$15
❏ 4540	There Was a Star/The Virgin Mary Had One Son	1962	$15

SHARP
| ❏ 603 | This May Be the Last Time/This Same Jesus | 1960 | $20 |

Number	Title	Yr	NM
STAX			
❏ 0248	Back Road Into Town/My Main Man	1975	$5
❏ 0164	Be What You Are/I Like the Things About Me	1973	$5
—B-side by Cal Starr			
❏ 0074	Brand New Day/God Bless the Children	1970	$6
❏ 0215	City in the Sky/That's What Friends Are For	1974	$5
❏ 0066	Give a Damn/God Bless the Children	1970	$6
❏ 0083	Heavy Makes You Happy (Sha-Na-Boom-Boom)/Love Is Plentiful	1970	$6
❏ 0179	If You're Ready (Come Go with Me)/Love Comes in All Colors	1973	$5
❏ 0125	I'll Take You There/I'm Just Another Soldier	1972	$5
❏ 0007	Long Walk to D.C./Stay with Us	1968	$6
❏ 0227	My Main Man/Who Made the Man	1974	$5
❏ 0156	Oh La De Da/We the People	1973	$5
❏ 0031	(Sittin' On) The Dock of the Bay/Top of the Mountain	1969	$6
❏ 0039	The Gardener/The Challenge	1969	$6
❏ 0019	The Ghetto/Got to Be Some Changes Made	1968	$6
❏ 0137	This World/Are You Sure	1972	$5
❏ 0196	Touch a Hand, Make a Friend/Tellin' Lies	1974	$5
❏ 0213	What's Your Thing/Whicha Way Did It Go	1974	$5
—B-side by Pops Staples			
❏ 0052	When Will We Be Paid/Tend to Your Own Business	1969	$6
❏ 0084	Who Took the Merry Out of Christmas/(Instrumental)	1970	$8
UNITED			
❏ 165	It Rained Children/Won't You Sit Down	1955	$400
VEE JAY			
❏ 881	Downward Road/So Soon	1959	$20
❏ 169	God's Wonderful Love/If I Could Hear My Mother	1956	$30
❏ 856	I Had a Dream/Help Me Jesus	1958	$20
❏ 870	I'm Leaving/Going Away	1959	$20
❏ 902	I've Been Scorned/Don't Knock	1961	$15
❏ 846	Let Me Ride/I'm Coming Home	1957	$30
❏ 866	Love Is the Way/On My Way to Heaven	1959	$20
❏ 893	Pray On/Too Close	1960	$15
❏ 912	Sit Down Servant/Swing Low	1962	$15
❏ 930	Swing Low Sweet Chariot/I'm So Glad	1963	$15
WARNER BROS.			
❏ 8748	Chica Boom/Handwriting on the Wall	1979	$4
❏ 49598	God Can/Unlock Your Mind	1980	$4
—Warner Bros. titles as "The Staples"			
❏ 8510	I Honestly Love You/Family Tree	1978	$4
❏ 8279	Love Me, Love Me, Love Me/Pass It On	1976	$4
❏ 8460	See a Little Further (Than My Bed)/Let's Go to the Disco	1977	$4
❏ 8317	Sweeter Than the Sweet/Making Love	1977	$4
STAPLES, GORDON, AND THE MOTOWN STRINGS			
MOTOWN			
❏ 1180 [DJ]	Strung Out (same on both sides)	1971	$40
—Red vinyl promo			
❏ 1180	Strung Out/Sounds of the Zodiac	1971	$40
STAPLES, MARK			
MARK STAPLES			
❏ 9547	A Mining City Christmas/Our Lady Of the Rockies	1984	$4
STAPLES, MAVIS			
CURTOM			
❏ 0132	A Piece of the Action/Till Blossoms Bloom	1977	$4
PAISLEY PARK			
❏ 22968	20th Century Express/All the Discomforts of Home	1989	$3
PHONO			
❏ 1051	Love Gone Bad/(B-side unknown)	1984	$5
VOLT			
❏ 4086	Endlessly/Don't Change Me Now	1972	$5

Number	Title	Yr	NM
❏ 4044	I Have Learned to Do Without You/Since I Fell for You	1970	$5
WARNER BROS.			
❏ PRO-S-3878 [DJ]	Christmas Vacation (same on both sides)	1989	$5
❏ 49054	Oh What a Feeling/If I Can't Have You	1979	$4
❏ 28765	Show Me How It Works/Half Time	1986	$3
❏ 8838	Tonight I Feel Like Dancing/If I Can't Have You	1979	$4
STAPLETON, CYRIL			
LONDON			
❏ 1895	I Saw Three Ships/Christmas Island	1959	$10
STAR FIRES, THE			
HARAL			
❏ 777	Each Night at Nine/What Good Is Money	1962	$125
STARCHER, BUDDY			
BOONE			
❏ 1038	History Repeats Itself/Sniper's Hill	1966	$12
COLUMBIA			
❏ 2-490(?)	Beyond the Sunset/Are You Facing the World All Alone	1949	$50
—Microgroove 33 1/3 rpm 7-inch single, small hole			
❏ 2-580(?)	Colored Child's Funeral/Oh Leave One Token of Your Love	1950	$60
—Microgroove 33 1/3 rpm 7-inch single, small hole			
❏ 4-20723	I'll Forgive Dear But Never Forget/My Old Pal of Yesterday	1950	$40
❏ 2-380(?)	I Planted a Rose/Isn't He Wonderful	1949	$50
—Microgroove 33 1/3 rpm 7-inch single, small hole			
DECCA			
❏ 32012	Fall of a Nation/The Last Supper	1966	$8
❏ 31975	Tax Payer's Lament/Day of Decision	1966	$8
HEART WARMING			
❏ 5069	When Payday Comes/What Then?	1967	$8
STARDAY			
❏ 471	Ace of Hearts/Cryin'	1959	$20
❏ 460	Billy the Kid/Running Away from the Blues	1959	$20
❏ 763	Little Red Riding Hood/Ace of Hearts	1966	$8
❏ 439	The Battle of New Orleans/Pale Wildwood Flower	1959	$20
STARDUST, ALVIN			
CHRYSALIS			
❏ 2835	So Near To Christmas/Alright - OK	1984	$6
❏ 2835 [PS]	So Near To Christmas/Alright - OK	1984	$6
—Both record and sleeve are U.K. imports			
❏ ALV3 [PS]	So Near To Christmas/Alright - OK/Clock On The Wall / Show You The Way	1983	$6
—Two-record set			
❏ ALV3	So Near To Christmas /Alright - OK/Clock On The Wall / Show You The Way	1983	$6
—Sleeve for two-record set; both of above are U.K. imports			
HONEY BEE			
❏ Honey13	Christmas/Executive	1989	$6
❏ Honey13 [PS]	Christmas/Executive	1989	$6
—Both record and sleeve are U.K. imports			
STARETTES			
VENETT			
❏ 101 [DJ]	Fifi The Christmas Fawn/Little Christmas Bells	1962	$15
STARFIRES, THE (1)			
APT			
❏ 25030	Fender Bender/Camel Walk	1959	$30
PACE			
❏ 101	Fender Bender/Camel Walk	1959	$50
STARFIRES, THE (2)			
ATOMIC			
❏ A-1912	Love Will Break Your Heart/The Dances	1961	$100

Number	Title	Yr	NM
BARGAIN			
❏ 5003	Love Will Break Your Heart/The Dances	1961	$70
D&H			
❏ 200	These Foolish Things/Let's Do the Pony	1961	$120
STARFIRES, THE (3)			
DECCA			
❏ 30916	Love Is Here to Stay/Tomorrow	1959	$60
❏ 30730	Three Roses/I Have Someone	1958	$50
STARFIRES, THE (4)			
DUEL			
❏ 518	Fools Fall in Love/Under the Stars	1962	$60
TRIUMPH			
❏ 61	Fink/Work Out Fine	1965	$30
STARFIRES, THE (5)			
G.I.			
❏ 4004	Cry for Freedom/(B-side unknown)	1965	$125
❏ 4001	I Never Loved Her/Linda	1965	$2500
STARFIRES, THE (7)			
ROUND			
❏ 1016	Space Needle/The Jordan Stomp	1962	$50
❏ 1016 [PS]	Space Needle/The Jordan Stomp	1962	$70
STARLAND VOCAL BAND			
WINDSONG			
❏ GB-10943	Afternoon Delight/California Day	1977	$3
—Gold Standard Series" reissue			
❏ CB-10588	Afternoon Delight/Starland	1976	$4
❏ CB-10785	California Day/War Surplus Baby	1976	$4
❏ CB-10855	Hail, Hail, Rock and Roll/Ain't It the Fall	1976	$4
❏ CB-11261	Late Nite Radio/Please Mrs. Newslady	1978	$4
❏ CB-11067	Light of My Life/Prism	1977	$4
❏ CB-11899	Loving You with My Eyes/Apartment for Rent	1980	$4
❏ CB-11168	Mr. Wrong/Too Long a Journey	1977	$4
❏ CB-12011	Thought I Would Never Find Love/Love Stuff	1980	$4
STARLETS, THE (1)			
ASTRO			
❏ 202/3	P.S. I Love You/Where Is My Love Tonight	1960	$40
STARLETS, THE (2)			
CHESS			
❏ 2038	I Wanna Be Good to You/Watered Down	1968	$30
❏ 1997	My Baby's Real/Loving You Is Something New	1967	$30
STARLETS, THE (3)			
LUTE			
❏ 5909	I'm So Young/He's Got It	1960	$30
PAM			
❏ 1003	Better Tell Him No/You Are the One	1961	$30
❏ 1004	My Last Cry/Money Hungry	1961	$30
STARLETTES, THE			
CHECKER			
❏ 895	Please Ring My Phone/Jungle Love	1958	$200
STARLIGHTERS, THE			
CRYSTALETTE			
❏ 662	Christmas Won't Be the Same (With You Away)/La Pinata (Mexican Christmas Song)	1952	$40
❏ 661	Sweetheart of Sigma Chi/Don't Call Me Coach, Call Me George	1952	$30
END			
❏ 1072	A Story of Love/Let's Take a Stroll	1960	$120
❏ 1049	I Cried/You're the One to Blame	1959	$100
❏ 1031	It's Twelve O'Clock/The Birdland	1958	$500
IRMA			
❏ 101	Love Cry/Last Night	1956	$400
LAMP			
❏ 2014	Slipping Out/Rocking Too Much	1958	$60
WHEEL			
❏ 1004	Hot Licks/Creepin'	1960	$20

Number	Title	Yr	NM

STARLINGS, THE (1)
DAWN
❏ 213	A-Loo, A-Loo/I Gotta Go Now	1955	$400
❏ 212	I'm Just a Crying Fool/ Hokey-Smokey Mama	1955	$600

JOSIE
❏ 760	My Plea for Love/Music, Maestro, Please	1954	$500

STARLINGS, THE (2)
WORLD PACIFIC
❏ 809	All I Want/That's Me	1959	$50

STARLITES, THE
PEAK
❏ 5000	Missing You/Give Me a Kiss	1957	$200

STARR, ANDY
KAPP
❏ 190	Do It Right Now/I Waited for You to Remember	1957	$30

MGM
❏ 12315	She's a-Going, Jessie/ Old Deacon Jones	1956	$200

STARR, EDWIN
20TH CENTURY
❏ 2396	Contact/Don't Waste Your Time	1978	$4
❏ 2455	Get Up-Whirlpool/ Better and Better	1980	$4
❏ 2408	H.A.P.P.Y. Radio/My Friend	1979	$4
❏ 2338	I Just Wanna Do My Thing/ Mr. Davenport and Mr. James	1977	$4
❏ 2389	I'm So Into You/Don't Waste Your Time	1978	$4
❏ 2423	It's Called the Rock/ H.A.P.P.Y. Radio	1979	$4
❏ 2441	It's Called the Rock/ H.A.P.P.Y. Radio	1980	$4
❏ 2420	It's Called the Rock/Patiently	1979	$4
❏ 2445	Stronger Than You Think I Am/(Instrumental)	1980	$4
❏ 2450	Tell-A-Star/Boop Boop Song	1980	$4
❏ 2477	Twenty-Five Miles/Never Turn My Back on You	1980	$4

GORDY
❏ 7107	Funky Music Sho Nuff Turns Me On/Cloud Nine	1971	$6
❏ 7066	Gonna Keep On Tryin' Til I Win Your Love/I Want My Baby Back	1967	$6
❏ 7071	I Am the Man for You Baby/ My Weakness Is You	1968	$6
❏ 7087	I'm Still a Struggling Man/ Pretty Little Angel	1969	$6
❏ 7090	Oh How Happy/Ooh Baby Baby	1969	$6
— With Blinky			
❏ 7104	Stop the War Now/Gonna Keep On Tryin' Til I Win Your Love	1970	$6
❏ 7097	Time/Running Back and Forth	1970	$6
❏ 7083	Twenty-Five Miles/Love Is the Destination	1969	$6
❏ 7083 [DJ]	Twenty-Five Miles (same on both sides)	1969	$30
— Promo only on red vinyl			
❏ 7101	War/He Who Picks a Rose	1970	$6
❏ 7078	Way Over There/If My Heart Could Tell the Story	1968	$6

GRANITE
❏ 532	Abyssinia Jones/Beginning	1975	$5
❏ 522	Pain/I'll Never Forget You	1975	$5
❏ 528	Stay with Me/Party	1975	$5

MONTAGE
❏ 1216	Tired of It/(B-side unknown)	1982	$4

MOTOWN
❏ 1284	Ain't It Hell Up in Harlem/Don't It Feel Good to Be Free	1973	$5
❏ 1300	Big Papa/Like We Used to Do	1974	$5
❏ 1326	Who's Right or Wrong/Lonely Rainy Days in San Diego	1974	$5

RIC-TIC
❏ 103	Agent Double-O-Soul/ (Instrumental)	1965	$20
❏ 107	Back Street/(Instrumental)	1965	$20
❏ 114	Headline News/Harlem	1966	$20
❏ 118	It's My Turn Now/Girls Are Getting Prettier	1967	$20
❏ 109X [DJ]	Scott's On Swingers (S.O.S.)/I Have Faith in You	1966	$60
❏ 109	Stop Her on Sight (S.O.S.)/I Have Faith in You	1966	$20

SOUL
❏ 35096	Take Me Clear from Here/ Ball of Confusion	1972	$6
❏ 35103	There You Go/(Instrumental)	1973	$6
❏ 35100	Who Is the Leader of the People/Don't Tell Me I'm Crazy	1972	$6

STARR, KAY
ABC
❏ 11049	My Melancholy Baby/ Some Sweet Tomorrow	1968	$5
❏ 11013	When the Lights Go On Again (All Over the World)/ Only When You're Lonely	1967	$5

CAPITOL
❏ F936	Bonaparte's Retreat/ Someday Sweetheart	1950	$30
❏ F1652	Bonaparte's Retreat/ The Honeymoon	1951	$15
—Reissue			
❏ 4894	Bossa Nova Casanova/ Swingin' at the Hungry-O	1962	$8
❏ F2657	Changing Partners/I'll Always Be in Love with You	1953	$15
❏ F1256	Christopher Robin/The Man with the Bag	1950	$20
❏ F1492	Come Back Darling/Then You've Never Been Blue	1951	$20
❏ F1710	Come On-a My House/ Hold Me, Hold Me	1951	$20
❏ F2213	Comes A-Long A-Love/ Three Letters	1952	$15
❏ F1796	Don't Tell Him What's Happened to Me/Angry	1951	$20
❏ F2151	Fool, Fool, Fool/ Kay's Lament	1952	$15
❏ 4542	Foolin' Around/Kay's Lament	1961	$8
❏ F2887	Fortune in Dreams/Am I a Toy or Treasure	1954	$15
❏ 4835	Four Walls/Oh Lonesome Me	1962	$8
❏ 4835 [PS]	Four Walls/Oh Lonesome Me	1962	$15
❏ F2464	Half a Photograph/ Allez-Vous-En	1953	$15
❏ 5386	Happy/I Forgot to Forget	1965	$6
❏ F980	Hoop-Dee-Doo/A Woman Likes to Be Told	1950	$30
❏ F2769	If You Love Me (Really Love Me)/The Man Upstairs	1954	$15
❏ F1124	I'll Never Be Free/Ain't Nobody's Business But My Own	1950	$30
— With Tennessee Ernie Ford			
❏ 4583	I'll Never Be Free/Nobody	1961	$8
❏ F1649	I'm the Lonesomest Gal in Town/You've Got to See Mama Every Night	1951	$15
— Reissue			
❏ 5492	I Never Dreamed I Could Love You/I Know That You Know That We…	1965	$6
❏ 5194	It's Happening All Over Again/Dancing on My Tears	1964	$6
❏ F2062	I Waited a Little Too Long/Me Too	1952	$15
❏ 54-681	I Wish I Had a Wishbone/ There's Yes! Yes! In Your Eyes	1949	$40
❏ 5328	Look on the Brighter Side/Lorna's Here	1965	$6
❏ F1357	Lovesick Blues/Evenin'	1951	$20
❏ F1205	Mama Goes Everywhere Papa Goes/Please Love Me	1950	$20
— With Tennessee Ernie Ford			
❏ F1072	Mississippi/He's a Good Man to Have Around	1950	$30
❏ F1567	Oceans of Tears/ You're My Sugar	1951	$20
— With Tennessee Ernie Ford			
❏ F1278	Oh Babe/Everybody's Somebody's Fool	1950	$20
❏ 5601	Old Records/Tears and Photographs	1966	$6
❏ 4419	Out in the Cold Again/ Just for a Thrill	1960	$8
❏ F1688	Side by Side/Breeze	1954	$10
— Reissue			
❏ F2334	Side by Side/Noah	1953	$15
❏ F1902	So Help Me/Hold Me, Hold Me	1951	$20
❏ F811	Stormy Weather/You're the One I Care For	1950	$30
❏ 5046	To Each His Own/ Make a Circle	1963	$8
❏ 5259	Together Again/Friends	1964	$6
❏ F1856	Two Brothers/On Honky Tonk Hardwood Floor	1951	$20
❏ 4620	Well I Ask Ya/Rough Riders	1961	$8
❏ F1964	Wheel of Fortune/I Wanna Love You	1952	$20
❏ F2595	When My Dreamboat Comes Home/Swamp Fire	1953	$20
❏ F1152	When You're a Long Way from Home/Is There Anything Wrong with Texas (The Texas Song)	1950	$20

DOT
❏ 17183	Something Happened to Me/12th Street Marching Band	1968	$5

GNP CRESCENDO
❏ 488	Tie a Yellow Ribbon Round the Ole Oak Tree/ Something's Missing	1974	$4

❏ 493	What Can I Say After I Say I'm Sorry/What Is This Thing Called Love	1975	$4

RCA VICTOR
❏ 47-6079	For Better or Worse/ Foolishly Yours	1955	$10
❏ 47-6146	Good and Lonesome/ Where, What or When	1955	$10
❏ 47-7414	He Cha-Cha'd Me/Oh How I Miss You Tonight	1958	$12
❏ 47-6247	Home Sweet Home on the Range/Without a Song	1955	$12
❏ 47-7521	I Couldn't Care Less/ Only Love Me	1959	$10
❏ 47-6981	My Heart Reminds Me/ Flim Flam Floo	1957	$10
❏ 47-6541	Second Fiddle/ Love Ain't Right	1956	$10
❏ 47-7218	Stroll Me/Rockin' Chair	1958	$10
❏ 47-6748	The Brass Ring/ Touch and Go	1956	$12
❏ 47-6617	The Good Book/The Things I Never Had	1956	$10
❏ 47-7114	The Last Song and Dance/Help Me	1957	$10
❏ 47-5999	Turn Right/If Anyone Finds This, I Love You	1955	$10

RCA VICTOR
❏ EPB-1149 [PS]	The One and Only Kay Starr	1955	$20
— Cover for 2-EP set (547-0719, 547-0720)			
❏ 547-0719	Wrap Your Troubles in Dreams/Fit as a Fiddle// Georgia on My Mind// Jump for Joy	1955	$15
— One record of 2-EP set EPB-1149			

STARR, RAY
KING
❏ 5652	I Have to Laugh to Keep from Crying/In the Middle of Two Hearts	1962	$10

STARR, RICHARD
CAMEO
❏ 340	Witchcraft Love/ Singing the Blues	1965	$20

STARR, RINGO
Also see THE BEATLES; GEORGE HARRISON AND FRIENDS.

APPLE
❏ 1849	Back Off Boogaloo/Blindman	1972	$8
— Green-background label			
❏ 1849	Back Off Boogaloo/Blindman	1972	$80
— Blue-background label			
❏ 1849 [PS]	Back Off Boogaloo/Blindman	1972	$20
— Black paper with flat finish			
❏ 1849 [PS]	Back Off Boogaloo/Blindman	1972	$50
— Glossy black paper on both sides			
❏ 1849 [PS]	Back Off Boogaloo/Blindman	1972	$50
— Glossy black on one side, gray on the other			
❏ 1849 [DJ]	Back Off Boogaloo/Blindman	1972	$200
— White label			
❏ 2969	Beaucoups of Blues/ Coochy-Coochy	1970	$30
— With small Capitol logo on bottom of B-side label and star on A-side label			
❏ 2969	Beaucoups of Blues/ Coochy-Coochy	1970	$50
— With "Mfd. by Apple" on label and star on A-side label			
❏ 2969	Beaucoups of Blues/ Coochy-Coochy	1970	$8
— With "Mfd. by Apple" on label and no star on A-side label			
❏ 1826 [PS]	Beaucoups of Blues/ Coochy-Coochy	1970	$50
— Sleeve with wrong catalog number (actually 2969)			
❏ 2969 [PS]	Beaucoups of Blues/ Coochy-Coochy	1970	$60
— Sleeve with correct catalog number			
❏ 1831	It Don't Come Easy/ Early 1970	1971	$8
❏ 1831	It Don't Come Easy/ Early 1970	1971	$15
— With star on A-side label			
❏ 1831 [PS]	It Don't Come Easy/ Early 1970	1971	$40
❏ 1831	It Don't Come Easy/ Early 1970	1975	$40
— With "All rights reserved" on label			
❏ P-1882 [DJ]	It's All Down to Goodnight Vienna (mono/stereo)	1975	$50
❏ 1882	It's All Down to Goodnight Vienna/Oo-Wee	1975	$6
— Custom nebula label			
❏ 1882 [PS]	It's All Down to Goodnight Vienna/Oo-Wee	1975	$30
❏ P-1872 [DJ]	Oh My My (Edited Mono)/ Oh My My (Long Stereo)	1974	$60

Number	Title	Yr	NM
❏ 1872	Oh My My/Step Lightly	1974	$6
—Custom star label			
❏ 1872	Oh My My/Step Lightly	1974	$8
—Regular Apple label			
❏ 1876	Only You/Call Me	1974	$6
—Custom nebula label			
❏ 1876	Only You/Call Me	1974	$8
—Regular Apple label			
❏ 1876 [PS]	Only You/Call Me	1974	$30
❏ P-1876 [DJ]	Only You (mono/stereo)	1974	$50
❏ P-1882 [DJ]	Oo-Wee/Oo-Wee	1975	$75
❏ 1865	Photograph/Down and Out	1973	$6
—Custom star label			
❏ 1865 [PS]	Photograph/Down and Out	1973	$30
❏ P-1865 [DJ]	Photograph (mono/stereo)	1973	$60

ATLANTIC

Number	Title	Yr	NM
❏ 3361	A Dose of Rock 'N' Roll/Cryin'	1976	$10
❏ 3361 [DJ]	A Dose of Rock 'N' Roll (With Intro)/(Without Intro)	1976	$125
—All-white label with no Atlantic logo at top			
❏ 3361 [DJ]	A Dose of Rock 'N' Roll (With Intro)/(Without Intro)	1976	$20
—Light blue label with Atlantic logo at top			
❏ 3412	Drowning in the Sea of Love/Just a Dream	1977	$120
❏ 3412 [DJ]	Drowning in the Sea of Love (mono/stereo)	1977	$30
❏ 3371 [DJ]	Hey Baby/(B-side blank)	1976	$300
—Light blue label			
❏ 3371	Hey Baby/Lady Gaye	1976	$40
❏ 3371 [DJ]	Hey Baby (mono/stereo)	1976	$125
—All-white label with no Atlantic logo at top			
❏ 3371 [DJ]	Hey Baby (mono/stereo)	1976	$20
—Red and white label on mono side, light blue label on stereo side			
❏ 3429	Wings/Just a Dream	1977	$40
❏ 3429 [DJ]	Wings (mono/stereo)	1977	$125
—All-white label with no Atlantic logo at top			
❏ 3429 [DJ]	Wings (mono/stereo)	1977	$20
—Red and white label on mono side, light blue label on stereo side			

BOARDWALK

Number	Title	Yr	NM
❏ NB7-11-134 [DJ]	Private Property (same on both sides)	1982	$20
❏ NB7-11-134	Private Property/Stop and Take the Time to Smell the Roses	1982	$15
❏ NB7-11-130	Wrack My Brain/Drumming Is My Madness	1981	$5
❏ NB7-11-130 [PS]	Wrack My Brain/Drumming Is My Madness	1981	$5
❏ NB7-11-130 [DJ]	Wrack My Brain (mono/stereo)	1981	$20

CAPITOL

Number	Title	Yr	NM
❏ B-44409	Act Naturally/Key's in the Mailbox	1989	$20
—A-side with Buck Owens; B-side is Owens solo			
❏ P-B-44409 [DJ]	Act Naturally (same on both sides)	1989	$40
—With Buck Owens			
❏ 1849	Back Off Boogaloo/Blindman	1976	$40
—Orange label			
❏ 1849	Back Off Boogaloo/Blindman	1978	$8
—Purple late-1970s label			
❏ 2969	Beaucoups of Blues/Coochy-Coochy	1976	$50
—Orange label			
❏ 1831	It Don't Come Easy/Early 1970	1976	$30
—Orange label			
❏ 1831	It Don't Come Easy/Early 1970	1978	$6
—Purple late-1970s label			
❏ 1831	It Don't Come Easy/Early 1970	1983	$6
—Black colorband label			
❏ 1831	It Don't Come Easy/Early 1970	1988	$5
—Purple late-1980s label (wider)			
❏ 1882	It's All Down to Goodnight Vienna/Oo-Wee	1978	$8
—Purple late-1970s label			
❏ 1876	Only You/Call Me	1978	$8
—Purple late-1970s label			
❏ 1876	Only You/Call Me	1983	$125
—Black colorband label			
❏ 1865	Photograph/Down and Out	1978	$8
—Purple late-1970s label			
❏ 1865	Photograph/Down and Out	1983	$8
—Black colorband label			
❏ 1865	Photograph/Down and Out	1988	$6
—Purple late-1980s label (wider)			

PORTRAIT

Number	Title	Yr	NM
❏ 6-70018 [DJ]	Heart on My Sleeve (mono/stereo)	1978	$30
❏ 6-70018	Heart on My Sleeve/Who Needs a Heart	1978	$20
❏ 6-70015 [DJ]	Lipstick Traces (On a Cigarette) (mono/stereo)	1978	$30
❏ 6-70015	Lipstick Traces (On a Cigarette)/Old Time Relovin'	1978	$20

STARR, SALLY
7-Inch Extended Plays

CLYMAX

Number	Title	Yr	NM
❏ EP-1001	Cuckoo in the Clock/Sing a Song of Happiness//TV Pal/A.B.C. Rock	1959	$35
—Second record of 3-EP set; master numbers are JB 142/JB 143			
❏ EP-1001/2/3 [PS]	Our Gal Sal	1959	$50
—Triple gatefold cover for all three EP-1001 records (despite what the cover says, the records are each numbered 1001)			
❏ EP-1001	Toy Shop in the Town/Happy Birthday//Candy Red/Blue Ranger	1959	$35
—First record of 3-EP set; master numbers are JB-140/JB-141			

STARS OF FAITH

VEE JAY

Number	Title	Yr	NM
❏ 915	Go Where I Send Thee/Poor Little Jesus Boy	1962	$10

STARSHIP

ELEKTRA

Number	Title	Yr	NM
❏ 69349	Wild Again/Laying It on the Line	1988	$3

GRUNT

Number	Title	Yr	NM
❏ 5308-7-R	Beat Patrol/Girls Like You	1987	$3
❏ 5308-7-R [PS]	Beat Patrol/Girls Like You	1987	$3
❏ PB-14393	Before I Go/Cut You Down to Size	1986	$3
❏ PB-14393 [PS]	Before I Go/Cut You Down to Size	1986	$5
❏ 5225-7-R	It's Not Over ('Til It's Over)/Babylon	1987	$3
❏ 5225-7-R [PS]	It's Not Over ('Til It's Over)/Babylon	1987	$3
❏ PB-14253	Sara/Hearts of the World (Will Understand)	1985	$8
—Originals on blue vinyl			
❏ PB-14253	Sara/Hearts of the World (Will Understand)	1985	$3
❏ PB-14253 [PS]	Sara/Hearts of the World (Will Understand)	1985	$5
❏ PB-14332	Tomorrow Doesn't Matter Tonight/Love Rusts	1986	$3
❏ PB-14332 [PS]	Tomorrow Doesn't Matter Tonight/Love Rusts	1986	$60
❏ PB-14170	We Built This City/Private Room	1985	$3
❏ PB-14170 [PS]	We Built This City/Private Room	1985	$5
❏ JK-14170 [DJ]	We Built This City (Short)/We Built This City (Long)	1985	$8
❏ JB-14200 [DJ]	We Built This City (Special Non-DJ Rock Radio Version)/We Built This City	1985	$10

RCA

Number	Title	Yr	NM
❏ 9032-7-R	It's Not Enough/Love Among the Cannibals	1989	$3
❏ 9032-7-R [PS]	It's Not Enough/Love Among the Cannibals	1989	$3
❏ 6964-7-R	Set the Night to Music/I Don't Know Why	1988	$4

STARZ

CAPITOL

Number	Title	Yr	NM
❏ 4546	(Any Way That You Want It) I'll Be There/Texas	1978	$4
❏ 4546 [PS]	(Any Way That You Want It) I'll Be There/Texas	1978	$5
❏ 4399	Cherry Baby/Rock Six Times	1977	$10
—Originals on yellow vinyl			
❏ 4399	Cherry Baby/Rock Six Times	1977	$4
❏ 4399 [PS]	Cherry Baby/Rock Six Times	1977	$6
❏ 4566	Hold On to the Night/Texas	1978	$4
❏ 4671	Last Night I Wrote a Letter/Coliseum Rock	1979	$5
❏ 4343	Monkey Business/(She's Just A) Fallen Angel	1976	$5
❏ 4434	Sing It, Shout It/Subway Terror	1977	$10
—Originals on yellow vinyl			
❏ 4434	Sing It, Shout It/Subway Terror	1977	$4
❏ 4434 [PS]	Sing It, Shout It/Subway Terror	1977	$6
❏ 4637	So Young, So Bad/Coliseum Rock	1978	$4
❏ 4637 [PS]	So Young, So Bad/Coliseum Rock	1978	$5

STATENS, THE

MARK-X

Number	Title	Yr	NM
❏ 8011	Summertime Is the Time for Love/That Certain Kind	1961	$100

STATESMEN QUARTET, THE

CAPITOL

Number	Title	Yr	NM
❏ F40263	White Christmas/Santa Claus Song	1949	$20

STATLER BROTHERS, THE

COLUMBIA

Number	Title	Yr	NM
❏ 43315	Flowers on the Wall/Billy Christian	1965	$10
❏ 43315 [DJ]	Flowers on the Wall (same on both sides)	1965	$30
—Promo only on red vinyl			
❏ 43146	I Still Miss Someone/You're a Foolish Game	1964	$15
❏ 44899	Oh Happy Day/How Great Thou Art	1969	$8
❏ 44608	Sissy/I Am the Boy	1968	$8
❏ 43868	That'll Be the Day/Makin' Rounds	1966	$8
❏ 43526	The Doodlin' Song/My Darling Hildegarde	1966	$8
❏ 43069	The Wreck of the Old 97/Hammer and Nails	1964	$15

MERCURY

Number	Title	Yr	NM
❏ 76184	A Child of the Fifties/I'll Love You All Over Again	1982	$3
❏ 73665	All American Girl/A Few Old Memories	1975	$5
❏ 870442-7	Am I Crazy?/Beyond Romance	1988	$3
❏ 818700-7	Atlanta Blue/If It Makes Any Difference	1984	$3
❏ 818700-7 [PS]	Atlanta Blue/If It Makes Any Difference	1984	$4
❏ 73141	Bed of Rose's/The Last Goodbye	1970	$5
❏ 73415	Carry Me Back/I Wish I Could Be	1973	$5
❏ 57031	Charlotte's Web/One Less Day to Go	1980	$4
❏ 884320-7	Christmas Eve (Kodia's Theme)/Mary's Sweet Smile	1985	$3
❏ 884721-7	Count On Me/Will You Be There?	1986	$3
❏ 57037	Don't Forget Yourself/We Got Paid by Cash	1980	$4
❏ 876112-7	Don't Wait on Me/A Hurt I Can't Handle	1989	$3
❏ 57051	Don't Wait on Me/Chet Atkins' Band	1981	$4
❏ PRO790-7 [DJ]	Don't Wait on Me (Live Edited Version/Live with Intro)	1989	$8
—US 99 10-In-a-Row Country Commemorative Edition" at top (other similar pressings may exist)			
❏ 55022	Do You Know You Are My Sunshine/You're the First	1978	$4
❏ 73275	Do You Remember These/Since Then	1972	$5
❏ 814881-7	Elizabeth/Class of '57	1983	$3
❏ 888219-7	Forever/More Like Daddy Than Me	1986	$3
❏ 812988-7	Guilty/I Never Want to Kiss You Goodbye	1983	$3
❏ 880685-7	Hello Mary Lou/Remembering You	1985	$3
❏ 55066	Here We Are Again/Mr. Autry	1979	$4
❏ 73732	How Great Thou Art/Noah Found Grace in the Eyes of the Lord	1975	$5
❏ 55057	How to Be a Country Star/A Little Farther Down the Road	1979	$4
❏ 55046	I Believe in Santa's Cause/Who Do You Think	1978	$4
❏ 888650-7	I'll Be the One/Deja Vu	1987	$3
❏ 57012	(I'll Even Love You) Better Than I Did Then/Almost in Love	1980	$4
❏ 73687	I'll Go to My Grave Loving You/You've Been Like a Mother to Me	1975	$5
❏ 76130	I Never Spend A Christmas That I Don't Think Of You/Who Do You Think?	1981	$4
❏ 57048	In the Garden/How Are Things in Clay, Kentucky	1981	$4
❏ 73906	I Was There/Somebody New Will Be Coming Along	1977	$5
❏ 870681-7	Let's Get Started If We're Gonna Break My Heart/Guilty	1988	$3
❏ 888920-7	Maple Street Mem'ries/Jesus Showed Me So	1987	$3
❏ 73360	Monday Morning Secretary/Special Song for Wanda	1973	$5
❏ 872604-7	Moon Pretty Moon/I'll Be the One	1989	$3
❏ 874196-7	More Than a Name on the Wall/Atlanta Blue	1989	$3
❏ 880411-7	My Only Love/Let's Just Take One Night at a Time	1984	$3
❏ 811488-7	Oh Baby Mine (I Get So Lonely)/I'm Dyin' a Little Each Day	1983	$3
❏ 880130-7	One Takes the Blame/Give It Your Best	1984	$3
❏ 888042-7	Only You/We Got the Mem'ries	1986	$3
❏ 73229	Pictures/Making Memories	1971	$5

Number	Title	Yr	NM
❏ 55000	Silver Medals and Sweet Memories/The Regular Saturday Night Setback Card Game	1977	$4
❏ 55013	Some I Wrote/Carried Away	1977	$4
❏ 73625	Susan When She Tried/She's Too Good	1974	$5
❏ 73846	Thank God I've Got You/Hat and Boots	1976	$5
❏ 73485	Thank You World/The Blackwood Brothers by the Statler Brothers	1974	$5
❏ 870164-7	The Best I Know How/I Lost My Heart to You	1988	$3
❏ 73315	The Class of '57/Every Time I Trust a Gal	1972	$5
❏ 73877	The Movies/You Could Be Coming to Me	1976	$5
❏ 55048	The Official Historian on Shirley Jean Berrell/The Best That I Can Do	1978	$4
❏ 884016-7	Too Much on My Heart/Her Heart or Mine	1985	$3
❏ 76162	Whatever/Do You Know You Are My Sunshine	1982	$3
❏ 73448	Whatever Happened to Randolph Scott/The Strand	1974	$5
❏ 55037	Who Am I to Say/I Dreamed About You	1978	$4
❏ 73392	Woman Without a Home/I'll Be Your Baby Tonight	1973	$5

7-Inch Extended Plays

Number	Title	Yr	NM
❏ DJ577 [DJ]	I Never Spend a Christmas That I Don't Think of You/Jingle Bells//Away in a Manger/The Carols Those Kids Used to Sing	1978	$6

STATON, DAKOTA
CAPITOL

Number	Title	Yr	NM
❏ F3181	Abracadabra/I Never Dreamt	1955	$15
❏ 4512	All in My Mind/Hey Lawdy Mama	1961	$10
❏ F4012	Confessin' the Blues/Blues in My Heart	1958	$10
❏ F3128	Don't Leave Me Now/Little You	1955	$15
❏ 4465	First Things First/I Don't Worry	1960	$10
❏ F3059	For the Rest of My Life/No Mama, No Papa	1955	$15
❏ F3361	How High the Moon/Weak for the Man	1956	$15
❏ F3958	Invitation/The Party's Over	1958	$10
❏ F3293	It Feels So Nice/Dangerous Age	1955	$15
❏ 4372	My Babe/Romance in the Dark	1960	$10
❏ F3489	My Friend/Don't Mean Maybe	1956	$15
❏ F3010	My Heart's Delight/What Do You Know About Love	1955	$15
❏ 4910	Once There Lived a Fool/You'd Better Go Now	1963	$10
❏ 4790	Porgy/On Chapel Hill	1962	$12
❏ F3876	The Late Late Show/Trust in Me	1958	$10
❏ PRO408/9 [DJ]	Trust in Me/The Late, Late Show	1957	$30

— White label "Special DJ Album Highlights"

Number	Title	Yr	NM
❏ 4673	When I Grow Too Old to Dream/Mean and Evil Blues	1961	$10
❏ F4299	Where Did You Go?/Avalon	1959	$10

GROOVE MERCHANT

Number	Title	Yr	NM
❏ 1019	How Did He Look/Girl Talk	1973	$5
❏ 1017	(I Want a) Country Man/I Love You More Than You'll Ever Know	1973	$5
❏ 1011	Let It Be Me/Losing Battle	1972	$5

UNITED ARTISTS

Number	Title	Yr	NM
❏ 611	When It's Sleepy Time Down South/Massachusetts	1963	$8

7-Inch Extended Plays

CAPITOL

Number	Title	Yr	NM
❏ EAP 1-876	*Broadway/Trust in Me/Moonray/Ain't No Use	1958	$20
❏ EAP 1-1170	*Crazy He Calls Me/Idaho/How Does It Feel?/How High the Moon	1959	$20
❏ EAP 2-1170	(contents unknown)	1959	$20
❏ EAP 1-1170 [PS]	Crazy He Calls Me, Part 1	1959	$20
❏ EAP 2-1170 [PS]	Crazy He Calls Me, Part 2	1959	$20
❏ EAP 2-876	Summertime/Misty/Give Me the Simple Life/You Showed Me the Way	1958	$20
❏ EAP 1-876 [PS]	The Late, Late Show, Part 1	1958	$20
❏ EAP 2-876 [PS]	The Late, Late Show, Part 2	1958	$20

STATON, MERRILL, CHOIR
EPIC

Number	Title	Yr	NM
❏ 9429	Sidewalk Santa/The Carillon	1960	$10

STATUES, THE
LIBERTY

Number	Title	Yr	NM
❏ 55245	Blue Velvet/Keep the Hall Light Burning	1959	$30
❏ 55363	Ten Commandments of Love/Love at First Sight	1961	$30
❏ 55292	White Christmas/Jeannie with the Light Brown Hair	1960	$30

STATUS CYMBAL, THE
RCA VICTOR

Number	Title	Yr	NM
❏ 47-9344	Blang-Dang (Yesterday and Tomorrow)/Takin' My Time	1967	$10
❏ 47-9598	From My Swing/With a Little Love	1968	$10
❏ 47-9419	In the Morning/Having Fun Again	1967	$10

STATUS QUO
A&M

Number	Title	Yr	NM
❏ 1510	Carolina/Softer Ride	1974	$5
❏ 1425	Don't Waste My Time/All the Reasons	1973	$5
❏ 1445	Paper Plane/All the Reasons	1973	$5

BELL

Number	Title	Yr	NM
❏ 45417	Gerdundula/(B-side unknown)	1973	$5

CADET CONCEPT

Number	Title	Yr	NM
❏ 7015	Black Veils of Melancholy/To Be Free	1969	$8
❏ 7006	Ice in the Sun/When My Mind Is Not Live	1968	$8
❏ 7001	Pictures of Matchstick Men/Gentleman Joe's Sidewalk Café	1968	$10
❏ 7010	Technicolor Dreams/Spicks and Specks	1969	$8
❏ 7017	The Price of Love/Little Miss Nothing	1969	$8

CAPITOL

Number	Title	Yr	NM
❏ 4125	Bye Bye Johnny/Down Down	1975	$4
❏ 4407	Wild Side of Life/All Through the Night	1977	$4

JANUS

Number	Title	Yr	NM
❏ 127	Down the Dustpipe/Face Without a Soul	1970	$6
❏ 141	Gerdundula/In My Chair	1970	$6

PYE

Number	Title	Yr	NM
❏ 65000	Good Thinking/Tuned to the Music	1971	$6
❏ 65017	Mean Girl/Everything	1971	$6

RIVA

Number	Title	Yr	NM
❏ 206 [DJ]	Living on an Island/(B-side unknown)	1980	$15

STEAGALL, RED
ABC

Number	Title	Yr	NM
❏ 12337	Hang On Feelin'/Bob's Got a Swing Band in Heaven	1978	$5
❏ 12381	Hot Roasted Peanuts/About Horses and Wars	1978	$5

ABC DOT

Number	Title	Yr	NM
❏ 17709	Freckles Brown/My Adobe Hacienda	1977	$5
❏ 17670	Her L-O-V-E's Gone/Take Me Back to Texas	1977	$5
❏ 17684	I Left My Heart in San Francisco/Texas Red	1977	$5
❏ 17610	Lone Star Beer and Bob Wills Music/I've Never Been This Loved Before	1976	$5
❏ 17726	The Devil Ain't a Lonely Woman's Friend/The Rain Don't Stop in Oklahoma	1977	$5
❏ 17634	Truck Drivin' Man/Neons and Nylons	1976	$5

CAPITOL

Number	Title	Yr	NM
❏ 3375	Beer Drinkin' Music/You Came Awful Close to Lovin' Me	1972	$6
❏ 3913	Finer Things in Life/Tight Levis and Yellow Ribbons	1974	$6
❏ 4107	God Only Knows (Who'll Take Her Home)/Party Dolls and Wine	1975	$6
❏ 3651	If You've Got the Time/Ol' Helen	1973	$6
❏ 3825	I Gave Up Good Mornin' Darling/Ballad of Billy's Lady	1974	$6
❏ 4162	Lone Star Beer and Bob Wills Music/Cold Beer Signs and Country Songs	1975	$8
❏ 3318	Oklahoma Promise/Texas Silver Zephyr	1972	$6
❏ 3244	Party Dolls and Wine/Middle Tennessee Country Boy's Blues	1971	$6
❏ 4042	She Worshiped Me/April's Paintings	1975	$6
❏ 3965	Someone Cares for You/Throw Away Heart	1974	$6
❏ 3461	Somewhere, My Love/Give Me One More Chance	1972	$6
❏ 3724	The Fiddle Man/Neon Playboy	1973	$6
❏ 3797	This Just Ain't My Day (For Lettin' Darlin' Down)/Little Old Heartbreaker You	1973	$6
❏ 3562	True Love/Something Nice and Easy	1973	$6

DOT

Number	Title	Yr	NM
❏ 17360	Alabama Woman/That Time Has Come and Gone	1970	$10

ELEKTRA

Number	Title	Yr	NM
❏ 46590	3 Chord Country Song/Jackson Hole, Wyoming	1980	$4
❏ 46633	Dim the Lights and Pour the Wine/He Ain't Got Nothin' on Me	1980	$4
❏ 46527	Goodtime Charlie's Got the Blues/Songs About People in Love	1979	$4
❏ 47014	Hard Hat Days and Honky Tonk Nights/Last Call for Alcohol	1980	$4

STEALERS WHEEL
A&M

Number	Title	Yr	NM
❏ 1450	Everyone's Agreed That Everything Will Turn Out Fine/Next to Me	1973	$4
❏ 2075	(Everyone's Agreed That) Everything Will Turn Out Fine/Who Cares	1978	$5
❏ 1483	Star/What More Could You Want	1973	$4
❏ 1483 [PS]	Star/What More Could You Want	1973	$6
❏ 1416	Stuck in the Middle with You/Jose	1973	$5
❏ 1675	This Morning/Found My Way to You	1975	$4

STEARNS, JUNE
DECCA

Number	Title	Yr	NM
❏ 32986	Man/In Case of a Storm	1972	$6
❏ 32828	Sweet Baby on My Mind/How's My Ex Treating You	1971	$6
❏ 32726	Tyin' Strings/Don't Trouble Trouble	1970	$6

STARDAY

Number	Title	Yr	NM
❏ 660	Family Man/We've Got Things in Common	1963	$15

— With Gene Martin

STEELE, DON
CAMEO

Number	Title	Yr	NM
❏ 399	Tina Delgado Is Alive/Hole in My Soul	1966	$30

PATCHES

Number	Title	Yr	NM
❏ 102	Cecil, the Unwanted French Fry/(B-side unknown)	1969	$30

STEELE, LARRY
AIR STREAM

Number	Title	Yr	NM
❏ 004	Daylight Losing Time/Watermelon Man	1974	$8
❏ 006	Funny How Time Slips Away/Somethin' Ain't Home	1975	$8
❏ 002	Heart Pepper Upper/A Little at a Time	1974	$8
❏ 003	Hold On/Little Wine, Little Gin	1974	$8
❏ 001	Things Money Won't Do/Goody Goody People	1973	$8

ASSAULT

Number	Title	Yr	NM
❏ 1847/8	My Own True Love/I Can't Help It	1963	$15

K-ARK

Number	Title	Yr	NM
❏ 648	Baby Workout/My Lucky Day	1965	$12
❏ 802	Hard Times/The Apple or the Pair	1968	$8
❏ 659	I Ain't Crying Mister/Ramblin Man	1965	$10

STEELE, TOMMY
BUENA VISTA

Number	Title	Yr	NM
❏ 457	Fortuosity/I'm a Brass Band Today	1967	$8

LONDON

Number	Title	Yr	NM
❏ 1735	Butterfingers/Teenage Party	1957	$20
❏ 1706	Doomsday Rock/Elevator Rock	1957	$20
❏ 1838	Hey You/Number 22 Across the Way	1959	$20
❏ 1950	She's My Baby/Happy-Go-Lucky Blues	1960	$20
❏ 1824	Swaller Tail Coat/The Only Man Across the Way	1959	$20
❏ 1878	The Trail/Give, Give, Give	1959	$20
❏ 1760	Water, Water/A Handful of Songs	1958	$20

RCA VICTOR

Number	Title	Yr	NM
❏ 47-8602	Half a Sixpence/If the Rain's Got to Fall	1965	$10
❏ 47-9458	Half a Sixpence/If the Rain's Got to Fall	1968	$8

WAM

Number	Title	Yr	NM
❏ 45-1	Doomsday Rock/Elevator Rock	1956	$40

Number	Title	Yr	NM

STEELY DAN

ABC
❑ 12101	Black Friday/Throw Back the Little Ones	1975	$4
❑ 12128	Chain Lightning/ Bad Sneakers	1975	$4
❑ 11323	Dallas/Sail the Waterway	1972	$40

—Neither of these songs has appeared on a U.S. Steely Dan album -- not even the "complete" CD box set!

❑ 12355	Deacon Blues/Home at Last	1978	$4
❑ 11338	Do It Again/Fire in the Hole	1972	$4
❑ 11396	My Old School/Pearl of the Quarter	1973	$4
❑ 12320	Peg/I Got the News	1977	$4
❑ 12033	Pretzel Logic/ Through with Buzz	1974	$4
❑ 11382	Show Biz Kids/Razor Boy	1973	$4
❑ 12222	The Fez/Sign In Stranger	1976	$4

MCA
❑ 40894	FM (No Static at All)/ (Instrumental)	1978	$4
❑ 51036	Hey Nineteen/Bodhisattva	1980	$4
❑ 51082	Time Out of Mind/ Bodhisattva	1981	$4

7-Inch Extended Plays

ABC
❑ PRO-779 [PS]	Countdown to Ecstasy	1973	$20

—Part of "Little LP" series (#225)

❑ PRO-779	My Old School/Pearl of the Quarter/King of the World	1973	$20

—Stereo jukebox issue; small hole, plays at 33 1/3 rpm

❑ PRO-40015 [PS]	Pretzel Logic	1974	$25

—Part of "Little LP" series (#QD 255)

❑ PRO-40015	With a Gun/Rikki Don't Lose That Number//Barrytown/Pretzel Logic	1974	$25

—Quadraphonic jukebox issue; small hole, plays at 33 1/3 rpm

STEFFIN SISTERS

WINDWARD
❑ 7	I Still Need You/ Guitar Fiddlin' Joe	1989	$6
❑ 7 [PS]	I Still Need You/ Guitar Fiddlin' Joe	1989	$10

STEIN, FRANK N., AND THE TOMBSTONES

MARCO
❑ 03	Mess Around/ Graveyard Giggle	1962	$50

STEIN, FRANKIE, AND THE GHOULS

KING
❑ 6414	Franken Boogie/All She Wants to Do Is Boogie	1972	$10

POWER
❑ 338	Goon River/Weerdo the Wolf	1964	$30
❑ 338 [PS]	Goon River/Weerdo the Wolf	1964	$40

STEIN, LOU

BRUNSWICK
❑ 9-80229	Poinciana/Tenderly	1952	$20

EPIC
❑ 5-9134	Butterfly Cha-Cha-Cha/Lou's Tune	1955	$20
❑ 5-9156	The Phonograph Song/ There'll Be Some Changes Made	1956	$20

MERCURY
❑ 71328	Got a Match?/Who Slammed the Door	1958	$10
❑ 71368	I'm Looking Over a Four Leaf Clover/I'll Be With You in Apple Blossom Time	1958	$10

MURBO
❑ 1033	That Old Time Flavour/ Winds of Change	1969	$8

RKO UNIQUE
❑ 385	Almost Paradise/Soft Sands	1957	$15
❑ 403	The Little Spinet/ Song of the East	1957	$15

STENMARK-MUELLER BAND

ENVELOPE
❑ 7004	Lover to Lover/ (B-side unknown)	1987	$8

STEPHENS, OTT

CHART
❑ 1205	Enough Man for You/ Never Tired of Loving You	1965	$12
❑ 1032	Hard Times (Are My Kind of Times)/Snow White Cloud	1968	$8
❑ 1145	I Still Love Y-O-U/ Little Bit of Blue	1964	$10

PEACH
❑ 749	Only a Friend/Oh Broken Hearted Me	1961	$30

REPRISE
❑ 0272	Be Quiet Mind/ Hard Luck Story	1964	$15

STEPPENWOLF
Also see SPARROW.

ABC
❑ 1436	The Pusher/Born to Be Wild	1970	$4

—Goldies 45" series

❑ 1436 [PS]	The Pusher/Born to Be Wild	1970	$6

ABC DUNHILL
❑ 4138	Born to Be Wild/ Everybody's Next One	1968	$8
❑ 4292	For Ladies Only/ Sparkle Eyes	1971	$5
❑ 4234	Hey Lawdy Mama/Twisted	1970	$6
❑ 4192	It's Never Too Late/ Happy Birthday	1969	$6
❑ 4161	Magic Carpet Ride/ Sookie Sookie	1968	$8
❑ 4221	Monster/Berry Rides Again	1969	$6
❑ 4205	Move Over/Power Play	1969	$6
❑ 4248	Screaming Night Hog/ Spiritual Fantasy	1970	$6
❑ 4269	Snow Blind Friend/ Hippo Stomp	1971	$5
❑ 4261	Who Needs Ya/ Earschplittenloudenboomer	1970	$6

ALLEGIANCE
❑ 3909	Hot Night in a Cold Town/ Every Man for Himself	1983	$4

—As "John Kay and Steppenwolf"

DUNHILL
❑ 4123	Sookie Sookie/Take What You Need	1968	$12
❑ 4109	The Ostrich/A Girl I Know	1967	$10

MUMS
❑ 6040	Caroline (Are You Ready for the Outlaw)/Angel Drawers	1975	$4
❑ 6036	Fool's Fantasy/Smokey Factory Blues	1975	$4
❑ 6034	Get Into the Wind/ Morning Blue	1974	$4
❑ 6031	Straight Shootin' Woman/ Justice, Don't Be Slow	1974	$4
❑ 6031 [PS]	Straight Shootin' Woman/ Justice, Don't Be Slow	1974	$6

STEREOS, THE

CUB
❑ 9095	I Really Love You/Please Come Back to Me	1961	$30

STEVENS, APRIL

A&M
❑ 1636	Marry Me Again/Gotta Leave You Baby	1974	$4

ATCO
❑ 6380	Lovin' Valentine/No Hair Say	1965	$8
❑ 6346	Teach Me Tiger 1965/ Morning Till Midnight	1965	$8

IMPERIAL
❑ 5907	Fly Me to the Moon/ That's My Name	1963	$20
❑ 5666	In Other Words/Jonny	1960	$20
❑ 5626	Teach Me, Tiger/That Warm Afternoon	1959	$30

KING
❑ 5826	Soft Warm Lips/How Could Red Riding Hood	1963	$12

RCA VICTOR
❑ 47-4283	And So to Sleep Again/Aw, C'mon	1951	$30
❑ 47-4208	Gimme a Little Kiss, Will Ya, Huh?/Dreamy Melody	1951	$30

—With Henri Rene

❑ 47-4876	I Like to Talk to Myself/ That Naughty Waltz	1952	$30
❑ 47-4567	I Love the Way You're Breaking My Heart/ Meant to Tell You	1952	$30
❑ 47-4148	I'm in Love Again/ Roller Coaster	1951	$30

—With Henri Rene

❑ 47-4381	Put Me in Your Pocket/ The Tricks of the Trade	1951	$30

STEVENS, CAT

A&M
❑ 1602	Another Saturday Night/ Home in the Sky	1974	$4
❑ 1602 [PS]	Another Saturday Night/ Home in the Sky	1974	$6
❑ 2109	Bad Brakes/Nascimento	1979	$4
❑ 1785	Banapple Gas/Ghost Town	1976	$4
❑ 1785 [PS]	Banapple Gas/Ghost Town	1976	$15

❑ 2711 [DJ]	Father and Son (same on both sides)	1985	$10

—No stock copies issued

❑ 2683	If You Want to Sing Out, Sing Out/I Want to Live in a Wigwam	1984	$4
❑ 1924	(I Never Wanted) To Be a Star/Land O' Freelove and Goodbye	1977	$4
❑ 1211	Lady D'Arbanville/ Time -- Fill My Eyes	1970	$5
❑ 1265	Moon Shadow/I Think I See the Light	1971	$4
❑ 1265 [PS]	Moon Shadow/I Think I See the Light	1971	$6
❑ 1335	Morning Has Broken/I Want to Live in a Wigwam	1972	$4
❑ 1335 [PS]	Morning Has Broken/I Want to Live in a Wigwam	1972	$6
❑ 1503	Oh Very Young/100 I Dream	1974	$4
❑ 1503 [PS]	Oh Very Young/100 I Dream	1974	$6
❑ 1291	Peace Train/Where Do the Children Play	1971	$4
❑ 1291 [PS]	Peace Train/Where Do the Children Play	1971	$6
❑ 1396	Sitting/Crab Dance	1972	$4
❑ 1396 [PS]	Sitting/Crab Dance	1972	$6
❑ 1418	The Hurt/Silent Sunlight	1973	$4
❑ 1418 [PS]	The Hurt/Silent Sunlight	1973	$6
❑ 1700	Two Fine People/Bad Penny	1975	$4
❑ 1971	Was Dog a Doughnut/ Sweet Jamaica	1977	$4
❑ 1231	Wild World/Miles from Nowhere	1970	$5

DERAM
❑ 7501	I Love My Dog/ Portobello Road	1966	$10
❑ 85006	I'm Gonna Get Me a Gun/School Is Out	1967	$10
❑ 85015	Laughing Apple/Bad Night	1967	$12
❑ 7505	Matthew and Son/Granny	1967	$10

7-Inch Extended Plays

A&M
❑ LLP-4391 [PS]	Foreigner	1973	$8

—Part of "Little LP" series (LLP #227)

❑ LLP-4391	Foreigner Suite (Part 1)/(Part 2)	1973	$8

—Jukebox issue; small hole, plays at 33 1/3 rpm

STEVENS, CONNIE

BELL
❑ 866	She'll Never Understand Him/5:30 Plane	1970	$5
❑ 45234	Simple Girl/(B-side unknown)	1972	$5

MGM
❑ 13906	Cinderella Could Have Saved Us All/Wouldn't It Be Nice (To Have Wings and Fly)	1968	$6

WARNER BROS.
❑ 5425	A Girl Never Knows/ They're Jealous of Me	1964	$10
❑ 5804	All of My Life/That's All I Want from You	1966	$10
❑ 5092	Apollo/Why Do I Cry for Joey	1959	$30
❑ 5691	Don't You Want to Love Me/ In My Room (El Amor)	1966	$12
❑ 5318	Hey, Good Lookin'/Nobody's Lonesome for Me	1962	$15
❑ 5834	How Bitter the Taste of Love/Most of All	1966	$10
❑ 5232	If You Don't, Somebody Else Will/Greenwood Tree	1961	$15
❑ 5656	In the Deep of Night/ Something Beautiful	1965	$10
❑ 5872	It'll Never Happen Again/ What Will I Tell Him	1966	$10
❑ 5380	Little Miss Understood/ There Goes Your Guy	1963	$12
❑ 5217	Make Believe Lover/ And This Is Mine	1961	$15
❑ 5238	Man Soil Such So Schwell Nicht Uberliebe/La Le Lu	1961	$40

—German release only

❑ 5289	Mr. Songwriter/I Couldn't Say No	1962	$15
❑ 5137	Sixteen Reasons/Little Sister	1960	$20

—First pressing has pink labels

❑ 5137	Sixteen Reasons/Little Sister	1960	$15

—Second pressing has red label with arrows

❑ 7128	Sixteen Reasons/ Make Believe Lover	1968	$5

—Back to Back Hits" series -- originals have green labels with "W7" logo

❑ 5159	Too Young to Go Steady/A Little Kiss Is a Kiss Is a Kiss	1960	$15
❑ 5159 [PS]	Too Young to Go Steady/A Little Kiss Is a Kiss Is a Kiss	1960	$40
❑ 5265	Why'd You Wanna Make Me Cry/Just One Kiss	1962	$15

Number	Title	Yr	NM
STEVENS, DEBBIE			
ABC-PARAMOUNT			
☐ 10034	Billy Boy's Theme/I Sit and Cry	1959	$20
APT			
☐ 25027	If You Can't Rock Me/What Will I Tell My Heart	1959	$30
STEVENS, DODIE			
CRYSTALETTE			
☐ 724	Pink Shoe Laces/Coming of Age	1959	$30
DOLTON			
☐ 88	Sailor Boy/Does Goodnight Mean Goodbye	1964	$15
DOT			
☐ 16139	Am I Too Young/So Let's Dance	1960	$20
☐ 16067	Candy Store Blues/Gringo's Guitar	1960	$20
☐ 16339	I Cried/Dancing on My Ceiling	1962	$20
☐ 16200	I Fall to Pieces/Turn Around	1961	$20
☐ 16259	Let Me Tell You About Johnny/You Are the Only One	1961	$20
☐ 16166	Merry Christmas Baby/Jingle Bells	1960	$30
☐ 15975	Miss Lonely Heart/Poor Butterfly	1959	$30
☐ 16389	Pink Shoelaces/Yes-Sir-Ee	1962	$20
☐ 16002	Steady Date/Mairzy Doats	1959	$30
☐ 16279	The In-Between Years/Trade Winds	1961	$20
IMPERIAL			
☐ 5908	Don't Send Me No Roses/Daddy Could Get Me One of These	1963	$20
☐ 5930	Hello Stranger/For a Little While	1963	$20
STEVENS, GERALDINE			
WORLD PACIFIC			
☐ 77927	Billy, I've Got to Go to Town/It's Not Their Heartache, It's Mine	1969	$8
☐ 77934	Love Is Gonna Get You/You Ain't Goin' Nowhere	1970	$8
☐ 77930	Play Me a Song/I've Got to Have More	1969	$8
STEVENS, JEFF, AND THE BULLETS			
ATLANTIC AMERICA			
☐ 99494	Darlington County/Tamed by Love	1986	$3
☐ 99433	Geronimo's Cadillac/Tamed by Love	1987	$3
STEVENS, JOHNNY			
FORD			
☐ 123	Oh Yeah/Last Chicken in the Shack	1963	$40
PARKWAY			
☐ 805	Apple Taffy/Mm, Baby, Mm	1959	$30
STEVENS, MARK, AND THE CHARMERS			
ALLISON			
☐ 921	Magic Rose/Come Back to My Heart	1962	$70
STEVENS, NEIL			
BRUNSWICK			
☐ 55095	More and More/What Could Be Better	1958	$40
— With the Dee-Vines			
GOLDISC			
☐ 3019	Ballad of Love/Tonight My Heart She Is Crying	1961	$30
— With the Temptations			
GONE			
☐ 5067	Ballad of Love/Gambler's Game	1959	$60
STEVENS, RAY			
☐ 2039	All My Trials/Have a Little Talk with Myself	1971	$5
☐ 2029	A Mama and a Papa/Melt	1971	$5
☐ 2016	America, Communicate with Me/Monkey See, Monkey Do	1970	$5
☐ 2024	Bridget the Midget (The Queen of the Blues)/Night People	1970	$5
☐ 2024 [PS]	Bridget the Midget (The Queen of the Blues)/Night People	1970	$10
☐ 610	Everybody Needs a Rainbow/Inside	1974	$4
☐ 2011	Everything Is Beautiful/A Brighter Day	1970	$6

Number	Title	Yr	NM
☐ 5020	Golden Age/Nashville	1973	$4
☐ 616	Indian Love Call/Piece of Paradise	1975	$4
☐ 619	Lady of Spain/Mockingbird Hill	1976	$4
☐ 2065	Losing Streak/Inside	1972	$5
☐ 2058	Love Lifted Me/Glory Special	1972	$5
☐ 2058	Love Lifted Me/Monkey See, Monkey Do	1972	$5
☐ 5028	Love Me Longer/Float	1973	$4
☐ 614	Misty/Sunshine	1975	$4
☐ 604	Moonlight Special/Just So Proud to Be Here	1974	$4
☐ 2021	Sunset Strip/Islands	1970	$5
☐ 600	The Streak/You've Got the Music Inside	1974	$5
— White label (not a promo)			
☐ 600	The Streak/You've Got the Music Inside	1974	$4
— Multicolor label			
☐ 2048	Turn Your Radio On/Loving You on Paper	1971	$5
CAPITOL			
☐ F4030	Cat Pants/Love Goes On Forever	1958	$40
☐ F3967	Chickie Chickie Wah Wah/Crying Goodbye	1958	$30
☐ F4101	The School/The Clown	1958	$30
MCA			
☐ 53007	Can He Love You Half As Much As I Do/Dudley Doright (Of the Highway Patrol)	1987	$3
☐ 53007 [DJ]	Can He Love You Half As Much As I Do (same on both sides)	1987	$10
— Blue vinyl promo			
☐ 53661	I Saw Elvis in a U.F.O./I Used to Be Crazy	1989	$10
☐ 52548	It's Me Again, Margaret/Joggin'	1985	$3
☐ 52492	Mississippi Squirrel Revival/Ned Nostril	1984	$4
☐ 52924	People's Court/Dudley Doright (Of the Highway Patrol)	1986	$3
☐ 52738	Santa Claus Is Watching You/Armchair Quarterback	1985	$3
☐ 52738 [PS]	Santa Claus Is Watching You/Armchair Quarterback	1985	$4
☐ 53232	Sex Symbols/The Ballad of Cactus Pete and Lefty	1987	$3
☐ 53372	Surfin' U.S.S.R./Language, Nudity, Violence & Sex	1988	$3
☐ 52906	The Camping Trip/Southern Air	1986	$3
☐ 53423	The Day I Tried to Teach Charlene MacKenzie How to Drive/I Don't Need None of That	1988	$3
☐ 52657	The Haircut Song/Punk Country Love	1985	$3
☐ 53178	Three-Legged Man/Doctor, Doctor (Have Mercy on Me)	1987	$3
☐ 53101	Would Jesus Wear a Rolex?/Cool Down Willard	1987	$4
MERCURY			
☐ 71966	Ahab, the Arab/It's Been So Long	1962	$20
☐ 71966 [PS]	Ahab, the Arab/It's Been So Long	1962	$40
☐ 72307	Bubble Gum the Bubble Dancer/Laughing Over My Grave	1964	$20
☐ 72255	Butch Barbarian (Sure Footed Mountain Climber World Famous Yodeling Champion)/Don't Say Anything	1963	$20
☐ 72098	Funny Man/Just One of Life's Little Tragedies	1963	$20
☐ 72816	Funny Man/Just One of Life's Little Tragedies	1968	$15
☐ 72039	Further More/Saturday Night at the Movies	1962	$20
☐ 72125	Harry the Hairy Ape/Little Stone Statue	1963	$20
☐ 72125 [PS]	Harry the Hairy Ape/Little Stone Statue	1963	$30
☐ 814196-7	Love Will Beat Your Brains Out/Game Show Love	1983	$4
☐ 72430	Mr. Baker the Undertaker/Old English Surfer	1965	$30
☐ 812906-7	My Dad/Game Show Love	1983	$5
☐ 818057-7	My Dad/Me	1984	$4
☐ 812496-7	Pice of Paradise Called Tennessee/Mary Lou Nights	1983	$4
☐ 72058	Santa Claus Is Watching You/Loved and Lost	1962	$20
☐ 72058 [PS]	Santa Claus Is Watching You/Loved and Lost	1962	$30
☐ 71888	Scratch My Back/When You Wish Upon a Star	1961	$20
☐ 72189	Speed Ball/It's Party Time	1963	$20
MONUMENT			
☐ 911	A-B-C/Party People	1966	$10
☐ 1150	Along Came Jones/Yakety Yak	1969	$8
☐ 927	Devil-May-Care/Make a Few Memories	1966	$12

Number	Title	Yr	NM
☐ 946	Freddy Feelgood (And His Funky Little Five Piece Band)/There's One in Every Crowd	1966	$10
☐ 1131	Gitarzan/Bagpipes-That's My Bag	1969	$8
☐ 1171	Have a Little Talk with Myself/Little Woman	1969	$6
☐ 1187	I'll Be Your Baby Tonight/Fool on the Hill	1970	$6
☐ 1099	Isn't It Lonely Together/The Great Escape	1968	$8
☐ 1001	Mary, My Secretary/Answer Me, My Love	1967	$8
☐ 1083	Mr. Businessman/Face the Music	1968	$8
☐ 1163	Sunday Mornin' Comin' Down/The Minority	1969	$6
NRC			
☐ 063	Happy Blue Year/White Christmas	1960	$30
☐ 031	High School Yearbook (Deck of Cards)/Truly True	1959	$30
☐ 057	Sergeant Preston of the Yukon/Who Do You Love	1960	$30
☐ 042	What Would I Do Without You/My Heart Cries for You	1959	$30
PREP			
☐ 122	Five More Steps/Tingle	1957	$30
RCA			
☐ GB-12368	Everything Is Beautiful/Gitarzan	1981	$3
— Gold Standard Series			
☐ PB-12170	One More Last Chance/I Believe You Love Me	1981	$4
☐ PB-11911	Shriner's Convention/You're Never Goin' to Tampa With Me	1980	$4
☐ GB-12370	Shriner's Convention/You're Never Goin' to Tampa With Me	1981	$3
— Gold Standard Series			
☐ PB-12185	The Streak/Misty	1981	$4
☐ PB-13207	Where the Sun Don't Shine/Why Don't We Go Somewhere and Love	1982	$4
☐ PB-13038	Written Down in My Heart/Country Boy, Country Club Girl	1981	$4
WARNER BROS.			
☐ 8603	Be Your Own Best Friend/With a Smile	1978	$4
☐ 8393	Dixie Hummingbird/Feel the Music	1977	$4
☐ 8318	Get Crazy with Me/Dixie Hummingbird	1977	$4
☐ 8237	Honky Tonk Waltz/Om	1976	$4
☐ 8785	I Need Your Help Barry Manilow/Daydream Romance	1979	$4
☐ 8785 [PS]	I Need Your Help Barry Manilow/Daydream Romance	1979	$6
☐ 8301	In the Mood/Classical Cluck	1976	$6
— As "Henhouse Five Plus Too"			
☐ 8849	The Feeling's Not Right Again/Get Crazy with Me	1979	$4
STEVENS, TERRI			
RCA VICTOR			
☐ 47-6300	All I Want Is You/I've Always Loved You	1955	$30
☐ 47-6393	Dood-ly Dood-ly/I'll Come When You Call	1956	$30
☐ 47-7014	Pick-Up Girl/Untouched Heart	1957	$30
☐ 47-6633	Sweet World/That's How I Cried Over You	1956	$30
☐ 47-6165	Why Am I to Blame/What Am I Trying to Forget	1955	$30
STEWART, ANDY			
WARWICK			
☐ 665	Donald Where's Your Troosers?/The Battle's Over	1961	$15
☐ 627	The Scottish Soldier/The Muckin' O' Georgie's Brye	1961	$15
STEWART, BILLY			
ARGO			
☐ 5256	Billy's Blues (Part 1)/Billy's Blues (Part 2)	1956	$50
CHESS			
☐ 1948	Because I Love You/Mountain of Love	1965	$12
☐ 1625	Billy's Blues (Part 1)/Billy's Blues (Part 2)	1956	$70
☐ 2080	By the Time I Get to Phoenix/We'll Always Be Together	1969	$10
☐ 1888	Count Me Out/A Fat Boy Can Cry	1964	$12
☐ 2002	Cross My Heart/Why (Do I Love You So)	1967	$12

Number	Title	Yr	NM
❏ 1991	Every Day I Have the Blues/Ol' Man River	1967	$12
❏ 1941	How Nice It Is/No Girl	1965	$10
❏ 1922	I Do Love You/Keep Loving	1965	$10
❏ 2063	I'm in Love (Oh Yes I Am)/Crazy 'Bout You Baby	1969	$10
❏ 1960	Love Me/Why Am I Lonely	1966	$10
❏ 1852	Scramble/Oh What Can the Matter Be	1963	$15
❏ 1978	Secret Love/Look Back and Smile	1966	$10
❏ 1932	Sitting in the Park/Once Again	1965	$12
❏ 1868	Strange Feeling/Sugar and Spice	1963	$15
❏ 1966	Summertime/To Love, To Love	1966	$20

— Black label

Number	Title	Yr	NM
❏ 1966	Summertime/To Love, To Love	1966	$15

— Blueish label

Number	Title	Yr	NM
❏ 1905	Tell It Like It Is/My Sweet Senorita	1964	$10
❏ 2053	Tell Me the Truth/What Have I Done	1968	$10
❏ 1835	True Fine Lovin'/Wedding Bells	1962	$15

OKEH

Number	Title	Yr	NM
❏ 7095	Baby, You're My Only Love/Billy's Heartache	1957	$300

UNITED ARTISTS

Number	Title	Yr	NM
❏ 340	This Is a Fine Time/Young in Years	1961	$20

STEWART BROTHERS, THE

KEEN

Number	Title	Yr	NM
❏ 2113	Sleep on the Porch/Yum Yum	1960	$125

STEWART, GARY

CORY

Number	Title	Yr	NM
❏ 101	Walk On By/(B-side unknown)	1964	$30

DECCA

Number	Title	Yr	NM
❏ 32880	She's the Next Best Thing/Something to Believe In	1971	$8

HIGHTONE

Number	Title	Yr	NM
❏ 507	An Empty Glass/Lucretia	1988	$5
❏ 506	Brand New Whiskey/Son of a Honky Tonk Woman	1988	$5

KAPP

Number	Title	Yr	NM
❏ 934	Here Comes That Feeling Again/Merry-Go-Round	1968	$8
❏ 2008	Sweet Tater and Cisco/Little Old Love	1969	$8

RCA

Number	Title	Yr	NM
❏ PB-12081	Are We Dreamin' the Same Dream/Roarin'	1980	$4
❏ PB-11960	Cactus and a Rose/Staring Each Other Down	1980	$4
❏ PB-12203	Let's Forget That We're Married/Honky Tonk Man	1981	$4
❏ PB-11623	Mazelle/One More	1979	$4
❏ PB-11534	Shady Streets/Everything a Good Little Girl Needs	1979	$4
❏ PB-12343	She's Got a Drinking Problem/Memories Swim in Whiskey	1981	$4
❏ PB-13261	She Sings Amazing Grace/Cold Turkey	1982	$4
❏ PB-11297	Single Again/Little Junior	1978	$4
❏ PB-11416	Stone Wall (Around Your Heart)/I Got Mine	1978	$4
❏ PB-10957	Ten Years of This/I Ain't Living Long Like This	1977	$4
❏ PB-11224	Whiskey Trip/Williamson County	1978	$4

RCA VICTOR

Number	Title	Yr	NM
❏ APBO-0281	Drinkin' Thing/I See the Want To in Your Eyes	1974	$5
❏ GB-10516	Drinkin' Thing/I See the Want To in Your Eyes	1976	$4

— Gold Standard Series" reissue

Number	Title	Yr	NM
❏ PB-10351	Flat Natural Born Good-Timin' Man/This Old Heart Won't Let Go	1975	$5
❏ PB-10351 [PS]	Flat Natural Born Good-Timin' Man/This Old Heart Won't Let Go	1975	$8
❏ PB-10680	In Some Room Above the Street/Easy People	1976	$5
❏ PB-10550	Oh, Sweet Temptation/Hank Western	1976	$5
❏ PB-10061	Out of Hand/Draggin' Shackles	1974	$5
❏ GB-10515	Out of Hand/Draggin' Shackles	1976	$4

— Gold Standard Series" reissue

Number	Title	Yr	NM
❏ PB-10222	She's Acting Single (I'm Drinking Doubles)/Williamson County	1975	$5
❏ GB-10514	She's Acting Single (I'm Drinking Doubles)/Williamson County	1976	$4

— Gold Standard Series" reissue

RED ASH

Number	Title	Yr	NM
❏ 8403	Hey, Bottle of Whiskey/Roadhouse Romances	1984	$5
❏ 8406	I Got a Bad Attitude/Life's a Game	1984	$5

STEWART, JOHN
Also see THE KINGSTON TRIO.

CAPITOL

Number	Title	Yr	NM
❏ 2605	Armstrong/Anna on a Memory	1969	$6
❏ 2842	Clack Clack/Marshall Wind	1970	$6
❏ 2711	Earth Rider/The Lady and the Outlaw	1969	$6
❏ 2469	Mother Country/Shackles and Chains	1969	$6
❏ 2712	World of No Return/Wild Is Love	1969	$8

— B-side by Patti Drew

RCA VICTOR

Number	Title	Yr	NM
❏ APBO-0109	Anna on a Memory/Wheatfield	1973	$5
❏ 74-0970	Chilly Winds/Durango	1973	$5
❏ PB-10227	Survivors/Josie	1975	$5
❏ PB-10268	Survivors/Josie	1975	$5

RSO

Number	Title	Yr	NM
❏ 931	Gold/Comin' Out of Nowhere	1979	$4
❏ 1016	Lost Her in the Sun/Heart of the Dream	1979	$4
❏ 1000	Midnight Wind/Somewhere Down the Line	1979	$4
❏ 1031	(Odin) Spirit of the Water/Love Has Tied My Wings	1980	$4
❏ 894	Promise the Wind/Morning Thunder	1978	$4

WARNER BROS.

Number	Title	Yr	NM
❏ 7592	An Accent of Halley's Comet/Arkansas Breakout	1972	$5
❏ 7525	Daydream Believer/Sweet Lizard	1971	$5
❏ 7552	Light Come Shine/A Little Road and a Stone to Roll	1972	$5
❏ PRO504 [PS]	The Bad Old Daysr/Just an Old Love Song	1971	$20

— Promo only

STEWART, REDD

DO-RA-ME

Number	Title	Yr	NM
❏ 1422	Levi Lady/River Road Rock Twist	1962	$30

HICKORY

Number	Title	Yr	NM
❏ 1584	And the Rain Comes Down/Ballad of the Country Song Writer	1970	$8
❏ 1572	Better Man/My Home Is the Dust of the Road	1970	$8
❏ 1543	Bimbo/Big, Big Show	1969	$8
❏ 1658	Bonaparte's Retreat/Where Love Doesn't Live Anymore	1973	$8
❏ 1554	Cold, Cold Heart/Dreaming Again	1969	$8
❏ 1603	My Friend/Sunshine Over the Hill	1971	$8
❏ 1640	Plain Ole Country Me/Tennessee Waltz	1972	$8

HICKORY/MGM

Number	Title	Yr	NM
❏ 325	Banjo/Talk to the Angels	1974	$6
❏ 356	Bimbo/Cold, Cold Heart	1975	$6
❏ 334	Cold, Cold Heart/I Remember	1974	$6
❏ 343	Having Second Thoughts/Sunshine Over the Hill	1975	$6

RCA VICTOR

Number	Title	Yr	NM
❏ 47-5928	I Did/Down Stream	1954	$30
❏ 47-6036	Which One of Us Is to Blame/Don't Make Me Fall in Love with You	1955	$30

STEWART, ROD

GEFFEN

Number	Title	Yr	NM
❏ 28303	Twistin' the Night Away/Let's Get Small	1987	$4

— B-side by Steve Martin

Number	Title	Yr	NM
❏ 28303 [PS]	Twistin' the Night Away/Let's Get Small	1987	$4

MERCURY

Number	Title	Yr	NM
❏ 73344	Angel/Lost Paraguayos	1972	$5
❏ 73196	Country Comfort/Gasoline Alley	1971	$6
❏ 73156	Cut Across Shorty/Gasoline Alley	1970	$12
❏ 73802	Every Picture Tells a Story/What's Made Milwaukee Famous (Has Made a Loser Out of Me)	1976	$5
❏ 73009	Handbags and Gladrags/An Old Raincoat Won't Ever Let You Down	1970	$12
❏ 73031	Handbags and Gladrags/Man of Constant Sorrow	1970	$8
❏ 73244	(I Know) I'm Losing You/Mandolin Wind	1971	$5
❏ 73095	It's All Over Now/Joe's Lament	1970	$10

Number	Title	Yr	NM
❏ 73660	Let Me Be Your Car/Sailor	1974	$6
❏ 73224	Maggie May/Reason to Believe	1971	$6
❏ 73636	Mine for Me/Farewell	1974	$5
❏ 73175	My Way of Giving/Lady Day	1971	$6
❏ 73426	Oh No Not My Baby/Jodie	1973	$5
❏ 73426 [PS]	Oh No Not My Baby/Jodie	1973	$6
❏ 73115	Only a Hero/Gasoline Alley	1970	$10
❏ 73412	Twistin' the Night Away//True Blue-Lady Day	1973	$5
❏ 73412 [PS]	Twistin' the Night Away//True Blue-Lady Day	1973	$6

PRESS

Number	Title	Yr	NM
❏ 9722	Good Morning Little Schoolgirl/I'm Gonna Move to the Outskirts of Town	1965	$50

PRIVATE STOCK

Number	Title	Yr	NM
❏ 45,130	Shake/Bright Lights, Big City	1976	$6

WARNER BROS.

Number	Title	Yr	NM
❏ 8810	Ain't Love a Bitch/Last Summer	1979	$4
❏ 8810 [PS]	Ain't Love a Bitch/Last Summer	1979	$5
❏ 29122	All Right Now/Dancin' Alone	1984	$4
❏ 28631	Another Heartache/You're In My Heart (The Final Acclaim)	1986	$3
❏ 28631 [PS]	Another Heartache/You're In My Heart (The Final Acclaim)	1986	$3
❏ 8066	As Long As You Tell Him/You Can Make Me Dance, Sing or Anything	1975	$5

— As "Rod Stewart and Faces"

Number	Title	Yr	NM
❏ 8102	As Long As You Tell Him/You Can Make Me Dance, Sing or Anything	1975	$4

— As "Rod Stewart and Faces

Number	Title	Yr	NM
❏ 29608	Baby Jane/Ready Now	1983	$4
❏ GWB 0469	Baby Jane/What Am I Gonna Do (I'm So in Love with You)	1984	$3

— Back to Back Hits" series

Number	Title	Yr	NM
❏ 27657	Crazy About Her/Dynamite	1989	$3
❏ GWB 0382	Da Ya Think I'm Sexy?/Ain't Love a Bitch	1980	$3

— Back to Back Hits" series

Number	Title	Yr	NM
❏ 8724 [DJ]	Da Ya Think I'm Sexy? (Edited Version 4:16)/(Full Version 5:21)	1978	$6
❏ 8724	Da Ya Think I'm Sexy?/Scarred and Scared	1978	$4

— Off-white label

Number	Title	Yr	NM
❏ 8724 [PS]	Da Ya Think I'm Sexy?/Scarred and Scared	1978	$5
❏ 8724	Da Ya Think I'm Sexy?/Scarred and Scared	1978	$12

— Burbank" palm trees label

Number	Title	Yr	NM
❏ 22685	Downtown Train/The Killing of Georgie (Part 1 and 2)	1989	$3
❏ 22685 [PS]	Downtown Train/The Killing of Georgie (Part 1 and 2)	1989	$8
❏ 28625	Every Beat of My Heart/Trouble	1986	$3
❏ 28625 [PS]	Every Beat of My Heart/Trouble	1986	$3
❏ 27796	Forever Young/Days of Rage	1988	$3
❏ 27796 [PS]	Forever Young/Days of Rage	1988	$3
❏ 29874	Guess I'll Always Love You/Rock My Plimsoul	1982	$4
❏ 29874 [PS]	Guess I'll Always Love You/Rock My Plimsoul	1982	$5
❏ 8535	Hot Legs/You're Insane	1978	$4
❏ 8535 [PS]	Hot Legs/You're Insane	1978	$5
❏ 50051 [DJ]	How Long (Edit 3:48)/(LP Version 4:12)	1982	$6
❏ 50051	How Long/Jealous	1982	$4
❏ 50051 [PS]	How Long/Jealous	1982	$5
❏ 49138	I Don't Want to Talk About It/Best Days of My Life	1979	$4
❏ 49138 [PS]	I Don't Want to Talk About It/Best Days of My Life	1979	$5
❏ 29256	Infatuation/She Won't Dance with Me	1984	$4
❏ 29256 [PS]	Infatuation/She Won't Dance with Me	1984	$4
❏ GWB 0522	Infatuation/Some Guys Have All the Luck	1985	$3

— Back to Back Hits" series

Number	Title	Yr	NM
❏ 29256	Infatuation/Three Time Loser	1984	$4
❏ 8568	I Was Only Joking/Born Loose	1978	$4
❏ 8568 [PS]	I Was Only Joking/Born Loose	1978	$5
❏ GWB 0371	I Was Only Joking/The Killing of Georgie (Part 1 and 2)	1979	$3

— Back to Back Hits" series

Number	Title	Yr	NM
❏ 27927	Lost in You/Almost Illegal	1988	$3
❏ 27927 [PS]	Lost in You/Almost Illegal	1988	$3
❏ 28668	Love Touch (Love Theme from Legal Eagles)/Heart Is on the Line	1986	$3
❏ 28668 [PS]	Love Touch (Love Theme from Legal Eagles)/Heart Is on the Line	1986	$3

Number	Title	Yr	NM
❏ 21976	Love Touch (Love Theme from Legal Eagles)/Hot Legs	1988	$3

— Back to Back Hits" series

Number	Title	Yr	NM
❏ 27729	My Heart Can't Tell You No/The Wild Horse	1988	$3
❏ 27729 [PS]	My Heart Can't Tell You No/The Wild Horse	1988	$3
❏ 49617	Passion/Better Off Dead	1980	$4
❏ 49617 [PS]	Passion/Better Off Dead	1980	$5
❏ 49617 [DJ]	Passion (Edit 4:45) (Full Version 5:29)	1980	$6
❏ GWB 0404	Passion/Somebody Special	1981	$3

— Back to Back Hits" series

Number	Title	Yr	NM
❏ 8146	Sailing/All in the Name of Rock and Roll	1975	$4
❏ 49686	Somebody Special/She Won't Dance with Me	1981	$4
❏ 29215	Some Guys Have All the Luck/I Was Only Joking	1984	$4
❏ 29215 [PS]	Some Guys Have All the Luck/I Was Only Joking	1984	$4
❏ 8321	The First Cut Is the Deepest/Ball Trap	1977	$4
❏ 8170	This Old Heart of Mine/Still Love Again	1975	$5
❏ 49886	Tonight I'm Yours (Don't Hurt Me)/Tora, Tora, Tora	1981	$4
❏ 49886 [PS]	Tonight I'm Yours (Don't Hurt Me)/Tora, Tora, Tora	1981	$5
❏ 8262	Tonight's the Night (Gonna Be Alright)/Fool for You	1976	$4
❏ GWB 0349	Tonight's the Night (Gonna Be Alright)/The First Cut Is the Deepest	1978	$3

— Back to Back Hits" series

Number	Title	Yr	NM
❏ 29564	What Am I Gonna Do (I'm So in Love with You)/Dancin' Alone	1983	$4
❏ 29564 [PS]	What Am I Gonna Do (I'm So in Love with You)/Dancin' Alone	1983	$4

7-Inch Extended Plays

MERCURY

Number	Title	Yr	NM
❏ MEPL-28 [DJ]	I'd Rather Go Blind/What's Made Milwaukee Famous//Italian Girls/Twistin' the Night Away	1972	$10

STEWART, SANDY

20TH CENTURY

Number	Title	Yr	NM
❏ 5014	I'm Goin' Home/Saturday Night	1954	$15
❏ 5007	The Game of Love/Do Ya Do Ya	1954	$15

ATCO

Number	Title	Yr	NM
❏ 6137	Playmates/Heavenly Father	1959	$10

COLPIX

Number	Title	Yr	NM
❏ 704	I Know He Needs Her/Please Don't Fall in Love with Me Again	1963	$8
❏ 669	My Coloring Book/I Heard You Cried Last Night	1962	$8
❏ 669 [PS]	My Coloring Book/I Heard You Cried Last Night	1962	$20
❏ 669	My Coloring Book (Without Verse)/(With Verse)	1962	$10
❏ 681	My Favorite Song/Promise of Love	1963	$8

DCP

Number	Title	Yr	NM
❏ 1004	Draw Me a Circle/Little Child (Mommy Dear)	1964	$8

EASTWEST

Number	Title	Yr	NM
❏ 122	To My Love/Music, Music, Music	1958	$10

OKEH

Number	Title	Yr	NM
❏ 6967	If My Heart Had a Window/Punch Brother Punch	1953	$15
❏ 6991	Loved and Lost/Please Come Home	1953	$15
❏ 6941	Since You Went Away from Me/Before	1953	$15

UNITED ARTISTS

Number	Title	Yr	NM
❏ 232	Indoor Sports/Time Waits for No One	1960	$10
❏ 287	Past the Age of Innocence/Richest Girl in the World	1961	$10

X

Number	Title	Yr	NM
❏ 0176	Could It Be?/I'll Take Care of You	1955	$15
❏ 0156	Puddin' 'n' Pie/In Nuevo Laredo	1955	$15

STEWART, SLY

A&M

Number	Title	Yr	NM
❏ 2890	Eek-Ah-Bo-Static Automatic/Black Girls	1986	$3

— B-side by Rae Dawn Chong

Number	Title	Yr	NM
❏ 2896	Love and Affection/Black Girls	1986	$3

— A-side as "Sly Stone and Martha Davis"; B-side by Rae Dawn Chong

AUTUMN

Number	Title	Yr	NM
❏ 14	Buttermilk -- Part 1/Buttermilk -- Part 2	1965	$30

— As "Sly

Number	Title	Yr	NM
❏ 3	I Just Learned How to Swim/Scat Swim	1964	$30

— Sylvester Stewart, later "Sly" of The Family Stone

Number	Title	Yr	NM
❏ 26	Temptation Walk/Temptation Walk -- Part 2	1966	$30

EPIC

Number	Title	Yr	NM
❏ 50795	Dance to the Music/Sing a Simple Song	1979	$5

— As "Sly Stone

G&P

Number	Title	Yr	NM
❏ 901	Help Me With My Heart/A Long Time Away	1962	$250

— As "Sylvester Stewart

LUKE

Number	Title	Yr	NM
❏ 1008	A Long Time Alone/I'm Just a Fool	1961	$250

— As "Danny Stewart

STEWART, VERNON

CHART

Number	Title	Yr	NM
❏ 501	The Way It Feels to Die/You're Not All Here	1962	$20

PEACH

Number	Title	Yr	NM
❏ 740	I'm Tired of Make Believe/I'll Still Love You	1961	$30
❏ 751	Mean, Mean Baby/Heal This Old Heart	1961	$70

STEWART, WYNN, AND JAN HOWARD

CHALLENGE

Number	Title	Yr	NM
❏ 59264	How the Other Half Lives/We'll Never Love Again	1964	$15
❏ 59071	Wrong Company/We'll Never Love Again	1960	$20

JACKPOT

Number	Title	Yr	NM
❏ 48014	How the Other Half Lives/Yankee Go Home	1960	$30

STEWART, WYNN

ATLANTIC

Number	Title	Yr	NM
❏ 4025	When/Why Don't You Come to Me	1974	$5

CAPITOL

Number	Title	Yr	NM
❏ 5593	Angels Don't Lie/The Tourist	1966	$8
❏ 3080	Baby, It's Yours/I Was the First One to Know	1971	$6
❏ 5937	'Cause I Love You/That's the Only Way to Cry	1967	$8
❏ 5937 [PS]	'Cause I Love You/That's the Only Way to Cry	1967	$15
❏ 5271	Half of This, Half of That	1964	$8
❏ 5271 [PS]	Half of This, Half of That	1964	$20
❏ 3000	Heavenly/You're No Secret of Mine	1970	$6
❏ 3157	Hello Little Rock/You Can't Take It With You	1971	$6
❏ F3651	Hold Back Tomorrow/New Love	1957	$30
❏ 5485	I Keep Forgettin' That I Forgot About You/My Rosalie	1965	$8
❏ 2240 [PS]	In Love/My Own Little World	1968	$15
❏ 2888	It's a Beautiful Day/Prisoner on the Run	1970	$6
❏ 5831	It's Such a Pretty World Today/Ol' What's Her Name	1967	$8
❏ 2012 [PS]	Love's Gonna Happen to Me/Waltz of the Angels	1967	$15
❏ 2012	Love's Gonna Happen to Me/Waltz of the Angels	1967	$8
❏ 5397	Sha Marie/Does He Love You Like I Do	1965	$8
❏ 2137 [PS]	Something Pretty/Built in Love	1968	$15
❏ F3594	That Just Kills Me/You Took Her Off My Hands	1956	$30
❏ F3408	The Waltz of the Angels/Why Do I Love You So	1956	$30

CHALLENGE

Number	Title	Yr	NM
❏ 9164	Another Day, Another Dollar/Donna on My Mind	1962	$20
❏ 9121	Big Big Love/One More Memory	1961	$20
❏ 59216	Big City/One Way to Go	1963	$20
❏ 9155	Don't Look Back/Loversville	1962	$20
❏ 59379	Girl in White/Fallin' for You	1967	$8
❏ 59084	Heartaches for a Dime/Playboy	1960	$20
❏ 59095	If You See My Baby/I'd Rather Have America	1960	$20
❏ 9192	Slightly Used/I'm Not the Man I Used to Be	1963	$20
❏ 59061	Wishful Thinking/Uncle Tom Got Caught	1958	$70

— The B-side is sought after by rockabilly collectors

FOUR STAR

Number	Title	Yr	NM
❏ 8001	Inflation Blues/Heartbreak Mountain	1980	$6

JACKPOT

Number	Title	Yr	NM
❏ 48005	Come On/School Bus Love Affair	1959	$300
❏ 48019	Open Up My Heart/Above and Beyond	1960	$30

PLAYBOY

Number	Title	Yr	NM
❏ 6080	After the Storm/Don't Monkey with My Widow	1976	$5
❏ 6060	I'm Gonna Kill You/Seasons of My Heart	1976	$6
❏ 6035	Lonely Rain/Just Now Thought of You	1975	$5
❏ 6091	Sing a Sad Song/It's Such a Pretty World Today	1976	$5

PRETTY WORLD

Number	Title	Yr	NM
❏ 001	Wait Till I Get My Hands on You/Would You Want the World to End	1985	$8

RCA VICTOR

Number	Title	Yr	NM
❏ 74-0891	Everything Needs a Little Woman's Touch/Search Through the Ashes	1973	$5
❏ APBO-0114	It's Raining in Seattle/If I Were You	1973	$5
❏ APBO-0004	Love Ain't Worth a Dime Unless It's Free/Me and My Jesus Would Know	1973	$5
❏ 74-0819	Paint Me a Rainbow/I Know They'll Make Room for You	1972	$5

WIN

Number	Title	Yr	NM
❏ 127	Could I Talk You Into Loving Me Again/I Was Raised Down on the Farm	1979	$6
❏ 126	Eyes Big as Dallas/Such a Perfect Day for Making Love	1978	$6

STILLROVEN, THE

AUGUST

Number	Title	Yr	NM
❏ 101	Little Picture Playhouse/Cast Thy Burden Upon the Stone	1968	$60

FALCON

Number	Title	Yr	NM
❏ 69	Hey Joe/Sunny Day	1967	$80
❏ 7296	She's Your Woman/I'm Not Your Steppin' Stone	1966	$200

ROULETTE

Number	Title	Yr	NM
❏ 4748	Hey Joe/Sunny Day	1967	$30

STILLS, STEPHEN

ATLANTIC

Number	Title	Yr	NM
❏ 89611	Can't Let Go/Grey to Green	1984	$4

— With Walter Finnegan

Number	Title	Yr	NM
❏ 2806	Change Partners/Relaxing Town	1971	$5
❏ 2806 [PS]	Change Partners/Relaxing Town	1971	$6
❏ 2917	Down the Road/Guaguanco De Vero	1972	$5

— With Manassas

Number	Title	Yr	NM
❏ 2876	It Doesn't Matter/Rock & Roll's Crazy Medley	1972	$5
❏ 2778	Love the One You're With/To a Flame	1970	$5
❏ 2820	Marianne/Nothin' to Do But Today	1971	$5
❏ 89597	Only Love Can Break Your Heart/Love Again	1984	$4
❏ 2790	Sit Yourself Down/We Are Not Helpless	1971	$5
❏ 2959	So Many Times/Isn't It About Time	1973	$5
❏ 89633	Stranger/No Hiding Place	1984	$4
❏ 89633 [PS]	Stranger/No Hiding Place	1984	$4

COLUMBIA

Number	Title	Yr	NM
❏ 10369	Buyin' Time/Soldier	1976	$5
❏ 10804	Lowdown/Can't Get No Booty	1978	$5
❏ 10872	Thoroughfare Gap/Lowdown	1978	$5
❏ 10179	Turn Back the Pages/Shuffle Just as Bad	1975	$5

7-Inch Extended Plays

ATLANTIC

Number	Title	Yr	NM
❏ SD 7-7206	Bluebird Revisited/Ecology Song//Sugar Babe/Marianne/Relaxing Town	1971	$15

— Jukebox issue; small hole, plays at 33 1/3 rpm

Number	Title	Yr	NM
❏ SD 7-7206 [PS]	Stephen Stills 2	1971	$15

— Part of "Little LP" series (LLP #157)

STIMULATORS, THE

CB

Number	Title	Yr	NM
❏ 0(# unknown)	Loud Fast Rules!/Run Run Run	1979	$50
❏ 0(# unknown) [PS]	Loud Fast Rules!/Run Run Run	1979	$50

— A very difficult sleeve to find in near-mint, as the top inch or so of the oversized sleeve is usually mangled

Number	Title	Yr	NM
STING			
Also see THE POLICE.			
❏ 2992	Be Still My Beating Heart/ Ghost in the Strand	1987	$3
❏ 2992 [PS]	Be Still My Beating Heart/ Ghost in the Strand	1987	$3
❏ 1200	Englishman in New York/If You're There	1988	$3
❏ 1200 [PS]	Englishman in New York/If You're There	1988	$3
❏ 2767	Fortress Around Your Heart/Consider Me Gone	1985	$3
❏ 2767 [PS]	Fortress Around Your Heart/Consider Me Gone	1985	$3
❏ 1211	Fragile/Gragilidad	1988	$3
❏ 2738	If You Love Somebody Set Them Free/Another Day	1985	$4
—Blue custom label			
❏ 2738	If You Love Somebody Set Them Free/Another Day	1985	$3
—Normal red and black label			
❏ 2738 [PS]	If You Love Somebody Set Them Free/Another Day	1985	$3
❏ 2765	If You Love Somebody Set Them Free/Another Day	1985	$5
❏ 2765 [PS]	If You Love Somebody Set Them Free/Another Day	1985	$5
❏ 2787	Love Is the Seventh Wave/The Dream of the Blue Turtles	1985	$3
❏ 2787 [PS]	Love Is the Seventh Wave/The Dream of the Blue Turtles	1985	$3
❏ 2501	Spread a Little Happiness/Only You	1982	$4
❏ 1242	They Dance Alone (Gueca Solo)/They Dance Alone (Gueca Solo)	1988	$3
❏ 2983	We'll Be Together/ Conversation with a Dog	1987	$3
❏ 2983 [PS]	We'll Be Together/ Conversation with a Dog	1987	$3
STINIT, DANE			
SUN			
❏ 402	Always on the Go/ Don't Knock What You Don't Understand	1966	$20
❏ 405	Sweet Country Girl/ That Muddy Ole River	1967	$20
STITES, GARY			
CARLTON			
❏ 516	A Girl Like You/Hey Little Girl	1959	$30
❏ 529	Gloria Lee/Hey, Hey	1960	$30
❏ 525	Lawdy Miss Clawdy/Don't Wanna Say Goodbye	1960	$30
❏ 508	Lonely for You/ Shine That Ring	1959	$30
❏ 521	Starry Eyed/Without Your Love	1959	$30
EPIC			
❏ 10064	Hurting/Thinking of You	1966	$15
MADISON			
❏ 155	Honey Girl/Little Lonely One	1961	$20
STITT, SONNY			
ARGO			
❏ 5493	Flame and Frost/ My Main Man	1965	$8
—With Bennie Green			
❏ 5403	It All Depends on You (Part 1)/It All Depends on You (Part 2)	1961	$10
CADET			
❏ 5701	Mr. Bojangles/Blue Monsoon	1974	$4
❏ 5708	Theme from The Godfather Part II/Ocho Nos	1974	$5
❏ 5705	Will You Love Me Tomorrow/Satan	1974	$4
ENTERPRISE			
❏ 9001	Private Number/ Heads or Tails	1969	$6
IMPULSE!			
❏ 230	Salt and Pepper (Part 1)/ Salt and Pepper (Part 2)	1964	$8
—With Paul Gonsalves			
❏ 710	Candy/Lover Man	1969	$6
❏ 304	Shangri-La/Soul Shack	1964	$10
❏ 282	Thirty-Three Ninety-Six (Part 1)/Thirty-Three Ninety-Six (Part 2)	1963	$10
ROULETTE			
❏ 4713	Stardust (Part 1)/ Stardust (Part 2)	1966	$8
❏ 4701	What's New/Morgan's Song	1966	$8
WINGATE			
❏ 011	Stitt's Groove/Marr's Groove	1966	$8
—With Hank Marr			
❏ 006	The Double-O-Soul of Sonny Stitt (Part 1 and 2)	1965	$8

Number	Title	Yr	NM
WORLD PACIFIC			
❏ 398	My Mother's Eyes/ Summer Special	1963	$10
STOECKLEIN, VAL			
DOT			
❏ 17234	All the Way Home/I Wonder Who I'll Be Tomorrow	1969	$20
❏ 17200	Sounds of Yesterday/ Say It's Not Over	1969	$20
STOLOFF, MORRIS			
COLPIX			
❏ 103	Wild One/Bell, Book and Candle	1959	$8
❏ 103	Wild One/Bell, Book and Candle	1959	$8
DECCA			
❏ 9-30064	Exactly Like You & Wanna Go Back to You/You Can't Run Away from It	1956	$10
❏ 9-30388	Harmonica Theme from "Fire Down Below"/ Half of My Heart	1957	$12
❏ 9-30030	Manhattan Romance & Sweet Sue, Just You/ The Solid Gold Cadillac	1956	$10
❏ 9-29888	Moonglow and Theme from "Picnic"/Theme from "Picnic	1956	$10
—B-side by George Duning			
MERCURY			
❏ 70428X45	Memphis Blues/ Wagon Wheels	1954	$30
❏ 70472X45	Stars Fell Over Alabama/By the Waters of Minnetonka	1954	$30
REPRISE			
❏ 0339	Sylvia/None But the Brave	1965	$8
WARNER BROS.			
❏ 5227	Fanny/Panisse and Son	1961	$8
STOMPERS, THE			
GONE			
❏ 5120	Stompin' Round the Christmas Tree/Forgive Me	1961	$200
LANDA			
❏ 684	Foolish One/Quarter to Four Stomp	1962	$30
❏ 684	Foolish One/Surf Stompin'	1962	$30
MERCURY			
❏ 72111	Frump/Blacksmith Blues	1963	$20
—As "The Ski Stompers			
SOUVENIR			
❏ 1003	I Miss You So/Blue Moon of Kentucky	1960	$125
STONE CIRCUS, THE			
MAINSTREAM			
❏ 694	Mister Grey/(B-side unknown)	1969	$30
STONE, CLIFFIE			
CAPITOL			
❏ F1406	Amen, Brother Ben/ Red Head Polka	1951	$30
❏ F40198	Bird in the Cage, Seven Hands Around/The Lady Goes Half Way Round	1949	$30
❏ F4141	Blood on the Saddle/ Cool Water	1959	$15
❏ F2910	Blue Moon of Kentucky/ Please, Please	1954	$40
❏ F1834	Bored of Education/ The Grunt Song	1951	$30
❏ F40265	Can I Canoe You Up the River/Just One Little Lie	1950	$40
❏ F1960	Carolina Waltz/ Dead End Street	1952	$30
❏ F40191	Catch All Eight/The Inside Out, The Outside In	1950	$30
❏ F1265	Christmas Waltz/Here Comes Santa Claus	1950	$30
❏ F3323	Copenhagen/Milenberg Joys	1956	$20
❏ F40161	Devil's Dream/Old Joe Clark/ Down Yonder/Buffalo Gals	1950	$40
—78 first issued in 1949; other 45s in the 40000 series, in addition to those listed, may exist			
❏ F2291	Dirty Dishes/Everyone's Sweetheart	1952	$30
❏ F1167	Fireball Mail/Blue Canadian Rockies	1950	$30
❏ F2362	Listen to the Mockingbird/ When the Bloom Is On the Sage	1953	$30
❏ 2270	Little Girl (With Calls)/ Little Girl (Without Calls)	1968	$8
❏ 2270 [PS]	Little Girl (With Calls)/ Little Girl (Without Calls)	1968	$15
❏ F4079	Maybe/I Don't Want to Walk Without You	1958	$15
❏ F3039	Melody of Love/Darling Je Vous Aime Beaucoup	1955	$20

Number	Title	Yr	NM
❏ F1606	Missouri Waltz/The Waltz You Saved for Me	1951	$30
—Reissue			
❏ F40190	Special Instructions for Square Dancing/The Arizona Double Star	1950	$30
❏ F40192	Swing in the Center, Swing on the Side/Forward Six, Don't You Blunder	1950	$30
❏ F1354	Tater Pie/With a Kiss	1951	$30
❏ F2497	The Bunny Hop/In a Shanty in Old Shanty Town	1953	$30
❏ F986	The Dipsey Doodle/ Rubber Knuckle Sam	1950	$30
❏ F2407	The Last Roundup/Pretend	1953	$30
❏ F40196	The Three Ladies Chain/ Four-Gent Star	1949	$30
❏ F966	Twilight Time in Texas/ Steel Strike	1950	$30
❏ F1109	Westphalia Waltz/ Put Your Little Foot	1950	$30
TOWER			
❏ 361	There Goes My Everything/Del Rio	1967	$8
STONE COUNTRY			
RCA VICTOR			
❏ 47-9534	Wheels on Fire/ Million Dollar Bash	1968	$8
STONE, JIMMY			
CROSS COUNTRY			
❏ 523	Found/Mine	1956	$300
GONE			
❏ 5001	Found/Mine	1957	$200
STONE, JUDY			
CAMEO			
❏ 330	4,003,221 Tears from Now/Hello Faithless	1964	$30
STONE PONEYS			
Also see LINDA RONSTADT.			
CAPITOL			
❏ 5838	All the Beautiful Things/ Sweet Summer Blue and Gold	1967	$10
❏ 2004	Different Drum/I've Got to Know	1967	$20
❏ 2195	Hobo (Mornin' Glory)/ Some of Shelly's Blues	1968	$12
❏ 5910	One for One/Evergreen	1967	$10
SIDEWALK			
❏ 937	So Fine/Everyone Has Their Own Ideas	1968	$200
STONEMANS, THE			
MGM			
❏ 13667	Back to Nashville, Tennessee/Bottle of Wine	1967	$8
❏ 13945	Christopher Robin/The Love I Left Behind	1968	$8
❏ 13896	Cimarron/Tell It to My Heart Sometime	1968	$8
❏ 13557	The Five Little Johnson Girls/Goin' Back to Bowling Green	1966	$8
❏ 13466	Tupelo County Jail/Spell of the Freight Train	1966	$8
❏ 13755	West Canterbury Subdivision Blues/The Three Cent Opera	1967	$8
STARDAY			
❏ 599	That Pal of Mine/ Talking Fiddle Blues	1962	$20
—As "The Stoneman Family			
WORLD PACIFIC			
❏ 413	Groundhog/Take Me Home	1964	$15
—As "The Stoneman Family			
STONES, THE			
SULLY			
❏ 928	She Said Yeah/Watch Me	1966	$80
—Reissued with group renamed "The Tracers			
STOOGES, THE			
See IGGY AND THE STOOGES.			
ELEKTRA			
❏ 45695 [B]	Down on the Street/I Feel Alright	1970	$40
—As "The Stooges			
❏ 45664 [B]	I Wanna Be Your Dog (mono)/I Wanna Be Your Dog (stereo)	1970	$80
—As "The Stooges			

Number	Title	Yr	NM

STORIES
KAMA SUTRA
Number	Title	Yr	NM
❑ 594	Another Love/Love Is In Motion	1974	$4
❑ 577	Brother Louie/Changes Have Begun	1973	$6
❑ 577	Brother Louie/What Comes After	1973	$5
❑ 588	Circles/If It Feels Good	1974	$4
❑ 566	Darling/Take Cover	1972	$4
❑ 545	I'm Coming Home/ You Told Me	1972	$4
❑ 574	Love in Motion/Changes Have Begun	1973	$4
❑ 584	Mammy Blue/Travelling Underground	1973	$4
❑ 558	Top of the City/Stepback	1972	$4

STORM, BILLY
ATLANTIC
Number	Title	Yr	NM
❑ 2112	Honey Love/A Kiss from Your Lips	1961	$15
❑ 2076	In the Chapel in the Moonlight/Sure As You're Born	1960	$15
❑ 2098	When You Dance/Dear One	1961	$15

BUENA VISTA
Number	Title	Yr	NM
❑ 418	'Deed I Do/Lonely People Do Foolish Things	1963	$20
❑ 415	Double Date/Good Girl	1963	$20
❑ 424	He Knows How Much We Can Bear/Motherless Child	1963	$30
❑ 413	Love Theme from El Cid/Cee Cee Rider	1962	$20
❑ 403	Puppy Love Is Here to Stay/Push Over	1962	$20
❑ 429	Since I Fell for You/ Body and Soul	1964	$30

COLUMBIA
Number	Title	Yr	NM
❑ 41431	Easy Chair/You Just Can't Plan These Things	1959	$20
❑ 41545	Enchanted/When the Whole World Smiles Again	1959	$20
❑ 41494	I Can't Stop Crying for You/Emotion	1959	$20
❑ 4-41356	This Is Always/I've Come of Age	1959	$20

GREGMARK
Number	Title	Yr	NM
❑ 9	3000 Tears/Who'll Keep an Eye on Jane	1961	$15

HANNA-BARBERA
Number	Title	Yr	NM
❑ 474	Please Don't Mention Her Name/The Warmest Love	1966	$30
❑ 474 [PS]	Please Don't Mention Her Name/The Warmest Love	1966	$30

INFINITY
Number	Title	Yr	NM
❑ 023	I Can't Help It/Educated Fool	1963	$15
❑ 013	Love Theme from El Cid/Don't Let Go	1962	$15
❑ 018	Since I Fell for You/A Million Miles from Nowhere	1963	$15

LOMA
Number	Title	Yr	NM
❑ 2001	Baby, Don't Look Down/I Never Want to Dream Again	1964	$12
❑ 2009	Goldfinger Theme/ Debbie and Mitch	1965	$10

ODE
Number	Title	Yr	NM
❑ 120	Coal Mine/Tonight I'll Be Staying Here with You	1968	$8

STORM, GALE
DOT
Number	Title	Yr	NM
❑ 15691	A Farewell to Arms/I Get That Feeling	1958	$10
❑ 15734	Angry/You	1958	$10
❑ 15558	Dark Moon/A Little Too Late	1957	$12
❑ 16032	Dark Moon/Memories Are Made of This	1960	$8
❑ 15666	Go 'Way from My Window/Winter Warm	1957	$10
❑ 16031	I Hear You Knocking/ Ivory Tower	1960	$8
❑ 15412	I Hear You Knocking/ Never Leave Me	1955	$30
❑ 15528	I Need You So/On Treasure Island	1957	$10
❑ 15458	Ivory Tower/I Ain't Gonna Worry	1956	$20
❑ 15515	My Heart Belongs to You/ Orange Blossoms	1956	$10
❑ 15861	Oh, Lonely Crowd/ Happiness Left Yesterday	1958	$10
❑ 15606	On My Mind Again/Love by the Jukebox Light	1957	$10
❑ 16057	On Treasure Island/I Need You So	1960	$8
❑ 15539	On Treasure Island/ Lucky Lips	1957	$10
❑ 16111	Please Help Me, I'm Falling/He's There	1960	$8
❑ 15783	South of the Border/ Soon I'll Wed My Love	1958	$10
❑ 15436	Teen-Age Prayer/Memories Are Made of This	1955	$20
❑ 15474	Tell Me Why/Don't Be That Way	1956	$20
❑ 15448	Why Do Fools Fall in Love/I Walk Alone	1956	$20

STORM, RORY, AND THE HURRICANES
COLUMBIA
Number	Title	Yr	NM
❑ 43018	I Can Tell/Let's Stomp	1964	$30

—B-side by Faron's Flamingos

STORM, TOM, AND THE PEPS
GE GE
Number	Title	Yr	NM
❑ 501	I Love You/That's the Way Love Is	1965	$40

STORME, ROBB
AURORA
Number	Title	Yr	NM
❑ 162	Here Today/Don't Cry	1966	$15

CAPITOL
Number	Title	Yr	NM
❑ 5452	Love Is Strange/Shy Guy	1965	$10

STORMS, THE
SUNDOWN
Number	Title	Yr	NM
❑ 114	Thunder/Tarantula	1959	$60

—This was re-recorded on Indigo 127

STORY, CARL
COLUMBIA
Number	Title	Yr	NM
❑ 4-21282	A Million Years in Glory/ On the Other Shore	1954	$30
❑ 4-21137	Lonesome Hearted Blues/ Love and Wealth	1953	$30
❑ 4-21327	Love Me Like You Used to Do/It's a Lonesome Road	1954	$30
❑ 4-21205	My Lord Keeps a Record/ Someone to Lean On	1954	$30
❑ 4-21250	Step It Up and Go/Have You Come to Say Goodbye	1954	$30
❑ 4-21444	What a Line/You've Been Tom-Cattin' Around	1955	$30

MERCURY
Number	Title	Yr	NM
❑ 71218	Family Reunion/Banjolina	1957	$20
❑ 70785	Get On Board, Little Children/God Put the Rainbow in the Clouds	1956	$20
❑ 71143	Got a Lot to Tell Jesus/ Banjo on the Mountain	1957	$20
❑ 71088	The Light at the River/ Mocking Banjo	1957	$20
❑ 71268	The Saviour's Love/ Fire on the Banjo	1958	$20
❑ 70932	Waiting for Me/Everybody Will Be Happy Over There	1956	$20

STARDAY
Number	Title	Yr	NM
❑ 619	A Picture from Life's Other Side/Rank Stranger	1963	$15
❑ 531	Get Religion/ Jerusalem Moan	1960	$20
❑ 465	I Heard My Mother Weeping/I'll Be a Friend	1959	$20
❑ 492	(I Heard My Name) On the Radio/Sweeter Than the Flowers	1960	$20
❑ 411	Old Country Baptizing/ Angel Band	1958	$20
❑ 449	Set Your House in Order/ The Old Gospel Ship	1959	$20
❑ 427	Shout and Shine/A Beautiful City	1959	$20
❑ 514	Someone's Last Day/The Ship That's Sailing Down	1960	$20
❑ 688	The Old Country Preacher/ Listen to Your Radio	1964	$10

STORYTELLERS, THE
CAPITOL
Number	Title	Yr	NM
❑ 5042	I Don't Want an Angel/ Down in the Valley	1964	$30

DIMENSION
Number	Title	Yr	NM
❑ 1014	When Two People/ Time Will Tell	1963	$30

RAMARCA
Number	Title	Yr	NM
❑ 501	When Two People/ Time Will Tell	1963	$40

STACK
Number	Title	Yr	NM
❑ 500	Hey Baby/You Played Me for a Fool	1959	$200

STOVALL, VERN
CREST
Number	Title	Yr	NM
❑ 1080	Long Black Limousine/ Loving on Borrowed Time	1961	$30
❑ 1090	My Best Wasn't Good Enough/That's All It Takes	1961	$20
❑ 1111	The World Had Too Much to See/Just Another Way to Get the Blues	1962	$20

LONGHORN
Number	Title	Yr	NM
❑ 581	Dallas/Movin' Round	1967	$12
❑ 584	Elbow Bender/ Everybody Has a Price	1968	$12
❑ 579	(I Didn't Know) Angels Flew This Close to the Ground/ Funny Sense of Humor	1967	$10

Number	Title	Yr	NM
❑ 588	Sittin' Pretty/You Can't Roll a Seven Every Time	1968	$12

MONUMENT
Number	Title	Yr	NM
❑ 1097	Cloud Burner/Honky Tonkers	1968	$8
❑ 1126	Love Is/Brought On by the Wine	1969	$8
❑ 1149	Pay Day/Code Alarm 7	1969	$8

STRAIT, GEORGE
MCA
Number	Title	Yr	NM
❑ 53693	Ace in the Hole/Oh Me, Oh My Sweet Baby	1989	$5
❑ 52225	A Fire I Can't Put Out/ Honky Tonk Crazy	1983	$4
❑ 53087	All My Ex's Live in Texas/I'm All Behind You Now	1987	$4
❑ 53087 [DJ]	All My Ex's Live in Texas (same on both sides)	1987	$20
—Promo only on yellow vinyl			
❑ 52162	Amarillo by Morning/ Lover in Disguise	1983	$4
❑ 53165 [DJ]	Am I Blue (same on both sides)	1987	$20
—Promo only on blue vinyl			
❑ 53165	Am I Blue/Someone's Walkin' Around Upstairs	1987	$3
❑ 53340	Baby Blue/Back to Bein' Me	1988	$3
❑ 53486	Baby's Gotten Good at Goodbye/Bigger Man Than Me	1988	$3
❑ 52458	Does Fort Worth Ever Cross Your Mind/Love Comes from the Other Side of Town	1984	$3
❑ 51170	Down and Out/Blame It on Mexico	1981	$4
❑ 53248	Famous Last Words of a Fool/It's Too Late Now	1988	$3
❑ 52066	Fool Hearted Memory/ Steal of the Night	1982	$4
❑ S45-17451 [DJ]	For Christ's Sake, It's Christmas/When It's Christmas Time in Texas	1987	$20
—Promo only on white vinyl			
❑ 53400	If You Ain't Lovin' (You Ain't Livin')/Is It That Time Again	1988	$3
❑ 51228	If You're Thinking You Want a Stranger (There's One Coming Home)/Her Goodbye Hit Me in the Heart	1982	$4
❑ 52914	It Ain't Cool to Be Crazy About You/ Rhythm of the Road	1986	$3
❑ 52392	Let's Fall to Pieces Together/You're the Cloud I'm On (When I'm High)	1984	$3
❑ 52120	Marina Del Rey/I Can't See Texas from Here	1982	$4
❑ S45-17234 [DJ]	Merry Christmas Strait to You/White Christmas	1986	$30
—Promo only on red vinyl			
❑ S45-17234 [DJ]	Merry Christmas Strait to You/White Christmas	1986	$30
—Promo only on red vinyl			
❑ 53021	Ocean Front Property/ My Heart Won't Wander Very Far from You	1987	$4
❑ 53021 [DJ]	Ocean Front Property (same on both sides)	1987	$20
—Promo only on yellow vinyl			
❑ 53755	Overnight Success/ Hollywood Squares	1989	$4
❑ 52667	The Chair/In Too Deep	1985	$3
❑ 52667 [PS]	The Chair/In Too Deep	1985	$5
❑ 52667 [DJ]	The Chair (same on both sides)	1985	$20
—Promo only on blue vinyl			
❑ 52526	The Cowboy Rides Away/Any Old Time	1985	$3
❑ 52586	The Fireman/What Did You Expect Me to Do	1985	$3
❑ 53648	What's Going On in Your World/Let's Get Down to It	1989	$3

STRANGE, BILLY
BUENA VISTA
Number	Title	Yr	NM
❑ 406	I'll Remember April/ The Mooncussors	1962	$10

COLISEUM
Number	Title	Yr	NM
❑ 605	A Lotta Limbo (Part 1)/A Lotta Limbo (Part 2)	1963	$15

GNP CRESCENDO
Number	Title	Yr	NM
❑ 374	Caliente/Have Tequila	1966	$8
❑ 309	Charade/Where's Baby Gone	1964	$8
❑ 477	Chattanooga Choo Choo/Track Walkin'	1974	$4
❑ 390	Go Ahead and Cry/Yours Is a World I Can't Live In	1967	$6
❑ 334	Goldfinger/(Theme from) The Munsters	1965	$8
❑ 413	Hang 'Em High/ Five Card Stud	1968	$6
❑ 367	Our Man Flint/Run, Spy, Run	1966	$8
❑ 800	Star Trek/Theme from "Jaws	1975	$5
❑ 417	The High Chaparral/ Gunsmoke	1968	$6

Number	Title	Yr	NM
❏ 341	The Man with the Golden Arm/Raunchy	1965	$8
❏ 308	Wildwood Flower/Wabash Cannonball	1964	$8

LIBERTY

Number	Title	Yr	NM
❏ 55414	A Life of Pretend/I'm Still Crying	1962	$10
❏ 55362	Long Steel Road/Soft Chains of Love	1961	$10

TOWER

Number	Title	Yr	NM
❏ 515	De Sade/Nocturne Permission	1969	$8

STRANGELOVES, THE
BANG

Number	Title	Yr	NM
❏ 508	Cara-Lin/(Roll On) Mississippi	1965	$15
❏ 524	Hand Jive/I Gotta Dance	1966	$15
❏ 501	I Want Candy/It's About My Baby	1965	$20

SIRE

Number	Title	Yr	NM
❏ 4102	I Wanna Do It/Honey Do	1968	$10

SWAN

Number	Title	Yr	NM
❏ 4192	Love Love (That's All I Want from You)/I'm on Fire	1964	$30

STRANGERS, THE
CAPITOL

Number	Title	Yr	NM
❏ 3376	I'm a Light Boy/Shoulder to Cry On	1972	$10
❏ 3144	Song from Sleepwalk/Slow 'n Easy	1971	$8

— By "Merle Haggard's Strangers"

STRANGERS, THE (1)
TITAN

Number	Title	Yr	NM
❏ 1704	Boogie Man/Young Maggie	1960	$30
❏ 1702	Hill Stomp/A Lost Soul	1959	$30
❏ 1701	The Caterpillar Crawl/Rockin' Rebel	1959	$40

STRANGERS, THE (2)
CHATTAHOOCHIE

Number	Title	Yr	NM
❏ 710	Like a Stranger/Can't Get the Water from My Eye	1966	$15

JUBILEE

Number	Title	Yr	NM
❏ 5514	Plan On Someone New/What's the Matter Baby	1965	$15

STRANGERS, THE (3)
CHECKER

Number	Title	Yr	NM
❏ 1010	Darlin'/Pa and Billie	1962	$20

STRANGERS, THE (4)
CHOICE

Number	Title	Yr	NM
❏ 5	Bart" Maverick/"Bret" Maverick	1960	$30

STRANGERS, THE (5)
CHRISTY

Number	Title	Yr	NM
❏ 107	We're in Love, We're in Love, We're in Love/Crab Louie	1959	$40

STRANGERS, THE (6)
LIBERTY

Number	Title	Yr	NM
❏ 55550	Card Shark/Mindreader	1963	$30
❏ 55481	Toy Soldier/Loco	1962	$30

STRANGERS, THE (7)
KING

Number	Title	Yr	NM
❏ 4709	Blue Flowers/Beg and Steal	1954	$500
❏ 4745	Drop Down to My Place/Get It One More Time	1954	$300
❏ 4728	Hoping You'll Understand/Just Don't Care	1954	$400
❏ 4766	How Long Must I Wait/Dreams Came True	1955	$250
❏ 4697	My Friends/I've Got Eyes	1954	$400
❏ 4821	Without a Friend/Think Again	1955	$70

— With "High Fidelity" on label

Number	Title	Yr	NM
❏ 4821	Without a Friend/Think Again	1955	$250

— Without "High Fidelity" on label (original)

STRANGERS, THE (8)
LINDA

Number	Title	Yr	NM
❏ 118	Easy Livin'/Tell Me	1965	$40

STRANGERS, THE (9)
MGM

Number	Title	Yr	NM
❏ 11980	Strange Lady in Town/North Dakota	1955	$50

STRANGLERS, THE
A&M

Number	Title	Yr	NM
❏ 1973 [DJ]	Hanging Around/Grip (Get a Grip on Yourself)/Something Better Change/Straighten Out	1977	$4

— With pink and white marbled vinyl; "totally safe" promo versions

Number	Title	Yr	NM
❏ 1973	Hanging Around/Grip (Get a Grip on Yourself)/Something Better Change/Straighten Out	1977	$5

— With pink and white marbled vinyl

Number	Title	Yr	NM
❏ 1973 [PS]	Hanging Around/Grip (Get a Grip on Yourself)/Something Better Change/Straighten Out	1977	$5
❏ 1973 [DJ]	Hanging Around/Grip (Get a Grip on Yourself)/Something Better Change/Straighten Out	1977	$4

— With pink and white marbled vinyl; "totally safe" promo versions

Number	Title	Yr	NM
❏ 1973 [PS]	Hanging Around/Grip (Get a Grip on Yourself)/Something Better Change/Straighten Out	1977	$4

— Promo sleeve accompanying the "totally safe" 45

EPIC

Number	Title	Yr	NM
❏ 06990	Always the Sun/Mayan Skies	1987	$3
❏ 07205	Dreamtime/Ghost Train	1987	$3

7-Inch Extended Plays

I.R.S.

Number	Title	Yr	NM
❏ SP-70952	White Room/Straighten Out/Do the European/Choosey Suzie	1980	$6

— Bonus with early copies of LP "Stranglers IV"; no picture sleeve

STRASSMAN, MARCIA
UNI

Number	Title	Yr	NM
❏ 55056	Star Gazer/Self-Analysis	1968	$10
❏ 55006	The Flower Children/Out of the Picture	1967	$10
❏ 55023	The Groovy World of Jack and Jill/The Flower Shop	1967	$10
❏ 55023 [PS]	The Groovy World of Jack and Jill/The Flower Shop	1967	$20

STRATAVARIOUS
ROULETTE

Number	Title	Yr	NM
❏ 7191	I Got Your Love Part I/Part II	1976	$30
❏ 7200	Let Me Be Your Lady Tonight/Love Me	1976	$12

— A-side as "Stratavarious & Lady"

STRAWBERRY ALARM CLOCK
ALL AMERICAN

Number	Title	Yr	NM
❏ 373	Incense and Peppermints/The Birdman of Alcatrash	1967	$200

UNI

Number	Title	Yr	NM
❏ 55076	Barefoot in Baltimore/Angry Young Man	1968	$12
❏ 55218	California Day/Three	1970	$30
❏ 55158	Desiree/Changes	1969	$8
❏ 55241	Girl from the City/Three	1970	$30
❏ 55125	Good Morning Starshine/Me and the Township	1969	$8
❏ 55190	I Climbed the Mountain/Three	1969	$8
❏ 55018	Incense and Peppermints/The Birdman of Alcatrash	1967	$15
❏ 55093	Paxton's Back Street Carnival/Sea Shell	1968	$10
❏ 55055	Pretty Song from Psych-Out/Sit with the Guru	1968	$10
❏ 55185	Small Package/Starting Out the Day	1969	$8
❏ 55113	Stand By/Miss Attraction	1969	$8
❏ 55046	Tomorrow/Birds in My Tree	1967	$10

STRAWBERRY CHILDREN
SOUL CITY

Number	Title	Yr	NM
❏ 758	Love Years Coming/One Stands Here	1967	$30

STRAWBS, THE
A&M

Number	Title	Yr	NM
❏ 1364	Heavy Disguise/Benedictus	1972	$5
❏ 1451	Lay Down/The Winter and the Summer	1973	$5
❏ 1747	Little Sleepy/Golden Salamander	1975	$4
❏ 944	Oh How She Changed/Or Am I Dreaming	1968	$5
❏ 1419	Part of the Union/Tomorrow	1973	$5
❏ 998	Poor Jimmy Wilson/The Man Who Called Himself Jesus	1968	$5
❏ 1476	Shine On Silver Sun/And Wherefore	1973	$5

Number	Title	Yr	NM
❏ 1687	Where Do You Go/Lemon Pie	1975	$4
❏ 1242 [DJ]	Where Is This Dream of Your Youth (mono/stereo)	1971	$6

— No stock copies known

Number	Title	Yr	NM
❏ 1242 [DJ]	Where Is This Dream of Your Youth (mono/stereo)	1971	$6

— No stock copies known

ARISTA

Number	Title	Yr	NM
❏ 0327	I Don't Want to Talk About It/Words of Wisdom	1978	$4

OYSTER

Number	Title	Yr	NM
❏ 705	Burning for Me/Heartbreaker	1977	$4
❏ 702	I Only Want My Love to Grow on You/(Wasting My Time) Thinking of You	1976	$4
❏ 704	So Close and Yet So Far Away/(B-side unknown)	1977	$4

STRAY CATS
Also see BRIAN SETZER.
EMI AMERICA

Number	Title	Yr	NM
❏ BB-8169-2	Cruisin'/Lucky Charm	1983	$5

— Paired with 8169-1

Number	Title	Yr	NM
❏ B-8185	I Won't Stand In Your Way/(Acappella Version)	1983	$3
❏ B-8194	Look at That Cadillac/Lucky Charm	1984	$5
❏ B-8194 [PS]	Look at That Cadillac/Lucky Charm	1984	$5
❏ BB-8169-1/2 [PS]	(She's) Sexy + 17/Lookin' Better Every Beer/Cruisin'/Lucky Charm	1983	$5

— Gatefold sleeve for two-record set

Number	Title	Yr	NM
❏ B-8168	(She's) Sexy + 17/Lookin' Better Every Beer	1983	$3
❏ B-8168 [PS]	(She's) Sexy + 17/Lookin' Better Every Beer	1983	$3
❏ BB-8169-1	(She's) Sexy + 17/Lookin' Better Every Beer	1983	$5

— Paired with 8169-2

Number	Title	Yr	NM
❏ B-8122	Stray Cat Strut/You Don't Believe Me	1982	$3
❏ B-8122 [PS]	Stray Cat Strut/You Don't Believe Me	1982	$8

STREAMERS, THE
DOT

Number	Title	Yr	NM
❏ 16648	Slip-Stream/Blue Mountain	1964	$40

STREET CLEANERS, THE
AMY

Number	Title	Yr	NM
❏ 914	Garbage City/That's Cool, That's Trash	1964	$40

STREET CORNERS, THE
PARKWAY

Number	Title	Yr	NM
❏ 997	My Generation/I Don't Care	1966	$10

STREET, MEL
GRT

Number	Title	Yr	NM
❏ 109	An Old Christmas Card/You Cared Enough To Send Me The Very Best	1976	$6
❏ 025	Even If I Have to Steal/Country Pride	1975	$6
❏ 012	Forbidden Angel/Don't Lead Me On	1974	$6
❏ 057	I Met a Friend of Yours Today/She Boogies While He's Gone	1976	$6
❏ 083	Looking Out My Window Through the Pain/Virginia's Song	1976	$6
❏ 017	Smokey Mountain Memories/Let's Put Out the Fire	1975	$6
❏ 043	The Devil in Your Kisses (And the Angel in Your Eyes)/Baby Don't Save Your Love for a Rainy Day	1976	$6
❏ 030	(This Ain't Just Another) Lust Affair/Strange Empty World	1975	$6

METROMEDIA COUNTRY

Number	Title	Yr	NM
❏ 901	Lovin' on Back Streets/Who'll Turn Out the Lights	1972	$6
❏ BMBO-0143	Lovin' on Borrowed Time/Moonshine Man	1973	$6
❏ BMBO-0018	The Town Where You Live/Body Man	1973	$6
❏ 906	Walk Softly on the Bridges/Spoiled Lonely Man	1973	$6

POLYDOR

Number	Title	Yr	NM
❏ 14399	Barbara Don't Let Me Be the Last to Know/My Friend the Jukebox	1977	$5
❏ 14421	Close Enough for Lonesome/If This Is Having a Good Time	1977	$5
❏ 14448	If I Had a Cheating Heart/Memory Eraser	1977	$5
❏ 14468	Shady Rest/She's No Honky Tonk Angel	1978	$5

Number	Title	Yr	NM

ROYAL AMERICAN
Number	Title	Yr	NM
❏ 64	Borrowed Angel/House of Pride	1972	$8

SUNBIRD
❏ 7568	Slip Away/Let's Put Out the Fire	1981	$5

— With Sandy Powell
❏ 103	Tonight Let's Sleep on It Baby/Muddy Mississippi	1980	$5
❏ 7555	Who'll Turn Out the Lights/Lust Affair	1980	$5

SUNSET
❏ 100	The One Thing My Lady Never Puts Into Words/Borrowed Angel	1979	$5

STREISAND, BARBRA

ARISTA
Number	Title	Yr	NM
❏ 0123	How Lucky Can You Get/More Than You Know	1975	$6

COLUMBIA
❏ 38-08026	All I Ask of You/On My Way to You	1988	$4
❏ 38-08026 [PS]	All I Ask of You/On My Way to You	1988	$4
❏ 46024	All in Love Is Fair/My Buddy-How About Me	1974	$5
❏ 18-02621	Comin' In and Out of Your Life/Lost Inside of You	1981	$4
❏ 45739	Didn't We/On a Clear Day	1972	$5
❏ 44704	Don't Rain on My Parade/My Man	1968	$6
❏ 38-04707	Emotion/Here We Are at Last	1984	$3
❏ 38-04707 [PS]	Emotion/Here We Are at Last	1984	$4
❏ 45384	Flim Flam Man/Maybe	1971	$5
❏ 43808	Free Again/I've Been Here	1966	$6
❏ 43127	Funny Girl/Absent Minded Me	1964	$10
❏ 44622	Funny Girl/I'd Rather Be Blue Over You	1968	$5
❏ 42937	Gotta Move/Make Believe	1964	$20
❏ 11-11390	Guilty/Life Story	1980	$4

— A-side with Barry Gibb
❏ 42631	Happy Days Are Here Again/When the Sun Comes Out	1962	$30
❏ 44351	Have Yourself a Merry Little Christmas/The Best Gift	1967	$12
❏ 44351 [PS]	Have Yourself a Merry Little Christmas/The Best Gift	1967	$30
❏ 43403	He Touched Me/I Like Him	1965	$8
❏ 44921	Honey Pie/Little Tin Soldier	1969	$5
❏ 45780	If I Close My Eyes/(Instrumental)	1973	$5
❏ JZSP79183/4 [DJ]	I'm All Smiles/Autumn	1964	$40

— White label promo only
❏ 44354	I Wonder As I Wander/The Lord's Prayer	1967	$40
❏ 43739	La Mer/C'est Rien	1966	$8
❏ 38-04605	Left in the Dark/Here We Are at Last	1984	$3
❏ 38-04605 [PS]	Left in the Dark/Here We Are at Last	1984	$4
❏ 10130	Let the Good Times Roll/Jubilation	1975	$5
❏ 10075	Love in the Afternoon/Guava Jelly	1974	$5
❏ 45072	Love Is Only Love/Before the Parade Passes By	1970	$5
❏ 44331	Lover Man (Oh, Where Can You Be)/My Funny Valentine	1967	$6
❏ 3-10450	Love Theme from "A Star Is Born" (Evergreen)/I Believe in Love	1976	$5
❏ 3-10450 [PS]	Love Theme from "A Star Is Born" (Evergreen)/I Believe in Love	1976	$6
❏ 3-10777	Love Theme from "Eyes of Laura Mars" (Prisoner)/Laura and Nevil	1978	$4
❏ 38-04695	Make No Mistake, He's Mine/Clear Sailing	1984	$3

— A-side with Kim Carnes
❏ 38-04695 [PS]	Make No Mistake, He's Mine/Clear Sailing	1984	$4
❏ 18-02717	Memory/Evergreen (Love Theme from "A Star Is Born")	1982	$4
❏ 44532	Morning After/Where Is the Wonder	1968	$5
❏ 45471	Mother/The Summer Knows	1971	$5
❏ 42648	My Coloring Book/Lover Come Back to Me	1962	$20
❏ 10198	My Father's Song/By the Way	1975	$5
❏ 44352	My Favorite Things/The Christmas Song	1967	$40
❏ 44352 [PS]	My Favorite Things/The Christmas Song	1967	$50
❏ 3-10555	My Heart Belongs to Me/Answer Me	1977	$5
❏ 43323	My Man/Where Is the Wonder	1965	$8
❏ 45511	One Less Bell to Answer-A House Is Not a Home/Space Captain	1971	$5
❏ 44474	Our Corner of the Night/He Could Show Me	1968	$5
❏ 38-04357	Papa Can You Hear Me?/Will Someone Ever Look at Me That Way	1984	$3
❏ 38-04357 [PS]	Papa Can You Hear Me?/Will Someone Ever Look at Me That Way	1984	$4

Number	Title	Yr	NM
❏ 42965	People/I Am Woman	1964	$10
❏ 11-02065	Promises/Make It Like a Memory	1981	$4
❏ 44775	Punky's Dilemma/Frank Mills	1969	$5
❏ 43612	Sam, You Made the Pants Too Long/The Minute Waltz	1966	$6
❏ 43469	Second Hand Rose/The Kind of Man a Woman Needs	1965	$8
❏ 38-05837	Send In the Clowns/Being Alive	1986	$4
❏ 38-05837 [PS]	Send In the Clowns/Being Alive	1986	$8
❏ 10272	Shake Me, Wake Me, When It's Over/Widescreen	1975	$5
❏ 45686	Sing a Song-Make Your Own Kind of Music/Starting Here-Starting Now	1972	$5
❏ 43896	Sleep in Heavenly Peace (Silent Night)/Gounod's Ave Maria	1966	$12
❏ 43896 [PS]	Sleep in Heavenly Peace (Silent Night)/Gounod's Ave Maria	1966	$30
❏ 38-05680	Somewhere/Not While I'm Around	1985	$3
❏ 38-05680 [PS]	Somewhere/Not While I'm Around	1985	$4
❏ 3-10756	Songbird/Honey Can I Put On Your Clothes	1978	$4
❏ 45236	Stoney End/I'll Be Home	1970	$5
❏ 44225	Stout-Hearted Men/Look	1967	$6
❏ 3-10931	Superman/A Man I Loved	1979	$4
❏ 45626	Sweet Inspiration-Where You Lead/Didn't We	1972	$5
❏ 45147	The Best Thing You've Ever Done/Summer Me, Winter Me	1970	$5
❏ 3-11008	The Main Event/Fight//(Instrumental)	1979	$4
❏ 38-04177	The Way He Makes Me Feel (Studio)/(Film Version)	1983	$3
❏ 38-04177 [PS]	The Way He Makes Me Feel (Studio)/(Film Version)	1983	$4
❏ 45944	The Way We Were/What Are You Doing the Rest of Your Life	1973	$5

—A-side contains a different vocal than most of the album versions
❏ 38-08062	Till I Loved You/Two People	1988	$3

—A-side with Don Johnson
❏ 38-08062 [PS]	Till I Loved You/Two People	1988	$4
❏ 45341	Time and Love/No Easy Way Down	1971	$5
❏ 73016	We're Not Makin' Love Anymore/Here We Are at Last	1989	$3
❏ 45040	What About Today/What Are You Doing the Rest of Your Life	1969	$5
❏ 11-11430	What Kind of Fool/The Love Inside	1981	$4

— A-side with Barry Gibb
❏ 68691	What Were We Thinking Of/Why Let It Go	1989	$3
❏ 43518	Where Am I Going?/You Wanna Bet	1966	$6
❏ 45414	Where You Lead/Since I Fell for You	1971	$5
❏ 43248	Why Did I Choose You/My Love	1965	$8
❏ 1-11364	Woman in Love/Run Wild	1980	$4

7-Inch Extended Plays
❏ 7-30378 [PS]	Stoney End	1971	$15
❏ 7-30378	Stoney End/Just a Little Lovin' (Early in the Mornin')/Maybe//I Don't Know Where I Stand/If You Could Read My Mind	1971	$15

—Jukebox issue; small hole, plays at 33 1/3 rpm

COLUMBIA MASTERWORKS
❏ 7-3220 [PS]	Funny Girl	1964	$20
❏ 7-3220	Funny Girl/My Man/People//Roller Skate Rag/I'd Rather Be Blue Over You/Don't Rain on My Parade	1964	$20

—Jukebox issue; small hole, plays at 33 1/3 rpm

STRENGTH, "TEXAS" BILL

CAPITOL
Number	Title	Yr	NM
❏ F3394	It Ain't Much, But It's Home/When the Bright Lights Grow Dim	1956	$20
❏ F3701	Six Fools/I Wanna Ride On Your Merry-Go-Round	1957	$20
❏ F3282	When Love Comes Knockin'/Turn Around	1955	$30
❏ F3477	Where Did My Heart Go/Gotta Lotta Love	1956	$20

CORAL
❏ 9-64171	Alone/Country Love	1954	$30
❏ 9-64117	Cherry Pie/Is Someone Else the Lucky One Tonight	1952	$30
❏ 9-64139	I Found My Love/It's a Shame	1952	$30
❏ 9-64177	Let's Make Love or Go Home/You Can't Have My Love	1954	$30

— With Tabby West
❏ 9-64133	Paper Boy Boogie/I Was Only Teasin' You	1952	$30

SUN
❏ 346	Guess I'd Better Go/Senorita	1960	$30

— As "Bill Strength

STRIDERS, THE (1)

APOLLO
Number	Title	Yr	NM
❏ 480	I Wonder/Hesitating Fool	1955	$300

DERBY
❏ 857	Come Back to Me Tomorrow/Rollin'	1954	$200

STRIDERS, THE (2)

COLUMBIA
❏ 43948	Am I On Your Mind/There's a Storm Comin'	1966	$30
❏ 43738	Sorrow/Say You Love Me	1966	$30
❏ 44143	When You Walk In the Room/Do It Now	1967	$20

LAVETTE
❏ 5008	Sorrow/When You Walk in the Room	1966	$50

STRIKES, THE

IMPERIAL
❏ 5433	Baby I'm Sorry/If You Can't Rock Me	1957	$60

LIN
❏ 5006	Baby I'm Sorry/If You Can't Rock Me	1957	$80

STRING-A-LONGS, THE

7 ARTS
❏ 700	Tell the World/For My Angel	1961	$20

— As "Mickey Boyd and the Plain Viewers

ATCO
❏ 6694	Popi/Places I Remember	1969	$8

DOT
❏ 16592	Beatles, You Bug Me/Bloomin' Bird	1964	$20

— As "The Bug Men
❏ 16708	Caravan/Mathilda	1965	$10
❏ 16448	Heartaches/Happy Melody	1963	$12
❏ 16393	Matilda/Replica	1962	$10
❏ 16575	Myna Bird/My Babe	1964	$10
❏ 16379	Spinnin' My Wheels/My Blue Heaven	1962	$10
❏ 16331	Twistwatch/Sunday	1962	$10

WARWICK
❏ 625	Brass Buttons/Panic Button	1961	$20
❏ 668	Myna Bird/Scottie	1961	$20
❏ 654	Take a Minute/Should I	1961	$20
❏ 606	Tell the World/For an Angel	1960	$20
❏ 675	Theme for Twisters/Nearly Sunrise	1962	$20
❏ 603	Wheels/Am I Asking Too Much	1960	$20
❏ 603	Wheels/Tell the World	1960	$30

— Red label
❏ 603	Wheels/Tell the World	1960	$30

— White label (not marked as a promo)

STRODE, LANCE

BOOTSTRAP
❏ 0416	Dangerous Ground/(B-side unknown)	1989	$8

STRONG, BARRETT

ANNA
❏ 1111	Money (That's What I Want)/Oh I Apologize	1960	$40

ATCO
❏ 6225	Seven Sins/What Went Wrong	1962	$50

CAPITOL
❏ 4223	Gonna Make It Right/The Man Up in the Sky	1976	$5
❏ 4052	Is It True/Anywhere	1975	$5
❏ 4120	Surrender/There's Something About You	1975	$5

EPIC
❏ 11011	Stand Up and Cheer for the Preacher (Part 1)/Stand Up and Cheer for the Preacher (Part 2)	1973	$5

TAMLA
❏ 54033	I'm Gonna Cry/Whirl Wind	1960	$60
❏ 54022	Let's Rock/Do the Very Best You Can	1960	$2000

— VG 1000; VG+ 1500
❏ 54027	Money (That's What I Want)/Oh I Apologize	1960	$120

— Horizontal lines label
❏ 54027	Money (That's What I Want)/Oh I Apologize	1962	$60

— Globe label
❏ 54043	Two Wrongs Don't Make a Right/Misery	1961	$60

TOLLIE
❏ 9023	Make Up Your Mind/I Better Run	1964	$40

Number	Title	Yr	NM
STRONG, BENNIE			
CAPITOL			
❏ 54-90039	The Merry Christmas Polka/Here Comes Santa Claus (Right Down Santa Claus Lane)	1949	$30
STRONG, NOLAN, AND THE DIABLOS			
FORTUNE			
❏ 509/10	Adios, My Desert Love/(I Want) An Old Fashioned Girl	1954	$125
❏ 564	Are You Making a Fool Out of Me/You're My Happiness	1964	$20
❏ 544	Blue Moon/I Don't Care	1962	$30
❏ 525	Can't We Talk This Over/The Mambo of Love	1957	$100
❏ 516	Daddy Rockin' Strong/Do You Remember What You Did Last Night	1955	$125
❏ 529	For Old Times' Sake/My Heart Will Always Belong to You	1959	$50
❏ 514	Hold Me Until Eternity/Route 16	1955	$125
❏ 531	I Am With You/Goodbye Matilda	1959	$50
❏ 532	If I Could Be with You Tonite/I Wanna Know	1959	$50
❏ 553	I Really Love You/You're My Love	1963	$30
❏ 546	Mind Over Matter (I'm Gonna Make You Mine)/Beside You	1962	$30
❏ 536	Since You're Gone/What You Gonna Do	1960	$40
❏ 522	Teardrop from Heaven/Try Me One More Time	1956	$100
❏ 518	The Way You Dog Me Around/Jump, Shake and Move	1955	$125
❏ 574	The Way You Dog Me Around/Jump with Me	1980	$20
❏ 511	The Wind/Baby, Be Mine	1954	$125
❏ 569	(What Did That Genie Mean When He Said) Ali-Coochie/(You're Not Good Looking But) You're Presentable	1964	$20
STRUMMER, JOE			
Also see THE CLASH.			
VIRGIN			
❏ 99381	Filibustero/Straight Shooter	1988	$4
STRUNK, JUD			
AD-MEDIA			
❏ 6416	The Santa Song/A Special Christmas Tree	1969	$10
❏ 6416 [PS]	The Santa Song/A Special Christmas Tree	1969	$20
CAPITOL			
❏ 3960	My Country/The Will	1974	$6
COLUMBIA			
❏ 4-45121	David's Place/Lion in the Park	1970	$8
❏ 4-45189	Self-Eating Watermelon/Children at Play	1970	$8
MCA			
❏ 40872	Tell Me Where I Am Tonight/Fool on My Shoulder	1978	$4
MELODYLAND			
❏ 6027	Pamela Brown/They're Tearing Down a Town	1975	$5
❏ 6015	The Biggest Parakeets in Town/I Wasn't Wrong About You	1975	$5
STRYPER			
Christian metal pioneers.			
ENIGMA			
❏ B-75009	Honestly/Sing-Along-Song	1986	$3
❏ B-75009 [PS]	Honestly/Sing-Along-Song	1986	$8
❏ 061	Winter Wonderland/Reason For The Season	1984	$8
STUART, CHAD			
SIDEWALK			
❏ 944	Good Morning Sunrise/Paxton's Song	1968	$8
❏ 944 [PS]	Good Morning Sunrise/Paxton's Song	1968	$20
STUART, CHAD AND JILL			
COLUMBIA			
❏ 43467	The Cruel War/I Can't Talk to You	1965	$8
❏ 43467 [PS]	The Cruel War/I Can't Talk to You	1965	$20
STUART, MARTY			
COLUMBIA			
❏ 38-06230	All Because of You/Maria (Love to See You Again)	1986	$4

Number	Title	Yr	NM
❏ 38-05724	Arlene/Midnight Moonlight	1985	$4
❏ 38-05724 [PS]	Arlene/Midnight Moonlight	1985	$8
❏ 38-06425	Do You Really Want My Lovin'/Heart of Stone	1986	$4
❏ 38-05897	Honky Tonker?/Anyhow I Love You	1986	$4
❏ 38-07914	Matches/Old Hat	1988	$4
❏ 38-07729	Mirrors Don't Lie/Freight Train Boogie	1988	$4
MCA			
❏ 53687	Cry Cry Cry/The Wild One	1989	$3
❏ 53751	Don't Leave Her Lonely Too Long/The Coal Mine Blues	1989	$3
STUCKEY, NAT			
MCA			
❏ 40752	Buddy, I Lied/Don't You Believe Her	1977	$5
❏ 40693	Fallin' Down/Please James	1977	$5
❏ 40808	I'm Coming Home to Face the Music/Linda on My Mind	1977	$5
❏ 40519	Sun Comin' Up/Honky Tonk Dreams	1976	$5
❏ 40855	That Lucky Old Sun (Just Rolls Around Heaven All Day)/I'm Coming Home	1978	$5
❏ 40608	That's All She Ever Said Except Goodbye/After the Lovin' Has Passed	1976	$5
❏ 40923	The Days of Sand and Shovels/Mexican Divorce	1978	$5
❏ 40658	The Shady Side of Charlotte/They'd Love to Be Children Again	1976	$5
❏ 40568	The Way He's Treated You/At Least One Time	1976	
PAULA			
❏ 276	Adorable Woman/I Knew Her When	1967	$10
❏ 267	All My Tomorrows/You're Puttin' Me On	1967	$10
❏ 288	Blue Christmas/How Can Christmas Be Merry	1967	$10
❏ 233	Don't You Believe Her/Round and Round	1966	$12
❏ 228	Hurtin' Again/Two Together	1965	$15
❏ 300	Leave This One Alone/I Never Knew	1968	$12
❏ 1230	Mental Revenge/Waitin' in Your Welfare Line	1970	$8
❏ 287	My Can Do Can't Keep Up With My Want To/If There's No Other Way	1967	$10
❏ 257	Oh! Woman/On the Other Hand	1966	$10
❏ 1217	Pop a Top/Love of the Common People	1970	$8
❏ 1204	She Thinks I Still Care/Two Together	1968	$8
❏ 243	Sweet Thang/Paralyze My Mind	1966	$10
❏ 243 [PS]	Sweet Thang/Paralyze My Mind	1966	$30
RCA VICTOR			
❏ PB-10307	Boom Boom Barroom Man/Ain't Nothing Bad About Feeling Good	1975	$6
❏ 74-0163	Cut Across Shorty/Understand Your Man	1969	$8
❏ APBO-0115	Got Leaving on Her Mind/Now Lonely Is Only a Word	1973	$6
❏ APBO-0288	It Hurts to Know the Feeling's Gone/Plans for the Future	1974	$6
❏ 47-9631	Plastic Saddle/Woman of Hurt	1968	$8
❏ 47-9786	Sittin' in Atlanta Station/Don't Wait for Me	1969	$8
❏ 74-0238	Sweet Thang and Cisco/Son of a Bum	1969	$8
❏ 47-9884	Whiskey, Whiskey/What Am I Doing in L.A.	1970	$8
SIMS			
❏ 206	Leave the Door Open/Wills Crossing	1964	$30
STUDENT TEACHERS			
ORK			
❏ NYC5 [B]	Christmas Weather/Channel 13	1978	$20
STUDENTS, THE			
ARGO			
❏ 5386	I'm So Young/Every Day of the Week	1961	$30
CHECKER			
❏ 902	I'm So Young/Every Day of the Week	1958	$50
❏ 1004	My Vow to You/That's How I Feel	1962	$20
NOTE			
❏ 10012	I'm So Young/Every Day of the Week	1958	$500
❏ 10019	My Vow to You/That's How I Feel	1959	$400

Number	Title	Yr	NM
RED TOP			
❏ 100	My Heart Is an Open Door/Mommy and Daddy	1958	$200
—Blue label			
❏ 100	My Heart Is an Open Door/Mommy and Daddy	1958	$50
—Red label			
STYLE COUNCIL, THE			
GEFFEN			
❏ 29359	My Ever Changing Moods/Mixed Company	1984	$3
❏ 29359 [PS]	My Ever Changing Moods/Mixed Company	1984	$3
❏ 28941	The Boy Who Cried Wolf/Our Favourite Shop	1985	$3
❏ 28941 [PS]	The Boy Who Cried Wolf/Our Favourite Shop	1985	$3
❏ 28674	(When You) Call Me/Internationalists	1986	$3
❏ 28674 [PS]	(When You) Call Me/Internationalists	1986	$3
POLYDOR			
❏ 885707-7	Heaven's Above/It Didn't Matter	1987	$3
❏ PRO 617-7 [DJ]	How She Threw It All Away (Edit) (same on both sides)	1988	$4
❏ PRO617-7 [DJ]	How She Threw It All Away (Edit) (same on both sides)	1988	$4
❏ 815276-7	Long Hot Summer/Le Depart	1983	$4
STYLERS, THE (1)			
JUBILEE			
❏ 5168	Believe It or Not/The World Is Yours	1954	$50
❏ 5279	Breaker of Hearts/Miracle in Milan	1957	$40
❏ 5253	Confession of a Sinner/Gonna Tell 'Em	1956	$50
❏ 5246	Lost John/Huffin' and Puffin'	1956	$50
❏ 5188	Shoo Shoo Sha La La/Love Ya Like Crazy	1955	$50
STYLERS, THE (U)			
GORDY			
❏ 7018	Going Steady Anniversary/Pushing Up Daisies	1963	$70
KICKS			
❏ 2	Gentle as a Teardrop/There Were Others	1954	$500
STYLES, THE (1)			
JOSIE			
❏ 920	I Love You for Sentimental Reasons/School Bells to Chapel Bells	1964	$70
SERENE			
❏ 1501	Scarlet Angel/Gotta Go, Go, Go	1961	$200
STYLES, THE (2)			
MODERN			
❏ 1048	I Know You Know That I Know/Baby You're Alive	1967	$15
SWAN			
❏ 4258	I Do Love You/Hush Little Girl	1966	$15
STYLETTES, THE			
CAMEO			
❏ 337	On Fire/Packing Up My Memories	1964	$70
SAN-DEE			
❏ 1010/1	On Fire/Packing Up My Memories	1964	$120
STYLISTS, THE			
V.I.P.			
❏ 25066	What Is Love/Where Did the Children Go	1970	$30
STYX			
A&M			
❏ 2188	Babe/I'm O.K.	1979	$4
❏ 2087	Blue Collar Man (Long Nights)/Superstars	1978	$4
❏ 2087 [PS]	Blue Collar Man (Long Nights)/Superstars	1978	$6
❏ 1818	Born for Adventure/Light Up	1976	$5
❏ 2228	Borrowed Time/Eddie	1980	$4
❏ 1977	Come Sail Away/Put Me On	1977	$4
❏ 1977 [PS]	Come Sail Away/Put Me On	1977	$6
❏ 1931	Crystal Ball/Put Me On	1977	$5
❏ 2543	Don't Let It End/Rockin' the Paradise	1983	$3
❏ 2543 [PS]	Don't Let It End/Rockin' the Paradise	1983	$3
❏ 2560	Double Life/Haven't We Been Here Before	1983	$3

Number	Title	Yr	NM
2007	Fooling Yourself (The Angry Young Man)/The Grand Finale	1978	$4
2007 [PS]	Fooling Yourself (The Angry Young Man)/The Grand Finale	1978	$6
2568	High Time/Double Life	1983	$3
1786	Lorelei/Midnight Ride	1976	$4
1877	Mademoiselle/Light Up	1976	$5
2525	Mr. Roboto/Snowblind	1983	$3
2525 [PS]	Mr. Roboto/Snowblind	1983	$3
2625	Music Time/Heavy Metal Poisoning	1984	$3
2625 [PS]	Music Time/Heavy Metal Poisoning	1984	$3
2110	Sing for the Day/Queen of Spades	1979	$5
2300	The Best of Times/Lights	1981	$4
2300 [PS]	The Best of Times/Lights	1981	$4
2323	Too Much Time on My Hands/Queen of Spades	1981	$4
2206	Why Me/Lights	1979	$4

WOODEN NICKEL

Number	Title	Yr	NM
WB-10329	Best Thing/Havin' a Ball	1975	$5
65-0106	Best Thing/What Has Come Between	1972	$5
65-0111	I'm Gonna Make You Feel It/Quick Is the Beat of My Heart	1972	$5
WB-10102	Lady/Children of the Land	1974	$5
GB-10492	Lady/Children of the Land	1975	$4

— Gold Standard Series

65-0116	Lady/You Better Ask	1973	$12
WB-10027	Lies/22 Years	1974	$5
WB-11205	Winner Take All/Best Thing	1978	$5

STYX (2)
ABC

| 10848 | Don't Bring Me Down/MacDougal Street | 1966 | $15 |

STYX (U)
ONYX

| 2200 | Puppetmaster/Hey, I'm Lost | 1966 | $30 |

PARAMOUNT

| 0104 | Promised Land/Soul Flow | 1971 | $6 |

SUDDENS, THE
SUDDEN

| 103 | Garden of Love/Childish Ways | 1961 | $125 |

SUGAR BEARS, THE
KIM CARNES was in this group.

BIG TREE

| 151 | Some Kind of a Summer/Put Some Love Into It | 1972 | $6 |
| 122 | Someone Like You/You Are the One | 1971 | $6 |

SUGAR CANES, THE
KING

| 5157 | Poor Boy/Sioux Rock | 1958 | $30 |

SUGAR HILL GANG
SUGAR HILL

774	Apache/Rapper's Delight	1981	$10
755	Here I Am/Rapper's Delight	1980	$20
92016	The Down Beat/(B-side unknown)	1984	$10

SUGARLOAF
BRUT

| 815 | I Got a Song/Myra, Myra | 1973 | $5 |
| 815 [PS] | I Got a Song/Myra, Myra | 1973 | $6 |

CLARIDGE

408	Boogie Man/I Got a Song	1975	$5
402	Don't Call Us, We'll Call You/Texas Two-Lane	1974	$5
415	Have a Good Time/You Set My Dreams to Music	1976	$5
422	Last Dance, Take a Chance/Satisfaction Guaranteed	1976	$5
405	Stars in My Eyes/Myra, Myra	1975	$5

LIBERTY

56183	Green-Eyed Lady/West of Tomorrow	1970	$6
56218	Tongue in Cheek/Woman	1970	$5
56218 [PS]	Tongue in Cheek/Woman	1970	$10

UNITED ARTISTS

| 50784 | Chest Fever/Mother Nature's Wine | 1971 | $5 |
| 0062 | Green-Eyed Lady/Tongue in Cheek | 1973 | $4 |

— Silver Spotlight Series" reissue

SUGGS, BRAD
METEOR

| 5034 | Charcoal Suit/Bop Baby Bop | 1956 | $400 |

PHILLIPS INT'L.

3554	Cloudy/Partly Cloudy	1960	$30
3571	Elephant Walk/Catching Up	1961	$30
3549	I Walk the Line/Ooh-Wee	1959	$30
3545	Low Outside/706 Union	1959	$30
3563	My Gypsy/Sam's Tune	1960	$30

SUICIDE COMMANDOS
P.S.

0 (# unknown)	Emisson Control/Cliche Ole/Monster Au Go Go	1976	$20
0 (# unknown) [PS]	Emisson Control/Cliche Ole/Monster Au Go Go	1976	$20
0 (# unknown)	Match Mismatch/Mark He's a Terror	1977	$5
0 (# unknown) [PS]	Match Mismatch/Mark He's a Terror	1977	$5

SULLIVAN, GENE
COLUMBIA

4-20902	Good Gosh Almighty/Walkin' and Talkin'	1952	$30
4-40971	Please Pass the Biscuits/Wash Your Feet Before Going to Bed	1957	$20
4-20977	Would You Forgive Me/Inflated Love	1952	$30

SULLIVAN, JIM
LONDON

| 9585 | Back and Forth/Toad Stool | 1963 | $15 |

SULLIVAN, NIKI
DOT

| 15751 | Three Steps to Heaven/It's All Over | 1958 | $125 |

SULLIVAN, PHIL
STARDAY

437	Hearts Are Lonely/Rich Man -- Po' Boy	1959	$30
462	I Could Never Be Alone/You Get a Thrill	1959	$30
410	Love Never Dies/The Luckiest Man in Town	1958	$30

SULTANS, THE (1)
ASCOT

| 2228 | I Wanna Know/Gloria | 1967 | $30 |

SULTANS, THE (2)
DUKE

135	Boppin' with the Mambo/What Makes Me Feel This Way	1954	$125
125	Good Thing/How Deep Is the Ocean	1954	$125
133	I Cried My Heart Out/Baby Don't Put Me Down	1954	$125
178	My Love Is So High/If I Could Tell	1957	$60

SULTANS, THE (3)
GUYDEN

| 2079 | Someone You Can Trust/Christina | 1963 | $20 |

JAM

107	Mary, Mary/How Far Does a Friendship Go	1963	$40
113	Poor Boy/Don't Tie Me Down	1964	$40
103	Toss in My Sleep/I Feel Your Love Growing Cold	1962	$40

TILT

| 782 | It'll Be Easy/You Got Me Goin' | 1961 | $125 |

— Yellow label

| 782 | It'll Be Easy/You Got Me Goin' | 1961 | $50 |

— Black label

SULTANS, THE (4)
JUBILEE

| 5077 | Blues at Dawn/Don't Be Angry | 1952 | $800 |
| 5054 | Lemon Squeezing Daddy/You Captured My Heart | 1951 | $250 |

SUMAC, YMA
CAPITOL

F2079	Babalu/Wimoweh	1952	$30
F1819	Birds/Najalas Lament	1951	$30
F1819 [PS]	Birds/Najalas Lament	1951	$50

CORAL

| 60742 | Cholitas Punenas/The Hummingbird | 1952 | $30 |
| 60744 | La Benita/I Love Only You | 1952 | $30 |

— The above four comprise a box set

| 60743 | One Love/Indian Love | 1952 | $30 |
| 60741 | The Sun Maidens/Beautiful Eyes | 1952 | $30 |

7-Inch Extended Plays

CAPITOL

EAP 1-299	(contents unknown)	1955	$30
EAP 2-299	(contents unknown)	1955	$30
EAP 1-564	(contents unknown)	1955	$30
EAP 2-564	(contents unknown)	1955	$30
EAP 1-770	(contents unknown)	1956	$25
EAP 2-770	(contents unknown)	1956	$25
EAP 3-770	(contents unknown)	1956	$25
EAP 1-770 [PS]	Legend of the Jivaro, Part 1	1956	$25
EAP 2-770 [PS]	Legend of the Jivaro, Part 2	1956	$25
EAP 3-770 [PS]	Legend of the Jivaro, Part 3	1956	$25
EAP 1-299 [PS]	Legend of the Sun Virgin, Part 1	1955	$30
EAP 2-299 [PS]	Legend of the Sun Virgin, Part 2	1955	$30
EAP 1-564 [PS]	Mambo!	1955	$30
EAP 2-564 [PS]	Mambo!	1955	$30

CORAL

EC81050	(contents unknown)	1954	$60
EC81051	(contents unknown)	1954	$60
EC81050 [PS]	Presenting Yma Sumac	1954	$60
EC81051 [PS]	Presenting Yma Sumac	1954	$60

SUMMER, DONNA
ATLANTIC

88792	Breakaway/Thinkin' Bout My Baby	1989	$4
88840	Love's About to Change My Heart (PWL 7" Mix)/(Clivilles & Cole 7" Mix)	1989	$3
88899	This Time I Know It's for Real/If It Makes You Feel Good	1989	$3
88899 [PS]	This Time I Know It's for Real/If It Makes You Feel Good	1989	$4

CASABLANCA

| 988 | Bad Girls/On My Honor | 1979 | $4 |
| 884 | Can't We Just Sit Down (And Talk It Over)/I Feel Love | 1977 | $6 |

— Original copies have "Can't We Just Sit Down" labeled as "Side A"

884 [DJ]	Can't We Just Sit Down (And Talk It Over) (stereo/mono)	1977	$10
2201	Dim All the Lights/There Will Always Be a You	1979	$4
959	Heaven Knows/Only One Love	1979	$4

— A-side with Brooklyn Dreams

| 978 | Hot Stuff/Journey to the Center of Your Heart | 1979 | $4 |
| 884 | I Feel Love/Can't We Just Sit Down (And Talk It Over) | 1977 | $5 |

— Second pressings have "I Feel Love" listed as "Side A"

| 884 [DJ] | I Feel Love (stereo/mono) | 1977 | $8 |

— Both sides are shorter than the version on the stock 45

907	I Love You/Once Upon a Time	1977	$5
926	Last Dance/With Your Love	1978	$4
939	Mac Arthur Park/Once Upon a Time	1978	$4
2236	On the Radio/There Will Always Be a You	1980	$4
2273	Our Love/Sunset People	1980	$5
872	Spring Affair/Come with Me	1976	$5
2300	Walk Away/Could It Be Magic	1980	$4
874	Winter Melody/Spring Affair	1977	$5

GEFFEN

49634	Cold Love/Grand Illusion	1980	$4
49634 [PS]	Cold Love/Grand Illusion	1980	$5
28418	Dinner with Gershwin/(Instrumental)	1987	$4
28418 [PS]	Dinner with Gershwin/(Instrumental)	1987	$4
27939	Fascination/All Systems Go	1988	$4
29982	Love Is In Control (Finger on the Trigger)/Sometimes Like Butterflies	1982	$4
29982 [PS]	Love Is In Control (Finger on the Trigger)/Sometimes Like Butterflies	1982	$5
28165	Only the Fool Survives/Love Shock	1987	$4

— A-side with Mickey Thomas

| 28165 [PS] | Only the Fool Survives/Love Shock | 1987 | $4 |

— A-side with Mickey Thomas

29895	State of Independence/Love Is Just a Breath Away	1982	$4
29895 [PS]	State of Independence/Love Is Just a Breath Away	1982	$4
29142	Supernatural Love/Face the Music	1984	$4
29142 [PS]	Supernatural Love/Face the Music	1984	$4

Number	Title	Yr	NM
❏ 29291	There Goes My Baby/ Maybe It's Over	1984	$4
❏ 29291 [PS]	There Goes My Baby/ Maybe It's Over	1984	$4
❏ 49563	The Wanderer/Stop Me	1980	$4

— Second pressings have WB logo replaced by Geffen logo

❏ 49563 [PS]	The Wanderer/Stop Me	1980	$5
❏ 29805	The Woman in Me/ Livin' in America	1982	$4
❏ 29805 [PS]	The Woman in Me/ Livin' in America	1982	$4
❏ 49664	Who Do You Think You're Foolin'/Runnin' for Cover	1981	$4

MERCURY

❏ 814922-7	Love Has a Mind of Its Own/ Stop, Look and Listen	1983	$4

— A-side with Matthew Ward

❏ 812370-7	She Works Hard for the Money/I Do Believe (I'll Fall in Love)	1983	$4
❏ 812370-7 [PS]	She Works Hard for the Money/I Do Believe (I'll Fall in Love)	1983	$5

OASIS

❏ 405	Could It Be Magic/ Whispering Waves	1976	$6
❏ 401AA/BB	Love to Love You Baby (4:55)/Love to Love You Baby (3:24)	1975	$6

— Both sides are remixed compared to the original 45 mix

❏ 401A /B	Love to Love You Baby/ Need-A-Man Blues	1975	$15

— Love to Love You Baby" has a radically different mix on the above first pressing

❏ 406	Try Me, I Know We Can Make It/Wasted	1976	$6
❏ 406 [PS]	Try Me, I Know We Can Make It/Wasted	1976	$8

WARNER BROS./GEFFEN

❏ 49563	The Wanderer/Stop Me	1980	$6

— Original pressings have a WB logo on the left side and "Geffen Records" in a box at the top of the label

SUMMER, SCOTT

CON BRIO

❏ 146	Flip Side of Today/I'm in Love	1979	$5
❏ 152	I Don't Wanna Want You/ Old Fashioned Lady	1979	$5

SUMMERHILL

TETRAGRAMMATON

❏ 1528	Soft Voice/The Last Day	1969	$12

SUMMERS, ANDY
Guitarist for The Police. Also see The Police.

A&M

❏ 2704	2010/To Hal and Back	1984	$3
❏ 2704 [PS]	2010/To Hal and Back	1984	$4
❏ 2513 [DJ]	I Advance Masked (same on both sides)	1982	$4

— With Robert Fripp; no stock copy was issued

❏ 2513 [DJ]	I Advance Masked (same on both sides)	1982	$4

— With Robert Fripp; no stock copy was issued

❏ 2699	Parade/Train	1984	$3

— With Robert Fripp

MCA

❏ 53112	Love Is the Strangest Way/XYZ	1987	$3

SUMMERS, DAVEY, AND THE SINGING ANTS

DORE

❏ 684	Gonna Climb That Big Ole Hill/Doin' the Davey Drag	1963	$50

SUMMERS, ED

SOYA

❏ 1001	I Can Tell/Prepare Yourself	1980	$100

SUMMERS, GENE

CAPRI

❏ 507	Alabama Shake/ Just Because	1964	$70

JAMIE

❏ 1273	Blue Diamond/You Said You Loved Me	1964	$20

JAN

❏ 100	School of Rock 'N' Roll/Straight Skirt	1958	$70
❏ 106	Twixteen/I'll Never Be Lonely	1959	$70

MERCURY

❏ 72606	Green-Eyed Monster/ The Clown	1966	$20

Number	Title	Yr	NM
TEARDROP			
❏ 3405	Goodbye Priscilla (Bye Bye Baby Blue)/ Down on the Farm	1977	$8
❏ 3405 [DJ]	Goodbye Priscilla (Bye Bye Blue Baby)	1977	$15

— Single-sided promo copies have erroneous subtitle

❏ 3405 [DJ]	Goodbye Priscilla (Bye Bye Blue Baby)	1977	$15

— Single-sided promo copies have erroneous subtitle

SUMMERS, J.B.

GOTHAM

❏ 209	I Want A Present For Christmas/My Baby Left Me	1952	$30

SUMMITS, THE

TIMES SQUARE

❏ 422	Go Back Where You Came From/(B-side unknown)	1961	$30

SUN-RAYS, THE

SUN

❏ 293	Love Is a Stranger/ The Lonely Hours	1958	$50

SUNBEAMS, THE (1)

ACME

❏ 109	Please Say You'll Be Mine/ You've Got to Rock and Roll	1957	$3000

HERALD

❏ 451	Tell Me Why/Come Back Baby	1955	$300

SUNBEAMS, THE (2)

DOT

❏ 1280	How About It/Wrap It Up and Save It	1956	$40
❏ 1271	I'm Gonna Go Home to Mama/Blue Mountain Waltz	1955	$40

SUNBEAMS, THE (3)

TOLLIE

❏ 9022	Sing a Song/Good Old Days	1964	$15

SUNBEAR

FILLMORE

❏ ZS77004	(When Everybody In the World Is) Friends/ Anywhere at All	1971	$8

SUNDAY FUNNIES, THE

CAPITOL

❏ 5614	Another Time, Another Place/Headlines	1966	$15

MERCURY

❏ 72571	Wonder Woman/She's Not at All Like You	1966	$15

RARE EARTH

❏ 5035	Walk Down the Path of Freedom/It's Just a Dream	1971	$8

UNI

❏ 55157	Baby, I Could Be So Good at Loving You/ See Things My Way	1969	$12

SUNDIALS, THE

GUYDEN

❏ 2065	Chapel of Love/ Whether to Resist	1962	$200

SUNDOWN PLAYBOYS, THE

APPLE

❏ 1852	Saturday Night Special/ Valse De Soleil Coucher	1972	$20

SUNDOWNERS, THE

JAMIE

❏ 1271	A Shot of Rhythm 'N' Blues/Come On In	1964	$15

SUNLINERS, THE

GOLDEN WORLD

❏ 31	The Swingin' Kind/All Alone	1965	$200

MGM

❏ 13809	Land of Nod/Well One	1967	$30

SUNLOVERS, THE

BREAKTHROUGH

❏ 1002	My Poor Heart/This Love of Ours	1967	$300

Number	Title	Yr	NM
MUTT & JEFF			
❏ 21	I'll Treat You Right/ (B-side unknown)	1967	$200
❏ 17	My Poor Heart/This Love of Ours	1967	$200
REVUE			
❏ 11045	Main Street/Main Street Shuffle	1969	$200

SUNNY AND THE SUNLINERS

DISCO GRANDE

❏ 1021	Peanuts (La Cacahuata)/ Fallaste Corazon	1965	$30

— A later issue than first pressings of Sunglow 107

KEY-LOC

❏ 1010	I Want to Come Home for Christmas Part 1/Part 2	1966	$8

OKEH

❏ 7143	Golly Gee/Touring	1962	$15

— As "Sunny and the Sunglows

SUNGLOW

❏ 103	A Dream/The Lasso	1961	$20
❏ 125	Again/Roly Poly	1967	$20
❏ 119	Baby I Apologize/ Cut Across Shorty	1965	$20
❏ 109	Close Your Eyes/ Ooo Poo Pa Doo	1963	$20
❏ 122	Fly Me to the Moon/ La Macarena	1966	$20
❏ 104	Golly Gee/Touring	1961	$20
❏ 116	Guess Who/Just as I Thought	1964	$20
❏ 123	If You Don't Love Me/ (B-side unknown)	1966	$20
❏ 127	It's Okay/99 + 1	1968	$20

— All Sunglow releases as "The Sunglows"

❏ 107	La Cacahuata/ Fallaste Corazon	1962	$40

— Original issue of this record; no mention of "Peanuts" on label; composer listed as "Desconocido" (Spanish for "Unknown")

❏ 117	Love Me/Honey Child	1964	$20
❏ 120	Oh Heart/Latin Trumpet	1965	$20
❏ 105	Once in a While/ Ho Ho Ha Ha	1962	$20
❏ 107	Peanuts (La Cacahuata)/ Fallaste Corazon	1962	$30
❏ 107	Peanuts (La Cacahuata)/ Happy Hippo	1963	$20
❏ 107	Peanuts (La Cacahuata)/ Love Me (All My Love Belongs to You)	1965	$15
❏ 118	Popcorn/All Night Worker	1965	$20
❏ 118	Popcorn/The Circus	1964	$20
❏ 102	Sylvia/(B-side unknown)	1961	$20
❏ 110	Talk to Me/Pony Time	1963	$30
❏ 112	The Dog/You Can Make It If You Try	1963	$20
❏ 115	Till the End of Time/ La Bamba	1964	$20
❏ 106	Won't You Tell Me/ (B-side unknown)	1962	$20

TEAR DROP

❏ 3016	Carino Nuevo/ (B-side unknown)	1963	$15
❏ 3025	Cuando El Destino/ (B-side unknown)	1963	$15
❏ 3066	El Ta Conazo/La Diudades	1965	$15
❏ 3094	Fly Me to the Moon/ Short Short Shorty	1966	$8
❏ 3067	Hitch Hike/That Night in San Antonio	1965	$12
❏ 3035	It's Too Late/You Gave Me a True Love	1964	$10
❏ 3027	Out of Sight, Out of Mind/ No One Else Will Do	1964	$10
❏ 3031	Pa Que Sientas, Lo Que Sientex Que Tal Te Sientes/ De Mi Nada Mas, Usted	1964	$15

— As "Sunny Ozuna

❏ 3045	Something's Got a Hold on Me/Teenage Promise-I'm Not a Fool Anymore	1964	$12
❏ 3014	Talk to Me/Every Week, Every Month, Every Year	1963	$10

— A-side as "Sunny and the Sunglows

❏ 3056	Token of Love/Little Dancing Girl	1965	$10

— As "Sunny Ozuna

❏ 3071	Too Young/The Very Thought of You	1965	$10
❏ 3079	Trick Bag/Cheatin' Traces	1965	$10
❏ 3096	Tristie Y Lastimado/ (B-side unknown)	1966	$15
❏ 3037	Tu Nueva Viva/Dime Como Le Haces	1964	$15
❏ 3183	Wonderful Girl/ Talk That Trash	1966	$8

WHITE WHALE

❏ 324	It's Okay/99 + 1	1969	$8

— As "The Sunglows

Number	Title	Yr	NM

SUNRAYS, THE

TOWER

Number	Title	Yr	NM
❏ 191	Andrea/You Don't Phase Me	1966	$15
❏ 256	Don't Take Yourself Too Seriously/I Look Baby, I Can't See	1966	$15
❏ 256 [PS]	Don't Take Yourself Too Seriously/I Look Baby, I Can't See	1966	$30
❏ 290	Hi, How Are You/Just 'Round the River Bend	1966	$20
❏ 148	I Live for the Sun/ Bye Baby Bye	1965	$15
❏ 340	Loaded with Love/Time (A Special Thing)	1967	$20
❏ 101	Outta Gas/Car Party	1964	$30
❏ 224	Still/When You're Not There	1966	$15

WARNER BROS.

Number	Title	Yr	NM
❏ 5253	Talk to Him/Gideon	1962	$20

SUNSETS, THE (1)

CHALLENGE

Number	Title	Yr	NM
❏ 9186	C.C. Rider/The Chug-a-Lug	1963	$50
❏ 9198	Lonely Surfer Boy/ Playmate of the Year	1963	$50
❏ 9208	My Little Beach Bunny/ My Little Surfin' Woody	1963	$60

PETAL

Number	Title	Yr	NM
❏ 1040	Lydia/Only You, Only Me	1963	$60

SUNSETS, THE (2)

RAE COX

Number	Title	Yr	NM
❏ 102	How Will I Remember/ Sittin' and Cryin'	1959	$50

SUNSHINE BOYS QUARTET, THE

DECCA

Number	Title	Yr	NM
❏ 9-46395	Angels Watch/ Happy Rhythm	1952	$30
❏ 9-46316	Everyone Is Welcome/God, Please Protect America	1951	$30
❏ 9-46348	My Home/Go Down to Jordan	1951	$30
❏ 9-46328	Where Could I Go/Checking Up on My Payments	1951	$30

SUNSHINE COMPANY, THE

IMPERIAL

Number	Title	Yr	NM
❏ 66260	Back on the Street Again/I Just Want to Be Your Friend	1967	$12
❏ 66247	Happy/Blue May	1967	$12
❏ 66298	Let's Get Together/Sunday Brought the Rain	1968	$12
❏ 66280	Look, Here Comes the Sun/It's Sunday	1968	$10
❏ 66324	Love Poem/Willie Jean	1968	$10
❏ 66308	On a Beautiful Day/ Darcy Farrow	1968	$10
❏ 66399	The Only Thing That Matters/Bolaro	1969	$10

UNITED ARTISTS

Number	Title	Yr	NM
❏ 0132	Happy/Back on the Street Again	1973	$4

—*Silver Spotlight Series" reissue*

SUNSHINE RUBY

RCA VICTOR

Number	Title	Yr	NM
❏ 47-5374	Datin'/Nobody Asked Me to Dance	1953	$30
❏ 47-5582	I Got My First Kiss Last Night/That Ain't in Any Catalogue	1954	$30
❏ 47-5806	I'm So Bashful/I Think He Winked at Me	1954	$30
❏ 47-5474	I Wanna Do Something for Santa Claus/Too Fat for the Chimney	1953	$30
❏ 47-5931	My Daddy Has Two Sweethearts/I Don't Care What the General Said	1954	$30
❏ 47-5467	Too Old for Toys/ Little Girl Love	1953	$30
❏ 47-5250	Too Young to Tango/Hearts Weren't Meant to Be Broken	1953	$30

SUPER K GENERATION, THE

LAURIE

Number	Title	Yr	NM
❏ 3413	Heartful O'Soul (Part 1)/ Heartful O'Soul (Part 2)	1967	$12

SUPER STOCKS, THE

CAPITOL

Number	Title	Yr	NM
❏ 5153	Thunder Road/ Wheel Stands	1964	$30

SUPERCHUNK

MERGE

Number	Title	Yr	NM
❏ MR 004	What Do I/My Noise/ Train from Atlantic City	1989	$60

—*As "Chunk"; gold vinyl*

Number	Title	Yr	NM
❏ MR 004	What Do I/My Noise/ Train from Atlantic City	1989	$30

—*As "Chunk"; black vinyl*

Number	Title	Yr	NM
❏ MR 004 [PS]	What Do I/My Noise/ Train from Atlantic City	1989	$30

—*As "Chunk*

SUPERFINE DANDELION, THE

MAINSTREAM

Number	Title	Yr	NM
❏ 673	Crazy Town/Janie's Tomb	1967	$15
❏ 672	People in the Street/ (B-side unknown)	1967	$15

SUPERIORS, THE (1)

ATCO

Number	Title	Yr	NM
❏ 6106	Lost Love/Don't Say Goodbye	1957	$75

MAIN LINE

Number	Title	Yr	NM
❏ 104	Lost Love/Don't Say Goodbye	1958	$600

—*With Fairmount Ave., Philadelphia street address on label*

Number	Title	Yr	NM
❏ 104	Lost Love/Don't Say Goodbye	1962	$50

—*No address on label or only "Philadelphia, Pennsylvania" address on label*

SUPERIORS, THE (2)

FAL

Number	Title	Yr	NM
❏ 301	What Is Love/Flee the Scene	1961	$100

FEDERAL

Number	Title	Yr	NM
❏ 12436	I'm Sorry Baby (I Didn't Mean to Do You Wrong)/ Dance of Love	1961	$40

SUPERIORS, THE (3)

MGM

Number	Title	Yr	NM
❏ 13503	Can't Make It Without You/ Let Me Make You Happy	1966	$15

SUE

Number	Title	Yr	NM
❏ 12	Heavenly Angel/I'd Rather Die	1969	$8

VERVE

Number	Title	Yr	NM
❏ 10370	Tell Me to Go/What Would I Do	1965	$30

SUPERTRAMP

A&M

Number	Title	Yr	NM
❏ 2760	Better Days/No In-Between	1985	$3
❏ 1660	Bloody Well Right/Dreamer	1975	$5
❏ 2292	Breakfast in America/ You Started Laughing	1980	$4
❏ 2731	Cannonball/Every Open Door	1985	$3
❏ 2731 [PS]	Cannonball/Every Open Door	1985	$3
❏ 1981	Dreamer/From Now On	1977	$5
❏ 1981 [PS]	Dreamer/From Now On	1977	$6
❏ 2269	Dreamer/From Now On	1980	$4
❏ 2269 [PS]	Dreamer/From Now On	1980	$5
❏ 1305	Forever/Your Poppa Don't Mind	1971	$6
❏ 2996	Free as a Bird/Thing for You	1987	$3
❏ 1938	Give a Little Bit/Downstream	1977	$4
❏ 1938 [PS]	Give a Little Bit/Downstream	1977	$6
❏ 2162	Goodbye Stranger/Even in the Quietest Moments	1979	$4
❏ 2162 [PS]	Goodbye Stranger/Even in the Quietest Moments	1979	$5
❏ 2985	I'm Beggin' You/ No Inbetween	1987	$3
❏ 2985 [PS]	I'm Beggin' You/ No Inbetween	1987	$3
❏ 2502	It's Raining Again/Bonnie	1982	$4
❏ 2502 [PS]	It's Raining Again/Bonnie	1982	$4
❏ 1793	Lady/You Started Laughing When I Held You in My Arms	1976	$5
❏ 2517	My Kind of Lady/ Know Who You Are	1983	$4
❏ 2517 [PS]	My Kind of Lady/ Know Who You Are	1983	$4
❏ 1814	Sister Moonshine/ Ain't Nobody But Me	1976	$5
❏ 2193	Take the Long Way Home/Ruby	1979	$4
❏ 2193 [PS]	Take the Long Way Home/Ruby	1979	$4

—*With yellow maze*

Number	Title	Yr	NM
❏ 2193 [PS]	Take the Long Way Home/Ruby	1979	$5

—*With green maze*

Number	Title	Yr	NM
❏ 2193 [PS]	Take the Long Way Home/Ruby	1979	$5

—*With red maze. Other colors may exist as well.*

Number	Title	Yr	NM
❏ 2128	The Logical Song/Just Another Nervous Wreck	1979	$4
❏ 2128 [PS]	The Logical Song/Just Another Nervous Wreck	1979	$5

SUPREMES FOUR, THE

SARA

Number	Title	Yr	NM
❏ 1032	I Lost My Job/I Love You Patricia	1958	$2000

SUPREMES, THE, DIANA ROSS AND, AND THE TEMPTATIONS

MOTOWN

Number	Title	Yr	NM
❏ 1137 [PS]	I'm Gonna Make You Love Me/A Place in the Sun	1968	$30

SUPREMES, THE

EEOC

Number	Title	Yr	NM
❏ 0 [DJ]	Things Are Changing (same on both sides)	1965	$200
❏ SL4M-3114 [DJ]	Things Are Changing (same on both sides)	1965	$200
❏ SL4M-3114 [PS]	Things Are Changing (same on both sides)	1965	$200

—*Promotional item for the Equal Employment Opportunity Commission (number not on sleeve)*

GEORGE ALEXANDER INC.

Number	Title	Yr	NM
❏ 1079 [DJ]	The Only Time I'm Happy/ Supremes Interview	1965	$70
❏ 1079 [DJ]	The Only Time I'm Happy/ Supremes Interview	1965	$70

MOTOWN

Number	Title	Yr	NM
❏ 1044	A Breath Taking, First Sight Soul Shaking, One Night Love Making, Next Day Heart Breaking Guy/Rock and Roll Banjo Band	1963	$125

—*Original pressing with long title. This does exist on stock copies as well as on promos.*

Number	Title	Yr	NM
❏ 1044	A Breath Taking Guy/Rock and Roll Banjo Band	1963	$30
❏ 1200	Automatically Sunshine/ Precious Little Things	1972	$5
❏ 1066	Baby Love/Ask Any Girl	1964	$30
❏ 1066 [PS]	Baby Love/Ask Any Girl	1964	$40
❏ 1075	Back in My Arms Again/ Whisper You Love Me Boy	1965	$20
❏ 1075 [PS]	Back in My Arms Again/ Whisper You Love Me Boy	1965	$40
❏ 1225	Bad Weather/Oh Be My Love	1973	$5
❏ 1085 [DJ]	Children's Christmas Song/ Twinkle, Twinkle Little Me	1965	$30

—*Promo only on red vinyl*

Number	Title	Yr	NM
❏ 1085	Children's Christmas Song/ Twinkle, Twinkle Little Me	1965	$30
❏ 1085 [DJ]	Children's Christmas Song/ Twinkle, Twinkle Little Me	1965	$30

—*Promo only on red vinyl*

Number	Title	Yr	NM
❏ 1085 [PS]	Children's Christmas Song/ Twinkle, Twinkle Little Me	1965	$40
❏ 1068	Come See About Me/ Always in My Heart	1964	$30
❏ 1167	Everybody's Got the Right to Love/But I Love You More	1970	$6
❏ 1195	Floy Joy/This Is the Story	1972	$5
❏ 1122	Forever Came Today/ Time Changes Things	1968	$8
❏ 1357	He's My Man/Give Out But Don't Give Up	1975	$5
❏ 1213	I Guess I'll Miss the Man/Over and Over	1972	$5
❏ 1083	I Hear a Symphony/Who Could Ever Doubt My Love	1965	$20
❏ 1391	I'm Gonna Let My Heart Do the Walking/ Early Morning Love	1976	$5
❏ 1139	I'm Livin' in Shame/I'm So Glad I Got Somebody	1969	$8
❏ 1116	In and Out of Love/I Guess I'll Always Love You	1967	$8
❏ 1008	I Want a Guy/Never Again	1961	$300
❏ 1034	Let Me Go the Right Way/ Time Changes Things	1962	$60
❏ 1415	Let Yourself Go/You Are the Heart of Me	1977	$5
❏ 1135	Love Child/Will This Be the Day	1968	$8
❏ 1103	Love Is Here and Now You're Gone/There's No Stopping Us Now	1967	$15
❏ 1094	Love Is Like an Itching in My Heart/He's All I Got	1966	$20
❏ 1488	Medley of Hits/Where Did We Go Wrong	1980	$4

—*As "Diana Ross and the Supremes*

Number	Title	Yr	NM
❏ 1523	Medley of Hits/Where Did We Go Wrong	1981	$4

—*As "Diana Ross and the Supremes*

Number	Title	Yr	NM
❏ 1040	My Heart Can't Take It No More/You Bring Back Memories	1963	$50
❏ 1089	My World Is Empty Without You/Everything Is Good About You	1966	$20
❏ 1156	Someday We'll Be Together/ He's My Sunny Boy	1969	$8
❏ 1126	Some Things You Never Get Used To/You've Been So Wonderful to Me	1968	$8
❏ 1172	Stoned Love/Shine on Me	1970	$6

Number	Title	Yr	NM
❏ 1074	Stop! In the Name of Love/I'm in Love Again	1965	$20
❏ 1074 [PS]	Stop! In the Name of Love/I'm in Love Again	1965	$40
❏ 1146	The Composer/The Beginning of the End	1969	$8
❏ 1107	The Happening/All I Know About You	1967	$15
❏ 1190	Touch/It's So Hard for Me to Say Goodbye	1971	$6
❏ 1051	When the Lovelight Starts Shining Through His Eyes/Standing at the Crossroads of Love	1963	$30
❏ 1060	Where Did Our Love Go/He Means the World to Me	1964	$30
❏ 1060 [PS]	Where Did Our Love Go/He Means the World to Me	1964	$40
❏ 1374	Where Do I Go from Here/Give Out But Don't Give Up	1975	$5

TAMLA

Number	Title	Yr	NM
❏ 54045	Buttered Popcorn/Who's Lovin' You	1961	$70

— *Globes label*

Number	Title	Yr	NM
❏ 54045	Buttered Popcorn/Who's Lovin' You	1961	$125

— *Lines label*

Number	Title	Yr	NM
❏ 54038	I Want a Guy/Never Again	1961	$125

— *Lines label*

Number	Title	Yr	NM
❏ 54038	I Want a Guy/Never Again	1961	$70

— *Globes label*

TOPPS/MOTOWN

Number	Title	Yr	NM
❏ 1	Baby Love	1967	$80

— *Cardboard record*

Number	Title	Yr	NM
❏ 15	Come See About Me	1967	$80

— *Cardboard record*

Number	Title	Yr	NM
❏ 16	My World Is Empty Without You	1967	$80

— *Cardboard record*

Number	Title	Yr	NM
❏ 2	Stop in the Name of Love	1967	$80

— *Cardboard record*

Number	Title	Yr	NM
❏ 3	Where Did Our Love Go	1967	$80

— *Cardboard record*

7-Inch Extended Plays

MOTOWN

Number	Title	Yr	NM
❏ S621 [S]	He Means the World to Me/Baby Love/Ask Any Girl//Where Did Our Love Go/Come See About Me/Run, Run, Run	1965	$30

— *33 1/3 rpm, small hole*

Number	Title	Yr	NM
❏ S621 [PS]	Where Did Our Love Go	1965	$30

SUPREMES, THE (3)

APT

Number	Title	Yr	NM
❏ 25055	Another Chance to Love/Fidgety	1961	$50

SUPREMES, THE (4)

KITTEN

Number	Title	Yr	NM
❏ 6969	Could This Be You/Margie	1956	$500

SUPREMES, THE (6)

MASCOT

Number	Title	Yr	NM
❏ 126	Little Sally Walker/Just Yell	1960	$125

SUPREMES, THE (7)

OLD TOWN

Number	Title	Yr	NM
❏ 1024	Tonight/My Babe	1956	$125
❏ 1024	Tonight/She Don't Want Me No More	1956	$200

SURE CURE, THE

PARKWAY

Number	Title	Yr	NM
❏ 145	Anything You Want/I Wanna Do It	1967	$10

SURF BOYS, THE

KARATE

Number	Title	Yr	NM
❏ 526	Da Doo Ron Ron/Hurt	1966	$30

SCEPTER

Number	Title	Yr	NM
❏ 12180	Stuck in the Chimney/I Told Santa Claus I Want You	1966	$30

SURF BREAKERS, THE

MERCURY

Number	Title	Yr	NM
❏ 72174	Hang Ten/Ridin' In #9	1963	$60

SURF BUNNIES, THE

DOT

Number	Title	Yr	NM
❏ 16523	Our Surfer Boys/Surf Bunny Beach	1963	$40

GOLIATH

Number	Title	Yr	NM
❏ 1352	Our Surfer Boys/Surf Bunny Beach	1963	$60
❏ 1353	Surf City High/Met the Boy I Adore	1963	$60

SURF RIDERS, THE

DECCA

Number	Title	Yr	NM
❏ 31477	The Birds/Blues for the Birds	1963	$40

NASCO

Number	Title	Yr	NM
❏ 6008	I'm Out/Rocko Socko	1958	$70

SURFARIS, THE

DOT

Number	Title	Yr	NM
❏ 144 [DJ]	Wipe Out (same on both sides)	1966	$125

— *Red vinyl*

Number	Title	Yr	NM
❏ 144 [DJ]	Wipe Out (same on both sides)	1966	$200

— *Red vinyl; error pressing with "Surfer Joe" on both sides*

SURFARIS, THE (1)

DECCA

Number	Title	Yr	NM
❏ 31561	A Surfer's Christmas List/Santa's Speed Shop	1963	$40
❏ 31731	Beat '65/Black Denim	1965	$30
❏ 31641	Bossa Barracuda/Dune Buggy	1964	$20
❏ 31835	Catch a Little Ride with Me/Don't Hurt My Little Sister	1965	$30
❏ 31954	Hey Joe Where Are You Going/So Get Out	1966	$30
❏ 31682	Hot Rod High/Karen	1964	$20
❏ 31581	I Wanna Take a trip to the Islands/Scatter Shield	1964	$30
❏ 31605	Murphy the Surfie/Go Go Go For Louie's Place	1964	$20
❏ 31538	Point Panic/Waikiki Run	1963	$20
❏ 31784	Theme of the Battle Maiden/Somethin' Else	1965	$30
❏ 32003	Wipe Out/I'm a Hog for You	1966	$10

DFS

Number	Title	Yr	NM
❏ 11/12	Wipe Out/Surfer Joe	1963	$3000

— *VG 1500; VG+ 2250*

DOT

Number	Title	Yr	NM
❏ 17008	Shake/The Search	1967	$10
❏ 16966	Show Biz/Chicago Green	1966	$10
❏ 16757	Surfer Joe/Can't Sit Down	1965	$40

— *B-side by the Challengers, but credited to the Surfaris*

Number	Title	Yr	NM
❏ 16757	Surfer Joe/Can't Sit Down	1965	$60

— *B-side by the Challengers, and credited correctly*

Number	Title	Yr	NM
❏ 144 [DJ]	Wipe Out (same on both sides)	1966	$125

— *Red vinyl*

Number	Title	Yr	NM
❏ 144 [DJ]	Wipe Out (same on both sides)	1966	$200

— *Red vinyl; error pressing with "Surfer Joe" on both sides*

Number	Title	Yr	NM
❏ 16479	Wipe Out/Surfer Joe	1963	$20
❏ 144	Wipe Out/Surfer Joe	1966	$10

— *Black label, script "Dot" in multicolor letters*

Number	Title	Yr	NM
❏ 144	Wipe Out/Surfer Joe	1969	$6

— *Muilticolor label, "DOT" in all capital letters in box at top*

PRINCESS

Number	Title	Yr	NM
❏ 52	Spanish Moon/She's Got the Blues	1963	$125

— *Reissued on Vault 911 credited to THE TRAVELERS; we don't know if Princess 52 exists credited to the Travelers, but we know this version exists*

Number	Title	Yr	NM
❏ 50	Wipe Out/Surfer Joe	1963	$400

— *With long versions of both songs. No "RE-1" is in the trail-off area.*

Number	Title	Yr	NM
❏ 50	Wipe Out/Surfer Joe	1963	$200

— *With short versions of both songs. "RE-1" is in the trail-off area.*

SURFARIS, THE (2)

CHANCELLOR

Number	Title	Yr	NM
❏ 1142	The Midnight Surf/Psyche-Out	1963	$60

DEL-FI

Number	Title	Yr	NM
❏ 4219	Surfari/Bombora	1963	$125

FELSTED

Number	Title	Yr	NM
❏ 8688	Tor-Chula/Psyche-Out	1964	$60

NORTHRIDGE

Number	Title	Yr	NM
❏ 1001	Moment of Truth/Church Key	1963	$70

— *B-side by the Biscaynes*

REGANO

Number	Title	Yr	NM
❏ 1062	Surfin' '63/Boss Beat	1963	$60

— *As "The Original Surfaris*

REPRISE

Number	Title	Yr	NM
❏ 20180	Moment of Truth/Church Key	1963	$40

— *B-side by the Biscaynes*

SURFARI

Number	Title	Yr	NM
❏ 301	Gum Dipped Slicks/High Time	1964	$125

— *As "The Original Surfaris*

SURVIVOR

CASABLANCA

Number	Title	Yr	NM
❏ 880053-7	Moment of Truth/It Doesn't Have to Be This Way	1984	$4

SCOTTI BROS.

Number	Title	Yr	NM
❏ ZS468526	Across the Miles/Burning Bridges	1989	$4
❏ ZS4 03213	American Heartbeat/Silver Girl	1982	$4
❏ ZS4 03213 [PS]	American Heartbeat/Silver Girl	1982	$5
❏ ZS4 05663	Burning Heart/Feels Like Love	1985	$3
❏ ZS4 05663 [PS]	Burning Heart/Feels Like Love	1985	$4
❏ ZS4 04074	Caught in the Game/Slander	1983	$4
❏ ZS4 04074 [PS]	Caught in the Game/Slander	1983	$5
❏ ZS4 08067	Didn't Know It Was Love/Rhythm of the City	1988	$3
❏ ZS5 02912	Eye of the Tiger/Take You on a Saturday	1982	$4
❏ ZS5 02912 [PS]	Eye of the Tiger/Take You on a Saturday	1982	$6
❏ ZS4 05579	First Night/Feels Like Love	1985	$3
❏ ZS4 05579 [PS]	First Night/Feels Like Love	1985	$4
❏ ZS4 04685	High on You/Broken Promises	1984	$3
❏ ZS4 04685 [PS]	High on You/Broken Promises	1984	$4
❏ ZS4 06705	How Much Love/Backstreet Love Affair	1987	$3
❏ ZS4 04603	I Can't Hold Back/I See You in Everyone	1984	$3
❏ ZS4 04603 [PS]	I Can't Hold Back/I See You in Everyone	1984	$4
❏ ZS4 04347	I Never Stopped Loving You/Ready for the Real Thing	1984	$4
❏ ZS4 06381	Is This Love/Can't Let You Go	1986	$3
❏ ZS4 06381 [PS]	Is This Love/Can't Let You Go	1986	$4
❏ ZS4 07070	Man Against the World/Oceans	1987	$3
❏ ZS4 07070 [PS]	Man Against the World/Oceans	1987	$4
❏ ZS5 02560	Poor Man's Son/Love Is On My Side	1981	$4
❏ 511	Somwhere in America/Freelance	1980	$5
❏ ZS5 02435 [DJ]	Summer Nights (3:07)/(3:23)	1981	$6
❏ ZS5 02435	Summer Nights/Love Is On My Side	1981	$5
❏ ZS5 02700	Summer Nights/Take You on a Saturday	1982	$4
❏ ZS4 03485	The One That Really Matters/Hesitation Dance	1983	$4
❏ ZS4 04871	The Search Is Over/It's the Singer, Not the Song	1985	$3
❏ ZS4 04871 [PS]	The Search Is Over/It's the Singer, Not the Song	1985	$4

SURVIVORS, THE

CAPITOL

Number	Title	Yr	NM
❏ 5102	Pamela Jean/After the Game	1963	$1000

SUSIE AND THE FOUR TRUMPETS

UNITED ARTISTS

Number	Title	Yr	NM
❏ 471	Starry Eyes/Blue Little Girl	1962	$70

SUTCH, SCREAMING LORD

CAMEO

Number	Title	Yr	NM
❏ 341	She's Fallen in Love with the Monster Man/Bye Bye Baby	1964	$20

COTILLION

Number	Title	Yr	NM
❏ 44149	Gotta Keep a-Rocking/Country Club	1972	$10

— *As "Lord Sutch*

SUTTON, GLENN

EPIC

Number	Title	Yr	NM
❏ 5-10163	I Ain't Built That Way/Too Many Honky Tonks (Behind Her)	1967	$10

MERCURY

Number	Title	Yr	NM
❏ 76188	Football Blues/The Football Card	1982	$4
❏ 884974-7	I'll Go Steppin' Too/Hulk-A-Mania	1986	$3
❏ 888544-7	I'm Gone This Time/Wild	1987	$3

Number	Title	Yr	NM
❑ 55056	Should Old Acquaintance Be Forgot/The Spaceship	1979	$5
❑ 888564-7	Super Bowl Trip/T.V. Preacher Man Blues	1987	$3

—B-side by Blue Water Dave

Number	Title	Yr	NM
❑ 884563-7	Super Bowl Trip/Wild	1986	$3
❑ 55064	Super Drunk/Under Pressure Like That	1979	$5
❑ 57009	The Football Card/ (B-side unknown)	1979	$4
❑ 55052	The Football Card/The Ballad of the Blue Cyclone	1978	$5

MGM

❑ 13333	Clarence, the Cross-Eyed Lion/Maurice the Police	1965	$15
❑ 13352	Gee-Whopper/I Don't Wanna Go	1965	$15

SUZUKI, PAT
7-Inch Extended Plays

RCA VICTOR

❑ SP-45-60	A Sunday Kind of Love/ Lazy Afternoon//I Enjoy Being a Girl/Just for Once	1959	$20

SUZY AND THE RED STRIPES
CAPITOL

❑ B-5608	Seaside Woman/B-Side to Seaside	1986	$40

EPIC

❑ 50403	Seaside Woman/B-Side to Seaside	1977	$10
❑ 50403 [DJ]	Seaside Woman (mono/stereo)	1977	$125

—Advance Promotion" label, black vinyl

❑ 50403 [DJ]	Seaside Woman (mono/stereo)	1977	$30

—Red vinyl, orange label on one side, white on the other

❑ 50403 [DJ]	Seaside Woman (mono/stereo)	1977	$125

—Black vinyl, orange label on one side, white on the other

❑ 50403 [DJ]	Seaside Woman (mono/stereo)	1977	$125

—Advance Promotion" label, black vinyl

❑ 50403 [DJ]	Seaside Woman (mono/stereo)	1977	$30

—Red vinyl, orange label on one side, white on the other

❑ 50403 [DJ]	Seaside Woman (mono/stereo)	1977	$125

—Black vinyl, orange label on one side, white on the other

SVEN AND CHARLOTTE
MGM

❑ 14779	Dance (While the Music Still Goes On)/He Is Your Brother	1975	$6

MORNINGSTAR

❑ 507	Bang-a-Boomerang/ Roly Poly Girl	1974	$12

—As "Svenne and Lotta

SVENSON, OLE
HAMILTON

❑ 50014	I Vant a Christmas Drum/Yingle Yingle Yumping Beans	1959	$15

SWAGMEN, THE
PARKWAY

❑ 854	By the Yonder Tree/ East Virginia	1962	$15

SWALLOWS, THE
AFTER HOURS

❑ 104	My Baby/Good Time Girls	1954	$2400

—VG 800; VG+ 1600

FEDERAL

❑ 12329	Beside You/Laughing Boy	1958	$50
❑ 12333	Itchy Twitchy Feeling/ Who Knows, Do You?	1958	$50
❑ 12319	Oh Lonesome Me/ Angel Baby	1958	$50
❑ 12328	We Want to Rock/Rock-a-Bye-Baby Rock	1958	$50

KING

❑ 4525	Beside You/You Left Me	1952	$400
❑ 4501	Eternally/It Ain't the Meat	1952	$800

—Black vinyl

❑ 4501	Eternally/It Ain't the Meat	1952	$2500

—Blue vinyl

❑ 4501	Eternally/It Ain't the Meat	1952	$2500

—Green vinyl

❑ 4676	I'll Be Waiting/It Feels So Good	1953	$400
❑ 4612	Laugh (Though You Want to Cry)/Our Love Is Dying	1953	$500

Number	Title	Yr	NM
❑ 4515	Tell Me Why/Roll, Roll, Pretty Baby	1952	$2000

—VG 1000; VG+ 1500

❑ 4656	Trust Me/Pleading Blues	1953	$400
❑ 4579	Where Do I Go from Here/ Please, Baby, Please	1952	$800
❑ 4458	Will You Be Mine/Dearest	1951	$1500

SWALLOWS, THE (2)
GUYDEN

❑ 2023	How Long Must a Fool Go On/You Must Try	1959	$60

—Reissued credited to "The Guides

SWAMP RATS, THE
CO & CE

❑ 245	In the Midnight Hour/ It's Not Easy	1967	$30

ST. CLAIR

❑ 711711	It's Not Easy/No Friend of Mine	1966	$60
❑ 69	Louie Louie/Hey Joe	1966	$60
❑ 2222	Psycho/Here, There and Everywhere	1966	$200
❑ 3333	Two Tymes Two/ (B-side unknown)	1966	$60

SWAMPWATER
KING

❑ 6345	Louisiana Woman/ River People	1971	$8
❑ 6376	Take a City Bride/It's Your Game, Mary Jane	1971	$8

SWAN, BILLY
A&M

❑ 2046	Hello! Remember Me/ Never Go Lookin' Again	1978	$4

COLUMBIA

❑ 10443	Shake, Rattle and Roll/I Got It for You	1976	$4
❑ 10486	Swept Away/California Song (For Malibu)	1977	$4

EPIC

❑ 51000	Do I Have to Draw a Picture/I Want to Change Your Life	1981	$3
❑ 02196	I'm Into Lovin' You/ Not Far from Forty	1981	$3
❑ 02601	Stuck Right in the Middle of Your Love/Soft Touch	1981	$3
❑ 02841	With Their Kind of Money and Our Kind of Love/Lay Down and Love Me Tonight	1982	$3

MERCURY

❑ 888320-7	I'm Gonna Get You/Three Chord Rock & Roll	1987	$3

MGM

❑ 14008	El Paso/The Sweet Sound of Your Name	1968	$12

MONUMENT

❑ 940	Breakin' Up/Out of Her System	1966	$15
❑ 8651	Come By/Woman Handled My Mind	1975	$4
❑ 45-275	Don't Be Cruel/Vanessa	1979	$4
❑ 8661	Everything's the Same (Ain't Nothing Changed)/ Overnite Thing (Usually)	1975	$4
❑ 8621	I Can Help/The Ways of a Woman in Love	1974	$5
❑ 8641	I'm Her Fool/I'd Like to Work for You	1975	$4
❑ 988	I've Got to Have You/Below Average Everyday Girl	1966	$15
❑ 8597	Wedding Bells/P.M.S.	1974	$5

RISING SONS

❑ 702	Friendship/You Got Me Laughing	1967	$10

SWAN SILVERTONES, THE
VEE-JAY

❑ 869	Great Day In December/ The Lord's Prayer	1958	$70

SWANN, BETTYE
ABET

❑ 9453	Don't Wait Too Long/I Can't Stop Loving You	1973	$12
❑ 9450	Make Me Yours/I Will Not Cry	1973	$10
❑ 9455	The Heartache Is Gone/ Fall in Love with Me	1973	$10

ATLANTIC

❑ 3262	All the Way In or All the Way Out/Doing for the One I Love	1975	$15
❑ 3352	Heading in the Right Direction/Be Strong Enough to Hold On	1976	$20

Number	Title	Yr	NM
❑ 3019	The Boy Next Door/Kiss My Love Goodbye	1974	$250
❑ 3019 [DJ]	The Boy Next Door (stereo/mono)	1974	$30
❑ 2950	Till I Get It Right/Yours Until Tomorrow	1973	$15
❑ 3211	Time to Say Goodbye/When the Game Is Played on You	1974	$30
❑ 2921	Today I Started Loving You Again/I'd Rather Go Blind	1972	$30

BIG TREE

❑ 16054	Storybook Children/ Just As Sure	1976	$125

—With Sam Dees

CAPITOL

❑ 2850	Ain't That Peculiar/Don't Let It Happen to Us	1970	$20
❑ 2515	Angel of the Morning/ No Faith No Love	1969	$30
❑ 2382	Don't Touch Me/(My Heart Is) Closed for the Season	1969	$40
❑ 2382 [PS]	Don't Touch Me/(My Heart Is) Closed for the Season	1969	$40
❑ 2606	Don't You Ever Get Tired (Of Hurting Me)/Willie and Laura Mae Jones	1969	$15
❑ 2263	I'm Lonely for You/(My Heart Is) Closed for the Season	1968	$40
❑ 2723	Little Things Mean a Lot/Just Because You Can't Be Mine	1970	$30

FAME

❑ 1479	I Can't Let You Break My Heart/I'm Just Living a Lie	1971	$50

MONEY

❑ 108	Don't Wait Too Long/What Is My Life Coming To	1965	$40
❑ 129	Fall in Love with Me/ Lonely Love	1967	$30
❑ 136	I Think I'm Falling in Love/ Don't Take My Mind	1968	$30
❑ 126	Make Me Yours/I Will Not Cry	1967	$40
❑ 118	The Heartache Is Gone/Our Love	1966	$40
❑ 113	What Can It Be/The Man That Said No	1965	$40

SWANS, THE (1)
BALLAD

❑ 1007	Happy/The Santa Claus Boogie	1955	$600
❑ 1003/6	It's a Must/Night Train	1954	$600

FORTUNE

❑ 822	I'll Forever Love You/ Mister Cool Breeze	1955	$800

STEAMBOAT

❑ 101	Believe in Me/In the Morning	1956	$2500

SWANS, THE (2)
CAMEO

❑ 302	The Boy with the Beatle Hair/Please Hurry Home	1964	$50

PARKWAY

❑ 881	Daydreamin' of You/ The Promise	1963	$40

SWAN

❑ 4151	He's Mine/You Better Be a Good Girl Now	1963	$40

SWANS, THE (3)
ROULETTE

❑ 4213	He Wasn't On the Air Again Today/If I Could Stop Every Clock	1959	$30

SWANSON, BOBBY
DONNA

❑ 1326	Tom and Susie/China Doll	1960	$30
❑ 1356	Twisting at the Top/ Hello There Lover Doll	1962	$30

SWATLEY, HANK
AARON

❑ 101	Oakie Boogie/I Can't Help It	1957	$500

SWEET, RACHEL, AND REX SMITH
STIFF/COLUMBIA

❑ 18-02169 [PS]	Everlasting Love	1981	$12

—Demonstration -- Not for Sale" on rear

❑ 18-02169	Everlasting Love// Still Thinking of You/ Billy and the Gun	1981	$10

—B-side features one song each by Rex Smith and Rachel Sweet

❑ 18-02169 [PS]	Everlasting Love// Still Thinking of You/ Billy and the Gun	1981	$15

Number	Title	Yr	NM

SWEET, RACHEL

COLUMBIA
| 38-68580 | Life Ain't Worth Living (When You're Dead)/Romance (Love Theme from "Sing") | 1989 | $4 |

— B-side by Paul Carrack and Terri Nunn

DERRICK
117	Any Port in a Storm/(B-side unknown)	1978	$6
111	I Believe What I Believe/(B-side unknown)	1976	$6
115	Overnight Success/Bluer Than the Dress	1977	$6
109	The Ballad of Mabel Ruth Miller and John Wesley Pritchett/All the Love We Had	1976	$6
1000	We Live in Two Different Worlds/Paper Airplane	1976	$6

MCA
| 53303 | (Theme from) Hairspray/Hairspray (Instrumental) | 1988 | $4 |
| 53303 [PS] | (Theme from) Hairspray/Hairspray (Instrumental) | 1988 | $4 |

STIFF/COLUMBIA
1-11100	B-A-B-Y/Stranger in the House	1979	$15
1-11052	I Go to Pieces/Suspended Animation	1979	$15
1-11245	Lover's Lane/Take Good Care of Me	1980	$15
11-11314	Lover's Lane/Tonight Ricky	1980	$15
1-11272	Spellbound/Tonight	1980	$15
18-02537	Then He Kissed Me/Be My Baby//Streetheart	1981	$12

SWEET SICK TEENS, THE

RCA VICTOR
| 47-7940 | The Pretzel/Agnes, the Teenage Russian Spy | 1961 | $50 |
| 37-7940 | The Pretzel/Agnes, the Teenage Russian Spy | 1961 | $100 |

— Compact Single 33" (small hole, plays at LP speed)

SWEET TEENS, THE

FLIP
| 311 | Forever More/Don't Worry About a Thing | 1955 | $70 |

GEE
| 1030 | My Valentine/With This Ring | 1957 | $70 |

SWEET, THE (1)

20TH CENTURY
| 2033 | It's Lonely Out There/I'm On My Way | 1973 | $10 |

— U.S. issue of 1968 material that was on Fontana in the U.K.

BELL
45361	Blockbuster/Need a Lot of Lovin'	1973	$5
45126	Co-Co/You're Not Wrong for Loving Me	1971	$6
45106	Funny, Funny/You're Not Wrong for Loving Me	1971	$8
45251	Little Willy/Man from Mecca	1972	$6
45184	Poppa Joe/Jeanie	1972	$6
45408	Wig-Wam Bam/New York Connection	1973	$5

CAPITOL
4220	Action/Medussa	1976	$5
4055	Ballroom Blitz/Restless	1975	$5
4610	California Nights/Dream On	1978	$5
4429	Fever of Love/Heartbreak Today	1977	$5
4157	Fox on the Run/Burn On the Flame	1975	$5
4454	Funk It Up (David's Song)/Stairway to the Stars	1977	$5
4549	Love Is Like Oxygen/Cover Girl	1978	$5
4730	Mother Earth/Why Don't You	1979	$4
4908	Sixties Man/Water's Edge	1980	$4

PARAMOUNT
| 044 | All You'll Ever Get from Me/The Juicer | 1970 | $30 |

SWEET, THE (2)

SMASH
| 2136 | Broken Heart Attack/Don't Do It | 1967 | $20 |
| 2116 | Got to Have More Love/You Can't Win at Love | 1967 | $20 |

SWEET THREE, THE

CAMEO
| 463 | Don't Leave Me Now/I Would If I Could | 1967 | $20 |

DECCA
| 32005 | Big Lovers Come in Small Packages/That's the Way It Is (When a Girl's in Love) | 1966 | $60 |
| 31938 | Spring Fever (Part 1)/(Part 2) | 1966 | $30 |

SWEETHEARTS OF THE RODEO

COLUMBIA
38-07985	Blue to the Bone/You Never Talk Sweet	1988	$3
38-07023	Chains of Gold/Gotta Get Away	1987	$3
38-07314	Gotta Get Away/Since I Found You	1987	$3
38-05824	Hey Doll Baby/Everywhere I Turn	1986	$3
38-05824 [PS]	Hey Doll Baby/Everywhere I Turn	1986	$3
38-08504	I Feel Fine/Until I Stop Dancing	1988	$3
38-68684	If I Never See Midnight Again/Gone Again	1989	$3
38-06525	Midnight Girl/Sunset Town/I Can't Resist	1986	$3
38-07757	Satisfy You/One Time, One Night	1988	$3
38-06166	Since I Found You/Chosen Few	1986	$3
38-73213	This Heart/So Sad (To Watch Good Love Go Bad)	1989	$3

SWEETHEARTS, THE

BRUNSWICK
| 55265 | Have You Ever Fell in Love/No No (I Won't Break My Lover's Heart) | 1964 | $30 |

SWEETIES, THE

END
| 1110 | After You/Paul's Love | 1962 | $30 |

SWIFT, BASIL, AND THE SEEGRAMS

MERCURY
| 72386 | Farmer's Daughter/Shambles | 1965 | $200 |

SWIFT, DICK

HIT
| 21 | Sealed with a Kiss/Breaking Up Is Hard to Do | 1962 | $8 |

— B-side by Bill Arndt

SWIMMING POOL Q'S, THE

DB
| 64 | Little Misfit/Stingray | 1979 | $3 |
| 64 [PS] | Little Misfit/Stingray | 1979 | $3 |

SWINGIN' MEDALLIONS

4 SALE
| 02 | Double Shot (Of My Baby's Love)/Here It Comes Again | 1966 | $125 |

1-2-3
| 1723 | We're Gonna Hate Ourselves in the Morning/It's Alright | 1970 | $8 |

CAPITOL
| 2338 | Sun, Sand and Sea/Hey, Hey Baby | 1968 | $8 |

DOT
| 16721 | Bye Bye, Silly Girl/I Want to Be Your Guy | 1965 | $15 |

SMASH
2129	Bow and Arrow/Where Can I Go to Get Soul	1967	$10
2084	Don't Cry No More!/Found a Rainbow	1967	$12
2033	Double Shot (Of My Baby's Love)/Here It Comes Again	1966	$20
2075	I Don't Want to Lose It for You Baby/Night Owl	1966	$15
2050	She Drives Me Out of My Mind/You Gotta Have Faith	1966	$15
2107	Turn On the Music/Summer's Not the Same This Year	1967	$10

SWINGING BLUE JEANS, THE

IMPERIAL
66154	Don't Make Her Over/What Can I Do Today	1966	$15
66030	Good Golly Miss Molly/Shaking Feeling	1964	$15
66021	Hippy Hippy Shake/Now I Must Go	1964	$20
66090	It Isn't There/One of These Days	1965	$15
66049	Shake, Rattle and Roll/You're No Good	1964	$15
66255	Something's Coming Along/Tremblin'	1967	$12
66059	Tutti Frutti/Promise You'll Tell Her	1964	$15

SWINGING EMBERS, THE

ACE
| 644 | Winter Wonderland/I'm So Lonely | 1961 | $20 |

SWINGING HEARTS, THE

620
| 1002 | How Can I Love You/(B-side unknown) | 1963 | $200 |

NRM
| 1002 | How Can I Love You/(B-side unknown) | 1963 | $300 |

SWINGING TIGERS

TAMLA
| 54024 | Snake Walk (Part 1)/Snake Walk (Part 2) | 1960 | $300 |

SYCAMORES, THE

GROOVE
| 0121 | I'll Be Waiting/Darling, Is It True | 1955 | $200 |

SYDELLS, THE

BELTONE
| 2032 | In the Night/The Hokey Pokey | 1963 | $20 |

SYKES, BOBBY

STARDAY
| 654 | I Should Start Running/Good Girl Bad | 1963 | $20 |

SYLVIA (1)

ALL PLATINUM
| 2303 | I Can't Help It!/It's a Good Life | 1969 | $8 |
| 2350 | Sho Nuff Boogie (Part 1)/Sho Nuff Boogie (Part 2) | 1974 | $5 |

— With the Moments

JUBILEE
| 5093 | Drive, Daddy, Drive/I Found Somebody to Love | 1952 | $60 |

— As "Little Sylvia

STANG
| 5015 | Have You Had Any Lately/Anytime | 1970 | $6 |

SUGAR HILL
| 781 | It's Good to Be the Queen/(B-side unknown) | 1982 | $4 |

VIBRATION
527	Alfredo/Lay It On Me	1973	$5
576	Automatic Lover/Stop Boy	1978	$5
524	Didn't I/Had Any Lately	1973	$5
530	Easy Evil/Give It Up in Vain	1974	$5
567	L.A. Sunshine/Taxi	1976	$5
570	Lay It On Me (Vocal)/(Instrumental)	1977	$5
572	Lollipop Man/Lay It On Me	1977	$5
521	Pillow Talk/My Thing	1973	$6
528	Private Performance/If You Get the Notion	1974	$5
536	Pussy Cat (Part 1)/Pussy Cat (Part 2)	1975	$5
525	Soul Je T'Aime/Sunday	1973	$5

— With Ralfi Pagan

| 529 | Sweet Stuff/Had Any Lately | 1974 | $5 |

SYLVIA (2)

RCA
PB-14107	Cry Just a Little Bit/Only the Shadow Knows	1985	$3
PB-12164	Drifter/Missin' You	1981	$4
PB-12164 [PS]	Drifter/Missin' You	1981	$5
GB-12312	Drifter/Tumbleweed	1981	$3

— Gold Standard Series" reissue

PB-13997	Fallin' in Love/True Blue	1985	$3
PB-12302	Heart on the Mend/Rainbow Rider	1981	$4
PB-13689	I Never Quite Got Back (From Loving You)/So Complete	1983	$3
PB-11958	It Don't Hurt to Dream/No News Is Good News	1980	$4
PB-13330	Like Nothing Ever Happened/Drifter	1982	$3
PB-13838	Love Over Old Times/I Just Don't Have the Heart	1984	$3

Number	Title	Yr	NM
❏ PB-13501	Snapshot/Tonight I'm Gettin' Friendly with the Blues	1983	$3
❏ 5127-7-R	Straight from My Heart/Makes You Wanna Slow Down	1987	$3
❏ PB-13020	Sweet Yesterday/I Feel Cheated	1981	$4
❏ PB-13589	The Boy Gets Around/Who's Kidding Who	1983	$3
❏ PB-12214	The Matador/Cry Baby Cry	1981	$4
❏ PB-12214 [PS]	The Matador/Cry Baby Cry	1981	$5
❏ PB-12077	Tumbleweed/Anytime, Anyplace	1980	$4

SYMBOLS, THE (1)
DORE
❏ 666	Last Year About This Time/Better Get Your Own One Buddy	1963	$20

SYMBOLS, THE (2)
IMPERIAL
❏ 66382	I Will Still Be There/The Wrong Girl	1969	$8

SYMBOLS, THE (3)
MGM
❏ 13463	Don't Go/Oo Wee Baby	1966	$12
❏ 13348	One Fine Girl/Don't Go	1965	$10

SYMBOLS, THE (4)
VINTAGE
❏ 1007	Bye Bye/I Love You	1973	$5

SYMBOLS, THE (U)
LAURIE
❏ 3401	Bye Bye Baby/The Things You Do to Me	1967	$10
❏ 3435	The Best Part of Breaking Up/Again	1968	$12
PRESIDENT
❏ 102	Canadian Sunset/The Gentle Art of Loving	1966	$10

SYMPHONICS, THE (1)
ABC
❏ 11068	Boy (Please Help Me)/It's Gonna Be Real Hard	1968	$8
BRUNSWICK
❏ 55303	Don't Fail Me Now/Silent Kind of Guy	1966	$12

SYMPHONICS, THE (2)
ENRICA
❏ 1002	Come On Honey/A Blessing to You	1959	$30

SYNDICATE OF SOUND
BELL
❏ 655	Goodtime Music/Keep It Up	1966	$20
❏ 640	Little Girl/You	1966	$30
❏ 666	Mary/That Kind of Man	1967	$20
BUDDAH
❏ 156	Brown Paper Bag/Reverb Beat	1970	$10
❏ 183	Mexico/First to Love You	1970	$10
DEL-FI
❏ 4304	Prepare for Love/Tell the World	1965	$80
HUSH
❏ 228	Little Girl/You	1966	$200
PHILCO-FORD
❏ HP-29	Little Girl/Rumors	1968	$30
—4-inch plastic "Hip Pocket Record" with color sleeve
SCARLET
❏ 503	Prepare for Love/Tell the World	1965	$80

SYNDICATE, THE
DORE
❏ 743	My Baby Is Barefoot/Love Will Take Away	1965	$200
DOT
❏ 16807	Egyptian Thing/She Haunts You	1965	$50

T

T-BIRDS, THE
CHESS
❏ 1778	Green Stamps/Come On Dance with Me	1961	$30
❏ 1792	Hog Wild/Taco Harry	1961	$30
GONE
❏ 5141	Wild Stomp/Soft Smoke	1962	$30
T-BIRD
❏ 101	Green Stamps/Come On Dance with Me	1961	$50

T-BONES, THE
Members of this group later formed HAMILTON, JOE FRANK AND REYNOLDS.
LIBERTY
❏ 55925	Balboa Blues/Walkin' My Cat Named Dog	1966	$12
❏ 55677	Draggin'/Rail-Vette	1964	$30
❏ 55906	Let's Go Get Stoned/Farre Thee Well	1966	$12
❏ 55867	Sippin' & Chippin'/Moment of Softness	1966	$10
❏ 55951	Tee Hee Hee (My Life Seems Different Now)/Proper Thing to Do	1967	$10
❏ 55814	That's Where It's At/Pearlin'	1965	$20
❏ 55885	Wherever You Look, Wherever You Go/Underwater	1966	$10
7-Inch Extended Plays
❏ LST-4-7439	*Hole in the Wall/Let's Hang On/Lies/Fever/Don't Think Twice, It's Alright	1966	$25
—Jukebox issue; small hole, plays at 33 1/3 rpm

T.C. ATLANTIC
AESOP'S LABEL
❏ 6044	Once Upon a Melody/I Love You So, Little Girl	1965	$30
B. SHARP
❏ 272	Mona/My Babe	1966	$50
CANDY FLOSS
❏ 101	I'm So Glad/Twenty Years Ago	1968	$50
PARROT
❏ 330	I'm So Glad/Twenty Years Ago	1968	$30
❏ 338	Love Is Just/Faces	1969	$30
TURTLE
❏ 1103	Faces/Baby, Please Don't Go	1966	$200
❏ 1105	Shake/Spanish Harlem	1967	$50

T.I.M.E.
LIBERTY
❏ 56020	Take Me Along/Make It Right	1968	$10
❏ 56020 [PS]	Take Me Along/Make It Right	1968	$20
❏ 56060	Tripping Into Sunshine/What Would Life Be Without You	1968	$10

T'PAU
VIRGIN
❏ 99417	Bridge of Spies/No Sense of Pride	1987	$3
❏ 99417 [PS]	Bridge of Spies/No Sense of Pride	1987	$3
❏ 99369	China in Your Hands/Friends Like These	1988	$4
❏ 99369 [PS]	China in Your Hands/Friends Like These	1988	$4
❏ 99466	Heart and Soul/On the Wing	1987	$3
❏ 99466 [PS]	Heart and Soul/On the Wing	1987	$3

T. REX
Featuring Marc Bolan.
A&M
❏ 955	Child Star/Debora	1968	$100
—As "Tyrannosaurus Rex"
BLUE THUMB
❏ 212	By the Light of the Magical Moon/Find a Little Wood	1971	$40
CASABLANCA
❏ 810	Precious Star/(B-side unknown)	1974	$15
LYNTONE
❏ (# unknown)	Christmas Time/Wanna Spend My Christmas with You/Christmas/Everybody Knows It's Christmas	1972	$100
—Fan-club flexidisc
❏ (# unknown) [PS]	Christmas Time/Wanna Spend My Christmas with You/Christmas/Everybody Knows It's Christmas	1972	$150

—Brown envelope and letter with above flexi; both are U.K. imports
MARC ON WAX
❏ SBOLAN12PD	Christmas Bop/Shy Boy/Ride A White Swan (live)	1983	$12
—U.K.-only picture disc
REPRISE
❏ 1032	Bang a Gong (Get It On)/Raw Ramp	1971	$10
❏ 1150	Bang a Gong (Get It On)/Telegram Sam	1972	$4
—Back to Back Hits" series
❏ 1161	Born to Boogie/The Groover	1973	$10
❏ 1161 [PS]	Born to Boogie/The Groover	1973	$30
❏ 1006	Hot Love//One Inch Rock/Seagull Woman	1971	$12
❏ 1170	Hot Love/Rip Off	1973	$10
❏ 1095	Metal Guru/Lady	1972	$12
❏ 1078	Telegram Sam/Cadillac	1972	$6
❏ 1122	The Slider/Rock On	1972	$6

T.S.U. TORONADOES, THE
ATLANTIC
❏ 2579	Getting the Corners/What Good Am I!	1968	$8
❏ 2614	Got to Get Through to You/The Goose	1969	$8
VOLT
❏ 4030	My Thing Is a Moving Thing/Still Love You	1969	$6
❏ 4038	One Flight Too Many/Play the Music Toronadoes	1970	$6

TABS, THE
DOT
❏ 15887	Avenue of Tears/The First Star	1959	$40
NASCO
❏ 6016	Will We Meet Again/Still Love You Baby	1958	$40
NOBLE
❏ 720	Oops/My Girl Is Gone	1959	$400
VEE JAY
❏ 418	Dance All By Myself/Dance Party	1961	$30
❏ 446	Mash Dem Taters/But You're My Baby	1962	$30
WAND
❏ 139	I'm with You/Take My Love Along with You	1963	$20
❏ 130	Two Stupid Feet/Footsteps	1962	$20

TABUCHI, SHOJI
ABC DOT
❏ 17561	Devil's Dream/Somewhere My Love	1975	$5
DOT
❏ 17505	Colinda/A Man Needs a Woman	1974	$5
TARGET
❏ 0151	Made in the U.S.A./Over the Waves	1972	$6
❏ 0153	San Antonio Rose/Sukiyaki	1973	$6

TACKETT, MARLOW
PALACE
❏ 1008	Midnight Fire/(B-side unknown)	1980	$8
❏ 1006	Would You Know Love/South Bound Train	1979	$8
RCA
❏ PB-13347	634-5789/She Couldn't Take It Anymore	1982	$4
❏ PB-13255	Ever-Lovin' Woman/Hang In There Teardrop	1982	$4
❏ PB-13471	I Know My Way to You by Heart/Big Old Teardrops	1983	$4
❏ JK-13471 [DJ]	I Know My Way to You by Heart (same on both sides)	1983	$10
—Promo only on blue vinyl
❏ PB-13579	I Spent the Night in the Heart of Texas/Way Back When	1983	$4

TACO
RCA
❏ PB-13646	Cheek to Cheek/After Eight	1983	$3
❏ PB-13777	Let's Face the Music (And Dance)/Lassiter's Theme: Beware of the Winners	1984	$3
❏ GB-13791	Puttin' On the Ritz/Cheek to Cheek	1984	$3
—Gold Standard Series
❏ PB-13574	Puttin' On the Ritz/Livin' in My Dream World	1983	$4

TAD

Number	Title	Yr	NM
SUB POP			
❏ 37	Damaged 1/Damaged 2	1989	$20
—B-side by Pussy Galore			
❏ 37 [PS]	Damaged 1/Damaged 2	1989	$20
—B-side by Pussy Galore; #8 in Sub Pop Singles Club series			
TADS, THE			
REV			
❏ 3513	Wolf Call/She Is My Dream	1958	$60
TAFFYS, THE			
AMY			
❏ 933	Bongo Man/The Game Called Love	1965	$20
FAIRMOUNT			
❏ 610	Everybody South Street/Key to My Heart	1963	$12
PAGEANT			
❏ 608	Can't We Just Be Friends/Peter Cottontail	1963	$10
PARKWAY			
❏ 872	Everybody South Street/Can't We Just Be Friends	1963	$20
TAGES, THE			
VERVE			
❏ 10626	Halcyon Days/I Read You Like an Open Book	1968	$30
TAKERS, THE			
INTERPHON			
❏ 7709	Think/If You Don't Come Back	1964	$10
TALK TALK			
EMI AMERICA			
❏ B-8326	Give It Up/Pictures of Bernadette	1986	$5
❏ B-8195	It's My Life/Again, a Game ... Again	1984	$4
❏ B-8195 [PS]	It's My Life/Again, a Game ... Again	1984	$4
❏ B-8303	Life's What You Make It/It's Getting Late in the Evening	1986	$3
❏ B-8303 [PS]	Life's What You Make It/It's Getting Late in the Evening	1986	$3
❏ B-8215	Such a Shame/Call In the Night Boy	1984	$4
❏ B-8136	Talk Talk/Mirror Man	1982	$5
❏ B-8244	Why Is It So Hard/It's My Life	1984	$5
TALKING HEADS			
❏ 28917 [PS]	And She Was/And She Was (Dub)	1985	$4
❏ 27948 [PS]	Blind/Still	1988	$4
❏ 29565	Burning Down the House/I Get Wild-Wild Gravity	1983	$3
❏ 29565 [PS]	Burning Down the House/I Get Wild-Wild Gravity	1983	$4
❏ 49734	Houses in Motion/The Overload	1981	$4
❏ 49075	Life During Wartime (This Ain't No Party...This Ain't No Disco...This Ain't No Foolin' Around)/Electric Guitar	1979	$4
❏ 737	Love Goes to Bulding on Fire/New Feeling	1977	$10
❏ 737 [PS]	Love Goes to Bulding on Fire/New Feeling	1977	$10
❏ 49649	Once in a Lifetime/Seen and Not Seen	1981	$4
❏ 29163	Once in a Lifetime/This Must Be the Place (Naive Melody)	1984	$3
❏ 29163 [PS]	Once in a Lifetime/This Must Be the Place (Naive Melody)	1984	$3
❏ 1013	Psycho Killer/Psycho Killer (Acoustic)	1978	$8
❏ 1013 [PS]	Psycho Killer/Psycho Killer (Acoustic)	1978	$8
❏ 29080	Stop Making Sense (Girlfriend Is Better)/Heaven	1985	$3
❏ 29080 [PS]	Stop Making Sense (Girlfriend Is Better)/Heaven	1985	$4
❏ 1032	Take Me to the River/Thank You for Sending Me an Angel (Version)	1978	$4
❏ 1032 [PS]	Take Me to the River/Thank You for Sending Me an Angel (Version)	1978	$4
❏ 29451	This Must Be the Place (Naive Melody)/Moon Rocks	1983	$3
❏ 29451 [PS]	This Must Be the Place (Naive Melody)/Moon Rocks	1983	$4
❏ 28629 [PS]	Wild Wild Life/People Like Us (Movie Version)	1986	$4
TALL, TOM			
CHART			
❏ 1370	Bad, Bad Tuesday/A Little Miracle	1966	$12
❏ 1225	Gravy Train/I've Seen Enough	1965	$10

Number	Title	Yr	NM
❏ 1305	Hill Above the City/Eyes Look Away	1966	$12
❏ 1170	I Want You/In the Shadows of the Night	1965	$10
— With Ginny Wright			
❏ 1085	Walk Tall/Eyes Look Away	1964	$10
CREST			
❏ 1052	High School Love/To Be Alone	1958	$40
❏ 1038	Stack-a-Records/Mary Jo	1957	$125
DECCA			
❏ 31240	One Thing's Wrong/You Call Everybody Darlin'	1961	$20
❏ 31151	The Fool's Side of Me/Was It Easy	1960	$20
FABOR			
❏ 139	Don't You Know/If You Know What	1956	$30
— With Ruckus Tyler			
❏ 125	Give Me a Chance/Remembering You	1955	$40
❏ 132	Hot Rod Is Her Name/Why Must I Wonder	1956	$50
❏ 115	I Want to Walk with You/You Loved Another One Better	1954	$40
❏ 108	Please Be Careful/I Gave My Heart to Two People	1954	$40
PETAL			
❏ 1210	Bad, Bad Tuesday/Oohin' and Aahin'	1963	$20
SAGE			
❏ 305	Three Walls/This Ireland	1959	$30
❏ 0514	She Knew How to Love Me/I Believe I'm Gonna Love You	1976	$6
TALLEY, JOHNNY T.			
MERCURY			
❏ 70902	Lonesome Train/(I've Changed My) Wild Mind	1956	$300
TALLEY, RUTH			
MGM			
❏ K12307	Don't Feel Guilty/Tell Me How Long	1956	$30
❏ K12505	Heartaches to Bear/The Last Time	1957	$30
❏ K12241	Let Me/Ever by the Side of Me	1956	$30
— With Bob Jennings			
❏ K12406	Ordinary/Just What You Want Me To	1957	$30
— With Skeets Yaney			
TALLYSMEN, THE			
TALLY			
❏ 200688	Little By Little/You Don't Care About Me	1966	$70
TALMADGE, BILLY			
DECCA			
❏ 9-28166	Blue Yodel #3/Blue Monday Blues	1952	$30
❏ 9-46397	'Tis Sweet to Be Remembered/I Made a Mistake	1952	$30
TAMANEERS, THE			
BRAMLEY			
❏ 102	Searching/Be Anything (But Be Mine)	1960	$400
TAMBLYN, LARRY			
FARO			
❏ 601	Patty Ann/Dearest	1960	$30
❏ 603	The Lie/My Bride-to-Be	1960	$30
❏ 612	This Is the Night/Destiny	1961	$30
TAMMI AND THE BACHELORS			
BANGAR			
❏ 0610	My Summer Love/My Love	1964	$30
TAMMYS, THE			
UNITED ARTISTS			
❏ 678	Egyptian Shamba/What's So Sweet About Sweet Sixteen	1963	$15
❏ 632	Take Back Your Ring/Part of Growing Up	1963	$15
VEEP			
❏ 1210	Gypsy/Hold Back the Light of Dawn	1965	$15
❏ 1220	His Actions Speak Louder Than Words/Blues Sixteen	1965	$15

Number	Title	Yr	NM
TAMPA RED			
RCA VICTOR			
❏ 50-0084	1950 Blues/Love Her with a Feelin'	1950	$125
— Gray label, orange vinyl			
❏ 47-5134	All Mixed Up Over You/Too Late Too Long	1953	$50
❏ 47-4275	Boogie Woogie Women/I Won't Let Her Do It	1951	$60
❏ 47-4722	But I Forgive You/I'm Gonna Put You Down	1952	$60
❏ 50-0019	Come On If You're Coming/When Things Go Wrong with You	1950	$120
— Gray label, orange vinyl			
❏ 47-5594	If She Don't Come Back/Big Stars Falling	1954	$50
❏ 50-0002	If You Ever Change Your Ways/Chicago Breakdown	1949	$120
— Gray label, orange vinyl; With Big Maceo			
❏ 50-0041	I'll Find My Way/That's Her Own Business	1950	$120
— Gray label, orange vinyl			
❏ 47-5273	I'll Never Let You Go/Got a Mind to Leave This Town	1953	$50
❏ 50-0027	It's a Brand New Boogie/Put Your Money Where Your Mouth Is	1950	$120
— Gray label, orange vinyl			
❏ 50-0094	It's Good Like That/New Deal Blues	1950	$125
— Gray label, orange vinyl			
❏ 50-0071	It's Too Late Now/Please Try to See It My Way	1950	$125
— Gray label, orange vinyl			
❏ 50-0112	Midnight Boogie/I Miss My Lovin' Blues	1951	$100
❏ 50-0136	Pretty Baby Blues/Since My Baby's Been Gone	1951	$100
❏ 47-4399	She's a Cool Operator/Green and Lucky Blues	1951	$60
❏ 50-0123	She's Dynamite/Early in the Morning	1951	$100
❏ 47-5523	So Craazy About You Baby/So Much Trouble	1953	$50
❏ 50-0107	Sweet Little Angel/Don't Blame Shorty for That	1951	$100
❏ 47-4898	True Love/Look-a There, Look-a There	1952	$60
TAMS, THE			
1-2-3			
❏ 1726	How Long Love/Too Much Foolin' Around	1970	$6
ABC			
❏ 11019	All My Heard Times/A Little More Soul	1967	$8
❏ 11228	Be Young, Be Foolish, Be Happy/Love, Love, Love	1969	$8
❏ 11066	Be Young, Be Foolish, Be Happy/That Same Old Song	1968	$8
❏ 10929	Breaking Up/How 'Bout It	1967	$8
❏ 11358	Don't You Just Know It/Making Music	1973	$5
❏ 10956	Everything Else Is Gone/Mary, Mary, Row Your Boat	1967	$8
❏ 10825	Holding On/Is It Better to Have Loved a Little	1966	$8
❏ 11128	Laugh at the World/Trouble Maker	1968	$8
❏ 10885	Shelter/Get Away (Leave Me Alone)	1966	$8
❏ 11183	Sunshine, Rainbow, Blue Sky, Brown Eyed Girl/There's a Great Big Change in Me	1969	$8
ABC DUNHILL			
❏ 4290	Hey Girl Don't Bother Me/Weep Little Girl	1971	$6
❏ 4290 [PS]	Hey Girl Don't Bother Me/Weep Little Girl	1971	$12
— Title sleeve with "#1 in England"			
ABC-PARAMOUNT			
❏ 10741	Carryin' On/I've Been Hurt	1965	$10
❏ 10702	Concrete Jungle/Till the End of Time	1965	$10
❏ 10779	Got to Get Used to a Broken Heart/Riding for a Fall	1966	$10
❏ 10573	Hey Girl Don't Bother Me/Take Away	1964	$15
❏ 10533	It's All Right (You're Just in Love)/You Lied to Your Daddy	1964	$15
❏ 10601	Silly Little Girl/Weep Little Girl	1964	$15
❏ 10614	The Truth Hurts/Why Did My Little Girl Cry	1965	$10
❏ 10635	What Do You Do/Unlove You	1965	$10
❏ 10502	What Kind of Fool (Do You Think I Am)/Laugh It Off	1963	$20
APT			
❏ 26010	Long Distance Operator/Numbers	1970	$6

Number	Title	Yr	NM
ARLEN			
❑ 717	Deep Inside Me/If You're So Smart (Why Do You Have a Broken Heart)	1962	$15
❑ 729	Don't Ever Go/Find Another Love	1963	$15
CAPITOL			
❑ 3050	The Tams Medley/Wire Help	1971	$6
COMPLEAT			
❑ 109	My Baby Sure Can Shag/ Making True Love	1983	$4
GENERAL AMERICAN			
❑ 714	My Baby Loves Me/ Find Another Love	1962	$20
SWAN			
❑ 4055	Sorry/Valley of Love	1960	$20
TAMS, THE (2)			
MINK			
❑ 22	Memory Lane/Teenage Kids	1959	$50
—Originally issued as "The Stereos"			
PARKWAY			
❑ 863	Memory Lane/A Lovely Piano	1963	$30
—The same record was reissued as "The Hippies"			
TAN GEERS			
OKEH			
❑ 4-7319	Let My Heart and Soul Be Free/What's the Use of Me Trying	1968	$400
TANDY, SHARON			
ABC-PARAMOUNT			
❑ 10742	Perhaps Not Ever/I've Found Love	1965	$10
TANEGA, NORMA			
NEW VOICE			
❑ 810	A Street That Rhymes at 6 A.M./Treat Me Right	1966	$10
❑ 815	Bread/Waves	1966	$10
❑ 807	Walkin' My Cat Named Dog/I'm the Sky	1966	$15
TANGERINE DREAM			
MCA			
❑ 40740	Betrayal (Sorcerer's Theme)/Grind	1977	$12
VIRGIN			
❑ 9516 [DJ]	Moonlight/Cherokee Lane	1977	$10
❑ 9516 [DJ]	Moonlight/Cherokee Lane	1977	$10
❑ 9516 [DJ]	Moonlight/Desert Dream	1977	$10
❑ 9516 [DJ]	Moonlight/Desert Dream	1977	$10
❑ 9516	Moonlight (Part 2)/ Coldwater Canyon (Part 2)	1977	$10
❑ 9516 [DJ]	Moonlight (Part 2) (mono/stereo)	1977	$10
❑ 9516 [DJ]	Moonlight (Part 2) (mono/stereo)	1977	$10
TANGERINE ZOO, THE			
MAINSTREAM			
❑ 682	A Trip to the Zoo/One More Heartache	1968	$30
❑ 690	Like People/(B-side unknown)	1968	$30
TANGIERS, THE			
A-J			
❑ 905	The Plea/The Waddle	1962	$30
CLASS			
❑ 224	School Days Will Be Over/Don't Try	1958	$40
DECCA			
❑ 29603	I Won't Be Around/Tabarin	1955	$200
STRAND			
❑ 25039	Ping Pong/Don't Stop the Music	1961	$40
TANTONES, THE			
LAMP			
❑ 2008	So Afraid/Tell Me	1957	$200
TAPP, DEMETRISS			
ABC			
❑ 11401	Ain't You Gettin' Tired of Us, God/Takin' His Love Away from Me	1973	$6
❑ 11115	How Could He Do This to Me/Love Will Come Your Way	1968	$10
❑ 11362	Love Me/I'm Missing You	1973	$6

Number	Title	Yr	NM
❑ 11160	Ordinary Man/What Did Sister Do	1968	$10
❑ 11383	Skinny Dippin'/Just Let Me Make Believe	1973	$6
❑ 11201	Strain on My Heart/I'm All Alone Again	1969	$8
BRUNSWICK			
❑ 55251	If You Find Love/Lipstick Paint a Smile on Me	1963	$20
❑ 55257	Let Go of My Heart/Is This the Beginning of the End	1964	$20
❑ 55264	What Kind of Girl/I Turn Blue	1964	$20
COLUMBIA			
❑ 4-42362	Am I the Keeper/ Another Victory	1962	$20
❑ 4-42603	It Isn't the End of the World/Act Your Age	1962	$20
MONUMENT			
❑ 908	The First Word/I'm in Love with You	1965	$20
TARANTULA			
A&M			
❑ 1156	Billy the Birdman/ Love Is for Peace	1969	$8
TARANTULAS, THE			
ATLANTIC			
❑ 2102	Tarantula/Black Widow	1961	$30
STOP			
❑ 102	Herky Jerky/Vera Brown	1964	$12
TARGETS, THE			
KING			
❑ 5538	It Doesn't Matter/ Girls, Girls, Girls	1961	$50
TARRIERS, THE			
DECCA			
❑ 31470	Casey Jones/Mary Ann	1963	$10
❑ 31387	Last Night I Had the Strangest Dream/ Lonesome Traveler	1962	$12
❑ 31524	Lonesome Traveller/ Seven Daffodils	1963	$10
❑ 31631	San Francisco Bay Blues/Guantanamera	1964	$10
GLORY			
❑ 264	Dunya/Quinto	1957	$20
❑ 255	I Know Where I'm Going/Pretty Boy	1957	$20
❑ 271	Lonesome Traveler/ East Virginia	1958	$20
❑ 249	The Banana Boat Song/ No Hidin' Place	1956	$30
❑ 254	Those Brown Eyes/Chaucon	1957	$20
❑ 286	Tom Dooley/Everybody Loves Saturday Night	1958	$20
❑ 246	Wishing Well Song/ East Virginia	1956	$20
UNITED ARTISTS			
❑ 168	Hard Travelin'/Times Are Getting Hard	1959	$15
TASSELS, THE			
AMY			
❑ 946	To a Soldier Boy/ The Boy for Me	1966	$10
MADISON			
❑ 117	To a Soldier Boy/ The Boy for Me	1959	$30
❑ 121	To a Young Lover/ My Guy and I	1959	$30
TASTE OF HONEY, A			
CAPITOL			
❑ 4565	Boogie Oogie Oogie/ World Spin	1978	$4
❑ 4565 [PS]	Boogie Oogie Oogie/ World Spin	1978	$5
❑ 4668	Disco Dancin'/Sky High	1978	$4
❑ 4744	Do It Good/I Love You	1979	$4
❑ B-5099	I'll Try Something New/ Good-Bye Baby	1982	$4
❑ B-5099 [PS]	I'll Try Something New/ Good-Bye Baby	1982	$5
❑ 4932	I'm Talkin' 'Bout You/ Don't You Lead Me On	1980	$4
❑ 4953	Sukiyaki/Don't You Lead Me On	1980	$4
❑ 4953 [PS]	Sukiyaki/Don't You Lead Me On	1980	$5
❑ B-5132	We've Got the Groove/ This Love of Ours	1982	$4
TATE, BILLY			
IMPERIAL			
❑ 5337	Single Life/You Told Me	1955	$200
—Script logo			

Number	Title	Yr	NM
PEACOCK			
❑ 1671	Don't Call My Name/ Right from Wrong	1957	$40
TATE, HOWARD			
ATLANTIC			
❑ 2894	Eight Days on the Road/ Girl of the North Country	1972	$6
❑ 2860	She's a Burglar/You Don't Know Nothing About Love	1972	$6
EPIC			
❑ 11118	Can You Top This/Ain't Got Nobody to Give It To	1974	$5
TURNTABLE			
❑ 1018	My Soul's Got a Hole In It/It's Too Late	1970	$8
❑ 505	These Are the Things That Make Me Know You're Gone/That's What Happens	1969	$8
UTOPIA			
❑ 510	Half a Man/(B-side unknown)	1966	$30
VERVE			
❑ 10420	Ain't Nobody Home/ How Come My Bull Dog Don't Bark	1966	$8
❑ 10525	Baby I Love You/How Blue Can You Get	1967	$8
❑ 10496	Get It While You Can/ Glad I Knew Better	1967	$8
❑ 10547	I Learned It All the Hard Way/Part-Time Love	1967	$8
❑ 10625	I'm Your Servant/ Sweet Love Child	1968	$8
❑ 10464	Look at Granny Run, Run/Half a Man	1966	$8
❑ 10573	Stop/Shoot 'Em All Down	1967	$8
TATE, MICHAEL			
OAK			
❑ 47102	Mexican Girl/True Love	1981	$6
TATE, TOMMY			
ABC-PARAMOUNT			
❑ 10626	What's the Matter/Ordinarily	1965	$30
KOKO			
❑ 722	Hardtimes S.O.S./Always	1976	$6
❑ 2114	I Ain't Gonna Worry/ More Power To You	1972	$6
❑ 723	If You Ain't Man Enough/ Revelations	1976	$6
❑ 727	I'm So Satisfied/If You Ain't Man Enough	1977	$6
❑ 2109	I Remember/Help Me Love	1971	$6
❑ 2112	School of Life/I Remember	1972	$6
OKEH			
❑ 7242	Are You From Heaven/I'm Taking On Faith	1966	$30
❑ 7253	Big Blue Diamonds/ Lover's Reward	1967	$30
TAVARES			
CAPITOL			
❑ 4811	Bad Times/Got to Have Your Love	1979	$4
❑ 3674	Check It Out/The Judgment Day	1973	$5
❑ 4348	Don't Take Away the Music/Guiding Star	1976	$5
❑ 4184	Free Ride/In the Eyes of Love	1975	$5
❑ 4453	Goodnight My Love/Watchin' the Woman's Movement	1977	$5
❑ 4781	Hard Core Poetry/Stabilize	1979	$4
❑ 4270	Heaven Must Be Missing An Angel (Part 1)/Heaven Must Be Missing An Angel (Part 2)	1976	$5
❑ 4846	I Can't Go On Living Without You/Why Can't We Fall in Love	1980	$4
❑ 4880	I Don't Want You Anymore/Paradise	1980	$4
❑ 4111	It Only Takes a Minute/I Hope She Chooses Me	1975	$5
❑ 4969	Loneliness/Break Down for Love	1981	$4
❑ A-5043	Loveline/Right On Time	1981	$4
❑ 4933	Love Uprising/Not Love	1980	$4
❑ 4500	More Than a Woman/ Keep in Touch	1977	$4
❑ 4738	One Telephone Call Away/ Let Me Heal the Bruises	1979	$4
❑ 3957	She's Gone/To Love You	1974	$5
❑ 4703	Straight from the Heart/I'm Back for You	1979	$4
❑ 3794	That's the Sound That Lonely Makes/Little Girl	1973	$5
❑ 4544	The Ghost of Love (Part 1)/ The Ghost of Love (Part 2)	1978	$4
❑ 4221	The Love I Never Had/In the City	1976	$5
❑ 4583	Timber/Feel So Good	1978	$4
❑ 3882	Too Late/Leave It Up to the Lady	1974	$5
❑ A-5019	Turn Out the Nightlight/ House of Music	1981	$4

Number	Title	Yr	NM
❑ 4398	Whodunit/Fool of the Year	1977	$5
RCA			
❑ PB-13530	Abra-Ca-Dabra Love You Too/Mystery Lady	1983	$4
❑ GB-13799	A Penny for Your Thoughts/Got to Find My Way Back to You	1984	$3

— Gold Standard Series

❑ PB-13292	A Penny for Your Thoughts/The Skin You're In	1982	$4
❑ PB-13611	Deeper in Love/I Really Miss You Baby	1983	$4
❑ PB-13433	Got to Find My Way Back to You/I Hope You Will Be Very Unhappy Without Me	1983	$4
❑ PB-13684	Words and Music/I'll Send Love (We Go Together)	1983	$4

TAVARES, ERNIE, TRIO
DOOTONE
| ❑ 325 | I'm Alone Tonight/It's Christmas | 1953 | $200 |

— B-side by the Bonairs

TAYLOR, MERLE "RED
DECCA
| ❑ 9-28741 | Gimme a Little Sugar/Suppose We Try | 1953 | $30 |
| ❑ 9-28496 | Most of All/You Can't Be a Bride | 1952 | $30 |

TAYLOR, ANDREW
GONE
| ❑ 5109 | That's How I Feel About You/Never Bite Off More Than You Could Chew | 1961 | $200 |

TAYLOR, BILL, AND SMOKEY JO
FLIP
| ❑ 502 | Split Personality/Lonely Sweetheart | 1955 | $1500 |

TAYLOR, BILLY
CITATION
| ❑ 5002 | Income Taxes and You/Lullaby to Carolyn | 1962 | $20 |
FELCO
| ❑ 101 | Wombie Zombie/I'm Young | 1959 | $30 |
FELSTED
| ❑ 8564 | Bandstand Baby/Cat with No Future | 1959 | $30 |
TOWER
| ❑ 421 | Sunny/I Wish I Knew How I Would Feel to Be Free | 1968 | $8 |

TAYLOR, BOBBY, AND THE VANCOUVERS
GORDY
❑ 7069	Does Your Mama Know About Me/Fading Away	1968	$30
❑ 7073	I Am Your Man/If You Love Her	1968	$30
❑ 7079	Malinda/It's Growing	1968	$30
❑ 7092	My Girl Is Gone/It Should Have Been Me Loving Her	1969	$30
❑ 7088	Oh I've Been Blessed/It Should Have Been Me Loving Her	1969	$600
INTEGRA
| ❑ 103 | This Is My Woman/(B-side unknown) | 1968 | $125 |
MOWEST
| ❑ 5006 | Hey Lordy/Just a Little Bit Closer | 1971 | $20 |
PLAYBOY
| ❑ 6046 | Why Play Games/Don't Wonder Why | 1975 | $5 |
SUNFLOWER
| ❑ 126 | There Are Roses Somewhere in the World/It Was a Good Time | 1972 | $30 |
V.I.P.
| ❑ 25053 | Oh I've Been Blessed/Blackmail | 1969 | $30 |

TAYLOR, CARMEN
APOLLO
| ❑ 489 | Oh Please/Teen Age Ball | 1956 | $70 |
ATLANTIC
❑ 1015	Big Mamou Daddy/Mamma Me and Johnny Free	1953	$60
❑ 1041	Freddie/Ooh I	1954	$120
❑ 1002	Lovin' Daddy/Ding Dong	1953	$60
GUYDEN
| ❑ 100 | Let Me Go Lover/No More, No Less | 1954 | $50 |

KAMA SUTRA
| ❑ 206 | My Son/You're Puttin' Me On | 1966 | $15 |
KING
| ❑ 5085 | So What/Why Did You Leave Me Alone | 1957 | $60 |

TAYLOR, CARMOL
COUNTRY INT'L.
❑ 151	Don't Tempt Me Woman/Sugar Creek Bottom	1980	$5
❑ 160	Georgia Soul/Honky Tonk at Home	1981	$5
❑ 171	Hard to Love a Woman/Georgia Soul	1982	$5
ELEKTRA
❑ 45255	Back in the U.S.A./I'd Like to Sleep Til I Get Over You	1975	$5
❑ 45409	Good Cheatin' Songs/I Don't Want My Country Funky	1977	$5
❑ 45312	I Really Had a Ball Last Night/Good Cheatin' Songs	1976	$5
❑ 45299	Play the Saddest Song on the Jukebox/I'd Like to Sleep Til I Get Over You	1976	$5
❑ 45342	That Little Difference/Love What's Left of Me	1976	$5
❑ 45366	What Would I Do Then?/You're Looking at a Happy Man	1976	$5
❑ 45277	Who Will I Be Loving Now/So Fine	1975	$5
EPIC
| ❑ 5-10615 | Mama, Take Me Home/Someday I'll Leave You | 1970 | $8 |
GOLDWAX
| ❑ 324 | Here Comes the Fool/Did She Ask About Me | 1967 | $15 |

TAYLOR, CHIP
BUDDAH
| ❑ 325 | Angel of the Morning/(B-side unknown) | 1972 | $6 |
| ❑ 344 | Londonderry Company/(B-side unknown) | 1973 | $6 |
CAPITOL
| ❑ 4692 | Saint Sebastian/One Night Out with the Boys | 1979 | $4 |
| ❑ 4840 | Stealin' Each Other Blind/He Ain't Makin' Music Anymore | 1980 | $4 |
COLUMBIA
❑ 10446	Hello Atlanta/Farmer's Daughter	1976	$4
❑ 44736	It's Such a Lonely Time of Year/(Instrumental)	1968	$15
❑ 10520	Three Younger Bandits/Nothing Like You Girl	1977	$4
EPIC
| ❑ 10567 | It's Such a Lonely Time of Year/(Instrumental) | 1969 | $10 |
MALA
| ❑ 476 | On My World/Joanie's Blues | 1964 | $15 |
| ❑ 489 | Suzannah (Comin' Home to Louisiana)/(B-side unknown) | 1964 | $15 |
MGM
| ❑ 12993 | Foolin' Around/Innocent Eyes | 1961 | $30 |
| ❑ 13040 | If You Don't Want Me Now/Sad Songs | 1961 | $30 |
WARNER BROS.
❑ 8128	Big River/John Tucker's On the Wagon Again	1975	$4
❑ 8159	Circle of Tears/You're Alright, Charlie	1975	$4
❑ 8090	Early Sunday Morning/Shickshinny	1975	$4
❑ 5314	Here I Am/I Love You But I Know	1962	$20
❑ 5333	Lucky Star/A Guy Don't Need a Lot of Time	1963	$20
❑ 8050	Me As I Am/Comin' From Behind	1974	$4

TAYLOR, DEBBIE
ARISTA
| ❑ 0144 | I Don't Wanna Leave You/Just Don't Pay | 1975 | $10 |
DECCA
| ❑ 32259 | Check Yourself/Wait Until I'm Gone | 1968 | $20 |
GWP
| ❑ 510 | Don't Let It End/How Long Can This Last | 1969 | $20 |
| ❑ 512 | Momma Look Sharp/No Brag, Just Fact | 1969 | $20 |
GWP'S GRAPEVINE
| ❑ 202 | Don't Nobody Mess with My Baby/Stop | 1970 | $20 |
POLYDOR
| ❑ 14219 | I Have Learned to Do Without You/Cheaper in the Long Run | 1974 | $40 |
TODAY
| ❑ TLP-1007 | Comin' Down on You | 1972 | $75 |

TAYLOR, EDDIE
VEE JAY
❑ 149	Bad Boy/E.T. Blues	1955	$120
❑ 185	Big Town Playboy/Ride 'Em On Down	1956	$100
❑ 267	I'm Gonna Love You/Looking for Trouble	1958	$50
VIVID
| ❑ 104 | I'm Sitting Here/Do You Want Me to Cry | 1964 | $30 |

TAYLOR, FAITH, AND THE SWEET TEENS
BEA & BABY
| ❑ 104 | I Need Him to Love Me/I Love You Darling | 1959 | $60 |

TAYLOR, FELICE
KENT
| ❑ 488 | Captured by Your Love/New Love | 1968 | $20 |
| ❑ 483 | Good Luck/I Can Feel Your Love | 1967 | $20 |
MUSTANG
| ❑ 3026 | I'm Under the Influence of Love/Love Theme | 1967 | $30 |
| ❑ 3024 | It May Be Winter Outside (But In My Heart It's Spring)/Winter Again | 1966 | $20 |

TAYLOR, FRANK
CHART
❑ 1150	Blue Part of the Blues/Tears and Tears to Pay	1964	$15
❑ 502	Bubbles in the Glass/A Part of You	1963	$20
❑ 1235	Forty Winks/I Can't Stand This Living Alone	1965	$15
❑ 1055	From Brown to Blue/You Didn't Leave Me Much to Live For	1964	$15
❑ 1095	Lost, Strayed or Stolen/She Used to Be My Girl	1964	$15
PARKWAY
| ❑ 869 | Snow White Cloud/Send Her Back to Me | 1963 | $20 |

TAYLOR, GLORIA
COLUMBIA
| ❑ 4-45986 | Deep Inside You/World That's Not Real | 1974 | $15 |
| ❑ 493 | Poor Unfortunate Me/You Might Need Me Another Day | 1968 | $70 |
MERCURY
| ❑ 73186 | Don't Want to Be a Girl That Cries/Total Disaster | 1970 | $70 |
SILVER FOX
| ❑ 19 | Grounded Part 1/Part 2 | 1970 | $20 |

TAYLOR, JAMES
APPLE
| ❑ 1805 | Carolina in My Mind/Something's Wrong | 1970 | $10 |

— With star on A-side label

| ❑ 1805 | Carolina in My Mind/Something's Wrong | 1970 | $8 |

— Without star on A-side label

| ❑ 1805 | Carolina in My Mind/Taking It In | 1969 | $300 |
| ❑ 1805 [DJ] | Carolina on My Mind/Something's Wrong | 1970 | $40 |

— Promo with error in title on A-side

| ❑ 1805 [DJ] | Carolina on My Mind/Something's Wrong | 1970 | $40 |

— Promo with error in title on A-side

COLUMBIA
❑ 07948	Baby Boom Baby/Letter in the Mail	1988	$3
❑ 05681	Everyday/Limousine Driver	1985	$3
❑ 05681 [PS]	Everyday/Limousine Driver	1985	$4
❑ 10557	Handy Man/Bartender's Blues	1977	$4
❑ 02093	Hard Times/Summer's Here	1981	$3
❑ 02093 [PS]	Hard Times/Summer's Here	1981	$4
❑ 60514	Her Town Too/Believe It or Not	1981	$4

— A-side: James Taylor and J.D. Souther

❑ 10689	Honey Don't Leave L.A./Another Grey Morning	1978	$4
❑ 06278	Only a Dream in Rio/Turn Away	1986	$3
❑ 05785	Only One/Mona	1986	$3
❑ 05785 [PS]	Only One/Mona	1986	$3
❑ 08493	Sweet Potato Pie/First of May	1988	$3
❑ 05884	That's Why I'm Here/Going Around One More Time	1986	$3
❑ 10676	(What a) Wonderful World/Wooden Planes	1978	$6

— By Art Garfunkel with Paul Simon and James Taylor; B-side is Garfunkel solo

Number	Title	Yr	NM

WARNER BROS.
Number	Title	Yr	NM
❑ 7460	Country Road/Sunny Skies	1970	$6
❑ 7655	Don't Let Me Be Lonely Tonight/Wow, Don't You Know	1972	$5
❑ 7423	Fire and Rain/Anywhere Like Heaven	1970	$8
❑ 8109	How Sweet It Is (To Be Loved By You)/Sarah Maria	1975	$5
❑ 7695	Hymn/Fanfare	1973	$5
❑ 8015	Let It All Fall Down/ Daddy's Baby	1974	$5
❑ 7521	Long Ago and Far Away/Let Me Ride	1971	$5
❑ 8137	Mexico/Gorilla	1975	$5
❑ 7682	One Man Parade/ Nobody But You	1973	$5
❑ 8222	Shower the People/I Can Dream of You	1976	$5
❑ 7387	Sweet Baby James/ Suite for 20G	1970	$8
❑ 8028	Walking Man/Daddy's Baby	1974	$5
❑ 8278	Woman's Gotta Have It/ You Make It Easy	1976	$5

7-Inch Extended Plays
Number	Title	Yr	NM
❑ S2561 [PS]	Mud Slide Slim	1971	$12

—Part of "Little LP" series (LLP #150)

Number	Title	Yr	NM
❑ S2561	Places in My Past/Love Has Brought Me Around/ Hey Mister, That's Me Up on the Jukebox/Mud Slide Slim/Isn't It Nice to Be Home Again/Riding on a Railroad	1971	$10

—Jukebox issue; small hole, plays at 33 1/3 rpm

TAYLOR, JOHNNIE
BEVERLY GLEN
Number	Title	Yr	NM
❑ 2004	I'm So Proud/I Need a Freak	1982	$4
❑ 2016	Seconds of Your Love/ Shoot for the Stars	1983	$4
❑ 2003	What About My Love/ Reaganomics	1982	$4

COLUMBIA
Number	Title	Yr	NM
❑ 10610	Disco 9000/Right Now	1977	$4
❑ 10281	Disco Lady/You're the Best in the World	1976	$5
❑ 10776	Give Me My Baby/ Ever Ready	1978	$4
❑ AE71153 [DJ]	God Is Standing By/ God Is Amazing	1977	$8

—B-side by Deniece Williams; promo with "Suggested Christmas Programming" on label

Number	Title	Yr	NM
❑ AE71153 [DJ]	God Is Standing By/ God Is Amazing	1977	$8

—B-side by Deniece Williams; promo with "Suggested Christmas Programming" on label

Number	Title	Yr	NM
❑ 11315	I Got This Thing for Your Love/Signing Off with Love	1980	$4
❑ 11373	I Wanna Get Into You/ Baby Don't Hesitate	1980	$4
❑ 10478	Love Is Better in the A.M. (Part 1)/Love Is Better in the A.M. (Part 2)	1977	$5
❑ 11084	(Ooh-Wee) She's Killing Me/Play Something Pretty	1979	$4
❑ 10334	Somebody's Gettin' It/ Please Don't Stop (That Song from Playing)	1976	$5

DERBY
Number	Title	Yr	NM
❑ 1006	Baby, We've Got Love/ In Love with You	1963	$20
❑ 1010	I Need Lots of Love/ Getting Married Soon	1964	$20
❑ 101	Shine, Shine, Shine/ Dance What You Wanna	1963	$20

MALACO
Number	Title	Yr	NM
❑ 2128	Can I Love You/There's Nothing I Wouldn't Do	1986	$3
❑ 2135	Don't Make Me Late/ Happy Time	1987	$3
❑ 2143	Everything's Out in the Open/Got to Leave This Woman	1988	$3
❑ 2111	Good with My Hips/ This Is Your Night	1985	$3
❑ 2140	If I Lose Your Love/ Something Is Going Wrong	1987	$3
❑ 2153	In Control/I Found a Love	1989	$3
❑ 2107	Lady, My Whole World Is You/L-O-V-E	1984	$3
❑ 2118	Still Called the Blues/ She's Cheatin' on Me	1985	$3
❑ 2159	Still Crazy for You/ (B-side unknown)	1989	$3
❑ 2125	Wall to Wall/(B-side unknown)	1986	$3

RCA
Number	Title	Yr	NM
❑ PB-11137	I Want You Back Again/ Heaven Bless This Home	1977	$5

SAR
Number	Title	Yr	NM
❑ 114	A Whole Lotta Woman/ Why Oh Why	1961	$30
❑ 156	Oh, How I Love You/ Run, But You Can't Hide	1964	$20

STAX
Number	Title	Yr	NM
❑ 209	Ain't That Loving You/ Outside Love	1967	$10
❑ 0176	Cheaper to Keep Her/I Can Read Between the Lines	1973	$6
❑ 0122	Doing My Own Thing (Part 1)/Doing My Own Thing (Part 2)	1972	$6
❑ 0155	Don't You Fool with My Soul (Part 1)/Don't You Fool with My Soul (Part 2)	1973	$6
❑ 0096	Hijackin' Love/Love in the Streets	1971	$6
❑ 253	I Ain't Particular/Where There's Smoke There's Fire	1968	$10
❑ 0078	I Am Somebody (Part 1)/I Am Somebody (Part 2)	1970	$6
❑ 0161	I Believe in You (You Believe in Me)/Love Depression	1973	$6

—With A-side time listed at 4:37

Number	Title	Yr	NM
❑ 0161	I Believe in You (You Believe in Me)/Love Depression	1973	$6

—With A-side time listed at 3:58

Number	Title	Yr	NM
❑ 0046	I Could Never Be President/It's Amazing	1969	$8
❑ 0089	I Don't Wanna Lose You/Party Life	1971	$6
❑ 226	If I Had It to Do Over/You Can't Get Away from It	1967	$10
❑ 193	I Got to Love Somebody's Baby/Just the One I've Been Looking For	1966	$10
❑ 186	I Had a Dream/Changes	1966	$10
❑ 3201	It Don't Pay to Get Up in the Mornin'/Just Keep On Loving Me	1977	$5
❑ 0226	It's September/Just One Moment	1974	$6
❑ 0208	I've Been Born Again/ At Night Time	1974	$6
❑ 202	Little Bluebird/Toe Hold	1967	$12
❑ 0055	Love Bones/Mr. Nobody Is Somebody	1969	$8
❑ 235	Somebody's Sleeping in My Bed/Strange Thing	1967	$12
❑ 0114	Standing In for Jody/ Shackin' Up	1972	$6
❑ 0068	Steal Away/Friday Night	1970	$6
❑ 0142	Stop Doggin' Me/ Stop Teasin' Me	1972	$6
❑ 0023	Take Care of Your Homework/Hold On This Time	1969	$6
❑ 0033	Testify (I Wanna)/I Had a Fight with Love	1969	$8
❑ 0241	Try Me Tonight/Free	1975	$6
❑ 0193	We're Getting Careless with Our Love/Poor Make Believer	1974	$6
❑ 0009	Who's Making Love/I'm Trying	1968	$8

TAYLOR, KATE
COLUMBIA
Number	Title	Yr	NM
❑ 10787	It's Growin'/Slow and Steady	1978	$4
❑ 10596	It's In His Kiss (The Shoop Shoop Song)/Jason and Ida	1977	$4
❑ 11017	It's the Same Old Song/ Champagne and Wine	1979	$4

COTILLION
Number	Title	Yr	NM
❑ 44112	Handbags and Gladrags/ You Can Close Your Eyes	1971	$5
❑ 44124	Lo and Behold-Jesus Is Just Alright/Home Again	1971	$5

TAYLOR, KATHY
HIT
Number	Title	Yr	NM
❑ 86	I Can't Stay Mad at You/ Wonderful! Wonderful!	1963	$8

—B-side by Wayne Harris

Number	Title	Yr	NM
❑ 55	The End of the World/ Our Day Will Come	1963	$8

—B-side by Clara and the Cleftones

TAYLOR, KOKO
CHECKER
Number	Title	Yr	NM
❑ 1106	Don't Mess with the Messer/Whatever I Am You Made Me	1965	$20
❑ 1191	Fire/Insane Asylum	1968	$20
❑ 1148	Good Advice/Tell Me the Truth	1966	$20
❑ 1140	Good Advice/When I Think of My Baby	1966	$20
❑ 1174	(I Got) All You Need/ All Money Spent (On Feeling Good)	1967	$20
❑ 1092	I Got What It Takes/What Kind of Man Is This	1964	$20
❑ 1230	Separate or Integrate/I Don't Care	1968	$20
❑ 1135	Wang Dang Doodle/ Blues Heaven	1966	$20

U.S.A.
Number	Title	Yr	NM
❑ 745	Like Heaven to Me/ Honky Tonky	1963	$30

TAYLOR, LAURA
GOOD SOUNDS
Number	Title	Yr	NM
❑ 9506	All Through Me/Some Love	1979	$8
❑ 9505	Dancin' in My Feet (Theme from Disco Magic)/Lady Scorpio	1979	$15

TAYLOR, LEROY
BRUNSWICK
Number	Title	Yr	NM
❑ 55345	Oh Linda/Nobody Can Love You	1967	$70

COLPIX
Number	Title	Yr	NM
❑ 739	Dr. Fix-It/Time (Brings About a Change)	1964	$30

COLUMBIA
Number	Title	Yr	NM
❑ 4-42258	Dooley Walk/Hey, I Like It	1962	$30

SHRINE
Number	Title	Yr	NM
❑ 0101	Takin' My Time/I'll Understand	1965	$300

—As "Leroy Taylor and the Four Kays"

TAYLOR, LITTLE JOHNNY, AND TED TAYLOR
RONN
Number	Title	Yr	NM
❑ 89	Pretending Love/ Funky Ghetto	1976	$6
❑ 75	Walking the Floor/ Cry It Out Baby	1973	$6

TAYLOR, LITTLE JOHNNY
GALAXY
Number	Title	Yr	NM
❑ 764	Double or Nothing/ Sometimey Woman	1968	$8
❑ 756	Driving Wheel/Darling Believe in Me	1967	$8
❑ 729	First Class Love/ If You Love Me	1964	$10
❑ 735	For Your Precious Love/I've Never Had a Woman Like You Before	1965	$8
❑ 736	Help Yourself/ Somebody's Got to Pay	1965	$8
❑ 752	I Know You Hear Me Calling/ Big Blue Diamonds	1967	$8
❑ 745	My Love Is Real/ All I Want Is You	1966	$8
❑ 739	One More Chance/ Looking at the Future	1965	$8
❑ 722	Part Time Love/Somewhere Down the Line	1963	$30
❑ 743	Please Come Home For Christmas/Miracle Maker	1965	$8
❑ 725	Since I Found a New Love/ My Heart Is Filled with Pain	1963	$15
❑ 733	True Love/I Smell Trouble	1964	$10

ICHIBAN
Number	Title	Yr	NM
❑ 174	Christmas Is Here Again/I Enjoy You	1989	$6
❑ 169	Christmas Is Here Again/Ugly Man	1988	$6

RONN
Number	Title	Yr	NM
❑ 88	A Hard Head Makes a Sore Behind/The Future	1976	$6
❑ 66	As Long As I Don't See You/Strange Bed with a Bad Head	1972	$6
❑ 55	Everybody Knows About My Good Thing Pt. 1/Pt. 2	1971	$6
❑ 85	Found a New Love/Oh, How I Love My Baby	1975	$6
❑ 51	How Are You Fixed for Love/Keep On Keepin' On	1971	$6
❑ 48	How Can a Broke Man Survive/Make Love to Me Baby	1970	$6
❑ 83	I Don't Want It All/I Can't See Myself As a One-Woman Man	1974	$6
❑ 69	I'll Make It Worth Your While/ You're Not the Only One	1973	$6
❑ 59	It's My Fault Darling/There Is Something On Your Mind	1972	$6
❑ 43	Make Love to Me Baby/ Sweet Soul Woman	1970	$6
❑ 73	My Special Rose/A Thousand Miles Away	1973	$6
❑ 64	Open House at My House (Part 1)/Open House at My House (Part 2)	1972	$6
❑ 87	True Love/When Are You Coming Home	1975	$6

TAYLOR, LIVINGSTON
CAPRICORN
Number	Title	Yr	NM
❑ 8012	Carolina Day/Sit On Back	1971	$5
❑ 8025	Get Out of Bed/Mom, Dad	1971	$5
❑ 0045	I Can Dream of You/Loving Be My New Horizon	1974	$4
❑ 0032	Somewhere Over the Rainbow/Lady Tomorrow	1973	$4

CRITIQUE
Number	Title	Yr	NM
❑ 99255	City Lights/Louie	1989	$3

EPIC
Number	Title	Yr	NM
❑ 50894	First Time Love/Pajamas	1980	$4

Number	Title	Yr	NM
❑ 50667	I'll Come Running/No Thank You Skycap	1979	$4
❑ 50604	I Will Be in Love with You/How Much Your Sweet Love Means to Me	1978	$4

TAYLOR, MARY
CAPITOL

Number	Title	Yr	NM
❑ 5776	Don't Waste Your Time/We Fooled 'Em Again	1966	$8
❑ 5484	Finders Keepers/Before He Was Yours, He Was Mine	1965	$8
❑ 5379	He Believes Me/If You Think You Feel Lonesome	1965	$8
❑ 5107	He's Coming Home/Little Bobby Bear	1964	$12
❑ 5582	I'm Gonna Slip Around on You/Today Is Not the Day	1966	$8
❑ 5210	Please Don't Tell Them About Me/Johnny's Not the Only Boy	1964	$8

TAYLOR, MICK
Also see THE ROLLING STONES.
COLUMBIA

Number	Title	Yr	NM
❑ 3-11065	Leather Jacket/Show Blues	1979	$6

TAYLOR, R. DEAN
20TH CENTURY

Number	Title	Yr	NM
❑ 2510	Let's Talk It Over/Add Up the Score	1981	$4

AUDIO MASTER

Number	Title	Yr	NM
❑ 1	At the High School Dance/How Wrong Can You Be?	1960	$200

FARR

Number	Title	Yr	NM
❑ 001	We'll Show Them All/Magdalena	1976	$5

MALA

Number	Title	Yr	NM
❑ 444	I'll Remember/It's a Long Way to St. Louis	1962	$125

RARE EARTH

Number	Title	Yr	NM
❑ 5023	Ain't It a Sad Thing/Back Street	1970	$5
❑ 5023 [PS]	Ain't It a Sad Thing/Back Street	1970	$10
❑ 5030	Candy Apple Red/Woman Alive	1971	$5
❑ 5026	Gotta See Jane/Back Street	1971	$5
❑ 5013	Indiana Wants Me/Love's Your Name	1970	$6
❑ 5041	Taos New Mexico/Shadow	1972	$5

STRUMMER

Number	Title	Yr	NM
❑ 3748	Let's Talk It Over/(B-side unknown)	1982	$6

V.I.P.

Number	Title	Yr	NM
❑ 25042	Don't Fool Around/There's a Ghost in My House	1966	$30
❑ 25045	Gotta See Jane/Don't Fool Around	1967	$30
❑ 25027	Let's Go Somewhere/Poor Girl	1965	$30

TAYLOR, RENEE
FELSTED

Number	Title	Yr	NM
❑ 8620	His Pigs/I'm in Love with Jack	1961	$15

TAYLOR, ROGER
CAPITOL

Number	Title	Yr	NM
❑ B-5364	Man on Fire/Killing Time	1984	$4
❑ B-5364 [PS]	Man on Fire/Killing Time	1984	$5
❑ B-5420	Strange Frontier/I Cry for You (Love, Hope and Confusion)	1984	$4

ELEKTRA

Number	Title	Yr	NM
❑ 47151	Let's Get Crazy/Laugh Or Cry	1981	$5

TAYLOR, SHERRI
MOTOWN

Number	Title	Yr	NM
❑ 1004	Lover/That's Why I Love You So Much	1960	$50

— With Singin' Sammy Ward

TAYLOR, TED
ALARM

Number	Title	Yr	NM
❑ 110	Everybody's Stealing/Caught Up in a Good Woman's Love	1975	$8
❑ 117	Ghetto Disco/You Can Make It If You Try	1977	$8
❑ 114	Gonna Hate Myself/Stick By Me	1976	$8
❑ 2119	Paying for My Love Mistakes/Two Minute Warning	1977	$8
❑ 2124	Spanish Harlem/Paying for My Love Mistakes	1978	$8
❑ 112	Steal Away/Somebody's Gettin' It	1976	$8

Number	Title	Yr	NM
❑ 2123	Talk to Me/You Made Loving You Easy	1978	$8

APT

Number	Title	Yr	NM
❑ 25063	Little Things Mean a Lot/My Days and Nights	1962	$30

ATCO

Number	Title	Yr	NM
❑ 6481	Baby Come Back to Me/Feed the Flame	1967	$20
❑ 6388	Dancing Annie/Try Me Again	1965	$20
❑ 6434	Help the Bear/Thank You for Helping Me See the Light	1966	$20
❑ 6408	Long Distance Love/River's Invitation	1966	$10

DADE

Number	Title	Yr	NM
❑ 5000	I Lost the Best Thing I Ever Had/Darling If You Must Leave	1963	$50

DUKE

Number	Title	Yr	NM
❑ 304	Be Ever Wonderful/Since You're Mine	1959	$30
❑ 308	Count the Stars/Hold Me Tight	1959	$30

EBB

Number	Title	Yr	NM
❑ 113	Days Are Dark/Everywhere I Go	1957	$40
❑ 132	If I Don't See You Again/Keep Walking On	1958	$40

JEWEL

Number	Title	Yr	NM
❑ 748	Days Are Dark/Very Truly Yours	1965	$12

LAURIE

Number	Title	Yr	NM
❑ 3082	I Don't Want to Love You/Lovin' Hands	1961	$20

— As "Austin Taylor

Number	Title	Yr	NM
❑ 3095	I Love Being Loved by You/Together Forever	1961	$20

— As "Austin Taylor

Number	Title	Yr	NM
❑ 3067	Push Push/A Heart That's True	1960	$20

— As "Austin Taylor

MCA

Number	Title	Yr	NM
❑ 40977	Chase the World Away/Double My Money Bag	1978	$20

OKEH

Number	Title	Yr	NM
❑ 4-7171	Be Ever Wonderful/That's Life I Guess	1963	$30
❑ 4-7252	Big Wheel/No One But You	1966	$20
❑ 4-7240	Daddy's Baby/Mercy Have Pity	1966	$20
❑ 4-7206	Don't Deceive Me (Please Don't Go)/If It Wasn't for You	1964	$30
❑ 4-7154	Don't Lie/Pretending Love	1962	$30
❑ 4-7165	I'll Release You/Can't Take No More	1962	$20
❑ 4-7179	It Ain't Like That No More/I'll Make It Up to You	1963	$30
❑ 4-7222	(Love Is Like a) Ramblin' Rose/I'm So Satisfied	1965	$30
❑ 4-7190	So Hard/Need You Home	1964	$20
❑ 4-7214	So Long, Bye Bye/Love You, Yes I Do	1965	$30
❑ 4-7198	Somebody's Always Trying/Top of the World	1964	$70
❑ 4-7231	Stay Away from My Baby/Walking Out of Your Life	1965	$20
❑ 74	Break of Day/Fair Weather Woman	1973	$8
❑ 49	Can't Take No More/Singing Man	1971	$10
❑ 106	Cummin's Prison Farm/Houston Town	1984	$6
❑ 82	For All the Days in My Life/I've Got to Find Somebody New	1974	$8
❑ 25	Honey Lou/Without a Woman	1968	$12
❑ 63	Houston Town/I'm Just a Crumb in Your Breadbox	1972	$10
❑ 57	How Do You Walk Away from Fear/Only the Lonely Knows	1971	$10
❑ 52	How's Your Love Life Baby/(This Is a) Troubled World	1971	$10
❑ 37	I'm Lonely Tonight/If I Thought You Needed Me	1969	$10
❑ 46	It's a Funky Situation/I'm Glad You're Home	1970	$10
❑ 34	It's Too Late/The Road of Love	1969	$10
❑ 65	I Want to Be Part of You Girl/Going in the Hole	1972	$10
❑ 33	Long Ago/I'm Gonna Send You Back to Oklahoma	1969	$10
❑ 40	Loving Physician/I Feel a Chill	1970	$10
❑ 15	Miss You So/I'm Gonna Get Tough	1967	$10
❑ 21	Ollie Mae/I Need Your Love So Bad	1968	$10
❑ 77	She Loves to Do It As Well As You/Ready for the Heartbreak	1974	$8
❑ 44	Something Strange Is Goin' On in My House/Funky Thing	1970	$12
❑ 29	Strangest Feeling/You Got to Feel It	1969	$10

Number	Title	Yr	NM
❑ 72	What a Fool/Make Up for Lost Time	1973	$8

TOP RANK

Number	Title	Yr	NM
❑ 2076	Darling Take Me Back/Look Out	1960	$40
❑ 2011	I'm Saving My Love/Chanta-Lula	1959	$30
❑ 2048	I Need You So/Has My Love Grown Cold	1960	$30

TAYLOR, VERNON
DOT

Number	Title	Yr	NM
❑ 15632	I've Got the Blues/The Losing Game	1957	$125
❑ 15697	Satisfaction Guaranteed/Why Must You Leave Me	1958	$60

SUN

Number	Title	Yr	NM
❑ 310	Breeze/Today Is a Blue Day	1958	$30
❑ 325	Sweet and Easy to Love/Mystery Train	1959	$40

TAYLOR, VINCE
PALETTE

Number	Title	Yr	NM
❑ 5065	I'll Be Your Hero/Jet Black Machine	1960	$15
❑ 5084	Move Over Tiger/What Cha Gonna Do	1961	$15

TAYLOR, ZOLA
RPM

Number	Title	Yr	NM
❑ 405	Make Love to Me/Oh My Dear	1954	$300

TAZMEN, THE
ABC-PARAMOUNT

Number	Title	Yr	NM
❑ 9812	Easy Pickin'/The Chicken	1957	$20

TEA COMPANY, THE
SMASH

Number	Title	Yr	NM
❑ 2176	Come and Have Some Tea with Me/Flowers	1968	$20

TEACHER'S PET
CLONE

Number	Title	Yr	NM
❑ CL-008 [B]	Hooked On You/To Kill You	1978	$25

TEAM MATES, THE
ABC-PARAMOUNT

Number	Title	Yr	NM
❑ 10760	If Only I Had Known/You Must Pay	1965	$15
❑ 707	Once There Was a Time/Come On Baby	1962	$30

PAULA

Number	Title	Yr	NM
❑ 220	Most of All/Please Believe Me	1965	$40

PHILIPS

Number	Title	Yr	NM
❑ 40029	Once There Was a Time/Never Believed in Love	1962	$15

TEARDROPS, THE (1)
DORE

Number	Title	Yr	NM
❑ 679	Little Orphan Boy/(Instrumental)	1963	$15

TEARDROPS, THE (2)
DOT

Number	Title	Yr	NM
❑ 15669	Bridge of Love/Jellyfish	1957	$30

RENDEZVOUS

Number	Title	Yr	NM
❑ 102	Catch Me, I'm Falling Again/Sugar Baby	1958	$40

TEARDROPS, THE (3)
JOSIE

Number	Title	Yr	NM
❑ 771	My Heart/Ooh Baby	1954	$500
❑ 766	The Stars Are Out Tonight/Oh Stop It	1954	$300

PORT

Number	Title	Yr	NM
❑ 70019	The Stars Are Out Tonight/Oh Stop It	1960	$30

TEARDROPS, THE (4)
JOSIE

Number	Title	Yr	NM
❑ 862	Cry No More/You're My Hollywood Star	1959	$30
❑ 873	Daddy's Little Girl/Always You	1960	$30
❑ 856	We Won't Tell/Al Chiar Di Luna (Porto Fortuna)	1959	$30

TEARDROPS, THE (5)
KING

Number	Title	Yr	NM
❑ 5037	After School/Don't Be Afraid to Love	1957	$30
❑ 5004	My Inspiration/I Prayed for Love	1956	$30

Number	Title	Yr	NM

TEARDROPS, THE (6)
MUSICOR
| ❏ 1218 | I Will Love You Dear Forever/Bubblegummers | 1966 | $20 |
| ❏ 1139 | Tears Come Tumbling/You Won't Be There | 1965 | $20 |

SAXONY
❏ 1008	I'm Gonna Steal Your Boyfriend/Call Me and I'll Be Happy	1965	$30
❏ 1009	Tears Come Tumbling/You Won't Be There	1965	$30
❏ 1007	Tonight I'm Gonna Fall in Love Again/That's Why I'll Get By	1964	$100

TEARDROPS, THE (7)
SAMPSON
| ❏ 634 | Come Back to Me/Sweet Lovin' Daddy-O | 1952 | $400 |

TEARDROPS, THE (8)
LAURIE
| ❏ 3660 | Goodnight Elvis/Hey Gingerbread | 1977 | $8 |
| ❏ 3642 | Welcome Back Kotter/Champagne Lady | 1976 | $8 |

TEARS FOR FEARS
FONTANA
| ❏ 874710-7 | Sowing the Seeds of Love/Tears Roll Down | 1989 | $3 |
| ❏ 874710-7 [PS] | Sowing the Seeds of Love/Tears Roll Down | 1989 | $3 |

MERCURY
❏ 812677-7	Change/The Conflict	1983	$8
❏ 880659-7	Everybody Wants to Rule the World/Pharaohs	1985	$3
❏ PRO342-7 DJ [DJ]	Everybody Wants to Rule the World (same on both sides)	1985	$12
❏ -70 [DJ]	Head Over Heels (Live) (same on both sides)	1985	$12
❏ PRO392-7 DJ [DJ]	Head Over Heels (Live) (same on both sides)	1985	$12
❏ 880899-7	Head Over Heels/When in Love with a Blind Man	1985	$3
❏ 880899-7 [PS]	Head Over Heels/When in Love with a Blind Man	1985	$3
❏ 812213-7	Mad World/Ideas As Opiates	1983	$8
❏ 812213-7 [PS]	Mad World/Ideas As Opiates	1983	$8
❏ 884636-7	Mothers Talk/Sea Song	1986	$3
❏ 884636-7 [PS]	Mothers Talk/Sea Song	1986	$3
❏ 880294-7	Shout/The Big Chair	1985	$3
❏ 880294-7 [PS]	Shout/The Big Chair	1985	$4

TEASERS, THE
CHECKER
| ❏ 800 | I Was a Fool to Love You/How Could You Hurt One So | 1954 | $600 |
| ❏ 800 | I Was a Fool to Love You/How Could You Hurt One So | 1954 | $1200 |

—Red vinyl

TECHNICS, THE
CHEX
| ❏ 1012 | Because I Really Love You/A Man's Confusion | 1963 | $40 |
| ❏ 1010 | Has He Told You/Workout With a Pretty Girl | 1963 | $40 |

—As "Tony and the Technics

| ❏ 1013 | Hey Girl Don't Leave Me/I Met Her on the First of September | 1963 | $50 |

TECHNIQUES, THE (1)
ROULETTE
❏ 4030	Hey! Little Girl/In a Round-About Way	1957	$30
❏ 4097	The Wisest Man You Know/Moon Tan	1958	$30
❏ 4048	(Why Did I Ever) Let Her Go/Marindy	1958	$30

STARS
| ❏ 551 | Hey Little Girl/In a Round-About Way | 1957 | $50 |

TECHNIQUES, THE (2)
VENUS
| ❏ RK4M-8540/1 | Dream Theme/Autumn Rain | 1964 | $30 |

TECHNOTRONIC
SBK
| ❏ B-07311 | Pump Up the Jam/(Instrumental) | 1989 | $10 |

—As "Technotronic featuring Felly

| ❏ B-07311 [PS] | Pump Up the Jam/(Instrumental) | 1989 | $20 |

—Both the record and sleeve received limited distribution

TEDDY AND HIS PATCHES
CHANCE
❏ 669	Haight Ashbury/It Ain't Nothin'	1967	$125
❏ 100	Suzy Creamcheese/From Day to Day	1967	$200
❏ 668	Suzy Creamcheese/It Ain't Nothin'	1967	$200

TEDDY AND THE CONTINENTALS
PIK
| ❏ 235 | Tick Tick Tock/Everybody Pony | 1961 | $30 |

RAGO
| ❏ 201 | Tick Tick Tock/Wild Christening Party | 1962 | $30 |

—B-side by the Teen Kings

RICHIE
| ❏ 453 | Crying Over You/Crossfire With Me Baby | 1963 | $60 |
| ❏ 445 | Do You/Tighten Up | 1961 | $125 |

—With no mention of Roulette distribution on label

| ❏ 445 | Do You/Tighten Up | 1961 | $50 |

—With Roulette Records distribution mentioned on label

| ❏ 1001 | Tick Tick Tock/Everybody Pony | 1961 | $70 |

TEDDY AND THE FRAT GIRLS
7-Inch Extended Plays
FFD
| ❏ 0(# unknown) | Audio Suicide | 1980 | $35 |

—Label calls them "Sheer Smegma

| ❏ 0(# unknown) [PS] | Audio Suicide | 1980 | $35 |

—Original had a rubber-stamped plain sleeve

| ❏ 0(# unknown) [PS] | Audio Suicide | 1980 | $75 |

—Sleeve with "Teddy and the Frat Girls" on it, added later

TEDDY AND THE TWILIGHTS
SWAN
| ❏ 4126 | I'm Just Your Clown/Bimini Bimbo | 1962 | $30 |
| ❏ 4102 | Woman Is a man's Best Friend/Goodbye to Love | 1962 | $30 |

TEDDY BEARS, THE
DORE
| ❏ 503 | To Know Him, Is to Love Him/Don't You Worry My Little Pet | 1958 | $40 |
| ❏ 520 | Wonderful Loveable You/Till You'll Be Mine | 1959 | $30 |

IMPERIAL
| ❏ 5562 | Oh Why/I Don't Need You Anymore | 1959 | $40 |
| ❏ 5594 | Seven Lonely Days/Don't Go Away | 1959 | $40 |

TEDDY BOYS, THE
CAMEO
| ❏ 448 | Mona/Good Morning Blues | 1966 | $30 |
| ❏ 433 | Where Have All the Good Times Gone/La La | 1966 | $30 |

TEE, WILLIE
A.F.O.
| ❏ 307 | All for One/Always Accused | 1962 | $20 |
| ❏ 311 | Why Lie/I Found Out You Are My Cousin | 1963 | $20 |

ATLANTIC
❏ 2302	I Want Somebody/You Better Say Yes	1965	$10
❏ 2273	Teasin' You/Walkin' Up a One-Way Street	1965	$10
❏ 2287	Thank You John/Dedicated to You	1965	$10

CAPITOL
| ❏ 2369 | Walk Tall (Baby, That's What I Need)/I'm Only a Man | 1968 | $8 |

NOLA
| ❏ 708 | Teasin' You/Walkin' Up a One-Way Street | 1964 | $250 |

UNITED ARTISTS
| ❏ XW910 | I'd Give It to You/Look Out World | 1976 | $5 |

TEEGARDEN AND VAN WINKLE
PLUMM
| ❏ 68102 | God, Love, and Rock & Roll (We Believe)/Work Me Tomorrow | 1970 | $20 |

WESTBOUND
| ❏ 210 | Carry On/Ride Away with Me | 1972 | $5 |

❏ 171	Everything Is Going to Be All Right/You Do	1970	$5
❏ 170	God, Love and Rock & Roll/Work Me Tomorrow	1970	$5
❏ 170 [PS]	God, Love and Rock & Roll/Work Me Tomorrow	1970	$6
❏ 200	Passing Gas/Ride Away with Me	1971	$5
❏ 187	Stoned on the Love for Jesus/I Need You	1971	$5

TEEL, LEO
DECCA
| ❏ 9-46336 | Fertilizer/He's Gazing at Daisy Boots Now | 1951 | $30 |

TEEMATES, THE
AUDIO FIDELITY
| ❏ 104 | Dream On Little Girl/Moving Out | 1964 | $20 |

TEEN ANGELS, THE
SUN
| ❏ 388 | Ain't Gonna Let You (Break My Heart)/Tell Me My Love | 1964 | $40 |

TEEN CLEFS, THE
DICE
| ❏ 98/99 | Sputnik/Hiding My Tears with a Smile | 1959 | $200 |

TEEN IDLES
7-Inch Extended Plays
DISCHORD
| ❏ 1 | Minor Disturbance | 1980 | $40 |
| ❏ 1 [PS] | Minor Disturbance | 1980 | $50 |

—Heavy stock

| ❏ 1 [PS] | Minor Disturbance | 1980 | $40 |

—Thin paper stock. Both versions include poster and lyric insert.

TEEN-KINGS, THE
BEE
| ❏ 1114/5 | That's a Teen-Age Love/Tell Me If You Know | 1959 | $1500 |

—Legitimate original copies are on black vinyl

WILLETT
| ❏ 118 | Don't Just Stand There/My Greatest Wish | 1959 | $250 |

TEEN QUEENS, THE
ANTLER
❏ 4016	Donny (Part 1)/Donny (Part 2)	1960	$20
❏ 4017	I Hear Violins/Magoo Can See	1960	$20
❏ 4015	Politician/I'm a Fool	1959	$20
❏ 4014	There's Nothing on My Mind (Part 1)/There's Nothing on My Mind (Part 2)	1959	$20

KENT
| ❏ 359 | Eddie My Love/Just Goofed | 1961 | $15 |

RCA VICTOR
| ❏ 47-7206 | Dear Tommy/You Good Boy-You Get Cookie | 1958 | $20 |
| ❏ 47-7396 | Movie Star/First Crush | 1958 | $20 |

RPM
| ❏ 464 | Billy Boy/Until the Day I Die | 1956 | $30 |
| ❏ 453 | Eddie My Love/Just Goofed | 1956 | $40 |

—Black label

| ❏ 453 | Eddie My Love/Just Goofed | 1956 | $120 |

—Red label

❏ 500	I Miss You/Two Loves and Two Lives	1957	$30
❏ 480	My First Love/(B-side unknown)	1956	$30
❏ 460	So All Alone/Baby Mine	1956	$30

TEEN TONES, THE
DANDY DAN
| ❏ 2 | Darling I Love You/My Sweet | 1958 | $100 |

DECCA
| ❏ 30895 | Don't Call Me Baby, I'll Call You/Yes You May | 1959 | $40 |

SWAN
| ❏ 4040 | My Little Baby/Head Strong Baby | 1959 | $40 |

TRI-DISC
| ❏ 102 | I'm So Happy/Shoutin' Twist | 1961 | $20 |

WYNNE
| ❏ 107 | Faded Love/Gypsy Boogie | 1958 | $30 |

Number	Title	Yr	NM

TEENAGE JESUS AND THE JERKS
MIGRAINE/LUST UNLUST

CC-334	Baby Doll/Freud in Flop/Race Mixing	1979	$13
CC-334 [PS]	Baby Doll/Freud in Flop/Race Mixing	1979	$13
CC-333	Orphans/Less of Me	1978	$13
CC-333 [PS]	Orphans/Less of Me	1978	$13

TEENAGE MOONLIGHTERS
MARK

134	Sorry Sorry/I Want to Cry	1960	$2000

— VG 1000; VG+ 1500

TEENAGERS, THE
These are records by the original group without FRANKIE LYMON. Also see FRANKIE LYMON AND THE TEENAGERS.
END

1076	Can You Tell Me/A Little Wiser Now	1960	$50
1071	Crying/Tonight's the Night	1960	$70

GEE

1046	Flip Flop/Everything to Me	1957	$40

ROULETTE

4086	My Broken Heart/ Momma Wanna Rock	1958	$100

TEENBEATS, THE
TEENBEAT

0(no cat #)	Surfbound/Mr. Moto	1963	$100

TEENETTES, THE
BRUNSWICK

55125	I Want a Boy with a Hi-Fi Supersonic Stereophonic Bloop Bleep/ From the Word Go	1959	$30

JOSIE

830	My Lucky Star/Too Young to Fall in Love	1958	$70

TELEVISION
Also see TOM VERLAINE.
ELEKTRA

45516	Ain't That Nothin'/Glory	1978	$5
45516 [DJ]	Ain't That Nothin' (mono/stereo)	1978	$30

— Radically different recording than on LP; unknown whether this also appears on stock copy

45516 [DJ]	Ain't That Nothin' (mono/stereo)	1978	$30

— Radically different recording than on LP; unknown whether this also appears on stock copy

ORK

81975	Little Johnny Jewel Pt. 1/ Little Johnny Jewel Pt. 2	1975	$60

TELSTARS, THE
IMPERIAL

5903	Continental Mash/ Stomp Happy	1962	$30

TEEN

510	Continental Mash/ Stomp Happy	1962	$50
513	Pow Wow/Lovina	1963	$40
516	Topless/Spaghetti Strap	1964	$40
517	Tough George/'Cause I Really Do	1964	$40

TEMPLE, BOB
KING

4958	Come Back, Come Back/ Vam Vam Vamoose	1956	$40

TEMPLE, SEBASTIAN
CAPITOL

5313	A Great Day in Bethlehem/A Perfect Family	1964	$8

TEMPO-TONES, THE
ACME

718	Come Into My Heart/ Somewhere There Is Sunshine	1957	$500
713	Get Yourself Another Fool/Ride Along	1957	$200
715	In My Dreams/My Boy Sleep Pete	1957	$500
722	The Day I Met You/ Wishing All the Time	1957	$400

TEMPO, NINO, AND APRIL STEVENS
A&M

1394	Love Story/Hoochy Coochy -- Wing Dang Doo	1972	$4

Number	Title	Yr	NM
1443	Put It Where You Want It/I Can't Get Over You Baby	1973	$4

ATCO

6410	Bye Bye Blues/King Kong	1966	$8
6273	Deep Purple/I've Been Carrying a Torch for You So Long That I Burned a Great Big Hole in My Heart	1963	$15
6391	Hey Baby/The Poison of Your Kisses	1965	$8
6375	I Love How You Love Me/Tears of Sorrow	1965	$8
6248	Indian Love Call/Paradise	1962	$10
6306	I Surrender Dear/Who	1964	$8
6314	Melancholy Baby/Ooh La La	1964	$8
6325	Our Love/Honeywell Rose	1964	$8
6897	She's My Baby/Tomorrow Is Soon a Memory	1972	$6
6286	Stardust/I-45	1964	$8
6224	Sweet and Lovely/True Love	1962	$10
6350	Swing Me/Tomorrow Is Soon a Memory	1965	$8
6294	Tea for Two/I'm Confessin' (That I Love You)	1964	$8
6368	That's My Desire/King Kong	1965	$8
6337	These Arms of Mine/The Coldest Night of the Year	1965	$8
6360	Think of You/I'm Sweet on You	1965	$8
6263	(We'll Always Be) Together/ Baby Weemus	1963	$10
6281	Whispering/Tweedlee Dee	1963	$10

BELL

769	Did I or Didn't I/Yesterday I Heard the Rain	1969	$8
823	Seas of Love-Dock of the Bay/Twilight	1969	$8

CHELSEA

3052	What Kind of Fool Am I/ (B-side unknown)	1976	$4

MGM

13825	Falling in Love Again/ Wanting You	1967	$8
14266	How About Me/Makin' Love to Rainbow Colors	1971	$6

UNITED ARTISTS

272	Ooeah (That's What You Do to Me)/High School Sweetheart	1960	$10

WHITE WHALE

236	All Strung Out/I Can't Go On Living Baby Without You	1966	$8
252	I Can't Go On Living Baby Without You/Little Child	1967	$8
252	I Can't Go On Living Without You Baby/Little Child	1967	$15

— Some copies have the above erroneous A-side title

268	Let It Be Me/Words of Love	1968	$8
271	Ooh Poo Pa Doo/ Let It Be Me	1968	$8
246	Wings of Love/ My Old Flame	1967	$8

TEMPO, NINO
A&M

1625	Gettin' Off/Don't Stop Now	1974	$10
1532	High on the Music/Come See Me 'Round Midnight	1974	$12
2131	Hooked on Young Stuff/ Ronan's Road	1979	$4
1461	Sister James/Clair De Lune (In Jazz)	1973	$70

RCA VICTOR

47-7424	15 Girl Friends/ Loonie 'Bout Junie	1958	$15
47-7647	Ding-a-Ling/When You Were Sweet Sixteen	1959	$15

TOWER

369	Boys Town/Boys Town (Sing Along)	1967	$6

UNITED ARTISTS

256	What Is Love to a Teenager/ Lipstick on Your Lips	1960	$10

TEMPOS, THE
ASCOT

2173	I Wish It Were Summer/ My Barbara Ann	1965	$30
2167	When You Loved Me/ My Barbara Ann	1965	$30

CANTERBURY

504	Here I Come (Countdown) Part 1/Here I Come (Countdown) Part 2	1967	$20

CLIMAX

102	See You in September/ Bless You My Love	1959	$30
105	The Crossroads of Love/ Whatever Happens	1959	$30

FAIRMOUNT

611	Oh Play That Thing/ Monkey Doo	1963	$15

Number	Title	Yr	NM

HI-Q

100	It's Tough/Sham-Rock	1959	$50

KAPP

213	I Got a Job/Strollin' with My Baby	1958	$30
199	Prettiest Girl in School/ Never You Mind	1957	$30

MONTEL

955	I Gotta Make a Move/ It Was You	1966	$20

PARIS

550	Look Homeward, Angel/ Under Ten Flags	1960	$30

RHYTHM

121	Promise Me/Never Let Me Go	1958	$500

RILEY'S

8781	Don't Leave Me/I Need You	1966	$40

U.S.A.

810	Why Don't You Write Me/A Thief in the Night	1965	$30

TEMPREES
EPIC

50192	I Found Love on a Disco Floor/There Ain't a Dream Been Dreamed	1976	$5

WE PRODUCE

1810	A Thousand Miles Away/ Chalk It Up to Experience	1973	$8
1808	Dedicated to the One I Love/I Love You, You Love Me	1972	$8
1807	Explain It to Her Mama/ Love Can Be So Wonderful	1972	$8
1803	(Girl) I Love You/I Love You, You Love Me	1971	$8
1801	I'm for You, You for Me/ Rules and Regulations	1971	$8
1811	Love's Maze/Wrap Me in Love	1973	$8
1805	My Baby Love/If I Could Say What's On My Mind	1972	$8

TEMPTATIONS, THE
The famous Detroit/Motown male vocal group.
Also see EDDIE KENDRICKS; DAVID RUFFIN; THE SUPREMES AND THE TEMPTATIONS.

ATLANTIC

3517	Bare Back/I See My Child	1978	$4
3538	Ever Ready Love/ Touch Me Again	1978	$4
3436	In a Lifetime/I Could Never Stop Loving You	1977	$4
3567	Mystic Woman/I Just Don't Know How to Let You Go	1979	$4
3461	Think for Yourself/ Let's Live in Place	1978	$4

GORDY

7208	Aiming at Your Heart/ Life of a Cowboy	1981	$50
7054	Ain't Too Proud to Beg/ You'll Lose a Precious Love	1966	$20
7061	All I Need/Sorry Is a Sorry Word	1967	$10
7099	Ball of Confusion (That's What the World Is Today)/It's Summer	1970	$6
7099 [PS]	Ball of Confusion (That's What the World Is Today)/It's Summer	1970	$30
7055	Beauty Is Only Skin Deep/ You're Not an Ordinary Girl	1966	$20
7055 [PS]	Beauty Is Only Skin Deep/ You're Not an Ordinary Girl	1966	$50
7081	Cloud Nine/Why Did She Have to Leave Me	1968	$8
7086	Don't Let the Joneses Get You Down/Since I've Lost You	1969	$8
1818	Do You Really Love Your Baby/I'll Keep My Light in My Window	1985	$4
7001	Dream Come True/ Isn't She Pretty	1962	$50
7049	Get Ready/Fading Away	1966	$20
7035	Girl (Why You Wanna Make Me Blue)/Baby, Baby I Need You	1964	$20
7144	Glasshouse/The Prophet	1975	$6
7138	Happy People/(Instrumental)	1974	$6
7135	Heavenly/Zoom	1974	$6
7131	Hey Girl (I Like Your Style)/Ma	1973	$6
1789	How Can You Say That It's Over/I'll Keep My Light in My Window	1985	$4
7093	I Can't Get Next to You/ Running Away (Ain't Gonna Help You)	1969	$8
7072	I Could Never Love Another (After Loving You)/Gonna Give Her All the Love I've Got	1968	$10
7057	(I Know) I'm Losing You/I Couldn't Cry If I Wanted To	1966	$20

Number	Title	Yr	NM
❏ 7032	I'll Be in Trouble/The Girl's Alright with Me	1964	$20
❏ 7040	It's Growing/What Love Has Joined Together	1965	$20
❏ 7109	It's Summer/I'm the Exception to the Rule	1971	$6
❏ 7015	I Want a Love I Can See/The Further You Look, The Less You See	1963	$30
❏ 7068	I Wish It Would Rain/I Truly, Truly Believe	1967	$10
❏ 1856	Lady Soul/Put Us Together Again	1986	$4
❏ 7152	Let Me Count the Ways (I Love You)/Who Are You (And What Are You Doing the Rest of Your Life)	1976	$6
❏ 7133	Let Your Hair Down/Ain't No Justice	1973	$6
❏ 7065	(Loneliness Made Me Realize) It's You That I Need/Don't Send Me Away	1967	$10
❏ 1666	Love on My Mind Tonight/Bring Your Body Here	1983	$4
❏ 1683	Made in America/Surface Thrills	1983	$4
❏ 7126	Masterpiece/(Instrumental)	1973	$6
❏ 7020	May I Have This Dance?/Farewell, My Love	1963	$30
❏ 1707	Miss Busy Body (Get Your Body Busy)/(Instrumental)	1983	$4
❏ 1631	More on the Inside/Money's Hard to Get	1982	$4
❏ 7119	Mother Nature/Funky Music Sho Nuff Turns Me On	1972	$6
❏ 7047	My Baby/Don't Look Back	1965	$20
❏ 7038	My Girl/Nobody But My Baby	1965	$20
❏ 7038 [PS]	My Girl/Nobody But My Baby	1965	$120
❏ 1781	My Love Is True (Truly for You)/Set Your Love Right	1985	$4
❏ 7213	Oh What a Night/Isn't the Night Fantastic	1981	$4
❏ 7121	Papa Was a Rollin' Stone/(Instrumental)	1972	$6
❏ 7010	Paradise/Slow Down Heart	1962	$40
❏ 7129	Plastic Man/Hurry Tomorrow	1973	$6
❏ 7074	Please Return Your Love to Me/How Can I Forget	1968	$10
❏ 7183	Power/Power (Part 2)	1980	$4
❏ 7183 [DJ]	Power (same on both sides)	1980	$30
—Promo only on red vinyl			
❏ 7096	Psychedelic Shack/That's the Way Love Is	1970	$6
❏ 1720	Sail Away/Isn't the Night Fantastic	1984	$4
❏ 7142	Shakey Ground/I'm a Bachelor	1975	$6
❏ 1654	Silent Night/Everything for Christmas	1982	$6
❏ 1713	Silent Night/Everything for Christmas	1983	$5
❏ 7082	Silent Night/Rudolph, the Red-Nosed Reindeer	1968	$15
❏ 7043	Since I Lost My Baby/You've Got to Earn It	1965	$20
❏ 1881	Someone/Love Me Right	1987	$4
❏ 1616	Standing on the Top-Part 1/Part 2	1982	$4
—With Rick James			
❏ 7188	Struck by Lightning Twice/I'm Coming Home	1980	$4
❏ 7111	Superstar (Remember How You Got Where You Are)/Gonna Keep On Tryin' Till I Win Your Love	1971	$6
❏ 7115	Take a Look Around/Smooth Sailing (From Now On)	1972	$6
❏ 7028	The Way You Do the Things You Do/Just Let Me Know	1964	$20
❏ 1871	To Be Continued/You're the One	1986	$4
❏ 1871 [PS]	To Be Continued/You're the One	1986	$6
❏ 1834	Touch Me/Set Your Love Right	1986	$4
❏ 1765	Treat Her Like a Lady/Isn't the Night Fantastic	1984	$4

MIRACLE

Number	Title	Yr	NM
❏ 12	Check Yourself/Your Wonderful Love	1961	$125
❏ 5	Oh, Mother of Mine/Romance Without Finance	1961	$125

MOTOWN

Number	Title	Yr	NM
❏ 1837	A Fine Mess/Wishful Thinking	1986	$4
❏ 1837 [PS]	A Fine Mess/Wishful Thinking	1986	$6
❏ 1974	All I Want from You/(Instrumental)	1989	$3
❏ 1933	Do You Wanna Go with Me/Put Your Foot Down	1988	$3
❏ 1908	I Wonder Who She's Seeing Now/Girls (They Like It)	1987	$3
❏ 1908 [PS]	I Wonder Who She's Seeing Now/Girls (They Like It)	1987	$4
❏ 1920	Look What You Started/More Love, Your Love	1987	$3
❏ 2004	Special/O.A.O. Lover	1989	$4
❏ 1501	Take Me Away/There's More Where That Came From	1980	$4

MOTOWN YESTERYEAR

Number	Title	Yr	NM
❏ Y-690F	Silent Night/Give Love at Christmas	1985	$4

TOPPS/MOTOWN

Number	Title	Yr	NM
❏ 4	My Girl	1967	$80
—Cardboard record			
❏ 13	The Way You Do the Things You Do	1967	$80
—Cardboard record			

7-Inch Extended Plays

GORDY

Number	Title	Yr	NM
❏ G-60914	My Baby/Since I Lost My Baby/Girl (Why You Wanna Make Me So Blue)//The Girl's Alright with Me/Just Another Lonely Night/Don't Look Back	1966	$60
—Stereo jukebox issue; small hole, plays at 33 1/3 rpm			
❏ G-60914 [PS]	The Temptin' Temptations	1966	$60

TEMPTATIONS, THE (2)

GOLDISC

Number	Title	Yr	NM
❏ 3001	Barbara/Someday	1960	$40
—All-black label			
❏ 3001	Barbara/Someday	1960	$30
—Multicolor (black, red, gold) label			
❏ 3007	Letter of Devotion/Fickle Little Girl	1960	$30

TEMPTATIONS, THE (3)

KING

Number	Title	Yr	NM
❏ 5118	Standing Alone/Roaches Rock	1958	$300

TEMPTATIONS, THE (4)

PARKWAY

Number	Title	Yr	NM
❏ 803	Temptations/Birds N' Bees	1959	$40

TEMPTATIONS, THE (5)

P&L

Number	Title	Yr	NM
❏ 1001	Blue Surf/Egyptian Surf	1963	$70

TEMPTATIONS, THE (6)

SAVOY

Number	Title	Yr	NM
❏ 1550	I Love You/Don't You Know	1958	$30
❏ 1532	Mister Juke Box/Mad at Love	1958	$30

TEMPTONES, THE

ARCTIC

Number	Title	Yr	NM
❏ 130	Girl, I Love You/Good-Bye	1967	$50
❏ 136	Say These Words of Love/This Could Be the Start of Something Good	1967	$50

TEN BROKEN HEARTS

DIAMOND

Number	Title	Yr	NM
❏ 123	Ten Lonely Guys/Shining Star	1962	$50

10CC

MERCURY

Number	Title	Yr	NM
❏ 73725	Art for Art's Sake/Get It While You Can	1975	$5
❏ 73725 [PS]	Art for Art's Sake/Get It While You Can	1975	$8
❏ 73943	Good Morning Judge/I'm So Laid Back I'm Laid Out	1977	$5
❏ 73779	I'm Mandy Fly Me/How Dare You	1976	$5
❏ 73678	I'm Not in Love/Channel Swimmer	1975	$5
❏ 73917	People in Love/Don't Squeeze Me Like Toothpaste	1977	$5
❏ 73875	The Things We Do for Love/Hot to Trot	1976	$5

POLYDOR

Number	Title	Yr	NM
❏ 14511	Dreadlock Holiday/Nothing Can Move Me	1978	$5
❏ 14528	For You and I/Take These Chains	1978	$5

UK

Number	Title	Yr	NM
❏ 49005	Donna/Hot Sun Rock	1972	$6
❏ 49019	Headline Hustler/Speed Kills	1973	$6
❏ 49023	The Wall Street Shuffle/Gismo My Way	1974	$6

WARNER BROS.

Number	Title	Yr	NM
❏ 49266	It Doesn't Matter Anymore/Strange Lover	1980	$5
❏ 29973	Power of Love/Action Man in Motown Suit	1982	$5

10,000 MANIACS

ELEKTRA

Number	Title	Yr	NM
❏ 69439	Don't Talk/City of Angels	1987	$4
❏ 69439 [PS]	Don't Talk/City of Angels	1987	$4
❏ 69279	Eat for Two/The Big Parade	1989	$5
❏ 69418	Like the Weather/A Campfire Song	1988	$4
❏ 69418 [PS]	Like the Weather/A Campfire Song	1988	$4
❏ 69457	Peace Train/Painted Desert	1987	$4
❏ 69457 [PS]	Peace Train/Painted Desert	1987	$4
❏ 69298	Trouble Me/The Lion's Share	1989	$4
❏ 69298 [PS]	Trouble Me/The Lion's Share	1989	$4
❏ 69388	What's the Matter Here?/Cherry Tree	1988	$4
❏ 69388 [PS]	What's the Matter Here?/Cherry Tree	1988	$4

TEN WHEEL DRIVE
Featuring Genya Ravan.

CAPITOL

Number	Title	Yr	NM
❏ 3700	Monsoon Rain/Close Up the Cheese	1973	$5

POLYDOR

Number	Title	Yr	NM
❏ 14052	Don't Blame Me/20 Miles from Home	1971	$5
❏ 14024	Eye of the Needle/I Am a Want Ad	1970	$5
❏ 14037	Morning Much Better/Stay with Me	1970	$5
❏ 14015	Tightrope/Lapidary	1969	$5

TEN YEARS AFTER
Also see ALVIN LEE.

COLUMBIA

Number	Title	Yr	NM
❏ 45530	Baby Won't You Let Me Rock 'N' Roll You/Once There Was a Time	1972	$5
❏ 45457	I'd Love to Change the World/Let the Sky Fall	1971	$5
❏ 45915	I'm Going Home/You Give Me Loving	1973	$5
❏ 46061	It's Getting Harder/I Wanted to Boogie	1974	$5
❏ 45787	Tomorrow, I'll Be Out of Town/Convention Prevention	1973	$5

DERAM

Number	Title	Yr	NM
❏ 85035	Hear Me Calling/I'm Going Home	1968	$8
❏ 7529	If You Should Love Me/Love Like a Man	1970	$8
❏ 85027	Portable People/The Sounds	1968	$8

TENDER SLIM

GREY CLIFF

Number	Title	Yr	NM
❏ 723	Teenage Hayride/Hey Joe!	1959	$20

HERALD

Number	Title	Yr	NM
❏ 571	Don't Cut Out on Me/I'm Checkin' Up	1962	$20

TENDER TONES, THE

DUCKY

Number	Title	Yr	NM
❏ 713	I Love You So/Just for a Little While	1959	$800

TENDERFOOTS, THE

FEDERAL

Number	Title	Yr	NM
❏ 12219	My Confession/Save Me Some Kisses	1955	$70
❏ 12228	Sindy/Sugar Ways	1955	$120
❏ 12225	Those Golden Bells/I'm Yours Anyhow	1955	$100

TENNESSEE DRIFTERS, THE

DOT

Number	Title	Yr	NM
❏ 1166	Boogie Woogie Baby/Drive Those Blues Away	1953	$40
❏ 1187	Corrine, Corrina/Somebody Loves You	1954	$40

TENNESSEE EXPRESS

RCA

Number	Title	Yr	NM
❏ PB-12277	Big Like a River/Now	1981	$4
❏ PB-13526	Cotton Fields/Good for Nothing	1983	$4
❏ JK-13526 [DJ]	Cotton Fields (same on both sides)	1983	$12
—Promo only on red vinyl			
❏ PB-13423	How Long Will It Take/Lead Me Into Love	1983	$4
❏ JK-13423 [DJ]	How Long Will It Take (Long Version 2:23)/(Short Version 1:52)	1983	$10
—Promo only on yellow vinyl			
❏ PB-12362	Little Things/How Much I Love You	1981	$4
❏ PB-13265	Operator/Let Me In and Let Me Love You	1982	$4
❏ PB-13078	The Arms of a Stranger/Someone Just Like You	1982	$4

Number	Title	Yr	NM
TERMITES, THE			
BEE			
❏ 1825	Give Me Your Heart/ Carrie Lou	1964	$60
TERRACETONES, THE			
APT			
❏ 25016	Words of Wisdom/ Ride of Paul Revere	1958	$125
TERRELL, ERNIE			
ARGO			
❏ 5511	Dear Abbie/I Can't Wait	1965	$15
TERRELL, TAMMI			
MOTOWN			
❏ 1095	Come On and See Me/ Baby Don'tcha Worry	1966	$10
❏ 1086	I Can't Believe You Love Me/ Hold Me Oh My Darling	1965	$10
❏ 1138	This Old Heart of Mine (Is Weak for You)/Just Too Much to Hope For	1968	$10
❏ 1115	What a Good Man He Is/There Are Things	1967	$10
TERRI AND THE KITTENS			
IMPERIAL			
❏ 5728	Wedding Bells/You Cheated	1961	$30
TERRI AND THE VELVETEENS			
KERWOOD			
❏ 711	Bells of Love/You've Broken My Heart	1962	$50
TERRI-TONES, THE			
CORTLAND			
❏ 105	Go/The Sinner	1962	$60
REGENCY			
❏ 929	Go/The Sinner	1962	$40
TERRY, AL			
FEATURE			
❏ 1061	I Wonder If I Can Lose the Blues This Way/Walking and Crying with the Blues	1953	$60
❏ 1075	Say a Prayer for Me/I Nearly Made a Fool of My Heart	1953	$60
❏ 1079	Will Christmas Be a Happy Day for Me/Santa Claus Is On His Way	1953	$60
HICKORY			
❏ 1056	Am I Seeing Things/ Roughneck Blues	1956	$40
❏ 1071	Coconut Girl/Bring Me Some Rain	1957	$40
❏ 1045	Follow Me/Lesson of Love	1956	$40
❏ 1029	Gone Again/No No John	1955	$40
❏ 1037	Goodbye Mr. Sunshine/I Love Her So	1955	$40
❏ 1075	Good Deal, Lucille/ Because I'm Yours	1958	$40
❏ 1003	Good Deal, Lucille/ Say a Prayer for Me	1954	$50
❏ 1017	Hey Whatta Y'Say/Let's Postpone Our Wedding	1954	$50
❏ 1012	House of Glass/Show Me That You Love Me	1954	$40
❏ 1082	I'm Not the Girl/ It's Just As Well	1958	$40
— With Wilma Lee (Cooper)			
❏ 1093	It's Better Late Than Never/Then You're Living Just Like Me	1958	$40
❏ 1066	It's What You Are to Me/Last Date	1957	$40
❏ 1061	Money/If I Win, I Win	1957	$40
— B-side by Rusty & Doug (Kershaw)			
❏ 1088	My Baby Knows/ Your Sweet Lies	1958	$40
❏ 1022	The Wall Around My Heart/Hate Me Not	1955	$40
❏ 1111	Watch Dog/Passing the Blues Around	1960	$30
TERRY AND THE MACS			
ABC-PARAMOUNT			
❏ 9668	Baby-O-Mine/Love Is a Beautiful Thing	1956	$30
❏ 9753	Please Don't Tease/ The Mystery of Love	1956	$30
TERRY AND THE PIRATES			
CHESS			
❏ 1696	Talk About the Girl/ What Did He Say	1958	$50

Number	Title	Yr	NM
TERRY, DOSSIE			
KING			
❏ 5890	Thunderbird/Be-Bop Wino	1964	$20
— B-side by the Lamplighters			
❏ 5072	Thunderbird/I Got a Watch Dog	1957	$60
RCA VICTOR			
❏ 47-4474	Didn't Satisfy You/24 Years	1952	$70
❏ 47-4864	Lost My Head/ Sad, Sad Affair	1952	$70
❏ 47-4648	When I Hit the Number/ My Love Is Gone	1952	$70
TERRY, GENE			
GOLDBAND			
❏ 1088	Cinderella, Cinderella/Guy with a Million Dreams	1959	$40
❏ 1066	Cindy Lou/Teardrops in My Eyes	1958	$120
SAVOY			
❏ 1559	This Should Go On Forever/Fine, Fine, Fine	1959	$30
TERRY, GORDON			
CADENCE			
❏ 1343	If You Don't Know It/I Lost Her to Somebody New	1958	$30
❏ 1317	Orange Blossom Special/ Black Mountain Rag	1957	$30
❏ 1316	Service with a Smile/ Johnson's Old Gray Mule	1957	$30
❏ 1334	Wild Honey/Run Little Joey	1957	$30
CHART			
❏ 1030	Baby Gets All Her Lovin' from Me/That's What Tears Me Up	1968	$12
❏ 5005	Charlie's Pride/Vision of Blindness	1969	$8
❏ 1014	Easy Way Out/Togetherness	1967	$12
❏ 1049	Holding Trouble/A Little Bit	1968	$12
❏ 5028	The Ballad of Biggersville/ Day of the Gun	1969	$8
EPIC			
❏ 5-9803	Almost Alone/My Teardrops Get Bigger Every Day	1965	$10
❏ 5-9855	My Blues Are Turning Gray/Whipping Post	1965	$10
LIBERTY			
❏ 55533	I Wish I'd Said That/ In a Moment	1963	$15
❏ 55558	Most of All/We've Got a Lot in Common	1963	$15
❏ 55630	Sitting Just One Car from You/Almost Gone	1963	$15
❏ 55500	Wild Honey/For Old Times' Sake	1962	$15
PLANTATION			
❏ 156	Disco Mule/Tennessee Waltz	1977	$5
❏ 146	Orange Blossom Special/ Smoking Violin	1977	$5
RCA VICTOR			
❏ 47-7632	A Lotta Lotta Woman/ Lonely Road	1959	$50
❏ 47-7875	And Then I Heard the Bad News/I Had a Talk with Me	1961	$20
❏ 47-7788	Gonna Go Down to the River/When They Ring Those Wedding Bells	1960	$20
❏ 47-7428	It Ain't Right/The Saddest Day	1958	$30
❏ 47-7989	Long Black Limousine/ Wild Desire	1962	$20
❏ 47-7741	Trouble on the Turnpike/ Almost Alone	1960	$20
TERRY, LARRY			
TESTA			
❏ 006	Hep Cat/Why Did She Go	1960	$1200
TERRY, NAT			
IMPERIAL			
❏ 5150	Take It Easy/I Don't Know Why	1951	$125
TERRY, SONNY			
CAPITOL			
❏ F931	Telephone Blues/Dirty Mistreater Don't You Know	1950	$120
CHESS			
❏ 1860	Dangerous Woman/ Hootenanny Blues	1963	$30
CHOICE			
❏ 15	Hootin'/Dupre	1961	$30
GOTHAM			
❏ 517	Baby Let's Have Some Fun/Four O'Clock Blues	1951	$50
❏ 518	Harmonica Rhumba/ Lonesome Room	1951	$50

Number	Title	Yr	NM
GRAMERCY			
❏ 1004	Hootin' Blues/ (B-side unknown)	1952	$60
—Black vinyl			
❏ 1004	Hootin' Blues/ (B-side unknown)	1952	$125
—Colored vinyl			
GROOVE			
❏ 015	Lost Jawbone/Louise	1954	$40
HARLEM			
❏ 2327	Dangerous Woman/I Love You Baby	1954	$300
RCA VICTOR			
❏ 47-5492	Hootin' and Jumpin'/ Hooray, Hooray	1953	$125
❏ 47-5577	Sonny Is Drinking/I'm Gonna Rock My Wig	1954	$125
RED ROBIN			
❏ 110	Harmonica Hop/Doggin' My Heart Around	1952	$300
TEX AND THE CHEX			
20TH FOX			
❏ 411	Beach Party/Now (Love Me)	1963	$40
ATLANTIC			
❏ 2116	I Do Love You/My Love	1961	$70
NEWTOWN			
❏ 5010	Watching Willie Wobble/Be on the Lookout for My Girl	1963	$30
TEX, JOE			
ACE			
❏ 674	Boys Will Be Boys/ Baby You're Right	1963	$20
❏ 591	Boys Will Be Boys/ Grannie Stole the Show	1960	$50
❏ 559	Charlie Brown Got Expelled/ Blessed Are These Tears	1959	$70
❏ 544	Cut It Out/Just for You and Me	1958	$70
❏ 572	Don't Hold It Against Me/Yum, Yum, Yum	1959	$70
❏ 550	Mother's Advice/You Little Baby Face Thing	1958	$100
ANNA			
❏ 1119	All I Could Do Was Cry (Part 1)/All I Could Do Was Cry (Part 2)	1960	$50
❏ 1128	Baby, You're Right/ Ain't It a Mess	1961	$50
❏ 1124	I'll Never Break Your Heart (Part 1)/I'll Never Break Your Heart (Part 2)	1960	$50
ATLANTIC			
❏ 2874	I'll Never Fall in Love Again (Part 1)/I'll Never Fall in Love Again (Part 2)	1972	$6
CHECKER			
❏ 1104	Baby, You're Right/All I Could Do Was Cry (Part 2)	1965	$15
DIAL			
❏ 1021	All the Heaven a Man Really Needs/Let's Go Somewhere and Talk	1973	$6
❏ 4022	A Sweet Woman Like You/Close the Door	1965	$10
❏ 4006	A Woman Can Change a Man/Don't Let Your Left Hand Know	1965	$10
❏ 4061	A Woman's Hands/ See See Rider	1967	$8
❏ 1156	Baby, It's Rainin'/ Have You Ever	1975	$6
❏ 1001	Bad Feet/I Know Him	1971	$6
❏ 4090	Buying a Book/ Chicken Crazy	1969	$8
❏ 4079	Chocolate Cherry/ Betwixt and Between	1968	$8
❏ 2802	Discomania/Fat People	1979	$5
❏ 4096	Everything Happens on Time/You're Right, Ray Charles	1970	$8
❏ 1008	Give the Baby Anything the Baby Wants/Takin' a Chance	1971	$6
❏ 4001	Hold What You've Got/ Fresh Out of Tears	1964	$20
❏ 4033	I Believe I'm Gonna Make It/Better Believe It, Baby	1966	$10
❏ 4095	I Can't See You No More (When Johnny Comes Marching Home Again)/Sure Is Good	1969	$8
❏ 3020	I'd Rather Have You/ Old Time Lover	1964	$15
❏ 1010	I Gotcha/A Mother's Prayer	1972	$6
❏ 3023	I Had a Good Thing But I Left (Part 1)/I Had a Good Thing But I Left (Part 2)	1964	$15
❏ 3009	I Let Her Get Away/ The Peck	1963	$15
❏ 4068	I'll Make Every Day Christmas (For My Woman)/Don't Give Up	1967	$15

Number	Title	Yr	NM
❏ 4076	I'll Never Do You Wrong/Wooden Spoon	1968	$8
❏ 4098	I'll Never Fall in Love Again/The Only Way I Know to Love You	1970	$8
❏ 1155	I'm Goin' Back Again/My Body Wants You	1975	$6
❏ 4045	I've Got to Do a Little Bit Better/What in the World	1966	$10
❏ 3016	I Wanna Be Free/Blood's Thicker Than Water	1963	$200
❏ 4016	I Want To (Do Everything For You)/Funny Bone	1965	$10
❏ 3019	Looking for My Pig/Say Thank You	1964	$15
❏ 2800	Loose Caboose/Music Ain't Got No Color	1979	$5
❏ 1157	Mama Red/Love Shortage	1975	$6
❏ 3007	Meet Me in Church/Be Your Own Judge	1962	$15
❏ 4069	Men Are Gettin' Scarce/You're Gonna Thank Me, Woman	1968	$8
❏ 3002	One Giant Step/The Rib	1961	$15
❏ 4011	One Monkey Don't Stop No Show/Build Your Love on a Solid Foundation	1965	$10
❏ 1003	Papa's Dream/I'm Comin' Home	1971	$6
❏ 4051	Papa Was Too/Truest Woman in the World	1966	$10
❏ 3003	Popeye Johnny/Hand Shakin', Love Makin', Girl Talkin', Son-of-a-Gun From Next Door	1962	$15
❏ 1154	Sassy Sexy Wiggle/Under Your Powerful Love	1975	$6
❏ 4055	Show Me/A Woman Sees a Hard Time (When Her Man Is Gone)	1967	$8
❏ 4063	Skinny Legs and All/Watch the One	1967	$12
❏ 3013	Someone to Take Your Place/I Should Have Kissed You More	1963	$15
❏ 4028	S.Y.S.L.J.F.M. (Letter Song)/I'm a Man	1966	$10
❏ 4093	That's the Way/Anything You Wanna Know	1969	$8
❏ 4089	That's Your Baby/Sweet, Sweet Woman	1968	$8
❏ 4026	The Love You Save (May Be Your Own)/If Sugar Was As Sweet As You	1966	$10
❏ 1024	Trying to Win Your Love/I've Seen Enough	1973	$6
❏ 4094	We Can't Sit Down Now/It Ain't Sanitary	1969	$8
❏ 3000	What Should I Do/The Only Girl I've Ever Loved	1961	$15
❏ 2801	Who Gave Birth to the Funk/If You Don't Want the Man	1979	$5
❏ 4059	Woman Like That, Yeah/I'm Going and Get It	1967	$8
❏ 1020	Woman Stealer/Cat's Got Her Tongue	1973	$6
❏ 1020 [PS]	Woman Stealer/Cat's Got Her Tongue	1973	$8

EPIC

Number	Title	Yr	NM
❏ 50313	Ain't Gonna Bump No More (With No Big Fat Woman)/I Mess Up Everything I Get My Hands On	1976	$5
❏ 50530	Get Back, Leroy/You Can Be My Star	1978	$5
❏ 50426	Hungry for Your Love/I Almost Got to Heaven Once	1977	$5

HANDSHAKE

Number	Title	Yr	NM
❏ 02565	Don't Do Da Do/Here Comes No. 34 (Do the Earl Campbell)	1981	$4

KING

Number	Title	Yr	NM
❏ 4840	Come In This House/Davy, You Upset My Home	1955	$70
❏ 5981	Come In This House/I Want to Have a Talk with You	1965	$10
❏ 4980	Get Way Back/Pneumonia	1956	$60
❏ 5064	I Want to Have a Talk with You/Ain't Nobody's Business	1957	$60
❏ 4884	My Biggest Mistake/Right Back to My Arms	1956	$60
❏ 4911	She's Mine/I Had to Come Back to You	1956	$60

TEXANS, THE

GOTHIC

Number	Title	Yr	NM
❏ 01	Old Reb/Rockin' Johnny Home	1961	$40

INFINITY

Number	Title	Yr	NM
❏ 01	Green Grass of Texas/Bloody River	1961	$40

JOX

Number	Title	Yr	NM
❏ 01	Old Reb/Rockin' Johnny Home	1965	$40

VEE JAY

Number	Title	Yr	NM
❏ 658	Green Grass of Texas/Bloody River	1965	$30

TEXAS PLAYBOYS, THE

CAPITOL

Number	Title	Yr	NM
❏ 4437	Bring It On Down to My House/Lily Dale	1977	$5
❏ 4401	Gambling Polka Dot Blues/Osage Stomp	1977	$5
❏ 4332	Ida Red/Don't Let the Deal Go Down	1976	$5

RIC

Number	Title	Yr	NM
❏ 182	Footsteps to Nowhere/Livin', Laughin', and Lovin'	1966	$15
❏ 163	I'll See You to the Door/Someday I'll Sober Up	1965	$15

TEXAS TROUBADOURS, THE

DECCA

Number	Title	Yr	NM
❏ 32185	Almost to Tulsa/Oklahoma Hills	1967	$10
❏ 31770	Cain's Corner/Honky Tonks and You	1965	$10
❏ 32065	E.T. Blues/Walking the Floor Over You	1966	$12
❏ 32121	Gardenia Waltz/Honey Fingers	1967	$10
❏ 31837	Highway Man/Leon's Guitar Boogie	1965	$12
❏ 31627	Honey Love/Last Letter	1964	$12
❏ 31699	Pan Handle Rag/Rhodes-Bud Boogie	1964	$10

TEXAS VOCAL COMPANY

RCA

Number	Title	Yr	NM
❏ PB-13566	It Had to Be You/Backsliding	1983	$4
❏ JK-13566 [DJ]	It Had to Be You (same on both sides)	1983	$10

—*Promo only on yellow vinyl*

Number	Title	Yr	NM
❏ JK-13504 [DJ]	Two Hearts (same on both sides)	1983	$10

—*Promo only on green vinyl*

Number	Title	Yr	NM
❏ PB-13504	Two Hearts/You Did It Again	1983	$4
❏ PB-13338	Why Did You Have to Be So Good/Didn't We Love	1982	$4

THARPE, SISTER ROSETTA

DECCA

Number	Title	Yr	NM
❏ 48328	In Bethlehem/When Jesus Was Born	1954	$15

THAT PETROL EMOTION

VIRGIN

Number	Title	Yr	NM
❏ 99238	Groove Check/Smooth	1989	$3

THE THE

EPIC

Number	Title	Yr	NM
❏ ES7 02718 [DJ]	Heartland/Slow Train to Dawn	1987	$8
❏ ES7 02718 [PS]	Heartland/Slow Train to Dawn	1987	$8

—*Promo item for Record World chain*

Number	Title	Yr	NM
❏ 68883	The Beat(en) Generation/Angel	1989	$5
❏ 04478	This Is the Day/The Sinking Feeling	1984	$8

THEE MIDNITERS

CHATTAHOOCHIE

Number	Title	Yr	NM
❏ 706	Are You Angry/I Found a Peanut	1966	$20
❏ 695	Brother, Where Are You/Heat Wave	1966	$20
❏ 693	I Need Someone/Empty Heart	1965	$30
❏ 666-2	Land of a Thousand Dances (Part 1)/Ball O' Twine	1965	$20
❏ 666	Land of a Thousand Dances (Part 1)/Land of a Thousand Dances (Part 2)	1965	$20
❏ 674	Sad Girl/Heat Wave	1965	$20
❏ 675	Sad Girl/Heat Wave	1965	$20
❏ 684	Whittier Blvd./Evil Love	1965	$20

UNI

Number	Title	Yr	NM
❏ 55170	She Only Wants What She Can't Get/I've Come Alive	1969	$10

WHITTIER

Number	Title	Yr	NM
❏ 509	Breakfast on the Grass/Dreaming Casually	1967	$30
❏ 513	Chicano Power/Never Goin' to Give You Up	1968	$30
❏ 508	Chile Con Soul/Tu Despedida	1967	$30
❏ 503	Dragon Fly/The Big Ranch	1966	$30
❏ 694	It's Not Unusual/It's Not Unusual	1969	$15
❏ 500	Love, Special Delivery/Don't Go Away	1966	$30
❏ 500 [PS]	Love, Special Delivery/Don't Go Away	1966	$60
❏ 674	Sad Girl/Heat Wave	1968	$15
❏ 512	The Ballad of Cesar Chavez/The Ballad of Cesar Chavez (Spanish)	1968	$30
❏ 501	The Midnite Feeling/It'll Never Be Over for Me	1966	$30

Number	Title	Yr	NM
❏ 501 [PS]	The Midnite Feeling/It'll Never Be Over for Me	1966	$60

THEE PROPHETS

KAPP

Number	Title	Yr	NM
❏ 2087	Little Bit of Love/Come to Me Girl	1970	$12
❏ 962	Playgirl/Patricia Ann	1969	$10
❏ 997	Some Kind of Wonderful/They Call Her Sorrow	1969	$12

THEM

Also see BELFAST GYPSIES; VAN MORRISON.

A&M

Number	Title	Yr	NM
❏ 1201	Baby Please Don't Go/Danger Heartbreak Dead Ahead	1988	$4

—*B-side by the Marvelettes*

Number	Title	Yr	NM
❏ 1201 [PS]	Danger Heartbreak Dead Ahead/Baby Please Don't Go	1988	$4

—*Good Morning Vietnam" sleeve*

HAPPY TIGER

Number	Title	Yr	NM
❏ 525	Lonely Weekends/I Am Waiting	1969	$20
❏ 534	Memphis Lady/Nobody Cares	1970	$15

PARROT

Number	Title	Yr	NM
❏ 9819	Call My Name/Bring 'Em On In	1966	$20
❏ 3006	Don't Start Crying Now/I Can Only Give You Everything	1966	$20
❏ 9702	Don't Start Crying Now/One, Two Brown Eyes	1964	$30
❏ 9727	Gloria/Baby, Please Don't Go	1965	$20
❏ 365	Gloria/Bring 'Em On In	1971	$10
❏ 9784	Gonna Dress in Black/Half As Much	1965	$20
❏ 9749	Here Comes the Night/All By Myself	1965	$20
❏ 9796	Mystic Eyes/If You and I Could Be As Two	1965	$20

RUFF

Number	Title	Yr	NM
❏ 1088	Walking in the Queen's Garden/I Happen to Love You	1967	$30

TOWER

Number	Title	Yr	NM
❏ 407	But It's Alright/Square Room	1968	$15
❏ 493	Corina/Dark Are the Shadows	1969	$15
❏ 384	Walking in the Queen's Garden/I Happen to Love You	1967	$15
❏ 384 [PS]	Walking in the Queen's Garden/I Happen to Love You	1967	$40
❏ 461	Waltz of the Flies/We've All Agreed to Help	1969	$15
❏ 461 [PS]	Waltz of the Flies/We've All Agreed to Help	1969	$30

—*Promo only picture sleeve*

THEM (2)

KING

Number	Title	Yr	NM
❏ 5967	Don't Look Now/A Girl Like You	1964	$20

THEMES, INC.

VEE JAY

Number	Title	Yr	NM
❏ 635	Theme from Petyon Place/Paula's Percussion	1964	$20

THERRIEN, JOE, JR.

BRUNSWICK

Number	Title	Yr	NM
❏ 9-55005	Hey Babe, Let's Go Downtown/Come Back to Me Darling	1957	$50
❏ 9-55017	Wheels/You're Long Gone	1957	$100

JAT

Number	Title	Yr	NM
❏ 101	I Ain't Gonna Be Around/Play Me a Blue Song	1958	$100

LIDO

Number	Title	Yr	NM
❏ 505	Hey Babe, Let's Go Downtown/Come Back to Me Darling	1957	$120

THEY MIGHT BE GIANTS

EVA-TONE

Number	Title	Yr	NM
❏ 8506475	Everything Right Is Wrong/You'll Miss Me	1985	$8

—*Flexidisc*

Number	Title	Yr	NM
❏ 8506475 [PS]	Everything Right Is Wrong/You'll Miss Me	1985	$8

—*Also known as "Wiggle Diskette"; sleeve is two pieces of paper wrapped around a piece of cardboard, with a woman at a loom on the front*

Number	Title	Yr	NM
THIN LIZZY			
Also see PHIL LYNOTT; MOTORHEAD; WHITESNAKE.			
LONDON			
❏ 20078	Broken Dreams/Randolph's Tango	1973	$20
❏ 20082	Little Darling/The Rocket	1973	$20
❏ 20076	Whiskey in the Jar/Black Boys on the Corner	1972	$20
MERCURY			
❏ 73945	Bad Reputation/Dancing in the Moonlight (It's Caught Me in the Spotlight)	1977	$5
❏ 73841	Cowboy Song/Angel from the Coast	1976	$5
❏ 73892	Don't Believe a Word/Boogie Woogie Dance	1977	$5
❏ 73882	Old Flame/Johnny the Fox Meets Jimmy the Weed	1977	$5
❏ 73786	The Boys Are Back in Town/Jailbreak	1976	$5
VERTIGO			
❏ 205	Wild One/Freedom Song	1975	$20
WARNER BROS.			
❏ 8648	Cowboy Song/Johnny the Fox Meets Jimmy the Weed	1978	$5
❏ 49078	Got to Give It Up/With Love	1979	$5
❏ 50056	Hollywood/Pressure Will Blow	1982	$4
❏ 49019	S & M/Do Anything You Want To	1979	$5
❏ 49679	We Will Be Strong/Sweetheart	1981	$5
THIN MEN, THE			
PARKWAY			
❏ 916	Indian Love Call/Guitar Blues	1964	$20
THINGS TO COME			
DUNWICH			
❏ 124	I'm Not Talkin'/'Til the End	1966	$60
STARFIRE			
❏ 103	Sweet Gina/(B-side unknown)	1966	$50
WARNER BROS.			
❏ 7164	Come Alive/Dancer	1968	$20
❏ 7228	Cool Day/Hello	1968	$20
THIRD PARTY, THE			
SCEPTER			
❏ 12340	What Do You Want For Christmas?/Everybody	1971	$15
THIRD RAIL, THE			
CAMEO			
❏ 445	The Subway Train That Came to Life/Train Rush Hour Stomp	1966	$20
EPIC			
❏ 10240	Boppa Do Down Down/Invisible Man	1967	$8
❏ 10285	Overdose of Love/It's Time to Say Goodbye	1968	$8
❏ 10323	Shape of Things to Come/She Ain't No Choir Girl	1968	$8
❏ 10457	The Ballad of General Humpty/Beggin' Me to Stay	1969	$8
THIRTEENTH FLOOR ELEVATORS, THE			
INTERNATIONAL ARTISTS			
❏ 121	Baby Blue/She Lives	1968	$50
❏ 113	Before You Accuse Me/Levitation	1968	$50
❏ 130	Livin' On/Scarlet and Gold	1969	$50
❏ 126	May the Circle Remain Unbroken/I'm Gonna Love You Too	1968	$50
❏ 122	Slip Inside This House/Splash 1	1968	$50
31ST OF FEBRUARY, THE			
VANGUARD			
❏ 35087	In the Morning When I'm Real/Porcelain Mirrors	1969	$10
❏ 35066	Sandcastles/Pick a Gripe	1968	$10
.38 SPECIAL			
A&M			
❏ 2955	Back to Paradise/Hold On Loosely	1987	$3
❏ 2955 [PS]	Back to Paradise/Hold On Loosely	1987	$3
❏ 2615	Back Where You Belong/Undercover Lover	1984	$3
❏ 2615 [PS]	Back Where You Belong/Undercover Lover	1984	$3
❏ 2412	Caught Up in You/Firestarter	1982	$4
❏ 2412 [PS]	Caught Up in You/Firestarter	1982	$4
❏ 2505	Chain Lightnin'/Back on the Track	1982	$4

Number	Title	Yr	NM
❏ 1424	Comin' Down Tonight/Chauahoocie	1989	$3
❏ 2330	Fantasy Girl/Honky Tonk Dancer	1981	$4
❏ 2330 [PS]	Fantasy Girl/Honky Tonk Dancer	1981	$4
❏ 2316	Hold On Loosely/Throw Out the Line	1981	$4
❏ 2594	If I'd Been the One/Twentieth Century Fox	1983	$3
❏ 2594 [PS]	If I'd Been the One/Twentieth Century Fox	1983	$3
❏ 2051	I'm a Fool for You/Travelin' Man	1978	$4
❏ 2831	Like No Other Night/Hearts on Fire	1986	$3
❏ 2831 [PS]	Like No Other Night/Hearts on Fire	1986	$3
❏ 2633	Long Distance Affair/One Time for Old Times	1984	$3
❏ 1946	Long Time Gone/Four Wheels	1977	$4
❏ 2873	One in a Million/Last Time	1986	$3
❏ 1273	Second Chance/Comin' Down Tonight	1989	$3
❏ 2854	Somebody Like You/Against the Night	1986	$3
❏ 2854 [PS]	Somebody Like You/Against the Night	1986	$3
❏ 2242	Stone Cold Believer/Stone Cold Believer (Part 2)	1980	$4
❏ 1964	Tell Everybody/Play a Simple Song	1977	$4
CAPITOL			
❏ B-5405	Teacher Teacher/Twentieth Century Fox	1984	$3
❏ B-5405 [PS]	Teacher Teacher/Twentieth Century Fox	1984	$3
THOMAS, B.J.			
ABC			
❏ 12054	(Hey, Won't You Play) Another Somebody Done Somebody Wrong Song/City Blues	1974	$4
❏ 12121	We Are Happy Together/Help Me Make It (To My Rockin' Chair)	1975	$4
BRAGG			
❏ 103	Billy and Sue/Never Tell	1964	$30
CLEVELAND INT'L.			
❏ 04608	From This Moment On/The Girl Most Likely To	1984	$4
❏ 03492	Whatever Happened to Old Fashioned Love/I Just Sing	1983	$4
COLUMBIA			
❏ 05771	America Is/Broken Toys	1986	$3
❏ 05771 [PS]	America Is/Broken Toys	1986	$4
❏ 05647	A Part of Me That Needs You Most/Northern Lights	1985	$3
❏ 04431	The Whole World's in Love When You're Lonely/We're Here to Love	1984	$3
❏ 04237	Two Car Garage/Beautiful World	1983	$4
HICKORY			
❏ 1395	Billy and Sue/Never Tell	1966	$10
LORI			
❏ 9561	For Your Precious Love/Here I Am Again	1964	$30
❏ 9547	I've Got a Feeling/Hey Judy	1963	$30
MCA			
❏ 40735	Don't Worry Baby/My Love	1977	$4
❏ 40854	Everybody Loves a Rain Song/Dusty Roads	1978	$4
❏ 41281	Everything Always Works Out for the Best/No Limit	1980	$4
❏ 41134	God Bless the Children/On This Christmas Night	1979	$4
❏ 41134 [PS]	God Bless the Children/On This Christmas Night	1979	$5
❏ 52053	I Really Got the Feeling/But Love Me	1982	$4
❏ 51087	Some Love Songs Never Die/There Ain't No Love	1981	$4
❏ 40812	Still the Lovin' Is Fun/Play Me a Little Traveling Music	1977	$4
❏ 40914	Sweet Young America/Aloha	1978	$4
❏ 51151	The Lovin' Kind/I Recall a Gypsy Woman	1981	$4
❏ 40986	We Could Have Been the Closest of Friends/In My Heart	1979	$4
MYRRH			
❏ 166	Home Where I Belong/Hallelujah	1977	$5
❏ 176	Without a Doubt/(B-side unknown)	1977	$5
PACEMAKER			
❏ 234	Bring Back the Time/I Don't Have a Mind of My Own	1965	$20
❏ 256	I Can't Help It (If I'm Still in Love with You)/Baby Cried	1965	$20
❏ 253	I'm Not a Fool Anymore/Baby Cried	1965	$20
❏ 227	I'm So Lonesome I Could Cry/Candy Baby	1964	$30
❏ 231	Mama/Wendy	1965	$20

Number	Title	Yr	NM
❏ 247	Plain Jane/My Home Town	1965	$20
❏ 259	Pretty Country Girl/Houston Town	1965	$20
❏ 239	Tomorrow Never Comes/Your Tears Leave Me Cold	1965	$20
PARAMOUNT			
❏ 0277	Play Something Sweet (Brickyard Blues)/Talkin' Confidentially	1974	$5
❏ 0218	Songs/Goodbye's a Long, Long Time	1973	$5
❏ 0218 [PS]	Songs/Goodbye's a Long, Long Time	1973	$6
❏ 0239	Sunday Sunrise/Early Morning Rush	1973	$5
❏ 0239	Sunday Sunrise/Talkin' Confidentially	1973	$5
REPRISE			
❏ 22837	Don't Leave Love (Out There All Alone)/One Woman	1989	$3
SCEPTER			
❏ 12154	Bring Back the Time/I Don't Have a Mind of My Own	1966	$8
❏ 12277	Everybody's Out of Town/Living Again	1970	$6
❏ 12364	Happier Than the Morning Sun/We Have Got to Get Out Ship Together	1972	$5
❏ 12230	Hooked on a Feeling/I've Been Down This Road Before	1968	$8
❏ 12194	I Can't Help It (If I'm Still in Love with You)/Baby Cried	1967	$8
❏ 12283	I Just Can't Help Believing/Send My Picture to Scranton, Pa.	1970	$6
❏ 12129	I'm So Lonesome I Could Cry/Candy Baby	1966	$10
❏ 12244	It's Only Love/You Don't Love Me Anymore	1969	$6
❏ 12335	Long Ago Tomorrow/Burnin' a Hole in My Mind	1971	$5
❏ 12139	Mama/Wendy	1966	$8
❏ 12320	Mighty Clouds of Joy/Life	1971	$5
❏ 12299	Most of All/The Mask	1970	$5
❏ 12255	Pass the Apple Eve/Fairy Tale of Time	1969	$6
❏ 12179	Plain Jane/My Home Town	1966	$8
❏ 12379	Sweet Cherry Wine/Roads	1973	$5
❏ 12354	That's What Friends Are For/I Get Enthused	1972	$5
❏ 12219	The Eyes of a New York Woman/I May Never Get to Heaven	1968	$8
❏ 12205	The Girl Can't Help It/Walkin' Back	1967	$8
❏ 12165	Tomorrow Never Comes/Your Tears Leave Me Cold	1966	$8
❏ 12201	Wisdom of a Fool/Human	1967	$8
VALERIE			
❏ 226	I've Got a Feeling/Hey Judy	1963	$30
WARNER BROS.			
❏ 5491	Billy and Sue/Never Tell	1964	$30
THOMAS, BUELL			
DOOTONE			
❏ 318	Green Christmas/For My Bride At Christmas Time	1953	$40
❏ 316	Santa Claus Walks Just Like Daddy/You're My Christmas	1953	$40
—B-side by Gerri Goodley			
THOMAS, CARLA			
ATLANTIC			
❏ 2101	A Love of My Own/Promises	1961	$15
❏ 2258	A Woman's Love/Don't Let the Love Light Leave	1964	$15
❏ 2212	Gee Whiz, It's Christmas/All I Want for Christmas Is You	1963	$20
❏ 2086	Gee Whiz (Look at His Eyes)/For You	1960	$20
❏ 2272	How Do You Quit (Someone You Love)/The Puppet	1965	$15
❏ 2163	I'll Bring It On Home to You/I Can't Take It	1962	$15
❏ 2238	I've Got No Time to Lose/A Boy Named Tom	1964	$15
❏ 2132	The Masquerade Is Over/I Kinda Think He Does	1962	$15
❏ 2189	What a Fool I've Been/The Life I Live	1963	$15
❏ 2113	Wish Me Good Luck/In Your Spare Time	1961	$15
GUSTO			
❏ 816	All I Want for Christmas Is You/Gee Whiz, It's Christmas	1979	$10
—A Canadian import ($5) from 1986 exists on King			
SATELLITE			
❏ 104	Gee Whiz (Look at His Eyes)/For You	1960	$500
STAX			
❏ 251	A Dime a Dozen/I Want You Back	1968	$10

Number	Title	Yr	NM
❏ 0067	All I Have to Do Is Dream/ Leave the Girl Alone	1970	$5

— With William Bell

Number	Title	Yr	NM
❏ 206	All I Want for Christmas Is You/Winter Snow	1966	$15
❏ 195	B-A-B-Y/What Have You Got to Offer Me	1966	$20
❏ 183	Comfort Me/I'm for You	1966	$15
❏ 0056	Guide Me Well/Some Other Man (Is Beating Your Time)	1970	$8
❏ 0080	Hi De Ho (That Old Sweet Roll)/I Loved You Like I Love My Very Life	1970	$6
❏ 0044	I Can't Stop/I Need You Woman	1969	$5

— With William Bell

Number	Title	Yr	NM
❏ 0173	I Have a God Who Loves/ Love Among People	1973	$6
❏ 0024	I Like What You're Doing (To Me)/Strung Out	1969	$8
❏ 222	I'll Always Have Faith in You/Stop Thief	1967	$10
❏ 0149	I May Not Be All You Want/Sugar	1972	$6
❏ 0011	I've Fallen in Love/ Where Do I Go	1968	$8
❏ 188	Let Me Be Good to You/Another Night Without My Man	1966	$15
❏ 188 [PS]	Let Me Be Good to You/Another Night Without My Man	1966	$125
❏ 239	Pick Up the Pieces/ Separation	1967	$10
❏ 207	Something Good (Is Going to Happen to You)/ It's Starting to Grow	1967	$12
❏ 172	Stop! Look What You're Doing/Every Ounce of Strength	1965	$15
❏ 0133	Sugar/You've Got a Cushion to Fall On	1972	$6
❏ 0061	The Time for Love Is Anytime/Living in the City	1970	$6

THOMAS, DANNY
DECCA
Number	Title	Yr	NM
❏ 9-29641	Bring Back Our Beale Street/It's Wonderful When	1955	$15

RCA VICTOR
Number	Title	Yr	NM
❏ 47-5142	Oh Moon/Hush-a-Bye	1952	$20
❏ 47-9342	The First Christmas/ Christmas Story	1967	$10
❏ 47-9342 [PS]	The First Christmas/ Christmas Story	1967	$10

THOMAS, DARRELL
OZARK OPRY
Number	Title	Yr	NM
❏ 101	Waylon, Sing to Mama/ The Conquered King	1979	$8

THOMAS, DICK
DECCA
Number	Title	Yr	NM
❏ 9-46301	I'm Tying the Leaves So They Won't Come Down/Esmereldy	1951	$30
❏ 9-46229	One Man's Loss Is Another Man's Gain/You Better Stop	1950	$40

JUBILEE
Number	Title	Yr	NM
❏ 5208	Anytime Is Lovin' Time/ When Uncle Joe Plays a Rag on His Old Piano	1955	$30

MERCURY
Number	Title	Yr	NM
❏ 5864	Don't Believe a Word They Say/Wonder	1952	$30
❏ 5808	Mistakes/The Little Boy I Knew	1952	$30

MGM
Number	Title	Yr	NM
❏ K11510	Call of the Far Away Hills/Brass Ring Love	1953	$30

THOMAS, GENE
UNITED ARTISTS
Number	Title	Yr	NM
❏ 640	Baby's Gone/Stand By Love	1963	$15
❏ 871	Down the Road/ It's a Sad World	1965	$12
❏ 799	Half the Time/I'd Rather Not Talk About It	1964	$10
❏ 501	It's Make Believe/So Wrong	1962	$15
❏ 583	Peace of Mind/The Puppet	1963	$15
❏ 771	Playing Those Old Records/Together Again	1964	$10
❏ 338	Sometime/Everyday	1961	$15
❏ 725	The Last Song/Bobby and the Boys	1964	$10

VENUS
Number	Title	Yr	NM
❏ 1444	Down the Road/ (B-side unknown)	1962	$100
❏ 1445	It's Make Believe/So Wrong	1962	$70
❏ 1441	Lamp of Love/Two Lips	1961	$30
❏ 1443	Mysteries of Love/That's What You Are to Me	1962	$30
❏ 1439	Sometime/Every Night	1961	$40

THOMAS, IAN
ATLANTIC
Number	Title	Yr	NM
❏ 3470	Coming Home/Clear Sailing	1978	$5
❏ 3505	Sally/(B-side unknown)	1978	$5

CHRYSALIS
Number	Title	Yr	NM
❏ 2116	Liars/(B-side unknown)	1976	$6

JANUS
Number	Title	Yr	NM
❏ 224	Painted Ladies/Will You Still Love Me	1973	$6

THOMAS, IRMA
CANYON
Number	Title	Yr	NM
❏ 31	I'll Do It All Over You/ We Won't Be In Your Way Anymore	1970	$6
❏ 21	Save a Little Bit for Me/ That's How I Feel About You	1970	$6

CHESS
Number	Title	Yr	NM
❏ 2017	A Woman Will Do Wrong/I Gave You Everything	1967	$8
❏ 2010	Cheater Man/ Somewhere Crying	1967	$8
❏ 2036	Good to Me/We Got Something Good	1968	$8

COTILLION
Number	Title	Yr	NM
❏ 44144	Full Time Woman/ She's Taken My Part	1972	$6

IMPERIAL
Number	Title	Yr	NM
❏ 66080	He's My Guy/(I Want a) True, True Love	1964	$12
❏ 66120	Hurts All Over/It's Starting to Get Me Now	1965	$10
❏ 66178	It's a Man-Woman's World (Part 1)/It's a Man-Woman's World (Part 2)	1966	$10
❏ 66095	Some Things You Better Get Used To/You Don't Miss a Good Thing	1965	$12
❏ 66137	Take a Look/What Are You Trying to Do	1965	$10
❏ 66041	Time Is On My Side/ Anyone Who Knows What Love Is (Will Understand)	1964	$15
❏ 66069	Times Have Changed/ Moments to Remember	1964	$10
❏ 66013	Wish Someone Would Care/Break-A-Way	1964	$15

MINIT
Number	Title	Yr	NM
❏ 625	Cry On/Girl Needs Boy	1961	$15
❏ 642	Gone/Done Got Over It	1962	$15
❏ 653	It's Raining/I Did My Part	1962	$15
❏ 633	It's Too Soon to Know/ That's All I Ask	1961	$15
❏ 660	Somebody Told Me/ Two Winters Long	1963	$15

RON
Number	Title	Yr	NM
❏ 328	Don't Mess with My Man/Set Me Free	1960	$20
❏ 330	Good Man/I May Be Wrong	1960	$20

UNITED ARTISTS
Number	Title	Yr	NM
❏ 0088	Wish Someone Would Care/Take a Look	1973	$4

— Silver Spotlight Series" reissue

THOMAS, JAMO
CHESS
Number	Title	Yr	NM
❏ 1971	Must I Holler/I'll Be Your Fool	1966	$20

DECCA
Number	Title	Yr	NM
❏ 32406	Bahama Mama (Part I)/(Part II)	1968	$20
❏ 32293	Education Is Where It's At (Part 1)/(Part 2)	1968	$20

SOUND STAGE 7
Number	Title	Yr	NM
❏ 2596	Bahama Mama (Part I)/(Part II)	1967	$20

THOMAS
Number	Title	Yr	NM
❏ 304	Arrest Me/Jamo's Soul	1966	$30
❏ 304 [PS]	Arrest Me/Jamo's Soul	1966	$60
❏ 303	I Spy (For the FBI)/ Snake Hip Mama	1966	$20
❏ 303 [PS]	I Spy (For the FBI)/ Snake Hip Mama	1966	$40

THOMAS, JON
ABC-PARAMOUNT
Number	Title	Yr	NM
❏ 10238	Boss Hoss/Flip, Flop, Fly	1961	$15
❏ 10122	Heartbreak (It's Hurtin' Me)/Tearin'	1960	$20
❏ 10140	Hey Hey Baby/Buffalo Blues	1960	$20
❏ 10190	The Snake/Story Telling	1961	$15
❏ 10274	The Thomas Twist/So Good	1961	$15

MERCURY
Number	Title	Yr	NM
❏ 71078	Hard Head (Part 1)/ Hard Head (Part 2)	1957	$40
❏ 71151	St. Louis Blues/Fat Back	1957	$30

THOMAS, MILLIE
CAMEO
Number	Title	Yr	NM
❏ 358	All Over Again/ Take Me Home	1965	$20

THOMAS, PAT
MGM
Number	Title	Yr	NM
❏ K13102	Desafinado (Slightly Out of Tune)/One Note Samba	1962	$8
❏ K13102 [PS]	Desafinado (Slightly Out of Tune)/One Note Samba	1962	$15
❏ K13124	Home in the Meadow/Where There's Love, There's Hope	1963	$30
❏ K13171	I'm in the Mood for Love/ Just Say Auf Wiederseh'n	1963	$10

VERVE
Number	Title	Yr	NM
❏ 10269	Desafinado (Slightly Out of Tune)/One Note Samba	1962	$12
❏ 10269 [PS]	Desafinado (Slightly Out of Tune)/One Note Samba	1962	$15
❏ 10333	Long Long Night/I Can't Wait Until I See My Baby's Face	1964	$10

THOMAS, RUFUS
ARTISTS OF AMERICA
Number	Title	Yr	NM
❏ 126	If There Were No Music/ Blues in the Basement	1976	$5

AVI
Number	Title	Yr	NM
❏ 178	I Ain't Gettin' Older, I'm Gettin' Better (Part 1)/I Ain't Gettin' Older, I'm Gettin' Better (Part 2)	1977	$4
❏ 149	Who's Makin' Love to Your Old Lady/Hot Grits	1977	$4

HI
Number	Title	Yr	NM
❏ 78520	Fried Chicken/I Ain't Got Time	1978	$4

METEOR
Number	Title	Yr	NM
❏ 5039	I'm Steady Holdin' On/ The Easy Livin' Plan	1956	$200

STAX
Number	Title	Yr	NM
❏ 167	Baby Walk/Little Sally Walker	1965	$8
❏ 0219	Boogie Ain't Nothin' (But Gettin' Down) (Part 1)/ Boogie Ain't Nothin' (But Gettin' Down) (Part 2)	1974	$6
❏ 144	Can Your Monkey Do the Dog/I Want to Get Married	1964	$15
❏ 178	Chicken Scratch/The World Is Round	1965	$8
❏ 0236	Do the Double Bump/ Do the Double Bump	1975	$6
❏ 0059	Do the Funky Chicken/ Turn Your Damper Down	1969	$6
❏ 0112	Do the Funky Penguin (Part 1)/Do the Funky Penguin (Part 2)	1971	$6
❏ 0079	(Do the) Push and Pull Part I/(Do the) Push and Pull Part II	1970	$6
❏ 240	Down Ta My House/ Steady Holding On	1968	$8
❏ 0010	Funky Mississippi/So Hard to Get Along With	1968	$6
❏ 0153	Funky Robot (Part 1)/ Funky Robot (Part 2)	1973	$6
❏ 0022	Funky Way/I Want to Hold You	1969	$6
❏ 0177	I Know You Don't Want Me No More/I'm Still in Love with You	1973	$6
❏ 0187	I'll Be Your Santa Baby/ That Makes Christmas Day	1973	$6
❏ 0140	Itch and Scratch (Part 1)/ Itch and Scratch (Part 2)	1972	$6
❏ 126	It's Aw-Rite/Can't Ever Let You Go	1962	$20
❏ 0129	Love Trap/6-3-8	1972	$6
❏ 0071	Sixty Minute Man/The Preacher and the Bear	1970	$6
❏ 149	Somebody Stole My Dog/I Want to Be Loved	1964	$15
❏ 221	Sophisticated Sissy/ Grasy Spoon	1967	$8
❏ 200	Talkin' 'Bout True Love/ Sister's Got a Boyfriend	1967	$8
❏ 0098	The Breakdown (Part 1)/ The Breakdown (Part 2)	1971	$6
❏ 130	The Dog/Did You Ever Love a Woman	1963	$20
❏ 0192	The Funky Bird/Steal a Little	1974	$6
❏ 250	The Memphis Train/I Think I Made a Boo-Boo	1968	$6
❏ 0090	The World Is Round/ (I Love You) For Sentimental Reasons	1971	$6
❏ 140	Walking the Dog/ Fine and Mellow	1963	$40
❏ 140	Walking the Dog/You Said	1963	$15
❏ 173	Willy Nilly/Sho' Gonna Mess Him Up	1965	$8

SUN
Number	Title	Yr	NM
❏ 181	Bear Cat (The Answer to Hound Dog)/ Walking in the Rain	1953	$350

— With subtitle on A-side

Number	Title	Yr	NM
❏ 181	Bear Cat/Walking in the Rain	1953	$200

— No subtitle on A-side

Number	Title	Yr	NM
❏ 188	Tiger Man (King of the Jungle)/Save Your Money	1953	$500

THOMAS, TIMMY

GLADES

Number	Title	Yr	NM
1721	Deep in You/Spread Us Around	1974	$5
1758	Drown in My Own Tears (Part 1)/Drown in My Own Tears (Part 2)	1980	$5
1730	Ebony Affair/It's What They Can't See	1975	$5
1749	Freak In, Freak Out/Say Love, Can You Chase	1978	$5
1723	I've Got to See You Tonight/You're the Song (I've Always Wanted to Sing)	1974	$5
1712	Let Me Be Your Eyes/Cold Cold People	1973	$6
1735	Love Shine/Running Out of Time	1976	$5
1719	One Brief Moment/Rio Girl	1974	$6
1709	People Are Changin'/Rainbow Power	1973	$6
1727	Sexy Woman/Sweet Brown Sugar	1975	$5
1740	Stone to the Bone/Watch It! Watch It!	1977	$5
1748	Touch to Touch/When a House Got Music	1978	$5
1717	What Can I Tell Her/Opportunity	1973	$6
1703	Why Can't We Live Together/Funky Me	1972	$6

GOLD MOUNTAIN

Number	Title	Yr	NM
82004	Gotta Give a Little Love (Ten Years After)/Same Old Song	1984	$4
82008	Love Is Never Too Late/Let It Flow	1984	$4

GOLDWAX

Number	Title	Yr	NM
320	Have Some Boogaloo/Liquid Mood	1967	$20
327	It's My Life/Whole Lotta Shakin' Goin' On	1967	$20

MARLIN

Number	Title	Yr	NM
3348	Are You Crazy??? (Pt. 1)/Are You Crazy??? (Pt. 2)	1981	$4

THOMPSON, BILLY

COLUMBUS

Number	Title	Yr	NM
1043	Black Eyed Girl/Kiss Tomorrow Goodbye	1965	$200

WAND

Number	Title	Yr	NM
1108	Black Eyed Girl/Kiss Tomorrow Goodbye	1966	$70

THOMPSON, HANK

ABC

Number	Title	Yr	NM
12447	Dance with Me Molly/Point of No Return	1979	$5
12409	I'm Just Gettin' By/I Hear the South Callin' Me	1978	$5

ABC DOT

Number	Title	Yr	NM
17612	Asphalt Cowboy/Fifteen Miles to Clarksville	1976	$6
17649	Big Band Days/Forgive Me	1976	$6
17673	Honky Tonk Girl/Another Shot of Today	1976	$6
17535	Mama Don't 'Low/Wait a Little Longer Baby	1974	$6
17583	Mona Lisa/Too Young	1975	$6
17556	That's Just My Truckin' Luck/After You Have Made Me Over	1975	$6

CAPITOL

Number	Title	Yr	NM
F1327	A Broken Heart and a Glass of Beer/If I Cry	1950	$40
F2758	A Fooler, a Faker/Breakin' the Rules	1954	$30
F876	All That Goes Up Must Come Down/Standing on the Outside	1950	$40
F4182	Anybody's Girl/Total Strangers	1959	$30
4334	A Six Pack to Go/What Made Her Change	1960	$30
4722	Blue Skirt Waltz/Westphalia Waltz	1962	$20
F2998	Dardanelle/Johnson Rag	1954	$30
F3275	Don't Take It Out on Me/Honey, Honey Bee Ball	1955	$30
F3709	Girl in the Night/Quicksand	1957	$30
F40264	Give a Little, Take a Little/A Cat Has Nine Lives	1949	$40
F1118	Green Light/Mary Had a Little Lamb	1950	$30
4605	Hangover Tavern/Give the World a Smile	1961	$30
F2823	Honky-Tonk Girl/We've Gone Too Far	1954	$30
4871	Honky Tonk Town/I'd Look Forward to Tomorrow	1963	$20
F2169	How Cold Hearted Can You Get/It's Better to Have Loved a Little	1952	$30
F3950	How Do You Hold a Memory/Li'l Liza Jane	1958	$30
4786	How Many Teardrops Will It Take/I Cast a Lonesome Shadow	1962	$20
F1198	Humpty Dumpty Boogie/Daddy Blues	1950	$40
F1113	Humpty Dumpty Heart/California Women	1950	$30
F1632	Humpty Dumpty Heart/Green Light	1951	$30

— Reissue of hit A-sides from 1948

Number	Title	Yr	NM
F1528	I Ain't Crying Over You/Hangover Heart	1951	$30
F4269	I Didn't Mean to Fall in Love/I Guess I'm Gettin' Over You	1959	$30
F1121	I Find You Cheatin' on Me/You Remembered Me	1950	$30
F3030	If Lovin' You Is Wrong/Annie Over	1955	$30
5344	I'm Gonna Practice Freedom/Life's Sweetest Moment	1965	$20
F3536	It Makes No Difference Now/Taking My Chances	1956	$30
4454	It's Got to Be a Habit/Will We Start It All Over Again	1960	$30
F4085	I've Run Out of Tomorrows/You're Going Back to Your Old Ways Again	1958	$30
4968	I Wasn't Even in the Running/The More in Love Your Heart Is	1963	$20
5535	Little Christmas/Gonna Wrap My Heart in Angel Ribbons	1965	$20
4649	Lost John/I've Convinced Everyone But Myself	1961	$30
4649 [PS]	Lost John/I've Convinced Everyone But Myself	1961	$40
F1745	Love Thief/How Do You Feel	1951	$30
F3188	Most of All/Simple Simon	1955	$30
5310	Mr. and Mrs. Snowman/I'd Like to Have an Elephant for Christmas	1964	$20
F1120	My Front Door Is Open/A Cat Has Nine Lives	1950	$30
4556	Oklahoma Hills/Teach Me How to Lie	1961	$30
5507	Paper Doll/You Only Hurt the One You Love	1965	$20
5599	Pick Me Up on Your Way Down/You Nearly Lose Your Mind	1966	$15
F1117	Second Hand Gal/Don't Flirt with Me	1950	$30
4386	She's Just a Whole Lot Like You/There My Future Goes	1960	$30
F1114	Soft Lips/Give a Little, Take a Little	1950	$30
F4017	Squaws Along the Yukon/Gathering Flowers	1958	$30
F1116	Swing Wide/Tomorrow Night	1950	$30
F1016	Take a Look at This Broken Heart/She's a Girl Without a Sweetheart	1950	$40
F1870	Teardrops on the Tea Leaves/I'll Be Your Sweetheart	1951	$30
F3781	Tears Are Only Rain/Under the Double Eagle	1957	$30
4694	That's the Recipe for a Heartache/Drop Me Gently	1962	$20
F3347	The Blackboard of My Heart/I'm Not Mad, Just Hurt	1956	$30
F1119	The Grass Looks Greener/Rock in the Ocean	1950	$30
5422	Then I'll Start Believing in You/In the Back of Your Mind	1965	$20
F1942	The Wild Side of Life/Cryin' in the Deep Blue Sea	1952	$30
5008	Too in Love/Blackboard of My Heart	1963	$30
F4138	Tuxedo Junction/The Cocoanut Grove	1959	$30
5071	Twice As Much/Reaching for the Moon	1964	$20
F2063	Waiting in the Lobby of Your Heart/Don't Make Me Cry Again	1952	$30
F2646	Wake Up, Irene/Go Cry Your Heart Out	1953	$30
F3440	Weeping Willow/You Can Give Me Back My Heart	1956	$30
F3235	Westphalia Waltz/Red Skin Gal	1955	$30
5217	Whatever Happened to Mary/Luckiest Heartache in Town	1964	$20
F1163	When God Calls His Children Home/I Can't Feel at Home	1950	$40
F1444	Where's Your Heart Tonight/Those Things Money Can't Buy	1951	$30
F2178	Whoa Sailor/Mary Had a Little Lamb	1952	$30
F1115	Whoa Sailor/Today	1950	$30
F3106	Wildwood Flower/Breakin' In Another Heart	1955	$30

—A-side with Merle Travis

CHURCHILL

Number	Title	Yr	NM
94003	Cocaine Blues/Drop Me Gently	1982	$5
94009	Driving Nails in My Coffin/What Ever Happened to Mary	1982	$5
94026	Once in a Blue Moon/Let's Stop What We Started	1983	$5
94026 [PS]	Once in a Blue Moon/Let's Stop What We Started	1983	$6

DOT

Number	Title	Yr	NM
17347	But That's All Right/Take It All Away	1970	$8
17207	I See Them Everywhere/Today	1969	$8
17307	Oklahoma Home Brew/Let's Get Drunk and Be Somebody	1969	$8
17354	One of the Fortunate Few/I'm Afraid I Lied	1970	$8
17108	On Tap, In the Can, or In the Bottle	1968	$8
17163	Smoky the Bar/Clubs, Spades, Diamonds and Hearts	1968	$8
17262	The Pathway of My Life/At Certain Times	1969	$8

MCA

Number	Title	Yr	NM
41079	I Hear the South Callin' Me/Through the Bottom of the Glass	1979	$4
41176	Tony's Tank-Up, Drive-In Cafe/Point of No Return	1980	$4

STEP ONE

Number	Title	Yr	NM
382	Here's to Country Music/The Hand I'm Holding Now	1988	$4
394	If I Were You I'd Fall in Love with Me/(B-side unknown)	1988	$4

WARNER BROS.

Number	Title	Yr	NM
5886	He's Got a Way with Women/Let the Four Winds Choose	1967	$12
5858	Where Is the Circus/Love Walked Out Long Before She Did	1966	$10

7-Inch Extended Plays

CAPITOL

Number	Title	Yr	NM
EAP 2-826	(contents unknown)	1957	$20
EAP 1-975	(contents unknown)	1958	$20
EAP 2-975	(contents unknown)	1958	$20
EAP 3-975	(contents unknown)	1958	$20
EAP 2-1111	(contents unknown)	1959	$20
EAP 3-1111	(contents unknown)	1959	$20
EAP 1-1246	(contents unknown)	1960	$20
EAP 2-1246	(contents unknown)	1960	$20
EAP 3-1246	(contents unknown)	1960	$20
EAP 1-975 [PS]	Dance Ranch, Part 1	1958	$20
EAP 2-975 [PS]	Dance Ranch, Part 2	1958	$20
EAP 3-975 [PS]	Dance Ranch, Part 3	1958	$20
EAP 2-729	Don't Flirt with Me/The Grass Looks Greener//Swing Wide Your Gate of Love/I Find You Cheatin' on Me	1957	$20
EAP 1-1111 [PS]	Favorite Waltzes by Hank Thompson, Part 1	1959	$20
EAP 2-1111 [PS]	Favorite Waltzes by Hank Thompson, Part 2	1959	$20
EAP 3-1111 [PS]	Favorite Waltzes by Hank Thompson, Part 3	1959	$20
EAP 1-826	Hang Your Head in Shame/Someone Can Steal Your Love from Me//You'll Be the One/Don't Be That Way	1957	$20
EAP 1-826 [PS]	Hank! Part 1	1957	$20
EAP 2-826 [PS]	Hank! Part 2	1957	$20
EAP 3-826 [PS]	Hank! Part 3	1957	$20
EAP 1-729	Humpty Dumpty Heart/Today//You Remembered Me/I'll Be Your Sweetheart for a Day	1957	$20
EAP 3-729	My Front Door Is Open/Standing on the Outside//Whoa Sailor/Tomorrow Night	1957	$20
EAP 3-826	Ole Napoleon/Across the Alley from the Alamo//Don't Get Around Much Anymore/Prosperity Special	1957	$20
EAP 1-1111	Shenandoah Waltz/Wednesday Night Waltz//In the Valley of the Moon/Fifty Year Ago Waltz	1959	$20
EAP 1-1246 [PS]	Songs for Rounders, Part 1	1960	$20
EAP 2-1246 [PS]	Songs for Rounders, Part 2	1960	$20
EAP 3-1246 [PS]	Songs for Rounders, Part 3	1960	$20

THOMPSON, JUNIOR

METEOR

Number	Title	Yr	NM
5029	Mama's Little Baby/Raw Deal	1956	$400

THOMPSON, KAY

CADENCE

Number	Title	Yr	NM
CCS3	Eloise/Just One of Those Things	1956	$15
CCS3 [PS]	Eloise/Just One of Those Things	1956	$30

MGM

Number	Title	Yr	NM
K11888	It's All Right with Me/I Hadn't Anyone Till You	1954	$15
K12075	Moonglow/How Deep Is the Ocean	1955	$15

VERVE

Number	Title	Yr	NM
10052	Bazazz/Light Up the Candle on the Birthday Cake	1957	$15

Number	Title	Yr	NM

THOMPSON, LORETTA
SKOOP
| ❏ 1050 | Buddy-Big Bopper-Ritchie/ Square from Nowhere | 1959 | $60 |

UNITED
| ❏ 214 | He Do Ho Rock 'N' Roll/ Let's Change the Alphabet | 1958 | $50 |

THOMPSON, PEGGY
HIT
| ❏ 15 | I Sold My Heart to the Junkman/Snap Your Fingers | 1962 | $8 |

—B-side by Benny Lattimore
| ❏ 04 | Love Letters/Soldier Boy | 1962 | $8 |
| ❏ 07 | Mashed Potato Time/ (B-side unknown) | 1962 | $8 |

THOMPSON, SUE
DECCA
| ❏ 29545 | Day Dreaming/Your Mommie and Your Daddy | 1955 | $30 |
| ❏ 29314 | Walkin' in the Snow/ Come a Little Bit Closer | 1954 | $30 |

— With Hank Penny
| ❏ 30435 | Walkin' to Missouri/Red Hot Honey Brown | 1957 | $30 |

HICKORY
❏ 1328	Afraid/It's Break-Up Time	1965	$15
❏ 1255	Bad Boy/Toys	1964	$15
❏ 1587	Because You Love Me/ Take a Little Time	1971	$6
❏ 1240	Big Daddy/I'd Like to Know You Better	1964	$15
❏ 1270	Big Hearted Me/Looking for a Good Boy	1964	$15
❏ 1652	Candy and Roses/ Full Time Job	1972	$6
❏ 1234	'Cause I Ask You To/ It's Twelve Thirty-Five	1963	$15
❏ 1488	Dear Boy/Love Has Come My Way	1967	$12
❏ 1457	Don't Forget to Cry/ Ferris Wheel	1967	$12
❏ 1524	Don't Try to Change Me/The Real Me	1968	$8
❏ 1174	Have a Good Time/ If the Boy Only Knew	1962	$20
❏ 1596	Here's To Forever/What You See Is What You Get	1971	$6
❏ 1493	How Do You Start Over/Why Not	1968	$8
❏ 1669	How I Love Them Old Songs/Just Two Young People	1973	$5
❏ 1403	I Can't Help It/Put It Back	1966	$10
❏ 1560	I Just Keep Hangin' On/Lost Highway	1970	$6
❏ 1431	Language of Love/ Let Me Down Hard	1967	$12
❏ 1622	Let Your Thoughts Be Sweet/What a Woman in Love Won't Do	1972	$6
❏ 1547	Pair of Broken Hearts/ You Two-Timed Me One Time Too Often	1969	$8
❏ 1284	Paper Tiger/Mama, Don't Cry at My Wedding	1964	$20
❏ 1153	Sad Movies (Make Me Cry)/Nine Little Teardrops	1961	$30
❏ 1423	Someone/From My Balcony	1966	$12
❏ 1308	Stop Th' Music/What I'm Needin' Is You	1965	$15
❏ 1641	Sweet Memories/ Take Me As I Am	1972	$6
❏ 1612	Swiss Cottage Place/ Thanks to Rumors	1971	$6
❏ 1534	Tennessee Waltz/Who's Gonna Mow Your Grass	1969	$8
❏ 1469	That's Just Too Much!/ Straight to Helen	1967	$12
❏ 1144	Throwin' Kisses/Angel, Angel	1961	$30
❏ 1221	Too Hot to Dance/I Like Your Kind of Love	1963	$15

— With Bob Luman
❏ 1217	True Confession/Suzie	1963	$20
❏ 1217 [PS]	True Confession/Suzie	1963	$30
❏ 1166	Two of a Kind/It Has to Be	1962	$20
❏ 1359	Walkin' My Baby/I'm Lookin' (For a World)	1965	$15
❏ 1381	What Should I Do/ After the Heartache	1966	$10
❏ 1204	What's Wrong Bill/I Need a Harbor	1963	$20
❏ 1204 [PS]	What's Wrong Bill/I Need a Harbor	1963	$30
❏ 1577	Whole Lot of Walkin'/ Guess Who's Coming to Dinner Tonight	1970	$6
❏ 1196	Willie Can/Too Much in Love	1962	$20

HICKORY/MGM
❏ 370	Baby's Not Home/I Want It All	1976	$4
❏ 354	Big Mabel Murphy/ Big Daddy	1975	$4
❏ 313	Find Out/Stay Another Day	1974	$5
❏ 346	I Can't Stop Loving You/ Any Other Morning	1975	$4

❏ 320	Making Love to You Is Just Like Eating Peanuts/ Sweet Memories	1974	$5
❏ 339	The Thought of Losing You/Tennessee Waltz	1975	$4
❏ 330	Trains/And Love Me	1974	$5

MERCURY
❏ 70309	Donna Wanna/Gee But I Hate to Go Home Alone	1954	$30
❏ 70066	How Many Tears/If You Should Change	1953	$30
❏ 70152	I'm Not That Kind of Girl/I Long to Tell You	1953	$30
❏ 70084	Take Care My Love/Things I Might Have Been	1953	$30

THOMPSON TWINS
ARISTA
❏ 9622	Bush Baby/Follow Your Heart	1987	$8
❏ 9209 [DJ]	Doctor! Doctor! (3:46)/(4:29)	1984	$5
❏ 9209	Doctor! Doctor!/Nurse Shark	1984	$3
❏ 9209 [PS]	Doctor! Doctor!/Nurse Shark	1984	$3
❏ 9577	Get That Love/Perfect Day	1987	$3
❏ 9577 [PS]	Get That Love/Perfect Day	1987	$3
❏ 9164 [DJ]	Hold Me Now (4:44)/(3:58)	1984	$5
❏ 9164	Hold Me Now/Let Loving Start	1984	$3
❏ 9164 [PS]	Hold Me Now/Let Loving Start	1984	$3
❏ 0671	In the Name of Love/ Coastline	1982	$8
❏ 9396 [DJ]	Lay Your Hands on Me (Fade 3:44)/ (Cold Ending 3:44)	1985	$6
❏ 9396 [DJ]	Lay Your Hands on Me (Special A/C Mix 3:52) (same on both sides)	1985	$6
❏ 9396	Lay Your Hands on Me/The Lewis Carol (Adventures in Wonderland)	1985	$3
❏ 9396 [PS]	Lay Your Hands on Me/The Lewis Carol (Adventures in Wonderland)	1985	$3
❏ 1024	Lies/Beach Culture	1982	$5
❏ 9609	Long Goodbye/Dancin' in Your Shoes	1987	$5
❏ 9609 [PS]	Long Goodbye/Dancin' in Your Shoes	1987	$5
❏ 1056	Love On Your Side/ Love On Your Back	1983	$5
❏ 1056 [PS]	Love On Your Side/ Love On Your Back	1983	$5
❏ 9013	Love On Your Side/ Love On Your Back	1983	$3

—Reissue of 1056
| ❏ 9013 [PS] | Love On Your Side/ Love On Your Back | 1983 | $3 |

— Same sleeve as 1056 except for new number
| ❏ 9290 | The Gap/Out of the Gap | 1984 | $10 |

FLASHBACK
| ❏ 9347 | Hold Me Now/ Doctor! Doctor! | 1985 | $3 |

—Reissue
| ❏ 9238 | In the Name of Love/ Coastline | 1984 | $3 |

—Reissue
| ❏ 9485 | Lay Your Hands on Me/King for a Day | 1986 | $3 |

—Reissue
| ❏ 9237 | Lies/Love on Your Side | 1984 | $3 |

—Reissue

WARNER BROS.
| ❏ 7-22819 | Sugar Daddy/Monkey Man | 1989 | $3 |
| ❏ 7-22819 [PS] | Sugar Daddy/Monkey Man | 1989 | $3 |

THOR-ABLES, THE
TITANIC
| ❏ 1002 | My Reckless Heart/ Batman and Robin | 1962 | $300 |
| ❏ 1001 | Our Love Song/ Get That Bread | 1962 | $300 |

THORINSHIELD
PHILIPS
| ❏ 40521 | Family of Man/Lonely Mountain Again | 1968 | $8 |
| ❏ 40492 | The Best of All/ Life Is a Dream | 1967 | $8 |

THORNE, DAVID
ADMIRAL
❏ 772	Dearest/Turning Point	1965	$20
❏ 768	If You Were Mine Again/Where'll I Be Tomorrow Night	1965	$20
❏ 756	I Love You, Yes I Do/ Send a Little My Way	1964	$20
❏ 750	Time Out for Tears/ Since You Went Away	1964	$20

RIVERSIDE
❏ 4552	Don't Let It Get Away/ One More Fool, One More Broken Heart	1963	$15
❏ 4520	I'll Be There/If You Should Ever Need Me	1962	$15
❏ 4530	The Alley Cat Song/ The Moon Was Yellow	1962	$15

THORNE, WOODY
GNP
| ❏ 169 | Teenagers in Love/ Sadie Lou | 1961 | $30 |

THORNTON, FRADKIN AND UNGER
ESP-DISK
| ❏ 63019 | God Bless California/ Sometimes | 1972 | $40 |

—Paul McCartney appears on this record

THORNTON, BIG MAMA
ARHOOLIE
| ❏ 520 | Ball and Chain/ Wade in the Water | 1968 | $8 |
| ❏ 512 | Swing It On Home/ My Heavy Load | 1968 | $8 |

GALAXY
| ❏ 749 | Life Goes On/ Because It's Love | 1966 | $12 |

KENT
| ❏ 424 | Before Day/Me and My Chauffeur | 1965 | $12 |

MERCURY
| ❏ 72981 | Hound Dog/Let's Go Get Started | 1969 | $8 |

PEACOCK
❏ 1626	Big Change/I Ain't No Fool Either	1953	$125
❏ 1603	Everytime I Think of You/ Mischievous Boogie	1952	$125
❏ 1612	Hound Dog/Nightmare	1953	$180
❏ 1612	Hound Dog/Rock-a-Bye Baby	1953	$200
❏ 1632	I've Searched the Whole World/I Smell a Rat	1954	$70
❏ 1642	Stop Hoppin' on Me/ Story of My Blues	1954	$70
❏ 1650	The Fish/Laugh, Laugh, Laugh	1955	$70
❏ 1621	They Call Me Big Mama/ Cotton Pickin' Blues	1953	$125
❏ 1647	Walking Blues/ Rock-a-Bye Baby	1955	$70

SOTOPLAY
| ❏ SO-0033/34 | Summer Time/The Truth'll Come to the Light | 1965 | $20 |

THORNTON, BUDDY
4 STAR
| ❏ 1668 | Ole Santa Claus Is Coming to Town/Lonely Christmas Eve | 1954 | $30 |

THOROGOOD, GEORGE, AND THE DESTROYERS
EMI AMERICA
❏ B-8140	Bad to the Bone/No Particular Place to Go	1982	$5
❏ B-8140 [PS]	Bad to the Bone/No Particular Place to Go	1982	$6
❏ B-8270	I Drink Alone/Willie & the Hand Jive	1985	$4

EMI MANHATTAN
| ❏ B-50121 | Treat Her Right/You Can't Catch Me | 1988 | $4 |
| ❏ B-50121 [PS] | Treat Her Right/You Can't Catch Me | 1988 | $4 |

MCA
| ❏ 41136 | In the Night Time/Nadine | 1979 | $6 |
| ❏ 41117 | My Way/You're Gonna Miss Me | 1979 | $6 |

ROUNDER
❏ 4536	Bottom of the Sea/ Kids from Philly	1980	$10
❏ 4536 [PS]	Bottom of the Sea/ Kids from Philly	1980	$10
❏ 4540	I'm Wanted/Restless	1980	$10
❏ 4514	Madison Blues/Ride On Josephine	1977	$20
❏ 4518	Move It On Over/ It Wasn't Me	1978	$10
❏ 4519	Who Do You Love/I'll Change My Style	1978	$10

THRASHER BROTHERS, THE
MCA
❏ 52357	A Good Love Died Tonight/ Southern Swing	1984	$4
❏ 51175	As Long As We Keep Believing/Waitin' on Love	1981	$4
❏ 51227	Best of Friends/The Captain and the Delta Queen	1982	$4

Number	Title	Yr	NM
❏ 52192	I've Got Country in My Soul/I Wanna Be with You Tonight	1983	$4
❏ 51049	Lovers Love/Wouldn't It Make a Good Country Song	1980	$4
❏ 52242	Some Other Time/So Good	1983	$4
❏ 52093	Still the One/Long Tall Texan	1982	$4
❏ 52047	Sweet Country Music/I Think I Feel a Love Comin' On	1982	$4
❏ 51032	To Make a Long Story Longer/Wouldn't It Make a Good Country Song	1980	$4
❏ 51123	Waitin' on Love/Smooth Southern Highway	1981	$4
❏ 52297	Whatcha Got Cookin' in Your Oven Tonight/Southern Swing	1983	$4
❏ 52153	Wherever You Are/Heart to Heart	1983	$4

VULCAN

| ❏ 10004 | A Message to Khomeini/Maharishi | 1979 | $6 |

—As "Roger Hallmark and the Thrasher Brothers

3 1/2
CAMEO

❏ 485	Angel Baby (Don't You Ever Leave Me)/You Turned Your Back on Love	1967	$30
❏ 425	Don't Cry to Me Babe/R&B in C	1966	$20
❏ 451	Hey Gyp/Hey Kitty, Cool Kitty	1967	$20
❏ 442	Problem Child/Hey Mom, Hey Dad	1966	$20

THREE BELLS, THE
LAWN

| ❏ 251 | He Doesn't Love Me/Softly in the Night | 1965 | $15 |

THREE BLONDE MICE
ATCO

| ❏ 6353 | Alley Cat/What Did I Say | 1965 | $10 |

THREE CHUCKLES, THE
VIK

❏ 0186	Anyway/The Funny Little Things We Used to Do	1956	$30
❏ 0232	Fallen Out of Love/Midnight 'Til Dawn	1956	$30
❏ 0216	Gypsy in My Soul/We're Still Holding Hands	1956	$30
❏ 0194	Tell Me/And the Angels Sing	1956	$30
❏ 0244	Won't You Give Me a Chance/We're Gonna Rock Tonight	1956	$30

X

❏ 0186	Anyway/The Funny Little Things We Used to Do	1956	$30
❏ 0150	Blue Lover/Realize	1955	$30
❏ 095	Foolishly/If I Should Love Again	1955	$30
❏ 0216	Gypsy in My Soul/We're Still Holding Hands	1956	$30
❏ 0134	So Long/You Should Have Told Me	1955	$30
❏ 0194	Tell Me/And the Angels Sing	1956	$30
❏ 0162	Times Two, I Love You/Still Thinking of You	1955	$30

7-Inch Extended Plays

❏ EXA-193	(contents unknown)	1955	$50
❏ EXA-194	(contents unknown)	1955	$50
❏ EXA-192 [PS]	The Three Chuckles (Vol. 1)	1955	$50
❏ EXA-193 [PS]	The Three Chuckles (Vol. 2)	1955	$50
❏ EXA-194 [PS]	The Three Chuckles (Vol. 3)	1955	$50
❏ EXA-192	To Each His Own/Solitude//In the Still of the Night/It's Been a Long, Long Time	1955	$50

THREE DEGREES, THE
ARIOLA AMERICA

❏ 7721	Giving Up, Giving In/Woman in Love	1978	$4
❏ 801	My Simple Heart/Hot Summer Night	1980	$4
❏ 7742	Woman in Love/Out of Love Again	1979	$4

EPIC

| ❏ 50330 | In Love We Grow/Standing Up for Love | 1977 | $4 |
| ❏ 50283 | What I Did for Love/Macaronie Man | 1976 | $4 |

ICHIBAN

| ❏ 89-167 | Tie U Up/(B-side unknown) | 1989 | $5 |

METROMEDIA

| ❏ 109 | Down in the Boondocks/Warm Weather Music | 1969 | $8 |
| ❏ 128 | Feeling of Love/Warm Weather Music | 1969 | $8 |

PHILADELPHIA INT'L.

❏ 3534	Dirty Ol Man/Can't You See What You're Doing to Me	1973	$6
❏ 3585	Free Ride/Loving Cup	1976	$5
❏ 3561	I Didn't Know/Dirty Ol Man	1975	$5
❏ 3568	Take Good Care of Yourself/Here I Am	1975	$5
❏ 3550	When Will I See You Again/Year of Decision	1974	$5

ROULETTE

❏ 7105	Ebb Tide/Low Down	1971	$6
❏ 7125	Find My Way/I Wanna Be Your Baby	1972	$6
❏ 7088	I Do Take You/You're the Fool	1970	$6
❏ 7137	I Won't Let You Go/Through Misty Eyes	1972	$6
❏ 7079	Maybe/Collage	1970	$6
❏ 7079	Maybe/Sugar on Sunday	1970	$6
❏ 7072	Melting Pot/The Grass Will Sing for You	1970	$6
❏ 7102	There's So Much Love All Around/Yours	1971	$6
❏ 7117	Trade Winds/I Turn to You	1972	$6

SWAN

❏ 4224	Close Your Eyes/Gotta Draw the Line	1965	$15
❏ 4197	Gee Baby (I'm Sorry)/Do What You're Supposed to Do	1965	$15
❏ 4214	I'm Gonna Need You/Just Right for Love	1965	$15
❏ 4253	I Wanna Be Your Baby/Tales Are True	1966	$15
❏ 4235	Look in My Eyes/Drivin' Me Mad	1965	$15
❏ 4267	Love of My Life/Are You Satisfied	1967	$15
❏ 4245	Maybe/Yours	1966	$15

WARNER BROS.

| ❏ 7198 | Contact/Oh No Not Again | 1968 | $10 |

THREE DOG NIGHT
ABC

| ❏ 12192 | Everybody Is a Masterpiece/Drive On, Ride On | 1976 | $4 |
| ❏ 12114 | 'Til the World Ends/Yo Te Quiero Hablo (Take You Down) | 1975 | $4 |

ABC DUNHILL

❏ 4294	An Old Fashioned Love Song/Jam	1971	$5
❏ 4317	Black and White/Freedom for the Stallion	1972	$5
❏ 4229	Celebrate/Feeling Alright	1970	$6
❏ 4203	Easy to Be Hard/Dreaming Isn't Good for You	1969	$8
❏ 4215	Eli's Coming/Circle for a Landing	1969	$8
❏ 4370	Let Me Serenade You/Storybook Feeling	1973	$4
❏ 4282	Liar/Can't Get Enough of It	1971	$5
❏ 4239	Mama Told Me (Not to Come)/Rock and Roll Widow	1970	$6
❏ 4239 [PS]	Mama Told Me (Not to Come)/Rock and Roll Widow	1970	$15
❏ 4191	One/Chest Fever	1969	$8
❏ 4262	One Man Band/It Ain't Easy	1970	$6
❏ 4250	Out in the Country/Good Time Living	1970	$6
❏ 4331	Pieces of April/The Writings on the Wall	1972	$5
❏ 15013	Play Something Sweet (Brickyard Blues)/I'd Be So Happy	1974	$4
❏ 4352	Shambala/Our "B" Side	1973	$5

—First pressings have "Dunhill" spelled out in children's blocks

| ❏ 4352 | Shambala/Our "B" Side | 1973 | $5 |

— Transitional pressings have "Dunhill" in children's blocks on one label and "Dunhill" in a box on the other label

| ❏ 4352 | Shambala/Our "B" Side | 1973 | $4 |

—Later pressings have "Dunhill" in a box on both labels (1968-72 style)

❏ 15001	Sure As I'm Sittin' Here/Anytime Babe	1974	$4
❏ 4306	The Family of Man/Going in Circles	1972	$5
❏ 4382	The Show Must Go On/On the Way Back Home	1974	$4
❏ 15010	The Show Must Go On/On the Way Back Home	1974	$8
❏ 4177	Try a Little Tenderness/That No One Ever Hurt So Bad	1969	$8

PASSPORT

| ❏ 7921 | It's a Jungle Out There/Somebody's Gonna Get Hurt | 1983 | $5 |

7-Inch Extended Plays
ABC

| ❏ PRO-40014 [PS] | Hard Labor | 1974 | $25 |

—Part of "Little LP" series (#QD 257)

| ❏ PRO-40014 | The Show Must Go On/Sure As I'm Sitting Here//Anytime Babe/Put Out the Light | 1974 | $25 |

— Quadraphonic jukebox issue; small hole, plays at 33 1/3 rpm

ABC DUNHILL

| ❏ LLP-231 [PS] | Cyan | 1973 | $15 |
| ❏ LLP-231 | Happy Song/Play Children Play//Storybook Feeling/Ridin' Thumb | 1973 | $15 |

—Jukebox issue; small hole, plays at 33 1/3 rpm

| ❏ PRO-50108 [PS] | Harmony | 1971 | $15 |
| ❏ PRO-50108 | My Impersonal Life/An Old Fashioned Love Song//Never Dreamed You'd Leave in Summer/Jam | 1971 | $15 |

—Jukebox issue; small hole, plays at 33 1/3 rpm

THREE DOTS AND A DASH
IMPERIAL

| ❏ 5164 | I'll Never Love Again/Let's Do It | 1951 | $500 |

THREE D'S, THE (1)
PARIS

| ❏ 511 | Baby Doll/Crazy Little Woman | 1958 | $30 |
| ❏ 503 | Little Billy Boy/Let Me Know | 1957 | $30 |

PILGRIM

| ❏ 719 | Broken Dreams/Tell Me That You Love Me | 1956 | $30 |

SQUARE

| ❏ 502 | Squeeze/Graveyard Cha-Cha | 1959 | $100 |

THREE D'S, THE (2)
CAPITOL

| ❏ 5249 | Chim Chim Cheree/Crayon Box | 1964 | $10 |
| ❏ 5188 | Sinner Man/Give, Said the Little Stream | 1964 | $10 |

THREE D'S, THE (U)
DEAN

| ❏ 521 | Broken Hearted/I Love You So | 1961 | $30 |

THREE FRIENDS, THE (1)
CAL-GOLD

| ❏ 169 | Walkin' Shoes/Blue Ribbon Baby | 1961 | $200 |

IMPERIAL

| ❏ 5763 | Dedicated (To the Songs I Love)/Happy as a Man Can Be | 1961 | $40 |

THREE FRIENDS, THE (2)
LIDO

| ❏ 500 | Baby I'll Cry/Blanche | 1956 | $70 |

— Gray label

| ❏ 500 | Baby I'll Cry/Blanche | 1956 | $50 |

—Blue label

| ❏ 502 | I'm Only a Boy/Jinx | 1957 | $60 |

THREE G'S, THE
COLUMBIA

❏ 4-41513	Barbara/Don't Cry Kathy	1959	$20
❏ 4-41584	Eeny-Meeny-Miny-Moe/Take That Step	1960	$20
❏ 4-41955	Foolish Tears/Blueberry Hill	1961	$20
❏ 4-41256	I'll Wait Forever/Sweet Thing	1958	$20
❏ 4-41678	Let's Go Steady for the Summer/Love Call	1960	$20
❏ 4-41175	Let's Go Steady for the Summer/Wild Man	1958	$30
❏ 4-41868	She's Mine/Take My Love	1960	$20
❏ 4-41292	These Are the Little Things/Wonder	1958	$20
❏ 4-41383	When It's Summer Again/Oh, Suzette	1959	$20

RIP

| ❏ 138 | Toy Telephone/Going Steady | 1958 | $40 |

THREE PENNIES, THE
B.T. PUPPY

| ❏ 501 | A Penny for Your Thoughts/Why Am I So Shy | 1964 | $15 |
| ❏ 511 | A Penny for Your Thoughts/Why Am I So Shy | 1965 | $20 |

—As "The English Muffins"; these are the same recordings as on 501

THREE PLAYMATES, THE
SAVOY

❏ 1537	(Do-oo, Do-oo) I Dreamer/Give Your Love to Me	1958	$30
❏ 1523	Giddy-Up-a-Ding-Dong/It Must Be Love	1957	$30
❏ 1528	Sugah Wooga/Lovey Dovey Pair	1958	$30

Number	Title	Yr	NM

THREE SOULS, THE

ARGO

Number	Title	Yr	NM
5472	Hi-Heel Sneakers/ Dangerous Dan Express	1964	$20
5369	The Horse/Madisonville	1960	$30

THREE SUNS, THE

RCA VICTOR

Number	Title	Yr	NM
WP313 [PS]	3/4 Time	1951	$12

— Box for 3-record set (47-4128, 47-4129, 47-4130)

Number	Title	Yr	NM
47-3786	Abide with Me/Ave Maria	1950	$10
47-3057	Adeste Fideles/Santa Claus Is Coming to Town	1949	$10
47-4010	After You've Gone/ Remember Me in Your Dreams	1950	$15
47-5246	Anna/Little Red Monkey	1953	$15
47-4464	April in Paris/Moonglow	1952	$10
47-6273	Arrividerci Roma/ Cha Cha Joe	1955	$10
47-4200	Auf Wiedersehn/Hands Across the Table	1951	$12
47-4201	Autumn Leaves/ La Vie En Rose	1951	$12
47-3788	Beautiful Isle of Somewhere/ In the Garden	1950	$12

— The above three comprise box set WP-285, "The Three Suns Present Your Favorite Hymns

Number	Title	Yr	NM
47-3105	Beyond the Sunset/The Game of Broken Hearts	1949	$40

— With Rosalie Allen and Elton Britt

Number	Title	Yr	NM
47-4790	Birds 'n' Bees/Sky-High	1952	$15
47-3722	Blue Prelude/I May Hate Myself in the Morning	1950	$15
47-2759	Canadian Capers/The Wedding of the Painted Doll	1949	$10

— The above four comprise a box set

Number	Title	Yr	NM
47-3079	Close Your Eyes and Dream/Merry Maiden Polka	1949	$15
47-4199	Come On-a My House/Hula Blues	1951	$10
47-4510	Cool, Cool Kisses/ Stolen Love	1952	$15
47-3272	Cruising Down the River/Allah's Holiday	1949	$15
47-2756	Dancing Tambourine/ Stumbling	1949	$12
47-2840	Deep Purple/Dardanella	1949	$12
47-4677	Delicado/Plink, Plank, Plunk	1952	$15
47-2757	Dizzy Fingers/Eccentric	1949	$12
47-5961	For You/Perdido	1954	$15
47-3824	Gone Fishin'/So Tall a Tree	1950	$15
47-3230	Goofus/Ragging the Scale	1949	$10
47-7970	Honey Bee/Fun in the Sun	1961	$8
47-2996	Hop Scotch Polka/The Windmill's Turning	1949	$15
47-2898	Hurry! Hurry! Hurry!/ Ballin' the Jack	1949	$15
47-2842	I'll Never Wish for More Than This/The Breeze and I	1949	$10

— The above four comprise a box set

Number	Title	Yr	NM
47-4465	Intermezzo/ Moonlight Sonata	1952	$10
47-5417	Invisible Hands/One Step	1953	$15
47-3976	It Is No Secret (What God Can Do)/To Think You've Chosen Me	1950	$15
47-6084	I Wonder, I Wonder, I Wonder/Dancing with Tears in My Eyes	1955	$10
47-4463	Laura/My Reverie	1952	$12
47-3787	Lead Kindly Light/ Whispering Hope	1950	$12
47-4287	Little Jumping Jack/Painting Clouds with Sunshine	1951	$15
47-2964	Lover's Gold/In a Shady Nook by a Babbling Brook	1949	$15
47-3817	Miaianne/When the Saints Go Marching In	1950	$15
47-5768	Moonlight and Roses (Bring Mem'ries of You)/Crazy Legs	1954	$15
47-8373	My Man/Happy Wedding Song	1964	$8
47-4466	My Silent Love/Smoke Rings	1952	$10

— The above four comprise a box set

Number	Title	Yr	NM
47-5463	Peg o' My Heart/Jealous	1953	$15
47-3095	Penthouse Serenade/ Frasquita Serenade	1949	$15
47-6713	Postmark: Vienna/ Wind River Valley	1956	$12
47-6202	Satan Takes a Holiday/ You and You Alone	1955	$10
47-3096	Serenade from the Student Prince/Serenade in the Night	1949	$10

— The above three comprise a box set

Number	Title	Yr	NM
47-3924	Sleigh Ride/I'll Find You	1949	$20
47-4323	Sleigh Ride/Uncle Mistletoe	1951	$20
47-3025	Soft Lips/Give Me Some Sugar, Sugar Baby	1949	$15
47-3202	Sugar Blues/The French Can-Can Song	1949	$15
47-2841	Sunrise Serenade/ When Day Is Done	1949	$10

— The above three comprise box set WP 185, "The Three Suns Present

Number	Title	Yr	NM
47-4385	Sunshower/Sleepy Serenade	1951	$15

Number	Title	Yr	NM
47-6461	The Beautiful Girls of Vienna/Petite Papillon	1956	$12
47-4221	The Bird of Happiness/ At the End of Day	1951	$15
47-5553	The Creep/Just One More Chance	1953	$15
47-3232	The Darktown Strutters' Ball/The Glow-Worm	1949	$12

— The above three comprise a box set

Number	Title	Yr	NM
47-3094	The Donkey Serenade/ Serenade	1949	$10
47-3768	The Flying Red Horse Polka/ Leicester Square Rag	1950	$15
47-6881	The Lovers/Wailin' Guitar	1957	$10
47-6574	Theme from The Proud Ones/Haunted Guitar	1956	$10
47-4130	The Sleeping Beauty Waltz/Coppelia Waltz	1951	$10

— The above three comprise box set WP 313, "3/4 Time

Number	Title	Yr	NM
47-4090	The Syncopated Clock/ March of Cards	1951	$10
WP185 [PS]	The Three Suns Present	1949	$10

— Box for three-record set (47-2839, 47-2840, 47-2841)

Number	Title	Yr	NM
WP-285 [PS]	The Three Suns Present Your Favorite Hymns	1950	$10

— Box for set containing 47-3786, 47-3787, 47-3788

Number	Title	Yr	NM
47-2924	Ting-a-Ling/Everybody Kiss the Bride	1949	$15
47-4150	Tom's Tune/These Things I Offer You	1951	$15
47-5874	Touch/Southern Star	1954	$15
47-7072	Tumbling Tumbleweeds/ Sentimental Journey	1957	$10
47-5082	Twilight Boogie/Junga-Junga	1952	$15
47-2839	Twilight Time/Hindustan	1949	$10
47-5185	Waggashoe/Ecstacy Tango	1953	$10
47-4128	Waltz Serenade/ Waltz in A-Flat	1951	$15
47-4122	What Will I Tell My Heart/I Whistle a Happy Tune	1951	$15
47-3058	Winter Wonderland/ White Christmas	1949	$10

7-Inch Extended Plays

Number	Title	Yr	NM
EPA-618 [PS]	Autumn Leaves	1955	$15
EPA-618	Autumn Leaves/Waltz Serenade//La Vie En Rose/Waltz in A Flat	1955	$15
EPA736	My Reverie/Intermezzo// Tenderly/Laura	1956	$10
547-0087	My Reverie/Moon Glow// Intermezzo/Smoke Rings	1952	$15

— One record of 2-EP set EPB 3012

Number	Title	Yr	NM
547-0088	My Silent Love/Moonlight Sonata//April in Paris/Laura	1952	$15

— One record of 2-EP set EPB 3012

Number	Title	Yr	NM
EPB1041 [PS]	Soft and Sweet	1954	$12
547-1041	Stars Fell on Alabama/ The Touch of Your Lips//Moonlight in Vermont/Flamingo	1954	$10

— One record of 2-EP set EPB 1041

Number	Title	Yr	NM
547-0032	Sunrise Serenade/I'll Never Wish for More Than This// Deep Purple/Hindustan	1952	$15

— One record of 2-EP set EPB 3034

Number	Title	Yr	NM
547-1040	There Is No Greater Love/A Sinner Kissed an Angel//Autumn Nocturne/Blue Orchids	1954	$10

— One record of 2-EP set EPB 1041

Number	Title	Yr	NM
EPA653 [PS]	The Sounds of Christmas	1955	$15
EPA-5021 [PS]	The Three Suns (Gold Standard Series)	1958	$12
EPB3034 [PS]	The Three Suns Present	1952	$15

— Two-pocket jacket for two-EP set

Number	Title	Yr	NM
EPA736 [PS]	(title unknown)	1956	$12
EPB3012 [PS]	Twilight Moods	1952	$15

— Two-pocket jacket for two-EP set

Number	Title	Yr	NM
LPC-110 [PS]	Twilight Time	1961	$12
547-0031	Twilight Time/Dardarnella// When Day Is Done/ The Breeze and I	1952	$15

— One record of 2-EP set EPB 3034

Number	Title	Yr	NM
LPC-110	Twilight Time/Don't Take Your Love from Me//Peg o' My Heart/Arrividerci Roma	1961	$10

— Compact 33 Double"; small hole, plays at 33 1/3 rpm

Number	Title	Yr	NM
EPA-5021	Twilight Time/Hindustan// Peg o' My Heart/ Canadian Capers	1958	$15
EPA655 [PS]	White Christmas	1955	$15
EPA655	White Christmas/Santa Claus Is Coming to Town/ Der Tannenbaum//It Came Upon a Midnight Clear/ Greensleeves/God Rest Ye Merry Gentlemen	1955	$15

THREE VALES, THE

CINDY

Number	Title	Yr	NM
3007	Blue Lights/Ay, Ay, Ay	1957	$120

THREE WISE MEN, THE

VIRGIN

Number	Title	Yr	NM
642	Thanks For Christmas/ Countdown To Christmas Party Time	1983	$10
642 [PS]	Thanks For Christmas/ Countdown To Christmas Party Time	1983	$10

— Record and sleeve are U.K. imports; band is actually XTC

THREETEENS, THE

REV

Number	Title	Yr	NM
3516	Dear 53310761/Doowaddie	1958	$50

THRILLERS, THE (1)

BIG TOWN

Number	Title	Yr	NM
109	The Drunkard/Mattie, Leave Me Alone	1953	$400

HERALD

Number	Title	Yr	NM
432	Lizabeth/Please Talk to Me	1954	$400

THRILLER

Number	Title	Yr	NM
3530	Lessie Mae/I'm Going to Live My Life Alone	1953	$1000

THRILLERS, THE (2)

UPTOWN

Number	Title	Yr	NM
715	Come What May/This I Know Little Girl	1965	$15

THRILLS, THE

CAPITOL

Number	Title	Yr	NM
5719	Here's a Heart/Bring It On Home to Me	1966	$30
5871	Show the World Where It's At/Underneath My Make-Up	1967	$30
5631	What Can Go Wrong/No One	1966	$30

THROWING MUSES
7-Inch Extended Plays

SPEWING MOUSES

Number	Title	Yr	NM
0(# unknown)	Stand Up/Dirt Is On the Floor/The Party + 1	1984	$75
0(# unknown) [PS]	Stand Up/Dirt Is On the Floor/The Party + 1	1984	$75

— Oversized 9-inch sleeve

THROWN-UPS, THE
7-Inch Extended Plays

AMPHETAMINE REPTILE

Number	Title	Yr	NM
SCALE10	Eat My Dump	1988	$35
SCALE10 [PS]	Eat My Dump	1988	$35

— 600 made

Number	Title	Yr	NM
SCALE4	Felch	1986	$43

— With Steve Turner, later of Mudhoney

Number	Title	Yr	NM
SCALE4 [PS]	Felch	1986	$43

— 500 made

Number	Title	Yr	NM
SCALE7	Smiling Panties	1987	$38
SCALE7 [PS]	Smiling Panties	1987	$38

— 600 made

THUDPUCKER, JIMMY

Fictional singing star from Garry Trudeau's "Doonesbury" comic strip.

WARNER BROS.

Number	Title	Yr	NM
8245	Ginny's Song (Part 1)/ Ginny's Song (Part 2)	1976	$6
8245 [PS]	Ginny's Song (Part 1)/ Ginny's Song (Part 2)	1976	$6

THUNDER AND ROSES

UNITED ARTISTS

Number	Title	Yr	NM
50536	Country Life/I Love a Woman	1969	$15

THUNDER HEADS, THE

CARTWHEEL

Number	Title	Yr	NM
100	Thunder Head/ Unemployment	1966	$40

THUNDER, JOHNNY

CALLA

Number	Title	Yr	NM
161	I'm Alive/Verbal Expressions of T.V.	1969	$6

DIAMOND

Number	Title	Yr	NM
222	Am I Right or Am I Wrong/You Send Me	1967	$8
206	Bewildered/Just Me and You	1966	$8
152	Constitution of Love/ Good Morning Sadness	1964	$8
192	Everybody Do the Sloopy/Beautiful	1965	$8

Number	Title	Yr	NM
❑ 155	Everybody Likes to Dance with Johnny/Zoo-Lee-Oh	1964	$8
❑ 148	Hey Child/Darling Je Vous Aime Beaucoup	1963	$12
❑ 129	Loop De Loop/Don't Be Ashamed	1962	$20
❑ 218	Make Love to Me/ Teach Me Tonight	1967	$8

— With Ruby Winters

Number	Title	Yr	NM
❑ 169	More, More More Love, Love, Love/ Shout It to the World	1964	$8
❑ 196	My Prayer/A Broken Heart	1966	$8
❑ 246	Put It in Motion/ Groovy Two Shoes	1968	$8
❑ 175	Send Her to Me/Shout It to the World	1964	$8
❑ 185	Suzie-Q/Dear John, I'm Going to Leave You	1965	$8
❑ 137	The Outlaw/Jailer, Bring Me Water	1963	$10
❑ 238	We Only Have One Life (Let's Live It Together)/ Teach Me Tonight	1968	$8

— With Ruby Winters

EPIC

Number	Title	Yr	NM
❑ 9329	Ever Your Man/Horror Show	1959	$20

UNITED ARTISTS

Number	Title	Yr	NM
❑ 50736	Power to the People/ Love Trip	1971	$6

THUNDERBOLTS, THE

DOT

Number	Title	Yr	NM
❑ 16496	Lost Planets/March of the Spacemen	1963	$30

THUNDERCLAP NEWMAN

TRACK

Number	Title	Yr	NM
❑ 2656	Something in the Air/Wilhelmina	1969	$12
❑ 2769	Something in the Air/Wilhelmina	1970	$6

THUNDERGRIN

EPIC

Number	Title	Yr	NM
❑ 10215	Women in the Street/ Mr. Simms	1967	$10

THUNDERKLOUD, BILLY, AND THE CHIEFTONES

20TH CENTURY

Number	Title	Yr	NM
❑ 2239	Pledging My Love/I Will Love You Until I Die	1975	$5
❑ 2181	What Time of Day/ When Love Is Right	1975	$5

POLYDOR

Number	Title	Yr	NM
❑ 14321	Indian Nation (The Lament of the Cherokee Reservation Indian)/I'm Going Right to Where I Do Wrong	1976	$5
❑ 14362	It's Alright/The Wanderer	1976	$5
❑ 14383	Let Me Be Your Man/A Hundred Years from Now	1977	$5
❑ 14449	Let Me Love You/My Lady	1977	$5
❑ 14412	Oklahoma Wind/The Trouble with Angels	1977	$5
❑ 14338	Try a Little Tenderness/A Natural Feelin' for You	1976	$5

THUNDERTONES, THE

DONNA

Number	Title	Yr	NM
❑ 1343	Thunder Rhythm/Pay Day	1961	$40

DOT

Number	Title	Yr	NM
❑ 16177	The Street Beat/ Happy Little Jug	1961	$40

— As "Lenny and the Thundertones"

THURMOND, DUFF

NEW VOICE

Number	Title	Yr	NM
❑ 816	If You Love Me Baby/ Now That You Left Me	1966	$70

THURSDAY'S CHILDREN

INTERNATIONAL ARTISTS

Number	Title	Yr	NM
❑ 110	Air Conditioned Man/ Sominoes	1967	$200
❑ 115	Help, Murder, Police/You Can't Forget About That	1967	$200

THYME

A-SQUARE

Number	Title	Yr	NM
❑ 201	Somehow/Shame, Shame	1969	$50
❑ 202	Time of the Season/I Found a Love	1969	$50

BANG

Number	Title	Yr	NM
❑ 546	Love to Love/Very Last Day	1967	$30

TICO AND THE TRIUMPHS

AMY

Number	Title	Yr	NM
❑ 876	Cards of Love/Noise	1963	$200
❑ 860	Cry, Lil' Boy, Cry/Get Up and Do the Wobble	1962	$125
❑ 835	Motorcycle/I Don't Believe Them	1961	$125
❑ 845	Wildflower/Express Train	1962	$125

MADISON

Number	Title	Yr	NM
❑ 169	Motorcycle/I Don't Believe Them	1961	$200

TIDES, THE

HIT

Number	Title	Yr	NM
❑ 42	Telstar/The Lonely Bull	1962	$10

— B-side by the Dan Rubin Orchestra

TIFFANY

MCA

Number	Title	Yr	NM
❑ 53371	All This Time/Can't Stop a Heartbeat	1988	$3
❑ 53371 [PS]	All This Time/Can't Stop a Heartbeat	1988	$3
❑ 53231	Could've Been/The Heart of Love	1987	$3
❑ 53231 [PS]	Could've Been/The Heart of Love	1987	$3
❑ 53076	Danny/No Rules	1987	$12
❑ 53325	Feelings of Forever/ Out of My Heart	1988	$3
❑ 53325 [PS]	Feelings of Forever/ Out of My Heart	1988	$3
❑ 53612	Hold an Old Friend's Hand/Ruthless	1989	$5
❑ 53285	I Saw Him Standing There/Mr. Mambo	1988	$3
❑ 53285 [PS]	I Saw Him Standing There/Mr. Mambo	1988	$3
❑ 53147	I Think We're Alone Now/No Rules	1987	$3
❑ 53147 [PS]	I Think We're Alone Now/No Rules	1987	$3
❑ 53704	It's the Lover (Not the Love)/Ruthless	1989	$6

TIFFANY SHADE, THE

MAINSTREAM

Number	Title	Yr	NM
❑ 680	An Older Man/Sam	1968	$20
❑ 677	One Good Reason/Would You Take My Mind Out for a Walk	1968	$20

TIFFANYS, THE

ARCTIC

Number	Title	Yr	NM
❑ 101	Love Me/Happiest Girl in the World	1964	$30

ATLANTIC

Number	Title	Yr	NM
❑ 2240	Please Tell Me/Gossip	1964	$30

JOSIE

Number	Title	Yr	NM
❑ 952	Heaven on Earth/Take Another Look at Me	1966	$15
❑ 942	I Feel the Same Way Too/I Just Wanna Be a Girl	1965	$15

KR

Number	Title	Yr	NM
❑ 120	He's Good for Me/It's Got to Be a Great Song	1967	$30

— As "The Tiffanies"

MRS

Number	Title	Yr	NM
❑ 777	Please Tell Me/Gossip	1964	$100

RKO

Number	Title	Yr	NM
❑ 120	He's Good for Me/It's Got to Be a Great Song	1967	$12

— Are the KR and RKO releases one and the same? We don't know

ROCKIN' ROBIN

Number	Title	Yr	NM
❑ 1	I've Got a Girl/I Don't Dig Western Movies	1963	$300

SWAN

Number	Title	Yr	NM
❑ 4104	Atlanta/The Pleasure of Love	1962	$30

TIGERS, THE

COLPIX

Number	Title	Yr	NM
❑ SPEC-773 [PS]	GeeTO Tiger/The Big Sounds of the GeeTO Tiger	1965	$200

— Sleeve appears to have been available only with the promotional B-side

Number	Title	Yr	NM
❑ SPEC-773	GeeTO Tiger/The Big Sounds of the GeeTO Tiger	1965	$100

— Special promotional issue

Number	Title	Yr	NM
❑ 773	GeeTO Tiger/The Prowl	1965	$60

TIKIS, THE, AND THE FABULONS

PANORAMA

Number	Title	Yr	NM
❑ 13	Take a Look/For Your Love	1965	$30

TOWER

Number	Title	Yr	NM
❑ 181	Take a Look/Cherry Pie	1965	$15

TIKIS, THE

Probably two different groups.

ASCOT

Number	Title	Yr	NM
❑ 2204	High School Dropout Blues/Whole Lotta Soul	1966	$12
❑ 2186	Stop-Look-Listen/ Cream in My Coffee	1965	$10

AUTUMN

Number	Title	Yr	NM
❑ 28	Bye Bye Bye/Lost My Love Today	1966	$10

— As "The Other Tikis"

Number	Title	Yr	NM
❑ 18	If I've Been Dreaming/ Pay Attention to Me	1965	$10

— As "The Other Tikis"

DIAL

Number	Title	Yr	NM
❑ 4048	Somebody's Sun/ Little Miss Lovelight	1966	$12

WARNER BROS.

Number	Title	Yr	NM
❑ 5818	Bye Bye Bye/Lost My Love Today	1966	$10

TIL, SONNY

Also see THE ORIOLES.

JUBILEE

Number	Title	Yr	NM
❑ 5118	(Danger) Soft Shoulders/ Congratulations to Someone	1953	$200
❑ 5066	Fool's World/For All We Know	1951	$300

— Black vinyl

Number	Title	Yr	NM
❑ 5066	Fool's World/For All We Know	1951	$800

— Red vinyl

Number	Title	Yr	NM
❑ 5099	Good/Picadilly	1952	$100

— With Edna McGriff

Number	Title	Yr	NM
❑ 5112	Have You Heard/ Lonely Wine	1953	$200
❑ 5060	I Never Knew (I Could Love Anybody)/My Prayer	1951	$300
❑ 5090	Once in Awhile/I Only Have Eyes for You	1952	$60

— With Edna McGriff

RCA VICTOR

Number	Title	Yr	NM
❑ 74-0432	Colours/Love Is What It's All About	1971	$8
❑ 74-0606	Crying in the Chapel/ What Are You Doing New Year's Eve	1971	$8
❑ 74-0390	Don't Feel No Pain/One Big Happy Family	1970	$8
❑ 47-9759	Tears and Misery/I Better Leave Love Alone	1969	$8
❑ 74-0529	'Til Then/Love or Desire	1971	$8

ROULETTE

Number	Title	Yr	NM
❑ 4079	Shy/First Blush	1958	$30

'TIL TUESDAY

EPIC

Number	Title	Yr	NM
❑ 34-08059	(Believed You Were) Lucky/Limits to Love	1988	$4
❑ 34-08059 [PS]	(Believed You Were) Lucky/Limits to Love	1988	$4
❑ 34-06571	Coming Up Close/ Angels Never Call	1986	$4
❑ 34-06571 [PS]	Coming Up Close/ Angels Never Call	1986	$8
❑ 34-04935	Looking Over My Shoulder (Single Mix)/ Don't Watch Me Bleed	1985	$4
❑ 34-04935 [PS]	Looking Over My Shoulder (Single Mix)/ Don't Watch Me Bleed	1985	$4
❑ 34-05673	Love in a Vacuum/ No More Crying	1985	$5
❑ 34-05673 [PS]	Love in a Vacuum/ No More Crying	1985	$5
❑ 34-05673 [DJ]	Love in a Vacuum (Single Remix)/(Long Version)	1985	$5
❑ 34-06289	What About Love/Will She Just Fall Down	1986	$3
❑ 34-06289 [PS]	What About Love/Will She Just Fall Down	1986	$3

TILLER, FLOYD

HIT

Number	Title	Yr	NM
❑ 275	Born Free/Winchester Cathedral	1966	$8

— B-side by the New Orleans Band

TILLIS, MEL

COLUMBIA

Number	Title	Yr	NM
❑ 4-40904	Case of the Blues/ It's My Life	1957	$30
❑ 4-41277	Finally/The Brooklyn Bridge	1958	$20
❑ 4-41986	Hearts of Stone/That's Where the Hurt Comes In	1961	$30
❑ 4-41632	It's So Easy/Loco Weed	1960	$20
❑ 4-40845	It Takes a Worried Man to Sing a Worried Song/ Honky Tonk Song	1957	$30
❑ 4-42262	Party Girl/If I Lost Your Love	1962	$30

Number	Title	Yr	NM
❏ 4-41863	Say/Walk On, Boy	1960	$20
❏ 4-41115	Teen Age Wedding/ Lonely Street	1958	$40
❏ 4-41038	This Heart/Take My Hand	1957	$30

DECCA

Number	Title	Yr	NM
❏ 31528	Couldn't See the Forest for the Trees/It's No Surprise	1963	$12
❏ 31474	Don't Tell Mama/Half Laughing, Half Crying	1963	$12
❏ 31623	It'll Be Easy/I'm Gonna Act Right	1964	$10

ELEKTRA

Number	Title	Yr	NM
❏ 47116	A Million Old Goodbyes/ Louisiana Lonely	1981	$4
❏ 46536	Blind in Love/Blackjack, Water Back	1979	$4
❏ 47412	It's a Long Way to Daytona/ Always You, Always Me	1982	$4
❏ 46583	Lying Time Again/Fooled Around and Fell in Love	1980	$4
❏ 47178	One-Night Fever/Time Has Treated You Well	1981	$4
❏ 47082	Southern Rains/Forgive Me for Giving You the Blues	1980	$4
❏ 69963	Stay a Little Longer/ Dream of Me	1982	$4
❏ 47015	Steppin' Out/ Whiskey Chasin'	1980	$4
❏ 47453	The One That Got Away/ Why Ain't Life the Way It's S'posed to Be	1982	$4
❏ 47233 [DJ]	White Christmas/ Blue Christmas	1981	$6

—B-side by Eddy Raven

KAPP

Number	Title	Yr	NM
❏ 881	All Right (I'll Sign the Papers)/Helpless, Hopeless Fool	1968	$8
❏ 941	Destroyed by Man/I Haven't Seen Mary in Years	1968	$8
❏ 837	Goodbye Wheeling/ At the Sight of You	1967	$8
❏ 804	Life Turned Her That Way/ If I Could Only Start Over	1967	$8
❏ 804 [PS]	Life Turned Her That Way/ If I Could Only Start Over	1967	$20
❏ 764	Mental Revenge/Guide Me Home My Georgia Moon	1966	$10
❏ 986	Old Faithful/Sorrow Overtakes the Wine	1969	$8
❏ 905	Something Special/ You Name It	1968	$8
❏ 772	Stateside/Home Is Where the Hurt Is	1966	$8
❏ 867	Survival of the Fittest/ The Old Gang's Gone	1967	$8
❏ 959	Who's Julie/Give Me One More Day	1968	$8

MCA

Number	Title	Yr	NM
❏ 52247	A Cowboy's Dream/ After All This Time	1983	$3
❏ 40946	Ain't No California/What Comes Natural to a Fool	1978	$5
❏ 40710	Burning Memories/Golden Nugget Gambling Casino	1977	$5
❏ 41041	Coca Cola Cowboy/ Cottonmouth	1979	$5
❏ 40627	Good Woman Blues/You Can't Trust a Crazy Man	1976	$5
❏ 40667	Heart Healer/It's Just Not That Easy to Say	1976	$5
❏ 40900	I Believe in You/It's Don't Trust You Daddy	1978	$5
❏ 40764	I Got the Hoss/It's Been a Long Time	1977	$5
❏ 52182	In the Middle of the Night/Even at Her Worst (She's Still the Best)	1983	$3
❏ 40559	Love Revival/Gator Bar	1976	$5
❏ 40983	Send Me Down to Tucson/Charlie's Angel	1978	$5
❏ 52285	She Meant Forever When She Said Goodbye/Try It Again	1983	$3
❏ KFC-001 [DJ]	There's No Turning Back/A Brandy Alexander	1977	$15

—Promo only; "America's Country Good Music from Kentucky Fried Chicken" on label

Number	Title	Yr	NM
❏ 40836	What Did I Promise Her Last Night/Woman, You Should Be in the Movies	1977	$5

MGM

Number	Title	Yr	NM
❏ 14850	Always Just a Memory Away/Come On Home	1976	$6
❏ 14782	Best Way I Know How/ Honey Dew Melon	1975	$6
❏ 14275	Brand New Mister Me/ Brand New Wrapper	1971	$6
❏ 14176	Commercial Affection/I Thought About You	1970	$6
❏ 14148	Heaven Everyday/How You Drink the Wine	1970	$6
❏ 14418	I Ain't Never/Burden of Love	1972	$6
❏ 14835	Lookin' for Tomorrow (And Findin' Yesterdays)/ Tennessee Banjo Man	1975	$6
❏ 14744	Memory Maker/Second Best	1974	$6
❏ 14846	Mental Revenge/My Bad Girl Treats Me Good	1976	$6
❏ 14689	Midnight, Me and the Blues/ Modern Home Magazine	1974	$6

Number	Title	Yr	NM
❏ 14585	Sawmill/Mama's Gonna Pray	1973	$6
❏ 14720	Stomp Them Grapes/Hang My Pictures in Your Heart	1974	$6
❏ 14522	Thank You for Being You/Over the Hill	1973	$6
❏ 14211	The Arms of a Fool/ Veil of White Lace	1971	$6
❏ 14804	Woman in the Back of My Mind/Kissing Your Picture (Is So Cold)	1975	$6
❏ 14372	Would You Want the World to End/Things Have Changed a Lot	1972	$6

RADIO

Number	Title	Yr	NM
❏ 001	City Lights/Who's Julie	1989	$6

RCA

Number	Title	Yr	NM
❏ PB-14175	California Road/ One More Time	1985	$3

RIC

Number	Title	Yr	NM
❏ 178	Bring On the Blues/ Mr. Dropout	1965	$15
❏ 150	Ode to the Little Brown Shack Out Back/Not in Front of the Kids	1965	$15
❏ 158	Wine/Buried Alive	1965	$15

TILLIS, MEL, AND SHERRY BRYCE

MGM

Number	Title	Yr	NM
❏ 14365	Anything's Better Than Nothing/Then It Will Be All Over	1972	$6
❏ 14472	Back to Life/Happyville	1972	$6
❏ 14714	Don't Let Go/Why Not Do the Things (They Think We've Done)	1974	$6
❏ 14660	Let's Go All the Way Tonight/In the Vine	1973	$6
❏ 14303	Living and Learning/ Tangled Vines	1971	$6
❏ 14803	Mr. Right and Mrs. Wrong/ Just Two Strangers Passing in the Night	1975	$6
❏ 14255	Take My Hand/Life's Little Surprises	1971	$6

TILLIS, MEL, WITH GLEN CAMPBELL

MCA

Number	Title	Yr	NM
❏ 52474	Slow Nights/Midnight Love	1984	$3

TILLIS, MEL, AND BILL PHILLIPS

COLUMBIA

Number	Title	Yr	NM
❏ 4-41530	Georgia Town Blues/Till I Get Enough of These Blues	1959	$20
❏ 4-41416	Sawmill/You Are the Reason	1959	$20

TILLIS, MEL, AND WEBB PIERCE

DECCA

Number	Title	Yr	NM
❏ 31445	How Come Your Dog Don't Bite Nobody But Me/So Soon	1962	$10

TILLIS, MEL, AND NANCY SINATRA

ELEKTRA

Number	Title	Yr	NM
❏ 47247	Play Me or Trade Me/ Where Would I Be	1981	$5
❏ 47157	Texas Cowboy Night/ After the Lovin'	1981	$5

TILLIS, PAM

ELEKTRA

Number	Title	Yr	NM
❏ 47171	Every Home Should Have One/Holding On to What Is Gone	1981	$15

WARNER BROS.

Number	Title	Yr	NM
❏ 29155	Goodbye Highway/ Somebody Else's	1984	$6
❏ 28676	I Thought I'd About Had It with You/Drawn to the Fire	1986	$5
❏ 28444	I Wish She Wouldn't Treat You That Way/ Drawn to the Fire	1987	$5
❏ 29517	Love Is Sneakin' Up on You/ Wish I Was in Love Tonight	1983	$10
❏ 28984	One of Those Things/ One Way Ticket	1985	$6
❏ 28346	There Goes My Love/ Drawn to the Fire	1987	$5
❏ 28806	Those Memories of You/ Drawn to the Fire	1986	$5

TILLMAN, BERTHA

BRENT

Number	Title	Yr	NM
❏ 7032	I Wish/(I Believe) Something Funny Is Going On	1962	$50
❏ 7029	Oh My Angel/Lovin' Time	1962	$40

TILLMAN, FLOYD

CIMARRON

Number	Title	Yr	NM
❏ 4056	Daisy Mae/Let's Make Memories Tonight	1962	$15

COLUMBIA

Number	Title	Yr	NM
❏ 4-20894	Don't Say You Love Me/I'll Still Be Loving You	1952	$30
❏ 4-20771	Each Night at Nine/I'm Falling for You	1951	$40
❏ 4-21004	Goodbye Tomorrow, Hello Yesterday/I Finally Saw the Light	1952	$30
❏ 2-535	I Almost Lost My Mind/ Precious Memories	1950	$50

—Microgroove 33 1/3 rpm 7-inch single, small hole

Number	Title	Yr	NM
❏ 2-404	I Gotta Have My Baby Back/ It Had to Be That Way	1949	$50

—Microgroove 33 1/3 rpm 7-inch single, small hole

Number	Title	Yr	NM
❏ 4-20860	I'll Be Playing the Field From Now On/Why Do I Drink	1951	$30
❏ 4-21257	I'll Never Be the Same/Call on Me	1954	$30
❏ 2-330(?)	I'll Never Slip Around Again/ This Cold War with You	1949	$50

—Microgroove 33 1/3 rpm 7-inch single, small hole

Number	Title	Yr	NM
❏ 4-20793	I Love You/I Don't Care Anymore	1951	$30
❏ 4-20956	It's Over, All Over/Take My Love With You Too	1952	$30
❏ 4-21200	More Than Anything/ Just One More Time	1954	$30
❏ 4-21303	One More Day Wasted/ Sometime, Somewhere, Somehow	1954	$30
❏ 4-21372	She's Long Gone/Let's Make Memories Tonight	1955	$30
❏ 4-33058	Slipping Around/I Love You So Much It Hurts	1961	$8

—Columbia Hall of Fame" series; red label

Number	Title	Yr	NM
❏ 4-33031	Slipping Around/I Love You So Much It Hurts	1961	$12

—Columbia Hall of Fame" series; red label

Number	Title	Yr	NM
❏ 2-216	Slipping Around/You Made Me Live, Love and Die	1949	$60

—Microgroove 33 1/3 rpm 7-inch single, small hole

Number	Title	Yr	NM
❏ 4-21076	Small Little Town/The Worm Has Turned	1953	$30
❏ 4-20746	The Grandest Prize/I've Got the Craziest Feeling	1950	$40
❏ 2-810	The Grandest Prize/I've Got the Craziest Feeling	1950	$50

—Microgroove 33 1/3 rpm 7-inch single, small hole

Number	Title	Yr	NM
❏ 6-810	The Grandest Prize/I've Got the Craziest Feeling	1950	$50

—Original issue; reissued on 4-20746

LIBERTY

Number	Title	Yr	NM
❏ 55280	It Just Tears Me Up/ The Song of Music	1960	$20
❏ 55323	Whatever You Do/The Record Goes 'Round	1961	$15

MUSICOR

Number	Title	Yr	NM
❏ 1292	At Four O'Clock Each Morning/I Gotta Get Outta This House	1968	$8
❏ 1342	Autumn Song (I'm Losing You)/It Hurts So Hard So Long	1968	$8
❏ 1304	Each Night at Nine/ Dream On	1968	$8
❏ 1254	Fightin' and Kissin'/A Memory's a Handy Thing to Have	1967	$10
❏ 1279	I Didn't Keep My Big Mouth Shut/I Reap What I Sow	1967	$10
❏ 1355	It Makes No Difference Now/A Rainbow Is the Color of Love	1969	$8
❏ 1196	Lonely Where I Stand/ Green Hills of Earth	1966	$10
❏ 1230	One for the Money/ You Won't Even Know That I Am Gone	1967	$10
❏ 1316	Pour Me a Heartache/ Because You're Gone	1968	$8

RCA VICTOR

Number	Title	Yr	NM
❏ 47-7157	Slipping Around/I Love You So Much It Hurts	1958	$20

SARG

Number	Title	Yr	NM
❏ 137	Save a Little for Me/ Baby I Just Want You	1956	$40

SIMS

Number	Title	Yr	NM
❏ 150	Gotta Have My Baby Back/I'll Never Get Over You	1963	$15

TILLOTSON, JOHNNY

AMOS

Number	Title	Yr	NM
❏ 146	I Don't Believe In It Anymore/ Kansas City, Kansas	1970	$6
❏ 136	Susan/Love Waits for Me	1970	$6
❏ 117	Tears on My Pillow/ Remember When	1969	$6
❏ 125	What Am I Living For/ Joy to the World	1969	$6

BUDDAH

Number	Title	Yr	NM
❏ 279	Make Me Believe/The Flower Kissed the Shoes That Jesus Wore	1972	$5
❏ 232	Star Spangled Bus/ Apple Bend	1971	$5

Number	Title	Yr	NM
❑ 256	Welfare Hero/The Flower Kissed the Shoes That Jesus Wore	1971	$5

CADENCE

Number	Title	Yr	NM
❑ 1353	Dreamy Eyes/Well, I'm Your Man	1958	$30
❑ 1409	Dreamy Eyes/Well, I'm Your Man	1961	$20
❑ 1377	Earth Angel/Pledging My Love	1960	$30
❑ 1377 [PS]	Earth Angel/Pledging My Love	1960	$40
❑ 1441	Funny How Time Slips Away/A Very Good Year for Girls	1963	$20
❑ 1432	I Can't Help It (If I'm Still in Love with You)/I'm So Lonesome I Could Cry	1962	$20
❑ 1354	I'm Never Gonna Kiss You/Cherie, Cherie	1958	$30

—With Genevieve

❑ 1418	It Keeps Right On a-Hurtin'/She Gave Sweet Love to Me	1962	$20
❑ 1434	Out of My Mind/Empty Feelin'	1963	$20
❑ 1384	Poetry in Motion/Princess, Princess	1960	$30
❑ 1424	Send Me the Pillow You Dream On/What'll I Do	1962	$20
❑ 1365	True True Happiness/Love Is Blind	1959	$30
❑ 1372	Why Do I Love You So/Never Let Me Go	1959	$30
❑ 1404	Without You/Cutie Pie	1961	$20

COLUMBIA

❑ 10125	Big Ole Jean/Mississippi Lady	1975	$5
❑ 45984	So Much of My Life/I Love How She Needs Me	1973	$5
❑ 45842	Sunshine of My Life/If You Wouldn't Be My Lady	1973	$5
❑ 46065	Till I Can't Take It Anymore/Sunday Kind of Woman	1974	$5

MGM

❑ 13316	Angel/Little Boy	1965	$10
❑ 13316 [PS]	Angel/Little Boy	1965	$30
❑ 13633	Christmas Country Style/Christmas Is the Best of All	1966	$10
❑ 13738	Don't Tell Me It's Raining/Takin' It Easy	1967	$12
❑ 13376	Heartaches by the Number/Your Mem'ry Comes Along	1965	$12
❑ 13376 [PS]	Heartaches by the Number/Your Mem'ry Comes Along	1965	$30
❑ 13445	Hello Enemy/I Never Loved You Anyway	1966	$12
❑ 13888	I Can Spot a Cheater/It Keeps Right On a-Hurtin'	1968	$8
❑ 13924	I Haven't Begun to Love You Yet/Why So Lonely	1968	$8
❑ 13232	I Rise, I Fall/I'm Watching My Watch	1964	$10
❑ 13232 [PS]	I Rise, I Fall/I'm Watching My Watch	1964	$30
❑ 13977	Letter to Emily/Your Mem'ry Comes Along	1968	$8
❑ 13499	Me, Myself and I/Country Boy, Country Boy	1966	$10
❑ 13598	More Than Before/Baby's Gone	1966	$10
❑ 13598	More Than Before/Open Up Your Heart	1966	$10
❑ 13408	Our World/(Wait 'Till You See) My Gidget	1965	$10
❑ 13284	She Understands Me/Tomorrow	1964	$10
❑ 13284 [PS]	She Understands Me/Tomorrow	1964	$30
❑ 13684	Strange Things Happen/Tommy Jones	1967	$10
❑ 13181	Talk Back Trembling Lips/Another You	1963	$15
❑ 13181 [PS]	Talk Back Trembling Lips/Another You	1963	$30
❑ 13344	Then I'll Count Again/One's Yours, One's Mine	1965	$10
❑ 13344 [PS]	Then I'll Count Again/One's Yours, One's Mine	1965	$30
❑ 13193	Worried Guy/Please Don't Go Away	1963	$10
❑ 13193 [PS]	Worried Guy/Please Don't Go Away	1963	$30
❑ 13255	Worry/Sufferin' from a Heartache	1964	$10
❑ 13255 [PS]	Worry/Sufferin' from a Heartache	1964	$30

REWARD

❑ 03327	Baby You Do It for Me (And I'll Do It for You)/She's Not As Married As She Used to Be	1982	$4
❑ 04123	Burnin'/What's Another Year	1983	$4
❑ 03901	Crying/You're a Beautiful Place to Be	1983	$4
❑ 04346	Lay Back (In the Arms of Somebody)/What's Another Year	1984	$4

SCEPTER

| ❑ 12389 | Song for Hank Williams (mono/stereo) | 1973 | $8 |

—With John Edward Beland; may be promo-only

UNITED ARTISTS

Number	Title	Yr	NM
❑ XW860	It Could've Been Nashville/Summertime Lovin'	1976	$5
❑ XW986	Toy Hearts/Just An Ordinary Man	1977	$5

7-Inch Extended Plays

CADENCE

| ❑ CLLP 33-1 | Poetry in Motion/Jimmy's Girl/True, True Happiness//Earth Angel/Why Do I Love You So/Pledging My Love | 1961 | $25 |

—Jukebox issue; small hole, plays at 33 1/3 rpm

| ❑ CLLP 33-1 [PS] | This Is Johnny Tillotson | 1961 | $35 |

—Cardboard insert in heavy vinyl envelope

| ❑ CEP-114 | True True Happiness/Love Is Blind//Dreamy Eyes/Well I'm Your Man | 1960 | $30 |
| ❑ CLLP 33-2 | Without You/Much Beyond Compare/Well I'm Your Man//Princess Princess/Dreamy Eyes/Cutie Pie | 1961 | $25 |

—Jukebox issue; small hole, plays at 33 1/3 rpm

| ❑ CLLP 33-2 [PS] | Words and Music by Johnny Tillotson | 1961 | $35 |

—Cardboard insert in heavy vinyl envelope

TIM TAM AND THE TURN-ONS

PALMER

Number	Title	Yr	NM
❑ 5003	Cheryl Ann/Sealed with a Kiss	1966	$40
❑ 5014	Don't Say Hi/(Instrumental)	1967	$30
❑ 5002	Wait a Minute/Ophelia	1965	$30

TIMBUK 3

I.R.S.

Number	Title	Yr	NM
❑ 53221	All I Want for Christmas/Medley: Blue Christmas-I Love You x 3	1987	$6
❑ 53221 [PS]	All I Want for Christmas/Medley: Blue Christmas-I Love You x 3	1987	$6
❑ 53338	Easy/I Love You in the Strangest Way	1988	$3
❑ 53338 [PS]	Easy/I Love You in the Strangest Way	1988	$3
❑ 53054	Hairstyles and Attitudes/I Just Want to Make Love to You	1987	$3
❑ 53017	Life Is Hard/I Love You in the Strangest Way	1987	$3
❑ 52940	The Future's So Bright, I Gotta Wear Shades/I'll Do All Right	1986	$3
❑ 52940 [PS]	The Future's So Bright, I Gotta Wear Shades/I'll Do All Right	1986	$5

—Title in small print

| ❑ 52940 [PS] | The Future's So Bright, I Gotta Wear Shades/I'll Do All Right | 1986 | $3 |

—Title in larger print

TIMETONES, THE

ATCO

Number	Title	Yr	NM
❑ 6201	I've Got a Feeling/Pretty Pretty Girl	1961	$30
❑ 526	The House Where Lovers Dream/Get a Hold of Yourself	1985	$10

TIMES SQUARE

❑ 26	A Sunday Kind of Love/Angels in the Sky	1964	$30
❑ 421	Here in My Heart/My Love	1961	$40
❑ 421	In My Heart/My Love	1961	$30
❑ 34	The House Where Lovers Dream/Get a Hold of Yourself	1964	$40

TIMMONS, PATSY

D

Number	Title	Yr	NM
❑ 1079	Answer to Life to Go/I've Got It	1959	$30
❑ 1109	Branded for Life/My Philosophy	1960	$30
❑ 1033	Step Aside Old Heart/I Understand Him	1958	$40

TIN HOUSE

EPIC

Number	Title	Yr	NM
❑ 10739	I Want Your Baby/Be Good and Be Kind	1971	$8

TIN HUEY

CLONE

Number	Title	Yr	NM
❑ CL-010	English Kids/Sister Rose	1980	$15
❑ CL-012 [PS]	English Kids/Sister Rose	1980	$20

—some copies numbered 011

WARNER BROS.

Number	Title	Yr	NM
❑ 49001	I'm a Believer/New York's Finest Dining Experience	1979	$4

7-Inch Extended Plays

CLONE

❑ CL-004	Breakfast with the Hueys	1978	$20
❑ CL-004 [PS]	Breakfast with the Hueys	1978	$20
❑ CL-002	Puppet Wipes/Cuyahoga Creeping Bent//Poor Alphonso/The Tin Huey Story	1977	$15
❑ CL-002 [PS]	Puppet Wipes/Cuyahoga Creeping Bent//Poor Alphonso/The Tin Huey Story	1977	$15

TINDLEY, GEORGE

EMBER

Number	Title	Yr	NM
❑ 1058	The Gypsy/I Wish	1960	$20
❑ 1060	Wedding Bells/No Lonely Nights	1960	$20

HERALD

| ❑ 558 | Close Your Eyes/Heart of Gold | 1961 | $15 |

PARKWAY

| ❑ 834 | Fairy Tales/Just For You | 1962 | $15 |

WAND

❑ 11205	Ain't That Peculiar/It's All Over But the Shouting	1969	$8
❑ 11208	Honky Tonk Women/So Help Me Woman	1969	$8
❑ 11215	Wan-Tu-Wah-Zuree/Pity the Poor Man	1970	$8

TINGLING MOTHER'S CIRCUS

MUSICOR

Number	Title	Yr	NM
❑ 1359	I Found a New Love/Happy Bubble	1969	$10
❑ 1335	Positively Negative/Sunday Kind of Feeling	1968	$12

ROULETTE

| ❑ 4758 | Face in My Mind/Isn't It Strange | 1967 | $20 |

TINY TIM

20TH CENTURY

Number	Title	Yr	NM
❑ U-30528M	I'll Never Get Married Again/The Chicken Dance	1988	$10
❑ 88-1	I Saw Mr. Presley Tip-Toeing Through the Tulips/Sam	1988	$30

—Came with Tiny's picture on promo envelope

BLUE CAT

| ❑ 127 | April Showers/Little Girl | 1966 | $15 |

BOUQUET

| ❑ B-101 | Be My Love/Oh How I Miss You Tonight | 1968 | $30 |
| ❑ B-102 | On the Good Ship Lollipop/Don't Take Your Love From Me | 1968 | $30 |

BROKEN

| ❑ 101 [PS] | Mr. Ed/Memory | 1984 | $30 |

—Colored vinyl

| ❑ 101 [PS] | Mr. Ed/Memory | 1984 | $10 |

—Black vinyl

CLONE

| ❑ CRI111 | I'm Just a Lonesome Clone/I'm the One (That They're Crazy About) | 1984 | $10 |

CLOUDS

| ❑ 17 [PS] | Tip-Toe to the Gas Pumps/The Hicky (On Your Neck) | 1979 | $10 |

GAS 'ER UP

| ❑ -1001T [B] | Tip-Toe to the Gas Pumps (stereo)/Tip-Toe to the Gas Pumps (mono) | 1979 | $20 |

—This 45 was given away by a gas station chain for filling your tank

KAMA

| ❑ OV567 | Howard Cosell (We Think You're Swell)/The Bi-Centennial Song (I Believe in America) | 1976 | $20 |

NLT

❑ 1993	Leave Me Satisfied/I Wanna' Get Crazy with You	1988	$8
❑ 1993	Leave Me Satisfied/I Wanna' Get Crazy with You	1988	$12
❑ 1993	Leave Me Satisfied/I Wanna' Get Crazy with You	1988	$12

—Came with Tiny's picture on promo envelope

| ❑ 1993 | Leave Me Satisfied/I Wanna' Get Crazy with You | 1988 | $12 |
| ❑ 1993 | Leave Me Satisfied/Leave Me Satisfied | 1988 | $30 |

—Red vinyl promo

Number	Title	Yr	NM

REPRISE

Number	Title	Yr	NM
☐ 20174	Bring Back Rockabye Baby Days/Just Say I Love Her	1963	$15

— B-side by Johnny Prophet

Number	Title	Yr	NM
☐ 0760	Bring Back Those Rock-A-Bye Baby Days/Hello, Hello	1968	$6
☐ 0760	Bring Back Those Rock-A-Bye Baby Days/This Is All I Ask	1968	$6
☐ 0939	Don't Bite the Hand That's Feeding You/What Kind of American Are You	1970	$6
☐ 0802 [S]	Great Balls of Fire/As Time Goes By	1968	$30
☐ 0802	Great Balls of Fire/As Time Goes By	1969	$6
☐ 0769	Hello, Hello/The Other Side	1968	$6
☐ 0867	I'm a Lonesome Little Raindrop/What the World Needs Now Is Love	1969	$6
☐ 0855	Mickey the Monkey/Neighborhood Children	1969	$6
☐ 0837	On the Good Ship Lollipop/America I Love You	1969	$6
☐ PRO-276	Tiny Tim Radio Spots	1968	$30

— Plays four ads for "God Bless Tiny Tim" album; sent to radio stations only

Number	Title	Yr	NM
☐ 0740	Tip-Toe Thru' the Tulips with Me/Don't Bite the Hand That's Feeding You	1971	$4

— Back to Back Hits" series

Number	Title	Yr	NM
☐ 0679	Tip-Toe Thru' the Tulips with Me/Fill Your Heart	1968	$8
☐ 0985	Why/Spaceship Song	1971	$20

— The label on the A-side label has a heart with arrow through it and "TINY TIM & MISS VICKI" written inside

SCEPTER

Number	Title	Yr	NM
☐ 12351	Am I Just Another Pretty Face/The Movies	1972	$10

SOLID BRASS

Number	Title	Yr	NM
☐ 101	Comic Strip Man/Tell Me That You Love Me (My Sweetheart)	1981	$10

— Without insert

Number	Title	Yr	NM
☐ 101	Comic Strip Man/Tell Me That You Love Me (My Sweetheart)	1981	$10

— With insert; a printed insert note from Tiny was included in some copies; the record has no promo markings, but the picture sleeve has "special promotional copy" on it; the picture sleeve also lists two album titles (Tell Me That You Love Me and I Won't Dance), but neither of these albums was ever released

Number	Title	Yr	NM
☐ 103 [PS]	Telll Me That You Love Me/Honest, Dear Honest	1981	$10

STARDUST

Number	Title	Yr	NM
☐ URC1225	Tip-Toe Through the Tulips With Me/Alley Oop	1988	$8

TCC

Number	Title	Yr	NM
☐ 2343	Tip-Toe Disco (Part I)/Tip-Toe Disco (Part 2 Instrumental)	1977	$10

TOILET

Number	Title	Yr	NM
☐ RB101	I Ain't Got No Money/Alice Blue Gown	1973	$20

TRUE

Number	Title	Yr	NM
☐ 109 [PS]	I'm Gonna Be a Country Queen/I Ain't No Cowboy (I Just Found This Hat)	1977	$10
☐ 109 [PS]	I'm Gonna Be a Country Queen/I Ain't No Cowboy (I Just Found This Hat)	1977	$10

— This 45 was given away by a gas station chain when you filled your tank

VIC TIM

Number	Title	Yr	NM
☐ 1007	Delilah/Sunshine	1972	$30
☐ 100?	Maggie May/When You and I Were Young, Maggie	1972	$30
☐ 778	The Ballad of Attica Prison/The Prisoners Song	1971	$30
☐ 778	The Ballad of Attica Prison/The Prisoners Song	1971	$30
☐ 777	Why Did They Have to Die So Young/Letter Edged in Black	1971	$30

— Vic Tim was a label that Tiny Tim started after leaving Reprise Records in 1971; the A-side is dedicated to Jimi Hendrix, Janis Joplin, and Jim Morrison

TINY TIM AND THE HITS

ROULETTE

Number	Title	Yr	NM
☐ 4123	Wedding Bells/Doll Baby	1958	$60

TIP TOPS, THE

PARKWAY

Number	Title	Yr	NM
☐ 868	Oo-Kook-a-Boo/He's a Braggin'	1963	$15

ROULETTE

Number	Title	Yr	NM
☐ 4684	Meetcha at the Cheetah/A Little Bit More	1966	$120

TITANS, THE

BANGAR

Number	Title	Yr	NM
☐ 0611	Surfer's Lullaby/Motivation	1964	$30

DUFF'S

Number	Title	Yr	NM
☐ 111	Little Girl/Pretty Young Thing	1969	$15
☐ 112	Ode to Billy Martin/Please Don't Be Angry	1970	$15

FIDELITY

Number	Title	Yr	NM
☐ 3016	What Have I Done/Everybody Happy?	1960	$40

NOLTA

Number	Title	Yr	NM
☐ 351	A-Rab/Marquette	1961	$30

SOMA

Number	Title	Yr	NM
☐ 1402	A Summer Place/Tchaikovsky Rides Again	1963	$30

SPECIALTY

Number	Title	Yr	NM
☐ 632	Arlene/Love Is a Wonderful Thing	1958	$30
☐ 625	Don't You Just Know It/Can It Be	1958	$30
☐ 614	Sweet Peach/Free and Easy	1957	$30

VITA

Number	Title	Yr	NM
☐ 158	G'Wan Home Calypso/Look What You're Doing Baby	1957	$70

TITONES, THE

SCEPTER

Number	Title	Yr	NM
☐ 1206	Symbol of Love/The Movies	1960	$60

— White label

Number	Title	Yr	NM
☐ 1206	Symbol of Love/The Movies	1960	$30

— Red label

WAND

Number	Title	Yr	NM
☐ 105	Symbol of Love/My Movie Queen	1960	$30

TJADER, CAL

(no label)

Number	Title	Yr	NM
☐ 552	Cool/Maria	1960	$12

— Black vinyl

Number	Title	Yr	NM
☐ 552	Cool/Maria	1960	$20

— Red vinyl (possibly promo only)

Number	Title	Yr	NM
☐ 659	Evil Ways/First There Is a Mountain	1971	$6

SAVOY

Number	Title	Yr	NM
☐ 1120	I Want to Be Happy/Minority	1954	$30
☐ 1117	Love Me or Leave Me/Tangerine	1953	$30

SKYE

Number	Title	Yr	NM
☐ 4510	My Little Red Book/Moneypenny	1968	$8
☐ 452	Ode to Billie Joe/Solar Heat	1968	$8

VERVE

Number	Title	Yr	NM
☐ 10431	Guajira en Azul/Modesty	1966	$8
☐ 10325	People/Poor Butterfly	1964	$10
☐ 10315	Sake and Greens/Shoji	1964	$10
☐ 10364	Soul Bird/The Whiffenpoof Song	1965	$8
☐ 10397	Soul Burst/Cuchy Frito Man	1966	$8
☐ 10345	Soul Sauce (Guacha Guaro)/Somewhere in the Night	1965	$8
☐ 10300	The Fakir/China Nights	1963	$10
☐ 10552	Trick or Treat/Quando Quando Que Sera	1967	$8
☐ 10275	Weeping Bossa Nova/Silenciosa	1962	$10

TOAD HALL

BARNABY

Number	Title	Yr	NM
☐ ZS72052	Hallelujah! I'm a Bum/I'm Leaving You Louisiana	1971	$8

TOBY BEAU

RCA

Number	Title	Yr	NM
☐ PB-11964	If I Were You/If You Believe	1980	$4
☐ PB-11388	Into the Night/Wink of an Eye	1978	$4
☐ PB-11250	My Angel Baby/California	1978	$5
☐ PB-12098	Ships in the Night/Little Miss American Dream	1980	$4
☐ PB-11670	Then You Can Tell Me Goodbye/Boogie Woogie Melody	1979	$4

TODAY AND TOMORROW

NOOSE

Number	Title	Yr	NM
☐ 812	Dooley Swings (Part 1)/Dooley Swings (Part 2)	1959	$50

TODAY'S PEOPLE

20TH CENTURY

Number	Title	Yr	NM
☐ 2032	He/I Didn't Know	1973	$6
☐ 2079	I Belong/Come Back to Save Us	1974	$6

TODD, ART AND DOTTY

ABBOTT

Number	Title	Yr	NM
☐ 3006	Busy Signal/Oh Honey Why Don't Cha	1955	$30

CAPITOL

Number	Title	Yr	NM
☐ 4778	Sweet Someone/Ring-a-Ding	1962	$8

DART

Number	Title	Yr	NM
☐ 51986	Blueberry Hill/Wonderful, Loveable You	1959	$10
☐ 405	Chop Chop/Say You	1956	$15
☐ 404	Wait for Me/Joie de Vivre	1956	$15

DECCA

Number	Title	Yr	NM
☐ 31227	Ca C'est La Vie/Drifting and Dreaming	1961	$10

DOT

Number	Title	Yr	NM
☐ 16939	I'll Take Care of Your Cares/Bodie Tree	1966	$6

ERA

Number	Title	Yr	NM
☐ 1076	Au Revoir Amour/Der Glockenspiel	1958	$12
☐ 1064	Chanson D'Amour (Song of Love)/Along the Trail with You	1957	$15
☐ 3001	Paradise/Ayuh Ayuh	1959	$10
☐ 1087	Pray/Don't You Worry My Little Pet	1958	$12
☐ 1088	Straight as an Arrow/Stand There Mountain	1959	$10

RCA VICTOR

Number	Title	Yr	NM
☐ 47-5029	Heavenly-Heavenly/Broken Wings	1952	$20

SIGNET

Number	Title	Yr	NM
☐ 2020	Bernadette Soubirous/Bodie Tree	1965	$8

TODD, DICK

DECCA

Number	Title	Yr	NM
☐ 32168	Big Wheel Cannonball/Return of the Double Eagle	1967	$8
☐ 9-29361	Columbus Stockade/Sweethearts or Strangers	1954	$30

— With Grady Martin

Number	Title	Yr	NM
☐ 32251	Pennsylvania Turnpike, I Love You/White House Waltz	1968	$8
☐ 9-28314	Too Old to Cut the Mustard/Waiting in the Lobby of Your Heart	1952	$30

— With Grady Martin

TODD, DYLAN

RCA VICTOR

Number	Title	Yr	NM
☐ 47-6463	The Ballad of James Dean/More Precious Than Gold	1956	$40
☐ 47-6463 [PS]	The Ballad of James Dean/More Precious Than Gold	1956	$60
☐ 47-6711	Timber/Golden Spurs and a Silver Saddle	1956	$30

TODD, FULLER

KING

Number	Title	Yr	NM
☐ 5048	Old Fashioned/Proud Lady Heart Stealer	1957	$30
☐ 5111	Top Ten Rock/Jeannie Marie	1958	$30

TODD, JOHNNY

MODERN

Number	Title	Yr	NM
☐ 1003	Pink Cadillac/What's Up	1956	$120

TODD, NICK

DOT

Number	Title	Yr	NM
☐ 15675	At the Hop/I Do	1957	$30
☐ 16109	Each Moment/Your Love's Gotta Grip on Me	1960	$20
☐ 15772	Forever and a Day/Too Much Rosita	1958	$30
☐ 15981	Invisible Man/Sayin' Something	1959	$20
☐ 15860	My Little Girl/Does Your Heart Beat for Me?	1958	$30
☐ 15643	Plaything/The Honey Song	1957	$30
☐ 15688	Teen-Age Cutie/Ever Since I Met Lucy	1958	$30
☐ 15951	Tiger/Twice As Nice	1959	$20

TOE FAT

RARE EARTH

Number	Title	Yr	NM
☐ 5019	Bad Side of the Moon/Just Like Me	1970	$6

TOGGERY FIVE, THE

TOWER

Number	Title	Yr	NM
☐ 119	I'm Gonna Jump/Bye Bye Bird	1965	$20

Number	Title	Yr	NM

TOKAYS, THE
BONNIE
| 102 | Lost and Found/Fatty-Boom Bi Laddy | 1962 | $125 |

BRUTE
| 001 | Hey Senorita/Baby Baby Baby | 1967 | $120 |

TOKENS, THE
ATCO
| 7009 | The Lord Can't Sing a Solo/Penny Whistle Band | 1974 | $6 |

B.T. PUPPY
500	A Girl Named Arlene/Swing	1964	$15
507	A Message to the World/Sylvie Sleepin'	1965	$10
519	Breezy/Greatest Moments of a Girl's Life	1966	$10
519 [PS]	Breezy/Greatest Moments of a Girl's Life	1966	$30
525	Green Plant/Saloogy	1967	$10
502	He's in Town/Oh Cathy	1964	$15
518	I Hear Trumpets Blow/Don't Cry, Sing Along with the Music	1966	$10
512	Only My Friend/Cattle Call	1965	$10
552	Please Say You Want Me/Get a Job	1969	$10
513	The Bells of St. Mary/Just One Smile	1966	$12
515	The Three Bells/Message to the World	1966	$10

BUDDAH
174	Both Sides Now/I Could See Me (Dancin' with You)	1970	$5
159	Don't Worry Baby/If the Shoe Fits Ya Baby	1970	$5
159	Don't Worry Baby/Some People Sleep	1970	$5
187	Listen to the Words (Listen to the Music)/Groovin' On the Sunshine	1970	$5
151	She Lets Her Hair Down (Early in the Morning)/Oh to Get Away	1970	$6

DATE
| 2737 | Oh What a Night/(Hey Hey) Juanita | 1961 | $60 |

GARY
| 1006 | Doom-Lang/Come Dance with Me | 1961 | $125 |

LAURIE
| 3180 | I'll Always Love You/Please Write | 1963 | $30 |

MELBA
| 104 | While I Dream/I Love My Baby | 1956 | $60 |

RCA VICTOR
47-8114	A Bird Flies Out of Sight/Wishing	1962	$30
47-8114 [PS]	A Bird Flies Out of Sight/Wishing	1962	$50
47-7991	B'wa Nina/Weeping River	1962	$30
47-7991 [PS]	B'wa Nina/Weeping River	1962	$60

—No mention of "The Lion Sleeps Tonight" LP on sleeve

| 47-7991 [PS] | B'wa Nina/Weeping River | 1962 | $40 |

—"The Lion Sleeps Tonight" LP mentioned on sleeve

| 37-7991 | B'wa Nina/Weeping River | 1962 | $50 |

—Compact Single 33" (small hole, plays at LP speed)

47-8210	Hear the Bells/ABC 1-2-3	1963	$20
47-8210 [PS]	Hear the Bells/ABC 1-2-3	1963	$40
47-8089	I'll Do My Crying Tomorrow/Dream Angel Goodnight	1962	$30
47-8089 [PS]	I'll Do My Crying Tomorrow/Dream Angel Goodnight	1962	$50
47-8052	La Bomba/A Token of Love	1962	$30
47-8052 [PS]	La Bomba/A Token of Love	1962	$50
47-7925	Sincerely/When the Summer Is Through	1961	$30
37-7925	Sincerely/When the Summer Is Through	1961	$50

—Compact Single 33" (small hole, plays at LP speed)

| 47-7954 | The Lion Sleeps Tonight/Tina | 1961 | $30 |
| 37-7954 | The Lion Sleeps Tonight/Tina | 1961 | $60 |

—Compact Single 33" (small hole, plays at LP speed)

47-8148	Tonight I Met An Angel/Hindi Lullabye	1963	$20
47-8148 [PS]	Tonight I Met An Angel/Hindi Lullabye	1963	$40
47-8309	Two Cars/Let's Go to the Drag Strip	1963	$20
47-8309 [PS]	Two Cars/Let's Go to the Drag Strip	1963	$100
47-7896	When I Go to Sleep at Night/Dry Your Eyes	1961	$30
47-7896 [PS]	When I Go to Sleep at Night/Dry Your Eyes	1961	$50
37-7896	When I Go to Sleep at Night/Dry Your Eyes	1961	$50

—Compact Single 33" (small hole, plays at LP speed)

ROULETTE
| 4230 | Can't You Tell/Your Mother Said So | 1960 | $40 |

—As "Darrell and the Oxfords"

RUST
| 5094 | Arlene/Rumble in the Park | 1965 | $10 |

WARNER BROS.
7099	Ain't That Peculiar/Bye, Bye, Bye	1967	$6
7202	Animal/Bathroom Wall	1968	$6
7280	Go Away Little Girl-Young Girl/I Want to Make Love to You	1969	$6
7233	Grandfather/The Banana Boat Song	1968	$6
7323	I Could Be/End of the World	1969	$6
7056	It's a Happening World/How Nice	1967	$6
7183	Mister Swail/Needles of Evergreen	1968	$10

—As "Margo, Margo, Medress and Siegel"

| 7118 | Portrait of My Love/It's a Happening World | 1968 | $5 |

—Back to Back Hits" series -- originals have green labels with "W7" logo

5900	Portrait of My Love/She Comes and Goes	1967	$8
5900 [PS]	Portrait of My Love/She Comes and Goes	1967	$30
7255	The World Is Full of Wonderful Things/Some People Sleep	1968	$6
7169	Till/Poor Man	1968	$6

WARWICK
| 615 | Tonight I Fell in Love/I'll Always Love You | 1961 | $40 |

TOLBERT, ISRAEL
WARREN/STAX
| 106 | Big Leg Woman (With a Short Short Mini Skirt)/I Got Love | 1970 | $8 |
| 107 | Shake Your Big Hips/Lost Love | 1971 | $10 |

TOM AND JERRIO
ABC-PARAMOUNT
10638	Boo-Ga-Loo/Boomerang	1965	$15
10704	Great Goo-Ga Moo-Ga/Come On and Love Me	1965	$15
10787	Oolya-Coo/Bacardi	1966	$15

TOM AND JERRY (1)
ABC-PARAMOUNT
| 10363 | Surrender, Please Surrender/Fightin' Mad | 1962 | $50 |
| 10788 | That's My Story/Tia-Juana Blues | 1966 | $30 |

—As "Simon and Garfunkel" (may have been reissued as "Tom and Jerry," but we don't know)

BELL
| 120 | Baby Talk/I'm Gonna Get Married | 1959 | $60 |

—B-side by Ronnie Lawrence

| 120 [PS] | Baby Talk/I'm Gonna Get Married | 1959 | $125 |

BIG
| 613 | Hey, Schoolgirl/Dancin' Wild | 1957 | $60 |

—With songwriting credits as "Tommy Graph-Jerry Landis"

| 613 | Hey, Schoolgirl/Dancin' Wild | 1957 | $60 |

—With songwriting credits as "Paul Simon-Art Garfunkel"

| 616 | Our Song/Two Teen Agers | 1958 | $60 |
| 618 | That's My Story/Don't Say Goodbye | 1958 | $60 |

EMBER
| 1094 | I'm Lonesome/Looking at You | 1959 | $60 |

HUNT
| 319 | That's My Story/Don't Say Goodbye | 1959 | $60 |

KING
| 5167 | Hey, Schoolgirl/Dancin' Wild | 1958 | $100 |

TOM AND JERRY (2)
Tommy Tomlinson and Jerry Kennedy, a country instrumental duo.

MERCURY
71753	Golden Wildwood Flower/South	1961	$30
71930	I'll Drown in My Tears/French Twist	1961	$30
71827	Swing Low/Sugarfoot Rag	1961	$30

TOM TOM CLUB
SIRE
49882	Genius of Love/Lorelei	1981	$4
7-29437	Pleasure of Love/Never Took a Penny	1983	$4
7-29437 [PS]	Pleasure of Love/Never Took a Penny	1983	$4
7-22998	Suboceana/Devil Does Your Dog Bite	1989	$5
7-29549	The Man with the 4-Way Hips/(Dub)	1983	$4
7-29549 [PS]	The Man with the 4-Way Hips/(Dub)	1983	$4
49813	Wordy Rappinghood (edit)/(You Don't Stop) Wordy Rappinghood	1981	$5
DSRE50067	Wordy Rappinghood (edit)/(You Don't Stop) Wordy Rappinghood	1982	$4

TOMBOYS, THE
SWAN
| 4181 | I'd Rather Fight Than Switch/Mary Had a Little Kiss | 1964 | $10 |

TOMBSTONES, THE
CAPITOL
| 5997 | Times Will Be Hard/Mary Jane | 1967 | $10 |

TOMLIN, LILY
POLYDOR
| 14180 | 20th Century Blues/Blues | 1973 | $5 |
| 14283 | Edith Ann/Detroit City | 1975 | $5 |

TOMMY AND THE HUSTLERS
FANTASY
| 573 | Diggin' Out/The Right Size | 1963 | $50 |

—Green vinyl

| 573 | Diggin' Out/The Right Size | 1963 | $30 |

TOMMY AND THE RIVIERAS
CAMEO
| 461 | Messin' with the Kid/(Make It to) Detroit City | 1967 | $30 |

TOMMY AND THE TWISTERS
REGENT
| 205 | Mr. Twist/Hucklebuck Twist | 1962 | $15 |

TOMMY TUTONE
COLUMBIA
02646	867-5309/Jenny//Not Say Goodbye	1981	$4
11278	Angel Say No/The Blame	1980	$3
11333	Cheap Date/Dancing Girl	1980	$3
04235	Get Around Girl/Imaginary Heart	1983	$3
11353	Girl on the Back Seat/Am I Supposed to Live	1980	$3
03002	Which Man Are You/Only One	1982	$3

TOMPALL AND THE GLASER BROTHERS
DECCA
31632	A Girl Like You/I've Got Troubles	1964	$10
31736	Baby, They're Playing Our Song/Winner Take All	1965	$12
31809	Back in Each Other's Arms Again/Teardrops 'Til Dawn	1965	$12
31551	Blow Out the Candles/Mr. Lonesome	1963	$10
31051	Careless Love, Goodbye/Alibi	1960	$15
31447	False Hearted Lover/Odds and Ends (Bits and Pieces)	1962	$15
31398	I Can't Remember/I'm Losing Again	1962	$15
31011	I'll Never Tell/21 Miles from Home	1959	$15
9-30805	Oh Little Mary/Lay Down the Gun	1959	$20
9-30900	Ooie-Gooie/She Loves the Love I Give Her	1959	$15
31180	Same Old Memories/Sweet Love, Goodbye	1960	$15
31494	Stand Beside Me/Trackin' Me Down	1963	$10
31322	Tired of Crying Over You/Let Me Down Easy	1961	$15

ELEKTRA
47461	I Still Love You (After All These Years)/Feelin' the Weight of My Chains	1982	$4
47405	It'll Be Her/A Mansion on the Hill	1982	$4
47134	Lovin' Her Was Easier (Than Anything I'll Ever Do Again)/United We Fall	1981	$4
69947	Maria Consuela/I Can Never Live Alone Again	1982	$4
47230 [DJ]	Silver Bells/Please Come Home for Christmas	1981	$6

—B-side by Johnny Lee

Number	Title	Yr	NM
❏ 47056	Sweet City Woman/Tryin' to Outrun the Wind	1980	$4
❏ 46595	Weight of My Chains/The Ballad of Lucy Jordan	1980	$4

MGM

Number	Title	Yr	NM
❏ 14462	A Girl Like You/Delta Lost	1972	$6
❏ 14390	Ain't It All Worth Living For/Blue Ridge Mountain	1972	$6
❏ 14516	Charlie/Lovin' You Again	1973	$6
❏ 14249	Faded Love/Pretty Eyes	1971	$6

— With Leon McAuliffe and the Cimarron Boys

Number	Title	Yr	NM
❏ 13611	Gone, On the Other Hand/Streets of Baltimore	1966	$8
❏ 13954	One of These Days/Where Has All the Love Gone	1968	$8
❏ 14349	Sweet, Love Me Good Woman/Stand Beside Me	1971	$6
❏ 13531	The Last Thing on My Mind/More or Less	1966	$10
❏ 13880	The Moods of Mary/No End of Love	1967	$8
❏ 13754	Through the Eyes of Love/She Loved the Wrong Man	1967	$8

ROBBINS

Number	Title	Yr	NM
❏ 1006	Sweet Lies/Yakety Yak	1958	$40

TONE LOC

DELICIOUS VINYL

Number	Title	Yr	NM
❏ 104	Funky Cold Medina/(Instrumental)	1989	$4
❏ 104 [PS]	Funky Cold Medina/(Instrumental)	1989	$4
❏ 106	I Got It Goin' On/The Homies	1989	$4
❏ 101	On Fire/(B-side unknown)	1987	$10
❏ 102	Wild Thing/Loc'ed After Dark	1988	$10

— Original issue has a white label

Number	Title	Yr	NM
❏ 102	Wild Thing/Loc'ed After Dark	1988	$4

— Second pressing has a red label

TONETTES, THE

ABC-PARAMOUNT

Number	Title	Yr	NM
❏ 9905	Oh What a Baby/Howie	1958	$30

DOE

Number	Title	Yr	NM
❏ 101	Oh What a Baby/Howie	1958	$100

MODERN

Number	Title	Yr	NM
❏ 997	Tonight You Belong to Me/Don't Fall in Love Too Soon	1956	$30

VOLT

Number	Title	Yr	NM
❏ 101	Please Don't Go/No Tears	1962	$30
❏ 104	Stolen Angel/Teardrop Sea	1963	$30

TONEY, OSCAR, JR.

BELL

Number	Title	Yr	NM
❏ 672	For Your Precious Love/Ain't That True Love	1967	$10
❏ 681	Turn On Your Love Light/Any Day Now	1967	$10
❏ 699	Without Love (There Is Nothing)/Love That Never Grows Old	1968	$10

CAPRICORN

Number	Title	Yr	NM
❏ 8005	Down on My Knees/Seven Days Tomorrow	1970	$8
❏ 0005	I Do What You Wish/Thank You, Honey Chile	1972	$6
❏ 8010	I Wouldn't Be a Poor Boy/Person to Person	1970	$8
❏ 8018	Workin' Together/Baby Is Mine	1971	$8

KING

Number	Title	Yr	NM
❏ 5906	Can It All Be Love/You Are Going to Need Me	1964	$30

TONGUE AND GROOVE

FONTANA

Number	Title	Yr	NM
❏ 1640	Cherry Ball/Devil	1969	$8
❏ 1653	Come On in My Kitchen/Mailman's Sack	1969	$8

TONY AND JOE

DORE

Number	Title	Yr	NM
❏ 688	The Freeze/Gonna Get a Little Kissin' Tonight	1963	$20
❏ 619	Twist and Freeze/Long Black Stockings	1961	$20

ERA

Number	Title	Yr	NM
❏ 1083	Play Something Sentimental Mr. D.J./Where Can You Be?	1958	$30
❏ 1075	The Freeze/Gonna Get a Little Kissin' Tonight	1958	$30

FLYTE

Number	Title	Yr	NM
❏ 106	Fairytale Love/(B-side unknown)	1959	$20

GARDENA

Number	Title	Yr	NM
❏ 103	Instant Love/The Duck Walk	1960	$20

TONY AND THE DAYDREAMS

PLANET

Number	Title	Yr	NM
❏ 1054	Christmas Lullaby/Handin' Hand	1961	$200
❏ 1008	Why Don't You Be Nice/I'll Never Tell	1958	$125

TONY AND THE HOLIDAYS

ABC-PARAMOUNT

Number	Title	Yr	NM
❏ 10295	There Goes My Heart Again/My Love Is Real	1962	$200

TONY AND THE MASQUINS

RUTHIE

Number	Title	Yr	NM
❏ 1000	My Angel Eyes/Fuji Womma	1961	$125

TONY AND THE RAINDROPS

CHESAPEKE

Number	Title	Yr	NM
❏ 609	While Walking/Our Love Is Over	1961	$70

CROSLEY

Number	Title	Yr	NM
❏ 340	Tina/My Heart Cried	1962	$200

TONY AND THE TWILIGHTERS

JALYNNE

Number	Title	Yr	NM
❏ 106	Be My Girl/Did You Make Up Your Mind	1960	$100

TONY AND TYRONE

ATLANTIC

Number	Title	Yr	NM
❏ 2458	Please Operator/Apple of My Eye	1967	$40

COLUMBIA

Number	Title	Yr	NM
❏ 43432	Turn It On/Talkin' About the People	1965	$20

TOOMORROW

KIRSHNER

Number	Title	Yr	NM
❏ 63-5005	Goin' Back/You're My Baby Now	1970	$70

TOOTIE AND THE BOUQUETS

PARKWAY

Number	Title	Yr	NM
❏ 887	The Conqueror/You Done Me Wrong	1963	$30

TOP HITS, THE

NORMAN

Number	Title	Yr	NM
❏ 504	Love No One/Thum-A-Lum-A	1961	$200

TOP NOTES, THE

ABC-PARAMOUNT

Number	Title	Yr	NM
❏ 10399	I Love You So Much/It's Alright	1963	$10

ATLANTIC

Number	Title	Yr	NM
❏ 2066	A Wonderful Time/Walkin' with Love	1960	$20
❏ 2097	Hearts of Stone/The Basic Things	1961	$20
❏ 2080	Say Man/Warm Your Heart	1960	$20
❏ 2115	Twist and Shout/Always Late (Why Lead Me On)	1961	$30

TOPICS, THE (1)

CARNIVAL

Number	Title	Yr	NM
❏ 520	She's So Fine/I Don't Have to Cry	1966	$125

— Counterfeit identification: Run-out groove is extremely wide; sound quality is poor; "clown" logo is incomplete and blurry

CHADWICK

Number	Title	Yr	NM
❏ 102	Hey Girl (Where Are You Going)/If Love Comes Knocking	1967	$800

HEAVY DUTY

Number	Title	Yr	NM
❏ 3	Try a Little Love/All Good Things Must End	1972	$50

MERCURY

Number	Title	Yr	NM
❏ 73447	Booking Up Baby/Giving Up	1974	$500

TOPICS, THE (2)

PERRI

Number	Title	Yr	NM
❏ 1007	The Girl in My Dreams/(B-side blank)	1961	$200

— One-sided record

TOPPERS, THE

ABC-PARAMOUNT

Number	Title	Yr	NM
❏ 9667	George Washington/Honey, Honey	1956	$30
❏ 9699	God Bless Kids and Little Animals/Tornado	1956	$30
❏ 9759	Three Roads/Lonely	1956	$30

AVALON

Number	Title	Yr	NM
❏ 63707	I Love You, I Love You/Bow-Legged Boy	1954	$50

DECCA

Number	Title	Yr	NM
❏ 30297	Pots and Pans/It Was Twice As Big As I Thought It Was	1957	$20
❏ 30209	The Purple Hills/Stashu Pandowski	1957	$20

JUBILEE

Number	Title	Yr	NM
❏ 5136	Let Me Bang Your Box/You're Laughing 'Cause I'm Crying	1954	$200

STACY

Number	Title	Yr	NM
❏ 927	Tell Me Why/All Around	1962	$15

TOPPS, THE

RED ROBIN

Number	Title	Yr	NM
❏ 131	I've Got a Feeling/Won't You Come Home Baby	1954	$300
❏ 126	What Do You Do (To Make Me Love You So)/Tippin'	1954	$300

TOPS, THE

SINGULAR

Number	Title	Yr	NM
❏ 712	An Innocent Kiss/Walkin' with My Baby	1957	$120

TOPSIDERS, THE

JOSIE

Number	Title	Yr	NM
❏ 907	Heartbreak Hotel/Let the Good Times Roll	1963	$15

TORME, MEL

ATLANTIC

Number	Title	Yr	NM
❏ 2219	42nd Street/Sunday in New York	1964	$10
❏ 2183	Cast Your Fate to the Wind/The Gift	1963	$10
❏ 2165	Comin' Home Baby/Right Now	1962	$30
❏ 2187	Gravy Waltz/My Gal's Back in Town	1963	$10

BETHLEHEM

Number	Title	Yr	NM
❏ 11008	Lulu's Back in Town/Keeping Myself for You	1958	$15

CAPITOL

Number	Title	Yr	NM
❏ F1383	Around the World/Sidewalk Shufflers	1951	$30
❏ F1662	Bewitched/Blue Moon	1951	$20

— Reissue

Number	Title	Yr	NM
❏ F1000	Bewitched/Piccolino	1950	$30
❏ F2263	Casually/Anywhere I Wander	1952	$30
❏ F2131	Don't Leave Me/Black Moonlight	1952	$30
❏ F1864	Foolish Rumors/You're a Heavenly Thing	1951	$30
❏ 2613	Games People Play/Willie and Laura Mae Jones	1969	$6
❏ F1237	I Owe a Kiss/Say No More	1950	$30
❏ F1761	My Buddy/Take My Heart	1951	$30
❏ F1712	One for Me/Love Is Such a Cheat	1951	$30
❏ F1291	Skylark/Lullaby of the Leaves	1950	$30
❏ F1524	The World Is Yours/Bundle of Love	1951	$30

COLUMBIA

Number	Title	Yr	NM
❏ 43677	All That Jazz/Hang On to Me	1966	$8
❏ 43230	Do I Love You Because You're Beautiful/That's All	1965	$8
❏ 43167	Every Day's a Holiday/One Little Snowflake	1964	$15
❏ 43167 [DJ]	Every Day's a Holiday/One Little Snowflake	1964	$20

— Promo only on green vinyl

Number	Title	Yr	NM
❏ 43383	Ho-Ba-La-Ba/My Romance	1965	$8
❏ 43022	I Know Your Heart/You Better Love Me	1964	$8
❏ 44180	Lover's Roulette/I Remember Suzanne	1967	$8
❏ 43087	Once in a Lifetime/I See It Now	1964	$8
❏ 45283	The Christmas Song/(B-side unknown)	1970	$6
❏ 43550	The Power of Love/Dominique's Discotheque	1966	$8
❏ 44399	Wait Until Dark/Lima Lady	1967	$8

CORAL

Number	Title	Yr	NM
❏ 61295	All of You/Spellbound	1954	$20
❏ 61136	Anything Can Happen Mambo/Just One More Chance	1954	$20
❏ 61507	Goody Goody/Jeepers Creepers	1955	$20

Number	Title	Yr	NM
❏ 61452	It Don't Mean a Thing/Rose O'Day	1955	$20
LIBERTY			
❏ 56022	A Day in the Life of Bonnie and Clyde/Brother Can You Spare a Dime	1968	$10
❏ 56066	Didn't We/Five-Four	1968	$8
LONDON			
❏ 180	A Phone Call to the Past/I Cried for You	1972	$6
❏ 171	Whose Garden Was This?/Morning Star	1971	$6
VERVE			
❏ 10232	Her Face/Yes Indeed	1961	$15
❏ 10174	The Crossroads/Frensei	1959	$15
❏ 10211	Wayfaring Stranger/Walk Like a Dragon	1960	$15

TORNADOES, THE (1)

DATE

Number	Title	Yr	NM
❏ 1519	Hey Baby!/Next Stop Kansas City	1966	$15
LONDON			
❏ 9579	Globetrottin'/Like Locomotion	1963	$30
❏ 9599	Life on Venus (Telstar II)/Robot	1963	$30
❏ 11003	Telestar/Jungle Fever	1964	$30

—*Gold label "Demand Performance" with misspelled A-side*

Number	Title	Yr	NM
❏ 9561	Telstar/Jungle Fever	1962	$30
❏ 9614	Theme from "The Scales of Justice"/The Ice Cream Man	1963	$30
TOWER			
❏ 171	Stingray/Aqua Marina	1965	$20
❏ 152	Stompin' Through the Rye/Early Bird	1965	$20

TORNADOES, THE (2)

AERTAUN

Number	Title	Yr	NM
❏ 100	Bustin' Surfboards/Beyond the Surf	1962	$50
❏ 102	Inebriated Surfer/Moon Dawg	1963	$40

—*As "The Hollywood Tornadoes*

Number	Title	Yr	NM
❏ 103	Phantom Surfer/Lightnin'	1964	$30

—*B-side is same recording as "Shootin' Beavers" but retitled*

Number	Title	Yr	NM
❏ 103	Phantom Surfer/Shootin' Beavers	1963	$40
❏ 101	The Gremmie (Part 1)/The Gremmie (Part 2)	1963	$30

—*As "The Hollywood Tornadoes*

TORNADOES, THE (3)

ABC-PARAMOUNT

Number	Title	Yr	NM
❏ 10174	Cora/Like a Frog	1960	$30

TORNADOES, THE (4)

CUCA

Number	Title	Yr	NM
❏ 1104	Hey There/Standing Watch	1963	$40
❏ 1099	Loneliest Guy in the World/It Always Makes Me Cry	1962	$40
❏ 1092	Scalping Party/7-0-7	1962	$50

TOROK, MITCHELL

ABBOTT

Number	Title	Yr	NM
❏ 140	Carribean/Weep Away	1953	$40

—*All copies we've seen misspell the A-side title as above*

Number	Title	Yr	NM
❏ 162	Dancerette/Haunting Waterfall	1954	$30
❏ 156	Edgar the Eager Easter Bunny/Living on Love	1954	$30
❏ 150	Hootchy Kootchy Henry (From Hawaii)/Gigolo	1953	$30
❏ 136	Little Hoo-Wee/Judalina	1953	$30
CAPITOL			
❏ 4946	Mighty Mighty Man/For Someone Who's Supposed to Be Hurtin'	1963	$8
DECCA			
❏ 30599	Be Kind to Me/How Much Do I Love You	1958	$15
❏ 30742	Date with a Teardrop/These Things I Hold Dear	1958	$15
❏ 30859	Go Ahead and Be a Fool/Memories of You Haunting Me Night and Day	1959	$15
❏ 29661	Marching My Blues Away/Country and Western	1955	$20
❏ 29408	Peasant's Guitar/The World Keeps Turning Around	1955	$20
❏ 30230	Pledge of Love/What's Behind That Strange Door	1957	$20
❏ 30901	PTA Rock and Roll/Teenie Weenie Bikini	1959	$30
❏ 30661	Sweet Revenge/Love Me Like You Mean It	1958	$15
❏ 30134	Take This Heart/Drink Up and Go Home	1956	$20
❏ 29576	Too Late Now/Smooth Talk	1955	$20

Number	Title	Yr	NM
❏ 30424	Two Words/You're Tempting Me	1957	$20
❏ 9-29986	When Mexico Gave Up the Rhumba (To Do the Rock and Roll)/I Wish I Was a Little Bit Younger (And Knew What I Know Now)	1956	$20
GUYDEN			
❏ 2018	Caribbean/Hootchy Kootchy Henry (From Hawaii)	1959	$15
❏ 2032	Guardian Angel/I Want to Know Everything	1960	$10
❏ 2040	Happy Street/Little Boy in Love	1960	$12
❏ 2034	Pink Chiffon/What You Don't Know	1960	$10
❏ 2034 [PS]	Pink Chiffon/What You Don't Know	1960	$30
INETTE			
❏ 105	Are You Trying to Tell Me Something/Love Is Magic	1963	$10
MERCURY			
❏ 71816	El Tigre/Eating My Heart Out	1961	$12
PARJO			
❏ 1003	Acupuncture/Pledge of Love	1972	$8

—*As "Mitch Torok"; B-side with Ramona Redd*

Number	Title	Yr	NM
RCA VICTOR			
❏ 47-8703	Caribbean/Witch Woman	1965	$8
❏ 47-8646	I Needed All the Help I Can Get/Man with a Golden Hand	1965	$8
REPRISE			
❏ 0568	Falling in Love Again/Baby, Baby, Baby	1967	$6
❏ 0541	Instant Love/Put Me in the Driver's Seat	1966	$6

TORQUAYS, THE

AERTAUN

Number	Title	Yr	NM
❏ 1020	Turmoil/Crying in the Chapel	1964	$40
COLPIX			
❏ 782	Image of a Girl/Stolen Moments	1965	$30
GEE CEE			
❏ 8163	Escondido/Surfer's City	1963	$60
GYPSY			
❏ 265	Busting Point/The Other Side	1965	$60
ORIGINAL SOUND			
❏ 66	Harmonica Man/Our Teenage Love	1967	$30
ROCK-IT			
❏ 1005	Hooked on Her/Harmonica Man	1965	$40
❏ 1004	Image of a Girl/Stolen Moments	1965	$40

TORQUES, THE

DIAL

Number	Title	Yr	NM
❏ 4060	Merry Maker/You Make Me Feel So Good	1967	$30
LEMCO			
❏ 1007	I've Been Hurt/Bumpin'	1966	$30
❏ 890	Mercy Mercy/Bumpin'	1966	$40
❏ 880	Tidal Wave/Harlem Nocturne	1965	$40

TORRENCE, GEORGE

DUO DISC

Number	Title	Yr	NM
❏ 117	Together at Last/Fine Foxy Frame	1965	$30
EPIC			
❏ 5-9453	Such a Fool Was I/Way Over Yonder	1961	$30
KING			
❏ 5376	Go Away/So Good to Me	1960	$30
SHOUT			
❏ 224	(Mama Come Quick and Bring Your) Licking Stick/So Long Goodbye	1968	$15

TORRENCE, JOHNNY

IMPERIAL

Number	Title	Yr	NM
❏ 5230	Sad Day/Bad Habit	1953	$120

TOTO

COLUMBIA

Number	Title	Yr	NM
❏ 1-11173	99/Hydra	1980	$4
❏ CNR-03399	Africa/(B-side blank)	1982	$6

—*One-sided budget release*

Number	Title	Yr	NM
❏ 38-03335	Africa/Good for You	1982	$4
❏ 1-11238	All Us Boys/Hydra	1980	$5
❏ 38-08010 [DJ]	Anna (4:03)/(4:55)	1988	$5
❏ 38-08010	Anna/The Seventh One	1988	$8

—*Scarce as stock copy*

Number	Title	Yr	NM
❏ 3-10944	Georgy Porgy/Child's Anthem	1979	$5
❏ 11-11437	Goodbye Elenore/Turn Back	1981	$6
❏ 3-10830	Hold the Line/Takin' It Back	1978	$5
❏ 0(no cat #)	Hold the Line/Takin' It Back	1978	$20

—*Picture disc in plastic sleeve; made for Licorice Pizza; price includes insert*

Number	Title	Yr	NM
❏ 38-04752	Holyanna/Mr. Friendly	1985	$3
❏ 38-04752 [PS]	Holyanna/Mr. Friendly	1985	$4
❏ 38-04844	How Does It Feel/Mr. Friendly	1985	$3
❏ 38-06280	I'll Be Over You/In a Word	1986	$3
❏ 38-06280 [PS]	I'll Be Over You/In a Word	1986	$3
❏ 3-10898	I'll Supply the Love/You Are the Flower	1979	$5
❏ 11-01056	It's the Last Night/Turn Back	1981	$6
❏ 38-03597	I Won't Hold You Back/Afraid of Love	1983	$3
❏ 38-03597 [PS]	I Won't Hold You Back/Afraid of Love	1983	$4
❏ CNR-03267	Make Believe/(B-side blank)	1982	$6

—*One-sided budget release*

Number	Title	Yr	NM
❏ 18-03143	Make Believe/We Made It	1982	$4
❏ 18-03143 [PS]	Make Believe/We Made It	1982	$5
❏ 38-07715	Pamela/The Seventh One	1988	$3
❏ 38-07715 [PS]	Pamela/The Seventh One	1988	$3
❏ 38-07945	Straight for the Heart/The Seventh One	1988	$3
❏ 38-07945 [PS]	Straight for the Heart/The Seventh One	1988	$3
❏ 38-04672	Stranger in Town/Change of Heart	1984	$3
❏ 38-04672 [PS]	Stranger in Town/Change of Heart	1984	$3
❏ 38-07030	Till the End/Don't Stop Me Now	1987	$4
❏ 38-07030 [DJ]	Till the End (Edited Version)/(Long Version)	1987	$5
❏ 38-03981	Waiting for Your Love/Lovers in the Night	1983	$3
❏ 38-06570	Without Your Love/Can't Stand It Any Longer	1987	$3
❏ 38-06570 [PS]	Without Your Love/Can't Stand It Any Longer	1987	$3
POLYDOR			
❏ 881628-7	Dune (Desert Theme)/Theme from Dune	1985	$5

TOURISTS, THE

EPIC

Number	Title	Yr	NM
❏ 50850	I Only Want to Be with You/In My Mind (There's Sorrow)	1980	$10

TOUSSAINT, ALLEN

ALON

Number	Title	Yr	NM
❏ 9021	Go Back Home/Poor Boy, Got to Move	1965	$10
BELL			
❏ 732	Get Out of My Life, Woman/Gotta Travel On	1968	$8
❏ 748	Hans Christian Anderson/I've Got That Feeling Now	1968	$8
❏ 782	Tequila/We the People	1969	$8
RCA VICTOR			
❏ 47-7192	Whirlaway/Happy Times	1958	$30

—*As "Al Tousan*

Number	Title	Yr	NM
REPRISE			
❏ 1132	Am I Expecting Too Much/Out of the City	1972	$5
❏ 1334	Country John/When the Party's Over	1975	$4
❏ 1109	Soul Sister/She Once Belonged to Me	1972	$5
SCEPTER			
❏ 12317	From a Whisper to a Scream/Secret Touch of Love	1971	$5
❏ 12334	Working in a Coal Mine/What Is Success	1971	$6
SEVILLE			
❏ 113	A Blue Mood/Moo Moo	1961	$20
❏ 110	Back Home in Indiana/Naomi	1960	$20
❏ 103	Chico/Sweetie-Pie	1960	$20

—*All Seville releases as "Al Tousan*

Number	Title	Yr	NM
❏ 124	Twenty Years Later/Real Churchy	1962	$20
WARNER BROS.			
❏ 8609	Happiness/Lover of Love	1978	$4

TOWER OF POWER

COLUMBIA

Number	Title	Yr	NM
❏ 10461	Ain't Nothin' Stoppin' Us Now/Because I Think the World of You	1976	$5
❏ 11157	In Due Time/And You Know It	1979	$4
❏ 10780	Love Bug/We Came to Play	1978	$4
❏ 10718	Lovin' You Is Gonna See Me Through/I Am a Fool	1978	$4

Number	Title	Yr	NM

WARNER BROS.

Number	Title	Yr	NM
❏ 7828	Don't Change Horses (In the Middle of a Stream)/I Got the Chop	1974	$6
❏ 7635	Down to the Nightclub/What Happened to the World That Day	1972	$6
❏ 8055	Only So Much Oil in the Ground/Give Me the Proof	1974	$6
❏ 8151	Soul of a Child/Treat Me Like Your Man	1975	$5
❏ 7687	So Very Hard to Say/Clean Slate	1973	$6
❏ 7733	This Time It's Real/Soul Vaccination	1973	$6
❏ 7796	Time Will Tell/Oakland Stroke	1974	$6
❏ 7748	What is Hip?/Clever Girl	1973	$6
❏ 8083	Willing to Learn/Walkin' Up Hip Street	1975	$5

TOWNE CHOIR, THE

CAPITOL
| ❏ 5538 | African Noel/Papa Noel | 1965 | $8 |

TOWNS, CHRIS, AND THE TOWNSMEN

COTILLION
| ❏ 44016 | Soul of My Sister/Sop It Up | 1968 | $30 |
| ❏ 44027 | Stuff/Earthy | 1969 | $20 |

TOWNSEND, BOB

MINARET
| ❏ 106 | Christmas Message From Space/The Night Before New Year's | 1962 | $10 |

TOWNSEND, ED

ALADDIN
| ❏ 3373 | Every Night/Love Never Dies | 1957 | $30 |
CAPITOL
❏ 4314	Be My Love/With No One to Love	1959	$15
❏ F4171	Don't Ever Leave Me/Lover Come Back to Me	1959	$15
❏ F3926	For Your Love/Over and Over Again	1958	$20
❏ F4240	This Little Love of Mine/Hold On	1959	$15
❏ F3994	What Shall I Do/Please Never Change	1958	$15
❏ F4048	When I Grow Too Old to Dream/You Are My Everything	1958	$15
CHALLENGE
| ❏ 9129 | And Then Came Love/Little Bitty Dave | 1961 | $15 |
| ❏ 9118 | Ed Townsend's Boogie Woogie (Part 1)/Ed Townsend's Boogie Woogie (Part 2) | 1961 | $15 |
DOT
| ❏ 15596 | Tall Grows the Sycamore/My Need for You | 1957 | $30 |
LIBERTY
❏ 55516	Tell Her/Down Home	1962	$15
❏ 55516	Tell Her/Hard Way to Go	1962	$15
❏ 55542	That's What I Get for Loving You/There's No End	1963	$15
MAXX
| ❏ 325 | I Love You/I Might Like It | 1964 | $10 |
MGM
| ❏ 13784 | Mommy's Never Comin' Back Again/Who Would Deny Me | 1967 | $10 |
WARNER BROS.
| ❏ 5200 | Cherrigale/Dream World | 1961 | $15 |
| ❏ 5174 | Stay with Me/I Love Everything About You | 1960 | $15 |

TOWNSEND, SHERRELL

GONE
| ❏ 5135 | He Thinks I Still Care/Glass of Tears | 1962 | $30 |
LITTLE STAR
| ❏ 115 | I Love You Alone/Summer Days Are Here | 1962 | $50 |
LUTE
| ❏ 6015 | I Love You Alone/Summer Days Are Here | 1961 | $40 |

TOWNSHEND, PETE, AND RONNIE LANE

MCA
| ❏ 40818 | My Baby Gives It Away/April Fool | 1977 | $4 |

TOWNSHEND, PETE
Also see THE WHO.

ATCO
❏ 7312	A Little Is Enough/Cat's in a Cupboard	1980	$4
❏ 99499	Barefootin'/Behind Blue Eyes	1986	$3
❏ 99499 [PS]	Barefootin'/Behind Blue Eyes	1986	$4
❏ 99884	Bargain/Dirty Water	1983	$4
❏ 99884 [PS]	Bargain/Dirty Water	1983	$4
❏ 99989	Face Dances Part Two/Man Watching	1982	$4
❏ 99989 [PS]	Face Dances Part Two/Man Watching	1982	$4
❏ 99590	Face the Face/Hiding Out	1985	$3
❏ 99590 [PS]	Face the Face/Hiding Out	1985	$4
❏ 99577	Give Blood/Magic Bus	1986	$3
❏ 99577 [PS]	Give Blood/Magic Bus	1986	$4
❏ 7217	Let My Love Open the Door/And I Moved	1980	$4
❏ 99553	Secondhand Love/White City Fighting	1986	$3
❏ 99973	Slit Skirts/Uniforms	1982	$4
ATLANTIC
| ❏ 88875 | A Friend Is a Friend/Man Machines | 1989 | $3 |
| ❏ 88875 [PS] | A Friend Is a Friend/Man Machines | 1989 | $4 |

TOWNSMEN, THE

COLUMBIA
| ❏ 43207 | Please Don't Say Goodbye/Gotta Get Moving | 1965 | $10 |
HERALD
| ❏ 585 | Is It All Over/Just a Little Bit | 1963 | $20 |
JOEY
| ❏ 6202 | Moonlight Was Made for Lovers/I'm in the Mood for Love | 1963 | $30 |
PJ
| ❏ 1341 | That's All I'll Ever Need/I Can't Let Go | 1963 | $200 |
VANITY
| ❏ 579/80 | It's Time/Little Jeanie | 1960 | $30 |

TOXIC REASONS

BENIT
| ❏ 4057 | War Hero/Somebody Help Me | 1980 | $60 |
| ❏ 4057 [PS] | War Hero/Somebody Help Me | 1980 | $60 |

TOY DOLLS, THE

ERA
| ❏ 3093 | Little Tin Soldier/Fly Away | 1962 | $20 |

TOYS, THE

DYNO VOICE
❏ 209	A Lover's Concerto/This Night	1965	$15
❏ 214	Attack/See How They Run	1965	$12
❏ 222	Baby Toys/Happy Birthday Broken Heart	1966	$12
❏ 219	Can't Get Enough of You Baby/Silver Spoon	1966	$10
❏ 218	My My Heart Be Cast Into Stone/On Backstreet	1966	$10
DYNO VOX
| ❏ 209 | A Lover's Concerto/This Night | 1965 | $30 |
MUSICOR
| ❏ 1319 | Sealed with a Kiss/I Got My Heart Set on You | 1968 | $8 |
PHILIPS
| ❏ 40432 | Ciao Baby/I Got Carried Away | 1967 | $10 |
| ❏ 40456 | My Love Sonata/I Close My Eyes | 1967 | $10 |

TRACERS, THE

SULLY
| ❏ 928 | She Said Yeah/Watch Me | 1966 | $60 |
—*Originally released under the name "The Stones;" produced with both blue and white labels*

TRACEY TWINS, THE

EASTWEST
| ❏ 108 | Heartbreak Hill/Don't Mean Maybe Baby | 1958 | $30 |
| ❏ 110 | Tonight You Belong to Me/(B-side unknown) | 1956 | $30 |

TRACEY, WREG

ANNA
| ❏ 1126 | All I Want for Christmas (Is Your Love)/Take Me Back | 1960 | $50 |
| ❏ 1105 | All I Want Is You/Take Me Back | 1959 | $50 |

TRACY, BILL

DEL-FI
| ❏ 4132 | I'm So Happy/January Love | 1959 | $30 |
DOT
| ❏ 15868 | Flame Out/Disappointed | 1958 | $50 |
| ❏ 15797 | One Chance/Hold Me, Thrill Me, Kiss Me | 1958 | $70 |
RADIANT
| ❏ 1504 | High School Hero/Lost Love | 1961 | $20 |

TRADE WINDS, THE

KAMA SUTRA
❏ 218	I Believe in Her/Catch Me in the Meadow	1966	$15
❏ 212	Mind Excursion/Little Susan's Dreamin'	1966	$15
❏ 234	Mind Excursion/Only When I'm Dreamin'	1967	$15
RED BIRD
| ❏ Oct-0028 | Girl from Greenwich Village/There's a Rock and Roll Show in Town | 1965 | $30 |
| ❏ Oct-0033 | Summertime Girl/The Party Starts at Nine | 1965 | $50 |

TRADEWINDS, THE

RCA VICTOR
| ❏ 47-7553 | Furry Murray/Crossroads | 1959 | $30 |
| ❏ 47-7511 | Toni/Twins | 1959 | $30 |

TRADITIONS, THE

ARTCO
| ❏ 45-102 | On Fire/My Heart | 1966 | $2000 |
BAR CLAY
| ❏ 19678 | My Life with You/Something Gone Wrong | 1967 | $75 |
| ❏ 19671 | Oh My Love/Girls | 1967 | $70 |

TRAFFIC
Also see JIM CAPALDI; DAVE MASON; STEVE WINWOOD.

ASYLUM
| ❏ 45207 | Walking in the Wind/(Instrumental) | 1974 | $5 |
UNITED ARTISTS
❏ 50692	Empty Pages/Stranger to Himself	1970	$6
❏ 50460	Feelin' Alright?/Withering Tree	1968	$8
❏ 50841	Gimme Some Lovin' (Part 1)/Gimme Some Lovin' (Part 2)	1971	$6
—*By "Traffic, Etc.*
❏ 50883	Glad (Part 1)/Glad (Part 2)	1972	$6
❏ 50261	Heaven Is In Your Mind/No Face, No Name and No Number	1968	$8
❏ 50232	Here We Go 'Round the Mulberry Bush/Coloured Rain	1967	$12
❏ 50218	Hole in My Shoe/Smiling Phases	1967	$12
❏ 50500	Medicated Goo/Pearly Queen	1969	$6
❏ 0129	Paper Sun/Empty Pages	1973	$4
—*Silver Spotlight Series" reissue*
| ❏ 50195 | Paper Sun/Giving to You | 1967 | $10 |

TRAITS, THE

ASCOT
| ❏ 2108 | Linda Lou/Little Mama | 1962 | $40 |
PACEMAKER
| ❏ 254 | Too Good to Be True/Gotta Keep Cool | 1967 | $30 |
RENNER
| ❏ 229 [DJ] | Got My Mojo Working/Woe Woe | 1962 | $50 |
—*Promo only on colored vinyl*
| ❏ 229 | Got My Mojo Working/Woe Woe | 1962 | $30 |
—*Black vinyl*
| ❏ 229 [DJ] | Got My Mojo Working/Woe Woe | 1962 | $50 |
—*Promo only on colored vinyl*
| ❏ 221 | Linda Lou/Little Mama | 1962 | $50 |
SCEPTER
| ❏ 12169 | Harlem Shuffle/Somewhere | 1966 | $12 |
| ❏ 12169 | Harlem Shuffle/Strange Lips Start Old Memories | 1966 | $8 |
TNT
❏ 175	Live It Up/Yes I Do	1960	$30
❏ 177	My Baby's Fine/Here I Am in Love Again	1960	$30
❏ 164	One More Time/Don't Be Blue	1959	$30
—*Later reissued on TNT 194 credited to "Roy Head*
| ❏ 181 | Summer Time Love/Your Turn to Cry | 1960 | $30 |
UNIVERSAL
| ❏ 30494 | Harlem Shuffle/Somewhere | 1966 | $40 |

Number	Title	Yr	NM

TRAMMELL, BOBBY LEE
ABC-PARAMOUNT
| ❏ 9890 | Shirley Lee/I Sure Do Love You Baby | 1958 | $100 |

ALLEY
| ❏ 1004 | Come On Baby/I Tried Not to Cry | 1963 | $30 |
| ❏ 1001 | It's All Your Fault/Arkansas Twist | 1962 | $30 |

ATLANTIC
| ❏ 2332 | Shimmy Loo/You Make Me Feel So Fine | 1966 | $15 |

CAPITOL
| ❏ 3718 | Love Don't Let Me Down/I Couldn't Believe My Eyes | 1973 | $8 |

CINNAMON
| ❏ 797 | The Warmth of Your Love/Marion County Tradition | 1974 | $6 |

FABOR
| ❏ 4038 | Shirley Lee/I Sure Do Love You Baby | 1957 | $200 |

HOT
| ❏ 102 | Betty Jean/(B-side unknown) | 1959 | $50 |
| ❏ 101 | Shimmy Lou/(B-side unknown) | 1959 | $50 |

RADIO
| ❏ 114 | My Susie Jane/Should I Make Amends | 1958 | $50 |

SIMS
❏ 195	Come On and Love Me/If You Don't Wanna, You Don't Have To	1964	$15
❏ 183	Good Lovin'/New Dance in France	1964	$15
❏ 241	I Tried/Am I Satisfying You	1965	$15
❏ 254	Long Tall Sally/The Saints Go Marchin' In	1965	$15
❏ 225	Twenty-Four Hours/Just Let Me Move You One More Time	1965	$15

SOUNCOT
❏ 1104	24 Hours a Day/I Lost the Girl I Love Tonight	1970	$6
❏ 1128	Don't Let the Stars Get In Your Eyes/Sheila	1971	$6
❏ 1143	I Believe in You/My Love Keeps Growing	1972	$6
❏ 1100	I Dare America to Be Great/A Gift from God	1970	$6
❏ 1135	Love Isn't Love (Till You Give It Away)/Tell Me That You Want Me	1972	$6
❏ 1119	My Shoes Keep Walkin' Back to You/Let's Wash the World and Make It Clean	1971	$6

WARRIOR
| ❏ 1554 | Woe Is Me/Open Up Your Heart | 1959 | $100 |

TRAMMPS, THE
ATLANTIC
| ❏ 3654 | Dance Contest/Hard Rock and Disco | 1980 | $4 |
| ❏ 3389 | Disco Inferno/That's Where the Happy People Go | 1978 | $5 |

—Reissue in conjunction with the success of "Saturday Night Fever

❏ 3389	Disco Inferno/You Touch My Hot Line	1977	$6
❏ 3389 [PS]	Disco Inferno/You Touch My Hot Line	1977	$8
❏ 3286	Hooked for Life/I'm Alright	1975	$5
❏ 3797	I Don't Want to Ever Lose Your Love/Breathtaking View	1981	$4
❏ 3403	I Feel Like I've Been Livin' (On the Dark Side of the Moon)/Don't Burn Bridges	1977	$5
❏ 3777	Mellow Out/Looking for You	1980	$4
❏ 3573	More Good Times to Remember/Teaser	1979	$5
❏ 3669	Music Freek/V.I.P.	1980	$4
❏ 3460	Seasons for Girls/Body Contact Contract	1978	$5
❏ 3460	Seasons for Girls/Love Ain't Been Easy	1978	$5
❏ 3537	Soul Bones/Love Magnet	1978	$5
❏ 3345	Soul Searchin' Time/Love Is a Funky Thing	1976	$5
❏ 3306	That's Where the Happy People Go (Short)/That's Where the Happy People Go (Long)	1975	$5

BUDDAH
| ❏ 507 | Hold Back the Night/Tom's Song | 1975 | $5 |
| ❏ 321 | Sixty Minute Man/Scrub Board | 1972 | $6 |

GOLDEN FLEECE
❏ 3251	Love Epidemic/I Know That Feeling	1973	$6
❏ 3255	Trusting Heart/Down These Dark Streets	1974	$6
❏ 3253	Where Do We Go from Here/Shout	1974	$6

TRAPEZE
Includes future JUDAS PRIEST drummer Dave Holland plus multi-band bassist/vocalist GLENN HUGHES.
THRESHOLD
❏ 67005 [DJ]	Black Cloud (mono/stereo)	1971	$10
❏ 67005 [DJ]	Black Cloud (mono/stereo)	1971	$10
❏ 67011	Coast to Coast/Your Love Is Alright	1972	$8
❏ 67001	Send Me No More Letters/Another Day	1970	$8

TRAPP, SANDY
PARKWAY
| ❏ 840 | Love Sickness/I Don't Know | 1962 | $10 |

TRASH
APPLE
| ❏ 1811 | Golden Slumbers-Carry That Weight/Trash Can | 1969 | $20 |

—A-side listed as "Golden Slumbers/Carry That Weight"

| ❏ 1811 | Golden Slumbers-Carry That Weight/Trash Can | 1969 | $30 |

—A-side listed as "Golden Slumbers and Carry That Weight"

| ❏ 1811 | Golden Slumbers-Carry That Weight/Trash Can | 1969 | $30 |

—A-side listed as "Golden Slumbers Carry That Weight"

TRASHMEN, THE
ARGO
| ❏ 5516 | Bird '65/Ubangi Stomp | 1965 | $60 |

GARRETT
❏ 4005	Bad News/On the Move	1964	$30
❏ 4003	Bird Dance Beat/A-Bone	1964	$30
❏ 4013	Dancing with Santa/Real Live Doll	1964	$30
❏ 4013 [PS]	Dancing with Santa/Real Live Doll	1964	$250
❏ 4010	Peppermint Man/New Generation	1964	$30
❏ 4002	Surfin' Bird/King of the Surf	1963	$40
❏ 4012	Whoa Dad/Walkin' My Baby	1964	$30
❏ 4012 [PS]	Whoa Dad/Walkin' My Baby	1964	$250

METROBEAT
| ❏ 7927 | Green, Green Backs of Home/Address Enclosed | 1968 | $20 |

OLDIES 45
| ❏ 301 | Surfin' Bird/King of the Surf | 1965 | $15 |

—Early reissue

SOMA
| ❏ 1469 | Surfin' Bird/Liar, Liar | 1966 | $15 |

—B-side by the Castaways

TRIBE
| ❏ 8315 | Hanging On Me/Some Lies | 1966 | $50 |

TRASK, DIANA
ABC DOT
❏ 17587	Cry/I Can Take a Little Heartache	1975	$5
❏ 17536	Oh Boy/Alone Again	1974	$5
❏ 17555	There Has to Be a Loser/Sunshine	1975	$5

COLUMBIA
❏ 4-41623	A Guy Is a Guy/Theme from "Our Man in Havana	1960	$20
❏ 4-41821	I'm So Lonesome I Could Cry/Our Language of Love	1960	$20
❏ 4-41711	Long Ago Last Summer/Turn to Me	1960	$20
❏ 4-41943	Waltzing Matilda/I Loved You Once in Silence	1961	$20

DIAL
| ❏ 4077 | Lock, Stock and Tear Drops/Precious Time | 1968 | $5 |

DOT
❏ 17342	Beneath Still Waters/Heartbreak Hotel	1970	$6
❏ 17520	(If You Wanna Hold On) Hold On to Your Man	1974	$6
❏ 17424	It Meant Nothing to Me/How Much Have I Hurt Thee	1972	$6
❏ 17467	It's a Man's World (If You Had a Man Like Mine)/World of the Missing	1973	$6
❏ 17496	Lean It All on Me/The King	1974	$6
❏ 17448	Say When/Old Southern Cotton Town	1973	$6
❏ 17384	The Chokin' Kind/Let's Keep Her Free (America)	1971	$6
❏ 17369	The Last Person to See Me Alive/A Stronger Hand to Hold	1970	$6
❏ 17404	We've Got to Work It Out Between Us/I Keep It Hid	1972	$6
❏ 17486	When I Get My Hands on You/Shadow of My Man	1973	$6

KARI
| ❏ 123 | Stirrin' Up Feelings/Give My Heart a Break | 1981 | $6 |

| ❏ 121 | This Must Be My Ship/Give My Heart a Break | 1981 | $6 |

ROULETTE
| ❏ 4184 | Soldier Won't You Marry Me/Love Is Just Another Name for a Fool | 1959 | $30 |

TRAVELERS, THE
ANDEX
❏ 34012	He's Got the Whole World in His Hands/Green Town Girl	1957	$40
❏ 4033	I Go for You/I'll Always Be in Love with You	1959	$40
❏ 2011	I'll Be Home for Christmas/Katie the Kangaroo	1958	$40
❏ 34006	Why/Teenage Machine Age	1957	$40

DECCA
| ❏ 31215 | Ivy on the Old School Wall/Cadwallader 0002 | 1961 | $50 |
| ❏ 31282 | White Rose/Oh My Love (Love Me) | 1961 | $50 |

DON RAY
| ❏ 5965 | Traveler/Seven Minutes Till Four | 1963 | $60 |

MAGIC LAMP
| ❏ 516 | Big House/Goin' Home | 1964 | $15 |

VAULT
| ❏ 911 | Spanish Moon/She's Got the Blues | 1964 | $20 |

YELLOW SAND
❏ 451	Groovy/(B-side unknown)	1965	$40
❏ 452	Malibu Sunset/Hang On	1965	$40
❏ 2	Windy and Warm/Last Date	1963	$60

TRAVELING SALESMEN
RCA VICTOR
| ❏ 47-9167 | I'm Alive/Days of My Years | 1967 | $30 |

TRAVELING WILBURYS
Also see BOB DYLAN; GEORGE HARRISON; JEFF LYNNE; ROY ORBISON; TOM PETTY AND THE HEARTBREAKERS.
WILBURY
❏ 27637	End of the Line/Congratulations	1989	$20
❏ 27637 [PS]	End of the Line/Congratulations	1989	$30
❏ 27637 [DJ]	End of the Line (same on both sides)	1989	$30
❏ 27637 [DJ]	End of the Line (same on both sides)	1989	$30
❏ 27732	Handle with Care/Margarita	1988	$8
❏ 27732 [PS]	Handle with Care/Margarita	1988	$8
❏ 27732 [DJ]	Handle with Care (same on both sides)	1988	$20
❏ 27732 [DJ]	Handle with Care (same on both sides)	1988	$20

TRAVELLERS, THE
GASS
| ❏ 1000 | Tie Me Surfer Board Down, Sport/In the Pines | 1963 | $50 |

TRAVERS, MARY
CHRYSALIS
| ❏ 2367 | Freedom/(B-side unknown) | 1979 | $4 |
| ❏ 2202 | The Air That I Breathe/You Turn Me Around | 1977 | $5 |

WARNER BROS.
❏ 7790	Circles/I'll Have to Say I Love You in a Song	1974	$5
❏ 7731	Five Hundred Miles/Oh, What a Feeling	1973	$5
❏ 7481	Follow Me/I Guess He'd Rather Be in Colorado	1971	$5
❏ 7588	Morning Glory/That's Enough for Me	1972	$5
❏ 7517	The Song Is Love/Ericka with the Windy Yellow Hair	1971	$5
❏ 7675	Too Many Mondays/That Year There Was No Winter	1972	$5

TRAVIS AND BOB
BIG TOP
| ❏ 3054 | Pocahontas/Day Dreams | 1960 | $20 |

MERCURY
| ❏ 71797 | Give Your Love to Me/Stay Close to Me | 1961 | $20 |
| ❏ 71866 | The Spider and the Fly/What a Change | 1961 | $20 |

SANDY
❏ 1024	Lover's Rendezvous/Oh Yeah	1959	$30
❏ 1019	Teenage Vision/Little Bitty Johnny	1959	$30
❏ 1017	Tell Him No/We're Too Young	1959	$30

—With no mention of Dot Records on label

Number	Title	Yr	NM
❏ 1017	Tell Him No/We're Too Young	1959	$30

—With Dot Records distribution mentioned on label

Number	Title	Yr	NM
❏ 1029	That's How Long/Wake Up and Cry	1960	$30

TRAVIS, MCKINLEY
PRIDE

Number	Title	Yr	NM
❏ 2	Baby, Is There Something on Your Mind/You've Got It and I Want It	1970	$12

SOULTOWN

Number	Title	Yr	NM
❏ 109	Baby, Is There Something on Your Mind/You've Got It and I Want It	1970	$30

TRAVIS, MERLE
CAPITOL

Number	Title	Yr	NM
❏ F2136	Ain't That a Cryin' Shame/A Too Fast Past	1952	$30
❏ F2336	Bayou Baby/Knee Deep in Trouble	1953	$30
❏ F3194	Beer Barrel Polka/Cuddle Up a Little Closer	1955	$30
❏ 5965	Country Joe/You're a Little Bit Cuter	1967	$12
❏ F1800	Done Rovin'/Faithful Fools	1951	$30
❏ F1337	Dry Bread/Woncha Be My Baby	1950	$40
❏ F1241	El Reno/Trouble, Trouble	1950	$40
❏ F2544	Gambler's Guitar/Shut Up and Drink Your Beer	1953	$30
❏ F1029	Guitar Rag/Cane Bottom Chair	1950	$40
❏ F3247	Hunky Dory/If You Want It I've Got It	1955	$30
❏ F2176	I Am a Pilgrim/Nine Pound Hammer	1952	$30
❏ F965	I Got a Mean Old Woman/Start Even	1950	$40
❏ F2453	I'll Have Myself a Ball/Green Cheese	1953	$30
❏ F2245	I'll See You in My Dreams/Cannonball Rag	1952	$30
❏ F3362	Lazy River/Turn My Picture Upside Down	1956	$30
❏ F1737	Lost John Boogie/Let's Settle Down	1951	$30
❏ F2902	Louisiana Boogie/Love Must Be Ketchin'	1954	$30
❏ 5764	Moon Over the Motel/That Tennessee Beat	1966	$10
❏ F40272	Petticoat Fever/I'm Pickin' Up the Pieces of My Heart	1950	$50
❏ F1146	Spoonin' Moon/Too Much Sugar for a Dime	1950	$40
❏ F2175	Steel Guitar Rag/Merle's Boogie Woogie	1952	$30
❏ 2624	Super Highway/World Full of Roses	1969	$10
❏ F1519	The Deep South/Boogie in A Minor	1951	$30
❏ 5876	Wildwood Flower/Farther On Down the Road	1967	$10

TRAVIS, RANDY
PAULA

Number	Title	Yr	NM
❏ 429	Dreamin'/I'll Take Any Willing Woman	1978	$30

—As "Randy Traywick"

Number	Title	Yr	NM
❏ 431	She's My Woman/(Instrumental)	1978	$30

—As "Randy Traywick"

WARNER BROS.

Number	Title	Yr	NM
❏ 28828	1982/Reasons I Quit	1985	$4
❏ 27707 [PS]	An Old Time Christmas/How Do I Wrap My Heart Up for Christmas	1988	$5
❏ 27707	An Old Time Christmas/How Do I Wrap My Heart Up for Christmas	1988	$5
❏ 27689	Deeper Than the Holler/It's Out of My Hands	1988	$4
❏ 27689 [PS]	Deeper Than the Holler/It's Out of My Hands	1988	$5
❏ 28649	Diggin' Up Bones/There'll Always Be a Honky Tonk Somewhere	1986	$4
❏ 28384	Forever and Ever, Amen/Promises	1987	$5
❏ 28384 [PS]	Forever and Ever, Amen/Promises	1987	$5
❏ 27833	Honky Tonk Moon/Young Guns	1988	$3
❏ 27833 [PS]	Honky Tonk Moon/Young Guns	1988	$5
❏ 27551	Is It Still Over?/Here in My Heart	1989	$4
❏ 27969	I Told You So/Good Intentions	1988	$3
❏ 27969 [PS]	I Told You So/Good Intentions	1988	$5
❏ 22841	It's Just a Matter of Time/This Day Was Made for You and Me	1989	$4
❏ 22841 [PS]	It's Just a Matter of Time/This Day Was Made for You and Me	1989	$8

Number	Title	Yr	NM
❏ 28246	I Won't Need You Anymore (Always and Forever)/Tonight I'm Walking Out on the Blues	1987	$4
❏ 22766	Oh, What a Silent Night/Winter Wonderland	1989	$4
❏ 28962	On the Other Hand/Can't Stop Now	1985	$4

—Reissued in 1986 with the same label and number

Number	Title	Yr	NM
❏ 22917	Promises/Written in Stone	1989	$3
❏ 28286	Too Gone Too Long/My House	1987	$4
❏ 28286 [PS]	Too Gone Too Long/My House	1987	$5
❏ 28556	White Christmas Makes Me Blue/Pretty Paper	1986	$5
❏ PRO-S-2842 [DJ]	White Christmas Makes Me Blue/Sleigh Ride	1987	$6

—B-side by Mark O'Connor

WARNER BROS

Number	Title	Yr	NM
❏ PRO02842 [DJ]	White Christmas Makes Me Blue/Sleigh Ride	1987	$4

—B-side by Mark O'Connor

TRAVOLTA, JOHN, AND OLIVIA NEWTON-JOHN
RSO

Number	Title	Yr	NM
❏ 906	Summer Nights/Rock 'N' Roll Party Queen	1978	$4

—B-side by Louis St. Louis

TRAVOLTA, JOHN
MIDLAND INT'L.

Number	Title	Yr	NM
❏ MB-10907	All Strung Out on You/Easy Evil	1977	$5
❏ MB-10907 [PS]	All Strung Out on You/Easy Evil	1977	$6
❏ MB-10623	Let Her In/Big Trouble	1976	$5
❏ MB-10623 [PS]	Let Her In/Big Trouble	1976	$8

—Picture sleeve with stock copies, has "RE" in lower left corner

Number	Title	Yr	NM
❏ JB-10623 [PS]	Let Her In/Big Trouble	1976	$20

—Picture sleeve with promo copies, completely different from stock sleeve

Number	Title	Yr	NM
❏ MB-10780	Whenever I'm Away from You/Razzamatazz	1976	$5
❏ MB-10780 [PS]	Whenever I'm Away from You/Razzamatazz	1976	$6

MIDSONG INT'L.

Number	Title	Yr	NM
❏ 1000	Big Trouble/Can't Let You Go	1978	$5
❏ MB-10977	Slow Dancin'/Moonlight	1977	$5
❏ MB-10977 [PS]	Slow Dancin'/Moonlight	1977	$6
❏ MB-11206	What Would They Say/Razzamatazz	1978	$5
❏ MB-11206 [PS]	What Would They Say/Razzamatazz	1978	$6

RCA

Number	Title	Yr	NM
❏ GB-10945	Let Her In/Whenever I'm Away from You	1977	$4

—Gold Standard Series

RSO

Number	Title	Yr	NM
❏ 909	Greased Lightnin'/Rock and Roll Is Here to Stay	1978	$4

—B-side by Sha Na Na

Number	Title	Yr	NM
❏ 909 [PS]	Greased Lightnin'/Rock and Roll Is Here to Stay	1978	$4
❏ 930	Sandy/Blue Moon	1979	$4

—B-side by Sha Na Na

TRAYNOR, JAY
ABC

Number	Title	Yr	NM
❏ 10809	Come On/The Merry-Go-Round Is Slowing You Down	1966	$20

CORAL

Number	Title	Yr	NM
❏ 62396	How Sweet It Is/I Rise, I Fall	1964	$15

—As "JAY, formerly of Jay & the Americans"

Number	Title	Yr	NM
❏ 62420	I've Known You All My Life/Little Sister	1964	$15

TREADWELL, IRENE
JAY DEE

Number	Title	Yr	NM
❏ 782	Church Bells Are Ringing on Christmas Morning/Dear Santa Bring Back My Daddy to Me	1953	$30

TREASURERS, THE
CROWN

Number	Title	Yr	NM
❏ 005	Story of Love/I Walk with An Angel	1961	$300

TREASURES, THE
SHIRLEY

Number	Title	Yr	NM
❏ 500	Hold Me Tight/Pete Meets Vinnie	1964	$40

VALOR

Number	Title	Yr	NM
❏ 0(# unknown)	Minor Chaos/Valley of the Broken Hearts	1964	$400

—Marbled vinyl

Number	Title	Yr	NM
❏ 0(# unknown)	Minor Chaos/Valley of the Broken Hearts	1964	$200

—Green vinyl

Number	Title	Yr	NM
❏ 0(# unknown)	Minor Chaos/Valley of the Broken Hearts	1964	$125

—Sources differ as to what the number of this record is, and we've never seen a copy, so we haven't listed one.

TREBELAIRES, THE
NESTOR

Number	Title	Yr	NM
❏ 16	There Goes That Train/I Gotta	1954	$125

TREBLE CHORDS, THE
DECCA

Number	Title	Yr	NM
❏ 31015	Teresa/My Little Girl	1959	$125

TREE SWINGERS, THE
BIG TOP

Number	Title	Yr	NM
❏ 3058	Only Forever/Kissin' and Cookin'	1960	$20

TREMAINES, THE
KANE

Number	Title	Yr	NM
❏ 08	Heavenly/Wonderful, Marvelous	1959	$60

V-TONE

Number	Title	Yr	NM
❏ 507	Heavenly/Wonderful, Marvelous	1959	$30

TREMELOES, THE
DJM

Number	Title	Yr	NM
❏ 1008	Hard Woman/My Friend Delaney	1976	$5
❏ 1016	September, November, December/(B-side unknown)	1976	$5

EPIC

Number	Title	Yr	NM
❏ 10621	Breakheart Motel/By the Way	1970	$10
❏ 10548	(Call Me) Number One/Instant Whip	1969	$8
❏ 10233	Even the Bad Times Are Good/Jenny's All Right	1967	$8
❏ 10233 [PS]	Even the Bad Times Are Good/Jenny's All Right	1967	$20
❏ 10328	Girl from Nowhere/Helule, Helule	1968	$8
❏ 10075	Good Day Sunshine/What a State I'm In	1966	$15
❏ 10139	Here Comes My Baby/Gentlemen of Pleasure	1967	$12
❏ 10437	I Shall Be Released/I Miss My Baby	1969	$8
❏ 10682	Me and My Life/Try Me	1970	$8
❏ 10376	My Little Lady/All the World to Me	1968	$8
❏ 10807	My Woman/Hello Buddy	1971	$6
❏ 10184	Silence Is Golden/Let Your Hair Hang Down	1967	$10
❏ 10184 [PS]	Silence Is Golden/Let Your Hair Hang Down	1967	$20
❏ 10293	Suddenly You Love Me/Suddenly Winter	1968	$8

7-Inch Extended Plays

Number	Title	Yr	NM
❏ 5-26388	Peggy Sue/The Lion Sleeps Tonight/Willy and the Hand Jive//Everyday/Rag Doll/Ain't Nothing But a House Party	1968	$20

—Jukebox issue; small hole, plays at 33 1/3 rpm

Number	Title	Yr	NM
❏ 5-26388 [PS]	World Explosion	1968	$20

TREMELOES, THE/THE HOLLIES
EPIC

Number	Title	Yr	NM
❏ 10184/0 [DJ]	Silence Is Golden/Carrie-Anne	1967	$125

—Promo only on red vinyl

Number	Title	Yr	NM
❏ 10184/0 [PS]	Silence Is Golden/Carrie-Anne	1967	$300

—"There's Room for Two at the Top!" across top of sleeve; has photos of both bands; all the print is in red

TREMONTS, THE
BRUNSWICK

Number	Title	Yr	NM
❏ 55217	Believe My Heart/Legend of Love	1961	$40

PAT RICCIO

Number	Title	Yr	NM
❏ 101	Believe My Heart/Legend of Love	1961	$125

TREN-DELLS, THE
JAM

Number	Title	Yr	NM
❏ 111	Hey Da-Da Dow/Tough Little Buggy	1962	$30

Number	Title	Yr	NM
SOUND STAGE 7			
❏ 2508	Mr. Doughnut Man/Ain't That Funny	1963	$15
TILT			
❏ 779	I'm So Young/Don't You Hear Me Calling Baby	1961	$40
—As "The Trend-Els			
❏ 788	Moments Like This/I Miss You So	1962	$40

TREN-TEENS, THE
CARNIVAL

Number	Title	Yr	NM
❏ 501	My Baby's Gone/Your Yah Yah Is Gone	1964	$125

TRENDS, THE (1)
ABC

Number	Title	Yr	NM
❏ 10944	Check My Tears/Don't Drop Out of School	1967	$30
❏ 11091	Soul Clap/Big Parade	1968	$30
❏ 10993	Thanks for a Little Lovin'/I Never Knew How Good I Had It	1967	$30
SMASH			
❏ 1914	Dance with My Baby/To Be Happy Enough	1964	$30
❏ 1933	Get Something Going/That's the Way the Story Goes	1964	$30

TRENDS, THE (2)
ARGO

Number	Title	Yr	NM
❏ 5341	I'll Be True/Class Ring	1959	$40
SCOPE			
❏ 102	Gone Again/Silly Grin	1959	$100

TRENDS, THE (U)
RCA VICTOR

Number	Title	Yr	NM
❏ 47-7733	The Beard/Chug-a-Lug	1960	$20

TRENIERS, THE
BRUNSWICK

Number	Title	Yr	NM
❏ 55047	Goodnight Irene/Rubbing Noses in the Midnight Sun	1958	$30
❏ 55014	Holy Mackerel Andy/Rock Calypso Joe	1957	$30
❏ 55033	Pennies from Heaven/Ooh-La-La	1957	$30
DOM			
❏ 410	Gotta Travel On/Let It All Hang Out	1968	$8
EPIC			
❏ 9162	Boodie Green/Good Rockin' Tonight	1956	$30
❏ 9127	Go! Go! Go!/Doin' 'Em Up	1955	$30
OKEH			
❏ 7035	Bald Head/Come On Let's Face It	1954	$50
❏ 7057	Devil's Mambo/Do, Do, Do (Do-Be-Oo-Be-Oo)	1955	$40
❏ 6804	Go! Go! Go!/Plenty of Money	1951	$60
❏ 6876	Hadacol, That's All/Long Distance Blues	1952	$50
❏ 6826	Hey, Little Girl/Old Woman Blues	1951	$50
❏ 6932	Hi-Yo Silver/Poon-Tang!	1953	$50
❏ 6984	I'd Do Nothin' But Grieve/This Is It	1953	$50
❏ 6853	It Rocks, It Rolls, It Swings/Taxi Blues	1952	$50
❏ 6937	The Moondog/Poon-Tang!	1953	$60
❏ 7050	Who Put the "Ungh" in the Mambo/Get Out of the Car	1955	$40
VIK			
❏ 0214	Lover Come Back to Me/Sorrento	1956	$30

7-Inch Extended Plays
EPIC

Number	Title	Yr	NM
❏ EG-7014	(contents unknown)	1955	$60
❏ EG-7014 [PS]	Go! Go! Go!	1955	$60

TRENT, JACKIE
A&M

Number	Title	Yr	NM
❏ 1022	Hollywood/Don't Send Me Away	1969	$6
KAPP			
❏ 583	Only One Such As You/If You Love Me, Really Love Me	1964	$15
❏ 630	Somewhere in the World/I Heard Someone Say	1964	$15
NASCO			
❏ 6012	Little Andy/What's He Got	1958	$30
PARKWAY			
❏ 941	Don't Stand in My Way/How Soon	1965	$15
❏ 963	To Show I Love Him/When Summertime Is Over	1965	$15

Number	Title	Yr	NM
❏ 955	Where Are You Now My Love/On the Other Side of the Tracks	1965	$15

WARNER BROS.

Number	Title	Yr	NM
❏ 7178	7:10 to Suburbia/Stop Me and Buy One	1968	$8
❏ 7022	Hummingbird/I'll Be with You	1967	$8
❏ 5865	If You Ever Leave Me/Take Me Away	1966	$10
❏ 7189	I'll Be With You/Two of Us	1968	$8
❏ 5683	It's All in the Way You Look at Life/Time After Time	1965	$10
❏ 7070	It's Not Easy Loving You/Your Love Is Everywhere	1967	$8

TRENTONS, THE
SHEPHERD

Number	Title	Yr	NM
❏ 2204	All Alone/Star Bright	1962	$100

TREVOR, VAN
ATLANTIC

Number	Title	Yr	NM
❏ 2175	Tuesday Girl/I Want to Cry	1963	$10
BAND BOX			
❏ 367	Born to Be in Love with You/It's So Good to Be Loved	1966	$8
❏ 373 [DJ]	Christmas In The Country/Holiday Driving (PSA Announcements)	1966	$10
❏ 373 [DJ]	Christmas In The Country/PSA Announcements	1966	$10
❏ 374	He's Losing His Mind/A Fool Called Me	1967	$8
❏ 371	Our Side/When You've Lost Your Baby	1966	$8
CANADIAN AMERICAN			
❏ 181	Louisiana Hot Sauce/Satisfaction Is Guaranteed	1964	$30
❏ 188	The Girl from the Main Street Diner/For This Girl	1965	$20
CLARIDGE			
❏ 305	Christmas in Washington Square/Melting Snow	1965	$20
COUNTRY INT'L.			
❏ 114	It All Adds Up to Love/Goodbye My Son, Goodbye	1976	$6
❏ 131	Luziana River/Virgil Benson's Rude Awakening	1978	$6
❏ 112	Sticky Situation/Love Is Like a Red, Red Rose	1976	$6
❏ 126	Who's Cheatin' Who/I'll Be Home	1977	$6
DATE			
❏ 1594	Take Me Along with You/Guitar	1968	$8
ROYAL AMERICAN			
❏ 283	A Man Away from Home/I've Got Today to Live For	1969	$6
❏ 289	Funny Familiar Forgotten Feelings/Daddy's Little Man	1969	$6
❏ 31	Lonely Looking Woman/Johnnie and Annie	1971	$5
❏ 9	Luziana River/Sweet Diana	1970	$5
❏ 3	Mercy Hospital/Something Missing in Me	1970	$5
❏ 67	Shiny New Penny/You and Only You	1972	$5
❏ 280	The Things That Matter/Band of Gold	1969	$6
❏ 23	Wish I Was Home Instead/Did I Have a Good Time	1970	$5
VIVID			
❏ 1004	C'mon Now Baby/A Fling of the Past	1963	$40
—Backing group is The Four Seasons			

TREXLER, GARY
RCA VICTOR

Number	Title	Yr	NM
❏ 47-7258	I Flipped/Turn About	1958	$20
❏ 47-7420	The Look/You Made Up for Everything	1958	$20
REV			
❏ 3507	Teen Baby/Cloud Full of Tears	1957	$30

TRIANGLE, THE
AMARET

Number	Title	Yr	NM
❏ 108	Music, Music, Music/Magic Touch	1969	$10

TRIANGLES, THE
FARGO

Number	Title	Yr	NM
❏ 1023	Dance the Magoo/Step-Up-and-Go	1962	$20
FIFO			
❏ 107	My Oh My/Really I Do	1964	$200
HERALD			
❏ 549	Savin' My Love/'Tis a Pity	1960	$50

TRIBULATIONS, THE
IMPERIAL

Number	Title	Yr	NM
❏ 66416	Mama's Love/You Gave Me Up for Promises	1969	$40

TRICKELS, THE
GONE

Number	Title	Yr	NM
❏ 5078	With Each Step a Tear/Outside the Chapel Door	1959	$125
POWER			
❏ 250	With Each Step a Tear/When I Fall in Love	1958	$200

TRIDELS, THE
SAN-DEE

Number	Title	Yr	NM
❏ 1009	Land of Love/Image of My Love	1963	$60

TRINIDADS, THE
FORMAL

Number	Title	Yr	NM
❏ 1005	Don't Say Goodbye/On My Happy Way	1959	$200
❏ 1006	One Lonely Night/When We're Together	1959	$200

TRIOLO, FRANK
FLAGSHIP

Number	Title	Yr	NM
❏ 106	Ice Cream Baby/Pretty Little Woman	1958	$400

TRIPLETS, THE
ELEKTRA

Number	Title	Yr	NM
❏ 69542	Boys/Message of Love	1986	$3
❏ 69556	Translate	1986	$3

TRIPP, ALLEN
NASHVILLE

Number	Title	Yr	NM
❏ 1001	Love Is/Lady Sorrow	1982	$6

TRIPP, PAUL
MUSICOR

Number	Title	Yr	NM
❏ 1125	An Old-Fashioned Christmas/I've Got a Date with Santa	1965	$15

TRIPP, TOM
HIT

Number	Title	Yr	NM
❏ 93	Since I Fell for You/Dominique	1963	$8
—B-side by Betty Coleson			

TRITT, TRAVIS
WARNER BROS.

Number	Title	Yr	NM
❏ 7-22882	Country Club/Sign of the Times	1989	$4

TRIUMVIRAT
CAPITOL

Number	Title	Yr	NM
❏ 4700	Waterfall/Jo Ann Walker	1979	$5

TROGGS, THE
ATCO

Number	Title	Yr	NM
❏ 6444	I Can't Control Myself/Gonna Make You	1966	$20
❏ 6415	Wild Thing/I Want You	1966	$30
❏ 6415	Wild Thing/With a Girl Like You	1966	$30
—Wild Thing" writer is incorrectly credited as "Presley.			
❏ 6415	Wild Thing/With a Girl Like You	1966	$30
—Wild Thing" writer is correctly credited as "Taylor.			
BELL			
❏ 45405	Listen to the Man/Queen of Sorrow	1973	$8
❏ 45426	Strange Movies/I'm on Fire	1973	$8
FONTANA			
❏ 1585	6-5-4-3-2-1/Anyway That You Want Me	1967	$8
❏ 1634	Hip Hip Hooray/Say Darlin'	1968	$8
❏ 1557	I Can't Control Myself/Gonna Make You	1966	$10
❏ 1607	Love Is All Around/When Will the Rain Come	1967	$10
❏ 1630	Surprise, Surprise/Cousin Jane	1968	$8
❏ 1548	Wild Thing/From Home	1966	$10
❏ 1552	With a Girl Like You/I Want You	1966	$10
PAGE ONE			
❏ 21032	Come Now/Lover	1970	$6
❏ 21030	Easy Lovin'/Give Me Something	1970	$6
❏ 21026	Evil Woman/Heads Or Tails	1969	$6
PYE			
❏ 65011	Feels Like a Woman/Everything's Funny	1972	$8
❏ 71015	Good Vibrations/Push It Up to Me	1975	$5
❏ 71054	Satisfaction/(B-side unknown)	1975	$5
❏ 71035	Summertime/Jerry Come Down	1975	$5

TROLL, THE

SMASH

Number	Title	Yr	NM
❏ 2208	Satin City News/Professor Potts' Pornographic Projector	1969	$15

TROLLS, THE

ABC

Number	Title	Yr	NM
❏ 10952	Baby. What You Ain't Got (I Ain't in Need)/Who Was That Boy	1967	$12
❏ 10823	Every Day and Every Night/Are You the One	1966	$15
❏ 10884	Laughing All the Way/Someone Here Inside	1966	$12
❏ 10916	They Don't Know/There Was a Time	1967	$10

RUFF

Number	Title	Yr	NM
❏ 1010	Into My Arms/That's the Way My Love Is	1966	$300

U.S.A.

Number	Title	Yr	NM
❏ 905	I Got to Have You/Don't Come Around	1968	$30

WARRIOR

Number	Title	Yr	NM
❏ 173	Stupid Girl/I Don't Recall	1967	$60
❏ 173 [PS]	Stupid Girl/I Don't Recall	1967	$80

TROMBONES UNLIMITED

LIBERTY

Number	Title	Yr	NM
❏ 55874	The Phoenix Love Theme/Daydream	1966	$8

TROPHIES, THE

CHALLENGE

Number	Title	Yr	NM
❏ 9133	Desire/Doggone It	1962	$70
❏ 9149	Peg O' My Heart/I Laughed So Hard I Cried	1962	$20
❏ 9170	That's All I Want from You/Felicia	1962	$20

KAPP

Number	Title	Yr	NM
❏ 714	Everywhere I Go/Baby Don't Live Here Anymore	1965	$20
❏ 750	Leave My Girl Alone/You're the Queen	1966	$20

TROWER, ROBIN

Also see JACK BRUCE/ROBIN TROWER; PROCOL HARUM.

CHRYSALIS

Number	Title	Yr	NM
❏ 2122	Caledonia/Messin' the Blues	1976	$6
❏ 2272	It's for You/Birthday Boy	1979	$4
❏ 2009	Man of the World/Take a Fast Train	1973	$6
❏ 2238	My Love (Burning Love)/(B-side unknown)	1978	$4
❏ 2206	Somebody Calling/Bluebird	1978	$4
❏ 2172	Sweet Wine of Love/In City Dreams	1977	$4
❏ 2113	Too Rolling Stoned (Part 1)/Too Rolling Stoned (Part 2)	1976	$6

TROY, BILLY

BARNABY

Number	Title	Yr	NM
❏ ZS72054	Isn't It Lonely Together/Sally's Sayin' Somethin'	1971	$8
❏ ZS72035	Longer Than Awhile/My Nancy's Love	1971	$8

TROY, DORIS

APPLE

Number	Title	Yr	NM
❏ 1820	Ain't That Cute/Vaya Con Dios	1970	$8

ATLANTIC

Number	Title	Yr	NM
❏ 2269	Hurry/He Don't Belong to Me	1965	$15
❏ 2222	One More Chance/Please Little Angel	1964	$15
❏ 2206	Tomorrow Is Another Day/What'cha Gonna Do About It	1963	$15

CALLA

Number	Title	Yr	NM
❏ 114	Heartaches/I'll Do Anything	1966	$30

CAPITOL

Number	Title	Yr	NM
❏ 2043	Face Up to the Truth/He's Qualified	1967	$8

MIDLAND INT'L.

Number	Title	Yr	NM
❏ MB-11082	Can't Hold On/Another Look	1977	$5
❏ MB-10806	Lyin' Eyes/Give God Glory	1976	$5

TRU-TONES, THE

CHART

Number	Title	Yr	NM
❏ 634	Tears in My Eyes/Magic	1957	$800

TRUELEERS, THE

CHECKER

Number	Title	Yr	NM
❏ 1026	Forget About Him/Waiting for You	1962	$15

TRUMPETEERS, THE (1)

IMPERIAL

Number	Title	Yr	NM
❏ 5972	Milky White Way/Leave That Lie Alone	1963	$20
❏ 5994	Seven Angels/Just a Little Walk with Jesus	1963	$20

JUBILEE

Number	Title	Yr	NM
❏ 5654	Milky White Way/Prayer for Today	1969	$10

—As "The CBS Trumpeeters"

NASHBORO

Number	Title	Yr	NM
❏ 805	Everything Moves/My Heart Bubbles Over	1964	$20

—As "The CBS Trumpeeters"

Number	Title	Yr	NM
❏ 788	God Is Coming/One Day I Was Walking	1963	$20

—As "The CBS Trumpeeters"

Number	Title	Yr	NM
❏ 887	Little Wooden Church/Lord, Ease My Weary Mind	1966	$20

—As "The CBS Trumpeeters"

OKEH

Number	Title	Yr	NM
❏ 6871	Don't Miss That Train/Home Don't Seem Like Home	1952	$125
❏ 6890	I'll Fly Away/Leave It in His Hands	1953	$125

TUBB, ERNEST, AND LORETTA LYNN

DECCA

Number	Title	Yr	NM
❏ 32570	I Chased You Till You Caught Me/If We Put Our Heads Together	1969	$8
❏ 31643	Mr. and Mrs. Used to Be/Love Was Right Here All the Time	1964	$10
❏ 31793	Our Hearts Are Holding Hands/We're Not Kids Anymore	1965	$10
❏ 32091	Sweet Thang/Beautiful, Unhappy Home	1967	$10
❏ 32496	Who's Gonna Take the Garbage Out/Somewhere Between	1969	$8

TUBB, ERNEST

CACHET

Number	Title	Yr	NM
❏ 4507	Walking the Floor Over You/Let's Say Goodbye Like We Said Hello	1979	$6

—A-side with Merle Haggard

Number	Title	Yr	NM
❏ 4501	Waltz Across Texas/Jealous Loving Heart	1979	$6

DECCA

Number	Title	Yr	NM
❏ 9-28837	A Dear John Letter/The Mean Gun, In Between Age Blues	1953	$30

—As "Bill and Ernest Tubb"

Number	Title	Yr	NM
❏ 32022	Another Story/There's No Room in My Heart (For the Blues)	1966	$10
❏ 9-46309	Any Old Time/A Drunkard's Child	1951	$30

— The above four comprise a box set

Number	Title	Yr	NM
❏ 33014	Baby, It's So Hard to Be Good/In This Corner	1972	$8
❏ 9-29103	Baby Your Mother (Like She Babies You)/Your Mother, Your Darling, Your Friend	1954	$30
❏ 31614	Be Better to Your Baby/Think of Me, Thinking of You	1964	$12
❏ 7-34273 [S]	Blue Christmas/Merry Texas Christmas, You All	1963	$30
❏ 7-34275 [S]	C-H-R-I-S-T-M-A-S/I'm Trimming the Christmas Tree with Teardrops	1963	$30

— The above five were a set issued to jukebox operators; each has a small hole and plays at 33 1/3 rpm

Number	Title	Yr	NM
❏ 31334	Christmas Is Just Another Day for Me/Rudolph the Red-Nosed Reindeer	1961	$15
❏ 9-46268	Christmas Island/Christmas	1950	$40

—Black label, lines on either side of "Decca

Number	Title	Yr	NM
❏ 32690	Dear Judge/A Good Year for the Wine	1970	$8
❏ 9-28550	Dear Judge/I Will Miss You When You Go	1953	$30
❏ 9-28869	Divorce Granted/Counterfeit Kisses	1953	$30
❏ 32849	Don't Back a Man Up in a Corner/Shenandoah Waltz	1971	$8
❏ 9-28777	Don't Brush Them on Me/My Wasted Past	1953	$30
❏ 9-30219	Don't Forbid Me/God's Eye	1957	$20
❏ 9-46296	Don't Stay Too Long/If You Want Some Lovin'	1951	$30
❏ 31742	Do What You Do Well/Turn Around, Walk Away	1965	$12
❏ 9-46377	Driftwood on the River/I'm Stepping Out of the Picture	1951	$30
❏ 9-31119	Ev'rybody's Somebody's Fool/Let the Little Girl Dance	1960	$15
❏ 9-28310	Fortunes in Memories/So Many Times	1952	$30
❏ 9-30526	Geisha Girl/I Found My Girl in the U.S.A.	1957	$20

(continued, right column)

Number	Title	Yr	NM
❏ 31196	Girl from Abilene/Little Old Band of Gold	1961	$15
❏ 31357	Go to Sleep Conscience (Don't Hurt Me This Time)/I Could Never Say No	1962	$15
❏ 9-30685	Half a Mind/The Blues	1958	$20
❏ 9-28630	Hank It Will Never Be the Same Without You/Beyond the Sunset	1953	$40
❏ 9-46144	Have You Ever Been Lonely? (Have You Ever Been Blue)/Let's Say Goodbye Like We Said Hello	1950	$50

—First 45 issue of 78 from 1948; black label, lines on either side of "Decca

Number	Title	Yr	NM
❏ 9-46144	Have You Ever Been Lonely? (Have You Ever Been Blue)/Let's Say Goodbye Like We Said Hello	1955	$30

—Black label, star under "Decca

Number	Title	Yr	NM
❏ 9-30610	Hey, Mr. Bluebird/How Do We Know	1958	$20
❏ 9-46338	Hey La La/Precious Little Baby	1951	$30
❏ 9-46308	Hobo's Meditation/Why Should I Be Lonely	1951	$30
❏ 9-29011	Honky Tonk Heart/I'm Not Looking for an Angel	1954	$30
❏ 9-30549	House of Glass/Heaven Help Me	1958	$20
❏ 31428	House of Sorrow/No Letter Today	1962	$15
❏ 9-30872	I Cried a Tear/I'd Rather Be	1959	$20
❏ 7-34274 [S]	I'll Be Walking the Floor This Christmas/Lonely Christmas	1963	$30
❏ 9-29350	I'll Be Walkin' the Floor This Christmas/Lonely Christmas Eve	1954	$30
❏ 9-46213	I Love You Because/Unfaithful One	1950	$50
❏ 9-29624	I Met a Friend/When Jesus Calls	1955	$20
❏ 32315	I'm Gonna Make Like a Snake/Mama, Who Was That Man	1968	$8
❏ 31399	I'm Looking High and Low for My Baby/Show Her Lots of Gold	1962	$15
❏ 9-28946	I'm Trimming My Christmas Tree with Teardrops/We Need God for Christmas	1953	$30
❏ 32131	In the Jailhouse Now/Yesterday's Winner Is a Loser Today	1967	$10
❏ 9-29520	It's a Lonely World/Have You Seen My Boogie Woogie Baby	1955	$20
❏ 32632	It's America/Somebody Better Than Me	1970	$8
❏ 31861	It's for God, and Country, and You Mom (That's Why I'm Fighting in Viet Nam)/After the Boy Gets the Girl	1965	$10
❏ 9-31082	Live It Up/Accidentally on Purpose	1960	$15
❏ 9-28453	Merry Texas Christmas, You All/Blue Snowflakes	1952	$30
❏ 9-46389	Missing in Action/A Heartsick Soldier on Heartbreak Ridge	1952	$30
❏ 9-30305	Mister Love/Leave Me	1957	$20
❏ 9-46306	Mother, Queen of My Heart/I'm Lonely and Blue	1951	$30
❏ 31476	Mr. Juke Box/Walking the Floor Over You	1963	$15
❏ 9-30422	My Treasure/Go Home	1957	$20
❏ 32800	One Sweet Hello/Once Ole Going Gets a-Goin'	1971	$8
❏ 31706	Pass the Booze/(A Memory) That's All You'll Ever Be to Me	1964	$10
❏ 32448	Saturday Satan Sunday Saint/Tommy's Doll	1969	$8
❏ 32943	Say Something Nice to Sarah/Teach My Daddy How to Pray	1972	$8
❏ 9-29836	So Doggone Lonesome/If I Never Have Anything Else	1956	$20
❏ 9-28448	Somebody Loves You/Don't Trifle on Your Sweetheart	1952	$30
❏ 9-28067	Somebody's Stolen My Honey/My Mother Must Have Been a Girl Like You	1952	$30
❏ 31526	Thanks a Lot/The Way That You're Living	1963	$15
❏ 9-29731	Thirty Days (To Come Back Home)/Answer the Phone	1955	$30
❏ 31241	Thoughts of a Fool/Don't Just Stand There	1961	$15
❏ 31300	Through That Door/What Will You Tell Them	1961	$15
❏ 9-46243	Throw Your Love My Way/Give Me an Old Fashioned Love	1950	$50
❏ 31908	Till Me Getup Has Gotup and Gone/Just One More	1966	$10
❏ 9-46289	Tomorrow Never Comes/Are You Waiting Just for Me	1951	$30
❏ 32237	Too Much of Not Enough/Nothing Is Better Than You	1968	$8
❏ 9-30098	Treat Her Right/Loving You Is My Weakness	1956	$20
❏ 9-29220	Two Glasses, Joe/Journey's End	1954	$30

Number	Title	Yr	NM
❑ 9-46006	Walking the Floor Over You/I'll Always Be Glad to Take You Back	1950	$50

— One of three discs included in "Album No. 9-146"; 78 first issued with this number in 1946; black label with lines on either side of "Decca

Number	Title	Yr	NM
❑ 31824	Waltz Across Texas/ Lots of Luck	1965	$10
❑ 9-30759	What Am I Living For/ Goodbye Sunshine, Hello Blues	1958	$20
❑ 9-46295	When It's Prayer Meetin' Time in the Hollow/ May the Good Lord Bless and Keep You	1951	$30
❑ 9-46186	White Christmas/ Blue Christmas	1950	$40

— 78 first issued in 1949; black label, lines on either side of "Decca

Number	Title	Yr	NM
❑ 7-34272 [S]	White Christmas/ Christmas Island	1963	$30
❑ 31161	White Silver Sands/A Guy Named Joe	1960	$15
❑ 31866	Who's Gonna Be Your Santa Claus This Year/ Blue Christmas Tree	1965	$10
❑ 9-46307	Why Did You Give Me Your Love/I'm Free from the Blues	1951	$30

DECCA FAITH SERIES

Number	Title	Yr	NM
❑ 9-14532	Farther Along/The Old Rugged Cross	1951	$40
❑ 9-14506	Stand By Me/When I Take My Vacation in Heaven	1950	$50
❑ 9-14515	What a Friend We Have in Jesus/The Wonderful City	1950	$50
❑ 9-14561	When It's Prayer Meetin' Time in the Hollow/ May the Good Lord Bless and Keep You	1951	$40

MCA

Number	Title	Yr	NM
❑ 40222	Anything But This/Don't Water Down the Bad News	1974	$6
❑ 40436	If You Don't Quit Checkin' on Me (I'm Checkin' Out on You)/I'd Like to Live It Again	1975	$6
❑ 40056	I've Got All the Heartaches I Can Handle/The Texas Troubadour	1973	$6
❑ 60078	Waltz Across Texas/Walking the Floor Over You	1973	$5

— Reissue

Number	Title	Yr	NM
❑ 65024	White Christmas/ Blue Christmas	1973	$4

— Black label with rainbow

Number	Title	Yr	NM
❑ 65024	White Christmas/ Blue Christmas	1980	$3

— Blue label with rainbow

7-Inch Extended Plays

DECCA

Number	Title	Yr	NM
❑ ED2691	*Ev'rybody's Somebody's Fool/Let the Little Girl Dance/Live It Up/ Accidentally on Purpose	1960	$25
❑ ED2357	*Have You Ever Been Lonely/Let's Say Goodbye Like We Said Hello/ Try Me One More Time/ Soldier's Last Letter	1956	$25
❑ ED 7-2655 [S]	*Have You Ever Been Lonely/Rainbow at Midnight/ Careless Darlin'/You Nearly Lost Your Mind	1959	$35
❑ ED2680	*He'll Have to Go/White Silver Sands/Am I That Easy to Forget/Guy Named Joe	1960	$25
❑ ED2643	*I'm a Long Gone Daddy/ San Antonio Rose/Your Cheatin' Heart/It Makes No Difference Now	1959	$25
❑ ED2627	*Mister Love/Leave Me/Hey Mr. Bluebird/How Do I Know	1959	$25
❑ ED2739	*No Letter Today!/ Women Make a Fool Out of Me/House of Sorrow/Go On Home	1963	$30
❑ ED2728	*Show Her Lots of Gold/I'm Looking High and Low for My Baby/I Walk the Line/Crazy Arms	1962	$30
❑ ED2774	*Thanks a Lot/Mr. Juke Box/Last Letter/Just Call Me Lonesome	1964	$30
❑ ED2718	*What Will You Tell Them/ Thoughts of a Fool/Go to Sleep Conscience/I Never Could Say No	1961	$25
❑ ED2787 [PS]	Be Better to Your Baby	1965	$35
❑ 7-4518 [PS]	Blue Christmas	1964	$20
❑ 7-34373 [PS]	By Request	1966	$25
❑ ED2706	(contents unknown)	1962	$25
❑ 7-4518 [S]	(contents unknown)	1964	$20

— 33 1/3 rpm, small hole jukebox edition

Number	Title	Yr	NM
❑ ED2769	(contents unknown)	1964	$30
❑ ED2787	(contents unknown)	1965	$35
❑ ED2797	(contents unknown)	1965	$35
❑ ED2522 [PS]	Encores	1957	$25
❑ ED2626 [PS]	Ernest Tubb	1959	$25
❑ ED2691 [PS]	Ernest Tubb	1960	$25

Number	Title	Yr	NM
❑ ED2718 [PS]	Ernest Tubb	1961	$25
❑ ED2706 [PS]	Ernest Tubb	1962	$25
❑ ED2739 [PS]	Ernest Tubb	1963	$30
❑ ED2769 [PS]	Ernest Tubb	1964	$30
❑ ED2627 [PS]	Ernest Tubb and the Wilburn Brothers	1959	$25
❑ ED2356 [PS]	Ernest Tubb Favorites, Vol. 1	1956	$25
❑ ED2357 [PS]	Ernest Tubb Favorites, Vol. 2	1956	$25
❑ 7-34417 [PS]	Ernest Tubb Sings Country Hits Old & New	1967	$25
❑ ED2563 [PS]	Ernest Tubb Sings the Hits	1958	$25
❑ ED2563	Geisha Girl/I Found My Girl in the U.S.A.//Home of the Blues/Tangled Mind	1958	$25
❑ ED2655 [M]	Have You Ever Been Lonely (Have You Ever Been Blue)/Rainbow at Midnight//Careless Darlin'/ You Nearly Lose Your Mind	1959	$25
❑ ED2626	House of Glass/My Treasure//Treat Her Right/Don't Forbid Me	1959	$25
❑ ED2522	I Dreamed of an Old Love Affair/Mississippi Gal//When a Soldier Knocks and Finds Nobody Home/Daisy May	1957	$25
❑ ED2523	I Knew the Moment I Lost You/You're the Only Good Thing (That's Happened to Me)//My Hillbilly Baby/There's No Fool Like a Young Fool	1957	$25
❑ 7-34417	Memphis//Under Your Spell Again/I'm Gonna Tie One On Tonight//Remember Me/Holdin' Hands/Waitin' in Your Welfare Line	1967	$25

— Stereo jukebox issue; small hole, plays at 33 1/3 rpm

Number	Title	Yr	NM
❑ ED2655 [PS]	More Ernest Tubb	1959	$25
❑ ED2523 [PS]	My Hillbilly Baby	1957	$25
❑ ED2797 [PS]	Pass the Booze	1965	$35
❑ ED2728 [PS]	Show Her Lots of Gold	1962	$30
❑ ED2774 [PS]	Thanks a Lot	1964	$30
❑ ED2521 [PS]	The Daddy of 'Em All	1957	$25
❑ ED2680 [PS]	The Ernest Tubb Record Shop	1960	$25
❑ ED 7-2655 [PS]	The Ernest Tubb Story	1959	$35
❑ ED2643	The Importance of Being Ernest	1959	$25
❑ ED2356	Walking the Floor Over You/I'll Always Be Glad to Take You Back//Rainbow at Midnight/I Don't Blame You	1956	$25

TUBB, JUSTIN

CHALLENGE

Number	Title	Yr	NM
❑ 59081	Big Fool of the Year/ Believing It Yourself	1960	$20

DECCA

Number	Title	Yr	NM
❑ 9-30792	Almost Lonely/Mine Is a Lonely Life	1958	$20
❑ 9-30930	Buster's Gang/I Know You Do	1959	$20
❑ 9-29401	I Gotta Go Get My Baby/ Chuga-Chuga, Chica-Mauga (Choo-Choo Train)	1955	$30
❑ 9-30229	I'm a Big Boy Now/The Life I Have to Live	1957	$20
❑ 9-29169	I'm Lookin' for a Date Tonight/Sufferin' Heart	1954	$30
❑ 9-29498	I'm Sorry I Stayed Away So Long/My Heart's Not for Little Girls to Play With	1955	$30
❑ 9-30062	It Takes a Lot o' Heart/I'm Just Fool Enough	1956	$20
❑ 9-29895	Lucky Lucky Someone Else/ You Nearly Lost Your Mind	1956	$20
❑ 9-28865	Ooh-La La/The Story of My Life	1953	$30
❑ 9-29720	Pepper Hot Baby/ Who Will It Be	1955	$30
❑ 9-29029	Somebody Ugghed On You/ Something Called the Blues	1954	$30
❑ 9-30606	Sugar Lips/Rock It On Down to My House	1958	$40
❑ 9-30408	The Party Is Over/ If You'll Be My Love	1957	$20
❑ 9-29590	Within Your Arms/All Alone	1955	$20

DOT

Number	Title	Yr	NM
❑ 17224	Blackjack County Chain/The Great River Road Mystery	1969	$8

GROOVE

Number	Title	Yr	NM
❑ 58-0024	As Long As There's a Sunday/When Love Goes Wrong	1963	$10
❑ 58-0034	If I Miss You (Half As Much As I Have Loved You)/ John Mason Whitney III	1964	$10
❑ 58-0019	Little Miss Lonesome/Sorry About the World Out There	1963	$12
❑ 58-0019 [PS]	Little Miss Lonesome/Sorry About the World Out There	1963	$40
❑ 58-0047	Prematurely Blue/You'll Never Get a Better Chance	1964	$12
❑ 58-0017	Take a Letter, Miss Gray/ Here I Sit a-Waiting	1963	$10
❑ 58-0017 [PS]	Take a Letter, Miss Gray/ Here I Sit a-Waiting	1963	$50

RCA VICTOR

Number	Title	Yr	NM
❑ 47-9428	A Funny Thing Happened/ I'm Going Back to Louisian	1968	$8
❑ 47-9082	But Wait There's More/The Second Thing I'm Gonna Do	1967	$8

STARDAY

Number	Title	Yr	NM
❑ 549	My Heart Keeps Getting in the Way/One for You, One for Me	1961	$15
❑ 530	One Eyed Red/I'd Know You Anywhere	1960	$20
❑ 582	Walking the Floor Over You/They Painted a Picture for Me	1962	$15

TUBB, JUSTIN, AND GOLDIE HILL

DECCA

Number	Title	Yr	NM
❑ 9-29145	Looking Back to See/I Miss You So	1954	$30
❑ 9-29349	Sure Fire Kisses/ Fickle Heart	1954	$30

TUBES, THE

A&M

Number	Title	Yr	NM
❑ 1826	Don't Touch Me There/ Proud to Be an American	1976	$6
❑ 2149	Love's a Mystery (I Don't Understand)/Telecide	1979	$6
❑ 2120	Prime Time/No Way Out	1979	$6
❑ 2037	Show Me a Reason/I Saw Her Standing There	1978	$6
❑ 1956	This Town/I'm Just a Mess	1977	$6
❑ 1733	White Punks on Dope (Part 1)/White Punks on Dope (Part 2)	1975	$8
❑ 1733 [PS]	White Punks on Dope (Part 1)/White Punks on Dope (Part 2)	1975	$15

CAPITOL

Number	Title	Yr	NM
❑ A-5007	Don't Want to Wait Anymore/Think About Me	1981	$3
❑ A-5007 [PS]	Don't Want to Wait Anymore/Think About Me	1981	$4
❑ B-5091	Gonna Get It Next Time/Sports Fans	1982	$6
❑ B-5443	Piece by Piece/Night People	1985	$3
❑ B-5443 [PS]	Piece by Piece/Night People	1985	$4
❑ SPRO-9909 [DJ]	She's a Beauty (same on both sides)	1983	$15
❑ B-5217	She's a Beauty/When You're Ready to Come	1983	$4

— First pressing has a purple label

Number	Title	Yr	NM
❑ B-5217	She's a Beauty/When You're Ready to Come	1983	$3

— Second pressing has a black label with colorband

Number	Title	Yr	NM
❑ B-5217 [PS]	She's a Beauty/When You're Ready to Come	1983	$8
❑ SPRO-9740 [DJ]	Sports Fans (same on both sides)	1982	$5
❑ A-5016	Talk To Ya Later/Power Tools	1981	$6
❑ B-5254	The Monkey Time/ Sports Fans	1983	$3
❑ B-5254 [PS]	The Monkey Time/ Sports Fans	1983	$4
❑ B-5258	Tip of My Tongue/ Keyboard Kids	1983	$4

TUBES

Number	Title	Yr	NM
❑ 833502XS	Happy Holidaze	1983	$60

— Fan club flexidisc

Number	Title	Yr	NM
❑ 12682XS	Tubular Holiday	1982	$60

— Fan club flexidisc

TUCKER, BILLY JOE

DOT

Number	Title	Yr	NM
❑ 16240	Boogie Woogie Bill/ Mail Train	1961	$125

MAHA

Number	Title	Yr	NM
❑ 103	Boogie Woogie Bill/ Mail Train	1961	$300

TUCKER, RICK

COLUMBIA

Number	Title	Yr	NM
❑ 4-41041	Patty Baby/Don't Do Me This Way	1957	$125

HITSVILLE

Number	Title	Yr	NM
❑ 6035	I Heard a Song/Plans That We Made	1976	$6

OAK

Number	Title	Yr	NM
❑ 1066	Honey I'm Just Walking Out the Door/(B-side unknown)	1989	$5

Number	Title	Yr	NM

TUCKER, TANYA
ARISTA
Number	Title	Yr	NM
❏ 9046	Baby I'm Yours/I Don't Want You to Go	1983	$3
❏ 1053	Changes/Too Long	1983	$4
❏ 9006	Changes/Too Long	1983	$3
❏ 0677	Feel Right/Cry	1982	$4

CAPITOL
Number	Title	Yr	NM
❏ B-44348	Call on Me/Daddy and Home	1989	$3
❏ B-44401	Daddy and Home/ Playing for Keeps	1989	$3
❏ B-44271	Highway Robbery/ Lonesome Town	1989	$3
❏ B-44142	If It Don't Come Easy/I'll Tennessee You in My Dreams	1988	$3
❏ B-5652	I'll Come Back As Another Woman/Somebody to Care	1986	$3
❏ B-5694	It's Only for You/ Girls Like Me	1987	$5

— First pressing had erroneous A-side title

Number	Title	Yr	NM
❏ B-5694	It's Only Over for You/ Girls Like Me	1987	$3
❏ B-44100	I Won't Take Less Than Your Love/Heartbreaker	1987	$3

— With Paul Davis and Paul Overstreet

Number	Title	Yr	NM
❏ B-44036	Love Me Like You Used To/If I Didn't Love You	1987	$3
❏ B-44036 [PS]	Love Me Like You Used To/If I Didn't Love You	1987	$3
❏ B-44469	My Arms Stay Open All Night/Love Me Like You Used To	1989	$3
❏ 7PRO-79810	My Arms Stay Open All Night (same on both sides)	1989	$5

— Originally promo only; stock copy on 44469

Number	Title	Yr	NM
❏ B-5533	One Love at a Time/ Fool Fool Heart	1985	$3
❏ B-5533 [PS]	One Love at a Time/ Fool Fool Heart	1985	$3
❏ B-44188	Strong Enough to Bend/ Back on My Feet	1988	$3
❏ 4986	Why Don't We Just Sleep on It Tonight/It's Your World	1981	$4

— With Glen Campbell

COLUMBIA
Number	Title	Yr	NM
❏ 45892	Blood Red and Goin' Down/The Missing Piece of the Puzzle	1973	$5
❏ 45588	Delta Dawn/I Love the Way He Loves Me	1972	$5
❏ 45588 [PS]	Delta Dawn/I Love the Way He Loves Me	1972	$12
❏ 10236	Greener Than the Grass (We Laid On)/Guess I'll Have to Love Him More	1975	$5
❏ 10069	I Believe the South Is Gonna Rise Again/Old Dan Tucker's Daughter	1974	$5
❏ 45721	Love's the Answer/The Jamestown Ferry	1972	$5
❏ 10127	Spring/Bed of Roses	1975	$5
❏ 46047	The Man That Turned My Mama On/Satisfied with Missing You	1974	$5
❏ 45799	What's Your Mama's Name/Rainy Girl	1973	$5
❏ 45991	Would You Lay with Me (In a Field of Stone)/ No Man's Land	1974	$5
❏ 51037	Can I See You Tonight/ Let Me Count the Ways	1980	$4
❏ 40755	Dancing the Night Away/ Let's Keep It That Way	1977	$4
❏ 40497	Don't Believe My Heart Can Stand Another You/ Depend on You	1975	$4
❏ 41323	Dream Lover/Bronco	1980	$4

— A-side with Glen Campbell

Number	Title	Yr	NM
❏ 40598	Here's Some Love/The Pride of Franklin County	1976	$4
❏ 41005	I'm the Singer, You're the Song/Lover Goodbye	1979	$4
❏ 40708	It's a Cowboy Lovin' Night/Morning Comes	1977	$4
❏ 41144	Lay Back in the Arms of Someone/By Day By Day	1979	$4
❏ 40402	Lizzie and the Rainman/ Traveling Salesman	1975	$4
❏ 51096	Love Knows We Tried/ Somebody (Trying to Tell You Something)	1981	$4
❏ 41305	Pecos Promenade/ King of Country Music	1980	$4
❏ 40444	San Antonio Stroll/The Serenade That We Played	1975	$4
❏ 40902	Save Me/Slippin' Away	1978	$4
❏ 40902 [PS]	Save Me/Slippin' Away	1978	$6
❏ 51131	Should I Do It/Lucky Enough for Two	1981	$4
❏ 52017	Somebody Buy This Cowgirl a Beer/Delta Dawn	1982	$4
❏ 41194	Tear Me Apart/Better Late Than Never	1980	$4
❏ 40976	Texas (When I Die)/ Not Fade Away	1978	$4
❏ 40976 [PS]	Texas (When I Die)/ Not Fade Away	1978	$6

TUCKER, TOMMY
CHECKER
Number	Title	Yr	NM
❏ 1112	Alimony/All About Melanie	1965	$20
❏ 1186	A Whole Lot of Fun Before the Weekend Is Done/Real True Love	1967	$8
❏ 1133	Chewing Gum/I've Been a Fool	1966	$10
❏ 1067	Hi-Heel Sneakers/I Don't Want 'Cha	1964	$30
❏ 1178	I'm Shorty/Sitting Home Alone	1967	$8
❏ 1075	Long Tall Shorty/Mo' Shorty	1964	$20

HI
Number	Title	Yr	NM
❏ 2014	Loving Lil/A Man in Love	1959	$40
❏ 2020	Miller's Cave/The Strangers	1960	$30

MGM
Number	Title	Yr	NM
❏ 10854	Christmas In Killarney/ Jing-A-Ling	1950	$20

SUNBEAM
Number	Title	Yr	NM
❏ 128	My Blue Heaven/That Man Comes Around	1959	$20

TUDOR MINSTRELS, THE
LONDON
Number	Title	Yr	NM
❏ 1012	Love in the Open Air/A Theme from "The Family Way"	1966	$60

TUFFS, THE
DORE
Number	Title	Yr	NM
❏ 757	I Only Cry Once a Day Now/The Moon Out There	1966	$30

DOT
Number	Title	Yr	NM
❏ 16304	Surfer Stomp (Part 1)/ Surfer Stomp (Part 2)	1962	$30

TULLY, LEE, AND MILT MOSS
FLAIR-X
Number	Title	Yr	NM
❏ 3007	Around the World with Elwood Pretzel (Part 1)/ Around the World with Elwood Pretzel (Part 2)	1956	$60

TUNE ROCKERS, THE
UNITED ARTISTS
Number	Title	Yr	NM
❏ 0145	The Green Mosquito/ Bust Out	1973	$4

— Silver Spotlight Series" reissue; B-side by the Busters

Number	Title	Yr	NM
❏ 139	The Green Mosquito/ Warm Up	1958	$30

TUNE WEAVERS, THE
CASA GRANDE
Number	Title	Yr	NM
❏ 4037	Happy, Happy Birthday Baby/Ol' Man River	1957	$200
❏ 4038	I Remember Dear/ Pamela Jean	1957	$40
❏ 101	Little Boy/Look Down That Lonesome Road	1959	$50
❏ 3038	My Congratulations Baby/ This Can't Be Love	1960	$40
❏ 4040	There Stands My Love/I'm Cold	1958	$50

CHECKER
Number	Title	Yr	NM
❏ 1007	Congratulations on Your Wedding/Your Skies of Blue	1962	$30
❏ 872	Happy, Happy Birthday Baby/Ol' Man River	1957	$30
❏ 872	Happy, Happy Birthday Baby/Yo Yo Walk	1957	$30

— B-side by Paul Gayten

Number	Title	Yr	NM
❏ 880	Ol' Man River/Tough Enough	1957	$30

— B-side by Paul Gayten

CLASSIC ARTISTS
Number	Title	Yr	NM
❏ 104	Come Back to Me/I've Tried	1988	$4

— As "Margo Sylvia and Tune Weavers

Number	Title	Yr	NM
❏ 107	Merry, Merry Christmas Baby/What Are You Doing New Year's Eve	1988	$4

— As "Margo Sylvia and Tune Weavers

TUNEDROPS, THE
GONE
Number	Title	Yr	NM
❏ 5072	Smoothie/Jumpin' Jellybeans	1959	$30

METRO
Number	Title	Yr	NM
❏ 20028	Smoothie/Jumpin' Jelly Beans	1959	$50

TUNEMASTERS, THE
MARK
Number	Title	Yr	NM
❏ 7002	Sending This Letter/ It's All Over	1957	$300

TUNESMITHS, THE
COLUMBIA
Number	Title	Yr	NM
❏ 4-21485	Outlaw/Snowdeer	1956	$30
❏ 4-21386	There's a Bottle Where She Used to Be/Oh Stop	1955	$30

TURBANS, THE
HERALD
Number	Title	Yr	NM
❏ 478	B-I-N-G-O (Bingo)/I'm Nobody's	1956	$40
❏ 510	Congratulations/ The Wadda-Do	1957	$30
❏ 486	It Was a Nite Like This/ All of My Love	1956	$40
❏ 469	Sister Sookey/I'll Always Watch Over You	1956	$40
❏ 458	When You Dance/ Let Me Show You (Around My Heart)	1955	$60

— Yellow label, script print inside flag

IMPERIAL
Number	Title	Yr	NM
❏ 5847	I Wonder (I Wanna Know)/ The Damage Is Done	1962	$30
❏ 5807	Six Questions/The Lament of Silver Gulch	1962	$50
❏ 5828	This Is My Story/ Clicky Clicky Clack	1962	$30

MONEY
Number	Title	Yr	NM
❏ 209	Tick Tock Awoo/ Nest Is Warm	1955	$200
❏ 209	Tick Tock Awoo/ No No Cherry	1955	$200

PARKWAY
Number	Title	Yr	NM
❏ 820	When You Dance/ Golden Rings	1961	$30

RED TOP
Number	Title	Yr	NM
❏ 115	I Promise You Love/ Curfew Time	1959	$60

ROULETTE
Number	Title	Yr	NM
❏ 4281	Diamonds and Pearls/Bad Man	1960	$30
❏ 4326	Three Friends (Two Lovers)/ I'm Not Your Fool Anymore	1961	$30

TURKS, THE
BALLY
Number	Title	Yr	NM
❏ 1017	This Heart of Mine/ Why Did You	1956	$40

CASH
Number	Title	Yr	NM
❏ 1042	It Can't Be True/ Wagon Wheels	1956	$40

— As "The Original Turks

CLASS
Number	Title	Yr	NM
❏ 256	Hully Gully/Rockville U.S.A.	1959	$30

IMPERIAL
Number	Title	Yr	NM
❏ 5783	I'm a Fool/It Can't Be True	1961	$15

KEEN
Number	Title	Yr	NM
❏ 3-4016	Father Time/Okay	1958	$30

KNIGHT
Number	Title	Yr	NM
❏ 2005	I'm a Fool/It Can't Be True	1958	$30

MONEY
Number	Title	Yr	NM
❏ 215	I'm a Fool/I've Been Accused	1956	$50

TURKS, THE / THE TURBANS
MONEY
Number	Title	Yr	NM
❏ 211	Emily/When I Return	1955	$70

TURLEY, RICHARD
DOT
Number	Title	Yr	NM
❏ 16231	I Wanna Dance/ Since I Met You	1961	$50

FRATERNITY
Number	Title	Yr	NM
❏ 845	Makin' Love with My Baby/All About Ann	1959	$50

TURNER, GRANT
CHART
Number	Title	Yr	NM
❏ 1275	Old North Star/Maco Light	1965	$15
❏ 1130	The Bible in Her Hand/ Lord Don't Let Me Down	1964	$20

SCORPION
Number	Title	Yr	NM
❏ 0532	I Remember (A Father's Day Card)/Old North Star	1977	$6

TURNER, IKE
Also see IKE AND TINA TURNER.
ARTISTIC
Number	Title	Yr	NM
❏ 1504	(I Know) You Don't Love Me/Down and Out	1958	$40

COBRA
Number	Title	Yr	NM
❏ 5033	Box Top/Walking Down the Aisle	1959	$40

Number	Title	Yr	NM
FEDERAL			
❏ 12297	Do You Mean It/She Made My Blood Run Cold	1957	$125
FLAIR			
❏ 1059	Cuban Getaway/Go To It	1955	$70
❏ 1040	Cubano Jump/Loosely	1954	$70
KING			
❏ 5553	The Big Question/She Made My Blood Run Cold	1961	$20
LIBERTY			
❏ 56194	Takin' Back My Name/Love Is a Game	1970	$5
RPM			
❏ 446	As Long As I Have You/I Wanna Make Love to You	1955	$50
❏ 362	My Heart Belongs to You/Lookin' for My Baby	1952	$70

— As "Bonnie and Ike Turner"

Number	Title	Yr	NM
SUE			
❏ 722	My Love/That's All I Need	1959	$30
UNITED ARTISTS			
❏ 51102	Dust My Broom/You Won't Let Me Go	1973	$5
❏ 50930	Lawdy Miss Clawdy/Tacks in My Shoes	1972	$5
❏ XW460	Take My Hand, Precious Lord/Father Alone	1974	$5

TURNER, IKE AND TINA
Also see IKE TURNER; TINA TURNER.

Number	Title	Yr	NM
A&M			
❏ 1170	A Love Like Yours/Save the Last Dance for Me	1970	$10
BLUE THUMB			
❏ 104	Bold Soul Sister/I Know	1969	$6
❏ 202	I've Been Loving You Too Long/Crazy 'Bout You Baby	1971	$30
❏ 101	I've Been Loving You Too Long/Grumbling	1969	$6
❏ 102	The Hunter/Crazy 'Bout You Baby	1969	$6
CENCO			
❏ 112	Get It-Get It/You Weren't Ready (For My Love)	1967	$20
INNIS			
❏ 6666	Betcha Can't Kiss Me/Don't Lie to Me	1968	$12
❏ 6667	So Fine/So Blue Over You	1968	$12
KENT			
❏ 409	Am I a Fool in Love/Please, Please, Please	1964	$10
❏ 418	Chicken Shack/He's the One	1965	$10
❏ 402	I Can't Believe What You Say (For Seeing What You Do)/My Baby Now	1964	$10
❏ 4514	Plaese, Please, Please (Part 1)/Please, Please, Please (Part 2)	1970	$6
LIBERTY			
❏ 56177	I Want to Take You Higher/Contact High	1970	$6
❏ 56216	Proud Mary/Funkier Than a Mosquito's Tweeter	1970	$6
❏ 56207	Workin' Together/The Way You Love Me	1970	$6
LOMA			
❏ 2011	I'm Thru with Love/Tell Her I'm Not Home	1965	$10
❏ 2015	Somebody Needs You/Just to Be with You	1965	$12
MINIT			
❏ 32087	Come Together/Honky Tonk Women	1970	$6
❏ 32060	I'm Gonna Do All I Can (To Do Right By My Man)/You've Got Too Many Ties That Bind	1969	$6
❏ 32077	I Wanna Jump/Treating Us Funky	1969	$6
❏ 32068	I Wish It Would Rain/With a Little Help from My Friends	1969	$6
MODERN			
❏ 1007	Good Bye, So Long/Hurt Is All You Gave Me	1965	$10
❏ 1012	I Don't Need/Gonna Have Fun	1965	$10
PHILLES			
❏ 136	I Idolize You/A Love Like Yours	1967	$20
❏ 135	I'll Never Need More Love Than This/The Cash Box Blues Or (Oops We Printed the Wrong Story Again)	1967	$20
❏ 134	Two to Tango/A Man Is a Man Is a Man	1966	$20
POMPEII			
❏ 7003	Betcha Can't Kiss Me/Cussin', Cryin', and Carryin' On	1969	$8
❏ 66675	It Sho' Ain't Me/We Need An Understanding	1968	$8
❏ 66700	Shake a Tail Feather/Cussin', Cryin', and Carryin' On	1969	$8
SONJA			
❏ 2001	If I Can't Be First/I'm Going Back Home	1968	$15

Number	Title	Yr	NM
SUE			
❏ 730	A Fool in Love/The Way You Love Me	1960	$40
❏ 146	Dear John/I Made a Promise Up Above	1966	$15
❏ 784	Don't Play Me Cheap/Wake Up	1963	$20
❏ 749	Gonna Work Out Fine/Won't You Forgive Me	1961	$60

— With erroneous A-side title

Number	Title	Yr	NM
❏ 735	I Idolize You/Letter from Tina	1960	$30
❏ 740	I'm Jealous/You're My Baby	1961	$30
❏ 749	It's Gonna Work Out Fine/Won't You Forgive Me	1961	$40

— With correct A-side title

Number	Title	Yr	NM
❏ 774	Please Don't Hurt Me/Worried and Hurtin' Inside	1962	$20
❏ 753	Poor Fool/You Can't Blame Me	1961	$30
❏ 760	Prancing/It's Gonna Work Out Fine	1962	$20
❏ 139	Stagger Lee and Billy/Can't Chance a Breakup	1965	$20
❏ 772	The Argument/Mind in a Whirl	1962	$20
❏ 768	Tina's Dilemma/I Idolize You	1962	$20
❏ 757	Tra La La La/Puppy Love	1962	$20
❏ 135	Two Is a Couple/Tin Top House	1965	$20
TANGERINE			
❏ 963	Beauty Is Only Skin Deep/Anything You Wasn't Born With	1966	$12
❏ 967	Dust My Broom/I'm Hooked	1966	$12
UNITED ARTISTS			
❏ 0119	A Fool in Love/I Idolize You	1973	$4
❏ XW598X	Baby, Get It On/Baby, Get It On (Disco Version)	1975	$5
❏ 50881	Do Wah Ditty (Got to Get Ya)/Up in Heah	1972	$5
❏ 50939	Games People Play/Pick Me Up	1972	$5
❏ XW409	Get it Out of Your Mind/Sweet Rhode Island Red	1974	$5
❏ 50837	I'm Yours/Doin' It	1971	$5
❏ 0120	It's Gonna Work Out Fine/Poor Fool	1973	$4
❏ 0121	I Want to Take You Higher/Come Together	1973	$4
❏ SP-48 [DJ]	I Want to Take You Higher/Ooh Poo Pah Doo	1971	$10
❏ 50955	Let Me Touch Your Mind/Chopper	1972	$5
❏ 50782	Ooh Poo Pah Doo/I Wanna Jump	1971	$5
❏ 50913	Outrageous/Feel Good	1972	$5
❏ 0122	Proud Mary/Tra La La La La	1973	$4

—0119 through 0122 are "Silver Spotlight Series" reissues

Number	Title	Yr	NM
❏ XW528	Sexy Ida (Part 1)/Sexy Ida (Part 2)	1974	$5
❏ XW174	With a Little Help from My Friends/Early One Morning	1973	$5
❏ XW257	Work On Me/Born Free	1973	$5
WARNER BROS.			
❏ 5433	A Fool for a Fool/No Tears to Cry	1964	$15
❏ 5433 [PS]	A Fool for a Fool/No Tears to Cry	1964	$50
❏ 5461	It's All Over/Finger Poppin'	1964	$15
❏ 5493	Ooh Poop A Doo/Merry Christmas Baby	1964	$15

TURNER, JACK

Number	Title	Yr	NM
HICKORY			
❏ 1050	Everybody's Rockin' But Me/I'm Gonna Get You If I Can	1956	$30
❏ 1057	It's My Foolish Pride/Looking for Love	1956	$30
MGM			
❏ K12690	Shake My Hand/An Indication of Love	1958	$20
❏ K12603	Weary Blues from Waitin'/Got a Heart	1957	$20
RCA VICTOR			
❏ 47-6163	Bama Bamboo Boy/The Story of the Smokey Mountain	1955	$30
❏ 47-5384	Gambler's Guitar/Butterfly Love	1953	$40
❏ 47-5267	Hound Dog/I Couldn't Keep from Crying	1953	$40
❏ 47-5815	If I Could Only Win Your Love/I'm Getting Married Tonight	1954	$30
❏ 47-5901	I'm Not Jealous/Put It Down on Paper	1954	$30
❏ 47-5997	Model T Baby/Hitchhikin' a Ride	1955	$40
❏ 47-5682	Walkin' a Chalk Line/Honey, I Reckon I Love You	1954	$30
78s			
❏ 20-5997	Model T Baby/Hitchhikin' a Ride	1955	$15

TURNER, JESSE LEE

Number	Title	Yr	NM
CARLTON			
❏ 509	Baby Please Don't Tease/Thinkin'	1959	$30
❏ 509 [PS]	Baby Please Don't Tease/Thinkin'	1959	$50
❏ 496	The Little Space Girl/Shake, Baby, Shake	1959	$30
FRATERNITY			
❏ 855	Teen-Age Misery/That's My Girl	1959	$30
❏ 855 [PS]	Teen-Age Misery/That's My Girl	1959	$50
GNP CRESCENDO			
❏ 184	All You Gotta Do (Is Ask Me To)/Voice Changing Song	1962	$15
❏ 188	Shotgun Boogie/Ballad of Billy Sol Estes	1962	$70
IMPERIAL			
❏ 5649	I'm the Little Space Girl's Father/Valley of Lost Soldiers	1960	$30
❏ 5635	Slippin' Around/Early in the Morning	1960	$20
TOP RANK			
❏ 2064	Do I Worry/All Right, Be That Way	1960	$30

TURNER, JOE

Number	Title	Yr	NM
ATLANTIC			
❏ 1184	Blues in the Night/Jump for Joy	1958	$40
❏ 939	Chains of Love/After My Laughter Came Tears	1951	$500
❏ 2054	Chains of Love/My Little Honey Dripper	1960	$30
❏ 1088	Corinne, Corrina/Boogie Woogie Country Girl	1956	$40
❏ 970	Don't You Cry/Poor Lover's Blues	1952	$125
❏ 1053	Flip, Flop, and Fly/Ti-Ri-Lee	1955	$60
❏ 2034	Got You On My Mind/Love, Oh Careless Love	1959	$30
❏ 1069	Hide and Seek/Midnight Cannonball	1955	$60
❏ 1001	Honey Hush/Crawdad Hole	1953	$200
❏ 1155	I Need a Girl/Trouble in Mind	1957	$40
❏ 1146	Love Roller Coaster/A World of Trouble	1957	$40
❏ 1122	Midnight Special Train/Feeling Happy	1957	$40
❏ 1080	Morning, Noon and Night/The Chicken and the Hawk	1956	$60
❏ 2072	My Reason for Living/Sweet Sue	1960	$30
❏ 1026	Shake, Rattle, and Roll/You Know I Love You	1954	$100
❏ 982	Still in Love/Baby I Still Want You	1953	$125
❏ 960	Sweet Sixteen/I'll Never Stop Loving You	1952	$120
❏ 1167	Teen-Age Letter/Wee Baby Blues	1957	$40
❏ 949	The Chill Is On/Bump Miss Suzie	1951	$800
❏ 2044	Tomorrow Night/Honey Hush	1959	$30
❏ 1016	TV Mama/Oke-She-Moke-She-Pop	1954	$120
❏ 1040	Well All Right/Married Woman	1954	$75
BAYOU			
❏ 015	The Blues Jumped the Rabbit/The Sun Is Shining	1951	$300
BLUESWAY			
❏ 61009	Big Wheel/Bluer Than Blue	1967	$8
CORAL			
❏ 62408	I Walk a Lonely Mile/I'm Packin' Up	1964	$20
❏ 62429	Shake, Rattle and Roll/There'll Be Some Tears Falling	1964	$20
DECCA			
❏ 29924	Corrine, Corrina/It's the Same Old Story	1956	$50
❏ 29711	Piney Brown Blues/I Got a Gal for Every Day of the Week	1955	$50
KENT			
❏ 4561	Chains of Love/Battle Hymn of the Republic	1971	$6
❏ 512	Love Ain't Nothin'/10-20-25-30	1969	$6
❏ 4569	One Hour in Your Garden/You've Been Squeezin' My Lemons	1972	$6
MGM			
❏ 10719	Moody Baby/Feeling So Sad	1951	$300
OKEH			
❏ 6829	Cherry Red/Joe Turner Blues	1951	$200
RONN			
❏ 35	Morning Glory/Night-Time Is the Right Time	1969	$6
❏ EP536	Honey Hush/Sweet Sixteen//Chains of Love/T.V. Mama	1955	$175
❏ EP565	Shake, Rattle and Roll/Flip, Flop and Fly//In the Evenin'/When the Sun Goes Down	1956	$175

Number	Title	Yr	NM

TURNER, ODELLE
ATLANTIC
❏ 964	Alarm Clock Boogie/ Draggin' Hours	1952	$200

TURNER, SAMMY
20TH FOX
❏ 6610	For Your Love I'll Die/ The House I Live In	1965	$10

BIG TOP
❏ 3029 [M]	Always/Symphony	1959	$30
❏ 3029 [S]	Always/Symphony	1959	$60
❏ 3089	Falling/Raincoat in the River	1961	$30
— B-side produced by Phil Spector			
❏ 3061	Falling/The Things I Love	1961	$20
❏ 3049	Fools Fall in Love/ Stay My Love	1960	$30
❏ 3038	Goodnight Irene/I Want to Be Loved	1960	$30
❏ 3016 [M]	Lavender-Blue/Wrapped Up in a Dream	1959	$30
❏ 3016 [S]	Lavender-Blue/Wrapped Up in a Dream	1959	$70
❏ 3065	Little Sir Echo/Love Keeps Calling	1961	$20
❏ 3032	Paradise/I'd Be a Fool Again	1960	$30
❏ 3082	Pour It On/The Fool of the Year	1961	$20
❏ 3070	Starlight, Starbright/ Let's Donkey On Down	1961	$20
❏ 3007	Thunderbolt/Sweet Annie Laurie	1959	$30

MILLENNIUM
❏ 616	Do You Know (What Life Is All About)/ Nothing Can Separate Me (From Your Love)	1978	$5

MOTOWN
❏ 1055	Only You/Right Now	1964	$40

PACIFIC
❏ 3016	Lavender-Blue/Wrapped Up in a Dream	1959	$50
—Despite label name, Pacific Records was in North Carolina!			

VERVE
❏ 10465	A Child Was Born/Come to Me Comf'tably	1966	$40

TURNER, SPYDER
KWANZA
❏ 7688	Since I Don't Have You/Happy Days	1973	$6

MGM
❏ 13692	Don't Hold Back/I Can't Take It Anymore	1967	$8
❏ 13739	For Your Precious Love/I Can't Wait to See My Baby's Face	1967	$8
❏ 14263	I Can't Make It Anymore/I'm Alive with a Lovin' Feeling	1971	$6
❏ 13617	Stand By Me/You're Good Enough for Me	1966	$10

WHITFIELD
❏ 8596	Get Down/Is It Love You're After	1978	$4
❏ 8526	I've Been Waiting/ Tomorrow's Only Yesterday	1978	$4

TURNER, TINA
Also see IKE AND TINA TURNER.
CAPITOL
❏ B-44111	Afterglow/(B-side unknown)	1987	$4
❏ B-5387	Better Be Good to Me/ When I Was Young	1984	$3
❏ B-5387 [PS]	Better Be Good to Me/ When I Was Young	1984	$4
❏ B-44003	Break Every Rule/ Take Me to the River	1987	$3
❏ B-44003 [PS]	Break Every Rule/ Take Me to the River	1987	$3
❏ B-5322	Let's Stay Together/I Wrote a Letter	1984	$3
❏ B-5322 [PS]	Let's Stay Together/I Wrote a Letter	1984	$5
❏ B-5518	One of the Living/One of the Living (Dub)	1985	$3
❏ B-5518 [PS]	One of the Living/One of the Living (Dub)	1985	$4
❏ B-5433	Private Dancer/ Nutbush City Limits	1984	$3
❏ B-5433 [PS]	Private Dancer/ Nutbush City Limits	1984	$4
❏ B-5461	Show Some Respect/Let's Pretend We're Married	1985	$3
❏ B-5461 [PS]	Show Some Respect/Let's Pretend We're Married	1985	$4
❏ B-44473	Steamy Windows/The Best	1989	$3
❏ B-44473 [PS]	Steamy Windows/The Best	1989	$3
❏ B-44442	The Best/Undercover Agent for the Blues	1989	$3
❏ B-44442 [PS]	The Best/Undercover Agent for the Blues	1989	$3
❏ B-5644	Two People/Havin' a Party	1986	$3
❏ B-5644 [PS]	Two People/Havin' a Party	1986	$3

Number	Title	Yr	NM
❏ B-5615	Typical Male/Don't Turn Around	1986	$3
❏ B-5615 [PS]	Typical Male/Don't Turn Around	1986	$3
❏ B-5491	We Don't Need Another Hero (Thunderdome)/ (Instrumental)	1985	$3
❏ B-5491 [PS]	We Don't Need Another Hero (Thunderdome)/ (Instrumental)	1985	$4
❏ B-5354	What's Love Got to Do with It/Rock 'N' Roll Widow	1984	$3
❏ B-5354 [PS]	What's Love Got to Do with It/Rock 'N' Roll Widow	1984	$4
❏ B-5668	What You Get Is What You See/What You Get Is What You See (Live)	1987	$3
❏ B-5668 [PS]	What You Get Is What You See/What You Get Is What You See (Live)	1987	$3

FANTASY
❏ 948	Lean On Me/Shame, Shame, Shame	1984	$4

POLYDOR
❏ PRO-2 [DJ]	Acid Queen/Pinball Wizard	1975	$50
— B-side by Elton John; promo-only			
❏ PRO-002 [DJ]	Acid Queen/Pinball Wizard	1975	$50
— B-side by Elton John; promo-only			

POMPEII
❏ 66682	Too Hot to Hold/You Got What You Wanted	1968	$10

UNITED ARTISTS
❏ XW920	Come Together/I Want to Take You Higher	1977	$6
❏ XW730	Delilah's Power/ That's My Power	1975	$6
❏ XW1265	Fire Down Below/ Viva La Money	1979	$5
❏ XW724	Whole Lotta Love/ Rockin' 'N' Rollin'	1975	$6

TURNER, TITUS
ATCO
❏ 6310	Baby Girl (Part 1)/ Baby Girl (Part 2)	1964	$8

ATLANTIC
❏ 1127	A-Knockin' at My Baby's Door/Hungry Man	1957	$30

COLUMBIA
❏ 42947	Make Someone Love You/ I'm a Fool About My Mama	1964	$10

ENJOY
❏ 2010	Bow Wow/I Love You Baby	1963	$10
❏ 1005	People Sure Act Funny/ My Darkest Hour	1962	$10
❏ 1015	Soulville/My Darkest Hour	1963	$12

GLOVER
❏ 201	We Told You Not to Marry/ Taking Care of Business	1959	$30
❏ 202	When the Sergeant Comes Marching Home/ Up Jumps the Devil	1960	$30

JAMIE
❏ 1184	Hey Doll Baby/I Want a Steady Girl	1961	$15
❏ 1189	Horsin' Around/ Chances Go Around	1961	$15
❏ 1177	Pony Train/Bla, Bla, Cha Cha Cha	1961	$15
❏ 1202	Shake the Hand of a Fool/ Beautiful Stranger	1961	$15
❏ 1174	Sound-Off/Me and My Lonely Telephone	1960	$20
❏ 1213	Walk on the Wild Twist/ Twistin' Train	1962	$10

JOSIE
❏ 1012	His Funeral, My Trial/ Do You Dig It	1969	$6
❏ 990	I Just Can't Keep It to Myself/People Sure Are Funny	1968	$6

KING
❏ 5243	Bonnie Baby/Miss Rubberneck Jones	1959	$15
❏ 5140	Coralee/Tears of Joy Fill My Eyes	1958	$15
❏ 5129	Follow Me/Way Down Yonder	1958	$15
❏ 5067	Have Mercy Baby/You Turned Lamps Too	1957	$15
❏ 5095	Hold Your Loving/ Stop the Rain	1957	$15
❏ 5213 [M]	Tarzan/Fall Guy	1959	$15
❏ S-5213 [S]	Tarzan/Fall Guy	1959	$40
❏ 5465	Way Down Yonder/Miss Rubberneck Jones	1961	$10

MURBO
❏ 1001	Huckle Buckle Beanstalk/ Hoop Hoop Hoop a Hoopa Doo	1965	$8

OKEH
❏ 6961	Big Mary's/Living in Misery	1953	$30
❏ 6929	Christmas Morning/ Be Sure You Know	1952	$40

Number	Title	Yr	NM
❏ 7244	Eye to Eye/What Kinda Deal Is This	1966	$8
❏ 7038	Hello Stranger/ Devilish Woman	1954	$30
❏ 6938	My Plea/It's Too Late Now	1953	$30
❏ 7027	Over the Rainbow/ My Lonely Room	1954	$30
❏ 6844	Same Old Feeling/ Don't Take Everybody to Be Your Friend	1951	$40
❏ 6883	What'cha Gonna Do for Me/Got So Much Trouble	1952	$40

PHILIPS
❏ 40445	(I'm Afraid the) Masquerade Is Over/Mary Mack	1967	$8

WING
❏ 90006	All Around the World/ Do You Know	1955	$30
❏ 90058	Get on the Right Track, Baby/I'll Wait Forever	1956	$30
❏ 90033	Sweet and Low/Big John	1955	$30

TURNER, ZEB
KING
❏ 950	Chew Tobacco Rag/ No More Nothin'	1951	$50
❏ 1001	Crazy Heart/I Got Loaded	1951	$40
❏ 960	I Got a Lot of Time for Lots of Things/Back, Back to Baltimore	1951	$40
❏ 5492	It Just Tears Me All to Pieces/I Hung My Head and Cried	1961	$20
❏ 999	Sissy Song/Lonely Little Robin	1951	$40
❏ 1009	Traveling Boogie/Oh She's Gone, Gone, Gone	1951	$40

TURNPIKES, THE
CAPITOL
❏ 2234	Cast a Spell/Nothing But Promises	1968	$30

TURRENTINE, STANLEY
BLUE NOTE
❏ 1948	Always Something There (To Remind Me)/When I Look Into Your Eyes	1970	$6
❏ 1936	Love Is Blue/Spooky	1969	$6
❏ 1940	The Look of Love/This Guy's in Love with You	1969	$6

CTI
❏ 10	I Told Jesus/(B-side unknown)	1972	$5
❏ 1	Sugar (Part 1)/Sugar (Part 2)	1971	$5

ELEKTRA
❏ 47245	After the Love Is Gone/I'll Give My Love	1981	$4
❏ 46576	Betcha/Hamlet (So Peaceful)	1980	$4
❏ 46533	Concentrate on You/ Together Again	1979	$4
❏ 47074	Deja Vu/Don't Misunderstand	1981	$4
❏ 47156	Having Fun with Mr. T/World Chimes	1981	$4
❏ 47008	Is It You/Inflation	1980	$4
❏ 46509	Take Me Home/ Long Time Gone	1979	$4

FANTASY
❏ 772	All By Myself/ There Is a Place	1976	$5
❏ 834	Disco Dancing/Heritage	1978	$5
❏ 790	Evil Ways/Love Hangover	1977	$5
❏ 778	Hope That We Can Be Together Soon/ There Is a Place	1976	$5
❏ 804	Papa "T" (Part 1)/ Papa "T" (Part 2)	1977	$5
❏ 745	Spaced/Naked as the Day I Was Born	1975	$5
❏ 816	Walkin'/Ann, Wonderful One	1977	$5

IMPULSE!
❏ 256	Let It Go/Good Looking Out	1967	$8

TURTLES, THE
RHINO
❏ RNOR74406	Happy Together/There You Sit Lonely	1987	$4
❏ RNOR74406 [PS]	Happy Together/There You Sit Lonely	1987	$4

WHITE WHALE
❏ 238	Can I Get to Know You Better?/Like the Seasons	1966	$10
❏ 276	Elenore/Surfer Dan	1968	$8
❏ 276 [PS]	Elenore/Surfer Dan	1968	$15
❏ 355	Eve of Destruction/ Wanderin' Kind	1970	$8
❏ 231	Grim Reaper of Love/ Come Back	1966	$30
❏ 251	Guide for the Married Man/Think I'll Run Away	1967	$50
—Withdrawn shortly after release			

Number	Title	Yr	NM
❑ 244	Happy Together/Like the Seasons	1967	$8
❑ 244 [PS]	Happy Together/Like the Seasons	1967	$50
❑ 306	House on the Hill/Come Over	1969	$30
❑ 350	Is It Any Wonder?/Wanderin' Kind	1970	$8
❑ 222	It Ain't Me, Babe/Almost There	1965	$15
❑ 334	Lady-O/Somewhere Friday Nite	1969	$8
❑ 224	Let Me Be/Your Maw Said You Cried	1965	$12
❑ 326	Love in the City/Bachelor Mother	1969	$8
❑ 326 [PS]	Love in the City/Bachelor Mother	1969	$10
❑ 364	Me About You/Think I'll Run Away	1970	$8
❑ 237	Outside Chance/Making My Mind Up	1966	$10
❑ 249	She'd Rather Be with Me/The Walking Song	1967	$8
❑ 249 [PS]	She'd Rather Be with Me/The Walking Song	1967	$30
❑ 260	She's My Girl/Chicken Little Was Right	1967	$8

— White concentric circles on mostly blue label

Number	Title	Yr	NM
❑ 260 [PS]	She's My Girl/Chicken Little Was Right	1967	$30
❑ 260	She's My Girl/Chicken Little Was Right	1967	$10

— All-blue label

Number	Title	Yr	NM
❑ 264	Sound Asleep/Umbassa the Dragon	1968	$8
❑ 264 [PS]	Sound Asleep/Umbassa the Dragon	1968	$20
❑ 273	The Story of Rock and Roll/Can't You Hear the Cows	1968	$8
❑ 273 [PS]	The Story of Rock and Roll/Can't You Hear the Cows	1968	$60
❑ 234	We'll Meet Again/Outside Chance	1966	$20
❑ 341	Who Would Ever Think That I Would Marry Margaret?/We Ain't Gonna Party No More	1970	$20

TURTLES, THE (2)
RCA VICTOR

Number	Title	Yr	NM
❑ 47-6356	Mystery Train/Say You Care	1955	$30

TUSCON, ARIZONA BOYS CHORUS
UNITED ARTISTS

Number	Title	Yr	NM
❑ 783	African Noel/Sleep, Little Tiny King	1964	$10
❑ 682	Sing Noel/Sleep, Little Tiny King	1963	$15

TUTTLE, WESLEY
CAPITOL

Number	Title	Yr	NM
❑ F1992	Call of the Mountains/They Locked God Outside the Iron Curtain	1952	$30
❑ F2545	Crying in the Chapel/For Me, For Me	1953	$30
❑ F1804	Detour/With Tears in My Eyes	1951	$30
❑ F2408	Fill the Cup to Overflowing/I've Got a Round Trip Ticket	1953	$30
❑ F2091	Hillbilly Heaven/Devil's Heart	1952	$30
❑ F2768	I'll Have the Last Waltz with Mother/Sign Post	1954	$30
❑ F3072	Penny Love Affair/That Little Boy of Mine	1955	$30
❑ F1916	Tennessee Rose/Heartbreak Ridge	1952	$30
❑ F40271	Texas Yodel/A Picture in a Frame	1950	$50
❑ F1478	Too Bad About You/Before I'm Through	1951	$30
❑ F1266	White Christmas/What I Want for Christmas	1950	$30
❑ F2577	Wonderful Waltz/Don't You Remember	1953	$30

CORAL

Number	Title	Yr	NM
❑ 9-64076	One Diamond Ring/I'm Tired of Playing Second Fiddle to a Steel Guitar	1951	$30
❑ 9-64068	The Lightning Express/That Silver Haired Daddy of Mine	1950	$30
❑ 9-64056	When the Bloom Is On the Sage/Jealous Lies	1950	$40

TUTTLE, WESLEY AND MARILYN
CAPITOL

Number	Title	Yr	NM
❑ F2983	Higher and Higher and Higher/Tennessee Mambo	1954	$30
❑ F2242	Our Love Isn't Legal/Don't Break the Sixth Commandment	1952	$30

Number	Title	Yr	NM

TWEEDS, THE
CAMEO

Number	Title	Yr	NM
❑ 367	A Walk in the Black Forest/3 O'Clock in the Morning	1965	$15

CORAL

Number	Title	Yr	NM
❑ 62551	We Got Time/I Want Her to Know	1968	$10
❑ 62542	What's Your Name/A Thing of the Past	1967	$10

TWEETERS, THE
DECCA

Number	Title	Yr	NM
❑ 30725	Mascara Mama/The Campus Rock	1958	$40

TWENTIETH CENTURY ZOO, THE
VAULT

Number	Title	Yr	NM
❑ 961	Only Thing That's Wrong/Stallion of Fate	1969	$15

21ST CREATION, THE
GORDY

Number	Title	Yr	NM
❑ 7158	Funk Machine/Girls, Let's Keep Dancing Close	1978	$10
❑ 7154	Mr. Disco Radio/Tailgate	1977	$10

21ST CENTURY, THE
GOSPEL TRUTH

Number	Title	Yr	NM
❑ 1209	Who's Supposed to Be Raising Who/If the Shoe Fits, Wear It	1973	$20

RCA VICTOR

Number	Title	Yr	NM
❑ PB-10364	Child/See My Love Growin' Old	1975	$6

TWICE AS MUCH
MGM

Number	Title	Yr	NM
❑ 13530	Sittin' on a Fence/Baby I Want You	1966	$20

— A-side is a Mick Jagger-Keith Richards song that only later was released by the Rolling Stones.

Number	Title	Yr	NM
❑ 13530 [PS]	Sittin' on a Fence/Baby I Want You	1966	$40
❑ 13600	Step Out of Line/Simplified	1966	$10

TWIGGY
CAPITOL

Number	Title	Yr	NM
❑ 5903	Over and Over/When I Think of You	1967	$10
❑ 5903 [PS]	Over and Over/When I Think of You	1967	$40

MERCURY

Number	Title	Yr	NM
❑ 73923	I Lie Awake and Dream of You/Woman in Love	1977	$6

TWILIGHTERS, THE (1)
BELL

Number	Title	Yr	NM
❑ 624	Be Faithful/Thumper	1965	$30

TWILIGHTERS, THE (2)
BUBBLE

Number	Title	Yr	NM
❑ 1334	My Silent Prayer/Little Bitty Bed Bug	1962	$50

CHESS

Number	Title	Yr	NM
❑ 1803	Scratchin'/Tears	1961	$30

CHOLLY

Number	Title	Yr	NM
❑ 712	Let There Be Love/Eternally	1957	$1000

DOT

Number	Title	Yr	NM
❑ 15526	Eternally/I Believe	1957	$50

EBB

Number	Title	Yr	NM
❑ 117	Pride and Joy/Live Like a King	1957	$50

IMPERIAL

Number	Title	Yr	NM
❑ 66238	I Still Love You/Meat Ball	1967	$15
❑ 66201	Shake a Tail Feather/Road to Fortune	1966	$15

JVB

Number	Title	Yr	NM
❑ 83	How Many Times/Water-Water	1957	$800

MGM

Number	Title	Yr	NM
❑ 55011	Little Did I Dream/Gotta Get On the Train	1955	$300
❑ 55014	Lovely Lady/Half Angel	1955	$400

PICO

Number	Title	Yr	NM
❑ 2801	Eternally/I Believe	1957	$100

TWILIGHTERS, THE (3)
CADDY

Number	Title	Yr	NM
❑ 103	Eternally/I Believe	1955	$250

Number	Title	Yr	NM

TWILIGHTERS, THE (4)
FRATERNITY

Number	Title	Yr	NM
❑ 889	To Love in Vain/The Beginning of Love	1961	$30

— As "The Twi-Lighters

TWILIGHTERS, THE (5)
MARSHALL

Number	Title	Yr	NM
❑ 702	Please Tell Me You're Mine/Wondering	1953	$200

— Black vinyl

Number	Title	Yr	NM
❑ 702	Please Tell Me You're Mine/Wondering	1953	$1000

— Red vinyl

TWILIGHTERS, THE (6)
SPECIALTY

Number	Title	Yr	NM
❑ 548	It's True/Wha-Bop-Sh-Wah	1955	$70

TWILIGHTERS, THE (U)
GROOVE

Number	Title	Yr	NM
❑ 0154	Sittin' in a Corner/It's a Cold, Cold, Rainy Day	1956	$70

— As "The Twi-Lighters

RICKI

Number	Title	Yr	NM
❑ 907	Help Me/Rockin' Mule	1961	$50

VANCO

Number	Title	Yr	NM
❑ 204	Out of My Mind/I Need Your Lovin'	1968	$10

TWILLEY, DWIGHT
ARISTA

Number	Title	Yr	NM
❑ 0311	Looking for the Magic/Invasion	1978	$5
❑ 0415	Out of My Hands/Nothing's Ever Gonna Change So Fast	1979	$4
❑ 0478	Somebody to Love/Money (That's What I Want)	1979	$4
❑ 0299	Trying to Find My Baby/Here She Comes	1977	$5

CBS ASSOCIATED

Number	Title	Yr	NM
❑ 06050	Sexual/Wild Dogs	1986	$3
❑ 06050 [PS]	Sexual/Wild Dogs	1986	$3

EMI AMERICA

Number	Title	Yr	NM
❑ 8196	Girls/To Get to You	1984	$3
❑ 8196 [PS]	Girls/To Get to You	1984	$4
❑ 8115	I Found the Magic/I'm Back Again	1982	$4
❑ 8109	Later That Night/Somebody to Love	1982	$4
❑ 8206	Little Bit of Love/Mad Dog	1984	$3
❑ 8206 [PS]	Little Bit of Love/Mad Dog	1984	$4
❑ 8235	Why You Wanna Break My Heart/Chilly D's Theme	1984	$3
❑ 8235 [PS]	Why You Wanna Break My Heart/Chilly D's Theme	1984	$3

SHELTER

Number	Title	Yr	NM
❑ 62003	Could Be Love/Feeling in the Dark	1976	$5
❑ 62003 [PS]	Could Be Love/Feeling in the Dark	1976	$8
❑ 40380	I'm on Fire/Did You See What Happened	1975	$5
❑ 40380 [PS]	I'm on Fire/Did You See What Happened	1975	$10
❑ 40450	Sincerely/You Were So Warm	1975	$5
❑ 40450 [PS]	Sincerely/You Were So Warm	1975	$5

TWINKLE
AURORA

Number	Title	Yr	NM
❑ 163	The End of the World/What Am I Doing Here with You	1966	$10

TOLLIE

Number	Title	Yr	NM
❑ 9047	Ain't Nobody Home But Me/Golden Lights	1965	$15
❑ 9040	The Boy of My Dreams/Terry	1965	$20

TWINS, THE
LANCER

Number	Title	Yr	NM
❑ 106	Heart of Gold/Buttercup	1959	$20
❑ 106 [PS]	Heart of Gold/Buttercup	1959	$40

— Number not on sleeve

RCA VICTOR

Number	Title	Yr	NM
❑ 47-7382	Classroom Rock/Gee Whiz	1958	$30
❑ 47-7148	My Dear/The Flip Skip	1958	$30

— As "The Twin-Tones

7-Inch Extended Plays

Number	Title	Yr	NM
❑ EPA-4237	My Dear/The Flip Skip//I Want a Girl/Together Forever	1958	$25
❑ EPA-4237 [PS]	Teenagers Love the Twins	1958	$25

Number	Title	Yr	NM

TWISTED SISTER
ATLANTIC
Number	Title	Yr	NM
☐ 89215	Hot Love/Tonight	1987	$3
☐ 89617	I Wanna Rock/The Kids Are Back	1984	$3
☐ 89617 [PS]	I Wanna Rock/The Kids Are Back	1984	$3
☐ 89478	Leader of the Pack/I Wanna Rock	1985	$3
☐ 89478 [PS]	Leader of the Pack/I Wanna Rock	1985	$3
☐ 89591	The Price/S.M.F.	1985	$3
☐ 89641	We're Not Gonna Take It/ You Can't Stop Rock 'N' Roll	1984	$3
☐ 89641 [PS]	We're Not Gonna Take It/ You Can't Stop Rock 'N' Roll	1984	$3

(NO LABEL)
Number	Title	Yr	NM
☐ 0(no cat #)	Bad Boys (Of Rock 'n' Roll)/Ladys Boy	1980	$15
☐ 0(no cat #) [PS]	Bad Boys (Of Rock 'n' Roll)/Ladys Boy	1980	$15

TWISTERS, THE
APT
Number	Title	Yr	NM
☐ 25045	Come Go with Me/Pretty Little Girl Next Door	1960	$30

CAMPUS
| ☐ 125 | Elvis Leaves Sorrento/ Street Dance | 1961 | $40 |

CAPITOL
| ☐ 4451 | Turn the Page/ Dancing Little Clown | 1960 | $30 |

DUAL
| ☐ 502 | Silly Chilli/Peppermint Twist Time | 1962 | $15 |

FELCO
| ☐ 103 | Count Down 1-2-3/ Speed Limit | 1959 | $30 |

SUN-SET
| ☐ 501 | Please Come Back/ This Is the End | 1961 | $600 |

TWISTIN' KINGS
MOTOWN
Number	Title	Yr	NM
☐ 1023	Congo (Part 1)/ Congo (Part 2)	1962	$50

TWITTY, CONWAY, AND LORETTA LYNN
MCA
Number	Title	Yr	NM
☐ 40251	As Soon As I Hang Up the Phone/A Lifetime Before	1974	$5
☐ 40420	Feelin's/You Done Lost Your Baby	1975	$5
☐ 41232	Hit the Road Jack/ It's True Love	1980	$4
☐ 51114	I Still Believe in Waltzes/Oh Honey	1981	$4
☐ 60183	Louisiana Woman, Mississippi Man/As Soon As I Hang Up the Phone	1976	$4

—Reissue series; black label with rainbow
☐ 40079	Louisiana Woman, Mississippi Man/Living Together Alone	1973	$5
☐ 51050	Lovin' What Your Lovin' Does to Me/Silent Partners	1981	$4
☐ 53417	Making Believe/As Soon As I Hang Up the Phone (The Telephone Song)	1988	$4
☐ 40728	The Bed I'm Dreaming On/I Can't Love You Enough	1977	$5
☐ 40572	The Letter/God Bless America Again	1976	$5
☐ 41141	The Sadness of It All/You Know Just What I'd Do	1979	$5
☐ 40283	Trouble in Paradise/We've Already Tasted Love	1974	$5

TWITTY, CONWAY
ABC-PARAMOUNT
Number	Title	Yr	NM
☐ 10507	Go On and Cry/ She Loves Me	1963	$20
☐ 10550	Such a Night/My Baby Left Me	1964	$30

DECCA
☐ 32424	Darling, You Know I Wouldn't Lie/Table in the Corner	1968	$8
☐ 32147	Don't Put Your Hurt in My Heart/Walk Me to the Door	1967	$8
☐ 32208	Funny (But I'm Not Laughing)/Working Girl	1967	$8
☐ 31897	Guess My Eyes Were Bigger Than Her Heart/ Honky Tonk Man	1966	$8
☐ 32081	I Don't Want to Be with Me/ Before I'll Set Her Free	1967	$8
☐ 32481	I Love You More Today/Bad Girl	1969	$8
☐ 31983	Look Into My Teardrops/ If You Were Mine to Lose	1966	$8
☐ 32599	That's When She Started to Stop Loving You/I'll Get Over Losing You	1969	$8

Number	Title	Yr	NM
☐ 32272	The Image of Me/Dim Lights, Thick Smoke (And Loud, Loud Music)	1968	$8
☐ 31833	Together Forever/ That Kind of Girl	1965	$10
☐ 32546	To See My Angel Cry/I Did the Best I Could	1969	$8

ELEKTRA
☐ 47443	Slow Hand/When Love Was Something Else	1982	$4
☐ 47302	The Clown/The Boy Next Door	1982	$4
☐ 47302 [PS]	The Clown/The Boy Next Door	1982	$5
☐ 69964	We Did But Now You Don't/A Good Love Died Tonight	1982	$4

MCA
☐ 51011	A Bridge That Just Won't Burn/You'll Be Back	1980	$4
☐ 40534	After All the Good Is Gone/I Got a Good Thing Going	1976	$5
☐ 40027	Baby's Gone/Dim Lonely Places	1973	$5
☐ 41002	Don't Take It Away/ Draggin' Chains	1979	$4
☐ 53276	Goodbye Time/ Your Loving Side	1988	$4
☐ 41135	Happy Birthday Darlin'/ Heavy Tears	1979	$4
☐ 60180	Hello Darlin' (English Version)/(Russian Version)	1975	$12

—Reissue series; only 45 rpm issue of the version played in space during the joint U.S.-Soviet Apollo-Soyuz mission in 1975
☐ 40649	I Can't Believe She Gives It All to Me/I Can't Help It If She Can't Stop Loving Me	1976	$5
☐ 41174	I'd Just Love to Lay You Down/She Thinks I Still Care	1980	$4
☐ 41174	I'd Love to Lay You Down/ She Thinks I Still Care	1980	$5

—Note slightly different A-side title
☐ 41059	I May Never Get to Heaven/ Grand Ole Blues	1979	$4
☐ 40224	I'm Not Through Loving You Yet/Before Your Time	1974	$5
☐ 40857	I'm Used to Losing You/The Grandest Lady of Them All	1978	$5
☐ 40282	I See the Want To in Your Eyes/Girl from Tupelo	1974	$5
☐ 40754	I've Already Loved You in My Mind/I Changed My Mind	1977	$5
☐ 41271	I've Never Seen the Likes of You/Soulful Woman	1980	$4
☐ 53134	I Want to Know You Before We Make Love/Snake Boots	1987	$4
☐ 53456	I Wish I Was Still in Your Dreams/If You Were Mine to Lose	1988	$4
☐ 60184	Linda on My Mind/I See the Want To In Your Eyes	1976	$4

—Reissue series; black label with rainbow
☐ 40339	Linda on My Mind/She's Just Not Over You Yet	1974	$5
☐ 52032	Over Thirty (Not Over the Hill)/Love Salvation	1982	$4
☐ 40682	Play, Guitar, Play/ One in a Million	1977	$5
☐ 53373	Saturday Night Special/ If You Were Mine to Lose	1988	$4
☐ 53633	She's Got a Single Thing in Mind/Too White to Sing the Blues	1989	$4
☐ 40805	Talkin' 'Bout You/Georgia Keeps Pulling on My Ring	1977	$5
☐ 40929	That's All She Wrote/ Boogie Grass Band	1978	$5
☐ 53200	That's My Job/Lonely Town	1987	$4
☐ 40601	The Games That Daddies Play/There's More Love in the Arms You're Leaving	1976	$5
☐ 53688	The House on Old Lonesome Road/Nobody Can Fill Your Shoes	1989	$4
☐ 40173	There's a Honky Tonk Angel (Who'll Take Me Back In)/ Don't Let It Go to Your Heart	1973	$5
☐ 60185	There's a Honky Tonk Angel (Who'll Take Me Back In)/I'm Not Through Loving You Yet	1976	$4

—Reissue series; black label with rainbow
☐ 40492	This Time I've Hurt Her More Than She Loves Me/ She Did, It Did, I Didn't	1975	$4
☐ 51137	Tight Fittin' Jeans/I Made You a Woman	1981	$4
☐ 40407	Touch the Hand/ Don't Cry Joni	1975	$5
☐ 60182	Touch the Hand/ Don't Cry Joni	1976	$4

—Reissue series; black label with rainbow
| ☐ 52154 | We Had It All/Cheatin' Fire | 1983 | $4 |
| ☐ 53759 | Who's Gonna Know/ Private Part of My Heart | 1989 | $4 |

MERCURY
☐ 71086	I Need Your Lovin'/Born to Sing the Blues	1957	$50
☐ 71148	Maybe Baby/Shake It Up	1957	$50
☐ 71384	Why Can't I Get Through to You/Double Talk Baby	1958	$50

Number	Title	Yr	NM

MGM
☐ 14447	Boss Man/Fever	1972	$5
☐ 12969	C'est Si Bon (It's So Good)/Don't You Dare Let Me Down	1960	$20
☐ 12969 [PS]	C'est Si Bon (It's So Good)/Don't You Dare Let Me Down	1960	$60
☐ 12826 [M]	Danny Boy/Halfway to Heaven	1959	$30

—First pressings on yellow labels
| ☐ 12826 [M] | Danny Boy/Halfway to Heaven | 1959 | $30 |

—Second pressings on black labels
☐ SK-50130 [S]	Danny Boy/Halfway to Heaven	1959	$125
☐ 14582	Danny Boy/The Pickup	1973	$5
☐ 12785	Hey Little Lucy! (Don'tcha Put No Lipstick On)/ When I'm Not with You	1959	$30
☐ 13149	I Got My Mojo Working/ She Ain't No Angel	1963	$20
☐ 13112	I Hope, I Think, I Wish/The Pickup	1962	$20
☐ 13011	I'm in a Blue, Blue Mood/A Million Teardrops	1961	$20
☐ 12911	Is a Blue Bird Blue/ She's Mine	1960	$30
☐ 12911 [PS]	Is a Blue Bird Blue/ She's Mine	1960	$60
☐ 13034	It's Drivin' Me Wild/ Sweet Sorrow	1961	$20
☐ 13034 [PS]	It's Drivin' Me Wild/ Sweet Sorrow	1961	$50
☐ 12677 [M]	It's Only Make Believe/I'll Try	1958	$30
☐ SK-50107 [S]	It's Only Make Believe/I'll Try	1958	$125
☐ 14172	It's Only Make Believe/ Lonely Blue Boy	1970	$5
☐ 14355	It's Too Late/I Hope, I Think, I Wish	1972	$5
☐ 13072	Little Piece of My Heart/ Comfy N' Cozy	1962	$20
☐ 12857	Lonely Blue Boy/Star Spangled Heaven	1959	$40

—Yellow label
| ☐ 12857 | Lonely Blue Boy/Star Spangled Heaven | 1959 | $30 |

—Black label
☐ 12804	Mona Lisa/Heavenly	1959	$30
☐ 13050	Portrait of a Fool/ Tower of Tears	1961	$20
☐ 12943	Teasin'/I Need You So	1960	$20
☐ 13089	There's Something on Your Mind/Unchained Melody	1962	$20
☐ 12748	The Story of My Love/Make Me Know You're Mine	1959	$30
☐ 14408	Walk On By/Hey Miss Ruby	1972	$5
☐ 14274	What a Dream/ Long Black Train	1971	$5
☐ 12918	What a Dream/Tell Me One More Time	1960	$20
☐ 14205	What Am I Living For/I'll Try	1970	$5
☐ 12886	What Am I Living For/ The Hurt in My Heart	1960	$30
☐ 12886 [PS]	What Am I Living For/ The Hurt in My Heart	1960	$60
☐ 12962	Whole Lot of Shakin' Going On/The Flame	1960	$20

WARNER BROS.
☐ 29137	Ain't She Somethin' Else/The Games That Daddies Play	1984	$4
☐ 28966	Between Blue Eyes and Jeans/Baby's Gone	1985	$4
☐ 28692	Desperado Love/I Can't See Me Without You	1986	$4
☐ 29057	Don't Call Him a Cowboy/ After All the Good Is Gone	1985	$4
☐ 28577	Fallin' for You for Years/I'll Try	1986	$4
☐ 29505	Heartache Tonight/ Hello Darlin'	1983	$4
☐ 29227	I Don't Know a Thing About Love (The Moon Song)/Don't Cry Joni	1984	$4
☐ 29636	Lost in the Feeling/You've Never Been This Far Before	1983	$4
☐ 29308	Somebody's Needin' Somebody/(Lying Here with) Linda on My Mind	1984	$4
☐ 28866	The Legend and the Man/(I Can't Believe) She Gives It All to Me	1985	$4
☐ 29395	Three Times a Lady/I Think I'm in Love	1983	$4
☐ 29129	White Christmas/Happy the Christmas Clown	1984	$5
☐ 29129 [PS]	White Christmas/Happy the Christmas Clown	1984	$5

7-Inch Extended Plays
DECCA
| ☐ DL 734732 | Be Proud of Your Man/ Girl at the Bar/That's When She Started to Stop Loving You//Girl from Muskogee /I'd Rather Be Gone/The House of the Rising Sun | 1969 | $20 |

—Jukebox issue; small hole, plays at 33 1/3 rpm
| ☐ DL 734732 [PS] | To See an Angel Cry | 1969 | $20 |

Number	Title	Yr	NM
MGM			
❏ X-1641	(contents unknown)	1959	$125
❏ X-1642	(contents unknown)	1959	$125
❏ X-1679	(contents unknown)	1959	$125
❏ X-1680	(contents unknown)	1959	$125
❏ X-1701	(contents unknown)	1960	$125
❏ X-1640 [PS]	Conway Twitty Sings, Volume 1	1959	$125
❏ X-1641 [PS]	Conway Twitty Sings, Volume 2	1959	$125
❏ X-1642 [PS]	Conway Twitty Sings, Volume 3	1959	$125
❏ X-1678	Danny Boy/Heavenly// She's Mine/Blueberry Hill	1959	$125
❏ X-1623 [PS]	It's Only Make Believe	1958	$175
❏ X-1640	It's Only Make Believe/ Hallelujah, I Love Her So//First Romance/Make Me Know You're Mine	1959	$125
❏ X-1623	It's Only Make Believe/I'll Try//When/I Vibrate	1958	$175
❏ X-1701 [PS]	Lonely Blue Boy	1960	$125
❏ X-1678 [PS]	Saturday Night with Conway Twitty, Volume 1	1959	$125
❏ X-1679 [PS]	Saturday Night with Conway Twitty, Volume 2	1959	$125
❏ X-1680 [PS]	Saturday Night with Conway Twitty, Volume 3	1959	$125
TWO CHAPS, THE			
ATLANTIC			
❏ 1195	Forgive Me/No More	1958	$40
2 LIVE CREW, THE			
LUKE SKYYWALKER			
❏ LS-113 [DJ]	Me So Horny (same on both sides)	1989	$20
❏ LS-104 [DJ]	Move Somethin'/ (Dirty Version)	1988	$10
❏ LS-110 [DJ]	The Bomb Has Dropped (same on both sides)	1989	$12
TWO MISTER F'S, THE			
MERCURY			
❏ 5741	Mrs. Santa Claus/ Say a Prayer	1951	$20
2 OF CLUBS			
FRATERNITY			
❏ F972	Heart/My First Heartbreak	1966	$12
❏ F990	Let Me Walk with You/ You Love Me	1967	$12
❏ F999	Look Away/(B-side unknown)	1967	$20
❏ F975	Walk Tall Like a Man/ So Blue Is Fall	1966	$20
❏ F975	Walk Tall/So Blue Is Fall	1966	$15
TWO OF US, THE			
CAMEO			
❏ 390	We'll Build a New World/Get Together	1965	$15
TWO PEOPLE			
A&M			
❏ 776	Barbara/Everybody's Talkin'	1965	$20
LIBERTY			
❏ 55916	I Really Don't Want to Know/ You're Gonna Hurt Me	1966	$20
❏ 55896	Love Isn't Tears Only/We Don't Do That Anymore	1966	$20
❏ 55870	Me and My Shadow/Uphill Climb to the Bottom	1966	$20
REVUE			
❏ 11033	Stop, Leave My Heart Alone/Love Dust	1969	$200
TYGH AND THE CRITERIONS			
FLITE			
❏ 101	To Be Mine/(B-side unknown)	1963	$120
TYLER, BONNIE			
CHRYSALIS			
❏ 2130	Lost in France/Baby I Remember You	1976	$6
COLUMBIA			
❏ 38-06527	Band of Gold/Tears	1986	$4
❏ 38-04548	Here She Comes/Obsession	1984	$4
—B-side by Giorgio Moroder			
❏ 38-04548 [PS]	Here She Comes/Obsession	1984	$5
❏ 38-07758	Hide Your Heart/ The Fire Below	1988	$4
❏ 38-04370	Holding Out for a Hero/Faster Than the Speed of Night	1984	$4
❏ 38-04370 [PS]	Holding Out for a Hero/Faster Than the Speed of Night	1984	$5

Number	Title	Yr	NM
❏ 38-05839	If You Were a Woman (And I Was a Man)/ Under Suspicion	1986	$3
❏ 38-05839 [PS]	If You Were a Woman (And I Was a Man)/ Under Suspicion	1986	$4
❏ 38-06151	Loving You's a Dirty Job (But Somebody's Gotta Do It)/ Before This Night Is Through	1986	$4
—A-side with Todd Rundgren			
❏ 38-08497	Save Up All Your Tears/ It's Not Enough	1988	$4
❏ 38-04246 [PS]	Take Me Back	1983	$5
—Demonstration -- Not for Sale" on back of sleeve			
❏ 38-04246	Take Me Back/ Gettin' So Excited	1983	$4
❏ 38-04246 [PS]	Take Me Back/ Getttin' So Excited	1983	$5
❏ 38-04246 [DJ]	Take Me Back (Long Version 5:20)/(Short Version 4:32)	1983	$4
❏ AE71719 [DJ]	Total Eclipse of the Heart (4:36)/(5:21)	1983	$8
—The 5:21 length matches the stock 45, even though the stock 45 label says "4:29			
❏ 38-03906	Total Eclipse of the Heart/ Straight from the Heart	1983	$4
RCA			
❏ PB-11763	I Believe in Your Sweet Love/Come On, Give Me Loving	1979	$5
❏ PB-11349	If I Sing You a Love Song/Heaven	1978	$5
❏ PB-11349 [PS]	If I Sing You a Love Song/Heaven	1978	$6
❏ PB-11249	It's a Heartache/ It's About Time	1978	$5
❏ PB-11630	Married Men/If You Ever Need Me Again	1979	$5
❏ PB-11468	My Guns Are Loaded/ Baby I Just Love You	1979	$5
TYLER, JOEY			
REPRISE			
❏ 0269	All the Good Times Are Over/When You Got Nothin' Else, You Got the Blues	1964	$10
TYLER, KIP			
CHALLENGE			
❏ 1014	She Got Eyes/ Shadow Street	1957	$40
EBB			
❏ 156	Oh Linda/Kali Lou	1959	$60
❏ 154	She's My Witch/ Rumble Rock	1959	$60
GYRO DISC			
❏ 711	Surfer's Lament (Eternity)/Toledo	1963	$60
❏ 711 [PS]	Surfer's Lament (Eternity)/Toledo	1963	$125
TYLER, T. TEXAS			
4 STAR			
❏ 1669	A Million Teardrops/ Little Miss Muffet	1955	$30
❏ 1660	Courtin' in the Rain/Old Blue	1954	$30
❏ 1735	Deck of Cards/Dad Have My Dog Away	1959	$20
❏ 1597	Get Out of My Life/ Who's to Blame	1952	$30
❏ 1555	If You Had a Heart/To Prove My Love Is True	1951	$40
❏ 1565	Irma/Blue Kimono Blues	1951	$40
❏ 1682	I Tickled Her Under the Chin/ She Wouldn't Do for You	1955	$30
❏ 1612	It's My Heart, It's My Conscience/It's a Pity	1952	$30
❏ 1579	I Want to Learn to Do It/ Curley Headed Baby	1951	$40
❏ 1588	I Was the Last One to Know/When the White Azaleas Start Blooming	1952	$30
❏ 1621	Snow on the Mountain/ Electric Guitar Polka	1952	$30
❏ 1658	Tattler's Wagon/The Soldier's Prayer Book	1954	$30
❏ 1628	Wasted Tears/Let's Fly Away	1953	$30
DECCA			
❏ 9-28579	Bumming Around/ Jealous Love	1953	$30
❏ 9-28544	He Done Her Wrong/Much More Than the Past	1953	$30
❏ 9-29007	Hot Rod Rag/ Lighthearted Guy	1954	$30
❏ 9-28922	Pretender/Nothing at All	1953	$30
❏ 9-28760	Scratch and Itch/ Let's Get Married	1953	$30
❏ 9-29598	That's What You Mean to Me/Ten-Ten-Tennessee Line	1955	$20
KING			
❏ 5249	Deck of Cards/Dad Gave My Dog Away	1959	$20
❏ 5380	Oklahoma Hills/ Remember Me	1960	$20

Number	Title	Yr	NM
RCA VICTOR			
❏ 47-5710	Deck of Cards/Ida Red	1954	$30
❏ 47-5679	Pie A La Mode/Here Goes	1954	$30
❏ 806	Injun Joe/Crawdad Town	1967	$10
❏ 783	It's a Long Road Back Home/I Still Love You (By the Way)	1966	$10
❏ 759	Texas Boogie Woogie/ Just Like Dad	1966	$10
TYMES, THE			
CAPITOL			
❏ 3440	When I Look Around Me/ Smile a Tender Smile	1972	$6
COLUMBIA			
❏ 44917	Find My Way/If You Love Me Baby	1969	$6
❏ 44799	God Bless the Child/ The Love That You're Looking For	1969	$6
❏ 45078	Love Child/Most Beautiful Married Lady	1970	$6
❏ 44630	People/For Love of Ivy	1968	$8
❏ 45336	She's Gone/Someone to Watch Over Me	1971	$6
MGM			
❏ 13536	Pretend/Street Talk	1966	$30
❏ 13631	(Touch of) Baby/ What Would I Do	1966	$30
PARKWAY			
❏ 924	Here She Comes/Malibu	1964	$20
❏ 924 [PS]	Here She Comes/Malibu	1964	$30
❏ 7039	Isle of Love/I'm Always Chasing Rainbows	1964	$20
—Included as a bonus with album 7039			
❏ 871	So in Love/Roscoe James McClain	1963	$30
—Original title of A-side			
❏ 891	Somewhere/View from My Window	1963	$30
❏ 891 [PS]	Somewhere/View from My Window	1963	$30
❏ 871	So Much in Love/Roscoe James McClain	1963	$20
❏ 871 [PS]	So Much in Love/Roscoe James McClain	1963	$40
❏ 919	The Magic of Our Summer Love/With All My Heart	1964	$20
❏ 919 [PS]	The Magic of Our Summer Love/With All My Heart	1964	$30
❏ 933	The Twelfth of Never/ Here She Comes	1964	$20
❏ 908	To Each His Own/ Wonderland of Love	1964	$20
❏ 908 [PS]	To Each His Own/ Wonderland of Love	1964	$30
❏ 884	Wonderful! Wonderful!/ Come with Me to the Sea	1963	$20
❏ 884 [PS]	Wonderful! Wonderful!/ Come with Me to the Sea	1963	$30
RCA			
❏ PB-11136	I'll Take You There/How Am I to Know (The Things a Girl in Love Should Know)	1977	$4
❏ PB-10862	Love's Illusion/Savannah Sunny Sunday	1976	$4
RCA VICTOR			
❏ PB-10422	God's Gonna Punish You/ If I Can't Make You Smile	1975	$4
❏ PB-10713	Goin' Through the Motions/ Only Your Love	1976	$4
❏ PB-10561	Good Morning Dear Lord/It's Cool	1976	$4
❏ PB-10244	Interloop/Someday, Somehow I'm Keeping You	1975	$4
❏ PB-10128	Ms. Grace/The Crutch	1974	$4
WINCHESTER			
❏ 1002	These Foolish Things (Remind Me of You)/ This Time It's Love	1967	$10
TYNER, MCCOY			
COLUMBIA			
❏ 03151	Island Birdie/Love Surrounds Us Everywhere	1982	$4
IMPULSE!			
❏ 240	Duke's Place/Searchin'	1965	$8
TYSON, ROY			
DOUBLE L			
❏ 723	Oh What a Night for Love/Not Too Young	1963	$100
❏ 733	The Girl I Love/I Want to Be Your Boyfriend	1964	$125

U

U.K.

Prog rock supergroup.

POLYDOR

Number	Title	Yr	NM
❑ 14491	In the Dead of Night/ Mental Medication	1978	$5

U.K.'S, THE

CAMEO

Number	Title	Yr	NM
❑ 342	Ever Faithful Ever True/ Your Love Is All I Want	1965	$30

U-MEN

AMPHETAMINE REPTILE

Number	Title	Yr	NM
❑ Scale8	Freezebomb/That's Wild About Jack	1988	$30
❑ Scale8 [PS]	Freezebomb/That's Wild About Jack	1988	$30

—First sleeve has gray heavy paper

Number	Title	Yr	NM
❑ Scale8 [PS]	Freezebomb/That's Wild About Jack	1988	$30

—Second sleeve has white heavy paper

BLACK LABEL

Number	Title	Yr	NM
❑ BLR 001	Solid Action/Dig It a Hole	1987	$8
❑ BLR 001 [PS]	Solid Action/Dig It a Hole	1987	$30

—First sleeve has silver title

Number	Title	Yr	NM
❑ BLR 001 [PS]	Solid Action/Dig It a Hole	1987	$8

—Second sleeve has black title

7-Inch Extended Plays

BOMBSHELTER

Number	Title	Yr	NM
❑ SPY 007	Blight/Flowers DGIH// Shoot 'Em Down/Gila	1984	$60
❑ SPY 007 [PS]	Blight/Flowers DGIH// Shoot 'Em Down/Gila	1984	$60

U.S. 1

PRIVATE STOCK

Number	Title	Yr	NM
❑ 45,045	Bye Bye Baby/Creation	1975	$6

U2

ISLAND

Number	Title	Yr	NM
❑ 99199	All I Want Is You/ Unchained Melody	1989	$4
❑ 99199 [PS]	All I Want Is You/ Unchained Melody	1989	$4
❑ 99254	Angel of Harlem/A Room at the Heartbreak Hotel	1988	$3
❑ 99254 [PS]	Angel of Harlem/A Room at the Heartbreak Hotel	1988	$3
❑ 99250	Desire/Hallelujah Here She Comes	1988	$3
❑ 99250 [PS]	Desire/Hallelujah Here She Comes	1988	$6

—Cardboard gatefold sleeve

Number	Title	Yr	NM
❑ 99250 [PS]	Desire/Hallelujah Here She Comes	1988	$3

—Standard paper sleeve

Number	Title	Yr	NM
❑ 94974	Gloria/Sunday Bloody Sunday	1987	$6

—Gold label "Revival of the Fittest" series; only U.S. 45 release for either track; "Sunday Bloody Sunday" has a unique edit

Number	Title	Yr	NM
❑ 99384	In God's Country/ Bullet the Blue Sky	1988	$5

—Black label jukebox pressing; both sides play at 45 rpm

Number	Title	Yr	NM
❑ 99385	In God's Country// Bullet the Blue Sky/ Running to Stand Still	1988	$4

—A-side plays at 45 rpm, B-side at 33 1/3 rpm

Number	Title	Yr	NM
❑ 99385 [PS]	In God's Country// Bullet the Blue Sky/ Running to Stand Still	1988	$4

—Cardboard sleeve

Number	Title	Yr	NM
❑ 99385 [PS]	In God's Country// Bullet the Blue Sky/ Running to Stand Still	1988	$4

—Paper sleeve

Number	Title	Yr	NM
❑ 99431	I Still Haven't Found What I'm Looking For/ Spanish Eyes	1987	$15

—Black label jukebox pressing; both sides play at 45 rpm

Number	Title	Yr	NM
❑ 99430	I Still Haven't Found What I'm Looking For//Spanish Eyes/Deep in the Heart	1987	$3

—A-side plays at 45 rpm, B-side at 33 1/3 rpm

Number	Title	Yr	NM
❑ 99430 [PS]	I Still Haven't Found What I'm Looking For//Spanish Eyes/Deep in the Heart	1987	$4

—Cardboard sleeve

Number	Title	Yr	NM
❑ 99430 [PS]	I Still Haven't Found What I'm Looking For//Spanish Eyes/Deep in the Heart	1987	$3

—Paper sleeve

Number	Title	Yr	NM
❑ 99789	I Will Follow (Live)/Two Hearts Beat as One (Live)	1983	$6
❑ PR564 [DJ]	I Will Follow (Mini LP Cut)/ (Special Remix for Radio)	1983	$60
❑ 49716	I Will Follow/Out of Control (Live)	1980	$30
❑ 49716 [PS]	I Will Follow/Out of Control (Live)	1980	$30
❑ 49716 [PS]	I Will Follow/Out of Control (Live)	1980	$70

—Promo-only poster sleeve with tour dates

Number	Title	Yr	NM
❑ 94976	I Will Follow/Pride (In the Name of Love)	1987	$6

—Gold label "Revival of the Fittest" series

Number	Title	Yr	NM
❑ 99704 [PS]	Pride (In the Name of Love)/Boomerang	1984	$5
❑ 99704	Pride (In the Name of Love)/Boomerang II	1984	$5
❑ 99861	Two Hearts Beat as One/Endless Deep	1983	$8
❑ 99861 [PS]	Two Hearts Beat as One/Endless Deep	1983	$8
❑ 99225	When Love Comes to Town/Dancing Barefoot	1989	$3

—A-side with B.B. King

Number	Title	Yr	NM
❑ 99225 [PS]	When Love Comes to Town/Dancing Barefoot	1989	$3
❑ 99407	Where the Streets Have No Name/Silver and Gold	1987	$6

—Black label jukebox pressing; both sides play at 45 rpm

Number	Title	Yr	NM
❑ 99408	Where the Streets Have No Name//Silver and Gold/Sweetest Thing	1987	$3

—A-side plays at 45 rpm, B-side at 33 1/3 rpm

Number	Title	Yr	NM
❑ 99408 [PS]	Where the Streets Have No Name//Silver and Gold/Sweetest Thing	1987	$4

—Cardboard sleeve

Number	Title	Yr	NM
❑ 99408 [PS]	Where the Streets Have No Name//Silver and Gold/Sweetest Thing	1987	$3

—Paper sleeve

Number	Title	Yr	NM
❑ 94961	With or Without You/ In God's Country	1988	$5

—Gold label "Revival of the Fittest" series

Number	Title	Yr	NM
❑ 99469	With or Without You// Luminous Times (Hold On to Love)/Walk on the Water	1987	$3

—A-side plays at 45 rpm, B-side at 33 1/3 rpm

Number	Title	Yr	NM
❑ 99469 [PS]	With or Without You// Luminous Times (Hold On to Love)/Walk on the Water	1987	$4

—Cardboard sleeve

Number	Title	Yr	NM
❑ 99469 [PS]	With or Without You// Luminous Times (Hold On to Love)/Walk on the Water	1987	$3

—Paper sleeve

Number	Title	Yr	NM
❑ 99453	With or Without You/ Walk on the Water	1987	$30

—White label jukebox pressing, both sides play at 45 rpm

UB40

A&M

Number	Title	Yr	NM
❑ 1236	Breakfast in Bed/ (Album Version)	1988	$3
❑ 2961	Cherry Oh Baby/ (B-side unknown)	1987	$6
❑ 2649	Cherry Oh Baby/ Food for Thought	1984	$6
❑ 2792	Don't Break My Heart/ Mek Ya Rok	1985	$5
❑ 2681	If It Happens Again/ Nkomo A Go Go	1984	$5
❑ 2758	I Got You Babe/ Nkomo A Go Go	1985	$3

—A-side with Chrissie Hynde

Number	Title	Yr	NM
❑ 2758 [PS]	I Got You Babe/ Nkomo A Go Go	1985	$3

—Green sleeve

Number	Title	Yr	NM
❑ 2758 [PS]	I Got You Babe/ Nkomo A Go Go	1985	$3

—Brown sleeve

Number	Title	Yr	NM
❑ 2630	Please Don't Make Me Cry/ Food for Thought (Live)	1984	$6
❑ 2858	Sing Our Own Song/ (Instrumental)	1986	$4
❑ 2858 [PS]	Sing Our Own Song/ (Instrumental)	1986	$4
❑ 1270	Where Did I Go Wrong/ Dance with the Devil	1989	$4

UBANS, THE

RADIANT

Number	Title	Yr	NM
❑ 102	Gloria/On the Bridge	1964	$200

UGGAMS, LESLIE

ATLANTIC

Number	Title	Yr	NM
❑ 2313	Don't You Care/Who Killed Teddy Bear	1965	$20
❑ 2397	Hallelujah Baby/ My Own Morning	1967	$10
❑ 2727	He Can Do It/Walk Him Up the Stairs	1970	$8
❑ 2698	Home/Save the Country	1969	$8
❑ 2371	If My Friends Could See Me Now/We Can Work It Out	1967	$10
❑ 2469	I (Who Have Nothing)/ The House Built on Sand	1967	$10

COLUMBIA

Number	Title	Yr	NM
❑ 43012	A Legend in My Time/My Wish	1964	$10
❑ 4-43121	And I Love Him/Who Do You Think	1964	$10
❑ 41564	Carefree Years/Lullaby of the Leaves	1960	$10
❑ 42611	Each and Ev'ry Day/Is He the Only Man in the World	1962	$12
❑ 42255	Get Happy/Birth of the Blues	1961	$10
❑ 42055	He Doesn't Know/I Love Him	1961	$12
❑ 4-42948	Here and Now/A Fortune in Pennies	1964	$12
❑ 41654	I Grew Up Last Night/I'm Just a Little Sparrow	1960	$10
❑ 41798	Inherit the Wind/Love Is Like a Violin	1960	$10
❑ 43064	Little Bird/This Is My Prayer	1964	$12
❑ 41531	My Favorite Things/Sixteen Going on Seventeen	1959	$15
❑ 41451	One More Sunrise (Morgen)/ The Eyes of God	1959	$15

GORDY

Number	Title	Yr	NM
❑ 7149	I Want to Make It Easy on You/Two Shoes	1976	$6

MGM

Number	Title	Yr	NM
❑ 11437	Easter Sunny Day/Percy the Pale Faced Bear	1953	$30

—As "Lesley 'Uggams' Crayne

Number	Title	Yr	NM
❑ 11755	Ev'ry Little Piggy's Curley Tail/Palsy Walsy Land	1954	$30
❑ 11965	Meet My Friend, Mr. Sun/ Did You Ever Dream	1955	$20
❑ 11676	My Candy Apple/ Kickin' Up a Storm	1954	$30

—As "Lesley 'Uggams' Crayne

Number	Title	Yr	NM
❑ 11626	My Stocking Is Empty/ This Is Santa Claus	1953	$30

—As "Leslie 'Uggams' Crayne

UGLYS, THE

ABC-PARAMOUNT

Number	Title	Yr	NM
❑ 10748	It's Alright/A Friend	1965	$15
❑ 10707	Wake Up My Mind/ Ugly Blues	1965	$50

ULANO, SAM

MGM

Number	Title	Yr	NM
❑ SK-37	Santa & The Doodle-Li-Boop/The Story Of Santa Claus	1954	$10
❑ SK-37 [PS]	Santa & The Doodle-Li-Boop/The Story Of Santa Claus	1954	$30

ULTRAVOX

CHRYSALIS

Number	Title	Yr	NM
❑ VS4-42781	Dancing with Tears in My Eyes/Building	1984	$4
❑ VS4-42781 [PS]	Dancing with Tears in My Eyes/Building	1984	$5

UMILIANI, PIERO

ARIEL

Number	Title	Yr	NM
❑ 500	Mah-Na Mah-Na/You Tried to Warn Me	1969	$15

—From the movie "Swedish Heaven and Hell"; Umiliani's name is only in parentheses on the label, making it appear as if he is merely the composer

UNBEATABLES, THE

DAWN

Number	Title	Yr	NM
❑ 552	I Love Paris/What I Say	1964	$50

UNCHAINED MYNDS, THE

BUDDAH

Number	Title	Yr	NM
❑ 119	Every Day/(B-side unknown)	1969	$20
❑ 111	We Can't Go On This Way/ Going Back to Miami	1969	$20

TEEN TOWN

Number	Title	Yr	NM
❑ 106	We Can't Go On This Way/ Going Back to Miami	1969	$50

TRANSACTION

Number	Title	Yr	NM
❑ 705	Hole in My Shoe/ Warm Smoke	1969	$30
❑ 705	Hole in My Shoe/ Warm Smoke	1969	$30

—As The Takers

Number	Title	Yr	NM
❑ 705 [PS]	We Can't Go On This Way/ Going Back to Miami	1968	$50
❑ 705	We Can't Go On This Way/ Going Back to Miami	1968	$20

Number	Title	Yr	NM

UNDEAD
7-Inch Extended Plays
POST MORTEM

| ☐ 1001 | A Life of Our Own/My Kinda Town//When the Evening Comes/I Want You Dead | 1983 | $15 |

STIFF

| ☐ TEES-7-14 | A Life of Our Own/My Kinda Town//When the Evening Comes/I Want You Dead | 1982 | $25 |

— With Bobby Steele, ex-Misfits

UNDERBEATS, THE
BANGAR

| ☐ 0632 | Annie Do the Dog/Sweet Words of Love | 1964 | $30 |

—Red label

| ☐ 0632 | Annie Do the Dog/Sweet Words of Love | 1964 | $20 |

—Blue label

| ☐ 0657 [DJ] | Broken Arrow/Little Romance | 1964 | $50 |

GARRETT

| ☐ 4004 | Foot Stompin'/Route 66 | 1964 | $30 |

METROBEAT

| ☐ 4449 | Sweetest Girl in the World/It's Gonna Rain Today | 1967 | $30 |

SOMA

| ☐ 1449 | Book of Love/Darling Lorraine | 1966 | $20 |
| ☐ 1458 | I Can't Stand It/Shake It for Me | 1966 | $60 |

UNDERDOGS, THE
HIDEOUT

☐ 1004	Little Girl/Don't Pretend	1965	$50
☐ 1011	Surprise Surprise/Get Down on Your Knees	1966	$50
☐ 1001	The Man in the Glass/Friday at the Hideout (Judy Be Mine)	1965	$50

REPRISE

| ☐ 0446 | Little Girl/Don't Pretend | 1966 | $30 |
| ☐ 0422 | The Man in the Glass/Friday at the Hideout (Judy Be Mine) | 1965 | $30 |

V.I.P.

| ☐ 25040 | Love's Gone Bad/Mo Jo Hanna | 1966 | $30 |

UNDERGROUND SUNSHINE
INTREPID

| ☐ 75002 | Birthday/All I Want Is You | 1969 | $15 |
| ☐ ITDJ-3 [DJ] | Don't Shut Me Out (mono/stereo) | 1969 | $15 |

— Promo issue of 75012

| ☐ 75012 | Don't Shut Me Out/Take Me, Break Me | 1969 | $12 |

UNDERGROUND, THE
MAINSTREAM

| ☐ 660 | Easy/Satisfy'n Sunday | 1967 | $30 |
| ☐ 667 | Get Him Out of Your Mind/Take Me Back | 1967 | $30 |

UNDERTAKERS, THE
BLACK WATCH

| ☐ BW5545/6 | I Fell in Love (For the Very First Time)/Throw Your Love Away Girl | 1965 | $200 |

—As The Takers

INTERPHON

| ☐ IN-7709/6 | Think/If You Don't Come Back | 1964 | $30 |

UNFORGETTABLES, THE
COLPIX

| ☐ 192 | It Hurts/Was It All Right | 1961 | $40 |

PAMELA

| ☐ 204 | Oh Wishing Well/Daddy Must Be a Man | 1961 | $500 |

— Blue vinyl

| ☐ 204 | Oh Wishing Well/Daddy Must Be a Man | 1961 | $300 |

TITANIC

| ☐ 5012 | He'll Be Sorry/Oh There He Goes | 1963 | $50 |

UNHOLY SWILL
NOISEVILLE

| ☐ 10 | Satan Swill Santa/Armless Legless | 1989 | $60 |

| ☐ 10 [PS] | Satan Swill Santa/Armless Legless | 1989 | $60 |

—Box set, numbered edition of 100

| ☐ 2 | Wanna Be God/Where's That Damn Cat? | 1989 | $60 |

— Yellow vinyl (90 made)

| ☐ 2 | Wanna Be God/Where's That Damn Cat? | 1989 | $30 |

—Black vinyl (210 made)

| ☐ 2 | Wanna Be God/Where's That Damn Cat? | 1989 | $8 |

—Burgundy vinyl

| ☐ 2 [PS] | Wanna Be God/Where's That Damn Cat? | 1989 | $30 |

—Hand-painted sleeve (with either yellow or black vinyl version)

| ☐ 2 [PS] | Wanna Be God/Where's That Damn Cat? | 1989 | $8 |

—Printed cover

UNIFICS, THE
KAPP

☐ 935	Court of Love/Which One Should I Choose	1968	$15
☐ 2058	Got to Get You/Memories	1969	$15
☐ 985 [PS]	It's a Groovy World!/Memories	1969	$20
☐ 985	It's a Groovy World!/Memories	1969	$15
☐ 957 [PS]	The Beginning of My End/Sentimental Man	1968	$20
☐ 957	The Beginning of My End/Sentimental Man	1968	$15
☐ 2026	Toshisumasu/It's All Over	1969	$15

UNIQUE TEENS, THE
DYNAMIC

| ☐ 110 | Whatcha Know Now/Run Fast | 1959 | $40 |

UNIQUES, THE (1)
PARAMOUNT

☐ 0017	Eunice/No One But You	1970	$5
☐ 0116	Lucille/One Night with You	1971	$5
☐ 0058	Shadow of Love/Lazy Afternoon	1970	$5
☐ 0172	Will You Love Me Tomorrow/I Am a Gemini	1972	$5

PAULA

☐ 238	All These Things/Tell Me What to Do	1966	$8
☐ 332	All These Things/You Know That I Love You	1970	$5
☐ 275	Every Now and Then (I Cry)/Love Is a Precious Thing	1967	$8
☐ 245	Goodbye, So Long/Run and Hide	1966	$8
☐ 289	Go On and Leave/I'll Do Anything	1967	$8

—B-side by University of Utah Chamber Choir

☐ 264	Groovin' Out/Areba	1967	$8
☐ 313	How Lucky Can One Man Be/You Don't Miss Your Water	1968	$6
☐ 307	It Hurts Me to Remember/I Sure Feel More (Like I Do Then I Did When I Got Here)	1968	$6
☐ 299	It's All Over Now/All I Took Was Love	1968	$6
☐ 227	Lady's Man/Bolivar	1965	$8
☐ 324	My Babe/Toys Are Made for Children	1970	$5
☐ 255	Please Come Home for Christmas/(Instrumental)	1966	$15
☐ 320	Sha-La Love/You Know (That I Love You)	1970	$5
☐ 231	Strange/You Ain't Tuff	1966	$8
☐ 222	Too Good to Be True/Never Been in Love	1965	$8

UNIQUES, THE (2)
AMBER

| ☐ 2004 | Taboo/Ghost Riders in the Sky | 1961 | $60 |

UNIQUES, THE (3)
BANGAR

| ☐ 0609 | Baby Don't Cry/Little Angel | 1967 | $30 |

UNIQUES, THE (4)
BLISS

| ☐ 1004 | I'm So Unhappy/I'm Confessin' | 1961 | $500 |

END

| ☐ 1012 | Tell the Angels/Hey, Little Cupid | 1958 | $250 |

FLIPPIN'

| ☐ 202 | Come Marry Me/Do You Remember | 1959 | $60 |

GONE

| ☐ 5113 | I'm So Unhappy/I'm Confessin' | 1961 | $200 |
| ☐ 5113 | I'm So Unhappy/It's Got to Come | 1961 | $75 |

MR. CEE

| ☐ 100 | Look at Me/Bossa Nova Cha Cha | 1960 | $300 |

PRIDE

| ☐ 1018 | I'm So Unhappy/It's Got to Come | 1960 | $250 |

TEE KAY

| ☐ 112 | One Million Miles Away/All at Once | 1962 | $60 |

UNIQUES, THE (5)
CAPITOL

| ☐ 4949 | Loving You/Blue Skies | 1963 | $15 |

ROULETTE

| ☐ 4528 | Send Him to Me/This Little Boy of Mine | 1963 | $30 |

UNIQUES, THE (6)

☐ 3950	Merry Christmas Darling (And A Happy New Year Too)/Times Change	1963	$60
☐ 2936	Merry Christmas Darling/Rockin' Rudolph	1963	$100
☐ 2490	Times Change/Alright, OK, You Win	1964	$60

DOT

| ☐ 16533 | Merry Christmas Darling/Times Change | 1963 | $50 |

UNIQUES, THE (7)
PEACOCK

| ☐ 1695 | Mysterious/Picture of My Baby | 1960 | $30 |

UNIQUES, THE (U)
LUCKY FOUR

| ☐ 1024 | Silvery Moon/Chocolate Bar | 1962 | $200 |

UNIT FOUR PLUS TWO
LONDON

☐ 9751	Concrete and Clay/When I Fall in Love	1965	$20
☐ 9751	Concrete and Clay/Wild as the Wind	1965	$30
☐ 1009	I Was Only Playing Games/I Won't Let You Down	1966	$20
☐ 9732	Sorrow and Pain/Woman from Liberia	1965	$20
☐ 9790	Stop Wasting Your Time/Hark	1965	$20

UNITED FRUIT CO.
LAURIE

| ☐ 3408 | On the Good Ship Lollipop/Sunshine Street | 1967 | $10 |

UNIVERSAL ROBOT BAND
RED GREG

| ☐ 207 | Dance and Shake Your Tambourine/(Part 2) | 1977 | $12 |
| ☐ 217 | Freak with Me/(B-side unknown) | 1978 | $10 |

UNIVERSALS, THE
ASCOT

| ☐ 2124 | Dear Ruth/Gotta Little Girl | 1963 | $70 |

CORA-LEE

| ☐ 501 | The Picture/He's So Right | 1958 | $50 |

FESTIVAL

| ☐ 25001 | Dreaming/Love Bound | 1961 | $30 |
| ☐ 1601 | Dreaming/Love Bound | 1961 | $70 |

—No subtitle on A-side

MARK-X

| ☐ 7004 | Teenage Love/Again | 1957 | $200 |

SHEPHERD

| ☐ 2200 | A Love Only You Can Give/I'm in Love | 1962 | $60 |

SOUTHERN

| ☐ 102 | Dear Ruth/Prayer of Love | 1963 | $60 |

UNKNOWN, THE
AUTOGRAPH

| ☐ 206 | I Have Returned/Keep Talking, Baby | 1960 | $50 |

UNKNOWNS, THE (1)
PARROT

| ☐ 307 | Melody for an Unknown Girl/Keith's Song | 1966 | $30 |

Number	Title	Yr	NM

UNKNOWNS, THE (2)
X-TRA

| ❏ 102 | One More Chance/ You and Me | 1957 | $1000 |

UNKNOWNS, THE (U)
MARLIN

| ❏ 16008 | Tighter/Young Enough to Cry | 1966 | $30 |

UNLUV'D, THE
MGM

| ❏ K13903 | I Got It Bad/Steadfastly | 1968 | $15 |

PARKWAY

| ❏ 138 | Ain't Gonna Do You No Harm/An Exception to the Rule | 1967 | $30 |

TRUE LOVE

| ❏ 1000 | Ain't Gonna Do You No Harm/An Exception to the Rule | 1967 | $60 |

UNNATURAL AXE
VARULVEN

| ❏ 16 | The Man I Don't Wanna Be/ They Saved Hitler's Brain | 1982 | $30 |

—Copies not distributed by Taang! did not have a picture sleeve

VARULVEN/TAANG!

| ❏ 16 | The Man I Don't Wanna Be/ They Saved Hitler's Brain | 1982 | $30 |

—Roughly 100 have a "Taang!" rubberstamp on them

| ❏ 16 [PS] | The Man I Don't Wanna Be/ They Saved Hitler's Brain | 1982 | $30 |

7-Inch Extended Plays
VARULVEN

| ❏ 87-66 | They Saved Hitler's Brain/The Creeper/The Plug/Summertime | 1978 | $60 |

UNRELATED SEGMENTS, THE
HANNA-BARBERA

| ❏ 514 | It's Unfair/Story of My Life | 1967 | $50 |

LIBERTY

| ❏ 56052 | Cry, Cry, Cry/It's Not Fair | 1968 | $125 |
| ❏ 55992 | It's Gonna Rain/Where You Gonna Go | 1967 | $20 |

UNREST
7-Inch Extended Plays
TEEN BEAT

| ❏ 28 [PS] | Catchpellet | 1989 | $30 |

—Limited edition of 399

| ❏ 7 | (contents unknown) | 1987 | $60 |
| ❏ 28 | (contents unknown) | 1989 | $30 |

UNSANE
TREEHOUSE

| ❏ TR 020 | This Town/Urge to Kill | 1989 | $50 |

—Yellow vinyl

| ❏ TR 020 | This Town/Urge to Kill | 1989 | $20 |

—Black vinyl

| ❏ TR 020 [PS] | This Town/Urge to Kill | 1989 | $20 |

UNTAMED, THE
PLANET

| ❏ 117 | It's Not True/Gimme Gimme Some Shade | 1966 | $50 |

—Also reported to be Planet 103

UNTOUCHABLES, THE
ALAN K

| ❏ 6901 | Little Mary/Funny What a Little Kiss Can Do | 1962 | $200 |

DOT

| ❏ 16306 | Blues in the Night/Bondaru | 1962 | $20 |

LIBERTY

| ❏ 55423 | Papa/Medicine Man | 1962 | $30 |

MADISON

❏ 147	Do Your Best/Raisin' Cain	1961	$30
❏ 134	Goodnight Sweetheart Goodnight/Vickie Lee	1960	$30
❏ 128	Poor Boy Need a Preacher/New Fad	1960	$30
❏ 139	Sixty Minute Man/ Everybody's Laughin'	1960	$30

MCA/STIFF

| ❏ 52988 | Freak in the Street/ (B-side unknown) | 1986 | $15 |
| ❏ 52725 | I Spy (For the F.B.I.)/ Freak in the Street | 1985 | $12 |

| ❏ 52725 [PS] | I Spy (For the F.B.I.)/ Freak in the Street | 1985 | $15 |
| ❏ 52775 | What's Gone Wrong?/ The Lonely Bull | 1986 | $12 |

NAU VOO

| ❏ 809 | Blue Chip Bounce (Part 1)/ Blue Chip Bounce (Part 2) | 1960 | $20 |

WASP

| ❏ 105 | Don't Go, I'm Beggin'/ Baby, Let's Wait | 1967 | $30 |

UPBEATS, THE
JOY

❏ 223	Oh What It Seemed to Be/The Night We Both Said Goodbye	1958	$30
❏ 229	Satin Shoes/Teenie Weenie Bikini	1959	$30
❏ 233	To Me You're a Song/ Unbelievable Love	1959	$30

PREP

| ❏ 131 | Will You Be Mine?/ My Last Frontier | 1958 | $40 |

UPCHURCH, PHIL
MARLIN

| ❏ 3325 | Strawberry Letter 23/ (B-side unknown) | 1978 | $4 |

UNITED ARTISTS

❏ 417	Organ Grinder's Swing/ The Persian	1962	$10
❏ 355	Pink Lollipop/Straw Hat	1961	$10
❏ 385	The Hog/That's Where It Is	1961	$10
❏ 488	The Stonewall/Flap Jack	1962	$10

UPFRONTS, THE
LUMMTONE

❏ 114	Do the Beetle/Most of the Pretty Girls	1964	$70
❏ 108	It Took Time/Baby For Your Love	1962	$30
❏ 103	It Took Time/Betty Lou and the Lions	1960	$60
❏ 107	Send Me Someone to Love Who Will Love Me/ Baby For Your Love	1961	$60

—White label

| ❏ 107 | Send Me Someone to Love Who Will Love Me/ Baby For Your Love | 1961 | $40 |

—Black label

| ❏ 104 | Too Far to Turn Around/ Married Jive | 1960 | $50 |
| ❏ 106 | Why You Kiss Me/Little Girl | 1961 | $60 |

UPSETTERS, THE
ABC

| ❏ 11120 | Don't Be Cruel/Down Home | 1968 | $12 |
| ❏ 11081 | Tossin' and Turnin'/ Always in the Wrong Place at the Wrong Time | 1968 | $10 |

AUTUMN

| ❏ 4 | Autumn's Here/ Draggin' the Main | 1964 | $30 |

GEE

| ❏ 1055 | The Blues/Rollin' On | 1960 | $30 |

UPTONES, THE
LUTE

| ❏ 6229 | Be Mine/Dreamin' | 1962 | $50 |

MAGNUM

| ❏ 714 | Dreaming/Wear My Ring | 1963 | $30 |

WATTS

| ❏ 1080 | Dreaming/Wear My Ring | 1963 | $40 |

URGE OVERKILL
TOUCH & GO

| ❏ 27 | Wichita Lineman/Head On | 1987 | $8 |
| ❏ 27 [PS] | Wichita Lineman/Head On | 1987 | $8 |

URIAH HEEP
CHRYSALIS

| ❏ 2274 | Come Back to Me/ Love or Nothing | 1978 | $4 |

MERCURY

❏ 73145	Come Away Melinda/ Wake Up	1970	$8
❏ 73307	Easy Livin'/All My Life	1972	$8
❏ 73103	Gypsy/Real Turned On	1970	$8
❏ 73174	High Priestess/ (B-side unknown)	1970	$12
❏ 73154	I Wanna Be Free/What Should Be Done	1971	$8
❏ 73243	Look at Yourself/ Love Machine	1971	$8
❏ 73349	Sweet Lorraine/Blind Eye	1972	$6

❏ 73406	Tears in My Eyes/ July Morning	1973	$6
❏ 76177	That's the Way It Is/ Son of a Bitch	1982	$4
❏ 76177 [PS]	That's the Way It Is/ Son of a Bitch	1982	$5
❏ 73271	Why/The Wizard	1971	$8

WARNER BROS.

❏ 8581	Masquerade/Free Me	1978	$5
❏ 8132	Prima Dance/Stealin'	1975	$5
❏ 8013	Something or Nothing/ What Can I Do	1974	$5
❏ 7738	Stealin'/Sunshine	1973	$5

7-Inch Extended Plays

| ❏ S2724 | Dreamer/One Day//If I Had the Time/Circus | 1974 | $10 |

—Jukebox issue; small hole, plays at 33 1/3 rpm

| ❏ S2724 [PS] | Sweet Freedom | 1974 | $12 |

—Part of "Little LP" series (LLP #230)

URINALS, THE
HAPPY SQUID

| ❏ 03 [PS] | Sex/Go Away Girl | 1980 | $50 |

—Note: The above record and sleeve have been counterfeited

| ❏ 03 | Sex/Go Away Girl// (B-side blank) | 1980 | $50 |

7-Inch Extended Plays

| ❏ 02 [PS] | Another E.P. | 1979 | $50 |

—Note: The above record and sleeve have been counterfeited

| ❏ 02 | Black Hole/I'm a Bug/ Ack Ack Ack/I'm White and Middle Class | 1979 | $50 |
| ❏ 01 | Dead Flowers/Hologram/ Last Days of Man on Earth// Surfin' with the Shah | 1978 | $60 |

USA FOR AFRICA
COLUMBIA

| ❏ US7-04839 | We Are the World/Grace | 1985 | $3 |

—B-side by Quincy Jones

| ❏ US7-04839 [PS] | We Are the World/Grace | 1985 | $4 |

USHER, GARY
CAPITOL

| ❏ 5403 | It's a Lie/Jody | 1965 | $60 |
| ❏ 5193 | Sacramento/That's the Way I Feel | 1964 | $100 |

—Produced by Brian Wilson

| ❏ 5128 | The Beetle/Jody | 1964 | $60 |

DOT

| ❏ 16518 | Three Surfer Boys/ Milky Way | 1963 | $400 |

LAN-CET

| ❏ 144 | Tomorrow/Lies | 1961 | $70 |

TITAN

| ❏ 1716 | Driven Insane/You're the Girl | 1961 | $200 |

UTMOSTS, THE
PAN-OR

| ❏ 1123 | I Need You/Big Man | 1962 | $120 |

UTOPIA
Also see TODD RUNDGREN.

BEARSVILLE

❏ 49579	Always Late/I Just Want to Touch You	1980	$4
❏ 49247	Love Alone/Very Last Time	1980	$4
❏ 0321	Love Is the Answer/Marriage of Heaven and Hell	1977	$4
❏ 50062	One World/Special Interest	1982	$5
❏ 49545	Second Nature/You Make Me Crazy	1980	$4
❏ 49180	Set Me Free/Umbrella Man	1980	$5
❏ 0317	Sunburst Finish/ Communion with the Sun	1977	$4

NETWORK

| ❏ 69859 | Feet Don't Fail Me Now/ There Goes My Inspiration | 1982 | $4 |
| ❏ 69830 | Hammer in My Heart/I'm Looking at You But I'm Talking to Myself | 1983 | $4 |

PASSPORT

❏ 7923	Cry Baby/Winston Smith Takes It on the Jaw	1984	$4
❏ 7923 [PS]	Cry Baby/Winston Smith Takes It on the Jaw	1984	$5
❏ 7927	Stand for Something/Mated	1985	$4

UTOPIANS, THE
IMPERIAL

❏ 5876	Along My Lonely Way/ Hurry to Your Date	1962	$400
❏ 5861	Dutch Treat/Ain't No Such Thing	1962	$40
❏ 5921	Let Love Come Later/ Opera vs. the Blues	1963	$30

V

V-EIGHTS, THE

ABC-PARAMOUNT

Number	Title	Yr	NM
❑ 10201	Papa's Yellow Tie/My Heart	1961	$30

MOST

Number	Title	Yr	NM
❑ 711/3	Pretty Girl/Please Come Back	1959	$125

VIBRO

Number	Title	Yr	NM
❑ 4007	Let's Take a Chance/Hot Water	1961	$40
❑ 4005	Papa's Yellow Tie/My Heart	1960	$40

V.I.P.'S

BIG TOP

Number	Title	Yr	NM
❑ 100	Don't Pass Me By/You Ain't Good for Nothing	1965	$15
❑ 521	I'm On to You Baby/ If He Wants Me	1964	$15

CONGRESS

Number	Title	Yr	NM
❑ 211	My Girl Cried/Strange Little Girl	1964	$20

VACELS, THE

KAMA SUTRA

Number	Title	Yr	NM
❑ 204	Can You Please Crawl Out Your Window/I'm Just a Poor Boy	1965	$30

VAGRANTS, THE

ATCO

Number	Title	Yr	NM
❑ 6552	And When It's Over/I Don't Need Your Lovin'	1968	$20
❑ 6513	Beside the Sea/Sunny Summer Rain	1967	$20

SOUTHERN SOUND

Number	Title	Yr	NM
❑ 204	Oh, Those Eyes/ You're Too Young	1966	$30

VANGUARD

Number	Title	Yr	NM
❑ 35042	Final Hour/Your Hasty Heart	1966	$30
❑ 35038	I Can't Make a Friend/ Young Blues	1966	$60
❑ 35038 [PS]	I Can't Make a Friend/ Young Blues	1966	$125

VAL-AIRES, THE

CORAL

Number	Title	Yr	NM
❑ 62177	Laurie My Love/Which One Will It Be	1960	$100

WILLETTE

Number	Title	Yr	NM
❑ 114	Laurie My Love/Which One Will It Be	1959	$400

VAL-CHORDS, THE

GAME TIME

Number	Title	Yr	NM
❑ 104	Candy Store Love/ You're Laughing at Me	1957	$300

—With no sword logo

Number	Title	Yr	NM
❑ 104	Candy Store Love/ You're Laughing at Me	1957	$125

—With sword logo

VAL-TONES, THE

DELUXE

Number	Title	Yr	NM
❑ 6084	Tender Darling/Siam Sam	1955	$200

VALADIERS, THE

GORDY

Number	Title	Yr	NM
❑ 7013	I Found a Girl/You'll Be Sorry Someday	1963	$70
❑ 7003	While I'm Away/ Because I Love Her	1962	$70

MIRACLE

Number	Title	Yr	NM
❑ 6	Greetings/Take a Chance	1961	$100

—With no subtitle on A-side and 2:23 version of B-side

Number	Title	Yr	NM
❑ 6	Greeting (This Is Uncle Sam)/Take a Chance	1961	$60

—With subtitle on A-side and 2:15 version of B-side

VALAQUONS, THE

LAGUNA

Number	Title	Yr	NM
❑ 102	Teardrops/Madeleine	1964	$200

TANGERINE

Number	Title	Yr	NM
❑ 951	I Wanna Woman/Window Shopping on Girl's Avenue	1965	$30

VALE, JERRY

BUDDAH

Number	Title	Yr	NM
❑ 591	Toot Toot Tootsie (Goodbye)/ Now Is Forever	1978	$4

COLUMBIA

Number	Title	Yr	NM
❑ 42439	Ah, Camminare/One Paradise for Sale	1962	$8
❑ 42027	Al Di La/Thinking of Your Happiness	1961	$10
❑ 40825	All Dressed Up with a Brand New Broken Heart/ It Looks Like Love	1957	$15
❑ 40404	A Million Moons Ago/ Lolly Linger Longer	1955	$20
❑ 39929	And No One Knows/You Can Never Give Me Back Your Heart	1953	$30
❑ 42201	Another Time, Another Place/If He Leaves You	1961	$8
❑ 40058	Ask Me/A Tear, a Kiss, a Smile	1953	$30
❑ 41373	Bella, Bella Sue/The Heart Has Won the Game	1959	$12
❑ 43473	Big Wide World/Ashamed	1965	$6
❑ JZSP111776 [DJ]	Blue Christmas (same on both sides)	1965	$10
❑ 41942	Camelot/Thirteen Girls Too Much	1961	$10
❑ 44823	Close to Cathy/Fa Fa Fa (Live for Today)	1969	$5
❑ 43413	Deep in Your Heart/ If It Isn't in Your Heart	1965	$6
❑ 43774	Dommage, Dommage (Too Bad, Too Bad)/Promises	1966	$6
❑ 44432	Don't Tell My Heart to Stop Loving You/When I'm With You	1968	$5
❑ 40880	Don't You Know Me Anymore/ For You My Love	1957	$15
❑ 43232	For Mama/Ti Adora	1965	$6
❑ 39990	For Me/Tired of Waiting	1953	$30
❑ 45992	Free As the Wind/ Reason to Believe	1974	$4
❑ 42637	From the Bottom of My Heart/Here's to Us	1962	$8
❑ 41238	Go Chase a Moonbeam/ Around the Clock	1958	$10
❑ 43181	Have You Looked Into Your Heart/Andiamo	1964	$6
❑ 44027	Have You Seen the One I Love Go By/Signs	1967	$5
❑ 45797	He/If I Give My Heart to You	1973	$4
❑ 45118	Hello and Goodbye/ Look Homeward Angel	1970	$4
❑ 44914	He Who Loves/Close to You	1969	$5
❑ 40429	Hey Punchinello/I Live for Only You	1955	$20
❑ 41120	I Always Say/She	1958	$10
❑ 45216	I Climbed the Mountain/ Love Never Goes Away	1970	$4
❑ 42304	If Ever I Would Leave You/Who Knows	1962	$8
❑ 10042	If I Could Write a Song/ Woman of the World	1974	$4
❑ 41681	If/The Dawn of Love	1960	$10
❑ 40260	I'll Follow You/Go	1954	$20
❑ 45188	I'l Never Fall in Love Again/Lovin' Time	1970	$4
❑ 44185	I Love New England/In the Back of My Heart	1967	$5
❑ 40634	Innamorata (Sweetheart)/ Second Ending	1956	$15
❑ 44274	In Time/Blame It on Me	1967	$5
❑ 43696	It'll Take a Little Time/Palermo	1966	$6
❑ 43605	Less Than Tomorrow/ This Day of Days	1966	$6
❑ 44753	Life/Congratulations, I Guess	1969	$5
❑ 43105	Love Goddess/Where Love Has Gone	1964	$8
❑ 40941	Love in the Afternoon/I'm Not Ashamed	1957	$15
❑ 40322	Love Is a Circus/ For You, My Love	1954	$20
❑ 40541	Magic Night/Heaven Came Down to Earth	1955	$20
❑ 42872	Maria Elena/Mala Femina	1963	$8
❑ 41314	Me and My Shadow/A Warm Spot	1959	$10
❑ 40584	Miracle in the Rain/Adelaide	1955	$20
❑ 45677	Mister Good Times/ Till We Two Are One	1972	$4
❑ 45896	Mon Amour/The Circle Ends	1973	$4
❑ 4-40775	Mother Mine/Tell Me So	1956	$15
❑ 42508	My Geisha/It's My Way	1962	$8
❑ 45361	My Little Girl/Is It Asking Too Much	1971	$4
❑ 44512	My Love, Forgive Me/I Never Let a Day Go By	1968	$5
❑ 43656	My Melancholy Baby/It's Magic	1966	$6
❑ 42826	Old Cape Cod/Theme for Young Lovers (Where Is My Someone)	1963	$8
❑ 42783	One More Blessing/Doin' What I Said I'd Never Do	1963	$8
❑ 40499	Only Beautiful/How Do I Love You	1955	$20
❑ 45308	Point Me in the Direction of Albuquerque/Perfect Love	1971	$5
❑ 45545	Pretend/Too Young	1972	$4
❑ 41010	Pretend You Don't See Her/ The Spreading Chestnut	1957	$15
❑ 41503	Prima Donna/What Do I Care	1959	$10
❑ 44280	Santa Mouse/Silent Night, Holy Night	1967	$6
❑ JZSP79175/6 [DJ]	Silent Night, Holy Night/ Oh Holy Night	1963	$10
❑ 45597	Smile/All I Ever Wanted	1972	$4
❑ 41594	Solitaire/Please Believe Me	1960	$12
❑ 43895	Somewhere/I've Lost My Heart Again	1966	$6
❑ 44087	So Near, Yet So Far/ Time Alone Will Tell	1967	$5
❑ 45043	Stay Awhile/It's All in the Game	1969	$5
❑ 43252	Tears Keep On Falling/Now	1965	$6
❑ 41423	The Flame/The Moon Is My Pillow	1959	$10
❑ 40201	The Ghost in the Vine/I Live Each Day	1954	$20
❑ 42994	The Lights of Rome/As Sure As Night Must Fall	1964	$8
❑ 44572	The Look of Love/ With Pen in Hand	1968	$5
❑ 42951	The Peking Theme (So Little Time)/On and On	1964	$8
❑ 44687	There's a Baby/Where Are They Now	1968	$5
❑ 44969	This Is My Life/What's Wrong with My World	1969	$5
❑ 44615	Till Now/That Girl Would Be So Happy	1968	$5
❑ 31163 [S]	(titles unknown)	1961	$10
❑ 31164 [S]	(titles unknown)	1961	$10
❑ 31165 [S]	(titles unknown)	1961	$10
❑ 31166 [S]	(titles unknown)	1961	$10
❑ 31167 [S]	(titles unknown)	1961	$10
❑ 31468 [S]	(titles unknown)	1962	$10
❑ 31469 [S]	(titles unknown)	1962	$10
❑ 31470 [S]	(titles unknown)	1962	$10
❑ 31471 [S]	(titles unknown)	1962	$10
❑ 31472 [S]	(titles unknown)	1962	$10

—Anyone who can fill in these gaps -- the above 10 all are Columbia "Stereo 7" singles -- please let us know.

Number	Title	Yr	NM
❑ 40131	Two Purple Shadows/ And This Is My Beloved	1953	$20
❑ 45463	Two Purple Shadows/I Found You	1971	$4
❑ 44347	What a Wonderful World/ Love Me the Way I Love You	1967	$5
❑ 40463	When I Let You Go/ And No One Knows	1955	$20
❑ 43337	Where Were You When I Needed You/I Don't Wanna Go Home	1965	$6
❑ 45407	Which Way You Goin' Girl/Moonlight	1971	$4
❑ 41182	With You/Blue Tears	1958	$10

7-Inch Extended Plays

Number	Title	Yr	NM
❑ B-2568	*Innamorata/Two Purple Shadows/Pretend You Don't See Her/And This Is My Beloved	1958	$10
❑ 7-9073 [S]	Hey, Look Me Over/Lulu's Back in Town/With a Song in My Heart//If I Had You/I'm Always Chasing Rainbows/ Lonesome Road	1964	$10

—33 1/3 rpm, small hole, "Special Coin Operator Release

Number	Title	Yr	NM
❑ 7-9073 [PS]	Standing Ovation!	1964	$12
❑ B-11641	Sweet and Lovely/All of Me// Prisoner of Love/Just Friends	1958	$10
❑ 7-9187 [PS]	There Goes My Heart	1965	$12
❑ 7-9187	There Goes My Heart/Sogni D'Oro (Dreams of Gold/Can't You See I'm Sorry//Without Saying a Word/No One Will Ever Know/Somebody Else Is Taking My Place	1965	$10

—33 1/3 rpm, small hole, "Special Coin Operator Release

Number	Title	Yr	NM
❑ B-11641 [PS]	(title unknown)	1958	$12

VALENS, RITCHIE

DEL-FI

Number	Title	Yr	NM
❑ 4106	Come On, Let's Go/Framed	1958	$100
❑ 4110	Donna/La Bamba	1958	$75

—Blue/green/black label with circles

Number	Title	Yr	NM
❑ 4110	Donna/La Bamba	1958	$50

—Green label

Number	Title	Yr	NM
❑ 4110	Donna/La Bamba	1958	$40

—Light blue label

Number	Title	Yr	NM
❑ 4110	Donna/La Bamba	1958	$50

—White label, similar in style to the green and light blue labels (probably not a promo)

Number	Title	Yr	NM
❑ 4111	Fast Freight/Big Baby Blues	1959	$60

—As "Arvee Allens

Number	Title	Yr	NM
❑ 4111	Fast Freight/Big Baby Blues	1959	$50

—As "Ritchie Valens

Number	Title	Yr	NM
❑ 1287	La Bamba '87/La Bamba	1987	$5
❑ 4117	Little Girl/We Belong Together	1959	$40
❑ 4117 [PS]	Little Girl/We Belong Together	1959	$125
❑ 4128	Stay Beside Me/Big Baby Blues	1959	$30
❑ 4114	That's My Little Susie/ In a Turkish Town	1959	$50
❑ 4133	The Paddiwack Song/ Cry, Cry, Cry	1960	$30

7-Inch Extended Plays

DEL-FI

Number	Title	Yr	NM
❑ DFEP-101	(contents unknown)	1959	$175
❑ DFEP-111	(contents unknown)	1960	$175
❑ PR-1 [DJ]	La Bamba/We Belong Together//Donna/Framed	1960	$175

VALENTE, CATERINA

DECCA

Number	Title	Yr	NM
❑ 9-30689	All My Love/Kiss of Fire	1958	$10
❑ 9-30401	Anna/El Cumbanchero	1957	$10
❑ 9-29570	Babalu/This Must Be Wrong	1955	$15
❑ 9-30456	Baia/Take Me to Your Heart	1957	$12
❑ 9-30629	Be Mine Tonight/ Mine, Mine, Mine	1958	$12
❑ 9-29709	Fiesta Cubana/If Hearts Could Talk	1955	$15

Number	Title	Yr	NM
❏ 9-29951	Granada/There But For the Grace of God Go I	1956	$10
❏ 9-30025	I'll Remember April/Everytime We Say Goodbye	1956	$10
❏ 9-29394	Malaguena/Mambo from Chile	1954	$15
❏ 9-30778	Secret Love/Oho-Aha	1958	$10
❏ 9-29760	Temptation/Siboney	1955	$15
❏ 9-29467	The Breeze and I (Andalucia)/Jalousie	1955	$20
❏ 9-29846	The Way You Love Me/Similau	1956	$10
❏ 9-30978	Tipi Tipso/Mack the Knife	1959	$10
❏ 9609	Hindustan/Never Will I Marry	1963	$8
❏ 1018	Melodie/Underbar, Wie Schon Der Abend War	1969	$6
❏ 10007	Peppermint Twist/ Twistin' the Twist	1962	$8
❏ 10011	Port-au-Prince/Corporation	1962	$8
— With Silvio Francesco			
❏ 9667	When in Rome/With a Song in My Heart	1964	$8

LONDON PHASE 4

Number	Title	Yr	NM
❏ 90004	Be In (Hare Krishna)/O Meu Viol	1969	$6
— With Edmundo Ros			

RCA VICTOR

Number	Title	Yr	NM
❏ 47-7525	Where/La Strada Del' Amore	1959	$10
❏ 4507	Gondoli, Gondola/Tango Italiano	1962	$15
— Canadian issue only?			

VALENTI, DINO
ELEKTRA

Number	Title	Yr	NM
❏ 45012	Birdses/Don't Let It Down	1964	$20

VALENTINE, DICKIE
LONDON

Number	Title	Yr	NM
❏ 1620	Christmas Island/ Christmas Alphabet	1955	$15

VALENTINE, JOE
RONN

Number	Title	Yr	NM
❏ 30	A Woman's Love/Hands On, Hands Off	1969	$30
❏ 14	I Can't Stand to See You Go/ One Night of Satisfaction	1967	$40

VALERIE

Number	Title	Yr	NM
❏ 67119	I Can't Stand to See You Go/ One Night of Satisfaction	1967	$200

VALENTINE, PENNY
LIBERTY

Number	Title	Yr	NM
❏ 55774	I Want to Kiss Ringo Goodbye/ Show Me the Way to Love You	1964	$40

VALENTINES, THE (1)
BETHLEHEM

Number	Title	Yr	NM
❏ 3055	I'll Forget You/Yes, You Made It That Way	1962	$30

KING

Number	Title	Yr	NM
❏ 5830	I Have Two Loves/Camping Out	1963	$30
❏ 5338	Please Don't Leave, Please Don't Go/That's It Man	1960	$30
❏ 5433	That's How I Feel/Hey Ruby	1960	$30

UNITED ARTISTS

Number	Title	Yr	NM
❏ 764	Alone in the Night/Mink Coats and Sneakers	1964	$20

VALENTINES, THE (2)
OLD TOWN

Number	Title	Yr	NM
❏ 1009	Tonight Kathleen/Summer Love	1954	$800

RAMA

Number	Title	Yr	NM
❏ 186	Christmas Prayer/K-I-S-S Me	1955	$500
— Blue label			
❏ 186	Christmas Prayer/K-I-S-S Me	1955	$60
— Red label			
❏ 228	Don't Say Goodnight/I Cried Oh, Oh	1957	$200
❏ 181	I Love You Darling/ Hand Me Down Love	1955	$200
❏ 171	Lily Maebelle/Falling for You	1955	$200
— Blue label			
❏ 171	Lily Maebelle/Falling for You	1955	$60
— Red label			
❏ 201	Twenty Minutes (Before the Hour)/I'll Never Let You Go	1956	$125
❏ 196	Why/The Woo Woo Train	1956	$125
— Blue label			
❏ 196	Why/The Woo Woo Train	1956	$60
— Red label			

VALENTINES, THE (3)
SOUND STAGE 7

Number	Title	Yr	NM
❏ 2663	If You Love Me/Breakaway	1970	$15
❏ 2646	I'm Alright Now/Gotta Get Yourself Together	1969	$20

VALENTINO AND THE LOVERS
DONNA

Number	Title	Yr	NM
❏ 1345	One Teardrop Too Late/I'm Gonna Love	1961	$50

VALENTINO, DANNY
MGM

Number	Title	Yr	NM
❏ K12881	Biology/A Million Tears	1960	$20
❏ K12952	Pictures from the Past/ Till the End of Forever	1960	$20
❏ K12835	Stampede/(You Gotta Be a) Music Man	1959	$30

VALENTINO, MARK
SWAN

Number	Title	Yr	NM
❏ 4135	Hey You're Lookin' Good/Do It	1963	$15
❏ 4121	The Push and Kick/ Walking Alone	1962	$20

VALENTINO, SAL
FALCO

Number	Title	Yr	NM
❏ 306	Lisa Marie/I Wanna Twist	1962	$80

WARNER BROS.

Number	Title	Yr	NM
❏ 7268	An Added Attraction (Come and See Me)/Alligator Man	1969	$10
❏ 7289	Friends and Lovers/ Alligator Man	1969	$10
❏ 7368	Silkie/Going for Rochelle	1970	$10

VALENTINOS, THE
CHESS

Number	Title	Yr	NM
❏ 1952	Do It Right/What About Me	1966	$15
❏ 1977	Let's Get Together/Sweeter Than the Day Before	1966	$15

JUBILEE

Number	Title	Yr	NM
❏ 5636	Death of Love/Tired of Being Nobody	1968	$12
❏ 5650	Two Lovers' History/ You've Got the Kind of Love That's for Real	1969	$10

SAR

Number	Title	Yr	NM
❏ 144	Baby, Lots of Luck/ She's So Good to Me	1963	$30
❏ 155	Bitter Dreams/Everybody Wants to Fall in Love	1964	$20
❏ 137	I'll Make It Alright/Darling Come Back Home	1963	$30
❏ 152	It's All Over Now/Tired of Living in the Country	1964	$30
❏ 132	Lookin' for a Love/ Somewhere There's a Girl	1962	$30

VALENTYNE, RUDY
ROULETTE

Number	Title	Yr	NM
❏ 4619	And Now/Ev'rything Beautiful	1965	$8
❏ 4610	Don't Ever Leave Me/I Won't Cry Anymore	1965	$12
❏ 4618	When I Fall in Love/ When I Was a Child	1965	$8
❏ 4620	Who Can I Turn To/More Than This I Cannot Give	1965	$8

VALERY, DANA
ABC

Number	Title	Yr	NM
❏ 11161	A Girl Without Love/ Happy Birthday to Me	1968	$15
❏ 11214	Surround Yourself with Sorrow/Breakfast in Bed	1969	$15
❏ 11138	The Lamplighter's Psalm/Didn't I	1968	$15

COLUMBIA

Number	Title	Yr	NM
❏ 44004	Having You Around/ You Don't Know Where Your Interest Lies	1967	$30
— With Paul Simon			
❏ 44301	Imagine/You	1967	$15

LIBERTY

Number	Title	Yr	NM
❏ 56156	Clinging Vine/Get In Line Girl	1970	$8
❏ 56209	Point of No Return/Put Your Hand in the Hand	1970	$8

PHANTOM

Number	Title	Yr	NM
❏ HB-10566	Will You Love Me Tomorrow/I Never Had It So Good	1975	$5

SCOTTI BROS.

Number	Title	Yr	NM
❏ 509	I Don't Want to Be Lonely/ Rainbow Connection	1979	$4
❏ 612	I Gave You My Love/ Roses and Rainbows	1980	$4

VALETS, THE
JON

Number	Title	Yr	NM
❏ 4025	I Need Someone/ When I Met You	1958	$125
❏ 4219	Sherry/You and You Alone	1959	$40

VULCAN

Number	Title	Yr	NM
❏ 135	Sherry/You and You Alone	1959	$200

VALIANTS, THE (1)
ANDEX

Number	Title	Yr	NM
❏ 4026	Please Wait My Love/ Freida, Freida	1958	$120
— Some copies were pressed with this label in error (Keen 4026 is the "correct" issue)			

KEEN

Number	Title	Yr	NM
❏ 34007	Lover Lover/Walkin' Girl	1958	$50
❏ 4026	Please Wait My Love/ Freida, Freida	1958	$70
❏ 4008	Temptation of My Heart/ Freida, Freida	1958	$60
❏ 34004	This Is the Nite/Good Golly Miss Molly	1957	$50
❏ 82120	This Is the Nite/Walkin' Girl	1960	$30

SHAR-DEE

Number	Title	Yr	NM
❏ 703	Dear Cindy/Surprise	1959	$120
— No mention of London distribution on label			
❏ 703	Dear Cindy/Surprise	1959	$50
— With London distribution credit on label			

VALIANTS, THE (3)
DOT

Number	Title	Yr	NM
❏ 16884	I'll Return to You/Don't Make the Same Mistake	1966	$15

VALIANTS, THE (4)
FAIRLANE

Number	Title	Yr	NM
❏ 21007	Blue Jeans and a Pony Tail/See Saw	1961	$30

IMPERIAL

Number	Title	Yr	NM
❏ 5915	Living in Paradise/I'm in a World of My Own	1963	$20
❏ 5843	Love Comes in Many Ways/ You Are Sweeter Than Wine	1962	$20

KC

Number	Title	Yr	NM
❏ 108	Frankie's Angel/ Are You Ready	1962	$20

VALIANTS, THE (5)
SPECK

Number	Title	Yr	NM
❏ 1001	Wedding Bells/Velma	1958	$2500

VALIANTS, THE (U)
JOY

Number	Title	Yr	NM
❏ 235	Let Me Go Lover/ Let Me Ride	1960	$30

VALINO, JOE
BAND BOX

Number	Title	Yr	NM
❏ 261	Turn Back the Dawn/Now	1961	$10

CROSLEY

Number	Title	Yr	NM
❏ 216	Back to Your Eyes/ Hidden Persuasion	1958	$15
❏ 219	Game of Fools/ Vesta La Giubba	1959	$15

DEBUT

Number	Title	Yr	NM
❏ 143	Christmas Is Here/ In Old Judea	1967	$8

RCA VICTOR

Number	Title	Yr	NM
❏ 47-7723	Garden of Eden/Caravan	1960	$10
❏ AMAO-0132	Garden of Eden/Caravan	1973	$5
— Gold Standard Series reissue			
❏ 47-7535	Out of Darkness/Everything I Touched Turned to Gold	1959	$10

UNITED ARTISTS

Number	Title	Yr	NM
❏ 119	God's Little Acre/I'm Happy with What I've Got	1958	$15
❏ 101	Legend of the Lost/ Declaration of Love	1957	$15
❏ 101 [PS]	Legend of the Lost/ Declaration of Love	1957	$30

VIK

Number	Title	Yr	NM
❏ 0204	Buckets of Love (Zoop Zoop Do U Ba)/Four Seasons	1956	$15
❏ 0226	Garden of Eden/Caravan	1956	$20
❏ 0275	I'll Be Good/Tears (That I Cry Over You)	1957	$15
❏ 0257	The Wind in the Riggin'/ In the Arms of My Love	1957	$15

7-Inch Extended Plays

Number	Title	Yr	NM
❏ EXA-223 [PS]	Garden of Eden	1956	$25
❏ EXA-223	Garden of Eden/The Four Seasons//When the Sun Comes Out/Buckets of Love	1956	$25

Number	Title	Yr	NM

VALJEAN

CARLTON

❏ 586	For the Birds/ Hungarian Hash	1963	$8
❏ 582	Mr. Mozart's Mash/Newsette	1962	$10
❏ 573	Theme from Ben Casey/ Theme from Dr. Kildare	1962	$10
❏ 573 [PS]	Theme from Ben Casey/ Theme from Dr. Kildare	1962	$30
❏ 576	Till There Was You/18th Variation	1962	$10
❏ 576 [PS]	Till There Was You/18th Variation	1962	$20

VALLEY, JIM

DUNHILL

❏ 4103	Go-Go Round/Maintain	1967	$15
❏ 4096	Try, Try, Try/Invitations	1967	$15
❏ 4096 [PS]	Try, Try, Try/Invitations	1967	$30

JERDEN

❏ 814	I'm Real/There Is Love	1967	$30
❏ 814 [DJ]	I'm Real/There Is Love	1967	$30

VALLI

SCEPTER

❏ 1233	Hurry Home to Me (Soldier Boy)/Jimmy's in a Hurry	1962	$20

— With the Shirelles backing up

VALLI, FRANKIE, AND THE FOUR SEASONS

See THE FOUR SEASONS.

VALLI, FRANKIE

Also see THE FOUR SEASONS.
Includes records under numerous pseudonyms. Also see THE FOUR LOVERS; THE FOUR SEASONS.

ATLANTIC

❏ 89720	American Pop/Why	1983	$4

— With Manhattan Transfer

CAPITOL

❏ B-5115	Can't Say No to You/ You Make It Beautiful	1982	$4

— With Cheryl Ladd

❏ B-5115 [PS]	Can't Say No to You/ You Make It Beautiful	1982	$5

CINDY

❏ 3012	Come Si Bella/Real (This Is Real)	1958	$200

— As "Franke Valli and the Romans"

CORONA

❏ 1234	My Mother's Eyes/ The Laugh's on Me	1953	$1500

— As "Frank Valley"

DECCA

❏ 30994	It May Be Wrong/Please Take a Chance	1959	$200

— As "Frankie Vally"

MCA

❏ 41253	Doctor Dance/Where Did We Go Wrong	1980	$5

— With Chris Forde

MERCURY

❏ 70381	Forgive and Forget/ Somebody Else Took Her Home	1954	$300

— As "Frankie Valley"; maroon label

❏ 70381	Forgive and Forget/ Somebody Else Took Her Home	1954	$200

— As "Frankie Valley"; black label

MOTOWN

❏ 1279	The Scalawag Song (And I Will Love You)/ Listen to Yesterday	1973	$15

MOWEST

❏ 5011	Love Isn't Here/Poor Fool	1972	$15

OKEH

❏ 7103	I Go Ape/If You Care	1958	$300

— As "Frankie Tyler"

PHILIPS

❏ 40446	Can't Take My Eyes Off You/The Trouble with Me	1967	$10
❏ 40446 [PS]	Can't Take My Eyes Off You/The Trouble with Me	1967	$20
❏ 40680	Circles in the Sand/ My Mother's Eyes	1970	$10
❏ 40484	I Make a Fool of Myself/ September Rain (Here Comes the Rain)	1967	$10
❏ 40484 [PS]	I Make a Fool of Myself/ September Rain (Here Comes the Rain)	1967	$20

Number	Title	Yr	NM
❏ DJP-16 [DJ]	My Mother's Eyes (mono/stereo)	1967	$60

— Only issued as a promo; alternate number is 40460, but actual issue of 40460 is "C'mon Marianne" by the Four Seasons

❏ 40622	The Girl I'll Never Know (Angels Never Fly This Low)/A Face Without a Name	1969	$10
❏ 40622 [PS]	The Girl I'll Never Know (Angels Never Fly This Low)/A Face Without a Name	1969	$20
❏ 40407	The Proud One/Ivy	1966	$10
❏ 40407 [PS]	The Proud One/Ivy	1966	$20
❏ 40510	To Give (The Reason I Live)/ Watch Where You Walk	1967	$10
❏ 40510 [PS]	To Give (The Reason I Live)/ Watch Where You Walk	1967	$20

PRIVATE STOCK

❏ 45,109	Boomerang/Look at the World, It's Changing	1976	$5
❏ 45,140	Easily/What Good Am I Without You	1977	$5
❏ 45,074	Fallen Angel/Carrie (I Would Marry You)	1976	$5
❏ 45,180	I Could Have Loved You/Rainstorm	1978	$5
❏ 45,169	I Need You/I'm Gonna Love You	1977	$5
❏ 45,003	My Eyes Adored You/ Watch Where You Walk	1974	$5
❏ 45,043	Our Day Will Come/ You Can Bet	1975	$5
❏ 45,154	Second Thoughts/ So She Says	1977	$5
❏ 45,021	Swearin' to God/Why	1975	$5
❏ 45,098	We're All Alone/You to Me Are Everything	1976	$5

RSO

❏ 897	Grease/Grease (Instrumental)	1978	$6

SMASH

❏ 1995	The Sun Ain't Gonna Shine (Anymore)/This Is Goodbye	1965	$10

WARNER BROS.

❏ 8734	Fancy Dancer/Needing You	1979	$5

VALLI, JUNE

ABC-PARAMOUNT

❏ 10467	Catch Myself Crying/Silly Girl	1963	$8

DCP

❏ 1120	Empty Rooms/I'm Made for Love (Not for Hurtin')	1964	$8

MERCURY

❏ 71461X45	An Anonymous Letter/Bygones	1959	$10
❏ 71588X45 [M]	Apple Green/Oh Why	1960	$10
❏ 10029X45 [S]	Apple Green/Oh Why	1960	$30
❏ 71800	Come Back to Sorrento/ The World We Live In	1961	$10
❏ 71332X45	Dance with Me/ La Santa Venuta	1958	$12
❏ 71882	Everlastin'/So Long Loser	1961	$12
❏ 71750	Guess Things Happen That Way/Tell Him for Me	1961	$10
❏ 71653	I'll Step Aside/Looking at the World	1960	$10
❏ 71480X45	I Love You Truly/You Were Meant for Me	1959	$10
❏ 71688	Love in Bloom/Flittin' and a Flirtin'	1960	$10
❏ 71520X45	My Darling, My Darling/Shadows	1959	$10
❏ 71422X45	The Answer to a Maiden's Prayer/In His Arms	1959	$12
❏ 71382X45	The Wedding/Lunch Hour	1958	$10
❏ 71729	Weep for Me Lover/ Borrowed Kisses	1960	$10

RCA VICTOR

❏ 47-4298	Always, Always/ Now, Now, Now	1951	$20
❏ 47-7032	Baby Come Home/ Open Your Arms	1957	$15
❏ 47-6662	Beauty Isn't Everything/Now	1956	$15
❏ 47-5298	Brass Ring Love/ Many Are the Times	1953	$20
❏ 47-5177	Congratulations to Someone/Love and Hate	1953	$20
❏ 47-5368	Crying in the Chapel/Love Every Moment You Live	1953	$20
❏ 47-4388	Cry/The Three Bells	1951	$20
❏ 47-6331	Don't Tell Me Not to Love You/Oh! What a Day	1955	$20
❏ 47-5740	I Understand/Love, Tears and Kisses	1954	$20
❏ 47-6402	Madonna in Blue/ While There's Time	1956	$15
❏ 47-5488	Mystery Street/Don't Forget to Write	1953	$20
❏ 47-6215	Oh! My Love/A Kiss Like Yours	1955	$20
❏ 47-5924	Ole Pappy Time/Wrong, Wrong, Wrong	1954	$20
❏ 47-6552	Shangri-La/I've Got Something in My Eye	1956	$15
❏ 47-6464	Sleepy Head/From the Wrong Side of Town	1956	$15

Number	Title	Yr	NM
❏ 47-4759	Strange Sensation/ So Madly in Love	1952	$20
❏ 47-4900	Taboo/Mighty Lonesome Feeling	1952	$20
❏ 47-5837	Tell Me, Tell Me/Boy Wanted	1954	$20
❏ 47-5653	The Gypsy Was Wrong/Old Shoes and a Bag of Rice	1954	$20
❏ 47-6258	The Things They Say/Por Favor	1955	$20
❏ 47-5017	Why Don't You Believe Me/A Shoulder to Weep On	1952	$20
❏ 47-6852	Will You Love Me Still/ Strictly Sentimental	1957	$15

UNITED ARTISTS

❏ 466	Hush Little Baby/I'm Afraid	1962	$8
❏ 490	I Forgot More Than You'll Ever Know/Is It Right or Wrong	1962	$8

VALOR, TONY

MUSICTONE

❏ 1119	There's a Story in My Heart/So Tenderly	1963	$200

VALQUINS, THE

GAITY

❏ 161/2	My Dear/Falling Star	1959	$800
❏ 161/2	My Dear/Falling Star	1959	$1500

— Red vinyl

VALRAYS, THE

PARKWAY

❏ 880	Get A Board/Pee Wee	1963	$40

VALS, THE

ASCOT

❏ 2163	Too Late/I'm Stepping Out with My Memories	1964	$40

UNIQUE LABORATORIES

❏ 0(no cat #)	The Song of a Lover/ Compensation Blues	1962	$1000

VAMPIRES, THE

CARROLL

❏ 104	Why Didn't I Listen to Mother/Did Anybody Lose a Tear	1962	$200

VAN DYKE, CONNIE

MOTOWN

❏ 1041	Oh Freddie/It Hurt Me Too	1963	$60

VAN DYKE, EARL, AND THE SOUL BROTHERS

SOUL

❏ 35028	6 x 6/There Is No Greater Love	1967	$30

— By Earl Van Dyke and the Motown Brass

❏ 35009	All for You/Too Many Fish in the Sea	1965	$800
❏ 35014	I Can't Help Myself/ How Sweet It Is To Be Loved By You	1965	$30
❏ 35006	Soul Stomp/Hot 'N' Tot	1964	$30
❏ 35018	The Flick (Part 1)/ The Flick (Part 2)	1966	$30

VAN DYKE, LEROY

ABC DOT

❏ 17691	Texas Tea/Las Vegas Girl	1977	$4
❏ 17597	Who's Gonna Run the Truck Stop in Tuba City When I'm Gone?/There Ain't No Roses in My Bed	1975	$4

AUDIOGRAPH

❏ 468	Here Today, Here Tomorrow/ (B-side unknown)	1983	$5

DECCA

❏ 32825	Birmingham/What Am I Gonna Tell Them Now	1971	$6
❏ 32933	I'd Rather Be Wantin' Love/ My Mind Is On You	1972	$6
❏ 32866	I Get Lonely When It Rains/Party Girl	1971	$6
❏ 32999	I'll Be Around/Yesterday Will Come Again Tonight	1972	$6
❏ 32756	Mister Professor/People Gonna Turn You Off	1970	$6

DOT

❏ 15503	Auctioneer/I Fell in Love with a Pony Tail	1956	$30

— Originals have maroon labels

❏ 15503	Auctioneer/I Fell in Love with a Pony Tail	1956	$20

— Second pressings have black labels

❏ 16299	Auctioneer/I Fell in Love with a Pony Tail	1961	$12
❏ 15698	Leather Jacket/My Good Mind Went Bad	1958	$125

Number	Title	Yr	NM
❏ 15652	One Heart/Everytime I Ask My Heart	1957	$20
❏ 15561	The Pocket Book Song/ Honky Tonk Song	1957	$20

KAPP

Number	Title	Yr	NM
❏ 2091	Belle-O/An Old Love Affair Now Showing	1970	$6
❏ 2054	Crack in the World/ Try a Little Bit Harder	1969	$6
❏ 983	Goin' Back to Boston/ The Straw	1969	$6
❏ 908	Lonely Thing/One More Minute of Lonely	1968	$6
❏ 951	Lonesome Is/The Long Drive Home	1968	$6
❏ 2021	Steal Away/This Beginning of a Man	1969	$6

MCA

Number	Title	Yr	NM
❏ 40114	I'm O.K., You're O.K./ Everytime Seems Like the First Time	1973	$5

MERCURY

Number	Title	Yr	NM
❏ 72277	Afraid of a Heartbreak/ Your Money	1964	$10
❏ 72360	Anne of a Thousand Days/Poor Guy	1964	$10
❏ 72097	Be a Good Girl/The Other Boys Are Talking	1963	$15
❏ 72057	Black Cloud/Five Steps	1962	$15
❏ 71779	Faded Love/Big Man in a Big House	1961	$15
❏ 72198	Happy to Be Unhappy/ Now I Lay Me Down	1963	$15
❏ 72018	How Long Must You Keep Me a Secret/I Sat Back and Let It Happen	1962	$15
❏ 71926	If a Woman Answers (Hang Up the Phone)/A Broken Promise	1962	$15
❏ 71988	The Life You Offered Me/ Dim, Dark Corner	1962	$15
❏ 71834	Walk On By/My World Is Caving In	1961	$20
❏ 72155	Wrong Side of the Track/ What Are the Lips of Janet	1963	$15

PLANTATION

Number	Title	Yr	NM
❏ 192	Don't Bite the Hand That Feeds You/A Gay Ranchero	1978	$4

SUN

Number	Title	Yr	NM
❏ 1146	Save Me a Seat by the Fire/Rev. Edmond Giles	1979	$4

WARNER BROS.

Number	Title	Yr	NM
❏ 5692	Big Wide Wonderful World of Country/Ol' Man Moses	1966	$10
❏ 7064	I'll Make It Up to You/ What Am I Bid	1967	$8
❏ 5650	It's All Over Now, Baby Blue/Just a State of Mind	1965	$10
❏ 7001	I've Never Been Loved/Less of Me	1967	$8
❏ 7155	Louisville/There's Always Tomorrow	1967	$8

VAN DYKE, REGGIE

PARKWAY

Number	Title	Yr	NM
❏ 829	Sweetness/Happy Music	1961	$20

VAN DYKES, THE

BALDWIN

Number	Title	Yr	NM
❏ 8308	Christmas Forever/ Christmas Forever (Reprise)	1983	$6

VAN DYKES, THE (1)

DELUXE

Number	Title	Yr	NM
❏ 6193	The Bells Are Ringing/ The Meaning of Love	1960	$30

DONNA

Number	Title	Yr	NM
❏ 1333	Gift of Love/Guardian Angel	1961	$50

FELSTED

Number	Title	Yr	NM
❏ 8565	Once Upon a Dream/ Dame Tu Corazon	1959	$30

KING

Number	Title	Yr	NM
❏ 5158	The Bells Are Ringing/ The Meaning of Love	1958	$75

SPRING

Number	Title	Yr	NM
❏ 1113	Gift of Love/Guardian Angel	1961	$120

VAN DYKES, THE (2)

MALA

Number	Title	Yr	NM
❏ 566	A Sunday Kind of Love/I'm So Happy	1967	$30
❏ 530	I've Got to Go On Without You/What Will I Do If I Lose You	1966	$15
❏ 584	Tears of Joy/Save My Love for a Rainy Day	1967	$50

VAN DYKES, THE (3)

GREEN SEA

Number	Title	Yr	NM
❏ 108	Miracle After Miracle/ How Can I Forget Her	1966	$50

VAN DYKES, THE (4)

DECCA

Number	Title	Yr	NM
❏ 31036	Better Come Back to Me/I Don't Know What to Do	1959	$70
❏ 30762	Come On Baby/ Lambie Baby	1958	$50
❏ 30654	The Fixer/Run Betty, Run	1958	$50

VAN EATEN, LON AND DERREK

A&M

Number	Title	Yr	NM
❏ 1845	Loving You/Baby It's You	1976	$4
❏ 1696	The Harder You Pull... The Tighter It Gets/ Dancing in the Dark	1975	$5
❏ 1662	Who Do You Outdo/All You're Hungry For Is Love	1975	$5
❏ 1643	Wildfire/Music Lover	1974	$5

— All A&M records as "Lon and Derrek"

APPLE

Number	Title	Yr	NM
❏ 1845	Sweet Music/Song of Songs	1972	$8
❏ 1845 [PS]	Sweet Music/Song of Songs	1972	$10

VAN HALEN

Also see SAMMY HAGAR; DAVID LEE ROTH; CHICKENFOOT.

WARNER BROS.

Number	Title	Yr	NM
❏ 49501	And the Cradle Will Rock.../ Could This Be Magic	1980	$5
❏ 49035	Beautiful Girls/D.O.A.	1979	$5
❏ 28505	Best of Both Worlds/Best of Both Worlds (Live)	1986	$3
❏ 28505 [PS]	Best of Both Worlds/Best of Both Worlds (Live)	1986	$5
❏ 27891	Black and Blue/ Apolitical Blues	1988	$3
❏ 27891 [PS]	Black and Blue/ Apolitical Blues	1988	$5
❏ 8823	Dance the Night Away/ Outta Love Again	1979	$6
❏ 8823 [PS]	Dance the Night Away/ Outta Love Again	1979	$15
❏ 29986	Dancing in the Street/Full Bug	1982	$4
❏ 28702	Dreams/Inside	1986	$3
❏ 27565	Feels So Good/ Sucker in a 3-Piece	1989	$5
❏ 8707	Feel Your Love Tonight/ Ain't Talkin' 'Bout Love	1978	$10
❏ 27746	Finish What Ya Started/ Sucker in a 3-Piece	1988	$3
❏ 27746 [PS]	Finish What Ya Started/ Sucker in a 3-Piece	1988	$3
❏ 29199	Hot for Teacher/ Little Dreamer	1984	$3
❏ 29199 [PS]	Hot for Teacher/ Little Dreamer	1984	$8

— Special plastic sleeve with inserts

Number	Title	Yr	NM
❏ 29199 [PS]	Hot for Teacher/ Little Dreamer	1984	$4

— Regular picture sleeve

Number	Title	Yr	NM
❏ 29307	I'll Wait/Girl Gone Bad	1984	$3
❏ 29307 [PS]	I'll Wait/Girl Gone Bad	1984	$4
❏ 28626	Love Walks In/ Summer Nights	1986	$3
❏ 28626 [PS]	Love Walks In/ Summer Nights	1986	$3
❏ 50003	(Oh) Pretty Woman/ Happy Trails	1982	$4
❏ 50003 [PS]	(Oh) Pretty Woman/ Happy Trails	1982	$4
❏ 29250	Panama/Drop Dead Legs	1984	$3
❏ 29250 [PS]	Panama/Drop Dead Legs	1984	$3
❏ 50003	Pretty Woman/Happy Trails	1982	$5
❏ 50003 [PS]	Pretty Woman/Happy Trails	1982	$5

— Original copies of both record and sleeve have no subtitles

Number	Title	Yr	NM
❏ 29929	Secrets/Big Bad Bill	1982	$6
❏ 49751	So This Is Love/Read About It Later	1981	$5
❏ 49751 [PS]	So This Is Love/Read About It Later	1981	$8
❏ 27827	When It's Love/Cabo Wabo	1988	$3
❏ 27827 [PS]	When It's Love/Cabo Wabo	1988	$3
❏ 28740	Why Can't This Be Love/Get Up	1986	$3
❏ 28740 [PS]	Why Can't This Be Love/Get Up	1986	$3

VAN, HARVIE JUNE

KING

Number	Title	Yr	NM
❏ 1369	Can Can Skirt/My Sins of Yesterday	1954	$30
❏ 1482	Don't Offer Me the Stars/ Mama Don't Chase My Love Away	1955	$30
❏ 1497	False or True/I Found Out	1955	$30
❏ 1387	The Lights Are Growing Dim/I'm Jut Not That Kind	1954	$30

RCA VICTOR

Number	Title	Yr	NM
❏ 47-7548	Butcher Boy/Leaving Woman Blues	1959	$15
❏ 47-7668	When You Are Here/ Poor Wildwood Flower	1960	$15

TODD

Number	Title	Yr	NM
❏ 1078	Biggest Broken Heart in Town/Good Morning Mr. Echo	1962	$15

VAN LOAN, JOE

FORD

Number	Title	Yr	NM
❏ 122	Autumn Leaves/ Love Divided	1963	$30

PARKWAY

Number	Title	Yr	NM
❏ 828	Hurricane/Broken Shoes	1961	$30

V-TONE

Number	Title	Yr	NM
❏ 200	Forever/Give Me Your Heart	1958	$200

VAN ZANDT, ED

HIT

Number	Title	Yr	NM
❏ 28	Little Diane/Devil Woman	1962	$8

— B-side by Bill Murphy

VAN ZANDT, TOWNES

POPPY

Number	Title	Yr	NM
❏ 90104	Come Tomorrow/ Delta Momma Blues	1970	$8
❏ XW170	Fraulein/Don't Let the Sunshine Fool You	1973	$6
❏ 90108	Greensboro Woman/ Stand-In	1971	$8
❏ 90116	Honky Tonkin'/ Snow Don't Fall	1972	$8
❏ 90113	If I Needed You/ Sunshine Boy	1971	$8
❏ XW238	Pancho and Lefty/ (B-side unknown)	1973	$10
❏ 510	Second Lovers/ (B-side unknown)	1968	$8
❏ 506	Talking Karate Blues/ Waiting Around to Die	1968	$8

TOMATO

Number	Title	Yr	NM
❏ 10005	When She Don't Need Me/No Place to Fall	1978	$5
❏ 10003	Who Do You Love?/ (B-side unknown)	1977	$5

VANCE, FRANKIE

REVUE

Number	Title	Yr	NM
❏ 11048	Do You Hear Me Baby/ Can't Break the Habit (Of Your Love)	1969	$50

VANCE, VINCE, AND THE VALIANTS

PAID

Number	Title	Yr	NM
❏ 109	Bomb Iran/Bye Bye Baby	1980	$6

SCRATCHED

Number	Title	Yr	NM
❏ (# unknown)	Good-Bye Johnny/Sha-La-La-La, Goodbye	1982	$6

SMC

Number	Title	Yr	NM
❏ (# unknown)	Fortune Teller/You'd Better Move On	1972	$10

STONE MAVERICK

Number	Title	Yr	NM
❏ (# unknown)	The Silver and the Blue/ (B-side unknown)	1981	$6

VALIANT

Number	Title	Yr	NM
❏ 92689	All I Want for Christmas Is You/Exceptional Man	1989	$6
❏ 92689 [PS]	All I Want for Christmas Is You/Exceptional Man	1989	$8
❏ 62386	Amadago/You Don't Own Me	1986	$5

— Red vinyl

Number	Title	Yr	NM
❏ (# unknown)	Backseat Couch/Gloria	1975	$8
❏ 6580	Bomb Iran/Bye Bye Baby	1980	$10

— Blue vinyl

Number	Title	Yr	NM
❏ (# unknown)	The Houston Love Song/ Bye-Bye Steelers	1981	$6

VANDROSS, LUTHER

ATLANTIC

Number	Title	Yr	NM
❏ 89593	At Christmas Time/ Santa's Rap	1984	$5

— As "Luther"; B-side by the Treacherous Three

COTILLION

Number	Title	Yr	NM
❏ 44205	Funky Music (Is a Part of Me)/The 2nd Time Around	1976	$20

— As "Luther

Number	Title	Yr	NM
❏ 44200	It's Good for the Soul -- Pt. 1/Pt. 2	1976	$30

— As "Luther

Number	Title	Yr	NM
❏ 44216	This Close to You/Don't Wanna Be a Fool	1977	$100

— As "Luther

EPIC

Number	Title	Yr	NM
❏ 34-08047	Any Love/(Instrumental)	1988	$3
❏ ENR-03263	Bad Boy/Having a Party//(B-side blank)	1982	$6

— One-sided budget release

Number	Title	Yr	NM
❏ 14-03205	Bad Boy/Having a Party// Once You Know How	1982	$4
❏ 14-02658	Don't You Know That?/I've Been Working	1981	$4
❏ 34-68742	For You to Love/ (Instrumental)	1989	$3

Number	Title	Yr	NM
❏ 34-06129	Give Me the Reason/ Don't You Want My Love	1986	$3
❏ 34-06129 [PS]	Give Me the Reason/ Don't You Want My Love	1986	$4
❏ 13-08432	Give Me the Reason/ Other Side of the World	1988	$3
—Reissue			
❏ 34-73029	Here and Now/Come Back	1989	$15
❏ 34-05751	If Only for One Night/ Other Side of the World	1986	$4
❏ 34-04231	I'll Let You Slide/ (Instrumental)	1983	$4
❏ 34-04231 [PS]	I'll Let You Slide/ (Instrumental)	1983	$4
❏ 34-07201	I Really Didn't Mean It/(Instrumental)	1987	$3
❏ 34-04944	It's Over Now/(Instrumental)	1985	$4
❏ 34-04944 [PS]	It's Over Now/(Instrumental)	1985	$4
❏ 34-04494	Make Me a Believer/ Busy Body	1984	$4
❏ 34-03804	Promise Me/Better Love	1983	$4
❏ 34-08513	She Won't Talk to Me/ (Instrumental)	1988	$3
❏ 34-03487	Since I Lost My Baby/ You're the Sweetest One	1982	$4
❏ 34-07434	So Amazing/(Instrumental)	1987	$3
❏ 34-06523	Stop to Love/(Instrumental)	1986	$3
❏ 34-06523 [PS]	Stop to Love/(Instrumental)	1986	$3
❏ 13-08429	Stop to Love/So Amazing	1988	$3
—Reissue			
❏ 14-02842	Sugar and Spice (I Found Me a Girl)/ She's a Super Lady	1982	$4
❏ 34-04441	Superstar/I Wanted Your Love	1984	$4
❏ 34-06978	There's Nothing Better Than Love/(Instrumental)	1987	$3
—A-side with Gregory Hines			
❏ 34-06978 [PS]	There's Nothing Better Than Love/(Instrumental)	1987	$3
❏ 34-04760	'Til My Baby Comes Home/(Instrumental)	1985	$4
❏ 34-04760 [PS]	'Til My Baby Comes Home/(Instrumental)	1985	$4
❏ 34-05610	Wait for Love/My Sensitivity (Gets in the Way)	1985	$4

VANELLI, JOHNNY
LITTLE APPLES
Number	Title	Yr	NM
❏ 2801	Phroomf/Santa's Ride	1965	$15

VANGELIS
POLYDOR
Number	Title	Yr	NM
❏ 873550-7	Chariots of Fire/Hymne	1989	$4
—Timepieces" reissue			
❏ 2189	Chariots of Fire -- Titles/ Eric's Theme	1982	$4
❏ 2189 [PS]	Chariots of Fire -- Titles/ Eric's Theme	1982	$8
❏ 2189 [DJ]	Chariots of Fire -- Titles (same on both sides)	1982	$5
—White label promo			
❏ PRO458-7 [DJ]	Hymne (same on both sides)	1986	$10
❏ PRO204 [DJ]	L'Enfant (same on both sides)	1979	$12
❏ 2189	Titles/Eric's Theme	1981	$30
—Original issue of this single			
❏ 2189 [DJ]	Titles (same on both sides)	1981	$10
—Promo; red label			
❏ 2189 [DJ]	Titles (same on both sides)	1981	$15
—Promo; white label; "Special Edition for Adult Contemporary Radio" on label			

RCA
Number	Title	Yr	NM
❏ PB-10882	Pulstar/Alpha	1977	$20
❏ JH-10882 [DJ]	Pulstar (stereo/mono)	1977	$8
❏ JB-10733 [DJ]	So Long Ago, So Clear/ Heaven and Hell Theme	1976	$15
—May not exist as a stock copy; if it does, it would fetch at least twice this amount			
❏ PB-13402	To the Unknown Man Part I/Part II	1982	$8

VANGUARDS, THE (1)
LAMP
Number	Title	Yr	NM
❏ 653	Girl Go Away/Man Without Knowledge	1970	$15
❏ 652	It's To Late for Love/The Thought of Losing Your Love	1970	$15
—Yes, the label misspelled the A-side			

WHIZ
Number	Title	Yr	NM
❏ 612	Somebody Please/I Can't Use You Girl	1969	$12

VANGUARDS, THE (2)
DERBY
Number	Title	Yr	NM
❏ 854	Don't Let It Happen Again/So Live	1954	$400

VANGUARDS, THE (3)
IVY
Number	Title	Yr	NM
❏ 103	Moonlight/I'm Movin'	1958	$200
—With mention of "Billy Butler's Orchestra"			
❏ 103	Moonlight/I'm Movin'	1958	$80
—No mention of "Billy Butler's Orchestra"			

VANGUARDS, THE (4)
WARNER BROS.
Number	Title	Yr	NM
❏ 5800	Girl/A Stranger in Your Town	1966	$15

VANGUARDS, THE (U)
DOT
Number	Title	Yr	NM
❏ 15791	Baby Doll/My Friend Mary Ann	1958	$60

VANILLA FUDGE
Also see CACTUS, BECK, BOGERT & APPICE.
ATCO
Number	Title	Yr	NM
❏ 6655	Good Good Lovin'/Shot Gun	1969	$8
❏ 99729	Mystery/The Stranger	1984	$4
❏ 6679	People/Some Velvet Morning	1969	$8
❏ 6632	Season of the Witch (Part 1)/ Season of the Witch (Part 2)	1968	$8
❏ 6616	Take Me for a Little While/Thoughts	1968	$8
❏ 6554	The Look of Love/ Where Is My Mind	1968	$8
❏ 6728	Windmills of Your Mind/ Lord in the Country	1970	$6

7-Inch Extended Plays
Number	Title	Yr	NM
❏ SP-4516 [DJ]	Eleanor Rigby-Part 1/ You Keep Me Hanging On//Eleanor Rigby-Part 2/Ticket to Ride	1968	$25
—Promo only, white label			
❏ SP-4516 [PS]	(title unknown)	1968	$25
—Paper sleeve with above EP			

VANITY FARE
20TH CENTURY
Number	Title	Yr	NM
❏ 2036	Down Home/Take It, Shake It, Break My Heart	1973	$5

BRENT
Number	Title	Yr	NM
❏ 7067	Peter Who (Peter Pan)/ Salt Water Babies	1967	$8

DJM
Number	Title	Yr	NM
❏ 70029	Big Parade/Nowhere to Go	1971	$5
❏ 70024	Where Did All the Good Times Go/Stand	1971	$5

PAGE ONE
Number	Title	Yr	NM
❏ 21027	Early in the Morning/You Made Me Love You	1969	$8
❏ 21020	Highway of Dreams/ Waiting for the Nightfall	1969	$6
❏ 21029	Hitchin' a Ride/Man Child	1970	$8
❏ 21007	I Live for the Sun/On the Other Side of Life	1969	$6
❏ 21033	(I Remember) Summer Morning/Megowd (Something Tells Me)	1970	$6

VANN, TEDDY
CAPITOL
Number	Title	Yr	NM
❏ 5878	Theme from Coloredman/ Introduction to the Adventures of Coloredman	1967	$50

COLUMBIA
Number	Title	Yr	NM
❏ 4-41996	Lonely Crowd/I Was Born to Love You	1961	$20

END
Number	Title	Yr	NM
❏ 1059	There Is Someone/ Sweetheart	1959	$30

ROULETTE
Number	Title	Yr	NM
❏ 4300	Do You Love Me/Young and Pretty Woman	1960	$30

TRIPLE-X
Number	Title	Yr	NM
❏ 101	Cindy/I'm Waiting	1960	$30

VAPORS, THE
LIBERTY
Number	Title	Yr	NM
❏ 1364	Turning Japanese/Talk Talk	1980	$3

UNITED ARTISTS
Number	Title	Yr	NM
❏ 1364	Turning Japanese	1980	$20
—Oblong white vinyl with custom sleeve			
❏ 1364	Turning Japanese/Talk Talk	1980	$4

VAQUEROS, THE
AUDITION
Number	Title	Yr	NM
❏ 6102	Desert Wind/Echo	1964	$60

BANGAR
Number	Title	Yr	NM
❏ 0647	Birds and Bees/80-Foot Wave	1964	$50

VARE, RONNIE, AND THE INSPIRATIONS
DELL
Number	Title	Yr	NM
❏ 5203	Let's Rock, Little Girl/ Love Is Just for Two	1959	$60

VAREEATIONS, THE
DIONN
Number	Title	Yr	NM
❏ 510	Foolish One/It's the Loving Season	1969	$20
❏ 506	The Time/Ssab-Bbrom	1968	$20

VARISCO, PAUL, AND THE MILESTONES
DATE
Number	Title	Yr	NM
❏ 2-1650	Gotta Have Love/Look Around You People	1969	$8

VARNER, DON
QUINCY
Number	Title	Yr	NM
❏ 8002	Tear Stained Face/Meet Me in the Church	1969	$250

VEEP
Number	Title	Yr	NM
❏ 1296	Tear Stained Face/Meet Me in the Church	1969	$200

VASEL, MARIANNE, AND ERICH STORZ
MERCURY
Number	Title	Yr	NM
❏ 71286X45	The Little Train (Die Kleine Bimmelbahn)/ Sunny Lake Walk	1958	$20

VASSY, KIN
AMOS
Number	Title	Yr	NM
❏ 168	My First Night Alone Without You/Will the Circle Be Unbroken	1971	$8

BELL
Number	Title	Yr	NM
❏ 45316	Bayou Song/(B-side unknown)	1973	$8

EPIC
Number	Title	Yr	NM
❏ 5-10125	Gamblin' Man/Tracks Run Through the City	1967	$10

IA
Number	Title	Yr	NM
❏ 501	Do I Ever Cross Your Mind/Sometimes Love Is Better When It's Gone	1979	$6
❏ 502	Makes Me Wonder If I Ever Said Goodbye/ Fort Worth Featherbed	1980	$6
❏ 505	There's Nobody Like You/Nite Out	1980	$6

LIBERTY
Number	Title	Yr	NM
❏ 1458	Cast the First Stone/ Lonely Hearts	1982	$4
❏ 1407	Likin' Him and Lovin' You/ Hell and High Water	1981	$4
❏ 1427	Sneakin' Around/ Lonely Hearts	1981	$4
❏ 1488	Tryin' to Love Two/All for the Love of a Girl	1982	$4
❏ 1440	When You Were Blue and I Was Green/ Honky Tonk Heart	1981	$4
❏ 1469	Women in Love/Hell and High Water	1982	$4

UNI
Number	Title	Yr	NM
❏ 55114	Farewell/Hello L.A., Bye Bye Birmingham	1969	$8
❏ 55195	I Just Wanna Give My Love to You/Blue Bird	1970	$8
❏ 55139	I Think I Just Found My Mind/That's the Bag I'm In	1969	$8

UNITED ARTISTS
Number	Title	Yr	NM
❏ 1368	There's Nobody Like You/Nite Out	1980	$4
—Reissue of IA 505			

VAUGHAN, DENNY
CORAL
Number	Title	Yr	NM
❏ 9-60321	A Marshmallow World/ So Long, Sally	1950	$30
❏ 9-60316	Autumn Leaves/Patricia	1950	$30
❏ 9-60534	By the Light of the Silvery Moon/I'm Bringing a Red, Red Rose	1951	$20
—The above four comprise a box set			
❏ 9-60524	Do You Really Love Me?/I Want to Remember	1951	$30
❏ 9-60355	If/Wait for Them	1951	$30
❏ 9-60334	I Guess I'll Have to Dream the Rest/Gee, But I'm Lonesome Tonight	1950	$30
❏ 9-60432	Love Tales/Mellow Mood	1951	$30
❏ 9-60531	Moonlight and Roses/ Moonglow	1951	$20
❏ 9-60393	Too Young/I Love the Way You Say Goodnight	1951	$30

GLORY
Number	Title	Yr	NM
❏ 261	Heart Beats/Once Again	1957	$20
❏ 251	If You Believe/C'est Ca	1957	$20

Number	Title	Yr	NM
❑ 293	Lover's Lament/ Ma Vleur D'Amor	1959	$20
❑ 278	My Lost Love/ Thoughts of You	1958	$20
❑ 256	Wonderful, Wonderful!/ Since You Went Away	1957	$20

KAPP

❑ 143	Walk Hand in Hand/ Just Sing a Song	1956	$20

—As "Denny Vaughn

VAUGHAN, FRANKIE

COLUMBIA

❑ 41480	Ain't Gonna Lead This Life No More/Heart of a Man	1959	$20
❑ 41859	Do You Still Love Me/Milord	1960	$20
❑ 41638	Hey You with the Crazy Eyes/The Key	1960	$20
❑ 41406	Honey Bunny Baby/Big Deal	1959	$20
❑ 41279	One Thing Led to Another/ So Happy in Love	1958	$20

EPIC

❑ 9238	Pebble on the Beach/Isn't This a Lovely Evening	1957	$20
❑ 9265	We're Not Alone/Can't Get Along Without You	1958	$20

MALA

❑ 588	If I Didn't Care/So Tired	1968	$6

PHILIPS

❑ 40349	Forgotten Man/Wait	1965	$8
❑ 40070	Hercules/I'm Gonna Clip Your Wings	1962	$15

VAUGHAN, SARAH, AND BILLY ECKSTINE

MERCURY

❑ 71393	Alexander's Ragtime Band/No Limit	1959	$15
❑ 71122	Passing Strangers/ The Door Is Open	1957	$15

VAUGHAN, SARAH

ATLANTIC

❑ 3835	Fool on the Hill/Get Back	1981	$5
❑ 1012	It Might As Well Be Spring/ You Go to My Head	1953	$125

COLUMBIA

❑ 4-39494	After Hours/Out of Breath	1951	$30
❑ 4-39207	Ave Maria/A City Called Heaven	1951	$30
❑ 1-199	Black Coffee/As You Desire Me	1949	$50

—Microgroove 33 1/3 rpm single

❑ 1-385(?)	Fool's Paradise/Lonely Girl	1949	$50

—Microgroove 33 1/3 rpm single

❑ 1-395(?)	I Cried for You/You Say You Care	1950	$50

—Microgroove 33 1/3 rpm single

❑ 4-39719	If Someone Had Told Me/Corner to Corner	1952	$30
❑ 4-39124	I'll Know/Gas Pipe Leaking	1950	$30
❑ 1-757(?)	(I Love the Girl) I Love the Guy/Thinking of You	1950	$50

—Microgroove 33 1/3 rpm single

❑ 6-757(?)	(I Love the Girl) I Love the Guy/Thinking of You	1950	$40
❑ 4-38925	(I Love the Girl) I Love the Guy/Thinking of You	1950	$30
❑ 1-485	I'm Crazy to Love You/ Summertime	1950	$50

—Microgroove 33 1/3 rpm single

❑ 4-39576	I Ran All the Way Home/ Just a Moment More	1951	$30
❑ 4-39932	Lovers' Quarrel/I Confess	1953	$30
❑ 1-679	Our Very Own/ Don't Be Afraid	1950	$50

—Microgroove 33 1/3 rpm single

❑ 1-830(?)	Perdido/Whippa Whippa Woo	1950	$50

—Microgroove 33 1/3 rpm single

❑ 6-830(?)	Perdido/Whippa Whippa Woo	1950	$40
❑ 4-39001	Perdido/Whippa Whippa Woo	1950	$30
❑ 4-39634	Pinky/A Miracle Happened	1952	$30
❑ 4-39839	Say You'll Wait for Me/ My Tormented Heart	1952	$30
❑ 4-39873	Sinner or Saint/Mighty Lonesome Feeling	1952	$30
❑ 4-39963	Spring Will Be a Little Late This Year/A Blues Serenade	1953	$30
❑ 1-321	That Lucky Old Sun (Just Rolls Around Heaven All Day)/Make Believe (You Are Glad When You're Sorry)	1949	$50

—Microgroove 33 1/3 rpm single

❑ 4-39370	These Things I Offer You (For a Lifetime)/Deep Purple	1951	$30
❑ 4-40041	Time/Linger Awhile	1953	$30
❑ 4-39789	Time to Go/Street of Dreams	1952	$30

Number	Title	Yr	NM
❑ 1-258(?)	Tonight I Shall Sleep (With a Smile on My Face)/ While You're Gone	1949	$50

—Microgroove 33 1/3 rpm single

MAINSTREAM

❑ 5544	Alone Again (Naturally)/ Run to Me	1973	$5
❑ 5527	And the Feeling's Good/ Deep in the Night	1972	$5
❑ 5553	Do Away with April/I Need You More	1974	$5
❑ 5517	Imagine/Sweet Gingerbread Man	1971	$5
❑ 5521	Pieces of Dreams/Once You've Been in Love	1972	$5
❑ 5541	Send In the Clowns/ (B-side unknown)	1973	$5
❑ 5523	Summer Me, Winter Me/ The Story of a Frasier	1972	$5
❑ 5522	What Are You Doing the Rest of Your Life/ The Summer Knows	1972	$5

MERCURY

❑ 72543	A Lover's Concerto/First Thing Every Morning	1966	$8
❑ 70299x45	And This Is My Beloved/ Easy Come, Easy Go Lover	1954	$20
❑ 71407	Are You Certain/Cool Baby	1959	$15
❑ 71157x45	Band of Angels/ Please Mr. Brown	1957	$15
❑ 72249	Bluesette/You Got It Made	1964	$10
❑ 71477	Broken-Hearted Melody/Misty	1959	$15
❑ 70727x45	C'est La Vie/Never	1955	$20
❑ 71702	Close to You/Out of This World	1960	$15
❑ 72510	Darling/I'll Never Be Lonely Again	1965	$8
❑ 71562	Eternally/You're My Baby	1960	$15
❑ 72588	Everybody Loves Somebody/1-2-3	1966	$8
❑ 70646x45	Experience Unnecessary/ Slowly, With Feeling	1955	$20
❑ 70885x45	Fabulous Character/ The Other Woman	1956	$15
❑ 71669	For All We Know/ The Rough Years	1960	$15
❑ 71235x45	Gone Train/Next Time Around	1957	$15
❑ 70846x45	Hot and Cold Running Tears/That's Not the Kind of Love I Want	1956	$15
❑ 70534x45	How Important Can It Be/ Waltzing Down the Aisle	1955	$20
❑ 72300	How's the World Treating You/Sole, Sole, Sole	1964	$10
❑ 71380	I Ain't Hurtin'/Everything I Do	1958	$15
❑ 71742	If You Are But a Dream/ Mary Contrary	1960	$15
❑ 70947x45	It Happened Again/I Wanna Play Hanuka	1956	$15
❑ 70331x45	It's Easy to Remember/ Come Along with Me	1954	$20
❑ 71030x45	Leave It to Love/The Bashful Matador	1957	$15
❑ 70469x45	Make Yourself Comfortable/ Idle Gossip	1954	$20
❑ 71642	Maybe You'll Be There/Doodlin'	1960	$15
❑ 70777x45	Mr. Wonderful/You Ought to Have a Wife	1956	$15
❑ 70423x45	Ol' Devil Moon/Saturday	1954	$20
❑ 71303	Padre/Spin the Bottle	1958	$15
❑ 72417	Pawn Broker/Bye Bye (Theme from Peter Gunn)	1965	$8
❑ 71085x45	Poor Butterfly/April Give Me One More Day	1957	$15
❑ 71433	Separate Ways/Careless	1959	$15
❑ 71519 [M]	Smooth Operator/ Maybe It's Because (I Love You Too Much)	1959	$15
❑ 10020 [S]	Smooth Operator/ Maybe It's Because (I Love You Too Much)	1959	$30
❑ 71610	Some Other Spring/ Our Waltz	1960	$15
❑ 71020x45	The Banana Boat Song/I've Got a New Heartache	1956	$15
❑ 72381	The Other Side of Me/ We Almost Made It	1965	$8
❑ 70595x45	Whatever Lola Wants/Oh Yeah	1955	$20
❑ 71326	What's So Bad About It/ Too Much Too Soon	1958	$15

MGM

❑ K11068	Don't Blame Me/If You Could See Me Now	1951	$30
❑ K10819	I Cover the Waterfront/ Don't Worry 'Bout Me	1950	$40
❑ K10890	I'm Gonna Sit Right Down and Write Myself a Letter/I'm Through with Love	1951	$30
❑ K10705	Tenderly/Wait and Pray	1950	$40
❑ K10762	What a Difference A Day Made/I Can't Get Started	1950	$40

ROULETTE

❑ 4359	April/Oh Lover	1961	$10
❑ 4604	A Taste of Honey/ The Good Life	1965	$8
❑ 4482	Call Me Irresponsible/ There'll Be Other Times	1963	$8
❑ 4397	If Love Is Good to Me/A Great Day	1961	$10

Number	Title	Yr	NM
❑ 4497	Once Upon a Summertime/ Snowbound	1963	$8
❑ 4413	One Mint Julep/Mama (He Treats Your Daughter Mean)	1962	$10
❑ 4285	Serenata/Let's	1960	$10
❑ 4547	The Wallflower Waltz/Only	1964	$8
❑ 4325	True Believer/ What's the Use	1961	$10
❑ 4516	What'll I Do/I Believe in You	1963	$8

WARNER BROS.

❑ 49890	Theme from "Sharkey's Machine"/Sharkey's Theme	1981	$4

—B-side by Eddie Harris

❑ B-2588	*Perdido/Linger Awhile/ Time/Corner to Corner	1959	$25
❑ B-2588 [PS]	Sarah Vaughan (Hall of Fame Series)	1959	$25

MGM

❑ X1019	(contents unknown)	1953	$20
❑ X1019 [PS]	I've Got a Crush on You	1953	$20
❑ X1020 [PS]	The Man I Love	1953	$20
❑ X1020	The Man I Love/Body and Soul/I Can Make You Love Me/Once in a While	1953	$20

VAUGHAN, STEVIE RAY

EPIC

❑ 05731	Change It/Look at Little Sister	1985	$4
❑ 69025	Double Crossfire/ Travis Walk	1989	$4
❑ 07340	Pipeline/Love Struck Baby	1987	$4

—With Dick Dale

❑ 04031	Pride and Joy/Rude Mood	1983	$5
❑ 06601	Superstition/Pride and Joy	1987	$4
❑ 06696 [DJ]	Willie the Wimp (LP Version)/Willie the Wimp (Edit)	1987	$8
❑ 06696	Willie the Wimp/Superstition	1987	$4

VAUGHN, BILLY

DOT

❑ 16924	Alfie/Lara's Theme	1966	$5
❑ 15960	All Night Long/Blues Stay Away from Me	1959	$8
❑ 17215	A Mansion on the Hill/I've Got You on My Mind Again	1969	$5
❑ 15466	Angel, Angel/ Autumn Concerto	1956	$10
❑ 16774	Anniversary Song/Please	1965	$6
❑ 16374	A Swingin' Safari/ Indian Love Call	1962	$6
❑ 15444	A Theme from (The Three Penny Opera) "Moritat"/Little Boy Blue	1956	$10
❑ 16900	Because They're Young/Buckaroo	1966	$5
❑ 16262	Berlin Melody/Come September	1961	$8
❑ 16397	Blue Flame/Someone	1962	$6
❑ 15879	Blue Hawaii/Tico Tico	1958	$8
❑ 16220	Blue Tomorrow/Red Wing	1961	$8
❑ 16580	Boss/Blue Tango	1964	$6
❑ 16329	Chapel by the Sea/One Love, One Heartache	1962	$6
❑ 15836	Cimarron (Roll On)/ You're My Baby Doll	1958	$8
❑ 15836 [PS]	Cimarron (Roll On)/ You're My Baby Doll	1958	$15
❑ 17337	Coco/Always Mademoiselle	1970	$4
❑ 17314	Color It Cool/On Days Like This	1969	$5
❑ 17346	Come Saturday Morning/True Grit	1970	$4
❑ 16359	Continental Melody/ Born to Be with You	1962	$6
❑ 16549	Cumberland County Feud/ Chow Chow Amore	1963	$6
❑ 16883	Did You Ever Have to Make Up Your Mind/It's Over	1966	$5
❑ 16245	Down Yonder/Born to Be with Me	1961	$6
❑ 16417	Down Yonder/I'm Waitin'	1963	$6
❑ 16295	Everybody's Twisting Down in Mexico/ Melody in the Night	1961	$8
❑ 16622	Guitar Song/Chianti Song	1964	$6
❑ 16477	Happy Cowboy/Broken Date	1963	$6
❑ 15900	Hawaiian War Chant/ Trade Winds	1959	$8
❑ 15900 [PS]	Hawaiian War Chant/ Trade Winds	1959	$15
❑ 15430	I'd Give a Million Tomorrows/Calico Cathy	1955	$15
❑ 17021	I Love You/Yellow Roses Mean Goodbye	1967	$5
❑ 15993	It's No Sin/After Hours	1959	$8
❑ 15795	La Paloma/Here Is My Love	1958	$8
❑ 17054	Last Hearts of Kyoto/ The Last Safari	1967	$5
❑ 17074	Lolly/Moonlight Makes Memories	1968	$5
❑ 16106	Look for a Star/ He'll Have to Go	1960	$8
❑ 225 [S]	Look for a Star/ He'll Have to Go	1960	$15
❑ 16739	Making Other Plans/ Our Dream of Love	1965	$6
❑ 16664	Maybe/Pearly Shells	1964	$6

Number	Title	Yr	NM
❏ 16436	Meditation (Meditacao)/Release Me	1963	$6
❏ 15247	Melody of Love/Joy Ride	1954	$15
❏ 16026	Melody of Love/Sail Along Silvery Moon	1960	$6
—Reissue			
❏ 16706	Mexican Pearls/Woodpecker	1965	$6
❏ 16835	Mexican Shuffle/Organ Grinder's Swing	1966	$5
❏ 16809	Michelle/Elaine	1965	$6
❏ 16762	Moon Over Naples/Tonight	1965	$6
❏ 16604	One Rose/Lucky Duck	1964	$6
❏ 16647	People/The World I Used to Know	1964	$6
❏ 15506	Petticoats of Portugal/La La Colette	1956	$10
❏ 15661	Sail Along Silvery Moon/Raunchy	1957	$8
❏ 15347	Silver Moon/Baby o' Mine	1955	$15
❏ 15771	Singing Hills/Chimes of Arcady	1958	$8
❏ 16064	Skaters' Waltz/Beg Your Pardon	1960	$8
❏ 16064 [PS]	Skaters' Waltz/Beg Your Pardon	1960	$12
❏ 16670	Song of Peace/Billy's Theme	1964	$6
❏ 17111	St. James Infirmary/Soulitude	1968	$5
❏ 15530	Sugar Blues/Pennsylvania Waltz	1957	$10
❏ 16484	Sukiyaki/Theme from A Summer Place	1963	$6
❏ 15479	Sweetheart Polka/The Left Bank	1956	$10
❏ 15514	Sweet Leilani/Cradle Love Call	1956	$10
❏ 15575	Tell My Love/Ve'Borriquito	1957	$10
❏ 17000	That's Life/Pineapple Market	1967	$5
❏ 16121	Theme from The Apartment/(B-side unknown)	1960	$8
❏ 16985	There Goes My Everything/Sweet Maria	1966	$5
❏ 16686	There's a Star Spangled Banner Waving Somewhere/In the Ocean of Time	1965	$6
❏ 15409	The Shifting, Whispering Sands (Part 1)/The Shifting, Whispering Sands (Part 2)	1955	$15
❏ 16030	The Shifting, Whispering Sands (Part 1)/The Shifting, Whispering Sands (Part 2)	1960	$6
—Reissue			
❏ 15546	The Ship That Never Sailed/Song of the Nairobi Trio	1957	$10
❏ 16133	The Sundowners/Old Cape Cod	1960	$8
❏ 15374	The Waltz You Saved for Me/Billy Vaughn's Boogie	1955	$15
❏ 17229	The Windmills of Your Mind/The Way That I Live	1969	$5
❏ 16841	Things Go Better/James (Steady Does It)	1966	$5
❏ 15454	Till I Waltz Again with You/Sleep	1956	$10
❏ 16957	Tiny Bubbles/Too Many Hot Tacos	1966	$5
❏ 17295	True Grit/Odds and Ends	1969	$5
❏ 15710	Tumbling Tumbleweeds/Trying	1958	$8
❏ 15976	Wabash Blues/Carnival in Paris	1959	$8
❏ 16174	Wheels/Orange Blossom Special	1961	$8
❏ 15491	When the White Lilacs Bloom Again/Spanish Diary	1956	$10

PARAMOUNT

Number	Title	Yr	NM
❏ 0036	Boulevard Saint/Michelle	1970	$4
❏ 0156	Butterfly/To the End of This Day	1972	$4
❏ 0073	Look What They've Done to My Song, Ma/Rooftops of Tokyo	1971	$4
❏ DEP-1072 [PS]	Sail Along Silv'ry Moon	1958	$12
❏ DEP-1072	Sail Along Silv'ry Moon/Jealous//Raunchy/I'm Getting Sentimental Over You	1958	$10

VAUGHN, SHIRLEY

COLUMBIA

Number	Title	Yr	NM
❏ 4-44919	Escape/Society	1969	$200

FAIRMOUNT

Number	Title	Yr	NM
❏ 1023	Doesn't Everybody/Stop and Listen	1967	$100

VAUGHN, YVONNE

DOT

Number	Title	Yr	NM
❏ 16751	Lonely Little Girl/When You Gonna Tell Her About Me	1965	$200

VEACH, GAIL

CHOICE

Number	Title	Yr	NM
❏ 101	Deepest Shade of Blue/(B-side unknown)	1988	$6

PRAIRIE DUST

Number	Title	Yr	NM
❏ 128	Would You Catch Me Baby (If I Fell for You)/(B-side unknown)	1987	$6

VEE, BOBBY

COGNITO

Number	Title	Yr	NM
❏ 010	Tremble On/Always Be Each Other's Best Friend	1981	$5

LIBERTY

Number	Title	Yr	NM
❏ 55854	A Girl I Used to Know/Gone	1965	$8
❏ 56009	Beautiful People/I May Be Gone	1967	$8
❏ 55921	Before You Go/Here Today	1966	$8
❏ 55581	Be True to Yourself/A Letter from Betty	1963	$12
❏ 55581 [PS]	Be True to Yourself/A Letter from Betty	1963	$30
❏ 55530	Charms/Bobby Tomorrow	1963	$15
❏ 55530 [PS]	Charms/Bobby Tomorrow	1963	$30
❏ 55964	Come Back When You Grow Up/Swahili Serenade	1967	$8
❏ S-55964 [S]	Come Back When You Grow Up/Swahili Serenade	1967	$30
—Small hole, plays at 33 1/3 rpm; promo "Audition Record" only			
❏ 55964	Come Back When You Grow Up/That's All There Is to That	1967	$8
❏ 55761	Cross My Heart/This Is the End	1965	$8
❏ 55270	Devil or Angel/Since I Met You Baby	1960	$30
❏ 55270 [PS]	Devil or Angel/Since I Met You Baby	1960	$40
❏ 56057	Do What You Gotta Do/Thank You	1968	$6
❏ 56149	Electric Trains and You/In and Out of Love	1969	$6
❏ 55700	Hickory, Dick and Doc/I Wish You Were Mine Again	1964	$12
❏ 55325	How Many Tears/Baby Face	1961	$20
❏ 55325 [PS]	How Many Tears/Baby Face	1961	$40
❏ 55670	I'll Make You Mine/She's Sorry	1964	$10
❏ 56080	I'm Into Lookin' for Someone to Love Me/Thank You	1968	$6
❏ 55251	Laurie/One Last Kiss	1960	$20
❏ 56124	Let's Call It a Day Girl/I'm Gonna Make It Up to You	1969	$6
❏ 55877	Look at Me Girl/Save a Love	1966	$8
❏ 56014	Maybe Just Today/You're a Big Girl Now	1968	$6
❏ 56014 [PS]	Maybe Just Today/You're a Big Girl Now	1968	$15
❏ 56033	Medley: My Girl-Hey Girl/Just Keep It Up	1968	$6
❏ 55296	More Than I Can Say/Stayin' In	1961	$20
❏ 55296 [PS]	More Than I Can Say/Stayin' In	1961	$40
❏ 55419	Please Don't Ask About Barbara/I Can't Say Goodbye	1962	$20
❏ 55419 [PS]	Please Don't Ask About Barbara/I Can't Say Goodbye	1962	$30
❏ 55479	Punish Her/Someday (When I'm Gone from You)	1962	$30
❏ 55479 [PS]	Punish Her/Someday (When I'm Gone from You)	1962	$40
—With the Crickets			
❏ 55451	Sharing You/In My Baby's Eyes	1962	$20
❏ 55654	Stranger in Your Arms/1963	1963	$10
❏ 55654 [PS]	Stranger in Your Arms/1963	1963	$30
❏ 55208	Suzie Baby/Flyin' High	1959	$30
❏ 56208	Sweet Sweetheart/Rock and Roll Music and You	1970	$6
❏ 55354	Take Good Care of My Baby/Bashful Bob	1961	$20
❏ 55751	(There'll Come a Day When) Ev'ry Little Bit Hurts/Pretend You Don't See Her	1964	$10
❏ 55843	The Story of My Life/High Coin	1965	$8
❏ 56178	The Woman in My Life/No Obligations	1970	$6
❏ 55234	What Do You Want/My Love Loves Me	1959	$30
❏ 55726	Where Is She/How to Make a Farewell	1964	$10

SHADY BROOK

Number	Title	Yr	NM
❏ 45030	It's Good to Be Here/If I Needed You	1976	$5
❏ 45013	Saying Goodbye/(I'm) Lovin' You	1975	$5

SOMA

Number	Title	Yr	NM
❏ 1110	Suzie Baby/Flyin' High	1959	$70

UNITED ARTISTS

Number	Title	Yr	NM
❏ 0025	Come Back When You Grow Up/Beautiful People	1973	$4
—0020 through 0025 are "Silver Spotlight Series" reissues			
❏ 0020	Devil or Angel/Stayin' In	1973	$4
❏ 50755	Signs/Something to Say	1971	$5
❏ 50875	Sweet Sweetheart/Electric Trains and You	1972	$5
❏ XW199	Take Good Care of My Baby/Every Opportunity	1973	$5
—As "Robert Thomas Velline"			
❏ 0022	Take Good Care of My Baby/Please Don't Ask About Barbara	1973	$4
❏ XW1142	Well All Right/Something Has Come Between Us	1978	$5

7-Inch Extended Plays

LIBERTY

Number	Title	Yr	NM
❏ LSX-1013	*Run to Him/Take Good Care of My Baby/Walkin' with My Angel/How Many Tears	1961	$60
❏ LSX-1013 [PS]	Bobby Vee	1961	$60
❏ LSX-1010 [PS]	Bobby Vee's Hits	1960	$60
❏ LSX-1010	(contents unknown)	1960	$60
❏ LSX-1006 [PS]	Devil or Angel	1960	$60
❏ LSX-1006	Devil or Angel/One Last Kiss//What Do You Want/My Love Loves Me	1960	$60

VEERS, RUSS

TREND

Number	Title	Yr	NM
❏ 30010	Warm As Toast/The Answer	1958	$500

VEGA, SUZANNE

A&M

Number	Title	Yr	NM
❏ 2988	Gypsy/Left of Center	1987	$3
❏ 2988 [PS]	Gypsy/Left of Center	1987	$60
❏ 2834	Left of Center/Small Blue Thing	1986	$3
❏ 2937	Luka/Night Vision	1987	$3
❏ 2937 [PS]	Luka/Night Vision	1987	$4
❏ 2960	Solitude Standing/Tom's Diner	1987	$3
❏ 2960 [PS]	Solitude Standing/Tom's Diner	1987	$4

VEGA, TATA

QWEST

Number	Title	Yr	NM
❏ 7-28754	Miss Celie's Blues (Sister)/Celie Shaves Mr./Scarification Contest	1986	$5
❏ 7-28754 [PS]	Miss Celie's Blues (Sister)/Celie Shaves Mr./Scarification Contest	1986	$6
—The Color Purple" picture sleeve			

TAMLA

Number	Title	Yr	NM
❏ 54271	Full Speed Ahead/Just As Long As There Is You	1976	$6
❏ 54299	I Just Keep Thinking About You Baby/Music in My Heart	1979	$6
❏ 54304	I Need You Now/In the Morning	1979	$30

VEGAS, PAT AND LOLLY

Also see REDBONE.

APOGEE

Number	Title	Yr	NM
❏ 101	Don't You Remember/The Robot Walk	1964	$20

MERCURY

Number	Title	Yr	NM
❏ 72509	Walk On (Right Out of My Life)/Let's Get It On	1965	$15

REPRISE

Number	Title	Yr	NM
❏ 20199	Boom Boom/Two Figures (On the Wedding Cake)	1963	$30

VEJTABLES, THE

AUTUMN

Number	Title	Yr	NM
❏ 15	I Still Love You/Anything	1965	$15
❏ 23	The Last Thing on My Mind/Mansion of Texas	1965	$15

UPTOWN

Number	Title	Yr	NM
❏ 741	Feel the Music/Shadows	1967	$10

VEL-TONES, THE

COY

Number	Title	Yr	NM
❏ 101	Cal's Tune/Playboy	1959	$2000
—VG 1000; VG+ 1500			

GOLDWAX

Number	Title	Yr	NM
❏ 301	Darling/I Do	1966	$20

JIN

Number	Title	Yr	NM
❏ 107	Lover Blues/Take a Ride	1959	$50

KAPP

Number	Title	Yr	NM
❏ 268	Cal's Tune/Playboy	1959	$125

MERCURY

Number	Title	Yr	NM
❏ 71526	Fool in Love/Someday	1959	$40

SATELLITE

Number	Title	Yr	NM
❏ 100	Fool in Love/Someday	1959	$125

VEL

Number	Title	Yr	NM
❏ 9178	Broken Heart/Please Say You'll Be True	1960	$1500

WEDGE

Number	Title	Yr	NM
❏ 1013	My Dear/I Want to Know	1964	$200

VELAIRES, THE

JAMIE

Number	Title	Yr	NM
❏ 1211	It's Almost Tomorrow/Ubangi Stomp	1962	$20
❏ 1223	Memory Tree/Don't Wake Me Up	1962	$20
❏ 1203	Sticks and Stones/Dream	1961	$20

Number	Title	Yr	NM
VELEZ, MARTHA			
MCA			
❏ 41244	What Becomes of the Brokenhearted/Wild Night in Paradise	1980	$4
POLYDOR			
❏ 14158	Magic in His Hands/Black Rose	1973	$6
SIRE			
❏ 727	Disco Night/Come On In	1976	$5
❏ 722	Mockingbird/Aggravation	1975	$5
—With Pete Wingfield			
❏ 735	Money Man/There You Are	1976	$5
❏ 4111	Tell Mama/Swamp Man	1969	$10
❏ 1010	When You Were Beautiful/Up to You	1977	$5
VELLS, THE			
MEL-O-DY			
❏ 103	There He Is At My Door/You'll Never Cherish a Love So True	1962	$125
VELONS, THE			
BJM			
❏ 6568	Summer Love/Why Don't You Write	1965	$30
❏ 6569	That's What Love Can Do/That's All Right	1965	$30
BLAST			
❏ 216	Shelly/From the Chapel	1964	$125
VELOURS, THE			
CUB			
❏ 9029	Blue Velvet/Tired of Your Rock and Rollin'	1959	$30
❏ 9014	Crazy Love/I'll Never Smile Again	1958	$30
END			
❏ 1090	Lover Come Back/The Lonely One	1961	$30
GOLDISC			
❏ 3012	Daddy Warbucks/Sweet Sixteen	1960	$30
GONE			
❏ 5092	Can I Come Over Tonight/Where There's a Will (There's a Way)	1960	$30
MGM			
❏ 13780	Don't Pity Me/I'm Gonna Change	1967	$40
ONYX			
❏ 512	Can I Come Over Tonight/Where There's a Will (There's a Way)	1957	$200
❏ 501	My Love Come Back/Honey Drop	1956	$200
❏ 515	This Could Be the Night/Hands Across the Table	1957	$120
❏ 508	What You Do to Me/Romeo	1957	$800
RONA			
❏ 010	Woman for Me/(B-side unknown)	1966	$30
STUDO			
❏ 9902	I Promise/Little Sweetheart	1959	$60
VELVATONES, THE			
NU KAT			
❏ 110	Impossible/I'm Leaving Home	1959	$60
VELVELETTES, THE			
I.P.G.			
❏ 1002	There He Goes/That's the Reason Why	1963	$125
SOUL			
❏ 35025	These Things Will Keep Me Loving You/Since You've Been Loving Me	1966	$30
V.I.P.			
❏ 25021	A Bird in the Hand (Is Worth Two in the Bush)/(B-side unknown)	1965	$800
❏ 25030	A Bird in the Hand (Is Worth Two in the Bush)/Since You've Been Loving Me	1965	$30
❏ 25013	He Was Really Sayin' Somethin'/Throw a Farewell Kiss	1965	$30
❏ 25017	I'm the Exception to the Rule/Lonely, Lonely Girl Am I	1965	$30
❏ 25034	These Things Will Keep Me Loving You/Since You've Been Loving Me	1966	$40

Number	Title	Yr	NM
VELVET, JIMMY			
ABC-PARAMOUNT			
❏ 10528	To the Aisle/Lonely, Lonely Night	1964	$30
❏ 10488	We Belong Together/History of Love	1963	$30
BELL			
❏ 692	Let Me Keep Your Love/Woman in Bloom	1967	$8
CAMEO			
❏ 464	Take Me Tonight/Young Hearts	1967	$30
CORREC-TONE			
❏ 102	When I Needed You/Bouquet of Flowers	1962	$125
—As "James Velvet"; the Supremes sing backup			
CUB			
❏ 9100	Sometimes at Night/Look at Me	1961	$20
❏ 9111	When I Needed You/Bouquet of Flowers	1962	$20
DIVISION			
❏ 102	Sometimes at Night/Look at Me	1961	$30
PHILIPS			
❏ 40285	It's Almost Tomorrow/Blue Eyes (Don't Run Away)	1965	$30
❏ 40314	I Won't Be Back This Year/Young Hearts	1965	$30
ROYAL AMERICAN			
❏ 291	Blue Velvet/Missing You	1969	$8
❏ 286	It's You/A Woman	1968	$8
TOLLIE			
❏ 9037	Teen Angel/Mission Bell	1964	$20
UNITED ARTISTS			
❏ 50272	Good Good Lovin'/Heart Breakin' Misery	1968	$30
VELVET			
❏ 201	We Belong Together/You're Mine	1963	$125
—As "Jimmy Velvit"			
VELVET TONE			
❏ 102	It's Almost Tomorrow/Young Hearts	1965	$40
VELVET KEYS, THE			
KING			
❏ 5109	Don't Take My Picture, Take Me/The Truth About Youth	1958	$100
❏ 5090	My Baby's Gone/Let's Stay After School	1957	$100
VELVET MONKEYS			
BONA FIDE			
❏ 7002	Colors Part 1/Colors Part 2	1985	$6
❏ 7002 [PS]	Colors Part 1/Colors Part 2	1985	$6
VELVET SOUNDS, THE			
COSMOPOLITAN			
❏ 530/531	Hanging Up Christmas Stockings/Sing A Song Of Christmas Cheer	1953	$500
❏ 105/106	Pretty Darling/Who'll Take My Place	1953	$400
❏ 100/101	Silver Star/The Devil and the Stocker	1953	$600
VELVET UNDERGROUND, THE			
Also see JOHN CALE; LOU REED; MAUREEN TUCKER; NICO.			
COTILLION			
❏ 44107 [DJ]	Who Loves the Sun (mono/stereo)	1971	$125
—Promo copy; white label; three different label variations exist, each of equal value			
❏ 44107	Who Loves the Sun/Oh, Sweet Nothin'	1971	$1200
—Stock copy; red--orange label			
MGM			
❏ 14057 [DJ]	What Goes On/Jesus	1969	$200
—Promo copy; yellow label			
VERVE			
❏ 10427	All Tomorrow's Parties/I'll Be Your Mirror	1966	$600
—Stock copy; dark blue label			
❏ 10427 [DJ]	All Tomorrow's Parties/I'll Be Your Mirror	1966	$300
—Promo copy; light blue label			
❏ 10427 [PS]	All Tomorrow's Parties/I'll Be Your Mirror	1966	$8000
❏ 10466	Femme Fatale/Sunday Morning	1966	$400
—Stock copy; dark blue label			
❏ 10466 [DJ]	Femme Fatale/Sunday Morning	1966	$300

Number	Title	Yr	NM
—Promo copy; light blue label			
❏ 10560	White Light/White Heat//Here She Comes Now	1967	$300
—Stock copy; dark blue label			
❏ 10560 [DJ]	White Light/White Heat//I Heard Her Call My Name	1967	$200
—Promo copy; light blue label			
VELVETEENS, THE			
GOLDEN ARTISTS			
❏ 614	I Feel Sorry for You Baby/Ching Bam Bah	1965	$10
LAURIE			
❏ 3126	I Thank You/Meant to Be	1962	$20
STARK			
❏ 105	I Thank You/Meant to Be	1962	$30
❏ 101	Please Holy Father/Baby Baby	1961	$60
—Original title of A-side			
❏ 101	Teen Prayer/Baby Baby	1961	$30
—Slightly altered A-side title			
❏ 101	The Teen Prayer/Baby Baby	1961	$40
—New A-side title			
VELVETEERS, THE			
SPITFIRE			
❏ 15	Tell Me You're Mine/Boo Wacka Boo	1956	$4000
—VG 2000; VG+ 3000			
VELVETIERS, THE			
RIC			
❏ 958	Oh Baby/Feelin' Right Saturday Night	1958	$300
VELVETONES, THE (1)			
ALADDIN			
❏ 3372	Glory of Love/I Love Her So	1957	$200
❏ 3391	I Found My Love/Melody of Love	1957	$200
❏ 3463	My Every Thought/Little Girl I Love You So	1960	$300
D			
❏ 1049	Come Back/Penalty of Love	1959	$200
❏ 1072	Worried Over You/Space Man	1959	$125
DEB			
❏ 1008	Stars of Wonder/Who Took My Girl	1959	$200
IMPERIAL			
❏ 66020	The Glory of Love/I Found My Love	1964	$20
❏ 5878	The Glory of Love/I Love Her So	1962	$40
VELVETONES, THE (2)			
ASCOT			
❏ 2117	I Want Him So Bad/Yes I Will	1962	$20
❏ 2126	Starry Eyed/I'm Ashamed	1963	$20
VELVETONES, THE (3)			
GARP			
❏ 102	Mister X/(B-side unknown)	1965	$70
—Black vinyl			
❏ 102	Mister X/(B-side unknown)	1965	$120
—Red vinyl			
VELVETONES, THE (4)			
VERVE			
❏ 10514	What Can the Matter Be/Hairy Lumpty Bump	1967	$15
VELVETONES, THE (U)			
GLENN			
❏ 309	Doheny Run/Static	1965	$40
VELVET			
❏ 101	Doheny Run/Static	1965	$75

Number	Title	Yr	NM

VELVETS, THE (1)
MONUMENT

Number	Title	Yr	NM
❏ 961	Baby the Magic Is Gone/ Let the Fool Kiss You	1966	$20
❏ 810	Crying in the Chapel/Dawn	1963	$30
❏ 861	If/Let the Fool Kiss You	1964	$30
❏ 448	Lana/Laugh	1961	$40
❏ 464	Let the Good Times Roll/The Lights Go On, The Lights Go Off	1962	$30
❏ 435	That Lucky Old Sun/ Time and Again	1961	$40
❏ 458	The Love Express/Don't Let Him Take My Baby	1962	$30
❏ 441	Tonight (Could Be the Night)/Spring Fever	1961	$40

VELVETS, THE (2)
FURY

Number	Title	Yr	NM
❏ 1012	I-I-I (Love You So-So-So)/ Dance Honey Dance	1958	$60

PILGRIM

Number	Title	Yr	NM
❏ 706	I/At Last	1956	$60
❏ 710	Tell Her/I Cried	1956	$60

RED ROBIN

Number	Title	Yr	NM
❏ 122	I/At Last	1953	$200
❏ 127	Tell Her/I Cried	1954	$200
❏ 120	They Tried/She's Gotta Grin	1953	$200

VELVETS, THE (U)
20TH FOX

Number	Title	Yr	NM
❏ 165	Happy Days Are Here Again/ If I Could Be with You	1959	$30

PLAID

Number	Title	Yr	NM
❏ 101	Everybody Knows/ Hand Jivin' Baby	1959	$100

VENEERS, THE
PRINCETON

Number	Title	Yr	NM
❏ 102	Believe Me (My Angel)/I	1960	$50

TREYCO

Number	Title	Yr	NM
❏ 402	With All My Love/ Recipe of Love	1963	$20

VENET, NICK
DECCA

Number	Title	Yr	NM
❏ 31939	Theme from "Out of Sight"/Camp Side	1966	$10

IMPERIAL

Number	Title	Yr	NM
❏ 5522	Love In Be-Bop Time/ Honey Baby	1958	$30

VENTRILLS, THE
PARKWAY

Number	Title	Yr	NM
❏ 141	Alone in the Night/Confusion	1967	$15

VENTURES, THE
BLUE HORIZON

Number	Title	Yr	NM
❏ 102	Hold Me, Thrill Me, Kiss Me/No Next Time	1960	$200

— As "Scott Douglas and the Venture Quintet"

Number	Title	Yr	NM
❏ 101	Walk-Don't Run/Home	1960	$2500

DOLTON

Number	Title	Yr	NM
❏ 321	Arabesque/Ginza Lights	1966	$15
❏ 47	Blue Moon/Lady of Spain	1961	$30
❏ 320	Blue Star/Comin' Home Baby	1966	$15
❏ 320 [PS]	Blue Star/Comin' Home Baby	1966	$30
❏ 303	Diamond Head/Lonely Girl	1965	$15
❏ 68	El Cumbanchero/ Skip To M'Limbo	1963	$20
❏ 94	Fugitive/Scratchin'	1964	$20
❏ 323	Green Hornet Theme/ Fuzzy and Wild	1966	$15
❏ 323 [PS]	Green Hornet Theme/ Fuzzy and Wild	1966	$40
❏ 55	Instant Mashed/My Bonnie	1962	$30
❏ 311	La Bomba/Gemini	1965	$15
❏ 60	Lolita Ya-Ya/Lucille	1962	$30
❏ 41	Lullaby of the Leaves/Ginchy	1961	$30
❏ 306	Pedal Pusher/The Swingin' Creeper	1965	$15
❏ 325	Penetration/Wild Thing	1966	$15
❏ 325 [PS]	Penetration/Wild Thing	1966	$30
❏ 28	Perfidia/No Trespassing	1960	$30
❏ 28 [PS]	Perfidia/No Trespassing	1960	$60
❏ 316	Secret Agent Man/00-711	1966	$15
❏ 300	Slaughter on Tenth Avenue/Rap City	1964	$15
❏ 300 [PS]	Slaughter on Tenth Avenue/Rap City	1964	$30
❏ 312	Sleigh Ride/Snow Flakes	1965	$20
❏ 308	Ten Seconds to Heaven/ Bird Rockers	1965	$15
❏ 67	The 2,000 Pound Bee (Part 1)/The 2,000 Pound Bee (Part 2)	1962	$30
❏ 44	(Theme from) Silver City/Bluer Than Blue	1961	$30

Number	Title	Yr	NM
❏ 327	Theme from "The Wild Angels"/Kickstand	1967	$15
❏ 85	The Savage/The Chase	1963	$20
❏ 96	Walk... Don't Run '64/ The Cruel Sea	1964	$20
❏ 96 [PS]	Walk... Don't Run '64/ The Cruel Sea	1964	$40
❏ 25	Walk -- Don't Run/Home	1960	$30
❏ 25X	Walk -- Don't Run/ The McCoy	1960	$30

LIBERTY

Number	Title	Yr	NM
❏ 56153	Expo Seven-O/Swan Lake	1970	$6
❏ 56019	Flights of Fantasy/Vibrations	1968	$6
❏ 56068	Hawaii Five-O/Soul Breeze	1968	$8
❏ 56007	On the Road/Mirrors and Shadows	1967	$8
❏ 56189	Storefront Lawyers (Theme)/ Kern County Line	1970	$6
❏ 55967	Strawberry Fields Forever/ Endless Dream	1967	$8
❏ 56115	Theme from A Summer Place/A Summer Love	1969	$6
❏ 55977	Theme from "Endless Summer"/Strawberry Fields Forever	1967	$8
❏ 56169	The Wanderer/ The Mercenary	1970	$6
❏ 56044	Walk Don't Run-Land of 1000 Dances/Too Young to Know My Mind	1968	$6

TRIDEX

Number	Title	Yr	NM
❏ 501	Surfin' and Spyin'/ Rumble at Newport	1981	$5

— A-side with Charlotte Caffey and Jane Wiedlin of the Go-Go's, who did their own version on an early single

Number	Title	Yr	NM
❏ 501 [PS]	Surfin' and Spyin'/ Rumble at Newport	1981	$5

UNITED ARTISTS

Number	Title	Yr	NM
❏ XW333	Also Sprach Zarathustra (2001)/The Cisco Kid	1973	$6
❏ 50903	Beethoven's Sonata in C# Minor/Peter and the Wolf	1972	$6
❏ 0052	Hawaii Five-O/Walk--Don't Run '64	1973	$4
❏ 50925	Honky Tonk (Part 1)/ Honky Tonk (Part 2)	1972	$6
❏ 50800	Indian Sun/Squaw Man	1971	$6
❏ 50800 [PS]	Indian Sun/Squaw Man	1971	$8
❏ 50989	Last Night/Ram-Bunk-Shush	1972	$6
❏ XW207	Last Tango in Paris/ Prima Vera	1973	$6
❏ XW369	Main Theme from The Young and the Restless/Eloise	1973	$6
❏ XW392	Main Theme from The Young and the Restless/Eloise	1974	$6
❏ XW392 [PS]	Main Theme from The Young and the Restless/Eloise	1974	$8
❏ XW784	Moonlight Serenade (Part 1)/ Moonlight Serenade (Part 2)	1976	$8

— As "The New Ventures"

Number	Title	Yr	NM
❏ 0051	Perfidia/Telstar	1973	$4
❏ XW277	Skylab/The Little People	1973	$6
❏ XW687	Superstar Revue (Part 1)/ Superstar Revue (Part 2)	1975	$6
❏ XW578	Theme from "Airport 1975"/The Man with the Golden Gun	1974	$6
❏ XW942	Theme from "Charlie's Angels"/Theme from "Starsky and Hutch"	1977	$8
❏ 50851	Theme from "Shaft"/Tight Fit	1971	$6
❏ XW1100	Walk Don't Run '77/ Amanda's Theme	1977	$6
❏ 0050	Walk--Don't Run/ Ram-Bunk-Shush	1973	$4

— 0050, 0051 and 0052 are "Silver Spotlight Series" reissues

Number	Title	Yr	NM
❏ XW1161	Wipe Out/Nadia's Theme	1978	$4

— Reissue

7-Inch Extended Plays
DOLTON

Number	Title	Yr	NM
❏ 4-8031	House of the Rising Sun/ Night Train/Rap City// Walk Don't Run '64/One Mint Julep/The Creeper	1964	$20

— Jukebox single, small hole, plays at 33 1/3 rpm

Number	Title	Yr	NM
❏ BEP-503 [PS]	Walk -- Don't Run	1960	$100
❏ 4-8031 [PS]	Walk Don't Run '64	1964	$20
❏ BEP-503	Walk -- Don't Run/ The McCoy//Honky Tonk/Raunchy	1960	$100

VENUS, VIK
BUDDAH

Number	Title	Yr	NM
❏ 118	Moonflight/Everybody's On Strike	1969	$10
❏ 138	Moon Jack/Moon Welcome	1969	$8

VERA, BILLY, AND JUDY CLAY
ATLANTIC

Number	Title	Yr	NM
❏ 2480	Country Girl -- City Man/So Good	1968	$8
❏ 2515	Ever Since/When Do We Go	1968	$8

Number	Title	Yr	NM
❏ 2445	Storybook Children/ Really Together	1967	$8
❏ 2654	Tell It Like It Is/Reaching for the Moon	1969	$6

VERA, BILLY
ALFA

Number	Title	Yr	NM
❏ 7005	At This Moment/ Someone Will School You, Someone Will Cool You	1981	$5
❏ 7005 [PS]	At This Moment/ Someone Will School You, Someone Will Cool You	1981	$5

— As "Billy and the Beaters"

Number	Title	Yr	NM
❏ 7002	I Can Take Care of Myself/ Corner of the Night	1981	$4

— As "Billy and the Beaters"

Number	Title	Yr	NM
❏ 7012	Millie, Make Me Some Chili/ Someone Will School You, Someone Will Cool You	1981	$4

— As "Billy and the Beaters"

Number	Title	Yr	NM
❏ 7020	We Got It All/You Own It	1982	$4

ATLANTIC

Number	Title	Yr	NM
❏ 2628	Bible Salesman/Are You Coming to My Party	1969	$6
❏ 2555	I've Been Loving You Too Long/Are You Coming to My Party	1968	$8
❏ 2700	I've Never Been Loved Like This Before/J.W.'s Dream	1970	$6
❏ 2526	With Pen in Hand/ Good Morning Blues	1968	$8

CAPITOL

Number	Title	Yr	NM
❏ B-44149	Between Like and Love/Heart Be Still	1988	$3
❏ B-44149 [PS]	Between Like and Love/Heart Be Still	1988	$3

MACOLA

Number	Title	Yr	NM
❏ 8912	She Ain't Johnnie/ My Girl Josephine	1987	$4

MIDLAND INT'L.

Number	Title	Yr	NM
❏ MB-10639	Back Door Man/Run and Tell the People	1976	$5
❏ MB-11042	I've Had Enough/Something Like Nothing Before	1977	$5
❏ MB-10909	Private Clown/Billy, Meet Your Son	1977	$5
❏ 72014	She Ain't Johnnie/I've Had Enough	1977	$5

RHINO

Number	Title	Yr	NM
❏ 74403	At This Moment/I Can Take Care of Myself	1986	$5
❏ 74403	At This Moment/ Peanut Butter	1986	$3
❏ 74407	Hopeless Romantic/ (B-side unknown)	1987	$3
❏ 74404	I Can Take Care of Myself/ Millie, Make Some Chili	1987	$3
❏ 74404 [PS]	I Can Take Care of Myself/ Millie, Make Some Chili	1987	$5

RUST

Number	Title	Yr	NM
❏ 5051	My Heart Cries/All My Love	1962	$30

VERA, RICKY, AND STEVE ALLEN
CORAL

Number	Title	Yr	NM
❏ 61098	How Can Santa Come to Puerto Rico/Can I Wait Up for Santa Claus	1953	$40

VERNE, LARRY
ERA

Number	Title	Yr	NM
❏ 3044	Abdul's Party/Tubby Tilly	1961	$15
❏ 3065	Beatnik/Speck	1961	$15
❏ 3051	Charlie the Bat/Pow, Right in the Kisser	1961	$15
❏ 3075	Hoo-Ha/I'm a Brave Little Soldier	1962	$15
❏ 3034	Mister Livingston/ Roller Coaster	1960	$15
❏ 3034 [PS]	Mister Livingston/ Roller Coaster	1960	$30
❏ 3024	Mr. Custer/Okefenokee Two-Step	1960	$20
❏ 3091	The Coward Who Won the West/The Porcupine Patrol	1962	$15

VERNON GIRLS, THE
CHALLENGE

Number	Title	Yr	NM
❏ 59261	Only You Can Do It/ Stupid Little Girl	1964	$10
❏ 59234	We Love the Beatles/ Hey Lover Boy	1964	$40

VERNON, KENNY
CAPITOL

Number	Title	Yr	NM
❏ 3925	Another Word for You/ Your Steppin' Stone	1974	$5
❏ 3430	Every Day with You/I Bought the Shoes	1972	$5
❏ 3506	Feel So Fine/Would You Settle for Roses	1973	$5
❏ 3590	Lady/What Kind of Mood (Will She Be In Tonight)	1973	$5

Number	Title	Yr	NM
❏ 3691	Loversville/Woman, I Just Want to Love You More	1973	$5
❏ 3331	That'll Be the Day/I'd Go Right Back Again	1972	$5
❏ 3785	What Was Your Name Again?/Have I Ever Lied to You	1973	$5
CARAVAN			
❏ 123	It Makes Me Happy (To Know You Make Me Blue)/Too Much Loving Turned Her Bad	1966	$10
CHART			
❏ 5075	Country Music Circus/The Part Inbetween	1970	$6
❏ 1050	Free Born Man/I'll Tell You Where to Go	1968	$8
❏ 5038	Mississippi Woman/The Bridge Washed Out	1969	$6
❏ 1031	Oh Why Not Tonight/Woman, Won't You Make Up Your Mind	1968	$8
❏ 5015	The Ba-Ba Song/Raining On a Sunny Day with You	1969	$6
EPIC			
❏ 5-10192	Ain't That a Shame/Miles and Miles	1967	$8

VERONICA

PHIL SPECTOR

Number	Title	Yr	NM
❏ 1	So Young/Larry L.	1964	$200
❏ 2	Why Can't They Let Us Fall in Love/Chubby Danny D	1964	$600
— *Note slightly different A-side title*			
❏ 2	Why Don't They Let Us Fall in Love/Chubby Danny D	1964	$200

VERSATILES, THE

ATLANTIC

Number	Title	Yr	NM
❏ 2004	Passing By/Crying	1958	$50
PEACOCK			
❏ 1910	White Cliffs of Dover/Just Words	1963	$40
RAMCO			
❏ 3717	Blue Feeling/Just Pretending	1962	$200
RO-CAL			
❏ 1002	I'll Whisper in Your Ear/Lundee Dundee	1960	$125
SEA CREST			
❏ 6001	Lonely Boy/Moon Dawg	1964	$30

VERSATONES, THE

ALL STAR

Number	Title	Yr	NM
❏ 501	Tight Skirt and Sweater/Bila	1958	$50
ATLANTIC			
❏ 2211	Tight Skirt and Sweater/Bila	1963	$30
FENWAY			
❏ 7001	Tight Skirt and Sweater/Bila	1960	$30
RCA VICTOR			
❏ 47-6976	Lovely Teenage Girl/Bikini Baby	1957	$20
❏ 47-6917	Wait for Me/De Obeah Man	1957	$20

VERTIGO

AMPHETAMINE REPTILE

Number	Title	Yr	NM
❏ SCALE21	Bad Syd/Going to Pieces	1989	$20
❏ SCALE21 [PS]	Bad Syd/Going to Pieces	1989	$20
SKID MARK			
❏ SMT 004	Two Lives//Front End Loader/Phil 105	1988	$20
❏ SMT 004 [PS]	Two Lives//Front End Loader/Phil 105	1988	$60
— *First sleeve is a numbered edition of 300 -- all numbered #1!*			
❏ SMT 004 [PS]	Two Lives//Front End Loader/Phil 105	1988	$20
— *Second sleeve is unnumbered*			

VERTUES FOUR, THE

SEA SEVEN

Number	Title	Yr	NM
❏ 22	Angel Baby/Uphill, Downhill	1963	$50

VESPE, LITTLE JOE

PARKWAY

Number	Title	Yr	NM
❏ 877	Caravan/Conservative Twist	1963	$10

VESPERS, THE

SWAN

Number	Title	Yr	NM
❏ 4156	Cupid/When I Walk with My Angel	1963	$50

VESTELLES, THE

DECCA

Number	Title	Yr	NM
❏ 9-30733	Come Home/Ditta Wa Do	1958	$40

VETTES, THE

MGM

Number	Title	Yr	NM
❏ 13186	Little Ford Ragtop/Happy Hodaddy (With Ragtop Caddy)	1963	$60

VIBES, THE (1)

ABC-PARAMOUNT

Number	Title	Yr	NM
❏ 9810	Darling/Come Back Baby	1957	$60

VIBES, THE (2)

AFTER HOURS

Number	Title	Yr	NM
❏ 105	Stop Torturing Me/Stop Jibing, Baby	1954	$2000
CHARIOT			
❏ 105	Stop Torturing Me/Stop Jibing, Baby	1954	$1500

VIBES, THE (3)

ALLIED

Number	Title	Yr	NM
❏ 10007	Misunderstood/Let the Old Folks Talk	1959	$50
❏ 10006	What's Her Name/You Are	1958	$70

VIBES, THE (4)

PERSPECTIVE

Number	Title	Yr	NM
❏ 5858	Pretty Baby (I Saw You Last Night)/Crying for You	1960	$125

VIBRA-SONICS, THE

IDEAL

Number	Title	Yr	NM
❏ 94874	Thunder Storm/Drag Race	1964	$60

VIBRANAIRES, THE

AFTER HOURS

Number	Title	Yr	NM
❏ 103	Doll Face/Ooh, I Feel So Good	1954	$2500
CHARIOT			
❏ 103	Doll Face/Ooh, I Feel So Good	1954	$2000

VIBRATIONS, THE

ATLANTIC

Number	Title	Yr	NM
❏ 2204	Between Hello and Goodbye/Lonesome Little Lonely Girl	1963	$15
❏ 2221	My Girl Sloopy/Daddy Woo-Woo	1964	$15
BET			
❏ 1	So Blue/Love Me Like You Should	1960	$125
CHECKER			
❏ 987	All My Love Belongs to You/Stop Right Now	1961	$50
❏ 1061	Dancing Danny/(Instrumental)	1963	$20
❏ 967	Doing the Slop/So Little Time	1961	$30
❏ 982	Don't Say Goodbye/Stranded in the Jungle	1961	$30
❏ 961	Feel So Bad/Cave Man	1960	$30
❏ 1022	Hamburgers on a Bun/If He Don't	1962	$20
❏ 990	Let's Pony Again/What Made You Change Your Mind	1961	$30
❏ 1002	Over the Rainbow/Oh, Cindy	1962	$20
❏ 1038	Since I Fell for You/May the Best Man Win	1963	$20
❏ 954	So Blue/Love Me Like You Should	1960	$40
❏ 974	The Continental/The Junkeroo	1961	$30
❏ 969	The Watusi/Wallflower	1961	$30
CHESS			
❏ 2151	Shake It Up/Make It Last	1974	$6
EPIC			
❏ 10418	I Took an Overdose/Because You're Mine	1968	$30
MANDALA			
❏ 2511	Ain't No Greens in Harlem/Wind-Up Toy	1972	$6
❏ 2514	Man Overboard/(B-side unknown)	1972	$6
NEPTUNE			
❏ 19	Expressway to Your Heart/Who's Gonna Help Me Now	1969	$8
❏ 21	Smoke Signals/Who's Gonna Help Me Now	1970	$8
OKEH			
❏ 7257	And I Love Her/Soul a-Go-Go	1966	$10
❏ 7241	Canadian Sunset/The Story of a Starry Night	1966	$10
❏ 7220	End Up Crying/Ain't Love That Way	1965	$15
❏ 7249	Forgive and Forget/Gonna Get Along Without You Now	1966	$10
❏ 7212	Hello Happiness/Keep On Keeping On	1965	$15

Number	Title	Yr	NM
❏ 7311	Love in Them There Hills/Remember the Rain	1968	$10
❏ 7230	Misty/Finding Out the Hard Way	1965	$15
❏ 7276	Pick Me/You Better Beware	1967	$10
❏ 7205	Sloop Dance/Watusi Time	1964	$15
❏ 7228	Talkin' 'Bout Love/If You Only Knew	1965	$15
❏ 7297	Together/Come To Yourself	1967	$10

VICEROYS, THE (1)

ALADDIN

Number	Title	Yr	NM
❏ 3273	Please, Baby, Please/I'm Yours As Long As I Live	1955	$400

VICEROYS, THE (2)

BETHLEHEM

Number	Title	Yr	NM
❏ 3045	Seagrams/Moasin'	1962	$30
— *Original A-side title*			
❏ 3045	Sea Green/Moasin'	1962	$30
❏ 3070	The Fox/Buzz Bomb	1963	$30
— *Original A-side title*			

VICEROYS, THE (3)

BOLO

Number	Title	Yr	NM
❏ 750	Bacon Fat/Until	1965	$12
❏ 743	Dartell Stomp/Granny's Medley	1964	$12
❏ 739	Goin' Back to Granny's/Get Set	1963	$15
❏ 736	Granny's Pad/Blues Bouquet	1962	$15
❏ 749	Please, Please, Please/Tiger Shark	1964	$10
❏ 754	That Sound/Tired of Waiting for You	1965	$12
DOT			
❏ 16456	Granny's Pad/Blues Bouquet	1963	$8

VICEROYS, THE (4)

LITTLE STAR

Number	Title	Yr	NM
❏ 107	I'm So Sorry (It's Ending with You)/Uncle Sam Needs You	1961	$200
ORIGINAL SOUND			
❏ 15	Dreamy Eyes/Ball 'N' Chain	1961	$50
RAMCO			
❏ 3715	My Heart/I Need Your Love So Bad	1962	$4000
— *VG 2000; VG+ 3000*			
SMASH			
❏ 1716	I'm So Sorry (It's Ending with You)/Uncle Sam Needs You	1961	$30

VICEROYS, THE (U)

E'DEN

Number	Title	Yr	NM
❏ 9001	Don't Let Go/Down Beat Blues	1962	$15
IMPERIAL			
❏ 66058	Death of an Angel/Earth Angel	1964	$15

VICKERY, MACK

BOONE

Number	Title	Yr	NM
❏ 1073	Searching for a Baby/Jailbirds Can't Fly	1968	$10
MCA			
❏ 40291	Cardboard Pillow/Hold What You've Got	1974	$6
— *As "Atlanta James*			
❏ 40435	Honky Tonkin' Ladies/Meet Me at the Spring Annie	1975	$6
— *As "Atlanta James*			
❏ 40386	I'm the Only Hell My Mama Ever Raised/Down on the Levee	1975	$6
— *As "Atlanta James*			
❏ 40233	That Kind of Fool/Starting All Over Again	1974	$6
— *As "Atlanta James*			
MEGA			
❏ 0013	Meat Man/The Farther I Let Her Go	1970	$8
— *As "Atlanta James*			
PLAYBOY			
❏ 5814	Here's to the Horses/When It Counted, You Could Never Count on Me	1977	$5
❏ 5800	Ishabilly/Think It Over	1977	$5

VICTORIALS, THE

IMPERIAL

Number	Title	Yr	NM
❏ 5398	I Get That Feeling/The Prettiest Girl in the World	1956	$60

Number	Title	Yr	NM

VICTORIANS, THE

ARNOLD
❏ 571	Move In a Little Closer/Lovin'	1963	$30

BANG
| ❏ 550 | Merry-Go-Round/Wasn't the Summer Short | 1967 | $20 |

LIBERTY
❏ 55574	Climb Every Mountain/What Makes Little Girls Cry	1963	$30
❏ 55693	Happy Birthday Blues/Oh What a Night for Love	1964	$20
❏ 55728	If I Loved You/The Monkey Stroll	1964	$20
❏ 55656	The Monkey Stroll/You're Invited to a Party	1964	$20

REPRISE
| ❏ 0434 | I Saw My Girl/Baby Toys | 1965 | $20 |

SAXONY
| ❏ 103 | Heartbreaking Moon/I'm Rollin' | 1956 | $500 |

SELMA
| ❏ 1002 | Wedding Bells/Please Say You Do | 1956 | $300 |

VICTORY FIVE, THE

TERP
| ❏ 101 | I Never Knew/Swing Low | 1958 | $600 |
— All copies on colored vinyl

VIDALTONES, THE

JOSIE
| ❏ 900 | Forever/Someone to Love | 1962 | $50 |

VIDELS, THE

EARLY
| ❏ 702 | I Wish/Blow, Winds, Blow | 1960 | $400 |

JDS
| ❏ 5004 | Mr. Lonely/I'll Forget You | 1960 | $40 |
— Gray label
| ❏ 5004 | Mr. Lonely/I'll Forget You | 1960 | $30 |
— Multicolor label
| ❏ 5005 | She's Not Coming Home/Now That Summer Is Here | 1960 | $40 |
— Gray label
| ❏ 5005 | She's Not Coming Home/Now That Summer Is Here | 1960 | $30 |
— Multicolor label

KAPP
| ❏ 405 | A Letter from Ann/This Year's Mister New | 1961 | $50 |
| ❏ 361 | Streets of Love/I'll Keep On Waiting | 1960 | $30 |

MEDIEVAL
| ❏ 203 | Be My Girl/A Place in Your Heart | 1961 | $20 |

MUSICNOTE
| ❏ 117 | We Belong Together/It's All Over | 1963 | $60 |

RHODY
| ❏ 2000 | Be My Girl/A Place in Your Heart | 1959 | $60 |

TIC TAC TOE
| ❏ 5005 | She's Not Coming Home/Now That Summer Is Here | 1962 | $60 |

VIDEOS, THE

CASINO
| ❏ 105 | Love or Infatuation/Shoo-Be-Doo-Be Cha Cha Cha | 1959 | $300 |
| ❏ 102 | Trickle, Trickle/Moonglow You Know | 1958 | $60 |
— Casino" in shadow print; no playing cards; no mention of distribution by Gone
| ❏ 102 | Trickle, Trickle/Moonglow You Know | 1958 | $30 |
— With playing cards on label
| ❏ 102 | Trickle, Trickle/Moonglow You Know | 1958 | $40 |
— Casino" in normal print; no playing cards; no mention of distribution by Gone
| ❏ 102 | Trickle, Trickle/Moonglow You Know | 1961 | $30 |
— No playing cards; with distribution by Gone

VILLAGE PEOPLE

CASABLANCA
❏ 2261	Can't Stop the Music/Milkshake	1980	$4
❏ 2261 [PS]	Can't Stop the Music/Milkshake	1980	$8
❏ 984	Go West/Citizens of the World	1979	$5
❏ 973	In the Navy/Manhattan Woman	1979	$5
❏ 973 [PS]	In the Navy/Manhattan Woman	1979	$40
— Picture sleeve is promo only
❏ 922	Macho Man/Key West	1978	$5
❏ 2291	Magic Night/I Love You to Death	1980	$4
❏ 896	San Francisco (You've Got Me)/Village People	1977	$8
❏ 2213	Sleazy/Save Me (Uptempo)	1979	$4

RCA
❏ PB-12258	5 O'Clock in the Morning/Food Fight	1981	$5
❏ PB-12258 [PS]	5 O'Clock in the Morning/Food Fight	1981	$6
❏ PB-12331	Action Man/Jungle City	1981	$8

VILLAGE SOUL CHOIR, THE

ABBOTT
| ❏ 2013 | Love Everyday, Love Every Night/(B-side unknown) | 1970 | $10 |
| ❏ 2010 | The Cat Walk/The Country Walk | 1970 | $12 |

VILLAGE STOMPERS, THE

CAMEO
| ❏ 2000 | Sing All Together/(B-side unknown) | 1967 | $8 |

EPIC
❏ 9655	Blue Grass/The La-Dee-La Song	1964	$6
❏ 9655 [PS]	Blue Grass/The La-Dee-La Song	1964	$8
❏ 9785	Brother, Can You Spare a Dime/Magic Horn	1965	$6
❏ 9785 [PS]	Brother, Can You Spare a Dime/Magic Horn	1965	$8
❏ 10106	Chopsticks/Wilkommen	1966	$6
❏ 9740	Fiddler on the Roof/Moonlight on the Ganges	1964	$6
❏ 9674	From Russia with Love/The Bridges of Budapest	1964	$6
❏ 9702	Haunted House/Mozambique	1964	$6
❏ 9718	Oh, Marie/Limehouse Blues	1964	$6
❏ 10017	Second Hand Rose/The Poet and the Prophet	1966	$6
❏ 9868	The Bride of Bleecker Street/Call Me	1965	$6
❏ 9824	Those Magnificant Men in Their Flying Machines/Sweetwater Bay	1965	$6
❏ 9617	Washington Square/Turkish Delight	1963	$8
❏ 9617 [PS]	Washington Square/Turkish Delight	1963	$10

VINCE AND THE WAIKIKI RUMBLERS

BIG BEN
| ❏ 1003 | Waikiki Rumble/Pacifica | 1965 | $60 |

ZODIAC
| ❏ 1004 | Waikiki Rumble/Pacifica | 1965 | $100 |

VINCENT & PESCI

MAINSTREAM
| ❏ 5531 | Can You Fix The Way I Talk For Christmas?/Little People Blues | 1972 | $10 |

VINCENT, GENE

CAPITOL
❏ F3959	Baby Blue/True to You	1958	$60
❏ 3871	Be-Bop-a-Lula/Lotta Lovin'	1974	$20
❏ F3450	Be-Bop-a-Lula/Woman Love	1956	$75
— With large Capitol logo
| ❏ F3450 | Be-Bop-a-Lula/Woman Love | 1956 | $60 |
— With small Capitol logo; counterfeits exist on a white label with blue vinyl
❏ F3678	B-I-Bickey-Bi-Bo-Bo-Go/Five Days, Five Days	1957	$60
❏ F3558	Bluejean Bop/Who Slapped John	1956	$50
❏ F3617	Crazy Legs/Important Words	1956	$60
❏ F3839	Dance to the Bop/I Got It	1957	$40
❏ F4051	Little Lover/Git It	1958	$50
❏ F3763	Lotta Lovin'/Wear My Ring	1957	$60
❏ 4665 [B]	Lucky Star/Baby Don't Believe Him	1961	$30
❏ 4525	Mister Loneliness/If You Want My Lovin'	1961	$30
❏ F4153	Over the Rainbow/Who's Pushin' Your Swing	1959	$60
❏ 4442	Pistol Packin' Mama/Anna Annabella	1960	$50
❏ F4105	Say Mama/Be-Bop Boogie Boy	1958	$60
❏ F3874	Walkin' Home from School/I Gotta Baby	1958	$50
❏ 4313	Wild Cat/Right Here on Earth	1959	$60

CHALLENGE
❏ 59337	Bird Doggin'/Ain't That Too Much	1966	$30
❏ 59365	Born to Be a Rolling Stone/Pickin' Poppies	1967	$30
❏ 59347	Lonely Street/I've Got My Eyes on You	1966	$30

FOREVER
| ❏ 6001 | Story of the Rockers/Pickin' Poppies | 1969 | $60 |

KAMA SUTRA
| ❏ 518 | High On Life/The Day the World Turned Blue | 1971 | $15 |
| ❏ 514 | Sunshine/Geese | 1970 | $15 |

PLAYGROUND
| ❏ 100 | Story of the Rockers/Pickin' Poppies | 1968 | $200 |

7-Inch Extended Plays

CAPITOL
❏ EAP 2-970	*By the Light of the Silvery Moon/Flea Brain/Rollin' Danny/Your Cheatin' Heart	1958	$175
❏ EAP 2-811	*Cruisin'/You Better Believe/Double Talkin' Baby/Blues Stay Away from Me	1957	$175
❏ EAP 1-1059	*Five Feet of Lovin'/The Wayward Wind/Somebody Help Me/Keep It a Secret	1958	$175
❏ EAP 1-970	*Frankie and Johnnie/In My Dreams/You'll Never Walk Alone/Brand New Beat	1958	$175
❏ EAP 3-764	*Jump Back, Honey, Jump Back/Waltz of the Wind/I Flipped/Peg o' My Heart	1957	$175
❏ EAP 3-811	*Pink Thunderbird/Pretty, Pretty Baby/Cat Man/I Sure Miss You	1957	$175
❏ EAP 2-764	*Who Slapped John/Wedding Bells/Up a Lazy River/Bop Street	1957	$175
❏ EAP 1-1059 [PS]	A Gene Vincent Record Date, Part 1	1958	$175
❏ EAP 2-1059 [PS]	A Gene Vincent Record Date, Part 2	1958	$175
❏ EAP 3-1059 [PS]	A Gene Vincent Record Date, Part 3	1958	$175
❏ EAP 1-764	Bluejean Bop/Jezebel// Jumps, Giggles and Shouts/Ain't She Sweet	1957	$175
❏ EAP 1-764 [PS]	Bluejean Bop! Part 1	1957	$175
❏ EAP 2-764 [PS]	Bluejean Bop! Part 2	1957	$175
❏ EAP 3-764 [PS]	Bluejean Bop! Part 3	1957	$175
❏ EAP 1-811 [PS]	Gene Vincent and the Blue Caps, Part 1	1957	$175
❏ EAP 2-811 [PS]	Gene Vincent and the Blue Caps, Part 2	1957	$175
❏ EAP 3-811 [PS]	Gene Vincent and the Blue Caps, Part 3	1957	$175
❏ EAP 1-970 [PS]	Gene Vincent Rocks! And the Blue Caps Roll, Part 1	1958	$175
❏ EAP 2-970 [PS]	Gene Vincent Rocks! And the Blue Caps Roll, Part 2	1958	$175
❏ EAP 3-970 [PS]	Gene Vincent Rocks! And the Blue Caps Roll, Part 3	1958	$175
❏ EAP 2-1059	Git It/Teenage Partner//Hey, Good Lookin'/I Can't Help It	1958	$175
❏ EAP 1-985	Hot Rod Gang	1958	$250
❏ EAP 3-1059	I Love You/Peace of Mind//Summertime/Look What You Gone and Done to Me	1958	$175
❏ EAP 1-985	Lovely Loretta/Dance to the Bop//Dance in the Street/Baby Blue	1958	$250

VINEGAR JOE

ATCO
| ❏ 6912 | See the World/Circles | 1973 | $8 |
| ❏ 6922 | Whole Lotta Shakin' Goin' On/Rock 'n Roll Gypsies | 1973 | $8 |

VINSON, EDDIE "CLEANHEAD"

BETHLEHEM
| ❏ 11097 | Cherry Red/Kidney Stew | 1961 | $30 |

BLUESWAY
| ❏ 61005 | Cadillac Blues/Old Maid Got Married | 1967 | $15 |

KING
❏ 4563	Good Bread Alley/I Need You Tonight	1952	$70
❏ 4582	Lonesome Train/Person to Person	1952	$70
❏ 6305	Person to Person/Cherry Red Blues	1970	$6

MERCURY
❏ 70525	Anxious Heart/Suffer Fool	1954	$120
❏ 70334	Old Man Boogie/You Can't Have My Love No More	1954	$200
❏ 70621	Tomorrow May Never Come/Big Chief Rain in the Face	1955	$125

RIVERSIDE
| ❏ 4512 | Back Door Blues/Hold It | 1962 | $30 |

VINTON, BOBBY

ABC

Number	Title	Yr	NM
❏ 12308	All My Todays/Strike Up the Band for Love	1977	$4
❏ 12056	Beer Barrel Polka/Dick and Jane	1974	$4
❏ 12293	Hold Me, Thrill Me, Kiss Me/Her Name Is Love	1977	$4
❏ 12229	Love Is the Reason/Nobody But Me	1976	$4
❏ 12178	Moonlight Serenade/Why Can't I Get Over You	1976	$4
❏ 12131	My Gypsy Love/Midnight Show	1975	$4
❏ 12022	My Melody of Love/I'll Be Loving You	1974	$5

—Black label

Number	Title	Yr	NM
❏ 12022	My Melody of Love/I'll Be Loving You	1974	$4

—Multi-colored label

Number	Title	Yr	NM
❏ 12265	Only Love Can Break a Heart/Once More with Feeling	1977	$4
❏ 12186	Save Your Kisses for Me/Love Shine	1976	$4
❏ 12100	Wooden Heart/Polka Pose	1975	$4

ALPINE

Number	Title	Yr	NM
❏ 50	First Impression/You'll Never Forget	1959	$40
❏ 59	The Sheik/A Freshman and a Sophomore	1960	$30

BOBBY VINTON

Number	Title	Yr	NM
❏ 100	Santa Must Be Polish/Santa Claus Is Coming to Town	1987	$3
❏ 100 [PS]	Santa Must Be Polish/Santa Claus Is Coming to Town	1987	$3

CURB

Number	Title	Yr	NM
❏ 10560	It's Been One of Those Days/(Now and Then There's) A Fool Such As I	1989	$3
❏ 10541	Please Tell Her That I Said Hello/Getting Used to Being Loved Again	1989	$3
❏ 10512	The Last Rose/Sealed with a Kiss	1988	$3

DIAMOND

Number	Title	Yr	NM
❏ 121	I Love You the Way You Are/You're My Girl	1962	$30

—B-side by Chuck and Johnny

ELEKTRA

Number	Title	Yr	NM
❏ 45503	My First, My Only Love/Summerlove Sensation	1978	$4

EPIC

Number	Title	Yr	NM
❏ 10790	A Little Bit of You/God Bless America	1971	$5
❏ 10736	And I Love You So/She Loves Me	1971	$5
❏ 9593	Blue on Blue/Those Little Things	1963	$15
❏ 9593 [PS]	Blue on Blue/Those Little Things	1963	$20
❏ 9593 [DJ]	Blue on Blue/Those Little Things	1963	$40

—Promo only on blue vinyl

Number	Title	Yr	NM
❏ 34-06537	Blue Velvet/Blue on Blue	1986	$5
❏ 9614	Blue Velvet/Is There a Place (Where I Can Go)	1963	$15
❏ 9614 [PS]	Blue Velvet/Is There a Place (Where I Can Go)	1963	$20
❏ 10936	But I Do/When You Love	1972	$5
❏ 10936 [PS]	But I Do/When You Love	1972	$8
❏ 10689	Christmas Eve in My Home Town/The Christmas Angel	1970	$6
❏ 50169	Christmas Eve in My Home Town/The Christmas Angel	1975	$5
❏ 50080	Clinging Vine/I Can't Believe That It's All Over	1975	$5
❏ 9705	Clinging Vine/Imagination Is a Magic Dream	1964	$8
❏ 9705 [PS]	Clinging Vine/Imagination Is a Magic Dream	1964	$15
❏ 10090	Coming Home Soldier/Don't Let My Mary Go Around	1966	$6
❏ 10090 [PS]	Coming Home Soldier/Don't Let My Mary Go Around	1966	$10
❏ 9440	Corrina, Corrina/Little Lonely One	1961	$20
❏ 10014	Dum-De-Da/Blue Clarinet	1966	$6
❏ 10014 [PS]	Dum-De-Da/Blue Clarinet	1966	$12
❏ 10822	Every Day of My Life/You Can Do It to Me Anytime	1972	$5
❏ 10822 [PS]	Every Day of My Life/You Can Do It to Me Anytime	1972	$8
❏ 9551	Excerpts from "Roses Are Red"	1962	$15
❏ 9552	Excerpts from "Roses Are Red"	1962	$15
❏ 9553	Excerpts from "Roses Are Red"	1962	$15
❏ 9554	Excerpts from "Roses Are Red"	1962	$15
❏ 10136	For He's a Jolly Good Fellow/Sweet Maria	1967	$6
❏ 10136 [PS]	For He's a Jolly Good Fellow/Sweet Maria	1967	$10
❏ 10350	Halfway to Paradise/(My Little) Christie	1968	$6
❏ 10350 [PS]	Halfway to Paradise/(My Little) Christie	1968	$10
❏ 10350	Halfway to Paradise/(My Little) Kristie	1968	$10

—Note variation in B-side spelling

Number	Title	Yr	NM
❏ 9469	Hip-Swinging, High-Stepping, Drum Majorette/Will I Ask Ya	1961	$20
❏ 10397	I Love How You Love Me/Little Barefoot Boy	1968	$6
❏ 10397 [PS]	I Love How You Love Me/Little Barefoot Boy	1968	$10
❏ 10980	I Love You the Way You Are/Hurt	1973	$5
❏ 9791	L-O-N-E-L-Y/Graduation Tears	1965	$8
❏ 9791 [PS]	L-O-N-E-L-Y/Graduation Tears	1965	$15
❏ 9768	Long Lonely Nights/Satin	1965	$8
❏ 9768 [PS]	Long Lonely Nights/Satin	1965	$15
❏ 9730	Mr. Lonely/It's Better to Have Loved	1964	$10
❏ 9730 [PS]	Mr. Lonely/It's Better to Have Loved	1964	$15
❏ 10576	My Elusive Dreams/Over and Over	1970	$5
❏ 10576 [PS]	My Elusive Dreams/Over and Over	1970	$10
❏ 9662	My Heart Belongs to Only You/Warm and Tender	1964	$10
❏ 9662 [PS]	My Heart Belongs to Only You/Warm and Tender	1964	$20
❏ 9577	Over the Mountain (Across the Sea)/Faded Pictures	1963	$10
❏ 9577 [PS]	Over the Mountain (Across the Sea)/Faded Pictures	1963	$20
❏ 10048	Petticoat White (Summer Sky Blue)/All the King's Horses	1966	$6
❏ 10048 [PS]	Petticoat White (Summer Sky Blue)/All the King's Horses	1966	$10
❏ 3-9550 [S]	Please Help Me, I'm Falling/Sentimental Me	1962	$15

—Jukebox issue, but unlike most, it has a large hole and plays at 45

Number	Title	Yr	NM
❏ 10228	Please Love Me Forever/Miss America	1967	$8
❏ 10228 [PS]	Please Love Me Forever/Miss America	1967	$10
❏ 9417	Posin'/Tornado	1960	$20
❏ 9869	Satin Pillows/Careless	1965	$8
❏ 9869 [PS]	Satin Pillows/Careless	1965	$15
❏ 10861	Sealed with a Kiss/All My Life	1972	$5
❏ 10861 [PS]	Sealed with a Kiss/All My Life	1972	$8
❏ 10711	She Loves Me/I'll Make You My Baby	1971	$5
❏ 10305	Take Good Care of My Baby/Strange Sensations	1968	$6
❏ 10305 [PS]	Take Good Care of My Baby/Strange Sensations	1968	$10
❏ 9894	Tears/Go Away Pain	1966	$6
❏ 9687	Tell Me Why/Remembering	1964	$8
❏ 9687 [PS]	Tell Me Why/Remembering	1964	$20
❏ 9741	The Bell That Couldn't Jingle/Dearest Santa	1964	$12
❏ 10485	The Days of Sand and Shovels/So Many Lonely Girls	1969	$5
❏ 10485 [PS]	The Days of Sand and Shovels/So Many Lonely Girls	1969	$12
❏ 9814	Theme from "Harlow" (Lonely Girl)/If I Should Lose Your Love	1965	$8
❏ 9814 [PS]	Theme from "Harlow" (Lonely Girl)/If I Should Lose Your Love	1965	$15
❏ 9638	There! I've Said It Again/The Girl with the Bow in Her Hair	1963	$15
❏ 9638 [PS]	There! I've Said It Again/The Girl with the Bow in Her Hair	1963	$20
❏ 10461	To Know You Is to Love You/The Beat of My Heart	1969	$5
❏ 10461 [PS]	To Know You Is to Love You/The Beat of My Heart	1969	$10
❏ 9561	Trouble Is My Middle Name/Let's Kiss and Make Up	1962	$10
❏ 9561 [PS]	Trouble Is My Middle Name/Let's Kiss and Make Up	1962	$20
❏ 9846	What Color (Is a Man)/Love or Infatuation	1965	$8
❏ 11038	Where Are the Children/I Can't Believe That It's All Over	1973	$5
❏ 10554	Where Is Love/For All We Know	1969	$5
❏ 10651	Why Don't They Understand/Where Is Love	1970	$5
❏ 10651 [PS]	Why Don't They Understand/Where Is Love	1970	$8

MELODY

Number	Title	Yr	NM
❏ 5001/2	Always in My Heart/Harlem Nocturne	1960	$30

TAPESTRY

Number	Title	Yr	NM
❏ 4009	Bed of Roses/I Know a Goodbye	1984	$4
❏ 001	Disco Polka (Pennsylvania Polka)/I Could Have Danced All Night	1979	$4
❏ 007	Forever and Ever/Ain't That Lovin' You	1982	$4
❏ 003	He/My First and Only Love	1980	$4
❏ 010	It Hurts to Be in Love/Love Makes Everything Better	1985	$4
❏ 005	It Was Nice to Know You John/Ain't That Lovin' You	1981	$5
❏ 006	Let Me Love You, Goodbye/You Are Love	1981	$4
❏ 002	Make Believe It's Your First Time/I Remember Loving You	1979	$4
❏ 008	She Will Survive (Poland)/Love Is the Reason	1982	$4
❏ 008 [PS]	She Will Survive (Poland)/Love Is the Reason	1982	$5
❏ 1986	Sweet Lady of Liberty (same on both sides)	1986	$4
❏ 013	What Did You Do with Your Old 45s/(B-side unknown)	1986	$4

7-Inch Extended Plays

ABC

Number	Title	Yr	NM
❏ LLP-271 [PS]	Melodies of Love	1974	$12
❏ LLP-271	The Most Beautiful Girl/My Melody of Love/Never Ending Song of Love/You'll Never Know/Am I Losing You/Here in My Heart	1974	$10

—Jukebox issue; small hole, plays at 33 1/3 rpm

EPIC

Number	Title	Yr	NM
❏ 5-26437	If I Didn't Care/Shangri-La/It's No Sin/Why Don't You Believe Me/Together/Save the Last Dance for Me	1968	$10

—Jukebox issue; small hole, plays at 33 1/3 rpm

Number	Title	Yr	NM
❏ 5-26437 [PS]	I Love How You Love Me	1968	$12
❏ 7-31642	Our Day Will Come/Song Sung Blue/Come Softly to Me//Some Kind of Wonderful/Somebody's Breaking My Heart/I'm Leaving It Up to You	1972	$10

—Jukebox issue; small hole, plays at 33 1/3 rpm

Number	Title	Yr	NM
❏ 5-26341 [PS]	Please Love Me Forever	1967	$12
❏ 5-26341	Please Love Me Forever/It's All in the Game/Love Me with All Your Heart//Just As Much As Ever/P.S. I Love You/My Song of Love	1967	$10

—Stereo jukebox issue; small hole, plays at 33 1/3 rpm

Number	Title	Yr	NM
❏ 7-31642 [PS]	Sealed with a Kiss	1972	$12
❏ EG7215	Silver Bells/White Christmas//O Holy Night/The Christmas Song	1963	$10
❏ EG7215 [PS]	Songs of Christmas	1963	$12
❏ 5-26382 [PS]	Take Good Care of My Baby	1968	$12
❏ 5-26382	Take Good Care of My Baby/I Apologize/To Think You've Chosen Me//Sentimental Me/Serenade of the Bells/Forget Me Not	1968	$10

—Jukebox issue; small hole, plays at 33 1/3 rpm

Number	Title	Yr	NM
❏ 7-26081 [PS]	There! I've Said It Again	1964	$15

—Slightly different cover than on N7-26081

VIOLENT FEMMES

SLASH

Number	Title	Yr	NM
❏ 28683	Children of the Revolution/World Without Mercy	1986	$4
❏ 29521	Gone Daddy Gone/Good Feeling	1983	$4

VIOLINAIRES, THE

JEWEL

Number	Title	Yr	NM
❏ 222	Little Jesus Boy/White Christmas	1973	$30

VIPERS SKIFFLE GROUP, THE

CAPITOL

Number	Title	Yr	NM
❏ F3711	Cumberland Gap/Maggie Mae	1957	$20
❏ F3673	Don't You Rock Me Daddy-O/10,000 Years Ago	1957	$30

VIRTUES, THE

ABC-PARAMOUNT

Number	Title	Yr	NM
❏ 10071	Blues in the Cellar/Vaya Con Dios	1959	$20

ARCADE

Number	Title	Yr	NM
❏ 135	Ooh You Gotta/I Make a Mistake	1955	$40

—As "Frank Virtue"

FAYETTE

Number	Title	Yr	NM
❏ 1626	Guitar Boogie Shuffle '65/Moon Maid	1965	$20

HIGHLAND

Number	Title	Yr	NM
❏ 2505	Bye Bye Blues/Happy Guitar	1960	$30
❏ 2505X	Bye Bye Blues/Strollin' Again	1960	$30

HUNT

Number	Title	Yr	NM
❏ 331	Blues in the Cellar/Vaya Con Dios	1960	$30
❏ 327	Flippin' In/Shufflin' Along	1959	$30

Number	Title	Yr	NM
❏ 324 [M]	Guitar Boogie Shuffle/ Guitar in Orbit	1959	$30
❏ S-324 [S]	Guitar Boogie Shuffle/ Guitar in Orbit	1959	$60
❏ 328	Pickin' the Stroll/Virtue's Boogie Woogie	1959	$30
❏ 329	Pony Walk/Virtue's Boogie Woogie	1959	$30

LIBERTY
| ❏ 55706 | Dream World/Move On | 1964 | $15 |

— As "Frank Virtuoso"

SURE
❏ 501	Guitar Boogie Shuffle/ Guitar in Orbit	1959	$100
❏ 1733	Guitar Boogie Shuffle Twist/ Guitar Boogie Stomp	1962	$20
❏ 1779	Tel-Star Guitar/ Jersey Bounce	1962	$20

VIRNON
| ❏ 603 | Guitar Boogie Twist/ Guitar Shimmy | 1960 | $20 |

VIRTUE
| ❏ 190 | Cotton Candy/Love You | 1966 | $12 |
| ❏ 2503 | Guitar on the Wild Side/ Meditation of the Soul | 1970 | $6 |

WYNNE
| ❏ 123 | Highland Guitar/Pickin' Plankin' Boogie | 1960 | $20 |

VISCAYNES, THE
TROPO
| ❏ 101 | I Guess I'll Be/Stop What You're Doing | 1958 | $200 |

VISCOUNTS, THE (1)
AMY
| ❏ 940 | Harlem Nocturne/Dig | 1965 | $15 |
CORAL
| ❏ 62490 | Come, Come On Back/Off Shore | 1966 | $10 |
| ❏ 62520 | Moonlight in Vermont/ Sweet Georgia Brown | 1967 | $10 |
MADISON
❏ 165	Drag Race/ Sophisticated Lady	1961	$20
❏ 123	Harlem Nocturne/Dig	1959	$30
❏ 159	Little Brown Jug/Opus One	1961	$20
❏ 152	Shadrack/This Place	1961	$20
❏ 129	The Touch/Chug-a-Lug	1960	$20
❏ 140	Wabash Blues/So Slow	1960	$20
MR. PEACOCK
| ❏ 107 | The Continental Walk/Hully Gully | 1962 | $15 |
| ❏ 101 | When Johnny Comes Marching Home/ Mark's Mood | 1961 | $15 |

VISCOUNTS, THE (2)
MERCURY
| ❏ 71073 | My Girl/Raindrop | 1957 | $50 |

VISIONS, THE
BIG TOP
| ❏ 3119 | Secret Worlds of Tears/ Swingin' Wedding | 1962 | $30 |
| ❏ 3092 | Tell Me You're Mine/ All Through the Night | 1961 | $30 |
BRUNSWICK
| ❏ 55206 | So Close/There'll Be No Next Time | 1961 | $30 |
COED
| ❏ 598 | Down in My Heart/ Tell Her Now | 1964 | $15 |
ELGEY
| ❏ 1003 | Teenager's Life/Little Moon | 1960 | $50 |
LOST-NITE
| ❏ 102 | Teenager's Life/Little Moon | 1961 | $30 |

— Original pressing on pink label with no "street lamp" logo

MERCURY
| ❏ 72188 | Oh Boy What a Girl/ Tommy's Girl | 1963 | $20 |
ORIGINAL SOUND
| ❏ 32 | Look at Me Now/Cigarette | 1963 | $20 |
UNI
| ❏ 55031 | How Can I Be Down/ Threshold of Love | 1967 | $15 |
WARNER BROS.
| ❏ 5898 | Black and White Rainbow/ Bulldog Cadillac | 1967 | $10 |

VISITORS, THE (1)
DAKAR
| ❏ 613 | I'm Gonna Stay/Lonely One, Only Son | 1969 | $8 |

| ❏ 603 | I'm in Danger/Until You Came Along | 1969 | $8 |
TANGERINE
| ❏ 1010 | Anytime Is the Right Time/Nevertheless | 1970 | $8 |
| ❏ 1003 | My Love Is Ready and Waiting/What About Me | 1970 | $8 |

VISITORS, THE (2)
TOWER
| ❏ 268 | Theme from The Wild Angels/Is It Them or Me | 1966 | $20 |

VISTAS, THE
REBEL
| ❏ 77755 | Ghost Wave/Surfer's Minuet | 1963 | $60 |
VENPRO
| ❏ 1000 | Ghost Wave/Surfer's Minuet | 1963 | $100 |

VISUALS, THE
POPLAR
❏ 117	My Juanita/A Boy, a Girl, and a Dream	1963	$60
❏ 121	Please Don't Be Mad at Me/Blue Enough to Cry	1963	$300
❏ 115	The Submarine Race/ Maybe You	1962	$50

VITELLS, THE
DECCA
| ❏ 31362 | Shirley/The Dip | 1962 | $40 |

VITO AND THE SALUTATIONS
APT
| ❏ 25079 | High Noon/Walkin' | 1965 | $60 |
BOOM
| ❏ 60020 | Bring Back Yesterday/I Want You to Be My Baby | 1966 | $30 |
HAROLD
| ❏ 5009 | Gloria/Let's Untwist the Twist | 1962 | $60 |
HERALD
| ❏ 586 | Eenie Meenie/ Extraordinary Girl | 1964 | $30 |
RAYNA
| ❏ 5009 | Gloria/Let's Untwist the Twist | 1962 | $60 |
RED BOY
| ❏ 5009 | Gloria/Let's Untwist the Twist | 1962 | $40 |
| ❏ 1001 | So Wonderful (My Love)/I'd Best Be Going | 1966 | $30 |
REGINA
| ❏ 1320 | Get a Job/Girls I Know | 1964 | $40 |
RUST
| ❏ 5106 | Can I Depend on You/Hello Dolly | 1966 | $30 |
SANDBAG
| ❏ 103 | So Wonderful (My Love)/I'd Best Be Going | 1966 | $30 |
WELLS
| ❏ 1008 | Can I Depend on You/ Liverpool Bound | 1964 | $60 |

— Yellow vinyl

| ❏ 1008 | Can I Depend on You/ Liverpool Bound | 1964 | $30 |
| ❏ 1010 | The Banana Boat Song (Day-O)/Don't Count on Me | 1964 | $30 |

VITO, SONNY
ABC-PARAMOUNT
| ❏ 9958 | Cameo Ring/Teen-Age Blues | 1958 | $15 |
STRAND
| ❏ 25045 | An Angel Cries/ Mister Groovy | 1961 | $15 |

VKTMS
415 RECORDS
| ❏ S-0010 | 100% White Girl/No Long Goodbyes | 1980 | $12 |
| ❏ S-0010 [PS] | 100% White Girl/No Long Goodbyes | 1980 | $12 |

VOCAL MINORITY, THE
WIZDOM
| ❏ 1970 | We Love You Spiro (A Healthy, Normal American Boy from "Bye Bye Birdie")/A Vice Precedent | 1970 | $20 |

VOCALEERS, THE
OLD TOWN
| ❏ 1089 | This Is the Night/ Love and Devotion | 1960 | $30 |

PARADISE
| ❏ 113 | I Need Your Love So Bad/Have You Ever Loved Someone | 1959 | $50 |
RED ROBIN
❏ 132	Angel Face/Lovin' Baby	1954	$300
❏ 113	Be True/Oh! Where	1953	$600
❏ 114	Is It a Dream/Hurry Home	1953	$300
❏ 119	I Walk Alone/How Soon	1953	$400
❏ 125	Will You Be True/Love You	1954	$300
TWISTIME
| ❏ 11 | Cootie Snap/A Golden Tear | 1962 | $40 |
VEST
| ❏ 832 | Hear My Plea/The Night Is Quiet | 1960 | $100 |

VOGUES, THE
20TH CENTURY
❏ 2085	As Time Goes By/ Prisoner of Love	1974	$5
❏ 2041	My Prayer/I've Got to Learn to Live Without You	1973	$5
❏ 2060	Wonderful Summer/ Guess Who	1973	$5
ABC-PARAMOUNT
| ❏ 10672 | Big Man/Golden Locket | 1965 | $30 |
ASTRA
| ❏ 1030 | Five O'Clock World/Land of Milk and Honey | 1973 | $5 |
BELL
❏ 45158	An American Family/ Gotta Have You Back	1971	$5
❏ 991	Love Song/We're On Our Way	1971	$5
❏ 45127	Take Time to Tell Her/I'll Be with You	1971	$5
CO & CE
❏ 246	Brighter Days/Lovers of the World Unite	1967	$10
❏ 232	Five O'Clock World/ Nothing to Offer You	1965	$15
❏ 234	Magic Town/Humpty Dumpty	1966	$10
❏ 240	Please Mr. Sun/Don't Blame the Rain	1966	$10
❏ 244	Take a Chance on My Heart/Summer Afternoon	1967	$10
❏ 242	That's the Tune/ Midnight Dreams	1966	$12
❏ 238	The Land of Milk and Honey/True Lovers	1966	$10
MGM
| ❏ 13813 | Brighter Days/Lovers of the World Unite | 1967 | $8 |
REPRISE
❏ 0931	50's Medley/Come Into My Arms	1970	$6
❏ 0820	Earth Angel (Will You Be Mine)/P.S. I Love You	1969	$6
❏ 0741	Five O'Clock World/ Magic Town	1970	$6

— Back to Back Hits" series; "Five O'Clock World" has overdubbed strings

❏ 0887	God Only Knows/Moody	1970	$6
❏ 0844	Green Fields/Easy to Say	1969	$6
❏ 0663	I've Got You on My Mind/Just What I've Been Looking For	1968	$10
❏ 0831	Moments to Remember/ Once in a While	1969	$6
❏ 0766	My Special Angel/I Keep It Hid	1968	$8
❏ 0909	Over the Rainbow/ Hey, That's No Way to Say Goodbye	1970	$6
❏ 0856	See That Girl/If We Only Have Love	1969	$6
❏ 0969	Since I Don't Have You/I Know You as a Woman	1970	$6
❏ 0788	Till/I Will	1968	$8
❏ 0731	Turn Around, Look at Me/My Special Angel	1969	$5

— Back to Back Hits" series

❏ 0686	Turn Around, Look at Me/Then	1968	$8
❏ 0803	Woman Helping Man/I'll Know My Love	1969	$8
❏ 0803	Woman Helping Man/ No, Not Much	1969	$6

VOGUES, THE (2)
DOT
| ❏ 15798 | Love Is a Funny Little Game/ Which Witch Doctor | 1958 | $30 |
| ❏ 15859 | Try, Baby. Try/Falling Star | 1958 | $30 |

VOGUES, THE (U)
CASCADE
| ❏ 5908 | Ev'ry Day, Ev'ry Night/Now I Lay Me Down to Cry | 1959 | $30 |

Number	Title	Yr	NM

VOICE MASTERS, THE
ANNA
❏ 101	Hope and Pray/ Oop's I'm Sorry	1959	$200

BAMBOO
❏ 113	Dance Right Into My Heart/ If a Woman Catches a Fool	1970	$20

VOICES, THE
CASH
❏ 1014	Hey Now/My Love Grows Stronger	1955	$70
❏ 1015	I Want to Be Ready/Takes Two to Make a Home	1955	$70
❏ 1016	Santa Claus Boogie/ Santa Claus Baby	1955	$100
❏ 1011	Why/Two Things I Love	1955	$70

VOIGHT, WES
DELUXE
❏ 6180	I Want a Lover/Little Joan	1958	$50
❏ 6176	Midnight Blues/ Another Guy's Line	1958	$125

KING
❏ 5211 [M]	I'm Loving It/Everything's the Same	1959	$70
❏ S-5211 [S]	I'm Loving It/Everything's the Same	1959	$200
❏ 5231 [M]	I'm Ready to Go Steady/ The Wind and the Cold Black Night	1959	$50
❏ S-5231 [S]	I'm Ready to Go Steady/ The Wind and the Cold Black Night	1959	$125

VOLCANOES, THE
EPIC
❏ 9490	Shotgun/Stardust	1962	$15

VOLCANOS, THE
ARCTIC
❏ 111	Help Wanted/Make Your Move	1965	$15
❏ 115	(It's Against the) Laws of Love/(Instrumental)	1965	$15

— With correct song title as above

❏ 115	(It's Against the) Rules of Love/(Instrumental)	1965	$300

— With erroneous song title as above

❏ 125	Lady's Man/Help Wanted	1966	$12
❏ 103	Make Your Move/Baby	1965	$15
❏ 106	Storm Warning/Baby	1965	$15

VOLTAGE BROTHERS, THE
LIFESONG
❏ ZS81762	Feeling Good/Gone Too Far to Turn Around	1978	$6
❏ ZS81766	Happening in the Streets/ Working Together	1978	$6
❏ ZS81780	Throw Down/The Prophet	1978	$6

MTM
❏ B-72077	Insecure/(B-side unknown)	1986	$5
❏ B-72060	I Think I Miss You (After All)/Don't Jump the Gun	1985	$5
❏ B-72067	Love's a Criminal/ (B-side unknown)	1986	$5

VOLUMES, THE
AMERICAN ARTS
❏ 6	Gotta Give Her Love/I Can't Live Without You	1964	$40
❏ 18	I Just Can't Help Myself/ One Way Lover	1965	$40

CHEX
❏ 1005	Come Back Into My Heart/The Bell	1962	$50
❏ 1002	I Love You/Dreams	1962	$300

— With typographical error crediting "The Valumes

❏ 1002	I Love You/Dreams	1962	$50

— With no reference to Jay-Gee Records on label

❏ 1002	I Love You/Dreams	1962	$30

— With "Nationally Dist. by Jay-Gee Rec. Co. Inc." on label

IMPACT
❏ 1017	That Same Old Feeling/ The Trouble I've Seen	1966	$60

INFERNO
❏ 5001	Ain't That Lovin' You/I Love You Baby	1968	$30
❏ 2001	A Way to Love You/ You Got It Baby	1967	$30
❏ 2004	My Road Is the Right Road/My Kind of Girl	1967	$30

JUBILEE
❏ 5454	Our Song/Oh My Mother-in-Law	1963	$30
❏ 5446	Sandra/Teenage Paradise	1963	$30

KAREN
❏ 1551	Am I Losing You/Ain't Gonna Give You Up	1970	$8

OLD TOWN
❏ 1154	Why/Monkey Hop	1964	$30

VOMIT PIGS, THE
7-Inch Extended Plays
BAD WRECORS
❏ 0(# unknown)	Take One	1979	$175
❏ 0(# unknown) [PS]	Take One	1979	$175

VON DRAKE, LUDWIG
BUENA VISTA
❏ 386	I'm Ludwig Von Drake/ Green with Envy Blues	1961	$20

VONNS, THE
KING
❏ 5793	Leave Us Alone/ So Many Days	1963	$30

VONTASTICS, THE
CHESS
❏ 2024	Why Must We Part/I Will Always Love You	1967	$20

MOON SHOT
❏ 4702	Lady Love/When My Baby Comes Back Home	1967	$40

SATELLITE
❏ 2002	I'll Never Say Goodbye/ Don't Mess Around	1965	$120

ST. LAWRENCE
❏ 1014	Day Tripper/My Baby	1966	$30
❏ 1009	I Need You/Keep On Rolling	1966	$30
❏ 1007	Peace of Mind/ No Love for Me	1966	$20

TODDLIN' TOWN
❏ 115	Let Me Down Easy/I'm the One You Need	1968	$30

VOWS, THE
MARKAY
❏ 103	I Wanna Chance/ Have You Heard	1962	$50

— Black label

❏ 103	I Wanna Chance/ Have You Heard	1962	$400

— Orange label

STA-SET
❏ 402	Say You'll Be Mine/When a Boy Loves a Girl	1963	$70

TAMARA
❏ 760	Say You'll Be Mine/When a Boy Loves a Girl	1964	$30
❏ 506	The Things You Do to Me/Dottie	1963	$50

V.I.P.
❏ 25016	Buttered Popcorn/Tell Me	1965	$50

VOXPOPPERS, THE
AMP 3
❏ 1004	Wishing for Your Love/ The Last Drag	1958	$50

MERCURY
❏ 71315	Pony Tail/Ping Pong Baby	1958	$30
❏ 71282	Wishing for Your Love/ The Last Drag	1958	$30

POPLAR
❏ 107	Come Back Little Girl/A Love to Last a Lifetime	1959	$30

VERSAILLES
❏ 200	Can't Understand It/A Blessing After All	1959	$40

WARWICK
❏ 589	Lonely for You/ Helen Isn't Tellin'	1960	$15

— As "Freddie and the Voxpoppers

7-Inch Extended Plays
MERCURY
❏ EP 1-3391	Wishing for Your Love/ The Last Drag//Stroll Roll/Guitar Stroll	1958	$125

W

WADE, ADAM
COED
❏ 553	As If I Didn't Know/ Playin' Around	1961	$10
❏ 553 [PS]	As If I Didn't Know/ Playin' Around	1961	$20
❏ 560	Cold Cold Winter/ Preview of Paradise	1961	$10
❏ 539	For the Want of Your Love/ In Pursuit of Happiness	1960	$15
❏ 541	Gloria's Theme/Dreamy	1960	$15
❏ 541 [PS]	Gloria's Theme/Dreamy	1960	$20
❏ 565	How Are Things in Lover's Lane/It's Good to Have You Back with Me	1962	$10
❏ 530	I Can't Help It/I Had the Craziest Dream	1960	$15
❏ 567	Little Miss Lovely/For the First Time in My Life	1962	$12
❏ 536	Speaking of Her/ Black Out the Moon	1960	$15
❏ 536 [PS]	Speaking of Her/ Black Out the Moon	1960	$30
❏ 546	Take Good Care of Her/ Sleepy Time Gal	1961	$10
❏ 546	Take Good Care of Her/Too Far	1961	$15
❏ 520	Tell Her for Me/Don't Cry, My Love	1959	$15
❏ 566	Them There Eyes/ Prisoner's Song	1962	$20
❏ 550	The Writing on the Wall/ Point of No Return	1961	$10
❏ 550 [PS]	The Writing on the Wall/ Point of No Return	1961	$20
❏ 556	Tonight I Won't Be There/Linda	1961	$10
❏ 556 [PS]	Tonight I Won't Be There/Linda	1961	$20

EPIC
❏ 10112	A Man Alone/Wheels on the Highway	1966	$6
❏ 9639	Charade/Does Goodnight Mean Goodbye	1963	$8
❏ 9752	Crying in the Chapel/ Broken Hearted Stranger	1964	$8
❏ 9566	Don't Let Me Cross Over/ Rain from the Skies	1963	$8
❏ 9808	Garden in the Rain/ Play Some Music for Broken Hearts	1965	$8
❏ 9840	Garden of Eden/ Time for Dreams	1965	$8
❏ 10024	How Can I Leave You/Solitude	1966	$6
❏ 9521	I'm Climbin' (The Wall)/ They Didn't Believe Me	1962	$8
❏ 9521 [PS]	I'm Climbin' (The Wall)/ They Didn't Believe Me	1962	$30
❏ 9771	It's Been a Long Time Comin'/A Lover's Question	1965	$8
❏ 9609	Let's Make the Most of a Beautiful Thing/ Theme from "Irma La Douce" (Look Again)	1963	$8
❏ 9686	Love Song from "Flight to Ashiya"/Pencil and Paper	1964	$8
❏ 9659	Seven Loves for Seven Days/Whisper Away	1964	$8
❏ 9590	Teenage Mona Lisa/Why Do We Have to Wait So Long	1963	$8
❏ 9557	There'll Be No Teardrops Tonight/ Here Comes the Pain	1962	$8
❏ 9557 [PS]	There'll Be No Teardrops Tonight/ Here Comes the Pain	1962	$30

REMEMBER
❏ 7791	Half the World/My Time for Love	1969	$6

WARNER BROS.
❏ 7179	Everybody Is Looking for That Someone/Maybe	1968	$6
❏ 7225	Old Devil Woman/Rome	1968	$6

WADE AND DICK
SUN
❏ 269	Bop Bop Baby/Don't Need Your Lovin' Baby	1957	$40

WADE, BILLY, AND THE 3 DEGREES
ABC
❏ 45-10991	Tear It Up (Part 1)/ Tear It Up (Part 2)	1967	$10

WADE, DON
SAN
❏ 207	Forever Yours/Oh Love	1958	$40
❏ 206	Gone, Gone, Gone/ (B-side unknown)	1958	$300

Number	Title	Yr	NM

WADE, RONNY
KING
Number	Title	Yr	NM
❏ 5112	All I Want/A King and a Vow	1958	$60
❏ 5099	Annie Don't Work/I'll Sail My Ship Alone	1958	$60
❏ 5061	Gotta Make Her Mine/Let Me Cry	1957	$100
❏ 5078	I Know But I'll Never Tell/I Never Fall in Love Again	1957	$60

WAGNER, BOB
ACE
| ❏ 669 | Lonely Christmas Again/Blue Evening | 1962 | $15 |

WAGNER, DANNY, AND KINDRED SOUL
IMPERIAL
| ❏ 66327 | Harlem Shuffle/When Johnny Comes Marching Home | 1968 | $30 |
| ❏ 66305 | I Lost a True Love/My Buddy | 1968 | $40 |

WAGONER, PORTER, AND DOLLY PARTON
Also see each artist's individual listings.

FREEDOM TRAIN
| ❏ 5767 | Here Comes the Freedom Train/All Aboard America | 1973 | $125 |

— B-side by Porter Wagoner solo; special promotional record for the American Freedom Train Foundation

RCA
| ❏ PB-12119 | If You Go, I'll Follow You/Hide Me Away | 1980 | $4 |
| ❏ PB-11983 | Making Plans/Beneath the Sweet Magnolia Trees | 1980 | $4 |

RCA VICTOR
❏ 74-0172	Always, Always/No Need to Hurry Home	1969	$6
❏ 47-9958	Better Move It On Home/Two of a Kind	1971	$6
❏ 74-0565	Burning the Midnight Oil/More Than Words Can Tell	1971	$6
❏ 47-9875	Daddy Was An Old Time Preacher Man/Good Understanding	1970	$6
❏ 47-9490	Holding On to Nothing/Just Between You and Me	1968	$8
❏ 74-0981	If Teardrops Were Pennies/Come to Me	1973	$5
❏ PB-10652	Is Forever Longer Than Always/If You Say I Can	1976	$4
❏ 74-0675	Lost Forever in Your Kiss/The Fog Has Lifted	1972	$5
❏ 74-0104	Malena/Yours, Love	1969	$6
❏ PB-10010	Please Don't Stop Loving Me/Sounds of Nature	1974	$4
❏ GB-10506	Please Don't Stop Loving Me/Sounds of Nature	1975	$4

— Gold Standard Series
| ❏ PB-10328 | Say Forever You'll Be Mine/How Can I Help You Forgive Me | 1975 | $4 |
| ❏ GB-10675 | Say Forever You'll Be Mine/How Can I Help You Forgive Me | 1976 | $4 |

— Gold Standard Series
❏ 47-9369	The Last Thing on My Mind/Love Is Worth Living	1967	$8
❏ 74-0773	Together Always/Love's All Over	1972	$5
❏ 47-9799	Tomorrow Is Forever/Mandy Never Sleeps	1969	$6
❏ 74-0893	We Found It/Lord Have Mercy on Us	1973	$5
❏ 47-9577	We'll Get Ahead Someday/Jeannie's Afraid of the Dark	1968	$8

7-Inch Extended Plays
| ❏ 7-4305 | Forty Miles from Poplar Bluff/No Love Left/Each Season Changes You//Run That By Me One More Time/Silver Sandals/We Can't Let This Happen to Us | 1970 | $10 |

— Jukebox issue; small hole, plays at 33 1/3 rpm
| ❏ 7-4305 [PS] | Porter Wayne and Dolly Rebecca | 1970 | $12 |

WAGONER, PORTER
RCA
❏ PB-11671	Everything I've Always Wanted/No Bed of Roses	1979	$4
❏ PB-11771	Hold On Tight/Someone Just Like You	1979	$4
❏ PB-10974	I Haven't Learned a Thing/Hand Me Down My Walking Cane	1977	$4

— A-side with Merle Haggard
❏ PB-11998	Is It Only 'Cause You're Lonely/When She Was Mine	1980	$4
❏ PB-11491	I Want to Walk You Home/Old Love Letter	1979	$4
❏ PB-11186	Mountain Music/Natural Wonder	1977	$4
❏ PB-11411	Ole Slew Foot/I'm Gonna Feed 'Em Now	1978	$4

| ❏ PB-10803 | When Lea Jane Sang/Storm of Love | 1976 | $4 |

RCA VICTOR
❏ 47-6105	A Satisfied Mind/Itchin' for My Baby	1955	$30
❏ 74-0753	A World Without Music/Denise Mayree	1972	$6
❏ 48-1007	Be a Little Quieter/Watching	1971	$6
❏ 47-5754	Be Glad You Ain't Me/Love at First Sight	1954	$30
❏ 47-9530	Be Proud of Your Man/Wino	1968	$8
❏ 74-0168	Big Wind/Tennessee Stud	1969	$8
❏ 47-5430	Bringing Home the Bacon/An Angel Made for Love	1953	$30
❏ PB-10124	Carolina Moonshiner/Not a Cloud in the Sky	1974	$5
❏ 47-9979	Charley's Picture/As Simple As I Am	1971	$6
❏ 47-8026	Cold Dark Waters/Ain't It Awful	1962	$15
❏ 47-5848	Company's Comin'/Tricks of the Trade	1954	$30
❏ 47-7073	Doll Face/Your Love	1957	$30
❏ 47-6289	Eat, Drink and Be Merry (Tomorrow You'll Cry)/Let's Squiggle	1955	$30
❏ 47-7901	Everything She Touches Gets the Blues/Sugar Foot Rag	1961	$15
❏ 47-7770	Falling Again/An Old Log Cabin for Sale	1960	$20
❏ 47-5527	Flame of Love/Dig That Crazy Moon	1953	$30
❏ APBO-0187	George Leory Chickashea/Dooley	1973	$5
❏ 47-6844	Good Mornin', Neighbor/Who Will He Be	1957	$30
❏ 47-8622	Green, Green Grass of Home/Dooley	1965	$10
❏ 47-7279	Haven't You Heard/Tell Her Lies and Feed Her Candy	1958	$20
❏ 47-6030	Hey, Maw/How Quick	1955	$30
❏ APBO-0328	Highway Headin' South/Freda	1974	$5
❏ 47-8257	Howdy Neighbor Howdy/Find Out	1963	$15
❏ 47-8882	I Dreamed I Saw America on Her Knees/When I Reach That City	1966	$10
❏ 47-8800	I Just Came to Smell the Flowers/I'm a Long Way from Home	1966	$10
❏ 47-8432	I'll Go Down Swinging/Country Music Has Gone to Town	1964	$15
❏ 47-6803	I'm Day Dreamin' Tonight/I Should Be with You	1957	$30
❏ 47-8524	I'm Gonna Feed You Now/The Bride's Bouquet	1965	$10
❏ 47-7532	I'm Gonna Sing/I Thought of God	1959	$20
❏ PB-10411	Indian Creek/Thank You for the Happiness	1975	$5
❏ 47-6964	I Thought I Heard You Call My Name/Pay Day	1957	$30
❏ PB-10281	It's My Time (To Say I Love You)/Just for the Lonely Ones	1975	$6
❏ 47-8105	I've Enjoyed As Much of This As I Can Stand/One Way Ticket to the Blues	1962	$15
❏ 47-7708	Legend of the Big Steeple/Wakin' Up the Crowd	1960	$20
❏ 74-0923	Lightening the Load/Tomorrow Is Forever	1973	$6
❏ 47-9811	Little Boy's Prayer/Roses Out of Season	1970	$6
❏ 47-7457	Me and Fred and Joe and Bill/Out of Sight, Out of Mind	1959	$20
❏ 47-7967	Misery Loves Company/I Cried Again	1961	$15
❏ 47-8178	My Baby's Not Here (In Town Tonight)/In the Shadows of the Wine	1963	$15
❏ 47-8977	Old Slew-Foot/Let Me In	1966	$10
❏ 47-6697	Seeing Her Only Reminded Me of You/A Good Time Was Had by All	1956	$30
❏ 47-4996	Settin' the Woods on Fire/Headin' for a Weddin'	1952	$40
❏ 47-8723	Skid Row Joe/Love Your Neighbor	1965	$12
❏ 47-8338	Sorrow on the Rocks/The Life of the Party	1964	$15
❏ 47-5086	Takin' Chances/I Can't Live with You	1952	$40
❏ 47-5215	That's It/Don't Play That Song	1953	$30
❏ 47-7568	The Battle of Little Big Horn/Our Song of Love	1959	$20
❏ 47-9651	The Carroll County Accident/Sorrow Overtakes the Wine	1968	$8
❏ 47-9067	The Cold Hard Facts of Life/You Can't Make a Heel Toe the Mark	1967	$12
❏ 47-7638	The Girl Who Didn't Need Love/Your Kind of People	1959	$20
❏ 47-9939	The Last One to Touch Me/The Alley	1970	$6
❏ 47-7199	Tomorrow We'll Retire/Heaven's Just a Prayer Away	1958	$20
❏ APBO-0233	Tore Down/Nothing Between	1974	$5
❏ 47-5330	Trademark/A Beggar for Your Love	1953	$30

❏ 47-5631	Trinidad/Bad News Travels Fast	1954	$30
❏ 47-6598	Tryin' to Forget the Blues/I've Known You from Somewhere	1956	$30
❏ 47-7158	Turn It Over in Your Mind/As Long As I'm Dreaming	1958	$20
❏ APBO-0013	Wake Up, Jacob/Stella, Dear Sweet Stella	1973	$5
❏ 74-0648	What Ain't to Be, Just Might Happen/Little Bird	1972	$6
❏ 47-6421	What Would You Do? (If Jesus Came to Your House)/How Can You Refuse Him Now	1956	$30
❏ 74-0267	When You're Hot You're Hot/The Answer Is Love	1969	$8
❏ 47-9379	Woman Hungry/Out of the Silence (Came a Song)	1967	$10

WARNER BROS.
❏ 29596	That Was Then, This Is Now/Bottom of the Fifth	1983	$4
❏ 29772	This Cowboy's Hat/She Don't Have a License to Drive Me Up the Wall	1983	$3
❏ 29875	Turn the Pencil Over/Texas Moonbeam Waltz	1982	$4

— B-side by Johnny Gimble/Texas Swing Band

7-Inch Extended Plays
RCA VICTOR
| ❏ EPA-937 | A Satisfied Mind/I Like Girls// Living in the Past/Midnight | 1956 | $30 |
| ❏ VLP3389 | My Baby Turns the Lights On Uptown/Dim Lights, Thick Smoke and Loud Music/I'll Go Down Swinging//My Friends Are Gonna Be Strangers/Lovin' Lies/Sorrow on the Rocks | 1965 | $20 |

— Jukebox issue; small hole, plays at 33 1/3 rpm
| ❏ EPA-937 [PS] | Satisfied Mind | 1956 | $30 |
| ❏ VLP3389 [PS] | The Thin Man from West Plains | 1965 | $20 |

WAIKIKIS, THE
KAPP
❏ KJB-52	Hawaii Honeymoon/Remember Boa-Boa	1965	$8
❏ KJB-30	Hawaii Tattoo/Tahiti Tamoure	1964	$8
❏ 891	Pearly Shells/Tiny Bubbles	1968	$5

PALETTE
| ❏ 5091 | Hawaii Tattoo/Aloha Parade | 1962 | $15 |
| ❏ 5109 | Tikitiki Puki/Tanita Tamoure | 1963 | $10 |

WAILERS, THE
BELL
| ❏ 694 | Thinking Out Loud/You Can't Fly | 1967 | $10 |

ETIQUETTE
| ❏ 22 | Christmas Spirit/Don't Believe in Christmas | 1965 | $40 |

— B-side by the Sonics
❏ 19	Hang Up/Dirty Robber	1965	$50
❏ 24	It's You Alone/Tears	1966	$50
❏ 2	Mashi/Velva	1966	$20
❏ 21	Out of Our Tree/I Got Me	1966	$50
❏ 7	Seattle/Party Time U.S.A.	1963	$20
❏ 4	Stompin' Willie/Doin' the Seaside	1963	$20
❏ 9	Tall Cool One/Frenzy	1964	$20
❏ 6	We're Goin' Surfin'/Shakedown	1963	$20
❏ 545	Lucille/Scratchin'	1960	$30

— Photo of group on label
| ❏ 545 | Lucille/Scratchin' | 1964 | $15 |

— No photo of group
| ❏ 591 | Mau-Mau/Beat Guitar | 1964 | $10 |
| ❏ 526 | Mau-Mau/Dirty Robber | 1959 | $30 |

— Photo of group on label
| ❏ 526 | Mau-Mau/Dirty Robber | 1964 | $15 |

— No photo on label
| ❏ 518 | Tall Cool One/Roadrunner | 1959 | $40 |

— Photo of group on label
| ❏ 518 | Tall Cool One/Roadrunner | 1964 | $20 |

— No photo on label
| ❏ 532 | Wailin'/Shanghai'd | 1960 | $30 |

— Photo of group on label
| ❏ 532 | Wailin'/Shanghai'd | 1964 | $15 |

— No photo on label

IMPERIAL
| ❏ 66045 | Mashi/On the Rocks | 1964 | $20 |

UNITED ARTISTS
❏ 50065	End of the Summer/Think Kindly Baby	1966	$12
❏ 50110	Tears (Don't Have to Fall)/You Won't Lead Me On	1967	$10
❏ 50026	Tears/It's You Alone	1966	$10

VIVA
| ❏ 614 | I'm Determined/I Don't Want to Follow You | 1967 | $30 |

Number	Title	Yr	NM

WAILERS, THE (2)
COLUMBIA
| 40288 | Hot Love/Stop the Clock | 1954 | $120 |

WAINWRIGHT, LOUDON, III
ARISTA
| 0174 | Bicentennial/Talking Big Apple '75 | 1976 | $5 |
| 0340 | Final Exam/(B-side unknown) | 1978 | $5 |

COLUMBIA
| 45726 | Dead Skunk/Needless to Say | 1972 | $8 |

— Gray label
| 45726 | Dead Skunk/Needless to Say | 1973 | $6 |

— Orange label
| 45949 | Down Drinking at the Bar/I Am the Way | 1973 | $5 |
| 46064 | Swimming Song/Bell Bottom Pants | 1974 | $5 |

WAITE, JOHN
CHRYSALIS
| 2606 | Change/White Heat | 1982 | $5 |
| VS442606 | Change/White Heat | 1985 | $3 |

— Reissue of 2606
| VS442606 [PS] | Change/White Heat | 1985 | $3 |
| 2649 | Going to the Top/(B-side unknown) | 1982 | $5 |

EMI AMERICA
B-43040	Don't Lose Any Sleep/Wild One	1987	$3
B-43040 [PS]	Don't Lose Any Sleep/Wild One	1987	$3
B-8282	Every Step of the Way/No Brakes	1985	$3
B-8282 [PS]	Every Step of the Way/No Brakes	1985	$3
B-8315	If Anybody Had a Heart/Just Like Lovers	1986	$3
B-8315 [PS]	If Anybody Had a Heart/Just Like Lovers	1986	$3
B-8212	Missing You/For Your Love	1984	$3
B-8212 [PS]	Missing You/For Your Love	1984	$3
B-8238	Tears/Dreamtime-Shake It Up	1984	$3
B-8238 [PS]	Tears/Dreamtime-Shake It Up	1984	$3
B-43018	These Times Are Hard for Lovers/Wild One	1987	$3
B-43018 [PS]	These Times Are Hard for Lovers/Wild One	1987	$3
B-8278	Welcome to Paradise/You're the One	1985	$3
B-8278 [PS]	Welcome to Paradise/You're the One	1985	$3

WAITRESSES, THE
ANTILLES
| ANS-4504 | I Know What Boys Like/No Guilt | 1980 | $5 |
| ANS-105 | I Know What Boys Like/No Guilt | 1980 | $5 |

— Small center hole
| ANS-105 [PS] | I Know What Boys Like/No Guilt | 1980 | $5 |

CLONE
| CL-006 [B] | Slide/Clones | 1978 | $20 |

POLYDOR
PRO193 [DJ]	Christmas Wrapping (same on both sides)	1981	$10
2196	I Know What Boys Like/It's My Car	1982	$4
813394-7	Pleasure/Make the Weather	1983	$4
2225	Square Pegs/The Smartest Person I Know	1982	$4

ZE
| WIP6763 | Christmas Wrapping/Christmas Fever | 1981 | $30 |

— B-side by Charlelie Couture; U.K. import
| WIP6821 | Christmas Wrapping/Hangover 1-1-83 | 1982 | $10 |

— U.K. pressing with punch-out center intact
| WIP6821 [PS] | Christmas Wrapping/Hangover 1-1-83 | 1982 | $10 |

WAITS, TOM
ASYLUM
11014	Ol' 55/(B-side unknown)	1973	$6
45213	San Diego Serenade/Diamonds on My Windshield	1974	$5
45371	Step Right Up/The Piano Has Been Drinking	1976	$5

WAKEFIELD SUN
MGM
| 14072 | Tryst on Love/Sing a Simple Song | 1969 | $40 |
| 14028 | When I See You/Get Out | 1969 | $30 |

WAKELY, JIMMY
CAPITOL
| F1393 | Beautiful Brown Eyes/At the Close of a Long Day | 1951 | $30 |
| CCF9004 [PS] | Christmas on the Range | 1949 | $30 |
— Box for 3-record set (54-90014, 54-90015, 54-90016)
F90040	Christmas Polka/If Santa Claus Could Bring You Back To Me	1949	$30
F1472	Did You Write a Letter to Your Sweetheart/Cryin' Just for Youq	1951	$30
F1554	Don't Be Lonely/I'll Never Do a Thing	1951	$30
F1838	Each Step of the Way/Walk with the Lord	1951	$30
F2078	Forgive Me/Just Because	1952	$30
F2028	Goodbye Little Girl/Love Song of the Waterfall	1952	$30
F2126	If You Would Only Be Mine/My Heart Has Room for You	1952	$30
54-90016	It Came Upon a Midnight Clear/O Little Town of Bethlehem	1949	$30
— The above three are from "Album CCF-9004"
F2644	It's Christmas/Thanks	1953	$30
F2221	I Went to Your Wedding/Pale Moon	1952	$30
F2380	Lorelei/If You Knew What It Meant to Be Lonesome	1953	$30
F1936	Missing in Action/Just a Little Waiting	1952	$30
F1151	Mona Lisa/Steppin' Out	1950	$30
F1328	My Heart Cries for You/Music by the Angels	1950	$30
54-90015	O Come All Ye Faithful/Joy to the World	1949	$30
F1534	Old Soldiers Never Die/I Like Wide Open Spaces	1951	$30
F1630	One Has My Name (The Other Has My Heart)/I Love You So Much It Hurts	1951	$30
— Reissue of material first released on 78s
F929	Peter Cottontail/Mr. Easter Bunny	1950	$30
F1240	Pot of Gold/Bandera Waltz	1950	$30
54-90014	Silent Night/The First Nowell (The First Noel)	1949	$30
F1066	Sugar Plum Kisses/I Don't Have to Go to Heaven	1950	$30
F2484	The Orchid Means Goodbye/Out of Sight, Out of Mind	1953	$30
F2161	There's a Cloud in My Valley of Sunshine/Four Legged Friend	1952	$30
— B-side by Bob Hope
| F1762 | The Solid South/Another Fool Steps In | 1951 | $30 |
| F2172 | When I Say Goodnight/There's the Same Old Lovelight in Your Eyes | 1952 | $30 |

CORAL
9-61428	Are You Mine?/Yellow Roses	1955	$20
9-61143	Bimbo/Ain't She Sweet	1954	$30
9-61175	Bright Eyed and Bushy Tailed/Twilight Time in Tennessee	1954	$30
— With Eileen Barton
9-61220	Here Lies My Heart/It's Lonely on the Trail	1954	$30
9-61706	His Name Was Dean/Giant	1956	$30
9-61134	I Love You/I Stopped Lovin'	1954	$30
9-61320	Let Me Go Lover/Let the Rest of the World Go By	1954	$30
9-61341	Let's Walk into the Future/When He Grows Tired of You	1955	$20
9-61324	Punch/This-a-Way, That-a-Way	1954	$30
— With Eileen Barton
9-61389	Show Me the Way/What God Hath Joined Together	1955	$20
9-61509	Steal a Penny from a Beggar/Keep No Secrets	1955	$20
9-61460	Tattle Tale Blues/I'd Love to Live in Loveland	1955	$20

DECCA
32649	Any Way That You Want Me/That Silver-Haired Daddy of Mine	1970	$8
9-29756	Are You Satisfied/Mississippi Dreamboat	1955	$20
31267	Blue Nosed Mule/Midnight Mule	1961	$15
9-30270	Blue Nosed Mule/The Hand That Swept the Stars	1957	$20
32539	Brotherly Love/I Haven't Lived Enough	1969	$8
32271	Faded Love/Losing My Mind	1968	$8
9-29875	Folsom Prison Blues/That's What the Lord Can Do	1956	$20
9-30632	Foreign Love Affair/The Blue Canadian Rockies	1958	$20
9-29925	Goo Goo Da Da/Slow Down	1956	$20
32381	Heartaches/I Gotta Have My Baby Back	1968	$8
32459	I'll Steal Away in the Crowd/My Life Was Filled with Love	1969	$8
32727	I'm Walkin' By/Peace in the World	1970	$8
32595	I Wanta Go Home/My Sweet Lovin' Wife	1969	$8
9-30019	The Lord's On My Side/Roundup for the Lord	1956	$20
9-30372	Tweedle-O-Twill/The Image of Me	1957	$20
32324	Walking the Wet Streets/I Know How It Feels	1968	$8

DOT
16986	Midnight Wind/Cowboy	1966	$8
16873	The Shelter of Your Arms/Look Back	1966	$8
143	Come to Me/Cowboy	1960	$10
150	Goodnight Irene/Please Don't Hurt Me Anymore	1961	$10
140	High School Romance/Quail Hunt	1960	$12
127	Hoot and Holler/I Heard an Angel	1960	$10
113	I Know How It Feels/Out in the Cold	1959	$15
105	I've Got a Secret/Tomorrow	1958	$15
104	Lonesome Lover/By the Waters of the Minnetonka	1958	$15
128	My Heart Cries for You/Beautiful Brown Eyes	1960	$10
137	Please Help Me, I'm Falling/One Has My Name (The Other Has My Heart)	1960	$10
— With Jeanne McManus
107	Slippin' Around/I Love You So Much It Hurts	1959	$15
107 [PS]	Slippin' Around/I Love You So Much It Hurts	1959	$30
145	Snow Flakes/Wang Wang Blues	1960	$12
119	Sugar Candy/You Came Along	1959	$15
124	Swinging Jingle Bells/Silver Bells	1959	$15
106	That's Santa Claus/Lonely Is the Hunter	1958	$20
110	When It's Springtime in Alaska/Keeper of the Key	1959	$15

SHASTONE
| 103 | High School Love/Puppy Love | 1958 | $20 |

WAKEMAN, RICK
Also see YES.
A&M
1430	Catherine/Anne	1973	$6
1708	Merlin the Magician/Sir Galahad	1975	$5
1635	The Battle/And Now a Word from Our Sponsor	1974	$5
2010	The Birdman of Alcatraz/And Now a Word from Our Sponsor	1978	$8
1937	White Rock/After the Ball	1977	$5

WALCOS, THE
DRUM
| 011 | Tell Me Why/Moonlight Rock | 1959 | $125 |

WALES, HOWARD, AND JERRY GARCIA
DOUGLAS 7
| ZS76501 | South Side Strut/Uncle Martin's | 1971 | $20 |

WALKER, BILLY
CAPITOL
F1097	Alcohol Love/The Last Kiss Is the Sweetest	1950	$40
F941	Dirt 'Neath Your Feet/Too Many Times	1950	$40
54-40244	Don't Be Afraid to Call Me Darlin'/Headed for Heartaches	1949	$60
F40277	I'm Gonna Take My Heart Away from You/You Didn't Try and Didn't Care	1950	$50

CAPRICE
2059	A Little Bit Short on Love (A Little Bit Long on Tears)/I'm Gonna Leave You Tomorrow	1979	$5
2056	Lawyers/Why (Don't Ask Me Why)	1979	$5
2057	Sweet Lovin' Things/Rainbow and Roses	1979	$5

CASINO
| 124 | (If You Can) Why Can't I/The Magic Touch | 1977 | $5 |

COLUMBIA
4-41008	Anything Your Heart Desires/The Image of Me	1957	$20
4-20914	Anything Your Heart Desires/What Made Me Love You	1952	$30
4-41433	A Woman Like You/The Storm Within My Heart	1959	$20
4-21003	Back Street Affair/You Can Talk Me Out of Anything	1952	$30
4-20798	Beautiful Brown Eyes/I Ain't Got No Roses	1951	$30

Number	Title	Yr	NM
❏ 4-42287	Charlie's Shoes/ Wild Colonial Boy	1962	$15
❏ 4-43010	Circumstances/ It's Lonesome	1964	$10
❏ 4-43434	Come a Little Bit Closer/ Nobody But a Fool	1965	$8
❏ 4-43120	Cross the Brazos at Waco/ Down to My Last Cigarette	1964	$12
❏ 4-43120 [PS]	Cross the Brazos at Waco/ Down to My Last Cigarette	1964	$50

— Sleeve is promo only

Number	Title	Yr	NM
❏ 4-20874	Don't Tell a Soul/ Millie My Darling	1952	$30
❏ 4-40846	Especially for Fools/ If You're Happy	1957	$20
❏ 4-41872	Faded Lights and Lonesome People/Yes, I've Made It	1961	$15
❏ 4-21439	Fool That I Am/The Record	1955	$30
❏ 4-41548	Forever/Changed My Mind	1960	$15
❏ 4-42050	Funny How Time Slips Away/Joey's Back in Town	1961	$15
❏ 4-41226	Ghost of a Promise/It's Doggone Tough on Me	1958	$20
❏ 4-21290	Going, Going, Gone/I'm a Fool to Care	1954	$30
❏ S7-31188 [S]	Gonna Find Me a Bluebird/Molly Darling	1961	$20
❏ 4-42794	Heart, Be Careful/ Storm of Love	1963	$12
❏ 4-42794 [PS]	Heart, Be Careful/ Storm of Love	1963	$30
❏ 4-41519	I Call It Heaven/One Way Give and Take	1959	$20
❏ 4-20994	If I Should Live That Long/ One Heart's Beatin', One Heart's Cheatin'	1952	$30
❏ 4-43327	If It Pleases You/I'm So Miserable Without You	1965	$8
❏ 4-21191	I Got Lost Along the Way/I Can't Keep Girls Away	1953	$30
❏ 4-21037	I Had a Dream/The One You Hurt	1952	$30
❏ 4-41658	I'll Be True to You/Little Lover	1960	$15
❏ 4-21154	I'm Looking for Love/ Don't Let Your Pride Break Your Heart	1953	$30
❏ 4-41154	It'll Take Awhile/Where My Baby Goes	1958	$20
❏ 4-42664	I've Got a New Heartache/ Thank You for Calling	1963	$10
❏ 4-21531	I've Got Leavin' on My Mind/ I'll Never Stand in Your Way	1956	$30
❏ 4-41763	I Wish You Love/ Gotta Find a Way	1960	$15
❏ 4-21348	Let Me Hear from You/Hey!	1955	$30
❏ 4-21566	Little Baggy Britches/So Far	1956	$30
❏ 4-43223	Matamoros/I'm Nothing to You	1965	$8
❏ 4-21085	Mexican Joe/You Have My Heart Now	1953	$30
❏ 4-41319	Mr. Heartache/I Thought About You	1959	$20
❏ 4-40920	On My Mind Again/ Viva La Matador!	1957	$20
❏ 4-41099	Put Your Hand in Mine/I Need It	1958	$20
❏ 4-21256	Thank You for Calling/ Pretend You Don't Know Me	1954	$30
❏ 4-42891	The Morning Paper/ Coming Back for More	1963	$10
❏ S7-31189 [S]	There Stands the Glass/Jambalaya	1961	$20

— The above five are "Stereo Seven" 33 1/3 rpm jukebox singles from set "JS 7-36" entitled "Everybody's Hits But Mine"

Number	Title	Yr	NM
❏ 4-21122	Time Will Tell/I Didn't Have the Nerve	1953	$30
❏ 4-20847	Ting-a-Ling/Fifteen Hugs Past Midnight	1951	$30
❏ S7-31185 [S]	titles unknown	1961	$20
❏ S7-31186 [S]	titles unknown	1961	$20
❏ S7-31187 [S]	titles unknown	1961	$20
❏ 4-21499	Whirlpool/Go Ahead and Make Me Cry	1956	$30
❏ 4-42492	Willie the Weeper/ Beggin' for Trouble	1962	$15

DIMENSION

Number	Title	Yr	NM
❏ 1042	One Away from One Too Many/Looking Through the Eyes of Love (Will Make You Blind)	1983	$5

MGM

Number	Title	Yr	NM
❏ 14268	Don't Let Him Make a Memory Out of Me/A Fool and His Love	1971	$6
❏ 14742	Fine As Wine/The Honky Tonks Are Calling Me Again	1974	$6
❏ 14377	Gone (Our Endless Love)/ All I Have to Offer You Is Me	1972	$6
❏ 14717	How Far Our Love Goes/ Love Me Back to Heaven (One More Time)	1974	$6
❏ 14693	I Changed My Mind/ Heart Be Careful	1974	$6
❏ 14210	I'm Gonna Keep On Lovin' You/It's a Long Way Down from Riches to Rags	1970	$6
❏ 14239	It's Time to Love Her/ She's Feeling Like a New Man Tonight	1971	$6
❏ 14655	Margarita/I'll Still Be There	1973	$8
❏ 14488	My Mind Hangs On to You/Charlie's Shoes	1973	$6

Number	Title	Yr	NM
❏ 14173	She Goes Walking Through My Mind/It's Your Fault I'm Cheating	1970	$6
❏ 14422	Sing Me a Love Song to Baby/The Day I Was Out and He Was In	1972	$6
❏ 14565	The Hand of Love/Ranada	1973	$6
❏ 14669	Too Many Memories/ Margarita	1973	$6
❏ 14305	Traces of a Woman/You Gave Me a Mountain	1971	$6
❏ 14134	When a Man Loves a Woman (The Way That I Love You)/She's As Close As I Can Get (To Loving You)	1970	$6

MONUMENT

Number	Title	Yr	NM
❏ 943	A Million and One/ Close to Linda	1966	$8
❏ 997	Anything Your Heart Desires/I Gotta Get Me Feelin' Better	1967	$8
❏ 980	Bear With Me a Little Longer/It's Beginning to Hurt	1966	$8
❏ 1013	In Del Rio/Wish I Could Love That Much Again	1967	$8
❏ 1024	I Taught Her Everything She Knows/I Treat Her Like a Baby	1967	$8
❏ 932	The Old French Quarter (In New Orleans)/ How Do You Ask?	1966	$8
❏ 932 [PS]	The Old French Quarter (In New Orleans)/ How Do You Ask?	1966	$30

MRC

Number	Title	Yr	NM
❏ 1009	Carlena and Jose Gomez/Every Cheatin' Thing She Knows	1977	$5
❏ 1003	It Always Brings Me Back Around to You/ (B-side unknown)	1977	$5
❏ 1014	It's Not Over Till It's Over/ Don't Let the Morning Sun Shine Shame on You	1978	$5

RCA

Number	Title	Yr	NM
❏ PB-10821	Instead of Givin' Up (I'm Givin' In)/Curtains on the Windows	1976	$5

RCA VICTOR

Number	Title	Yr	NM
❏ PB-10466	Don't Stop in My World (If You Don't Mean to Stay)/Honky Tonkitis	1975	$5
❏ PB-10613	(Here I Am) Alone Again/ When the Song Is Gone (The Music Dies)	1976	$5
❏ PB-10345	If I'm Losing You/I'd Love to Feel You Loving Me Again	1975	$5
❏ PB-10729	Love You All to Pieces/ Sierra Nevada	1976	$5
❏ PB-10205	Word Games/I Can't Say No If She Keeps Saying Yes	1975	$5

TALL TEXAN

Number	Title	Yr	NM
❏ 52	Beautiful Texas/Your Ever Leavin' Lovin'	1984	$6
❏ 57	Coffee Brown Eyes/Jesse	1985	$6
❏ 56	He Sang the Song About El Paso/Welcome Back to My Heart	1985	$6
❏ 55	Soap and Water/ Someone Loves You	1985	$6
❏ 58	Welcome Back to My Heart/(B-side unknown)	1986	$6
❏ 60	Wild Texas Rose/Sweet Spanish Melodies	1988	$6

WALKER BROTHERS, THE

KAY-Y

Number	Title	Yr	NM
❏ 66785	Beautiful Brown Eyes/ Ninety-Seven	1960	$60

SMASH

Number	Title	Yr	NM
❏ 2063	Another Tear Falls/Saddest Night in the World	1966	$15
❏ 2048	(Baby) You Don't Have to Tell Me/Young Man Cried	1966	$15
❏ 1952	Doin' the Jerk/Pretty Girls Everywhere	1964	$15
❏ 1976	Love Her/Seventh Dawn	1965	$15
❏ 2000	Make It Easy on Yourself/But I Do	1965	$20
❏ 2009	Make It Easy on Yourself/ Doin' the Jerk	1965	$15
❏ 2009 [PS]	Make It Easy on Yourself/ Doin' the Jerk	1965	$30
❏ 2016	My Ship Is Comin' In/ You're All Around Me	1966	$15
❏ 2016 [PS]	My Ship Is Comin' In/ You're All Around Me	1966	$30
❏ 2032	The Sun Ain't Gonna Shine (Anymore)/After the Lights Go Out	1966	$15

TOWER

Number	Title	Yr	NM
❏ 218	I Only Came to Dance with You/Greens	1966	$15

WALKER, CHARLIE

CAPITOL

Number	Title	Yr	NM
❏ 3813	I Do My Cryin' at Night/ Wantin' My Woman Again	1974	$6

Number	Title	Yr	NM
❏ 3922	Odds and Ends (Bits and Pieces)/Society's Got Us	1974	$5
❏ 4040	Say You're Gone/ The Last Supper	1975	$5

COLUMBIA

Number	Title	Yr	NM
❏ 4-41820	Facing the Wall/I Walked Out on Heaven (When I Walked Out on You)	1961	$15
❏ 4-42176	Good Deal, Lucille/ Louisiana Bell	1961	$15
❏ 4-41388	I'll Catch You When You Fall/I Don't Mind Saying	1959	$15
❏ 4-42454	Life Goes On/Only Meant to Borrow	1962	$15
❏ 4-41211	Pick Me Up on Your Way Down/Two Empty Arms	1958	$20
❏ 4-42669	What's Wrong with Me/ One in Every Crowd	1963	$15
❏ 4-41467	When My Conscience Hurts the Most/Bow Down Your Head and Cry	1959	$15
❏ 4-41633	Who Will Buy the Wine/I Go Anywhere	1960	$15

DECCA

Number	Title	Yr	NM
❏ 9-30282	Cheaters Never Win/ Stepping Stones	1957	$30
❏ 9-29715	Only You, Only You/Can't Get There from Here	1955	$30
❏ 9-29154	Tell Her Lies and Feed Her Candy/You Don't Need No Other Daddy But Me	1954	$30
❏ 9-29416	The Chocolate Song/ Hurry Back Home	1955	$30
❏ 9-29334	When You Know You Have Lost (And You Know You Still Care)/It Takes That to Satisfy Me	1954	$30

EPIC

Number	Title	Yr	NM
❏ 5-9727	Close All the Honky Tonks/ Truck Driving Man	1964	$10
❏ 5-10063	Daddy's Coming Home (Next Week)/I'm Gonna Hang Up My Gloves	1966	$8
❏ 5-9852	He's a Jolly Good Fellow/Memory Killer	1965	$12
❏ 5-9759	Honky Tonk Song/Pick Me Up on Your Way Down	1965	$10
❏ 5-10021	I'm Gonna Live (As Long As I Can)/Little Old Wine Drinker	1966	$8
❏ 5-9875	The Man in the Little White Suit/Fraulein	1966	$8
❏ 5-10118	The Town That Never Sleeps/The Way to Say Goodbye	1967	$8
❏ 5-9799	Wild as a Wildcat/Out of a Honky Tonk	1965	$10

IMPERIAL

Number	Title	Yr	NM
❏ X8173	A Flock of Memories/What You Savin' Your Lovin' For	1952	$40
❏ X8155	Flaming Bell/ Two Red Lips	1952	$40
❏ X8146	I'm Looking for Another You/Stolen Kisses	1952	$40
❏ X8161	Out of My Arms/By Nights You Belong to Me	1952	$40
❏ X8185	Stay Away from My Heart/I've Never Been Out of Texas	1953	$40

MERCURY

Number	Title	Yr	NM
❏ 71081	Gentle Love/Dancing Mexican Boy	1957	$30
❏ 71111	I'll Never Let It Show/ Take My Hand	1957	$30
❏ 71405	I'm Not Mixed Up Anymore/ No Sorrow Tonight	1959	$30

PLANTATION

Number	Title	Yr	NM
❏ 185	Don't Sing a Song About Texas/Please Mr. Please	1979	$5
❏ 165	I've Had a Beautiful Time/ Truck Driving Man	1977	$5
❏ 168	T for Texas/Pick Me Up on Your Way Down	1978	$5
❏ 180	Tonight My Solitaire Turns Into Gin/My Shoes Keep Walking Back to You	1979	$5

RCA VICTOR

Number	Title	Yr	NM
❏ 74-0929	Gonna Drink Milwaukee Dry/ Time Changes Everything	1973	$6
❏ 74-0730	I Don't Mind Goin' Under (If It'll Get Me Over You)/ Honky Tonk Heart	1972	$6
❏ 74-0870	Soft Lips and Hard Liquor/It's Better Than Going Home Alone	1973	$6

WALKER, CINDY

COLUMBIA

Number	Title	Yr	NM
❏ 4-21045	Oh How Sweet It Is to Know/Hold to God's Unchanging Hand	1952	$40

WALKER, CLINT

WARNER BROS.

Number	Title	Yr	NM
❏ 5133	Silver Bells/Love at Home	1959	$15

Number	Title	Yr	NM

WALKER, DUSTY
COLUMBIA
❏ 1-687	My Castle Just Tumbled/ Someday You'll Cry	1950	$40

—*Microgroove 33 1/3 rpm 7-inch single*

❏ 4-21011	My Heart Cries for You Like a Baby/Bird with a Broken Wing	1952	$30
❏ 1-755(?)	Silver River/Proud Little Heart	1950	$40

—*Microgroove 33 1/3 rpm 7-inch single*

❏ 4-38924	Silver River/Proud Little Heart	1950	$30

IMPERIAL
❏ 8193	Our Vow/I'm So Glad	1953	$40
❏ 8179	Peaches and Cream/I Don't Need a Diary	1953	$40

WALKER, JERRY JEFF
Also see CIRCUS MAXIMUS.

ATCO
❏ 6767	I'm Gonna Tell on You/ But For the Time	1970	$6
❏ 6594	Mr. Bojangles/Round and Round	1968	$10

ELEKTRA
❏ 46016	Comfort and Crazy/Eastern Ave. River Railway Blues	1979	$4

MCA
❏ 40570	Dear John Letter Lounge/ It's a Good Night for Singing	1976	$4
❏ 40167	Desperadoes Waitin' for a Train/Gettin' By	1973	$4
❏ 40389	Goodbye Easy Street/ Salvation Army Band	1975	$4
❏ 40054	L.A. Freeway/Charlie Dunn	1973	$4
❏ 40622	(Looking for the) Heart of Saturday Night/Stoney	1976	$4
❏ 40760	Mr. Bojangles/Don't It Make You Wanna Dance	1977	$4
❏ 40250	Sangria Wine/Hill Country Rain	1974	$4

SOUTH COAST
❏ 52122	Don't Think Twice, It's Alright/Laying My Life on the Line	1982	$4
❏ 51146	Got Lucky Last Night/ Maybe Mexico	1981	$4
❏ 51215	Take It As It Comes/She Knows Her Daddy Sings	1981	$4

TRIED & TRUE
❏ 1690	I Feel Like Hank Williams Tonight/Mr. Bojangles	1989	$5
❏ 1695	The Pickup Truck Song/ The Pickup Truck Song (Long Version)	1989	$5
❏ 1698	Trashy Women/I Feel Like Hank Williams Tonight	1989	$5

WALKER, JR., AND THE ALL STARS
HARVEY
❏ 117	Cleo's Mood/Brain Washer	1963	$30
❏ 119	Good Rockin'/Brain Washer	1963	$30
❏ 113	Willie's Blues/Twist Lackawanna	1962	$30

MOTOWN
❏ 1689	Blow the House Down/Ball Baby	1983	$4
❏ 1352	Country Boy/What Does It Take (To Win Your Love)	1975	$5

SOUL
❏ 35017	Cleo's Mood/Baby You Know It Ain't Right	1966	$8
❏ 35041	Come See About Me/Sweet Soul	1967	$8
❏ 35110	Dancing Like They Do on Soul Train/I Ain't That Easy to Love	1973	$6
❏ 35012	Do the Boomerang/Tune Up	1965	$12
❏ 35073	Do You See My Love (For You Growing)/ Groove and More	1970	$6
❏ 35104	Gimme That Beat (Part 1)/ Gimme That Beat (Part 2)	1973	$6
❏ 35070	Gotta Hold On to This Feeling/Clinging to the Theory That She's Coming Back	1970	$6
❏ 35097	Groove Thang/Me and My Family	1972	$6
❏ 35048	Hip City -- Part 1/ Hip City -- Part 2	1968	$8
❏ 35081	Holly Holy/Carry Your Own Load	1970	$6
❏ 35055	Home Cookin'/Mutiny	1969	$8
❏ 35118	Hot Shot/You're No Ordinary Woman	1976	$5
❏ 35024	How Sweet It Is (To Be Loved By You)/ Nothing But Soul	1966	$8
❏ 35024 [PS]	How Sweet It Is (To Be Loved By You)/ Nothing But Soul	1966	$30
❏ 35106	I Don't Need No Reason/ Country Boy	1973	$6

❏ 35015	(I'm a) Road Runner/ Shoot Your Shot	1965	$10
❏ 35116	I'm So Glad/Soul Clappin'	1975	$5
❏ 35026	Money (That's What I Want) Part I/Money (That's What I Want) Part II	1966	$8
❏ 35003	Monkey Jump/Satan's Blues	1964	$20
❏ 35108	Peace and Understanding (Is Hard to Find)/ Soul Clappin'	1973	$6
❏ 35030	Pucker Up Buttercup/ Anyway You Wanna	1967	$8
❏ 35013	Shake and Fingerpop/ Cleo's Back	1965	$10
❏ 35036	Shoot Your Shot/ Ain't That the Truth	1967	$8
❏ 35008	Shot Gun/Hot Cha	1965	$125

—*Not only is the A-side title listed as two words, but the record is credited to "Jr. Walker and All The Stars"!*

❏ 35008	Shotgun/Hot Cha	1965	$20
❏ 35008 [PS]	Shotgun/Hot Cha	1965	$30
❏ 35084	Take Me Girl, I'm Ready/ Right On Brothers and Sisters	1971	$6
❏ 35067	These Eyes/Got to Find a Way to Win Maria Back	1969	$6
❏ 35095	Walk in the Night/I Don't Want to Do Wrong	1972	$6
❏ 35090	Way Back Home/ (Instrumental)	1971	$6
❏ 35062	What Does It Take (To Win Your Love)/ Brainwasher -- Part 1	1969	$8
❏ 35122	Whopper Bopper Show Stopper/Hard Love	1977	$5

WHITFIELD
❏ 8861	Back Street Boogie/ Don't Let Me Go Away	1979	$4
❏ 49052	Wishing on a Star/ Hole in the Wall	1979	$4

WALKER, T-BONE
ATLANTIC
❏ 1045	Papa Ain't Salty/T-Bone Shuffle	1955	$60
❏ 1074	Why Not/Play On Little Girl	1955	$50

BLUESWAY
❏ 61008	Confusion Blues/Every Night I Have to Cry	1967	$8

CAPITOL
❏ F799	Go Back to the One You Love/On Your Way Blues	1950	$200
❏ F944	Too Much Trouble Blues/She's My Old Time Used to Be	1950	$200

IMPERIAL
❏ 5216	Blue Mood/Got No Use for You	1953	$200
❏ 5284	Bye Bye Baby/ Wanderin' Heart	1954	$100
❏ 5962	Doin' Time/Cold, Cold Water	1963	$15
❏ 5247	Everytime/Tell Me What's the Reason	1953	$200
❏ 5832	Evil Hearted Woman/ Life Is Too Short	1962	$20
❏ 5330	I'll Understand/ The Hard Way	1955	$60
❏ 5261	I'm About to Lose My Mind/I Miss You Baby	1954	$125
❏ 5311	Love Is Just a Gamble/ High Society	1954	$100
❏ 5239	Party Girl/You're Here in the Dark	1953	$300
❏ 5264	Pony Tail/When the Sun Goes Down	1954	$100
❏ 5202	Street Walkin' Woman/ The Blues Is a Woman	1952	$400

—*Note: T-Bone Walker records on Imperial before 5202 are unconfirmed on 45 rpm.*

❏ 5299	Teenage Baby/ Strugglin' Blues	1954	$100
❏ 5695	Travelin' Blues/ Strollin' with Bones	1960	$20

JETSTREAM
❏ 730	T-Bone's Back/She's a Hit	1967	$10

MODERN
❏ 1004	Should I Let Her Go/ Hey Hey Baby	1965	$10

POST
❏ 2002	I Get So Weary/Tell Me What's the Reason	1955	$70

7-Inch Extended Plays
CAPITOL
❏ EAP 1-370 [PS]	Classics in Jazz	1953	$250
❏ EAP 1-370	(contents unknown)	1953	$250

WALKER, WAYNE
ABC-PARAMOUNT
❏ 9735	It's My Way/All I Can Do Is Cry	1956	$70

BRUNSWICK
❏ 55133	Little Ole You/What Kind of God Do You Think You Are	1959	$50

COLUMBIA
❏ 40905	A Teenage Love Affair/ Whatever You Desire	1957	$30
❏ 41042	Bo-Bo Sha Diddle Diddle/ Come Away from His Arms	1957	$30
❏ 41130	I'm Finally Free/It's Written in Your Arms	1958	$30

CORAL
❏ 62328	Battle of the Bulge/Reaching for the Impossible	1962	$20

EVEREST
❏ 19380	Love, Love, Love/ Sweet Chains of Love	1960	$20

WALLACE, BILLY
DEB
❏ 1003	Don't Flirt with My Baby/You'll Never Cheat Me Anymore	1958	$200
❏ 883	Wolf Call/(B-side unknown)	1957	$200

MERCURY
❏ 70957	Mean Mistrteating Baby/ Burning the Wind	1956	$300
❏ 70876	What'll I Do/That's My Reward	1956	$200

WALLACE, CEDRIC, ORCHESTRA
DERBY
❏ 786	White Christmas/ Lonely Christmas	1952	$20

WALLACE, JERRY
4 STAR
❏ 1035	I Wanna Go to Heaven/After You	1978	$5

ALLIED
❏ 5015	Little Miss One/Petrillo	1954	$60

—*B-side by Eddie Oliver and the Oliver Twisters*

❏ 5019	That's What a Woman Can Do/I Hate to Go Home Alone	1954	$50

BMA
❏ 8-006	At the End of a Rainbow/ Looking for a Memory	1978	$5
❏ 7-005	I'll Promise You Tomorrow/ You're on the Run	1977	$5
❏ 7-002	I Miss You Already/At the End of a Rainbow	1977	$5
❏ 8-008	My Last Sad Song/ Wickenburg Way	1978	$5

CHALLENGE
❏ 59040	A Touch of Pink/Off Stage	1959	$20
❏ 59223	Auf Wiedesehn/If I Make It Through Today	1963	$12
❏ 1003	Blue Jean Baby/ Fool's Hall of Fame	1957	$30
❏ 59027	Diamond Ring/All My Love Belongs to You	1958	$30
❏ 59205	Empty Arms Again/ Bambola (My Darling One)	1963	$15
❏ 59265	Even the Bad Times Are Good/Spanish Guitars	1964	$12
❏ 9117	Eyes (Don't Give My Secrets Away)/Lonesome	1961	$15
❏ 9152	Here I Go/You'll Never Know	1962	$15
❏ 59013	How the Time Flies/ With This Ring	1958	$30
❏ 59246	In the Misty Moonlight/ Cannon Ball	1964	$20

—*B-side by the Soul Surfers*

❏ 59246	In the Misty Moonlight/Even the Bad Times Are Good	1964	$10
❏ 9107	Life's a Holiday/I Can See an Angel Walking	1961	$15
❏ 59060	Little Coco Palm/ Mission Bell Blues	1959	$20
❏ 59060 [PS]	Little Coco Palm/ Mission Bell Blues	1959	$50
❏ 9139	Little Miss Tease/Mr. Lonely	1962	$15
❏ 9185	Move Over/On a Merry-Go-Round	1963	$15
❏ 59047	Primrose Lane/By Your Side	1959	$20
❏ 9171	Shutters and Boards/Am I That Easy to Forget	1962	$15
❏ 59082	Swingin' Down the Lane/ Teardrops in the Rain	1960	$20
❏ 59000	The Other Me/ Good and Bad	1958	$30
❏ 59098	There She Goes/Angel on My Shoulder	1960	$20

CLASS
❏ 502	Taj Mahal/Autumn Has Come and Gone	1955	$30

DOOR KNOB
❏ 127	Cling to Me/Paper Madonna	1980	$5
❏ 134	If I Could Set My Love to Music/Cling to Me	1980	$5

GLENOLDEN
❏ 159	Are You Ready/That's the Fool in Me	1968	$6

LIBERTY
❏ 56028	Another Time, Another Place, Another World/ That's What Fools Are For	1968	$6

Number	Title	Yr	NM
❏ 56155	Even the Bad Times Are Good/For All We Know	1970	$6
❏ 56147	Honey Eyed Girl/Glory of My Girl	1969	$6
❏ 56059	Sweet Child of Sunshine/Our House on Paper	1968	$6
❏ 56130	Swiss Cottage Place/With Aging	1969	$6
❏ 56095	Temptation/Son	1969	$6
❏ 56001	This One's on the House/A New Sun Risin'	1967	$8

MCA

Number	Title	Yr	NM
❏ 40037	A Song Nobody Sings/Sound of Goodbye	1973	$5
❏ 40111	Don't Give Up on Me/You Look Like Forever	1973	$5
❏ 40183	Guess Who/All I Ever Want from You	1974	$5
❏ 40321	Make Hay While the Sun Shines/I Wonder Whose Baby	1974	$5
❏ 40248	My Wife's House/A Better Way to Say I Love You	1974	$5

MERCURY

Number	Title	Yr	NM
❏ 72258	Butterfly/Let the Tears Begin	1964	$10
❏ 72356	Careless Hands/San Francisco d'Assisi	1964	$10
❏ 72529	Diamonds and Horseshoes/Will the Pain Fade Away	1966	$12
❏ 72246	In the Misty Moonlight/Even the Bad Times Are Good	1964	$15
❏ 72292	It's a Candy Cotton World/Keep a Lamp Burning	1964	$10
❏ 72461	Life's Gone and Slipped Away/Twelve Little Roses	1965	$12
❏ 70812	One Night When Flowers Were Dancing/Gloria	1956	$30
❏ 70684	Taj Mahal/Autumn Has Come and Gone	1955	$30
❏ 70758	The Greatest Magic of All/Walking in the Rain	1955	$30
❏ 72589	Wallpaper Roses/Son of a Green Beret	1966	$10

MGM

Number	Title	Yr	NM
❏ 14788	Comin' Home to You/The River St. Marie	1975	$5
❏ 14832	Georgia Rain/In the Garden	1975	$5
❏ 14809	Wanted Man/Your Love	1975	$5

POLYDOR

Number	Title	Yr	NM
❏ 14322	The Fool I've Been Today/Jenny Angel	1976	$4

TOPS

Number	Title	Yr	NM
❏ 369	P.S. I Love You/Vaya Con Dios (May God Be With You)	1953	$50

—B-side by Betty Ford

UNITED ARTISTS

Number	Title	Yr	NM
❏ 50971	Funny How Time Slips Away/Thanks to You for Loving Me	1972	$5
❏ XW239	Take Me As I Am/Touch Me	1973	$5
❏ XW618	With Pen in Hand/All I Want Is You	1975	$5

WING

Number	Title	Yr	NM
❏ 90065	Eyes of Fire, Lips of Wine/Monkey See, Monkey Do	1956	$30

WALLACE, SONNY

YUCCA

Number	Title	Yr	NM
❏ 127	Black Cadillac/If a Man Could See	1961	$125

WALLIS, RUTH

DECCA

Number	Title	Yr	NM
❏ 9-30336	A Sad Calypso/Donkey Is a Jackass	1957	$10

KING

Number	Title	Yr	NM
❏ 6024	I'd Rather Be a Broad/I'm the Sexiest Gal in Town	1966	$10

MONARCH

Number	Title	Yr	NM
❏ 3005	Dear Mr. Godfrey/Say Hello to Joe	1953	$30

WALLS, TOM

HIT

Number	Title	Yr	NM
❏ 10	Funny Way of Laughin'/PT 109	1962	$8

—B-side by Johnny Keaton

Number	Title	Yr	NM
❏ 20	Speedy Gonzales/The Stripper	1962	$8

—B-side by the Music City Orchestra

WALLS, VAN

ATLANTIC

Number	Title	Yr	NM
❏ 980	After Midnight/Blue Sender	1952	$125

WALSH, JOE

Also see EAGLES; THE JAMES GANG (1)

ABC

Number	Title	Yr	NM
❏ 12115	Time Out/Help Me Through the Night	1975	$5
❏ 12187	Walk Away/Help Me Through the Night	1976	$5

ABC DUNHILL

Number	Title	Yr	NM
❏ 4327	I'll Tell the World About You/Mother Says	1972	$5
❏ 4373	Meadows/Bookends	1973	$5
❏ 15026	Turn to Stone/All Night Laundromat Blues	1974	$5

ASYLUM

Number	Title	Yr	NM
❏ 47144	A Life of Illusion/Rockets	1981	$4
❏ 45536	At the Station/Over and Over	1978	$4
❏ 45493	Life's Been Good/Theme from Boat Weirdos	1978	$4
❏ 47197	Made Your Mind Up/Things	1981	$4

FULL MOON

Number	Title	Yr	NM
❏ 69951	Waffle Stomp/Things	1982	$4
❏ 69951 [PS]	Waffle Stomp/Things	1982	$4

FULL MOON/ASYLUM

Number	Title	Yr	NM
❏ 46639	All Night Long/Orange Blossom Special	1980	$4

—B-side by Gilley's Urban Cowboy Band

Number	Title	Yr	NM
❏ 46639 [PS]	All Night Long/Orange Blossom Special	1980	$5

WARNER BROS.

Number	Title	Yr	NM
❏ 28910	Good Man Down/I Broke My Leg	1985	$4
❏ 29519	Here We Are Now/I Can Play That Rock and Roll	1983	$4
❏ 29454	I.L.B.T.'s/Love Letters	1983	$4
❏ 28225	In My Car/How Ya Doin'?	1987	$3
❏ 29611	Space Age Whiz Kids/Theme from Island Weirdos	1983	$4
❏ 29611 [PS]	Space Age Whiz Kids/Theme from Island Weirdos	1983	$5

WANDERERS, THE (1)

CUB

Number	Title	Yr	NM
❏ 9003	A Teenage Quarrel/My Shining Hour	1958	$40
❏ 9019	Collecting Hearts/Two Hearts on a Window Pane	1958	$50
❏ 9089	For Your Love/Sally Goodheart	1961	$40
❏ 9094	I'll Never Smile Again/A Little Too Long	1961	$40
❏ 9075	I Need You More/I Could Make You Mine	1960	$40
❏ 9054	I Walked Through a Forest/I'm Waiting for Green Pastures	1959	$40
❏ 9035	Only When You're Lonely/I'm Not Ashamed	1959	$40
❏ 9023	Please/Shadrack, Meshack, and Abednego	1959	$40
❏ 9099	She Wears My Ring/Somebody Else's Sweetheart	1961	$60
❏ 9109	There Is No Greater Love/As Time Goes By	1962	$40

MGM

Number	Title	Yr	NM
❏ 13082	There Is No Greater Love/As Time Goes By	1962	$30

ONYX

Number	Title	Yr	NM
❏ 518	Thinking of You/Great Jumpin' Catfish	1957	$70

ORBIT

Number	Title	Yr	NM
❏ 9003	A Teenage Quarrel/My Shining Hour	1958	$70

SAVOY

Number	Title	Yr	NM
❏ 1109	We Could Find Happiness/Holy Mae Ethel	1953	$500

UNITED ARTISTS

Number	Title	Yr	NM
❏ 570	After He Breaks Your Heart/Run, Run Senorita	1963	$20
❏ 648	I'll Know/You Can't Run Away from Me	1963	$40

WANDERERS, THE (U)

GONE

Number	Title	Yr	NM
❏ 5005	Mask Off/My Lady Chocaonine	1957	$40

WANDERERS THREE, THE

DOLTON

Number	Title	Yr	NM
❏ 59	Cry I Do/Toro	1962	$15
❏ 66	My Glory Land/Turn Around	1962	$15
❏ 82	Wanderin'/Hi-De-Ink-Tum	1963	$10

MGM

Number	Title	Yr	NM
❏ K13257	Gimmie Some/Long Time Man	1964	$20

WANG CHUNG

A&M

Number	Title	Yr	NM
❏ 2728	Fire in the Twilight/The Reggae (Instrumental)	1985	$5

—B-side by Keith Forsey

Number	Title	Yr	NM
❏ 2728 [PS]	Fire in the Twilight/The Reggae (Instrumental)	1985	$5

ARISTA

Number	Title	Yr	NM
❏ 1012 [DJ]	Hold Back the Tears (same on both sides)	1983	$8

—As "Huang Chung"; stock copy appears not to exist

GEFFEN

Number	Title	Yr	NM
❏ 7-29310	Dance Hall Days/Ornamental Elephant	1984	$3
❏ 7-29310 [PS]	Dance Hall Days/Ornamental Elephant	1984	$3
❏ 7-29193	Don't Be My Enemy/The Waves	1984	$5
❏ 7-29377	Don't Let Go/There Is a Nation	1984	$3
❏ 7-29377 [PS]	Don't Let Go/There Is a Nation	1984	$3
❏ 7-28562	Everybody Have Fun Tonight/Fun Tonight: The Early Years	1986	$3
❏ 7-28562 [PS]	Everybody Have Fun Tonight/Fun Tonight: The Early Years	1986	$3
❏ 7-28359	Hypnotize Me/Lullaby	1987	$3
❏ 7-28359 [PS]	Hypnotize Me/Lullaby	1987	$3
❏ 7-28531	Let's Go!/Betrayal	1987	$4
❏ 7-28531 [PS]	Let's Go!/Betrayal	1987	$4

—We don't know if the back of the sleeve contains a reference to the revised B-side or no reference at all to the B-side

Number	Title	Yr	NM
❏ 7-28531	Let's Go!/The World in Which We Live	1986	$3
❏ 7-28531 [PS]	Let's Go!/The World in Which We Live	1986	$3
❏ 7-22969	Praying to a New God/Tall Trees in a Blue Sky	1989	$3
❏ 7-22969 [PS]	Praying to a New God/Tall Trees in a Blue Sky	1989	$3
❏ 7-28891	To Live and Die in L.A./Black-Blue-White	1985	$3
❏ 7-28891 [PS]	To Live and Die in L.A./Black-Blue-White	1985	$3

WAR

Also see ERIC BURDON AND WAR.

BLUE NOTE

Number	Title	Yr	NM
❏ 1009	L.A. Sunshine/Slowly We Walk Together	1977	$5

COCO PLUM

Number	Title	Yr	NM
❏ 2002	Groovin'/(Instrumental)	1985	$4

LAX

Number	Title	Yr	NM
❏ 02120	Cinco de Mayo/Don't Let No One Get You Down	1981	$5

MCA

Number	Title	Yr	NM
❏ 41158	Don't Take It Away/The Music Band 2 (We Are the Music Band)	1979	$5
❏ 40820	Galaxy (Part 1)/Galaxy (Part 2)	1977	$5
❏ 40820 [PS]	Galaxy (Part 1)/Galaxy (Part 2)	1977	$6
❏ 40995	Good, Good Feelin'/Baby Face (She Said Do Do Do Do)	1979	$5
❏ 40883	Hey Senorita/Sweet Fighting Lady	1978	$5
❏ 41209	I'll Be Around/The Music Band 2 (We Are the Music Band)	1980	$5
❏ 41061	I'm the One Who Understands/Corns & Callouses	1979	$5

RCA

Number	Title	Yr	NM
❏ JH-13426 [DJ]	Baby, It's Cold Outside (same on both sides)	1982	$5
❏ PB-13544	Life (Is So Strange)/W.W. III	1983	$4
❏ PB-13239	Outlaw/I'm About Somebody	1982	$4

UNITED ARTISTS

Number	Title	Yr	NM
❏ 50815	All Day Music/Get Down	1971	$8
❏ XW432	Ballero/Slippin' Into Darkness	1974	$5
❏ XW281	Gypsy Man/Deliver the Word	1973	$5
❏ 50746	Lonely Feelin'/Sun Oh Sun	1971	$8
❏ 50746 [PS]	Lonely Feelin'/Sun Oh Sun	1971	$15
❏ XW706	Low Rider/So	1975	$5
❏ XW706 [PS]	Low Rider/So	1975	$6
❏ XW350	Me and Baby Brother/In Your Eyes	1973	$5
❏ XW1247	Sing a Happy Song/This Funky Music Makes You Feel Good	1978	$5
❏ 50867	Slippin' Into Darkness/Happy Head	1971	$6
❏ XW834	Summer/All Day Music	1976	$5
❏ XW163	The Cisco Kid/Beetles in the Bog	1973	$5
❏ 50975	The World Is a Ghetto/Four Cornered Room	1972	$6
❏ XW629	Why Can't We Be Friends?/In Mazatlin	1975	$5
❏ XW629 [PS]	Why Can't We Be Friends?/In Mazatlin	1975	$6

7-Inch Extended Plays

Number	Title	Yr	NM
❏ SP-92 [PS]	Edited Versions from The World Is a Ghetto	1972	$12
❏ SP-92 [DJ]	Where Was You At/City, Country, City//Beetles in the Bog/Four Cornered Room	1972	$10

Number	Title	Yr	NM

WAR BABIES, THE
UNI
❑ 55164	War Baby/Together Forever	1969	$8

WARD, BILLY, AND THE DOMINOES
DECCA
❑ 30043	Come On, Shake, Let's Crawl/Will You Remember	1956	$40
❑ 30149	Half a Love (Is Better Than None)/Evermore	1956	$40
❑ 30514	September Song/When the Saints Go Marching In	1957	$40
❑ 29933	St. Therese of the Roses/Home Is Where You Hang Your Hat	1956	$40
❑ 30420	To Each His Own/I Don't Stand a Ghost of a Chance	1957	$40

FEDERAL
❑ 12193	Above Jacob's Ladder/Little Black Train	1954	$60
❑ 12263	Bobby Sox Baby/How Long, How Long Blues	1956	$60
❑ 12209	Can't Do Sixty No More/If I Never Get to Heaven	1955	$125
❑ 12001	Do Something For Me/Chicken Blues	1951	$800

— Note: Federal 12010 and 12016 were issued only on 78s

❑ 12184	Handwriting on the Wall/One Moment with You	1954	$200
❑ 12068AA	Have Mercy Baby/Deep Sea Blues	1952	$250
❑ 12308	Have Mercy Baby/Love, Love, Love	1957	$50
❑ 12036	Heart to Heart/Looking for a Man to Satisfy My Soul	1951	$500

— With Little Esther

❑ 12039	I Am with You/Weeping Willow Blues	1951	$400
❑ 12105	I'd Be Satisfied/No Room	1952	$180
❑ 12106	I'm Lonely/Yours Forever	1952	$180
❑ 12072	Love, Love, Love/That's What You're Doing to Me	1952	$200
❑ 12218	Love Me Now or Let Me Go/Cave Man	1955	$60
❑ 12022AA	Sixty Minute Man/I Can't Escape from You	1951	$500
❑ 12301	St. Louis Blues/One Moment with You	1957	$60
❑ 12059	That's What You're Doing to Me/When the Swallows Come Back to Capistrano	1952	$400
❑ 12114	The Bells/Pedal Pushin' Papa	1952	$200
❑ 12129	These Foolish Things Remind Me of You/Don't Leave Me This Way	1953	$300

— Green label, gold top

❑ 12129	These Foolish Things Remind Me of You/Don't Leave Me This Way	1954	$125

— Green label, silver top

❑ 12129	These Foolish Things Remind Me of You/Don't Leave Me This Way	1955	$40

— All-green label

❑ 12178	Tootsie Roll/Move to the Outskirts of Town	1954	$125

JUBLIEE
❑ 5163	Gimme, Gimme, Gimme/Come to Me, Baby	1954	$40
❑ 5213	Sweethearts on Parade/Take Me Back to Heaven	1955	$40

KING
❑ 1281	Christmas in Heaven/Ringing In a Brand New Year	1953	$125
❑ 6002	I'm Walking Behind You/This Love of Mine	1965	$30
❑ 5463	Lay It on the Line/That's How You Know You're Growing Old	1961	$30
❑ 1492	Learnin' the Blues/May I Never Love	1955	$50
❑ 1368	Little Things Mean a Lot/I Really Don't Want to Know	1954	$50
❑ 6016	O Holy Night/What Are You Doin' New Year's Eve	1965	$30
❑ 1502	Over the Rainbow/Give Me You	1955	$50
❑ 5322	Sixty Minute Man/Have Mercy Baby	1960	$30
❑ 1342	Tenderly/Little Lie	1954	$60
❑ 1364	Three Coins in the Fountain/Lonesome Road	1954	$60

LIBERTY
❑ 55099	Deep Purple/Do It Again	1957	$30
❑ 55111	My Proudest Possession/Someone Greater Than I	1957	$30
❑ 55181	Please Don't Say No/Behave, Hula Girl	1959	$30
❑ 55126	Solitude/You Grow Sweeter As the Years Go By	1958	$30
❑ 55071	Star Dust/Lucinda	1957	$30
❑ 55071 [PS]	Star Dust/Lucinda	1957	$125

RO-ZAN
❑ 10001	Man in the Stain Glass Window/My Fair Weather Friend	1961	$30

UNITED ARTISTS
❑ 0017	Stardust/These Foolish Things	1973	$5

— Silver Spotlight Series" reissue

7-Inch Extended Plays
DECCA
❑ ED2549 [PS]	Billy Ward and His Dominoes	1958	$250
❑ ED2549	(contents unknown)	1958	$250

FEDERAL
❑ 262	*The Bells/Pedal Pushin' Papa/I'd Be Satisfied/That's What You're Doing to Me	1957	$400

— Green label, silver top

❑ 262	*The Bells/Pedal Pushin' Papa/I'd Be Satisfied/That's What You're Doing to Me	1957	$125

— All-green label

❑ 269	*These Foolish Things Remind Me of You/Rags to Riches/When the Swallows Come Back to Capistrano/Harbor Lights	1957	$400

— Green label, silver top

❑ 269	*These Foolish Things Remind Me of You/Rags to Riches/When the Swallows Come Back to Capistrano/Harbor Lights	1957	$125

— All-green label

❑ 212 [PS]	Billy Ward and His Dominoes, Vol. 1	1956	$125
❑ 262 [PS]	Billy Ward and His Dominoes, Vol. 2	1957	$125
❑ 269 [PS]	Billy Ward and His Dominoes Singing the All Time Hit Standards	1957	$125
❑ 212	Sixty Minute Man/Do Something for Me//Have Mercy Baby/Don't Leave Me This Way	1956	$400

— Green label, silver top

❑ 212	Sixty Minute Man/Do Something for Me//Have Mercy Baby/Don't Leave Me This Way	1956	$125

— All-green label

LIBERTY
❑ LEP-1-3056	(contents unknown)	1959	$125
❑ LEP-3-3056	(contents unknown)	1959	$125
❑ LEP-2-3083	Deep Purple/Lucinda//These Foolish Things/Don't Say I Love You	1959	$125
❑ LEP-2-3056	Deep River/By and By//The House of the Lord/The Lullaby Divine	1959	$125
❑ LEP-2-3056 [PS]	Sea of Glass (Part 2)	1959	$125
❑ LEP-3-3056 [PS]	Sea of Glass (Part 3)	1959	$125
❑ LEP-1-3056 [PS]	Sea of Glass (Part One)	1959	$125
❑ LEP-3-3083	Smoke Gets in Your Eyes/Do It Again//If You Please/Yours Forever	1959	$125
❑ LEP-1-3083	Stardust/Eatin' and Sleepin'//Music, Maestro, Please//I'll Never Ask for More Than This	1959	$125

WARD, BURT
MGM
❑ 13632	Boy Wonder I Love You/Orange Colored Sky	1966	$200

— Written and produced by Frank Zappa

WARD, DALE
BOYD
❑ 118	Here's Your Hat/Big Dale Trust	1962	$30
❑ 153	I Didn't Know/Pennies and Guitar Picks	1965	$10
❑ 152	I Tried/Living on Coal	1965	$10
❑ 150	Shake, Rattle and Roll/You Gotta Let Me Know	1965	$10

DOT
❑ 16520	A Letter from Sherry/Oh Julie	1963	$20
❑ 16590	Crying for Laura/I Got a Girl Friend	1964	$15
❑ 16704	Dirty Old Town/River Goodbye	1965	$15
❑ 16672	Fortune Teller/One Last Kiss Cherie	1964	$15
❑ 16632	I'll Never Love Again (After Loving You)/Young Lovers After Midnight	1964	$15
❑ 16759	Lonely Mary Ann/You Little Flirt	1965	$15

MONUMENT
❑ 945	Back in That World Again/Just Because I'm Lonely	1966	$12
❑ 1052	Don't Be Giving Away Your Love/Mama Don't Cry for Me	1968	$8
❑ 920	Hey You (I'm the One)/Kiss Him Goodbye	1966	$12
❑ 1101	How Much Can I Give/Saturday's Fool	1968	$8
❑ 1094	If Loving You Means Anything/River of Regret	1968	$8
❑ 1014	Operator/Your Seventeenth Year	1967	$8

WARD, HERB
ARGO
❑ 5510	Strange Change/Why Do You Want to Leave	1965	$100

RCA VICTOR
❑ 47-9688	Honest to Goodness/If You Got to Leave Me	1968	$70

WARD, JACKY, AND REBA MCENTIRE
MERCURY
❑ 55054	That Makes Two of Us/Good Friends	1979	$8
❑ 55026	Three Sheets in the Wind/I'd Really Love to See You Tonight	1978	$8

WARD, JACKY
ASYLUM
❑ 47468	Take the Mem'ry When You Go/Get Rhythm	1982	$4
❑ 47424	Travelin' Man/Save a Little Love	1982	$4

CINNAMON
❑ 811	Baby Let's Do Something/(B-side unknown)	1974	$8

— Quickly reissued on Mercury

❑ 800	Good Wine/Reachin' for You	1974	$6
❑ 783	Smoky Places/Living Again	1974	$6
❑ 776	The One I Sing My Love Songs To/I've Got to Burn	1973	$6

ELECTRIC
❑ 105	Can't Get to You from Here//(B-side unknown)	1987	$5
❑ 108	I Just Want to Be Your Santa Claus/The Greatest Gift of All	1987	$6

LUV
❑ 119	Georgia Blue Eyes/Handing Out Emotions	1986	$6

MEGA
❑ 0112	Dream Weaver/Biggest Piece of Me	1973	$6
❑ 0099	Words/Pretty Girl, Pretty Clothes, Pretty Sad	1973	$6

MERCURY
❑ 55018	A Lover's Question/She Belongs to Me	1978	$5
❑ 73640	Baby Let's Do Something/No Guarantee	1974	$5
❑ 73716	Dance Her By Me (One More Time)/Just Because	1975	$5
❑ 55003	Fools Fall in Love/Big Blue Diamond	1977	$5
❑ 57013	I'd Do Anything for You/Ain't It Just Like Me	1979	$5
❑ 73826	I Never Said It Would Be Easy/Nobody's Perfect	1976	$5
❑ 55038	I Want to Be in Love/Hey Friend	1978	$5
❑ 57022	Save Your Heart for Me/It Doesn't Matter Anymore	1980	$5
❑ 73783	She'll Throw Stones at You/One Pillow Between Us	1976	$5
❑ 57044	Somethin' on the Radio/Let Me Be Your Man	1981	$5
❑ 73667	Stealin'/I Can't Stand the Pain	1975	$5
❑ 73880	Texas Angel/Just Out of Reach	1976	$5
❑ 57032	That's the Way a Cowboy Rocks and Rolls/I Just Can't Help Believing	1980	$5
❑ 73918	Why Not Tonight/The Feelin's Right	1977	$5
❑ 55055	Wisdom of a Fool/One Day and a Night	1979	$5

MURCO
❑ 1021	I Want You/Little Boy with a Lonely Heart	1960	$30

WARD, ROBIN
DOT
❑ 16624	In His Car/Wishing	1964	$30
❑ 16578	Winter's Here/Bobby	1963	$10
❑ 16530	Wonderful Summer/Dream Boy	1963	$15

WARD, SINGIN' SAMMY
MOTOWN
❑ 1004	Lover/That's Why I Love You So Much	1960	$50

— With Sherri Taylor

SOUL
❑ 35004	Bread Winner/You've Got to Change	1964	$60

TAMLA
❑ 54057	Everybody Knew It/Big Joe Moe	1962	$60
❑ 54071	Part Time Love/Someday Pretty Baby	1962	$60
❑ 54049	What Makes You Love Him/Don't Take It Away	1961	$60

Number	Title	Yr	NM
❑ 54030	What Makes You Love Him/ The Child Is Really Wild	1960	$200

— *With lines label*

Number	Title	Yr	NM
❑ 54030	What Makes You Love Him/ The Child Is Really Wild	1960	$80

— *With globe label*

WARD, WALTER, AND THE CHALLENGERS
MELATONE
❑ 1002	I Can Tell/The Mambo Beat	1957	$400

WARDELL AND THE SULTANS
IMPERIAL
❑ 5886	I Need Your Love/I'm Broke	1962	$20
❑ 5812	The Original Popeye/ Dance Time	1962	$30

WARE, CURTIS, AND THE FOUR DO-MATICS
KAYBEE
❑ 101	Flame in My Heart/ Am I in Love	1961	$500

WARE, EDDIE
STATES
❑ 130	That's the Stuff I Like/ Lonely Broken Heart	1954	$120

WARINER, STEVE
MCA
❑ 53287	Baby I'm Yours/ All That Matters	1988	$3
❑ 53586	Baby I'm Yours/ Starting Over Again	1989	$3

— *Double Play* reissue

❑ 52562	Heart Trouble/As Long As Love's Been Around	1985	$3
❑ 53583	Heart Trouble/You Can Dream of Me	1989	$3

— *Double Play* reissue

❑ 53419	Hold On (A Little Longer)/Runnin'	1988	$3
❑ 53665	I Got Dreams/The Loser Wins	1989	$3
❑ 53347	I Should Be with You/ Caught Between Your Duty and Your Dream	1988	$3
❑ 52786	Life's Highway/She's Crazy for Leaving	1986	$3
❑ 53584	Life's Highway/ Small Town Girl	1989	$3

— *Double Play* reissue

❑ 53160	Lynda/There's Always a First Time	1987	$3
❑ 53006 [DJ]	Small Town Girl (same on both sides)	1987	$12

— *Promo only on blue vinyl*

❑ 53006	Small Town Girl/ When It Rains	1987	$3
❑ 52644	Some Fools Never Learn/You Can't Cut Me Any Deeper	1985	$3
❑ 52837 [DJ]	Starting Over Again (same on both sides)	1986	$10

— *Promo only on red vinyl*

❑ 52837	Starting Over Again/She's Leaving Me All Over Again	1986	$3
❑ 53068	The Weekend/Fastbreak	1987	$3
❑ 53585	The Weekend/I Should Be with You	1989	$3

— *Double Play* reissue

❑ 53582	What I Didn't Do/Some Fools Never Learn	1989	$3

— *Double Play* reissue

❑ 52506	What I Didn't Do/Your Love Has Got a Hold on Me	1984	$3
❑ 52506 [PS]	What I Didn't Do/Your Love Has Got a Hold on Me	1984	$4
❑ 53738	When I Could Come Home to You/Do You Want to Make Something Of It	1989	$3
❑ 53504	Where Did I Go Wrong/ Plano Texas Girl	1989	$3

RCA
❑ PB-12307	All Roads Lead to You/Here We Are	1981	$4
❑ PB-12204	By Now/Beverly (Take Care of Your Baby)	1981	$4
❑ JK-13308 [DJ]	Don't It Break Your Heart (same on both sides)	1982	$12

— *Promo only on green vinyl*

❑ PB-13308	Don't It Break Your Heart/ We'll Never Know	1982	$4
❑ PB-13395	Don't Plan on Sleepin' Tonight/Your Memory	1982	$4
❑ PB-13862	Don't You Give Up on Love/ When Is It All Gonna End	1984	$4
❑ JK-13515 [DJ]	Don't Your Mem'ry Ever Sleep at Night (same on both sides)	1983	$12

— *Promo only on blue vinyl*

Number	Title	Yr	NM
❑ PB-13515	Don't Your Mem'ry Ever Sleep at Night/ Well, Hello Again	1983	$4
❑ PB-14289	Drawn to the Fire/Those Memories of You	1986	$4
❑ PB-11658	Forget Me Not/Beside Me	1979	$5
❑ PB-11173	I'm Already Taken/ Daytime Dreamer	1978	$5
❑ PB-11173 [PS]	I'm Already Taken/ Daytime Dreamer	1978	$8
❑ PB-13691	Lonely Women Make Good Lovers/I Can Hear Kentucky Calling Me	1983	$4
❑ PB-11447	Marie/One Song in Everybody	1979	$5
❑ PB-13588	Midnight Fire/You Turn It All Around	1983	$4
❑ PB-11336	So Sad (To Watch Good Love Go Bad)//Atlanta/ My Greatest Moment	1978	$5
❑ PB-12029	The Easy Part's Over/ It's Your Move	1980	$5
❑ JH-12029 [DJ]	The Easy Part's Over (stereo/mono)	1980	$15

— *Promo only on green vinyl*

❑ PB-13968	When We're Together/You Make Me Feel So Right	1984	$4
❑ PB-13768	Why Goodbye/Don't You Give Up on Love	1984	$4

WARING, FRED, AND THE PENNSYLVANIANS
CAPITOL
❑ F3901	Christmas Was Meant for Children/I Heard the Bells on Christmas Day	1958	$15
❑ 4289	Inch Worm/The Donkey Song	1959	$8

DECCA
❑ 27150	A Cigarette, Sweet Music and You/So Beats My Heart for You	1950	$15
❑ 9-23644	Adeste Fideles/ Cantique de Noel	1950	$15

— *Black label, lines on either side of "Decca"; Sides 5 and 6 of "Album No. 9-67"*

❑ 9-23727	All the Things You Are/ The Song Is You	1950	$10

— *Black label, lines on either side of "Decca"; part of "Album No. 9-51"*

❑ 9-27284	A Musical Christmas Card/O Christmas Tree//Christmas Wassailsong/Parade Of The Wooden Soldiers	1950	$15

— *Black label, lines on either side of "Decca"; Sides 3 and 4 of "Album No. 9-97"*

❑ 27146	Ave Maria/The Rosary	1950	$15
❑ 27295	A Wonderful Guy/People Will Say We're in Love	1950	$15
❑ 27294	Bali Ha'i/Some Enchanted Evening	1950	$15
❑ 29305	Be Kind to Your Parents/I Have to Tell You	1954	$12
❑ 27152	Besame Mucho/Marcheta	1950	$15
❑ 27153	Beyond the Blue Horizon/My Ideal	1950	$15

— *The above four comprise a box set*

❑ 28400	Bibbidi-Bobbidi-Boo/ Zip-a-Dee-Doo-Dah	1952	$15
❑ 32323	Big Man/Kites Are Fun	1968	$5
❑ 9-97 [PS]	Christmas Time	1950	$15

— *Box for 4-record set (27283, 27284, 27285, 27286)*

❑ 29063	Easter Parade/ Say It with Music	1954	$12
❑ 27496	Faithful/My Lost Melody	1951	$15
❑ 27149	Faith of Our Fathers/Blest Be the Tie That Binds	1950	$15

— *The above four comprise a box set*

❑ 29304	Fanny/Restless Heart	1954	$10
❑ 9-51 [PS]	Fred Waring Music, Jerome Kern Songs	1950	$15

— *Box for 4-record set (23727, 23728, 23729, 23730)*

❑ 28512	God Bless America/ Where in the World	1952	$15
❑ 9-27285	Heigh Ho the Holly/ See Amid the Winter's Snow//Behold That Star/ Carol of the Bells	1950	$15

— *Black label, lines on either side of "Decca"; Sides 5 and 6 of "Album No. 9-97"*

❑ 27988	Heigh-Ho/Whistle While You Work	1952	$15
❑ 28449	High Noon (Do Not Forsake Me)/Outside of Heaven	1952	$15
❑ 27293	If I Loved You/What's the Use of Wond'rin'	1950	$15
❑ 29619	(I'll Be With You) In Apple Blossom Time/ Drug Store Cowboy	1955	$10
❑ 28235	It Happened in Monterey/You	1952	$15
❑ 27297	It Might As Well Be Spring/A Fellow Needs a Girl	1950	$15
❑ 27600	I Whistle a Happy Tune/ We Kiss in the Shadows	1951	$15
❑ 28402	Lavender Blue/Tico Tico	1952	$15
❑ 25698	Lollytoodum/On Top of Old Smoky	1966	$5

Number	Title	Yr	NM
❑ 9-23729	Long Ago (And Far Away)/ Can't Help Lovin' Dat Man	1950	$10

— *Black label, lines on either side of "Decca"; part of "Album No. 9-51"*

❑ 9-23730	Look for the Silver Lining/Poor Pierrot	1950	$10

— *Black label, lines on either side of "Decca"; part of "Album No. 9-51"*

❑ 28559	Mamie/Ike, Mr. President	1953	$30
❑ 27855	Monastery Bells/A Little Foolish Pride	1951	$15
❑ 29192	My Friend/He Was There	1954	$10
❑ 28305	My Gal Sal/I Do, I Do, I Do	1952	$15
❑ 27291	Oklahoma!/The Surrey with the Fringe on Top	1950	$15
❑ 28600	One to Remember/Just a Dream of You Dear	1953	$10
❑ 27465	Palms/Before the Crucifix	1951	$15
❑ 28298	Peace in the Valley/Just a Closer Walk with Thee	1952	$15
❑ 9-23643	Silent Night/Oh Gathering Clouds	1950	$15

— *Black label, lines on either side of "Decca"; Sides 3 and 4 of "Album No. 9-67"*

❑ 9-23728	Smoke Gets In Your Eyes/Yesterdays	1950	$12

— *Black label, lines on either side of "Decca"; part of "Album No. 9-51"*

❑ 28527	Somebody Loves You/ True, Be True, My Love	1953	$12
❑ 27581	Something Wonderful/ Hello, Young Lovers	1951	$15
❑ 27147	The Bells of St. Mary's/ In a Monastery Garden	1950	$15
❑ 28020	The Caissons Go Rolling Along/Army Air Corps	1952	$15
❑ 9-23645	The First Noel/O Little Town of Bethlehem//Carol of the Bells/Beautiful Saviour	1950	$15

— *Black label, lines on either side of "Decca"; Sides 7 and 8 of "Album No. 9-67"*

❑ 27148	The Lord's Prayer/Were You There When They Crucified My Lord	1950	$15
❑ 27507	The Loveliest Night of the Year/Tulips and Heather	1951	$15
❑ 27480	The Place Where I Worship/A Home That's Filled with Love	1951	$15
❑ 9-74	The Song of Christmas	1950	$50

— *Includes records and box*

❑ 27292	This Was A Real Nice Christmas/You'll Never Walk Alone	1950	$15
❑ 9-67 [PS]	'Twas the Night Before Christmas	1950	$15

— *Box for four-record set (23642, 23643, 23644, 23645)*

❑ 9-23642	Twas the Night Before Christmas (Part 1)/ Twas the Night Before Christmas (Part 2)	1950	$15

— *Black label, lines on either side of "Decca"; Sides 1 and 2 of "Album No. 9-67"*

❑ 29451	We'll Go a Long Way Together/He Was the Happiest	1955	$10
❑ 9-27283	When Angels Sang Of Peace/The Christmas Song (Merry Christmas To You)	1950	$15

— *Black label, lines on either side of "Decca"; Sides 1 and 2 of "Album No. 9-97"*

❑ 28401	When You Wish Upon a Star/One Song	1952	$15
❑ 9-24500	White Christmas/Twelve Days Of Christmas	1950	$15

— *Black label, lines on either side of "Decca"; 78 originally released in 1948*

❑ 24500	White Christmas/Twelve Days Of Christmas	1960	$8

— *Black label with color bars*

❑ 28970	Winter Wonderland/ Snow, Snow	1953	$15
❑ 29331	Without Love/Silk Stockings	1954	$10

REPRISE
❑ 0315	It's Christmas Time Again/ Christmas Candles	1964	$15

— *With Bing Crosby*

❑ 0316	The 12 Days of Christmas/ Do You Hear What I Hear	1964	$12

7-Inch Extended Plays
CAPITOL
❑ EAP 1-896	*Now Is the Caroling Season/We Three Kings/ Winter Wonderland/It Was a Night of Wonder/ White Christmas	1957	$15
❑ EAP 3-896	(contents unknown)	1957	$15
❑ EAP 2-845	(contents unknown)	1957	$15
❑ EAP 3-845	(contents unknown)	1957	$15
❑ EAP 1-845 [PS]	Fred Waring and the Pennsylvanians in Hi-Fi, Part 1	1957	$15
❑ EAP 2-845 [PS]	Fred Waring and the Pennsylvanians in Hi-Fi, Part 2	1957	$15

Number	Title	Yr	NM
❏ EAP 3-845	Fred Waring and the Pennsylvanians in Hi-Fi, Part 3	1957	$15
❏ EAP 2-896	O Christmas Tree/Silver Bells/Angels We Have Heard on High/In Sweetest Jubilee/I Heard the Bells on Christmas Day/The Christmas Song	1957	$15
❏ EAP 1-845	Whiffenpoof Song/So Beats My Heart for You/Sleep/I Hear Music/Ol' Man River	1957	$15
❏ 91224	I Believe/My Cathedral//One Little Candle/No Man Is an Island	1954	$10

—Part of 2-EP set ED 635

Number	Title	Yr	NM
❏ 91225	Somebody Bigger Than You and I/There'll Be Peace in the Valley for Me//He Was There/You'll Never Walk Alone	1954	$10

—Part of 2-EP set ED 635

Number	Title	Yr	NM
❏ ED635 [PS]	Songs of Inspiration	1954	$12

—Cover for 2-EP set (91224, 91225)

WARLOCKS, THE (1)
ARA

Number	Title	Yr	NM
❏ 1017	If You Really Want Me to Stay/Good Time Trippin'	1968	$200

WARLOCKS, THE (2)
DECCA

Number	Title	Yr	NM
❏ 31806	I'll Go Crazy/Temper Tantrum	1965	$30

WASHINGTON SQUARE

Number	Title	Yr	NM
❏ 2023	Hey Joe/Girl	1966	$30

WARMEST SPRING, THE
PARKWAY

Number	Title	Yr	NM
❏ 990	Suddenly (You Find Love)/Hard, Hard Girl	1966	$10

WARNER, PETE
POLYDOR

Number	Title	Yr	NM
❏ 14278	I Just Want to Spend My Life with You/Hands	1975	$200

WARNER, SANDY
SIGNATURE

Number	Title	Yr	NM
❏ 12018	All I Want for Christmas Is Your Love/Girl With The Long Black Hair	1960	$10

WARNES, JENNIFER
Includes records as "Jennifer."
Also see JOE COCKER; BILL MEDLEY.

ARISTA

Number	Title	Yr	NM
❏ 0670	Come to Me/I'm Restless	1982	$4
❏ 0611	Could It Be Love/I'm Restless	1982	$4
❏ 0455	Don't Make Me Over/I'm Restless	1979	$4
❏ 0430	I Know a Heartache When I See One/Frankie in the Rain	1979	$4
❏ 0252	I'm Dreaming/Don't Lead Me On	1977	$5
❏ 0497	When the Feeling Comes Around/Shot Through the Heart	1980	$4

CASABLANCA

Number	Title	Yr	NM
❏ 814603-7	All the Right Moves/Theme -- All the Right Moves	1983	$4

—A-side with Chris Thompson; B-side by David Campbell

CYPRESS

Number	Title	Yr	NM
❏ 661111-7	Ain't No Cure for Love/Famous Blue Raincoat	1986	$4
❏ 661111-7 [PS]	Ain't No Cure for Love/Famous Blue Raincoat	1986	$5
❏ 661115-7	First We Take Manhattan/Famous Blue Raincoat	1987	$4
❏ 661115-7 [PS]	First We Take Manhattan/Famous Blue Raincoat	1987	$4

PARROT

Number	Title	Yr	NM
❏ 328	Chelsea Morning/The Park	1969	$10
❏ 336	Easy to Be Hard/Let the Sunshine In	1969	$12
❏ 324	Here, There and Everywhere/Sunny Day Blue	1968	$15
❏ 333	I Am Waiting/The Leaves	1969	$10
❏ 346	Old Folks/Cajun Train	1970	$8

—All of the above as "Jennifer

Number	Title	Yr	NM
❏ 343	We're Not Gonna Take It/The Weather's Better	1970	$8

REPRISE

Number	Title	Yr	NM
❏ 1070	Last Song/These Days	1972	$8

—As "Jennifer

WARREN, BEVERLY
B.T. PUPPY

Number	Title	Yr	NM
❏ 526	He's So Fine/March	1967	$12
❏ 521	Would You Believe/So Glad You're My Baby	1966	$10

RUST

Number	Title	Yr	NM
❏ 5098	Baby Hullabaloo/Let Me Get Close to You	1964	$15

UNITED ARTISTS

Number	Title	Yr	NM
❏ 543	It Was Me Yesterday/Like a Million Years	1963	$20

WARREN, DOUG
IMAGE

Number	Title	Yr	NM
❏ 1013	Ain't Gonna Wait No Longer/Ain't That Love	1960	$40
❏ 1011	Around Midnight/If the World Don't End Tomorrow	1960	$50

WARREN, JOE
DOT

Number	Title	Yr	NM
❏ 45-1142	Amazing Grace/Softly and Tenderly	1953	$30
❏ 45-1143	How Firm a Foundation/Sweet Hour of Prayer	1953	$30

WARREN, RUSTY
JUBILEE

Number	Title	Yr	NM
❏ 5473	Lil' Lizzy Beth/Life Is Really Worth Living	1964	$15

WARREN, TOMMY
COLUMBIA

Number	Title	Yr	NM
❏ 4-21017	I'm Just in Time to Be Too Late/Do You Care for Me	1952	$40
❏ 4-21141	I'm Trying to Tell My Heart/I'm Gonna Fall Out of Love	1953	$40
❏ 4-21182	One Last Look at You/Fading Away	1953	$40

WARWICK, DEE DEE
ATCO

Number	Title	Yr	NM
❏ 6796	Cold Night in Georgia/Searchin'	1971	$6
❏ 6840	Everybody's Got to Believe in Somebody/Signed, Dee Dee	1971	$6
❏ 6769	I'm Only Human/If This Was the Last Song	1970	$6
❏ 6754	Make Love to Me/She Didn't Know (She Kept On Talkin')	1970	$6
❏ 6810	Suspicious Minds/I'm Glad I'm a Woman	1971	$6

BLUE ROCK

Number	Title	Yr	NM
❏ 4032	Baby I's Yours/Gotta Get a Hold of Myself	1965	$20
❏ 4008	Do It with All Your Heart/Happiness	1965	$20
❏ 4027	We're Doing Fine/I Want to Be with You	1965	$20

MERCURY

Number	Title	Yr	NM
❏ 72738	Don't You Ever Give Up on Me/We've Got Everything Going for Us	1967	$8
❏ 72880	Foolish Fool/Thank You Girl	1969	$8
❏ 72788	Girls Need Love/It's Not Fair	1968	$8
❏ 73397	I Haven't Got Anything Better to Do/All That Love Went to Waste	1973	$8
❏ 72834	I'll Be Better Off (Without You)/Monday, Monday	1968	$8
❏ 72638	I'm Gonna Make You Love Me/Yours Until Tomorrow	1966	$8
❏ 72584	I Want to Be with You/Lover's Chant	1966	$8
❏ 72966	I (Who Have Nothing)/Where Is That Rainbow	1969	$8
❏ 72710	Locked in Your Love/Alfie	1967	$8
❏ 72927	That's Not Love/It's Not Fair	1969	$8
❏ 72667	When Love Slips Away/House of Gold	1967	$8

PRIVATE STOCK

Number	Title	Yr	NM
❏ 45,011	Get Out of My Life/Funny How We Change Places	1975	$5
❏ 45,033	This Time May Be My Last/Funny How We Change Places	1975	$5

SUTRA

Number	Title	Yr	NM
❏ 134	Move with the World/The Way We Used to Be	1984	$4
❏ 134 [PS]	Move with the World/The Way We Used to Be	1984	$4

WARWICK, DIONNE
ARISTA

Number	Title	Yr	NM
❏ 0498	After You/Out of My Hands	1980	$4
❏ 9032	All the Love in the World/You Are My Love	1983	$4
❏ 9652	Another Chance for Love/Cry on Me	1987	$3

—A-side with Howard Hewett

Number	Title	Yr	NM
❏ 9652 [PS]	Another Chance for Love/Cry on Me	1987	$3
❏ 0459	Deja Vu/All the Time	1979	$4
❏ 0572	Easy Love/You Never Said Goodbye	1980	$4
❏ 9281	Finder of Lost Loves/It's Love	1984	$4

—A-side with Glen Jones

Number	Title	Yr	NM
❏ 0701	For You/What Is This	1982	$4
❏ 0673	Friends in Love/What Is This	1982	$4

—A-side with Johnny Mathis

Number	Title	Yr	NM
❏ 9145	Got a Date/Two Ships Passing in the Night	1984	$4
❏ 1015	Heartbreaker/I Can't See Anything But You	1982	$4
❏ 9073	How Many Times Can We Say Goodbye/What Can a Miracle Do	1983	$4

—With Luther Vandross

Number	Title	Yr	NM
❏ 0419	I'll Never Love This Way Again/In Your Eyes	1979	$4
❏ 9567	Love Power/In a World Such As This	1987	$3

—A-side with Jeffrey Osborne

Number	Title	Yr	NM
❏ 9567 [PS]	Love Power/In a World Such As This	1987	$3
❏ 0602	Some Changes Are For Good/This Time Is Ours	1981	$4
❏ 9901	Take Good Care of You and Me/Heartbreak of Love	1989	$3

—A-side with Jeffrey Osborne; B-side with June Pointer

Number	Title	Yr	NM
❏ 1040	Take the Short Way Home/Just One More Night	1983	$4
❏ 0630	There's a Long Road Ahead of Me/Medley of Hits	1981	$4
❏ 9460	Whisper in the Dark/Extravagant Gestures	1986	$3
❏ 9460 [PS]	Whisper in the Dark/Extravagant Gestures	1986	$3

ATLANTIC

Number	Title	Yr	NM
❏ 3029	Then Came You/Just As Long As We Have Love	1974	$6

—With the Spinners

Number	Title	Yr	NM
❏ 3202	Then Came You/Just As Long As We Have Love	1974	$5

—With the Spinners

MUSICOR

Number	Title	Yr	NM
❏ 6303	If I Ruled the World/Only Love Can Break a Heart	1977	$5

SCEPTER

Number	Title	Yr	NM
❏ 12187	Alfie/The Beginning of Loneliness	1967	$8
❏ 12326	Amanda/He's Moving On	1971	$6
❏ 12181	Another Night/Go with Love	1966	$8
❏ 1262	Anyone Who Had a Heart/The Love of a Boy	1963	$15
❏ 12122	Are You There (With Another Girl)/If I Ever Make You Cry	1965	$10
❏ 1239	Don't Make Me Over/I Smiled Yesterday	1962	$15
❏ 12216	Do You Know the Way to San Jose?/Let Me Be Lonely	1968	$8
❏ 12104	Here I Am/They Long to Be Close to You	1965	$12
❏ 12167	I Just Don't Know What to Do with Myself/In Between the Heartaches	1966	$8
❏ 12352	I'm Your Puppet/Don't Make Me Over	1972	$6
❏ 12203	I Say a Little Prayer/(Theme from) Valley of the Dolls	1967	$8
❏ 12276	Let Me Go to Him/Loneliness Remembers What Happiness Forgets	1970	$6
❏ 12111	Looking with My Eyes/Only the Strong, Only the Brave	1965	$10
❏ 12294	Make It Easy on Yourself/Knowing When to Leave	1970	$6
❏ 1253	Make the Music Play/Please Make Him Love Me	1963	$15
❏ 12383	Medley: Reach Out and Touch (Somebody's Hand)-All Kinds of People/The Good Life	1973	$6
❏ 12133	Message to Michael/Here Where There Is Love	1966	$8
❏ 12285	Paper Mache/The Wine Is Young	1970	$6
❏ 12300	The Green Grass Starts to Grow/They Don't Give Medals to Yesterday's Heroes	1970	$6
❏ 12336	The Love of My Man/Hurts So Bad	1971	$6
❏ 12196	The Windows of the World/Walk Little Dolly	1967	$8
❏ 1247	This Empty Place/Wishin' and Hopin'	1963	$15
❏ 1247 [PS]	This Empty Place/Wishin' and Hopin'	1963	$30
❏ 12153	Trains and Boats and Planes/Don't Go Breaking My Heart	1966	$8
❏ 1274	Walk On By/Any Old Time of Day	1964	$15
❏ 1298	Who Can I Turn To/Don't Say I Didn't Tell You Something	1965	$10
❏ 12309	Who Gets the Guy/Walk the Way You Talk	1971	$6

Number	Title	Yr	NM
❏ 12226	Who Is Gonna Love Me?/ (There's) Always Something There to Remind Me	1968	$8

WARNER BROS.

Number	Title	Yr	NM
❏ 8530	Don't Ever Take Your Love Away/Do I Have to Cry	1978	$4
❏ 7669	Don't Let My Teardrops Bother TYou/I Think You Need Love	1973	$5
❏ 8419	Do You Believe in Love at First Sight/Do I Have to Cry	1977	$5
❏ 8183	His House and Me/ Ronnie Lee	1976	$5
❏ 8280	I Didn't Mean to Love You/He's Not for You	1976	$5
❏ 7560	If We Only Have Love/ Close to You	1972	$5
❏ 7693	(I'm) Just Being Myself/ You're Gonna Need Me	1973	$5
❏ 8154	Once You Hit the Road/ World of My Dreams	1975	$5
❏ 8026	Sure Thing/Who Knows	1974	$5
❏ 8088	Take it from Me/It's Magic	1975	$5

7-Inch Extended Plays

SCEPTER

Number	Title	Yr	NM
❏ SGS565 [PS]	Dionne Warwick's Golden Hits, Part One	1968	$15
❏ SGS565	Don't Make Me Over/ Anyone Who Had a Heart/ Wishin' and Hopin'//This Empty Place/(There's) Always Something There to Remind Me/ Any Old Time of Day	1968	$15

— Jukebox issue; small hole, plays at 33 1/3 rpm

Number	Title	Yr	NM
❏ SGS568	Do You Know the Way to San Jose/Let Me Be Lonely/ As Long As There's an Apple Tree//Up, Up and Away/Where Would I Go	1968	$15

— Jukebox issue; small hole, plays at 33 1/3 rpm

WAS (NOT WAS)

Number	Title	Yr	NM
❏ 23350	Papa Was a Rollin' Stone/Ballad of You	1989	$3

GEFFEN

| ❏ 29477 | Smile/The Party Broke Up | 1983 | $4 |

ISLAND

| ❏ 49756 | Out Come the Freaks/ Out Come the Freaks (Dub Version) | 1981 | $5 |

WASHINGTON, BABY

ABC-PARAMOUNT

Number	Title	Yr	NM
❏ 10223	My Time to Cry/ Let Love Go By	1961	$20

— As Jeanette "Baby" Washington

| ❏ 10245 | There You Go Again/ Don't Cry, Foolish Heart | 1961 | $20 |

AVI

| ❏ 253 | I Wanna Dance/I Can't Get Over Losing You | 1978 | $5 |

— As Jeanette "Baby" Washington

CHECKER

| ❏ 918 | I Hate to See You Go/ Knock Yourself Out | 1959 | $30 |

CHESS

| ❏ 2099 | Happy Birthday/Is It Worth It | 1970 | $6 |

COTILLION

❏ 44086	Don't Let Me Lose This Dream/I'm Good Enough for You	1970	$6
❏ 44047	I Don't Know/I Can't Afford to Lose Him	1969	$6
❏ 44065	Let Them Talk/I Love You Brother	1970	$6

J&S

❏ 1656	Every Day/Smitty's Rock	1961	$70
❏ 1632	I Hate to See You Go/ Knock Yourself Out	1958	$40
❏ 1604	There Must Be a Reason/ Congratulations Honey	1957	$60

LIBERTY

| ❏ 1393 | Silent Night/Merry Christmas Baby | 1980 | $5 |

— B-side by Charles Brown

MASTER 5

| ❏ 3500 | Can't Get Over Losing You//(B-side unknown) | 1974 | $6 |
| ❏ 9103 | Forever/(B-side unknown) | 1973 | $6 |

— With Don Gardner

| ❏ 9107 | I've Got to Break Away/ You (Just a Dream) | 1973 | $6 |

NEPTUNE

| ❏ 120 | Medicine Man/Tears Fall | 1961 | $30 |

— As "Jeanette B. Washington

| ❏ 104 | The Bells (On Our Wedding Day)/(B-side unknown) | 1959 | $40 |

Number	Title	Yr	NM
❏ 101	The Time/You Never Could Be Mine	1959	$40
❏ 107	Work Out/Let's Love in the Midnight	1960	$40

SUE

❏ 150	Either You're With Me (Or Either You're Not)/ You Are What You Are	1967	$20
❏ 767	Handful of Memories/ Careless Hands	1962	$12
❏ 794	Hey Lonely One/Doodlin'	1963	$12
❏ 764	Hey Lonely One/No Tears	1962	$15
❏ 769	Hush Heart/I've Got a Feeling	1962	$10
❏ 797	I Can't Wait Until I See My Baby/Who's Going to Take Care of Me	1964	$10

— As Justine Washington

| ❏ 124 | I Can't Wait Until I See My Baby/Who's Going to Take Care of Me | 1965 | $8 |

— As Justine Washington

❏ 114	It'll Never Be Over for Me/Move On Drifter	1964	$8
❏ 790	Leave Me Alone/You and the Night and the Music	1963	$100
❏ 129	Only Those in Love/The Ballad of Bobby Dawn	1965	$8
❏ 149	Silent Night/White Christmas	1967	$30
❏ 783	That's How Heartaches Are Made/There He Is	1963	$12
❏ 104	The Clock/Standing on the Pier	1964	$8

UNITED ARTISTS

| ❏ 0143 | That's How Heartaches Are Made/Leave Me Alone | 1973 | $5 |

— Silver Spotlight Series" reissue

VEEP

| ❏ 1274 | Silent Night/White Christmas | 1967 | $30 |
| ❏ 1297 | Think About the Good Times/Hold Back the Dawn | 1969 | $8 |

WASHINGTON, DINAH, AND BROOK BENTON

MERCURY

Number	Title	Yr	NM
❏ 71565	Baby (You Got What It Takes)/I Do	1960	$20

WASHINGTON, DINAH

MERCURY

Number	Title	Yr	NM
❏ 71087	Ain't Nobody Home/I'm Gonna Keep My Eyes on You	1957	$20
❏ 8231	Ain't Nobody's Bizness If I Do/Please Send Me Someone to Love	1951	$30
❏ 70125	Ain't Nothing Good/You Let My Love Grow Old	1953	$30
❏ 71018	All Because of You/To Love and Be Loved	1956	$20
❏ 70868	Cat on a Hot Tin Roof/ The First Time	1956	$20
❏ 72040	Cold, Cold Heart/I Don't Hurt Anymore	1962	$8
❏ 72040 [PS]	Cold, Cold Heart/I Don't Hurt Anymore	1962	$20
❏ 5728	Cold, Cold Heart/ Mixed Emotions	1951	$30
❏ 71958	Dream/Such a Night	1962	$12
❏ 71958 [PS]	Dream/Such a Night	1962	$20
❏ 71778	Early Every Morning (Early Every Evening Too)/Do You Want It That Way	1961	$12
❏ 71778 [PS]	Early Every Morning (Early Every Evening Too)/Do You Want It That Way	1961	$20
❏ 71220	Everybody Loves My Baby/Blues Down Home	1957	$20
❏ 8207	Fast Movin' Mama/Juice Head Man of Mine	1950	$30
❏ 5488	Harbor Lights/I Cross My Fingers	1950	$30
❏ 8257	Hey Good Lookin'/Out in the Cold Again	1951	$100

— With The Ravens

❏ 5510	How Deep Is the Ocean/ Harbor Lights	1950	$30
❏ 8192	How Deep Is the Ocean/Why Don't You Think Things Over	1950	$30
❏ 5842	I Can't Face the Music/ Mad About the Boy	1952	$30
❏ 70694	I Concentrate on You/ Not Without You	1955	$30
❏ 70046	I Cried for You/ Gambler's Blues	1953	$30
❏ 70439	I Don't Hurt Anymore/Dream	1954	$30
❏ 8206	If I Loved You/My Kind of Man	1950	$30
❏ 70600	If It's the Last Thing I Do/I Diddie	1955	$30
❏ 70653	I Hear Those Bells/ The Cheat	1955	$30
❏ 8187	I'll Never Be Free/Big Deal	1950	$30
❏ 5665	I'm a Fool/If You Don't Believe I'm Leaving	1951	$30
❏ 70728	I'm Lost Without You Tonight/ You Might Have Told Me	1955	$30

Number	Title	Yr	NM
❏ 8232	I'm So Lonely I Could Cry/Fine Fine Daddy	1951	$30
❏ 71560	It Could Happen to You/ Age of Miracles	1960	$10
❏ 8195	It Isn't Fair/I'll Never Be Free	1950	$30
❏ 8181	I Wanna Be Loved/ Love with Misery	1950	$50

— Note: Earlier Dinah Washington 45s in the Mercury 8000 series may exist

❏ 72015	I Want to Be Loved/ Am I Blue	1962	$8
❏ 72015 [PS]	I Want to Be Loved/ Am I Blue	1962	$20
❏ 8211	I Won't Cry Anymore/Don't Say You're Sorry Again	1951	$30
❏ 70833	Let's Get Busy Too/Let's Go Around Together	1956	$20
❏ 71696	Love Walked In/I'm in Heaven Tonight	1960	$10
❏ 71377	Make Me a Present of You/All of Me	1958	$20
❏ 8209	My Heart Cries for You/I Apologize	1951	$30
❏ 8194	My Kind of Man/I Wanna Be Loved by You	1950	$30
❏ 70175	My Lean Baby/Never Never	1953	$30
❏ 8294	My Song/Half As Much	1952	$30
❏ 71557	Ol' Santa/The Light	1959	$15
❏ 71812	Our Love Is Here to Stay/ Congratulations to Someone	1961	$10
❏ 71812 [PS]	Our Love Is Here to Stay/ Congratulations to Someone	1961	$20
❏ 8292	Pillow Blues/Double Dealin' Daddy	1952	$30
❏ 8249	Saturday Night/ Be Fair to Me	1951	$30
❏ 71876	September in the Rain/Wake the Town and Tell the People	1961	$10
❏ 71876 [PS]	September in the Rain/Wake the Town and Tell the People	1961	$20
❏ 70329	Short John/Feel Like I Wanna Cry	1954	$30
❏ 70263	Silent Night/The Lord's Prayer	1953	$30
❏ 70284	Since My Man Has Gone and Went/My Man's an Undertaker	1953	$30
❏ 70906	Soft Winds/Tears to Burn	1956	$20
❏ 5906	Stormy Weather/Make Believe Dreams	1952	$30
❏ 70336	Such a Night/Until Sunrise	1954	$30
❏ 70497	Teach Me Tonight/ Wishing Well	1954	$30
❏ 71922	Tears and Laughter/ If I Should Lose You	1962	$10
❏ 71922 [PS]	Tears and Laughter/ If I Should Lose You	1962	$20
❏ 70537	That's All I Want from You/ You Stay on My Mind	1955	$30
❏ 70776	The Show Must Go On/I Just Couldn't Stand It No More	1956	$20
❏ 71635	This Bitter Earth/I Understand	1960	$10
❏ 5503	Time Out for Tears/ Only a Moment Ago	1950	$30
❏ 8269	Trouble in Mind/New Blowtop Blues	1952	$30
❏ 70214	TV Is the Thing (This Year)/Fat Daddy	1953	$30
❏ 71744	We Have Love/ Looking Back	1960	$10
❏ 71744 [PS]	We Have Love/ Looking Back	1960	$20
❏ 10008 [S]	What a Diff'rence a Day Made/Come On Home	1959	$30

— The A-side title is listed differently on the stereo 45 than on the mono 45 (71435)

| ❏ 71435 | What a Diff'rence a Day Makes/Come On Home | 1959 | $20 |
| ❏ 8267 | Wheel of Fortune/ Tell Me Why | 1952 | $30 |

ROULETTE

❏ 4538	Call Me Irresponsible/ Funny Thing	1963	$8
❏ 4444	For All We Know/I Wouldn't Know (What to Do)	1962	$8
❏ 4490	Soulsville/Let Me Be the First to Know	1963	$8
❏ 4534	That Sunday (That Summer)/A Stranger on Earth	1963	$8
❏ 4520	The Show Must Go On/I'll Drown in My Own Tears	1963	$8
❏ 4424	Where Are You/ You're Nobody 'Til Somebody Loves You	1962	$8

7-Inch Extended Plays

EMARCY

❏ EP-1-6080	*Lover Come Back to Me/ I've Got You Under My Skin/ There Is No Greater Love	1955	$30
❏ EP-1-6080 [PS]	Dinah Jams	1955	$30
❏ EP-1-6119 [PS]	For Those in Love -- Vol. II	1956	$30

WASHINGTON, GINO

ATAC

| ❏ 101 | Doin' the Popcorn/ What Can a Man Do | 1969 | $40 |
| ❏ 102 | I'll Be Around/ (B-side unknown) | 1969 | $50 |

Number	Title	Yr	NM
❏ 7823	Like My Baby/(B-side unknown)	1969	$50

CONGRESS

Number	Title	Yr	NM
❏ 273	Beach Bash/Hi Hi Hazel	1966	$15

CORREC-TONE

Number	Title	Yr	NM
❏ 503	Gino Is a Coward/Puppet on a String	1962	$70

KAPP

Number	Title	Yr	NM
❏ 796	All I Need/Whatever Will Be, Will Be	1966	$10

MALA

Number	Title	Yr	NM
❏ 12029	Like My Baby/I'll Be Around When You Want Me	1968	$50

RIC-TIC

Number	Title	Yr	NM
❏ 100	Gino Is a Coward/Puppet on a String	1964	$30

SONBERT

Number	Title	Yr	NM
❏ 3770	Gino Is a Coward/Puppet on a String	1963	$30

WAND

Number	Title	Yr	NM
❏ 147	Out of This World/Come Monkey with Me	1964	$30

WASHINGTON, GROVER, JR.

COLUMBIA

Number	Title	Yr	NM
❏ 38-07240	Summer Nights/Strawberry Moon	1987	$5
❏ 38-07621	The Look of Love/Shwaree Ride	1987	$5

ELEKTRA

Number	Title	Yr	NM
❏ 47246	Be Mine (Tonight)/Reaching Out	1981	$4
❏ 47246 [PS]	Be Mine (Tonight)/Reaching Out	1981	$5
❏ 7-69834	Brazilian Memories/I'll Be with You	1983	$5
❏ 7-69708	Inside Moves/Sassy Stew	1984	$4
❏ 47071	Let It Flow (For Dr. J.)/Winelight	1980	$5
❏ 46060	Tell Me About It Now/Feel It Comin'	1979	$5
❏ 7-69887	The Best Is Yet to Come/More Than Meets the Eye	1982	$4

—With Patti LaBelle

Number	Title	Yr	NM
❏ 7-69680	When I Look at You/Secret Sounds	1984	$4
❏ 47140	Winelight/Take Me There	1981	$5

KUDU

Number	Title	Yr	NM
❏ 937	A Secret Place (Part 1)/A Secret Place (Part 2)	1977	$8
❏ 902	Inner City Blues/Ain't No Sunshine	1972	$8
❏ 916	Masterpiece (Part 1)/Masterpiece (Part 2)	1973	$8
❏ 903	Mercy Mercy Me (Part 1)/Mercy Mercy Me (Part 2)	1972	$8
❏ 924	Mister Magic/Black Frost	1975	$8
❏ 942	Summer Song/Juffere	1978	$8
❏ 912	Where Is the Love (Part 1)/Where Is the Love (Part 2)	1973	$8

MOTOWN

Number	Title	Yr	NM
❏ 1454	Do Dat/Reed Seed (Trio Tune)	1978	$6
❏ 1454 [DJ]	Do Dat (stereo/mono)	1978	$15

—Promo only on yellow vinyl

Number	Title	Yr	NM
❏ 1486	Snake Eyes/Love	1979	$4

WATCHPOCKET

TMI

Number	Title	Yr	NM
❏ 75-0100	Love Will Be the Answer/People All Around Me	1972	$6

WATERS, MUDDY

CHESS

Number	Title	Yr	NM
❏ 1509	All Night Long/Country Boy	1952	$2500

—Note: Muddy Waters records on Chess before 1509 are unconfirmed on 45 rpm

Number	Title	Yr	NM
❏ 1704	Close to You/She's Nineteen Years Old	1958	$40
❏ 1630	Don't Go No Farther/Diamonds at Your Feet	1956	$60
❏ 1862	Five Long Years/Twenty-Four Hours	1963	$20
❏ 1620	Forty Days and Forty Nights/All Aboard	1956	$50
❏ 2143	Garbage Man/Can't Get No Grindin'	1973	$6
❏ 2085	Going Home/I Feel So Good	1970	$8
❏ 1819	Going Home/Tough Times	1962	$30
❏ 1667	Good News/Come Home Baby	1957	$40
❏ 1652	Got My Mojo Working/Rock Me	1957	$60
❏ 1774	Got My Mojo Working/Woman Wanted	1960	$30
❏ 1748	I Feel So Good/When I Get to Thinking	1960	$30
❏ 1644	I Got to Find My Baby/Just to Be with You	1956	$50
❏ 1680	I Live the Life I Love/Evil	1958	$40
❏ 1579	I'm Ready/I Don't Know Why	1954	$70

Number	Title	Yr	NM
❏ 1752	I'm Your Doctor/Ready Way Back	1960	$30
❏ 1973	I'm Your Hoochie Coochie Man/Corrina, Corrina	1966	$15
❏ 1560	I'm Your Hoochie Coochie Man/You're So Pretty	1954	$125
❏ 1596	I Want to Be Loved/My Eyes Keep Me in Trouble	1955	$60
❏ 1692	I Won't Go/She's Got It	1958	$40
❏ 1758	Love Affair/Look What You've Done	1960	$30
❏ 1585	Lovin' Man/I'm a Natural Born Lover	1955	$60
❏ 1550	Mad Love/Blow, Wind, Blow	1953	$120
❏ 2107	Making Friends/Two Steps Forward	1971	$8
❏ 1602	Manish Boy/Young Fashion Ways	1955	$75
❏ 1718	Mean Mistreater/Walking Thru the Park	1959	$30
❏ 1796	Messin' with the Man/Lonesome Room Blues	1961	$30
❏ 1827	Muddy Waters Twist/You Shook Me	1962	$30
❏ 1937	My Dog Can't Bark/I Got a Rich Man's Woman	1965	$15
❏ 1724	Ooh Wee/Clouds in My Heart	1959	$30
❏ 1514	Please Have Mercy/Looking for My Baby	1952	$800
❏ 1921	Put Me in Your Lay-A-Way/Still a Fool	1965	$15
❏ 1537	She's All Right/Sad, Sad Day	1953	$400
❏ 1914	Short Dress Woman/My John the Conqueror	1964	$20
❏ 1526	Standing Around Crying/Gone to Main St.	1952	$700
❏ 1733	Take the Bitter with the Sweet/She's Into Somethin'	1959	$30
❏ 1895	The Same Thing/You Can't Lose What You Never Had	1964	$20
❏ 1765	Tiger in Your Tank/Meanest Woman	1960	$30
❏ 1612	Trouble, No More/Sugar Sweet	1955	$100
❏ 2018	When the Eagle Flies/Birdnest on the Ground	1967	$10
❏ 1542	Who's Gonna Be Your Sweet Man/Turn the Lamp Down Low	1953	$300

WATERS, ROGER
Also see PINK FLOYD.

COLUMBIA

Number	Title	Yr	NM
❏ 38-04455	5:01 A.M. (The Pros and Cons of Hitch Hiking)/4:30 A.M. (Apparently They Were Travelling Abroad)	1984	$3
❏ 38-04566	5:06 A.M. (Every Stranger's Eyes)/4:56 A.M. (For the First Time Today, Part 1)	1984	$3
❏ 38-07364	Sunset Strip/Money	1987	$3
❏ 38-07364 [PS]	Sunset Strip/Money	1987	$3
❏ 38-07617	Who Needs Information/Molly's Song	1987	$3

WATKINS, LOVELACE

GROOVE

Number	Title	Yr	NM
❏ 58-0023	I Won't Believe It/He'[s Lookin' Out for the World	1963	$40
❏ 58-0016	Tender Love/Ma Cherie Au Revoir	1963	$40
❏ 58-0016 [PS]	Tender Love/Ma Cherie Au Revoir	1963	$100

MGM

Number	Title	Yr	NM
❏ 12875	Hello Young Lovers/When I Fall in Love	1960	$20

SUE

Number	Title	Yr	NM
❏ Oct-003	Who Am I/Dreams	1968	$15

UNI

Number	Title	Yr	NM
❏ 55211	Fool on the Hill/Je Vous Aime Beaucoup	1970	$15

WATLEY, JODY

MCA

Number	Title	Yr	NM
❏ 53162	Don't You Want Me/(Instrumental)	1987	$3
❏ 53162 [PS]	Don't You Want Me/(Instrumental)	1987	$3
❏ 53714	Everything/(Instrumental)	1989	$3
❏ 53660	Friends/Private Life	1989	$3
❏ 52956	Looking for a New Love/Looking for a New Love (Acapella)	1987	$3
❏ 52956 [PS]	Looking for a New Love/Looking for a New Love (Acapella)	1987	$3
❏ S45-17291 [DJ]	Looking for a New Love (same on both sides)	1987	$5
❏ S45-17291 [PS]	Looking for a New Love (same on both sides)	1987	$10

—Fold-out poster sleeve (not used on stock copies)

Number	Title	Yr	NM
❏ 53258	Most of All/(Instrumental)	1988	$3
❏ 53258 [PS]	Most of All/(Instrumental)	1988	$3
❏ 53235	Some Kind of Lover/(Instrumental)	1988	$3
❏ 53235 [PS]	Some Kind of Lover/(Instrumental)	1988	$3

Number	Title	Yr	NM
❏ 53081	Still a Thrill/Looking for a New Love	1987	$3
❏ 53081 [PS]	Still a Thrill/Looking for a New Love	1987	$3

WATSON, JOHNNY "GUITAR", AND LARRY WILLIAMS

OKEH

Number	Title	Yr	NM
❏ 7300	Find Yourself Someone to Love/Nobody	1967	$30

—Backed by Kaleidoscope

Number	Title	Yr	NM
❏ 7274	Mercy, Mercy, Mercy/A Quitter Never Wins	1967	$10
❏ 7281	Two for the Price of One/Too Late	1967	$10
❏ 7281 [PS]	Two for the Price of One/Too Late	1967	$30

WATSON, JOHNNY "GUITAR"

A&M

Number	Title	Yr	NM
❏ 2383	Planet Funk/First Timothy Six	1981	$4
❏ 2398	That's What Time It Is/First Timothy Six	1982	$4

CACTUS

Number	Title	Yr	NM
❏ 118	Let's Rock/(B-side unknown)	1959	$200

CLASS

Number	Title	Yr	NM
❏ 246	The Bear/One More Kiss	1959	$40

—As "Johnny Watson

DJM

Number	Title	Yr	NM
❏ 1020	Ain't That a Bitch/Won't You Forgive Me Baby	1977	$6
❏ 1020 [PS]	Ain't That a Bitch/Won't You Forgive Me Baby	1977	$8
❏ 1101	Gangster of Love/Guitar Disco	1978	$5
❏ 1013	I Need It/Since I Met You Baby	1976	$5
❏ 1304	Love Jones/(B-side unknown)	1980	$5
❏ 1029	Lover Jones/Tarzan	1977	$5
❏ 1034	Love That Will Not Die/A Damn Shame	1978	$5
❏ 1019	Superman Lover/We're No Exception	1976	$5
❏ 1305	Telephone Bill/(B-side unknown)	1980	$5
❏ 1106	What the Hell Is This?/Can You Handle It	1979	$5

FANTASY

Number	Title	Yr	NM
❏ 739	I Don't Want to Be a Lone Ranger/You Can Stay But the Noise Must Go	1975	$6
❏ 752	It's Too Late/Tripping	1975	$6
❏ 721	Like I'm Not Your Man/You Bring Love	1974	$6

FEDERAL

Number	Title	Yr	NM
❏ 12183	Gettin' Drunk/You Can't Take It With You	1954	$200

—All Federal 45s as "Young John Watson

Number	Title	Yr	NM
❏ 12175	Half Pint of Whiskey/Space Guitar	1954	$250
❏ 12120	Highway 60/No I Can't	1953	$200
❏ 12143	I Got Eyes/Walkin' to My Baby	1953	$200
❏ 12131	Motor Head Baby/Sad Fool	1953	$200
❏ 12157	What's Going On/Thinking	1953	$200

KEEN

Number	Title	Yr	NM
❏ 3-4023	Deana Baby/Honey	1957	$40
❏ 3-4005	Gangster of Love/One Room Country Shack	1957	$40

KENT

Number	Title	Yr	NM
❏ 328	Those Lonely, Lonely Nights/(B-side unknown)	1959	$30

KING

Number	Title	Yr	NM
❏ 5579	Broke and Lonely/Cuttin' In	1961	$30
❏ 5716	Cold, Cold Heart/That's the Chance You've Got to Take	1963	$20
❏ 5774	Gangster of Love/In the Evening	1963	$20
❏ 5833	I Say, I Love You/You Better Love Me	1964	$20
❏ 5536	Posin'/Embraceable You	1961	$30
❏ 5666	What You Do to Me/Sweet Lovin' Mama	1962	$20

OKEH

Number	Title	Yr	NM
❏ 7270	Hold On, I'm Comin'/Wolfman	1967	$15

RPM

Number	Title	Yr	NM
❏ 423	Hot Little Mama/I Love to Love You	1955	$60
❏ 447	Oh Baby/Give a Little	1955	$50
❏ 471	She Moves Me/Love Me Baby	1956	$50
❏ 436	Those Lonely, Lonely Nights/Someone Cares for Me	1955	$50
❏ 455	Three Hours Past Midnight/Ruben	1956	$50
❏ 431	Too Tired/Don't Touch Me	1955	$60

VALLEY VUE

Number	Title	Yr	NM
❏ 769	Strike On Computers/(B-side unknown)	1984	$5

Number	Title	Yr	NM

WATSON, CLAYTON
LAVENDER
| ❏ 2454 | Everybody's Boppin'/Tall Skinny Annie | 1958 | $400 |

WATSON, DOC
Includes records by the father-son duo of "Doc and Merle Watson."
POPPY
| ❏ XW276 | Bottle of Wine/Corinna, Corinna | 1973 | $4 |

— With Merle Watson
| ❏ 90110 | Freight Train Boogie/Going Down the Road Feeling Bad | 1971 | $5 |
| ❏ XW169 | If I Needed You/Bonaparte's Retreat | 1973 | $4 |

— With Merle Watson
| ❏ XW414 | Poor Boy Blues/Doc's Rag | 1974 | $4 |

— With Merle Watson
| ❏ 90114 | Summertime/I Couldn't Believe It Was True | 1972 | $5 |

— With Merle Watson
UNITED ARTISTS
| ❏ 1275 | All I Have to Do Is Dream/'Rangement Blues | 1979 | $4 |

— With Merle Watson
| ❏ 1231 | Don't Think Twice, It's All Right/Under the Double Eagle | 1978 | $4 |

— With Merle Watson
❏ XW824	I Can't Help But Wonder (Where I'm Bound)/Southbound Passenger Train	1976	$4
❏ XW894	Little Maggie/Cypress Grove Blues	1976	$4
❏ XW713	Make Me a Pallet/Shady Grove	1975	$4
❏ XW1020	My Creole Belle/Minglewood Blues	1977	$4

— With Merle Watson
VANGUARD
| ❏ 35079 | Peach Picking Time in Georgia/Memphis Blues | 1968 | $6 |

WATSON, GENE
CAPITOL
❏ 4279	Because You Believed in Me/When My World Left Town	1976	$5
❏ 4854	Bedroom Ballad/After the Party	1980	$4
❏ 4556	Cowboys Don't Get Lucky All the Time/I'd Love to Live with You Again	1978	$4
❏ 4680	Farewell Party/I Don't Know How to Tell Her (She Don't Love Me Anymore)	1979	$4
❏ 4331	Her Body Couldn't Keep You (Off My Mind)/If I'm a Fool for Leaving	1976	$5
❏ 4513	I Don't Need a Thing at All/Hey Barnum and Bailey	1977	$5
❏ 4076	Love in the Hot Afternoon/Through the Eyes of Love	1975	$5
❏ 4616	One Sided Conversation/I Know What It's Like in Her Arms	1978	$4
❏ 4378	Paper Rosie/Don't Look at Me (In That Tone of Voice)	1976	$5
❏ 4723	Pick the Wildwood Flower/Mama Sold Roses	1979	$4
❏ 4772	Should I Come Home (Or Should I Go Crazy)/Beautiful You	1979	$4
❏ 4458	The Old Man and His Horn/Just at Dawn	1977	$5
❏ 4143	Where Love Begins/Long Enough to Care	1975	$5
EPIC
❏ 34-06057	Bottle of Tears/Stranger in Our House Tonight	1986	$3
❏ 34-05817	Carmen/The New York Times	1986	$3
❏ 34-05407	Cold Summer Day in Georgia/The Note	1985	$3
❏ 34-07308	Everybody Needs a Hero/When She Touched Me	1987	$3
❏ 34-06290	Everything I Used to Do/I Saved Your Place	1986	$3
❏ 34-06987	Honky Tonk Crazy/Starting New Memories Today	1987	$3
❏ 34-05633	Memories to Burn/Get Along Little Doggie	1985	$3
MCA
❏ 51039	Between This Time and the Next Time/I'm Tellin' Me a Lie	1981	$3
❏ 52309	Drinkin' My Way Back Home/My Memories of You	1983	$3
❏ 52356	Forever Again/Growing Apart	1984	$3
❏ 51183	Fourteen Carat Mind/Lonely Me	1981	$4
❏ 52410	Little by Little/The Ballad of Richard Lindsey	1984	$3

Number	Title	Yr	NM
❏ 51127	Maybe I Should Have Been Listening/I'm Gonna Kill You	1981	$3
❏ 52243	Sometimes I Get Lucky and Forget/You Put Out an Old Flame Last Night	1983	$3
❏ 52009	Speak Softly (You're Talking to My Heart)/'Til Melinda Comes Around	1982	$3
❏ 52074	This Dream's On Me/This Torch That I Carry for You	1982	$3
❏ 52131	What She Don't Know Won't Hurt Her/Fightin' Fire with Fire	1982	$3

MCA CURB
| ❏ 52457 | Got No Reason Now for Goin' Home/A Memory Away | 1984 | $3 |
| ❏ 52533 | One Hell of a Heartache/Sailing Home to Me | 1985 | $3 |

RESCO
❏ 630	Bad Water/I'll Run Right Back to You	1974	$8
❏ 619	Burning Memories/Do You Have Any Plans for Me	1974	$8
❏ 634	Love in the Hot Afternoon/Through the Eyes of Love	1975	$8
❏ 627	Shadows on the Wall/I Told a Lie	1974	$8
❏ 616	To Have Conquered/Through the Eyes of Love	1974	$8

TRI-DEC
| ❏ 8357 | My Rockin' Baby/Drummer Boy Rock | 1958 | $800 |

WARNER BROS.
❏ 49648	Any Way You Want Me/Those Eyes That Lie to Me	1981	$4
❏ 7-27532	Back in the Fire/Just How Little I Know	1989	$3
❏ 7-27692	Don't Waste It on the Blues/I Picked a San Antonio Rose	1988	$3
❏ 7-22751	The Great Divide/Ain't No Fun to Be Alone in San Antone	1989	$3

WIDE WORLD
❏ 1001	Autumn in June/I'll Run Right Back to You	1970	$15
❏ 1002	Before the Next Teardrop Falls/I Told a Lie	1970	$15
❏ 1016	Eli Funkelby/When My Daddy Danced	1971	$15
❏ 1003	Florence Jean/John's Back in Town	1970	$15
❏ 1010	I Feel a Sin Coming On/Lie to Me	1970	$15
❏ 1019	I Feel Fine/I'm Not Strong Enough	1971	$15
❏ 1014	If I'm a Fool for Leaving/The Only Difference	1971	$15
❏ 1007	I Went All to Pieces/Two Right People (In the Wrong Frame of Mind)	1970	$15
❏ 1021	The Birds and the Bees/My Eyes Are Jealous	1972	$15

WATSON, JOHN L., AND THE HUMMELFUGS
PARKWAY
| ❏ 946 | Lookin' for Love/I Only Came to Dance with You | 1965 | $15 |

WATTS, CLEM
MERCURY
| ❏ 5695x45 | A Half Fast Waltz/Down Yonder | 1951 | $40 |

WATTS, JAKE
MERCURY
| ❏ 6341x45 | Too Late to Regret/I Never Want to See You Cry | 1952 | $30 |

WATTS, NOBLE
BATON
❏ 246	Easy Going (Part 1)/Easy Going (Part 2)	1957	$30
❏ 266	Flap Jack/Hot Tamales	1959	$20
❏ 257	Great Times/The Creep	1958	$20
❏ 249	Hard Times (The Slop)/Midnite Flight	1957	$20
❏ 254	The Slide/Shakin'	1958	$20
❏ 249	The Slop/Midnite Flight	1957	$30
BRUNSWICK
| ❏ 55382 | Thingamajig/F.L.A. | 1968 | $8 |
CUB
| ❏ 9078 | The Beaver/Frog Hop | 1960 | $15 |
DELUXE
| ❏ 6066 | Mashing Potatoes/Pig Ears and Rice | 1954 | $40 |
SIR
| ❏ 273 | Boogie Woogie/Mashed Potatoes | 1959 | $20 |
VEE JAY
| ❏ 268 | South Shore Drive/Big Two Four | 1956 | $40 |

Number	Title	Yr	NM

WAYLON (JENNINGS) AND JESSI (COLTER)
RCA
| ❏ PB-12176 | Storms Never Last/I Ain't the One | 1982 | $4 |
| ❏ PB-12245 | Wild Side of Life/It Wasn't God Who Made Honky Tonk Angels | 1982 | $4 |
RCA VICTOR
| ❏ 47-9920 | Suspicious Minds/I Ain't the One | 1970 | $6 |
| ❏ PB-10653 | Suspicious Minds/I Ain't the One | 1976 | $5 |

WAYLON AND WILLIE
For convenience's sake, we've listed all the variations of their credits here, including "Willie Nelson and Waylon Jennings." Also see WAYLON JENNINGS; WILLIE NELSON.
COLUMBIA
| ❏ 04131 | Take It to the Limit/Till I Gain Control Again | 1983 | $4 |
| ❏ 04131 [PS] | Take It to the Limit/Till I Gain Control Again | 1983 | $5 |
RCA
| ❏ PB-11198 | Mammas Don't Let Your Babies Grow Up to Be Cowboys/I Can Get Off on You | 1978 | $4 |
| ❏ GB-11996 | Mammas Don't Let Your Babies Grow Up to Be Cowboys/I Can Get Off on You | 1980 | $3 |

— Gold Standard Series
| ❏ GB-11499 | Mammas Don't Let Your Babies Grow Up to Be Cowboys/Luckenbach, Texas (Back to the Basics of Love) | 1979 | $4 |

— Gold Standard Series
| ❏ PB-13319 | (Sittin' On) The Dock of the Bay/Luckenbach, Texas | 1982 | $4 |
RCA VICTOR
| ❏ PB-10529 | Good Hearted Woman/Heaven or Hell | 1975 | $5 |

WAYLON AND WILLIE/WAYLON AND JESSI
RCA
| ❏ GB-10928 | Good Hearted Woman/Suspicious Minds | 1977 | $3 |

— Gold Standard Series

WAYLORS, THE
RCA VICTOR
| ❏ PB-10738 | Crazy Arms/Shopping | 1976 | $5 |

WAYNE, ALVIS
ROLLIN' ROCK
| ❏ 32 | I Wanna Eat Your Pudding/It's Your Last Chance to Dance Tonight | 1975 | $20 |
WESTPORT
| ❏ 138 | Don't Mean Maybe Baby/I'd Rather Be with You | 1957 | $200 |

— As "Tony Wayne"
| ❏ 138 | Don't Mean Maybe Baby/I'd Rather Be with You | 1958 | $125 |

— As "Alvis Wayne"
| ❏ 132 | Swing Bop Boogie/Sleep, Rock-a-Roll Rock-a-Baby | 1956 | $200 |

WAYNE AND DEE
HIT
| ❏ 221 | I Got You Babe/Eve of Destruction | 1965 | $15 |

— B-side by the Roamers

WAYNE, BERNIE
20TH CENTURY FOX
| ❏ 559 | Christmas Is Over/Christmas Is Over | 1964 | $8 |

— B-side by the Hushtones
ABC-PARAMOUNT
❏ 9752	Flirtango/Maracaibo	1956	$30
❏ 9815	Leaky Faucet/Theme from "Abner the Baseball"	1957	$30
❏ 9727	Shalimar/South of Saigon	1956	$30
❏ 9967	The Telegraph Operator and the Chorus Girl/Cool Caballero	1958	$30
IMPERIAL
| ❏ 5575 | The Whistling Pixie/Soft Shoe Rock | 1959 | $20 |
RUST
| ❏ 5063 | 38-24-38/Martinique | 1963 | $15 |

Number	Title	Yr	NM
WAYNE, BILLY			
FEDORA			
❏ 1008	Telegram/Heartbreak and Blues	1962	$30
HILLCREST			
❏ 778	I Love My Baby/Walkin' n' Strollin'	1960	$800
WAYNE, BOBBY			
EPIC			
❏ 9595	Big Train/The Valley	1963	$15
MERCURY			
❏ 70268	Snow, Snow, Beautiful Snow/The Jones Boy	1953	$20
WAYNE, BUDDY			
GARDENA			
❏ 132	Artificial Christmas/Heartbreak Ahead	1962	$15
WAYNE, CARL, AND THE VIKINGS			
ABC-PARAMOUNT			
❏ 10752	Shimmy Shammy Jingle/My Girl	1965	$40
WAYNE, DOTTIE			
VEE JAY			
❏ 482	Silent Night/Little Church Bell	1962	$20
WAYNE, FARLEY			
HIT			
❏ 18	That's Old Fashioned/Wolverton Mountain	1962	$8
WAYNE, JOHN			
CASABLANCA			
❏ 1002	I Have Faith/The Prayer	1979	$6
LIBERTY			
❏ 55389	I Have Faith/Walk with Him	1961	$15
WAYNE, THOMAS			
CAPEHART			
❏ 5009	Tragedy/No More, No More	1961	$40
FERNWOOD			
❏ 111	Eternally/Scandalizing My Name	1959	$40
❏ 122	Girl Next Door/Because of You	1960	$40
❏ 113	Gonna Be Waitin'/Just Beyond	1959	$40
❏ 120	Guilty of Love/Pancho Villa	1960	$40
❏ 128	Tragedy/No More, No More	1961	$40
❏ 109	Tragedy/Saturday Date	1959	$40
PHILLIPS INT'L.			
❏ 3577	I've Got It Made/The Quiet Look	1962	$30
SANTO			
❏ 9053	Stop the River/Eighth Wonder of the World	1962	$30
❏ 9057	Tragedy/Gonna Be Waiting	1962	$30
WAYNE, WANDA			
KING			
❏ 45-1290	Don't Forget to Write/Take Your Tears	1953	$30
❏ 45-1437	I Gotta Go Get My Baby/The Light Across the River	1955	$30
❏ 45-1466	Turn Your Fire Down/Catch Your Lover	1955	$30
❏ 45-1291	Who Would You Cry To/These Three Little Words	1953	$30
— With Johnny Grimes			
WE FIVE			
A&M			
❏ 894	High Flying Bird/What Do I Do	1967	$6
❏ 784	Let's Get Together/Cast Your Fate to the Wind	1965	$8
❏ XMAS1 [DJ]	My Favorite Things/The 12 Days Of Christmas	1968	$15
—B-side by the Baja Marimba Band			
❏ XMAS1 [PS]	My Favorite Things/The 12 Days Of Christmas	1968	$20
—B-side by the Baja Marimba Band			
❏ 800	Somewhere/There Stands the Door	1966	$20
❏ 1072	Walk On By/It Really Doesn't Matter	1969	$6
❏ 820	What's Goin' On/The First Time	1966	$8
MGM			
❏ 14618	Seven Day Change/Natural Way	1973	$5

Number	Title	Yr	NM
VAULT			
❏ 969	Catch the Wind/Oh, Lonesome Me	1970	$6
VERVE			
❏ 10716	Bandstand Dancer/Rejoice	1973	$5
7-Inch Extended Plays			
A&M			
❏ SP438	Let's Get Together/Make Someone Happy/Somewhere//The First Time/Our Day Will Come/The Inch Worm	1966	$20
— Stereo jukebox issue; small hole, plays at 33 1/3 rpm			
❏ SP438 [PS]	Make Someone Happy	1966	$20
WE THE PEOPLE (1)			
CHALLENGE			
❏ 59351	In the Past/St. John's Shop	1966	$125
❏ 59333	Mirror of Your Mind/The Color of Love	1966	$125
HOTLINE			
❏ 3680	My Brother, The Man/Proceed with Caution	1966	$200
RCA VICTOR			
❏ 47-9292	Follow Me Back to Louisville/Fluorescent Hearts	1967	$30
❏ 47-9393	Love Is a Beautiful Thing/The Day She Dies	1967	$30
❏ 47-9498	When I Arrive/Ain't Gonna Find Nobody (Better Than You)	1968	$80
REENA			
❏ 116	Back Street Thoughts/Who Am I?	1967	$60
❏ 105	For No One to See/Feelings of My Emptiness	1967	$60
WE THE PEOPLE (2)			
LION			
❏ 148	Forgotten Man/Left in the Lost & Found	1973	$30
❏ 164	Making My Daydream Real/Whatcha Done for Me, I'm Gonna Do for You	1974	$200
MAP CITY			
❏ 305	Cat and Mouse (Round and Round)/We Can Survive	1969	$15
VERVE			
❏ 10665	We Done Threw It Away/Right Now	1971	$30
WE THE PEOPLE (U)			
IMPERIAL			
❏ 66404	Moonstep/Earthrise	1969	$20
WE TWO			
ABC			
❏ 10930	Magic Moments/Way Down Deep Inside	1967	$30
WEASELS, THE			
SIAMESE			
❏ 02	Beat Her with a Rake/I'm the Commander	1978	$20
❏ 02 [PS]	Beat Her with a Rake/I'm the Commander	1978	$20
WEATHER REPORT			
ARC			
❏ 11166	Birdland/Brown Street	1979	$4
COLUMBIA			
❏ 45964	125th Street Congress/Will	1973	$5
❏ 45883	Adios/Boogie Woogie Waltz	1973	$5
❏ 10004	American Tango/(B-side unknown)	1974	$5
❏ 10215	Between the Thighs/Lusitano	1975	$5
❏ 10532	Birdland/Palladium	1977	$5
WEATHERLY, JIM			
20TH CENTURY FOX			
❏ 565	I'm Gonna Make It/Wise Men Never Speak	1965	$20
ABC			
❏ 12288	All That Keeps Me Going/I Hope It Never Rains Like That Again	1977	$5
❏ 12193	(Apples Won't Grow In) Colorado Snow/To a Gentler Time	1976	$5
❏ 12213	Gonna Shine It On Again/People Some People Choose to Love	1976	$5
❏ 12252	Storms of Troubled Times/(B-side unknown)	1977	$5

Number	Title	Yr	NM
BUDDAH			
❏ 444	I'll Still Love You/My First Day Without Her	1974	$5
❏ 467	It Must Have Been the Rain/Mississippi	1975	$5
❏ 505	What's One More Time/How'd We Ever Get This Way	1975	$5
ELEKTRA			
❏ 46592	Gift from Missouri/All I Need to Know	1980	$4
❏ 47096	Love That Went Away/(B-side unknown)	1980	$4
❏ 47027	Safe in the Arms of Your Love (Cold in the Streets)/All I Need to Know	1980	$4
❏ 46547	Smooth Sailin'/Let Me Love It Away	1979	$4
RCA VICTOR			
❏ PB-10134	High on Love/Like a First Time Thing	1974	$5
❏ APBO-0020	Leavin' Dallas/It Must Be Love This Time	1973	$5
❏ 74-0822	Loving You Is Just an Old Habit/Between His Goodbye and My Hello	1972	$6
❏ 74-0897	Old Kentucky Moon/Until Your Ship Comes In	1973	$6
❏ 74-0949	Where Peaceful Waters Flow/Like a First Time Thing	1973	$6
WEAVER, DENNIS			
CASCADE			
❏ 5906	Girls (Wuz Made to Be Loved)/Michael Finnigan	1959	$30
CENTURY CITY			
❏ 701	Days Like These/Cobwebs of Your Mind	1969	$8
EVA			
❏ 103	The Apes/Chicken Mash	1963	$15
IM'PRESS			
❏ 716	20th Century Man/No Name	1973	$6
OVATION			
❏ 1056	Hubbardville Store/Prairie Dog Blues	1975	$4
❏ 1056 [PS]	Hubbardville Store/Prairie Dog Blues	1975	$5
WARNER BROS.			
❏ 5352	The Sinking of the Reuben James/Genesis Through Exodus	1963	$20
WEAVERS, THE			
DECCA			
❏ 28054	Around the Corner (Beneath the Berry Tree)/The Gandy Dancer's Ball	1952	$20
❏ 28434	Clementine/True Love	1952	$20
❏ 28542	Down in the Valley/The Bay of Mexico	1953	$20
❏ 27728	Drinking Gourd/Easy Rider Blues	1951	$20
❏ 28272	Goodnight Irene/Midnight Special	1952	$20
❏ 9-27077	Goodnight Irene/Tzena, Tzena, Tzena	1950	$30
—Co-credited with Gordon Jenkins and His Orchestra			
❏ 27818	Go Tell It on the Mountain/Poor Little Jesus	1951	$20
— Sides 5 and 6 of "Album No. 9-284			
❏ 27727	I Know Where I'm Going-Hush Little Baby/Suliram	1951	$20
❏ 27819	Lulloo Lullay-It's Almost Day/Burgundian Carol-God Rest Ye Merry Gentlemen	1951	$20
— Sides 7 and 8 of "Album No. 9-284			
❏ 9-27515	On Top of Old Smoky/Across the Wide Missouri	1951	$30
— With Terry Gilkyson			
❏ 27376	So Long (It's Been Good to Know Yuh)/Lonesome Traveller	1951	$20
❏ 28637	Taking It Easy/Benoni	1953	$20
❏ 27726	The Frozen Logger/Darling Corey	1951	$20
❏ 27817	The Seven Blessings of Mary/The Twelve Days of Christmas	1951	$20
— Sides 3 and 4 of "Album No. 9-284			
❏ 9-27053	Tzena, Tzena, Tzena/Around the World	1950	$30
❏ 9-284 [PS]	We Wish You a Merry Christmas	1951	$20
— Empty box for 27783, 27817, 27818, 27819			
❏ 27783	We Wish You a Merry Christmas/One for the Little Bitty Baby	1951	$20
— Sides 1 and 2 of "Album No. 9-284			
❏ 27928	Wimoweh/Old Paint	1952	$20

Number	Title	Yr	NM
WEBB, BOOGIE BILL			
IMPERIAL			
❏ 5257	Bad Dog/I Ain't For It	1953	$250
WEBB, JACK			
WARNER BROS.			
❏ 5003	Try a Little Tenderness/You'd Never Know the Old Place Now	1958	$30
7-Inch Extended Plays			
RCA VICTOR			
❏ EPB3199 [PS]	The Christmas Story	1953	$50
— Cover for 2-EP set			
❏ 547-0342	The Christmas Story (Part 1)/The Christmas Story (Part 4)	1953	$35
❏ 547-0343	The Christmas Story (Part 2)/The Christmas Story (Part 3)	1953	$35
WEBB, JAY LEE			
DECCA			
❏ 32710	Bloomin' Fools/If I Go On a-Livin'	1970	$6
❏ 32145	Bottle Turn Her Off/You Never Were Mine	1967	$8
❏ 32087	I Come Home a-Drinking (To a Worn-Out Wife Like You)/Since You Made a Wreck Out of Me	1967	$10
—As "Jack Webb"			
❏ 32798	I Was Ready for the World/Whole Lot of Nothin'	1971	$6
WEBB, JUNE			
HICKORY			
❏ 1086	A Mansion on the Hill/Friendly Enemy	1958	$30
❏ 1096	Conscience/You Take the Table	1959	$30
❏ 1079	I'm So Lonesome I Could Cry/Love	1958	$30
❏ 1105	I Wonder If You Know/What a Price to Pay	1959	$30
❏ 1120	Love Has Come My Way/Sweeter Than Flowers	1960	$20
❏ 1129	Take Me Home (To My Lover)/I Was Just Meant to Be Lonely	1960	$20
RCA VICTOR			
❏ 47-7022	Crew Cut Romeo/Final Affair	1957	$40
WEBB, SKEETER			
KING			
❏ 45-1302	Fool's Folly/I Could Hardly Wait	1954	$30
❏ 45-1278	Was It a Bad Dream/Your Secret's Not a Secret Anymore	1953	$30
WEBER, HENRY			
MERCURY			
❏ 5514	Christmas Carols (Part 1)/Christmas Carols (Part 2)	1950	$20
WEBER, JOAN			
COLUMBIA			
❏ 4-40535	Anything, Everything for Love/Don't Throw My Love Away	1955	$10
❏ 4-40440	Call Me Careless/It May Sound Silly	1955	$10
❏ 4-40852	Gone/A Love That's a Lie	1957	$10
❏ 4-40366	Let Me Go, Lover!/Marionette	1954	$15
❏ 4-40474	Lover, Lover, Why Must We Part/Tell the Lord	1955	$10
❏ 4-40898	Saturday Lover, Sunday Stranger/Who'll Be My Love	1957	$10
❏ 4-40709	What Should a Teen Heart Do/Goodbye Lollipops, Hello Lipstick	1956	$10
WEBS, THE (1)			
ATLANTIC			
❏ 2415	Let's Party/Keep Your Love Strong	1967	$15
MGM			
❏ 13602	People Sure Act Funny/You Pretty Fool	1966	$15
POPSIDE			
❏ 4595	Give In/It's So Hard to Break a Habit	1968	$10
❏ 4593	This Thing Called Love/Tomorrow	1967	$10
VERVE			
❏ 10610	We Belong Together/I Want You Back	1968	$10

Number	Title	Yr	NM
WEBS, THE (2)			
HEART			
❏ 333	Blue Skies/Lost (Cricket in My Ear)	1962	$50
LITE			
❏ 9004	Blue Skies/Lost (Cricket in My Ear)	1962	$30
WEBSTER BROTHERS, THE			
COLUMBIA			
❏ 4-21473	Looking Through the Windows of Heaven/Walking in God's Sunshine	1955	$30
❏ 4-21503	Only One Heart/Watching the Clock	1956	$30
❏ 4-21421	Seven Year Blues/Road of Broken Hearts	1955	$30
❏ 4-21563	Where We Never Grow Old/Somebody Touched Me	1956	$30
WEBSTER, CHASE			
CAMEO			
❏ 312	Cry Cry Darling/Suit Cash	1964	$15
DOT			
❏ 16270	Could This Be Magic/Sweethearts in Heaven	1961	$20
❏ 16318	For Sale/Patty Cake	1961	$20
❏ 16367	Handful of Friends/I Can't Walk Away	1962	$20
❏ 16384	I'll Light a Candle/Like I've Never Been Gone	1962	$20
HICKORY			
❏ 1303	Cry Cry Darling/Find Out	1965	$12
❏ 1283	Life Can Have Meaning/Where Is Your Heart Tonight	1964	$12
SHOW BIZ			
❏ 237	Happy in the Morning/Love or the Wine	1970	$12
❏ 241	Honky Tonkin'/I'll Just Have to Pay	1970	$10
❏ 233	Moody River/Turn Out the Lights	1970	$10
WEBTONES, THE			
MGM			
❏ 12724	My Lost Love/Walk, Talk and Kiss	1958	$30
WEIR, BOB			
Also see THE GRATEFUL DEAD.			
Arista			
❏ 0315	Bombs Away/Easy to Slip	1978	$6
❏ 0336	I'll Be Doggone/Shade of Grey	1978	$15
— May be promo only			
WARNER BROS.			
❏ 7611	One More Saturday Night/Cassidy	1972	$15
WEIRDOS			
BOMP!			
❏ 112	Destroy All Music/Why Do You Exist?/A Life of Crime	1977	$50
— Black label, pressed on styrene			
❏ 112	Destroy All Music/Why Do You Exist?/A Life of Crime	1977	$30
— White label, pressed on styrene			
❏ 112 [PS]	Destroy All Music/Why Do You Exist?/A Life of Crime	1977	$12
❏ 112	Destroy All Music/Why Do You Exist?/A Life of Crime	1977	$10
— White label, pressed on vinyl			
DANGERHOUSE			
❏ 1063	We Got the Neutron Bomb/Solitary Confinement	1978	$30
❏ 1063 [PS]	We Got the Neutron Bomb/Solitary Confinement	1978	$30
(NO LABEL)			
❏ 0(no cat #)	Skateboards to Hell/Adult Hood	1979	$13
❏ 0(no cat #) [PS]	Skateboards to Hell/Adult Hood	1979	$13
WEISBERG, TIM			
A&M			
❏ 1680	Dion Blue/The Visit	1975	$4
❏ 1493	Do Dah/A Night for Crying	1973	$5
❏ 1330	Fog and Spice/For Those Who Never Dream	1972	$5
❏ 1318	Long Ago and Far Away/Hard Way to Go	1971	$5
❏ 1397	Our Thing/Tyme Cube	1972	$5
❏ 1520	Streak-Out/A Night for Crying	1974	$5
MCA			
❏ 41307	I'm the Lucky One/Magic Lady	1980	$4
❏ 41036	Midsummer's Dream/Moonchild	1979	$4

Number	Title	Yr	NM
❏ 51163	Sleep Walk/Paula	1981	$4
❏ 51042	What's Going On/Page One	1981	$4
UNITED ARTISTS			
❏ XW1083	Cascade/Gene, Jean	1977	$4
❏ 1227	Every Time I See Your Smile/So Good to Me	1978	$4
❏ XW933	Gonna Fly Now (Theme from "Rocky")/Just for Fun	1976	$4
WEISSBERG, ERIC, AND STEVE MANDELL			
WARNER BROS.			
❏ 7659	Dueling Banjos/End of a Dream	1972	$12
—A-side listed as "from the Warner Bros. motion picture Deliverance" with no artist mentioned on the B-side; "Dueling Banjos" time is 3:17			
❏ 7659	Dueling Banjos/End of a Dream	1972	$4
— Later pressings credit the musicians; "Dueling Banjos" time is 2:12			
❏ 7659	Dueling Banjos/End of a Dream	1973	$6
—A-side listed as "from the Warner Bros. motion picture Deliverance" with no artist mentioned on the B-side; "Dueling Banjos" time is 2:12			
7-Inch Extended Plays			
❏ S2683 [PS]	Dueling Banjos	1973	$12
— Part of "Little LP" series (LLP #210)			
❏ S2683	Eight More Miles to Louisville/Dueling Banjos/Little Maggie/Pony Express/Buffalo Gals/Eighth of January	1973	$10
—Jukebox issue; small hole, plays at 33 1/3 rpm			
WELCH, BOB			
CAPITOL			
❏ 4719	Church/Here Comes the Night	1979	$4
❏ 4719 [PS]	Church/Here Comes the Night	1979	$5
❏ 4926	Don't Rush the Good Things/Reason	1980	$4
❏ 4543	Ebony Eyes/Outskirts	1978	$4
❏ 4954	Girl Can't Stop/Those Days Are Gone	1980	$4
❏ 4588	Hot Love, Cold World/Danchiva	1978	$4
❏ 4588 [PS]	Hot Love, Cold World/Danchiva	1978	$6
❏ 4745	Oh Jenny/Three Hearts	1979	$4
❏ 4833	Oneonone/Don't Let Me Fall	1980	$4
❏ 4685	Precious Love/Something Strong	1979	$4
❏ 4479	Sentimental Lady/Hot Love, Cold World	1977	$4
RCA			
❏ PB-13569	Fever/Can't Hold Your Love Back	1983	$4
❏ PB-13669	I'll Dance Alone/Stay	1983	$4
❏ PB-12356	Imaginary Fool/Two to Do	1981	$4
WELCH, LENNY			
ATCO			
❏ 6894	A Sunday Kind of Love/I Wish You Could Know Me	1972	$5
❏ 6915	Goodnight My Love/Fancy Meeting You Here Baby	1973	$5
BIG TREE			
❏ 16107	Six Million Dollar Woman/(B-side unknown)	1977	$5
CADENCE			
❏ 1428	A Taste of Honey/The Old Cathedral	1962	$10
❏ 1399	Changa Rock/Boogie Cha Cha	1961	$10
❏ 1386	Darlin'/Three Handed Woman	1960	$12
❏ 1422	Ebb Tide/Congratulations Baby	1962	$30
— The A-side was the hit, but this is sought after for its group sound on the B-side			
❏ 1394	I'd Like to Know/Darlin'	1960	$10
❏ 1446	If You See My Love/Father Sebastian	1964	$10
❏ 1416	It's Just Not That Easy/Mama Don't You Hit That Boy	1962	$10
❏ 1439	Since I Fell for You/Are You Sincere	1963	$15
COLUMBIA			
❏ 44007	Since I Fell for You/A Taste of Honey	1967	$8
COMMONWEALTH UNITED			
❏ 3004	Breaking Up Is Hard to Do/Get Mommy to Come Back Home	1969	$6
❏ 3011	To Be Loved and Glory of Love/My Heart Won't Let Me	1970	$6

Number	Title	Yr	NM
DECCA			
30829	Blessing of Love/Last Star of the Evening	1959	$15
KAPP			
662	Darling Take Me Back/Time After Time	1965	$8
778	If You Love Me, Really Love Me/Once Before I Die	1966	$8
648	I'm Dreaming Again/My Fool of a Heart	1965	$8
854	I'm Over You/Coronet Blue	1967	$8
827	Let's Start All Over Again/Love Don't Live Here Anymore	1967	$8
761	Please Help Me I'm Falling/Just One Smile	1966	$8
689	Two Different Worlds/I'll Be There	1965	$8
751	What Now My Love/Gonna Hear from Me	1966	$8
MAINSTREAM			
5560	A Hundred Pounds of Pain/The Iguana	1974	$5
5554	Eyewitness News/I Need You More	1973	$5
5545	Since I Don't Have You/Right in the Next Room	1973	$5
5561	When There's No Such Thing As Love/Minx	1974	$5
MERCURY			
72777	Darling Stay with Me/Wait a While Longer	1968	$8
72866	Halfway to Your Arms/You Can't Run Away	1968	$8
72811	Tennessee Waltz/He Who Loves	1968	$8

WELK, LAWRENCE

Number	Title	Yr	NM
CORAL			
61081	Angel on the Christmas Tree/Are My Ears On Straight	1953	$20
—With Sara Berner			
61741	Around the World/Champagne Time	1956	$8
61318	At the Junior Prom/Home Again Blues	1954	$12
61442	Ball of Fire/Go 'Way, Go 'Way	1955	$8
61515	Bonnie Blue Gal/Sam the Old Accordian Man	1955	$8
60689	Bubbles in the Wine/Josephine	1952	$20
60998	Bubbling Over/The La-De-Da Song	1953	$10
61849	By the Bend of the River/Keyboard Serenade	1957	$8
60974	Canadian Capers/Did I Remember	1953	$10
62056	Cha Cha Polka/I Never Should Have Let You Go	1958	$8
61508	Champagne Waltz/Musette	1955	$8
61095	Christmas Carols (Part 1)/Christmas Carols (Part 2)	1953	$15
61746	Christmas Waltz/Santa from Santa Fe	1956	$15
—With the Lennon Sisters			
61765	Cinco Robles/Whispering Heart	1956	$8
61784	Dance Around a Stack of Barley/When Irish Eyes Are Smiling	1957	$8
60619	Dolores/Emaline	1952	$12
60752	Dream House/Small Talk	1952	$12
61075	Ebb Tide/Beautiful Ohio	1953	$12
61372	Elephant's Tango/Lazy Gondolier	1955	$8
60519	Every Little Moment/Till We Meet Again	1951	$15
61786	Falling Star/It Was That Kiss	1957	$8
60975	Good Morning, Mr. Zip Zip Zip/Just Once Again	1953	$10
62091	Gunsmoke/The Ballad of Paladin	1959	$15
61017	Hallelujah Brother/"O	1953	$10
61629	Helena Polka/Hot Pretzels	1956	$8
61408	Hey, Mr. Banjo/Love Me or Leave Me	1955	$8
61003	High Life Polka/Town and Country Polka	1953	$12
60976	I'll See You in My Dreams/Peggy O'Neill	1953	$10
65604	I'll See You in My Dreams/Till We Meet Again	1966	$5
61387	I See God/Pray for Me	1955	$8
61524	It's Almost Tomorrow/Rice	1955	$8
61958	I Want a Girl/When My Baby Smiles at Me	1958	$8
61900	Lichtenstein Polka/You Know Too Much	1957	$8
61595	Lisbon Antigua/Chain Gang	1956	$8
60621	Louise/Sweet Eloise	1952	$10
62031	Mary Ann/Indiana Holiday	1958	$8
60620	Mary Lou/Annabelle	1952	$10
61783	McNamara's Band/Wild Colonial Boy	1957	$8
60828	Meet Mister Callaghan/Flirtation Waltz	1952	$10
61914	Merry Christmas from Our House to Your House/Santa Claus Is Here Again	1957	$15
—With the Lennon Sisters			
61597	Mickey Mouse Mambo/Hi! to You	1956	$15
60947	Minnie the Mermaid/Say It Isn't So	1953	$10
60444	Moonlight Bay/Boomp! Pa-Deedle Doodle	1951	$15
61893	Moon Love/We'll Be There	1957	$8
61574	Moritat (A Theme from the Threepenny Opera)/Stompin' at the Savoy	1956	$8
60618	My Extraordinary Gal/Irene	1952	$10
61894	My Reverie/Fool Moon and Empty Arms	1957	$8
60893	Oh Happy Day/Your Mother and Mine	1952	$10
60973	Ohio/It's Love	1953	$10
61937	One Note Polka/The Lovers on the Park Bench	1958	$8
61644	On the Street Where You Live/I Could Have Danced All Night	1956	$8
62053	Outer Space Santa/All Around The Merry Christmas Tree	1958	$15
—As "Lawrence Welk's Little Band			
60806	Padam Padam (How It Echoes the Beat of My Heart)/Your Eyes So Lovely	1952	$10
61621	Practice, Practice What You Preach/What a Heavenly Night for Love	1956	$8
60514	Sad and Lonely/Irving	1951	$15
60905	She Looked Down from Her Window/I'm Gonna Ring the Bell Tonight	1953	$10
—Vocalist: Jack Smith			
60405	Shenandoah Waltz/Metro Polka	1951	$15
—Note: Earlier Lawrence Welk 45s on Coral may exist			
60516	Slow Drive/Moonlight Bay	1951	$15
60575	Sweetheart Waltz/I Wanna Say Hello	1951	$15
60630	Swingin' Down the Lane/You're Somebody	1952	$10
60517	Tell Me/Cuddle Up a Little Closer, Lovey Mine	1951	$15
61806	Ten Little Trees/The Bridge of Saint Lo	1957	$8
61135	The Darktown Strutter's Ball/In the Mood	1954	$12
60677	The Gandy Dancer's Ball/Ivory Rag	1952	$10
61240	The Greatest Feeling in the World/Luxembourg Polka	1954	$10
61174	The Man with the Banjo/Until Sunrise	1954	$10
61592	The Poor People of Paris/Nobody Knows But the Lord	1956	$8
61701	Tonight You Belong to Me/When the White Lilacs Bloom Again	1956	$10
—With the Lennon Sisters			
61477	Wake the Town and Tell the People/I Hear Those Bells	1955	$8
62018	Walk with Me/Be Thankful	1958	$8
60784	Watermelon Weather/Busybody	1952	$10
61670	Weary Blues/In the Alps	1956	$10
—With the McGuire Sisters			
61670 [PS]	Weary Blues/In the Alps	1956	$20
61645	With a Little Bit of Luck/I've Grown Accustomed to Her Face	1956	$8
DECCA			
23858	Barbara Polka/Friendly Tavern Polka	1950	$12
—Reissue of 78; part of "Album No. 9-24			
23855	Beer Barrel Polka/Pennsylvania Polka	1950	$12
—Reissue of 78; part of "Album No. 9-24			
24442	Bubbles in the Wine/Kentucky Waltz	1950	$30
—78 originally released in 1948; original 45 has black label with "rays" on either side of the word "Decca			
24442	Bubbles in the Wine/Kentucky Waltz	1955	$15
—Second 45 has star under "Decca			
24442	Bubbles in the Wine/Kentucky Waltz	1960	$8
—Third 45 has color bars on label			
23857	Clarinet Polka/Pound Your Table Polka	1950	$10
—Reissue of 78; part of "Album No. 9-24			
DOT			
16697	Apples and Bananas/Theme from "The Addams Family	1965	$8
16364	Baby Elephant Walk/Theme from the Brothers Grimm	1962	$8
16526	Blue Velvet/Fiesta	1963	$6
16981	Born Free/Winchester Cathedral	1966	$5
16161	Calcutta/My Grandfather's Clock	1960	$8
16017	Christmas Moon/Peppy the Peppermint Bear	1959	$15
—With the Lennon Sisters			
16810	Currier and Ives/Tia-Juana	1965	$6
16764	Down, Down, Down, Down/Jenny Dear	1965	$6
15995	Every Night When You Say a Prayer/Thank the Lord for This Thanksgiving	1959	$12
—With the Lennon Sisters			
16943	Family Affair/Tarzan (Tarzan's March)	1966	$8
15967	Goodnight Sweetheart/This Night Is Young and You're So Beautiful	1959	$8
—By "The Lawrence Welk Glee Club			
16603	Hello, Dolly/Clair de Lune	1964	$6
16063	Hour of Parting/Summer Set	1960	$8
16114	It Started in Naples/I Get So Lonely (Oh Baby Mine)	1960	$8
16145	Last Date/Remember Lolita	1960	$6
16794	Moonlight and Roses/Send Me the Pillow You Dream On	1965	$6
16620	Poodle Walk/Do I Need You	1964	$6
16488	Scarlett O'Hara/Breakwater	1963	$6
16680	Sixteen Reasons/Little Things Mean a Lot	1964	$6
16582	Stockholm/Girl from Barbados	1964	$6
16778	Summer Nights/La Bamba	1965	$6
17001	The Beat Goes On/Then You Can Tell Me Goodbye	1967	$5
16153	The Cradle to the Cross/Laura-Jean	1960	$6
16198	Theme from My Three Sons/Out of a Clear Blue Sky	1961	$10
16741	There's No One Like You/Schatzie	1965	$6
15924	The Swingin' Burglar/Bell Boogie	1959	$8
—By "Lawrence Welk's Little Band			
16885	Wabash Cannonball/Tennessee Waltz	1966	$5
MERCURY			
70735	Amilia Polka/Tinker Polka	1955	$10
5666	Bubbles in the Wine/Back Home in Illinois	1951	$30
70737	Dakota Polka/Kit Kat Polka	1955	$12
5434	Dakota Polka/Windy River	1950	$20
5440	Deep Freezer Dinah/Fancy Free	1950	$20
5411	Doo-Wacka-Doo/Pizzacata	1950	$20
—Note: Earlier Lawrence Welk 45s on Mercury may exist			
5518	Emilia Polka/Tinker Polka	1950	$20
70149	Fiddle-Dee-Dee/Dancing Doll	1953	$15
70734	Hoop-De-Dee/Bar Room Polka	1955	$10
5419	Hoop-De-Dee/If You Can Get a Drum with a Boom, Boom, Boom	1950	$20
5469	Mama's Samba/Skaters Waltz in Springtime	1950	$20
—Vocalist: Roberta Linn			
5735	Merry Christmas Polka/Julida Polka	1951	$20
70738	Merry Christmas Polka/Laughing Polka	1955	$15
5487	Petite Waltz/The Middle of a Riddle	1950	$20
70739	Tiger Rag/Chopsticks Polka	1955	$10
5529	Tiger Rag/Military Polka	1950	$20
RANWOOD			
874	Applause/Smiles	1970	$4
888	Candida/Endlessly	1971	$4
1091	Christmas in Los Angeles/Carol Of The Bells	1980	$4
—By "The Lawrence Welk Christmas Chorale			
1039	Fantastic, That's You/Oh Harry	1975	$3
—With Henry Questa			
842	Galveston/Gentle on My Mind	1969	$4
801	Green Tambourine/Watch What Happens	1968	$4
865	Hello Dolly/Southtown U.S.A.	1970	$4
845	Land of Dreams/Chee Chee Kookaroo	1969	$4
814	Let's Make America What It Used to Be/To America with Love	1968	$4
920	Melody of Love (Parody)/Melody of Love	1972	$8
—With Bob Hudson (of Hudson and Landry) on A-side			
915	Theme from Summer of '42/Adios, Au Revoir, Auf Wiedersehn	1971	$4
83057	A Little Bit of Heaven (Shure They Call It Ireland)/Ireland Must Be Heaven For My Mother Came from There//Shamrocks, Shillelaghs and Shenanigans/Dance Aroun' a Stack of Barley	1956	$10
—Part of 2-EP set EC 82026			
83068	(contents unknown)	1956	$10

Number	Title	Yr	NM
—Part of 2-EP set EC 82032			
❏ EC 781181	Gunsmoke/Maverick//Ballad of Paladin/The Legend of Wyatt Earp	1959	$20
— Stereo			
❏ EC81133	I Could Have Danced All Night/I've Grown Accustomed to Her Face//On the Street Where You Live/With a Little Bit of Luck	1956	$10
❏ EC81133 [PS]	My Fair Lady	1956	$12
❏ 83069	Santa Claus Is Comin' To Town/Winter Wonderland//Christmas Dreaming (A Little Early This Year)/The Twelve Gifts Of Christmas	1956	$10
—Part of 2-EP set EC 82032			
❏ EC82027 [PS]	Say It With Music	1956	$12
—Cover for 2-EP set (83058 and 83059)			
❏ 83058	Say It With Music/Tea for Two/Thou Swell/I Found a Million Dollar Baby in a Five and Ten Cent Store/Pretty Baby/Yes Sir, That's My Baby//Oh Lady Be Good/Somebody Loves Me/S'Wonderful/Sleepy Time Gal/My Blue Heaven/Doodle Doo Doo	1956	$10
—Part of 2-EP set EC 82027			
❏ 83059	The Gypsy in My Soul/Exactly Like You//Anything Goes/Was That the Human Thing to Do/Cecilia/I Can't Believe It's True//Wabash Blues/September Song/Mood Indigo/Sympathy/L'Amour Toujours L'Amour (Love Everlasting)/Giannina Mia	1956	$10
—Part of 2-EP set EC 82027			
❏ EC 781181 [PS]	TV Western Theme Songs	1959	$20
❏ 83056	When Irish Eyes Are Smiling/My Heart Danced an Irish Jig/Irish Alphabet/McNamara's Band	1956	$10
—Part of 2-EP set EC 82026			

WELLER, FREDDY
ABC DOT

Number	Title	Yr	NM
❏ 17554	Love You Back to Georgia/Show Me the Way to Your Love	1975	$5
❏ 17577	Stone Crazy/Still Making Love to You	1975	$5

APT
| ❏ 25096 | Walk Away Slowly/You Better Go Join the Campfire | 1966 | $10 |

COLUMBIA
❏ 11221	A Million Old Goodbyes/Sleep with Me	1980	$4
❏ 45451	Another Night of Love/Always Something Special	1971	$5
❏ 10300	Ask Any Old Cheater Who Knows/A Legend in My Home	1976	$4
❏ 45542	Ballad of a Hillbilly Singer/Good Old-Fashioned Music	1972	$5
❏ 10769	Bar Wars/One of the Mysteries of Love	1978	$4
❏ 45026	Down in the Boondocks/Amarillo, Texas	1969	$5
❏ 10890	Fantasy Island/Take a Little Bit	1979	$4
❏ 44800	Games People Play/Home	1969	$5
❏ 11149	Go for the Night/Two Makes One Wonderful	1979	$4
❏ 45388	Indian Lake/Over You	1971	$5
❏ 45087	I Shook the Hand/We Gotta All Get Together	1970	$5
❏ 45968	I've Just Got to Know (How Loving You Would Be)/Georgia Girl	1973	$5
❏ 10682	Let Me Fall Back in Your Arms/Snuff Queens	1978	$4
❏ 10352	Liquor, Love and Life/Celia Brown	1976	$4
❏ 45138	Listen to the Young Folks/That Little Boy	1970	$6
❏ 11266	Lost in Austin/Explosion!	1980	$4
❏ 10837	Love Got in the Way/You Win Again	1978	$4
❏ 10539	Merry-Go-Round/One Man Show	1977	$4
❏ 46040	Sexy Lady/Bobby Crabtree's Grave	1974	$5
❏ 45723	She Loves Me (Right Out of My Mind)/Angel on My Shoulder	1972	$5
❏ 11394	Still Your Fool/Tonight I'm Drinkin'	1980	$4
❏ 10482	Strawberry Curls/When You Were Mine	1977	$4
❏ 11044	That Run-Away Woman of Mine/Atlanta	1979	$4
❏ 45902	The Perfect Stranger/Betty Ann and Shirley Cole	1973	$5
❏ 45276	The Promised Land/Goodnight Sandy	1970	$5

Number	Title	Yr	NM
❏ 44916	These Are Not My People/Never Knew Julie	1969	$5
❏ 45827	Too Much Monkey Business/It Sure Feels Good	1973	$5

WELLES, ORSON
GNP CRESCENDO

| ❏ 8345 | I Know What It Is to Be Young/Love Is a Lovely Word | 1984 | $8 |

WELLS, BILLY, AND THE CRESCENTS
RESERVE

| ❏ 105 | I Love Only You/Julie | 1956 | $600 |

WELLS, CHUCK
COLUMBIA

❏ 4-21224	Barroom Girl/Three Memories	1954	$30
❏ 4-21312	Foot Loose and Fancy Free/Marryin' Preacher Man	1954	$30
❏ 4-21134	I'm Not Ashamed/I'm Setting You Free	1953	$30
❏ 4-21275	I Saw the Lord/Heavenly Road	1954	$30
❏ 4-21360	Is This the Day/Someone Cares	1955	$30

WELLS, KENNY
NEW VOICE

| ❏ 812 | Isn't It Just a Shame/I Can't Stop | 1966 | $700 |

WELLS, KITTY, AND ROY DRUSKY
DECCA

| ❏ 31523 | Another Chance to Fall in Love/My World's Losing You | 1963 | $10 |
| ❏ 31164 | I Can't Tell My Heart That/When Do You Love Me | 1960 | $15 |

WELLS, KITTY, AND RED FOLEY
DECCA

❏ 9-29390	As Long As I Live/Make Believe ('Til We Can Make It Come True)	1955	$30
❏ 32126	Happiness Means You/Hello Number One	1967	$8
❏ 32427	Have I Told You Lately That I Love You?/We Need One More Chance	1968	$8
❏ 32223	Living as Strangers/Loved and Wanted	1967	$8
❏ 9-29065	One by One/I'm a Stranger in My Home	1954	$30
❏ 9-29228	Skinnie Minnie (Fishtart)/Thank You for Calling	1954	$30
❏ ED2667	I'm a Stranger in My Home/One by One//As Long As I Live/Make Believe (Till We Can Make It Come True)	1959	$30

WELLS, KITTY, AND WEBB PIERCE
DECCA

❏ 31663	Finally/He Made You for Me	1964	$10
❏ 9-30183	Oh So Many Years/Can You Find It in Your Heart	1957	$20
❏ 9-30489	One Week Later/When I'm with You	1957	$20

7-Inch Extended Plays
| ❏ ED2666 | *Oh So Many Years/One Week Later/When I'm With You/Can You FInd It in Your Heart | 1959 | $30 |

WELLS, KITTY, AND JOHNNY WRIGHT
DECCA

| ❏ 32604 | There Won't Be Any Tree This Christmas/White Christmas | 1969 | $8 |
| ❏ 32294 | We'll Stick Together/Heartbreak Waltz | 1968 | $8 |

WELLS, KITTY

Number	Title	Yr	NM
CAPRICORN			
❏ 0240	Anybody Out There Wanna Be a Daddy/Somewhere Down the Road (There's a Country Girl)	1975	$6
❏ 0226	I've Been Loving You Too Long/Too Stubborn	1975	$6
❏ 0264	Mary Hartman, Mary Hartman/Nickel Candy Bar	1976	$6
❏ 0208	Too Much Love Between Us/What About You	1974	$6
DECCA			
❏ 32976	A Bridge I Just Can't Burn/Love Is the Answer	1972	$8
❏ 9-30987	Amigo's Guitar/Lonely Is a Word	1959	$20
❏ 31881	A Woman Half My Age/When Your Little High Horse Runs Down	1966	$10
❏ 31123	Carmel by the Sea/The Man I Used to Know	1960	$15
❏ 9-28931	Cheatin's a Sin/I Gave My Wedding Dress Away	1953	$30
❏ 31441	Christmas Ain't Like Christmas Anymore/Dancer (With the Light Upon His Tail)	1962	$20
❏ 31457	Cold and Lonely (Is the Forecast for Tonight)/Is It Asking Too Much	1963	$10
❏ 7-34185 [S]	Dasher (With the Light Upon His Tail)/C-H-R-I-S-T-M-A-S	1962	$30
—Small hole, plays at 33 1/3 rpm			
❏ 31313	Day Into Night/Our Mansion Is a Prison Now	1961	$15
❏ 9-28525	Divided by Two/The Things I Might Have Been	1953	$30
❏ 33047	Full Grown Man/Every Step of the Way	1973	$8
❏ 32455	Guilty Street/Shape Up or Get Out	1969	$8
❏ 32455 [PS]	Guilty Street/Shape Up or Get Out	1969	$30
— Her only known Decca picture sleeve			
❏ 32343	Gypsy King/When Hearts Grow Hard and Cold	1968	$8
❏ 32389	Happiness Hill/You're No Angel Yourself	1968	$8
❏ 31246	Heartbreak U.S.A./There Must Be Another Way to Live	1961	$15
❏ 9-28797	Hey Joe/My Cold Cold Heart Is Melted Now	1953	$30
❏ 9-29823	How Far Is Heaven/Dust on the Bible	1956	$30
—A-side with Carol Sue			
❏ 9-30551	I Can't Stop Loving You/She's No Angel	1958	$20
❏ 9-28753	I Don't Claim to Be an Angel/The Life They Live in Songs	1953	$30
❏ 32629	I Don't See What I Say/Gonna Find Me a Bluebird	1970	$8
❏ 31501	I Gave My Wedding Dress Away/A Heartache for a Keepsake	1963	$10
❏ 9-28432	I Heard the Juke Box Playing/A Wedding Ring Ago	1952	$30
❏ 9-30415	(I'll Always Be Your) Fraulein/What I Believe	1957	$20
❏ 31705	I'll Repossess My Heart/Kill Him with Kindness	1964	$10
❏ 32763	I Love You/That Ain't a Woman's Way	1970	$8
❏ 32889	I'm the Wreck of Number Two/Reno Airport Nashville Plane	1971	$8
❏ 31957	It's All Over (But the Crying)/You Left Your Mark on Me	1966	$10
❏ 9-28232	It Wasn't God Who Made Honky Tonk Angels/I Don't Want Your Money, I Want Your Time	1952	$40
❏ 33016	I've Got Yesterday/Less Than a Lady	1972	$8
❏ 31065	Left to Right/Memory of Love	1960	$20
❏ 9-29728	Lonely Side of Town/I've Kissed You My Last Time	1955	$30
❏ 32088	Love Makes the World Go Around/I'm Just Not Smart	1967	$8
❏ 9-29419	Makin' Believe/Whose Shoulder Will You Cry On	1955	$30
❏ 31817	Meanwhile, Down at Joe's/Leavin' Town Tonight	1965	$10
❏ 9-30804	Mommy for a Day/All the Time	1959	$20
❏ 32247	My Big Truck Drivin' Man/You Want Her Not Me	1967	$8
❏ 7-34189 [S]	Ole Kris Kringle/(B-side unknown)	1962	$30
—Small hole, plays at 33 1/3 rpm			
❏ 32024	Only Me and My Hairdresser Know/A Woman Never Forgets	1966	$10
❏ 31622	Password/I've Thought of Leaving You	1964	$10
❏ 9-28578	Paying for That Back Street Affair/Crying Steel Guitar Waltz	1953	$30
❏ 32840	Pledging My Love/Thank You for Loving Me	1971	$8
❏ 9-46409	Precious Memories/Gloryland March	1952	$50

Number	Title	Yr	NM
❏ 7-34186 [S]	Santa's On His Way/(B-side unknown)	1962	$30
—Small hole, plays at 33 1/3 rpm			
❏ 9-29956	Searching (For Someone Like You)/I'd Rather Stay Home	1956	$30
❏ 32931	Sincerely/J.J. Sneed	1972	$8
❏ 31192	The Other Cheek/Fickle Fun	1961	$15
❏ 9-29577	There's Poison in Your Heart/I'm in Love with You	1955	$30
❏ 32795	They're Stepping All Over My Heart/Your Old Love Letters	1971	$8
❏ 31580	This White Circle on My Finger/(I Didn't Have to) Break Up Someone's Home	1964	$10
❏ 9-29313	Thou Shalt Not Steal/I Hope My Divorce Is Never Granted	1954	$30
❏ 9-30288	Three Ways (To Love You)/A Change of Heart	1957	$20
❏ 7-34187 [S]	titles unknown	1962	$30
—Small hole, plays at 33 1/3 rpm			
❏ 9-30736	Touch and Go Heart/He's Lost His Love for Me	1958	$20
❏ 31422	We Missed You/Wicked World	1962	$15
❏ 31392	Will Your Lawyer Talk to God/The Big Let Down	1962	$15

MCA

Number	Title	Yr	NM
❏ 40057	Easily Persuaded/It Doesn't Say	1973	$6
❏ 40123	If I Was a Bottle/Mississippi Missus	1973	$6

RCA VICTOR

Number	Title	Yr	NM
❏ 47-5539	Gathering Flowers for the Master's Banquet/Don't Wait for the Last Minute to Pray	1953	$30
❏ 48-0384	How Far Is Heaven/My Mother	1950	$60
—Originals on green vinyl			
❏ 48-0084	Love or Hate/Don't Wait for the Last Minute to Pray	1949	$70
—Originals on green vinyl			
❏ 48-0333	Make Up Your Mind/All Smiles Tonight	1950	$60
—Originals on green vinyl			

RUBOCA

Number	Title	Yr	NM
❏ 124	I Can't Help It/I'll Hold You in My Heart	1980	$8
❏ 123	Old Milwaukee Talking/I Never Told Him I Loved Him	1979	$8
❏ 122	Thank You for the Roses/Loving You Was All I Ever Needed	1979	$8

7-Inch Extended Plays

DECCA

Number	Title	Yr	NM
❏ ED2646 [M]	*Dust on the Bible/I Dreamed I Searched Heaven for You/Lonesome Valley/My Loved Ones Are Waiting for Me	1959	$25
❏ ED2519	*Each Day/She's No Angel/Broken Marriage Vows/Change of Heart	1957	$25
❏ ED2699	*Heartbreak U.S.A./Heart to Heart Talk/This Old Heart/Cold, Cold Heart	1961	$25
❏ ED2749	*I Can't Stop Loving You/All the Time/Wild Life's Gonna Get You Down/Hey Joe	1963	$25
❏ ED2763	*I Gave My Wedding Dress Away/A Heartache for a Keepsake/Cold and Lonely/Is It Asking Too Much	1963	$25
❏ ED2520	*Mansion on the Hill/Standing Room Only/I Guess I'll Go On Dreaming/Stubborn Heart	1957	$25
❏ ED2780	*Password/B.J. the D.J./Old Records/As Usual	1964	$25
❏ ED2684	*Seasons of My Heart/Lonely Is a Word/Send Me the Pillow You Dream On/Amigo's Guitar	1960	$25
❏ ED2677	*Sugartime/Dark Moon/Bonaparte's Retreat/When the Moon Comes Over the Mountain	1960	$25
❏ ED2777	*Talk Back Trembling Lips/Busted/Ring of Fire/Guilty	1964	$30
❏ ED2737	*Wicked World/We Missed You/Your Old Love Letters/Slowly	1963	$25
❏ ED2732	*Will Your Lawyer Talk to God/The Big Let Down/I'm Couting on You/I've Got a New Heartache	1962	$25
❏ ED2518	*Winner of Your Heart/Right or Wrong/Pace That Kills/Dancing with a Stranger	1957	$25
❏ ED2749 [PS]	All the Time	1963	$25
❏ ED2804 [PS]	Burning Memories	1965	$35
❏ ED2363	(contents unknown)	1956	$25
❏ ED2692	(contents unknown)	1961	$25
❏ ED2710	(contents unknown)	1962	$25
❏ ED2717	(contents unknown)	1962	$25
❏ ED2804	(contents unknown)	1965	$35

Number	Title	Yr	NM
❏ ED2781	(contents unknown)	1965	$35
❏ ED2646 [PS]	Dust on the Bible	1959	$25
❏ ED 7-2646 [PS]	Dust on the Bible	1959	$35
❏ ED 7-2646 [S]	Dust on the Bible/I Dreamed I Searched Heaven for You//Lonesome Valley/My Loved Ones Are Waiting for Me	1959	$35
❏ ED2699 [PS]	Heartbreak U.S.A.	1961	$25
❏ ED2163	It Wasn't God Who Made Honky Tonk Angels/The Things I Might Have Been//Paying for That Back Street Affair/I Don't Claim to Be an Angel	1955	$30
❏ ED2584 [PS]	Lonely Street	1958	$25
❏ ED2361	Makin' Believe/Release Me//I'm Too Lonely to Smile/Searching for a Soldier's Grave	1956	$25
❏ ED2780 [PS]	Password	1964	$30
❏ ED2684 [PS]	Seasons of My Heart	1960	$25
❏ ED2777 [PS]	Talk Back Trembling Lips	1964	$30
❏ ED2584	That's Me Without You/Waltz of the Angels//Lonely Street/Love Me to Pieces	1958	$25
❏ ED2362	There's Poison in Your Heart/Whose Shoulder Will You Cry On//Cheatin's a Sin/I've Kissed You My Last Time	1956	$25
❏ ED2781 [PS]	This White Circle	1965	$35
❏ ED2737 [PS]	Wicked World	1963	$25
❏ ED2518 [PS]	Winner of Your Heart, Vol. 1	1957	$25
❏ ED2519 [PS]	Winner of Your Heart, Vol. 2 (Change of Heart)	1957	$25
❏ ED2520 [PS]	Winner of Your Heart, Vol. 3 (Stubborn Heart)	1957	$25

WELLS, MARY

20TH CENTURY FOX

Number	Title	Yr	NM
❏ 544	Ain't It the Truth/Stop Takin' Me for Granted	1964	$20
❏ 590	He's a Lover/I'm Learnin'	1965	$20
❏ 590 [PS]	He's a Lover/I'm Learnin'	1965	$40
❏ 6619	I Should Have Known Better/Please Please Me	1965	$30
❏ 6606	Me Without You/I'm Sorry	1965	$20

ATCO

Number	Title	Yr	NM
❏ 6469	Coming Home/Hey You Set My Soul on Fire	1967	$15
❏ 6392	Dear Lover/Can't You See	1965	$15
❏ 6436	Fancy Free/Me and My Baby	1966	$15

EPIC

Number	Title	Yr	NM
❏ 02664	Gigolo/I'm Changing My Ways	1982	$4
❏ 02855	These Arms/Spend the Night With Me	1982	$4

JUBILEE

Number	Title	Yr	NM
❏ 5629	Can't Get Away From Your Love/A Woman in Love	1968	$20
❏ 5684	Dig the Way I Feel/Love Shooting Bandit	1969	$15
❏ 5639	Don't Look Back/500 Miles	1968	$20
❏ 5676	Mind Reader/Never Give a Man the World	1969	$15
❏ 5718	Mr. Tough/Never Give a Man the World	1971	$15
❏ 5695	Sweet Love/It Must Be	1970	$15
❏ 5621	The Doctor/Two Lovers' History	1968	$20

MOTOWN

Number	Title	Yr	NM
❏ 1003	Bye Bye Baby/Please Forgive Me	1960	$60
❏ 1011	I Don't Want to Take a Chance/I'm Sorry	1961	$40
—Pink "lines" label			
❏ 1011	I Don't Want to Take a Chance/I'm Sorry	1961	$30
—Blue "map" label			
❏ 1011 [PS]	I Don't Want to Take a Chance/I'm Sorry	1961	$100
❏ 1039	Laughing Boy/Two Wrongs Don't Make a Right	1963	$30
❏ 1056	My Guy/Oh Little Boy (What Did You Do to Me)	1964	$30
❏ 1016	Strange Love/Come to Me	1961	$30
❏ 1016 [PS]	Strange Love/Come to Me	1961	$100
❏ 1024	The One Who Really Loves You/I'm Gonna Stay	1962	$30
❏ 1024 [PS]	The One Who Really Loves You/I'm Gonna Stay	1962	$100
❏ 1035	Two Lovers/Operator	1962	$30
❏ 1061	When I'm Gone/Guarantee for a Lifetime	1964	$600

REPRISE

Number	Title	Yr	NM
❏ 1031	I Found What I Wanted/I See a Future in You	1971	$10
❏ 1308	If You Can't Give Her Love (Give Her Up)/Cancel My Subscription	1974	$10

WENDIGO

SCEPTER

Number	Title	Yr	NM
❏ 12211	Gimmie Some Lovin' (Part 1)/Gimmie Some Lovin' (Part 2)	1968	$15

WESLEY, FRED

KING

Number	Title	Yr	NM
❏ 6317	The Grunt (Part 1)/The Grunt (Part 2)	1970	$10
—As "The J.B.'s"			
❏ 6333	These Are the J.B.'s (Part 1)/These Are the J.B.'s (Part 2)	1970	$10
—As "The J.B.'s"			

PEOPLE

Number	Title	Yr	NM
❏ 663	All Aboard the Funky Soul Train/Thank You for Lettin' Me Be Myself and You Be Yourself	1976	$5
❏ 617	Alone Again (Naturally)/Watermelon Man	1973	$6
❏ 614	Backstabbers/J.B. Shout	1972	$6
❏ 648	Breakin' Bread/Funky Music Is My Style	1974	$5
❏ 638	Damn Right I Am Somebody-Part 1/Damn Right I Am Somebody-Part 2	1974	$6
❏ 621	Doing It to Death/Everybody Got Soul	1973	$6
❏ 602	Gimme Some More/The Rabbit Got the Gun	1972	$6
—As "The J.B.'s"			
❏ 610	Givin' Up Food for Funk (Part 1)/Givin' Up Food for Funk (Part 2)	1972	$6
—As "The J.B.'s"			
❏ 627	If You Don't Get It the First Time, Back Up and Try It Again, Party/You Can Have Watergate, Just Give Me Some Bucks and I'll Be Straight	1973	$6
❏ 616	If You Don't Get It the First Time/You Can Have Her Boogie	1973	$6
❏ 655	(It's Not the Express) It's the J.B.'s Monaurail, Part 1/(It's Not the Express) It's the J.B.'s Monaurail, Part 2	1975	$5
❏ 646	Little Boy Black/Rockin' Funky Watergate (Part 2)	1974	$6
❏ 651	Makin' Love/Rice and Ribs	1975	$5
❏ 2502	My Brother (Part 1)/My Brother (Part 2)	1971	$6
—As "The J.B.'s"			
❏ 607	Pass the Peas/Hot Pants Road	1972	$6
—As "The J.B.'s"			
❏ 632	Same Beat - Part 1/Same Beat - Part 2	1974	$6
❏ 619	Sportin' Life/Dirty Harri	1973	$6
❏ 654	Thank You for Lettin' Me Be Myself and Be Yours (Part 1)/Thank You for Lettin' Me Be Myself and Be Yours (Part 2)	1975	$5
❏ 660	Thank You for Lettin' Me Be Myself (Part 1)/Thank You for Lettin' Me Be Myself (Part 2)	1975	$5

RSO/CURTOM

Number	Title	Yr	NM
❏ 1037	House Party/I Make Music	1980	$4

WESLEY, GATE

ATLANTIC

Number	Title	Yr	NM
❏ 2319	Do the Batman/Do the Thing	1966	$30

WEST COAST POP ART EXPERIMENTAL BAND, THE

AMOS

Number	Title	Yr	NM
❏ 119	Free As a Bird/Where's My Daddy	1969	$20

REPRISE

Number	Title	Yr	NM
❏ 0582	Help, I'm a Rock/Transparent Day	1967	$30
❏ 0552	Shifting Sands/1906	1967	$30
❏ 0776	Smell of Incense/Unfree Child	1968	$30

WEST, DOTTIE, AND DON GIBSON

RCA VICTOR

Number	Title	Yr	NM
❏ 74-0178	Sweet Memories/How's the World Treating You	1969	$6
❏ 74-0291	There's a Story (Goin' 'Round)/Lock, Stock and Teardrops	1969	$6
❏ 47-9867	Till I Can't Take It Anymore/I Love You Because	1970	$6

WEST, DOTTIE

LIBERTY

Number	Title	Yr	NM
❏ 1392	Are You Happy Baby/Right or Wrong	1980	$3
❏ 1392 [PS]	Are You Happy Baby/Right or Wrong	1980	$5
❏ 1490	If It Takes All Night/Try to Win a Friend	1982	$3
❏ 1490 [PS]	If It Takes All Night/Try to Win a Friend	1982	$4

Number	Title	Yr	NM
❏ 1419	(I'm Gonna) Put You Back on the Rack/Sorry Seems to Be the Hardest Word	1981	$3
❏ 1436	It's High Time/Don't Be Kind	1981	$3
❏ 1479	She Can't Get My Love Off the Bed/Hurt	1982	$3
❏ 1500	Tulsa Ballroom/A Woman in Love with You	1983	$3
❏ 1404	What Are We Doin' in Love/ Choosin' Means Losin'	1981	$3

—Duet with Kenny Rogers, who is not credited on the label

PERMIAN

Number	Title	Yr	NM
❏ 82007	Let Love Come Lookin' for You/Blue Fiddle Waltz	1984	$4
❏ 82010	We Know Better Now/Let Love Come Lookin' for You	1985	$4
❏ 82006	What's Good for the Goose (Is Good for the Gander)/Tell Me Again	1984	$4

RCA

Number	Title	Yr	NM
❏ PB-12284	Once You Were Mine/ Dream Baby (How Long Must I Dream)	1981	$4

RCA VICTOR

Number	Title	Yr	NM
❏ 47-8702	Before the Ring on Your Finger Turns Green/Wear Away	1965	$12
❏ 47-9957	Careless Hands/Only One Thing Left to Do	1971	$6
❏ 47-9377	Childhood Places/No One	1967	$8
❏ 74-0239	Clinging to My Baby's Hand/Don't Say a Word	1969	$6
❏ 74-0601	Cold Hand of Fate/You're the Other Half of Me	1971	$6
❏ 47-9497	Country Girl/That's Where Our Love Must Be	1968	$8
❏ APBO-0072	Country Sunshine/Wish I Didn't Love You Any More	1973	$8
❏ 47-8467	Didn't I/In Its Own Little Way	1964	$12
❏ 47-9911	Forever Yours/Cold Hand of Fate	1970	$6
❏ 47-8525	Gettin' Married Has Made Us Strangers/ It Just Takes Practice	1965	$10
❏ 47-8374	Here Comes My Baby/ (How Can I Face) These Heartaches Alone	1964	$12
❏ PB-10553	Here Come the Flowers/ He's Not for You	1976	$5
❏ APBO-0321	House of Love/Love As Long As We Can	1974	$5
❏ PB-10699	If I'm a Fool for Loving You/Home Made Love	1976	$5
❏ 74-0828	If It's All Right with You/ Special Memory	1972	$5
❏ 47-9792	I Heard Our Song/ Makin' Memories	1969	$6
❏ 74-0711	I'm Only a Woman/ Baby, I Tried	1972	$5
❏ 47-9872	It's Dawned on Me You're Gone/Love's Farewell	1970	$6
❏ APBO-0231	Last Time I Saw Him/ Everybody Bring a Song	1974	$5
❏ PB-10125	Lay Back Lover/ Good Lovin' You	1974	$5
❏ 47-8225	Let Me Off at the Corner/I Wish You Wouldn't Do That	1963	$12
❏ 47-9267	Like a Fool/Everything's a Wreck	1967	$8
❏ 47-9982	Lonely Is/Cancel Tomorrow	1971	$6
❏ 47-8324	Love Is No Excuse/ Look Who's Talking	1964	$10

—With Jim Reeves

Number	Title	Yr	NM
❏ 47-8900	Mommy, Can I Still Call Him Daddy/Suffertime	1966	$8
❏ 47-9118	Paper Mansions/ Someone's Gotta Cry	1967	$8
❏ 48-1012	Six Weeks Every Summer (Christmas Day)/Wish I Didn't Love You Anymore	1971	$5
❏ 47-9947	Slowly/Sweet Thang	1971	$6

—With Jimmy Dean

Number	Title	Yr	NM
❏ 47-8166	Touch Me/More Than I Meant To	1963	$15
❏ 47-9011	What's Come Over My Baby/How Many Lifetimes Will It Take	1966	$8
❏ 47-8770	Would You Hold It Against Me/You're Just the Only World I Know	1965	$8

STARDAY

Number	Title	Yr	NM
❏ 517	Angel on Paper/No Time Will I Ever	1960	$30
❏ 724	I'd Be Lying/Walking in the Dark	1965	$10
❏ 547	I Lost, You Win, I'm Leavin'/I Should Start Runnin'	1961	$30
❏ 574	My Big John/Men with Evil Hearts	1961	$30

UNITED ARTISTS

Number	Title	Yr	NM
❏ 1339	A Lesson in Leavin'/ Love's So Easy for Two	1980	$4
❏ XW1209	Come See Me and Come Lonely/Decorate Your Conscience	1978	$4
❏ XW946	Every Word I Write/ We Love Each Other	1977	$4
❏ 1352	Leavin's for Unbelievers/ Blue As I Want To	1980	$4
❏ XW1084	That's All I Wanted to Know/ Who's Gonna Love Me Now	1977	$4

Number	Title	Yr	NM
❏ XW1010	Tonight You Belong to Me/Tiny Fingers	1977	$4
❏ XW898	When It's Just You and Me/ We Love Each Other	1976	$4

7-Inch Extended Plays

RCA VICTOR

Number	Title	Yr	NM
❏ VLP3587	Baby/Before the Ring on Your Finger Turns Green/ Wear Away//Would You Hold It Against Me/Just Out of Reach/What's Come Over My Baby	1966	$25

—Jukebox issue; small hole, plays at 33 1/3 rpm

Number	Title	Yr	NM
❏ VLP3587 [PS]	Suffering Time	1966	$25

WEST, MAE

20TH CENTURY FOX

Number	Title	Yr	NM
❏ 6718	Hard to Handle/You Gotta Taste All the Fruit	1968	$12
❏ 6718 [PS]	Hard to Handle/You Gotta Taste All the Fruit	1968	$30

DAGONET

Number	Title	Yr	NM
❏ 6	Put the Loot in the Boot, Santa/With Love from Me to You	1966	$20

DECCA

Number	Title	Yr	NM
❏ 29452	Love Is the Greatest Thing/All of Me	1955	$20
❏ 32738	The Sayings of Mae West/ More Sayings of Mae West	1970	$10

MGM

Number	Title	Yr	NM
❏ 14491	Great Balls of Fire/ Naked Ape	1973	$8

PLAZA

Number	Title	Yr	NM
❏ 506	Am I Too Young/ He's Good for Me	1962	$15

TOWER

Number	Title	Yr	NM
❏ 260	Day Tripper/Treat Him Right	1966	$12
❏ 260 [PS]	Day Tripper/Treat Him Right	1966	$30
❏ 261	Shakin' All Over/ If You Gotta Go	1966	$10
❏ 261 [PS]	Shakin' All Over/ If You Gotta Go	1966	$30

WEST, MARSHALL

PARKWAY

Number	Title	Yr	NM
❏ 878	This House Is Gonna Live/I Hurt Myself	1963	$15

WEST, RED

DOT

Number	Title	Yr	NM
❏ 16268	Midnight Ride/Unforgiven	1961	$30

JARO

Number	Title	Yr	NM
❏ 77031	FBI Story/What Must I Do	1960	$60

SANTO

Number	Title	Yr	NM
❏ 9006	Bossa Nova Mamza/ My Babe	1963	$20

WEST, SPEEDY, AND JIMMY BRYANT

CAPITOL

Number	Title	Yr	NM
❏ F2892	Bustin' Thru/Our Paradise	1954	$30
❏ F3150	Cotton Pickin'/ Sleepwalkers' Lullaby	1955	$30
❏ F2964	Deep Water/ Stratosphere Boogie	1954	$30
❏ F3276	Frettin' Fingers/Chatterbox	1955	$30
❏ F3454	Pickin' Peppers/ Pushin' the Blues	1956	$30
❏ F2444	Serenade to a Frog/ Bryant's Bounce	1953	$30
❏ F3348	Shuffleboard Rag/ Yankee Clover	1956	$30
❏ F2519	Speedin' West/ Skiddle Dee Boo	1953	$30
❏ F3208	Steelin' Moonlight/ Caffeine Patrol	1955	$30
❏ F3537	Water Baby Blues/ Sand Canyon Swing	1956	$30
❏ F3026	West of Samoa/ Flippin' the Lid	1955	$30

IMPERIAL

Number	Title	Yr	NM
❏ 66219	Shinbone/Tabasco Road	1966	$8

—As "Orville and Ivy"

Number	Title	Yr	NM
❏ 66249	Slow Poke/Please Pass the Biscuits	1967	$8

—As "Orville and Ivy"

WEST, SPEEDY, AND CLIFFIE STONE

CAPITOL

Number	Title	Yr	NM
❏ F2620	Steel Guitar Rag/One Rose	1953	$30

WEST, SPEEDY

CAPITOL

Number	Title	Yr	NM
❏ F1991	Crackerjack/Roadside Rag	1952	$30
❏ F1805	Hub Cap Roll/Truck Drivers Ride	1951	$30
❏ F2448	Lover Man/Pennies from Heaven	1953	$30
❏ F3669	On the Alamo/Shawnee Trot	1957	$20

WEST, TED

MGM

Number	Title	Yr	NM
❏ 11539	Call of the Devil's Rider/ On the Wrong Side	1953	$30

WESTON, KIM

ENTERPRISE

Number	Title	Yr	NM
❏ 9101	Beautiful People/ Goodness Gracious	1974	$5

GORDY

Number	Title	Yr	NM
❏ 7050	Helpless/A Love Like Yours (Don't Keep Knocking Every Day)	1966	$30
❏ 7041	I'll Never See My Love Again/A Thrill a Moment	1965	$30
❏ 7046	Take Me in Your Arms (Rock Me A Little While)/ Don't Compare Me to Her	1965	$30

MGM

Number	Title	Yr	NM
❏ 13720	I Got What You Need/ Someone Like You	1967	$30
❏ 13720 [PS]	I Got What You Need/ Someone Like You	1967	$50
❏ 13992	I Will Understand/Thankful	1968	$20
❏ 13927	Lift Every Voice and Sing/This Is America	1968	$30
❏ 13804	That's Groovy/Land of Tomorrow	1967	$30
❏ 13928	The Impossible Dream/ When Johnny Comes Marching Home	1968	$20

PEOPLE

Number	Title	Yr	NM
❏ 1001	Danger, Heartbreak Ahead/I'll Be Thinkin'	1970	$12

PRIDE

Number	Title	Yr	NM
❏ 1	Lift Every Voice and Sing/This Is America	1970	$12

TAMLA

Number	Title	Yr	NM
❏ 54106	A Little More Love/Go Ahead and Laugh	1964	$125
❏ 54110	I'm Still Loving You/Go Ahead and Laugh	1964	$70
❏ 54076	It Should Have Been Me/ Love Me All the Way	1963	$60
❏ 54100 [DJ]	Looking for the Right Guy	1964	$80

—One-sided white-label promo (B-side blank)

Number	Title	Yr	NM
❏ 54100	Looking for the Right Guy/ Feel Alright Tonight	1964	$60

VOLT

Number	Title	Yr	NM
❏ 1502	If I Had My Way/ Gonna Be Alright	1971	$20
❏ 1503	Little By Little, Bit By Bit/ (B-side unknown)	1971	$20

WESTON, PAUL

CAPITOL

Number	Title	Yr	NM
❏ F1251	Autumn Leaves/ No Other Love	1950	$20
❏ F833	Big Movie Show in the Sky/Little Gray House	1950	$20
❏ 54-687	Clair de Lune/Prelude, Op. 28, No. 4 in E Minor	1949	$30
❏ F1640	Deep Purple/Etude	1951	$20

—Reissue of 78 rpm from 1948

Number	Title	Yr	NM
❏ F826	Fairy Tales/Am I Wasting My Time	1950	$20

—Note: Earlier Paul Weston 45s on Capitol may exist

Number	Title	Yr	NM
❏ F1495	Hot Canary/La Raspa	1951	$20
❏ F1022	I'll Get By/Blue Prelude	1950	$20
❏ F1670	Laura/Intermezzo	1951	$20

—Reissue

Number	Title	Yr	NM
❏ F890	La Vie En Rose/Les Feviles Mortes	1950	$20
❏ F918	Orchids in the Moonlight/I'll Be Seeing You	1950	$20
❏ F949	Panama/Original Dixieland One-Step	1950	$20
❏ 4350	The Thrill Is Gone/I Love You	1960	$8

COLUMBIA

Number	Title	Yr	NM
❏ 39968	Anna/Dutch Treat	1953	$15
❏ 40484	A Streetcar Named Desire/ For Whom the Bell Tolls	1955	$15
❏ 40152	Autumn in Rome/Indiscretion	1954	$12
❏ 40292	Bimbo/Champagne Wine	1954	$10
❏ 39465	Bonne Nuit/Maybe It's Because	1951	$15
❏ 39616	Charmaine/At Dawning	1951	$15
❏ 39662	Charmaine/Jealousy (Jalousie)	1952	$15

—B-side by Frankie Laine; part of a box set

Number	Title	Yr	NM
❏ 39646	Embraceable You/ Pennies from Heaven	1952	$12
❏ 39864	Forgetting You/Wonderful Copenhagen	1952	$15
❏ 40901	High Society/ Riverfront Blues	1957	$12
❏ 39647	How High the Moon/ Over the Rainbow	1952	$10

—The above four comprise a box set

Number	Title	Yr	NM
❏ 39610	I'll Follow My Secret Heart/All Alone	1951	$10
❏ 39210	Lonesome Gal/Never Let the Sun Set on a Quarrel	1951	$15

Number	Title	Yr	NM
❏ 39666	Low in Lehigh Valley/Flapperette	1952	$15
❏ 40876	Mardi Gras/Storyville	1957	$10
❏ 40605	Memories of You/Naked Sea	1956	$10
❏ 39509	Moon Song/Among My Souvenirs	1951	$10
❏ 39424	Morningside/What Will I Tell	1951	$15
❏ 40014	Shane/Gigi	1953	$15
❏ 39736	So Help Me/Beautiful Ohio	1952	$15
❏ 39160	So Long/Across the Wide Missouri	1951	$15
❏ 39000	So Long Sally/These Foolish Things	1950	$20
❏ 39508	Stardust/When Your Lover Has Gone	1951	$10
❏ 39569	Story of Love/And So to Sleep	1951	$15
❏ 40385	Tara's Theme/Love Letters	1954	$15
❏ 40861	Ten Minutes Ago!/Where Is Cinderella	1957	$10
❏ 40237	The Bells of Notre Dame/I Went Out of My Way	1954	$12
❏ 40737	The Kentuckian Song/Love Theme from "La Strada"	1956	$10
❏ 40675	Theme from My Foolish Heart/Infatuation	1956	$10
❏ 39510	Then I'll Be Tired of You/My Silent Love	1951	$10
❏ 40359	The Song from Desiree/Maria, Maria, Maria	1954	$15
❏ 39645	This Can't Be Love/Why Shouldn't I?	1952	$10
❏ 39611	Together/I'll See You Again	1951	$10

— The above four comprise a box set

Number	Title	Yr	NM
❏ 39608	What'll I Do/One Night of Love	1951	$10
❏ 39114	When You Return/In Your Arms	1950	$20
❏ 39609	Wonderful One/Sweethearts	1951	$10

7-Inch Extended Plays

Number	Title	Yr	NM
❏ B-9091	*Moonlight Becomes You/But Not for Me/It Never Entered My Mind/I Remember You from Somewhere	1956	$10
❏ B-9092	(contents unknown)	1956	$10
❏ B-9093	(contents unknown)	1956	$10
❏ B-9091 [PS]	Moonlight Becomes You, Vol. 1	1956	$12
❏ B-9092 [PS]	Moonlight Becomes You, Vol. 2	1956	$12
❏ B-9093 [PS]	Moonlight Becomes You, Vol. 3	1956	$12

WHAM!
Also see GEORGE MICHAEL.

COLUMBIA

Number	Title	Yr	NM
❏ 38-03932	Bad Boys/(Instrumental)	1983	$6

— As "Wham! U.K.

| ❏ 38-03932 | Bad Boys/(Instrumental) | 1983 | $4 |

— As "Wham!

| ❏ 38-04691 [PS] | Careless Whisper | 1984 | $10 |

— As "Wham! featuring George Michael"; color sleeve; "Demonstration -- Not for Sale" on rear

| ❏ 38-04691 | Careless Whisper/(Instrumental) | 1984 | $3 |

— As "Wham! featuring George Michael

| ❏ 38-04691 [PS] | Careless Whisper/(Instrumental) | 1984 | $8 |

— As "Wham! featuring George Michael"; color sleeve

| ❏ 38-04691 [PS] | Careless Whisper/(Instrumental) | 1984 | $5 |

— As "Wham! featuring George Michael"; black & white sleeve

| ❏ 38-68713 | Careless Whisper/(Instrumental) | 1988 | $3 |

— Reissue

Number	Title	Yr	NM
❏ 38-04840	Everything She Wants/Like a Baby	1985	$3
❏ 38-04840 [PS]	Everything She Wants/Like a Baby	1985	$3
❏ 38-68715	Everything She Wants/Like a Baby	1988	$3

— Reissue

Number	Title	Yr	NM
❏ 38-05409	Freedom/Heartbeat	1985	$3
❏ 38-05409 [PS]	Freedom/Heartbeat	1985	$3
❏ 38-05721	I'm Your Man/Do It Right	1985	$3
❏ 38-05721 [PS]	I'm Your Man/Do It Right	1985	$3
❏ 38-05721 [PS]	I'm Your Man/Do It Right	1985	$6

— Demonstration -- Not for Sale" on rear

Number	Title	Yr	NM
❏ CS72591 [DJ]	Last Christmas (4:24)/(6:43)	1986	$20
❏ 38-06182	The Edge of Heaven/Blue (Live in China)	1986	$3
❏ 38-06182 [PS]	The Edge of Heaven/Blue (Live in China)	1986	$3
❏ 38-04552	Wake Me Up Before You Go-Go/(Instrumental)	1984	$3
❏ 38-04552 [PS]	Wake Me Up Before You Go-Go/(Instrumental)	1984	$8
❏ 38-68712	Wake Me Up Before You Go-Go/(Instrumental)	1988	$3

— Reissue

Number	Title	Yr	NM
❏ 38-06294	Where Did Your Heart Go?/Wham! Rap '86	1986	$3
❏ 38-06294 [PS]	Where Did Your Heart Go?/Wham! Rap '86	1986	$3

EPIC

Number	Title	Yr	NM
❏ GA4949	Last Christmas/Everything She Wants	1984	$5
❏ GA4949 [PS]	Last Christmas/Everything She Wants	1984	$8

— Gatefold sleeve; sleeve and record are U.K. imports

| ❏ (no #) | Merry Xmas from Wham! | 1984 | $30 |

— Fan club single, no sleeve; U.K. import

WHAT FOUR, THE
CAPITOL

Number	Title	Yr	NM
❏ 5449	Anything for a Laugh/Baby Can't You Hear Me Call Your Name	1965	$15

COLUMBIA

| ❏ 43711 | Baby, I Dig Love/It's Hard to Live on Promises | 1966 | $15 |
| ❏ 43711 [PS] | Baby, I Dig Love/It's Hard to Live on Promises | 1966 | $30 |

DESTINATION

| ❏ 633 | We Could Be Happy/Where Love Can Go | 1967 | $15 |

— As "What For

ESP-DISK'

| ❏ 109 | Our Love Should Last Forever/(B-side unknown) | 1966 | $60 |

MERCURY

| ❏ 72716 | Dandelion Wine/You're Wishin' I Was Someone Else | 1967 | $30 |

— As "Whatt Four

REPRISE

| ❏ 0387 | Gemini 4/Night Surf | 1965 | $30 |

TOWER

| ❏ 404 | Asparagus/Stop in the Name of Love | 1968 | $15 |

WHAT-KNOTS, THE
DIAL

Number	Title	Yr	NM
❏ 4067	I Ain't Dead Yet/Talkin' 'Bout Our Breakup	1967	$30

WHEEL MEN, THE
WARNER BROS.

| ❏ 5480 | Hon-Da Beach/School Is a Gas | 1964 | $60 |

WHEELER, JOE
KING

Number	Title	Yr	NM
❏ 45-993	A Country Boy Goes to Town/Out of the Skillet	1951	$40
❏ 45-1013	I'd Walk a Country Mile/Red Heads and Blondes	1951	$40
❏ 45-1096	Shut My Mouth Wide Open/Ain't That Just Like a Woman	1952	$40
❏ 45-1127	Why Don't You Make Believe/Do I Love Her	1952	$30

WHEELER, ONIE
CHARTA

Number	Title	Yr	NM
❏ 122	I Don't Believe We're Through/Pick Up the Pieces	1978	$6
❏ 129	Lucie Ann's Song/I Don't Believe We're Through	1978	$6
❏ 148	Onie's Bop/I'd Rather Scratch with the Chickens	1979	$6

COLUMBIA

Number	Title	Yr	NM
❏ 4-40787	A Beggar for Your Love/A Booger Gonna Getcha	1956	$60
❏ 4-21454	Cut It Out/I'm Satisfied with My Dreams	1955	$30
❏ 4-21371	Little Mama/She Wiggled and Giggled	1955	$30
❏ 4-21418	My Home Is Not a Home at All/That's What I Like	1955	$30
❏ 4-21523	Onie's Bop/I Wanna Hold My Baby	1956	$70
❏ 4-40911	Steppin' Out/Going Back to the City	1957	$20

EPIC

| ❏ 9540 | What About Tomorrow/Sunnyland Farmer | 1962 | $10 |

JAB

| ❏ 9013 | Dirt Behind My Years/Burn Another Honky Tonk Down | 1968 | $8 |
| ❏ 671 | Too Hot to Handle/I Need to Go Home | 1966 | $10 |

MUSICOR

❏ 1121	Her Porch Came Up to My Knees/Pretty Little Tomboy	1965	$12
❏ 1096	I'm Gonna Hang My Britches Up/You're Too Good for Me	1965	$10
❏ 18022	When We All Get There/Run 'Em Off	1952	$40
❏ 18058	Would You Like to Wear a Crown/I Saw Mother with God Last Night	1954	$30

RANWOOD

Number	Title	Yr	NM
❏ 1025	EIO (The Sawmill Man)/Train to Louisville	1975	$6

ROYAL AMERICAN

| ❏ 85 | Shuckin' My Way to the Hall of Fame/I Can't Pass an Orchard | 1973 | $5 |

STARDAY

| ❏ 767 | Mr. Free/Dancing | 1966 | $10 |
| ❏ 785 | Playing Tricks/I Closed My Book Last Night | 1966 | $10 |

UNITED ARTISTS

| ❏ 716 | Wanted for Robbery/Who Put Out the Fire | 1964 | $15 |

WHEELS, THE (1)
AURORA

| ❏ 157 | Bad Little Woman/Don't You Know | 1966 | $30 |

WHEELS, THE (2)
FOLLY

| ❏ 800 | Clap Your Hands (Part 1)/Clap Your Hands (Part 2) | 1959 | $20 |

WHEELS, THE (3)
IMPACT

| ❏ 1029 | Dancing in the Streets/A Taste of Money | 1967 | $30 |

WHEELS, THE (4)
PREMIUM

Number	Title	Yr	NM
❏ 410	I Can't Forget/How Could I Ever Leave Me	1956	$200
❏ 405	My Heart's Desire/Let's Have a Ball	1956	$70
❏ 408	Teasin' Heart/Loco	1956	$100

WHEELS, THE (U)
TIME

| ❏ 1003 | Where Were You/So Young and So In Love | 1958 | $100 |

WHIPPOORWILLS, THE
JOSIE

| ❏ 892 | Deep Within/Going to a Party | 1961 | $70 |

WHIPS, THE
FLAIR

| ❏ 1025 | Pleadin' Heart/She Done Me Wrong | 1954 | $800 |

MGM

| ❏ 13401 | Whip It on Me, Baby/First Dance Fear | 1965 | $15 |

WHIRLERS, THE
PORT

| ❏ 70025 | Tonight and Forever/Magic Mirror | 1961 | $30 |

WHIRLIN' DISC

| ❏ 108 | Tonight and Forever/Magic Mirror | 1956 | $100 |

WHIRLWINDS, THE
GUYDEN

| ❏ 2052 | Angel Love/The Mountain | 1961 | $40 |

PHILIPS

| ❏ 40139 | Heartbeat/At the Party | 1963 | $125 |

WHISPERS, THE
CANADIAN AMERICAN

Number	Title	Yr	NM
❏ 179	It's Rainin', It's Pourin'/Tomorrow's On Your Side	1964	$40

DORE

❏ 740	As I Sit Here/Shake It, Shake It	1965	$30
❏ 751	Doctor Love/Lonely Avenue	1966	$30
❏ 724	It Only Hurts for a Little While/The Happy One	1964	$30
❏ 729	Slow Jerk/Never Again	1965	$30
❏ 768	Take a Lesson from the Teacher/Claire De Looney	1966	$30
❏ 842	The Dip/It Only Hurts for a Little While	1970	$12
❏ 735	The Dip/Weirdo	1965	$30
❏ 758	Walkin' the Fat Man/I Was Born When You Kissed Me	1966	$30

FONTANA

| ❏ 1564 | My Long and Sleepless Night/Knowin' | 1966 | $30 |

JANUS

| ❏ 247 | All I Ever Do (Is Dream of You)/Here Comes Tomorrow | 1975 | $6 |

Number	Title	Yr	NM
231	A Mother for My Children/What More Can a Girl Ask For	1973	$6
238	Bingo/Once More with Feeling	1974	$6
174	Can't Help But Love You/A Hopeless Situation	1971	$6
222	Feel Like Comin' Home/I Love the Way You Make Me Feel	1973	$6
184	I Only Meant to Wet My Feet/You Fill My Life with Music	1972	$6
212	POW-MIA/Does She Care	1973	$6
200	Somebody Loves You/Can We Love Forever	1972	$6
140	There's a Love for Everyone/It Sure Ain't Pretty	1970	$6
244	What More Can a Girl Ask For/Broken Home	1974	$6

SOLAR

Number	Title	Yr	NM
YB-11894	And the Beat Goes On/Can You Do the Boogie	1980	$4
GB-12230	And the Beat Goes On/Lady	1981	$3

— *Gold Standard Series*

Number	Title	Yr	NM
YB-11739	A Song for Donny/(Instrumental)	1979	$4
YB-11739 [PS]	A Song for Donny/(Instrumental)	1979	$6
YB-11590	Can't Do Without Love/Headlights	1979	$4
69683	Contagious/(B-side unknown)	1984	$4
69639	Don't Keep Me Waiting/Suddenly	1985	$4
48008	Emergency/Only You	1982	$4
48008 [PS]	Emergency/Only You	1982	$6
YB-11449	Happy Holidays to You/Try and Make It Better	1978	$6
YB-11685	Homemade Lovin'/You'll Never Get Away	1979	$4
YB-12232	I Can Make It Better/Say You (Would Love for Me Too)	1981	$4
YB-13005	I'm the One for You/I'm Gonna Love You More	1981	$4
B-70017	In the Mood/(Instrumental)	1987	$3
47961	In the Raw/Small Talkin'	1982	$4
YB-12154	It's a Love Thing/Girl I Need You	1981	$4
GB-13486	It's a Love Thing/Make That Move	1983	$3

— *Gold Standard Series; B-side by Shalamar*

Number	Title	Yr	NM
YB-11928	Lady I Love You	1980	$4
YB-11246	(Let's Go) All the Way/Chocolate Girl	1978	$4
GB-11977	(Let's Go) All the Way/Lost and Turned Out	1980	$3

— *Gold Standard Series*

Number	Title	Yr	NM
GB-11328	Living Together (In Sin)/One for the Money	1978	$3

— *Gold Standard Series*

Number	Title	Yr	NM
69965	Love Is Where You Find It/Say Yes	1982	$4
YB-11353	(Olivia) Lost and Turned Out/Try and Make It Better	1978	$4
YB-12050	Out the Box/Welcome Into My Dream	1980	$4
69658	Some Kinda Lover/Never Too Late	1985	$4
YB-12295	This Kind of Lovin'/What Will I Do	1981	$4
69809	This Time/Love for Real	1983	$4
69842	Tonight/Small Talkin'	1983	$4

SOUL CLOCK

Number	Title	Yr	NM
104	Great Day/I Can't See Myself Leaving	1969	$10
1001	I Can Remember/Planets of Life	1970	$8
1005	I'm the One/You Must Be Doing All Right	1970	$8
1004	Seems Like I Gotta Do Wrong/Needle in a Haystack	1970	$8
107	The Time Will Come/Flying High	1969	$10
109	What Will I Do/Remember	1969	$10

SOUL TRAIN

Number	Title	Yr	NM
SB-11139	I'm Gonna Make You My Wife/You Never Miss Your Water	1977	$5
SB-10430	In Love Forever/Fairytale	1975	$5
SB-10773	Living Together (In Sin)/I've Got a Feeling	1976	$5
SB-10996	Make It with You/You Are Number One	1977	$5
SB-10700	One for the Money (Part 1)/One for the Money (Part 2)	1976	$5

WHISPERS, THE (2)

GOTHAM

Number	Title	Yr	NM
312	Are You Sorry/We're Getting Married	1953	$1500
309	Fool Heart/Don't Fool with Lizzie	1953	$250

WHISPERS, THE (3)

LAURIE

Number	Title	Yr	NM
3344	Here Comes Summer/If You Don't Care	1966	$30

WHITCOMB, IAN

JERDEN

Number	Title	Yr	NM
735	Soho/Bony Moronie	1964	$20
747	This Sporting Life/Soho	1964	$20

TOWER

Number	Title	Yr	NM
170	18 Whitcomb St./Fizz	1965	$12
385	Groovy Day/Sally Sails the Sky	1967	$10
385 [PS]	Groovy Day/Sally Sails the Sky	1967	$50
192	High Blood Pressure/Good Hard Rock	1966	$12
212	Lover's Prayer/Your Baby Has Gone Down the Plug Hole	1966	$10
120	This Sporting Life/Fizz	1965	$10
134	Turn On Song/Poor But Honest	1965	$30
274	Where Did Robinson Crusoe Go (With Friday on Saturday Night)/Poor Little Bird	1966	$15
274 [PS]	Where Did Robinson Crusoe Go (With Friday on Saturday Night)/Poor Little Bird	1966	$30

UNITED ARTISTS

Number	Title	Yr	NM
XW162	They Go Wild, Simply Wild Over Me/Yaaka Hula Hickey Dula	1973	$6

WHITE, BARRY

20TH CENTURY

Number	Title	Yr	NM
2298	Baby, We Better Try to Get It Together/If You Know, Won't You Tell Me	1976	$5
2120	Can't Get Enough of Your Love, Babe/Just Not Enough	1974	$5
2309	Don't Make Me Wait Too Long/Can't You See It's Only You I Want	1976	$5
2077	Honey Please Can't You See/Honey Please Can't You See	1974	$5
2433	How Did You Know It Was Me?/Oh Me Oh My	1979	$5
2208	I'll Do for You Anything You Want Me To/Anything You Want Me To	1975	$5
2416	I Love to Sing the Songs I Sing/Oh Me Oh My	1979	$5
2018	I'm Gonna Love You Just a Little More Baby/Just a Little More Baby	1973	$5
2328	I'm Qualified to Satisfy You/(Instrumental)	1977	$5
2350	It's Ecstasy When You Lay Down Next to Me/I Never Thought I'd Fall in Love with You	1977	$5
2042	I've Got So Much to Give/I've Got So Much to Give	1973	$5
2265	Let the Music Play/(Instrumental)	1975	$5
2365	Oh What a Night for Dancing/You're So Good You're Bad	1978	$5
2361	Playing Your Game, Baby/Of All the Guys in the World	1977	$5
2177	What Am I Gonna Do with You/What Am I Gonna Do with You, Baby	1975	$5
0(no cat #) [PS]	With Love from Barry White	1975	$30

—*Pink and white sleeve issued with some stock copies of "What Am I Gonna Do with You"*

A&M

Number	Title	Yr	NM
3000	For Your Love (I'd Do Most Anything)/I'm Ready for Love	1987	$3
3000 [PS]	For Your Love (I'd Do Most Anything)/I'm Ready for Love	1987	$3
2943	Sho' You Right/You're What's On My Mind	1987	$3
2943 [PS]	Sho' You Right/You're What's On My Mind	1987	$3
1459	Super Lover/I Wanna Do It Good to Ya	1989	$3

FARO

Number	Title	Yr	NM
613	Tracy/Flame of Love	1964	$20

—*B-side by the Atlantics*

UNLIMITED GOLD

Number	Title	Yr	NM
03957	America/Life	1983	$4
1401	Any Fool Could See (You Were Meant for Me)/You're the One I Need	1979	$4
02580	Beware/Tell Me Who Do You Love	1981	$4
02956	Change/I Like You, You Like Me	1982	$4
04098	Don't Let 'Em Blow Your Mind/Dreams	1983	$4
1420	I Believe in Love/You're the One I Need	1980	$4
1404	It Ain't Love, Babe (Until You Give It)/Hung Up in Your Love	1979	$4
02425	Louie Louie/Ghetto Letto	1981	$4
1411	Love Ain't Easy/I Found Love	1980	$4
1418	Love Makin' Music/Ella Es Todo Mi (She's Everything to Me)	1980	$4
03379	Passion/It's All About Love	1982	$4
1415	Sheet Music/(Instrumental)	1980	$4

WHITE, DANNY

GRAND PRIX

Number	Title	Yr	NM
4	Then You Can Tell Me Goodbye/(B-side unknown)	1983	$15

WHITE, JOHNNY

VERVE

Number	Title	Yr	NM
10187	The Christmas Seal Song/Seal Boogie	1959	$20

WHITE, PAUL

COUNTRY JUBILEE

Number	Title	Yr	NM
0101	Elvis, Christmas Won't Be Christmas Without You/(B-side unknown)	1977	$15

SPIN CHECK

Number	Title	Yr	NM
(no #)	Merry Christmas Elvis/I'm So Lonesome I Could Cry	1978	$15

WHITE, ROGER

BIG A

Number	Title	Yr	NM
103	Mystery of Tallahatchie Bridge/Wild Roses	1967	$15

WHITE, STEVE, QUARTET

PACIFIC JAZZ

Number	Title	Yr	NM
629	My New Jet Plane/Swing Easy	1955	$20

WHITE, YOLANDA

DECCA

Number	Title	Yr	NM
31340	My Brother Wants a Doll for Christmas/What I Want for Christmas (Is Six More Years)	1961	$30

WHITEHAWK, JOHN

LITTLE DARLIN'

Number	Title	Yr	NM
071	Is It Love/You Live Your Life, I'll Live Mine	1970	$10
064	It Shows on Your Face/I Need Love, Love, Love	1970	$10

WHITEMAN, PAUL

CAPITOL

Number	Title	Yr	NM
F1668	Travelin' Light/The General Jumped at Dawn	1951	$30

—*Reissue of 78 rpm hit from 1942*

Number	Title	Yr	NM
F2999	Wang Wang Blues/San	1954	$10

CORAL

Number	Title	Yr	NM
61516	Charleston/Black Bottom	1955	$10
61254	I Love You/Japanese Sandman	1954	$10
61336	Mississippi Mud/Then and Now	1955	$10
61273	Saw Your Eyes/There's a Small Hotel	1954	$10
61403	Three O'Clock in the Morning/Jukin'	1955	$10
61228	Whispering/You're Driving Me Crazy	1954	$10

7-Inch Extended Plays

Number	Title	Yr	NM
EC81095 [PS]	All Time Dance Party, Vol. 2	1954	$15

WHITESNAKE

Also see DEEP PURPLE; THIN LIZZY.

GEFFEN

Number	Title	Yr	NM
7-28103	Give Me All Your Love/Straight for the Heart	1988	$3
7-28103 [PS]	Give Me All Your Love/Straight for the Heart	1988	$3
7-28339	Here I Go Again/Children of the Night	1987	$4

—*A radically different version than that on the LP*

Number	Title	Yr	NM
7-28339 [PS]	Here I Go Again/Children of the Night	1987	$4
7-28233	Is This Love/Bad Boys	1987	$3
7-28233 [PS]	Is This Love/Bad Boys	1987	$3
7-29171	Love Ain't No Stranger/Guilty of Love	1984	$4
7-29171 [PS]	Love Ain't No Stranger/Guilty of Love	1984	$5
7-28331	Still of the Night/Don't Turn Away	1987	$4

Number	Title	Yr	NM

MIRAGE

Number	Title	Yr	NM
❏ 3794 [DJ]	Ain't No Love in the Heart of the City (same on both sides)	1981	$10

— May be promo only

| ❏ 3844 | Don't Break My Heart Again/ Lonely Days, Lonely Nights | 1981 | $12 |
| ❏ 3672 [PS] | Fool for Your Loving/ Black and Blue | 1980 | $8 |

UNITED ARTISTS

| ❏ UA-X1240#NAME? [DJ] | Ain't No Love in the Heart | 1978 | $15 |

— May be promo only; as "David Coverdale's Whitesnake"

| ❏ 1323 | Long Way from Home/ We Wish You Well | 1979 | $10 |
| ❏ UA-X1291#NAME? | The Time Is Right for Love/ Belgian Tom's Hot Trick | 1979 | $10 |

WHITFIELD, DAVID

LONDON

| ❏ 1508 | Santo Natale/Adeste Fideles | 1954 | $20 |

WHITING, MARGARET, AND JIMMY WAKELY

CAPITOL

❏ F1234	A Bushel and a Peck/ Beyond the Reef	1950	$20
❏ F800	Broken Down Merry-Go-Round/The Gods Were Angry with Me	1950	$30
❏ F1065	Close Your Pretty Eyes/ Fools' Paradise	1950	$30
❏ F1382	Easter Parade/Let's Go to Church	1951	$30
❏ F1965	Give Me More, More, More/Let Old Mother Nature Have Her	1952	$20
❏ F2402	Gomen Nasai/I Learned to Love You Too Late	1953	$20
❏ 54-40246	I'll Never Slip Around Again/Six Times a Week and Twice on Sunday	1949	$40
❏ F960	Let's Go to Church (Next Sunday Morning)/Why Do You Say Those Things	1950	$30
❏ F1816	Let's Live a Little/I Don't Want to Be Free	1951	$20
❏ F2528	My Heart Knows/When Love Goes Wrong	1953	$20
❏ F1255	Silver Bells/ Christmas Candy	1950	$30
❏ F3905	Silver Bells/ Christmas Candy	1958	$15
❏ 54-40224	Slipping Around/ Wedding Bells	1949	$50
❏ F1634	Slipping Around/ Wedding Bells	1951	$20

— Reissue of 78 rpm hits from 1948

❏ F1555	Star of Hope/Why Am I Losing You	1951	$20
❏ F2689	Tennessee Church Bells/ There's a Silver Moon on Golden Gate	1953	$20
❏ F1500	When You and I Were Young Maggie Blues/ Till We Meet Again	1951	$20

WHITING, MARGARET

CAPITOL

❏ F2913	All I Want Is All There Is And Then Some/ Can This Be Mine	1954	$20
❏ F2217	Alone Together/ Outside of Heaven	1952	$20
❏ F1784	And So to Sleep/ Beer Barrel Polka	1951	$20
❏ 54-546	A Wonderful Guy/Younger Than Springtime	1949	$30

— Note: Earlier Margaret Whiting 45s on Capitol may exist

| ❏ F1801 | Bill/More More More | 1951 | $20 |
| ❏ F1042 | Blind Date/Home Cookin' | 1950 | $40 |

— With Bob Hope

❏ F879	Come Rain or Come Shine/ Dream Peddler's Serenade	1950	$30
❏ 54-709	Dime a Dozen/Whirlwind	1949	$30
❏ F1160	Don't Rock the Boat/I'm in Love with You	1950	$20

— With Dean Martin

❏ F1585	Everlasting/The End of a Love Affair	1951	$20
❏ F1391	Faithful/Lonesome Gal	1951	$20
❏ F1984	Foggy River/Try Me One More Time	1952	$20
❏ F1702	Good Morning, Mr. Echo/ River Road Two-Step	1951	$20
❏ F1566	Happy, Topper and Me/This Little Pig	1951	$20
❏ F3509	Hello Young Lovers/ We Kiss in a Shadow	1956	$15
❏ F2869	How Long Has It Been/ Affair of the Heart	1954	$20
❏ F1103	I Didn't Know What Time It Was/This Can't Be Love	1950	$30
❏ F2599	I Just Love You/The Night Holds No Fear	1953	$20
❏ F2000	I'll Walk Alone/I Could Write a Book	1952	$20

❏ F3314	I Love a Mystery/ Bidin' My Time	1956	$15
❏ F841	I Said My Pajamas (And Put On My Pray'rs)/Be Mine	1950	$30
❏ F2717	I Speak to the Stars/It's Nice to Have You Home	1954	$20
❏ F874	It Might As Well Be Spring/ How Deep Is the Ocean	1950	$30
❏ F1645	It Might As Well Be Spring/ How Deep Is the Ocean	1951	$20

— Reissue of 78 rpm hit of 1945

❏ 54-724	It's a Most Unusual Day/St. Louis Blues	1949	$30
❏ F1213	I've Never Been in Love Before/The Best Things for You	1950	$20
❏ F1132	Let's Do It Again/ Friendly Star	1950	$30
❏ F3232	Lover Lover/I Kiss You a Million Times	1955	$15
❏ F3189	Mama's Pearls/Man	1955	$15
❏ F1671	Moonlight in Vermont/ My Ideal	1951	$20

— Reissue

❏ F934	My Foolish Heart/Stay with the Happy People	1950	$30
❏ F2996	My Son, My Son/ My Own True Love	1954	$20
❏ F1309	Once You Find Your Guy/Man Ain't Nothin' But a Nothin'	1950	$20
❏ 4638	On Second Thought/ Who Can You Can	1961	$10
❏ F1343	Over and Over and Over/ The Moon Was Yellow	1950	$20
❏ F3412	Second Time in Love/ Old Enough	1956	$15
❏ F1041	Shawl of Galway Gray/ If You Were Only Mine	1950	$30
❏ F2331	Singing Bells/Take Care My Love	1953	$20
❏ F851	Solid As a Rock/Sure Thing	1950	$30
❏ F2489	Something Wonderful Happens/Where Did He Go	1953	$20
❏ F1491	Something Wonderful/ Hello Young Lovers	1951	$20
❏ F3067	Stowaway/Allah Be Praised	1955	$15
❏ F1845	That's For Sure/ If I Can Love You	1951	$20
❏ F3586	The Money Tree/ Maybe I Love Him	1956	$15
❏ 54-776	The Sun Is Always Shining/Sorry	1949	$30
❏ 54-748	Three Rivers/(It Happened at the) Festival of Roses	1949	$30
❏ F2177	Till We Meet Again/The Gods Were Angry with Me	1952	$20
❏ F3666	Tippy Toe/Spring in Maine	1957	$15
❏ F3473	True Love/Haunting Love	1956	$15
❏ F2550	Waltz to the Blues/C.O.D.	1953	$20
❏ F1469	We Kiss in a Shadow/ Make Man Love Me	1951	$20
❏ F2292	Why Don't You Believe Me/ Come Back to Me Johnny	1952	$20

DOT

❏ 15973	Half As Much/My Ideal	1959	$10
❏ 15680	I Can't Help It (If I'm Still in Love with You)/ That's Why I Was Born	1957	$10
❏ 15826	I Love You Because/ The Waiting Game	1958	$10
❏ 15931	I'm Alone Because I Love You/Top of the Moon	1959	$10
❏ 15742	I'm So Lonely I Could Cry/Hot Spell	1958	$10

LONDON

❏ 122	Faithfully/Am I Losing You	1968	$6
❏ 115	I Almost Called Your Name/Let's Pretend	1968	$6
❏ 119	I Hate to See Me Go/It Keeps Right On a Hurtin'	1968	$6
❏ 128	Love Has a Way/At the End of the Ocean	1969	$6
❏ 126	Love's the Only Answer/ Where Was I	1969	$6
❏ 124	Maybe Just One More/Can't Get You Out of My Mind	1968	$6
❏ 108	Only Love Can Break a Heart/Where Do I Stand	1967	$6
❏ 132	Theme from Z/Life Goes On	1970	$5
❏ 101	The Wheel of Hurt/ Nothing Lasts Forever	1966	$6

VERVE

| ❏ 10230 | Hey, Look Me Over/ What's New at the Zoo | 1960 | $12 |

— With Mel Torme

| ❏ 10212 | Why Was I Born/You Couldn't Be Cuter | 1960 | $10 |

WHITLEY, RAY (2)

1-2-3

| ❏ 1707 | Don't Throw Your Love to the Wind/Underdose of Faith | 1969 | $12 |

APT

| ❏ 25086 | I'll Tell the Robin/Runaway | 1965 | $15 |

COLUMBIA

| ❏ 4-43980 | Here Today, Gone Tomorrow/Take Back Your Mind | 1967 | $12 |

TRX

| ❏ 5007 | Gotta Go There/1983 | 1968 | $10 |

VEE JAY

❏ 448	It Hurts/Deeper in Love	1962	$20
❏ 521	Teenage Crush/ Your Heartache	1963	$20
❏ 414	There Goes a Teardrop/I Wasn't Sure	1961	$20
❏ 591	Walking Back to You/ Weep Little Girl Weep	1964	$20

WHITMAN, SLIM

CLEVELAND INT'L.

❏ 02402	Can't Help Falling in Love with You/Oh My Darlin' (I Love You)	1981	$4
❏ 02544	If I Had My Life to Live Over/Flowers	1981	$4
❏ 50971	I Remember You/Where Do I Go from Here	1981	$4
❏ 02779	My Melody of Love/ Open Up Your Heart	1982	$4
❏ 50946	That Silver-Haired Daddy of Mine/If I Could Only Dream	1980	$4
❏ 50912	When/Since You Went Away	1980	$4
❏ 50957	Where Is the Christ in Christmas/Sleep My Child (All Through the Night)	1980	$4
❏ 03370	Where Is the Christ in Christmas/Sleep My Child (All Through the Night)	1982	$4

EPIC

| ❏ 04358 | Blue Memories/ Cry Baby Heart | 1983 | $4 |
| ❏ 04549 | Four Walls/Tryin' to Outrun the Wind | 1984 | $4 |

IMPERIAL

❏ 8322	A Fool Such As I/The Prisoner's Song	1959	$20
❏ 8328	A Lonesome Heart/ The Wind	1960	$15
❏ 8321	A Tree in the Meadow/ What Kind of God	1959	$20
❏ 8319	At the End of Nowhere/ Wherever You Are	1958	$20
❏ 8144	Bandera Waltz/ End of the World	1952	$30
❏ 8257	Beautiful Dreamer/ Ride Away	1954	$30
❏ 5871	Blues Stay Away from Me/ You Have My Heart	1962	$10
❏ 5966	Broken Down Merry-Go-Round/Never	1963	$10
❏ 8163	By the Waters of the Winnetonka/In Amateur in Love	1952	$30
❏ 8317	Candy Kisses/Tormented	1958	$20
❏ 8309	Careless Love/I Must Have Been Blind	1957	$20
❏ 8281	Cattle Call/When I Grow Too Old to Dream	1954	$30
❏ 8147	Cold Empty Arms/In a Hundred Years or More	1952	$30
❏ 8201	Danny Boy/There's a Rainbow in Every Teardrop	1953	$30
❏ 66311	Happy Street/My Heart Is In the Roses	1968	$6
❏ 8180	How Can I Tell/All That I'm Asking Is Sympathy	1953	$30
❏ 5859	I Forgot More Than You'll Ever Know (About Her)/ Backward, Turn Backward	1962	$10
❏ 66040	I'll Hold You in My Heart (Till I Can Hold You in My Arms)/No Other Arms, No Other Lips	1964	$8
❏ 8298	I'll Never Stop Loving You/I'll Never Take You Back Again	1955	$30
❏ 8310	I'll Take You Home Again Kathleen/Lovesick Blues	1957	$20
❏ 66248	I'm a Fool/North Wind	1967	$8
❏ 8305	I'm a Fool/Serenade	1956	$30
❏ 8156	Indian Love Call/China Doll	1952	$30

— Black vinyl

| ❏ 8156 | Indian Love Call/China Doll | 1952 | $60 |

— Opaque red vinyl

❏ 8323	Indian Love Call/ Haunted Hungry Heart	1960	$15
❏ 66181	I Remember You/ Travelin' Man	1966	$10
❏ 66384	Irresistible/Flower of Love	1969	$6
❏ 66337	Livin' On Lovin' (And Lovin' Livin' with You)/ Heaven Says Hello	1968	$6
❏ 5919	Love Letters in the Sand/ You're the Only One	1963	$10
❏ 8134	Love Song of the Waterfall/ My Love's Growing Stale	1951	$30
❏ 66077	Love Song of the Waterfall/Virginia	1964	$8
❏ 66103	Mansion on the Hill/ Reminiscing	1965	$8
❏ 66002	Maria Elena/Gortamona	1963	$10
❏ 66130	More Than Yesterday/ La Golondrina	1965	$8
❏ 66358	My Happiness/Promises	1969	$6
❏ 5990	My Wild Irish Rose/ Chime Bells	1963	$10
❏ 8194	Once Before/Have Mercy on Me	1953	$30

Number	Title	Yr	NM
❏ 5766	Once in a Lifetime/When I Call on You	1961	$10
❏ 66212	One Dream/Jerry	1966	$8
❏ 8223	Secret Love/Why	1954	$30
❏ 8267	Singing Hills/I Hate to See You Cry	1954	$30
❏ 8308	Smoke Signals/Curtain of Tears	1956	$30
❏ 8299	Song of the Wild/You Have My Heart	1955	$30
❏ 8327	Sunrise/I'll Walk with God	1960	$15
❏ 66012	Tell Me Pretty Words/Only You And You Alone	1964	$8
❏ 5746	The Bells That Broke My Heart/I'd Climb the Highest Mountain	1961	$12
❏ 8320	The Letter Edged in Black/I Never See Maggie	1959	$20
❏ 5778	The Old Spinning Wheel/In a Hundred Years	1961	$10
❏ 66153	The Twelfth of Never/Straight from Heaven	1966	$8
❏ 5900	The Wayward Wind/Straight from Heaven	1962	$10
❏ 8307	The Whiffenpoof Song/Dear Mary	1956	$30
❏ 66441	Tomorrow Never Comes/Come Take My Hand	1970	$6
❏ 8304	Tumbling Tumbleweeds/Tell Me	1955	$30
❏ 5938	What'll I Do/So Long Mary	1963	$10
❏ 66226	What's This World a-Comin' To/You Bring Out the Best in Me	1967	$8
❏ 8318	When It's Springtime in the Rockies/Put Your Trust in Me	1958	$20
❏ 66411	When You Were 16/Love Song of the Waterfall	1969	$6

RCA VICTOR

Number	Title	Yr	NM
❏ 47-5557	Birmingham Jail/Wabash Waltz	1953	$30
❏ 48-0145	I'll Never Pass This Way Again/Birmingham Jail	1949	$70
—Green vinyl			
❏ 47-5724	I'll Never Pass This Way Again/Please Paint a Rose on the Garden Wall	1954	$30
❏ 48-0358	I'm Crying for You/Wabash Waltz	1950	$70
—Green vinyl			
❏ 48-0069	Please Paint a Rose on the Garden Wall/Tears Can Never Drown the Flame	1949	$70
—Green vinyl			
❏ 47-5431	There's a Rainbow in Every Teardrop/I'm Casting My Lasso	1953	$30

UNITED ARTISTS

Number	Title	Yr	NM
❏ XW690	Everything Leads Back to You/I'm Beginning to Love You	1975	$4
❏ 50731	Guess You/From Heaven to Heartache	1970	$5
❏ XW530	Happy Anniversary/What I Had with You	1974	$4
❏ XW178	Hold Me/So Close to Home	1973	$5
❏ 0138	Indian Love Call/China Doll	1973	$4
—Silver Spotlight Series" reissue			
❏ XW402	It's All in the Game/Make Believe	1974	$5
❏ 50806	It's a Sin to Tell a Lie/That's Enough for Me	1971	$5
❏ 50952	(It's No) Sin/(B-side unknown)	1972	$5
❏ 50899	Little Drops of Silver/Tammy	1972	$5
❏ 50852	Loveliest Night of the Year/Near You	1971	$5
❏ XW731	Mexicali Rose/As You Take a Walk Through My Mind	1975	$4
❏ 50697	Shutters and Boards/I Pretend	1970	$5
❏ 50775	Something Beautiful (To Remember)/Jerry	1971	$5
❏ XW619	The Most Beautiful Girl/Foolish Question	1975	$4
❏ XW269	Where the Lilacs Grow/Something Beautiful	1973	$5

7-Inch Extended Plays

IMPERIAL

Number	Title	Yr	NM
❏ IMP106 [PS]	America's Favorite Folk Artist	1954	$60
—With original back cover			
❏ IMP106 [PS]	America's Favorite Folk Artist	1956	$25
—We've found a copy of this cover that lists Imperial EPs to IMP-133, which we presume is a reissue and is priced accordingly			
❏ IMP106	China Doll/Indian Love Call//Keep It a Secret/My Heart Is Broken in Three	1954	$60
—Red label			
❏ IMP106	China Doll/Indian Love Call//Keep It a Secret/My Heart Is Broken in Three	1958	$25
—Black label			
❏ IMP-134	(contents unknown)	1956	$50
❏ IMP-136	(contents unknown)	1956	$50

Number	Title	Yr	NM
❏ IMP-131	In a Hundred Years or More/Why//Secret Love/Singing Hills	1956	$50
❏ IMP-130	Love Song of the Waterfall/Bandera Waltz//Beautiful Dreamer/Rose Marie	1956	$50
❏ IMP-135	Ride Away (With a Song in Your Heart)/We Stood at the Altar//An Amateur in Love/I Hate to See You Cry	1956	$50
❏ IMP-135 [PS]	Slim Whitman	1956	$50
❏ IMP-137 [PS]	Slim Whitman	1956	$50
❏ IMP-130 [PS]	Slim Whitman Singing…	1956	$50
❏ IMP-131 [PS]	Songs by Slim Whitman	1956	$50
❏ IMP-132 [PS]	Songs by Slim Whitman	1956	$50
❏ IMP-133 [PS]	Songs by Slim Whitman	1956	$50
❏ IMP-134 [PS]	Songs by Slim Whitman	1956	$50
❏ IMP-136 [PS]	Songs by Slim Whitman	1956	$50
❏ IMP-132	When I Grow Too Old to Dream/Cattle Call//Cold Empty Arms/By the Waters of the Minnetonka	1956	$50
—Red label			
❏ IMP-132	When I Grow Too Old to Dream/Cattle Call//Cold Empty Arms/By the Waters of the Minnetonka	1958	$25
—Black label			
❏ IMP-133	When My Blue Moon Turns to Gold/Blue Eyes Crying in the Rain//That Silver Haired Daddy of Mine/A Petal from a Faded Rose	1956	$50

WHITNEY, JILL
CORAL

Number	Title	Yr	NM
❏ 61082	Little Johnny Jingle Bells/Ragamuffin Doll	1953	$20

WHITNEY, TY
20TH FOX

Number	Title	Yr	NM
❏ 448	Surfin' Santa Claus/Winner's Wonderland	1963	$40

WHO, THE
Also see ROGER DALTREY; JOHN ENTWISTLE; KEITH MOON; PETE TOWNSHEND.

ATCO

Number	Title	Yr	NM
❏ 6409	Substitute/Waltz for a Pig	1966	$60
❏ 6509	Substitute/Waltz for a Pig	1967	$30

DECCA

Number	Title	Yr	NM
❏ 734610 [DJ]	Amazing Journey/The Acid Queen	1970	$30
❏ 31801	Anyway, Anyhow, Anywhere/Anytime You Want Me	1965	$60
❏ 32888	Behind Blue Eyes/My Wife	1971	$12
❏ 32288	Call Me Lightning/Dr. Jeckyll & Mr. Hyde	1968	$30
❏ 734610/3 [DJ]	Excerpts from Tommy	1970	$200
—Promo-only four-record box set with box and 4-page insert. As the records are sometimes found separately, they are also priced individually below.			
❏ 734611 [DJ]	Go to the Mirror Boy/Tommy Can You Hear Me	1970	$30
❏ 34444 [DJ]	Happy Jack (same on both sides)	1967	$50
—Promo-only number, pink label			
❏ 32114	Happy Jack/Whiskey Man	1967	$40
❏ 32114 [PS]	Happy Jack/Whiskey Man	1967	$60
❏ 32206	I Can See for Miles/Mary-Anne with the Shaky Hands	1967	$30
❏ 31725	I Can't Explain/Bald Headed Woman	1965	$40
❏ 32058	I'm a Boy/In the City	1966	$40
❏ 32519	I'm Free/We're Not Gonna Take It	1969	$10
❏ 32362	Magic Bus/Someone's Coming	1968	$20
❏ 31877	My Generation/Out in the Street (You're Going to Know Me)	1965	$40
❏ 32156	Pictures of Lily/Doctor, Doctor	1967	$30
❏ 34470 [DJ]	Pictures of Lily (same on both sides)	1967	$50
—Promo-only number, pink label			
❏ 732465	Pinball Wizard/Dogs Part Two	1969	$10
❏ 732465 [PS]	Pinball Wizard/Dogs Part Two	1969	$30
❏ 734613 [DJ]	Sally Simpson/I'm Free	1970	$30
❏ 732729	See Me, Feel Me/Overture from Tommy	1970	$15
—With custom gold label			
❏ 732729 [PS]	See Me, Feel Me/Overture from Tommy	1970	$30
❏ 734612 [DJ]	Smash the Mirror/Sensation	1970	$30
❏ 32708	Summertime Blues/Heaven and Hell	1970	$15
❏ 32670	The Seeker/Here for More	1970	$15
❏ 32846	Won't Get Fooled Again/I Don't Even Know Myself	1971	$10

MCA

Number	Title	Yr	NM
❏ L45-1809 [DJ]	Had Enough (same on both sides)	1978	$10

Number	Title	Yr	NM
❏ 60110	I Can't Explain/Bald Headed Woman	1973	$5
—Reissue; black label with rainbow			
❏ 41053	Long Live Rock/My Wife	1979	$5
❏ 60174	Pinball Wizard/Dogs Part Two	1974	$5
—Reissue; black label with rainbow			
❏ 60174	Pinball Wizard/Dogs Part Two	1980	$3
—Reissue; blue label with rainbow			
❏ 60106	See Me, Feel Me/Overture from Tommy	1973	$5
—Reissue; black label with rainbow			
❏ 40603	Slip Kid/Dreaming from the Waist	1976	$5
❏ 40475	Squeeze Box/Success Story	1975	$5
❏ 40475 [PS]	Squeeze Box/Success Story	1975	$40
—Sleeve is promo only			
❏ 40978	Trick of the Light/9:05	1978	$5
❏ 40948	Who Are You/Had Enough	1978	$5
❏ 40948 [DJ]	Who Are You (Short 3:22)/(Long 6:11)	1978	$10
—Promo only; the long version has two lines deleted from the LP version			

MERCURY

Number	Title	Yr	NM
❏ DJ-570 [DJ]	I'm the Face/Zoot Suit	1980	$5
❏ DJ-570 [PS]	I'm the Face/Zoot Suit	1980	$6
—As "The High Numbers			

POLYDOR

Number	Title	Yr	NM
❏ 2022	5:15/I'm One	1979	$4
❏ 2022 [PS]	5:15/I'm One	1979	$6

TRACK

Number	Title	Yr	NM
❏ 40152	Love, Reign O'er Me/Water	1973	$8
❏ 40330	Postcard/Put the Money Down	1974	$50

WARNER BROS.

Number	Title	Yr	NM
❏ 29905	Athena/It's Your Turn	1982	$4
❏ 29905 [PS]	Athena/It's Your Turn	1982	$5
❏ 49743	Don't Let Go the Coat/You	1981	$4
❏ 29814	Eminence Front/One at a Time	1983	$5
❏ 29731	It's Hard/Dangerous	1983	$5

WICHITA TRAIN WHISTLE, THE
DOT

Number	Title	Yr	NM
❏ 17152	Tapioca Tundra/Don't Cry Now	1968	$20

WIEDLIN, JANE
I.R.S.

Number	Title	Yr	NM
❏ 52674	Blue Kiss/My Traveling Heart	1985	$3
❏ 52674 [PS]	Blue Kiss/My Traveling Heart	1985	$3
❏ 52674 [PS]	Blue Kiss/Somebody's Going to Get Into This House	1985	$30
—Copies of the picture sleeve were printed, but the B-side was not pressed onto vinyl; a few were used as WLP, but not on stock copies with official B-side "My Traveling Heart			

WIER, RUSTY
20TH CENTURY

Number	Title	Yr	NM
❏ 2219	Don't It Make You Wanna Dance/I Believe in the Way That You Love Me	1975	$5
❏ 2273	I Don't Want to Lay This Guitar Down/Long and Lonesome Highway Blues	1976	$5
❏ 2188	I Heard You Been Layin' My Old Lady (Apologies to Susie)/Aqua Dulce	1975	$5

ABC

Number	Title	Yr	NM
❏ 12019	Stoned, Slow and Rugged/Jeremiah Black	1974	$6

BLACK HAT

Number	Title	Yr	NM
❏ 102	Close Your Eyes/Kum-Back Bar and Grill	1987	$6
❏ 103	(Lover of the) Other Side of the Hill/I Kept Thinkin' About You	1987	$6

COLUMBIA

Number	Title	Yr	NM
❏ 3-10445	I Think It's Time (I Learned How to Let Her Go)/Me and Daisy on the Run	1976	$4

COMPLEAT

Number	Title	Yr	NM
❏ 107	Don't It Make You Wanna Dance/You Gave Me a Reason	1983	$5
❏ 121	Lone Star Lady/I Still Believe in You	1984	$5

LONGHORN

Number	Title	Yr	NM
❏ 101	(Lover of the) Other Side of the Hill/(B-side unknown)	1965	$20

Number	Title	Yr	NM

WIGGINS, JAY
AMY
Number	Title	Yr	NM
❑ 955	Sad Girl/No, Not Me	1966	$10

WIGGINS, ROY
DOT
Number	Title	Yr	NM
❑ 15053	It's a Sin/Cimarron	1953	$30
❑ 584	Through the Night/Love Theme	1962	$15

WIGGINS, WALLY
MERCURY
Number	Title	Yr	NM
❑ 71645	I Need You/Maybe Someday	1960	$100
❑ 71713	Maybellene/Sweeter Than Sweet	1960	$30
❑ 71953	The Habit of Loving You/Little Old Lady Who Lives in a Shoe	1962	$40

WILBURN BROTHERS, THE
DECCA
Number	Title	Yr	NM
❑ 32921	Arkansas/Santa Fe Rolls Royce	1972	$8
❑ 30968	A Woman's Intuition/A Town That Never Sleeps	1959	$20
❑ 31276	Blue Blue Day/No Legal Right	1961	$15
❑ 29277	Carefree Moments/Let Me Be the First to Know	1954	$30
❑ 30686	Cry Baby Cry/Till I'm the Only One	1958	$20
❑ 32597	Gift of the Blues/Tag Along	1969	$8
❑ 30087	Go Away with Me/Great Big Love	1956	$30
❑ 32169	Goody, Goody Gumdrop/You're Standing in the Way	1967	$8
❑ 31578	Hangin' Around/Never Alone	1964	$12
❑ 32038	Hurt Her Once for Me/Just to Be Where You Are	1966	$10
❑ 31974	I Can't Keep Away from You/I'm Gonna Dress Up	1966	$10
❑ 30428	I Close My Eyes/I Got Over the Blues	1957	$20
❑ 29190	If You Love Me/A Little Time Out for Love	1954	$30
❑ 31764	I Had One Too Many/Left Out	1965	$10
❑ 31674	I'm Gonna Tie One On Tonight/Making Plans	1964	$10
❑ 32225	I'm Leavin'/Wastin' My Time	1967	$8
❑ 31625	Impossible/I'll Take What's Left of Me	1964	$10
❑ 29887	I'm So in Love with You/Deep Elem Blues	1956	$30
❑ 32449	It Looks Like the Sun's Gonna Shine/Make My Heart Die Away	1969	$8
❑ 31819	It's Another World/My Day Won't Be Complete	1965	$10
❑ 29459	I Wanna Wanna Wanna/My Heart or My Mind	1955	$30
❑ 32683	Lilacs in Winter/Country Boy (Sing Your Heart Out)	1970	$8
❑ 32771	Little Eyes That Look at Me/I've Gotta Hang My Hat Up on the Wind	1971	$8
❑ 32608	Little Johnny from Down the Street/Which Side's the Wrong Side	1970	$8
❑ 30591	Oo Bop Sha Boom/My Baby Ain't My Baby No More	1958	$40
❑ 32978	Opryland/Hard Times Have Been There	1972	$8
❑ 31062	Sentenced to Die/You Can't Take It With You	1960	$15
❑ 32292	Shakiest Gun in the West/She'll Walk All Over You	1968	$8
❑ 32531	Signs Are Everywhere/Who Could Ask for More	1969	$8
❑ 30871	Somebody's Back in Town/I Love Everybody	1959	$20
❑ 31894	Someone Before Me/Something About You	1966	$12
❑ 31333	Tag Along/Gift of the Blues	1961	$15
❑ 31520	Tell Her So/Here Comes a Million Memories	1963	$15
❑ 29614	Temptation Go Away/Mixed-Up Medley	1955	$30
❑ 32835	That She's Leaving Feeling/Everything I Am	1971	$8
❑ 31152	The Best of All My Heartaches/Someone Else's Love	1960	$15
❑ 33027	The City's Goin' Country/Minds of Lonely Men	1972	$8
❑ 31214	The Flame's Still Burning/The Legend of the Big River Train	1961	$15
❑ 31425	The Sound of Your Footsteps/Day After Day	1962	$15
❑ 32909	The War Keeps Draggin' On/Bloomin' Fools	1971	$8
❑ 31363	Trouble's Back in Town/Young But True Love	1962	$15
❑ 32386	We Need a Lot More Happiness/If You're with Me	1968	$8
❑ 31114	When Will You Know It/Big Heartbreak	1960	$15
❑ 30787	Which One Is to Blame/The Knoxville Girl	1958	$20

MCA
Number	Title	Yr	NM
❑ 40473	Country Honey/Milwaukee, You're in Trouble	1975	$5
❑ 40577	Country Kind of Feeling/Goin' and Comin'	1975	$5
❑ 40042	Simon Crutchfield's Grave/Treat the Dog Like a Dog	1973	$5
❑ 40264	There Must Be More to Love Than This/You've Still Got a Place in My Heart	1974	$5

SCORPION
Number	Title	Yr	NM
❑ 0558	Mama's Shoe Box/What a Way to Go	1978	$4

7-Inch Extended Plays
DECCA
Number	Title	Yr	NM
❑ ED2588	*If It's Wrong to Love You/One Has My Name, The Other Has My Heart/You Can't Break the Chains of Love/Much Too Often	1958	$25
❑ ED2617	*Need Someone/A Boy's Faithful Friend/Faded Love/Great Speckled Bird	1959	$25
❑ ED2681	*Never Be Anyone Else But You/Big Heartbreak/Empty Arms/I Almost Lost My Mind	1960	$25
❑ ED2782	*Roll Muddy River/Talk Back Trembling Lips/Hangin' Around/A Fool Never Learns	1964	$30
❑ ED2537	*That's When I Miss You/Cry, Cry Darling/I Know You Don't Love Me Anymore/Always Alone	1957	$30
❑ ED2727	*Trouble's Back in Town/Young But True Love/Roll On Buddy, Roll On/Michael	1962	$25
❑ ED2689	*When Will You Know It/A Town That Never Sleeps/Sentenced to Die/You Can't Take It With You	1961	$25
❑ ED2551	*You Win Again/I'll Sail My Ship Alone/Don't Sweetheart Me/Time Changes Everything	1957	$30
❑ ED2681 [PS]	Big Heartbreak	1960	$25
❑ ED2783	(contents unknown)	1964	$30
❑ ED2803	(contents unknown)	1965	$30
❑ ED2803 [PS]	I'm Gonna Tie One on Tonight	1965	$30
❑ ED2617 [PS]	Side by Side	1959	$25
❑ ED2783 [PS]	Take Up Thy Cross	1964	$30
❑ ED2537 [PS]	The Wilburn Brothers	1957	$30
❑ ED2551 [PS]	The Wilburn Brothers	1957	$30
❑ ED2588 [PS]	The Wilburn Brothers	1958	$25
❑ ED2689 [PS]	The Wilburn Brothers	1961	$25
❑ ED2756 [PS]	The Wilburn Brothers	1963	$25
❑ ED2727 [PS]	Trouble's Back in Town	1962	$25
❑ ED2756	Which One Is to Blame/No Legal Right//Blue Blue Day/Day After Day	1963	$25

WILCOX, HARLOW
IMPEL
Number	Title	Yr	NM
❑ 68-002	Groovy Grubworm/Sad Is the Lonely	1969	$30
❑ 68-002 [PS]	Groovy Grubworm/Sad Is the Lonely	1969	$60

PLANTATION
Number	Title	Yr	NM
❑ 28	Groovy Grubworm/Moose Trot	1969	$8
❑ 28 [PS]	Groovy Grubworm/Moose Trot	1969	$10

WILD BEES, THE
RCA VICTOR
Number	Title	Yr	NM
❑ 47-7275	Doctor Rock/Bamboozled	1958	$40

WILD-CATS, THE
UNITED ARTISTS
Number	Title	Yr	NM
❑ 169	Dancing Elephants/King Size Guitar	1959	$30
❑ 154	Gazachstahagen/Billy's Cha Cha	1958	$30

WILD, JACK
BUDDAH
Number	Title	Yr	NM
❑ 241	(Holy Moses) Everything's Coming Up Roses/Bring Yourself Back to Me	1971	$8

CAPITOL
Number	Title	Yr	NM
❑ 2742	Some Beautiful/A Picture of You	1970	$6
❑ 2742 [PS]	Some Beautiful/A Picture of You	1970	$15
❑ 2868	Wait for Summer/Melody	1970	$6

WILD ONES, THE (1)
MAINLINE
Number	Title	Yr	NM
❑ 500	Caught in the Cookie Jar/Super Fox	1965	$10

MALA
Number	Title	Yr	NM
❑ 564	High-Ho/Valerie	1967	$8

UNITED ARTISTS
Number	Title	Yr	NM
❑ 50043	For Your Love (I Would Do Almost Anything)/Never Givin' Up (On Your Love)	1966	$10
❑ 971	My Love/Lord Love a Duck	1966	$10
❑ 971 [PS]	My Love/Lord Love a Duck	1966	$20
❑ 947	Wild Thing/Just Can't Cry Anymore	1965	$15

WILD ONES, THE (2)
SEARS
Number	Title	Yr	NM
❑ 2180	Come On Back/(Instrumental)	1966	$10
❑ 2180 [PS]	Come On Back/(Instrumental)	1966	$40

WILD ONES, THE (3)
S.P.Q.R.
Number	Title	Yr	NM
❑ 3316	A Little Bit o' Soul/I've Been Crying	1964	$30

WILDCATS, THE (2)
REPRISE
Number	Title	Yr	NM
❑ 0253	3625 Groovy Street/What Are We Gonna Do in '64	1964	$30

WILDE, KIM
EMI AMERICA
Number	Title	Yr	NM
❑ B-8139	Chequered Love/Everything We Know	1982	$5

MCA
Number	Title	Yr	NM
❑ 53192	Another Step (Closer to You)/Hold Back	1987	$4
❑ 53192 [PS]	Another Step (Closer to You)/Hold Back	1987	$4
❑ 53480	Four Letter Word/She Hasn't Got Time for You	1988	$5
❑ 52513	Go For It/Lovers on a Beach	1984	$4
❑ 52513 [PS]	Go For It/Lovers on a Beach	1984	$10
—Fold-out poster sleeve			
❑ 52952	Say You Really Want Me/(Instrumental)	1986	$5
❑ 52952 [PS]	Say You Really Want Me/(Instrumental)	1986	$6
—Photo of Kim at left, light green background at right			
❑ 52925 [PS]	Say You Really Want Me (same on both sides)	1986	$8
—Running Scared movie scene sleeve (possibly promo only)			
❑ 52925	Say You Really Want Me (same on both sides)	1986	$6
—Possibly promo only			
❑ 53130	Say You Really Want Me/She Hasn't Got Time for You	1987	$3
❑ 53130 [PS]	Say You Really Want Me/She Hasn't Got Time for You	1987	$5
—Photo of Kim at left, dark blue background at right			

WILDE, MARTY
BELL
Number	Title	Yr	NM
❑ 45603	All Night Girl/(B-side unknown)	1974	$5

EPIC
Number	Title	Yr	NM
❑ 9400	Angry/My Baby Is Gone (Stop This World)	1960	$15
❑ 9356	Bad Boy/Teenage Years	1960	$15
❑ 9392	Little Girl/Your Seventeenth Spring	1960	$15
❑ 9291	My Lucky Love/Misery's Child	1958	$20

HERITAGE
Number	Title	Yr	NM
❑ 814	Abergavenny/Alice in Blue	1969	$6
—As "Shannon			
❑ 814 [PS]	Abergavenny/Alice in Blue	1969	$10
—As "Shannon			

WILDER BROTHERS, THE
WING
Number	Title	Yr	NM
❑ 90039	I Want a Goat for Christmas/That Old Chimney	1955	$20

X
Number	Title	Yr	NM
❑ 0169	Timber/Yes and No	1955	$30

WILDING, BOBBY
ABC-PARAMOUNT
Number	Title	Yr	NM
❑ 10275	Mama/You Give Me No Choice	1961	$15

DCP
Number	Title	Yr	NM
❑ 1009	I Want to Be a Beatle/Since I've Been Wearing My Hair Like a Beatle	1964	$30
❑ 1106	I Want You/Too Young to Fall in Love	1964	$15

MAY
Number	Title	Yr	NM
❑ 125	Slide (Part 1)/Slide (Part 2)	1962	$15

Number	Title	Yr	NM

WILDWOODS, THE
CAPRICE
| 101 | When the Swallows Come Back to Capistrano/Heart of Mine | 1961 | $200 |
MAY
| 106 | Golden Sunset/Here Comes Big Ed | 1961 | $40 |

WILEY AND GENE
COLUMBIA
| 4-20750 | I'm Sorry for the One Who's Losing You/My Prison | 1950 | $40 |
| 4-20729 | Stolen Kisses/Tear Drop Waltz | 1950 | $40 |

WILEY, CHUCK
JAX
| 1004 | I Love You So Much/I Begin to Miss You | 1959 | $125 |
UNITED ARTISTS
| 113 | Tear It Up/Shake Up the Dance | 1958 | $80 |

WILKENS, ARTIE, AND THE PALMS
STATES
| 157 | Darling Patricia/Please Come Back | 1956 | $600 |

WILLET, SLIM
4 STAR
1614	Don't Let the Stars (Get In Your Eyes)/Hadacol Corners	1952	$40
1645	Don't Waste Your Heart/Shibuya	1953	$30
1643	Hard to Love Just One/Little Bluebird Keeps Singin'	1953	$30
1642	Hungry Slim/Villa Cuna	1953	$30
1698	It Ain't Gonna Rain/(B-side unknown)	1956	$30
1625	Let Me Know/My Love Song for You	1953	$30
1663	Lonely Tide/Don't Laugh at Me Now	1954	$30
1672	Love Me Baby/When Lovers Go By	1955	$30
1677	Mata Hari/Tell Me Now	1955	$30
1679	When Nobody Cares/Tall Men	1955	$30
1653	Will There Be Stars in My Crown/Life Today As You Know	1954	$30
DECCA
| 9-29066 | Leave Me Alone Now/Starlight Waltz | 1954 | $30 |
EDMORAL
| 1010 | I've Been a-Wonderin'/Don't Be Afraid of the Moonlight | 1956 | $30 |
WINSTON
1043	Abilene Waltz/Blue Eagle	1959	$30
1038	Billy Tremain/Marching Down	1959	$30
1036	Boom Town Man/Tool Pusher (On a Rotary Rig)	1959	$30
1019	Pandemonium/Crazy Crazy	1957	$30
1044	Sweet Sally/Smell That Sweet Perfume	1959	$30

WILLIAMS, ALAINE
PARKWAY
| 923 | When Are We Getting Married/So This Is Goodbye | 1964 | $30 |

WILLIAMS, ANDRE
CHECKER
1205	Cadillac Jack/Mrs. Mother USA	1968	$15
1214	Do the Popcorn/It's Gonna Be Fine in '69	1969	$15
1219	Girdle Up/(Instrumental)	1969	$15
1187	The Stroke/Humpin' Bumpin' and Trumpin'	1967	$15
EPIC
| 9196 | Bacon Fat/Just Because of a Kiss | 1956 | $30 |
FORTUNE
831	Bacon Fat/Just Because of a Kiss	1956	$40
828	Bobby Jean/It's All Over	1956	$50
839	Come On Baby/The Greasy Chicken	1957	$40
— With Gino Park
| 839 | Don't Touch/Please Pass the Biscuits | 1957 | $100 |
— With Gino Park
| 851 | (Georgia May Is) Movin'/(Mmmm -- Andre Williams Is) Movin' | 1960 | $70 |
— With Gino Park

834	Mean Jean/You Are My Sunshine	1957	$40
827	Mozelle/Just Want a Little Lovin'	1956	$50
842	My Last Dance with You/Hey! Country Girl	1958	$40
824	Pulling Time/Going Down to Tia-Juana	1955	$100
847	Put a Chain on It/I'm All For You	1959	$40
839	The Greasy Chicken/Please Pass the Biscuits	1957	$70
— With Gino Park
SPORT
| 105 | Pearl Time/Soul Groove | 1967 | $30 |
WINGATE
| 021 | Do It! (Part 1)/Do It! (Part 2) | 1966 | $30 |
| 014 | Loose Juice/Sweet Little Pussycat | 1966 | $20 |

WILLIAMS, ANDY
CADENCE
1340	Are You Sincere/Be Mine Tonight	1957	$15
1303	Baby Doll/Since I've Found My Baby	1956	$15
1308	Butterfly/It Doesn't Take Very Long	1957	$15
1297	Canadian Sunset/High Upon a Mountain	1956	$15
1282	Christmas Is a Feeling in Your Heart/The Wind, The Sand and The Stars	1955	$20
1381	Do You Mind?/Dreamsville	1960	$12
1323	I Like Your Kind of Love/Stop Teasin' Me	1957	$15
1389	In the Summertime (You Don't Want My Love)/Don't Go to Strangers	1960	$10
1447	Let It Be Me/Under Paris Skies	1964	$12
1336	Lips of Wine/Straight from the Heart	1957	$15
1370	Lonely Street/Summer Love	1959	$10
1351	Promise Me, Love/Your Hand, Your Heart, Your Love	1958	$10
1398	The Bilbao Song/How Wonderful to Know	1961	$12
1358	The Hawaiian Wedding Song/House of Bamboo	1958	$10
1433	Twilight Time/So Rare	1962	$10
1378	Wake Me When It's Over/We Have a Date	1960	$10
1288	Walk Hand in Hand/Not Anymore	1956	$15
COLUMBIA
42950	A Fool Never Learns/Charade	1963	$8
43358	Ain't It True/Loved One	1965	$6
10029	A Mi Esposa Con Amor (To My Wife with Love)/Another Lonely Song	1974	$4
43257	…And Roses and Roses/My Carousel	1965	$6
43257 [PS]	…And Roses and Roses/My Carousel	1965	$8
3-10471	Are You In There?/(Disco Version)	1977	$4
JZSP76322/3 [DJ]	Away In A Manger/O Holy Night	1963	$12
44650	Battle Hymn of the Republic/Ave Maria	1968	$5
44650 [PS]	Battle Hymn of the Republic/Ave Maria	1968	$6
44102	Born Free/Alfie	1967	$10
— Possibly yellow-label promo only
43519	Bye Bye Blues/You're Gonna Hear from Me!	1966	$6
S731972 [S]	Canadian Sunset/Sing a Rainbow	1964	$15
4-42674	Can't Get Used to Losing You/Days of Wine and Roses	1963	$8
4-42674 [PS]	Can't Get Used to Losing You/Days of Wine and Roses	1963	$10
4-42674 [DJ]	Can't Get Used to Losing You (same on both sides)	1963	$20
— Promo only on red vinyl
45094	Can't Help Falling in Love/Sweet Memories	1970	$5
10054 [PS]	Christmas Present/The Lord's Prayer	1974	$5
10054	Christmas Present/The Lord's Prayer	1974	$4
10113	Cry Softly/You Lay So Easy on My Mind	1975	$4
42199	Danny Boy/Fly by Night	1961	$8
42199 [PS]	Danny Boy/Fly by Night	1961	$15
4-42674 [DJ]	Days of Wine and Roses (same on both sides)	1963	$30
— Promo only on yellow vinyl
43180	Dear Heart/Emily	1964	$6
42523	Don't You Believe It!/Summertime	1962	$8
42523 [PS]	Don't You Believe It!/Summertime	1962	$12
43458	Do You Hear What I Hear/Some Children See Him	1965	$8
S731973 [S]	Dream/Wives and Lovers	1964	$15

10144	Feelings/Quits	1975	$4
44818	Happy Heart/Our Last Goodbye	1969	$5
JZSP111911/2 [DJ]	Have Yourself a Merry Little Christmas/The Bells of St. Mary's	1966	$8
— Yellow label
| JZSP111911/2 [DJ] | Have Yourself a Merry Little Christmas/The Bells of St. Mary's | 1966 | $8 |
— White label, black vinyl
| JZSP111911/2 [DJ] | Have Yourself a Merry Little Christmas/The Bells of St. Mary's | 1966 | $20 |
— White label, green vinyl
45494	Help Me Make It Through the Night/Love Is All	1971	$4
42784	Hopeless/The Peking Theme (So Little Time)	1963	$8
43456	I'll Remember You/Quiet Nights of Quiet Stars	1965	$6
43737	In the Arms of Love/The Many Faces of Love	1966	$6
S731462 [S]	It Might As Well Be Spring/Three Coins in the Fountain	1962	$15
— The above five are "Stereo Seven" 33 1/3 rpm jukebox singles from set "JS 7-55" and the album "Moon River and Other Great Movie Themes"
| AE71108 [DJ] | It's the Most Wonderful Time of the Year/Kay Thompson's Jingle Bells | 1976 | $10 |
— Special radio promo for Christmas Seals. Also contains public service announcements for Christmas Seals by Williams on each side.
AE71108 [PS]	It's the Most Wonderful Time of the Year/Kay Thompson's Jingle Bells	1976	$10
45814	Last Tango in Paris/I'll Never Be the Same	1973	$4
44929	Live and Learn/You Are	1969	$5
S731458 [S]	Love Is a Many-Splendored Thing/A Summer Place	1962	$15
10078	Love Said Goodbye/One More Time	1974	$4
46049	Love's Theme/You're the Best Thing That's Ever Happened to Me	1974	$4
45533	Love Story (Spanish Version)/Music from Across the Way (Spanish Version)	1972	$6
3-10952	Love Story (Where Do I Begin)/Love Theme from "Oliver's Story"	1979	$4
3-10878	Love Theme from "Oliver's Story"/Everytime I See Laureen	1979	$4
45579	Love Theme from "The Godfather" (Speak Softly Love)/Home for Thee	1972	$4
45647	MacArthur Park/Amazing Grace	1972	$4
S731459 [S]	Maria/Never on Sunday	1962	$15
45757	Marmalade, Molenaisse and Honey/Who Was It	1973	$4
44202	More and More/I Want to Be Free	1967	$5
44065	Music to Watch Girls By/The Face I Love	1967	$5
45175	One Day of Your Life/Long Time Blues	1970	$5
43128	On the Street Where You Live/Almost There	1964	$6
S731974 [S]	Pennies from Heaven/First Born	1964	$15
10208	Sad Eyes/Quits	1975	$4
45936	Solitaire/My Love	1973	$4
42451	Stranger on the Shore/I Want to Be Wanted	1962	$8
42451 [PS]	Stranger on the Shore/I Want to Be Wanted	1962	$10
44527	Sweet Memories/You Are Where Everything Is	1968	$5
10263	Tell It Like It Is/Goin' Through the Motions	1975	$4
44709	The Christmas Song (Chestnuts Roasting On An Open Fire)/It's The Most Wonderful Time Of The Year	1968	$6
42894	The Christmas Song (Chestnuts Roasting On An Open Fire)/White Christmas	1963	$8
— Stock copy or black vinyl promo
| 42894 [DJ] | The Christmas Song (Chestnuts Roasting On An Open Fire)/White Christmas | 1963 | $15 |
— Promo only on green vinyl
S731460 [S]	The Exodus Song/Moon River	1962	$15
45531	The Last Time I Saw Her/Music from Across the Way	1972	$4
43650	The Summer of Our Love/How Can I Tell Her It's Over	1966	$6
42265	The Wonderful World of the Young/Help Me	1962	$8
42265 [PS]	The Wonderful World of the Young/Help Me	1962	$10
31495 [S]	(titles unknown)	1962	$15
31496 [S]	(titles unknown)	1962	$15
31497 [S]	(titles unknown)	1962	$15
31498 [S]	(titles unknown)	1962	$15
31499 [S]	(titles unknown)	1962	$15

Number	Title	Yr	NM
❏ S731976 [S]	(titles unknown)	1964	$15

— *The above five are 33 1/3 rpm jukebox singles with small holes and are taken from the album "The Wonderful World of Andy Williams*

Number	Title	Yr	NM
❏ S731461 [S]	Tonight/The Second Time Around	1962	$15
❏ 45985	Walk Right Back/Remember	1974	$4

— *With Noelle*

Number	Title	Yr	NM
❏ 45003	What Am I Living For/A Woman's Way	1969	$5
❏ 44325	When I Look in Your Eyes/Holly	1967	$5
❏ 45317	(Where Do I Begin) Love Story/Something	1971	$4
❏ 45246	Whistling Away the Dark/Home Lovin' Man	1970	$5
❏ 45716	Who Was It?/Home Lovin' Man	1972	$4
❏ 43015	Wrong for Each Other/Madrigal	1964	$6

MGM

Number	Title	Yr	NM
❏ 11076	Gentle Hands/From the Manger to the Cross	1951	$30

X

Number	Title	Yr	NM
❏ 036	Why Should I Cry Over You/You Can't Buy Happiness	1954	$30

7-Inch Extended Plays

CADENCE

Number	Title	Yr	NM
❏ CEP-103	*Canadian Sunset/Baby Doll/Butterfly/I Like Your Kind of Love	1957	$15
❏ CEP-120	Aloha Oe/A Song of Old Hawaii//Song of the Islands/Love Song of Kalua	1959	$15
❏ CEP-103 [PS]	Andy Williams	1957	$15
❏ CEP-112 [PS]	Andy Williams	1959	$15
❏ CEP-116	It's All in the Game/My Happiness//Twilight Time/Love Letters in the Sand	1959	$15
❏ CEP-120 [PS]	Song of the Islands	1959	$15
❏ CEP-112	The Hawaiian Wedding Song/Sail Along Silv'ry Moon//Blue Hawaii/Sweet Leilani	1959	$15
❏ CEP-119 [PS]	To You Sweetheart, Aloha	1959	$15
❏ CEP-119	To You Sweetheart, Aloha/The Moon of Manakoora//I'll Weave a Lot of Stars for You/Beyond the Reef	1959	$15
❏ CEP-116 [PS]	Two Time Winners	1959	$15
❏ 7-9138 [PS]	Dear Heart	1965	$12
❏ 7-9138	Dear Heart/Red Roses for a Blue Lady/Who Can I Turn To//You're Nobody 'Til Somebody Loves You/Everybody Loves Somebody/I Can't Stop Loving You	1965	$10

— *Special Coin Operator Release"; small hole, plays at 33 1/3 rpm*

Number	Title	Yr	NM
❏ 7-9299 [PS]	The Shadow of Your Smile	1966	$12
❏ 7-9299	The Shadow of Your Smile/Try to Remember/Yesterday//Michelle/A Taste of Honey/Somewhere	1966	$10

— *Special Coin Operator Release"; small hole, plays at 33 1/3 rpm*

COLUMBIA SPECIAL PRODUCTS

Number	Title	Yr	NM
❏ CSM679 [PS]	Andy Williams	1968	$20

— *Produced Exclusively for Kentucky Fried Chicken Corp.*

Number	Title	Yr	NM
❏ CSM679	A Taste of Honey/(Corcovado) Quiet Nights of Quiet Stars/Holly//You Are Where Everything Is/Noelle/May Each Day	1968	$10

— *Small hole, plays at 33 1/3 rpm*

WILLIAMS, BARRY

PARAMOUNT

Number	Title	Yr	NM
❏ 0122	Sweet Sweetheart/Sunny	1971	$20
❏ 0122 [PS]	Sweet Sweetheart/Sunny	1971	$30

WILLIAMS, BERNIE

BELL

Number	Title	Yr	NM
❏ 768	Ever Again/Next to You	1969	$1200

WILLIAMS, BILLY

CORAL

Number	Title	Yr	NM
❏ 62230	Begin the Beguine/For You	1960	$8
❏ 61795	Butterfly/The Pied Piper	1957	$10
❏ 61576	Cry Baby/A Crazy Little Place	1956	$12
❏ 61932	Don't Let Go/Baby, Baby	1958	$12
❏ 61346	Fools Rush In/He Follows She	1955	$15
❏ 61462	Glory of Love/Wonderful, Wonderful One	1955	$15
❏ 62101	Goodnight Irene/Red Hot Love	1959	$10
❏ 61886	Got a Date with an Angel/The Lord Will Understand	1957	$10

Number	Title	Yr	NM
❏ 62131	Go to Sleep, Go to Sleep, Go to Sleep/Telephone Conversation	1959	$8

— *With Barbara McNair*

Number	Title	Yr	NM
❏ 62218	I Cried for You/The Lover of All Lovers	1960	$8
❏ 61999	I'll Get By/It's Prayin' Time	1958	$10
❏ 61830	I'm Gonna Sit Down and Write Myself a Letter/Date with the Blues	1957	$15
❏ 62029	It Hurts So Much/So Long	1958	$10
❏ 61264	Love Me/The Honeydripper	1954	$15
❏ 61639	Pray/You'll Reach Your Star	1956	$12
❏ 61730	Shame, Shame, Shame!/Don't Cry on My Shoulder	1956	$10
❏ 61212	Sh-Boom (Life Could Be a Dream)/Whenever Wherever	1954	$15
❏ 62140	Smack Dab in the Middle/I Wonder	1959	$8
❏ 61751	Stormy/Follow Me	1956	$10
❏ 61961	There! I've Said It Again/Steppin' Out Tonight	1958	$10
❏ 61684	This Planet Earth/I Guess I'll Be On My Way	1956	$10
❏ 62438	Why Do I Love You So/Raise Your Hand	1964	$6
❏ 62438	Why Do I Love You So/The Honeydripper	1964	$6

MERCURY

Number	Title	Yr	NM
❏ 70376	Go Home, Joe/You're the Only One I Adore	1954	$20
❏ 70012	I Don't Know Why/Mad About 'Cha	1952	$20
❏ 70271	If I Ever Get to Heaven/Ask Me No Questions	1953	$20
❏ 70324	Invitation to Dance/I'll Close My Eyes	1954	$20
❏ 70094	Pour Me a Glass of Teardrops/It's a Miracle	1953	$20
❏ 5866	Stay/Azure-Te (Paris Blues)	1952	$20
❏ 5902	That's What I'm Here For/Some Folks Do, Some Folks Don't	1952	$20
❏ 70180	This Side of Heaven/You're the One for Me	1953	$20
❏ 5884	Who Knows/It's Best We Say Goodbye	1952	$20
❏ 70210	Why Do You Have to Go?/Cattle Call	1953	$20

MGM

Number	Title	Yr	NM
❏ 11184	Confetti/Don't Grieve	1952	$20
❏ 10928	Gaucho Serenade/I Won't Cry Anymore	1951	$20
❏ 11117	I'll Never Find You/Busy Line	1951	$20
❏ 10764	Longing/I Didn't Slip	1950	$30
❏ 10967	Pretty Eyed Baby/You Made Me Love You	1951	$20
❏ 10998	Shang-Hai/A Wondrous Word	1951	$20
❏ 12537	Shang-Hai/Gaucho Serenade	1957	$10
❏ 11066	Sin/It's Over	1951	$20
❏ 11172	Wheel of Fortune/What Can I Say	1952	$20

7-Inch Extended Plays

CORAL

Number	Title	Yr	NM
❏ EC81164	*I'm Gonna Sit Right Down and Write Myself A Letter/Lucy Lou/The Lord Will Understand (And Say "Well Done")/The Honeydripper	1957	$15
❏ EC81164 [PS]	(title unknown)	1957	$15

WILLIAMS BROS.

DEL-MAR

Number	Title	Yr	NM
❏ 1008	Bad Old Memories/The Last Time	1963	$30

WILLIAMS, CORA/SHIRLEY HAVEN AND THE FOUR JACKS

FEDERAL

Number	Title	Yr	NM
❏ 12079	I Ain't Coming Back Anymore/Sure Cure for the Blues	1952	$600

WILLIAMS, CURLEY

COLUMBIA

Number	Title	Yr	NM
❏ 2-380(?)	Barbecue Rag/No Not Now	1949	$50

— *Microgroove 33 1/3 rpm 7-inch single, small hole*

Number	Title	Yr	NM
❏ 4-20797	Between a Rock and a Hard Place/Good Ol' Alabam	1951	$40
❏ 4-20757	Fiddlin' Boogie/Shy Baby	1951	$40
❏ 2-820(?)	Honey Do You Love Me/Whole Hog or None	1950	$50

— *Microgroove 33 1/3 rpm 7-inch single, small hole*

Number	Title	Yr	NM
❏ 4-20879	Louisiana Serenade/Half As Much	1952	$40
❏ 4-21096	On the Okefenokee/What's the Matter with My Heart	1953	$40
❏ 2-740(?)	Saturday Night Rag/Mississippi	1950	$50

— *Microgroove 33 1/3 rpm 7-inch single, small hole*

Number	Title	Yr	NM
❏ 4-20849	String Steeling/All You Gotta Do Is Whistle	1951	$40

Number	Title	Yr	NM
❏ 4-20918	We've Come a Long Way Together/Texas Swing	1952	$40
❏ 4-21039	When You're Tired of Breaking Other Hearts/Time and a Half	1952	$40

WILLIAMS, DANNY

UNITED ARTISTS

Number	Title	Yr	NM
❏ 860	All's Fair in Love and War/Masquerade	1965	$10
❏ 50020	Blue on White/It's Not for Me to Say	1966	$8
❏ 825	How Soon/The Seventh Dawn	1965	$10
❏ 762	I Watched a Flower Grow/Forget Her, Forget Her	1964	$10
❏ 348	Lonely/We Will Never Be As Young As This Again	1961	$15
❏ 601	More (Theme from Mondo Cane)/Rhapsody	1963	$15
❏ 480	Something's Gotta Give/Miracle of You	1962	$15
❏ 493	Tears/Miracle of You	1962	$15
❏ 959	The Stranger/I Can't Believe I'm Losing You	1965	$10
❏ 729	The Truth Hurts/Little Toy Balloon	1964	$10
❏ 685	White on White/The Comedy Is Ended	1964	$20

WILLIAMS, DENIECE

ARC

Number	Title	Yr	NM
❏ 3-11063	I Found Love/Are You Thinking?	1979	$5
❏ 18-02812	It's Gonna Take a Miracle/A Part of Love	1982	$4
❏ 13-03242	It's Gonna Take a Miracle/Silly	1982	$4

— *Reissue*

Number	Title	Yr	NM
❏ 11-02108	It's Your Conscience/Sweet Surrender	1981	$5
❏ 3-10971	I've Got the Next Dance/When Love Comes Calling	1979	$5
❏ 18-02406	Silly/My Melody	1981	$4
❏ 18-03015	Waiting by the Hotline/Love Notes	1982	$4
❏ 18-03261	Waiting/How Does It Feel	1982	$6
❏ 11-60504	What Two Can Do/Suspicious	1981	$4

COLUMBIA

Number	Title	Yr	NM
❏ 3-10648	Baby, Baby My Love's All for You/Be Good to Me	1977	$5
❏ 38-04641	Black Butterfly/Blind Dating	1984	$5
❏ 38-03807	Do What You Feel/Love, Peace and Unity	1983	$4
❏ 38-03807 [PS]	Do What You Feel/Love, Peace and Unity	1983	$4
❏ 3-10429	Free/Cause You Love Me Baby	1976	$5
❏ AE71153 [DJ]	God Is Amazing/God Is Standing By	1977	$8

— *B-side by Johnnie Taylor; promo with "Suggested Christmas Programming" on label*

Number	Title	Yr	NM
❏ 3-10770	God Is Amazing/Season	1978	$5
❏ 38-06318	Healing/I Feel the Night	1986	$4
❏ 38-04218	Heaven in Your Eyes/Love, Peace and Unity	1983	$4
❏ 38-07704	I Believe in You/(Instrumental)	1988	$5
❏ 38-08014	I Can't Wait/(Instrumental)	1988	$3
❏ 38-08014 [PS]	I Can't Wait/(Instrumental)	1988	$3
❏ 38-07357	I Confess/(Instrumental)	1987	$3
❏ 38-04037	I'm So Proud/It's Okay	1983	$4
❏ 38-04417	Let's Hear It for the Boy/(Instrumental)	1984	$3
❏ 38-04417 [PS]	Let's Hear It for the Boy/(Instrumental)	1984	$4
❏ 13-08425	Let's Hear It for the Boy/(Instrumental)	1988	$3

— *Reissue*

Number	Title	Yr	NM
❏ 3-10556	That's What Friends Are For/It's Important to Me	1977	$5
❏ 38-08507	This Is As Good As It Gets/Don't Stop the Love	1988	$4
❏ 38-07633	Water Under the Bridge/Love Finds You	1987	$4
❏ 38-06157	Wiser and Weaker/(Instrumental)	1986	$3
❏ 38-06157 [PS]	Wiser and Weaker/(Instrumental)	1986	$3

MCA

Number	Title	Yr	NM
❏ 53707	Every Moment/Do You Hear What I Hear?	1989	$5

SPARROW

Number	Title	Yr	NM
❏ SGL-11741 [DJ]	Healing (same on both sides)	1986	$5
❏ SGL-11741 [PS]	Healing (same on both sides)	1986	$5
❏ SGL-11212 [DJ]	I Surrender All/Personal Testimony	1986	$5
❏ SGL-11211 [DJ]	My Soul Desire/Personal Testimony	1986	$5
❏ SGL-11211 [PS]	My Soul Desire/Personal Testimony	1986	$5
❏ SGL-11213 [DJ]	So Glad I Know/I Surrender All	1986	$5
❏ SGL-11215 [DJ]	Wings of an Eagle (same on both sides)	1986	$8

— *Pink vinyl*

Number	Title	Yr	NM
❑ SGL-11215 [PS]	Wings of an Eagle (same on both sides)	1986	$8

TODDLIN' TOWN

Number	Title	Yr	NM
❑ 113	Hey Baby/Glorious Feeling	1968	$50

— As "Deniece Chandler"; with Lee Sain

| ❑ 118 | I Don't Wanna Cry/ Goodbye Cruel World | 1969 | $50 |

— As "Deniece Chandler

| ❑ 107 | Love Is Tears/I'm Walkin' Away | 1968 | $50 |

— As "Deniece Chandler

| ❑ 127 | Shy Boy/Come On Home to My Baby | 1969 | $40 |

— As "Deniece Chandler

WILLIAMS, DON

ABC

Number	Title	Yr	NM
❑ 12332	I've Got a Winner in You/Overlookin' and Underthinkin'	1978	$4
❑ 12458	Lay Down Beside Me/I Would Like to See You Again	1979	$5
❑ 12425	Tulsa Time/When I'm With You	1978	$5

ABC DOT

❑ 17717	I'm Just a Country Boy/ It's Gotta Be Magic	1977	$4
❑ 17631	Say It Again/I Don't Want the Money	1976	$4
❑ 17658	She Never Knew Me/Ramblin'	1976	$4
❑ 17683	Some Broken Hearts Never Mend/I'll Forgive But I'll Never Forget	1977	$4
❑ 17531	The Ties That Bind/Goodbye Isn't Really Good at All	1974	$4
❑ 17604	Till the Rivers All Run Dry/ Don't You Think It's Time	1976	$4
❑ 17568	(Turn Out the Light And) Love Me Tonight/ Reason to Be	1975	$4

CAPITOL

❑ B-44131	Another Place, Another Time/Running Out of Reasons to Run	1988	$3
❑ B-44216	Desperately/You Loved Me Through It All	1988	$3
❑ B-5588	Heartbeat in the Darkness/ Light in Your Eyes	1986	$3
❑ B-44019	I'll Never Be in Love Again/Send Her Roses	1987	$3
❑ B-44066	I Wouldn't Be a Man/ Light in Your Eyes	1987	$3
❑ B-44274	Old Coyote Town/You Loved Me Through It All	1988	$3
❑ B-5683	Senorita/Send Her Roses	1987	$3
❑ B-5638	Then It's Love/ It's About Time	1986	$3
❑ B-5526	We've Got a Good Fire Goin'/Shot Full of Love	1985	$3

DOT

| ❑ 17516 | I Wouldn't Want to Live If You Didn't Love Me/Fly Away | 1974 | $5 |

JMI

❑ 32	Atta Way to Go/I Recall a Gypsy Woman	1973	$6
❑ 24	Come Early Morning/ Amanda	1973	$6
❑ 7	Don't You Believe/ You Have a Star	1972	$6
❑ 42	Down the Road I Go/She's in Love with a Rodeo Man	1974	$6
❑ 12	The Shelter of Your Eyes/Playin' Around	1972	$6
❑ 36	We Should Be Together/ Miller's Cave	1974	$6

MCA

❑ S45-1763 [DJ]	A Special Message from Don Williams For Your Radio Station and Audience	1982	$15
❑ 51065	Falling Again/I Keep Putting Off Getting Over You	1981	$3
❑ 41205	Good Ole Boys Like Me/ We're All the Way	1980	$3
❑ 41304	I Believe in You/It Only Rains on Me	1980	$4
❑ 52152	If Hollywood Don't Need You/Help Yourselves to Each Other	1982	$3
❑ 41069	It Must Be Love/ Not a Chance	1979	$3
❑ 52692	It's Time for Love/I'll Never Need Another You	1985	$3
❑ 12458	Lay Down Beside Me/I Would Like to See You Again	1979	$3

— Reissue of ABC 12458

❑ 52037	Listen to the Radio/ Only Love	1982	$3
❑ 51207	Lord, I Hope This Day Is Good/Smooth Talking Baby	1981	$3
❑ 52205	Love Is on a Roll/I'll Take Your Love Anytime	1983	$3
❑ 41155	Love Me Over Again/ Circle Driveway	1979	$3
❑ 52448	Maggie's Dream/Leavin'	1984	$3

Number	Title	Yr	NM
❑ 51134	Miracles/I Don't Want to Love You	1981	$3
❑ 52097	Mistakes/Fool, Fool Heart	1982	$3
❑ 52310	Stay Young/Pressure Makes Diamonds	1983	$3
❑ 52389	That's the Thing About Love/I'm Still Looking for You	1984	$3
❑ 52514	Walkin' a Broken Heart/ True Blue Hearts	1984	$3

RCA

| ❑ 9017-7-R | I've Been Loved by the Best/If You Love, Won't You Love Me | 1989 | $4 |
| ❑ 8867-7-R | One Good Well/ Flowers Won't Grow (In a Field of Stone) | 1989 | $4 |

WILLIAMS, ELLY

RAINBOW

| ❑ 253 | Worry, Worry, Worry/ Oh-Dee-Dong | 1954 | $20 |

WILLIAMS, HANK, JR., AND LOIS JOHNSON

MGM

❑ 14356	Send Me Some Lovin'/What We Used to Hang On To	1972	$8
❑ 14164	So Sad (To Watch Good Love Go Bad)/Let's Talk It Over Again	1970	$8
❑ 14443	Whole Lotta Loving/Why Should We Try Anymore	1972	$8

WILLIAMS, HANK, JR.

ELEKTRA

❑ 47257	A Country Boy Can Survive/Weatherman	1982	$5
❑ 47191	All My Rowdy Friends (Have Settled Down)/ Everytime I Hear That Song	1981	$5
❑ 47137	Dixie on My Mind/ Ramblin' Man	1981	$5
❑ 46046	Family Tradition/ Paying On Time	1979	$5
❑ 69846	Gonna Go Huntin' Tonight/ Twodot, Montana	1983	$4
❑ 47462	Honky Tonkin'/High and Pressurized	1982	$5
❑ 47012	If You Don't Like Hank Williams/Outlaw Women	1980	$6
❑ 47231 [DJ]	Little Drummer Boy/ The Christmas Song	1981	$8

—B-side by Sonny Curtis

❑ 47016	Old Habits/Won't It Be Nice	1980	$5
❑ 47102	Texas Women/You Can't Find Many Kisses	1981	$5
❑ 69960	The American Dream/If Heaven Ain't a Lot Like Dixie	1982	$4
❑ 46018	To Love Somebody/We Can Work It All Out	1979	$5
❑ 46535	Whiskey Bent and Hell Bound/O.D.'d in Denver	1979	$5
❑ 46593	Women I've Never Had/Tired of Being Johnny B. Goode	1980	$5

MGM

❑ 14024	A Baby Again/Swim Across a Tear	1969	$10
❑ 14277	After All They All Used to Belong to Me/Happy Kind of Sadness	1971	$8
❑ 14486	After You/Knoxville Courthouse Blues	1973	$6
❑ 14317	Ain't That a Shame/ End of a Bad Day	1971	$8
❑ 14152	All for the Love of Sunshine/ Ballad of the Moonshine	1970	$8
❑ 14755	Angels Are Hard to Find/ Getting Over You	1974	$6
❑ 14062	Be Careful of Stones That You Throw/ Book of Memories	1969	$12

— As "Luke the Drifter, Jr.

| ❑ 14047 | Cajun Baby/My Heart Won't Let Me Go | 1969 | $10 |
| ❑ 14020 | Custody/My Home Town Circle "R | 1968 | $15 |

— As "Luke the Drifter, Jr.

❑ 14371	Eleven Roses/Richmond Valley Breeze	1972	$8
❑ 13278	Endless Sleep/My Bucket's Got a Hole In It	1964	$15
❑ 13253	Guess What, That's Right, She's Gone/Goin' Steady with the Blues	1964	$15
❑ 13253 [PS]	Guess What, That's Right, She's Gone/Goin' Steady with the Blues	1964	$30
❑ 14550	Hank (Part 2)	1973	$6
❑ 13640	I Can't Take It No Longer/ You Can Hear a Tear Drop	1966	$15
❑ 14077	I'd Rather Be Gone/ Try, Try Again	1969	$10
❑ 14731	I'll Think of Something/ Country Music Lover	1974	$6
❑ 13730	I'm In No Condition/I'm Gonna Break Your Heart	1967	$15
❑ 13318	I'm So Lonesome I Could Cry/Is It That Much Fun to Hurt Someone	1965	$15

Number	Title	Yr	NM
❑ 13318 [PS]	I'm So Lonesome I Could Cry/Is It That Much Fun to Hurt Someone	1965	$30
❑ 14120	It Don't Take But One Mistake/Goin' Home	1970	$8

— As "Luke the Drifter, Jr.

❑ 13968	It's All Over But the Crying/ Rock in My Shoes	1968	$10
❑ 14240	I've Got a Right to Cry/Jesus Loved the Devil Out of Me	1971	$8
❑ 14107	I Walked Out on Heaven/ Your Love's One Thing	1970	$8
❑ 14002	I Was With Red Foley (The Night He Passed Away)/On Trial	1968	$15

— As "Luke the Drifter, Jr.

❑ 13353	I Went to All That Trouble for Nothin'/Mule Skinner Blues	1965	$15
❑ 13857	I Wouldn't Change a Thing About You (But Your Name)/ No Meaning and No End	1967	$15
❑ 14845	Living Proof/Brothers of the Road	1976	$6
❑ 13208	Long Gone Lonesome Blues/Doesn't Anybody Know My Name	1964	$15
❑ 13208 [PS]	Long Gone Lonesome Blues/Doesn't Anybody Know My Name	1964	$30
❑ 13392	Pecos Jail/You're Ruinin' My Life	1965	$15
❑ 13392 [PS]	Pecos Jail/You're Ruinin' My Life	1965	$30
❑ 14421	Pride's Not Hard to Swallow/Hamburger Steak, Holiday Inn	1972	$8
❑ 14095	Something to Think About/(There Must Be) A Better Way to Love	1969	$12

— As "Luke the Drifter, Jr.

❑ 13504	Standing in the Shadows/It's Written All Over Your Face	1966	$15
❑ 14833	Stoned at the Jukebox/ The Devil in the Bottle	1975	$6
❑ 14656	The Last Love Song/Those Tear Jerking Songs	1973	$6
❑ 13922	The Old Ryman/I Wonder Where You Are Tonight	1968	$10
❑ 14813	The Same Old Story/ Country Love	1975	$6
❑ 14794	Where He's Going, I've Already Gone/The Kind of Woman I've Got	1975	$6

VERVE

| ❑ 10572 | Mental Revenge/ Splish Splash | 1967 | $50 |

— As "Bocephus

| ❑ 10540 | Meter Reader Maid/ Just a Dream | 1967 | $60 |

— As "Bocephus

WARNER BROS.

❑ 28794	Ain't Misbehavin'/I've Been Around	1986	$4
❑ 29184	All My Rowdy Friends Are Coming Over Tonight/Video Blues	1984	$4
❑ PRO-S-3838 [DJ]	All My Rowdy Friends (Are Here on Monday Night) (same on both sides)	1989	$20
❑ 29253	Attitude Adjustment/ Knoxville Courthouse Blues	1984	$4
❑ 28369	Born to Boogie/What It Boils Down To	1987	$3
❑ 28691	Country State of Mind/Fat Friends	1986	$4
❑ 27722	Early in the Morning and Late at Night/I'm Just a Man	1988	$3
❑ 27722 [PS]	Early in the Morning and Late at Night/I'm Just a Man	1988	$4
❑ 8507	Feelin' Better/Once and For All	1977	$5
❑ 22945	Finders Are Keepers/ What You Don't Know (Won't Hurt You)	1989	$3
❑ 28227	Heaven Can't Be Found/ Doctor's Song	1987	$3
❑ 28227 [PS]	Heaven Can't Be Found/ Doctor's Song	1987	$4
❑ 8641	I Fought the Law/It's Different with You	1978	$5
❑ 27862	If the South Woulda Won/Wild Streak	1988	$3
❑ 27862 [PS]	If the South Woulda Won/Wild Streak	1988	$4
❑ 29022	I'm for Love/Lawyers, Guns and Money	1985	$4
❑ 8410	I'm Not Responsible/ (Honey, Won't You) Call Me	1977	$5
❑ 29633	Leave Them Boys Alone/ The Girl in the Front Row at Fort Worth	1983	$4
❑ 29095	Major Moves/Mr. Lincoln	1985	$4
❑ 29382	Man of Steel/Now I Know How George Feels	1984	$4
❑ 28581	Mind Your Own Business/ My Name Is Bocephus	1986	$4
❑ 8361	Mobile Boogie/She's the Star (On the Stage of My Mind)	1977	$5
❑ 8715	Old Flame, New Fire/ Payin' On Time	1978	$5
❑ 8451	One Night Stands/I'm Not Responsible	1977	$5

Number	Title	Yr	NM
❑ 8345	She's the Star (On the Stage of My Mind)/Call Me, Honey, Won't You	1977	$5
❑ 27584	There's a Tear in My Beer/You Brought Me Down to Earth	1989	$4

— A-side with Hank Williams Sr.

❑ 27584 [PS]	There's a Tear in My Beer/You Brought Me Down to Earth	1989	$4
❑ 28912	This Ain't Dallas/I Really Like Girls	1985	$4
❑ 28452	When Something Is Good (Why Does It Change)/ Loving Instructor	1987	$3

7-Inch Extended Plays

MGM

| ❑ SLM-4316 [PS] | Ballads of the Hills and Plains | 1966 | $20 |
| ❑ SLM-4316 | Cowpoke/Big Twenty/ The Blizzard//Streets of Laredo/The River | 1966 | $20 |

— Jukebox issue; small hole, plays at 33 1/3 rpm

WILLIAMS, HANK

MGM

Number	Title	Yr	NM
❑ 11861	Angel of Death/(I'm Gonna) Sing, Sing, Sing	1954	$30
❑ 12029	A Teardrop on a Rose/ Alone and Forsaken	1955	$30
❑ 11100	Baby, We're Really in Love/I'd Still Want You	1951	$40
❑ 11309	Be Careful of Stones That You Throw/Why Don't You Make Up Your Mind	1952	$50

— As "Luke the Drifter"

| ❑ 10630 | Beyond the Sunset/ The Funeral | 1950 | $70 |

— As "Luke the Drifter"

❑ 12332	Blue Love (In My Heart)/ Singing Waterfall	1956	$30
❑ 12185	California Zephyr/ Thy Burdens Are Greater Than Mine	1956	$30
❑ 11628	Calling You/When God Comes and Gathers His Jewels	1953	$30
❑ 10904	Cold, Cold Heart/Dear John	1951	$40
❑ 13359	Cold, Cold Heart/Pale Horse and His Rider	1965	$15
❑ 11054	Crazy Heart/ Lonesome Whistle	1951	$40
❑ 10434	Dear Brother/Lost on the River	1949	$70
❑ 10718	Everything's OK/ Too Many Parties	1950	$70

— As "Luke the Drifter"

❑ 11202	Half As Much/Let's Turn Back the Years	1952	$40
❑ 11000	Hey, Good Lookin'/My Heart Would Know	1951	$40
❑ 11160	Honky Tonk Blues/I'm Sorry for You My Friend	1952	$40
❑ K10171	Honky Tonkin'/I'll Be a Bachelor 'Til I Die	1950	$60

— Yellow label; 78 first issued in 1948

❑ 11707	How Can You Refuse Him Now/A House of Gold	1954	$30
❑ 11768	I Ain't Got Nothin' But Time/I'm Satisfied with You	1954	$30
❑ 10961	I Can't Help It (If I'm Still in Love with You)/ Howlin' at the Moon	1951	$40
❑ 11017	I Dreamed About Mama Last Night/I've Been Down That Road Before	1951	$60

— As "Luke the Drifter"

❑ 10813	I Heard My Mother Praying for Me/Jesus Remembered Me	1950	$60
❑ 10609	I Just Don't Like This Kind of Lovin'/May You Never Be Alone	1950	$50
❑ 11366	I'll Never Get Out of This World Alive/I Could Never Be Ashamed	1952	$40
❑ 13489	I'm So Lonesome I Could Cry/You Win Again	1966	$15
❑ 12244	I Wish I Had a Nickel/There's No Room in My Heart	1956	$30
❑ 11533	I Won't Be Home No More/My Love for You	1953	$30
❑ 12484	Leave Me Alone with the Blues/With Tears in My Eyes	1957	$30
❑ 11083	Leave Us Women Alone/ If You See My Baby	1951	$50
❑ 13717	Long Gone Lonesome Blues/Hang On the Bell, Nellie	1967	$15
❑ 10645	Long Gone Lonesome Blues/My Son Calls Another Man Daddy	1950	$50
❑ 8010	Lovesick Blues/Never Again (Will I Knock on Your Door)	1949	$75
❑ K10352	Lovesick Blues/Never Again (Will I Knock on Your Door)	1950	$60

— Reissue has original 45 rpm number in parentheses under this number

Number	Title	Yr	NM
❑ K10328	Mansion on the Hill/I Can't Get You Off of My Mind	1950	$60

— Yellow label; 78 first issued in 1949

❑ 11975	Message to My Mother/ Mother Is Gone	1955	$30
❑ 10461	Mind Your Own Business/There'll Be No Teardrops Tonight	1949	$70
❑ 10832	Moanin' the Blues/Nobody's Lonesome for Me	1950	$50
❑ K10033	Move It On Over/(Last Night) I Heard You Cryin' in Your Sleep	1950	$60

— Yellow label; 78 first issued in 1947

❑ 10560	My Bucket's Got a Hole In It/I'm So Lonesome I Could Cry	1949	$70
❑ 11928	Please Don't Let Me Love You/Faded Love and Winter's Roses	1955	$30
❑ 11318	Settin' the Woods On Fire/You Win Again	1952	$40
❑ 12077	Someday You'll Call My Name/The First Fall of Snow	1955	$30
❑ 11479	Take These Chains from My Heart/Ramblin' Man	1953	$30
❑ 12127	The Battle of Armageddon/ Thank God	1955	$30
❑ 12394	The Pale Horse and His Rider/A Home in Heaven	1956	$30

— As "Hank and Audrey Williams"

❑ 13630	There'll Be No Teardrops Tonight/They'll Never Take Her Love from Me	1966	$15
❑ 10760	They'll Never Take Her Love from Me/Why Should We Try Anymore	1950	$50
❑ 11574	Weary Blues from Waitin'/I Can't Escape from You	1953	$30
❑ K10401	Wedding Bells/I've Just Told Mama Goodbye	1949	$70
❑ 12635	We Live in Two Different Worlds/My Bucket's Got a Hole In It	1958	$30
❑ 10696	Why Don't You Love Me/A House Without Love	1950	$50
❑ 12611	Why Don't You Love Me/I Can't Help It (If I'm Still in Love with You)	1958	$30
❑ 14849	Why Don't You Love Me/Ramblin' Man	1976	$6

7-Inch Extended Plays

| ❑ X-1235 | *Honky Tonkin'/Mind Your Own Business/ Rootie Tootie/I Ain't Got Nothing But Time | 1956 | $50 |

— Yellow label

| ❑ X-1235 | *Honky Tonkin'/Mind Your Own Business/ Rootie Tootie/I Ain't Got Nothing But Time | 1960 | $20 |

— Black label

| ❑ X-1637 | *I Can't Get You Off My Mind/I Don't Care (If Tomorrow Never Comes)/ Dear John/My Love for You (Has Turned to Hate) | 1959 | $35 |

— Yellow label

| ❑ X-1637 | *I Can't Get You Off My Mind/I Don't Care (If Tomorrow Never Comes)/ Dear John/My Love for You (Has Turned to Hate) | 1959 | $20 |

— Black label

| ❑ X-1644 | Be Careful of Stones That You Throw/I Dreamed About Mama Last Night// Funeral/Beyond the Sunset | 1959 | $35 |

— Yellow label

| ❑ X-1644 | Be Careful of Stones That You Throw/I Dreamed About Mama Last Night// Funeral/Beyond the Sunset | 1960 | $20 |

— Black label

| ❑ X-4103 | Cold, Cold Heart/Kaw-Liga//I Could Never Be Ashamed of You/Half As Much | 1953 | $50 |

— One record of "X202

| ❑ X-1613 | Cold, Cold Heart/Kaw-Liga//I Could Never Be Ashamed of You/Half As Much | 1959 | $35 |

— Yellow label

| ❑ X-1613 | Cold, Cold Heart/Kaw-Liga//I Could Never Be Ashamed of You/Half As Much | 1960 | $20 |

— Black label

❑ X-1698	(contents unknown)	1960	$20
❑ X-1700	(contents unknown)	1960	$20
❑ X-1014 [PS]	Crazy Heart	1953	$25
❑ X-1014	Crazy Heart/Baby We're Really in Love//My Heart Would Know/I Can't Help It (If I'm Still in Love with You)	1953	$100

— Yellow label

Number	Title	Yr	NM
❑ X-1014	Crazy Heart/Baby We're Really in Love//My Heart Would Know/I Can't Help It (If I'm Still in Love with you)	1960	$25

— Black label

| ❑ X-1636 | Crazy Heart/Move It On Over//My Heart Would Know/I'm Sorry for You My Friend | 1959 | $35 |

— Yellow label

| ❑ X-1636 | Crazy Heart/Move It On Over//My Heart Would Know/I'm Sorry for You My Friend | 1960 | $20 |

— Black label

❑ X-1047 [PS]	Hank Williams as Luke the Drifter	1954	$25
❑ X-1643 [PS]	Hank Williams as Luke the Drifter	1959	$20
❑ X-1644 [PS]	Hank Williams as Luke the Drifter	1959	$20
❑ X-1612 [PS]	Hank Williams Memorial Album Vol. 1	1959	$20
❑ X-1613 [PS]	Hank Williams Memorial Album Vol. 2	1959	$20
❑ X-1636 [PS]	Hank Williams Memorial Album Vol. 3	1959	$20
❑ X-1101 [PS]	Hank Williams Sings	1955	$25
❑ X-1102 [PS]	Hank Williams Sings Vol. 2	1955	$25
❑ X-242 [PS]	Honky Tonkin'	1954	$50

— Cover for X4108 and X4109

| ❑ X-1235 [PS] | Honky Tonkin' | 1956 | $20 |
| ❑ X-4108 | Honky Tonkin'/Howlin' at the Moon//My Bucket's Got a Hole in It/Baby, We're Really in Love | 1954 | $50 |

— One record of "X242

| ❑ X-1318 | Honky Tonkin'/Howlin' at the Moon//My Bucket's Got a Hole in It/Baby, We're Really in Love | 1957 | $50 |

— Yellow label

| ❑ X-1318 | Honky Tonkin'/Howlin' at the Moon//My Bucket's Got a Hole in It/Baby, We're Really in Love | 1960 | $20 |

— Black label

❑ X-1317 [PS]	Honky Tonkin' Vol. 1	1957	$20
❑ X-1318 [PS]	Honky Tonkin' Vol. 2	1957	$20
❑ X-1319 [PS]	Honky Tonkin' Vol. 3	1957	$20
❑ X-1492	I Heard You Crying in Your Sleep/Blue Love//Mansion on the Hill/They'll Never Take Her Love from Me	1958	$35

— Yellow label

| ❑ X-1492 | I Heard You Crying in Your Sleep/Blue Love//Mansion on the Hill/They'll Never Take Her Love from Me | 1960 | $20 |

— Black label

| ❑ X-1699 | I'm Free at Last/Roly Poly//The Old Home/Rock My Cradle (Once Again) | 1960 | $20 |
| ❑ X-1218 | I'm Gonna Sing/Message to My Mother//Thank God/ The Angel of Death | 1956 | $50 |

— Yellow label

| ❑ X-1218 | I'm Gonna Sing/Message to My Mother//Thank God/ The Angel of Death | 1960 | $20 |

— Black label

| ❑ SLM-4377 | I'm So Lonesome I Could Cry/You Win Again//Kaw-Liga//Lovesick Blues/Let's Turn Back the Years/I'm Sorry for You, My Friend | 1966 | $30 |

— Jukebox issue; small hole, plays at 33 1/3 rpm

| ❑ X-1218 [PS] | I Saw the Light | 1956 | $20 |
| ❑ X-1101 | I Saw the Light/Mansion on the Hill//Six More Miles/Wedding Bells | 1955 | $70 |

— Yellow label

| ❑ X-1101 | I Saw the Light/Mansion on the Hill//Six More Miles/Wedding Bells | 1960 | $25 |

— Black label

| ❑ X-1493 | I've Just Told Mama Goodbye/House Without Love//Six More Miles/ Singing Waterfall | 1958 | $35 |

— Yellow label

| ❑ X-1493 | I've Just Told Mama Goodbye/House Without Love//Six More Miles/ Singing Waterfall | 1960 | $20 |

— Black label

| ❑ X-1555 | I Wish I Had a Nickel/ Fly Trouble//Please Don't Let Me Love You/I'm Satisfied with You | 1958 | $35 |

— Yellow label

| ❑ X-1555 | I Wish I Had a Nickel/ Fly Trouble//Please Don't Let Me Love You/I'm Satisfied with You | 1960 | $20 |

Number	Title	Yr	NM
— Black label			
❏ X-1136	Lonesome Whistle/I Jus' Don't Like This Kind of Livin'//Take These Chains from My Heart/Why Don't You Love Me?	1955	$50
— Yellow label			
❏ X-1136	Lonesome Whistle/I Jus' Don't Like This Kind of Livin'//Take These Chains from My Heart/Why Don't You Love Me?	1960	$20
— Black label			
❏ X-1102	Lost Highway/I've Just Told Mama Goodbye//Wealth Won't Save Your Soul/A House Without Love	1955	$70
— Yellow label			
❏ X-1102	Lost Highway/I've Just Told Mama Goodbye//Wealth Won't Save Your Soul/A House Without Love	1960	$25
— Black label			
❏ X-4042	Lovesick Blues/The Blues Come Around//I'm a Long Gone Daddy/Long Gone Lonesome Blues	1953	$50
— One record of "X168			
❏ X-1217	Lovesick Blues/The Blues Come Around//I'm a Long Gone Daddy/Long Gone Lonesome Blues	1956	$50
— Yellow label			
❏ X-1217	Lovesick Blues/The Blues Come Around//I'm a Long Gone Daddy/Long Gone Lonesome Blues	1960	$20
— Black label			
❏ X-1215	Low Down Blues/Someday You'll Call My Name//Alone and Forsaken/Weary Blues From Waitin'	1956	$50
— Yellow label			
❏ X-1215	Low Down Blues/Someday You'll Call My Name//Alone and Forsaken/Weary Blues From Waitin'	1960	$20
— Black label			
❏ X-1165 [PS]	Luke the Drifter	1955	$20
❏ X-1319	Mind Your Own Business/Rootie Tootie//I Ain't Got Nothin' But Time/You Better Keep It on Your Mind	1957	$50
— Yellow label			
❏ X-1319	Mind Your Own Business/Rootie Tootie//I Ain't Got Nothin' But Time/You Better Keep It on Your Mind	1960	$20
— Black label			
❏ X-168 [PS]	Moanin' the Blues	1953	$50
— Cover with X-4041 and X-4042			
❏ X-4041	Moanin' the Blues/I'm So Lonesome I Could Cry//My Sweet Love Ain't Around/Honky Tonk Blues	1953	$50
— One record of "X168			
❏ X-1216	Moanin' the Blues/I'm So Lonesome I Could Cry//My Sweet Love Ain't Around/Honky Tonk Blues	1956	$50
— Yellow label			
❏ X-1216	Moanin' the Blues/I'm So Lonesome I Could Cry//My Sweet Love Ain't Around/Honky Tonk Blues	1960	$20
— Black label			
❏ X-1215 [PS]	Moanin' the Blues Vol. 1	1956	$20
❏ X-1216 [PS]	Moanin' the Blues Vol. 2	1956	$20
❏ X-1217 [PS]	Moanin' the Blues Vol. 3	1956	$20
❏ X-1076 [PS]	Move It On Over	1954	$25
❏ X-1076	Move It On Over//Fly Trouble/Window Shopping/Pan American	1954	$75
— Yellow label			
❏ X-1076	Move It On Over//Fly Trouble/Window Shopping/Pan American	1960	$25
— Black label			
❏ X-1638	On the Banks of the Old Ponchartrain/We Live in Two Different Worlds//I'll Be a Bachelor 'Til I Die/Let's Turn Back the Years	1959	$35
— Yellow label			
❏ X-1638	On the Banks of the Old Ponchartrain/We Live in Two Different Worlds//I'll Be a Bachelor 'Til I Die/Let's Turn Back the Years	1960	$20
— Black label			

Number	Title	Yr	NM
❏ X-1047	Pictures from Life's Other Side/Men with Broken Hearts//Help Me Understand/Too Many Parties (And Too Many Pals)	1954	$75
— Yellow label			
❏ X-1643	Pictures from Life's Other Side/Men with Broken Hearts//Help Me Understand/Too Many Parties and Too Many Pals	1959	$35
— Yellow label			
❏ X-1643	Pictures from Life's Other Side/Men with Broken Hearts//Help Me Understand/Too Many Parties and Too Many Pals	1960	$20
— Black label			
❏ X-1047	Pictures from Life's Other Side/Men with Broken Hearts//Help Me Understand/Too Many Parties (And Too Many Pals)	1960	$25
— Black label			
❏ X-1491 [PS]	Sing Me a Blue Song Vol. 1	1958	$20
❏ X-1492 [PS]	Sing Me a Blue Song Vol. 2	1958	$20
❏ X-1493 [PS]	Sing Me a Blue Song Vol. 3	1958	$20
❏ X-202 [PS]	The Hank Williams Memorial Album	1953	$50
— Cover with X-4102 and X-4103			
❏ X-1554 [PS]	The Immortal Hank Williams Vol. 1	1958	$20
❏ X-1555 [PS]	The Immortal Hank Williams Vol. 2	1958	$20
❏ X-1556 [PS]	The Immortal Hank Williams Vol. 3	1958	$20
❏ SLM-4377 [PS]	The Legend Lives Anew -- Hank Williams with Strings	1966	$30
❏ X-1698 [PS]	The Lonesome Sound of Hank Williams Vol. 1	1960	$20
❏ X-1699 [PS]	The Lonesome Sound of Hank Williams Vol. 2	1960	$20
❏ X-1700 [PS]	The Lonesome Sound of Hank Williams Vol. 3	1960	$20
❏ X-1082 [PS]	There'll Be No Teardrops Tonight	1954	$25
❏ X-1082	There'll Be No Tear-Drops Tonight/You're Gonna Change (Or I'm Gonna Leave)//Nobody's Lonesome for Me/Mind Your Own Business	1954	$75
❏ X-1082	There'll Be No Tear-Drops Tonight/You're Gonna Change (Or I'm Gonna Leave)//Nobody's Lonesome for Me/Mind Your Own Business	1960	$25
— Black label			
❏ X-1554	There's No Room in My Heart/Waltz of the Wind//Pan American/With Tears in My Eyes	1958	$35
— Yellow label			
❏ X-1554	There's No Room in My Heart/Waltz of the Wind//Pan American/With Tears in My Eyes	1960	$20
— Black label			
❏ X-1491	Wedding Bells/May You Never Be Alone//Lost Highway/Why Should We Try Anymore	1958	$35
— Yellow label			
❏ X-1491	Wedding Bells/May You Never Be Alone//Lost Highway/Why Should We Try Anymore	1960	$20
— Black label			
❏ X-1165	Why Don't You Make Up Your Mind/I've Been Down That Road Before//Just Waitin'/Everything's Okay	1955	$50
— Yellow label			
❏ X-1165	Why Don't You Make Up Your Mind/I've Been Down That Road Before//Just Waitin'/Everything's Okay	1960	$20
— Black label			

WILLIAMS, HERB

MGM

Number	Title	Yr	NM
❏ 12431	Alimony Blues/Because You've Been Away	1957	$30

— This record was erroneously listed in the past as a HANK Williams record

WILLIAMS, JIM

SUN

Number	Title	Yr	NM
❏ 270	Please Don't Cry Over Me/That Depends on You	1957	$40

WILLIAMS, JIMMY

ABC-PARAMOUNT

Number	Title	Yr	NM
❏ 10523	Green Pastures (23rd Psalm)/I'm Strung Out Over You, Baby	1964	$15
❏ 10471	I Gave My Love a Cherry/Half Man	1963	$15

ATLANTIC

Number	Title	Yr	NM
❏ 2296	Walking on Air/I'm So Lost	1965	$10

CUB

Number	Title	Yr	NM
❏ 9039	C'mon Baby (What's Your Name)/Don't Put It Off (Do It Now)	1959	$20
❏ 9031	My Pledge and My Promise/Keep Me with You	1959	$20

DYNO VOICE

Number	Title	Yr	NM
❏ 931	Mushroom City/Standing There	1969	$8

HULL

Number	Title	Yr	NM
❏ 765	I Can't Help Falling in Love/Smile	1964	$10

LIMELIGHT

Number	Title	Yr	NM
❏ 3038	Mrs. Cherry/Keoto'To	1964	$10

MGM

Number	Title	Yr	NM
❏ 12262	Alpha and Omega/Where Will I Shelter My Sheep	1956	$30
❏ 12362	Throwing My Life Away/We're Drifting Further Apart	1956	$30

ROULETTE

Number	Title	Yr	NM
❏ 4303	There Is No Doubt/What a Change	1960	$20

WILLIAMS, JOHNNY

CINNAMON

Number	Title	Yr	NM
❏ 812	Love Me for a While/That's All That Matters	1974	$6

COLUMBIA

Number	Title	Yr	NM
❏ 4-42777	Black Knight/Augie's Great Piano	1963	$10

WILLIAMS, JUANITA

GOLDEN WORLD

Number	Title	Yr	NM
❏ 18	Baby Boy/You Knew What You Was Gettin'	1964	$40

WINGATE

Number	Title	Yr	NM
❏ 08	Some Things You Never Get Used To/You Knew What You Were Gettin'	1965	$40

WILLIAMS, LARRY

BELL

Number	Title	Yr	NM
❏ 813	I Could Love You Baby/Can't Find No Substitute for Love	1969	$10

— With Johnny Watson

CHESS

Number	Title	Yr	NM
❏ 1745	Get Ready/Baby, Baby	1959	$30
❏ 1761	I Wanna Know/Like a Gentle Man	1960	$30
❏ 1805	Lawdy Mama/Fresh Out of Tears	1961	$30
❏ 1736	My Baby's Got Soul/Every Day I Wonder	1959	$30
❏ 1764	Oh Baby/I Hear My Baby	1960	$30

EL BAM

Number	Title	Yr	NM
❏ 69	Call on Me/Boss Lovin'	1965	$15

FANTASY

Number	Title	Yr	NM
❏ 806	Doing the Best I Can (With What I Got)/Gimme Some	1977	$5
❏ 810	One Thing or the Other (Part 1)/One Thing or the Other (Part 2)	1977	$5

MERCURY

Number	Title	Yr	NM
❏ 72147	Woman/Can't Help Myself	1963	$20

OKEH

Number	Title	Yr	NM
❏ 7280	I Am the One/You Ask for One Good Reason	1967	$10
❏ 7259	This Old Heart (Is So Lonely)/I'd Rather Fight Than Switch	1966	$10

SMASH

Number	Title	Yr	NM
❏ 2035	Call on Me/Boss Lovin'	1966	$15

SPECIALTY

Number	Title	Yr	NM
❏ 658	Bad Boy/She Said "Yeah"	1959	$40
❏ 658	Bad Boy/She Said "Yeah"	1984	$4
— Orange vinyl			
❏ 615	Bony Moronie/You Bug Me, Baby	1957	$50
❏ 615	Bony Moronie/You Bug Me, Baby	1984	$4
— Red vinyl			
❏ 626	Dizzy, Miss Lizzy/Slow Down	1958	$50
❏ 626 [PS]	Dizzy, Miss Lizzy/Slow Down	1958	$100
❏ 626	Dizzy, Miss Lizzy/Slow Down	1984	$4
— Blue vinyl			

Number	Title	Yr	NM
❑ 677	Give Me Your Love/Teardrops	1959	$30
❑ 634	Hootchy-Koo/The Dummy	1958	$30
❑ 634	Hootchy-Koo/The Dummy	1984	$4

—Green vinyl

Number	Title	Yr	NM
❑ 647	I Was a Fool/Peaches and Cream	1958	$30
❑ 608	Short Fat Fannie/High School Dance	1957	$50
❑ 608	Short Fat Fannie/High School Dance	1984	$4

—Gold vinyl

Number	Title	Yr	NM
❑ 665	Steal a Little Kiss/I Can't Stop Loving You	1959	$30
❑ 682	Ting-a-Ling/Little Schoolgirl	1960	$30
❑ 682	Ting-a-Ling/Little Schoolgirl	1984	$4

—Gold vinyl

VENTURE

Number	Title	Yr	NM
❑ 622	Shake Your Body Girl/Love I Can't Seem to Find It	1968	$10
❑ 627	Wake Up (Nothing Comes to a Sleeper But a Dream)/Love I Can't Seem to Find It	1968	$10

WILLIAMS, LAWTON

D

Number	Title	Yr	NM
❑ 1120	I Don't Care Who Knows/Satan's Bell	1960	$20

DECCA

Number	Title	Yr	NM
❑ 9-30839	Iron Curtain/House Full of Love	1959	$20
❑ 9-30709	Texas vs. Alaska/Don't Let Anybody Tell You	1958	$20

GROOVE

Number	Title	Yr	NM
❑ 58-0011	The Carpetbaggers/Mama Pinch a Penny	1963	$15

MERCURY

Number	Title	Yr	NM
❑ 71867	Anywhere There's People/Ploughed Ground	1961	$15
❑ 71780	The Big Fire/John and Mary Doe	1961	$15

RCA VICTOR

Number	Title	Yr	NM
❑ 47-7188	Casino on the Hill/If You're Waitin' on Me	1958	$30
❑ 47-8142	Don't Destroy Me/Rock of Gibraltar	1963	$12
❑ 47-8407	Everything's OK on the LBJ/Don't Look Down	1964	$10
❑ 47-7105	Foreign Love/Don't Burn the Bridge Behind You	1957	$30
❑ 47-8359	I'm Not All Here/Stay on the Ball	1964	$10
❑ 47-8203	Mountain of a Man/In Love with You	1963	$10
❑ 47-8300	Squawlein/It Looks Like You Love Me	1963	$10
❑ 47-8514	War on Poverty/Power of Love	1965	$10

WILLIAMS, LESTER

DUKE

Number	Title	Yr	NM
❑ 131	Crazy 'Bout You Baby/Don't Take Your Love from Me	1954	$50
❑ 123	Let's Do It/Good Lovin' Baby	1954	$60

IMPERIAL

Number	Title	Yr	NM
❑ 5402	McDonald's Daughter/Daddy Loves You	1956	$60

SPECIALTY

Number	Title	Yr	NM
❑ 450	Brand New Baby/If I Knew How Much I Loved You	1953	$125
❑ 422	I Can't Lose with the Stuff I Use/My Home Ain't Here	1952	$125
❑ 431	Let Me Tell You a Thing or Two/Tryin' to Forget	1952	$200
❑ 437	Sweet Lovin' Daddy/Lost Gal	1952	$200

WILLIAMS, LEW

IMPERIAL

Number	Title	Yr	NM
❑ 5411	Bop Bop Ba Doo Bop/Something I Said	1956	$120
❑ 5394	Cat Talk/Gone Ape Man	1956	$120
❑ 5429	Centipede/Abra Cadabra	1957	$120
❑ 8306	Don't Mention My Name/I'll Play Your Game	1956	$200

WILLIAMS, MASON

MERCURY

Number	Title	Yr	NM
❑ 72603	Exciting Accident/Love Our Wine	1966	$10

WARNER BROS.

Number	Title	Yr	NM
❑ 7235	Baroque-a-Nova/Wanderlove	1968	$5
❑ 7245	Cinderella Rockafella/Generatah-Oscillath	1968	$5
❑ 7190	Classical Gas/Long Time Blues	1968	$6
❑ 7402	Find a Reason to Believe/Jose's Piece	1970	$5
❑ 7301	Gift of Song/Major Thang	1969	$5
❑ 7272	Greensleeves/13 Dollar Stella	1969	$5
❑ 7513	Here I Am Again/Train Ride in G	1971	$5
❑ 7248	Saturday Night at the World/One Minute Commercial	1968	$5

7-Inch Extended Plays

Number	Title	Yr	NM
❑ S1729	Overture/All the Time/Baroque-a-Nova//She's Gone Away/The Prince's Panties/Long Time Blues	1968	$10

—Jukebox issue; small hole, plays at 33 1/3 rpm

Number	Title	Yr	NM
❑ S1729 [PS]	The Mason Williams' Phonograph Record	1968	$12

WILLIAMS, MAURICE, AND THE ZODIACS

ATLANTIC

Number	Title	Yr	NM
❑ 2199	Funny/Loneliness	1963	$20

—As "The Zodiacs

Number	Title	Yr	NM
❑ 2741	Sweetness/Whirlpool	1970	$5

COLE

Number	Title	Yr	NM
❑ 100	Golly Gee/"I" Town	1959	$60
❑ 101	Lover (Where Are You)/She's Mine	1959	$50

DEESU

Number	Title	Yr	NM
❑ 302	Baby Baby/Being Without You	1967	$30
❑ 311	Don't Be Half Safe/How to Pick a Winner	1967	$30
❑ 309	Don't Ever Leave Me/Surely	1967	$30
❑ 304	May I/This Feeling	1967	$30
❑ 307	Ooh Poo Pa Doo (Part 1)/Ooh Poo Pa Doo (Part 2)	1967	$30
❑ 318	Stay '68 (Live Version)/Dance, Dance, Dance	1968	$20

HERALD

Number	Title	Yr	NM
❑ 556	Always/I Remember	1961	$20
❑ 559	Do I/Come Along	1961	$20
❑ 572	It's Alright/Here I Stand	1962	$20
❑ 565	Please/High Blood Pressure	1961	$20
❑ 563	Someday/Come and Get It	1961	$20
❑ 552	Stay/Do You Believe	1960	$30

RCA

Number	Title	Yr	NM
❑ 5363-7-R	Stay/She's Like the Wind	1987	$3

—B-side by Patrick Swayze

SEA HORN

Number	Title	Yr	NM
❑ 503	My Baby's Gone/Return	1964	$20

SELWYN

Number	Title	Yr	NM
❑ 5121	Say Yeah/College Girl	1959	$60

SPHERE SOUND

Number	Title	Yr	NM
❑ 707	So Fine/The Winds	1965	$15

VEE JAY

Number	Title	Yr	NM
❑ 678	May I/Lollipop	1965	$30

VEEP

Number	Title	Yr	NM
❑ 1294	My Reason for Living/The Four Corners	1969	$8

WILLIAMS, OTIS, AND HIS CHARMS

DELUXE

Number	Title	Yr	NM
❑ 6187	Blues Stay Away from Me/Funny What True Love Can Do	1959	$30
❑ 6105	Blues Stay Away from Me/Pardon Me	1957	$30
❑ 6165	Burnin' Lips/Red Hot Love (Do This Love)	1958	$30
❑ 6158	Could This Be Magic/Oh Julie	1958	$30
❑ 6174	Don't Wake Up the Kids/You'll Remain Forever	1958	$30
❑ 6149	Dynamite Darling/Well Oh Well	1957	$30
❑ 6090	Gum Drop/Save Me, Save Me	1955	$40

—As "Otis Williams and His New Group

Number	Title	Yr	NM
❑ 6098	Gypsy Lady/I'll Remember You	1956	$40
❑ 6097	I'd Like to Thank You Mr. D.J./Whirlwind	1956	$40
❑ 6185	I Knew It All the Time/Tears of Happiness	1959	$30
❑ 6186	In Paradise/Who Knows	1959	$30
❑ 6093	Ivory Tower/In Paradise	1956	$40
❑ 6160	Let Some Love in Your Heart/Baby-O	1958	$30
❑ 6088	Miss the Love/Tell Me Now	1955	$40

—As "Otis Williams and His New Group

Number	Title	Yr	NM
❑ 6178	My Friends/The Secret	1958	$30
❑ 6183	My Prayer Tonight/Watch Dog	1959	$30
❑ 6095	One Night Only/It's All Over	1956	$40
❑ 6181	Pretty Little Things Called Girls/Welcome Home	1959	$30
❑ 6137	Talking to Myself/One Kind Word from You	1957	$30
❑ 6091	That's Your Mistake/Too Late I Learned	1955	$40
❑ 6115	Walkin' After Midnight/I'm Waiting Just for You	1957	$30

KING

Number	Title	Yr	NM
❑ 6034	Bye Bye Baby/Please Believe in Me	1966	$20
❑ 5323	Chief Um (Take It Easy)/It's a Treat	1960	$30
❑ 5372	Image of a Girl/Wait a Minute Baby	1960	$60
❑ 5816	It Just Ain't Right/It'll Never Happen Again	1963	$20
❑ 5455	Little Turtle Dove/So Can I	1961	$30
❑ 5527	Pardon Me/Panic	1961	$30
❑ 5332	Silver Star/Rickety Rickshaw Man	1960	$30
❑ 5389	The First Sign of Love/So Be It	1960	$30
❑ 5558	Two Hearts/The Secret	1961	$30
❑ 5421	Wait/And Take My Love	1960	$30
❑ 5682	When We Get Together/Only Young Once	1962	$20

OKEH

Number	Title	Yr	NM
❑ 7261	Ain't Gonna Walk Your Dog No More/Your Sweet Love (Rained Over Me)	1966	$20
❑ 7225	Baby, You Turn Me On/Love Don't Grow on Trees	1965	$20
❑ 7235	I Fall to Pieces/Gotta Get Myself Together	1965	$20
❑ 7248	I Got Loving/Welcome Home	1966	$20

SCEPTER

Number	Title	Yr	NM
❑ 12376	Here Lie the Bones of Nellie Jones/When You Turn On the Love	1973	$8

STOP

Number	Title	Yr	NM
❑ 301	Begging to You/(B-side unknown)	1968	$12
❑ 306	Begging to You/Everybody's Got a Song But Me	1968	$12
❑ 388	I Wanna Go Country/Rocky Top	1971	$8

—As "Otis Williams and the Midnight Cowboys

Number	Title	Yr	NM
❑ 360	Ling, Ting, Tong/For the Love	1970	$12

7-Inch Extended Plays

DELUXE

Number	Title	Yr	NM
❑ EP-385	*That's Your Mistake/Too Late I Learned/Miss the Love/Gum Drop	1956	$300
❑ EP-385 [PS]	Otis Williams and His Charms	1956	$300

WILLIAMS, ROGER

KAPP

Number	Title	Yr	NM
❑ 299	Adeste Fideles/Hark the Herald Angels Sing	1959	$10
❑ 175	Almost Paradise/For the First Time	1957	$8
❑ 2110	America the Beautiful/Ain't No Mountain High Enough	1970	$4
❑ 169	Anastasia/A Serenade for Joy	1956	$10
❑ 210	Arrivederci Roma/Sentimental Touch	1958	$8
❑ 707	Autumn Leaves 1965/Autumn Leaves 1955	1965	$6

—Black label stock copy

Number	Title	Yr	NM
❑ 707	Autumn Leaves 1965/Autumn Leaves 1955	1965	$8

—Special gold label promotional copy with "Celebrrating the 10th Anniversary" at right

Number	Title	Yr	NM
❑ 116	Autumn Leaves/Take Care	1955	$12
❑ 116 [PS]	Autumn Leaves/Take Care	1955	$30
❑ 767	Born Free/Jimmie's Train	1966	$6
❑ 560	Cardinal/Walking Alone	1963	$6
❑ 505	Cold, Cold Heart/San Antonio Rose	1963	$6
❑ 545	Danke Schoen/Look Again	1963	$6
❑ 257	Dearer Than Dear/The Key to the Kingdom	1959	$8
❑ 949	Elvira Madigan Theme/Only for Lovers	1968	$5
❑ 574	Felicia/Takewood Nocturne	1964	$6
❑ 2007	Galveston/Mini Minuet	1969	$4
❑ 144	Hi-Lili, Hi-Lo/My Dream Sonata	1956	$12
❑ 2148	How Can You Mend a Broken Heart/Bach Talk	1971	$4
❑ 224	Indiscreet/Young and Warm and Wonderful	1958	$8
❑ 2189	Lady Sings the Blues/Play Me	1972	$4
❑ 138	La Mer (Beyond the Sea)/Song of Devotion	1956	$12
❑ 738	Lara's Theme from "Dr. Zhivago"/Dulcinea	1966	$6
❑ 2064	Let It Be Me/Fill the World with Love	1969	$4
❑ 607	Lollipops and Roses/Whistlin'	1964	$6
❑ 821	Love Me Forever/Sweet Pea	1967	$5
❑ 975	Love Theme from La Strada/Gentle on My Mind	1969	$5
❑ 995	Love Theme from Romeo and Juliet/As Long As He Needs Me	1969	$5
❑ 2165	Love Theme from The Godfather/Life Is What You Name It	1972	$4
❑ 437 [PS]	Maria/Even Tide	1961	$15
❑ 300	Mary's Little Boy Child/Winter Wonderland	1959	$10
❑ 265	Mockin' Bird Hill/Memories Are Made of This	1959	$8
❑ 186	Moonlight Love/Every Little Movement	1957	$8
❑ 440	Santa Claus, Santa Claus (We Love You)/Jingle Bells	1961	$10
❑ 890	Spinning Song/Glory of Love	1968	$5
❑ 2084	Suicide Is Painless/The Time for Love Is Anytime	1970	$4
❑ 2140	Summer Knows/Your Song	1971	$4
❑ 801	Sunrise, Sunset/Edelweiss	1966	$5
❑ 301	Sunrise Serenade/Cool Water	1959	$8
❑ 301 [PS]	Sunrise Serenade/Cool Water	1959	$15
❑ 907	The Impossible Dream/If You Go	1968	$5
❑ 2078	The Lonely Ones/I'm a Believer	1970	$4
❑ 533	Theme from "11th Hour"/Janie Is Her Name	1963	$6
❑ 2123	Theme from Love Story/For All We Know	1971	$4
❑ 2177	The Way of Love/Tchaikovsky '73	1972	$4

Number	Title	Yr	NM
❏ 2043	The Windmills of Your Mind/ Fill the World with Love	1969	$4
❏ 246	The World Outside/ Tchaikovsky Piano Concerto	1958	$8
❏ 587	This Is My Prayer/ Roger's Bumble Bee	1964	$6
❏ 197	Till/Big Town	1957	$8
❏ 843	Tiny Bubbles/More Than a Miracle	1967	$5
❏ KJB-48	Try to Remember/ (B-side unknown)	1965	$6
❏ 156	Tumbling Tumbleweeds/I'll Always Walk with You	1956	$10
❏ 161	Two Different Worlds/ Nights in Verona	1956	$10

— With Jane Morgan

Number	Title	Yr	NM
❏ 522	Walking Alone/On the Trail	1963	$6
❏ 2135	Wandering Star/Your Song	1971	$4
❏ 127	Wanting You/Night Wind	1955	$10
❏ 929	Who Killed Ezra Brymay/Marlena	1968	$5

MCA

Number	Title	Yr	NM
❏ 40529	Country Comfort/Roger's Bumble Bee (Latter Day)	1976	$3
❏ 40185	Dark Lady/Solace	1974	$3
❏ 40571	God Bless America/ Grieg's You Know What By Roger You Know Who	1976	$3
❏ 40725	Love Theme from "A Star Is Born"/Theme from "Airport '77"	1977	$3
❏ 40669	Main Title from "King Kong"/Love Song	1976	$3
❏ 40044	Theme from "Baxter"/ Rain Song	1973	$3
❏ 40155	Theme from "Exodus"/ Hungarian Dance No. 5	1973	$3
❏ 40341	Theme from "Murder on the Orient Express"/Half-Breed	1974	$3
❏ 40741	Theme from "New York, New York"/Me	1977	$3
❏ 40451	Theme from "Rollerball"/Bolero	1975	$3
❏ 40373	Theme from "The Young and the Restless"/ Melody to Dawn	1975	$4
❏ 40098	Tie a Yellow Ribbon Round the Ole Oak Tree/Rain Song	1973	$3

WARNER BROS.

Number	Title	Yr	NM
❏ 49584	Somewhere in Time/ Bee Side	1980	$3
❏ KE-751	*Till/Marcheta/Always/ The Merry Widow Waltz	1958	$8
❏ KE-753	April Love/Que Sera, Sera//Fascination/ Brahms' A Flat Waltz	1958	$8
❏ KE-708	Autumn Leaves/Take Care// Summertime/'Til Roses Cry	1955	$8
❏ KE-738	Buttons and Bows/Sunday, Monday or Always//Oh, What It Seemed to Be/ Zip-a-Dee Doo-Dah	1957	$8
❏ KE-738 [PS]	Songs of the Fabulous Forties Vol. 2	1957	$8
❏ KE-754	Tammy/Oh, My Papa// Arrivaderci Roma/The High and the Mighty	1958	$8
❏ KE-757 [PS]	(title unknown)	1958	$8
❏ KE-753 [PS]	(title unknown)	1958	$8
❏ KE-754 [PS]	(title unknown)	1958	$8

WILLIAMS, TEX

BOONE

Number	Title	Yr	NM
❏ 1044	Another Day, Another Dollar in the Hole/The Big Man	1966	$8
❏ 1032	Big Tennessee/My Last Two Tens	1965	$8
❏ 1059	Black Jack County/Ain't Gonna Walk Your Dog	1967	$8
❏ 1040	Bottom Land/First Step Down	1966	$8
❏ 1036	Bottom of a Mountain/ Tears Are Only Rain	1965	$8
❏ 1052	Crazy Life/The Toy Piano	1966	$8
❏ 1072	Here's to You and Me/If Not for You There Could Go Me	1968	$8
❏ 1065	Mother's Flower Garden/ She's Somebody Else's Heartache Now	1967	$8
❏ 1069	Smoke, Smoke, Smoke -- '68/Lonely One	1968	$8
❏ 1080	The Tail's Been Wagging/ Look Beyond Your Dreams	1969	$8
❏ 1028	Too Many Tigers/ Winter Snow	1965	$8

CAPITOL

Number	Title	Yr	NM
❏ 4690	A Hundred Years from Now/ How Do You Lie to a Heart	1962	$10
❏ F1286	Alimony/I Want Gold	1950	$30
❏ 4479	Are You Sure?/Think It Over Boys	1960	$15
❏ F40184	Beer Barrel Polka/ Banjo Polka	1950	$30
❏ F1006	Birmingham Bounce/ Great Big Needle	1950	$30
❏ F40185	Capitol Polka/Milkman Polka	1950	$30
❏ F1345	Cheaters Never Prosper/ Don't Make Love	1950	$30
❏ F1799	Cocker Spaniel Polka/I Want to Be Near You	1951	$30

Number	Title	Yr	NM
❏ F40186	Cow Bell Polka/ Yodeling Polka	1950	$30

— The above four, which comprise a box set entitled "Polkas!", were issued on 78 in 1948

Number	Title	Yr	NM
❏ F40183	Cowboy Polka/ Big Bass Polka	1950	$30
❏ F1087	Happy Feet/You Two Time Me, I'll Two Time You	1950	$30
❏ F1475	I Lost My Gal from Memphis/One Way Ticket	1951	$30
❏ F1700	Love and Devotion/ Black Strap Molasses	1951	$30
❏ F940	My San Fernando Rose/ Was Yesterday a Dream	1950	$30
❏ F1390	She Didn't Even Kiss Me Goodbye/Tulsa Trot	1951	$30
❏ F40001	Smoke! Smoke! Smoke! (That Cigarette)/ Roundup Polka	1949	$50
❏ 4413	Smoke! Smoke! Smoke! (That Cigarette)/That's What I Like About the West	1960	$15
❏ F1540	Sugar Coated Love/ Goodnight Cincinnati, Good Morning Tennessee	1951	$30
❏ F1437	That's What I Like About the West/Smoke! Smoke! Smoke! (That Cigarette)	1951	$30
❏ F1166	Wild Card/Tamburitza Boogie	1950	$30
❏ F40276	With Men Who Know Tobacco Best (It's Women Two to One)/Three Little Girls Dressed in Blue	1950	$40

DECCA

Number	Title	Yr	NM
❏ 9-29385	Air Mail Special/ Williams Rag	1954	$30
❏ 9-30037	Artichokes/Reno, Town of Broken Hearts	1956	$20
❏ 9-28660	Big Big Lie/Changeable	1953	$30
❏ 9-30328	Every Night/Talkin' to the Blues	1957	$20
❏ 9-30553	False Face/Danny Boy of San Angelo	1958	$20
❏ 9-28721	Hey Mister Cotton-Picker/ Don't Call My Name	1953	$30

— With Roberta Lee

Number	Title	Yr	NM
❏ 9-29077	If You'd Believe in Me/Honey	1954	$30
❏ 9-30459	Let's Go Rockabilly/ Long Lost Love	1957	$30
❏ 9-29578	Old Betsy/Be Sure You're Right (Then Go Ahead)	1955	$30
❏ 9-29900	Shake the Hand of a Stranger/Revival Is On Its Way	1956	$20
❏ 9-29308	Sidetracked/Can I Say the Same About You	1954	$30
❏ 9-30672	The Ballad of Thunder Road/Bad Man's Country	1958	$20
❏ 9-28809	The Deck of Cards/ Seven Days in Heaven	1953	$30
❏ 9-29202	They Were Doing the Mambo/That's the Good Lord Saying "Good Morning	1954	$30
❏ 9-30161	When I Call the Roll/ You're Cold, So Cold	1956	$20

DOT

Number	Title	Yr	NM
❏ 16850	Bummin' Around/ Keeper of Boot Hill	1966	$8

GRANITE

Number	Title	Yr	NM
❏ 512	Bum, Bum, Bum/Mother Was a Sideman	1974	$6
❏ 505	Is This All You Hear/ Roll, Muddy River	1974	$6
❏ 507	Those Lazy, Hazy, Crazy Days of Summer/ Nowhere, West Virginia	1974	$6

LIBERTY

Number	Title	Yr	NM
❏ 55711	Empty Letter/Closer, Closer, Closer	1964	$12
❏ 55652	Late Movies/Long John	1963	$12
❏ 55698	Mr. All Alone/Pickin' White Gold	1964	$10
❏ 55760	Smokey Hollow/Between Today and Tomorrow	1965	$12
❏ 55537	Where the Sad People Are/ Five Foot Deep in Teardrops	1963	$10

RCA VICTOR

Number	Title	Yr	NM
❏ 47-4561	Double Shuffle/Senator from Tennessee	1952	$30

— With Dinah Shore

Number	Title	Yr	NM
❏ 47-4897	Miracle Waltz/Sweet Little Boogalie	1952	$30
❏ 47-4506	Only Politickin'/ Shame on You	1952	$30
❏ 47-4409	Shrimp Boats/Urn on the Mantel	1951	$30
❏ 47-4708	Sinful/Bronco Buster's Ball	1952	$30

SHASTA

Number	Title	Yr	NM
❏ 122	Bummin' Around/ Keeper of Boot Hill	1959	$15
❏ 116	The Battle of New Orleans/ Keeper of Boot Hill	1959	$15
❏ 130	Where Do We Go from Here/Blue Ribbons	1960	$15

— With Bonnie Sloan

7-Inch Extended Plays

DECCA

Number	Title	Yr	NM
❏ ED2174 [PS]	All Time Greats	1955	$30
❏ ED2229	(contents unknown)	1955	$30
❏ ED2229 [PS]	Dance-O-Rama	1955	$30
❏ ED2174	Smoke! Smoke! Smoke! (That Cigarette)/Wild Card// The Leaf of Love/That's What I Like About the West	1955	$30

WILLIAMS, TIMMY

MALA

Number	Title	Yr	NM
❏ 515	Competition/Wipe Away Your Tears	1965	$1200

WILLIAMS, TONY

Lead singer of THE PLATTERS when they were having their biggest hits in the 1950s. Also see THE PLATTERS.

DOT

Number	Title	Yr	NM
❏ 16806	Endless Street/Smoke, Drink, Play 21	1965	$8

MERCURY

Number	Title	Yr	NM
❏ 71532	Charmaine/Peg o' My Heart	1959	$30
❏ 71158	Let's Start All Over Again/ When You Return	1957	$30

PHILIPS

Number	Title	Yr	NM
❏ 40069	Chloe/Second Best	1962	$10
❏ 40141	How Come/When I Had You	1963	$10
❏ 40123	Twenty-Four Lonely Hours/Save Me	1963	$10

REPRISE

Number	Title	Yr	NM
❏ 20067	Come Along Now/ That's More Like It	1962	$20
❏ 20136	Dream/Loving You	1963	$50

— Released only in Italy

Number	Title	Yr	NM
❏ 20056	It's So Easy to Surrender/ That's More Like It	1962	$50

— Released only in Italy

Number	Title	Yr	NM
❏ 20030	Miracle/My Prayer	1961	$20
❏ 20073	Sing, Lover, Sing/Mandalino	1962	$50

— Released only in Hong Kong

Number	Title	Yr	NM
❏ 20019	Sleepless Nights/Movin' In	1961	$20

WILLIAMSON, SONNY BOY (1)

RCA VICTOR

Number	Title	Yr	NM
❏ 50-0005	Little Girl/Bring Another Half a Pint	1949	$300

— Orange vinyl

Number	Title	Yr	NM
❏ 50-0030	Southern Dream/I Love You For Myself	1949	$300

— Orange vinyl

WILLIAMSON, SONNY BOY (2)

ACE

Number	Title	Yr	NM
❏ 511	Boppin' with Sonny/ No Nights By Myself	1955	$120

CHECKER

Number	Title	Yr	NM
❏ 883	Born Blind/Ninety-Nine	1958	$50
❏ 1134	Bring It On Home/ Down Child	1966	$30
❏ 1036	Bye Bye Bird/Help Me	1963	$40
❏ 910	Cross My Heart/Dissatisfied	1958	$50
❏ 824	Don't Start Me Talkin'/ All My Love In Vain	1955	$125
❏ 864	I Don't Know/Fattening Frogs for Snakes	1957	$60
❏ 834	Let Me Explain/ Your Imagination	1956	$70
❏ 927	Let Your Conscience Be Your Guide/Unseeing Eye	1959	$50
❏ 1080	My Younger Days/I Want You Close to Me	1964	$40
❏ 1003	One Way Out/Nine Below Zero	1962	$40
❏ 956	Temperature 110/ Lonesome Cabin	1960	$40
❏ 943	The Goat/It's Sad to Be Alone	1960	$40
❏ 975	The Hurt/Stop Right Now	1961	$40
❏ 963	Trust My Baby/Too Close Together	1960	$40
❏ 1065	Trying to Get Back on My Feet/Decoration Day	1963	$40

TRUMPET

Number	Title	Yr	NM
❏ 212	Cat Hop/Too Close Together	1952	$100
❏ 228	From the Bottom/ Empty Bedroom	1953	$75
❏ 215	Gettin' Out of Town/ She Brought Life Back to the Dead	1952	$100
❏ 168	Stop Now Baby/ Mr. Downchild	1952	$125
❏ 144	West Memphis Blues/I Cross My Heart	1951	$125

WILLIE AND THE WHEELS

DUNHILL

Number	Title	Yr	NM
❏ 4002	Skateboard Craze/ Do What You Do	1965	$50

WILLING, FOY, AND THE RIDERS OF THE PURPLE SAGE

Number	Title	Yr	NM
CAPITOL			
❏ F1070	Texas Blues/Sometime	1950	$50
CHALLENGE			
❏ 1011	Cool Water/No One to Cry To	1958	$30
DECCA			
❏ 9-46365	Detour/Address Unknown	1951	$30
ROULETTE			
❏ 4055	Cowboy/Soft Winds	1958	$20

WILLIS BROTHERS, THE

Number	Title	Yr	NM
STARDAY			
❏ 782	Ain't It Funny/Goin' to Town	1966	$10
❏ 863	Alcohol and No. 2 Diesel/My Ramblin' Boy	1969	$8
❏ 713	A Six Foot Two by Four/Strange Old Town	1965	$10
❏ 570	Big Daddy/It's the Miles	1961	$20
❏ 703	Blazing Smokestack/Too Early to Get Up	1964	$10
❏ 796	Bob/Show Her Lots of Gold	1967	$8
❏ 874	Buyin' Popcorn/1,000 Acres	1969	$8
❏ 884	Cold North Wind/Gypsy Rose and Me	1969	$8
❏ 848	Diesel Driving Donut Dunkin' Dan/A Moonlight Ride in a Diesel	1968	$8
❏ 555	Everlovin' Dixieland/Tattooed Lady	1961	$20
❏ 681	Give Me 40 Acres (To Turn This Rig Around)/Gonna Buy Me a Juke Box	1964	$10
❏ 662	Linda Do the Bubble Up/Wash Up	1964	$15
❏ 532	Little Footprints in the Snow/Y'All Come	1960	$20
❏ 830	Ode to Big Joe/Drivin's in My Blood	1968	$8
❏ 730	Pinball Anonymous/When I Came Driving Through	1965	$10
❏ 518	Pretty Diamonds/Billy the Kid	1960	$20
❏ 625	Private Lee/Ax Cabin	1963	$15
❏ 592	Sally's Bangs/Honey, Do You Love Your Man	1962	$15
❏ 812	Somebody Knows My Dog/The End of the Road	1967	$8
❏ 748	Swing 'Til My Rose Breaks/Love Thy Neighbor	1965	$10
❏ 760	Three Sheets in the Wind/Waltzing with Sin	1966	$10
❏ 645	Truck Driver's Queen/Who's Next on Your List	1963	$15

WILLIS, CHUCK

Number	Title	Yr	NM
ATLANTIC			
❏ 1168	Betty and Dupree/My Crying Eyes	1958	$30
❏ 1130	C.C. Rider/Ease the Pain	1957	$30
❏ 1098	It's Too Late/Kansas City Woman	1956	$30
❏ 1148	Love Me, Cherry/That Train Has Gone	1957	$30
❏ 2029	My Baby/Just One Kiss	1959	$30
❏ 1192	Thunder and Lightning/My Life	1958	$30
❏ 1179	What Am I Living For/Hang Up My Rock And Roll Shoes	1958	$40
OKEH			
❏ 7041	Change My Mind/My Heart's Been Broke Again	1954	$50
❏ 7067	Come On Home/It Were You	1956	$50
❏ 6985	Don't Deceive Me/I've Been Treated Wrong Too Long	1953	$60
❏ 7048	Give and Take/I've Been Away Too Long	1954	$50
❏ 6952	Going to the River/Baby Has Left Me Again	1953	$60
❏ 7055	I Can Tell/One More Break	1955	$50
❏ 7029	I Feel So Bad/Need One More Chance	1954	$70
❏ 6810	I Tried/I Rule My House	1951	$125
❏ 7051	Lawdy Miss Mary/Love-Struck	1955	$50
❏ 6841	Let's Jump Tonight/It's Too Late	1951	$100
❏ 6873	Lud Mouth Lucy/Here I Come	1952	$100
❏ 7004	My Baby's Coming Home/When My Day Is Over	1953	$60
❏ 6905	My Story/Caldonia	1952	$60
❏ 6930	Salty Tears/Wrong Lake to Catch a Fish	1953	$60
❏ 7062	Search My Heart/Ring-Ding-Doo	1955	$50
❏ 7070	Two Spoons of Tears/Charged with Cheating	1956	$50

7-Inch Extended Plays

Number	Title	Yr	NM
ATLANTIC			
❏ EP609	C.C. Rider/Ease the Pain//That Train Has Gone/Love Me, Cherry	1958	$120
❏ EP591 [PS]	Chuck Willis	1957	$250
❏ EP612 [PS]	What Am I Living For	1958	$250
❏ EP612	What Am I Living For/Hang Up My Rock and Roll Shoes//Betty and Dupree/My Crying Eyes	1958	$175
EPIC			
❏ 7070 [PS]	Chuck Willis Sings the Blues	1956	$250
❏ 7070	(contents unknown)	1956	$250

WILLIS, HAL

Number	Title	Yr	NM
ATHENS			
❏ 704	Crazy Little Mama/Walkin' Dream	1958	$200
ATLANTIC			
❏ 1114	Bop-A-Dee, Bop-A-Doo/My Pink Cadillac	1956	$200
DECCA			
❏ 30949	Poor Little Jimmy/That's the Way It Goes	1959	$15
MERCURY			
❏ 71933	Bayou Pierre/I Love You (Around the World)	1962	$15
SIMS			
❏ 250	Creole Rose/When It's Springtime in Alaska	1965	$15
❏ 288	Doggin' in the U.S. Mail/The Battle of Viet Nam	1966	$15
❏ 307	Parson from Paint Rock/Private Dick	1966	$15
❏ 207	The Lumberjack/Dig Me a Hole	1964	$15
❏ 224	The One I Love/What's Left of Me	1965	$15
❏ 243	Thumb and Shoes/Nopper the Topper	1965	$15

WILLIS SISTERS, THE

Number	Title	Yr	NM
RENOWN			
❏ 126	Doodley Duck/It's Christmas Again	1960	$15

WILLOWS, THE (1)

Number	Title	Yr	NM
MELBA			
❏ 102	Church Bells Are Ringing/Beby Tell Me	1956	$300
— Original A-side title			
❏ 102	Church Bells May Ring/Baby Tell Me	1956	$125
❏ 106	Do You Love Me/My Angel	1956	$70
❏ 115	Little Darlin'/My Angel	1957	$100

WILLOWS, THE (2)

Number	Title	Yr	NM
4-STAR			
❏ 1753	There's a Dance Goin' On/Now That I Have You	1961	$300

WILLOWS, THE (3)

Number	Title	Yr	NM
HEIDI			
❏ 103	It's Such a Shame/Tears in Your Eyes	1964	$20
❏ 107	Sit by the Fire/Such a Night	1965	$20

WILLOWS, THE (4)

Number	Title	Yr	NM
MGM			
❏ 13484	Hurtin' All Over/My Kinda Guy	1966	$15
❏ 13714	Snow Song/Outside the City	1967	$15

WILLS, BOB

Number	Title	Yr	NM
COLUMBIA			
❏ 2-158	Goodbye Liza Jane/I'm Feelin' Bad	1949	$60
— Microgroove 33 1/3 rpm 7-inch single, small hole			
❏ 2-220	Misery/You're There	1949	$60
— Microgroove 7-inch 33 1/3 single, small hole			
DECCA			
❏ 9-30367	I'll Always Be in Love with You/Oh Monah	1957	$30
❏ 9-30165	It's the Bottle Talking/Lily Dale	1956	$30
❏ 9-29604	San Antonio Rose/I'll Follow Wherever You Go	1955	$30
❏ 9-29432	Sincerely/Cornball Rag	1955	$30
❏ 9-29909	So Let's Rock/Sugar Baby	1956	$30
❏ 9-30068	Texas Fiddler/My Shoes Keep Walking Back to You	1956	$30
❏ 9-29453	The Boston Fancy/Don't Keep It a Secret	1955	$30
KAPP			
❏ 918	Across the Alley from the Alamo/I'm Living in the Middle of Nowhere	1968	$10
❏ 886	Born to Love You/Fiddle Bird	1968	$10
❏ 825	Eight'r from Decatur/Let's Be Sure We Know	1967	$12
❏ 842	I Wish I Felt This Way at Home/Looking Over My Shoulder	1967	$10
— With Mel Tillis			

Number	Title	Yr	NM
❏ 988	Milk Cow Blues/It's a Good World	1969	$10
❏ 744	She's Killin' Me/She Won't Let Me Forget Her	1966	$10
❏ 2067	Southwestern Waltz/If I Just Had a Home to Go Home To	1969	$10
❏ 2019	What Kind of Girl Are You/Look What Trouble Left Behind	1969	$10
LIBERTY			
❏ 55311	After All/It May Be Too Late	1961	$20
❏ 55260	Heart to Heart Talk/What's the Matter with the Mill	1960	$20
❏ 55450	Oklahoma Gals/Tomorrow I'll Cry	1962	$20
❏ 55378	Siesta/I'm Crying My Heart Out	1961	$20
❏ 55264	The Image of Me/Goodbye Liza Jane	1960	$20
LONGHORN			
❏ 545	All Night Long/You Can't Break a Heart	1964	$15
❏ 544	Buffalo Twist/Sooner or Later (You'll Fall)	1964	$20
❏ 560	Faded Love/Wills Junction	1965	$15
❏ 550	If He's Movin' In/Let's Get It Over and Done With	1965	$15
MGM			
❏ K11635	As I Sit Broken-Hearted/Bottle Baby Boogie	1953	$30
❏ K11377	Awake But Dreaming/Steamboat Stomp	1952	$30
❏ K11119	Brown Skin Gal/Send Me a Red Rose	1951	$30
❏ K11883	Cadillac in Model "A"/Waltzing in Ole San Antone	1954	$30
❏ K10980	Cross My Heart/I'm Dotting Every I	1951	$30
❏ K10898	End of the Line/Anything	1951	$30
❏ K10786	Faded Love/Boot Heel Rag	1950	$40
❏ K11213	Hubbin' It/I'll Be Lucky Someday	1952	$30
❏ K10934	I Betcha My Heart I Love You/I Laugh When I Think	1951	$30
❏ K10570	Ida Red Likes the Boogie/A King Without a Queen	1949	$40
❏ K11288	I'm All Alone/Three Miles South of Cash in Arkansas	1952	$30
❏ K11241	I Want to Be Wanted/Snatchin' Grabbin'	1952	$30
❏ K11516	I Want to Go to Mexico/Broken Heart for a Souvenir	1953	$30
❏ K11568	I Won't Be Back Tonight/B. Bowman Hop	1953	$30
❏ K11452	Little Girl, Little Girl/Sittin' on Top of the World	1953	$30
❏ K11024	Plain Jane/I'm Tired of Living	1951	$30
❏ K10620	She's Gone/Mean Woman with Green Eyes	1950	$40
❏ K11709	She's the Quarter Horse Type (Of a Gal)/(Everyone Is Callin' You) A Fallen Angel	1954	$30
❏ K11082	Silver Bells/Last Goodbye	1951	$30
❏ K11985	So Long, I'll See You Later/I Live for You	1955	$30
❏ K11832	St. Louis Blues/I Got a New Road	1954	$30
❏ K10836	Tater Pie/I Didn't Realize	1950	$40
❏ K11767	Texas Blues/I Hit the Jackpot	1954	$30
❏ K11163	Twinkle Star/Can't Stand Loneliness	1952	$30
UNITED ARTISTS			
❏ XW556	San Antonio Rose/Faded Love	1974	$6
UNITED ARTISTS			
❏ SP-102 [PS]	For the Last Time	1974	$20
❏ SP-102 [DJ]	San Antonio Rose/Faded Love//Stay All Night (Stay a Little Longer)/Yearning (Just for You)	1974	$12

WILLS, DAVID

Number	Title	Yr	NM
EPIC			
❏ 8-50090	From Barrooms to Bedrooms/I'll Be More Than Happy	1975	$5
❏ 8-50260	(I'm Just Pouring Out) What She Bottled Up in Me/The Happy Hour	1976	$5
❏ 34-08043	Paper Thin Walls/Honey Baby	1988	$3
❏ 8-50154	She Deserves My Very Best/Lady of the Evening	1975	$5
❏ 8-50118	The Barmaid/Make Me Hate You	1975	$5
❏ 8-50036	There's a Song on the Jukebox/I Can't Even Drink It Away	1974	$6
❏ 8-50228	Woman/Paint Me a Picture	1976	$5
RCA			
❏ PB-13737	Lady in Waiting/First Time Feeling	1984	$3
❏ PB-13940	Macon Love/Racin' Down the Highway	1984	$4
❏ PB-13653	Miss Understanding/First to Make It Last	1983	$3
❏ JK-13653 [DJ]	Miss Understanding (same on both sides)	1983	$10
— Promo only on blue vinyl			

Number	Title	Yr	NM
❏ PB-13833	Thank God for Friday/Racin' Down the Highway	1984	$4
❏ JK-13833 [DJ]	Thank God for Friday (same on both sides)	1984	$10

— Promo only on blue vinyl

Number	Title	Yr	NM
❏ PB-13541	The Eyes of a Stranger/Give Her a Break	1983	$3
❏ JK-13541 [DJ]	The Eyes of a Stranger (same on both sides)	1983	$10

— Promo only on yellow vinyl

Number	Title	Yr	NM
❏ JK-13460 [DJ]	Those Nights, These Days (same on both sides)	1983	$10

— Promo only on red vinyl

Number	Title	Yr	NM
❏ PB-13460	Those Nights, These Days/Tennessee Moon	1983	$3

UNITED ARTISTS

Number	Title	Yr	NM
❏ XW1042	Cheatin' Turns Her On/I'm Gonna Save It for My Baby	1977	$4
❏ XW1097	Do You Wanna Make Love/The Fool Strikes Again	1977	$4
❏ XW1319	Endless/One, Two, Three, We Were Lovers	1979	$4
❏ XW1271	I'm Being Good/Women Have a Feeling ('Bout These Things)	1979	$4
❏ XW1350	She's Hangin' In There (I'm Hangin' Out)/Take It Back	1980	$4
❏ XW988	The Best Part of My Days (Are My Nights with You)/I'm Gonna Save It for My Baby	1977	$4
❏ X1375	The Light of My Life (Has Gone Out Again Tonight)/Marriage on the Rocks	1980	$4

WILLS, JOHNNIE LEE

SIMS

Number	Title	Yr	NM
❏ 129	Blue Twist/Your Love for Me Is Losing Light	1962	$20
❏ 133	Lazy John/Milk Cow Blues	1963	$20

WILLS, TOMMY

COUNTRY INT'L.

Number	Title	Yr	NM
❏ 108	Georgia on My Mind/Help Me Make It Through the Night	1975	$6
❏ 103	Green, Green Grass of Home/Saxy Boogie	1975	$6

GOLDEN MOON

Number	Title	Yr	NM
❏ 004	Wildwood Flower/Ram-Bunk-Shush	1978	$8

TERRY

Number	Title	Yr	NM
❏ 110	Aw Shucks/Tuffer Than Tuff	1962	$20
❏ 106	Mr. Movin' Is Groovin'/Third Man Theme "Rock	1962	$20

WILMER AND THE DUKES

APHRODISIAC

Number	Title	Yr	NM
❏ 263	Get Out of My Life, Women/I Do Love You	1969	$10
❏ 260	Give Me One More Chance/Git It	1968	$8
❏ 261	Heavy Time/I'm Free	1969	$8
❏ 261 [PS]	Heavy Time/I'm Free	1969	$15
❏ 262	Living in the U.S.A./Count on Me	1969	$8

WILSON, AL

CAROUSEL

Number	Title	Yr	NM
❏ 30052	Falling/Bachelor Man	1971	$6
❏ 30051	I Hear You Knocking/Sugar Cane Girl	1971	$6

PLAYBOY

Number	Title	Yr	NM
❏ 6076	Baby I Want Your Body/Stay with Me	1976	$5
❏ 6076 [PS]	Baby I Want Your Body/Stay with Me	1976	$6
❏ 6062	I've Got a Feeling (We'll Be Seeing Each Other Again)/Be Concerned	1976	$5

ROADSHOW

Number	Title	Yr	NM
❏ PB-11583	Count the Days/Is This the End	1979	$4
❏ PB-11714	Earthquake/You Got It	1979	$4

ROCKY ROAD

Number	Title	Yr	NM
❏ 30067	Born on the Bayou/(B-side unknown)	1972	$6
❏ 30060	Heavy Church/(B-side unknown)	1972	$6
❏ 30202	I Won't Last a Day Without You-Let Me Be the One/Willoughbry Brook Road	1974	$6
❏ 30200	La La Peace Song/Keep On Loving You	1974	$6
❏ 30073	Show and Tell/Listen to Me	1973	$6
❏ 30076	Touch and Go/Settle Me Down	1974	$6

SOUL CITY

Number	Title	Yr	NM
❏ 761	Do What You Gotta Do/Now I Know What Love Is	1968	$8
❏ 773	I Stand Accused/Shake Me, Wake Me	1969	$8
❏ 775	Lodi/By the Time I Get to Phoenix	1969	$8

Number	Title	Yr	NM
❏ 771	Poor Side of Town/The Dolphins	1969	$8
❏ 767	The Snake/Getting Ready for Tomorrow	1968	$8
❏ 759	When You Love, You're Loved Too/Who Could Be Lovin' You	1967	$10

WAND

Number	Title	Yr	NM
❏ 1135	Help Me/(Instrumental)	1966	$40

WILSON, ANN, AND THE DAYBREAKS

TOPAZ

Number	Title	Yr	NM
❏ 1311	Standin' Watchin' You/Wonder How I Managed	1967	$120
❏ 1312	Through Eyes and Glass/I'm Gonna Drink My Hurt Away	1967	$120

WILSON, BRIAN, AND MIKE LOVE

BROTHER

Number	Title	Yr	NM
❏ 1002	Gettin' Hungry/Devoted to You	1967	$40

WILSON, BRIAN

Also see THE BEACH BOYS.

CAPITOL

Number	Title	Yr	NM
❏ 5610	Caroline, No/Summer Means New Love	1966	$30

— Actually a Beach Boys recording released as a solo Brian record

SIRE

Number	Title	Yr	NM
❏ 28350	Let's Go to Heaven in My Car/Too Much Sugar	1987	$12

— Promo copies go for 50% of this price

Number	Title	Yr	NM
❏ 28350 [PS]	Let's Go to Heaven in My Car/Too Much Sugar	1987	$5

— Accompanied both stock and promo copies

Number	Title	Yr	NM
❏ 27814	Love and Mercy/He Couldn't Get His Poor Old Body to Move	1988	$10

— Promo copies go for 50% of this price

Number	Title	Yr	NM
❏ 27814 [PS]	Love and Mercy/He Couldn't Get His Poor Old Body to Move	1988	$5

— Accompanied both stock and promo copies

Number	Title	Yr	NM
❏ 27694	Melt Away/Being with the One You Love	1988	$30

WILSON, CARL

Also see THE BEACH BOYS.

CARIBOU

Number	Title	Yr	NM
❏ 04020	Givin' You Up/Too Early to Tell	1983	$5
❏ 02136	Heaven/Hurry Love	1981	$5
❏ 01049	Hold Me/Hurry Love	1981	$5
❏ 03590	What You Do to Me/Time	1983	$5

WILSON, COLEMAN

KING

Number	Title	Yr	NM
❏ 5596	A Green Truck Driver's First Experience/Hot Rod Baby	1962	$30
❏ 5512	Passing Zone Blues/Flat-Footed Mama	1961	$30

WILSON, FRANK

SOUL

Number	Title	Yr	NM
❏ 35019	Do I Love You (Indeed I Do)/Sweeter As the Days Go By	1966	$20000

— VG 10000; VG+ 15000

WILSON, J. FRANK, AND THE CAVALIERS

CHARAY

Number	Title	Yr	NM
❏ 13	Last Kiss '69/Black Car	1969	$6

JOSIE

Number	Title	Yr	NM
❏ 931	Dreams of a Fool/Open Your Eyes	1965	$12
❏ 938	Forget Me Not/A White Sport Coat (And a Pink Carnation)	1965	$10
❏ 926	Hey Little One/Speak to Me	1964	$12
❏ 923	Last Kiss/That's How Much I Love You	1964	$15
❏ 929	Say It Now/Six Boys	1965	$10
❏ 924	Tears of Happiness/Summertime	1964	$10

— As "The Cavaliers"

LE CAM

Number	Title	Yr	NM
❏ 722	Last Kiss/Carla	1964	$40

SOLLY

Number	Title	Yr	NM
❏ 927	Me and My Teardrops/Unmarked and Uncovered with Sand	1966	$10

TAMARA

Number	Title	Yr	NM
❏ 761	Last Kiss/That's How Much I Love You	1964	$30

WILSON, JACKIE

BRUNSWICK

Number	Title	Yr	NM
❏ 55170	Alone at Last/Am I the Man	1960	$30
❏ 55170 [PS]	Alone at Last/Am I the Man	1960	$60
❏ 9-55070	As Long As I Live/I'm Wanderin'	1958	$30
❏ 55250	Baby Get It (And Don't Quit It)/The New Breed	1963	$15
❏ 55239	Baby Workout/I'm Going Crazy	1963	$30
❏ 55490	Beautiful Day/What 'Cha Gonna Do About Love	1973	$6
❏ 55495	Because of You/Go Away	1973	$200
❏ 55266	Big Boss Line/Be My Girl	1964	$12
❏ 55263	Call Her Up/The Kickapoo	1964	$10
❏ 55373	Chain Gang/Funky Broadway	1968	$8
❏ 55277	Danny Boy/Soul Time	1965	$8
❏ 55522	Don't Burn No Bridges/(Instrumental)	1975	$6

— With the Chi-Lites

Number	Title	Yr	NM
❏ 55233	Forever and a Day/Baby That's All	1962	$20
❏ 55392	For Once in My Life/You Brought About a Change in Me	1968	$8
❏ 55365	For Your Precious Love/Uptight	1968	$8
❏ 55260	Haunted House/I'm Travelin' On	1964	$12
❏ 55225	Hearts/Sing (And Tell the Blues So Long)	1962	$20
❏ 55418	Helpless/Do It the Right Way	1969	$8
❏ 55294	I Believe/Be My Love	1966	$8
❏ 55283	I Believe I'll Love On/Lonely Teardrops	1965	$8
❏ 55443	(I Can Feel Those Vibrations) This Love Is Real/Love Uprising	1970	$6
❏ 55309	I Don't Want to Lose You/Just Be Sincere	1967	$8
❏ 55224	I Found Love/There's Nothing Like Love	1962	$15

— With Linda Hopkins

Number	Title	Yr	NM
❏ 55381	I Get the Sweetest Feeling/Nothing But Heartaches	1968	$8
❏ 55229	I Just Can't Help It/My Tale of Woe	1962	$20
❏ 55136	I'll Be Satisfied/Ask	1959	$30
❏ 55216	I'm Comin' On Back to You/Lonely Life	1961	$20
❏ 55402	I Still Love You/Hum De Dum De Do	1969	$8
❏ 55504	It's All Over/Shake a Leg	1973	$6
❏ 55289	I've Got to Get Back/3 Days, 1 Hour, 30 Minutes	1966	$8
❏ 55321	I've Lost You/Those Heartaches	1967	$8
❏ 55435	Let This Be a Letter (To My Baby)/Didn't I	1970	$6
❏ 55435 [PS]	Let This Be a Letter (To My Baby)/Didn't I	1970	$15
❏ 9-55105	Lonely Teardrops/In the Blue of Evening	1958	$40
❏ 55461	Love Is Funny That Way/Try It Again	1971	$6
❏ 55201	My Empty Arms/The Tear of the Year	1961	$20
❏ 55201 [PS]	My Empty Arms/The Tear of the Year	1961	$50
❏ 55208	Please Tell Me Why/Your One and Only Love	1961	$20
❏ 55454	Say You Will/(B-side unknown)	1971	$6
❏ 55243	Shake a Hand/Say I Do	1963	$15

— With Linda Hopkins

Number	Title	Yr	NM
❏ 55246	Shake! Shake! Shake!/He's a Fool	1963	$15
❏ 55254	Silent Night/Oh Holy Night	1963	$20
❏ 55354	Since You Showed Me How to Be Happy/The Who Who Song	1967	$8
❏ 55499	Sing a Little Song/No More Goodbyes	1973	$6
❏ 55290	Soul Galore/Brand New Things	1966	$8
❏ 55269	Squeeze Her-Tease Her (But Love Her)/Give Me Back My Heart	1964	$10
❏ 55165	Talk That Talk/Only You, Only Me	1959	$30
❏ 55165 [PS]	Talk That Talk/Only You, Only Me	1959	$70
❏ 55121	That's Why (I Love You So)/Love Is All	1959	$30
❏ 55121 [PS]	That's Why (I Love You So)/Love Is All	1959	$70
❏ 55475	The Girl Turned Me On/Forever and a Day	1972	$8
❏ 55221	The Greatest Hurt/There'll Be No Next Time	1962	$20
❏ 55221 [PS]	The Greatest Hurt/There'll Be No Next Time	1962	$50
❏ 55220	The Way I Am/My Heart Belongs to Only You	1961	$20
❏ 55220 [PS]	The Way I Am/My Heart Belongs to Only You	1961	$50
❏ 55287	Think Twice/Please Don't Hurt Me	1965	$8

— With LaVern Baker

Number	Title	Yr	NM
❏ 55449	This Guy's in Love with You/Say You Will	1971	$6

Number	Title	Yr	NM
❏ 9-55052	To Be Loved/Come Back to Me	1958	$30
❏ 55273	Watch Out/She's All Right	1964	$10
❏ 9-55086	We Have Love/ Singing a Song	1958	$30
❏ 55480	What a Lovely Way/You Left the Fire Burning	1972	$6
❏ 55236	What Good Am I Without You/A Girl Named Tamiko	1962	$20
❏ 55236 [PS]	What Good Am I Without You/A Girl Named Tamiko	1962	$40
❏ 55300	Whispers (Gettin' Louder)/ The Fairest of Them All	1966	$8
❏ 55423	With These Hands/Why Don't You (Do Your Thing)	1969	$8

7-Inch Extended Plays

Number	Title	Yr	NM
❏ EB71103 [PS]	Baby Workout	1963	$75
❏ EB71103	Baby Workout/Say You Will// Kickapoo/Yeah Yeah Yeah	1963	$75
❏ EB71047	(contents unknown)	1960	$75
❏ EB71104	(contents unknown)	1963	$75
❏ EB71102	I Just Can't Help It/My Tale of Woe//Bad News Travels Fast/ You Ought to Be Ashamed	1962	$70
❏ EB71042	Lonely Teardrops/It's Too Bad We Had to Say Goodbye// Someone to Need Me/Joke	1960	$70
❏ EB71047 [PS]	Mr. Excitement	1960	$75
❏ EB71104 [PS]	Shake a Hand	1963	$75
❏ EB71048	So Much/Only You, Only Me// Happiness/Magic of Love	1960	$75
❏ EB71046 [PS]	Talk That Talk	1960	$75
❏ EB71046	Talk That Talk/Ask//I'll Be Satisfied/Wishing Well	1960	$75
❏ EB71045 [PS]	That's Why (I Love You So)	1960	$75
❏ EB771045 [PS]	That's Why (I Love You So)	1960	$100
❏ EB71045 [M]	That's Why/Love Is All//You Better Know It/Each Time	1960	$75
❏ EB771045	That's Why/Love Is All//You Better Know It/Each Time	1960	$100
❏ EB71101	The Greatest Hurt/I Don't Know You Anymore// Tear of the Year/There'll Be No Next Time	1962	$75
❏ EB71040	To Be Loved/Reet Petite// Danny Boy/As Long As I Live	1959	$75

WILSON, JIM
MERCURY

Number	Title	Yr	NM
❏ 70755	Daddy, Who Is Santa Claus?/Round, Round the Christmas Tree	1955	$30
❏ 70635	Daddy, You Know What?/ Plans for Divorce	1955	$30
❏ 70702	I Wonder When We'll Ever Know/Don't Point Your Finger	1955	$30
❏ 70859	Thank You, Lord, for Dinner/ My Greatest Possession	1956	$30

REED

Number	Title	Yr	NM
❏ 1032	Have a Tear on Me/Just for You	1959	$20

WILSON, JUSTIN
TOWER

Number	Title	Yr	NM
❏ 299	Santa Claus Gonna Brought Himself to Town/Randolph the Rouge-Nosed Reindeer	1966	$15
❏ 380	Whitey, the Snow White Lamb/ When Christmas Angels Sing	1967	$10

—B-side by Whitney Snow

WILSON, MARTY
DECCA

Number	Title	Yr	NM
❏ 30644	Po-Go/Hey Eula	1958	$40
❏ 30544	Super Sonic/I'm All Woke Up	1958	$40

TEL

Number	Title	Yr	NM
❏ 1008	Stroll Me/Hot Foot	1959	$30

WILSON, MARY
MOTOWN

Number	Title	Yr	NM
❏ 1467	Midnight Dancer/Red Hot	1979	$5

WILSON, MERI
BNA

Number	Title	Yr	NM
❏ 8248	Peter the Meter Reader/ (B-side unknown)	1981	$10

GRT

Number	Title	Yr	NM
❏ 127	Telephone Man/Itenerary	1977	$5

WMOT

Number	Title	Yr	NM
❏ WS9 02405	Peter the Meter Reader/ My Heat Walkin'	1981	$5

WILSON, MURRY
Father of Brian, Carl and Dennis Wilson of the Beach Boys.
CAPITOL

Number	Title	Yr	NM
❏ 2063	Leaves/Plumber's Tune	1967	$15

WILSON, NANCY, AND CANNONBALL ADDERLEY
CAPITOL

Number	Title	Yr	NM
❏ 4693	Save Your Love for Me/ Never Will I Marry	1962	$8

WILSON, NANCY
CAPITOL

Number	Title	Yr	NM
❏ 2644	Can't Take My Eyes Off You/Do You Know Why	1969	$6
❏ 5340 [PS]	Don't Come Running Back to Me/Love Has Many Faces	1965	$15
❏ 4189	Don't Let Me Be Lonely Tonight/Happy Tears	1975	$5
❏ 5133	Don't Rain on My Parade/ The Grass Is Greener	1964	$8
❏ 2136	Face It Girl, It's Over/ The End of Our Love	1968	$6
❏ 2555	Got It Together/One Soft Night	1969	$6
❏ 4117	He Called Me Baby/Like a Circle Never Stops	1975	$5
❏ 4578	I'm Gonna Let Ya/Light	1978	$4
❏ 2361	In a Long White Room/ Only Love	1968	$6
❏ 4359	In My Loneliness (When We Were One)/He Never Had It So Good	1976	$4
❏ 4476	I've Never Been to Me/ Here It Comes	1977	$4
❏ 4741	Life, Love and Harmony/Open Up Your Heart and Take Me In	1979	$4
❏ 4509	My Foolish Heart/Seventh Son	1961	$20
❏ 2061	Ode to Billie Joe/I'm Always Drunk in San Francisco	1967	$6
❏ 2283	Peace of Mind/This Bitter Earth	1968	$6
❏ 4816	Put On a Happy Face/You Don't Know What Love Is	1962	$8
❏ 3956	Streetrunner/Ocean of Love	1974	$5
❏ 4801	Sunshine/This Is Our Song	1979	$4
❏ 4991	Tell Me the Truth/ My Sweet Thing	1963	$8
❏ 5084	That's What I Want for Christmas/What Are You Doing New Year's Eve	1963	$12
❏ 3212	The Greatest Performance of My Life/Everybody Knows	1971	$6
❏ 2831	This Girl Is a Woman Now/Trip with Me	1970	$6
❏ 2749	Waitin' for Charlie to Come Home/Words and Music	1970	$6
❏ 4839	Welcome Home/Let's Hold On to Love	1980	$4

COLUMBIA

Number	Title	Yr	NM
❏ 07037	Forbidden Lover/A Song for You	1987	$3

7-Inch Extended Plays

CAPITOL

Number	Title	Yr	NM
❏ SU-2555 [S]	Don't Go to Strangers/Like Someone in Love/Tender Loving Care//Gee Baby, Ain't I Good to You/Close Your Eyes/As You Desire Me	1966	$10

—33 1/3 rpm, small hole

Number	Title	Yr	NM
❏ SXA-2351 [PS]	Gentle Is My Love	1965	$12
❏ SU-2555 [PS]	Tender Loving Care	1966	$12
❏ SXA-2351 [S]	Who Can I Turn To/Gentle Is My Love/There Will Never Be Another You/ Funnier Than Funny/More/ If Ever I Would Leave You	1965	$10

—33 1/3 rpm, small hole

WILSON, NANCY (2)
WTG

Number	Title	Yr	NM
❏ 68678	All for Love/Taste the Rain	1989	$10

—B-side by Red Hot Chili Peppers

WILSON, NORRO
CAPITOL

Number	Title	Yr	NM
❏ 3886	Loneliness (Can Break a Good Man Down)/I Want to Hold You in My Arms	1974	$6
❏ 4004	Thanks But No Thanks/ Come On, Come On, Pour Your Lovin' on Me	1974	$6

HICKORY

Number	Title	Yr	NM
❏ 1379	Let's Think About Living/ Oh Lonesome Me	1966	$15

—As "Norris Wilson

MGM

Number	Title	Yr	NM
❏ 14038	Chantilly Lace/Love Hurts	1969	$8

—As "Norris Wilson

Number	Title	Yr	NM
❏ 13323	Chantilly Lace/Where the Action Is	1965	$15

—As "Norris Wilson

MONUMENT

Number	Title	Yr	NM
❏ 466	For a Little While/Honolulu	1962	$20

—As "Norris Wilson

Number	Title	Yr	NM
❏ 453	Ma Baker's Island/(My Heart's in) Mexico	1962	$20

—As "Norris Wilson

Number	Title	Yr	NM
❏ 813	Top Dog/Blink Away	1963	$20

—As "Norro

RCA VICTOR

Number	Title	Yr	NM
❏ 74-0677	A Gift of Love/Sweet Lips That Kiss Me Good Morning	1972	$6
❏ APBO-0062	Ain't It Good (To Feel This Way)/It's All in the Game	1973	$6
❏ 74-0909	Darlin' Raise the Shade/ Keep Me from Blowin' Away	1973	$6
❏ 74-0824	Everybody Needs Lovin'/ The Strange Little Girl	1972	$6
❏ 74-0762	Times Like These Make the Roses Sweet/Little Old Lady	1972	$6

SMASH

Number	Title	Yr	NM
❏ 2262	In the Loneliness of the City/Roses in the Snow	1970	$8
❏ 2210	Love Comes But Once in a Lifetime/All the Time	1969	$8
❏ 2192	Only You/Hey Mister	1968	$8
❏ 2236	Shame on Me/Let Me Go Back	1969	$8
❏ 2151	Stranger to Me/ Mama McCluskie	1968	$8
❏ 2184	Sunset and Vine/I'd Rather Do It Than Eat	1968	$8

WILSON, PEANUTS
BRUNSWICK

Number	Title	Yr	NM
❏ 55039	Cast Iron Arm/You've Got Love	1957	$200

WILSON SISTERS, THE
KING

Number	Title	Yr	NM
❏ 5724 [PS]	Little Klinker/All I Want For Christmas Is My Two Front Teeth	1962	$30
❏ 5724	Little Klinker/All I Want For Christmas Is My Two Front Teeth	1962	$30

WILSON, SONNY
CANDIX

Number	Title	Yr	NM
❏ 327	I Ain't Givin' Up Nothin'/ Troubled Time	1962	$30

SUN

Number	Title	Yr	NM
❏ 341	The Great Pretender/I'm Gonna Take a Walk	1960	$30

WILSON, WALLY
SABRE

Number	Title	Yr	NM
❏ 106	If You Don't Love Me/The Hunt	1954	$600

WIMBERLEY, MAGGIE SUE
SUN

Number	Title	Yr	NM
❏ 229	Daydreams Come True/How Long	1956	$70

WINCHELL, DANNY
MGM

Number	Title	Yr	NM
❏ 11335	Carolina in the Morning/ There Goes My Heart	1952	$40

RECORTE

Number	Title	Yr	NM
❏ 415	Come Back Baby/I've Chosen You	1959	$50
❏ 410	We're Gonna Have a Rockin' Party/Don't Say You're Sorry	1959	$60

WINDING, KAI
A&M

Number	Title	Yr	NM
❏ 1035	Wichita Lineman/ Betwixt and Between	1969	$6

COLUMBIA

Number	Title	Yr	NM
❏ 41330	Manhattan/Cha Cha Chicago	1959	$10

IMPULSE!

Number	Title	Yr	NM
❏ 201	Theme from Picnic/ Side by Side	1961	$10

—With J.J. Johnson

VERVE

Number	Title	Yr	NM
❏ 10455	All/More	1966	$6
❏ 10372	A Sign of the Times/You've Lost That Lovin' Feelin'	1965	$6
❏ 10258	Baby Elephant Walk/ Experiment in Terror	1963	$8
❏ 10335	Dear Heart/Wolverton Mountain	1964	$8
❏ 10407	Dirty Dog/Sunrise	1966	$6
❏ 10328	Don't Blow Your Cool (In the Merry Old Summertime)/ New Song of India	1964	$8
❏ 10301	Ice Cream Man/ The Lonely One	1963	$8
❏ 10343	I Will Wait for You/ Baker Street Mystery	1965	$6
❏ 10348	Marriage, Italian Style/My Hands Reach Out to You	1965	$6
❏ 10295	More/Comin' Home Baby	1963	$10
❏ 10488	Penny Lane/Time	1967	$6
❏ 10313	Portrait of My Love/ Mondo Cane #2	1964	$8
❏ 10313 [PS]	Portrait of My Love/ Mondo Cane #2	1964	$15
❏ 10355	Singin' in the Rain/Half a Crown	1965	$6
❏ 10334	Theme from The Luck of Ginger Coffey/Do Anything You Wanna	1964	$8
❏ 10433	The Sidewinder/ Something You Got	1966	$6
❏ 10307	Time Is On My Side/Baby Don't Come On with Me	1963	$8

Number	Title	Yr	NM

WINDSORS, THE (2)
BACK BEAT
| ❏ 506 | My Gloria/Cool Seabreeze | 1958 | $8000 |

— VG 4000; VG+ 6000

WINDSORS, THE (U)
UNITED ARTISTS
| ❏ 128 | Saki Rock/Caramba | 1958 | $30 |

WIG WAG
| ❏ 203 | Carol Ann/Keep Me from Crying | 1959 | $200 |

WINE, TONI
ATCO
| ❏ 6736 | Sisters in Sorrow/Take a Little Time Out for Love | 1970 | $6 |

COLPIX
❏ 742	A Boy Like You/Funny Little Heart	1964	$15
❏ 732	I Love That Boy/The Thirteenth Hour	1964	$15
❏ 715	My Boyfriend's Coming Home for Christmas/What a Pity	1963	$20
❏ 756	Only Fools/A Girl Is Not a Girl	1964	$15

WINGS
See PAUL McCARTNEY.

WINSTON, HATTIE
PARKWAY
| ❏ 956 | Pass Me By/Pictures Don't Lie | 1965 | $100 |
| ❏ 928 | Pictures Don't Lie/Please Write Back to Me | 1964 | $30 |

WINTER, EDGAR
BLUE SKY
❏ 2786	Above and Beyond/(Instrumental)	1980	$4
❏ 2762	Cool Dance/People Music	1975	$4
❏ 2763	Diamond Eyes/Infinite Peace in Rhythm	1976	$4
❏ 2780	Forever in Love/It's Your Life to Live	1979	$4
❏ 70068	Love Is Everywhere/Everyday Man	1981	$4
❏ 2758	One Day Tomorrow/Jasmine Nightdream	1975	$4
❏ 2761	Outa Control/I Always Wanted You	1975	$4
❏ 2769	Stickin' It Out/Puttin' It Back	1977	$4

EPIC
| ❏ 50034 | Easy Street/Do Like Me | 1974 | $4 |
| ❏ JBQ506 [Q] | Frankenstein/Free Ride | 1973 | $25 |

— Special Coin Operator Release" in quadraphonic; contains single edit of "Frankenstein" and unknown version of "Free Ride"

| ❏ 10945 | Frankenstein/Hangin' Around | 1973 | $8 |
| ❏ 10967 | Frankenstein/Undercover Man | 1973 | $6 |

— Yellow label

| ❏ 10967 | Frankenstein/Undercover Man | 1973 | $4 |

— Orange label

❏ 10903	Free Ride/Catchin' Up	1972	$8
❏ 11024	Free Ride/When It Comes	1973	$4
❏ 10762	Give It Everything You've Got/You Were My Light	1971	$6
❏ 10740	Good Morning Music/Where Would I Be	1971	$8
❏ 11069	Hangin' Around/We All Had a Real Good Time	1973	$4
❏ 10855	I Can't Turn You Loose/Cool Fool	1972	$6
❏ 50060	Miracle of Love/Someone Take My Heart Away	1975	$4
❏ 10618	Tobacco Road/Now Is the Time	1970	$8
❏ 10750	Where Would I Be/Feeling Like a Woman	1971	$6

— B-side by Patsy Sledd

WINTER, JOHNNY
ATLANTIC
| ❏ 2248 | Gangster of Love/Eternally | 1964 | $10 |

BLUE SKY
| ❏ 2756 | Golden Olden Days of Rock 'N' Roll/Stranger | 1975 | $4 |

BUDDAH
| ❏ 168 | Out of Sight/Bad News | 1970 | $10 |

COLUMBIA
❏ 46006	Bad Luck Situation/Stone County	1974	$5
❏ 46036	Boney Moroney/Hurtin' So Bad	1974	$5
❏ 45899	Can't You Feel It/Rock and Roll	1973	$5
❏ 44900	I'll Drown in My Tears/I'm Yours and I'm Here	1969	$5
❏ 45860	Silver Train/Rock and Roll	1973	$5

FROLIC
| ❏ 509 | Gangster of Love/Eternally | 1963 | $60 |
| ❏ 512 | Gone for Bad/I Won't Believe It | 1963 | $70 |

| ❏ 501 | That's What Love Does/Shed So Many Tears | 1962 | $60 |

GRT
| ❏ 9 | Gangster of Love/Roadrunner | 1969 | $8 |

IMPERIAL
| ❏ 66376 | Forty-Four/Rollin' & Tumblin' | 1969 | $8 |

MGM
| ❏ 13380 | Gone for Bad/I Won't Believe It | 1965 | $8 |

PACEMAKER
| ❏ 243 | Leavin' Blues/Birds Can't Row Boats | 1966 | $30 |

WINTER, JOHNNY AND EDGAR
Also see each artist's individual listings.

BLUE SKY
| ❏ 2764 | Soul Man/Let the Good Times Roll | 1976 | $4 |

WINTERHALTER, HUGO
ABC-PARAMOUNT
| ❏ 10485 | Blue Concerto/Indian Summer | 1963 | $8 |
| ❏ 10432 | Snowfall/I'll Remember April | 1963 | $8 |

COLUMBIA
| ❏ 1-401 | Blue Christmas/You're All I Want For Christmas | 1949 | $40 |

— Microgroove 33 1/3 rpm, 7-inch single, small hole

| ❏ 1-478 | My Foolish Heart/Leave It to Love | 1950 | $40 |

— Microgroove 7-inch, 33 1/3 record, small hole

| ❏ 1-489 | (Put Another Nickel In) Music! Music! Music!/The Glow-Worm | 1950 | $40 |

— Microgroove 7-inch, 33 1/3 record, small hole

| ❏ 1-402(?) | There's No Tomorrow/When the Wind Was Green | 1949 | $40 |

— Microgroove 7-inch, 33 1/3 record, small hole

| ❏ 1-492 | The Third Man Theme/Come Into My Heart | 1950 | $40 |

— Microgroove 7-inch, 33 1/3 record, small hole

MUSICOR
| ❏ 1327 | For Love of Ivy/Love Theme from Romeo and Juliet | 1968 | $8 |

RCA VICTOR
❏ 47-4017	Across the Wide Missouri/The Seven Wonders of the World	1951	$20
❏ 47-4087	Alice in Wonderland/I'll Never Know Why	1951	$20
❏ 47-6701	All That I Ask Is Love/The Boulevard of Love	1956	$10
❏ 47-3807	Babes in the Woods/Here Comes the Bride on a Pinto Pony	1950	$30
❏ 47-5729	Banana Buggyride/Windsor Melody	1954	$15
❏ 47-4288	Beyond the Blue Horizon/I Never Was Loved by Anyone Else	1951	$20
❏ 47-4412	Blue December/I'll See You in My Dreams	1951	$20
❏ 47-4518	Blue Tango/The Gypsy Trail	1952	$20
❏ 47-4997	Blue Violins/Fandango	1952	$20
❏ 47-6537	Canadian Sunset/This Is Real (We're in Love, We're in Love)	1956	$10
❏ 47-3221	Count Every Star/The Flying Dutchman	1950	$30
❏ 47-7329	Crazy Little Tune/I Haven't Met the Right One Yet	1958	$8
❏ 47-3943	Cross My Heart, I Love You/My Bouquet	1950	$20
❏ 47-7674	Crying Guitar/Hide Me in Your Arms	1960	$8
❏ 47-8141	Diamond Head/Brazilian Barn Dance	1963	$8
❏ 47-4851	Hesitation/Tic-Tac-Toe	1952	$20
❏ 47-7939	I Believe in You/Viennese Nightingale	1961	$8
❏ 47-3857	I'll See You in My Dreams/Why Can't This Night Go On	1950	$20
❏ 47-3858	It Had to Be You/You've Got Me Crying Again	1950	$20
❏ 47-5655	Latin Lady/(I Left My Heart in) Heidelberg	1954	$15
❏ 47-5326	Limelight/Symphony for a Starry Night	1953	$15
❏ 47-5369	Lover's Waltz/Music Box in Blue	1953	$15
❏ 47-4212	Make Believe Land/Blow, Blow, Winds of the Sea	1951	$20
❏ 47-6299	Melancholy Serenade/Serenade for a Wealthy Widow	1955	$10
❏ 47-6339	Memories of You/Autumn Rhapsody	1955	$10
❏ 47-3893	Memories of You/Just an Echo in the Valley	1950	$20
❏ 47-7182	Midnight/Tango Boogie	1958	$8
❏ 47-7113	Moonlight in Capri/Blue Lover's Lament	1957	$10
❏ 47-3913	Mr. Touchdown, U.S.A./The Red We Want Is the Red We've Got (In the Old Red, White and Blue)	1950	$30
❏ 47-8043	My Geisha/The Honey Bucket Brigade	1962	$8
❏ 47-4873	On Army Team/Girls Are Marching	1952	$20
❏ 47-7454	On a Slow Boat to China/You're So Far Away Blues	1959	$8
❏ 47-3856	On the Alamo/There Is No Greater Love	1950	$20
❏ 47-6003	Say It Isn't the Night/Un Grand Amour	1955	$10
❏ 47-7033	Search for Paradise/Kashmir	1957	$10
❏ 47-3951	Something to Dance About/Once Upon a Time Today	1950	$30
❏ 47-5888	Song of the Barefoot Contessa/Land of Dreams	1954	$15
❏ 47-4586	Star Gazing/What Does It Take	1952	$20
❏ 47-5547	Stella by Starlight/High on a Windy Hill	1953	$15
❏ 47-6982	Swingin' Sweethearts/The Happy Cobbler	1957	$10
❏ 47-3737	Symphony of Spring/As We Are Today	1950	$30
❏ 47-7824	The Girl from Amsterdam/Theme from an Unfilmed Movie	1960	$8
❏ 47-6459	The Little Musicians/Flaherty's Beguine	1956	$10
❏ 47-5769	The Little Shoemaker/Magic Tango	1954	$20

— Credited to "Hugo Winterhalter's Orchestra and Chorus and a Friend"; the "friend" is Eddie Fisher

❏ 47-7599	Theme from A Summer Place/Blue Strings	1959	$15
❏ 47-6889	Theme from New Girl in Town/It's Good to Be Alive	1957	$10
❏ 47-5124	Thumbelina/Anywhere I Wander	1953	$15
❏ 47-3937	White Christmas/Blue Christmas	1950	$20
❏ 47-5209	Will of the Wisp Romance/Magic Touch	1953	$15

RCA VICTOR
❏ EPA-413	*I'll See You in My Dreams/A Kiss to Build a Dream On/Why Can't This Night Go On Forever/Love Makes the World Go 'Round	1953	$10
❏ EPA-452 [PS]	Blue Violins	1953	$12
❏ EPA495	Carol of the Bells/Christmas Island//Deck the Halls with Boughs of Holly-Wassail Song/Away in a Manger-I Saw Three Ships	1953	$10
❏ EPA-452	(contents unknown)	1953	$10
❏ EPA-983	(contents unknown)	1956	$8
❏ EPA-984	(contents unknown)	1956	$8
❏ EPA495 [PS]	Deck the Halls	1953	$12

— Ornament-shaped cover

❏ EPA-413 [PS]	Dream Time	1953	$12
❏ EPA-983 [PS]	The Eyes of Love, Vol. 1	1956	$8
❏ EPA-984 [PS]	The Eyes of Love, Vol. 2	1956	$8

WINTERS, DON
DECCA
❏ 31352	Disappointed/Blue Sun Down	1962	$15
❏ 31067	Someday Baby/That's All I Need	1960	$15
❏ 31253	Too Many Times/Shake Hands with a Loser	1961	$15

WINTERS, JUNE
MERCURY
| ❏ 5502 | Christmas in My Heart/Charms for Sale | 1950 | $20 |

WINWOOD, STEVE
Also see BLIND FAITH; THE SPENCER DAVIS GROUP; TRAFFIC.

ISLAND
❏ 49726	Arc of a Diver/Dust	1981	$4
❏ 49726 [PS]	Arc of a Diver/Dust	1981	$5
❏ 7-28472	Back in the High Life Again/Night Train	1987	$3
❏ 7-28472 [PS]	Back in the High Life Again/Night Train	1987	$3
❏ 7-28595	Freedom Overspill/Help Me Angel	1986	$3
❏ 7-28595 [PS]	Freedom Overspill/Help Me Angel	1986	$3
❏ 7-28710	Higher Love/And I Go	1986	$3
❏ 7-28710 [PS]	Higher Love/And I Go	1986	$3
❏ 7-29940	Still in the Game/Dust	1982	$5
❏ 7-28122	Talking Back to the Night/There's a River	1988	$4
❏ 7-28122 [PS]	Talking Back to the Night/There's a River	1988	$4
❏ 7-28498	The Finer Things/Night Train	1987	$3
❏ 7-28498 [PS]	The Finer Things/Night Train	1987	$3
❏ 091	Time Is Running Out/Hold On	1977	$10
❏ 091 [DJ]	Time Is Running Out (same on both sides)	1977	$5
❏ 49656	While You See a Chance/Vacant Chair	1981	$4
❏ 49656 [PS]	While You See a Chance/Vacant Chair	1981	$5

VIRGIN
❏ 7-99290	Don't You Know What the Night Can Do/(Instrumental)	1988	$3
❏ 7-99290 [PS]	Don't You Know What the Night Can Do/(Instrumental)	1988	$3
❏ 7-99234	Hearts On Fire (7" Remix)/(Instrumental)	1989	$3
❏ 7-99234 [PS]	Hearts On Fire (7" Remix)/(Instrumental)	1989	$3
❏ 7-99261	Holding On/(Instrumental)	1988	$3
❏ 7-99261 [PS]	Holding On/(Instrumental)	1988	$3

WIPERS, THE

PARK AVE.

Number	Title	Yr	NM
❑ PA-10	Alien Boy//Image of Man/Telepathic Love/ Voices in the Rain	1980	$13
❑ PA-10 [PS]	Alien Boy//Image of Man/Telepathic Love/ Voices in the Rain	1980	$13

TRAP

Number	Title	Yr	NM
❑ 810x44	Better Off Dead//Up in Flames/Does It Hurt?	1978	$20
❑ 810x44 [PS]	Better Off Dead//Up in Flames/Does It Hurt?	1978	$30

—Red and black on yellow sleeve, printed on both sides

Number	Title	Yr	NM
❑ 810x44 [PS]	Better Off Dead//Up in Flames/Does It Hurt?	1978	$20

—Black on orange sleeve, printed on one side, address on rear

WISDOMS, THE

GAITY

Number	Title	Yr	NM
❑ 169	Two Hearts Make One Love/Lost in Dreams	1959	$600

WISEMAN, MAC

CAPITOL

Number	Title	Yr	NM
❑ 4781	Bluegrass Fiesta/What's Gonna Happen to Me	1962	$10
❑ 4701	Footprints in the Snow/ Just Outside	1962	$10
❑ 5256	Heads You Win, Tails I Lose/Old Pair of Shoes	1964	$12
❑ 4854	Pistol Packin' Preacher/ Sing Little Birdie	1962	$10
❑ 5116	Scene of the Crime/'Tis Sweet to Be Remembered	1964	$10
❑ 4898	Wildfire/I Like Good Bluegrass Music	1963	$10

CHURCHILL

Number	Title	Yr	NM
❑ 7735	My Blue Heaven/ It Must Be True	1979	$6

—With Woody Herman

Number	Title	Yr	NM
❑ 7738	Scotch and Soda/Dancing Bear	1979	$6

DOT

Number	Title	Yr	NM
❑ 1062	Are You Coming Back to Me/'Tis Sweet to Be Remembered	1951	$30
❑ 1131	By the Side of the Road/ Waiting for the Boys	1953	$30
❑ 1168	Crazy Blues/Rainbow in the Valley	1953	$30
❑ 16194	Dark as a Dungeon/Darling, How Can You Forget So Soon	1961	$15
❑ 16107	Darling Nelly Gray/There's a Star Spangled Banner Waving Somewhere	1960	$15
❑ 1192	Dreams of Mother and Home/Reveille in Heaven	1954	$30
❑ 16045	Drifting on the River/ One Mint Julep	1960	$15
❑ 15929	Each Ring of the Hammer/Did You Stop to Pray This Morning	1959	$20
❑ 1266	Fire Ball Mail/When the Roses Bloom Again	1955	$30
❑ 1126	Fire in My Heart/Going to See My Baby	1952	$30
❑ 1092	Georgia Waltz/Dreaming of a Little Cabin	1952	$30
❑ 16148	Glad Rags/Now That You Have Me	1960	$15
❑ 1230	I Didn't Know/Don't Blame It All on Me	1954	$30
❑ 1273	I Hear You Knockin'/ Camptown Races	1955	$30
❑ 15638	I'll Still Write Your Name in the Sand/'Tis Sweet to Be	1957	$20
❑ 1202	I Saw Your Face in the Moon/ You Can't Judge a Book	1954	$30
❑ 1091	I Still Write Your Name in the Sand/Four Walls Around Me	1952	$30
❑ 1115	I Wonder How the Old Folks Are/You're the Girl of My Dreams	1952	$30
❑ 16980	Little Bird/This Is Where I Came In	1966	$8
❑ 1075	Little White Church/I'm a Stranger	1951	$30
❑ 15578	Love Letters in the Sand/ Because We Are Young	1957	$20
❑ 1282	Meanest Blues in the World/Be Good Baby	1956	$30
❑ 1194	My Little Home in Tennessee/I Haven't Got the Right	1954	$30
❑ 1149	My Little Home in Tennessee/I Haven't Got the Right to Love You	1953	$30
❑ 15497	One Mint Julep/I'm Waiting for the Ships That Never Come	1956	$20
❑ 15731	Put Me in Your Pocket/ When the Work's All Done	1958	$20
❑ 1150	Shackles and Chains/ Going Like Wildfire	1953	$30
❑ 1146	Six More Miles/It's Goodbye and So Long to You	1953	$30
❑ 1285	Smilin' Through/I'm Drifting Back to Dreamland	1956	$30
❑ 15544	Step It Up and Go/Sundown	1957	$40
❑ 1240	The Ballad of Davy Crockett/ Danger Heartbreak Ahead	1955	$30
❑ 16008	The Preacher and the Bear/ When It's Lamp Lightin' Time in the Valley	1959	$20
❑ 1276	These Hands/I'm Eatin' High on the Hog	1956	$30
❑ 1191	The Waltz You Saved for Me/ Love Letters in the Sand	1954	$30
❑ 15796	Thinkin' About You/ Promise of Things	1958	$20
❑ 1236	When I Get Money Made/The Little Old Church in the Valley	1955	$30

GUSTO

Number	Title	Yr	NM
❑ 814	Christmas Time's a-Coming/ Nuttin' for Christmas	1979	$4

—B-side by Joe Ward

MGM

Number	Title	Yr	NM
❑ 13986	Got Leavin' on Her Mind/ She Simply Left	1968	$8

RCA VICTOR

Number	Title	Yr	NM
❑ APBO-0034	At the Crossroad/You Can't Go in the Red Playin' Bluegrass	1973	$6
❑ APBO-0276	It Comes and Goes/I've Got to Catch That Train	1974	$6

WISHBONE ASH

ATLANTIC

Number	Title	Yr	NM
❑ 3381	Lorelei/Lorelei	1977	$5

DECCA

Number	Title	Yr	NM
❑ 32826	Blind Eye/Queen of Torture	1971	$8
❑ 33004	Blowin' Free/No Easy Road	1972	$8

MCA

Number	Title	Yr	NM
❑ 40829	Front Page News/Goodbye Baby, Hello Friends	1977	$4
❑ 40362	Persephone/Silver Shoes	1975	$6

WISNER, JIMMY

ATLANTIC

Number	Title	Yr	NM
❑ 2315	Choppin' Around/Juliet's Theme	1966	$40

CAMEO

Number	Title	Yr	NM
❑ 373	A Walk in Space/El Senor Jose	1965	$20

COLUMBIA

Number	Title	Yr	NM
❑ 4-44558	Theme from "The Swimmer"/Music	1967	$8

WITHERS, BILL

COLUMBIA

Number	Title	Yr	NM
❑ 10459	Close to Me/I'll Be with You	1976	$5
❑ 10892	Don't It Make It Better/Love Is	1979	$4
❑ 10357	Family Table/Hello Like Before	1976	$5
❑ 10420	If I Didn't Mean You Well/ My Imagination	1976	$5
❑ 02071	I Want to Spend the Night/ Memories Are That Way	1981	$4
❑ 10308	I Wish You Well/She's Lonely	1976	$5
❑ 10627	Lovely Day/It Ain't Because of Me Baby	1977	$5
❑ 10702	Lovely Night for Dancing/I Want to Spend the Night	1978	$5
❑ 10255	Make Love to Your Mind/I Love You Dawn	1975	$5
❑ 04841	Oh Yeah!/Just Like the First Time	1985	$4
❑ 05424	Something That Turns You On/You Tried to Find a Love	1985	$4
❑ 05424 [PS]	Something That Turns You On/You Tried to Find a Love	1985	$4
❑ 05675	We Could Be Sweet Lovers/ You Just Can't Smile It Away	1985	$4

SUSSEX

Number	Title	Yr	NM
❑ 219	Ain't No Sunshine/Harlem	1971	$6
❑ 257	Friend of Mine/Lonely Town, Lonely Street	1973	$5
❑ 227	Grandma's Hands/ Sweet Wanomi	1971	$5
❑ 227 [DJ]	Grandma's Hands (with Monologue)/ (without Monologue)	1971	$10
❑ 629	Heartbreak Road/Ruby Lee	1974	$5

—Heartbreak Road" was the side that charted, though at least some copies of the stock 45 have it labeled as the B-side

Number	Title	Yr	NM
❑ 235	Lean On Me/Better Off Dead	1972	$6
❑ 247	Let Us Love/The Gift of Giving	1972	$5
❑ 247 [PS]	Let Us Love/The Gift of Giving	1972	$8
❑ 513	The Same Love That Made Me Laugh/Make a Smile for Me	1974	$5
❑ 638	Who Is He (And What Is He to You)/Harlem	1975	$5

WITHERSPOON, JIMMY

ABC

Number	Title	Yr	NM
❑ 11288	Handbags and Gladrags/ Stay with Me Baby	1971	$6

BLUE NOTE

Number	Title	Yr	NM
❑ XW716	Pearly Whites/Sign on the Building	1975	$5

CAPITOL

Number	Title	Yr	NM
❑ 3998	Love Is a Five Letter Word/ Other Side of Love	1974	$5

CHECKER

Number	Title	Yr	NM
❑ 798	Big Daddy/When the Lights Go Out	1954	$40
❑ 826	It Ain't No Secret/Why Do I Love You Like I Do	1955	$40
❑ 810	Time Brings About a Change/ Waiting for Your Return	1955	$40

FEDERAL

Number	Title	Yr	NM
❑ 12173	24 Sad Hours/Just for You	1954	$40
❑ 12138	Back Door Blues/Last Mile	1953	$40
❑ 12107	Don't Tell Me Now/ Corn Whiskey	1952	$40
❑ 12155	Fast Women and Sloe Gin/Miss Mistreater	1953	$40
❑ 12095	Foolish Prayer/Two Little Girls	1952	$40
❑ 12180	It/Highway to Happiness	1954	$40
❑ 12099	Lucille/Blues in Trouble	1952	$40
❑ 12189	Oh Boy/I Done Told You	1954	$40
❑ 12128	One Fine Gal/Back Home	1953	$40
❑ 12156	Sad Life/Move Me Baby	1953	$60

—With the Lamplighters

GNP CRESCENDO

Number	Title	Yr	NM
❑ 156	Ain't Nobody's Business/ No Rollin' Blues	1959	$15

HIFI

Number	Title	Yr	NM
❑ 594	Everytime I Feel the Spirit/ Oh Mary Don't You Weep	1960	$15

KENT

Number	Title	Yr	NM
❑ 4551	Ain't Nobody's Business (Part 1)/Ain't Nobody's Business (Part 2)	1971	$6
❑ 343	Stormy Monday Blues/ Your Cheating Heart	1960	$30

KING

Number	Title	Yr	NM
❑ 5997	Foolish Prayer/Two Little Girls	1965	$10

MODERN

Number	Title	Yr	NM
❑ 895	Baby Baby/Slow Your Speed	1953	$50
❑ 903	Each Step of the Way/ Let Jesus Fix It for You	1953	$50
❑ 877	Love My Baby/Daddy Pinocchio	1952	$50
❑ 909	Oh Mother, Dear Mother/I'll Be Right On Down	1953	$50
❑ 857	The Wind Is Blowin'/My Baby Make a Change	1952	$50

—Note: Earlier Jimmy Witherspoon 45s on Modern are not known to exist

PACIFIC JAZZ

Number	Title	Yr	NM
❑ 327	Ain't Nobody's Business/ Times Have Changed	1961	$10
❑ 298	I Had a Dream/S.K. Blues	1963	$10
❑ 340	I Never Will Marry/Happy Blues	1964	$10
❑ 307	Money's Gettin' Cheaper/Ever In	1963	$10
❑ 341	Some of My Best Friends Are the Blues/You're Next	1964	$12

RCA VICTOR

Number	Title	Yr	NM
❑ 47-6977	Ain't Nobody's Business/ Who Baby Who	1957	$30
❑ 47-7377	Confessin' the Blues/Ooo Wee, Then the Lights Go Out	1958	$30

REPRISE

Number	Title	Yr	NM
❑ 20013	The Masquerade Is Over/I Don't Know	1961	$10
❑ 20029	Warm Your Heart/ Hey Mrs. Jones	1961	$10

VEE JAY

Number	Title	Yr	NM
❑ 322	Everything But You/I Know, I Know	1959	$15

VERVE

Number	Title	Yr	NM
❑ 10495	Fast Forty Blues/ My Baby Quit Me	1967	$8
❑ 10439	It's All Over But the Crying/My Blue Tears	1966	$8

WORLD PACIFIC

Number	Title	Yr	NM
❑ 814	Ain't Nobody's Business/ There's Good Rockin' Tonight	1960	$15

WIZZARD

HARVEST

Number	Title	Yr	NM
❑ 05517	I Wish It Could Be Christmas Everyday/Rob Roy's Nightmare	1973	$15
❑ 5079 [PS]	I Wish It Could Be Christmas Everyday/Rob Roy's Nightmare	1973	$15

—Gatefold sleeve; Harvest logo stuck over Warner Bros. logo

Number	Title	Yr	NM
❑ 05517 [PS]	I Wish It Could Be Christmas Everyday/Rob Roy's Nightmare	1973	$30

—European (non-U.K.) import

Number	Title	Yr	NM
❑ 5079	I Wish It Could Be Christmas Everyday/Rob Roy's Nightmare	1973	$15

WARNER BROS.

Number	Title	Yr	NM
❑ K16336	I Wish It Could Be Christmas Everyday/Rob Roy's Nightmare	1973	$20

—Original U.K. pressing

Number	Title	Yr	NM
❑ K16336 [PS]	I Wish It Could Be Christmas Everyday/Rob Roy's Nightmare	1973	$20

—Gatefold sleeve; both sleeve and record withdrawn and moved to Harvest

Number	Title	Yr	NM
WOLFE, DANNY			
DOT			
❏ 15715	I'd Rather Be Lucky/ Pucker Paint	1958	$50
❏ 15667	Let's Flat Get It/I'm Glad I Waited	1957	$70
❏ 15591	Pretty Blue Jean Baby/ Once with You	1957	$50
WOMACK, BOBBY			
ARISTA			
❏ 0421	How Could You Break My Heart/I Honestly Love You	1979	$4
BEVERLY GLEN			
❏ 2000	If You Think You're Lonely Now/Secrets	1981	$4
❏ 2023	I'm So Proud/Searching for My Love	1985	$4
❏ 2018	It Takes a Lot of Strength to Say Goodbye/Who's Foolin' Who	1984	$4
—A-side with Patti LaBelle			
❏ 2012	Love Has Finally Come at Last/American Dream	1984	$4
—With Patti LaBelle			
❏ 2021	Someday We'll All Be Free/I Wish I Had Someone to Go Home To	1985	$4
❏ 2014	Tell Me Why/Through the Eyes of a Child	1984	$4
—B-side with Patti LaBelle			
❏ 2001	Where Do We Go from Here/ Just My Imagination	1982	$4
CHECKER			
❏ 1122	Lonesome Man/I Found a True Love	1965	$20
COLUMBIA			
❏ 10437	Home Is Where the Heart Is/ We've Only Just Begun	1976	$5
❏ 10493	Standing in the Safety Zone/A Change Is Gonna Come	1977	$5
❏ 10672	Trust Your Heart/When Love Begins, Friendship Ends	1978	$5
❏ 10732	Wind It Up/Stop Before We Start	1978	$5
LIBERTY			
❏ 56186	I'm Gonna Forget About You/Don't Look Back	1970	$8
❏ 56206	Something/Everybody's Talkin'	1970	$8
MCA			
❏ 52793	Gypsy Woman/What Evert Happened to the Times	1986	$3
❏ 52955	(I Wanna) Make Love to You/The Launch	1986	$3
❏ 52955 [PS]	(I Wanna) Make Love to You/The Launch	1986	$3
❏ 52624	I Wish He Didn't Trust Me So Much/Got to Be with You Tonight	1985	$4
❏ 52624 [PS]	I Wish He Didn't Trust Me So Much/Got to Be with You Tonight	1985	$4
❏ 52709	Let Me Kiss It Where It Hurts/Check It Out	1985	$4
❏ 53190	Living in a Box/I Can't Stay Mad	1987	$3
❏ 53263	Outside Myself/A Woman Likes to Hear Than	1988	$3
MINIT			
❏ 32024	Baby, I Can't Stand It/Trust Me	1967	$12
❏ 32055	California Dreamin'/Baby, You Oughta Think It Over	1968	$10
❏ 32048	Fly Me to the Moon/Take Me	1968	$10
❏ 32081	How I Miss You Baby/ Tried and Convicted	1969	$8
❏ 32059	I Left My Heart in San Francisco/Love, The Time Is Now	1969	$8
❏ 32071	It's Gonna Rain/Thank You	1969	$8
❏ 32093	More Than I Can Stand/ Arkansas State Prison	1970	$8
❏ 32030	Somebody Special/ Broadway Walk	1967	$12
❏ 32037	What Is This/What You Gonna Do (When Your Love Is Gone)	1968	$10
SOLAR			
❏ 74006	Save the Children/(Instrumental)	1989	$3
UNITED ARTISTS			
❏ XW196	Across 110th Street/ Hang On In There	1973	$5
❏ XW527	California Dreamin'/ Fly Me to the Moon	1974	$5
❏ XW621	Check It Out/Interlude No. 2	1975	$5
❏ 50816	Communication/Fire and Rain	1971	$6
❏ XW763	Daylight/Trust Me	1976	$5
❏ 50988 [DJ]	Harry Hippie (mono/stereo)	1972	$8
—Apparently, no stock copy exists			
❏ XW526	Harry Hippie/Sweet Caroline	1974	$4
—Reissue			
❏ 50946	Harry Hippie/Sweet Caroline (Good Times Never Seemed So Good)	1972	$6
❏ XW561	I Don't Know/Yes, Jesus Loves Me	1974	$5
❏ XW804	I Feel a Groove Comin' On/Trust Me	1976	$5
❏ XW674	It's All Over Now/Git It	1975	$5
❏ XW375	Lookin' for a Love/ Let It Hang Out	1973	$5

Number	Title	Yr	NM
❏ XW525	Lookin' for a Love/ Nobody Wants You When You're Down and Out	1974	$4
— Reissue			
❏ 50847	That's the Way I Feel About 'Cha/Come L'Amore	1971	$6
❏ 0123	That's the Way I Feel About Cha/Woman's Gotta Have It	1973	$4
—Silver Spotlight Series" reissue			
❏ 50773	The Preacher/More Than I Can Stand	1971	$6
❏ XW735	Where There's a Will, There's a Way/Everything's Gonna Be Alright	1975	$5
❏ 50902	Woman's Gotta Have It/Give It Back	1972	$6
WOMB			
DOT			
❏ 17250	Hang On/My Baby Thinks About the Good Things	1969	$15
WONDER, STEVIE, AND MICHAEL JACKSON			
MOTOWN			
❏ 1930	Get It/(Instrumental)	1988	$3
❏ 1930 [PS]	Get It/(Instrumental)	1988	$3
WONDER, STEVIE			
GORDY			
❏ 7076	Alfie/More Than a Dream	1968	$30
—As "Eivets Rednow" (read it backwards)			
MOTOWN			
❏ 1745	I Just Called to Say I Love You//(Instrumental)	1984	$3
❏ 1745 [PS]	I Just Called to Say I Love You//(Instrumental)	1984	$50
—Sleeve is labeled promo only, though it has been found on the (very) occasional stock copy			
❏ 1769	Love Light in Flight/ It's More Than You	1984	$3
❏ 1769 [PS]	Love Light in Flight/ It's More Than You	1984	$4
❏ 1946	My Eyes Don't Cry/ (Instrumental)	1988	$3
❏ 1946 [PS]	My Eyes Don't Cry/ (Instrumental)	1988	$4
❏ 1907	Skeletons//(Instrumental)	1987	$3
❏ 1907 [PS]	Skeletons//(Instrumental)	1987	$4
❏ 1953	With Each Beat of My Heart/(Instrumental)	1989	$3
MOTOWN YESTERYEAR			
❏ Y621F	Another Star/As	1978	$3
—Reissue			
❏ Y685F	Don't Drive Drunk/(Instrumental)	1985	$3
—First U.S. edition of this song on 45			
❏ Y647F	I Ain't Gonna Stand For It/Lately	1982	$3
—Reissue			
❏ Y684F	I Just Called to Say I Love You/Love Light in Flight	1985	$3
—Reissue			
❏ Y620F	I Wish/Sir Duke	1978	$3
—Reissue			
❏ Y646F	Master Blaster (Jammin')/ Master Blaster (Dub)	1982	$3
—Reissue			
❏ Y657F	That Girl/Do I Do	1983	$3
—Reissue			
TAMLA			
❏ 54286	Another Star/Creepin'	1977	$5
❏ 54139	A Place in the Sun/Sylvia	1966	$15
❏ 54139 [PS]	A Place in the Sun/Sylvia	1966	$30
❏ 54291	As/Contusion	1977	$3
❏ 54136	Blowin' in the Wind/Ain't That Asking for Trouble	1966	$15
❏ 54136 [PS]	Blowin' in the Wind/Ain't That Asking for Trouble	1966	$30
❏ 54254	Boogie On Raggae Woman/ Seems So Long	1974	$6
—With incorrect spelling of A-side			
❏ 54254	Boogie On Reggae Woman/ Seems So Long	1974	$5
—With correct spelling of A-side			
❏ 54090	Castles in the Sand/Thank You (For Loving Me All the Way)	1964	$20
—Up to and including this, as "Little Stevie Wonder			
❏ 54074	Contract on Love/Sunset	1963	$30
❏ 54328	Did I Hear You Say You Love Me/As If You Read My Mind	1981	$4
❏ 1612	Do I Do/Rocket Love	1982	$4
❏ 54245	Don't You Worry 'Bout a Thing/Blame It on the Sun	1974	$5
❏ 54080	Fingertips -- Pt. 2/ Fingertips -- Pt. 1	1963	$30
❏ 54080 [PS]	Fingertips -- Pt. 2/ Fingertips -- Pt. 1	1963	$60
❏ 54174	For Once in My Life/Angie Girl	1968	$8
❏ 1817	Go Home//(Instrumental)	1985	$3
❏ 1817 [PS]	Go Home//(Instrumental)	1985	$4
❏ 54200	Heaven Help Us All/I Gotta Have a Song	1970	$6
❏ 54096	Hey Harmonica Man/ This Little Girl	1964	$20

Number	Title	Yr	NM
❏ 54096 [PS]	Hey Harmonica Man/ This Little Girl	1964	$50
❏ 54235	Higher Ground/Too High	1973	$5
❏ 54119	High Heel Sneakers/Funny How Time Slips Away	1965	$30
❏ 54119	High Heel Sneakers/Music Talk	1965	$15
❏ 54320	I Ain't Gonna Stand For It/ Knocks Me Off My Feet	1980	$4
❏ 54061	I Call It Pretty Music But The Old People Call It the Blues (Part 1)/I Call It Pretty Music But The Old People Call It the Blues (Part 2)	1962	$40
❏ 54061 [PS]	I Call It Pretty Music But The Old People Call It the Blues (Part 1)/I Call It Pretty Music But The Old People Call It the Blues (Part 2)	1962	$100
❏ 54180	I Don't Know Why/ My Cherie Amour	1969	$10
❏ 54208	If You Really Love Me/Think of Me As Your Soldier	1971	$6
❏ 54157	I'm Wondering/Every Time I See You I Go Wild	1967	$10
❏ 54151	I Was Made to Love Her/Hold Me	1967	$10
❏ 54274	I Wish/You and I	1976	$5
❏ 1846	Land of La La/(Instrumental)	1986	$3
❏ 1846 [PS]	Land of La La/(Instrumental)	1986	$4
❏ 54323	Lately/If It's Magic	1981	$4
❏ 54070	Little Water Boy/La La La La La	1962	$30
❏ 54242	Living for the City/Visions	1973	$5
❏ 54317	Master Blaster (Jammin')/ (Instrumental)	1980	$4
❏ 54317 [PS]	Master Blaster (Jammin')/ (Instrumental)	1980	$6
❏ 54180	My Cherie Amour/Don't Know Why I Love You	1969	$8
—Re-release with A and B side switched and new title on B-side			
❏ 54308	Outside My Window/ Same Old Story	1980	$4
❏ 54308 [PS]	Outside My Window/ Same Old Story	1980	$6
❏ 1832	Overjoyed//(Instrumental)	1986	$3
❏ 1832 [PS]	Overjoyed//(Instrumental)	1986	$4
❏ 1808	Part-Time Lover/(Instrumental)	1985	$3
❏ 1808 [PS]	Part-Time Lover/(Instrumental)	1985	$4
❏ 54103	Sad Boy/Happy Street	1964	$30
❏ 54303	Send One Your Love/ (Instrumental)	1979	$4
❏ 54303 [PS]	Send One Your Love/ (Instrumental)	1979	$6
❏ 54165	Shoo-Be-Doo-Be-Doo-Da-Day/Why Don't You Lead Me to Love	1968	$8
❏ 54196	Signed, Sealed, Delivered, I'm Yours/I'm More Than Happy	1970	$6
❏ 54281	Sir Duke/He's Misstra Know-It-All	1977	$5
❏ 54281 [PS]	Sir Duke/He's Misstra Know-It-All	1977	$10
❏ 54142	Some Day at Christmas/ The Miracles of Christmas	1966	$20
❏ 54226	Superstition/You've Got It Bad Girl	1972	$5
❏ 54216	Superwoman (Where Were You When I Needed You)/I Love Every Little Thing About You	1972	$6
❏ 1602	That Girl/All I Do	1982	$4
❏ 54147	Travlin' Man/Hey Love	1967	$10
❏ 54202	We Can Work It Out/ Never Dreamed You'd Leave in Summer	1971	$6
❏ 54214	What Christmas Means to Me/Bedtime for Toys	1971	$6
❏ 54086	Workout Stevie, Workout/ Monkey Talk	1963	$20
TOPPS/MOTOWN			
❏ 8	Fingertips Part 2	1967	$80
—Cardboard record			
7-Inch Extended Plays			
TAMLA			
❏ T340EP	Saturn/Ebony Eyes//All Day Sucker/Easy Goin' Evening (My Mama's Call)	1976	$4
—Called "A Something's Extra for Songs in the Key of Life," this was issued with the 2-LP set of the same name and is sometimes found separately, though it was never sold separately; not issued with picture sleeve			
WONDERETTES, THE			
ENTERPRISE			
❏ 5025	Love's Got a Hold on Me/Work Out Fine	1964	$30
RUBY			
❏ 5065	I Feel Strange/Wait Until Tonight	1965	$50
UNITED ARTISTS			
❏ 944	I Feel Strange/Wait Until Tonight	1965	$30
❏ 997	Mend My Broken Heart/ And If I Had My Way	1966	$30
—By "Rose St. John and the Wonderettes			
VEEP			
❏ 1231	Fool Don't Laugh/I Know the Meeting	1966	$30
—As "Rose St. John and the Wonderettes			

WOOD, ANITA

SUN

Number	Title	Yr	NM
❏ 361	I'll Wait Forever/I Can't Show How I Feel	1961	$40

WOOD, BOBBY

CHALLENGE

Number	Title	Yr	NM
❏ 9160	The Day After Forever/Everybody's Searchin'	1962	$12

CINNAMON

Number	Title	Yr	NM
❏ 790	I'm a Fool for Loving You/Secret Love Affair	1974	$4

JOY

Number	Title	Yr	NM
❏ 295	Bed of Roses/Show Me	1965	$8
❏ 279	Do Darlin' (Do Remember Me)/That's All I Need	1963	$12
❏ 301	Fool's Paradise/What Am I Gonna Tell Myself	1965	$8
❏ 298	Human Emotions/When a Lonely Boy Meets a Lonely Girl	1965	$8
❏ 285	If I'm a Fool for Loving You/My Heart Went Boing! Boing! Boing!	1964	$10
❏ 277	I Still Hurt/Just the Same	1963	$10
❏ 291	So Cruel/I'd Do It Again	1964	$12
❏ 288	That's All I Need to Know/This Time	1964	$12

LUCKY ELEVEN

Number	Title	Yr	NM
❏ 361	One Day Behind/Sound of Sadness	1973	$5

MALA

Number	Title	Yr	NM
❏ 526	My Special Angel/I'd Rather Forgive You	1966	$8

MGM

Number	Title	Yr	NM
❏ 13797	Break My Mind/This Thing Called Love	1967	$6
❏ 13912	Is That All There Is To It/Say It's Not You	1968	$6
❏ 14051	(Margie's at the) Lincoln Park Inn/I'm the Name of Her Game	1969	$6
❏ 13952	Mary/Big Buildup	1968	$6
❏ 13729	My Last Date (With You)/Everybody's Baby	1967	$6

SUN

Number	Title	Yr	NM
❏ 369 [DJ]	Everybody's Searchin'/Human Emotions	1961	$600

—No stock copies known; should one be discovered, it would be worth much more

WOOD, BRENTON

BRENT

Number	Title	Yr	NM
❏ 7057	Cross the Bridge/Sweet Molly Malone	1966	$30
❏ 7052	Good Lovin'/I Want to Love	1966	$20
❏ 7068	I Want Love/Sweet Molly Malone	1967	$10

CREAM

Number	Title	Yr	NM
❏ 7602	All That Jazz/Bless Your Little Heart	1976	$4
❏ 7716	Come Softly to Me/You're Everything I Need	1977	$4
❏ 7833	Let's Get Crazy Together/Love Is Free	1978	$4

DOUBLE SHOT

Number	Title	Yr	NM
❏ 121	Baby You Got It/Catch You on the Rebound	1967	$8
❏ 150	Bogaloosa, Lousiana/I Need Your Love So Bad	1970	$6
❏ 147	Can You Dig It/Great Big Bubble of Love	1970	$6
❏ 116	Gimme Little Sign/I Think You've Got Your Fools Mixed Up	1967	$10
❏ 126	Lovey Dovey Kinda Lovin'/Two-Time Loser	1968	$8
❏ 156	Sad Little Song/Who But a Fool	1971	$6
❏ 130	Some Got It, Some Don't/Me and You	1968	$8
❏ 111	The Oogum Boogum Song/I Like the Way You Love Me	1967	$10
❏ 135	Trouble/It's Just a Game, Love	1968	$8
❏ 137	Where Are You/A Change Is Gonna Come	1969	$8
❏ 142	Whoop It On Me/Take a Chance	1969	$8

PHILCO-FORD

Number	Title	Yr	NM
❏ HP-38	Gimme Little Sign/Oogum Boogum	1969	$30

—4-inch plastic "Hip Pocket Record" with color sleeve

PROPHESY

Number	Title	Yr	NM
❏ 3003	Another Saturday Night/(B-side unknown)	1973	$5
❏ 3002	Sticky Boom Boom Too Cold (Part 1)/Sticky Boom Boom Too Cold (Part 2)	1973	$5

WAND

Number	Title	Yr	NM
❏ 145	Mr. Schemer/Hide-A-Way	1963	$50

WARNER BROS.

Number	Title	Yr	NM
❏ 8079	All That Jazz/Rainin' Love	1975	$5
❏ 8144	Better Believe It/It Only Makes Me Want It More	1975	$5

WOOD, DEL

DECCA

Number	Title	Yr	NM
❏ 9-28795	Listen to the Mockingbird/Margie	1953	$30
❏ 9-28611	The Eyes of Texas Are Upon You/Washington and Lee Swing	1953	$30

MERCURY

Number	Title	Yr	NM
❏ 72158	Columbus Georgia Blues/Old Piano Roll Blues	1963	$15
❏ 71899	Creole Fandango/My Adobe Hacienda	1961	$15
❏ 71972	Down Yonder/Lady of Spain	1962	$15
❏ 72351	I Walk the Line/Night Train to Memphis	1964	$10

RCA VICTOR

Number	Title	Yr	NM
❏ 47-6613	Are You from Dixie/Intermission at the Opry	1956	$30
❏ 47-6489	Down Yonder/Tie Me to Your Apron	1956	$30
❏ 47-6080	Home Sweet Home/That Naughty Waltz	1955	$30
❏ 47-7088	Maggie Blues/Whirl-A-Way	1957	$30
❏ 47-6725	On the Sunny Side of the Street/Crazy	1956	$30
❏ 47-6978	Piano Roll Waltz/Chicka-Boo	1957	$30
❏ 47-7421	Shortcake/Sunday Down South	1958	$20
❏ 47-7594	Swanee River Soft Shoe/Gismo Rag	1959	$20

REPUBLIC

Number	Title	Yr	NM
❏ 7105	Are You from Dixie/There's a Tavern in the Town	1955	$30
❏ 7070	Columbus Stockade Blues/Bye Bye Blackbird	1954	$30
❏ 7043	Elmer's Tune/Jersey Bounce	1953	$30
❏ 7085	It's a Grand Old Flag/When I Lost You	1954	$30
❏ 7087	It's a Sin/I Like Mountain Music	1954	$30
❏ 7036	Pickin' and Grinnin'/12th Street Rag	1953	$30

TENNESSEE

Number	Title	Yr	NM
❏ 775	Down Yonder/Dreamy Eyes	1951	$40

WOOD, RONNIE

Also see FACES; THE ROLLING STONES.

COLUMBIA

Number	Title	Yr	NM
❏ 1-11014	Seven Days/Breakin' My Heart	1979	$6

WARNER BROS.

Number	Title	Yr	NM
❏ 8036	Breathe on Me/I Can Feel the Fire	1974	$6
❏ 8131	I Got a Feeling/If You Don't Want My Love	1975	$6

WOOD, ROY

Also see ELECTRIC LIGHT ORCHESTRA; THE MOVE. (45)

UNITED ARTISTS

Number	Title	Yr	NM
❏ XW792	Any Old Time Will Do/Why Does Such a Pretty Girl Sing Those Sad Songs	1976	$10
❏ XW160	Ball Park Incident/Carlsberg Special	1973	$12

—As "Wizzard"

Number	Title	Yr	NM
❏ XW320	Dear Elaine/Song of Praise	1973	$12
❏ XW394	Forever/Woodbe	1974	$10
❏ XW272	See My Baby Jive/Bend Over Beethoven	1973	$10

WOODALL, BOOTS

CAPITOL

Number	Title	Yr	NM
❏ F2670	Bet'cha I'm in Love/You're Waiting in My Place	1953	$30
❏ F2851	I'm Gonna Start at the Top/You're Gonna Learn to Love Me	1954	$30
❏ F2559	I Might Have Been/Only Three Days	1953	$30
❏ F2739	Salt Water River/Lovely Little Darling	1954	$30

MERCURY

Number	Title	Yr	NM
❏ 6398	It's Sweet of You/You Asked Me for Some Loving	1952	$40
❏ 6380	There'll Be No Cripples Up There/They Locked God Outside the Iron Curtain	1952	$40

WOODS, BENNIE

ATLAS

Number	Title	Yr	NM
❏ 1040	I Cross My Fingers/Wheel Baby Wheel	1955	$800

—As "Bennie Woods and the Five Dukes"

Number	Title	Yr	NM
❏ 1040	I Cross My Fingers/Wheel Baby Wheel	1955	$500

—As "Bennie Woods and Rockin' Townies

WOODS, BILLY

DOT

Number	Title	Yr	NM
❏ 16053	Falling Rain/Friendly Mr. Wendley	1960	$50

SUSSEX

Number	Title	Yr	NM
❏ 213	Let Me Make You Happy/That Was the Love That Was	1971	$1500

VERVE

Number	Title	Yr	NM
❏ 10451	I Don't Want to Lose Your Love/No One to Blame	1966	$60
❏ 10484	I Found Satisfaction/If I Could Only See	1967	$60

WOODS, DONALD

ALADDIN

Number	Title	Yr	NM
❏ 3412	Memories of an Angel/That Much of Your Love	1958	$40

FLIP

Number	Title	Yr	NM
❏ 306	Death of an Angel/Man from Utopia	1955	$50

WOODS, GENE

HAP

Number	Title	Yr	NM
❏ 1004	The Ballad of Wild River/Afraid	1960	$30

WOODS, KENNI

PHILIPS

Number	Title	Yr	NM
❏ 40156	Back with My Baby/Do You Really Love Me	1963	$12
❏ 40112	Can't He Take a Hint/That Guy Is Mine	1963	$10

WOODS, MARTY

HIT

Number	Title	Yr	NM
❏ 248	Secret Agent Man/Time Won't Let Me	1966	$8

—B-side by the Chellows

WOODS, MICKEY

TAMLA

Number	Title	Yr	NM
❏ 54052	Please Mr. Kennedy/(They Call Me) Cupid	1962	$50
❏ 54039	They Rode Through the Valley/Poor Sam Jones	1961	$60

WOOLEY, SHEB

Includes records by his comedic alter ego, "Ben Colder."

BLUE BONNET

Number	Title	Yr	NM
❏ 125	Peeping Thru the Keyhole/Time Won't Heal an Achin' Heart	1954	$75
❏ 130	Too Long with the Wrong Mama/Your Papa Ain't Steppin' Anymore	1954	$70
❏ 124	Wooley's Polka/Lazy Mary	1954	$75

MGM

Number	Title	Yr	NM
❏ 11910	38-24-35/I Flipped	1955	$20
❏ 11308	A Cowboy Had Ought to Be Single/You Never Can Tell	1952	$40
❏ 13897	Ain't It Funny How Wine Sips Away/The Doo-Hickey Song	1968	$8

—As "Ben Colder"

Number	Title	Yr	NM
❏ 13590	Almost Persuaded No. 2/A Packet of Pencils	1966	$8

—As "Ben Colder"

Number	Title	Yr	NM
❏ 12114	Are You Satisfied/Humdinger	1955	$20
❏ 11180	Backroom Boogie/Down in the Toolies	1952	$40
❏ 14639	Behind Cloe's Door/Satin Sheets	1973	$5

—As "Ben Colder"

Number	Title	Yr	NM
❏ 13395	Big Land/Sally's Arms	1965	$8
❏ 14111	Big Sweet John/Games People Play	1970	$6

—As "Ben Colder"

Number	Title	Yr	NM
❏ 13241	Blue Guitar/Natchez Landing	1964	$8
❏ 11717	Blue Guitar/Panama Pete	1954	$30
❏ 13477	Buba Hoo Boba Dee/I'll Leave the Singin' to the Bluebirds	1966	$8
❏ 13152	Buildin' a Railroad/Cowboy Hero	1963	$10
❏ 13914	By the Time I Get to Phoenix No. 2/Skip a Rope No. 2	1968	$8

—As "Ben Colder"

Number	Title	Yr	NM
❏ 12817	Careless Hands/Pigmy Love	1959	$10
❏ 12743	Cherry Street/Star of Love	1958	$15
❏ 14123	Daddy's Home/The Will	1970	$6
❏ 13167	Detroit City No. 2/Ring of Smoke	1963	$12

—As "Ben Colder"

Number	Title	Yr	NM
❏ 13104	Don't Go Near the Eskimos/Louisiana Trapper	1962	$12

—As "Ben Colder"

Number	Title	Yr	NM
❏ 11665	Don't Stop Kissing Me Goodnight/Knew I Had Lost	1954	$30
❏ 14610	Early in the Morning/Getting High on Love	1973	$6
❏ 14327	Easy Loving No. 2/Sing a Drinkin' Song	1971	$6

—As "Ben Colder"

Number	Title	Yr	NM
❏ 14209	Fifteen Beers Ago/Sunday Mornin' Fallin' Down	1970	$6

—As "Ben Colder"

Number	Title	Yr	NM
❏ 12328	First Day of School/The Lonely Man	1956	$20

Number	Title	Yr	NM
□ 14471	Glossy 8 x 10/Moontan	1972	$5
—As "Ben Colder			
□ 11640	Goodbye Texas, Hello Tennessee/I'll Rerturn the Letters	1953	$30
□ 14287	Goodbye Wabash Cannonball/Joy	1971	$6
□ 13997	Harper Valley P.T.A. (Later That Same Day)/Folsom Prison Blues No. 1 1/2	1968	$12
—As "Ben Colder			
□ 11403	Heart Bound in Chains/Freight Train Cinders	1953	$30
□ 13122	Hello Wall No. 2/Shudders and Screams	1963	$12
—As "Ben Colder			
□ 14247	Help Me Fake It Through the Night/Rose Garden	1971	$6
—As "Ben Colder			
□ 11836	Hillbilly Mambo/I Go Outta My Mind	1954	$30
□ 12382	Honey I'm Lonesome/Let the Big Winds Blow	1956	$20
□ 10960	Hoot Owl Boogie/Country Kisses	1951	$40
□ 12853	It's Almost Time/Roughneck	1959	$10
□ 12060	It Takes a Heap of Livin'/Listen for Your Footsteps	1955	$20
□ 13197	I Walk the Line No. 2/Talk Back Blubberin' Lips	1963	$10
—As "Ben Colder			
□ 13065	Laughin' the Blues/Somebody Please	1962	$12
□ 13705	Letter to Daddy/Draggin' the River	1967	$8
□ 14384	Life Is a Fountain/Somebody Gonna Come Along	1972	$6
□ 12048	Listening to Your Footsteps/Love Is a Prayer	1955	$20
□ 13125	Little Bitty Bilbo Abernathy Nathan Allen Quincy Jones/Daddy Kiss and Make It Well	1963	$12
□ 14015	Little Green Apples No. 2/It's Such a Pretty World Tonight	1968	$8
—As "Ben Colder			
□ 11580	Love Is a Merry-Go-Round/Texas Tango	1953	$30
□ 12851	Love Like Mine/Josie	1959	$10
□ 12882	Luke the Spook/My Only Treasure	1960	$10
□ 13938	Make 'Em Laugh/Tie a Tiger Down	1968	$6
□ 13444	Make the World Go Away No. 2/May the Bird of Paradise Fly Up Your Snoot	1966	$8
—As "Ben Colder			
□ 12778	More/Deep Goes the Love	1959	$10
□ 10697	Mule Boogie/Changing Your Name	1950	$40
□ 14044	Ode to the Little Shack Out Back/You're a Real Good Friend	1969	$6
—As "Ben Colder			
□ 13166	Old Rag Joe/Hootenanny Hoot	1963	$10
□ 13166 [PS]	Old Rag Joe/Hootenanny Hoot	1963	$50
□ 14085	One Man Band/You Still Turn Me On	1969	$6
□ 14165	One of Them Roarin' Songs/I Don't Belong in Her Arms	1970	$6
□ 11059	Over the Barrel/Air Castles	1951	$40
□ 13195	Papa's Ole Fiddle/She Called Me Baby	1963	$10
□ 12467	Plenty of Love/I Won't Come Back	1957	$15
□ 12733	Santa and the Purple People Eater/Star of Love	1958	$30
□ 12733 [PS]	Santa and the Purple People Eater/Star of Love	1958	$50
□ 13351	Silver (The Wonder Horse)/Blistered	1965	$8
□ 13013	Skin Tight, Pin Striped, Pink Pedal Pushers/Till the End of the World	1961	$12
□ 13013 [PS]	Skin Tight, Pin Striped, Pink Pedal Pushers/Till the End of the World	1961	$50
□ 12584	So Close to Heaven/I Found Me An Angel	1957	$15
□ 11976	Speak of the Devil/Love at First Sight	1955	$20
□ 13147	Still No. 2/Goin' Surfin'	1963	$20
—As "Ben Colder			
□ 12781	Sweet Chile/More	1959	$10
□ 12931	Taste of Ashes/Reach for the Moon	1960	$10
□ 14133	Tennessee Bird Talk/What Is Youth	1970	$6
—As "Ben Colder			
□ 14005	That Girl/I Remember Loving You	1968	$6
□ 13079	That's My Ma/Land of No Love	1962	$12
□ 13046	That's My Pa/Meet Mr. Lonely	1961	$12
□ 12202	The Birth of the Rock 'N' Roll/A King or a Clown	1956	$20
□ 14065	The Carroll County Accident No. 2/His Lincoln's Parked at Margie's Again	1969	$6
—As "Ben Colder			
□ 12704	The Chase/Monkey Jive	1958	$15
□ 13094	The Leged of Echo Mountain/Give That Ball to Willie B	1962	$10
□ 13827	The Love-In/Wildwood Flower on the Autoharp	1967	$8
□ 12651	The Purple People Eater/I Can't Believe You're Mine	1958	$20
□ 14647	The Purple People Eater/I Can't Believe You're Mine	1973	$10
□ 13771	The Purple People Eater No. 2/Undertaker's Love Lament	1967	$8
—As "Ben Colder			
□ 13668	There Goes My Everything No. 2/Great Men Repeat Themselves	1967	$8
—As "Ben Colder			
□ 13556	Tonight's the Night My Angel's Halo Fell/Anchors Aweigh	1966	$8
□ 13262	TV Westerns/Dobro's Catchin' On Again (And I'm Gonna Be a Star)	1964	$8
—As "Ben Colder			
□ 11792	White Lightnin'/Fool About You	1954	$30
□ 13294	Wild and Wooley, Big Unruly Me/Sittin' and Thinkin'	1964	$8

SCORPION

□ 0556	Lucille No. 2/Senior Citizen's Lament	1978	$4

—As "Ben Colder

SUNBIRD

□ 109	Flower of the County (Censored Version)/Flower of the County (Uncensored Version)	1980	$4

—As "Ben Colder

□ 7566	The Belly Button Song/Jack Hammer Man	1981	$4

WORK, JIMMY

CAPITOL

Number	Title	Yr	NM
□ F2565	Crazy Moon/Out of My Mind	1953	$30
□ F2682	How Can I Love You/I'm Lonesome for Someone	1953	$30
□ F2372	If I Should Lose You/Don't Play with My Heart	1953	$30

DOT

□ 1284	Blind Heart/You've Got a Heart Like a Merry-Go-Round	1956	$20
□ 1287	Digging My Own Grave/That Cold, Cold Look in Your Eyes	1957	$20
□ 1267	Don't Knock, Just Come On In/Let 'Em Talk	1955	$30
□ 1221	Making Believe/Just Like Downtown	1954	$30
□ 1277	My Old Stomping Ground/Hands Away from My Heart	1956	$30
□ 1245	That's What Makes the Juke Box Play/Don't Give Me a Reason	1955	$30
□ 1272	There's Only One You/When She Said You All	1955	$30

WORLD OF OZ, THE

DERAM

□ 85043	Mandy-Ann/Beside the Fire	1969	$10
□ 85029	The Muffin Man/Peter's Birthday	1968	$10

WORTH, MARION, AND GEORGE MORGAN

COLUMBIA

□ 4-43020	Slipping Around/I Love You So Much It Hurts	1964	$20
□ 4-43874	The Wheel of Hurt/Married	1966	$20
□ 4-43543	Too Busy Saying Goodbye/Saving All My Love (For You)	1966	$20

WORTH, MARION

CHEROKEE

□ 503	Are You Willing, Willie/This Heart of Mine	1959	$40

COLUMBIA

□ 4-42703	Crazy Arms/Lovers' Lane	1963	$20
□ 4-43308	Does the Sun Rise in the East/Seven Roses	1965	$15
□ 4-43686	Don't Count on Tomorrow/Overtime	1966	$15
□ 4-42184	Go On Home/Imitation	1961	$20
□ 4-42848	In His Own Quiet Way/Play a Blue Guitar (For Me)	1963	$20
□ 4-41799	I Think I Know/Tomorrow at a Quarter Till Nine	1960	$20
□ 4-41799 [PS]	I Think I Know/Tomorrow at a Quarter Till Nine	1960	$40
□ 4-42453	It's So Funny I Could Cry/Lover's Hymn	1962	$20
□ 4-43405	I Will Not Blow Out the Light/Twenty-One Days of Darkness	1965	$15
□ 4-42904	Shake Me I Rattle (Squeeze Me I Cry)/My Dolly Has a Pain in Her Sawdust	1963	$15
□ 4-42640	Shake Me I Rattle (Squeeze Me I Cry)/Tennessee Teardrops	1962	$20
□ 4-42640 [PS]	Shake Me I Rattle (Squeeze Me I Cry)/Tennessee Teardrops	1962	$30
□ 4-43119	The French Song/Kentucky Waltz	1964	$15
□ 4-43214	The Hands You're Holding Now/I'm Not Myself	1965	$15
□ 4-41972	There'll Always Be Sadness/I'm Not at All Sorry for You	1961	$20

DECCA

□ 32195	A Woman Needs Love/I've Got That Sad and Lonely Feeling	1967	$8
□ 32150	Baby For You/Only You Can Make Me Cry	1967	$8
□ 32457	Love Is a Very Strange Thing/Wonder What to Do	1969	$8
□ 32278	Mama Sez/Then I'll Be Over	1968	$8
□ 32579	Sock It To 'Em Sister Nell/He's Mean to Me	1969	$8
□ 32398	Spreadin' My Wings/Are You Sleeping Well at Night	1968	$8

GUYDEN

□ 2026	Are You Willing, Willie/This Heart of Mine	1959	$8

—Reissue of Cherokee 503

□ 2033	That's My Kind of Love/I Lost Johnny	1960	$30

WRAY, LINK

EPIC

□ 9321	Comanche/Lillian	1959	$30
□ 9454	El Toro/Tijuana	1961	$30
□ 9419	Mary Ann/Ain't That Lovin' You Baby	1960	$30
□ 9361	Trail of the Lonesome Pine/Golden Strings	1960	$30

KAY

□ 3690	I Sez Baby/(B-side unknown)	1958	$125

MALA

□ 458	There's a Hole in the Middle of the Moon/Dancing Party	1963	$30

POLYDOR

□ 14096	Fallin' Rain/Juke Box Mama	1971	$8
□ 14084	Fire and Brimstone/June Box Mama	1970	$8
□ 14256	I Got to Ramble/She's That Kind of Woman	1974	$6
□ 14188	Shine the Light/Lawdy Miss Clawdy	1973	$6

SWAN

□ 4261	Ace of Spades/Hidden Charms	1966	$30
□ 4244	Batman Theme/Alone	1966	$30
□ 4211	Branded/Hang On	1965	$30
□ 4187	Deuces Wild/Summer Dream	1964	$30
□ 4232	Girl from the North Country/You Hurt Me So	1965	$30
□ 4201	Good Rockin' Tonight/I'll Do Anything for You	1965	$30
□ 4239	The Fuzz/Ace of Spades	1966	$30
□ 4171	The Shadow Knows/My Alberta	1964	$30
□ 4154	Weekend/Turnpike U.S.A.	1963	$30

TRANS ATLAS

□ 687	Big City Stomp/Poppin' Popeye	1962	$30

WRECKLESS ERIC

STIFF/EPIC

□ 50870	Broken Doll/A Little Bit More	1980	$15

WRENS, THE

RAMA

□ 194	C'est La Vie/C'est La Vie	1956	$400

—B-side by Jimmy Wright and His Orchestra

□ 65	Come Back My Love/Beggin' for Love	1955	$200
□ 65	Come Back My Love/Eleven Roses	1955	$400
□ 174	Hey Girl/Serenade of the Bells	1955	$400
□ 184	I Won't Come to Your Wedding/What Makes You Do the Things That You Do	1956	$400
□ 53	Love's Something That's Made for Two/Beggin' for Love	1955	$1500
□ 110	Love's Something That's Made for Two/Eleven Roses	1955	$300

WRIGHT, BOBBY

ABC

□ 12028	Baby's Gone/Love Look (At Us Now)	1974	$5
□ 11363	Burning Memories/Live and Let Live	1973	$5
□ 11443	Everybody Needs a Rainbow/I'll Surely Fall in Love with You	1974	$5
□ 12062	I Just Came Home to Count the Memories/No One Has Ever Loved Me Like You	1975	$5
□ 12093	It's for You Hon/You Won't Find Another Fool Like Me	1975	$5
□ 11390	Lovin' Someone on My Mind/This Time	1973	$5
□ 11418	Seasons in the Sun/Live and Let Live	1974	$5

DECCA

□ 9-29221	Cry Baby/Little Paper Boy	1954	$30
□ 32839	Here I Go Again/If You Don't Swing...Don't Ring	1971	$6

Number	Title	Yr	NM
❏ 32705	Hurry Home to Me/My Home Away from Home	1970	$6
❏ 33034	If Not for You/Searching	1972	$6
❏ 32792	If You Want Me To I'll Go/Rain Falling on Me	1971	$6
❏ 31229	I Need Sleep/Wonderful One	1961	$15
❏ 32107	Lay Some Happiness on Me/How Much Lonelier Can Lonely Be	1967	$6
❏ 9-29033	My Momma Didn't Raise No Foolish Children/You Better Not Do That	1954	$30
❏ 32367	Old Before My Time/Shutting Out the Light	1968	$6
❏ 32903	Search Your Heart/I'll Walk on Water	1971	$6
❏ 32564	Sing a Song About Love/If You Don't Swing -- Don't Ring	1969	$6
❏ 32280	Something Called Happiness/It Happens in the Best of Families	1968	$6
❏ 32633	Take Me Back to the Goodtimes, Sally/Something Called Happiness	1970	$6
❏ 32193	That See Me Later Look/Nail My Shoes to the Floor	1967	$6
❏ 32954	There She Goes/Somebody's Breakin' My Heart	1972	$6
HICKORY			
❏ 1360	I'll Put My Boots On Backwards/No Not Right	1965	$10
❏ 1330	Singing Country Music/Ashes of Love	1965	$10
UNITED ARTISTS			
❏ XW1197	Caroline's Footsteps/I'm Comin' Down Lonely	1978	$4
❏ XW1281	Gettin' Down, Gettin' Together, Gettin' in Love/Same Old Song	1979	$4
❏ X1300	I'm Turning You Loose/Going Home	1979	$4
❏ XW963	In Our Room/Lay Down Beside Me	1977	$4
❏ X1337	I Wish You Could Have Turned My Head (And Left My Heart Alone)/I'm Comin' Down Lonely	1980	$4
❏ XW1051	Playing with the Baby's Mama/Lay Down Beside Me	1977	$4
❏ XW1238	Takin' a Chance/I Don't Know What to Tell Her	1978	$4

WRIGHT, CHARLES, AND THE WATTS 103RD STREET RHYTHM BAND

Number	Title	Yr	NM
ABC			
❏ 12127	Is It Real/One Lie	1975	$4
—Charles Wright solo			
ABC DUNHILL			
❏ 15027	Don't Rush Tomorrow/Is It Real	1974	$4
❏ 4363	Liberated Lady/You Threw It All Away	1973	$4
❏ 4381	The Weight of Hate/You Threw It All Away	1974	$4
❏ 4364	(Well I'm) Doing What Cums Naturally Part 1/Part 2	1973	$4
KEYMEN			
❏ 108	Spreadin' Honey/Charlie	1967	$10
—As "The Watts 103rd Street Rhythm Band"			
WARNER BROS.			
❏ 7222	Bottomless/65 Bars and a Taste of Soul	1968	$10
❏ 7175	Brown Sugar/Caesar's Palace	1968	$10
—Through 7298, as "The Watts 103rd Street Rhythm Band"			
❏ 7250	Do Your Thing/A Dance, a Kiss, and a Song	1969	$8
❏ 7417	Express Yourself/Living on Borrowed Time	1970	$6
❏ 7630	Here Comes the Sun/You Gotta Know Whatcha Doin'	1972	$5
❏ 7577	I've Got Love/Let's Make Love -- Not War	1972	$5
❏ 7365	Love Land/Sorry Charlie	1970	$6
❏ 7338	Must Be Your Thing/Comment	1969	$6
❏ 7600	Soul Train/Run Judy Run	1972	$5
❏ 7298	Till You Get Enough/Light My Fire	1969	$8

WRIGHT, DOYLE

Number	Title	Yr	NM
IMPERIAL			
❏ X8157	Ask the Lord/Don't You Know or Don't You Care	1952	$40
❏ X8250	Someday You'll Return/Ache in My Heart	1954	$30

WRIGHT, GARY

Number	Title	Yr	NM
A&M			
❏ 1319	Love to Survive/Fascinating Things	1972	$5
❏ 1228	Over You Now/Get On the Right Road	1970	$5
❏ 1267	Stand for Our Rights/I Can't See the Reason	1971	$5
❏ 1344	Two-Faced Man/I Know	1972	$5
WARNER BROS.			
❏ 8598	Can't Get Above Losing You/Starry Eyed	1978	$4
❏ 49836	Comin' Apart/Heartbeat	1981	$4
❏ 8167	Dream Weaver/Let It Out	1975	$4

Number	Title	Yr	NM
❏ 8383	Empty Inside/Water Sign	1977	$4
❏ 8809	Follow Next to You/I'm the One Who'll Be At Your Side	1979	$4
❏ 49879	Got the Feelin'/Close to You	1981	$4
❏ 8426	Light of Smiles/Silent Fury	1977	$4
❏ 8143	Love Is Alive/Much Higher	1975	$4
—Reissued in 1976 with the same number			
❏ 8250	Made to Love You/Power of Love	1976	$4
❏ 8331	Phantom Writer/Child of Light	1977	$4
❏ 8548	Something Very Special/Starry Eyed	1978	$4

WRIGHT, GINNY, AND TOM TALL

Number	Title	Yr	NM
FABOR			
❏ 117	Are You Mine/I've Got Somebody New	1954	$40
❏ 121	Out of Line/Boom Boom Boomerang	1955	$40
❏ 127	Will This Dream of Mine Come True/Come with Me	1955	$40
ZERO			
❏ 106	Are You Mine/I've Got Somebody New	1960	$30

WRIGHT, GINNY

Number	Title	Yr	NM
FABOR			
❏ 101	I Love You/I Want You Yes (You Want Me No)	1953	$50
— With Jim Reeves			
❏ 110	Indian Moon/Your Eyes Feasted Upon Her	1954	$40
❏ 105	My Chihuahua Dog/I Saw Esau	1954	$40
❏ 130	Please Leave My Darling Alone/I Could Still Tell You	1955	$40
❏ 114	Turn Around My Darling/How to Get Married	1954	$40
❏ 102	Wait/Lonesome Seagull	1954	$40
— With Jerry Rowley			
❏ 133	Where Were You/Whirlwind	1956	$30

WRIGHT, O.V.

Number	Title	Yr	NM
ABC			
❏ 12119	What More Can I Do (To Prove My Love to You)/Henpecked Man	1975	$6
BACK BEAT			
❏ 615	Ace of Spade/Afflicted	1970	$8
❏ 544	Don't Want to Sit Down/Can't Find True Love	1965	$12
❏ 626	Drowning on Dry Land/I'm Gonna Forget About You	1973	$6
❏ 580	Eight Men, Four Women/Fed Up with the Blues	1967	$8
❏ 558	Gone for Good/How Long Baby	1966	$10
❏ 583	Heartaches-Heartaches/Treasured Moments	1967	$8
❏ 625	He Made Woman for Man/Don't Let My Baby Ride	1972	$6
❏ 628	I'd Rather Be (Blind, Cripple and Crazy)/Please Forgive Me	1973	$6
❏ 607	I'll Take Care of You/Why Not Give Me a Chance	1969	$8
❏ 551	I'm In Your Corner/Poor Boy	1965	$10
❏ 5103	I'm In Your Corner/Poor Boy	1974	$6
❏ 631	I've Been Searching/I'm Going Home	1974	$6
❏ 597	I Want Everyone to Know/I'm Gonna Forget About You	1968	$8
❏ 611	Love the Way You Love/Blowin' in the Wind	1970	$8
❏ 604	Missing You/This Must Be Real	1969	$8
❏ 591	Oh Baby Mine/Working Your Game	1968	$8
❏ 586	What About You/What Did You Tell This Girl of Mine	1967	$8
❏ 620	When You Took Your Love from Me/I Was Born All Over	1971	$6
GOLDWAX			
❏ 106	That's How Strong My Love Is/There Goes My Used to Be	1964	$15
HI			
❏ 78514	I Don't Do Windows/I Feel Love Growin'	1978	$6
❏ 77501	Into Something (Can't Shake Loose)/The Time We Have	1977	$6
❏ 77506	Precious, Precious/You Gotta Have Love	1977	$6
❏ 79531	We're Still Together/I Don't Know Why	1979	$6

WRIGHT, OSCAR

Number	Title	Yr	NM
FAIRMOUNT			
❏ 1011	Fell in Love/Leave Me Alone	1966	$60
HEMISPHERE			
❏ 100	Fell in Love/Leave Me Alone	1966	$200

WRIGHT, RANDY

Number	Title	Yr	NM
ATLANTIC			
❏ 1115	What My Heart Didn't Know/Snake in the Grass	1956	$30

Number	Title	Yr	NM
MCA			
❏ 52358	If You're Serious About Cheating/Times Like This	1984	$4
❏ 52273	There's Nobody Lovin' at Home/Times Like This (Make Me Want Times Like That)	1983	$4

WRIGHT, RUBY (1)

Number	Title	Yr	NM
COLUMBIA			
❏ 4-41807	Wasn't the Summer Short/Fooled	1960	$30
FRATERNITY			
❏ 787	Let's Light the Christmas Tree/Merry Merry Christmas	1957	$20
KING			
❏ 1293	Boy You Got Yourself a Girl/Bimbo	1953	$30
❏ 5225	Don't Take Me for Granted/I Only Have One Lifetime	1959	$30
❏ 4850	Do You Believe/I Fall in Love with You Every Day	1955	$30
❏ 5297	Free-Hearted/When You're Away	1959	$30
❏ 1411	God Loves You Child/What Have They Told You	1954	$30
❏ 5208	Goodbye, Jimmy, Goodbye/Don't Take Me for Granted	1959	$30
❏ 1288	Santa's Little Sleigh Bells/Toodle Oo To You	1953	$40
❏ 5261	Sweet Night of Love/You're Just a Flower from an Old Bouquet	1959	$30
❏ 1305	Tennessee Churchbells/I Had the Funniest Feeling	1954	$30
❏ 5192	Three Stars/I Only Have One Lifetime	1959	$30

WRIGHT, RUBY (2)

Number	Title	Yr	NM
CHART			
❏ 5171	He's a Night Owl/The Fire That Burns at Home	1973	$6
EPIC			
❏ 5-10150	(I Can Find) A Better Deal Than That/Everything, All the Time	1967	$10
RIC			
❏ 166	Adios Aloha/Smile on My Lips	1965	$20
❏ 145	Billy Broke My Heart at Walgrains/You're Not Really Leaving Me	1964	$20
❏ 126	Dern Ya/Such a Silly Notion	1964	$20
❏ 157	Webster, You Wrote the Book/Up the Path (and In My Door)	1965	$20

WRIGHT, SONNY (1)

Number	Title	Yr	NM
ATLANTIC			
❏ 45-2045	Heaven Help Me/Lullaby with a Beat	1960	$40

WRIGHT, SONNY (2)

Number	Title	Yr	NM
COLUMBIA			
❏ 4-44320	Leftover Love/Running Drunk	1967	$8
❏ 4-44496	Pain Remover/Hung to Another Man	1968	$8
COUNTRY INT'L.			
❏ 178	Don't Leave Without Taking Your Silver/(B-side unknown)	1982	$5
DOOR KNOB			
❏ 076	If This Isn't It/Same Old Highway	1978	$5
❏ 128	Molly (And the Texas Rain)/It Wasn't Me Who Said I Owned a Gold Mine	1980	$5
❏ 040	Motel Mourning/When I Start Drinking	1977	$5
❏ 057	Same Old Highway/Motel Mourning	1978	$5
KAPP			
❏ 2040	Hung Over/The Trash You Threw Away	1969	$8
❏ 2009	I Love You, Loretta Lynn/Rose	1969	$10
❏ 2090	My Long Gone Reason/Mama Didn't Bend the Twig	1970	$8

WRIGHT, STEVE

Number	Title	Yr	NM
LIN			
❏ 5024	Silver Bells/Keep The Christ In Christmas	1960	$40

WRITIS, ARTHUR, AND THE NAGGING PAINS

Number	Title	Yr	NM
REPRISE			
❏ 0589	Say What/Welcome to San Francisco	1967	$10

WYATT, GENE

Number	Title	Yr	NM
DOLLIE			
❏ 502	Fightin' for the Free Land/Searching for a New Love Affair	1966	$10
EBB			
❏ 123	Love Fever/Lover Boy	1957	$125
LUCKY SEVEN			
❏ 101	Prettiest Girl at the Dance/Music and Arithmetic	1959	$70

Number	Title	Yr	NM

MERCURY
| ❏ 72752 | I Stole the Flowers/I'm a One Woman Man | 1967 | $10 |

PAULA
❏ 1224	Go Together/As Long As I Live	1970	$8
❏ 308	I Just Ain't Got (As Much As He's Got Going for Me)/Chains Around My Heart	1968	$10
❏ 1206	Little Liza Jane/Country Music Peyton Place	1968	$12
❏ 1216	Milk and Honey Memories/Failure of T Crop	1969	$10
❏ 1211	My Story of Love/Evangeline	1969	$10
❏ 1223	Twelve Men/Back Door of My Mind	1970	$8

WYLIE, RICHARD "POPCORN"

ABC
| ❏ 12124 | Georgia's After Hours/E.S.P. | 1975 | $8 |
| ❏ 12067 | Lost Time/Trust in Me | 1975 | $8 |

CARLA
| ❏ 715 | Move Over Babe (Here Comes Henry)/(Instrumental) | 1973 | $10 |
| ❏ 715 [PS] | Move Over Babe (Here Comes Henry)/(Instrumental) | 1973 | $15 |

EPIC
❏ 5-9575	Brand New Man/So Much Love in My Heart	1963	$30
❏ 5-9543	Come to Me/Weddin' Bells	1962	$30
❏ 5-9543 [PS]	Come to Me/Weddin' Bells	1962	$30
❏ 5-9663	Do You Still Care for Me/Marlene	1964	$60
❏ 5-9611	Greater Than Anything/Head Over Heels in Love	1963	$30

MOTOWN
| ❏ 1009 | Money (That's What I Want)/I'll Be Around | 1961 | $250 |

SOUL
| ❏ 35087 | Funky Rubber Band/(Instrumental) | 1971 | $20 |

WYMAN, BILL
Also see THE ROLLING STONES.

A&M
| ❏ 2367 | (Si Si) Je Suis Un Rock Star/Rio De Janeiro | 1981 | $5 |
| ❏ 2367 [PS] | (Si Si) Je Suis Un Rock Star/Rio De Janeiro | 1981 | $10 |

ROLLING STONES
| ❏ 19303 | Apache Woman/Soul Satisfying | 1975 | $5 |
| ❏ 19111 | White Lightning/I Wanna Get Me a Gun | 1974 | $5 |

WYNETTE, TAMMY

EPIC
❏ 03384	A Good Night's Love/I'm Going On with Everything Gone	1982	$4
❏ 06263	Alive and Well/I'll Be Thinking of You	1986	$3
❏ 02770	Another Chance/What's It Like to Be a Woman	1982	$4
❏ 5-11079	Another Lonely Song/The Only Time I'm Really Me	1973	$6
❏ 5-10095	Apartment No. 9/I'm Not Mine to Give	1966	$10
❏ 5-10818	Bedtime Story/Reach Out Your Hand	1971	$6
❏ 07788	Beneath a Painted Sky/Some Things Will Never Change	1988	$3
❏ 51011	Cowboys Don't Shoot Straight (Like They Used To)/You Brought Me Back	1981	$4
❏ 02439	Crying in the Rain/Bring Back My Baby to Me	1981	$4
❏ 5-10315	D-I-V-O-R-C-E/Don't Make It Now	1968	$8
❏ 5-10759	Good Lovin' (Makes It Right)/I Love You, Mr. Jones	1971	$6
❏ 5-10612	He Loves Me All the Way/One Last Night Together	1970	$6
❏ 50868	He Was There (When I Needed You)/Only the Names Have Been Changed	1980	$5
❏ 50538	I'd Like to See Jesus (On the Midnight Special)/Love Doesn't Always Come (On the Night It's Needed)	1978	$5
❏ 5-10211	I Don't Wanna Play House/Soakin' Wet	1967	$8
❏ 03811	I Just Heard a Heart Break (And I'm So Afraid It's Mine)/Back to the Wall	1983	$4
❏ 5-10571	I'll See Him Through/Enough of a Woman	1970	$6
❏ 50145	I Still Believe in Fairy Tales/Your Memory's Gone to Rest	1975	$5
❏ 50349	(Let's Get Together) One Last Time/Hardly a Day Goes By	1977	$5
❏ 04467	Lonely Heart/(I'm Not) A Candle in the Wind	1984	$3
❏ 5-10909	My Man/Things I Love to Do	1972	$6
❏ 5-10690	One Happy Christmas/(Merry Christmas) We Must Be Having One	1970	$8
❏ 50450	One of a Kind/Loving You, I Do	1977	$5
❏ 5-10462	Singing My Song/Too Far Gone	1969	$6

Number	Title	Yr	NM
❏ 5-10462 [PS]	Singing My Song/Too Far Gone	1969	$10
❏ 5-10398	Stand By Your Man/I Stayed Long Enough	1968	$10
❏ 50915	Starting Over/I'll Be Thinking of You	1980	$5
❏ 04101	Still in the Ring/Midnight Love	1983	$4
❏ 5-10269	Take Me to Your World/Good	1967	$8
❏ 07635	Talkin' to Myself Again/A Slow Burning Fire	1987	$3
❏ 68894	Thank the Cowboy for the Ride/We Called It Everything But Quits	1989	$3
❏ 5-10512	The Ways to Love a Man/Still Around	1969	$6
❏ 5-10687	The Wonders You Perform/Gentle Shepherd	1970	$6
❏ TW1 [DJ]	The Wonders You Perform (stereo/mono)	1969	$30

—Red vinyl; included with some early copies of the LP "Inspiration"

❏ 50661	They Call It Making Love/Let Me Be Me	1979	$5
❏ 50196	'Til I Can Make It on My Own/Love Is Something Good for Everybody	1976	$5
❏ 5-10940	'Til I Get It Right/The Bridge of Love	1973	$6
❏ 5-10707	We Sure Can Love Each Other/Fun	1971	$6
❏ AS60 [DJ]	White Christmas/One Happy Christmas	1973	$8

—1973 Christmas Seals promotional record

❏ AS60 [PS]	White Christmas/One Happy Christmas	1973	$10
❏ 50574	Womanhood/50 Words or Less	1978	$5
❏ 50008	Woman to Woman/Love Me Forever	1974	$5

7-Inch Extended Plays
| ❏ 5-26392 [PS] | D-I-V-O-R-C-E | 1968 | $15 |
| ❏ 5-26392 | D-I-V-O-R-C-E/Kiss Away/Lonely Street//Honey/Sweet Dreams/Yesterday | 1968 | $15 |

—Jukebox issue; small hole, plays at 33 1/3 rpm

| ❏ 5-30213 | I Wish I Had a Mommy Like You/He's Still My Man/Playin' Around with Love//True and Lasting Love/ I Never Once Stopped Loving You/The Lovin' Kind | 1970 | $15 |

—Jukebox issue; small hole, plays at 33 1/3 rpm

| ❏ 5-26451 [PS] | Stand By Your Man | 1969 | $15 |
| ❏ 5-26451 | Stand By Your Man/It's My Way/I Stayed Long Enough//My Arms Stay Open Late/I've Learned/Cry, Cry Again | 1969 | $15 |

—Jukebox issue; small hole, plays at 33 1/3 rpm

| ❏ 5-30213 [PS] | The First Lady | 1970 | $15 |

WYNTER, MARK

GUYDEN
| ❏ 2115 | Answer Me/Only You | 1964 | $10 |

LONDON
❏ 1973	Dream Girl/Two Little Girls	1961	$20
❏ 1997	Exclusively Yours/Warm and Willing	1961	$20
❏ 9522	Heaven's Plan/You Are Everything	1962	$20

SCEPTER
| ❏ 1299 | Am I Living in a Dream/Can I Get to Know You Better | 1965 | $10 |

WYNTERS, GAIL

HICKORY
❏ 1644	Basic Blue/Bring the Boys Around	1972	$8
❏ 1530	Crawling Back/It's Daytime	1968	$8
❏ 1461	Have a Good Time/You've Got the Power	1967	$12
❏ 1591	Help Me Make it Through the Night/Rainbow Sign	1971	$8
❏ 1548	I Like Your Kind of Love/Who Am I	1969	$8
❏ 1625	I'll Sing for You/Young Tears Don't Fall Forever	1972	$8
❏ 1478	My Man/You Don't Have to Be in Love	1967	$10
❏ 1453	Snap Your Fingers/Find Myself a New Love	1967	$12
❏ 1613	Snap Your Fingers/Going Out of My Head	1971	$8
❏ 1520	When I Stop Dreaming/You Don't Even Know the Meaning of the Word	1968	$8

RCA
| ❏ PB-10973 | Gonna Love You, Love You, and Love You Some More/Remember | 1977 | $5 |

Number	Title	Yr	NM

X

X

CURB
| ❏ 10538 [DJ] | Wild Thing/Wild Thing, Part 2 | 1988 | $40 |

—Does not exist as stock copy

DANGERHOUSE
| ❏ D-88 [B] | Adult Books/We're Desperate | 1978 | $70 |
| ❏ D-88 [PS] | Adult Books/We're Desperate | 1978 | $70 |

—Folded picture sleeve in plastic bag; authentic sleeves are black, white and yellow (photocopies in black and white exist and have no collector value)

ELEKTRA
❏ 69462	4th of July/Positively 4th Street	1987	$4
❏ 69462 [PS]	4th of July/Positively 4th Street	1987	$4
❏ 69885	Blue Spark/Dancing with Tears in My Eyes	1982	$15
❏ 69885 [PS]	Blue Spark/Dancing with Tears in My Eyes	1982	$15
❏ 69825	Breathless/Riding with Mary	1983	$6
❏ 69825 [PS]	Breathless/Riding with Mary	1983	$6
❏ 69626 [DJ]	Burning House of Love (edit) (same on both sides)	1985	$4
❏ 69626	Burning House of Love/Love Shack	1985	$8
❏ 69626 [PS]	Burning House of Love/Love Shack	1985	$4
❏ 69709	Wild Thing/Devil Doll	1984	$5

SLASH
| ❏ SRS-106 | White Girl/Your Phone's Off the Hook (But You're Not) | 1980 | $10 |
| ❏ SRS-106 [PS] | White Girl/Your Phone's Off the Hook (But You're Not) | 1980 | $10 |

—Blue and white sleeve

| ❏ SRS-106 [PS] | White Girl/Your Phone's Off the Hook (But You're Not) | 1980 | $30 |

—Green and white sleeve

X-CELLENTS, THE

SMASH
| ❏ 1996 | Hey Little Willie/I'll Always Be On Your Side | 1965 | $30 |

X-CITERS UNLIMITED

ABC
| ❏ 11029 | Soul to Fillie Joe/Hang On Sloopy | 1967 | $12 |

X. LINCOLN

DOT
| ❏ 17170 | Anywhere I Happen to Be/You're Everything | 1968 | $10 |
| ❏ 17101 | In the Freedom of My Mind/What Am I Gonna Do Now | 1968 | $10 |

X-TERMINATORS

RADIO ACTIVE
| ❏ 1 | Microwave Radiation/Occasional Lay | 1978 | $70 |

X-TREMES, THE

STAR TREK
| ❏ 1221 | Substitute/Facts of Life | 1966 | $30 |

X-25 BAND

H.C.R.C.
| ❏ WS9 01396 | Black Hole Bop/Jam It | 1982 | $6 |

—This record was supposed to be "03196," but all the labels have the above typographical error!

XAVIER

LIBERTY
| ❏ B-1464 | Do It to the Max/(Instrumental) | 1982 | $4 |
| ❏ 1445 | Work That Sucker to Death/Love Is on the One | 1981 | $6 |

Number	Title	Yr	NM

YOUNGSTERS, THE
EMPIRE

Number	Title	Yr	NM
❏ 109	Christmas In Jail/Dreamy Eyes	1956	$70
❏ 109	Dreamy Eyes/I'm Sorry Now	1956	$125
❏ 104	Shattered Dreams/Rock'n Roll'n Cowboy	1956	$125

YOUNGTONES, THE
BRUNSWICK

❏ 55089	Come On Baby/Oh Tell Me	1958	$70

YOUTH BRIGADE
BYO

❏ 06	What Price Happiness/Where Are We Going/Who Can You Believe In	1984	$40

—*Red vinyl (fewer than 200 made)*

❏ 06	What Price Happiness/Where Are We Going/Who Can You Believe In	1984	$75

— *Yellow vinyl*

❏ 06	What Price Happiness/Where Are We Going/Who Can You Believe In	1984	$10

—*Black vinyl*

❏ 06 [PS]	What Price Happiness/Where Are We Going/Who Can You Believe In	1984	$12

YUM YUMS, THE
ABC-PARAMOUNT

❏ 10697	Looky, Looky (What I Got)/Gonna Be a Big Thing	1965	$1000

—*Black label stock copy*

❏ 10697 [DJ]	Looky, Looky (What I Got)/Gonna Be a Big Thing	1965	$500

—*White label promo*

YURO, TIMI
LIBERTY

❏ 55701	A Legend in My Time/Should I Ever Love Again	1964	$8
❏ 55665	Call Me/Permanently Lonely	1964	$8
❏ 55634	Gotta Travel On/Down in the Valley	1963	$10
❏ 55343	Hurt/I Apologize	1961	$20
❏ 55400	I Believe/A Mother's Love	1961	$10

—*With Johnnie Ray*

❏ 55432	I Know (I Love You)/Count Everything	1962	$10
❏ 55747	I'm Movin' On (Part 1)/I'm Movin' On (Part 2)	1964	$8
❏ 56061	I Must Have Been Out of My Head/Interlude	1968	$6
❏ 55552	Insult to Injury/Just About the Time	1963	$10
❏ 55410	Let Me Call You Sweetheart/Satan Never Sleeps	1962	$12
❏ 55587	Make the World Go Away/Look Down	1963	$10
❏ 55375	Smile/She Really Loves You	1961	$15
❏ 55519	The Love of a Boy/I Ain't Gonna Cry No More	1962	$10
❏ 55469	What's a Matter Baby (Is It Hurting You)/Thirteenth Hour	1962	$15
❏ 56049	Wrong/Something Bad on My Mind	1968	$6

MERCURY

❏ 72478	Big Mistake/Teardrops Till Dawn	1965	$8
❏ 72431	Can't Stop Running Away/Get Out of My Life	1965	$8
❏ 72391	Could This Be Magic/You Can Have Him	1965	$8
❏ 72601	Don't Keep Me Lonely Too Long/You Took My Happy Away	1966	$8
❏ 72316	If/The Masquerade Is Over	1964	$8
❏ 72355	I Got It Bad and That Ain't Good/Johnny	1964	$8
❏ 72515	Once a Day/Pretend	1966	$8
❏ 72628	Turn the World Around the Other Way/Just a Ribbon	1966	$8
❏ 72674	Why Not Now/Cuttin' In	1967	$8

PLAYBOY

❏ 6050	Southern Lady/Lovin' You Is All I Ever Had	1975	$5

UNITED ARTISTS

❏ 0042	Hurt/What's a Matter Baby (Is It Hurting You)	1973	$4

—*Silver Spotlight Series" reissue*

Z

Z'LOOKE
ORPHEUS

Number	Title	Yr	NM
❏ B-72654	Can U Read My Lips/(Remix)	1988	$4
❏ B-72678	Gitchi U/Take Away the Heartache	1989	$4
❏ B-72650	Lovesick (The Cure)/(Doctor's Groove)	1989	$4

ZABACH, FLORIAN
CADENCE

❏ 1406	Oceans of Love/Theme from "Carnival"	1961	$8

DECCA

❏ 9-29047	Callaghan's Monkey/Solfaggio	1954	$20
❏ 9-27775	Ida (Sweet as Apple Cider)/Cold Turkey	1951	$20
❏ 9-27614	Tea for Two/Running After the Rails	1951	$20
❏ 9-28916	The Funny Fiddle/Plink, Plank, Plunk	1953	$20
❏ 9-28090	The Happy Whistler/Jazz Legato-Jazz Pizzicato	1952	$20
❏ 9-27509	The Hot Canary/Jalousie	1951	$20
❏ 9-27729	The Waltzing Cat/The Whistler and His Dog	1951	$20

MERCURY

❏ 70975X45	Petticoats of Portugal/Rainbow Trail	1956	$15
❏ 70936X45	When the White Lilacs Bloom Again/Fiddler's Boogie	1956	$15

ZACA CREEK
COLUMBIA

❏ 38-73096	Ghost Town/Time's Up	1989	$3
❏ 38-69062	Sometimes Love's Not a Pretty Thing/Rock Me Back	1989	$3

ZACHARIAS AND THE TREE PEOPLE
VIKING

❏ 1004	We're All Paul Bearers (Part 1)/We're All Paul Bearers (Part 2)	1969	$30

ZACHARIAS, HELMUT
DECCA

❏ 31296	Bermuda Shorts/Adios My Love	1961	$8
❏ 9-29849	China-Boogie/The Big Bell and the Little Bell	1956	$15
❏ 9-30795	Crazy Violins/The Tipsy Piano	1958	$12
❏ 9-31101	La Montana/Mare Nostrum	1960	$8
❏ 9-30102	Spanish Violins/The Whistler and His Dog	1956	$10
❏ 31715	Tokyo Melody/Teatime in Tokyo	1964	$8
❏ 31259	Tres Jolie/Innocence Abroad	1961	$8
❏ 9-30039	When the White Lilacs Bloom Again/Blue Blues	1956	$15

ZACHERLEY, JOHN
CAMEO

❏ 130	Dinner with Drac (Part 1)/Dinner with Drac (Part 2)	1958	$40

—*Orange label*

❏ 130	Dinner with Drac (Part 1)/Dinner with Drac (Part 2)	1960	$30

—*Red and black label*

❏ 130	Igor/Dinner with Drac	1958	$50
❏ 145	I Was a Teenage Caveman/Dummy Doll	1958	$40
❏ 139	Lunch with Mother Goose/82 Tombstones	1958	$40

COLPIX

❏ 743	Monsters Have Problems Too/Hello Dolly	1964	$30

PARKWAY

❏ 885	Clementine/Surfboard 109	1963	$30

—*As "Zacherley*

❏ 853	Dinner with Drac/Hurry Bury Baby	1962	$30
❏ 888	Scarey Tales from Mother Goose/Monster Monkey	1963	$30

—*As "Zacherley*

ZACK, EDDIE, AND COUSIN RICHIE
COLUMBIA

❏ 4-21441	I'm Gonna Rock and Roll/Foolish Me	1955	$200
❏ 4-21199	I've Lost Again/I Never Saw Her Again	1954	$60
❏ 4-21261	Positively No Dancing/Dancing Country Style	1954	$60

ZACK, EDDIE
COLUMBIA

Number	Title	Yr	NM
❏ 4-21148	Little Donkey/You Knew Men When You Were Lonely	1953	$50

DECCA

❏ 9-46302	Beautiful Brown Eyes/Shenandoah Waltz	1951	$50
❏ 9-28082	Call of the Mountains/Words	1952	$50
❏ 9-46245	Dill Pickles/That Silver Haired Daddy of Mine	1950	$50
❏ 9-28329	Draggin' the Bow/Lights Out	1952	$50
❏ 9-46284	Land Beyond the Sun/Heaven's TV Screen	1951	$50
❏ 9-46330	The Clouds Will Soon Roll By/You Remind Me of So Much	1951	$50

ZADORA, PIA
CBS ASSOCIATED

❏ ZS4-05717	Come Rain or Come Shine/Smile Though Your Heart Is Breaking	1985	$4
❏ ZS4-06322	I Am What I Am/For Once in My Life	1986	$4

ELEKTRA

❏ 47428	I'm in Love Again/It's Wrong for Me to Love You	1982	$4
❏ 69889	The Clapping Song/Lovin' Things	1982	$4

MCA CURB

❏ 52521	When the Rain Begins to Fall/Substitute	1984	$3

—*A-side with Jermaine Jackson*

❏ 52521 [PS]	When the Rain Begins to Fall/Substitute	1984	$3

WARNER BROS.

❏ 49148	Baby It's You/Roses Ain't Red	1979	$4
❏ 8766	Bedtime Stories/Tell Him	1979	$4
❏ 8612	Come Share My Love/Just Make Believe You Love Me	1978	$4
❏ 49065	I Know a Good Thing When I Feel It/Trouble	1979	$4

ZAGER AND EVANS
RCA VICTOR

❏ 47-9816	Help One Man Today/Year 32	1969	$5
❏ 74-0174	In the Year 2525 (Exordium & Terminus)/Little Kids	1969	$6
❏ 74-0299	Listen to the People/She Never Sleeps Beside Me	1969	$5
❏ 74-0246	Mr. Turnkey/Cary Lynn Jones	1969	$5
❏ 74-0359	Plastic Park/Crutches	1970	$5

TRUTH

❏ 0(# unknown)	In the Year 2525 (Exordium & Terminus)/Little Kids	1967	$30

VANGUARD

❏ 35125	Hydra 15,000/I Am	1971	$5
❏ 35125 [PS]	Hydra 15,000/I Am	1971	$30

ZAGER, MICHAEL
CBS ASSOCIATED

❏ ZS4-04546	Shot in the Dark/(Instrumental)	1984	$4

COLUMBIA

❏ 1-11273	Don't Sneak on Me/Bring Me Love	1980	$4

PRIVATE STOCK

❏ 45,184	Let's All Chant/Love Express	1978	$5
❏ 45,202	Soul to Soul/Freak	1978	$5

ZAHND, RICKY, AND THE BLUE JEANERS
COLUMBIA

❏ 40576	(I'm Getting) Nuttin' For Christmas/Something Barked On Christmas Morning	1955	$20
❏ 4-263	(I'm Getting) Nuttin' For Christmas/Something Barked On Christmas Morning	1955	$20

—*Yellow-label Children's Series edition*

❏ 40670	My Church Is My Palace/You Got to Go to Church	1956	$15

Number	Title	Yr	NM

MERCURY
| ❏ 72752 | I Stole the Flowers/I'm a One Woman Man | 1967 | $10 |

PAULA
❏ 1224	Go Together/As Long As I Live	1970	$8
❏ 308	I Just Ain't Got (As Much As He's Got Going for Me)/Chains Around My Heart	1968	$10
❏ 1206	Little Liza Jane/Country Music Peyton Place	1968	$12
❏ 1216	Milk and Honey Memories/Failure of T Crop	1969	$10
❏ 1211	My Story of Love/Evangeline	1969	$10
❏ 1223	Twelve Men/Back Door of My Mind	1970	$8

WYLIE, RICHARD "POPCORN"

ABC
| ❏ 12124 | Georgia's After Hours/E.S.P. | 1975 | $8 |
| ❏ 12067 | Lost Time/Trust in Me | 1975 | $8 |

CARLA
| ❏ 715 | Move Over Babe (Here Comes Henry)/(Instrumental) | 1973 | $10 |
| ❏ 715 [PS] | Move Over Babe (Here Comes Henry)/(Instrumental) | 1973 | $15 |

EPIC
❏ 5-9575	Brand New Man/So Much Love in My Heart	1963	$30
❏ 5-9543	Come to Me/Weddin' Bells	1962	$30
❏ 5-9543 [PS]	Come to Me/Weddin' Bells	1962	$30
❏ 5-9663	Do You Still Care for Me/Marlene	1964	$60
❏ 5-9611	Greater Than Anything/Head Over Heels in Love	1963	$30

MOTOWN
| ❏ 1009 | Money (That's What I Want)/I'll Be Around | 1961 | $250 |

SOUL
| ❏ 35087 | Funky Rubber Band/(Instrumental) | 1971 | $20 |

WYMAN, BILL
Also see THE ROLLING STONES.

A&M
| ❏ 2367 | (Si Si) Je Suis Un Rock Star/Rio De Janeiro | 1981 | $5 |
| ❏ 2367 [PS] | (Si Si) Je Suis Un Rock Star/Rio De Janeiro | 1981 | $10 |

ROLLING STONES
| ❏ 19303 | Apache Woman/Soul Satisfying | 1975 | $5 |
| ❏ 19111 | White Lightning/I Wanna Get Me a Gun | 1974 | $5 |

WYNETTE, TAMMY

EPIC
❏ 03384	A Good Night's Love/I'm Going On with Everything Gone	1982	$4
❏ 06263	Alive and Well/I'll Be Thinking of You	1986	$3
❏ 02770	Another Chance/What's It Like to Be a Woman	1982	$4
❏ 5-11079	Another Lonely Song/The Only Time I'm Really Me	1973	$6
❏ 5-10095	Apartment No. 9/I'm Not Mine to Give	1966	$10
❏ 5-10818	Bedtime Story/Reach Out Your Hand	1971	$6
❏ 07788	Beneath a Painted Sky/Some Things Will Never Change	1988	$3
❏ 51011	Cowboys Don't Shoot Straight (Like They Used To)/You Brought Me Back	1981	$4
❏ 02439	Crying in the Rain/Bring Back My Baby to Me	1981	$4
❏ 5-10315	D-I-V-O-R-C-E/Don't Make It Now	1968	$8
❏ 5-10759	Good Lovin' (Makes It Right)/I Love You, Mr. Jones	1971	$6
❏ 5-10612	He Loves Me All the Way/One Last Night Together	1970	$6
❏ 50868	He Was There (When I Needed You)/Only the Names Have Been Changed	1980	$5
❏ 50538	I'd Like to See Jesus (On the Midnight Special)/Love Doesn't Always Come (On the Night It's Needed)	1978	$5
❏ 5-10211	I Don't Wanna Play House/Soakin' Wet	1967	$8
❏ 03811	I Just Heard a Heart Break (And I'm So Afraid It's Mine)/Back to the Wall	1983	$4
❏ 5-10571	I'll See Him Through/Enough of a Woman	1970	$6
❏ 50145	I Still Believe in Fairy Tales/Your Memory's Gone to Rest	1975	$5
❏ 50349	(Let's Get Together) One Last Time/Hardly a Day Goes By	1977	$5
❏ 04467	Lonely Heart/(I'm Not) A Candle in the Wind	1984	$3
❏ 5-10909	My Man/Things I Love to Do	1972	$6
❏ 5-10690	One Happy Christmas/(Merry Christmas) We Must Be Having One	1970	$8
❏ 50450	One of a Kind/Loving You, I Do	1977	$5
❏ 5-10462	Singing My Song/Too Far Gone	1969	$6

Number	Title	Yr	NM
❏ 5-10462 [PS]	Singing My Song/Too Far Gone	1969	$10
❏ 5-10398	Stand By Your Man/I Stayed Long Enough	1968	$10
❏ 50915	Starting Over/I'll Be Thinking of You	1980	$5
❏ 04101	Still in the Ring/Midnight Love	1983	$4
❏ 5-10269	Take Me to Your World/Good	1967	$8
❏ 07635	Talkin' to Myself Again/A Slow Burning Fire	1987	$3
❏ 68894	Thank the Cowboy for the Ride/We Called It Everything But Quits	1989	$3
❏ 5-10512	The Ways to Love a Man/Still Around	1969	$6
❏ 5-10687	The Wonders You Perform/Gentle Shepherd	1970	$6
❏ TW1 [DJ]	The Wonders You Perform (stereo/mono)	1969	$30

—Red vinyl; included with some early copies of the LP "Inspiration

❏ 50661	They Call It Making Love/Let Me Be Me	1979	$5
❏ 50196	'Til I Can Make It on My Own/Love Is Something Good for Everybody	1976	$5
❏ 5-10940	'Til I Get It Right/The Bridge of Love	1973	$6
❏ 5-10707	We Sure Can Love Each Other/Fun	1971	$6
❏ AS60 [DJ]	White Christmas/One Happy Christmas	1973	$8

— 1973 Christmas Seals promotional record

❏ AS60 [PS]	White Christmas/One Happy Christmas	1973	$10
❏ 50574	Womanhood/50 Words or Less	1978	$5
❏ 50008	Woman to Woman/Love Me Forever	1974	$5

7-Inch Extended Plays
| ❏ 5-26392 [PS] | D-I-V-O-R-C-E | 1968 | $15 |
| ❏ 5-26392 | D-I-V-O-R-C-E/Kiss Away/Lonely Street//Honey/Sweet Dreams/Yesterday | 1968 | $15 |

—Jukebox issue; small hole, plays at 33 1/3 rpm

| ❏ 5-30213 | I Wish I Had a Mommy Like You/He's Still My Man/Playin' Around with Love//True and Lasting Love/I Never Once Stopped Loving You/The Lovin' Kind | 1970 | $15 |

—Jukebox issue; small hole, plays at 33 1/3 rpm

| ❏ 5-26451 [PS] | Stand By Your Man | 1969 | $15 |
| ❏ 5-26451 | Stand By Your Man/It's My Way/I Stayed Long Enough//My Arms Stay Open Late/I've Learned/Cry, Cry Again | 1969 | $15 |

—Jukebox issue; small hole, plays at 33 1/3 rpm

| ❏ 5-30213 [PS] | The First Lady | 1970 | $15 |

WYNTER, MARK

GUYDEN
| ❏ 2115 | Answer Me/Only You | 1964 | $10 |

LONDON
❏ 1973	Dream Girl/Two Little Girls	1961	$20
❏ 1997	Exclusively Yours/Warm and Willing	1961	$20
❏ 9522	Heaven's Plan/You Are Everything	1962	$20

SCEPTER
| ❏ 1299 | Am I Living in a Dream/Can I Get to Know You Better | 1965 | $10 |

WYNTERS, GAIL

HICKORY
❏ 1644	Basic Blue/Bring the Boys Around	1972	$8
❏ 1530	Crawling Back/It's Daytime	1968	$8
❏ 1461	Have a Good Time/You've Got the Power	1967	$12
❏ 1591	Help Me Make it Through the Night/Rainbow Sign	1971	$8
❏ 1548	I Like Your Kind of Love/Who Am I	1969	$8
❏ 1625	I'll Sing for You/Young Tears Don't Fall Forever	1972	$8
❏ 1478	My Man/You Don't Have to Be in Love	1967	$10
❏ 1453	Snap Your Fingers/Find Myself a New Love	1967	$12
❏ 1613	Snap Your Fingers/Going Out of My Head	1971	$8
❏ 1520	When I Stop Dreaming/You Don't Even Know the Meaning of the Word	1968	$8

RCA
| ❏ PB-10973 | Gonna Love You, Love You, and Love You Some More/Remember | 1977 | $5 |

Number	Title	Yr	NM

X

X

CURB
| ❏ 10538 [DJ] | Wild Thing/Wild Thing, Part 2 | 1988 | $40 |

—Does not exist as stock copy

DANGERHOUSE
| ❏ D-88 [B] | Adult Books/We're Desperate | 1978 | $70 |
| ❏ D-88 [PS] | Adult Books/We're Desperate | 1978 | $70 |

—Folded picture sleeve in plastic bag; authentic sleeves are black, white and yellow (photocopies in black and white exist and have no collector value)

ELEKTRA
❏ 69462	4th of July/Positively 4th Street	1987	$4
❏ 69462 [PS]	4th of July/Positively 4th Street	1987	$4
❏ 69885	Blue Spark/Dancing with Tears in My Eyes	1982	$15
❏ 69885 [PS]	Blue Spark/Dancing with Tears in My Eyes	1982	$15
❏ 69825	Breathless/Riding with Mary	1983	$6
❏ 69825 [PS]	Breathless/Riding with Mary	1983	$6
❏ 69626 [DJ]	Burning House of Love (edit) (same on both sides)	1985	$4
❏ 69626	Burning House of Love/Love Shack	1985	$8
❏ 69626 [PS]	Burning House of Love/Love Shack	1985	$4
❏ 69709	Wild Thing/Devil Doll	1984	$5

SLASH
| ❏ SRS-106 | White Girl/Your Phone's Off the Hook (But You're Not) | 1980 | $10 |
| ❏ SRS-106 [PS] | White Girl/Your Phone's Off the Hook (But You're Not) | 1980 | $10 |

—Blue and white sleeve

| ❏ SRS-106 [PS] | White Girl/Your Phone's Off the Hook (But You're Not) | 1980 | $30 |

—Green and white sleeve

X-CELLENTS, THE

SMASH
| ❏ 1996 | Hey Little Willie/I'll Aways Be On Your Side | 1965 | $30 |

X-CITERS UNLIMITED

ABC
| ❏ 11029 | Soul to Fillie Joe/Hang On Sloopy | 1967 | $12 |

X. LINCOLN

DOT
| ❏ 17170 | Anywhere I Happen to Be/You're Everything | 1968 | $10 |
| ❏ 17101 | In the Freedom of My Mind/What Am I Gonna Do Now | 1968 | $10 |

X-TERMINATORS

RADIO ACTIVE
| ❏ 1 | Microwave Radiation/Occasional Lay | 1978 | $70 |

X-TREMES, THE

STAR TREK
| ❏ 1221 | Substitute/Facts of Life | 1966 | $30 |

X-25 BAND

H.C.R.C.
| ❏ WS9 01396 | Black Hole Bop/Jam It | 1982 | $6 |

— This record was supposed to be "03196," but all the labels have the above typographical error!

XAVIER

LIBERTY
| ❏ B-1464 | Do It to the Max/(Instrumental) | 1982 | $4 |
| ❏ 1445 | Work That Sucker to Death/Love Is on the One | 1981 | $6 |

Number	Title	Yr	NM
XIT			
MOTOWN			
❏ 1304	I Need Your Love (Git It To Me)/Movin' from the City	1974	$8
XTC			
EVA-TONE			
❏ 113824XS	Blame the Weather/Tissue Tigers	1982	$30
—Red flexi-disc included in April 1982 edition (#72) of "Trouser Press"; second song by the Arguers			
GEFFEN			
❏ 28394	Dear God/Mermaid Smiled	1987	$4
❏ 27552	The Mayor of Simpleton/One of the Millions	1989	$3
❏ 27552 [PS]	The Mayor of Simpleton/One of the Millions	1989	$3
❏ 29351	Wonderland/Jump	1984	$5
VIRGIN			
❏ PR344	Limelight/Day In Day Out/Chain of Command	1979	$8
—7-inch 33 1/3 record with small center hole; only issued with first 15,000 copies of album 13134, though often found separately			
❏ 67009 [DJ]	Making Plans for Nigel (mono/stereo)	1980	$5
❏ 67009	Making Plans for Nigel//This Is Pop/Meccanik Dancing	1980	$15
❏ 67009 [PS]	Making Plans for Nigel//This Is Pop/Meccanik Dancing	1980	$5
—Sleeve came with both stock and promo copies			
❏ 67004	Ten Feet Tall//Helicopter/The Somnabulist	1980	$15
❏ 67004 [PS]	Ten Feet Tall//Helicopter/The Somnabulist	1980	$5
—Sleeve came with both stock and promo copies			
❏ 67004 [DJ]	Ten Feet Tall (mono/stereo)	1980	$5
VIRGIN/EPIC			
❏ 14-02875	Senses Working Overtime/English Roundabout	1982	$10
VIRGIN/RSO			
❏ 300	Generals and Majors/Living Through Another Cuba	1981	$8
XYMOX			
WING			
❏ 871707-7	Obsession/(B-side unknown)	1989	$5

Y

Number	Title	Yr	NM
Y KANT TORI READ			
Lead singer is Tori Amos.			
ATLANTIC			
❏ 89021 [PS]	Cool on Your Island/Heart Attack at 23	1988	$100
❏ 89021	Cool on Your Island/Heart Attack at 23	1988	$120
—Copies of this have been documented			
❏ 89021 [DJ]	Cool on Your Island (same on both sides)	1988	$60
❏ 89086 [DJ]	The Big Picture (same on both sides)	1988	$60
—Lead vocal: Tori Amos			
❏ 89086	The Big Picture/You Go to My Head	1988	$120
—Copies of this have been documented			
❏ 89086 [PS]	The Big Picture/You Go to My Head	1988	$100
YANKEE DOLLAR, THE			
DOT			
❏ 17123	City Sidewalks/Sanctuary	1968	$20
❏ 17155	Live and Let Live/Sanctuary	1968	$20
❏ 17213	Mucky Truckee River/Reflections of a Shattered Mind	1969	$20
YANKOVIC, FRANKIE			
COLUMBIA			
❏ 39594	Christmas Chopsticks/The Merry Christmas Polka	1951	$15
❏ 43173	There'll Always Be a Santa Claus/Jing-a-Ling (Christmas Time Is Here Again)	1964	$8
SMASH			
❏ 888196-7	Old Fashioned Christmas Polka/Christmas Chimes	1986	$3
YANKOVIC, "WEIRD AL"			
CAPITOL			
❏ 4816	My Bologna/School Cafeteria	1980	$30
PLACEBO			
❏ 3626	Another One Rides the Bus (Live)/Happy Birthday/ + 2	1980	$10
❏ 3626 [PS]	Another One Rides the Bus (Live)/Happy Birthday/ + 2	1980	$10
ROCK N ROLL			
❏ 06588	Christmas At Ground Zero/One of Those Days	1986	$5
❏ 06588 [PS]	Christmas At Ground Zero/One of Those Days	1986	$5
❏ 06207	Dare to Be Stupid/The Touch	1986	$3
❏ 05483	Eat It/I Lost on Jeopardy	1985	$3
—Reissue			
❏ 04374	Eat It/That Boy Could Dance	1984	$3
❏ 04374 [PS]	Eat It/That Boy Could Dance	1984	$3
❏ 07769	Fat/You Make Me	1988	$3
❏ 07769 [PS]	Fat/You Make Me	1988	$3
❏ 04469	I Lost on Jeopardy/I'll Be Mellow When I'm Dead	1984	$3
❏ 04469 [PS]	I Lost on Jeopardy/I'll Be Mellow When I'm Dead	1984	$3
❏ 03998	I Love Rocky Road/Happy Birthday	1983	$5
❏ CL-18046	I Think I'm a Clone Now/(This Song's Just) Six Words Long	1988	$3
❏ 05578	I Want a New Duck/Cable TV	1985	$3
❏ 05578 [PS]	I Want a New Duck/Cable TV	1985	$3
❏ 07961	Lasagna/Velvet Elvis	1988	$3
❏ 07961 [PS]	Lasagna/Velvet Elvis	1988	$3
❏ 04937 [PS]	Like a Surgeon	1985	$6
—Demonstration Only -- Not for Sale" on rear			
❏ 06435	Like a Surgeon/King of Suede	1986	$3
—Reissue			
❏ 04937	Like a Surgeon/Slime Creatures from Outer Space	1985	$3
❏ 04937 [PS]	Like a Surgeon/Slime Creatures from Outer Space	1985	$3
❏ 06400	Living with a Hernia/Don't Wear Those Shoes	1986	$3
❏ 06400 [PS]	Living with a Hernia/Don't Wear Those Shoes	1986	$3
❏ 69019	Money for Nothing-Beverly Hillbillies/Generic Blues	1989	$3
❏ 05606	One More Minute/Midnight Star	1985	$3
❏ 05606 [PS]	One More Minute/Midnight Star	1985	$3
❏ 04708	This Is the Life (Theme from Johnny Dangerously)/Buy Me a Condo	1984	$3
❏ 04708 [PS]	This Is the Life (Theme from Johnny Dangerously)/Buy Me a Condo	1984	$3

Number	Title	Yr	NM
TK			
❏ 1043	Another One Rides the Bus/Gotta Boogie	1981	$30
YANOVSKY, ZALMAN			
Also see THE LOVIN' SPOONFUL.			
BUDDAH			
❏ 12	As Long As You're Here/Ereh Er'uoy Sa Gnol Sa	1967	$10
❏ 12 [PS]	As Long As You're Here/Ereh Er'uoy Sa Gnol Sa	1967	$40
YARBROUGH, BOB			
MUSIC MILL			
❏ 186	50 Ways to Leave Your Lover/You Only Look Me Up When You're Down	1976	$6
SUGAR HILL			
❏ 024	Before I Knew Love Was Here/Eight O'Clock Saturday Night	1972	$8
❏ 016	Cause God Made You Mine/(B-side unknown)	1971	$8
❏ 023	Eight O'Clock Saturday Night/You Make My Day	1972	$8
❏ 018	When's the Last Time/(B-side unknown)	1971	$8
YARBROUGH, GLENN			
PRIDE			
❏ 1020	Back Roads/(B-side unknown)	1972	$5
RCA VICTOR			
❏ 47-9452	A Face in the Crown/Times Gone By	1968	$6
❏ 47-8745	Ain't No Way/You Can't Ever Go Home Again	1965	$8
❏ 47-8447	An Acre of Gal to a Foot of Ground/Jenny's Gone And I Don't Care	1964	$8
❏ 47-8498	Baby the Rain Must Fall/I've Been to Town	1965	$12
❏ 47-8498 [PS]	Baby the Rain Must Fall/I've Been to Town	1965	$20
❏ 47-9187	Golden Under the Sun/Gently Here Beside Me	1967	$6
❏ 47-9309	Honey and Wine/Ain't You Glad You're Livin', Joe	1967	$6
❏ 47-8619	It's Gonna Be Fine/She	1965	$8
❏ 47-8796	Lonely Things/Changing Way No. 2	1966	$6
❏ 47-9019	Spin, Spin/Love Are Wine	1966	$6
❏ 47-8366	The Honey Wind Blows/San Francisco Bay Blues	1964	$8
STANYAN			
❏ 34	Simple Christmas/A Hand To Hold At Christmas	1974	$5
—B-side by Rod McKuen			
STAX			
❏ 0204	Everybody's Reaching Out for Someone/Freedom to Stay	1974	$5
❏ 0185	I See America/Holy Creation	1973	$5
WARNER BROS.			
❏ 7335	(Don't Let the Sun Shine On You) In Tulsa/Wisconsin	1969	$6
❏ 7196	Downtown L.A./Until You Happened to Pass By	1968	$6
❏ 7448	Gentle Hearts and Gentle People/A Friend of Jesus	1970	$5
❏ 7382	Goodbye Girl/Sunshine Fields of Love	1970	$5
❏ 7427	I Wish I Knew How It Would Feel to Be Free/Jubilee	1970	$5
❏ 7247	Let Me Choose Life/I'll Catch the Sun	1968	$6
❏ 7478	Lonesome Cities/Ivy That Clings to the Wall	1971	$5
❏ 7269	Somehow, Someway (I'm Gonna Get to You)/Child of the Night Time	1969	$6
YARDBIRDS, THE			
Also see JEFF BECK; ERIC CLAPTON; JIMMY PAGE; KEITH RELF. Ex-members of the group formed BOX OF FROGS; LED ZEPPELIN; and RENAISSANCE. (45)			
EPIC			
❏ 5-9790	For Your Love/Got to Hurry	1965	$20
❏ 5-10303	Goodnight Sweet Josephine/Think About It	1968	$60
❏ 5-10204	Ha Ha Said the Clown/Tinker, Tailor, Soldier, Sailor	1967	$30
❏ 5-10094	Happenings Ten Years Time Ago/The Nazz Are Blue	1966	$20
❏ 5-10094 [PS]	Happenings Ten Years Time Ago/The Nazz Are Blue	1966	$60
❏ 5-9823	Heart Full of Soul/Steeled Blues	1965	$20
❏ 5-9823 [PS]	Heart Full of Soul/Steeled Blues	1965	$60
❏ 5-9857	I'm a Man/Still I'm Sad	1965	$20
❏ 5-9709	I Wish You Could/A Certain Girl	1964	$50
—With typographical error on A-side			

Number	Title	Yr	NM
❏ 5-9709 [PS]	I Wish You Could/A Certain Girl	1964	$800

—*Promo-only picture sleeve used by Esquire Socks, Burlington, N.C.; the back of the sleeve advertises "Denim Tones" by Esquire Socks; some copies of the sleeve also contain an insert, through which a store could order multiple copies of the Yardbirds record for use as a giveaway in the store (double the value if included)*

Number	Title	Yr	NM
❏ 5-9709	I Wish You Would/A Certain Girl	1964	$60

—*With correct A-side title; also includes "Radio Station Copy" versions, some of which were used as giveaways in stores*

Number	Title	Yr	NM
❏ 5-10156	Little Games/Puzzles	1967	$30
❏ 5-10035	Over Under Sideways Down/Jeff's Boogie	1966	$20
❏ 5-10035 [PS]	Over Under Sideways Down/Jeff's Boogie	1966	$60
❏ 5-9881	Shapes of Things/I'm Not Talking	1966	$20
❏ 5-10006	Shapes of Things/New York City Blues	1966	$30
❏ 5-10248	Ten Little Indians/Drinking Muddy Water	1967	$30

YARROW, PETER
WARNER BROS.

Number	Title	Yr	NM
❏ 7567	Don't Ever Take Away My Freedom/Greenwood	1972	$5
❏ 7236	Don't Remind Me Now of Time/Teenage Fair	1968	$8

—*B-side by Rosko*

Number	Title	Yr	NM
❏ 7761	Old Father Time/Isn't That So	1973	$4
❏ 8114	Wanderin'/Another Chain Unbound	1975	$4
❏ 7587	Weave Me the Sunshine/Wings of Time	1972	$5

YATES, BILL
SUN

Number	Title	Yr	NM
❏ 399	Big Big World/I Dropped My M & M's	1966	$20
❏ 397	Carleen/Too Late to Right My Wrong	1965	$20
❏ 390	Stop, Wait and Listen/Don't Step on My Dog	1964	$20

YATES, TOMMY
VERVE

Number	Title	Yr	NM
❏ 10556	Darling, Something's Gotta Give/If You're Looking for a Fool	1967	$30

YAZ
SIRE

Number	Title	Yr	NM
❏ 7-29844	Only You/Winter Kills	1982	$5
❏ 7-29953	Situation/(Dub)	1982	$12

—*As "Yazoo*

Number	Title	Yr	NM
❏ 7-29953 [PS]	Situation/(Dub)	1982	$20

—*Yazoo" on sleeve*

Number	Title	Yr	NM
❏ 7-29953	Situation/(Dub)	1982	$4

—*As "Yaz*

Number	Title	Yr	NM
❏ 7-29953 [PS]	Situation/(Dub)	1982	$12

—*Yaz" on sleeve*

YEAWORTHS, THE
RCA VICTOR

Number	Title	Yr	NM
❏ 47-8480	The Ballad of the Christmas Donkey/Oky Doky Tokyo	1964	$15

YELLOW BALLOON, THE
CANTERBURY

Number	Title	Yr	NM
❏ 513	Good Feeling Time/I've Got a Feeling for Love	1967	$10
❏ 516	Stained Glass Window/Can't Get Enough of Your Love	1967	$10

YELLOW PAYGES, THE
SHOWPLACE

Number	Title	Yr	NM
❏ 217	Love in the Making/Jezebel	1967	$30
❏ 216	Sleeping Minds/Never See the Good in Me	1967	$30

UNI

Number	Title	Yr	NM
❏ 212/3	Finger Poppin' Party/Moonfire	1970	$30

—*Though not marked as such, this appears to be a promo; no regular Uni number; both sides have custom labels*

Number	Title	Yr	NM
❏ 55225	I'm a Man/Home Again	1970	$20
❏ 55192	Little Women/Follow the Bouncing Ball	1970	$10
❏ 55043	Our Time Is Running Out/Sweet Sunrise	1967	$10
❏ 55176	Slow Down/Fresco Annie	1969	$12
❏ 55107	The Two of Us/Never Put Away My Love for You	1969	$10
❏ 55153	Would You Mind If I Loved You/Vanilla on My Mind	1969	$10

YELVINGTON, MALCOLM
SUN

Number	Title	Yr	NM
❏ 211	Drinkin' Wine Spo-Dee-O-Dee/Just Rolling Along	1954	$125

YEOMEN, THE
CUCA

Number	Title	Yr	NM
❏ 1188	I Never Will Marry/This Little Light of Mine	1964	$15

YES
Also see STEVE HOWE; RICK WAKEMAN; ALAN WHITE.

ATCO

Number	Title	Yr	NM
❏ 99745	It Can Happen/It Can Happen (Live)	1984	$3
❏ 99745 [PS]	It Can Happen/It Can Happen (Live)	1984	$3
❏ 99787	Leave It/Leave It (Acapella)	1984	$3
❏ 99787 [PS]	Leave It/Leave It (Acapella)	1984	$3
❏ 99449	Love Will Find a Way/Holy Lamb	1987	$3
❏ 99449 [PS]	Love Will Find a Way/Holy Lamb	1987	$3
❏ 99817	Owner of a Lonely Heart/Our Song	1983	$3
❏ 99817 [PS]	Owner of a Lonely Heart/Our Song	1983	$3

ATLANTIC

Number	Title	Yr	NM
❏ 2899	America/Total Mass Retain	1972	$5
❏ 2920	And You And I (Part 1)/And You And I (Part 2)	1972	$5
❏ 3416	Awaken (Part 1)/Wonderful Stories	1977	$5
❏ 3534	Don't Kill the Whale/Release, Release	1978	$5
❏ 2709	Every Little Thing/Sweetness	1970	$6
❏ 3767	Into the Lens/Does It Really Happen	1980	$5
❏ 3242	Sound Chaser/Soon	1975	$5

YESTER, JERRY
DUNHILL

Number	Title	Yr	NM
❏ 4061	I Can Live Without You/Garden of Imagining	1967	$10
❏ 4042	The Sound of Summer Showers/Ashes Have Turned	1966	$10

YIN AND YAN
GULL

Number	Title	Yr	NM
❏ 26	The 12 Days Of Christmas/Breakfast Conversations	1975	$8

—*U.K. import*

YO LA TENGO
COYOTE

Number	Title	Yr	NM
❏ 87104	For Turnstiles/Asparagus Song	1987	$8
❏ 87104 [PS]	For Turnstiles/Asparagus Song	1987	$8

YOAKAM, DWIGHT
REPRISE

Number	Title	Yr	NM
❏ 7-27994	Always Late with Your Kisses/1,000 Miles	1988	$3
❏ 7-27994 [PS]	Always Late with Your Kisses/1,000 Miles	1988	$4
❏ 7-22944	Buenas Noches from a Lonely Room (She Wore Red Dresses)/What I Don't Know	1989	$3
❏ 7-28688	Guitars, Cadillacs/I'll Be Gone	1986	$3
❏ 7-28688 [PS]	Guitars, Cadillacs/I'll Be Gone	1986	$8
❏ 7-28793	Honky Tonk Man/Miner's Prayer	1986	$3
❏ 7-27567	I Got You/South of Cincinnati	1989	$3
❏ 7-27715	I Sang Dixie/Floyd County	1988	$3
❏ 7-27715 [PS]	I Sang Dixie/Floyd County	1988	$4
❏ 7-21868	I Sang Dixie/Long White Cadillac	1989	$3

—*Back to Back Hits" reissue*

Number	Title	Yr	NM
❏ 7-28565	It Won't Hurt/Bury Me (Duet with Maria McKee)	1986	$3
❏ 7-28432	Little Sister/This Drinkin' Will Kill Me	1987	$3
❏ 7-28432 [PS]	Little Sister/This Drinkin' Will Kill Me	1987	$4
❏ 7-28310	Little Ways/Readin', Rightin', Rt. 23	1987	$3
❏ 7-28310 [PS]	Little Ways/Readin', Rightin', Rt. 23	1987	$4
❏ 7-22799	Long White Cadillac/Little Ways	1989	$3
❏ 7-22799 [PS]	Long White Cadillac/Little Ways	1989	$4
❏ 7-28174	Please, Please Baby/Throughout All Time	1987	$3
❏ 7-28156	Santa Claus Is Back in Town/Christmas Eve With The Babylonian Cowboys: Jingle Bells	1987	$5

Number	Title	Yr	NM
❏ 7-28156 [PS]	Santa Claus Is Back in Town/Christmas Eve With The Babylonian Cowboys: Jingle Bells	1987	$5
❏ 7-27964	Streets of Bakersfield/One More Name	1988	$5

—*A-side with Buck Owens*

Number	Title	Yr	NM
❏ 7-27964 [PS]	Streets of Bakersfield/One More Name	1988	$5

—*With Buck Owens*

WARNER BROS.

Number	Title	Yr	NM
❏ PRO02424 [DJ]	This Drinkin' Will Kill Me (Live)/Miner's Prayer (Live)	1985	$8
❏ PRO-S-2424 [DJ]	This Drinkin' Will Kill Me (Live)/Miner's Prayer (Live)	1985	$15

YORGESSON, YOGI
CAPITOL

Number	Title	Yr	NM
❏ F2978	Be Kind to the Street Corner Santa/I Give Up, What Is It	1954	$20
❏ F1831	Christmas Party/I Was Santa at the Schoolhouse	1951	$20
❏ F781	I Yust Go Nuts At Christmas/Yingle Bells	1949	$30
❏ F3904	I Yust Go Nuts At Christmas/Yingle Bells	1958	$20
❏ 3904	I Yust Go Nuts At Christmas/Yingle Bells	1983	$4

—*Black label, rainbow ring along edge (reissue)*

YORK, BETTY
HIT

Number	Title	Yr	NM
❏ 174	Downtown/Have You Been There	1965	$8

—*B-side by the Chords (2)*

Number	Title	Yr	NM
❏ 238	My Love/Michelle	1966	$10

—*B-side by Bobby and Buddy*

YORK, FRED
HIT

Number	Title	Yr	NM
❏ 104	A Fool Never Learns/I Want to Hold Your Hand	1964	$15

—*B-side by the Doodles*

Number	Title	Yr	NM
❏ 249	A Sign of the Times/I'm So Lonesome I Could Cry	1966	$8

—*B-side by Leroy Jones*

Number	Title	Yr	NM
❏ 82	Blue Velvet/You Can Never Stop Me Loving You	1963	$8

—*B-side by Bill Austin*

Number	Title	Yr	NM
❏ 139	Clinging Vine/A Broken Hearted Fool Like Me	1964	$8
❏ 59	Don't Be Afraid Little Darling/Puff the Magic Dragon	1963	$8

—*B-side by Jimmy, Joe and Betty*

Number	Title	Yr	NM
❏ 43	Go Away Little Girl/My Coloring Book	1962	$8

—*B-side by Connie Landers*

Number	Title	Yr	NM
❏ 239	Lightnin' Strikes/Crying Time	1966	$8

—*B-side by Leroy Jones*

Number	Title	Yr	NM
❏ 208	Lonely Girl/10 Little Bottles	1965	$8

—*B-side by Jack White*

Number	Title	Yr	NM
❏ 163	Mr. Lonely/Two Plus Two	1964	$8

—*B-side by the Chords (2)*

Number	Title	Yr	NM
❏ 179	My Love, Forgive Me/Anything	1965	$8

—*B-side by Joanie Key*

Number	Title	Yr	NM
❏ 157	Pay It No Mind/Ask Me	1964	$8

—*B-side by Ed Hardin*

Number	Title	Yr	NM
❏ 29	Send Me the Pillow You Dream On/Ramblin' Rose	1962	$8

—*B-side by Frank Clark*

Number	Title	Yr	NM
❏ 96	There! I've Said It Again/You Don't Have to Be a Baby to Cry	1963	$8

—*B-side by the Belles*

Number	Title	Yr	NM
❏ 113	White on White/Can't Buy Me Love	1964	$15

—*B-side by the Beagles*

YORK, RUSTY
CAPITOL

Number	Title	Yr	NM
❏ 4663	That's What I Need/Just Like You	1961	$20

CHESS

Number	Title	Yr	NM
❏ 1730	Sugaree/Red Rooster	1959	$30

GAYLORD

Number	Title	Yr	NM
❏ 6428	Sally Was a Good Old Girl/I Might Just Walk Right Back Again	1962	$20

KING

Number	Title	Yr	NM
❏ 5511	Love Struck/Goodnight Cincinnati, Good Morning Tennessee	1961	$20
❏ 5103	Peggy Sue/Shake 'Em Up Baby	1958	$30

Number	Title	Yr	NM
❑ 5587	Tramblin'/Tore Up Over You	1961	$20

NOTE

Number	Title	Yr	NM
❑ 10021	Sugaree/Red Rooster	1959	$30

P.J.

Number	Title	Yr	NM
❑ 100	Sugaree/Red Rooster	1959	$40

SAGE AND SAND

Number	Title	Yr	NM
❑ 266	Sadie May/Margaret Ann	1960	$30

YOUNG, NEIL

Also see BUFFALO SPRINGFIELD; CROSBY, STILLS, NASH AND YOUNG; THE STILLS-YOUNG BAND.

GEFFEN

Number	Title	Yr	NM
❑ 29433	Cry, Cry, Cry/Payola Blues	1983	$4
❑ 28883	Get Back to the Country/Misfits	1985	$3
❑ 29887	Little Thing Called Love/ We Are In Control	1982	$4
❑ 29887 [PS]	Little Thing Called Love/ We Are In Control	1982	$4
❑ 28196	Mideast Vacation/ Long Walk Home	1987	$3
❑ 29707	Mr. Soul/Mr. Soul	1983	$4
❑ 28753	Old Ways/Once an Angel	1986	$3
❑ 28623	Weight of the World/ Pressure	1986	$3
❑ 28623 [PS]	Weight of the World/ Pressure	1986	$3
❑ 29574	Wonderin'/Payola Blues	1983	$4
❑ 29574 [PS]	Wonderin'/Payola Blues	1983	$4

REPRISE

Number	Title	Yr	NM
❑ 1023	Brave Belt/Rock and Roll Band	1971	$5
—With Graham Nash			
❑ 0911	Cinnamon Girl/ Sugar Mountain	1970	$5
❑ 1395	Comes a Time/ Motorcycle Mama	1978	$4
❑ 1395 [PS]	Comes a Time/ Motorcycle Mama	1978	$4
❑ 0836	Down By the River/(When You're On the) Losing End	1969	$60
❑ 1350	Drive Back/Stupid Girl	1976	$4
❑ 819 [DJ]	Everyone Knows This Is Nowhere/The Emperor of Wyoming	1969	$300
—Alternate acoustic version of A-side			
❑ 819 [DJ]	Everyone Knows This Is Nowhere/The Emperor of Wyoming	1969	$30
—Standard version of A-side, with "RE-1" in trail-off wax			
❑ 0819 [DJ]	Everyone Knows This Is Nowhere/The Emperor of Wyoming	1969	$500
—Alternate acoustic version of A-side			
❑ 0819 [DJ]	Everyone Knows This Is Nowhere/The Emperor of Wyoming	1969	$40
—Standard version of A-side, with "RE-1" in trail-off wax			
❑ 0819	Everyone Knows This Is Nowhere/The Emperor of Wyoming	1969	$125
❑ 1396	Four Strong Winds/ Human Highway	1979	$4
❑ 49555	Hawks and Doves/ Union Man	1980	$3
❑ 49555 [PS]	Hawks and Doves/ Union Man	1980	$3
❑ 1152	Heart of Gold/Old Man	1972	$3
—Back to Back Hits" release			
❑ 1065	Heart of Gold/ Sugar Mountain	1971	$4
—Without reference to "Harvest" LP on label			
❑ 1065	Heart of Gold/ Sugar Mountain	1971	$5
—With reference to "Harvest" LP on label			
❑ 1390	Hey Baby/Homegrown	1977	$4
❑ 0898	I've Been Waiting for You/ Oh, Lonesome Me	1970	$60
❑ 1391	Like a Hurricane/Hold Back the Tears	1978	$4
❑ 1344	Lookin' for a Love/ Sugar Mountain	1976	$4
❑ 0861	Oh, Lonesome Me/ Sugar Mountain	1969	$60
❑ 1084	Old Man/The Needle and the Damage Done	1972	$4
❑ 0958	Only Love Can Break Your Heart/Birds	1970	$5
❑ 0746	Only Love Can Break Your Heart/Cinnamon Girl	1971	$3
—Back to Back Hits" release			
❑ 50014	Opera Star/Surfer Joe and Moe the Sleaze	1982	$3
❑ 49870	Southern Pacific/Motor City	1981	$3
❑ 49641	Stayin' Power/ Captain America	1980	$3
❑ 1393	Sugar Mountain/The Needle and the Damage Done	1978	$4
❑ 27908	Ten Men Workin'/I'm Goin'	1988	$3
❑ 27908 [PS]	Ten Men Workin'/I'm Goin'	1988	$8
❑ 49189	The Loner/Cinnamon Girl	1980	$4
❑ 0785	The Loner/Sugar Mountain	1968	$120
❑ 27848	This Note's For You (LP Version)/This Note's For You (Edited Live Version)	1988	$4
❑ 27848 [PS]	This Note's For You (LP Version)/This Note's For You (Edited Live Version)	1988	$4
❑ 1184	Time Fades Away/The Last Train to Tulsa (Live)	1973	$10
❑ 1209	Walk On/For the Turnstiles	1974	$4
❑ 1209 [DJ]	Walk On (same on both sides)	1974	$20
—Small hole			
❑ 1209 [DJ]	Walk On (same on both sides)	1974	$10
—Large hole			
❑ 1209 [DJ]	Walk On (same on both sides)	1974	$20
—Small hole			
❑ 1209 [DJ]	Walk On (same on both sides)	1974	$10
—Large hole			
❑ 1099	War Song/The Needle and the Damage Done	1972	$4
—With Graham Nash			
❑ 0992	When You Dance I Can Really Love/Sugar Mountain	1971	$5

7-Inch Extended Plays

Number	Title	Yr	NM
❑ SR2032 [PS]	Harvest	1972	$25
—Part of "Little LP" series (LLP #183)			
❑ SR2032	Old Man/The Needle and the Damage Done/Heart of Gold//Harvest/Alabama	1972	$25
—Jukebox issue; small hole, plays at 33 1/3 rpm			

YOUNG AMERICANS, THE

ABC

Number	Title	Yr	NM
❑ 10977	Beautiful, Beautiful World/Little Girl	1967	$6
❑ 10940	Born to Be with You/ One by One	1967	$6
❑ 11044	Happiness/Oh, What a Lovely Day	1968	$6
❑ 10998	Here I Am (Billy Guy)/ As Quiet As It's Kept	1967	$6
❑ 11220	On the Blue Cloud Sky/ Blackberry Organ	1969	$6

YOUNG, BARRY

COLUMBIA

Number	Title	Yr	NM
❑ 43584	A Heart Without a Home/ He'll Have to Go	1966	$8
❑ 43723	I Love You So Much It Hurts/Cryin' Street	1966	$8

DOT

Number	Title	Yr	NM
❑ 16756	One Has My Name (The Other Has My Heart)/ Show Me the Way	1965	$10
❑ 16819	Since You Have Gone from Me/Nashville, Tennessee	1966	$8

YOUNG, BOBBY

GUYDEN

Number	Title	Yr	NM
❑ 2087	To Each His Own/ The Only Girl for Me	1963	$250

YOUNG, CATHY

MAINSTREAM

Number	Title	Yr	NM
❑ 703	Spoonful/Circus	1969	$20

YOUNG, FARON

CAPITOL

Number	Title	Yr	NM
❑ F3169	All Right/Go Back You Fool	1955	$30
❑ F3982	Alone with You/Every Time I'm Kissing You	1958	$30
❑ F4113	A Long Time Ago/ Last Night at a Party	1959	$30
❑ F2859	A Place for Girls Like You/In the Chapel in the Moonlight	1954	$30
❑ 4616	Backtrack/I Can't Find the Time	1961	$20
❑ 4616 [PS]	Backtrack/I Can't Find the Time	1961	$40
❑ F4233	Country Girl/I Hear You Talkin'	1959	$30
❑ 4868	Down by the River/ Safely in Love Again	1962	$20
❑ F2133	Foolish Pride/I Knew You When	1952	$40
❑ 4463	Forget the Past/A World So Full of Love	1960	$20
❑ F2299	Goin' Steady/Just Out of Reach (Of My Two Open Arms)	1952	$30
❑ 4533	Hello Walls/Congratulations	1961	$20
❑ F2461	I Can't Wait (For the Sun to Go Down)/What's the Use to Love You	1953	$30
❑ F2953	If You Ain't Lovin' (You Ain't Livin')/If That's the Fashion	1954	$30
❑ F3611	I Miss You Already (And You're Not Even Gone)/I'm Gonna Live Some Before I Die	1957	$30
❑ F3258	It's a Great Life (If You Don't Weaken)/For the Love of a Woman Like You	1955	$30
❑ F3056	Live Fast, Love Hard, Die Young/Forgive Me, Dear	1955	$30
❑ F3753	Love Has Finally Come My Way/Moonlight Mountain	1957	$30
❑ F2171	Saving My Tears/What Can I Do with My Sorrow	1952	$40
❑ F3443	Sweet Dreams/ Until I Met You	1956	$30
❑ F2039	Tattle Tale Tears/Have I Waited Too Long	1952	$50
❑ F4050	That's the Way I Feel/I Hate Myself	1958	$30
❑ F4164	That's the Way It's Gotta Be/We're Talking It Over	1959	$30
❑ F2570	That's What I'd Do for You/Baby My Heart	1953	$30
❑ 4754	The Comeback/Over Lonely and Under Kissed	1962	$20
❑ F3855	The Locket/Snowball	1957	$30
❑ 4410	There's Not Any Like You Left/is She All You Thought She'd Be	1960	$20
❑ F3696	The Shrine of St. Cecilia/ He Was There	1957	$30
❑ F2780	They Made Me Fall in Love with You/You're Right	1954	$30
❑ 4696	Three Days/I Let It Slip Away	1962	$20
❑ 4696 [PS]	Three Days/I Let It Slip Away	1962	$40
❑ F3549	Turn Her Down/I'll Be Satisfied with Love	1956	$30
❑ F3107	Where Could I Go/ God Bless God	1955	$30

MCA

Number	Title	Yr	NM
❑ 41177	(If I'd Only Known) It Was the Last Time/Free and Easy	1980	$4
❑ 51176	Pull Up a Pillow/Ain't Your Memory Got No Pride at All	1981	$4
❑ 41292	Tearjoint/I May Lose You Tomorrow	1980	$4
❑ 41046	That Over Thirty Look/ Second Hand Emotion	1979	$4
❑ 41004	The Great Chicago Fire/Old Songs	1979	$5

MERCURY

Number	Title	Yr	NM
❑ 73633	Another You/God's Been Good to Me	1974	$6
❑ 73925	Crutches/The Last Goodbye	1977	$6
❑ 73731	Feel Again/Some Old Rainy Mornin'	1975	$6
❑ 73692	Here I Am in Dallas/Too Much of Not Enough of You	1975	$6
❑ 73782	I'd Just Be Fool Enough/ What You See Is What You Get	1976	$6
❑ 72656	I Guess I Had Too Much to Dream Last Night/I Just Don't Know How to Say No	1967	$10
❑ 72827	I Just Came to Get My Baby/Missing You Is All I Did Today	1968	$8
❑ 72889	I've Got Precious Memories/You Stayed Just Long Enough	1969	$8
❑ 55019	Loving Here and Living There and Lying In Between/City Lights	1978	$6
❑ 72490	My Dreams/You Had a Call	1965	$10
❑ 72313	My Friend on the Right/ The World's Greatest Love	1964	$15
❑ 72774	She Went a Little Bit Farther/Stay, Love	1968	$8
❑ 72774 [PS]	She Went a Little Bit Farther/Stay, Love	1968	$20
❑ 72576	Sweet Love and Happiness/ You Don't Treat Me Right	1966	$10
❑ 73847	(The Worst You Ever Gave Me Was) The Best I Ever Had/You Get the Feelin'	1976	$6
❑ 72375	Walk Tall/Heartbreak Valley	1965	$10
❑ 72375	Walk Tall/The Weakness of a Man	1965	$10
❑ 72167	We've Got Something in Common/Think About the Old Days	1963	$15
❑ 72936	Wine Me Up/That's Where My Baby Feels at Home	1969	$8
❑ 72728	Wonderful World of Women/All I Can Stand	1967	$10

STEP ONE

Number	Title	Yr	NM
❑ 408	After the Lovin'/Let Me Walk	1989	$5
❑ 397	Here's to You/You're Just Another Beer Drinking Song	1989	$5
❑ 390	Stop and Take the Time/ Misty Morning Rain	1988	$5

7-Inch Extended Plays

CAPITOL

Number	Title	Yr	NM
❑ EAP 1-921	(contents unknown)	1958	$25
❑ EAP 2-921	(contents unknown)	1958	$25
❑ EAP 3-921	(contents unknown)	1958	$25
❑ EAP 1-1096	(contents unknown)	1959	$25
❑ EAP 2-1096	(contents unknown)	1959	$25
❑ EAP 3-1096	(contents unknown)	1959	$25
❑ EAP 1-1185	(contents unknown)	1959	$25
❑ EAP 2-1185	(contents unknown)	1959	$25
❑ EAP 3-1185	(contents unknown)	1959	$25
❑ EAP 1-1245	(contents unknown)	1959	$25
❑ EAP 2-1245	(contents unknown)	1959	$25
❑ EAP 3-1245	(contents unknown)	1959	$25

Number	Title	Yr	NM
❏ EAP 1-921 [PS]	Country Music Holiday, Part 1	1958	$25
❏ EAP 2-921 [PS]	Country Music Holiday, Part 2	1958	$25
❏ EAP 3-921 [PS]	Country Music Holiday, Part 3	1958	$25
❏ EAP 1-611 [PS]	Faron Young	1956	$35
❏ EAP 1-450	Goin' Steady/Tattle Tale Tears//Saving My Tears (For Tomorrow)/I Knew You When	1954	$35
❏ EAP 1-450 [PS]	Goin' Steady with Faron Young	1954	$35
❏ EAP 1-611	If You Ain't Lovin' (You Ain't Livin')/A Place for Girls Like You//Live Fast, Love Hard, Die Young/If That's the Fashion	1956	$35
❏ EAP 3-778	I'm a Poor Boy/I Can't Help It/You Are My Sunshine/That's What It's Like to Be Lonesome	1957	$30
❏ EAP 1-1185 [PS]	My Garden of Prayer, Part 1	1959	$25
❏ EAP 2-1185 [PS]	My Garden of Prayer, Part 2	1959	$25
❏ EAP 3-1185 [PS]	My Garden of Prayer, Part 3	1959	$25
❏ EAP 1-778 [PS]	Sweethearts or Strangers, Part 1	1957	$30
❏ EAP 2-778 [PS]	Sweethearts or Strangers, Part 2	1957	$30
❏ EAP 3-778 [PS]	Sweethearts or Strangers, Part 3	1957	$30
❏ EAP 1-778	Sweethearts or Strangers/Your Cheatin' Heart//Shame on You/I Can't Tell My Heart	1957	$30
❏ EAP 1-1245 [PS]	Talk About Hits, Part 1	1959	$25
❏ EAP 2-1245 [PS]	Talk About Hits, Part 2	1959	$25
❏ EAP 3-1245 [PS]	Talk About Hits, Part 3	1959	$25
❏ EAP 1-869 [PS]	The Shrine of St. Cecilia	1957	$30
❏ EAP 1-869	The Shrine of St. Cecilia/Mansion Over the Hilltop//He Was There/How Long Has It Been	1957	$30
❏ EAP 1-1096 [PS]	This Is Faron Young, Part 1	1959	$25
❏ EAP 2-1096 [PS]	This Is Faron Young, Part 2	1959	$25
❏ EAP 3-1096 [PS]	This Is Faron Young, Part 3	1959	$25

YOUNG GENERATION, THE
RED BIRD
| ❏ Oct-0065 | Hideaway/Hymn of Love | 1966 | $20 |

YOUNG, GEORGIE
CAMEO
| ❏ 166 | Feels So Good/Two Weeks with Pay | 1959 | $30 |
| ❏ 168 | Georgie Porgie/Where Is Your Heart | 1959 | $30 |
CHANCELLOR
| ❏ 1066 | Autumn Lovers/Indian Summer | 1960 | $20 |
| ❏ 1069 | Birdland Hully Gully/Marie | 1961 | $20 |
COLUMBIA
| ❏ 42773 | Supercar/Chicken Scratch | 1963 | $40 |
FORTUNE
| ❏ 524 | Shakin' Shelley/Buggin' Baby | 1957 | $30 |
MERCURY
| ❏ 71259 | Can't Stop Me/Come Back to Me | 1958 | $100 |
PARKWAY
| ❏ 809 | Gold Rush/That's Tough | 1960 | $30 |

YOUNG, JESSE COLIN
Also see THE YOUNGBLOODS.
ELEKTRA
| ❏ 46026 | Sanctuary/City Boy | 1979 | $4 |
WARNER BROS.
❏ 7816	Cuckoo/Light Shine	1974	$5
❏ 7749	Evenin'/Morning Sun	1973	$5
❏ 8398	Fool/Higher and Higher	1977	$5
❏ 7581	Good Times/Peace Song	1972	$5
❏ 7581 [PS]	Good Times/Peace Song	1972	$10
❏ 7618	It's a Lovely Day/Sweet Little Child	1972	$5
❏ 8352	Love on the Wing/(B-side unknown)	1977	$5
❏ 7404	Peace Song/Pretty in the Fair	1970	$6
❏ 8106	Songbird/'Til You Come Back Home	1975	$5
❏ 8129	Sugar Babe/Motorhome	1975	$5
❏ 8225	Sunlight/Peace Song	1976	$5
❏ 8053	Susan/Barbados	1974	$5

YOUNG JESSIE
ATLANTIC
| ❏ 2003 | Margie/That's Enough for Me | 1958 | $30 |

YOUNG, KATHY, AND THE INNOCENTS
INDIGO
Number	Title	Yr	NM
❏ 108	A Thousand Stars/Eddie My Darling	1960	$40
❏ 137	Baby, Oh Baby/The Great Pretender	1961	$30
❏ 115	Happy Birthday Blues/Someone to Love	1961	$30
❏ 115 [PS]	Happy Birthday Blues/Someone to Love	1961	$60
❏ 146	Lonely Blue Nights/I'll Hang My Letters Out to Dry	1962	$30
❏ 125	Magic Is the Night/Du Du'nt Du	1961	$30
❏ 125 [PS]	Magic Is the Night/Du Du'nt Du	1961	$60
❏ 121	Our Parents Talked It Over/Just As Though You Were Here	1961	$30
❏ 147	Send Her Away/Dream Awhile	1962	$30
❏ 141	Time/Dee Dee Di Oh	1962	$30
MONOGRAM
| ❏ 506 | Dreamboy/I'll Love That Man | 1962 | $30 |
STARFIRE
| ❏ 112 | Sparkle and Shine/Please Love Me Forever | 1979 | $5 |

7-Inch Extended Plays
INDIGO
| ❏ 1001 | Sparkle and Shine/Eddie My Darling//Happy Birthday Blues/Angel on My Shoulder | 1961 | $250 |

YOUNG LADS, THE
FELICE
| ❏ 712 | Graduation Kiss/Night After Night | 1963 | $125 |
NEIL
| ❏ 100 | Moonlight/I'm in Love | 1956 | $75 |

YOUNG, LEON
ATCO
| ❏ 6274 | Sea Winds/Spinning Jenny | 1963 | $8 |

YOUNG LIONS, THE (U)
DOT
| ❏ 16172 | Little Girl/It Would Be | 1960 | $60 |

YOUNG, PAUL
COLUMBIA
❏ 38-04313	Come Back and Stay/Yours	1984	$3
❏ 38-04313 [PS]	Come Back and Stay/Yours	1984	$4
❏ 38-05712	Everything Must Change/Give Me My Freedom	1985	$3
❏ 38-05712 [PS]	Everything Must Change/Give Me My Freedom	1985	$4
❏ 38-04867	Everytime You Go Away/This Means Anything	1985	$3
❏ 38-04867 [PS]	Everytime You Go Away/This Means Anything	1985	$5
❏ 38-05577	I'm Gonna Tear Your Playhouse Down/Broken Man	1985	$3
❏ 38-05577 [PS]	I'm Gonna Tear Your Playhouse Down/Broken Man	1985	$4
❏ 38-04453	Love of the Common People/Behind Your Smile	1984	$3
❏ 38-04453 [PS]	Love of the Common People/Behind Your Smile	1984	$4
❏ 38-06423	Some People/Steps to Go	1986	$3
❏ 38-06423 [PS]	Some People/Steps to Go	1986	$3
❏ AE71757 [DJ]	Wherever I Lay My Hat (That's My Home) (same on both sides)	1983	$6
❏ 38-04071	Wherever I Lay My Hat (That's My Home)/The Tender Trap	1983	$4
❏ 38-04071 [PS]	Wherever I Lay My Hat (That's My Home)/The Tender Trap	1983	$4
❏ 38-06630	Why Does a Man Have to Be Strong/A Matter of Fact	1987	$3
❏ 38-06630 [PS]	Why Does a Man Have to Be Strong/A Matter of Fact	1987	$3

YOUNG, SHERRY
HIT
| ❏ 206 | Goldfinger/Something's Happened | 1965 | $8 |
—B-side by Fred Hess
| ❏ 274 | Single Girl/Sugar Town | 1966 | $8 |
—B-side by Connie Dee

YOUNG, STEVE
A&M
| ❏ 1083 | Seven Bridges Road/I'm a One Woman Man | 1969 | $30 |
BLUE CANYON
| ❏ 135 | My Oklahoma/The White Trash Song | 1973 | $8 |

Number	Title	Yr	NM
❏ 135 [PS]	My Oklahoma/The White Trash Song	1973	$15
RCA
❏ PB-10823	Broken Hearted People (Take Me to a Barroom)/Light of My Life	1976	$5
❏ PB-11233	Don't Think Twice, It's All Right/Montgomery in the Rain	1978	$5
❏ PB-10868	It's Not Supposed to Be That Way/Lonesome, On'ry and Mean	1976	$5
❏ PB-11361	Whiskey/Mid-Nite Fever	1978	$5
REPRISE
❏ 1001	Call Me Up in Dreamland/I Can't Hold Myself in Line	1971	$8
❏ 1013	Come Sit By My Side/Golden Rocket	1971	$8
❏ 0946	Crash on the Levee/Sea Rock City	1969	$8
❏ 1100	Seven Bridges Road/Many Rivers	1972	$15

YOUNGBLOOD, JACK
COLUMBIA
| ❏ 4-21103 | Bile Dem Cabbage Down/Wednesday Night Waltz | 1953 | $30 |
| ❏ 4-21298 | Hitch-Hiker's Blues/Twinkle, Twinkle, Little Star | 1954 | $30 |

YOUNGBLOOD, LONNIE
CALLA
| ❏ 109 | Let My Love Bring Out the Woman in You/Right Back Where We Started | 1976 | $50 |
CAMEO
| ❏ 374 | Come On Let's Strut/Youngblood Feeling | 1965 | $60 |
FAIRMOUNT
| ❏ 1002 | Go Go Shoes/Go Go Place | 1966 | $60 |
—Jimi Hendrix plays guitar on this record (both sides)
| ❏ 1022 | Soul Food (That's What I Like)/Goodbye Bessie Mae | 1967 | $70 |
—Jimi Hendrix plays guitar on this record (both sides)
| ❏ 1016 | The Grass (Will Sing for You)/Wooly Bully | 1966 | $50 |
LOMA
| ❏ 2081 | African Twist Pt. 1/Pt. 2 | 1967 | $30 |
RADIO
| ❏ 3866 | Feelings and Expressions Medley/Try Love | 1981 | $8 |
| ❏ 3820 | The Best Way to Break a Habit/Reasons | 1981 | $8 |
SHAKAT
| ❏ 708 | Man to Woman/(Instrumental) | 1974 | $6 |
TURBO
❏ 050	Gonna Fly Now (Rocky Theme)/Happiness Is You	1977	$6
❏ 013	Let's Party/(B-side unknown)	1971	$20
❏ 029	Super Cool/Black Is So Bad	1973	$20
❏ 026	Sweet Sweet Tootie/In My Lonely Room	1972	$20

YOUNGBLOODS, THE
Also see JESSE COLIN YOUNG.
MERCURY
| ❏ 72583 | Sometimes/Rider | 1966 | $30 |
—As "Jesse Colin and the Youngbloods"
| ❏ 73068 | Sometimes/Rider | 1969 | $12 |
RCA VICTOR
❏ 47-9422	Dreamer's Dream/Quicksand	1967	$12
❏ 47-9360	Fool Me/I Can Tell	1967	$10
❏ 47-9264	Get Together/All My Dreams Blue	1967	$20
❏ 47-9752	Get Together/Beautiful	1969	$8
❏ 47-9015	Grizzly Bear/Tears Are Falling	1966	$10
❏ 47-9015 [PS]	Grizzly Bear/Tears Are Falling	1966	$40
❏ 47-9142	Merry-Go-Round/Foolin' Around (The Waltz)	1967	$10
❏ 74-0129	On Sir Francis Drake/Darkness, Darkness	1969	$8
❏ 74-0380	On Sir Francis Drake/Darkness, Darkness	1970	$6
❏ 74-0270	Sunlight/Trillium	1969	$8
❏ 47-9222	The Wine Song/Euphoria	1967	$10
WARNER BROS.
❏ 7639	Dreamboat/Kind Hearted Woman	1972	$5
❏ 7445	Hippie from Olema/Misty Roses	1970	$5
❏ 7499	It's a Lovely Day/Ice Bag	1971	$5
❏ 7563	Will the Circle Be Unbroken/Light Shine	1972	$5

Number	Title	Yr	NM

YOUNGSTERS, THE
EMPIRE
Number	Title	Yr	NM
❏ 109	Christmas In Jail/ Dreamy Eyes	1956	$70
❏ 109	Dreamy Eyes/I'm Sorry Now	1956	$125
❏ 104	Shattered Dreams/ Rock'n Roll'n Cowboy	1956	$125

YOUNGTONES, THE
BRUNSWICK
| ❏ 55089 | Come On Baby/Oh Tell Me | 1958 | $70 |

YOUTH BRIGADE
BYO
| ❏ 06 | What Price Happiness/ Where Are We Going/ Who Can You Believe In | 1984 | $40 |

— Red vinyl (fewer than 200 made)
| ❏ 06 | What Price Happiness/ Where Are We Going/ Who Can You Believe In | 1984 | $75 |

— Yellow vinyl
| ❏ 06 | What Price Happiness/ Where Are We Going/ Who Can You Believe In | 1984 | $10 |

— Black vinyl
| ❏ 06 [PS] | What Price Happiness/ Where Are We Going/ Who Can You Believe In | 1984 | $12 |

YUM YUMS, THE
ABC-PARAMOUNT
| ❏ 10697 | Looky, Looky (What I Got)/ Gonna Be a Big Thing | 1965 | $1000 |

— Black label stock copy
| ❏ 10697 [DJ] | Looky, Looky (What I Got)/ Gonna Be a Big Thing | 1965 | $500 |

— White label promo

YURO, TIMI
LIBERTY
❏ 55701	A Legend in My Time/ Should I Ever Love Again	1964	$8
❏ 55665	Call Me/Permanently Lonely	1964	$8
❏ 55634	Gotta Travel On/ Down in the Valley	1963	$10
❏ 55343	Hurt/I Apologize	1961	$20
❏ 55400	I Believe/A Mother's Love	1961	$10

— With Johnnie Ray
❏ 55432	I Know (I Love You)/ Count Everything	1962	$10
❏ 55747	I'm Movin' On (Part 1)/I'm Movin' On (Part 2)	1964	$8
❏ 56061	I Must Have Been Out of My Head/Interlude	1968	$6
❏ 55552	Insult to Injury/Just About the Time	1963	$10
❏ 55410	Let Me Call You Sweetheart/ Satan Never Sleeps	1962	$12
❏ 55587	Make the World Go Away/Look Down	1963	$10
❏ 55375	Smile/She Really Loves You	1961	$15
❏ 55519	The Love of a Boy/I Ain't Gonna Cry No More	1962	$10
❏ 55469	What's a Matter Baby (Is It Hurting You)/Thirteenth Hour	1962	$15
❏ 56049	Wrong/Something Bad on My Mind	1968	$6

MERCURY
❏ 72478	Big Mistake/Teardrops Till Dawn	1965	$8
❏ 72431	Can't Stop Running Away/ Get Out of My Life	1965	$8
❏ 72391	Could This Be Magic/ You Can Have Him	1965	$8
❏ 72601	Don't Keep Me Lonely Too Long/You Took My Happy Away	1966	$8
❏ 72316	If/The Masquerade Is Over	1964	$8
❏ 72355	I Got It Bad and That Ain't Good/Johnny	1964	$8
❏ 72515	Once a Day/Pretend	1966	$8
❏ 72628	Turn the World Around the Other Way/Just a Ribbon	1966	$8
❏ 72674	Why Not Now/Cuttin' In	1967	$8

PLAYBOY
| ❏ 6050 | Southern Lady/Lovin' You Is All I Ever Had | 1975 | $5 |

UNITED ARTISTS
| ❏ 0042 | Hurt/What's a Matter Baby (Is It Hurting You) | 1973 | $4 |

— Silver Spotlight Series" reissue

Z

Z'LOOKE
ORPHEUS
❏ B-72654	Can U Read My Lips/(Remix)	1988	$4
❏ B-72678	Gitchi U/Take Away the Heartache	1989	$4
❏ B-72650	Lovesick (The Cure)/ (Doctor's Groove)	1989	$4

ZABACH, FLORIAN
CADENCE
| ❏ 1406 | Oceans of Love/Theme from "Carnival | 1961 | $8 |

DECCA
❏ 9-29047	Callaghan's Monkey/Solfaggio	1954	$20
❏ 9-27775	Ida (Sweet as Apple Cider)/Cold Turkey	1951	$20
❏ 9-27614	Tea for Two/Running After the Rails	1951	$20
❏ 9-28916	The Funny Fiddle/ Plink, Plank, Plunk	1953	$20
❏ 9-28090	The Happy Whistler/Jazz Legato-Jazz Pizzicato	1952	$20
❏ 9-27509	The Hot Canary/Jalousie	1951	$20
❏ 9-27729	The Waltzing Cat/The Whistler and His Dog	1951	$20

MERCURY
| ❏ 70975X45 | Petticoats of Portugal/ Rainbow Trail | 1956 | $15 |
| ❏ 70936X45 | When the White Lilacs Bloom Again/Fiddler's Boogie | 1956 | $15 |

ZACA CREEK
COLUMBIA
| ❏ 38-73096 | Ghost Town/Time's Up | 1989 | $3 |
| ❏ 38-69062 | Sometimes Love's Not a Pretty Thing/Rock Me Back | 1989 | $3 |

ZACHARIAS AND THE TREE PEOPLE
VIKING
| ❏ 1004 | We're All Paul Bearers (Part 1)/ We're All Paul Bearers (Part 2) | 1969 | $30 |

ZACHARIAS, HELMUT
DECCA
❏ 31296	Bermuda Shorts/Adios My Love	1961	$8
❏ 9-29849	China-Boogie/The Big Bell and the Little Bell	1956	$15
❏ 9-30795	Crazy Violins/The Tipsy Piano	1958	$12
❏ 9-31101	La Montana/Mare Nostrum	1960	$8
❏ 9-30102	Spanish Violins/The Whistler and His Dog	1956	$10
❏ 31715	Tokyo Melody/Teatime in Tokyo	1964	$8
❏ 31259	Tres Jolie/Innocence Abroad	1961	$8
❏ 9-30039	When the White Lilacs Bloom Again/Blue Blues	1956	$15

ZACHERLEY, JOHN
CAMEO
| ❏ 130 | Dinner with Drac (Part 1)/ Dinner with Drac (Part 2) | 1958 | $40 |

— Orange label
| ❏ 130 | Dinner with Drac (Part 1)/ Dinner with Drac (Part 2) | 1960 | $30 |

— Red and black label
❏ 130	Igor/Dinner with Drac	1958	$50
❏ 145	I Was a Teenage Caveman/Dummy Doll	1958	$40
❏ 139	Lunch with Mother Goose/82 Tombstones	1958	$40

COLPIX
| ❏ 743 | Monsters Have Problems Too/Hello Dolly | 1964 | $30 |

PARKWAY
| ❏ 885 | Clementine/Surfboard 109 | 1963 | $30 |

— As "Zacherley
| ❏ 853 | Dinner with Drac/ Hurry Bury Baby | 1962 | $30 |
| ❏ 888 | Scarey Tales from Mother Goose/Monster Monkey | 1963 | $30 |

— As "Zacherley

ZACK, EDDIE, AND COUSIN RICHIE
COLUMBIA
❏ 4-21441	I'm Gonna Rock and Roll/Foolish Me	1955	$200
❏ 4-21199	I've Lost Again/I Never Saw Her Again	1954	$60
❏ 4-21261	Positively No Dancing/ Dancing Country Style	1954	$60

ZACK, EDDIE
COLUMBIA
| ❏ 4-21148 | Little Donkey/You Knew Men When You Were Lonely | 1953 | $50 |

DECCA
❏ 9-46302	Beautiful Brown Eyes/ Shenandoah Waltz	1951	$50
❏ 9-28082	Call of the Mountains/Words	1952	$50
❏ 9-46245	Dill Pickles/That Silver Haired Daddy of Mine	1950	$50
❏ 9-28329	Draggin' the Bow/Lights Out	1952	$50
❏ 9-46284	Land Beyond the Sun/ Heaven's TV Screen	1951	$50
❏ 9-46330	The Clouds Will Soon Roll By/ You Remind Me of So Much	1951	$50

ZADORA, PIA
CBS ASSOCIATED
| ❏ ZS4-05717 | Come Rain or Come Shine/Smile Though Your Heart Is Breaking | 1985 | $4 |
| ❏ ZS4-06322 | I Am What I Am/For Once in My Life | 1986 | $4 |

ELEKTRA
| ❏ 47428 | I'm in Love Again/It's Wrong for Me to Love You | 1982 | $4 |
| ❏ 69889 | The Clapping Song/ Lovin' Things | 1982 | $4 |

MCA CURB
| ❏ 52521 | When the Rain Begins to Fall/Substitute | 1984 | $3 |

— A-side with Jermaine Jackson
| ❏ 52521 [PS] | When the Rain Begins to Fall/Substitute | 1984 | $3 |

WARNER BROS.
❏ 49148	Baby It's You/Roses Ain't Red	1979	$4
❏ 8766	Bedtime Stories/Tell Him	1979	$4
❏ 8612	Come Share My Love/Just Make Believe You Love Me	1978	$4
❏ 49065	I Know a Good Thing When I Feel It/Trouble	1979	$4

ZAGER AND EVANS
RCA VICTOR
❏ 47-9816	Help One Man Today/Year 32	1969	$5
❏ 74-0174	In the Year 2525 (Exordium & Terminus)/Little Kids	1969	$6
❏ 74-0299	Listen to the People/She Never Sleeps Beside Me	1969	$5
❏ 74-0246	Mr. Turnkey/Cary Lynn Jones	1969	$5
❏ 74-0359	Plastic Park/Crutches	1970	$5

TRUTH
| ❏ 0(# unknown) | In the Year 2525 (Exordium & Terminus)/Little Kids | 1967 | $30 |

VANGUARD
| ❏ 35125 | Hydra 15,000/I Am | 1971 | $5 |
| ❏ 35125 [PS] | Hydra 15,000/I Am | 1971 | $30 |

ZAGER, MICHAEL
CBS ASSOCIATED
| ❏ ZS4-04546 | Shot in the Dark/(Instrumental) | 1984 | $4 |

COLUMBIA
| ❏ 1-11273 | Don't Sneak on Me/ Bring Me Love | 1980 | $4 |

PRIVATE STOCK
| ❏ 45,184 | Let's All Chant/Love Express | 1978 | $5 |
| ❏ 45,202 | Soul to Soul/Freak | 1978 | $5 |

ZAHND, RICKY, AND THE BLUE JEANERS
COLUMBIA
| ❏ 40576 | (I'm Getting) Nuttin' For Christmas/Something Barked On Christmas Morning | 1955 | $20 |
| ❏ 4-263 | (I'm Getting) Nuttin' For Christmas/Something Barked On Christmas Morning | 1955 | $20 |

— Yellow-label Children's Series edition
| ❏ 40670 | My Church Is My Palace/ You Got to Go to Church | 1956 | $15 |

Number	Title	Yr	NM

ZANG, TOMMY
CANADIAN AMERICAN
| ❏ 107 | Break the Chain/I'll Put a String on Your Finger | 1959 | $20 |
| ❏ 102 | Lonely As an Island/Jennings St. Near Falcon Square | 1959 | $20 |

HICKORY
❏ 1148	Every Hour, Every Day/I'm Gonna Slip You Offa My Mind	1961	$15
❏ 1133	Hey Good Lookin'/With Love (For You)	1960	$15
❏ 1122	I Can't Stop Loving You/Truly, Truly	1960	$15
❏ 1180	I Love You Because/Just Call My Name	1962	$15
❏ 1205	I Take the Chance/Wall to Wall Love	1963	$10
❏ 1109	I Wonder When We'll Ever Know/Nashville Blues	1959	$15
❏ 1165	She's Getting Married/I Can't Hold Your Letters (In My Arms)	1962	$15
❏ 1114	Take These Chains from My Heart/Under Your Spell Again	1960	$15

MARK
| ❏ 128 | Miranda/Tommy's Gonna Get Ya | 1958 | $30 |
| ❏ 116 | White Silence/With the Good Lord Willing | 1957 | $30 |

ZANIES, THE
DORE
❏ 734	Bless 'Em All/Last Dance at the Prom	1965	$20
❏ 683	Chicken Surfer/London Rick	1963	$30
❏ 655	Comin' Down the Track/Hello Jackie	1962	$30
❏ 962	Curvacious Cora and Carlos Condo/Percolator	1980	$4
❏ 875	Do the 1-2-3/Mr. President-to-Be	1972	$12
❏ 893	Flakey/(Instrumental)	1974	$6
❏ 968	From Peanuts to Jelly Beans/For He's a Jolly Good Fellow	1981	$4
❏ 912	Frustration/Roller Coaster	1975	$5
❏ 979	Gesundheit/Darlin' Come Back	1983	$4
❏ 974	I Hate Baseball/Dancing with Ronnie Cey	1982	$5
— With "A. Player"			
❏ 963	I Love Life, Men, Candy and Paree/I Love Life, Men, Candy and Paree (X-Rated Adult Version)	1981	$4
❏ 978	Is There An Echo in the Joint/Doin' the Head	1983	$4
❏ 597	It's Lovely/Saxophone Safari	1961	$30
❏ 889	Let Out a Scream (Part 1)/Let Out a Scream (Part 2)	1973	$8
❏ 638	London Rock/Stalled	1962	$30
❏ 900	Los Angeles, Los Angeles/Let Out a Scream	1974	$6
❏ 920	Old Man River/Los Angeles, Los Angeles	1976	$5
❏ 647	Sleepwalker/Alexander's Ragtime Band	1962	$30
❏ 705	Slinky/Camel Walk	1964	$20
❏ 509	The Blob/Do You Dig Me, Mr. Pygmy	1958	$30
❏ 515	The Mad Scientist/She's a Winner	1958	$30
❏ 959	The Song of the Masochist/Special	1980	$4
❏ 959	The Song of the Masochist/What Is a One	1980	$4
❏ 959	What Is a One/Louie's Market	1980	$4
❏ 853	Will the Real Dr. Frankenstein Please Stand Up/Frankenstein's Laboratory	1971	$20

ZAPP
REPRISE
| ❏ 22849 | Ooh Baby Baby/(Instrumental) | 1989 | $3 |
| ❏ 22849 [PS] | Ooh Baby Baby/(Instrumental) | 1989 | $5 |

WARNER BROS.
❏ 49623	Be Alright -- Part I/Part II	1980	$5
❏ 28805	Computer Love Part I/Part II	1985	$4
❏ 29961	Dance Floor Part I)/(Part II)	1982	$5
❏ 29891	Doo Wa Ditty (Blow That Thing)/Come On	1982	$5
❏ 29779	Do You Really Want an Answer?/Playin' Kind of Ruff	1983	$5
❏ 29462	Heartbreaker (Part I)/(Part II)	1983	$5
❏ 29553	I Can Make You Dance (Part I)/(Part II)	1983	$5
❏ 28719	Itchin' for Your Twitchin'/(Long Version)	1986	$4
❏ 28879	It Doesn't Really Matter/Make Me Feel Good	1985	$5
❏ 49534	More Bounce to the Ounce Part I/Part II	1980	$6
❏ 29380	Spend My Whole Life/Play Some Blues	1984	$5

ZAPPA, DWEEZIL
BARKING PUMPKIN
❏ B-74204	Let's Talk About It/Electric Hoedown	1987	$6
❏ B-74204 [PS]	Let's Talk About It/Electric Hoedown	1987	$6
❏ WS9-03366	My Mother Is a Space Cadet/Crunchy Water	1982	$4
❏ WS9-03366 [PS]	My Mother Is a Space Cadet/Crunchy Water	1982	$4

ZAPPA, FRANK
Includes his work leading The Mothers of Invention. The label credit, if other than "Frank Zappa," is listed under each record.

BIZARRE
❏ 1127	Cletus Awreetus-Awrightus/Eat That Question	1972	$40
— The Mothers			
❏ 0840	My Guitar/Dog Breath	1969	$60
— The Mothers of Invention			
❏ 0889	Peaches En Regalia/Little Umbrellas	1970	$60
❏ 1052	Tears Began to Fall/Junior Mintz Boogie	1971	$60
—Frank Zappa and The Mothers of Invention			
❏ 1027	Tears Began to Fall/Junior Mintz Boogie	1971	$60
—Junior Mintz			
❏ 0967	Tell Me You Love Me/Would You Go All the Way for the U.S.A.?	1970	$60
❏ 0892	WPLJ/My Guitar	1970	$60
— The Mothers of Invention			

DISCREET
❏ 1312	Don't Eat the Yellow Snow/Cosmic Debris	1974	$20
❏ 1180	I'm the Slime/Montana	1973	$30
— The Mothers			

UNITED ARTISTS
| ❏ 50857 | Magic Fingers/Daddy, Daddy, Daddy | 1971 | $60 |

VERVE
❏ 10418	How Could I Be Such a Fool/Help I'm a Rock (3rd Movement: It Can't Happen Here)	1966	$200
— The Mothers of Invention			
❏ 10418 [DJ]	How Could I Be Such a Fool/Help I'm a Rock (3rd Movement: It Can't Happen Here)	1966	$125
— The Mothers of Invention			
❏ 10570	Mother People/Lonely Little Girl	1967	$200
— The Mothers of Invention			
❏ 10570 [DJ]	Mother People/Lonely Little Girl	1967	$125
— The Mothers of Invention			
❏ 10458 [DJ]	Who Are the Brain Police/Trouble Comin' Every Day	1966	$125
— The Mothers of Invention			
❏ 10458	Who Are the Brain Police/Trouble Comin' Every Day	1966	$200
— The Mothers of Invention			
❏ 10513	Why Don't You Do Me Right/Big Leg Emma	1967	$200
— The Mothers of Invention			
❏ 10513 [DJ]	Why Don't You Do Me Right/Big Leg Emma	1967	$125
— The Mothers of Invention			

WARNER BROS.
| ❏ 8342 | Disco Boy/Miss Pinky | 1977 | $30 |
| ❏ 8296 | Find Her Finer/Zoot Allures | 1976 | $30 |

ZAPPA
❏ Z-10	Dancin' Fool/Baby Snakes	1979	$12
❏ ZR1001	I Don't Wanna Get Drafted/Ancient Armaments (Live)	1980	$5
❏ ZR1001 [PS]	I Don't Wanna Get Drafted/Ancient Armaments (Live)	1980	$10
❏ ZRP-21 [DJ]	I Don't Wanna Get Drafted (Stereo)/(Mono)	1980	$20
— Sold at Zappa concerts around 1980			

ZEBRA, THE
BLUE THUMB
| ❏ 109 | Christmas Morning (Part 1)/Christmas Morning (Part 2) | 1969 | $10 |

PHILIPS
| ❏ 40535 | Groovy Personality/Miss Ann (Ain't That Kind of Man) | 1968 | $15 |

WHITE WHALE
| ❏ 305 | Bring Me to My Knees/(B-side unknown) | 1969 | $10 |

ZEBULONS, THE
CUB
| ❏ 9069 | Falling Water/Wo-Ho-La-Tee-Da | 1960 | $70 |

ZEITGEIST, THE
RCA VICTOR
| ❏ 47-9852 | I Want to Walk to San Francisco/(Herein Lie) The Seeds of Revolution | 1970 | $20 |

ZEKLEY, GARY
AVA
| ❏ C151 | Other Towns, Other Girls/When I Go to Sleep | 1963 | $80 |
| —($180 on eBay auction 3/2008) | | | |

ZELLA, DANNY
DIAL
| ❏ 100 | Sapphire/You Made Me Blue | 1959 | $200 |

FOX
❏ F #1	Black Saxs/Wicked Ruby	1959	$40
❏ ZTSC10056/7	Black Saxs/Wicked Ruby	1959	$40
— Some copies of this 45 do not have a catalog number; these are the master numbers of each side			

RED ROCKET
| ❏ 475 | Black Saxs/Wicked Ruby | 1959 | $50 |

ZENTNER, SI
LIBERTY
❏ 55240	Armen's Theme/The Swinging Eye	1960	$10
❏ 55609	Broken Date/Fink	1963	$8
❏ 55955	Dear John/Haven't Been to Church	1967	$6
❏ 55499	Desafinado/Elephant's Tango	1962	$8
❏ 55683	From Russia with Love/James Bond Theme	1964	$10
❏ 55408	Hollywood Twist/Nice 'N Easy	1962	$8
❏ 55675	I'm Getting Sentimental Over You/Sentimental Journey	1964	$8
❏ 55476	Shadrack/Boogie Woogie Maxine	1962	$8
❏ 55204	Sock Hop/Two Guitars	1959	$12
❏ 55420 [DJ]	The Goulash (Shufflin' Blues)	1962	$20
—One-sided promo-only release			
❏ 55538	Waltz in Jazz Time/A La Mode	1963	$8
❏ 55941	Warning Shot/Mona Lisa	1967	$6

RCA VICTOR
❏ 47-8779	Baby, Take Another Bow/Mr. Nashville	1966	$6
❏ 47-8550	Dear Heart/In a Little Spanish Town	1965	$6
❏ 47-8634	Fat Cat/My Devotion	1965	$6
❏ 47-8454	Theme from Max/Spanish Rice	1964	$6

7-Inch Extended Plays
| ❏ VLP3484 [PS] | Put Your Head on My Shoulder | 1966 | $12 |

ZEPHYR
PROBE
| ❏ 475 | Sail On/Cross the River | 1970 | $15 |

WARNER BROS.
| ❏ 7444 | Going Back to Colorado/Radio Song | 1970 | $10 |

ZEPHYRS, THE
ROTATE
| ❏ 5009 | Let Me Love You Baby/Wonder What I'm Gonna Do | 1965 | $40 |
| ❏ 5006 | She's Lost You/There's Something About You | 1965 | $30 |

ZEPPA, BENN JOE
AWARD
| ❏ 124/5 | Shame on You, Miss Lindy/Terry Lou | 1958 | $100 |

ERA
| ❏ 1042 | Topsy Turvy/Mom and Dad | 1957 | $60 |

HUSH
| ❏ 1000-0.75 | Louise/Doctor, Doctor | 1958 | $40 |

METROL
| ❏ 9001X45 | Shame on You, Miss Lindy/Terry Lou | 1958 | $200 |

SPECIALTY
| ❏ 577 | A Foolish Fool/Baby I Need (Ting-a-Ling) | 1956 | $100 |
| —As "Ben Zeppa and the Zephyrs | | | |

Number	Title	Yr	NM
ZERO BOYS			
7-Inch Extended Plays			
Z-DISK			
❏ 0(# unknown)	Livin' in the 80's	1980	$125
[PS]			
— The above has been counterfeited, but it also has been reissued on Lookout and Panic Button			
❏ 0(# unknown)	Livin' in the 80's/Stoned to Death/Stick to Your Guns/I'm Bored/Piece of Me	1980	$125
ZEROES, THE			
TY-TEX			
❏ 105	Flossie Mae/Twisting with Crazee Babee	1963	$200
ZEROS			
BOMP!			
❏ 110	Don't Push Me Around/Wimp	1977	$50
❏ 110 [PS]	Don't Push Me Around/Wimp	1977	$50
❏ 118	Wild Weekend/Beat Your Heart Out	1978	$50
❏ 118 [PS]	Wild Weekend/Beat Your Heart Out	1978	$50
TEST TUBE			
❏ 03	They Say That Everything's Alright/Getting Nowhere Fast	1980	$50
❏ 03 [PS]	They Say That Everything's Alright/Getting Nowhere Fast	1980	$50
ZEVON, WARREN			
ASYLUM			
❏ 46610	A Certain Girl/Empty-Handed Heart	1980	$5
❏ 45356	Hasten Down the Wind/Mohammad's Radio	1976	$8
❏ 47118 [DJ]	Lawyers, Guns and Money (Clean)/(Dirty)	1981	$12
❏ 47118	Lawyers, Guns and Money/Werewolves of London	1981	$5
❏ 69946	Let Nothing Come Between You/The Hula Hula Boys	1982	$6
❏ 69966	Looking for the Next Best Thing/The Hula Hula Boys	1982	$5
❏ 69509	Werewolves of London/Jesus Mentioned	1986	$5
❏ 45472	Werewolves of London/Roland the Headless Thompson Gunner	1978	$5
ELEKTRA			
❏ 45091	Werewolves of London/Lawyers, Guns and Money	1979	$4
— Spun Gold" reissue series			
VIRGIN			
❏ 99440	Leave My Monkey Alone/(Latin Rascals Dub)	1987	$3
❏ 99440 [PS]	Leave My Monkey Alone/(Latin Rascals Dub)	1987	$5
ZILL, PAT			
BIG C			
❏ 119	Air Mail to Heaven/Two Empty Arms	1962	$20
BOONE			
❏ 1031	All I Have to Do Is Wait/Heartaches by the Number	1965	$10
INDIGO			
❏ 126	Bouquet of Roses/Hold Tight	1961	$20
❏ 119	Pick Me Up on Your Way Down/La Marida	1961	$20
SAND			
❏ 336	Pick Me Up on Your Way Down/La Marida	1961	$30
STOP			
❏ 236	The Things You Should Do/Lonesome 7-7203	1969	$8
ZIMBALIST, EFREM, JR.			
WARNER BROS.			
❏ 5126	Adeste Fideles//Deck the Halls with Boughs of Holly/Caroling, Caroling	1959	$15
— B-side by The Guitars Inc.			
❏ 5126 [PS]	Adeste Fideles//Deck the Halls with Boughs of Holly/Caroling, Caroling	1959	$30

Number	Title	Yr	NM
ZIMMERMAN, GEORGE, AND THE THRILLS			
JAB			
❏ 103	Whose Baby Are You?/I Ain't Got the Money to Pay for This Drink	1956	$400
ZIP AND THE ZIPPERS			
PAGEANT			
❏ 607	Where You Goin' Little Boy/Gig	1963	$30
ZIRCONS, THE			
AMBER			
❏ 851	One Summer Night/The Lone Stranger	1966	$20
BAGDAD			
❏ 1007	Going Places/Surfing in the Sunset	1963	$100
CAPITOL			
❏ 2667	Finders Keepers/You Ain't Comin' Back	1969	$50
COOL SOUND			
❏ 1030	Silver Bells/You Are My Sunshine	1964	$40
DOT			
❏ 15724	Only One Love/I Need It	1958	$30
FEDERAL			
❏ 12478	Get Up and Go to School/Mr. Jones	1962	$30
HEIGH HO			
❏ 645/6	Go On and Cry/Was It Meant to Be This Way	1967	$50
❏ 608/9	I Couldn't Stop Crying/Sit Down Girl	1967	$50
❏ 607	Where There's a Will/Don't Put Off for Tomorrow	1967	$50
MELLOMOOD			
❏ 1000	Lonely Way/Your Way	1963	$30
OLD TIMER			
❏ 603	Stormy Weather/Sincerely	1964	$20
SIAMESE			
❏ 403	Stormy Weather/Sincerely	1964	$15
WINSTON			
❏ 1022	Crazy Crazy/Return My Love	1958	$100
❏ 1020	I Need It/Only One Love	1957	$70
ZOE, ALPHA			
HIT			
❏ 229	A Lover's Concerto/Keep On Dancing	1965	$30
— B-side by the Gentrys			
❏ 65	Da Doo Ron Ron/Foolish Little Girl	1963	$8
— B-side by Clara Wilson and the Cleftones			
❏ 44	Everybody Loves a Lover/Love Came to Me	1962	$8
— B-side by Ed Hardin			
❏ 70	Hello Stranger/Sukiyaki	1963	$8
— B-side by the Music City Chorus and Orchestra Featuring Samayami			
❏ 54	Let's Turkey Trot/One Broken Heart for Sale	1963	$8
— B-side by Ed Hardin			
ZOMBIES, THE			
COLUMBIA			
❏ 44363	Care of Cell 44/Maybe After He's Gone	1967	$125
DATE			
❏ 1612	Butcher's Tale (Western Front 1914)/This Will Be Our Year	1968	$10
❏ 1612 [PS]	Butcher's Tale (Western Front 1914)/This Will Be Our Year	1968	$30
❏ 1648	If It Don't Work Out/Don't Cry for Me	1969	$10
❏ 1644	Imagine the Swan/Conversation of Floral Street	1969	$10
❏ 1628	Time of the Season/Friends of Mine	1968	$15
❏ 1604	Time of the Season/I'll Call You Mine	1968	$50
❏ 2-1203	Time of the Season/Imagine the Swan	1970	$5
— Hall of Fame" series			
EPIC			
❏ 11145	Time of the Season/Imagine the Swan	1974	$5

Number	Title	Yr	NM
PARROT			
❏ 9821	Don't Go Away/Is This the Dream	1966	$20
❏ 9786	I Love You/Whenever You're Ready	1965	$15
❏ 3004	Indication/How We Were Before	1966	$20
❏ 9769	I Want You Back Again/Once Upon a Time	1965	$15
❏ 9747	She's Coming Home/I Must Move	1965	$15
❏ 9747 [PS]	She's Coming Home/I Must Move	1965	$40
❏ 9695	She's Not There/You Make Me Feel So Good	1964	$20
❏ 9723	Tell Her No/Leave Me Be	1965	$20
❏ 9723 [PS]	Tell Her No/Leave Me Be	1965	$40
ZOO, THE (1)			
SUNBURST			
❏ 775	One Night Man/(Standing On) The Sunset Strip	1968	$10
ZOO, THE (U)			
PARKWAY			
❏ 147	Good Day Sunshine/Where Have All the Good Times Gone	1967	$15
ZOOM			
POLYDOR			
❏ 2197	Love Seasons/Bye Bye Baby	1982	$8
❏ 2186	Saturday, Saturday Night/Distant Destiny	1981	$8
ZULEMA			
LEJOINT			
❏ 5N-34001	Change/Hanging On to a Memory	1978	$5
❏ 5N-34002	I'm Not Dreaming/(B-side unknown)	1979	$5
RCA			
❏ PB-10815	Hungry for Your Love/Suddenly There Was You	1976	$5
RCA VICTOR			
❏ PB-10541	Half of Your Heart/What Kind of Person Are You	1976	$5
❏ PB-10704	Pity for the Children/I Love You Baby	1976	$5
❏ PB-10246	Standing in the Back Row of Your Heart/Hail, Hail America	1975	$5
❏ PB-10116	Wanna Be Where You Are/No Time Next Time	1974	$5
SUSSEX			
❏ 504	Telling the World Good-Bye (Try to Find Yourself)/Tree	1973	$5
❏ 242	This Child of Mine/Don't Be Afraid	1972	$6
ZZ TOP			
LONDON			
❏ 5N-252	Enjoy and Get It On/El Diablo	1977	$12
❏ 45-179	Francene/Francene (Spanish)	1972	$10
❏ 5N-241	It's Only Love/Asleep in the Desert	1976	$8
❏ 5N-241 [PS]	It's Only Love/Asleep in the Desert	1976	$10
❏ 45-203	La Grange/Just Got Paid	1973	$8
❏ 45-131	Salt Lick/Miller's Farm	1970	$10
❏ 5N-220	Tush/Blue Jean Blues	1975	$8
❏ 5N-220 [PS]	Tush/Blue Jean Blues	1975	$15
SCAT			
❏ 500	Salt Lick/Miller's Farm	1969	$200
WARNER BROS.			
❏ 49220	Cheap Sunglasses/Esther Be the One	1980	$4
❏ 29693	Gimme All Your Lovin/If I Could Only Flag Her Down	1983	$4
❏ 29693 [PS]	Gimme All Your Lovin/If I Could Only Flag Her Down	1983	$5
❏ 49163	I Thank You/Fool for Your Stockings	1980	$4
❏ 29272	Legs/Bad Girl	1984	$4
❏ 29272 [PS]	Legs/Bad Girl	1984	$4
❏ 49782	Leila/Don't Tease Me	1981	$4
❏ 29576	Sharp Dressed Man/I Got the Six	1983	$4
❏ 28884	Sleeping Bag/Party on the Patio	1985	$3
❏ 28884 [PS]	Sleeping Bag/Party on the Patio	1985	$3
❏ 28810	Stages/Can't Stop Rockin'	1986	$3
❏ 28810 [PS]	Stages/Can't Stop Rockin'	1986	$3
❏ 49865	Tube Snake Boogie/Heaven, Hell or Houston	1981	$5